Dictionary of Upriver Halkomelem

Volume I

Dictionary of Upriver Halkomelem

Volume I

Brent D. Galloway

UNIVERSITY OF CALIFORNIA PRESS
Berkeley • Los Angeles • London

University of California Press, one of the most distinguished university presses in the United States, enriches lives around the world by advancing scholarship in the humanities, social sciences, and natural sciences. Its activities are supported by the UC Press Foundation and by philanthropic contributions from individuals and institutions. For more information, visit www.ucpress.edu.

University of California Publications in Linguistics, Volume 141

University of California Press
Berkeley and Los Angeles, California

University of California Press, Ltd.
London, England

Printed in the United States of America

10 9 8 7 6 5 4 3 2
28 27 26 25 24

Cataloging-in-Publication data for this title is on file with the Library of Congress.

ISBN 978-0-520-09872-5 (pbk. : alk. paper)

The paper used in this publication meets the minimum requirements of ANSI/NISO Z39.48-1992 (R 1997) (Permanence of Paper).

CONTENTS

Introduction

Quick Start ix

Sample entries xi

About the language xvii

About the elders xx

Abbreviations of related Salish languages and dialects cited in the dictionary xxvi

How to Use the Dictionary (an introduction for those with linguistic training) xxvii

Labels used for each different type of information xxix

Spelling and orthography xxxv

References xxxvii

Abbreviations for references cited xlix

Halkomelem-to-English

a 1

ch 27

ch’ 48

e 61

h 96

i 110

k 136

k’ 140

kw 141

kw’ 170

l 201

lh 246

m 296

n 344

o 345

ō 365

p 368

p’ 401

q 419

q’ 460

qw 499

qw’ 533

R (reduplication) 548

s 556

sh 653

t 664

t’ 710

th 744

th’ 765

tl’ 805

Volume 2

ts 838

ts’ 845

u 877

w 878

x 899

xw 918

x̲ 953

x̲w 1003

y 1021

' or ’ 1057

English-to-Halkomelem Index 1059

a 1060

b 1084

c 1131

d 1185

e 1212

f 1227

g 1260

h 1285

i 1317

j 1327

k 1332

l 1338

m	1368
n	1396
o	1410
p	1426
q	1471
r	1472
s	1503
t	1591
u	1626
v	1634
w	1642
x	1668
y	1669
z	1673

Introduction

Quick Start

For those who are already oriented to the language and its dialects here is a quick way to get started using this dictionary. The dictionary begins with the Halq'eméylem-to-English section where you can look up words in alphabetical order by Halq'eméylem, the same order as English except that some sounds are written with two or three characters and are treated and alphabetized as single characters. So, **q** will be found before **q'**, **q'** will be found before **qw**, and **qw** will be found before **qw'**. The plain character (for ex. **q**) is always alphabetized before the glottalized version (**q'**), and those sounds made with lips rounded (labialized) are found after the versions not labialized (so **qw** follows **q'**, and **qw'** follows **qw**). (Most entries use ' to show glottalization and glottal stop, but ' is also quite acceptable in the Stó:lō writing system and is usually preferable for clarity in handwritten Halq'eméylem.) So to look things up by Halq'eméylem, follow this order: (**a, ch, ch', e, h, i, k, k', kw, kw', l, lh, m, n, o,** ō, **p, p', q, q', qw, qw', R** (reduplication or doubling)**, s, sh, t, t', th, th', tl', ts, ts', u, w, x, xw, x̱, x̱w, y, '**).

To look up words by their English translations, look in the English-to-Halq'eméylem section which is the second main section of the book. If you find the Halq'eméylem word you're looking for, to get more information about it (what are its meaningful parts, root, suffixes, prefixes, infixes, example sentences, details of all sorts) then look the word up in the Halq'eméylem-to-English section. If you don't know its root, look it up where you'd normally expect it and you'll find where to find the whole family of words with the same root. Every word is cross-referenced in that way. If you know the word has a prefix (for ex. **s-** or **shxw-** which make nouns from verbs, since 95% of all roots are verbs) you can look it up either under the **s** or **sh** or under the next letter in the word which is usually where the root starts.

In the Halq'eméylem-to-English section the entry with no indent from the margin is root or other headword. Under each root is an entry indented once, a word derived from the root and called a stem. If there is an entry under that which is indented twice, it is derived from the word above it with one fewer indent (i.e. takes that previous word as its stem or starting point and adds something to it–an affix stuck on at the beginning (prefix), inserted inside the root (infix) or stuck on at the end (suffix). Looking down at the words derived from the same root, they are generally arranged going down from simpler to more complex forms (using more affixes) in sets using the same stems. When a word is derived from a stem (always a root plus at least one affix), the meaning of the affix is shown in the entry for the stem, but is not usually repeated in the entries for words derived from that stem. The stems are not otherwise arranged in any fixed order among themselves, except that often they are in alphabetical order or by the suffixes added. So if one stem is derived from a root by adding <**=es**>, the next stem may be one derived from a root by added <**=st**>. This is not always the case, so look through the whole family derived from a particular root if you know from the English index that the word you seek is found under that root. This teaches a lot about how words are formed and about the related meanings behind each word. You will find many interesting and often surprising things; I did myself. (As a reader learns more about forming words, one can soon make up new words for things that are modern technology, etc., which are not known or listed yet in this dictionary! This is a skill all elders and fluent speakers have.)

Rarely a word begins in **s-** or **shxw-** and is followed by a consonant which seems the first letter of the root and yet is not. This is sometimes the case when the root is one beginning in **s-** or **xw-**. For example, <**sqá:la**> *red huckleberry* is derived from <**seq**> *hang under* and <**=á:la**> *container*, since they are harvested by hanging the berry basket container under the clusters of berries and hitting the branch with the cluster on the container so they fall into the basket–a very efficient means of harvesting them.
In these kinds of words, the root vowel is dropped and a vowel later in the word normally has or here gets a higher stress or tone (high tone or mid tone). The elders did not tell me this in all cases but showed many other words that work like this, and when one tries to account for every affix and root and their meanings, to make sense of the literal meanings behind the words, one finds examples like this which

don't make sense any other way. The root of *red huckleberry* is not <**qél**> *bad*, or <**qá:l**> *steal*, or <**qí:l ~ qéy**> *put away, save*, or <**qó:**> *water*, as they contribute meanings that make no sense for <**sqá:la**> with either <**=á:la**> *container* or <**=á**> *living thing* added to finish the word.

It's important that this dictionary have lots of cross-references (entries that are alphabetized by the whole word, for ex. and show which root it has and thus where to find all the detailed information on the word). Cross-references usually just have the word, its meaning, and the root (*see* <**tó:l**> for ex.). However, in some interesting cases I have included fuller information (the International Phonetic Alphabet spelling and analysis) and sometimes the literal meaning of the word. It takes too much space and time to do this for all cross-references but shows the type of information that can be found under the full entry filed under the word's root.

There are sometimes differences of tones in a given word's pronunciation (and spelling) between one dialect or another or one speaker and another. I have tried to be as accurate and faithful to the elders' pronunciations as possible with these and to show all variants. I have relative pitch myself (and compose classical music) so that plus 37 years of experience should help make the tones accurately reflected by the spelling. The three phonemic tones are sometimes called high-stress, mid-stress, and unstressed, but actually are high tone, mid tone, and low tone (each about a major third apart on a musical scale). These tones can make a difference in meaning between words otherwise spelled exactly the same (for example, <**qwá:l**> *mosquito* and <**qwà:l**> *talk, speak*)(with high tone and mid tone respectively). Many examples can be found contrasting between low tone and high or mid tone. Each vowel has its own tone in the word. <pípehò:m> *frog*, has high tone, then low tone, then mid tone (like the U.S. Marine song, "Over Hill, Over Dale" or 5-1-3 in relative musical pitches). (Downriver Halkomelem and Island Halkomelem do not have such phonemic tones so far as is known, they have instead phonemic stress plus some intonation.)

A few words about the English-to-Halq'eméylem section:

1) it is organized by showing the English meaning you want to find. If the word only has that meaning, the entry will show the English, then two colons (::), a few spaces, then the Halq'eméylem word, then if that word is not a root by itself it will be followed by a comes from sign (<) a space and the root the word will be found under in the Halq'eméylem-to-English section. If there is no root shown like this, just look up the word by its own spelling. You can usually do this anyway since all words are cross-referenced.

2) they are in alphabetical order by English, of course, but personal names or place names all begin with capital letters, and if they are spelled the same way as a regular word (like Raven, the name of the character in stories, and raven, the bird), the capitalized name precedes the regular word which is not capitalized.

3) Though this section is an English-to-Halq'eméylem section, you will find a number of terms in another language. These are scientific names which identify the scientific species, genus, and sometimes family or order of a plant or creature. They are mostly Latin terms (a few are Greek terms mixed in), and they are so that one can look up the plant or creature in books or the Internet and get pictures, full details of when plants are ripe, what habits or descriptions are given there, for each plant and animal known to the elders I worked with. Sometimes from the English name alone (for example hlueberry or whale) one cannot be sure of the precise plant or creature and all the details. However, with the scientific name identified one can be sure that the exact species or variety of that plant or creature exists in the Stó:lō area and get information exactly about that type or the variety of types the word means.

4) The computer program which I used to create the English-to-Halq'eméylem section is a very good one but created entries only where I inserted a star (*) before the word in my original computer entry of the dictionary. I've added any words I found that were missed (for ex. by my forgetting to add a star before it before I ran the program), but there might be a few I still missed. In such cases the word and meaning will be in the Halq'eméylem-to-English section but that meaning may not be in the English-to-

Halq’eméylem section. If you have a rough idea of the form’s Halq’eméylem spelling or root, try looking there to see if a word with that meaning is found there.

Sample entries

This dictionary has a large number of different types of information about each word in the Halq’eméylem-to-English section. The English-to-Halq’eméylem section is mainly an index or finder-list. Later in this introduction is a complete list of all types of information given and all the abbreviations for them, in various tables and charts. For now, I will show you how to read the first three entries under q’.

The first entry is:

<**=q'**>, da //=q’//, DIR /'*on something else, within something else*'/, TIB; found in <**q'elq'élq'**>, //C_1əC_2=q’ə́l=q’//, /'*tangled on s-th else, snagged (as a net on a log or branch)*'/, <**q'elq'élq't**>, //C_1əC_2=q’ə́l=q’=t//, /'*coil it*'/, <**x̱éyq'et**>, //x̣ɛ́y=q’=ət//, /'*scratch it (to itch it)*'/ (compare with <**x̱éy=m=et**> *grab it*).

Angle brackets show forms in the Stó:lō writing system. To make it easier to find, forms in the Stó:lō writing system are shown in bold-face type. These are first in every entry, since the speakers and learners of the language will located them easier. Linguists can use the key (pp.xxxv-xxxvii) to quickly learn the writing system’s equivalents to IPA characters and can find the IPA characters given for each word, closely following the word spelled in the writing system. If a hyphen or equals sign precedes a Halq’eméylem form, the form is a suffix, an affix added after the root or after another suffix on the root. The equals sign shows it is derivational, that is, changes the meaning of the word or the word class of the word (for ex. from a verb to a noun); some roots cannot occur as words by themselves and these are sometimes indicated by ending them with an equals sign as well. A hyphen shows the affix is inflectional, so that it allows the word to be used in a sentence (for ex. adds a subject to the verb, makes it plural, etc.). The first entry, given above, is <**=q’**>, a derivational suffix, written in the International Phonetic Alphabet (IPA) also a //=q’//. Its main semantic area (domain or subdomain) is in DIRECTION and it means *on something else*, or *within something else*. (Translations are given in italics.) This meaning also belongs in the semantic area or domain of TRANSITIVIZERS, INTRANSITIVIZERS, BENEFACTIVES (TIB), suffixes that show what the verb is acting on or affecting; it isn’t actually such a suffix but is closely related semantically, since getting tangled on something else shows an action on something else or affecting something else. When an entry is an affix, typically some examples are given of some words in which it is found; these are shown after the words “as in” in this entry.

The examples are given first in the Stólō writing system used for Upriver Halq’eméylem, then in the IPA used by linguists. The IPA form here shows all the prefixes, infixes and suffixes added to the root, separated by hyphens or equals signs and within double slashes, which linguists use to show morphophonemic transcriptions (versions of the word with the affixes shown divided from the root and from each other). The first example under <**=q’**> begins with doubling or reduplication, where the first consonant (C_1) and the second consonant (C_2) are copied, separated by a vowel (/ə/, called schwa by linguists and written as <**e**> in the Stólō writing system) and prefixed to the root. In this case, the root is followed directly by the suffix we have looked up, <**=q’**>. This example means *tangled on something else, snagged (as a net on a log or branch)*; in linguistics, translations are usually shown within single quotes, as here, but to highlight them, they are also put in italics throughout the dictionary; in certain systematic places the single quotes are omitted. Other examples follow, in the same order. The last one has a form to compare which shows the root without the suffix; by contrasting this we can show clearly what part of the word’s meaning belongs to the root and what part to the affixes.

The second entry or root after **q’** is:

<**q'a ~ qa ~ qe**>, free root //q’ɛ ~ qɛ ~ qə//, CJ ['*or*'], syntactic analysis: conjunction, attested by AC, example: <**lí chòkw te lálems q'a lí stetís? ~ lí chòkw te lálems qa lí stetís?**>, //lí cákʷ tə lɛ́ləm-s

q'ɛ/qɛ lí s=tə[=C_1əAí=]s//, /'*Is his house far or is it nearby?*'/, attested by AC, <**tsel má:ythome kw'e tseláqelhelh qe lhulhá.**>, //c-əl mɛ́·y=T-ámə k'ʷə cəlɛ́q=əɬ=əɬ qə ɬuɬɛ́//, /'*I helped you yesterday or the day before yesterday.*'/, attested by AC.

This word has several variant pronunciations (~ means "varies with"); it is a free root (can occur as a word by itself without affixes. The IPA spelling follows next with the variants given in the same order. The word belongs to the semantic domain of CONJUNCTIONS (abbreviated CJ) and means *or*. If there are comments about the pronunciation (phonological comments), the word structure (morphological comments), the word order (syntactic analysis), or the meaning (semantic comments SMC or ASM), they follow next, as here. The word is given or attested by Amy Cooper (abbreviations of speaker's names, and other abbreviations, are listed later in this introduction); then examples in sentences may be given, as here, if available. In the IPA version, full morphological analysis is given, breaking all the words down into their morphemes, whether prefixes, infixes, suffixes, or roots; infixes are shown in square brackets and both preceded and followed by equals signs or hyphens, stuck in the correct place within the root (usually after the first vowel of the root). The speaker or speakers who gave the sentences are identified after the meaning is given.

The third entry or root after **q'** is:

<**q'á:l**>, free root //q'ɛ́·l//, EFAM ['*believe*'], syntactic analysis: intransitive verb, attested by Elders Group, AC, EB, example: <**skw'áy kw'els q'á:l kwes lúwes.**>, //s=k'ʷɛ́y k'ʷ-əl-s q'ɛ́·l kʷə-s lúwə-s//, /'*I couldn't believe it was you.*'/, literally /'it can't be that -I -subordinate nominalizer believe that -subordinate nominalizer is you -it (third person subord. subject)'/, attested by AC, <**ốwelhtsellh q'à:l.**>, //ʔówə=ɬ-c-əl-ɬ q'ɛ́·l//, /'*I don't/didn't believe.*'/, Elder's comment: "there's no word for doubt", attested by EB.

This headword is **<q'á:l>**, a free root whose meaning belongs in the semantic area or semantic domain of EMOTIONS, FEELINGS, ATTITUDES, MOODS (abbreviated EFAM), and it means *believe*. If a root is a bound root (cannot occur as a separate word without added affixes), then it is sometimes hard or impossible to identify its meaning–one must subtract the meanings of the affixes to see what meaning is left, but this must be done for all the words it appears in and a common or shared meaning or set of related meanings found for the root. Here, however, there is no problem. The word is an intransitive verb (that is, doesn't have to have a stated object which it acts upon). It was attested by the Elders Group, Amy Cooper, and Edna Bobb (no dates recorded, or attested on multiple dates). A sentence example follows next, and after its meaning is given, a literal meaning is given which shows the meaning of each morpheme in the order it occurs in each word, separated by a hyphen. This helps to show how native speakers organize the words and their meanings and think about the phrase subconsciously. The first example was given by Amy Cooper, the second example sentence by Edna Bobb, who commented, when asked for the Halq'eméylem word for *doubt*, said there is no single word, so this phrase would be a way to express it.

This root has a number of words derived from it which are shown as indented sub-entries under it. Whenever a word is indented further from the left margin than the word above it, it is derived or inflected from the word above it indented less. Thus:

<**q'á:l**>, free root //q'ɛ́·l//, EFAM ['*believe*'], syntactic analysis: intransitive verb, attested by Elders Group, AC, EB, example: <**skw'áy kw'els q'á:l kwes lúwes.**>, //s=k'ʷɛ́y k'ʷ-əl-s q'ɛ́·l kʷə-s lúwə-s//, /'*I couldn't believe it was you.*'/, literally /'it can't be that -I -subordinate nominalizer believe that -subordinate nominalizer is you -it (third person subord. subject)'/, attested by AC, <**ốwelhtsellh q'à:l.**>, //ʔówə=ɬ-c-əl-ɬ q'ɛ́·l//, /'*I don't/didn't believe.*'/, Elder's comment: "there's no word for doubt", attested by EB.

<**q'áq'el**>, cts //q'ɛ́[-C_1ə-]l//, EFAM ['*believing*'], (<-**R1-**> *continuative*), phonology: reduplication, syntactic analysis: intransitive verb, attested by Elders Group.

<**lheq'él:exw ~ lhq'él:exw ~ lhq'élexw**>, ncs //ɬ(ə)=q'ɛ[=Aə́=]l=l-əx^{w}//, EFAM /'*know s-th, know s-o*'/, (<**lhe= ~ lh=**> *use, extract, extract a portion*), root <**q'á:l**> *believe*, (<**=l**> *non-control transitivizer, accidentally, happen to, manage to*, é-ablaut *resultative* or *durative*), (<**-exw**> *third person object*), phonology: consonant merger, ablaut, syntactic analysis: transitive verb, dialects: *Cheh., Tait*, attested by IHTTC, EB, AC, JL, other sources: ES /ɬəq'əl·əx^{w}/ *know*, also <**slhéq'el:exw ~ lhéq'el:exw ~ slhéq'elexw**>, //s=ɬə= ´=q'ɛl=l=əx^{w} ~ ɬə= ´=q'ɛl=l-əx^{w}//, (<**s=**> *stative*, lhe= *use, extract, extract a portion*), (<**= ´= (stress-shift)**> *derivational*), phonology: vowel-reduction to schwa-grade in root after stress-shift, dialects: *Chill.*, attested by IHTTC, AC, JL, also <**slhéq'awelh ~ slhéq'ewelh**>, //s=ɬə= ´=q'ɛl=wəɬ//, dialects: *Pilalt (Chilliwack town) and Chill. (Sardis)*, attested by EB, AC; example: <**líchxw lheq'él:exw?**>, //lí-c-x^{w} ɬə=q'ɛ[=Aə́=]l=l-əx^{w}//, /'*Do you know?, (Do you know it?)*'/, attested by AC; found in <**lhéq'el:exwtsel.**>, //ɬə= ´=q'ɛl=l-əx^{w}-c-əl//, /'*I know.*'/, example: <**líchexw slhéq'awelh kw'as ch'eqw'ōwelh?**>, //lí-c-əx^{w} s=ɬə= ´=q'ɛl=əwəɬ k'^{w}-ɛ-s c'əq'^{w}=ówəɬ//, /'*Do you know how to make a basket?*'/, attested by AC, <**qe ōwétal slhéq'elexw; tsel we xwlálá: el.**>, //qə ʔowə= ´tɛ-l s-ɬə= ´=q'ɛl=l-əx^{w}; c-əl əw x^{w}lɛ́lɛ́·ʔəl//, /'*I didn't know/understand; I just listened.*'/, attested by AC, <**ōwétal slhéq'elexw.**>, //ʔowə= ´tɛ-l s-ɬə= ´=q'ɛl=l-əx^{w}//, /'*I don't know.*'/, attested by AC, <**ōwéta slhéq'el:exwes.**>, //ʔowə= ´tɛ s-ɬə= ´=q'ɛl=l-əx^{w}-əs//, /'*She doesn't know.*'/, attested by AC, <**tsel slhéq'elexw (kwses spá:th, kws spá:ths).**>, //c-əl s=ɬə= ´=q'ɛl=l-əx^{w} (k^{w}-s-əs s=pɛ́·θ, k^{w}-s s=pá·θ-s)//, /'*I know it was a bear.*'/, attested by AC, <**ōwéta slhéq'elexw wetemtámescha kw'es álhtelchet qelát.**>, //ʔowə= ´tɛ s=ɬə= ´=q'ɛl=l-əx^{w} wə-təm=tɛ́m-əs-cɛ k'^{w}ə-s ʔi[=Aɛ́=]ɬ=təl-c-ət qəlɛ́t//, /'*No-one knows when we'll be able to eat again.*'/, literally /'nobody knows it when/if- time= is what -it (subjunctive) -will be/future that -subord.cl. eat meal -we again.'/, usage: story of the Flood, attested by AC, <**ōwéta slhéq'elexw te skwíxs te "cave".**>, //ʔowə= ´tɛ s=ɬə= ´=q'ɛl=l-əx^{w} tə s=k^{w}íx^{y}-s tə "cave"//, /'*Nobody knows the cave's name., (Nobody knows the name of the cave.)*'/, usage: story of the Flood, attested by AC, <**chel we lhq'élexw westámes kw'e le kwú:tes.**>, //c-əl wə ɬ=q'ɛ[=Aə́=]l=l-əx^{w} wə-s=tɛ́m-əs k'^{w}ə lə k^{w}ú·=T-əs//, /'*I know what he took.*'/, literally /'non-subord.subj.- I contrastive know it if- is what -it (subjunct. subject) what (the (remote)) third person past he takes it'/, attested by EB, <**(chel we, chu) lhq'élexw wetewátes kw'e x̱t'ástxw tethá.**>, //(c-əl wə, c(-əl)-u) ɬ=q'ɛ[=Aə́=]l=l-əx^{w} wə-tə=wɛ́t-əs k'^{w}ə x̣t'ɛ́=sT-əx^{w} tə=θɛ́//, /'*I know who did it.*'/, literally /'I contrastive know it if/when- is who -3subj. that do s-th that'/, attested by EB, <**wétal slhéq'ewelh**>, //ʔowə= ´tɛ-l s=ɬə= ´=q'ɛl=wəɬ//, /'*I don't know.*'/, dialects: *Pilalt and Chill. (Chilliwack and Sardis)*, attested by EB (5/18/76), <**wétal lhq'élexw**>, //ʔəwə= ´tɛ-l ɬ=q'ə[=Aə́=]l=l-əx^{w}//, /'*I don't know.*'/, dialects: *Cheh.*, attested by EB, <**líchxw lhq'él:àx?**>, //lí-c-x^{w} ɬ=q'ɛ[=Aə́=]l=l-áx^{y}//, /'*Do you know me?*'/, dialects: *Cheh., Tait*, attested by IHTTC, also <**líchxw slhéq'el:òx?**>, //lí-c-x^{w} s=ɬə= ´=q'ɛl=l-áx^{y}//, dialects: *Chill.*, attested by IHTTC (8/8/77).

<**lheq'elómet**>, ncrs //ɬə=q'ɛl=l-áməT//, EFAM /'*know oneself, be confident*'/, (<**-ómet**> *reflexive*), phonology: consonant merger, vowel-reduction to schwa-grade of root from stress-shift to affix, syntactic analysis: intransitive verb, attested by Elders Group (4/6/77), also <**slheq'el:ó:met**>, //s=ɬə=q'ɛl=l-á·mət//, also /'*understand*'/, phonology: consonant merger, dialects: *Chill.*, attested by AC (10/8/71), example: <**ōwetsel líl slheq'el:ó:met**>, //ʔówə-c-əl lí-l s=ɬə=q'ɛl=l-á·mət//, /'*I don't understand.*'/, attested by AC.

<**q'élmet**>, iecs //q'ɛ[=Aə́=]l=məT//, EFAM /'*believe s-o, trust s-o*'/, (<**é-ablaut**> *non-continuative*), (<**=met**> *indirect effect control transitivizer*), phonology: ablaut, syntactic analysis: transitive verb, attested by Elders Group (2/16/77, 2/8/78), AC, example: <**ōwetsellh q'élmethóme.**>, //ʔówə-c-əl-ɬ q'ɛ[=Aə́=]l=məT-ámə//, /'*I don't (didn't) believe you.*'/, attested by AC.

<**q'áq'elmet**>, cts //q'ɛ́[-C$_{1}$ə-]l=məT//, EFAM ['*believing s-o*'], (<**-R1-**> *continuative*), phonology:

reduplication, syntactic analysis: transitive verb, attested by Elders Group (2/8/78).

<**q'elstá:xw**>, caus //q'ɛl=sT-ə[=Aɛ́·=]x^{w}//, durs, EFAM /'*fool s-o, deceive s-o, (lie to s-o [SJ])*'/, (<**=st**> *causative control transitivizer*), probably <**á:-ablaut on suffix**> *durative* or possibly to dissimilate from <**q'élstexw**> *return it, bring it back, give it back* which has root <**q'ó:**> *together* or possibly <**q'ál**> *go over/around, go back on oneself, coil,* (<**-exw**> *third person object*), phonology: ablaut, syntactic analysis: transitive verb, attested by EB, Deming, also /'*lie to s-o*'/, attested by SJ (Deming 4/27/78), example: <**tsel q'elstá:xw.**>, //c-əl q'ɛl=sT-ə[=Aɛ́·=]x^{w}//, /'*I fooled him.*'/, attested by EB; found in <**q'elstá:xwes.**>, //q'ɛl=sT-ə[=Aɛ́·=]x^{w}-əs//, /'*He fooled someone.*'/, attested by EB, example: <**q'elstá:xwes qesu q'á:l.**>, //q'ɛl=sT-ə[=Aɛ́·=]x^{w}-əs qə=s=u q'ɛ́·l//, /'*He fooled him and he believed.*'/, attested by EB, <**q'elstá:xwes á:lhtel te Lawéchten.**>, //q'ɛl=sT-ə[=Aɛ́·=]x^{w}-əs ʔɛ́·ɬtəl tə lɛw(=)ə́c=tən//, /'*They fooled Lawéchten., They lied to Lawéchten.*'/, comment: Lawéchten is a Nooksack language proper name; Charlie Lewiston, an Indian doctor from the area of Nooksack, Wash., had that name till his death ca. 1920 (pronounced by non-Indians as Lewiston); the name was formally passed to Brent Galloway by Alice Hunt (AH) and Louisa George (LG) at a naming ceremony 10/9/77 at Chehalis, B.C.), attested by Deming (4/27/78 and 1974-1977 as well); found in <**q'elstá:xwesthòx**>, //q'ɛl=sT-ə[=Aɛ́·=]x^{w}=sT-áx^{y}//, (irregular), comment: in this form =stá:xw is used as part of the root and a second causative =st is added, then the object pronoun suffix -òx *me*; it is not clear whether this is an error or is required and allowed to maintain the root vowel shifted into =stá:xw; normally the -exw is present only when a third person object is intended (even if it is reanalyzed and considered part of the causative and non-control suffixes, as =stexw and =lexw, as do Suttles and Hukari in other dialects of Halkomelem); but here both the e (though moved) and the xw are retained with the third person object superceded by the -òx *second person singular object* suffix, phonology: the last vowel has stress downstepped to `, attested by Deming (4/27/78).

<**q'íq'elstá:xw**>, cts and dmv //C_1í=q'ɛl=sT-ə[=Aɛ́·=]x^{w}//, EFAM /'*fooling s-o, (fool s-o as a joke, April-fool s-o [Deming])*'/, attested by Deming (2/7/80), (<**R4=**> *diminutive continuative*), phonology: reduplication, metathesis or ablaut plus vowel-reduction, morphological note: causative durative continuative, syntactic analysis: transitive verb, attested by Elders Group (3/29/78), also <**q'íq'elstaxw**>, //C_1í=q'ɛl=sT-ə[=Aɛ=]x^{w}//, [q'éq'əlstʊx^{w}], also /'*fool s-o as a joke, April-fool s-o*'/, (<**R4=**> *diminutive*), morphological note: causative durative diminutive, attested by Deming (2/7/80); found in <**q'éyq'elsthome**>, //C_1í=q'ɛl=sT-ámə//, /'*to April-fool you*'/, attested by Deming, <**q'íq'elsthòm.**>, //C_1í=q'ɛl=sT-àm//, /'*You're being fooled.*'/, attested by Elders Group (3/29/78).

So this root has four sub-entries (words derived or inflected from it directly), and the last three of these each have a sub-entry of its own. The four are <**q'áq'el**> '*believing*', <**lheq'él:exw ~ lhq'él:exw ~ lhq'élexw**> '*know s-th, know s-o*' (which has a form derived from it: <**lheq'elómet**> '*know oneself, be confident*'), <**q'élmet**> '*believe s-o, trust s-o*' (which has a form inflected from it: <**q'áq'elmet**> '*believing s-o*'), and <**q'elstá:xw**> '*fool s-o, deceive s-o, (lie to s-o [SJ])*' (which has a form derived from it: <**q'íq'elstá:xw**> '*fooling s-o, (fool s-o as a joke, April-fool s-o [Deming])*').

<**q'áq'el**> is a continuative stem (cts); later in the introduction there is a list of all such abbreviations and what they stand for. It has infixed doubling or reduplication to make it continuative (i.e. adds the -ing, thus *believing*). The infix consists of a copy of the first consonant of the root (C_1) followed by /ə/ (called schwa by linguists, spelled <e> in the Stó:lō orthography); it is inserted or infixed inside the root, after the first vowel.

<**lheq'él:exw ~ lhq'él:exw ~ lhq'élexw**> '*know something, know someone*' is the next word derived from the root. It has a prefix, <**lhe= ~ lh=**> '*use, extract, extract a portion* ', added before the root. And it has two suffixes, <**=l**> *non-control transitivizer, accidentally, happen to, manage to* and <**-exw**> *third*

person object (the *someone* or *something*) added after the root. A non-control transitivizer means that the subject doesn't have full control over what or who he/she knows, in this case, but the verb can have an object. The root vowel <**á**> is also changed in this word to <**é**>: this is called **é-ablaut** and adds the meaning *resultative* or *durative*. *Resultative* shows the meaning emphasizes the result of the action (for ex. *do* + *resultative* becomes *done*). This vowel change could also mean *durative* (continued for a long time or long duration). Putting the meanings of these morphemes together gives a literal meaning something like "happen to or managed to have used or extracted a portion of belief about someone or something" which becomes '*know something or someone*'. Halq'eméylem (and this dictionary) is filled with this kind of interesting information, which shows how words were and are made up in the language.

The entry for this word is a complicated one with lots more information about the word. There is consonant merger when the last <**l**> of the root is combined with the <**l**> of the suffix; the result is an <**l**> which is held for twice as long as a single <**l**> in the first two variants (shown by <**l:**> in the writing system); in the last variant, the second <**l**> is just dropped. These three variants are found in the Chehalis and Tait dialects, attested by the elders in the Intermediate Halkomelem Teachers Training Class (IHTTC) and by Edna Bobb, Amy Cooper, and Joe Lorenzetto (EB, AC, JL). Another place where one of these variants is attested is in the Elmendorf and Suttles article from 1960; that form is given next in the IPA. There is another variant set of pronunciations in the Chilliwack dialect, <**slhéq'el:exw ~ lhéq'el:exw ~ slhéq'elexw**>, attested by IHTTC, AC, JL, and another variant set <**slhéq'awelh ~ slhéq'ewelh**>, //s=ɬə= ́=q'ɛl=wəɬ//, subdialects: *Pilalt (Chilliwack town)* and *Chill. (Sardis)*, attested by EB, AC. This last set means *know* but lacks the <**-l-exw**> suffixes and has instead the suffix <**=welh**> which is probably <**=welh ~ =ulh ~ welh**> meaning *already*. One version leaves the root vowel unchanged, the other changes it to <**e**>, but both shift the high tone to the first syllable, and both sets of variants add a prefix <**s-**> stative (which means *be in a state of*); the literal meaning of this last variant set is "to be in a state of already extracted or used believing", thus yielding *to know someone or something.*).

The entry continues with a large number of example sentences, each with the Stó:lō orthography first, then the IPA, the meaning, then the person who attested it, and where specified, the dialect or dialects the speakers reported it to be in.

The next entry, <**lheq'elómet**> '*know oneself, be confident*', is derived from the word just discussed, <**lheq'él:exw ~ lhq'él:exw ~ lhq'élexw**>, and is a non-control reflexive stem; the suffix <**-ómet**> is *reflexive, do to oneself.* The meaning *be confident* is developed from "know oneself" and is an alloseme. There are also dialect variants in the entry for the Chilliwack dialect with *stative* <**s-**> prefixed. There is also the same consonant merger as in the previous word that <**lheq'elómet**> is derived from, and since the reflexive has a vowel with a high tone (also called high stress in lessons), the root vowel <**á**> or <**é**> is changed to low tone <**e**> (called by linguists here zero grade or schwa). The Chilliwack form is also used to mean '*understand*'. The verb is used as an intransitive verb that can't have a further object. (You can't "be confident the dogs." for example. If you want to say *know/understand the dogs,* you would use the transitive verb <**slhéq'el:exw ~ lhéq'el:exw ~ slhéq'elexw**> in the Chilliwack dialect.) There is one example sentence to conclude the entry.

The next entry or stem is <**q'élmet**>, an *indirect effect control* stem (iecs), meaning '*believe s-o, trust s-o*'. It is derived directly from the root <**q'á:l**> with a vowel change (<**é-ablaut**> *non-continuative*) and a suffix (<**=met**> *indirect effect control transitivizer*). (The reason we know this vowel change has a different meaning than the same vowel change seen in <**lheq'él:exw ~ lhq'él:exw ~ lhq'élexw**>, is because the next word is <**q'áq'elmet**> which is *continuative* and keeps the root vowel by contrast.) The suffix meaning *indirect effect control transitive* shows that believing or trusting someone has only an indirect effect on that someone (unlike *chopping carrots* which has a direct effect on the carrots). This word is a transitive verb and was attested by the Elders Group (2/16/77, 2/8/78 [U.S.-style dates]) and by Amy Cooper. A sentence example follows, showing the typical change of <**=met**> to <**=meth**> before certain pronoun suffixes.

The next form <**q'áq'elmet**> '*believing s-o*', derives from the last stem. It is a continuative stem with infixed doubling or reduplication (copies the first consonant of the root, adds <**e**> and infixes this after the first vowel of the root and before the next root consonant (<**l**>). It's also a transitive verb, attested by Elders Group (2/8/78).

The next entry or stem is <**q'elstá:xw**> *fool s-o, deceive s-o,* a causative stem (caus) and also durative (durs), and according to Susan Jimmy, [SJ], it also can mean *lie to s-o.* It has a suffix, <**=st**> *causative control transitivizer,* which applied to the root *believe* gives it a literal meaning of "cause someone to believe", thus *fool s-o, deceive s-o.* It probably has <**á:-ablaut**> *durative* on the suffix <**-exw**> (*third person object*), thus changing the <**e**> to <**á:**>; this vowel change morpheme is the only one that is applied to change vowels in suffixes–the others only change the vowel in the root. There is a possibility that the change is also to dissimilate (make the word different) from <**q'élstexw**> *return it, bring it back, give it back* which either has root <**q'ó:**> *together* or possibly <**q'ál**> *go over/around, go back on oneself, coil.* There are then a number of example sentences (labelled "example") and words (labelled "found in") of this word in use. There is a comment and history in passing of the name <**Lawéchten**> which is used in one of the sentences (the author was given this name in a formal naming ceremony in Chehalis, B.C. in 1977). This is followed by an odd example that seems to have another causative added onto this word, and some discussion about the form and alternate analyses of the causative suffix as <**=stexw**> instead of <**=st**> and my arguments against that. There is also a comment about a tone change in the last vowel of the odd form, that the tone or pitch stress is lowered (downstepped) from high to mid.

The last form in this excerpt from the dictionary is <**q'íq'elstá:xw**>, a diminutive continuative stem (all diminutive verbs are also continuative, i.e. *doing s-th a little*)(cts and dmv) and means *fooling s-o,* and according to the Deming elders also *fool s-o as a joke, April-fool s-o.* It was attested by the Deming elders on Feb.7, 1980 (2/7/80). It has prefixed reduplication (<**R4=**> *diminutive continuative*), which is made by copying the first consonant of the root, adding <**í**> and prefixing this right before the root. The word is derived from <**q'elstá:xw**>, the stem or entry before it in the dictionary. It keeps the *durative* vowel change on the suffix <**á:-ablaut**>, so there is a morphological note: causative durative and diminutive continuative. The literal meaning is "fooling someone a little for a while".

These sample entries do not show examples of every abbreviation or type of information or type of entry, but give an idea how entries are constructed and what to get out of them. To interpret the rest of the entries check out the abbreviations given later in this introduction. They show best the types of other information that can be found in various entries, and the lists can be used to look up all abbreviations. Sometimes there are entries which have words from related languages. These are given because they are cognates or words that are related to the word in Halq'eméylem and in most cases to cognate words in other sister Salish languages; linguists can follow the sound correspondences within such cognate sets and reconstruct what the word looked like in the parent language, either Proto-Central Salish or Proto-Salish for example–both are ancestors of Halq'eméylem. These cognate words are similar in shape and in meaning and follow regular sound shifts or correspondences between sister languages. They also often help us to see what the meaning of the root is or was in Halq'eméylem and confirm the spelling of the word in Halq'eméylem. For example if Squamish, Lushootseed and Nooksack have **q'** in the word and the Halq'eméylem speakers have some variation between <**q'**> and <**qw'**>, the cognates help to show that the <**q'**> is probably the correct sound in spelling the word and <**qw'**> is a recent or older variant.

The English-to-Halq'eméylem portion of this dictionary is much simpler to use. Here is a brief example. This whole portion of the dictionary is in 10-point type instead of 11-point to maintain the original headers provided by the sorting program. The English is on the left, but all the variant meanings of the Halq'eméylem word are also given to show all the allosemes and the range of meaning of each word, affix or idiom. After these allosemes, the word itself in Stó:lō orthography appears after two colons (::). Where the main entry of the word is under a root, that is shown after a < (comes from) sign.

a

the (distant and out of sight, remote), (definite but distant and out of sight, remote), the (abstract), a (remote, abstract), some, (indefinite):: kw'e.

the (male, present, visible), the (gender or presence and visibility unspecified), a (male, present and visible), a (gender or presence and visibility unspecified):: te.

abandon

leave s-o, leave s-th, go away from s-o/s-th, abandon s-o, leave s-o behind:: áyeles < á:y.

Abies amabilis or Abies grandis

prob. Abies lasiocarpa, if sample is mistaken poss. Abies amabilis or Abies grandis, if term balsam is mistaken poss. a variety of Pseudotsuga menziesii:: q'et'emá:yelhp < q'át'em.

Abies grandis:: t'ó:xw ~ t'óxw ~ t'óx̲w.

branch of probably Abies grandis:: t'óx̲wtses < t'ó:xw ~ t'óxw ~ t'óx̲w.

prob. Abies lasiocarpa, if sample is mistaken poss. Abies amabilis or Abies grandis, if term balsam is mistaken poss. a variety of Pseudotsuga menziesii:: q'et'emá:yelhp < q'át'em.

probably Abies grandis:: t'ó:xw ~ t'óxw ~ t'óx̲w.

Abies lasiocarpa

prob. Abies lasiocarpa, if sample is mistaken poss. Abies amabilis or Abies grandis, if term balsam is mistaken poss. a variety of Pseudotsuga menziesii:: q'et'emá:yelhp < q'át'em.

able

be alright, be okay, it's alright, it's okay, can, be able, it's enough, be right, be correct, that's right:: iyólem ~ iyó:lem < éy ~ éy:.

aboard

be aboard, be in (a conveyance):: eló:lh < ó:lh.

get in a canoe, get aboard:: ó:lh.

get s-th aboard (a canoe, car, conveyance):: eló:lhstexw < ó:lh.

put s-th/s-o aboard, put it on-board:: ó:lhstexw < ó:lh.

About the language

Halkomelem is an endangered Central Salish language of the Pacific Northwest (B.C. and Washington) with dialects of Upriver, Downriver, and Island Halkomelem (Elmendorf and Suttles 1960 discusses the differences between dialects as do Hill-Tout 1902 and 1904, Duff 1952, and Kava 1972). Each dialect had subdialects, and for Upriver and Island some of these remain. Gerdts (1977, 1996, 1997, and 1999 for ex.) describes some of the subdialect differences. Island Halkomelem was and is spoken on Vancouver Island from Malahat to Nanoose. Downriver Halkomelem was spoken in the downriver end of the Fraser Valley, from Vancouver to Matsqui; there are still several first language speakers of the Musqueam subdialect in Vancouver, but the last first language speaker of the Matsqui subdialect (a member of the Nooksack tribe, Alice Hunt) passed away June 2004 in Washington. Upriver Halkomelem was and is spoken between Abbotsford and Yale, B.C. and by a few speakers in Whatcom Co., Washington, members of the Nooksack Tribe there.

There are probably less than six fluent elders left who spoke Upriver Halkomelem as their first language; the same is true of Downriver Halkomelem, but the situation is somewhat better for Island

Halkomelem with probably about 50 such speakers left. Fortunately, for all three dialects, English speaking tribal members have been actively trying to learn and revive the language with the help of five or six linguists and the remaining fluent elders, and there are now some moderately fluent speakers of each. A group of about eight students, three or four years ago, finished a three-year language immersion course in Upriver Halkomelem, and there is a similar number of graduates from an earlier three-year sequence of courses given through Simon Fraser University extensions. The Stó:lō Shxwelí language department, at the Stó:lō Nation, have given classes from pre-school to adult for 15 to 20 years and for at least 10 years have also used increasingly sophisticated computer lessons which have also been developed (by Dr. Strang Burton); from about 2002 similar work has been done for Upriver Halkomelem by the Nooksack Tribe (coordinated by Catalina Renteria (a graduate of the Simon Fraser University extension program) and now for the Nooksack language by George Adams). Similar efforts have shown good success for Musqueam and Cowichan. The dialects are sufficiently different that separate full grammars have been written for them (Leslie 1979, and Hukari, In preparation for Island or Cowichan; Suttles 2004 for Musqueam (Downriver Halkomelem), and for Upriver Halkomelem (including Chilliwack, Chehalis, Pilaltxw, Sumas, and Tait subdialects) Galloway 1977a and 1993a (for people with linguistic training) and Galloway 1980a (for those without linguistic training). There are also separate dictionaries either done or being completed for each, also based on original fieldwork (Hukari and Peters 1996, and Gerdts, Compton, Edwards, Thorne, & Ulrich 1997), Suttles posthumous, in preparation by Gerdts, and the present work by Galloway).

The Upriver Halkomelem subdialects share certain phonological, morphological, syntactic, and lexical features which allow them to be considered as a unit in contrast to Downriver and Island dialects of Halkomelem. Within the Upriver area are the Chilliwack, Chehalis, Pilaltxw, Sumas, and Tait subdialects. I believe Tait includes speakers native to the following areas: Yale, Hope-Katz, Seabird Island, and Laidlaw-Cheam; Chehalis includes Chehalis and Scowlitz; Chilliwack River includes Chilliwack Landing-Rosedale (Pilaltxw), Sardis-Tzeachten, and Soowahlie-Cultus Lake (Pilaltxw includes Chilliwack Landing-Rosedale and is often considered part of the Chilliwack subdialect).. In the Nooksack-Everson-Deming area of Washington, some members of the Nooksack Tribe speak the Chilliwack River dialect (Sardis-Tzeachten), and some speak a dialect more downriver (Kilgard-Sumas and Matsqui microdialects); these last two microdialects probably form a single subdialect and seem to have some distinctive linguistic features of both Upriver and Downriver dialects. With the establishment of an ethnic curriculum and a writing system, the upriver people now refer to themselves and the downriver people in writing as the Stó:lō and politically all those except the Musqueam as the Stó:lō Nation, though in fact some reserves opt in and out of the Stó:lō Nation politically, and the more downriver groups are not politically part of the Stó:lō Nation. Linguistically, Upriver Halkomelem, Downriver Halkomelem, and Island Halkomelem will refer to the groupings of dialects.

I began work on the language in August 1970 with Mrs. Amy (Lorenzetto) (Commodore) Cooper on the Soowahlie Reserve near Vedder Crossing. I worked with her each summer (or fall) in 1970, 1971, 1972, and 1973, funded by the Survey of California and Other Indian Languages at the University of California, Berkeley. My thesis supervisor was Mary Haas. In 1972 I had only a week in the area but met the Stalo Heritage Project's Elders Group (a group of most of the fluent speakers of Upriver Halkomelem who spoke it as a first language) and worked with the group and with some individual elders twice. In 1973, Amy and I worked together from August to December; during that period, on several occasions, I also visited Mrs. Mary Charles of Seabird Island and with Mrs. Cecilia Thomas of Seabird Island (near Agassiz), who was able to tell me a number of stories in Halkomelem. I also met with Mrs. Nancy Phillips of Chehalis (on Harrison River), who was teaching the language in the Chehalis Reserve federally-funded elementary school.

Amy, her husband Albert, and I also made a trip to Yale and visited with Mrs. Margaret Emory of

Yale, who spoke only Halkomelem and Thompson. At the end of the year (Dec. 1973), I gave a speech in Halkomelem at a large spirit dance at Tzeachten; the speech was in honor of chief Richie Malloway, who put on the dance, and it also encouraged the preservation and revival of the language. I constructed the speech in Halq'eméylem, then Amy corrected my grammar in the speech and gave me stylistic pointers. Amy was good to work with--patient, diligent, always willing to work, and always willing to travel with me to visit others. She would even call people up (for ex. Elizabeth Herrling and Joe Lorenzetto) to track down particular words she could not remember. In 1974 I self-funded a short trip and was also hired by the Nooksack Tribe in Deming, Wash. to work with their Halkomelem Workshop, which had about 15 fluent speakers of Upriver Halkomelem and the last fluent speaker of Nooksack.

In 1974 I applied to the newly started Coqualeetza Education Training Centre in Sardis, B.C. to set up a Halkomelem program for them, develop a writing system, classes, train teachers, and train an elder to replace me to head the program. I was hired and moved to Chilliwack in Jan.1975. Working with both the Elders Group and the Nooksack Tribe's Halkomelem Workshop, as well as a full-time research assistant elder, through daily and weekly field work plus card files from my work with Amy Cooper (which I began in 1970), we amassed a dictionary card file of 15,000 cards of Halkomelem words with example sentences. Through several grants at different times Coqualeetza was able to employ Wilfred Charlie, Mrs. Tillie Gutierrez, Mrs. Edna Bobb, and Mrs. Amelia Douglas to help with language research and file-slipping. Tillie is and Amelia was fluent in the Tait dialect; Edna was fluent in the Chehalis dialect; and Wilfred knew a little of the Chilliwack (Sardis) dialect. Edna and I, especially, worked together from November 1975 to October 1976. As a result, I elicited, transcribed, and analyzed and she file-slipped several thousand Chehalis forms from her, as well as all the forms from the weekly elders' meetings since 1975; we also transcribed a number of songs and stories. Wilfred, Edna, and Amelia also helped me transcribe some tapes of elders' meetings going back to 1972, though many remain to be transcribed (I understand Elizabeth Phillips has since done those). Amelia and I worked together from May to September 1978 and from November 1979 to July 1980, obtaining several thousand Tait forms and transcribing more songs, conversations, and stories We made a copy of this whole set of file cards before I left the program in the hands of Mrs. Amelia Douglas, one of the graduates of the three Halkomelem Teacher Training courses for elders (Beginning, Intermediate and Advanced, abbreviated as BHTTC, IHTTC, and AHTTC). These courses taught literacy, curriculum development, phonics, grammatical structure, and also were occasions for transcribing a great many new words for the dictionary in the process. Galloway 1979a, 1988b, 2001b, 2002a and 2007a have accounts of this program and the Nooksack program in some detail.

From 1978 to 1982 I worked with Ralph Maud and Marie Weeden to transcribe and annotate all of the 50 tapes Marie's father Oliver Wells had recorded with speakers of Upriver Halkomelem (Maud, Galloway & Weeden 1978-1982), and good portions of the transcripts are published in Maud, Galloway and Weeden 1987. Mrs. Edna Bobb, my elder research assistant during this period, helped me transcribe and translate difficult recorded passages of Halkomelem. Thus, a number of speakers who were already dead when I began my work (Dan Milo, Bob Joe, Albert Louie, Harry Edwards, Mrs. Margaret Jim, and others) have contributed their knowledge to this dictionary; all their recorded words are in this dictionary, as well.

In 1984 I received a grant from the National Endowment for the Humanities to compile an Upriver Halkomelem dictionary and enter data towards a Nooksack language dictionary, learning how to enter and sort the data on computers with Dr. Bob Hsu of the University of Hawaii. Dr. Laurence Thompson and his wife, Terry, as well as Dr. Thom Hess and Vi Hilbert (táqʷšəblu) had been working on similar projects for the Thompson and Lushootseed languages, respectively. I learned the basics and a little programming in Hawaii, with their help, and thanks also to linguists at the University of Washington I was able to get started on the mainframe there. Thanks to Dr. Tim Montler and Pam Cahn, who assisted in the computer programming on the mainland and helped me progress from entering data on a Terak computer (before p.c.'s) and sorting it on the mainframe, to converting everything to a p.c. and updated programs. Thanks also to Bob Hsu who, having retired to Seattle with his wife Pam Cahn, continued working with me through the final sorts, and formatting programs to convert the results from DOS to WordPerfect 4, then WordPerfect 8, the dictionary reached a stage where it was ready for final proofing and editing. Having gotten a professorship in 1988 at Saskatchewan Indian Federated College (now First Nations University of Canada in Regina, Saskatchewan), complicated matters a bit, leaving less time for editing. In 1991 the English-to-Halkomelem sort was done. As I got to stages where the whole thing was printed out, I made copies available to the Stó:lō Shxwelí for use in classes from 1999 on. In summer 2002, the Nooksack Tribe funded recording of the English-to-Halq'eméylem portion with Mrs. Elizabeth Phillips, on digital camera. Much editing is required to get those files into shape for a CD. The 2004 edition was the first copy completely printed in WordPerfect. I gave copies of that print-out to the both the Stó:lō Shxwelí and the Nooksack language department. Bob Hsu's Lexware program, his cross-referencing program, and formatting program, which he taught me to use and helped me program, debug, and fine-tune for Halq'eméylem, have produced a dictionary I am satisfied with and have allowed me to search for and correct inconsistencies, formatting errors caused by inconsistent data entry, etc. Galloway 1984c, 1985a, 1985b, 1986d, 1987a , 1989c, 1991d, and 1992a describe the use and progress of these programs and my dictionary projects. Thanks also to the Social Sciences and Research Council of Canada for several grants to allow the conversion of all my reel-to-reel and cassette tapes of Halkomelem, Nooksack, Samish, and some of Nakoda to CDs and presentation of these to the Stó:lō Nation Archives, the Nooksack tribe, the Samish tribe, and the First Nations University Indian Languages department, respectively. Thanks also to my research assistants, Mary Wilde, Darren Okemaysim, and Sonja van Eijk, who computerized all the Nooksack data and Sonja who converted all the tapes to CD's, allowing the start of the revival of the Nooksack language and the Samish language.

About the elders

A dictionary of this scope would not have been possible without the wonderful knowledge, help, and good humor of the elders I was able to work with on both sides of the border and the elders who contributed information to earlier linguists before I began my studies (for ex. "Captain John" Sualis of Soowahlie who worked with Charles Hill-Tout ca 1900-1902; Amy Cooper lived with Captain John when she married his son Commodore). Galloway 1980 and 1993 both have photos of most (if not all) of the elders whose knowledge contributed to this dictionary; Maud, Galloway and Weeden 1987 has photos of those elders whom Oliver Wells recorded, whose knowledge also contributed to this dictionary.

What follows are several lists of elders I worked with or transcribed tapes of: 1) alphabetically by last name with their affiliations and Indian names, 2) a compilation, organized by subdialect, of which elders spoke which subdialects of Halq'eméylem, 3) a list alphabetized by abbreviations used for them, abbreviations used (basically their first initial and last initial), and 4) a list of all the sister languages of Halkomelem, classified into branches and showing their dialects and the abbreviations used for their names in this dictionary and in the field of Salishan linguistics in general.

Then follows a brief technical section for those trained in linguistics on how to use the dictionary. After that, follows a list of abbreviations for each different type of information, then a list of syntactic abbreviations used in the syntactic analysis sections of each entry. After that is a section giving a key to convert from the Stó:lō writing system or orthography to the IPA. Finally is a bibliography of the references used (plus a few referred to but not actually seen by me on Downriver and Island Halkomelem).

COQUALEET7A ELDERS GROUP:	INDIAN NAMES (SO FAR AS KNOWN)
Louise Bolan	Xwiyéym
Tillie Bordon	
Danny Charlie	Tísele, nickname Sp'éqw'oya from sp'éqw 'proud'
Madeline Charlie	Temitátkwō, Thompson name
Wilfred Charlie	Kwethómet
Mandy Charnley	Tá:wtelót, Katzie name
Amy Cooper	Óyewòt
Amelia Douglas	Siyamíya, nickname Táneki
Dolly Felix	Tselx̲át, a Boothroyd Thompson name
Rosaleen George*	Yamelót
Al Gutierrez	Swolésiya
Tillie Gutierrez	Xwiyálemot, from xwayólem 'gift one really makes use of'
Elizabeth Herrling*	Ts'ats'elexwót
Lucy Jackson	
Lawrence James	Teméxwtel
Lizzie Johnson	Siyámíya
Flora Julian	
Agnes Kelly	Siyámiyò;t
Francis Kelly	
Philornena Kelly	Siyó:mót
Ed Leon Sr.	Swelímeltxw, name from Soowahlie Púlemqen, Port Douglas name
Joe Lorenzetto	Páthiyetel
Jeanne McIntyre	Selhámiya
Teresa Michell	Siyámtelòt, Tl'pá'a, Port Douglas name
Shirley Norris*	Tselóyóthelwet
Hank Pennier	nicknames Swék'ten and Sénde
Maggie Pennier	T'esóts', Port Douglas name
Evangeline Pete	Nickname Ta's
Bertha Peters	
Mabel Peters	Kweláxtelot
Mary Peters	Málí
Susan (Josh) Peters	Siyámò:t, Th'atísiya
Albert Phillips	
Elizabeth Phillips	Siyámiyatéliyòt
Nancy Phillips	Sí:le Qwet'óselwet
Alice Point	Th'ith'exwemlómét, name from Soowahlie, her grandmother's name
Roy Point	Siyólewethet
Jean Silver	
Cecilia Thomas	Slóx̲iya, Ow'elóxwelwet (name of Thunder too), Ts'símteló:t (daughter of Mt. Cheam)
Henry Thomas	Chewóteleq

(*joined group after it was no longer called Coqualeetza Elders Group; this group still meets weekly)

STALO HERITAGE PROJECT ELDERS GROUP: (besides most of those already listed)

Peter Bolan	Has 2 names: Xwelíkw'eltel and one other
Mary Charles	Láime', Thompson name
Seraphine Dick	Ts'esqílwet
Adeline Lorenzetto	Ow'et'ósiya, X̲éyelwet, Tesyákw'ō (Thompson name

OTHERS WHO CONTRIBUTED HALKOMELEM AT ELDERS MEETINGS AT SARDIS

Joe Alec	
Andy Alex	
Clara Campbell	
Annie Grace Chapman	
Ben James	
Flossie Joe (dau. of Isaac Joe, Bob Joe's brother)	
Rose Jones	
Stanley Jones	
Delphine Kelly	
Ed Kelly Sr. (Sumas/Matzqui dial.)	
Richie Malloway Sr.	Th'eláchiyatel
Jimmy Peters (Katz subdial.)	
P.D. Peters (Katz subdial.)	
Mary Lou Sepass	
Johnny Williams Sr. (Scowlitz subdial.)	

HALKOMELEM WORKSHOP ELDERS GROUP (NOOKSACK TRIBE)-,

Martha Castillo	Ts'etósiya
George Cline	Lex̲é:ym (Nooksack name)
Martha Cline	Siyamelhót (Tzeachten name)
Norma Cline	Thxwólemòt (Tzeachten name)
Mamie Cooper	Ts'átsesamíya (Musqueam name)
Esther Fidele	Sthő:nelh (Nooksack name)
Louisa George	Tsisxwísalh, Tsisyúyud (Skagit name)
Mabel Hicks	Sló'met (Deroche name)
Alice Hunt	Gyi'xdémqe (a Cape Mudge Kwakwala name), Soyó:lhéwet, Siyáme (name of Agnes James)
Sindick Jimmy	X̲á:x̲wemelh (a Nooksack name)
Susan Jimmy	Chúchowelwet (Yakweakwioose name from Squamish)
Joe Louie	Sákwelti, spelled Sacquilty by him
Ernie Paul	Gwítsideb (Skagit name)
Helen Paul	Tsetósiya (Shxway or Skway name)
Ella Reid	X̲ó:lelh
Bill Roberts	Snúlhem'qen (Nooksack name) lyésemqel (Stó:1ō name)
Matilda Sampson	Xwélhiya
Philoniena Solomon	(name not remembered)
Dan Swaneset	Selhámeten (Nooksack name)

Elizabeth Jane Swaneset	Lísepet
Maria Villanueva	Siyémchesót (Yakweakwioose name)
Clara Williams	Iyálh (Soowahlie name)
Ollie (Olive) Williams	Swolesót (Soowahlie name)
Walt Williams	Dedíchbed (Skagit name from "Dutchman")

ELDERS ON WELLS TAPES:

Bob Joe	X̱welx̱wé:yleq
Dan Milo	Lhó:kw'elàlèxw
Mrs. Margaretta Jim (Mrs. August Jim)	Sqewóthelwet
Edmund Joe Peters (husband of Mary Peters)	
Harry Edwards	
Albert Louie	(wasn't given an Indian name)
John Wallace	
Mrs. Lena Hope	
Mrs. Maggie Emory	

<u>Chilliwack dialect:</u> Mrs. Amy (Mary Amy Lorenzetto) Cooper (1886-1975), Vedder Crossing, Soowahlie Reserve (AC); Mrs. Nancy Phillips, Sardis, late of Chehalis (NP); Lawrence James, Chilliwack Landing (LJ1); Danny Charlie, Sr., Chilliwack Landing (DC); Mrs. Susan Jimmy, Sardis, late of Everson, Washington (SJ1); Mrs. Marie Villanueva, Sardis, late of Everson (MV); Mrs. Mamie Cooper, Sardis, late of Everson (MC); Roy Point, Sardis (RP); Richard Malloway, Sr., Sardis (RM); Mrs. Philomena Solomon, late of Everson (PS1); Dan Milo, Sardis, Scowkale Reserve (DM); Bob Joe, Sardis, Tzeachten Reserve (BJ), Albert Louie, Yeqwyeqwíws Res. (AL), Ben James (some Chill.) (BJ2), Bill Roberts (BR), Esther Fidele (also some Nooksack)(EF), Elizabeth Herrling* (EH), Flossie Joe (FJ), Joe Louie, John Wallace, Soowahlie (JW), Louisa George, (also Skagit & Nooksack)(LG), Martha Cline (MC), Mabel Hicks (MH), Mabel Peters some Chilliwack and Downriver, Olive ("Ollie") Williams (dau. of AC)(OW), Shirley (Julian) Norris, (also Cowichan & some Chehalis) (SN), Wilfred Charlie, some Chilliwack, late of Scowkale, Martha Castillo* (Nooksack Tribe), Francis Kelly of Soowahlie, Tillie Bordon late of Chilliwack (TB).

<u>Chehalis dialect:</u> Ed Leon, Sr., Chehalis (EL); Mrs. Dolly Felix, Scowlitz, late of Chehalis (DF); Hank Pennier, Scowlitz (HP) and wife Mrs. Maggie Pennier, formerly from Chehalis (MP1); Mrs. Lizzie Johnson, late of Seabird Island (LJ2); Mrs. Edna Bobb, Chehalis, late of Seabird Island (EB); Mrs. Teresa Michell, Chehalis, late of Cheam Reserve (TM); Mrs. Philomena Kelly, Deroche (PK), Adeline Lorenzetto, Ohamil (AL), Albert Phillips, Chehalis (AP), Alice Point, Chehalis, Rosaleen George (RG), Seraphine Dick, Scowlitz (SD).

<u>Tait dialect:</u> Mrs. Cecilia Thomas, Cheam, late of Seabird Island (CT); her husband Henry Thomas, Cheam, late of Seabird Island (HT); Mrs. Susan (Josh) Peters, Union Bar, late of Seabird Island (SP); Mrs. Amelia Douglas, American Bar, late of Cheam Reserve #2 (AD); Mrs. Tillie Gutierrez* and husband Al Gutierrez, both of Katz (TG, AG); Mrs. Agnes Kelly, Laidlaw (AK); Joe Lorenzetto, Laidlaw, late of Boston Bar (JL); Mrs. Mary Peters, American Bar, late of Chilliwack (MP2); Mrs. Philomena Seymour, late of Seabird Island (PS2); Mrs. Maggie Emery, Yale (ME); Stanley Jones, Laidlaw, some Tait (SJ2); tapes of Mrs. Margaret Jim, Laidlaw (MJ), Adeline Lorenzetto, Ohamil (AL), Edmund Joe Peters (husband of Mary Peters), Skw'átets (EJP), Elizabeth Phillips* (also some Chehalis) (EP), Harry Edwards, Cheam (HE), Mrs. Lena Hope, Spuzzum (also Thompson, some Tait

(LH), P.D. Peters (Peter D. Peters), Katz (PDP), Rose Jones, Ohamil, some Tait (RJ)

Sumas/Kilgard dialect: Mrs. Jeanne Silver, Kilgard (JS); Peter "Speedy" Bolan (PB); Mrs. Ella (Cline) Reid, Kilgard, late of Everson (ER); Mrs. Alice (Cline) Hunt, Matsqui, of Everson, late of Bellingham (AH), Ed Kelly Sr. (EK), Delphine Kelly (DK).

Downriver Halkomelem dialects: GC George Cline, Matqui (GC), Norma Cline, Matsqui, Alice Hunt some Chilliwack (AH), perhaps Matilda Sampson, also some Lummi, Mandy Charnley, Katzie, Evangeline Pete, some Katzie, some Tait.

All those in the dialect list above but RM, DM, and BJ are or were members of the Coqualeetza Elders Group (more recently the Stó:lō Elders Group) or the Halkomelem Workshop at Deming. All of those listed were or are fluent speakers (except where "some" appears before the dialect), but this is not a complete list of the members of the two groups, nor of all the fluent speakers. It is a list of those from whom I have had specific forms or with whom I have had interviews. MP2 and her sister ME spoke Halkomelem and Thompson but little or no English. MJ spoke only Halkomelem and no English. Only those with asterisks by the names in the list above were still alive in 2008.

Elders' names by abbreviations in dictionary
AC Amy Cooper
AD Amelia Douglas
AG Al Gutierrez
AH Alice Hunt
AK Agnes Kelly
AL Albert Louie*
AL Adeline Lorenzetto
AP Albert Phillips
AP Alice Point*
BJ Bob Joe
BJ2 Ben James
BR Bill Roberts
CT Cecilia Thomas
CW Clara Williams
DC Danny Charlie
DF Dolly Felix
DK Delphine Kelly
DM Dan Milo
DS Dan Swaneset
EB Edna Bobb
EF Esther Fidele
EH Elizabeth Herrling
EJP Edmund Joe Peters (husband of Mary Peters)
EJS Elizabeth Jane Swaneset
EK Ed Kelly Sr.
EL Ed Leon Sr.
EP Ernie Paul*
EP Evangeline Pete*
EP Elizabeth Phillips

ER Ella Reid
FJ Flossie Joe (dau. of Isaac Joe, Bob Joe's brother)
FK Francis Kelly
GC George Cline
HE Harry Edwards
HP Helen Paul*
HP Hank Pennier
HT Henry Thomas
JL Joe Lorenzetto
JL Joe Louie*
JS Jean Silver
JW John Wallace
LB Louise Bolan
LG Louisa George
LH Mrs. Lena Hope
LJ Lizzie Johnson
LJ Lawrence James*
MC Martha Cline
MC Mandy Chamley*
MC Mamie Cooper*
MC Madeline Charlie*
MC Mary Charles*
ME Mrs. Maggie Emory
MH Mabel Hicks
MJ Mrs. Margaretta Jim (Mrs. August Jim)
MP Mabel Peters*
MP Mary Peters*
MP Maggie Pennier
MS Matilda Sampson*
MV Maria Villa nueva
NC Norma Cline*
NP Nancy Phillips
OW Olive ("Ollie") Williams
PB Peter Bolan
PDP P.D. Peters (Peter D. Peters)
PK Philomena Kelly
PS Philomena Solomon*
PS2 Philomena Seymour
RG Rosaleen George
RJ Rose Jones
RM Richie Malloway Sr.
RP Roy Point
SD Seraphine Dick
SJ Susan Jimmy
SJ2 Stanley Jones*
SN Shirley Norris
SP Susan (Josh) Peters
TB Tillie Bordon

TG Tillie Gutierrez
TM Teresa Michell
WC Wilfred Charlie
WW Walt Williams

80 names in this list
*not cited in dictionary by abbreviation but by full name to prevent ambiguity with abbreviations of those cited more often.

Abbreviations of related Salish languages and dialects cited in the dictionary
(where no abbreviation was used in dictionary none is given here)
I Bella Coola Division
1) Bella Coola (BC)
II Central [Coast] Division (Central Salish)
2) Comox (Cx) (Island Comox [ICx], Mainland Comox [MCx])
3) Pentlatch (Pt)
4) Sechelt (Se)
5) Squamish (Sq)
6) Halkomelem (Hk)(3 dialect groups listed below)
a) Upriver Halkomelem (UHk) (Chilliwack [Chill.], Chehalis [Cheh.], Tait)
b) Downriver Halkomelem (DHk)(Musqueam [Ms], Kwantlen, Katzie)
c) Island Halkomelem (IHk)(Nanaimo, Chemainus, Cowichan [Cw])
7) Nooksack (Nk)
8) Northern Straits (Saanich [Sn or Saan], Sooke [So], Songish [Sg], Lummi [Lm], Samish [Sm or Sam][with subdialects Sma Samish-a[Suttles], Smb Samish-b) (Galloway)], Semiahmoo)
9) Southern Straits (SSt) = Clallam or Klallam (Cl)
10) Lushootseed [Puget (Sound) Salish] (Ld) (Northern incl. Skagit, etc., Southern)
11) Twana (Tw)
III Tsamosan [Olympic] Division
12) Quinault (Queets, Quinault)
13) Lower Chehalis
14) Upper Chehalis
15) Cowlitz
IV Oregon Division
16) Tillamook (Tillamook, Siletz)
V Interior Division
A) Northern
17) Lillooet [St'át'imcets] (Lill.)(Upper [Lillooet-Fountain], Lower [Mount Currie-Douglas])
18) Shuswap (Sh) (Western, Eastern)
19) Thompson
B) Southern
20) Colville-Okanagan (Ok) (Northern, Southern)
21) Columbian (Cb)
22) Spokane-Kalispel-Flathead (Spokane, Kalispel, Flathead ["Selish"])
23) Coeur d'Alene (Cd)

How to Use the Dictionary (an introduction for those with linguistic training)

The Quick-Start section in the beginning of this introduction shows how to use the dictionary, how it is set up, and gives some simple and complex examples of entries and how to read and use them. It is written for those wishing to use the dictionary who aren't linguists. A few more details are given here in technical language for linguists.

The Halq'eméylem-to-English section is a root dictionary, with cross-references to show each word and which root it has (where more information is given about that word). All affixes are also given with examples of words in which they occur. I have tried to discover the root of every word, but some resist further analysis (unanalyzed stems). Cognates have assisted with this derivation.

Each headword (or entry) begins with a transcription of the word in the Stó:lō orthography, which I developed in 1975 from slight modifications of the Bouchard orthography. Then the morphological category (abbreviation in table below) come next. IPA transcriptions, morphophonemic (with all affixes segmented), then sometimes phonemic and/or phonetic transcriptions, where notable, follow next. All variant meanings are given (allosemes) and semantic domains and subdomains are given for each in all-caps; these domains and subdomains also provide the semantic environment of allosemes of surrounding words in the sentence or nearby text or conversation, which help speakers and learners to predict which alloseme is most likely for each word. Full information is given about any dialect limitations of forms or variants. The source of each word (the speaker or speakers) is given for each word and example sentence. Most entries have example sentences obtained in linguistic field-work. I have not included any forms I have made up, except for a handful (less than 15) which have been verified by named speakers. Other sources are given for words obtained by earlier linguists from Gibbs (1858-1863) to as late as data from Su Urbanczyk in 2002. Cognates have been found for a huge number of words and are given; many were obtained from the work of Aert Kuipers and others before his published Salish Etymological Dictionary. I have not rechecked all those, but obtained many from other published sources or the linguists themselves by personal correspondence in the 1970's.

There is a wide range of phonological processes, morphological comments, syntactic comments, and semantic comments, the latter including cultural information. The morphological and syntactic categories of each word are given as well. Since the Proto-Central Salish stative prefix /ʔas-/ has become /s-/ in Upriver Halkomelem, and since the nominalizer /s=/ has the same shape, there are a huge number of words beginning with <s> (angle brackets enclose graphemes). I have put them all under their roots but have also cross-referenced them all under the letter <**s**>. The nominalizer <**shxw=**> also has many words cross-referenced to the roots where the words are found in more detail. A similar process was followed with all other words with prefixes. Scientific names are given for all flora and fauna (based on earlier work I did and aided by work on other languages by Nancy Turner, Randy Bouchard, Dorothy Kennedy, and others, see References).

There is an extensive English-to-Halkomelem section after the Halkomelem-to-English section just discussed; it is a finder-list or index (some 667 pages or so) for looking up each meaning of each morpheme, affix, word, and idiom. Thus it doesn't have detail on the analysis of the Halkomelem forms except to list what root or stem they may be found under; since they are cross-referenced one can just look up the word directly in the first section of the dictionary to find the root where more information is given.

The Halq'eméylem-to-English section is arranged in alphabetical order by the Stó:lō or Halq'eméylem orthography (**a, ch, ch', e, h, i, k, k', kw, kw', l, lh, m, n, o, ō, p, p', q, q', qw, qw', R** (reduplication)**, s, sh, t, t', th, th', tl', ts, ts', u, w, x, xw, x̲, x̲w, y, '**). I have found the articulatory order used in dictionaries by some Dutch linguists to be more difficult to use myself, and it would require additional linguistic training for beginning students of the language who have not yet studied linguistics. Angle brackets (for graphemes) show that an entry or example is in the Halq'eméylem orthography. Square brackets enclose phonetic transcriptions, single slashes enclose phonemic transcriptions, double slashes enclose segmented morphophonemic transcriptions and allomorphs–all of these are in the International Phonetic Alphabet or IPA. Violin brackets sometimes enclose morphemes. Square brackets with single quotes enclose allosemes, the semantically similar, variant meanings of a morpheme, word, or idiom which are predictable in degree of likelihood from the semantic environment (especially from matching subdomains of the allosemes) of the surrounding words, sentences, or speech event and shared culture and other shared information between speaker and hearer. Slashes with single quotes enclose sememes (shortened summaries or lists of all or the most common meanings of a morpheme, word, or idiom). Each sememe (as in the work of Bloomfield and Nida separately) is the sum total of all the allosemes or variant meanings of a morpheme, word, or idiom. Double slashes plus single quotes enclose morphosememic transcriptions (which show alternations of sememes, much as double slashes alone show alternations of phonemes). These levels and notations are discussed in my work on Three-Dimensional Semantics (for ex. Galloway 1971, 1977a, 1987b, 1989b, c, d, 1992a, 1993a, b, c), more recently called Multidimensional Semantics or Integrated Cognitive Semantics (Galloway 2000b, 2001a).

The types of information included in the Halq'eméylem-to-English portion are included in the following order:

1) roots, affixes, or words in the orthography;
2) after some affixes come the International Phonetic Alphabet (Americanist) phonemic transcription,
3) second in the other entries is the morphemic class (abbreviated) of the head entry (free root, da = derivational affix, ia = inflectional affix, iecs = indirect effect control stem, etc., see below for list with all these);
4) the semantic domain or subdomain of the first alloseme (in all caps, abbreviated in most cases, PRON = PRONOUNS, ABDF = ANIMAL BODY DYSFUNCTIONS, SPRD = SPIRIT DANCING, etc., see below for a complete list);
5) the alloseme or sememic transcription of the first meaning of the entry;
6) sometimes another domain or subdomain name where the alloseme has membership in more than one domain (domain names show the semantic context which makes the alloserne most likely in that context);
7) where there are allosemes in different domains the new domain name is next followed by the alloseme;
8) a phonetic or phonological comment, if any;
9) morphological comment, if any;
10) syntactic comment, if any;
11) other sources of this word or affix in any dialect of Halkomelem;
12) cognates in related languages (with abbreviated language name, IPA transcription, abbreviation of source for this word)
13) dialect variants, if any, with initials of the elders or elders groups which attested the entry (for ex., AC = Mrs. Amy Cooper; IHTTC = Intermediate Halq'eméylem Teacher Training Course with ten elders, etc., see lists above);
14) examples of the morpheme (in words or sentences) or examples of the word (in phrases or sentences, whenever available, first in the Halq'eméylem orthography, then in the IPA (Americanist) transcription;
15) the translation of the word, phrase or sentence;
16) the initials of the elder or elder's group that attested the word, phrase, or sentence;.
17) after the root entries are complete, next come derivations of the root, with the 16 types of information just listed for roots listed for each derivation, each derivation is indented once from the entry it derives from;
18) next come derivations of the previous derivation with information in the same order--if there are no such subderivations then the next derivation from the root or word follows.

The following is a list of abbreviations used for all semantic domains and subdomains and other abbreviations (in all cases these were labels for particular types of information). All abbreviations in all-capital letters are for information in English; most are domain or subdomain names. All abbreviations in all-small letters have information in Halq'eméylem. A number of these abbreviations have been replaced by the full terms throughout the dictionary. Although this may add a few pages, it makes the dictionary much easier to use; a dictionary where every other term has to be looked up in charts of abbreviations is difficult to use. Since the language is so endangered, I hope it will be used extensively by learners and teachers, so ease of use is crucial if the language is to survive. Even if the dictionary can't be used all the time by learners, it will hopefully serve to document and preserve the large amount of knowledge the elders have passed on here.

Labels used for each different type of information (fields or bands, Band labels)

A attested by
ABDF animal body dysfunctions (incl. human)(subdomain)
ABFC animal body functions (incl. human)(subdomain)
ABI animal (incl. human) body insults (subdomain)
ACL acculturated (post-contact) meaning
alt alternative name
ANA anatomy
ANAA anatomy--animal (subdomain)
ANAB anatomy--bird (subdomain)
ANAF anatomy--fish (subdomain)
ANAH anatomy--human (subdomain)
ANAR anatomy--reptile (subdomain)
ant antonym
asin as in (example of affix in a word)
ASM alloseme
ASP aspect (subdomain of TIME)
bens benefactive stem
BLDG buildings (names, parts, functions, how to make them)(subdomain)
BOT botanical scientific name (in Latin)
BSK basketry (types, parts, functions, how to make)(subdomain)
CAN canoes and other transportation (types, parts, functions, verbs for making, repairing and canoeing [strokes, etc.])(subdomain)
caus causative control stem
cdia see dialect form (fewer dialects have this form or dialects which are not the original source of the main form)
cf compare with form
cfr compare with root
cfs compare with stem
CH Christianity (subdomain)
chrs characteristic stem
CJ conjunctions and logical operators
ck check Indian form
CK check English form
CLO clothing and ornaments (names, parts, functions, how to make, may incl. WV as subsubdomain)(subdomain)
CM linguist's commentary
cmdf see main dialect form (this form is found in more dialects or in a dialect which is the original source of the word)

CONV conversation and speech (domain)
cpds compound stem
cpvs comparative stem
CST change of physical state (inanimate)(domain?)
CSR constructions other than buildings (names, parts, functions, how to construct them)(subdomain)
ctr contrast (with following word or words of similar meaning)
cts continuative stem
D dialectal limitation
DEM demonstrative (domain)(prob. subsumed under DIR)
DESC descriptive words (incl. diminutive)(domain)
df derived form (root or derivational affix unclear)
di derivational infix
DIR directions (general adverbs, prepositions and demonstratives)(domain)
dmn diminutive nominal
dms diminutive stem
dmv diminutive verb
dnom derived nominal
dp derivational prefix
drs derivational suffix
ds derived stem
durs durative stem
EB ethnobotany (common names)(domain of flora)
EFAM emotions, feelings, attitudes, mental processes, interjections (domain)
ETH ethnographic information
EZ ethnozoology (common names)(domain of fauna, incl. man)
FIRE fire features and functions (domain)
FOLK folk classification (groupings and hierarchies)
FOOD food (domain)
FR borrowed from (lists language name, then ^Indian word^)(^ = cap6)
FRP possibly borrowed from
frqs frequentative stem
FSH fishing (devices, parts, functions, processing the catch, making the devices)(subdomain)
G gloss (of single-word example)
GA grammatical analysis
GAM games (domain)
GC grammatical comment (incl. morphological categories)
HARV harvesting (devices, parts and functions, techniques, how to make the devices, processing the harvest)(subdomain)
HAT human age terms (subdomain)
HHG household goods (names, parts, functions, how to make)(subdomain, prob. subsubdomain under BLDG)
HUMC categories of humans (domain)(includes subdomains: HAT, KIN, SOC, N)
HUNT hunting (devices, parts, functions, techniques, how to make devices, processing the catch)(subdomain)
IC informant's commentary
IDOC Indian doctoring (subdomain)
ie in-context example (phrase or sentence)
iecs indirect effect control stem

ii inflectional infix
IL illustration (to show source)?
incs. inceptive stem
inss instrumental stem
ip inflectional prefix
irg irregular form(s)
is inflectional suffix
its iterative stem
izs intransitivized stem
KIN kinterms (subdomain)
LAND land features and functions (domain)
LIT (=SMM) literal meaning (triggers sememic notation /' '/)
LO loanword (probably not needed, FR band will suffice)?
LT qualities of light (subdomain)
lx lexical affix (not to replace semological band as main entry)
MC material culture (domain)(incl. subdomains: BLDG, BSK, CAN, CLO, CSR, FSH, HARV, HHG, HUNT, MUS, TOOL, WV)
mdls middle voice stem
MED medical information (techniques, medicines, functions, how to prepare, mainly secular) (subdomain, merges at edge with REL:IDOC)
MOOD moods: interrog., subjunct., imperative, declarative (domain)
mos motion stem (in ye-)
mpcl modal particle
MUS music (names, parts, functions, devices, techniques, techniques for making the devices and using them)(subdomain)
MYC myth character name (subsubdomain of N)
N personal names (inherited, nicknames)(subdomain of HUMC)
nca numeral classifier affix
ncr non-control root
ncrs non-control reflexive stem
ncs non-control stem
NOG no gloss
NUM numerals, their functions, and plurals (domain)
numc numeral compound ?
numr numeral root
nums numeral stem
o orthography
OS other sources (gives source ref. and form)
pbf probable form
PBG probable gloss
pbr probable root
PC phonological comment (incl. phonological processes: backing or fronting (bof), consonant alternation (ca), consonant merger (cmrg), glottalization and deglottalization (gl), labialization and delabialization (lab), metathesis (M), ablaut (A), vowel merger (vmrg), stress-shift (- ´- or = ´=), lengthening (-:-, =:=), stressed transitivizer (stz), stressed intransitivizer (siz), etc.)
pcr purposeful control root
pcrs purposeful control reflexive stem
pcs purposeful control stem

phm	phonemic transcription
phn	phonetic transcription
pln	plural nominal
PLN	place name (subdomain)
plr	plural root
pls	plural stem
plv	plural verb
pncs	psychological non-control stem
posf	possible form
POSG	possible gloss
posr	possible root
POW	spirits and powers
prcs	Proto-Central Salish
PRON	pronouns (definite, indefinite, etc.)(domain)
prr	perhaps related to root
psal	Proto-Salish
Q	questionable ?
QUAL	qualifiers (general adverbial)(domain)
r	root (bound root form)
rcps	reciprocal stem
rej	rejected form
REL	religion (domain)(incl. subdomains: CH, IDO, POW, SPD)
rfls	reflexive stem
rsls	resultative stem
rf	root form (free root form)
S	source reference
sas	structured activity stem
SCG	Salish cognate
SD	sound (subdomain)
SENS	senses and perceptions (domain)(incl. subdomains: LT, SD, SM, TAST, TCH)
SM	smell (subdomain)
SMC	semantic comment
SME	semantic environment (which conditions allosemes)(=old SMC band)
SMM	morphosememic development (triggers //' '// notation; used only where a combination of sememes (meanings of morphemes or words or phrases) produces a meaning different that the sum of its parts)
SMN	semantic transcription (narrow semantic info., semantic components, triggers semantic notation [' '])(allosemes could be listed here but are usually listed under domains as subentries)
SPRD	spirit dancing (subdomain) (could use SPD)
SQ	posited source
STA	syntactic analysis
SOC	social terms (status, occupational, tribal, national, social transactions, etc.) (subdomain)
STC	syntactic comment
stca	stative causative control stem
stie	stative indirect effect control stem
stnc	stative non-control stem
stpc	stative purposeful control stem
stpn	stative psychological non-control stem

stvi stative intransitive verb stem
strs stative resultative ? stem
su see under stem
syn synonym
TAST taste (subdomain)
TCH touch (subdomain)
TIB transitivizers, intransitivizers, benefactives (subdomain)
TIME time periods and tenses (domain)
tlcs translocational? stem
TN translation of sentence example
TOOL tools for making things (names, parts, techniques for making and using)(subdomain)
TVMO travel and motion (domain)
uf underlying form (morphophonemic, triggers // // notation)
us unanalyzable stem
US usage (sociolinguistic comments, etc.)
UX unexplained form or problem
UXB unexplained botanical identification or info.
UXG unexplained grammatical detail
UXH historical or comparative notes
UXP unexplained phonological detail
UXPN unexplained place name info.
UXQ adjustments required between files ?
UXZ unexplained zoological identification or info.
VALJ value judgements (domain)
vir intransitive verb root
vis intransitive verb stem
VOIC voice (active, middle, reflexive, reciprocal, passive)(subdomain)
WATR water features and functions
WETH weather features and functions
WV weaving (techniques, devices, parts, dyeing, designs, functions) (subsubdomain)
ZOO scientific zoological name (in Latin)

SYNTACTIC ABBREVIATIONS
adem adverbial demonstrative
apas ambiguous past
apcl adverbial particle
aug augmentative
avop active verb object pronoun
avps past adverbial
cau causative control (purposeful)
chr characteristic
cj conjunction
cptv completive aspect
cpv comparative
ct continuative aspect
dema demonstrative article
demc demonstrative conjunction
demp demonstrative pronoun

dm	diminutive
drv	directive (may only be in Nooksack)?
dst	distributive
dur	durative aspect
frq	frequentative aspect
fut	future tense
hbt	habitual aspect
hpas	historical past tense
icsp	independent clause subject pronoun
iec	indirect effect control
ij	interjection
imp	imperative
inc	inceptive aspect
ind	indirective ?
inom	indefinite nominal
inp	independent nominal pronoun
ins	instrumental (creates words for devices, etc.)(need better label) ?
iopv	independent object of prepositional verb
ipp	independent possessive pronoun
it	iterative aspect
ivp	independent verbal pronoun
mdl	middle voice
ncm	non-control middle ?
nct	non-control transitive
nctv	non-continuative aspect
ndem	nominal demonstrative
nmps	nominal past
nom	nominal
np-a	nominal phrase minus article
npa	nominal phrase with apposition
npas	negative habitual past
npc	nominal phrase with conjoining
npm	nominal phrase with modifier(s)
nps	simple nominal phrase
nqps	negative interrogative past
oc	out-of-control
pasf	past affixed
pass	passive
pcl	particle
pcsa	purposeful control structured activity
pcsi	purposeful control stem inanimate object preferred
per	persistent
pers	persistent stem
pl	plural
pnc	psychological non-control
ppl	participle (=stative)
pres	present tense
prof	professional

psv possessive
psvf possessive pronoun affix
qaf interrogative affix
qpas interrogative past
rcp reciprocal
rfl reflexive
rlcl relative clause
rpt repetitive aspect
rsl resultative
sa structured activity
sbcl subordinate clause
scjs sentence + coordinating conjunction + sentence
scpv sentence comparative
sij sentence with interjection
siz stressed intransitivizer
sjsp subjunctive subject pronoun
sna sentence with nominal in apposition
spp sentence with prepositional phrase
ssjp sentence with subjunctive phrase
sspv sentence superlative
st stative aspect (=ppl)
stz stressed transitivizer
svpa sentence with verb phrase in apposition
tlc translocational ?
vadv adverbial verb
vaj adjectival verb
vaux auxiliary verb
vdem demonstrative verb
vpad verb phrase with adverbial verb, adverbial particle, or adverbial demonstrative
vpmd verb phrase with modal particle
vpn verb phrase with negative
vppa verb phrase with past tense
vpq verb phrase with yes/no interrogative
vpro pronominal verb, = verbal pronoun
vprp prepositional verb
vpx verb phrase with auxiliary
vq interrogative verb
xpas auxiliary past

Spelling and orthography

The Key below gives the International Phonetic Alphabet (Americanist) equivalents for each symbol in the Stó:lō orthography. Orthographic symbols which are made up of two or three characters (digraphs and trigraphs resp.) are always pronounced as a single sound, a unit and almost never occur as clusters to two or more sounds. When they do (as in éts-'ets *stutter*), a hyphen separates them. Notice that the writing system is phonemic in almost every case. Only /c/ and /s/ have allophones which are written differently from each other in the Stó:lō orthography.

Key to the Official Orthography of Upriver Halkomelem

Stó:lō Orthography	IPA equivalents
<a>	= /ɛ/ [æ] before length or under high or mid tone (<a:, á, à>) with rare exceptions
<a>	= /ɛ/ [ɛ] elsewhere, i.e., under low tone (unmarked) and short (<a>)
<ch>	= /c/ [č]
<ch'>	= /c'/ [č']
<e>	= /ə/ [ɪ] between or next to palatal sounds <l, lh, x, y, s, ts, ts'>[l, ɬ, x^{y}, y, s, ¢, ¢']
<e>	= /ə/ [ʊ] between or next to labial(ized) sounds <m,w, kw, kw', qw, qw', xw, xw> [m,w, k^{w}, k'^{w}, q^{w}, q'^{w}, x^{w}, x̣^{w}]
<e>	= /ə/ [ʌ ~ ə] elsewhere
<h>	= /h/ [h]
<i>	= /i/ [i]
<k>	= /k/ [k ~ k^{y}] after <s>
<k>	= /k/ [k^{h} ~ k^{yh}] elsewhere (aspirated except after /s/)
<k'>	= /k'/ [k']
<kw>	= /k^{w}/ [k^{w}] after <s>
<kw>	= /k^{w}/ [k^{wh}] elsewhere (aspirated except after /s/)
<kw'>	= /k'^{w}/ [k'^{w}]
<l>	= /l/ [l]
<lh>	= /ɬ/ [ɬ]
<m>	= /m/ [m]
<n>	= /n/ [n]
<o>	= /a/ [a]
<ō>	= /o/ [o]
<p>	= /p/ [p] after <s>
<p>	= /p/ [p^{h}] elsewhere (aspirated except after /s/)
<p'>	= /p'/ [p']
<q>	= /q/ [q] after <s>
<q>	= /q/ [q^{h}] elsewhere (aspirated except after /s/)
<q'>	= /q'/ [q']
<qw>	= /q^{w}/ [q^{w}] after <s>
<qw>	= /q^{w}/ [q^{wh}] elsewhere (aspirated except after /s/)
<qw'>	= /q'^{w}/ [q'^{w}]
<s>	= /s/ [s] everywhere except before <xw>
<sh>	= /s/ [š] only before <xw> except in a few loan words from French or English
<t>	= /t/ [t] after <s>
<t>	= /t/ [t^{h}] elsewhere (aspirated except after /s/)
<t'>	= /t'/ [t']
<th>	= /θ/ [θ]
<th'>	= /θ/ [t^{θ}']
<tl'>	= /ƛ'/ [ƛ']
<ts>	= /c/ [¢]
<ts'>	= /c'/ [¢']
<u>	= /u/ [u]
<w>	= /w/ [w]
<x>	= /x^{y}/ [x̭ ~ x̭^{y}]

<xw> = /x^w/ [x^w]
<x̲> = /x̣/ [x̣]
<x̲w> = /$ẋ^w$/ [$ẋ^w$]
<y> = /y/ [y]
<'> = /ʔ/ [ʔ] except after stops (<p, t, k, q> where the mark glottalizes the consonant)
<:> = /·/ [·] (length, one mora)
<´> = /´/ [^{5}] (high tone, usually a pitch 5 whole tones above low tone)
<`> = /`/ [^{3}] (mid tone, usually a pitch 3 whole tones above low tone)
no mark on vowel = / / [^{1}] (low tone)

References

Abbreviations used below
AA = American Anthropologist
AL = Anthropological Linguistics
BCILP = British Columbia Indian Language Project
ICSL = International Conference on Salish Languages (after 1983 International Conference on Salish and Neighboring Languages)
IJAL = International Journal of American Linguistics
UCPL = University of California Publications in Linguistics
UHWPL = University of Hawaii Working Papers in Linguistics
UMOPL = University of Montana Occasional Papers in Linguistics
UWPA = University of Washington Publications in Anthropology
WCCSL = Working Conference on Central Salish Languages

Adams, George, Brent Galloway, and Catalina Renteria. 2005. "A Nooksack Story from 1956; How to Become an Indian Doctor." A paper presented at the 40th ICSL and published in University of British Columbia Working Papers in Linguistics, 16:1-31.

Amoss, Pamela (Thorsen). 1955-1956, 1969-1970. Nooksack language field notes. Unpublished ms.

__________. 1961. "Nuksack phonemics". Unpublished M.A. thesis, University of Washington.

__________. 1978. Coast Salish Spirit Dancing: The Survival of an Ancestral Religion. Seattle: University of Washington Press.

Bates, Dawn, Thom Hess, and Vi Hilbert. 1994. Lushootseed Dictionary. Ed. by Dawn Bates. Seattle: University of Washington Press

Beaumont, Ronald C. 1980. Personal communication

Beaumont, Ronald C. 1983. Personal communication.

Beaumont, Ronald C. 1985. She Shashishalhem: The Sechelt Language. Theytus Books, Penticton, B.C.

Boas, Franz. 1886. "Pentlatch materials" [Pentlatch language field notes, esp. Pentlatch-English, English-Pentlatch, and Pentlatch-German word lists]. Unpublished ms., #APS-L 30(S2j.3, in the Boas Collection, American Philosophical Society Library, Philadelphia.

__________. 1890 (or 1886b). "Scowlitz materials" [handwritten ms. field notes, a short word list] in the Boas Collection, American Philosophical Society Library, Philadelphia.

__________. 1895a. Indianische Sagen von der nordpacifischen Küste Amerikas. Berlin: A. Asher

__________ (Bouchard & Kennedy). 2002. Indian Myths & Legends from the North Pacific Coast of America: A Translation of Franz Boas' 1895 Edition of Indianische Sagen Von Der Nord-Pacifischen Kuste Amerikas (by Dietrich Bertz), Edited by Randy Bouchard and Dorothy Kennedy. Vancouver: Talonbooks.

Bouchard, Randy. 1974a. "Classified word list for B.C. Indian languages, Straits (Saanich) version". Unpublished ms., BCILP, Victoria, B.C.
__________. 1974b. "Classified word list for B.C. Indian languages, Halkomelem (Cowichan) version". Unpublished ms., BCILP, Victoria, B.C.
__________. 1974c. "Classified word list for B.C. Indian languages, Thompson version" Unpublished ms., BCILP, Victoria, B.C.
__________. 1975. "Classified word list for B.C. Indian languages, Mainland Comox (Tl'úhus dialect) version (preliminary version)". Unpublished ms., BCILP, Victoria, B.C.
__________. 1977. "Classified word list for B.C. Indian languages, Sechelt version". Unpublished ms., BCILP, Victoria, B.C.
__________. 1978a. "Classified word list for B.C. Indian languages, Squamish (corrected) version (corrections largely by Louis Miranda)". Unpublished ms., BCILP, Victoria, B.C.
__________. 1978b. A portion of the "Classified word list for B.C. Indian languages, Island Comox version (preliminary version)". Unpublished ms., BCILP, Victoria, B.C.
__________. 1982, 1983. Personal communications.
Bouchard, Randy, and Nancy J. Turner. 1976. "Ethnobotany of the Squamish Indian People of British Columbia." Unpublished report for the Squamish Indian Band North Vancouver, B.C. BCILP.
Charles, Al, Richard A. Demers, and Elizabeth Bowman. 1978. " Introduction to the Lummi language". Unpublished ms., University of Arizona, Western Washington University and Lummi Indian Reservation.
Davis, John H. 1970. " Some phonological rules in Mainland Comox". Unpublished M.A. thesis, University of Victoria.
__________. 1981, 1982. Personal communications.
Demers, Richard A. 1972. "Stress assignment in ablauting roots in Lummi". Paper presented at the 7th ICSL, Bellingham, Washington.
__________. 1980a. "The category AUX in Lummi". Paper presented at the l5th ICSL, Vancouver, B.C.
__________. 1980b. "ʔuʔ in Lummi". Handout circulated at the 1st WCCSL, Vancouver, B.C.
__________. 1982. Personal communication.
Duff, Wilson. 1952. The Upper Stalo Indians of the Fraser Valley, British Columbia. (Anthropology in British Columbia Memoir 1.) Victoria: British Columbia Provincial Museum, Department of Education.
Efrat, Barbara S. 1969. "A grammar of non-particles in Sooke, a dialect of Straits Coast Salish". Unpublished Ph.D. dissertation, University of Pennsylvania.
__________. 1970-1972, 1974. Nooksack language field notes. Unpublished ms.
Elmendorf, William W. and Wayne Suttles. 1960. " Pattern and change in Halkomelem Salish dialects". AL 2.7:1-32.
Galloway, Brent D. 1970-2002. Upriver Halkomelem field notes. Unpublished ms.
__________. 1971. "Some Similarities Between Semology and Phonology (With Illustrations from Chilliwack Halkomelem)," a paper given at the 6th ICSL, Victoria, B.C., Aug. 16-18, 1971 (all ICSL papers after 1973, except late papers, are printed in a collection of working papers distributed in advance to the participants).
__________. 1973a. "Reduplication in the Chilliwack Dialect of Halkomelem," a paper given at the Group in American Indian Languages, U.C. Berkeley, May 10, 1973.
__________. 1973b. "Reduplication in the Chilliwack Dialect of Halkomelem (With a Sketch of Phonemics)," a paper given at the 8th ICSL, Eugene, Oregon, Aug. 13-15, 1973.
__________. 1973c. "Practical Phonetic System (PPS), Part 3," (written for Casey Wells to give

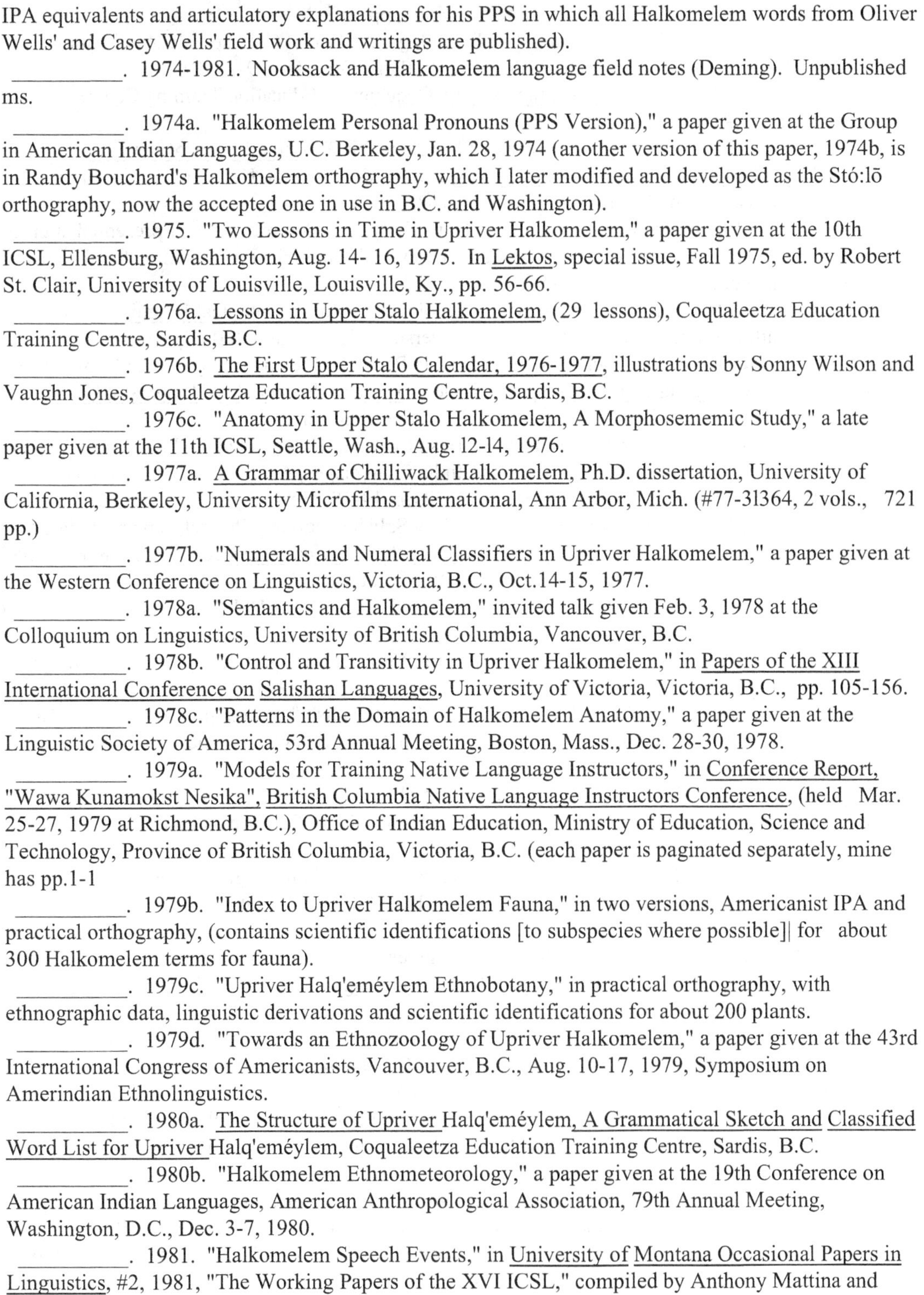

IPA equivalents and articulatory explanations for his PPS in which all Halkomelem words from Oliver Wells' and Casey Wells' field work and writings are published).

__________. 1974-1981. Nooksack and Halkomelem language field notes (Deming). Unpublished ms.

__________. 1974a. "Halkomelem Personal Pronouns (PPS Version)," a paper given at the Group in American Indian Languages, U.C. Berkeley, Jan. 28, 1974 (another version of this paper, 1974b, is in Randy Bouchard's Halkomelem orthography, which I later modified and developed as the Stó:lō orthography, now the accepted one in use in B.C. and Washington).

__________. 1975. "Two Lessons in Time in Upriver Halkomelem," a paper given at the 10th ICSL, Ellensburg, Washington, Aug. 14- 16, 1975. In Lektos, special issue, Fall 1975, ed. by Robert St. Clair, University of Louisville, Louisville, Ky., pp. 56-66.

__________. 1976a. Lessons in Upper Stalo Halkomelem, (29 lessons), Coqualeetza Education Training Centre, Sardis, B.C.

__________. 1976b. The First Upper Stalo Calendar, 1976-1977, illustrations by Sonny Wilson and Vaughn Jones, Coqualeetza Education Training Centre, Sardis, B.C.

__________. 1976c. "Anatomy in Upper Stalo Halkomelem, A Morphosememic Study," a late paper given at the 11th ICSL, Seattle, Wash., Aug. 12-14, 1976.

__________. 1977a. A Grammar of Chilliwack Halkomelem, Ph.D. dissertation, University of California, Berkeley, University Microfilms International, Ann Arbor, Mich. (#77-31364, 2 vols., 721 pp.)

__________. 1977b. "Numerals and Numeral Classifiers in Upriver Halkomelem," a paper given at the Western Conference on Linguistics, Victoria, B.C., Oct.14-15, 1977.

__________. 1978a. "Semantics and Halkomelem," invited talk given Feb. 3, 1978 at the Colloquium on Linguistics, University of British Columbia, Vancouver, B.C.

__________. 1978b. "Control and Transitivity in Upriver Halkomelem," in Papers of the XIII International Conference on Salishan Languages, University of Victoria, Victoria, B.C., pp. 105-156.

__________. 1978c. "Patterns in the Domain of Halkomelem Anatomy," a paper given at the Linguistic Society of America, 53rd Annual Meeting, Boston, Mass., Dec. 28-30, 1978.

__________. 1979a. "Models for Training Native Language Instructors," in Conference Report, "Wawa Kunamokst Nesika", British Columbia Native Language Instructors Conference, (held Mar. 25-27, 1979 at Richmond, B.C.), Office of Indian Education, Ministry of Education, Science and Technology, Province of British Columbia, Victoria, B.C. (each paper is paginated separately, mine has pp.1-1

__________. 1979b. "Index to Upriver Halkomelem Fauna," in two versions, Americanist IPA and practical orthography, (contains scientific identifications [to subspecies where possible]| for about 300 Halkomelem terms for fauna).

__________. 1979c. "Upriver Halq'eméylem Ethnobotany," in practical orthography, with ethnographic data, linguistic derivations and scientific identifications for about 200 plants.

__________. 1979d. "Towards an Ethnozoology of Upriver Halkomelem," a paper given at the 43rd International Congress of Americanists, Vancouver, B.C., Aug. 10-17, 1979, Symposium on Amerindian Ethnolinguistics.

__________. 1980a. The Structure of Upriver Halq'eméylem, A Grammatical Sketch and Classified Word List for Upriver Halq'eméylem, Coqualeetza Education Training Centre, Sardis, B.C.

__________. 1980b. "Halkomelem Ethnometeorology," a paper given at the 19th Conference on American Indian Languages, American Anthropological Association, 79th Annual Meeting, Washington, D.C., Dec. 3-7, 1980.

__________. 1981. "Halkomelem Speech Events," in University of Montana Occasional Papers in Linguistics, #2, 1981, "The Working Papers of the XVI ICSL," compiled by Anthony Mattina and

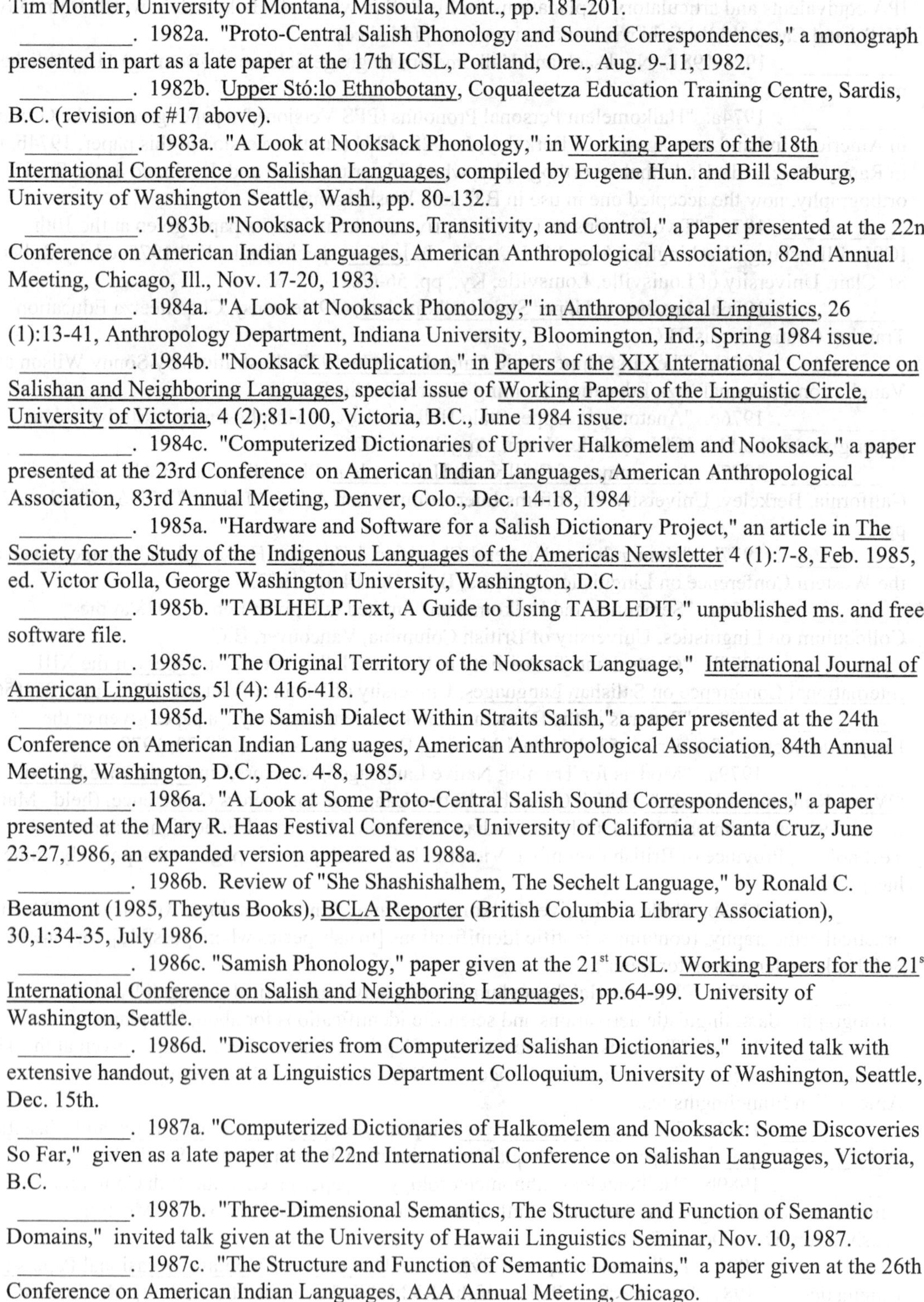

Tim Montler, University of Montana, Missoula, Mont., pp. 181-201.

__________. 1982a. "Proto-Central Salish Phonology and Sound Correspondences," a monograph presented in part as a late paper at the 17th ICSL, Portland, Ore., Aug. 9-11, 1982.

__________. 1982b. Upper Stó:lo Ethnobotany, Coqualeetza Education Training Centre, Sardis, B.C. (revision of #17 above).

__________. 1983a. "A Look at Nooksack Phonology," in Working Papers of the 18th International Conference on Salishan Languages, compiled by Eugene Hun. and Bill Seaburg, University of Washington Seattle, Wash., pp. 80-132.

__________. 1983b. "Nooksack Pronouns, Transitivity, and Control," a paper presented at the 22nd Conference on American Indian Languages, American Anthropological Association, 82nd Annual Meeting, Chicago, Ill., Nov. 17-20, 1983.

__________. 1984a. "A Look at Nooksack Phonology," in Anthropological Linguistics, 26 (1):13-41, Anthropology Department, Indiana University, Bloomington, Ind., Spring 1984 issue.

__________. 1984b. "Nooksack Reduplication," in Papers of the XIX International Conference on Salishan and Neighboring Languages, special issue of Working Papers of the Linguistic Circle, University of Victoria, 4 (2):81-100, Victoria, B.C., June 1984 issue.

__________. 1984c. "Computerized Dictionaries of Upriver Halkomelem and Nooksack," a paper presented at the 23rd Conference on American Indian Languages, American Anthropological Association, 83rd Annual Meeting, Denver, Colo., Dec. 14-18, 1984

__________. 1985a. "Hardware and Software for a Salish Dictionary Project," an article in The Society for the Study of the Indigenous Languages of the Americas Newsletter 4 (1):7-8, Feb. 1985, ed. Victor Golla, George Washington University, Washington, D.C.

__________. 1985b. "TABLHELP.Text, A Guide to Using TABLEDIT," unpublished ms. and free software file.

__________. 1985c. "The Original Territory of the Nooksack Language," International Journal of American Linguistics, 51 (4): 416-418.

__________. 1985d. "The Samish Dialect Within Straits Salish," a paper presented at the 24th Conference on American Indian Lang uages, American Anthropological Association, 84th Annual Meeting, Washington, D.C., Dec. 4-8, 1985.

__________. 1986a. "A Look at Some Proto-Central Salish Sound Correspondences," a paper presented at the Mary R. Haas Festival Conference, University of California at Santa Cruz, June 23-27,1986, an expanded version appeared as 1988a.

__________. 1986b. Review of "She Shashishalhem, The Sechelt Language," by Ronald C. Beaumont (1985, Theytus Books), BCLA Reporter (British Columbia Library Association), 30,1:34-35, July 1986.

__________. 1986c. "Samish Phonology," paper given at the 21st ICSL. Working Papers for the 21st International Conference on Salish and Neighboring Languages, pp.64-99. University of Washington, Seattle.

__________. 1986d. "Discoveries from Computerized Salishan Dictionaries," invited talk with extensive handout, given at a Linguistics Department Colloquium, University of Washington, Seattle, Dec. 15th.

__________. 1987a. "Computerized Dictionaries of Halkomelem and Nooksack: Some Discoveries So Far," given as a late paper at the 22nd International Conference on Salishan Languages, Victoria, B.C.

__________. 1987b. "Three-Dimensional Semantics, The Structure and Function of Semantic Domains," invited talk given at the University of Hawaii Linguistics Seminar, Nov. 10, 1987.

__________. 1987c. "The Structure and Function of Semantic Domains," a paper given at the 26th Conference on American Indian Languages, AAA Annual Meeting, Chicago.

__________. 1988a. "Some Proto-Central Salish Sound Correspondences," pp. 293-343 in a refereed subset of the conference papers, entitled, In Honor of Mary Haas, From the Haas Festival Conference on Native American Linguistics, edited by William Shipley, Mouton de Gruyter, Berlin.

__________. 1988b. "The Upriver Halkomelem Language Program at Coqualeetza," Human Organization, 47,4:291-297.

__________. 1988c. "Metaphor in a Salish Language or Two," a paper given at the 27th Conference on American Indian Languages, AAA Annual Meeting, Phoenix.

__________. 1988d. "The 1987 Salish Conference," IJAL 54:365-366.

__________. 1989a. "Review of The Bella Coola Language by Hank F. Nater", IJAL, 55.1:97-105, (Jan. 1989).

__________. 1989b. "Metaphors, Allosemes, and Semantic Domains in Salish and Algonquian Languages," an invited paper given at the Session on Cognitive Grammar and American Indian Languages, Southwestern Anthropological Association, 60th Annual Meeting, Riverside, Calif., April 27-29, 1989.

__________. 1989c. "3-D Semantics and the First Halkomelem Dictionary," a paper given at the 28th Conference on American Indian Languages, American Anthropological Assoc. Annual Meeting, Washington, D.C.

__________. 1989d. "Three-Dimensional Semantics: Language, Culture and Cognition", First DILLL Lunchbox Talk, given with handout Nov. 1989.

__________. 1990a. A Phonology, Morphology, and Classified Word List for the Samish Dialect of Straits Salish (Mercury Series, National Museum of Man, Canadian Ethnology Service, Ottawa, Ont.).

__________. 1990b. "3-D Semantics Meets Discourse Analysis," a paper given at the 29th Conference on American Indian Languages, American Anthropological Assoc. Annual Meeting, New Orleans.

__________. 1991a. "Some Cognate Words to Halkomelem Words on Economy", exhibits 31 and 32 in HMQ v. Alfred Hope et al, Fishing Rights case.

__________. 1991b. "Review of Colville Okanagan Dictionary by Anthony Mattina", IJAL, 57.1:402-405, (July, 1991).

__________. 1991c. "A Salish Language with Tone and Other Interesting Phonological Complexities," a paper given at the 30th Conference on American Indian Languages, American Anthropological Assoc. Annual Meeting, Chicago.

__________. 1991d. "Upriver Halkomelem Dictionary," English-to-Halkomelem, 667 pages, manuscript.

__________. 1992a. "Computerized Dictionaries of Upriver Halkomelem and Nooksack," and "3-D Semantics and the Halkomelem Dictionary," in Amerindia, Revue d'Ethnolinguistique Amérindienne, numéro special 7, "Amerindian Languages and Informatics, The Pacific Northwest, ed. by Guy Buchholtzer, pp.47-82, Paris

__________. 1992b. "Aspects of Color in Halkomelem, " a paper given in a session, "Light on Color Ethnography", at the 91st Annual Meeting, American Anthropological Association, San Francisco

__________. 1992c. "The Samish Dialect and Straits Salish: Dialect Death and Dialect Survival," in a special issue of the International Journal of the Sociology of Language, guest editor, Allan R. Taylor, 93:37-51.

__________. 1993a. A Grammar of Upriver Halkomelem, University of California Press, Publications in Linguistics, vol. 96, Berkeley, Calif.

__________. 1993b. "Nooksack Reduplication," in American Indian Linguistics and Ethnography in Honor of Laurence C. Thompson, Anthony Mattina and Timothy Montler, eds., University of

Montana Occasional Papers in Linguistics, no. 10, pp. 93-112.
_________. 1993c. "Three-Dimensional Semantics," unpublished manuscript.
_________. 1993d. "Nooksack Reduplication," paper given at the 32nd Conference on American Indian Languages, American Anthropological Assoc. 92nd Annual Meeting, Washington, D.C.
_________. 1994a. "The Life or Death of Indian Languages: Prescriptions for Survival," invited talk, given May 13, 1994 at the University of Alberta, Edmonton.
_________. 1994b. "Indian Language Classes Help People of All Ages", in Starblanket First Nation Newsletter, 4:6-7.
_________. 1994c. "An Etymological Analysis of the 32 Place Names Sent by Harry Slade by Letter Dated Nov. 5, 1993." to be used in evidence in Mathias v. HMQ, Grant, and George; Grant v. HMQ and Mathias; and George v. HMQ and Mathias; land claims cases.
_________. 1995, "Review of the Lushootseed Dictionary by Dawn Bates, Thom Hess, and Vi Hilbert". American Indian Culture and Research Journal, 19.4:293-296, University of California at Los Angeles.
_________. 1996a. "An Upriver Halkomelem Mink Story: Mink and Miss Pitch" (30 pages), to appear in One People's Stories: A Collection of Salishan Myths and Legends, ed. by M. Terry Thompson and Steven M. Egesdal, published later as Galloway 2007d (see below).
_________. 1996b. "A Samish Story: The Maiden of Deception Pass" (29 pages), to appear in One People's Stories: A Collection of Salishan Myths and Legends, ed. by M. Terry Thompson and Steven M. Egesdal, published later as Galloway 2007d (see below).
_________. 1996c. "An Upriver Halkomelem Mink Story: Ethnopoetics and Discourse Analysis". In Papers for the 31st International Conference on Salishan and Neighboring Languages, eds. M. Dale Kinkade and Henry Davis, University of British Columbia Linguistics Department, University of British Columbia, Vancouver, B.C., pp.159-174.
_________. 1996d. "An Etymological Analysis of the 59 Squamish and Halkomelem Place Names on Burrard Inlet Analyzed in Suttles Report of 1996." filed in evidence in the land claims cases of Mathias v. HMQ, Grant, and George; Grant v. HMQ and Mathias; and George v. HMQ and Mathias.
_________. 1996e. "A Look At Some Nooksack Stories" A paper presented at the 35th Conference on American Indian Languages, 95th American Anthropological Association Annual Meeting, San Francisco, Calif.
_________. 1996f. "Review of the Spokane Dictionary, compiled by Barry F. Carlson and Pauline Flett" in International Journal of American Linguistics, 62 (4):415-418.
_________. 1997b. "Nooksack Pronouns, Transitivity, and Control," in Papers for the 32nd International Conference on Salish and Neighboring Languages, Peninsula College, Port Angeles, Wash., compiled by Timothy Montler, Denton: University of North Texas, pp. 197-243.
_________. 1997c. "Recollections of Mary Haas as Teacher, Supervisor, and Inspiration." In Anthropological Linguistics, 39.4:636-641.
_________. 1998a. "Semantic Structure and Constituency in Amerindian Languages", a paper given at the Workshop on Structure and Constituency in the Native Languages of the Americas, Mar. 27-29, 1998, SIFC/University of Regina.
_________. 1998c. "Proto-Salish Sound Correspondences", a paper given at the 37th Conference on American Indian Languages at the American Anthropological Society Annual Meetings, Philadelphia, Pa.
_________. 2000a. "Review of Salish Languages and Linguistics, edited by Ewa Czaykowska-Higgins and M. Dale Kinkade" in International Journal of American Linguistics, 66 (2):257-266.
_________. 2000b. "Cognitive Semantics in Halkomelem", a paper given at the 39th Conference on American Indian Languages at the American Anthropological Society Annual Meetings, San Francisco, Ca.

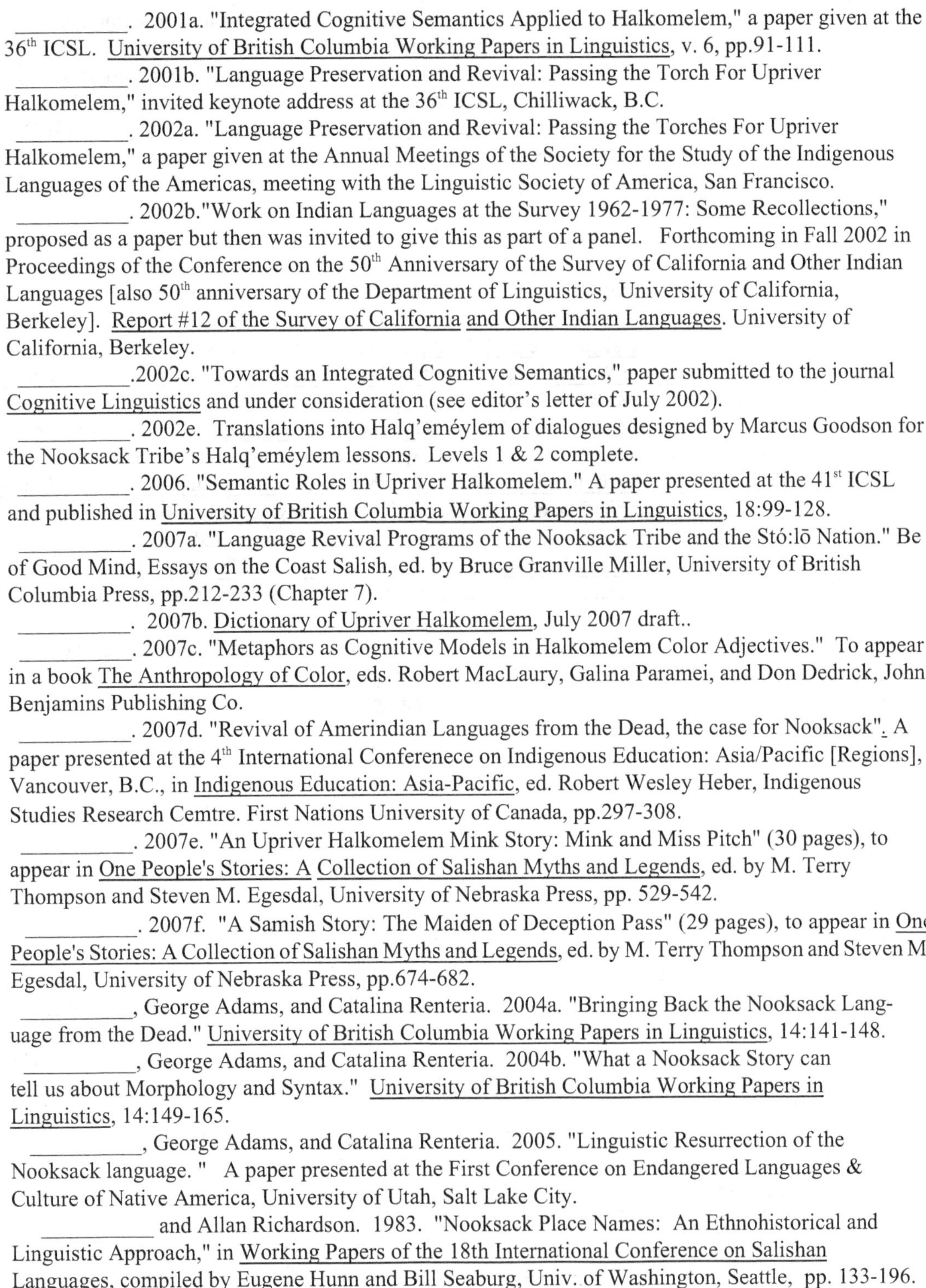

__________. 2001a. "Integrated Cognitive Semantics Applied to Halkomelem," a paper given at the 36th ICSL. University of British Columbia Working Papers in Linguistics, v. 6, pp.91-111.

__________. 2001b. "Language Preservation and Revival: Passing the Torch For Upriver Halkomelem," invited keynote address at the 36th ICSL, Chilliwack, B.C.

__________. 2002a. "Language Preservation and Revival: Passing the Torches For Upriver Halkomelem," a paper given at the Annual Meetings of the Society for the Study of the Indigenous Languages of the Americas, meeting with the Linguistic Society of America, San Francisco.

__________. 2002b."Work on Indian Languages at the Survey 1962-1977: Some Recollections," proposed as a paper but then was invited to give this as part of a panel. Forthcoming in Fall 2002 in Proceedings of the Conference on the 50th Anniversary of the Survey of California and Other Indian Languages [also 50th anniversary of the Department of Linguistics, University of California, Berkeley]. Report #12 of the Survey of California and Other Indian Languages. University of California, Berkeley.

__________.2002c. "Towards an Integrated Cognitive Semantics," paper submitted to the journal Cognitive Linguistics and under consideration (see editor's letter of July 2002).

__________. 2002e. Translations into Halq'eméylem of dialogues designed by Marcus Goodson for the Nooksack Tribe's Halq'eméylem lessons. Levels 1 & 2 complete.

__________. 2006. "Semantic Roles in Upriver Halkomelem." A paper presented at the 41st ICSL and published in University of British Columbia Working Papers in Linguistics, 18:99-128.

__________. 2007a. "Language Revival Programs of the Nooksack Tribe and the Stó:lō Nation." Be of Good Mind, Essays on the Coast Salish, ed. by Bruce Granville Miller, University of British Columbia Press, pp.212-233 (Chapter 7).

__________. 2007b. Dictionary of Upriver Halkomelem, July 2007 draft..

__________. 2007c. "Metaphors as Cognitive Models in Halkomelem Color Adjectives." To appear in a book The Anthropology of Color, eds. Robert MacLaury, Galina Paramei, and Don Dedrick, John Benjamins Publishing Co.

__________. 2007d. "Revival of Amerindian Languages from the Dead, the case for Nooksack". A paper presented at the 4th International Conferenece on Indigenous Education: Asia/Pacific [Regions], Vancouver, B.C., in Indigenous Education: Asia-Pacific, ed. Robert Wesley Heber, Indigenous Studies Research Cemtre. First Nations University of Canada, pp.297-308.

__________. 2007e. "An Upriver Halkomelem Mink Story: Mink and Miss Pitch" (30 pages), to appear in One People's Stories: A Collection of Salishan Myths and Legends, ed. by M. Terry Thompson and Steven M. Egesdal, University of Nebraska Press, pp. 529-542.

__________. 2007f. "A Samish Story: The Maiden of Deception Pass" (29 pages), to appear in One People's Stories: A Collection of Salishan Myths and Legends, ed. by M. Terry Thompson and Steven M. Egesdal, University of Nebraska Press, pp.674-682.

__________, George Adams, and Catalina Renteria. 2004a. "Bringing Back the Nooksack Language from the Dead." University of British Columbia Working Papers in Linguistics, 14:141-148.

__________, George Adams, and Catalina Renteria. 2004b. "What a Nooksack Story can tell us about Morphology and Syntax." University of British Columbia Working Papers in Linguistics, 14:149-165.

__________, George Adams, and Catalina Renteria. 2005. "Linguistic Resurrection of the Nooksack language. " A paper presented at the First Conference on Endangered Languages & Culture of Native America, University of Utah, Salt Lake City.

__________ and Allan Richardson. 1983. "Nooksack Place Names: An Ethnohistorical and Linguistic Approach," in Working Papers of the 18th International Conference on Salishan Languages, compiled by Eugene Hunn and Bill Seaburg, Univ. of Washington, Seattle, pp. 133-196.

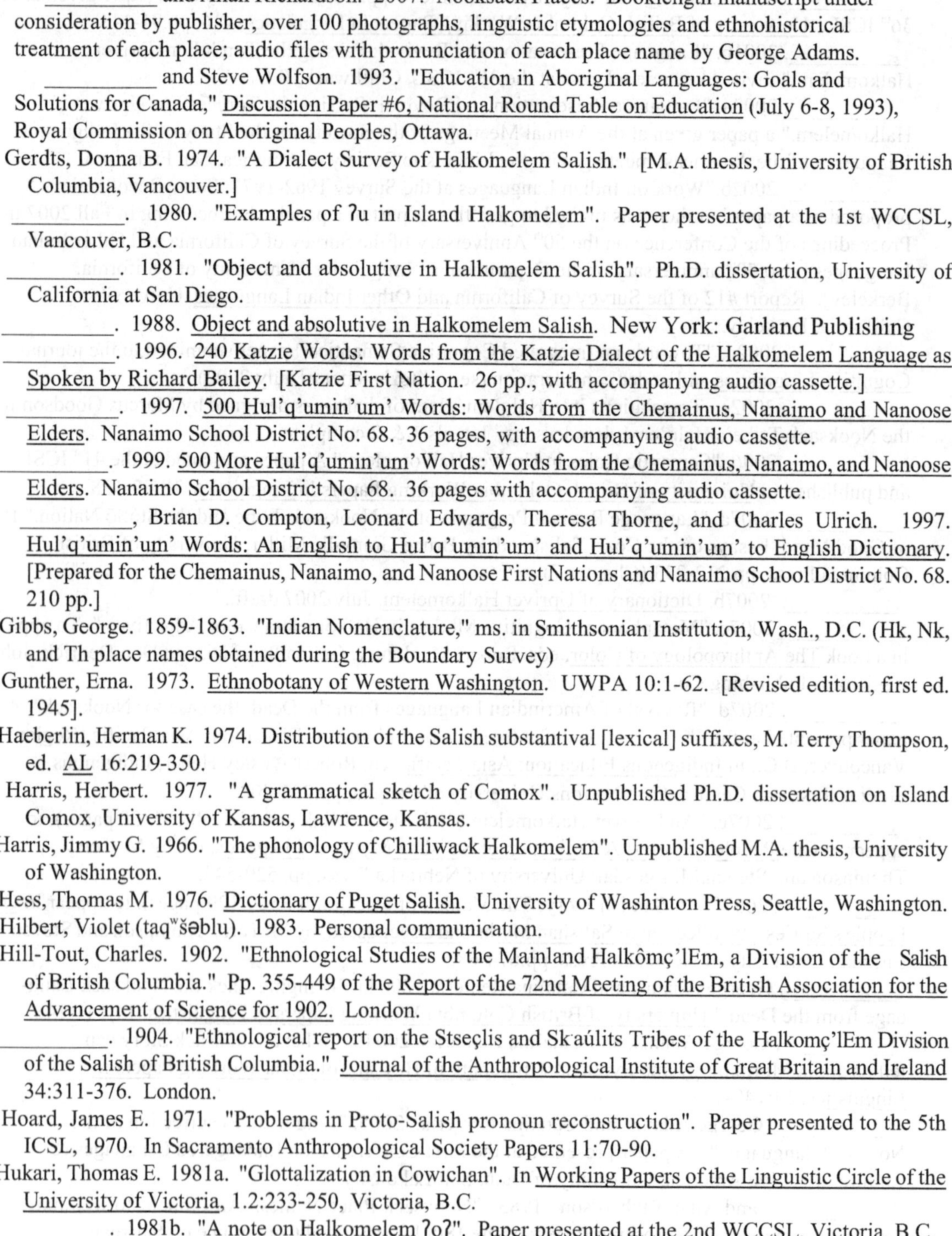

__________ and Allan Richardson. 2007. Nooksack Places. Booklength manuscript under consideration by publisher, over 100 photographs, linguistic etymologies and ethnohistorical treatment of each place; audio files with pronunciation of each place name by George Adams.

__________ and Steve Wolfson. 1993. "Education in Aboriginal Languages: Goals and Solutions for Canada," Discussion Paper #6, National Round Table on Education (July 6-8, 1993), Royal Commission on Aboriginal Peoples, Ottawa.

Gerdts, Donna B. 1974. "A Dialect Survey of Halkomelem Salish." [M.A. thesis, University of British Columbia, Vancouver.]

__________. 1980. "Examples of ʔu in Island Halkomelem". Paper presented at the 1st WCCSL, Vancouver, B.C.

__________. 1981. "Object and absolutive in Halkomelem Salish". Ph.D. dissertation, University of California at San Diego.

__________. 1988. Object and absolutive in Halkomelem Salish. New York: Garland Publishing

__________. 1996. 240 Katzie Words: Words from the Katzie Dialect of the Halkomelem Language as Spoken by Richard Bailey. [Katzie First Nation. 26 pp., with accompanying audio cassette.]

__________. 1997. 500 Hul'q'umin'um' Words: Words from the Chemainus, Nanaimo and Nanoose Elders. Nanaimo School District No. 68. 36 pages, with accompanying audio cassette.

__________. 1999. 500 More Hul'q'umin'um' Words: Words from the Chemainus, Nanaimo, and Nanoose Elders. Nanaimo School District No. 68. 36 pages with accompanying audio cassette.

__________, Brian D. Compton, Leonard Edwards, Theresa Thorne, and Charles Ulrich. 1997. Hul'q'umin'um' Words: An English to Hul'q'umin'um' and Hul'q'umin'um' to English Dictionary. [Prepared for the Chemainus, Nanaimo, and Nanoose First Nations and Nanaimo School District No. 68. 210 pp.]

Gibbs, George. 1859-1863. "Indian Nomenclature," ms. in Smithsonian Institution, Wash., D.C. (Hk, Nk, and Th place names obtained during the Boundary Survey)

Gunther, Erna. 1973. Ethnobotany of Western Washington. UWPA 10:1-62. [Revised edition, first ed. 1945].

Haeberlin, Herman K. 1974. Distribution of the Salish substantival [lexical] suffixes, M. Terry Thompson, ed. AL 16:219-350.

Harris, Herbert. 1977. "A grammatical sketch of Comox". Unpublished Ph.D. dissertation on Island Comox, University of Kansas, Lawrence, Kansas.

Harris, Jimmy G. 1966. "The phonology of Chilliwack Halkomelem". Unpublished M.A. thesis, University of Washington.

Hess, Thomas M. 1976. Dictionary of Puget Salish. University of Washinton Press, Seattle, Washington.

Hilbert, Violet (taqʷšəblu). 1983. Personal communication.

Hill-Tout, Charles. 1902. "Ethnological Studies of the Mainland Halkõmç'lEm, a Division of the Salish of British Columbia." Pp. 355-449 of the Report of the 72nd Meeting of the British Association for the Advancement of Science for 1902. London.

__________. 1904. "Ethnological report on the Stseçlis and Sk'aúlits Tribes of the Halkomç'lEm Division of the Salish of British Columbia." Journal of the Anthropological Institute of Great Britain and Ireland 34:311-376. London.

Hoard, James E. 1971. "Problems in Proto-Salish pronoun reconstruction". Paper presented to the 5th ICSL, 1970. In Sacramento Anthropological Society Papers 11:70-90.

Hukari, Thomas E. 1981a. "Glottalization in Cowichan". In Working Papers of the Linguistic Circle of the University of Victoria, 1.2:233-250, Victoria, B.C.

__________. 1981b. "A note on Halkomelem ʔoʔ". Paper presented at the 2nd WCCSL, Victoria, B.C.

__________. In Preparation. Hul'qumi'num' Grammar. Cowichan Tribes.

__________(ed.) and Ruby Peter (assoc. ed.). 1996. Hul'qumi'num' Dictionary. Duncan, B.C.: Cowichan Tribes.

Jenness, Diamond. 1955. The Faith of a Coast Salish Indian. Ed. by Wayne Suttles, Anthropology in British Columbia Memoir 3. Victoria: British Columbia Provincial Museum, Department of Education.

Johnson, Samuel V. 1978. " Chinook Jargon: a computer assisted analysis of variation in an American Indian pidgin". Unpublished Ph.D. dissertation, University of Kansas.

Jones, Michael K. 1976. " Morphophonemic properties of Cowichan actual aspect". Unpublished M.A. thesis, University of Victoria.

Kava, Tiiu. 1969. "A Phonology of Cowichan." M.A. thesis, University of Victoria, Victoria, B.C.

__________. 1972. "A Consideration of Historical Implications in an Idiosyncratic Development of Vowel Length in the Chilliwack Dialect." A paper given at the 7th ICSL, Bellingham, Washington. Also distributed as UHWPL 4(3).

Kennedy, Dorothy I.D. and Randy Bouchard. 1976. Utilization of Fish, Beach Foods, and Marine Mammals by the Squamish Indian people of British Columbia. Unpublished report for the Squamish Indian Band North Vancouver, B.C. BCILP.

Kinkade, M. Dale. 1980. " Pentlatch possessives". Paper and handout presented at the 1st WCCSL, Vancouver, B.C.

__________. 1981. Dictionary of the Moses-Columbia Language. Nespelem, Washington: Colville Confederated Tribes.

__________. 1982. "Pentlatch and Boas' early transcriptions practices". Paper presented at the 21st Conference on American Indian Languages, Washington, D.C.

__________. 1983a. "More on nasal loss in the Northwest coast". In Working Papers for the 18th International Conference on Salish and Neighboring Languages, comp. by Eugene Hunn and Bill Seaburg, University of Washington, Seattle, Washington.

__________. 1983b. "Pentlatch cedars and allied technology, salmon names, and orientation domain". Handout presented at the 4th WCCSL, Vancouver, B.C.

__________. 1984. "Pentlatch negatives (total repertoire)"., "Pentlatch questions (total repertoire)"., "Pentlatch reduplication"., and "Pentlatch color terms". Four handouts presented at the 5th WCCSL, Victoria, B.C.

__________ and Laurence C. Thompson. 1974. "Proto-Salish *r". IJAL 40:22-28.

Kuipers, Aert H. 1967a. "On divergence, interaction and mergin of Salish language-communities". Paper presented at the 2nd ICSL, Seattle, Washington.

__________. 1967b. The Squamish Language: Grammar, Texts, Dictionary. Mouton Press, Janua Linguarum, Series Practica 73, The Hague.

__________. 1969. The Squamish Language: Grammar, Texts, Dictionary, Part 2. Mouton Press, Janua Linguarum, Series Practica 73:2, The Hague.

__________. 1970. "Towards a Salish etymological dictionary". Lingua 26:46-72.

__________. 1973. "About evidence for Proto-Salish *r". Paper presented at the 8th ICSL, Eugene, Oregon. In Dutch Contributions to the 8th ICSL,1:1-19, University of Leiden, Leiden, Netherlands.

__________. 1974. The Shuswap Language: Grammar, Texts, Dictionary. Janua Linguarum, Series Practica 225. The Hague: Mouton.

__________. 1975. A Classified English-Shuswap Word-List. PdR Publications on Salish Languages 3. Lisse, The Netherlands: Peter de Ridder Press.

__________. 1980. "Corrections to 'The Shuswap Language,'" The Hague 1974.' In Working Papers of the 15th ICSL pp.283-284, Vancouver, B.C.

__________. 1981. "On Reconstructing the Proto-Salish Sound System." IJAL 47:323-335.

__________. 1982. "Towards a Salish etymological dictionary II". Lingua 57:71-92.

__________. 1995. "Towards a Salish Etymological Dictionary III." A paper and handout given at the 30th ICSL 30, Victoria, B.C.

__________. 1996. "Towards a Salish Etymological Dictionary IV." In Papers for the 31st International Conference on Salishan and Neighboring Languages, eds. M. Dale Kinkade and Henry Davis, University of British Columbia Linguistics Department, University of British Columbia, Vancouver, B.C., pp.203-210, Vancouver, B.C.

__________. 1998. "Towards a Salish Etymological Dictionary V." In Working Papers of the 33rd ICSNL 33:296-306, Seattle, Washington.

__________. 2002. Salish Etymological dictionary. UMOPL 16.

Leslie, Adrian Roy. 1979. "A grammar of the Cowichan dialect of Halkomelem Salish". Unpublished Ph.D. dissertation, University of Victoria.

MacLaury, Robert E. and Brent Galloway. 1988. "Color Categorization and Color Qualifiers in Halkomelem, Samish, Lushootseed, Nooksack, and Yakima," in Working Papers of the 23rd ICSL, pp.166-199, Eugene, Oregon

Mattina, Anthony. 1973. Colville Grammatical Structure. UHWPL 5. Honolulu. [Ph.D. dissertation, University of Hawaii, Honolulu.]

Maud, Ralph, Brent Galloway, and Marie Weeden Wells (eds.) , Oliver N. 1987 (posthumous). The Chilliwacks and Their Neighbors, Talonbooks, Vancouver, B.C.

Maud, Ralph, Brent Galloway, and Marie Weeden. 1978-1982. The Oliver Wells tapes relating to Salish Indians. Unpublished ms. transcriptions of all the tapes, annotated.

Mitchell, Marjorie R. 1968. "A dictionary of Songish, a dialect of Straits Salish". Unpublished M.A. thesis, University of Victoria.

Montler, Timothy R. 1984. "Saanich Morphology and Phonology". Ph.D. dissertation, University of Hawaii at Manoa. Subsequently published in 1985 as An Outline of the Morphology and Phonology of Saanich, North Straits Salish. UMOPL 4, Missoula, Montana.

__________. 1991. Saanich, North Straits Salish. Classified Word List. Canadian Museum of Civilization. Canadian Ethnology Service Paper No. 119, Mercury Series.) Hull, Quebec.

Nater, Henk F. 1977. Stem List of the Bella Coola Language. Peter de Ridder Press, Lisse, Netherlands.

__________. 1984. The Bella Coola Language. Mercury Series, Ethnology Service paper 92. Ottawa: National Museum of Man.

__________. 1990. A Concise Nuxalk-English Dictionary. Mercury Series, Ethnology Service paper 115. Ottawa: Canadian Museum of Civilization.

__________ et al. 1973. "Bella Coola etymologies". Paper presented at the 8th ICSL, Eugene, Oregon. In Dutch Contributions to the 8th ICSL, 3:1-9.

Newman, Stanley. 1976. "Salish and Bella Coola prefixes". IJAL 42:228-242.

__________. 1977. "The Salish independent pronoun system". IJAL 43:302-314.

__________. 1979a. "A history of the Salish possessive and subject forms". IJAL 45:207-223.

__________. 1979b. "The Salish object forms". IJAL 45:299-308.

__________. 1980. "Functional changes in the Salish pronominal system". IJAL 46:155-167.

Norris, Shirley. 1988. [Transcriptions by Shirley Norris of terms for modern foods in Upriver Halkomelem by Elizabeth Herrling, Rosaleen George, and Shirley Norris].

Pidgeon, Michael W. 1970. "Lexical suffixes in Saanich, a dialect of Straits Coast Salish". Unpublished M.A. thesis, University of Victoria.

Raffo, Yolanda A. 1972. "A phonology and morphology of Songish, a dialect of Straits Salish". Unpublished Ph.D. dissertation, University of Kansas.

Reichard, Gladys A. 1958-1960. "A comparison of five Salish languages", ed. by Florence M. Voegelin. IJAL 24:293-300, 25:8-15, 90-96, 154-167, 239-253, 26:50-61.

Suttles, Wayne. 1948. Excerpts from Samish field notes. Unpublished ms. made available to Thompson,

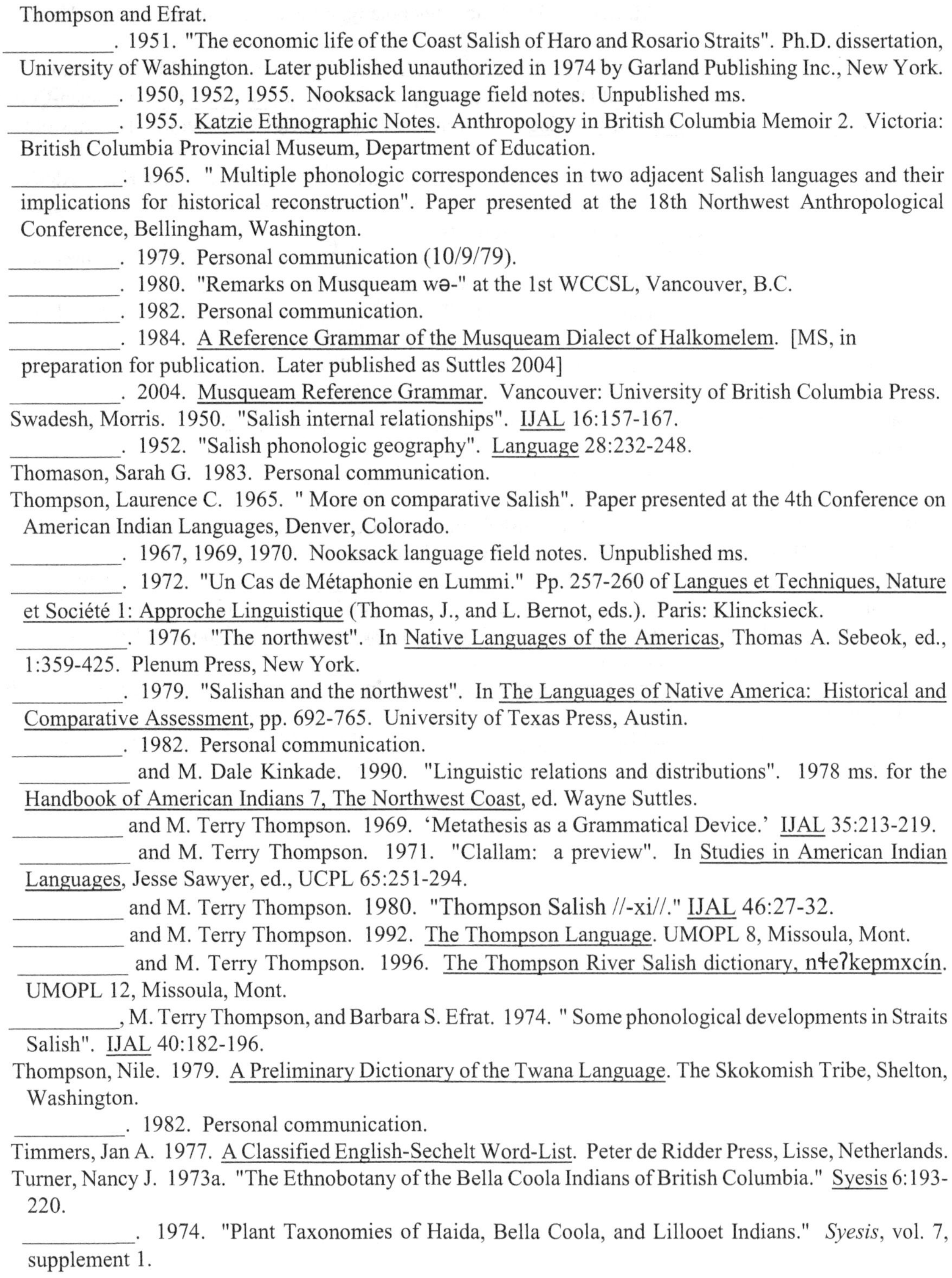

Thompson and Efrat.
__________. 1951. "The economic life of the Coast Salish of Haro and Rosario Straits". Ph.D. dissertation, University of Washington. Later published unauthorized in 1974 by Garland Publishing Inc., New York.
__________. 1950, 1952, 1955. Nooksack language field notes. Unpublished ms.
__________. 1955. Katzie Ethnographic Notes. Anthropology in British Columbia Memoir 2. Victoria: British Columbia Provincial Museum, Department of Education.
__________. 1965. " Multiple phonologic correspondences in two adjacent Salish languages and their implications for historical reconstruction". Paper presented at the 18th Northwest Anthropological Conference, Bellingham, Washington.
__________. 1979. Personal communication (10/9/79).
__________. 1980. "Remarks on Musqueam wə-" at the 1st WCCSL, Vancouver, B.C.
__________. 1982. Personal communication.
__________. 1984. A Reference Grammar of the Musqueam Dialect of Halkomelem. [MS, in preparation for publication. Later published as Suttles 2004]
__________. 2004. Musqueam Reference Grammar. Vancouver: University of British Columbia Press.
Swadesh, Morris. 1950. "Salish internal relationships". IJAL 16:157-167.
__________. 1952. "Salish phonologic geography". Language 28:232-248.
Thomason, Sarah G. 1983. Personal communication.
Thompson, Laurence C. 1965. " More on comparative Salish". Paper presented at the 4th Conference on American Indian Languages, Denver, Colorado.
__________. 1967, 1969, 1970. Nooksack language field notes. Unpublished ms.
__________. 1972. "Un Cas de Métaphonie en Lummi." Pp. 257-260 of Langues et Techniques, Nature et Société 1: Approche Linguistique (Thomas, J., and L. Bernot, eds.). Paris: Klincksieck.
__________. 1976. "The northwest". In Native Languages of the Americas, Thomas A. Sebeok, ed., 1:359-425. Plenum Press, New York.
__________. 1979. "Salishan and the northwest". In The Languages of Native America: Historical and Comparative Assessment, pp. 692-765. University of Texas Press, Austin.
__________. 1982. Personal communication.
__________ and M. Dale Kinkade. 1990. "Linguistic relations and distributions". 1978 ms. for the Handbook of American Indians 7, The Northwest Coast, ed. Wayne Suttles.
__________ and M. Terry Thompson. 1969. 'Metathesis as a Grammatical Device.' IJAL 35:213-219.
__________ and M. Terry Thompson. 1971. "Clallam: a preview". In Studies in American Indian Languages, Jesse Sawyer, ed., UCPL 65:251-294.
__________ and M. Terry Thompson. 1980. "Thompson Salish //-xi//." IJAL 46:27-32.
__________ and M. Terry Thompson. 1992. The Thompson Language. UMOPL 8, Missoula, Mont.
__________ and M. Terry Thompson. 1996. The Thompson River Salish dictionary, nɬeʔkepmxcín. UMOPL 12, Missoula, Mont.
__________, M. Terry Thompson, and Barbara S. Efrat. 1974. " Some phonological developments in Straits Salish". IJAL 40:182-196.
Thompson, Nile. 1979. A Preliminary Dictionary of the Twana Language. The Skokomish Tribe, Shelton, Washington.
__________. 1982. Personal communication.
Timmers, Jan A. 1977. A Classified English-Sechelt Word-List. Peter de Ridder Press, Lisse, Netherlands.
Turner, Nancy J. 1973a. "The Ethnobotany of the Bella Coola Indians of British Columbia." Syesis 6:193-220.
__________. 1974. "Plant Taxonomies of Haida, Bella Coola, and Lillooet Indians." *Syesis*, vol. 7, supplement 1.

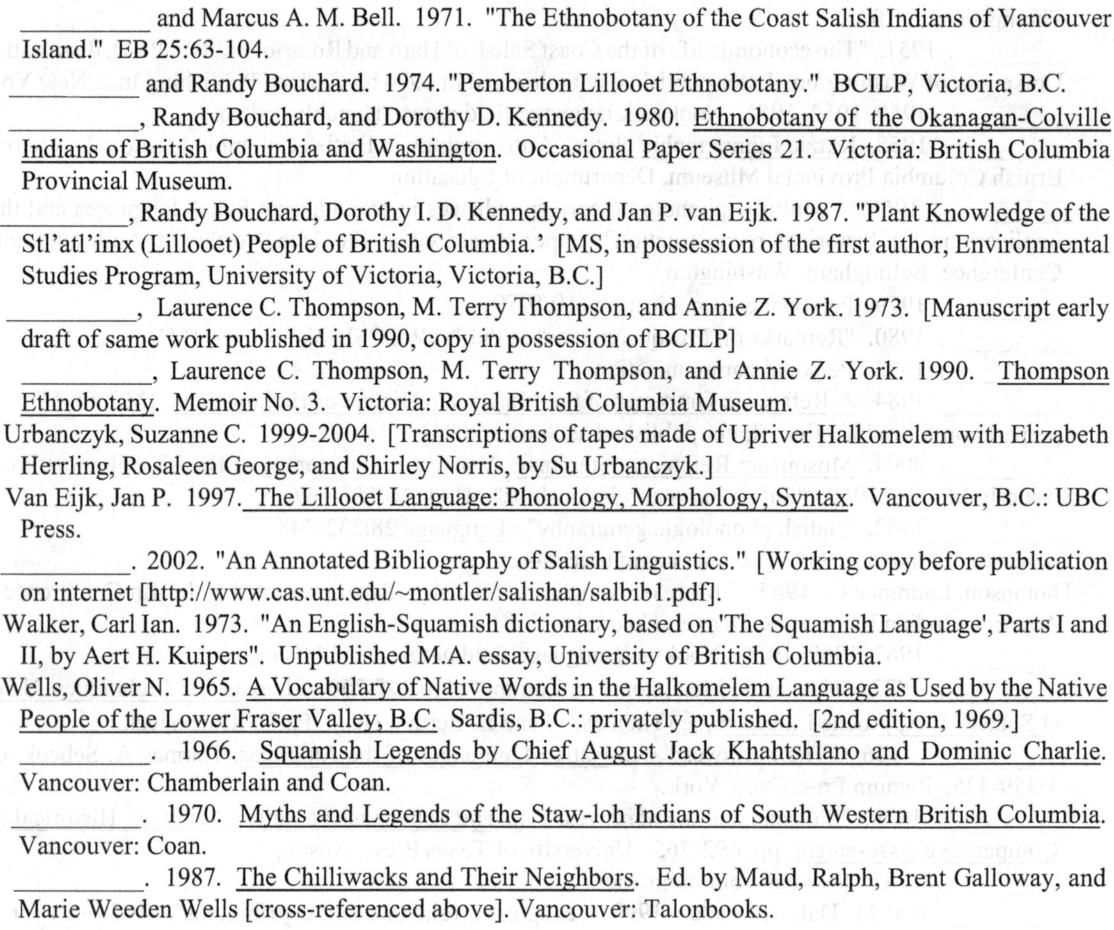

__________ and Marcus A. M. Bell. 1971. "The Ethnobotany of the Coast Salish Indians of Vancouver Island." EB 25:63-104.

__________ and Randy Bouchard. 1974. "Pemberton Lillooet Ethnobotany." BCILP, Victoria, B.C.

__________, Randy Bouchard, and Dorothy D. Kennedy. 1980. Ethnobotany of the Okanagan-Colville Indians of British Columbia and Washington. Occasional Paper Series 21. Victoria: British Columbia Provincial Museum.

__________, Randy Bouchard, Dorothy I. D. Kennedy, and Jan P. van Eijk. 1987. "Plant Knowledge of the Stl'atl'imx (Lillooet) People of British Columbia.' [MS, in possession of the first author, Environmental Studies Program, University of Victoria, Victoria, B.C.]

__________, Laurence C. Thompson, M. Terry Thompson, and Annie Z. York. 1973. [Manuscript early draft of same work published in 1990, copy in possession of BCILP]

__________, Laurence C. Thompson, M. Terry Thompson, and Annie Z. York. 1990. Thompson Ethnobotany. Memoir No. 3. Victoria: Royal British Columbia Museum.

Urbanczyk, Suzanne C. 1999-2004. [Transcriptions of tapes made of Upriver Halkomelem with Elizabeth Herrling, Rosaleen George, and Shirley Norris, by Su Urbanczyk.]

Van Eijk, Jan P. 1997. The Lillooet Language: Phonology, Morphology, Syntax. Vancouver, B.C.: UBC Press.

__________. 2002. "An Annotated Bibliography of Salish Linguistics." [Working copy before publication on internet [http://www.cas.unt.edu/~montler/salishan/salbib1.pdf].

Walker, Carl Ian. 1973. "An English-Squamish dictionary, based on 'The Squamish Language', Parts I and II, by Aert H. Kuipers". Unpublished M.A. essay, University of British Columbia.

Wells, Oliver N. 1965. A Vocabulary of Native Words in the Halkomelem Language as Used by the Native People of the Lower Fraser Valley, B.C. Sardis, B.C.: privately published. [2nd edition, 1969.]

__________. 1966. Squamish Legends by Chief August Jack Khahtshlano and Dominic Charlie. Vancouver: Chamberlain and Coan.

__________. 1970. Myths and Legends of the Staw-loh Indians of South Western British Columbia. Vancouver: Coan.

__________. 1987. The Chilliwacks and Their Neighbors. Ed. by Maud, Ralph, Brent Galloway, and Marie Weeden Wells [cross-referenced above]. Vancouver: Talonbooks.

Abbreviations for references cited (language or dialect is listed in parentheses)
A78 for Amoss 1978 (Nk)
B74a for Bouchard 1974a (Saan)
B74b for Bouchard 1974b (Cw)
B74c for Bouchard 1974c (Th)
B75prelim for Bouchard 1975 (MCx)
B77 for Bouchard 1977 (Se)
B78 for Bouchard 1978a (Bouchard's corrected Squamjsh Classified Word List (largely with LM)
B80pc for Beaumont 1980 personal communication (Se)
B83pc for Beaumont 1983 personal communication (Se)
Beaumont 1985 or B85 for Beaumont 1985 (Se)
BG83-84 Samish and Saanich field notes for Galloway 1983-1984 (Sam & Saan)
Boas 1890 Scowlitz ms.field notes in APS library
Boas 1886 Pentlatch field notes (copy in B.C. Provincial Archives, orig, APS lib. Philadelphia)
Boas 1895 (Indianische Sagen ..., 1977 Bertz translation) or Boas 1895 (Bertz 1977 translation) for Boas (Bouchard & Kennedy) 2002.
Boas 1895 (Bertz)(1980 version), later published as Boas (Bouchard & Kennedy) 2002.
Bouchard 1978b (ICx)
Bouchard and Turner 1976 (Sq)
CDB78 for Charles, Demers, & Bowman 1978
Davis 1970
Davis 1981pc for Davis 1981 personal communication
Demers 1982 p.c. or D82pc for Demers 1982 personal communication
Deming (6/21/79) for a place & date of elicitation by Galloway of Nk terms in Galloway 1974-80
DJ: WS 1955 for Diamond Jenness ed. by Wayne Suttles 1955 (The Faith of a Coast Salish Indian) with Katzie ethnographic notes by Suttles; Victoria: Anthropology in British Columbia)
Diamond Jenness's field notes on Wm. Sepass (copy in collection of Stó:lō Nation)
Duff 1952
E69 for Efrat 1969 (Sooke)
Elders Group 6/11/75 for the date and source of elicitation by Galloway of Th & UHk terms in Galloway 1970-2002
ES for Elmendorf and Suttles 1960
Galloway 1974-80 (Nk & UHk field notes)
G82 or G82a or Galloway 1982 for Galloway 1982a (PCS)
G83b or G83 for Galloway 1983b (Nk)(Pron., Transit. & Control)
G84a for Galloway 1984a (Nk)
G84b for Galloway 1984b (Nk also)
G85: field notes for Galloway 1985 ms. field notes (Sam)
G86 or G86a for Galloway 1986a (PCS)
G88a or G88 for Galloway 1988a (PCS)
Galloway 1990 for Galloway 1990a
Galloway, Adams & Renteria 2004a
GC 9/7/77 for the partial speaker (George Cline) & date of elicitation of some Nk terms in Galloway 1974-80
Gibbs for Gibbs (1859-1863) ms. "Indian Nomenclature" (Smithsonian)(Hk, Nk, and Th place names)
Gunther 73 for Gunther 1973
H-T 1902 or H-T 02 for Hill-Tout 1902 (UHk)

H-T 1904 or H-T04 for Hill-Tout 1904 (UHk, Cheh. & Scowlitz dials.)
H76 for Hess 1976
Haeberlin (Thompson) 1974
Harris77 for Herbert Harris 1977 (ICx)
JH or JH66 for Jimmy Gene Harris 1966
Johnson 1978 (CJ or Chinook Jargon)
K1980 for Kinkade 1980, 1982, 1983a, 1983b and 1984 (Pentlatch)
K67 for Kuipers 1967 (Sq)
K69 for Kuipers 1969 (Sq)
K74 for Kuipers 1974 (Sh)
KB76 for Kennedy and Bouchard 1976 (Sq)
Kinkade 1981 (Columbian)
LT:GS for Thompson 1967, 1969, 1970. Nooksack language field notes and tapes unpublished, words transcribed from George Swanaset (Nk)
M68 for Mitchell 1968 (Song.)
M87 for Mattina 1987 (Colville-Okanagan)
M86 for Montler 1986 (Saan.)
Nater 1977 (BC)
Newman 1979 for Newman 1977, 1979a, 1979b, and 1980 (Proto-Salish)
NT79 for Nile Thompson 1979
NT82pc for Nile Thompson 1982 personal communication
PA:GS for file cards from Amoss, Pamela T. 1955-1956, 1969-1970. Nooksack language field notes and tapes, unpublished (Nk)
PA61 for Amoss 1961
PA78 for Amoss 1978
place names reference file # for place names files by Reuben Ware (in collection of Stó:lō Nation)
Raffo 1972
S79pc for Suttles p.c. 10/9/79
S82pc or WS82pc for Suttles 1982 personal communication
Suttles 1950 (Nk)
Suttles 1955 (Katzie dial. of Downriver Halkomelem)
Suttles65 for Suttles 1965
Suttles ca1984
Thompson and Thompson71 for Thompson and Thompson 1971 (Clallam)
T72 for Thompson 1972 (Lummi, some Sq)(in Bouchard & Turner 76)
T77 for Timmers 1977 (Se)
Thompson, Turner and Thompson 1973
TTE74 for Thompson, Thompson and Efrat 1974
Turner 1974 (Haida, BC & Lillooet)
Turner and Bouchard: Pemberton Lillooet Ethnobotany (ms.)(1974) for Turner and Bouchard 1974
Turner, Bouchard and Kennedy 1980 (Ok)
Turner and Bell 1971
VH83pc for Vi Hilbert 1983 personal communication (Ld)
W73 for Walker 1973 (Sq)
Wells 1965 for Wells 1965 (lst ed.)
Wells 1966

Galloway: Upriver Halkomelem Dictionary

Halkomelem to English

A

<á>, free root //ʔɛ́ ~ ʔə́//, TIME ['*recent past tense*'], phonology: free variation, free variant: <é>, //ʔə́//, syntactic comment: subject pronouns are suffixed to this verb to form ambiguous past, example: <**átst álhtel**>, //ʔɛ́-ct ʔɛ́ɬtəl//, /'*we ate*'/, attested by AC, <**échap mő́kw' álhtel cheláqelh(elh)**>, //ʔə́-cɛp mók'ʷ ʔɛ́ɬtəl cəlɛ́qəɬ(-əɬ)//, /'*you all ate yesterday*'/, <**étsel lhíts'**>, //ʔə́-cəl ɬíc'//, /'*I got cut*'/, <**ét'wōlh lám**>, //ʔə́-t'wə-wəɬ lɛ́m//, /'*he must have gone*'/ (grammatical analysis: t'we *must, I guess, evidential*; -welh *already)*, <**átsel totí:lt**>, //ʔɛ́-cəl tá·[-C_1ə-]l=í·l=T//, /'*I used to think*'/, syntactic analysis: auxiliary verb, attested by AC.

<**-á**>, (/-ɛ́/), MOOD ['*interrogative*'], phonology: combination of -e *interrogative* with e at end of preceding morpheme (by regular morphophonemic rule, e-e → **á** or //ə-ə// → ɛ́), vowel merger, syntactic analysis: interrogative affix; found in <**ōwáchap lámelep ~ ōwáchap lámélep**>, //ʔə́wə-ə-c-ɛp lɛ́m-ələp//, /'*Aren't you folks going?*'/, attested by IHHTC, <**ōwálh**>, //ʔə́wə-ə-ɬ//, /'*didn't he (or she) ?*'/ (syntactic analysis: negative interrogative past), <**ōwá:ta**>, //ʔəwə́-ə-tɛ//, /'*is it none?, is it nobody?, didn't anybody?*'/, <**lewá:, Lópet**>, //ləwə-ə́, lápət//, /'*Is it you, Robert?*'/.

<**-à**>, //-ɛ̀//, TIME ['*later*'], usage: found in the speech of a few older monolinguals as well as that of SP, prob. archaic, phonology: appears as a suffix though not a tense suffix, syntactic comment: semantically similar to the class of adverbial particles and used like them but suffixed unlike them, syntactic analysis: suffixed adverbial particle, dialects: *Tait only so far*, attested by SP, MP, MJ (Mrs. August Jim); found in <**maythométsta**>, //mɛy=T-amə́-cət-ɛ̀//, /'*we'll help you later*'/ (grammatical analysis: root -purposeful control transitivizer-2so-1ps-adverbial particle), attested by SP.

<**=á:**>, da //=ɛ́·//, QUAL ['*overly ?*'], MOOD, syntactic analysis: lexical suffix, derivational suffix; found in <**kw'esá:**>, //k'ʷəs=ɛ́·//, /'*overheated*'/ (contrast <**kw'ó:kw'es**> *hot*, contrast <**kw'és=**> *get burned*), perhaps <**selá:**>, //səl=ɛ́· (but more likely that is s=hə=lɛ́·)//, /'*tight*'/ (contrast possibly <**sí:l= ~ sel**> *spin)*.

<**-a ~ -a'**>, ia & fr //**-ɛ(ʔ)** ~ ʔɛ//, PRON /'*your (sg.), second person sg. possessive pronoun, second person sg. subordinate subject pronoun*'/, syntactic comment: affixed to the word (usu. demonstrative article) which precedes the nominal possessed or verb subordinated, syntactic analysis: possessive pronoun affix, dialects: *Sumas, Tait, and Cheh. speakers seem to prefer -a', Chill. speakers seem to prefer -a*, see dialect form <**-a (Chill.)**>, also <**a**>, //ʔɛ// occurs sentence initial or following li *interrogative* or li or i verbal auxiliaries or tl'ó *that's*, and in some other constructions, -a(') occurs elsewhere, also <**-a**>, //-ɛ//, dialects: *Chill.*, example: <**lí a stl'í kw'e tí**>, //lí ʔɛ s=ƛ'í k'ʷə tí//, /'*do you want some tea?*'/ (grammatical analysis: yes-no question your want some tea), <**ta(') má:l**>, //t-ɛ(ʔ) mɛ́·l//, /'*your father*'/, <**tha(') tá:l**>, //θ-ɛ(ʔ) tɛ́·l//, /'*your mother*'/, <**tl'ó a swá**>, //ƛ'á ʔɛ swɛ́//, /'*that's yours*'/, <**skw'áy kw'a(')s kw'étslexw**>, //s=k'ʷɛ́y k'ʷ-ɛ(ʔ)-s k'ʷə́c=l-əxʷ//, /'*you can't see it*'/, literally /'it's impossible that you see it'/ (syntactic analysis: nominal.-impossible demonstrative article-possessive pronoun affix-nominal./subord. see-non-control transitive-3o), <**li a sqwá:lewel kwes xwe'í:s wáy:eles**>, //li ʔɛ s=qɛ̀·l=əwəl kʷə-s xʷə=ʔí·-s wɛ́y:əl=əs//, /'*Do you think they'll come tomorrow?*'/, literally /'is it your thought that they arrive tomorrow?'/, attested by AC.

<**-a -elep ~ -a' -elep**>, (/**-ɛ -əl-əp ~ -ɛʔ -əl-əp**/), PRON /'*your (pl.), you folks's, second person plural possessive pronoun, second person plural subordinate subject*'/, (the <**-el**> portion is probably the same as the infix <**=el=**> *plural*), syntactic analysis: is, syntactic comment: also used as subordinate subject by possessing a nominalized clause, the -a is suffixed to the first element of the nominal phrase or clause (usually the demonstrative article) and the -elep is suffixed to the next word in the clause or phrase, example: <**ta má:lelep**>, //t-ɛ mɛ́·l-əl-əp//, /'*you folks's father*'/, <**a' stl'íyelep kw'a's lámelep.**>, //ʔɛʔ s=ƛ'í·y-əl-əp k'ʷ-ɛʔ-s lɛ́=m-əl-əp//, /'*You folks want to go.*'/, literally /'(it) is you folks' want that you folks go'/.

<**ahíw**>, free root //ʔɛhíw//, DIR /'*(be) upstream, east (in some contexts)*'/, semantic environment ['*going east* for a speaker anywhere on the Fraser River from Vancouver, B.C. to about Laidlaw, B.C., since the river flows east to west on this stretch'], syntactic analysis: adverb/adverbial verb, also <**ehí(:)w**>, //ʔəhí(·)w// in faster speech, example: <**lám kw'e ahíw**>, //lɛ́m k'ʷə ʔɛhíw//, /'*he's going upstream*'/, attested by EB, <**lámtsel kw'e ehí:w**>, //lɛ́m-c-əl k'ʷə ʔəhí·w//, /'*I'm going east.*'/, attested by EB.

<**xwehíwel**>, incs //xʷə=əhíw=əl//, DIR ['*go upstream*'], literally /'get=upstream=go'/, (<**xwe=**> *get, become*), (<**=el**> *go, come*), syntactic analysis: intransitive verb, adverb/adverbial verb.

<**ák'**>, free root //ʔɛ́k'//, probably /'*cute.*'/, EFAM, usage: expression when playing with a baby and the baby is cute, phonology: diminutive fronting (yielding k'), syntactic analysis: interjection, dialects: *Tait; unknown whether in other dialects*, attested by AD.

<**ákwelex**>, HUNT ['*shooting*'], *see* kwél.

<**-ál**>, is, //-ɛ́l//, PRON ['*first person singular subjunctive subject*'], syntactic comment: can be suffixed to forms prefixed with <we-> *when, if* or to the first subordinate verb after a negative verb, can also add the *when/if* meaning even without the we- prefix being present, also <**-l**>, //-l// after auxiliary verbs ending in i (í, lí, mí, lhí); as in <**welámàl**>, //wə-lɛ́=m-ɛ́l//, /'*if/when I go*'/, phonology: downstepping, example: <**yó:swe welámàl.**>, //yá·swə wə-lɛ́=m-ɛ́l//, /'*I might go., I don't know if I could go.*'/, <**éwetsel lámàl.**>, //ʔə́wə-c-əl lɛ́=m-ɛ́l//, /'*I don't go., I won't go.*'/, <**chexw maythóx kw'els éwe líyemál.**>, //c-əxʷ mɛy=T-áxʸ k'ʷ-əl-s ʔə́wə líy=əm-ɛ́l//, /'*You helped me not to laugh.*'/, <**éwetsel lí:l lám.**>, //ʔə́wə-c-əl lí·-l lɛ́=m//, /'*I didn't/don't go.*'/.

<**=á:l**> ds, //=ɛ́·l//, DESC ['*similar to, -like, or part/portion* ']; found in <**xaweqá:l**>, ds //xɛw(=)əq=ɛ́·l//, EB /'*yarrow, also parsely fern*'/, ['*Achillea millefolium*, also *Cryptogramma crispa*'], lit. "carrot like, similar to a carrot", <**sx̱wewál**>, df //s=x̣ʷəwɛ́l or s=x̣ʷɛ́w=ə[=M2=]l or more likely x̣ʷ[=F=]əw(=)ə=ɛ́l//, EZ ['*fox*'], ['*Vulpes fulva cascadensis*'], most likely lit. "cougar-like, similar to a cougar".

<**'ál ~ ál**>, bound root, //ʔɛ́l(=)əm//, root could mean *pole/shaft/length*

<**s'álem**>, dnom //s=ʔɛ́ləm//, [sʔɛ́ləm], FSH /'*spear, shaft (of spear/harpoon/gaff-hook), gaff-hook pole*'/, HUNT /'*spear, shaft of spear*'/, (<**s=**> nominalizer), probably root <**'ál**> *pole/shaft/length*?, possibly <**=em**> *place to have/get*, syntactic analysis: nominal, attested by BHTTC, (compare with <**s'aléts**> *bottom of a tree, trunk of a tree* with same possible root (=lets 'on the bottom')), also <**s'álém**>, //s=ʔɛ́lə́m//, [sʔɛ́lə́m], dialects: *Cheh.*, attested by EL.

<**s'aléqs ~ s'eléqs**>, dnom //s=ʔɛl=ə[=´=]qs//, MC ['*point*'], (<**s= nominalizer**>), probably root <**'al**> *pole/shaft/length*?, lx <**=eqs**> *on the nose, on the point*, probably <= ´=> *derivational*, phonology: vowel-reduction, stress-shift, geminate consonant (unusual word finallly), syntactic analysis: nominal, attested by DM (Chill.), example: <**s'eléqs: te lháts'tel**>, //s=ʔəl=ə́qs-s tə ɬɛ́c'=təl//, [sʔələ́qs· tə ɬǽc'təl], /'*point of a knife*'/, attested by DM.

<**s'álqsel**>, dnom //s=ʔɛ́l=qsəl//, [sʔɛ́lqsəl], ANA ['*tip or point of one's nose*'], LAND ['*point of land*'], semantic environment ['semantic environments determine which alloseme is selected (those with components of ['land'] select the second, those with ['animate'] select the first listed'], (<**s=**> *nominalizer*), probably root <**'ál**> *pole, shaft, length*?, lx <**=qsel**> *on the nose, on the point*, syntactic analysis: nominal.

<**s'aléts**> dnom //s=ʔɛ(l)=lə́c//, EB ['*bottom of a tree, trunk of a tree*'], (<**s=**> *nominalizer*, <=lets> *on the bottom*), syntactic analysis: nominal, attested by BHTTC

<**s'alétsmel**>, dnom //s=ʔɛlə́c=məl//, BLDG /'*foundation of a house, bottom of a tree*'/, EB ['*bottom of a tree*'], (<**s= nominalizer**>), (<**=mel**> *part, portion*; prob. also =lets *on the bottom*), syntactic analysis: nominal, attested by BHTTC, also <**alétsmel**>, //ʔɛlə́c=məl//, phonology: free variant.

<**shxw'állhelh**>, dnom //sxʷ=ʔɛ́l=ɬəɬ//, [šxʷʔɛ́lɬəɬ], ANA ['*front of the neck*'], (<**sxw=**> *nominalizer*), probably root <**'ál**> *pole/shaft/length*, lx <**=lhelh** (or poss. **=llhelh)**> *on the throat, on the front of the neck*, syntactic analysis: nominal.

<**=á:lá ~ =álá ~ =àlà ~ =ela**>, da //=ɛ́·lɛ́ ~ =əlɛ//, SH /'*container for, receptacle for*'/, MC, numc, syntactic analysis: lexical suffix, derivational suffix; found in <**shxwhéyqwala**>, //sxʷ=hɛ́=yəqʷ=ɛlɛ//, /'*firepit*'/, literally /'container for burning'/, <**shxwetl'qelá:lá**>, //s=xʷəƛ̓=qəl=ɛ́·lɛ́//, /'*pillow case, container for pillow, pillow*'/, literally /'container for rolled thing under head'/, <**sqelxwá:lá**>, //sqəlxʷ=ɛ́·lɛ́//, /'*throat, gullet*'/, literally /'greedy + container'/, <**shxwiymálá**>, //s=xʷiy=əm=ɛ́lɛ́//, /'*store*'/, literally /'nominal + sell + container for'/, <**shxwlámálá**>, //sxʷlɛ́m=ɛ́lɛ́//, /'*bottle*'/, <**shxwmálahá:lá**>, //sxʷ=mɛ́lɛ=hɛ́·lɛ́//, /'*fishing basket, bait basket*'/, literally /'nominal + bait + container for'/, <**lhà:ts'telálá**>, //ɬɛ̀·c'=təl=ɛ́lɛ́//, /'*knife handle*'/, literally /'cutting + device + container for'/, <**sp'òtl'emálá**>, //s=p'àƛ̓'əm=ɛ́lɛ́//, /'*(tobacco) pipe*'/, literally /'smoke + container for'/, <**sp'otl'emá:látel**>, //s=p'aƛ̓'əm=ɛ́·lɛ́=təl//, /'*smokehole*'/, <**smōkw'e'á:lá**>, //smok'ʷə=ʔɛ́·lɛ́//, /'*graveyard*'/ (compare <**smṓkw'a**> *grave)*, <**spotelálá**>, //spatəl=ɛ́lɛ́//, /'*mast*'/ (compare <**s=pót=(t)el**> *sail)*, <**sts'axtálá**>, //sc'ɛxʸt=ɛ́lɛ́//, /'*knothole*'/, literally /'branch + container for'/, <**S<u>x</u>wá:yehà:là**>, //sx̣ʷɛ́·yə=hɛ̀·lɛ̀//, /'*Squia=a=ala (Chilliwack Indian Reserve #7, a village in pre-contact times also)*'/ (compare <**<u>x</u>wá:y**> *many people perished together)*, <**se<u>x</u>we'álá**>, //səx̣ʷə=ʔɛ́lɛ́//, /'*bladder*'/, literally /'urine + container for'/, <**kw'él(:)a**>, //k'ʷə́l(·)ɛ//, /'*stomach*'/, <**<u>x</u>elwéla**>, //x̣əlw=ə́lɛ//, /'*horn rings for dip nets*'/ (compare <**<u>x</u>álew**> *spoon.*

<**Alámex**>, us //ʔɛlɛ́məxʸ//, PLN /'*the whole Agassiz (B.C.) area (JL), Agassiz Mountain (AK), place near Agassiz where Hamersley Hopyards were*'/, syntactic analysis: nominal, attested by JL, AK, possibly other speakers, other sources: Duff 1952 /ɛlɛ́mɪx/, example: <**lámtsel te Alámex kwsetst lhím te hóps.**>, //lɛ́m-cəl tə ʔɛlɛ́məxʸ kʷsə-ct ɬím tə háps//, /'*I'm going to Alámex so that we (can) pick hops.*'/, attested by JL.

<**Alámex Smámelt**>, //ʔɛlɛ́məxʸ s=mɛ́·[=C_1ə=]lt//, PLN ['*Agassiz Mountain*'], syntactic analysis: nominal phrase with modifier(s), attested by JL, AK.

<**=ále**>, da //=ɛ́lə//, HUMC ['*people*'], semantic environment ['with numerals 3-99, kw'í:l'], syntactic comment: obligatory, syntactic analysis: lexical suffix, derivational suffix; found in <**lhq'á:tsále**>, //ɬq'ɛ́·c=ɛ́lə//, /'*five people*'/.

<**álel**>, chrs //ʔɛ́ləl//, [ʔɛ́ləl], EZ ['*black-billed magpie*'], ['*Pica pica*'], possibly <**-eC2**> *out-of-control*, probably old <**=R2**> *characteristic* in BJ's pronunciation, phonology: old reduplication, syntactic analysis: nominal, dialects: *Tait + other elders*, attested by ME, AD, others, also <**ál'el**>, //ʔɛ́l=C_1əC_2//, [ʔɛ́lʔəl], dialects: *Chill.*, attested by BJ.

<**alelí'**>, us //ʔɛləlíʔ//, EFAM /'*yipes., eek.*'/, usage: said to oneself or to someone else when scared, syntactic analysis: interjection.

<**-àlèm**>, is, //-ɛ̀lə̀m or -ɛ̀l=əm//, PRON [*'first person singular patient or object of passive'*], VOIC, comment: historically may be connected with **-ál** *first person sing. subject*, probably <**-em**> *passive*, phonology: possible updrifting, syntactic analysis: inflectional suffix; found in <**ó:thàlèm**>, //ʔá·=T-ɛ̀lə̀m//, /*'I was called.'*/, <**kw'étslàlèm.**>, //k'ʷə́c=l-ɛ̀lə̀m//, /*'I was seen.'*/, <**éysthàlem.**>, //ʔɛ́y=sT-ɛ̀lə̀m//, /*'I was liked.'*/, example: <**éwe lís yéthesthàlèm.**>, //ʔə́wə lí-s yə́θə=sT-ɛ̀lə̀m//, /*'I wasn't told.'*/, syntactic comment: note the third person subordinate subject/agent in lí-s.

<**=á:leq ~ =eleq**>, da //=ɛ́·ləq ~ =ələq//, WATR [*'waves'*], SH, syntactic analysis: lexical suffix, derivational suffix, also <**=eleq**>, //=ələq//; as in <**thithehá:leq**>, //θiθəh=ɛ́·ləq//, /*'waves are getting bigger'*/ (compare <**thíthe**> *bigger*, <**-h**> epenthetic), dialects: *Seabird Island dialect*; found in <**smá:yeleq**>, //smɛ́·y=ələq//, /*'wave'*/, root meaning unknown unless sméya *bay*, <**xetáléqetel**>, //xʸət=ɛ́lə́q(ə)=təl or xʸət=ɛ́lə́qə(l)=təl//, /*'sinker line'*/ (compare <**xá:t**> *a sinker, lead weight, lead*), <**stl'epá:leq**>, //sƛ'əp=ɛ́·ləq//, /*'underskirt, underslip'*/, literally /'underwaves'/.

<**aleqá:y**>, EZ /*'slow-worm ("a slow-moving foot-long snake")*, actually *a species of blind legless lizard'*/, compare <**álhqey ~ álhqay**> *snake* from which it derives.

<**=áléqel**>, da //=ɛ́lə́qəl//, ANA [*'(in) the head'*], syntactic analysis: lexical suffix, derivational suffix; found in <**x̱elháléqel**>, //x̣əɬ=ɛ́lə́qəl//, /*'headache'*/, <**tesáléqel**>, //təs=ɛ́lə́qəl//, /*'bump one's head'*/, <**smeltáléqel**>, //sməlt=ɛ́lə́qəl//, /*'kidneys'*/, root probably <**smált**> *stone*, literally /"stone in its head"/.

<**=áléqep ~ =áleqep**>, da //=ɛ́lə́qəp ~ =ɛ́ləqəp//, SM /*'fragrance, smell, odor'*/, SD [*'sound'*], syntactic analysis: lexical suffix, derivational suffix, phonetic & semantic comment: it seems most likely there has been a recent phonological convergence of two separate morphemes here, perhaps {**=(ál)eqep**} 'fragrance, smell, odor' and {**=aléqep**} 'sound' since the former examples (smell) rarely have the next to last <e> with high tone while the latter examples (sound) almost always have the next to last <e> with high tone (<é>), but there has been some phonological and synthesethic convergence where examples of each have //**=áléqep**//; as in <**eyáleqep ~ iyáleqep**>, //ʔɛy=ɛ́ləqəp//, /*'good smell'*/, <**qéleqep**>, //qə́l=əqəp//, /*'bad smell'*/, <**selchímáléqep**>, //səlcím=ɛ́lə́qəp//, /*'how does it smell?;'*/ (compare <**selchím**> *how is it?, how?)*, <**qelqéyláléqep**>, //qəlqɛ́yl=ɛ́lə́qəp//, /*'turn bad in smell'*/ (compare <**qelqéyl**> *turn bad)*, <**simáléqep ~ simáleqep**>, //s=(ʔ)ɛy=əm=ɛ́lə́qəp or s=(ʔ)i(y)=(ə)m=ɛ́ləqəp//, /*'bad stink'*/ (compare < **ey=ém**> *strong*, with <**s=**> *nominal or stative*), <**stáléqep**>, //sɛt=ɛ́lə́qəp//, /*'a distant sound'*/, <**sasetáléqep**>, //sɛ[=C_1ə=]t=ɛ́lə́qəp//, /*'keep on hearing a distant sound'*/ (compare <**stáléqep**> *a distant sound*), <**eháléqep**>, //ʔəh=ɛ́lə́qəp//, /*'a faint sound carried by the air, sound within earshot or hearing range or distance'*/ (compare <**eh=ó:t**> *wrap s-th up)*, <**thxwáléqep**>, //θəxʷ=ɛ́lə́qəp//, /*'a steady sound that's been stopped for a while'*/ (compare <**théxw**> *disappear*), <**théxweleqep**>, //θə[-´-]xʷ=ɛləqəp//, /*'sound gettting softer'*/, example: <**welóy théxweleqep**>, //wə=láy θə[-´-]xʷ=ɛləqəp//, /*'sound getting softer'*/; also found in <**chqwáléqep**>, //cqʷ=ɛ́lə́qəp//, /*'a loud sound'*/, example: <**mí xwe chqwáléqep.**>, //mí xʷə cqʷ=ɛ́lə́qəp//, /*'sound getting louder'*/; found in <**iyotháléqep**>, //ʔɛy=aθ=ɛ́lə́qəp//, /*'sharp sound'*/ (compare <**iyóth**> *sharp)*, <**x̱wemx̱wemaléqep**>, //x̣ʷəm=C_1əC_2=ɛ́lə́qəp//, /*'talks fast (*perhaps also for *"fast sounds"?)'*/ (compare <**x̱wém**> *fast, hurry*).

<**alétsa**>, free root //ʔɛlə́cɛ//, DIR [*'where (is it)?'*], syntactic analysis: interrogative verb, dialects: *Chill., Sumas, Tait, most Cheh.*, other sources: ES /likʷɛʔəlɛ́cɛ/ (but Musqueam /ə́nəcɛ/) *where?*, also <**létsa**>, //lə́cɛ//, attested by EB (of Cheh.), example: <**alétsa ta' lálém?**>, //ʔɛlə́cɛ tɛʔ lɛ́lə́m//, /*'where's your house?'*/, attested by Deming, <**alétsa kw'as lé thìyt?**>, //ʔɛlə́cɛ k'ʷ-ɛ-s lə́ θìy=T//, /*'where did you make it?'*/, attested by AC, <**létsa kw'asé thìyt?**>, //lə́cɛ k'ʷ-ɛ-s-ə́ θìy=T//, /*'where did you make it?'*/, attested by EB, <**kwe elétsa?**>, //kʷə ʔələ́cɛ//, /*'where is he?'*/, attested by EB, <**chel**

ōlhq'élexw we'ís létsa.>, //cəl ʔəw-ɬ=q'əl=l-əxʷ wə-ʔí-s ləcɛ//, /*'I know where it is.'*/, attested by EB, <**í:lhchexw alétsa?**>, //ʔí·-ɬ-c-əxʷ ʔɛləcɛ//, /*'where have you been?'*/, attested by AC.

<**alétsestxwes**>, caus //ʔɛləcɛ=sT-əxʷ-əs//, DIR [*'wherever he's got it'*], (<**=st**> *causative control transitivizer*, <**-exw**> *third person object*, <**-es**> *third person subject*), syntactic analysis: transitive verb, attested by AD.

<**tel'alétsa**>, ds //təl=ʔɛləcɛ ~ təl=ʔələcɛ ~ təl=·əcɛ//, DIR /*'where is he/she/it from?, from where?'*/, (<**tel=**> *from*), phonology: tel'elétsa and tel:étsa are variants at increasing speed, syntactic analysis: interrogative verb, also <**tel:écha ~ te'elécha**>, //təl=·əcɛ ~ tə=ʔələcɛ//, dialects: *EB of Cheh.*, example: <**tel'alétsechexw?**>, also <**tel:étsechexw?**> is found in faster speech, //təl=ləcɛ-c-əxʷ ~ təl=ʔɛləcɛ-c-əxʷ//, /*'where are you from?'*/, attested by IHTTC, <**tel'elétsa tútl'ò?**>, //təl=ʔələcɛ t=ú=ƛ'à//, /*'where is he from?'*/, attested by CT, HT, <**chel ōlhq'élexw we'ís te'elécha kwses xwe'í.**>, //cəl ʔow=ɬ=q'əl=l-əxʷ wə-ʔí-s tə=ʔələcɛ kʷ-s-əs xʷə=ʔí//, /*'I know where he came (arrived) from.'*/ (syntactic analysis: sentence with subjunctive phrase, also with relative indefinite pronoun) attested by EB.

<**álex**>, free root //ʔɛ́ləxʸ//, HUMC, KIN /*'sibling, brother, sister'*/, (semological comment: sex gender is indicated in the demonstrative article or other semantic context external to this word), syntactic analysis: nominal, usage: this word has a limited distribution; more speakers use only forms meaning either *elder sibling* or *younger sibling*, i.e., they must specify the relative age, dialects: *Chill.*, attested by AC, other sources: ES /ʔɛ́ləxʸ/ *sibling*, S82pc 'sibling of opposite sex', Salish cognate: Squamish /ʔáyiš/ 'cousin or sibling of opposite sex W73:68, K67:394, also /*'brother'*/, dialects: *Tait (and poss. Cheh.)*, example: <**lí: skwetáxw kwtha álex?**>, //lí· s-kʷətɛ́xʷ kʷ-θ-ɛ ʔɛ́ləxʸ//, /*'Is your brother/sister in?'*/, attested by AC, <**álexs**>, //ʔɛ́ləxʸ-s//, /*'her brother'*/, attested by AC.

<**el'álex**>, pln //C$_1$əC$_2$-ʔɛ́ləxʸ//, HUMC, KIN /*'(siblings), brothers'*/, (<**R3-**> *plural*), phonology: reduplication, syntactic analysis: nominal, dialects: *Chill.*, attested by AC.

<**shxw'álex**>, dnom //sxʷ=ʔɛ́ləxʸ//, HUMC, KIN /*'sister-in-law, husband's sister, brother's wife, wife's sister (EB)'*/, syntactic analysis: nominal, dialects: *Cheh., Chill.*, attested by EB, AC, other sources: ES /šxʷʔɛ́ləxʸ/ *husband's sister, woman's brother's wife*, also <**shxw'áléx**>, //sxʷ=ʔɛ́ləxʸ//, dialects: *Tait*, attested by CT, also /*'wife's sister'*/, attested by EB, example: <**tl'ól shxw'álex**>, //ƛ'á-l šxʷ=ʔɛ́ləxʸ//, /*'That's my sister-in-law.'*/, attested by AC.

<**shxw'el'álex**>, pln //sxʷ=C$_1$əC$_2$-ʔɛ́ləxʸ//, HUMC, KIN [*'sisters-in-law'*], phonology: reduplication, syntactic analysis: nominal, example: <**tl'ó: a shxw'el'álex**>, //ƛ'á-: ʔɛ šxʷ=C$_1$əC$_2$-ʔɛ́ləxʸ//, /*'Are those your sisters-in-law?'*/, attested by AC.

<**=á:lews**>, da //=ɛ́·ləws//, EB /*'leaf, leaves'*/, syntactic analysis: lexical suffix; found in <**p'elp'àlq'emá:lews**>, //p'əlp'ɛ̀lq'əm=ɛ́·ləws// or //C$_1$əC$_2$=p'ɛ̀lq'əm=ɛ́·ləws//,, /*'poplar, cottonwood, trembling aspen; sparkling leaves'*/, literally /'many=glittering/sparkling=leaf'/, attested by SP, AD (compare <**p'álq'em**> *sparkling)*, <**xwesá:lews**>, //xʷəs=ɛ́·ləws//, /*'fallen leaves'*/ (compare <**xwís=et**> *shake leaves or fruit off a tree or bush)*, attested by SP, AD, <**ch'okw'e'á:lews**>, //c'ak'ʷə=ʔɛ́·ləws//, /*'skunk cabbage leaf or leaves'*/, attested by SP, AD (compare <**ch'ókw'e**> *skunk cabbage)*, <**q'emō:welhpá:lews**>, //q'əmó·w=əɬp=ɛ́·ləws//, /*'big-leaf maple tree leaf'*/, attested by SP, AD (compare <**q'emṓ:w=elhp**> *maple tree)*, <**chewō:welhpá:lews**>, //cəwó·w=əlp=ɛ́·ləws//, /*'cottonwood leaf or leaves'*/ (compare <**chew=ṓ:w=elhp**> *cottonwood tree)*, <**pipehomá:lews**>, //pipəham=ɛ́·ləws//, /*'plantain'*/, (semological comment: the plant is always translated "frog leaf" by the speakers, never as "plantain" an unfamiliar term).

<**alíliyem ~ elíliyem**>, ABFC [*'laughter'*], *see* líyém ~ leyém.

<**=á:lí:ya**>, da //=ɛ́·lí·yɛ//, ANA /*'on the ear, in the ear'*/, syntactic analysis: lexical suffix, derivational

suffix; found in <**kw'qwá:lí:ya**>, //k'ʷqʷ=ɛ́·lí·yɛ//, /'*hit on the ear with a stick-like object or club*'/, <**s=lhellhelp'á:lí:ya**>, //s=C_1əC_2=ɬəl=p'=ɛ́·lí·yɛ//, /'*sloppy or flabby ears*'/, <**sqwelqwelá:lí:ya**>, //s=C_1əC_2=qʷəl=ɛ́·lí·yɛ//, /'*hair in the ears*'/, <**t'emxá:lí:ya**>, //t'əmxʸ=ɛ́·lí·yɛ//, /'*braid hair*'/, literally /'over the ears or side of head'/.

<**álíy ~ 'álíy**>, VALJ /'*more than one is good, good (of many things or people)*'/, *see* **éy ~ éy:**.

<**aliyólés**>, ABFC /'*(have) quick eyes, (have) peeping-Tom eyes*'/, *see* **éy ~ éy:**.

<**álmelh**>, ds //ʔɛ́lm=əɬ//, KIN ['*to baby-sit one's own children*'], possibly root related to that in <**ó:lmets=t**> *wait for someone*, lx <**=əɬ**> *child, baby*, syntactic analysis: intransitive verb, attested by so far Tait: AD, AK.

<**á:lmelh**>, cts //ʔɛ́[-·-]lm=əɬ//, KIN /'*baby-sitting, the one baby-sitting, baby-sitter*'/, SOC, (<**-:-**> *continuative*), phonology: lengthening, syntactic analysis: intransitive verb, nominal after demonstrative article, attested by AD, example: <**tsel á:lmelh**>, //c-əl ʔɛ́·lməɬ//, /'*I'm baby-sitting.*'/, attested by AD, <**tset á:lmelh**>, //c-ət ʔɛ́·lməɬ//, /'*We're baby-sitting.*'/, attested by AD, <**lichxw á:lmelh?**>, //li-c-xʷ ʔɛ́·lməɬ//, /'*Are you the one baby-sitting?*'/, attested by AD.

<**alqá:ls ~ alqáls**>, SOC /'*buy (as structured activity), He bought (as structured activity).*'/, *see* **iléq**.

<**=álqel ~ =élqel**>, da //=ɛ́lqəl ~ =ə́lqəl or =ɛ́l=qəl//, ANA ['*wool*'], WV, ANA ['*feather*'], possibly <**=qel**> *in the head*, syntactic analysis: lexical suffix, derivational suffix, also <**=élqel**>, //=ə́l(=)qəl//; found in <**metú:'álqel ~ metú:lqel**>, //mətú·=ʔɛ́lqəl ~ mətú·lqəl//, /'*sheep wool*'/, root <**lemetú: ~ metú:**> *sheep*, <**sqwemá:yalqel ~ sqwmá:yalqel**>, //sqʷ(ə)mɛ́·y=ɛlqəl//, /'*dog wool*'/, <**p'q'élqel**>, //p'q'=ə́lqəl//, /'*mountain goat*'/, literally /'white wool'/, <**stl'p'álqel**>, //sƛ'p'=ɛ́lqəl//, /'*long feathers*'/, literally /'deep (derivational glottalization as in *tail*) wool'/.

<**á:lqem**>, mdls //ʔɛ́·lq=əm//, cts, ANAA ['*charging (of an angry grizzly for ex.)*'], possibly <**-:-**> *continuative*, (<**=em**> *middle voice*), syntactic analysis: intransitive verb, attested by AD.

<**i'á:lqem**>, mos //ʔi-ʔɛ́·lq=əm (or yi=ʔɛ́·lq=əm)//, mdls, cts, ANAA ['*charging (of an angry grizzly for ex.)*'], (<**i= ~ yi=**> *in motion, travelling while*), syntactic analysis: intransitive verb, attested by AD.

<**álq't**>, pcs //ʔɛ́l(=)q'=T//, HUNT /'*scrape hair off it, scrape hide off of it*'/, possibly <**=q'**> *on something else*, (<**=t**> *purposeful control transitivizer*), syntactic analysis: transitive verb.

<**=á:ls**>, da //=ɛ́·ls//, ASP ['*structured activity non-continuative*'], (semological comment: the activity is usually done for a while, often ceremonial or occupational), syntactic analysis: derivational suffix; found in <**yeqwá:ls**>, //yəqʷ=ɛ́·ls//, /'*burn at a ritual, perform a burning*'/, <**thiyqwá:ls**>, //θiy=qʷɛ=ɛ́·ls//, /'*dig*'/, <**kwxwáls ~ kwxwà·ls**>, //kʷáxʷ-M1=ɛ́ls//, /'*knock, rap*'/, <**thq'á:ls**>, //θɛ́q'=M1=ɛ́·ls//, /'*to spear*'/, <**ts'ekwx̲áls**>, //c'ɛkʷ=x̣=ɛ́ls//, /'*to fry (as an activity)*'/.

<**=á:ltel**>, da //=ɛ́·l(=)təl//, MED ['*medicine*'], possibly <**=tel**> *device, thing*, syntactic analysis: lexical suffix, derivational suffix; found in <**xweqw'ele'á:ltel**>, //xʷəq'ʷələ=ʔɛ́·ltəl//, /'*hangover medicine*'/ (compare probably <**xweqw'éle**> *scouring rush, horsetail fern*), <**th'el'á:ltel**>, //θ'əl=ʔɛ́·ltəl//, /'*heart medicine, juniper*'/ (compare <**th'ále**> *heart*), <**syeqwlhá:ltel**>, //s=yəqʷ=ɬ=ɛ́·ltəl//, /'*tinder*'/ (compare root <**yéqw**> *burn*.

<**=á:ltxw**>, da //=ɛ́·l(=)txʷ//, KIN ['*wives*'], semantic environment ['numeral 2'], possibly <**=txw**> *building, house*, syntactic analysis: lexical suffix, derivational suffix; found in <**islá:ltexw**>, //ʔisl=ɛ́·ltəxʷ//, /'*man with two wives*'/ and <**ts'elá́ltxw**>, ds //c'əl=ɛ́ltxʷ//, SOC ['*steal someone's spouse*'], Salish cognate: Musqueam /=ɛ́·ltəxʷ/ *spouse* Suttles ca1984:14.5.15.

<**áltha ~ álthe**>, free root //ʔɛ́lθɛ ~ ʔɛ́lθə//, PRON /'*it's me, that's me, I do, I am*'/, dialects: *Chill.*, syntactic analysis: independent verbal pronoun, pronominal verb/verbal pronoun, other sources: ES

/ɛ́·lθɛ/ *I*, dialects: *Cheh.*, example: <**álthe qas taléwe**>, //ʔɛ́lθɛ qɛs tɛlə́wə//, /'*It's me and you.*'/, attested by AC, <**álthacha le máyt**>, //ʔɛ́lθɛ-cɛ lə mɛ́y=t//, /'*I'll [underlined] go and help [s-o].*'/, attested by AC.

<**ta'áltha**>, ds //tɛ=ʔɛ́lθɛ//, PRON /'*me, I*'/, (<**ta=**> *demonstrative article*), syntactic analysis: inp, nominal phrase not needing further article, dialects: *Chill., Tait*, attested by AC, BJ, MJ, EB, also <**ta'álthe**>, //tɛ=ʔɛ́lθə//, dialects: *Chill., Tait, Cheh.*, example: <**lúwe qas ta'áltha**>, //lúwə qɛs tɛ=ʔɛ́lθɛ//, /'*It's you and me.*'/, attested by AC.

<**á'altha**>, ds //C_1ɛ́=ʔɛ́lθɛ//, PRON /'*it's me., that's me., I* do, *I* am (ls emphatic)'/, (<**R7=**> *emphatic*), phonology: reduplication, phonology: **á**'altha (slow), **á**'althe (normal speed), **á**'elthe (fast), syntactic analysis: independent verbal pronoun, pronominal verb/verbal pronoun, dialects: *Chill.*, attested by AC, example: <**á'althacha**>, //C_1ɛ́=ʔɛ́lθɛ-cɛ//, /'*It will be me.*'/, attested by IHTTC.

<**ta'á'altha**>, ds //tɛ=C_1ɛ́=ʔɛlθɛ//, PRON /'*me myself, I myself (emphatic)*'/, phonology: reduplication, syntactic analysis: inp, nominal phrase minus article, dialects: *Chill.*, attested by AC, also <**ta'á'altha** (slow), **ta'á'althe ~ te'á'althe** (normal)>, //tɛ=C_1ɛ́=ʔɛlθɛ, tɛ=C_1ɛ́=ʔɛlθə ~ tə=C_1ɛ́=ʔɛlθə//, attested by AC, dialects: also attested by EB, *Cheh.*, as <**ta'á'althe**>, //tɛ=C_1ɛ́=ʔɛlθə//, example: <**welóy ta'á'altha ~ welóy ta'á'althe**>, //wə=láy tɛʔɛ́ʔɛlθɛ ~ wə=láy tɛʔɛ́ʔɛlθə//, /'*just me, (only me)*'/, attested by AC, <**lúwe qas te'á'altha**>, //lúwə qɛs təʔɛ́ʔɛlθɛ//, /'*It's you and me.*'/, attested by AC.

<**tl'á'altha**>, ds //ƛ'-C_1ɛ́=ʔɛ́lθɛ//, PRON /'*me (after prepositional verbs), I (after prepositional verbs)*'/, phonology: reduplication, syntactic analysis: independent object of prepositional verb, nominal phrase minus article, syntactic comment: only occurs after prepositional verbs, example: <**yeláwel lós telí tl'á'altha**>, //yəlɛ́w=əl lás tə=líƛ'-C_1ɛ́=ʔɛ́lθɛ//, /'*He's fatter than me.*'/, syntactic comment: telí *from, than* is a prepositional verb, <**ístexwchxw ó í tl'á'althe**>, //ʔí=st-əx^w-c-x^w ʔá ʔíƛ'-C_1ɛ́=ʔɛ́lθə//, /'*You leave it with me.*'/, attested by EB, literally /'be here=causative-3obj-indep.subj.-2ssubj just be here [with]-me'/, syntactic comment: the idiom, ístexw ó í ~ ístexwò (í), means *leave it* and either the final í *be here* is functioning as a prepositional verb, *with*, or the prepositional inflection, tl'=, alone implies the *with*, <**míchxw stetís tl'a'á'altha**>, //mí-cx^w s=C_1ə=tə[=Aí=]sƛ'ɛ-C_1ɛ́=ʔɛ́lθɛ//, /'*Come close to me.*'/, attested by AC.

<**=á:lts' ~ =á:lth'ts**>, da //=ɛ́·lc' ~ =ɛ́·lθ'c//, TIME (perhaps) ['*month*'], syntactic analysis: lexical suffix,also <**=á:lth'ts**>, //=ɛ́·lθ'c//; found in <**lhqá:lts'**>, //ɬq=ɛ́·lc'//, /'*moon*'/, <**lhxwá:lth'ts**>, //ɬx^w=ɛ́·lθ'c//, /'*third month since*'/, attested by AK (in IHTTC).

<**alts'elít**>, DIR ['*to separate things or objects*'], *see* halts'elí. under root <lats'>

<**álwem**>, mdls //ʔɛ́lw=əm//, [ʔɛ́lwʊm], TVMO ['*to stay at home*'], (<**=em**> *middle voice*), syntactic analysis: intransitive verb, dialects: *Tait*, attested by AD, AK, also /'*to stay at home alone*'/, dialects: *Chill.*, attested by SJ, MV.

<**=á:lwes ~ =élwes**>, da //=ɛ́·lwəs ~ =ə́lwəs//, ANA /'*in the stomach, on the stomach*'/, EFAM ['*courage (lit. in the stomach)*'], syntactic analysis: lexical suffix, also <**=élwes**>, //=ə́lwəs//; found in <**x̲elhá:lwes**>, //x̣əɬ=ɛ́·lwəs//, /'*(have a) stomach-ache*'/, <**th'qw'á:lwestem**>, //θ'q'^{w}=ɛ́·lwəs=t-əm//, /'*he was punched in the stomach*'/, <**qelélwes**>, //qəl=ə́lwəs//, /'*cowardly, afraid to try*'/, <**iyá:lwes**>, //ʔiy=ɛ́·lwəs//, /'*brave*'/, literally /'good in the stomach'/, possibly <**lhéx̲weláw**>, //ɬə́x̣^{w}=əláw or ɬə́x̣^{w}=ɛ́lə[=M2=]w(s)//, /'*ruptured belly-button*'/, root maybe <**lhex̲w**> *spit out.* Salish cognate: Lushootseed /=g^{w}as/ as in /s-ʔác-g^{w}əs/ 'waistline' and /ƛ'uc'ə-g^{w}aθs-əb/ 'tighten your belt' H76:161.

<**Alwís Lhqéletel**>, npc //ʔɛlwís-s ɬqə́lətəl//, PLN /'*name of second creek below (here south of) Suka Creek (as of 8/30/77), creek called Alwís's Bow-line*'/, ASM ['on the CN side (east side) of the Fraser River'], literally /'Alwís's bow-line (line from the bow of a canoe), named after Alwís, a man who tied

his canoe to the mountain above this creek in the great flood; the CN railway has a bridge over it'], source: place name file reference #246, syntactic comment: the proper name Alwís is functioning as an adjectival modifier of the nominal, lhq**é**letel *bow-line*, in this two-word (binomial) place name, attested by SP, AK, AD.

<**=á:lxw**>, da //=ɛ́·lx^w//, EB ['*leaves*'], syntactic analysis: lexical suffix, derivational suffix; found in <**temhilá:lxw**>, //təm=hil=ɛ́·lx^w//, /'*autumn, fall*'/, compare with <**hí:l=em**> *(to) fall (tumbling).*

<**alxwítsel**>, dnom //ʔɛlx^w=íc(=)əl//, DIR /'*middle (in age or spatial position), between*'/, possibly <**=íts(el)**> *in back*, attested by AC, syntactic analysis: adverb/adverbial verb, adjective/adjectival verb, also <**al<u>x</u>wítsel**>, //ʔɛlx̣^{w}=íc(=)əl//, attested by AC, example: <**lí te alxwítsel**>, //lí tə ʔɛlx̣^{w}=íc(=)əl//, /'*in the middle*'/, attested by AC.

<**S'alxwítsel**>, dnom //s=ʔɛlx^w=íc(=)əl//, PLN /'*Camp Slough, Camp River*'/, literally /'middle (stream), the center (stream)'/, syntactic analysis: nominal, attested by Wells 1966, source: place name file reference #263; Wells 1966; photo list 6/20/78.

<**á:l<u>x</u>em**>, mdls //ʔɛ́·lx̣=əm//, LANG /'*(make) a murmur, to murmur*'/, possibly root <**as in ó:l=thet**> *to groan*, possibly <**=<u>x</u>**> *distributive, all around*, (<**=em**> *middle voice*), syntactic analysis: intransitive verb.

<**al'álíy**> (sometimes written <**'al'álíy**>), VALJ ['*all good*'], *see* **é**y ~ **é**y:.

<**=álh ~ =áxw ~ =á**>, da //=ɛ́ɬ ~ =ɛ́x^w ~ =ɛ́//, TIME /'*times, occasions*'/, lexical suffix, derivational suffix, semantic environment ['with numerals 1-10, kw'í:l'], phonology: =alh occurs after numbers 3 through 10, <**=áxw**>, //=ɛ́x^w// occurs after l**é**ts'e *one*, <**=á**>, //=ɛ́// occurs after *two, second*, syntactic comment: obligatory; found in <**lhq'átsesálh**>, //ɬq'ɛ́cəs=ɛ́ɬ//, /'*five times*'/.

<**=à:lh ~ =elh**>, da, ia //=ɛ̀·ɬ ~ =əɬ//, TIME /'*late (deceased);, past tense*'/, syntactic analysis: lexical suffix/derivational suffix with nouns, inflectional suffix with verbs; found in <**sí:là:lh**>, //sí·lɛ̀·ɬ//, /'*late grandparent, deceased grandparent*'/ (compare <**sí:le**> *grandparent*, <**mélà:lh**>, //mə́l=ɛ̀·ɬ//, /'*late or deceased child*'/ (compare <**méle**> *child*, <**sí:selà:lh**>, //sí·səl=ɛ̀·ɬ//, /'*late grandmother*'/ (compare <**sísele**> used by AC for *grandmother)*, <**selsí:là:lh**>, //səlsí·l=ɛ̀·ɬ//, /'*late grandparents*'/ (compare <**selsí:le**> *grandparents)*, <**shxwemthiyà:lh**>, //sx^{w}əmθiy=ɛ̀·ɬ//, /'*deceased uncle or aunt or grandparent or someone responsible for you directly or indirectly*'/, <**shxwemxwemthiyá:lh**>, //s=C$_1$əC$_2$=x^{w}əmθiy=ɛ̀·ɬ//, /'*deceased uncles or aunts or grandparents responsible for someone*'/, <**smestiyálh**>, //s=məstiy=ɛ́ɬ//, /'*sibling of deceased parent*'/ (compare <**mestíy=exw**> *person)*, <**swelmáylh**>, //s=wɛ́ləm=ə[=M3=]yɬ or s=wɛləm=ə́yɬ//, /'*child of a dead sibling*'/, root <**swálém**> *orphan*, <**lá:telh**>, //lɛ́·t=əɬ//, /'*morning*'/, literally /'night + past'/, <**xwelá́ltelh**>, //x^{w}ə=lɛ́[=C$_1$ə=]t=əɬ//, /'*last night*'/ (compare <**xwe=lált**> *evening* from < **lá:t**> *night)*, <**welhí:thelh**>, //wə=ɬí·θ=əɬ//, /'*a long time ago*'/, root <**lhí:th**> *a long time*, with <**=lh**> *past tense* on verbs).

<**-alha**>, //-ɛɬɛ//, MOOD ['*command imperative second person plural*'], ASM ['ordering the listeners to do something'], semantic environment ['cannot be used with non-control transitives (for ex. in =l) since the actor has no control over doing it), also cannot be used with some intransitive verbs (prepositional, adverbial, interrogative, personal pronoun, demonstrative, and some verbs whose action a subject cannot do on command, thus non-control imperatives such as *kw'**é**tslexwalha *See it.* and *kw**é**l:exwalha *Get/Catch/Find it.* are not allowed (EB, AC, etc.), also this imperative is not allowed with auxiliary verbs like me ~ mi *come to, start to* and la ~ l**á**m *go to, going to* (-tlh *coaxing imperative* is used with them)--however when mí ~ emí or l**á**m are used as main verbs the command imperative is allowed'], syntactic analysis: is, contrast <**-lhqwe**> *polite imperative*, contrast <**-chexw**> and <**-chap**> *mildly urging imperative*, contrast <**-tlh**> and <**-atlha**> *coaxing imperative*; found in

<**míyalha.**>, //míy-ɛɬɛ//, /'*You folks come.*'/, <**emétalha.**>, //ʔəmə́t-ɛɬɛ//, /'*You folks sit., Sit up, you guys., Sit down, you guys.*'/, <**meythóxalha.**>, //mɛy=T-áx^y-ɛɬɛ//, /'*You folks help me., Help me, you folks/you guys.*'/.

<**Alhqá:yem**>, dnom //ʔɛɬqɛ[=´·=]y=əm//, PLN /'*a snake rock in the Fraser River just north of Strawberry Island which had snakes sunning themselves and covering the rock; also the name of the village on Strawberry Island*'/, see álhqey ~ álhqay

<**álhqey ~ álhqay**>, possibly root //ʔɛ́ɬqəy ~ ʔɛ́ɬqɛy (or poss.) ɬɛ[=M1=]q=ɛy//, [ʔɛ́ɬqəy ~ ʔɛ́ɬqey], EZ ['*snake (generic)*'], possibly root <**lháq**> *whisper, hiss*??, possibly <**metathesis type 1**> *derivational*?, possibly <**=ay**> *bark, wood*??, syntactic analysis: nominal, other sources: ES /ʔɛ́ɬqɛy/, JH /ʔə́ɬqey/, H-T <Étlkai> *snake (Coluber Lin. sp.)*, example: <**lhálheqem te álhqey**>, //ɬɛ́[-C_1ə-]qəm tə ʔɛ́ɬqəy//, /'*The snake is hissing.*'/, literally /'The snake is whispering.'/.

<**slálem álhqey**>, cpds //s=lɛ́·[=C_1ə=]m ʔɛ́ɬqəy//, EZ //'*turtle*'//, lit. /"snake with a house, housed snake"/, <**s=**> *stative*, <**=R1=**> *resultative*, attested by RG & EH (4/10/99 Ling332)

<**sth'íms te álhqey**>, cpds //s=θ'ím-s tə ʔɛ́ɬqəy//, EB /'*"snakeberry",* including *False Solomon's seal, star-flowered Solomon's seal,* and probably *Twisted-stalk* and *Hooker's fairy bells*'/, ['respectively *Smilacina racemosa, Smilacina stellata, Streptopus amplexifolius* (and *Streptopus roseus*), and *Disporum hookerii*'], literally /'berry of the snake'/, syntactic analysis: nominal phrase with modifier(s), trinomial expression.

<**sp'áq'ems te álhqey**>, npc //s=p'ɛ́q'=əm-s tə ʔɛ́ɬqəy//, EB /'*"snake's flower",* prob. *same plant as "snakeberry", q.v.*'/, , MED ['roots are eye medicine; berries are squashed and put in cloth and in hot water for medicine (SJ,MV, and others in Deming)'], literally /'flower of the snake'/, attested by Deming: SJ, MV, others.

<**Alhqá:yem**>, dnom //ʔɛɬqɛ[=´·=]y=əm//, PLN /'*a snake rock in the Fraser River just north of Strawberry Island which had snakes sunning themselves and covering the rock; also the name of the village on Strawberry Island*'/, ASM ['SP and AK saw the snakes on this island; if one passed by very quietly in a canoe then made a loud noise they would all dump into the water at once; Strawberry Island is about two miles north of American Bar Indian Reserve'], (<**=´:=**> *derivational, continuative?, emphatic?*), phonology: stress shift (consonant alternation), ablaut, lengthening, lx <**=em**> *place to have/get*, syntactic analysis: nominal, attested by SP, AK, source: place name reference #38 and #48; also Wells 1966 (lst ed):25 village #16; and Duff 1952:32, also <**I'alhqá:yem**>, //C_1í=ʔɛɬqɛ[=´·=]y=əm//, literally /'little snake place'/, (<**R4= (C1í=)**> *diminutive*), lx <**=em**> *place of*, phonology: reduplication, attested by SP, AD, MP, also <**Elqá:yem**>, //ʔɛ[=lə=]ɬqɛ[=´·=]y=əm//, possibly <**=le=**> *plural*, phonology: if not the plural infix with vowel-loss then consonant merger (llh > l) or an error for lh, the change to l is a derivational consonant-shift (consonant alternation), or it may instead be from <**aleqá:y**>*slow-worm ("a slow-moving foot-long snake"), actually a species of blind legless lizard*'/, ['*Anguis fragilis*'], attested by SP, AD, MP.

<**sílhqey**>, dnom //is[=M1=]=ɛ́ɬqəy//, EZ ['*two-headed supernatural snake*'], POW, ASM ['a **stl'áleqem** creature (with supernatural power), it had characteristics of a duck (could fly and float coiled up in the water) and of a snake; one BJ reported lived in swamps near Chilliwack; Harrison Lake had a huge one, and Pitt Lake had one. A man caught the one in Pitt Lake in a deadfall trap and ground its bones to powder and painted a likeness of it on the rafters of his longhouse at Chilliwack to protect him from enemies; they'd die if they entered, twisting horribly like a snake. A Stó:lō man, brother of an elder living in 1979, saw the one in Harrison Lake and got xó:lís (a sickness from seeing **stl'áleqem** creatures); he got scales all over his body and died soon thereafter.'], (derivational metathesis of the root/first syllable in <**isá:le**> *two*; this seems more

likely than ablaut and nominalizer s= since that would keep the initial glottal stop in the root for *snake*), phonology: metathesis, vowel merger after loss of glottal stop, syntactic analysis: nominal, other sources: Duff 1952, Wells 1970, Maud, Galloway, and Weeden 1987, Galloway 1979.

<**aleqá:y**>, df //ʔɛləqɛ́·y//, EZ /'*slow-worm ("a slow-moving foot-long snake"), actually a species of blind legless lizard*'/, ['*Anguis fragilis*'], (consonant-shift *derivational* (lh → l)), phonology: derivational consonant shift (consonant alternation), ASM ['classed as a snake by Halkomelem speakers, as a lizard by zoologists'], Elder's comment: "Someone related or close to you will die soon after you see it unless you throw it over your shoulder and tell it to go to someone else and you name them.", syntactic analysis: nominal, Salish cognate: Squamish /ʔlqáyʔ/ 'mythological being poss. identical with /č'ínk'ʷu/ (both said to be what the thunderbird feeds on; it moved along by rolling itself sideways along the hills; a person crossing its path would get sick with crippled swollen feet; said to have been eaten by pigs; striking similarity to Squamish word /ʔə́ɬqayʔ/)' K67:336, K69:73, LM believes it to be 'a real creature something like a snake (approx. two feet long, blunt on both ends, capable of digging into hard ground simultaneously with both ends, and propelled itself by rolling sideways along the ground; a /sƛ'álqəm/ creature to the Squamish)' KB76:127.

<**álhtel**>, pcrs //ʔi[=Aɛ́=]ɬ=T-əl//, [ʔɛ́ɬtl], FOOD ['*eat (a meal)*'], literally /'feed each other, eat purposely with each other'/, Elder's comment: "One can't say álhtel te Bill te s'álhtel *Bill eats the food.* nor álhtel te steqóye te Bill *The wolf ate Bill.* for two reasons: a) one would use lép'exes *he eats it* instead of álhtel here, and b) wolves don't eat people. (EB)", (<**á-ablaut**> *derivational*), (<**=t**> *purposeful control transitivizer*), (<**-el**> *reciprocal*), phonology: ablaut, syntactic analysis: intransitive verb, other sources: ES /ʔə́ɬtəl/, example: <**íchap álhtel?**>, //ʔí-c-ɛp ʔɛ́ɬtəl//, /'*Did you folks eat?*'/, attested by Deming: MH, <**míchap álhtel ~ míyalha álhtel**>, //mí-c-ɛp ʔɛ́ɬtəl ~ míy-ɛɬɛ ʔɛ́ɬtəl//, /'*Come eat, you folks.*'/, attested by Deming, <**líchxw welh álhtel?**>, //lí-c-xʷ wəɬ ʔɛ́ɬtəl//, /'*Have you already eaten?*'/, attested by EB, <**le álhtel chelá:qelhelh**>, //lə ʔɛ́ɬtəl čəlɛ́qəɬ-əɬ//, /'*He ate yesterday.*'/, attested by AC, <**álhtelcetcha wàyèlès**>, //ʔɛ́ɬtəl-c-ət-cɛ wɛ̀yə̀l-ə̀s//, /'*We'll eat tomorrow.*'/, attested by AC.

<**í:lhtel**>, cts //ʔí[-·-]ɬtəl//, FOOD ['*eating (a meal)*'], (<**-:-**> *continuative*), phonology: lengthening, attested by AC, MH, example: <**le í:lhtel**>, //lə ʔí·ɬtəl//, /'*He's eating.*'/, attested by AC, <**tsel xwel í:lhtel**>, //c-əl xʷəl ʔí·ɬtəl//, /'*I'm still eating.*'/, attested by MH.

<**s'álhtel**>, dnom //s=ʔɛ́ɬtəl//, ds, FOOD ['*food*'], ACL ['*groceries*'], (<**s=**> *nominalizer, something to*), syntactic analysis: nominal, example: <**x̱éytl' s'álhtel ~ x̱ítl' s'álhtel**>, //x̣ə́yƛ' s=ʔɛ́ɬtəl ~ x̣íƛ' s=ʔɛ́ɬtəl//, [x̣éƛ' sʔɛ́ɬtl], /'*cold food*'/, attested by AC, <**x̱ítl' te s'álhtel**>, //x̣íƛ' tə sʔɛ́ɬtəl//, /'*The food is cold.*'/, attested by AC, <**lechxw tsesá:t kws las kwél:em kw s'álhtel?**>, //lə-c-xʷ cəsɛ́·=T kʷ-s lɛ-s kʷə́l=l-əm kʷ s=ʔɛ́ɬtəl//, /'*Did you send him to get food?*'/, attested by EB, <**ewálhtsel mí:l alqá:ls kw s'álhtel**>, //ʔəwə-ɛ́ɬ-c-əl mí·-l ʔɛlq-ɛ́·ls kʷ s=ʔɛ́ɬtəl//, /'*I wasn't going to buy groceries (but I did).*'/, attested by EB, variant <**s'élhtel**> attested by RG,EH 6/16/98 could be a better spelling than <**s'álhtel**> for speakers who have [ɪ] or [ə́] as the stressed vowel instead of [ɛ́].

<**smómeleqw spíls s'élhtel sqe'óleqw**>, FOOD *V8 juice* (lit. mixed + planted + food + fruit juice), (attested by RG,EH 6/16/98 to SN, edited by BG with RG,EH 6/26/00)

<**spíls s'élhtel sqe'óleqw**>, FOOD *vegetable juice* (lit. planted + food + fruit juice), (attested by RG,EH 6/16/98 to SN, edited by BG with RG,EH 6/26/00)

<**xwelítemelh x̱eyeslótel** (or) **kw'ókw'es kwémlexw s'élhtel**>, EB, FOOD *ginger* (lit. white man style + wild ginger (or) hot + root + food), (attested by RG,EH 6/16/98 to SN, edited by BG with RG,EH 6/26/00)

<**alhteláwtxw**>, dnom //ʔɛɬtəl=ɛ́wtxʷ//, BLDG ['*restaurant*'], ACL, lx <**=áwtxw**> *building, house,*

syntactic analysis: nominal, attested by Deming.

<**á:lhtel**>, ds //ʔɛ́·ɬtəl//, PRON /'*they (known to the speaker), them (known to the speaker)*'/, possibly <**=t-el**> *reciprocal*, syntactic analysis: nominal demonstrative, example: <**ts'its'kwiyóls á:lhtel**>, //c'i[=C_1ə=]kʷiy=áls ʔɛ́·ɬtəl//, /'*They're playing pool.*'/, attested by Deming.

<**alht'éqw'**>, NUM ['*half*'], *see* t'éqw'.

<**=ám ~ =á** (or merely **=em)**>, da //=ɛ́m ~ =ɛ́ or =əm//, TIB ['*using a (?)*'], phonology: **á** may be ablaut from regular **e** or **á** + **e** → **á**: morphophonemic rule, syntactic analysis: lexical suffix, derivational suffix, also <**=á**>, //=ɛ́//; found in <**q'ewá ~ q'ewám**>, //q'əwə=ɛ́ ~ q'əwə=ɛ́m or q'əwə=əm//, /'*using a cane, walk with a cane*'/, <**sq'ewá**>, //s=q'əw=ɛ́//, /'*person with a cane*'/ (compare <**q'éwe**> *cane, staff*), <**texwmelámtsel ~ smelámtsel**>, //təxʷ=məl=ɛ́m-cəl ~ s=məl=ɛ́m-cəl//, /'*I adopt a child*'/ (compare <**texw=méle**> *step-child*), <**th'áyám**>, //θ'ɛ́yɛ=ɛ́m or θ'ɛ́yə=əm//, /'*marry a sibling of deceased spouse*'/ (compare <**th'áya**> *sibling of deceased spouse).*

<**=á:m ~ =ém**>, da //=ɛ́·m ~ =ə́m//, ANA ['*strength*'], syntactic analysis: lexical suffix, derivational suffix; found in <**eyém**>, //ʔɛy=ə́m//, /'*strong*'/ (compare <**éy**> *good*), <**qelá:m**>, //qəl=ɛ́·m//, /'*weak*'/ (compare <**qél**> *bad)*, <**x̱lhém**>, //x̣ɬ=ə́m//, /'*tired*'/ (compare <**x̱élh**> *(to) hurt, ache).*

<**á:m (?)**>, free root //ʔɛ́·m (?)//, TIB ['*give*'], compare <**ámeq't**> *bring s-o/s-th back*?, syntactic analysis: intransitive verb, attested by EB.

<**=á:mel**>, da //=ɛ́·məl//, CJ /'*part, member, nick-*'/, NUM, compare <**=ó:mél**> *part, member*, syntactic analysis: lexical suffix; found in <**kwekwxá:mel**>, //kʷəkʷxʸ=ɛ́·məl//, /'*nickname*'/ (compare <**s=kwíx**> *a name*, literally /'a part name'/).

<**ámeq't**>, pcs //ʔɛ́məq'=T (or perhaps) ʔɛ́m=q'=T//, TVMO ['*bring s-o/s-th back*'], possibly root <**á:m**> *give, (bring)*, possibly <**=q'**> *on sth/s-o else*, (<**=t**> *purposeful control transitivizer*), syntactic analysis: transitive verb, example: <**ewálhtsel mí:l ámeq't, qetsel(we) th'éx̱metò**>, //ʔəwə-ɛ́ɬ-c-əl mí·-l ʔɛ́məq'=T qə-c-əl(-wə) θ'ə́x̣ʷ=mə=T à//, /'*I wasn't going to bring him/her back, but I felt sorry for him/her.*'/, attested by EB.

<**=ámets' ~ =ámeth' ~ =ó:meth' ~ =emeth'**>, da //=ɛ́məc' ~ =ɛ́məθ' ~ =á·məθ' ~ =əməθ'//, SH /'*upright, standing, height, stature, pole*'/, ANA, MC, DESC, DIR, semantic environment ['with numeral 2 so far, non-numerals'], phonology: ts' from idiolects which usually replace th' with ts' in most words (EL, TM), syntactic comment: obligatory, syntactic analysis: lexical suffix, derivational suffix; found in <**isálámets'**>, //ʔisɛ́l=ɛ́məc'//, /'*two poles standing upright*'/, <**isálámets'**>, //ʔisɛ́l=ɛ́məc'//, /'*two poles standing up*'/ (compare <**isá:le**> *two)*, <**xelkw'ámeth'**>, //xʸəlk'ʷ=ɛ́məθ'//, /'*round (of a pole)*'/ (compare <**xelkw'=ó:ls**> *spherical)*, <**sqewá:meth'**>, //s=qəw=ɛ́·məθ'//, /'*side of tree first warmed (by sun)*'/, its root <**qew**> means *warmed*, <**sx̱á:lts'emeth'**>, //s=x̣ɛ́·lc'=əməθ'//, /'*grown twisted (of a tree)*'/ (compare <**s=**> *stative*, plus <**x̱á:lts'**> *twist*), <**eyá:meth' ~ eyá:mets'**>, //ʔɛy=ɛ́·məθ' ~ ʔɛy=ɛ́·məc'//, /'*good figure, good shape, straight (of stick), smooth (of wood, etc.)*'/, <**tl'eqtó:meth'**>, //ƛ'əqt=á·məθ'//, /'*tall (of a person)*'/ (compare <**tl'á:qt**> *long*), <**ts'í:tl'emeth'**>, //c'í·ƛ'=əməθ'//, /'*short person*'/ (compare <**ch'í·ch'etl'**> *short*), <**x̱omó:th'iya**>, //x̣am=á·θ'=iyɛ//, /'*baby sister of Mt. Cheam*'/ (with <**=iya**> *diminutive*, literally perhaps /'little standing tears'/), possibly <**ch'áléléth'xel**>, //c'ɛ́(=)l(=)ə́l=ə́θ'=xʸəl//, /'*short-legged runt (insulting)*'/ (root form unclear unless <**ts'á:**> *on top of, astride.*

<**-áp ~ -elep**>, ia //-ɛ́p ~ -əl-əp//, PRON ['*second person plural subjunctive subject*'], syntactic comment: can be suffixed to forms prefixed with we- *when, if* or to the first subordinate verb after a negative verb, can also add the *when/if* meaning even without the we- prefix being present, also <**-p**>, //-p//, phonology: after auxiliary verbs ending in i (í, lí, mí, lhí), also <**-elep**>, //-əl-əp//; found in

<**welámàp**>, //wə-lɛ́=m-ɛ̀p//, /'*if/when you folks go*'/, phonology: downstepping, example: <**éwechap sts'eláxwemáp.**>, //ʔə́wə-c-ɛp s=c'ələ[=Aɛ́=]xʷ=əm-ɛ́p//, /'*You're not spirit-dancers.*'/, <**éwechap lámàp.**>, //ʔə́wə-c-ɛp lɛ́=m-ɛ́p//, /'*You folks don't/won't go., Don't you folks go.*'/, <**éwechap líp tl'ílsòx**>, //ʔə́wə-c-ɛp lí-p ƛ'í·=ləs-áxʸ//, /'*You folks don't like me.*'/.

<**á:pel**>, free root //ʔɛ́·pəl//, EZ ['*maggot(s)*'], MED ['If you put your hands or feet in a fish crawling with maggots and leave them there for a couple of minutes your hands or feet will never get cold; this must be done before you become a woman or a man. (EB)'], syntactic analysis: nominal, attested by BJ, AC.

<**á:p' ~ áp'**>, bound root //ʔɛ́·p' ~ ʔɛ́p'// *wipe*.

<**á:p'et ~ áp'et**>, pcs //ʔɛ́·p'=əT ~ ʔɛ́p'=əT//, MC ['*wipe s-th/s-o*'], CLO, REL, MED, ABDF, ABFC, syntactic analysis: transitive verb, other sources: ES /ɛ́·p'ət/, JH /ʔép'ət/, AC reported (10/13/71) this word as a Cowichan dialect form but wasn't a speaker of Cowichan (she used it in an example, <**léwe á:p'et.**>, //léwə ʔɛ́·p'=əT//, /'*You wipe it.*'/, dialects: *Cowichan*, attested by AC, other Upriver speakers probably use it too since the root is attested with <ap'> as root in derived forms used by some speakers for '*dish towel*'.

<**shxw'áp'ewí:ls**>, dnom //s(=)xʷ=ʔɛ́p'=əwí·ls//, HHG ['*dish-towel*'], literally /'dish wiper, thing to wipe dishes'/, (<**sxw=**> *nominalizer, something to*), lx <**=ewí:ls**> *dishes*, syntactic analysis: nominal, attested by AD (Aug. 1980), attested by Elders Group, Elder's comment: "some say this rather than shxwiqw'ewí:ls". also <**shxwiqw'ewí:ls**>, //s(=)xʷ=ʔiq'ʷ=əwí·ls//, literally /'dish rubber, thing to rub dishes'/, attested by AD (Aug. 1980), example: <**íkw'elò te shxw'áp'ewí:ls.**>, //ʔí=k'ʷə=là tə sxʷ=ʔɛ́p'=əwí·ls//, /'*Here's the dish-towel.*'/, attested by AD.

<**óp'esem**>, mdls //ʔɛ[=Aá=]p'=əs=əm//, ABFC ['*wipe one's face*'], PE, (<**ó-ablaut**> *derivational* but triggered automatically by suffix), lx <**=es**> *on the face*, (<**=em**> *middle voice*), phonology: **ó**-ablaut on root **á** triggered automatically by =es suffix, syntactic analysis: intransitive verb, attested by Deming, also <**ep'ósem**>, //ʔɛ[=Aə=]p'=ás=əm//, /'*clean one's face* '/, attested by RG & EH (4/10/99 Ling332).

<**s'ep'ó:s**>, dnom //ʔɛ[=Aə=]p'=á·s=əm//, SPRD /'*people without paint on face (non-dancers)*'/, attested by RG & EH (4/10/99 Ling332)

<**áp'eqselem**>, dnom //ʔɛ́·p'=əqsel=em//, PE /'*handkerchief for nose*'/, attested by RG & EH (4/10/99 Ling332)

<**shxw'óp'estel**>, dnom //s(=)xʷ=ʔɛ[=Aá=]p'=əs=təl//, HHG ['*large towel*'], literally /'device/thing to wipe on the face'/, (<**shxw=**> *nominalizer*), (<**ó-ablaut**> *derivational* but triggered automatically by suffix), lx <**=es**> *on the face*, lx <**=tel**> *device to, something to*, phonology: **ó**-ablaut on root **á** triggered automatically by =es suffix, syntactic analysis: nominal, attested by Elders Group (6/1/77).

<**shxwep'életstel ~ shxwp'életstel**>, ds //s(=)xʷ=(ə)p'=ə́ləc=təl or s(=)xʷ=ʔɛp'=ə́ləc=təl//, [šxʷʊp'ə́lɪctəl ~ šxʷp'ə́lɪctəl], HHG ['*toilet paper*'], PE, literally /'device/thing to wipe on the rump/bottom'/, (<**shxw=**> *nominalizer*), lx <**=élets**> *on the rump, on the bottom*, lx <**=tel**> *device to, something to*, phonology: vowel-reduction or vowel-loss in root due to stressed suffix, consonant-loss of first consonant in root after shxw=, or just as likely: root allomorph ep' ~ p' here, syntactic analysis: nominal, attested by Elders Group (6/1/77), AD (9/21/78, Aug. 1980), EB (9/21/78), example: <**alétsa te shxwep'életstel?**>, //ʔɛlə́cɛ tə sxʷ=ʔɛp'=ə́ləc=təl//, /'*Where's the toilet paper?*'/, attested by AD (Aug. 1980).

<**ep'ó:yethel? or epó:yethel?**>, df //ʔɛp'=á·yθəl? or ʔəp=á·yθəl?//, EZ ['*butterfly (medium- and small-sized)*'], ['*Papilio spp.*'], possibly root <**áp'**> *wipe*, possibly <**=ó:y(e)thel**> *on the lips*, phonology:

possible deglottalization, syntactic analysis: nominal, source: H-T <apai'EsEl> (circumflex over first a) *butterfly (Papilio)(medium- and small-sized)*, comment: Papilio includes primarily swallowtail butterflies in the Stó:lō area.

<**=á:q ~ =aq ~ =eq**>, da //=ɛ́·q ~ =ɛq ~ =əq//, ANA /'*on the penis, in the penis, on the genitals, on the male*'/, syntactic analysis: lexical suffix, derivational suffix; found in <**qwéyleq** (or better) **qwíleq**>, //qʷíl=əq//, /'*pubic hair*'/, <**thá:q**>, //θ=ɛ́·q//, /'*big penis*'/, <**weth'áqt**> /'*tease s-o's penis*'/, <**thekw'áqt**> /'*pull s-o's penis*'/, <**xwíqweqt**> /'*press & rub his penis, massage s-o's penis*'/, <**th'óth'eqweqtes**> *she was sucking his penis*, <**iyéseq**>, //ʔiyə́s=əq//, /'*dear male friend, (male pal, male chum, buddy)*'/, contrast <**ʔiyə́s**> *dear female friend.*

<**áq'**>, free root //ʔɛ́q'//, EFAM /'*yechh., (expression of disgust used by some elders on seeing or smelling something disgusting)*'/, syntactic analysis: interjection, attested by AD.

<**áq'elh**>, us //ʔɛ́q'(=)əɬ//, ABDF ['*choke on bone or s-th solid*'], syntactic analysis: intransitive verb, <**áq'elh**>, [ʔǽq'ʌɬ], '*choked on a bone*', attested by (EH,RG) 7/27/99 (SU transcription, tape 3)[BG: probably past tense translation by context, not resultative].

<**á:q'elh**>, cts //ʔɛ[=·=]q'(=)əɬ//[ʔǽ·q'ʌɬ], ABDF '*always choking on food*', attested by (EH,RG) 7/27/99 (SU transcription, tape 3) [BG: probably <=:=> continuative, the *always* is probably not always required in the translation].

<**Aseláw**>, us //ʔɛsəlɛ́w//, PLN /'*Esilao villacage, Siwash Creek village*'/, ASM ['area just north of mouth of Siwash Creek into the Fraser River; the pre-contact village area was at the base of the hill; on top of the hill was a graveyard (AD, AK); the hill is across the Fraser (on east bank) from the village of Eayem. Long ago a big gathering was held here with a tl'etl'áxel feast for a wedding; that night an old man heard a rumble of a slide and warned everyone. But the newlyweds didn't hear the warning. Everyone else woke and dashed across the creek in the dark, but the newlyweds were buried in the slide. Every year after that, they had wá:ls *scramble-giving* for them; these were eventually stopped years ago. (SP, AK)'], syntactic analysis: nominal, source: place name file #136; Wells lst ed.:25, village #28.

<**Aseláw Smált**>, cpds //ʔɛsəlɛ́w s=mɛ́lt//, PLN /'*mountain above Esilao, Siwash Creek Mountain*'/, literally /'Esilao mountain'/, syntactic analysis: nominal phrase with modifier(s), attested by AD, AK, source: place name file #138.

<**Aseláw Stótelō**>, cpds //ʔɛsəlɛ́w s=tá[=C_1ə=]l=əw//, PLN /'*Siwash Creek, on the CN (east) side of the Fraser River*'/, literally /'Esilao creek'/, (<=**R1**=> *diminutive*), phonology: reduplication, syntactic analysis: nominal phrase with modifier(s), attested by AD, AK, source: place name file #137, also <**Aseláw Stó:lō**>, //ʔɛsəlɛ́w s=tá·l=əw//, attested by AD, AK.

<**áshxw**>, free root //ʔɛ́sxʷ//, EZ ['*hair seal*'], ['*Phoca vitulina richardi*'], ASM ['hair seals came up the Fraser and Harrison Rivers even to Harrison Lake where I saw several of them in 1977; they were hunted by the Chehalis people with special spears or harpoons'], syntactic analysis: nominal, attested by ME, AK, BJ, others, other sources: ES /ʔɛ́·sxʷ/, JH /ʔé·sxʷ/, H-T <**ácuH**> (umlaut over a) *(hair) seal (Phoca vitulina)*, contrast <**skwló ~ sqwló**> *seal fat* (EL of Cheh.), also <**á:shxw**>, //ʔɛ́·sxʷ//, attested by AC, example: <**slós te áshxw**> (Tait: CT), //s=lás-s tə ʔɛ́sxʷ//, /'*fat of the seal, the seal's fat*'/, attested by CT.

<**Áshxwetel**>, dnom //ʔɛ́sxʷ=(ə)təl l//, PLN ['*name of a seal-shaped rock formerly on the Harrison or Chehalis River*'], ASM ['a seal hunter and seal on the Chehalis or Harrison River were both turned to stone by X̲á:ls, the Transformer, in one story; the seal rock was removed from its location for safety about 1977-early 1978 by a Chehalis resident and at last report rested on the lawn of Bill Phillips'], lx <**=tel**> *something for*, syntactic analysis: nominal, attested by Cheh.: DF, others,

source: place name file #73.

<**Áshxwetel**>, dnom //ʔɛ́sx^{w}=(ə)təl2//, PLN /'*name of a seal bay on Harrison River just before Pretty's house going to Chehalis; lots of seals were there sometimes*'/, lx <**=tel**> *something for*, syntactic analysis: nominal, attested by prob. DF, poss. others.

<**ate**>, free root //ʔɛtə//, QUAL ['*right (in the sense of exactly or just)*'], syntactic analysis: adverb/adverbial verb, Elder's comment: "an old word", attested by AD, EB, example: <**ate íkw'elò**>, //ʔɛtə ʔí=k'^{w}ə=là//, /'*It's right here.*'/, attested by AD, EB.

<**-atlha**>, ia //-ɛtɬɛ//, MOOD ['*coaxing imperative plural*'], syntactic analysis: is, syntactic comment: used mainly with auxiliary verbs, contrast <**-lhqwe**> *polite imperative*, contrast <**-chexw**> and <**-chap**> *mildly urging imperative*, contrast <**-lha**> and <**-alha**> *command imperative*; found in <**héyatlha**>, //hɛ́y-ɛtɬɛ//, /'*Let's (coaxing several persons)*'/, <**x̲wématlha.**>, //x̣^{w}ə́m-ɛtɬɛ//, /'*Hurry up, you folks (coaxing).*'/.

<**áthelets**>, dnom //ʔɛ́θ=(ə)ləc1//, [ʔɛθəlɪc], DIR /'*the bottom (of a waterfall, body of water, basket, anything)*'/, (semological comment: functions as member of several semantic domains: WATR, LAND, WETH, MC (+ each subdomain), EB, ANA, as well as DIR), possibly root <**áth**> *edge*?, lx <**=lets**> *on the bottom*, syntactic analysis: nominal, also <**shxw'áthelets**>, //sx^{w}=ʔɛ́θ=ələc//.

<**shxw'étselets**>, //sx^{w}=ʔɛ́[=Aə́=]c=(ə)ləc//, [šx^{w}ʔícɪlɪc], LAND ['*base of mountain or something high*'], EB ['*base of a tree*'], phonology: **é**-ablaut derivational, syntactic analysis: nominal, attested by EB, historical/comparative detail: note EB's use of /c/ for /θ/ here; this may be influence from the Thompson language in which she is also fluent, compare <**áthelets**> *the bottom*.

<**Áthelets**>, dnom //ʔɛ́θ=(ə)ləc2//, PLN ['*Atchelitz village and now Chilliwack Indian reserve #8*'], ASM ['the village was at the junction of Chilliwack River and Atchelitz Creek; the chief in the 1890's was a man named Swoyús'], literally /'bottom (of Chilliwack Mountain)'/, syntactic analysis: nominal, source: place name file #81; also Hill-Tout 1902.

<**Áthelets**>, dnom //ʔɛ́θ=(ə)ləc3//, PLN /'*Atchelitz Creek, an old Chilliwack River channel*'/, syntactic analysis: nominal, source: Wells 1966 (lst ed.).

<**Áthelets**>, dnom //ʔɛ́θ=(ə)ləc4//, PLN /'*Othello, (B.C.), a village on the Coquihalla River, on the west side across from the most northwest point above the mouth of Nicolum Creek, up nine miles from Hope on the Kettle Valley Railroad*'/, syntactic analysis: nominal, dialects: *Tait*, attested by LJ2.

<**átheqel**>, dnom //ʔɛ́θ(=)əqəl//, DIR ['*front*'], possibly root <**áth**> *edge*, possibly <**=eqel**> *on the front of the neck, on the throat*?, syntactic analysis: nominal, example: <**lí kw'e átheqel**>, //lí k'^{w}ə ʔɛ́θ(=)əqəl//, /'*in front of (s-o or s-th, in canoe or anywhere), at the front*'/, <**lí kw'el átheqel**>, //lí k'^{w}ə-l ʔɛ́θ(=)əqəl//, /'*in front of me, at my front*'/, attested by EB.

<**áth'el**>, us //ʔɛθ'əl//, QUAL ['*be really*'], possibly <**=el**> *go, come, get, become*, syntactic analysis: adverb/adverbial verb, attested by EB, example: <**áth'elchxw x̲wém**>, //ʔɛθ'əl-c-x^{w} x̣^{w}ə́m//, /'*You're really fast.*'/, attested by EB, <**áth'elchxw óyém**>, //ʔɛθ'əl-c-x^{w} ʔáy=əm//, /'*You're really slow.*'/, attested by EB.

<**átl'q**>, bound root //ʔɛ́ƛ'q *outside*//.

<**s'átl'q**>, ds //s=ʔɛ́ƛ'q//, DIR ['*the outside*'], (<**s=**> *nominalizer*), syntactic analysis: nominal, also <**shxw'átl'q**>, //sx^{w}=ʔɛ́ƛ'q//, attested by EB, example: <**lí kw'e s'átl'q qe ő̃we ís chókw**>, //lí k'^{w}ə s=ʔɛ́ƛ'q qə ʔówə ʔí-s cák^{w}//, /'*It's outside but not far.*'/, literally /'it's at the (remote) outside but is not aux-it is far'/, syntactic analysis: preposition/prepositional verb demonstrative article(remote) nominal-adverb/adverbial verb conjunction vneg auxiliary verb-3subjunctive subject pronoun adjective/adjectival verb, attested by EB, <**xwémxel li te s'átl'q**>, //x^{w}ə́m=x^{y}əl li tə s=ʔɛ́ƛ'q//, /'*It's*

raining hard outside.'/ (lx <**=xel**> *precipitation*, literally /'it's fast=precipitation at the(present + visible) outside'/), attested by Deming, <**lá kw'e shxw'átl'q**>, //lɛ́ k'ʷə sxʷ=ʔɛ́ƛ'q//, /'*go outside*'/, attested by EB.

<**átl'qel**>, incs //ʔɛ́ƛ'q=əl//, DIR ['*get outside*'], (<**=el ~ =íl**> *go, come, become, get*), attested by AC, syntactic analysis: intransitive verb, <kwekwíl kws atl'qel>, [kʷʊkʷíl kʷʊs æƛ'qəl], 'He's sneaking out', attested by (EH,RG,SN 7/16/99 (SU transcription, tape 1)

<**atl'qílt**>, pcs //ʔɛƛ'q=íl=T//, DIR ['*bring s-th/s-o outside (purposely), put s-o/s-th out(side)*'], (<**=t**> *purposeful control transitivizer*), syntactic analysis: transitive verb, ASM ['take it out (outside/outside of a container'] (attested by RG & EH 4/9/99 Ling332), ASM ['kick s-o out']; found in <**atl'qílthóxes**>, //ʔɛƛ'q=íl=T-axʸ-əs//, /'*He kicked me out.*'/, ASM ['outside=get-purposely-me-he/she/it/they'], <**atl'qílthò:m**>, //ʔɛƛ'q=íl=T-à·m//, /'*You got kicked out.*'/, ASM ['outside=get-purposely-2spassive'], ASM ['reveal s-th'], example: <**atl'qílt ta' sqwá:lewel**>, //ʔɛƛ'q=íl=T t-ɛʔ s=qʷɛ́·l=əwəl//, /'*Reveal your thoughts.*'/, syntactic comment: one form of imperative is: transitive verb demonstrative article-2posspron nominal, <alhqílt>, (BG: should be <**atl'qílt**>), [ɛɬqéyltʰ] (BG: should be [ɛƛ'qéyltʰ]), 'put s.o. out', attested by (EH,RG,SN 7/16/99 (SU transcription, tape 1), <la tsel cha alhqílt> (BG: should be <**la tsel cha atl'qílt**>), [lɛ čɪl čæ ɛɬqéyltʰ] (BG: should be [lɛčɪlčæ ɛƛ'qéyltʰ]), 'I'm putting him out' [BG: not actually continuative, actually future intentive], attested by (EH,RG,SN 7/16/99 (SU transcription, tape 1), <**atl'qílt s'álhte**l> //ʔɛƛ'q=íl=T s=ʔɛ́ɬtəl//, /'*take-out food*'/, attested by RG & EH (4/9/99 Ling332)

<**atl'qeláwtxw**>, dnom //ʔɛƛ'q=əl=ɛ́wtxʷ//, BLDG /'*outhouse, toilet, bathroom*'/, literally /'outside=go=house'/, lx <**=áwtxw**> *house, building*, syntactic analysis: nominal, example: <**líchxw welh lám kw'e atl'qeláwtxw?**>, //li-c-xʷ wəɬ lɛ́=m k'ʷə ʔɛƛ'q=əl=ɛ́wtxʷ//, /'*Did you already go to the outhouse?*'/, attested by AD.

<**s'átl'qmel**>, dnom //s=ʔɛ́ƛ'q=məl//, BLDG ['*the outside part of a house*'], lx <**=mel**> *part of, member*, syntactic analysis: nominal.

<**átl'qt**>, pcs //ʔɛ́ƛ'q=T//, DIR ['*take it outside (outside of a building or car)*'], (<**=t**> *purposeful control transitivizer*), syntactic analysis: transitive verb, attested by EB, example: <**láchxw átl'qt**>, //lɛ́-c-xʷ ʔɛ́ƛ'q=T//, /'*Go take it outside.*'/, attested by EB.

<**átl'qel**>, DIR ['*get outside*'], see átl'q.

<**atl'qeláwtxw**>, BLDG /'*outhouse, toilet, bathroom*'/, see átl'q.

<**atl'qílt**>, DIR ['*bring s-th/s-o outside (purposely)*'], see átl'q.

<**átl'qt**>, DIR ['*take it outside (outside of a building or car)*'], see átl'q.

<**áts**>, bound root //ʔɛ́c//, ABFC /'*hear*'/

<**átsele**>, free root or stem //ʔɛ́c(=)ələ//, EFAM /'*gee., good grief., well. (said when surprised), goodness., gee whiz.*'/, phonology: The stressed vowel is subject to emphatic lengthening with : and :: as in **á:tsele** and **á::tsele**. Most speakers have an unusual [ɛ́] here, even when lengthened; JL has [ǽ·] when lengthened., syntactic analysis: interjection, example: <**átsele méle.**>, //ʔɛ́cələ mələ//, /'*Goodness, child., Gee whiz, child.*'/, syntactic comment: notice the vocative where the nominal is not preceded by an article. An interesting possible etymology might relate this word to the root in <**átslexw**> /'*hear about it, (hear about s-o)*'/, with lx <-ele> /'*lack of*'/, thus expressing surprise through "lack of hearing about s-th/s-o" or less likely with lx <**=éla**> /'*on the side of the head, on the temples, around the ear, on the cheek*'/. Salish cognates: Lushootseed /ʔəčədá/, Nooksack /æčənǽ/ *oh my what a pity, alas, gee whiz* (PAC715, 717).

<**átslexw**>, ncs //ʔɛ́c=l-əxʷ//, LANG /'*hear about it, (hear about s-o)*'/, syntactic analysis: transitive

verb, attested by Deming.

<**éts-'ets**>, chrs //ʔə́c=C₁əC₂//, LANG ['*to stutter*'], ABDF, (<=**R2**> *characteristic* or *iterative*), perhaps <**áts**>, bound root //ʔɛ́c//, ABFC /'*hear*'/, phonology: reduplication, syntactic analysis: intransitive verb, Elder's comment: "AC said it has this form because you can't stutter just once" (compare probably <**áts=l-exw**> *hear about s-th/s-o*, Salish cognate: Lushootseed /ʔə́čʔəč/ *stutter, stammer* H76:655, Sechelt /ʔáčʔəč/ *to stutter* T77:34, B77:93 Squamish /ʔəs-ʔə́č-ʔəč/ *stuttering* W73:257, K67:387, *see* <áts>.

<**s'éts-'ets**>, chrs //s=ʔə́c=C₁əC₂//, [sʔɪ́cʔɪc (normal speed), sʔɛ́cʔɛc (hyper-slow speed)], LANG /'*stuttering, to stutter*'/, (<**s=**> *stative*), possibly root <**áts**> *hear* as in <**átslexw**> *hear about it*, (<=**R2**> *characteristic*), phonology: reduplication, syntactic analysis: intransitive verb, attested by AC, compare <**átslexw**> *hear about it*, example: <**s'éts-'ets swíyeqe**>, //s=ʔə́c=ʔəc s=wíyəqə//, /'*stuttering man*'/, attested by AC.

<**atse**>, free root or stem //ʔɛ(=)cɛ//, TIME /'*next, again*'/, QUAL, grammatical analysis: possibly contains -cha ~ -tsa *future*, grammatical comment: usually appears followed by ew ~ ōw *contrastive, emphasis*, attested by IHTTC, AC, syntactic analysis: adverbial particle, also <**ásche**>, //ʔɛ́scɛ or ʔɛ-s-cɛ//, dialects: *EB*, example: <**stámcha skw'exós kw'e atse ōw me pélekw?**>, //s=tɛ́m-cɛ s=k'ʷəxʸ=ás k'ʷə ʔɛcɛ ʔəw mə pə́ləkʷ//, /'*What is the next moon to appear?*'/, attested by IHTTC, <**atsa ew lám**>, //ʔɛcɛ ʔəw lɛ́=m//, /'*(Yes,) he's going too [next?].*'/, attested by AC.

<**a'áchewlh**>, cpds //ʔɛ[=R9=]cɛ=wɬ or ʔɛ=ʔɛ́=cə=wɬ//, TIME /'*until, unless*'/, CJ, possibly <**R8=** or **=R9**> *derivational*, possibly root <**atsa ~ ache**> *next, again*, possibly <**-cha**> *future tense*, possibly <**-(e)wlh ~ welh**> *already*, possibly root <**a'á**> *oh-oh*, phonology: reduplication, syntactic analysis: conjunction, example: <**ő́wechexw lámexwcha xwa siyólexwe a'áchewlh x̱áp'kw'tem ta' sth'eth'elòm**>, //ʔəwə-c-xʷ lɛ́m-əxʷ xʷɛ s=iyáləxʷə ʔɛʔɛ́cəwɬx̣ɛ́p'k'ʷ(-)t(-)əm t-ɛʔ s=C₁ə-θ'[-əl-]àm//, /'*You're not going to get (become) old until (unless) your bones are aching.*'/, usage: This is a saying of the old people, a proverb. (AD), grammatical analysis: vneg-independent clause subject pronoun-2s auxiliary verb-2ssjsp particle (stat=)adjective/adjectival verb conjunction adjective/adjectival verb(-pc?)-middle voice demonstrative article-2spsvp (nominal=)dim-root[-pl-]root, ASM ['are not-(subject)-you going to-you(subjunct. subj.) become old until(-fut-contr-past/already) are aching (the)-your little-many-bone'].

<**átsele**>, free root or stem //ʔɛ́c(=)ələ//, EFAM /'*gee., good grief., well. (said when surprised), goodness., gee whiz.*'/, *see* áts.

<**átslexw**>, ncs //ʔɛ́c=l-əxʷ//, LANG /'*hear about it, (hear about s-o)*'/, *see* áts.

<**=á:w ~ =í:w ~ =ew ~ =ú:w**>, da //=ɛ́·w ~ =í·w ~ =əw ~ =ú·w//, ANA /'*on the body, on top of itself*'/, DIR, comment: rare variant of =í:ws ~ =ews *on the body*, predictable before =et *purposeful control transitivizer*, syntactic analysis: lexical suffix,<**q'álq'elp'í:w**>, //q'ɛ́l=C₁əC₂=p'=í·w(s)//, /'*inchworm*'/; found in <**sq'elá:w**>, //s=q'ɛ́l=ə[=M2=]w(s) or s=q'əl=ɛ́·w//, /'*coiled (and ready to strike, for ex. a snake)*'/, <**sq'elq'elá:w**>, //s=C₁əC₂=q'əl=ɛ́·w or s=q'əl=C₁əC₂=ɛ́·w//, /'*coiling (of a snake)(ready to strike)*'/ (compare <**q'elq'él=q'=t**> *coil it*, <**q'elq'él=q'**> *tangled on s-th else*, and <**q'elq'él=p'**> *tangled on itself*), <**qwemchíwet**>, //qʷəm=c(əs)=íw(s)=əT//, /'*hug s-o around*'/, <**qwsá:wiyel**>, //qʷəs=ɛ́·w=iyəl or qʷɛ́s=M1=əw(s)=iyəl or qʷɛ́·s=ə[=M2=]w(s)=iyəl//, /'*set a net and drift with it*'/, <**q'ewú:w**>, //q'ə́wə=ú·w//, SPRD /new spirit dancer's cane (compare <q'éwe> 'cane').

<**á:we**>, free root //ʔɛ́·wə//, EZ ['*seagull (generic)*'], syntactic analysis: nominal, dialects: *Chill., Tait*,also <**slílōwya**>, //s=líləwyɛ//, dialects: *Cheh.*, also <**qw'elíteq**>, //q'ʷəlítəq//, dialects: *Chill., Katzie.*

<**áwélh ~ (-)àwèlh ~ (-)òwèlh**>, //ʔɛ́wə́ɬ ~ ʔɛ̀wə̀ɬ ~ -ɛ̀wə̀ɬ~ -àwə̀ɬ//, MOOD ['*polite imperative*'], syntactic analysis: is ~ particle, dialects: *Cheh., Tait*, also <**(-)òwèlh**>, //(-)àwə̀ɬ//, dialects: *Chill.*;

found in Chill. **<hóyòwèlh>,** Cheh. + Tait **<hóyàwèlh ~ hóy àwèlh>**, //Chill. háy-àwə̀ɬ, Cheh. + Tait háy-ɛ̀wə̀ɬ ~ háy ʔɛ̀wə̀ɬ//, root probably **<hóy>** *it's finished*, LANG, /'*goodbye (said to one staying), (stay well, well done)*'/, Chill. **<lámòwèlh>,** Cheh. + Tait **<lámàwèlh ~ lám àwèlh>**, Chill. //lɛ́màwə̀ɬ//, Cheh. + Tait //lɛ́mɛ̀wə̀ɬ ~ lɛ́m ʔɛ̀wə̀ɬ//, root **<lám>** *go*, LANG, /'*goodbye (said to one leaving), (go well)*'/, example: Cheh. + Tait **<á'á àwèlh>,** Chill. **<á'á òwèlh>**, Cheh. + Tait //ʔɛ́ʔɛ ʔɛ̀wə̀ɬ//, Chill. //ʔɛ́ʔɛ́ ʔàwə̀ɬ//, root **<á:'a>** *yes*, LANG, /'*You're welcome., Yes, thanks.*'/, semantic environment ['said in answer to a person who just said "Look after yourself." while leaving (for ex. Thehíthetchxw. or xólhmethetchxw.)'], dialects: *Cheh., Tait, Chill.*, attested by EB, AD, AC, also **<le áwélh>**, //lə ʔɛ́wə́ɬ//, attested by NP (usu. Chill., but knows some Cheh. as here), **<ṓ'òwèlh>**, //ʔóʔàwə̀ɬ//, LANG, /'*I'm listening*'/, root **<ō>** *oh* or root something like *I'm listening* or root as also in **< ō siyám>,** said while a prominent speaker is doing public speaking, **<siyám>** *respected person, leader, chief, boss*), attested by AC, usage: Said periodically by those listening to a story, to show they're attentive; most dialects also use i'ó:y for this too., **<lí'àwèlh>**, //lí-ʔɛ̀wə̀ɬ//, LANG, /'*Yes of course.*'/, root **<lí>** *it is there, it is, yes,* attested by EB, AD.

<á:wkw'>, free root //ʔɛ́·wk'ʷ//, HHG ['*belongings (AC)*'], CLO ['*clothes*'], syntactic analysis: nominal, example: **<l swá á:wkw'>**, //l swɛ́ ʔɛ́·wk'ʷ//, /'*That belongs to me.*'/, literally /'It's my own belonging.'/, attested by AC, **<iyóqthetchxw ta' á:wkw'>**, //ʔiyáq=θət-c-xʷ t-ɛʔ ʔɛ́·wk'ʷ//, /'*Change your clothes.*'/, attested by EB, **<lemlémetchxw mékw' yel á:wkw'>**, //C_1əC_2-lə́m=əT-c-xʷ mə́k'ʷ yə-l ʔɛ́·wk'ʷ//, /'*Fold all my clothes.*'/.

<shxw'awkw'ála>, dnom //sxʷ=ʔɛwk'ʷ=ɛ́lɛ//, HHG ['*clothes basket*'], CLO, BSK, (**<shxw=>** *nominalizer, something for*), lx **<=ála>** *container of*, syntactic analysis: nominal.

<awkw'áwtxw>, dnom //ʔɛwk'ʷ=ɛ́wtxʷ//, BLDG ['*clothes store*'], CLO, lx **<=áwtxw>** *building for*, syntactic analysis: nominal, contrast **<ith'emáwtxw>** *clothes store.*

<á:wkw'mal>, dnom //ʔɛ́·wk'ʷ=mɛl//, TOOL ['*tool case*'], lx **<=mal>** *part, portion*, syntactic analysis: nominal, attested by EB.

<áwkw'emálá>, dnom //ʔɛ́wk'ʷ=əm=ɛ́lɛ́//, HHG /'*suitcase (Deming), luggage (Deming), clothingcontainer, clothes bag, trunk (for clothes), etc.*'/, CLO, (**<=em>** *place to have/get*), lx **<=álá>** *container of*, syntactic analysis: nominal, also **<shxw'áwkw'emálá>**, //sxʷ=ʔɛ́wk'ʷ=əm=ɛ́lɛ́//, HHG ['*suitcase*'], also **<shxw'á:wkw'emálá ~ shxw'á:wkw'álá>**, //sxʷ=ʔɛ́·wk'ʷ=əm=ɛ́lɛ́ ~ sxʷ=ʔɛ́·wk'ʷ=ɛ́lɛ́//, HHG /'*clothes container, suitcase, clothes case*'/, attested by EB.

<awkw'áwtxw>, BLDG ['*clothes store*'], see á:wkw'.

<áwkw'emálá>, HHG /'*suitcase (Deming), luggage (Deming), clothing container, clothes bag, trunk (for clothes), etc.*'/, see á:wkw'.

<á:wkw'mal>, TOOL ['*tool case*'], see á:wkw'.

<=á:wtxw ~ =áwtxw ~ =ewtxw ~ =(á)ltxw ~ =(el)txw>, da //=ɛ́(·)w(=)txʷ ~ =əw(=)txʷ ~ =(ɛ́)l(=)txʷ ~ =(əl=)txʷ//, BLDG /'*building, house*'/, semantic environment ['with numerals 2-5, kw'í:l, non-numerals oblig. for single owner'], possibly **<=á:w>** *on the body* possibly here *over people*, syntactic analysis: lexical suffix, derivational suffix, found in **<lhq'átsesá:wtxw>**, //ɬq'ɛ́cəs=ɛ́·wtxʷ//, /'*five houses or buildings (belonging to one person)*'/, **<xwelmexwáwtxw>**, //xʷəlməxʷ=ɛ́wtxʷ//, /'*smokehouse, longhouse*'/, literally /'Indian house'/, **<atl'qelá:wtxw>**, //ʔɛƛ'qəl=ɛ́·wtxʷ//, /'*outhouse, bathroom*'/, literally /'outside house'/, **<lámá:wtxw>**, //lɛ́m=ɛ́·wtxʷ//, /'*bar, pub, liquor store*'/, comment: **lám** *liquor* from English "rum", **<chálhteláwtxw>**, //cɛ́ɬtəl=ɛ́wtxʷ//, /'*smoke-house, dried fish house*'/, literally /'dried fish house'/, **<íltexwáwtxw>**, //ʔíltəxʷ=ɛ́wtxʷ//, /'*plank house*'/, literally /'plank house'/, **<tsaháyelháwtxw>**, //cɛhɛ́yəɬ=ɛ́wtxʷ//, /'*church building*'/, literally /'prayer house'/,

<**tále'áwtxw**>, //tɛ́lə=ɛ́wtxʷ//, /'*bank*'/, literally /'money house'/, comment: **tále** *money* is Chinook Jargon from English "dollar", <**siláwtxw**>, //sil=ɛ́wtxʷ//, /'*tent*'/, literally /'cloth house'/, comment: síl *cloth* is Chinook Jargon from English "sail", <**slexwelhá:wtxw**>, //sləxʷəɬ=ɛ́·wtxʷ//, /'*canoe shed*'/, <**siyólhá:wtxw**>, //siyáɬ=ɛ́·wtxʷ//, /'*woodshed*'/, <**sokw'emáwtxw**>, //sak'ʷəm=ɛ́wtxʷ//, /'*bark house*'/, <**qw'eyíléxáwtxw**>, //q'ʷəyíləxʸ=ɛ́wtxʷ//, /'*dance hall*'/, <**smílha'áwtxw**>, //smíɬɛ=ʔɛ́wtxʷ//, /'*spirit dancing house*'/, <**wá:cháwtxw**>, //wɛ́·c=ɛ́wtxʷ//, /'*out-house (for solid waste)*'/, <**mekw'emáwtxw**>, //mək'ʷəm=ɛ́wtxʷ//, /'*second-hand store*'/, root <**mékw'em**> *use second-hand*, <**ítetá:wtxw**>, //ʔítət=ɛ́·wtxʷ//, /'*hotel, bedroom*'/, <**spepíláwtxw**>, //spəpíl=ɛ́wtxʷ//, /'*root cellar (covered with earth, separate from house, kept potatoes, apples, etc.)*'/, <**thí:yáwtxwem**>, //θí·y=ɛ́wtxʷ=əm//, /'*build a house*'/, literally /'make + house + middle voice'/, <**lá:ts'áwtxw**>, //lɛ́·c'=ɛ́wtxʷ//, /'*next-door, different house*'/, <**lá:ts'awtxwem**>, //lɛ́·c'=ɛwtxʷ=əm//, /'*visit*'/, <**tslháltxw**>, //cɬ=ɛ́ltxʷ//, /'*upper portion of pit house or any house*'/, <**s'í:ltexw**>, //sʔí·ltəxʷ//, /'*cedar planks on roof or side of house*'/, <**Swelímeltxw**>, //swəlím=əltxʷ//, /'*(Indian name of Ed Leon Sr. of Chehalis*'/, <**qiq'áwtxw**>, //qiq'=ɛ́wtxʷ//, /'*jail*'/.

<**áwth**>, bound root //ʔɛ́wθ *hurry, haste*//.

<**s'ówth**>, strs //s=ʔɛ[=Aá=]wθ//, ABFC ['*be in a hurry*'], (<**s=**> *stative*), (<**ó-ablaut**> on root <**á**> *resultative*), phonology: ablaut, syntactic analysis: intransitive verb, attested by Deming (1/18/79), also <**s'ówts**>, //s=ʔɛ[=Aá=]wc//, phonology: possible Nooksack or Lushootseed influence, dialects: *Deming (some speakers)*, attested by Deming (1/18/79), Salish cognate: Squamish /ʔawʔíc/ *fast* as also in /nəxʷ-s-awʔíc-i/ *rush work, fast work* W73:97, K67:310, example: <**s'ówthtsel.**>, //s=ʔɛ́wθ-c-əl//, /'*I'm in a hurry.*'/, attested by Deming, also <**s'ówtstsel.**>, //s=ʔɛ[=Aá=]wc-c-əl//, attested by Deming (some speakers).

<**ówthet**>, pcrs //ʔɛ[=Aá=]wθ=T-ət//, ABFC /'*to hurry, hurry up, move fast*'/, (<**ó-ablaut**> on root <**á**> *resultative*), (<**=t**> *purposeful control transitivizer*), (<**-et**> *reflexive*), phonology: ablaut, consonant merger, syntactic analysis: intransitive verb, attested by BHTTC, NP (6/4/80), EB or Deming or IHTTC (fall 1977), example: <**ówthetchap kw'as í:lhtelelep.**>, //ʔɛ[=Aá=]wθ=T-ət-c-ɛp k'ʷ-ɛ-s ʔɛ[=Aí·=]ɬ=təl-ələp//, /'*Hurry up and eat (folks).*'/, literally /'hurry =purposely -oneself -you folks that -you -subord. are eating a meal =with each other -you plural'/, attested by NP, <**tu ówthetlha.**>, //tu ʔɛ[=Aá=]wθ=T-ət-ɬɛ//, /'*Move a little faster.*'/, attested by EB or Deming or IHTTC (fall 1977).

<**axelés**>, us //ʔɛxʸələ́s or ʔɛxʸ(=)əl=əs//, DIR /'*front, in front of*'/, possibly <**=el**> *go, come, get,become*, possibly <**=es**> *on the face*, syntactic analysis: adverb/adverbial verb?.

<**axelésmel**>, dnom //ʔɛxʸələs=məl//, BLDG ['*front of a house*'], lx <**=mel**> *part, portion*, syntactic analysis: nominal.

<**áxw**>, free root //ʔɛ́xʷ//, FOOD ['*give me s-th (to eat)*'], SOC, usage: slang or shortcut for axwesthóx, syntactic analysis: transitive verb, syntactic comment: transitive verb in spite of the dropping of the transitivizer, attested by AHTTC (2/15/80), MH (2/8/79), example: <**mítlh éxw.**>, //mí-tɬ ʔɛ́xʷ//, /'*Give me some.*'/, literally /'come -mildly urging imperative 2s give (me) food'/, attested by MH, <**mítlh áxw kópi.**>, //mí-tɬ ʔɛ́xʷ kápi//, /'*Give me coffee.*'/, syntactic comment: dropping of tie article here may be English influence, (irregular), attested by MH.

<**áxwe ~ s'áxwe**>, stvi //ʔɛ́xʷ(=)ə ~ s=ʔɛ́xʷ(=)ə//, FOOD ['*(food) given*'], SOC, (<**s=**> *stative*), possibly <**=e**> meaning uncertain if not *living thing*, syntactic analysis: adjective/adjectival verb, attested by AD (3/6/79), also <**s'áxwem?**>, //s=ʔɛ́xʷ=əm//, Elder's comment: "may be the same as **áxwe** and s'áxwe", attested by AD, Salish cognate: Squamish /ʔə́xʷaʔ-t/ *give to, hand to (tr.) (obj. destinee)*.

<**á:xwem**>, cts //ʔɛ́[-·-]xʷ=əm//, FOOD ['*giving (food)*'], SOC, (<**-:-**> *continuative*), (<**=em**> *intransitivizer*), phonology: lengthening, syntactic analysis: intransitive verb, attested by EB,

example: <**tl'émes á:xwem.**>, //ƛ'ə́ mə-s ʔɛ́[-·-]xʷ=əm//, /'*That's what he gave.*'/, literally /'it's that come to -he dependent (be) giving'/, attested by EB.

<**s'áxwem**>, df //s=ʔɛ́xʷ=əm//, FOOD ['*(food) given*'], SOC, (<**s=**> *nominalizer* or *stative*), (<**=em**> *intransitivizer* or *resultative* or *passive*??), syntactic analysis: adjective/adjectival verb?, nominal?, attested by AD, example: <**qéx̱ tel s'áxwem.**>, //qə́x̣ tə-l s=ʔɛ́xʷ=əm//, /'*I was given a lot of food.*'/, attested by AD.

<**áxwest**>, df //ʔɛ́xʷ=əs=T//, pcs, SOC /'*give an equal share or amount to s-o, give (food?) to s-o, share with s-o*'/, FOOD, possibly <**=es**> *money, dollars*?, (<**=t**> *purposeful control transitivizer*), syntactic analysis: transitive verb, attested by Deming (SJ, MC, MV, LG) (3/15/79), Elders Group (3/72), example: <**ōwéta shxwlís kws axwesthóxs.**>, //ʔəwə= ´=tɛ s(=)xʷ=lí-s kʷ-s ʔɛxʷ(=)ə(=)sT-áxʸ-s//, /'*It's free., (What (food) he gives me is (costs) nothing there.)*'/, literally /'what's there is nothing that he gives me (food)'/, attested by Deming (SJ, MC, MV, LG), <**lhíxw áxwest kw'e mőkw'ewátes**>, //ɬí-xʷ ʔɛ́xʷ=əs=T k'ʷə mok'ʷ=wɛ́t=əs//, /'*when you give everyone equal amounts or equal share*'/, attested by Elders Group (3/72).

<**óxwest**>, df //ʔɛ[=Aá=]xʷ=əs=T//, SOC /'*give it to s-o, give to s-o*'/, (<**ó-ablaut**> on root <**é**> *derivational*), lx <**=es**> probably *money*, (<**=t**> *purposeful control transitivizer*), phonology: **ó**-ablaut on root **á** automatic with =es suffix, syntactic analysis: transitive verb, attested by AC, Elders Group (3/15/72, 1/19/77, 3/14/79), IHTTC, EB, AD, RG & EH (4/9/99 Ling332), also <**ó:xwest**>, //ʔɛ[=Aá·=]xʷ=əs=T//, attested by AC, BJ (5/64); found in <**ó:xwesthòxes. ~ óxwesthòxes.**>, //ʔɛ[=Aá(·)=]xʷ=əs=T-axʸ-əs//, /'*He gave it to me.*'/, attested by AC, example: <**óxwesthométsel.**>, //ʔɛ[=Aá=]xʷ=əs=T-ámə-c-əl//, /'*I give it to you.*'/, attested by Elders Group (3/15/72), <**l stl'í kw'els óxwesthòmè.**>, //l s=ƛ'í k'ʷə-l-s ʔɛ[=Aá=]xʷ=əs=T-ámə//, /'*I want to give you (this).*'/, attested by Elders Group (3/15/72); found in <**oxwestólxwes.**>, //ʔɛ[=Aá=]xʷ=əs=T-á[=l=]xʷ-əs//, /'*He gave us (lots of people) something.*'/, ASM ['*us* here is lots of people, i.e. has plural infix'], attested by IHTTC (8/8/77), comment: comparison of -ólxw *us (many)* and -óxw *us (few)* from the next example (and a few others) with cognates shows that the =l= element is may be the plural affix, but this has not been clear before since -óxw was used very rarely and perhaps only by a few elders, the next generation of elders (1990's) use -óxw in preference & rarely use -ólxw at all now, Salish cognate: Songish /-əl-xʷ/, Coeur d'Alene and Shuswap /-el/, Columbian /-al/, Thompson /-ey/, etc. *first person plural object* in the neutral object paradigm Newman 1979:300ff, <**oxwestóxwes.**>, //ʔɛ[=Aá=]xʷ=əs=T-áxʷ-əs//, /'*He gave us (maybe a couple of people) something.*'/, ASM ['*us* here is not pluralized (perhaps us exclusive)'], attested by IHTTC (8/8/77), example: <**ó(:)xwest mőkw'**>, //ʔɛ[=Aá=]xƛ'=əs=T mók'ʷ//, /'*give it to all (of them)*'/, attested by AC; found in <**ó:xwestlha.**>, //ʔɛ[=Aá=]xʷ=əs=T-ɬɛ//, /'*Give it to him!.*'/, attested by AC, example: <**óxwestchexw telí tl'elhlímelh.**>, //ʔɛ[=Aá=]xƛ'=əs=T-c-əxʷ təlí ƛ'ə=ɬlíməɬ//, /'*Give it to him from ts.*'/, attested by Elders Group (1/19/77), also <**óxwestbhexw xwelá tl'elhlímelh.**>, //ʔɛ[=Aá=]xʷ=T-c-əxʷ xʷə=lɛ́ ƛ'ə=ɬlíməɬ//, usage: idiom, attested by Elders Group (1/19/77), <**óxwestchexw xwelá tl'á'altha.**>, //ʔɛ[=Aá=]xʷ=əs=T-c-əxʷ xʷə=lɛ́ƛ'=(ʔ)ɛ́ʔɛlθɛ//, /'*Give it to him from me.*'/, attested by EB (3/1/76), <**óxwest kw'e mékw'ewátes**>, //ʔɛ[=Aá=]xʷ=əs=T k'ʷə mə́k'ʷ=wɛ́t=əs//, /'*give it to everybody*'/, attested by Elders Group (3/15/72), <**le óxwestes.**>, //lə ʔɛ[=Aá=]xʷ=əs=T-əs//, /'*He gives it to s-o.*'/, attested by AC, <**óxwestlha te lepót.**>, //ʔɛ[=Aá=]xʷ=əs=T-ɬɛ tə ləpát//, /'*Give him the cup.*'/, attested by AD, <**óxwest ta syó:ys.**>, //ʔɛ[=Aá=]xʷ=əs=T t-ɛ s=yá·ys//, /'*Turn in (to s-o) your work., Give (s-o) your work.*'/, SCH, ECON, MC, attested by Elders Group (3/14/79).

<**óxw**>, ds //ʔɛ[=Aá=]xʷ//, SOC ['*give it to me*'], usage: slang or short form (clipped form) for oxwesthóx, syntactic analysis: transitive verb, attested by AHTTC (2/15/80).

<**ó:xwest**>, cts //ʔɛ[=Aá=][-·-]xʷ=əs=T//, SOC ['*giving it to s-o*'], (<-:-> *continuative*), phonology: lengthening, syntactic analysis: transitive verb, attested by AC (8/11/70), example: <**le ó:xwestes.**>, //lə ʔɛ[=Aá=][-·-]xʷ=əs=T-əs//, /'*He is giving it (to s-o).*'/, attested by AC.

<**áxwet**>, pcs //ʔɛ́xʷ=əT//, FOOD ['*share food with s-o*'], SOC, ASM ['*give s-o food, bring s-o food,pass food to s-o*'], ASM ['*serve s-o (food)*'] (RG & EH 4/10/99 Ling332), (<**=et**> *purposeful control transitivizer*), syntactic analysis: transitive verb, compare <**áxwem**> *share, give*, and compare <**óxwest**> *give it to s-o* which seems to show **o-ablaut** derivation, or **o-ablaut** conditioned by derivational suffix **=es**, attested by AD, DC, Ben James, EB, Salish cognate: Squamish root in /ʔə́xʷaʔ-t/ *give to, hand to (tr.) (obj. destinee)* and /ʔíxʷ-n/ *give, make a present of (tr.)* W73:117, K67:388, K69:96, example: <**axwethóxchexw; echulh me kw'à:y.**>, //ʔɛxʷ=əT-áxʸ-c-əxʷ; ʔə-c-əl-uɬ mə k'ʷɛ̀·y//, /'*Give me some food; I'm hungry.*'/, literally /'you give me food; ambiguous past -I - already become hungry'/, attested by AD, <**axwethóxchexw kw'e qwe'óp.**>, //ʔɛxʷ=əT-áxʸ-c-əxʷ k'ʷə qʷəʔáp//, /'*Give me an apple.*'/, attested by DC, Ben James,AD, <**axwethóxchexw tel sq'éyle.**>, //ʔɛxʷ=əT-áxʸ-c-əxʷ tə-l s=q'ílə//, /'*Give me my wind dried salmon.*'/, literally /'you give me food the -my dried fish/dried meat'/, attested by AD, <**axwethóxchexw kw' tí, ő̱we slíts'es.**>, //ʔɛxʷ=əT-áxʸ-c-əxʷ k'ʷə tí, ʔówə s=lə[=Aí=]c'-əs//, /'*Give me some tea, not full.*'/, attested by EB, <**áxwethòmè**> //ʔɛ́xʷ=əT-àmə̀//, /'*serve you (food)*'/, attested by RG & EH (4/10/99 Ling332), *<**áxwetlha te lepót**>. *Give him the cup.* rejected by AD, comment: rejected because of semantic co-occurence restrictions, **áxwet** is *giving food* and a cup is not food, <**metlh áxwet te seplí:l**>, //mə-tɬ ʔɛ́xʷ=əT tə səplí·l//, /'*Pass the bread (please).*'/, (<**-tlh**> *polite imperative*), attested by Deming: MH, <**metlh áxwethòx te th'áles te músmes**>, //mə-tɬ ʔɛ́xʷ=əT-àxʸ tə θ'ɛ́lə-s tə mús=C_1əC_2//, /'*Please give me the heart of the cow.*'/, grammatical analysis: auxiliary verb-polimp2s r-pc-1soj demonstrative article nominal-3possessive demonstrative article r=characteristic, attested by AC, <**tsel me áxwet ta sqwéqwemey te sth'ò:m**>, //c-əl mə ʔɛxʷ=əT t-ɛ s=C_1í[-Aə́-]-qʷəmɛ́y tə s=θ'à·m//, /'*I brought up a bone for your dogs.*'/, literally /'I came to bring food to them the-your (sg) little-pl.-dog the bone'/, grammatical analysis: isb-1ssb auxiliary verb r-pc demonstrative article-2spsv nominal=dim[-pl-]-r demonstrative article nominal-r, syntactic comment: preposed pronoun *ambiguous past tense*, syntactic analysis of sentence: subjpron + auxiliary verb + transitive verb + dirobj np + indirobj np, attested by AC, <**tset áxwet mékw' ta sqwéqwemey te sth'ò:m**>, //c-ət ʔɛxʷ=əT mək'ʷ t-ɛ s=C_1í[-Aə́-]-qʷəmɛ́y tə s=θ'à·m//, /'*We gave all your dogs a bone.*'/, syntactic comment: vadj mékw' *all* precedes the article of its np, attested by AC, <**lhí:xw e(l) kwthels áxwet**>, //ɬí·xʷ ʔə(l) kʷθ-əl-s ʔɛ́xʷ=əT//, /'*I just gave him three (items of food).*'/, ASM ['it's three just that(near but not visible)-I-nom give food-to him'], attested by AC.

<**áxwe ~ s'áxwe**>, FOOD ['*(food) given*'], *see* áxw.

<**á:xwem**>, FOOD ['*giving (food)*'], *see* áxw.

<**áxwest**>, SOC /'*give an equal share or amount to s-o, give (food?) to s-o, share with s-o*'/, see áxw.

<**áxwet**>, FOOD ['*share food with s-o, give s-o food, bring s-o food,pass food to s-o*'], *see* áxw.

<**axwíl**>, us //ʔɛxʷ(=)íl//, VALJ /'*small (AC, BJ), little (AC), a little bit (Deming: EF, MC, Cheh.: EB)*'/, semantic environment ['*a little bit* used if someone is going to pour a drink for ex. (AD); *little* used in contexts the opposite of *big* (AD)'], Elder's comment: "some use axwíl for *less* but it's not really proper (AD); yeláwel axwíl could work for *less* but is a poor substitute (AD)", possibly <**=íl**> *inceptive, go, come, get, become*, syntactic analysis: adjective/adjectival verb, dialects: *some speakers contrast* <**axwíl**> *small, little* with <**emémel ~ emímel**> *a little bit* (AC for ex.); some speakers maintain the contrast but reverse the meanings (EB for ex̲.); some speakers use <**ax̲wíl**> with both meanings (AD for ex̲.), other sources: ES /ʔɛmí·məl/ *small* (Cw,Ms /ʔəx̲ʷínʔ/), JH /ʔex̲ʷí·l/, example:

<**tu ax̲wíl è kw'a's óx̲westhòx̲**>, //t=əw ʔɛx^{w}íl ʔə̀ k'^{w}-ɛʔ-s ʔáx^{w}əs=T-àx^{y}//, /'*You gave me too little.*'/, attested by AD, <**l stl'í kw'els qwà:l kw'e axwí:l òl**>, //l s=ƛ'í k'^{w}ə-l-s q^{w}ɛ̀·l k'^{w}ə ʔɛx^{w}í·l ʔàl//, /'*I would like to say just a few words.*'/, attested by Deming, <**axwíl tsqwáy**>, //ʔɛx^{w}íl c=q^{w}ɛ́y//, /'*a little yellow, a little green*'/, ASM ['P1 through V1 on Berlin and Kay color chart'], compare <**tsqwá:y**> *yellow, green*, attested by TM.

<**í:'axwì:l ~ í:'axwí:l**>, dms //C$_{1}$í=ʔɛx^{w}í[=·=]l//, VALJ /'*small (smaller than axwíl), little*'/, DESC, (<**R4=**> *diminutive*), (<**=:=**> *emphatic*), phonology: reduplication, phonology: lengthening, optional downstepping, syntactic analysis: adjective/adjectival verb, dialects: *Chill.*, attested by AC, example: <**í:'axwì:l mestíyéxw**>, //C$_{1}$í=ʔɛx^{w}ì·l məstíyə́x^{w}//, /'*small person*'/, attested by AC, <**i'axwí:l mí:meqw**>, //C$_{1}$í=ʔɛx^{w}í·l C$_{1}$í=má·q^{w}//, phonology: doubling prefix with i= attracts stress normally; found in mí:meqw where **á:** → e also, /'*tiny bird*'/, attested by AC, <**í:'axwìl smá:lt**>, //C$_{1}$í=ʔɛx^{w}ìl s=mɛ́·lt//, /'*little rock*'/, attested by AC, also <**a'axwíl ~ a'axwí:l**>, //C$_{1}$ɛ=ʔɛx^{w}íl ~ C$_{1}$ɛ=ʔɛx^{w}í[=·=]l//, dialects: *Cheh.: EB; Tait: CT*, <**a'axwí:l tel sts'áletstel telí ta' swá**>, //C$_{1}$ɛ=ʔɛx^{w}í·l tə-l s=c'ɛ́=ləc=təl təlí t-ɛʔ s=wɛ́//, /'*My chair is smaller than yours.*'/, <**a'axwíl o**>, //C$_{1}$ɛ=ʔɛx^{w}íl ʔà//, /'*just a few (for ex. of berries, but not of people)*'/, attested by EB.

<**a'axwíleqel**>, dnom //C$_{1}$ɛ=ʔɛx^{w}íl=əqəl//, HHG ['*small container*'], (<**R8=**> *diminutive*), lx <**=eqel**> *container* lx <**[from**> *throat*], phonology: reduplication, syntactic analysis: nominal, attested by CT.

<**a'axwíyelhp**>, dnom //C$_{1}$ɛ=ʔɛx^{w}íl=əɬp//, EB ['*small tree*'], (<**R8=**> *diminutive*), lx <**=elhp**> *tree, plant*, phonology: reduplication, phonology: consonant-shift (consonant alternation, l → y stem-finally before =elhp), syntactic analysis: nominal, attested by CT.

<**áx̲ ~ yáx̲**>, free root //ʔɛ́x̣ ~ yɛ́x̣//, EFAM ['*(bad)*'], usage: said to a child (crawling age) to teach him something is bad; baby talk, syntactic analysis: interjection, attested by AD.

<**áx̲e**>, free root //ʔɛ́x̣ə//, EZ ['*Canada goose*'], ['*Branta canadensis*'], ASM ['goose that comes just before winter'], syntactic analysis: nominal, Salish cognate: Squamish /ʔə́x̣/ 'wild goose, Canada goose' W73:122, K67:389, K69:93, Lushootseed /ʔəx̣áʔ/ 'snowgoose' H76:662.

<**Áx̲etel**>, dnom //ʔɛ́x̣ə=təl//, PLN /'*a goose-shaped rock near Hamisley Mt. and near Hooknose Mountain or Lhílhkw'elqs, west of Agassiz, B.C.*'/, ASM ['the half of the top of the rock with the goose on it was blasted off for a quarry there; the goose can't be seen now; the rock was close by Harry Bouchard's place (AK, AP)'], lx <**=tel**> *device, thing*, syntactic analysis: nominal, attested by AK, also <**S'áx̲etxel**>, //s=ʔɛ́x̣ə=t(əl?)=x^{y}əl//, PLN /'*where B.C. Hopyard used to be at Agassiz,* (probably *the same place as Áx̲etel)*'/, lx <**=xel**> *foot*, attested by AK, prob. LJ2 (of Tait), source: place name file reference #198.

<**=áx̲el ~ =ex̲el**>, da //=ɛ́x̣əl ~ =əx̣əl//, BLDG ['*end or side of a house (inside/outside)*'], DIR, SH ['*angular or perpendicular extension*'], comment: prob. source of =eláx̲el *arm, wing*, syntactic analysis: lexical suffix, derivational suffix, also <**=ex̲el**>, //=əx̣əl//; found in <**stiytáx̲el**>, //s=tiyt=ɛ́x̣əl//, /'*upper (upriver) end of house (inside or out)*'/ (root <**tíyt**> *upriver)*, <**sewqw'áx̲el ~ sōwqw'áx̲el**>, //s=əwq'^{w}=ɛ́x̣əl//, /'*lower (downriver) end of house (inside or out)*'/ (root <**wṓqw'**> *drift downriver, drown)*, <**chuchuwáx̲el** or **chewchewáx̲el**>, //cucuw=ɛ́x̣əl or cəw=C$_{1}$əC$_{2}$=ɛ́x̣əl//, /'*front end of house (inside or out)*'/, root <**cúcuw**> *away from shore, towards the middle of the river, in front*, <**stselkwáx̲el**>, //s=cəlk^{w}=ɛ́x̣əl//, /'*back end of house (inside or out)*'/, root <**chó:lekw (kw ~ qw)**> *toward the woods, away from the river, in the backwoods*, <**chelkwáx̲elmel**>, //cəlk^{w}=ɛ́x̣əl=məl//, /'*behind or back of a house*'/, <**q'eléx̲el**>, //q'əl=ə́x̣əl//, /'*fence*'/, <**st'elt'eláx̲el**>, //s=t'əlt'əl=ɛ́x̣əl//, /'*a square*'/, <**sélts'ex̲el**>, //sə́lc'=əx̣əl//, /'*to circle around the outside of a house*'/, root <**sə̀lc'**> *go around in a circle.*

<**áx̲elqel**>, dnom //ʔi[=Aɛ́=]x̣=əlqəl or ʔi[=Aə́=]x̣=əlqəl//, [ʔɛ́x̣əlqəl], HUNT /'*buckskin, rawhide, tanned buckskin*'/, root <**íx̲**> *scrape off*, (<**á-ablaut**> of root <**í**> *resultative*), lx <**=elqel**> *wool, feathers*, phonology: derivational ablaut Aɛ if root /ʔíx̣/, syntactic analysis: nominal.

<**Áx̲etel**>, PLN /'*a goose-shaped rock near Hamisley Mt. and near Hooknose Mountain or Lhilhkw'elqs, west of Agassiz, B.C.*'/, see áx̲e.

<**áx̲eth**>, free root //ʔɛ́x̣əθ//, TVMO ['*lie down*'], syntactic analysis: intransitive verb, attested by AC, BHTTC, EB, LJ2, CT, HT, example: <**lhéq' me sélts'tem tel sx̲óyes lhíl áx̲eth**>, //ɬə́q' mə sə́lc'=təm tə-l s=x̣áy(=)əs ɬí-l ʔɛ́x̣əθ//, /'*Sometimes my head spins when I lay down.*'/, attested by LJ2 (of Tait), <**áx̲eth í ta' s'éqwelets**>, //ʔɛ́x̣əθ ʔí t-ɛʔ s=ʔə́qʷə=ləc//, /'*Lie down on your back.*'/, attested by EB, <**áx̲eth lí tel éqwelets**>, //ʔɛ́x̣əθ lí tə-l ʔə́qʷə=ləc//, /'*lie on my back*'/, attested by CT, HT.

<**á:x̲eth**>, cts //ʔɛ́[-·-]x̣əθ//, TVMO ['*lying down*'], (<-:-> *continuative*), phonology: length infixing, syntactic analysis: intransitive verb, attested by EB, BHTTC.

<**i'ax̲íth**>, dmv //C_1í=ʔɛx̣ə[=Aí=]θ//, TVMO ['*little baby lying down*'], (<**R4=**> *diminutive*), (<**í-ablaut**> *diminutive*), phonology: diminutive reduplication and ablaut, syntactic analysis: intransitive verb, attested by BHTTC.

<**shxw'áx̲eth**>, dnom //sx̲ʷ=ʔɛ́x̲əθ//, HHG ['*bed*'], literally /'what one lies down on'/, syntactic analysis: nominal, attested by CT, DM, AC, other elders, also <**shxw'á:x̲eth**>, //sxʷ=ʔɛ́[-·-]x̣əθ//, literally /'what one is lying down on'/, attested by NP.

<**shxw'álex̲eth(')**>, pln //sxʷ=ʔɛ́[-lə-]x̣əθ'//, HHG ['*beds*'], phonology: consonant alternation (th' /θ'/ in my notes is probably in error for th /θ/, as is also **shxwáx̲eth'** /sxʷɛ́x̣əθ'/ [šwǽx̣ətθ'] *bed* in my early notes from a DM tape; but these may also be a legitimate derivational glottalization), syntactic analysis: nominal, attested by EB (5/5/78).

<**á:y**>, free root //ʔɛ́·y//, TVMO ['*keep on going*'], syntactic analysis: intransitive verb, Salish cognate: Lushootseed /ʔáy'/ 'change' H76:652, example: <**qe tl'o sésuw á::y qa lís te kw'íl "hour" kwses á:y yi qwóqwel**>, //qə ƛ'a s-ʔə-s-əw ʔɛ́·[=·=]y qɛ líy-ə-s tə k'ʷíl "hour" kʷ-s-əs ʔɛ́·y yi qʷɛ[-Aa-C_1ə-]l//, /'*Then it went on, I don't know how many hours the talking/speakers went on.*'/, literally /'and then it went on and is it the how many hours that it went on the (pl.) talking/speakers'/, (semological comment: qwóqwel means *talking*, but dema <yi> usually has components +human and +plural, thus yi qwóqwel probably means *the speakers* (and is attested elsewhere with this meaning) though it was translated by AC as *the talking*), grammatical analysis: (conjunction) (demonstrative verb) (nominal-auxiliary verb-3sj-contr) (intransitive verb[-emph-]) (conjunction) (aux-interrogative affix-3subordinate subject pronoun) (demonstrative article) (interrogative verb) (nominal) (demonstrative conjunction-nominal-3possessive pronoun affix(=3depsj)) (intransitive verb) (demonstrative article(plhum)) (intransitive verb[-ctv-ctv]), attested by AC, <**chexw xwel á:y**>, //c-əxʷ xʷəl ʔɛ́·y//, /'*You're still going.*'/, attested by EB, <**ō áy el te sqwóqwels**>, //ʔo ʔɛ́y ʔəl tə s-qʷɛ[-AáC_1ə-]l-s//, /'*He's talking without making any sense; he keeps on talking (in spite of the fact no one is listening).*'/, literally /'his talking really just keeps on going'/ Salish cognate: Nooksack //ʔǽyʔ// *continuative* (Galloway 1997).

<**i'ó:y**>, dmv //C_1í=ʔɛ́[=Aá=]·y//, LANG ['*keep on a little*'], ASM ['a murmur that you're still awake listening to a bedtime story'], (<**R4=**> *diminutive*), (<**ó-ablaut**> *derivational*), phonology: reduplication, ablaut, syntactic analysis: intransitive verb, attested by AC, EB, AD, Salish cognate: Squamish /ʔiʔáy ~ yaʔáy ~ yəh/ '(interjection expressing interest, used by listeners to a story) I see; well, well; indeed.' K67:381.

<**á:yel**>, incs //ʔɛ́·y=əl//, TVMO /'*get away, leave,* (perhaps just) *away*'/, lx <**=el**> *go, come, get, become*, syntactic comment: usually attested preceded by auxiliary verb <**la**> *go* or <**me**> *come,*

syntactic analysis: intransitive verb, example: <**tl'ésu la á:yel**>, //ƛ'ə́=s-əw lɛ ʔɛ́·y=əl//, /'*So he went away*'/, attested by EB, <**tsel me á:yel**>, //c-əl mə ʔɛ́·y=əl//, /'*I left.*'/, attested by EB, <**latsel á:yel**>, //lɛ-c-əl ʔɛ́·y=əl//, /'*I'm going to leave.*'/, (semological comment: here la functions as a future auxiliary), attested by EB, <**lalh á:yel <u>x</u>wém ~ <u>x</u>wém lalh á:yel**>, //lɛ-ɬ ʔɛ́·y=əlx̣ʷə́m ~x̣ʷə́m lɛ-ɬ ɛ́·y=əl//, /'*Go away quickly.*'/, grammatical comment: -lh *imperative 2s* is an allomorph of -lha and appears only with auxiliaries, attested by AC, <**latset mékw' áyel tl'ekwtset t'át'iyeq'**>, //lɛ-c-ət mə́k'ʷ ʔɛ́·y=əl ƛ'ə=kʷ-c-ət t'ɛ[-C_1ə-]yəq'//, /'*We all left because we were mad.*'/, attested by Deming (MC, others).

<**áyeles**>, pncs //ʔɛ́y=ələs//, TVMO /'*leave s-o, leave s-th, go away from s-o/s-th, abandon s-o, leave s-o behind*'/, ASM, syntactic analysis: transitive verb, example: <**áyeles te héyeqw**>, //ʔɛ́y=ələs tə hɛ́=yəqʷ//, /'*go away from the fire*'/, attested by EF, <**tsel le (me) áyeles te s'álhtel**>, //c-əl lə (mə) ʔɛ́y=ələs tə s=ʔɛ́ɬtəl//, /'*I left the food.*'/, attested by CT, HT, <**mōkw'ewát le áyeles**>, //mək'ʷ=əwɛ́t lə ʔɛ́y=ələs//, /'*Everyone left (him alone).*'/, attested by EB, <**le á:yelesóxes álhtel**>, //lə ʔɛ́·y=ələs-áxʸ-əs ʔɛ́(·)ɬtəl//, /'*They left me.*'/, grammatical comment: rare example of non-third person psychological non-control inflection, attested by EB, <**látsel áyelesóme**>, //lɛ́-c-əl ʔɛ́y=ələs-ámə//, /'*I'm going to leave you.*'/, grammatical comment: rare example of non-third person psychological non-control inflection, <**le áyelesem**>, //lə ʔɛ́y=ələs-əm//, /'*They left him., They abandoned him.*'/, (<**-em**> *passive*), also <**le á:yelésem**>, //lə ʔɛ́·y=ələ́s-əm//, attested by EB, also <**le áyelésem**>, //lə ʔɛ́y=ələ́s-əm//, attested by LG, <**le áyelésem tethá**>, //lə ʔɛ́y=ələs-əm tə-θɛ́//, /'*That's left behind.*'/, attested by Deming: LG.

<**á:ystexw**>, caus //ʔɛ́·y=sT-əxʷ//, TVMO /'*chase s-o, chase s-th, chasing s-o/s-th*'/, syntactic analysis: transitive verb, example: <**tló: tethá, la á:ystexw(es) tel sqwemá:y**>, //ƛ'á-ə tə-θɛ́ lɛ ʔɛ́·y=sT-əxʷ(-əs) t-əl s=qʷəm=ɛ́·y//, /'*Is that the one that was chasing my dog?*'/, syntactic comment: due to lack of a demonstrative article to form a relative clause in Halkomelem, this may be two sentences in apposition *Is that the one? He was chasing my dog.*, attested by AC, <**á:ystexwes te músmes**>, //ʔɛ́·y=sT-əxʷ-əs tə mús=C_1əC_2//, /'*He's chasing the cow.*'/, attested by IHTTC, for ex. NP, ASM ['chase s-o to have sex'], ABFC, semantic environment ['often used when the participants are husband and wife (NP); probably also used for other people or for animate beings of the opposite sex'], usage: double entendre, attested by IHTTC, <**á:ysthòx**>, //ʔɛ́·y=sT-àxʸ//, /'*chase me (in normal sense), chase me (sexually, to try to get me to have sex)*'/, attested by IHTTC, <**á:ystexwes the stó:les**>, //ʔɛ́·y=sT-əxʷ-əs θə s=tá·ləs-s//, /'*He's chasing after his wife (sexually).*'/, attested by NP has heard this lots..

<**eyát**>, pcs //ʔɛ́y-M1=T or ʔɛ́y=ə[=M2=T//, TVMO /'*go after s-th/s-o, chase s-o/s-th (not stopping or slowing tillit's caught)*'/, possibly <**metathesis type 1**> *non-continuative*, possibly metathesis type 2 *derivational*, (<**=t ~ =et**> *purposeful control transitivizer*), phonology: metathesis, possible stressed transitivizer, syntactic analysis: transitive verb, example: <**eyátes**>, //ʔɛ́y=ə[=M2=T-əs//, /'*He went after it/s-o., It chased it (not stopping or slowing till it was caught).*'/, attested by IHTTC.

<**iy'iyátes**>, pls //C_1əC_2-ʔɛ́y=ə[=M2=T-əs//, if, TVMO ['*He's chasing them/it repeatedly.*'], (<**R3-**> *plural*), phonology: reduplication, syntactic analysis: intransitive verb, attested by IHTTC.

<**s'i'á:ytses**>, pls //s=C_1əC_2=ʔɛ́·y=cəs//, ABFC ['*he's holding s-th in each hand*'], (<**s=**> *stative*), (<**R3=**> *plural*), da //=tses *in the hand*//, phonology: reduplication, syntactic analysis: intransitive verb, attested by IHTTC.

<**=á:y ~ =ey ~ =iy**>, da //=ɛ́·y ~ =əy ~ =iy//, EB /'*bark, wood, plant*'/, ANA /'*wool, fur*'/, syntactic analysis: lexical suffix, derivational suffix; found in <**pqwá:y**>, //p(ə)qʷ=ɛ́·y//, /'*rotten wood*'/, root <**péqw**> *split, broken, busted*, <**pqwá:ythet**>, //p(ə)qʷ=ɛ́·y=θət//, /'*wood decays*'/ (compare <**póqwthet**> *get mouldy, decayed)*, <**qwlhá:y**>, //qʷɬ=ɛ́·y//, /'*driftwood*'/, root <**qwélh**> *fall in water, tip over in canoe*, <**<u>x</u>epá::y ~ <u>x</u>pá:y**>, //x̣(ə)p=ɛ́·y//, /'*red cedar wood*'/, <**slewíy**>, //s=ləw=íy//,

/'inner cedar bark'/, root <**lew**> *inside or into an opening*, <**lhqw'á:y**>, //ɬq'ʷ=ɛ́·y//, */'cedar bark skirt or cedar bark mat (or peeled bark)'/* (compare <**lheqw'ót**> *peel any bark)*, <**slá:y**>, //s=lɛ́·y//, */'Douglas fir bark'/*, <**lá:yelhp**>, //lɛ́·y=əɬp//, */'Douglas fir tree'/*, <**ts'sá:y**>, //c's=ɛ́·y//, */'fir log or wood'/*, <**th'á:x̱ey**>, //θ'ɛ́·x̣=əy//, */'bleached grass for basketry designs'/* (compare <**th'á:x̱=et**> *scald it)*, <**q'et'emá:yelhp**>, //q'ət'əm=ɛ́·y=əɬp//, */'balsam, larch'/* (compare <**q'áq'et'em**> *sweet-tasting* (showing the root (the tree has sweet sap on outside of bark)), <**sékw'emiy**>, //sə́k'ʷəm=iy//, */'birch'/*, <**qwéqwelhiy**>, //qʷə́qʷəɬ=iy//, */'lots of little pieces of driftwood'/*.

<**=á:yel ~ =iyel ~ =ú:yel**>, da //=ɛ́·y=əl ~ =iy(=)əl ~ =ú·yəl//, FSH */'net, trap'/*, HUNT */'trap, net'/*, possibly <**=á:y ~ =iy**> *bark, wool*, possibly <**=el**> *go, come, get, become*, syntactic analysis: lexical suffix, derivational suffix, //=ú·y(=)əl or =ə́w=iy=əl//; found in <**míliyel**>, //míl=iyəl//, */'set a net'/*, <**semláliyel**>, //səmlɛ́l=iyəl//, */'a set net, stationary net'/* (compare <**seml=óth(=)el**> *riverbank)*, <**mesíyeltel**>, //məs=íyəl=təl//, */'anchor (probably for nets)'/*, <**qwsá:yel**>, //qʷs=ɛ́·yəl//, */'throw a net out'/* (compare <**qwés**> *fall overboard, fall in the water)*, <**qwsá:wiyel**>, //qʷs=ɛ́·w=iyəl//, */'set a net and drift with it'/*, (semological comment: the =ɛ́·w may mean *on the body/on top of itself*), <**qwáseliyel**>, //qʷɛ́s=əl=iyəl//, */'drifting a net in different places'/* (with <**=el=**> probably *plural)*, <**qwesú:yel**>, //qʷəs=ú·yəl//, */'drop net into water'/*, <**istéytiyel**>, //ʔis=tɛ́yt=iyəl//, */'group of canoes travelling upstream (moving to fish drying camp)'/* (compare <**tíyt**> *upriver)*, <**pathú:yel**>, //pɛθ=ú·yəl//, */'bear trap'/* (compare <**s=pá:th**> *bear)*, <**kw'echú:yel**>, //k'ʷəc=ú·yəl//, */'check a trap or net (for animal or fish [or bird])'/*.

<**á:yel**>, TVMO */'get away, leave,* (perhaps just) *away'/*, see á:y.

<**áyeles**>, TVMO */'leave s-o, leave s-th, go away from s-o/s-th, abandon s-o, leave s-o behind'/*, see á:y.

<**á:yelexwlexw**>, ABFC */'save s-o, (EB) bring s-o back to life'/*, see áylexw ~ **á**yelexw.

<**á:yelexwstexw**>, ABFC [*'keep s-o/s-th alive'*], see áylexw ~ **á**yelexw.

<**á:yelexwt**>, ABFC */'revive s-o, bring s-o back to life, heal s-o, (EB) give s-o medicine to make him better?'/*, see áylexw ~ **á**yelexw.

<**=áyiws ~ =éyiws ~ =áyews**>, da //=ɛ́y=iws//, CLO [*'pants'*], semantic environment ['with numeral 5 so far, non-numerals'], (<**=áy**> *covering, bark, wool*), (<**=iws**> *on the body*), syntactic comment: optional, syntactic analysis: lexical suffix, derivational suffix; found in <**lhq'atsesáyiws**>, //ɬq'ɛcəs=ɛ́yiws//, */'five pairs of pants'/*, <**seqí:ws** or **sqí:ws** or **sqéyiws**>, //s(ə)q=í·ws or sq=ɛ́yiws (or even) s=həq=ɛ́y=əws//, */'pants'/*, possibly root <**heq=**> *underneath* (compare with <**eqílem**> *crawl/go underneath* and <**Híqelem**> (a placename that means *go underneath)(*probably with vowel metathesis), <**siseqí:ws** or **siseqéyiws**>, //sisəq=í·ws or sisəq=ɛ́yiws//, */'short pants'/*, <**heqí(y)wsem**>, //həq=íyəws=əm//, */'put on one's pants'/* (prob. also with root <**heq=**> *underneath)*, <**tl'itl'eplà·yìws**>, //ƛ'íƛ'əp=l=ɛ̀·yìws//, */'man's underpants'/* (with root <**tl'ép**> *down, deep under-*, prefixed reduplication *diminutive*, <**=l=**> possibly *plural*), <**lhosemáyiws**>, //ɬas=əm=ɛ́yiws//, */'pants sliding down'/* (compare <**lhósem**> *slide down (of clothes))*.

<**Á:yiya**>, us //ʔɛ́·y(=)iyɛ//, N [*'Mack (EB's great grandfather)'*], SPRD also [*'the words of Mack's spirit song'*], ASM ['Mack was a "good" Indian doctor; he was called this name because **á:yiya** were the words of his spirit song'], lx <**=iya**> *personal name ending,* fits the end of this name but may be coincidental according to EB's account of the name's origin as words to the owner's spirit song, syntactic analysis: nominal, attested by EB.

<**áylexw ~ áyelexw**>, df //ʔɛ́y(=)əl=(l)əxʷ ~ ʔɛ́y(=)ləxʷ//, ABFC */'be alive, be living, be in good health, be healthy, be well'/*, possibly literally */'manage/happen to keep on going* or *manage/happen to be good'/*, possibly root <**á:y**> *keep on going*, possibly root <**éy**> *be good*, possibly <**=el**> *go, come, get,*

become, comment: poss. contains a crystallized partial-control transitivizer =lexw which has lost its transitivity but kept the partial control component, syntactic analysis: intransitive verb, also <**á:yelexw**>, //ʔɛ́·yələx^{w}//, attested by BJ, EB, TM, some others, also <**á:'yelxw**>, //ʔɛ́·[-ʔ-]yəlx^{w}//, dialects: *Matsqui*, attested by AH, example: <**lí xwel áyelexw**>, //lí x^{w}əl ʔɛ́yələx^{w}//, /'*Is he still alive?*'/, attested by AC, <**skw'áy kw'es áyelexws**>, //s=k'^{w}ɛ́y k'^{w}ə-s ʔɛ́yələx^{w}-s//, /'*He can never be well.*'/, attested by AC, <**me á:yelexw ~ me á:ylexw**>, //mə ʔɛ́·yələx^{w} ~ mə ʔɛ́·yləx^{w}//, ASM ['come alive, come back to life, get better (from sickness), get well, revive'], usage: used in slang as well as serious sentences, <**me á:ylexw te spoleqwíth'a**>, //mə ʔɛ́·yləx^{w} tə s=paləq^{w}(=)íθ'ɛ//, /'*The corpse came back to life.*'/, attested by EB, <**lí me áyelexw**>, //lí mə ʔɛ́yələx^{w}//, /'*Did he get well?*'/, attested by AC, <**lichxw wélh me á:yelexw**>, //lí-c-x^{w} wə́ɬ mə ʔɛ́·yələx^{w}//, /'*Are you better from your sickness?*'/, <**li á:'yelxw ta' shxwewálí**>, //li ʔɛ́·ʔyəlx^{w} t-ɛʔ sx^{w}=(ə)wɛ́lí//, /'*Are your parents still living?*'/, dialects: *Matsqui*, attested by AH.

<**á:yelexwlexw**>, ncs //ʔɛ́·yələx^{w}=l-əx^{w}//, ABFC /'*save s-o, (EB) bring s-o back to life*'/, syntactic analysis: transitive verb, example: <**me á:yelexwlexw**>, //mə ʔɛ́·yələx^{w}=l-əx^{w}//, /'*save s-o, (EB) bring s-o back to life*'/; found in <**á:yelexwlòmè**>, //ʔɛ́·yələx^{w}=l-àmə̀//, <**2soj**>, no translation given but probably *save you, bring you back to life.*

<**á:yelexwstexw**>, caus //ʔɛ́·yələx^{w}=sT-əx^{w}//, ABFC ['*keep s-o/s-th alive*'], syntactic analysis: transitive verb, example: <**tset me á:yelexwstexw**>, //c-ət mə ʔɛ́·yələx^{w}=sT-əx^{w}//, /'*We kept him alive.*'/, attested by EB, <**me á:yelexwstem**>, //mə ʔɛ́·yələx^{w}=sT-əm//, (<**-em**> *passive*), /'*He was kept alive.*'/, <**stl'ítset kws me á:yelexwstexwtset te sqwá:ltset**>, //s=ƛ'í-c-ət k^{w}-s mə ʔɛ́·yələx^{w}=sT-əx^{w}-c-ət tə s=q^{w}ɛ́·l-cət//, /'*We want to keep our language alive.*'/, literally /'it is our want that come/start to we cause it to be alive the our language'/, attested by EB.

<**á:yelexwt**>, pcs //ʔɛ́·yələx^{w}=T//, ABFC /'*revive s-o, bring s-o back to life, heal s-o, (EB) give s-o medicine to make him better?*'/, (<**=t**> *purposeful control transitivizer*), syntactic analysis: transitive verb; found in <**á:yelexwthòme**>, //ʔɛ́·yələx^{w}=T-àmə//, /'*heal you*'/, source: Elders 3/15/72, example: <**me á:yelexwtem**>, //mə ʔɛ́·yələx^{w}=T-əm//, (<**-em**> *passive*), /'*He was brought back to life.*'/, attested by EB.

<**=á(:)ylh ~ =á(:)lh ~ =elh (~ =iylh ~ =ó:llh ?)**>, da //=ɛ́(·)yɬ, =ɛ́(·)ɬ, =ə́ɬ//, HHG /'*bed, (child, young)*'/, syntactic analysis: lexical suffix, compare with <**=iylh ~ =ó:llh**> *child, young*; found in <**thiyá:lhem**>, //θiy=ɛ́·ɬ=əm//, /'*make a bed or place to sleep or lay or rest*'/, compare with <**thíy**> *make, fix*, <**chewélhem**>, //cəw=ə́ɬ=əm//, /'*spawning*'/ (compare <**cháchew**> *beach),* <**tl'xwá:ylhem**>, //ƛ'x^{w}=ɛ́·yɬ=əm//, /'*sit on eggs*'/ (compare <**tl'éxw**> *cover over),* <**sqelá:lh**>, //s=qəl=ɛ́·ɬ//, /'*diaper*'/ (compare <**qél**> *bad; dirty*, which is used as euphemism for *dung), feces.*

<**á:ystexw**>, TVMO /'*chase s-o, chase s-th, chasing s-o/s-th*'/, see á:y.

<**á:yt ~ é:yt**>, free root //ʔɛ́·yt//, [ʔǽ·yt ~ ʔé·yt], EZ ['*ling-cod*'], ['*Ophiodon elongatus*'], syntactic analysis: noun, nominal, compare? <**eyát**> *go after s-th/s-o, chase s-o/s-th (not stopping or slowing tillit's caught)* which is quite similar in form, (perhaps because a) it is a voracious predator, and b) it spawns in mid-winter under the ice in a writhing ball about 2 ft. in diameter made up of 10 or 12 individuals)

<**á:yx̱**>, free root //ʔɛ́·yx̣//, EZ ['*crab*'], ['probably *the tribe Brachyura (a tribe is intermediate between a family and a suborder)*'], possible root <**á:y**> *keep on going* + lx <**=x̱**> *all over*, Salish cognate: the Squamish cognate <óy'x̱> (/ʔáy'x̣/) is identified by Kennedy and Bouchard 1976 as *Dungeness crab, Cancer magister*, syntactic analysis: noun, nominal, attested by AC, others, other sources: JH /ʔé·yəx̣/ *crab*, WS (pc) may also be *crayfish.*

<**á:'a**>, us possibly //C_1ɛ́[=·=]=ʔɛ//, CJ ['*yes*'], possibly <**R7=**> *emphatic*, probably <=:=> *emphatic*, possibly root <**á**> *yes* as in Cheh. <**li á** or **li'á**> *yes*; RM of Chill. comment: Chill. dialect also uses lí (AC) and lhéq' (RM) as answer *yes* to yes-no questions), phonology: reduplication, syntactic analysis: interjection, attested by AC, BJ, AD, others, also <**á'a**>, //C_1ɛ́=ʔɛ//, attested by NP, AC, some at Deming, example: <**á'á'àwèlh ~ á'á àwèlh**>, //ʔɛ́ʔɛ́ʔɛ̀wəɬ ~ ʔɛ́ʔɛ́ ʔɛ̀wəɬ//, LANG ['*You're welcome.*'], semantic environment ['said in reply to Yálh lixw kw'a'as hò:y *Thank you.*'], (<**(-)àwèlh**> *polite imperative*), dialects: *Tait, Cheh.*, also <**á'a'òwèlh.**>, //ʔɛ́ʔɛ-ʔàwə̀ɬ// ['*Yes (certainly).*'], dialects: *Chill.*, attested by AD, semantic environment ['said in reply to Qw'óqw'ele**x̲** *Excuse me.* or in reply after someone has just said xólhmethetchxw *Look after yourself.*'], attested by AD, Salish cognate: Nooksack //ʔɛ́·ʔɛ// *yes* (NKF1.202).

<**a'á**>, us //ʔɛʔɛ́ or C_1ɛ=ʔɛ́ or C_1ɛ́=ʔɛ-´//, EFAM ['*oh-oh.*'], possibly <**R8=**> *derivational*, possibly <**R7=**> *emphatic*, possibly root <**á**> *yes*, possibly <-´-> *derivational*, phonology: reduplication, possible stress-shift, syntactic analysis: interjection, example: <**a'á te swék'**>, //ʔɛʔɛ́ tə s=wə́k'//, /'*Oh-oh, [here comes] the dandy.*'/, attested by Deming.

<**a'áchewlh**>, cpds //ʔɛ[=R9=]cɛ=wɬ or ʔɛ=ʔɛ́=cə=wɬ//, TIME /'*until, unless*'/, CJ, possibly <**R8=** or **=R9**> *derivational*, possibly root <**atsa ~ ache**> *next, again*, possibly <**-cha**> *future tense*, possibly <**-(e)wlh ~ welh**> *already*, possibly root <**a'á**> *oh-oh*, phonology: reduplication, syntactic analysis: conjunction, example: <**ő́wechexw lámexwcha xwa siyólexwe a'áchewlh x̲áp'kw'tem ta' sth'eth'elòm**>, //ʔəwə-c-xʷ lɛ́m-əxʷ xʷɛ s=iyáləxʷə ʔɛʔɛ́cəwɬx̣ɛ́p'k'ʷ(-)t(-)əm t-ɛʔ s=C_1ə-θ'[-əl-]àm//, /'*You're not going to get (become) old until (unless) your bones are aching.*'/, usage: This is a saying of the old people, a proverb. (AD), grammatical analysis: vneg-independent clause subject pronoun-2s auxiliary verb-2ssjsp particle (stat=)adjective/adjectival verb conjunction adjective/adjectival verb(-pc?)-middle voice demonstrative article-2spsvp (nominal=)dim-root[-pl-]root, ASM ['are not-(subject)-you going to-you(subjunct. subj.) become old until(-fut-contr-past/already) are aching (the)-your little-many-bone'], *see* atsa ~ ache or a'á.

<**á'altha**>, PRON /'*it's me., that's me., I* do, *I* am (ls emphatic)'/, see áltha ~ **á**lthe.

<**a'axwíleqel**>, HHG ['*small container*'], *see* axwíl.

<**a'axwíyelhp**>, EB ['*small tree*'], *see* axwíl.

<**á'iy ~ 'á'iy**>, VALJ ['*cute little one*'], *see* **é**y ~ **é**y:.

CH

<**ch**>, comment: The Stó:lō orthography uses both <**ch**> ([č]) and <**ts**> ([c]), for two allophones of a single Halkomelem phoneme, /c/. This has the advantage of showing phonetic preferences of the speakers which are difficult to predict purely from environments; in linguistic terms [č] and [c] are evolving from a state of free variation to conditioned variation (or vice versa)(see Galloway 1993:18-20 for a statement of the environments, dialects, and idiolects conditioning these two sounds). As it happens, few cases of initial <**ts**> [c] occur except when it is a prefix. Therefore if a reader is looking up a word spelled or sounded with an initial <**ts**>, he should be sure to check under ch as well, as more speakers may pronounce it with <**ch**>.

<**ch=**>, da //c=//, SENS, LT /'*stative (with color terms), have/get (elsewhere)*'/, phonology: since most roots begin with a consonant and there is a phonemic rule that /c/ → [c] <**ts**> between word boundary and a consonant, this suffix is only rarely found as [č] <**ch**>, see main dialect form <**ts=**>.

<**-cha**>, //**-cɛ**//, [-čæ ~ -čɛ ~ -cɛ], TIME ['*future tense*'], ASM ['not immediate future but after a while; immediate future is expressed by the present non-continuative'], syntactic analysis: is, syntactic comment: this suffix follows all others in a verb; it is word-final; found in <**p'ékwcha**>, //p'ə́kʷ-cɛ//, /'*it will float*'/, syntactic analysis: intransitive verb, <**tl'ócha**>, //ƛ'á-cɛ//, /'*that will be, it will be (him/her/them/that)*'/, syntactic analysis: demonstrative verb, conjunction, <**selchí:mcha**>, //səlcí·m-cɛ//, /'*how shall it be?, how should it be?*'/, syntactic analysis: interrogative verb, example: <**lhwélepcha lám**>, //ɬw=ə́l=əp-cɛ lɛ́=m//, /'*It will be you folks that go.*'/, syntactic analysis: pronominal verb/verbal pronoun, attested by AC, <**skw'áytsa kw'els málqles**>, //s=k'ʷɛ́y-cɛ k'ʷ-əl-s mɛ́lq=ləs//, /'*I'll never forget him/her/it/them.*'/, syntactic analysis: nominal phrase minus article, literally /'it's impossible that I forget him/her/it/them'/, <**lítsa sp'ap'ákw**>, //lí-cɛ s=C_1ɛ=p'ə́[=Aɛ́=]kʷ//, /'*Will it float?*'/, syntactic analysis: interrogative verb, stvi, <**líy-e-tsa lám**>, //lí(y)-ə-cɛ lɛ́=m//, /'*Will he go?*'/, grammatical analysis: interrogative verb-interrogative affix-future tense auxiliary verb=itz, <**éwetsa me kw'étslàlèmèt**>, //ʔə́wə-cɛ mə k'ʷə́c=l-ɛ̀lə̀m-ə̀t//, /'*I won't be seen., Nobody will see me.*'/, grammatical analysis: vneg-future tense auxiliary verb r=non-control transitive-1spass-passive sbor to neg, <**wátsa lamál yewá:**>, //ʔə́wə-ə-cɛ lɛ=m-ɛ́l yəwɛ́·//, /'*Will you take me along?, Can I go along?, (Won't you take me along?)*'/, grammatical analysis: vneg-interrogative affix-future tense auxiliary verb=itz-1ssbsj adverb/adverbial verb; found in <**sta'ástexwescha**>, //s=tɛʔɛ́=sT-əxʷ-əs-cɛ//, /'*They will follow him., They will do like him.*'/, grammatical analysis: stative=intransitive verb=causative-3object pronoun-3sj-future tense, <**el'éliyamethométselcha**>, //C_1əC_2-ʔəliyɛ=məT-ámə-c-əl-cɛ//, /'*I'll dream about you (repeatedly).*'/, phonology: stress-shift on object pronoun due to suffixation with subject, grammatical analysis: pl-intransitive verb=indirect effect control-2soj-independent clause subject pronoun-1ssj-future tense, <**lhíts'elhtsthométselcha**>, //ɬíc'-əɬc=T-ámə-c-əl-cɛ//, /'*I'll cut it off for you.*'/, grammatical analysis: r-ben-pc-2soj-independent clause subject pronoun-1ssj-future tense, <**malqí:wsemtselcha**>, //mɛlq=í·ws=əm-c-əl-cɛ//, /'*I'll faint.*'/, grammatical analysis: r=lexical suffix=middle voice-independent clause subject pronoun-1ssj-future tense, <**x̲éywethò:mcha**>, //x̣íw-əT-à·m-cɛ//, /'*You'll be warned., Someone will warn you.*'/, grammatical analysis: r-pc-2spass-future tense, example: <**líchxw slhéq'el:exw welámescha**>, //lí-c-əxʷ s=ɬə́q'əl=l-əxʷ wə-lɛ́m-əs-cɛ//, /'*Do you know if he'll go?*'/, grammatical analysis: interrogative verb-independent clause subject pronoun-2ssj stative?=r-nc-3object pronoun sb-auxiliary verb=itz-3subordinate subject pronoun-future tense.

<**chácha**>, us //cɛ́cɛ//, EFAM ['*be tender (in emotions)*'], phonology: perhaps an old *characteristic* reduplication, syntactic analysis: adjective/adjectival verb, dialects: *Tait only*, attested by TG, some

others; found in <**cháchachexw**>, //cɛ́cɛ-c-əxʷ//, /'*Be tender (mildly urging imperative).*'/, dialects: *Tait*, example: <**chácha te swíyeqe**>, //cɛ́cɛ tə s=wíyəqə//, /'*The man is tender.*'/, also <**tsátsa te swíyeqe**>, dialects: *Tait*, <**chácha te sqwálewels**>, //cɛ́cɛ tə s=qʷɛ́l=əwəl-s//, /'*He's/She's emotional (cries easy when happy or sad, etc.).*'/, literally /'are tender the his/her thoughts/feelings'/, (semological comment: one of a series of idioms which combine vaj + dema + sqwálewel).

<**cháchelh**>, cts //cɛ́[-C_1ə-]ɬ//, ABDF ['*it's aching of arthritis*'], *see* chálh

<**Cháchelut**> [or better, <**Cháchelówt**>], [čǽčʌlót], *Elixabeth Herrling's (EH's) grandfather's brother's name*, *see* chaléwt

<**cháchew ~ cháchu**>, dnom //cɛ[=C_1ə=]w or C_1ɛ́=cəw//, LAND /'*beach, shore*'/, *see* chew ~ cháw

<**chachí:lhtel ~ chachíyelhtel**>, pls possibly //C_1ɛ-cíɬ=ʔɛ[-Aí·-]ɬtəl//, FSH ['*hanging lots of fish to dry*'], *see* chílh

<**chachí:q'el**>, dnom //C_1ɛ=cí·q'əl//, EZ ['*mink*'], ['*Mustela vison energumenos*'], ASM ['The story-character Mink is known from many stories in which he tries to marry or have sex with all manner of creatures (and plants, etc.) before and during the time of the Transformers; he usually fails for comic reasons.'], (<**R8=**> *derivational*), phonology: reduplication, also <**chachíq'el**>, //C_1ɛ=cíq'əl//, attested by ME, AK.

<**cháchket**>, dms //cɛ́[=C_1ə=]kət//, CLO ['*small jacket*'], (<**=R1=**> *diminutive*), phonology: reduplication, attested by Deming.

<**cháket**>, dnom //cɛ́kət//, [čǽkʸɪt], CLO /'*jacket, vest*'/, borrowed from English *jacket*, attested by Deming.

<**chákw**>, bound root //cɛ́kʷ//, meaning uncertain, probably interrogative and verbal

<**schákwel**>, stvi //s=cɛ́kʷ(=)əl//, MOOD ['*how is s-o/s-th?*'], (<**s=**> *stative*), possibly <**=el**> *go, come, get, become*, example: <**schákwel talúwe**>, //s=cɛ́kʷ(=)əl tɛ=lə́wə//, /'*How are you?*'/, attested by unrecorded.

<**chá:l ~ chó:l**>, probably root //cɛ́·l or cá·l or cá·=əl or cɛ[=Aá=]=əl *follow behind, go a distance*//, possibly root <**chó(:)**> as in <**chó:kw ~ chókw**> *far, distant*, possibly <**=el**> *go, come, get, become, inceptive*.

<**xwechà:l**>, incs //xʷə=cɛ̀·l//, TVMO /'*where did he go?, where is he/she/etc.?*'/, MOOD, semantic environment ['used after you've gone different places looking for someone in the house, example'], lx <**xwe=**> *go, get, become*, possibly <**=el**> *go, get, become, come*, attested by AD, also <**xwchà:l**>, //xʷ(ə)=cɛ̀·l//, attested by EB, example: <**le xwchà:l**>, //lə xʷ=cɛ̀·l//, /'*Where is he going?*'/, attested by EB, also <**xwechá:l**>, //xʷə=cɛ́·l//, attested by AC, EB; found in <**xwechálchexw**>, //xʷə=cɛ́l-c-əxʷ//, /'*Where are you going?*'/, attested by AC, <**xwechá:lchxw ~ xwchá:lchexw**>, //xʷə=cɛ́·l-c-əxʷ ~ xʷ=cɛ́·l-c-əxʷ//, /'*Where are you going?*'/, attested by EB, example: <**chelō lhq'élexw wexwchá:les**>, //c-əl-əw ɬ=q'ə́l=l-əxʷ wə-xʷ=cɛ́·l-əs//, /'*I know where he's going.*'/, grammatical analysis: independent clause subject pronoun-1ssj-contr lexical suffix=r-nc-3object pronoun sb-inceptive aspect=r-3subordinate subject pronoun, syntactic analysis: pro transitive verb indefinite nominal(< sb-interrogative verb-subordinate subject pronoun), attested by EB.

<**xwchókwel**>, cts //xʷ=cɛ́[-AáAkʷə-]l//, TVMO /'*where is s-o going?, where is s-o travelling?, where is s-o headed for?*'/, DIR, lx <**xwe=**> *go, get, become*, <-=R1-> *continuative* (a → o bef. -R1- is regular. and ch → kw in -R1- is found in three or four examples),, possibly <**=el**> *go, get, become, come*, phonology: ablaut, reduplication, consonant ablaut or replacement of <**ch**> by <**kw**> in reduplication (also reported in Musqueam by WS), syntactic analysis: interrogative verb, semantic environment ['asked example as you see the person heading for his car, wondering

where he is going today'], attested by AD, EB, AC, others; found in <**xwchókwelchexw**>, //x^w=cák^w=əl-c-əx^w//, /*'Where are you travelling?, Where are you going?'*/, attested by EB, also <**xwchó:kwelchexw**>, example: <**echxw ye xwchókwel**>, //ʔə-c-x^w yə x^w=cák^w=əl//, /*'Where are you headed for?'*/, attested by EB, <**echxw yálh xwchókwel ~ échxw kw'e úlh xwchókwel**>, //ʔə-c-x^w yɛ́ɬ x^w=cák^w=əl ~ ʔə-c-x^w k'^{w}ə ʔúɬ x^w=cák^w=əl//, /*'Where are you going now (this time)?'*/, attested by EB, <**li xwechókwel**>, //li x^w(ə)=cák^w=əl//, /*'Where is he going?'*/, attested by AC.

<**chó:lqem**>, mdls //cɛ́[=Aa=]·l=q=əm or cá(·)=əl=(ələ)q=əm//, TVMO /*'follow, follow along after (the one ahead knows)'*/, possibly <**ó(:)-ablaut**> *derivational*, possibly <**=q**> meaning uncertain, possibly <**=el**> *go, come, get, become, inceptive*, possibly <**=eleq**> *occupational*, (<**=em**> middle voice or intransitivizer), phonology: derivational ablaut, syntactic analysis: intransitive verb, attested by IHTTC, EB, Salish cognate: Squamish /čáy-aq-m/ *follow, pursue (intr.)* has -aq as a formative suffix with no clear meaning (Kuipers 1967:133); the cognate confirms the connection of the above root with that in xwch**à**:l /x^w=cɛ̀·l/ *where is s-o going?* because Squamish /a/ corresponds to Halkomelem /ɛ/ and /ɛ/ is attested in the Halkomelem root; the Squamish /y/ here corresponds to Halkomelem /l/ (as do a number of Squamish /y/'s, see Galloway 1982:59-64); also cf. Squamish /čáy-n/ *follow, pursue, chase (transitive)* with Halkomelem chó:lt /čá·l-t/ *follow s-o/s-th* below, where Squamish -n and Upriver Halkomelem =T are both *purposeful control transitivizers.* Halkomelem now has derivational ablaut of the vowel from /ɛ/ to /a/; historically that may be influence or borrowing from neighboring languages such as Nooksack, Squamish, Lushootseed, or Thompson, which didn't undergo the historical sound shift from PCS *a to /e/ or /ɛ/ as did Halkomelem and Straits., example: <**me chó:lqem**>, //mə cá·lqəm//, /*'come along after (the person followed is aware of it)'*/, attested by EB, <**latsel chó:lqem.**>, //lɛ-c-əl cá·l=q=əm//, also <**lamtsel chó:lqem.**>, //lɛ́=m-c-əl cá·lq=əm//, /*'I'll go follow., I'm going to follow.'*/, attested by IHTTC, also <**látselcha choléqem.**>, //lɛ́-c-əl-cɛ cal[-ə́-]q=əm//, (<**-é-**> *continuative*), phonology: stress-shift, infix, attested by EB.

<**chelchó:lqem**>, pls //C$_1$əC$_2$=cɛ́[=Aa=]·l=q=əm//, TVMO [*'lots following'*], (semological comment: note that pluralizing a verb automatically makes it continuative in most cases), (<**R3=**> *plural*), (<**ó-ablaut**> *continuative or derivational*), phonology: reduplication, attested by IHTTC.

<**chichelóqtel**>, pcrs //C$_1$í=cá=lə[=M2=]q=T-əl//, dms, TVMO [*'walking single-file'*], (<**R4=** (here **chi=)**> *diminutive*), lx <**=eleq**> *occupational*, lx <**=metathesis2**> (switches preceding two vowels) *continuative*, (<**-t**> *purposeful control transitivizer*, <-el> *reflexive*), phonology: reduplication, phonology: metathesis, syntactic analysis: transitive verb-reflexive, literally /'following after each other purposely'/, attested by IHTTC.

<**chó:lt**>, pcs //cɛ́[=Aa=]·l=T or cá(·)=əl=T//, TVMO /*'follow s-th/s-o (on foot, in a car, or on a horse, for ex.), follow behind s-o'*/, (<**=t**> *purposeful control transitivizer*), syntactic analysis: transitive verb; found in <**chó:lthóxes**>, //cá·l=T-áx^y-əs//, /*'he's following me (on foot or in a car)*(continuative prob. wrong here)'/, attested by Elders 3/15/72, /*'he followed me'*/, attested by IHTTC, example: <**lechxw chó:lt**>, //lə-c-x^w cá·l-t//, /*'You follow something (on foot or horse)'*/, attested by EB.

<**chochí:lt**>, cts //cɛ́[=Aa=][-C$_1$ə-]·l-í·l-t//, TVMO [*'go following s-o'*], (<**-R1-**> *continuative aspect*), (<**-í:l**> *inceptive, go, come, get, become*), phonology: reduplication, ablaut, phonology: when -í:l is suffixed to a form ending in ...el, the el drops, to be replaced by the -í:l, syntactic analysis: transitive verb.

<**chichelót**>, cts //C$_1$í=cá(=)l-ə[=M2=]T//, pcs, dms, TVMO /*'running after s-o, running after s-th'*/, (<**R4=**> *diminutive*), phonology: metathesis, reduplication, stress-shift, syntactic analysis:

transitive verb, attested by IHTTC; found in <**chichelóthóxes**>, //C_1í=cá(=)l-ə[=M2=]T-áx^y-əs//, /'*He was running after me.*'/, attested by IHTTC, <**chichelótel**>, //C_1í=cá(=)l-ə[=M2=]T-əl//, /'*running after each other*'/, (<-et> *purposeful control transitivizer*).

<**chél:exw**>, ncs //cɛ́·[=Aə́=]l=l-əx^w//, /'catch up with someone'/, prob. <**=Aé=**> *resultative*, <**=l**> *non-control transitivizer*, <**-exw**> *3rd person object*, attested by RG & EH (4/10/99 Ling332), found in <**chél:òmè**>, //cɛ́·[=Aə́=]l=l-àmə̀//, /catch up with you/, attested by RG & EH (4/10/99 Ling332)

<**chó:leqw**>, us //possibly cá·(=ə)l=əq^w//, DIR /'*in the backwoods, toward the woods, away from the river, in the bush*'/, literally possibly /'get (a distance) behind a river mouth'/, lx possibly <**=el**> *go, come, get*, lx possibly <**=eqw**> *on top of the head (mouth of a river)*, syntactic analysis: adverb/adverbial verb, attested by EB, RP, SP, AK, AC, BHTTC, also <**chóleqw**>, attested by SP, AK, AC, example: <**le yéqw kw'e tsóleqw**>, //lə yə́q^w k'^{w}ə cáləq^w//, /'*The backwoods are burnt.*'/.

<**chóleqwmel**>, ds //cá(=)l=əq^w=məl//, DIR /'*part away from the river, side away from the river*'/, LAND, WATR, lx <**=mel**> *location, part, location around a house*, syntactic analysis: nominal, attested by JL, others, example: <**chóleqwmels te x̲wox̲welálhp**>, //cá(=)l=əq^w=məl-s//, /'*away from the river from X̲wox̲welálhp (a village just below Yale Creek)*'/, literally /'the away-from-the-river-side of **X̲**wox̲welálhp'/, (<**-s**> *psvf3*), attested by SP, AK, <**esesu x̲óx̲cha the'ít tethá lí te chóleqwmels**>, //ʔə-s-əs-əw x̣á[-C_1ə-]cɛ θəʔít tə-θɛ́ lí tə cá(=)l=əq^w=məl-s//, /'*It's really a little lake there on the side away from the river.*'/, attested by JL.

<**telchó:leqwtel**>, ds //təl=cá(=)l=əq^w=təl//, DIR ['*from away from the river*'], semantic environment ['where EL's people came from, from away from the Harrison River and back toward Chehalis Lake'], (<**tel=**> *from*), syntactic analysis: adverb/adverbial verb, attested by EL.

<**tselqwáx̲el**>, ds //cá(=)l=əq^w=ɛ́x̣əl//, DIR ['*(in) back of a house*'], BLDG, literally /'away-from-the-river end of a house'/, lx <**=áx̲el**> *end of a house (inside or outside)*, syntactic analysis: adverb/adverbial verb.

<**stselqwáx̲el**>, dnom //s=cá(=)l=əq^w=ɛ́x̣əl//, BLDG /'*back end of a house (inside or outside), back part of a house*'/, (<**s=**> *nominalizer*), syntactic analysis: nominal, attested by AC, EB, others, example: <**stselqwáx̲els te lálem**>, //s=cá(=)l=əq^w=ɛ́x̣əl-s tə lɛ́ləm//, /'*back of the house*'/.

<**tselqwáx̲elmel**>, ds //cá(=)l=əq^w=ɛ́x̣əl=məl//, DIR /'*in back of a house, behind a house*'/, BLDG, lx <**=mel**> *location around a house*, syntactic analysis: adverb/adverbial verb.

<**Chelqwílh ~ Chelqwéylh**>, df //ca(=)l=əq^w=wə[=Aí=]ɬ or ca(=)l=əq^w=íɬ ~ ca(=)l=əq^w=ə́yɬ//, PLN ['*an area up the mountainside from X̲wox̲welálhp (Yale)*'], ASM ['there was a village there with lots of pit-houses, lots of pits from them are still there, the place name refers to the whole area--not just the village'], literally /'up the mountainside from'/, possibly <**=welh**> *canoe*, possibly <**í-ablaut** on suffix **e**> *durative*, possibly <**=ílh ~ =éylh**> *offspring* or possibly <**=elh**> *past*, syntactic analysis: nominal, adverb/adverbial verb, attested by SP, AK, other source: place names file reference #142.

<**stselqwóthel**>, dnom //s=cá(=)l=əq^w=áθəl//, DIR (maybe) ['*the backwoods side*'], lx <**=óthel**> *in the mouth*, syntactic analysis: nominal, attested by Elders 9/7/77.

<**stselqwá:ls**>, ds //s=cá(=)l=əq^w=ɛ́·ls//, REL (possibly) ['*clean out brush from a graveyard or the ceremony of graveyard cleaning*'], Elder's comment: "something to do with a graveyard", literally /'do a structured activity in the backwoods'/, lx <**=á:ls**> *do as a structured activity*, syntactic analysis: intransitive verb or nominal, attested by EB.

<**chaléwt**>, pcs //cɛlə́w=T//, MC /'*turn s-th/s-o over, flip it over (of fish for ex.), turn it inside out*'/, ASM, syntactic analysis: transitive verb, also <**chelő́wt**>, Salish cognate: Lushootseed /dzal-/ 'reverse the side of, turn over/around, go over/around some obstruction' as in /dzál-qs/ 'go around a point',

/dzál-q-əd/ 'turn it over' (-q 'bottom), /s-dzə́l-č'/ (Skagit dial.) 'year, turning of the seasons' H76:212-213 (if so cf UHk syilólem *year* perhaps a doublet; found in <**chelő́wtlha**>, //cəlów=T-ɬɛ ~ cələ́w=T-ɬɛ//, /'*Turn it inside out.*'/, (<**-t**> *purposeful control transitivizer*, <**-lha**> *imperative sg.*), attested by EB, <**chelő́wtes**>, also <**chelé́wtes**>, //cəlów=T-əs ~ cələ́w=T-əs//, /'*He turns s-th inside out.*'/, attested by EB, <chelút> [BG: to be faithful to the phonetic transcription this should be spelled <**chelő́wt**>], [čʌlót], '*turn s.t. inside out*', attested by (EH,RG,SN) 8/13/99 (SU transcription, tape 5), there is more properly a <**w**> before the final t also, see the stative form below which requires a <**w**>.

<**chelchelút**> [or better, <**chelchelő́wt**>], plv [čʌ́lčɪlót], '*turning lots of things inside out*', attested by (EH,RG,SN) 8/13/99 (SU transcription, tape 5)

<*chálút>, [*čǽlót], *'turning s.t. inside out', rejected by EH,RG,SN 8/13/99 (SU transcription, tape 5)

<**Cháchelut**> [or better, <**Cháchelő́wt**>], [čǽčʌlót], *Elixabeth Herrling's (EH's) grandfather's brother's name*, attested by (EH,RG,SN) 8/13/99 (SU transcription, tape 5) - not a regular word referring to 'turning s.t. inside out'.

<**schelá:w**>, stvi //s=cɛlə́[-M2·-]w//, MC ['*be turned inside out*'], (<**s=**> *stative aspect*), (**metathesis and lengthening** *resultative or durative*), phonology: metathesis and lengthening, syntactic analysis: adjective/adjectival verb, example: <**schelá:w te swétas**>, //s=cəlɛ́·w//, /'*Her sweater is turned inside out.*'/, attested by EB.

<**chálé́x**>, dnom //cɛ́lə́x^{y}//, ANA ['*hand*'], attested by AC, BJ, others, syntactic analysis: nominal, other sources: ES /cɛ́lə́x^{y}/, H-T <tcáliH> (umlaut over a), also <**chálex**>, //cɛ́ləx^{y}//, attested by AC. others, <**le kwelá:tes li te s'eyí:ws chálexs**>, //lə k^{w}əl-ɛ́·T-əs li tə s=ʔəy=í·ws cɛ́ləx^{y}-s//, /'*He's holding it in his right hand.*'/, attested by AC.

<**chelchálé́x**>, pls //C$_1$əC$_2$-cɛ́lə́x^{y}//, ANA ['*hands*'], (<**R3-**> *plural*), syntactic analysis: nominal, phonology: reduplication, attested by BHTTC.

<**chéchelex**>, dms //C$_1$í=Aə́-cɛ́lə́x^{y}//, pls, EB /'*Prince's pine, pipsessewa*'/, ['*Chimaphila umbellata*'], literally /'many little hands'/, ASM ['the plant is named "many little hands" because the leaves are shaped like fingers, usually joined together with a short stem, resembling hands sticking out of the ground.'], MED ['The whole plant can be steeped for tea which is tasty and is also a medicine.'], (<**R4=**> *diminutive*), (<**-Aə́-**> *plural of diminutive*), phonology: ablaut, reduplication, attested by TG.

<**chá:lmel**>, dnom //cɛ́·lməl//, SOC ['*Chinese person*'], borrowed from English *Chinaman*, prob. through Chinook Jargon, syntactic analysis: nominal, attested by BHTTC, AC, also <**cháchelmel**>, //cɛ́[=C$_1$ə=]lməl//, (<**=R1=**> *diminutive or derivational or plural*), phonology: reduplication, attested by Ed Kelly Sr. (Sumas or Matsqui dialect).

<**tsálmalqel ~ chálmalqel**>, dnom //cɛ́lmɛl=qəl//, LANG ['*Chinese language*'], lx <**=qel**> *language, in the throat*, attested by AC, <**chálmelqel**>, attested by RG & EH (4/10/99 Ling332)

<**chólmelelh tl'álhem**>, FOOD *soy sauce* (lit. Chinese style + salt), (attested by RG,EH 6/16/98 to SN, edited by BG with RG,EH 6/26/00).

<**chálmalqel**>, dnom //cɛ́lmɛl=qəl//, LANG ['*Chinese language*'], *see* chá:lmel

<**chá:lq**>, cts //cə́[-Aɛ·-]lq//, TVMO ['*falling*'], *see* chélq ~ tsélq.

<**chálh**>, free root //cɛ́ɬ//, ABDF ['*it aches of arthritis*'], syntactic analysis: intransitive verb, attested by Deming: including SJ (Chill./Pil.), others.

<**cháchelh**>, cts //cɛ́[-C$_1$ə-]ɬ//, ABDF ['*it's aching of arthritis*'], (<**-R1-**> *continuative*), phonology: reduplication, syntactic analysis: intransitive verb, attested by Deming: incl. SJ, others.

<**chálhtel**>, df //cíɬ=ʔɛ́ɬtəl//, FSH ['*hang fish (especially salmon) for drying*'], *see* chílh

<**chá:lhtel**>, cts //probably cíɬ=ʔɛ[-·-]´ɬtəl//, FSH /'*smoking salmon, (hanging fish up to smoke)*'/, *see* chílh

<**chalhteláwtxw**>, dnom //cíɬ=ʔɛ́ɬtəl=ɛ́wtx^w//, BLDG ['*fish smokehouse*'], *see* chílh

<**chám**>, bound root //cɛ́m *pack, carry with strap*//.

<**chámem**>, mdls //cɛ́m=əm//, TVMO /'*pack on one's back, carry on one's back*'/, syntactic analysis: intransitive verb; found in <**chámemlha**>, //cɛ́m=əm-ɬɛ//, /'*Pack some., Pack a bit.*'/, attested by EB, example: <**me chámem**>, //mə cɛ́m=əm//, /'*He packed it on his back.*'/, attested by EB, <**xw'ít kw'as éwelh ō chámem**>, //x^{w}ʔít k'^{w}-ɛ-s ʔəwə-ɬ ʔəw cɛ́m=əm//, /'*Why don't you pack?*'/, attested by EB.

<**chmà:m**>, cts //cɛ́m-M1·`=əm (or cɛ́m=ə[-M1·`-]m)//, TVMO /'*carrying on one's back, packing on one's back*'/, (<**-M`:-**> *continuative*), phonology: metathesis plus lengthening and stress-shift *continuative aspect*, syntactic analysis: intransitive verb, also <**chmá:m ~ chemá:m**>, attested by EB.

<**iychmà:m ~ iytsmà:m**>, mos //ʔi(y)=cɛ́m-M1·`=əm//, TVMO ['*travelling by and packing on his back (might be said of a passer-by)*'], semantic environment ['might be said of a passer-by or others'], lx <**ye= ~ yi= ~ i(y)=**> *travelling while, moving while, going along doing an action*, syntactic analysis: intransitive verb (and adverb/adverbial verb).

<**chmaméleqw**>, cts //cɛ́m-M1=əm=ə́ləq^w//, TVMO ['*carry[ing] a packstrap around the head*'], lx <**=eleqw**> *on the top of the head*, syntactic analysis: intransitive verb, attested by IHTTC.

<**chámet**>, pcs //cɛ́m-əT//, [čɛ́mət], TVMO /'*carry s-th on one's back, pack s-th on one's back*'/, syntactic analysis: transitive verb, also <**chémat**>, //cə́m=əT//, attested by EB; found in <**chámetlha**>, //cɛ́m-əT-ɬɛ//, /'*Pack it.*'/, attested by EB, example: <**tsel chámet**>, //c-əl cɛ́m-əT//, /'*I pack it (for ex. a child) on my back.*'/, attested by EB, <**le chámetes**>, //lə cɛ́m-əT-əs//, /'*He packed it on his back.*'/, attested by EB, <**chémet**>, [čɪ́mɪt], '*carry on back*', attested by (EH,RG) 7/27/99 (SU transcription, tape 3), <**chámet**>, //cɛ́m-əT// /'to pack it '/, attested by RG & EH (4/9/99 Ling332)(BG transcription)

<**chmá:t**>, cts //cɛ́m-M1´·-əT//, TVMO /'*carrying s-th/s-o on one's back, packing it on one's back*'/, (<**-M1:´-**> *continuative*), also <**chemá:t**>, attested by EB, example: <**tsel chmá:t**>, //c-əl cɛ́m-M1´:-əT//, /'*I was packing it on my back.*'/, attested by EB, <**chemá:tes te mímeles**>, //cɛ́m-M1´·-əT-əs tə C_1í=mələ-s//, /'*She's carrying her child on her back., He's packing his child.*'/, attested by EB, <**chmá:tes te á:wkw's**>, //cɛ́m-M1´·-ət-əs tə ʔɛ́·wk'^{w}-s//, /'*He's packing his baggage or belongings.*'/, attested by EB, <**chemát**>, [čɪmǽt], '*packing on back*', attested by (EH,RG) 7/27/99 (SU transcription, tape 3) (a different continuative was cited in the previous session, <**chechémet**>, [čʌčɪ́mɪt], '*packing it*', attested by (EH,RG 7/23/99) (SU transcription, tape 2), but <**chemát**> given the next time may have been a correction, along with several other corrections)

<**chím ~ chí:m**>, ds //cɛ́m=í·m//, TVMO ['*to pack*'], lx <**=í:m**> *repeatedly*, phonology: consonant alternation, vmrgr: when =í:m is suffixed to a stem ending in m, the stem m is dropped and the stem vowel merges with the suffix's í: (yielding í:), syntactic analysis: intransitive verb, attested by IHTTC and RG & EH (4/9/99 Ling332).

<**schí:m**>, dnom //s=cɛ́m=í·m//, TVMO ['*a pack*'], phonology: since a pack is something used repeatedly the suffix =í·m *repeatedly* seem quite plausible here; the alternative would require a derivation with í·-ablaut, /s=cɛ́[=Aí·=]m/, which seems less likely, attested by IHTTC, example:

<**xet'éla tel schí:m**>, //x^{y}ət'(=)əĺɛ tə-l s=cɛ́m=í·m//, /'*My pack is slack or loose (the straps are loose).*'/, attested by IHTTC.

<**chámatel**>, dnom //cɛ́mɛ=təl//, [čɛ́mætəl], TVMO /'*tumpline, packstrap*'/, MC, lx <**=tel**> *something for, device for*, phonology: note the appearance of two full (non-schwa) vowels in the root with this suffix (including the less common stressed [ɛ́] and the rare unstressed [æ]); this may indicate that the other instances of this root should be reanalyzed with /cɛ́mɛ/ and merely stress-shift, not metathesis; with schí:m *pack*, however, the root allomorph lacks the final vowel or the m would not drop before =í:m, dialects: *used by some Upriver speakers and by Katzie Downriver speakers;* other Upriver speakers use q'síyeltel (see under q'), syntactic analysis: nominal, also <**tsématel**>, [cɪ́mætəl], dialects: *DM.*

<**chámatel**>, dnom //cɛ́mɛ=təl//, [čɛ́mætəl], TVMO /'*tumpline, packstrap*'/, *see* chám

<**chá:mel**>, free root //cɛ́·məl//, SOC ['*German person*'], borrowed from English *German*, syntactic analysis: nominal, attested by BHTTC.

<**chámet**>, pcs //cɛ́m-əT//, [čɛ́mət], TVMO /'*carry s-th on one's back, pack s-th on one's back*'/, *see* chám

<**-chap**>, is, //**-c-ɛp**//, PRON /'*you folks (subj. of independent verb phrase), you (pl.) (subj. of independent verb phrase), you people (subj. of independent verb phrase)*'/, syntactic analysis: is, example: <**"éwechap lamáp hélem tel slhx̱wélhcha."**>, //ʔə́wə-c-ɛp lɛm-ɛ́p hə́-ləm tə-l s=ɬx̣^{w}=ə́ɬcɛ//, /'*"Don't you people go to my spit."*'/ (a pun made by Paul Webster's wife on the place name Th'qwélhcha, a little lake in back of Paul Webster's house on Hicks Road), attested by LJ (Tait).

<**chaplí**>, free root //cɛplí//, SOC ['*Japanese person*'], borrowed from English *Japanese*, syntactic analysis: nominal, attested by BHTTC.

<**chá:xw**>, free root //cɛ́·x^w//, SOC /'*wife (not respectful), the "old lady", "squaw", mistress*'/, KIN, syntactic analysis: nominal, usage: informal term, slangy, not respectful, attested by AC, other sources: JH /cé·x̣^{w}/ *wife*, Salish cognate: Squamish /čuáš/ 'wife' W73:289, K67:317, Lushootseed (Northern) /čəg^{w}áš/ 'wife', (Southern) /čə́g^{w}əš/ 'wife' H76:92, Twana /čuʔwáš ~ /cúwaš/ 'wife' NT79 & NT82, also <**cháxw ~ chá:x̱w**>, //cɛ́x^w ~ cɛ́·x̣^{w}//, attested by AC, example: <**thel chá:xw**>, //θə-l cɛ́·x^w//, /'*my wife, my woman, my squaw*'/, attested by AC.

<**scháchexw**>, stvi //s=cɛ́·[-C_1ə-]x^w//, SOC ['*got married to a wife*'], (<**s=**> *stative*), (<**-R1-**> (here **<-che->)** probably *continuative*), phonology: reduplication, syntactic analysis: adjective/adjectival verb, attested by EB, AD, JS, others, example: <**éwe ís scháchexw**>, //ʔə́wə ʔí-s s=cɛ́·[-C_1ə-]x^w//, /'*He's got no wife (got wife).*'/, attested by JS.

<**scháchxwelmel**>, ds //s=cɛ́·[-C_1ə-]x^w=əlməl//, SOC /'*want to get a wife, He wants to get a wife.*'/, lx <**=elmel**> *in the mind, want to,* phonology: reduplication, syntactic analysis: intransitive verb, attested by Deming.

<**chxwélmel**>, ds //cɛ́·x^w=ə́lməl//, SOC /'*want a wife, He wants a wife.*'/, lx <**=élmel**> *in the mind, want,* syntactic analysis: intransitive verb, example: <**x̱elx̱ólqemoles te chítmexw lhís chxwélmel**>, //C_1əC_2-x̣álq=əm=áləs tə cítməx^w ɬi-s cɛ́·x^w=ə́lməl//, /'*The owl rolls his eyes when he wants a wife.*'/, usage: a saying or proverb.

<**schéxwmet**>, iecs //s=cɛ́[=Aə́=]x^w=məT//, SOC ['*to propose to someone*'], syntactic analysis: transitive verb, attested by AD.

<**tscháxw**>, ds //c-cɛ́x^w//, KIN ['*get a wife*'], syntactic analysis: intransitive verb, attested by AC, Salish cognate: Nooksack /ččwǽš/ 'wife' PA61.

<**chéchelex**>, dms //C_1í=Aə́-cɛ̀lə́x^y//, pls, EB /'*Prince's pine, pipsessewa*'/, ['*Chimaphila umbellata*'], literally /'many little hands'/, *see* chálex

possibly <**Chéchem**>, ds possibly //cə́[=C_1ə=]m//, PLN ['*Mt. MacFarlane Creek*'], phonology: reduplication, source: Wells 1966.

<**chechíxw**>, rsls //C_1ə=cíx^w//, ABDF ['*(be) swollen*'], *see* =chíxw ~ chxw=

<**Chechí<u>x</u>em**> possibly, ds probably //C_1ə=cíx̣=əm//, PLN ['*Depot Creek (off upper Chilliwack River)*'], *see* chí<u>x</u>em

<**chek chek chek**>, cpds //cək cək cək//, [čɪk čɪk čɪk], EZ ['*(calling a chicken)*'], borrowed from English *chick chick chick*, syntactic analysis: interjection, attested by DC.

<**chéke chéke chéke chéke**>, cpds //cə́kə cə́kə cə́kə cə́kə//, [číkə číkə číkə číkə (in high notes)], EZ ['*(this cry of a bluejay [Steller's jay] warns you of bad news)*'], ASM ['one name for the Steller's jay means *sacred fortune-teller; another cry,* ***q'éy q'éy q'éy,*** *predicts good news'],* syntactic analysis: interjection.

<**chékel**>, free root //cə́kəl ~ cə́kəls//, [čík^{y}ɪl ~ čík^{y}ɪls], EZ ['*chicken*'], borrowed from English *chicken,* syntactic analysis: nominal, example: <**sqwóqwiyel te chékels**>, //s=q^{w}ɛ[=AáC$_1$ə=]y=əl tə cə́kəls//, /'*The chicken is tan., The chicken is yellow.*'/, attested by Deming, esp. SJ, <**sqw'él:em chékel**>, FOOD *roast chicken* (lit. roasted/barbecued + chicken), (attested by RG,EH 6/16/98 to SN, edited by BG with RG,EH 6/26/00), <**s<u>x</u>éles te chékel**>, ANAB, FOOD *chicken drumstick* (lit. leg of + the + chicken), (attested by RG,EH 6/16/98 to SN, edited by BG with RG,EH 6/26/00)

<**chèkelélets**>, dnom //cə̀kəl=ə́ləc//, ABFC ['*chicken dung*'], lx <**=élets**> *on the bottom, rump,* syntactic analysis: nominal, attested by SP, AK.

<**chelichkelsó:llh**>, dms //C_1í[-əl-]-cə́kəls=á·lɬ//, pls, EZ ['*baby chicks*'], (<**R4=**> *diminutive*), (<**-el-**> *plural*), lx <**=ó:llh**>, phonology: the plural is infixed into the reduplication, syntactic analysis: nominal.

<**chèkelélets**>, dnom //cə̀kəl=ə́ləc//, ABFC ['*chicken dung*'], *see* chékel

<**chekwílem**>, mdls //cák^w=íl-əm//, incs, TVMO ['*go far away*'], *see* chó:kw

<**chelà:l**>, us //cəlɛ̀·l//, EFAM /'*what a lot., it's sure a lot*'/, NUM, DESC, syntactic analysis: adjective/adjectival verb and possibly interjection, attested by EB from LJ (Tait), example: <**chelà:l yexw ye me xwe'í**>, //cəlɛ̀·l yəx^w yə mə x^{w}ə=ʔí//, /'*A lot of people came.*'/, attested by EB.

<**chelà:lqwlha**>, ds //cəlɛ̀·l=q^{w}ɬɛ//, EFAM ['*it's sure a lot*'], NUM, DESC, lx <**=qwlha**> *intensifier,* syntactic analysis: adjective/adjectival verb and possibly interjection, attested by EB, example: <**chelà:lqwlha te sxélchas**>, //cəlɛ̀·l=q^{w}ɬɛ tə s-x^{y}ə́lcɛ-s//, /'*He sure caught a lot.*'/, literally /'it's sure a lot the nom-catch-his'/, attested by EB, <**chelà:lqwlha kwa te slhíms**>, //cəlɛ̀·l=q^{w}ɬɛ k^{w}ɛ tə s-ɬím-s//, /'*He was going to pick a lot.*'/, literally /'it's sure a lot anyway the nom-pick-his'/, attested by EB.

<**cheláqelh**>, ds //cəlɛ́q(=)əɬ//, TIME /'*yesterday, it was yesterday*'/, possibly root <**chó:l**> as in <**chó:lq=em**> *follow along after* and <**chó:l=t**> *follow behind s-o,* possibly <**=elh**> perhaps a reduced form of <**=elhlàt**> *day* as in <**s<u>x</u>á<u>x</u>elhlàt**> *Sunday ("sacred day")* and <**yiláwelhlàt**> *Monday ("day after")* or perhaps the past tense affix <=elh> now used derivationally, syntactic analysis: probably adverb/adverbial verb, intransitive verb, also <**chelá:qelh**>, //cəlɛ́·q(=)əɬ//, usage: citation form, also <**tseláqelh**>, //cəlɛ́q(=)əɬ//, usage: less common, example: <**stámelh swàyèl kw'e cheláqelhelh**>, //s=tɛ́m-əɬ s=wɛ̀y=ə̀l k'^{w}ə cəlɛ́qəɬ-əɬ//, /'*What day was yesterday?*'/, literally /'nom=what?-past nom=be day=come the remote/abstract yesterday-past'/, usage: Answer: example, Yilá**w**elh(l)**à**t.

Monday., attested by IHTTC, <**yeláwel x̲ítl' tlówàyèl telí kw'e cheláqelh(elh)**>, //yəlɛ́w=əl x̣íƛ' təlá=wɛ̀y=ə̀l təlí k'ʷə cəlɛ́qəɬ(=əɬ)//, /'*Today is colder than yesterday.*'/, literally /'it goes past cold this day from/than the remote yesterday'/, <**himqáxel kw'e tseláqelhelh**>, //hi=mɛqɛ́=xʸəl k'ʷə cəlɛ́qəɬ-əɬ//, /'*It rained and snowed together yesterday.*'/, literally /'pl?=fallen snow=precipitation the abstract yesterday-past'/, attested by Deming, <**tsel mí kw'e lò kw cheláqelhelh qe ő̓wechxw íxw xwe'í**>, //c-əl mí k'ʷə là kʷ cəlɛ́qəɬ-əɬ qə ʔə́wə-c-xʷ ʔí-xʷ xʷə=ʔí//, /'*I came here yesterday and you weren't here (hadn't arrived).*'/, literally /'icsp-1ssj come the remote here the near yesterday-past and did not-icsp-2ssj here(aux)-2ssbsj get=here'/, attested by EB, <**ilh x̲ét'esthò:m kw' cheláqelhelh kw'a's ő̓we x̲et'áxw tethá**>, //ʔi-ɬ x̣ət'ə=sT-à·m k'ʷ cəlɛ́qəɬ-əɬ k'ʷ-ɛʔ-s ʔə́wə x̣ət'ɛ́-xʷ tə=θɛ́//, /'*You were told yesterday not to do that.*'/, literally /'be here (aux)-past say=caus-2sojpass the abstract yesterday-past that-your sg-nom not do like that-2ssbsj the=that'/, attested by IHTTC, <**ílhtsel li kwe tseláqelh**>, //ʔí-ɬ-c-əl lí kʷə cəlɛ́qəɬ//, /'*I was there yesterday.*'/, literally /'be here-past-icsp-1ssj on/in the near yesterday'/, attested by AC, <**tsel má:ythòme kw'e tseláqelhelh qa lhulhá**>, //c-əl mɛ́·y=T-àmə k'ʷə cəlɛ́qəɬ-əɬ qɛ ɬ(=)əwɬ(-)ɛ̀//, /'*I helped you yesterday or the day before yesterday.*'/, literally /'icsp-1ssj help=purposely-2soj the abstract yesterday-past or ?(=already)(-later?)'/, attested by AC, <**léts'e swáyel iwá:lmels kw' cheláqelhelh**>, //lə́c'ə s=wɛ́y(=)əl ʔiwɛ́·l(=)məls k'ʷ cəlɛ́qəɬ-əɬ//, /'*(It's) one day before yesterday.*'/, literally /'it's one day before the abstract/remote yesterday-past'/, attested by DM, also <**yewálmels kw'e tseláqelh(elh)**>, //yəwɛ́l=məl-s k'ʷə cəlɛ́q(=)əɬ(-əɬ)//, also /'*the day before yesterday*'/, attested by AC, literally /'before the yesterday'/.

<**chelchálé x**>, pls //C_1əC_2-cɛ́lə́xʸ//, ANA ['*hands*'], *see* chálé x

<**Chelchálíth**>?, dnom //possibly C_1əC_2-cɛ́líθ//, PLN ['*Elk Creek falls on west side of Elk Mountain*'], literally /'water falling or rolling (according to Wells)'/, compare with root <**chélq**> *fall (of water and other things)* compare with root and its continuative, <**chá:lq**> *falling*, (<**R3-**> *plural*), phonology: reduplication, syntactic analysis: nominal?, source: Wells 1965:13, Wells 1966 map,

<**chelchélq**>, plv [čɪlčɪ́lq] EH, [¢ɪl¢ɪ́lq] RG, 'fall all over the place', *see* chélq ~ tsélq

<**chelchelút**> [or better, <**chelchelő̓wt**>], plv [čʌ́lčɪlót], '*turning lots of things inside out*', *see* chaléwt

<**chelchó:lqem**>, pls //C_1əC_2=cɛ́[=Aa=]·l=q=əm//, TVMO ['*lots following*'], *see* chá:l or chó:l

<**chelichkelsó:llh**>, dms //C_1í[-əl-]-cə́kəls=á·lɬ//, pls, EZ ['*baby chicks*'], *see* chékel

<**chélq ~ tsélq**>, free root //cə́lq//, TVMO /'*to fall (of a person, waterfall, etc.), stumble*'/, ASM, syntactic analysis: intransitive verb, other sources: ES /c'ə́lq/ *fall*, example: <**le tsélq**>, //lə cə́lq//, /'*He fell in (caught his foot and fell).*'/, attested by AC, <**chelq**>, [čɪ́lq] EH, [¢ɪ́lq] RG, '*fall over; trip accidentally*', attested by (EH,RG 7/30/99)(SU transcription, tape 4).

<**chá:lq**>, cts //cə́[-Aɛ·-]lq//, TVMO ['*falling*'], (<**-Aa:-**> *continuative aspect*), phonology: continuative ablaut and lengthening, attested by BJ, example: <**chá:lq qó:**>, //cɛ́·lq qá·//, /'*falling water, waterfall*'/, WATR, attested by BJ, also <**qó: me chá:lq**>, attested by BJ, syntactic comment: syntax probably in error.

<**Tsólqthet te Skwówech**>, pcs //cə́[-Aɛ·-][Aá]lq=Tət tə s=kʷáw(=)əc//, PLN ['*Rainbow Falls on the east side of Harrison Lake*'], literally /'the sturgeon fell (or dropped himself)'/, ASM ['so named after Indians found a sturgeon at the foot of Rainbow Falls; they said it fell from the lake at the top; EL thought it must have gotten stuck there feeding after a high-water time.'], <**-Aá-**> *resultative* changed automatically to <**Aó**> by following <**=thet**> *purposeful control reflexive* or *become, get*), phonology: ablaut, grammatical comment: tsólqthet not attested so far as a regular reflexive form, not attested outside of this placename so far, dialects: *Cheh.*, attested by EL.

<**chelchélq**>, plv [čɪlčílq] EH, [¢ɪl¢ílq] RG, 'fall all over the place', attested by (EH,RG 7/30/99)(SU transcription, tape 4)

<**tselqó:mé**>, dnom //cəlq=á·mə́//, EB ['*blackcap berry*'], ['*Rubus leucodermis*'], MED ['leaf tea is medicine for stomach ache'], ASM ['the berries are out in early July but often not ripe till late summer; the berries are eaten fresh; young sprouts are peeled and eaten raw in spring (see <sthát hqi>)'], literally /'fall-berry (perhaps because they come off easily)'/, lx <**=ó:mé**> *berry*, syntactic analysis: nominal.

<**tselqó:má:lhp**>, dnom //cəlq=á·mə́=ɛ·ɬp//, EB ['*blackcap plant*'], lx <**=á:lhp**> *tree, plant*, phonology: the suffix =elhp takes the form =**á**:lhp after stems ending in a vowel (or stays =elhp and e + e combine to become a: in vowel merger processes, syntactic analysis: nominal.

<**chelqó:mé ~ tselqó:mé**>, dnom //cəlq=á·mə́//, EB ['*blackcap berry*'], ['*Rubus leucodermis*'], *see* chélq ~ tsélq

<**chelqó:má:lhp ~ tselqó:má:lhp**>, dnom //cəlq=á·mə́=ɛ·ɬp//, EB ['*blackcap plant*'], *see* chélq ~ tsélq

<**Chelqwílh ~ Chelqwéylh**>, df //ca(=)l=əqʷ=wə[=Aí=]ɬ or ca(=)l=əqʷ=íɬ ~ ca(=)l=əqʷ=ə́yɬ//, PLN ['*an area up the mountainside from X̲woxweláIhp (Yale)*'], *see* chá:l or chó:l

<**chélhmel**>, ds //cí[=Aə́=]ɬ=məl//, BLDG ['*on top of the house*'], *see* chílh

<**chelhó:lemelh**>, dnom //cíɬ=á·ləməɬ//, ANA /'*upper circle over the eye,* (probably) *upper eyelid*'/, *see* chílh

<**chélhqel**>, ds //cí[=Aə́=]ɬ=qəl//, ANA ['*(have a) high voice*'], *see* chílh

<**chelhqí:l ~ chelhqéyl**>, ds //cíɬ=qəl=í·l or cíɬ=qə[=Aí·=]l//, ANA /'*roof of the mouth, inside of upper lip, palate*'/, *see* chílh

<**chélhta**>, us //cə́ɬtɛ//, SOC ['*borrow*'], root <**chá:l ~ chó:l**> //cɛ́·l ~ cá·l or cá·=əl or cɛ[=Aá=]=əl *follow behind, go a distance*//, possibly root <**chó(:)**> as in <**chó:kw ~ chókw**> *far, distant,* plus <**=el**> *go, come, get, become, inceptive*, plus devoicing to <lh>, lx <**=´ta**> *thing*, syntactic analysis: intransitive verb, also <**chélhte**>, //cə́ɬtə//, Salish cognate: Lushootseed /čul'-/ 'borrow, lend items other than money' Bates, Hess & Hilbert 1994:293, attested by EB; found in <**chélhtatsel**>, //cə́ɬtɛ-c-əl//, /'*I borrow.*'/, <**chélhte**>, [čʌ́ɬtʌ], '*borrow*', attested by (EH,RG) 7/27/99 (SU transcription, tape 3).

<**chókwelhta** (or **chókwellhta)**>, cts //cá[-kʷə-]ɬ=tɛ//, SOC ['*borrowing*'], root <**chélhta**> *lend, let s-o borrow* with <-R1-> reduplication *continuative* except with <**kw**> replacing the <**ch**> (consonant ablaut (-Akw-) or replacement--this is attested in Musqueam, and Upriver also since when <x> is reduplicated in <-R1-> it is sometimes done with <xw> replacing the <x> (also consonant ablaut)), syntactic analysis: intransitive verb, attested by EB, AC; found in <**chókwelhtatsel**>, //cákʷəɬtɛ-c-əl//, /'*I'm borrowing.*'/.

<**chélhtat ~ chélhtet**>, pcs //cə́ɬ=tɛ=T ~ cə́ɬ=tə=T//, SOC /'*lend it to s-o, let s-o borrow it*'/, syntactic analysis: transitive verb; found in <**chelhtethóme**>, //cəɬ=tə=T-ámə//, /'*let you borrow something*'/, attested by EB, <**chèlhtathóx**>, //cə̀ɬ=tɛ=T-áxʸ//, /'*lend me something*'/, attested by AC, example: <**chelhtethóx ta' lháts'tel**>, //cəɬ=tə=T-áxʸ t-ɛʔ ɬɛ́c'=təl//, /'*Let me borrow your knife.*'/, syntactic comment: a second person imperative ending is not necessary when the second person possessive ta' tells who is being addressed, attested by EB.

<**schókwelelh**>, strs //s=cá[-kʷə-]l=əɬ//, SOC ['*be borrowed*'], (<**s=**> *stative*), root <**chélhta**> *lend, let s-o borrow* with <-R1-> reduplication *continuative* except with <**kw**> replacing the <**ch**> (consonant ablaut (-Akw-), final consonant in root revoices before <**=elh**> *resultative* probably

either a rare survival from PCS or borrowed with the form from another Salish language, lx <= ´**ta**> *thing* appears to be clipped or dropped, the root of this word may be related (or identical) to that in chó(:)(=)kw *be far away, distant,* syntactic analysis: adjective/adjectival verb, example: <**tl'ól schókwelelh**>, //ƛ'á-l s=cákʷ=əl=əɬ//, /*'That's what I borrowed.'*/, attested by EB, <**schókwelelh ò te skwí:xs**>, //s=cákʷ=əl=əɬ ʔà tə s=kʷí·xʸ-s//, /*'He's borrowed his name.'*/, attested by EB.

<**chélhtat ~ chélhtet**>, pcs //cə́ɬ=tɛ=T ~ cə́ɬ=tə=T//, SOC /*'lend it to s-o, let s-o borrow it'*/, *see* chélhta

<**chémlexw ~ chemléxw**>, ncs //cá[=Aə́=]m=l-əxʷ ~ cá(=)m=l-ə[= ´=]xʷ//, SOC [*'elope with s-o or meet up with s-o'*], TVMO, KIN, literally possibly /'manage to get s-o away from the river'/, *see* chó:m

<**chémq ~ tsémq**>, us //cə́mq//, [čímq ~ címq], WETH [*'stop blowing (of the wind)'*], syntactic analysis: intransitive verb, dialects: *Cheh. (Chill.* uses **líqwel** *get calm)*, example: <**lí le chémq ~ lí le tsémq**>, //lí lə cə́mq//, /*'Is the wind stopped?'*/, <**chémq te spehá ls**>, //cə́mq tə s=pəh=ɛ́ls//, /*'The wind has stopped.'*/, dialects: *Cheh. (Chill.* uses **Líqwel te spehá ls** *The wind has stopped.)*, syntactic analysis: historical past tense, <**le chémq te spehá:ls**>, //lə cə́mq tə s=pəh=ɛ́·ls//, /*'The wind stopped.'*/, (semological comment: note the contrast in past tenses in the last two examples: the ambiguous past with <**le**> seems here to indicate a more sudden action that the historical past without <**le**> in the next-to-last example), syntactic analysis: ambiguous past.

<**chew ~ cháw**>, bound root //cəw ~ cɛ́w//, LAND /*'beach, shore'*/.

<**cháchew ~ cháchu**>, dnom //cɛ́[=C_1ə=]w or C_1ɛ́=cəw//, LAND /*'beach, shore'*/, (<**=R1=**> (may be an old) *stative*) or more likely <R7=>*augmentative*, phonology: reduplication, syntactic analysis: nominal, also <**tsá:tsō**>, //cɛ́cəw//, dialects: *Chill.: AC*, other sources: ES /cɛ́·cəw/, JH /cé·cu/.

<**chúchu ~ chúwchuw ~ chéwchew**>, ds //cə́w=C_1əC_2//, LAND /*'away from the shore, toward the river'*/, WATR, (<**=R2**> *characteristic*), phonology: reduplication, syntactic analysis: adverb/adverbial verb, example: <**lámtset kwe chúchu**>, //lɛ́=m-c-ət kʷə cə́w=C_1əC_2//, /*'We'll go down to the river (near but out of sight).'*/, <**lám kwe chúchu [qesésu] lhó:s**>, //lɛ́=m kʷə cə́w=C_1əC_2 [qə-s-ə́s-əw] ɬá·s//, /*'He's going to the river to drift-net.'*/.

<**Chuchuwálets**>, dnom //cəw=C_1əC_2=ɛ́ləc (or possibly? C_1əC_2=cəwɛ́=ləc)//, PLN /*'Fraser River (way out at the end), mouth of the Fraser River'*/, phonology: reduplication, attested by Cheh., other source: place name file reference #107, also <**Chōchō'álets**>, //cəwcəwʔɛ́ləc//, [čočoʔǽləc], dialects: *Sumas.*

<**chuchuwá<u>x</u>el**>, dnom //cəw=C_1əC_2=ɛ́x̣əl//, BLDG [*'front end of a house (inside or outside)'*], literally /'side of a house/building toward the river'/, lx <**=á<u>x</u>el**> *side (of a building, a square, or a river),* phonology: reduplication, syntactic analysis: nominal.

<**chuchuwó:ythel**>, ds //cəw=C_1əC_2=á·yθəl//, WATR [*'out in the middle of the river'*], literally /'toward the river from the lip/edge'/, lx <**=ó:ythel**> *on the lip, on the jaw*, phonology: reduplication, attested by BHTTC.

<**chewélhem ~ tsewélhem ~ tsōwélhem**>, mdls //cə́w=ə[- ´-]ɬ-əm//, cts, ABFC [*'to spawn'*], literally /'to beach one's offspring'/, lx <**=elh**> *offspring, child,* (<**-em**> *middle voice*), syntactic analysis: intransitive verb, dialects: *Deming* (report meaning as *be spawning*), example: <**chewélhem te sth'óqwi**>, //cə́w=ə[- ´-]ɬ-əm//, /*'The fish are spawning.'*/, attested by Deming, also <**thewélhem**>, //θəw=ə́ɬ-əm//, ABFC [*'to spawn'*], dialects: *AD*, also <**thōwélhem**>, //θəw-ə́ɬ-əm//, ABFC [*'a fish that's going to spawn'*], dialects: *IHTTC*, phonology: the form given here can be analyzed in two ways: AD and the IHTTC speakers here have a weak-grade root with the derivational suffix required to take the stress or there is inflection for the non-continuative form here by stress-shift (less likely). The stress-shift patterns for aspect are reversed from those of the Deming speakers for this word. Another difference between dialects/speakers is that AD and IHTTC speakers reporting

this form have a th /θ/ where Deming speakers have ch /c/. The Squamish cognate is /ʔa-č-čáwam/ *to spawn*. Halkomelem ch /c/ corresponds to Squamish /č/ and Halkomelem th /θ/ corresponds to Squamish /c/. Unless the Squamish root /čáwam/ had an initial /c/ which assimilated to the preceding /č/ prefix, it seems like the Halkomelem form with ch corresponds to the Squamish form., syntactic analysis: intransitive verb, <**chowlh tu thewélhem kw'e sth'elóth'qwi**>, //cɛ-əwɬ tu θəw=ə́ɬ-əm k'ʷə s=θ'[-əl-]á[-C_1ə-]qʷi//, /'*Soon the fishes will spawn.*'/, grammatical analysis: future tense-already really beach=offspring-one's own(middle voice) the (remote) nominal-fish[-pl.-][-pl./dim.?-], attested by AD.

<**théwelhem**>, cts //cə[-´-]w=əɬ-əm//, ABFC ['*spawning (in action when you see them)*'], grammatical comment: AD was specific that this was a continuative form; she was correcting a word list entry where it was listed as non-continuative; at the same time she also said that thewélhem should be listed as *spawn (non-continuative)*, attested by AD, syntactic analysis: intransitive verb, also <**thő̂welhem**>, //θə[-´-]w=əɬ-əm//, ABFC ['*spawning*'], attested by IHTTC.

<**chewő:lhp**>, dnom //c[=əC_2=]ə́w=(ə)ɬp//, EB ['*black cottonwood tree*'], ['*Populus balsamifera trichocarpa*'], ASM ['the sweet cambium, sx̱á:meth or ts'its'emá:welh, was scraped or licked off of the peeled bark and eaten fresh; the cotton from the catkins was gathered and mixed with dog and goat wool to whiten it and make it go further'], literally /'many shores tree or little shore tree (so named since it grows mainly on the shores of rivers or lakes)'/, (<**=R6= (here =ew=)**> either *plural* or *diminutive*), phonology: reduplication, syntactic analysis: nominal, other sources: ES /cəw·ə́w·ɬp/, JH /cəwú·ɬp/, H-T <tcEwólp> all *cottonwood*.

<**Chewő:lhp**>, dnom //cəw=ə́w=ɬp//, PLN ['*Cottonwood Beach (in the southern quarter of Harrison Lake)*'], ASM ['located north of Eagle Falls (Walian Creek) and south of Lhó:leqwet'], literally /'cottonwood tree, so called because there are lots of cottonwoods here'/, syntactic analysis: nominal, attested by EL, other source: place name file reference #117.

<**Lexwchéwő̂lhp**>, dnom //ləxʷ=cəw=ə́w=ɬp//, PLN /'*village between Yale Creek and Mary Ann Creek on the CP side (west bank of the Fraser R.) where lots of cottonwoods grow/grew (near Yale, B.C.)*'/, syntactic analysis: nominal, attested by SP, AK, other sources: ES čiwiɬp.

<**Chowéthel**>, dnom //cəw=á[=M2´=]θəl//, PLN /'*village at what's now Katz Reserve, Katz Landing*'/, literally /'beach at the mouth (of a creek)'/, ASM ['so called because at the mouth of a little creek there a sand bar extends way out (perhaps half a mile) into the Fraser R. in low water'], (semological comment: the English name Katz (Landing) is said to be from the fact that riverboats landed here and that a cat of one ferry once jumped off here), (<**=óthel**> *in the mouth*), (<**metathesis**> *place name* (used to separate it from chewóthel which would be a word meaning *beach at the mouth of a river*), syntactic analysis: nominal, attested by PDP, SP, others, other source: place name file reference #22; Wells 1965.

<**chichewós**>, dms //C_1í=cəw=ás//, LAND /'*sit facing a river and watch it, sit on a riverbank and sunbathe*'/, WATR, ASM ['sunbathing is not required according to AD'], (<**R4=** (here **chi=**)> *diminutive*), lx <**=ós**> *on the face*, attested by IHTTC, AD, also <**ch'ich'ewós**>, df //C_1í=c[=G=]əw=ás//, cts, ABFC ['*sunning oneself*'], , phonology: reduplication, attested by IHTTC (8/4/77).

<**chichewóthel**>, dms //C_1í=cəw=áθəl//, LAND ['*a little below the mouth of a creek or slough*'], WATR, (<**R4=**> *diminutive*), (<**=óthel**> *at the mouth*), phonology: reduplication, syntactic analysis: nominal (?) or intransitive verb (?).

(probably) <**Schāchewxel ~ Cháchewxel**>, dnom //s=cɛ́cəw=xʸəl ~ cɛ́cəw=xʸəl//, PLN ['*a village of the Pilalt people*'], syntactic analysis: nominal, source: Wells 1965, Wells 1966, H-T <tsátcu_Hil>

(umlaut on a), literally probably /'beach at the foot or beach trail'/, source: Wells 1966 <s'CH.AH-choo-k ihl> , literally /'a going down'/,

(possibly) <**Chuwtí:l**>, dnom (possibly) //cəw=təl=í·l//, PLN ['*another village of the Pilalt people*'], (possibly <**=tel**> *something for, device for,* <**=í:l**> *go, come, get, become*), syntactic analysis: nominal, source: Wells 1965, Wells 1966, H-T <tcu_tíl>.

(possibly) <**Schewíts**>, dnom (possibly) //s=cəw=íc//, PLN ['*Lindeman Lake or Post Lake*'], lx (possibly) <**=íts**> *in/on the back*, phonology: ch could also be ch', ts could also be ts' or th', syntactic analysis: nominal, source: place names file reference #261; Wells 1965 <s'ch-WEETZ>, PLN /'*Lindeman Creek below Chilliwack Lake, on the north side of Chilliwack River*'/, source: Wells 1965 <s'ch-WEETZ>.

<**chewélhem ~ tsewélhem ~ tsōwélhem**>, mdls //cə́w=ə[-´-]ɬ-əm//, cts, ABFC ['*to spawn*'], literally /'to beach one's offspring'/, *see* chew ~ cháw

<**chewót**>, bound root or stem //cəwát//, root meaning unknown

<**schewót**>, stvi //s=cəwát//, DESC /'*smart, know how, good at it*'/, syntactic analysis: intransitive verb, also <**sthewót**>, [sθəwát], dialects: idiolectal for EB only; found in <**schewótchexw**>, //s=cəwát-c-əx^w//, /'*You're smart.*'/, example: <**ts'áts'el ō sthewót**>, //c'ɛ[=C_1ə=]l ʔəw sθəwát//, /'*(he's/she's) very smart*'/, attested by EB, <**líchxw schewót**>, //lí-c-x^w s=cəwát//, /'*Are you good at it?*'/, attested by AC, <**líchxw schewót kw'as t'ít'ets'em**>, //lí-c-x^w s=cəwát k'^{w}-ɛ-s t'i[-C_1ə-]c'=əm//, /'*Do you know how to swim?*'/, attested by Deming: MC, SJ, MV, LG (all Chill.), <**ő́wetsel il schewót kw'els t'í:ts'em**>, //ʔə́wə-c-əl ʔí-l s=cəwát k'^{w}ə-l-s t'í·c'=əm//, /'*I don't know how to swim.*'/, attested by Deming: MC, SJ, MV, LG, <**stsewó:t kw's kwél:éxs**>, //s=cəwá[=·=]t k'^{w}-s k^wə́l=ə́x^y-s//, /'*He knows how to shoot.*'/, attested by AC, <**schewót kw'es st'ít'elems**>, //s=cəwát k'^{w}ə-s s-t'í[-C_1ə-]l=əm-s//, /'*He's good at singing.*'/, attested by AC, <**schewót kw'es qw'eyílexs**>, //s=cəwát k'^{w}ə-s q'^{w}əy(=)íl=əx^y-s//, /'*He's good at dancing.*'/, <**stsewó:t kwthel mál kw'es kwel:éxs lhlá:mes há:we**>, //s=cəwá[=·=]t k^w=θə-l mɛ́l k'^{w}ə-s k^wəl=əx^y-s ɬ-lɛ́·m-əs hɛ́·wə//, /'*My father knows how to shoot when he goes hunting.*'/, literally /'stative=know[=emphasis=] near + visible-my father that-nom hold (weapon)=upright-he (i.e. shoots-he) when-go-he (sbsj) hunt'/, attested by AC,

<**schéchewòt**>, dms //s=C_1í[-Aə́-]-cəwát//, DESC ['*little smart one*'], (<**s=**> *stative*), (<**R4=**> *diminutive*), (<**é-ablaut**> *plural?*), phonology: reduplication, syntactic analysis: nominal, attested by BHTTC.

<**schewétmet**>, iecs //s=cəwa[=Aə́=]t=məT//, DESC ['*be good at s-th*'], (<**=met**> *indirect effect control transitivizer, do with an indirect effect on s-o/s-th*), syntactic analysis: transitive verb, example: <**schewétmet te syó:ys**>, //s=cəwa[=Aə́=]t=məT tə s=yá·ys(-s)//, /'*He's good at his work., He's good at that work.*'/.

<**schechwétiyethel**>, stvi //s=cə[=C_1ə=]wá[=Aə=]t=iyəθəl//, LANG ['*fluent (at speaking)*'], (<**s=**> *stative*), (<**=R1= (here =che=)**> *continuative with stative*, derivational ablaut (here =**é**=)(further meaning unknown)), lx <**=iyethel**> *in the jaw, in speaking*, phonology: reduplication, syntactic analysis: participle, stvi, attested by AD.

<**chewő́:lhp**>, dnom //c[=əC_2=]ə́w=(ə)ɬp//, EB ['*black cottonwood tree*'], ['*Populus balsamifera trichocarpa*'], *see* chew ~ cháw

<**Chewő́:lhp**>, dnom //cəw=ə́w=ɬp//, PLN ['*Cottonwood Beach (in the southern quarter of Harrison Lake)*'], *see* chew ~ cháw

<**-chexw ~ -chxw**>, is, //**-c-əx^w ~ -c-x^w**//, PRON /'*you (sg.) (subject of an independent clause), second peron sg.*'/, (<**-ch**> *subject of an independent clause*), phonology: <**-chxw**> is used in more rapid pronunciation, syntactic analysis: is, example: <**ő́wechxw swiyeqáxw, qe xixpó:mchexw**>, //ʔə́wə-c-

x^w s=wíyəqə-ɛ́x^w, qə C_1í=x^yá·p[-M1-]=əm-c-əx^w//, /'*You're not a man, but you're whistling (with pursed lips).*'/, phonology: methathesis, reduplication, syntactic analysis: vneg-independent clause subject pronoun-2ssj nominal=root-2ssbsj conjunction dim-root[-ctv-]=middle voice-independent clause subject pronoun-2ssj, literally /'are not-subj.-you sg. be a man-you sg. but dim.-whistle-contin.=middle voice (to oneself)-subj.-you sg.'/, usage: This is a proverb or saying to a young girl around puberty to stop her from whistling., attested by MV.

<**chexw**>, bound root, meaning unknown

<**schéxwem**>, dnom //s=cə́x^w=əm//, WETH ['*west wind*'], syntactic analysis: nominal, attested by BJ, numerous other elders, WETH /'*south wind, warm wind*'/, attested by Deming.

<**chée̲xtemet**>, [čʌ́x̣tʌmʌt], 'ask for s.t.', attested by (EH,RG 7/23/99) (SU transcription, tape 2); <*cháchex̲temet>, [čǽčʌx̣tʌmʌt], *'asking for s.t.' rejected by EH,RG 7/23/99 (SU transcription, tape 2)

<**chhémkw'**>, ctv //c=hə́-m ək'^{w}//, MC /'*finding things*'/, *see* mékw'.

<**chichelóqtel**>, pcrs //C_1í=cá=lə[=M2=]q=T-əl//, dms, TVMO ['*walking single-file*'], *see* chá:l or chó:l

<**chichelót**>, cts //C_1í=cá(=)l-ə[=M2=]T//, pcs, dms, TVMO /'*running after s-o, running after s-th*'/, *see* chá:l or chó:l

<**chíchelh**>, cts //cí[=C_1ə=]ɬ//, DESC /'*be above, be high, top, up above, way high*'/, *see* chílh

<**Chíchelh Siyá:m ~ Chíchelh Siyám**>, npc //cí[=C_1ə=]ɬ siyɛ́·m ~ cí[=C_1ə=]ɬ siyɛ́m//, CH /'*God, the Lord*'/, REL, literally /'high respected leader, respected leader above, chief (way) above, chief up high'/, *see* chílh

<**chíchelh téméxw**>, npc //cí[=C_1ə=]ɬ tə́mə́x^w//, CH ['*heaven*'], literally /'high land, land way above'/, *see* chílh

<**chichewós**>, dms //C_1í=cəw=ás//, LAND /'*sit facing a river and watch it, sit on a riverbank and sunbathe*'/, *see* chew ~ cháw

<**chichewóthel**>, dms //C_1í=cəw=áθəl//, LAND ['*a little below the mouth of a creek or slough*'], *see* chew ~ cháw

<**chíchex̲em**>, mdls //cí[=C_1ə=]x̣=əm//, SENS, TAST /'*bitter, rancid*'/, *see* chíx̲em

<**chíkmel**>, us //cíkməl//, LAND /'*iron (the metal), silver*'/, borrowed from Chinook Jargon *chickamin* iron, silver, metal of all kinds, syntactic analysis: nominal, adjective/adjectival verb, also <**chí:kmal**>, //cí·kmɛl//, attested by BJ, /'*iron (the metal)*'/, example: <**chíkmel tále**>, //cíkməl tɛ́lə//, /'*silver money*'/, literally /'iron money, silver money'/, <**kw'óqwet te chíkmel**>, //k'^{w}áq^w=əT tə cíkməl//, /'*use a telephone, to phone*'/, literally /'club the iron'/, (semological comment: idiom (morphosememic shifts)).

<**chílh**>, bound root //cíɬ//, DESC /'*high, upper, above*'/.

<**schí:lh**>, dnom //s=cí·ɬ//, SOC ['*first-born*'], KIN, syntactic analysis: nominal, adjective/adjectival verb, attested by AC.

<**chíchelh**>, cts //cí[=C_1ə=]ɬ//, DESC /'*be above, be high, top, up above, way high*'/, (<**=R1=**> *continuative* in a derivational use), phonology: reduplication, syntactic analysis: adjective/adjectival verb, example: <**chíchelh smá:lt**>, //cí[=C_1ə=]ɬ s=mɛ́·lt//, /'*high mountain*'/, attested by AC, <**le xwe chíchelh te qó:**>, //lə x^wə cí[=C_1ə=]ɬ tə qá·//, /'*The water is high.*'/, attested by CT, <**kw'e chíchelh**>, //k'^{w}ə cí[=C_1ə=]ɬ//, /'*the sky*'/, literally /'the (remote, distant, abstract) above'/, dialects: EB; others use swàyèl *day* also for *sky*.

<**Chíchelh Siyá:m ~ Chíchelh Siyám**>, npc //cí[=C_1ə=]ɬ siyɛ́·m ~ cí[=C_1ə=]ɬ siyɛ́m//, CH /'*God, the Lord*'/, REL, literally /'high respected leader, respected leader above, chief (way) above, chief up high'/.

<**swáyels te Chíchelh Siyám**>, npc //s=wɛ́yəl-s tə cí[=C_1ə=]ɬ siyɛ́m//, CH ['*Christmas day*'], TIME, literally /'the day of the Lord'/.

<**lúwe ts'ít te Chíchelh Siyám**>, npc //lə́wə c'í=T tə cí[=C_1ə=]ɬ siyɛ́m//, CH /'*It's you to thank the Lord, (Please say grace)*'/, syntactic analysis: sentence with verb phrase in apposition, attested by Deming.

<**chíchelh téméxw**>, npc //cí[=C_1ə=]ɬ tə́mə́x^{w}//, CH ['*heaven*'], literally /'high land, land way above'/, attested by EB, AC, NP, Deming.

<**schelhá:liya**>, dnom //s=cəɬ=ɛ́·liyɛ//, ANA ['*top of the ear*'], lx <**=á:liya**> *on the ear*, syntactic analysis: nominal, attested by IHTTC.

<**tslháltxw**>, dnom //cíɬ=ɛ́ltx^{w}//, BLDG /'*upper part or top of a house, upper part or top of a pit-house*'/, lx <**=áltxw**> *house, building*, syntactic analysis: nominal.

<**chílheqw**>, ds //cíɬ=əq^{w}//, ANA ['*(have) bushy and uncombed hair, "bed hair"*'], literally /'high hair'/, lx <**=eqw**> *on top of the head, (in the) hair*, syntactic analysis: probably adjective/adjectival verb, intransitive verb, example: <**chílheqw st'á kw'e x̲eyímelets**>, //cíɬ=əq^{w} s=t'ɛ́ k'^{w}ə x̲əy(=)ím=ələc//, /'*(he/she has) messy hair like floating tree roots*'/.

<**tslhítselxel**>, dnom //cíɬ=ícəl=x^{y}əl//, ANA ['*top of the foot*'], lx <**=ítsel**> *on the back*, lx <**=xel**> *on the foot, on the leg*, syntactic analysis: nominal.

<**chlhíth'a**>, dnom //cíɬ=íθ'ɛ//, CLO /'*upper clothing, clothing on upper half of the body*'/, lx <**=íth'a**> *clothing*, syntactic analysis: nominal, also <**chelhíth'a**>.

<**chélhmel**>, ds //cí[=Aə́=]ɬ=məl//, BLDG ['*on top of the house*'], (<**é-ablaut**> *derivational*), lx <**=mel**> part of a house, portion of a house, syntactic analysis: intransitive verb, possibly also nominal.

<**chelhó:lemelh**>, dnom //cíɬ=á·ləməɬ//, ANA /'*upper circle over the eye,* (probably) *upper eyelid*'/, lx <**=ó:lemelh**> *on the eyelid?,* syntactic analysis: nominal, attested by IHTTC.

<**schelhó:les**>, dnom //s=cíɬ=á·ləs//, ANA /'*upper circle over the eye,* (probably) *upper eyelid*'/, lx <**=ó:les**> *on the eye*, syntactic analysis: nominal, attested by IHTTC.

<**schelhóyethel**>, dnom //s=cíɬ=áyəθəl//, ANA ['*upper lip*'], lx <**=óyethel**> *on the lip, on the jaw or mouth,* syntactic analysis: nominal, attested by AC, other source: ES /scɬá·yθəl/, JH /scɬáyθəl/, H-T <stlEtláitsEl>.

<**chélhqel**>, ds //cí[=Aə́=]ɬ=qəl//, ANA ['*(have a) high voice*'], LANG, (<**é-ablaut**> *derivational*), lx <**=qel**> *in the throat, in the voice, in the inside of the mouth, language*, syntactic analysis: probably intransitive verb, possibly nominal, attested by IHTTC.

<**chelhqí:l ~ chelhqéyl**>, ds //cíɬ=qəl=í·l or cíɬ=qə[=Aí·=]l//, ANA /'*roof of the mouth, inside of upper lip, palate*'/, lx <**=qel**> *in the inside of the mouth, in the throat*, syntactic analysis: nominal, attested by BHTTC: Chill., IHTTC, also <**chélhqel**>, //cə́ɬqəl//, attested by BHTTC: Tait.

<**stselhsó:lwelh**>, ds //s=cíɬ=s=á·lwəɬ//, DIR /'*over, in the air over, above*'/, (prob. <**s=**> *stative*), lx <**=s**> uncertain**,** <**=ó:lwelh**> *side, -ward*, syntactic analysis: preposition/prepositional verb, attested by EB.

<**chálhtel**>, df //cíɬ=ʔɛ́ɬtəl//, FSH ['*hang fish (especially salmon) for drying*'], FOOD, (most likely a blend-word with <**chílh**> *be high* and <**á**lhtel> *eat a meal, food*), syntactic analysis: intransitive verb, attested by RP, EB.

<**chalhteláwtxw**>, dnom //cíɬ=ʔɛ́ɬtəl=ɛ́wtxʷ//, BLDG [*'fish smokehouse'*], FSH, lx <**=áwtxw**> *building, house*, syntactic analysis: nominal; found in <**chalhteláwtxws**>, //cɛɬtəlɛ́wtxʷ-s//, /*'his smokehouse'*/, ASM ['an outbuilding with tall walls in which raw specially-trimmed fish is hung over racks over a smoking fire to smoke-cure the fish'].

<**chá:lhtel**>, cts //probably cíɬ=ʔɛ[-·-] ́ɬtəl//, FSH /*'smoking salmon, (hanging fish up to smoke)'*/, FOOD, (probably <**-:-**> *continuative*), syntactic analysis: intransitive verb, attested by EB.

<**schá:lhtel ~ stsá:lhtel**>, dnom //probably s=cíɬ=ʔɛ[-·-] ́ɬtəl//, FSH [*'dried fish'*], FOOD, (<**s=**> *nominalizer*), syntactic analysis: nominal, attested by AC, DM, other source: ES /scɛ́·ɬtəl/, example: <**lí qéx̱ ta stsá:lhtel**>, //lí qə́x̣ t-ɛ s=cɛ́·ɬtəl//, /*'Do you have a lot of dried fish?'*/, attested by AC.

<**temchálhtel**>, ds //təm=cíɬ=ʔɛ́ɬtəl//, [tɪmčǽɬtəl], TIME /*'time to dry fish, first of July (at Yale), October (at Chehalis)'*/, FSH, FOOD, ASM ['first of July'], semantic environment ['at Yale: TIME, FSH, FOOD'], ASM ['October'], semantic environment ['at Chehalis: TIME, FSH, FOOD'], (<**tem=**> *time for, season to*), syntactic analysis: probably nominal.

<**chachí:lhtel ~ chachíyelhtel**>, pls possibly //C_1ɛ-cíɬ=ʔɛ[-Aí·-]ɬtəl//, FSH [*'hanging lots of fish to dry'*], (possibly <**R8-**> *plural,* possibly <**í:-ablaut**> *continuative*), phonology: reduplication, syntactic analysis: intransitive verb, attested by RP, EB, also <**chaché:yelhtel**>, //cɛcɛ́·yəɬtəl ~ cɛcí·ɬtəl//, FSH [*'fish ready for drying'*], syntactic analysis: possibly nominal, probably intransitive verb, attested by DM.

<**chílheqw**>, ds //cíɬ=əqʷ//, ANA [*'(have) bushy and uncombed hair, "bed hair"'*], literally /'high hair'/, *see* chílh

<**chím ~ chí:m**>, ds //cɛ́m=í·m//, TVMO [*'to pack'*], *see* chám

<**chí:s** (or) **tl'éxw ts'íyxw sqemó:**>, nom., np, FOOD *cheese* (lit. cheese or hard + dry + milk), (attested by RG,EH 6/16/98 to SN, edited by BG with RG,EH 6/26/00)

<**chítmexw**>, ds possibly //cít=məxʷ//, EZ /*'horned owl, great horned owl'*/, [*'Bubo virginianus occidentalis, Bubo virginianus saturatus,* and perhaps other *Bubo virginianus* subspecies; possibly also the following other horned owls found in the area: long-eared owl *Asio otus* and spotted owl *Strix occidentalis*'], ASM ['owls cover one's mouth if they catch one person in the woods; owls can predict the future'], PLAY [*'name of a cat's-cradle pattern (lit. horned owl)'*], ASM, lx possibly <**=mexw**> *person*, syntactic analysis: nominal, also <**chí:tmexw ~ chítmexw**>, attested by AC, IHTTC, other source: ES, JH /cí·tməxʷ/.

<**Chítmexw**>, ds //cít(=)məxʷ//, PLN /*'horned owl-shaped rock (beside Spá:th, a bear-shaped rock) up on a cliff on the south side above Echo Point bay on Echo Island in Harrison Lake'*/, syntactic analysis: nominal, attested by EL.

<**chiwt**>, possible bound root or stem //ciw(=)t//, meaning unknown

<**schiwtálh**>, dnom //s=ciwt=ɛ́ɬ//, KIN /*'child's spouse, son-in-law, daughter-in-law, (man's) sister's husband'*/, lx <**=álh**> *child, offspring*, syntactic analysis: nominal, KIN /*'son-in-law, daughter-in-law'*/, attested by AC, KIN /*'sister's husband, daughter's husband'*/, other source: ES /scutɛ́ɬ/ *child's spouse, man's sister's husband*; H-T <tsútatl>(macron over u) *sister's husband.*

<**schí:wetálh**>, pls //s=ci[- ́·-]wt=ɛ́ɬ//, KIN /*'sons-in-law, daughters-in-law, children's spouses'*/, (<- ́:-> *plural*), syntactic analysis: nominal, attested by AC.

<**=chíxw ~ chxw=**>, bound root //=cíxʷ ~ cxʷ=//, ABDF [*'to swell (of a body part)'*].

<**chxwélqsel**>, ds //cxʷ=ə́lqsəl//, ABDF [*'(have a) swollen nose'*], lx <**=elqsel**> *on the nose*, syntactic analysis: intransitive verb, attested by Deming.

<**schxwó:les**>, stvi //s=cxʷ=á·ləs//, ABDF /'*(be) swollen on the eye, (have a) swollen eye*'/, lx <**=ó:les**> *on the eye, around the eye, on the eyelid*, syntactic analysis: intransitive verb, attested by Deming.

<**chechíxw**>, rsls //C_1ə=cíxʷ//, ABDF ['*(be) swollen*'], (<**R5=**> plus <**í-ablaut**> of root <**é**> *resultative*), phonology: reduplication, syntactic analysis: intransitive verb, attested by AC.

<**chxwétem**>, ds //cxʷ=ə́t=əm (or) cxʷə́=təm//, ABDF /'*be swollen, swelled up (EB), swelling (AC)*'/, ASM, semantic environment ['infected sore, bloated dead animal unbled, balloon, perhaps others (all given by AC)'], (possibly <**=et**> *purposeful control transitivizer* + stress-shift *resultative* + <=em> *intransitivizer* (or) <=tem> *participial*), syntactic analysis: participle, attested by AC, EB, JL, NP, Deming, other source: ES /cxʷə́təm/ *swell*, example: <**chxwétem te s'ó:thes**>, //cxʷə́təm tə s=ʔá·θ=əs//, /'*The face is swollen.*'/, attested by Deming, JL, NP.

<**chíxem**>, bound root //cíx̣=əm//, SENS, TAST /'*bitter, rancid*'/, Salish cognate: Lushootseed /číx̣əm/ rancid Bates, Hess & Hilbert 1994:66.

<**chíchexem**>, mdls //cí[=C_1ə=]x̣=əm//, SENS, TAST /'*bitter, rancid*'/, ASM ['bitter'], semantic environment ['of dried fish or anything'], ASM ['rancid'], semantic environment ['of butter or other oily things'], (<**=R1=**> *continuative, participial*), (<**=em**> *middle voice*), phonology: reduplication, syntactic analysis: Vaj, attested by BHTTC.

<**chxí:mthet**>, incs //cíx̣[=M1]=əm=θət//, SENS, TAST /'*got rancid, got bitter*'/, (<**=metathesis type 1**> (switches preceding consonant and vowel) *completive*, <**=em**> *middle voice*, <**=thet**> *get, become, inceptive*, phonology: metathesis, vowel merger (íe /íə/ → í: /í·/), syntactic analysis: intransitive verb.

<**Chechíxem**> possibly, ds probably //C_1ə=cíx̣=əm//, PLN ['*Depot Creek (off upper Chilliwack River)*'], (probably <**R5=**> (here <**che=**>) possibly *continuative, diminutive, plural* or *diminutive plural*, <**=em**> possibly *place of* or =em *intransitivizer* or *middle voice*), phonology: reduplication, source: Wells 1966,

<**chí:ya**>, bound root //cí·yɛ//, meaning unknown

<**schí:ya**>, dnom //s=cí·yɛ//, EB ['*wild strawberry*'], ACL ['*domestic strawberry*'], ['*Fragaria vesca, Fragaria virginiana*'], ASM ['berries ripen in May and June; leaf tea is good'], MED ['plant is used for diarrhea medicine'], (<**s=**> *nominalizer*), syntactic analysis: nominal, attested by AC, BJ, many others, other source: ES /scí·yɛ/, example: <**schíya sqe'óleqw**>, FOOD *strawberry juice* (lit. strawberry + fruit juice), (attested by RG,EH 6/16/98 to SN, edited by BG with RG,EH 6/26/00)

<**schí:yà:lhp**>, dnom //s=cí·yɛ=əɬp//, EB /'*strawberry vine, strawberry plant, strawberry patch*'/, lx <**=elhp**> *plant, tree*, phonology: vowel merger, syntactic analysis: nominal, dialects: *Chill., Cheh., Tait*, attested by AC, IHTTC, also <**chí:yà:lhp**>, dialects: *Tait: SP,* perhaps *others*, example: <**ílhtsel lí kwthe schí:yà:lhp**>, //ʔí-ɬ-c-əl lí kʷ-θ-ə s=cí·yɛ=əɬp//, /'*I was at the strawberry patch.*'/.

<**schíyeláxel**>, ds //s=cíyɛ=əlɛ́x̣əl//, ANAH ['*strawberry birthmark on the arm*'], ASM ['so named because of the strawberry color of the mark'], lx <**=eláxel**> *on the arm*, syntactic analysis: nominal or possibly stvi, attested by NP.

<**xwchí:yò:m**>, dnom //xʷ=chí·yɛ=əm//, PLN /'*Cheam Island (my name for an island in the Fraser River across from Cheam Indian Reserve #2), Cheam village, Cheam Indian Reserve #1*'/, ASM ['the island I'm calling Cheam Island is unnamed on the maps; LJ pointed it out upstream from the Agassiz-Rosedale bridge; it was the first place to be named for the strawberries and was full of wild strawberries many years ago; the island was planted with trees to be harvested some years ago; there may be some strawberries left; it is now a small and long island more like a gravel bar with some trees on it; the village got its name from the island; then the Indian Reserve got its name from the village; Mt. Cheam was named in English after the village but actually in Halkomelem has an

entirely different name, Lhílheqey.'], lx <**xw=**> *always*, lx <**=em**> *place where, (place) to get*, syntactic analysis: nominal, attested by Tait: LJ, phonology: vowel merger, syntactic analysis: nominal, other source: place name reference file #60, also <**Shxwchí:yò:m**>, //s=x^{w}=cí·yɛ=əm//, literally /'place to pick strawberries'/, attested by SP, also <**Lexwchíyò:m**>, //ləx^{w}=cí·yɛ=əm//, literally /'where wild strawberries grow'/, lx <**lexw=**> *always*, lx <**a free variant with xw=**, attested by Pilalt: HE, ASM ['Cheam village was originally not up on the hill where Cheam I.R. #1 is now; Harry Edwards' (HE's) parents were the first to move up there and were there when the missionaries came (ca 1860)'], also <**Chí:yò:m**>, //cí·yɛ=əm//, literally /'wild strawberry patch'/, attested by DM.

<**chiyólh**>, [čiyáɬ], 'go out and get wood', *see* yolh.

<**chí'**>, us //ciʔ//, EZ /'*something scary, monster*'/, usage: slang, phonology: final glottal stop is unusual for these dialects, syntactic analysis: nominal, attested by BHTTC, also <**schichí'**>, //s=C_1í=cíʔ//, (<**s=**> *nominalizer*), lx possibly <**R4=**> *diminutive*, phonology: reduplication, attested by BHTTC, example: <**Don't go out there, the schichí' will get you.**>, usage: one elder used this with her children or grandchildren (who don't speak Halkomelem); code-switching, also <**schí'**>, //s=cíʔ//, (<**s=**> *nominalizer*), attested by Deming.

<**chlhíth'a**>, dnom //cíɬ=íθ'ɛ//, CLO /'*upper clothing, clothing on upper half of the body*'/, *see* chílh

<**chmà:m**>, cts //cɛ́m-M1·\`=əm (or cɛ́m=ə[-M1·\`-]m)//, TVMO /'*carrying on one's back, packing on one's back*'/, *see* chám

<**chmaméleqw**>, cts //cɛ́m-M1=əm=ə́ləq^{w}//, TVMO ['*carry[ing] a packstrap around the head*'], *see* chám

<**chmá:t**>, cts //cɛ́m-M1´·-əT//, TVMO /'*carrying s-th/s-o on one's back, packing it on one's back*'/, *see* chám

<**chmékw'**>, //c=mék'^{w}//, MC /'*find*'/, *see* mékw'.

<**chóchekw**>, cpvs possibly //cá[=C_1ə=]k^{w}//, DIR ['*(being far?)*'], *see* chó:kw

<**chochí:lt**>, cts //cɛ́[=Aa=][-C_1ə-]·l-í·l-t//, TVMO ['*go following s-o*'], *see* chá:l or chó:l

<**chochkwó:les**>, dnom //cá[=C_1ə=]k^{w}=á·ləs//, EB ['*goatsbeard*'], ['*Aruncus sylvester*'], *see* chó:kw

<**chó:kw**>, free root //cá·k^{w}//, DIR /'*far, be far away, far off, way in the distance*'/, syntactic analysis: adverb/adverbial verb, attested by EB, BJ, AC, others, other source: ES, JH /cá·k^{w}/, also <**chókw**>, //cák^{w}//, attested by AC, EB, others, example: <**lí: chókw**>, //lí-ə cák^{w}//, phonology: by a regular morphophonemic rule a stressed full vowel + schwa (here *interrogative, yes/no question* suffix -e /-ə/) → the full vowel + length, /'*Is it far?*'/, attested by AC, <**lí te chókw**>, //lí tə cák^{w}//, /'*It's far away., It's there (distant).*'/, attested by AC, EB, usage: this would be the answer to the question in the example just previous, <**lí(:) chòkw te lálems qa (~ q'a) lí: stetís**>, //lí-ə cák^{w} tə lɛ́ləm-s qɛ (~ q'ɛ) lí-ə s=C_1ə=tə́[=Aí=]s//, /'*Is his house far or is it nearby?*'/, phonology: sentence-stress changes the stress from <**chókw**> to <**chòkw**> after stressed interrogative <**lí(:)**>; length on <**lí**> is dropped in allegro speech; in slow pronunciations by AC <**lí**> is attested as <**líye**>, showing the <**-e**> *yes/no question* suffix.

<**chóchekw**>, cpvs possibly //cá[=C_1ə=]k^{w}//, DIR ['*(being far?)*'], possibly <**=R1=**> *continuative*, phonology: reduplication, example: <**ley xwchóchekw ~ ley kw'e chóchekw**>, possibly //lɛ x^{w}=cá[=C_1ə=]k^{w} ~ lɛ k'^{w}ə cá[=C_1ə=]k^{w}//, Elder's comment: "speakers are unsure about the form of this sentence", /'*It's going farther.*'/.

<**chochkwó:les**>, dnom //cá[=C_1ə=]k^{w}=á·ləs//, EB ['*goatsbeard*'], ['*Aruncus sylvester*'], ASM ['a plant with white blooms in June which can be seen from far away, thus its name, literally *farther*

in the eyes or *far away in the eyes*'], MED ['used as eye medicine'], (<**=R1=**> *continuative*), lx <**=ó:les**> *in the eyes*, phonology: reduplication, syntactic analysis: nominal, attested by SP, AD.

<**telchókw**>, ds //təl=cákʷ//, DIR ['*from far away*'], lx <**tel=**> *from*, syntactic analysis: adverb/adverbial verb, attested by BHTTC.

<**chekwílem**>, mdls //cákʷ=íl-əm//, incs, TVMO ['*go far away*'], DIR, lx <**=íl**> *go, come, get, become, inceptive*, (<**-em**> *middle voice*), syntactic analysis: intransitive verb, example: <**éwechexw we'ol chekwílem**>, //ʔə́wə-c-əxʷ wə-ʔal cəkʷ=íl-əm//, /'*Don't go too far (away).*'/, literally /'don't-you contrast-just/too far=go-oneself'/.

<**xwetskwí:lem**>, incs //xʷə=cákʷ=í·l-əm//, TVMO ['*(go) far away*'], DIR, lx <**xwe=**> *go, come*, syntactic analysis: intransitive verb, attested by AC.

<**chokwí:lt**>, pcs //cákʷ=í·l=T//, TVMO /'*follow behind s-o, trail s-o*'/, DIR, lx <**=í:l**> *go, come, get, become*, (<**-t**> *purposeful control transitivizer*), syntactic analysis: transitive verb, attested by IHTTC, also <**chokwú:lt**>, //cákʷ=í[=Aú=]·l=T//, dialects: *Chill., Tait: Peters and Lorenzetto families on Peters Reserve or Squatits Reserve (Skw'átets)*, attested by AC, JL, MJ; found in <**chokwí:lthóxes**>, //cákʷ=í·l=T-áxʸ-əs//, /'*He followed me.*'/, also <**chokwú:lthóxes**>, //cákʷ=í[=Aú=]·l=T-áxʸ-əs//, dialects: *Chill., Tait: Peters and Lorenzetto families at Skw'átets*, attested by IHTTC.

<**chokwú:lt**>, cts //cákʷ=í[-Aú-]·l=T//, TVMO ['*following s-o*'], DIR, (<**ú-ablaut**> *continuative*), syntactic analysis: transitive verb, dialects: *Chill., Tait: Peters and Lorenzetto families at Skw'átets*; found in <**chokwú:ltes**>, //cákʷ=í[-Aú-]·l=T-əs//, /'*He was following it*'/, attested by AC, <**chokwú:lthóxes**>, //cákʷ=í[-Aú-]·l=T-áxʸ-əs//, /'*He's following me.*'/, attested by Elders 3/15/72 (prob. JL), <**chokwú:lthòme**>, //cákʷ=í[-Aú-]·l=T-àmə//, /'*chasing after me (following me, trailing me)*'/.

<**chokwelélqem**>, ds //cákʷ=əl=ə́ləq=əm//, HUNT ['*tracking an animal*'], DIR, lx <**=el**> *go, come, get, become, inceptive*, lx <**=eleq**> *occupational*, lx <**=em**> *middle voice or intransitivizer*, syntactic analysis: intransitive verb, attested by IHTTC, TVMO /'*follow after, coming behind (the one ahead knows)*'/, attested by EB.

<**chokwelélqem**>, ds //cákʷ=əl=ə́ləq=əm//, HUNT ['*tracking an animal*'], *see* chó:kw

<**chókwelhta (or chókwellhta)**>, cts //cá[-kʷə-]ɬ=tɛ//, SOC ['*borrowing*'], root <**chélhta**> *lend, let s-o borrow* with <-R1-> reduplication *continuative* except with <**kw**> replacing the <**ch**> (consonant ablaut (-Akw-) or replacement--this is attested in Musqueam, and Upriver also since when <x> is reduplicated in <-R1-> it is sometimes done with <xw> replacing the <x> (also consonant ablaut)), syntactic analysis: intransitive verb, attested by EB, AC; found in <**chókwelhtatsel**>, //cákʷəɬtɛ-c-əl//, /'*I'm borrowing.*'/, *see* chélhta.

<**chokwí:lt**>, pcs //cákʷ=í·l=T//, TVMO /'*follow behind s-o, trail s-o*'/, *see* chó:kw

<**chokwú:lt**>, cts //cákʷ=í[-Aú-]·l=T//, TVMO ['*following s-o*'], *see* chó:kw

<**chó:leqw**>, us //possibly cá·(=ə)l=əqʷ//, DIR /'*in the backwoods, toward the woods, away from the river, in the bush*'/, *see* chá:l or chó:l

<**chóleqwmel**>, ds //cá(=)l=əqʷ=məl//, DIR /'*part away from the river, side away from the river*'/, *see* chá:l or chó:l

<**choléxwem**>, mdls //calə́xʷ=əm//, ABFC ['*bleed*'], syntactic analysis: intransitive verb, also <**tsoléxwem**>, //calə́xʷ=əm//, attested by RP, also <**choléx̱wem**>, //calə́x̣ʷ=əm//, attested by AC.

<**chó:lxwem**>, cts //ca[-´·-]lə́xʷ=əm//, ABFC ['*bleeding*'], (<**stress-shift and lengthening**> *continuative*), phonology: stress-shift, lengthening, syntactic analysis: intransitive verb, also <**tsó:lxwem**>, //cá[-´·-]lə́xʷ=əm//, attested by RP, others.

<**scholéx̱wem**>, dnom //s=calə́x̣ʷ=əm//, ANA ['*blood*'], ABFC, syntactic analysis: nominal, attested by AC, example: <**qéx̱ scholéx̱wem**>, //qə́x̣ s=calə́x̣ʷ=əm//, /'*a lot of blood*'/, attested by AC.

<**chólmelelh tl'álhem**>, FOOD *soy sauce* (lit. Chinese style + salt), *see* chá:lmel

<**chó:lqem**>, mdls //cɛ́[=Aa=]·l=q=əm or cá(·)=əl=(ələ)q=əm//, TVMO /'*follow, follow along after (the one ahead knows)*'/, *see* chá:l ~ chó:l.

<**chó:lt**>, pcs //cɛ́[=Aa=]·l=T or cá(·)=əl=T//, TVMO /'*follow s-th/s-o (on foot, in a car, or on a horse, for ex.), follow behind s-o*'/, *see* chá:l ~ chó:l.

<**chó:lxwem**>, cts //ca[-´·-]lə́xʷ=əm//, ABFC ['*bleeding*'], *see* choléxwem

<**chó:m**>, izs possibly //cá·=əm or cá=əm//, DIR ['*go away from the river*'], WATR, LAND, TVMO, (possibly <**=em**> *intransitivizer*), syntactic analysis: intransitive verb, attested by BHTTC, also <**chóm**>, attested by BHTTC.

<**chémlexw ~ chemléxw**>, ncs //cá[=Aə́=]m=l-əxʷ ~ cá(=)m=l-ə[=´=]xʷ//, SOC ['*elope with s-o or meet up with s-o*'], TVMO, KIN, literally possibly /'manage to get s-o away from the river'/, (<**é-ablaut** or **stress-shift**> *derivational*), (<**=l**> *non-control transitivizer, happen to, accidentally, manage to*), (<**-exw**> *3oj (3rd person object)*), phonology: ablaut or stress-shift, syntactic analysis: transitive verb, example: <**le chemléxwes**>, //lə cá(=)m=l-ə[=´=]xʷ-əs//, /'*He met up with her.*'/.

<**chó:mtel**>, pcrs //cá·(=)m=T=əl//, KIN /'*elope, run away together*'/, TVMO, (<**=t**> *purposeful control transitivizer*, <**=el**> *reflexive*), syntactic analysis: transitive verb=reflexive, (semological comment: the reflexive here appears derivational rather tian inflectional as the meaning is more than just 'get each other away from the river'; the elopement implication is present perhaps because most dwellings or villages were located on a river), literally /'get each other away from the river purposely'/, example: <**le chemléxwes the q'é:mi qesu le chó:mtel**>, //lə cá(=)m=l-ə[=´=]xʷ-əs θə q'ɛ́·mi qə-s-əw lə cá·(=)m=T=əl//, /'*He met up with the (adolescent virgin) girl and they eloped (or ran away together).*'/.

<**xwchém:és**>, ds //xʷ=cá[=Aə́=](=)m[=·]=əs//, TVMO ['*they met*'], (<**xw=**> (meaning uncertain here, perhaps *go, come, get, become*) but often found with suffix <**=es**>), (<**é-ablaut**> *derivational*), (<**=:**> (meaning uncertain here), <**=es**> *face, on the face*, perhaps here *face-to-face*), syntactic analysis: intransitive verb, attested by EB.

<**xwchém:est**>, pcs //xʷ=cá[=Aə́=]m[=·]=əs=T//, TVMO ['*meet s-o*'], (<**-t**> *purposeful control transitivizer*), syntactic analysis: transitive verb, attested by EB, Salish cognate: Squamish /čə́mʔ-us/ '*meet, come together, double*' and /čə-čmʔ-ús-n/ '*meet (transitive)*' (no meaning is suggested for the Squamish -ús on this word) (W73, K67), example: <**le xwchém:estes te stó:les**>, //lə xʷcə́m·əs=T-əs tə s=tá·ləs-s//, /'*He met his wife.*'/, attested by EB, *<**xwchém:és tútl'o te stó:les**> rejected.<**chóxw**>, us //cáxʷ// (or possibly // cá=xʷ//? with root as in //cá·m, cá·kʷ//, etc.)//, TVMO ['*go down to the river*'], WATR, lx possibly <**=xw**>, unattested elsewhere; it would have to have a meaning of *negative* which seems unlikely, syntactic analysis: intransitive verb, attested by BHTTC.

<**chó:mtel**>, pcrs //cá·(=)m=T=əl//, KIN /'*elope, run away together*'/, *see* chó:m

<**Chowéthel**>, dnom //cəw=á[=M2´=]θəl//, PLN /'*village at what's now Katz Reserve, Katz Landing*'/, literally /'beach at the mouth (of a creek)'/, *see* chew ~ cháw

<**chóxwxel**>, dnom //cáx^w=x^{y}əl//, CLO /'*cloth or warm material to wrap around the foot, stockings*'/, ASM ['stockings'], ACL, semantic environment ['post-contact times, acculturated dress'], lx <**=xel**> *on the leg, on the foot*, syntactic analysis: nominal.

<**chó:ythet**>, incs //cá·y=θət//, WETH /'*get quiet (of wind), stop (of wind)*'/, semantic environment ['wind'], lx <**=thet**> *become, get*, syntactic analysis: intransitive verb, attested by AD,

<**chő:wqwela**>, dnom //có·wq^w=əlɛ//, EZ ['*Canada lynx*'], Elder's comment: "a big white cat about a foot and a half long that is found on the highest mountains", ['*Lynx canadensis canadensis*'], lx probably <**=ela**> *on the side of the head, by the ears* (since they have a tuft of hair there), syntactic analysis: nominal, attested by Jimmy Peters of Katz Reserve, also <**thő:qwela**>, //θó·q^w=əlɛ//, attested by JL.

<**chqwáléqep**>, ds //cq^w=ɛ́lə́qəp//, SENS, SD /'*be loud in sound, a loud sound (?)*'/, lx <**=áléqep**> *sound, in sound*, syntactic analysis: probably adjective/adjectival verb, example: <**mí xwe chqwáléqep**>, //mí x^{w}ə cq^w=ɛ́lə́qəp//, /'*sound getting louder*'/.

<**chth'éylem**>, incs //cθ'=íl=əm//, mdls, FSH ['*spearing sqwéx̲em (silver spring salmon) in clear water after waiting for them*'], (<**=íl**> *come, go, get, become, inceptive*, <=em> *middle voice*), syntactic analysis: intransitive verb, attested by EL.

<**Chth'éylem**>, dnom //cθ'=íl=əm//, PLN ['*a point or bald hill on Harrison River where people waited to spear silver spring salmon*'], phonology: zero derivation, syntactic analysis: nominal, attested by EL,

<**chúchu ~ chúwchuw ~ chéwchew**>, ds //cə́w=C_1əC_2//, LAND /'*away from the shore, toward the river*'/, *see* chew ~ cháw

<**Chuchuwálets**>, dnom //cəw=C_1əC_2=ɛ́ləc (or possibly? C_1əC_2=cəwɛ́=ləc)//, PLN /'*Fraser River (way out at the end), mouth of the Fraser River*'/, *see* chew ~ cháw

<**chuchuwáx̲el**>, dnom //cəw=C_1əC_2=ɛ́x̣əl//, BLDG ['*front end of a house (inside or outside)*'], *see* chew ~ cháw

<**chuchuwó:ythel**>, ds //cəw=C_1əC_2=á·yθəl//, WATR ['*out in the middle of the river*'], *see* chew ~ cháw

<**Chuwtí:l**>, PLN ['*another village of the Pilalt people*'], *see* chá**chew ~ chá**chu.

<**chxílche**>, [čx^{y}ílčʌ], '*catch a fish*', *see* xélcha.

<**chxólcho**>, [čx^{y}álča], '*always catching fish*', *see* xélcha.

<**chxw= ~ =chíxw**>, bound root //=cíx^w ~ cx$^{w=}$//, ABDF ['*to swell (of a body part)*'], *see* chíxw.

<**-chxw ~ -chexw**>, //**-c-əx^w ~ -c-x^w**//, PRON /'*you (sg.) (subject of an independent clause), second peron sg.*'/, *see* -chexw.

<**chxwélmel**>, ds //cɛ́·x^w=ə́lməl//, SOC /'*want a wife, He wants a wife.*'/, *see* cháxw.

<**chxwélqsel**>, ds //cx^w=ə́lqsəl//, ABDF ['*(have a) swollen nose*'], *see* chixw

<**chxwétem**>, ds //cx^w=ə́t=əm (or) cx^{w}ə́=təm//, ABDF /'*be swollen, swelled up (EB), swelling (AC)*'/, *see* chixw.

<**chx̲í:mthet**>, incs //cíx̣[=M1]=əm=θ(=)ət//, SENS, TAST /'*got rancid, got bitter*'/, *see* chix̲

CH'

<**ch'**>, comment: The Stó:lō orthography uses both ch' ([č']) and ts' ([c']), for two allophones of a single
Upriver Halkomelem phoneme, /c'/. ts' occurs more frequently in initial position than ch', so for most forms look under ts' first. Those forms which have a frequent variant in ch' will also be found here. In Musqueam and Cowichan dialects of Halkomelem Wayne Suttles informs me that both /c/ and /č/ must be set up as phonemes (Suttles 1982 p.c.), contrary to Elmendorf and Suttles 1960; he did not mention both /c'/ and /č'/ being required. Kava 1969 and Jones 1976 both give /c/ and /č/, but Kava has only /c'/ while Jones sets up both /c'/ and /č'/ (the latter in only one root)., comment: Leslie 1979 has a very brief section on Cowichan phonology with four phonemes here, /c, č, c', č'/ but derives this analysis from Jones 1976 and Hukari 1977. None of these sources, however, contains a tabulation of the environments in which the four sounds [c, č, c', č'] occur. Galloway 1977 & 1993 do have such a tabulation and show that for Upriver Halkomelem [c] and [č] are allophones of /c/ and [c'] and [č'] are allophones of /c'/ all predictable in part from the environments in which they occur and in part in free variation.

<**ch'á: ~ ts'á:**>, bound root //c'ɛ́· *on top of*//, several derivations from this root are only attested with **ts'** pronunciations, all are listed under ts'; those given here show frequent **ch'** attestations.

<**ch'alech'á (~ ts'alets'á)**>, plv //C_1ɛ[=lə=]=c'ɛ́//, TVMO ['*they came on (top of)*'], (<**R8=**> *resultative*), (<**=le=**> *plural*), phonology: reduplication, infixed plural, syntactic analysis: intransitive verb, attested by AC, example: <**ch'alech'á te stiqíw.**>, //C_1ɛ[=lə=]=c'ɛ́ tə s=tiqíw//, /'*They came on a horse.*'/, attested by AC (8/28/70).

<**xwch'alech'á:ls**>, sas //x^w=C_1ɛ[=lə=]=c'ɛ́=ɛ́ls//, FOOD ['*put on the stove (water/food)*'], HHG, literally /'(towards) many things put on top of in a structured activity'/, <**xw=**> *towards*, (<**=á:ls**> *structured activity non-continuative*), phonology: reduplication, infixed plural, vowel merger, syntactic analysis: intransitive verb, attested by IHTTC (9/2/77).

<**shxwch'ech'áls**>, dnom //s(=)x^w=C_1əC_2=c'ɛ́=əls//, sas, cts, HHG ['*shelf*'], literally /'something for putting on top of in a structured activity'/, (<**shxw=**> *something for*), (<**R2=**> *continuative*), lx <**=els**> *structured activity continuative nominal/tool*, phonology: reduplication, vowel merger, syntactic analysis: nominal, attested by Elders Group (6/1/77), AD (8/80), example: <**lí te shxwch'ech'áls.**>, //lí tə sx^w=C_1əC_2=c'ɛ́=əls//, /'*It's on the shelf.*'/, attested by AD.

<**sts'á:ltexw**>, ds //s=c'ɛ́=ɛ́ltəx^w//, BLDG /'*top of roof, roof planks*'/, literally /'something to put/go on top of the building'/, (<**s=**> *nominalizer, something to*), lx <**=áltexw ~ =áwtxw**> *building, house*, phonology: vowel merger, syntactic analysis: nominal, attested by Elders Group (9/17/75).

<**ts'ech'ó:lwelh**>, ds //C_1ə=c'ɛ́=á·lwəɬ//, HHG ['*(being/put) on the top shelf*'], BLDG, literally /'(being/put) on the top side'/, (<**R2=**> *continuative or resultative*), lx <**=ó:lwelh**> *side*, phonology: reduplication, vowel merger, syntactic analysis: adverb/adverbial verb, attested by EB (12/18/75).

<**ts'ílem**>, mdls //c'ɛ=íl=əm//, TVMO ['*get on top of something*'], literally /'go/come/get oneself on top'/, (<**=íl**> *go, come, get, become*), (<**=em**> *middle voice*), phonology: vowel merger, syntactic analysis: intransitive verb, attested by EB (4/2/76), example: <**ts'ílem te stiqíw**>, //c'ɛ=íl=əm tə s=tiqíw//, /'*mount a horse*'/, attested by EB, <**ts'ílemchxw í te sch'áletstel.**>, //c'ɛ=íl=əm-c-x^w ʔí tə s=c'ɛ́=ləc=təl//, /'*You get on top of the chair.*'/, attested by EB.

<**ts'ílém**>, cts //c'ɛ=íl=ə[-´-]m//, TVMO /'*mounting a horse, mounting a person*'/, (<-´-> *continuative*), phonology: vowel merger, stress-shift, syntactic analysis: intransitive verb, attested by Elders Group (3/5/80).

<**ch'áletstel ~ sch'á(:)letstel ~ shxwch'áletstel**>, dnom //c'ɛ́=ləc=təl ~ s=c'ɛ́(·)=ləc=təl ~ sx^{w}=c'ɛ́=ləc=təl//, HHG /'*chair, bench, seat, something to sit on*'/, literally /'device to put the rump on top of ~ something to put the rump on top of device ~ something that put the rump on top of device'/, (<**s=**> *something to, nominalizer*), (<**shxw=**> *something for/that, nominalizer*), lx <**=lets**> *rump, bottom*, (semological comment: here the body part is the subject/object and not locative), lx <**=tel**> *device to, thing to*, syntactic analysis: nominal, attested by AC (1023/71, 12/8/71), AD and NP (1/23/80), TG (Elders Group 3/1/72), Elders Group (3/1/72, 1/7/76), EB (4/2/76, 2/11/76), IHTTC (9/15/77), example: <**emét li te sts'áletstel**>, //ʔəmə́t li tə s=c'ɛ́=ləc=təl//, /'*sit down on the chair*'/, attested by AC, <**lí tí te sts'áletstel.**>, //lí tí tə s=c'ɛ́=ləc=təl//, /'*The chair is over there.*'/, attested by AC, <**emétlha lam te shxwch'áletstel.**>, //ʔəmə́t-ɬɛ lɛ=m tə sx^{w}=c'ɛ́=ləc=təl//, /'*Go sit in the chair.*'/, attested by IHTTC.

<**ch'álechem**>, mdls //c'ɛ́=ləc=əm//, ABFC /'*find a seat, have a seat, sit down*'/, SOC, usage: more polite than <**emét**>, lx <**=lets ~ =lech**> *rump, bottom*, (<**=em**> *middle voice*), syntactic analysis: intransitive verb, attested by Elders Group (3/1/72, 2/26/75), Deming (12/15/77), example: <**ch'álechemchap.**>, //c'ɛ́=ləc=əm-c-ɛp//, /'*You folks have a seat.*'/, attested by Deming.

<**xwch'áletsem**>, mdls //x^{w}=c'ɛ́=ləc=əm//, ABFC ['*have a seat*'], SOC, (<**xw=**> *towards*, syntactic analysis: intransitive verb, attested by IHTTC (9/15/77).

<**Ts'a'í:les**>, ds //c'ɛʔ=í·ləs//, PLN /'*Chehalis village on Harrison River, the Heart Rock for which Chehalis, B.C. was named (at the mouth of Chehalis River)*'/, ASM ['the Heart Rock was about 14 ft. around, was shaped like a heart, was supported by a great root probably a willow (possibly a cottonwood) with lots of solid earth and grasses, it went up and down with the river's rise and fall (beating like a heart), the wash from the logging tugs washed it out about 4 or 5 years ago [i.e. 1973-1974], it was probably a little upstream [north][on Harrison River] from the Chehalis River mouth and close to the village, Ed Leon knew the location, his son Rudy knows it also (EL with Ken McRae, November 1978)'], literally /'on top on the chest'/, (semological comment: the word and place name is not related at all to Chehalis, Washington, that is in another language and has a totally different meaning), lx <**=í:les**> *on the chest*, phonology: glottal stop final in root or epenthetic, such glottal stops vary rarely with h in the speech of some of the oldest elders and so it is possible that an alternate old pronunciation was accurately reflected in the English spelling Chehalis, such a pronunciation also might have had the older historical features of **ch'** instead of **ts'** and <**éy**> [éy] allophone of /**i**/ after [h], thus ***Ch'ahéyles** /č'ɛh=í·ləs/ [č'ɛhɛ́ylɪs], syntactic analysis: nominal, attested by EL with Ken McRae (11/78), AC (1973 for the form), also some say it means instead literally /'over the top (when canoeing)'/, ASM ['so named after the place of rough water past Chehalis on the way to Harrison Lake'], attested by John Williams of Scowlitz (1/29/79), also /'*Chehalis River*'/, source: Wells 1965 (lst ed.):14.

<**sts'áts'elstexw**>, caus //s=c'ɛ́[=C$_{1}$ə=]=əl=sT-əx^{w}//, TVMO /'*carry it carefully, handle it with care*'/, ABFC, literally /'make/cause it to be going/coming on top'/, (<**s=**> *stative*), probably root <**ts'á**> *on top*, (<**=R1=**> *continuative or derivational*), possibly <**=el**> *go, come, get, become*, (<**=st**> *causative control transitivizer*), (<**-exw**> *third person object*), phonology: reduplication, syntactic analysis: transitive verb, attested by IHTTC (9/9/77).

<**ch'álechem**>, mdls //c'ɛ́=ləc=əm//, ABFC /'*find a seat, have a seat, sit down*'/, *see* ch'á: ~ ts'á:.

<**ch'alech'á (~ ts'alets'á)**>, plv //C$_{1}$ɛ[=lə=]=c'ɛ́//, TVMO ['*they came on (top of)*'], *see* ch'á: ~ ts'á:.

<**ch'áléléth'xel**> ~ <**ts'eléletl'xel**>, df //c'[=əl=]i[=Aə́=lə=]ƛ'=x^yəl//, BPI [*'has short legs'*], *see* ch'í:tl' ~ ts'í:tl' ~ ts'ítl'.

<**ch'áletstel ~ sch'á(:)letstel ~ shxwch'áletstel**>, dnom //c'ɛ=ləc=təl ~ s=c'ɛ(·)=ləc=təl ~ sx^w=c'ɛ=ləc=təl//, HHG /*'chair, bench, seat, something to sit on'*/, *see* ch'á: ~ ts'á:.

<**ch'ám ~ ts'ám ~ ts'ém**>, bound root //c'ɛm ~ c'ə́m// *bite*

<**ch'ámet ~ ts'ámet ~ ts'émet**>, pcs //c'ɛm=əT ~ c'ə́m=əT//, [c'ɛ́mət ~ c'ə́mət], ABFC /*'put s-th between the teeth, put it in one's mouth, bite on s-th (not into it)'*/, possibly related to th'ám *chew*, (<**=et**> *purposeful control transitivizer*), syntactic analysis: transitive verb, attested by AC (8/15/70, 9/30/71), EB (3/22/76), Salish cognate: Squamish /č'ə́mʔ/ *bite (itr.)(dog, fish, fly, etc.)* and /č'əmʔ-t/ *bite (tr.)* W73:38, K67:319, perhaps not Shuswap /c'm-em/ and /c'm-nt-es/ and /s-c'm-st-es/ *to bite and suck blood (of mosquito, sand fly, etc.)* K74:177, nor Shuswap root /k'em/ *surface* in many body parts K74 (but the latter may be cognate with Upriver Halkomelem /c'əmx^yá·yθəl/ *jaw*, contrast <**th'ám**> *chew*.

<**ch'mát**>, cts //c'ɛm=M1=T//, ABFC [*'biting on s-th'*], (<**metathesis type 1**> *continuative* (irregular)), phonology: metathesis, syntactic analysis: transitive verb, attested by Elders Group (2/8/78).

<**ch'emá:ls**>, sas //c'əm=ɛ·ls//, dnom, ABFC [*'a thing that bites'*], (<**=á:ls**> *structured activity non-continuative nominal*), syntactic analysis: nominal, attested by IHTTC (9/2/77).

<**ch'ech'émels**>, cts //C_1ə=c'ə́m=əls//, sas, dnom, ABFC /*'a biter (animal, fish, etc.), a thing that is (always) biting'*/, (<**R5=**> *continuative*), (<**=els**> *structured activity continuative nominal*), phonology: reduplication, syntactic analysis: nominal, attested by IHTTC (9/2/77), example: <**ch'ech'éméls te sqwemáy.**>, //C_1ə=c'ə́m=əls//, /*'The dog is a biter.'*/, attested by IHTTC.

<**ch'ámet ~ ts'ámet ~ ts'émet**>, pcs //c'ɛm=əT ~ c'ə́m=əT//, [c'ɛ́mət ~ c'ə́mət], ABFC /*'put s-th between the teeth, put it in one's mouth, bite on s-th (not into it)'*/, *see* ch'ám ~ ts'ám ~ ts'ém.

<**ch'átxwels ~ ts'átxwels**>, df //c'ɛ́t(=)x^w=əls//, sas, ABFC /*'(mice) chewing (a wall, box, etc.)'*/, possibly root <**ts'á:(t)**> *chew (s-th)*, possibly <**=xw**> *round/lump-like*?, (<**=els**> *structured activity continuative*), syntactic analysis: intransitive verb, attested by Elders Group (10/27/76), Salish cognate: possibly Squamish /č'ít-inʔ/ *gnaw* W73:117, K69:68, possibly Lushootseed /č'ít'-id/ *chewed it up, destroyed it as would an insect* H76:118, Sechelt /c'əʔ-át/ *chew [s-th]* T77:26.

<**ts'á:txwels**>, dnom //c'ɛ́·t=x^w=əls//, sas, EZ /*'a big rat (*prob. the introduced *Norway rat,* probably *native species of large vole* which may include any or all of the following that are found in the area: *creeping vole, long-tail vole, mountain heather vole, boreal redback vole),* possibly also the introduced *roof rat*'/, ['prob. the introduced *Rattus norvegius,* native species possibly including any/all of these four: *Microtus oregoni serpens, Microtus longicaudus macrurus, Phenacomys intermedius oramontis*, and *Clethrionomys gapperi cascadensis*, possibly also the introduced *Rattus rattus*'], literally /'something chewing (as a structured activity like a mouse on a wall or box)'/, (<**=els**> *structured activity continuative nominal*), syntactic analysis: nominal, attested by Elders Group (7/27/75).

<**ch'á:tl'em ~ ts'á:tl'em ~ ts'átl'em**>, ABFC /*'jumping, hopping'*/, *see* ts'tl'ám ~ ts'tl'ém.

<**ch'áwq'em**>, df //c'ɛw(=)q'=əm//, SD [*'sizzling'*], FOOD, semantic environment ['of grease in a frying pan or in roasting meat'], root meaning unknown, possibly <**=q'**> *on something else*?, (<**=em**> *have/get/intransitivizer*), syntactic analysis: intransitive verb, attested by Elders Group (12/15/76).

<ch'**áxw ~ ts'áxw**>, bound root //c'ɛx^w *quiet/silent (after noise)*//.

<**ts'áxws**>, if //c'ɛ́xʷ-s//, LANG ['*everyone got quiet*'], SD, (<**-s**> *third person possessive/subordinate*), syntactic analysis: intransitive verb, attested by Elders Group (3/23/77).

<**sts'áxw**>, stvi //s=c'ɛ́xʷ//, LANG /'*quiet or silent (after noise) (used of people), (be/have) a lull in conversation*'/, SD, (<**s=**> *stative*), syntactic analysis: adjective/adjectival verb, attested by AD (12/7/79).

<**sts'áts'exw ~ sch'ách'exw**>, strs //s=c'ɛ́[=C_1ə=]xʷ//, LANG /'*(be) silent, quiet, keep quiet*'/, SD, (<**=R1=**> *resultative*), phonology: reduplication, syntactic analysis: adjective/adjectival verb, attested by AD (12/9/79), EB (12/18/75), Elders Group (3/3/76); found in <**sch'ách'exwchexwo.**>, //s=c'ɛ́[=C_1ə=]xʷ-c-əxʷ-a//, /'*You keep quiet.*'/, attested by Elders Group.

<**ch'áxwel ~ ts'áxwel**>, incs //c'ɛ́xʷ=əl//, LANG /'*shut up, (go or get or become quiet)*'/, SD, (<**=el**> *go, come, get, become*), syntactic analysis: intransitive verb, usage: not polite, attested by Elders Group (2/19/75), EB (5/3/76); found in <**ch'áxwellha.**>, //c'ɛ́xʷ=əl-ɬɛ//, /'*Shut up.*'/, attested by Elders Group, *<**ts'áxwellha ta' thóthel.**> rejected by EB.

<**ch'exweló:ythel ~ ts'exweló:ythel**>, ds //c'ɛxʷ=əl=á·yθəl or c'ɛ[=Aə=]xʷ=əl=á·yθəl//, LANG /'*stop talking, shut up (the lips or jaw)*'/, literally /'go/get silent on the lips/jaw'/, possibly <**e-ablaut**> *derivational/resultative/durative*, lx <**=ó:ythel**> *on the jaw, on the lips*, phonology: vowel-reduction or ablaut, syntactic analysis: intransitive verb, attested by IHTTC, Elders Group; found in <**ch'exweló:ythellha.**>, //c'ɛxʷ=əl=á·yθəl-ɬɛ//, /'*Stop talking.*'/, attested by IHTTC (9/15/77), example: <**skw'áy kw'es ts'exweló:ythels.**>, //s=k'ʷɛ́y k'ʷ-əs c'ɛxʷ=əl=á·yθəl-s//, /'*(He/She/They) can't shut up.*'/, attested by Elders Group (2/25/75); found in <**ch'exweló:ythelalha.**>, //c'ɛxʷ=əl=á·yθəl-ɛɬɛ//, /'*Stop talking you guys., Stop talking you folks.*'/, attested by IHTTC.

<**ch'exwí:lt**>, pcs //c'ɛxʷ=í·l=T//, KIN /'*hush a baby from crying, (hush s-o (a baby) from crying)*'/, LANG, (<**=el ~ =í:l**> *go, come, get, become*), (<**=t**> *purposeful control transitivizer*), phonology: vowel-reduction, syntactic analysis: transitive verb, attested by IHTTC (9/15/77).

<**ts'exwí:lthet**>, pcrs //c'ɛxʷ=í·l=T-ət//, LANG ['*one gets silent*'], literally /'hush oneself, get oneself quiet'/, (<**-et**> *reflexive*), phonology: vowel-reduction, syntactic analysis: transitive verb, attested by Elders Group (3/23/77).

<**ts'xwó:ythel**>, ds //c'(ɛ)xʷ=á·yθəl//, LANG /'*silence the mouth, keep the mouth quiet*'/, literally /'quiet the jaw/lips'/, lx <**=ó:ythel**> *(on the) jaw, lips*, phonology: vowel-loss, syntactic analysis: intransitive verb, attested by EB (5/3/76); found in <**ts'xwó:ythellha.**>, //c'(ɛ)xʷ=á·yθəl-ɬɛ//, /'*Silence your mouth., Keep your mouth quiet.*'/, *<**ts'xwó:ythellha ta' thóthel.**> rejected by EB.

<**ch'áxwel ~ ts'áxwel**>, incs //c'ɛ́xʷ=əl//, LANG /'*shut up, (go or get or become quiet)*'/, *see* ch'áxw ~ ts'áxw.

<**ch'áyxwt**>, cts //c'i[-Aɛ́-]yxʷ=T//, HARV ['*drying s-th*'], *see* ch'íyxw ~ ts'íyxw ~ ts'éyxw.

<**ch'ech'émels**>, cts //C_1ə=c'ə́m=əls//, sas, dnom, ABFC /'*a biter (animal, fish, etc.), a thing that is (always) biting*'/, *see* ch'ám ~ ts'ám ~ ts'ém.

<**ch'ékwx̲ ~ ts'ékwx̲**>, pcs //c'ə́kʷ(=)x̣=T//

<**ts'ékwx̲t**>, pcs //c'ə́kʷ(=)x̣=T//, FOOD ['*fry s-th*'], possibly <**=x̲**> *distributive*, (<**=t**> *purposeful control transitivizer*), syntactic analysis: transitive verb, Salish cognate: Squamish /čəkʷx̣-án/ *fry (tr.)* beside /čəkʷx̣-ímʔ/ *fry (act. itr.)* W73:109, K67:316, Songish dial. of NSt /č'kʷə́x̣t/ *to fry (tr.)* M68:39, also <**ts'éqwx̲wt**>, //c'ə́qʷx̣ʷ=T//, comment: probably mistranscribed for ts'ékwx̲t; attested by AC (9/18/71), EB (12/15/75), example: <**ts'eqwx̲wt te stsél:èm**>, //c'ə́qʷx̣ʷ=T tə s=cə́l·əm//, /'*fry the liver*'/, comment: ts'eqwx̲wt prob. mistranscribed, attested by AC; found in

<**ts'ékwx̲chexw. ~ ts'ékwx̲tlha.**>, //c'ə́kʷx̣=T-c-əxʷ ~ c'ə́kʷx̣=T-ɬɛ//, /'*Fry it.*'/, attested by EB (3/1/76).

<**ts'ákwx̲t**>, cts //c'ə[-Aɛ́-]kʷ(=)x̣=T//, FOOD ['*(be) frying s-th*'], (<**á-ablaut**> *continuative*), phonology: ablaut, syntactic analysis: transitive verb, attested by EB (5/3/76), example: <**ílhtsel ts'ákwx̲t.**>, //ʔí-ɬ-c-əl c'ə[-Aɛ́-]kʷx̣=T//, /'*I was frying it.*'/, attested by EB, <**ts'ákwx̲tes te chékel.**>, //c'ə[-Aɛ́-]kʷx̣=T-əs tə cə́kəl//, [c'ǽkʷx̣tɪs tə čɪ́kʸɪl], /'*She's frying the chicken.*'/, attested by EB (3/1/76).

<**sts'ákwx̲ ~ sch'ákwx̲**>, strs //s=c'ə[=Aɛ́=]kʷx̣//, FOOD ['*(already) fried*'], (<**s=**> *stative*), (<**á-ablaut**> *resultative*), phonology: ablaut, syntactic analysis: adjective/adjectival verb, attested by IHTTC (8/24/77), AD (12/19/78), also <**sch'ékwx̲**>, //s=c'ə́kʷx̣//, attested by Danny Charlie Sr. (12/19/78), <**sch'ákwx̲ seplíl**>, //s=c'ə[=Aɛ́=]kʷx səplíl//, /'*fried bread*'/, attested by AD, also <**sch'ékwx̲ seplíl**>, //s=c'ə́kʷx̣ səplíl//, attested by DC.

<**ts'ekwx̲á:ls ~ ts'ekwx̲áls**>, sas //c'əkʷx̣=ɛ́·ls//, FOOD ['*to fry (as a structured activity)*'], (<**=á:ls**> *structured activity non-continuative*), syntactic analysis: intransitive verb, attested by EB (3/1/76, 5/3/76), example: <**ílhtsel ts'ekwx̲áls te seplí:l.**>, //ʔí-ɬ-c-əl c'əkʷx̣=ɛ́ls tə səplí·l//, /'*I fried bread.*'/, attested by EB; found in <**ts'ekwx̲á:lslha.**>, //c'əkʷx̣=ɛ́·ls-ɬɛ//, /'*Fry some.*'/, ASM ['meaning do the work for awhile'], attested by EB, example: <**ts'ekwx̲á:lslha kw seplí:l. ~ ts'ekwx̲álschexw kw seplì:l.**>, //c'əkʷx̣=ɛ́·ls-ɬɛ kʷ səplí·l ~ c'əkʷx̣=ɛ́ls-c-əxʷ kʷ səplí·l//, /'*Fry some bread.*'/, attested by EB (3/1/76, 5/3/76).

<**ts'ákwx̲els**>, cts //c'ə[-Aɛ́-]kʷx̣=əls//, sas, FOOD ['*frying*'], (<**á-ablaut**> *continuative*), (<**=els**> *structured activity continuative*), phonology: ablaut, syntactic analysis: intransitive verb, attested by EB (5/3/76 corrects 12/15/75), example: <**ílhtsel ts'ákwx̲els te seplí:l**>, //ʔí-ɬ-c-əl c'ə[-Aɛ́-]kʷx̣=əls tə səplí·l//, /'*I was frying bread.*'/, attested by EB (5/3/76).

<**ts'ákwx̲els**>, dnom //c'ə[=Aɛ́=]kʷx̣=əls//, FOOD ['*frying pan*'], TOOL, HHG, (<**á-ablaut**> *continuative*), (<**=els**> *structured activity continuative nominal*), phonology: ablaut, syntactic analysis: nominal, attested by Deming Elders at Ft. Langley, B.C. museum (3/9/78), also <**sch'ákwx̲els**>, //s=c'ə[=Aɛ́=]kʷx̣=əls//, attested by Elders Group (6/1/77), AD (8/80), example: <**alétsa te sch'ákwx̲els?**>, //ʔɛlə́cɛ tə s=c'ə[=Aɛ́=]kʷx̣=əls//, /'*Where's the frying pan?*'/, attested by AD.

<**ts'ékwx̲elhtst**>, bens //c'ə́kʷx̣-əɬc=T//, pcs, FOOD ['*fry it for s-o*'], (<**-elhts**> *benefactive*), (<**=t**> *purposeful control transitivizer*), syntactic analysis: transitive verb, attested by Elders Group (3/24/76), also <**ts'ékwx̲elht**>, //c'ə́kʷx̣=əɬ=T//, attested by EB (3/1/76); found in <**ts'ekwx̲elhtsthó:x**>, //c'əkʷx̣-əɬc=T-áxʸ//, /'*fry it for me*'/, attested by Elders Group, example: <**ts'ekwx̲elhthó:xchexw.**>, //c'əkʷx̣-əɬ=T-áxʸ-c-əxʷ//, /'*Fry it for me.*'/, attested by EB.

<**ch'el ~ ts'el**>, bound root //c'əl *turn, turn around*//, the **ts'** pronunciation prevails in all but a few derivations from this root, so most will be found under **ts'**; it may be that since the words for *Chilliwack* and the **Ch'élexwoqwem** language (see below under <**ts'éléxw**>) have the **ch'** pronunciation quite frequently,, this is probably a conservative retention from influence of the Nooksack and **Ch'élexwoqwem** languages, precisely most adjacent to the Chilliwack area (the latter had a village on Cultus Lake and the former had villages on Chilliwack Lake and the upper parts of that river. Salish cognate: Lushootseed root /č'ə́lp/ *twist, turn, sprain* [perhaps with /=p/ *on itself* as in Upriver Halkomelem /=p'/ *on itself* but with loss of glottalization] as in Lushootseed /ʔəs-č'ə́lp/ *it's turned*, /č'ə́lp-əd/ *turn it, twist it*, /č'əlp-ús-əd/ *turn the head (of a horse when riding)* H76:110-111.

<**ts'eláltxw**>, ds //c'əl=ɛ́ltxʷ//, SOC ['*steal someone's spouse*'], literally /'turn/turn around the spouse/home'/, lx <**=áltxw**> *spouse, home*, comment: this use contrasts with that of =áwtxw *house, building*, clearly a related suffix, syntactic analysis: intransitive verb, attested by Deming (4/26/79).

<ts'ólesem ~ ts'ólésem>, mdls //c'ə[=Aá=]l=əs=əm ~ c'ə[=Aá=]l=ə[=´=]s=əm//, ABFC /'*turn one's face, (turn one's body away [IHTTC])*'/, DIR, probably <**ó-ablaut**> *derivational*, lx <**=es**> *on the face*, possibly <=´=> *derivational*, (<**=em**> *middle voice*), phonology: probable ablaut, possible updrifting, syntactic analysis: intransitive verb, attested by EF (9/21/78), also /'*turn one's body away*'/, attested by IHTTC (9/16/77), example: <**ts'ólésem, ts'ólésem telúwe q'ámi. l stl'í kw'els kw'atsethóme. Pshaw, it's only my cousin.**>, //c'ə[=Aá=]l=əs=əm, c'ə[=Aá=]l=əs=əm, tɛ=lúwə q'ɛ́miy. l s=ƛ'í k'ʷ-əl-s k'ʷɛc=əT-ámə.//, /'*Turn your face, turn your face, you, girl. I want to see you. Pshaw, it's only my cousin.*'/, usage: love song, attested by EF (9/21/78).

<ts'ó:lexeth'>, df //c'ə[=Aá=]l=ləx̣əθ' or c'ə[=Aá=](l)=ɛ́ləx̣əθ'//, ABFC /'*roll over in bed, turn over in bed*'/, DIR, (<**ó-ablaut**> *derivational*), lx <**=(a)lexeth'**> (*in*) *bed*, phonology: possible vowel-loss in suffix and consonant merger (l+l→:l), or possible consonant-loss in root and vowel merger, (semological comment: the non-body-part suffix here seems clearly locative and has the =el= ~ =ál= like many body-part suffixes, could this indicate that the =el= ~ =ál= element was originally *locative*? and then that meaning element spread to the other body part suffixes by analogy even when =el=/=ál= was not added?), syntactic analysis: intransitive verb, attested by NP (Elders Group 3/5/80), also <**ch'ó:lexeth'**>, //c'ə[=Aá=]l=ləx̣əθ'//, attested by H-T (Elders Group 3/5/80).

<ts'elqéylt or **ts'elqí:lt>**, pcs //c'əl=q=í·l=T//, DIR ['*turn s-th around*'], possibly <**=q ~ =q'**> *(on) something else*, (<**=í:l**> *go, come, get, become*), (<**=t**> *purposeful control transitivizer*), phonology: allomorph or deglottalization of =q', syntactic analysis: transitive verb, attested by Deming (4/17/80).

<ts'elqéylém>, mdls //c'əl=q=í·l=əm//, DIR /'*turn (oneself) around, make a U-turn*'/, TVMO, literally /'turn oneself around (on) something else'/, lx <**=q ~ =q'**> *(on) something else*, (<**=í:l**> *go, come, get, become*), (<**=em**> *middle voice*), phonology: syllable-loss, updrifting, allomorph or deglottalization of =q', syntactic analysis: intransitive verb, attested by Deming (4/17/80), example: <**ts'elqéylém ta' (wákel, stiqíw, kyó, péki).**>, //c'əl=q=í·l=əm t-ɛʔ (wɛ́kəl, s=tiqíw, kʸá, pə́ki)//, /'*Turn your (wagon, horse, car, buggy) around.*'/, attested by Deming (4/17/80).

<sts'élqes>, ds //s=c'ə́l=q=əs or s=c'ə́l=q'=D=əs//, HUNT ['*whirled slingshot*'], ASM ['whirled from one end'], literally /'something to turn around something else on the face (or) something round to turn around something else'/, (<**s=**> *nominalizer, something to*), lx <**=q ~ =q'**> *(on) something else*, lx <**=es**> *on the face, round object*, phonology: allomorph or deglottalization of =q', syntactic analysis: nominal, attested by Deming (7/27/78), also <**tsélqes**>, //c'ə́l=q=əs or c'[=D=]ə́l=q=əs//, comment: ts probably mistranscribed for ts', phonology: possible deglottalization, attested by Elders Group (2/11/76), also <**th'élqos**>, //θ'ə́=q=as//, attested by Elders Group (11/26/75).

<ts'á:lq'em>, cts //c'ə[-Aɛ́·-]l=q'=əm//, TVMO /'*spinning (while hanging), (twirling)*'/, DIR, literally /'go/come/get turning around on something else (or) turning itself around on something else'/, (<**á:-ablaut**> *continuative*), lx <**=q'**> *on something else*, (<**=em**> *go/come/get/become or middle voice*), phonology: ablaut, syntactic analysis: intransitive verb, attested by Elders Group (10/13/76).

<ts'élexw>, df //c'ə́l=əxʷ//, TVMO /'*turn back into a quiet slough from the river, be going into a slough from the river*'/, CAN, DIR, possibly <**=exw**> *round, around*, syntactic analysis: intransitive verb, attested by Elders Group (2/26/75), also <**ts'éléxw**>, //c'ə́l=əxʷ//, also /'*(a fish) going into a quieter stream*'/, attested by Elders Group (7/20/77), example: <**ts'élexw te sthóqwi.**>, //c'ə́l=əxʷ tə s=θáqʷi//, /'*The fish is going into a slough from the river.*'/, attested by Elders Group (2/26/75), <chélexw>, [čʌ́lʊxʷ] EH, [¢ʌ́lʊxʷ1 RG,'*go upstream*', attested by (EH,RG 7/23/99) (SU transcription, tape 2) [BG: initial consonant should be glottalized].

<sts'élexw>, dnom //s=c'ə́l=əxʷ//, WATR /'*slough, backwater, ((*also*) eddy* [AC])'/, literally /'something to go into quieter water'/, (<**s=**> *nominalizer, something to*), syntactic analysis:

nominal, attested by EB (6/14/78), also <**sts'èlèxw**>, //s=c'ə́lə́x^{w}//, also /'*eddy, backwater*'/, attested by AC (9/1/71).

<**Sts'elxwíqw ~ Ts'elxwíqw ~ Ts'elxwéyeqw**>, ds //s=c'əl=(ə)x^{w}=íq^{w} ~ c'əl=(ə)x^{w}=íq^{w}//, PLN ['*Chilliwack River*'], SOCT ['*Chilliwack Indian people*'], ASM ['there are traditions that these people lived on the Chilliwack River from Chilliwack Lake to Soowahlie (the headquarters) and spoke a language closer to the Nooksack language than to Halkomelem, a language DM called ch'**é**lexwoqwem (Wells tapes, new transcript p.), sometime about the 1790's they began to mix with and adopt Upriver Halkomelem, a few placenames only survived (Th'ewálí, St'ept'ő̄p, Stútelō) and these are discussed in Galloway 1985c'], literally /'slough/backwater/quieter water at the top of the head (or) something to go into slough/quieter water from the river at the top of the head'/, (semological comment: perhaps so named because of the many (named) sloughs at the mouth of (top of the head of) the Chilliwack river where it formerly hit the Fraser River), lx <**=íqw**> *on the top of the head*, phonology: vowel-loss, phonology: this name is the source of the modern names of Chilliwack, B.C. and the former municipality of Chilliwhack nearby, syntactic analysis: nominal, attested by AC (8/4/70, 10/31/73), Elders Group (7/20/77), other sources: JH /c'ilx^{w}í·q^{w}/ *slough, Chilliwack*, place names reference file #79, also <**Ch'elxwíqw ~ Ch'elxwí:qw ~ Ch'elxwéyeqw**>, //c'əl=x^{w}=í(·)q^{w}//, (semological comment: Wells glosses it as *Chilliwack River* and says it literally means *going back upstream, a backwater*, but on the same page also gives it as the names for Dolly Varden Creek as well as Chilliwack Creek (= Chilliwack River), later he also says it was the name for a village below Centre Creek, an old village destroyed by a slide), attested by Wells 1965 (lst ed.):13, 19.

<**Ch'élexwoqwem ~ ch'élexwoqwem**>, ds //c'ə́l=əx^{w}=aq^{w}=əm or c'ə́l=əx^{w}=i[=Aa=]q^{w}=əm//, LANG /'*the old Chilliwack language,* ([also prob.] *to speak the old Chilliwack language*'/, SOCT, (semological comment: this language was either midway between Halkomelem and Nooksack languages or was a dialect of lh**é**chelesem, the Nooksack language), possibly <**=íqw ~ =aqw ~ =eqw**> *on top of the head*, possibly <**o-ablaut**> *derivational*, (<**=em**> *intransitivizer/have/get, speak*), phonology: possible ablaut, syntactic analysis: nominal, (also prob. intransitive verb), attested by DM (Wells tapes, new transcripts p.),

<**sts'elxwíwel**>, ds //s=c'əl=(ə)x^{w}=íwəl//, ANA /'*insides (animal or human or other?), (internal organs, guts, etc.), (stomach [inside] [DM])*'/, ASM ['(includes the guts, stomach, heart, liver, etc.)'], literally /'backwater/slough in the insides'/, lx <**=íwel**> *in the insides*, syntactic analysis: nominal, attested by AC (11/11/71), Deming (esp. SJ 5/3/79), other sources: ES /šc'əlx^{w}íwəl/ *guts*, also /'*stomach [inside]*'/, attested by DM (12/4/64), example: <**tsqwá:y te sts'elxwíwels te st'élém.**>, //c=q^{w}ɛ́·y tə s=c'əl=əx^{w}=íwəl-s tə s=t'ə́l=əm//, /'*The inside/inner cherry bark is green.*'/, attested by Deming (esp. SJ).

<**ts'elxwí:wsem**>, mdls //c'əl=(ə)x^{w}=í·ws=əm//, ABFC ['*relieved (in one's body)*'], literally /'turn into quieter water on (in?) one's body'/, lx <**=í:w**> *on the body*, (<**=em**> *middle voice*), syntactic analysis: intransitive verb, attested by Elders Group (3/23/77).

<**Ch'élexwoqwem ~ ch'élexwoqwem**>, ds //c'ə́l=əx^{w}=aq^{w}=əm or c'ə́l=əx^{w}=i[=Aa=]q^{w}=əm//, LANG /'*the old Chilliwack language,* ([also prob.] *to speak the old Chilliwack language*'/, *see* ch'el ~ ts'el.

<**Ch'elxwíqw ~ Ch'elxwí:qw ~ Ch'elxwéyeqw**> ~ <**Sts'elxwíqw ~ Ts'elxwíqw ~ Ts'elxwéyeqw**>, ds //s=c'əl=(ə)x^{w}=íq^{w} ~ c'əl=(ə)x^{w}=íq^{w}//, PLN ['*Chilliwack River*'], SOCT ['*Chilliwack Indian people*'], *see* ch'el ~ ts'el.

<**ch'emá:ls**>, sas //c'əm=ɛ́·ls//, dnom, ABFC ['*a thing that bites*'], *see* ch'ám ~ ts'ám ~ ts'ém.

<**ch'éqw' ~ ts'éqw'**>, probable root //c'ə́q'ʷ// *poke, pierce*, see under ts' for all derivations from this root; only those with frequent ch' pronunciation are listed here

<**sts'éqw' ~ sch'éqw'**>, dnom //s=c'ə́q'ʷ//, BSK /'*fine cedar root weaving, fine cedar root work*'/, literally /'something that got pierced/poked'/, (semological comment: prob. so named because one uses an awl to poke holes in the roots in the basket as one weaves, and the roots are poked through each other in places), (<**s=**> *nominalizer*), syntactic analysis: nominal, attested by Elders Group (6/11/75, 3/24/76), example: <**sts'éqw' syó:ys**>, //s=c'ə́q'ʷ s=yá·ys//, /'*fine cedar root work (only roots used)*'/, attested by Elders Group (6/11/75).

<**ts'eqw'ő:welh ~ ts'eqw'őwelh ~ ch'eqw'őwelh**>, ds //c'əq'ʷ=ó·wəɬ ~ c'əq'ʷ=ówəɬ//, BSK ['*to weave a cedar root basket*'], literally /'pierce/poke into vessel/canoe/?basket'/, lx <**=ő:welh ~ =őwelh ~ =ewelh**> *canoe, vessel, basket?*, syntactic analysis: intransitive verb, attested by Elders Group (6/11/75), AC (8/13/70), <**ch'qwőwélh**>, [č'qʷówʊ́ɬ], '*make a cedar basket*', attested by (EH,RG) 7/27/99 (SU transcription, tape 3), also <**ts'qw'őwelh ~ ts'qw'őwélh ~ th'qw'őwelh**>, //c'əq'ʷ=ówəɬ ~ θ'əq'ʷ=ówəɬ//, attested by EB (IHTTC 9/2/77, 12/19/75), example: <**líchexw slhéq'alexw kw'as ch'eqw'őwelh?**>, //lí-c-əxʷ s=ɬə́=q'ɛl=l-əxʷ k'ʷ-ɛ-s c'əq'ʷ=ówəɬ//, /'*Do you know how to make a basket?*'/, literally /'do you have knowledge of it that you weave a basket'/, attested by AC, <**yalhòlse ts'qw'őwélh.**>, //yɛɬ=à-l-s-ə c'əq'ʷ=ówəɬ//, /'*I started to make a basket.*'/, attested by EB (12/19/75), <**yálho'ó kw'a'sé ts'qw'őwelh.**>, //yɛ́ɬ=a à k'ʷ-ɛʔ-s-ə c'əq'ʷ=ówəɬ//, /'*You just start to make a basket.*'/, attested by EB (12/19/75), <**qá:ysò le ts'eqwőwélh.**>, //qɛ́·ys-à lə c'əq'ʷ=ówəɬ//, /'*He just now made a basket.*'/, attested by EB (12/19/75), <**totí:ltes te syó:ys te ts'qw'ő:welhs.**>, //ta[-C_1ə-]l=í·l=T-əs tə s=yá·ys-s tə c'əq'ʷ=ó·wəɬ-s//, /'*He/She is learning basketwork.*'/, literally /'he/she is learning s-th the work -of the his/her make a basket'/, attested by Elders Group (3/16/77), also <**totí:ltes kws thíytes te ts'qw'ő:welh.**>, //ta[-C_1ə-]l=í·l=T-əs kʷ-s θíy=T-s tə c'əq'ʷ=ó·wəɬ//, attested by EB (Elders Group 3/16/77).

<**th'éqw'ōwelh ~ ch'éqw'ōwelh**>, cts //θ'ə[-´-]q'ʷ=owəɬ ~ c'ə[-´-]q'ʷ=əwəɬ//, BSK /'*making a basket, (weaving a cedar root basket)*'/, (<**-´-**> *continuative*), phonology: stress-shift, <**ch'éqw'ōwelh**>, [č'ʌ́qʷowʊɬ], '*always making cedar baskets*' (BG: *always* here is probably optional, overemphasizing the plain *continuative*), attested by (EH,RG) 7/27/99 (SU transcription, tape 3), EB's pronunciation is probably also erroneous or idiolectal shift to **th'** by EB here based on her knowledge of Thompson as well as Halq'emeylem, syntactic analysis: intransitive verb, attested by EB (IHTTC 9/27/77).

<**sch'eqw'őwelh**>, dnom //s=c'əq'ʷ=ówəɬ//, BSK ['*basket-weaving*'], (<**s=**> *nominalizer*), syntactic analysis: nominal, attested by AC (11/17/71), example: <**hókwixtsel li tel sch'eqw'őwelh.**>, //hákʷ=əxʸ-c-əl li t-əl s=c'əq'ʷ=ówəɬ//, /'*I'm using it on my basket-weaving.*'/, attested by AC.

<**ch'éqw'ōwelh ~ th'éqw'ōwelh**>, cts //θ'ə[-´-]q'ʷ=owəɬ ~ c'ə[-´-]q'ʷ=əwəɬ//, BSK /'*making a basket, (weaving a cedar root basket)*'/, see ch'éqw' ~ ts'éqw'.

<**ch'eqw'őwelh ~ ts'eqw'ő:welh ~ ts'eqw'őwelh**>, ds //c'əq'ʷ=ó·wəɬ ~ c'əq'ʷ=ówəɬ//, BSK ['*to weave a cedar root basket*'], see ch'éqw' ~ ts'éqw'.

<**ch'étem**>, [č'ítɪm], '*crawling*', attested by (EH,RG 7/30/99)(SU transcription, tape 4), variant of <**ts'átem**>, *see* ch'tá:m> ~ <ts'tá:m.

<**ch'exweló:ythel ~ ts'exweló:ythel**>, ds //c'ɛxʷ=əl=á·yθəl or c'ɛ[=Aə=]xʷ=əl=á·yθəl//, LANG /'*stop talking, shut up (the lips or jaw)*'/, literally /'go/get silent on the lips/jaw'/, *see* ch'áxw ~ ts'áxw.

<**ch'exwélhchat**>, ds //c'əxʷ=ə́ɬcɛ=T//, WATR ['*add some water [to s-th]*'], *see* ts'xwót (or *ch'xwót).

<**ch'exwí:lt**>, pcs //c'ɛx^{w}=í·l=T//, KIN /*'hush a baby from crying, (hush s-o (a baby) from crying)*'/, *see* ch'áxw ~ ts'áxw.

<**ch'ich'ewós**>, df //c'i[-C_1ə-]w=ás//, cts, ABFC [*'sunning oneself'*], a variant of <**chichewós**>, dms //C_1í=cəw=ás//, LAND /*'sit facing a river and watch it, sit on a riverbank and sunbathe*'/, see root <**chew ~ cháw**>, bound root //cəw ~ cɛ́w//, LAND /*'beach, shore*'/, <**R4=** (here **chi=**)> prob. *continuative diminutive*, lx <**=ós**> *on the face*, phonology: reduplication, glottalization, syntactic analysis: intransitive verb, attested by IHTTC (8/4/77), comment: translation omitted in original notes.

<**ch'í:t ~ ts'ít**>, pcs //c'íy=T//, SOC /*'greet s-o, thank s-o*'/, (<**=t**> *purposeful control transitivizer*), phonology: vocalization, syntactic analysis: transitive verb, attested by Elders Group (5/19/76, 7/21/76), Elder's comment: "the root may be ts'á *on top of* especially considering ts'itóléstexw *pile it up* (EB (4/23/76)", comment: EB may be right or the two roots may be unconnected, Salish cognate: Sechelt /č'íy-it/ *to thank* T77:35, B85:296, also <**th'í:t**>, //θ'íy=T or θ'í[=·=]y=T//, also /*'praise s-o (with words), thank s-o*'/, attested by EB (4/23/76), also <**th'ít ~ ch'ít**>, //θ'íy=T ~ c'íy=T//, attested by Deming (4/20/78), example: <**ch'í:t te syúwel**>, //c'íy=T tə s=yə́w=əl//, SPRD, /*'thank a spirit song, ((also) thank a spirit power)*'/, ASM ['done before you sing it'], attested by Elders Group (7/21/76), <**lúwe ts'ít te Chíchelh Siyám.**>, //lúwə c'íy=T tə cí[=C_1ə=]ɬ s=iy=ɛ́m//, /*'It's you to thank the Lord.*'/, attested by Deming (12/15/77), <**ts'ítchxw ta' siyáye.**>, //c'íy=T-c-əx^{w} t-ɛʔ s=yɛ́yə//, /*'Thank your friend.*'/, attested by AD (12/17/79), <**ts'í:tchexw ta' siyáye.**>, //c'í[=·=]y=T-c-əx^{w} t-ɛʔ s=yɛ́yə//, /*'Really thank your friend.*'/, attested by AD (12/17/79), <**tsel th'í:thòmè.**>, //c-əl θ'íy=T-ámə//, /*'I praised you (with words)., I thanked you.*'/, attested by EB; found in <**ch'ítolétsel. ~ th'ítolétsel.**>, //c'íy=T-álə-c-əl ~ θ'íy=T-álə-c-əl//, /*'I thank you folks., I thank you all very much., I praise you folks.*'/, attested by Deming (12/15/77, 4/20/78), example: <**ch'íthométset lám kw's mōkw'stám.**>, //c'íy=T-amə-c-ət lɛ́=m k'^{w}-s mok'^{w}=s=tɛ́m//, /*'We thank you for everything.*'/, usage: blessing a meeting, attested by AD (1/17/80).

<**xwth'í:t**>, df //x^{w}=θ'íy=T//, SOC /*'thank s-o (for a cure, for pall-bearing, a ceremony, being a witness)*'/, REL, ASM ['one thanks a witness with a token wrapped in a colored scarf, the token is often a quarter'], (<**xw=**> *towards*), syntactic analysis: transitive verb, usage: it is an insult to translate this word as *pay s-o (for a cure, for pall-bearing, etc.)*, attested by EB (4/23/76); found in <**xwth'í:tes.**>, //x^{w}=θ'íy=T-əs//, /*'He thanked him (for a cure, pall-bearing, etc.)*'/, attested by EB, <**xwth'í:thóxes.**>, //x^{w}=θ'íy=T-áx^{y}-əs//, /*'He thanked me (for a cure, pall-bearing, a ceremony).*'/, attested by EB, example: <**á:xwesthoxes te tále tl'óles shxwth'í:thóxes.**>, //ʔɛ́·x^{w}əs=T-áx^{y}-əs tə tɛ́lə ƛ'á lə-s sx^{w}=θ'íy=T-áx^{y}-əs//, /*'He gave me money, that's how he thanked me. (give it to s-o)*'/, attested by EB; found in <**shxwth'í:tèmèt.**>, //sx^{w}=θ'íy=T-ə̀m-ə̀t//, /*'They thanked someone (for a cure, pall-bearing, being a witness).*'/, attested by EB.

<**ts'itóléstexw**>, df //c'iy=tálə́=sT-əx^{w}//, caus, SOC /*'pile it up (blankets, rocks, anything)*'/, possibly <**=tólé**> meaning unknown, (<**=st**> *causative control transitivizer*), (<**-exw**> *third person object*), Elder's comment: "derived from ts'á *on top*", syntactic analysis: transitive verb, attested by EB (4/23/76).

<**ch'í:tl' ~ ts'í:tl' ~ ts'ítl'**>, bound root //c'í·ƛ' ~ c'íƛ' *short*//, most derivations from this root have ts' pronunciation (see under ts' for all derivations); the two below do not, in the speech of AC

<**ch'í:tl'emeth'**>, ds //c'í·ƛ'=əməθ'//, BPI /*'short person, short (in stature)*'/, DESC, lx <**=emeth'**> *in height, stature*, syntactic analysis: nominal?, adjective/adjectival verb?, attested by AC (11/11/71).

<**ts'í:ts'tlemeth'**>, dmv //c'í·[=C_1ə=]ƛ'=əməθ'//, BPI /*'short (of a person), shorty*'/, DESC, ABFC [*'call of a little bird (chickadee?)*'], Elder's comment: "probably call of the chickadee (AD)",

(**<=R1=>** *diminutive or resultative*), phonology: reduplication, syntactic analysis: nominal?, adjective/adjectival verb?, attested by EB (12/1/75), IHTTC (8/23/77), AD (IHTTC 8/23/77).

<**ts'eléletl'xel**>, df //c'[=əl=]i[=Aə́=lə=]ƛ'=xʸəl//, BPI [*'has short legs'*], possibly **<=el=>** *plural*, possibly **<é-ablaut>** *durative or derivational*, possibly **<=le=>** *plural*, phonology: double infixed plural?, ablaut, syntactic analysis: adjective/adjectival verb, attested by EB (9/18/78), also <**ch'áléléth'xel**>, //c'ɛ́lə́lə́θ'=xʸəl//, also /*'short-legged runt'*/, Elder's comment: "a swear-word", attested by AC (11/11/71).

<**ch'í:tl'emeth'**>, ds //c'í·ƛ'=əməθ'//, BPI /*'short person, short (in stature)'*/, *see* ch'í:tl' ~ ts'í:tl' ~ ts'ítl'.

<**ch'iyáq ~ ts'iyáq**>, us //c'iyɛ́q//

<**sts'iyáq**>, dnom //s=c'iyɛ́q//, FSH /*'fish trap, weir'*/, (**<s=>** *nominalizer*), syntactic analysis: nominal, attested by Deming (3/25/76), Salish cognate: Squamish /č'iáq/ *salmon weir* W73:286, K67:322, also /*'trapping animals'*/, attested by AC (8/28/70).

<**Sch'iyáq**>, dnom //s=c'iyɛ́q//, PLN [*'creek with its mouth on the south side of Chilliwack River and above the mouth of Middle Creek'*], (semological comment: Wells says it means *place of fish weir*), syntactic analysis: nominal, source: Wells 1965 (lst ed.):13.

<**ch'iyáqtel**>, ds //c'iyɛ́q=təl//, FSH /*'salmon weir, fish trap'*/, root **<ch'iyáq>** *to trap fish*, lx **<=tel>** *device to*, syntactic analysis: nominal, attested by DM (12/4/64).

<**Ch'iyáqtel**>, dnom //c'iyɛ́q=təl//, PLN /*'Tzeachten, a (recent) settlement on the upper reaches of the lower Chilliwack River, now Chilliwack Indian Reserve #13 near Sardis'*/, literally /'device to trap fish'/, (semological comment: Wells says it means *place of the fish weir*), lx **<=tel>** *device to, something to*, phonology: the in the Anglicized spelling of the name either reflects the pronunciation at first recording by whites (Gibbs) in which case the sound change of Downriver /n/ to Upriver /l/ was not complete consonant alternation 1858, or it reflects a recording of this name by Downriver speakers to Gibbs about the same time, none of the Elders from the 1890's to the present pronounce it with /n/, syntactic analysis: nominal, attested by AC, BJ (5/10/64), DM (12/4/64), other sources: Wells 1965 (lst ed.):19, Wells 1966, H-T <TciáktEl>, source: place names reference file #181.

<**ch'iyáqtel**>, ds //c'iyɛ́q=təl//, FSH /*'salmon weir, fish trap'*/, *see* ch'iyáq ~ ts'iyáq.

<**Ch'iyáqtel**>, dnom //c'iyɛ́q=təl//, PLN /*'Tzeachten, a (recent) settlement on the upper reaches of the lower Chilliwack River, now Chilliwack Indian Reserve #13 near Sardis'*/, literally /'device to trap fish'/, *see* ch'iyáq ~ ts'iyáq.

<**ch'íyxw ~ ts'íyxw ~ ts'éyxw**>, free root //c'íyxʷ ~ c'ə́yxʷ//, DESC /*'be dry, get dry, to dry'*/, possibly **<í-ablaut** or **é-ablaut>** *resultative*, syntactic analysis: intransitive verb, attested by AC, BHTTC (10/76), EB (12/1/75, 2/6/76), Deming (1/31/80), Salish cognate: Squamish root /č'iʔ ~ č'ayʔ/ *dry out, wither* K69:68 as in /č'iʔxʷ/ *dry* K67:322, K69:68 and /č'áyʔ-i/ *dry out (ab. living things), die (ab. tree)* K69:68, all W73:86, example: **<lulh ts'éyxw.>**, //lə=uɬ c'ə́yxʷ//, /*'It's dry.'*/, literally /'past - already is dry'/, attested by AC, **<ts'íyxw tel thóthel.>**, //c'íyxʷ t-əl θ=áθəl//, /*'My mouth is dry.'*/, attested by Deming, **<lulh le ts'íyxw te stó:lō.>**, //lə=uɬ lə c'íyxʷ tə s=tá·l=əw//, /*'The river is getting dry.'*/, literally /'past -already past 3rd person subject get dry the river'/, attested by EB.

<**ts'áyxw**>, cts //c'i[-Aɛ́-]yxʷ//, DESC [*'drying'*], (**<á-ablaut>** *continuative*), phonology: ablaut, syntactic analysis: intransitive verb, attested by Deming (1/31/80), other sources: ES and JH /c'ɛ́·yxʷ/ *dry*.

<**shxwch'á:yxwels**>, dnom //sxʷ=c'i[=Aɛ́·=]yxʷ=əls//, sas, FSH [*'fish-drying rack'*], literally /'something for drying fish as a structured activity continuative'/, (**<shxw=>** *something for*),

(<**=els**> *structured activity continuative nominal*), phonology: ablaut, syntactic analysis: nominal, attested by DM (12/4/64 new transcript new p. 187).

<**sch'á:yxw**>, strs //s=c'i[=Aɛ́·=]yxʷ//, DESC ['*(be) dried*'], FOOD, (<**s=**> *stative*), (<**á:-ablaut**> *resultative*), phonology: ablaut, syntactic analysis: adjective/adjectival verb, attested by DM (12/4/64 new transcript new p.191), example: <**sch'á:yxw (swí:wa, sth'í:m)**>, //s=c'i[=Aɛ́·=]yxʷ (s=wí·wɛ, s=θ'í·m)//, /'*dried (eulachons, berries)*'/, attested by DM.

<**sch'á:yxwels**>, dnom //s=c'i[=Aɛ́·=]yxʷ=əls//, sas, FOOD ['*dried meat*'], (<**s=**> *nominalizer*), (<**ó:-ablaut**> *resultative*), (<**=els**> *structured activity continuative*), phonology: ablaut, syntactic analysis: nominal, attested by DM (12/4/64 new transcript new p.190).

<**ts'íyxwt ~ ts'éyxwt**>, pcs //c'íyxʷ=T ~ c'ə́yxʷ=T//, FSH ['*dry s-th*'], HUNT, HARV /'*spread them out to dry (berries, bulrushes, etc.)*'/, MC, (<**=t**> *purposeful control transitivizer*), syntactic analysis: transitive verb, attested by AC (10/1/71, 10/13/71), EB (4/28/76), example: <**éwechexw ts'íyxwtexw.**>, //ʔə́wə-c-əxʷ c'íyxʷ=T-əxʷ//, /'*Don't dry it.*'/, attested by AC, <**lachxw ch'éyxwt te qwe'óp.**>, //lɛ-c-xʷ c'ə́yxʷ=T tə qʷəʔáp//, /'*You go dry the apple.*'/, attested by AC, <**léwe ts'éyxwt ta s'óthes.**>, //lə́wə c'ə́yxʷ=T t-ɛ s=ʔáθ=əs//, /'*You dry your face.*'/, attested by AC, <**th'exwót q'e éwechxw ts'éyxwtexw.**>, //θ'əx̣ʷ=áT q'ə ʔə́wə-c-xʷ c'ə́yxʷ=T-əxʷ//, /'*Wash it but don't dry it.*'/, attested by AC.

<**ch'áyxwt**>, cts //c'i[-Aɛ́-]yxʷ=T//, HARV ['*drying s-th*'], HUNT, FSH, MC, (<**á-ablaut**> *continuative*), phonology: ablaut, syntactic analysis: transitive verb, attested by AC (8/24/70, 10/13/71); found in <**ch'áyxwtes.**>, //c'i[-Aɛ́-]yxʷ=T-əs//, /'*He/She is drying it (clothes, fruit, dishes, etc.).*'/, attested by AC, example: <**tsel ts'áyxwt.**>, //c-əl c'i[-Aɛ-]yxʷ=T//, /'*I'm drying it.*'/, attested by AC (8/24/70).

<**ch'íyxweqel**>, ds //c'íyxʷ=əqəl//, ABDF ['*dry in the throat*'], lx <**=eqel**> *in the throat*, syntactic analysis: adjective/adjectival verb, attested by Deming (1/31/80).

<**ts'iyxweqthàlèm**>, df //c'iyxʷ=əq(əl)=T-ɛ̀lə̀m//, if, ABDF ['*my throat is dry*'], literally /'my throat was dried out (on purpose)'/, possibly <**=t**> *purposeful control transitivizer*, (<**-àlèm**> *first person singular passive*), phonology: syllable-loss predictable, syntactic analysis: transitive verb - passive, attested by EB (12/19/75), example: <**me ts'íyxweqthàlèm, tsel me lhqó:le.**>, //mə c'íyxʷ=əq(əl)=T-ɛ̀lə̀m, c-əl mə ɬ=qá·-lə//, /'*My throat is dry, I'm thirsty.*'/, attested by EB.

<**ch'iyxwíwel**>, ds //c'iyxʷ=íwəl//, ABDF ['*really constipated*'], literally /'dry in the rectum, dry in the insides'/, lx <**=íwel**> *in the rectum, in the insides, in the bottom*, syntactic analysis: adjective/adjectival verb, attested by JL (3/31/78).

<**ch'íyxweqel**>, ds //c'íyxʷ=əqəl//, ABDF ['*dry in the throat*'], *see* ch'íyxw ~ ts'íyxw ~ ts'éyxw.

<**ch'iyxwíwel**>, ds //c'iyxʷ=íwəl//, ABDF ['*really constipated*'], *see* ch'íyxw ~ ts'íyxw ~ ts'éyxw.

<**ch'mát**>, cts //c'ɛm=M1=T//, ABFC ['*biting on s-th*'], *see* ch'ám ~ ts'ám ~ ts'ém.

<**ch'ó:kw'e ~ ts'ó:kw'e ~ ts'ó:kw'a**>, possibly root //c'á·k'ʷə ~ c'á·k'ʷɛ or c'á·k'ʷ=ɛ//, EZ ['*skunk cabbage*'], ['*Lysichitum americanum*'], ASM ['leaves used to wrap food for cooking and as waxed paper'], MED ['roots used for spring tonic (AC), leaf put on head for antidote for baldness, roots used as medicine for rheumatism (wash limbs in it) (EF), leaves are medicine for swelling and arthritis and put on the chest for emphysema (EF)'], possibly <**=a ~ =e**> *living thing*, syntactic analysis: noun, nominal, attested by AC, EF (Deming 9/21/78), other sources: ES /c'ák'ʷa/ *skunk cabbage*, JH /c'á·k'ʷe/ *skunk cabbage*, Salish cognate: Northern Lushootseed /č'ú(ʔ)k'ʷ/ *skunk cabbage* H76:119, Squamish /č'úk'ʷa/ *skunk cabbage* W73:237, K67:321, K69:68, also <**ts'ókw'elets**>, //c'ák'ʷ=ələc//, lx <**=elets**> *on the bottom*, attested by Deming (4/12/79).

<**Ts'okw'á:m ~ Lexwts'okw'á:m ~ Lexwch'okw'á:m**>, ds //c'ak'ʷ(=)ɛ=əm ~ ləxʷ=c'ak'ʷ(=)ɛ=əm//, PLN /'*village at Five-Mile Creek (five miles above Yale), (village about half a mile above mouth of Sawmill Creek* [SP and AK (Fish Camp 8/2/77)], *Five-Mile Creek, Saddle Rock* [Halkomelem Instructors Association 10/26/77], *area of skunk cabbages right across the Fraser River from Five-Mile Creek, a low area at the swampy south end of Q'alelíktel* [AK (Trip to Five-Mile Creek 4/30/79)], *area along the banks of Five-Mile Creek, the original area is a quarter mile north from SLAHEECH CEMETERY No. 3 (marked by sign and white picket fence of west side of highway) and a quarter mile west* [Albert Phillips (Trip to Five-Mile Creek 4/30/79)])'/, lx <**=em**> *place to have/get*, lx <**lexw=**> *always*, phonology: vowel merger, syntactic analysis: nominal, attested by AK (Trip to Five-Mile Creek 4/30/79), other sources: Wells 1965 (lst ed.):25, other source: place names reference file #133,.

<**ch'ó:lh ~ ts'ó:lh**>, bound root or stem //c'á·ɬ or /c'á·ɬ//, meaning unknown but possibly composed of <**ch'á: ~ ts'á:**>, bound root //c'ɛ́· *on top of*// + <**=lh**>, da //=ɬ//, MC ['*(material for)*'] (in the general sense not the cloth sense), thus poss. lit. 'material for on top of (plants)'.

<**sch'ó:lha ~ sts'ó:lha ~ sts'ólha**>, df //s=c'á·ɬ(=)ɛ ~ s=c'áɬ(=)ɛ//, EB ['*leaf*'], LT ['*leaf-green*'], ASM ['the following color terms are used by AK before sts'ólha to specify shades of the color: tsxwíkw', xwíxwekw'el, tsqw'í*x*w, tsqwáy, sqwóqwiyel, stl'ítl'esel'], (<**s=**> *nominalizer*), root meaning possibly *material for on top of (plants)*, possibly <**=a**> *living thing*, syntactic analysis: nominal, attested by AC, BJ (5/10/64, 12/5/64), EB (2/16/76), Elders Group (5/16/79), other sources: ES /sc'áɬa/ (Cw /sc'áɬɛʔ/, Ms /sc'áɬaʔ/) *leaf*, Salish cognate: Squamish /sč'úɬaʔ/ *leaf (of any tree)* W73:158, K67:288, Lushootseed /s-č'úɬəyʔ/ *leaf (in general)* H76:119, see charts by Rob MacLaury, example: <**ts'ats'í:ts'etl' sts'ó:lha *x*wá:lá:lhp**>, //C_1ɛ=c'í·ƛ'[=C_1ə=]ƛ' s=c'ɛ́·ɬɛ *x*ʷɛ́·lɛ=ɛ́ɬp//, EB, /'*short leaf willow, short-leaf willow, Sitka willow*'/, /'*Salix sitchensis*'/ (compare with <***x*wá:lá:lhp**> *short-leaf willow, Sitka willow*), attested by AC (11/26/71), <**tl'áqt sts'ó:lha *x*wá:lá:lhp**>, //ƛ'ɛ́qt s=c'á·ɬɛ*x*ʷɛ́·lɛ=ɛ́ɬp//, EB, /'*long leaf willow, Pacific willow*'/, /'*Salix lasiandra*'/ (compare with <**xélts'epelhp**> *Pacific willow, long-leaf willow)*, attested by AC (11/26/71), <**tsqwá:y te hilálxw sch'ó:lha.**>, //c=qʷɛ́·y tə hil=álxʷ s=c'á·ɬɛ//, /'*The Fall leaves are yellow.*'/, attested by Elders Group (5/16/79), <**tsqwá:y te sts'ólha.**>, //c=qʷɛ́·y tə s=c'áɬɛ//, /'*The leaf is green.*'/, attested by Deming (5/3/79, SJ esp.).

<**ts'tá:m**>, ds //c'ɛ́t-M1=əm//, ABFC ['*crawl*'], (<**metathesis type 1**> *non-continuative*), (<**=em**> *middle voice*), phonology: metathesis, vowel merger, syntactic analysis: intransitive verb, attested by EB (12/11/75), AC (8/6/70), <**ch'tá:m**>, [č'ʰtǽ·m] EH, [tᶿ'tǽ·m] RG, '*crawl*', attested by (EH,RG 7/30/99)(SU transcription, tape 4), Salish cognate: Samish dial. of NSt /č'tə́ŋ/ *crawl* (beside /č'ə́tŋ'/ *crawling*) G86a:93, Cowichan dial. of Halkomelem /c'tém/ *crawl* B74b:59, possibly Squamish /č'ít-n/ *bring close (tr.)* W73:61, K67:321, also <**ts'tám**>, //c'ɛ́t=M1=(ə)m//, attested by Deming (3/16/78), example: <**lulh ts'tá:m tel mímele.**>, //lə=uɬ c'ɛ́t=M1=əm t-əl C_1í=məlɛ//, /'*My baby is already crawling.*'/, literally /'my little child has already crawled'/, attested by EB.

<**ts'átem**>, cts //c'ɛ́t=əm//, [c'ɛ́təm], ABFC ['*crawling*'], (lack of metathesis here means *continuative*), syntactic analysis: intransitive verb, attested by AC (8/6/70), EB (12/11/75), Deming (3/16/78), IHTTC (7/28/77), <**ch'étem**>, [č'ítɪm], '*crawling*', attested by (EH,RG 7/30/99)(SU transcription, tape 4), Salish cognate: Samish dial. of NSt /č'ə́tŋ'/ *crawling* G86a:93, also <**ts'étem ~ ch'étem**>, //c'ə́t=əm//, attested by NP (9/30/75), example: <**ts'átem stim:ōt**>, //c'ɛ́t=əm stim=mót//, CAN, /'*train*'/, literally /'crawling steamboat'/, attested by IHTTC (7/28/77), also <**ts'étem stim:ōt ~ ch'étem stim:ōt**>, //c'ə́t=əm stim=mót//, attested by NP (9/30/75).

<**ts'tl'ám ~ ts'tl'ém**>, mdls //c'ɛ́ƛ'-M1=m ~ c'ə́ƛ'-M1=m or c'ɛƛ'=ə[-´-]m//, [c'ƛ'ɛ́m ~ c'ƛ'ə́m], ABFC /'*jump, hop (once)*'/, TVMO, (<**metathesis type 1**> *non-continuative*), (<**=em**> *middle voice*),

phonology: metathesis, vowel-loss or vowel merger, most derivations from this root have **ts'** pronunciation, all are found under ts'; syntactic analysis: intransitive verb, attested by AC (8/7/70), Elders Group (3/1/72, 3/15/72), EB (12/12/75), JL (5/5/75), <**ch'tl'ém**>, [č'ƛ'ɪm] EH, [¢'ƛ'ɪm] RG, *'jump'*, attested by RG,EH 8/27/99 (SU transcription, tape 6), example: <**le ts'tl'ám.**>, //lə c'ɛ́ƛ'=M1=m//, /*'He jumped.'*/, attested by AC, JL.

<**ch'á:tl'em ~ ts'á:tl'em ~ ts'átl'em**>, cts //c'ɛ́[-·-]ƛ'=əm//, ABFC /*'jumping, hopping'*/, TVMO, (<**-:- and lack of metathesis**> *continuative*), phonology: lengthening, syntactic analysis: intransitive verb, attested by AC (8/7/70), Elders Group (3/15/72), JL (5/5/75), example: <**le ts'átl'em.**>, //lə c'ɛ́ƛ'=əm//, /*'He's jumping.'*/, attested by AC, <**ch'ech'etl'ím**>, [č'ɪč'ɪƛ'ím] EH, [¢'ɪ¢'ɪƛ'ím] RG, *'jumping'*, attested by RG,EH 8/27/99 (SU transcription, tape 6).

<**ts'xwót**> (*<**ch'xwót**>), pcs //c'xʷá=T or c'áxʷ=M1=T or c'xʷ=áT//, TIB /*'add some, add it, (do it again [AD])'*/, possibly <**metathesis type 1**> *non-continuative*, (<**=t**> *purposeful control transitivizer*), phonology: metathesis or allomorph of suffix, syntactic analysis: transitive verb, attested by Elders Group (3/16/77), Salish cognate: Lushootseed /č'xʷ-úd/ *add it to something* H76:696, Squamish root /č'ixʷ ~ č'əxʷ/ *increase* as in /č'xʷ-ut/ *increase (tr.)* W73:149, K67:319,320, K69:68, also /*'do it again'*/, attested by AD (11/19/79).

<**ch'exwélhchat**>, ds //c'əxʷ=ə́ɬcɛ=T//, WATR [*'add some water [to s-th]'*], TIB, FOOD, lx <**=élhcha**> *water, unclear liquid*, syntactic analysis: transitive verb, attested by IHTTC (8/17/77).

E

<é>, free root //ʔə́//, MOOD [*'is that okay? (interrogative tag-question)'*], phonology: related to <-e> *interrogative* by addition of glottal stop /ʔ/ at beginning (not written word-initially in the orthography) so that it can occur as an independent word in a position where <-e> cannot; may be a separate morpheme also however as the meaning is slightly more than just interrogative, syntactic analysis: interrogative particle, tag-question, used at end of sentence to ask if it's okay, syntactic comment: occurs in position similar to <étlh> *isn't it?, tag-question*, attested by AD, dialects: *maybe only Tait.*

<**-e**>, //-ə//, MOOD /*'interrogative, yes/no question'*/, phonology: occurs often after li, yielding lí: ~ líye, syntactic analysis: interrogative suffix, syntactic comment: occurs after the first word in a sentence and before the subject pronoun suffix and non-subordinate suffix -ts ~ -ch, example: <**lámechexw**>, //lɛ́-m-ə-c-əxw//, /*'Are you (sg.) going?'*/, attested by AC, <**lámetsel**>, //lɛ́-m-ə-c-əl//, /*'Am I going?'*/, attested by AC, <**láme á:lhtel**>, //lɛ́-m-ə ʔɛ́·ɬtəl//, /*'Are they going?'*/, attested by AC, <**lhéq'e t'ít'ets'em**>, //ɬə́q'-ə t'í[-C_1ə-]c'=əm//, /*'Does he swim?'*/, literally /'is he sometimes swimming?'/, (<-**R1-**> *continuative*), (semological comment: lhéq' *sometimes*), <**lí: chókw**>, //lí-ə cákw//, /*'Is it far?'*/, attested by AC.

<**=e ~ =a**>, da //=ə ~ =ɛ//, EZ [*'living thing'*], syntactic analysis: derivational suffix, as in <**swíyeqe ~ swí:qe**>, //s=wí·q=ə//, /*'man, male'*/, <**sqáqele**>, //s=qɛ́qəl=ə or s=C_1ɛ́=qəl=ə//, /*'baby'*/, <**mél:e ~ mél:a**>, //mə́l·=ə ~ mə́l·=ɛ//, /*'(someone's) child'*/, <**syéw:e ~ syúw:e**>, //s=yə́w·=ə//, /*'fortune-teller, seer'*/, comment: possibly also as in <**shxwéwe**> *cougar*, <**(s)t'ít'ele**> *fawn*, <**stqóye ~ stqóye**> *wolf*, <**á<u>x</u>e**> *Canada goose*, <**smő qw'e**> *great blue heron*, <**á:we**> *seagull*, <**s<u>x</u>wő<u>x</u>wtha ~ s<u>x</u>wő<u>x</u>wtsa**> (beside Katzie <**s<u>x</u>wéth<u>x</u>weth**>) *sparrow*, <**swí:we**> *eulachon, oolichen*, <**s'ó<u>x</u>we**> *clam*, <**<u>x</u>we<u>x</u>wá:ye**> *big fly, blowfly*, <**yó:le**> *cow parsnip*, <**t'emó:sa**> *western dock, wild rhubarb, domestic rhubarb*,< **th'ékwa**> *mountain fern with wide top,* probably *spiny wood fern*, <**welékwsa**> *poison fern that grows in swampy places,* probably *water hemlock, poison hemlock*, <**t'áqa**> *salal berry*, <**elíle**> *salmonberry*, <**ts'ókwe**> *skunk cabbage*, <**sts'ó:lha**> *leaf.*

<**ehálēqep**>, SD /*'(made) a faint sound carried by the air, sound within hearing distance, sound within earshot'*/, *see* ehó.

<**ehó**>, bound root //ʔəhá//, MC [*'wrap up'*].

<**ehó:t**>, pcs //ʔəhá·=T//, MC /*'wrap s-th up (a present, etc.)'*/, SOC /*'wrap s-th up (a baby, etc.)'*/, ASM, (<**=T**> *purposeful control transitivizer*), phonology: length seems to be conditioned here by the transitivizer rather than being part of the transitivizer or aspect, it probably corresponds to a root final glottal stop in Musqueam, syntactic analysis: transitive verb, attested by EB, Elders meeting.

<**s'ehó**>, stvi //s=ʔəhá//, MC [*'wrapped up'*], syntactic analysis: participle, attested by Deming.

<**s'i'hó**>, dmv //s=C_1í=ʔəhá//, EFAM [*'wrapped up (in stupidity)'*], (<**s=**> *stative*), (<**R4=**> *diminutive*), phonology: reduplication, syntactic analysis: participle, example: <**s'i'hó ta' s<u>x</u>éyes**>, //s=C_1í=ʔəhá t-ɛʔ s=x̣ə́y=əs//, /*'Your head is wrapped up (in stupidity).'*/.

<**ehálēqep**>, ds //ʔəhá=ɛ́lə́qəp//, SD /*'(made) a faint sound carried by the air, sound within hearing distance, sound within earshot'*/, lit. "a wrapped up sound", SENS, (<**=áléqep**> *sound*), phonology: vowel combination, syntactic analysis: intransitive verb probably, poss. nominal, also <**ehálеqep**>, //ʔəhá=ɛ́ləqəp//, SD [*'a sound heard starting up again in the distance'*], attested by AD.

<**s'ehólets**>, dnom //s=ʔəhá=ləc//, CLO [*'pocket'*], literally /'wrapped up on the bottom'/, lx <**=lets**> *on the bottom*, syntactic analysis: nominal, attested by RJ (Rose Jones), example: <**epóles qas te isóles i ta' s'ehólets tl'esu sóles**>, //ʔápə[=M2=]l=əs qɛs tə ʔisɛ́[=Aá=]lə=əs ʔi t-ɛʔ s=ʔəhá=ləc ƛ'a-s=əw sí[=Aá=]l=əs//, /*'Ten dollars and two dollars in your pocket and you're drunk.'*/, phonology: metathesis, ablaut (triggered by =es *dollars*), stress-shifting, vowel combination, usage: a rhyme (not traditional), attested by RJ.

<**sxwehóthes**>, dnom //s(=)xʷ=əhá=aθəs//, CLO [*'a veil'*], literally /'something wrapped on the face'/, lx <**=óthes**> an unusually full form of *on the face* lx <**=es**> is the more usual form) (also found in the independent word, <**s'óthes**> *face*, phonology: TG's idiolect consistently has [sxʷ] where other speakers have [šxʷ]; also in this citation the initial glottal stop of the root has been dropped, syntactic analysis: nominal, attested by TG.

<**ehó:les**>, ds //ʔəhál(=)əs//, DIR /*'facing towards, facing me (sic?)'*/, probably lx <**=es**> *face*, syntactic analysis: intransitive verb, adjective/adjectival verb?.

<**ehó:t**>, MC /*'wrap s-th up (a present, etc.)'*/, *see* ehó.

<**ehó:yt**>, pcs //ʔəhá·y=T//, SOC [*'cheat s-o (in slahal for ex.)'*], PLAY, (<**=T**> *purposeful control transitivizer*), syntactic analysis: transitive verb, also <**ehóyt**>, attested by Deming; found in <**ehóythóxes**>, //ʔəháy=T-áxy-əs//, /*'he cheated me'*/, attested by Deming.

<**íhóyt**>, cts //ʔə[-Aí-]háy=T//, SOC [*'cheating s-o'*], (<**í-ablaut**> *continuative*), phonology: ablaut, stress-shift, syntactic analysis: transitive verb, attested by Deming; found in <**íhóytes**>, //ʔə[-Aí-]háy=T-əs//, /*'he's cheating someone'*/, attested by Deming.

<**=ekw ~ =íkw**>, possibly //=əkʷ ~ =íkʷ//, possibly /*'(perhap) round'*/, SH, syntactic analysis: lexical suffix, also <**=íkw**>; found in <**th'íkwekw**>, //θ'íkʷ=əkʷ//, /*'blue elderberry'*/, literally (perhaps) /'round prickle (referring to taste)'/, <**th'eth'emíkw**>, //C_1ə=θ'am=íkʷ//, /*'little tiny beads'*/, literally (perhaps) /'many little round bones'/.

<**ékwiyeqw**>, df //ʔə́kʷ(=)iyəqʷ//, KIN /*'great great grandparent; great great grandchild; sibling/cousin of great great grand-parent/-child'*/, ASM, lx possibly <**=iyeqw**> (perhaps related to <**=iqw ~ =eqw**> *on the head, hair*); found in the words for *great grandparent/child, great great great grandparent/-child*, and *great great great great grandparent/-child*, perhaps since each of the parent allosemes is at the head of at least 4 generations of descendants, syntactic analysis: nominal, also <**ékwiyeqw**>, KIN /*'great great great grandparent/-child; sibling/cousin of great great great grandparent/-child'*/, dialects: *a smaller number of speakers use the word with this meaning and use* θ'ə́p'*ayəqʷ* ~ θ'ə́p'*iyəqʷ for great great grandparent/-child, etc.*, attested by AC, some others incl. Hill-Tout's teacher, Captain John Suwalis (whom AC lived with when married to his son, Commodore), other sources: ES /ʔə́kʷəyəqʷ/ *great great grandparent, great great grandchild*; H-T <ō'kwiuk·> (macron over the i) *great great great grandparent, great great great grandchld.*

<**ekw'ólem**>, DIR /*'lose (s-th, an object, etc.)'*/, *see* íkw' ~ í:kw'.

<**=el**>, da //=əl//, QUAL [*'-ish'*], syntactic analysis: lexical suffix, derivational suffix, (semological comment: this semantic element may be signalled by reduplication in the examples; then <=el> would have to be *verbal* or from <**=í:l ~ =el**> *go*); found in <**tsqw'íqw'exwel**>, //c=q'ʷíq'ʷəx̣ʷ=əl//, /*'brownish-black'*/ (compare <**ts=qw'íxw**> *brown)*, <**sq'íq'exel**>, //s=q'íq'əx̣=əl//, /*'getting blackish'*/, <**qeyqeyxeló**>, //qɛyqɛyx̣=əl=á//, /*'shadow'*/ (compare <**ts'=q'éyx**> *black*), <**sqwóqweyel**>, //s=qʷáqʷiy=əl//, /*'yellowish'*/ (compare <**qwóy=el**> *get yellow, be yellow,* has <**=el**> from <**=í:l**> *got, come get* and <**a-ablaut**> from <**ts=qwá:y**> *color yellow)*, <**stítethel**>, //stítəθ=əl//, /*'puny'*/ (compare <**stí:th**> *thin, skinny).*

<**-el ~ -l ~ l**>, is //**-əl ~ -l ~ l**//([-əl ~ -ɪl ~ -ʊl ~ -l ~ l̩]), PRON /'*my, first person singular possessive pronoun, first person subordinate subject*'/, phonology: appears as syllabic l at sentence beginning before nominal verbs such as stl'í: *want*, syntactic analysis: is, syntactic comment: also used as subordinate subject by possessing a nominalized clause, also <**-l**>, //-l//, example: <**thel tà:l**>, //θə-l tɛ̀·l//, /'*my mother*'/, also <**l**>, //l//, [syllabic l], <**l stl'í: kw'els lám.**>, //l s=ƛ'í· k'ʷ-əl-s lɛ́=m//, /'*I want to go.*'/, literally /'(it) is my want that I go (or) is my want the (abstract)-my-nominal go (or) my go(ing) is my want'/.

<**=el ~ =a(:)l ~ =o(:)l**>, da //=əl, =ɛ(·)l =a(·)l//, possibly /'*locative, on the*'/, DIR, comment: one-fourth of all the lexical suffixes begin with <=el, =a(:)l =o(:)l>, including: <**=áléqel, =élmél, =ó:les, =á:lí:ya, =(e)(l)qs(el), =él:es** (~ **=elís), =elá<u>x</u>el, =á:lwes ~ =élwes, =(e)lets, =álq<el ~ =elqel, =elsxá, =elwet, =á:ltexw, =(a)ltxw ~ =(el)txw** (~ **=á:wtxw), =ó:lkwlh, =elep ~ =í:lep** (etc.) ~ **=ép** (etc.), **=(el)tsep, =áléqep, =álews, =á:ltel, =eló:t, =elácha, =elálexw, =eleq** (*male name* and *one who*), **=eletsá:ls, =ó:lwelh, =á:lts' ~ =elts', =á:leq ~ =eleq,** and **=ó:llh**>. Some of the initial vowel + l elements show signs of being optional. It seems like the vowel plus l may bave been a grammatical marker of some kind whose meaning can no longer be recovered. Semantically it could have meant *locative, on* and then been extended by analogy without the meaning surviving., syntactic analysis: lexical suffix.

<**=éla**>, da //=ə́lɛ//, ANA /'*on the side of the head, on the temples, around the ear, on the cheek*'/, syntactic analysis: lexical suffix, derivational suffix; found in <**th'iyaméla**>, //θ'iyɛm=ə́lɛ//, /'*side of the head, temples*'/, <**s<u>x</u>elpéla**>, //s=x̣əl=p=ə́lɛ//, /'*sideburns*'/, <**tl'alqtéle**>, //ƛ'ɛlqt=ə́lə//, /'*deer*'/ (root <**tl'áqt**> *long*, with <**-l-**> infix *plural*).

<**=elácha**>, da //=əlɛ́cɛ//, N ['*male name*'], syntactic analysis: lexical suffix, derivational suffix; found in <**Q'ewq'ewelácha**>, //q'əwq'əw=əlɛ́cɛ//, /'*male loon of Kawkawa Lake in a story*'/, <**T'ixwelátsa**>, //t'ixʷ=əlɛ́cɛ//, /'*Indian name of second oldest Wealick brother*'/, <**Th'eláchiyetel**>, //θ'=əlɛ́c=iyətəl//, /'*Indian name of Richard Malloway Sr. (of Sardis)*'/, <**Lá<u>x</u>elácha**>, //lɛ́x̣=əlɛ́cɛ//, /'*Indian name of Jimmie Swíweles*'/.

<**=elálexw ~ =elàlè<u>x</u>w**>, da //=əlɛ́ləxʷ ~ =əlɛ̀lə̀x̣ʷ//, N ['*male name*'], syntactic analysis: lexical suffix, derivational suffix; found in <**Siyomelálexw**>, //siyam=əlɛ́ləxʷ//, /'*Indian name of Charlie Siyomelálexw, (said to mean) head of the house, superior of the house*'/, <**Lhó:kw'elàlèxw**>, //ɬá·k'ʷ=əlɛ̀lə̀xʷ//, /'*Indian name of Dan Milo's great grandfather*'/ (root <**lhó:kw'**> *(to) fly*, **the** man was said to have arrived one day in the village by flying there.

<**=elá<u>x</u>el**>, da //=əlɛ́x̣əl//, ANA /'*on the arm, in the arm, on or in the wing*'/, (semological comment: prob. source of <**=á<u>x</u>el**> *side (of a house, a square, a river)*), syntactic analysis: lexical suffix, derivational suffix; found in <**kw'qwelá<u>x</u>el**>, //k'ʷqʷ=əlɛ́x̣əl//, /'*hit on the arm (with a stick-like object)*'/, <**shxw'ilá<u>x</u>el**>, //sxʷ=ʔi=lɛ́x̣əl//, /'*armpit*'/, <**sth'emxwelá<u>x</u>el**>, //s=θ'əm=xʷ=əlɛ́x̣əl//, /'*elbow*'/, literally /'bone--lump-like--in arm'/, <**lhets'elá<u>x</u>el**>, //ɬəc'=əlɛ́x̣əl//, /'*cut one's arm*'/, <**lekwelá<u>x</u>el**>, //ləkʷ=əlɛ́x̣əl//, /'*break an arm*'/, <**skw'elyá<u>x</u>el**>, //sk'ʷəly=ɛ́x̣əl or sk'ʷ=əlyɛ́x̣əl//, /'*bat*'/, <**p'íp'eth'elá<u>x</u>el**>, //p'íp'əθ'=əlɛ́x̣əl//, /'*bat*'/, literally /'squeezing arm'/, <**Spotpetelá<u>x</u>el**>, //s=pat=C_1əC_2=əlɛ́x̣əl//, /'*thunder-wind (wind that precedes a thunderstorm)*'/, (semological comment: thunder is thought of as a bird--the thunderbird, shxwexwó:s), probably <**s=**> *nominal*, probably root <**pó:t**> *blow*, probably <**=R2**> *iterative*, possibly <**=á<u>x</u>el**> *end or side of a house (inside or outside)*.

<**=élchep ~ =éltsep**>, da //=ə́lcəp//, FIRE ['*firewood*'], HARV, syntactic analysis: lexical suffix, derivational suffix; found in <**th'iqw'éltsep**>, //θ'iq'ʷ=ə́lcəp//, /'*split (fire)wood*'/ (compare <**th'íqw'=et**> *punch s-o or s-th*), <**yéqwelchep**>, //yə́qʷ=əlcəp//, /'*make a fire, burn wood*'/ (root <**yéqw**> *burn)*, <**sí:lcheptel**>, //sí·lcəp=təl//, attested by DM, /'*a firedrill*'/ (root <**sel=**> *spin)*,

<**qw'á:ychep**>, //q'ʷɛ́·y=cəp//, /'*cinders, real fine powdery ashes (light, soft dust-like)*'/ (compare <**qw'á:y=t**> *burning pitch onto a canoe).*

<**=éleq**>, da //=ə́ləq or =ə[=´=]l=əq//, SOC /'*one who, -er, one who does as an occupation*'/, syntactic analysis: lexical suffix, derivational suffix; found in <**í:weséleq**>, //ʔí·wəs=ə́ləq//, /'*a guide*'/ (compare <**í:wes=t**> *guide s-o, teach s-o, show s-o),* <**lhalhewéleq**>, //ɬɛɬəw=ə́ləq//, /'*a healer, an Indian doctor or medicine man at work*'/ (compare <**lhálhew**> *working or curing (of an Indian doctor on a patient)),* <**skwukwelstéleq**>, //skʷukʷəl(=)st=ə́ləq//, /'*school teacher*'/ (root <**skwú:l**> *school),* perhaps <**slets'éleq**>, //sləc'=ə́ləq//, /'*spouse's sibling's spouse ~ step-sibling*'/ (root <**láts' ~ lets'=**> *different).*

<**=eleq**>, da //=ələq or =əl=əq//, N ['*male name*'], comment: poss. related to <**=éleq**> *one who does as an occupation,* possibly <**=el**> *go, come, get, become,* possibly <**=eq**> *male,* syntactic analysis: lexical suffix, derivational suffix; found in <**X̲éyteleq**>, //xɛ́yt=ələq//, /'*Indian name of an old man from Kilgard (a strong warrior and Indian dancer, in a battle he once punched through a man's chest)*'/ (compare <**x̲éyléx̲**> *war, fight war* and <**x̲éy=t=em**> *growl (of a person)).*

<**=eles ~ =les**>, da //=(ə)ləs//, TIB ['*psychological non-control transitivizer*'], syntactic analysis: derivational suffix, also <**=les**>, //=ləs//, also <**=es**>, //=əs//; found in <**málqeles**>, //mɛ́lq=ələs//, /'*forget s-o/s-th*'/, example: <**skw'á:y kw'els málqelesóme.**>, //s=k'ʷɛ́·y k'ʷ-əl-s mɛ́lq=ələs-ámə//, /'*I'll never forget you.*'/; found in <**hákw'eles**>, //hɛ́k'ʷ=ələs//, /'*remember s-o/s-th*'/, <**hákw'elesóxes.**>, //hɛ́k'ʷ=ələs-áxʸ-əs//, /'*He remembered me.*'/, <**tl'í:lsóxes.**>, //ƛ'í·=ləs-áxʸ-əs//, /'*He/She loves me., He/She likes me.*'/, <**á:yelesóxes.**>, //ʔɛ́·y=ələs-áxʸ-əs//, /'*He left me. (leave s-o)*'/, <**á:yeleses.**>, //ʔɛ́·y=ələs-əs//, /'*He/She/It/They went away from s-o/s-th. (go away from s-o/s-th)*'/, <**pétemesòxes.**>, //pə́təm=(l)əs-áxʸ-əs//, /'*He asked for me. (ask for s-o)*'/.

<**=eletsá:ls, =elesà:ls**>, da //=ələcɛ́·ls, =ələsɛ̀·ls//, EB /'*plants, grass*'/, syntactic analysis: lexical suffix; found in <**lhéts'eletsá:ls**>, //ɬə́c'=ələcɛ́·ls//, /'*(to) cut hay*'/ (root <**lhíts'**> *(to) cut),* <**lhá:lteletsá:ls**>, //ɬɛ́·lt=ələcɛ́·ls//, /'*spraying water on the garden*'/ (compare <**lhó:lt**> *(to) spray* and <**lhélt=es=t**> *splash/spray/flip s-o with water in the face),* <**spópex̲welá:ls**>, //Chwk. s=pá[=C₁ə=]x̣ʷ=əlsɛ́·ls//, /'*spray-gun (for plants)*'/ (compare <**póx̲w=et**> *blow spray on patient (done by Indian doctor)),* dialects: *Chill.*, also <**shxwpópex̲welsà·ls**>, //sxʷ=pá[=C₁ə=]x̣ʷ=əlsɛ́·ls//, dialects: *Tait.*

<**=elétsel ~ =átsel**>, da //=ələ́cəl ~ =ɛ́cəl//, ANA ['*on the testicles*'], syntactic analysis: lexical suffix, Salish cognate: Musqueam /-ələcən ~ -éləcən ~ -écən/ *testicles* (Suttles ca 1985: 14.5.68), Lushootseed /báčəd/ *testicles* and /=álačəd/ *testicles* H76:692, 689; found in <**ma'elétstem**>, //mɛʔ=ələ́c(əl)=T-əm//, /'*castrated, he was castrated*'/, attested by DF (on Banff trip 8/30/78), <**mátsel**>, //mɛ́cəl or m=ɛ́cəl//, /'*testicle*'/.

<**=élets ~ =lets**>, da //=ə́ləc ~ =ləc//, ANA /'*on the rump, on the bottom, on the buttock(s)*'/, DIR ['*on the bottom (of anything)*'], syntactic analysis: lexical suffix, derivational suffix, also <**=lets**>, //=ləc//; found in <**kw'qwélets**>, //k'ʷqʷ=ə́ləc//, /'*hit on the rump (with club or stick)*'/, <**skw'íylets**>, //s=k'ʷíy=ləc//, /'*lame; to limp*'/, literally /'nominal climb rump'/, <**lheq'láts**>, //ɬəq'=lɛ́c or ɬɛ́q'=lə[=M2=]c//, /'*hip, hind leg*'/, literally /'wide of rump'/, <**ó:qwelets ~ éqwelets ~ ő̃qwelets**>, //ʔá·qʷ=ələc ~ ʔə́qʷ=ələc ~ ʔóqʷ=ələc//, /'*back*'/, literally /'comes out above rump'/, <**kw'esélets**>, //k'ʷɛ[=Aə=]s=ə́ləc//, /'*burned on the rump*'/, <**slhél:ets ~ slhl:ets**>, //s=ɬə́l=ləc//, /'*ass, butt, rump*'/, (semological comment: translated with less refined terms *ass, butt* to reflect the same shock value this word has for many elders as the two English words), root <**lhél**> *folded over,* <**stl'ep'élets**>, //s=ƛ'əp'=ə́ləc//, /'*tail*'/, literally /'deep in rump'/, <**sch'á:letstel ~ sch'áletstel ~ sts'á:letstel**>, //s=c'ɛ́(·)=ləc=təl//, /'*chair, bench*'/, literally /'nominal on top of rump (subject) device > "device the rump is on top of"'/, <**yáqeletsem**>, //yɛ́q=ələc=əm//, /'*change one's seat, change one's chair*'/, literally /'change rump one's (middle voice)'/, <**shxw'áthelets**>, //sxʷ=ʔɛ́θ=ələc//, /'*bottom of*

anything'/, <**tl'epláts**>, //ƛ'əp=lɛ́c or ƛ'əp=lə[=Aɛ́=]c//, /'*bottom of creek*'/, <**sq'epláts**>, //s=q'əp=lɛ́c or s=q'əp=lə[=Aɛ́=]c//, /'*bush bunched up tight at bottom, thick crowded tight underbrush*'/, <**skwélets**>, //skʷ=ə́ləc (or skʷə́(l)=ləc)//, /'*coiled bottom of basket before the sides are on*'/, <**spà:thélets**>, //spɛ̀·θ=ə́ləc//, /'*bear dung*'/, <**chèkelélets**>, //cə̀kəl=ə́ləc//, /'*chicken dung, chicken shit*'/, <**Th'émexwlats**>, //θ'ə́məxʷ=lɛc//, /'*tail of Seabird Island*'/.

<**elílá:lhp ~ elílà:lhp**>, EB ['*salmonberry plant*'], *see* elíle.

<**elíle**>, us //ʔəlílə//, EB ['*salmonberry (the berry itself)*'], ['*Rubus spectabilis*'], (semological comment: both the golden and the ruby form are eaten fresh, usually the first berry out; the sweet tender shoots are peeled in early spring and eaten raw as one kind of stháthqiy (also see under stháthqiy)), syntactic analysis: nominal, also <**alíle**>, //ʔɛlílə//, phonology: at slow speed, attested by AC, also <**alílé ~ elílá**>, //ʔɛlílə́ ~ ʔəlílɛ́//, phonology: at slow speed, attested by BJ, other sources: ES /əlí·lɛ̀/, H-T <ele'la> (macron over second e), example: <**elíle stháthqiy ~ alíle stháthqiy**>, //ʔəlílə s=θɛ́θq=iy ~ ʔɛlílə s=θɛ́θq=iy//, /'*salmonberry sprouts, salmonberry shoots*'/, attested by AC, <**yewál qw'él sth'í:m te elíle**>, //yəwɛ́l qʼʷə́l s=θ'í·m tə ʔəlílə//, /'*The salmonberry is the first ripe berry.*'/, attested by EB.

<**elílá:lhp ~ elílà:lhp**>, dnom //ʔəlílə=əɬp//, EB ['*salmonberry plant*'], lx <**=elhp**> *tree, plant,* phonology: vowel-merger, length and stress addition, syntactic analysis: nominal, also <**alílà:lhp**>, //ʔɛlílɛ̀·ɬp//, attested by AC.

<**tem'elíle**>, dnom //təm=ʔəlílə//, TIME /'*salmonberry time, (usually) May*'/, (semological comment: usually in May when the first salmonberries get ripe; used more generally for the Stó:lō month/moon that begins after the first sliver of moon appearing after a "burnt-out" or dark moon [English new moon]), syntactic analysis: nominal, other sources: Diamond Jenness's field notes on Wm. Sepass (Chill.) tem'elí:le *April-May, berry moon.*

<**lí:latses**>, dnom //(ʔə)lí·lɛ=cəs//, BSK ['*little berry basket*'], ASM ['tied around waist in front when harvesting, made in same design and shape as the big berry basket, when full the little basket is dumped into the big berry basket'], HARV, (morphosememic development: //'salmonberries in the hand → little berry basket'//), (<**=tses**> *in the hand*), phonology: syllable-loss, compensatory vowel lengthening, syntactic analysis: nominal, dialects: *Tait* (compare (Chill.) <**skw'álhem**> *little berry basket).*

<**=elís ~ =él:es**> /=əlís ~ =ə́l·əs//, da, ANA ['*(on the) tooth, teeth; on the buttons*'], ASM the last meaning or alloseme ['*on the buttons*'] since buttons were made out of teeth sometimes in precontact times, syntactic analysis: derivational affix, lexical suffix, found in <**silís**> //s=ʔɛy=əlís//, /'*(have) sharp teeth, (have) fangs*'/, literally /'be good teeth'/, (<**s=**> *stative*, root <**éy**> *be good*, lx <**=elís**> *(on the) teeth),* <**yél:és**> //y=ə́l·ə́s *or* yə́l·ə́s//, /'*tooth*'/, <**slheqwél:es**> //sɬəqʷ=ə́l·əs//, /'*gums*'/ (lit. "flesh on the teeth"), <**x̱ax̱elts'elísem**> //x̣ɛx̣əl=c'=əlís=əm//, /'*grinding one's teeth*'/, <**spex̱elís**> //s=pɛx̣=əlís//, /'*(be) tight-fitting (of clothes, can't be quite buttoned)*'/, semantic environment ['of pants, shirt, etc.'], literally /'be spread apart on the buttons'/.

<**élíyá**>, df //ʔə́lí(ʔ=í)yɛ́//, REL /'*to dream, have a vision*'/, possibly <**=íya**> *diminutive*?, poss. same root as in <shxwelí> *soul, spirit of a living person*, syntactic analysis: intransitive verb, attested by Elders (March 1972, tape 33), also <**èlìyà**>, //ʔə̀lìyɛ̀//, attested by EB, also <**ó:liya**>, //ʔá·liyɛ//, REL ['*have a vision before you become an experienced spirit dancer (a sts'eláxwem)*'], attested by AL (March 1972), <**élíyá**> REL /'*to dream, have a vision; prophet*'/, attested by BJ 12/5/64, also <**el'éliya**>, //$C_1əC_2$=ʔə́liyɛ//, REL /'*to dream, dreaming*'/, literally /'have visions (plural)'/, (<**R3=**> *plural*), phonology: reduplication, attested by AC, Salish cognate: Squamish root /ʔə́li/ *to dream* does not occur alone, see Squamish /ʔl-ʔə́li/ *to dream*, /ʔə́li-nit/ and /ʔl-ʔə́li-nit/ both *dream about (tr.)*, and /s-

ʔə́li/ *dream, vision, guardian spirit* W73:84, K67:302, 336, 388, Salish cognate: Nooksack /s-ʔə́liyə/ *a dream, vision'* A78:77.

<**el'èlìyà**>, cts //C_1əC_2-ʔəlìyɛ̀//, REL [*'dreaming'*], literally /'have visions (plural)'/, (<**R3-**> *continuative* from R3= *plural*), syntactic analysis: intransitive verb, attested by Elders (Mar. 1972, tape 33), EB 12/15/75, also <**el'éliya ~ el'élya**>, //C_1əC_2-ʔə́liyɛ ~ C_1əC_2-ʔə́lyɛ//, REL /*'dream, dreaming'*/, attested by AC, also <**él'eliya**>, //ʔə́l[-C_1əC_2-]iyɛ//, REL [*'dreaming'*], attested by Elders (Mar. 1972, tape 33), Salish cognate: Squamish /ʔl-ʔə́li/ *to dream*, example: <**tsel el'él(i)ya**>, //cəl ʔəlʔə́l(i)yɛ//, /*'I dreamed.'*/, attested by AC.

<**el'éliyemet**>, iecs //C_1əC_2-ʔə́liyə=məT//, REL [*'dreaming about s-o/s-th'*], (<**=met**> *indirect effect control transitivizer*), syntactic analysis: transitive verb, attested by AC; found in <**el'éliyemethométselcha**>, //C_1əC_2-ʔə́liyə=məT-amə[´]-c-əl-cɛ//, [ʔəlʔə̀liyəməθamə́cɪlčæ], /*'I'll be dreaming about you.'*/, attested by AC.

<**s'élíyá**>, dnom //s=ʔə́líyɛ́//, REL /*'spirit dream, vision, (any) dream'*/, syntactic analysis: nominal, attested by EB, BJ, JL (Elders Mar. 1972), also <**s'el'éliya**>, //s=C_1əC_2=ʔə́liyɛ//, REL [*'a dream'*], literally /'multiple visions'/, attested by AC, Salish cognate: Nooksack /s-ʔə́liyə/ *a dream, vision* A78:77; Squamish /s-ʔə́li/ *dream, vision, guardian spirit* W73:84, K67:302 ?Samish /səlí/ *soul* G86:81 (compare <**shxwelí**> *life spirit, soul)*, example: <**l s'élíyá**>, //l (or ʔl) s=ʔə́líyɛ́//, /*'my spirit dream'*/, attested by JL (Elders Mar. 1972).

<**éliyels**>, free root //ʔə́liyəls//, EB, FOOD [*'domestic onion'*], [*'Alium cepa'*],, syntactic analysis: nominal, (attested by RG,EH 6/16/98 to SN, edited by BG with RG,EH 6/26/00),, borrowed from English /ʔə́n(i)yənz/ *onions*, (semological comment: introduced by Caucasians, bulb eaten cooked or raw; the meaning can be singular though the term is borrowed from the English plural form), syntactic analysis: nominal.,see also <**éniyels**>

<**séyem éliyels**>, EB, FOOD *garlic* (lit. strong + [domestic] onion), (attested by RG,EH 6/16/98 to SN, edited by BG with RG,EH 6/26/00)

<**elíyliyem te híyqw.**>, FIRE [*'the fire is laughing'*], *see* yéqw.

<**=élmél**>, da //=əlmə́l//, EFAM [*'in the mind'*], syntactic analysis: lexical suffix, derivational suffix, as in <**télmél**>, //t=ə́lmə́l//, /*'the mind'*/, <**héyetélmél**>, //hɛ́yət=ə́lmə́l//, /*'nauseated'*/, literally /'vomiting in the mind'/, <**t'ekw'élmél**>, //t'ək'ʷ=ə́lmə́l//, /*'home-sick'*/, literally /'go home in the mind'/.

<**eló:lh**>, TVMO /*'be aboard, be in (a conveyance)'*/, *see* ó:lh.

<**eló:lhstexw**>, TVMO /*'get s-th aboard (a canoe, car, conveyance)'*/, *see* ó:lh.

<**=elò:t ~ =eló:t**>, da //=əl=à·t ~ =əl=á·t//, N [*'female name'*], possibly <**=el**> *come, go, get, become?*, (<**=ò:t**> *female name*), syntactic analysis: lexical suffix, derivational suffix; found in <**Q'ewq'eweló:t**>, //q'əw=C_1əC_2=əl(=)á·t//, /*'name of female loon in a story'*/ (compare <**q'ow=el**> *howl* and <**q'ewq'ew=el(=)ácha**> *name of the male loon in a story* and <**Q'éwq'ewe**> *Kawkawa Lake* where they lived and gave name to the lake), <**qewástelòt**>, //qəwɛ́stəlàt//, /*'kind of deer (probably female)'*/, <**Ts'símtelòt**>, //c'sím=t(=)əl(=)àt//, /*'name of one of Mt. Cheam's sisters,* also *a name of Mrs. Celia Thomas'*/ (compare <**ts'sím=t**> *grow s-th)*, <**Siyámtelòt**>, //siyɛ́m=təlàt//, /*'Indian name of Teresa Michell and Mrs. Shirley Leon'*/ (compare <**siyám**> *leader, chief*), <**Th'tístelot**>, //θ'tístəlat//, /*'Indian name of Mary Andrew (Susan Peter's deceased sister, wife of David Andrew of American Bar)'*/, <**Kweláxtelot**>, //kʷəlɛ́xʸ=təlat//, /*'Indian name of Mabel Peters'*/ (compare <**kwelxóme**> *fine snow that drifts in windows or doors)*; all examples but the first probably are better analyzed with =tel (gloss uncertain here) + =ó(:)t or =ot> *female name*.

<**Elqá:yem**>, PLN /'*a snake rock in the Fraser River just north of Strawberry Island which had snakes sunning themselves and covering the rock;* also *the name of the village on Strawberry Island*'/, *see* <**Alhqá:yem**> under álhqey ~ álhqay.

<**=els**>, da //=əls//, ASP /'*structured activity continuative, structured activity continuative nominal or tool or person*'/, MC /'*device, tool, thing for doing something [as a structured activity]), person doing something [as structured activity]*'/, comment: used mostly with continuative forms of the verb, related to =á:ls ~ =els *structured activity intransitivizer*, (semological comment: the activity is usually done for a while, often ceremonial or occupational), syntactic analysis: lexical suffix, derivational suffix; found in <**héyeqwels**>, //hɛ́-yəqʷ=əls//, /'*burning at a ritual, performing a burning*'/, <**thóyqwels**>, //θi[-Aá-]y=qʷɛ=əls//, /'*dig*'/, <**kwókwexwels**>, //kʷá[-C_1ə-]xʷ=əls//, /'*knocking, rapping*'/, <**thá:q'els**>, //θɛ́·q'=əls//, /'*spearing*'/, <**ts'ákwx̱els**>, //c'ɛ́kʷ=x̣=əls//, /'*frying (as an activity)*'/, <**lhílhets'els ~ slhílhets'els ~ shxwlhílhets'els**>, //ɬí[=C_1ə=]c'=əls ~ s=ɬí[=C_1ə=]c'=əls ~ sxʷ=ɬí[=C_1ə=]c'=əls//, /'*a saw*'/ (compare <**lhíts'=et**> *cut it)*, <**xíxepels**>, //xʸí[=C_1ə=]p=əls//, /'*a plane (tool)*'/ (compare <**xí:p=et**> *carve s-th, plane it)*, <**t'et'émels**>, //C_1ə=t'ə́m=əls//, /'*a chisel*'/ (root <**t'em=**> *to chip or chop with sharp tool)*, <**st'et'émels**>, //s=C_1ə=t'ə́m=əls//, /'*an adze,* (prob.) *D-adze*'/, <**qíqeq'els**>, //qí[=C_1ə=]q'=əls//, /'*policeman*'/ (root <**qíq'**> *apprehend*), <**híyeqwels ~ héyeqwels**>, //hə́=yəqʷ=əls ~ hɛ́=yəqʷ=əls//, /'*one who burns at a burning ceremony*'/ (compare <**híyeqw ~ héyeqw**> *burning)*, <**sch'ó:qw'els ~ sts'ó:qw'els**>, //sc'á·q'ʷ=əls//, /'*a fork (utensil)*'/ (root <**ts'éqw'**> *poke, spear, pierce)*, <**shxwth'ámqels**>, //s=xʷɛ́θ'ə[=M2=]m(=)q=əls//, /'*scissors*'/, <**sqweqwá:ls**>, //s=C_1ə=qʷɛ́·=əls or s=C_1ə=qʷɛ́·=ɛ́·ls//, /'*a borer (tool for making holes)*'/ (compare <**sqweqwá:**> *hole* + <**=els ~ =á:ls**>**)**, <**swá:ls**>, //s=wɛ́·l=əls//, /'*scramble-giving, scramble*'/ (compare <**wá:l=x**> *throw it upwards* and <**swél=tel**> *net)*.

<**=elwet ~ =élwet**>, da //=əlwət ~ =ə́lwət//, CLO /'*garment, clothing*'/, semantic environment ['with numerals 2-5, non-numerals'], N ['*female name (garment)*'], syntactic analysis: lexical suffix, derivational suffix; found in <**lhq'átsesélwet**>, //ɬq'ɛ́cəs=ə́lwət//, /'*five garments*'/, <**th'éx̱welwetem**>, //θ'ə́x̣ʷ=əlwət=əm//, /'*wash(ing) ones clothes*'/ (root <**th'éx̱w**> *wash)*, <**shxwth'éx̱welwetem**>, //sxʷ=θ'ə́x̣ʷ=əlwət=əm//, /'*washtub, washing machine*'/, <**shxwótqwelwetem**>, //s=xʷátqʷ=əlwət=əm//, /'*washboard*'/ (compare <**xwótqw=em**> *rumble*), <**tl'ítl'eplèlwèt**>, //ƛ'íƛ'əp=l=ə̀lwə̀t//, /'*men's underclothes*'/ (compare *diminutive* <**R4=**> plus <**tl'ép**> *deep, under-* plus probably <**=le=**> *plural*), <**yáqelwétem**>, //yɛ́q=əlwə́t=əm//, /'*change clothes*'/ (root <**yáq**> *change* plus <**=em**> *middle voice*), also appears as a numeral classifier affix and may appear as a woman's personal name suffix, both q.v., <**Olóxwelwet**>, //ʔaláxʷ=əlwət//, /'*sister of Mt. Cheam*'/, <**T'elíxwelwet**>, //t'əlíxʷ=əlwət//, /'*Indian name of Isabel (Mrs. Jimmy Church), now Indian name of Darlene Guttierrez (daughter of Tillie and Al Guttierrez)*'/, <**Qw'otóselwet**>, //q'ʷatás=əlwət//, /'*Indian name of Mary Anne (of Chehalis), now Indian name of Jennie Peters (daughter of Nancy Phillips)*'/, <**Pelóqw'elwet**>, //pəláq'ʷ=əlwət//, /'*Indian name of Annie, wife of Charlie Siyomelálexw.*'/.

<**el'álex**>, KIN /'*brothers, (siblings)*'/, *see* álex.

<**el'èlìyà**>, REL ['*dreaming*'], *see* **é**líyá.

<**el'éliyemet**>, REL ['*dreaming about s-o/s-th*'], *see* **é**líyá.

<**=elh**>, da //=əɬ//, MOOD /'*according to the ways of the, in the way of the*'/, syntactic analysis: lexical suffix, derivational suffix; found in <**shxwelméxwelh**>, //s=xʷəlmə[=´=]xʷ=əɬ//, /'*according to the ways of the Indian, in the way of the Indian, in the Indian way*'/, <**shxwelítemelh**>, //s=xʷəlítəm=əɬ//, /'*in the white man's way, according to the ways of the white man*'/.

<**=elh**>, da //=əɬ//, WV /'*weaving, mat*'/ as in <**wṓl=á:lh**> *bulrush/tule mat*, and <**swṓqw'elh**>, df //s=wóq'ʷ=əɬ//, WV /'*woven goat-wool blanket, (twilled weave (JL))*'/ possibly lit. /'downriver weaving'/.

<**elhápt**>, df //ʔə(=)ɬɛ́p=T or ʔəɬ(=)ɛ́p=T//, pcs, ABFC ['*slip it out*'], semantic environment ['of penis from vagina (in the only example I have)'], Elder's comment: "what a woman will tell a man if she doesn't want to get pregnant", possibly <**e=**> unknown meaning (not likely *continuative), <***=t**> *purposeful control transitivizer*, syntactic analysis: transitive verb, attested by JL (7/20/79) (compare <**x̱wlhép**> *slip off* and <**x̱welhx̱wélhepxel**> *slip with both feet* and <**xwlhépelets**> *sat down (with plop), (slip of on rump)*, if these are related they would have to have been reanalyzed and <**x̱w**> would have to be an error for <**xw=**> *become, get*), Salish cognate: perhaps Squamish /ɬup/ *be out of reach, be away from the edge, be way off* (corresponding with Halkomelem /ɬap/ with =Aɛ́= needed to explain) and Squamish /ɬúp-n/ *put away (tr.)* and /ɬúp-cut/ *move away* K67:329-330.

<**=elhcha**>, da //=əɬcɛ//, WATR /'*unclear liquid, water, juice*'/, syntactic analysis: lexical suffix, derivational suffix; found in <**lhex̱wélhcha**>, //ɬəx̣ʷ=ə́ɬcɛ//, /'*(to) spit*'/, <**lhéx̱welhcha**>, //ɬə́x̣ʷ=əɬcɛ//, /'*spitting*'/, <**slhéx̱welhcha**>, //s=ɬə́x̣ʷ=əɬcɛ//, /'*spit, saliva*'/ (compare <**lh(e)x̱w=ó:t**> *(to) spit)*, <**th'eqwélhcha**>, //θ'əqʷ=ə́ɬcɛ//, /'*mudpuddle, dirty pond* '/ *(*root meaning unclear), <**qó:lhcha**>, //qá·=ə́ɬcɛ//, /'*juicy*'/ (root <**qó:**> *water)*, <**Swí:lhcha**>, //s=wí·ɬcɛ//, /'*Cultus Lake*'/.

<**=elhlát ~ =lhát**>, da //=əɬ=lɛ́t ~ =ɬɛ́t//, TIME ['*day of the week*'], possibly <**=elh**> *times* or *past*, possibly <**=lát**> *night*, literally /'past night'/, syntactic analysis: lexical suffix, derivational suffix, also <**=lhát**>, //=ɬɛ́t//; found in <**Sx̱ex̱elhlát ~ Sx̱ex̱elhát**>, //sx̣əx̣=əɬ=lɛ́t//, /'*Sunday*'/, literally /'sacred + day of the week'/, <**Yilá:welhlàt ~ Yelá:welhàt**>, //yilɛ́·w=əɬ=lɛ̀t//, /'*Monday*'/, literally /'passed or after + day of the week'/, Salish cognate: Musqueam /=əɬnét/ *day*.

<**=élhelh ~ =lhelh** ~ poss. **=elhlelh**> , da //=ə́ɬəɬ ~ =ɬəɬ ~ =əɬləɬ//, ANA /*in the windpipe, throat*/, found in <**t'eqw'élhelh**>, ds //t'əq'ʷ=ə́ɬəɬ//, ABDF /'*pass out, faint*'/, literally /'break (flexible obj.)/run out of breath/cut off in the windpipe'/, (compare cognate Nooksack //t'k'ʷ=ə́ɬniɬ// *faint* (PA:SJ), and <**shxwehómélllhelh**>, df //sxʷ=qʷəhɛ́=áməl=ɬəɬ or s=xʷəh=áməl=ɬəɬ//, ANA ['*adam's apple*'], literally perhaps /'something that goes through a tunnel/hole part of in the windpipe/throat'/ (root xwehó).

<**=elhót**>, da //=əɬ=át//, N ['*female name*'], syntactic analysis: lexical suffix, derivational suffix; found in <**Xwóylhot**>, //xʷáyɬat//, /'*Indian name of Amy Cooper's mother's mother*'/, <**Ólmelhót ~ Élmelhò:t**>, //ʔálm=əɬát ~ ʔə́lmə=ɬà·t//, /'*Indian name of Amy Cooper's father's mother and of Amy's granny Lorenzetto's oldest twin*'/, <**Kwoxwilhót**>, //kʷaxʷ=iɬ=át//, /'*Indian name of Miss Susanna Jim from Katz, grandmother of Mrs. Duncan (Dorothy) Wealick*'/ (perhaps from root <**kwoxw**> *knock, rap* + <=iylh> *child, offspring* + =ot *female name*)–this raises the possibility that the <elh ~ ilh> part of the affix is the morpheme {=iylh ~ =elh} *child, offspring.*

<**=elhp**>, da //=əɬp//, EB /'*tree, plant*'/, semantic environment ['with numerals 1-5, kw'í:l, non-numerals'], phonology: e + e rule predicts =á:lhp allomorph, comment: very productive, over 50 examples found so far, syntactic comment: obligatory with numerals for single owner, syntactic analysis: lexical suffix, derivational suffix, also <**=á:lhp**>, //=ɛ́·ɬp//, phonology: this form is not an allomorph but just the result of a final root vowel combining with =elhp by regular phonological rules; found in <**lhq'atsesálhp**>, //ɬq'ɛcəs=ɛ́ɬp//, /'*five trees (belonging to one person)*'/, <**x̱é:yth'elhp ~ x̱éyth'elhp**>, //x̣ɛ́(·)yθ'=əɬp//, /'*alder tree*'/ (root <**x̱é(:)yth'**> *unripe*), <**qwe'ó:pelhp**>, //qʷəʔá·p=əɬp//, /'*(crab)apple tree*'/ (root <**qwe'óp**> *(crab)apple),*

<**skw'ő:lmexwelhp**>, //sk'ʷó·lməxʷ=əɬp//, /'*blackberry vine (or bush)*'/ (compare <**skw'ő:l=mexw**> *blackberry*), (semological comment: if a plant has fruit, the =elhp can be dropped to obtain the word for the fruit), <**tselqó:má:lhp**>, //cəlq=á·mə=əɬp//, /'*blackcap bush*'/ (compare <**tselq=ó:me**> *blackcap)*, <**mats'íyelhp**>, //mɛc'əl=əɬp//, /'*black hawthorne tree*'/ (root <**máts'el**> *black haw berry*, phonology: el → íy before =elhp), <**x̱pá:yelhp ~ x̱páyelhp**>, //x̣pɛ́(·)y=əɬp//, /'*red cedar tree*'/ (compare <**x̱pá:y**> *red cedar bark and wood*), <**qá:lqelhp**>, //qɛ́·lq=əɬp//, /'*wild rose bush*'/ (root <**qá:lq**> *rose hip)*, <**chewő:welhp**>, //cəwó·w=əɬp//, /'*cottonwood tree*'/, <**t'á:ts'elhp**>, //t'ɛ́·c'=əɬp//, /'*pink spirea*'/, (semological comment: so named because it is used for t'á:ts' *crosspieces for drying fish*), <**ts'qw'élhp**>, //c'q'ʷ=əɬp//, /'*spruce tree*'/ (root <**ts'éqw'**> *poke, pierce, stab)*, <**elílà:lhp**>, //ʔəlílə=əɬp//, /'*salmonberry plant*'/ (root <**elíle**> *salmonberry)*, <**th'estíyelhp**>, //θ'əs=təl=əɬp//, /'*poplar tree*'/ (compare <**th'és=tel**> *metal nail*, phonology: el → íy before =elhp), <**sthá:lhp**>, //s=θ=ɛ́·ɬp//, /'*big tree*'/ (root <**th ~ thí=**> *big)*.

<**=elhsxá ~ =elsxá**>, da //=əɬ=sxʸɛ ~ =əlsxʸɛ́//, NUM /'*times ten, -ty (multiple of ten)*'/, semantic environment ['with numerals 3-9'], TIME ['*first time*'], semantic environment ['snow'], possibly <**=elh**> *times*, syntactic comment: obligatory, syntactic analysis: lexical suffix, derivational suffix; found in <**lhèxwelsxá**> //ɬi[=Aə̀=]xʷ=əlsxʸɛ́// (attested by AC, BJ (12/5/64), MC (9/5/73)) ~ <**lhèxwelhsxá**>, //ɬi[=Aə̀=]xʷ=əɬsʸɛ́// (attested by DM (12/4/64), CT (9/5/73), others) *thirty*, <**lhéq'etselsxá**>, //ɬə́q'əc=əlsxʸɛ́//, /'*fifty*'/, <**yíqelsxáy**>, //yíq=əlsxʸɛ́=y//, /'*first snow of winter*'/ (root <**yíq**> *to fall (of snow))*.

<**-em**>, is //**-əm**//, PRON ['*third person patient or object of passive*'] (or that could be seen as zero /-Ø/), VOIC ['*passive*'], syntactic analysis: is, syntactic comment: there is no first person plural passive form, the active form is used instead with a third person subject and first person plural object (<**ó:tólxwes**> *we were called, he/she/it/they called us*), but there are passive forms for all other person & number combinations, a passive conjugation; found in <**ó:tem.**>, //ʔá·=T-əm//, /'*He/She/It was called., They were called.*'/, <**kw'étslem.**>, //k'ʷə́c=l-əm//, /'*He/She/It was seen., They were seen.*'/, <**skwetáxwstem.**>, //s=k'ʷətɛ́xʷ=sT-əm//, /'*They were brought inside. (bring s-o inside)*'/, example: <**éwe lís yéthestem.**>, //ʔə́wə lí-s yə́θə=sT-əm//, /'*He/She wasn't told., They weren't told. (tell s-o)*'/, syntactic comment: note the third person subordinate subject/agent in lí-s.

<**-em**>, is //**-əm**//, PRON ['*intransitive*'], VOIC ['*antipassive*'], syntactic analysis: is, syntactic comment: this works well as an intransitivizer when there is no object np, when there is an object np following it has the alloseme antipassive which means that while there is an object, the focus is on the action instead–it is the opposite of a passive in that there is no transitivizer but there is an object np; there is no antipassive conjugation; found in <**íx̱em**>, izs //ʔíx̣=əm//, SOC ['*get credit*'], (<**=em**> *have, get, intransitivizer*), <**íweltàlem**>, ds //ʔíwəl=tə[=Aɛ̀=]l=əm//, HUNT ['*set a snare trap*'], lx <**=tel**> *device, thing for*, (<**à-ablaut**> *derivational*, <**=em**> *intransitivizer*), <**kwókwexwem**>, izs //kʷá[-C$_1$ə-]xʷ=əm//, ABFC /'*knocking, rapping (in the distance), tapping*'/, (<**-R1-**> *continuative*), (<**=em**> *intransitivizer*), <**kwél:em ~ kwélem**> //kʷə́l=l=əm// /'*get, fetch*'/; example: <**lámtlh kwélem te siyólh**>, //lɛ́=m-tɬ kʷə́l=l=əm tə si=yáɬ//, /'*Go fetch some wood.*'/, phonology: si= allomorph of s= before roots beginning in y, (<**-tlh**> *coaxing imperative, 2nd person sing.*), attested by EB, <**lalh kwélem kw'e sth'óqwi**>, //lɛ-ɬ kʷə́l=l=əm k'ʷə s=θáqʷi//, /'*Go get some fish.*'/, (<**-lh**> *ordering imperative*), phonology: -lh allomorph of -lha after auxiliary verbs such as mi and la, attested by MH, <**lachxw tsesá:t kws las (kwél:em, qó:m) kw qó:**>, //lɛ-c-xʷ cəs=ɛ́·=T kʷ-s lɛ-s (kʷə́l=l=əm, qá·=m) kʷ qá·//, /'*Send him to (get, pack) water.*'/.

<**-em**>, is //**-əm**// or <**=em**>, //**=əm**//, VOIC ['*middle voice*'], PRON, syntactic analysis: is or ds, semantic comment: the middle voice expresses an action or process done by an agent to part of himself (as in scratch one's nose) or an action or process done as a natural force without human instigation, in the

former context it seems more like a required inflection, in the latter context it seems more derivational; there is no middle voice conjugation; found in <**chewélhem ~ tsewélhem ~ tsōwélhem**>, mdls //cə́w=ə[- ́-]ɬ-əm//, cts, ABFC ['*to spawn*'], literally /'to beach one's offspring'/, lx <**=elh**> *offspring, child*, (<**-em**> *middle voice*), <**chekwílem**>, mdls //cákʷ=íl-əm//, incs, TVMO ['*go far away*'], DIR, lx <**=íl**> *go, come, get, become, inceptive*, (<**-em**> *middle voice*), <**kwelkwímelésem**>, plv //C_1ə=əl=kʷím=əl=ə́s=əm//, cts, ABDF /'*one's face is red, one is blushing*'/, (<**R5=**> *continuative*), (<**=el=**> *plural*), (<**=el**> *sort of, -ish*, <**=es**> *on the face*, <**=em**> *middle voice*), <**kwótx̱wem ~ kwótxwem**>, mdls //kʷátx̣ʷ=əm ~ kʷátxʷ=əm//, SD /'*to rumble, to roar*'/, semantic environment ['especially of water, also of thunder, earthquake, rockslide, etc.'], (<**=em**> *middle voice*), <**kwíythesem**>, mdls //kʷíyθ=əs=əm//, ABFC ['*shake one's head side to side (as in saying no)*'], LANG, lx <**=es**> *on the face*, (<**=em**> *middle voice*), <**qweloythí:lem**>, //qʷəl=ayθ=í·l=əm//, /'*making music; March moon*'/ (compare root <**qwà:l ~ qwel**> *talk, speak* and <**=ó:ythel**> *in the lips or jaw* and <**=em**> *middle voice)*, <**imexósem**>, mdls //ʔim=əxʸ=ás=əm//, TVMO /'*go for a walk, take a stroll, stroll*'/, lx <**=ós**> *face*, (<**=em**> *middle voice*), literally /'walk one's face (or walk oneself in a circle, walk oneself around)'/, <**íqw'esem**>, mdls //ʔíq'ʷ=əs=əm//, ABFC ['*wipe one's face*'], MC, CLO, PE, REL, MED , lx <**=es**> *on the face*, (<**=em**> *middle voice*).

<**=em**>, //**=əm**//, PLN ['*place to get or have or gather or find*'], phonology: often attracts stress to the preceding vowel, grammatical comment: probably developed from <-em> *intransitivizer* in the context of place-names; found in <**Alhqá:yem**>, //ʔɛ́ɬqə[=Aɛ́·=]y=əm//, phonology: ablaut, stress shift, /'*snake island north of Strawberry Island in the Fraser River*'/, <**Íyem**>, //ʔíy=əm//, /'*Eayem, a village site and fishing place above (upriver of) Yale, B.C.*'/, <**Lkwőxwethem**>, //l=kʷóxʷəθ=əm//, /'*Six-Mile Creek and bay on west side of Harrison Lake*'/, <**(Lexw)popeleqwith'á:m**>, //(ləxʷ=)pa[=C_1ə=]ləqʷ=íθ'ɛ=əm//, phonology: vowel-merger, stress shift, /'*rocky place between two CPR tunnels above and about half a mile east of Haig*'/, <**Qíwex̱em**>, //qíwəx̣=əm//, /'*steelhead fishing spot at CPR tunnel near mouth of Hogg Slough*'/, <**Qiwéx̱em**>, //qíwə[= ́=]x̣=əm//, phonology: stress shift, /'*Sakwi Creek, about 1/3 mi. above Weaver Creek fish hatchery*'/, <**Skwiyó:m**>, //s-kʷíyà=əm//, phonology: stress shift, /'*place of Joe and Louie Punch just east of Lakahahmen (Nicomen) band reserve #10 now known as Skweam (Joe Punch's father was known as Skweam)*'/, <**Temélhem**>, //təmə[= ́=]ɬ=əm//, phonology: stress shift, /'*a spring-water stream south of Skowkale*'/, <**T'ít'x̱elhchò:m**>, //C_1í-t'əx̣=əɬcɛ=Aà=əm//, phonology: ablaut, stress shift, /'*Yale Creek where it divides*'/, <**(Lexw)thíthesem**>, //(ləxʷ=)θí[=C_1ə=]=á·ls=əm//, phonology: vowel-merger, /'*place of big stones at Ruby Creek or on mountain above it*'/, <**(Lexw)tl'átl'ekw'em**>, //(ləxʷ=)ƛ'ɛ́[-C_1ə-]k'ʷ=əm//, /'*Klaklacum, peaked waves place at Union Bar Indian Reserve #12 of the same name*'/, <**(Lexw)ts'okw'á:m**>, //(ləxʷ=)c'ak'ʷɛ[= ́=]=əm//, phonology: stress shift, /'*village above Five-Mile Creek near where skunk cabbages grew*'/, <**(Lexw)wex̱ésem**>, //(ləxʷ=)wəx̣ə́s=əm//, /'*Bill Bristol Island*'/, <**Lexwchíyò:m**>, //ləxʷ=cí·yɛ=Aà=əm//, phonology: ablaut, stress shift, /'*village at Cheam Indian Reserve #1*'/, <**Xwth'kw'ém**>, //xʷ=θ'ik'ʷ=ə[= ́=]m//, phonology: stress shift, vowel-loss, /'*small spring-water creek near American Bar*'/.

<**=em**>, da //=əm//, CJ ['*(nominalizer)*'], syntactic analysis: lexical suffix; found in <**kw'qwém**>, //k'ʷqʷ=ə́m//, /'*small hatchet, small axe*'/ (compare <**kw'ó·qw'=et**> *club s-th or s-o, hit s-th (or s-o) with stick-like object)*, <**tsqwá:yem**>, //c=qʷɛ́·y=əm//, /'*lemon extract*'/, literally /'color + yellow + whatever =em means'/, <**ts'q'éyx̱em**>, //c'=q'ɛ́yx̣=əm//, /'*vanilla extract*'/ (compare <**ts'=q'éyx̱**> *black* + <**=əm**//, <**s=yelyelísem**>, //s=yəl=C_1əC_2=(əl)ís=əm//, /'*icicle*'/, <**yelyelísem**>, //C_1əC_2=yəlís=əm//, /'*many icicles*'/ (compare <**yélés**> and <**=elís**> *tooth, teeth)*, <**q'elsyáqem**>, //q'əls=yɛ́q=əm//, /'*snowdrift*'/, literally /'twisting + snow + ?'/, <**qeyqeyx̱eló:sem**>, //qɛyqɛyx̣=əlá=ás=əm//, /'*ray of sun from between clouds*'/ (compare <**qeyqeyx̱=eló**> *shadow* +

<=ós> *on the face* + **<=em>**), possibly <u><**x**</u>**wéylem ~ <u>x</u>wí:lem**>, //x̣^{w}í:l=əm//, /'*rope, thread, string*'/, and a few others.

<**em**>, possible bound root, meaning unclear unless related to <**emét**> *sit.*

<**s'émqsel**>, stvi //s=ʔə́m=qsəl//, LANG ['*nasal-sounding*'], lx <**=qsel**> *in the nose*, syntactic analysis: participle, attested by BHTTC.<**emémel**>, DESC /'*small (in quantity), a little*'/, *see* emímel ~ amí:mel.

<**emémel**>, DESC /'*small (in quantity), a little*'/, *see* emímel ~ amí:mel.

<**emémeles**>, DESC ['*tiny round things*'], *see* emímel ~ amí:mel.

<**emét**>, probably root //ʔəmə́t from ʔamə́t//, ABFC /'*sit, sit down, sit up, arise (from lying or sitting), get up (from lying down, from bed or chair)*'/, *see* **omét**.

<**emí: ~ emí**>, TVMO ['*come*'], *see* mí ~ **mé** ~ me.

<**emíls**>, TVMO /'*come near s-o, (come to s-o)*'/, *see* mí ~ **mé** ~ me.

<**emímel ~ amí:mel**>, dmn //ʔəmíməl ~ ʔɛmí·məl, prob. ʔə(=)[C_1í=]məl//, DESC /'*a little bit, small bit, a few*'/, (<**R4=**> *diminutive* probably, added (since it is a prefix only) before the initial <e> /ʔə/ was added (historically); <e> /ʔə/ is perhaps attested elsewhere as a prefix but with uncertain meaning), phonology: the pronunciation amí:mel by AC is probably slow or careful speech, with initial "a" /ɛ/ being a slow variant occasionally for "e" /ə/ and "í:" /í·/ being a slow variant of "í" /í/ in diminutive reduplication, syntactic analysis: nominal probably, possibly adjective/adjectival verb or adverb/adverbial verb, attested by AC, EB, example: <**Did they give you a lot? No, just amí:mel.**>, /'*Did they give you a lot? No, just a small bit.*'/, usage: code-switching, attested by AC, <**axwethóxchxw kw' emímel**>, //ʔɛx^w=əT-áxy-c-x^w k'w ʔəmíməl//, /'*Give me a few., Give me a little bit (milk or raisins, for ex., from a couple to half full)*'/, attested by EB.

<**emémel**>, dmv //ʔəmə́məl, prob. ʔə(=)[C_1í=][=Aə́=]məl//, DESC /'*small (in quantity), a little*'/, (<**é-ablaut**> here may well be *plural* as is normal with diminutive reduplication and as is hinted at by the glosses), phonology: reduplication, syntactic analysis: adjective/adjectival verb, attested by AC, AD, EB, example: <**emémelò kw'a's thíyt**>, //ʔəmə́məl-à k'w-ɛʔ-s θíy=T//, /'*(You only made/fixed a little.)*'/, attested by AD, <**ő̂we lís u óle qé<u>x</u> emémelò**>, //ʔówə lís ʔu ʔálə qə́x̣ ʔəmə́məl-à//, /'*(It's not very much, just a little.)*'/, literally /'is not aux(there)-3sb contrast very much a little-just'/, attested by AD, ASM ['little, small'], attested by EB, (semological comment: other speakers use axwíl in this way; EB uses axwíl for *a little bit* (as in emémel skw'ő:lmexw *a little blackberries, a few blackberries*)); found in <**emémel kó**>, //ʔəmə́məl kyá//, /'*small car, little car*'/, attested by EB, <**emémel stl'ítl'eqelh**>, //ʔəmə́məl s=ƛ'i=ƛ'əq=əɬ//, /'*small child*'/, attested by EB, ASM ['a bunch of little ones'], attested by Deming: EF, MC.

<**emémeles**>, plv //ʔə(=)[C_1í=][=Aə́=]məl=əs//, DESC ['*tiny round things*'], literally /'(?=)diminutive=plural=small=round thing'/, lx <**=es**> *round thing, fruit, rock*, phonology: reduplication, syntactic analysis: adjective/adjectival verb, attested by AD, example: <**emémeles smelmá:lt**>, //ʔəmə́məl=əs s=C_1əC_2-mɛ́·lt//, /'*tiny rocks*'/, attested by AD.

<**=emòt**>, da //=əm=àt//, N ['*female name*'], syntactic analysis: lexical suffix, derivational suffix; may well be merely two affixes, <=em> or <-em> plus <=òt> *female name*, found in <**Xwiyálemot**>, //x^{w}iyɛ́l=əmat//, /'*Indian name of Tillie Guttierrez*'/, <**Siyámót**>, //siyɛ́m=át//, /'*Indian name of Susan Peters*'/, <**Siyó:mót**>, //siyá·m=át//, /'*Indian name of Philomena Kelly*'/, <**Ts'ekwlhólemot**>, //c'ək^{w}ɬál=əmat//, /'*Indian name of Mary (of Tzeachten, wife of Casimir of Chehalis, great grandmother of Nancy Phillips of Chehalis)*'/.

<**em'í:meth**>, KIN ['*grandchildren*'], *see* í:meth.

<**éniyels**>, free root //ʔə́niyəls//, EB [*'domestic onion'*], [*'Alium cepa'*], borrowed from English /ʔə́niyənz/ *onions*, (semological comment: introduced by Caucasians, bulb eaten cooked or raw; the meaning can be singular though the term is borrowed from the English plural form), syntactic analysis: nominal.

<**=ep ~ =ép ~ =lep ~ =í:lep**> da //=əp ~ =ə́p ~ =ləp//, LAND /*'ground, earth, dirt, on the ground'*/, syntactic analysis: lexical suffix, derivational suffix; found in <**sqel:ép ~ sqél:ep**>, ds //s=qə́l=lə́p//, LAND /*'a lot of dirt, weeds, nuisance, something that's no good, garbage, trash'*/, literally /'something bad/dirty on the ground'/, perhaps <**sqoyép**>, df //s(=)qay(=)ə́p//, EZ /*'unidentified animal with marks on its face,* perhaps *badger or wolverine'*/, see under main allomorph **=ílép**.

<**epále**>, NUM [*'ten people'*], *see* ó:pel.

<**epálemets'**>, NUM /*'ten ropes, ten threads, ten sticks, ten poles'*/, *see* ó:pel.

<**epálōwes**>, NUM [*'ten paddles'*], *see* ó:pel.

<**epálōws**>, NUM [*'ten leaves'*], *see* ó:pel.

<**epálōws**>, NUM [*'ten birds'*], *see* ó:pel.

<**epóles**>, NUM /*'ten dollars, (ten Indian blankets [Boas])'*/, *see* ó:pel.

<**epóléstel**>, TIME /*'(first lunar month beginning in) July, (tenth month)'*/, *see* ó:pel.

<**epoléstexw**>, NUM [*'cost ten dollars'*], *see* ó:pel.

<**=épsem**>, da //=ə́psəm//, ANA /*'on the back of the head, back of the neck'*/, LAND [*'neck of land'*], syntactic analysis: lexical suffix, derivational suffix; found in <**tépsem**>, //t=ə́psəm//, /*'back of head and back of neck'*/, <**temélhépsem**>, //təmə́ɬ=ə́psəm//, /*'red-headed woodpecker'*/, literally /'red ochre/Indian paint fungus on back of head and neck'/, <**tl'éqtepsem**>, //ƛ'ɛ[=Aə́=]qt=əpsəm//, /*'long neck'*/, <**qwe'íqwepsem**>, //q^{w}əʔíq^{w}=əpsəm//, /*'scrawny neck, thin neck'*/, <**thehápsem**>, //θəh=ɛ́psəm//, /*'big neck'*/, <**lekwépsem**>, //lək^{w}=ə́psəm//, /*'break one's neck'*/.

<**=eqel**>, da //=əqəl//, ANA /*'in the throat, in the esophagus, in the voice'*/, LAND [*'throat of a cliff or mountain'*], LANG [*'language'*], syntactic analysis: lexical suffix, derivational suffix; found in <**ch'í:yxweqel ~ ts'í:yxweqel**>, //c'í·yx^{w}=əqəl//, /*'dry in the throat'*/, <**kw'éseqel**>, //k'^{w}ɛ[=Aə́=]s=əqəl//, /*'burned in the mouth and throat'*/, <**smélqw ~ smélqweqel**>, //smə́lq^{w} ~ smə́lq^{w}=əqəl//, /*'uvula'*/, <**sthí:qel**>, //s=θí·=əqəl//, /*'loud (voice)'*/, literally /'big in throat'/, <**xwiyétheqel**>, //x^{w}ə=yə́θ=əqəl//, /*'interpret, repeat what is said'*/, <**xwéytheqel**>, //x^{w}ə=yə́[-M2-]θ=əqəl//, /*'interpreting'*/, <**xweyétheqethòx**>, //x^{w}ə=yə́θ=əqəl=T-àx^{y}//, /*'interpret for me'*/, phonology: l → zero here before //T//, <**xwetíyéqel**>, //x^{w}ə=tíy=ə́qəl//, /*'to answer, reply, answer back'*/ (compare <**xwtíy=tses**> *fight back)*, <**xwtélqethóx**>, //x^{w}=tə́l=əqəl=T-áx^{y}//, /*'repeat after me'*/, <**xwelméxwqel**>, //x^{w}əlmə́x^{w}=qəl//, /*'Indian language'*/, <**xwelítemqel**>, //x^{w}əlítəm=qəl//, /*'white man's language, English'*/, <**chálmalqel**>, //cɛ́lmɛl=qəl//, /*'Chinese language'*/, <**shxwmáth'elqel**>, //s=x^{w}=mɛ́θ'əl=qəl//, /*'liar'*/, <**máth'elqéylem**>, //mɛ́θ'əl=qel=íl=əm//, /*'to tell a lie'*/, probably root <**máth'el**> *be proud,* comment: the last five examples may show suffix =qel *language* possibly from =qel *in the head* instead of from =eqel *in the throat*, but in *loud* we see loss of the first <e>and in *interpret* and *answer* we see the =eqel suffix referring to *language*. Further figurative extension of =eqel can be seen in kw'íy=eqel *climb a hill or mountain* (if this is not =qel *in the head* used figuratively) and (s)qw'el=éqel *cliff, vertical rock face*.

<**=eqel**>, da //=əqəl//, MC [*'container(s)'*], semantic environment ['with numeral 5 so far, non-numerals, oblig.?'], (semological comment: possibly related to? =eqel *in the throat*), syntactic

analysis: lexical suffix, derivational suffix; found in <**lhq'átseqel**>, //ɬq'ɛ́c=əqəl//, /'*five containers (like baskets, etc.)*'/, <**i'axwíleqel**>, //ʔiʔɛxʷíl=əqəl// (compare Tait and Cheh. <**a'axwíleqel**>, /'*small container*'/), <**mímeleqel**>, //míməl=əqəl//, /'*small container*'/ (compare <**emímel**> *a little bit*), <**mémeleqel**>, //mi[=Aə́=]məl=əqəl//, /'*small containers*'/, phonology: e-ablaut plural of i in diminutive reduplication is regular, <**t'iléqel**>, //t'il=ə́qəl//, /'*salmon after spawning when its eggs are loose*'/, literally /'?lonely + container'/.

<**eqéylem ~ yeqílem**>, mdls //yəq=íl=əm~ ʔəq=íl=əm//, incs, TVMO /'*crawl underneath, (go underneath)*'/, *see* yeqílem ~ eqéylem.

<**=eqs ~ =éqsel ~ =élqsel ~ =elqs**>, da //=əqs ~ =ə́qs(=)əl ~ =ə́l(=)qs(=)əl ~ =əl(=)qs//, ANA /'*on the nose, in the nose*'/, SH /'*point or tip of a long object (pole, tree, knife, candle, land)*'/, LAND ['*point of geog. features like island or mountain or land*'], syntactic analysis: lexical suffix, derivational suffix; found in <**lhts'élqel**>, //ɬc'=ə́lqsəl//, /'*cut on the tip of the nose*'/, <**méqsel**>, //m=ə́qsəl//, /'*nose*'/, <**Lhí:lhkw'elqs**>, //ɬí·[=C₁ə=]k'ʷ=əlqs//, /'*hook-nose (of people/creatures), Hooknose (the name of a mountain near Agassiz)*'/, <**x̱éyp'eqsel**>, //x̣íy=p'=əqsəl//, /'*scraped on the nose*'/, <**shxweqw'eléqstel**>, //s=xʷəq'ʷ=ələ́qs=təl//, /'*nose-ring*'/, <**sth'émqsel**>, //sθ'ə́m=qsəl//, /'*bridge of nose*'/, <**smétóqsel ~ smétéqsel**>, //smə́tá=qsəl or smə́t=ə́qsəl//, /'*snot*'/, <**s'éleqs ~ s'álqsel**>, //sʔə́l=əqs ~ sʔɛ́=əqsəl//, /'*point of a knife*'/, <**témkweqsel**>, //tə́mkʷ=əqsəl//, /'*blunt (of poles)*'/, <**yéqweqsí:lstsel**>, //yə́qʷ=əqs=í·ls=cəl//, /'*I'm lighting the light (candle, lantern, etc.)*'/, literally /'burn point go, come or device I (subject)'/, <**xépqst**>, //xʸə́p=qs=t//, /'*sharpen a point*'/, <**éx̱qst**>, //ʔə́x̣=qs=t//, /'*strike it (of a match)*'/, literally /'scratch on the point 3rd person object)'/, also <**=éqsel**>, //=ə́qs(=)əl//, also <**=elqsel**>, //=əl(=)qs(=)əl//, also <**=elqs**>, //=əl(=)qs//.

<**éq''eq'esem**>, chrs //ʔə́q'=C₁əC₂=əs=əm//, its //?//, EZ ['*turkey vulture*'], ['*Cathartes aura*'], Elder's comment: "the name means "moving its head"", literally /'moving=characteristically=face=middle voice, or characteristically moving its own face'/, (<**=R2**> *characteristic*), lx <**=es**> *on the face*, (<**=em**> *middle voice*), phonology: reduplication, rare case of glottalized consonant followed by glottal stop, attested by EL, JL.

<**=eqw ~ =(e)leqw ~ =íqw ~ =ó:qw**>, da //=əqʷ ~ =(ə)ləqʷ ~ =íqʷ ~ =á·qʷ//, ANA /'*on top of the head, on the hair*'/, WATR ['*head of a river*'], KIN ['*head of descendants*'], EZ ['*fish (=heads)*'], semantic environment ['with numerals 2-9, non-numerals'], (semological comment: optional?), phonology: =eqw occurs after íC(C), syntactic analysis: lexical suffix, derivational suffix; found in <**kw'qwélqwt**>, //k'ʷqʷ=ə́ləqʷ=t//, /'*hit s-o on top of the head (with a club or stick-like object)*'/, <**yethéleqw**>, //yəθ=ə́ləqʷ//, /'*pointed head*'/, literally /'sharp/good edge on top of the head'/, <**sqwóteleqw**>, //s=qʷát=ələqʷ//, /'*crown of head*'/, <**st'émleqw**>, //s=t'ə́m=ləqʷ//, /'*scalp, top of head*'/, <**x̱éymleqwt ~ x̱íymleqwt**>, //x̣ɛ́ym=ləqʷ=t//, /'*grab s-o by the hair*'/, <**tskwí:meqw**>, //c=kʷí·m=əqʷ//, /'*red-headed, red hair*'/, <**yó:seqw**>, //yá·s=əqʷ//, /'*hat*'/, <**chílheqw**>, //cíɬ=əqʷ//, /'*bushy and uncombed hair*'/, literally /'high on top of the head/hair'/, <**tl'xwíqwtel**>, //ƛ'xʷ=íqʷ=təl//, /'*kerchief*'/, literally /'cover on top of head device'/, <**lhíts'eqwem**>, //ɬíc'=əqʷ=əm//, /'*get one's hair cut*'/, <**xwthó:qw**>, //xʷ=θ=á·qʷ//, /'*big head*'/, <**thítheqw**>, //θíθ=əqʷ//, /'*big heads*'/, <**sts'ó:meqw**>, //s=c'á·m=əqʷ//, /'*great grandparent/-child*'/, <**ékwiyeqw**>, //ʔə́kʷiy=əqʷ//, /'*great grandparent/-child*'/, <**th'ep'eyeqw ~ th'ep'oyeqw**>, //θ'əp'əy=əqʷ//, /'*great grandparent/-child*'/, <**tómiyeqw**>, //támiy=əqʷ//, /'*great grandparent/-child*'/, <**lhq'atsesíqw**>, //ɬq'ɛcəs=íqʷ//, /'*five fish*'/, also <**=eleqw**>, //=ələqʷ//, also <**=íqw**>, //=íqʷ//, also <**=ó:qw**>, //=á·qʷ//.

<**eqw'ewílt**>, HHG /'*dry them (dishes), dry s-th (dish)*'/, *see* íqw'.

<**-es**>, ia //-əs//, PRON ['*third person subject (of transitive verbs)*'], syntactic analysis: is; found in <**kw'átsetes.**>, //k'ʷə[=Aɛ́=]c=əT-əs//, /'*He/She/It/They look at s-o.*'/, <**kw'étslexwes.**>, //k'ʷə́c=l-

əxʷ-əs//, /'*He/She/It/They see s-o.*'/, <**imexsthóxes.**>, //ʔim=əxʸ=sT-áxʸ-əs//, /'*He made me walk.*'/, <**léwexes.**>, //lə́w=əxʸ-əs//, /'*He put it in.*'/, <**th'íwélmetes.**>, //θ'=íwəl=məT-əs//, /'*He/She is fed up with s-o.*'/, <**tl'í:lsóxes.**>, //ƛ'í·=ləs-áxʸ-əs//, /'*He/She loves me.*'/.

<**-es**>, ia //**-əs**//, PRON ['*third person subjunctive subject*'], syntactic comment: can be suffixed to forms prefixed with we- *when, if* or to the first subordinate verb after a negative verb, can also add the *when/if* meaning even without the we- prefix being present, also <**-s**>, //-s//, phonology: after auxiliary verbs ending in i (í, lí, mí, lhí); found in <**welámes**>, //wə-lɛ́=m-əs//, /'*if/when he/she/it goes, if/when they go*'/, example: <**yó:swe weskw'áyes kw'els lám.**>, //yá·swə wə-s=k'ʷɛ́y-əs k'ʷ-əl-s lɛ́=m//, /'*It might be impossible for me to go., I don't know if I could go., I don't know if it's impossible for me to go.*'/, <**éwe (kw'es) lámes.**>, //ʔə́wə k'ʷə-s lɛ́=m-əs//, /'*He/She/It doesn't/won't/don't go., They don't/won't go.*'/, <**éwe sts'eláxwemes.**>, //ʔə́wə s=c'əl[=Aɛ́=]xʷ=əm-əs//, /'*He/She is not a spirit-dancer., They're not spirit-dancers.*'/, <**éwe lís lám.**>, //ʔə́wə lí-s lɛ́=m//, /'*He/She/It didn't/doesn't go., They don't/didn't go.*'/.

<**esáp'**>, possibly root //ʔəsɛ́p' or ʔəsə́[-Aɛ́-]p'//, cts //?//, LANG ['*ending a story (citation gloss) ~ it's ended(?)*'], *see* esép'.

<**esép'**>, possibly root //ʔəsə́p' or ʔəsɛ[=Aə́=]p'//, rsls //?//, LANG ['*end a story (citation gloss) ~ is ended (of a story) (in context)*'], possibly <**é-ablaut**> *resultative,* syntactic analysis: intransitive verb, participle?, attested by AD, example: <**esép' tel s<u>x</u>wō<u>x</u>wiyám**>, //ʔəsə́p' t-əl s=xʷəxʷiyɛ́m//, /'*My story is ended.*'/, attested by AD.

<**esáp'**>, prob. rsls and cts //ʔəsɛ́p' or ʔəsə́[-Aɛ́-]p'//, cts //?//, LANG ['*ending a story* (citation gloss) ~ *it's ended(?)*'], possibly <**á-ablaut**> *continuative or resultative* depending on which gloss is correct, syntactic analysis: intransitive verb, participle?, attested by AD.

<**ésqthet**>, pcrs //ʔə́sq=T-ət//, ABFC ['*grunt*'], semantic environment ['when lifting something (for ex.)'], (<**-thet**> *purposeful control reflexive*), syntactic analysis: intransitive verb, attested by IHTTC.

<**ésta**>, us //ʔə́stɛ//, ASP probably /'*start to (no citation gloss, just in context)*'/, syntactic analysis: mpcl?, attested by Deming, example: <**ésta welh lhémexw**>, //ʔə́stɛ wəɬ ɬə́məxʷ//, /'*It's started to rain.*'/, literally /'start to? already rain'/, attested by Deming.

<**ésh**>, free root //ʔə́š//, [ʔíš], LANG ['*You're kidding.*'], usage: slang popular at hop-picking about the 1940's, possibly borrowed from English perhaps itself from Yiddish (see "ish-ka-bibble", etc. of the same era), syntactic analysis: particle.

<**-èt**>, ia //**-ə̀t**//, MOOD ['*subjunctive of passive*'], VOIC (probably also) ['*subordinate or dependent (with passive)*'], syntactic analysis: is, syntactic comment: added to passive words that follow (are subordinated to) negatives or skw'á(:)y kw'es (*impossible/can't) or subjunctive we- when, if,* since there is no first person plural passive (-tólxw-es /-tóxʷ-əs/ the active form *he/she/they [did s-th to] us* is used instead) -**èt** is not added to the active form (skw'áy kw'es maytólxwes. *We can't be helped., They can't help us.*), example: <**skw'áy kw'es máythàlèmèt.**>, //s=k'ʷɛ́y k'ʷə-s mɛ́y=T-ɛ̀ləm-ə̀t//, /'*I can't be helped.*'/, <**skw'áy kw'es máythòmèt.**>, //s=k'ʷɛ́y k'ʷə-s mɛ́y=T-à·m-ə̀t//, /'*You can't be helped.*'/, <**skw'áy kw'es máytèmèt.**>, //s=k'ʷɛ́y k'ʷə-s mɛ́y=T-əm-ə̀t//, /'*He/She/It/They can't be helped.*'/, <**skw'áy kw'es máytòlèmèt.**>, //s=k'ʷɛ́y k'ʷə-s mɛ́y=T-àlə̀m-ə̀t//, /'*You folks can't be helped.*'/, <**skw'áy kw'es (kw'étslàlèmèt., kw'étslò:mèt., kw'étslèmèt., kw'etslólxwes., kw'étslòlèmèt.)**>, //s=k'ʷɛ́y k'ʷə-s (k'ʷə́c=l-ɛ̀ləm-ə̀t, k'ʷə́c=l-à·m-ə̀t, k'ʷə́c=l-əm-ə̀t, k'ʷəc=l-álxʷ-əs, k'ʷə́c=l-àlə̀m-ə̀t)//, /'*(I, you, he/she/it/they, we, you folks) can't be seen.*'/, <**skw'áy kw'es (qwélstàlèmèt., qwélstò:mèt., qwélstèmèt., qwelstólxwes., qwélstòlèmèt.)**>, //s=k'ʷɛ́y k'ʷə-s (qʷɛ[=Aə́=]l=sT-ɛ̀ləm-ə̀t, qʷɛ[=Aə́=]l=sT-à·m-ə̀t, qʷɛ[=Aə́=]l=sT-əm-ə̀t, qʷəl=sT-álxʷ-əs, qʷɛ[=Aə́=]l=sT-àlə̀m-ə̀t)//, /'*(I, you, he/she/it/they, we, you folks) can't be spoken*

to. (speak to s-o)'/, <**ewéta skwíyex̱tèmèt.**>, //ʔəwə= ´tɛ s=kʷíy=x̣=T-əm-èt//, /'*Nothing could be done.*'/, <**ewétalh slheq'él:èmèt te skwíxs.**>, //ʔəwə= ´tɛ=ɛɬ s=ɬə=q'ɛ[=Aə́=]l=l-əm-èt tə s=kʷɛ[=Aí=]xʸ-s//, /'*Nobody knows his name.*'/, <**wiyóth kws wetsésetémet kws láms xó:kw'em.**>, //wə=yáθ kʷ-s wə-cə́s=əT-əm-èt kʷ-s lɛ́=m-s xʸá·k'ʷ=əm//, /'*He was always told to go bathe.*'/, literally /'(it) is always that if he was told that he go bathe himself'/, <**skw'áy kw'es xwlálá·ms tútl'ò kws las x̱íx̱ewetèmèt welámes th'x̱wó·sem.**>, //s=k'ʷɛ́y k'ʷə-s xʷlɛ́lɛ́=əm-s tə=w=ƛ'á kʷ-s x̣í[-C_1ə-]w=əT-əm-èt wə-lɛ́m-əs θ'x̣ʷ=á·s=əm//, /'*He wouldn't listen to being warned not to go wash his face.*'/.

<**-et**>, ia //**-ət**//, PRON [*'first person plural subjunctive subject'*], syntactic comment: can be suffixed to forms prefixed with we- *when, if* or to the first subordinate verb after a negative verb, can also add the *when/if* meaning even without the we- prefix being present, also <**-t**>, //-t//, phonology: after auxiliary verbs ending in i (í, lí, mí, lhí); found in <**welámet**>, //wə-lɛ́=m-ət//, /'*if/when we go*'/, example: <**éwetset sts'eláxwemet.**>, //ʔə́wə-c-ət s=c'ələ[=Aɛ́=]xʷ=əm-ət//, /'*We're not spirit-dancers.*'/, <**éwetset lámet.**>, //ʔə́wə-c-ət lɛ́=m-ət//, /'*We don't go., We won't go.*'/, <**chexw maytólxw kw's éwetst líyemet.**>, //c-əxʷ mɛy=T-álxʷ k'ʷ-s ʔə́wə-c-ət líy=əm-ət//, /'*You helped us not to laugh.*'/, <**éwetset lí:t lám.**>, //ʔə́wə-c-ət lí·-t lɛ́=m//, /'*We didn't/don't go.*'/.

<**=et** or **-et**>, ia or da //**-ət**// or //**=ət**//, PRON [*'reflexive'*], phonology: triggers o-ablaut of root a, syntactic analysis: derivational suffix or possibly is; found in <**q'óythet**>, //q'áy=T=ət//, /'*kill oneself*'/, <**qelqelí:lthet**>, //C_1əC_2=qəl=í·l=T=ət//, /'*go get oneself dirty*'/, <**x̱élts'thet**>, //x̣ə́l=c'=T=ət//, /'*turn over, turn around*'/, literally /'turn around purposely oneself'/, <**xó:lhmethet**>, //xʸá·ɬ=məT=ət//, /'*take care of oneself*'/, <**x̱ehó:methet**>, //C_1ə-x̣ɛ[=Aá=](·)m=məT=ət or C_1ə-x̣ɛ[=Aá=]·m=əT=ət//, /'*cry for oneself*'/, <**kw'qweméthet**>, //k'ʷə́qʷ=M1=məT=ət or k'ʷqʷ=mə[= ´=]T=ət//, /'*drop onself into a seat angrily, throw oneself on the ground or floor in a tantrum, throw a tantrum*'/.

<**étlh**>, ds //ʔə́(-)tɬ//, LANG /'*tag-question, isn't it? (often pronounced like "in it"), ain't it?, right?*'/, possibly root <**e**> /ʔə/ *interrogative*, (probably <**-tlh**> *coaxing imperative*), attested by EB, RM, AD, example: <**lám tútl'o, étlh**>, //lɛ́=m t=ú=ƛ'a, ʔə́-tɬ//, /'*He went, didn't he?, He left, right?, He left, ain' it/i'n' it?*'/, usage: one answer to this is <**á'a**> *yes* (but not <lí> *he did*), attested by AD, <**xwá:lq chexw lám, étlh**>, //xʷɛ́lq c-əxʷ lɛ́m, ʔə́-tɬ//, /'*You almost went, didn't you?*'/, attested by EB, <**éwe ís lám, étlh**>, //ʔə́wə ʔí-s lɛ́=m, ʔə́-tɬ//, /'*He didn't leave, did he?*'/, usage: the answer to this is <**éwe**> *no* (<**á'a**> *yes* is not acceptable), attested by AD, <**éwechxw íxw lám, étlh**>, //ʔə́wə-c-xʷ ʔí-xʷ lɛ́=m, ʔə́-tɬ//, /'*You didn't go, did you?, You didn't go, ain' it/i'n' it?*'/, usage: the answer to this is **éwe** *no* (neither **lí** *(I) did* nor **á'a** *yes* are acceptable), attested by AD, <**ewéte kw stámes láme tl'éltl'elmet, étlh**>, //ʔəwə́=tɛ kʷ s=tɛ́m=əs lɛ́mə ƛ'ə́l=C_1əC_2=məT, ʔə́-tɬ//, /'*You never get used to it, do you?*'/, attested by EB.

<**=étmel ?**>, da //=ə́t=məl//, ANA [*'fin'*], possibly <**=mel**> *part, portion*, syntactic analysis: lexical suffix, derivational suffix; found in <**q'étmel**>, //q'=ə́tməl or q'ə́t=məl//, /'*fin, neck fin*'/, <**th'étmel**>, //θ'=ə́tməl or θ'ə́t=məl//, /'*belly fin, (ventral fin)*'/, however the affix is questionable if the two examples have roots that include the <et> (for ex. <**q'et**> meaning uncertain unless *rattling sound, scraping sound* perhaps as made when taken out of water and thrown on deck or ground; and <**th'át**>*chew s-th* (see root th'a)).

<**etqwt**>, pcs //ʔətqʷ=T//, SOC [*'caress s-o'*], ABFC, (<**=t**> *purposeful control transitivizer*), syntactic analysis: transitive verb, attested by IHTTC.

<**ótqwt**>, cts //ʔə[-Aá-]tqʷ=T//, SOC [*'caressing s-o'*], ABFC, (<**ó-ablaut**> *continuative*), phonology: ablaut, syntactic analysis: transitive verb, attested by IHTTC.

<**ét"et'**>, DESC /'*(be) stretchy, (be) elastic*'/, *see* ót'.

<**=eth ?**>, da //=əθ//, DESC ['*(stripes)*'], syntactic analysis: lexical suffix, derivational suffix; found in <**skwímeth**>, //s=k^{w}ím=əθ//, /'*little round-mouthed sucker-fish (many have red stripes)*'/ (compare <**ts=kwí:m**> *red color)*, <**sx̱á:meth ~ ts'its'emá:welh**>, //s=x̣έ·m=əθ ~ c'ic'əm=έ·wəɬ//, /'*cottonwood sap*'/ (root perhaps **x̱**à:m *crying* or stem sáx̱=em *bitter* as the sweet sap turns bitter if left out in the air for a while).

<**eth'íwsem**>, CLO ['*put on a dress*'], *see* íth'a.

<**éts-'ets**>, chrs //ʔə́c=C$_1$əC$_2$//, LANG ['*to stutter*'], ABDF, (<=**R2**> *characteristic* or *iterative*), perhaps <**áts**>, bound root //ʔέc//, ABFC /'*hear*'/, phonology: reduplication, syntactic analysis: intransitive verb, Elder's comment: "AC said it has this form because you can't stutter just once" (compare probably <**áts=l-exw**> *hear about s-th/s-o*, Salish cognate: Lushootseed /ʔə́čʔəč/ *stutter, stammer* H76:655, Sechelt /ʔáčʔəč/ *to stutter* T77:34, B77:93 Squamish /ʔəs-ʔə́č-ʔəč/ *stuttering* W73:257, K67:387, *see* <áts>.

<**s'éts-'ets**>, chrs //s=ʔə́c=C$_1$əC$_2$//, [sʔícʔɪc (normal speed), sʔέcʔεc (hyper-slow speed)], LANG /'*stuttering, to stutter*'/, (<**s=**> *stative*), possibly root <**áts**> as in <**átslexw**> *hear about it*, (<=**R2**> *characteristic*), phonology: reduplication, syntactic analysis: intransitive verb, attested by AC , example: <**s'éts-'ets swíyeqe**>, //s=ʔə́c=ʔəc s=wíyəqə//, /'*stuttering man*'/, attested by AC.

<**Ets'íts'a** or **Eth'íth'a** or **Ets'íth'a**>, possibly root //ʔəc' or ʔəθ'//, PLN /'*Ford Creek, (=Foley Creek?)*'/, lx <=**íθ'ε**> *clothes, blankets* probably, syntactic analysis: nominal, source: Wells 1966 uht-ZEET-zah,

<**éw**>, free root //ʔə́w//, DESC ['*too heavy to lift*'], syntactic analysis: adjective/adjectival verb?, particle?, attested by BHTTC.

<**ew**>, free root //ʔəw//, TIME ['*again*'], syntactic analysis: mpcl, attested by EB, example: <**áscha ew me xw'í látselcha yesq'ó**>, //ʔέ-s-cε ʔəw mə x^{w}ə=ʔí lέ-c-əl-cε yə=s=q'á//, /'*If he comes again, I'll go along.*'/, attested by EB, <**atselcha ew mi xw'í:lsòmè**>, //ʔε-c-əl-cε ʔəw mi x^{w}ə=ʔí·=ls-àmə̀//, /'*I'll come and see you again.*'/, comment: note pncs (psychological non-control stem) xwe='í:=ls, attested by EB, also <**atselcha ew me xw'í:lmethome**>, //ʔε-c-əl-cε ʔəw mə x^{w}ə=ʔí·=əl=məT-amə//, /'*I'll come and see you again.*'/, comment: note iecs (indirect effect control stem) xwe='í:=el=met, with inceptive =el, attested by EB.

<**ewá:lh ~ wá:lh**>, CJ /'*wasn't?, weren't?, didn't?*'/, *see* **é**we ~ ṓwe.

<**ewá ~ ōwá ~ wá**>, CJ /'*isn't?, aren't?, don't?, doesn't?, (be not?)*'/, *see* **é**we ~ ṓwe.

<**ewás**>, CJ /'*unless he, if he doesn't*'/, *see* **é**we ~ ṓwe.

<**éwe ~ ṓwe**>, free root //ʔə́wə ~ ʔówə//, CJ /'*no, not be, be not*'/, ASM, LANG ['*say no*'], semantic environment ['subject pronoun and no other verb in sentence (at most li *interrogative*), conversation where opinions are being polled'], syntactic analysis: vneg, dialects: *Chill. speakers (for ex. AC, BJ, NP, MV) and Deming speakers (for ex. MH, MC) seem to have ṓwe as a more frequent variant than speakers further from the Nooksack area, i.e. Tait and Cheh. speakers (for ex. AD, LJ, CT, SP, AK, and EB); this may be influence from Nooksack /o/; some speakers (for ex. BJ and AC) occasionally even have ówe /ʔáwə/ as a variant (which would correspond with Nooksack /o/)*, attested by AC, BJ, NP, MV, MH, MC, AD, LJ, CT, SP, AK, EB, others; found in <**éwechexw**>, //ʔə́wə-c-əx^w//, /'*Don't.*'/, grammatical analysis: vneg-nonsubord.sj.-2ssj = vneg-mild imperative, attested by AC, also <**uwchxw**>, //ʔuw-c-x^w//, /'*Don't.*'/, usage: short for **é**wechxw, attested by EB, AD, example: <**éwe lís qéx̱**>, //ʔə́wə lí-s qə́x̣//, /'*There are not many.*'/, attested by AC, <**ṓwe lís the'í:t, sta'á**

kw'e sx̱wōx̱wiyám>, //ʔówə lí-s θəʔí·t, s=t-ɛʔɛ́ k'wə s=x̣^{w}ox̣^{w}iyɛ́m//, /'*It's not true, (it's) like a fable.*'/, attested by AC, <**axwethóxchxw kw' tí, ő̄we slíts'es; ōwéchxw lets'étexw**>, //ʔɛx^w=əT-áxy-c-əx^w k'w tí, ʔówə s=líc'-əs; ʔowə́-c-x^w ləc'-ə́T-əx^w//, /'*Give me some tea, not full; don't fill it.*'/, attested by EB, <**lámelhtsel qe tsel ő̄we o**>, //lɛ́=m-əɬ-c-əl qə c-əl ʔówə ʔa//, /'*I was going but I'm not now.*'/, <**ő̄we lámes**>, //ʔówə lɛ́=m-əs//, /'*He's not going., He won't go.*'/, attested by Deming: MC, <**éwe ís xwélalà:m**>, //ʔə́wə ʔí-s x^w[-ə́-]lɛlɛ̀·-m//, /'*He's not listening.*'/, attested by EB, <**ő̄wechap lámáp ~ ő̄wechap lámélép**>, //ʔówə-c-ɛp lɛ́=m-ɛ́p ~ ʔówə-c-ɛp lɛ́=m-ə́ləp//, /'*Don't you folks go.*'/, attested by IHTTC, <**ő̄wechap halemáp ~ ő̄wechap halemélep**>, //ʔówə-c-ɛp hɛ-lə=m-ɛ́p ~ ʔówə-c-ɛp hɛ-lə=m-ə́ləp//, /'*Don't you folks go (be going).*'/, attested by IHTTC, <**"éwechap lamáp hélem tel slhx̱wélhcha."**>, //ʔə́wə-c-ɛp lɛ=m-ɛ́p hə́-lə=m t-əl s=ɬx̣^{w}=ə́ɬcɛ//, /'*"Don't you people go to my spit."*'/, usage: reporting what Paul Webster's wife said, a pun, playing on the word spit, slhx̱wélhcha, and the placename where Paul Webster lived, Th'qw'élhcha., attested by Tait: LJ, <**"ő̄wechxw swiyeqáxw, qe xixpó:mchexw"**>, //ʔówə-c-x^w s=wiyəqə-ɛ́x^w, qə C_1í-xyá:pə[-M2-]m-c-əx^w//, /'*"You're not a man, but you're whistling."*'/, phonology: methathesis, usage: a saying to a young girl around puberty, to stop her from whistling, attested by Deming: MV, <**tl'o éwe í tí kwíxelexwt te thá**>, //ƛ'a ʔə́wə ʔí tí k^{w}íxyə=l-əx^w-ət tə θɛ́//, /'*We didn't have a name for that (right here).*'/, attested by CT, HT, <**éwe stl'íses meytóxwes welámet súwq'tòlè**>, //ʔə́wə s=ƛ'í-s-əs mɛy=T-áx^w-əs wə-lɛ́=m-ət súwq'=T-àlə̀//, /'*He doesn't want to help us (when we) find you folks.*'/, dialects: *Tait*, attested by SP, AK, AD, also <**éwe stl'íses kws meytóxwes welámet súwq'tòlè**>, //ʔə́wə s=ƛ'í-s-əs k^w-s mɛy=T-áx^w-əs wə-lɛ́-m-ət súwq'=T-àlə̀//, dialects: *Cheh.*, attested by EB, also <**ewe stl'ís kw'es meytólxws welámet ső̄wq'tòlè**>, //ʔəwə s=ƛ'í-s k'wə-s mɛy=T-álx^w-s wə-lɛ́=m-ət sówq'=T-àlə̀//, dialects: *Chill.*, attested by NP, ASM ['say no'], <**chap ő̄we ~ lichap ő̄we**>, //c-ɛp ʔówə ~ li-c-ɛp ʔówə//, /'*Do you folks say no?*'/, attested by IHTTC.

<**ewá ~ ōwá ~ wá**>, //ʔəwə-ə ~ ʔowə-ə ~ wɛ́//, CJ /'*isn't?, aren't?, don't?, doesn't?, (be not?)*'/, phonology: vowel-merger, stress-shift, syntactic analysis: vneg-interrog., example: <**ōwáchap lámelep ~ ōwáchap lámélep**>, //ʔow-ɛ́-c-ɛp lɛ́=m-ə(́)ləp//, /'*Aren't you folks going?*'/, *<**ōwáchap halemélep**> rejected by IHTTC, <**ōwáchxw lámexw**>, //ʔow-ɛ́-c-x^w lɛ́=m-əx^w//, /'*Will you go?*'/, literally /'Aren't you going?'/, attested by Deming: MC (Chill.), <**ōwáchxw t'ílemexw**>, //ʔow-ɛ́-c-x^w t'íl=əm-əx^w//, /'*Will you sing?*'/, literally /'Is it not you sing?'/, attested by Deming: MC, <**wátsa lamál yewá:**>, //w-ɛ́-cɛ lɛ=m-ɛ́l yə=wɛ́·//, /'*Will you take me along?, Can I go along?*'/, literally /'will it not be I go along?'/, syntactic analysis: vneg-interrog-future tense go=izs-subjunc1ssb (travelling by=)along, attested by AC.

<**ewás**>, //ʔəwə-əs//, CJ /'*unless he, if he doesn't*'/, phonology: vowel-merger, stress-shift, syntactic analysis: vneg-subjunctive3s, example: <**mícha xwe'í ewás lís málqelexwes**>, //mí-cɛ x^{w}ə=ʔí ʔəw-ɛ́s lí-s mɛ́lqə=l-əx^w-əs//, /'*He's coming unless he forgets.*'/.

<**éwelh**>, //ʔə́wə-ɬ//, CJ /'*never, not ever*'/, syntactic analysis: vneg-past, example: <**éwelhtsel làm**>, //ʔə́wə-ɬ-c-əl lɛ̀=m//, /'*I never go.*'/, attested by EB, also possibly <**éwetsellh làm**>, //ʔə́wə-c-əl-ɬ lɛ̀=m//, *<**ewetsellh í:l làm**> rejected by EB, <**éwelhtsel lám ye mímelha**>, //ʔə́wə-ɬ-c-əl lɛ́=m yə mí[-C_1ə-]ɬɛ//, /'*I never go to spirit dances.*'/, attested by EB, <**éwelh x̱à:m ~ ő̄welh x̱à:m**>, //ʔə́wə-ɬx̣ɛ̀·m ~ ʔówə-ɬx̣ɛ̀·m//, /'*He never cries (cry).*'/, attested by EB, (irregular)éwe'lh x̱à:m, //ʔə́wə-ʔɬx̣ɛ̀·m//, /'*He never cried.*'/, attested by AD, <**éwelh xwlalà:m**>, //ʔə́wə-ɬ x^{w}lɛlɛ̀·m//, /'*He never listens.*'/, attested by EB, <**éwelhtsel xwlalà:m**>, //ʔə́wə-ɬ-c-əl x^{w}lɛlɛ̀·m//, /'*I never listen.*'/, attested by EB, <**éwelh t'ílemesthò:m té syùwèls**>, //ʔə́wə-ɬ t'íl=əm=sT-à·m tə s=yə̀wə̀l-s//, /'*He never sang you his spirit song.*'/, syntactic analysis: vneg-past sing=izs-causative-passive2s demonstrative article nominal=spirit song-his, attested by AD, <**mő̄kw'tset éwelh teló:met welí:xw xwe'í:t.**>, //mók'w-c-ət ʔə́wə-ɬ təl=l-á·mət wə-lí·-x^w x^{w}əʔí·t//, /'*We don't understand what you're saying.*'/,

literally /'all -we don't -past learn =happen/manage to -oneself when/if- (there) -you subjunctive what is someone saying?'/, attested by AC.

<**ewá:lh ~ wá:lh**>, //ʔəwə-ə-ɬ//, CJ /'*wasn't?, weren't?, didn't?*'/, ASM, TIME /'*weren't ever?, wasn't ever?, didn't ever?, does s-o ever?, never used to, not going to (but did anyway)* [perhaps in the sense of *never usually do X but did this time*]'/, syntactic analysis: vneg-interrogative affix-past affixed (vneg-interrog.-past), example: <**ewá:lhchexw lhì:m**>, //ʔəw-ɛ́·-ɬ-c-əxʷ ɬí·m//, /'*Weren't you going to pick (fruit/leaves)?*'/, attested by EB, ASM ['weren't ever?, wasn't ever?, didn't ever?'], <**ewálhchxw kwáxw stl'ítl'qelh**>, //ʔəw-ɛ́-ɬ-c-xʷ kʷɛ́-xʷ s=C_1í=ƛ'əq=əɬ//, /'*Weren't you ever a child?*'/, syntactic comment: shows subjunctive subject pronoun2s -xw attached to kwá *anyway* which is a mpcl, attested by EB, ASM ['does s-o ever?'], <**ewá:lh me kw'átsethò:m**>, //ʔəw-ɛ́·-ɬ mə k'wɛ́c=əT-à·m//, /'*Does he ever come to see you?*'/, syntactic analysis: vneg-interrogative affix-past affixed auxiliary verb see-purposeful control transitivizer-passive2s, attested by EB, (irregular)ewá:'lh x̣à:m, //ʔəw-ɛ́·-ʔɬx̣ɛ̀·m//, /'*Does he ever cry?*'/, attested by AD, also <**ewá:lh x̱à:m**>, //ʔəw-ɛ́·-ɬx̣ɛ̀·m//, attested by EB, <**walh me x̱élh kw'a' sqwálewel lhíxw me p'élh**>, //(ʔə)w-ɛ́-ɬ mə x̣ə́ɬ k'w-ɛʔ s=qʷɛ́l=əwəl ɬí-xʷ mə p'ə́ɬ//, /'*Do you ever feel sorry when you sober up?*'/, attested by Elders Meeting, ASM ['never used to'], <**ewá:lh qó:qe**>, //ʔəw-ɛ́·-ɬ qá·=C_1ə//, /'*He never used to drink.*'/, attested by EB, <**ewálhtsel xwlalà:m**>, //ʔəw-ɛ́-ɬ-c-əl xʷlɛlɛ̀·m//, /'*I never used to listen., I never listened.*'/, attested by EB, <**ewá:lh x̱à:m**>, //ʔəw-ɛ́·-ɬx̣ɛ̀·m//, /'*He never cried (cry).*'/, ASM ['*not going to (but did anyway)*, [perhaps in the sense of: *never usually do X but did this time*]'], <**ewálhtsel lámàl**>, //ʔəw-ɛ́-ɬ-c-əl lɛ́=m-ɛ̀l//, /'*I wasn't going to go (but went anyway).,* [perhaps: *I never go (but went anyway).]*'/, attested by EB, <**ewálhtsel mí:l alqá:ls kws s'álhtel**>, //ʔəw-ɛ́-ɬ-c-əl mí·-l ʔɛlq=ɛ́·ls kʷ-s s=ʔɛ́ɬtəl//, /'*I wasn't going to buy groceries (but I did).*'/, attested by EB, <**ewá:lhtsel í:l làm**>, //ʔəw-ɛ́·-ɬ-c-əl ʔí·-l lɛ̀m//, /'*I wasn't going to go (but I did).*'/, attested by EB, also <**ewá:lhtsel lí:l làm**>, attested by EB, also <**ewá:lhtsel lámàl**>, attested by EB, (semological comment: all three alternatives are in free variation, except that the forms with vaux lí:-l (root lí: *be there*) may imply going further to pick than the forms with vaux í:-l (root í: *be here*)), syntactic analysis: -l and -àl are alternative forms of 1s subordinate subjunctive subject; the former is used with auxiliary verb's ending in i, the latter is used with the subordinated verb itself (see Galloway 1977, 1980, etc.).

<**ő westexw ~ éwestexw**>, caus //ʔówə=sT-əxʷ ~ ʔə́wə=sT-əxʷ//, LANG /'*deny it; say no; tell s-o to say no*'/, syntactic analysis: transitive verb, ASM ['deny it'], attested by Elders Meetings 6/16/76, 3/29/78; found in <**ő westexwlha**>, //ʔówə=sT-əxʷ-ɬɛ//, /'*Deny it.*'/, example: <**lúw xwel ő westexw**>, //lə-əw xwəl ʔówə=sT-əxʷ//, /'*He's still denying someone.*'/, ASM ['say no'], <**tsel wel ő westexw**>, //c-əl wəl ʔówə=sT-əxʷ//, /'*I really say no.*'/, ASM ['tell s-o to say no to s-o'], Elder's comment: "this is correcting the translations *deny it* and *say no* given earlier", attested by AD 10/9/79.

<**ewéta**>, cpds //ʔə́wə=M2=tɛ//, CJ /'*there's none, there's nothing, there's nobody, there's no, be none, be nothing, be nobody*'/, phonology: metathesis or stress-shift, syntactic analysis: vneg, syntactic comment: occupies first position in sentence nearly all the time, even when functioning as a subject or object (in the English translation); also it precedes main verbs directly in sentences though often serving as a subject or object of that verb in English translation; it may be that it originated as te **éwe** *that which is no* (which doesn't seem to occur itself now), but shifted the article and stress when it compounded--thus when it precedes a nominal no article is required and it can serve as a subject or object but occurs in sentence-initial position (since the verbal part is now in front), ASM ['there's none, be none'], <**la ōwéte tl'oqá:ys**>, //lɛ ʔowə́tɛ tə=la=qɛ́·ys//, /'*Now (there's) no more.*'/, attested by ME, ASM ['there's nothing, is nothing'], example: <**ewéta kw'e kw'étslexwes te swíyeqe**>, //ʔəwə́tɛ k'wə k'wə́c=l-əxʷ-əs tə s=wíyəqə//, /'*The man saw (see) nothing., The man didn't see anything.*'/, attested by EB, also <**ewéta kw'étslexwes te swíyeqe**>, //ʔəwə́tɛ k'wə́c=l-

əxʷ-əs tə s=wíyəqə//, attested by EB, <**ōwéta kw totí:ltá:l**>, //ʔowə́tɛ kʷ ta[=C_1ə=]l=í·l=T-ɛ́·l//, /'*I've got nothing to think about.*'/, syntactic analysis: vneg demonstrative article understand[=?=]=go/come/get-purposeful control transitivizer-sbdsj1ssb, attested by Deming, <**ōwéta shxwlís kws axwesthóxes**>, //ʔowə́tɛ sxʷ=lí-s kʷ-s ʔɛxʷə=sT-áxy-əs//, /'*There's nothing that he has to give me., It's free.*'/, attested by Deming, <**ewéta kwstám íl kw'étslexw**>, //ʔəwə́tɛ kʷ=s=tɛ́m ʔí-l k'wə́c=l-əxʷ//, /'*I saw (see) nothing.*'/, attested by Elders Meeting, <**ewéta kwstáms slí:w**>, //ʔəwə́tɛ kʷ=s=tɛ́m-s s=lí·w//, /'*There's nothing in(side) it.*'/, attested by EB, <**ōwéta stáms s'álhtels**>, //ʔowə́tɛ s=tɛ́m-s s=ʔɛ́ɬtəl-s//, /'*He/She didn't have anything to eat.*'/, attested by Deming, ASM ['there's nobody, be nobody']; found in <**ōwéta**>, //ʔəwə́tɛ//, /'*There's nobody.*'/, semantic environment ['example in reply to a question meaning Is your grandfather in?'], attested by AC, example: <**ewéta mé xwe'í**>, //ʔəwə́tɛ mə́ xʷə=ʔí//, /'*Nobody came.*'/, attested by EB, <**ewéte kwstámes láme tl'éltl'elmet, etlh**>, //ʔəwə́tə kʷ=s=tɛ́m-əs lɛ́=m-ə ƛ'əl=C_1əC_2=məT, ʔə-tɬ//, /'*You never get used to it, do you?*'/, literally /'Nobody ever gets used to it, does one?'/, attested by EB, <**ewéta kw'étslexw te swíyeqe**>, //ʔəwə́tɛ k'wə́c=l-əxʷ tə s=wíyəqə//, /'*Nobody saw (see) the man., Nothing saw the man.*'/, attested by EB, <**ewéta tewát kw'étslexwes te swíyeqe**>, //ʔəwə́tɛ tə=wɛ́t k'wə́c=l-əxʷ-əs tə s=wíyəqə//, /'*The man saw nobody.*'/, syntactic comment: tewát is *who*, tewátes is *somebody*, attested by Elders Meeting 3/29/77, <**ewéte tewátes**>, //ʔəwə́tə tə=wɛ́t=əs//, /'*nobody*'/, attested by EB, <**ewéta tewát íl kw'étslexw**>, //ʔəwə́tɛ tə=wɛ́t ʔí-l k'wə́c=l-əxʷ//, /'*I saw nobody.*'/, attested by Elders Meeting 3/29/77, also <**ewéta tewát líl kw'étslexw**>, //ʔəwə́tɛ tə=wɛ́t lí-l k'wə́c=l-əxʷ//, attested by Elders Meeting 3/29/77, <**ewéte kw'ewát q'óq'ey**>, //ʔəwə́tə k'wə=wɛ́t q'á[=C_1ə=]y//, /'*There's nobody sick.*'/, attested by JL.

<**wá:ta**>, //ʔə́wə[-ə-]=tɛ//, CJ /'*is there none?, isn't there any?*'/, phonology: vowel merger, syntactic analysis: vneg[-interrogative affix-], syntactic comment: contains interrogative affix -e merging with the root vowel before the =ta suffix, example: <**wá:ta á sméyéth**>, //wɛ́·tɛ ʔɛ́ smɛ́yəθ//, /'*Have you got any meat?*'/, literally /'Is there none, your meat?'/, syntactic comment: this is a common type of construction in AC's speech, attested by AC.

<**ő̄wethelh**>, ds //ʔówə=θ-əɬ or ʔówə-θ-əɬ//, CJ /'*never did, he/she/they never did*'/, possibly <**=th**> which seems to here mean *ever* or *time* ("it was not ever", "there was no time that"), (<**-elh**> *past tense*), syntactic analysis: vneg, attested by EB, AD, example: <**ő̄wethelhtsel**>, //ʔówə=θ-əɬ-c-əl//, /'*I never did.*'/, attested by EB, AD.

<**xwewá**>, ds //xʷ=ʔə́wə=Aɛ́//, CJ /'*not yet be, be not yet*'/, (<**á-ablaut**> *derivational*), phonology: ablaut, syntactic analysis: vneg, Salish cognate: Squamish /xʷəwʔáxʷ/ *(be) not yet (the case)* K67:349, Songish /xʷəwʔéʔ/ *(be not yet)* M68; Sechelt and Pentlatch /xʷá/ *(be) not, no* and Mainland Comox /xʷáʔ/ *no* show that the stressed vowel may be inherited from the plain negative root (G82:23), example: <**xwewáchxw í:xw q'e'íl:ém**>, //xʷ=ʔəwɛ́-c-xʷ ʔí-xʷ q'əʔíl-ə́m//, /'*You're not old yet.*'/, phonology: hyperslow pronunciation adds length in two places, attested by AC, <**xwewátsel íl álhtel**>, //xʷ=ʔəwɛ́-c-əl ʔí-l ʔɛ́ɬtəl//, /'*I haven't eaten yet.*'/, attested by Deming: MH, <**xwewá ís me t'ókw' thel tàl**>, //xʷ=ʔəwɛ́ ʔí-s mə t'ák'w θ-əl tɛ̀l//, /'*My mother hasn't come home yet.*'/, attested by EB, AD, <**xwewá ís slíts'**>, //xʷ=ʔəwɛ́ ʔí-s s=líc'//, /'*It's not yet full (fill).*'/, attested by AD, <**xwewá lís x̱à:m**>, //xʷ=ʔəwɛ́ lí-sx̣ɛ̀·m//, /'*He hasn't cried (cry) yet.*'/, attested by AD, <**ts'áts'el tsqwá:y, (xw)ewás lép'ex.**>, //c'ɛ́[=C_1ə=]l c=qʷɛ́·y (xʷ=)ʔəwə-ɛ́s lə́p'=əxy//, /'*It's very green, one doesn't eat it (yet).*'/, attested by Deming (esp. SJ 5/3/79).

<**xwewá:**>, //xʷ=ʔə́wə=Aɛ́-ə//, CJ /'*isn't s-o yet?, isn't it yet?, hasn't s-o yet?*'/, phonology: vowel merger, syntactic analysis: vneg-interrogative affix, example: <**xwewá: ís me t'ókw' thel tàl**>, //xʷ=əwɛ́-ə ʔí-s mə t'ák'w θ-əl tɛ̀l//, /'*Hasn't my mother come home yet?*'/, attested by EB, AD, <**xwewá lís x̱à:m**>, //xʷ=əwɛ́-ə lí-sx̣ɛ̀·m//, /'*Hasn't he cried yet?, He hasn't cried yet.*'/, phonology: for AD here length on xwewá: to show interrogative is optional, attested by AD,

<**xwewá ta' swáqeth**>, //xʷ=əwɛ́(-ə) t-ɛʔ s=wɛ́q=əθ//, /'*You haven't got a husband yet?*'/, literally /'your husband is not yet?, (or perhaps instead) your husband is not yet.'/, phonology: if there is an interrogative here, its reflex (length here on xwewá:) is optionally deleted here; another interpretation is that the sentence is only a rhetorical question, not literally a question meant to be answered, and thus has no interrogative -e affix, attested by DC, BJ, AD, <**xwewá ta' swíyeqe**>, //xʷ=əwɛ́(-ə) t-ɛʔ s=wíyəqə//, /'*You haven't got a man yet?*'/, attested by DC, BJ, AD, <**xwewá is me qw'él te sth'í:m?**>, //xw=əwɛ́(-ə) ʔi-s mə q'wə́l tə s=θ'í·m//, /'*Is the fruit ripened yet?*'/, literally /'is not yet? here -it become ripe the berry'/, attested by AC (11/19/71).

<**ewelti:l**>, df //ʔəw=əl=T-ə[=Aí·=]l or ʔəw=əl=T-əl=í·l or ʔəw=əl=t[=Aí·=]əl//, PLAY /'*to race (on foot), a race (any kind)*'/, literally possibly /'go hurry each other purposely for a long time'/, possibly root <**ʔəw**> *hurry*, possibly <**=el**> *go, come, get, become*, possibly <**=t**> *purposeful control transitivizer*, possibly <**-el**> *reciprocal*, possibly <**=í:l**> *go, come, get, become*, possibly <**í:-ablaut**> *durative*, phonology: vowel loss in root, consonant merger in root, possible ablaut or syllable-loss, syntactic analysis: intransitive verb, nominal (compare root in <**ów=thet**> *to hurry, be in a hurry)*, attested by EB (4/27/76, 3/1/76), also <**õtí:l**>, //ʔəw=tə[=Aí·=]l//, also /'*race (any kind/horse/foot/etc.)*'/, attested by NP (10/10/75), example: <**ewelti:lchelcha.**>, //ʔəw=əl=T-ə[=í·=]l-c-əl-cɛ//, /'*I'll race.*'/, attested by EB (4/27/76), possible variant pronunciation: <**àweltí:l**>, [ǣwʌltí˙l], '*any kind of racing*', attested by (EH,RG,SN 7/16/99 (SU transcription, tape 1) and <**ilh àweltí:l**>, [iɬ ǣwʌltí˙l], '*He raced*', attested by (EH,RG,SN 7/16/99 (SU transcription, tape 1).

<**óweltì:l**>, cts //ʔə[-Aá-]w=əl=T-ə[=í·=]l//, PLAY /'*racing, (a race (on foot/canoe/horse) (Elders Group))*'/, (<**ó-ablaut**> *continuative*), phonology: ablaut, possible syllable-loss, syntactic analysis: intransitive verb, attested by EB, also /'*a race (on foot/canoe/horse)*'/, attested by Elders Group (4/28/76), example: <**látsel óweltì:l.**>, //lɛ́-c-əl ʔə[-Aá-]w=əl=T-ə[=í·=]l//, /'*I'm going to be racing., I'll be racing.*'/, attested by EB, also /'*I'm going to race.*'/, attested by Elders Group (4/28/76), <**òweltí:l tútl'ò**>, [āwʌltí:l túƛ'à], '*He was racing*', attested by (EH,RG,SN 7/16/99 (SU transcription, tape 1).

<**sweltì:l**>, dnom //s=ʔəw=əl=T-ə[=Aí·=]l//, PLAY ['*a race*'], (<**s=**> *nominalizer*), phonology: vowel-loss in root, consonant merger (ʔw → w), possible ablaut, syntactic analysis: nominal, attested by EB (4/27/76), example: <**híkw sweltì:l**>, //híkʷ s=ʔəw=əl=T-ə[=Aí·=]l//, /'*(It's) a big race.*'/, attested by EB.

<**éwelh**>, CJ /'*never, not ever*'/, *see* éwe ~ õwe.

<**ewéta**>, CJ /'*there's none, there's nothing, there's nobody, there's no, be none, be nothing, be nobody*'/, *see* éwe ~ õwe.

<**ewéta shxwlístexw**>, EFAM /'*not care about s-o, have no use for s-o, be impassive*'/, *see* shxwlí.

<**ewétò shxwlís**>, EFAM /'*useless, no special use, ordinary*'/, *see* shxwlí.

<**=ewí:ls**>, da //=əwí·ls or =əw=í·ls//, HHG ['*dishes*'], possibly <**=í:ls**> *tool, device*, syntactic analysis: lexical suffix, derivational suffix; found in <**th'e<u>x</u>w(e)wí:ls**>, //θ'əx̣ʷ=(ə)wí·ls//, /'*wash dishes*'/ (root <**th'é<u>x</u>w**> *wash)*, <**shxwth'o<u>x</u>wewí:ls (**or **shxwth'e<u>x</u>wewí:ls)**>, //sxʷ=θ'ax̣ʷ=əwí·ls (a probably sic for ə)//, /'*sink, dishpan*'/, <**xwe'íqw'ewí:ls**>, //xʷə=ʔíq'ʷ=əwí·ls//, /'*drying dishes*'/ (compare <**íqw'=es=em**> *wipe one's face)*.

<**=ewíts ~ =íts ~ =ích ~ =ech**>, da //=əw(=)íc ~ =íc ~ =əc//, ANA ['*on the back*'], DIR ['*on the back of something*'], possibly <**=ew**> *on the body*, those allomorphs without <=ew> also have extended allosemes/meanings DIR ['*on the surface, on top*'] (fuller discussion see under <**=í:tsel ~ =etsel**>, syntactic analysis: lexical suffix, derivational suffix, also <**=ewích**>, //=əw(=)íc//, also <**=í:tsel**>,

//=í·cəl//, also <**=etsel**>, //=əcəl//; found in <**kw'qwewíts**>, //kʼʷqʷ=əwíc//, /'*hit on the back (with stick-like object)*'/, <**x̲ekw'ólesewíts ~ x̲ekw'óles**>, //x̣əkʼʷ=áləs=əwíc ~ x̣əkʼʷ=áləs//, /'*backbone*'/, <**lekwewíts**>, //ləkʷ=əwíc//, /'*break the spine or back; have a hunchback*'/, <**kw'etsewítsem**>, //kʼʷəc=əwíc=əm//, dialects: *Tait*, /'*look back*'/, <**sx̲ep'í:tsel**>, //sx̣əpʼ=í·cəl//, /'*chipmunk*'/, literally /'scratch or scrape on back'/, <**sx̲ex̲ep'í:tsel**>, //s=x̣əx̣əpʼ=í·cəl//, /'*chipmunk with multiple stripes on his back*'/, <**sqwómàtsel**>, //sqʷám=ὲcəl//, /'*hunchback, lump on the back*'/, root <**qʷem**> *lump*, possibly <**tslhítselxel**>, //cɬ=ícəl=xʸəl//, /'*top of the foot*'/, literally /'upper back/surface/top of foot)'/, <**pálétst**>, df //pɛ́l(=)əc=T or pɛ́l=ə[=´=]c=T//, /'*skim it off*'/ (root meaning unknown but <**=ets**> *on the surface/top)*, <**q'áwetsel**>, //qʼɛ́w=əcəl//, /'*dorsal fin (long fin on back of fish)*'/, literally perhaps /'turn in river on back'/, <**láts'ewets**>, //lɛ́cʼ=əwəc//, /'*one hundred, hundred*'/, root <**láts'**> *different*, also see <**=í:tsel ~ =etsel**>.

<**ewól**>, bound root //ʔəwál//, PLAY /'*play (games, etc.)*'/.

<**ewólem**>, mdls //ʔəwál=əm//, PLAY /'*play (games, etc.)*'/, syntactic analysis: intransitive verb, attested by AC, Deming, also <**ewó:lem**>, //ʔəwá·l=əm//, attested by AC, other sources: ES /ʔəwá·ləm/, example: <**lámalha ewólem e**>, //lɛ́=m-ɛɬɛ ʔəwál=əm ʔə//, /'*Go play (you guys).*'/, syntactic comment: imperative2p, attested by Deming.

<**iwólem ~ í:wólem**>, cts //ʔə[-Ai(·´)-]wál=əm//, PLAY ['*playing*'], (<**i-ablaut ~ í:-ablaut**> *continuative*), phonology: ablaut, syntactic analysis: intransitive verb, attested by AC, example: <**wiyóth kw'es í:wólems te stá:xwelh, t'ít'elem kw'es í:wólems**>, //wiyáθ kʼʷ-əs ʔə[-Aí·-]wál=əm-s tə s=tɛ́·xʷ=əɬ, tʼí[-C_1ə-]l=əm kʼʷə-s ʔə[-Aí·-]wál=əm-s//, /'*The children are playing all the time, singing as they're playing.*'/, attested by AC.

<**sewólem**>, dnom //s=ʔəwál=əm//, PLAY ['*a game*'], phonology: loss of the root glottal stop after s= nominalizer is irregular, (irregular), syntactic analysis: nominal, attested by EB.

<**sewsewólem**>, pln //C_1əC_2=səwál=əm//, PLAY ['*games*'], (<**R3=**> *plural*), phonology: the reduplication even of the nominalizer is very irregular, showing that EB considers the initial /s/ part of the root now, (irregular), syntactic analysis: nominal, attested by EB.

<**lexwsewólem**>, ds //ləxʷ=s=ʔəwál=əm//, EFAM ['*playful*'], PLAY, lx <**lexw=**> *always*, syntactic analysis: adjective/adjectival verb, attested by Elders Group 2/16/76.

<**ewólemstexw**>, caus //ʔəwál=əm=sT-əxʷ//, PLAY ['*play with s-o*'], (<**=em**> *middle voice*, <**=st**> *causative control transitivizer*), syntactic analysis: transitive verb, attested by Deming.

<**eywéylaq** or **iwílaq**>, ds //ʔə[-Ai-]wál=í(·)l=ɛq//, cts, incs, PLAY ['*play-dancing*'], (<**i-ablaut**> *continuative*), (<**=í(:)l**> *come, go, get, become*, <**=aq**> *male*? or more likely <**=éleq**> *as an occupation*), syntactic analysis: intransitive verb?, attested by EB after LJ.

<**iwá:ltses**>, ds //ʔə[-Ai-]wa[=Aɛ́·=]l=cəs//, PLAY ['*cat's-cradle*'], ASM ['game of making designs in string strung between one's hands; the designs or patterns include: the flea (t'ót'elhem), the whirlpool in the Fraser (Hémq'eleq), the owl (chítmexw), diamonds (either one, two, four, eight or sixteen diamonds), and slip-away (cut fingers, cut neck)'], (<**i-ablaut**> *continuative*), (<**á:-ablaut**> *derivational*), lx <**=tses**> *on the hand*, phonology: ablaut, syntactic analysis: intransitive verb?, nominal?, attested by IHTTC 9/14/77, also <**siwá:ltses**>, //s=ʔiwɛ́·lcəs//, attested by NP has also heard this form.

<**ewólemstexw**>, PLAY ['*play with s-o*'], *see* ewólem.

<**=ewòt**>, da //=əw=àt//, N ['*female name*'], syntactic analysis: lexical suffix, derivational suffix; found in <**Óyewot**>, //ʔáy=əwat//, /'*baby sister of Mt. Cheam,* also *Indian name of Amy Cooper.*'/.

<**=ex**>, da //=əxʸ//, TIB ['*purposeful control transitivizer inanimate object preferred*'], syntactic analysis: derivational suffix; found in <**léwexes.**>, //lə́w=əxʸ-əs//, /'*He put it in.*'/, <**léwexem.**>,

//lə́w=əxʸ=əm//, /'*It was put in.*'/, <**lép'ex**>, //lə́p'=əxʸ//, /'*eat s-th*'/, <**tá:lx**>, //tɛ́·l=xʸ//, /'*track s-th/s-o*'/, <**kwá:lx**>, //kʷɛ́·l=xʸ//, /'*hide s-th (an object, not a person)*'/, <**tl'pì:lx**>, //ƛ'əp=í·l=xʸ//, /'*bring s-th down (from upper shelf or upstairs)*'/, <**wá:lxes.**>, //wɛ́·l=xʸ-əs//, /'*He threw it (upwards). (throw s-th upwards)*'/, <**hó:kwexes.**>, //há·kʷ=əxʸ-əs//, /'*He used it. (use s-th)*'/, <**xwálxes.**>, //xʷɛ́=l=xʸ-əs//, /'*He lifted it. (lift s-th)*'/, <**máx**>, //mɛ́=xʸ//, /'*take it off (from s-th it is attached to)*'/, <**xwemáx**>, //xʷə=mɛ́=xʸ//, /'*open s-th (a door for ex.)*'/, <**memáx**>, //C_1ə=mɛ́=xʸ//, /'*to separate/split up people fighting*'/, <**témex**>, //tə́m=əxʸ//, /'*desire s-th, wish for s-th*'/, <**t'ámex**>, //t'ɛ́m=əxʸ//, /'*braid it*'/.

<**=ex**>, da //=əxʸ//, SH /'*upright, erect*'/, DIR, syntactic analysis: lexical suffix, derivational suffix; found in <**ímex**>, //ʔím=əxʸ//, /'*walk*'/ (compare <**í(:)m=et**> *step on s=th*, literally /'step upright'/), <**lhex̲éyléx** or better **lhex̲íléx**>, //ɬəx̣=íl=ə́xʸ//, /'*stand up*'/ (root <**lhex̲=**> *stiff* plus <**=i:l**> *go, come get* and <**=éx**> *upright)*, <**xwexwíléx**>, //C_1ə=xʷíy=əl=ə́xʸ//, /'*get up with quick motion*'/ (compare <**R5=**> *resultative* and <**xwiy**> *rise, climb* + <**=el**> *go, come, get* + <**=éx**>, <**qw'eyíléx**>, //q'ʷəy=íl=ə́xʸ//, /'*dance*'/, <**kwéléxt**>, //kʷə́l=ə́xʸ=t//, /'*shoot s-th*'/ (root <**kwel=**> *hold in hand)*, <**wá:lx**>, //wɛ́·l=xʸ//, /'*throw upward*'/ (compare <**s=wá:ls**> *a scramble, scramble-giving (gifts are thrown upward towards a crowd and they scramble for them))*, <**t'áméx**>, //t'ɛ́m=ə́xʸ//, /'*to braid* '/ (root unclear).

<**éxel**>, possibly root //ʔə́xʸəl//, [ʔɪ́xʸɪl], CAN /'*to paddle, paddling a canoe (in rough water)*'/, possibly <**=el**> *come, go, get*, syntactic analysis: intransitive verb, attested by AC, BJ, Elders Group, EB, Salish cognate: Squamish /ʔísun/ *make strokes, to paddle* and /ʔíʔsun/ *(making strokes, paddling)* W73:256, K67:398, also <**éyxel**>, //ʔɛ́yxʸəl//, attested by Elders Group; found in <**éxellha**>, //ʔə́xʸəl-ɬɛ//, /'*Paddle (in rough water).*'/, example: <**li éxel?**>, //li ʔə́xʸəl//, /'*Did he paddle?*'/, attested by AC, <**latsel éxel**>, //lɛ-c-əl ʔə́xʸəl//, /'*I'm going to paddle.*'/, attested by AC, <**éwelh éxel**>, //ʔə́wə-ɬ ʔə́xʸəl//, /'*He didn't paddle.*'/, attested by AC (text), <**lóy kwsu xwéms kw'as éxel**>, //láy kʷ-s-u xʷəm-s k'ʷ-ɛ-s ʔə́xʸəl//, /'*You have to paddle fast.*'/, literally /'it's only fast that you paddle'/, syntactic comment: note adverb/adverbial verb as main verb, attested by EB, *<**tsel éxel te (sléxwelh, tl'elá:y, q'x̲wő:welh)**> rejected, /'*I paddled a (canoe, shovel-nose canoe, big-bowed canoe)*'/, rejected by EB.

<**í:xel**>, cts //ʔə[-Aí·-]xʸəl//, CAN ['*paddling*'], (<**í:-ablaut**> *continuative*), phonology: ablaut, lengthening, syntactic analysis: intransitive verb, attested by AC, also <**íxel**>, //ʔə[-Aí-]xʸəl//, also /'*paddling a canoe (in smooth water)*'/, attested by Elders Group 3/26/75.

<**-exw**>, ia //-əxʷ//, PRON /'*him, her, it, them, third person object*'/, syntactic analysis: is; found in <**qelstexwtsel**>, //qə́l=sT-əxʷ-cəl//, /'*I don't like it/him/her/them. (dislike s-o/s-th)*'/, <**kw'étslexwes.**>, //k'ʷə́c=l-əxʷ-əs//, /'*He/She/It/They see s-o.*'/.

<**-exw**>, ia //-əxʷ//, PRON ['*second person singular subjunctive subject*'], syntactic comment: can be suffixed to forms prefixed with we- *when, if* or to the first subordinate verb after a negative verb, can also add the *when/if* meaning even without the we- prefix being present, also <**-xw**>, //-xʷ//, phonology: after auxiliary verbs ending in i (í, lí, mí, lhí); found in <**welámexw**>, //wə-lɛ́=m-əxʷ//, /'*if/when you go*'/, example: <**éwechexw sts'eláxwemexw.**>, //ʔə́wə-c-əxʷ s=c'ələ[=Aɛ́=]xʷ=əm-əxʷ//, /'*You're not a spirit-dancer.*'/, <**éwechexw lámexw.**>, //ʔə́wə-c-əxʷ lɛ́=m-əxʷ//, /'*You don't/won't go.*'/, <**éwechexw íxw lám.**>, //ʔə́wə-c-əxʷ ʔí·-xʷ lɛ́=m//, /'*You didn't/don't go., Don't go.*'/.

<**éxw**>, free root //ʔə́xʷ//, SM ['*(said when something smells bad)*'], EFAM, syntactic analysis: interjection, attested by AHTTC.

<**exwá:ls**>, sas //ʔəxʷ=ɛ́·ls//, ABFC ['*scratch around*'], (<**=á:ls**> *as a structured activity (non-continuative))*, syntactic analysis: intransitive verb, attested by IHTTC.

<**íxwels**>, cts //ʔə[-Aí-]x^w=əls//, sas, ABFC ['*scratching around*'], (<**=els**> *as a structured activity (continuative)),* syntactic analysis: intransitive verb, attested by IHTTC.

<**=éxwthelh**>, da //=ə́x^{w}θəɬ//, ANA ['*on the tongue*'], syntactic analysis: lexical suffix, derivational suffix, possibly <**=exw**> *lump, round, around*, possibly <**=thel**> *in the mouth*, possibly final devoicing of <**l**> to <**lh**> *derivational* or possibly diachronic, phonology: possible devoicing; found in <**téxwthelh**>, //tə́x^w=x^{w}θəɬ or t=ə́x^{w}θəɬ//, /'*tongue*'/, <**sx̱àmeléxwthelh**>, //s=x̣ɛ̀m=əl=ə́x^{w}θəɬ//, /'*wild tiger lily*'/, literally /'nominal bitter on the tongue'/.

<**éx̱**>, free root //ʔə́x̣//, EFAM ['*(said when you are disgusted)*'], syntactic analysis: interjection, attested by AHTTC: AD, NP.

<**ex̱ímels**>, SOC ['*to put on credit ??*'], *see* íx̱em.

<**ex̱ímstexw**>, SOC ['*lend s-o money*'], *see* íx̱em.

<**ex̱ímt**>, SOC /'*lend money to s-o, [give s-o credit]*'/, *see* íx̱em.

<**ex̱ó:ythelem**>, HHG ['*shave (the face)*'], *see* íx̱.

<**éx̱qst**>, FIRE ['*strike s-th pointed (esp. a match)*'], *see* íx̱.

<**éx̱wtel**>, HHG ['*broom*'], *see* íx̱w.

<**éy ~ éy:**>, free root //ʔɛ́y ~ ʔɛ́y·//, VALJ /'*be good, good, well, nice, fine, better, better (ought to), it would be good if, may it be good, let it be good, happy, glad, clean, well-behaved, polite, virgin, popular, comfortable (with furniture, other things?),*'/, EFAM, SOC, syntactic analysis: adjective/adjectival verb, other sources: ES /ʔɛ́y·/, JH /ʔí·/, ASM ['be good, good'], example: <**é:ychexw swíyeqe**>, //ʔɛ́·y-c-əx^w s=wíyəqə//, /'*You're a good man.*'/, attested by AC, <**éy slháli**>, //ʔɛ́y s=ɬɛ́li//, /'*She's a good woman.*'/, attested by AC, <**éytsel**>, //ʔɛ́y-c-əl//, /'*I'm good.*'/, attested by Deming, <**éy swàyèl**>, //ʔɛ́y s=wɛ̀y=ə̀l//, /'*Good day.*'/, usage: a greeting, attested by Deming, <**éy kw'els kw'etslòmè**>, //ʔɛ́y k'w-əl-s k'wəc=l-àmə̀//, /'*It's good to see you.*'/, attested by RP, EB, <**ts'áts'eltsel xwoyíwel tel sqwálewel kw'els me xwe'í sq'ó talhlúwep, éy l sí:yáye**>, //c'ɛ́[=C_1ə=]l-c-əl x^w=ɛ[=a=]y=íwəl t-əl s=q^{w}ɛ́l=əwəl k'w-əl-s mə x^{w}ə=ʔí s=q'á tɛ=ɬ=lúwə=p, ʔɛ́y l si[=´·]yɛ́yə//, /'*I'm very happy to come here at this gathering my good friends.*'/, attested by Deming, syntactic comment: the possessive /l/ *my* follows the adjective /éy/ *good*, and occurs alone with no article in the vocative use here, <**éy xwlá(m) tl'eléwe te tselqómé**>, //ʔɛ́y x^w=lɛ́(m) ƛ'ə-lə́wə tə cəlq=ámə́//, /'*Blackcaps are good for you.*'/, attested by EB, <**éy xwlá(m) tl'eléwe te st'élmexw**>, //ʔɛ́y x^w=lɛ́(m) ƛ'ə-lə́wə tə s=t'ə́lməx^w//, /'*The medicine is good for you.*'/, <**le xwe éy**>, //lə x^{w}ə ʔɛ́y//, /'*It was good., He's/She's satisfied (of sex or many other things).*'/, semantic environment ['sex, other things also'], attested by JL, ASM ['may it be good'], <**éy ta' sleq'áleq'el**>, //ʔɛ́y t-ɛʔ s=lə(=)q'ɛ́lə=C_1əC_2(?)//, /'*May your travelling be good.*'/, attested by EB, ASM ['good feelings, glad, happy'], <**éy kw'el sqwá:lewel**>, //ʔɛ́y k'w-əl s=q^{w}ɛ̀·l=əwəl//, /'*I have good feelings., I have good thoughts.,I'm glad., I'm happy. I'm grateful., I'm thankful.*'/, also <**éy tel sqwálewel**>, //ʔɛ́y t-əl s=q^{w}ɛ́l=əwəl//, <**thá:ytes te éy sqwálewel**>, //θí[=Aɛ́·=]y=T-əs tə ʔɛ́y s=q^{w}ɛ̀·l=əwəl//, /'*It's making good feelings.*'/, attested by EB, <**éy tel sqwálewel kw'etslóle mőkw' í(kw'elò)**>, //ʔɛ́y t-əl s=q^{w}ɛ́l=əwəl [k'w-əl-s] k'wəc=l-álə mók'w ʔí(=k'wə=là)//, /'*I'm glad to see you all here.*'/, attested by Deming, <**éy t'we kw'el sqwálewel we'emís**>, //ʔɛ́y t'wə k'w-əl s=q^{w}ɛ́l=əwəl wə-ʔəmí-s//, /'*I'll be glad if he comes*'/, ASM ['better'], <**éy telí tl'á'altha**>, //ʔɛ́y təlíƛ'-C_1ɛ́-ʔɛ́lθɛ//, /'*He's better than me.*'/, literally /'He's good from (obj. of prep.-)me.'/, <**le xwá éy**>, //lə x^{w}ɛ́ ʔɛ́y//, /'*It got better.*'/, <**yeláwel éy**>, //yəlɛ́w=əl ʔɛ́y//, /'*It's better., He's/She's better.*'/, <**yeláwel éy telí tl'á'altha**>, //yəlɛ́w=əl ʔɛ́y təlíƛ'-C_1ɛ́-ʔɛ́lθɛ//, /'*(It's/He's/She's) better than me.*'/, <**Tl'ó yeláwel éy**>, //ƛ'á yəlɛ́w=əl ʔɛ́y//, /'*That's the best., That's better.*'/, <**éy, tl'ó yewál éy**

st'élmexw; welí kw'e li te éqwelets te thqát éwe lís eyém>, //ʔɛ́y, ƛ'á yəwɛ́l ʔɛ́y s=t'əlməx^{w}; wəlí k'wə li tə ʔə́q^{w}ə=ləc tə θqɛ́t ʔə́wə lí-s ʔɛy=ə́m//, /'*It's good; it's the best medicine; if it's on the back (side away from the rising sun) of the tree it's not as strong.*'/, attested by CT, <**éy t'wa**>, //ʔɛ́y t'wɛ//, also <**éy t'we**>, (morphosememic development: //'it would be better, it would be good, it ought to be, it should be, it needs to be'//), literally /'it's good evidently, it's good I guess, it must be good'/, <**éy t'we kw'as th'e<u>x</u>wewíls tloqá:ys**>, //ʔɛ́y t'wə k'w-ɛ-s θ'ə́x̣^{w}=əwíls tla=qɛ́·ys//, /'*You better wash the dishes now.*'/, attested by AD, <**éy t'we kws p'áth'etemet**>, //ʔɛ́y t'wə k^{w}-s p'ɛ́θ'=əT-əm-ət//, /'*It better be sewed., It needs to be sewed.*'/, attested by AD, <**éy t'wa kw'els lám**>, //ʔɛ́y t'wɛ k'w-əl-s lɛ́m//, /'*I should go.*'/, literally /'it should be that I go'/, ASM ['let it be'], <**éy kw'ómkw'emcha telí s'ólh sqwálewel xwlam kw'e ít totí:lt tlówàyèl**>, //ʔɛ́y k'^{w}ám=C_1əC_2-cɛ təlí s=ʔáɬ s=q^{w}ɛ́l=əwəl x^{w}=lɛ-m k'wə ʔí-t ta[-C_1ə-]l=í·l=T tlá=wɛ̀y=ə̀l//, /'*Let our thoughts be strong toward what we are studying today.*'/, attested by AD, <**éy kws hákw'eleschet te s'í:wes te siyolexwálh**>, //ʔɛ́y k^{w}-s hɛ́k'w=ələs-c-ət tə s=ʔí·wəs-s tə s=iyáləx^{w}ə-əɬ//, /'*Let us remember the teaching of the elders past.*'/, phonology: vowel merger, consonant merger, attested by AD, <**éy kws ste'ás**>, //ʔɛ́y k^{w}-s s=t=əʔɛ́-s//, /'*Amen.*'/, (morphosememic development: //'Amen'//), literally /'let it be like that'/, attested by AD, NP, Deming, ASM ['well'], <**li éy ta' s'ítet**>, //li ʔɛ́y t-ɛʔ s-ʔítət//, /'*Did you sleep well?*'/, literally /'Was it good your sleep'/, attested by Fish Camp 1978, also <**líchxw we'ítet kw'e éy**>, //li-c-x^{w} wə-ʔítət k'wə ʔɛ́y//, attested by Fish Camp 1978, ASM ['nice, well-behaved, good'], <**é:y ta sqwmà:y**>, //ʔɛ́[-·-]y t-ɛ s=q^{w}əm=ɛ́·y//, /'*You've got a nice dog.*'/, literally /'it's very good your dog, your dog is very good'/, phonology: stress shift (high to mid in sentence intonation), attested by AC, <**éychap mámele**>, //ʔɛ́y-c-ɛp C_1ɛ́-mələ//, /'*You are good children.*'/, semantic environment ['(said to someone's children)'], attested by AD, ASM ['polite'], <**éy ~ ts'áts'el éy**>, //ʔɛ́y ~ c'ɛ́c'əl ʔɛ́y//, /'*polite, good, very good*'/, literally /'good ~ very good'/, attested by Deming, ASM ['is popular'], <**éy mestíyexw; mekw'ewát tl'íls**>, //ʔɛ́y məstíyəx^{w}; mək'w=əwɛ́t ƛ'í=ls//, /'*He's popular., He's a good person; everyone likes him.*'/, ASM ['is clean, good'], <**éy te lálems**>, //ʔɛ́y tə lɛ́ləm-s//, /'*Her house is clean.*'/, attested by AC, ASM ['virgin'], <**Éy Máli**>, //ʔɛ́y mɛ́li//, /'*Virgin Mary*'/, attested by EB, /'*the Hail Mary*'/, ASM, semantic environment ['Catholic prayer, words to a Catholic prayer'], attested by EB, ASM ['comfortable'], semantic environment ['furniture, perhaps other environments'], <**welá:wel éy**>, //wə=yəlɛ́·w=əl ʔɛ́y//, /'*it's comfortable*'/, ASM ['fine'], <**ō éy**>, //ʔow ʔɛ́y//, /'*it's fine, he's/she's fine*'/, attested by BJ (Ben James), ASM ['it would be good'], <**éyelh**>, //ʔɛ́y-əɬ//, /'*it would be good*'/, (<**-elh**>), syntactic analysis: intransitive verb-past affixed, <**éyelh lílelh welám**>, //ʔɛ́y-əɬ lí-l-əɬ wə-lɛ́m//, /'*It would be good if I went.*'/, syntactic comment: note 1s subordinate subjunctive here followed by the past tense, both on the auxiliary; note too the subjunctive prefix we- *if, when* on the verb following the aux and the subjunctive subject marker; also note that both the main verb éy and the adjacent auxiliary lí-l are inflected with past tense markers -elh; all three structures seem a little unusual.

<**í'iy**>, dmv //C_1í=ʔɛy//, VALJ /'*cute, a little one is good, good (of s-th little)*'/, (<**R4=**> *diminutive*), phonology: reduplication, syntactic analysis: adjective/adjectival verb, attested by BHTTC, IHTTC.

<**é'iy ~ á'iy**>, dmpv //C_1í[-Aə́-]-ʔɛy ~ C_1ɛ́-ʔɛy//, VALJ /'*good (of little ones), cute (of many of them)*'/, (<**é-ablaut of R4=**> *plural of diminutive*), phonology: stress shift, ablaut, reduplication, vowel change (**éy** → unstressed iy), syntactic analysis: adjective/adjectival verb-diminutive-pl, attested by IHTTC.

<**í'istexw**>, caus //C_1í=ʔɛy=sT-əx^{w}//, EFAM ['*find it funny*'], (<**R4=**> *diminutive*), phonology: reduplication, syntactic analysis: transitive verb, attested by BHTTC.

<**á'iy ~ 'á'iy**>, dmn //ʔɛ́[=C_1ə=]y or C_1ɛ́=ʔɛy//, VALJ ['*cute little one*'], probably <**-R1-**> *diminutive*, possibly <**R7=**> *diminutive*, phonology: reduplication, vowel-raising (ey > iy), syntactic analysis: nominal, attested by AD.

<**álíy ~ 'álíy**>, plv //ʔ[-əl-]ɛ́y//, VALJ /'*more than one is good, good (of many things or people)*'/, (<**-el-**> *plural*), phonology: infixed plural, syntactic analysis: adjective/adjectival verb-pl, attested by IHTTC.

<**'al'álíy**>, plv //C_1əC_2-ʔ[-əl-]ɛ́y//, VALJ ['*all good*'], (irregular)double plural?, (<**R3-**> *plural*), (<**-el-**> *plural*), phonology: reduplication, infixed plural, syntactic analysis: adjective/adjectival verb-pl-pl?, attested by IHTTC.

<**shxw'éy**>, dnom //sx^w=ʔɛ́y//, VALJ ['*what s-o/s-th is good for*'], syntactic analysis: nominal, relative clause, example: <**mekw'stám shxw'éys**>, //mək'w=stɛ́m sx^w=ʔɛ́y-s//, /'*(It's) good for everything.*'/, attested by EB, <**ōwéte shxw'éys**>, //ʔowə=´tə sx^w=ʔɛ́y-s//, /'*(It's) good for nothing., He's good for nothing.*'/, attested by EB, Elders, <**ewétal shxw'éy**>, //ʔəwə=´tɛ-l sx^w=ʔɛ́y//, /'*I'm good for nothing.*'/, <**lóy kws shxw'íys kws qwíqwelats**>, //láy k^w-s sx^w=ʔɛ́y-s k^w-s C_1í=q^{w}ɛ̀·l=lə[=M2=]c//, /'*All he's good for is calling s-o down (call s-o down, gossip)*'/, literally /'is only that he what he's good for that he is calling down/gossiping'/, phonology: reduplication, metathesis, attested by EB.

<**siyachís**>, dnom //s=ʔɛy=ɛcə[=Aí=]s//, ANAH ['*right arm*'], lx <**=(a)chís**> *arm* from lx <**=tses**> *hand* plus **í-ablaut**, phonology: ablaut, stress shift, syntactic analysis: nominal.

<**eyáléqep ~ iyáléqep**>, ds //ʔɛy=ɛ́lə́qəp//, SM /'*have a fragrance, have a good smell, smell good*'/, lx <**=áléqep**> *smell, in smell*, phonology: vowel shift, syntactic analysis: intransitive verb, attested by Elders 3/15/72, Deming, also <**eyáleqep**>, //ʔɛy=ɛ́ləqəp//, attested by NP, example: <**eyáleqep te sp'á:q'em**>, //ʔɛy=ɛ́ləqəp tə s=p'ɛ́·q'əm//, /'*The flower smells good.*'/.

<**iyáléqepthet**>, incs //ʔɛy=ɛ́lə́qəp=θət//, SM ['*starting to smell good*'], syntactic analysis: intransitive verb.

<**iyálewes**>, ds //ʔɛy=ɛ́ləwəs//, EFAM ['*(be) brave*'], syntactic analysis: adjective/adjectival verb.

<**iyálewet**>, pcs //ʔɛy=ɛ́ləwə(s)=T//, EFAM ['*do s-th oneself*'], syntactic analysis: transitive verb, attested by AC, example: <**léwecha o iyálewet**>, //lə́wə-cɛ ʔa ʔɛy=ɛ́ləwə(s)=T//, /'*You'll do it (yourself).*'/, attested by AC, <**lhlímèlhcha o iyálewet**>, //ɬlímə̀ɬ-cɛ ʔa ʔɛy=ɛ́ləwə(s)=T//, /'*We'll do it ourselves.*'/, attested by AC, <**lhwélepcha o iyálewet**>, //ɬwə́ləp-cɛ ʔa ʔɛy=ɛ́ləwə(s)=T//, /'*You people will do it yourselves.*'/, attested by AC.

<**iyálewethet**>, incs //ʔɛy=ɛ́ləwə(s)=T=ət//, EFAM /'*try to do something (no matter what, anyway)*'/, phonology: consonant loss, vowel shift, syntactic analysis: intransitive verb, dialects: *Cheh.*, attested by EB, AD, also <**iyólewethet**>, //ʔɛy=ɛ́[=Aá=]ləwə(s)=T=ət//, phonology: ablaut automatic before <=thet>, consonant loss, vowel shift, dialects: *Chill.*, attested by EB,AD, also <**iyólwéthet**>, //ʔɛy=ɛ́[=Aá=]lwə[=´=](s)=T=ət//, phonology: ablaut, consonant loss, stress shift, vowel shift, dialects: *Chill.*, attested by NP, example: <**lachxw iyólwéthet**>, //lɛ-c-x^w ʔɛy=ɛ́lwə́=θət//, /'*You're going to try it (anyway, no matter what).*'/, (semological comment: see also *independent*), attested by NP.

<**eyámeth'**>, ds //ʔɛ́y=ɛ́məθ'//, DESC /'*smooth (of pole, stick, or wood)*'/, semantic environment ['pole, stick, wood, stature'], ANAH /'*good figure, good shape*'/, VALJ, semantic environment ['human'], lx <**=ámeth'**> *pole, stick, upright, stature, height*, syntactic analysis: adjective/adjectival verb, attested by BHTTC, Elders Meeting, example: <**eyámeth' siyó:lh**>, //ʔɛy=ɛ́məθ' s=yá·ɬ//, /'*smooth wood*'/, ASM ['good figure, good shape'], also <**eyámets'**>, //ʔɛy=ɛ́məc'//, attested by EL or TM, phonology: these speakers (from Chehalis) often show <ts'> /c'/ where all other Upriver speakers attested have <th'> /θ'/--consonant shift.

<**iyá:q**>, df //ʔɛy=ɛ́·q or ʔəy=ɛ́·q//, KIN ['*girl's younger brother (pet name)*'], root <**éy ~ iy**> *good*, possibly <**=á:q**> *male; penis*, phonology: éy → iy unstressed often, syntactic analysis: nominal, attested by Elders Group (1/7/76).

<**i'éyel**>, dmv //C₁í=ʔɛ́y=əl//, incs, ABFC /'*recover, be better*'/, (<**R4=**> *diminutive*), (<**=el**> *go, come, get, become*), phonology: reduplication, syntactic analysis: intransitive verb, attested by EB, example: <**tsel i'éyel**>, //c-əl ʔi=ʔɛ́y=əl//, /'*I'm recovered.*'/, attested by EB, <**tsel ma i'éyel**>, //c-əl mɛ ʔi=ʔɛ́y=əl//, /'*I got better.*'/ (compare <**me**> *get, become, inceptive)*, attested by EB, <**líchxw me tu i'éyel**>, //li-c-xʷ mə tu ʔi=ʔɛ́y=əl//, /'*Are you getting better?*'/, also <**líchxw welh me tu á:yelew**>, //li-c-xʷ wəɬ mə tu ʔɛ́·y=əl=əw (w sic for xʷ?)//, usage: less preferred than líchxw me tu i'éyel.

<**á'áyal**> (BG: better spelled <**éy'éyel**> or <**á'éyel**> or <**í'éyel**>), [éʔéyel], '*got better; recovered*', attested by RG,EH 8/27/99 (SU transcription, tape 6), [BG: if the initial vowel is <**á**>, this could be a *resultative* form, if it is <**éy**> it could be *resultative, characteristic*, or *plural*, if it is <**í**> then this form may be a *non-continuative* just translated in a past tense manner due to context].

<**i'éyelstexw**>, caus //C₁í=ʔɛ́y=əl=sT-əxʷ//, IDOC ['*make s-o well*'], (<**=st**> *causative control transitivizer*), (<**-exw**> *third person object*), phonology: reduplication, syntactic analysis: transitive verb, attested by EB, example: <**mí i'éyelstem te shxwlám**>, //mí ʔi=ʔɛ́y=əl=sT-əm tə sxʷlɛ́m//, /'*The Indian doctor made him/her well.*'/, literally /'get/become he/she was caused to be well (by) the Indian doctor'/, syntactic analysis: auxiliary verb transitive verb-passive demonstrative article nominal (agent of passive), attested by EB.

<**éyeles**>, pncs //ʔɛ́y=ələs//, EFAM ['*agree*'], syntactic analysis: transitive verb or adjective/ adjectival verb, example: <**l éyeles sqwálewel**>, //l ʔɛ́y=ələs s=qʷɛ̀·l=əwəl//, /'*I agree with you.*'/, literally /'my agree(ing) thoughts/feelings'/, (morphosememic development: //'I agree with you'//).

<**éyelew**>, incs //ʔɛ́y=əl=əw//, EFAM ['*oh my gosh.*'], (<**=ew**> *contrastive*), syntactic analysis: interjection.

<**eyeléwthelh**>, df //ʔɛy=əl=ə[=´=]w=θəɬ//, EFAM ['*for goodness sakes.*'], (<**=thelh**> meaning unknown unless related to <**=exwthelh**> *tongue*), phonology: stress shift, syntactic analysis: interjection, attested by EB, AD, example: <**eyeléwthelh te qél**>, //ʔɛy=əl=ə́w=θəɬ tə qə́l//, /'*For goodness sakes., the bad person.*'/, attested by EB, AD.

<**xw'í'àlh**>, df //xʷ=ʔɛ́y=ʔɛ̀ɬ//, LANG ['*talk quietly*'], literally perhaps /'be good in the manner of the voice [head or become good in the voice'/, possibly <**xw=**> *pertaining to the head*, possibly <**xw(e)=**> *become, get*, possibly <**=elh ~ ='alh**> *according to, in the manner of*, possibly <**='àlh**> *in voice*, syntactic analysis: intransitive verb, attested by Elders 12/15/76.

<**shxw'í'àlh**>, stvi //s=xʷ=ʔɛ́y=ʔɛ̀ɬ//, LANG /'*soft voice, have a soft voice*'/, ABFC, syntactic analysis: nominal?, adjective/adjectival verb?, attested by Elders 12/15/76.

<**shxw'éyelh**>, stvi //s=xʷ=ʔɛ́y=əɬ//, ABFC /'*be in clear voice, be in good voice, be in good health, healthy*'/, VALJ, (<**s=**> *stative*), possibly <**xw=**> *pertaining to the head*, possibly <**xw(e)=**> *get, become*, lx <**=elh ~ ='alh**> *according to, in the manner of* or *in voice*?, syntactic analysis: adjective/adjectival verb, attested by NP, ASM ['be in clear voice, be in good voice'], <**atsel shxw'éyelh tel qwóqwel**>, //ʔɛ-c-əl s=xʷ=ʔɛ́y=əɬ t-əl qʷɛ̀·[-Aá-C₁ə-]l//, /'*My voice is clear.*'/, literally /'my talking is in good/clear voice'/, phonology: ablaut, reduplication, syntactic comment: ambiguous past, attested by JL, ASM ['be in good health, be healthy'], dialects: *NP, JL ("hardly used"), never heard by EB*, <**lí u shxw'éyelh el líye**>, //lí ʔu s=xʷ=ʔɛ́y=əɬ ʔəl lí-ə//, /'*How's his health?*'/, semantic environment ['asking after your child's health (for ex.)'], dialects: *NP*, ASM ['somebody that's healthy'], dialects: *Cheh.*, attested by NP.

<**ey'éyelh**>, plv //C₁əC₂=ʔɛ́y=əɬ//, LANG ['*talking good*'], VALJ, (<**R3=**> *plural*), lx <**=elh ~ ='alh**> *according to, in the manner of* or *in voice*?, phonology: reduplication, syntactic analysis: adjective/adjectival verb, attested by HT.

<**shxw'iy'éyelh**>, stvi //s=xʷ=C₁əC₂=ʔɛ́y=əɬ//, LANG ['*be in clear voice*'], VALJ, (<**s=**> *stative*),

possibly <**xw=**> *relating to the face or head*, (<**R3=**> *plural*), lx <**=elh ~ ='alh**> *according to, in the manner of* or *in voice*?, phonology: reduplication, syntactic analysis: adjective/adjectival verb, attested by JL, example: <**atsel shxwiy'éyelh tel qwóqwel**>, //ʔɛ-c-əl s=x^w=C_1əC_2=ʔέy=əɬ t-əl q^{w}á[-q^{w}ə-]l//, /*'My voice is clear.*'/, chrs //s=xw=C_1əC_2='éy=elh//, phonology: vowel shift (ey → iy), attested by JL, <**xwey'éyelhs yé qweqwà:l**>, //x^w=C_1əC_2=ʔέy=əɬ-s yə́ C_1ə=q^{w}έ·l//, /*'He's talking good.*'/, attested by JL.

<**eyelhómex**>, ds //ʔɛy=əɬ=áməxy//, DESC ['*good-looking*'], VALJ, lx <**=elh**> meaning uncertain unless *in health* lx as above, <**=ómex**> *in appearance, in looks, -looking*, syntactic analysis: adjective/adjectival verb, dialects: *Deming*, attested by EF.

<**eyém ~ iyém**>, ds //ʔɛy=ə́m ~ ʔiy=ə́m//, DESC ['*be strong*'], VALJ, semantic environment ['of persons, animates, sickness, medicine, health, words, stick (but not of table)'], literally /'good in strength'/, lx <**=ém**> *in strength*, phonology: optional vowel shift, syntactic analysis: adjective/adjectival verb, attested by AC, BJ, EB, ME, Elders Group, CT, JL, NP, example: <**olew eyém**>, //ʔal=əw ʔɛy=ə́m//, /*'(It's) too strong*'/, semantic environment ['of medicine or strength of a person or thing'], <**eyém sq'óq'ey**>, //ʔɛy=ə́m s=q'á·[=C_1ə=]y//, /*'(It's a) real bad sickness.*'/, literally /'it's a strong sickness'/, attested by ME, <**eyém sqwà:l**>, //ʔɛy=ə́m s=q^{w}έ·l//, /*'(They're) strong words*'/, ASM ['used by a chief or high councillor when he talked to his people, good words that were respected'], <**éy, tl'ó yewál éy st'élmexw; welí kw'e lí te éqwelets te thqát éwe lís eyém**>, //ʔέy, ƛ'á yəwέl ʔέy s=t'ə́lməx^w; wə-lí k'wə lí tə ʔə́q^{w}ə=ləc tə θqέt ʔə́wə lí-s ʔɛy=ə́m//, /*'It's good, it's the best medicine; if it's on the back of the tree (side away from the rising sun) it's not as strong.*'/, MED ['*be strong*'], attested by CT, <**ő́we ís eyém**>, //ʔówə ʔí-s ʔɛy=ə́m//, /*'He/she/it is not strong., He/she/it is weak.*'/, attested by EB, <**atsu eyém**>, //ʔɛ-c-əl-əw ʔɛy=ə́m//, /*'I'm healthy., I'm strong., My health is good.*'/, grammatical comment: in the speech of JL, TM and EB -el *first person sg. subject* is sometimes dropped before -ew *contrastive*, -el dropping, syntactic analysis: ambiguous past, attested by JL, TM, also <**áchu eyémò**>, //ʔέ-c-əl-əw ʔɛy=ə́m-à//, attested by JL, <**tsel u eyém ò**>, //c-əl ʔu ʔɛy=ə́m ʔà//, attested by EB, <**su mékw' tsu eyémò**>, //s-əw mə́k'w c-əl-əw ʔɛy=ə́m-à//, /*'(So they are all strong/healthy.)*'/, attested by JL, also <**su mékw'ò kwsu eyémes**>, //s-əw mə́k'w-à k^w-s-əw ʔɛy=ə́m-əs//, attested by JL, <**eyém u ól**>, //ʔɛy=ə́m ʔu ʔál//, /*'strongest*'/, attested by NP.

<**eyémstexw**>, caus //ʔɛy=ə́m=sT-əx^w//, IDOC /*'make it strong, make him/her/them strong*'/, VALJ, syntactic analysis: transitive verb, attested by Deming, Elders Group, example: <**ő́wechxw eyémstexw**>, //ʔówə-c-x^w ʔɛy=ə́m=sT-əx^w//, /*'Don't make it strong.*'/, syntactic comment: irregular negative construction in that it lacks the 2s subjunctive pronoun either on a auxiliary verb or on eyémstexw, syntactic analysis: imperative, negative, <**eyémstexw ta sqwálewel**>, //ʔɛy=ə́m=sT-əx^w tɛ s=q^{w}έ·l=əwəl//, /*'Make your mind strong., Make your feelings strong.*'/, syntactic comment: imperative (though no imperative nor 2s subject pronoun inflections are present) due to the 2s possessive pronoun on the object np.

<**xwe'éyem ~ xw'éyem**>, incs //x^{w}ə=ʔɛ[=´=]y=ə́m//, WATR /*'be clear (of water), be smooth (AC)*'/, semantic environment ['water'], syntactic analysis: adjective/adjectival verb, attested by EB, JL, AC, Deming, example: <**xwe'éyem te stólō**>, //x^{w}ə=ʔέy=əm tə s=tá·low//, /*'The river is clear., The river is smooth.*'/, attested by AC,

<**Xwe'éyem**>, dnom /x^{w}ə=ʔέy=əm//, PLN /*'Deming (Wash.), South Fork of Nooksack River and village nearest Deming*'/, probably borrowed from Nooksack nox^{w}ʔíyəm ~ x^{w}ʔíyəm *South Fork of Nooksack River and village at its mouth near modern village of Deming; now used for Deming*, <**li te Xwe'éyem**>, //li tə x^{w}ə=ʔέy=əm//, /*'at Deming*'/, attested by Deming.

<**séyem**>, stvi //s=ʔɛy=ə́[=M2=]m//, DESC [*'be strong'*], found in <**séyem éliyels**>, EB, FOOD *garlic* (lit. strong + [domestic] onion), (attested by RG,EH 6/16/98 to SN, edited by BG with RG,EH 6/26/00)

<**simáléqep**>, stvi //s=ʔɛy=ə́m=ɛ́ləqəp, simɛ́lə́qəp//, SM /*'strong smell, bad stink, smell that can't be located'*/, (<**s=**> prob. *stative*), lx <**=ém**> *in strength*, lx <**=áléqep**> *smell*, phonology: consonant-loss (glottal stop), vowel-loss (**é**), syntactic analysis: stvi, attested by Elders Group, AC, also <**simáleqep**>, //s=ʔɛy=ə́m=ɛ́ləqəp//, /*'bad stink'*/, attested by AC.

<**simíwél**>, stvi //s=ʔɛy=ə́m=íwə́l//, EFAM /*'strong feelings, mad all the time but won't fight'*/, (semological comment: ['one is scared of such a person']), syntactic analysis: stvi.

<**siyá:m**>, dnom, probably //s=iy=ɛ́·m//, SOC /*'chief, leader, respected person, boss, rich, dear'*/, VALJ, probably literally "nominal/someone/something that=is strong", (<**s=**> *nominalizer*), root <**éy ~ iy**> *good*, probably lx <**=ém ~ =á:m**> *in strength,* compare <**ey=ém ~ iy=ém**> *strong*, and <**qel=á:m**> *weak*, syntactic analysis: nominal. See main entry under letter s, for much more information and derived forms from <**siyá:m**>.

<**Íyem ~ Íyém**>, dnom //ʔíy=əm ~ ʔíy=ə́m//, PLN /*'Eayem, a village site and fishing place above (upriver of) Yale, B.C.'*/, ASM ['located 3 miles north of Yale and two miles south of Five-Mile Creek, on the west side of the Fraser River; site now marked by a sign off the highway calling it Eayem and giving some details, toward the end of the road is access to the Fraser River where a smooth potholed rock shore may show where the Stó:lō fished (and still fish) and made fish oil in the holes; the name is said to mean "lucky place to catch fish"'], literally /'good place'/, lx <**=em**> *place*, syntactic analysis: nominal, attested by BHTTC, AD, AK.

<**xw'éyeqel**>, ds //xʷ=ʔɛ́y=əqəl//, ABFC [*'(have) a clear voice'*], LANG, syntactic analysis: intransitive verb, poss. adjective/adjectival verb.

<**iyés**>, dnom //ʔɛy=ə́s//, SOC /*'ma'am, female friend, chum (female), little girl'*/, phonology: vowel shift (unstressed ey → iy), syntactic analysis: nominal, ASM ['ma'am'], semantic environment ['used with a female adult stranger as polite term of address'], usage: polite, example: <**éy swàyèl, iyés**>, //ʔɛ́y s=wɛ̀y=əl, ʔiy=ə́s//, /*'Good day, ma'am.'*/, attested by Deming, ASM ['female friend'], semantic environment ['used with or of a friend'], <**láw iyés**>, //lɛ́w ʔɛy=ə́s//, /*'Hello friend (to a female)., Hi chum (girl).'*/, attested by AC, NP, ASM ['little girl'], semantic environment ['used with a female child stranger as polite term of address'], <**éy swàyèl, iyés**>, //ʔɛ́y s=wɛ̀y=ə̀l, ʔiy=ə́s//, /*'Good day, little girl.'*/, attested by Deming.

<**iyéseq**>, dnom //ʔɛy=ə́s=əq//, SOC /*'sir, male friend, chum (male), sonny'*/, lx <**=eq**> *male*, LANG, syntactic analysis: nominal, attested by Deming, Elders Group, AC, NP, ASM ['sir'], semantic environment ['used with an adult male stranger as a polite form of address'], usage: polite, example: <**éy swàyèl, iyéseq**>, //ʔɛ́y s=wɛ̀y=əl, ʔiy=ə́s=əq//, /*'Good day, sir.'*/, attested by Deming, ASM ['male friend'], semantic environment ['used with or of a male friend'], <**láw iyéseq**>, //lɛ́w ʔiy=ə́s=əq//, /*'Hello friend (to a male).'*/, attested by AC, ASM ['(male) chum'], semantic environment ['used with or of a male friend'], <**láw iyéseq**>, //lɛ́w ʔiy=ə́s=əq//, /*'Hi chum (to a boy).'*/, attested by NP, <**éy swàyèl, iyéseq**>, //ʔɛ́y s=wɛ̀y=ə̀l, ʔiy=ə́s=əq//, /*'Good day, chum (to a male).'*/, attested by Deming, ASM ['sonny'], semantic environment ['used with a young boy stranger as a polite form of address'], <**éy swàyèl, iyéseq**>, //ʔɛ́y s=wɛ̀y=əl, ʔiy=ə́s=əq//, /*'Good day, sonny.'*/, attested by Deming.

<**íyes ~ éyes**>, ds //ʔíy=əs ~ ʔɛ́y=əs//, SOC /*'be fun, have (lots of) fun, have amusement, having lots of fun, be pleasant'*/, VALJ, EFAM, lx <**=es ~ =ó:s**> probably *cyclic period, time period,* literally /'be good time, have good time'/, syntactic analysis: vii, poss. also adjective/adjectival verb, attested by EB, Elders Group, AC, ASM ['be fun'], <**íyes te'ílé**>, //ʔíy=əs tə=ʔí=lə́//, /*'This is fun.'*/, attested by EB, ASM ['have fun'], example: <**éyes te stá:xwelh**>, //ʔɛ́y=əs tə s=tɛ́·xʷ=əɬ//, /*'The kids had a lot*

of fun.'/, attested by AC, <**eyéschxwò ta' x̲áws syó:ys**>, //ʔɛ́y=əs-c-xʷ-à t-ɛʔ x̣ɛ́ws s=yá·ys//, /'*Have fun in your new work.*'/, phonology: stress shift perhaps due to suffixing of **-à**, attested by EB, <**eyéstset**>, //ʔɛ́y=əs-c-ət//, /'*We have fun.*'/, phonology: stress shift unexplained, attested by EB, <**tset éyes**>, //c-ət ʔɛ́y=əs//, /'*We had fun.*'/, syntactic analysis: ambiguous past, attested by EB, ASM ['having lots of fun'], <**áth'elchet we'éyes kwsu mékw'tset**>, //ʔɛ́θ'əl-c-ət wə-ʔɛ́y=əs kʷ-s-əw mə́k'w-c-ət//, /'*Everybody is really having lots of fun., We are all really having lots of fun.*'/, attested by Elders Group.

<**í:yó:sem**>, cts //ʔí[-·-]y=á·s=əm//, mdls, SOC ['*having fun*'], VALJ, EFAM, ds <=em> *middle voice*, phonology: length infixing, syntactic analysis: intransitive verb, attested by EB, example: <**í:yó:semtset**>, //ʔí·y=á·s=əm-c-ət//, /'*We're having fun.*'/, attested by EB.

<**eyéstem**>, stpc //ʔɛ́y=əs=təm or ʔɛ́y=əs=Təm or ʔɛ́y=əs=T-əm//, SOC /'*he was fun, he was enjoyed, they enjoyed him*'/, VALJ, EFAM, phonology: stress shift unexplained, syntactic analysis: participle or passive?, attested by EB.

<**í'eyó:stem**>, plv //ʔíy[=C_1əC_2]=á·s=təm//, chrs, SOC /'*having lots of fun, it's a lot of fun*'/, VALJ, EFAM, (<**=R2**> *plural or characteristic*), phonology: reduplication, attested by EB, example: <**í'eyó:stem kw'e la imexósem**>, //ʔíy-ʔəy=á·s=təm k'wə lɛ ʔim=əxy=ás=əm//, /'*It's a lot of fun to go for a walk.*'/, attested by EB.

<**eyó:sthet ~ iyósthet**>, pcrs //ʔɛ́y=á·s=T-ət ~ ʔiy=ás=T-ət//, SOC /'*a whole bunch having fun; having lots of fun, having a good time*'/, VALJ, EFAM, syntactic analysis: intransitive verb.

<**iyésqel**>, ds //ʔɛ́y=əs=qəl//, ABFC ['*(have a) pleasant voice*'], LANG, VALJ, lx <**=qel**> *in the throat; voice; language*, phonology: stress shift probably triggered by second affix, syntactic analysis: adjective/adjectival verb.

<**éystexw ~ éy:stexw**>, caus //ʔɛ́y=sT-əxʷ ~ ʔɛ́y·=sT-əxʷ//, SOC /'*like s-o [his/her personality], like s-th [its taste, its idea], be interested in s-th/s-o, enjoy s-o sexually*'/, VALJ, EFAM, syntactic analysis: transitive verb, ASM ['be interested in s-th/s-o'], <**éy:stexwes**>, //ʔɛ́y·=sT-əxʷ-əs//, /'*he is interested in it, he was interested in it*'/, ASM ['like it [its idea/concept; its taste]'], example: <**tsel éystexw**>, //c-əl ʔɛ́y=sT-əxʷ//, /'*I like it*'/, semantic environment ['also used to express agreement with someone's idea or statement'], Elder's comment: ""also used for 'I agree with you'", lit. *I like it*", <**tsel éystexw te skw'õlmexw**>, //c-əl ʔɛ́y=sT-əxʷ tə s=k'wólməxʷ//, /'*I like blackberries.*'/, attested by NP, <**éystexwtsel te halq'eméylem sqwéltel**>, //ʔɛ́y=sT-əxʷ-c-əl tə hɛ=ləq'ɛ́[=Aə=]məl=í·l=əm s=qʷɛ̀·[=Aə́=]l=təl//, /'*I like the Halkomelem language.*'/, phonology: vowel shift, ablaut, el-loss, attested by AC, ASM ['like s-o [his/her personality]'], <**éystexwes**>, //ʔɛ́y–sT-əxʷ-əs//, /'*he/she/it/they like him/her/them*'/, attested by AC, ASM ['enjoy s-o sexually'], <**éysthòx**>, //ʔɛ́y=sT-àxy//, /'*like me [my personality]; like me [my taste]; enjoy me sexually*'/, attested by IHTTC 9/9/77.

<**éystelómet ~ éy:stelómet**>, //ʔɛ́y=sT-əlámət//, SOC /'*pretending to be good, want to be accepted*'/, EFAM, VALJ, (<**-elómet**> *reflexive of causative*), phonology: the second (e) is epenthetic if it needs to be written at all, syntactic analysis: intransitive verb, refl, attested by Elders Group.

<**éyetses**>, ds //ʔɛ́y=əcəs//, DESC ['*clean hands*'], VALJ, ANAH, lx <**=(e)tses**> *on the hands, in the hands*, syntactic analysis: adjective/adjectival verb.

<**eyétses**>, ds //ʔɛ́y=ə[=´=]cəs//, DESC /'*clean [in everything: clothes, house, person, etc.], clean in one's person and what one owns*'/, VALJ, (morphosememic development: //'clean hands → clean in one's person and what one owns'//), phonology: stress shift, syntactic analysis: adjective/adjectival verb.

<**lexw'éy**>, ds //ləxʷ=ʔɛ́y//, SOC ['*generous*'], VALJ, EFAM, lx <**lexw=**> *always*, syntactic analysis: adjective/adjectival verb, attested by EB.

<**xw'éywelh ~ xwe'éywelh ~ xwe'éy:welh**>, ds //xʷ=ʔɛ́y=wəɬ ~ xʷə=ʔɛ́y=wəɬ ~ xʷə=ʔɛ́y·=wəɬ//, EFAM /'*good-hearted, kind-hearted, kind, generous, helpful, easy-going, good-natured*'/, SOC, VALJ, lx <**=welh**> *canoe, vessel, container* or lx <**=ó:lwelh**> *side, -ward,* syntactic analysis: adjective/adjectival verb, attested by Elders Group, AC, also <**shxw'éywelh**>, //s=xʷ=ʔɛ́y=wəɬ//, attested by Elders Group 4/6/77, also <**lexwe'éywelh ~ xwe'éywelh**>, //ləxʷ=ʔɛ́y=wəɬ ~ xʷ=ʔɛ́y=wəɬ//, lx <**lexw= ~ xw=**> *always*, attested by Elders Group 2/16/77.

<**iyílem**>, incs //ʔɛy=íl=əm//, mdls, WETH /'*clear up (of weather), turn fine (after a hard storm)*'/, VALJ, semantic environment ['of weather, for ex. after a hard storm'], literally /'get/become good on its own'/, lx <**=íl ~ =í:l**> *get, become, go, come*, (<**=em**> *middle voice, on its own*), syntactic analysis: intransitive verb, attested by EB.

<**Lexw'á:yí:les**>, ds //ləxʷ=ʔɛ́[=·=]y=í·l=əs//, PLN ['*a bay on west side of Harrison Lake*'], ASM ['above Qwélés and below Lkwőxwethem, this bay has a shore which is all sandy in low water; Indians always came here to swim after berry-picking, etc.'], Elder's comment: "the name means "always a pleasant place" from **éyes** *fun, pleasant*", literally /'always get/become a good time'/, lx <**lexw=**> *always*, lx <**=í:l**> *get, become, go, come*, lx <**=es**> *time, cycle*, phonology: lengthening, syntactic analysis: nominal, attested by EL 6/27/78.

<**s'eyí:ws**>, dnom //s=ʔɛy=í·ws//, ANAH ['*right side*'], DIR, lx <**s=**> *nominal*, lx <**=í:ws**> *on the body, on the skin, on the covering*, syntactic analysis: nominal, adjective/adjectival verb, attested by Elders Group, AC, EB, other sources: ES /sʔɛy·íus/ *right (side)*, H-T <c'ye'wus> (macron over e) *right hand*, example: <**lámchxw ta' s'eyí:ws**>, //lɛ́=m-c-xʷ t-ɛʔ s=ʔɛy=í·ws//, /'*You go to your right., Go to your right.*'/, attested by EB, <**s'eyí:ws í:lwelh**>, //s=ʔɛy=í·ws ʔí·lwəɬ//, /'*right side of the body*'/, <**le kwelá:tes li te s'eyí:ws chálexs**>, //lə kʷəl=ɛ́·T-əs li tə s=ʔɛy=í·ws cɛ́ləxy-s//, /'*He's holding it in his right hand.*'/, attested by AC.

<**s'eyí:wtses**>, dnom //s=ʔɛy=í·ws=cəs//, ANAH ['*right hand*'], phonology: consonant merger (s-ts → ts), syntactic analysis: nominal, attested by AC, Elders Group, also <**s'eyíwatses**>, //s=ʔɛy=íw=ɛcəs//, usage: not used often, attested by Elders Group, example: <**tl'ó te s'eyí:wtses**>, //ƛ'á tə s=ʔɛy=í·ws=cəs-s//, /'*It's his right hand.*'/, phonology: consonant merger or loss (s-ts → ts, and s-s → s), attested by AC.

<**s'iyláx̱el**>, dnom //s=ʔɛy=əlɛ́x̣əl//, ANAH ['*right arm*'], lx <**=eláx̱el**> *arm, on the arm*, phonology: vowel shift (unstress ey to iy), vowel loss, syntactic analysis: nominal, attested by BHTTC, also <**shxw'iláx̱el**>, //sxʷ=ʔɛy=əlɛ́x̣əl//, lx <**shxw=**> *nominalizer*, attested by DM.

<**silís**>, stvi //s=ʔɛy=əlís//, ANA /'*(have) sharp teeth, (have) fangs*'/, literally /'be good on the teeth'/, (<**s=**> *stative*), root <**éy**> *be good*, lx <**=elís**> *on the teeth*, phonology: vowel shift, vowel loss, consonant loss (' dropped), syntactic analysis: adjective/adjectival verb, example: <**silís tel sqwemá:y**>, //s=i=lís t-əl s=qʷəm=ɛ́·y//, /'*My dog has sharp teeth.*'/.

<**Selísi**>, dnom //s=i[=Aə=]=(ə)lís=iy//, PLN /'*Mt. Slesse; village at mouth of Slesse Creek onto Chilliwack R.*'/, probably borrowed from Nooksack or Chilliwhokwum senísiy *Mt. Slesse* (Boundary Survey records by Gibbs and others show variation of the l with n; n and =iy *place* both reflect Nooksack (or Chilliwhokwum) rather than Halkomelem (see Galloway and Richardson 1983 and Galloway 1985a), (<**e-ablaut**> *derivational*), phonology: ablaut, Elder's comment: "the name means "fang"", other sources: Wells 1965:13: the name means "fangs, teeth", source: place names file reference #225, attested by AC.

<**Selísi (Stótelō)**>, dnom //s=i[=Aə=]=(ə)lís=iy//, PLN ['*Slesse Creek*'], source: Wells 1965:13,

<**i'é:ymet**>, iecs //C_1əC_2=ʔɛ́y·=məT or C_1əC_2=ʔɛ́[=·=]y=məT//, EFAM ['*getting to like somebody*'], SOC, (<**R3=**> *continuative* or *plural*), phonology: reduplication, poss. length-infixing, syntactic analysis: transitive verb, attested by EB.

<**ō éy ~ ōw'éy**>, ds //ʔow ʔɛ́y ~ ʔow=ʔɛ́y//, ABFC [*'fine (in health)'*], VALJ, (morphosememic development from literally /'really be good'/, (<**ō ~ ōw= ~ =ew ~ ew= ~ we=**> *contrastive*), syntactic analysis: intransitive verb, attested by BJ (Ben James).

<**éy òl ~ éyòl ~ éyò**>, ds //ʔɛ́y ʔàl ~ ʔɛyàl ~ ʔɛ́yà//, VALJ /*'be alright, be well, be fine, be okay'*/, syntactic analysis: intransitive verb particle ~ intransitive verb.

<**we'éy òl ~ we'éyòl ~ we'éyò ~ u éyò ~ u'éyò**>, ds //wə=ʔɛy ʔàl ~ wə=ʔɛ́y=àl ~ wəʔɛ́yà ~ ʔu ʔɛ́yà ~ ʔu=ʔɛ́yà//, ABFC /*'be fine (in health), be alright (in health), be well'*/, VALJ, phonology: òl *just, simply* tends to combine phonetically with the previous word; we= ~ ew ~ u ~ ō *contrastive* usually combines phonetically with either the previous word or the following word, syntactic analysis: intransitive verb or intransitive verb particle, example: <**líchxw we'éy òl**>, //li-c-xʷ wə=ʔɛ́y ʔàl//, /*'How are you?, Are you well?'*/, literally /'Are you fine?, Are you well?, Are you alright?'/, usage: the answer is usually: lí *(I) am.*, but may also be: éy òl or éyò or tsel tu éyò (see below), dialects: *Chill.*, attested by AC, NP, Deming, also <**líchxw we'éyòl**>, dialects: *Deming*, also <**líchxw we'éyò**>, Elder's comment: "I think people also used this for *Will you be alright? (like when they are about to be doing something dangerous)*", attested by AD, also <**líchxw u éyò**>, attested by JL, also <**líchexw éyòl**>, dialects: *Deming: OW (Olive Williams, AC's daughter)*, also <**íchexw éyòl**>, dialects: *Deming: MH*, <**lichxw we'éy el qwóqwel kw'es me kwetxwílem (te xwelítem, kwtha siyáya)?**>, //li-c-xʷ wə=ʔɛ́y ʔəl qʷɛ[-AáC₁ə]l k'w-əs mə kʷət(ɛ)xʷ=íl=əm (tə xʷəlítəm, kʷ=θ-ɛ s(i)=yɛ́(=)yɛ)//, /*'Were you still talking when your friend came in?'*/, attested by AC, <**tsel we'éy òl**>, //c-əl wə=ʔɛ́y ʔàl//, /*'I'm alright., I'm well.'*/, attested by AC, also <**éy òl ~ éyò**>, attested by Deming, also <**tsel tu éyò**>, root <**tu**> *very, really*, attested by Deming, also <**chu tu éyò**>, phonology: chu is a collapse in rapid speech of chel=ew heard in the speech of some Chehalis and Tait speakers (EB, TM, JL), attested by TM, also <**tu éyò**>, attested by NP, also <**áchu tu éyò**>, phonology: collapse in rapid speech of achelew //ʔɛ-c-əl=əw//, attested by TM, JL, also <**tsu tu éyò ~ chu tu éyò**>, attested by JL, also <**áchu éyò**>, attested by JL, <**líchap we'éy òl ~ líchap we'éyò**>, //lí-c-ɛp wə=ʔɛ́y ʔàl ~ lí-c-ɛp wə=ʔɛ́yà//, /*'Are you folks well?'*/, usage: one answer is: lí. á'a. *We are. Yes.*, attested by IHTTC, <**áchxw u éyò**>, //ʔɛ́-c-xʷ ʔu ʔɛ́y=à//, /*'You are fine.'*/, attested by JL, <**ew tu éyò á:lhtel**>, //ʔəw tu ʔɛ́y=à ʔɛ́·ɬtəl//, /*'They are well.'*/, attested by TM, <**we'íxw u éyò**>, //wə-ʔí-xʷ ʔu ʔɛ́y=à//, /*'if you are fine'*/, attested by EB, <**ṓwetsel íl tu éyò**>, //ʔówə-c-əl ʔí-l tu ʔɛ́yà//, /*'I don't feel very well.'*/, attested by NP, also <**ṓwetsel tu éy**>, attested by JS, <**ṓwetsel welól ol éy**>, //ʔówə-c-əl wə=lá-l ʔàl ʔɛ́y//, /*'I'm not very well.'*/, attested by Deming, <**líchxw kwo tuw éyò talṓwe**>, //li-c-xʷ kʷɛ tuw ʔɛ́y=à tɛ=lə́wə//, [líčx^{w4} k^{wh}æ^{2} t^{h}uw^{2} ʔɛ́y^{5}à^{2} t^{h}ɛ^{2} lò^{3}wə̀^{3}], /*'(How are you really anyway?)'*/, attested by AC, <**éyò kw'a sqwálewel ~ éyò ta sqwálewel**>, //ʔɛ́y=à k'w-ɛ s=qʷɛ̀·l=əwəl ~ ʔɛ́y=à t-ɛ s=qʷɛ̀·l=əwəl//, /*'Be brave., Don't take it so hard.'*/, EFAM, (morphosememic development: //'Be brave., Don't take it so hard.'//), literally /'may your feelings /thoughts /emotions be well'/, attested by AD, EB 9/22/78; Elders Group 4/6/77, <**tu éychxwò kwá**>, //tu ʔɛ́y-c-xʷ-à kʷɛ́//, /*'Have courage.'*/, EFAM, (morphosememic development: //'Have courage.'//), literally /'you be very good anyway.'/, attested by Elders Group 4/6/77, <**tu éychxw òl**>, //tu ʔɛ́y-c-xʷ ʔàl//, /*'Go gently., Go slowly.'*/, EFAM, (morphosememic development: //'Go gently., Go slowly.'//), literally /'you be very good.'/, attested by AC.

<**tu s'éy ~ u s'éyò**>, stvi //tu s=ʔɛ́y ~ ʔu s=ʔɛ́yà//, EFAM [*'be careful'*], (morphosememic development from literally /'be in a state of being very good'/, syntactic analysis: particle intransitive verb, attested by EB, example: <**tu s'éychexw**>, //tu s=ʔɛ́y-c-əxʷ//, /*'You be careful.'*/, attested by EB, <**tu s'éytsel**>, //tu s=ʔɛ́y-c-əl//, /*'I'm careful.'*/, attested by EB, <**chelu s'éyò**>, //c-əl=əw s=ʔɛ́y=à//, /*'I was careful.'*/, syntactic analysis: ambiguous past, attested by EB.

<**iyólem ~ iyó:lem**>, izs //ʔɛy=à[=´·=]l=əm//, VALJ /'*be alright, be okay, it's alright, it's okay, can, be able, it's enough, be right, be correct, that's right*'/, phonology: stress shift, lengthening, syntactic analysis: intransitive verb, attested by AC, BJ, ASM ['be alright, be okay, it's alright, it's okay'], example: <**le iyó:lem**>, //lə ʔiy=á·l=əm//, /'*It's alright., It's okay., It's right.*'/, attested by AC, <**li iyó:lem**>, //li#ʔiy=á·l=əm//, /'*Is it alright?, Is it okay?, Is it right?*'/, attested by AC, <**lí. iyó:lem.**>, //lí##ʔiy=á·l=əm//, /'*Yes. It's alright.*'/, usage: answer to the previous question, attested by AC, <**tu iyó:lem**>, //tu ʔiy=á·l=əm//, /'*It's alright.*'/, <**lí iyólem kw'els kwú:t ò**>, //lí ʔiy=ál=əm k'w-əl-s kʷú·=T ʔà//, /'*Is it alright if I (just) take it?*'/, attested by Elders Group, <**luw iyó:lem ~ lew iyó:lem**>, //lə=w ʔiy=á·l=əm//, /'*It's alright, yes.*'/, attested by BJ, <**luw iyó:lem kw'es kw'étslexw**>, //lə=w ʔiy=á·l=əm k'wə-s k'wə́c=l-əxʷ//, /'*It's alright to see it.*'/, attested by AC, ASM ['can, be able'], <**luw iyólem**>, //lə=w ʔiy=ál=əm//, /'*I am able., I can.*'/, literally /'it's alright ("I" is not present)'/, semantic environment ['in answer to a question'], attested by Elders Group 3/1/72, <**luw iyó:lem kw'es kw'étslexwtset**>, //lə=w ʔiy=á·l=əm k'wə-s k'wə́c=l-əxʷ-c-ət//, /'*We can see it., It's alright, we can see it.*'/, attested by AC, <**luw iyó:lem kw'es kw'étslexwelep**>, //lə=w ʔiy=á·l=əm k'wə-s k'wə́c=l-əxʷ-ələp//, /'*(It's alright) you can all see it.*'/, attested by AC, <**luw iyó:lem kw'es kw'étslexws**>, //lə=w ʔiy=á·l=əm k'wə-s k'wə́c=l-əxʷ-s//, /'*(It's alright) he can see it.*'/, <**luw iyó:lem kw'es kw'étslexws á:lhtel**>, //lə=w ʔiy=á·l=əm k'wə-s k'wə́c=l-əxʷ-s ʔɛ́·ɬtəl//, /'*(It's alright) they can see it.*'/, <**í:lh iyó:lem kw'es álhtels**>, //ʔí·-ɬ ʔiy=á·l=əm k'wə-s ʔɛ́ɬtəl-s//, /'*He could have eaten.*'/, literally /'it was alright that he eat (a meal)'/, attested by AC, <**í:lh iyó:lem kw'els álhtel**>, //ʔí·-ɬ ʔiy=á·l=əm k'w-əl-s ʔɛ́ɬtəl//, /'*I could have eaten.*'/, attested by AC, <**í:lh iyó:lem kw'as álhtel**>, //ʔí·-ɬ ʔiy=á·l=əm k'w-ɛ-s ʔɛ́ɬtəl//, /'*You could have eaten.*'/, attested by AC, <**í:lh iyó:lem kw'(e)s álhteltset**>, //ʔí·-ɬ ʔiy=á·l=əm k'w(ə)-s ʔɛ́ɬtəl-c-ət//, /'*We could have eaten.*'/, ASM ['be enough'], <**welh iyó:lem**>, //wəɬ ʔiy=á·l=əm//, /'*enough*'/, literally /'it's already alright'/, attested by EB, also <**lulh iyólem**>, attested by Elders Group (Mar. 1972), <**welh iyó:lem kw'e mékw'ewátes**>, //wəɬ ʔiy=á·l=əm k'wə mə́k'w=əwɛ́t=əs//, /'*(There's) enough for everybody.*'/, attested by EB, <**xwōwá ís iyó:lem te s'álhtel**>, //xʷə=(ʔ)ówə-Aɛ́ ʔí-s ʔiy=á·l=əm tə s=ʔɛ́ɬtəl//, /'*It's not enough to eat.*'/, literally /'the food (meal) is not yet alright/enough'/, attested by EB, ASM ['be right, be correct'], <**echxw we'iyó:lem**>, //ʔə-c-xʷ wə=ʔiy=á·l=əm//, /'*You're right.*'/, syntactic analysis: auxiliary past, <**ốwe lís iyó:lem**>, //ʔówə lí-s ʔiy=á·l=əm//, /'*He's not right., It's not alright.*'/, <**iyólem kw'els sqwálewel**>, //ʔiy=ál=əm kʷ-əl-s s=qʷɛ̀·l=əwəl//, /'*My mind is in the right place., My mind is alright., I agree.*'/, attested by DF, <**íxwō iyólem**>, //ʔí-xʷ=əw ʔiy=ál=əm//, /'*Is it right?, if it's right*'/, literally /'If you are right.'/, syntactic analysis: auxiliary verb-2ssjsp=contrastive intransitive verb, attested by AHTTC, <**tex̲wō'iyó:lem**>, //təxʷ=əw ʔiy=á·l=əm//, /'*it fits*'/, (morphosememic development: //'it fits'//), literally /'later =really alright/correct/okay'/, attested by EB.

<**iyó:lemstexw**>, caus //ʔiy=á·l=əm=sT-əxʷ//, EFAM ['*obey s-o*'], SOC, syntactic analysis: transitive verb, attested by CT, example: <**iyó:lemstxwes**>, //ʔiy=á·l=əm=sT-əxʷ-əs//, /'*he obeys him*'/, phonology: vowel-loss in faster speech, attested by CT.

<**iyálewet ~ eyálewet**>, pcs //ʔiy=à[=Aɛ́=]l=əw=əT ~ ʔəy=à[=Aɛ́=]l=əw=əT//, TIB /'*do it, do it oneself, manage*'/, SOC, REL, EFAM, FOOD, MED, TVMO, (<**á-ablaut**> *derivational*), <**=ew**> *contrastive*, phonology: stress shift, ablaut, vowel reduction, syntactic analysis: transitive verb, attested by AC, example: <**álthecha ò iyálewet**>, //ʔɛ́lθə-cɛ ʔà ʔiy=ɛ́l=əw=əT//, /'*I'll do it myself., I'll manage.*'/, literally /'it will be me just/only to do it'/, phonology: i ~ e, attested by AC, <**tl'ócha tethá ò iyálewet**>, //ƛ'á-cɛ tə=θɛ́ ʔà ʔiy=ɛ́l=əw=əT//, /'*He will do it himself.*'/, literally /'it will be that one (male) just/only to do it'/, phonology: i ~ e, attested by AC, <**tl'óchasu tl'ós e thútl'o eyálewet**>, //ƛ'á-cɛ-s-əw ƛ'á-s ʔà θ=ə́w=ƛ'a ʔəy=ɛ́l=əw=əT//, /'*She will do it herself., She's the*

one to do it herself.'/, literally /'thus it will be contrastive that it is just her to do it'/, attested by AC, <**tl'ócha yethá o iyálewet**>, //ƛ'á-cɛ yə=θɛ́ ʔà ʔiy=ɛ́l=əw=əT//, /'*They will do it themselves., They're the ones to do it themselves.*'/, literally /'it will be those (people) just/only to do it'/, attested by AC.

<**iyóleweéthet**>, pcrs //ʔiy=à[=´=]l=əw=ə́T-ət//, FOOD /'*manage by oneself (in food or travel), try to do it by oneself, try to be independent, do the best one can*'/, TVMO, SOC, EFAM, VALJ, phonology: stress shift, stressed transitivizer, syntactic analysis: reflexive verb, attested by AHTTC: NP, AD, ASM ['do the best one can'], <**lámtsel iyóleweéthet**>, //lɛ́=m-c-əl ʔiy=ál=əw=ə́T-ət//, /'*I'm going to do the best I can.*'/, attested by AD, ASM ['try to be independent'], <**lámchexw iyól(e)wéthet**>, //lɛ́=m-c-əxʷ ʔiy=ál=əw=əT-ət//, /'*Go try to be independent.*'/, attested by NP.

<**óyó:lwethet**>, cts //ʔi[=Aá=]y=à[=´·=]l=əw=əT-ət//, SOC /'*be totally independent, doing the best one can*'/, FOOD, TVMO, EFAM, VALJ, (<**ó-ablaut**> *durative?*, stress & length infix *continuative*), phonology: ablaut, stress shift, lengthening, vowel loss, syntactic analysis: intransitive verb, attested by NP, ASM ['be totally independent'], <**tsel óyó:lwethet**>, //c-əl ʔáy=á·l=əw=əT-ət//, /'*I'm totally independent.*'/, attested by NP, ASM ['doing the best one can'], <**oliyólwéthet**>, //ʔá[-lə-]y=ál=əw=ə́T-ət//, /'*doing the best they can*'/, plv, attested by AD.

<**eyólés ~ eyó:les**>, ds //ʔɛy=álə́s ~ ʔɛy=á·ləs//, ABFC /'*(have) good eyes, (have) good sight, soft on the eyes, easy on the eyes*'/, VALJ, LT ['*yellow?*'], lx <**=ólés ~ =ó:les**> *in the eyes*, syntactic analysis: intransitive verb, poss. adjective/adjectival verb, attested by Elders Group, EB, DM, Deming, ASM ['yellow?'], <**eyó:les syátl'qels**>, //ʔəy=á·ləs s=yɛ́ƛ'=q=əls//, /'*yellow paint*'/, dialects: *DM 12/4/64.*

<**aliyólés**>, plv //ʔɛ[-lə-]y=álə́s//, ABFC /'*(have) quick eyes, (have) peeping-Tom eyes*'/, VALJ, (morphosememic development from literally /'be good in the eyes'/, (<**-le-**> *plural*), syntactic analysis: intransitive verb, poss. adjective/adjectival verb, attested by Elders Group.

<**xw'elyó:les**>, plv //xʷ=ʔɛ[-lə-]y=á·ləs//, ABFC ['*(have) good sight*'], VALJ, (morphosememic development from literally /'become/get good in the eyes'/), syntactic analysis: intransitive verb, poss. adjective/adjectival verb, attested by Deming.

<**ey'ó:les**>, ds //ʔɛy=ʔá·ləs//, DESC ['*smooth (of wood)*'], VALJ, (morphosememic development from literally /'good on the eye'/, semantic environment ['wood'], lx <**='ó:les** > prob. *on the eye* but possibly another affix, syntactic analysis: adjective/adjectival verb, attested by EB.

<**iyó:mex ~ iyóméx ~ iyómex**>, ds //ʔiy=á·məxy ~ ʔiy=ámə́xy ~ ʔiy=áməxy//, VALJ /'*good-looking, beautiful, pretty, handsome, looks good*'/, DESC, syntactic analysis: adjective/adjectival verb, attested by AC, BJ, Elders Group, EB, NP, also <**eyó:mex ~ eyó:méx**>, //ʔəy=á·məxy ~ ʔəy=á·mə́xy//, attested by BJ, example: <**iyómex slhálí**>, //ʔɛy=áməxy s=ɬɛ́lí//, /'*beautiful woman*'/, attested by AC, also <**iyóméx slhálí**>, //ʔiy=ámə́xy s=ɬɛ́lí//, attested by EB, <**iyómex swíqe**>, //ʔiy=áməxy s=wíqə//, /'*handsome man*'/, attested by AC, <**iyóméx thqá:t**>, //ʔiy=ámə́xy θqɛ́·t//, /'*beautiful tree*'/, attested by EB, <**iyómex u ól**>, //ʔiy=áməxy ʔu ʔàl//, /'*She's the prettiest.*'/, literally /'(he's/she's) good-looking contrastive just'/, attested by NP, <**yeláwel iyómex q'á:mi**>, //yəlɛ́w=əl ʔiy=áməxy q'ɛ́·mi//, /'*the prettiest girl*'/, <**iyómex telí kwsu mőkw'tset**>, //ʔiy=áməxy təlí kʷ-s=əw mók'w-c-ət//, /'*She's the prettiest of all of us.*'/, <**é:yòmèx swíyeqe**>, //ʔɛ[=´·=]y=ámə́xy//, /'*(very) handsome man*'/, (<**=´:=**> *very, intensive*), phonology: lengthening, stress shifts, attested by EB, ASM ['looks good'], <**st'á kw'u éyòmèx te skúks**>, //s=t=ɛʔɛ́ k'w-əw ʔɛy=ámə́xy tə s=kúk-s//, /'*Her cooking looks good.*'/, phonology: s=t=a'á → s=t='á → st'á in rapid speech, attested by EB.

<**eyó:th ~ iyóth**>, ds //ʔɛy=á·θ ~ ʔiy=áθ//, DESC /'*be sharp, have a sharp edge*'/, VALJ, lx <**=ó:th**> *edge*, syntactic analysis: adjective/adjectival verb, attested by Elders Group, EB, AC, DM, other sources: ES /ʔɛyá·θ/ (MsCw /ʔayáʔθ/), JH /ʔí·yaθ/, example: <**eyó:th tel lhá:ts'tel**>, //ʔɛy=á·θ t-əl ɬɛ́·c'=təl//, /'*My knife is sharp.*'/, attested by AC, <**stá:més t'we eyó:th x̱íp'et kw'el óqwelets**>, //s=tɛ́·m=ə́s t'wə ʔɛy=á·θ x̣íp'=əT k'w-əl ʔáq^{w}ə=ləc//, /'*Something sharp (must have) scraped /scratched my back.*'/, attested by AC, <**es'iyó:ths te lhá:ts'tel**>, //ʔəs=ʔiy=á·θ-s tə ɬɛ́·c'=təl//, /'*the sharp edge of a knife*'/, attested by DM 12/4/64.

<**eyotháléqep**>, ds //ʔɛy=áθ=ɛ́lə́qəp//, SD /'*be a sharp sound, have a sharp sound, make a sharp sound*'/, lx <**=áléqep**> *sound*, syntactic analysis: adjective/adjectival verb.

<**yethéleqw**>, ds //(ʔɛ)y=á[=ə=]θ=ə́ləq^{w}//, ABDF ['*(have a) pointed head*'], BPI, lx <**=éleqw**> *on top of the head*, syntactic analysis: adjective/adjectival verb.

<**s'ó:ytheqw**>, dnom //s=ʔ(ɛ)y=á·[=M2=]θ=əq^{w}//, EB /'*wild red raspberry, domestic red raspberry*'/, lx <**=ó:th**> *edge*, lx <**=eqw**> *on top of the head*, phonology: metathesis, vowel-loss, syntactic analysis: nominal, attested by AC, ASM ['wild red raspberry'], ['*Rubus idaeus malanolasius*'], semantic environment ['rare but eaten when found'], ACL, ASM ['domestic red raspberry'], ['*Rubus idaeus var. strigosus*'], <**s'óytheqw sqe'óleqw**>, FOOD *raspberry juice* (lit. raspberry + fruit juice), (attested by RG,EH 6/16/98 to SN, edited by BG with RG,EH 6/26/00)

<**s'ó:ytheqwelhp**>, dnom //s=ʔ(ɛ)y=á·[=M2=]θ=əq^{w}=əɬp//, EB /'*wild red raspberry plant, domestic red raspberry plant*'/, lx <**=ó:th**> *edge*, lx <**=eqw**> *on top of the head*, lx <**=elhp**> *plant, tree*, phonology: metathesis, (stress shift), vowel-loss, syntactic analysis: nominal, attested by AC, SP, also <**ó:ytheqwelhp**>, //ʔ(ɛ)y=á·[=M2=]θ=əq^{w}=əɬp//, attested by IHTTC.

<**xwiyótheqel**>, ds //x^{w}=ʔiy=áθ=əqəl//, MUS /'*(have a) high pitch (voice or melody), (have a) sharp voice*'/, SD, ABFC, LANG, syntactic analysis: adjective/adjectival verb.

<**Iy'óythel**>, df //ʔiy=ʔá·yθəl or $C_1əC_2$=ʔ(ɛ)y=á·[=M2=]θ=əl//, PLN /'*a place on Chilliwack River, a little above Anderson Flat and Allison's (between Tamihi Creek and Slesse Creek), a village at deep water between Tamihi Creek and Slesse Creek*'/, ASM ['a trail to this place in 1978 was at top of hill near two signs: on the river side the sign said, "SLIDE AREA 60 km/h", on the cliff side the sign said, "END SLIDE AREA"; there are good fishing rocks at the end of the trail'], lx poss. <**=ó:ythel**> *(on the) lips, jaw* (with root for *good*) or <**R3=**> *characteristic or plural* plus lx <**=el**> *get, go, come, become* (with stem for *sharp*), phonology: possibly reduplication and metathesis, syntactic analysis: nominal, literally /'good lips /chin /jaw or characteristically get sharp or getting sharp many times'/, attested by Duff:1952:38, source: place name reference file #232; photos + location 6/19/78 notes, other sources: Wells 1965:19 says it means "rock wall to rock wall".

<**éyqwlha**>, ds //ʔɛ́y=q^{w}ɬɛ//, DESC ['*beautiful.*'], EFAM, lx <**=qwlha**> *really., emphatically.*, syntactic analysis: adjective/adjectival verb, interjection, attested by EB 1/19/76.

<**eyáléqep ~ iyáléqep**>, SM /'*have a fragrance, have a good smell, smell good*'/, *see* **éy** ~ **éy**:.

<**eyámeth'**>, DESC /'*smooth (of pole, stick, or wood)*'/, *see* **éy** ~ **éy**:.

<**eyát**>, TVMO /'*go after s-th/s-o, chase s-o/s-th (not stopping or slowing tillit's caught)*'/, *see* á:y.

<**éyeles**>, EFAM possibly ['*agree*'], *see* **éy** ~ **éy**:.

<**éyelew**>, EFAM ['*oh my gosh.*'], *see* **éy** ~ **éy**:.

<**eyeléwthelh**>, EFAM ['*for goodness sakes.*'], *see* **éy** ~ **éy**:.

<**eyelhómex**>, DESC ['*good-looking*'], *see* **éy** ~ **éy**:.

<**eyém ~ iyém**>, DESC ['*be strong*'], *see* **éy** ~ **éy**:.

<**eyémstexw**>, IDOC /*'make it strong, make him/her/them strong'*/, *see* **éy** ~ **éy**:.

<**eyéstem**>, SOC /*'he was fun, he was enjoyed, they enjoyed him'*/, *see* **éy** ~ **éy**:.

<**éyetses**>, DESC [*'clean hands'*], *see* **éy** ~ **éy**:.

<**eyétses**>, DESC /*'clean [in everything: clothes, house, person, etc.], clean in one's person and what one owns'*/, *see* **éy** ~ **éy**:.

<**=éylém ~ =ílém**>, da //=íləm ~ =íl=əm//, N [*'male name'*], possibly <**=íl**> *come, go, get, become*, possibly <**=ém**> *strength* or <**=em**> *have, get* or <**=em**> *middle voice*, syntactic analysis: lexical suffix, derivational suffix, also <**=ílém**>, //=íl=əm//; found in <**Ye<u>x</u>wéylém**> (or better) <**Ye<u>x</u>wílém**>, //yəx̣^{w}=ɛyləm//, /*'Indian name of the third from oldest original Wealick brother'*/ (root <**yé<u>x</u>w**> *untied)*, <**Qeypílém**> (or better) <**Qipílém**>, //qɛyp=íləm//, /*'Indian name of August Billie'*/.

<**eyólés ~ eyó:les**>, ABFC /*'(have) good eyes, (have) good sight, soft on the eyes, easy on the eyes'*/, *see* **éy** ~ **éy**:.

<**éy òl ~ éyòl ~ éyò**>, VALJ /*'be alright, be well, be fine, be okay'*/, *see* **éy** ~ **éy**:.

<**=(e)yó:lhe**>, da //=(ə)y(=)á·ɬə//, ANA [*'on the stomach or ventral surface of a body'*], possibly <**=ey**> *covering, bark*??, syntactic analysis: lexical suffix, derivational suffix; found in <**qeyqep'(e)yó:lhe**>, //qɛyqəp'=(ə)yá·ɬə//, /*'lay on one's stomach'*/, comment: this suffix is fairly rare, root <**qep'**> *cover*, (semological comment: the gloss should probably be continuative).

<**eyó:sthet ~ iyósthet**>, SOC /*'a whole bunch having fun; having lots of fun, having a good time'*/, *see* **éy** ~ **éy**:.

<**eyó:th ~ iyóth**>, DESC /*'be sharp, have a sharp edge'*/, *see* **éy** ~ **éy**:.

<**eyothálḗqep**>, SD /*'be a sharp sound, have a sharp sound, make a sharp sound'*/, *see* **éy** ~ **éy**:.

<**éyqwlha**>, DESC [*'beautiful.'*], *see* **éy** ~ **éy**:.

<**éystelómet ~ éy:stelómet**>, SOC /*'pretending to be good, want to be accepted'*/, *see* **éy** ~ **éy**:.

<**éystexw ~ éy:stexw**>, SOC /*'like s-o [his/her personality], like s-th [its taste, its idea], be interested in s-th/s-o, enjoy s-o sexually'*/, *see* **éy** ~ **éy**:.

<**eywéylaq** or **iwílaq**>, PLAY [*'play-dancing'*], *see* ewólem.

<**ey'éyelh**>, LANG [*'talking good'*], *see* **éy** ~ **éy**:.

<**ey'ó:les**>, DESC [*'smooth (of wood)'*], *see* **éy** ~ **éy**:.

<**é'iy ~ á'iy**>, VALJ /*'good (of little ones), cute (of many of them)'*/, *see* **éy** ~ **éy**:.

H

<**há- ~ hé-**>, ia //**hɛ́- ~ hə́-**//, ASP /'*continuative, resultative*'/, NUM ['*plural (rare)*'], phonology: predictable allomorphy before a limited set of roots: hɛ́- → hɛ́- /_y, l in certain roots and → hə́- /_m, w in certain roots; this morpheme cannot be used with most roots to express *continuative* as can reduplication -doubling infix #1 with e- (see examples like yíyəq *snowing*, lɛ́ləc'ə̀wtxʷəm *visiting*, mɛmíyət *helping s-o* and wíwəqəs *yawning*)., syntactic analysis: ip; found in <**héyeqw**>, //hɛ́yqʷ ~ hɛ́yəqʷ//, /'*burning, fire*'/(root <**yéqw**> *burn)*, <**héyet**>, //hɛ́yət//, /'*vomiting*'/(root <**yá:t**> *to vomit)*, <**hé(:)ytht**>, //hɛ́(·)yθt//, /'*talking about s-o*'/(compare <**yétht**> *talk about s-o)*, <**hé(:)ythest**>, //hɛ́(·)yθəst//, /'*telling it*'/(compare <**yéthest**> *tell it)*, <**hé:yó:t**>, //hɛ́·yá·t//, /'*warning s-o*'/(root <**yó:t**> *warn s-o*), <**héyq'es**>, //hɛ́yq'əs//, /'*filing*'/(compare <**yéq'es**> *file (abrasively))*, <**héythet**>, //hɛ́yθət//, /'*backing up*'/(compare <**yóthet**> *back up)*, <**hálp'ex**>, //hɛ́lp'əxʸ//, /'*eating*'/(compare <**lép'ex**> *eat)*, <**hálx̱eywa**>, //hɛ́lx̣ɛywɛ//, /'*spearing fish by torchlight*'/(compare <**lex̱éywa**> *spear fish by torchlight)*, <**hálts'elí**>, //hɛ́lc'əlí(y)//, /'*by themselves*'/(root <**léts'e**> *one,* compare <**lólets'e**> *one person; alone')*:, <**hálqem**>, //hɛ́lqəm//, /'*diving*'/(compare <**léqem**> *dive)*, <**hálkw**>, //hɛ́lkʷ//, /'*pocket knife; being broken*'/(root <**lékw**> *broken (of bone or stick))*, <**hálx̱eywa**>, //hɛ́lx̣ɛywɛ//, /'*torchlighting, spearing fish by torchlight, etc.*'/(compare <**lex̱éywa**> *to torchlight, spear fish from canoe by torchlight, lantern or firelight, pitlamp for fish)*, <**hámq'et**>, //hɛ́mq'ət//, /'*swallowing*'/(compare <**méq'et**> *to swallow)*, <**hámex**>, //hɛ́məxʸ//, /'*taking it off (a button, example)*'/(compare <**máx**> *take it off*), <**héwts'etl'**>, //hə́wc'əƛ'//, /'*falling*'/(compare <**wets'étl'**> *fall, drop (intransitive))*, <**héwqw'**>, //hə́wq'ʷ//, /'*floating downstream*'/(root <**wő̄qw'**> *drown, float downstream)*, <**hewth'át**>, //həwθ'ɛ́t//, /'*teasing s-o*'/(compare <**weth'át**> *tease s-o*), <**hewts'á:**>, //həwc'ɛ́·//, /'*getting to the summit of a mountain*'/(compare <**wets'á:**> *get to the summit of a mountain*), <**héwqw'elem**>, //hə́wq'ʷələm//, /'*drifting downstream*'/(compare <**wō̄qw'éylem**> *drift downstream)*.

<**hahà:y**>, CAN ['*making a canoe*'], *see* hà:y.

<**haheláwt**>, EZ ['*a few little rats*'], *see* há:wt.

<**hahíkwthet**>, DESC /'*rising, getting big*'/, *see* híkw.

<**hákw'eles**>, pncs //hɛ́k'ʷ=ələs//, EFAM /'*remember s-o, remember s-th*'/, syntactic analysis: transitive verb, attested by EB, Deming, example: <**tsel me hákw'eles**>, //c-əl mə hɛ́k'ʷ=ələs//, /'*I just remembered.*'/, syntactic analysis: ambiguous past, attested by EB, <**tsel hákw'eles kwstámés**>, //c-əl hɛ́k'ʷ=ələs kʷ=s=tɛ́m=əs//, /'*I remembered something.*'/, syntactic comment: ambiguous past, indef. nominal. obj., attested by EB, <**éy kws hákw'eleschet te s'í:wes te siyolexwálh**>, //ʔɛ́y kʷ-s hɛ́k'ʷ=ələs-c-ət tə s-ʔí·wəs-s tə s=yáləxʷə-ɛ́ɬ//, /'*Let us remember the teaching of the elders past.*'/, syntactic comment: imperative-1p, attested by AD, <**líyechexw hákw'eles**>, //lí-(y)ə-c-əxʷ hɛ́k'ʷ=ələs//, /'*Do you remember?*'/, dialects: *Chill.*, attested by Deming, also <**líyechexw wehákw'eles**>, //li-(y)ə-c-əxʷ wə-hɛ́k'ʷ=ələs//, dialects: *Matsqui*, attested by Deming, (<**we-**> prob *suddenly*), <**líyechexw hákw'elesóx**>, //lí-(y)ə-c-əxʷ hɛ́k'ʷ=ələs-áxʸ//, /'*Do you remember me?*'/, dialects: *Chill.*, attested by Deming, also <**líyechexw hákw'elesómx**>, //lí-(y)ə-c-əxʷ hɛ́k'ʷ=ələs-ámxʸ//, dialects: *Matsqui*, attested by Deming, <**tsel xwel hákw'elesóme**>, //c-əl xʷəl hɛ́k'ʷ=ələs-ámə//, /'*I (still) remember you.*'/, usage: answer to the previous example question, attested by Deming; found in <**hákw'elesométsel**>, //hɛ́k'ʷ=ələs-amə-´-c-əl//, /'*I remember you.*'/, attested by Deming, <**hákw'elesólxw**>, //hɛ́k'ʷ=ələs-álxʷ//, /'*remember us*'/, attested by Deming, <**hákw'elesóle**>, //hɛ́k'ʷ=ələs-álə//, /'*remember you folks*'/, attested by Deming, example: <**hákw'eleses kwthá**>,

//hɛ́k'^{w}=ələs-əs k^{w}-θɛ́//, /'*he remembered it*'/, attested by EB; found in <**hákw'elesem**>, //hɛ́k'^{w}=ələs-əm//, /'*they remembered him, he was remembered*'/, syntactic analysis: pncs-passive, attested by EB, <**hákw'elesemcha**>, //hɛ́k'^{w}=ələs-əm-cɛ//, /'*he'll (future) be remembered*'/, attested by EB, <**me xwpósem te hákw'elesem**>, /mə x^{w}p=ós=əm tə hɛ́k'^{w}=ələs=əm/, /'come show a picture of those remembered'/, attested by RG & EH (4/10/99 Ling332)

<**há:kw'eles**>, cts //hɛ́[-·-]k'^{w}=ələs//, EFAM /'*remembering s-o, remembering s-th*'/, phonology: length infix, syntactic analysis: transitive verb, attested by EB, example: <**xw'ít kw'a'as ő̋welh há:kw'eles**>, //x^{w}ʔít k'^{w}-ɛʔ(ɛ)-s ʔówə-ɬ hɛ́[-·-]k'^{w}=ələs//, /'*Why don't you remember?*'/, syntactic comment: interrogative verb, attested by EB.

<**há:kw'elem ?**>, df //hɛ́·k'^{w}ələm ?//, possibly /'*remember*'/, attested by EB, possibly /'*something like a hiccough ?*'/, attested by AD.

<**há:kw'eles**>, EFAM /'*remembering s-o, remembering s-th*'/, *see* hákw'eles.

<**hálém**>, TVMO /'*be on one's way, be going*'/, *see* la.

<**halemélmel**>, EFAM ['*feel like going*'], *see* la.

<**halíyches**>, CAN /'*all the equipment for making a canoe, canoe-making equipment*'/, *see* hà:y.

<**hálíytel**>, CAN /'*adze with handle for canoe-making, elbow-adze*'/, *see* hà:y.

<**hálkw**>, PE ['*pocket knife*'], *see* **lé**kw.

<**hálkweletsem**>, ABDF ['*limp in the hip*'], *see* **lé**kw.

<**hálma'à:ls**>, ABFC ['*kicking*'], *see* lemá'.

<**hálpetsel**>, TVMO /'*riding with someone, (riding along)*'/, *see* **lé**pets.

<**hálp'ex**>, ABFC ['*eating s-th (short of a meal)*'], *see* **lé**p'ex.

<**hálqem**>, ABFC ['*diving*'], *see* **lé**qem.

<**hálqem**>, SOCT ['*a diver*'], *see* **lé**qem.

<**Halq'eméylem**>, LANG /'*Halkomelem language, to speak Halkomelem*'/, *see* Leq'á:mél.

<**halts'elíthet**>, DIR ['*a group separating themselves from another group*'], *see* láts'.

<**hálx̱eywa ~ hálx̱iwa**>, FSH ['*spearing fish by torchlight*'], *see* lex̱éywa ~ lex̱íwa.

<**hà:m**>, possibly root //hɛ̀·m//, TIME /'*finished, over*'/, possibly <**a-ablaut**> *resultative or durative*, possibly <**=em**> *intransitivizer*, phonology: possible vowel merger, possible ablaut, comment: connection with hóy *finish, end* would require very irregular loss of its final root consonant and so is unlikely, syntactic analysis: intransitive verb, usage: sometimes used at the end of a story, Salish cognate: Squamish /hámʔ/ *come home, be covered* W73:69, K67:374, example: <**le hà:m.**>, //lə hɛ̀·m//, /'*It's over., It's finished (of a story).*'/, (semological comment: perhaps; found in Squamish, *It's covered.* as in English at the end of a narrative, "Well, that covers it.").

<**hámelet**>, ABFC ['*placing s-th (prob. in water)*'], *see* mí:l ~ míl.

<**hám:et**>, pcs //hɛ́m·ə=T//, MC /'*nail s-th, hammer s-th*'/, borrowed from English /hǽmr/, syntactic analysis: transitive verb, attested by EB.

<**hámex**>, MC ['*taking s-th off*'], *see* má ~ má'-.

<**hásem**>, mdls //hɛ́s=əm//, ABFC ['*to sneeze*'], syntactic analysis: intransitive verb, attested by EB, Salish cognate: Lushootseed /hásəb/ *sneeze* H76:178, Sechelt /hásam/ *to sneeze* T77:33, also <**hás:em**>, //hɛ́s·=əm//, attested by AC.

<**háshuw**>, possibly root //hɛ́šuw//, ABFC ['*to sneeze*'], syntactic analysis: intransitive verb, possibly root <**hás-**> as in <**hásem**> *to sneeze*, attested by AC, Salish cognate: Squamish /ʔə́šuʔ-n/ *to sneeze* K67:388, <**la háshuw**>, //lɛ hɛ́šuw//, /'*he sneezed*'/, syntactic analysis: ambiguous past, attested by AC.

<**háwe**>, free root //hɛ́wə//, HUNT ['*to hunt*'], syntactic analysis: intransitive verb, attested by AC, example: <**latsel háwe kw'e tl'alqtéle**>, //lɛ-c-əl hɛ́wə k'ʷə ƛ'ɛ[=l=]qt=ə́lə//, /'*I'm going to hunt deer.*'/, syntactic comment: auxiliary verb, demonstrative article, attested by AC, also /'*to hunt, hunting*'/, attested by AD, <**le háwe álhtel**>, //lə hɛ́wə ʔɛ́ɬtəl//, /'*They're gone out hunting.*'/, syntactic comment: ambiguous past, attested by AD, <**háwe te tl'alqtéle**>, //hɛ́wə təƛ'ɛ[=l=]qt=ə́lə//, /'*The deer is hunting.*'/, attested by AD, <**háwe te sméyeth**>, //hɛ́wə tə s=mɛ́yəθ//, /'*The animal is hunting.*'/, attested by AD.

<**há:we**>, cts //hɛ́[-·-]wə//, HUNT ['*hunting*'], phonology: length infixing, (<**-:-**> *continuative aspect*), syntactic analysis: intransitive verb, example: <**la há:we**>, //lɛ hɛ́[-·-]wə//, /'*He's gone hunting.*'/, attested by AC, <**latst há:we**>, //lɛ-c-ət hɛ́[-·-]wə//, /'*Let's go hunting.*'/, phonology: vowel lengthening, syntactic comment: imperative, attested by AC, <**lhlá:mes há:we**>, //ɬ-lɛ́·=m-əs hɛ́[-·-]wə//, /'*when he goes hunting*'/, (<**lh- ~ lhi (vaux)**> *when* + subjunctive), (<**-es**> *3s subjunctive subject*), attested by AC, <**ílh la há:we**>, //ʔí-ɬ lɛ hɛ́[-·-]wə//, /'*He went hunting.*'/ *(go past)*, attested by AC, <**la há:we kw'e spá:th**>, //lɛ hɛ́[-·-]wə k'ʷə s=pɛ́·θ//, /'*He went hunting for bear.*'/ *(go past)*, syntactic comment: intransitive verb with oblique object, attested by AC, also /'*to hunt, hunting*'/, attested by JL, EB, <**le há:we ~ la há:we**>, //lə hɛ́·wə ~ lɛ hɛ́·wə//, /'*go hunt*'/, attested by EB, also /'*to hunt*'/, attested by JL, <**lítsel welh hó:y kw'els há:we**>, //lí-c-əl wəɬ há·y k'ʷ-əl-s hɛ́·wə//, /'*Yes, I have finished my hunting.*'/, literally /'yes (to answer yes/no question)-I already have finish remote-my-nominal hunting'/, attested by EB, <**lílhtsel há:we**>, //lí-ɬ-c-əl hɛ́·wə//, /'*I've been hunting.*'/, syntactic comment: auxiliary verb-past affixed, attested by EB.

<**lexws-há:wa**>, dnom //ləxʷ=s=hɛ́·wə//, HUNT /'*a person that always hunts, hunter*'/, syntactic analysis: nominal, literally /'always=nominal=hunt(ing)'/, <s-h> shows each is pronounced /sh/, in contrast to <sh> which shows a single pronounced sound /š/.

<**há:we**>, HUNT ['*hunting*'], *see* háwe.

<**há:wt**>, free root //hɛ́·wt//, EZ /'*rat, vole (short-tailed mouse),* may include any or all of the following which occur in this area*: creeping vole, long-tail vole, mountain heather vole, boreal redback vole, Norway rat (intro.),* and perhaps *roof rat,* also includes *bushy-tailed wood rat (packrat)* which has its own name below'/, ['may include any or all of the following which occur in this area: creeping vole *Microtus oregoni serpens*, long-tail vole *Microtus longicaudus macrurus*, mountain heather vole *Phenacomys intermedius oramontis*, boreal redback vole *Clethrionomys gapperi cascadensis*, Norway rat (intro.) *Rattus norvegicus*, and perhaps roof rat *Rattus rattus*, also includes bushy-tailed wood rat (packrat) *Neotoma cinerea occidentalis* which has its own name below'], syntactic analysis: nominal, attested by Elders Group (1972, 1975, 1976), AC, other sources: ES /hɛ́wt/, JH /hé·wət/ both *rat*.

<**qélqel há:wt**>, dnom //qə́l=C_1əC_2 hɛ́·wt//, EZ /'*packrat, i.e. bushy-tailed wood rat*'/, ['*Neotoma cinerea occidentalis*'], phonology: reduplication, syntactic analysis: nominal phrase with modifier(s), attested by Elders Group 2/11/76.

<**hiháwt**>, dmn //C_1í=hɛ́wt//, EZ /'*small rat, small vole*'/, phonology: reduplication, phonology: length loss, syntactic analysis: nominal.

<**haheláwt**>, dmpn //C_1ɛ=h[-əl-]ɛ́wt//, EZ ['*a few little rats*'], phonology: reduplication, phonology: length loss, syntactic analysis: nominal, syntactic comment: note change of reduplication type *diminutive* before adding plural infix.

<**hà:y**>, free root //hɛ̀·y//, CAN /'*make a canoe, making a canoe*'/, syntactic analysis: intransitive verb, example: <**ílhtsel hà:y**>, //ʔí-ɬ-c-əl hɛ̀·y//, /'*I made a canoe.*'/, syntactic analysis: auxiliary verb-past affixed-non-subordinate subject marker-subject pronoun intransitive verb, <**tsel xwel hà:y**>, //c-əl x^{w}əl hɛ̀·y//, /'*I'm still canoe-making.*'/, syntactic analysis: ambiguous past, non-subordinate subject marker-subject pronoun adverb/adverbial verb intransitive verb.

<**s-há:y**>, dnom //s=hɛ̀[=´=]·y//, CAN /'*canoe-work, canoe-making*'/, phonology: stress shift, orthographic hyphen here is to separate graphemes s anan h from the grapheme sh, it does not mean inflection rather than derivation in this case, syntactic analysis: nominal, example: <**tel s=há:y**>, //t-əl s=hɛ̀·y//, /'*my canoe-work*'/.

<**hahà:y**>, cts //C$_1$ɛ-hɛ̀·y//, CAN ['*making a canoe*'], (<**R8-**> *continuative*), phonology: reduplication, syntactic analysis: intransitive verb, attested by EB.

<**halíyches**>, pln //hɛ̀·[=lə=´]y=cəs//, CAN /'*all the equipment for making a canoe, canoe-making equipment*'/, phonology: stress shift, length loss, syntactic analysis: nominal, attested by IHTTC.

<**hálíytel**>, pln //hɛ̀·[=´=lə=´]y=təl//, CAN /'*adze with handle for canoe-making, elbow-adze*'/, lx <**=le=**> *plural*, lx <**=tel**> *device for*, literally /'device for making many canoes'/, phonology: stress shift, length loss, syntactic analysis: nominal.

<**Shxwhá:y**>, dnom //sx^{w}=hɛ̀[=´=]·y//, PLN /'*village at outlet of old Chilliwack River on Fraser River, now known as Skway reserve (Chilliwack Indian Reserve #5)*'/, literally /'place to make canoes'/, phonology: stress shift, syntactic analysis: nominal, Elder's comment: "this is the true pronunciation and meaning, but Shxwá:y is the most common pronunciation and was even common amongst the old people who taught many of today's elders, for ex. amongst grandparents of NP, DF, and CT", attested by LJ (Lawrence James), source: place name reference file #84, 7/20/77, other sources: Wells 1965:19, also <**Shxwá:y**>, //sx^{w}ɛ́·y//, attested by NP, DF, CT, AC, BJ.

<**hék'elh ~ hékw'elh**>, free root //hə́k'əɬ ~ hə́k'^{w}əɬ//, [hɪ́k'əɬ ~ hɪ́k'^{w}əɬ], ABFC /'*to hiccough, hiccup*'/, syntactic analysis: intransitive verb, Elder's comment: "hékw'elh is less common", attested by Elders Group 3/15/72, IHTTC, also <**hék'alh**>, //hə́k'ɛɬ//, [hɪ́k'ɛɬ], attested by EB.

<**héleméstem**>, EFAM ['*he's gone (mentally)*'], *see* la.

<**hélmethet**>, IDOC ['*jumping up and down or bouncing up and down (of an Indian doctor training)*'], *see* lá:m.

<**hel-hílém**>, TVMO ['*rolling down*'], *see* híl.

<**hemhémetheqw**>, FSH ['*a group making (fish) oil*'], *see* mótheqw or metheqw.

<**Hemhémetheqw**>, PLN ['*flat rocks (bedrock) with holes at Hill's Bar where they used to make smótheqw (prepared fish oil) from sockeye heads*'], *see* mótheqw or metheqw.

<**hemó:**>, free root //həmá·//, EZ /'*pigeon, dove,* including *band-tailed pigeon, mourning dove,* and possibly *passenger pigeon,* also (introduced) *domestic pigeon, rock dove*'/, ['including *Columba fasciata, Zenaidura macroura,* possibly *Ectopistes migratorius,* also *Columbia livia* (introduced)'], (semological comment: a passenger pigeon was killed at Chilliwack June 29, 1859 for ex. and in 1917 was in the U.S. National Museum (Brooks 1917)), syntactic analysis: nominal, comment: this word has been widely diffused in the Northwest Coast between unrelated languages and language families in pre-contact times but seems reconstructable for Proto-Salish (see Seaburg 1985), attested by Elders Group 3/1/72, 6/4/75, AC, also <**homó:**>, //hamá·//, [hamá·], attested by Elders Group 2/18/76, [hamɔ́·], attested by BJ 12/5/64, other sources: ES /həmá·/, JH /həmá·/, H-T <hama'> (macrons over both vowels) (his gloss: pigeon *Columba fasciata*), example: <**qé<u>x</u> te hemó:**>, //qə́x̣ tə həmá·//, /'*(There are) a lot of pigeons.*'/, attested by AC.

<**Hémq'eleq**>, PLN ['*large whirlpool in the Fraser River just above Hill's Bar and near the west (CPR) side*'], *see* méq'.

<**hémq'et**>, ABFC ['*swallowing s-th*'], *see* méq'.

<**héwqw'elem ~ hó̸wqw'elem**>, DIR /'*(going) downstream, drift downstream, (drifting downstream)*'/, *see* wó̸qw' ~ wéqw'.

<**hewth'át**>, SOC ['*teasing s-o*'], *see* weth'át.

<**hewth'eláq**>, SOC ['*teasing*'], *see* weth'át.

<**hewts'á:**>, DIR ['*getting to the summit of a mountain*'], *see* ts'á:.

<**héy**>, free root //hə́y ~ híy//, LANG /'*let's, (coaxing)*'/, MOOD, syntactic analysis: auxiliary verb, attested by EB, SJ, EF; found in <**héytlh**>, //hə́y-tɬ//, /'*let's (coaxing one person, imperative 1p exclusive)*'/, syntactic analysis: auxiliary verb-imperative(1p excl. coaxing), attested by EB, example: <**héytlh lám**>, //hə́y-tɬ lɛ́=m//, /'*Let's go (coaxing one person).*'/, (<**-tlh**> *coaxing imperative, mildly urging imperative*), attested by EB; found in <**héyatlha**>, //hə́y-ɛtɬɛ//, /'*let's (coaxing a group, imperative 1p inclusive)*'/, syntactic analysis: auxiliary verb-imperative(1p incl. coaxing), attested by EB, <**héylha**>, //hə́y-ɬɛ//, /'*let's (demanding one person, imperative 2s)*'/, syntactic analysis: auxiliary verb-imperative(2s demanding), attested by EB, SJ, EF, example: <**héylha lám**>, //hə́y-ɬɛ lɛ́=m//, /'*Let's go (demanding).*'/, (<**-lha**> *demanding imperative, strong imperative*), attested by Deming: SJ, EF, <**héylha t'ó:kw'**>, //hə́y-ɬɛ t'á·k'ʷ//, /'*Let's go home.*'/, attested by Deming: EF; found in <**héyalha**>, //hə́y-ɛɬɛ//, /'*let's (demanding a group, imperative 2p)*'/, syntactic analysis: auxiliary verb-imperative(2p demanding), attested by EB.

<**híqwt**>, pcs //híy=qʷ=T//, LANG /'*coax s-o, persuade s-o, invite s-o (on trip, hunt, etc.)*'/, SOC, (<**=qw**> *(meaning uncertain)*), syntactic analysis: transitive verb, Salish cognate: Musqueam /hə́yqwt/ *recruit s-o* Suttles ca1984: ch.7 [p.90], contrast <**yákw'(e)met**> *hire s-o*, also <**hí:qwt**> (or better, <**híyqwt**>), //hí·qʷ=T (or híyqʷ=T)//, ASM ['coax s-o'], <**híqwtlha**>, //híy=qʷ=T-ɬɛ//, /'*Coax him.*'/, (<**-lha**> *imperative*), ASM ['persuade s-o'], <**hiqwthóxes**>, //hiy=qʷ=θ-áxʸ-əs//, /'*He persuaded me., He coaxed me.*'/.

<**hóyeqwt**>, cts //hi[-Aá-]y=qʷ=T//, LANG ['*coaxing s-o*'], SOC, syntactic analysis: transitive verb; found in <**hóyeqwthóxes**>, //hi[-Aá-]y=qʷ=θ-áxʸ-əs//, /'*He's coaxing me.*'/, <**hóyeqwthòm**>, //hi[-Aá-]y=qʷ=θ-àm//, /'*They're coaxing you.*'/, (<**-òm**> *passive, 2s obj.*).

<**híqwelhtel**>, bens //híy=qʷ=əɬ(c)=T-əl//, rcps, LANG /'*(coaxing to go,) Let's go.*'/, literally /'coax for each other'/, (<**=elh(ts)**> *benefactive*), (<**=t**> *purposeful control transitivizer*), (<**-el**> *reciprocal*), syntactic analysis: intransitive verb, attested by LJ (Tait) as reported by EB, also /'*hiring(?)*'/, Elder's comment: "unsure of translation", attested by EB and AD (2/15/78).

<**hóyqwelhtel**>, cts //hi[-Aá-]y=qʷ-əɬ(c)-təl//, rcps, LANG /'*coaxing to go, let's go*'/, syntactic analysis: intransitive verb.

<**hóyeqwels**>, sas //hi[-Aá-]y=qʷ=əls//, cts, LANG ['*coaxing (as a structured activity)*'], SOC, syntactic analysis: intransitive verb.

<**héyeq'et ~ héyq'et**>, MC ['*filing s-th*'], *see* yéq'.

<**héyeqw**>, FIRE ['*be burning*'], *see* yéqw.

<**héyeqw**>, FIRE /'*fire, (*(also) *flame* [EB, Elders Group])'/, *see* yéqw.

<**heyeqwá:la**>, FIRE ['*fireplace*'], *see* yéqw.

<**héyetélmel**>, ABDF ['*nauseated*'], *see* yá:t.

<**héyethet ~ héythet**>, TVMO ['*backing up*'], *see* yóthet.

<**hé:yó:t**>, LANG ['*warning s-o*'], *see* yó:t ~ yót.

<**héyót**>, LANG ['*warned s-o*'], *see* yó:t ~ yót.

<**héyq'es**>, MC ['*filing*'], *see* yéq'.

<**heywí:leqw**>, REL /'*a category of religious songs including* ***sx̲wó:yx̲wey*** *songs and burning songs, a burning song*'/, *see* yéw: ~ yéw.

<**hiháwt**>, EZ /'*small rat, small vole*'/, *see* há:wt.

<**híheltu**>, SOC /'*a small Hindu, a small East Indian*'/, *see* híltu.

<**híhòkwexes**>, CLO ['*he (a small child) is wearing it.*'], *see* hókwex.

<**híkw**>, free root //híkʷ//, DESC /'*be big, be large, be high (of floodwater), rise (of floodwater)*'/, syntactic analysis: adjective/adjectival verb, attested by AC, Elders Group, CT, EB, other sources: ES /hí·kʷ/, ASM ['be big, be large'], example: <**híkw thqá:t**>, //híkʷ θqɛ́·t//, /'*big tree*'/, attested by AC, <**híkw tel sts'áletstel telí ta' swá**>, //híkʷ t-əl s=c'ɛ́=ləc=təl təlí t-ɛʔ s=wɛ́//, /'*My chair is bigger than yours.*'/, attested by Elders Group 2/5/75, ASM ['be high, rise'], semantic environment ['of floodwater'], <**híkw te qó:**>, //híkʷ tə qá·//, /'*The water is high.*'/, attested by CT, also /'*The water rises.*'/, attested by EB, <**wulh me híkw te qó**>, //wəɬ mə híkʷ tə qá//, /'*The water is starting to rise.*'/, literally /'the water has already become big'/, attested by EB.

<**hí:kw ~ hí::kw**>, augs //hí[=·=]kʷ ~ hí[=··=]kʷ//, DESC /'*be very big; be great, be important*'/, syntactic analysis: adjective/adjectival verb, attested by AC, BJ, EB, ASM ['be very big'], example: <**hí::kw te stólō**>, //hí[=··=]kʷ tə s=tálo//, /'*The river is very big.*'/, attested by AC, <**hí:kw mestìyèxw**>, //hí[=·=]kʷ məstìyə̀xʷ//, /'*big person*'/, attested by AC, <**kwélhtu hí:kw**>, //kʷə́ɬt=əw hí[=·=]kʷ//, /'*It's very big.*'/, attested by EB, ASM ['be great, be important'], <**hí:kw siyá:m**>, //hí[=·=]kʷ s=iy=ɛ́·m//, /'*great chief*'/, attested by BJ.

<**híkwthet**>, incs //híkʷ=θət//, DESC /'*get big, rise (of floodwater)*'/, (<**=thet**> *get, become, inceptive*), syntactic analysis: intransitive verb, attested by AC, example: <**esésu me híkwthet te qó:s**>, //ʔə-sə́-s-əw mə híkʷ=θət tə qá·-s//, /'*And then its water got big.*'/, attested by AC, <**tés; me híkwthet te qó**>, //tə́s; mə híkʷ=θət tə qá//, /'*It got near; the water got big and rose/came up.*'/, attested by AC.

<**hahíkwthet**>, cts //C_1ɛ-híkʷ=θət//, DESC /'*rising, getting big*'/, (<**R3- (C1ɛ-)**> *continuative* or possibly <ha-> //hɛ-// *continuative* usually found only before sonorants), phonology: reduplication, syntactic analysis: intransitive verb, attested by CT, example: <**le qém:el kwses mi xwe hahíkwthet te qó:**>, //lə qə́m·=əl kʷ-s-əs mi xʷə C_1ɛ-híkʷ=θət tə qá·//, /'*The tide comes in and the water rises.*'/, literally /'the tide comes/came in when it came to become getting big the water'/, attested by CT.

<**Híkw Tl'tsás**>, cpds //híkʷ ƛ'cɛ́s//, PLN ['*Long Island (in Harrison Lake)*'], literally /'big island'/, syntactic analysis: nominal phrase with modifier(s), attested by EL 9/27/77, source: place name file reference #314.

<**Híkw Sméya**>, cpds //híkʷ s=mɛ́yɛ//, PLN ['*largest deepest bay on Harrison River (between Victor McDonald's place and Morris Mt.)*'], ASM ['located on east side of river upriver from Morris Mt. and below Dixon Point'], literally /'big bay'/, syntactic analysis: nominal phrase with modifier(s), attested by EL 6/27/78,

<**hí:kw ~ hí::kw**>, DESC /'*be very big; be great, be important*'/, *see* híkw.

<**Híkw Sméya**>, PLN ['*largest deepest bay on Harrison River (between Victor McDonald's place and Morris Mt.)*'], *see* híkw.

<**híkwthet**>, DESC /'*get big, rise (of floodwater)*'/, *see* híkw.

<**Híkw Tl'tsás**>, PLN ['*Long Island (in Harrison Lake)*'], *see* híkw.

<**híl**>, bound root //híl *roll, fall and roll*//.

<**hílém**>, ds //híl=ə́m//, TVMO ['*fall and roll*'], semantic environment ['off roof, down hill, etc.'], (<**=ém**> *intransitivizer*), possibly <**=em**> *middle* with unusual stress shift, phonology: stressed intransitivizer, syntactic analysis: intransitive verb, attested by EB, Elders Group Mar. 1972, AC, RG & EH (4/9/99 Ling332), example: <**le hílém**>, //lə híl=ə́m//, /'*He fell down.*'/, attested by AC, <**me hílém**>, //mə híl=ə́m//, /'*fall from a height*'/, literally /'come to fall (and roll)'/, attested by EB, <**chókw te shxwlís kw'es hílém qesu lékw te sx̲éles**>, //cákʷ tə sxʷ=lí=s k'ʷ-əs híl=ə́m qə-s=əw ɭə́kʷ tə s=x̣ə́lə-s//, /'*He fell from a long ways and broke (break) his leg.*'/, literally /'where he was at was far when he fell and so broke his leg/foot'/, attested by EB.

<**hel-hílém**>, its //$C_1əC_2$=híl=ə́m//, TVMO ['*rolling down*'], phonology: reduplication, syntactic analysis: intransitive verb, comment: l-h spelling in orthography needed rarely to show [lh] rather than [ɬ], attested by EB.

<**hí:lt**>, pcs //hí[=·=]l=T//, TVMO /'*roll s-o over, roll s-th over*'/, (<**=:=**> *derivational?*, <**=t**> *purposeful control transitivizer*), phonology: lengthening, syntactic analysis: transitive verb, Salish cognate: Squamish /híl-it/ *roll (tr.)(e.g. a tree)* W73:218, K67:375.

<**hí:lthet**>, pcrs //hí[=·=]l=T-ət//, TVMO ['*roll oneself (over and over usually)*'], phonology: lengthening, syntactic analysis: intransitive verb, attested by Elders Group 3/5/80.

<**temhilálxw**>, ds //təm=hil=ɛ́lxʷ//, TIME /'*autumn, fall (season)*'/, literally /'time of falling and rolling leaves'/, lx <**tem=**> *time of, time for*, possibly <**=álews**> *leaf*, phonology: =álews here possibly with loss of s and devoicing of w, syntactic analysis: nominal?, attested by AC, Elders Group 3/12/75, other sources: ES /təmʔilɛ́lxʷ/, Cowichan and Musqueam /hɛylɛ́nxʷ/ *autumn*, also <**hilálxw**>, //hil=ɛ́lxʷ//, attested by AC, Elders Group (5/16/79), also <**tem'ilálx̲w**>, //təm=ʔil=ɛ́lxʷ//, attested by Elders Group 3/1/72, example: <**tsqwá:y te hilálxw sch'ó:lha**>, //c-qʷɛ́·y tə hil=ɛ́lxʷ s=c'á·ɬɛ//, /'*The fall leaves are yellow.*'/, attested by Elders 5/16/79.

<**hilékw**>, free root //hilə́kʷ//, TVMO ['*get ready*'], syntactic analysis: intransitive verb, attested by EB, AD, BHTTC; found in <**hilékwchap**>, //hilə́kʷ-c-ɛp//, /'*You folks get ready., You folks get ready.*'/, attested by BHTTC, example: <**ulh iyólem kws hílékwchet kws látset t'ó:kw'**>, //ʔuwɬ ʔiy=ál=əm kʷ-s hilə́kʷ-c-ət kʷ-s lɛ́-c-ət t'á·k'ʷ//, /'*It's time we got ready to go home.*'/, literally /'it's already okay that we get ready that we go homeward'/, attested by EB.

<**hí:lekw ~ hílekw**>, cts //hi[-´·-]ləkʷ ~ hi[-´-]ləkʷ//, [héyləkʷ ~ hí·ləkʷ ~ híləkʷ], TVMO ['*getting ready to go*'], (<-´:- ~ -´-> *continuative*?), phonology: stress shift?, lengthening, syntactic analysis: intransitive verb, attested by Elders Group 3/15/72, contrast Downriver Halkomelem (Katzie dialect) <**hí:lékw**> *glad* Elders Group 3/15/72, example: <**líchap hílekw**>, //lí-c-ɛp híləkʷ//, /'*Are you folks ready?*'/, literally /'are you folks getting ready?'/, attested by AD.

<**s-hí:lekw ~ s-hílekw**>, stvi //s=hi[-´·-]ləkʷ ~ s=hi[-´-]ləkʷ//, TVMO ['*be ready*'], syntactic analysis: stvi, phonology: stress shift?, lengthening, syntactic comment: statives are usually built on a continuative stem; example: <**líchap welh s-hí:lekw**>, //lí-c-ɛp wəɬ s=hi[-´·-]ləkʷ//, /'*Are you folks ready?*'/, attested by BHTTC, <**líchxw xwel s-hílekw**>, //lí-c-xʷ xʷəl s=hi[-´-]ləkʷ//, /'*Are you still ready?*'/, attested by EB.

<**hí:lekw ~ hílekw**>, TVMO ['*getting ready to go*'], *see* hilékw.

<**hílém**>, TVMO ['*fall and roll*'], *see* híl.

<**hí:lt**>, TVMO /'*roll s-o over, roll s-th over*'/, *see* híl.

<**híltu**>, free root //híltu//, SOC /'*a Hindu, an East Indian*'/, borrowed from English /hĩndu/ *Hindu*, syntactic analysis: nominal, attested by BHTTC, example: <**híltu te mő̲xwoya**>, //híltu tə móx̣ʷayɛ//, /'*The belly button is an East Indian.*'/, usage: one line of a humorous song, ASM ['so said in the song due to the similarity of the convolutions in a navel or belly button and in a turban'], attested by BHTTC.

<**híheltu**>, dmn //C₁í=hiltu ~ hí[=C₁ə=]ltu//, SOC /'*a small Hindu, a small East Indian*'/, (<**R4=**> *diminutive* or <**=R1=**> *diminutive*), phonology: reduplication, vowel-reduction, syntactic analysis: nominal, attested by BHTTC, example: <**híheltu te mímx̲woya**>, //C₁í=hiltu tə C₁í=mox̣ʷayɛ//, /'*A little belly button is (like) a little Hindu.*'/, usage: a line of a humorous song, ASM ['comparing the convolutions of a belly button and a turban'], attested by BHTTC.

<**hí:lthet**>, TVMO ['*roll oneself (over and over usually)*'], *see* híl.

<**Híqelem**>, PLN /'*creek and bay on Harrison River just below the old native Chehalis Cemetery, on the east side of Harrison River*'/, *see* **y**eqílem ~ eqéylem.

<**híqwelhtel**>, LANG /'*(coaxing to go,) Let's go.*'/, *see* **h**é**y**.

<**híqwt**>, LANG /'*coax s-o, persuade s-o, invite s-o (on trip, hunt, etc.)*'/, *see* **h**é**y**.

<**hí:tel ~ hí:ytel**>, SOC /'*weapon (arrow, club, etc.), something used to defend oneself*'/, *see* iyó:tel.

<**híth**>, free root //híθ//, TIME /'*a long time, it's a long time*'/, possibly related to <**yóth**>, bound root //yáθ// *always*, perhaps by <he=> continuative, resultative (//hə[=´=]-yáθ//), syntactic analysis: adverb/adverbial verb, example: <**híth kw'as kwelát**>, //híθ k'ʷ-ɛ-s kʷəl=ɛ́T//, /'*You'll have it a long time.*'/, phonology: stressed transitivizer, attested by CT, HT, <**áth'elchu w(e)híth kw'as hókwex**>, //ʔɛ́θ'əl-cɛ-uw híθ k'ʷ-ɛ-s hákʷ=əxʸ//, /'*You'll use it a [very] long time.*'/, literally /'it's very-fut.-contrast a long time that-you-nom use=it'/, phonology: vowel merger, attested by CT, HT, <**kws híthscha kw'as hókwex**>, //kʷ-s híθ-s-cɛ k'ʷ-ɛ-s hákʷ=əxʸ//, /'*that you'll use it a long time*'/, attested by CT, HT, <**welh híth kwses míq'**>, //wəɬ híθ kʷ-s-əs míq'//, /'*He was underwater a long time.*'/, literally /'it's already a long time that-nom-he is underwater'/, attested by EB, <**welh híth ye me q'ép**>, //wəɬ híθ yə mə q'ə́p//, /'*The gathering lasted a long time.*'/, literally /'it's already a long time the pl. anim. come/become/start to gather'/, attested by EB, <**welhíth kw'es kwelát**>, //wəɬ=íθ k'ʷ-əs kʷəl=ɛ́t//, /'*He'll have it a long time (shoes, clothes, etc.).*'/, phonology: consonant merger of lh + h → lh, more common than the lack of merger here, attested by CT, HT, <**ő̄we híthes**>, //ʔówə híθ-əs//, /'*soon, not long*'/, (<**-es**> *subjunctive 3s sjsp*), attested by EB, <**míchxw q'ó:lthet kw'atsetólxw ō̄we híthes**>, //mí-c-xʷ q'á·l=T-ət k'ʷɛc=əT-álxʷ ʔówə híθ-əs//, /'*Come back and see us soon.*'/, literally /'come-you (imperative) return=oneself see-us not it is long time'/, grammatical analysis: auxiliary verb-independent clause subject pronoun-2s intransitive verb=pcr intransitive verb=pc-1pobj vneg adverb/adverbial verb-3subjunctive subject pronoun, syntactic analysis: auxiliary verb-imperative transitive verb-refl. transitive verb-lpobj vneg adverb/adverbial verb-3subjunctive subject pronoun, syntactic comment: note that the negative vp is functioning here syntactically like a single-word adverb/adverbial verb, postposed without any connecting demonstrative article, attested by EB.

<**welhíth**>, cpds //wəɬ=híθ//, [wəɬíθ], TIME ['*a long time ago*'], phonology: consonant merger, syntactic analysis: adverb/adverbial verb, attested by EB.

<**welhíthelh**>, cpds //wəɬ=íθ-əɬ//, (<**-elh**> *past tense*), TIME ['*a long time ago*'], syntactic analysis: adverb/adverbial verb; found in <**kw'ulhíthelh**>, //k'ʷə-wɬ=íθ-əɬ//, /'*a long time*'/, phonology: word boundary has been lost here between the article and the adverb, syntactic analysis: demonstrative article adverb/adverbial verb → np, attested by EB, also <**kw'ōlhíthelh**>, //k'ʷə-wɬ=íθ-əɬ//, [k'ʷoɬíθəɬ], attested by AC, others, also <**kw'e lhíthelh**>, //k'ʷ-wəɬ=íθ-əɬ//, [k'ʷə

ɬ=íθ-əɬ], also /'*long ago*'/, phonology: word boundary has shifted position here phonetically, obscuring welh, attested by CT, HT.

<**welhí:thelh**>, augs //wəɬ=í[=·=]θ-əɬ//, TIME ['*a long time ago*'], (<=:=> *augmentative*), phonology: lengthening, syntactic analysis: adverb/adverbial verb, attested by AC.

<**hiyeq'á:l**>, SOCT /'*a filer, someone that's filing (with a file)*'/, *see* yéq'.

<**híyeqwels**>, REL /'*the one who burns [at a burning ceremony], (ritualist at a burning)*'/, *see* yéqw.

<**híyeqwt**>, FIRE ['*burning s-th*'], *see* yéqw.

<**híyeqwtem siyólh**>, FIRE ['*firewood*'], *see* yéqw.

<**híyex̲wet**>, SH ['*unlacing it*'], *see* yíx̲w.

<**híyqwelchep**>, FIRE /'*making the fire, building the fire, (stoking a fire)*'/, *see* yéqw.

<**hí:ywes**>, REL ['*predicting the future*'], *see* yéw: ~ yéw.

<**hókwex**>, pcis //hák^w=əx^y//, MC /'*use it, wear it, put it on*'/, REL, syntactic analysis: transitive verb, Salish cognate: Squamish /x^{w}úk^w ~ x^{w}ə́k^w/ *be used* and causative /x^{w}ə́k^w-s/ *use (tr.)* K67:348, ASM ['use it'], example: <**lalh hókwex**>, //lɛ-ɬ hák^w=əx^y//, /'*Go use it.*'/, attested by AC, <**hókwexes te stl'eqéwtel**>, //hák^w=əx^y-əs tə s=ƛ'əqə́w=təl//, /'*He used the awl.*'/, attested by AC, <**le hókwexes thel tà:l te x̲wéylem kwses p'ówí:tes tel s'í:th'em**>, //lə hák^w=əx^y-əs θə-l tɛ̀·l tə x^{w}íyləm k^w-s-əs p'ówíy-t-əs tə-l s=ʔí·θ'=əm//, /'*My mother used the thread to patch up my dress.*'/, attested by AC, <**hókwextsel li tel scheqw'ő:welh**>, //hák^w=əx^y-c-əl li tə-l s=cəq'^{w}=ó·wəɬ//, /'*I'm using it on my basket-weaving.*'/, attested by AC, <**qesu mí hókwex te shxwch'óqw'els**>, //qə-s-u mí hák^w=əx^y tə sx^w=c'áq'^{w}=əls//, /'*and use a fork*'/, attested by CT, HT, <**qéx̲ te shxwhókwextset**>, //qə́x̣ tə sx^w-hák^w=əx^y-c-ət//, /'*We'll use it in many ways.*'/, semantic environment ['using plants for medicine'], literally /'are many the our uses for it'/, attested by TM (or DF or NP), ASM ['put it on'], semantic environment ['clothes, shoes'], <**hókwexchexw ta' s'íth'em**>, //hák^w=əx^y-c-əx^w t-ɛʔ s=ʔíθ'=əm//, /'*Put on your clothes.*'/, syntactic comment: polite imperative with 2s subj. pronoun, attested by AD, <**hókwexchxw ta' hólem swéta**>, //hák^w=əx^y-c-x^w t-ɛʔ háləm swə́tɛ//, /'*Put on your warm sweater.*'/, attested by AD, <**hókwexchxw ta' hólem kopú**>, //hák^w=əx^y-c-x^w t-ɛʔ háləm kapú//, /'*Put on your warm coat.*'/, attested by AD, <**hókwexlha ta' kopú**>, //hák^w=əx^y-ɬɛ t-ɛʔ kapú//, /'*Put on your coat.*'/, syntactic comment: command imperative with -lha, attested by EB, <**hókwex ta' (sqélxel, slewíws, kopú, seqí:ws, swéta, stl'epíwel)**>, //hák^w=əx^y t-ɛʔ (s=qə́l=x^{y}əl, s=ləw=íws, kapú, səq=í·ws, swə́tɛ, s=ƛ'əp=íwəl)//, /'*Put on your (moccasins, dress, coat, pants, sweater, shirt).*'/, syntactic comment: imperative marked only by 2s possessive pronoun modifying object, attested by AD, <**líchexw hókwex ta' qwlhíxel**>, //lí-c-əx^w hák^w=əx^y t-ɛʔ q^{w}ɬí=x^{y}əl//, /'*Did you put on your shoes?*'/, attested by AD, <**hókwextsel tel stókel**>, //hák^w=əx^y-c-əl t-əl stákəl//, /'*I put on my socks.*'/, attested by AD, ASM ['wearing it']; found in <**hókwexes**>, //hák^w=əx^y-əs//, /'*He's wearing it., He put it on.*'/, attested by AD, example: <**ílh hókwexes**>, //ʔíɬ hák^w=əx^y-əs//, /'*He wore it .*'/, syntactic analysis: auxiliary past, attested by AD.

<**híhòkwexes**>, dmv //C$_1$í=hák^w=əx^y-əs//, if, CLO ['*he (a small child) is wearing it.*'], (<**R4=**> *diminutive*), phonology: reduplication, syntactic analysis: transitive verb, attested by AD.

<**hó:kwt**>, df //há·k^{w}t//, SD ['*make a high hooting call (maybe only of spirits)*'], syntactic analysis: intransitive verb?.

<**hólem**>, df //hál=əm//, CLO ['*warm (of clothing)*'], DESC, semantic environment ['clothing'], possibly <**=em**> *middle voice*?, syntactic analysis: adjective/adjectival verb, attested by AD, example: <**hókwexchxw ta' hólem (swéta, kopú)**>, //hák^w=əx^y-c-x^w t-ɛʔ hál=əm (swə́tɛ, kapú)//, /'*Put on your warm (sweater, coat).*'/, attested by AD.

<**hómkw**>, probable root or stem //hám(=)k^w//, root meaning unknown

<**s-hómkw**>, stvi //s=hámk^w//, WETH /'*sultry, humid*'/, (<**s=**> *stative*), syntactic analysis: adjective/adjectival verb, comment: this is one of the few words requiring a hyphen in the Stó:lō writing system to show that both s and h are pronounced separately (as in English "misheard"), not together as a digraph for a single sound ([š]) as it usually is (as in English "mush"), attested by IHTTC.

<**s-hómkwstem**>, stca //s=hámk^w=sT=əm//, SOC ['*(someone) standing in the middle of a crowd*'], (<**s=**> *stative*), probably <**=st**> *causative*, probably <**=em**> *middle voice*, or possibly <**=em**> *intransitivizer*, or <**=tem ~ =em**> *participial*, possibly root as in <**s-hómkw**> *sultry, humid*??, syntactic analysis: intransitive verb, comment: another rare word requiring a hyphen in the Stó:lō writing system to show s and h are pronounced separately (not as in English "mush"), attested by IHTTC.

<**homiyósem**>, ABFC ['*drink without using hands*'], *see* homò:y.

<**homò:y**>, probably root //hamà·y//, EZ ['*shrimp*'], ['suborder *Natantia,* probably *Crago* and other genera, especially *Crago vulgaris*, *Pandalus danae* were identified by AD from a photo as the kind AD's parents got dried from the Chinese and called by this name'], syntactic analysis: nominal, attested by IHTTC, AD, also <**hómò:y**>, //hámà·y//.

<**homiyósem**>, df //hamiy=ás=əm//, ABFC ['*drink without using hands*'], literally /'shrimp in one's face'/, lx <**=ós**> *on the face*, (<**=em**> *middle voice*), syntactic analysis: intransitive verb, attested by IHTTC.

<**hóps**>, free root //háps//, EB ['*domestic hops*'], ['*Humulus lupulus*'], borrowed from English /háps/ *hops*, ASM ['introduced and cultivated in large fields in the Sardis and Agassiz areas; Indians from all over the northwest came to the fields as pickers each summer, socializing, singing, gambling, etc. in their off-hours ca 1920's to 1950's'], syntactic analysis: noun, nominal.

<**hóqw**>, bound root //háq^w *smell*//.

<**hóqwem**>, mdls //háq^w=əm//, SM /'*it smells, give off a smell, smell bad*'/, (<**=em**> *middle voice*), syntactic analysis: intransitive verb, example: <**ts'áts'elō hóqwem**>, //c'ɛ́c'əl-ow háq^w=əm//, /'*real strong smell*'/.

<**s-hóqwem**>, dnom //s=háq^w=əm//, SM ['*a smell*'], syntactic analysis: nominal, attested by NP, Elders, example: <**ewéta s-hóqwems**>, //ʔəwə=´=tɛ s=háq^w=əm-s//, /'*It has no smell.*'/.

<**hó:qwem**>, cts //há[-·-]q^w=əm//, SM /'*giving off a smell, to smell*'/, syntactic analysis: intransitive verb, attested by EB.

<**hóqwels**>, sas //háq^w=əls//, SM /'*smelling, sniffing (of an animal like a dog, etc.)*'/, syntactic analysis: intransitive verb.

<**hóqwlexw ~ héqwlexw**>, ncs //háq^w=l-əx^w ~ hə́q^w=l-əx^w//, SM ['*happen to smell s-th*'], syntactic analysis: transitive verb, attested by NP, AC, example: <**tsel héqwlexw ~ tsel háqwlexw**>, //c-əl hə́q^w=l-əx^w ~ c-əl háq^w=l-əx^w//, /'*I smelled it.*'/, syntactic analysis: ambiguous past, attested by AC, <**tsel héqwlexw te sp'ó:tl'ems te swíyeqe**>, //c-əl hə́q^w=l-əx^w tə s=p'á·ƛ'=əm-s tə s=wíyəqə//, /'*I smelled the man's smoke.*'/, syntactic analysis: ambiguous past, attested by AC, <**étsel héqwlexw te skú:ks**>, //ʔə́-c-əl hə́q^w=l-əx^w tə s=kú·k-s//, /'*[I smelled her cooking.]*'/, syntactic analysis: auxiliary past, attested by AC, <**tsel héqwlexw te s'álhtels; le qwó:lstes**>, //c-əl hə́q^w=l-əx^w tə s=ʔɛ́ɬtəl-s lə q^{w}á·ls=T-əs//, /'*I smelled her food boiling.*'/, literally /'I smelled her meal; it was boiling.'/, syntactic analysis: sentence with verb phrase in apposition, attested by AC, <**achxw héqwlexw**>, //ʔə-ə-c-x^w hə́q^w=l-əx^w//, /'*Did you smell it?*'/, syntactic analysis: interrogative affix, auxiliary past, attested by AC.

<**hó:qwlexw**>, cts //há[-·-]q^{w}=l-əx^{w}//, SM ['*smelling s-th*'], (<**-:-**> *continuative aspect*), syntactic analysis: transitive verb, attested by AC, example: <**ílhtsel hó:qwlexw**>, //ʔíɬ-c-əl há[-·-]q^{w}=l-əx^{w}//, /'*I was smelling something.*'/, syntactic analysis: auxiliary past, attested by AC, <**ílh há:qwlexwes te sp'ó:tl'em**>, //ʔíɬ há[-·-]q^{w}=l-əx^{w}-əs tə s=p'á·ƛ'=əm//, /'*He was smelling the smoke.*'/, syntactic analysis: auxiliary past, attested by AC.

<**hóqwet**>, pcs //háq^{w}=əT//, SM ['*smell s-th on purpose*'], syntactic analysis: transitive verb, attested by NP, AC, example: <**hóqwet te sp'á:q'em**>, //háq^{w}=əT tə s=p'ɛ́q'=əm//, /'*smell the flower*'/, attested by AC.

<**hó:qwet**>, cts //há[-·-]q^{w}=əT//, SM ['*smelling s-th*'], syntactic analysis: intransitive verb, attested by AC, example: <**hó:qwetes**>, //há[-·-]q^{w}=əT-əs//, /'*She's smelling [s-th].*'/, attested by AC, <**hó:qwetes te sp'á:q'em**>, //há[-·-]q^{w}=əT-əs tə s=p'ɛ́q'=əm//, /'*She's smelling the flower.*'/, attested by AC.

<**hóqwels**>, SM /'*smelling, sniffing (of an animal like a dog, etc.)*'/, *see* hóqw.

<**hóqwem**>, SM /'*it smells, give off a smell, smell bad*'/, *see* hóqw.

<**hó:qwem**>, SM /'*giving off a smell, to smell*'/, *see* hóqw.

<**hóqwet**>, SM ['*smell s-th on purpose*'], *see* hóqw.

<**hó:qwet**>, SM ['*smelling s-th*'], *see* hóqw.

<**hóqwlexw ~ héqwlexw**>, SM ['*happen to smell s-th*'], *see* hóqw.

<**hó:qwlexw**>, SM ['*smelling s-th*'], *see* hóqw.

<**hóts**>, free root //hác//, PLAY ['*hearts (in cards)*'], semantic environment ['card games'], borrowed from English /há(r)ts/ *hearts,* syntactic analysis: nominal.

<**hótl'**>, bound root //háƛ'// probably *blunt*.

<**s-hótl'eqw**>, dnom //s=háƛ'=əq^{w}//, HUNT ['*blunt-headed arrow*'], PLAY, ASM ['the head is made of cloth or hide, etc.; the shaft may be feathered or not'], lx <**=eqw**> *on the head*, syntactic analysis: nominal, attested by Deming.

<**hóxwethílém**>, mdls //háx^{w}=əθəl=íl=əm//, incs, ABFC /'*to sigh, breathe out whew*'/, lx <**=ethel**> *in the mouth, in the lips*, (<**=em**> *middle voice*), phonology: =íl as usual replaces preceding el, syntactic analysis: intransitive verb, attested by IHTTC.

<**hò:y ~ hó:y ~ hóy**>, free root //hà·y ~ há·y ~ háy//, ASP /'*finish, stop, quit, get done, be finished, have enough, be done, be ready*'/, syntactic analysis: intransitive verb, adjective/adjectival verb, ASM ['finish'], example: <**islá tel hóy**>, //ʔisɛ́lə[=M2] t-əl háy//, /'*I finished two things.*'/, literally /'it's two things the-my finish'/, (irregular)k'^{w}-əl-s háy would be more expected here with the remote demonstrative k'^{w}ə and -s nominalizer always used to subordinate and nominalize a verb phrase, attested by IHTTC, <**stám te hó:y**>, //s=tɛ́m tə há·y//, /'*What did you get done? (sarcastically)*'/, usage: sarcastic, attested by Deming evening class 5/18/78, ASM ['stop']; found in <**hóylha**>, //háy-ɬɛ//, /'*Stop. (for ex. filling a cup), Stop it.*'/, syntactic analysis: command imperative, attested by AC, IHTTC, <**hóyálha**>, //háy-ɛɬɛ//, /'*Stop it you guys.*'/, syntactic analysis: pl command imperative, (semological comment: the command imperative here seems to encourage the less polite translation *you guys* instead of the more usual 2p *you folks*; it also allows the use of *stop it* which is more forceful than *stop*), attested by IHTTC, example: <**le hóy kw'es qwóqwels**>, //lə háy k'^{w}ə-s q^{w}ɛ̀·[-Aá-C_1ə-]l-s//, /'*They stopped talking.*'/, syntactic analysis: ambiguous past, attested by AC, ASM ['quit'], <**hóylha**>, //háy-ɬɛ//, /'*Quit it.*'/, syntactic analysis: command imperative, (semological comment: command imperative allows *quit it* which is more forceful than *quit*), attested by Elders, ASM ['be

finished'], <**lé hò:y**>, //lə́ hà·y//, /'*It's finished.*'/, syntactic analysis: ambiguous past, attested by Elders 3/15/72, also <**lé hó:y ~ le hó:y**>, //lə́ há·y ~ lə há·y//, attested by BJ, also <**le hò:y**>, //lə hà·y//, attested by EB, AD, <**lí hó:y**>, //lí há·y//, /'*Is it finished?*'/, attested by BG checked with AD, <**líchxw hó:y ta' sq'óq'ey**>, //lí-c-x^{w} há·y t-ɛʔ s=q'á[=C$_{1}$ə=]y//, /'*Are you finished your sickness?, Are you finished coming?, Are you finished climaxing?*'/, attested by JL, <**kws wetl'e hó:y te skw'ókw'es**>, //k^{w}-s wə-ƛ'a há·y tə s=k'^{w}ɛ[=Aa=C$_{1}$ə=]s//, /'*that's when the hot [weather] is finished, autumn*'/, attested by DM 12/4/64, ASM ['have enough'], <**chel hóy**>, //c-əl háy//, /'*I've had enough.*'/, syntactic analysis: ambiguous past, attested by AC, <**iyó:lem kw'els hò:y**>, //ʔiy=á·l=əm k'^{w}-əl-s hà·y//, /'*I've had enough., I'm finished.*'/, literally /'it's alright that I'm finished.'/, attested by Elders Mar. 1972, ASM ['be done'], <**stám te hó:y**>, //s=tɛ́m tə há·y//, /'*What did you get done?*'/, usage: sarcastic, literally /'What is it that's finished (present and visible)?'/, (semological comment: note effective use of te *the (present and visible)*), (irregular)one would expect -s preceding hó:y to nominalize, attested by Deming (evening class), ASM ['be ready'], <**téxwcha kws hóy te s'álhteltset**>, //tə́x^{w}-cɛ k^{w}-s háy tə s=ʔɛ́ɬtəl-c-ət//, /'*Our food will soon be ready.*'/, attested by Deming (prompted), <**xwewá is hóy te s'álhtel**>, //x^{w}=əwə=ɛ́ ʔi-s háy tə s=ʔɛ́ɬtəl//, /'*The food is not yet ready.*'/, attested by Deming; found in <**ihó:y**>, //ʔi=há·y//, /'*finished, ready*'/, attested by EB.

<**yálh yuw kw'a's hò:y**>, df //yɛ́ɬ yuw k'^{w}-ɛʔ-s hà·y//, LANG /'*I thank you (deeply), I thank you (deeply)., Thank you.*'/, literally /'(only now/only then)(praise for beauty)(that-you-nom are done/finished'/, (morphosememic development), ASM ['deep thanks, not used for ex. after food is passed'], attested by AC, also see <**yuw**> *praising something beautiful*, examples: <**yálh yuxw kw'a's hò:y**>, //yɛ́ɬ yux^{w} k'^{w}-ɛʔ-s hà·y//, attested by AD, Elder's comment: "this is a better spelling than yálh lixw kw'a's hò:y", also <**yálh yuw kw'a'as hò:y**>, //yɛ́ɬ yuw k'^{w}-ɛʔɛ-s hà·y//, attested by AC, Deming, also <**kw'a's hò:y**>, //k'^{w}-ɛʔ-s hà·y//, attested by Annie Grace Chapman, Elder's comment: "this is a shortcut for yálh yuxw kw'a's hò:y", example: <**yalh yuw kwa'as hó:yelep**>, //yɛɬ yuw k^{w}-ɛʔɛ-s há·y-ələp//, /'*Thank you folks.*'/, attested by Deming, <**yálh yuw kw'a's hó:yelep, mámele**>, //yɛ́ɬyuw k'^{w}-ɛʔ-s há·y-ələp C$_{1}$ɛ́-mələ//, /'*Thank you, children.*'/, attested by BG checked with AD, <**welóy kw'els ch'ítòle qetl'olsu thét, "yálh yuw kw'as hóyelép."**>, //wə=láy k'^{w}-əl-s c'í=T-àlə qə-ƛ'a-l-su θə́t yɛ́ɬ yuw k'^{w}-ɛ-s háy-ələ́p//, /'*just that I praise you folks and so I said, "I thank you all."*'/, attested by AC, Salish cognate:Nooksack <yalh qémalh ashó:y or yalh qwómalh ashó:y or yalh kwómalh ashó:y> GA

<**yiláwel kw'a's hò:y**>, df //yilɛ́w=əl k'^{w}-ɛʔ-s hà·y//, LANG /'*thank you very much, Thank you very much.*'/, attested by Annie Grace Chapman, also <**yiláwél kw'a's hò:y**>, //yilɛ́w=ə́l k'^{w}-ɛʔ-s hà·y//, attested by Annie Grace Chapman.

<**hóyòwèlh**>, df //háy=à=wə̀ɬ//, LANG /'*goodbye, Goodbye.*'/, usage: said by the person leaving to the person staying, literally /'it's just already finished'/, dialects: *Chill., Deming*, see main dialect form <**hóyàwèlh**>, attested by AC, Deming, example: <**hóyòwèlh, tátel**>, //háy=àwə̀ɬ tɛ́[=C$_{1}$ə=]l//, /'*Goodbye, Mom.*'/, phonology: reduplication, attested by BG checked with AD.

<**hóyàwèlh**>, df //háy=ɛ̀wə̀ɬ//, LANG /'*goodbye, Goodbye.*'/, usage: said by the person leaving to the person staying, dialects: *Tait and Cheh.*, see dialect form <**hóyòwèlh**>, attested by EB, Elders Group, AD.

<**ílhulhòy**>, df //ʔí-ɬ-uɬ-hày//, TIME ['*the last time*'], phonology: ílh welh hò:y but pronounced as one word using the following phonological processes: loss of word boundaries, schwa-deletion (e-deletion), vocalization of w to u, consonant merger of h with lh (loss of h), literally /'it was already finished'/, grammatical analysis: auxiliary verb-past affixed-particle-intransitive verb, syntactic analysis: verb phrase with modal particle, attested by BHTTC, example: <**ílhulhòy kw'étslòmè**>, //ʔí-ɬ-uɬ-hày k'^{w}ə́c=l-àmə̀//, /'*the last time I saw you*'/, (irregular)there is no 1s subj. pronoun present, attested by BHTTC.

<**hóystexw**>, caus //háy=sT=əxw//, /'*make s-th/s-o finish, cause it to finish*'/, <**=st**> *causative*, <-exw> *3rd person object*, attested by RG & EH (4/10/99 Ling332), example: SPRD <**le hóystexw tel sxwexwá**>, REL, ABFC //lə háy=sT=əxw təl s=C_1ə-x^wɛ́//, /I broke my fast/ (lit. "past - cause to finish it - my - starving"), phonology: rare exception (or error) to phonemic rule /s/ → [š]/_x^w, attested by RG & EH (4/10/99 Ling332)

<**hó:ythel**>, ds //há·y=(ə)θəl//, FOOD /'*finish eating, be done eating*'/, lx <**=(e)thel ~ =ó:thel**> *on the mouth, in the mouth*, syntactic analysis: intransitive verb, attested by AC, MH (Deming), AD, example: <**líchap hó:ythel**>, //lí-c-ɛp há·y=θəl//, /'*Are you folks done eating?*'/, attested by MH (Deming), AD, <**étsel hó:ythel**>, //ʔə́-c-əl há·y=θəl//, [ʔɪ́cl há·yθl], /'*I'm finished eating.*'/, syntactic analysis: ambiguous past, attested by AC, <**átset hó:ythel**>, //ʔɛ́-c-ət há·y=θəl//, /'*We've had enough (food).*'/, syntactic analysis: ambiguous past, attested by AC.

<**hà:m**>, possibly free root //hɛ̀·m// or possible stem ///há[=Aɛ̀=]]·y=m//, TIME /'*finished, over*'/, possibly <**a-ablaut**> *resultative or durative*, possibly <**=em**> *intransitivizer*, phonology: possible vowel merger, possible ablaut, comment: connection with hóy *finish, end* would require very irregular loss of its final root consonant and so is unlikely phonologically but is semantically quite plausible, syntactic analysis: intransitive verb, usage: sometimes used at the end of a story, Salish cognate: Squamish /hámʔ/ *come home, be covered* W73:69, K67:374, example: <**le hà:m.**>, //lə hɛ̀·m//, /'*It's over., It's finished (of a story).*'/, (semological comment: perhaps; found in Squamish, *It's covered* as in English at the end of a narrative, "Well, that covers it.").

<**hóyàwèlh**>, LANG /'*goodbye, Goodbye.*'/, *see* hò:y ~ hó:y ~ hóy.

<**hóyeqwels**>, LANG ['*coaxing (as a structured activity)*'], *see* **héy**.

<**hóyeqwt**>, LANG ['*coaxing s-o*'], *see* **héy**.

<**hóyiws**>, bound stem //háy=iws// root meaning uncertain

<**s-hóyiws**>, dnom //s=háy=iws//, SPRD /'*spirit-dancing costume, wool hat for spirit-dancer (Deming)*'/, (<**s=**> *nominalizer*), poss. root <**hóy**> *finish, stop, quit, get done, be finished, have enough, be done, be ready*, perhaps relating to the dancer's rebirth on becoming a dancer, lx <**=iws**> *on the body, on the skin*, phonology: one of the few words requiring a hyphen in the Stó:lō writing system to show that s and h are here pronounced separately as in English "misheard" and not together as in English "mush", syntactic analysis: nominal, attested by Elders, CLO /'*dancer's uniform, (any) coordinated outfit*'/, attested by RG & EH (4/10/99 Ling332) example: SPRD <**s-hó:yiws te xawsólkwlh**>, //s=há·y=iws-s təx̣ɛws=álkʷɬ//, /'*whole costume of a new spirit-dancer*'/, syntactic analysis: nominal phrase with modifier(s), attested by Elders 11/26/75, also /'*wool hat for spirit-dancer*'/, attested by Deming, SPRD <**s-hóyiws máqel**>, //s=háy=iws-s mɛ́=qəl//, /'*hair hat for experienced spirit-dancer*'/, lit. "it's costume - hair" or "hair of the costume", syntactic analysis: nominal phrase with modifier(s), attested by Deming, *see* hóyiws.

<**hóyòwèlh**>, LANG /'*goodbye, Goodbye.*'/, *see* hò:y ~ hó:y ~ hóy.

<**hóyqwelhtel**>, LANG /'*coaxing to go, let's go*'/, *see* **héy**.

<**hó:ythel**>, FOOD /'*finish eating, be done eating*'/, *see* hò:y ~ hó:y ~ hóy.

<**hó'i'**>, df //há=ʔiʔ//, EFAM ['*(expression of amazement)*'] root <**í'**>, syntactic analysis: interjection, attested by AD.

<**hṓ:liya**>, dnom //hó·l=iyɛ//, EZ /'*humpback salmon, pink salmon, humpy*'/, ['*Oncorhynchus gorbuscha*'], ASM ['return to spawning area in Fraser tributaries in September every two years, larger run every four years, called "humpy" years or jokingly called "Indian leap year"'], syntactic analysis: nominal,

dialects: *Chill.*, other sources: ES /hə́w·ləyɛ/, H-T <hō'lia> *humpback salmon (Oncorhynchus Gorbusca)*, also <**húliya ~ hú:liya**>, //húl=iyɛ ~ hú·l=iyɛ//, dialects: *Tait, Cheh.*.

<**húheliya**>, dmn //hú[=C_1ə=]l=iyɛ//, EZ ['*small-sized humpback salmon*'], ['*Oncorhynchus gorbuscha*'], (<=**R1**=> *diminutive*), root *see* hṓ:liya *humpback salmon*, phonology: reduplication, syntactic analysis: nominal, attested by BHTTC.

<**húheliya**>, dmn //hú[=C_1ə=]l=iyɛ//, EZ ['*small-sized humpback salmon*'], ['*Oncorhynchus gorbuscha*'], *see* hṓ:liya .

I

<í>, free root //ʔí//, DIR /'*here, be here, be in (i.e. here)*'/, syntactic analysis: adverb/adverbial verb; example: <**luw í**>, //lə-uw ʔí//, /'*He's here.*'/, phonology: vowel merger, grammatical analysis: 3ambiguous past-contrastive be here, attested by EB, <**líchap ole í**>, //lí-c-ɛp ʔalə ʔí//, /'*You folks are here, eh?*'/, attested by RP, EB, <**li í thel tàl**>, //li ʔí θ-əl tɛ̀l//, /'*Is my mother in?*'/, attested by AC.

<**te í ~ te'í**>, dnom //tə ʔí//, DIR ['*this (speaker is not holding it but is close enough to touch it)*'], syntactic analysis: demonstrative article adverb/adverbial verb → demonstrative pronoun, np, attested by FJ (Flossie Joe, dau. of Isaac Joe, Bob Joe's brother), AD, also <**te í:**>, //tə ʔí·//, attested by BJ 12/5/64; example: <**stám te'í**>, //s=tɛ́m tə ʔí//, /'*What's this (the speaker is not holding it but is close enought to touch it)?*'/, attested by AD, also <**stam te'í**>, //s=tɛm tə ʔí//, also /'*What's this?*'/, attested by FJ.

<**te'íle ~ te'í:le**>, dnom //tə ʔí=lə ~ tə ʔí·=lə//, DIR /'*this (speaker is holding it), this one, this thing here*'/, syntactic analysis: demonstrative article adverb/adverbial verb-adverb/adverbial verb, np; example: <**stám te'íle**>, //s=tɛ́m tə ʔí=lə//, /'*What's this (the speaker is holding it)?*'/, attested by AD, also /'*What's this?*'/, attested by FJ, RP, EB, <**tl'ó: te'í:le**>, //ƛ'á· tə ʔí·=lə//, /'*It's this one., That's this one.*'/, attested by AC, other sources: ES /ƛ'atiʔílɛ/ *this (it's this one)*, <**tewát te í:le**>, //tə=wɛ́t tə ʔí·=lə//, /'*Who owns this?*'/, attested by AC, <**l stl'í: te í:le**>, //l=s=ƛ'í· tə ʔí·=lə//, /'*This is the one I want.*'/, attested by AC, <**tl'ó te í:le sakweláx le q'éylexw te mó:qw**>, //ƛ'á tə ʔí·=lə sɛ=kʷələ[=Aɛ́=]xʸ lə q'ó[=Aə́=]y=l-əxʷ tə má·qʷ//, /'*This is the gun that killed the bird.*'/, attested by AC, <**máqel te'í:le**>, //mɛ́=qəl tə ʔí·=lə//, /'*This is hair (can be used if holding one's own hair).*'/, attested by AD, <**th'emxweláx̲el te'íle**>, //θ'əm=xʷ=əlɛ́x̣əl tə ʔí=lə//, /'*This is an elbow.*'/, syntactic comment: when naming a number of body parts like this the s= *nominalizer* is left off; the s= is present when the body part is possessed (inalienable possession); the following body parts work this way: (s=)th'emxweláx̲el*elbow*, Cheh. (s=)th'emeláx̲el *arm bone, point of elbow*,(s=)qep'ó:lthetel *knee*, (sh-)xw'ílàmàlà ~ (sh-)xw'ílámálá *shoulder*, and perhaps others, attested by IHTTC.

<**ye'íle**>, dnom //yə ʔí=lə//, DIR ['*these*'], syntactic analysis: pl.demonstrative article adverb/adverbial verb=adverb/adverbial verb, attested by FJ; example: <**stám ye'íle**>, //s=tɛ́m yə ʔí=lə//, /'*What are these?*'/, attested by FJ.

<**íkw'elò ~ ikw'eló ~ íkw'elo**>, ds //ʔí=k'ʷə=là ~ ʔi=k'ʷə=lá ~ ʔí=k'ʷə=la//, DIR /'*here, be here*'/, syntactic analysis: adverb/adverbial verb, attested by EB, BJ, AC, Deming, Elders; example: <**tsel íkw'elò**>, //c-əl ʔí=k'ʷə=là//, /'*I'm here.*'/, attested by EB, <**ōwéta slhéq'elexw kw'e sq'épscha kw'e í:kw'elo**>, //ʔowə= ́=tɛ s=ɬə́q'ə=l-əxʷ k'ʷə s=q'ə́p-s-cɛ k'ʷə ʔí·=k'ʷə=la//, /'*I didn't know there was a gathering here.*'/, attested by AC, <**sth'áth'elh te íkw'elò**>, //s=θ'ɛ́[=C$_1$ə=]ɬ tə ʔí=k'ʷə=là//, /'*It's cool here.*'/, <**éy tel sqwálewel kw'etslóle mőkw' íkw'elò**>, //ʔɛ́y t-əl s=qʷɛ́l=əwəl k'ʷəc=l-álə mók'ʷ ʔí=k'ʷə=là//, /'*I'm glad to see you (pl.) all here.*'/, attested by Deming, also <**éy tel sqwálewel kw'etslóle mőkw' í**>, //ʔɛ́y t-əl s=qʷɛ́l=əwəl k'ʷəc=l-álə mók'ʷ ʔí//, (semological comment: this shows that í and íkw'elò are largely synonymous), attested by Deming.

<**í ò**>, ds //ʔí ʔà ~ ʔí -à//, DIR /'*stay here, stay, remain at a place*'/, phonology: ʔà *just, simply* here, as elsewhere, often becomes a suffix -a, losing its glottal stop, syntactic analysis: adverb/adverbial verb particle; example: <**íchxwò**>, //ʔí-c-xʷ-à//, /'*Stay here.*'/, syntactic analysis: imperative, literally /'you are just here, you be just here.'/, also /'*You stay., You remain at a place.*'/, attested by EB,

<**lámtsel t'ó:kw' qe chelew í ò**>, //lɛ́=m-c-əl t'á·k'ʷ qə c-əl-əw ʔí ʔà//, /'*I was going home but instead I stayed.*'/, (semological comment: note -ew *contrastive* is here beautifully translated by *instead*).

<**í ò kw'eló**>, ds //ʔí ʔà k'ʷə=lá//, DIR /'*stay right here, staying right here*'/, syntactic analysis: adverb/adverbial verb particle demonstrative article=adverb/adverbial verb/particle → verb phrase with adverbial (verb/particle/demonstrative); example: <**íchxwò kw'eló**>, //ʔí-c-xʷ-à k'ʷə=lá//, /'*Stay right here.*'/, syntactic analysis: imperative, <**ítsel o kw'eló**>, //ʔí-c-əl ʔa k'ʷə=lá//, /'*I'm staying right here.*'/.

<**ístexw ó**>, caus //ʔí=sT-əxʷ ʔá//, DIR /'*leave this here, leave s-th here*'/, TVMO, syntactic analysis: transitive verb, attested by EB; example: <**ístexwchelcha ó**>, //ʔí=sT-əxʷ-c-əl-cɛ ʔá//, /'*I'm going to leave this here.*'/, attested by EB.

<**íchelstexw**>, df //ʔí=cəl=sT-əxʷ//, DIR ['*leave s-th here*'], TVMO, syntactic analysis: transitive verb, attested by EB; example: <**íchelstexwtselcha o te s'álhtel**>, //ʔí=cəl=sT-əxʷ-c-əl-cɛ ʔa tə s=ʔɛ́ɬtəl//, /'*I'm going to leave the food.*'/, attested by EB.

<**xwe'í**>, incs //xʷə=ʔí//, TVMO /'*arrive, arriving, come here, have come, get here, get back, come in (in a race)*'/, syntactic analysis: intransitive verb, ASM ['arrive'], ASM ['come in (in a race)'], <**yelhyó:qwt kwes xwe'í**>, //yə=ɬiyá·qʷt kʷ-əs xʷə=ʔí//, /'*He arrived last., He came in last (in a race).*'/, attested by EB, ASM ['get here']; example: <**wexwe'í:s**>, //wə-xʷə=ʔí-əs//, /'*when he gets here*'/, phonology: vowel merger, syntactic analysis: when/if-intransitive verb-3subordinate subject pronoun, attested by AC, <**yálhòlse me xwe'í**>, //yɛ́ɬ-à-l-s mə xʷə=ʔí//, /'*I just got here.*'/, attested by EB, also <**yalholsú xwe'í**>, //yɛɬ-à-l-s-əw xʷə=ʔí//, attested by EB, <**me txwém xwe'í**>, //mə txʷ=xʷə́m xʷə=ʔí//, /'*got here early*'/, <**lulh xwe'í te (swíwe, sth'óqwi, kwő̱xweth)**>, //lə-uɬ xʷə=ʔí tə (s=wíwə, s=θ'áqʷi, kʷóxʷ=əθ)//, /'*The (eulachons, fish, cohoes) are running., The (eulachons, fish, cohoes) have gotten here/arrived.*'/, attested by AC, ASM ['get back'], <**yalhtsel xwe'í:**>, //yɛɬ-c-əl xʷə=ʔí·//, /'*I got back.*'/, ASM ['come here, come (here)'], <**ts'áts'eltsel xwoyíwel tel sqwálewel kw'els me xwe'í sq'ó talhlúwep, (ey l sí:yáye, l sí:yáye sí:yám)**>, //c'ɛ́c'əl-c-əl xʷ-ɛ[=Aa=]y=íwəl t-əl s=qʷɛ́l=əwəl k'ʷ-əl-s mə xʷə=ʔí s=q'á tɛ=ɬ=lə́wə=p, (ʔɛ́y l si[-´·-]yɛ́yə, l si[-´·-]yɛ́yə s=i[-´·-]yɛ́m)//, /'*I'm very happy to come here gathering with you folks, my (good friends, dear (pl.) friends (pl.)).*'/, phonology: length and stress infixing *plural* in example sentence, syntactic analysis: adverb/adverbial verb-non-subordinate subject marker-1s adjective/adjectival verb demonstrative article-possessive pronoun affix1s nominal demonstrative conjunction-1s-nominal auxiliary verb intransitive verb preposition/prepositional verb independent object of prepositional verb2p, (adjective/adjectival verb possessive pronoun affix1s nominal-pl, possessive pronoun affix-1s adjective/adjectival verb-pl nominal-pl), usage: public-speaking, formal longhouse style, attested by Deming, <**le xwe'í ta skw'á:lho**>, //lə xʷə=ʔí t-ɛ s=k'ʷí[-Aɛ́·-]ɬəw//, /'*Your in-laws (pl.) have come.*'/, phonology: ablaut, attested by AC, <**áscha ew me xw'í látselcha yesq'ó**>, //ʔɛ́-s-cɛ ʔəw mə xʷə=ʔí lɛ́-c-əl-cɛ yə-s-q'á//, /'*If he comes again, I'll go along.*'/, attested by EB (compare <**atse**> *next*), <**xwe'í te sqwélqwel**>, //xʷə=ʔí tə s=qʷɛ[=Aə=] ´l=C_1əC_2//, /'*News has come., to report news, to bring news*'/, attested by EB, <**lí a sqwá:lewel kwes xwe'í:s wéy:eles**>, //lí ʔɛ s=qʷɛ̀·l=əwəl kʷ-s xʷə=ʔí·-s wɛ́y·=əl=əs//, /'*Do you think they'll come tomorrow?*'/, attested by AC.

<**xwe'ílòmèt**>, ncrs //xʷə=ʔí=l-àmə̀t//, TVMO ['*manage to get here*'], syntactic analysis: intransitive verb, attested by BHTTC, RP, EB; example: <**líchap xwe'ílomet**>, //lí-c-ɛp xʷə=ʔí=l-amət//, /'*Have you folks all got here?*'/, attested by RP, EB.

<**xw'í:lmet**>, iecs //xʷ=ʔí=íl=məT//, incs, TVMO ['*reach s-o here*'], (<**=íl**> *come, go, inceptive*, <**=met**> *indirect effect control transitivizer*), syntactic analysis: transitive verb, attested by EB; found in <**xw'í:lmethome**>, //xʷ=ʔí=íl=məT-amə//, /'*reach you here*'/, attested by EB; example:

<**atselcha ew me xw'í:lmethome**>, //ʔɛ-c-əl-cɛ ʔəw mə x^w=ʔí=íl=məT-amə//, /'*I'll come and see you again.(sic), I'll come reach you here again.*'/, attested by EB.

<**xw'í:ls**>, pncs //x^w=ʔí=ələs//, TVMO ['*manage to get to s-o here*'], (<**=les**> *psychological non-control transitivizer*), syntactic analysis: transitive verb, attested by EB; example: <**atselcha ew mi xw'í:lsòmè**>, //ʔɛ-c-əl-cɛ ʔəw mi x^w=ʔí=ələs-àmə̀//, /'*I'll come and see you again.(sic), I'll manage to come get to you here again.*'/, syntactic analysis: auxiliary verb-non-subordinate subject marker-1s-future tense contrastive auxiliary verb transitive verb=pncs-object pronoun2s, attested by EB.

<**xwe'í:lstexw**>, caus //x^{w}ə=ʔí=íl=sT-əx^w//, incs, TVMO ['*bring s-o/s-th here*'], (<**=íl**> *come, go, get, become, inceptive*, <**=st**> *causative control transitivizer*), syntactic analysis: transitive verb, attested by EB; found in <**xwe'í:lsthóxes**>, //x^{w}ə=ʔí=íl=sT-áx^y-əs//, /'*He brought me here.*'/, attested by EB, <**xwe'í:lsthàlèm**>, //x^{w}ə=ʔí=íl=sT-ɛ̀lə̀m//, /'*I was brought here.*'/, grammatical analysis: incs=caus-passive1s, syntactic comment: passive, attested by EB.

<**í**>, free root //ʔí//, DIR ['*with*'], syntactic analysis: preposition/prepositional verb, syntactic comment: like most prepositional verbs when preceding independent pronouns this one takes the tl'e- prefixed pronoun set, attested by EB; example: <**í tl'léwe**>, //ʔí ƛ'-lə́wə//, /'*with you*'/, attested by EB, <**ístexwchelcha ó í (kw'e tewátes, tútl'ò, tl'eléwe)**>, //ʔí=sT-əx^w-c-əl-cɛ ʔà ʔí (k'^{w}ə tə=wɛ́t=əs, t=ú=ƛ'à, ƛ'ə-lə́wə)//, /'*I'll leave it (with somebody, with him, with you).*'/, attested by EB, <**ístexwchxw ó í (tl'á'althe, tl'elhlímelh)**>, //ʔí=sT-əx^w-c-x^w ʔà ʔí (ƛ'-C_1ɛ́=ʔɛ́lθə, ƛ'ə-ɬíməɬ)//, /'*You leave it (with me, with us).*'/, attested by EB, <**ístexwchel ó í tl'elhléwep**>, //ʔí=sT-əx^w-c-əl ʔà ʔí ƛ'ə-ɬ=lə́wə=p//, /'*I leave it with you folks.*'/, attested by EB.

<**í**>, free root //ʔí//, DIR ['*on*'], syntactic analysis: preposition/prepositional verb, attested by EB; example: <**sq'óq'ey te pús í kw'e xálh**>, //s=q'a[=C_1ə=]y tə pús ʔí k'^{w}ə x^{y}ɛ́ɬ//, /'*There's a dead cat on the road.*'/, attested by EB.

<**í**>, free root //ʔí//, CJ ['*yes/no question*'], syntactic analysis: interrogative verb, attested by AD, MH (Deming), AHTTC; example: <**i hó:y**>, //ʔi há·y//, /'*Is it finished?*'/, attested by AD, <**íchxw álhtel**>, //ʔí-c-x^w ʔɛ́ɬtəl//, /'*Did you eat?*'/, attested by MH (Deming); found in <**íxw**>, //ʔí-x^w//, /'*Do you?*'/, attested by AHTTC.

<**í**>, free root //ʔí//, CJ /'*(auxiliary verb), (*[may also imply] *here)*'/, syntactic analysis: auxiliary verb, syntactic comment: found in three places: as auxiliary verb (vaux) after negative verbs (vneg); as auxiliary verb carrying the subject person marker of a subordinate clause whose object corefers to the subject of the main clause; and as auxiliary verb carrying the past tense suffix -lh; examples of each type are listed below as examples of three allosemes (though some exx. may not differ in translation but more in function), semantic environment ['negative verbs']; example: <**éwe is wel ól éy**>, //ʔə́wə ʔi-s wəl ʔál ʔɛ́y//, /'*He's not very good.*'/, phonology: <í-s> loses stress here due to an optional rule of sentence stress, attested by Deming, <**éwe ís xwélalà:m**>, //ʔə́wə ʔí-s x^{w}ə[=´=]lɛlɛ́[=`=]·m//, /'*He's not listening.*'/, attested by EB, <**tl'ó; éwe ít í kwíxelexwt te thá**>, //ƛ'á; ʔə́wə ʔí-t ʔí k^{w}íx^y=l-əx^w-t tə θɛ́//, /'*We didn't have a name for that.*'/, attested by CT, HT, <**xwewátsel í:l xwá siyó:lexwe**>, //x^w=əwə=ɛ́-c-əl ʔí·-l x^{w}ɛ́ s=yá·ləx^{w}ə//, /'*I'm not old yet ., I haven't become old yet.*'/, attested by AC, <**xwewáchap í:p xwá siyó:lexwe**>, //x^w=əwə=ɛ́-c-ɛp ʔí·-p x^{w}ɛ́ s=yá·ləx^{w}ə//, /'*You folks are not old yet .*'/, attested by AC, <**xwewátst í:t xwá siyó:lexwe**>, //x^w=əwə=ɛ́-c-t ʔí·-t x^{w}ɛ́ s=yá·ləx^{w}ə//, /'*We're not old yet .*'/, attested by AC, <**xwewá ís xwá siyó:lexwe**>, //x^w=əwə=ɛ́ ʔí-s x^{w}ɛ́ s=yá·ləx^{w}ə//, /'*He's not old yet .*'/, attested by AC, <**xwewáchxw íxw xwá siyó:lexwe**>, //x^w=əwə=ɛ́-c-x^w ʔí-x^w x^{w}ɛ́ s=yá·ləx^{w}ə//, /'*You're not old yet .*'/, attested by AC, <**xwewáchxw í:xw toteló:met**>, //x^w=əwə=ɛ́ ʔí·-x^w ta[=C_1ə=]l=l=á·mət//, /'*You don't understand yet .*'/, attested by AC, <**ewálhtsel íl stl'ítl'eqelh**>, //ʔəwə-ɛ́ɬ-c-əl ʔí-l s=ƛ'íƛ'əq=əɬ//, /'*I wasn't a child.*'/, attested by AC, semantic environment ['subject

of subordinate verb whose object corefers to main verb subject'], <**tewát kw'e íxw tháyelhtset te swéltel**>, //tə=wɛ́t k'ʷə ʔí-xʷ θi[=Aɛ́=]y-əɬc-ət tə s=wə́l=təl//, /'*Who are you making the fish net for?*'/, syntactic analysis: object of subordinate verb corefers to subject of main verb, attested by AC, <**stám te í:xw thá:yt**>, //s=tɛ́m tə ʔí·-xʷ θi[=Aɛ́=]y=T//, /'*What are you making?*'/, syntactic analysis: object of subordinate verb corefers to subject of main verb, attested by AC, semantic environment ['past tense + existential']; found in <**ílh ~ í:lh**>, //ʔí-ɬ ~ ʔí·-ɬ//, /'*he was, she was, it was, they were*'/, attested by AC; example: <**ílh éy**>, //ʔí-ɬ ʔɛ́y//, /'*It was good.*'/, attested by AC, <**í:lh lí**>, //ʔí·-ɬ lí//, /'*He was there.*'/, attested by AC, <**í:lh lí te thá**>, //ʔí·-ɬ lí tə θɛ́//, /'*He was there (pointing).*'/, attested by AC, <**í:lhtsel lí**>, //ʔí·-ɬ-c-əl lí//, /'*I was there.*'/, attested by AC, <**í:lhchap lí tàlhwélep**>, //ʔí·-ɬ-c-ɛp lí tɛ̀=ɬwə́ləp//, /'*You people were there.*'/, attested by AC, <**í:lh lí yethá.**>, //ʔí·-ɬ lí yə=θɛ́//, /'*They were there.*'/, attested by AC, <**í:lh ikw'eló kw'e cheláqelhelh**>, //ʔí·-ɬ ʔi=k'ʷə=là k'ʷə cəlɛ́q=əɬ=əɬ//, /'*He was here yesterday.*'/, attested by AC, <**í:lh í:kw'elo li kw'the Christmas**>, //ʔí·-ɬ ʔí·=k'ʷə=là li k'ʷ=θə krísməs//, /'*He was here on Christmas.*'/, attested by AC.

<**-í ~ í-**>, da //-í ~ í-// (meaning uncertain); example: <**tl'o; éwe ítí kwíxelexwt te thá**>, //ƛ'á; ʔə́wə ʔí-t-í kʷíxʸ=l-əxʷ-t tə θɛ́//, /'*(That); we didn't have a name for that.*'/, attested by CT, HT, <**ewe isí kw'étslexwes tl' Bill**>, //ʔə́wə ʔís-i k'ʷə́c=l-əxʷ-əsƛ' Bill//, /'*Bill didn't see it .*'/, attested by EB.

<**íchelstexw**>, DIR ['*leave s-th here*'], *see* í.

<**íhóyt**>, SOC ['*cheating s-o*'], *see* ehó:yt.

<**íkw' ~ í:kw'**>, free root //ʔík'ʷ ~ ʔí·k'ʷ//, DIR /'*become lost, get lost*'/, syntactic analysis: intransitive verb; example: <**le íkw'**>, //lə ʔík'ʷ//, /'*It got lost.*'/, attested by AC, <**skw'áycha kw'es í:kw's**>, //s=k'ʷɛ́y-cɛ kʷ-əs ʔí·k'ʷ-s//, /'*It will never get lost.*'/, attested by AC.

<**s'í:kw'**>, stvi //s=ʔí·k'ʷ//, DIR /'*lost and presumed dead, perished*'/, SOC, ABDF, (<**s=**> *stative*), syntactic analysis: adjective/adjectival verb, attested by EB; example: <**le s'í:kw' te lólets'e**>, //lə s=ʔí·k'ʷ tə C_1á=ləc'ə//, /'*One person was lost.*'/, attested by EB, <**s'í:kw' ye kw'í:làs**>, //s=ʔí·k'ʷ yə k'ʷí·l=ɛ̀s//, /'*Several persons were lost., Several people were lost.*'/, grammatical analysis: stative-intransitive verb demonstrative article(pl.human) interrogative verb=person classifier, attested by EB.

<**s'ekw''í:kw'**>, plv //s=C_1əC_2-ʔí·k'ʷ//, ABDF ['*to perish (of a lot of people)*'], SOC, (<**s=**> *stative*), (<**R3-**> *plural subject*), phonology: reduplication, syntactic analysis: adjective/adjectival verb, attested by EB.

<**ókw'elexw**>, ncs //ʔi[=Aá=]k'ʷ=əl-əxʷ//, DIR ['*lose s-th*'], SOC, (<**ó-ablaut**> *derivational*), (<**=(e)l**> *non-control transitivizer*), phonology: ablaut, syntactic analysis: transitive verb, attested by EB.

<**ekw'ólem**>, izs //ʔi[=Aá=]k'ʷ=ə[=M2=]l=əm//, DIR /'*lose (s-th, an object, etc.)*'/, (<**ó-ablaut**> *derivation*, metathesis *derivation*), (<**=em**> *intransitivizer*, perhaps *middle voice?*), phonology: since there is no suffix =ól attested elsewhere the ó must be metathesized from the ó added by ablaut; both vowels and =l *non-control transitivizer* are attested in their original positions in ókw'elexw, syntactic analysis: intransitive verb, syntactic comment: here at last is an example of an intransitive verb, transitivized with a non-control transitivizer, then intransitivized again; it is intransitive morphologically in that it lacks the -exw *third person object*; syntactically and semantically it is or can be transitive with an np object, attested by Elders Group 3/16/77; example: <**tsel ekw'ólem tel lepót**>, //c-əl ʔi[=Aá=]k'ʷ=ə[=M2=]l=əm//, [cɪl ʔək'ʷáləm tʰɪl ləpʰátʰ], /'*I lost my cup.*'/, attested by Elders Group 3/16/77.

<**íkw'et**>, pcs //ʔík'ʷ=əT//, DIR /'*throw s-th away, discard s-th, throw s-o away, discard s-o*'/, MC, SOC, syntactic analysis: transitive verb, attested by EB, AH, Elders Group, ASM ['throw s-th away, discard s-th'], <**íkw'et te sqélep**>, //ʔík'ʷ=əT tə s=qə́l=əp//, /'*throw away the garbage*'/, attested by AH, ASM ['throw someone away, discard someone']; example: <**íkw'etem**>, //ʔík'ʷ=əT-əm//, /'*He*

was thrown away.'/, syntactic analysis: intransitive verb=pcs-passive, attested by Elders Group, <**le íkw'etòlèm**>, //lə ʔík'^{w}=əT-àlə̀m//, /'*They threw you folks away., You folks were thrown away.*'/, syntactic analysis: ambiguous past intransitive verb=pcs-passive2p, attested by Elders Group.

<**íkw'eló ~ íkw'elo**>, DIR /'*here, this place*'/, *see* ló.

<**íkw'elò ~ ikw'eló ~ íkw'elo**>, DIR /'*here, be here*'/, *see* í.

<**íkw'et**>, DIR /'*throw s-th away, discard s-th, throw s-o away, discard s-o*'/, *see* íkw' ~ í:kw'.

<**=í:l ~ =íl ~ =el**>, da //=í·l ~ =il ~ =əl//, ASP /'*go, come, get, become*'/, CST, phonology: conditions preceding =əl → zero, syntactic analysis: lexical suffix, derivational suffix, also <**=el**>, //=əl//; found in <**xets'í:lem**>, //x^{y}əc'=í·l=əm//, /'*(go) through the woods*'/ (compare <**s=xí:xets'**> *woods),* <**kwetxwí:lem**>, //k^{w}ətx^{w}=í·l=əm//, /'*come inside, go inside*'/ (compare <**s=kwetáxw**> *inside (a house)),* <**tl'pí:l**>, //ƛ'p=í·l//, /'*descend*'/ (compare root <**tl'ép**> *down, deep)* <**q'axí:lt**>, //q'á·=x^{y}əl=í·l=T//, /'*go with, come with, be partner with s-o*'/ (compare <**s=q'ó:=xel**> *partner),* <**sq'eq'ó:**>, //s=C$_{1}$ə=q'á·//, /'*together with*'/, <**sqemí:l**>, //sqəm=í·l//, /'*inside a pit house*'/ (compare <**sqémél**> *pit house),* <**thetí:l**>, //θɛt=í·l//, /'*gone dark*'/ (compare root <**thá:t**> *darkness),* <**kwí:mel**>, //k^{w}í·m=əl//, /'*go red, get red*'/ (compare <**ts=kwí:m**> *red),* <**qwá:yel**>, //q^{w}ɛ́·y=əl//, /'*go yellow (or green), get yellow*'/ (compare <**ts=qwá:y**> *yellow, green),* <**p'eq'éyl** (or better) **p'eq'í:l**>, //p'əq'=í·l//, /'*go white, get white*'/ (compare root <**p'éq'**> *white),* <**q'éyxel** (or better) **q'íxel**>, //q'íx̣=əl//, /'*go black, get black*'/ (compare <**ts'=q'éyx**> *black),* <**meth'í:l**>, //məθ'=í·l//, /'*go blue, get blue*'/ (compare <**ts=méth'**> *blue*), <**meth'í:lt**>, //məθ'=í·l=t//, /'*make it blue, dye it, color it (any color)*'/, <**lewí:lem**>, //ləw=í·l=əm//, /'*go into an opening*'/, <**iyí:lem**>, //ʔiy=í·ləm//, /'*clear up, turn fine*'/ (root <**ʔɛy**> *good),* <**syeqwí:l**>, //s=yəq^{w}=í·l//, /'*lamp, lantern*'/, <**yíyeqwí:l**>, //yíyəq^{w}=í·l//, /'*small light, candle*'/, literally /'thing that comes/goes burning'/, <**q'esí:ltel**>, //q'əs=í·l=təl//, /'*tumpline*'/, literally /'a device that goes tied'/ (compare <**q'éyset**> *tie s-th),* possibly <**qeliythí:lem**>, //qəl=iyθ=í·l=əm//, /'*say bad words, swear, curse*'/, <**qweloythí:lem**>, //q^{w}əl=ayθ=í·l=əm//, /'*making music; March moon*'/ (compare root <**qwà:l ~ qwel**> *talk, speak* and <**=ó:ythel**> *in the lips or jaw* and <**=em**> *middle voice).*

<**ílàm**>, probably root //ʔílɛ̀m//, ABFC ['*carry on one's shoulder*'], possibly <**=m**> *middle voice*, grammatical comment: if present, =m would have to be an old crystallized middle since a transitivizer can be suffixed to it, as can a lexical suffix (see below); in present-day Halkomelem the middle =em is word-final (unless =met *indirectly affecting control transitivizer* is analyzed as an old middle + =et *purposeful control transitivizer*), syntactic analysis: intransitive verb.

<**í:lá:mt**>, pcs //ʔí·lɛ́·m=T//, ABFC ['*carry s-th on one's shoulder*'], (<**=t**> *purposeful control transitivizer*), syntactic analysis: transitive verb.

<**xw'ílámálá ~ xw'ílàmàlà**>, dnom //x^{w}=ʔílɛ́m=ɛ́lɛ́ ~ x^{w}=ʔílɛ̀m=ɛ̀lɛ̀//, ANA /'*shoulder (name of body part, unpossessed)*'/, lx <**xw=**> *(meaning unclear: towards the face?)*, lx <**=álá ~ =àlà**> *container for*, syntactic analysis: nominal, attested by IHTTC.

<**shxw'ílámálá ~ shxw'ílàmàlà**>, dnom //s=x^{w}=ʔílɛ́m=ɛ́lɛ́ ~ s=x^{w}=ʔílɛ̀m=ɛ̀lɛ̀//, ANA /'*shoulder (especially the top), shoulder (someone's, possessed)*'/, HARV ['*yoke*'], (<**s=**> *nominalizer*), syntactic analysis: nominal, attested by BHTTC, IHTTC, also <**shxw'í:lá:má:lá:**>, attested by DM (12/4/64), Elders Group 7/27/75.

<**xw'ilamő́welh**>, ds //x^{w}=ʔilɛm=ówəɬ//, CAN /'*carry a canoe on one's shoulders, to portage*'/, lx <**xw=**> *(meaning unclear)*, lx <**=ő́welh**> *canoe*, syntactic analysis: intransitive verb.

<**Shxw'ílamő́welh**>, dnom //s=x^{w}=ʔílɛm=ówəɬ//, PLN /'*rocky place across from and just above Emory Creek, on east/CN side of Fraser River*'/, ASM ['across the Fraser above Frank Malloway's drying rack; this was a portage place since in high-water time (like early summer) the river is too

rough to pass here'], also at this place are two or three people turned to stone in the rocks that can still be seen lying on their sides; they got hit with logs in the back and this is was given by AK as a reason why the place is called by its name, because xwelemṓwelh or xwlemṓwelh means *get hit on the back* [I wonder if she meant xw(e)lemṓwech since =ṓwech is *on the back*], we visited this magical place on the raft trip down the Fraser 8/30/77 with AK, SP, AD, AP, myself, and the hired raft man; AK had me reach up into a crevice to check for her fish-knife from where she had put it when butchering fish here 30 years before, and I felt it and pulled it out, somewhat rusted, a knife in the form of a half-circle with a wooden haft on the radius, it was made from a filed down circular saw blade but in the style of an old-time Stó:lō fish-knife., (<**s=**> *nominalizer*), syntactic analysis: nominal, source: place name reference file #11.

<**xwelemṓwelh ~ xwlemṓwelh**>, ds //xʷələm=ówəɬ ~ xʷləm=ówəɬ//, possibly /*'get hit on the back'*/, comment: perhaps mistranscribed for <**xwelemṓwech ~ xwlemṓwech**>, syntactic analysis: intransitive verb, attested by AK, (or possibly SP) 8/30/77, *see* ló:m ~ lóm.

<**í:lá:mt**>, ABFC [*'carry s-th on one's shoulder'*], *see* ílàm.

<**iláq**>, possibly root //ʔilɛ́q//, CAN /*'stern of canoe, stern-man among paddlers'*/, syntactic analysis: nominal, Salish cognate: Lushootseed /ʔílaq/ *stern, back seat of a car* H76:666 and its ultimate root /laq/ *last, behind* H76:265-266 as in /ʔu-yáyus čəd ʔal ti làq s-ɬukʷàlb/ *I worked last month.*, /ad-ɬəq-bíd/ *behind you*, and /ʔəs-láq-il/ *late.*

<**íláxel**>, bound stem //ʔí=lɛ́x̣əl or ʔíl=əlɛ́x̣əl or ʔílɛ́=ɛ́x̣əl// probably root <i(:)l> *surface*, automatic syllable deletion.

<**shxw'íláxel**>, dnom //s=xʷ=ʔí=lɛ́x̣əl or s=xʷ=ʔíl=ɛ́x̣əl or s=xʷ=ʔílɛ́=ɛ́x̣əl//, ANA [*'armpit'*], (<**s=**> *nominalizer*), lx <**xw=**> *(meaning unclear)*, lx <**=(e)láxel**> *on the arm*, root <**í** or **íl** or **ílá**>, syntactic analysis: nominal.

<**í:lchel**>, free root //ʔí·lcəl//, CAN /*'engine, motor'*/, MC, ACL, borrowed from English "engine", syntactic analysis: nominal, dialects: *Chilliwack Landing.*

<**=ílép ~ =í:lep ~ =éylép ~ =elep ~ =áp ~ =íp ~ =ép**>, da //=íl=ə́p ~ =í·ləp ~ =əl=əp ~ =ɛ́p ~ =íp ~ =ə́p//, LAND /*'dirt, ground'*/, possibly <**=íl ~ =əl**>, (semological comment: =ep and =ap are cognate with forms meaning *on the rump* in other Salish languages, though that meaning has been taken over by =elets in Upriver Halkomelem and =ep, =ap, =í:lép now clearly has the meaning of *dirt, ground*, there still are perhaps a few cases of survival of that meaning in Upriver Halkomelem), phonology: allomorphy seems to be =**éylép** and =**áp** after postvelars, the other allomorphs elsewhere, =í:lep after CV́CV̆C and other stressed roots, =elep after a stressed syllable, but two of the 16 examples don't fit this pattern, syntactic analysis: lexical suffix, derivational suffix, also <**=éylép**>, //=íl=ə́p//, also <**=elep**>, //=əl=əp//, also <**=áp**>, //=ɛ́p//, also <**=íp**>, //=íp//, also <**=ép**>, //=ə́p//; found in <**leq'éylép**>, //ləq'=í·lə́p//, /*'level ground'*/ (compare root <**léq'**> *level)*, <**tl'xwéylép**>, //ƛ'x̣ʷ=í·lə́p//, /*'hard ground'*/ (compare root <**tl'éxw**> *hard)*, <**lhexéyléptel**>, //ɬəx̣=í·lə́p=təl//, /*'floor'*/, comment: this is an alternate analysis to that given in lexical prefixes under the prefix lh= (compare <**lhex=ōwélh=tel**> *thwarts, crosspieces of a canoe* and <**lháx=xe=tel**> *rug* and <**lhex=í:l=éx**> *stand up)*, <**syíts'emílép**>, //syíc'əm=ílə́p//, /*'sand bar'*/ (compare <**syíts'em**> *sand)*, <**sqótemílep**>, //sqátəm=íləp//, /*'hill'*/, root meaning unknown, <**tewálehí:lép**>, //təwɛ́lə(=)h=í·lə́p//, /*'sloping ground'*/ (compare <**tewále**> *sloping)*, <**xéyxep'í:lep ~ xíxep'í:lep**>, //x̣í[=C₁ə=]p'=í·ləp//, /*'a rake'*/ (compare <**xéy=p'=et**> *scratch or scrape s-th and leave a mark*), <**thóyxwí:leptes**>, //θáyxʷ=í·ləp=t-əs//, /*'he was softening the ground (this was done to some places to insure a good growth of wild vegetables)'*/ (compare <**thóyqwels**> *digging)*, <**ts'esémelep**>, //c'isə[=´=]m=ələp//, /*'weeds'*/ (compare <**ts'ísem**> *grow*) literally /'growing dirt'/, <**shxwtl'éxelep**>, //sxʷ=ƛ'ə́xʸ=ələp//, /*'a plow'*/ (compare root <**tl'éx**> *rip or break apart)*, <**sqwelíp**>, //s=qʷíl=ə[=M2=]p//, /*'(black) beard moss,*

black moss bread'/, literally /'nom. + hair + dirt'/, (semological comment: this moss is cooked underground and becomes a sweet licorice-tasting loaf), <**tl'asíp**>, //ƛ'ɛs=íp//, /'*licorice fern*'/, (semological comment: the roots are edible and grow in dirt-like accumulations on the bark of maple trees), root meaning unknown, <**sq'exáp**>, //s=q'əx̣=ɛ́p//, /'*stump (of tree)*'/, <**Sqwá:p**>, //s=qʷɛ́·=(ɛ́)p//, /'*hole with water at (foot of?) Mt. Cheam on the side away from the Fraser River, lake or waterhole on Mt. Cheam*'/ (compare <**s=qwá:**> *hole*, <**sthíyép ~ sthiyáp**>, //sθíy=ə́p ~ sθiy=ɛ́p//, /'*loincloth*'/, literally /'nom. + θíy *make, fix*? + *dirt* or *on the rump*'/, <**sqelép ~ sqélép**>, //s=qəl=ə́p or s=qə́l=ə́p//, /'*garbage*'/ (compare root <**qél**> *bad, dirty)*.

<**iléq**>, bound root //ʔilə́q *buy*//.

<**iléqet**>, pcs //ʔilə́q=əT//, SOC ['*buy s-th*'], (<**=et**> *purposeful control transitivizer*) (compare root possibly <**iláq**> *stern of canoe, stern-man* because some trade goods were exchanged in early days from boats and canoes), syntactic analysis: transitive verb, attested by EB, Elders Group; found in <**iléqtes**>, //ʔilə́q=T-əs//, /'*He bought it.*'/, attested by EB; example: <**tsel iléqet te seplí:l**>, //c-əl ʔilə́q=əT tə səplí·l//, /'*I bought the bread.*'/, syntactic analysis: ambiguous past.

<**iléqelhtst**>, bens //ʔilə́q=əɬc=T//, SOC ['*buy it for s-o*'], (<**=elhts**> *benefactive*, <**=t**> *purposeful control transitivizer*), syntactic analysis: transitive verb; found in <**iléqelhtsthó:x**>, //ʔilə́q=əɬc=T-á·xʸ//, /'*buy it for me*'/, attested by Elders Group, <**iléqelhtchexw**>, //ʔiləq=əɬc=T-c-əxʷ//, /'*You buy it for him.*'/, phonology: the ts in =elhts has been dropped here (irregular assimilation), attested by EB, *<**iléqelhchetchexw**> rejected, *<**ileqelhthetchexw**> rejected, <**iléqelhthó:xchexw**>, //ʔilə́q=əɬc=T-á·xʸ-c-əxʷ//, /'*You buy it for me., You buy it for me.*'/, phonology: the ts in =elhts has been dropped here (irregular assimilation), attested by EB.

<**alqá:ls ~ alqáls**>, sas //ʔi[=Aɛ=]ləq=ɛ́·ls ~ ʔi[=Aɛ=]ləq=ɛ́ls//, SOC /'*buy (as structured activity), He bought (as structured activity).*'/, possibly <**a-ablaut**> *derivational*? or merely vowel-reduction, (<**=á:ls**> *structured activity intransitivizer*), phonology: length apparently can be dropped here by EB in faster speech, ablaut or vowel-reduction with shift of stress, (semological comment: this intransitivizer is actually neutral in transitivity; it allows the presence or absence of third person objects syntactically and semantically), syntactic analysis: intransitive verb, attested by EB; example: <**tsel alqáls te seplí:l**>, //c-əl ʔɛlq=ɛ́ls tə səplí·l//, /'*I bought the bread (as a structured activity).*'/, attested by EB, <**ewá:lhtsel mí:l alqá:ls**>, //ʔəwə-əɬ-c-əl mí·-l ʔɛlq=ɛ́·ls//, /'*I wasn't going to buy (but did).*'/, phonology: vowel merger, grammatical analysis: vneg-past affixed-non-subordinate subject marker-1ssj auxiliary verb-subjunctive subject pronoun1s intransitive verb=structured activity, syntactic comment: shows subjunctive pronoun attached to mí: *come, coming to*, (semological comment: shows implication), attested by EB, Elder's comment: "possibly okay", <**ewálhtsel mí:l alqá:ls kw s'álhtel**>, //ʔəwə-əɬ-c-əl mí·-l ʔɛlq=ɛ́·ls kʷ s=ʔɛ́ɬtəl//, /'*I wasn't going to buy groceries)but I did).*'/, phonology: vowel merger, grammatical analysis: vneg-past affixed-nrs-1s vatx-subjunctive subject pronoun1s intransitive verb=structured activity demonstrative article nominal, syntactic comment: shows subjunctive pronoun attached to mí: *come, coming to*, (semological comment: shows implication), attested by EB.

<**íleqels**>, cts //ʔi[=´=]ləq=əls//, SOC /'*buying (as structured activity), He's buying (it) [as structured activity].*'/, (<**=els**> *structured activity continuative*), phonology: it also could be said that =els is not continuative but that =á:ls just automatically becomes =els when it loses stress (here due to *continuative* stress-insertion), syntactic analysis: intransitive verb, attested by EB; example: <**íleqels te stámes**>, //ʔi[=´=]ləq=əls tə s=tɛ́m=əs//, /'*[He's/She's] buying something.*'/, syntactic comment: note indefinite nominal, syntactic analysis: intransitive verb[=continuative aspect=]=structured activity demonstrative article indefinite nominal, attested by EB.

<**íleqels**>, SOC /'*buying (as structured activity), He's buying (it) [as structured activity].*'/, *see* iléq.

<**iléqelhtst**>, SOC ['*buy it for s-o*'], *see* iléq.

<**iléqet**>, SOC ['*buy s-th*'], *see* iléq.

<**=í:les**>, da //=í·ləs//, ANA /'*on the chest, in the chest*'/, syntactic analysis: lexical suffix, derivational suffix; found in <**kw'qwí:les**>, //k'ʷqʷ=í·ləs//, /'*hit on the chest (with a stick-like object)*'/, <**s'í:les**>, //sʔí·ləs//, /'*(human) chest*'/, <**t'kwí:lés**>, //t'ə́kʷ=M1=í·ləs//, /'*choke on food*'/, <**t'ékweles**>, //t'ə́kʷ=iləs//, /'*choking on food*'/, literally /'t'ə́kʷ *mired*'/, <**t'lhí:léstel ~ st'lhí:léstel**>, //(s)=t'ɛɬ=í·lə́s=təl//, /'*collarbone*'/, root <**t'alh**> *(go) across, span*, <**qwemth'í:les**>, //qʷəm=θ'=í·ləs//, /'*big breasts; name of Mt. Ogilby near Hope*'/, root <**qwem**> *large lump*, <**slheqwí:les**>, //s=ɬiqʷ=í·ləs//, /'*breast*'/, root <**slhíqw**> *flesh*.

<**s'í:les ~ s'í:lés**>, dnom //s=ʔ=í·ləs ~ s=ʔ=í·lə́s//, ANA ['*chest (human or animal thorax)*'], (<**s=**> *nominalizer*), lx <**=í:les**> *(on the) chest*, root <**'**> (empty root to form nominals from lexical affixes) or the affix may have derived instead from the nominal here, syntactic analysis: nominal, attested by AC, DM, MH, LJ (Tait), other sources: ES /sʔí·ləs/ *chest (animal or human thorax),* JH /sʔí·ləs/, H-T <se'lis> (macron over e); example: <**th'ex̲wót tel s'í:lés**>, //θ'əx̣ʷ=áT t-əl s=ʔ=í·lə́s//, /'*wash my chest*'/, attested by AC, <**x̲élh tel s'í:les**>, //x̣ə́ɬ t-əl s=ʔ=í·ləs//, /'*I have heartburn.*'/, literally /'I hurt in my chest.'/, attested by MH (Deming), <**x̲élh tel s'íles lhíl kw'à:y**>, //x̣ə́ɬ t-əl s=ʔ=í·ləs ɬi-l k'ʷɛ̀·y//, /'*My chest hurts when I get hungry.*'/, syntactic comment: note auxiliary lhí *when* which takes subjunctive subject pronoun, attested by LJ (Tait).

<**ilólets'e ~ hilólets'e**>, SOC ['*alone*'], *see* léts'a ~ léts'e.

<**=í:ls**>, da //=í·ls or =ə[=Aí·=]ls//, MC /'*device, tool*'/, possibly <**=els**> *structured activity continuative device/person for*, possibly <**í:-ablaut on e in suffix**> *durative*, phonology: possible ablaut, phonology: replaces preceding el, syntactic analysis: lexical suffix, derivational suffix (compare <**=els**>; found in <**sxó:xwí:ls**>, //s=xʸá·[=C_1ə-W]l=í·ls//, /'*a borer or auger*'/ (compare <**xó:l=t**> *to bore)*, phonology: this root is one of a small group beginning in x that reduplicate with labialization (shown here as [-W] in the analysis, so doubling infix #1 with e is xwe rather than xe (the e of the reduplicated syllable and the final l are replaced with the í:ls of the suffix later), <**yéqweqsí:lstsel**>, //yə́qʷ=əqs=í·ls-cəl//, /'*I'm lighting the light*'/, literally /'burn + pointed object, nose + device? + I (subj.)'/.

<**í:ltexw**>, stem //ʔí·l(=)təxʷ or ʔí·(=)ltəxʷ//, *house surface*

<**s'í:ltexw**>, dnom //s=ʔí·l(=)təxʷ or s=ʔí·(=)ltəxʷ//, BLDG /'*thick plank for side of house, thick shake for longhouse roof, covering over hole in roof of pit-house*'/, may contain <**=eltxw**> *house* on a root <i(:)l> *surface*, (semological comment: made of cedar in pre-contact days, might be 10 feet or longer, fastened horizontally to posts before contact, later nailed vertically; pre-contact roof planks were sometimes made a little differently from wall planks in that they were sometimes made in a shallow u-shape and overlapped (bottom layer u's up, top layer u's down) for drainage; sometimes flat planks were overlapped as on non-Indian roofs; some were put on with no overlap (roof plank info. from AD); when a family or village moved they could unlash the planks from walls and roof, and carry them via canoe to their new (or old) house site where the posts were erected or were already up from before; this word does not refer to non-Indian style lumber (see leplós *board*)), syntactic analysis: nominal, other sources: ES /sí·ltəxʷ/ (Cw,Ms /sʔíltəxʷ/) *plank*, also <**shxw'í:ltexw ~ s'í:ltexw**>, attested by DM 12/4/64, Salish cognate: Nooksack /sʔil-ɛ́ltxʷ/ *plank* (compare Nooksack /sʔil-ínwəs/ *chest (anatomy), surface of chest.*

<**s'iltexwáwtxw ~ iltexwáwtxw**>, dnom //s=ʔiltəxʷ=ɛ́wtxʷ ~ ʔiltəxʷ=ɛ́wtxʷ//, BLDG ['*plank house*'], lx <**=áwtxw**> *house, building*, syntactic analysis: nominal.

<**s'iltexwím**>, dnom //s=ʔiltəxʷ=ím//, BLDG ['*plank building*'], lx <**=ím**> *repeatedly*, syntactic analysis: nominal.

<**í:lwelh**>, df //ʔí·lwəɬ//, ANA [*'side (of the body)'*], root <i(:)l> *surface*, lx <**=ó:lwelh**> *side of the body*, syntactic analysis: noun, nominal.

<**s'í:lwelh**>, dnom //s=ʔí·lwəɬ//, ANA [*'one side of the body (*probably *someone's)'*], (<**s=**> *nominalizer (*probably *inalienable possession* also here*)),* syntactic analysis: nominal, dialects: *Tait.*

<**í:lwelh**>, df //ʔí·lwəɬ//, EB /*'short unidentified plant, about 3 ft. tall with red berries like a short mountain ash, the berries are bitter but the plant is used as medicine,* possibly *red baneberry'*/, [*'Actaea rubra* if red baneberry is correct identification'], (semological comment: probably named after the homophonous word for *side (of the body)*, especially if this medicine is used for pain or illness of the side), syntactic analysis: noun, nominal, attested by SP, or perhaps AK or AD.

<**í:lhtel**>, FOOD [*'eating (a meal)'*], *see* álhtel.

<**ílhulhòy**>, TIME [*'the last time'*], *see* hò:y ~ hó:y ~ hóy.

<**=í:m**>, da //=í·m//, ASP [*'repeatedly'*], TIME, syntactic analysis: lexical suffix, derivational suffix; found in <**ts'áts'etl'í:m**>, //c'ɛ́c'əƛ'=í·m//, /*'jumping up and down, jumping along'*/ (compare <**ts'á:tl'em**> *jumping*), <**tàtí:m**>, //tɛ̀tí·m//, /*'hollering more than once'*/ (compare root <**tá:m**> *holler, yell*), <**shxwtatí:m**>, //sx^w=tɛtí·m//, /*'telephone'*/, <**t'áts'exelí:m**>, //t'ɛ́c'=əxəl=í·m//, /*'mistake in splitting roots (for basketry) by making them uneven'*/ (compare root <**t'áts'**> *split stick for stretching salmon to dry)*, <**xwtiytí:m**>, //x^w=tiyt=í·m//, /*'eddy water (where one sets nets)'*/ (compare root <**tíyt**> *upriver*), <**xwelkw'í:m**>, //x^{w}əlk'^{w}=í·m//, /*'an eddy'*/ (compare <**xwélkw'**> *to eddy)*, <**slets'í:mél**>, //s=ləc'=í·m=él//, /*'a comb'*/, <**stl'eqtí:m ~ stl'eqtí:ms**>, //s=ƛ'əqt=í·m(s) *length*// (compare root <**tl'á:qt**> *long)*, <**xts'í:mthet**>, //xts'=í:m=thet//, /*'(smell oneself) always smell bad'*/ (compare <**xíxets'=em**> *stinking).*

<**ím**>, bound root //ʔím *step*//.

<**ímex ~ (rare) íméx**>, //ʔím=əx^y ~ (rare) ʔíméx^y//, TVMO [*'walk'*], ABFC, lx <**=ex**> *upright*, syntactic analysis: intransitive verb, other sources: ES /i·míx^y/ (but Ms /ímix^y/, Cw /ímiš/), JH /ʔíməx/, attested by AC, Deming, Elders Group; found in <**iméxlha**>, //ʔim=ə[=´=]x^y-ɬɛ//, /*'Walk.'*/, phonology: stress-shift conditioned by -lha following, usage: said to a child for ex., attested by AC; example: <**skw'á:y kw'es ímexs; q'óq'eyxel**>, //s=k'^{w}ɛ́·y k'^{w}-əs ʔím=əx^y-s; q'á[=C$_1$ə=]y=x^{y}əl//, /*'He can't walk; he's lame.'*/, attested by AC, <**ímex te (q'alq'elp'í:w, ts'ayíye<u>x</u>, slhets'ímels te pítxel, sth'ékw')**>, //ʔím=əx^y tə (q'ɛl[=q'əl=]p'=í·w, c'ɛyíyəx̣, s=ɬəc'=ím=əls tə pít=x^{y}əl, s=θ'ək'^{w})//, /*'The (inchworm, lizard, centipede, worm) walks.'*/, attested by Deming, <**ímex á:yel**>, //ʔím=əx^y ʔɛ́·y=əl//, /*'walk away'*/, <**ta'á:'altha qas talúwe, látst ímex**>, //tɛ=C$_1$ɛ́=ʔɛlθɛ qɛs tɛ=lə́wə, lɛ́=c-t ʔím=əx^y//, [3t^{h}5ʔæ$_2$ʔɛl2θɛ 3q^{h}ɛs 3tɛ4lú4wə 5lɛ́ct 3ʔí3mɪx^y], phonology: intonation transcribed, /*'Let's you and I go for a walk.'*/, syntactic analysis: conjoined pronouns, imperative1p, attested by AC, <**qé<u>x</u> te ímex mestíyexw**>, //qə́x̣ tə ʔím=əx^y məstíyəx^w//, /*'(There's) lots of people walking.'*/, attested by Ed and Delphine Kelly, phonology: í:mex would be expected for *walking* here.

<**í:mex**>, cts //ʔí[-·-]m=əx^y//, TVMO [*'walking'*], syntactic analysis: intransitive verb, attested by AC, EB; example: <**lí: welh í:mex**>, //lí=ə wəɬ ʔí[-·-]m=əx^y//, /*'Is he (already) walking?'*/, attested by AC, <**í:mex te mestíyexw**>, //ʔí[-·-]m=əx^y tə məstíyəx^w//, /*'A person is walking.'*/, attested by AC, <**í:mex; qé<u>x</u> te mestíyexw ~ qé<u>x</u> te mestíyexw; í:mex**>, //ʔí[-·-]m=əx^y, qə́x̣ tə məstíyəx^w ~ qə́x̣ tə məstíyəx^w, ʔí[-·-]m=əx^y//, /*'A lot of people are walking.'*/, attested by AC.

<**ye'í:mex**>, mos //yə=ʔí[-·-]m=əx^y//, TVMO /*'coming by foot, travelling by walking, already walking, travelling on foot'*/, (<**ye=**> *travel(ling) by means of*), syntactic analysis: intransitive verb, attested by EB; example: <**tsel ye'í:mex**>, //c-əl yə=ʔí[-·-]m=əx^y//, /*'I travelled by foot.'*/, attested by EB.

<**s'ímex**>, dnom //s=ʔím=əx^{y}//, ABFC /'*gait, a walk*'/, (<**s=**> *nominalizer*), syntactic analysis: nominal, (semological comment: note minimal contrast with shxw'ímex), attested by Elders Group 5/3/78; example: <**xwáyq'esem s'ímex**>, //x^{w}ɛ́yq'=əs=əm s=ʔím=əx^{y}//, /'*a wobbly walk*'/.

<**shxw'ímex**>, dnom //s=x^{w}=ʔím=əx^{y} or sx^{w}=ʔím=əx^{y}//, TVMO /'*what one walks on (trail, board sidewalk, cement sidewalk, etc.)*'/, MC, ACL /'*board sidewalk, cement sidewalk*'/, (<**s=**> *nominalizer*, xw= (from the minimal contrast several glosses are possible; since s= nominalizes, the gloss for xw= need not be nominalizing necessarily) *used for* and *man-made* are both possible), syntactic analysis: nominal, attested by AD, NP.

<**imexósem**>, mdls //ʔim=əx^{y}=ás=əm//, TVMO /'*go for a walk, take a stroll, stroll*'/, lx <**=ós**> *face*, (<**=em**> *middle voice*), literally /'walk one's face (or walk oneself in a circle, walk oneself around)'/, syntactic analysis: intransitive verb, attested by AC, EB, NP, AD; example: <**latst imexósem**>, //lɛ-c-t ʔim=əx^{y}=ás=əm//, /'*We're going to go for a walk.*'/, attested by EB.

<**ts'lhimexóstel**>, rcps //c'ɬ=ʔim=əx^{y}=ás=T-əl//, SOC /'*go with each other (romantically), go for a walk with each other (romantically)*'/, TVMO, literally /'going for a walk close to/next to each other'/, lx <**ts'lh=**> probably *close to, next to*, (<**=tel**> *purposeful control reciprocal*), syntactic analysis: nominal, transitive verb??; example: <**tl'ó yewá:lelh ts'lhimexóstels**>, //ƛ'á yəwɛ́·l-əɬ c'ɬ=im=əx^{y}=ás=T-əl-s//, /'*That's the first one he was going with (romantically).*'/, literally /'that's the one was first/before his going for a walk close to each other'/, grammatical analysis: demonstrative verb adverb/adverbial verb-pasx rcps-possessive pronoun affix3, attested by MV, <**le'ówelh láts' te ts'lhimexóstels**>, //lə-ʔáwəɬ lɛ́c' tə c'ɬ=ʔim=əx^{y}=ás=T-əl-s//, /'*He went (romantically) with a different girl., He went (to walk) (romantically) with a different girl.*'/, attested by MV.

<**ímet**>, pcs //ʔím=əT//, ABFC /'*step on s-th, step on it*'/, (<**=et**> *purposeful control transitivizer*), syntactic analysis: transitive verb, attested by CT, HT, AC, RG & EH (4/9/99 Ling332); found in <**ímetlha**>, //ʔím=əT-ɬɛ//, /'*Step on it.*'/, attested by AC; example: <**le ímet kw'es le tl'pì:lx**>, //lə ʔím=əT k'^{w}-əs lə ƛ'p=í·l=x^{y}//, /'*He stepped on it to press it down.*'/, attested by CT, HT.

<**ómeléxw**>, ncs //ʔi[=Aá=]m=l-əx^{w}//, ABFC ['*step on it accidentally*'], (<**o-ablaut**> *derivational*), (<**=l-exw**> *non-control transitivizer*), phonology: ablaut, epenthesis (e inserted between resonants m and l), syntactic analysis: transitive verb; found in <**omeléxwes**>, //ʔi[=Aa=]m=l-əx^{w}-əs//, /'*He stepped on it (accidentally).*'/, attested by Elders Group at Fish Camp 7/11/78.

<**=ímeltxw**>, da //=ím=əl(=)tx^{w}//, N /'*male name, (*prob.*) repeatedly gets wives/houses*'/, possibly <**=ím**> *repeatedly*, possibly <**=el**> *go, come, get, become*, possibly <**=eltxw**> *wives, houses*, syntactic analysis: lexical suffix, derivational suffix, also <**=eltxw**>, //=əl(=)tx^{w}//, also /'*male name, (*prob.*) wives, houses*'/; found in <**Swelímeltxw**>, //swəlím=əltx^{w}//, /'*Indian name of Ed Leon Sr. (of Chehalis, B.C.)*'/.

<**ímet**>, ABFC /'*step on s-th, step on it*'/, *see* ím.

<**í:meth**>, free root //ʔí·məθ//, KIN /'*grandchild, grandchild of sibling, grandchild of cousin (esp. in the old days)*'/, syntactic analysis: noun, nominal, other sources: ES /ʔí·məθ/ *grandchild*, attested by AC, BJ, Elders Group.

<**em'í:meth**>, pln //C$_1$əC$_2$-ʔí·məθ//, KIN ['*grandchildren*'], (<**R3-**> *plural (many)*), phonology: reduplication, syntactic analysis: noun, nominal; found in <**em'í:meths**>, //ʔəm-ʔí·məθ-s//, /'*his grandchildren*'/, attested by AC.

<**ímex ~ (rare) íméx**>, TVMO ['*walk*'], *see* ím.

<**í:mex**>, TVMO ['*walking*'], *see* ím.

<**imexósem**>, TVMO /'*go for a walk, take a stroll, stroll*'/, *see* ím.

<**í ò**>, DIR /'*stay here, stay, remain at a place*'/, *see* í.

<**í ò kw'eló**>, DIR /'*stay right here, staying right here*'/, *see* í.

<**í:pel**>, free root //ʔí·pəl//, CLO ['*apron*'], ACL, borrowed from English /éprən/ *apron*, syntactic analysis: nominal.

<**=íqw ~ =eqw ~ =(e)leqw ~ =ó:qw**>, da //=íqʷ ~ =əqʷ ~ =(ə)ləqʷ ~ =á·qʷ//, ANA /'*on top of the head, on the hair*'/, WATR ['*head of a river*'], KIN ['*head of descendants*'], EZ ['*fish (=heads)*'], semantic environment ['with numerals 2-9, non-numerals'], see <=eqw>.

<**íqw'**>, bound root //ʔíq'ʷ *rub*//.

<**íqw'em**>, mdls //ʔíq'ʷ=əm//, MC /'*get rubbed off, to smudge (a line), to smear, to fade (of material)*'/, CLO, DESC, PE, HHG, SCH, MED, REL, TCH, ABFC, (<**=em**> *middle voice*), syntactic analysis: intransitive verb, attested by EB, Elders Group; example: <**le íqw'em**>, //lə ʔíq'ʷ=əm//, /'*It smeared., etc.*'/.

<**íqw'et**>, pcs //ʔíq'ʷ=əT//, MC /'*rub s-th off, wipe s-th*'/, CLO, FIRE, PLAY, DESC, PE, HHG, SCH, REL, MED , TCH, ABFC, syntactic analysis: transitive verb, attested by EB, Elders Group, AC.

<**íqw'ethet**>, pcrs //ʔíq'ʷ=əT-ət//, ABFC ['*wipe oneself off*'], MC, CLO, FIRE, REL, MED , PE, syntactic analysis: intransitive verb, attested by IHTTC.

<**shxw'íqw'els**>, sas //s=xʷ=ʔíq'ʷ=əls//, SCH ['*eraser (for pencil or blackboard)*'], ACL, (<**s=**> *nominalizer*, xw= *used for* or *man-made*), lx <**=els**> *structured activity*, syntactic analysis: nominal, attested by BHTTC.

<**íqw'esem**>, mdls //ʔíq'ʷ=əs=əm//, ABFC ['*wipe one's face*'], MC, CLO, PE, REL, MED , lx <**=es**> *on the face*, (<**=em**> *middle voice*), syntactic analysis: intransitive verb.

<**shxwíqw'estel**>, dnom //s=xʷ=ʔíq'ʷ=əs=təl//, HHG ['*face-cloth*'], PE, (<**s=**> *nominalizer*, xw= *used for, man-made*), lx <**=es**> *on the face*, lx <**=tel**> *something for*, phonology: consonant merger, syntactic analysis: nominal, attested by Elders Group, AD; example: <**alétsa te shxwíqw'estel**>, //ʔɛlécɛ tə s=xʷ=ʔíq'ʷ=əs=təl//, /'*Where's the face-cloth?*'/, attested by AD.

<**iqw'wí:ls**>, //**ʔiq'ʷ=(ə)wí·ls**//, HHG /'*dry dishes, wipe off dishes*'/, FOOD, lx <**=(e)wí:ls**> *dishes*, syntactic analysis: intransitive verb, attested by MH (Deming), also <**eqw'ewíls**>, //ʔiq'ʷ=(ə)wí·ls//, phonology: vowel-reduction (i → e before stressed suffix), attested by AD, <**eqw'ewílschap**>, //ʔiq'ʷ=əwí·ls-c-ɛp//, /'*You folks dry the dishes.*'/, syntactic analysis: imperative2p, attested by AD; example: <**metlh iqw'wí:ls**>, //mə=tɬ ʔiq'ʷ=wí·ls//, /'*Come dry dishes.*'/, (<**-tlh**> *mildly urging imperative, coaxing imperative*), attested by MH.

<**xwe'í:qw'wí:ls ~ xwe'íyeqw'wí:ls**>, cts //xʷə=ʔí[-·-]q'ʷ=(ə)wí·ls//, HHG ['*drying dishes*'], FOOD, (<**-:-**> *continuative aspect*), phonology: lengthening, syntactic analysis: intransitive verb, attested by AC, Salish cognate: Musqueam /ʔiʔq'ʷət/ *wiping it* shows cognate continuative Suttles ca1984:ch.7 [p.37].

<**eqw'ewílt**>, pcs //ʔiq'ʷ=əwíls=T//, HHG /'*dry them (dishes), dry s-th (dish)*'/, FOOD, phonology: vowel-reduction due to stress-shift, consonant merger, syntactic analysis: transitive verb, attested by AD; example: <**eqw'ewíltchexw te lethlóthel**>, //ʔiq'ʷ=əwíls=T-c-əxʷ tə $C_1əC_2$=láθəl//, /'*Dry the plates.*'/, syntactic analysis: imperative2s, attested by AD.

<**shxwiqw'ewí:ls**>, dnom //s=xʷ=ʔiq'ʷ=əwí·ls//, HHG ['*dish towel*'], (<**s=**> *nominalizer*, xw= *used for, man-made*), syntactic analysis: nominal, attested by Elders Group, also <**shxw'áp'ewí:ls**>, //s=xʷ=ʔɛ́p'=əwí·ls//, attested by Elders Group 6/1/77, Elder's comment: "some say this"; example: <**íkw'elò te shxwiqw'ewí:ls ~ íkw'elò te shxw'áp'ewí:ls**>, //ʔí=k'ʷə=là tə

s=xʷ=ʔiq'ʷ=əwí·ls ~ ʔí=k'ʷə=là tə s=xʷ=ʔɛ́p'=əwí·ls//, /'*Here's the dish towel.*'/, attested by AD.

<**ó:leqw'**>, plv //ʔi[-Aá·-][-lə-]q'ʷ//, MC ['*a lot got rubbed off*'], CLO, DESC, FIRE, LAND, WATR, PLAY, REL, MED , ABFC, ABDF, (<**ó:-ablaut**> *plural*, <**-le-**> *plural*), syntactic analysis: intransitive verb, attested by EB, Elders Group; example: <**le ó:leqw'**>, //lə ʔ-á·[-lə-]q'ʷ//, /'*It rubbed off [a lot of it].*'/, attested by Elders Group 12/10/75.

<**íqw'em**>, MC /'*get rubbed off, to smudge (a line), to smear, to fade (of material)*'/, *see* íqw'.

<**íqw'esem**>, ABFC ['*wipe one's face*'], *see* íqw'.

<**íqw'et**>, MC /'*rub s-th off, wipe s-th*'/, *see* íqw'.

<**íqw'ethet**>, ABFC ['*wipe oneself off*'], *see* íqw'.

<**iqw'wí:ls**>, HHG /'*dry dishes, wipe off dishes*'/, *see* íqw'.

<**isá:le ~ isále ~ isá:la**>, free root //ʔisɛ́·lə ~ ʔisɛ́lə ~ ʔisɛ́·lɛ//, NUM ['*two*'], syntactic analysis: num, adjective/adjectival verb, other sources: ES /isɛ́·la/; example: <**isále spáth**>, //ʔisɛ́lə s=pɛ́θ//, /'*two bears*'/, attested by AC, <**isále sásq'ets**>, //ʔisɛ́lə sɛ́sq'əc//, /'*two sasquatches*'/, attested by HT, AK, also <**yáysele sásq'ets**>, attested by other Elders, <**isále stl'ítl'leqem**>, //ʔisɛ́lə s=C$_1$í=ƛ'ɛləqəm//, /'*two little supernatural creatures, two stl'áleqems*'/, attested by Elders Group, also <**yáysele stl'ítl'leqem**>, attested by some use, <**tsel thíyt kw'e isále**>, //c-əl θíy=T k'ʷə ʔisɛ́lə//, /'*I made two .*'/, attested by AC, <**isále te sléxwelhs; xwe'í:lxwes**>, //ʔisɛ́lə tə s=lə́xʷəɬ-s; xʷə=ʔí·=l-əxʷ-əs//, /'*He has two canoes; he managed to bring them.*'/, attested by AC, <**ó:pel qas kwe isá:le**>, //ʔá·pəl qɛs kʷə ʔisɛ́·lə//, /'*twelve*'/, attested by AC, also <**ópel qas kwe isá:le**>, //ʔápəl qɛs kʷə ʔisɛ́·lə//, attested by BJ, also <**ó:pel qas te isá:la**>, //ʔá·pəl qɛs tə ʔisɛ́·lɛ//, attested by CT 9/5/73, <**ts'kw'éx qas kwe isále**>, //c'=k'ʷə́xʸ qɛs kʷə ʔisɛ́lə//, /'*twenty-two*'/, attested by AC, also <**ts'kw'éx qas te isá:la**>, //c'=k'ʷə́xʸ qɛs tə ʔisɛ́·lɛ//, attested by CT 9/5/73, <**láts'ewets qas kwe isále**>, //lɛ́c'=əwəc qɛs kwə isɛ́lə//, /'*one hundred and two*'/, attested by AC, <**isále mít**>, //ʔisɛ́lə mít//, /'*twenty cents*'/, literally /'two dimes'/, attested by AC, <**xwel isá:le**>, //xʷəl ʔisɛ́·lə//, /'*There's only two., There's just two., [There's still two.]*'/, attested by EB, <**isále tel s'íth'em**>, //ʔisɛ́lə t-əl s=ʔíθ'ə=m//, /'*I have two clothes., I have two blankets., I have two garments.*'/, attested by Elders Group.

<**isáles**>, dnom //ʔisɛ́lə=s//, TIME /'*two o'clock, two hours*'/, NUM, lx <**=s**> *o'clock, hours, cyclic periods*, syntactic analysis: nominal, attested by AC; example: <**wetéses te isáles**>, //wə-tə́s-əs tə ʔisɛ́lə=s//, /'*when it gets to two o'clock, when it's two o'clock*'/, syntactic analysis: when-intransitive verb-subjunctive subject pronoun3 demonstrative article num=o'clock, attested by AC, <**wetéses te s'ó:pels qas kwe isále**>, //wə-təs-əs tə s=ʔá·pəl=s qɛs kʷə ʔisɛ́lə//, /'*when it gets to twelve o'clock*'/, literally /'when it gets to/reaches the ten=o'clock and the two'/, syntactic comment: note that in *eleven o'clock* and *twelve o'clock* (compound numerals) only the first part of the numeral needs to be inflected for *o'clock*, attested by AC.

<**islá**>, dnom //ʔisɛlə[=M2]//, NUM ['*two things*'], (<**metathesis**> *things*), phonology: metathesis, syntactic analysis: nominal, attested by IHTTC; example: <**islá tel sxélcha**>, //ʔisɛ́lə=M2 t-əl s=xʸə́lcɛ//, /'*I caught two things .*'/, literally /'is two things my catch'/, attested by IHTTC, <**islá tel hóy**>, //ʔisɛ́lə=M2 t-əl háy//, /'*I finish*ed two things.'/, literally /'is two things what-I finish(ed)'/, attested by IHTTC.

<**islálews**>, dnom //ʔisl=ɛ́ləws//, EB ['*two leaves*'], NUM, lx <**=álews**> *leaf*, phonology: ʔisɛ́lə[=M2]=ɛ́ləws is less likely (metathesis required here by lexically-determined morphophonemic rule) than just an allomorph, //ʔisl//, produced historically by 1) loss of root stress (variable stress valence) to the stressed suffix (strong stress valence), 2) subsequent vowel-loss in normal-to-rapid speech; more examples below, syntactic analysis: nominal, attested by AD, Elder's comment: "may be correct".

<**islá:ltexw**>, dnom //ʔisl=ɛ́·ltəxʷ//, SOC ['*man with two wives*'], NUM, lx <**=á:ltexw**> *man with multiple wives* may be related **to** <**=á:wtxw**> *house,* phonology: strong-stress-valenced suffix attracts stress from variable-stress-valenced root and root allomorph then loses its last two vowels, syntactic analysis: nominal, attested by Elders Group 7/27/75.

<**isá:lhp ~ s'isá:lhp**>, dnom //ʔisɛ́·=əɬp ~ s=ʔisɛ́·=əɬp//, EB ['*two trees*'], NUM, lx <**=elhp**> *tree,* phonology: loss of final root syllable is allomorphic rule here which probably developed from *isá:l=lhp through consonant merger, syntactic analysis: nominal, attested by Elders Group 3/19/75; example: <**tsel xáq'et tel isá:lhp**>, //c-əl xʸɛ́q'=əT t-əl ʔisɛ́·=əɬp//, /'*I felled my two trees.*'/, attested by Elders Group 3/19/75,

<**isalámeth'**>, dnom //ʔisɛlə=ɛ́məθ'//, MC /'*two ropes, two threads, two sticks, two poles, two poles standing up*'/, NUM, lx <**=ámeth'**> *pole, stick, pole standing, rope, thread,* syntactic analysis: nominal, attested by AD, also <**isalámets'**>, //ʔisɛlə=ɛ́məc'//, attested by some elders in the Elders Group 2/5/75.

<**islá:wes**>, dnom //ʔisl=ɛ́·wəs//, CAN /'*two paddles; two paddlers*'/, NUM, lx <**=á:wes ~ =ő́wes**> *canoe paddles, paddlers,* syntactic analysis: nominal.

<**islá:wtxw**>, dnom //ʔisl=ɛ́·wtxʷ//, BLDG ['*two houses*'], NUM, lx <**=á:wtxw**> *house, building,* syntactic analysis: nominal.

<**isláyiws**>, dnom //ʔisl=ɛ́yiws//, CLO ['*two pants*'], NUM, lx <**=áyiws**> *pants* from < **=áy**> *bark, wool, covering* + lx <**=íws**> *on the body,* syntactic analysis: nominal, attested by AD.

<**Isléleqw**>, dnom //ʔisl=ə́ləqʷ//, PLN ['*Isolillock Mountain (this spelling on topographic map)*'], ASM ['this mountain is by Silver Creek on the C.N. side of the Fraser R., can be seen from Hope and above'], literally /'double-headed'/, ANA, NUM, lx <**=éleqw**> *on top of the head, head,* syntactic analysis: nominal, attested by MP, AD, SP, source: place name file reference #32, also called <**Tl'ítl'xeleqw**>, //C_1í=ƛ'əxʸ=ələqʷ//, attested by AK, ME, others, see latter name for more traditions about the mountain.

<**islélwet**>, dnom //ʔisl=ə́lwət//, CLO /'*two garments, two (items of) clothes*'/, NUM, lx <**=élwet**> *clothing,* syntactic analysis: nominal.

<**isáleqel**>, dnom //ʔisɛ́lə=əqəl//, MC ['*two containers*'], NUM, HHG, lx <**=eqel**> *containers,* syntactic analysis: nominal, attested by AD.

<**iselíqw**>, dnom //ʔisələ[=M2]=íqʷ//, FSH ['*two fish*'], EZ, NUM, lx <**=íqw**> *fish; on top of the head,* syntactic analysis: nominal, attested by BHTTC.

<**iselíws**>, dnom //ʔisələ=íws//, EZ ['*two birds*'], NUM, lx <**=íws**> *bird; on the body, on the skin, on the covering,* syntactic analysis: nominal, attested by Elders 3/29/77, also <**islíws**>, //ʔisl=íws//, attested by TM.

<**isálemó:t**>, dnom //ʔisɛ́lə=má·t//, NUM ['*two kinds*'], lx <**=mó:t**> *kinds, piles of things,* syntactic analysis: nominal, adjective/adjectival verb, attested by Elders 7/27/75, also <**isálemò:t**>, //ʔisɛ́lə=mà·t//, also /'*two kinds*'/, attested by IHTTC 7/28/77.

<**isòls** >**?** possibly, dnom //ʔis=àls//, EB ['*two fruit in a group (as they grow on a plant)*'], NUM, lx <**=ó:ls**> *fruit, rocks, spherical things,* phonology: the root allomorph is not a very common one, syntactic analysis: nominal, attested by AD unsure.

<**islóqw**>, dnom //ʔisl=áqʷ or ʔis=láqʷ//, EZ ['*two birds*'], NUM, lx <**=áqw**> *?bird* elsewhere ~ <**=íqw**> *on top of head, hair, head of river, head of descendants,* syntactic analysis: nominal, attested by Elders Group 1/30/80.

<**isó:les**>, dnom //ʔisɛ́[=Aá(·)=]lə=əs//, MC /'*two dollars,* [Boas] *two Indian blankets*'/, NUM, lx <**=es**> *face, dollar,* phonology: this suffix (but not <**=es**> *hours, o'clock*) triggers ablaut of a to o

(/ɛ/ to /a/), syntactic analysis: nominal, attested by EB, also /'*two Indian blankets, two dollars*'/, source: Boas 1890 ["Sk·'au'lits (Scowlitz dialect) = Lower Fraser" word list, field notes; APS Library]; example: <**ílhchel x̱ethós te isó:les**>, //ʔi-ɬ-c-əl x̣əθ=ás tə ʔisɛ[=Aá·=]lə=əs//, /'*I bet (past tense) two dollars.*'/, attested by EB, <**epóles qas te isóles i ta' s'ehólets tl'esu sóles**>, //ʔápə[=M2=]l=əs qɛs tə ʔisɛ́[=Aá=]lə=əs ʔi t-ɛʔ s=ʔəhá=ləc ƛ'a-s=əw sí[=Aá=]l=əs//, /'*Ten dollars and two dollars in your pocket and you're drunk.*'/ (a kind of rhyming joke), phonology: metathesis, ablaut (triggered by =es *dollars*), stress-shifting, vowel combination, usage: a rhyme (not traditional), attested by RJ, <**epóles qas kwe isále**>, //ʔápə[=M2=]l=əs qɛs kʷə ʔisɛ́lə//, /'*twelve dollars*'/, attested by AC.

<**islṓwelh ? or isṓwelh ?**>, possibly //ʔisl=ówəɬ or ʔis=ówəɬ//, CAN /'*two canoes, two boats*'/, lx <**=ōwelh**> *canoe, boat*, syntactic analysis: nominal, attested by AD unsure.

<**yáysele ~ yéysele**>, dnom //ʔi=ʔisɛ́[=M2=]lə//, [yǽysələ ~ yéysələ], HUMC ['*two people*'], EZ ['*two supernatural creatures*'], NUM, lx <**metathesis and irregular type of reduplication**> *people (classifier)*, phonology: /yɛ́ysələ/ < //i=ɛ́=isələ// (with the second /i/ probably epenthetic and the first /ə/ by vowel-reduction from an unstressed /i/ metathesized to that position), thus probably < //i=ɛ́silə// < //ʔi=ʔisɛ́[=M2=]lə// (with consonant-loss of both glottal stops and an unusual reduplication type, C1V1= (R11), which could be called doubling prefix #1 with same vowel= but is not attested elsewhere); when both glottal stops were lost both /i/'s became /y/'s; the reduplication type is not attested elsewhere, but neither is doubling prefix with ó=, the reduplication type for lólets'e /lá=ləc'ə/ 'one person', in the same set of classified numerals) thus from //R11=ʔisɛ́[=M2=]lə//, syntactic analysis: nominal, attested by Elders Group, AC, NP, EB, Deming, ASM ['two people']; found in <**yéyseletset**>, //yɛ́ysələ-c-ət//, /'*two of us*'/, attested by AC, ASM ['two supernatural creatures']; example: <**yéysele sásq'ets**>, //yɛ́ysələ sɛ́sq'əc (or C_1ɛ́=səq'=əc)//, /'*two sasquatches*'/, attested by NP, EB, <**yáysele te sásq'ets**>, //yɛ́ysələ tə sɛ́sq'əc//, /'*There's two sasquatches.*'/, attested by Deming, <**yáysele shxwexwós**>, //yɛ́ysələ s=xʷəxʷ=ás//, /'*two Thunderbirds*'/, attested by Elders Group 1/30/80, <**yáysele te stl'áléqem**>, //yɛ́ysələ tə s=ƛ'ɛ́lə́qəm//, /'*There's two stl'áleqems (supernatural creatures).*'/, attested by Deming, <**yáysele s'ó:lmexw (?)**>, //yɛ́ysələ s=ʔá·l=məxʷ//, /'*two black water babies*'/, attested by Elders Group 1/30/80, <**yáysele te th'ōwx̱eye**>, //yɛ́ysələ tə θ'ówəx̣=ɛyə//, /'*There are two cannibal ogresses.*'/, attested by Elders Group 1/30/80, contrast <**isále te sílhqey**>, //ʔisɛ́lə tə síɬqəy//, /'*There's two double-headed snakes.*'/, attested by Deming.

<**sílhqey**>, cpds //ʔis[=M1=]=(ʔɛ)ɬqəy//, EZ ['*supernatural double-headed snake*'], syntactic analysis: nominal, attested by Deming.

<**isalámeth'**>, MC /'*two ropes, two threads, two sticks, two poles, two poles standing up*'/, *see* isá:le ~ isále ~ isá:la.

<**isálemó:t**>, NUM ['*two kinds*'], *see* isá:le ~ isále ~ isá:la.

<**isáleqel**>, MC ['*two containers*'], *see* isá:le ~ isále ~ isá:la.

<**isáles**>, TIME /'*two o'clock, two hours*'/, *see* isá:le ~ isále ~ isá:la.

<**isá:lhp ~ s'isá:lhp**>, EB ['*two trees*'], *see* isá:le ~ isále ~ isá:la.

<**iselíqw**>, FSH ['*two fish*'], *see* isá:le ~ isále ~ isá:la.

<**iselíws**>, EZ ['*two birds*'], *see* isá:le ~ isále ~ isá:la.

<**islá**>, NUM ['*two things*'], *see* isá:le ~ isále ~ isá:la.

<**islálews**>, EB ['*two leaves*'], *see* isá:le ~ isále ~ isá:la.

<**islá:ltexw**>, SOC [*'man with two wives'*], *see* isá:le ~ isále ~ isá:la.

<**islá:wes**>, CAN /*'two paddles; two paddlers'*/, *see* isá:le ~ isále ~ isá:la.

<**islá:wtxw**>, BLDG [*'two houses'*], *see* isá:le ~ isále ~ isá:la.

<**isláyiws**>, CLO [*'two pants'*], *see* isá:le ~ isále ~ isá:la.

<**Isléleqw**>, PLN [*'Isolillock Mountain (this spelling on topographic map)'*], *see* isá:le ~ isále ~ isá:la.

<**islélwet**>, CLO /*'two garments, two (items of) clothes'*/, *see* isá:le ~ isále ~ isá:la.

<**islóqw**>, EZ [*'two birds'*], *see* isá:le ~ isále ~ isá:la.

<**islő̃welh**> **?** or <**iső̃welh** > **?**, CAN /*'two canoes, two boats'*/, *see* isá:le ~ isále ~ isá:la.

<**isó:les**>, MC /*'two dollars, [Boas] two Indian blankets'*/, *see* isá:le ~ isále ~ isá:la.

<**isòls** > **?**, EB [*'two fruit in a group (as they grow on a plant)'*], *see* isá:le ~ isále ~ isá:la.

<**ístexw ó**>, DIR /*'leave this here, leave s-th here'*/, *see* í.

<**ítet**>, free root //ʔítət//, ABFC /*'sleep, go to sleep, asleep'*/, syntactic analysis: intransitive verb, attested by AC, BJ, AD, EB, AH, other sources: ES /ʔí·tət/, JH /ʔítət/, ASM ['sleep']; example: <**éwelh ítet**>, //ʔə́wə=ɬ ʔítət//, /*'He never sleeps.'*/, attested by EB, <**éwelhtsel ítet**>, //ʔə́wə=ɬ-c-əl ʔítət//, /*'I never sleep.'*/, attested by EB, <**tsel we'ólwe ítet**>, //c-əl wə=ʔál=wə ʔítət//, /*'I overslept ., I slept too much.'*/, attested by EB, <**li éy ta' s'ítet**>, //li ʔɛ́y t-ɛʔ s-ʔítət//, /*'Did you sleep well?'*/, attested by Elders at Fish Camp, also <**lichxw we'ítet kw'e éy**>, //li-c-x^w wə=ʔítət k'^{w}ə ʔɛ́y//, attested by Elders at Fish Camp, also <**i uw'éy el s'ítet ?**>, //ʔi ʔəw=ɛ́y ʔəl s-ʔítət//, attested by AH, ASM ['go to sleep'], <**lámtselcha ítet welámescha tu lhóp**>, //lɛ́=m-c-əl-cɛ ʔítət wə-lɛ́=m-əs-cɛ tu ɬáp//, /*'I'm going to go to sleep later in the night.'*/, literally /'I am going to go to sleep when it is going to be a little later in the night.'/, attested by AD, ASM ['asleep'], <**welh tu ítet**>, //wəɬ tu ʔítət//, /*'nearly asleep'*/, literally /'already a little asleep'/, attested by EB.

<**í:tet**>, cts //ʔí[-·-]tət//, ABFC /*'sleeping, asleep'*/, (<-:-> *continuative*), syntactic analysis: intransitive verb, attested by AC, EB, other sources: JH /ʔí·tət/ *sleeping* vs. /ʔítət/ *to sleep*, ASM ['asleep']; example: <**la í:tet**>, //lɛ ʔí[-·-]tət//, /*'He's asleep.'*/, attested by AC, ASM ['sleeping'], <**t'wa í:tet, th'íth'eplexw**>, //t'wɛ ʔí[-·-]tət, C_1í=θ'əp=l-əx^w//, /*'He must be sleeping, his eyes are closed., He must be sleeping, he's closed his eyes.'*/, literally /'it must be he's sleeping, closed them (his eyes) a little'/, attested by EB.

<**lexwshxw'í:tet**>, dnom //ləx^w=s=x^w=ʔí[-·-]tət//, ABFC [*'sleepy-head'*], EFAM, (<**lexw=**> *always*, s= *nominalizer*, xw= *one who*), syntactic analysis: nominal, attested by IHTTC.

<**ítetem**>, stvi //ʔítət=təm//, ABFC [*'sleepy'*], <=tem> *stative*, phonology: consonant deletion of same consonant (//t=t// → /t/), syntactic analysis: intransitive verb, attested by AC, AD, others, also <**í:tetem**>, //ʔí[-·-]tət=(t)əm//, attested by EK, DK (the Kellys); example: <**tsel xwel ítetem**>, //c-əl x^{w}əl ʔítət=əm//, /*'I'm still sleepy.'*/, attested by AD.

<**itetlómet**>, ncrs //ʔitət=l-ámət//, ABFC [*'fall asleep'*], syntactic analysis: intransitive verb; example: <**lích(e)xw itetlómet**>, //lí-c-(ə)x^w ʔitət=l-ámət//, /*'Did you fall asleep?'*/.

<**itetáwtxw**>, dnom //ʔitət=ɛ́wtx^w//, BLDG /*'bedroom, hotel'*/, lx <**=áwtxw**> *building*, syntactic analysis: nominal, attested by CT, HT, EB, Deming.

<**ítey**>, possible bound root //ʔítəy//, meaning unknown

<**s'íteyí:les**>, stvi //s=ʔítəy=í·ləs//, BSK [*'carry a packstrap around the shoulders and across the chest at the collarbone'*], CLO, FSH, HARV, HUNT, SOC, TVMO, (<**s=**> *stative*), lx <**=í:les**> *on the chest*, syntactic analysis: intransitive verb, attested by IHTTC.

<**íth'a**>, bound root //ʔíθ'ɛ *clothing*//.

<**=íth'a**>, //**=íθ'ɛ**//, lx <, CLO /'*clothing, material*'/, WV, HHG, syntactic analysis: derivational suffix, also <**=íth'e**>, //=íθ'ə//; found in <**papíth'a**>, //C_1έ(=)pɛ=íθ'ɛ//, /'*flannelette, velvet, woolly material, soft material*'/, root <**pápa**> *woolly*, phonology: reduplication, attested by IHTTC, <**lhewíth'a**>, //ɬɛw=íθ'ɛ//, [ɬəwíθ'ɛ], /'*be naked*'/, phonology: the vowel change /ɛ/ → /ə/ is a result of the morphophonemic rule that changes vowels in weak-grade or medium-grade roots or affixes to /ə/ in the presence of a stronger-grade root or affix within the word; less likely is the possibility that the vowel change is derivational ablaut, [=Aə=], root <**lhá:w**> *abandon, escape from, run away from*, attested by AC, EB, <**lhuwth'ám**>, //ɬuw=iθ'ɛ=´=əm//, /'*take off clothes, (undress)*'/, phonology: stress shift, also /u/ from /əw/, attested by EB (compare root <**lhaw**> *abandon, escape from, run away from)*; found also in <**Kw'eqwálíth'**à ~ **Kw'ōqwálíth'a**>, //k'^{w}əq^w=έl=íθ'ὲ (ə ~ o)//, /'*Coqualeetza (a place in present day Sardis, B.C.)*'/, literally /'club + ? + clothes; at least two different stories account for the origin of this placename from *club*'/, <**lhōwíth'e ~ lhewíth'**à>, //(AC) ɬow=íθ'ə ~ (DM) ɬəw=íθ'ὲ//, /'*naked*'/, <**lhōwth'ám**>, //ɬow=θ'έ=m//, /'*to undress*'/, <**íth'em**>, //ʔíθ'əm//, /'*get dressed*'/, <**s'íth'em**>, //s=ʔíθ'əm//, /'*clothes, clothing*'/, <**spoleqwíth'**à>, //spaləq^w=íθ'ὲ//, /'*corpse, ghost*'/, literally /'(probably clothing of the spirit)'/, <**sqeló:líth'a**>, //s=qəl[=Aá·=l=]=íθ'ɛ//, /'*west wind*'/, literally possibly /'something that dirties clothes'/.

<**íth'em**>, mdls //ʔíθ'ɛ=əm//, [ʔíθ'əm], CLO /'*to dress, get dressed*'/, (<**=em**> *middle voice*), syntactic analysis: intransitive verb, also <**í:th'em**>, //ʔí·θ'əm//, attested by AC; found in <**íth'emchexw**>, //ʔíθ'ɛ=əm-c-əx^w//, /'*Get dressed.*'/, attested by AD.

<**ith'emáwtxw**>, dnom //ʔiθ'ɛ=əm=έwtx^w//, BLDG /'*clothes store, clothing store*'/, CLO, lx <**=áwtxw**> *house, building*, syntactic analysis: nominal.

<**s'íth'em**>, dnom //s=ʔíθ'ɛ=əm//, //sʔíθ'əm//, CLO /'*clothes, clothing (esp. Indian clothing, men's or women's), something to wear, dress, gown*'/, literally /'something to clothe oneself'/, (<**s=**> *nominalizer, something to*), syntactic analysis: nominal, attested by AD, Elders Group, also <**s'í:th'em ~ s'íth'em**>, //s=ʔí·θ'ɛ=əm ~ s=ʔíθ'ɛ=əm//, attested by AC, ES, other sources: ES /sʔí·θ'əm/; example: <**ewá:ta a s'íth'em**>, //ʔəwə=ə[=´=]=tɛ ʔɛ s=ʔíθ'əm//, /'*Have you got anything to wear?*'/, literally /'Is there none, your something to wear/clothes?'/, attested by AC.

<**s'oth'ó:mes**>, dnom //s=ʔi[=Aa=]θ'ɛ[=Aá·=]m=əs or s=ʔi[=Aa=]θ'ɛ=m=á·[=M2=]s//, CLO ['*big shawl*'], ASM ['made of woven wool before the White man came'], literally /'something to wear/clothing on the face'/, possibly <**o-ablaut**> *derivational*, possibly <**metathesis**> *derivational*, lx <**=es ~ =ó:s**> *on the face*, phonology: possible double ablaut (the second perhaps automatically triggered by =əs ~ =ó:s *on the face* as is attested in many other places), or ablaut on V1 plus possible metathesis between V2 and V3, syntactic analysis: nominal, also <**s'ath'ó:mes**>, //s=ʔi[=Aɛ=]θ'ɛ[=Aá·=]m=əs or s=ʔiθ'ɛ[=M2=]=əm=á·[=M2=]s//, phonology: phonologically very complex with double ablaut, double methathesis or double assimilation; it is possible that a principle of vowel-preservation is behind metathesis and examples like this, that is, "preserve" the root and/or affix vowels by trading them to show derivation rather than by changing them with no trace of the original vowels which help show the semantic connection; thus here one could imagine that the second vowel <a> /ɛ/ was moved to first position, and the suffix vowel was moved to second position, attested by Elders Meeting ll/26/75, also <**s'oth'ómes**> attested by RG & EH (4/10/99 Ling332), contrast <**sxwehóthes**> *veil* (TG 4/23/75).

<**s'oth'ó:mő̄sem**>, mdls //s=ʔi[=Aa=]θ'ɛ[=Aá·=]m=ə́ws=əm or s=ʔi[=Aa=]θ'ɛ[=Aá·=]m=ə[=Aó=]s=əm//, CLO ['*put on a shawl*'], possibly <**ő-ablaut**> *derivational*? (unlikely), probably <**o-ablaut and ó:-ablaut**> *derivational*, lx <**=ews ~ =ōws**> *on*

the body, phonology: one unlikely derivation of this word has the suffix =es *on the face* retained here with a third ablaut added; the other possibility is that the suffix for *face* is replaced by the one for *body* for the implication of a *body-shawl* here rather than a head-shawl, double ablaut retained from s'oth'ó:mes, syntactic comment: note that there are two layers of middle voice here; the earliest was applied to made the words *get dressed* and *clothing* from which the word for *shawl* was created; then *shawl* was inflected with another middle voice to yield *put on a shawl*, attested by Elders Meeting 1/21/76.

<**eth'íwsem**>, mdls //ʔíθ'ɛ=ə[=M2=]ws=əm//, CLO ['*put on a dress*'], lx <**=ews**> *on the body*, phonology: metathesis, syntactic analysis: intransitive verb, attested by AD.

<**(=)l=íth'e**>, //**(=)l=íθ'**ə//, WV ['*processed fiber*'], ASM ['from dog or goat wool; fluff from fireweed and cottonwood might be added'], (semological comment: this word or suffix seems to apply to processed fiber since =álqel refers to *raw wool*), CLO, HHG, ANAA, (semological comment: =el is sometimes proven to be a *pluralizer* in Upriver Halkomelem lexical suffixes and it may serve that function here too), syntactic analysis: derivational suffix or nominal??; found in <**qweqwemaylíth'e**>, //C_1í[-Aə-]=qʷəm=ɛy=l=íθ'ɛ//, /'*dog wool fiber*'/, ASM ['sometimes mixed with cedar fiber or perhaps nettle fiber to make it soft and warm for clothes'], (<**R4=**> *diminutive*), (<**e-ablaut on R4**> *plural of diminutive*), phonology: reduplication, ablaut, attested by AD.

<**íth'em**>, CLO /'*to dress, get dressed*'/, *see* íth'a.

<**ith'emáwtxw**>, BLDG /'*clothes store, clothing store*'/, *see* íth'a.

<**=í(:)tsel**> da //=í(·)cəl//, ANA *on the back, on the surface, on the top,* clearly related to <**=ewíts ~ =íts ~ =ích ~ =ech**>, da //=əw(=)íc ~ =íc ~ =əc//, ANA ['*on the back*'], DIR ['*on the back of something*'] (first allomorph possibly has <**=ew**> *on the body),* see that main entry under allomorph <**=ewits**> where <**=í(:)tsel**> and <**=etsel**> are reported as allomorphs (however without <**=ew**> *body* and with a probable add <**=el**>, <**=í(:)tsel**> and <**=etsel**> may have the broader allosemes *on the surface, on the top* (see examples here), syntactic analysis: lexical suffix, derivational suffix; found in <**sx̱ep'í:tsel**>, //sx̣əp'=í·cəl//, /'*chipmunk*'/, literally /'scratch or scrape on back'/, <**sx̱ex̱ep'í:tsel**>, //s=x̣əx̣əp'=í·cəl//, /'*chipmunk with multiple stripes on his back*'/, <**sqwómàtsel**>, //sqʷám=ɛ̀cəl//, /'*hunchback, lump on the back*'/, root <**qʷem**> *lump,* possibly <**tslhítselxel**>, //cɬ=ícəl=xʸəl//, /'*top of the foot*'/, literally /'upper back/surface/top of foot)'/, <**q'áwetsel**>, //q'ɛ́w=əcəl//, /'*dorsal fin (long fin on back of fish)*'/, literally perhaps /'turn in river on back/surface/top'/, <**qw'es=í:tsel**> *swallow (bird)* lit. *go in the water on the surface?* referring to its flight skimming surfaces)(cf. also Suttles ca1984:14.5.67 where Musqueam /=ícən ~ =əcən/ is given this range of meanings, *surface, top, back* with convincing examples

<**í:ts'el**>, incs //ʔí·c'=əl//, SOC ['*temporarily lazy*'], DESC, (<**=el**> *inceptive, get, become, go, come*), syntactic analysis: intransitive verb, attested by Deming, Elders Group; example: <**tsel í:ts'el**>, //c-əl ʔí·c'=əl//, /'*I'm lazy.*'/, usage: , semantic environment ['if someone comes by to ask you to go with him you can answer this'], attested by Elders Group.

<**lexws'í:ts'el**>, dnom //ləxʷ=s=ʔí·c'=əl//, SOC ['*person who is always lazy*'], (<**lexw=**> *always*, s= *nominalizer*), syntactic analysis: nominal, attested by EB, also <**lexws'ú:met**>, //ləxʷ=s=ʔa[=Aú·=]mət//, attested by EB (compare <**lexws'ú:met**>).

<**=í:wa ~ =í:wá: ~ =el=áwa**>, da //=í·wɛ ~ =í·wɛ́· ~ =əl=ɛ́wɛ//, MC possibly /'*cord, rope*'/, ANA, syntactic analysis: lexical suffix, derivational suffix; found in <**thelí:wá:xel**>, //θəlí·wɛ́·=xʸəl//, /'*snowshoes*'/, literally /'cover/pad under rope/cord on the foot'/, possibly root <**thél**> ?*cover under/pad under*, lx <**=xel**> *on the foot*, <**xixweláwa**>, //xʸi[=C_1ə=W=]ə=əl=ɛ́wɛ//, /'*fish air bladder*'/ (possible root <**xíwe**> *urinate)*, possibly <**=R1= plus labialization**> *continuative.*

<**iwá:ltses**>, PLAY [*'cat's-cradle'*], *see* ewólem.

<**=í:wel ~ =íwel ~ =ewel**>, da //=í·wəl ~ =íwəl ~ =əwəl//, ANA /*'in the rump, in the anus, in the rectum, in the bottom; on the insides, inside parts, core, inside the head'*/, EB [*'inside or core of a plant or fruit (or canoe or anything)'*], CAN [*'inside/core of a canoe'*], DIR [*'inside/core of anything'*], (semological comment: =í:wel ~ =íwel may refer mainly to rump/anus--=ewel to the more general inside of anything--check this in examples), syntactic analysis: lexical suffix, derivational suffix, also <**=ewel**>, //=əwəl//; found in <**ch'iyxwí:wel ~ ts'iyxwí:wel**>, //c'iyxʷ=í·wəl//, /*'constipated'*/, literally /'dry in the rump'/, <**xaxekw'í:wel**>, //x̣ɛx̣ək'ʷ=í·wəl//, /*'constipated'*/, literally /'wedged tight in the rump'/, <**t'ekwí:wel**>, //t'əkʷ=í·wəl//, /*'constipated'*/, literally /'mired in the rump'/, <**(s)ts'ep(x)í:wel**>, //(s)c'əp(x̣)=í·wəl//, /*'dirty asshole'*/, (semological comment: this translation by several elders captures the shocking tone of the word), usage: crude, <**sq'eyxí:wel**>, //sq'ix̣=í·wəl//, /*'black asshole'*/, (semological comment: these last two translations by several elders capture the shock-value of the word), usage: crude, <**th'qw'í:wel**>, //θ'q'ʷ=í·wəl//, /*'open sores in rump, hemorrhoids'*/, <**st'elmexwí:wel**>, //st'əlməxʷ=í·wəl//, /*'love medicine, (aphrodisiac)'*/, literally /'medicine for genitals)'/, <**sts'elxwíwel**>, //s=c'ələxʷ=íwəl//, /*'insides (all the organs inside an animate being)'*/, <**méth'elhqìwèl**>, //mə́θ'əɬ=q=íwəl//, /*'woodtick'*/, literally /'pus closable container inside'/, phonology: dowstepping, updrifting,(perhaps) <**t'emewí:lt**>, //t'əm=əwí·l=t//, /*'chop the inside of it out'*/, (perhaps) <**xepewí:lt**>, //xʸəp=əwí·lt//, /*'plane it out inside'*/, <**sth'emíwél**>, //sθ'əm=íwəl//, /*'core, pith, seed, nut, center (of rock or anything)'*/, <**sqwa'í:wel**>, //sqʷɛ=ʔí·wəl//, /*'hollow'*/, literally /'hole on inside'/, <**sqwehí:wel**>, //sqʷəh=í·wəl//, /*'tunnel, hole, hollow'*/, <**(s)tl'epí:wel ~ tl'pí:wel**>, //(s)ƛ'(ə)p=í·wəl//, /*'shirt, undershirt, bra'*/, literally /'below or deep on inside'/, <**simíwél**>, //s=(ʔ)iy=(ə)m=íwə́l//, /*'strong feelings or mad all the time but won't fight'*/, literally /'strong on insides'/, <**lhekw'í:wel**>, //ɬək'ʷ=í·wəl//, /*'be surprised'*/, literally /'fly on insides'/, <**xwoyí:wel**>, //xʷay=í·wəl//, /*'happy, happy inside'*/, <**sqwálewel**>, //sqʷɛ́l=əwəl//, /*'thoughts, feelings'*/, literally /'talk or speech on insides'/.

<**íwel**>, bound root //íwəl//.

<**íweltàlem**>, ds //ʔíwəl=tə[=Aɛ̀=]l=əm//, HUNT [*'set a snare trap'*], lx <**=tel**> *device, thing for*, (<**à-ablaut**> *derivational*, <**=em**> *intransitivizer*), phonology: ablaut, downstepping, syntactic analysis: intransitive verb.

<**s'eweltá:l**>, dnom //s=ʔí[=Aə=]wəl=tə[=Aɛ́·=]l//, HUNT /*'snare, snare trap'*/, (<**e-ablaut and á:-ablaut**> *derivational*), (<**s=**> *nominalizer*), (<**=tel**> *device, thing for*), phonology: ablaut, syntactic analysis: nominal, attested by Elders Group 3/15/78, also <**íweltàlt**>, //ʔíwəl=tɛ̀l=t//, HUNT [*'spring snare trap'*], (semological comment: no derivational affix =t is known elsewhere; it may be that the suffix is -t *purposeful control transitivizer* and that the translation of íweltàlt should be *set it (snare trap), set a snare),* attested by Elders Group 10/20/76, also <**íweltà:lt**>, //ʔíwəl=tɛ́·l=t//, HUNT /*'snare, deadfall'*/, (semological comment: see comment on íweltàlt above), attested by Elders Group 11/26/75, also <**weltá:lt**>, //wəl=tə[=Aɛ́·=]l=t or better wɛ́·l=tə[=M2=]l=t//, HUNT [*'spring snare'*] (compare root <**wá:l=x**> *lift it* which shows the possible root of this word, phonology: if wá:l= *lift* is the root, then the form is better analyzed derivationally with metathesis, as /wɛ́·l=tə[=M2=]l=t/; the initial í, if not a prefix (ye= *travelling by*), otherwise is part of the root; attested by Deming 4/13/78, also <**t'í:tsel**>, //t'í·c(=)əl//, HUNT [*'spring snare'*], attested by Deming (compare root <**t'í:tsel**).

<**íweltàlem**>, HUNT [*'set a snare trap'*], *see* íwel.

<**íwes**>, free root //ʔíwəs//, SOC /*'teach how to do something, teach, guide, direct, show'*/, LANG, DIR, SCH, SENS, TVMO, ABFC, syntactic analysis: intransitive verb, attested by EB, Salish cognate:

Lushootseed /ʔúgʷus/ *teach, give directions, show, demonstrate* H76:680.

<**í:wes**>, cts //ʔi[-·-]´wəs//, SOC /'*directing, training, teaching, guiding*'/, MC, (<-:-> *continuative*), phonology: length-infixing, syntactic analysis: intransitive verb, attested by EB.

<**s'í:wes**>, dnom //s=ʔi[-·-]´wəs//, SOC /'*training, teaching, upbringing*'/, syntactic analysis: nominal, attested by Elders Group, AD; example: <**ewéta s'í:wes ta mámele**>, //ʔəwə= ´tɛ s=ʔi[-·-]´wəs t-ɛ C$_1$ɛ́-mələ//, /'*Your children have no training.*'/, attested by Elders Group, <**éy kws hákw'eleschet te s'í:wes te siyolexwálh**>, //ʔɛ́y kʷ-s hɛ́k'ʷ=ələs-c-ət tə s=ʔi[-·-]´wəs tə siyáləxʷə=ə́ɬ//, /'*Let us remember the teachings of the elders past.*'/, phonology: vowel merger, lengthening, syntactic comment: note the nominal past, attested by AD.

<**í:wesà:ls**>, sas //ʔi[-·-]´wəs=ɛ̀·ls//, TVMO ['*a guide*'], HUNT, HARV, FSH, CAN, lx <**=à:ls**> *structured activity (non-continuative)*, phonology: length after the i here as *continuative* is unusual since the suffix, =à:ls, usually has the form =els in the continuative and =á:ls in the non-continuative aspect, syntactic analysis: nominal with zero derivation (but preceded by a demonstrative article), attested by Elders Group 3/15/72.

<**íwest**>, pcs //ʔíwəs=T//, SOC /'*advise s-o, teach s-o, show s-o*'/, syntactic analysis: transitive verb, attested by Elders Group, AC; example: <**íwesthox ta sqwéltel**>, //ʔíwəs=T-axʸ t-ɛ s=qʷɛ[=Aə́=]l=təl//, /'*Teach me your language.*'/, syntactic comment: imperative subject is implied by the 2s possessive pronoun and therefore can be omitted as a verb inflection, attested by AC; found in <**iwesthométsel**>, //ʔiwəs=T-ámə-c-əl//, /'*I advise you.*'/, phonology: stress-shift automatically conditioned by following subject suffix, attested by Elders Group, <**iwesthométselcha**>, //ʔiwəs=T-ámə-c-əl-cɛ//, /'*I will advise you.*'/, attested by Elders Group.

<**í:west**>, cts //ʔi[-·-]´wəs=T//, MC /'*showing s-o (how to do it), teaching s-o, advising s-o, guiding s-o, directing s-o*'/, syntactic analysis: transitive verb, attested by AC, Elders Group 11/9/77, 12/7/77, 3/15/72; example: <**tsel xwel í:west**>, //c-əl xʷəl ʔi[-·-]´wəs=T//, /'*I'm still teaching him.*'/, attested by Elders 11/9/77.

<**iwestéleq**>, dnom //ʔíwəs=T=ə́ləq//, SOC /'teacher'/, lx <**=éleq**> one who, attested by Elders Group, BHHTC, AC

<**iwesáwtxw**>, dnom //ʔiwəs=ɛ́wtxʷ//, BLDG ['*schoolhouse*'], lx <**=áwtxw**> *building, house*, syntactic analysis: nominal, attested by Deming, also <**iwes-háltxw**>, //ʔiwəs=hɛ́ltxʷ//, phonology: epenthetic /h/, and /l/ instead of /w/ are two unusual features of this variant of the suffix =áwtxw, attested by Deming (SJ, LG both present).

<**s'iwesá:ylhem**>, dnom //s=ʔiwəs=ɛ́·yɬ=əm//, SOC /'*teachings for children, what is taught to one's children*'/, MC, (<**s=**> *nominalizer*), lx <**=á:ylh**> *children*, (<**=em**> *middle voice*), syntactic analysis: nominal, attested by Elders Group, also <**í:wesè:ylhem**>, //ʔi[-·-]´wəs=ɛ̀·yɬ=əm//, phonology: once pronounced í:wesà:ylhem, syntactic comment: without the s= nominalizer this pronunciation would be relativized instead by the preceding demonstrative article, attested by Deming (SJ, MC, MV, LG) 3/15/79; example: <**skw'á:y te s'iwesá:ylhem**>, //s=k'ʷɛ́·y tə s=ʔiwəs=ɛ́·yɬ=əm//, /'*teachings for children that are wrong*'/, attested by Elders Group.

<**í:weséleq**>, ds //ʔi[-·-]´wəs=ə́ləq//, MC ['*guiding*'], SOC, (<-:-> *continuative*), lx <**=éleq**> *as an occupation*, syntactic analysis: intransitive verb, attested by Elders Group 3/15/72.

<**í:wes**>, SOC /'*directing, training, teaching, guiding*'/, *see* íwes.

<**í:wesà:ls**>, TVMO ['*a guide*'], *see* íwes.

<**iwesáwtxw**>, BLDG ['*schoolhouse*'], *see* íwes.

<**í:weséleq**>, MC ['*guiding*'], *see* íwes.

<**íwest**>, SOC /'*advise s-o, teach s-o, show s-o*'/, *see* íwes.

<**í:west**>, MC */'showing s-o (how to do it), teaching s-o, advising s-o, guiding s-o, directing s-o'/*, *see* íwes.

<**iwestéleq**>, SOC /'teacher'/, *see* íwes

<**iwólem ~ í:wólem**>, PLAY [*'playing'*], *see* ewólem.

<**Iwówes**>, df //ʔiwáwəs//, PLN */'village at Union Bar,* now also *Hope Indian Reserve #5 (#15 in Duff 1952), Ay-wa-wis'/*, ASM ['located about 2 mi. above Hope on the east side of the Fraser River'], syntactic analysis: nominal, attested by Elders Group, PDP (Katz class), source: placenames reference file #14, other sources: Wells 1965:25.

<**=í:ws ~ =ews**>, da //=í·ws ~ =əws//, ANA */'on the body, on the skin, on the covering'/*, syntactic analysis: lexical suffix, derivational suffix; found in <**lhq'í:ws**>, //ɬq'=í·ws//, */'half the body'/*, <**slexwí:ws**>, //sləxʷ=í·w//, */'(living) body'/*, <**kw'sí:ws**>, //k'ʷs=í·ws//, */'singe hairs off skin'/*, <**qetí:wsem**>, //qət=í·ws=əm//, */'take a sweatbath'/*, literally /'steam/warm one's body'/, <**qw'emí:ws**>, //q'ʷəm=í·ws//, */'plucked (of a bird)'/*, <**qw'eméwst ~ qw'emṓwst**>, //q'ʷəm=ə́ws=t//, */'pluck it (of a bird)'/*, <**séqw'emí:ws**>, //sə́q'ʷəm=í·ws//, */'cedar bark skirt'/*, root <**síqw'em**> *peel cedar bark*, <**seqí:ws ~ sqí:ws**>, //səq=í·ws ~ sq=í·ws//, */'pants'/*, <**slewí:ws**>, //sləw=í·ws//, */'(woman's) dress'/*, literally (probably) /'opening on the body/covering'/, <**p'elyí:ws**>, //p'əly=í·ws//, */'bark of tree'/*, <**Yeqwyeqwí:ws**>, //yəqʷyəqʷ=í·ws//, */'Yakweakwioose (a village near Sardis)'/*, literally /'covering (of grass) burnt out repeatedly'/, <**s-hóyews**>, //s=háy=əws//, */'spirit-dancing costume'/*, literally perhaps */'final covering'/* from <**hóy**> *finish*)'/.

<**í:wth'elàq**>, SOC */'a teaser, somebody that teases to get one's goat'/*, *see* weth'át.

<**í:xel**>, CAN [*'paddling'*], *see* éxel.

<**íxwels**>, ABFC [*'scratching around'*], *see* exwá:ls.

<**íx̱**>, free root //ʔíx̣//, ABFC */'scratch, get scratched, scrape, get scraped'/*, syntactic analysis: intransitive verb, attested by AHTTC, EB; example: <**íx̱ te chálexs te Málí**>, //ʔíx̣ tə cɛ́ləxʸ-s tə mɛ́lí//, */'Mary scraped her arm., [Mary's lower arm got scraped.]'/*, attested by EB.

<**íx̱et**>, pcs //ʔíx̣=əT//, MC */'scrape it (of hide or anything), scrape s-o, erase it'/*, ABFC, BSK, FSH, HARV, HHG, HUNT, SCH, TCH, syntactic analysis: transitive verb, attested by EB, Elders Group, AHTTC, ASM ['erase it'], semantic environment ['writing implements, blackboard, paper, etc.'], attested by AHTTC.

<**í:x̱et**>, cts //ʔí[-·-]x̣=əT//, MC [*'scraping it'*], semantic environment ['like a pot one is scrubbing, etc.'], syntactic analysis: transitive verb, attested by EB.

<**ex̱ó:ythelem**>, mdls //ʔix̣=á·yθəl=əm or ʔi[=Aə=]x̣=á·yθəl=əm//, HHG [*'shave (the face)'*], possibly <**e-ablaut**> *derivational*, lx <**=ó:ythel**> *on the jaw, chin, lip*, (<**=em**> *middle voice*), phonology: the initial e probably shows a weaker vowel grade in the root than in the suffix, thus automatically changing root full i /i/ to e /ə/; less likely but possible is ablaut, syntactic analysis: intransitive verb, attested by EB, also <**ex̱ó:ythem**>, //ʔix̣=á·yθəl=əm//, (irregular)loss of el /əl/ is not expected, attested by EB, *<**ex̱ó:ythem tutl'o te s'óthes**> rejected, */'He shaved his face.'/*, attested by EB, also <**ex̱ó:ythìlèm ~ ex̱ó:ythílém**>, //ʔəx̣=á·yθəl=íl=əm//, also */'shave, shave oneself'/*, (<**=il**> *go, come, get*, <**=em**> *middle voice*), attested by EB, Elder's comment: "correct this to ex̱ó:ythem".

<**íx̱iyethílem**>, mdls //ʔíx̣=əyəθəl=íl=əm//, HHG [*'shaving'*], phonology: stress-shift changes suffix vowels to e /ə/, =íl causes preceding el to drop automatically, syntactic analysis: intransitive verb, attested by JL at Fish Camp 7/20/79.

<**éx̱qst**>, pcs //ʔi[=Aə́=]x̣=qs=T//, FIRE [*'strike s-th pointed (esp. a match)'*], (<**é-ablaut**> *derivational*), lx <**=qs**> *on the point, on the nose*, (<**=t**> *purposeful control transitivizer*),

phonology: ablaut, syntactic analysis: transitive verb, attested by CT, HT; example: <**éx̲qst te máches qesu yéqwt kw'e sísq' or kw'estámés**>, //ʔə́x̣=qs=T tə mɛ́cəs qə-su yə́qʷ=T k'ʷə C_1í=sq' or[English] k'ʷə=s=tɛ́m=ə́s//, /'*strike the match and light the kindling or something*'/, attested by CT, HT.

<**íx̲em**>, izs //ʔíx̣=əm//, SOC ['*get credit*'], (<**=em**> *have, get, intransitivizer*), possibly root <**íx̲**> *scrape, scratch*??, syntactic analysis: intransitive verb, dialects: *Chill., Pilalt*, attested by RM; example: <**látsel íx̲em**>, //lɛ́-c-əl ʔíx̣=əm//, /'*I'm going to get credit.*'/, attested by RM.

<**ex̲ímels**>, sas //ʔíx̣=ə[=M2=]m=əls//, SOC ['*to put on credit ??*'], (<**metathesis type 2**> *derivational*), (<**=em**> *intransitivizer*, <**=els**> *as a structured activity (continuative aspect)*), syntactic analysis: intransitive verb, attested by Deming.

<**ex̲ímt**>, pcs //ʔíx̣=ə[=M2=]m=T//, SOC /'*lend money to s-o, [give s-o credit]*'/, (<**metathesis type 2**> *derivational*), (<**=t**> *purposeful control transitivizer*), syntactic analysis: transitive verb, dialects: *Chill. (Sardis)*, attested by RM; example: <**melh ex̲ímthòx**>, //mə=ɬ ʔəx̣ím=T-àxʸ//, /'*Lend me money.*'/, (<**-lh**> *imperative 2s polite* after me *come*, <**-òx**> *lst person singular object*), dialects: *Chill. (Sardis)*, attested by RM.

<**ex̲ímstexw**>, caus //ʔíx̣=ə[=M2=]m=sT-əxʷ//, //ʔəx̣ímstəxʷ//, SOC ['*lend s-o money*'], (<**metathesis type 2**> *derivational*), (<**=st**> *causative control transitivizer*), syntactic analysis: transitive verb, attested by EB; example: <**ex̲ímsthoxes**>, //ʔíx̣=ə[=M2=]m=sT-axʸ-əs//, [ʔəx̣émsθaxʸɪs], /'*He lent me money.*'/, attested by EB.

<**íx̲et**>, MC /'*scrape it (of hide or anything), scrape s-o, erase it*'/, *see* íx̲.

<**í:x̲et**>, MC ['*scraping it*'], *see* íx̲.

<**íx̲iyethílem**>, HHG ['*shaving*'], *see* íx̲.

<**íx̲w**>, bound root //ʔíx̣ʷ//.

<**íx̲wet**>, pcs //ʔíx̣ʷ=əT//, BLDG ['*sweep it*'], FIRE, MC, syntactic analysis: transitive verb, attested by AC, M.H.; example: <**íx̲wet te lálem**>, //ʔíx̣ʷ=əT tə lɛ́ləm//, /'*sweep the house*'/, attested by AC, <**íx̲wet ta' sqel:ép**>, //ʔix̣ʷ=əT t-ɛʔ s=qəl=lə́p//, /'*Sweep up your trash.*'/, syntactic comment: 2s imperative sj implied by possessive pronoun affix used to modify the nominal object, thus no imperative inflection is required at all, attested by MH.

<**íx̲wethet**>, rfls //ʔíx̣ʷ=əT=ət//, //ʔíx̣ʷəθət//, BLDG /'*to sweep up, the sweep-up (last spirit dance of season in a given longhouse)*'/, FIRE, SPRD, syntactic analysis: intransitive verb, attested by RM, ASM ['the sweep-up (last spirit dance of season in a given longhouse)'], semantic environment ['spirit-dancing, winter gatherings'], ASM ['another name for the same spirit dance is yekw'ólhem "breaking the canoe (since the winter travelling is over)'], attested by RM.

<**s'íx̲w**>, stvi //s=ʔíx̣ʷ//, BLDG ['*be swept*'], FIRE, MC, DESC, syntactic analysis: adjective/adjectival verb, attested by AHTTC; example: <**li wulh s'íx̲w**>, //li wu=lh s=ʔíx̣ʷ//, /'*Is it swept?*'/, attested by AHTTC.

<**éx̲wtel**>, dnom //ʔi[=Aə=]´x̣ʷ=təl//, HHG ['*broom*'], (<**e-ablaut**> *derivational*), lx <**=tel**> *device, thing for*, phonology: ablaut, syntactic analysis: nominal, other sources: ES /ʔə́x̣ʷtəl/.

<**íx̲wet**>, BLDG ['*sweep it*'], *see* íx̲w.

<**íx̲wethet**>, BLDG /'*to sweep up, the sweep-up (last spirit dance of season in a given longhouse)*'/, *see* íx̲w.

<**=iya ~ =óya**>, da //=iyɛ ~ =áyɛ//, EFAM ['*affectionate diminutive*'], DESC, syntactic analysis: lexical suffix, derivational suffix, also <**=óya**>, //=áyɛ//; found in <**iyésiya or tá'iya**>, //ʔiyə́s=iyɛ or táʔ=iyɛ//, /'*darling, dear (mother to little girl)*'/ (compare <**iyés**> *dear female friend* and <**tó'**> *dear*

mother), <**Sqayéx̱iya**>, //sqɛyə́x̣=iyɛ//, /'*pet name of Mink*'/, <**wíthiya ~ wéthweth**>, //wíθ=iyɛ ~ wə́θ=C₁əC₂//, /'*snipe*'/, <**t'ámiya**>, //t'ɛ́m=iyɛ//, /'*little winter wren*'/, <**t'ámiya**>, //t'ɛ́m=iyɛ//, /'*hermaphrodite baby*'/, phonology: homophonous with *wren*, <**q'oyátl'iya**>, //q'ayɛ́ƛ'=iyɛ//, /'*snail*'/, <**sth'ímiya**>, //sθ'ím=iyɛ//, /'*small (landlocked) coho salmon*'/, comment: said to hatch from berry that drops in lake (compare <**sth'í:m**> *berry* and <**=iya**> *diminutive)*, possibly <**hő:liya ~ hú:liya**>, possibly //hó·l=iyɛ (o· ~ u)//, /'*humpback salmon*'/, possibly <**swetíya ~ swet'íya**>, //swət=íyɛ (t ~ t')//, /'*porcupine*'/, <**siyámiyam**>, //siyɛ́miyɛm//, dialects: *CT (ɛ́ ~ AC'sə́ here)*, /'*pregnant*'/, comment: possibly /**siyɛ́m**/ *leader, chief* + /=iyɛ/ *little* + /=ɛm/ *carry, use*, <**St'ít'ex̱eya**>, //s=C₁í=t'əx̣=əyɛ//, /'*Ruby Creek (near Seabird Island)*'/ (compare <**st'éx̱**> *fork in s-th*), <**X̱omó:th'iya**>, //x̣am=á·θ'=iyɛ//, /'*youngest sister of Mt. Cheam*'/ (compare <**x̱à:m**> *weep, cry* + <**=ó:meth'**> *standing, height* + <**=iya**>) (semological comment: so called because lots of creeks run together from her because she cries since she can't see the Fraser River), <**Slóx̱iya**>, //sláx̣=iyɛ//, /'*Indian name of Celia Thomas*'/, <**Xwemítsiya**>, //xʷəmíc=iyɛ//, /'*Indian name of Lucy, mother or other close relative of Celia Thomas*'/, <**Swolésiya**>, //swalə́s=iyɛ//, /'*Indian name of Al Guttierrez and his great grandfather Bill Swolésiya*'/, <**Selhámíya**>, //səɬɛ́m=íyɛ//, /'*Indian name of Jeanne McIntire (of Seabird)*'/, <**sisemóye**>, //sisəm=áyə//, /'*bee*'/ (compare possibly <**sí(:)sem**> *feel creepy, fear s-th behind*, <**sxó:ya**>, //s(=)xʸ=á·yɛ//, /'*co-wife, female rival of wife*'/ (compare <**s=**> *nominalizer* + <**x=**> *genitals* and compare <**=ó:ya**> *little)*, <**sxoyá:seq**>, //s=xʸ=ayɛ́·=s(=)əq//, /'*ex-wife's husband, wife's ex-husband, male rival of husband*'/ (compare <**=eq**> or perhaps here <**=seq**> *male*)..

<**iyáléqepthet**>, SM ['*starting to smell good*'], *see* **éy** ~ **éy**:.

<**iyálewes**>, EFAM ['*(be) brave*'], *see* **éy** ~ **éy**:.

<**iyálewet**>, EFAM ['*do s-th oneself*'], *see* **éy** ~ **éy**:.

<**iyálewet ~ eyálewet**>, TIB /'*do it, do it oneself*'/, *see* **éy** ~ **éy**:.

<**iyálewethet**>, EFAM /'*try to do something (no matter what, anyway)*'/, *see* **éy** ~ **éy**:.

<**iyá:q**>, ds //ʔiy(=)ɛ́·q//, KIN ['*girl's younger brother (pet name)*'], usage: pet name, possibly root <**ey**> *good*, possibly <**=á:q**> *male*, possibly root <**qá:q**> as in <**sqá:q**> *younger sibling* (compare <**kyá:ky**> *younger sister (pet name)*), syntactic analysis: nominal, attested by Elddrs 1/7/76.

<**iyá:q**>, free root //ʔiyɛ́·q//, CST ['*change*'], EFAM, syntactic analysis: intransitive verb, also <**yá:q**>, //yɛ́·q//, phonology: this rare variant probably occurs with lors of the initial vowel /i/ in rapid speech, yielding an initial /ʔy/ which must simplify to /y/; vowel-loss, consonant merger, attested by Elders Group 1/26/77, ASM ['change s-th (mental/emotional)'], semantic environment ['emotions, feelings, attitudes'], <**yá:q tel sqwálewel**>, //yɛ́·q tə-l s=qʷɛ́l=əwəl//, /'*change my mind,)my mind changed)*'/, attested by Elders Group 1/26/77.

<**iyá:qt ~ iyáqt**>, pcs //ʔiyɛ́·q=T ~ ʔiyɛ́q=T//, CST /'*change s-th (purposely), change s-o, transform s-o/s-th, trade s-th, replace s-th*'/, EFAM, SOC, MC, CLO, syntactic analysis: transitive verb, attested by Elders Group, Deming, EB, AD, ASM ['change s-o/s-th (into something else), transform s-o/s-th'], semantic environment ['myth character, Transformer, magic, religion'], <**iyá:qtes te shxwlá:m te spó:l tl'ésu mé xwe swíyeqe**>, //ʔiyɛ́·q=T-əs tə s=xʷlɛ́·m tə s=pá·l ƛ'ə́-su mə́ xʷə s=wíyəqə//, /'*The Indian doctor changed a crow into a man.*'/, attested by EB, ASM ['change s-th (physically), replace'], semantic environment ['material culture, two or more physical objects']; example: <**iyáqtchexw ta' s'íth'em**>, //ʔiyɛ́q=T-c-əxʷ t-ɛʔ s=ʔíθ'ə=m//, /'*Ciange your clothes.*'/, syntactic comment: imperative with independent clause subject pronoun, attested by AD, <**iyáqt te sqelálhs te sqáqele**>, //ʔiyɛ́q=T tə s=qəl=ɛ́ɬ-s tə s=qɛ́qələ//, /'*change the baby's diaper*'/, attested by AD, <**skw'áye kw'els iyáqt tel tále**>, //s=k'ʷɛ́y-ə k'ʷə-l-s ʔiyɛ́q=T tə-l tɛ́lə//, /'*Can't I change my money?*'/, attested by Deming, <**l stl'í kw'els iyáqt tel tále**>, //l s=ƛ'í k'ʷə-l-s ʔiyɛ́q=T tə-l tɛ́lə//, /'*I*

want to change my money.'/, attested by Deming, <**iyáqtes te sqwà:ls**>, //ʔiyɛ́q=t-əs tə s=q^{w}ɛ̀·l-s//, /'*He changed the subject.*'/, literally /'he changed his words'/, attested by Elders 3/3/76.

<**iyóqthet**>, rfls //ʔiyɛ[=Aa=]´q=T=ət//, [ʔiyáqθət], CST /'*change oneself (purposely), change oneself into something else, change s-th on oneself*'/, MC, SOC, (<**o-ablaut**> *derivational*), phonology: ablaut, syntactic analysis: intransitive verb, attested by EB, ASM ['change into s-th else'], <**iyóqthet te skwówech esu xwe mestíyexw**>, //ʔiyáq=θ=ət tə s=k^{w}áwəc ʔə-su x^{w}ə məstíyəx^{w}//, /'*The sturgeon changed into a person.*'/, literally /'he changed himself purposely the sturgeon and so became person'/, attested by EB, ASM ['change s-th on oneself'], <**iyóqthetchexw ta' á:wkw'**>, //ʔiyáq=θ=ət-c-əx^{w} t-ɛʔ ʔɛ́·wk'^{w}//, /'*Change your clothes.*'/, literally /'you change on yourself your belongings'/, attested by EB.

<**íyeqthet**>, rfls //ʔi[=´=]yɛq=T=ət//, [ʔíyəqθət], CST /'*get out of the way, get off the way, dodge*'/, (<**stress-shift**> *derivational*), phonology: stress-shift, syntactic analysis: intransitive verb, attested by EB; example: <**le íyeqthet**>, //lə ʔi[=´=]yɛq=T=ət//, /'*He got out of the way., He got off the way.*'/, attested by EB, ABFC.

<**iyáqestexw**>, caus //ʔiyɛ́qə=sT-əx^{w}//, SOC ['*trade with s-o*'], syntactic analysis: transitive verb; found in <**iyáqesthòmè**>, //ʔiyɛ́qə=sT-àmə̀//, [ʔiyǽqəsθàmə̀], /'*trade (with) you*'/, literally /'cause you to trade/exchange'/.

<**iyáqelhtst**>, bens //ʔiyɛ́q=əɬc=T//, SOC ['*trade with s-o*'], (<**=elhts**> *benefactive*, <**=t**> *purposeful control transitivizer*), syntactic analysis: transitive verb, attested by EB; found in <**yáqelhtstes**>, //yɛ́q=əɬc=T-əs//, /'*He traded with her.*'/, attested by EB, <**yáqelhtsthòxes**>, //yɛ́q=əɬc=T-àx^{y}-əs//, [yǽqəɬcθàx^{y}ɪs], /'*He traded with me.*'/, attested by EB.

<**iyóqelhtsthet**>, bens //ʔiyɛ[=Aa=]´q=əɬc=T=ət//, rfls, [ʔiyáqəɬcθət], SOC ['*change it (money) for s-o*'], (<**o-ablaut**> *derivational*), phonology: ablaut; found in <**iyóqelhtsthetes**>, //ʔiyáq=əɬc=θ=ət-əs//, /'*He changed it for her (money only).*'/, attested by EB.

<**siyóqelhtsthet**>, dnom //s=ʔiyɛ[=Aa=]´q=əɬc=T=ət//, [siyáqəɬcθət], SOC ['*change (money)*'], literally /'what one changes for oneself'/, (<**s=**> *nominalizer*), syntactic analysis: nominal, attested by EB; example: <**wá:ta' siyóqelhtsthet**>, //ʔəwə-ə́-tə-ɛʔ s=ʔiyɛ[=Aa=] ´q=əɬc=T=ət//, [wǽ·tɛʔ siyáqəɬcθət], /'*Have you got any change?*'/, literally /'is it none? your what one changes for oneself'/, attested by EB.

<**iyáqest**>, pcs //ʔiyɛ́q=əs=T//, SOC ['*change it (of money)*'], lx <**=es**> *money, dollars, round things, blankets*, (<**=t**> *purposeful control transitivizer*), syntactic analysis: transitive verb, attested by Deming; example: <**skw'áye kw'els iyáqest**>, //s=k'^{w}ɛ́y-ə k'^{w}-əl-s ʔiyɛ́y=əs=T//, /'*Can't I change my money?*'/, attested by Deming.

<**xwe'íyáqepem**>, mdls //x^{w}ə=ʔíyɛ́q=əp=əm//, LANG ['*to joke*'], literally /'get changed on one's (bottom?)'/, (<**xwe=**> *inceptive, become, get*), lx <**=ep**> *on the bottom(?), dirt(?)*, (<**=em**> *middle voice*), syntactic analysis: intransitive verb, attested by AD (3/6/79), also <**xwe'í:yá:qepem**>, //x^{w}ə=ʔí·yɛ́·q=əp=əm//, attested by JL (5/5/75); example: <**le xwe'í:yá:qepem**>, //lə x^{w}ə=ʔí·yɛ́·q=əp=əm//, /'*He (or she) joked.*'/, attested by JL, Salish cognate: Cowichan /x^{w}iy'**é**qəpəm/ *to joke* B74b:66, Saanich /x^{w}iy'**é**qəč/ *to joke* (-əč *on the back*) B74a:66, but not Sechelt /ʔiyal-uc-ím/, /ʔiyál-uc-əm/ *to joke* T77:29, B77:79.

<**iyáqelhtst**>, SOC ['*trade with s-o*'], *see* iyá:q.

<**iyáqest**>, SOC ['*change it (of money)*'], *see* iyá:q.

<**iyáqestexw**>, SOC ['*trade with s-o*'], *see* iyá:q.

<**iyá:qt ~ iyáqt**>, CST /'*change s-th (purposely), change s-o, transform s-o/s-th, trade s-th, replace s-th*'/, *see* iyá:q.

<**iychmà:m ~ iytsmà:m**>, TVMO ['*travelling by and packing on his back (might be said of a passer-by)*'], *see* chám.

<**Íyem ~ Íyém**>, PLN /'*Eayem, a village site and fishing place above (upriver of) Yale, B.C.*'/, *see* **éy** ~ **éy**:.

<**íyeqthet**>, CST /'*get out of the way, get off the way, dodge*'/, *see* iyá:q.

<**iyés**>, SOC /'*ma'am, female friend, chum (female), little girl*'/, *see* **éy** ~ **éy**:.

<**íyes ~ éyes**>, SOC /'*be fun, have (lots of) fun, have amusement, having lots of fun, be pleasant*'/, *see* **éy** ~ **éy**:.

<**iyéseq**>, SOC /'*sir, male friend, chum (male), sonny*'/, *see* **éy** ~ **éy**:.

<**iyésqel**>, ABFC ['*(have a) pleasant voice*'], *see* **éy** ~ **éy**:.

<**=iyetel**>, da //=iyɛ=təl//, N ['*male name*'], possibly <**=iya**> *affectionate diminutive*, possibly <**=tel**> *device, thing*, syntactic analysis: lexical suffix, derivational suffix; found in <**Olóxwiyetel**>, //ʔaláxʷ=iyətəl//, /'*male name version of Olóxw=elwet*'/, <**X̱emóth'iyetel**>, //x̣əmáθ'=iyətəl//, /'*male version of Indian name X̱omóth'iya*'/, <**Saláq'oyetel**>, //sɛlɛ́q'=ayətəl//, /'*Indian name of David (Matilda David's husband)*'/, <**Th'eláchiyetel**>, //θ'əlɛ́c=iyətəl//, /'*Indian name of Richard Malloway Sr. (prominent chief in Sardis in 1960's and earlier)*'/.

<**iyílem**>, WETH /'*clear up (of weather), turn fine (after a hard storm)*'/, *see* **éy** ~ **éy**:.

<**iyólem ~ iyó:lem**>, VALJ /'*be alright, be okay, it's alright, it's okay, can, be able, it's enough, be right, be correct, that's right*'/, *see* **éy** ~ **éy**:.

<**iyó:lemstexw**>, EFAM ['*obey s-o*'], *see* **éy** ~ **éy**:.

<**iyóleweéthet**>, FOOD /'*manage by oneself (in food or travel), try to do it by oneself, try to be independent, do the best one can*'/, *see* **éy** ~ **éy**:.

<**iyó:mex ~ iyóméx ~ iyómex**>, VALJ /'*good-looking, beautiful, pretty, handsome, looks good*'/, *see* **éy** ~ **éy**:.

<**iyóqelhtsthet**>, SOC ['*change it (money) for s-o*'], *see* iyá:q.

<**iyóqthet**>, CST /'*change oneself (purposely), change oneself into something else, change s-th on oneself*'/, *see* iyá:q.

<**=iyó:s**>, da //=iy(=)á·s//, SH ['*(in a) circle*'], possibly <**=iy**> *covering, bark*, possibly <**=ó:s**> *(on a) round object*, syntactic analysis: lexical suffix, derivational suffix; found in <**q'eyq'elts'iyósem spehá:ls**>, //q'ɛyq'əlc'=iyás=əm spəhɛ́·ls//, /'*whirlwind*'/ (compare <**spehá:ls**> *wind*), <**siselts'iyósem**>, //sisəlc'=iyás=əm//, /'*turn around in a circle*'/ (compare <**sísel-**> *spinning* and <**=(el)ts'**> *around, over, turning* and <**=iyó:s**> *in a circle*, and <**=em**> *middle voice)*, <**x̱éylx̱eliyó:sem**>, //x̣ɛ́ylx̣əl=iyá·s=əm//, /'*it is written (in the sky) (as striped clouds)*'/.

<**í:yó:sem**>, SOC ['*having fun*'], *see* **éy** ~ **éy**:.

<**iyó:tel**>, df //ʔi=yá·=təl//, rcps, SOC ['*to fight*'], possibly <**i= ~ yi=**> *in motion, travelling along* or possibly epenthetic, possibly root <**yó:**> *warn* possibly root as in <**yó:=t**> *warn s-o*, (<**=tel**> *reciprocal*), contrast <**siyá:ye**> *friend*, <**yáyetel**> *they've made (make) friends*, <**yóyatel**> *they're making friends*, phonology: i perhaps to make pronunciation easier (epenthetic); this can be seen from its absence in other occurences of the same root (ó:ytel, etc.) and from my transcriptions of AC's pronunciations of iyó:tel sometimes with a phonetic superscript [i], syntactic analysis: intransitive verb, attested by Elders Group 3/15/72, AC, other sources: ES /ʔəyá·təl/; example: <**le iyó:tel**

qetl'os'ésu x̲á:m>, //lə ʔiyá·=təl qə-ƛ'a-s-ʔə-s-əwx̣ɛ́·m//, /*'They had a fight and she cried.*'/, attested by AC.

<**ó:ytel**>, cts //ʔiyá·[-M2-]=təl//, SOC [*'fighting*'], (<**metathesis type 2**> *continuative*), phonology: metathesis, syntactic analysis: intransitive verb, attested by Elders Group 3/15/72, AC; example: <**qéx̲ yi ó:ytel**>, //qə́x̣ yi ʔá·ytəl//, /*'There's a lot of them fighting., (There's) many people fighting.*'/, attested by AC, also <**qéx̲ mestíyexw ó:ytel**>, //qə́x̣ məstíyəxʷ ʔá·y=təl//, /*'a lot of people fighting*'/, syntactic analysis: nominal phrase with apposition, also /*'fight*'/, attested by EB.

<**hí:tel ~ hí:ytel**>, dnom //hə́=iy(á·)=təl or hə́=á·y=təl//, SOC /*'weapon (arrow, club, etc.), something used to defend oneself*'/, literally perhaps /'device/thing for warning'/, (<**hé=**> *continuative*), possibly root <**yó(:)**> *warn* possibly root as in <**hé:yó:t**> *warning s-o*, (<**=tel**> *device, thing for*), phonology: vowel merger, consonant-loss, vowel-loss, grammatical comment: =tel *reciprocal* is dropped and =tel *device, thing for* is added also nominalizing the word, syntactic analysis: nominal.

<**iyóthet**>, df //ʔiyá=θət//, CST /*'start, started*'/, (<**=thet**> *inceptive, get, become* (probably not =thet *reflexive*)), syntactic analysis: intransitive verb, attested by EB, AD; example: <**íkw'elò kw'a's iyóthet**>, //ʔí=k'ʷə=là k'ʷ-ɛʔ-s ʔiyá=θət//, /*'Start here.*'/, literally /'it's here that you start'/, attested by AD, <**uwlh iyóthet ye mímelha**>, //wəɬ ʔiyá=θət yə mí[-C₁ə-]ɬɛ//, [ʔu(w)ɬ ʔiyáθət yɪ míməɬæ], /*'They started spirit-dancing already., They started spirit-dancing again.*'/, literally /'already they start the (human plural) spirit-dancing'/, attested by EB.

<**íy'eyòm**>, TIME [*'(be) slower*'], *see* óyém.

<**iy'eyómthet**>, TIME [*'delay oneself*'], *see* óyém.

<**iy'iyátes**>, TVMO [*'He's chasing them/it repeatedly.*'], *see* á:y.

<**Iy'óythel**>, PLN /*'a place on Chilliwack River, a little above Anderson Flat and Allison's (between Tamihi Creek and Slesse Creek), a village at deep water between Tamihi Creek and Slesse Creek*'/, *see* **éy ~ éy**:.

<**í' ~ i'**>, free root //ʔíʔ//, EFAM /*'close to danger., danger., stop.*'/, syntactic analysis: interjection, usage: slang, semantic environment ['used with alarm; example if someone is close to a cliff-edge'], attested by BHTTC.

<**i'á:lqem**>, ANAA [*'charging (of an angry grizzly for ex.)*'], *see* á:lqem.

<**I'alhqá:yem**>, PLN /*'a snake rock in the Fraser River just north of Strawberry Island which had snakes sunning themselves and covering the rock;* also *the name of the village on Strawberry Island*'/, literally /'little snake place'/, *see* Alhqá:yem under álhqey ~ álhqay.

<**í:'axwì:l ~ í:'axwí:l**>, VALJ /*'small (smaller than axwíl), little*'/, *see* axwíl.

<**i'ax̲íth**>, TVMO [*'little baby lying down*'], *see* áx̲eth.

<**i'éyel**>, ABFC /*'recover, be better*'/, *see* **éy ~ éy**:.

<**i'éyelstexw**>, IDOC [*'make s-o well*'], *see* **éy ~ éy**:.

<**i'é:ymet**>, EFAM [*'getting to like somebody*'], *see* **éy ~ éy**:.

<**i'eyó:stem**>, SOC /*'having lots of fun, it's a lot of fun*'/, *see* **éy ~ éy**:.

<**í'istexw**>, EFAM [*'find it funny*'], *see* **éy ~ éy**:.

<**í'iy**>, VALJ /*'cute, a little one is good, good (of s-th little)*'/, *see* **éy ~ éy**:.

<**i'ó:lthet ò**>, ABFC [*'keeps on groaning*'], *see* ó:lthet.

<**i'ó:y**>, LANG (probably) [*'keep on a little'*], *see* á:y.

<**i'oyóm** or **i'eyóm**>, TVMO [*'to walk slow'*], *see* óy**é**m.

K

<**k**>, phonology: The sound k is found mainly in borrowings from English, French, Chinook Jargon, and other Indian languages; it is also found in some words which normally have q in the same position in the word but have undergone a process of sound symbolism to produce diminutives or pet names. Where borrowings are found, the source word and source language will be listed, where known; where sound symbolism is identified that will be shown. The sound k often is palatalized ([k^y]), and the most consistently palatalized are sometimes spelled with ky in the orthography..

<**ká:k ~ kyá:ky**>, KIN ['*younger sibling (pet name)*'], *see* sqá:q.

<**kalipốli**>, free root //kɛlipóli//, PLN ['*California*'], borrowed from English /kælɪfɔ́rnyə/ *California*, syntactic analysis: nominal, attested by IHTTC, source: place names file reference #191a.

<**kálti**>, free root //kɛ́lti//, FOOD ['*candy*'], borrowed from English <candy>/kǽndi/ or Chinook Jargon <**kánti**> /kánti/ *candy* (Johnson 1978:285), syntactic analysis: nominal, attested by EK,DK.

<**kápech**>, free root //kɛ́pəc//, [kǽpɪč], EB ['*cabbage*'], ['*Brassica oleracea*'], borrowed from Chinook Jargon /kápac/ *cabbage* (Johnson 1978:284), syntactic analysis: nominal.

<**mémeles kápech**>, EB, FOOD *brussel sprouts* (lit. many little children of + cabbage), (attested by RG,EH 6/16/98 to SN, edited by BG with RG,EH 6/26/00)

<**p'éq' sp'áq'em kápech**>, EB, FOOD *cauliflower* (lit. white + flower + cabbage), (attested by RG,EH 6/16/98 to SN, edited by BG with RG,EH 6/26/00)

<**tsqwá:y p'áp'eq'em kápech**>, EB, FOOD *broccoli* (lit. green + flowering/flowered + cabbage), (attested by RG,EH 6/16/98 to SN, edited by BG with RG,EH 6/26/00)

<**ká(t) ~ ke'át**>, df //kɛ́(t) ~ k(=)əʔɛ́(=)t//, TIME /'*wait, be later*'/, possibly <**=e'á**> *comparative*, possibly **<fronting>** *diminutive*, phonology: possible fronting, syntactic analysis: adverb/adverbial verb, attested by EB, Deming, AH; found in <**káchxwò**>, //kɛ́-c-x^w=à//, /'*Wait a while.*'/, possibly root <qa> /qɛ/ *and*, syntactic analysis: imperative, attested by EB, example: <**ke'áts el**>, //k(=)əʔɛ́(=)t-s ʔəl or k(=)əʔɛ́(=)c ʔəl//, /'*Wait a bit.*'/, attested by Deming 1/18/79.

<**keke'át**>, ds //C_1ə=kəʔɛ́t//, TIME ['*a little later (??)*'], (<**reduplication**> *diminutive*), phonology: reduplication, syntactic analysis: adverb/adverbial verb, attested by AH (Deming 2/8/79).

<**katkasyéthem**>, us //kɛtkɛsyə́θəm//, [kætkæsyíθəm], CH ['*catechism*'], borrowed from French catéchisme /katešísm/ *catechism*, syntactic analysis: intransitive verb?, nominal?, attested by IHTTC, also <**katesíth'em**>, //kɛtəsíθ'əm//, attested by EB.

<**Káthlek**>, free root //kɛ́θlək//, CH ['*Catholic*'], borrowed from English /kǽθlɪk/ *Catholic*, syntactic analysis: nominal, adjective/adjectival verb.

<**Katsesló:y**>, df //kɛcəslá·y or kɛt=cəs=əl=ɛ[=Aá=]·y or q[=K=]ɛt=cəs=əl=ɛ[=Aá·=]y//, PLN /'*Kateseslie, a spring-water stream east of Coqualeetza, part of the Kw'eqwá:líth'a [property or stream?] that went through Sardis and came out to the Cottonwood Corner*'/, possibly root <**kát**> *wait, be later* or possibly root <**qát**> *cook or heat with steam, put on a poultice*, possibly <**fronting**> *diminutive*, possibly <**=tses**> *on the hand*, possibly <**=el**> *get, become, come, go*, possibly <**=á(:)y**> *bark, covering*, possibly <**ó(:)-ablaut**> on <**á**> in suffix *resultative*, phonology: possible fronting, possible ó(:)-ablaut on á in suffix, possible vowel-loss in suffix before stressed suffix, syntactic analysis: nominal, attested by DM (1/8/62)(new p.5 of transcripts), other sources: Wells 1965 (lst ed.):13.

<**káwpōy**>, free root //kɛ́wpoy//, SOC ['*cowboy*'], borrowed from English /kɛ́wbɔy/ *cowboy*, syntactic analysis: nominal, adjective/adjectival verb.

<**kawpōyóweq(w)**>, dnom //kɛwpoy=áwəq(^{w})//, CLO ['*cowboy hat*'], lx <**=óweqw**> *hat* (incl. <**=eqw**> *on the top of the head, on the hair*), contrast <**yóseqw**> *hat*, syntactic analysis: nominal phrase with modifier(s), Salish cognate: Musqueam /=áw'əq^{w}/ *hat* Suttles ca1984:14.5.86.

<**kéchel**>, free root //kə́cəl//, [kɪ́čɪl], BLDG ['*kitchen*'], borrowed from English /kɪ́čən/ *kitchen*, syntactic analysis: nominal, attested by Elders Group, EB, example: <**alétsa te kéchel**>, //ʔɛlə́cɛ tə kə́cəl//, /'*Where's the kitchen?*'/, attested by AD.

<**keke'át**>, TIME ['*a little later (??)*'], *see* **ká**(t) ~ ke'**át**.

<**kelchóch ~ kyelchóch**>, ds //kəl=các ~ k^{y}əl=coc//, SOC /'*Englishman, English, Canadian, Canada, Anglican*'/, CH, borrowed from Chinook Jargon /kin cóc/ *English, Scotch, Irish, Canadian* (Johnson 1978:311-312), syntactic analysis: nominal, adjective/adjectival verb, attested by Elders Group, Deming 3/15/79 (SJ, MC, MV, LG), ASM ['English, Englishman'], semantic environment ['in Canada'], ASM ['Canada, Canadian'], semantic environment ['speaker living in the United States'], <**telí kw'e Kelchóch**>, //təlí k'^{w}ə kəl=các//, /'*from Canada*'/, attested by Deming 3/15/79 (SJ, MC, MV, LG), ASM ['Anglican'], semantic environment ['religion'], <**Kyelchóch ts'ahéyelh**>, //k^{y}əl=các c'ɛhɛ́yəɬ//, /'*Anglican church (institution)*'/, also compare <**Kíl Chóch**>, ds //kíl các//, N ['*King George*'], borrowed from Chinook Jargon /kin cóc/ *King George*.

<**kelchochéleqw**>, ds //kəl=cac=ə́ləq^{w}//, ANAH /'*part the hair on the right side (left side as people look at you), have the hair parted on the right side*'/, lx <**=éleqw**> *hair, top of the head*, syntactic analysis: adjective/adjectival verb, attested by IHTTC.

<**kemí(')**>, possible root //kəmí(ʔ)//, meaning unknown

<**skemí'iya**>, dnom //s=kəmíʔ=iyɛ//, EZ /'*a white-headed duck, [*could be *bufflehead, snow goose, emperor goose,* poss. *oldsquaw,* or *hooded merganser,* other duck-like birds with white heads do not occur in the Stó:lō area and the emperor goose would be only an occasional visitor*]*'/, (<**s=**> *nominalizer*), (<**=iya**> *diminutive*), (possibly <**fronting**>, i.e., **q → k** *diminutive*), phonology: possibly fronting, syntactic analysis: nominal, source: JH:DM.

<**ke'át ~ ká(t)**>, df //kɛ́(t) ~ k(=)əʔɛ́(=)t//, TIME /'*wait, be later*'/, possibly <**=e'á**> *comparative*, possibly <**fronting**> *diminutive*, phonology: possible fronting, syntactic analysis: adverb/adverbial verb, attested by EB, Deming, AH; found in <**káchxwò**>, //kɛ́-c-x^{w}=à//, /'*Wait a while.*'/, possibly root <qa> /**q**ɛ/ *and*, syntactic analysis: imperative, attested by EB, example: <**ke'áts el**>, //k(=)əʔɛ́(=)t-s ʔəl or k(=)əʔɛ́(=)c ʔəl//, /'*Wait a bit.*'/, attested by Deming 1/18/79.

<**keke'át**>, ds //C_1ə=kəʔɛ́t//, TIME ['*a little later (??)*'], (<**reduplication**> *diminutive*), phonology: reduplication, syntactic analysis: adverb/adverbial verb, attested by AH (Deming 2/8/79).

<**kíks**>, free root //kíks//, FOOD ['*cake*'], borrowed from English /kéyks/ *cakes*, syntactic analysis: nominal, attested by Elders Group, also /'*cakes*'/, attested by EB, <**t'át'ets'em qwíqwòyèls kíks seplíl**>, FOOD *lemon cake* (lit. lemon (itself from sour little yellowish fruit) + cake + bread), (attested by RG,EH 6/16/98 to SN, edited by BG with RG,EH 6/26/00), <**xáweq kíks seplíl**>, FOOD *carrot cake* (lit. carrot + cake + bread), (attested by RG,EH 6/16/98 to SN, edited by BG with RG,EH 6/26/00)

<**Kíl Chóch**>, ds //kíl các//, N ['*King George*'], borrowed from Chinook Jargon /kin cóc/ *King George*, syntactic analysis: nominal, attested by EB.

<**Kíl Ítewet**>, ds //kíl ʔítəwət//, N ['*King Edward*'], borrowed from back-formation from Chinook Jargon /kin cóc/ *King George* with Ítewet *Edward*, the common name, from British English /ʔɛ́dwəd/

Edward, syntactic analysis: nominal, attested by EB.

<**klekleklék**> perhaps, df //klək=klək=klək// [klʌk=klʌk=klʌk], SD ['*glug glug glug*'], syntactic analysis: intransitive verb, prob. borrowed from English, attested by Elders Group.

<**klép**>, free root //klə́p//, PLAY ['*club (in cards)*'], semantic environment ['cards'], borrowed from English [klʌb] *club*, syntactic analysis: nominal.

<**kópi**>, free root //kápi ~ kʸápi//, FOOD ['*coffee*'], borrowed from Chinook Jargon <kau´py>/kɔ́pi/ *coffee* or English /kɔ́fi/, syntactic analysis: nominal, attested by Deming, Elders Group, AD, example: <**éy te kópitset**>, //ʔɛ́y tə kápi-c-ət//, /'*We have good coffee., Our coffee is good.*'/, attested by Deming.

<**kópi'álá**>, dnom //kápi=ɛ́lɛ́//, HHG ['*coffee-pot*'], FOOD, lx <**=álá**> *container of*, syntactic analysis: nominal, attested by AD, example: <**alétsa te kópi'álá**>, //ʔɛlə́cɛ tə kápi=ɛ́lɛ́//, /'*Where is the coffee-pot?*'/, attested by AD.

<**kopú**>, free root //kapú//, CLO ['*coat*'], borrowed from Chinook Jargon <kapo> /kapó/ *coat* itself from French <capote> *hooded cloak*, syntactic analysis: nominal, attested by EB, AC.

<**kúkumels**>, EB /'*cucumber*'/, see **kwúkwemels.**

<**kú:l**>, free root //kú·l//, LAND ['*gold*'], borrowed from Chinook Jargon <gold>/kól/ *gold* or English /góld/, syntactic analysis: nominal, attested by Elders Group 5/28/75, Deming, also <**kő:l**>, //kó·l//, attested by Elders Group 3/72, example: <**atsel kwéléxw te kő:l**>, //ʔɛ-c-əl kʷə́l=ləxʷ tə kó·l//, /'*I discovered gold.*'/, attested by Elders Group 3/72, <**tsel thexláxw te kő:l**>, //c-əl θəx̣=lə[=Aɛ́=]xʷ//, /'*I discovered gold.*'/, attested by Elders Group 3/15/72.

<**Kúshen**>, free root //kúšən//, PLN ['*Goshen*'], ASM ['name of a small town near Deming, Wash. in Nooksack territory'], borrowed from English /gósən/ *Goshen*, syntactic analysis: nominal, attested by Deming, example: <**li te Kúshen Xálh**>, //li tə kúšən xʸɛ́ɬ//, /'*on Goshen Road*'/, attested by Deming.

<**kyá:ky ~ ká:k**>, KIN ['*younger sibling (pet name)*'], *see* sqá:q.

<**kyal:ám**>, free root //kʸɛl·ɛ́m//, [kʸæl·ǽm], CH /'*fasting for Lent,* prob. also *Lent*'/, borrowed from French **carême** *Lent*, Elder's comment: "all Catholic people over 21 used to have to abstain from meals for Lent; now they just fast one hour before", syntactic analysis: intransitive verb?, attested by Elders Group 1/30/80.

<**kyépe=**>, bound root //kʸə́pə=//, borrowed from possibly Thompson or Lillooet, Salish cognate: Shuswap /kʔep/ *sick* (Kuipers 1974:205).

<**kyépetses**>, df //kʸə́pə=cəs//, [kʸɪ́pɪcɪs], ABDF ['*in-grown finger-nail*'], lx <**=tses**> *on the hand,* syntactic analysis: intransitive verb, attested by BHTTC.

<**kyépexel**>, df //kʸə́pə=xʸəl//, [kʸɪ́pəxʸɪl], ABDF ['*in-grown toe-nail*'], lx <**=xel**> *on the foot,* borrowed from possibly Thompson or Lillooet, Salish cognate: Shuswap /kʔəp=xʸén'/ *to have a sore leg* (Kuipers 1974:205), syntactic analysis: intransitive verb, attested by BHTTC.

<**kyépetses**>, ABDF ['*in-grown finger-nail*'], *see* kyépe=.

<**kyépexel**>, ABDF ['*in-grown toe-nail*'], *see* kyépe=.

<**kyó**>, free root //kʸá ~ kʸá·//, CAN /'*car, automobile*'/, borrowed from English /kár/ *car*, syntactic analysis: nominal, attested by EB, Elders Group, example: <**xwá:lq i tós te kyó**>, //xʷɛ́·lq yi-tás tə kʸá//, /'*He almost got hit by a car.*'/, literally /'he almost got hit by something moving the car'/, attested by EB, <**sle'ó:lwelhs te kyó**>, //s=ləʔ=á·lwəɬ-s tə kʸá//, /'*It's on the other side of the car.*'/, attested by EB, <**tsel sle'ólwelh te kyó**>, //c-əl s=ləʔ=álwəɬ tə kʸá//, /'*I'm on the other side of the car.*'/.

<**kyóxàlh**> or better <**kyó xàlh**>, cpds //kyá=x^{y}ɛ̀ɬ// or better //kyá x^{y}ɛ̀ɬ//, CAN ['*railroad*'], literally /'car road'/, syntactic analysis: nominal phrase with modifier(s), attested by Elders Group 3/2/77, *also see* xálh ~ xá:lh.

K'

<**k'**>, phonology: The sound k' /k'/ is found in borrowings from Interior Salish Indian languages (Thompson, perhaps Lillooet and Okanagan) and perhaps in words with *diminutive* fronting of q' /q'/ → k' /k'/. As with the sound k, these origins will be indicated in each entry, where known. Unlike k, k' is not palatalized often with a glide, i.e. [k'ʸ]; it is more often velar or palatal and less often palatalized.

<**k'áxwe**>, possible bound root or stem //k'ɛ́xʷ(=)ə// from Thompson language, the borrowed word may have been borrowed with or without the **s=** nominalizer, research into older records of UHk is needed (Boas, Hill-Tout, etc. have not been checked yet)

<**sk'ak'áxwe**>, df //s=C₁ɛ=k'ɛ́xʷə//, EB [*'dried saskatoon berries'*], [*'Amelanchier alnifolia'*], ASM ['ripe in July, the best ones are found north of Hope, B.C.; fresh berries are eaten and have a separate name; the dried berries are obtained in cakes or sheets from the Thompson and other Interior Salish Indians; saskatoons can be mixed with bulbs of the sx̲ameléxwthelh *tiger lily* and kw'épan [k'ʷʊ́pɛn] (a Thompson word, a white root, like a sweet potato in taste) and then either with sugar or with fish eggs'], borrowed from Thompson /s=k'ɛ́x=əm/ *dried berries* (Thompson /x/ is velar and corresponds to Upriver Halkomelem velar /xʷ/ in this word), (<**R8=**> *diminutive* or *resultative* or *derivational*), possibly <**=e ~ =a**>, da //=ə ~ =ɛ//, EZ [*'living thing'*], phonology: reduplication, syntactic analysis: nominal, attested by Elders Group, Deming (M.H.), AC, DM 12/4/64; unclear whether borrowed with the reduplication and s= nominalizer from Thompson or borrowed as the root <k'axwe> or stem <k'axw> and then these were added from UHk.

<**k'ák'elha**>, df //k'ɛ́[=C₁ə=]ɬɛ//, EZ [*'pill-bug'*], ['class *Crustacea*, order *Isopoda, Armadillidium vulgare*'], semantic environment ['sowbug that rolls up [therefore a pill-bug, since they and not true sowbugs, roll up], found in damp areas and on bacon and dried fish, black and grey striped bug with lots of legs, real tiny bug found with decayed meat, oval-shaped bug smaller than a lady-bug'], possibly <**=R1=**> *diminutive* or *continuative* or *resultative*, possibly <**=a**> *living thing*, phonology: reduplication, syntactic analysis: nominal.

<**k'ámets ~ k'ámeth**>, possible bound root //k'ɛ́məc ~ k'ɛ́məθ//, the borrowed word may have been borrowed with or without the **s=** nominalizer, research into older records of UHk is needed (Boas, Hill-Tout, etc. have not been checked yet)

<**sk'ámets ~ sk'ámeth**>, dnom //s=k'ɛ́məc ~ s=k'ɛ́məθ//, EB /*'blue camas, yellow dog-tooth violet = yellow avalanche lily'*/, ['resp. *Camassia leichtlinii and Camassia quamash, Erythronium grandiflorum*'], semantic environment ['wild sweet potatoes, obtained in trade, don't grow here; camas, like sweet potatoes with little sausage-shaped potatoes on root; dried bulbs of both camas and avalanche lily were obtained in trade probably both from the Interior and the Coast Indian peoples'], borrowed from Thompson /sk'ém'ec/ *dog-tooth violet, blue camas, white easter lily, Indian potato*, syntactic analysis: nominal, attested by Elders Group, also <**sk'ámeth'**>, //sk'ɛ́məθ'//, attested by Deming, may have been borrowed with or without the **s=** nominalizer of Thompson.

KW

<**kw**>, free root //kʷ//, DEM /'*the (remote, not visible, abstract), some (indefinite)*'/, phonology: may be a rapid speech alternant of kwe, syntactic analysis: demonstrative article, dialects: *EB uses both kw and kw'e, while AC prefers kw'e and only very rarely (if ever) uses kw*, attested by EB, also /'*some (indefinite)*'/, example: <**la há:we kw (s'álhtel, stámés).**>, //lɛ hɛ́·wə kʷ (s=ʔɛ́ɬtəl, s=tɛ́m=ə́s)//, /'*He went hunting for (some food, something).*'/, attested by EB, contrast <**la há:we kw'e spá:th**>, //lɛ hɛ́·wə k'ʷə s=pɛ́·θ//, /'*He went hunting for bear.*'/, attested by AC, contrast <**l stl'í kw'e qó:**>, //l s=ƛ'í k'ʷə qá·//, /'*I want some water.*'/, attested by AC, others, also /'*the (remote, abstract, not visible, distant)*'/, <**kw (spelwálh, cheláqelh(elh))**>, //kʷ (s=pəl(=)w=ɛ́ɬ, cəlɛ́q=əɬ(=əɬ))//, /'*last year, yesterday*'/, attested by EB, contrast <**kw'e (spelwálh, cheláqelh(elh))**>, //k'ʷə (s=pəl(=)w=ɛ́ɬ, cəlɛ́q=əɬ(=əɬ))//, /'*last year, yesterday*'/.

<**kws ...-s ~ kwses ~ kw'es ...-s**>, if //kʷ-s ...-s ~ kʷ-s-əs ~ k'ʷ-əs ...-s//, CJ /'*that he, that she, that it, that they*'/, (the first <**-s** (**-es** after **kw'**)> *nominalizes following phrase*, the second -s ~ -es *third person subordinate subject*), phonology: kws ...-s, kwses, and kw'es ...-s are in free variation for most speakers, syntactic analysis: demonstrative conjunction, sbsp (possessive pronoun affix), syntactic comment: used to attach (conjoin) subordinate phrases or subordinate sentences with third person subjects to main verbs; the -s closest to kw (or kw') is the nominalizer, since ...-s is attached to the first word in the su subordinate phrase or sentence in the same position as a third person possessive pronoun and since possessive pronouns are used in the same way to show first and second person subordinate subjects;, syntactic comment: with first or second person subjects only kw'e (not kw) can be used to attach subordinate phrases or sentences with first or second person subjects to main verbs (example, **kw'-el-s** *that I*, **kw'-a(')-s** *that you (sg.)*, **kw'-s ...-tset** *that we*, and **kw'-a(')-s ...-elep** *that you folks*;, syntactic comment: often an adverb or adjective is focussed upon by being made the main verb and the rest of the phrase or sentence is subordinated; -u *contrastive* can also be attached at the end of any of these conjunctions, as in kwsu ...-s, kwsesu, kw'esu ...-s, kw'elsu, kw'a(')su, etc.; (-u is often not translated in English directly, more by tone of voice and implication; see under -u), attested by Elders Group, AC, EB, others, example: <**tsel slhéq'elexw kwses spá:th**>, //c-əl s=ɬə́q'=ələxʷ kʷ-s-əs s=pɛ́·θ//, /'*I know (that) it was a bear.*'/, attested by AC, also <**tsel slhéq'elexw kws spá:ths**>, //c-əl s=ɬə́q'=ələxʷ kʷ-s s=pɛ́·θ-s//, attested by AC, <**lachxw tsesá:t kws las kwél:em kw s'álhtel**>, //lɛ-c-xʷ cəs=ɛ́·=T kʷ-s lɛ-s kʷə́l=l-əm kʷ s=ʔɛ́ɬtəl//, /'*Send him to get food.*'/, literally /'go-you send-him that go-he get some food'/, attested by EB, <**x̱wém (kwses, kw'els, kw'as) me áyelexw**>, //x̣ʷə́m (kʷ-s-əs, k'ʷ-əl-s, k'ʷ-ɛ-s) mə ʔɛ́yələxʷ//, /'*(He, She, It, They; I; you (sg.)) got well fast.*'/, attested by AC, <**skw'á:y kw'els q'á:l kw'es léwes**>, //s=k'ʷɛ́·y k'ʷ-əl-s q'ɛ́·l k'ʷ-əs lə́wə-s//, /'*I couldn't believe it was you.*'/, literally /'it can't be that I believe that is you-it'/, (semological comment: note the semantic focus), syntactic comment: note the second person pronominal verb/verbal pronoun with third person subject, attested by AC, <**wiyóth kwsu qéls te sqwálewels te lólets'e**>, //wiyáθ kʷ-s-u qə́l-s tə s=qʷɛ́l=əwəl-s tə C$_1$á=ləc'ə//, /'*a pessimist, a person whose thoughts are always bad*'/, literally /'it's always that the thoughts of the one person are bad'/, attested by Elders Group, <**wiyóth kwsu éys te sqwálewels te lólets'e**>, //wiyáθ kʷ-s-u ʔɛ́y-s tə s=qʷɛ́l=əwəl-s tə C$_1$á=ləc'ə//, /'*an optimist, a person whose thoughts are always good*'/, attested by Elders Group.

<**kwe**>, ds //kʷ=ə or kʷə//, DEM /'*the (present, not visible, gender unspecified), the (remote, abstract)*'/, poss. lx <**=e**> *living thing*, syntactic analysis: demonstrative article, example: <**li kwe í skwetáxw tha sísele**>, //li kʷə ʔí s-kʷətɛ́xʷ (kʷ)θə-ɛ sí·[=C$_1$ə=]lə//, /'*Is your grandmother in?, Is*

your granny in?'/, (<=**R1**=> *affectionate diminutive*), phonology: length-loss happens automatically before =doubling infix #1 with e= reduplication, attested by AC.

<**kwse**>, ds //kʷ=sə//, DEM /'*the (female, near but not visible), (female, near but not in sight) (translated by gender specific words in English, like aunt, etc.)*'/, phonology: in fast speech kw is sometimes dropped (consonant-loss), leaving se /sə/, syntactic analysis: demonstrative article, attested by AC, CT, others, example: <**tsel kw'étslexw kwsa (sí:sele, stó:les, shxwemlí:kw, stí:wel).**>, //c-əl k'ʷə́c=ləxʷ kʷ=s=ɛ (sí·[=C_1ə=]lə, s=tá·ləs, s=xʷəmlí·kʷ, s=tí·wəl)//, /'*I saw (see, past) your (grandmother, wife, aunt, niece).*'/, attested by AC, <**kwsel sí:selà:lh**>, //kʷ=s=əl sí·[=C_1ə=]lə-ɛ́(·)ɬ//, /'*my deceased grandmother, my late grandmother*'/, attested by CT, <**líye skwetáxw se Mary**>, //lí-ə s=kʷətɛ́xʷ sə mɛ́riy//, /'*Is Mary inside?*'/, attested by AC, <**lí í: sel tà:l**>, //lí ʔí· sə-l tɛ̀·l//, /'*Is my mother here?*'/, attested by AC.

<**kwsú:tl'ò**>, cpds //kʷ=s=ú·=ƛ'à//, PRON ['*that's her (absent)*'], DEM, (<**=s**> *(female near but not visible)*, <**=ú:**> *contrastive*, <(=)**tl'ó'** *that's*), syntactic analysis: inp, attested by AC, others.

<**kwsú:tl'ò:lh**>, ds //kʷ=s=ú·=ƛ'à-əɬ//, PRON ['*that was her (deceased)*'], DEM, (<**-elh**> *past tense, deceased*), phonology: vowel merger, syntactic analysis: inp, nominal past, attested by AC, others.

<**kwthe**>, ds //kʷ=θə//, DEM /'*the (male or gender unspecified, near but not in sight)*'/, phonology: in fast speech kw is lost after xw and perhaps other labialized consonants, syntactic analysis: demonstrative article, attested by AC, EB, Elders Group, others, example: <**li í skwetáxw kwtha (màl, sí:le)**>, //li ʔí s-kʷətɛ́xʷ kʷθə-ɛ (mɛ̀l, sí·lə)//, /'*Is your (father, grandfather) in?*'/, literally /'is he? here inside the (male or gender unspecified near but not visible) (father, grandfather)'/, phonology: vowel merger, attested by AC, <**li í skwetáxw (tha selsí:le, kwthá í:méth, ta am'í:méth)**>, //li ʔí s-kʷətɛ́xʷ (kʷθə-ɛ C_1əC_2-sí·lə, kʷθə-ɛ ʔí·məθ, tə-ɛ C_1əC_2-ʔí·məθ)//, /'*Are your (grandparents, grandchild, grandchildren) in?*'/, ASM ['the grandparents and grandchild are near but not visible; the grandchildren are either present and visible or unspecified as to presence and visibility'], phonology: the first article, tha, shows consonant-loss in fast speech, the stress on the second article, kwthá, shows iterative aspect is hyper-slow speech since articles are not so stressed at normal speeds; all the articles show vmerg of e with -a (possessive pronoun suffix) → a, attested by AC, <**me stetís kwthe yewál**>, //mə s=C_1ə=tís kʷθə yəwɛ́l//, /'*He came close to the first., (He was next to the first.)*'/, attested by AC, <**li i tl'eláxw kwtha màl**>, //li ʔí ƛ'əlɛ́xʷ kʷθə-ɛ mɛ̀l//, /'*Is your father in (home).*'/, usage: less formal than li i skwetáxw kwtha màl, attested by AC, <**etset tl'élexw li te shxwlís kwtha màl**>, //ʔə-c-ət ƛ'ə́ləxʷ li tə s(=)xʷ=lí-s kʷθə-ɛ mɛ̀l//, /'*We stopped at the place your father is at.*'/, literally /'We stopped at the where he is your father'/, attested by AC, <**kwthel mà:l ~ kwthel màl ~ kwthel mál**>, //kʷθ-əl mɛ̀·l (mɛ̀·l ~ mɛ̀l ~ mɛ́l)//, [kʷθí6l mæ̀₃l], /'*my father*'/, phonology: articles often get higher pitch than normal high stress, this is a fact of phrase- or sentence intonation and so is not written in the writing system or phonemically, attested by AC, <**lí: skwetáxw kwtha álex**>, //lí· s-kʷətɛ́xʷ kʷθə-ɛ ʔɛ́ləxʸ//, /'*Is your brother/sister in?, Is your sibling in?*'/, phonology: length here may reflect vowel merger of li-e, attested by AC, contrast <**skwetáxw te lálem**>, //s=kʷətɛ́xʷ tə lɛ́ləm//, /'*in the house*'/, attested by AC, also <**skwetáxw li te lálem**>, //s-kʷətɛ́xʷ li tə lɛ́ləm//, /'*inside the house*'/, literally /'inside in the house'/, attested by EB, contrast <**líye skwetáxw se Mary**>, //lí-ə s-kʷətɛ́xʷ kʷ=sə Mary//, /'*Is Mary home?*'/, literally /'Is she there? inside the (female near but not visible) Mary'/, semantic environment ['the speaker is near to Mary's residence'], (<**-e**> *interrogative (yes/no question)* (optional after sentence-initial li, as in examples below)), phonology: consonant-loss; se is short for kwse *the (female near but not visible)*; iterative aspect loses the kw here after xw (and perhaps after other labialized consonants) in rapid speech, attested by AC, <**lichxw we'éy el qwóqwel kw'es me kwetxwílem kwtha siyáya**>, //li-c-xʷ wə=ʔɛ́y ʔəl qʷɛ[-AáC_1ə-]l k'ʷ-əs mə kʷətxʷ=íl=əm kʷ=θ=ɛ si=yɛ́yɛ//, /'*Were you still talking when*

your friend came in?'/, attested by AC, contrast <**li skwetáxw tha (màl, sí:le)**>, //li s-kʷətɛ́xʷ kʷ=θə-ɛ (mɛ̀l, sí·lə)//, /'*Is your (father, grandfather) in?*'/, semantic environment ['the speaker is outside the building'], phonology: consonant-loss; <tha>/θə-ɛ/ is short for <kwtha>/kʷθ-ɛ/ *the (male or gender unspecified near but not visible)*; iterative aspect loses the kw here after xw (+ other labialized consonants?) in rapid speech; the article <tha>/θə-ɛ/ here cannot be from <the>/θə/ *the (female present and visible or presence and visibility unspecified)* because the nominals are male (for ex. *father*) and not visible; vowel merger is also present here (<ea> → <a>, /əɛ/ → /ɛ/), attested by AC, contrast <**líye skwetáxw kw'e John**>, //lí-ə s-kʷətɛ́xʷ k'ʷə ǰán//, /'*Is John home?*'/, literally /'is there - interrogative (yes/no) inside the (distant, remote) John'/, semantic environment ['speaker is distant from John's home'], phonology: vowel merger, attested by AC.

<**kwthú:tl'ò**>, cpds //kʷ=θ=ú·=ƛ'à//, PRON /'*that's him (absent), that's her (absent), it's him (absent), it's her (absent)*'/, DEM, (<**=th**> *(male, near not visible or gender and visibility unspecified)*, <**=ú:**> *contrastive*, <(=)**tl'ó**> *that's*), phonology: down-drift or down-stepping, syntactic analysis: inp, demonstrative pronoun, attested by AC, others.

<**kwthú:tl'òlem**>, pls //kʷ=θ=ú·=ƛ'à=lə=m//, PRON /'*that's them (absent, not present)*'/, DEM, (<**=le=**> *plural*, <**=m**> meaning unclear), syntactic analysis: inp, demonstrative pronoun, attested by AC.

<**kwthú:tl'òlèmèlh**>, ds //kʷ=θ=ú·=ƛ'à=lə=m=əɬ//, PRON ['*that was them (deceased)*'], DEM, (<**=elh**> *past tense, deceased*), syntactic analysis: inp, demonstrative pronoun, attested by AC.

<**kwethá ~ kwe thá**>, ds //kʷə=θɛ́ ~ kʷə θɛ́//, DEM /'*him (there, near but not visible), that one*'/, syntactic analysis: nominal demonstrative, attested by AC, others, example: <**tló: kwethá**>, //ƛ'á· kʷəθɛ́//, /'*It IS him., It's him (right out there, barely visible).*'/, semantic environment ['said for ex. after someone says "Oh, it's not him."'], attested by AC.

<**kwá**>, free root //kʷɛ́//, MOOD /'*anyway, ever, (new information* as in NStraits*)*'/, syntactic analysis: mpcl, attested by EB, others, Salish cognate: probably Musqueam /kʷə/ *consequential (then)* Suttles ca1984: 15.1.17, Saanich dial. of NSt /kʷəʔ/ postclitic *informative,* [perhaps] *new information* Montler 1986, Samish dial. of NSt /kʷəʔ/ (same meaning as in Saanich) Galloway 1990:59-60, example: <**ewálhchxw kwáxw stl'itl'qelh**>, //ʔəwə-ə́ɬ-c-xʷ kʷɛ́-xʷ s=C_1í=ƛ'əq=əɬ//, /'*Weren't you ever a child?*'/, attested by EB, <**tsel kwá welh lám**>, //c-əl kʷɛ́ wəɬ lɛ́=m//, /'*I began to go.*'/, literally /'I anyway already go'/, attested by EB.

<**kwá:**>, bound root //kʷɛ́·=//.

<**kwá:t ~ kwát**>, pcs //kʷɛ́·=T ~ kʷɛ́=T//, ABFC /'*let go of s-th/s-o, drop s-th, set s-o free, turn s-o/s-th loose, let it go, release it*'/, SOC, syntactic analysis: transitive verb, attested by EB, Elders Group, RG & EH (4/9/99 Ling332), example: <**tsel le kwá:t**>, //c-əl lə kʷɛ́·=T//, /'*I set him free., [I turned him loose.]*'/, attested by EB, <**lachxw kwát te staméstʼwo**>, //lɛ-c-xʷ kʷɛ́=T tə s=tɛm=ə́s-t'wa//, /'*Let go of something.*'/, literally /'you're going to. let go of it whatever it must be'/, phonology: <**t'wo**> *evidently, must be, I guess* is usually pronounced <**t'wa**> by most speakers; the <**o**> /a/ here may be Thompson influence since Thompson /a/ (<o>) corresponds to Halkomelem <a>/ɛ/ historically in a number of words, attested by EB (who was also fluent in Thompson), <**le kwá:tem**>, //lə kʷɛ́·=T-əm//, /'*He got turned loose., He was set free.*'/, syntactic analysis: auxiliary past, passive, attested by EB, <**ŏwechxw lámexw temkwát**>, //ʔówə-c-xʷ lɛ́=m-əxʷ təm=kʷɛ́=T//, /'*Don't let him go yet.*'/, attested by EB 6/24/76 correcting, also *Don't go yet., Hold on.*, attested by Elders Group 6/16/76.

<**kwó:thet**>, pcrs //kʷɛ[=Aa=]´·=T-ət//, ABFC ['*to gallop*'], literally /'set oneself free, loose oneself'/, (<**o-ablaut**> *derivational*), (<**=t**> *purposeful control transitivizer*), (<**-et**> *reflexive*), phonology: ablaut, syntactic analysis: intransitive verb, attested by AC.

<**kwekwó:thet**>, cts //C$_1$ə-k^{w}ɛ[=Aa=] ˊ·=T-ət//, [k^{w}ʊk^{w}á·θət], ABFC ['*galloping*'], (<**R5-**> *continuative*), phonology: ablaut, reduplication, syntactic analysis: intransitive verb, attested by AC, also <**kwekwóthet**>, //C$_1$ə-k^{w}ɛ[=Aa=] ˊ=T-ət//, example: <**kwekwóthet te stiqíw**>, //k^{w}ək^{w}áθət tə s=tiqíw//, /'*The horse is galloping.*'/, attested by EB.

<**kwikwe'át**>, dmv //C$_1$í=k^w[=əʔ=]á=T//, [k^{w}ik^{w}əʔǽt], SOC /'*leave s-o alone, stop pestering s-o*'/, (<**R4=**> *diminutive*), (<**=e'(á)=**> *comparative* or this may be merely a phonological alternative to á: (preserving ' for : and metathesizing)), (<**=t**> *purposeful control transitivizer*), phonology: reduplication, example: <**skw'áy kws tu kwikwe'átes te sqiqáqs**>, //s=k'^{w}ɛ́y k^w-s tu C$_1$í=k^{w}əʔɛ́=T-əs tə s=C$_1$í=qɛ́q-s//, /'*He never stops pestering his little brother., He never leaves his little brother alone.*'/, literally /'it can't be that he really he stops pestering him/he leaves him alone the male his little younger sibling'/, attested by AD, EB.

<**skwekwó:tel**>, rcps //s-C$_1$ə=k^{w}ɛ[=Aa=] ˊ·=T=əl//, stpc, [sk^{w}ʊk^{w}á·təl], KIN ['*separated in marriage*'], SOC, (<**s-**> *stative*), (<**R5=**> *completive?*), (<**o-ablaut**> *derivational*), (<**=t**> *purposeful control transitivizer*, <**=el**> *reciprocal*), phonology: ablaut, reduplication, syntactic analysis: intransitive verb, attested by Elders Group, also <**skwekwótel**>, //s-C$_1$ə=k^{w}ɛ[=Aa=] ˊ=T=əl//, attested by EB.

<**kwò:lxw**>, ncs //k^{w}ɛ[=Aà=]·=ləx^w//, ABFC /'*drop s-th (accidentally), let s-o go*'/, (<**ò-ablaut**> *derivational*), (<**=lexw**> *non-control transitivizer*), phonology: ablaut, syntactic analysis: transitive verb, attested by AD, also <**kwólxw**>, //k^{w}ɛ=Aá=ləx^w//, attested by EB; found in <**kwólxwes**>, //k^{w}ɛ=Aá=ləx^w-əs//, [k^{w}álx^{w}əs], /'*He dropped it.*'/, attested by EB, <**kwólòmè**>, //k^{w}ɛ=Aá=l-àmə̀//, /'*let me go*'/, attested by DF, also <**kwálòmè**>, //k^{w}ɛ́=l-àmə̀//, attested by EB.

<**kwólòmèt**>, ncrs //k^{w}ɛ=Aá=l=àmə̀t//, TVMO /'*escape (from slavery for ex.), get out (from being snowed in or snagged in river for ex.)*'/, ASM ['may be used for people other than the speaker in contrast to kwálòmèt which may be used by the speaker escaping himself/herself'], Elder's comment: "probably used for others [than oneself] (AD)", semantic environment ['previously trapped by the physical or social environment: snowed in, snagged in a river in one's canoe, as a slave, etc.'], (<**ó-ablaut**> *derivational*), (<**=l**> allomorph of <**=lexw**> *non-control transitivizer*, <**=òmèt**> *reflexive*), phonology: ablaut, syntactic analysis: intransitive verb, attested by AD, Elders Group 3/72, example: <**kwólòmèt á:lhtel**>, //k^{w}ɛ=Aá=l=àmə̀t ʔɛ́·ɬtəl//, /'*They escaped.*'/, attested by AD, Elder's comment: "she has heard this used"; found in <**qwó:lómet**> or probably mistranscribed for <**kwó:lòmet**>, //q^{w}á·lámət or k^{w}ɛ=Aá=l=àmət//, /'*make it through the winter*'/, attested by Elders 2/19/75.

<**kwálòmèt**>, ncrs //k^{w}ɛ́=l=àmə̀t//, TVMO /'*escape, get out*'/, ASM ['may be used by the speaker about him/herself, in contrast to kwólòmèt which may be used about people other than the speaker'], Elder's comment: "probably used for oneself", semantic environment ['previously trapped by physical or social environment: snowed in, snagged in the river in one's canoe, as a slave, etc.'], (<**=l**> allomorph of <**=lexw**> *non-control transitivizer*, <**=òmèt**> *reflexive*), syntactic analysis: intransitive verb, attested by AD.

<**kwetl'éthet**>, incs //k^{w}ɛ́=Aə=ƛ'=ə́θət//, [k^{w}əƛ'ə́θət], ABFC /'*start to struggle, start to flip around to escape (fish esp.)*'/, (<**e-ablaut**> *derivational*, <**=tl'**> meaning unknown (stem-extender?), <**=éthet**> *inceptive, start to*), phonology: ablaut, syntactic analysis: intransitive verb, attested by IHTTC.

<**kwótl'thet**>, cts //k^{w}ɛ[-Aa-] ˊ=ƛ'=θət//, ABFC /'*flipping around (of fish), struggling (of anything alive trying to get free)*'/, FSH, HUNT, (<**o-ablaut**> *continuative*), syntactic analysis: intransitive verb, attested by IHTTC.

<**kwetl'kwótl'thetōws**>, plv //C$_1$əC$_2$=k^{w}ɛ[-Aa-] ˊ=ƛ'=θət=əws//, [k^{w}əƛ'k^{w}áƛ'θətows], WATR ['*water jumping (as it goes over a rough bottom in a river)*'], (<**R3=**> *plural* or *frequentative* or

iterative), (<**o-ablaut**> *continuative*), (<**=tl'**> meaning unclear**,** <**=t**> *purposeful control transitivizer*, <**=et**> *reflexive*, <**=ōws**> *on the skin, on the covering*), phonology: reduplication, ablaut, syntactic analysis: intransitive verb, nominal?, attested by SP, AK, AD (all on raft trip).

<**Kwetl'kwótl'thetōws**>, ds //C_1əC_2=k^wɛ[-Aa-] ´=ƛ'=T=ət=əws//, PLN ['*a stretch of water in the Fraser River on the C.N. side by Strawberry Island*'], phonology: reduplication, ablaut, syntactic analysis: nominal, attested by AK, SP, AD, IHTTC, source: place names file reference #248.

<**kwíkwexel**>, bound stem //C_1í=k^wɛ=x^yəl or C_1í=k^wɛ=Aə=x^yəl//, meaning uncertain

<**skwíkwexel**>, dnom //s=C_1í=k^wɛ=x^yəl or s=C_1í=k^wɛ=Aə=x^yəl//, EZ ['*baby sockeye salmon*'], ['*Oncorhynchus nerka*'], (<**s=**> *nominalizer*, R4= *diminutive*), possibly root <**kwá**> *let go*, lx <**=xel**> *on the foot, foot, tail (of fish)*, possibly <**e-ablaut**> *derivational*, phonology: either a shift to schwa-grade in the root due to the stressed prefix, or derivational ablaut, reduplication, syntactic analysis: nominal, attested by AC.

<**temkwíkwexel**>, dnom //təm=C_1í=k^wɛ=x^yəl or təm=C_1í=k^wɛ=Aə=x^yəl//, TIME /'*time of the baby sockeye's coming, early spring (usually April), April moon*'/, EZ, literally /'time the little one gets free (his) tail'/, Elder's comment: "means "time when the baby sockeye free their feet"", (<**tem=**> *time of, season of*, R4= *diminutive*), lx <**=xel**> *foot, tail (of fish)*, possibly <**e-ablaut**> *derivational*, phonology: either a shift to schwa-grade in the root due to the stressed prefix, or derivational ablaut, reduplication, syntactic analysis: nominal, attested by AC, Elders Group 3/12/75.

<**kwáchem ~ kwátsem**>, mdls //k^wɛ́c=əm//, ABFC /'*to scream, holler (of a spirit-dancer)*'/, SD, (<**=em**> *middle voice*), syntactic analysis: intransitive verb, attested by EB.

<**skwátsem ~ skwáchem**>, dnom //s=k^wɛ́c=əm//, ABFC ['*a scream*'], SD, (<**s=**> *nominalizer*), syntactic analysis: nominal, attested by EB, Elders Group.

<**kwekwchám**>, cts //C_1ə-k^wɛ́c=ə[-M2-]m//, [k^wʊk^wčǽm], ABFC /'*screaming, crying (of a baby)*'/, SD, phonology: reduplication, metathesis, syntactic analysis: intransitive verb, attested by Elders Group, also <**kwekwchá:m**>, //C_1ə-k^wɛ́c=ə[-M2·-]m//, [k^wʊk^wčǽ·m], phonology: reduplication, metathesis, lengthening, attested by EB, example: <**kwekwchá:m kwá**>, //k^wək^wcɛ́·m k^wɛ́//, /'*Serves her right she's screaming now., [She's screaming anyway.]*'/, semantic environment ['used when someone has done something the speaker dislikes and is getting his/her come-uppance'], usage: , attested by EB.

<**kwíkwekwchá:m**>, dmv //C_1í=C_1ə-k^wɛ́c=ə[-M·-]m//, cts, [k^wik^wʊk^wčǽ·m], ABFC ['*squealing (like a pig for ex.)*'], (<**R4=**> *diminutive*), (<**R5-**> *continuative*), (<**metathesis type 2 plus lengthening**> *continuative*), (<**=em**> *middle voice*), phonology: double reduplication, metathesis, lengthening, syntactic analysis: intransitive verb, attested by BHTTC, usage: appears in a children's song featuring diminutive reduplication, but presumably also occurs elsewhere in normal speech.

<**kwechmí:l ~ kwetsmí:l**> dnom //k^wɛ́c=əm=í·l//, /'*stick holding deer hooves*'/, prob. <**=í:l ~ =íl ~ =el**>, *go, come, get, become* (thus perhaps lit. "(thing to) come/go/get holler of a spirit-dancer") or poss. <**=mel**> *location around a house, part* or <**=ó:mél**> *member, part, portion* with <**=Aí:**> *derivational*, attested by RG & EH (4/10/99 Ling332)

<**kwà:l**>, free root //k^wɛ̀·l//, SOC /'*to hide, hide oneself*'/, syntactic analysis: intransitive verb, attested by Elders Group 3/15/72, EB.

<**kwekwí:l ~ kwokwí:l**>, cts //C_1ə-k^wɛ[-Aí-]·l ~ C_1á-k^wɛ[-Aí-]·l//, [k^wʊk^wí·l ~ k^wɔk^wí·l], SOC /'*hiding, hiding oneself*'/, (<**R5-** or **R10-**> *continuative*), (<**í-ablaut**> *durative*), phonology: reduplication, ablaut, syntactic analysis: intransitive verb, attested by Elders Group 3/15/72, EB; found in <**kwekwí:ltsel**>, //C_1ə-k^wɛ[-Aí-]·l-c-əl//, /'*I'm hiding.*'/, attested by Elders Group 3/15/72, also

<**kwékwì:l**>, //C_1ə́-k^{w}ɛ[-Ai-] ^·l//, [k^{w}ʊ́k^{w}ì·l], attested by Elders Group 3/15/72, example: <**tsel kwékwì:l**>, //c-əl k^{w}ə́k^{w}ì·l//, /*'I'm hiding.'*/, syntactic analysis: ambiguous past, also <**kwókwì:l**>, //C_1á-k^{w}ɛ[-Ai-] ^·l//, [k^{w}ɔ́k^{w}ì·l], attested by Elders Group 3/15/72, <**atsel kwókwì:l**>, //ʔɛ-c-əl k^{w}ák^{w}ì·l//, /*'I'm hiding.'*/, syntactic analysis: ambiguous past, attested by Elders Group 3/15/72.

<**kwokwílàlà**>, dnom //C_1á-k^{w}ɛ[-Ai-] ´l=ɛ̀lɛ̀//, SOC /*'hiding place, refuge, hide-out'*/, (<**R10-**> *continuative*), (<**i-ablaut**> *durative*), lx <**=àlà**> *container of*, phonology: reduplication, syntactic analysis: nominal, attested by Elders Group at Fish Camp 8/2/77.

<**Skwokwílàla**>, dnom //s=r-k^{w}ɛ[-Aa-] ´l=ɛ́lɛ//, PLN [*'several places where there were pit-houses in which to hide from enemy raids (place to hide)'*], ASM ['three refugeswere above Yale Creek, one was around Chilliwack Mountain, one was on Seabird Island, among those remembered'], syntactic analysis: nominal, attested by Elders Group at Fish Camp 8/2/77, source: place names file reference #143.

<**kwekwí:lh**>, df //C_1ə-k^{w}ɛ[-Aí-]·l=ɬ ?//, SOC /*'someone's hiding, (a child is hiding ?)'*/, possibly <**=(iy)lh**> *child*, phonology: possible vowel loss and l + lh →lh or possibly just irregular devoicing (and spirantization) of /l/, reduplication, syntactic analysis: intransitive verb, attested by Elders Group 2/26/75.

<**shxwkwál**>, dnom //s(=)x^w=k^{w}ɛ́l//, SOC [*'a hiding'*], syntactic analysis: nominal, attested by EB.

<**kwà:lx**>, pcis //k^{w}ɛ̀·l=x^y//, SOC /*'hide an object, hide s-th'*/, (<**=x**> *purposeful control transitivizer inanimate object preferred*), syntactic analysis: transitive verb, attested by Elders Group (3/15/72), JL (Tait), also <**kwá:lx**>, //k^{w}ɛ́·l=x^y//, attested by EB, Deming, example: <**tsel kwá:lx**>, //c-əl k^{w}ɛ́·l=x^y//, /*'I hide an object.'*/, attested by EB; found in <**kwá:lxes**>, //k^{w}ɛ́·l=x^y-əs//, /*'He hides an object.'*/, attested by EB, Elders Group 3/15/72, example: <**tsel kwá:lx tel shxwtále'ále**>, //c-əl k^{w}ɛ́·l=x^y tə-l s(=)x^w=tɛ́lə=ʔɛ́lə//, /*'I hid my moneybag (purse, wallet, etc.).'*/, attested by EB; found in <**kwá:lxlha**>, //k^{w}ɛ́·l=x^y-ɬɛ//, /*'Hide it.'*/, syntactic analysis: imperative, attested by EB, example: <**kwá:lxlha tel tála**>, //k^{w}ɛ́·l=x^y-ɬɛ tə-l tɛ́lɛ//, /*'Hide my money.'*/, attested by EB, <**kwá:lxchexw ta' méqsel**>, //k^{w}ɛ́·l=x^y-c-əx^w t-ɛʔ mə́qsəl//, /*'Hide your nose (polite imperative).'*/, attested by Deming, <**atsel kwà:lx**>, //ʔɛ-c-əl k^{w}ɛ̀·l=x^y//, /*'I hide an object'*/, syntactic analysis: auxiliary past, attested by Elders Group 3/15/72.

<**kwokwí:lx**>, cts //C_1á-k^{w}ɛ[-Aí-]·l=x^y//, //k^{w}ak^{w}í·lx^y//, SOC [*'hiding an object'*], phonology: reduplication, ablaut, syntactic analysis: transitive verb, attested by Elders Group 3/15/72.

<**kwókwelx**>, rsls //k^{w}ɛ[=Aá=][-C_1ə-]l=x^y or C_1á-k^{w}ɛ[=Aə=]l=x^y//, cts, //k^{w}ák^{w}əlx^y//, SOC [*'hiding an object real well'*], (<**ó-ablaut**> *resultative*), (<**-R1-**> *continuative*), <**R10-**> *continuative,* <**e-ablaut**> *resultative,* possibly vice versa, phonology: ablaut, reduplication, syntactic analysis: transitive verb, attested by Elders Group 3/15/72, EB, example: <**kwókwelxes te sqá:ls**>, //k^{w}ák^{w}əl=x^y-əs tə s-qɛ́·l-s//, /*'He's hiding what he stole (steal).'*/, attested by EB.

<**kwá:lxelht**>, bens //k^{w}ɛ́·l=x^y=əɬ(c)=T//, SOC [*'hide it for s-o'*], (<**=x**> *purposeful control transitive inanimate object preferred*, <**=elh(ts)**> *benefactive*, <=**t**> *purposeful control transivitizer*), phonology: the ts /c/, usually found in the benefactive suffix has been dropped in this form (probably to simplify pronunciation), grammatical comment: <=**t**> must be used, besides <=**x**>, so that a person, rather than an inanimate object, can be the beneficiary indirect object, syntactic analysis: transitive verb, attested by EB, Elders Group 3/24/76; found in <**kwá:lxelhthóme**>, //k^{w}ɛ́·l=x^y=əɬ(c)=T-ámə//, [k^{w}ǽ·lx^{y}ɪɬθámə], /*'hide it for you'*/, attested by EB 3/1/76, example: <**kwá:lxelhthométsel**>, //k^{w}ɛ́·l=x^y=əɬ(c)=T-amə́-c-əl//, [k^{w}ǽ·lx^{y}ɪɬθamə́cɪl], /*'I hide it for you.'*/, attested by Elders Group 3/24/76, <**kwá:lxelhthóxlha**>, //k^{w}ɛ́·l=x^y=əɬ(c)=T-áx^y-ɬɛ//, [k^{w}ǽ·lx^{y}ɪɬθáx^{y}ɬæ], /*'Hide it for me.'*/, syntactic analysis: imperative.

<**skwálepel**>, dnom //s=k^{w}ɛ́l=əp(=)əl//, SOC [*'something hidden away'*], (<**s=**> *nominalizer*), lx <**=ep**>

in the dirt or at the bottom, lx <**=el**> *inceptive, get, become*, syntactic analysis: nominal, attested by Elders Group, also <**skwá:lpel**>, //s=kʷɛ́·l=p=əl//, attested by EB; found in <**skwá:lpels**>, //s=kʷɛ́·l=p=əl-s//, /'*something he hid (hide) away*'/, attested by EB.

<**Skwálepel**>, dnom //s=kʷɛ́l=əp=əl//, PLN ['*Skwellepil Creek*'], ASM ['flows into Chehalis Lake'], syntactic analysis: nominal, attested by Elders Group, Elder's comment: "this name is spelled Skwellepil Creek on maps, and the pronunciation and meaning *something hidden away* seem likely, though no one remembers it being used for sure with this creek", source: place names file reference #237.

<**kwáléws ~ kwálṓws**>, ds //kʷɛ́l=ə́ws ~ kʷɛ́l=ó́ws//, SOC ['*to murder*'], literally /'hide the body'/, lx <**=ó́ws ~ -ews**> *body*, syntactic analysis: intransitive verb, attested by IHTTC.

<**skwálṓws**>, strs //s-kʷɛ́l=óws//, SOC ['*got murdered*'], (<**s-**> *stative*), syntactic analysis: adjective/adjectival verb, participle, attested by IHTTC.

<**kwókwelōws ~ kwókwelews**>, rsls //C_1á-kʷɛ[=Aə=]l=əws or C_1á=kʷɛ[-Aə-]l=əws//, cts, SOC /'*murdering, murderer (of more than one)*'/, (<**R10-**> *continuative* and <**e-ablaut**> *resultative* or possibly <**R10=**> *resultative* and <**e-ablaut**> *continuative*, phonology: ablaut, reduplication, syntactic analysis: intransitive verb, nominal, attested by IHTTC.

<**kwelkwálṓws ~ kwelkwáléws**>, its //C_1əC_2=kʷɛ́l=ó́ws//, SOC ['*to murder*'], literally /'hide many bodies or hide bodies repeatedly'/, (<**R3=**> *iterative* or *frequentative*), phonology: reduplication, syntactic analysis: intransitive verb, attested by EB.

<**kwelkwálṓwst ~ kwelkwáléwst**>, pcs //C_1əC_2=kʷɛ́l=ó́ws=T//, SOC ['*murder s-o*'], phonology: reduplication, syntactic analysis: transitive verb, attested by EB; found in <**kwelkwáléwstem**>, //C_1əC_2=kʷɛ́l=ó́ws=T-əm//, /'*s-o was murdered*'/, syntactic analysis: passive, attested by EB.

<**kwáléws ~ kwálṓws**>, SOC ['*to murder*'], *see* kwà:l.

<**kwálòmèt**>, TVMO /'*escape, get out*'/, *see* kwá:.

<**kwà:lx**>, SOC /'*hide an object, hide s-th*'/, *see* kwà:l.

<**kwá:lxelht**>, SOC ['*hide it for s-o*'], *see* kwà:l.

<**kwá:m ~ kwám**>, bound root //kʷɛ́·m ~ kʷɛ́m *round*//.

<**skwá:m ~ skwám**>, dnom //s=kʷɛ́·m ~ s=kʷɛ́m//, BSK /'*storage basket (for oil, fruit, clothes), burial basket for twins, round basket (any size, smaller at top), clay jug (to store oil or fruit)*'/, (<**s=**> *nominalizer*), syntactic analysis: nominal, attested by Elders Group, AC, TG, ASM ['jug or basket to store oil or fruit'], attested by Elders Group 2/25/76, ASM ['round storage basket (any size, smaller at top)'], attested by Elders Group 3/26/80, ASM ['storage basket'], attested by TG, ASM ['round basket, clothes basket, burial basket for twins'], attested by AC.

<**kwamó:ythel**>, ds //kʷɛm=á·yθəl//, ANA ['*have a round mouth*'], lx <**=ó:ythel**> *mouth, jaw, lips, chin*, semantic environment ['used for ex. to describe sucker fish'], syntactic analysis: adjective/adjectival verb, dialects: *Yale*, attested by Elders Group, also <**kwemó:ythel**>, //kʷəm=á·yθəl//, dialects: *Chehalis*, phonology: a /ɛ/ → e /ə/ here since the suffix apparently has a stronger grade of vowel than the root in Chehalis, so the root loses stress and its vowel becomes schwa; in the Yale subdialect (Tait dialect), the root loses stress but the vowel isn't changed; other dialects are not attested yet with this word, attested by Elders Group.

<**kwamó:ythel**>, ANA ['*have a round mouth*'], *see* kwá:m ~ kwám.

<**kwá:t ~ kwát**>, ABFC /'*let go of s-th/s-o, drop s-th, set s-o free, turn s-o/s-th loose*'/, *see* kwá:.

<**Kwátexw**>, us //kʷɛ́təxʷ or possibly kʷətɛ́[=M2=]xʷ//, PLN ['*creek that runs into Yale Creek about two miles up (above the mouth of Yale Creek into the Fraser River)*'], ASM ['it is behind the mountain

called Tl'atl'eq'xélém'], possibly root <**kwetáxw**> *inside a house or enclosure*, possibly <**metathesis type 2**> *derivational*, phonology: metathesis?, syntactic analysis: nominal, attested by SP and AK at Fish Camp 8/2/77, Elders Group 9/13/77, source: place names file reference #155.

<**kwá:y**>, free root //kʷɛ́·y//, EZ /'*bluejay, Steller's jay*'/, ['*Cyanocitta stelleri paralia and Cyanocitta stelleri annectens*'], ASM ['also known as x̱ax̱esyúwes *sacred fortune-teller*, this bird predicts good news when it cries "q'ey, q'ey, q'ey" [q'ey q'ey q'ey] and bad news when it cries "chéke, chéke, chéke, chéke" [číkə číkə číkə číkə] in high notes; AC says its cry sounds like its name, loud and 4 or 5 times; AD says it tells you you'll have good luck fishing when it calls by making a "xwesh xwesh" [xʷɪš xʷɪš] sound like sharpening a knife'], syntactic analysis: nominal, attested by AC, BJ, Elders Group (3/1/72, 6/4/75, 2/18/76), AD 5/1/79, other sources: ES /kʷɛˇ·y/ (ˇ over the vowel, meaning rising tone).

<**kwe**>, DEM /'*the (present, not visible, gender unspecified), the (remote, abstract)*'/, *see* kw.

<**kwekwchám**>, ABFC /'*screaming, crying (of a baby)*'/, *see* kwátsem ~ kwáchem.

<**kwekweshú'ò:llh**>, EZ ['*piglet*'], *see* kweshú.

<**kwekwí:l ~ kwokwí:l**>, SOC /'*hiding, hiding oneself*'/, *see* kwà:l.

<**kwekwí:ltel**>, PLAY ['*play-fighting*'], *see* kwél.

<**kwekwí:lh**>, SOC /'*someone's hiding, (a child is hiding ?)*'/, *see* kwà:l.

<**kwekwó:thet**>, ABFC ['*galloping*'], *see* kwá:.

<**kwekwxá:mel**>, N ['*nickname*'], *see* kwí:x ~ kwíx.

<**kwél**>, bound root //kʷə́l//, meaning unknown

<**skwél**>, dnom //s=kʷə́l//, [skʷíl], WATR /'*waterfall, falls*'/, LAND, (<**s=**> *nominalizer*), syntactic analysis: nominal, attested by Elders Group 5/28/75.

<**skwíkwel**>, dmn //s=C_1í=kʷəl//, WATR ['*small waterfall*'], LAND, (<**R4=**> *diminutive*), phonology: reduplication, syntactic analysis: nominal, attested by Elders Group 5/28/75, for other words for *waterfall* see under stem <**chélq**> *fall*, see under stem <**wets'étl'**> *fall*.

<**kwél**>, bound root //kʷə́l *grasp, hold*//.

<**kwelát**>, durs //kʷəl=ə[=Aɛ́=]T//, pcs, ABFC /'*hold s-th (in one's grasp), holding s-th (in one's grasp), have s-th, grasp s-th*'/, SOC, (semological comment: apparently this form can be used for both continuative and non-continuative aspects (see examples below)), (<**=Aá**> *durative* or *continuative*, <**=et**> *purposeful control transitivizer*), also ABFC /'*hold it, carry s-o*'/, attested by RG & EH (4/9/99 Ling332), syntactic analysis: transitive verb, attested by Elders Group 3/15/72, AD, AC, EB, JL, Deming, other sources: ES /kʷəlɛ́·t/, also <**kwelá:t**>, //kʷəl=ə[=Aɛ́·=]T//, attested by AC, JL, example: <**le kwelá:tes li te s'eyí:ws chálexs**>, //lə kʷəl=ə[=Aɛ́·=]=T-əs li tə s=ʔɛy=í·ws cɛ́ləxʸ-s//, /'*He's holding it in his right hand.*'/, attested by AC, <**kwelátes te smált**>, //kʷəl=ə[=Aɛ́=]T-əs tə s=mɛ́lt//, /'*He's holding a rock.*'/, attested by AC, <**mí kwelátes te mímeles**>, //mí kʷəl=ə[=Aɛ́=]T-əs tə C_1í=mələ-s//, /'*She brought her baby.*'/, literally /'(he/she) came he/she held it the little child (baby)'/, attested by EB, <**ílh a kwelátes**>, //ʔí=ɬ ʔɛ kʷəl=ə[=Aɛ́=]T-əs//, /'*He held it (before)., He had it.*'/, attested by AD, <**lé xwel kwelátes**>, //lə́ xʷəl kʷəl=ə[=Aɛ́=]T-əs//, /'*He's still holding it.*'/, attested by AD, <**kwelátes te stámést'wa**>, //kʷəl=ə[=Aɛ́=]T-əs tə s=tɛ́m=ə́s-t'wɛ//, /'*He's holding something [evidently].*'/, attested by EB, <**kwelátchexw ta' méqsel**>, //kʷəl=ə[=Aɛ́=]T-c-əxʷ t-ɛʔ mə́qsəl//, /'*Hold your nose.*'/, attested by Deming, <**kwelá:tchxwò**>, //kʷəl=ə[=Aɛ́·=]T-c-xʷ-à//, /'*[You just] hold an object.*'/, attested by JL (Tait), <**tsel kwelát te sqwélqwel**>, //c-əl kʷəl=ə[=Aɛ́=]T tə s=qʷɛ̀·[=Aə́=]l=C_1əC_2//, /'*I've got*

news.'/, attested by AD.

<**kwikwelát**>, dmv //C_1í=kʷəl=ə[=Aɛ́=]T//, ABFC [*'someone small is holding (holds) it'*], SOC, (<**R4=**> *diminutive*), phonology: reduplication, syntactic analysis: transitive verb, attested by AD; found in <**kwikwelátes**>, //C_1í=kʷəl=ə[=Aɛ́=]T-əs//, /*'He (small child) is holding it.*'/, attested by AD.

<**kwelálhtst**>, bens //kʷəl=ə[=Aɛ́·=]ɬc=T//, SOC [*'owe s-o'*], literally /'hold for s-o'/, ds //=Aá *durative*, <=**elhts**> *benefactive*, <=**t**> *purposeful control transitivizer*//, phonology: vowel merger, syntactic analysis: transitive verb, attested by Deming, Elders Group; found in <**kwelálhtsthóxes**>, //kʷəl=ə[=Aɛ́=]ɬc=T-áxʸ-əs//, [kʷɪlǽɬcθáxʸɪs], /*'He owes me.*'/, attested by Deming, also <**kwelálhchethóxes**>, //kʷəl=ə[=Aɛ́=]ɬc=əT-áxʸ-əs//, attested by Elders Group 6/7/78.

<**skwelálhchiyelh**>, df //s=kʷəl=ə[=Aɛ́=]ɬc=iyəɬ//, SOC [*'what he owes'*], (<**s=**> *nominalizer*), possibly <**s-**> *nominalizer*, syntactic analysis: nominal, attested by Deming, example: <**qéx̲ te skwelálhchiyelh**>, //qə́x̣ tə s=kʷəl=ɛ́=əɬc=iyəɬ//, /*'He owes lots.*'/, literally /'it's lots the what he owes'/, attested by Deming.

<**kwelátelhtst**>, bens //kʷəl=ə[=Aɛ́·=]=T=əɬc=T//, **ABFC** /*'hold it for s-o'*/, morphological comment: this form contrasts with the benefactive above in both form and meaning, it has both purposeful control transitivizer and benefactive with transitivizer so that both objects are expressed, it contrasts semantically with the previous benefactive since it does not mean *owe s-o*, it is important since it shows how two forms can be developed to express and contrast the literal and figurative meanings, attested by RG & EH (4/9/99 Ling332)), found in <**kwelátelhtsthòxchexw**>, //kʷəl=ə[=Aɛ́·=]=T=əɬc=T-áxʸ-cəxʷ//, /*'hold it for me'*/, attested by RG & EH (4/9/99 Ling332)

<**kwelà:ls**>, sas //kʷəl=ɛ̀·ls//, ABFC /*'hang on (grab and hang on)'*/, <**=á:ls**> *structured activity non-continuative*, phonology: downstepping, attested by RG & EH (4/9/99 Ling332)

<**kwélexw ~ kwél:exw**>, ncs //kʷə́l=ləxʷ//, ABDF /*'get s-th, catch s-th, have s-th, find s-th'*/, FSH, HARV, HUNT, KIN, MC, MED, REL, SOC, (<**=lexw**> *non-control transitivizer*), phonology: stress-shift to next vowel when -es *third person subject* is added, syntactic analysis: transitive verb, attested by EB, AC, AD, BJ2 (Ben James), DC, ASM ['catch s-th'], example: <**kweléxwes te sth'épeq**>, //kʷəl=lə́xʷ-əs tə s=θ'ə́p=əq//, /*'He caught a skunk.*'/, attested by EB, <**kweléxwes te pó:l**>, //kʷəl=lə́xʷ-əs tə pá·l//, /*'He caught the ball.*'/, attested by EB, <**kweléxwes te (sth'ólhem, stó:qw'em)**>, //kʷəl=lə́xʷ-əs tə (s=θ'áɬ=əm, s=tá·q'ʷ=əm)//, /*'He caught a (cold, cough).*'/, attested by EB, ASM ['get s-th'], also <**kwó:lexwes**>, attested by AC, <**qethosésu kwó:lexwes te sthóqwi lhis me p'ékw li te qó:**>, //qə=ƛ'a-s-ə́-s-u kʷál=ləxʷ-əs tə s=θáqʷi ɬi-s mə p'ə́kʷ li tə qá·//, /*'And so they got fish when they surfaced on the water.*'/, usage: text, attested by AC, ASM ['have s-th'], <**líw iyólem kw'els kwélexw kw'e qwe'óp**>, //lí-w ʔiy=ál=əm k'ʷə-l-s kʷə́l=ləxʷ k'ʷə qʷəʔáp//, /*'Can I have an apple?*'/, literally /'is it? (contrastive) alright that I have/get some apple'/, attested by AD, DC, BJ2, <**stám kw'es sth'óqwi i kwélexw?**>, //s=tɛ́m k'ʷ-əs s=θ'áqʷi ʔi kʷə́l=l-əxʷ//, /*'What kind of fish do you have?*'/, attested by EB (12/15/75), ASM ['find s-th'], <**tsel kwélexw thél s'ekw'ò:lèm**>, //c-əl kʷə́l=ləxʷ θə́-l s-ʔi[=Aà=]k'ʷ=í[=M2=]·l=əm//, [cɪl kʷə́lʊxʷ θɪ́l sʔək'ʷà·lə̀m], /*'I found what I lost (nearby but not visible).*'/, phonology: thél shows consonant merger in the faster speech of EB of kwthe to the; also shown here are sentence stress-shifts where the article gets high-stress (one note higher than normal high-stress) and the following nominal gets its stress down-shifted to mid-stress at sentence end, grammatical comment: s- *nominalizer* is inflectional here because the verb is only incorporated into a relative clause, not permanently derived as an independent nominal word, attested by EB, also <**tsel kwélexw tel s'íkw'**>, //c-əl kʷə́l=ləxʷ tə-l s-ʔík'ʷ//, attested by EB, *<**kwélexwlha**> *Find it.* rejected, semantic environment ['non-control verbs

are seldom allowed with imperatives, one rarely orders someone to do something he has no control over completing'].

<**kwél:em ~ kwélem**>, izs //kʷə́l=l=əm//, TVMO /'*get, fetch*'/, (<**=l**> allomorph of <**=lexw**> *non-control transitivizer*, <**=em**> *intransitive (action-focused), antipassive*), syntactic analysis: intransitive verb? or better: antipassive verb, syntactic comment: such intransitive or antipassive verbs can have NP objects but the focus is upon the action rather than the object, (semological comment: focus upon the action rather than upon the object (if any)), attested by EB, MH, example: <**lámtlh kwélem te siyólh**>, //lɛ́=m-tɬ kʷə́l=l=əm tə si=yáɬ//, /'*Go fetch some wood.*'/, phonology: si= allomorph of s= before roots beginning in y, (<**-tlh**> *coaxing imperative, 2nd person sing.*), attested by EB, <**lalh kwélem kw'e sth'óqwi**>, //lɛ-ɬ kʷə́l=l=əm k'ʷə s=θáqʷi//, /'*Go get some fish.*'/, (<**-lh**> *ordering imperative*), phonology: -lh allomorph of -lha after auxiliary verbs such as mi and la, attested by MH, <**lachxw tsesá:t kws las (kwél:em, qó:m) kw qó:**>, //lɛ-c-xʷ cəs=ɛ́·=T kʷ-s lɛ-s (kʷə́l=l=əm, qá·=m) kʷ qá·//, /'*Send him to (get, pack) water.*'/, (<**-ch-xw**> *second person non-subordinate subject* used as *mildly urging imperative*), (<**=á:**> *durative*, <=**t**> *purposeful control transitivizer*, <=l> *non-control transitivizer*, <=em> *intransitivizer (action-focused)*), attested by EB.

<**kwélest**>, pcs //kʷə́l=əs=T//, HUNT /'*catch an animal, get an animal*'/, possibly <**=es**> *on the face*, (<**=t**> *purposeful control transitivizer*), syntactic analysis: transitive verb, attested by Deming.

<**kwéltsestel**>, dnom //kʷə́l=cəs=təl or kʷələ́=M2=cəs=təl//, HHG ['*pot-holder*'], literally /'holding in the hand device'/, lx <**=tses**> *in the hand*, lx <**=tel**> *device, thing for*, phonology: metathesis?, syntactic analysis: nominal, attested by IHTTC.

<kwe**létses**>, ds //kʷələ́=cəs or kʷəl=ə́=cəs//, SOC ['*shake hands*'], lx <**=(é)tses**> *on the hand*, possibly <**=é**> *derivational*? or it may be the stressed part of the suffix (<**=étses**>), syntactic analysis: intransitive verb, attested by Elders Group 3/15/72.

<**kwelátses**>, ds //kʷəl=ə[=Aɛ́=]cəs//, ABFC ['*holding a hand*'], SOC, (<**=Aá**> *durative* or *continuative*), lx <**=etses**> *hand* (alloseme of *on the hand*), syntactic analysis: intransitive verb, attested by Elders Group 3/15/72, compare with <**kwelétses**> *shake hands*.

<**kwelátsest**>, pcs //kʷəl=ə[=Aɛ́=]cəs=T//, ABFC ['*holding the hand of s-o*'], SOC, (<**=t**> *purposeful control transitivizer*), syntactic analysis: transitive verb, attested by Elders Group 3/15/72; found in <**kwelátsesthòmè**>, //kʷəl=ɛ́=cəs=T-àmə̀//, [kʷɪlǽcɪsθàmə̀], /'*holding your hand*'/, attested by Elders Group 3/15/72, example: <**kwelátsesthóxes**>, //kʷəl=ɛ́=cəs=T-áxʸ-əs//, /'*He's holding my hand.*'/, attested by Elders Group 6/7/78.

<**kweltssà:ls**>, sas //kʷəl=cəs=ɛ̀·ls//, SOC ['*shaking hands*'], (<**=á:ls ~ =à:ls**> *structured activity (non-continuative)*), ASM ['the -ing translation reflects the structured activity morpheme not a continuative stem, i.e. it was a structured activity, perhaps done with a number of people but is not continuing at present'], phonology: vowel loss of e in =tses due to speed of speech, syntactic analysis: intransitive verb, attested by EB.

<**kwéletsesà:ls**>, cts //kʷələ́-M2=cəs=ɛ̀·ls//, SOC ['*shaking a lot of hands*'], (<**metathesis type 2**> *continuative*), (<**=à:ls**> *structured activity*), ASM ['the structured activity morpheme rather than a plural morpheme is shown here by the translation: a lot of'], lx <**=tses**> *hand*, phonology: metathesis, syntactic analysis: intransitive verb, attested by AD.

<**kwelétsest**>, pcs //kʷələ́=cəs=T//, SOC ['*shake hands with s-o*'], (<**=t**> *purposeful control transitivizer*), syntactic analysis: transitive verb, attested by Elders Group 3/15/72, AD, also <**kweléchest**>, //kʷələ́=cəs=T//, [kʷɪlə́čɪst ~ kʷɪlíčɪst], attested by EB; found in <**kwelétsesthòmè**>, //kʷələ́=cəs=T-àmə̀//, /'*shake your hand*'/, attested by Elders Group 3/15/72,

example: <**tsel kwelétsest**>, //c-əl kʷələ́=cəs=T//, /'*I shook his hand.*'/, syntactic analysis: ambiguous past, attested by Elders Group 3/15/72, <**kwelétsestlha**>, //kʷələ́=cəs=T-ɬɛ//, /'*Shake his hand.*'/, syntactic analysis: imperative, attested by AD, <**kwelétsestlha ta' siyáye**>, //kʷələ́=cəs=T-ɬɛ t-ɛʔ si=yɛ́yə//, /'*Shake hands with your friend.*'/, syntactic analysis: imperative, attested by Elders Group 3/15/72.

<**kwéletsest**>, cts //kʷələ́-M2=cəs=T//, SOC /'*shaking the hand of s-o, shaking his hand*'/, (<**metathesis type 2**> *continuative*), phonology: metathesis, syntactic analysis: transitive verb, attested by AD, example: <**kwéletsesthóxes**>, //kʷələ́=M2=cəs=T-áxʸ-əs//, [kʷílɪcɪsθáxʸɪs], /'*He was shaking my hand.*'/, attested by AD.

<**kwú:ls**>, pncs //kʷə[=Aú=]l=ls//, ABFC ['*hang onto s-o*'], root <**kwél**> *grasp*, (<**ú-ablaut**> *derivational*), (<**=l(e)s**> *psychological non-control transitivizer*), phonology: ablaut, consonant change (l-l → :l), syntactic analysis: transitive verb, attested by Elders Group, example: <**kwú:lsóxes**>, //kʷə[=Aú·=]l=ls-áxʸ-əs//, [kʷú·lsáxʸɪs], /'*He hangs onto me.*'/, attested by Elders Group.

<**kweltó:l**>, rcps //kʷəl=tá·l//, PLAY ['*to wrestle*'], SOC, ABFC, root <**kwél**> *grasp*, (<**=tó:l**> *reciprocal*), phonology: allomorphy: weak-grade root with strong-grade suffix, syntactic analysis: intransitive verb, attested by EB, others.

<**kwú:ltel**>, cts //kʷə[-Aú·-]l=təl or kʷə[=Aú·=]l-təl//, PLAY /'*wrestling, fighting*'/, SOC, ABFC, root <**kwel**> *grasp*, (<**ú:-ablaut**> *continuative* or *derivational*), (<**=tel**> *reciprocal* or *reciprocal (continuative grade)*), phonology: weak-grade suffix may indicate continuative as in =els *structured activity (continuative)* ~ =á:ls *structured activity (non-continuative)*, ablaut, syntactic analysis: intransitive verb, attested by Elders Group, EB.

<**kwíkweltò:l ~ kwí:kweltò:l**>, cts //C_1í-kʷəl=tá·l//, PLAY ['*wrestling*'], SOC, ABFC, (<**R4-**> *continuative*), phonology: down-drifting or down-stepping shifts high-stress to mid-stress here; strong-grade suffix and strong-grade prefix, weak-grade root, reduplication, syntactic analysis: intransitive verb, attested by Elders Group, EB, BJ, also <**kwikweltó:l**>, //C_1í-kwəl=tá·l//, attested by EB, example: <**tset kwikweltó:l**>, //c-ət C_1í-kwəl=tá·l//, /'*We wrestled.*'/, attested by EB.

<**kwekwí:ltel**>, dmv //C_1í=kʷə[=M2=]l=təl//, cts, PLAY ['*play-fighting*'], SOC, ABFC, (<**R4=**> *diminutive*), (<**metathesis type 2**> *derivational* or *continuative*?), (<**weak-grade suffix tel**> *continuative*?), phonology: metathesis, weak-grade suffix *continuative*, reduplication, syntactic analysis: intransitive verb, attested by EB.

<**skwélemel**>, dnom //s=kʷə́l=əməl or s=kʷələ́=M2=əməl//, HHG ['*handle of a spoon*'], literally /'nominal hold/grasp part'/, lx <**=emel**> *part, member*, (<**metathesis**> *continuative*?), phonology: metathesis?, syntactic analysis: nominal.

<**skwélets**>, dnom //s=kʷə́l=ləc or s=kʷələ́=M2=ləc//, BSK ['*coiled bottom of a basket before the sides are on*'], literally /'something holding the bottom'/, lx <**=lets**> *(on the) bottom*, (<**metathesis**> *continuative*?), phonology: metathesis?, syntactic analysis: nominal.

<**kwelósel**>, dnom //kʷəl=ás=əl//, CAN /'*driver (of car, wagon, etc.)*'/, TVMO, literally /'grasp (by reins) =(on) the face =come/go'/, lx <**=ós**> *(on the) face*, possibly <**=el**> *come, go, get, become*, (<**zero derivation**> *nominalizer*), syntactic analysis: nominal, example: <**ōwéta kwelósels**>, //ʔowə= ́tɛ kʷəl=ás=əl-s//, /'*She has no driver.*'/, literally /'it is none her driver'/.

<**kwelél ~ kwel:éx**>, ds //kʷəl=ə́xʸ ~ kʷəl·=ə́xʸ//, HUNT /'*to shoot, shoot (with bow and arrow)*'/, SOC, ACL /'*shoot (gun, etc.)*'/, literally /'grasp upright'/, lx <**=ex** or **=éx**> *upright*, syntactic analysis: intransitive verb, attested by AC, Elders Group, Salish cognate: Musqueam /kʷə́lləxʸ/ *shoot* Suttles ca1984: ch.7 [p.96], also <**kwélex**>, //kʷə́l=əxʸ//, attested by EB, example: <**stsōwó:t kw's**

kweléxs>, //s=cəwá·t k'ʷ-s kʷəl=ə́xʸ-s//, /'*He knows how to shoot.*'/, attested by AC, <**stsōwó:t kwthel mál kw'es kweléxs lhlá:mes há:we**>, //s=cəwá·t kʷθə-l mɛ́l k'ʷə-s kʷəl=ə́xʸ-s ɬə-lɛ́·=m-əs hɛ́·wə//, /'*My (near but not visible) father knows how to shoot when he goes hunting.*'/, syntactic comment: subjunctive with lhe, attested by AC.

<**ákwelex**>, cts //ʔɛ́-kʷəl=əxʸ//, HUNT ['*shooting*'], (irregular)<á->//ʔɛ́-// *continuative*, syntactic analysis: intransitive verb, attested by AC (8/24/70), Salish cognate: Musqueam /ʔɛ́ʔkʷəl'ləxʸ/ *be shooting* Suttles ca1984: ch.7 [p.96].

<**sakwelá̖x ~ sekwelá̖x**>, dnom //s=ɛ=kʷəl=ə[=Aɛ=]´xʸ ~ s=ɛ́=kʷəl=ə[=M3=]xʸ//, HUNT /'*arrow, gun*'/, ACL ['*gun*'], (<**s=**> *nominalizer*, <á=> *continuative* here derivational), (<**a=ablaut** or **metathesis type 3**> *derivational*), phonology: ablaut, metathesis type 3 (switches first and third vowels), syntactic analysis: nominal, attested by Elders Group, AC, BJ, also <**sékwelá̖x**>, //s=ɛ́=kʷəl=ə[=M3 ´=]xʸ//, attested by Elders Group, also <**sékwelàx**>, //s=ɛ́=kʷəl=ə[=M3 ´=]xʸ//, attested by JL and grandmother MJ (Mrs. August Jim)--Elders Group 10/27/76, also <**sikwelá̖x**>, //s=ɛ=Ai=kʷəl=ə[=Aɛ=] ´xʸ//, phonology: double ablaut, metathesis type 3, attested by EB, also <**síkwelax**>, //s=ɛ[=Ai=] ´=kʷəl=ə[=Aɛ=]xʸ//, phonology: double ablaut, attested by BHTTC, comparative note: the unusual phonological form of the word may be show influence of one of the four Chinook Jargon words for *gun*, i.e. <sak-wá-la ~ suck-w ~ shuckwalála ~ sookwalash>, from such variant spellings it appears that the Halkomelem word could possibly even have been the source of the Chinook Jargon just as easily as vice versa, especially since the stem in UHk means to *shoot an arrow (or a gun)* and may be lit. /'hold upright'/, example: <**sékwelàxs te té<u>x</u>wets**>, //sə́kʷəlɛ̀xʸ-s tə tə́x̣ʷəc//, /'*arrow of a bow*'/, attested by JL and grandmother MJ--Elders Group 10/27/76, <**tl'e te'í:le sakwelá̖x, le q'éylexw te mó:qw**>, //ƛ'ə tə=ʔí·=lə s=ɛ=kʷəl=ɛ́xʸ, lə q'ɛ́y=ləxʷ tə má·qʷ//, /'*This is the gun that killed the bird.*'/, attested by AC, <**méstexw ta sakwelá̖x qe tl'olsuw kweléxt te mó:qw**>, //mə́=sTəxʷ t-ɛʔ s=ɛ=kʷəl=ɛ́xʸ qə ƛ'a-l-s-uw kʷəl=ə́xʸ=T tə má·qʷ//, /'*Give (lend) me your gun and I will shoot the bird.*'/, literally /'come=causative s-th (bring it, fetch it) your gun and then I shoot it the bird'/, syntactic comment: imperative by implication (when nominal. obj. is possessed by 2s possessive pronoun affix, and no subj. pronoun is present, 2s imperative is assumed by default), attested by AC.

<**kweléxt**>, pcs //kʷəl=ə́xʸ=T//, HUNT ['*shoot s-th/s-o*'], SOC, ABFC ['*sting s-o/s-th*'], (<**=t**> *purposeful control transitivizer*), syntactic analysis: transitive verb, attested by Elders Group, AC, other sources: ES /kʷələ́xʸt/, also <**kwélext**>, //kʷə́l=əxʸ=T//, attested by CT, HT, ASM ['shoot s-o/s-th'], example: <**táwet te tl'elqtéle kw'es le kwélext te (tl'elqtéle, sméyéth)**>, //tɛ́w=əT təƛ'ɛ[=əl=]qt=ə́lə k'ʷə-s lə kʷə́l=əxʸ=T tə (ƛ'ɛ[=əl=]qt=ə́lə, s=mɛ́yə́θ)//, /'*light up the deer to shoot the (deer, animal)*'/, attested by CT, HT, <**tsel kweléxt te móqw**>, //c-əl kʷəl=ə́xʸ=T tə máqʷ//, /'*I shot the bird.*'/, attested by AC, <**le kweléxtes te mó:qw**>, //lə kʷəl=ə́xʸ=T-əs tə má·qʷ//, /'*He shot the bird.*'/, attested by AC, ASM ['sting s-o/s-th'], <**kweléxthóxes te sisemóye**>, //kʷəl=ə́xʸ=T-áxʸ-əs tə C_1í=səmáyə//, /'*The bee stung me.*'/, attested by Elders Group 4/2/75.

<**Kwelxá:lxw**>, df //kʷəl=əxʸ=ɛ́·lxʷ//, PLN ['*Mount Baker*'], poss. lx <**=á:lxw**> *leaves*, (compare with <**hilá:lxw**> *autumn* (root <**hil=**> *fall, drop and roll* and <**=á:lxw**> *leaves*), borrowed from Nooksack /kʷəlš=ǽn/ *Mt. Baker, the slopes clear of underbrush where they hunted*, literally means *shooting place* (Suttles 1950: Nooksack field notes from George Swanaset interview 4/26/50)(UHk cognate of the Nooksack root is <**kweléx ~ kwel:éx**> *shoot*, the suffix could be a rare UHk cognate to Nooksack /=ǽn/ *place* or just using one that sounds similar), phonology: the final xw may have been added by analogy with the suffix on hilá:lxw, syntactic analysis: nominal, attested by Elders Group 4/16/75, source: place names file reference #123 and #318.

<**kweléqelh**>, df //kʷələ́qəɬ//, SOC ['*distribute*'], possibly root <**kwelé=**> *grasp, hold (in hand)*, probably <**=elhts**> *benefactive*, syntactic analysis: intransitive verb, attested by Elders Group 3/72,

Adaline Lorenzetto 3/72, Salish cognate: possibly Lushootseed /kʷə́lq/ *other things*? (Hess 1976:247), example: <**latselcha kweléqelh**>, //lɛ-c-əl-cɛ kʷələ́qəɬ//, /'*I will distribute*'/, attested by Elders Group 3/72, source: Stalo Heritage Proj. tape 33.

<**kweléqelh(t)st**>, pcs //kʷələ́q=əɬc=T//, bens, SOC ['*distribute to s-o*'], (<**=elhts**> *benefactive*, <**=t**> *purposeful control transitivizer*), phonology: the t in =elhts is not heard on the tape, perhaps not pronounced as a consonant-shift due to speed or dialect differences, perhaps pronounced but merely not heard on the tape or mistranscribed by me, syntactic analysis: transitive verb, attested by Elders Group 3/72; found in <**kweléqelhsthòmè**>, //kʷələ́q=əɬc=T-àmə̀//, /'*distribute to you*'/, attested by Elders Group 3/72, <**kw'els kweléqelhstòlè**>, //k'ʷə-l-s kʷələ́q=əɬc=T-àlə̀//, /'*that I distribute to you folks*'/, attested by AL (in Elders Group 3/72).

<**kwelálhtst**>, SOC ['*owe s-o*'], *see* kwél.

<**kwelát**>, ABFC /'*hold s-th (in one's grasp), holding s-th (in one's grasp), have s-th, grasp s-th*'/, *see* kwél.

<**kwelátses**>, ABFC ['*holding a hand*'], *see* kwél.

<**kwelátsest**>, ABFC ['*holding the hand of s-o*'], *see* kwél.

<**kweleleselqel**>, df //kʷələləs=ə́lqəl//, ANA ['*(have) fine hair*'], lx <**=élqel**> *wool, hair*, syntactic analysis: adjective/adjectival verb, nominal?, attested by BHTTC, Salish cognate: same root perhaps in Squamish /kʷə́l(=)məxʷ(=)us/ *fine-work basket*? (Kuipers 1967:341).

<**kwél:em ~ kwélem**>, TVMO /'*get, fetch*'/, *see* kwél.

<**kweléqelh**>, SOC ['*distribute*'], *see* kwel *grasp, hold (in hand),*

<**kweléqelh(t)st**>, SOC ['*distribute to s-o*'], *see* kwel.

<**kwélest**>, HUNT /'*catch an animal, get an animal*'/, *see* kwél.

<**kwelétses**>, SOC ['*shake hands*'], *see* kwél.

<**kwéletsesà:ls**>, SOC ['*shaking a lot of hands*'], *see* kwél.

<**kwéletsest**>, SOC /'*shaking the hand of s-o, shaking his hand*'/, *see* kwél.

<**kwelétsest**>, SOC ['*shake hands with s-o*'], *see* kwél.

<**kweléx ~ kwel:éx**>, HUNT /'*to shoot, shoot (with bow and arrow)*'/, *see* kwél.

<**kweléxt**>, HUNT ['*shoot s-th/s-o*'], *see* kwél.

<**kwélexw ~ kwél:exw**>, ABDF /'*get s-th, catch s-th, have s-th, find s-th*'/, *see* kwél.

<**kwelkwálő̃ws ~ kwelkwáléws**>, SOC ['*to murder*'], *see* kwà:l.

<**kwelkwálő̃wst ~ kwelkwáléwst**>, SOC ['*murder s-o*'], *see* kwà:l.

<**kwelkwelqéylém**>, LAND ['*caves*'], *see* kwelqéylém ~ kwelqílém.

<**Kwelkwelqéylém**>, PLN ['*name of the first mountain northwest of X̱ó:letsa Smá:lt (X̱ó:letsa Smá:lt a mountain with Frozen Lake as one of several lakes on it)*'], *see* kwelqéylém ~ kwelqílém.

<**kwelkwímelésem**>, ABDF /'*one's face is red, one is blushing*'/, *see* kwí:m.

<**kwelósel**>, CAN /'*driver (of car, wagon, etc.)*'/, *see* kwél.

<**kwelqéylém ~ kwelqílém**>, df //kʷəl(=)q(əl)=íl=ə́m//, incs, LAND ['*cave*'], literally perhaps? /'place to have/get hold on the head (or) go holding one's head ??'/, possibly root <**kwel=**> *hold, grasp*, possibly <**=qel**> *(on the) head*, (<**=íl**> *go, come, get, become, inceptive*), possibly <**=em**> *place to have/get* or

middle voice, phonology: consonant-loss and vowel merger of el before =íl, syntactic analysis: nominal, intransitive verb?.

<**kwelkwelqéylém**>, df //C_1əC_2=kʷəl(=)q(əl)=íl=ə́m//, LAND ['*caves*'], ASM ['there's a lot of them near Kw'ikw'iyále (the pools on the Coquihalla River that gave that river its name)'], (<**R3=**> *plural*), phonology: reduplication, syntactic analysis: intransitive verb?, nominal?.

<**Kwelkwelqéylém**>, df //C_1əC_2=kʷəl(=)q(əl)=íl=ə́m//, PLN ['*name of the first mountain northwest of X̱ó:letsa Smá:lt (X̱ó:letsa Smá:lt a mountain with Frozen Lake as one of several lakes on it)*'], literally /'caves'/, syntactic analysis: nominal, source: place names file reference #156, attested by SP and AK 8/2/77 at Fish Camp.

<**kweltó:l**>, PLAY ['*to wrestle*'], *see* kwél.

<**kwéltsestel**>, HHG ['*pot-holder*'], *see* kwél.

<**kweltssà:ls**>, SOC ['*shaking hands*'], *see* kwél.

<**Kwelxá:lxw**>, PLN ['*Mount Baker*'], *see* kwél.

<**kwém**>, free root //kʷə́m or kʷa[=Aə=] ´m//, SD /'*to thud (dull, outside)*'/, phonology: ablaut, syntactic analysis: intransitive verb, attested by Elders Group, Salish cognate: Squamish /kʷumʔ, kʷəmʔ/ *to thump; to rise; protuberance, lump* as in /kʷə́m-iʔn/ *to thump* (Kuipers 1967), example: <**le kwém**>, //lə kʷə́m//, /'*It thuds (dull, outside sound)., (It thudded.)*'/, syntactic analysis: ambiguous past.

<**kwómkwem**>, cts //kʷám=C_1əC_2 or kʷə[=Aa=] ´m=C_1əC_2//, chrs //?//, its //?//, frqs //?//, plv //?//, SD ['*thudding (of footsteps or horses hooves on ground)*'], semantic environment ['footsteps or horses hooves on ground'], possibly <**=R2**> *continuative or characteristic* or possibly *iterative or frequentative*, possibly <**o-ablaut**> *derivational*, phonology: reduplication, possible ablaut, syntactic analysis: intransitive verb, attested by BHTTC.

<**kwémléxw ~ kwemléxw ~ kwémlexw ~ kwèmlèxw**>, us //kʷə́mlə́xʷ ~ kʷəmlə́xw ~ kʷə́mləxʷ ~ kʷə̀mlə̀xʷ//, [kʷʊ́mlʊ́xʷ ~ kʷmlʊ́xʷ ~ kʷʊ́mlʊxʷ ~ kʷə́mlʊxʷ ~ kʷm´lʊxʷ ~ kʷʊ̀mlʊ̀xʷ], EB ['*root*'], possibly root <**kwám ~ kwem**> *round*, syntactic analysis: nominal, attested by AC, BJ, EB, other sources: ES /kʷə̀mlə̀xʷ/, H-T 1902 <kwo'mloq> prob. [kʷʊ̆mlʊxʷ], example: <**kwèmlèxws te theqát**>, //kʷə̀mlə̀xʷ-s tə θəqɛ́t//, /'*root of a tree, tree root*'/, attested by AC, <**kwémlexws te x̱epáy**>, //kʷə́mləxʷ-s tə x̣əp=ɛ́y//, /'*(red) cedar root, root of a red cedar*'/, attested by AC, <**xí:pet te kwemléxw**>, //xʸí·p=əT tə kʷəmlə́xʷ//, /'*peel the root*'/, attested by AC, also <**xí:pet te kwémlexw**>, //xʸí·p=əT tə kʷə́mləxʷ//, /'*peel roots, straighten unevenly split roots*'/, attested by EB, <**seq'át te kwémlexw**>, //səq'=ɛ́=T tə kʷə́mləxʷ//, /'*split a root*'/, attested by EB.

<**xwelítemelh x̱eyeslótel** (or) **kw'ókw'es kwémlexw s'élhtel**>, EB, FOOD *ginger* (lit. white man style + wild ginger (or) hot + root + food), (attested by RG,EH 6/16/98 to SN, edited by BG with RG,EH 6/26/00)

<**kweq'tál**>, df //kʷəq'tɛ́l or kʷəq'=tə[=Aɛ́=]l or kʷɛ́q'=tə[=M2=]l//, ANA ['*shoulder-blade*'], (<**=tel**> *device, thing for* or =tel *reciprocal*), (<**á-ablaut** or **metathesis type 2**> *derivational*), phonology: possible ablaut or metathesis, syntactic analysis: nominal, attested by SJ, also <**kwokwéq'tel**>, //kʷɛ[=Aa=C_1ə] ´q'=təl or C_1á=kʷə́q'=təl//, [kʷakʷə́q'təl], phonology: reduplication, possible ablaut, attested by Elders Group, also <**kweqw'tá:l**>, //kʷəq'ʷtɛ́·l or kʷəq'ʷ=tə[=Aɛ́·=]lor kʷɛ́·q'ʷ=tə[=M2=]l//, attested by Deming.

<**kwesúyex̱el**>, df //kʷəs(=)úy(=)əx̣əl//, LAND ['*valley*'], syntactic analysis: nominal, attested by SJ, MV, comment: this word may be a borrowing from Nooksack, since SJ and MV gave a word with a similar affix in two versions, súyéx̱el ~ sóyéx̱el *edge of the sky*, and Nooksack ú corresponds to Halkomelem ó /á/; the cases of Upriver Halkomelem ú /ú/ that are not in borrowed words usually

are found before w, seldom before y.

<**kweshú**>, free root //k^{w}əšú//, EZ ['*domestic pig*'], ['Genus *Sus*, introduced'], borrowed from Hudson's Bay Co. French <**cochon**> //košɔ̃// *pig* or Chinook Jargon /kúšu ~ kóšo/ *hog, pork, ham, bacon* (Johnson 1978:385) (possibly pronounced /kušú ~ košó/ in Chinook Jargon?), syntactic analysis: nominal, attested by AC, Elders Group, etc., also <**kweshú:**>, //k^{w}əšú·//, attested by AC, example: <**ló:s te kweshú:**>, //lá·s tə k^{w}əšú·//, /'*The pig is fat.*'/, attested by AC.

<**kwíkweshú**>, dmn //C_1í=k^{w}əšú//, EZ ['*little pig*'], (<**R4=**> *diminutive*), phonology: reduplication, syntactic analysis: nominal, attested by BHTTC, example: <**qí:qel te kwíkweshú**>, //C_1í=qəl tə C_1í=k^{w}əšú//, /'*The little pig is naughty.*'/, usage: in the Híltu Song, a fun song sung to "Jimmy Crack Corn", attested by BHTTC, <**ts'áts'ets'tl'ím te kwíkweshú**>, //C_1ɛ́=C_1ə=c'ƛ'ɛ́=m=ím tə C_1í=k^{w}əšú//, /'*The little pig is hopping.*'/, (<**R7=**> *continuative* or *emphatic*, R5= *diminutive*), (<**=m**> *middle voice*, <**=ím**> *iterative, repeatedly, repetitive*), phonology: double reduplication, consonant-loss of m before =ím, and vowel merger, usage: in the Híltu Song, attested by BHTTC.

<**kwekweshú'ò:llh**>, dnom //C_1ə=k^{w}əšú=ʔà·ɬ//, EZ ['*piglet*'], (<**R5=**> *diminutive*), (<**='ò:llh**> *offspring*), phonology: reduplication, syntactic analysis: nominal, attested by CT.

<**kwetáxw**>, bound root //k^{w}ətɛ́x^w *inside*//.

<**skwetáxw**>, stvi //s-k^{w}ətɛ́x^w//, [sk^{w}ʊtɛ́x^w ~ sk^{w}ətɛ́x^w], BLDG /'*be inside a house, be inside an enclosure*'/, DIR, (<**s-**> *stative*), syntactic analysis: adverb/adverbial verb, attested by Elders Group, IHTTC, AC, EB, example: <**skwetáxw te lálem**>, //s=k^{w}ətɛ́x^w tə lɛ́ləm//, /'*in the house*'/, attested by AC, also <**skwetáxw li te lálem**>, //s-k^{w}ətɛ́x^w li tə lɛ́ləm//, /'*inside the house*'/, literally /'inside in the house'/, attested by EB, <**líye skwetáxw se Mary**>, //lí-ə s-k^{w}ətɛ́x^w sə Mary//, /'*Is Mary home?*'/, literally /'Is she there? inside the (female near but not visible) Mary'/, semantic environment ['the speaker is near to Mary's residence'], (<**-e**> *interrogative (yes/no question)* (optional after sentence-initial li; found in examples below)), phonology: consonant-loss; se is short for kwse *the (female near but not visible)*; iterative aspect loses the kw here after xw (and perhaps after other labialized consonants) in rapid speech, attested by AC, <**li skwetáxw tha (màl, sí:le)**>, //li s-k^{w}ətɛ́x^w θ-ɛ (mɛ̀l, sí·lə)//, /'*Is your (father, grandfather) in?*'/, semantic environment ['the speaker is outside the building'], phonology: consonant-loss; <tha>//θə-ɛ// is short for <kwtha>/k^{w}θ-ɛ/ *the (male or gender unspecified near but not visible)*; it loses the kw here after xw (+ other labialized consonants?) in rapid speech; the article <tha> //θə-ɛ// here cannot be from <the> /θə/ *the (female present and visible or presence and visibility unspecified)* because the nominals are male (for ex. *father*) and not visible; vowel merger is also present here (<ea> → <a>, /əɛ/ → /ɛ/), attested by AC, <**líye skwetáxw kw'e John**>, //lí-ə s-k^{w}ətɛ́x^w k'^{w}ə ǰán//, /'*Is John home?*'/, literally /'is there - interrogative (yes/no) inside the (distant, remote) John'/, semantic environment ['speaker is distant from John's home'], phonology: vowel merger, attested by AC.ˇ

<**skwetáxwstexw**>, caus //s=k^{w}ətɛ́x^w=sTəx^w//, BLDG ['*leave s-o/s-th inside*'], TVMO, DIR, (<**=stexw**> *causative*), syntactic analysis: transitive verb, attested by IHTTC, example: <**skwetáxwstem**>, //s=k^{w}ətɛ́x^w=sTəx^w-əm//, /'*They were left inside.*'/, syntactic analysis: passive, attested by IHTTC.

<**skwetóxwes**>, stvi //s=k^{w}ətɛ́[=Aá=]x^w=əs//, SPRD /'*mask covering the face*'/, <**=es**> *face*, lit. /"face is inside"/, phonological comment <**=Aó**> automatically <**a**> → <**ó**> when word has suffix <**=es**> *face*, semantic comment: the only mask in Stó:lō area was <**s<u>x</u>wó:y<u>x</u>wey**>, attested by RG & EH (4/10/99 Ling332)

<**skwetóxwes sqw'eyílex**>, cpds //s=k^{w}ətɛ́[=Aá=]x^w=əs s=q'^{w}əy=íl=əx^y//, SPRD /'*mask dance*'/, semantic comment: the only mask in Stó:lō area was <**s<u>x</u>wó:y<u>x</u>wey**>, attested by RG & EH (4/10/99 Ling332)

<**kwetáxwt**>, pcs //kʷətɛ́xʷ=T//, BLDG /'*bring s-o/s-th in (to a house/enclosure), take s-o/s-th in(inside a house/enclosure), admit s-o (into a house/enclosure), let s-o/s-th in (to a house/enclosure), put s-o/s-th in (inside a house/enclosure*'/, DIR, TVMO, (<**=t**> *purposeful control transitivizer*), syntactic analysis: transitive verb, attested by IHTTC, Elders Group, EB, ASM ['bring s-o/s-th in (to a house or enclosure)'], <**kwtáxwtem**>, //kʷtɛ́xʷ=T-əm//, /'*Someone was brought in.*'/, phonology: vowel-loss in rapid speech, syntactic analysis: passive, attested by IHTTC, ASM ['let s-o/s-th in (to a house or enclosure)'], <**kwtáxwt te sqwemá:y**>, //kʷtɛ́xʷ=T tə s=qʷəm=ɛ́·y//, /'*let the dog in*'/, phonology: vowel-loss in rapid speech, syntactic comment: no subject given in this phrase, attested by EB, ASM ['put s-o/s-th inside (a house or enclosure)'], example: <**kwtáxwt lí te kyó**>, //kʷtɛ́xʷ=T lí tə kʸá//, /'*put it inside the car*'/, phonology: vowel-loss in rapid speech, syntactic analysis: no subject given in this phrase, attested by EB, <**lámtlh kwtáxwt**>, //lɛ́=m-tɬ kʷtɛ́xʷ=T//, /'*Go put it inside the house (coaxing).*'/, phonology: vowel-loss in rapid speech, syntactic analysis: coaxing imperative, attested by EB.

<**kwétexwt**>, cts //kʷə[-´-]tɛ́[-Aə-]xʷ or kʷətɛ́[-M2Aə-]xʷ//, BLDG /'*admitting s-o/s-th, letting s-o/s-th in, bringing s-o/s-th inside*'/, (<**stress-shift and e-ablaut**> *continuative* or <**metathesis and e-ablaut**> *continuative*), syntactic analysis: transitive verb, attested by Elders Group, NP.

<**kwetáxwstexw**>, caus //kʷətɛ́xʷ=sTəxʷ//, BLDG ['*keep s-o/s-th inside*'], (<**=stexw**> *causative*), syntactic analysis: transitive verb, attested by IHTTC, example: <**kwetáxwstem**>, //kʷətɛ́xʷ=sTəxʷ=əm//, /'*They were kept inside*'/, syntactic analysis: passive, attested by IHTTC.

<**kwtxwéltsep ~ kwetxwéltsep**>, ds //kʷtxʷ=ə́lcəp ~ kʷətxʷ=ə́lcəp//, FIRE /'*bring in firewood, bring wood in*'/, lx <**=éltsep**> *firewood*, phonology: note the vowel-loss in the root due to its ambivalent stress grade (variable stress grade) before the strong stress grade suffix, syntactic analysis: intransitive verb, attested by IHTTC, Elders Group, AHTTC.

<**kwetxwí:lem**>, mdls //kʷətxʷ=í·l=əm//, BLDG /'*go in (a house/enclosure), come in, come inside, enter a house or enclosure*'/, DIR, TVMO, (<**=í:l**> *come, go, get, become*, <**=em**> *middle voice*), syntactic analysis: intransitive verb, attested by IHTTC, AC, also <**kwetxwílém**>, //kʷətxʷ=íl=ə́m//, attested by EB, also <**kwetxwílem**>, //kʷətxʷ=íl=əm//, attested by Elders Group, example: <**qesu la kwetxwí:lem yutl'ólem; x̲ét'esexwes ye xwelítem "cave"**>, //qə=s=u lɛ kʷətxʷ=í:l=əm y=u=ƛ'á=lə=m; x̣ə́t'ə=sTəxʷ-əs yə xʷəlítəm "cave"//, /'*And so they went inside; White people call it "cave".*'/, attested by AC, usage: from the Story of the Flood, <**mís tl'ó kwetxwílém te sqwemá:y**>, //mí-s ƛ'á kʷətxʷ=íl=ə́m tə s=qʷəm=ɛ́·y//, /'*let the dog come in*'/, attested by EB, <**lichxw we'éy el qwóqwel kw'es me kwetxwílem (te xwelítem, kwtha siyáya)?**>, //li-c-xʷ wə-ʔɛ́y ʔəl qʷɛ̀·[-AáC₁ə-]l k'ʷ-əs mə kʷətxʷ=íl=əm (tə xʷəlítəm, kʷ=θ=ɛ si=yɛ́yɛ)//, /'*Were you still talking when (the white man came in, your friend came in)?*'/, attested by AC.

<**kwetexwí:lem**>, cts //kʷətɛ[-Aə-]xʷ=í·l=əm//, BLDG /'*(more than one) entering a house, going in (of a whole bunch)*'/, DIR, TVMO, (<**e-ablaut**> *continuative, plural subject*), syntactic analysis: intransitive verb, attested by IHTTC, AD, Elders Group, also <**kwetexwílem**>, //kʷətɛ[-Aə-]xʷ=íl=əm//, attested by Elders Group, AD.

<**skwetxwewílh**>, dnom //s=kʷətxʷ=əwíɬ//, MC ['*the inside (of a container)*'], semantic environment ['a canoe, a house, a can, a purse, etc.'], (<**s=**> *nominalizer*), (<**=ewílh**> *container*), phonology: vowel-loss, ambivalent stress grade root loses stress and vowel before a strong stress grade suffix, syntactic analysis: nominal, dialects: *Tait*, attested by IHTTC.

<**skwetxwó:lwelh**>, dnom //s=kʷətxʷ=á·lwəɬ//, BLDG /'*inner lining, inner side*'/, DIR, MC, (<**s=**> *nominalizer*), (<**=ó:lwelh**> *side, surface*), phonology: vowel-loss and stress-shift of ambivalent stress grade root before a strong stress grade suffix, syntactic analysis: nominal, dialects: *Chill., Cheh., Tait*, attested by IHTTC, example: <**skwetxwó:lwelhs te kopú**>, //s=kʷətxʷ=á·lwəɬ-s tə kapú//, /'*the inside of a coat, the lining of a coat*'/, attested by IHTTC, <**skwetxólwelh t'ómel**>,

//s=kʷətxʷ=álwəɬ t'áməl//, /'*inside wall*'/, dialects: *Chill., Cheh.*, attested by IHTTC, also <**skwetxwó:lwelh t'ó:mel**>, //s=kʷətxʷ=á·lwəɬ t'á·məl//, also /'*carved post inside longhouse*'/, attested by DM 12/4/64.

<**skwetxwós**>, dnom //s=kʷətxʷ=ás//, BLDG ['*ceiling*'], (<**s=**> *nominalizer*), (<**=ó:s**> *on the face*), syntactic analysis: nominal, example: <**skwetxwós te lálem**>, //s=kʷətxʷ=ás-s tə lɛ́ləm//, /'*ceiling of a house*'/, phonology: consonant merger, vowel-loss and stress-shift of root before strong stress grade suffix.

<**Skwtéxwqel**>, dnom //s=kʷtɛ[=Aə=] ´xʷ=qəl//, PLN /'*point on west side of Harrison River on which or across from which S*x̱*wó:y*x̱*wey is located (the rock formation resembling a s*x̱*wó:y*x̱*wey mask); the first point on Harrison River after it leaves Harrison Lake*'/, literally /'inside on the head'/, (<**s=**> *nominalizer*), (<**e-ablaut**> *derivational*), (<**=qel**> *on the head, at the head or source of a river*), phonology: ablaut, syntactic analysis: nominal, attested by EL 6/27/78.

<**kwétxwt**>, df //kʷə́txʷ=T//, pcs, FOOD ['*take someone's food or clothes*'], CLO, SOC, (<**=t**> *purposeful control transitivizer*), syntactic analysis: transitive verb, attested by IHTTC.

<**kwetáxwstexw**>, BLDG ['*keep s-o/s-th inside*'], *see* kwetáxw.

<**kwetáxwt**>, BLDG /'*bring s-o/s-th in (to a house/enclosure), take s-o/s-th in(inside a house/enclosure), admit s-o (into a house/enclosure), let s-o/s-th in (to a house/enclosure), put s-o/s-th in (inside a house/enclosure*'/, *see* kwetáxw.

<**kwetexwí:lem**>, BLDG /'*(more than one) entering a house, going in (of a whole bunch)*'/, *see* kwetáxw.

<**kwétexwt**>, BLDG /'*admitting s-o/s-th, letting s-o/s-th in, bringing s-o/s-th inside*'/, *see* kwetáxw.

<**kwetxwí:lem**>, BLDG /'*go in (a house/enclosure), come in, come inside, enter a house or enclosure*'/, *see* kwetáxw.

<**kwétxwt**>, SD ['*to rattle s-th inside*'], *see* kwótxwem ~ kwótx̱wem.

<**kwétxwt**>, df //kʷə́txʷ=T//, pcs, FOOD ['*take someone's food or clothes*'], *see* kwetáxw.

<**kwéth**>, bound root //kʷə́θ//, meaning unknown

<**skwéthqsel**>, df //s-kʷə́θ=qsəl//, stvi, BPI ['*(have) a big nose*'], (<**s-**> *stative* or *nominiazer,* probably both are attested, resp. by *'have a big nose'* and *'big nose'*), lx <**=qsel**> *on the nose*, syntactic analysis: adjective/adjectival verb, nominal?, attested by SJ, contrast <**sméqsel**> *have a big nose*, example: <**ō taléwe skwéthqsel**>, //ʔo tɛ=lə́wə s-kʷə́θ=qsəl//, /'*Oh you big nose.*'/, usage: body part insult, attested by SJ.

<**kwethá ~ kwe thá**>, DEM /'*him (there, near but not visible), that one*'/, *see* kw.

<**kwéth'**>, bound root //kʷə́θ'//, meaning unknown

<**skwéth' ~ skwéth'kweth'**>, dnom //s=kʷə́θ' ~ s=kʷə́θ'=C_1əC_2//, EZ /'*willow grouse, ruffed grouse*'/, ['*Bonasa umbellus sabini*'], (<**s=**> *nominalizer*), (<**=R2**> *characteristic* or *frequentative* or *iterative*), phonology: reduplication, syntactic analysis: nominal, attested by AC, BJ, others from Cheh., dialects: *apparently Chill., Cheh.*, other sources: ES /skʷə́θ'kʷaθ'/ (CwMs /skʷə́θ'/), JH:DM /skʷə́θ'/, Salish cognate: Squamish /skʷə́c'/ *willow grouse*, also <**sqwéth' ~ sqwéth'qweth'**>, //s=qʷə́θ' ~ s=qʷə́θ'=C_1əC_2//, phonology: reduplication, attested by BJ, others mainly Tait speakers, dialects: *largely Tait.*

<**th'ith'kwimelálews**>, df //θ'i[=C_1ə=]kʷ=əm=ím=əl=ɛ́ləws or C_1í=kʷθ'=M2=ím=əl=ɛ́ləws//, [θ'iθ'kʷiməlǽləws], EB ['*big-leaved avens*'], ['*Geum macrophyllum*'], probably root <**th'íth'ekwem**> *have an allergic reaction (esp. to bark powder of fir or cedar)*, possibly root <**kwéth'**> *willow grouse, ruffed grouse*, possibly <**=ím**> *repeatedly*, possibly <**=el**> *get, inceptive*

or pluralizes suffix or connective, possibly <**=álews**> *leaf*, Elder's comment: "means *grouse leaf* because the willow grouse eats it", phonology: if derived from kwéth', a very complex set of phonological changes are required: metathesis of consonants then reduplication with the switched consonant (not attested elsewhere for the language),, plus three suffixes; if derived from th'ith'ekwem (for which I have no evidence but the close resemblance of the words; the derivation from grouse would have to be a folk etymology) only the normal replacement of preceding em by the suffix =ím *repeatedly* plus two suffixes is required, MED ['part of the plant is rubbed on as a numbing medicine'], syntactic analysis: nominal, attested by SJ, contrast <**xwókw'eltel**> *big-leaved avens*, literally "thing for getting numb, numbing medicine".

<**kwetl'éthet**>, ABFC /'*start to struggle, start to flip around to escape (fish esp.)*'/, *see* kwá:.

<**kwetl'kwótl'thetōws**>, WATR ['*water jumping (as it goes over a rough bottom in a river)*'], *see* kwá:.

<**Kwetl'kwótl'thetōws**>, PLN ['*a stretch of water in the Fraser River on the C.N. side by Strawberry Island*'], *see* kwá:.

<**kwexáls**>, N ['*naming*'], *see* kwí:x ~ kwíx.

<**kwéyl**>, free root //kʷɛ́yl//, EZ /'*mountain quail*, possibly also *California quail*'/, ['*Oreortyx pictus*, possibly also *Lophortyx californicus*'], ASM ['introduced by non-Indians'], borrowed from English /kʷéyl/ *quail*, syntactic analysis: nominal, attested by AC.

<**kwíkwekwchá:m**>, ABFC ['*squealing (like a pig for ex.)*'], *see* kwátsem ~ kwáchem.

<**kwikwelát**>, ABFC ['*someone small is holding (holds) it*'], *see* kwél.

<**kwíkweltò:l ~ kwí:kweltò:l**>, PLAY ['*wrestling*'], *see* kwél.

<**kwíkwemel**>, LT ['*it's getting red*'], *see* kwí:m.

<**kwíkweshú**>, EZ ['*little pig*'], *see* kweshú.

<**Kwíkwetl'em**>, df //kʷíkʷəƛ’=əm, possibly C_1í=kʷaƛ’=əm//, PLN ['*Coquitlam*'], SOC ['*Coquitlam Indian people*'], literally /'stinking (of fish slime), smelly fish slime'/, ASM ['the people were called this according to Duff because the tribe sold themselves to a neighboring tribe as slaves when they were starving one winter and were covered with fish slime working for their masters during salmon season; Boas gives more of the early background (I have normalized his transcriptions here): the Kwíkwetl'em of Choních en (a village?), he says, "are descendants of slaves of Tl'pelqílen (prob. Tl'pelqílem), chief of the Kwantlen, who established a fishing station at the site of the Kwíkwetl'em village, and ordered part of his slaves to live at this place. Five generations ago, when wars were raging on this part of the coast, they became free, and continue to occupy their old village. They are, however, not con- sidered as equals of the other tribes, and never owned any land....Their present chief is named T'élq'es."'], phonology: possible reduplication, syntactic analysis: nominal, intransitive verb? also, attested by Elders Group, DF, EL, BJ 12/5/64, Elder's comment: "EL recalled that in the Kwantlen dialect of Downriver Halkomelem the word meant *stinking*", source: place name reference file #106, other sources: Duff 1952:27, Boas 1895:455.

<**kwikwe'át**>, SOC /'*leave s-o alone, stop pestering s-o*'/, *see* kwá:.

<**kwí:l**>, free root //kʷí·l//, SOC ['*queen*'], borrowed from English /kʷíyn/ *queen*, syntactic analysis: nominal, attested by Elders Group, also <**kwíl**>, //kʷíl//, attested by EB.

<**Kwíl Mektṓliya**>, cpds //kʷíl məktóliyɛ//, [kʷíl mɪktóliyɛ], N ['*Queen Victoria*'], borrowed from English /kʷíyn vɪktɔ́riyə/ *Queen Victoria*, attested by EB.

<**Kwíl Mektṓliya**>, N ['*Queen Victoria*'], *see* kwí:l.

<**kwí:m**>, bound root //kʷí·m//, comment: using derived forms of the root as a modifier of other color terms the following combinations were given by AK: kwíkwemel qálq, and skwíkwemel qálq.

<**tskwí:m**>, stvi //c=kʷí·m//, LT /'*be red, red, reddish-brown, copper-colored*'/, ASM ['squares circled on the color chart of Berlin and Kay (1969) (rows top to bottom = B-I, columns left to right = 1-40, side column of white to black = 0); individual speakers circled the following squares for tskwí:m, AK: E2, E3, E4, F3, F4; EL: F3, F4; TG (with RP after mentioning "red"): E1 (lower rt. diagonal), E2, E3, E4, E5, E6 (left half), F1, F2, F3, F4, F5, F6 (left half), G1, G2, G3, G4, G5, H1, H2, H3, H4, H5 (upper left diagonal); NP: F1, G1, H1; Evangeline Pete (Downriver Halkomelem): G4 LJ (Pilalt): E2'], semantic environment ['cow, cranberry, red-flowering currant, red elderberry, fish eggs, fox, red huckleberry, raspberry, rose, salmonberry, sky, strawberry, thimbleberry, clothes, crabapple, apple, rotten bark, red ochre (iron oxide soil and paint), red cedar, potato, flower, (copper) money (penny), mountain, paint, sugar, fur/animal hair, bear, human hair, eyes'], ASM ['the following color terms are used by AK before tskwím to specify shades of the color: tsxwíkw', tsq'íx̲, tsqw'íx̲w, qw'íqw'ex̲wel, stl'ítl'esel'], (<**ts=**> *stative with color terms*), syntactic analysis: adjective/adjectival verb, attested by EB, AC, BJ, DM, EL, NP, EP (Downriver Halkomelem), LJ (Pilalt), TG, SJ, AK (1987), TG (1987), EB (1987), NP (1987), AH (1987), other sources: ES /ckʷí·m/, JH /ckʷí·m/, chart by Rob McLaury, also <**tskwím**>, //c=kʷím//, attested by AK, TG, example: <**tskwí:m te (músmes, qwemchó:ls, qwelíyes, sth'íweq', qéléx̲, sx̲ewál, sqá:le, s'ó:ytheqw, qá:lq, elíle, swáyél, schí:ya, t'qwém, qwe'óp, pqwá:y, témelh, x̲pá:y, sqáwth, sp'áq'em)**>, //c=kʷí·m tə (músməs, qʷəmc=á·ls, qʷəlíyəs, s=θ'íwə́q', qə́lə́x̣, s=x̣əwɛ́l, s=qɛ́·lə, s=ʔɛy=á·[=M2=]θ=əqʷ, qɛ́·lq, ʔəlílə, s=wɛ́yə́l, s=cí·yɛ, t'qʷə́m, qʷəʔáp, pqʷ=ɛ́·y, tə́məɬ, x̣p=ɛ́·y, s=qɛ́wθ, s=p'ɛ́q'=əm//, /'*The (cow, cranberry, red-flowering currant, red elderberry, fish eggs, fox, red huckleberry, raspberry, rose, salmonberry, sky ~ day, strawberry, thimbleberry, crabapple ~ apple, rotten bark, red ochre soil or paint (iron oxide), red cedar, potato (domestic or wild varieties), flower) is red.*'/, attested by Elders Group, TG, SJ, NP, <**tskwí:m siyáth'qels**>, //c=kʷí·m si=yɛ́θ'q=əls//, /'*red paint*'/, attested by DM 12/4/64, <**lemlémetchxw mékw' ye tskwí:m l á:wkw'**>, //C_1əC_2=lə́m=əT-c-xʷ mə́k'ʷ yə c=kʷí·m l ʔɛ́·wk'ʷ//, /'*Fold all my red clothes.*'/, attested by Elders Group, <**tskwí:m tále**>, //c=kʷí·m tɛ́lə//, /'*penny*'/, literally /'red money'/, attested by Elders Group, <**léts'e tskwí:m tále**>, //lə́c'ə c=kʷí·m tɛ́lə//, /'*one penny*'/, <**isále tskwí:m tále**>, //ʔisɛ́lə c=kʷí·m tɛ́lə//, /'*two pennies*'/, attested by Elders Group, <**tskwí:m shúkwe**>, //c=kʷí·m šúkʷə//, /'*brown sugar*'/,

<**tskwí:m**>, ds //c=kʷí[=·=]m//, LT ['*[be especially red]*'], (semological comment: especially characteristic shades of red and, perhaps occasionally, surprise at a newly=glimpsed shade), (<**ts=**> *have, get, stative with colors*), (<**=:=**> *(emphatic, especially)*), phonology: emphatic lengthening, syntactic analysis: adjective/adjectival verb, attested by EB, see charts by Rob MacLaury.

<**tskwí::m**>, ds //c=kʷí[=··=]m//, LT ['*[be extra specially red]*'], (<**ts=**> *have, get, stative with colors*), (<**=::=**> *(very emphatic), really*), (semological comment: especially characteristic shades of red and, perhaps occasionally, surprise at a newly=glimpsed shade), phonology: emphatic lengthening, syntactic analysis: adjective/adjectival verb, attested by EB, see charts by Rob MacLaury.

<**Tskwím Smált**>, cpds //c=kʷím s=mɛ́lt//, PLN ['*third mountain behind X̲ó:letsa and northwest of Th'emth'ómels*'], ASM ['northwest of Yale, B.C.'], literally /'red mountain'/, (<**s=**> *nominalizer*, ts= *stative of color terms*), syntactic analysis: nominal phrase minus article, attested by SP, AK 8/2/77, source: place names file reference #159.

<**tskwíkwem**>, cts //c=kʷí[=C_1ə=]m//, LT ['*[being red]*'], (<**ts=**> *have, get, stative with colors*), (<**=R1=**> *continuative*), ASM ['it can be a darker shade or if preceded by tu it can be a lighter

shade of red'], ASM ['tskwímel is further from the focus of tskwím than tskwíkwem is, and tskwíkwemel is usually furthest of all from the focus (literally it means something like "going/coming/getting to have red")'], syntactic analysis: adjective/adjectival verb, attested by TG, see charts by Rob MacLaury.

<**tskwékwelim**>, dmpv //c=C$_1$ə́=kʷ[=əl=]ím//, LT [*'lots of little red'*], (<**ts=**> *stative, color term, R5´= diminutive, little*), (<**=el=**> *plural*), phonology: reduplication, infixed plural, syntactic analysis: adjective/adjectival verb, attested by ME, example: <**tskwékwelim yutl'étl'elòm**>, //c=C$_1$ə́=kʷ[=əl=]ím y=u=C$_1$ə́=ƛ'àlə[=M2=]m//, [ckʷʊ́kʷəlim yuƛ'ə́ƛ'əlàm], /*'(There were) lots of little red ones.'*/, attested by ME.

<**skwekwelím shxw'ólewù**>, EB, FOOD *radishes* (lit. little red ones + turnip), (attested by RG,EH 6/16/98 to SN, edited by BG with RG,EH 6/26/00)

<**tskwímelqel**>, ds //c=kʷím=əlqəl//, ANAA /*'have reddish-brown fur, have reddish-brown animal hair'*/, LT, lx <**=elqel**> *fur, animal hair, wool*, syntactic analysis: adjective/adjectival verb, attested by ME, example: <**tskwímelqel spá:th**>, //c=kʷím=əlqəl s=pɛ́·θ//, EZ [*'brown bear'*], [*'Ursus americanus altifrontalis, Ursus americanus cinnamomum'*], syntactic analysis: nominal phrase minus article, attested by ME 11/21/72, also <**tskwím spá:th**>, //c=kʷím spɛ́·θ//,

<**tskwí:meqw**>, ds //c=kʷí·m=əqʷ//, ANAH /*'have red hair, have reddish-brown hair'*/, lx <**=eqw**> *hair, on the hair, on top of the head*, syntactic analysis: adjective/adjectival verb, attested by NP.

<**tskwimó:les**>, ds //c=kʷim=á·ləs//, ANA [*'have red eyes'*], lx <**=ó:les**> *on the eyes, in the eyes*, syntactic analysis: adjective/adjectival verb, attested by EB.

<**kwí:mel**>, incs //kʷí·m=əl//, LT /*'got red, became red, gone red'*/, (<**=el**> *go, come, get, become, inceptive*), syntactic analysis: intransitive verb, attested by AC, example: <**kwí:mèl te s'ó:thes**>, //kʷí·m=əl tə s=ʔá·θ=əs-s//, /*'His face got red., The face is getting red (like blushing).'*/, phonology: consonant merger, attested by AC, <**lulh kwí:mel te swáyel**>, //lə=wɬ kʷí·m=əl tə s=wɛ́yəl//, /*'The sky is turning red.'*/, attested by AC.

<**tskwímel**>, incs //c=kʷím=əl//, LT [*'[be get/go/become red]'*], ASM ['tskwímel is further from the focus of tskwím than tskwíkwem is, and tskwíkwemel is usually furthest of all from the focus (literally it means something like "going/coming/getting to have red")'], (<**ts=**> *have, get, stative with colors*), (<**=el ~ =íl**> *go, come, get, become*), syntactic analysis: adjective/adjectival verb, attested by TG, see charts by Rob MacLaury.

<**kwíkwemel**>, cts //kʷí[-C$_1$ə-]m=əl//, LT [*'it's getting red'*], (<**-R1-**> *continuative*), phonology: reduplication, syntactic analysis: intransitive verb, adjective/adjectival verb, attested by AC, AD, NP (also 1987), see charts by Rob MacLaury, also /*'reddish'*/, ASM ['on Berlin and Kay color chart (1969) NP circled for this color: E37, E38, E39, E40'], attested by NP, example: <**stowlh ley kwíkwemel**>, //sta=wɬ lə-yə kʷí[-C$_1$ə-]m=əl//, /*'already turning red'*/, attested by AD.

<**tskwíkwemel**>, stvi //c=kʷí[-C$_1$ə-]m=əl//, incs, LT [*'reddish'*], ASM ['on Berlin and Kay color chart (1969), EL circled for this color: D1, D2, and E6, E7'], ASM ['tskwímel is further from the focus of tskwím than tskwíkwem is, and tskwíkwemel is usually furthest of all from the focus (literally it means something like "going/coming/getting to have red")'], (<**ts=**> *have, get, stative with colors*), lx <**=el**> *come, go, get, become, -ish*, phonology: reduplication, syntactic analysis: adjective/adjectival verb, attested by EL, TG (1987), EB (1987), NP (1987), AH (1987), see charts by Rob MacLaury.

<**skwíkwemel**>, cts //s=kʷí[=C$_1$ə=]m=əl//, incs, stvi, LT /*'[be getting red, be going red]'*/, (<**s=**> *stative*), (<**=R1=**> *continuative*), (<**=el ~ =íl**> *go, come, get, become*), syntactic analysis: adjective/adjectival verb, attested by AH, NP, see charts by Rob MacLaury.

<**skwekwíkwemel**>, dmv //s=C$_1$ə=kʷí[=C$_1$ə=]m=əl//, cts, stvi, incs, LT [*'[be getting/going a little*

red]'], ASM ['the very very lightest reds (actually more white tinged with pink, but not named as varieties of p'éq' or qálq)'], (<**s=**> *stative*), (<**R5=**> *diminutive*), (<**=R1=**> *continuative*), (<**=el ~ =íl**> *go, come, get, become*), phonology: double reduplication, syntactic analysis: adjective/adjectival verb, attested by NP, see charts by Rob MacLaury.

<**tskwekwíkwemel**>, dmv //c=C_1ə=kʷí[=C_1ə=]m=əl//, cts, incs, LT ['*[be getting/going a little red]*'], ASM ['the very very lightest reds (actually more white tinged with pink, but not named as varieties of p'éq' or qálq)'], (<**ts=**> *have, get, stative with colors*), (<**R5=**> *diminutive*), (<**=R1=**> *continuative*), (<**=el ~ =íl**> *go, come, get, become*), phonology: double reduplication, syntactic analysis: adjective/adjectival verb, attested by NP, see charts by Rob MacLaury.

<**tskwimómex**>, ds //c=kʷim=áməxʸ//, LT /'*[looks red, red-looking]*'/, (<**ts=**> *have, get, stative with colors*), (<**=ómex**> *looks, -looking, in color*), syntactic analysis: adjective/adjectival verb, attested by EB, NP, see charts by Rob MacLaury.

<**kwelkwímelésem**>, plv //C_1ə=əl=kʷím=əl=ə́s=əm//, cts, ABDF /'*one's face is red, one is blushing*'/, (<**R5=**> *continuative*), (<**=el=**> *plural*), (<**=el**> *sort of, -ish*, <**=es**> *on the face*, <**=em**> *middle voice*), phonology: reduplication, infixed plural, syntactic analysis: intransitive verb, attested by Elders Group 3/1/72.

<**skwímeth**>, dnom //s=kʷím=əθ//, EZ /'*little roundmouth suckerfish,* probably *longnose sucker*'/, ASM ['eulachon-sized, many with red stripes'], ['probably *Catostomus catostomus*'], (<**s=**> *nominalizer*), lx <**=eth**> *edge* or *on the mouth*, syntactic analysis: nominal, attested by Elders Group, JL, also <**skwímeth**>, //s=kʷə[=Aí=]m=əθ//, literally perhaps alternatively /'round mouth thing'/, attested by Elders Group.

<**kwí:mel**>, LT /'*got red, became red, gone red*'/, *see* kwí:m.

<**kwí:x ~ kwíx**>, bound root //kʷí·xʸ ~ kʷíxʸ *name*//.

<**skwí:x ~ skwíx**>, dnom //s=kʷí·xʸ ~ s=kʷíxʸ//, N ['*personal name*'], ASM ['personal names often have lexical suffixes (name endings) which mean something or may have meant something in addition to telling that the name is a name or a male name or a female name; these endings also can be changed to give a person of the opposite sex from the former owner the same name but with a slightly different sound or marked to show their gender; nicknames are given more freely, often in childhood, and can be used throughout a person's life, whether they are bestowed a formal name in a naming ceremony or not'], LANG /'*name or word for s-th, what s-th/s-o is called/named*'/, (<**s=**> *nominalizer*), syntactic analysis: nominal, attested by AC, BJ, EB, others, other sources: ES /skʷí·xʸ/, ASM ['personal name'], example: <**tewát (ta' ~ kw'a') skwíx**>, //tə=wɛ́t (t-ɛʔ ~ k'ʷ-ɛʔ) s=kʷíxʸ//, /'*What is your name?*'/, literally /'who is it? your name'/, attested by EB, <**tewát kw'a schókwelhta skwí:x**>, //tə=wɛ́t k'ʷ-ɛ s=cákʷ=əɬtɛ s=kʷí·xʸ//, /'*What's your nickname?*'/, literally /'who is it? your borrowed name'/, attested by EB, <**Sqeláw tel schókwelhta skwí:x**>, //s=qəlɛ́w tə-l s=cákʷ=əɬtɛ s=kʷí·xʸ//, /'*Sqeláw is my nickname.*'/, attested by EB, ASM ['name (word for something)'], <**stám te skwí:xs te'í:le**>, //s=tɛ́m tə s=kʷí·xʸ-s tə=ʔí·=lə//, /'*What is the name of this?, What's the word for this?*'/.

<**kwexáls**>, sas //kʷixʸ=ɛ́ls → kʷəxʸɛ́ls//, [kʷɪxʸǽls], N ['*naming*'], SOC, SCH ['*reading*'], (<**=áls**> *structured activity (non-continuative)*), syntactic analysis: intransitive verb, attested by BHTTC.

<**kwíxet**>, pcs //kʷíxʸ=əT//, N ['*name s-o (in a ceremony)*'], SOC, naming ceremonies are very formal, usually done in a longhouse, esp. in winter spirit-dancing season for dancers; the name is usually one held by an elder in the same extended family, but can also be one held by someone not related but close and lacking a descendant to give it to for any reason; often the name is of someone who has been deceased for several years at least; the person to be named should be similar in character to the person who had the name; the naming ceremony involves wrapping the person to be named in

a blanket and standing him or her on a blanket during the ceremony;, witnesses are called from representative areas to learn the name, watch the ceremony and spread the word of the naming and the name; then a spokesperson for the person bestowing the name tells the history of the name and its owner(s); then the witnesses each get up and speak to the newly named person, lecturing him to keep himself worthy of the name and to respect the name and the culture; others file by each witness as he/she speaks and give him a token to thank him;, LANG [*'call s-o's name'*], SCH [*'read it'*], (<**=et**> *purposeful control transitivizer*), syntactic analysis: transitive verb, attested by AC, BHTTC, Deming, ASM ['name s-o (in a ceremony)'], <**kwíxetem**>, //kʷíxʸ=əT-əm//, /*'He is named (in a ceremony)., He'll be named.'*/, syntactic analysis: passive, attested by EB, ASM ['call someone's name'], example: <**lítsel kwíxet kw'e mekw'ewát**>, //lí=c-əl kʷíxʸ=əT k'ʷə mək'ʷ(ə)=wɛ́t//, /*'Did I name everybody?, Did I call everybody's name?'*/, attested by Deming, <**tewát kw'e kwíkwexetem**>, //tə=wɛ́t k'ʷə kʷí[-C₁ə=] xʸ=əT-əm//, N /*'Who are they naming?'*/, attested by RG & EH (4/10/99 Ling332), <**tewát kw'e kwíxetem**>, //tə=wɛ́t k'ʷə kʷíxʸ=əT-əm//, N /*'Who was named?'*/, attested by RG & EH (4/10/99 Ling332).

<**skwíkwexetem**>, dnom //s=kʷí[-C₁ə=]]xʸ=əT-əm//, pass., cts, SPRD /*'a naming ceremony'*/, <s=> *nominalizer*, <**-R1-**> *continuative aspect*, <-em> *passive*, attested by RG & EH (4/10/99 Ling332)

<**kwíxelexw ~ kwéxwelexw**>, ncs //kʷíxʸ(ə)=ləxʷ ~ kʷi[=Aə=]´xʸ(ə)=ləxʷ//, N /*'get s-o's name, manage to get s-o's name'*/, SOC, LANG /*'manage to say s-o's name, have a name for s-th'*/, (<**=lexw**> *non-control transitivizer*), phonology: <e> /ə/ (epenthetic) is often added between a consonant and a following <l> or <m> (<e> (schwa) makes it easier to shift the tongue from <x> to <l> here), possible ablaut, syntactic analysis: transitive verb, attested by Deming, CT, HT, ASM ['have a name for s-th'], <**tl'o éwe í tí kwíxelexw tethá**>, //ƛ'a ʔə́wə ʔí-t-í kʷíxʸə=ləxʷ tə=θɛ́//, /*'We didn't have a name for that.'*/, attested by CT, HT.

<**kwekwxá:mel**>, dnom //kʷí[=AəC₁ə=]xʸ=ɛ́·məl//, [kʷʊkʷxʸæ̂·məl], N [*'nickname'*], SOC, LANG, (<**e-ablaut and =R1=**> *derivational*), lx <**=á:mel**> *part*, phonology: ablaut, reduplication, syntactic analysis: nominal, example: <**éy te kwekwxwá:mels**>, //ʔɛ́y tə kʷí[=AəC₁ə=]xʸ=ɛ́·məl-s//, /*'He had a good nickname.'*/, literally /'It is good the his nickname'/.

<**kwxő:mexw**>, df //s=kʷixʸ=ó·məxʷ//, PLN /*'place-name, name of a place'*/, N, (<**s=**> *nominalizer*), probably <**=ó:(=)mexw**> *people, place of people*, phonology: vowel-loss, the root loses its vowel (zero-grade) before the strong-grade suffix, syntactic analysis: nominal, attested by NP, JL (Tait), example: <**st'á kw te skwxő:mexws tá'a shxwlí**>, //s=t'ɛ́ kʷ tə s=kʷxʸ=ó·məxʷ-s t-ɛ́ʔɛ s(=)xʷ=lí//, /*'It's like the place-name of where you come from.'*/, phonology: consonant merger, glottalization and vowel-loss can be seen in stative'á /s=t'ɛ́/ *to be similar, like* which varies with ste'á /s=t=əʔɛ́/ (=e'á *comparative*), attested by JL (Tait), <**te skwxőmexws tel shxwlí tl'esu Skw'átets**>, //tə s=kʷxʸ=óməxʷ-s tə-l s(=)xʷ=lí ƛ'ə=s=u s=k'ʷɛ́t=əc//, /*'The name of the place I'm from is Skw'átets.'*/, literally /'the place-name of my where from so that is Skw'átets'/, attested by JL (Tait), also <**kwxő:mexw**>, //kʷixʸ=ó·(=)məxʷ//, attested by JL, <**kwxő:mexws ta' shxwlí**>, //kʷxʸ=ó·məxʷ-s t-ɛʔ s(=)xʷ=lí//, /*'name of the place where you come from'*/, attested by JL.

<**kwíxelexw ~ kwéxwelexw**>, N /*'get s-o's name, manage to get s-o's name'*/, *see* kwí:x ~ kwíx.

<**kwíxet**>, N [*'name s-o (in a ceremony)'*], *see* kwí:x ~ kwíx.

<**kwiy=**>, bound root, ABFC /*'move'*/, with continuative <**kwóy=**> /*'moving'*/, perhaps as in <**kwíythesem**> *'shake one's head side to side (as in saying no)'*, <**kwóythesem**> *'shaking one's head side to side (as in saying no)'*, <**kwíyx̲**> *'to move'*, <**kwó:yxthet ~ kwó:yex̲thet ~ kwó:yxethet**>,*'moving, moving oneself/itself'*, <**skwóye** or **Skwóye**> *'Douglas squirrel,* possibly *a character name, i.e. Squirrel'*, <**kwóyethet**> *'to duck'*.

<**kwiyáxqel**>, //kʷiyɛ́xʸ=qəl//, also /*'moose, rack of horns'*/, ANAA [*'rack of horns'*], attested by AL

(Elders Group 3/1/72), Salish cognate: Thompson (Lytton dial.) /laxʷáyaxkn/ *moose* B74c:8 (vs. Lytton dial. /sqʷáy'axkn/ *horn, antler* B74c:22, also <**kwiyáxchel**>, //kʷiyɛ́xʸ=cəl//, also /'*moose, rack of horns*'/, ANAA ['*rack of horns*'], attested by SP (Elders Group 3/1/72), *see* **xwiyáxkel**.

<**kwiyó:s**>, us //kʷiyá·s//, KIN /'*uncle, aunt*'/, possibly <**=ó:s**> *on the face*, syntactic analysis: nominal, usage: sometimes used in speeches instead of the normal word, shxwemlí:kw, attested by AC.

<**kwíythesem**>, mdls //kʷíyθ=əs=əm//, ABFC ['*shake one's head side to side (as in saying no)*'], LANG, lx <**=es**> *on the face*, (<**=em**> *middle voice*), possibly root <**kwíy=**> as in <**kwíyx̲**> *move*, possibly root <**kwóyx̲**> *moving*, possibly <**=thes**> *face* instead of usual **<=ó:s ~ =es>, see s'ó:thes**> *face*), syntactic analysis: intransitive verb, attested by IHTTC.

<**kwóythesem**>, cts //kʷi[=Aa=]´yθ=əs=əm//, ABFC ['*shaking one's head side to side (as in saying no)*'], LANG, (<**a-ablaut**> *continuative aspect*), lx <**=es**> *on the face*, (<**=em**> *middle voice*), phonology: ablaut, syntactic analysis: intransitive verb, attested by IHTTC.

<**kwíyx̲**>, df //kʷíy(=)x̣//, TVMO ['*to move*'], possibly <**=x̲**> *distributive, around*, possibly root <**kwiy=**> *move*?, syntactic analysis: intransitive verb, attested by AD.

<**kwíyx̲t**>, pcs //kʷíy(=)x̣=T//, TVMO ['*move s-th*'], semantic environment ['the eyebrows for ex.'], (<**=t**> *purposeful control transitivizer*), syntactic analysis: transitive verb, attested by AD.

<**kwíyx̲thet**>, pcrs //kʷíy(=)x̣=T-ət//, TVMO /'*move, move itself, move oneself*'/, ABFC, LAND, EB, WATR, WETH, (<**-et**> *reflexive* after =t ~ =th *purposeful control transitivizer*), phonology: =t //T// has allomorphs =th /θ/ before -et *reflexive*, -óx *first person object*, and -óme *second person sg. obj.*, and allomorph =t elsewhere, syntactic analysis: intransitive verb, attested by AD, also <**qwíyx̲thet**>, //qʷíy(=)x̣=T-ət//, attested by AC, etc., compare with <**qwíyx̲thet**, example: <**lí kwíyx̲thet**>, //lí kʷíy(=)x̣=T-ət//, /'*Did he move?*'/, attested by AD.

<**kwó:yxthet ~ kwó:yex̲thet ~ kwó:yxethet**>, cts //kʷi[-Aá·-]y(=)x̣=T-ət ~ kʷi[-Aá·-]y(=)əx̣=T-ət ~ kʷi[-Aá·-]y(=)x̣=əT-ət//, [kʷá·yx̣θət ~ kʷá·yəx̣θət ~ kʷá·yx̣əθət], TVMO /'*moving, moving oneself/itself*'/, ABFC, (<**ó:-ablaut**> *continuative*), possibly <**=(e)x̲**> *derivational*?, syntactic analysis: intransitive verb, attested by AD, example: <**lí kwó:yex̲thet**>, //lí kʷá·yəx̣=θ-ət//, /'*Is he moving?*'/, attested by AD.

<**skwó:yex̲thet ~ skwó:yx̲thet**>, dnom //s-kʷi[-Aá·-]y(=)əx̣=T-ət ~ s-kʷi[-Aá·-]y(=)x̣=T-ət//, [skʷá·yəx̣θət ~ skʷá·yx̣θət], TVMO ['*a doing*'], (<**s-**> *nominalizer*), syntactic analysis: nominal, attested by AD.

<**kwíyx̲t**>, TVMO ['*move s-th*'], *see* kwíyx̲.

<**kwíyx̲thet**>, TVMO /'*move, move itself, move oneself*'/, *see* kwíyx̲.

<**kwló ~ qwló**>, bound root //kʷlá ~ qʷlá//, meaning unknown

<**skwló ~ sqwló**>, df //s=kʷlá ~ s=qʷlá//, ANAA ['*seal fat*'], (<**s=**> *nominalizer*), syntactic analysis: nominal, attested by EL.

<**Skwló ~ Sqwló**>, dnom //s=kʷlá ~ s=qʷlá//, PLN ['*a rock along Harrison River which looks like layers of seal fat all along its bottom*'], ASM ['located above (upstream from) Th'éqwela ~ Ts'éqwela and below (downstream from) Híkw Sméya; the seal fat layers are usually underwater in June (as they were when we visited the site by boat 6/27/78)'], phonology: probably zero-derivation, syntactic analysis: nominal, attested by EL,

<**kwókwelōws ~ kwókwelews**>, SOC /'*murdering, murderer (of more than one)*'/, *see* kwà:l.

<**kwókwelx**>, SOC ['*hiding an object real well*'], *see* kwà:l.

<**kwókwexwels**>, ABFC /'*knocking, rapping*'/, *see* kwoxw.

<**kwókwexwem**>, ABFC /'*knocking, rapping (in the distance), tapping*'/, *see* kwoxw.

<**kwókwexwet**>, ABFC ['*knocking on s-th*'], *see* kwoxw.

<**kwókwexwetsesem**>, ABFC ['*knocking with one's hand*'], *see* kwoxw.

<**kwokwílàlà**>, SOC /'*hiding place, refuge, hide-out*'/, *see* kwà:l.

<**kwokwí:lx**>, SOC ['*hiding an object*'], *see* kwà:l.

<**Kwókwxwemels**>, PLN ['*village or area on north side of Suka Creek (which is on the east side of the Fraser River*'], *see* kwoxw.

<**kwól ~ kwó:l**>, free root //kʷál ~ kʷá·l//, ABFC ['*to be born*'], syntactic analysis: intransitive verb, attested by Elders Group 3/1/72, 4/16/75, contrast <**tsméle**> *having a child, giving birth*, example: <**lulh lhq'átses syilólem kwseslh kwó:l**>, //lə=wɬ ɬq'ɛ́cəs s=yiláləm kʷ-s-əs-ɬ kʷá·l//, /'*It's his (or her) fifth birthday.*'/, literally /'it has already become five years since his past be born'/, attested by Elders Group 4/16/75, <**xwoyíwel tel sqwálewel kw'es le tés te ílh a skwól**>, //xʷ=ɛ[=Aa=]y=íwəl tə-l s=qʷɛ́l=əwəl k'ʷ-əs lə tə́s tə ʔí-ɬ ʔɛ s-kʷá·l//, /'*I'm happy that it has reached your birthday., Happy Birthday to you.*'/, literally /'is happy my thoughts, feelings that it it did reach the past your birth'/, usage: used to sing the "Happy Birthday to You" song, attested by NP (and now taught to the Elders Group and to students), <**tsel t'í:lemet xwoxweyíwel te ílh á skwól**>, //c-əl t'í·l=əm=əT xʷ=ɛ[=Aa=-C$_1$ə-]y=íwəl tə ʔí-ɬ ʔɛ s-kʷál//, /'*I sang (sing it to s-o) "Happy Birthday to You" to someone.*'/, attested by EB approved this sentence constructed by a staff class member, Elder's comment: "one must say whose birthday it is [by inflecting t'í:lemet]".

<**kwól**>, free root //kʷál//, EB ['*corn*'], ['*Zea mais*'], ASM ['introduced by non-Indians (Hudson's Bay Co.), and since grown by some Stó:lō people, past and present'], borrowed from English /kɔ́rn ~ kɔ́·n/ *corn*, perhaps through Chinook Jargon, syntactic analysis: nominal, attested by IHTTC.
<**p'éq' q'áq'et'em kwó:l**>, EB, FOOD *white sweet corn* (lit. white + sweet + corn), (attested by RG,EH 6/16/98 to SN, edited by BG with RG,EH 6/26/00)

<**Kwó:le**>, free root //kʷá·lə//, PLN ['*Cottonwood Corner*'], ASM ['a corner in Sardis, B.C.'], ASM ['this name goes back to the 1890's at least but occurs only after white settlement in the area, so after 1858'], borrowed from English /kɔ́rnr ~ kɔ́·nə/ *Corner*, syntactic analysis: nominal, attested by DF 6/9/77.

<**kwólòmèt**>, TVMO /'*escape (from slavery for ex.), get out (from being snowed in or snagged in river for ex.)*'/, *see* kwá:.

<**kwò:lxw**>, ABFC /'*drop s-th (accidentally), let s-o go*'/, *see* kwá:.

<**kwómexw**>, us //kʷáməxʷ//, EZ /'*salmon after spawning, with no more eggs*'/, syntactic analysis: nominal.

<**kwómkwem**>, SD ['*thudding (of footsteps or horses hooves on ground)*'], *see* kwém.

<**kwósel**>, us //kʷásəl//, WETH ['*star*'], syntactic analysis: nominal, attested by AC, others, other sources: ES /kʷásəl/, also <**kwó:sel**>, //kʷá·səl//, attested by BJ.

<**kwótawi ~ kwótewi**>, us //kʷátɛwi ~ kʷátəwi//, EZ /'*eel, Pacific lamprey, western brook lamprey*'/, ['*Entosphenus tridentatus, Lampetra richardsoni*'], syntactic analysis: nominal.

<**kwóte**>, free root //kʷátə//, SOC ['*quarter (coin)*'], borrowed from Chinook Jargon <**quarter, kwata**> /kwáta/ *quarter* Johnson 1978:391, Thomas 1970:79, syntactic analysis: nominal.

<**kwótexwem**>, SD /'*roaring (of falls, for ex.), rumbling (of falls, thunder, quake, rockslide, etc.)*'/, *see* kwótxwem ~ kwótxwem.

<**kwótx̲wem ~ kwótxwem**>, mdls //kʷátx̣ʷ=əm ~ kʷátxʷ=əm//, SD /'*to rumble, to roar*'/, semantic environment ['especially of water, also of thunder, earthquake, rockslide, etc.'], (<**=em**> *middle voice*), syntactic analysis: intransitive verb, adjective/adjectival verb, attested by Elders Group, AD, also <**kwó:tx̲wem**>, //kʷá·tx̣ʷ=əm//, attested by Elders Group, also <**kwótxwem**>, //kʷátxʷ=əm//, SD ['*make a banging sound*'], semantic environment ['of waterfalls, of hammering or banging'], attested by EB, also <**kwótx̲wem**>, //kʷátx̣ʷ=əm//, also /'*be roaring*'/, semantic environment ['example of water'], attested by AD, example: <**kwótx̲wem te stó:lō**>, //kʷátx̣ʷ=əm tə s=tá·lo//, /'*The river is roaring.*'/, attested by AD.

<**Kwótxwem Stó:lō**>, cpds //kʷátxʷ=əm s=tá·lo//, PLN /'*"Eagle Falls" on the west side of Harrison Lake,* probably *Walian Creek falls*'/, ASM ['a waterfall where lots of eagles gather'], literally /'rumbling river'/, syntactic analysis: adjective/adjectival verb nominal, attested by EL, source: place names file reference #119.

<**kwótex̲wem**>, cts //kʷát[-ə-]x̣ʷ=əm//, SD /'*roaring (of falls, for ex.), rumbling (of falls, thunder, quake, rockslide, etc.)*'/, (<**e-infix**> *continuative*), phonology: vowel infix, syntactic analysis: intransitive verb, adjective/adjectival verb.

<**kwétxwt**>, pcs //kʷa[=Aə=]´txʷ=T//, SD ['*to rattle s-th inside*'], (<**e-ablaut**> *derivational*), phonology: ablaut, (<**=t**> *purposeful control transitivizer*), syntactic analysis: transitive verb, attested by BHTTC.

<**Kwótxwem Stó:lō**>, PLN /'*"Eagle Falls" on the west side of Harrison Lake,* probably *Walian Creek falls*'/, *see* kwótx̲wem ~ kwótxwem.

<**kwó:thet**>, ABFC ['*to gallop*'], *see* kwá:.

<**kwótl'thet**>, ABFC /'*flipping around (of fish), struggling (of anything alive trying to get free)*'/, *see* kwá:.

<**kwoxw**>, bound root //kʷaxʷ *knock, rap*//.

<**kwxwà:ls**>, sas //kʷaxʷ=ɛ̀·ls//, ABFC /'*knock (once), rap*'/, BLDG, HARV, (<**=à:ls**> *structured activity (non-continuative)),* phonology: vowel-loss, zero-grade root due to strong-grade suffix, syntactic analysis: intransitive verb, attested by EB, JL (Tait), also <**kwxwáls**>, //kʷaxʷ=ɛ́ls//, attested by Elders Group 10/27/76.

<**kwókwexwels**>, cts //kʷá[-C_1ə-]xʷ=əls//, ABFC /'*knocking, rapping*'/, BLDG, HARV, (<**-R1-**> *continuative*), (<**=els**> *structured activity (continuative)*), phonology: reduplication, syntactic analysis: intransitive verb, attested by Elders Group, also <**kwó:kwexwels**>, //kʷá·[-C_1ə-]xʷ=əls//, attested by JL, also <**kwokwxwá:ls**>, //kʷá[-C_1ə-]xʷ=ɛ́·ls//, also /'*knocking (like on a door)*'/, (irregular) <**-R1-**> *continuative* but <**=á:ls**> *structured activity (non-continuative)),* attested by EB.

<**kwókwexwem**>, izs //kʷá[-C_1ə-]xʷ=əm//, ABFC /'*knocking, rapping (in the distance), tapping*'/, (<**-R1-**> *continuative*), (<**=em**> *intransitivizer*), phonology: reduplication, syntactic analysis: intransitive verb, attested by EB.

<**kwóxwet**>, pcs //kʷáxʷ=əT//, ABFC ['*knock on s-th*'], BLDG, MC, **beat a drum* rejected, (<**=et**> *purposeful control transitivizer*), syntactic analysis: transitive verb, attested by EB, Elders Group, example: <**kwóxwet te q'éwet**>, //kʷáxʷ=əT tə q'ə́wət//, /'*beat a drum*'/, attested by EB.

<**kwókwexwet**>, cts //kʷá[-C_1ə-]xʷ=əT//, ABFC ['*knocking on s-th*'], BLDG, MC, (<**-R1-**> *continuative*), phonology: reduplication, syntactic analysis: transitive verb, attested by EB, example: <**kwókwexwet te q'éwet**>, //kʷá[-C_1ə-]xʷ=əT tə q'ə́wət//, attested by EB.

<**kwókwexwetsesem**>, mdls //kʷá[-C_1ə-]xʷ=əcəs=əm//, cts, ABFC ['*knocking with one's hand*'], (<**-R1-**> *continuative*), lx <**=etses**> *on the hand, with the hand*, (<**=em**> *middle voice*), phonology:

reduplication, syntactic analysis: intransitive verb, attested by Elders Group.

<**kwxwó:mels**>, sas //k^{w}ax^{w}=á·mə=əls//, EB /'*shiny black mountain huckleberry,* also called *a mountain blueberry* by the speakers'/, ['*Vaccinium membranaceum*'], ASM ['several varieties are known to the Stó:lō people: sour, or sweet; round, pear-shaped, or flatter [BHTTC]; tall, or shorter [AC]; they are picked at Hemlock Valley (summits of logged off sections especially) (above Chehalis) and many other spots (esp. logged-off areas nowadays); one harvesting technique was to rap or knock the branch and the berries would fall off--thus the name; shiny, deep-purple to black, glossy berries, real juicy, found high up in the mountains, right up on the mountain top; some describe them as wine-colored; ripe in August or early fall'], literally /'knock berry structured activity continuative'/, lx <**=ó:me**> *berry*, (<**=els**> *structured activity (continuative)*, sometimes used as *nominalizer* as here), syntactic analysis: nominal, attested by AC, Elders Group 3/1/72, also <**kwxwó:méls**>, //k^{w}ax^{w}=á·mə́=əls//, attested by BJ, also <**kwxwó:móls**>, //k^{w}ax^{w}=á·má=əls//, attested by AC, also <**kwxwóméls**>, //k^{w}ax^{w}=ámə́=əls//, attested by TM, BHTTC, Elders Group, also <**kwxwómels**>, //k^{w}ax^{w}=ámə=əls//, attested by Elders Group, Deming, EL.

<**Kwókwxwemels**>, pln //k^{w}əx^{w}=á[=M2=]mə=əls//, PLN ['*village or area on north side of Suka Creek (which is on the east side of the Fraser River*'], literally /'lots of black huckleberries'/, (<**metathesis type 2**> *plural*), syntactic analysis: nominal, attested by SP, AK, source: place names file reference #149.

<**kwóxwemal ~ kwóxwmal**>, df //k^{w}áx^{w}=(ə)mɛl or k'^{w}[=D=]áx^{w}=məl//, IDOC ['*hand rattle of Indian doctor or shaman*'], SPRD ['*deer hoof rattle of spirit-dancer (stick with deer hoof rattles tied onto it)*'], ASM ['made with deer hooves inside a leather bulb tied onto a stick'], also /'*deer hooves*'/ (attested by RG & EH (4/10/99 Ling332), possibly root <**kwóxw**> *knock, rap* or possibly root <**kw'óxwmel ~ kwóxwemal**> *hoof*, phonology: <=D=> deglottalization if derived from kw'óxwmel, syntactic analysis: nominal, attested by EB, Elders Group 4/5/78 and 3/21/79.

<**kwóxwemal ~ kwóxwmal**>, IDOC ['*hand rattle of Indian doctor or shaman*'], *see* kwoxw.

<**kwóxwet**>, ABFC ['*knock on s-th*'], *see* kwoxw.

<**kwóye**>, bound root or stem //k^{w}áy(=)ə//, root meaning uncertain but perhaps <**kwiy=**>, bound root, ABFC /'*move*'/, with continuative <**kwóy=**> /'*moving*'/, plus <**=e ~ =a**> '*living thing*'.

<**skwóye** or **Skwóye**>, df //s=k^{w}áyə//, EZ /'*Douglas squirrel,* possibly *a character name, i.e. Squirrel*'/, ['*Tamiasciurus douglasi mollipilosus*'], syntactic analysis: nominal, attested by Elders Meeting 2/11/76.

<**kwóyethet**>, pcrs //k^{w}i[=Aá=]y=əT=ət//, /'to duck'/, probable root <**kwiy=**> '*move*', with <=Aó=> *continuative* (as in <**kwóy=**> '*moving*'), (<**=t**> *purposeful control transitivizer*), (<**-et**> *reflexive*), attested by RG & EH (4/9/99 Ling332)

<**kwóythesem**>, ABFC ['*shaking one's head side to side (as in saying no)*'], *see* kwíythesem.

<**kwó:yx̲thet ~ kwó:yex̲thet ~ kwó:yx̲ethet**>, TVMO /'*moving, moving oneself/itself*'/, *see* kwíyx̲.

<**Kwōkwa'áltem ?**>, us //k^{w}ok^{w}ɛʔɛ́ltəm ?//, PLN ['*a tributary of Atchelitz Creek*'], source: Wells 1965:13 <koh-kwah-AHL-tuhm>; said to mean *place where a brave found his bride*, comment: if Wells' gloss has any validity the root could be kwà:l *to hide* and thus Kwekwà:ltem /R5=k^{w}ɛ̀·l=T=əm/ or /R5=k^{w}ɛ̀·l=təm/ could be *place where she was hidden* with R5= *resultative* or *continuative*, <=**t**>*purposeful control transitivizer* and <=**em**> *place of* or <=**tem**> *stative participle*, phonology: reduplication,

<**Kwṓkwelem ?**>, us //k^{w}ók^{w}ələm ?//, PLN ['*Post Creek*'], source: Wells 1966 <KOHK-oh-lum>, comment: if kw is right in both positions the root could be kwṓl *gold* if gold was found in historic

times, or kwà:l *to hide* if something was hidden here or if some Indian people hid here, or kwel= *grasp, hold* as in kwelá:t *grasp it, hold it* or kwél(:)em *get, fetch*, or the root in skwél *waterfall*, etc., etc.; =em could be *place of* or *middle* or *intransitive*; the reduplication could be of several types (infixed or prefixed with ablaut or stress shift) and could mean *continuative*, *plural*, *diminutive*, etc., or just *derivational*, Carlson, McHalsie & Perrier 2001:142 has "you think somebody is talking back there, but it's your own voice (echo)" but I have only found <wélwelàm ~ wélwelà:m> *to echo, echoing* and <X̲wix̲we'áqel ~ Xwixwe'áqel ~ Xwōxwe'áqel>.*Echo Point on Echo Island, Echo Bay on Echo Island*, literally /'imitating a voice'/ from <x̲wex̲we'á> *copy, imitate*. However, in light of the 2001 work above, most likely the root is kwà:l *to hide* as I speculated and the place name <Kwókwelem> (as the Stó:lō atlas (the 2001 work above) has it, meaning *place to get hidden* with <=em> *place to have/get*.

<**kwṓxweth**>, us //kʷóxʷəθ//, EZ /'*coho salmon, silver salmon*'/, ['*Oncorhynchus kisutch*'], syntactic analysis: nominal, attested by NP, AC, Elders Group 3/1/72, other sources: ES, JH /kʷə́xʷəθ/, H-T02 <kō'kwats>, also <**kwṓx̲weth**>, //kʷóx̣ʷəθ//, attested by AC, BJ, also <**kwéxweth**>, //kʷə́xʷəθ//, attested by AD.

<**temkwṓxweth**>, dnom //təm=kʷóxʷəθ//, TIME /'*coho salmon time, August to September*'/, (<**tem=**> *time for, season for*), syntactic analysis: nominal, source: DJ:WS of Sardis.

<**Lkwṓxwethem**>, dnom //l=kʷóxʷəθ=əm//, PLN ['*Six-Mile Creek and bay on west side of Harrison Lake*'], ASM ['a coho spawning ground'], literally /'coho salmon place'/, (<**l=** poss. ~ **lexw=**> *always*), lx <**=em**> *place of*, dialects: *Cheh.*, attested by EL, Salish cognate: Squamish /n- ~ nəxʷ-/ (n- before consonants proper, i.e. not before vowels or semivowels w, y) *(prefix referring to location) on, in, at, over (a surface), by way of; (in some body part words which are surfaces of others); (with root /ʔin-/ meaning 'one body part; the other body part'); nomina agentis (one who does X); in body part descriptions (incl. body part insults); (other uses too)* K67:310, 113-116.

<**kwṓxwethtel**>, dnom //kʷóxʷəθ=təl//, FSH ['*coho net*'], lx <**=tel**> *device, thing for*, syntactic analysis: nominal.

<**kwṓxwethtel**>, FSH ['*coho net*'], *see* kwṓxweth.

<**kwse**>, DEM /'*the (female, near but not visible), (female, near but not in sight) (translated by gender specific words in English, like aunt, etc.)*'/, *see* kw.

<**kws ...-s ~ kwses ~ kw'es ...-s**>, CJ /'*that he, that she, that it, that they*'/, *see* kw.

<**kwsú:tl'ò**>, PRON ['*that's her (absent)*'], *see* kw.

<**kwsú:tl'ò**>, PRON /'*that's her (absent), she (absent)*'/, *see* tl'ó ~ tl'o.

<**kwsú:tl'ò:lh**>, PRON ['*that was her (deceased)*'], *see* kw.

<**kwsú:tl'ò:lh**>, PRON /'*that was her (deceased), she (deceased)*'/, *see* tl'ó ~ tl'o.

<**kwtxwéltsep ~ kwetxwéltsep**>, FIRE /'*bring in firewood, bring wood in*'/, *see* kwetáxw.

<**kwthá**>, free root //kʷθɛ́//, MC ['*a pile*'], LAND, syntactic analysis: nominal, attested by JL, NP, Deming (Fish Camp 7/19/79).

<**kwthát**>, pcs //kʷθɛ́=T//, MC ['*pile it*'], LAND, (<**=t**> *purposeful control transitivizer*), syntactic analysis: transitive verb, attested by JL, NP, Deming (Fish Camp 7/19/79).

<**skwthá**>, stvi //s=kʷθɛ́//, MC ['*piled up*'], LAND, (<**s=**> *stative*), syntactic analysis: adjective/adjectival verb, attested by JL, NP, Deming (Fish Camp 7/19/79), example: <**ō li kwetlhew skwthá**>, //ʔo li kʷətɬ=əw s=kʷθɛ́//, /'*Oh look at how it's piled., Oh there's lots of piles.*'/, attested by JL, NP, Deming (Fish Camp 7/19/79).

<**kwthát**>, MC [*'pile it'*], *see* kwthá.

<**kwthe**>, DEM /*'the (male or gender unspecified, near but not in sight)'*/, *see* kw.

<**(kw)the tátí:m**>, SOC [*'the messenger'*], *see* tà:m.

<**kwthú:tl'ò**>, PRON /*'that's him (absent), that's her (absent), it's him (absent), it's her (absent)'*/, *see* kw.

<**kwthú:tl'ò**>, PRON /*'that's him (absent), that's her (absent), it's him/her (absent), he (absent), she (absent)'*/, *see* tl'ó ~ tl'o.

<**kwthú:tl'òlem**>, PRON /*'that's them (absent, not present)'*/, *see* kw.

<**kwthú:tl'òlem**>, PRON /*'that's them (absent, not present), they (absent)'*/, *see* tl'ó ~ tl'o.

<**kwthú:tl'ò:lèmèlh**>, PRON /*'that was them (deceased), they (deceased)'*/, *see* tl'ó ~ tl'o.

<**kwthú:tl'òlèmèlh**>, PRON [*'that was them (deceased)'*], *see* kw.

<**kwúkw**>, free root //k^{w}úk^{w}//, FOOD /*'to cook, cooking'*/, borrowed from Chinook Jargon <**cook**> /kúk/ *cook* itself < English /kʊ́k/ *cook* (Johnson 1978:295), syntactic analysis: intransitive verb, attested by Elders Group, also <**kú:k**>, //kú·k//, attested by EB, AC, example: <**le kú:k kw cheláqelhelh**>, //lə kú·k k^{w} cəlɛ́q=əɬ=əɬ//, /*'She cooked yesterday.'*/, syntactic analysis: ambiguous past3 intransitive verb demonstrative article adverb/adverbial verb, attested by EB.

<**skwúkw**>, dnom //s=k^{w}úk^{w}//, FOOD /*'cooking, (cooking) food'*/, (<**s=**> *nominalizer*), syntactic analysis: nominal, attested by MH, also <**skú:k**>, //s=kú·k//, attested by AC, example: <**etsel hó:qwlexw te skú:ks**>, //ʔə-c-əl há·q^{w}=ləx^{w} tə s=kú·k-s//, /*'(I smelled her cooking.)'*/, syntactic analysis: auxiliary past1s transitive verb demonstrative article nominal-possessive3, attested by AC, also <**skúk**>, //s=kúk//, attested by EB, <**qp'á:qet ta' skúk**>, //qp'=ɛ́·q=əT t-ɛʔ s=kúk//, /*'Put a lid on your cooking.'*/, attested by EB, <**yéqw ta' skwúkw**>, //yə́q^{w} t-ɛʔ s=k^{w}úk^{w}//, /*'Your cooking is burning.'*/, attested by MH (Deming).

<**kwukwáwtxw**>, dnom //k^{w}uk^{w}=ɛ́wtx^{w}//, BLDG /*'cookhouse, kitchen'*/, FOOD, lx <**=áwtxw**> *building, room*, phonology: variable-grade root, strong-grade suffix, syntactic analysis: nominal, attested by Elders Group, CT, HT, EB, AD, example: <**alétsa te kwukwáwtxw**>, //ʔɛlə́cɛ tə k^{w}uk^{w}=ɛ́wtxw//, /*'Where is the kitchen?, Where's the cookhouse.'*/, attested by AD.

<**kwukwáwtxw**>, BLDG /*'cookhouse, kitchen'*/, *see* kwúkw.

<**kwúkwemels**>, free root //k^{w}úk^{w}əməls//, EB [*'cucumber'*], [*'Cucumis sativus'*], ACL [*'introduced by non-Indians'*], FOOD [*'pickle'*], ACL, borrowed from probably English /kyúkəmbrz/ *cucumbers* or possibly an unattested Chinook Jargon word in turn from English /kyúkəmbrz/, grammatical comment: could easily be reanalyzed as fitting Halkomelem patterns, i.e., k^{w}ú[=R1=]m=əls with =əls *thing for* used in some derived nominals, syntactic analysis: nominal, attested by JL, NP, Deming (all at Fish Camp 7/19/79).

<**sth'íth'eqw kúkumels** or **sth'íth'eqw kwúkwemels**>, FOOD *relish* (lit. chopped + cucumber), (attested by RG,EH 6/16/98 to SN, edited by BG with RG,EH 6/26/00)

<**t'át'ets'em kúkumels** or **t'át'ets'em kwúkwemels**>, FOOD *pickles* (lit. sour + cucumber), (attested by RG,EH 6/16/98 to SN, edited by BG with RG,EH 6/26/00)

<**ts'áyxw kúkumels** or **ts'íyxw kwúkwemels**>, EB, FOOD *zucchini* (lit. dried + cucumber), (attested by RG,EH 6/16/98 to SN, edited by BG with RG,EH 6/26/00)

<**kwúkwewels**>, df //k^{w}ú[=C$_1$ə=]w=əls//, EB possibly /*'high-bush cranberry,* more likely *squashberry'*/, ['possibly *Viburnum opulus*, more likely *Viburnum edule*'], ASM ['sour edible berries found in a high bush in round bunches, used as medicine, sample from Chehalis village identified as high-bush cranberry or squashberry'], (<**=R1=**> meaning uncertain here), lx <**=els**> *device, tool, thing for or*

structured activity (non-continuative), phonology: reduplication, syntactic analysis: nominal, dialects: *Tait*, attested by CT, HT, also <**kwúkwels**>, //k^{w}úk^{w}əls//, dialects: *Chill., Cheh.*, attested by AC, NP, Elders Group, <**kwúkwewels sqe'óleqw** (or better: **qwemchó:ls sqe'óleqw**)>, FOOD *cranberry juice* (lit. highbush cranberry + fruit juice (or better:) bog cranberry + fruit juice), (attested by RG,EH 6/16/98 to SN, edited by BG with RG,EH 6/26/00)

<**kwúkwstú:p**>, HHG /'*pot-bellied stove, cook-stove*'/, *see* stú:p.

<**kwú:l**>, bound root //k^{w}ú·l//, reanalyzed from free root //sk^{w}ú·l//, SCH ['*school*'], *see* **skwú:l**.

<**kwú:ls**>, ABFC ['*hang onto s-o*'], *see* kwél.

<**kwú:ltel**>, PLAY /'*wrestling, fighting*'/, *see* kwél.

<**kwú:t**>, pcs //k^{w}ú·=T//, SOC /'*take s-th, accept s-th, get s-th, fetch s-th, pick s-th up*'/, MC, possibly root <**kwél**> *grab, grasp, hold*??, (<**=t**> *purposeful control transitivizer*), syntactic analysis: transitive verb, attested by Elders Group, AC, EB, ASM ['catch it, grab it'] (RG & EH (4/9/99 Ling332)), example: <**lí iyólem kw'els kwú:t ò**>, //lí ʔəy=ál=əm k'^{w}-əl-s k^{w}ú·=T ʔà//, /'*Is it alright if I (just) take it?*'/, attested by Elders Group, <**kwú:t (te, ta) sqwemá:y**>, //k^{w}ú·=T (tə, t-ɛ) s=q^{w}əm=ɛ́·y//, /'*take (the, your) dog*'/, attested by AC, <**kwútes telí te kw'óxwe**>, //k^{w}ú=T-əs təlí tə k'^{w}áx^{w}ə//, /'*He took it from the box.*'/, attested by EB, <**kwútes telí (tl'á'altha, tl'elówe)**>, //k^{w}ú=T-əs təlí (ƛ'-C$_{1}$ɛ́=ʔɛlθɛ, ƛ'ə-lówə)//, /'*He took it from (me, you (sg.)).*'/, syntactic comment: independent object of prepositional verb, attested by Elders Group, <**chel we lhqélexw westámes kw'e le kwú:tes**>, //c-əl wə ɬ=q'ə́l=ləx^{w} wə=s=tɛ́m=əs k'^{w}ə lə k^{w}ú·=T-əs//, /'*I know what he took.*'/, attested by EB, <**kwútes te lepál tl'esu kw'oqwethóxes**>, //k^{w}ú=T-əs tə ləpɛ́l ƛ'ə=s=u k'^{w}aq^{w}=əT-áx^{y}-əs//, /'*He took the shovel and hit me.*'/, attested by Elders Group, ASM ['get s-th, fetch s-th'], <**le kwú:tes**>, //lə k^{w}ú·=T-əs//, /'*He got it., He fetched it.*'/, attested by AC, ASM ['pick s-th up'], <**kwútes te smált qesesu lomethóxes**>, //k^{w}ú=T-əs tə s=mɛ́lt qə-s-əs-u lam=əT-áx^{y}-əs//, /'*He picked up the rock and threw it at me (throw it at s-o).*'/, attested by AC.

KW'

<**=kw' ~ =ekw'**>, possibly //=k'ʷ ~ =ək'ʷ//, perhaps /*'round, around in circles'*/, SH, syntactic analysis: lexical suffix, also <**=ekw'**>, //=ək'ʷ//; found in <**tl'ámkw'em**>, //ƛ'ə[=Aɛ́=]m=k'ʷ=əm//, /*'(have) sound of popping small round things'*/, <**xwélekw'**>, //xʷə́l=ək'ʷ//, /*'to wrap'*/ (compare root in <**xwél=p'**> *to fan* or <**xwà:l=x**> *lift s-th*), <**xwélkw'**>, //xʷə́l=k'ʷ//, /*'to eddy'*/, <**x̲ep'kw'á:ls**>, //x̣əp'=k'ʷ=ɛ́·ls//, /*'chew with a crunch'*/, <**xep'ékw'**>, //x̣əp'=ə[=´=]k'ʷ//, /*'make a crunch underfoot (bones, nut, glass, etc.)'*/, <**x̲et'kw'á:ls**>, //x̣ət'=k'ʷ=ɛ́·ls//, /*'carve wood, whittle'*/, <**xéykw'et**>, //x̣ə́y=k'ʷ=əT//, /*'chew s-th hard (apple, pill, etc.)'*/.

<**kw'á:lem**>, mdls //k'ʷɛ́·l=əm//, FOOD [*'serve oneself (mainly soup and liquids)'*], syntactic analysis: intransitive verb, attested by Elders Group, BHTTC, Salish cognate: Squamish /k'ʷan-ʔánʔ/ *to ladle (tr.)* W73:156, K69:77.

<**kw'áles**>, ABDF /*'both burned, (many got burned)'*/, *see* kw'ás.

<**kw'alqéyls**>, sas //k'ʷí=lq=ə[=M2=]ls or k'ʷ=ɛləq=íls or k'ʷɛl=ləq=íls//, FSH [*'hanging a net'*], possibly root <**kw'i(y)**> *climb*, possibly <**=aleq**> *net, wave*, (<**=els**> *structured activity continuative*), syntactic analysis: intransitive verb, attested by Elders Group, EB, example: <**kw'alqéyls te swéltel**>, //k'ʷɛlqíls tə s=wə́l=təl//, /*'hanging a net'*/, attested by EB.

<**kw'álx̲**> or <**s(i)kw'álx̲**>, possible root or stem //k'ʷɛ́l(=)x̣// or //sik'ʷ=ɛ́l(=)x̣//, meaning unclear but in the second possible etymology the root is <**síkw'**>, //sík'ʷ//, [*'get skinned'*] with vowel loss before <**=á:l**> *similar to, -like, or part/portion* and <**=x̲**> *distributive, all around* with the idea of the white feathers "skinned off like" or "skinned off part/portion" or "similar to skinned off" (metaphorically that they are not there leaving the brown head feathers).

<**skw'álx̲**>, df //s=k'ʷɛ́l(=)x̣// or more likely //sik'ʷ=ɛ́l(=)x̣//, EZ [*'immature bald eagle'*], ASM ['before the head feathers turn white, age one to three years'], [*'Haliaeetus leucocephalus'*], possibly <**s=**> *nominalizer*) or <**síkw'**>, //sík'ʷ//, [*'get skinned'*], possibly <**=x̲**> *distributive, all around*, syntactic analysis: nominal, attested by Elders Group 2/13/80, 3/15/78, also <**skw'àlx̲**>, attested by Elders Group 2/18/76, also <**skw'á:lx̲**>, attested by Elders Group 6/4/75, also <**sqw'á:lx̲**>, attested by Elders Group 3/1/72, also <**skw'álx̲ ~ sqw'álx̲**>, also /*'golden eagle'*/.

<**kw'á:lx̲w**> or <**sekw'á:lx̲w**>, possible root or stem //k'ʷɛ́·l=x̣ʷ or sík'ʷ=ɛ́·l(=)x̣ʷ//, meaning unclear, though perhaps for the second etymology root <sekw'> as in <**sékw'emiy**>, /*'birch, western white birch'*/ from <**síkw'**>, free root //sík'ʷ//, [*'get skinned'*], *see* síkw', plus <**=á:lx̲w**> *leaves* or <=altxw> *house*.

<**Skw'á:lx̲w**>, df //s=k'ʷɛ́·lx̣ʷ//, PLN [*'a little bay or eddy on Harrison River about two miles downriver from Chehalis'*], syntactic analysis: nominal, attested by Elders Group 9/7/77, other sources: H-T04:315 skwa^ltuq (macron over u, ^ over the a) *a camp about two miles below Chehalis village in a sunny bay, abandoned before 1904 but marked by an old logging camp of the early white settlers*, said to mean literally *sheltered* (the latter points to a form Skwáltxw perhaps (root <**kwá:l**> *hide*, <=**altxw**> *house*).

<**kw'álhem**>, df //k'ʷə[=Aɛ́=]ɬ=əm//, BSK [*'little berry basket'*], ASM ['tied around the waist in front, when full dumped into larger berry basket on ground, made of same design and shape as big berry basket (i.e. with two sides trapezoidal, tapering at bottom)'], HARV, probably root <**kw'élh**> *spill (into)*, (<**a-ablaut**> *derivational*), phonology: ablaut, syntactic analysis: nominal, dialects: *Chilliwack*, also <**lí:latses**>, dialects: *Tait*.

<**kw'aq**> bound root //k'ʷɛq// *lie on one's back*, Salish cognate: Lushootseed /k'ʷə́q/ *lie on back, fall on back* H76:256

<**kw'aqálém**>, mdls ///k'ʷɛq=i[=Aɛ́=]l=əm//, incs, ABFC [*'lie down on one's back'*], (<**=íl**> *go, get, become, come*, <**=em**> *middle voice*), phonology: i → a ablaut *derivational*, updrifting of stress on final syllable, syntactic analysis: intransitive verb, attested by IHTTC; found in <**kw'aqálémlha**>, /*'Lie down on your back.'*/, attested by IHTTC, contrast <**kw'e'íyeqel ~ kw'e'íqel**>, //k'ʷəʔí=qəl//, ABFC /*'lie on one's back, on his back'*/ from root <**kw'e'í ~ kw''í ~ kw'í**>, //k'ʷəʔí ~ k'ʷʔí ~ k'ʷí//, ABFC /*'lie? with surface facing up, sticking up, on the side? or edge?'*/ + <**=qel**> *head*.

<**skw'okw'qá:q ~ skw'okw'qáq ~ skw'ōkw'qáq**>, dnom //s=k'ʷak'ʷqɛ́·q ~ s=k'ʷak'ʷqɛ́q ~ sk'ʷək'ʷqɛ́q, probably s=k'ʷɛ[=AaC$_1$ə=]q=V1´C2//, EZ [*'American'*], [*'Turdus migratorius caurinus'*], ASM ['migrates south in winter unlike the varied thrush (s<u>x</u>wík')'], (<**s=**> *nominalizer*), probably root <**kw'aq**> *lie on one's back*, possibly <**o-ablaut plus =R1=**> *continuative* or *derivational*, possibly <**=áq**> *on the penis, male* or possibly an otherwise very rare =V1C2 reduplication perhaps cognate with *out-of-control* in other languages, phonology: possible ablaut, possible reduplication, syntactic analysis: nominal, attested by AC, BJ, EL, Elders Group (3/1/72, 2/18/76, 6/4/75, 3/19/75), other sources: ES /sk'ʷqɛ́q/ *robin, varied thrush*, H-T s'kukōkáq (macron over the u) *robin (Merula migratoria)*, Salish cognate: Squamish /s-k'ʷq-áq/ *robin* (derived from root /k'ʷəq/ *be split (ab. tree)(for ex. of a branch hanging from a tree) W73:218, K67:294, Lushootseed /s-k'ʷəqíq/ robin* (< root /k'ʷəq/ *fall/lie on back* so named because it tilts it head back when singing) H76:256, example: <**qweloythí:lem te skw'okw'qáq**>, //qʷɛl=ayθ(əl)=í·l=əm tə s=k'ʷak'ʷqɛ́q//, /*'Robins are singing (making music).'*/, attested by Elders Group.

<**kw'aqálém**>, ABFC [*'lie down on one's back'*], *see* kw'e'í ~ kw''í ~ kw'í.

<**kw'ás**>, free root //k'ʷɛ́s//, ABDF [*'get burned (of human or creature)'*], syntactic analysis: intransitive verb, attested by AC, EB, JL, example: <**le kw'ás**>, //lə k'ʷɛ́s//, /*'He got burnt., She got burnt.'*/, attested by AC, <**chexw kw'ás**>, //c-əxʷ k'ʷɛ́s//, /*'You got burnt.'*/, attested by AC, <**tsel kw'ás**>, //c-əl k'ʷɛ́s//, /*'I got burned.'*/, attested by EB, <**kw'ás te téxwthelh**>, //k'ʷɛ́s tə tə́xʷθəɬ//, /*'The tongue got burned.'*/, attested by EB.

<**kw'áles**>, plv //k'ʷɛ́[-lə-]s//, ABDF /*'both burned, (many got burned)'*/, syntactic analysis: intransitive verb, attested by JL.

<**kw'ásem**>, izs //k'ʷɛ́s=əm//, FOOD /*'to toast by a fire (of smoke-cured fish, dried fish), get toasted by fire (of smoke-dried fish)'*/, ASM ['often done before eating the fish, done till the skin gets toasted, the toasted skin is eaten too, also warms it and brings out the flavor and oil to make it moister'], (<**=em**> *intransitivizer*), syntactic analysis: intransitive verb, attested by Deming, AK.

<**kw'áset**>, pcs //k'ʷɛ́s=əT//, FOOD [*'toast it by a fire (of smoked fish)'*], (<**=et**> *purposeful control transitivizer*), syntactic analysis: transitive verb, attested by Deming.

<**kw'ósthet**>, incs //k'ʷɛ[=Aá=]s=θət//, WETH [*'get warm (of weather)'*], (<**=thet**> *inceptive, get, become*), phonology: =thet triggers o-ablaut of most root a-vowels, syntactic analysis: intransitive verb, attested by EB, Deming, also <**kw'ó:sthet**>, //k'ʷɛ[=Aá·=]s=θət//, attested by EB, example: <**me kw'ó:sthet**>, //mə k'ʷá·s=θət//, WETH [*'summer'*], literally /'It starts to get warm.'/, attested by EB, <**kw'ósthet te swáyel**>, //k'ʷá·s=θət tə s=wɛ́y=əl//, /*'The weather has gotten warm., The weather has gotten warmer.'*/, attested by EB, <**(le, ulh) kw'ósthet te swáyel**>, //(lə, ʔuɬ) k'ʷás=θət tə s=wɛ́y=əl//, /*'The day is getting warm.'*/, literally /'the day (it past tense, already) got warm'/, attested by Deming.

<**kw'ókw'es**>, stvi //k'ʷɛ[=Aá(=)C$_1$ə=]s//, DESC /*'be hot, be warm'*/, WETH, TCH, (<**ó-ablaut** and/or **reduplication type 1**> *stative*), phonology: ablaut, reduplication, syntactic analysis: intransitive verb, attested by EB, AC, BJ, RP, Deming, DM, Elders Group, other sources: ES /k'ʷá·k'ʷəs/ *warm*

*(*as in *warm day),* example: <**kw'okw'es qó:**>, //k'ʷák'ʷəs qá·//, /*'It's hot water.*'/, attested by EB, <**kw'ókw'es swáyel**>, //k'ʷák'ʷəs s=wɛ́y=əl//, /*'It's hot weather.*'/, attested by EB, <**kw'ókw'es speháls**>, //k'ʷák'ʷəs s=pəh=ɛ́ls//, /*'It's a warm wind., It's a hot wind.*'/, attested by AC, <**ts'áts'el kw'ókw'es telowáyel**>, //c'ɛ́c'əl k'ʷák'ʷəs təla=wɛ́y=əl//, /*'It's really hot today.*'/, dialects: *Chill.*, attested by EB, RP, also <**ts'áts'el ō kw'ókw'es telowáyel**>, //c'ɛ́c'əl ʔow k'ʷák'ʷəs təla=wɛ́y=əl//, dialects: *Cheh.*, attested by EB, RP, <**kw'ókw'es te swáyel**>, //k'ʷák'ʷəs tə s=wɛ́y=əl//, /*'The day is hot.*'/, attested by Deming, <**ő̄we ís ólew(e) kw'ókw'es**>, //ʔówə ʔí-s ʔál-əw k'ʷák'ʷəs//, /*'It's lukewarm.*'/, literally /'It's not too hot.'/, attested by EB, <**ő̄we olésu kw'ókw'es te qó:**>, //ʔówə ʔal-ə́s-u k'ʷák'ʷəs tə qá·//, /*'The water is not too hot., It's just lukewarm water.*'/, attested by EB.

<**xwelítemelh x̱eyeslótel** (or) **kw'ókw'es kwémlexw s'élhtel**>, EB, FOOD *ginger* (lit. white man style + wild ginger (or) hot + root + food), (attested by RG,EH 6/16/98 to SN, edited by BG with RG,EH 6/26/00)

<**skw'ókw'es**>, dnom //s=k'ʷɛ[=AáC₁ə=]s or s-k'ʷɛ[=AáC₁ə=]s//, WETH [*'heat'*], syntactic analysis: may be an inflected rather than derived nominal, phonology: reduplication, ablaut, attested by DM, example: <**kwes we tl'e hó:y te skw'ókw'es**>, //kʷə-s wə ƛ'a há·y tə s-k'ʷák'ʷəs//, /*'(which is when the heat is finished)*'/, semantic environment ['when asked for the word for autumn, fall'], attested by DM 12/4/64.

<**temkw'ókw'es**>, ds //təm=k'ʷɛ[=Aá=]s//, TIME [*'summer'*], WETH, literally /'time for hot, hot season'/, (<**tem=**> *time for, season, time*), syntactic analysis: intransitive verb, nominal, attested by AC, Elders Group, also <**temkw'ó:kw'es**>, //təm=k'ʷɛ[=Aá·(=)C_1ə=]s//, phonology: reduplication, attested by DM, Elders Group, also <**temkw'ólekw'es**>, //təm=k'ʷɛ[=Aá=lə=C_1ə=]s//, (<**-le-**> *plural*), literally /'time for many heats, hot seasons, hot times'/, attested by Elders Group 3/12/75.

<**kw'esélets**>, //**k'ʷɛ[=Aə=]s=ə́ləc**//, TCH /*'hot on the rump, hot seat'*/, ABDF [*'burned on the rump'*], lx <**=élets**> *on the rump*, (<**e-ablaut**> *resultative*), phonology: ablaut, syntactic analysis: intransitive verb, attested by SP, AK.

<**kw'síws**>, //**k'ʷɛs=íws**//, HUNT [*'singe the hairs off skin'*], ABDF, lx <**=íws**> *on the skin*, phonology: vowel-loss, syntactic analysis: intransitive verb, attested by EB.

<**kw'esó:ythel**>, //**k'ʷɛ[=Aə=]s=á·yθəl**//, ABDF [*'burned on the lips'*], lx <**=ó:ythel**> *on the lip(s), in the jaw, on the jaw or chin*, (<**e-ablaut**> *resultative*), phonology: reduplication, syntactic analysis: intransitive verb, attested by Elders Group, also /*'burn one's tongue or mouth* (poss. this gloss is an error for *burned on the lips or jaw or chin)*'/, attested by EB.

<**kw'ésqel**>, //**k'ʷɛ[=Aə́=]s=qəl**//, ABDF [*'burned in the throat'*], lx <**=eqel**> *in the throat*, (<**é-ablaut**> *resultative),* phonology: ablaut, syntactic analysis: intransitive verb, attested by Deming, also /*'burned on the mouth,* (or perhaps better: *burned in the throat, burned in the mouth)*'/, attested by Elders Group.

<**kw'éstses**>, //**k'ʷɛ[=Aə́=]s=cəs**//, ABDF /*'burned on the finger or hand, burnt the hand, a hand got burnt'*/, (<**é-ablaut**> *resultative*), lx <**=tses**> *on the hand, on the finger(s)*, phonology: ablaut, syntactic analysis: intransitive verb, attested by Elders Group 3/15/72, AC.

<**kw'ésxel**>, //**k'ʷɛ[=Aə́=]s=xʸəl**//, ABDF [*'burned on the foot'*], (<**é-ablaut**> *resultative*), lx <> *on the foot, on the leg below thigh*, phonology: ablaut, syntactic analysis: intransitive verb, attested by Elders Group 3/15/72, JL.

<**kw'síts**>, dnom //k'ʷs(=)íc//, EZ /*'rainbow trout,* prob. also *coastal cutthroat trout'*/, [*'Salmo gairdneri,* prob. also *Salmo clarki clarki'*], possibly root <**k'ʷɛs**> *burn*, possibly <**=íc**> *on the back*, since it has red stripes on its back, syntactic analysis: nominal, attested by Elders Group 7/9/75, JL

5/8/79, other sources: ES /k'ʷsí·c/ *cutthroat trout*, JH /k'ʷsí·c/ *cutthroat trout*, H-T k·ōse'tc (macron over e also) *trout (Salmo sp.)*, also <**kwesích**>, //kʷəsíc//, also /*'trout salmon, small spring salmon [sic?]'*/, attested by Elders Group 3/1/72, also <**qw'esíts ~ qw'esí:ts**>, //q'ʷəsíc ~ q'ʷəsí·c//, also /*'trout'*/, attested by BJ 12/5/64 p.304.

<**kw'ásem**>, FOOD /*'to toast by a fire (of smoke-cured fish, dried fish), get toasted by fire (of smoke-dried fish)'*/, *see* kw'ás.

<**kw'áset**>, FOOD [*'toast it by a fire (of smoked fish)'*], *see* kw'ás.

<**kw'át**> bound root, //k'ʷέt//, WATR *trickling*

<**kw'átem**>, df //k'ʷέt=əm//, WATR /*'trickling, dribbling, water bubbling up in a river, add water to a container, water running under'*/, (<**=em**> *intransitivizer* or *middle voice*), syntactic analysis: intransitive verb, attested by Elders Group 9/7/77, Salish cognate: perhaps Lushootseed /k'ʷád-ad/ *dip it out*, also <**kw'át'em**>, //k'ʷέt'=əm//, also /*'trickling, dribbling'*/, attested by IHTTC, also /*'trickling (of water)'*/, attested by SP (in Elders Group 7/13/77), also <**sqwátem**>, //s=qʷέt=əm//, also /*'trickling, running under'*/, attested by LJ (in Elders Group 7/13/77), example: <**sqwátem te qó:**>, //s=qʷέt=əm tə qá·//, /*'Water (of a river) is trickling (or running) under the tree.'*/.

<**kw'tómés**>, ds //k'ʷɛ[=Aá=]t=ə[=M2=]m=əs or k'ʷɛt=əm=á[=M2=]s//, WATR [*'(rain or sweat) trickling down one's face'*], root <**kw'át**> *trickling*. lx <**=es ~ =ós**> *on the face*, (<**metathesis type 2**> *derivational*), phonology: metathesis, perhaps ablaut a → o triggered by =es ~ =ós *on the face*, syntactic analysis: intransitive verb, attested by Elders Group 9/7/77.

<**Skw'átets**>, dnom //s=k'ʷέt=əc//, PLN /*'Squatits village on east bank of Fraser river across from the north end of Seabird Island, Peters Indian Reserves #1, 1a, and 2 on site of Squatits village'*/, literally /'trickling water in the back'/, ASM ['named after trickling water because trees grew on roots here above ground and water trickled under the trees in seasons when waterfalls were going'], root <**kw'át**> *trickling*. lx <**=ets ~ =íts**> *on the back*, syntactic analysis: nominal, attested by LJ and JL (History tape 4/7/78), IHTTC (AK, others), other sources: Wells 1965 (lst ed.):24, 25, also <**Sqwátets**>, //s=qʷέt=əc//, Elder's comment: "more modern pronunciation", example: <**esesu e Th'qwélhcha te lí te Skw'átets**>, //ʔə-s-əs-y=u ʔə θ'qʷ=əɬcɛ tə lí tə s=k'ʷέt=əc//, /*'and it's just Th'qwélhcha that's [the bay] at Skw'átets'*/, attested by JL (History tape #34, 4/7/78).

<**kw'át'el**>, probably root //k'ʷέt'əl//, EZ /*'mouse,* probably includes at least*: white-footed deer mouse, cascade deer mouse,* and the post-contact *house mouse,* respectively'/, ['*Peromyscus maniculatus, Peromyscus oreas,* and *Mus musculus domesticus*'], syntactic analysis: nominal, attested by AC, BJ (12/5/64), Elders Group 3/1/72, other sources: JH /kʷé·tel/ *mouse*, also <**kw'á:t'el**>, //k'ʷέ·t'əl//, attested by Elders Group (7/27/75).

<**kw'elókw't'el**>, ds //k'ʷ[-əl-]ɛ[=AáC_1ə=]t'əl//, EZ ['*a few mice*'], (<**-el-**> infix *plural*), (<**á-ablaut and R1**> *diminutive*), phonology: infixed plural, ablaut, reduplication, syntactic analysis: nominal.

<**kw'áth'eletsem**>, MC ['*wobbling on its bottom*'], *see* kw'eth'ém.

<**kw'átl'**>, free root //k'ʷέƛ'//, ABFC /*'have intercourse, fuck'*/, usage: a "bad word", taboo-word on par with English fuck, with same shock value, syntactic analysis: intransitive verb, Salish cognate: Squamish /k'ʷáƛ'/ *futuere [Latin for 'to have intercourse']* W73:110, K69:77, Lushootseed /k'ʷáƛ'/ as in /ləcu-k'ʷáƛ'/ *copulating* (Lushootseed /ləcu-/ is *continuative*), a less refined term than Lushootseed /qə́dəb/ H76:252; found in <**kw'átl'lha**>, //k'ʷέƛ'-ɬɛ//, /*'Fuck., Have intercourse.'*/, (<**-lha**> *imperative, 2s*).

<**kw'átl'et**>, pcs //k'ʷέƛ'=əT//, ABFC /*'have intercourse with s-o, fuck s-o'*/, usage: a taboo-word, syntactic analysis: transitive verb, Salish cognate in part: Squamish /k'ʷáƛ'-an/ *futuere (tr.) ['to have intercourse (tr.)']* W73:110, K69:77.

<**kw'okw'etl'élmel**>, cts //k'ʷɛ[=AaC₁ə=]ƛ'=ə́lməl//, ABFC ['*thinking about having intercourse*'], literally /'having intercourse in the mind'/, lx <**=élmel**> *in the mind, thinking about*, (<**o-ablaut and R1**> *continuative*), phonology: ablaut, reduplication, syntactic analysis: intransitive verb.

<**kw'átl'et**>, ABFC /'*have intercourse with s-o, fuck s-o*'/, *see* kw'átl'.

<**kw'áts ~ kw'éts**>, bound root //k'ʷɛ́c ~ k'ʷə́c// *see.*

<**skw'áts**>, dnom //s=k'ʷɛ́c//, ABFC /'*eyesight, sight*'/, LT, (<**s=**> *nominalizer*), syntactic analysis: nominal, attested by AC, example: <**stselá:l te skw'áts**>, //s=cəlɛ́·l tə s=k'ʷɛ́c//, /'*Her eyes are fading., [Her eyesight is fading.]*'/, attested by AC.

<**kw'átset**>, pcs //k'ʷɛ́c=əT//, ABFC /'*look at s-th/s-o, examine s-o/s-th*'/, MED ['*examine s-o (like a doctor)*'], SOC /'*come to see s-o/s-th, visit s-o*'/, SCH ['*read it (see well enough to read it)*'], (<**=et**> *purposeful control transitivizer*), syntactic analysis: transitive verb, attested by Elders Group, AC, Deming, SJ, EB, other sources: JH /k'ʷé·cət/ *to look, watch, see s-th*; found in <**kw'átsetlha**>, //k'ʷɛ́c=əT-ɬɛ//, /'*Look at it.*'/, (<**-lha**> *imperative 2s*), attested by AC, <**kw'átsethòx**>, //k'ʷɛ́c=əT-áxʸ//, [k'ʷǽcəθàxʸ], /'*look at me, examine me, come see me*'/, <**kw'átsethòmè**>, //k'ʷɛ́c=əT-ámə//, [k'ʷǽcəθàmə̀], /'*come to see you, come see you, look at you (like a doctor), examine you*'/, example: <**míchxw q'ó:lthet kw'atsetólxw ő́we híthes**>, //mí-c-xʷ q'á·=l=T-ət k'ʷɛ́c=əT-álxʷ ʔówə híθ=əs//, /'*Come back and see us soon.*'/, syntactic analysis: lack of conjunctions like kw'as or qésu seems unusual, attested by EB, <**milh kw'átsethò:m wàyèlès**>, //mi-ɬ k'ʷɛ́c=əT-à·m wɛ̀y=ə̀l=ə̀s//, /'*Come and seem me tomorrow.*'/, attested by Deming, <**ewá:lh me kw'átsethò:m**>, //ʔəwə-əɬ (or ʔəwə-ɛ́·ɬ) mə k'ʷɛ́c=əT-à·m//, /'*Does he ever come to see you?*'/, attested by EB, <**(s)kw'áy kw'els kw'átset te pípe**>, //(s)k'ʷɛ́y k'ʷə-l-s k'ʷɛ́c=əT tə pípə//, /'*I can't read the paper., I can't see the paper.*'/, attested by SJ (Deming).

<**kw'ókw'etset**>, cts //k'ʷɛ[-AáC₁ə-]c=əT//, ABFC ['*looking at s-th/s-o*'], SOC ['*seeing s-o (i.e. visiting s-o)*'], (<**ó-ablaut and R1**> *continuative*), phonology: ablaut, reduplication, syntactic analysis: transitive verb, attested by IHTTC, BJ, AC, example: <**líchxw wekw'ákw'etset**>, //lí-c-xʷ wə-k'ʷɛ[-AáC₁ə-]c=əT//, [líčxʷ wʊk'ʷɔ́k'ʷəcɪt], /'*Are you looking at it?*'/, attested by BJ 5/64.

<**kw'étslexw**>, ncs //k'ʷɛ[=Aə́=]c=l-əxʷ//, [k'ʷʊ́clʊxʷ ~ k'ʷə́clʊxʷ], ABFC /'*see s-o/s-th, catch sight of s-th/s-o*'/, LT, (<**é-ablaut**> *derivational* or *non-continuative*), comment: Suttles ca1984 shows such a vowel change as *perfective* in Musqueam (another name for what I'm calling here non-continuative) for a group of TAT roots including root /k'ʷɛ́c/, (<**=lexw**> or <**=l**> *non-control transitivizer*), phonology: ablaut, syntactic analysis: transitive verb, attested by AC, BJ, AD, EB, LJ (Tait), Elders Group, BHTTC, IHTTC, Deming, other sources: ES /k'ʷɛ́cələxʷ/ *see*, example: <**me kw'étslexw**>, //mə k'ʷə́c=l-əxʷ//, /'*to catch sight of s-th*'/, attested by EB, <**tsel kw'étslexw te spá:th tl'ésu lé me théxw**>, //c-əl k'ʷə́c=l-əxʷ tə s=pɛ́·θ ƛ'ə́-s-u lə mə θə́xʷ//, /'*I caught sight of a bear and it disappeared.*'/, attested by EB, <**(tsel, í:lhtsel) kw'étslexw**>, //(c-əl, ʔí·-ɬ-c-əl) k'ʷə́c=l-əxʷ//, /'*I saw it., I saw him., I saw her., I saw them.*'/, attested by BHTTC, Elders resp., <**tsel (kw'étslòmè, kw'étslòlè, kw'étslòlé talhwèlèp)**>, //c-əl (k'ʷə́c=l-ámə, k'ʷə́c=l-álə, k'ʷə́c=l-álə tɛ=ɬwə́lə́p)//, /'*I saw (you, you folks, you folks (crowd, the gang).)*'/, attested by AC, <**líchxw (kw'étslòx, kw'étslòlxw, kw'étslexw, kw'étslexw yithá, kw'étslexw yi í:mex)**>, //lí-c-xʷ (k'ʷə́c=l-áxʸ, k'ʷə́c=l-álxʷ, k'ʷə́c=l-əxʷ, k'ʷə́c=l-əxʷ yi-θɛ́, k'ʷə́c=l-əxʷ yi ʔí[-·-]m=əxʸ)//, /'*Did you (see me, see us, see it/him/her/them, see them, see them walking)?*'/, attested by AC, <**lí(:)tsel kw'étslòmè li té sq'èp**>, //lí(·)-c-əl k'ʷə́c=l-ámə lí tə s=q'ə́p//, [lícɪl k'ʷʊ́clàmə̀ li tɪ́ sq'ə̀p], /'*Did I see you in the crowd?, Did I see you at the gathering?*'/, attested by AC, <**lí tsel kw'étslòlè li té sq'ep**>, //lí-c-əl k'ʷə́c=l-álə lí tə s=q'ə́p//, /'*Did I see you people at the gathering?*'/, attested by AC, <**le kw'étslexwes**>, //lə k'ʷə́c=l-əxʷ-əs//, /'*He saw it., He can see it., (He, She, They, It) saw (him, her, it, them).*'/, attested by AC, <**étsel kw'étslexw**>, //ʔə́-c-əl k'ʷə́c=l-əxʷ//, [ʔícɪl k'ʷʊ́clʊxʷ], /'*I can*

see it., [I could see it., I saw it.]'/, attested by AC, <**tsel kw'éts(e)lexw te (qé<u>x</u> sthó:qwi, tl'alqtéle)**>, //c-əl k'ʷə́c=l-əxʷ tə (qə́x̣ s=θá·qʷi, ƛ'a[=l=]qt=ə́lə)//, /'*I saw (a lot of fish, a deer).*'/, attested by AC, <**kw'étslexwes thú:tl'ò**>, //k'ʷə́c=l-əxʷ-əs θ=ú·=ƛ'à//, /'*She saw it*'/, */'He saw her.'/ rejected, syntactic comment: shows this independent pronoun functions only as subject or shows that it is taken as subject even in syntactic object position when the verb has both 3rd person subject and 3rd person object, attested by IHTTC, *<**kw'étslexwes thú:tlò tú:tlò**> rejected, //k'ʷə́c=l-əxʷ-əs θ=ú·=ƛ'à t=ú·=ƛ'à//, /'*She saw him.*'/, syntactic comment: rejected as "broken" Halkomelem showing either that two independent pronouns are not tolerated syntactically adjacent or that both would have to be subject pronouns, attested by IHTTC, <**tsel kw'etslòmè qe Bob**>, //c-əl k'ʷəc=l-ámə qə báb//, /'*I saw you and Bob.*'/, syntactic comment: shows conjoining of pronoun affix and a nominal as object by embedding, attested by LJ (one of the most fluent Tait speakers)(Elders Meeting 7/5/78), *<**kw'étslexwlha**> rejected, //k'ʷə́c=l-əxʷ-ɬɛ//, /'*See it.*'/, Elder's comment: "This can't be said because kw'étslexw is not done on purpose.", syntactic comment: shows imperative and non-control transitives are semantically incompatible and not allowed together, attested by EB, <**éwechel íl kw'étslexw**>, //ʔə́wə-c-əl ʔí-l k'ʷə́c=l-əxʷ//, /'*I didn't see it.*'/, syntactic comment: subjunctive subject pronoun on auxiliary verb after vneg, attested by AD, <**eweche'átlh kw'étslexw**>, //ʔəwə-c-əl-ɛ́(t)ɬ k'ʷə́c=l-əxʷ//, /'*I haven't seen them.*'/, phonology: shows Tait dialect allows dropping of l from -tsel, attested by AD, <**skw'áy kw'es kw'étslexw te theqát**>, //s=k'ʷɛ́y k'ʷə-s k'ʷə́c=l-əxʷ tə θəqɛ́t//, /'*They couldn't see the trees.*'/, usage: from the Story of the Flood, attested by AC, <**skw'áy kw'as kw'étslexw ikw'eló; st'át'el; lí kw'e sle'ó:lwelh te lálem**>, //s=k'ʷɛ́y k'ʷ-ɛ-s k'ʷə́c=l-əxʷ ʔi=k'ʷə=lá; s=t'ɛ́[=C_1ə=]l; lí k'ʷə s=ləʔɛ́=álwəɬ tə lɛ́ləm//, /'*You can't see it; it's not showing; it's on the other side of the house.*'/, attested by EB, <**mekw'ewát kw'étslexwes te swíyeqe**>, //mək'ʷ=wɛ́t k'ʷə́c=l-əxʷ-əs tə s=wíyəqə//, /'*The man saw everyone., The man caught a glimpse of everyone (implying he saw each in a state of undress or the like).*'/, attested by EB, (semological comment: this alloseme is not obligatory, but is common; I used some sentences verbally and in lessons with kw'étslexw and found that it caused elders to chuckle; they advised I avoid it in the semantic environment /'one person sees another person (esp. of the opposite sex)'/ in lessons unless wanting to allow the ambiguity of ['X saw Y'] and ['X saw Y undressed']; this is perhaps stronger than the same ambiguity that might be present in English /'John caught a glimpse of Mary'/.).

<**kw'ókw'etslexw**>, cts //k'ʷɛ[-AáC_1ə-]c=l-əxʷ//, [k'ʷák'ʷəclʊxʷ], ABFC ['*seeing s-o*'], (<**ó-ablaut and R1**> *continuative*), phonology: reduplication, ablaut, syntactic analysis: transitive verb, attested by IHTTC.

<**kw'étskw'ets**>, chrs //k'ʷɛ[=Aə́=]c=C_1əC_2//, [k'ʷʊ́ck'ʷʊc ~ k'ʷə́ck'ʷəc], SOC ['*expect*'], literally /'characteristically looking'/, ds //=C_1əC_2 *characteristic*//, phonology: é-ablaut automatic before =doubling suffix with e, reduplication, syntactic analysis: intransitive verb, attested by Elders Group (Mar. 1972).

<**kw'étskw'etsmet**>, iecs //k'ʷɛ[=Aə́=]c=C_1əC_2=məT//, SOC ['*expect s-o*'], ds //=C_1əC_2 *characteristic*, <**=met**> *indirect effect control transitivizer*//, phonology: ablaut, reduplication, syntactic analysis: transitive verb, attested by Elders Group (Mar. 1972, 1/7/76), also <**kw'ókw'etsmet**>, //k'ʷɛ[=AáC_1ə=]c=məT//, phonology: reduplication, ablaut, attested by EB, example: <**etsel kw'étskw'etsmet**>, //ʔə-c-əl k'ʷɛ[=Aə́=]c=C_1əC_2=məT//, [ʔɪcɪl k'ʷʊ́ck'ʷʊcmət], /'*I expect someone.*'/, attested by Elders Group (Mar. 1972).

<**Kw'okw'echíwel**>, df //k'ʷɛ[=AáC_1ə=]c=íwəl//, [k'ʷak'ʷəčíwəl], PLN /'*Wahleach Bluff, a lookout mountain with rock sticking out over a bluff,* also *the lookout point on Agassiz Mountain*'/, ASM ['Wahleach Bluff divides Ruby Cr. and Wahleach; a ladder goes up the rock and major electric power lines cross the Fraser River there above Ruby Cr.; the Agassiz Mountain lookout is a

different bluff which is also used as a modern fire lookout today'], literally /'looking out (for s-o), looking (with binoculars)'/, probably <**o-ablaut** (or underlying **ó-ablaut**) and **R1**> *derivational* or *continuative*, lx <**=íwel**> *on the inside*, phonology: stress valence of the suffix here is stronger than that of the infix, ablaut, reduplication, syntactic analysis: nominal, attested by AK (History tape #34 4/7/78, also 8/30/77), IHTTC.

<**kw'ótsest**>, pcs //k'ʷɛ[=Aá=]c=əs=T//, [k'ʷácɪst], ABFC /'*stare at someone's face, look at s-o's face, stare at s-o, look at s-o*'/, SOC, lx <**=es**> *on the face*, (<**=t**> *purposeful control transitivizer*), phonology: ó-ablaut on root a triggered by =es, syntactic analysis: transitive verb, attested by Elders Group, also <**xwkw'ótsest**>, //xʷ=k'ʷɛ[=Aá=]c=əs=T//, (<**xw=**> *(meaning unclear, often used with =ós ~ =es 'on the face')*), attested by IHTTC, example: <**xwkw'ótsesthòmè**>, //xʷ=k'ʷɛ[=Aá=]c=əs=T-ámə//, [x̣ʷk'ʷácɪsθàmə̀], /'*stare at you*'/, phonology: downshifting, <**kw'otsesthóx**>, //k'ʷɛ[=Aá=]c=əs=T-áxʸ//, [k'ʷacɪsθáxʸ], /'*stare at me, look at me*'/, attested by Elders Group 5/26/76.

<**xwkw'ókw'etsest**>, cts //xʷ=k'ʷɛ[=Aá=][-C_1ə-]c=əs=T//, ABFC ['*staring at s-o*'], (<**-R1-**> *continuative*), phonology: ablaut, reduplication, syntactic analysis: transitive verb, attested by IHTTC; found in <**xwkw'ókw'etsesthòmè**>, //xʷ=k'ʷɛ[=Aá=][-C_1ə-]c=əs=T-ámə//, [xʷk'ʷák'ʷəcɪsθàmə̀], /'*staring at you*'/, phonology: downshifting, attested by IHTTC.

<**kw'okw'etsíls**>, sas //k'ʷɛ[=Aa=][-C_1ə-]c=íls//, cts, [k'ʷak'ʷəcíls ~ k'ʷɔk'ʷəcíls], ABFC ['*staring*'], (<**o-ablaut**> *derivational*), (<**-R1-**> *continuative aspect*), (<**=íls** (irregular for **=els**)> *structured activity continuative*), phonology: ablaut, reduplication, syntactic analysis: intransitive verb.

<**kw'echó:sem**>, mdls //k'ʷɛc=á·s=əm//, [k'ʷəčá·səm], ABFC ['*look at one's face*'], lx <**=ó:s**> *on the face, in the face*, (<**=em**> *middle voice*), phonology: stress-valence of lexical suffix here stronger than that of root, destressing of /ɛ/ converts it here to /ə/, syntactic analysis: intransitive verb, attested by BHTTC.

<**skw'ikw'echó:sem**>, dmn //s=C_1í=kʷɛc=á·s=əm//, HHG /'*mirror,* (probably *small mirror)*'/, literally /'something little to see one's face'/, (<**s=**> *nominalizer*, R4= *diminutive*), phonology: reduplication, syntactic analysis: nominal, attested by BHTTC.

<**skw'echó:stel**>, dnom //s=k'ʷɛc=á·s=təl//, BLDG ['*window*'], HHG ['*mirror*'], literally /'device to see face, thing to see in the face'/, (<**s=**> *nominalizer*), lx <**=ó:s**> *(in the)face*, lx <**=tel**> *device, thing to*, phonology: stress-valence of first suffix stronger than that of root, causing /ɛ/ to become /ə/, syntactic analysis: nominal, attested by Elders Group, also <**skw'echóstel**>, //s=k'ʷɛc=á·s=təl//, attested by IHTTC, example: <**lhx̱eyléxlha stetís te skw'echóstel**>, //ɬx̣=íl=ə́xʸ-ɬɛ s=C_1ə=tís tə s=k'ʷɛc=ás=təl//, /'*Stand near the window.*'/, attested by IHTTC.

<**skw'echó:steló:les**>, dnom //s=k'ʷɛc=á·s=təl=á·ləs//, CLO ['*eyeglasses*'], literally /'window(s) on the eyes, mirror(s) on the eyes, device on the eyes for seeing faces'/, (<**=ó:les**> *on the eyes*), syntactic analysis: nominal, attested by Elders Group 7/9/75.

<**kw'echú:yel**>, ds //k'ʷɛc=ú·yəl//, [k'ʷəčú·yɪl], FSH ['*check a net or trap (for fish)*'], HUNT ['*check a net or trap (for animal)*'], lx <**=ú:yel**> *net*, syntactic analysis: intransitive verb, attested by BHTTC, also <**kw'echő:yel**>, //k'ʷɛc=ó·yəl//, [k'ʷəčó·yɪl], /'*check fish nets*'/, dialects: *Upriver Halkomelem dialects [Nicomen]*, attested by PK (at Fish Camp 7/11/78), also <**kw'echá:yel**>, //k'ʷɛc=ɛ́·yəl//, /'*check fish nets*'/, dialects: *Matsqui*, attested by PK (at Fish Camp 7/11/78).

<**kw'ókw'etsxel**>, cts //k'ʷɛ[=Aá=][-C_1ə-]c=xʸəl//, [k'ʷák'ʷəcxʸɪl], HUNT /'*tracking, following prints*'/, literally /'examining foot(prints)'/, (<**ó-ablaut**> *derivational*), (<**-R1-**> *continuative*), lx <**=xel**> *on the foot, footprints*, phonology: ablaut, reduplication, syntactic analysis: intransitive verb, attested by IHTTC.

<**kw'átset**>, ABFC /'*look at s-th/s-o, examine s-o/s-th*'/, *see* kw'áts ~ kw'éts.

<kw'áx ~ kw'x ~ kw'xá>, bound root //k'ʷɛ́xʸ ~ k'ʷxʸ ~ k'ʷxʸɛ́// *count.*

<kw'xá:m>, izs //k'ʷɛ́xʸ[-M1-=əm//, NUM ['*count*'], (**<metathesis type 1>** *non-continuative*), (**<=em>** *intransitive*), phonology: metathesis, vowel merger, syntactic analysis: intransitive verb, attested by AC, other sources: ES /k'ʷxʸɛ́·m/ *count*, JH /k'ʷxé·m/ *to count*, Salish cognate: Squamish /k'ʷš-ímʔ/ *count (act.-itr.)*, k'ʷš-át *count (tr.)* W73:68, K69:76, also **<kw'xám>**, //k'ʷɛ́xʸ[-M1-=(ə)m//, attested by Deming (3/16/78), also /'*counting*'/, phonology: perhaps in error as continuative as stressed intransitivizer is usually non-continuative, attested by EB (5/4/76); found in **<kw'xá:mchexw>**, //k'ʷɛ́xʸ[-M1-=əm-c-əxʷ//, /'*Count.*'/, (**<-chexw>** *mild imperative 2s*), attested by AC, example: **<léwe kw'xá:m>**, //lə́wə k'ʷɛ́xʸ[-M1-=əm//, [lʊ́wə k'ʷxʸǽ·m], /'*You count.*'/, attested by AC, ASM ['different speakers count on their fingers in different ways:'], ASM ['1) left hand up, each finger touched with index finger of opposite hand, little finger one to thumb five, right hand down thumb six to little finger ten; 2) another way is both hands down, bend each finger down at its middle joint keeping the rest of the finger and hand held horizontal, left little finger one to thumb five, right thumb six to little finger ten'], attested by AD, ASM ['(left-handed): one = touch left little finger to left thumb, etc., five = hold out left thumb, six = touch right index finger to right thumb, ten = hold out right thumb'], attested by TM, ASM ['left hand facing person counting, one = touch little finger with right index, then fold down, etc., five = thumb, six = right thumb touched with index of hand facing away'], attested by NP, ASM ['right first, palms outward, fingers bent down, index finger raised = one, second finger raised also = two, third finger raised also = three, little finger also = four, thumb spread = five, thumb of left spread = six, seven = index left, ten = little finger'], attested by TG, ASM ['right first, hands horizontal like playing piano, little finger taps down = one, thumb taps = five, left thumb taps = six, little finger left = ten'], attested by PK, ASM ['right first, thumb holding fingers bent, little finger up = one, thumb out = five, bend fingers and repeat, little finger up right = six, etc.'], attested by Flossie Joe, ASM ['palms outward, right first, fingers held by thumb, little finger raised = one, five = thumb, six = left thumb, etc.'], attested by EB, ASM ['start with left (sic right?), fingers spread, one = fold down little finger, five = fold thumb, six = thumb of right (sic left?), seven = fold down index, etc.'], attested by Flora Julian (sister of NP), living at Matsqui, ASM ['one through five on hand facing person counting, six through ten on right hand facing away, right index points to left first, one = to index left, four = to little finger, five = to thumb left, six = to right thumb (with left index), seven = to right index, ten = to little finger right'], dialects: *Matsqui (Deming elders group)*, attested by GC (brother of AH), ASM ['(right-handed): hands facing person counting, touch right index to left hand first, one = to thumb, two = index, five = little, six = touch left index to right thumb, seven = to right index, etc.'], dialects: *Matsqui (Deming elders group)*, attested by AH, ASM ['hands face away from person counting, bend fingers down, little finger right hand = one, right thumb = five, left thumb = six, etc.'], dialects: *Katzie*, attested by EP, Salish cognate: Lillooet (Port Douglas dialect)(Wally Henry, young fluent speaker): right hand first, hand points up and is brought down with index finger pointing at hearer = one, arm is raised again at elbow to point up then brought down to point at hearer again with index and first finger = two, etc., thumb and whole hand points (hand held vertical with thumb on top and finger directly underneath) = five, six = index of left points, ten = thumb and whole hand brought down, Salish cognate: Thompson (Madeline Charlie): right hand faces away and left faces toward person counting, bend fingers down, right index finger = one, little finger right = four, left index = five, left little finger = eight, left thumb = nine, right thumb = ten, Salish cognate: Lushootseed (Skagit dialect)(LG)(right-handed): touch right index to left hand first, one = to left thumb, two = to left index, five = to left little, six = touch left index to right little finger, ten = to right thumb, Skagit numbers /dəč'úʔ/ [dəč'óʔ ~ dəč'úʔ] *one*, /sálíʔ/ *two*, /ɬíxʷ/ *three*, /bú·s/ [bú·s ~ bó·s] *four*, /c'əláč/ [c'əlǽc] *five*, /yəláč/ [yəlǽc] *six* (/yəláči/ *other hand*), /c'úkʷs/ *seven*, /tqáči/ *eight*, /x̣ʷə́l/ *nine*, /ʔúlub/ *ten*, Salish cognate: Squamish (Louise Bolan)(left-handed): hands face away from person counting, right hand folds little finger down = one, right thumb = five, left thumb = six.

<**kw'áxem**>, cts //k'ʷɛ́xʸ=əm//, NUM ['*counting*'], (<**lack of metathesis type 1**> *continuative*), syntactic analysis: intransitive verb, attested by Deming.

<**skw'exá:m**>, dnom //s=k'ʷɛ́xʸ=M1=əm//, NUM ['*number*'], (<**s=**> *nominalizer*), syntactic analysis: nominal, also <**ts'kw'éx**>, //c'-k'ʷə́xʸ//, comment: ts' may be error for ts; the form may be confusion with ts'kw'éx *twenty*, attested by AC, example: <**skw'í:l te ts'kw'éxs ta qwlhí:xel**>, //s=k'ʷí·l tə c'=k'ʷə́xʸ-s t-ɛ qʷɬ=íy=xʸəl//, /'*What is the number of your shoe?*'/, literally /'is how many of a cycle the number of the your shoe'/, attested by AC.

<**mekw'stám skw'xám ~ mekw'stám skw'áxem**>, cpds //mək'ʷ=s=tɛ́m s=k'ʷɛ́xʸ=M1=əm ~ mək'ʷ=s=tɛ́m s=k'ʷɛ́xʸ=əm//, NUM //'math, mathematics'//, morphosememic development (SMM), semantic comment: from lit. "everything (in) numbers"), attested by RG & EH (4/10/99 Ling332)

<**kw'xát**>, pcs //k'ʷɛ́xʸ[-M1-]=T//, NUM /'*count them, count s-th*'/, (<**metathesis type 1**> *non-continuative*), (<**=t**> *purposeful control transitivizer*), phonology: metathesis, syntactic analysis: transitive verb, attested by Deming, AC, Elders Group; found in <**kw'exátlha**>, //k'ʷɛ́xʸ[-M1-]=T-ɬɛ//, /'*Count it.*'/, attested by AC, example: <**l stl'í: kw'els kw'exá:t tel sth'í:m**>, //l s=ƛ'í· k'ʷə-l-s k'ʷɛ́xʸ[-M1-]=T t-əl s=θ'í·m//, /'*I want to count my berries.*'/, attested by AC, <**kw'xát á:lhtel**>, //k'ʷɛ́xʸ[-M1-]=T ʔɛ́·ɬtəl//, /'*count them*'/, attested by Elders Group, <**kw'xátes te staliqíw**>, //k'ʷɛ́xʸ[-M1-]=T-əs tə s=t[-əl-]iqíw//, /'*He counts horses.*'/, attested by EB.

<**kw'áxt**>, cts //k'ʷɛ́xʸ=T//, NUM /'*counting them, counting s-th*'/, (<**lack of metathesis type 1**> *continuative*), syntactic analysis: transitive verb, attested by Deming, also <**kw'íxat**>, //k'ʷɛ[-Aí-]xʸ=əT//, attested by EB, example: <**kw'íxates te staliqíw**>, //k'ʷɛ[-Aí-]xʸ=əT-əs tə s=t[-əl-]iqíw//, /'*He's counting horses.*'/, attested by EB, <**kw'áxtes te táles**>, //k'ʷɛ́xʸ=T-əs tə tɛ́lə-s//, /'*He's counting his money.*'/, attested by AC.

<**skw'ekw'íx**>, strs //s=C_1ə=k'ʷɛ[=Aí=]xʸ//, NUM ['*be counted*'], (<**s=**> *stative*, <R5=> *resultative*), (<**í-ablaut**> *derivational* or *stative*), phonology: reduplication, ablaut, syntactic analysis: adjective/adjectival verb, attested by JL (Joe Lorenzetto), example: <**lulh skw'ekw'íx**>, //lə=wɬ s=C_1ə=k'ʷɛ[=Aí=]xʸ//, /'*(They're) already counted.*'/, attested by JL.

<**ts'kw'éx**>, possibly root //c'k'ʷə́xʸ or c[=G=]=k'ʷɛ[=Aə́=]xʸ//, [c'k'ʷíxʸ], NUM ['*twenty*'], probably root <**kw'ɛ́x**> *count*, possibly <**ts=**> *have, get,* possibly <**=G= (glottalization)**> *derivational,* possibly <**é-ablaut**> *derivational*, phonology: possible glottalization, possible ablaut, syntactic analysis: num, adjective/adjectival verb, attested by AC, DM, BJ, CT, others, other sources: ES /c'k'ʷɛ́xʸ/, JH /c'k'ʷéx/, also <**tskw'éx ~ ts'kw'éx**>, //ck'ʷə́xʸ ~ c'k'ʷə́xʸ//, attested by AC; found in <**ts'kw'éxtset**>, //c'k'ʷə́xʸ-c-ət//, /'*We're twenty., There's twenty of us.*'/, attested by AC, example: <**ts'kw'éx qas kw'e léts'e**>, //c'k'ʷə́xʸ qɛs k'ʷə lə́c'ə//, /'*twenty-one*'/, attested by AC, BJ, also <**ts'kw'éx qas te léts'e**>, //c'k'ʷə́xʸ qɛs tə lə́c'ə//, attested by CT 9/5/73.

<**ts'ekw'xále**>, ds //c'k'ʷə[=M1=]xʸ=ɛ́lə//, NUM ['*twenty people*'], lx <**=ále**> *people*, syntactic analysis: nominal, attested by Elders Group, also <**ts'kw'éx mestíyexw**>, //c'k'ʷə́xʸ məstíyəxʷ//, attested by AC.

<**ts'kw'exáleqel**>, ds //c'k'ʷəxʸ=ɛ́ləqəl//, NUM ['*twenty containers*'], lx <**=áleqel**> *containers*, syntactic analysis: nominal, attested by AD.

<**ts'kw'xó:s**>, ds //c'k'ʷxʸ=á·s//, NUM ['*twenty dollars*'], lx <**=ó:s**> *on the face, round thing, dollar*, syntactic analysis: nominal, attested by Elders Group, also <**ts'ekw'xó:s**>, //c'k'ʷə[=M1=]xʸ=á·s//, attested by AC (11/30/71).

<**skw'exó:s ~ skw'xó:s**>, dnom //s=k'ʷəxʸ=á·s ~ s=k'ʷxʸ=á·s//, WETH ['*moon*'], semantic environment ['used when pointing or describing'], TIME ['*month*'], semantic environment ['used when counting'],

(<**s=**> *nominalizer*), probably root <**kw'ax**> *count*, also see under that root, lx <**=ó:s**> *on the face, round thing*, syntactic analysis: nominal, attested by AC, DM (12/4/64), BJ (12/5/64, 5/64), EB, Elders Group, IHTTC, NP, other sources: JH /sk'ʷxá·s/ ~ /ɬqé·lc'/ *moon*, (semological comment: many interesting morphosememic shifts can be seen in the expressions for the phases of the moon below), ASM ['moon'], example: <**lulh xelo:kw' te skw'exó:s**>, //lə=uɬ xʸəlá·k'ʷ tə s=k'ʷəxʸ=á·s//, /'*The moon is full.*'/, literally /'the moon past already is circular'/, attested by AC, <**selíts' te skw'exó:s**>, //s=(ə)lə[=Aí=]c' tə s=k'ʷəxʸ=á·s//, /'*It's full moon, The moon is full.*'/, ASM ['about the middle of the Stó:lō month'], attested by Elders Group 3/12/75, <**léts' skw'exó:s ~ slíts' skw'exó:s**>, //lə́c' s=k'ʷəxʸ=á·s ~ s=lə[=Aí=]c' s=k'ʷəxʸ=á·s//, /'*full moon*'/, attested by IHTTC, <**léts'e(s) skw'xó:s**>, //lə́c'ə(s) s=k'ʷxʸ=á·s//, /'*first quarter of the moon, new moon; one month*'/, ASM ['this is the beginning of the Stó:lō month'], attested by DM 12/5/65, <**x̱áws te skw'exó:s**>, //x̣ɛ́ws tə s=k'ʷəxʸ=á·s//, /'*It's first quarter moon.*'/, literally /'The moon is new.'/, (semological comment: this differs from the English "new moon" which is all dark; a drawing of this moon shows it as a crescent with horns facing left), attested by Elders Group 3/12/75, <**me pélekw te x̱áws skw'exós**>, //mə pə́ləkʷ təx̣ɛ́ws s=k'ʷəxʸ=ás//, /'*The new sliver of moon has appeared., The new crescent moon has appeared.*'/, literally /'the new moon has come to appear, come up on the horizon, come out from behind something'/, attested by IHTTC, <**lhséq' skw'xó:s**>, //ɬ=sə́q' s=k'ʷxʸ=á·s//, /'*a half-moon*'/, attested by DM 12/4/64, <**yuwál lhséq' te skw'exó:s**>, //yuwɛ́l ɬ=sə́q' tə s=k'ʷəxʸ=á·s//, /'*It's the first half-moon.*'/, literally /'The moon is first half.'/, ASM ['a drawing of this moon shows the right half visible'], attested by Elders Group, <**lhséq' te skw'exó:s**>, //ɬ=sə́q' tə s=k'ʷəxʸ=á·s//, /'*second half-moon, The moon is in second half., The moon is half.*'/, literally /'The moon is half.'/, ASM ['a drawing of this moon shows the left half visible, the expression is said to be the only way to refer to the second half-moon in contrast to the expression for the first half-moon, but it can also be used for any half-moon'], attested by Elders Group, <**th'éx̱ te skw'exó:s**>, //θ'ə́x̣ tə s=k'ʷəxʸ=á·s//, /'*It's a new moon (dark).*'/, literally /'The moon is burnt out.'/, attested by Elders Group, <**th'éth'ex̱ te skw'exó:s**>, //θ'ə́[-C_1ə-]x̣ tə s=k'ʷəxʸ=á·s//, /'*It's the last quarter moon.*'/, literally /'The moon is burning out.'/, attested by Elders Group 3/12/75, <**kw'e'ós skw'exó:s**>, //k'ʷəʔ=ás s=k'ʷəxʸ=á·s//, /'*It's a quarter moon with horns up.*'/, literally /'it's a face-up moon'/, attested by IHTTC, <**kw'élh skw'exó:s**>, //k'ʷə́ɬ s=k'ʷəxʸ=á·s//, /'*It's a quarter moon with horns down (straight down or down left or down right).*'/, literally /'it's a spilled moon'/, attested by IHTTC, <**lhékw'qsel te skw'exós**>, //ɬə́k'ʷ=qsəl tə s=k'ʷəxʸ=ás//, /'*The moon is in the day-time sky (when the sun is out too).*'/, literally /'The moon tripped., The moon hooked its nose.'/, attested by IHTTC, <**stámcha skw'exós kw'e atse ōw me pélekw**>, //s=tɛ́m-cɛ s=k'ʷəxʸ=ás k'ʷə ʔɛcɛ ʔəw mə pə́ləkʷ//, /'*What is the next moon to appear?*'/, literally /'what will be the moon that next comes to appear'/, attested by IHTTC, <**lálems te skw'exó:s**>, //lɛ́ləm-s tə s=k'ʷəxʸ=á·s//, /'*halo around the moon*'/, literally /'the house of the moon'/, attested by Elders Group, <**q'elóts'eqw(em te skw'exó:s)**>, //q'əlác'=əqʷ(=əm tə s=k'ʷəxʸ=á·s)//, /'*(the moon has a) halo*'/, literally /'(the moon has a) rainshelter'/, attested by Elders Group, ASM ['month'], ASM ['each month began with the first sliver of moon after the burnt out moon; Old Louie from Skw'átets (grandfather of Mrs. Steven Kelly, Agnes Kelly's grandmother) could tell time by the sun with a stick sun-dial or without; he also had knotted rags to tell days and months; he was first cousin to Joe Lorenzetto's grandmother (Fish Camp 7/19/78)'], <**kw'í:l skw'xó:s**>, //k'ʷí·l s=k'ʷxʸ=á·s//, /'*how many months*'/, semantic environment ['how many months (old) is that child?'], attested by AC, <**stám te skw'exó:s**>, //s=tɛ́m tə s=k'ʷəxʸ=á·s//, /'*What month is it?, What moon is it?*'/, (semological comment: a typical answer might be: Tem'elíle (May, salmonberry time)), attested by IHTTC (Calendar Lesson), <**kw'e les hó:ys te skw'xó:s**>, //k'ʷə lɛ-s há·y-s tə s=k'ʷəxʸ=á·s//, /'*the last day of the month*'/, literally /'what has-gone finished of the month'/, attested by EB, <**skw'exó:s sq'óq'ey**>, //s=k'ʷəxʸ=á·s s=q'ó[=C_1ə=]y//, /'*menstruation*'/, ABDF, literally /'moon sickness'/, attested by NP.

<kw'áxem>, NUM ['*counting*'], *see* kw'áx.

<kw'áxt>, NUM /'*counting them, counting s-th*'/, *see* kw'áx.

<kw'á:y ~ kw'áy>, bound root //k'ʷɛ́·y ~ k'ʷɛ́y//, EFAM /'*impossible, can't be*'/, VALJ ['*wrong*'], MOOD, CJ, syntactic analysis: intransitive verb, rarely a free form, Salish cognate: Squamish /k'ʷáy/ *be impossible, wrong* W73:294, K67:346, K69:77; found in **<kw'á:ya ~ kw'á:ye>**, //k'ʷɛ́·yɛ ~ k'ʷɛ́·yə//, /'*is it impossible, can't?, can?*'/, (**<-a ~ -e>** *interrogative, yes/no question*), attested by AC, example: **<kw'á:ya kw'as kw'étslexw>**, //k'ʷɛ́·y-ɛ k'ʷ-ɛ-s k'ʷə́c=l-əxʷ//, /'*Can you see it?*'/, attested by AC, **<kw'é:ye kw'as kw'ètslexwélep>**, //k'ʷɛ́·y-ə k'ʷ-ɛ-s k'ʷə̀c=l-əxʷ-ə́ləp//, /'*Can you all see it?*'/, attested by AC.

<**skw'á:y**>, stvi //s=k'ʷɛ́·y//, EFAM /'*it is impossible, it can't be, it never is*'/, VALJ ['*be wrong*'], MOOD, CJ, (**<s=>** *stative*), syntactic analysis: intransitive verb, adjective/adjectival verb, attested by AC, Elders Group, also **<skw'áy>**, //s=k'ʷɛ́y//, attested by EB, Deming, IHTTC (SP, NP, AD, AK, DC, EB), BHTTC, Elders Group, ASM ['it can't be'], example: **<skw'á:y kw'els kw'étslexw.>**, //s=k'ʷɛ́·y k'ʷ-əl-s k'ʷə́c=l-əxʷ//, /'*I can't see it.*'/, literally /'it can't be that I see it, my seeing it can't be'/, attested by AC, **<skw'á:y kw'els q'á:l kw'es lúwes>**, //s=k'ʷɛ́·y k'ʷ-əl-s q'ɛ́·l k'ʷ-əs lə́wə-s//, /'*I couldn't believe it was you.*'/, literally /'it can't be that I believe that it is you (present ~ recent past tense)'/, syntactic comment: note the 2nd person pronominal verb with 3rd person subject suffix -s, attested by AC, **<skw'á:y kw'as (kw'étslexw, kw'ètslexwélep, lám, mőkw'elep lám)>**, //s=k'ʷɛ́·y k'ʷ-ɛ-s (k'ʷə́c=l-əxʷ, k'ʷə́c=l-əxʷ-ə́ləp, lɛ́=m, mók'ʷ-ələp lɛ́=m)//, /'*You can't (see it, all see it, go, all go).*'/, attested by AC, **<skw'á:y kw'es (kw'étslexwtset, kw'étslexws, kw'étslexws á:lhtel).>**, //s=k'ʷɛ́·y k'ʷə-s (k'ʷə́c=l-əxʷ-c-ət, k'ʷə́c=l-əxʷ-s, k'ʷə́c=l-əxʷ-s ʔɛ́·ɬtəl).//, /'*We can't see it., He/She can't see it., They can't see it. (resp.)*'/, literally /'it can't be that (we see it, he/she/they see it, they see it)'/, attested by AC, **<skw'áye kw'els iyáqest>**, //s=k'ʷɛ́y-ə k'ʷ-əl-s ʔiyɛ́q=əs=T//, /'*Can't I change my money (change money)?*'/, attested by Deming, **<skw'áy kw'as qwéles>**, //s=k'ʷɛ́y k'ʷ-ɛ-s qʷə́ləs(?)//, /'*a secret, something you can't talk about*'/, (irregular **<qwéles>** *talk about)*, attested by EB, ASM ['it is impossible'], **<yó:swe weskw'áyes kw'els lám>**, //yá·swə wə-s=k'ʷɛ́y-əs k'ʷ-əl-s lɛ́=m//, /'*Maybe it's impossible for me to go.*'/, attested by IHTTC: SP, NP, AD, AK, DC, also **<yó:swe skw'áyes kw'els lám>**, //yá·swə s=k'ʷɛ́y-əs k'ʷ-əl-s lɛ́=m//, attested by IHTTC: EB, also AD, AK, DC, ASM ['it never is'], **<skw'áy kws léps>**, //s=k'ʷɛ́y kʷ-s lə́p-s//, /'*He never learns his lesson.*'/, attested by BHTTC, **<skw'áy kw'els su éyo>**, //s=k'ʷɛ́y k'ʷ-əl-s s-u ʔɛ́y=à//, /'*I'm never good.*'/, **<skw'áy kws tu kwikwe'átes te sqiqáqs>**, //s=k'ʷɛ́y kʷ-s tu C_1í=kʷəʔɛ́=T-əs tə s=C_1í=qɛ́q-s//, /'*He never stops pestering his little brother., He never leaves (leave alone) his little brother alone.*'/, literally /'it never is that he a little bit stops pestering his little brother'/, attested by EB, AD, ASM ['be wrong'], **<skw'á:y te s'iwesá:ylhem>**, //s=k'ʷɛ́·y tə s=ʔiwəs=ɛ́·yɬ=əm//, /'*teachings for children that are wrong, (The teachings for children are wrong.)*'/, attested by Elders Group (5/3/78), **<echxw skw'á:y>**, //ʔə-c-xʷ s=k'ʷɛ́·y//, /'*You're wrong.*'/, attested by Elders Group (10/1/75), **<tu skw'á:y>**, //tu s=k'ʷɛ́·y//, /'*a little bit wrong, not well upstairs (in the mind)*'/, attested by Elders Group (1/16/80).

<kw'à:y>, free root //k'ʷɛ̀·y//, ABFC ['*get hungry*'], syntactic analysis: intransitive verb, attested by EB, Elders Group (Mar. 1972), LJ, also **<kw'á:y>**, //k'ʷɛ́·y//, attested by Deming, LJ, Elders Group (6/28/78), Salish cognate: Squamish /k'ʷáyʔ/ *be hungry* and /k'ʷák'ʷayʔ/ *be very hungry* W73:146, K67:346, Lushootseed /k'y-úc-əb/ *starved* H76:240, and Samish /k'ʷéy'k'ʷiy'/ *be hungry* G86:91, example: **<étsulh kw'à:y>**, //ʔə́-c-(əl)-uɬ k'ʷɛ̀·y//, /'I'm hungry.'/, phonology: a few speakers drop the el in -tsel *I (non-subordinate subject)* in certain environments, largely before -u or -ulh, attested by Elders Group (Mar. 1972), **<éwelhtsel kw'à:y>**, //ʔə́wə-ɬ-c-əl k'ʷɛ̀·y//, /'*I'm never hungry.*'/, attested by EB; found in <**wekw'á:yàl**>, //wə-k'ʷɛ́·y-ɛ̀l//, /'*if I get hungry*'/, attested by Elders (6/28/78), example: <**x̱élh tel s'íles lhíl kw'à:y**>, //x̣ə́ɬ tə-l s=ʔíləs ɬi-l k'ʷɛ̀·y//, /'*My chest hurts when I get hungry*'/, attested by LJ (Elders Group 6/28/78), <**le qelámthet tel th'éle lhíl ólew le kw'á:y**>, //lə qəl=ɛ́m=θət tə-l θ'ɛ́lə ɬí-l ʔál=əw lə k'ʷɛ́·y//, /'*My heart gets weak when I get too hungry.*'/, attested by LJ (Elders Group 6/28/78); found in <**kw'á:ytsel**>, //k'ʷɛ́·y-c-əl//, /'*I'm getting hungry.*'/, attested by Deming.

<**kw'ókw'iy**>, stvi //k'ʷɛ[=AáC$_1$ə=]y//, ABFC ['*be hungry*'], FOOD, (<**ó-ablaut and -R1-**> *stative*), phonology: ablaut, reduplication, syntactic analysis: intransitive verb, attested by EB, Deming, AC, MH, AD, Elders (Mar. 1972), also <**kw'ó:kw'iy**>, //k'ʷɛ[=Aá·C$_1$ə=]y//, attested by JL; found in <**kw'ókw'iytsel**>, //k'ʷɛ[=AáC$_1$ə=]y-c-əl//, [k'ʷák'ʷiycɪl], /'*I'm hungry.*'/, attested by MH, AD, example: <**tsel kw'ókw'iy**>, //c-əl k'ʷɛ[=AáC$_1$ə=]y//, /'*I'm hungry.*'/, attested by Elders Group (Mar. 1972), <**latsullh kw'ókw'iy**>, //lɛ-c-əl-uɬ k'ʷɛ[=AáC$_1$ə=]y//, /'*I am hungry.*'/, literally /'I have already become hungry.'/, attested by Deming, <**wiyóthtsel kw'ókw'iy**>, //wə=yáθ-c-əl k'ʷɛ[=AáC$_1$ə=]y//, /'*I'm always hungry., I'm hungry all the time.*'/, attested by Deming, <**ő́wetsel kw'ókw'iy**>, //ʔə́wə-c-əl k'ʷɛ[=AáC$_1$ə=]y//, /'*I wasn't hungry.*'/, attested by EB, <**éwe ílhtsel kw'ókw'iy kw' cheláqelhelh**>, //ʔə́wə ʔi-ɬ-c-əl k'ʷɛ[=AáC$_1$ə=]y k'ʷ cəlɛ́qəɬ-əɬ//, /'*I wasn't hungry yesterday.*'/, attested by EB, <**éwelhtsel kw'ókw'iy**>, //ʔə́wə-ɬ-c-əl k'ʷɛ[=AáC$_1$ə=]y//, /'*I'm never hungry.*'/, attested by EB.

<**temkw'à:y**>, ds //təm=kʷɛ̀·y//, TIME /'*hungry time (about mid-April to mid-May), famine (Elders 3/72)*'/, FOOD, ASM ['time when people run out of stored food and can't get any fresh; all the spá:lx̱w (vegetable food, camas) and sq'éyle (dried meat) is gone, no fish running; all the lazy people have to bum food; only the sxwúxwe (ambitious) have enough'], lx <**tem=**> *time for, season for*, syntactic analysis: intransitive verb, nominal, attested by IHTTC, also /'*famine*'/, attested by Elders Group (Mar. 1972), comment: this translation may be too strong (see note above), compare <**temxwá**> *famine, starving time* with root <**xwá**> *starve*.

<**kw'e**>, free root //k'ʷə//, DEM /'*the (distant and out of sight, remote), (definite but distant and out of sight, remote), the (abstract), a (remote, abstract), some, (indefinite)*'/, CJ ['*that (abstract subordinating conjunction)*'], TIME /'*when (simultaneous subordinating conjunction), as*'/, syntactic analysis: demonstrative article, demonstrative conjunction, attested by AC, Elders Group, Deming, AD, EB, etc., also <**kw' ~ kw**>, //k'ʷ ~ kʷ//, attested by EB, ASM ['the (distant and out of sight, remote)'], <**li kw'e North**>, //li k'ʷə North//, /'*in the North*'/, attested by AC, ASM ['(definite but remote or distant and out of sight)'], semantic environment ['proper name'], <**líye skwetáxw kw'e John**>, //lí-ə s=kʷətɛ́xʷ k'ʷə John//, /'*Is John home?*'/, literally /'is there yes/no question the/definite (distant and out of sight, remote) John'/, attested by AC, ASM ['(the)(abstract)'], <**chap álhtel kw'e cheláqelh(elh)**>, //c-ɛp ʔɛ́ɬtəl k'ʷə cəlɛ́q=əɬ(-əɬ)//, /'*You (plural) ate yesterday.*'/, attested by AC, ASM ['(indefinite)'], <**lóy sqwálewels tl' Máli kw'e qó:**>, //láy s=qwɛ́l=əwəl-s-ƛ' mɛ́li k'ʷə qá·//, /'*Mary is only thinking of water.*'/, literally /'water (indefinite) is the only thought of Mary'/, syntactic comment: lóy *is only* adverb/adverbial verb modifies sqwálewel-s *her/his thought* and together form the main verb phrase with adverbial (verb/particle/demonstrative) of the sentence, *is her only thought*; the nominal phrase immediately following a 3rd person possessed form (here sqwálewel-s) is its possessor, thus *is Mary's only thought*; words closer to the beginning of the sentence are foregrounded, thus *only* and then *thought* are foregrounded or emphasized; *water* is syntactically the subject but is not syntactically foregrounded and so occurs at the end of the sentence in the speaker's translation rather than at the beginning where it would be emphasized in English, attested by EB, ASM ['some'], example: <**kw' seplì:l ~ kw seplì:l**>, //k'ʷ səplì·l ~ kʷ səplì·l//, /'*some bread*'/, attested by EB, <**axwethóxchxw kw' tí**>, //ʔɛxʷ=əT-áxʸ-c-xʷ k'ʷ tí//, /'*Give me some tea.*'/, attested by EB, ASM ['that (abstract coordinating conjunction)'], <**t'áyeq' kw'els ólmetsel**>, //t'ɛ́yəq' k'ʷə-l-s

ʔálməc-əl//, /'*mad that I have to wait*'/, attested by Elders Group, ASM ['when (simultanous coordinating conjunction)'], <**ílhtsel le qíq' kw'els e só:les**>, //ʔí-ɬ-c-əl lə qí=q' k'ʷə-l-s ʔə sá·ləs//, /'*I went to (go to) jail when I was drunk.*'/, attested by Elders Group, <**líchxw we'éy el qwóqwel kw'es me kwetxwílem kwtha siyáya**>, //lí-c-xʷ wə-ʔɛ́y ʔəl qʷɛ[=AáC_1ə=]l k'ʷə-s mə kʷətɛxʷ=íl=əm kʷ=θ-ɛ si=yɛ́yɛ//, /'*Were you still talking when your friend came in?*'/, attested by AC.

<**kw'é**>, free root //k'ʷə́//, EFAM /'*Look., See.*'/, semantic environment ['used when showing something to someone'], phonology: has rising tone when used this way, probable clipped form from root kw'éts *look, see*, syntactic analysis: interjection, syntactic comment: used as a sentence all by itself, attested by AD.

<**kw'è:**>, df //k'ʷə́= `· or k'ʷə́-ə̀//, EFAM ['*Really. (said in doubt)*'], semantic environment ['used when doubting someone'], (<= `:> *emphasis* or <-è> *interrogative, yes/no question*), phonology: mid-pitch stress is not a normal part of either the emphasis suffix nor the interrogative suffix; it may be derivational or may be a sentence stress feature; (if the interrogative suffix is correctly analyzed here it is violating the usual rule of vowel merger which makes e + e → a: and the phonotactic rule that e can only be lengthened by <=:> *emphasis* (schwa-lengthening)), syntactic analysis: interjection, syntactic comment: used as a sentence by itself, attested by AD.

<**kw'echó:sem**>, ABFC ['*look at one's face*'], *see* kw'áts ~ kw'éts.

<**kw'echú:yel**>, FSH ['*check a net or trap (for fish)*'], *see* kw'áts ~ kw'éts.

<**kw'ekw'élh**>, WATR ['*be flowing*'], *see* kw'élh.

<**kw'ekw'ém**>, ABFC ['*growing up*'], *see* kw'ém.

<**kw'ekw'e'íqw ~ kw'ekw'íqw**>, ABFC /'*facing up, head sticking up*'/, *see* kw'e'í ~ kw''í ~ kw'í.

<**Kw'ekw'e'í:qw ~ Kw'ekw'e'íqw ~ Kw'ekw'í:qw**>, PLN ['*Kilgard village on Upper Sumas River*'], *see* kw'e'í ~ kw''í ~ kw'í.

<**kw'ekw'í**>, TVMO /'*climbing, rising*'/, *see* kw'í ~ kw'íy.

<**kw'ekw'íxwxel**>, CLO /'*gumboots, rubber boots*'/, *see* kw'íxw.

<**kw'ekw'íythet**>, REL ['*training*'], *see* kw'í ~ kw'íy.

<**kw'ekw'qwá:lth'átel**>, HHG /'*stick for beating blankets or clothes or mat, blanket-beater, clothes-beater, mat-beater, rug-beater*'/, *see* kw'óqw.

<**kw'ekw'xwós**>, WETH ['*hailing (weather)*'], *see* kw'xwós.

<**kw'él**>, possible bound root //k'ʷə́l//, meaning uncertain but prob. *turn, twist*

<**skw'elkw'élxel**>, df //s=C_1əC_2=k'ʷə́l=xʸəl//, WETH ['*whirlwind*'], (<**s=**> *nominalizer*, R3= *plural* or *characteristic*), (<**=xel**> *precipitation; on the foot*), phonology: reduplication, syntactic analysis: nominal, attested by EB, Deming, compare <**q'eyq'elts'iyósem spehá:ls**> *whirlwind*.

<**kw'él:a ~ kw'éla**>, probably root //k'ʷə́l·ɛ ~ k'ʷə́lɛ//, ANA /'*belly, stomach*'/, syntactic analysis: nominal, noun, attested by AC, Elders Group, DM, other sources: ES /k'ʷə́l·ɛ/ *belly* vs. ES /spə́xʷ ~ sməq'tɛ̂l/ *stomach*, H-T<kōēla> *stomach*, Elder's comment: "stomach (inside and outside)(of animal, bird, human, etc.)", attested by AC, contrast <**spéxw**> *animal tripe (stomach, upper and lower), bowel*, Elder's comment: "some call it that", attested by AC, example: <**hí:kw te kw'él:es te músmesò:llh**>, //hí·kʷ tə k'ʷə́l·ɛ-s tə músməs=á·lɬ//, /'*The calf's belly is big.*'/, attested by AC.

<**skw'él:a**>, ds //s=k'ʷə́l·ɛ//, BPI /'*have a big belly, big-bellied person*'/, (<**s=**> *stative* ~ s= *nominalizer*), syntactic analysis: intransitive verb, nominal, example: <**chxw xwe'ít telúwe skw'él:a**>, //c-xʷ xʷəʔít tɛ=lə́wə s=k'ʷə́l·ɛ//, /'*What are you doing, you big-belly?*'/, attested by

Elders Group.

<**kw'elálh**>, NUM [*'how many times'*], *see* kw'í:l ~ kw'íl.

<**kw'eléw ~ kw'elṓw**>, probably root //k'ʷələ́w ~ k'ʷəlów//, ANA /*'skin, hide (with/without hair or fur), pelt, sinew'*/, HUNT, SPRD [*'dog-hair blanket dancing apron (DM 12/4/64)'*], MC, syntactic analysis: nominal, noun, attested by AC, DM, CT, HT, other sources: ES /k'ʷələ́w·/ *skin (hide)*, H-T kwElṓ *skin (human)* and kwElṓs tE smíyEts (macron over i) *skin of an animal*, also <**kw'elṓ:w**>, //k'ʷəló·w//, attested by BJ 12/5/64, also /*'dog-hair blanket dancing apron'*/, attested by DM 12/4/64, example: <**kw'elṓws te sméyeth**>, //k'ʷəlów-s tə s=mə́yəθ//, /*'the animal's hide, the skin of an animal'*/, attested by AC, CT, HT, <**hókwex kw'e lháts'tel kw'es máx te kw'eléws te sméyeth**>, //hákʷ=əxʸ k'ʷə ɬi[=Aɛ=]c'=təl k'ʷə-s mɛ=xʸ tə k'ʷələ́w-s tə s=mə́yəθ//, /*'use a knife to take off the skin of an animal'*/, attested by CT, HT, <**p'áth'et te kw'eléws te sméyeth li te st'elákw' siyólh**>, //p'ɛ́θ'=əT tə k'ʷələ́w-s tə s=mə́yəθ lí tə s=t'əlɛ́k'ʷ si=yáɬ//, /*'sew the hide of an animal on a circular frame'*/, attested by HT, <**kw'elṓ: sp'áp'eth'**>, //k'ʷəló(·)w s=pɛ́[=C_1ə=]θ'//, /*'sinew thread'*/, attested by DM 12/4/64.

<**kw'elōwáx̱el**>, ds //k'ʷəlow=ɛ́x̣əl//, ANA [*'skin of the arm'*], lx <**=áx̱el**> *on the arm*, syntactic analysis: nominal.

<**kw'elōwépsem**>, ds //k'ʷəlow=ə́psəm//, ANA [*'skin of the nape of the neck'*], lx <**=épsem**> *on the back of the neck, on the back of the head*, syntactic analysis: nominal.

<**kw'elṓweqw**>, ds //k'ʷəlów=əqʷ//, ANA /*'skin of the head, scalp'*/, lx <**=eqw**> *on top of the head*, syntactic analysis: nominal, also <**kw'élewōqw**>, //k'ʷə[=´=]ləw=əqʷ//, attested by IHTTC; found in <**skw'élewōqws**>, //s-k'ʷələw=əqʷ-s//, /*'his scalp'*/, (<**s-**> *inalienable possession*), (<**-s**> *third person possessive*), attested by IHTTC.

<**kw'elōwíles**>, ds //k'ʷəlow=íləs//, ANA [*'skin of the chest'*], lx <**=íles**> *on the chest*, syntactic analysis: nominal.

<**kw'elōwíts**>, ds //k'ʷəlow=íc//, ANA [*'skin of the back'*], lx <**=íts ~ =ewíts**> *on the back*, syntactic analysis: nominal.

<**kw'elṓwlhelh**>, ds //k'ʷəlów=ɬəɬ//, ANA [*'skin of the throat'*], lx <**=lhelh**> *on the throat*, syntactic analysis: nominal.

<**kw'elōwó:ythel**>, ds //k'ʷəlow=á·yθəl//, ANA /*'skin of the mouth, (*prob. also *skin of the chin or jaw or lips)'*/, lx <**=ó:ythel**> *on the chin, on the jaw, on the lips*, syntactic analysis: nominal.

<**kw'elókw'exwóles**>, MC [*'be box-shaped'*], *see* kw'óxwe.

<**kw'elókw't'el**>, EZ [*'a few mice'*], *see* kw'át'el.

<**kw'elōwáx̱el**>, ANA [*'skin of the arm'*], *see* kw'eléw ~ kw'elṓw.

<**kw'elōwépsem**>, ANA [*'skin of the nape of the neck'*], *see* kw'eléw ~ kw'elṓw.

<**kw'elṓweqw**>, ANA /*'skin of the head, scalp'*/, *see* kw'eléw ~ kw'elṓw.

<**kw'elōwíles**>, ANA [*'skin of the chest'*], *see* kw'eléw ~ kw'elṓw.

<**kw'elōwíts**>, ANA [*'skin of the back'*], *see* kw'eléw ~ kw'elṓw.

<**kw'elṓwlhelh**>, ANA [*'skin of the throat'*], *see* kw'eléw ~ kw'elṓw.

<**kw'elōwó:ythel**>, ANA /*'skin of the mouth, (*prob. also *skin of the chin or jaw or lips)'*/, *see* kw'eléw ~ kw'elṓw.

<**kw'elqwál**>, TCH /*'clubbing many times, hitting many times'*/, *see* kw'óqw.

<**kw'élwelh**>, df //k'ʷə́l=(ə́l)wəɬ or k'ʷ=ə́lwəɬ//, ABFC ['*step over something*'], possibly <**=élwelh**> *on the side*, syntactic analysis: intransitive verb.

<**Lexwskw'owő̂welh**>, dnom //ləxʷ=s=k'ʷaw(=)ówəɬ//, PLN /'*slough just east of T'ít'emt'ámex (which is at the railway tunnel north of Ruby Creek), slough near Sq'ewá:lxw and just east of Silhíxw (which is creek from Hick's Lake)*'/, lx <**lexw=s=**> *something that's always*, possibly <**=ő̂welh**> *canoe, vessel*, Elder's comment: "actually derives from kw'élwelh *step over something*", syntactic analysis: nominal, attested by IHTTC, source: place names reference file #200 and #252, also <**Kw'elewő̂welh**>, comment: perhaps in error, recorded later from memory, attested by AK.

<**kw'élwés**>, probable stem //k'ʷə́lwə́s//, root meaning unclear

<**skw'élwés**>, df //s=k'ʷə́lwə́s//, KIN /'*child's spouse's parent, child's spouse's sibling, child's in-laws*'/, (<**s=**> *nominalizer*), syntactic analysis: nominal, attested by AC, other sources: ES /sk'ʷə́lwə́s/ *relative's spouse's relative*, H-T skwóluis (macron over u) *sibling's spouse's relations*.

<**skw'ekw'ílwes**>, pln //s=C_1ə-k'ʷə[-Aí-]lwəs//, KIN ['*children's in-laws*'], (semological comment: note that it is the connecting relation that is pluralized here), (<**R5-**> *plural*), (<**í-ablaut**> (an unusual type) perhaps also *plural* here), phonology: reduplication, ablaut, syntactic analysis: nominal, attested by AC.

<**kw'ely**>, possible root or stem //k'ʷəly//, meaning unclear

<**skw'elyáx̲el**>, dnom //s=k'ʷəly=ɛ́x̣əl//, EZ ['*bat*'], ['order *Chiroptera*, family *Vespertilionidae*'], EZ /'may include any or all of the following (all of which occur in the area): *western big-eared bat, big brown bat, silver-haired bat, hoary bat, California myotis, long-eared myotis, little brown myotis, long-legged myotis, Yuma myotis,* and possibly *the keen myotis, respectively*'/, ['*Corynorhinus townsendi townsendi, Eptesicus fuscus bernardinus, Lasionycteris noctivagans, Lasiurus cinereus, Myotis californicus caurinus, Myotis evotis pacificus, Myotis lucifugus alascensis, Myotis volans longicrus, Myotis yumanensis saturatus,* and possibly *Myotis keeni keeni*'], ASM ['it is said if a bat urinates on your head you will die, so if bats are around, cover your head; a bat is classed as a type of bird by some of the most fluent speakers; other fluent speakers say that a bat is a different creature than a sméyeth (*animal*) or mímeqw (*little bird*)'], (<**s=**> *nominalizer*), <**=áx̲el**> *arm*, syntactic analysis: nominal, dialects: *Cheh., Tait*, attested by Elders Group, compare <**p'ip'eth'eláx̲el**> *bat* **(Chill. dialect))**, other sources: JH /sk'ʷilé·x̣ə/ *bat*, H-T petspasElákEl (macron over e, umlaut over the á) *bat (Vespertilio subulatus)*.

<**skw'íkw'elyàx̲el**>, dmn //s=C_1í=k'ʷəly=ɛ́x̣əl//, EZ ['*young bat*'], (<**R4=**> *diminutive*), phonology: reduplication, phonology: downstepping, syntactic analysis: nominal.

<**kw'élh**>, free root //k'ʷə́ɬ//, MC /'*tip over, spill (of liquid or solid), spilled, spill accidentally*'/, semantic environment ['liquid, solid, container'], HHG, FOOD, WATR ['*flow*'], CAN /'*tip over, capsize*'/, semantic environment ['canoe'], WETH ['*tip (from horizontal or vertical)*'], semantic environment ['crescent moon, moon less than full'], phonology: AC's pronunciation, [k'ʷɛɬ] could show an underlying /ɛ/ vowel; thus too perhaps the vowel in /k'ʷɬɛ́t/ *pour it out*, syntactic analysis: intransitive verb, attested by NP, AD, Deming, EB, AC, Salish cognate: Squamish /k'ʷə́ɬ/ *spill (itr.)* W73:245, K67:344, Lushootseed /k'ʷə́ɬ/ *spill, pour* H76:255, example: <**kw'élh te seplíl**>, //k'ʷə́ɬ tə səplíl//, /'*The flour spilled.*'/, literally /'the bread spilled'/, attested by AC, <**le kw'élh te qó:**>, //lə k'ʷə́ɬ tə qá·//, /'*The water spilled.*'/, attested by AC, <**kw'élh te sth'í:ms; q'pétlha**>, //k'ʷə́ɬ tə s=θ'í·m-s; q'p=ə́T-ɬɛ//, /'*His berries spilled; gather them.*'/, attested by EB, <**kw'élh te skw'exó:s**>, //k'ʷə́ɬ tə s=k'ʷəxʸ=á·s//, /'*The horns of the crescent or less-than-full moon are tipped.*'/, literally /'The moon is spilled., The moon is tipped.'/.

<**kw'ekw'élh**>, cts //C_1ə-k'ʷə́ɬ//, WATR ['*be flowing*'], semantic environment ['liquid'], (<**R5-**>

continuative), phonology: reduplication, syntactic analysis: intransitive verb, attested by Elders Group 3/15/72, AC, also <**kw'ékw'elh**>, //k'ʷə́[-C_1ə-]ɬ//, attested by AC, example: <**le kw'ekw'élh te qó:**>, //lə C_1ə-k'ʷə́ɬ tə qá·//, /'*The water is flowing.*'/, attested by Elders Group 3/15/72, <**li me kw'ékw'elh te stó:lō li te shxwlísalh**>, //li me k'ʷə́[-C_1ə-]ɬ tə s=tá·low lí tə sxʷ=lí-s-əɬ//, /'*Is the river coming (flowing) through the old riverbed?*'/, literally /'is it start flowing the river in the place where it was long past'/, attested by AC.

<**kw'lhát**>, pcs //k'ʷəɬ=ɛ́T or k'ʷɛ́ɬ=M1=T//, MC /'*pour s-th out, pour out s-th, spill it*'/, semantic environment ['liquid, solid if comprised of many particles or round objects'], HHG, WATR, FOOD, CAN, (<**=át**> or **metathesis type 1** and <**-t**> *purposeful control transitive*), phonology: possibly metathesis type 1, syntactic analysis: transitive verb, attested by EB, also <**kw'lhá:t**>, also /'*spill it, turn it on its side*'/, //k'ʷɬ=ɛ́·T//, attested by Deming, also <**kw'elhát**>, //k'ʷəɬ=ɛ́T or k'ʷɛ́ɬ=ə[=M2=]T//, phonology: possible metathesis type 2, attested by AC, example: <**kw'elhát te qó:**>, //k'ʷəɬ=ɛ́T tə qá·//, /'*spill the water*'/, attested by AC.

<**kw'lhó:s**>, ds //k'ʷə́ɬ=á·s//, WATR ['*spill (on the face?)*'], (<**=ó:s**> *on the face*), syntactic analysis: intransitive verb, attested by Deming.

<**kw'lhó:st**>, pcs //k'ʷə́ɬ=á·s=T//, WATR ['*pour water on s-th to keep it damp*'], semantic environment ['for ex. like on salmon under a sack in the hot weather'], (<**=t**> *purposeful control transitivizer*), syntactic analysis: transitive verb, attested by Deming.

<**skw'álhem**>, dnom //s=k'ʷɛ́ɬ=əm or s=k'ʷə[=Aɛ́=]ɬ=əm//, BSK ['*little berry basket*'], ASM ['tied around waist in front, made to same design and shape as the big berry basket, used for dumping handfuls then emptying into large basket on ground'], literally /'something spilled into'/, HARV, (<**s=**> *nominalizer*), possibly <**á-ablaut**> *derivational*, (<**=em**> *intransitivizer*), phonology: ablaut, syntactic analysis: nominal, dialects: *Chill.*, attested by Elders Group, compare <**lí:latses**> *little berry basket* **(Tait dial.)**.

<**kw'elhwát**>, PRON /'*who else?, who (of several)?, (anybody else (AC))*'/, *see* wát.

<**kw'ém**>, free root //k'ʷə́m//, ABFC ['*grow up*'], syntactic analysis: intransitive verb, attested by CT.

<**kw'ekw'ém**>, cts //C_1ə-k'ʷə́m//, ABFC ['*growing up*'], phonology: reduplication, syntactic analysis: intransitive verb, attested by CT.

<**kw'eqw=** ~ kw'qw= ~ kw'oqw>, TCH /'*hit with a stick-like object, clubbed*'/, *see free root* kw'oqw.

<**Kw'eqwálíth'a**>, PLN /'*Coqualeetza stream esp. where it joins Luckakuck Creek, later Coqualeetza (residential school, then hospital, then Indian cultural centre and Education Training Centre)*'/, *see* kw'óqw.

<**kw'eqwelá:x̱el**>, TCH ['*hit on the arm*'], *see* kw'óqw.

<**kw'eqwíwét**>, SOC ['*spank s-o*'], *see* kw'óqw.

<**kw'éqwxel**>, TCH /'*hit on the leg, [hit on the foot]*'/, *see* kw'óqw.

<**kw'és**>, possible root //k'ʷə́s//, root meaning unclear

<**skw'éstel**>, df //s=k'ʷə́s=təl//, CAN /'*homemade anchor, kilik, calik, (killick)*'/, ASM ['made by sharpening the ends of two hazelnut sticks or axe handles, tying them crossways (like an X), weaving a rock into the center with rope or wire, and fastening short hazelnut whips about an inch thick onto each of the pointed ends of the crossed sticks, see illustration'], FSH, probably <**s=**> *nominalizer*, lx <**=tel**> *device, something for*, syntactic analysis: nominal, attested by BHTTC, reproduce drawing from card.

<**kw'esélets**>, TCH /'*hot on the rump, hot seat*'/, *see* kw'ás.

<**kw'esó:ythel**>, ABDF ['*burned on the lips*'], *see* kw'ás.

<**kw'ésqel**>, ABDF ['*burned in the throat*'], *see* kw'ás.

<**kw'éstses**>, ABDF /'*burned on the finger or hand, burnt the hand, a hand got burnt*'/, *see* kw'ás.

<**kw'ésxel**>, ABDF ['*burned on the foot*'], *see* kw'ás.

<**kw'étxwt**>, pcs //k'ʷə́txʷ=T//, MC ['*loosen it (of a knot)*'], semantic environment ['knotted fibre'], WV, (<**=t**> *purposeful control transitivizer*), syntactic analysis: transitive verb, attested by BHTTC, IHTTC.

<**kw'ethí:lt** (possible error for **kw'eth'í:lt**)>, pcs //k'ʷəθ=í·l=T (or) k'ʷəθ'=í·l=T//, incs, MC ['*turn s-th right-side up*'], probably root <**kw'eth'**> *tip, turn over*, (<**=í:l**> *go, get, become, come*, <**=t**> *purposeful control transitivizer*), syntactic analysis: transitive verb, attested by Deming 4/17/80.

<**kw'eth'elíqwem**>, PLAY ['*do a somersault*'], *see* kw'eth'ém.

<**kw'eth'ém**>, mdls //k'ʷəθ'=ə́m//, MC /'*to tip (of canoe, etc.)*'/, semantic environment ['canoe, things normally upright'], CAN, WATR, LAND, (<**=em**> *middle voice*), phonology: root has weak-grade stress-valence, suffix has ambivalent-grade stress-valence, syntactic analysis: intransitive verb, attested by IHTTC.

<**kw'éth'em**>, ds //k'ʷə[=´=]θ'=əm//, CAN ['*tippy (of a canoe)*'], (<**=´=**> *continuative* or *derivational*), syntactic analysis: adjective/adjectival verb, perhaps just intransitive verb, attested by IHTTC.

<**kw'eth'elíqwem**>, mdls //k'ʷəθ'=əl=íqʷ=əm//, PLAY ['*do a somersault*'], ABFC, literally /'go/get/become tipped or turned over on top of one's head'/, probably <**=el**> *go, come, get, become*, lx <**=íqw**> or <**=elíqw**> *on top of the head*, (<**=em**> *middle voice*), syntactic analysis: intransitive verb, attested by IHTTC.

<**kw'eth'kw'eth'elíqwem**>, plv //C_1əC_2=k'ʷəθ'=əl=íqʷ=əm//, PLAY /'*doing somersaults, tumbling (like a gymnast)*'/, semantic environment ['play, gymnast (latter environment conditions the 'characteristic' alloseme of the reduplication)'], (<**R3=**> *plural ~ characteristic*), phonology: reduplication, syntactic analysis: intransitive verb, attested by IHTTC.

<**kw'áth'eletsem**>, mdls //k'ʷə[=Aɛ́=]θ'=ələc=əm//, MC ['*wobbling on its bottom*'], ABFC, (<**á-ablaut**> *continuative* or *derivational*), lx <**=elets**> *on the bottom*, (<**=em**> *middle voice*), phonology: ablaut, syntactic analysis: intransitive verb, attested by IHTTC.

<**kw'eth'elíqwem**>, mdls //k'ʷəθ'=əl=íqʷ=əm//, PLAY ['*do a somersault*'], *see* kw'eth'ém.

<**kw'éth'em**>, CAN ['*tippy (of a canoe)*'], *see* kw'eth'ém.

<**kw'eth'kw'eth'elíqwem**>, PLAY /'*doing somersaults, tumbling (like a gymnast)*'/, *see* kw'eth'ém.

<**kw'étskw'ets**>, SOC ['*expect*'], *see* kw'áts ~ kw'éts.

<**kw'étskw'etsmet**>, SOC ['*expect s-o*'], *see* kw'áts ~ kw'éts.

<**kw'étslexw**>, ABFC /'*see s-o/s-th, catch sight of s-th/s-o*'/, *see* kw'áts ~ kw'éts.

<**kw'éts'eles**>, ANAH /'*(have a) part in the hair, to part (hair)*'/, *see* kw'íts'.

<**kw'éts'elesem**>, ABFC ['*to part one's hair*'], *see* kw'íts'.

<**kw'éts'tel**>, FSH ['*fish butchering knife*'], *see* kw'íts'.

<**kw'ewátes**>, PRON ['*something*'], *see* wát.

<**kw'éxalhàlem ~ kw'exelhálém**>, df //k'ʷə́xʸɛ=ɬɛ̀l=əm ~ k'ʷəxʸə=ɬɛ́l=ə́m//, ABFC ['*panting*'], possibly root <**kw'exá**> *count*, lx <**=lhelh ~ =lhál ~ =lhàl**> *in the throat*, (<**=em**> *middle voice*), syntactic analysis: intransitive verb, attested by IHTTC.

<**kw'e'í ~ kw''í ~ kw'í**>, free root //k'ʷəʔí ~ k'ʷʔí ~ k'ʷí//, ABFC /*'lie? with surface facing up, sticking up, on the side? or edge?*'/, syntactic analysis: intransitive verb, attested by AD, example: <**í kw'í te thíthqet**>, //ʔí k'ʷí tə C_1í-θəqɛt//, /*'on the (side? or edge?) of the little tree*'/, attested by AD.

<**kw'e'íyeqel ~ kw'e'íqel**>, df //k'ʷəʔí=qəl or k'ʷəʔíq=əl//, ABFC /*'lie on one's back, on his back*'/, lx <**=qel**> *head* or lx <**=el**> *go, come, get*, possibly <**metathesis type 2**> *derivational*, phonology: possibly metathesis, syntactic analysis: intransitive verb, attested by AC, CT, HT, EB, contrast <**kw'aqálém**> lie on ones back under root <**kw'aq**>.

<**kw'e'í:qel**>, cts //k'ʷəʔí[-·-]=qəl or k'ʷəʔí[-·-]q=əl//, ABFC ['*lying on one's back*'], (<-:-> *continuative*), syntactic analysis: intransitive verb, attested by IHTTC.

<**kw'ekw'e'íqw ~ kw'ekw'íqw**>, cts //k'ʷə[-C_1ə-]ʔí=əqʷ or k'ʷə[-C_1ə-]ʔí=íqʷ or C_1ə-k'ʷəʔí=əqʷ//, ABFC /*'facing up, head sticking up*'/, possibly <**R5- or -R1-**> *continuative*, lx <**=eqw ~ =íqw**> *on top of the head*, phonology: reduplication, syntactic analysis: intransitive verb, attested by EB, DF, Elders Group.

<**Kw'ekw'e'í:qw ~ Kw'ekw'e'íqw ~ Kw'ekw'í:qw**>, ds //k'ʷə[-C_1ə-]ʔí=əqʷ or k'ʷə[-C_1ə-]ʔí=íqʷ or C_1ə-k'ʷəʔí=əqʷ//, PLN ['*Kilgard village on Upper Sumas River*'], ASM ['originally the village on north side of Vedder Mt. above Sumas Prairie'], phonology: reduplication, attested by DF, IHTTC, Elders Group, literally /'facing up'/, Elder's comment: "so called because you go over a hump of hill and slide down the other side face up", attested by DF, literally /'fish heads sticking up'/, attested by IHTTC, other sources: Wells 1965 (lst ed.):19 <kaw-kwi-UHK>, source: place names reference file #92.

<**kw'e'ós**>, ds //k'ʷəʔí=ás//, ABFC ['*face up*'], lx <**=ós**> *on the face, face*, syntactic analysis: intransitive verb, attested by IHTTC, example: <**kw'e'ós skw'exó:s**>, //k'ʷəʔí=ás s=k'ʷəxʸ=á·s//, /*'quarter moon with horns up*'/, attested by IHTTC.

<**kw'e'í:qel**>, ABFC ['*lying on one's back*'], *see* kw'e'í ~ kw''í ~ kw'í.

<**kw'e'íyeqel ~ kw'e'íqel**>, ABFC /*'lie on one's back, on his back*'/, *see* kw'e'í ~ kw''í ~ kw'í.

<**kw'e'ós**>, ABFC ['*face up*'], *see* kw'e'í ~ kw''í ~ kw'í.

<**kw'íkw'ets'**>, FSH ['*butchering*'], *see* kw'íts'.

<**kw'íkw'ets'**>, FSH ['*sides of butchered salmon with knife marks in them*'], *see* kw'íts'.

<**kw'íkw'ets'els**>, HUNT ['*cleaning or butchering a fish or animal*'], *see* kw'íts'.

<**kw'íkw'exwelhp**>, EB /*'"jack pine", lodgepole pine*'/, *see* kw'íxw.

<**Kw'íkw'exwelhp**>, PLN /*'next mountain above (north/upriver from) Títxwemqsel (Wilson's Point or Grouse Point),* possibly *Elbow Lake mountain [north of Harrison Mills, on west side of the Harrison River], Willoughby's Point [opposite Lhá:lt,* but does this mean across Harrison R. as I first thought and show on the topographic map "Harrison Lake 92H/5" where I have pencilled in all Chehalis place names) or does it mean on the opposite, i.e. south end of the same bay where Lhá:lt starts, i.e. both on the west side of Harrison R. as are Títxwemqsel and Elbow Lake mountain*?]*'/, *see* kw'íxw.

<**Kw'ikw'iyá:la**>, PLN ['*Coquihalla River*'], *see* kw'íy.

<**kw'íkw'xwòs**>, WETH ['*hail when it comes in sheets*'], *see* kw'xwós.

<**kw'í:l ~ kw'íl**>, free root //k'ʷí·l ~ k'ʷíl//, NUM ['*are how many?*'], syntactic analysis: interrogative verb, num, attested by AC, EB, BJ, Elders Group, BHTTC, IHTTC; found in <**kw'í:lchap**>, //k'ʷí·l-c-ɛp//, /*'How many of you?, How many of you are there?*'/, attested by AC, also <**kw'í:lchap talhwélép**>, //k'ʷí·l-c-ɛp tɛ=ɬwə́ləp//, attested by AC, example: <**kw'í:l (swáyel, sthóqwi, músmes)**>, //k'ʷí·l

(s=wɛ́yəl, s=θáqʷi, músməs)//, /'*How many (days, fish, cows/cattle)?*'/, attested by AC, <**kw'íl yé sléxwelh**>, //k'ʷíl yə s=lə́xʷəɬ//, /'*How many canoes?*'/, *<**kw'ílőwelh, kw'ílewelh**> rejected by EB, <**kw'íl yé lalàlèm**>, //k'ʷíl yə C_1ɛ-lɛ̀lə̀m//, /'*How many houses?*'/, *<**kw'íláwtxw**> rejected by EB, also <**kw'íl í te lálem**>, //k'ʷíl ʔí tə lɛ́ləm//, attested by Elders Group, also <**kw'íl te lálem**>, //k'ʷíl tə lɛ́ləm//, dialects: *Cheh.*, attested by Elders Group, also <**kw'íltxw**>, //k'ʷíl=ltxʷ//, dialects: *Tait*, attested by Elders Group, *<**kw'ilélwet**> rejected, /'*How many clothes?*'/, Elder's comment: "never heard", attested by EB, *<**kw'ilmó:t**> rejected, /'*How many piles?, How many kinds?*'/, Elder's comment: "never heard", attested by EB, <**lulh kw'íl syilólém**>, //l=uɬ k'ʷíl s=yilál=ə́m//, /'*How old is he?, How many years is he?*'/, attested by AC, <**achxw welh kw'íl máqa**>, //ʔɛ-c-xʷ wəɬ k'ʷíl mɛ́qɛ//, /'*How old are you?*'/, literally /'you were already how many snow(s)?'/, Elder's comment: "better than achxw welh kw'íl syilólem", attested by BHTTC, also <**achxw welh kw'íl syilólem**>, //ʔɛ-c-xʷ wəɬ k'ʷíl s=yilál=əm//, Elder's comment: "okay", attested by BHTTC, also <**achxw welh kw'í:l má:qa**>, //ʔɛ-c-xʷ wəɬ k'ʷí·l mɛ́·qɛ//, semantic environment ['a typical answer might be: t'x̲ém má:qa *six snows*'], attested by IHTTC, <**welh kw'íl syilólem kw'as yóyes**>, //wəɬ k'ʷíl s=yilál=əm k'ʷ-ɛ-s yáy[-ə-]s//, /'*How many years have you been working?*'/, attested by BHTTC.

<**kw'ílà**>, ds //k'ʷíl=ɛ́lə → k'ʷíl=ɛ̀//, NUM ['*how many people?*'], lx <**=ále ~ =à** > *people*, phonology: downstepping, syntactic analysis: interrogative verb, num, attested by EB, also <**kw'í:lá**>, //k'ʷí·l=ɛ́//, attested by BJ 5/64, also <**kw'íla**>, //k'ʷíl=ɛ//, attested by Deming, example: <**kw'ílà yé me xwe'í**>, //k'ʷíl=ɛ̀ yə mə xʷə=ʔí//, /'*How many people came?*'/, literally /'the (plural, human) ones who come to arrive/come here are how many people?'/, phonology: sentence-stress on the demonstrative article yé, attested by EB, <**kw'íla ye xwélmexw xwe'í**>, //k'ʷíl=ɛ yə xʷə́lməxʷ xʷə=ʔí//, /'*How many people got here?*'/, literally /'the (plural, human) Indian, person who get here are how many people?'/, attested by EB.

<**kw'í:làs ~ kw'ílàs**>, ds //k'ʷí·l=ɛ́s ~ k'ʷíl=ɛ́s//, NUM /'*several (people, animals) (exact number unknown)*'/, (<**=ás**> *subjunctive, 3p* used to derive indefinite nominals), phonology: downstepping, syntactic analysis: indefinite nominal, attested by EB, example: <**kw'ílàs t'we té músmes**>, //k'ʷíl=ɛ́s t'wə tə músməs//, /'*There must be several cows.*'/, phonology: sentence-stress on the demonstrative article té, attested by EB.

<**kw'í:les ~ kw'íles**>, ds //k'ʷí·l=əs ~ k'ʷíl=əs//, NUM ['*be how much money?*'], lx <**=es**> *on the face, round thing, dollar*, phonology: length present here in slow speech, optional at normal or fast speech, syntactic analysis: interrogative verb, num, attested by BJ, Elders Group, also <**kw'ílés**>, //k'ʷíl=əs//, phonology: updrifting or tone-harmony, attested by EB, example: <**kw'ílés tá' tále**>, //k'ʷíl=əs t-ɛʔ tɛ́lə//, /'*How much is your money?, How much money do you have?*'/, phonology: updrifting or tone-harmony (ta' is normally never stressed; it has low pitch), attested by EB, <**kw'í:les ta' tá:le**>, //k'ʷí·l=əs t-ɛʔ tɛ́·lə//, /'*How much money do you have?*'/, attested by Elders Group.

<**kw'ilőwelh**>, ds //k'ʷil=ówəɬ//, NUM ['*be how many canoes?*'], lx <**=őwelh**> *canoe, vessel*, syntactic analysis: interrogative verb, num, attested by Elders Group, but never heard by EB before.

<**kw'ilőwes**>, ds //k'ʷíl=ówəs//, NUM ['*how many paddles?*'], lx <**=őwes**> *canoe paddle*, syntactic analysis: interrogative verb, num, attested by Elders Group.

<**skw'í:ls**>, ds //s=k'ʷí·l=s//, NUM /'*be what hour?, be what time?*'/, lx <**s=...=s**> *hour, o'clock*, syntactic analysis: interrogative verb, num, attested by EB, AC, example: <**tés te skw'í:ls**>, //tə́s tə s=k'ʷí·l=s//, /'*What time is it? (approach, get up to, get near)*'/, attested by EB, AC.

<**skw'íles**>, ds //s=k'ʷíl=əs//, NUM ['*be what day?*'], lx <**s=...=es**> *day, cyclic period*, phonology: circumfix, syntactic analysis: interrogative verb, num, attested by BJ, example: <**e le skw'íles tlowáyel**>, //ʔə lə s=k'ʷíl=əs tla=wɛ́yəl//, /'*What day is this? (today, this day)*'/, attested by BJ 5/64.

<**kw'elálh**>, ds //k'ʷil=ɛ́ɬ//, NUM ['*how many times*'], lx <**=álh**> *times, occasions*, phonology: i → e after loss of root stress to strong-valenced suffix, syntactic analysis: interrogative verb, num, attested by EB, example: <**kw'elálh (kw'elsé, kw'a'asé) là:m**>, //k'ʷil=ɛ́ɬ (k'ʷə-l-s-ə́, k'ʷ-ɛʔɛ-s-ə́) lɛ̀·=m//, /'*How many times did (I, you) go?*'/, phonology: downstepping, syntactic comment: Cheh. dialect -é supposedly *past tense* here, attested by EB, <**kw'elálh (kwsét, kwsélep, kwsés) là:m**>, //k'ʷil=ɛ́ɬ (kʷ-s-ə́-t, kʷ-s-ə́-ləp, kʷ-s-ə́-s) lɛ̀·=m//, /'*How many times did (we, you folks, he) go?*'/, syntactic comment: unusual place for subordinating pronoun (normally 3, 1p, 2p persons follow the verb), Cheh. dialect -é *past tense* here, attested by EB.

<**kw'í:là:lhp ~ kw'ílà:lhp**>, ds //k'ʷí·l=ɛ̀·ɬp ~ k'ʷíl=ɛ̀·ɬp//, NUM ['*how many trees*'], lx <**=á:lhp ~ =álhp ~ =elhp**> *tree, plant*, phonology: downstepping, syntactic analysis: interrogative verb, num, attested by EB, example: <**kw'í:là:lhp ye theqthéqet íkw'elò**>, //k'ʷí·l=ɛ̀·ɬp yə $C_1əC_2$-θə[-´-]qɛt ʔí=k'ʷə=là//, /'*How many trees are there [here]?*'/, literally /'the (plural, human) trees here are how many trees?'/, attested by EB.

<**kw'ílà**>, NUM ['*how many people?*'], *see* kw'í:l ~ kw'íl.

<**kw'í:là:lhp ~ kw'ílà:lhp**>, NUM ['*how many trees*'], *see* kw'í:l ~ kw'íl.

<**kw'í:làs ~ kw'ílàs**>, NUM /'*several (people, animals) (exact number unknown)*'/, *see* kw'í:l ~ kw'íl.

<**kw'í:les ~ kw'íles**>, NUM ['*be how much money?*'], *see* kw'í:l ~ kw'íl.

<**kw'ilőwelh**>, NUM ['*be how many canoes?*'], *see* kw'í:l ~ kw'íl.

<**kw'ilőwes**>, NUM ['*how many paddles?*'], *see* kw'í:l ~ kw'íl.

<**kw'ílhew**>, probable root or stem //k'ʷíɬəw// /'*mother-in-law, father-in-law, spouse's parent, parent-in-law*'/, not attested as free form but may exist when not inalienably possessed

<**skw'ílhew**>, df //s=k'ʷíɬəw//, KIN /'*mother-in-law, father-in-law, spouse's parent, parent-in-law*'/, probably <**s=**> *nominalizer*, syntactic analysis: nominal, attested by AC, CT, other sources: ES /sk'ʷíɬəw/ *spouse's parent, wife's brother.*

<**skw'álhew**>, pln //s=k'ʷi[-Aɛ́-]ɬəw//, KIN /'*in-laws (?), parents-in-law, spouse's parents*'/, (<**á-ablaut**> *plural*), phonology: ablaut, syntactic analysis: nominal, attested by AC, example: <**le xwe'í: ta skw'álhew**>, //lə xʷə=ʔí· t-ɛ s=k'ʷi[-Aɛ́=]ɬəw//, /'*Your in-laws have come. (arrive, past tense)*'/, attested by AC.

<**kw'íqel**>, EB ['*to sprout (from root)*'], *see* kw'í ~ kw'íy.

<**kw'í:tsel**>, df //k'ʷí·cəl//, EZ ['*grizzly bear*'], ['*Ursus arctos horribilis*'], ASM ['grizzlies are said to be x̲áx̲e (sacred, taboo) because they are hard to kill--they must be shot in the ear; they can't climb trees, but they are not eaten because they sometimes eat people; in the grizzly's own language, which you can speak to him and he'll understand) the male grizzly's proper name is Syeqwílmetxw, and the female's is Syeqwílmetelòt (from yéqw burnt); if they are called by these names they will understand'], possible root <**qw'á:y**>, bound root //q'ʷɛ́·y *scorch, blacken near fire*// if fronted and vowel dropped, possibly <**=ítsel**> *on the back*, (a lit. meaning of *scorched on the back* would fit the grizzled/gray-tipped fur on the back), syntactic analysis: nominal, attested by NP, HT, DF, DM, also /'*small grizzly bear*'/, attested by DF, also <**kw'í:chel**>, //k'ʷí·cəl//, attested by BJ (12/5/64, 5/64), also <**kw'íchel**>, //k'ʷícəl//, attested by Elders Group 3/1/72.

<**kw'íts'**>, root, perhaps bound //k'ʷíc' *butcher, cut open and process*//, semantic environment ['fish, animal'].

<**kw'íkw'ets'**>, cts //k'ʷí[-C_1ə-]c'//, FSH ['*butchering*'], HUNT, (<**-R1-**> *continuative*), phonology: reduplication, syntactic analysis: intransitive verb, Elder's comment: "possibly the same word is used

for skinning", attested by EB.

<**kw'íkw'ets'**>, rsls //k’^{w}í[=C_1ə=]c’//, FSH ['*sides of butchered salmon with knife marks in them*'], (<**=R1=**> *resultative*), phonology: reduplication, syntactic analysis: nominal, attested by DM 12/4/64, example: <**kw'íkw'ets' te sx̲éwe**>, //k’^{w}í[-C_1ə-]c’ tə s=x̣ə́wə//, /'*backbone of fish (with meat left on)*'/, attested by DM 12/4/64.

<**kw'íts'et**>, pcs //k’^{w}íc’=əT//, HUNT /'*cut open and butcher it, clean it (of fish or animal)*'/, ASM ['take out the guts, etc., take the skin off where appropriate'], FSH, semantic environment ['animal or fish that is dead'], (<**=et**> *purposeful control transitivizer*), syntactic analysis: transitive verb, attested by AC, EB, CT, HT.

<**kw'íkw'ets'els**>, sas //k’^{w}í[-C_1ə-]c’=əls//, cts, HUNT ['*cleaning or butchering a fish or animal*'], FSH, (<**-R1-**> *continuative*), (<**=els**> *structured activity continuative*), phonology: reduplication, syntactic analysis: intransitive verb, attested by EB.

<**kw'éts'tel**>, dnom //k’^{w}i[=Aə́=]c’=təl//, FSH ['*fish butchering knife*'], ASM ['on our raft trip to get place names and photograph sites, Agnes Kelly had me reach into a crevice at Shxw'ílamōwelh to find her old fish knife she had left there years before; it was still there and had an old design, a thin, sharpened half-circle of metal (old circular saw-blade) mounted on a wooden haft); when rotated while cutting, this produced very efficient scoring and slicing of salmon; the pre-contact style behind this style of knife was probably a sharpened (chipped) semicircular stone mounted in a wooden haft'], (<**é-ablaut**> *derivational*), (<**=tel**> *device, thing for*), phonology: ablaut, syntactic analysis: nominal, attested by Elders Group.

<**kw'éts'eles**>, ds //k’^{w}i[=Aə́=]c’=əl=əs//, ANAH /'*(have a) part in the hair, to part (hair)*'/, probably root <**kw'íts'**> *cut and open and process, butcher*, (<**é-ablaut**> *derivational*), (<**=el**> *get, become*), lx <**=es**> *on the face*, phonology: ablaut, syntactic analysis: intransitive verb, attested by AK in IHTTC, MH in Deming, also <**skw'éts'eles**>, //s=k^{w}i[=Aə́=]c’=əl=əs//, also /'*a part in the hair*'/, attested by SP in IHTTC, also <**kw'éts'eleqw**>, //k’^{w}i[=Aə́=]c’=ələq^w//, lx <**=eleqw**> *on top of the head, in the hair*, attested by AK in IHTTC.

<**kw'éts'elesem**>, df //k’^{w}í[=Aə́=]c’=əl=əs=əm//, mdls, ABFC ['*to part one's hair*'], (<**=em**> *middle voice*), phonology: ablaut, syntactic analysis: intransitive verb, attested by IHTTC.

<**skw'íts'òlès**>, stvi //s=k’^{w}íc’=áləs//, ANAH /'*cross-eyed,* prob. also *cock-eyed*'/, probably root <**kw'íts'**> *butchered, cut open*, (<**s=**> *stative*), lx <**=óles**> *in the eye(s)*, phonology: downdrifting, syntactic analysis: intransitive verb, attested by AH, LG.

<**kw'íts'et**>, HUNT /'*cut open and butcher it, clean it (of fish or animal)*'/, *see* kw'íts'.

<**kw'íxw**>, free root //k’^{w}íx^w//, EB /'*pitch, sap, gum, chewing gum*'/, ASM ['some kinds of sap, esp. spruce, were chewed like chewing gum; SJ tells a wonderful story of Mink and Miss Pitch (who is called <the Kw'íxw> /θə k’^{w}íx^w/ in the story, *the (female) Pitch*)'], syntactic analysis: nominal, noun, attested by AC, Elders Group, other sources: ES /k’^{w}íx^w/ *pitch*, H-T kwe'Eq (macron over e) *gum, pitch*.

<**kw'íxwelhp**>, ds //k’^{w}íx^w=əɬp//, EB /'*pitchwood (esp. fir, pine, spruce)*'/, ASM ['burns with hotter flame, often preferred for fires, also used to burn pitch onto canoe hulls for waterproofing'], lx <**=elhp**> *tree, plant*, syntactic analysis: nominal.

<**kw'íkw'exwelhp**>, dmn //k’^{w}í[=C_1ə=]x^w=əɬp//, EB /'*"jack pine", lodgepole pine*'/, ['*Pinus contorta*'], (<**=R1=**> *diminutive*), phonology: reduplication, syntactic analysis: nominal, attested by EL.

<**Kw'íkw'exwelhp**>, dmn //k’^{w}í[=C_1ə=]x^w=əɬp//, PLN /'*next mountain above (north/upriver from) Títxwemqsel (Wilson's Point or Grouse Point),* possibly *Elbow Lake mountain [north of Harrison Mills, on west side of the Harrison River], Willoughby's Point [opposite Lhá:lt,* but

does this mean across Harrison R. as I first thought and show on the topographic map "Harrison Lake 92H/5" where I have pencilled in all Chehalis place names) or does it mean on the opposite, i.e. south end of the same bay where Lhá:lt starts, i.e. both on the west side of Harrison R. as are Títxwemqsel and Elbow Lake mountain?]'/, Elder's comment: "the mountain was called Kw'íkw'exwelhp because jack pines used to grow there long ago", syntactic analysis: nominal, attested by EL (9/27/77 with NP, EB; 3/1/78 tape), source: place names file reference #310.

<**kw'ekw'íxwxel**>, ds //C_1ə=k'ʷíxʷ=xʸəl//, CLO /'*gumboots, rubber boots*'/, (<**R5=**> *derivational*), lx <**=xel**> *on the foot*, phonology: reduplication, syntactic analysis: nominal, noun.

<**kw'íxwelhp**>, EB /'*pitchwood (esp. fir, pine, spruce)*'/, *see* kw'íxw.

<**kw'íy ~ kw'í**>, free root //k'ʷíy ~ k'ʷí//, TVMO /'*climb, get up a vertical surface*'/, ABFC, LAND, syntactic analysis: intransitive verb, attested by AC and RG & EH (4/9/99 Ling332), also /'*climb a tree*'/, attested by EB, ASM ['get up a vertical surface'], <**skw'áy kw'els la kw'í**>, //s=k'ʷέy k'ʷə-l-s lε k'ʷí//, /'*I can't get up (vertical surface).*'/, attested by AC, ASM ['climb'], <**lalh kw'í**>, //lε-ɬ k'ʷí//, /'*Go on, climb.*'/, attested by AC.

<**kw'ekw'í**>, df //C_1ə-k'ʷí//, TVMO /'*climbing, rising*'/, (<**R5-**> *continuative*), phonology: reduplication, syntactic analysis: intransitive verb, attested by AC, HT, example: <**mi kw'ekw'íy te qó:**>, //mi C_1ə-k'ʷíy tə qá·//, /'*spring tide has come., The water has started rising /climbing.*'/, Elder's comment: "some say this", attested by HT.

<**sh(xw)kw'ekw'í**>, dnom //sxʷ=C_1ə=k'ʷí//, BLDG ['*main rafters of longhouse*'], ASM ['poles going across the top of a longhouse'], (<**shxw=**> *nominalizer*, R5= *continuative* or *resultative*), phonology: reduplication, syntactic analysis: nominal, attested by DM (12/4/64).

<**kw'ekw'íythet**>, pcrs //C_1ə-k'ʷíy=T-ət//, cts, REL ['*training*'], literally /'purposely climbing oneself, purposely raising oneself'/, ASM ['done by a combination of fasting, exercise, religious rituals, morning baths in the river, abstinence, and spirit-seeking; done to train to be an Indian doctor or shaman, a ritualist, a seer, a spirit-dancer, a crewman in canoe races (a puller), a skilled slahal gambler, a skilled hunter or fisherman'], IDOC, SPRD, HUNT, FSH, PLAY, (<**R5-**> *continuative*), (<**=thet**> *purposeful control transitivizer* plus *reflexive*), phonology: reduplication, syntactic analysis: intransitive verb.

<**kw'íyeqel**>, //**k'ʷíy=əqəl**//, TVMO /'*climb a mountain, climb a hill, go up a mountain or hill*'/, LAND, semantic environment ['vertical or sloped rock, hill or mountain'], lx <**=eqel**> *on the throat, on a cliff*, syntactic analysis: intransitive verb, attested by EB, AC and RG & EH (4/9/99 Ling332), example: <**lámtsel kw'íyeqel(t) te smált**>, //lέ=m-c-əl k'ʷíy=əqəl(=T) tə s=mέlt//, /'*I'm going to climb up the mountain (or rock).*'/, attested by AC, <**latsel kw'íyeqel la(m) te smált; latsel háwe kw'e tlalqtéle**>, //lε-c-əl k'ʷíy=əqəl lε(=m) tə s=mέlt; lε-c-əl hέwə k'ʷəƛ'ε[=l=]qt=ə́lə//, /'*I'm going up the mountain to hunt deer.*'/, literally /'I'm going to go up on the mountain; I'm going to hunt some deer.'/, attested by AC.

<**kw'íqel**>, probably //k'ʷí=qəl//, EB ['*to sprout (from root)*'], probably <**=qel**> *on the head*, syntactic analysis: intransitive verb, source: H-T kwákEl (macron over a) *to sprout (from root).*

<**kw'íyles ~ kw'éyles**>, df //k'ʷíy=əl=əs ~ k'ʷə́y=əl=əs//, TIME /'*(be) Spring, [cyclic period] when everything comes up*'/, probably root <**k'ʷíy**> *climb, rise, get up*, probably <**=el**> *become, get, come, go*, probably <**=es**> *cyclic period, season, month*, syntactic analysis: intransitive verb, nominal?, attested by AC.

<**temkw'éyles**>, df //təm=k'ʷə́y=əl=əs//, TIME /'*(be) Spring, [time or season] when everything comes up*'/, (<**tem=**> *time for, season for*), syntactic analysis: intransitive verb, nominal?, attested by DM, also <**temkw'éylés**>, //təm=k'ʷíy=əl=əs//, phonology: updrifting, attested by AC.

<**skw'í:lets**>, stvi //s=k'^{w}íy=ləc//, ABDF /'*be lame (in hip, esp. from birth)*'/, literally /'be raised/climbing in the bottom/hip'/, (<**s=**> *stative*), lx <**=lets**> *on the bottom, on the rump, in the hip*, syntactic analysis: intransitive verb, adjective/adjectival verb, attested by AC.

<**Skw'iykw'íylets**>, ds //s=C$_1$əC$_2$=k'^{w}íy=ləc//, PLN ['*village at the confluence of Sweltzer and Soowahlie creeks with Chilliwack River*'], literally /'something that climbs/rises many times on the bottom'/, (<**s=**> *nominalizer*, R3= *plural, iterative*), lx <**=lets**> *on the bottom*, phonology: reduplication, syntactic analysis: nominal, source: Wells 1965:19, Wells 1966 <skwee-KWIY-lehts>, source: place names file reference #269.

<**skw'íytel**>, ds //s=k'^{w}íy=təl//, HHG /'*ladder, notched cedar pole ladder, rope ladder (pre-contact or later), modern ladder*'/, ASM ['notched cedar pole ladder'], semantic environment ['pit-house, keekwillie house, winter house'], ACL ['*modern ladder*'], semantic environment ['post-contact times'], (<**s=**> *nominalizer*), lx <**=tel**> *device, thing for*, syntactic analysis: nominal, attested by EB, AC, DM.

<**kw'íy**>, bound root //'*stingy, refuse*'//.

<**kw'íyà:m**>, izs //k'^{w}íy=ɛ̀·m//, EFAM /'*stingy of food, refuse (somebody something)*'/, (<**=à:m**> *intransitivizer*), phonology: stressed intransitivizer, syntactic analysis: intransitive verb, attested by EB.

<**kw'íyat**>, pcs //k'^{w}íy=ɛT//, EFAM ['*refuse s-o something*'], (<**=at**> *purposeful control transitivizer*), syntactic analysis: transitive verb, attested by EB; found in <**kw'íyates**>, //k'^{w}íy=ɛT-əs//, /'*He refuses s-o something.*'/, attested by EB.

<**skw'íkw'iy ~ skw'íkw'i**>, chrs //s=k'^{w}íy=C$_1$əC$_2$//, stvi, EFAM ['*be stingy*'], (<**s=**> *stative*), (<**=R2**> *characteristic* or *iterative*), phonology: reduplication, syntactic analysis: adjective/adjectival verb, attested by Elders Group, EB, example: <**ō telúwe skw'íkw'iy**>, //ʔo tɛ=lə́wə s=k'^{w}íy=C$_1$əC$_2$//, /'*Oh, you're stingy.*'/, attested by Elders Group.

<**Kw'ikw'iyá:la**>, dnom //k'^{w}íy=C$_1$əC$_2$=ɛ́·lɛ//, PLN ['*Coquihalla River*'], literally /'stingy container, stingy place'/, ASM ['so named because Indians would go to a deep pool named Skw'é<u>x</u>weq or Skw'e<u>x</u>wáq in the Coquihalla River to spear q'ó<u>x</u>el (suckerfish) which were plentiful in the pool; but when they thrust their spears in, black-haired, 2-foot tall, dark-skinned water-pygmies (called s'ó:lmexw) would grab the spears and hold onto them and so they were stingy with the fish; the pygmies left the pool after white people started to come around; the pool is located at the first wooden bridge over the Coquihalla (near Hope) that has the sign "To Union Bar"'], Reuben Ware was taken to the pool by some of the elders in about 1977 and took photographs of it for Coqualeetza's place names photo collection; there were two other pools farther up the Coquihalla where these water-pygmies or water-babies lived; the pool Skw'é<u>x</u>weq (place name #204) is just where Kawkawa Creek comes into the Coquihalla River; it may also have been called Skw'íkw'<u>x</u>weq by Susan Peters (or that may have been a different place); water-babies in Chilliwack Lake were also seen by a man living in the 1970's (contemporary of AC) and told about in a story in Halkomelem by Seraphine Dick on a Stalo Heritage Project tape, lx <**=á:la ~ =álé**> *container* lx <**(rarely, as here,**> *place*), phonology: reduplication, syntactic analysis: nominal, attested by Elders Group, AC, source: place names reference file #19, also <**Kw'ikw'iyálé**>, //k'^{w}iy=C$_1$əC$_2$=álə́//, attested by SP, also <**Kw'ikw'iy'álé**>, //k'^{w}iy=C$_1$əC$_2$=ʔɛ́lə́//, [k'^{w}ik'^{w}iʔǽlə́], phonology: variant ='álé ~ =hálé appear when the root is felt by the speaker to end in a vowel; it reflects the pronunciation given to Gibbs when he first spelled Coquihalla with an <h>, attested by P.D. Peters.

<**kw'íyat**>, EFAM ['*refuse s-o something*'], *see* kw'íy.

<**kw'íyeqel**>, TVMO /'*climb a mountain, climb a hill, go up a mountain or hill*'/, *see* kw'í ~ kw'íy.

<**kw'lhát**>, MC /'*pour s-th out, pour out s-th, spill it*'/, *see* kw'élh.

<**kw'lhó:s**>, WATR ['*spill (on the face?)*'], *see* kw'élh.

<**kw'lhó:st**>, WATR ['*pour water on s-th to keep it damp*'], *see* kw'élh.

<**Kw'okw'echíwel**>, PLN /'*Wahleach Bluff, a lookout mountain with rock sticking out over a bluff, also the lookout point on Agassiz Mountain*'/, *see* kw'áts ~ kw'éts.

<**kw'ókw'elem**>, cts //k'^{w}á[-C_1ə-]l=əm or possibly k'^{w}ɛ[=AáC$_1$ə=]ɬ=əm with voicing of ɬ to l//, izs, WATR ['*pouring a liquid*'], (<**=em**> *intransitivizer*), (<**-R1-**> *continuative*), probably root <**kw'élh**> *spill, pour*, phonology: reduplication, probably ablaut, possibly consonant change but probably the l is just an error for lh, syntactic analysis: intransitive verb.

<**kw'ókw'eleqw**>, df //k'^{w}ák'^{w}ələq^w, possibly k'^{w}á[=C_1ə=]l=əq^w//, EFAM ['*be curious*'], possibly <**=R1=**> *resultative* or *continuative*, possibly <**=eqw ~ =eleqw**> *on top of the head*, phonology: reduplication, syntactic analysis: intransitive verb, attested by Elders Group 5/19/76.

<**kw'ókw'eqwet**>, TCH /'*beating s-o/s-th with a stick, hitting s-o/s-th with a stick, clubbing it*'/, *see* kw'óqw.

<**kw'ókw'es**>, DESC /'*be hot, be warm*'/, *see* kw'ás.

<**kw'okw'etl'élmel**>, ABFC ['*thinking about having intercourse*'], *see* kw'átl'.

<**kw'ókw'etset**>, ABFC ['*looking at s-th/s-o*'], *see* kw'áts ~ kw'éts.

<**kw'okw'etsíls**>, ABFC ['*staring*'], *see* kw'áts ~ kw'éts.

<**kw'ókw'etslexw**>, ABFC ['*seeing s-o*'], *see* kw'áts ~ kw'éts.

<**kw'ókw'etsxel**>, HUNT /'*tracking, following prints*'/, *see* kw'áts ~ kw'éts.

<**kw'ókw'iy**>, ABFC ['*be hungry*'], *see* kw'à:y.

<**kw'ókw'qwōwsà:ls**>, HUMC ['*a whipper*'], *see* kw'óqw.

<**kw'ó:lexw**>, free root //k'^{w}á·ləx^w//, EZ /'*dog salmon, chum salmon*'/, ['*Oncorhynchus keta*'], syntactic analysis: nominal, attested by AC, Deming (Chill. speakers), Elders Group (3/1/72, 3/12/75), other sources: ES /k'^{w}á·ləx^w/ *dog (chum) salmon*, H-T kwálōq *dog salmon (Oncorhychus Keta)*, also <**kw'ó'lexw**>, //k'^{w}áʔləx^w//, dialects: *Sumas*, attested by Deming.

<**temkw'ó:lexw**>, ds //təm=k'^{w}á·ləx^w//, TIME /'*September to October, dog salmon time*'/, ASM ['each month begins roughly on the first quarter moon after the black (or new) moon, but must coincide generally with the time it names as well'], lx <**tem=**> *time, time for, season*, syntactic analysis: intransitive verb, nominal?, other sources: Diamond Jenness (Suttles ed.) WS 1955 (Faith of a Coast Salish Indian & Katzie ethnographic notes)

<**kw'olexwáwtxw**>, dnom //k'^{w}aləx^w=ɛ́wtx^w//, FSH /'*smokehouse, house for smoking fish*'/, ASM ['about 30 ft. by 30 ft. would make a good one'], BLDG, literally /'dog salmon house (because dog salmon are one of the best kinds of salmon to smoke)'/, lx <**=áwtxw**> *building*, syntactic analysis: nominal, attested by AC.

<**kw'olexwáwtxw**>, FSH /'*smokehouse, house for smoking fish*'/, *see* kw'ó:lexw.

<**kw'ómkw'em**>, chrs //k'^{w}ám=C_1əC_2//, DESC ['*be strong (of animates or inanimates)*'], semantic environment ['people, boat, table, etc.'], (<**=R2**> *characteristic*), phonology: reduplication, syntactic analysis: adjective/adjectival verb, attested by AC, EB, Elders Group, AD, example: <**yeláwel kw'ómkw'em swíyeqe**>, //yəlɛ́w=əl k'^{w}ám=C_1əC_2 s=wíyəqə//, /'*(He's the) strongest man.*'/, literally

/'(he is) past,beyond strong man'/, syntactic comment: superlative, attested by Elders Group, <**éy kw'ómkw'emcha telí s'ólh sqwálewel xwlam kw'e ít totí:lt tlówàyèl**>, //ʔɛ́y k'ʷám=C_1əC_2-cɛ təlí sʔáɬ s=qʷɛ̀l=əwəl xʷlɛ=m k'ʷə ʔi-t ta[-C_1ə-]l=í·l=T təlá=wɛ̀yə̀l//, /*'Let our thoughts be strong toward what we are studying today.'*/, literally /'it's good it will be strong from our thought toward what subjunctive subject we here are studying this day'/, attested by AD.

<**kw'óqw ~ kw'eqw= ~ kw'qw=**>, free root //k'ʷáqʷ//, TCH /*'hit with a stick-like object, clubbed'*/, syntactic analysis: intransitive verb, attested by JL, EB, example: <**kw'óqw (ta' t'álŏw, te óqwelets, te chálex, te sq'pó:lthtel)**>, //k'ʷáqʷ (t-ɛʔ t'ɛ́lə̆w, tə ʔáqʷə=ləc, tə cɛ́ləxʸ, tə s=q'p=á·lθ'=təl)//, /*'hit (with a stick-like object) on (your arm, the back, the hand, the kneecap)'*/, attested by JL, <**kw'óqw te méqsels**>, //k'ʷáqʷ tə mə́qsəl-s//, /*'hit on his nose'*/, attested by EB, <**le kw'óqw i te sqw'éméls**>, //lə k'ʷáqʷ ʔi tə s=q'ʷə́m=ə́ls//, /*'something hit one's forehead'*/, literally /'it past hit on the forehead'/, attested by JL, <**kw'óqw lí te yél:és**>, //k'ʷáqʷ lí tə yə́l·ə́s//, /*'hit on the teeth'*/, attested by EB.

<**kw'óqwet**>, pcs //k'ʷáqʷ=əT//, TCH /*'beat s-o/s-th with a stick, hit s-o/s-th with a stick, hit s-th (on purpose), hit s-o intentionally'*/, (<**=et**> *purposeful control transitivizer*), syntactic analysis: intransitive verb, attested by EB, AC, BHTTC, Elders Group, IHTTC; found in <**kw'eqwethóxes**>, //k'ʷəqʷ=əT-áxʸ-əs//, /*'He hit me intentionally.'*/, attested by AC, example: <**kw'oqwethóxes te lepà:l**>, //k'ʷáqʷ=əT-áxʸ-əs tə ləpɛ̀·l//, /*'He hit me with a shovel.'*/, attested by BHTTC, <**kw'óqwethóxes te q'éwe**>, //k'ʷáqʷ=əT-áxʸ-əs tə q'ə́wə//, /*'He hit me with a cane.'*/, attested by Elders Group, <**kwóqwetes te swáqeths thú:tlò**>, //k'ʷáqʷ=əT-əs tə s=wɛ́q=əθ-s θ=ú·=ƛ'à//, /*'She hit her husband (with a stick).'*/, attested by IHTTC, <**kwútes te lepál tl'esu kw'oqwethóxes**>, //kʷú=T-əs tə ləpɛ́l ƛ'ə=s=u k'ʷáqʷ=əT-áxʸ-əs//, /*'He took the shovel and hit me.'*/, attested by Elders Group; found in <**kw'óqwetem**>, //k'ʷáqʷ=əT-əm//, /*'He got hit., He got spanked.'*/, attested by EB.

<**kw'ókw'eqwet**>, cts //k'ʷá[-C_1ə-]qʷ=əT//, TCH /*'beating s-o/s-th with a stick, hitting s-o/s-th with a stick, clubbing it'*/, (<**-R1-**> *continuative*), phonology: reduplication, syntactic analysis: intransitive verb, attested by EB, BHTTC, IHTTC; found in <**kw'ókw'eqwetes**>, //k'ʷá[-C_1ə-]qʷ=əT-əs//, /*'He is clubbing or hitting someone with a stick-like object'*/, attested by IHTTC, EB.

<**kw'óqwlexw**>, ncs //k'ʷáqʷ=ləxʷ//, TCH /*'hit s-o unintentionally, hit s-o accidentally'*/, syntactic analysis: transitive verb, attested by AC; found in <**kw'eqwláxes**>, //k'ʷáqʷ=l-áxʸ-əs//, /*'He hit me unintentionally.'*/, phonology: root allomorph //k'ʷəqʷ ~ k'ʷqʷ// before stressed affixes, weak stress valence ~ zero grade, attested by AC, <**kw'éqwlòmè**>, //k'ʷə́qʷ=l-ámə//, /*'hit you accidentally'*/, phonology: downstepping, upstepping, high stress irregular on this root allomorph (//k'ʷəqʷ// expected unstressed), attested by AC.

<**kw'elqwál**>, plv //k'ʷə[-lə-]qʷ=ɛ́l(s)//, TCH /*'clubbing many times, hitting many times'*/, (<**-le-**> *plural*), (irregular) =ál for =áls *structured activity*, syntactic analysis: intransitive verb, Elder's comment: "(unsure)", attested by TM.

<**Kw'eqwálíth'a**>, df //k'ʷəqʷ=ɛ́l=íθ'ɛ//, PLN /*'Coqualeetza stream esp. where it joins Luckakuck Creek, later Coqualeetza (residential school, then hospital, then Indian cultural centre and Education Training Centre)'*/, there are several versions of why the stream was so-named; the most plausible is that it was used for washing clothes and blankets, which were beaten with sticks in the process; another version is told in Hill-Tout 1902 as a wonderful long story, involving a famine, men discovering fish in Coqualeetza stream and deciding to eat them on the spot and not bring home any for their wives and families, a little boy sneaking home to tell his mother and the wives approaching en masse beating their husbands' blankets in anger;, as the wives approach one man throws paint on several men one-by-one and they change into different birds and fly away, finally he throws the remaining paint on the rest and they change and fly away; they then proceed to another adventure;, the third version says the stream was called Kw'eqwálíth'a because the fish were so numerous in it

that they could be clubbed and tossed into the boat; EL and Wilfred Tommy went with their grandfather and pitch-forked fish here, all kinds: coho, sockeye, even steelhead; they spawned on Hulbert's place and there were a few small Indian houses or sheds there; Lawrence James said many people from all over the Fraser Valley went there in the Fall to catch fish; this version is supported by the root kw'eqw *to club* but not by the suffix =íth'a *clothes* not *fish*, possibly <**=ál**> *plural affix?*, lx <**=íth'a**> *clothes, blankets used for clothing*, syntactic analysis: nominal, attested by Elders Group, EL (in Chill. dialect), source: place names reference file #89, also <**Skw'ékw'qwòs**>, //s=kʷə́[-C_1ə-]qʷ=ás//, phonology: downstepping, reduplication, literally /'place for clubbing (salmon) in the face'/, (semological comment: this name supports the clubbing fish etymology but is only reported by EL and no-one else), dialects: *Cheh.*, attested by EL.

<**kw'qwá:lí:ya**>, ds //k'ʷqʷ=ɛ́·lí·yɛ//, TCH /'*hit on the ear, hit on the temple (side of the head)*'/, lx <**=á:lí:ya**> *on the ear, on the temple (side of the head),* syntactic analysis: intransitive verb, attested by JL.

<**kw'ekw'qwá:lth'átel**>, dnom //k'ʷə[-C_1ə-]qʷ=ɛ́·l=iθ'ɛ= ´=təl//, [k'ʷək'ʷqʷǽ·lθ'ǽtɪl], HHG /'*stick for beating blankets or clothes or mat, blanket-beater, clothes-beater, mat-beater, rug-beater*'/, (<**-R1-**> *continuative*), (<**=á:l(s)?**> *structured activity*), lx <**=ith'a**> *clothes, blanket*, lx <**=tel**> *ōdevice for, thing for*, phonology: reduplication, syntactic analysis: nominal, attested by ME (11/21/72 tape), IHTTC.

<**kw'oqwchí:ws**>, ds //k'ʷaqʷ=c(əs)=í·ws//, REL ['*to whip all over the body with cedar boughs*'], TCH, lx <**=tses ~ =ches**> *on the hand, hand, bough of tree*, lx <**=í:ws**> *on the body*, syntactic analysis: intransitive verb, attested by Elders Group.

<**kw'eqwelá:x̱el**>, ds //k'ʷəqʷ=əlɛ́·x̣əl//, TCH ['*hit on the arm*'], lx <**=elá:x̱el**> *on the arm, wing*, syntactic analysis: intransitive verb, attested by JL.

<**kw'qwéleqw**>, ds //k'ʷqʷ=ə́ləqʷ//, TCH ['*hit on the top of the head*'], lx <**=éleqw**> *on top of the head*, syntactic analysis: intransitive verb, attested by EB.

<**kw'qwéleqwt**>, pcs //k'ʷqʷ=ə́ləqʷ=T//, TCH /'*hit s-o on the head, club him on the head*'/, (<**-t**> *purposeful control transitivizer*), syntactic analysis: transitive verb, attested by JL, Elders Group.

<**kw'qwélets**>, ds //k'ʷqʷ=ə́ləc//, TCH ['*hit on the behind (with a stick-like object)*'], lx <**=élets**> *on the bottom, on the rump*, syntactic analysis: intransitive verb, attested by JL.

<**kw'óqweletstel ~ kw'óqwletstel**>, dnom //k'ʷáqʷ=ələc=təl//, TOOL /'*big axe, double-bladed heavy axe*'/, literally /'device to hit with stick-like object on the bottom (i.e. to cleave through to the bottom?)'/, lx <**=elets**> *on the bottom*, lx <**=tel**> *device for, thing for*, syntactic analysis: nominal, attested by Elders Group (3/1/72, 3/26/75).

<**kw'qwém**>, dnom //k'ʷqʷ=əm//, [k'ʷqʷʊ́m ~ k'ʷqʷm], TOOL /'*little hatchet, little axe*'/, phonology: this could be analyzed as a vowelless word, (<**=em**> *nominalizer?* prob. from -em *intransitivizer*), syntactic analysis: nominal, attested by Elders Group (3/1/72, 3/26/75), also <**kw'qwéb**>, also /'*axe*'/, //k'ʷqʷ=ə́b//, [k'ʷqʷə́b ~ k'ʷqʷb], phonology: DM, JL and his grandmother Mrs. August Jim all have /m/ with an allophone [b] with half-closure of the velum; it sounds somewhat like the speaker has a cold; upriver dialects have no /n/ and thus these speakers would have no [d] allophone; half-nasal [b] has been reported for some other B.C. Salish languages by Boas, Davis, and Kinkade; JH worked almost exclusively with DM and therefore reported [b] /b/ beside [m] /m/, attested by DM (12/4/64), also <**skw'qwém**>, also /'*axe*'/, //s=k'ʷqʷ=ə́m//, attested by BJ (5/64).

<**kw'qweméthet**>, pcrs //k'ʷqʷ=əm=ə́T-ət//, EFAM /'*drop oneself into a seat, throw oneself on the floor or ground in a tantrum, throw a tantrum*'/, literally /'(uncertain, perhaps) axe oneself, club oneself, club s-th with oneself'/, (<**=éthet**> *purposeful control transitivizer* with *reflexive*), syntactic analysis: intransitive verb.

<**kw'qwémést(exw?)**>, df //k'ʷqʷ=ə́m=ə́s=T or k'ʷqʷ=ə́m=ə́sT-əxʷ//, SOC ['*knock s-o down*'], probably <**=es**> *on the face*, and <**=t**> *purposeful control transitivizer*, possibly <**=stexw**> *causative control transitivizer*, syntactic analysis: transitive verb, comment: only the form with 2s obj. has been obtained, which could be accounted for by either the purposeful control suffix or the causative suffix, example: <**x̲wém kw'els kw'qwémésthòmè**>, //x̣ʷə́m k'ʷə-l-s k'ʷqʷ=ə́m=ə́s(=)T-ámə//, /'*I can knock you down fast.*'/, phonology: upshifting, downstepping, Elder's comment: "(unsure)", attested by Elders Group.

<**kw'qwépsem**>, ds //k'ʷqʷ=ə́psəm//, TCH /'*clubbed on the back of the neck, clubbed on the back of the head*'/, lx <**=épsem**> *on the back of the neck, on the back of the head*, syntactic analysis: intransitive verb, attested by Deming.

<**kw'óqwestel**>, dnom //k'ʷáqʷ=əs=təl or k'ʷəqʷ=á[=M2=]s=təl//, SOC /'*war club, club for any purpose*'/, FSH ['*salmon club*'], HUNT, ASM ['a short club'], lx <**=es**> *on the face*, lx <**=tel**> *device for, thing for*, syntactic analysis: nominal, attested by BHTTC, Elders Group, DM, also <**kw'ó:qwestel**>, also /'*club (for any purpose)*'/, //k'ʷəqʷ=á·[=M2=]s=təl//, phonology: metathesis since the root is not attested elsewhere with length but the suffix is often attested with length, attested by Elders Group.

<**kw'qwewíts**>, ds //k'ʷqʷ=əwíc//, TCH ['*hit on the back*'], lx <**=ewíts**> *on the back*, syntactic analysis: intransitive verb, attested by JL.

<**kw'qwí:les**>, ds //k'ʷqʷ=í·ləs//, TCH ['*hit on the chest*'], lx <**=í:les**> *on the chest*, syntactic analysis: intransitive verb, attested by JL.

<**kw'eqwíwét**>, pcs //k'ʷəqʷ=íwə́l=T//, SOC ['*spank s-o*'], TCH, lx <**=íwél**> *on the inside, in the rectum, in the bowels, on the rump; in the mind*, (<**=t**> *purposeful control transitivizer*), syntactic analysis: transitive verb, attested by AD.

<**kw'qwí:ws**>, ds //k'ʷqʷ=í·ws//, TCH ['*club on the body*'], lx <**=í:ws**> *on the body*, syntactic analysis: intransitive verb, attested by BHTTC.

<**kw'ókw'qwōwsà:ls**>, sas //k'ʷá[=C_1ə=]qʷ=əws=ɛ̀·ls//, HUMC ['*a whipper*'], SOC, ASM ['a man who whipped boys in keekwillie houses (pit-houses) every morning (to get them running outside to bathe) and knew how to not hurt them bad'], (<**=R1=**> *derivational*, perhaps *habitual*), lx <**=ōws ~ =ews ~ =í:ws**> *on the body*, (<**=á:ls**> *structured activity non-continuative*), possibly root <**qw'óqw**> //q'ʷáqʷ// *whip* rather than <**kw'óqw**> //k'ʷáqʷ// *hit with stick-like object* since there is some evidence in other words for this slight distinction and since cognates in other Salish languages show **/k'ʷəqʷ ~ q'ʷəqʷ/ roots**, phonology: reduplication, downstepping, syntactic analysis: nominal, Elder's comment: "(uncertain)", attested by BHTTC.

<**kw'oqwiyó:ls**>, ds //k'ʷaqʷ=iyá·ls//, PLAY ['*lacrosse*'], lx <**=iyó:ls ~ =ó:ls**> *round object, fruit, rock, ball*, syntactic analysis: nominal?, intransitive verb?, attested by Elders Group, also <**kw'okw'qwiyóls**>, //k'ʷa[=C_1ə=]qʷ=iyáls//, phonology: reduplication, attested by MC, MV, LG (Deming 3/15/79), ASM ['lacrosse sounds similar to the game of knobbies, in which spools or rocks are tied with string and players throw and catch them with notched vine maple sticks; the name for knobbies was not remembered'], attested by Deming (7/27/78).

<**kw'qwó:les ~ kw'qwóles**>, ds //k'ʷqʷ=á·ləs ~ k'ʷqʷ=áləs//, TCH ['*hit in the eye (on the eyelid)*'], lx <**=ó:les ~ =óles**> *in the eye, on the eyelid, in appearance, in color*, syntactic analysis: intransitive verb, attested by JL.

<**kw'qwó:ythel**>, ds //k'ʷqʷ=á·yθəl//, TCH /'*hit on the mouth, [hit on the chin, hit on the lip, hit on the jaw]*'/, lx <**=ó:ythel**> *on the chin, on the lip, on the jaw*, syntactic analysis: intransitive verb, attested by EB.

<**kw'óqwtses**>, dnom //k'ʷáqʷ=cəs//, EB ['*red huckleberry*'], ['*Vaccinium parvifolium*'], literally

/'clubbed on the hand'/, ASM ['so named because they can be gathered by doing this over a berry basket'], lx <**=tses**> *on the hand*, syntactic analysis: nominal, attested by Elders Group, Salish cognate: Squamish /sk'ʷəqʷč's/ *red huckleberry* W73:145, K67:294, K69:59, also <**skw'óqwtses**>, //s=k'ʷáqʷ=cəs//, attested by Elders Group (3/1/72), also <**skw'éqwtses**>, //s=k'ʷə́qʷ=cəs//, attested by SJ, AH, also <**sqále**>, //sqɛ́lə//, attested by Elders Group, AC, others.

<**kw'éqwxel**>, ds //k'ʷə́qʷ=xʸəl//, TCH /'*hit on the leg, [hit on the foot]*'/, lx <**=xel**> *on the leg, on the foot*, syntactic analysis: intransitive verb, attested by EB.

<**kw'oqwchí:ws**>, REL ['*to whip all over the body with cedar boughs*'], *see* kw'óqw.

<**kw'óqweletstel ~ kw'óqwletstel**>, TOOL /'*big axe, double-bladed heavy axe*'/, *see* kw'óqw.

<**kw'óqwestel**>, SOC /'*war club, club for any purpose*'/, *see* kw'óqw.

<**kw'óqwet**>, TCH /'*beat s-o/s-th with a stick, hit s-o/s-th with a stick, hit s-th (on purpose), hit s-o intentionally*'/, *see* kw'óqw.

<**kw'oqwiyó:ls**>, PLAY ['*lacrosse*'], *see* kw'óqw.

<**kw'óqwlexw**>, TCH /'*hit s-o unintentionally, hit s-o accidentally*'/, *see* kw'óqw.

<**kw'óqwtel**>, SOC ['*a whip*'], *see* qw'óqw.

<**kw'óqwtses**>, EB ['*red huckleberry*'], *see* kw'óqw.

<**kw'ósthet**>, WETH ['*get warm (of weather)*'], *see* kw'ás.

<**kw'ótl'kwa**>, probably root //k'ʷáƛ'kʷɛ//, WATR /'*sea, ocean, salt water*'/, syntactic analysis: nominal, noun, attested by EB, Deming, other sources: ES /k'ʷáƛ'kʷa/, H-T k·wátkwa (macron over á), Salish cognate: Squamish /k'ʷúƛ'kʷ/ *salt water* W73:283, K67:346, also <**kw'ótl'kwe**>, //k'ʷáƛ'kʷə//, attested by AC, example: <**ő́welh le thét yutl'ólem wetló:s te kw'ótl'kwe kwses me híkwthet te qó:**>, //ʔówə-ɬ lə θə́t yə=u=ƛ'á-lə=m wə-ƛ'á-əs tə k'ʷáƛ'kʷə kʷ-s-əs mə híkʷ=θət tə qá·//, /'*They didn't say if it was (if that is) salt water when the water got big.*'/, usage: Story of the Flood, attested by AC.

<**kw'ótsest**>, ABFC /'*stare at someone's face, look at s-o's face, stare at s-o, look at s-o*'/, *see* kw'áts ~ kw'éts.

<**kw'ó:wes ~ kw'ówes**>, probable bound root or stem //k'ʷá·wəs ~ k'ʷáwəs//, meaning uncertain.

<**skw'ó:wes ~ skw'ówes**>, dnom //s=k'ʷá·wəs ~ s=k'ʷáwəs//, HHG /'*pail, bucket, kettle (BJ, Gibbs)*'/, (<**s=**> *nominalizer*), syntactic analysis: nominal, attested by AC, EB, other sources: ES /sk'ʷá·wəs/ *bucket*, also /'*kettle*'/, attested by BJ, Gibbs, example: <**stám kw'es lí:w í te skw'ó:wes**>, //s=tɛ́m k'ʷə-s lí·w ʔí tə s=k'ʷá·wəs//, /'*What's in the pail? (inside)*'/, attested by EB, <**sqweqwá tel skw'ówes**>, //s=C_1ə=qʷɛ́ tə-l s=k'ʷáwəs//, /'*hole in my pail*'/, attested by AC.

<**skw'ékw'ewes**>, dmn //s=k'ʷa[=Aə́C_1ə=]wəs//, [sk'ʷʊ́k'ʷʊwəs], HHG ['*small pot*'], (<**é-ablaut and =R1=**> *diminutive*), phonology: ablaut, reduplication, syntactic analysis: nominal, attested by EB.

<**kw'óxwe**>, free root //k'ʷáxʷə//, HHG /'*box, trunk, grave box (old-style, not buried), coffin, casket*'/, syntactic analysis: nominal, noun, attested by AC, Elders Group, Deming, BJ, also <**kw'ó:xwe**>, //k'ʷá·xʷə//, attested by BJ, EB, example: <**qéx̱ te kw'óxwe**>, //qə́x̣ tə k'ʷáxʷə//, /'*a lot of boxes*'/, attested by AC, <**qp'á:qet te kw'ó:xwe**>, //qp'ɛ́·q=əT tə k'ʷá·xʷə//, /'*close the box*'/, attested by EB.

<**skw'ókw'exwe**>, stvi //s=k'ʷá[=C_1ə=]xʷə//, MC /'*It's boxed., It's in a box.*'/, (<**s=**> *stative*), (<**=R1=**> *stative* or *resultative*), phonology: reduplication, syntactic analysis: intransitive verb, attested by Elders Group (5/26/76).

<**kw'elókw'exwóles**>, plv //k'ʷ[=əl=]á[=C_1ə=]xʷə=áləs//, stvi, [k'ʷʊlák'ʷʊxʷálɪs], MC ['*be box-*

shaped'], literally /'be boxes in appearance, look like boxes'/, (<**=el=**> *plural*, <**=R1=**> *resultative*), lx <**=óles**> *on the eye, in the eye, in appearance, look like*, phonology: reduplication, syntactic analysis: intransitive verb, attested by Elders Group (6/1/77).

<**kw'óxwemel**>, df //k'ʷáxʷə=məl//, ANAA /'*hoof, esp. deer hoof (off deer or attached to stick as rattle)*'/, literally perhaps /'box portion of the body'/, lx <**=mel**> *part, portion of the body*, syntactic analysis: nominal, noun, attested by Elders Group.

<**kw'óxwemel**>, ANAA /'*hoof, esp. deer hoof (off deer or attached to stick as rattle)*'/, *see* kw'óxwe.

<**kw'ó:yx̱wem**>, mdls //k'ʷá·yx̣ʷ=əm//, ABFC ['*growling (of one's stomach)*'], (<**=em**> *middle voice*), syntactic analysis: intransitive verb, attested by Elders Group (3/3/76).

<**kw'ō wiyóth(cha) ò ~ kw'ō hélémcha ò**>, TIME ['*forever*'], *see* wiyóth.

<**kw'ṓ:la ~ kw'ú:la**>, free root //k'ʷó·lɛ ~ k'ʷú·lɛ//, FOOD ['*stink-eggs*'], FSH, ASM ['salmon eggs buried in cheese-cloth or burlap sack and left to ripen for several months, has the consistency of cheese and a strong smell, eaten as a delicacy'], syntactic analysis: nominal, noun.

<**kw'ōle'álá**>, dnom //k'ʷolɛ=ʔɛ́lɛ́//, BSK /'*stink-egg basket, stink salmon egg basket*'/, FOOD, FSH, lx <**=álá**> *container, container of*, syntactic analysis: nominal, noun, attested by Elders Group (3/24/76).

<**kw'ōle'álá**>, BSK /'*stink-egg basket, stink salmon egg basket*'/, *see* kw'ṓ:la ~ kw'ú:la.

<**kw'ṓ:l ~ qw'ṓ:l** or **kw'ṓ:w ~ qw'ṓ:w**>, possible root //k'ʷó·l or k'ʷów// or //q'ʷó·l or q'ʷów//, root meaning uncertain unless <**qw'él**> *ripe*.

<**skw'ṓ:lmexw ~ sqw'ṓ:lmexw**>, df //s=k'ʷó·l(=)mexw or s=k'ʷów=lməxʷ//, EB /'*blackberry (fruit),* before contact, only *wild trailing blackberry,* (now also) *evergreen blackberry,* (now also) *Himalaya blackberry*'/, ['before contact, only *Rubus ursinus,* now also *Rubus laciniatus,* and *Rubus procerus*'], ASM ['the berries of the trailing variety are ready as early as July, those of the evergreen somewhat later, those of the Himalaya in late August and even later'], MED ['a tea made from boiled roots is diarrhea medicine, a tea from the leaves is medicine for stomach ache'], (<**s=**> *nominalizer*), root meaning uncertain, possibly <**=mexw**> *people* or possibly <**=lmexw**> *medicine?? or on the breast??*, perhaps related to root in <**kw'ew=ítsel**> *grizzly bear* (where <**=ítsel**> may be *on the back),* phonology: labialization is sometimes less noticeable before ō here almost sk'ṓ:lmexw, syntactic analysis: nominal, attested by AC, other sources: ES /sk'ʷə́w·lməxʷ/ (CwMs /sk'ʷí·lməxʷ/) *blackberries*, H-T <skṓlmoq> *blackberry (trailing) (Rubus sp.)*, also <**sqw'ṓ:lmexw**>, //s=q'ʷów=lməxʷ//, attested by BJ (5/10/64, 12/5/64), example: <**sqw'ṓ:lmexw sqe'óleqw**>, FOOD *blackberry juice* (lit. blackberry + fruit juice), (attested by RG,EH 6/16/98 to SN, edited by BG with RG,EH 6/26/00)

<**skw'ṓ:lmexwelhp**>, ds //s=k'ʷó·lməxʷ=əɬp//, EB /'*blackberry vine, blackberry bush*'/, ['*Rubus ursinus, Rubus laciniatus, Rubus procerus*'], lx <**=elhp**> *plant, tree*, syntactic analysis: nominal, attested by AC, Elders Group.

<**shxwelméxwelh skw'ṓ:lmexwelhp**>, ds //s=xʷəl=mə[=´=]xʷ=əɬ s=k'ʷó·lməxʷ=əɬp//, EB ['*trailing blackberry vine*'], ['*Rubus ursinus*'], literally /'Indian kind of blackberry'/, ASM ['this was the pre-contact blackberry in the area'], (<**s=**> *stative*), lx <**=elh**> *style, kind of*, syntactic analysis: simple nominal phrase.

<**xwelítemelh skw'ṓ:lmexwelhp**>, ds //xʷəlítəm=əɬ s=k'ʷó·lməxʷ=əɬp//, EB /'*Himalaya blackberry bush, evergreen blackberry bush*'/, ['*Rubus procerus, Rubus laciniatus*'], literally /'White-man kind of blackberry'/, ASM ['both introduced by non-Indians'], lx <**=elh**> *kind of, style*, syntactic analysis: simple nominal phrase.

<**kw'ōwiyékw ~ kw'ōyékw**>, df //k'ʷowiyə́kʷ ~ k'ʷoyə́kʷ//, [k'ʷowiyʊ́kʷ ~ k'ʷoyʊ́kʷ], FSH /'*small fish-hook (for trout, etc.), trolling hook*'/, syntactic analysis: nominal, noun, attested by Elders Group (3/15/72), DM (12/4/64), BJ (5/64), other sources: ES /k'ʷə́wyəkʷ/ *trolling hook*, Salish cognate: Samish /k'ʷúyəkʷ/ *fish hook* G86:85, Sechelt /k'ʷúyukʷ/ *fish hook* T77:19, also <**kw'ṓwiyekw ~ kw'ṓyekw**>, //k'ʷówiyəkʷ ~ k'ʷóyəkʷ//, attested by Deming (3/25/76).

<**kw'pé<u>x</u>w**>, probably root //k'ʷpə́x̣ʷ//, SD /'*[make a bang, make a sudden hard thump sound]*'/, ASM ['sharp sound of something dropped, sudden sound that happens when something falls (not a dull sound, has echo to it from ground)'], semantic environment ['marble dropped on floor, kidnapped children dropped from the basket of the Basket Ogress, Th'ṓw<u>x</u>eya'], syntactic analysis: intransitive verb, attested by BHTTC, also /'*make a bang*'/, attested by EB, Elders Group (Mar. 1972), also /'*to thump*'/, attested by Elders Group (10/27/76), example: <**le wets'étl' qésu le kw'pé<u>x</u>w**>, //lə wə=c'ə́ƛ' qə=s=u lə k'ʷpə́x̣ʷ//, /'*It fell (fall suddenly) and made a bang (past tense).*'/, attested by Elders Group (Mar. 1972).

<**kw'qwá:lí:ya**>, TCH /'*hit on the ear, hit on the temple (side of the head)*'/, *see* kw'óqw.

<**kw'qwéleqw**>, TCH ['*hit on the top of the head*'], *see* kw'óqw.

<**kw'qwéleqwt**>, TCH /'*hit s-o on the head, club him on the head*'/, *see* kw'óqw.

<**kw'qwélets**>, TCH ['*hit on the behind (with a stick-like object)*'], *see* kw'óqw.

<**kw'qwém**>, TOOL /'*little hatchet, little axe*'/, *see* kw'óqw.

<**kw'qwémést(exw?)**>, SOC ['*knock s-o down*'], *see* kw'óqw.

<**kw'qweméthet**>, EFAM /'*drop oneself into a seat, throw oneself on the floor or ground in a tantrum, throw a tantrum*'/, *see* kw'óqw.

<**kw'qwépsem**>, TCH /'*clubbed on the back of the neck, clubbed on the back of the head*'/, *see* kw'óqw.

<**kw'qwewíts**>, TCH ['*hit on the back*'], *see* kw'óqw.

<**kw'qwí:les**>, TCH ['*hit on the chest*'], *see* kw'óqw.

<**kw'qwí:ws**>, TCH ['*club on the body*'], *see* kw'óqw.

<**kw'qwó:les ~ kw'qwóles**>, TCH ['*hit in the eye (on the eyelid)*'], *see* kw'óqw.

<**kw'qwó:ythel**>, TCH /'*hit on the mouth, [hit on the chin, hit on the lip, hit on the jaw]*'/, *see* kw'óqw.

<**kw'síts**>, dnom //k'ʷs(=)íc//, EZ /'*rainbow trout,* prob. also *coastal cutthroat trout*'/, ['*Salmo gairdneri,* prob. also *Salmo clarki clarki*'], possibly root <**k'ʷɛs**> *burn*, possibly <**=íc**> *on the back*, since it has red stripes on its back, syntactic analysis: nominal, attested by Elders Group 7/9/75, JL 5/8/79, other sources: ES /k'ʷsí·c/ *cutthroat trout*, JH /k'ʷsí·c/ *cutthroat trout*, H-T k·ōse'tc (macron over e also) *trout (Salmo sp.)*, also <**kwesích**>, //kʷəsíc//, also /'*trout salmon, small spring salmon [sic?]*'/, attested by Elders Group 3/1/72, also <**qw'esíts ~ qw'esí:ts**>, //q'ʷəsíc ~ q'ʷəsí·c//, also /'*trout*'/, attested by BJ 12/5/64 p.304, *see also under* <kw'as>

<**kw'síws**>, HUNT ['*singe the hairs off skin*'], *see* kw'ás.

<**kw'sí:ws**>, df //k'ʷs=í·ws//, ABDF ['*(have) measles*'], possibly root <**kw'as**> *burned, hot*, probably <**=í:ws**> *on the body, on the skin*, syntactic analysis: intransitive verb prob., attested by Deming.

<**kw'tómés**>, WATR ['*(rain or sweat) trickling down one's face*'], *see* kw'átem.

<**kw'ú:tl'ò:lh**>, PRON /'*that was him (deceased), he (deceased)*'/, *see* tl'ó ~ tl'o.

<**kw'xá:m**>, NUM ['*count*'], *see* kw'áx.

<**kw'xát**>, NUM /'*count them, count s-th*'/, *see* kw'áx.

<**kw'xwós**>, df //k’^{w}x^w=ás//, WETH ['*to hail (weather)*'], lx <**=ós**> *on the face, round thing*, syntactic analysis: intransitive verb, attested by EB.

<**kw'ekw'xwós**>, cts //C_1ə-k’^{w}x^w=ás//, WETH ['*hailing (weather)*'], (<**R5-**> *continuative*), phonology: reduplication, syntactic analysis: intransitive verb, attested by EB 3/11/76.

<**skw'ekw'xwós**>, dnom //s=C_1ə-k’^{w}x^w=ás//, WETH ['*the hail*'], (<**s=**> *nominalizer*), phonology: reduplication, syntactic analysis: nominal, attested by EB, BJ (5/64, 12/5/64), also <**kw'ekw'xwós**>, //C_1ə=k’^{w}x^w=ás//, attested by Elders Group 3/15/72, EB.

<**kw'íkw'xwòs**>, dmn //C_1í=k’^{w}x^w=ás//, WETH ['*hail when it comes in sheets*'], literally /'little hail'/, (<**R4=**> *diminutive*), phonology: reduplication, downstepping, syntactic analysis: nominal, perhaps intransitive verb, attested by Elders Group 3/15/72.

L

<**l ~ -l ~ -el**>, free root //l ~ -l ~ -əl//, [l̩ (syllabic) ~ -l ~ -ɪl ~ -əl ~ -ʊl], PRON ['*my*'], phonology: l occurs sentence initial, -l occurs after stressed vowel or (in fast speech) after a consonant, and -el occurs in slower speech after a consonant, -ɪl occurs after alveolars or palatals, -ʊl occurs after labialized consonants, -əl occurs in free variation in those locations and occurs elsewhere, syntactic analysis: possessive pronoun affix, syntactic comment: occurs before a head nominal or suffixed to the word immediately before it, even between an adjective and the nominal it modifies, more often found suffixed to the demonstrative article before the nominal, attested by Deming, Elders Group, AC, others, also <**n ~ -n**>, //n ~ -n//, dialects: *Matsqui*, attested by AH, example: <**siyám l siyáye**>, //s=iy=ɛ́m l si=yɛ́yə//, /'*my dear friends*'/, attested by Deming, <**ts'áts'eltsel xwoyíwel tel sqwálewel kw'els me xwe'í sq'ó talhlúwep (éy l sí:yáye, l sí:yáye sí:yám)**>, //c'ɛ́c'əl-c-əl x^w=ɛ[=Aa=]y=íwəl tə-l s=q^{w}ɛ́l=əwəl k'^{w}ə-l-s mə x^{w}ə=ʔí s=q'á tɛ=ɬlúwəp (ʔɛ́y l si[=´·=]=yɛ́yə, l si[=´·=]=yɛ́yə s=i[=´·]y=ɛ́m)//, /'*I'm very happy to come here at this gathering (my good friends, my dear friends).*'/, attested by Deming, <**talhwélep l siyáye**>, //tɛ=ɬwə́ləp l si=yɛ́yə//, /'*you people my friends*'/, attested by Deming, <**lemlémetchxw mékw' ye tskwí:m l á:wkw'**>, //C_1əC_2-lə́m=əT-c-x^w mə́k'^{w} yə c=k^{w}í·m l ʔɛ́·wk'^{w}//, /'*Fold all my red clothes.*'/, literally /'mild imperative fold them many all the (plural, human?) red my belongings'/, syntactic comment: note that mékw' *all* precedes the article, that the article which is normally only human plural is used with inanimate objects, that the pronoun occurs between the adjective tskwí:m *be red* and the nominal á:wkw' *belongings*, attested by Elders Group, <**lemlémetchxw mékw' yel á:wkw'**>, //C_1əC_2-lə́m=əT-c-x^w mə́k'^{w} yə-l ʔɛ́·wk'^{w}//, /'*Fold all my clothes.*'/, attested by Elders Group, <**l stl'í**>, //l s=ƛ'í//, /'*I want, my want*'/, <**n stl'í ten yóseqw**>, //n s=ƛ'í tə-n yás=əq^w//, /'*I want my hat.*'/, dialects: *Matsqui*, attested by AH.

<**=l**>, da //=l//, TIB /'*non-control transitivizer, accidentally, happen to, manage to do to s-o/s-th*'/, comment: this suffix could also be shown as <**=lexw**> (/=ləx^w/), cognate with Musqueam and Cowichan dialects /=nəx^w/ (as in work of Suttles, Hukari, etc.), however -exw can just as well be segmented as *third person object* here and from <**=stexw**> (/=sT-əx^w/, leaving //=sT// *causative control transitivizer*), besides setting up object suffixes for all persons this also eliminates the need for a rule deleting the <**exw**> in all other persons (though such a rule may be historically motivated, it is synchronically uneconomical and unmotivated), syntactic analysis: derivational suffix; found in <**kw'étslexwtsel.**>, //k'^{w}ə́c=l-əx^w-c-əl//, /'*I see him/her/it/them.*'/, <**héqwlòxes.**>, //hə́q^w=l-áx^y-əs//, /'*It smelled me.*'/, <**kw'etslolétsel.**>, //k'^{w}əc=l-álə-c-əl//, /'*I see you folks.*'/, example: <**líchxw slhéq'el:àx?**>, //lí-c-x^w s=ɬə́=q'ɛl=láx^y//, /'*Do you know me?*'/ and many more elsewhere in this work.

<**la**>, free root //lɛ//, TVMO /'*go, go to, going, going to, (go somewhere else to do the action), going to (in future)*'/, syntactic analysis: auxiliary verb, preposition/prepositional verb, syntactic comment: like another auxiliary, mi (come), la uses a special imperative -lh (see examples below), rather than -lha, attested by AC, EB, ASM ['go'], <**lí welh la áyel**>, //lí wəɬ lɛ ʔɛ́y=əl//, /'*Has he gone away?*'/, attested by AC, example: <**latst álhtel**>, //lɛ-c-t ʔɛ́ɬtəl//, /'*Let's go and eat.*'/, attested by AC, <**lalh (átl'qel, kwetxwílem, t'ó:kw', tl'epíl lám te qó:, áyel, áyeles te qó:, má:yt)**>, //lɛ-ɬ (ʔɛ́ƛ'q=əl, k^{w}ətɛx^w=íl=əm, t'á·k'^{w}, ƛ'əp=íl lɛ́=m tə qá·, ʔɛ́y=əl, ʔɛ́y=əl=əs tə qá·, mɛ́·y=T)//, /'*Go (outside, inside, home, down to the water, away, away from the water, and help him). (imperative)*'/, attested by AC, contrast <**lámtlh tl'epíl lám te qó:**>, //lɛ́=m-tɬ ƛ'əp=íl lɛ́=m tə qá·//, /'*Go down to the water.*'/, attested by AC, <**lí welás mílha**>, //lí wə-lɛ́-s míɬɛ//, /'*Is it when they go spirit-dance?*'/, attested by AC, ASM ['go to'], <**le kwetxwílem te spá:th la te lálémს**>, //lə kwətɛx^w=íl=əm tə s=pɛ́·θ lɛ tə

lɛ́lə́m-s//, /'*The bear goes into his den.*'/, literally /'past 3rdperson get oneself inside the bear go in the his house'/, syntactic comment: la functions as preposition/prepositional verb here, attested by EB, <**là kwe sle'óthels te x̱ó:tsa**>, //lɛ kʷə s=ləʔɛ=áθ=əl-s tə x̣á·cɛ//, /'*He went across the lake.*'/, literally /'(he) go to the (remote) nominal=across=edge=get-of the lake'/, *<**sle'óthels te stó:lō**> *across the river* rejected by EB, syntactic comment: la is preposition/prepositional verb here, <**ílhtsel la q'íq kw'els e só:les.**>, //ʔí-ɬ-c-əl lɛ q'íq k'ʷə-l-s ʔə sá·l=əs//, /'*I went to jail when I was drunk.*'/, literally /'I past go to get apprehended when/that I just be drunk'/, attested by Elders Group, ASM ['going'], <**latsel (xwehíwel, xwewqw'éylem)**>, //lɛ-c-əl (xʷə=híw=əl, xʷə=wq'ʷ=íl=əm)//, /'*I'm going (upstream, downstream).*'/, attested by AC, <**latsel t'ó:kw' (wets'ímeles te Christmas, tl'okwsesṓ:kw' kwthel tále).**>, //lɛ-c-əl t'á·k'ʷ (wə-c'ím=əl-əs tə krɪ́sməs, ƛ'a=kʷ-s-əs ʔó·k'ʷ kʷ=θ-əl tɛ́lə)//, /'*I'm going home ((when it is) near Christmas, because my money ran out (run out)).*'/, attested by AC, <**la xwehíwel yithá**>, //lɛ xʷə=híw=əl yi=θɛ́//, /'*They (those people) are going upstream.*'/, attested by AC, ASM ['going to (displacement and/or future)(immediate future is unmarked, like present tense)'], <**latsel (xwóyeqwem, lá:ts'ewtxwem)**>, //lɛ-c-əl (xʷáy=əqʷ=əm, lɛ́·c'=əwtxʷ=əm)//, /'*I'm going to (wash my head, drop in [visit]).*'/, attested by AC, contrast <**lámtsel lá:ts'ewtxwem**>, //lɛ́=m-c-əl lɛ́·c'=əwtxʷ=əm//, /'*I'm going to drop in.*'/, attested by AC, <**lachxw xwehíwel**>, //lɛ-c-xʷ xʷə=híw=əl//, /'*You're going upstream.*'/, literally /'you are going to go upstream.'/, attested by AC, ASM ['going to (future), will go and (do s-th)'], <**latsel t'ókw' wáy:élés**>, //lɛ-c-əl t'ák'ʷ wɛ́y·ə́l=ə́s//, /'*I'll go home tomorrow.*'/, attested by AC, <**(latsel, lámtsel) máythòme**>, //(lɛ-c-əl, lɛ́=m-c-əl) mɛ́y=T-ámə//, /'*I'll go and help you.*'/, attested by AC.

<**ley ~ lay**>, df //lɛ=y < lɛ + yə-//, TVMO /'*go travelling by way of, go via*'/, (<**ye-**> *travelling by way of*), phonology: the prefix combines phonologically with the preposed auxiliary and is no longer phonetically prefixed, syntactic comment: auxiliary verb, attested by Elders Group, others, example: <**ley lhe'á kw'e Sq'éwlets ~ lay lhe'á kw'e Sq'éwlets**>, //lɛ=y ɬəʔɛ́ k'ʷə s=q'ə́w=ləc//, /'*He went via Scowlitz.*'/, literally /'he went travelling by way of through Scowlitz.'/.

<**lám**>, mdls //lɛ́=m//, TVMO /'*go, go to, going, going to, go(ing) to (in future), be gone*'/, syntactic analysis: auxiliary verb, intransitive verb, preposition/prepositional verb, syntactic comment: a preposition/prepositional verb requires a following nominal phrase as its object and can be added right after another verb phrase without any subordinating conjunction, attested by AC, Elders Group, Deming, etc., ASM ['go'], example: <**tsel lám.**>, //c-əl lɛ́=m.//, /'*I went.*'/, syntactic analysis: ambiguous past, attested by AC, <**tsel lám tseláqelhelh.**>, //c-əl lɛ́=m cəlɛ́q=əɬ=əɬ//, /'*I went yesterday.*'/, syntactic analysis: ambiguous past, attested by AC, <**tsel lám kw'e látelh.**>, //c-əl lɛ́=m k'ʷə lɛ́t=əl//, /'*I went early this morning.*'/, attested by EB, <**lhíl lám**>, //ɬí-l lɛ́=m//, /'*when I go*'/, attested by Elders Group, <**lhíl ulh lám t'ókw'**>, //ɬí-l ʔu=wɬ lɛ́=m t'ák'ʷ//, /'*it's time for me to go home., when I'm going home (already)*'/, attested by Elders Group, <**ewá:lhtsel (l)í:l làm**>, //ʔəwə=ɛ́ɬ-c-əl lí·-l (~ ʔí·-l) lɛ́=m//, /'*I wasn't going to go (but did).*'/, Elder's comment: "possibly", attested by EB, <**lámtselcha látelh(es) wáyélés**>, //lɛ́=m-c-əl-cɛ lɛ́t=əɬ(-əs) wɛ́yə́l-ə́s//, /'*I'll go early tomorrow morning. (will, early morning)*'/, literally /'I will go (when it) is night=past tense tomorrow'/, attested by EB, <**éy kws lámtset**>, //ʔɛ́y kʷ-s lɛ́=m-c-ət//, /'*Let's go.*'/, literally /'it's good that-nominalizer our-go(ing)'/, attested by JL, <**lámalha ewólem e**>, //lɛ́=m-ɛɬɛ ʔəwál=əm ʔə//, /'*Go play (you guys). (imperative 2p)*'/, attested by Deming, ASM ['go to'], <**étset lám te sqw'eyílex**>, //ʔə́-c-ət lɛ́=m tə s=q'ʷəy=íl=əxʸ//, /'*We went to the dance.*'/, syntactic analysis: auxiliary past, attested by AC, <**xwemxálemlha la(m) te steqtál**>, //xʷəm=xʸ[=Aɛ́=]l=əm-ɬɛ lɛ(=m) tə s=təq=tə[=Aɛ́=]l (or s=təqɛ́=tə[=M2=]l)//, /'*Run to the door.*'/, literally /'run. go to the door'/, attested by IHTTC, <**lám kw'e sle'óthels te (x̱ó:tsa, stó:lō).**>, //lɛ́=m k'ʷə s=ləʔáθəl-s tə (x̣á·cɛ, s=tá·l=əw)//, /'*He went across the (lake, river).*'/, literally /'he went to the other side of the (lake, river)'/, attested by EB, <**lám kw'e láts'ewtxw**>, //lɛ́=m k'ʷə lɛ́c'=əwtxʷ//, /'*go to another*

room'/, attested by Elders Group, <**emétlha lam te shxwch'áletstel**>, //ʔəmə́t-ɬɛ lɛ=m tə s=xʷ=c'ɛ́=ləc=təl//, /'*Go sit in the chair.*'/, attested by IHTTC, <**lámchexw te theqthéqet qetl'ó:su (tés, xwelí:ls) te theqát**>, //lɛ́=m-c-əxʷ tə $C_1əC_2$=θə[=´=]qɛt qə=ƛ'á·=s=uw (tə́s, xʷə=lí·-ls) tə θəqɛ́t//, /'*Go through the thicket and get to the tree.*'/, attested by AC, ASM ['going'], <**(lámtsel, lámtset) xwehíwel**>, //(lɛ́=m-c-əl, lɛ́=m-c-ət) xʷə=híw=əl//, /'*(I'm, we're) going upstream.*'/, attested by AC, <**lámtsel tlówàyèl**>, //lɛ́=m-c-əl tlá=wɛ̀yə̀l//, /'*I'm going today.*'/, attested by AC, <**lámcha**>, //lɛ́=m-cɛ//, /'*They're going. (they)*'/, (<**-cha**> *future tense*), attested by AC, ASM ['going to'], <**lámtsel te (lamá:wtxw, shxwiymá:le, sq'ép).**>, //lɛ́=m-c-əl tə (lɛm=ɛ́·wtxʷ, s=xʷəyəm=ɛ́·lə, s=q'ə́p)//, /'*I'm going to (the beer parlor, the store, a gathering).*'/, attested by AC, <**lámtsel kwthe chí:yà:lhp**>, //lɛ́=m-c-əl kʷθə cí·yɛ=ɛ́ɬp//, /'*I'm going to the strawberry patch.*'/, phonology: vowel merger, downstepping, attested by AC, <**lámtset te sqw'eyílex**>, //lɛ́=m-c-ət tə s=q'ʷəy=íl=əxʸ//, /'*We're going to the dance.*'/, attested by AC, <**lámtset te Alámex kwsetst lhím te hóps**>, //lɛ́=m-c-ət tə ʔɛlɛ́məxʸ kʷ-sə-c-t ɬím tə háps//, /'*We're going to Agassiz area to pick hops.*'/, attested by JL, ASM ['go(ing) to (in future)'], <**lámtsel wéy:eles**>, //lɛ́=m-c-əl wɛ́y·əl=əs//, /'*I'll go tomorrow.*'/, *<**tsel lám wáy:eles**> rejected by AC, ASM ['be gone'], <**le lám**>, //lə lɛ́=m//, /'*He is gone., She is gone., It is gone., They are gone.*'/, attested by AC; found in <**lámechexw**>, //lɛ́=m-ə-c-əxʷ//, /'*Are you going?*'/, syntactic comment: interrogative affix, attested by Elders Group, AC, NP, example: <**lámechexw t'ó:kw'**>, //lɛ́=m-ə-c-əxʷ t'á·k'ʷ//, /'*Are you going home?*'/, attested by NP, <**lámechexw (kw'e táwn, xwehíwel)?**>, //lɛ́=m-ə-c-əxʷ (k'ʷə tɛ́wn, xʷə=híw=əl)//, /'*Are you going (to town, upstream)?*'/, <**lámechap**>, //lɛ́=m-ə-c-ɛp//, /'*Are you (pl.) going (present, immediate future)?*'/, attested by IHTTC, AC, <**lámechapcha**>, //lɛ́=m-ə-c-ɛp-cɛ//, /'*Are you (pl.) going (future)?*'/, attested by IHTTC, <**lámechap (mőkw' lám, xwehíwel)?**>, //lɛ́=m-ə-c-ɛp (mók'ʷ lɛ́=m, xʷə=híw=əl)//, /'*Are you (all going to go, going upstream)?*'/, attested by AC; found in <**lámàwèlh**>, //lɛ́=m-ɛ̀wə̀ɬ//, /'*Goodbye (to person leaving).*'/, dialects: *Tait, Cheh.*, attested by Elders Group (3/15/72), EB, also <**lámòwèlh**>, //lɛ́=m-à=wə̀ɬ//, dialects: *Chill., Pilalt, Deming,* literally /'just go already, go just already'/, attested by EB, Deming, AC, example: <**lámòwèlh, mámele**>, //lɛ́=m-àwə̀ɬ C_1ɛ́-mələ//, /'*Goodbye, children (to them leaving).*'/, syntactic comment: nominal phrase minus article *vocative*, dialects: *Chill.*, attested by AD, <**lámelhtsel qe tsel ő we o.**>, //lɛ́=m-əɬ-c-əl qə c-əl ʔówə ʔa//, /'*I was going but I'm not now.*'/, syntactic comment: past affixed, attested by Elders Group, <**éwe stl'ís kw'es meytólxws welámet séwq'tòlè**>, //ʔəwə s=ƛ'í-s k'ʷə-s mɛy=T-álxʷ-s wə-lɛ́=m-ət sə́wq'=T-álə//, /'*He doesn't want to help us (when we) go find (search for) you folks.*'/, phonology: downstepping, updrifting, syntactic comment: verb phrase with negative, nominal phrase minus article, auxiliary verb, sentence with subjunctive phrase, dialects: *Chill.*, attested by NP (in IHTTC), also <**éwe stl'íses kws meytóxwes welámet súwq'tòlè**>, //ʔə́wə s=ƛ'í-s-əs kʷ-s mɛy=T-áxʷ-əs wə-lɛ́=m-ət súwq'=T-álə//, dialects: *Cheh.*, attested by EB (in IHTTC), also <**éwe stl'íses meytóxwes welámet súwq'tòlè**>, //ʔə́wə s=ƛ'í-s-əs mɛy=T-áxʷ-əs wə-lɛ́=m-ət súwq'=T-álə//, dialects: *Tait*, attested by SP, AK, AD (in IHTTC), <**yóswe welámá:l**>, //yáswə wə-lɛ́=m-ɛ́·l//, /'*I might go.*'/, attested by AC, <**temtámcha welámexw t'ó:kw'**>, //təm=tɛ́m-cɛ wə-lɛ́=m-əxʷ t'á·k'ʷ//, /'*When are you going home?*'/, literally /'what time will it be when you are going home'/, attested by AC, <**tl'ótsasew qw'eyílex qa t'ílem tel siyáya welámet mílha**>, //ƛ'á-cɛ-s-uw q'ʷəy=íl=əxʸ qɛ t'íl=əm t-əl si=yɛ́yɛ wə=lɛ́=m-ət míɬɛ//, /'*My friends will sing and dance when we go to the spirit-dance.*'/, attested by AC, <**őwetsel lámá:l t'ó:kw'**>, //ʔówə-c-əl lɛ́=m-ɛ́·l t'á·k'ʷ//, /'*I'm not going home.*'/, attested by Elders Group, <**őwechxw lámexw temkwát**>, //ʔówə-c-xʷ lɛ́=m-əxʷ təm=kʷɛ́=T//, /'*Don't go yet.*'/, attested by Elders Group, also /'*Don't let him go yet.*'/, attested by EB, <**őwe lámes**>, //ʔówə lɛ́=m-əs//, /'*He's not going., He won't go.*'/, attested by MC, <**éwechap lamáp hélem tel slhx̲wélhcha**>, //ʔə́wə-c-ɛp lɛ=m-ɛ́p hə́-lɛm tə-l s=ɬxʷ=ə́ɬcɛ//, /'*Don't you people go to my spit.*'/, usage: pun on place name Th'qwélhcha, a stagnant lake or ponds at the downriver end of Squatits (Peters) Reserve, attested by LJ (Tait), **<ōwáchxw lámexw>**, //ʔowə-ɛ́-c-xʷ lɛ́=m-əxʷ//, /'*Will you go?*'/, literally /'won't you? go'/, attested by MC, **<ōwáchap lámelep ~ ōwáchap lámélep>**, //ʔowə-ɛ́-c-ɛp lɛ́=m-ə́ləp//, /'*Aren't you folks going?*'/, attested by IHTTC, **<ewá:lhtsel (lámàl ~ í:l làm ~ lí:l làm)>**, //ʔəwə-ɛ́·ɬ-c-əl (lɛ́=m-ɛ́l ~ ʔí·-l lɛ́=m ~ lí·-l lɛ́=m)//, /'*I wasn't going to go (but did).*'/, syntactic comment: verb phrase with negative, sentence with subjunctive phrase, verb phrase with auxiliary, attested by EB, **<ő̄we chókwes kw'el shxwlà:m.>**, //ʔówə cákʷ-əs kʷə-l sxʷ-lɛ̀·m//, /'*I'm not going far.*'/, attested by Elders Group.

<**shxwlàm**>, dnom //sxʷ=lɛ́=m//, TVMO ['*place to go to*'], (<**shxw=**> *nominalizer*), phonology: downstepping, syntactic analysis: nominal, attested by AD.

<**hálém**>, cts //hə́=lɛ[=M2=]=m or hɛ́=lɛ[=Aə́=]=m//, TVMO /'*be on one's way, be going*'/, (<**hé- ~ há-**> *continuative*), (<**metathesis (or é-ablaut)**> *derivational*), phonology: metathesis (or ablaut), syntactic analysis: intransitive verb, attested by IHTTC, EB, Elders Group, example: <**le q'ep'lóxes wiyóthe kwsu háléms ye mímelha**>, //lə q'ə́p'=l-áxʸ-əs wi=yáθ-ə kʷ-s-u hə́=lɛ́[=M2=]=m-s yə mí[-C₁ə-]ɬɛ//, /'*He got me addicted to always going to spirit-dances. (get s-o addicted, get s-o hooked on), He got me hooked on always going to spirit-dances.*'/, literally /'past 3rd person subject he gets me addicted to always-just consequently be going to the (plural, human?) spirit-dancing (continuative)'/, attested by EB, <**ő̄wechxw halémexw**>, //ʔówə-c-xʷ hə́-lɛ[=M2=]=m-əxʷ//, /'*Don't go.*'/, literally /'don't you be going'/, attested by IHTTC, <**ő̄wechap halemélep ~ ő̄wechap halemáp**>, //ʔówə-c-ɛp hɛləm-ə́ləp ~ ʔówə-c-ɛp hɛləm-ə́ləp//, /'*Don't you folks go.*'/, literally /'don't you folks be going'/, contrast <**ő̄wechap lámáp**> *Don't you folks go.*, attested by IHTTC, *<**ōwáchap halemélep**> rejected, contrast <**ōwáchap lámélep**>, //ʔowə-ɛ́-c-ɛp lɛ́=m-ə́ləp//, /'*Aren't you folks going?*'/, syntactic analysis: verb phrase with negative with interrogative affix, attested by IHTTC, <**kw'ō hálémcha ò**>, //k'ʷ-əw hɛ́ləm-cɛ ʔà//, /'*forever*'/, literally /'what (remote) will just be going on'/, attested by Elders Group, also <**kw'ō wiyóth(cha) ò**>, //k'ʷ-əw wi=yáθ-cɛ ʔà//, literally /'what will just be always'/, attested by Elders Group.

<**halemélmel**>, ds //hə=lɛ[=M2=]=m=ə́lməl//, EFAM ['*feel like going*'], TVMO, lx <**=élmel**> *in the mind, feel like, thinking about*, phonology: metathesis, suffix has strong stress-valence, syntactic analysis: intransitive verb, attested by IHTTC, example: <**líchap halemélmel**>, //lí-c-ɛp hɛləm=ə́lməl//, /'*Do you folks feel like going?*'/, attested by IHTTC.

<**héleméstem**>, caus //hə́=lɛm=ə[=´=]sT-əm//, EFAM ['*he's gone (mentally)*'], literally /'he's been caused to be on his way, he's been caused to be going'/, (<**=(é)st**> *causative*), (<**-em**> *passive*), phonology: presumably the penultimate stress is derivational, syntactic analysis: intransitive verb or participle?, attested by Elders Group.

<**shxwélem ~ shxwélém**>, dnom //sxʷ=hə́=lɛm ~ sxʷ=hə́=lɛ́[=Aə́=]=m//, TVMO /'*wandering, where someone goes*'/, (<**shxw=**> *nominalizer*), phonology: possible ablaut, optional updrifting, syntactic analysis: nominal, attested by EB, others, example: <**qéx̱ ta' shxwélem**>, //qə́x̣ t-ɛʔ sxʷ=hə́=lɛm//, /'*You're wandering a lot.*'/, literally /'your wandering is a lot'/, attested by EB, <**lécha kw'a' shxwélém**>, //ʔɛlə́cɛ k'ʷ-ɛʔ sxʷ=hə́=lə́m//, /'*Where are you wandering to?*'/, attested by EB, <**ő̄we mékw'es a shxwélém**>, //ʔówə mə́k'ʷ=əs ʔɛ sxʷ=hə́=lə́m//, /'*Don't go all over., Don't be all over in your wandering.*'/, literally /'is not every(where) your wandering'/, attested by EB, <**mekw'o shxwélems**>, //mə́k'ʷ-à sxʷ=hə́=lɛm-s//, /'*a wanderer, goes all over*'/, attested by EB.

<**lámtselh**>, ds //lɛ́=m=cə(s)=əɬ//, LANG ['*signal with the hand to go (or that you can go)*'], TVMO, lx <**=tses**> *in the hand*, lx <**=elh**> *according to, in the ways/fashion/style/manner of*, phonology: consonant-loss of s in =tses is irregular but happens in a few other cases, syntactic analysis: intransitive verb, attested by Elders Group (5/26/76).

<**xwelá ~ xwelám ~ xwlá ~ xwlám**>, incs //x^{w}ə=lɛ́ ~ x^{w}ə=lɛ́=m//, DIR /'*toward, towards, for*'/, (<**xwe=**> *go, come, get, become*), syntactic analysis: preposition/prepositional verb, attested by EB, BHTTC, Elders Group, AD, example: <**xwlám te máqa**>, //x^w=lɛ́=m tə mɛ́qɛ//, /'*through (towards) the (fallen) snow*'/, attested by EB, <**éy xwlá(m) tl'eléwe te st'élmexw.**>, //ʔɛ́y x^w=lɛ́(=m) ƛ'ə=lə́wə s=t'ə́lməx^w//, /'*The medicine is good for you.*'/, syntactic comment: independent object of prepositional verb, attested by EB, <**éy xwlá(m) tl'eléwe te tselqómé**>, //ʔɛ́y x^w=lɛ́(=m) ƛ'ə=lə́wə tə cəlq=ámə́//, /'*Blackcaps (blackcap berries) are good for you.*'/, syntactic comment: independent object of prepositional verb, attested by EB, <**qél xwlá(m) tl'eléwe**>, //qə́l x^w=lɛ́(=m) ƛ'ə=lə́wə//, /'*It's bad for you.*'/, syntactic comment: independent object of prepositional verb, attested by EB, <**le thékw' xwlá te s'em'oméla**>, //lə θə́k'^{w} x^w=lɛ́ tə s=C$_1$əC$_2$-ʔámə́lɛ//, /'*She was pulled towards the Thompsons (Thompson Indians)., She was influenced by the Thompsons.*'/, attested by BHTTC, <**éy kw'ómkw'emcha telí s'ólh sqwálewel xwlám kw'e ít totí:lt tlówàyèl.**>, //ʔɛ́y k'^{w}ám=C$_1$əC$_2$-cɛ təlí sʔáɬ s=q^{w}ɛ́l=əwəl x^w=lɛ́=m k'^{w}ə ʔí-t ta[-C$_1$ə-]l=í·l=T tlá=wɛ̀yə̀l//, /'*Let our thoughts be strong toward what we are studying today.*'/, attested by AD, <**le xwelá te Agassiz.**>, //lə x^{w}ə=lɛ́ tə Agassiz//, /'*He got to Agassiz., (He went toward Agassiz.)*'/, semantic environment ['like two people travelling together, and one maybe changes his mind and goes as far as Agassiz while his partner keeps on going to his (maybe original) destination'], attested by Elders Group (incl. NP), <**óxwestchexw xwelá tl'elhlímelh**>, //ʔáx^{w}əs=T-c-əx^w x^{w}ə=lɛ́ ƛ'ə=ɬlíməɬ//, /'*Give it to him from us.*'/, literally /'you (imperative 2s) give it to him towards us (towards our credit)'/, syntactic comment: iovp, attested by Elders Group, <**ch'íthométset (xw)lám kw'e mōkw'stám**>, //c'í=T-amə́-c-ət (x^w=)lɛ́=m k'^{w}ə mok'^{w}=s=tɛ́m//, /'*We thank you for everything.*'/, attested by AD.

<**lá ~ lá: ~ lah**>, bound root //lɛ́ or lɛ́h//, DESC //'*tight, put away*'//

<**slá ~ selá ~ slá:**>, strs //s=lɛ́ ~ s(ə)=lɛ́ ~ s=lɛ́·//, DESC /'*be tight, be secured tightly; be tucked away, put away so well you can't find it, be solid*'/, root <**lá:**> *tight, put away*, (<**s=**> *stative*), possibly <**he-**> *resultative*, comment: possible since resultatives are often like continuatives in form except often have the stative s- as well); other forms with such stative resultatives in s-(h)e- are found only on roots beginning in l or m so far, and he- 'continuative' occurs only before l, m, y, and w, phonology: h-loss would be expected after s-, syntactic analysis: participle, adjective/adjectival verb, attested by Elders Group, EB, AD, AC, Salish cognate: Squamish /yáʔ/ *tight, shut, tied tightly* and /yáʔ-n/ *put on tightly, hold tightly, tie tightly* W73:268, K67:381, 382, Musqueam /səl'éʔ/ 'put away' (resultative) beside /léʔ-x^y/ 'put it away' Suttles ca1984:7-164, example: <**q'éyset kw'es selá ~ selá kw'es q'éyset**>, //q'ís=əT k'^{w}ə-s s=lɛ́ ~ səlɛ́ k'^{w}ə-s q'ís=əT//, /'*tie it tightly*'/, syntactic comment: the sentence-initial position probably indicates semantic focus, attested by AC, <**éwe ís selá**>, //ʔə́wə ʔí-s s=lɛ́//, /'*It's not tight.*'/, attested by EB.

<**slálets**>, ds //s=lɛ́=ləc//, DESC ['*firmly planted in ground (can't be pulled out)*'], LAND, EB, lx <**=lets**> *on the bottom*, syntactic analysis: adjective/adjectival verb, attested by IHTTC.

<**Lohíts ~ Lahíts ~ Lahích ~ Slahích**>, df //la=híc ~ lɛ=híc ~ s=lɛ=híc//, PLN ['*Five-Mile Creek*'], ASM ['five miles above (upriver from, here north of) Yale, the creek is easy to locate; the Indian name can also be found on a sign, "Slaheech Yale Native Ancient Cemetery No. 3", by a little white picket fence around the cemetery, down a bank in the bush on the west side of the main highway from Yale north; the cemetery is located below the first bay above Íyém and above Aseláw (Esilao) and Aseláw Stótelō; we visited it 4/30/79 on a place names field trip to Five Mile Creek, which is said to be about the furthest north Stó:lō territory goes'], probably root <**lɛ́·**> *tight* or probably even stem <**s=lɛ́·**> *be tight*, lx <**=ích** ~ (after vowel) **=hích** or **='ích**> *on the back*, phonology: given with o (/a/) by Duff but pronounced after prompting with an <a> /ɛ/ as the first vowel, <ts ~ ch> here vary freely, syntactic analysis: nominal, attested by AK, AD, source: place names reference file

#135, other sources: Duff 1952:30 /lahíc/.

<**láxel**>, dnom //lɛ́=xʸəl or lɛ́xʸ=əl//, FSH [*'fishing platform'*], ASM ['plank and pole platform built extended out over eddy water from bank to stand on in dip-netting or other fishing from land for salmon'], Duff 1952:cover of 1973 printing, root <**lá:**> *tight, put away, secure tightly*, lx <**=xel**> *on the foot or =el*> *get, become, go, come*, syntactic analysis: nominal, attested by Elders Group (3/15/72, 3/26/75, 2/11/76).

<**lakwwí:l**>, free root //lɛkʷwí·l//, REL /*'a cross, grave cross, gravestone, cross one hangs up'*/, syntactic analysis: nominal, attested by CT, Salish cognate: Squamish /ləkʷín/ *cross* borrowed from French le coin? W73:71, K67:336, Musqueam Halkomelem /lɛkwín/ *cross* S79pc (Suttles p.c. 10/9/79), borrowed from Chinook Jargon <**la qhuen**> for *cross* Johnson 1978:297 (that form from Good 1880, the more usual CJ form is <**la clo-a**> from French <**la croix**>/lakɣwá/ *the cross*); probably as Kuipers suggests from French <**le coin**> *corner, nook, quoin (exterior angle of a building), cornerstone, wedge*, also <**lak-wíl**>, //lɛkwíl//, attested by AD 10/9/79, also <**lakw'wì:l**>, //lɛk'ʷwì·l//, attested by EB.

<**lílakw'wì:l**>, dmn //C_1í=lɛk'ʷwì·l//, REL ['*small cross*'], (<**R4=**> *diminutive*), phonology: downstepping, reduplication, syntactic analysis: nominal, attested by EB.

<**lá:la**>, df //lɛ́·lɛ//, EFAM /*'oh for goodness sakes., well. (in surprise)'*/, phonology: probable reduplication, syntactic analysis: interjection, attested by AD, EB, Salish cognate: possibly Squamish /na/ *there you are.* (interjection used when handing something over)(prob. related to /naʔ/ *be there*), K67:312, possibly Lushootseed /dáʔdaʔ/ *that which gives emotional support, satisfaction; that which is important to someone* H76:127, also <**lála**>, //lɛ́lɛ//, attested by Deming.

<**lalàlèm**>, BLDG ['*houses*'], *see* lá:lém.

<**lálàt**>, TIME ['*getting dark*'], *see* lá:t.

<**lá láw (or) lá:láw**>, LANG /*'say, Honey; hello, Honey; hello, Husband; hello, Wife'*/, *see* láw.

<**lálekw'em**>, df //lɛ́[=C_1ə=]k'ʷ=əm//, FOOD /*'not cooked enough (of fish), [undercooked]'*/, semantic environment ['fish'], (<**=R1=**> perhaps *stative* or *continuative*), (<**=em**> *middle voice* or *intransitivizer*), root meaning unknown, phonology: reduplication, syntactic analysis: intransitive verb, attested by IHTTC.

<**lá:lém**>, df //lɛ́·[=C_1ə=]m//, BLDG /*'house, home, den, lodge, hive'*/, (<**=R1=**> *derivational*), phonology: reduplication, phonology: this is not the most common pronunciation but the other pronunciations can be derived more easily from it than vice versa, syntactic analysis: nominal, noun, attested by BJ (5/64), other sources: ES /lɛ́·ləm/ (CwMs /lɛ́ləmʔ/), JH /lé·ləm/, Salish cognate: Squamish /námʔ/ *house* W73:145, K67:336, also <**lálém**>, //lɛ́lə́m//, attested by DM 12/4/64, EB, Elders Group (3/15/72), also <**lálem ~ (once) lá:lem**>, //lɛ́[=C_1ə=]m ~ lɛ́·[=C_1ə=]m//, attested by AC, Elders Group, example: <**qéx̱ te lá:lem ~ qéx̱ te lálem**>, //qə́x̣ tə lɛ́·ləm ~ qə́x̣ tə lɛ́ləm//, /*'There's a lot of houses., There's a group of houses.'*/, attested by AC, <**lulh q'e'í:lem ta lálem**>, //lə=wɬ q'əʔí·l=əm t-ɛ lɛ́ləm//, /*'Your house is (already) ancient.'*/, attested by AC, <**(hí:kw, tl'áqt) lálèm**>, //(hí·kʷ, ƛ'ɛ́qt) lɛ́lə̀m//, /*'It's a (big, long) house.'*/, phonology: downstepping, attested by DM (12/4/64), <**lálems te sisemóye**>, //lɛ́ləm-s tə sisəmáyə//, /*'beehive, hive of the bee'*/, literally /'house of the bee'/, attested by Elders Group, <**lálems te sqelá:w**>, //lɛ́ləm-s tə s=qəlɛ́·w//, /*'the beaver's lodge'*/, attested by Elders Group, <**lálémş te spá:th**>, //lɛ́lə́m-s tə s=pɛ́·θ//, /*'the bear's den, the bear's house'*/, attested by EB, <**lálems te skw'exó:s**>, //lɛ́ləm-s tə s=k'ʷəxʸ=á·s//, /*'halo around the moon'*/, literally /'the house of the moon'/.

<**lalàlèm**>, pln //l[-əl-]ɛ̀lə̀m//, BLDG ['*houses*'], (<**-el-**> *plural*), phonology: downshifting, syntactic

analysis: nominal, attested by EB.

<**lílem**>, dmn //C_1í=lɛm//, BLDG /'*little house, cabin (say 12 ft. x 10 ft. or less), small home, storage house (small shed-like house, enclosed with door), outhouse (slang), toilet (slang)*'/, (<**R4=**> *diminutive*), phonology: reduplication, syntactic analysis: nominal, noun, attested by AC, Elders Group (3/15/72, 6/1/77).

<**slálem álhqey**>, cpds //s=lɛ́·[=C_1ə=]m ʔɛ́ɬqəy//, EZ //'*turtle*'//, lit. /"snake with a house, housed snake"/, <**s=**> *stative*, <**=R1=**> *resultative*, semantic comment: this takes the verbal root <lá:m> (prob. meaning *to house*) and forms a *stative resultative* on it (strs) to show that the *turtle* is a *snake that is housed* or *a snake with a house,* attested by RG & EH (4/10/99 Ling332)

<**làlets'éwtxwem**>, SOC ['*be visiting*'], *see* láts'.

<**lale'úlem**>, mdls //lɛlə(=)ʔúl=əm//, EFAM /'*generalize, reminisce*'/, possibly <**R8=** or **=R1=**> uncertain form and function**, <=(ʔ)éw(ə)l>** *on the inside, in the mind,* (<**=em**> *middle voice*), phonology: reduplication, phonology: the /ú/ is unusual and since the form was obtained at Deming could be Nooksack influence (or a Nooksack form) though identified by both speakers as Halkomelem, comment: EF was one of the last partial speakers of Nooksack, MV is the daughter of the last fluent speaker of Nooksack (though very fluent in Halkomelem and not a speaker of Nooksack), syntactic analysis: intransitive verb, attested by EF, MV (both at Deming 4/27/78), Salish cognate: Lushootseed /lələʔúləb/ *recite the history of a people* H76:271.

<**lálwes**>, possibly root //lɛ́lwəs//, BLDG /'*platform (in house, etc.), bed platform, platform in bottom of canoe, flooring (the planks)*'/, syntactic analysis: nominal, noun, attested by Elders Group (5/3/78), SP (Elders Group 3/72), AD, LG, other sources: ES /lɛ́lwəs/ (CwMs /lɛ́·lʔwəs/) *bed platform*, Salish cognate: Squamish /yáyʔwas/ *bed platform* K67:382, also <**lál'wes**>, //lɛ́lʔwəs//, /'*platform, bed*'/, dialect: *Matsqui* attested by AH, example: <**kw'íles ta' lál'wes**>, //k'^{w}íl=əs t-ɛʔ lɛ́lʔwəs//, /'*How much (money) is your bed?*'/, attested by AH, <**qelés te (lálwes, lhx̱eyléptel).**>, //qəl=ə́s tə (lɛ́lwəs, ɬx̣=íl=ə́p=təl)//, /'*The floor is dirty.*'/, attested by Elders Group (3/72).

<**lám**>, TVMO /'*go, go to, going, going to, go(ing) to (in future), be gone*'/, *see* la.

<**lám**>, free root //lɛ́m//, FOOD /'*liquor, rum*'/, borrowed from Chinook Jargon /lə́m/ *alcohol, rum, whiskey, spirits* Johnson 1978:256, syntactic analysis: nominal, noun.

<**lamáwtxw**>, ds //lɛm=ɛ́wtx^w//, BLDG /'*liquor store, beer parlor* (AC)'/, lx <**=áwtxw**> *building, house*, syntactic analysis: nominal, noun, attested by Elders Group, EB, also <**lamá:wtxw**>, //lɛm=ɛ́·wtx^w//, also /'*beer parlor*'/, attested by AC.

<**shxwlámá:lá**>, ds //sx^w=lɛ́m=ɛ́·lɛ́//, HHG ['*bottle*'], literally /'something that is a container of liquor'/, (<**shxw=**> *nominalizer, something that is*), lx <**=á:lá ~ =ále**> *container of,* syntactic analysis: nominal, attested by CT, HT, also <**shxwlámále**>, //sx^w=lɛ́m=ɛ́lə//, attested by Elders Group, example: <**tsméth' shxwlámá:lá**>, //c=mə́θ' sx^w=lɛ́m=ɛ́·lɛ́//, /'*It's a blue bottle.*'/, attested by CT, HT.

<**lamélwelh**>, df //lɛm=ə́lwəɬ//, EZ ['*canvas-back duck*'], ['*Aythya valisineria*'], probably root <**lam**> *rum* from the brown rum color on the sides of their wings, <**=élwelh**> *on the side (of the body),* syntactic analysis: nominal, noun, attested by Elders Group (6/4/75), also <**lemélwélh**>, //ləm=ə́lwə́ɬ//, attested by Elders Group (2/18/76).

<**lá:m**>, bound root //lɛ́·m//, possibly same as root that means *go* (since Indian doctors/shamans go repeatedly to the spirit world to communicate with spirits) or poss. *function as shaman*

<**slá:m**>, df //s=lɛ́·m//, IDOC ['*spirit power of an Indian doctor or shaman*'], ASM ['example, thunderbird; the Indian doctor's power takes the longest quest, is often the most dangerous of spirits,

like stl'áleqem (supernatural creature) spirits, and may require sleeping in graveyards, etc. during the quest'], (<**s=**> *nominalizer*), syntactic analysis: nominal, attested by NP, Salish cognate: Squamish /s-náʔm/ *power possessed by the medicine man* perhaps from root /náʔ/ *name* W73:203, K67:287, K69:57, also <**slám**>, //s=lɛ́m//, attested by EB, example: <**te sláms**>, //tə s=lɛ́m-s//, /'*his (Indian doctor's) power*'/, attested by EB.

<**shxwlá:m**>, df //sxʷ=lɛ́·m//, IDOC /'*Indian doctor, shaman, medicine man, Indian doctor's spirit power (Elders Group 11/19/75)*'/, (<**shxw=**> *nominalizer*), syntactic analysis: nominal, attested by BJ, AD, EB, other sources: ES /šxʷlɛ́·m/ *shaman, shaman's spirit power*, Salish cognate: Samish dial. of NSt /šnéʔem/, (VU) /šxʷnéʔem/ *shaman, Indian doctor, medicine man* G86:81, also PCS cognate set 112 in G82:25 incl.: Musqueam /sxʷnɛ́ʔɛm/, Nooksack /šxʷnǽʔæ̀m/, Sechelt possibly /sxʷə́nam/ *monster*, Pentlatch /sxʷnáʔəm/, Lushootseed /dxʷ-dáʔəb/, Lummi /šxʷənə́m/, Saanich /šnéʔem/, Songish /šnéʔəm/, also <**shxwlám**>, //sxʷ=lɛ́m//, attested by AC, Elders Group, also /'*Indian doctor, Indian doctor's spirit power*'/, attested by Elders Group (11/19/75), example: <**iyá:qtes te shxwlá:m te spó:l tl'ésu mé xwe swíyeqe.**>, //ʔiyɛ́·q=T-əs tə sxʷ=lɛ́·m tə s=pá·l ƛ'ə́-s-u mə́ xʷə s=wíyəqə//, /'*The Indian doctor changed a crow into a man.*'/, attested by EB, <**mí i'éyelstem te shxwlám**>, //mí C_1əC_2=ʔɛ́y=əl=sT-əm tə sxʷ=lɛ́m//, /'*The Indian doctor made him/her well (make s-o well).*'/, attested by EB.

<**lemóthet**>, pcrs //lɛ́=m[=M2]Aá=T-ət or ləmɛ́ʔAá=T-ət//, IDOC ['*jump up and down (of Indian doctor training)*'], perhaps root <**lemá'**> *kick* with <**ó-ablaut**> automatic on root before <**=thet**>, (or more likely <**lá:m**> (root in *shaman* and in *shaman's spirit power*, meaning uncertain but may be *go* [since Indian doctors travel to the spirit world], with <**metathesis type 2**> and then <**ó-ablaut**> automatic on root before <**=thet**>,<**=th-et**> *purposeful control transitivizer* with *reflexive*), phonology: possible ablaut, syntactic analysis: intransitive verb, attested by IHTTC.

<**hélmethet**>, cts //hə́-ləmɛ=T-ət//, IDOC ['*jumping up and down or bouncing up and down (of an Indian doctor training)*'], (<**hé-**> *continuative* before resonants (l, m, w, y)), syntactic analysis: intransitive verb, attested by IHTTC.

<**shxwlemóthetále**>, dnom //sxʷ=ləmɛ=Aá=T-ət=ɛ́lə//, IDOC ['*place of training to become an Indian doctor (pit made from repeated jumping every year on the same spot)*'], (<**shxw=**> *nominalizer*), lx <**=ále**> *container of*, phonology: ablaut, syntactic analysis: nominal, attested by IHTTC.

<**lamáwtxw**>, BLDG /'*liquor store, beer parlor (AC)*'/, *see* lám.

<**lamá'íwét**>, ABFC /'*kick s-o in the behind, kick s-o in the rump*'/, *see* lemá'.

<**lamélwelh**>, df //lɛm(=)ə́lwəɬ//, EZ ['*canvas-back duck*'], ['*Aythya valisineria*'], probably root <lam> *rum* from the rum color on the sides of their wings, <**=élwelh**> *on the side (of the body)*, syntactic analysis: nominal, noun, attested by Elders Group (6/4/75), also <**lemélwélh**>, //ləm=ə́lwə́ɬ//, attested by Elders Group (2/18/76).

<**lámtselh**>, LANG ['*signal with the hand to go (or that you can go)*'], *see* la.

<**láqleqem**>, EZ /'*goldeneye duck* (probably both the *common goldeneye duck* and the *Barrow goldeneye duck*), *(a kind of diving duck* [Elders Group] *)*'/, *see* léqem.

<**Lasisélhp?**>, df //lɛsisə́ɬp?//, [læsisɪ́ɬp?], PLN /'*Ford Lake (sic Foley Lake), Ford Creek (sic Foley Creek) on north side of Chilliwack River below Post Creek*'/, possibly <**le= ~ lexw=**> *always*, lx <**=elhp**> *tree*, comment: close stems with this suffix are síts'elhp /síc'=əɬp/ *vine maple* and thíthelhp /θí=R1=əɬp/ *bigger tree(s)*; these would yield literal meaning for the place name of *always vine maples* or *always bigger tree(s)*; the correction of the English name is based on close comparisons of

Wells' maps and descriptions locating the place with topographic maps, phonology: the spelling given so far are transliterations of Oliver Wells' transcriptions, but in light of his other transcriptions may be off slightly; the =elhp on the end however is clearly correct and is the suffix for tree; the name is not found so far on the Wells tapes and may be from either Boundary Survey records or the Billy Sepass map, syntactic analysis: nominal, source: Wells 1965:11,13, Wells 1966 also; place names reference file #260.

<**lá:t**>, probably free form, root *//get dark//.*

<**slá:t ~ slát**>, dnom //s=lɛ́·t ~ s=lɛ́t//, TIME ['*night*'], (<**s=**> *nominalizer*), syntactic analysis: nominal, attested by AC, DM, BJ, other sources: ES /slɛ́·t/, JH /slé·t/, example: <**téxw slát ~ texwslát**>, //tə́x^w s=lɛ́t ~ təx^w=s=lɛ́t//, /'*midnight*'/, literally /'later night'/, attested by AC.

<**lálàt**>, cts //C_1ɛ́-lɛ̀t//, TIME ['*getting dark*'], (<**R7-**> *continuative*), phonology: reduplication, phonology: downstepping, syntactic analysis: intransitive verb, attested by Elders Group (3/72), example: <**welh lálàt**>, //wəɬ C_1ɛ́-lɛ̀t//, /'*evening*'/, literally /'already getting dark'/, attested by Elders Group (3/72).

<**xwelált**>, incs //x^wə=C_1ɛ́-lɛ̀t or x^wə=lɛ́[-C_1ə-]t//, TIME ['*become evening, evening*'], literally /'become getting dark'/, (<**xwe=**> *become, get*), phonology: perhaps vowel-loss, reduplication, syntactic analysis: intransitive verb, attested by EB, example: <**tlo xwelált**>, //tlá x^wə=lɛ́lt//, /'*tonight, this evening*'/, attested by EB, <**kw'e xwelált**>, //k'ʷə x^wə=lɛ́lt//, /'*yesterday evening, last night*'/, literally /'the (remote) evening'/, attested by EB, <**xwelá'elt s'álhtel**>, //x^wə=lɛ́ʔ=C_1ə=t s=ʔɛ́ɬ=təl//, /'*evening meal*'/, dialects: *Matsqui*, attested by AH; found in <**xweláltelh**>, //x^wə=lɛ́lt-əɬ//, /'*last night*'/, syntactic analysis: nominal past, attested by Elders Group, RG & EH (4/10/99 Ling332)

<**lá:telh**>, ds //lɛ́·t=əɬ//, TIME /'*be early morning, early morning*'/, ASM ['from maybe 5 or 5:30 a.m. to 8 a.m.'], literally /'it was dark, dark=past tense'/, (<**=elh**> *past tense*), syntactic analysis: intransitive verb, nominal?, syntactic comment: past tense is usually inflectional, but here is derivational, attested by DM (12/4/64), BJ (5/64), also <**látelh**>, //lɛ́t=əɬ//, attested by EB, example: <**éwe olésu látelh**>, //ʔə́wə ʔalə́-s-u lɛ́t=əɬ//, /'*not early morning (i.e. 9:00 a.m. or later)*'/, literally /'it's not too (contrastive) early morning'/, attested by EB, <**tsel lám kw'e látelh**>, //c-əl lɛ́=m k'ʷə lɛ́t=əɬ//, /'*I went early this morning.*'/, attested by EB, <**éy látelh**>, //ʔɛ́y lɛ́t=əɬ//, /'*Good morning.*'/, usage: not used much before the white came, attested by Deming, <**látelh wáyélés**>, //lɛ́t=əɬ wɛ́yə́lə́s//, /'*tomorrow morning, early tomorrow*'/, attested by EB, <**lámtselcha látelhes wáyélés**>, //lɛ́=m-c-əl-cɛ lɛ́t=əɬ-əs wɛ́yə́l=ə́s//, /'*I'll go early tomorrow morning.*'/, literally /'I will go when it is early morning tomorrow'/, attested by EB, <**látelh s'álhtel**>, //lɛ́t=əɬ s=ʔɛ́ɬ=təl//, /'*morning meal, breakfast*'/, literally /'early morning food, meal'/, attested by Deming.

<**lá:telh**>, TIME /'*be early morning, early morning*'/, *see* lá:t.

<**làtém**>, possibly root //lɛ̀tə́m//, SD ['*(make) a blast or boom (and the earth shakes afterward)*'], syntactic analysis: intransitive verb, attested by Elders Group (10/27/76).

<**láts**>, free root //lɛ́c//, TIME ['*sometimes*'], phonology: ts maybe error for ts', syntactic analysis: adverb/adverbial verb, attested by AC, example: láts kw'e(s) slhális, láts kw'e(s) swíyeqes kw' qwà:l, //lɛ́c k'ʷə s=ɬɛ́li-s, lɛ́c k'ʷə swíyəqə-s k'ʷ q^wɛ̀·l//, /'*Sometimes it's a woman, sometimes it's a man that spoke.*'/, attested by AC.

<**láts'**>, free root //lɛ́c'//, DESC ['*different*'], syntactic analysis: adjective/adjectival verb, attested by MV, Deming, Salish cognate: Squamish /náč'/ *different, several, some; go wrong* W73:78, K67:313, K69:65, also <**lá:ts'**>, //lɛ́·c'//, attested by AC, example: <**láts' tel stl'í**>, //lɛ́c' t-əl s=ƛ'í//, /'*I want*

something different.'/, attested by Deming, **<le'ówelh láts' te ts'lhimexóstels>**, //lə?ɛ=Aá=(l)wəɬ lɛ́c' tə c'ɬ=im=əxʸ=ás=T-əl-s//, /'*He went with a different girl., He went (to walk) with a different girl.*'/, literally /'be across be different the his take a walk next to each other'/, attested by MV.

<selá:ts'>, strs //s=hə=lɛ́·c'//, DESC ['*be different*'], (**<s=>** *stative*), (**<he=>** *resultative*), phonology: consonant merger, syntactic analysis: adjective/adjectival verb, attested by AC.

<selélets'>, plv //s=hə=lɛ[=Aə́=][-lə-]c'//, [sɪlílәc'], DESC ['*two different things*'], literally /'nominal/stative-plural-different'/, (**<s=>** *stative* or *nominalizer*), (**<é-ablaut>** *derivational*), (**<-le->** *plural*), phonology: ablaut, syntactic analysis: nominal, adjective/adjectival verb?, attested by AC.

<lets'emót>, ds //lɛ[=Aə=]c'=mát//, DESC ['*a different kind*'], (**<e-ablaut>** *derivational*), lx **<=mót>** *kind, pile*, phonology: ablaut and epenthetic e before resonant yields a form that is homophonous with lets'emót //lə́c'ə=mát// *one kind*, syntactic analysis: nominal, adjective/adjectival verb?, attested by ME (11/21/72).

<xwléts'eqel>, ds //xʷ=lɛ[=Aə́=]c'=əqəl//, LANG ['*different language*'], (**<xw=>** *always*), (**<e-ablaut>** *derivational*), lx **<=eqel>** *language, in speech, in the throat*, phonology: ablaut, syntactic analysis: nominal, intransitive verb?.

<láts'ewtxw>, ds //lɛ́c'=əwtxʷ//, BLDG /'*another room, different room*'/, lx **<=áwtxw ~ =á:wtxw ~ =ewtxw>** *building, house, room*, syntactic analysis: nominal, attested by Elders Group, Deming, example: **<lám kw'e láts'ewtxw>**, //lɛ́=m k'ʷə lɛ́c'=əwtxw//, /'*go to another room, he/she goes to another room*'/, attested by Elders Group, **<láts'ewtxw te sqwáléwéls.>**, //lɛ́c'=əwtxʷ tə s=qʷɛ́l=əwəl-s//, /'*His mind is somewhere else.*'/, literally /'his mind is (in) a different room'/, phonology: updrifting probably as a word-final sentence-intonation variable (most updrifting and downdrifting seems to happen on sentence final words), attested by Deming.

<lá:ts'ewtxwem>, mdls //lɛ́·c'=əwtxw=əm//, SOC /'*visit, be on a short visit*'/, BLDG, (**<=em>** *middle voice*), syntactic analysis: intransitive verb, attested by AC, example: **<ílhtsel lá:ts'ewtxwem>**, //?í-ɬ-c-əl lɛ́·c'=əwtxʷ=əm//, /'*I went on a short visit.*'/, attested by AC, **<metsel lá:ts'ewtxwem>**, //mə-c-əl lɛ́·c'=əwtxʷ=əm//, /'*I'm coming to visit (a short visit)., I'm coming on a short visit.*'/, attested by AC.

<làlets'éwtxwem>, cts //lɛ́[-C₁ə-]c'=ə[-´-]wtxʷ=əm//, SOC ['*be visiting*'], (**<-R1->** *continuative*, <-´-> *continuative* or *derivational*), phonology: reduplication, stress-shift, syntactic analysis: intransitive verb, attested by AC, example: **<í:lhtsel làlets'éwtxwem>**, //?í·-ɬ-c-əl lɛ̀[-C₁ə-]c'=ə́wtxʷ=əm//, /'*I've been visiting.*'/, attested by AC.

<lelts'ó:méx>, cts //lɛ[-C₁ə-]c'=á·məxʸ//, DESC ['*look different*'], possibly **<-R1->** *continuative*, lx **<=ó:méx>** *in appearance, -looking*, phonology: reduplication, syntactic analysis: intransitive verb.

<lets'ő:mexw>, ds //lɛc'=ó·məxʷ//, SOC /'*different person, stranger*'/, DESC, lx **<=ő:mexw ~ =mexw>** *person*, phonology: vowel-shift (a → e) due to stress-shift, ambi-valenced root and strong-valenced suffix, syntactic analysis: nominal, attested by BHTTC, AC (9/29/71, 11/10/71 text), other sources: ES /ləc'ə́wməxʷ/ *people, tribe (lit. one people)*, also **<xwlets'ő:mexw>**, //xʷ=lɛc'=ó·məxʷ//, attested by AC, example: **<lets'ő:mexw lí te thá, lets'ő:mexw lí kw'e thá>**, //ləc'=ó·məxʷ lí tə θɛ́, ləc'=ó·məxʷ lí k'ʷə θɛ́//, /'*There were different Indians from here, different Indians from there., There was one tribe from here, one tribe from there.*'/, comment: the second translation (one tribe) interprets the ambiguity of the form with another form with root léts'e *one*, attested by AC (11/10/71 text).

<lets'ő:lmexw>, pln //lɛc'=ó·[-l-]məxʷ//, SOC /'*different tribe, different people, strangers*'/, (**<-l->** *plural*), (semological comment: note the infix pluralizing the suffix), syntactic analysis: nominal, attested by AC, BHTTC, also <**lets'élmexw**>, //lɛc'=ə́[-l-]məxʷ//, attested by BHTTC.

<**lets'ő̃w(e)yelh ~ slets'ő̃weyelh**>, dnom //lɛc'=ə́w=(ə)yəɬ or lɛc'=óyəɬ ~ s=lɛc'=ə́w=əyəɬ or s=lɛc'=óyəɬ//, KIN /'*half-sibling, half-brother, half-sister*'/, possibly <**=ő̃w**> uncertain, probably not a separate affix, lx <**=ó:llh ~ =ó:ylh ~ =elh ~ =(e)yelh**> *child, offspring, young*, phonology: <**=ő̃yelh**> maybe Nooksack-influence, Salish cognate: Nooksack /=ólɬ (~ =óyɬ)/ *child, offspring, young*, syntactic analysis: nominal, attested by AC, other sources: ES /sləc'ə́wəyəɬ/ *half-sibling*; found in <**slets'ő̃weyelh(s?)**>, //s=lɛc'=óyəɬ(-s)//, /'*his half-sibling*'/, (semological comment: could show inalienable possession use of s= *nominalizer*), attested by AC.

<**slets'éleq**>, dnom //s=lɛc'=ə́ləq//, KIN /'*brother-in-law's wife, (spouse's sibling's spouse), (step-sibling, step-brother, step-sister [AC])*'/, (<**s=**> *nominalizer*), lx <**=éleq**> /'*occupational*'/ or /'*plural*'/ plus lx /'*male*'/, syntactic analysis: nominal, attested by NP, other sources: ES /sləc'ə́lə́q/ *spouse's sibling's spouse*, also <**slets'él:eq**>, also /'*step-sibling, step-brother, step-sister*'/, //s=lɛc'=ə́l·əq//, attested by AC.

<**lets'ló:ts'tel**>, plv //C₁əC₂=lɛ́[=Aá=]·c'=T-əl//, rcps, LT ['*(many) different colors*'], (<**R3=**> *plural*), (<**ó-ablaut**> *derivational*), (<**=tel**> *reciprocal*), phonology: reduplication, phonology: ablaut, syntactic analysis: nominal?, adjective/adjectival verb?, attested by Elders Group (6/16/76).

<**lá:ts'ewets ~ láts'ewets**>, ds //lɛ́·c'=əwəc ~ lɛ́c'=əwəc//, NUM /'*hundred, one hundred*'/, literally /'different on the back'/, lx <**=ewets**> *on the back*, syntactic analysis: adjective/adjectival verb, attested by AC, BJ, CT, Mary Charles, Elders Group, other sources: ES /lɛ́·c'əwəc/, example: <**láts'ewets qas kwe léts'e**>, //lɛ́·c'=əwəc qɛ=s kʷə lə́c'ə//, /'*one hundred and one*'/, attested by AC, also <**láts'ewets qas te léts'e**>, //lɛ́c'=əwəc qɛ=s tə lə́c'ə//, attested by BJ 12/5/64, <**(isále, lhíxw, x̱e'ó:thel, lhq'átses) láts'ewets**>, //(ʔisɛ́lə, ɬíxʷ, x̣əʔá·θəl, ɬq'ɛ́=cəs) lɛ́c'=əwəc//, /'*(two, three, four, five) hundred*'/, attested by AC, <**ópel kws láts'ewets**>, //ʔápəl kʷ-s lɛ́c'=əwəc//, /'*one thousand*'/, literally /'ten that is a hundred'/, attested by Elders Group (3/19/75), <**lá:ts'ewets mestíyexw**>, //lɛ́·c'=əwəc məstíyəxʷ//, /'*one hundred people*'/, attested by AC,

<**halts'elí**>, df //hɛ=lɛc'=əlí or hɛ=ləc'ə=əl=í//, DIR /'*get separated (by distance), be by themselves, be separate*'/, SOC, (<>), <**ha=**> *resultative*, probably root <**láts'**> *be different* with metathesis *derivational*, possibly <**=el**> *come, go, get, become*, possibly <**=í**> meaning unknown unless *durative*, phonology: epenthesis, syntactic analysis: intransitive verb, adjective/adjectival verb?, dialects: *Chill., Cheh.*, attested by AC, Elders Group, also <**alts'elí**>, //hɛ=lɛc'=əl=í or lɛ[=M1=]c'=əl=í//, phonology: consonant-change (h > '), possible epenthesis, possible metathesis, dialects: *Tait*, attested by Elders Group.

<**alts'elít**>, pcs //hɛ=lɛc'=əl=í=T or lɛ[=M1=]c'=əl=ə[=Aí=]T//, DIR ['*to separate things or objects*'], possibly root <**léts'e**> *one*, probably root <**láts'**> *be different* with metathesis *derivational*, í-ablaut or <=í> perhaps *durative*, (<**=et**> *purposeful control transitivizer*), phonology: possible ablaut, possible metathesis, possible epenthesis, syntactic analysis: transitive verb, attested by EB and AD (7/31/78), Elder's comment: "correction from <halts'elít>", Salish cognate: Saanich /nəč'əlíʔt/ *to separate objects* B74a:74, probably analyzable as root /neč'/ *different*, /=əl/ *go, come, get, become, inceptive*, /=ət/ *purposeful control transitivizer*, /=Aíʔ=/ *resultive*, for the latter suffix compare Musqueam /=Aí= ~ =Aɛ́=/ on affix schwas *durative* (Suttles ca1984), also <**halts'elít**>, //lɛ[=M1=]c'=əl=í=T//, attested by EB (3/30/78), sometimes AD (12/17/79), also <**thelts'elít**>, //θəlc'=əl=í=T//, attested by AD (12/17/79).

<**lets'elíthet**>, pcrs //lɛc'=əl=í=T-ət//, DIR /'*separate oneself from a group, separate oneself (from others)*'/, SOC, (<**-et**> *reflexive*), syntactic analysis: intransitive verb, attested by AD (1/8/80), also <**alts'elíthet**>, //lɛ[=M1=]c'=əl=í=T-ət//, Elder's comment: "corrected from halts'elíthet", attested by EB and AD (7/31/78), AD (12/17/79).

<**halts'elíthet**>, plv //hɛ-lɛ[=M1=]c'=əl=í=T-ət//, DIR ['*a group separating themselves from another group*'], SOC, possibly <**ha=**> *plural*, phonology: matathesis, epenthesis, syntactic analysis: intransitive verb, attested by AD (1/8/80), also /'*to separate*'/, attested by Elders Group (11/12/75); found in <**halts'elíthetlha.**>, //hɛ-lɛ[=M1=]c'=əl=í=T-ət-ɬɛ//, /'*Separate yourselves.*'/, attested by Elders Group (9/7/77).

<**lá:ts'ewets ~ láts'ewets**>, NUM /'*hundred, one hundred*'/, *see* láts'.

<**láts'ewtxw**>, BLDG /'*another room, different room*'/, *see* láts'.

<**lá:ts'ewtxwem**>, SOC /'*visit, be on a short visit*'/, *see* láts'.

<**láw**>, free root //lɛ́w//, [lǽw], LANG /'*say. (said to get someone's attention), (term of reference for spouse used with friends), hello*'/, KIN, SOC, syntactic analysis: interjection, attested by AC, EB, AD, Elders Group, Deming, ASM ['say. (said to get someone's attention)'], semantic environment ['used between husband and wife by either spouse to get their attention'], attested by HP, EB and used by EB's grandparents and great grandparents in this way, ASM ['Honey (term of address to one's spouse), Husband, Wife'], semantic environment ['can be used in talking to one's spouse'], attested by Deming, AD, example: <**(tel, ta') láw**>, //(tə-l, t-ɛʔ) lɛ́w//, /'*(my, your) spouse*'/, attested by AD, <**Lílhtsel yóyes, law.**>, //lí-ɬ-c-əl yáy[-ə-]s, lɛw//, /'*I was working, Honey.*'/, ASM ['hello'], semantic environment ['greeting'], usage: , ACL ['*now just sort of adopted as greeting like the English phrase*'], attested by AD, <**láw iyés.**>, //lɛ́w ʔiy=ə́s//, /'*Hello Mam., Hello (my)(female) friend.*'/, attested by Elders Group, <**láw iyéseq.**>, //lɛ́w ʔiy=ə́s=əq//, /'*Hello Mister., Hello (my)(male) friend.*'/, attested by Elders Group.

<**lá láw (or) lá:láw**>, df //lɛ́ lɛ́w (or) C_1ɛ́=lɛ́w (or) lɛ́[=C_1ɛ́(·)=]w//, LANG /'*say, Honey, hello, Honey, hello, Husband, hello, Wife*'/, possibly <**R7=** or **=R9=**> *emphasis?*, phonology: reduplication, syntactic analysis: interjection + nominal, or just interjection, attested by Deming, Elders Group, example: <**lá láw, alétsa te háme**>, //lɛ́ lɛ́w, ʔɛlə́cɛ tə hɛ́mə//, /'*Say, Honey, where's the hammer?*'/, attested by Deming, <**lí tí te háme, lá láw.**>, //lí tí tə hɛ́mə, lɛ́ lɛ́w//, /'*The hammer is over there, Honey.*'/, attested by Deming, <**lá láw, líchxw alétsa**>, //lɛ́ lɛ́w, lí-c-x^w ʔɛlə́cɛ//, /'*Hello, Honey, where were you?*'/, attested by Deming, <**lá láw.**>, //lɛ́ lɛ́w//, /'*Hello, Husband., Hello, Wife.*'/, attested by Elders Group.

<**láwa**>, plv //lɛ́w=ɛ//, LANG ['*hello (to a whole group)*'], SOC, semantic environment ['used example when one comes in late; everyone just answers láw'], (<**=a**> *plural* not attested elsewhere), syntactic analysis: intransitive verb < interjection, attested by HT, AD.

<**láwa**>, LANG ['*hello (to a whole group)*'], *see* láw.

<**Lawéchten**>, nom ////, N ['*Charlie Lewiston*, an Indian doctor from the area of Nooksack, Wash., had that name till his death ca. 1920 (pronounced by non-Indians as Lewiston); the name was formally passed to *Brent Galloway* by Alice Hunt (AH) and Louisa George (LG) at a naming ceremony 10/9/77 at Chehalis, B.C.)'], SMC ['Charlie Lewiston was an Indian doctor who did only good curing, when he came to a gathering, he could make his cane fly to people and they knew he would give them a coin if they tied up his horse or horses; in the late 1970's or early 1980's while documenting Nooksack place names with elders and Allan Richardson, the author visited his tombstone where he is buried with his wife and took a photo of the stones, still well tended '], attested by Deming (4/27/78 and as early as 1974), the root meaning is uncertain, there may be Nooksack suffix <**=ich ~ =ech**> *on the back* and certainly the word ends in Nooksack <**=ten ~ =tan**> *male name ending*.

<**láxel**>, dnom //lɛ́=x^yəl or lɛ́x^y=əl//, FSH ['*fishing platform*'], ASM ['plank and pole platform built extended out over eddy water from bank to stand on in dip-netting or other fishing from land for

salmon'], see root <**lá ~ lá: ~ lah**> *tight, put away, secure tightly.*

<**láx̱et**>, pcs //lɛ́x̣=əT//, LT ['*give s-o light*'], (<**=et**> *purposeful control transitivizer*), syntactic analysis: transitive verb.

<**láx̱etem**>, izs //lɛ́x̣=əT=əm//, LT ['*going out(side) with a light*'], TVMO, possibly <**=em**> *intransitivizer*, syntactic analysis: intransitive verb, example: <**lachxw láx̱etem.**>, //lɛ-c-xʷ lɛ́x̣=əT=əm//, /'*You're going out with a light.*'/, attested by Elders Group.

<**sláx̱et**>, dnom //s=lɛ́x̣=əT//, LT /'*any kind of light that one carries, torch (made from pitch), lantern, lamp, flashlight*'/, HHG, (<**s=**> *nominalizer*), syntactic analysis: nominal, attested by SJ, MV, Elders Group.

<**láx̱etem**>, LT ['*going out(side) with a light*'], *see* láx̱et.

<**Lá:x̱ewey**>, df //lɛ́·x̣(=)əw=əy//, PLN /'*Lackaway village, Lackaway Creek*'/, ASM ['village between Sumas River and Chilliwack Mountain; creek from Atchelitz Creek to Wilson's Creek'], (<**=ey**> *place* or *covering, bark*), syntactic analysis: nominal, attested by BJ (5/64), source: place names reference file #78, other sources: Wells 1965 (lst ed.):19, Wells 1966, also <**Láx̱ewey**>, //lɛ́x̣əw=əy//, attested by AC (1973), Elders Group (7/13/77).

<**lá:y**>, bound root //lɛ́·y *fir*//.

<**lá:yelhp**>, dnom //lɛ́·y=əɬp//, EB ['*Douglas fir*'], ['*Pseudotsuga menziesii*'], ASM ['used for firewood, especially the bark and pitchwood from rotten trees, pitch burned onto canoes for caulking, trees also used for poles, ordinary fir now used for lumber'], lx <**=elhp**> *tree*, syntactic analysis: nominal, attested by AC, Elders Group, other sources: ES /lá·yəɬp/ (and CwMs /lɛ́·yʔəɬp/) *Douglas fir.*

<**slá:y**>, dnom //s=lɛ́·y//, EB ['*fir bark*'], ASM ['slivers from the bark can be painful in the eyes and some people are allergic to them on the skin'], (<**s=**> *nominalizer*), syntactic analysis: nominal, attested by AC, BJ (12/5/64), other sources: ES /slá·y/, example: <**slá:ys te lá:yelhp**>, //s=lɛ́·y-s tə lɛ́·y=əɬp//, /'*bark of the Douglas fir*'/, attested by AC, <**xí:pet te slá:y**>, //xʸí·p=əT tə s=lɛ́·y//, /'*peel the bark of a fir tree*'/, attested by AC.

<**lá:yelhp**>, EB ['*Douglas fir*'], *see* lá:y.

<**lá:yem ~ láyem**>, ABFC ['*laughing*'], *see* líyém ~ leyém.

<**le**>, free root //lə//, TIME ['*recent past third person subject*'], PRON, syntactic analysis: mpcl, attested by AC, Elders Group, others, example: <**le álhtel chelá:qelhelh.**>, //lə ʔɛ́ɬ=təl cəlɛ́·q=əɬ-əɬ//, /'*He ate yesterday. (eat)*'/, attested by AC, <**le álhtel.**>, //lə ʔɛ́ɬ=təl//, /'*They ate.*'/, attested by AC, <**le éy.**>, //lə ʔɛ́y//, /'*They were good.*'/, attested by AC, also <**li éy**>, //li ʔɛ́y//, dialects: *Tait*, attested by AC.

<**lulh**>, (//lə=uɬ < lə=wəɬ//), TIME /'*he/she/it was (already), they were (already)*'/, cpds //welh *be already*//, phonology: vowel merger, syntactic analysis: mpcl, attested by Elders Group, AC, most others, example: <**lulh lhís kw'es me p'óp'etl'em**>, //lə=uɬ ɬí-s k'ʷə-s mə p'á[-C_1ə-]ƛ'=əm//, /'*It was smoking quite a while ago.*'/, literally /'it was already past when it becomes smoking'/, attested by Elders Group.

<**=le= ~ =el=**>, da //=lə= ~ =əl=//, NUM ['*plural*'], (semological comment: pluralizes nominals or agents or patients of verbs but not actions (Galloway 77:309)), phonology: <**=le=**> occurs after root vowel 1, <**=el=**> after root consonant 1, but the occurrence of these allomorphs is not predictable, syntactic analysis: derivational suffix, also <**=el=**>, //=əl=//; found in <**ó:leqw'**>, //ʔi[=Aá·=lə=]q'ʷ//, /'*a lot rubbed off*'/, root <**íqw'**> *rub*, <**th'elíth'eplexw**>, //C_1í[=əl=]=θ'əp=l-əxʷ//, /'*lots of eyes being closed; Japanese wineberries*'/ (compare <**th'íth'eplexw**> *one eye being closed, closing one's eye),*

<**lhóleqwet**>, //ɬá[=lə=]q^w=əT//, /'*wetting many things*'/ (compare <**lhóqwet**> *wet s-th* and <**lhéqw**> *wet)*, <**lháleq'et**>, //ɬɛ́[=lə=]q'=əT//, /'*put down several objects*'/ (compare <**lháq'et**> *lay/put s-th down, put down one object)*, <**q'á(:)lemi**>, //q'ɛ́·[=lə=]mi//, /'*adolescent girls*'/ (compare <**q'á:mi(y)**> *adolescent girl)*, <**sqelá:q**>, //s=q[=əl=]ɛ́·q//, /'*younger siblings*'/ (compare <**sqá:q**> *younger sibling)*, <**shxwemlá:lekw**>, //s(=)x^{w}əm=li[=Aɛ́·=lə=]k^w//, /'*parent's siblings*'/ (compare <**shxwemlí:kw**> *parent's sibling, uncle, aunt)*, <**sts'ólemeqw**>, //s=c'á[=lə=]m(=)əq^w//, /'*great grandparents, great grandchildren*'/, attested by AC (compare <**sts'ó:meqw**> *great grandparent, great grandchild*), also <**sts'eló:meqw ~ sts'ets'eló:meqw**>, //s=c'[=əl=]á·m(=)əq^w//, dialects: *Tait*, <**th'elí:p'oyeqw**>, //θ'[=əl=]í·p'ay(=)əq^w//, /'*great great grandparents/-children*'/ (compare <**th'ép'oyeqw**> *great great grandparent/-child)*, <**skw'álelhō ~ skw'á:lhō**>, //s(=)k'^{w}i[=Aɛ́·=lə=]ɬəw ~ s(=)k'^{w}i[=Aɛ́·=]ɬəw//, /'*in-laws*'/ (compare <**skw'ílhō**> or better <**skw'ílhew**> *in-law)*, <**sqelá:qele**>, //s=q[=əl=]ɛ́·q=ələ or s=C_1ɛ́[=əl=]=qəl=ə//, /'*babies*'/ (compare <**sqá:qele**> *baby)*, <**chá:lexw(s)**>, //cɛ́·[=lə=]x^w(-s)//, /'*wives*'/ (compare <**chá:xw**> *wife)*, <**swá:leqeth**>, //s=wɛ́·[=lə=]q=əθ or s=wi[=Aɛ́·=lə=]q=əθ//, /'*husbands*'/ (compare <**swá:qeth**> *husband)*, <**slélex̲tses**>, //s=lə́[=lə=]x̲=cəs//, /'*fingers*'/ (compare <**sléx̲tses**> *finger)*, <**slélex̲xel**>, //s=lə́[=lə=]x=x^{y}əl//, /'*toes*'/ (compare <**sléx̲xel**> *toe)*, <**steliqíw**>, //s=t[=əl=]iqíw//, /'*horses*'/ (compare <**stiqíw**> *horse)*, <**stelqóye**>, //s=t[=əl=]q(=)áyə//, /'*wolves*'/ (compare <**stqóye**> *wolf)*, <**tl'áleqtxel**>, //ƛ'ɛ́[=lə=]qt=x^{y}əl//, /'*long legs, long legged*'/ (compare root <**tl'áqt**> *long)*, <**tl'áleqtxel q'ésq'esetsel**> *daddy long legs, harvestman spider, long-legged spider*, <**tl'áleqtxel qwá:l**> *cranefly, leatherjacket, long-legged mosquito*, <**tl'elqtéle**>, //ƛ'ɛ[=lə=]qt=ə́lɛ//, /'*deer*'/, literally /'long ears'/, <**tl'elqtélets**>, //ƛ'ɛ[=lə=]qt=ə́ləc//, /'*pheasant*'/, literally /'long tail'/, <**q'eq'elá:mi**>, //C_1ə=q'[=əl=]ɛ́·mi//, /'*little girls*'/ (compare <**q'áq'emi**> *little girl)*, <**sts'emts'ó:lemeqw**>, //s=C_1əC_2=c'á·[=lə=]m(=)əq^w//, /'*eldest great grandchildren*'/ (compare <**sts'emts'ó:meqw**> *eldest great grandchild*), <**chelíchkelsó:llh**>, //C_1í[=əl=]=cəkəls=á·lɬ//, /'*baby chicks*'/ (*<**chichkelsó:llh**> unattested *baby chick(en):* compare root <**chékels**> *chicken)*, <**hahelá́wt** or **hehelá́wt**>, //C_1ɛ=h[=əl=]ɛ́wt or C_1ə=h[=əl=]ɛ́wt//, /'*a few little rats*'/ (compare <**hiháwt**> *little rat* and root <**há:wt**> *rat)*, <**telíleqsel**>, //C_1í[=əl=]=(ta)l=əqsəl//, /'*baby ducks*'/ (compare <**teléqsel**> *duck, mallard)*.

<**=le** or **=ele**>, da //=lə or =ələ//, SOC /'*lack, need*'/, syntactic analysis: lexical suffix, derivational suffix; found in <**tsqó:le ~ lhqó:le**>, //c=qá·=lə ~ ɬ=qá·=lə//, /'*thirsty*'/ (compare <**ts=**> *have* and <**lh=**> *use a portion of*, root <**qó:**> *water)*, comment: this seems to be the only example of =le, but it is a clear one.

<**lehà:l**>, free root //ləhɛ̀·l//, PLAY /'*play slahal, play the bone-game*'/, the game is a gambling game in which two teams compete at guessing the distribution of four hidden hand-held bones, two marked and two plain; initial guesses can determine who starts by holding and who by guessing; team members sit in a line facing the opposite team, many of the holding team drumming and singing special slahal songs some with spiritual power; two people mix the bones behind their backs then hold one in each hand; one the guess is made the holders slowly bring out their hands and open them palm up to show the bones; the marked bone is called the lady and the plain bone is called the man (or vice versa?);, if the opposite team guesser guesses the correct hand of each bone (he only gets one guess for the set) the bones are passed to the guessers to hold and the guessing is reversed; if only two bones are guessed right, the guessers pay the hiders a tally stick (?but receive two of the bones); if no bones are guessed right the guessers pay the hiders a tally stick; there is also a larger "kick stick" that is held as the final stick; sticks are laid or stuck in the dirt in front of the team that has them; bets are made before each guess by holding up money--if someone catches your eye and holds up the same amount you have bet;, bets can also be made on the final outcome; bone-games can take all night with the bones changing hands many times; psychology, singing, spirit power, intimidation, skill, and rarely cheating when revealing the bones are all attested; nowadays these games are usually held at the

summer canoe-races and big money can change hands;, guessing gestures in the Stó:lō area include tapping one's chest to indicate you are now going to guess, palms down moving one index finger in an arching motion pointing downward (both marked bones on inside hands), palm down pointing at the bones with thumb and index finger extended at right angles (both marked bones on outside hands), right hand held palm facing guesser's left and index finger pointing left (both marked bones on guesser's left), and right hand palm up fingers curled thumb thrusted pointing right (both marked bones on guesser's right), syntactic analysis: intransitive verb, borrowed from Chinook Jargon /lahál/ *hand game, gambling game* < Chinook Proper according to Gibbs 1863 (Johnson 1978:137), attested by Deming, Salish cognate: Sechelt /ləhál/ *slahal game* T77:15, Samish /ləhél'/ *the bone game, slahal game* and /ləhéʔel/ *playing slahal (gambling)* G86:81.

<**slehà:l**>, dnom //s=ləhɛ̀·l//, PLAY /'*the slahal game, the bone-game, (slahal sticks, gambling sticks [BJ])*'/, (<**s=**> *nominalizer*), syntactic analysis: nominal, attested by Deming, other sources: ES /slɛhɛ́·l/ *hand game*, also <**slehá:l**>, //s=ləhɛ́·l//, also /'*gambling sticks, slahal sticks*'/, attested by BJ 12/5/64, also <**slehál**>, //s=ləhɛ́l//, also /'*guessing game (with guessing sticks)*'/, attested by AC.

<**lílehà:l**>, dmv //C_1í=ləhɛ̀·l//, PLAY /'*starting to play slahal, (to gamble [Elders Group 3/15/72])*'/, (<**R4=**> *diminutive*), phonology: reduplication, syntactic analysis: nominal, attested by Deming, Elders Group (3/28/79), also /'*to gamble*'/, attested by Elders Group (3/15/72), Elder's comment: "loons do this underneath", attested by Elders Group (3/28/79), example: <**tsel lílehà:l**>, //c-əl C_1í=ləhɛ̀·l//, /'*I gamble*'/, attested by Elders Group (3/15/72).

<**lekaléstel**>, df //ləkɛlə́stəl//, CH ['*communion*'], borrowed from Chinook Jargon <**la-ka-lis-ti**> *Eucharist* Johnson 1978:312, itself < French <**l'eucharistie**>, syntactic analysis: nominal probably, possibly intransitive verb, attested by Elders Group (6/8/77).

<**lekelít ~ xwleklít**>, HHG ['*lock it with a key*'], *see* leklí ~ lekelí.

<**leklí ~ lekelí**>, free root //ləklí//, HHG ['*key*'], borrowed from Chinook Jargon <**la klee, le klee**> *key* Johnson 1978:351, itself < French <**la clef**> *key*, syntactic analysis: nominal.

<**lekelít ~ xwleklít**>, pcs //ləkəlí=T ~ x^w=ləklí=T//, HHG ['*lock it with a key*'], (<**xw=**> *derivational*), (<**=t**> *purposeful control transitivizer*), syntactic analysis: transitive verb; found in <**lekelíthò:m**>, //ləkəlí=T-à·m//, /'*You are locked in.*'/, syntactic analysis: passive 2s, <**lekelítòlèm**>, //ləkəlí=T-àləm//, /'*You are all locked in [with a key].*'/, syntactic analysis: passive 2p.

<**lekyó:lta**>, free root //lək^yá·ltɛ ~ lik^yá·ltɛ (bound)//, PLAY /'*cards, playing cards (noun), (one person playing cards (solitaire) [EB])*'/, ASM ['types of cards include: tó:ymel *diamond, diamonds*, klép *club, clubs*, spít *spade, spades*, hóts *heart, hearts*, pékcha *face card*'], borrowed from French <**la carte**> or more likely <**les cartes**>, syntactic analysis: nominal, attested by EB, Elders Group, also /'*one person playing cards (solitaire)*'/, syntactic analysis: intransitive verb?, attested by EB, example: <**alétse thel lekyó:lta**>, //ʔɛlə́cɛ k^w=θ-əl lək^yá·ltɛ//, /'*Where's my playing cards?*'/, attested by EB.

<**lilekyó:lta**>, pln //li[=C_1ə=]k^yá·ltɛ//, PLAY ['*a bunch playing cards*'], comment: root *<**likyó:lta**> is possible from French (esp. from <**les cartes**>) , this form is not attested so far by itself as a variant of <**lekyó:lta**> but seems likely since the alternative is to have <**li=**> as <R4=> *plural* when <R4=> is never attested anywhere else as a plural but only as a *diminutive*, phonology: reduplication, syntactic analysis: intransitive verb, attested by EB.

<**lilekó:ltel**>, pcs //li[-C_1ə-]ká·lt(=T)=əl//, /'*playing cards [verb]*'/, syntactic analysis: continuative aspect, reciprocal, attested by Elders Group.

<**lék' or léq'**>, possible bound root //lə́k' or lə́q'// meaning unclear, possibly *proud*, connection with <**léq'**> *level, even, flat* seems unlikely

<**slék'**>, dnom //s=lə́k' or s=lə́q'[=K=]//, EFAM ['*nickname for someone who is proud*'], (<**s=**> *nominalizer*), phonology: could have fronting q' → k' *diminutive*, syntactic analysis: nominal, attested by IHTTC (compare <**swék'**> *show-off, dandy*) or could be clipping of <**slek'iyáp**>, df //s=lək'(=)iy(=)ɛ́p//, EZ ['*coyote*'].

<**lek'iyáp ~ k'iyáp**>, bound stem //(lə)k'(=)iy(=)ɛ́p//, root meaning unclear, first alternate could have root <**léq'**> *level, even, flat,* possibly <**=iy**> *covering, (tree) bark* possibly <**=áp ~ =ep**> *on the rump* ("flat covering on the rump"?) or could be related to or the same root <**lék'** or **léq'**> possibly meaning *proud*

<**slek'iyáp**>, df //s=lək'(=)iy(=)ɛ́p//, EZ ['*coyote*'], ['*Canis latrans lestes*'], ASM ['one can sound like lots; it makes sounds for protection from other animals; it can tl'áwéls (*bark*) and q'áw (howl) like a wolf or a dog can'], (<**s=**> *nominalizer*), possibly <**=iy**> *covering, (tree) bark,* possibly <**=áp ~ =ep**> *on the rump*, syntactic analysis: nominal, attested by TG, AG, PS, JL, probably borrowed from Thompson /snk'y'ép/ *coyote* Thompson and Thompson 1980:58, also <**slek'eyáp**>, //s=lək'əyɛ́p//, attested by ME (11/21/72 tape), AK (11/21/72 tape), AC, DM, also <**snek'iyáp**>, //s=nək'iyɛ́p//, attested by Lawrence James, BJ (5/64, 12/5/64), also <**sk'ek'iyáp**>, //s=C_1ə=k'iy(=)ɛ́p or s=k'ə[=C_1ə=]y(=)ɛ́p//, phonology: reduplication, attested by NP, AG, DF, MP (Cheh.), AC, DM, also <**k'ek'iyáp**>, //C_1ə=k'iy(=)ɛ́p or k'ə[=C_1ə=]y(=)ɛ́p//, phonology: reduplication, attested by HT.

<**lilk'eyáp**>, dmn //C_1í=lək'əy(=)ɛ́p//, EZ ['*little coyote*'], (<**R4=**> *diminutive*), phonology: reduplication, syntactic analysis: nominal, attested by AK (11/21/72 tape).

<**lékw**>, free root //lə́kʷ//, ABDF ['*break (of a stick-like object)*'], EB, HHG, PE, semantic environment ['bone, stick, flora, fauna, pocket knife'], syntactic analysis: intransitive verb, attested by EB, example: <**lékw te léwex̱s.**>, //lə́kʷ tə lə́wəx̣-s//, /'*He broke his rib., His rib broke.*'/, attested by EB, <**me lékw (te hálkw)**>, //mə lə́kʷ (tə hɛ́=lkʷ)//, /'*(The pocket knife) gets broken.*'/, attested by CT.

<**lékwlekw**>, plv //lə́kʷ=C_1əC_2//, ABDF /'*all broken up (of sticks or bones, of the bones of a person who got in an accident)*'/, semantic environment ['sticks, bones, bones of person who got in an accident'], (<**=R2**> *characteristic or iterative*), phonology: reduplication, syntactic analysis: intransitive verb, attested by EB.

<**hálkw**>, rsls or cts //hɛ́=lkʷ//, PE ['*pocket knife*'], (semological comment: lit. "*broken (of stick-like object)*" so called because it *gets broken* to put it in one's pocket), (<**há=**> *resultative; continuative* here used derivationally), syntactic analysis: nominal, attested by CT.

<**lekwát**>, durs //ləkʷ=ə[=Aɛ́=]T//, pcs, MC ['*break s-th (stick-like)*'], EB, (<**á-ablaut**> *durative*), (<**=et**> *purposeful control transitivizer*), phonology: ablaut or stressed transitivizer, syntactic analysis: transitive verb, attested by BJ (5/64).

<**lekwlá:xw**>, ncs //ləkʷ=lə[=Aɛ́·=]xʷ//, ABDF ['*break s-th (stick-like)* (accidentally)'], MC, EB, (<**á:-ablaut**> *durative*), (<**=lexw**> *non-control transitivizer*), phonology: ablaut or stressed transitivizer, syntactic analysis: transitive verb, attested by AC, example: <**tsel lekwlá:xw tel (lheq'láts, sx̱él:e).**>, //c-əl ləkʷ=lɛ́·xʷ tə-l (ɬəq'=lɛ́c, s=x̣ə́l·ə)//, /'*I broke my (hip, foot or leg).*'/, attested by AC.

<**selí:kw**>, strs //s=hə=lə[=Aí·=]kʷ//, ABDF ['*be broken (of stick-like object)*'], MC, EB, (<**s=**> *stative*), (<**he= ~ ha=**> *resultative*), (<**í:-ablaut**> *resultative*), phonology: ablaut, consonant merger (s + h > s), syntactic analysis: intransitive verb, attested by AC, example: <**selí:kw te (t'álōws, sx̱él:es).**>, //s=lə[=Aí·=]kʷ tə (t'ɛ́low-s, s=x̣ə́l·ə-s)//, /'*Her (arm, leg) is broken.*'/, attested by AC.

<**lekwátses**>, durs //ləkʷ=ə[=Aɛ́=]cəs//, ABDF /'*she broke her hand, he broke his hand*'/, literally /'a bone got broken on the hand'/, (<**á-ablaut**> *durative*), lx <**=etses**> *on the hand*, phonology: ablaut,

syntactic analysis: intransitive verb, attested by AC.

<**selkwá:tses**>, rsls //s=hɛ=lkʷ=ə[=Aɛ́·=]cəs//, durs, ABDF /*'her hand is broken, his hand is broken'*/, (<**s=**> *stative*), (<**he=** ~ **ha=**> *resultative*), (<**á:-ablaut**> *durative*), phonology: ablaut, syntactic analysis: intransitive verb, attested by AC.

<**lekwátssá:ls**>, sas //ləkʷ=ə[=Aá=]cəs=ɛ́·ls//, HARV [*'break off branches of berries'*], ASM ['in the past this was often done to take as a treat to elders that couldn't travel to the berrying ground; some people harvest certain berries this way'], lx <**=etses**> *on the hand, on the bough of a tree*, (<**=á:ls**> *as a structured activity*), phonology: ablaut, syntactic analysis: intransitive verb, attested by Elders Group.

<**lekweláx̱el**>, ds //ləkʷ=əlɛ́x̣əl//, ABDF [*'break an arm'*], lx <**=eláx̱el**> *on the arm*, syntactic analysis: intransitive verb, attested by EB.

<**lekwépsem**>, ds //ləkʷ=ə́psəm//, ABDF [*'break one's neck'*], lx <**=épsem**> *on the neck*, syntactic analysis: intransitive verb, attested by EB.

<**lekwewíts**>, ds //ləkʷ=əwíc//, ABDF /*'break one's spine, break one's back, have a humpback/hunchback'*/, lx <**=ewíts**> *on the back*, syntactic analysis: intransitive verb, attested by EB.

<**slékwlets** ~ **slékwelets**>, stvi //s=lə[=´=]kʷ=ələc//, ABDF /*'be lame (esp. if deformed), be a cripple, to limp, have a limp'*/, (<**s=**> *stative*), (<=´=> *derivational*), lx <**=elets**> *on the rump, on the hip, on the bottom*, phonology: stress-shift, syntactic analysis: intransitive verb, attested by EB, BJ (5/64, 12/5/64), AC, example: <**tsel slékwlets.**>, //c-əl s=lə́kʷ=ləc//, /*'I limp.'*/, <**slékwlets tel siyáye.**>, //s=lə́kʷ=ləc tə-l si=yɛ́yə//, /*'My friend limps.'*/, attested by EB.

<**hálkweletsem**>, cts //hɛ́-lkʷ=ələc=əm//, ABDF [*'limp in the hip'*], literally /'breaking in one's hip/rump'/, (<**há-**> *continuative*), lx <**=elets**> *on the rump, on the bottom, on the hip*, (<**=em**> *middle voice*), syntactic analysis: intransitive verb, attested by Deming.

<**lekwxá:l** ~ **lekwxál**>, durs //ləkʷ=xʸə[=Aɛ́(·)=]l//, ABDF /*'break a leg, (have/get) a broken leg'*/, lx <**=xel**> *on the leg, on the foot*, (<**á(:)-ablaut**> *durative*), phonology: ablaut, syntactic analysis: intransitive verb, attested by AC, also <**lekwxà:l**>, //ləkʷ=xʸə[=A`·=]l//, attested by EB, example: <**xwómxelem qetl'osésu lhekw'xel qetl'osésu (wets'étl', tsélq) qetl'osésu lekwxál.**>, //xʷə[=Aá=]m=xʸəl=əm qə=ƛ'a=s-əs-əw ɬə́k'ʷ=xʸəl qə=ƛ'a=s-əs-əw (wə=c'ə́ƛ', cə́l=q) qə=ƛ'a=s-əs-əw ləkʷ=xʸə[=Aɛ́=]l//, /*'He was running and he tripped and fell and broke his leg.'*/, attested by AC.

<**lekwát**>, MC [*'break s-th (stick-like)'*], *see* lékw.

<**lekwátses**>, ABDF /*'she broke her hand, he broke his hand'*/, *see* lékw.

<**lekwátssá:ls**>, HARV [*'break off branches of berries'*], *see* lékw.

<**lekweláx̱el**>, ABDF [*'break an arm'*], *see* lékw.

<**lekwépsem**>, ABDF [*'break one's neck'*], *see* lékw.

<**lekwewíts**>, ABDF /*'break one's spine, break one's back, have a humpback/hunchback'*/, *see* lékw.

<**lekwlá:xw**>, ABDF [*'break s-th (stick-like) (accidentally)'*], *see* lékw.

<**lékwlekw**>, ABDF /*'all broken up (of sticks or bones, of the bones of a person who got in an accident)'*/, *see* lékw.

<**lekwxá:l** ~ **lekwxál**>, ABDF /*'break a leg, (have/get) a broken leg'*/, *see* lékw.

<**leléts'** ~ **laléts'**>, df //lələ́c' ~ lɛlə́c'//, ANA /*'gall-bladder, gall, bile, have bile trouble, be jaundiced,*

bilious'/, syntactic analysis: nominal, intransitive verb, attested by AC, contrast <**mésel**> *animal and bird gall-bladder* or poss. *fish gall-bladder* and <**méleqw**> *fish gall-bladder, fish heart.*

<**lelts'ó:méx**>, DESC ['*look different*'], *see* láts'.

<**lemá:t**>, ABFC ['*kick s-th/s-o*'], *see* lemá'.

<**lemá'**>, bound root //ləmɛ́ʔ *kick*//.

<**lema'à:ls**>, sas //ləmɛʔ=ɛ̀·ls//, ABFC ['*kick*'], (<**=á:ls**> *structured activity*), phonology: downstepping, syntactic analysis: intransitive verb, attested by IHTTC.

<**hálma'à:ls**>, cts //hɛ́-ləmɛʔ=ɛ̀·ls//, ABFC ['*kicking*'], (<**há-**> *continuative*), phonology: downstepping, vowel-loss, syntactic analysis: intransitive verb, attested by IHTTC.

<**lemá:t**>, pcs //ləmɛ́·=T//, ABFC ['*kick s-th/s-o*'], (<**=t**> *purposeful control transitivizer*), phonology: unusually good example of glottal stop becoming length before consonant (' → : or /ʔ/ → /·/ before consonant), syntactic analysis: transitive verb, attested by JL and RG & EH (4/9/99 Ling332), example: <**le lémates**>, //lə lə́mɛ=T-əs//, /'*He kicked sombody.*'/, phonology: irregular stress-shift, attested by JL.

<**lemlemá:t**>, its //$C_1əC_2$=ləmɛ́·=T//, ABFC ['*kick s-th around*'], (<**R3=**> *iterative*), phonology: reduplication, syntactic analysis: transitive verb, attested by EB, example: <**lemlemá:tes te qwlhí:xels.**>, //$C_1əC_2$=ləmɛ́·=T-əs tə qʷɬ=í·=xʸəl-s//, /'*He kicked his shoes around.*'/, attested by EB.

<**lamá'íwét**>, pcs //lɛmɛ́ʔ=íwə(l)=T//, ABFC /'*kick s-o in the behind, kick s-o in the rump*'/, lx <**=íwel**> *in the insides, in the rectum, in the rump*, (<**=t**> *purposeful control transitivizer*), phonology: consonant-loss (of l before =t), syntactic analysis: transitive verb, attested by JL.

<**lemóthet**>, pcrs //lɛ́=m[=M2]Aá=T-ət or ləmɛ́ʔAá=T-ət//, IDOC ['*jump up and down (of Indian doctor training)*'], probably root <**lemá'**> *kick* with <**ó-ablaut**> automatic on root before <**=thet**>, (or possibly <**lá:m**> (root in *shaman* and in *shaman's spirit power*, meaning uncertain but may be *go* [since Indian doctors travel to the spirit world], with <**metathesis type 2**> and then <**ó-ablaut**> automatic on root before <**=thet**>, <**=th-et**> *purposeful control transitivizer* with *reflexive*), phonology: possible ablaut, syntactic analysis: intransitive verb, attested by IHTTC.

<**hélmethet**>, cts //hə́-ləmɛ=T-ət//, IDOC ['*jumping up and down or bouncing up and down (of an Indian doctor training)*'], (<**hé-**> *continuative* before resonants (l, m, w, y)), syntactic analysis: intransitive verb, attested by IHTTC.

<**shxwlemóthetále**>, dnom //sxʷ=ləmɛ=Aá=T-ət=ɛ́lə//, IDOC ['*place of training to become an Indian doctor (pit made from repeated jumping every year on the same spot)*'], (<**shxw=**> *nominalizer*), lx <**=ále**> *container of*, phonology: ablaut, syntactic analysis: nominal, attested by IHTTC.

<**lema'à:ls**>, ABFC ['*kick*'], *see* lemá'.

<**lémet**>, pcs //lə́m=əT//, MC ['*fold s-th (once)*'], (<**=et**> *purposeful control transitivizer*), syntactic analysis: transitive verb, attested by EB, Elders Group.

<**lemlémet**>, plv //$C_1əC_2$-lə́m=əT//, MC /'*folding lots of things, fold s-th several times or many times*'/, (<**R3-**> *plural action, plural objects*), phonology: reduplication, syntactic analysis: transitive verb, attested by EB, Elders Group, example: <**lemlémetchxw mékw' yel á:wkw'.**>, //$C_1əC_2$-lə́m=əT-c-xʷ mə́k'ʷ yə-l ʔɛ́·wk'ʷ//, /'*Fold all my clothes.*'/, literally ["you fold lots of things all the (plural human?) belongings"], attested by Elders Group, <**lemlémetchxw mékw' ye tskwí:m l á:wkw'.**>, //$C_1əC_2$-lə́m=əT-c-xʷ mə́k'ʷ yə c=kʷí·m l ʔɛ́·wk'ʷ//, /'*Fold all my red clothes.*'/, literally ["you fold lots of things all the (plural human?) red my belongings"], attested by Elders Group,

<**lemlémetchxw mékw' tel th'x̱welwétem.**>, //C_1əC_2-lə́m=əT-c-x^w mə́k'^{w} tə-l θ'x̣^{w}=ə́lwət=əm//, /'*Fold all my laundry.*'/, literally ["you fold (mild imperative) all that (is) my wash one's clothes"], attested by EB.

<**Lém:i ~ Lexwlém:i**>, ds //lə́m·i ~ ləx^w=lə́m·i//, PLN ['*Lummi Reserve*'], HUMC /'*Lummi (person, people)*'/, lx <**lexw=**> *always (*or esp. in placenames outside Stó:lō territory: *place of),* lx if not borrowed from Lummi dialect of N. Straits, syntactic analysis: nominal, attested by Elders Group, Salish cognate: Lummi dial. of N. Straits /nəx^w=lə́m=i/ *Lummi people* from /x^w=lóləm=əs ~ nəx^w=lóləm=əs/ *name of a village crowded with houses,* said to mean lit. *they faced each other, to be at right angles* referring to the crowded houses CDB78:63; poss. Salish cognates in Nooksack or Musqueam /nəx^w= ~ x^w=/ *always,* /lǽləm/ *house,* /=iy/ *place.*

<**lemlemá:t**>, ABFC ['*kick s-th around*'], *see* lemá'.

<**lemlémet**>, MC /'*folding lots of things, fold s-th several times or many times*'/, *see* lémet.

<**lemóthet**>, IDOC ['*jump up and down (of Indian doctor training)*'], *see* lá:m & lemá'.

<**lép**>, free root //lə́p//, SOC /'*learn a lesson, give up*'/, syntactic analysis: intransitive verb, attested by BHTTC, example: <**skw'áy kws léps**>, //s=k'^{w}ɛ́y k^w-s lə́p-s//, /'*He never learns his lesson.*'/, attested by BHTTC.

<**lepét**>, pcs //ləp=ə́T//, SOC /'*beat up s-o as a lesson till he learns or gives up, teach s-o a lesson*'/, (<**=ét**> *purposeful control transitivizer*), phonology: weak-stress-valenced root and stressed transitivizer or stress-ambivalent suffix, syntactic analysis: transitive verb, attested by BHTTC.

<**lepál**>, free root //ləpɛ́l//, TOOL ['*shovel*'], HHG, syntactic analysis: nominal, attested by IHTTC, EB, Elders Group, borrowed from Chinook Jargon <**lapelle**> *spade,* itself from French <**la pelle**> *shovel, scoop,* contrast <**shxwoweth'ílep**> *shovel* (lit. ["*s-th for prying the dirt*"]), also <**lepà:l**>, //ləpɛ̀·l//, attested by BHTTC, example: <**sle'ó:lwelhs te kyó te lepál.**>, //s=ləʔɛ́=Aá=əlwəɬ-s tə k^{y}á tə ləpɛ́l//, /'*The shovel is on the other side of the car.*'/, attested by EB, <**kwútes te lepál tl'esu kw'oqwethóxes.**>, //k^{w}ú=T-əs tə ləpɛ́l ƛ'ə=s=u k'^{w}aq^w=əT-áx^y-əs//, /'*He took the shovel and hit me. (take s-th)*'/, attested by Elders Group, <**kw'oqwethóxes te lepà:l.**>, //k'^{w}aq^w=əT-áx^y-əs tə ləpɛ̀·l//, /'*He hit me with a shovel.*'/, syntactic comment: oblique simple nominal phrase with no oblique case /ʔə/, attested by BHTTC.

<**lepét**>, SOC /'*beat up s-o as a lesson till he learns or gives up, teach s-o a lesson*'/, *see* lép.

<**lépets**>, free root //lə́pəc//, TVMO ['*send*'], SOC, syntactic analysis: intransitive verb, attested by AC, EB, IHTTC, example: <**tsel lépets**>, //c-əl lə́pəc//, /'*I sent*'/.

<**slépets**>, dnom //s=lə́pəc//, TVMO ['*something sent*'], SOC, (<**s=**> *nominalizer*), syntactic analysis: nominal, attested by EB, example: <**tl'émes slépets.**>, //ƛ'ə́=m-əs s=lə́pəc//, /'*This is what he sent.*'/, attested by EB.

<**lépetst**>, pcs //lə́pəc=T//, TVMO ['*send s-th*'], SOC, */'send s-o'/ rejected, (<**=t**> *purposeful control transitivizer*), syntactic analysis: transitive verb, attested by EB, AD, AC, example: <**tsel lépetst tha tá:l te sthóqwi.**>, //c-əl lə́pəc=T θ-ɛ tɛ́·l tə s=θáq^{w}i//, /'*I sent your mother the salmon.*'/, attested by AC.

<**lépetsel**>, incs //lə́pəc=əl//, TVMO /'*to ride [along], hook a ride, get a ride, send oneself*'/, (<**=el ~ =íl**> *come, go, get, become*), syntactic analysis: intransitive verb, attested by IHTTC, AC, example: <**tsel lépetsel.**>, //c-əl lə́pəc=əl//, /'*I sent myself., I hooked a ride.*'/, attested by AC, <**latsel lépetsel.**>, //lɛ-c-əl lə́pəc=əl//, /'*(I'm going to get a ride.)*'/, attested by AC.

<**hálpetsel**>, cts //hɛ́-ləpəc=əl//, TVMO /'*riding with someone, (riding along)*'/, (<**há-**>

continuative), phonology: vowel-loss of weak-valence root, syntactic analysis: intransitive verb, attested by IHTTC.

<**lépetsel**>, TVMO /'*to ride [along], hook a ride, get a ride, send oneself*'/, *see* lépets.

<**lépetst**>, TVMO ['*send s-th*'], *see* lépets.

<**leplít**>, free root //ləplít//, CH /'*priest, minister*'/, SOCT, attested by AH, Elders Group, borrowed from Chinook Jargon <**le plate ~ le prate**> *priest* Johnson 1978:391 itself from French <**le prêtre**> *priest*, example: <**shíka leplít**>, //šíkɛ ləplít//, /'*Shaker minister*'/, attested by AH, <**leplít te Bill.**>, //ləplít tə Bill//, /'*Bill is a priest.*'/, syntactic comment: nominal as existential verb in sentence-initial position, attested by Elders Group.

<**lepílítòs**>, free root //ləpílítàs//, CH ['*punish*'], syntactic analysis: intransitive verb, attested by Elders Group (4/28/76), borrowed from French <**la pénitence**>/lapenitã́s/ *penitence, repentence; penance* (perhaps not through Chinook Jargon as it is not listed in Johnson 1978 a compilation of all known Chinook Jargon dictionaries.

<**lepót**>, free root //ləpát//, HHG ['*cup*'], syntactic analysis: nominal, attested by AC, AD, others, borrowed from Chinook Jargon <**le pot**> *pot* itself from French Canadian <**le pot**>(/lə pát/) Johnson 1978:389, example: <**lí te shxwlathílé te lepót.**>, //lí tə sxʷ=lá[=Aɛ=]θəl=ɛ̀lə́ tə ləpát//, /'*The cup is in the cupboard.*'/, phonology: ablaut, consonant-loss (el before =V́1... suffix), =álé → =ílé unexplained, attested by AD.

<**lép'ex**>, pcis //lə́p'=əxʸ//, ABFC ['*eat s-th (short of a social meal)*'], FOOD, ASM ['animals only eat this way, people can eat this way too'], (<**=ex**> *purposeful control inanimate object preferred*), syntactic analysis: transitive verb, attested by Elders Group, AC, Deming, SJ, MV, example: <**líchxw lép'ex te tl'álhem?**>, //lí-c-xʷ lə́p'=əxʸ tə ƛ'ɛ́ɬəm//, /'*Did you eat the salt?*'/, attested by AC, <**ts'áts'el tsqwá:y, (xw)ewás lép'ex.**>, //c'ɛ́[=C₁ə=]l c=qʷɛ́·y, (xʷ=əwə=ɛ́-s or) ʔəwə-əs lə́p'=əxʸ//, /'*It's very green, one doesn't eat it (yet).*'/, attested by Deming, SJ esp., <**le lép'exes te spáth tel qwe'óp.**>, //lə lə́p'=əxʸ-əs tə s=pɛ́θ tə-l qʷəʔáp//, /'*The bear ate my apple.*'/, attested by AC, <**mekw'ewát lép'exes te xeytl'áls.**>, //mək'ʷ=əwɛ́t lə́p'=əxʸ-əs tə x̣iƛ'ɛ́ls//, /'*The grizzly ate everybody.*'/, attested by Elders Group, <**"ítetlha, uwlh emí the Th'ő:wxeya, lep'exómecha."**>, //ʔítət-ɬɛ, ʔuwɬ ʔəmí θə θ'ó·wx̣=iyɛ, ləp'=əxʸ-ámə-cɛ//, /'*"Sleep or the Th'ő:wxeya (Cannibal Ogress) will come eat you."*'/, attested by Deming (SJ or MV), MV's grandmother said this to her.

<**hálp'ex**>, cts //hɛ́-lp'=əxʸ//, ABFC ['*eating s-th (short of a meal)*'], (<**há-**> *continuative*), syntactic analysis: intransitive verb, attested by AC, NP, Elders Group (3/72), example: <**líchxw hálp'ex te tl'álhem?**>, //lí-c-xʷ hɛ́-lp'=əxʸ təƛ'ɛ́ɬəm//, /'*Are you eating salt?*'/, attested by AC, <**tsel éystexw kw'els le hálp'ex.**>, //c-əl ʔɛ́y=sT-əxʷ k'ʷə-l-s lə hɛ́-lp'=əxʸ//, /'*I like eating it.*'/, attested by NP, <**lulh hálp'exes tloqá:ys.**>, //lə=uɬ hɛ́-lp'=əxʸ-əs tla=qɛ́·ys//, /'*He's eating it now.*'/, attested by Elders Group (3/72), <**xexekw'íwelchapcha hálp'exexw te elíle.**>, //x̣ɛ[=C₁ə=]k'ʷ=íwəl-c-ɛp-cɛ hɛ́-lp'=əxʸ-əxʷ tə ʔəlílə//, /'*You'll get constipated if you eat salmonberries.*'/, literally /'you'll be getting constipated if you're eating salmonberries'/, syntactic comment: subjunctive subject pronoun, usage: words to a berry-picking song, attested by EF.

<**leqàlèm**>, ABFC /'*dive (already in water), go underwater, sink oneself down*'/, *see* léqem.

<**léqem**>, mdls //lə́q=əm//, ABFC /'*dive, dive in*'/, (<**=em**> *middle voice*), syntactic analysis: intransitive verb, attested by EB, Elders Group (3/72), AC, also <**léq:em**>, //lə́q·=əm//, attested by AC, example: <**àtsel léqem.**>, //ʔɛ-c-əl lə́q=əm//, /'*I dove in.*'/, syntactic analysis: auxiliary past, attested by AC, <**lewéslha léq:em.**>, //ləwə-´s-ɬɛ lə́q·=əm//, /'*YOU dive in.*'/, literally /'let it be you to dive in'/, phonology: stress-shift on inflected independent verbal pronoun, syntactic comment: independent

verbal pronoun with 3rd person subject and imperative, attested by AC.

<**leqàlèm**>, incs //ləq=i[=Aɛ́=]l=əm//, durs, [ləqǽlə̀m], ABFC /'*dive (already in water), go underwater, sink oneself down*'/, (<**à-ablaut on suffix**> *durative*), probably <**=í:l ~ =íl ~ =el**> *go, come, get, become*, (<**=em**> *middle voice*), phonology: updrifting on final syllable, syntactic analysis: intransitive verb, attested by EB, also <**leqà:lèm**>, //ləq=i[=Aɛ̀·=]l=əm//, also /'*dive*'/, attested by AC.

<**hálqem**>, cts //hɛ́-lq=əm//, ABFC ['*diving*'], (<**há-**> *continuative*), phonology: vowel-loss due to stress shift from strong-valenced prefix, syntactic analysis: intransitive verb, attested by Elders Group (3/72).

<**hálqem**>, dnom //hɛ́=lq=əm//, SOCT ['*a diver*'], FSH, ASM ['in the old days a man would dive to fix méthelh (dogbane) nets when people were fishing for sturgeon'], possibly <**zero-derivation**> *nominalizer* or perhaps the form is merely the continuative as above but nominalized (actually relativized) by following a demonstrative article, i.e. <**te hálqem**> *the one who is diving*, syntactic analysis: nominal? or intransitive verb, attested by IHTTC.

<**leqléqem**>, chrs //C_1əC_2=lə́q=əm//, SOCT ['*a diver*'], (<**R3=**> *characteristic, occupational*), phonology: reduplication, syntactic analysis: nominal by zero-derivation?, attested by Elders Group (3/72).

<**láqleqem**>, dnom //lə[=Aɛ́=]q=ləq=əm//, EZ /'*goldeneye duck* (probably both the *common goldeneye duck* and the *Barrow goldeneye duck), (a kind of diving duck* [Elders Group] *)*'/, ['probably *Bucephala clangula and Bucephala islandica*'], (<**á-ablaut**> *derivational*), phonology: ablaut, reduplication, syntactic analysis: nominal, attested by EL, also /'*a kind of diving duck*'/, attested by Elders Group (2/11/76).

<**Leqémél**>, PLN ['*Harrison Bay*'], *see* qém:el.

<**leqléqem**>, SOCT ['*a diver*'], *see* léqem.

<**léq'**>, free root //lə́q'//, DESC ['*level*'], syntactic analysis: adjective/adjectival verb, attested by SP, AD, Elders Group, DESC /'*level, flat*'/, attested by SP, AD, example: <**léq' te sqwálewel**>, //lə́q' tə s=qʷɛ́l=əwəl//, /'*think alike*'/, (morphosememic development: literally /'thoughts/feelings are level/even'/, an orientational metaphor), EFAM, attested by Elders Group.

<**leq'éylep ~ leq'ílep**>, ds //ləq'=íləp//, LAND /'*level ground, flat (of ground)*'/, lx <**=ílep**> *ground, earth*, phonology: <**éy**> [é] expresses the allophone of /i/ after /q'/, syntactic analysis: adjective/adjectival verb?, nominal?, attested by CT, EB, also <**leq'éylép**>, //ləq'=ílə́p//, [ləq'élə́p], attested by Elders Group (3/15/72).

<**slíq'**>, strs //s=lə[=Aí=]q'//, DESC ['*to be even*'], semantic environment ['in a race, of a group of things in size, of two glasses of liquid, etc.'], (<**s=**> *stative*), (<í-ablaut > perhaps *resultative*), phonology: ablaut, syntactic analysis: adjective/adjectival verb, attested by Elders Group, comment: the case for resultative is not strong semantically here but phonologically í-ablaut and á-ablaut on roots with an e-vowel (root /ə/ → /í/ or /ɛ́/), esp. in statives are common and called resultives in Saanich as well (Montler 1986:131-132),

<**leq'éltsest**>, df //ləq'ə́l=cəs=T//, pcs, SOC ['*turn the tables on s-o*'], literally /'get even in the hand purposely with someone'/ (orientational metaphor), lx <**=tses**> *in the hand*, (<**=el**> *come, go, get, become*, <**=t**> *purposeful control transitivizer*), phonology: irregular stress-shift or avoidance of usual stressed allomorph (=íl) of =el, syntactic analysis: transitive verb, attested by Elders Group.

<**leq'á:lh**>, df //ləq'=ɛ́·ɬ//, DESC ['*be in the way*'], DIR, semantic environment ['of a tree fallen, a person, etc.'], VALJ ['*right (correct)*'])(orientational metaphor), lx <**=á:lh**> gloss uncertain,

perhaps related to <**=elh**> *aocording to, in the manner of*, comment: the suffix may be cognate with durative in Northern Straits, syntactic analysis: adjective/adjectival verb, attested by AC, Deming, Salish cognate: Lushootseed /ləq'áɬ-/ as in /ʔu=ləq'áɬ=il čəd/ *I'm correct.* and /ʔəs=ləq'áɬ=il=bi-c/ *You are in my way.* Hess 1976:274, also <**leq'álh**>, //ləq'=ɛ́ɬ//, attested by EB, example: <**xwe leq'á:lh**>, //xʷə ləq'=ɛ́·ɬ//, /'*get in the way*'/, attested by AC, <**tsel xwe leq'á:lh kwses lhékw'xel qetl'osesu kw'eqwlóxes.**>, //c-əl xʷə ləq'=ɛ́·ɬ kʷ-s-əs ɬə́k'ʷ=xʸəl qə=ƛ'a-s-əs-u k'ʷəqʷ=l-áxʸ-əs//, /'*I got in the way and he tripped and he hit me unintentionally.*'/, attested by AC, ASM ['right (correct)'], <**welí'àl leq'á:lh**>, //wə-lí-ʔɛ̀l ləq'=ɛ́·ɬ//, /'*if I am right*'/, literally /'if I am in the way'/, attested by AC.

<**leq'áleq'el (~ leq'áleqel (rare))**>, df //ləq'ɛ́ləq'əl (~ ləq'ɛ́ləqəl (rare))//, TVMO /'*travel (to a destination), be on a journey*'/, probably root <**léq'**> *level, flat* + <**=á:leq ~ =eleq**> *waves* + <**=el**> *come, go, get* (thus lit. "come/go on flat waves"), or less likely <**le-**> *always* + <**q'ó:l**> *return* + <**=R2**> *characteristic or iterative*?, phonology: reduplication, phonology: plain q may be in error but more likely some pronunciations kept it and others assimilated the glottalization from the root, syntactic analysis: intransitive verb, attested by AC, EB, also <leq'á:lqel> //ləq'ɛ́[-·-]lqəl//, /'*to travel*'/, morphological comment: note that the aspect is reversed from that of the other speakers, attested by RG & EH (4/10/99 Ling332) and <letsel leq'áléqel>, ////, /'I'm going travelling.'/, morphological comment: note that the aspect is reversed from that of the other speakers, attested by RG & EH (4/10/99 Ling332), example: <**skw'áy kws las leq'áleqel.**>, //s=k'ʷɛ́y kʷ-s lɛ-s ləq'ɛ́ləqəl//, /'*He can't travel.*'/, attested by AC, <**ōwe lámes híth kws las leq'áléq'el**>, //ʔówə lɛ́=m-əs híθ kʷ-s lɛ-s ləq'ɛ́lə́qəl//, /'*He's not going to be long on his travels.*'/, attested by EB, <**ílhtsel leq'áleq'el.**>, //ʔí-ɬ-c-əl ləq'ɛ́ləq'əl//, /'*I was on a journey.*'/, attested by AC, <**skw'áy kws las leq'áleqel; sí:simetes te sqwétxem.**>, //s=k'ʷɛ́y kʷ-s lɛ-s ləq'ɛ́ləqəl; sí·=C_1əC_2=məT-əs tə s=qʷət=xʸə=m//, /'*He can't travel; he's afraid of the fog.*'/, attested by AC, <**éy ta' sleq'áleq'el.**>, //ʔɛ́y t-ɛʔ s-ləq'ɛ́ləq'əl//, /'*May your travelling be good.*'/, syntactic comment: imperative 3rd person, attested by EB.

<**leq'á:l(e)q'el ~ leq'á:lqel**>, cts //ləq'ɛ́[-·-]ləq'əl ~ ləq'ɛ́[-·-]lqəl//, TVMO /'*travelling (without a destination), going out*'/, (<-:-> *continuative*), syntactic analysis: intransitive verb, attested by AC, EB, also <leq'á:lqel> //ləq'ɛ́[-·-]lqəl//, /'*to travel*'/, morphological comment: note that the aspect is reversed from that of the other speakers, attested by RG & EH (4/10/99 Ling332) and <letsel leq'áléqel>, ////, /'I'm going travelling.'/, morphological comment: note that the aspect is reversed from that of the other speakers, attested by RG & EH (4/10/99 Ling332), example: <**í:lhtsel la leq'álq'el.**>, //ʔí·-ɬ-c-əl lɛ ləq'ɛ́lq'əl//, /'*I went travelling.*'/, attested by AC, <**í:lhtsel leq'á:leq'el.**>, //ʔí·-ɬ-c-əl ləq'ɛ́[-·-]ləq'əl//, /'*I've been travelling.*'/, attested by AC, <**lámtsel leq'á:leq'el.**>, //lɛ́=m-c-əl ləq'ɛ́[-·-]ləq'əl//, /'*I'm going out., I'm going travelling (as you're leaving).*'/, attested by AC, <**látsel leq'á:leq'el.**>, //lɛ́-c-əl ləq'ɛ́[-·-]ləq'əl//, /'*I'm going (in future) travelling.*'/, attested by AC, <**latsel leq'á:leq'el way:eles.**>, //lɛ-c-əl ləq'ɛ́[-·-]ləq'əl wɛ̀y·ə̀l=ə̀s//, /'*I'm going travelling tomorrow.*'/, attested by AC.

<**lá:leqel**>, plv //lɛ́·[-lə-]q=əl//, cts, TVMO ['*lots of people visiting (one another)*'], (<**-le-**> *plural*), possibly <-:-> *continuative*, syntactic analysis: intransitive verb, attested by Elders Group.

<**leq'á:l(e)q'el ~ leq'á:lqel**>, TVMO /'*travelling (without a destination), going out*'/, *see* leq'áleq'el (~ leq'áleqel (rare)).

<**leq'á:lh**>, DESC ['*be in the way*'], *see* léq'.

<**Leq'á:mél**>, df //ləq'=ɛ́·məl or lɛ́q'=ə[=M2=]m=əl//, PLN /'*Nicomen Island (in the Fraser River near Deroche),* also *a specific place on northeast end of Nicomen Island where lots of people used to*

gather [now Sumas Indian Reserve #10]'/, possibly root <**léq'**> *level, flat,* probably <**=á:mél ~ =emél**> *part, portion (of body esp.),* possibly <**metathesis**> *derivational,* possibly <**=el**> *go, come,* syntactic analysis: nominal, attested by Elders Group, (semological comment: the first root and suffix would have a literal meaning like "level/flat part/portion", source: place names reference file #67 and #114, Salish cognate: Northern Straits /ləq'^{w}ə́ŋən/ *Songhees, a Songish village in what is now Victoria, B.C.* BG83-84 Samish and Saanich field notes, also <**Leq'ámel**>, //ləq'=ɛ́mə́l//, attested by EB.

<**Halq'eméylem**>, ds //hɛ́=lq'=ɛm(əl)=í·l=əm//, LANG /'*Halkomelem language, to speak Halkomelem*'/, SOC, literally /'going to Nicomen Island, getting to Nicomen Island, (possibly) going to the visiting (place), or going to the level place'/, (<**há=**> *continuative* before resonants (rarely *plural*)), (<**=í:l ~ =el ~ (rarely) =éyl**> *come, go, get, become,*), possibly <**=em**> *middle voice* or possibly <**=em**> *intransitivizer,* phonology: loss of el before =í:l, syntactic analysis: intransitive verb, nominal, attested by AC, Deming, TM, EB, LG, Salish cognate: Northern Straits /ləq'^{w}əŋ=ín=əŋ/ *the Northern Straits language* from /ləq'^{w}ə́ŋən/ *Songhees, a Songish village in Victoria* BG83-84 Samish and Saanich field notes, ASM ['Halkomelem language'], example: <**lichxw qwóqwel te Halq'eméylem.**>, //li-c-x^{w} q^{w}ɛ[-AáC$_1$ə-]l tə hɛ=lq'=əm=í·l=əm//, /'*Are you (speaking Halkomelem?, Do you speak Halkomelem?*'/, attested by Deming, <**toteló:mettsel te Halq'eméylem.**>, //ta[-C$_1$ə-]l=l-á·mət-c-əl tə hɛ=lq'=əm=í·l=əm//, /'*I understand Halkomelem.*'/, attested by Deming, <**lichexw toteló:met te Halq'eméylem?**>, //li-c-əx^{w} ta[-C$_1$ə-]l=l-á·mət tə hɛ=lq'=əm=í·l=əm//, /'*Do you understand Halkomelem?*'/, attested by Deming, <**éystexwtsel te Halq'eméylem sqwéltel.**>, //ʔɛ́y=sT-əx^{w}-c-əl tə hɛ=lq'=əm=í·l=əm s=q^{w}ɛ[=Aə́=]l=təl//, /'*I like the Halkomelem language.*'/, attested by AC, <**étsel tótí:lt te Halq'eméylem sqwàl tl'olsu xa̲x̲é:ylt.**>, //ʔə́-c-əl ta[-C$_1$ə-]l=í·l=T tə hɛ=lq'=əm=í·l=əm s=q^{w}ɛ̀·l ƛ'a-l-s-u C$_1$ɛ-x̣í·l=T//, /'*I'm learning the Halkomelem language/speech and I'm writing it.*'/, attested by AC, ASM ['to speak Halkomelem'], <**stsewót kw'es halq'eméylems.**>, //s=cəwát k'^{w}ə-s hɛ=lq'=əm=í·l=əm-s//, /'*He/She knows Halkomelem.*'/, literally /'he/she/they know how to that he/she/they talk Halkomelem (or that-nominalizer speak Halkomelem -his/her/their)'/, attested by AC, <**olsu halq'eméylem; tl'olsu thet "hoy siyáye."**>, //ʔa-l-s-u hɛ=lq'=əm=í·l=əm ƛ'a-l-s-u θə́t "hay si=yɛ́yɛ"//, /'*So I spoke Halkomelem; and so I said, "Hi friends."*'/, attested by AC, <**lichxw halq'eméylem?**>, //li-c-x^{w} hɛ=lq'=əm=í·l=əm//, /'*Do you speak Halkomelem?*'/, attested by LG (in Deming Elders Group), <**halq'eméylemtsel.**>, //hɛ=lq'=əm=í·l=əm-c-əl//, /'*I speak Halkomelem.*'/, attested by Deming, TM, EB, also <**tsel halq'eméylem.**>, //c-əl hɛ=lq'=əm=í·l=əm//, attested by TM, EB, *<**tsel qwà:l te Halq'eméylem.**> rejected by TM, EB, <**ő̌wetsel welol ol éy kw'els halq'eméylem.**>, //ʔówə-c-əl wəl-a-l ʔal ʔɛ́y k'^{w}ə-l-s hɛ=lq'=əm=í·l=əm//, /'*I'm not very good at speaking Halkomelem.*'/, attested by Deming.

<**leq'éltsest**>, SOC ['*turn the tables on s-o*'], *see* léq'.

<**leq'éylep ~ leq'ílep**>, LAND /'*level ground, flat (of ground)*'/, *see* léq'.

<**léqw**>, possibly root //lə́q^{w}// or perhaps //li[=Aə=]q^{w}//, ABFC ['*fall asleep*'], possibly <**é-ablaut**> *derivational or resultative* applied to root <**liqw**> //líq^{w}// *slacken,* phonology: possible ablaut, syntactic analysis: intransitive verb, attested by BHTTC, example: <**lí léqw?**>, //lí lə́q^{w}//, /'*Did he fall asleep?*'/, attested by BHTTC.

<**léqwem**>, mdls //lə́q^{w}=əm//, WETH ['*getting warmer*'], TCH, (<**=em**> *middle voice* or perhaps <**=em**> *intransitivizer, verbalizer*), syntactic analysis: intransitive verb, attested by Elders Group, Salish cognate: Squamish /nə́q^{w}-n/ *warm near fire* and /nəq^{w}-šn-ámʔ/ *warm one's feet* W73:281, K69:65, example: <**léqwem te swayel.**>, //lə́q^{w}=əm tə s=wɛ̀yəl//, /'*The day is getting warmer.*'/.

<**líqwem**>, rsls //lə[=Aí=]qʷ=əm//, WETH ['*got warm*'], TCH, (<**í-ablaut**> *resultative*), phonology: ablaut, syntactic analysis: intransitive verb, attested by EB.

<**leqw'ímőws**>, df //ləq'ʷ=ím=óws//, DESC /'*limber, supple, bend easily (of a person)*'/, lx <**=í:m ~ =ím**> *repeatedly*, lx <**=ő ws ~ =ews**> *in the body, in the skin*, syntactic analysis: adjective/adjectival verb.

<**lesák**>, free root //ləsɛ́k//, HHG ['*sack*'], syntactic analysis: nominal, attested by Deming, borrowed from Chinook Jargon <**le sac**> *sack, pocket* Johnson 1978:263, itself from French <**le sac**> *sack, bag, pouch*, example: <**léts'e lesák spólqw' seplí:l**>, //lə́c'ə ləsɛ́k s=pá[=lə=]q'ʷ səplí·l//, /'*a sack of flour*'/, literally /'one sack powdered bread'/, attested by Deming.

<**lesák swéltel**>, FSH /'*bag net, sack net*'/, *see* swéltel.

<**lésleseqw**>, DESC ['*greasy-headed*'], *see* ló:s ~ lós.

<**lesúpli**>, free root //ləsúpli//, CH ['*prayer beads*'], syntactic analysis: nominal, attested by JS, also <**losúpli**>, //lasúpli//, attested by Elders Group (2/18/76), borrowed from French <**le chapelet**> *lesser rosary (of 55 beads), string of beads* or French <**le suppliant**> *a supplicant, a prayer (person).*

<**letám**>, free root //lətɛ́m//, HHG /'*table, desk*'/, syntactic analysis: nominal, attested by Elders Group, borrowed from Chinook Jargon <**la table, la-tem**> *table* Johnson 1973:432 itself from French <**la table**> *table*, ASM ['desk'], semantic environment ['school, writing'], example: <**skwúl letám**>, //s=kʷúl lətɛ́m//, /'*school desk*'/, ASM ['table'], <**tl'álxchxw te s<u>x</u>el<u>x</u>éyles te letám.**>, //ƛ'ɛ́l=xʸ-c-xʷ tə s=C_1əC_2-x̣ə[=Aí=]lə-s tə lətɛ́m//, /'*Put the legs (back) on the table. (put s-th on, fasten s-th)*'/.

<**létqw'estem**>, df //lə́t=q'ʷ=əs=T=əm or lɛ[=Aə́=]t=q'ʷ=əs=təm//, ABFC ['*nodding (falling asleep)*'], root meaning uncertain unless <**lá:t**> *get dark*, lx <**=qw' ~ =eqw'**> *around in circles*, lx <**=es**> *on the face, face (obj.)*, or possibly <**=st**> *causative control transitive* and <**-em**> *middle voice* or possibly <**=tem**> *participial, stative*, syntactic analysis: intransitive verb.

<**lethló:thel**>, HHG ['*plates*'], *see* ló:thel.

<**léth'ilets**>, df //lə́θ'(=)i(y)=ləc//, EZ /'*tall gray mountain blueberry,* probably *Alaska blueberry*'/, ['*Vaccinium alaskaense*'], ASM ['berries tart with grayish dust on them; the word is said by some speakers to be used for both the berries and the plant']['the leaves are shiny on top with "whiskers" on the bottom'], root meaning unknown (unless possibly a doublet with <**láts'**> *different* or <**lets'**> *fill* or related to <**=líth'e**>*processed fiber*), lx <**=lets**> *on the bottom*, possibly <**=á:y ~ =ey ~ =i(y)**> *bark, plant, wood, covering, wool*, if the first root doublet is correct that would give lit. "different covering/wool on the bottom [of the leaves]", syntactic analysis: nominal, attested by Elders Group, TM, also <**léth'elets**>, //lə́θ'=ələc//, attested by EL, AC, Elders Group (3/1/72), other sources: H-T <lítcelEtc> (macron over e) *blueberry (Vaccinium sp.)*, Duff (1952) [lɪcaylɪc] *blue huckleberry (of lower elevations)*, Salish cognate: Lillooet (Pemberton dial.) /lə́c'iyəc/ *Alaska blueberry (V. alaskaense)* Turner and Bouchard: Pemberton Lillooet Ethnobotany (ms.)(1974), example: <**sth'íms te léth'ilets**>, //s=θ'ím-s tə lə́θ'(=)i=ləc//, /'*berry of the tall mountain blueberry (Alaska blueberry)*'/, attested by Elders Group.

<**léts'**>, free root //lə́c'//, [lɪ́c'], MC ['*fill (of container)*'], EB, LAND, WATR, syntactic analysis: intransitive verb, attested by AC, AHTTC, Salish cognate: Lushootseed /ləč'/ *full (container)* and /ləč'-íl/ *it's filling up* (H76), example: <**le léts'.**>, //lə lə́c'//, /'*It's filled.*'/, <**lulh léts' te skw'ówes te qó:**>, //lə=uɬ lə́c' tə s=k'ʷáwəs tə qá·//, /'*The bucket is full of water.*'/, literally /'the bucket already filled with water'/, attested by AC.

<**lets'ét**>, pcs //ləc'=ə́T//, MC /'*fill s-th (with liquid or solid), fill it up*'/, (<**=ét**> *purposeful control*

transitivizer), phonology: stressed transitivizer, syntactic analysis: transitive verb, attested by EB, AC, Salish cognate: Samish dial. of N. Straits /ləč'ə́t/ (VU) *fill s-th* and (VU) /s=léc'=əɬ/ ~ (LD) /s=léθ'=ɬ/ *it is full* G86:74, Squamish /yíč'-it/ *fill (tr.)* W73:99, K67:383, example: <**lets'ét te skw'ówes te sqáwth**>, //ləc'=əT tə s=k'ʷáwəs tə s=qɛ́wθ//, /'*fill the bucket with potatoes*'/, syntactic comment: note oblique nominal phrase with no special marking, only position further from the verb phrase than the object nominal phrase, attested by AC.

<**lets'éthet**>, pcrs //ləc'=ə́T-ət//, ABFC /'*fill oneself, fill oneself up*'/, (<**-et**> *reflexive*), phonology: stressed transitivizer, syntactic analysis: intransitive verb, attested by EB, Elders Group.

<**me lets'léts'**>, df //mə C_1əC_2=lə́c'//, WATR ['*high tide*'], literally /'come fill repeatedly/completely'/, (<**R3=**> *iterative* or *completive* or *plural*), phonology: reduplication, syntactic analysis: intransitive verb, attested by CT.

<**selíts' ~ slíts'**>, strs //s=hə=lə[=Aí=]c' ~ s=lə[=Aí=]c'//, MC ['*be full*'], WATR, LAND, ABFC, (<**s=**> *stative*), (<**he=**> *resultative*), (<**í-ablaut**> *resultative*), phonology: ablaut, syntactic analysis: adjective/adjectival verb, attested by EB, AC, other sources: ES /səlí·c'/ *full*, example: <**ólew slíts'**>, //ʔál=əw s=lə[=Aí=]c'//, /'*too full*'/, attested by EB, <**lulh selíts' te skw'ówes te sqáwth.**>, //lə-uɬ s=hə=lə[=Aí=]c' tə s=k'ʷáwəs tə s=qɛ́wθ//, /'*The bucket is full of potatoes.*'/, attested by AC, <**selíts' te skw'ówes.**>, //s=hə=lə[=Aí=]c' tə s=k'ʷáwəs//, /'*The pail is full.*'/, attested by AC, <**axwethóxchxw kw' tí, ő́we slíts'es, ő́wechxw lets'étexw.**>, //ʔɛxʷ=əT-áxʸ-c-xʷ k'ʷə tí, ʔówə s=lə[=Aí=]c'-əs, ʔówə-c-xʷ ləc'=əT-əxʷ//, /'*Give me some tea, not full, don't fill it.*'/, syntactic comment: vneg, subjunctive subject pronoun, sentence with verb phrase in apposition, attested by EB.

<**léts'a ~ léts'e**>, free root //lə́c'ɛ ~ lə́c'ə//, NUM ['*one*'], phonology: léts'a in slow and normal speed speech, léts'e at normal or faster speeds, syntactic analysis: adjective/adjectival verb, attested by AC, CT (9/5/73), NP (12/6/73), BJ (5/64), EB, DM (12/4/64), BHTTC, Elders Group, SP, AD, other sources: ES /lə́c'à·/, JH /lə́c'e/, example: <**tset áxwet ta sqwmáy te léts'e sth'ò:m.**>, //c-ət ʔɛ́xʷ=əT t-ɛ s=qʷəm=ɛ́y tə lə́c'ə s=θ'á·m//, /'*We gave your dog one bone.*'/, syntactic analysis: verb phrase with both direct object np and indirect object np, attested by AC, <**tl'ose kw'e léts'e a' stl'í**>, //ƛ'a-s-ə k'ʷə lə́c'ə ʔɛʔ s=ƛ'í//, /'*(that's) any one you want*'/, attested by EB, <**máx kw'e léts'e**>, //mɛ́=xʸ k'ʷə lə́c'ə//, /'*take one off (take s-th off)*'/, attested by Elders Group, <**ópel qas te léts'a**>, //ʔápəl qɛ-s tə lə́c'ɛ//, /'*eleven*'/, literally /'ten and the (present or unspecified location) one'/, attested by DM, CT, also <**ópel qas kw'e léts'e**>, //ʔápəl qɛ-s k'ʷə lə́c'ə//, literally /'ten and the (remote) one'/, attested by BJ, AC, <**wetéses te s'ópels qas kw'e léts'e**>, //wə-tə́s-əs tə s=ʔápəl=s qɛ-s k'ʷə lə́c'ə//, /'*when it gets to eleven o'clock*'/, grammatical comment: the hour affix (s=...=s cirumfix) need only be applied to the first numeral of a compound numeral in AC's speech, attested by AC, <**léts'e slà:t**>, //lə́c'ə s=lɛ̀·t//, /'*one night*'/, attested by AC, <**léts'e (máqa, syilólem)**>, //lə́c'ə (mɛ́qɛ, s=yil=óləm)//, /'*one (snow, year), one year*'/, attested by Elders Group, (semological comment: fish can be counted with the plain numeral also), attested by BHTTC, <**léts'e léxwtel**>, //lə́c'ə lə́xʷ=təl//, /'*one blanket*'/, attested by AC, <**lets'ó te spópiys**>, //ləc'ɛ-à tə s=pó[-C_1ə-]y-s//, /'*(It has) one bend., (It has) one crook.*'/, literally /'is one-just the its bend'/, attested by AC.

<**lets'álews**>, ds //ləc'ə=ɛ́ləws//, NUM ['*one leaf*'], HARV, lx <**=álews**> *leaf*, phonology: vowel merger, syntactic analysis: nominal, adjective/adjectival verb, attested by SP, AD.

<**lets'ámeth'**>, ds //ləc'ɛ=ɛ́məθ'//, NUM /'*one rope, one thread, one stick, one pole*'/, MC, HARV, lx <**=ámeth'**> *long thin object, rope, thread, stick, pole*, phonology: vowel merger, syntactic analysis: nominal, adjective/adjectival verb, attested by AD.

<**lets'á:wes**>, ds //ləc'ɛ=ɛ́·wəs//, NUM /'*one paddle, one paddler*'/, CAN, PLAY, lx <**=á:wes ~ =ő́wes**> *paddle*, phonology: vowel merger, syntactic analysis: nominal, adjective/adjectival verb,

attested by Elders Group.

<**lets'áxw**>, ds //ləc'ɛ=ɛ́xʷ//, NUM /'*once, one time*'/, TIME, lx <**=áxw**> **(only after <léts'a>) ~ =á (only after <them=>** allomorph of **<isále>) ~ =álh** (elsewhere)> *time(s)*, phonology: vowel merger, syntactic analysis: adverb/adverbial verb, attested by Elders Group, EB, Salish cognate: Lushootseed /dəč'áxʷ/ *once* H76:130, also <**lets'á:xw ~ lets'áxw**>, //ləc'ɛ=ɛ́·xʷ ~ ləc'ɛ=ɛ́xʷ//, attested by AC, example: <**lets'áxw kw'else qw'eyílex.**>, //ləc'ɛ=ɛ́xʷ k'ʷə-l-s-ə q'ʷəy=íl=əxʸ//, /'*I danced once.*'/, attested by EB, <**lets'áxwe ses yóyes.**>, //ləc'ɛ=ɛ́xʷ-ə s-əs yáyəs//, /'*He only (just) worked once.*'/, literally /'it's just once that he works'/, attested by AC, <**(te, kw'e) lech'áxw**>, //(tə, k'ʷə) ləc'ɛ=ɛ́xʷ//, /'*at one time, once*'/, attested by AD.

<**lets'áyiws**>, ds //ləc'ɛ=ɛ́y=iws//, NUM ['*one pair of pants*'], CLO, lx <**=áyiws**> *pants*, phonology: vowel merger, syntactic analysis: nominal, adjective/adjectival verb, attested by AD.

<**sléts'elhp**>, ds //s=lə́c'=əɬp//, NUM ['*one tree*'], EB, HARV, lx <**=elhp ~ =álhp**> *tree, plant*, phonology: vowel-loss probably rather than vowel merger, syntactic analysis: nominal, adjective/adjectival verb, attested by Elders Group.

<**lets'emó:t**>, ds //ləc'ə=má·t//, NUM /'*one kind, one pile*'/, DESC, lx <**=mó:t**> *kind, pile*, syntactic analysis: adjective/adjectival verb, nominal, attested by Elders Group, IHTTC, also <**lets'emót**>, //ləc'ə=mát//, attested by ME.

<**léts'eqel**>, ds //lə́c'=əqəl//, NUM ['*one container*'], MC, lx <**=eqel**> *container; throat, language*, phonology: vowel-loss, syntactic analysis: adjective/adjectival verb, vnom, attested by AD.

<**léts'es**>, ds //lə́c'=əs//, NUM /'*one dollar, one Indian blanket (Boas)*'/, SH ['*one round object*'], TIME ['*one cyclic period*'], DESC, SOC, lx <**=es**> *on the face; Indian blanket (in counting wealth) ~* (post-contact) *dollar(s)*, phonology: vowel-loss, syntactic analysis: nominal, adjective/adjectival verb, attested by AC, other sources: Boas Scowlitz field notes (ca 1886)(APS Library ms.) <le'tces> (double underline under each e) *one Indian blanket, one dollar*, comment: some examples follow which are questionable only because the following word begins with an "s" (which could be the only "s" heard or which could have combined phonetically (consonant merger) with the suffix final "s", example: <**tsel áxwet mékw' ta sqwéqwemiy léts'es sth'ó:m.**>, //c-əl ʔɛ́xʷ=əT mə́k'ʷ t-ɛ s=C_1í=Aə́=q'ʷəməy (k'ʷə) lə́c'əs s=θ'á·m//, /'*I gave (give) all your dogs one bone.*'/, attested by AC, <**léts'e(s) hiló:lém**>, //lə́c'ə(s) hilá·lə́m//, /'*one year, a whole year*'/, attested by DM (12/4/64), also <**lets'e(s) s(y)iló:lém**>, //lə́c'ə(s) s=yilá·lə́m//, attested by AC, <**léts'e(s) skw'xó:s**>, //lə́c'ə(s) s=k'ʷxʸ=á·s//, /'*one moon, one month, first quarter of moon, the new moon*'/, attested by DM (12/4/64), <**léts'e(s) sx̱éytl'**>, //lə́c'ə(s) s=x̣íƛ'//, /'*one winter*'/, literally /'one nominalizer-cold'/, attested by AC.

<**lets'íws**>, ds //ləc'ɛ=íws//, NUM ['*one bird*'], HUNT, lx <**=íws**> *bird (body); body, skin*, phonology: vowel merger, syntactic analysis: num, nominal, adjective/adjectival verb, attested by Elders Group.

<**lets'òls ~ léts'òls**>, ds //lə́c'ɛ=àls//, NUM ['*one fruit (as it grows singly on a plant)*'], HARV, EB, lx <**=ó:ls ~ =òls**> *fruit, spherical objects, rocks*, phonology: vowel merger, syntactic analysis: num, nominal, adjective/adjectival verb, attested by AD.

<**lets'ő́welh**>, ds //ləc'ɛ=ówəɬ//, NUM /'*one canoe, one boat*'/, CAN, lx <**=ő́welh**> *canoe, boat*, phonology: vowel merger, syntactic analysis: num, nominal, adjective/adjectival verb, attested by AD.

<**lólets'e**>, ds //C_1á=ləc'ə//, NUM /'*one person, be alone*'/, SOC, lx <**R10=**> *person* (only with this morpheme), phonology: reduplication, syntactic analysis: num, nominal, adjective/adjectival verb, attested by Elders Group, EB, also <**lólets'a ~ lólets'e**>, //C_1á=ləc'ɛ ~ C_1á=ləc'ə//, attested by AC, ASM ['one person'], example: <**lólets'e (~ lólets'a) (swíyeqe, slháli)**>, //lá=ləc'ə (~ lá=ləc'ɛ)

(s=wíyəqə, s=ɬɛ́li)//, /'*one (man, woman)*'/, attested by AC, <**lólets'e xwélmexw**>, //lá=ləc'ə xʷə́l=məxʷ//, /'*one Indian*'/, attested by Elders Group, <**ópel qas kw'e lólets'e**>, //ʔápəl qa-s k'ʷə lá=ləc'ə//, /'*eleven people, (There are) eleven people.*'/, attested by AC, <**lólets'etsel.**>, //lá=ləc'ə-c-əl//, /'*I'm one (person).*'/, attested by AC, <**le s'í:kw' te lólets'e.**>, //lə s=ʔí·k'ʷ tə lá-ləc'ə//, /'*One person was lost.*'/, attested by EB, <**wiyóth kwsu éys te sqwálewels te lólets'e.**>, //wə=yáθ kʷ-s-u ʔɛ́y-s tə s=qʷɛ́l=əwəl-s tə lá=ləc'ə//, /'*an optimist, a person whose thoughts are always good, a person who is always happy*'/, literally /'it's always so-that it's good the thoughts of the one person'/, syntactic comment: very interesting example of a complete sentence in Halkomelem which translates as an incomplete sentence (an np) in English, attested by Elders Group, <**wiyóth kwsu qéls te sqwálewels te lólets'e.**>, //wə=yáθ kʷ-s-u qə́l-s tə s=qʷɛ́l=əwəl-s tə lá=ləc'ə//, /'*a pessimist, a person whose thoughts are always bad*'/, attested by Elders Group, ASM ['be alone'], <**wiyóth we lólets'a e**>, //wə=yóθ wə lá=ləc'ɛ ʔə//, /'*(he/she is) always alone*'/, literally /'is always contrastive is alone just'/, attested by AC.

<**ilólets'e ~ hilólets'e**>, df //ʔi=C_1á=ləc'ə ~ hi=C_1á=ləc'ə//, SOC ['*alone*'], possibly <**i= ~ hi=**> *continuative*? (~ há- ~ hé-) or (~ yi=)> *travelling along by*, syntactic analysis: intransitive verb, num?, attested by Elders Group (3/1/72, 3/19/75), example: <**ilólets'e o**>, //ʔi=C_1á=ləc'ə ʔà//, /'*just alone*'/, attested by Elders Group (3/1/72).

<**ta'elólets'e**>, df //tɛ=ʔi=C_1á=ləc'ə or tə ʔi=lá=ləc'ə//, NUM ['*each (person)*'], (<**ta=**> (as in <**ta='áltha**> *me) nominalizer* or <**te**> *the* as *nominalizer*), syntactic comment: could be a prefixed form or a np, attested by Elders Group (3/72).

<**lets'álews**>, NUM ['*one leaf*'], *see* léts'a ~ léts'e.

<**lets'ámeth'**>, NUM /'*one rope, one thread, one stick, one pole*'/, *see* léts'a ~ léts'e.

<**lets'á:wes**>, NUM /'*one paddle, one paddler*'/, *see* léts'a ~ léts'e.

<**lets'áxw**>, NUM /'*once, one time*'/, *see* léts'a ~ léts'e.

<**lets'áyiws**>, NUM ['*one pair of pants*'], *see* léts'a ~ léts'e.

<**lets'elíthet**>, DIR /'*separate oneself from a group, separate oneself (from others)*'/, *see* halts'elí.

<**lets'emó:t**>, NUM /'*one kind, one pile*'/, *see* léts'a ~ léts'e.

<**lets'emót**>, DESC ['*a different kind*'], *see* láts'.

<**léts'eqel**>, NUM ['*one container*'], *see* léts'a ~ léts'e.

<**léts'es**>, NUM /'*one dollar, one Indian blanket (Boas)*'/, *see* léts'a ~ léts'e.

<**lets'ét**>, MC /'*fill s-th (with liquid or solid), fill it up*'/, *see* léts'.

<**lets'éthet**>, ABFC /'*fill oneself, fill oneself up*'/, *see* léts'.

<**lets'íws**>, NUM ['*one bird*'], *see* léts'a ~ léts'e.

<**lets'ló:ts'tel**>, LT ['*(many) different colors*'], *see* láts'.

<**lets'òls ~ léts'òls**>, NUM ['*one fruit (as it grows singly on a plant)*'], *see* léts'a ~ léts'e.

<**lets'ő:lmexw**>, SOC /'*different tribe, different people, strangers*'/, *see* láts'.

<**lets'ő:mexw**>, SOC /'*different person, stranger*'/, *see* láts'.

<**lets'őwelh**>, NUM /'*one canoe, one boat*'/, *see* léts'a ~ léts'e.

<**lets'őw(e)yelh ~ slets'őweyelh**>, KIN /'*half-sibling, half-brother, half-sister*'/, *see* láts'.

<**léw**>, bound root //lə́w *inside a hollow object*//.

<**léwex**>, pcis //lə́w=əxʸ//, DIR /'*put it in (and leave it), stick it into s-th hollow*'/, MC, ABFC, EB, LAND, (<**=ex**> *purposeful control transitivizer inanimate object preferred*), syntactic analysis: transitive verb, attested by EB, Elders Group, CT, HT, and RG & EH (4/9/99 Ling332), example: <**léwex li te kw'óxwe**>, //lə́w=əxʸ li tə k'ʷáxʷə//, /'*put it in a box*'/, attested by EB, <**léwex te (pípe, mail)**>, //lə́w=əxʸ tə (pípə, mail)//, /'*put in the mail*'/, attested by Elders Group, <**léwexes kwstámes li te shxwótkwewel.**>, //lə́w=əxʸ-əs kʷ=s=tɛ́m=əs li tə s=xʷátkʷ=əwəl//, /'*He sticks something into something hollow.*'/, attested by CT, HT, <**léwexes te chálexs li te shxwótkwewel.**>, //lə́w=əxʸ-əs tə cɛ́ləxʸ-s li tə s=xʷátkʷ=əwəl//, /'*He stuck his hand into something hollow.*'/, attested by CT, HT.

<**slíw**>, stvi //s=lə[=Aí=]w//, strs, DIR /'*be inside (a hollow object), be in (a hollow object)*'/, (<**s=**> *stative*), (<**í-ablaut**> *resultative*), phonology: ablaut, syntactic analysis: adjective/adjectival verb, attested by Elders Group, also <**slí:w**>, //s=lə[=Aí·=]w//, attested by EB, example: <**slí:w í te kw'óxwe.**>, //s=lə[=Aí·=]w ʔí tə k'ʷáxʷə//, /'*It's in the box.*'/, attested by EB, <**tsel slíw te kw'óxwe.**>, //c-əl s=lə[=Aí=]w tə k'ʷáxʷə//, /'*I'm inside a box.*'/, attested by Elders Group, <**ōwéta kw'e slíw ta' sx̱éyes.**>, //ʔowə=´tɛ k'ʷə s=lə[=Aí=]w t-ɛʔ s=x̣ə́yəs//, /'*There's nothing inside your head.*'/, attested by Elders Group.

<**slewí**>, dnom //s=lə[=Aí=]w=ə[=M2=]y or s=líw=ə[=M2=]y or s=ləw=i[=´=]y//, EB ['*inner cedar bark*'], literally /'inside bark'/, ASM ['used for diapers, etc., also made into strings usually, for shirts, and other things'], (<**s=**> *nominalizer*), lx <**=á:y ~ =ey**> *bark, wool, covering*, (<**í-ablaut**> *durative* or *resultative*), phonology: ablaut, metathesis, syntactic analysis: nominal, attested by Elders Group, also <**sléw:í**>, //s=líw·=ə[=M2=]y//, phonology: updrifting, consonant lengthening sometimes phonetic between high-stressed vowels, attested by Elders Group.

<**slewíws**>, df //s=ləw=íws ~ s=ləwí=íws//, CLO /'*a dress, woman's dress*'/, (<**s=**> *nominalizer*), lx <**=í:ws ~ =íws ~ =ews**> *body*, possibly root <**lew=**> *put inside an opening (*possibly lit. //"something with (an opening) for the body to be put inside"//) or from stem <**slewí**> *inner cedar bark* (which pre-contact clothing was oftten made of) + <**=í:ws ~ =íws ~ =ews**> *on the body*, syntactic analysis: nominal, attested by Elders Group.

<**slewómet ~ lewómet**>, df //s=ləw(=)ámət ~ ləw(=)ámət//, CLO ['*dancing costume*'], SPRD, REL, ASM ['whole costume from head to toe, includes those for spirit dancing, sx̱wó:yx̱wey dance or any other'], (<**s=**> *nominalizer*), possibly <lew> *inside a hollow*, possibly <=omet> *reflexive, onself*, (semological comment: if this etymology is right, the costume reflects the spirit that is inside the person, as we know it is supposed to from reports of dancers & ceremonialists), syntactic analysis: nominal, attested by Elders Group.

<**Te Lewómet**>, df //tə ləwámət//, WETH ['*The Milky Way*'], literally (probably) /'The Costume'/, (semological comment: some spirit-dancing costumes had mother of pearl shells attached which shone in the firelight, somewhat like stars in the dark) syntactic analysis: simple nominal phrase, source: Wells (1965, 2nd ed.):38 <tel-uh-WA-meht> [but the semantic comment is mine only] , I think also in H-T,

<**lewálh**>, probably root //ləwɛ́ɬ//, EFAM /'*be surprised, astonished*'/, syntactic analysis: adjective/adjectival verb, attested by AD, Elders Group (3/1/72, 3/15/72, 3/3/76), example: <**lewálh tútlo.**>, //ləwɛ́ɬ t=ú=ƛ'a//, /'*He was surprised.*'/, attested by AD.

<**lewálhlexw**>, ncs //ləwɛ́ɬ=l-əxʷ//, EFAM ['*(happen to) surprise s-o*'], (<**=l**> *non-control transitivizer*), (<**-exw**> *third person object*), syntactic analysis: transitive verb; found in <**lewálhlòx**>, //ləwɛ́ɬ=l-áxʸ//, /'*I'm surprised*'/, literally /'surprised me'/, phonology: downstepping,

example: <**ts'áts'el welewálhlòxes.**>, //c'ɛ́[=C_1ə=]l wə-ləwɛ́ɬ=l-áx^{y}-əs//, /'*I'm really surprised.*'/, literally /'very/really contrastive-it/he/she/they happened to surprise me'/.

<**lewálhmet**>, iecs //ləwɛ́ɬ=məT//, EFAM ['*be surprised by s-th/s-o*'], (<**=met**> *indirect effect control transitivizer*), syntactic analysis: transitive verb, attested by AD, example: <**ts'áts'eltsel lewálhmet.**>, //c'ɛ[=C_1ə=]l-c-əl ləwɛ́ɬ=məT//, /'*I was really surprised.*'/, literally /'I am very/really surprised by it/him/her/them'/, attested by AD, <**lewálhmetes te skwóyxthets.**>, //ləwɛ́ɬ=məT-əs tə s-k^{w}áyx̣=T-ət-s//, /'*He was surprised by what he is doing.*'/, literally /'he is surprised by it the his doings'/, syntactic analysis: relative clause obj. of transitive verb, attested by AD.

<**lewálhlexw**>, EFAM ['*(happen to) surprise s-o*'], *see* lewálh.

<**lewálhmet**>, EFAM ['*be surprised by s-th/s-o*'], *see* lewálh.

<**léwe**>, free root //lə́wə//, [lʊ́wə ~ lə́wə], PRON /'*it's you, you are the one. you (focus or emphasis)*'/, syntactic analysis: vpron, attested by IHTTC, Deming, AC, AD, example: <**léwe ó:le.**>, //lə́wə ʔá·lə//, /'*Oh, it's you. (said in surprise)*'/, attested by IHTTC, <**léwe ts'ít te Chíchelh Siyám.**>, //lə́wə c'íy=T tə cí[=C_1ə=]ɬ s=iy=ɛ́m//, /'*It's you to thank the Lord.*'/, literally /'it's you thank him the high leader'/, attested by Deming, <**léwecha o iyálewet.**>, //lə́wə-cɛ ʔa ʔiy=ɛ́ləw=əT//, /'*You'll do it yourself.*'/, attested by AC, <**skw'áy kw'els q'á:l kw'es léwes.**>, //s=k'^{w}ɛ́y k'^{w}ə-l-s q'ɛ́·l k'^{w}ə-s lə́wə-s//, /'*I couldn't believe it was you.*'/, syntactic comment: 2nd person vpron with 3rd person subject, attested by AC; found in <**lewá:**>, //ləwə-ə or ləwə-ɛ́·//, /'*Is it you?*'/, attested by AC, example: <**lewá: Edie?**>, //ləwə-ɛ́· Edie?//, /'*Is it you Edie?*'/, attested by AC, <**luwá óle?**>, //ləwə-ɛ ʔálə//, /'*Is that you?*'/, attested by AD.

<**taléwe**>, ds //tɛ=lə́wə//, PRON ['*you (sg.)*'], (<**ta=**> *nominalizer* from the demonstrative article te), syntactic analysis: inp, attested by AC, other sources: ES /tələ̀wə́/, also <**taléwé ~ tal:éwé**>, //tɛ=lə́wə́ ~ tɛ=l·ə́wə́//, attested by AC, BJ (12/5/64), example: <**(ta)léwe qas ta'á'altha**>, //(tɛ=)lə́wə qɛ-s tɛ=C_1ɛ́=ʔɛlθɛ//, /'*(it's) you and me*'/, attested by AC, <**welóy tàl:èwe.**>, //wə=láy tɛ=l·ə́wə//, /'*It's just you.*'/, phonology: updrifting, downstepping, attested by AC; found in <**taléwecha**>, //tɛ=lə́wə-cɛ//, /'*it will be you*'/, attested by IHTTC, example: <**chexw ó:met tal:éwe.**>, //c-əx^{w} ʔə[=Aá·=]mət tɛ=l·ə́wə//, /'*You're sitting down.*'/, attested by AC.

<**tl'eléwe ~ tl'léwe**>, ds //ƛ'ə=lə́wə ~ƛ'=lə́wə//, PRON ['*you (sg.) (object of preposition)*'], (<**tl'e= ~ tl'=**> *the (human, near/remote)* sometimes used as a catch all preposition plus article), syntactic analysis: independent object of prepositional verb, attested by AC, EB, others, example: <**stetís tl'(e)léwe.**>, //s=C_1ə=tís ƛ'(ə)=lə́wə//, /'*She is close to you.*'/, attested by AC, <**(éy, qél) xwlá(m) tl'eléwe.**>, //(ʔɛ́y, qə́l) x^{w}=lɛ́(-m) ƛ'ə=lə́wə//, /'*It's (good, bad) for you.*'/, semantic environment ['speaking of a kind of food, or medicine, or anything'], attested by EB, comment: attested with both xwlá and xwlám *towards* (no difference in meaning), <**éy xwlá(m) tl'eléwe te st'élmexw.**>, //ʔɛ́y x^{w}lɛ́(-m) ƛ'ə=lə́wə tə s=t'ə́lməx^{w}//, /'*The medicine is good for you.*'/, attested by EB, <**kwútes telí tl'léwe.**>, //k^{w}ú=T-əs təlíƛ'=lə́wə//, /'*He took it from you. (take s-th)*'/, attested by EB, <**ístexwchelcha ó í teléwe** (or **tl'léwe**)**.**>, //ʔí=sT-əx^{w}-c-əl-cɛ ʔà ʔí tə=lə́wə (orƛ'=lə́wə)//, /'*I'm going to leave this here with you.*'/, attested by EB.

<**léwex**>, DIR /'*put it in (and leave it), stick it into s-th hollow*'/, *see* léw.

<**lewéx̱ ~ lṓwéx̱**>, free root //ləwə́x ~ lówə́x̣//, ANA /'*rib, ribs*'/, possibly root <**lew=**> *put inside a hole*, possibly <**=x̱**> *distributive*, syntactic analysis: nominal, attested by AC, others, other sources: ES /ləwə́x̣/, H-T <lúwEq> (macron over u), example: <**th'ex̱wót ta lṓwéx̱.**>, //θ'əx̣^{w}=áT t-ɛ lówə́x̣//, /'*Wash your ribs.*'/, syntactic comment: imperative due to lack of subject pronoun but presence of 2s possessive pronoun, attested by AC.

<**léwlets ~ lṓwlets**>, df //lə́wləc ~ lówləc//, SOC /'*repay, pay a debt*'/, possibly root <**léw=**> *put inside something hollow*, possibly <=lets> *in the bottom*, syntactic analysis: intransitive verb, attested by Deming, IHTTC, Salish cognate: Squamish /nə́wʔ-n-ač-t/ *pay (a person)(tr.)* W73:195, K67:311.

<**Lewóxwemey** or **Lewó<u>x</u>wemey**>, df //lə(=)wáxʷ=əm=əy ~ lə(=)wáx̣ʷ=əm=əy//, PLN ['*mountain behind (west of) Tkwóthel near Yale (on the CPR side)*'], ASM ['Tkwóthel is the mountain with a natural tunnel above the highway at Yale, just south of Popelehó:ys (Yale Mt.); the CPR (Canadian Pacific Railroad) side of the Fraser River is the north side from roughly Vancouver east to about Seabird Island where the river turns north and the side is better called the west side; across the Fraser is often called the CN or CNR side (Canadian National Railroad); these describe where each national railroad system has its tracks'], possibly <**le= ~ lexw= ~ xw=**> *always*, possibly <**=em**> *middle voice or intransitivizer or place*, possibly <**=ey**> may be cognate with Nooksack <**=iy** ~ =ey> *place*, syntactic analysis: nominal, attested by IHTTC (esp. SP, AD, AK)(9/13/77), source: place names reference file #249.

<**lex**>, bound root //ləx̌ *lie on its side*//.

<**lexét**>, pcs //ləxʸ=ə́T//, DIR /'*turn it on its side, lay it on its side*'/, (<**=et**> *purposeful control transitivizer*), phonology: stressed transitivizer, syntactic analysis: transitive verb, attested by Deming, Salish cognate: Squamish /nə́š-n/ *put s-th on its side (tr.)* K69:64.

<**slíx**>, strs //s=lə[=Aí=]xʸ//, DIR ['*lying on its side*'], (<**s=**> *stative*), (<**í-ablaut**> *resultative*), phonology: ablaut, syntactic analysis: adjective/adjectival verb, attested by Deming.

<**lexósem**>, mdls //ləxʸ=ás=əm//, ABFC /'*put one's head to one side, lay on one side of the head*'/, lx <**=ós**> *on the face*, (<**=em**> *middle voice*), syntactic analysis: intransitive verb, attested by IHTTC.

<**lexét**>, DIR /'*turn it on its side, lay it on its side*'/, *see* lex.

<**lexósem**>, ABFC /'*put one's head to one side, lay on one side of the head*'/, *see* lex.

<**lexw= ~ xw=** ~ (rarely) **le=**>, da //**ləxʷ= ~ xʷ= ~ (rarely) lə=**//, TIME ['*always*'], syntactic analysis: derivational prefix; found in <**lexw'éy ~ xw'éywelh**>, //ləxʷ=ʔɛ́y ~ xʷ=ʔɛ́y=wəɬ//, /'*generous, always good*'/, <**lexwqélwelh**>, //ləxʷ=qə́ɬ=wəɬ//, /'*cranky, crabby, dirty-minded*'/ (root <**qél**> *bad; dirty)*, <**lexwmálqewelh**>, //ləxʷ=mɛ́lq=əwəɬ//, /'*forgetful; passed out (if drunk)*'/, <**lexwslhám**>, //ləxʷ=s=ɬɛ́m//, /'*always choking on liquid*'/, also <**lexwshxwlhám**>, //ləxʷ=sxʷ=ɬɛ́m//, /'*choking on liquid*'/, <**lexwstl'ép**>, //ləxʷ=s=ƛ'ə́p//, /'*always deep*'/, (<**s=**> *stative*), <**Lkwṓxwethem**>, //l(ə)=kʷóxʷəθ=əm//, /'*Six-Mile Creek and bay on west side of Harrison Lake*'/, literally /'always coho place or always catch coho since this is a coho spawning ground'/, attested by EL, <**Lexwyó:qwem ~ Xwyó:qwem**>, //ləxʷ=yá·qʷ=əm ~ xʷ=yá·qʷ=əm//, /'*mountain above Union Bar,* also prob. *Trafalgar Flat below it*'/, literally /'always (smells of) rotten fish (since spawned out salmon, yó:qwem, collect in the river nearby)'/, attested by SP, <**Xwchí:yò:m**>, PLN /'*Cheam Island (my name for an island in the Fraser River across from Cheam Indian Reserve #2), Cheam village, Cheam Indian Reserve #1*'/, literally /'always a place to get strawberries '/.

<**lexws=**>, (<**ləxʷ=s=**>), SOCT ['*a person that always*'], comment: contains <**s=**> *nominalizer*; found in <**lexwshá:wa**>, //ləxʷ=s=hɛ́·wɛ//, /'*a person that always hunts*'/, <**lexwst'í:lem**>, //ləxʷ=s=t'í·l=əm//, /'*a person that always sings*'/, <**lexwsí:si**>, //ləxʷ=s=síy=C$_1$əC$_2$//, /'*coward, a person who is always scared*'/.

<**Lexwchéwṓlhp**>, PLN /'*village between Yale Creek and Mary Ann Creek on the CP side (west bank of the Fraser R.) where lots of cottonwoods grow/grew (near Yale, B.C.)*'/, *see* cháchew ~ cháchu.

<**Lexwchmóqwem?**>, df //ləxʷ=c=máqʷəm?//, PLN ['*village on both sides of the Lower Sumas River*'], probably <**lexw=**> *always*, probably <**ch=**> *having*, probably root <**móqwem**> *dry swamp; swamp*

tea, Labrador tea, syntactic analysis: nominal, source: Wells 1965:23 (from Sepass map) <Lochchamaquim> (not in PPS), other sources: Gibbs Boundary Survey materials and maps show a similar name in a similar location; the Nooksacks have villages named <Chmóqwem> and <Mómeqwem> after their locations as sources of prized Labrador tea.

<**léxwelh**>, bound root or stem //lə́x^{w}əɬ or lə́=x^{w}=wəɬ or lə́x̣==wəɬ//, CAN /'*canoe (any kind)*'/, possibly root <**léx̲**>, *widened* or <**lá** ~ **le**> *go*, probably <**=x̲**> *distributive, all over, all around* or less likely <**=xw** ~ **=exw**>, *lump-like, round*, probably <**=welh**> *vessel, canoe, boat, bowl-like object*, the first root would give lit. /'widened vessel'/ and canoes were always widened with water & hot rocks inside when the thwarts were installed, the second root would give lit./'vessel that goes all over'/, both etymologies require *derivational* fronting of the uvular <**x̲w**> or <**x̲**> to velar <**xw**> before <**=welh**>. If the lexical affix existed before the stem these etymologies are fine; if it did not then the lexical affix would be a shortened form of the stem; Kuipers' etymological dictionary might help answer this.

<**sléxwelh**>, df //slə́x^{w}əɬ//, CAN /'*canoe (any kind), car, vehicle (any kind)*'/, possibly <**s=**> *nominalizer*, syntactic analysis: nominal, attested by AC, BJ (5/64), DM (12/4/64), Elders Group, EB, other sources: ES /slə́x^{w}əɬ/ *canoe; raid (homophonous forms)*, also /'*ordinary canoe*'/, ASM ['used like pick-up truck today, held about six to eight people, used especially around Soowahlie (Vedder Crossing to Cultus Lake area)'], attested by AC, example: <**kw'étslexw te sléxwelh, sq'émel, qas te sx̲wő qw'tel.**>, //k'^{w}ə́c=l-əx^{w} tə s=lə́x^{w}əɬ, s=q'ə́m=əl, qɛ-s tə s=x̣^{w}óq'^{w}=təl//, /'*He saw a canoe, a paddle, and a canoe pole. (see s-th)*'/, attested by EB.

<**slílxwelh**>, dmn //s=C$_{1}$í=ləx^{w}əɬ//, CAN ['*small canoe*'], (<**R4=**> *diminutive*), phonology: reduplication, phonology: vowel-loss, syntactic analysis: nominal, attested by SJ.

<**slexwelháwtxw**>, ds //s=ləx^{w}əɬ=ɛ́wtx^{w}//, CAN ['*canoe shed*'], BLDG, lx <**=áwtxw**> *building*, syntactic analysis: nominal, attested by Elders Group, also <**slexwelhá:wtxw**>, //s=ləx^{w}əɬ=ɛ́·wtx^{w}//, Elder's comment: "probably", attested by EB.

<**sléxwelhmet**>, iecs //s=lə́x^{w}əɬ=məT//, CAN ['*raid s-o in canoes*'], SOC, (<**=met**> *indirect effect control transitivizer*), syntactic analysis: transitive verb, attested by CT, example: <**me sléxwelhmetò:lxwes te sxemá:ltset.**>, //mə s=lə́x^{w}əɬ=məT-á·lx^{w}-əs tə s=x^{y}əmɛ́·l-cət//, /'*Our enemy comes to raid us in canoes.*'/, attested by CT.

<**lexw(=)íws**>, df //ləx^{w}//, root meaning uncertain unless a fronted version of root <**lex̲w**> *cover up*

<**slexwíws**>, df //s=ləx^{w}=íws//, ANA ['*body (while alive)*'], (<**s=**> *nominalizer*), lx <**=íws** ~ **=í:ws** ~ **=ews**> *on the body, on the skin*, syntactic analysis: nominal, attested by AC, other sources: ES /sləʔx^{w}íus/ (CwMs /sləʔx^{w}íws/), also <**slexwí:ws**>, //s=ləx^{w}=í·ws//, attested by EB, also <**sixwí:ws**>, attested by DM (12/4/64).

<**lexwmálqewelh**>, EFAM ['*forgetful*'], *see* mál ~ mél.

<**Lexwp'ép'eq'es**>, PLN ['*unnamed mountain on the northwest side of the Fraser River between Hope and Yale which has white mineral deposits visible from the river*'], *see* p'éq'.

<**Lexwp'oth'esála ~ Xwp'oth'esála**>, PLN /'*baby basket rock just below main bay and sand bar of Lexwtl'átl'ekw'em (Klaklacum, Indian Reserve #12, first village and reserve south of American Creek), on the west side of the Fraser River*'/, *see* p'ó:th'es ~ p'óth'es.

<**lexwqélwelh**>, EFAM /'*(be) cranky, crabby, dirty-minded*'/, *see* qél.

<**lexws=**>, da //ləx^{w}=s=//, TIME ['*someone that always*'], SOCT ['*a person that always*', syntactic analysis: derivational prefix; found in <**lexwshá:wa**>, //ləx^{w}s=hɛ́·wɛ//, /'*a person that always hunts*'/, <**lexwst'í:lem**>, //ləx^{w}s=t'í·ləm//, /'*a person that always sings*'/, <**lexws'ú:met**>, //ləx^{w}s=ʔú·mət//, /'*a person that's always lazy*'/, <**lexwshxwiyétheqel**>, //ləx^{w}s=x^{w}iyə́θəqəl//, /'*a gossip*'/, <**lexwsí:si**>,

//ləx^{w}s=sí·si//, /'*a person who is always scared, coward*'/, <**lexwsqw'eyíléx**>, //ləx^{w}s=q'^{w}əyíləx^{y}//, /'*a person that always dances, someone who likes to dance*'/, *see* lexw= ~ xw= ~ (rarely) le=.

<**Lexwsá:q**>, SOCT ['*Nooksack people*'], *see* sá:q.

<**lexwsewólem**>, EFAM ['*playful*'], *see* ewólem.

<**lexwsí:si**>, EFAM /'*coward, person that's always afraid*'/, *see* síy.

<**lexwsí:si ~ xwsí:si**>, EFAM ['*(be) always scared*'], *see* síy.

<**lexwslhém ~ lexwslhám**>, ABDF /'*choke on water, choked on liquid*'/, *see* lhém.

<**lexwspésqw**>, LANG ['*someone who always calls people names*'], *see* pésqw.

<**lexwsqwélqwel**>, LANG ['*tattletale*'], *see* qwà:l.

<**lexwsqw'eyíléx**>, PLAY /'*a person that likes to dance, a person that always dances*'/, *see* qw'eyílex ~ qw'eyíléx.

<**lexwst'í:lem**>, MUS ['*a person that always sings*'], *see* t'íl.

<**lexwstl'ép**>, DIR /'*deeper, always deep*'/, *see* tl'ép.

<**lexwsyóyes ~ lexwsiyó:yes**>, SOC ['*[someone] always working*'], *see* yó:ys.

<**lexws'í:ts'el**>, SOC ['*person who is always lazy*'], *see* í:ts'el.

<**lexws'ú:met**>, EFAM ['*a person that's always lazy*'], *see* emét.

<**lexws-há:wa**>, HUNT /'*a person that always hunts, hunter*'/, *see* háwe.

<**lexwshxwiyétheqel**>, LANG /'*a gossip, person that always gossips*'/, *see* yéth.

<**lexwshxwmó:mel**>, SOCT ['*beggar*'], *see* shxwmó:l.

<**lexwshxw'í:tet**>, ABFC ['*sleepy-head*'], *see* ítet.

<**Lexwtamílem?**>, PLN ['*Promontory Point above Vedder Crossing*'], *see* tà:m.

<**lexwtitití́yeqel** or **lexwtitiytíyeqel**>, LANG ['*a person always answering back*'], *see* tiy.

<**Lexwtl'íkw'elem**>, PLN ['*village at mouth of Stulkawhits Creek on Fraser River*'], *see* tl'íkw'el.

<**Lexwts'ístel**>, PLN ['*north and south sides of the mouth of Five-Mile Creek*'], *see* th'ís.

<**Lexwyó:qwem**>, PLN ['*place on Fraser River between first tunnel and Yale where rotten fish used to (always) pile up*'], *see* yó:qw.

<**Lexwyó:qwem Smá:lt**>, PLN ['*mountain on Fraser River between first tunnel and Yale where rotten fish used to (always) pile up*'], *see* yó:qw.

<**Lexw'á:yí:les**>, PLN ['*a bay on west side of Harrison Lake*'], *see* éy ~ éy:.

<**lexw'éy**>, SOC ['*generous*'], *see* éy ~ éy:.

<**léx̲**>, bound root //lə́x̣ *widened*//.

<**léx̲et**>, pcs //lə́x̣=əT//, DESC /'*widen it, move it wider*'/, semantic environment ['of canoes, carvings like plates (as on a shelf), etc., but not of a river'], (<**=et**> *purposeful control transitivizer*), syntactic analysis: transitive verb, attested by AC (10/15/71), other sources: JH /lə́x̣/ *to be widened* and /ləx̣ə́t/ *to widen*.

<**sléx̲tses**>, dnom //s=lə́x̣=cəs//, ANA ['*finger*'], literally /'(something to widen on the hand)'/, ASM

['each finger has its own name, sometimes two'], (<**s=**> *nominalizer*), lx <**=tses**> *on the hand*, syntactic analysis: nominal, attested by AC, BJ (5/64), DM (12/4/64), Elders Group (3/15/72), other sources: ES /slə́x̣cəs/, H-T <slúqtcis, elúqEl> (macron over e).

<**sléx̱xel**>, dnom //s=lə́x̣=xʸəl//, ANA ['*toe*'], literally /'(something that widens on the foot)'/, ASM ['the big toe and small toe are named'], (<**s=**> *nominalizer*), lx <**=xel**> *on the foot*, syntactic analysis: nominal.

<**léx̱et**>, DESC /'*widen it, move it wider*'/, *see* léx̱.

<**Lex̱ex̱éq**>, PLN ['*Luckakuck Creek*'], *see* x̱éq.

<**lex̱éywa ~ lex̱íwa**>, probably root //ləx̣íwɛ//, FSH /'*spear fish by torchlight, to torchlight, to pit-lamp*'/, HUNT ['*spear animals by torchlight*'], ASM ['done by canoe with a fire in the canoe, see under tl'áts'eq (platform and shield for fire when torchlighting for salmon) and swáts'et (bark shield for fire when torchlighting) for some details of how the fire was controlled in the canoe; the fire would draw fish to the surface and animals to the water but would hide the hunters'], syntactic analysis: intransitive verb, Salish cognate: Squamish /yəx̣íʔu/ *fish or hunt with fire in canoe* K69:90.

<**hálx̱eywa ~ hálx̱iwa**>, cts //hɛ́-lx̣iwɛ//, FSH ['*spearing fish by torchlight*'], HUNT, (<**há-**> *continuative*), phonology: vowel-loss, syntactic analysis: intransitive verb.

<**lex̱w**>, bound root //ləx̣ʷ *cover up*//.

<**léx̱wet**>, pcs //lə́x̣ʷ=əT//, HHG /'*cover s-o with a blanket, cover s-th, cover s-th/s-o up*'/, (<**=et**> *purposeful control transitivizer*), syntactic analysis: transitive verb, attested by Deming, EB.

<**léx̱wethet**>, pcrs //lə́x̣ʷ=əT-ət//, HHG ['*cover oneself up*'], (<**-et**> *reflexive*), syntactic analysis: intransitive verb, attested by Deming.

<**léx̱wtel**>, dnom //lə́x̣ʷ=təl//, HHG /'*blanket (modern), covering*'/, lx <**=tel**> *device, thing to*, syntactic analysis: nominal, attested by AC, BJ, EB, Elders Group (3/1/72), other sources: ES /ƛ'əxʷtɛ́·l/ *blanket (generic)* is apparently another word.

<**léx̱wet**>, HHG /'*cover s-o with a blanket, cover s-th, cover s-th/s-o up*'/, *see* lex̱w.

<**léx̱wethet**>, HHG ['*cover oneself up*'], *see* lex̱w.

<**lex̱wő:m ~ lex̱wőm**>, WATR /'*rapids, fast water, clear water, flowing fast, going fast, swift (water)*'/, *see* x̱wém ~ xwém.

<**léx̱wtel**>, HHG /'*blanket (modern), covering*'/, *see* lex̱w.

<**ley ~ lay**>, TVMO /'*go travelling by way of, go via*'/, *see* la.

<**le'á**>, bound root //ləʔɛ́ *facing away, on the other side*//.

<**sle'álets**>, stvi //s=ləʔɛ́=ləc//, DIR ['*be with behind facing toward something (like a fire)*'], ABFC, literally /'be with bottom facing away, be with bottom on the other side'/, (<**s=**> *stative*), lx <**=lets**> *(on the) bottom*, syntactic analysis: adverb/adverbial verb, attested by IHTTC.

<**sle'ó:les**>, stvi //s=ləʔɛ=á·ləs//, DIR /'*be watchful, be facing away*'/, ABFC, (<**s=**> *stative*), lx <**=ó:les**> *in the eyes, in sight, in appearance*, phonology: vowel merger, syntactic analysis: adverb/adverbial verb.

<**sle'ólwelh**>, stvi //s=ləʔɛ=álwəɬ//, DIR /'*be on the other side of, be on the side facing away*'/, (<**s=**> *stative*), lx <**=ílwelh ~ =ólwelh**> *on the side*, phonology: vowel merger, syntactic analysis: adverb/adverbial verb, attested by Elders Group, EB, also <**sle'ó:lwelh ~ sle'ólwelh**>, //s=ləʔɛ́=á·lwəɬ ~ s=ləʔɛ́=álwəɬ//, attested by EB, example: <**tsel sle'ólwelh te kyó.**>, //c-əl s=ləʔɛ́=álwəɬ tə kʸá//, /'*I'm on the other side of the car.*'/, attested by Elders Group, <**sle'ó:lwelhs**

te Bill>, //s=ləʔɛ́=á·lwəɬ-s tə Bill//, /'*(It's/He's/She's) behind Bill.*'/, literally /'it's on the other side of Bill, it's on Bill's other side'/, attested by EB, <**lám te sle'ólwelhs té xàlh.**>, //lɛ́=m tə s=ləʔɛ=álwəɬ-s tə x^{y}ɛ́ɬ//, [lǽ5m tə1 slə1ʔá5lwə1ɬs tə6 x^{y}ɛ̀3ɬ (with pitch transcription)], /'*He went across the road.*'/, phonology: extra high pitch on article, not infrequent, sentence intonation, downstepping, attested by EB.

<**le'ós**>, ds //ləʔɛ=ás//, DIR ['*be facing toward*'], lx <**=ós**> *on the face*, phonology: vowel merger, syntactic analysis: adverb/adverbial verb, attested by Deming, example: <**le'ós te xálh tel làlèm.**>, //ləʔɛ=ás tə x^{y}ɛ́ɬ tə-l lɛ̀lə̀m//, /'*My house is facing the road.*'/, attested by Deming.

<**sle'ó:thel**>, stvi //s=ləʔɛ́=á·θəl//, DIR /'*be across, be on the other side of*'/, literally /'be on the other side of the mouth'/, (<**s=**> *stative*), lx <**=ó:thel**> *on the mouth*, syntactic analysis: adverb/adverbial verb, attested by Elders Group (3/1/72, 1/19/77), EB, ASM ['across'], example: <**lám te sle'ó:thel**>, //lɛ́=m tə s=ləʔɛ́=á·θəl//, /'*He went across (a river, for ex.) (go).*'/, attested by EB, <**lám te sle'óthels te stó:lō.**>, //lɛ́=m tə s=ləʔɛ́=áθəl-s tə s=tá·l=ow//, /'*He went across the river. (go)*'/, attested by EB, ASM ['be on the other side of'], <**tsel sle'óthel te stó:lō.**>, //c-əl s=ləʔɛ́=áθəl tə s=tá·l=ow//, /'*I'm on the other side of the river.*'/, attested by Elders Group (1/19/77).

<**le'áméstexw**>, TVMO ['*bring s-th to someone*'], *see* mí ~ mé ~ me.

<**le'ós**>, DIR ['*be facing toward*'], *see* le'á.

<**lí ~ li**>, free root //lí ~ li//, DIR /'*be in, in, be on, on, be at, at, before (an audience), (untranslated)*'/, semantic environment ['"be" is omitted when the verb phrase (formed by the vprep and its object nominal phrase) is not a main verb phrase but modifies one in apposition'], syntactic analysis: preposition/prepositional verb,Salish cognate: Lushootseed in part /diʔ/ *to, at the side of, in* H76:138, ASM ['be in, in'], semantic environment ['large geographic area'], example: <**li kw'e north**>, //li k'^{w}ə north//, /'*in the north*'/, attested by AC, <**li te xálh tel méle.**>, //li tə x^{y}ɛ́ɬ tə-l mə́lə//, /'*My child is in the road.*'/, attested by Elders Group, <**lí te x̲ó:tsa**>, //lí tə x̣á·cɛ//, /'*in the lake*'/, attested by Elders Group, ASM ['be on, on'], semantic environment ['small area with surface something can rest on or adhere to'], <**lí te stúp.**>, //lí tə stúp//, /'*It's on the stove.*'/, attested by AD, <**éy, tl'ó yewál éy st'élmexw; welí kw'e li te éqwelets te thqát éwe lís eyém.**>, //ʔɛ́y, ƛ'á yəwɛ́l ʔɛ́y s=t'ə́lməx^{w}; wə=lí k'^{w}ə li tə ʔə́q^{w}ə=ləc-s tə θqɛ́t ʔə́wə lí-s ʔɛy=ə́m//, /'*It's good, it's the best medicine; if it's on the back of the tree it's not as strong.*'/, attested by CT, HT, ASM ['be at, at'], semantic environment ['social event, named place'], <**ilhtset li te sqw'eyílex.**>, //ʔi-ɬ-c-ət li tə s-q'^{w}əy=íl=əx^{y}//, /'*We were at the dance.*'/, attested by AC, <**li te Yex̲sá:y.**>, //li tə yəx̣sɛ́·y//, /'*(It's, He's, She's, They're) at Lawrence (Wash.).*'/, attested by Deming, usage: using a Nooksack placename but speaking in Upriver Halkomelem, <**ilhtsel lí kw'e Chilliwack.**>, //ʔi-ɬ-c-əl lí k'^{w}ə Chilliwack//, [ʔiɬcɪl lí k'^{w}ə číləwæk], /'*I was at Chilliwack (the modern non-Indian town).*'/, attested by AC, ASM ['before'], semantic environment ['an audience'], <**qwà:l li kw'e qéx̲ mestíyexw.**>, //q^{w}ɛ̀·l li k'^{w}ə qə́x̣ məstíyəx^{w}//, /'*announce before lots of people, announce at a gathering*'/, /'*speak before the (remote) many person*'/, attested by CT, HT, ASM ['(not translated)'], semantic environment ['when modifying a phrase with other locational adverbs'], <**lí kw'e s'átl'q qe ő we ís chókw.**>, //lí k'^{w}ə s=ʔɛ́ƛ'q qə ʔówə ʔi-s cák^{w}//, /'*It's outside but not far.*'/, literally /'it's on/at/in the (remote) outside but it's not far'/, attested by EB, <**ye líkw' mőkw' shxwelís li te B.C.**>, //yə lík'^{w} mók'^{w} sx^{w}=lí-s li tə B.C.//, /'*some from all over (in) B.C.*'/, attested by AC, <**lí tí**>, //lí tí//, /'*way over there, over there, there (a little further)*'/, attested by AC, EB, MP, ME, many others, <**li tethá**>, //li tə=θɛ́//, /'*(just) over there, (right) there*'/, attested by AC, EB, AD, many others.

<**shxwlí**>, ds //sx^{w}=lí//, DIR /'*where it's at, where it's from*'/, (<**shxw=**> *nominalizer*), syntactic analysis: nominal, attested by JL, Elders Group, AC, others, example: <**kwxőmexws ta' shxwlí**>,

//kʷəxʸ=ómәxʷ-s t-ɛʔ s=xʷ=lí//, /'*place name, name of the place where you come from*'/, attested by JL, <**te skwxő̄mexws tel shxwlí tl'esu Skw'átets**>, //tә s=kʷәxʸ=ómәxʷ-s tә-l sxʷ=lí ƛ̓ә-s-u s=kʼʷɛ́t=әc//, /'*The (place)name of the place I'm from is Skw'átets.*'/, literally /'the place-name of my where it's from, that's Skw'átets'/, attested by JL, <**ewétal shxwlís**>, //ʔәwә= ́tɛ-l sxʷ=lí-s//, /'*I don't care (what happens).*'/, literally /'it's nothing where I'm at'/, attested by Elders Group, <**ye líkw' mő̄kw' shxwlís li te B.C.**>, //yә líkʼʷ mókʼʷ sxʷ=lí-s li tә B.C.//, /'*some from all over B.C.*'/, literally /'the (plural, human) one all where they're from in B.C.'/, attested by AC, also *see under* xwlí.

<**shxwlístexw**>, caus //sxʷ=lí=sT-әxʷ//, EFAM ['*care about s-o/s-th*'], (<**=st**> *causative control transitivizer*), (<**-exw**> *third person object*) or could be instead related to <**shxwelí**> *life, soul*, syntactic analysis: transitive verb, attested by Elders Group, example: <**ewétal shxwlístexw.**>, //ʔәwә= ́tɛ-l sxʷ=lí=sT-әxʷ//, /'*I don't care about s-th or s-o.*'/, attested by Elders Group, <**ewéta shxwlístexw tewátes.**>, //ʔәwә= ́tɛ sxʷ=lí=sT-әxʷ tә=wɛ́t=әs//, /'*He doesn't care about anyone; he's got no use for anyone; he's impassive.*'/, attested by Elders Group, <**ewéta shxwlístexwes te mámele.**>, //ʔәwә= ́tɛ sxʷ=lí=sT-әxʷ-әs tә C_1ɛ́-mәlә//, /'*He doesn't care about the children.*'/, attested by Elders Group, also *see under* xwlí.

<**lí**>, free root //lí//, DIR ['*be there*'], syntactic analysis: demonstrative verb, attested by AC, others, example: <**í:lhtsel lí.**>, //ʔí·-ɬ-c-әl lí//, /'*I was there.*'/, attested by AC, <**lílhachxw lí?**>, //lí-ɬ-ɛ-c-xʷ lí//, /'*Were you there?*'/, grammatical analysis: yes/no question-past tense-interrogative-subj. of main cl.-2s demonstrative verb, syntactic analysis: interrogative past demonstrative verb, attested by AC, <**éy, tl'ó yewál éy st'élmexw; welí kw'e li te éqwelets te thqát éwe lís eyém.**>, //ʔɛ́y, ƛ̓á yәwɛ́l ʔɛ́y s=tʼә́lmәxʷ; wә-lí kʼʷә li tә ʔә́qʷә=lәc tә θqɛ́t ʔә́wә lí-s ʔɛy=ә́m//, /'*It's good, it's the best medicine; if it's (there) on the back of the tree it's not as strong.*'/, attested by CT, HT.

<**xwelí ~ xwlí**>, ds //xʷә=lí//, DIR /'*get there, arrive there, reach there*'/, TVMO, (<**xwe=**> *get, become*), syntactic analysis: intransitive verb, attested by EB, AC, example: <**máqa qetstu ló me xwlí te smá:lt.**>, //mɛ́qɛ qә-c-t-uw lá mә xʷ=lí tә s=mɛ́·lt//, /'*(There was) (fallen) snow all the way until we reached the mountain.*'/, attested by EB, also *see under* xwlí.

<**xwelí:ls**>, pncs //xʷә=lí=әlәs//, DIR /'*get to, reach there*'/, TVMO, (<**=eles**> *psychological non-control transitivizer*), syntactic analysis: intransitive verb, attested by AC, EB, example: <**lámchexw te théqet qetl'ó:su xwelí:ls te theqát.**>, //lɛ́=m-c-әxʷ tә θә[= ́=]qɛt qә-ƛ̓á-ɛ-s-u xʷә=lí=әlәs tә θәqɛ́t//, /'*Go through the thicket and get to the tree.*'/, attested by AC; found in <**xwelí:lsóxwes**>, //xʷә=lí=әlәs-á(l)xʷ-әs//, /'*He reached us there.*'/, attested by EB.

<**lí ~ lí: ~ li**>, free root //lí ~ lí· ~ li//, DIR /'*(there), (action distant or abstract)*'/, ASM ['the displacement of action is only weakly implied; contrast with the lack of displace when auxiliary í ~ i (here, action present) is used'], may be alloseme instead of separate morpheme of the previous morpheme <**lí**>, free root //lí//, DIR ['*be there*'], syntactic analysis: auxiliary verb used with vneg, attested by AC, EB, CT, others, example: <**ōwe lis the'í:t sta'á kw'e sx̱wōx̱wiyám.**>, //ʔówә li-s θәʔí·t s=t=ɛʔɛ́ kʼʷә s=C_1ә=x̱ʷiyɛ́m//, /'*It's not true, it's like a fable.*'/, attested by AC, <**welí kw'e li te éqwelets te thqát ewe lís eyém.**>, //wә-lí kʼʷә li tә ʔә́qʷә=lәc tә θqɛ́t ʔәwә lí-s ʔɛy=ә́m//, /'*if it's on the back of the tree it's not as strong.*'/, attested by CT, HT, <**ewá:lhtsel lí:l làm.**>, //ʔәwә-ɛ́·ɬ-c-әl lí·-l lɛ́=m//, /'*I wasn't going to go (but did)., (?I never go.)*'/, phonology: downstepping, syntactic analysis: negative habitual past, verb phrase with negative, verb phrase with auxiliary, attested by EB, <**éwechxw líxw tl'ílsthòx.**>, //ʔә́wә-c-xʷ lí-xʷ ƛ̓í=l=sT-áxʸ//, /'*You don't like me.*'/, phonology: downstepping, attested by AC, <**éwetst lí:t lám.**>, //ʔә́wә-c-t lí·-t lɛ́=m//, /'*We didn't go.*'/, attested by AC, <**éwechap lí:p qwélstòlxw.**>, //ʔә́wә-c-ɛp lí·-p qʷɛ[=Aә́=]l=sT-álxʷ//, /'*You folks didn't speak to us.*'/, phonology: downstepping, attested by AC, contrast <**xwewáchxw í:xw toteló:met.**>, //xʷә=әwә=ɛ́-c=xʷ ʔí·-xʷ

tə[=AáC$_1$ə=]l=l-á·mət//, /'*You don't yet understand.*'/, attested by AC, contrast <**stám te íxw (kwelá:t, thá:yt)?**>, //s=tɛ́m tə ʔí-xʷ (kʷəl=ɛ́·=T, θi[-Aɛ́·-]y=T//, /'*What are you (holding, making)?*'/, attested by AC.

<**lí**>, free root //lí//, LANG /'*yes (answer to yes/no question), do (affirmative), I/you/we/you folks/they do (affirmative), he/she/it does (affirmative), be (affirmative), I am (affirmative), you/we/you folks/they are (affirmative), he/she/it is (affirmative)*'/, CJ, syntactic analysis: auxiliary verb, attested by AC, AD, Deming, BJ, BHTTC, EB; found in <**lí.**>, //lí//, /'*Yes., I did., (Yes) We are., etc.*'/, attested by AD, also /'*Yes.*'/, attested by Deming, BJ (12/5/64), <**lítsel.**>, //lí-c-əl//, /'*I did.*'/, attested by AD, example: <**lí, chexw lám.**>, //lí, c-əxʷ lɛ́=m//, /'*Yes, you went.*'/, attested by AC, <**lí mà.**>, //lí mɛ̀//, /'*I guess so.*'/, semantic environment ['reply to líchxw we'éyòl (Are you doing well?)'], usage: conversational, dialects: *Seabird Island*, attested by BHTTC, also <**lí á.**>, //lí ʔɛ́//, dialects: *Cheh.*, attested by BHTTC; found in <**lí'àwèlh.**>, //lí=ʔɛwə̀ɬ//, /'*Yes of course.*'/, dialects: *Cheh., Tait*, attested by EB, AD, <**le'áwélh.**>, //li=ʔɛ́wə́ɬ or li=Aə=ʔɛ́wə́ɬ or lə=ʔɛ́wə́ɬ//, /'*Yes, thanks.*'/, semantic environment ['answer to a person who just said "Look after yourself." while leaving'], usage: conversational, attested by NP, also <**á'á'àwèlh.**>, //ʔɛ́ʔɛ́=ʔɛwə̀ɬ//, dialects: *Cheh., Tait*, attested by EB, AD, <**lí:lh.**>, //lí-əɬ//, /'*That's right.*'/, literally /'It was (affirmative).'/, syntactic analysis: past affixed, attested by EB, example: <**u lí ~ lu lí.**>, //ʔu lí ~ lə-u lí//, /'*Yes, there's some.*'/, literally /'contrastive yes ~ past third person -contrastive yes'/, <**u lí, lí. ~ wulí tethá.**>, //ʔu-lí, lí ~ wu-lí tə=θɛ́//, /'*(Yes) he's there.*'/, attested by EB.

<**lí ~ lí: ~ líye**>, if //lí ~ lí-ə//, CJ ['*yes/no question*'], literally /'is it yes?'/, (<**-e**> *interrogative, yes/no question*), syntactic analysis: interrogative verb, attested by AC, Elders at Fish Camp (7/11/78), AD, MC, BHTTC, example: <**lí éy?**>, //lí ʔɛ́y//, /'*Was it good?*'/, attested by AC, <**lí éy ta' s'ítet?**>, //lí ʔɛ́y t-ɛʔ s-ʔítət//, /'*Did you sleep well?*'/, literally /'is it good your nominal-sleep'/, attested by Elders at Fish Camp (7/11/78), also <**líchxw we'ítet kw'e éy?**>, //lí-c-xʷ wə=ʔítət k'ʷə ʔɛ́y//, attested by Elders at Fish Camp (7/11/78), <**lí chòkw te lálems qa (~ q'a) lí stetís?**>, //lí càkʷ tə lɛ́ləm-s qɛ (~ q'ɛ) lí s=tə[=C_1əAí=]s//, /'*Is his house far or is it nearby?*'/, attested by AC, <**líchxw eqw'í:wsem?**>, //lí-c-xʷ ʔəq'ʷ=í·ws=əm//, /'*Did you dry yourself off (with a towel)?*'/, attested by AD, <**líchxw tu éyò?**>, //lí-c-xʷ tu ʔɛ́y-à//, /'*How are you?*'/, literally /'are you a little good -just'/, attested by AD, <**líchap mőkw' álhtel?**>, //lí-c-ɛp mók'ʷ ʔɛ́ɬtəl//, /'*Did you (pl.) all eat?*'/, attested by AC, <**lí a stl'í**>, //lí ʔɛ s=ƛ'í//, /'*do you want ...*'/, literally /'is it your want'/, attested by AC, many others, <**lí lám kw'e Albert?**>, //lí lɛ́=m k'ʷə Albert//, /'*Did Albert go?*'/, attested by AC, <**líye qéx̱?**>, //lí(y)-ə qə́x̣//, /'*Is it a lot?*'/, attested by AC, <**líyecha lám?**>, //lí(y)-ə-cɛ lɛ́=m//, /'*Will he go?*'/, attested by MC (of Sardis), <**lílhachexw x̱à:m?**>, //lí-ɬ-ɛ-c-xʷx̣ɛ̀·m//, /'*Were you crying?*'/, usage: answer: ílhtsel x̱à:m (I was crying.), attested by BHTTC.

<**lí: ~ lí ~ líye**>, CJ ['*yes/no question*'], *see* lí.

<**lílakw'wì:l**>, REL ['*small cross*'], *see* lakwwí:l.

<**lí:latses**>, BSK ['*little berry basket*'], *see* elíle.

<**lílehà:l**>, PLAY /'*starting to play slahal, (to gamble [Elders Group 3/15/72])*'/, *see* lehà:l.

<**lilekyó:lta**>, PLAY ['*a bunch playing cards*'], *see* lekyó:lta.

<**lilekó:ltel**>, PLAY /'*playing cards [verb]*'/, *see* lekyó:lta.

<**lílem**>, BLDG /'*little house, cabin (say 12 ft. x 10 ft. or less), small home, storage house (small shed-like house, enclosed with door), outhouse (slang), toilet (slang)*'/, *see* lá:lém.

<**lílemas**>, CH ['*saying Mass*'], *see* lomá:s ~ lemá:s.

<**lí:leq**>, stvi //lí·[=C_1ə=]q//, DESC /*'it's easy, be easy, easy (to get)*'/, (<**=R1=**> *stative*), phonology: reduplication, syntactic analysis: adjective/adjectival verb, attested by AC, EB, Salish cognate: Sechelt /lilíq/ *cheap* T77:21, also <**líleqw**>, //lí[=C_1ə=]q^{w}//, comment: qw prob. sic for q as in cognates, attested by Elders Group (5/3/78), <**lí:leq syó:ys.**>, //lí·[=C_1ə=]q s=yá·ys//, /*'It's easy work.*'/, attested by AC.

<**líleqwesem**>, ABFC [*'nodding one's head*'], *see* líqw.

<**lilk'eyáp**>, EZ [*'little coyote*'], *see* slek'iyáp.

<**lílōt**>, free root //lílòt//, CAN /*'railroad, (railroad track [IHTTC])*'/, TVMO, borrowed from English <**railroad**> [ré:lrod], syntactic analysis: nominal, attested by Elders check song, also <**lílú:t**>, //lílú·t//, attested by Deming, also /*'railroad track*'/, attested by IHTTC.

<**líqw**>, bound root //líq^{w} *slacken*//.

<**líqwem**>, mdls //líq^{w}=əm//, WETH /*'slackened down, calmed down*'/, WATR, DESC, (<**=em**> *middle voice*), syntactic analysis: intransitive verb, attested by Elders Group.

<**líqwel**>, incs //líq^{w}=əl//, WETH /*'(get) calm, (become) calm, peaceful*'/, WATR, DESC, (<**=el**> *get, become, go, come*), syntactic analysis: intransitive verb, attested by Elders Group, Deming, example: <**líqwel te swáyel.**>, //líq^{w}=əl tə s=wɛ́yəl//, /*'The day is calm.*'/, attested by Elders Group, <**líqwel te qó:.**>, //líq^{w}=əl tə qá·//, /*'The water is calm.*'/, attested by Elders Group, <**líqwel te speháls.**>, //líq^{w}=əl tə s=pəh=ɛ́ls//, /*'The wind has stopped.*'/, dialects: *Chill.*, attested by Deming, also <**chémq te spehál s.**>, //cə́mq tə s=pəh=ɛ́ls//, dialects: *Cheh.*, attested by Deming.

<**líqwet**>, pcs //líq^{w}=əT//, MC /*'slacken it, let it out (of a rope), loosen it, (lower it (*prob. *of s-th suspended)*'/, (<**=et**> *purposeful control transitivizer*), syntactic analysis: transitive verb, attested by IHTTC, EB, and RG & EH (4/9/99 Ling332), also /*'lower it (*prob. *of something suspended)*'/, attested by Elders Group, example: <**we'ólwe thethá:kw', líqwetlha.**>, //wə=ʔál wə=θə[=C_1ə=Aɛ́·=]k'^{w}, líq^{w}=əT-ɬɛ//, /*'It's pulled too tight (pulled tight), loosen it.*'/, <**líqwet te <u>x</u>wéylem**>, //líq^{w}=əT təx̣^{w}íləm//, /*'let out a rope*'/, attested by IHTTC.

<**Líqwetem**>, df //líq^{w}=əT-əm//, N [*'name of a man from Yale who had seven wives*'], ASM ['he had supported all his wives, had them in different villages, and had 94 grandchildren; he lived at Yale and is buried there; he was part Stó:lō and part Thompson; he was Edna Bobb's husband's grand-uncle'], literally /'he was let loose (prob.)(prob. because he was described as always travelling from one wife and family to another)'/, (<**-em**> probably *passive*), syntactic analysis: nominal, attested by EB, and others.

<**líqwethet**>, pcrs //líq^{w}=əT-ət//, /*'to loosen up*'/, (<**=ét**> *purposeful control transitivizer*), (<**-et**> *reflexive*), attested by RG & EH (4/9/99 Ling332)

<**slí:leqw**>, stvi //s=lí·[=C_1ə=]q^{w}//, DESC /*'be slack, loose, too loose, hanging loose (of a slackened rope)*'/, semantic environment ['of rope, clothes, anything'], (<**s=**> *stative*), (<**=R1=**> *continuative* or *resultative*), phonology: reduplication, syntactic analysis: adjective/adjectival verb, attested by EB, Elders Group, IHTTC, also <**slíleqw**>, //s=lí[=C_1ə=]q^{w}//, attested by IHTTC.

<**líqwesem**>, mdls //líq^{w}=əs=əm//, ABFC /*'nod one's head, nod one's head (up and down for yes for ex.)*'/, lx <**=es**> *on the face*, (<**=em**> *middle voice*), syntactic analysis: intransitive verb, attested by EB, IHTTC, and RG & EH (4/9/99 Ling332).

<**líleqwesem**>, cts //lí[-C_1ə-]q^{w}=əs=əm//, ABFC [*'nodding one's head*'], (<**-R1-**> *continuative*), phonology: reduplication, syntactic analysis: intransitive verb, attested by EB.

<**léqw**>, possibly root //lə́q^{w} or perhaps li[=Aə=]q^{w}//, ABFC [*'fall asleep*'], possibly <**é-ablaut**>

derivational, phonology: possible ablaut, syntactic analysis: intransitive verb, attested by BHTTC, example: <**lí léqw?**>, //lí lə́q^w//, /'*Did he fall asleep?*'/, attested by BHTTC.

<**líqwel**>, WETH /'*(get) calm, (become) calm, peaceful*'/, *see* líqw.

<**líqwem**>, WETH ['*got warm*'], *see* léqwem.

<**líqwem**>, WETH /'*slackened down, calmed down*'/, *see* líqw.

<**líqwesem**>, ABFC /'*nod one's head, nod one's head (up and down for yes for ex.)*'/, *see* líqw.

<**líqwet**>, MC /'*slacken it, let it out (of a rope), loosen it, (lower it (*prob. *of s-th suspended)*'/, *see* líqw.

<**Líqwetem**>, N ['*name of a man from Yale who had seven wives*'], *see* líqw.

<**líqw'em**>, mdls //líq'^{w}=əm//, DESC ['*soft*'], semantic environment ['of sounds, material, hands, cloth'], (<**=em**> *middle voice*), syntactic analysis: adjective/adjectival verb, attested by Elders Group, BHTTC, IHTTC.

<**lisós**>, free root //lisás//, CH ['*angel*'], syntactic analysis: nominal, attested by Elders Group, also <**lísòs**>, //lísàs//, attested by EB, borrowed from Chinook Jargon <**lesash**> /lesás/ *angel* Johnson 1978:419 itself from French <**les anges**> [lezã̌ž] *the angels.*

<**=líth'e**>, WV ['*processed fiber*'], *see* íth'a.

<**líxw**>, bound root //líx^w//, root meaning uncertain

<**slílexwelh**>, stvi //s=lí[=C_1ə=]x^w=əɬ//, EFAM ['*be calm*'], (<**s=**> *stative*), possibly <**=R1=**> *continuative*, possibly <**=elh**> *according to the ways of*??, phonology: reduplication, syntactic analysis: adjective/adjectival verb, attested by Deming, comment: this word is suspiciously similar in form and meaning to slíleqw *be slack, loose* and the same root in líqwem *slackened down, calmed down*, example: <**atsel slílexwelh.**>, //ʔɛ-c-əl s=lí[=C_1ə=]x^{w}əɬ//, /'*I was calm.*'/.

<**silíxw**>, free stem //s-hi-líx^w// or free root //silíx^w//, TVMO /'*slow down, go slow*'/, syntactic analysis: intransitive verb, attested by Elders Group (3/29/78).

<**silíxwstexw**>, caus //s=hi=líx^w=sT-əx^w// or //silíx^w=sT-əx^w//, TVMO ['*making s-o slow*'], (<**=st**> *causative control transitivizer*), (<**-exw**> *third person object*), the continuative translation here makes it most likely the stem structure is //s-hi-líx^w// with continuative prefix <**hi-**>, stative prefix <**s-**> which causes the <**h**> to drop, and root <**líxw**> as in <**slílexwelh**>, stvi //s=lí[=C_1ə=]x^w(=)əɬ//, EFAM ['*be calm*'], syntactic analysis: transitive verb, attested by Elders Group; found in <**silíxwsthométsel.**>, //silíx^w=sT-ámə-c-əl//, /'*I'm making you slow.*'/.

<**líye ~ lí: ~ lí**>, CJ ['*yes/no question*'], *see* lí.

<**líyém ~ leyém**>, mdls //líy=ə́m ~ ləy=ə́m//, ABFC ['*to laugh*'], (<**=em**> *middle voice*), phonology: updrifting or stressed intransitivizer, syntactic analysis: intransitive verb, attested by Elders Group, AC, other sources: ES /layə́m/, Salish cognate: PCS cognate set #80 (*náyəm ~ *nə́yəm/) G82:20, thus SanSgCl dialect of N. Straits /nə́č'-əŋ/ *laugh*, Nooksack /nǽy-æm/ *laugh*, etc., example: <**leyémlha**>, //ləy=ə́m-ɬɛ//, /'*Laugh now.*'/, syntactic analysis: imperative, attested by AC.

<**lá:yem ~ láyem**>, cts //lə[-Aɛ́·-]y=əm ~ lə[-Aɛ́-]y=əm//, ABFC ['*laughing*'], (<**á(:)-ablaut**> *continuative*), phonology: ablaut, syntactic analysis: intransitive verb, attested by AC, Elders Group (12/10/75).

<**lívliyem**>, plv //líy=C_1əC_2=əm//, ABFC /'*lots of laughing, (many are laughing [AC])*'/, ds //=C_1əC_2 *plural (actions)*//, phonology: reduplication, syntactic analysis: intransitive verb, attested by Elders Group (12/10/75), also <**léyleyèm**>, //lə́y=C_1əC_2=ə̀m//, also /'*many are laughing*'/, attested by AC, <**léyleyèm te stá:xwelh.**>, //lə́y=C_1əC_2=ə̀m tə s=tɛ́·x^w=əɬ//, /'*The children are laughing.*'/, attested

by AC.

<**alíliyem ~ elíliyem**>, df //ʔɛ=líy=C_1əC_2=əm ~ ʔə=líy=C_1əC_2=əm//, ABFC ['*laughter*'], possibly <**a= ~ e=**> perhaps from <**há- ~ hé-**> *resultative or continuative*, phonology: reduplication, syntactic analysis: nominal, attested by IHTTC.

<**xwlíyémés**>, ds //xʷ=líy=ə́m=əs//, ABFC ['*to smile*'], (<**xw= ~ xwe=**> *become, get*), lx <**=es ~ =ó:s**> *on the face*, phonology: updrifting (since =es is the unstressed allomorph of =ó:s), syntactic analysis: intransitive verb, (semological comment: this example provides the first clear example of the inceptive function of the xw= prefix that so often occurs when a lexical suffix occurs which refers to some part of the head), attested by Elders Group.

<**xwló:yemes**>, cts //xʷ=li[-Aá·-]y=əm=əs//, ABFC ['*smiling*'], (<**á:-ablaut**> *continuative*), phonology: the added long vowel discourages updrifting on =em (middle voice) and without high-stress on =em, the final =es cannot updrift either, syntactic analysis: intransitive verb, attested by Elders Group.

<**líyliyem**>, ABFC /'*lots of laughing, (many are laughing [AC])*'/, *see* líyém ~ leyém.

<**líyóm**>, free root //líyám//, CH /'*devil, Satan*'/, syntactic analysis: nominal, attested by Elders Group, EB, DF, borrowed from Chinook Jargon <**le job, le jaub, le yom**> *devil* Johnson 1978:301, itself from French <**diable**> *devil.*

<**Líyómxetel**>, ds //líyám=xʸəl=təl//, PLN ['*Devil's Run*'], ASM ['a place on the Fraser River just west of Lackaway (Láx̱ewey), must be a recent name since it is based on a Chinook Jargon root, one inhabitant was a strong shaman, Charlie Seymour, who "owned" everything and everyone in the area and took whomever he wished for a wife (and had many wives) according to Reuben Ware's interview with DF'], literally /'devil's foot place'/, lx <**=xel**> *on the foot, on the leg*, lx <**=tel**> *device, thing for*, sometimes *place*, as said to be the meaning here, phonology: consonant-loss (=xel → =xe before =tel, =íl, and some other suffixes, syntactic analysis: nominal, attested by Elders Group (DF)(7/13/77), source: place names reference file #77, also <**S(e)má:th**>, //s=mɛ́·θ//, attested by Elders Group.

<**Líyómxetel**>, PLN ['*Devil's Run*'], *see* líyóm.

<**Lkwőxwethem**>, PLN ['*Six-Mile Creek and bay on west side of Harrison Lake*'], *see* kwőxweth.

<**ló**>, free root //lá//, DIR ['*here*'], ASM ['need not be present or even close'], syntactic analysis: demonstrative verb or adverb/adverbial verb, syntactic comment: invariably compounded with a preceding demonstrative article yielding a translation of: here, this (lit. "what's here" if considered as a relative clause), attested by NP, AD, AC, others, example: <**li s'ú:met te stó:les te ló?**>, //li s=ʔə[=Aú·-]mət tə s=tá·ləs tə lá//, /'*Is the wife lazy here?*'/, attested by NP, AD, <**tl'ó: the ló slháli?**>, //ƛ'á-ə θə lá s=ɬɛ́li//, /'*Is it this woman?*'/, literally /'is that the (female) here woman'/, ASM ['she need not be close to the speaker'], semantic environment ['said while pointing'], attested by AC, <**st'á kw'e lò**>, //st'ɛ́ k'ʷə là//, /'*(It's) like this.*'/, attested by EB, <**lí lhe'á kw'eló?**>, //lí ɬ=əʔɛ́ k'ʷəlá//, /'*Did he go through there?*'/, (semological comment: (is there sic for here)), attested by Elders Group, <**lí tl'o ló**>, //lí ƛ'a lá//, /'*(it's) way over there*'/, literally /'is there that's the one here'/, attested by Elders Group (3/72), AC.

<**íkw'eló ~ íkw'elo**>, cpds //ʔí=k'ʷə=lá//, DIR /'*here, this place*'/, literally /'here=the (abstract)=here → here=this'/, syntactic analysis: adverb/adverbial verb, demonstrative verb, attested by AC, Elders Group, many others, example: <**íkw'elo lálem**>, //ʔí=k'ʷə=la lɛ́ləm//, /'*this house*'/, attested by AC.

<**tloqá:ys**>, cpds //tə=la=qɛ́·ys//, TIME /'*now, this moment, this instant*'/, literally /'this now'/, syntactic analysis: adverb/adverbial verb, attested by AD, many others, example: <**éy t'we kw'as**

th'ex̲wewíls tloqá:ys.>, //ʔɛ́y t'wə k'ʷ-ɛ-s θ'əx̣ʷ=əwíls tə=la=qɛ́·ys//, /'*You better wash the dishes now.*'/, literally /'it's good evidently/must be that you wash dishes now'/, attested by AD.

<**tlowáyél ~ tlówàyèl**>, cpds //tə=la=wɛ́yə́l//, TIME /'*today, this day*'/, literally /'this day'/, syntactic analysis: adverb/adverbial verb, attested by AC, BJ (5.64), DM (12/4/64), many others, example: <**ílhtsel lí tlowáyél.**>, //ʔí-ɬ-c-əl lí tə=la=wɛ́yə́l//, /'*I was there today.*'/, attested by AC.

<**lók ~ làk**>, bound root //lák ~ lɛ̀k *log*//, borrowed from English <**log**>.

<**lokáwtxw**>, ds //lak=ɛ́wtxʷ//, BLDG /'*log house, log-cabin*'/, lx <**=áwtxw**> *house, building*, syntactic analysis: nominal, attested by Elders Group.

<**ts-hélàk**>, ds //c=hə́=lɛ̀k// or //c=hə́=lá[=Aɛ̀=]k//, CSTR ['*logging*'], BLDG, ACL, Elder's comment: "not based on a Halq'eméylem word, just made up after the white man", (<**ts=** ~ **ch=**> *have*, <hé= ~ há=> *continuative*, perhaps <**à**-ablaut> *derivational*), phonology: rare example where orthography requires hyphen to distinguish ts-h (/c + h/) from t-sh (/t + š/), syntactic analysis: nominal?, intransitive verb?, attested by Elders Group (RP), Deming, other sources: JH /cəshə́lèk/ *logging*, example: <**x̲wá:ytem te ts-hélak.**>, //x̣ʷɛ́·y=T-əm tə c=hə́=lɛ̀k//, /'*Logging killed him.*'/, literally /'he was killed in a group by logging'/, syntactic comment: passive with oblique agent unmarked, attested by Deming.

<**lokáwtxw**>, BLDG /'*log house, log-cabin*'/, *see* lók ~ làk.

<**lólemet**>, TVMO ['*throwing and hitting s-th*'], *see* ló:m ~ lóm.

<**lólets'e**>, NUM /'*one person, be alone*'/, *see* léts'a ~ léts'e.

<**lóli(y)** or **lóy**> possible bound root //láli(y) or láy//, *lean*

<**slóli**>, stvi //s=láli(y) or s=lá[=C_1ə=]y//, DESC ['*be leaning*'], (<**s=**> *stative*), possibly <**=R1=**> *continuative or durative*, phonology: reduplication?, syntactic analysis: adjective/adjectival verb, attested by NP.

<**slóliyes ~ slólí:s**>, df //s=lá[=C_1ə=]y(=/-)əs//, DESC ['*be leaning*'], possibly <**=es**> *on the face* or possibly <**-es**> *third person subject subjunctive*? or -s> *third person possessive*, syntactic analysis: adjective/adjectival verb, attested by Elders Group, SP (and AK, AD)(Raft trip), example: <**slóliyes te thqát.**>, //s=lá[=C_1ə=]yəs tə θqɛ́t//, /'*The tree is leaning.*'/, attested by Elders Group, also <**slólí:s te thqá:t.**>, //s=lálí·s tə θqɛ́·t//, attested by SP (and AK, AD).

<**sló:litses**>, df //s=lá·[=C_1ə=]y=cəs//, DESC ['*leaning to one side*'], literally /'leaning on the hand'/, lx <**=tses**> *on the hand*, syntactic analysis: adjective/adjectival verb?, intransitive verb, attested by Elders Group, also <**slólitses**>, //s=lá[=C_1ə=]y=cəs//, also /'*leaning a board or pole*'/, attested by TM, example: <**ye'í:mex te sló:litses.**>, //yə=ʔí[-·-]m=əxʸ tə s=lá[=C_1ə=]y=cəs//, /'*He's walking leaning to one side.*'/, attested by Elders Group.

<**ló:lt**> or <**lát**>, possible stem or root //lá·lt or lɛt//, *sad, sour,* or <**le'á**>, bound root //ləʔɛ́ *facing away, on the other side*//, see it above.

<**sló:ltes**>, df //s=lá·lt=əs or s=lɛ[=Aá·C_1ə=]t=əs//, EFAM /'*looking sad, (making a sour face [MV, EF])*'/, (<**s=**> *stative*), possibly stem <**ló:lt**> *sour, sad*, possibly root <**lát**> *dark, night* or <**le'á**>, //ləʔɛ́ *facing away, on the other side*//, possibly <**=R1=**> *continuative*, lx <**=es**> *on the face*, phonology: ó:-ablaut automatically triggered on root vowel <**a**> (/ɛ/) by <**=es**> *on the face*, possible reduplication, syntactic analysis: adjective/adjectival verb, attested by Deming (MV, EF), also <**xwló'eltes**>, //xʷ=lɛ́[=AáʔC_1ə=]t=əs// or less likely //xʷ=ləʔɛ́=Aá[=M2]=C_1ə=t=əs//, also /'*making a sour face*'/, phonology: the Matsqui dialect is often heard beside the Chilliwack dialect at Deming and is a Downriver dialect with <'> (glottal stop, /ʔ/) instead of length, before consonants, and infixed as *continuative*, attested by Deming (MV, EF).

<**ló:m ~ lóm**>, free root //lá·m ~ lám//, TVMO ['*get hit (by s-th thrown or airborne)*'], syntactic analysis: intransitive verb, attested by JL, also <lóm> //lám//, /'*it hit (what was aimed for)*'/, attested by RG & EH (4/9/99 Ling332), example: <**ló:m í te tépsems.**>, //lá·m ʔí tə tə́psəm-s//, /'*(He/She/It) got hit on the neck.*'/, literally /'third person got hit (by s-th airborne) on his/her/it's back of the neck or back of the head'/, attested by JL, <**lóm í te sqw'éméls.**>, //lám ʔí tə s=q'^{w}ə́m=ə́ls//, /'*(He) got hit on the forehead.*'/, attested by JL.

<**ló:met ~ lómet**>, pcs //lá·m=əT ~ lám=əT//, TVMO /'*throw and hit s-th/s-o, strike s-th/s-o (with something thrown)*'/, semantic environment ['lightning strikes, a snake strikes, a spear, arrow, rock strikes s-th'], (<**=et**> *purposeful control transitivizer*), also <**lómet**>, //lám=əT//, /'hit it (what was aimed for)'/, attested by RG & EH (4/9/99 Ling332), syntactic analysis: transitive verb, attested by EB, Deming, MV, AC; found in <**ló:metes.**>, //lá·m=əT-əs//, /'*He threw and hit s-o with a stick or rock.*'/, attested by EB, example: <**lómetes te shxwexwó:s.**>, //lám=əT-əs tə s=x^{w}əx^{w}á·s//, /'*Lightning strikes it., A thunderbolt strikes it.*'/, literally /'the thunderbird/thunder throws and hits s-th/s-o'/, attested by Deming, MV, <**kwútes te smált qesesu lómethóxes.**>, //k^{w}ú=T-əs tə s=mɛ́lt qə-s-əs-u lám=əT-áx^y-əs//, /'*He picked up the rock and threw it at me (and hit me).*'/, attested by AC.

<**lólemet**>, cts //lá[-C_1ə-]m=əT//, TVMO ['*throwing and hitting s-th*'], (<**-R1-**> *continuative*), phonology: reduplication, half-long vowel under stress, syntactic analysis: transitive verb, attested by EB.

<**ló:metsel**>, df //lá·m=əcəl//, ABFC ['*get carried away and sleepy from eating too rich food*'], EFAM, FOOD, probably <**=etsel**> *on the back*, probably root <**ló:m**> *struck or hit by s-th thrown*, syntactic analysis: intransitive verb, attested by Elders Group, also with this meaning is <**melmelő́ws**>, //məl=C_1əC_2=óws//, ['*get carried away and sleepy from eating too rich food*'], phonology: reduplication, attested by Elders Group.

<**xwelemő́welh ~ xwlemő́welh**>, ds //x^{w}ə=lom=ówəɬ//, TVMO ['*get hit on the back*'], (<**xwe= ~ xw=**> *become, get*), lx <**=ő́welh**> *canoe, bowl-like container*, syntactic analysis: intransitive verb, attested by AK or SP or AD (on Raft trip 8/30/77).

<**lomá:s ~ lemá:s**>, free root //lamɛ́·s ~ ləmɛ́·s//, CH /'*Mass, (to say Mass?)*'/, syntactic analysis: nominal?, intransitive verb?, attested by Elders Group, borrowed from Chinook Jargon <**la messe, la mass**> *ceremony of the Mass* Johnson 1978:363, itself from French <**la messe**> *the Mass.*

<**lílemas**>, cts //C_1í-ləmɛs//, CH ['*saying Mass*'], (<**R4-**> *continuative*), phonology: unusual meaning for this type of reduplication, syntactic analysis: intransitive verb, attested by Elders Group.

<**ló:met ~ lómet**>, TVMO /'*throw and hit s-th/s-o, strike s-th/s-o (with something thrown)*'/, *see* ló:m ~ lóm.

<**=l=ómet** or **=l-ómet ~ =l=ó:met**>, da //=l=ámət or =l-ámət ~ =l=á·mət//, PRON /'*non-control reflexive, happen to or manage to or accidentally do to oneself*'/, syntactic analysis: derivational suffix, or derivational suffix plus is, syntactic comment: the reflexive part of this combination has been shown as an inflection thoughout most of the dictionary, but could probably better be counted as derivational since it changes a transitive verb to an intransitive syntactically; found in <**ts'ísemlò:mèt**>, //c'ís=əm=l=á·mət//, /'*grow up, raise oneself*'/, phonology: downstepping, updrifting, <**x̲éyx̲elò:met**>, //x̣í=C_1ə=l=á·mət//, /'*shame oneself, be embarassed*'/, phonology: downstepping, updrifting, <**itetlómet**>, //ʔítət=l=ámət//, /'*fall asleep*'/, <**lhx̲eylexlómet**>, //ɬ=x̣íl=əx^y=l=ámət//, /'*stand up by oneself*'/.

<**ló:metsel**>, ABFC ['*get carried away and sleepy from eating too rich food*'], *see* ló:m ~ lóm.

<**lopál**>, free root //lapɛ́l//, TOOL /'*shovel, spade*'/, syntactic analysis: nominal, attested by AC, borrowed from Chinook Jargon <**la pell**> *spade, shovel* Johnson 1978:407, itself from French <**la pelle**> *shovel, scoop*.

<**lópe**x̲**wem**>, SD ['*making noise*'], *see* ló:px̲wem.

<**lópe**x̲**wemstexw**>, SD ['*making noise*'], *see* ló:px̲wem.

<**loplós ~ leplós**>, free root //laplás ~ ləplás//, BLDG /'*plank, board, lumber*'/, syntactic analysis: nominal, attested by AC, Elders Group, borrowed from Chinook Jargon <**laplash, laplosh**> *lumber* Johnson 1978:359, itself from French <**la planche**> *board, plank*, example: <**le xwálxes te x̲wétes (leplós, lesák, smá:lt).**>, //lə xʷɛ́l=xʸ-əs təx̣ʷə́təs (ləplás, ləsɛ́k, s=mɛ́·lt)//, /'*He lifted the heavy (plank, sack, rock).*'/, attested by AC, <**ts'q'éyx̲ leplós**>, //c'=q'íx̣ ləplás//, /'*black board, blackboard*'/, SCH, attested by Elders Group.

<**lopót**>, free root //lapát//, HHG ['*cup*'], syntactic analysis: nominal, attested by AC, also <**lepót**>, //ləpát//, attested by DM (12/4/64), borrowed from Chinook Jargon <**le pot**> *pot* Johnson 1978:387 itself from French <**le pot**> *pot, jug, can, jar, mug*, see main dialect form <**lepót**>.

<**lópōs**>, df //láp(=)ows//, CLO ['*cape*'], possibly <**=ōws**> *on the body*, syntactic analysis: nominal, attested by Elders Group (1/21/76), probably borrowed from Chinook Jargon or French but no source word has yet been found and in such borrowing the first syllable when ultimately from a French article <**le, la, les**> is rarely (if ever) stressed in Halkomelem; if the analysis with <=ōws> is correct this form is not a borrowing at all but has a Halkomelem root as well; more evidence seems to point to a Halkomelem origin than to a borrowing.

<**ló:px̲wem**>, mdls //lá·px̣ʷ=əm//, SD /'*make noise, be noisy, (a noise [EB], making noise [EB])*'/, ASM ['see Halkomelem words for the following noises: crackle, pop, crunch, gurgle, bang, thud, gnawing, scratching, knock, rap, roar, rumble, fall splat, suction sound of something being pulled out of mud, fizz, sizzle, whisper, hiss, whistle, echo, etc.'], (<**=em**> *middle voice*), syntactic analysis: intransitive verb, attested by Elders Group, AD, Salish cognate: Squamish /lə́-lʔəpx̣ʷm/ *noisy* W73:186, K69:74, also <**lópx̲wem**>, //lápx̣ʷ=əm//, also /'*a noise; making noise*'/, attested by EB, (semological comment: neither translation really seems justified by the form: there is no nominalizer to yield "a noise" and no continuative inflection to yield "making noise"), example: <**líchxw ts'lhámet kw'e lópx̲wem?**>, //lí-c-xʷ c'ɬɛ=məT k'ʷə lápx̣ʷ=əm//, /'*Did you hear a noise.*'/, attested by EB, <**ólewe lópx̲wem**>, //ʔálə=wə lápx̣ʷ=əm//, /'*making too much noise*'/, attested by EB, <**éwechxw we'ólew ló:px̲wem.**>, //ʔə́wə-c-xʷ wə=ʔál=əw lá·px̣ʷ=əm//, /'*Don't be so noisy.*'/, literally /'don't you too much be noisy'/, attested by AD.

<**lópex̲wem**>, cts //láp[-ə-]x̣ʷ=əm//, SD ['*making noise*'], (<**-e-**> unusual for *continuative*), phonology: infixed vowel, syntactic analysis: intransitive verb, attested by Elders Group.

<**lópx̲wemstexw**>, caus //lápx̣ʷ=əm=sT-əxʷ//, SD /'*make s-th be noisy, make noise with s-th*'/, (<**=st**> *causative control transitivizer*), (<**-exw**> *third person object*), syntactic analysis: transitive verb, attested by AD, EB; found in <**lópx̲wemstxwes**>, //lápx̣ʷ=əm=sT-əxʷ-əs//, /'*He made noise., He makes a noise.*'/, attested by EB, example: <**kwelhtstu lópx̲wemstxwes.**>, //kʷəɬctu lápx̣ʷ=əm=sT-əxʷ-əs//, /'*My, but he made a lot of noise.*'/, attested by EB, <**chap we'ólew lópx̲wemstexw ta' syó:yselep.**>, //c-ɛp wə=ʔál=əw lápx̣ʷ=əm=sT-əxʷ t-ɛʔ s=yá·ys-ələp//, /'*You folks are making too much noise with your work., You folks are making your work be too noisy.*'/, attested by AD.

<**lópex̲wemstexw**>, cts //láp[-ə-]x̣ʷ=əm=sT-əxʷ//, SD ['*making noise*'], (<**-e-**> unusual for

continuative), phonology: infixed vowel, syntactic analysis: transitive verb, attested by EB; found in <**lópex̱wemstexwes.**>, //láp[-ə-]x̣ʷ=əm=sT-əxʷ-əs//, /'*He's making noise.*'/, attested by EB.

<**lópx̱wemstexw**>, SD /'*make s-th be noisy, make noise with s-th*'/, *see* ló:px̱wem.

<**lopyúws**>, free root //lapyúws//, TOOL ['*hoe*'], HARV, ACL, syntactic analysis: nominal, attested by AC, borrowed from Chinook Jargon <**la pioche, la pe-osh**> /la-pe-ós/ *hoe, pick, mattock* Johnson 1978:343-344.

<**lóqwet**>, pcs //láqʷ=əT//, MC ['*stake it (for ex. of a horse)*'], TVMO, (<**=et**> *purposeful control transitivizer*), syntactic analysis: transitive verb, attested by Elders Group, example: <**lóqwet qesu q'éyset te stiqíw**>, //láqʷ=əT qə=s=u q'ís=əT tə s=tiqíw//, /'*stake and tie a horse*'/, attested by Elders Group.

<**ló:s ~ lós**>, free root //lá·s ~ lás//, ABFC ['*be fat*'], DESC, phonology: phonetically [a] here ~ [ɔ], syntactic analysis: adjective/adjectival verb, attested by AC, Elders Group (3/72, 1/19/77), EB; found in <**ló:schexw.**>, //lá·s-c-əxʷ//, /'*You're fat.*'/, attested by AC, example: <**ló:s te sqwmáy.**>, //lá·s tə s=qʷm=ɛ́y//, /'*The dog is fat.*'/, attested by AC, <**líy lós te músmes?**>, //lí-ə lás tə músməs//, /'*Is the cow fat?*'/, attested by AC, <**tsel yeláwel lós telí tl'elő we.**>, //c-əl yəlɛ́w=əl lás təlí ƛ'ə-lówə//, /'*I'm fatter than you.*'/, literally /'I'm gone past fat from you.'/, syntactic analysis: comparative, syntactic comment: independent object of prepositional verb, attested by Elders Group (1/19/77), <**yeláwel lós telí tl'á'altha.**>, //yəlɛ́w=əl lás təlíƛ'=C_1ɛ́=ʔɛlθɛ//, /'*He's fatter than me.*'/, syntactic analysis: comparative, syntactic comment: independent object of prepositional verb, attested by Elders Group, <**yeláwel lós telí kws mő kw's.**>, //yəlɛ́w=əl lás təlí kʷ-s mók'ʷ-s//, /'*He's fattest of all.*'/, literally /'(he's) gone past fat from who is everyone → he's fatter than everyone'/, syntactic analysis: comparative, attested by Elders Group, <**ts'áts'el welós telí tl'alhlímelh.**>, //c'ɛ́c'əl wə-lás təlíƛ'ɛ-ɬlíməɬ//, /'*He's fattest of us.*'/, literally /'(he's) very contrastive- fat from us'/, syntactic analysis: sentence superlative, syntactic comment: independent object of prepositional verb, attested by Elders Group.

<**ló:sthet ~ lósthet**>, incs //lá·s=θət lás=θət//, ABFC /'*get fat, put on weight, getting fat*'/, (semological comment: control status unclear), (<**=thet**> *become, get, inceptive*), possibly <**-:-**> *continuative*, syntactic analysis: intransitive verb, attested by EB, AC, example: <**chexw ma ló:sthet.**>, //c-əxʷ mɛ lá·s=θət//, /'*You're getting fat.*'/, literally /'you evidently are getting fat'/, (semological comment: ma translated as evidently by AC), attested by AC, <**tsel me lósthet.**>, //c-əl mə lás=θət//, /'*I'm getting fat.*'/, (semological comment: unclear here whether <**me**> is *become, come to* or *evidently*), attested by EB.

<**ló:st**>, pcs //lá·s=T//, MC ['*grease s-th*'], (<**=t**> *purposeful control transitivizer*), syntactic analysis: transitive verb, attested by EB, example: <**tsel ló:st.**>, //c-əl lá·s=T//, /'*I greased it.*'/, attested by EB, <**ló:stes te ts'ákwx̱els thútl'o.**>, //lá·s=T-əs tə c'ɛ́kʷx̣=əls θ=ú=ƛ'a//, /'*She greased the frying pan.*'/, attested by EB, also <**ulh slóstes te shxwts'ákwx̱els.**>, //ʔuɬ s-lós=T-əs tə s=xʷ=c'ɛ́kʷx̣=əls//, literally /'already she greased it the frying pan (device to=get fry=structured activity)'/, attested by EB.

<**sló:s ~ slós**>, dnom //s=lá·s ~ s=lás//, ANA /'*fat, grease, lard, (oil [EB], shortening [MH])*'/, FOOD, (<**s=**> *nominalizer*), syntactic analysis: nominal, attested by AC, EB, MH, other sources: ES /slá·s/ *fat*, JH /slá·s/ *fat, grease*, H-T <las, los> (macron over a) *fat*, also /'*grease, oil*'/, attested by EB, also /'*lard, shortening*'/, attested by MH.

<**slós qwóls sqá:wth**>, FOOD *French fries* (lit. fat + boiled + potato), (attested by RG,EH 6/16/98 to SN, edited by BG with RG,EH 6/26/00)

<**lésleseqw**>, chrs //lo[=Aə́=]s=C_1əC_2=əqʷ//, DESC ['*greasy-headed*'], ANA ['*fatty salmon head*'],

FOOD, (<**é-ablaut**> *derivational*), (<**=R2**> *characteristic*), lx <**=eqw**> *on the head; fish head,* phonology: ablaut, reduplication, syntactic analysis: adjective/adjectival verb, nominal, attested by IHTTC.

<**shxwlósàlà**>, dnom //s(=)xʷ=lás=ɛ̀lɛ̀//, HHG ['*grease bowl*'], (<**shxw=**> *thing for, device to*), lx <**=àlà**> *container of,* phonology: downdrifting, syntactic analysis: nominal, attested by DM (12/4/64).

<**slésxel**>, dnom //s=lá[=Aə́=]s=xʸəl//, ANA ['*bone marrow*'], (<**s=**> *nominalizer*), lx <**=xel**> *on the leg, on the foot,* phonology: ablaut, syntactic analysis: nominal, attested by Elders Group.

<**ló:st**>, MC ['*grease s-th*'], *see* ló:s ~ lós.

<**ló:sthet ~ lósthet**>, ABFC /'*get fat, put on weight, getting fat*'/, *see* ló:s ~ lós.

<**ló:thel**>, probably root //lá·θəl//, HHG /'*dish, big cooking and serving trough used in longhouse, feast dish, plate (of wood or basketry), (platter), tray*'/, possibly <**=ó:thel**> *in the mouth*?, syntactic analysis: nominal, noun, attested by AC, Elders Group, also <**ló:tsel**>, //lá·cəl//, dialects: *Cheh.*, attested by MP, TM, also <**lóthel ~ ló:thel**>, //láθəl lá·θəl//, attested by Elders Group (3/72), also <**lótsel**>, //lácəl//, dialects: *Matsqui*, attested by AH, WC, example: <**x̱epá:y ló:thel**>, //x̣əp=ɛ́·y lá·θəl//, /'*cedar dish*'/, attested by Elders Group (3/72), also <**x̱epyúwelh (or x̱epyíwelh)**>, //x̣əp=ɛy=ówəɬ (or x̣əp=ɛy=íwəɬ)//, also /'*cedar trough [feast dish]*'/, attested by Elders Group (3/72), <**q'emő:lhp lóthel**>, //q'əmə[=Aó·=]l=ɬp láθəl//, /'*maple-wood dish*'/, Elder's comment: "less good way of saying it", attested by Elders Group (3/72), also <**q'emő:lhpíwelh**>, //q'əmə[=Aó·=]l=ɬp=íwəɬ//, Elder's comment: "best way of saying it", attested by Elders Group (3/72), <**híkw lóthel**>, //híkʷ láθəl//, /'*big dish*'/, attested by Elders Group (3/72), <**ts'ékw' ló:thel** (or **sts'éqw' ló:thel?)**>, //c'ə́k'ʷ lá·θəl (or s=c'ə́q'ʷ lá·θəl)//, /'*woven tray, woven plate*'/, attested by Elders Group (6/11/75), <**alétsa te ló:thel?**>, //ʔɛlə́cɛ tə lá·θəl//, /'*Where's the plate?*'/, attested by AD.

<**lethló:thel**>, pln //C_1əC_2-lá·θəl//, HHG ['*plates*'], (<**R3-**> *plural*), phonology: reduplication, syntactic analysis: nominal, noun, attested by AD, example: <**alétsa te lethló:thel?**>, //ʔɛlə́cɛ tə C_1əC_2-lá·θəl//, /'*Where's the plates?*'/, attested by AD.

<**shxwlathílé**>, dnom //s(=)xʷ=lo[=Aɛ=]θ(əl)=ɛ́[=Aí=]lə́ or sxʷ=lo[=Aí=]θ(əl)=ɛ[=M2/M3=]lə́//, [šxʷlæθílə́], HHG ['*any kind of cupboard*'], literally /'device to contain dish/plate/tray'/, (<**shxw=**> *device to, thing for*), possibly <**a-ablaut, í-ablaut, metathesis type 2** or **3**> all *derivational*, lx <**=álá ~ =álé**> *container of,* phonology: ablaut, metathesis, consonant-loss (el before íl), syntactic analysis: nominal, attested by Elders Group, example: <**lí te shxwlathílé.**>, //lí tə sxʷ=laθ(əl)=ɛ[=Aí=]lə́//, /'*(They are) in the cupboard.*'/, attested by AD.

<**lóy**>, free root //láy//, CJ /'*be only, just*'/, syntactic analysis: adverb/adverbial verb, attested by EB, TG, AD, example: <**lóy sqwálewels tl' Máli kw'e qó:.**>, //láy s=qʷɛ́l=əwəl-sƛ' mɛ́li k'ʷə qá·//, /'*Mary is only thinking of water.*'/, attested by EB, <**lóy lóy lóy tes tes tes**>, //láy láy láy təs təs təs//, [lá5y lá5y lá5y tí1s tí1s tí1s], /'*only only only come near come near come near*'/, phonology: the numbers are song pitches, usage: lyrics from song of the Man in the Moon's blacksmith, in the story of the spider and the man who shot arrows at the moon to make a ladder of arrows and reach the man in the moon, attested by TG (Stó:lō Sítel tape of 5/2/79 meeting), <**ōwéta kw swíweles, lóy te siyó:lexwe.**>, //ʔowə= ́tɛ kʷ s=wíwələs, láy tə si=yá·ləxʷə//, /'*There's no young men, only old men.*'/, attested by AD, <**lóy kwsu xwéms kw'as éxel.**>, //láy kʷ-s-u xʷə́m-s k'ʷ-ɛ-s ʔə́xʸəl//, /'*You have to paddle faster.*'/, literally /'it's only that contrast it's fast that you paddle'/, attested by EB.

<**welóy**>, df //wə=láy//, CJ /'*be only (contrastive), be just (contrastive)*'/, (<**we=**> *contrastive*), syntactic analysis: adverb/adverbial verb, attested by AC, EB, AD, Deming, example: <**welóye**

talúwe>, //wə=láy tɛ=lúwə//, /'*only you*'/, attested by EB, AD, <**welóy te kópi qas te seplí:l l stl'í.**>, //wə=láy tə kápi qɛ-s tə səplí·l l s=ƛ'í//, /'*I just want coffee and bread.*'/, attested by Deming.

<**lóyéxwa**>, df //láy=əxʷ-ɛ//, EFAM /'*do I have to?, does one have to?*'/, ASM ['a question one asks oneself, so it does not need to change pronouns, it has an impersonal subject (third person, one) or refers to the speaker (I)'], possibly <**=éxw**> uncertain meaning, poss. from <**éwe**> *not* possibly <**with devoicing**, (<**-e ~ -a**> *yes/no question*), phonology: devoicing?, syntactic analysis: interrogative verb, syntactic comment: usually sentence initial, appears to require subjunctive third person subordinate subjects, thus may contain vneg, attested by EB, example: <**lóyéxwa x̱áwses kw kyó:s?**>, //láy=əxʷ-ɛx̣ɛ́ws-əs kʷ kʸá·-s//, /'*Do I have to have a new car?*'/, syntactic comment: third person subjunctive subject, attested by EB, <**lóyéxwa tstíqíwés?**>, //láy=əxʷ-ɛ c=tíqíw-əs//, /'*Do I have to have a horse?*'/, phonology: updrifting? or stressed subjunctive?, syntactic comment: third person subjunctive subordinate subject, also note ts= *have* replacing s= *nominalizer*, (semological comment: note clear gloss *have* for ts= here), attested by EB, <**lóyéxwa p'óp'eqw'émes kw séx̱wes?**>, //láy=əxʷ-ɛ p'á[=C₁ə=]q'ʷ=əm-əs kʷ sə́x̣ʷə//, /'*Does one have to have foamy urine?*'/, attested by EB.

<**Lóyaqwe'áth'**? or **Lóyaqw'e'áts'**? or more likely **Lóyeqw'e'áts**>, df //láyɛqʷəʔɛ́θ' or láyɛqʷəʔɛ́c' ?//, PLN ['*Middle Creek*'], ASM ['a creek which enters Chilliwack River on its south side above (east or upriver from) Slesse (Slesse Creek or Mt. Slesse)'], root possibly <**qw'á:ts**> *little suckerfish with big salmon-like mouth,* prob. *largescale sucker*, possibly compound beginning with <**lóye**> *be only, just*, since suckerfish were not highly prized as fish, if a name in the Ch'élexwoqwem language, the second root (cognate with the suckerfish in UHk could be *<qw'e'áts> syntactic analysis: nominal, source: Wells 1965:13 <LIY-ah-quh-'AHT'Z> in PPS,

<**lóyéxwa**>, EFAM /'*do I have to?, does one have to?*'/, *see* lóy.

<**Loyú:mthel ~ Loyúmthel**>, df //lə=(ʔ)ɛy=ə́[=Aú·=]m=θəl//, PLN /'*village on both sides of Liumchen Creek, Liumchen Creek, Liumchen Mountain*'/, ASM ['the creek enters Chilliwack River from the south about 2.5 miles east (upriver) from Vedder Crossing; Wells reports (BJ says) it means "water swirling out in gushes"; FK says there is a place on the river where water comes out of the rock in a spring; Liumchen Falls are also a well-known; NP says the word could be derived from root <**eyém**> (strong) and =thel (mouth) and I agree; the name probably first refered to the spring location, then to the village established on the river, then to the mountain'], possibly <**le= ~ lexw=**> *always*, possibly <**=thel**> *in the mouth*, possibly <**ú:-ablaut**> *derivational*, phonology: ablaut?, syntactic analysis: nominal, attested by BJ (12/5/64), AC (1973), probably borrowed from Ch'élexwoqwem dialect of Nooksack which was spoken in the area and which has /u/ (see Galloway 1985), source: place names reference file #224 village and creek, other sources: Wells 1965 (lst ed.):19, 13, photo 6/19/78, example: <**Loyúmthel (Smált)**>, //layúmθəl (s=mɛ́lt)//, /'*Liumchen Mountain*'/, source: Wells 1965:ll, place names reference file #171, <**Loyúmthel (X̱ótsa)**>, //loyúmθəl (x̣ácɛ)//, /'*Liumchen Lake*'/, source: Wells 1965:11,

<**lulh**>, TIME /'*he/she/it was (already), they were (already)*'/, *see* le.

<**lúste**>, free root //lústə//, EZ ['*rooster*'], syntactic analysis: nominal, noun, attested by AH, borrowed from English [rústə˞] *rooster.*

<**lúwe**>, free root //lúwə or lə́wə//, [lúwə or lʊ́wə ~ lə́wə], PRON /'*it's you, you are the one. you (focus or emphasis)*'/, see <**léwe**>

<**lúwe ts'ít te Chíchelh Siyám**>, CH /'*It's you to thank the Lord, (Please say grace)*'/, *see* =chílh ~ chílh=.

LH

<**lh- ~ lhé-**>, da //ɬ= ~ ɬə́=//, TIB /'*use, extract, extract a portion*'/, syntactic analysis: derivational prefix; found in <**lhp'ó:tl'em**>, //ɬ=p'á·ƛ'=əm//, /'*smoke a pipe*'/, literally /'use=/extract(portion)= smoke =middle voice'/, <**lhqó:le**>, //ɬ=qá·=lə//, /'*be thirsty*'/, literally /'use=/extract= water =derivational?'/, dialects: *Cheh.*, see main dialect form <**tsqó:le**>, <**lhq'él:exw**>, //ɬ=q'ɛ́[=Aə́=]l=l-əxʷ//, /'*know s-th*'/, literally /'use=/extract(portion)= believe =non-control transitivizer -third person obj.'/, attested by Elders Group, others, also <**s=lhéq'el:exw**>, //s=ɬə́=q'ɛ[=Aə=]l=l-əxʷ//, dialects: *Chill.*, attested by AC, others, example: <**chel lhq'él:exw kw'els tl'xwéléqcha.**>, //c-əl ɬ=q'ə́l=l-əxʷ k'ʷə-l-s ƛ'xʷ=ə́lə́q-cɛ//, /'*I know I'm going to win.*'/, attested by Elders Group; found in <**lhémxts'eltel**>, //ɬə́=məxʸc'əl=təl//, /'*delousing comb, fine-toothed comb*'/, literally /'extract= louse =device'/, <**lhséq'**>, //ɬ=sə́q'//, /'*half, be half, half-breed, half dollar*'/, literally /'use=/extract(portion)= split in half'/, attested by Elders Group, AC, ER (Deming), many others, example: <**slhíxws qas te lhséq'**>, //s=ɬíxʷ=s qɛ=s tə ɬ=sə́q'//, /'*half past three o'clock, 3:30 (three thirty)*'/, attested by ER of Deming (1/10/77); found in <**alht'éqw'**>, //ɬ=t'ə́q'ʷ or ʔɛɬ=t'ə́q'ʷ//, /'*half*'/, literally /'use=/extract(portion)= break (of s-th continuous, like rope, string, breathing, consciousness)'/, attested by Elders Fish Camp (7/19/78), example: <**alht'éqw' syiláws te slhéms.**>, //(ʔɛ)ɬ=t'ə́q'ʷ s=yil=ɛ́w-s tə s=ɬə́m=s//, /'*(It's) half (an hour) past eleven o'clock.*'/, literally /'use= break nominalizer=past-of/its the hour of= dew'/, attested by Elders Fish Camp (7/19/78); found in <**lhthéleq ~ lhtheléq**>, //ɬ=θə́ləq ~ ɬ=θələ́q//, /'*some*'/, literally /'extract(portion)= divided'/ (compare <**tseléqelhtst /cələ́q-əɬc-T/**> *divide it with s-o)*, Salish cognate: Musqueam /ɬ=θə́ləq/ *some, a part* and /θə́ləq=θət/ *separate* Suttles ca1984, example: <**lhtheléqchap**>, //ɬ=θələ́q-c-ɛp//, /'*some of you folks*'/, <**lhth'óméls**>, //ɬ=θ'ám=əls//, /'*to file (abrasively)*'/, root <**th'om**> *file*, also as in <**lhó:yel**>, //ɬ=á·y(=)əl//, /'*getting dusk*'/, literally /'extract a portion =daylight'/, attested by IHTTC.

<**=lh**>, da //=ɬ//, MC ['*(material for)*'?], syntactic analysis: lexical suffix, derivational suffix; found in <**syéqwlhàlà**>, //s=yə́qʷ=ɬ=ɛ̀lɛ̀//, /'*firepit, fire-place*'/, <**syeqwlhá:ltel**>, //s=yəqʷ=ɬ=ɛ́·ltəl//, /'*tinder, material used to start fire (fine dried cedar bark)*'/ (compare <**yeqw**> *burn,* <**=álá**> *container* <**=ɛ́·ltəl**> *medicine*).

<**-lha**>, (//-ɬɛ//), MOOD ['*command imperative second person singular*'], ASM ['ordering someone to do something'], semantic environment ['cannot be used with non-control transitives (for ex. in =l) since the actor has no control over doing it), also cannot be used with some intransitive verbs (prepositional, adverbial, interrogative, personal pronoun, demonstrative, and some verbs whose action a subject cannot do on command, thus non-control imperatives such as *kw'étslexwlha *See it.* and *kwél:exwlha *Get/Catch/Find it.* are not allowed (EB, AC, etc.), also this imperative is not allowed with auxiliary verbs like me ~ mi *come to, start to* and la ~ lám *go to, going to* (-tlh *coaxing imperative* is used with them)--however when mí ~ emí or lám are used as main verbs the command imperative is allowed'], syntactic analysis: is, contrast <**-lhqwe**> *polite imperative*, contrast <**-chexw**> and <**-chap**> *mildly urging imperative*, contrast <**-tlh**> and <**-atlha**> *coaxing imperative*; found in <**emílha. ~ mílha.**>, //ʔəmí-ɬɛ ~ mí-ɬɛ//, /'*Come.*'/, <**emétlha.**>, //ʔəmə́t-ɬɛ//, /'*Sit., Sit up., Sit down.*'/, <**meythóxlha.**>, //mɛy=T-áxʸ-ɬɛ//, /'*Help me.*'/, <**ólhstexwlha.**>, //ʔáɬ=sT-əxʷ-ɬɛ//, /'*Put it on board.*'/, <**áyelexwlha.**>, //ʔɛ́yələxʷ-ɬɛ//, /'*Get well.*'/, (semological comment: not =l *non-control* since that is áyelexwlexw *manage to keep s-o alive*), example: <**emétlha kwé.**>, //ʔəmə́t-ɬɛ kʷə́//, /'*Sit down then.*'/.

<**lhákw'**>, bound root //ɬɛ́k’^{w}//, ABFC [*'breathe'*]

<**slhákw'em**>, dnom //s=ɬɛ́k’^{w}=əm//, mdls, ABFC [*'breath (noun)'*], (<**s=**> *nominalizer*), (<**=em**> *middle voice*), syntactic analysis: nominal, attested by EB, also <**slháqwem**>, //s=ɬɛ́q^{w}=əm//, attested by AC, Salish cognate: Squamish /sɬák’^{w}am/ *breath* W73:45, K67:290, Nooksack /sɬǽq^{w}əm/ *breath* A78:44, example: <**x̲éytl' te slháqwems.**>, //x̣íƛ’ tə s=ɬɛ́q^{w}=əm-s//, /*'His breath is cold., (He's stopped breathing.)'*/, attested by AC, <**li xwel emí te slháqwems?**>, //li x^{w}əl ʔə-mí tə s=ɬɛ́q^{w}=əm-s//, /*'Is he/she/it still breathing?'*/, literally /'is it still coming the his breath'/, attested by AC, <**li xwelí kw'e slháqwems?**>, //li xw=əlí k’^{w}ə s=ɬɛ́q^{w}=əm-s//, /*'Is he/she/it still breathing?'*/, literally /'is he/she/it alive the (remote, abstract) his breath'/, attested by AC, <**tsel t'á:t kw'els xwemxálém kw'e le me t'éqw' tel slhákw'em.**>, //c-əl t’ɛ́·=T k’^{w}ə-l-s x^{w}əm=x^{y}ɛ́l=əm k’^{w}ə lə mə t’ə́q’^{w} tə-l s=ɬɛ́k’^{w}=əm//, /*'I tried to run but I ran out of breath.'*/, literally /'I try it that I run when it past become break (of continuous item) the-my breath. → I tried to run when my breath got broken.'/, attested by EB.

<**lhkw'ámő(w)s ~ lhkw'ámő:s**>, ds //ɬɛ́k’^{w}=ə[=M2=]m=óws//, ANA [*'pulse'*], literally /'breath(ing) on the body'/, (<**metathesis type 2**> *derivational*, possibly *continuative*), lx <**=ő̃ws**> *on the body*, phonology: metathesis, syntactic analysis: intransitive verb, attested by Elders Group (7/27/75, 10/8/75).

<**lhákw'els**>, FSH /*'gaff-hooking (all the time, catching a lot)'*/, *see* lhíkw' ~ lhí:kw'.

<**lhà:l**>, free root //ɬɛ̀·l//, CAN /*'pull ashore in a canoe, land a canoe'*/, syntactic analysis: intransitive verb, attested by EB.

<**lhál:omet**>, ncrs //ɬɛ́l=l-amət//, CAN /*'made it to shore, get to shore'*/, (<**=l**> *non-control transitivizer*), (<**-omet**> *reflexive*), phonology: consonant merger, syntactic analysis: intransitive verb.

<**lhá:lt**>, pcs //ɬɛ́·l=T//, CAN [*'to land s-th (from water)'*], semantic environment ['canoe, boat, etc., not a plane on land'], (<**=t**> *purposeful control transitivizer*), syntactic analysis: transitive verb.

<**Lhá:lt**>, ds //ɬɛ́·l=T//, PLN [*'big marsh below old Pretty's place and above modern Scowlitz'*], literally /'land a canoe, pull ashore in s-th'/, (<**=t**> *purposeful control transitivizer*), syntactic analysis: nominal, attested by EL, poss. NP and/or EB, source: place names reference file #307.

<**lheltálets**>, df //ɬɛ́l=tə[=M2=]l=əc or ɬɛ́l=t=ə[=M2=]ləc//, WATR /*'a channel that makes an island, inside channel'*/, literally perhaps /'something to land a canoe in the back (or) land a canoe on the bottom'/, (<**metathesis type 2**> *derivational*), possibly <**=elets**> *on the bottom* or possibly <**=tel**> *something to* plus <**=ets**> *on the back*, phonology: metathesis, syntactic analysis: nominal, attested by EL, NP, possibly EB, BHTTC.

<**lheltáletsem**>, mdls //ɬɛ́l=tə[=M2=]l=əc=əm or ɬɛ́l=t=ə[=M2=]ləc=əm//, WATR [*'go through a channel'*], CAN, (<**=em**> *middle voice*), phonology: metathesis, syntactic analysis: intransitive verb, attested by BHTTC.

<**Lheltá:lets ~ Lheltálets**>, df //ɬɛ́·l=tə[=M2=]l=əc (probably)//, PLN /*'a channel between an island and the main shore a) across Harrison River from where the Phillips smokehouse was at Chehalis village (slightly downriver from the mouth of Chehalis R. into Harrison R.),* also b) *at Harrison Lake where the hatchery was'*/, literally /'inside channel'/, syntactic analysis: nominal, attested by EL, NP, possibly EB, HHTTC.

<**Lhilheltálets**>, dmn //C$_1$í=ɬɛ́l=tə[=M2=]l=əc or C$_1$í=ɬɛ́l=t=ə[=M2=]ləc//, PLN [*'village with many pit-houses below Union Bar'*], ASM ['on the south end of an island in the Fraser River just above Hope and on the east bank of the Fraser, a creek forms this island in front of the village in high water and the water comes against it, the village was located across from where wild

onions grow'], PLN [*'island in front of Iwówes (Elders Group 7/9/75)'*], (<**R4=**> *diminutive*), phonology: reduplication, metathesis, syntactic analysis: nominal, attested by Elders Group, IHTTC, also <**Lhìlheltálets**>, //C_1í=ɬɛ́l=tə[=M2=]l=əc or C_1í=ɬɛ́l=t=ə[=M2=]ləc//, also /*'island in front of Iwówes'*/, ASM ['the creek forming the island dries up in winter'], attested by Elders Group (7/9/75), also <**Lhilheltálets**>, //C_1í=ɬɛ́l=t(əm)=ələc//, literally /'little spray on the bottom'/, Elder's comment: "from lháltem (spray) because the creek forms an island in front in high water and the water comes against it", attested by Elders Group (7/6/77)(incl. ME, MP, LJ, CT), source: place names file reference #16, other sources: Wells 1965 (lst ed.):25

<**lháléqet**>, df //ɬɛlə́q=əT or ɬɛ́l=ə́qəl=T//, pcs, ABFC /*'stick out one's tongue, (stick it out (the tongue))'*/, possibly <**=eqel**> *in the throat, voice, speech, language,* (<**=et ~ =t**> *purposeful control transitivizer*), possibly root <**lhá:l??**> *to land (from water)*, phonology: consonant-loss probably, possibly stress-shift, syntactic analysis: transitive verb, attested by MV, SJ.

<**lháleq'et**>, LAND [*'put them down (several objects)'*], *see* lháq'.

<**lhálétem**>, WETH /*'starting to sprinkle, start sprinkling'*/, *see* lhél.

<**lhál:omet**>, CAN /*'made it to shore, get to shore'*/, *see* lhà:l.

<**lhálqi**>, FOOD [*'soaking dried fish'*], *see* lhél.

<**lhá:lt**>, CAN [*'to land s-th (from water)'*], *see* lhà:l.

<**Lhá:lt**>, PLN [*'big marsh below old Pretty's place and above modern Scowlitz'*], *see* lhà:l.

<**lhá:ltelechá:ls**>, WATR [*'spraying (as a structured activity)'*], *see* lhél.

<**lhá:ltem**>, WATR [*'get splashed'*], *see* lhél.

<**lhálts'**>, free root //ɬɛlc'//, EFAM /*'cheeky, rough (of a person in conduct)'*/, syntactic analysis: adjective/adjectival verb, attested by Elders Group, Salish cognate: Squamish /(ʔə)s-ɬánč'/ *rough, careless (with things)* K69:99.

<**lhálheqem**>, ABFC [*'whispering'*], *see* lháqem.

<**lhálheqet**>, LANG [*'whispering to s-o'*], *see* lháqem.

<**lhálheq'**>, LAND [*'lying on the ground'*], *see* lháq'.

<**lhálheq'els**>, LAND /*'laying down, putting down'*/, *see* lháq'.

<**lhálheq'et**>, LAND [*'putting it down'*], *see* lháq'.

<**lhalhewéleq**>, IDOC /*'Indian doctor at work, shaman at work, healer'*/, *see* lhá:w.

<**lhálhewels**>, IDOC /*'(an Indian doctor or shaman) working, curing, chasing the bad things away'*/, *see* lhá:w.

<**lhálhewet**>, IDOC [*'curing s-o (as an Indian doctor)'*], *see* lhá:w.

<**lhalhí:lt**>, CAN [*'bailing'*], *see* lhí:lt ~ lhílt.

<**lhálhq'etxel**>, WETH [*'have wide snowflakes'*], *see* lheq'át ~ lhq'á:t.

<**lhámkiya**>, df //ɬɛ́m(=)k(=)iyɛ//, [ɬɛ́mkiyɛ], HHG [*'pot to boil in'*], ACL, possibly <**=iya**> *little*, possibly <**q → k**> *diminutive*, possibly sound symbolism, possibly root <**lhem**> *drops of liquid*, phonology: possible fronting, syntactic analysis: nominal, attested by AC, comment: the /k/ could also indicate a borrowing from Thompson, see main dialect form <**lhémkiya**>.

<**lhámth't**>, FOOD [*'pick food by one's fingers (before a meal)'*], *see* lhím.

<**lháp**>, bound root uncertain, possibly //ɬɛ́p//, possibly ABFC [*'slip out, put away'*], see also under *elhap* and *lhep*.

<**elhápt**>, df //ʔə(=)ɬɛ́p=T or ʔəɬ(=)ɛ́p=T//, pcs, ABFC [*'slip it out'*], semantic environment ['of penis from vagina (in the only example I have)'], Elder's comment: "what a woman will tell a man if she doesn't want to get pregnant", possibly <**e=**> unknown meaning (not likely *continuative), <=t> purposeful control transitivizer*, syntactic analysis: transitive verb, attested by JL (7/20/79) (compare <**x̲wlhép**> *slip off*, <**x̲welhx̲wélhepxel**> *slip with both feet*, and <**xwlhépelets**> *sat down (with plop), (slip of on rump)*, if these are related they would have to have been reanalyzed and <x̲w> would have to be an error for <xw=> *become, get*), Salish cognate: perhaps Squamish /ɬup/ *be out of reach, be away from the edge, be way off* (corresponding with Halkomelem /ɬap/ with //=Aɛ́=// needed to explain) and Squamish /ɬúp-n/ *put away (tr.)* and /ɬúp-cut/ *move away* K67:329-330.

<**lhapxálem**>, mdls //ɬɛp=x^yə[=Aɛ́=]l=əm//, durs, /*'to trot (animal or person), jog'*/, root meaning uncertain unless <**lháp**> *slip out*, <=xel> *leg, foot*, <=Aá=> *durative*, <=em> *middle voice*, attested by RG & EH (4/9/99 Ling332)

<**lháq**>, bound root //ɬɛ́q//, ABFC meaning uncertain perhaps *to whisper*.

<**lháqem**>, mdls //ɬɛ́q=əm//, ABFC [*'to whisper (once)'*], (<**=em**> *middle voice*), syntactic analysis: intransitive verb, attested by Elders Group.

<**lhálheqem**>, cts //ɬɛ́[-C_1ə-]q=əm//, ABFC [*'whispering'*], semantic environment ['human agent'], ABFC [*'hissing'*], semantic environment ['snake, probably other fauna'], (<**-R1-**> *continuative*), phonology: reduplication, syntactic analysis: intransitive verb, attested by Elders Group, EB, example: <**lhálheqem te álhqey.**>, //ɬɛ́[-C_1ə-]q=əm tə ʔɛ́ɬqəy//, /*'The snake is hissing (or whispering).'*/, attested by Elders Group.

<**lháqet**>, pcs //lɛ́q=əT//, LANG [*'whisper to s-o'*], ABFC, (<**=et**> *purposeful control transitivizer*), syntactic analysis: transitive verb, attested by AC.

<**lhálheqet**>, cts //ɬɛ́[-C_1ə-]q=əT//, LANG [*'whispering to s-o'*], ABFC, (<**-R1-**> *continuative*), phonology: reduplication, syntactic analysis: transitive verb, attested by AC, EB; found in <**lhálheqethóxes.**>, //ɬɛ́[-C_1ə-]q=əT-áx^y-əs//, /*'He's whispering to me.'*/, attested by EB, example: <**tset kwa (welh, ōlh) xwe'í:t tset lhálheqet?**>, //c-ət k^wɛ (wə=ɬ, ʔu=ɬ) x^wəʔí·t c-ət ɬɛ́[-C_1ə-]q=əT//, /*'What are we doing whispering (to s-o)?'*/, attested by EB.

<**lháqem**>, LANG [*'whisper (once)'*], *see* lháq.

<**lháqet**>, LANG [*'whisper to s-o'*], *see* lháq.

<**lháq'**>, bound root //lay (flat?), put down//.

<**lhálheq'**>, cts //ɬɛ́[-C_1ə-]q'//, LAND [*'lying on the ground'*], (<**-R1-**> *continuative*), phonology: reduplication, syntactic analysis: intransitive verb, attested by HT, example: <**lhálheq' te thqát lí tí.**>, //ɬɛ́[-C_1ə-]q' tə θqɛ́t lí tí//, /*'A tree is lying over there (if still growing along the ground).'*/, (semological comment: the still growing component is due to thqát *(living) tree*), attested by HT.

<**slhálheq'**>, stvi //s=ɬɛ́[-C_1ə-]q'//, LAND [*'be lying on the ground'*], semantic environment ['coat, sack, person, growing tree, log, etc.'], (<**s=**> *stative*), phonology: reduplication, syntactic analysis: adjective/adjectival verb, attested by CT, EB, HT, example: <**slhálheq' te syáyeq' lí tí.**>, //s=ɬɛ́[-C_1ə-]q' tə s=yɛ́[-C_1ə-]q' lí tí//, /*'A log is lying over there.'*/, attested by CT, <**slhálheq' te lesák lí tí.**>, //s=ɬɛ́[-C_1ə-]q' tə ləsɛ́k lí tí//, /*'The sack lies over there.'*/, attested by CT, HT.

<**lhálheq'els**>, sas //ɬɛ́[-C_1ə-]q'=əls//, LAND /*'laying down, putting down'*/, MC, DIR, semantic environment ['bricks, foundation, stone wall, etc.'], (<**=els**> *structured activity continuative*), phonology: reduplication, syntactic analysis: intransitive verb, attested by EB.

<**lháq'et**>, pcs //ɬɛ́q'=əT//, LAND /*'lay it down, put it down'*/, DIR, (<**=et**> *purposeful control transitivizer*), syntactic analysis: transitive verb, attested by EB, AC and RG & EH (4/9/99 Ling332), example: <**lháq'et íkw'elo**>, //ɬɛ́q'=əT ʔí=k'ʷə=la//, /*'put it down here, lay it down here'*/, attested by AC.

<**lhálheq'et**>, cts //ɬɛ́[-C_1ə-]q'=əT//, LAND [*'putting it down'*], DIR, (<**-R1-**> *continuative*), phonology: reduplication, syntactic analysis: transitive verb, attested by AC, EB; found in <**lhálheq'etes.**>, //ɬɛ́[-C_1ə-]q'=əT-əs//, /*'He's putting it down.'*/, attested by EB.

<**lháleq'et**>, plv //ɬɛ[-lə-]q'=əT//, LAND [*'put them down (several objects)'*], DIR, (<**-le-**> *plural*), phonology: infix, syntactic analysis: transitive verb, attested by EB.

<**lhóq'ethet**>, pcrs //ɬɛ[-Aá-]q'=əT-ət//, LAND [*'lie down'*], ABFC, <**ó-ablaut**> triggered by reflexive, (<**-et**> *reflexive*), phonology: ablaut, syntactic analysis: intransitive verb, attested by EB or Deming or IHTTC (fall 1977).

<**slháq'emex**>, df //s=ɬɛ́q'=aməxʸ or s=ɬəq'ɛ́=M2=aməxʸ//, LAND [*'a large portion of the earth'*], (<**s=**> *nominalizer*), possibly <**metathesis**> *derivational*, possibly <**=omex**> *in appearance*, possibly root <**lháq'**> *lay on the ground* or more likely <**lheq'á-**> *wide*, phonology: metathesis perhaps, syntactic analysis: nominal?, attested by BJ (12/5/64) (compare <**lheq'át**> *be wide)*, Salish cognate: root perhaps cognate with Squamish root /ɬəq'/ *wide, broad, flat* as in /ɬq'-át/ *wide, broad, flat* and with Coeur d'Alene and Kalispel /ɬáq'/ *wide, be wide* K67:328.

<**lháq'et**>, LAND /*'lay it down, put it down'*/, *see* lháq'.

<**lhátx̱tem**>, ABDF /*'be trembling, shiver'*/, *see* lhétx̱tem.

<**lhàth'**>, bound root //ɬɛ̀θ'// *make fun, (ridicule)*

<**lhílhàth'**>, dmv //C_1í=ɬɛ̀θ'//, cts, EFAM /*'making fun, (ridiculing)'*/, (<**R4=**> *diminutive → continuative*), phonology: reduplication, syntactic analysis: intransitive verb, attested by Elders Group (2/16/77), Salish cognate: Squamish /ɬi-ɬác'-t/ *ridicule, rile, belittle (tr.)* W73:216, K69:71, also <**lhílhà:lts'**>, //C_1í=ɬɛ̀·lc'//, attested by EB, comment: the /l/ may be influence from (confusion with) lhálts' *cheeky, rough (in conduct)* which is similar in meaning but not related historically; the /c'/ (ts') could show similar influence or confusion or could show the occasional archaic Cheh. preservation of ts' from PCS which is usually th' in other words and other dialects; or the ts' could show Thompson language influence since Thompson would have ts' not th' here and since EB speaks Thompson and Halkomelem.

<**lhílhàth't**>, pcs //C_1í=ɬɛ̀θ'=T//, EFAM /*'making fun of s-o, (ridiculing s-o)'*/, (<**=t**> *purposeful control transitivizer*), phonology: reduplication, syntactic analysis: transitive verb, attested by Elders Group (2/16/77), also <**lhílhà:lts't**>, //C_1í=ɬɛ̀·lc'=T//, attested by EB; found in <**lhílhàth'thòmè**>, //C_1í=ɬɛ̀θ'=T-àmə̀//, /*'making fun of you'*/, phonology: downdrifting, attested by Elders Group (2/16/77).

<**lhá:ts'tel**>, TOOL [*'knife'*], *see* lhíts' ~ lhí:ts'.

<**lhà:ts'telálá**>, TOOL /*'handle of a knife, knife-handle'*/, *see* lhíts' ~ lhí:ts'.

<**lhá:w**>, free root //ɬɛ́·w//, ABFC /*'heal, be cured'*/, semantic environment ['of sore, any sickness, possession'], TVMO [*'run away'*], SOC, syntactic analysis: intransitive verb, attested by Elders Group, JL, also <**lháw**>, //ɬɛ́w//, attested by EB, example: <**lulh lhá:w (ta, ta'a) sq'óq'eytses.**>, //lə=uɬ ɬɛ́·w (t-ɛ, t-ɛʔ(ɛ)) s=q'á[=C_1ə=]y=cəs//, /*'Your hand is healed.'*/, literally /'it past/already heals/is cured the-your sickness in the hand'/, attested by JL.

<**lhálhewels**>, sas //ɬɛ́[-C_1ə-]w=əls//, cts, IDOC /*'(an Indian doctor or shaman) working, curing, chasing the bad things away'*/, (<**-R1-**> *continuative*), (<**=els**> *structured activity continuative*),

phonology: reduplication, syntactic analysis: intransitive verb, attested by EB.

<**lhalhewéleq**>, dnom //ɬɛ[=C_1ə=]w=ə́ləq//, [ɬæƛ'əwɪ́ləq], cts, IDOC /'*Indian doctor at work, shaman at work, healer*'/, (<**=R1=**> *continuative*), (<**=éleq**> *one who, occupational*), phonology: reduplication, syntactic analysis: nominal, attested by Elders Group.

<**lhá:wet**>, pcs //ɬɛ́·w=əT//, IDOC /'*cure s-o, heal s-o by Indian doctoring*'/, semantic environment ['used only of an Indian doctor or shaman'], (<**=et**> *purposeful control transitivizer*), syntactic analysis: transitive verb, attested by EB, Deming, Elders Group (3/15/72); found in <**lhá:wetem**>, //ɬɛ́·w=əT-əm//, /'*cured (by Indian doctor)*'/, syntactic analysis: passive, attested by EB.

<**lhálhewet**>, cts //ɬɛ́[-C_1ə-]w=əT//, IDOC ['*curing s-o (as an Indian doctor)*'], (<**-R1-**> *continuative*), phonology: reduplication, syntactic analysis: transitive verb, attested by Deming.

<**Lhewálmel**>, ds //ɬɛ́w=ə[=M2=]lməl//, PLN /'*an old course of the Chilliwack River, now Vedder River*'/, ASM ['(where Vedder River is now, from Vedder Crossing to Sumas Lake)'], literally /'wanting to run away'/, (<**metathesis type 2**> *derivational*), lx <**=elmel**> *in the mind, wanting to, thinking about*, probably root <**lhá:w**> *run away*, phonology: metathesis, syntactic analysis: nominal, attested by BJ or DM, source: place names reference file #262, other sources: Wells 1965:13 and Wells 1966 gives the literal meaning as *river that changed its course.*

<**lhewíth'a**>, df //ɬɛw=íθ'ɛ or ɬɛ[=Aə=]w=íθ'ɛ//, CLO ['*be naked*'], probably root <**lhá:w**> *run away (from)*, lx <**=íth'a**> *clothes*, possibly <**e-ablaut**> *derivational* (unless result of valence rules), phonology: vowel-change from strong-valenced suffix and ambi-valent root or ablaut, syntactic analysis: adjective/adjectival verb, attested by EB, Salish cognate: Squamish /ɬi-ləwʔ-íc'/ *naked* and /ɬu-íc'-aʔm/ *undress (tr.)*, which may have schwa and zero grades of root /ɬáwʔ/ *recover; run away* W73:182, K67:329-331, K69:71, also <**lhōwíth'a**>, //ɬow=íθ'ɛ or ɬəw=íθ'ɛ//, attested by EB, also <**lhuwítha ~ lhewíth'a**>, //ɬuw=íθ'ɛ ~ ɬəw=íθ'ɛ//, [ɬuwíθ'æ ~ ɬʊwíθ'æ], attested by DM (12/4/64).

<**lhōwth'ám**>, mdls //ɬow=(i)θ'ɛ=əm or ɬ(ə)w=(i)θ'ɛ=ɛ́m or ɬəw=(i)θ'ɛ=´=əm or even ɬɛ́w=(i)θ'ɛ=ə[=M3=]m//, CLO /'*take off one's clothes, undress*'/, probably <**=em**> *middle voice* or probably < **=ám**> *intransitivizer*, possibly <= ´=> *derivational* (if not result of vowel merger attracting stress) or <**metathesis type 3**> *derivational*, phonology: vowel merger, vowel-loss, stress-shift or stressed intransitivizer, prob. complex interaction of stress-valences or vowel-grades: if <**lhá:w ~ lhew**> in '*naked*' then the root is ambi-valent (there strong-grade ~ weak-grade); as result of a derivational stress shift or a stress-intransitivizer being added or shift to syllable where there is vowel-merger, the normally strong-valenced lexical suffix <**=íth'a →** **=th'ám**> (with vowel-loss of the <**i**>); that leaves the schwa-grade root <**lhew**> to lose its vowel, then vocalize its <**w**> before the following consonant <**th'**>, to AC <**ō**>/o/, EB <**u**> (a good example of how /o/ and /u/ arise in Halkomelem); a different possible analysis has metathesis type 3 preserving the root vowel and its stress by switching with the final vowel, syntactic analysis: intransitive verb, attested by AC, also <**lhuwth'ám**>, //ɬ(ə)w=(i)θ'ɛ=ɛ́m//, attested by EB.

<**lhuwth'á:m**>, cts //ɬəw=(i)θ'ɛ= ´-·-əm or ɬəw=(i)θ'ɛ=ɛ́[-·-]m//, CLO ['*undressing*'], (<**-:-**> *continuative*), phonology: lengthening, vowel merger, vowel-loss, an alternate analysis would have metathesis type 3 preserving the stressed root vowel (and its length?) by switching it with the final vowel, lengthening is an attested continuative process however an needn't be preserved necessarily from root lhá:w, syntactic analysis: intransitive verb, attested by EB.

<**lhuwth'á:mestexw**>, caus //ɬ(ə)w=(i)θ'ɛ=ɛ́m=sT-əx^w//, CLO ['*undress s-o*'], (<**=st**> *causative control transitivizer*), (<**-exw**> *third person object*), phonology: lengthening is not continuative

here but prob. the result of vowel merger, syntactic analysis: transitive verb, attested by EB, example: <**lhuwth'á:mestexw ta' mímele.**>, //ɬ(ə)w=(i)θ'ɛ=ɛ́m=sT-əx^w t-ɛʔ C_1í=mələ//, /'*Undress your (little) child.*'/, syntactic comment: imperative through presence of second person possessed object and no subject pronoun, attested by EB, <**lhuwth'á:mestexwes te mímeles.**>, //ɬ(ə)w=(i)θ'ɛ=ɛ́m=sT-əx^w-əs tə C_1í=mələ-s//, /'*She undresses her child.*'/, *<**lhuwth'á:mestexwes te tá:l te mímeles**> 'The mother undresses her child.'> rejected by EB.

<**lhuwth'ím**>, its //ɬ(ə)w=(i)θ'ɛ=ím//, CLO /'*undress in front of someone, strip-tease*'/, SOC, lx <**=í:m ~ =ím**> *repeatedly, iterative*, phonology: vowel-loss, vowel merger, vocalization, syntactic analysis: intransitive verb, attested by EB, example: <**shxwó:xwth' wemí'o lhuwth'ím.**>, //s=x^wá·x^wθ' wə=mí=ʔà ɬ(ə)w=iθ'ɛ=ím//, /'*She's/He's crazy (if) she/he just came to take off her/his clothes in front of somebody.*'/, attested by EB (12/12/75).

<**lhá:wet**>, IDOC /'*cure s-o, heal s-o by Indian doctoring*'/, *see* lhá:w.

<**lhawét'em**>, mdls //ɬɛwə́t'=əm//, ABFC /'*twitch, flutter (of one's eye, hand, skin, etc.)*'/, semantic environment ['body part'], probably root <**lhawét'**> or <**lháwt'**> or <**lháwet'**> and <**=em**> *middle voice*, possibly root <**lhá:w**> *run away*, possibly <**=ét' ~ =t'**> meaning unknown, phonology: perhaps stress-shift to dissimilate from lhá:wetem *s-o was cured by a shaman*, with the loss of stress from the root comes automatic length-loss, syntactic analysis: intransitive verb, attested by BHTTC.

<**lhá:wt'em**>, cts //ɬɛ[-´·-]w=t'=əm//, ABFC /'*twitching (of one's eye, hand, skin, etc.), fluttering*'/, semantic environment ['body part'], (<**-´:-**> *continuative*), phonology: stress-shift, lengthening, vowel-loss (due to stress-shift), actually these processes are all probably restoring the original root shape, syntactic analysis: intransitive verb, attested by BHTTC, example: <**lhá:wt'em tel qélém.**>, //ɬɛ́[-´·]w=t'=əm tə-l qə́lə́m//, /'*My eye is fluttering., My eye is twitching.*'/, attested by BHTTC.

<**lhá:wt'em**>, ABFC /'*twitching (of one's eye, hand, skin, etc.), fluttering*'/, *see* lhá:w.

<**lhá:x̱ ~ lháx̱**>, bound root //*spread, lay out under*//.

<**lhá:x̱em ~ lháx̱em**>, mdls //ɬɛ́·x̣=əm ~ ɬɛ́x̣=əm//, FOOD /'*help oneself to food, serve oneself, serve oneself food (with a ladle), serve oneself a meal (food), (put on a dish [CT, HT])*'/, literally /'(spread/lay out under for oneself)'/, (<**=em**> *middle voice*), syntactic analysis: intransitive verb, attested by BHTTC, CT, HT, EB, also /'*put on a dish*'/, attested by CT, HT, example: <**ts'qw'ét(chxw) (kwthéstàmès, te sqá:wth) li kw'e sts'óqw'els qesu mi lhá:x̱em i tel lóthel.**>, //c'q'=ə́T(-c-x^w) (k^w=θə́=s=tɛ̀m=ə̀s, tə s=qɛ́·w=θ) li k'^{w}ə s=c'áq'^{w}=əls qə-s-u mi ɬɛ́·x̣=əm ʔi tə-l láθəl//, /'*Pick up (poke s-th) (something, a potato) on a fork and put it on my dish.*'/, attested by CT, also /'*(corrected to) Pick up (something, a potato) on a fork and serve yourself on my dish/plate.*'/, attested by EB.

<**slhálhex̱**>, strs //s=ɬɛ́[=C_1ə=]x̣//, FOOD ['*be served*'], literally /'(be spread/be laid out under)'/, (<**s=**> *stative*), (<**=R1=**> *resultative* (not *continuative*)), phonology: reduplication, syntactic analysis: intransitive verb, attested by EB, example: <**ulh slhálhex̱ te s'álhtel.**>, //ʔuɬ s=ɬɛ́[=C_1ə=]x̣ tə s=ʔɛ́ɬ=Təl//, /'*The food is served.*'/, attested by EB.

<**lháx̱elhtst**>, bens //ɬɛ́x̣=əɬc=T//, FOOD ['*serve s-o (food)*'], <=elhts> *benefactive*, <=t> *purposeful control transitivizer*, as in <**lháx̱elhtsthòmè**>, //ɬɛ́x̣=əɬc=T-àmə̀//, /'serve you '/, attested by RG & EH (4/10/99 Ling332) and <**lháx̱elhtsthométselcha**>, //ɬɛ́x̣=əɬc=T-amə́-c-əl-cɛ//, /'I'll serve you'/, attested by RG & EH (4/10/99 Ling332)

<**lháx̱eletstel**>, dnom //ɬɛ́x̣=ələc=təl//, HHG ['*cushion*'], literally /'(device to spread/lay out under the rump) or possibly (device to lay out under the bottom)'/, lx <**=elets**> *on the bottom, rump*, lx <**=tel**> *device to*, syntactic analysis: nominal, attested by CT, HT.

<**lhex̲elwélhtel**>, dnom //ɬɛx̣=əlwə[=´=]ɬ=təl//, CAN /'*crosspieces in a canoe, (thwarts)*'/, ASM ['these are inserted to spread apart the sides of a dugout canoe when it is adzed out and filled with water heated by steaming rocks to make the sides pliable enough to spread apart'], literally /'(device to spread/lay out under the sides) or (devices to spread the canoe)'/, lx <**=elwelh**> *side (of s-th), on the side*, lx <**=tel**> *device to*, possibly <**=el=**> *plural or formative* plus <**=welh**> *canoe* and <=´=> *derivational*, phonology: stress-shift, vowel-change due to stress shift or (less likely) ablaut, syntactic analysis: nominal, attested by Elders Group.

<**lhex̲éyléptel**>, dnom //ɬɛx̣=íl=ə́p=təl//, incs, HHG /'*floor, floor mat, floor covering, linoleum, rug*'/, literally /'device/thing to get spread/laid out under on the dirt/ground'/, SPRD ['floor (of longhouse or anywhere)'] (attested by RG & EH (4/10/99 Ling332)), (<**=íl**> *come, go, get, become, inceptive*), lx <**=ép**> *on the dirt, on the ground*, lx <**=tel**> *device to*, phonology: stress-shift due to strong-valenced suffixes, vowel-change due to stress shift (not due to ablaut probably because DM preserves the original root vowel even though unstressed), syntactic analysis: nominal, attested by AD, EB, Elders Group (3/72 tape 33, 2/26/75, 5/3/78), NP (1973), also <**lhax̲éyléptel**>, //ɬɛx̣=íl=ə́p=təl//, [ɬæx̣éylə́ptəl], attested by DM (12/4/64 p.177), example: <**qelés te (lhx̲eyléptel, lálwes).**>, //qəl=ə[=´=]s tə (ɬx̣=íl=ə́p=təl, lɛ́lwəs)//, /'*The floor is dirty.*'/, attested by Elders Group (3/72), <**íx̲wetlha ta' lhex̲éyleptel.**>, //ʔíx̣ʷ=əT-ɬɛ t-ɛʔ ɬəx̣=íl=ə́p=təl//, /'*Sweep your floor.*'/, attested by Elders Group (2/26/75).

<**lhex̲ōwéstel**>, dnom //ɬɛx̣=owə[=´=]s=təl//, CAN ['*boards in a canoe bottom*'], ASM ['used so that one doesn't have to put stuff directly on the bottom in water'], HHG ['*boards put under bed if moved outside*'], literally /'(device to spread the canoe paddle on) or (device to spread/lay out under the canoe paddles)'/, lx <**=ōwes**> *paddle*, lx <**=tel**> *device to*, possibly <=´=> *derivational*, phonology: stress-shift, vowel-change due to stress-shift or possibly to ablaut, syntactic analysis: nominal, attested by BHTTC.

<**lháx̲tsestel**>, dnom //ɬɛ́x̣=cəs=təl//, HHG ['*woven mat to put hot plates on*'], ASM ['made of cedar bark or cedar root strips or grass, woven'], FOOD, literally /'device to spread/lay out under the hands/boughs'/, lx <**=tses**> *on the hand, bough,*> *device to*, syntactic analysis: nominal, attested by IHTTC.

<**lháx̲xetel**>, dnom //ɬɛ́x̣=xʸə(l)=təl//, HHG ['*rug*'], literally /'device to spread/lay out under the feet '/, lx <**=xel ~ =xe** (before some suffixes)> *on the foot*, lx <**=tel**> *device to*, phonology: consonant-loss (allomorph of =xel before some suffixes), syntactic analysis: nominal, attested by BHTTC.

<**lhíx̲**>, ds //ɬɛ[=Aí=]x̣ or ɬíx̣//, REL /'*to paint red or black or white (spirit dancer, Indian doctor, etc.)*'/, SPRD, IDOC, ASM ['may include other colors (white is used rarely on spirit dancers), but red and black are the usual colors, they signify different powers or different quests, red is usually more powerful and is used by more ritualists'], semantic environment ['Indian religious participant or ceremony'], (<**í-ablaut**> *derivational*, perhaps *resultative*?), phonology: ablaut, probably not a separate root, (semological comment: probably a derived root since painting of the kind done here is done by spreading colored grease on the skin and root lháx̲ is *spread*), syntactic analysis: intransitive verb, attested by BHTTC.

<**slhílhex̲es**>, dnom //s=ɬɛ[=Aí=][=C₁ə=]]x̣=əs=əm or s=ɬí[=C₁ə=]x̣=əs=əm//, SPRD /'*the painted people (spirit-dancers)*'/, <**s=**> *nominalizer*, <**=R1=**> *resultative*, <**=es**> *on the face*, <**=em**> *middle voice* or *passive voice*, attested by RG & EH (4/10/99 Ling332)

<**lhíx̲esem**>, mdls //ɬɛ[=Aí=]x̣=əs=əm//, REL /'*paint one's face red or black or white (spirit dancer, Indian doctor, ritualist, etc.)*'/, SPRD, IDOC, lx <**=es**> *on the face*, (<**=em**> *middle voice*), phonology: ablaut, syntactic analysis: intransitive verb, attested by BHTTC and RG & EH (4/10/99 Ling332), example <**lámchxw lhíx̲esem**>, //lɛ́=m-c-əxʷ ɬɛ[=Aí=]x̣=əs=əm//, /'*Go*

paint yourself/., attested by RG & EH (4/10/99 Ling332).

<**lhíx̱et**>, pcs //ɬɛ[=Aí=]x̣=əT//, REL [*'spread red or black paint on s-th(?)/s-o'*], (<**=et**> *purposeful control transitivizer*), phonology: ablaut, syntactic analysis: transitive verb, attested by BHTTC.

<**lháx̱eletstel**>, HHG [*'cushion'*], *see* lhá:x̱ ~ lháx̱.

<**lhá:x̱em ~ lháx̱em**>, FOOD /*'help oneself to food, serve oneself, serve oneself food (with a ladle), serve oneself a meal (food), (put on a dish [CT, HT])'*/, *see* lhá:x̱ ~ lháx̱.

<**lháx̱tsestel**>, HHG [*'woven mat to put hot plates on'*], *see* lhá:x̱ ~ lháx̱.

<**lháx̱xetel**>, HHG [*'rug'*], *see* lhá:x̱ ~ lháx̱.

<**lháy**>, free root //ɬɛ́y// or rsls //ɬi[=Aɛ́=]y//, EFAM [*'be shamed'*], possibly <**á-ablaut**> *resultative*, phonology: ablaut possible, syntactic analysis: intransitive verb.

<**lháylexw**>, ncs //ɬɛ́y=l-əxʷ or ɬi[=Aɛ́=]y=l-əxʷ//, EFAM [*'make s-o ashamed [happen to or accidentally or manage to]'*], (<**=l**> *non-control transitivizer*), phonology: ablaut possibly resultative, syntactic analysis: transitive verb.

<**lhí(y)stexw**>, caus //ɬíy=sT-əxʷ or ɬɛ[=Aí=]y=sT-əxʷ//, EFAM [*'ashamed of s-th'*], (<**=st**> *causative control transitivizer*), (<**-exw**> *third person object*), possibly <**í-ablaut**> *derivational*, phonology: ablaut possible, syntactic analysis: transitive verb.

<**lhi(y)stélémét**>, //ɬɛ[-Ai-]y=sT-ə́lə́mə́t or ɬ(ɛ)y=sT-ə́lə́mət//, EFAM /*'feel embarrassed and shy because ashamed, be ashamed'*/, (<**-élémét** (allomorph after causative) ~ **-lómet**> *reflexive*), phonology: possibly vocalization of y to i, syntactic analysis: intransitive verb, attested by IHTTC, Elders Group.

<**lholhistélemet**>, cts //ɬɛ[-AaC$_1$ə-]y=sT-ə́lə́mət//, EFAM [*'feeling embarrassed'*], (<**o-ablaut** plus **-R1-** (or possibly **R10-**)> *continuative*), phonology: ablaut, vocalization of y to i, reduplication, syntactic analysis: intransitive verb, attested by SP (in IHTTC).

<**lháylexw**>, EFAM [*'make s-o ashamed [happen to or accidentally or manage to]'*], *see* lháy.

<**lhchí:ws**>, df //ɬc=í·ws//, EFAM [*'tired'*], lx <**=í:ws**> *on the body, on the skin*, possibly root <**lhéch**> *feel like singing a spirit song, be in a trance making sighs and crying sounds before singing a spirit song*, (semological comment: plausible since dancers sighing give the impression of being tired or bored outwardly (though most are not)), phonology: zero-grade of root, syntactic analysis: adjective/adjectival verb, Salish cognate: Squamish /ɬč-íws/ *be tired* W73:269, K67:326.

<**welhchí:ws**>, df //wəl=ɬc=í·ws or wə=ɬc=í·ws//, EFAM [*'real tired'*], (<**wel=** ~ **wel**> *really, intensive*), phonology: consonant-loss (l assimilated to lh), syntactic analysis: adjective/adjectival verb or adverb/adverbial verb adjective/adjectival verb.

<**lhchí:wsmet**>, iecs //ɬc=í·ws=məT//, EFAM /*'tired of s-th, bored with s-th'*/, (<**=met**> *indirect effect control transitivizer*), syntactic analysis: transitive verb.

<**lhchí:wsmet**>, EFAM /*'tired of s-th, bored with s-th'*/, *see* lhchí:ws.

<**lhéch**>, free root //ɬə́c//, SPRD /*'feel like singing a spirit song, be in a trance making sighs and crying sounds before singing a spirit song, be in the beginning of a trance before the spirit song is recognizable (the motions and sounds, crying out or wailing before singing)'*/, syntactic analysis: intransitive verb, attested by AD (7/23/79), also <**lhéts**>, //ɬə́c//, attested by PK (at Fish Camp 7/11/78).

<**Lhéchelesem**>, ds //ɬə[=Aə́=]c=ɛ́[=Aə=]los=em//, LANG /Nooksack language/, lit. "speak (like they do in) Lhechálōws village", phonological comment: the Nooksack language lacks ablaut and so this

may be the Upriver Halkomelem name or pronunciation of the name used in Nooksack, attested by AC, Deming.

<**lhéch'elechá:ls**>, HARV /'*cut (grass, hay)*'/, *see* lhíts' ~ lhí:ts'.

<**lhék'a**>, possibly root //ɬə́k'ɛ//, PLAY /'*the hooking game, the feather game*'/, ASM ['long feathers from ducks were burned till the ends curled over, each of two players would have one and hook it over his opponent's and pull; whoever's broke first lost; the game was also played by each player biting his index finger till it was numb, then hooking his index finger on the opponents and pulling till the loser's finger gave out'], phonology: note unusual final vowel and k' may show either borrowing from Thompson or Lillooet or diminutive fronting or unrounding, syntactic analysis: nominal?, intransitive verb?, (semological comment: Squamish /klə́xʷ/ *game in which two persons spit on their middle fingers, hook them up and see who can pull hardest* W73:110, K67:338 seems the same game but the name is not cognate (it also seems borrowed with unusual plain /k/)) (compare root <**lhékw'**> *hook*?), attested by Elders Group (2/25/76), IHTTC.

<**lhekw'á:ls**>, FSH /'*hook fish, catch fish (by hook), to gaff-hook fish*'/, *see* lhíkw' ~ lhí:kw'.

<**lhekw'í:wel**>, EFAM ['*surprise*'], *see* lhó:kw' ~ lhókw'.

<**lhékw'qsel**>, ABDF /'*get tripped, to trip*'/, *see* lhíkw' ~ lhí:kw'.

<**lhékw'tel**>, FSH ['*gaff-hook (a large pole-mounted hook)*'], *see* lhíkw' ~ lhí:kw'.

<**lhékw'xel**>, ABDF ['*to trip*'], *see* lhíkw' ~ lhí:kw'.

<**lhékw'xet**>, ABDF ['*to trip s-o*'], *see* lhíkw' ~ lhí:kw'.

<**lhél**>, bound root //hang folded over, hang in folds//, comment: may be related to lhí:l *weave*.

<**slhél:éts ~ slhél:ets ~ slhéléts ~ slhélets**>, dnom //s=ɬə́l=ləc//, ANAH /'*butt, ass, rump, buttocks*'/, literally /'(hang folded over on the rump/bottom)'/, (<**s=**> *nominalizer*), lx <**=lets**> *on the bottom, on the rump*, phonology: consonant merger, syntactic analysis: nominal, usage: has some shock-value, much like English ass or butt, so I've translated it with those terms though rump and buttocks are more refined, attested by Elders Group, AC, AK (4/30/79), IHTTC (Place names meeting 8/23/77).

<**Slhélets**>, dnom //s=ɬə́l=ləc//, PLN ['*four rocks in the Fraser River by Peqwchō:lthel (American Bar) that are shaped like rumps*'], ASM ['the Transformers, X̲ex̲éyls, changed four boys there into rocks; they were diving for slhélqi (rehydrated or soaked dried fish); they can be seen from the American Bar beach when the river is low'], syntactic analysis: nominal, attested by IHTTC (Place names meeting 8/23/77), AK (on Trip to Five-Mile Creek 4/30/79 with AD also), source: place names reference file #206, possibly #153.

<**lhélp'**>, ds //ɬə́l=p'//, ANA /'*a wrinkle, (have a wrinkle?)*'/, literally /'(hang folded over on itself)'/, lx <**=p'**> *on itself*, syntactic analysis: nominal?, prob. intransitive verb (have a wrinkle), attested by Elders Group.

<**slhellhelp'á:lí:ya**>, pln //s=C_1əC_2=ɬəl=p'=ɛ́·lí·yɛ//, plv, ANA /'*(have) sloppy ears, big ears*'/, BPI, literally /'(hanging folded over on itself many times on the ear(s))'/, (<**s=**> *stative* or *nominalizer*, R3= *plural*), lx <**=á:lí:ya**> *on the ear*, phonology: reduplication, syntactic analysis: adjective/adjectival verb, nominal?, attested by Elders Group.

<**slhellhélp'elets**>, plv //s=C_1əC_2=ɬə́l=p'=ələc//, HARV ['*sloppy pack*'], HUNT, TVMO, CLO ['*sloppy back*'], literally /'(hanging folded over on itself many times on the bottom)'/, (<**s=**> *stative*, R3= *plural*), lx <**=elets**> *on the bottom, on the rump* lx perhaps mistranscribed for <**=ewets**> *on the back*, phonology: reduplication, syntactic analysis: adjective/adjectival verb prob., attested by BHTTC, comment: contrast the following word (forming a minimal pair).

<**slhellhelp'élets**>, plv //s=C₁əC₂=ɬəl=p'=ə́ləc//, ANA ['*(have a) sloppy rump*'], BPI, literally /'(hanging folded over on itself many times on the rump)'/, (<**s=**> *stative* or *nominalizer*, R3= *plural*), lx <**=élets**> *on the bottom, on the rump*, phonology: reduplication, syntactic analysis: adjective/adjectival verb prob., poss. nominal, attested by BHTTC.

<**lhélp'es**>, ds //ɬə́l=p'=əs//, ANA ['*(have a) wrinkled face*'], BPI, possibly literally /'wrinkled on the face' from "folded over on itself in the face"/, lx <**=es**> *on the face*, syntactic analysis: adjective/adjectival verb, nominal?, attested by Elders Group (3/2/77).

<**lhellhélp'es**>, plv //C₁əC₂=ɬə́l=p'=əs//, ANA ['*(have a) wrinkled face with many wrinkles*'], probably BPI, (<**R3=**> *plural*), phonology: reduplication, syntactic analysis: adjective/adjectival verb, nominal?, attested by Elders Group (3/2/77).

<**slhelp'íwel**>, ds //s=ɬəl=p'=íwəl//, ANA ['*(have a) sloppy ass*'], BPI, literally /'(be folded over on itself in the insides/rectum)'/, (<**s=**> *stative* or poss. *nominalizer*), lx <**=íwel**> *on the insides, in the rump, in the rectum*, syntactic analysis: adjective/adjectival verb, poss. nominal, attested by Deming (6/24/76).

<**slhelp'ó:ythel**>, ds //s=ɬəl=p'=á·yθəl//, ANA /'*(have) flabby lips, (have) sloppy lips*'/, BPI, literally /'(be folded over on itself on the lips)'/, lx <**=ó:ythel**> *on the lips, on the chin, on the jaw*, syntactic analysis: adjective/adjectival verb, poss. nominal, attested by Elders Group (3/3/76).

<**lhelelméxwtel**>, ds //ɬəl=əlmə́xʷ=təl//, EB ['*wall lettuce*'], ['*Lactuca muralis*'], ASM ['a plant of the mustard family, gathered at Emory Creek example, used as a hot poultice on swollen breasts sore from nursing'], MED literally /'(something to hang folded over on the breast, or something for breasts hanging folded over [swollen])'/, lx <**=álmexw ~ =elméxw**> *(on the) breast*, lx <**=tel**> *device to, thing to*, syntactic analysis: nominal, attested by SP (at Fish Camp 7/29/77).

<**lhél**>, bound root //sprinkle, splash, spray//, a doublet/second version has root <lhélt>.

<**lhélt**>, pcs //ɬə́l=T//, WATR ['*sprinkle it (usually by hand)*'], (<**=t**> *purposeful control transitivizer*), syntactic analysis: transitive verb, attested by Elders Group (5/26/76).

<**lhá:ltem**>, rsls //ɬə[=Aɛ́·=]l=T-əm//, WATR ['*get splashed*'], WETH ['*(get sprinkled)*'], ASM ['with waves in speedboat, with rain, etc.'], (<**á:-ablaut**> *resultative*), (<**-em**> *passive*), phonology: ablaut, syntactic analysis: transitive verb, attested by EB (6/7/76), Elders Group (5/26/76), example: <**me lhá:ltem te slhémexw.**>, //mə ɬə[=Aɛ́·=]l=T-əm//, /'*get splashed by rain, (He got splashed by rain.)*'/, attested by Elders Group (5/26/76), Salish cognate: Lushootseed /ɬə́lt-əb/ *start raining, starting to rain* H76:297, 376.

<**lhélt**>, df //ɬə́l(=)t//, WATR ['*splash*'], (<**=t**> meaning lost, affix petrified from *purposeful control transitivizer*), syntactic analysis: intransitive verb, Salish cognate: Squamish /ɬít/ *splash, sprinkle* which can be transitivized as /ɬit-ánʔ/ *splash (tr.)(obj. the liquid)* W73:246, K69:71, Sechelt /ɬít-it/ *to sprinkle with water [tr.]* T77:34.

<**lhéltes**>, df //ɬə́l(=)t=əs//, WATR ['*splash on the face*'], lx <**=es**> *on the face*, syntactic analysis: intransitive verb, attested by Elders Group (5/26/76).

<**lhéltest**>, pcs //ɬə́l(=)t=əs=T//, WATR /'*splash s-o with water, spray s-o with water*'/, ASM ['like with canoe paddle playfully or flip water in s-o's face'], CAN, (<**=t**> *purposeful control transitivizer*), syntactic analysis: transitive verb, attested by Elders Group (5/28/75), Salish cognate: Squamish /ɬit-ús-n/ *splash water on, besprinkle* W73:246, K67:330, K69:71.

<**lhálétem**>, cts //ɬə[=Aɛ́=]l[-ə́-](=)t=əm//, WETH /'*starting to sprinkle, start sprinkling*'/, WATR, (<**á-ablaut**> *inceptive*), (<**-é-**> *continuative*), (<**=em**> *middle voice* or *intransitivizer*), phonology: ablaut, stress-shift, syntactic analysis: intransitive verb, attested by Deming (3/31/77), Elders Group (5/26/76), example: <**me lhálétem te slhémexw.**>, //mə ɬə[=Aɛ́=]l[-ə́-](=t)=əm tə

s=ɬə́m=əxʷ//, /'*It's starting to sprinkle.*'/, attested by Elders Group, <**uwlh me lhalétem.**>, //ʔu=wɬ mə ɬə[=Aɛ́=]l[-ə́-](=)t=əm//, /'*It started to sprinkle.*'/, literally /'contrast= already become/start sprinkling'/, attested by Deming.

<**lhélest**>, pcs //ɬə́l=əs=T//, WATR /'*splash s-o in the face, squirt s-o in the face*'/, semantic environment ['when swimming (for ex.)'], lx <**=es**> *on the face*, (<**=t**> *purposeful control transitivizer*), syntactic analysis: transitive verb, attested by EB (4/28/76), Elders Group (5/26/76).

<**lhélqwelhem**>, mdls //ɬə́l=əqʷ=əɬ=əm or better ɬə[=lə=]qʷ=əɬ=əm//, WATR /'*wet one's head (sic?), (wet one's bed repeatedly)*'/, if the meaning is *wet one's head* lx <**=eqw**> *on top of the head, on the hair* or if the meaning is *wet one's bed* the root is <**lhéqw**> *wet* as here, lx <**=elh**> *young, offspring; bed*, (<**=em**> *middle voice*), syntactic analysis: intransitive verb, attested by Elders Group (5/26/76).

<**lhá:ltelechá:ls**>, sas //ɬə[=Aɛ́·=]l(=)t=ələc=ɛ́·ls//, WATR ['*spraying (as a structured activity)*'], (<**á:-ablaut**> *resultative*), lx <**=elets**> *on the bottom*, (<**=á:ls**> *structured activity non-continuative*), phonology: ablaut, syntactic analysis: intransitive verb, attested by Elders Group (5/28/75).

<**lhó:ltes**>, rsls //lə[=Aɛ́·=]l(=)t=əs//, WATR ['*spray*'], (<**á:-ablaut**> *resultative*), lx <**=es**> *on the face*, phonology: ablaut, vowel-change: =es triggers a → o (even when the a is secondary), syntactic analysis: intransitive verb, attested by Elders Group (5/28/75).

<**lhélq**>, ds //ɬə́l=q *wet, soak*//, WATR /'*soaked, wet*'/, lx <**=q**> probably *intensive, intensively, thoroughly*, syntactic analysis: adjective/adjectival verb, attested by EB, Salish cognate: Nooksack /ɬə́lq/ *soaked* PA61, Sechelt /ɬə́lʔq/ *soaked* Nater 1977:37, Pentlatch /ɬə́lq/ *wet* K1980, all quoted in G82a:27, example: <**ét'wōwlh la lhélq thel slhálqi.**>, //ʔə=t'wə=u=wɬ lɛ ɬə́l=q (kʷ)θə-l s-ɬə[-Aɛ́-]l=q=i//, /'*What I'm soaking must be already soaked.*'/, literally /'ambig.past =evidential/it must be =contrast =already go(ne) soaked the (near but not visible)(relativizing) -my nominalizer-soaking'/, attested by EB.

<**lhélqt**>, pcs //ɬə́l=q=T//, WATR ['*wet s-th*'], (<**=q**> probably *intensive, intensively, thoroughly* (cf. Musqueam /-q/ meaning uncertain in Suttles ca1984: 14.6.37), <**=t**> *purposeful control transitivizer*), syntactic analysis: transitive verb.

<**lhélqesem**>, mdls //ɬə́l=q=əs=əm//, WATR ['*wet one's face*'], lx <**=es**> *on the face*, (<**=em**> *middle voice*), syntactic analysis: intransitive verb.

<**lhélqi**>, df //ɬə́l=q=i(y)//, FOOD /'*to soak (fish, beans, dried fruit, only food, not of cedar roots), rehydrate dried food, soak dried fish*'/, WATR, FSH, (<**=i(y) meaning uncertain unless**> *dry food* or *fish* (cf. Musqueam /-əy' ~ -ay'/ *fish?* Suttles ca1984: 14.6.43)), syntactic analysis: intransitive verb, dialects: *Chill., Tait, Cheh.*, attested by Elders Group (4/26/78), IHTTC, also <**lhelqí ~ lhalqí**>, //ɬəl=q=í ~ ɬɛl=q=í//, attested by AC.

<**lhálqi**>, cts/durs //ɬə[-Aɛ́-]l=q=i//, FOOD ['*soaking dried fish*'], WATR, FSH, (<**á-ablaut**> *continuative/durative*), phonology: ablaut, syntactic analysis: intransitive verb, attested by IHTTC, AC, also /'*to soak fish*'/, attested by Deming (3/25/76).

<**slhálqi**>, stcs //s-ɬə[-Aɛ́-]l=q=i//, FOOD ['*is soaking (dried fish)*'], WATR, FSH, (<**á-ablaut**> *continuative/durative*, <**s-**> *stative*), phonology: ablaut, syntactic analysis: intransitive verb, attested by IHTTC, AC, also /'*to soak fish*'/, attested by Deming (3/25/76), example: <**lí xwel slhálqi?**>, //lí xʷəl s-ɬə[-Aɛ́-]l=q=i//, /'*Is it still soaking?*'/, attested by DF.

<**slhálqi**>, dnom //s=ɬə[-Aɛ́-]l=q=i//, FOOD ['*what is soaking (dried fish)*'], WATR, FSH, (<**á-ablaut**> *continuative/durative*, <s-> *nominalizer*), phonology: ablaut, syntactic analysis: nominalized intransitive verb, attested by IHTTC, AC, also /'*to soak fish*'/, attested by Deming

(3/25/76), example: <**ét'wōwlh la lhélq thel slhálqi**>, //ʔə́=t'wə=u=wɬ lɛ ɬə́l=q (kʷ)θə-l s-ɬə[-Aɛ́-]l=q=i//, /'*What I'm soaking must be already soaked.*'/, attested by EB, <**lí xwel slhálqi?**>, //lí xʷəl s-ɬə[-Aɛ́-]l=q=i//, /'*Is it still soaking?*'/, attested by DF.

<**slhálqi**>, strs //s-ɬə[-Aɛ́-]l=q=i//, FOOD ['*already soaked dried fish*'], WATR, FSH, (<**á-ablaut**> *resultative,* <**s-**> *stative*), phonology: ablaut, syntactic analysis: intransitive verb, attested by IHTTC, AC, also /'*to soak fish*'/, attested by Deming (3/25/76), example: <**ét'wōwlh la lhélq thel slhálqi**>, //ʔə́=t'wə=u=wɬ lɛ ɬə́l=q (kʷ)θə-l s-ɬə[-Aɛ́-]l=q=i//, /'*What I'm soaking must be already soaked.*'/, attested by EB.

<**Slhálqi**>, ds //s=ɬə[=Aɛ́=]l=q=i//, PLN /'*village on west bank of old course of Chilliwack River near Tzeachton,* also *the place nearby where the Stó:lō used to soak dried fish*'/, ASM ['the old soaking place was at the turn of what's now Bailey Rd. (where it splits to go to Tzeachten); this place is in the dip where the old course of the Chilliwack River went and was a place where they used to soak fish; even after the river changed course there was still water there; Hill-Tout lists a chief for the village (ca 1890's) as <weúsElu>k (macron over e, umlaut over u) in the Stó:lō orthography <Wiyúseleq> (/wiyús=ələq/), now spelled Uslick'], literally /'place where dried salmon was soaked'/, (<**s=**> *nominalizer*), (<**á-ablaut**> *continuative/durative* (derivational in place names)), phonology: ablaut, syntactic analysis: nominal, attested by Elders Group (4/26/78, 1/15/75), AC (8/28/70), source: place names reference file #177, other sources: Wells 1965:19, H-T 1902 <C'lálki> (umlaut over the a).

<**slhélqi**>, dnom //s=ɬə́l=q=i//, FSH ['*dried fish that's been soaked (rehydrated)*'], FOOD, WATR, (<**s=**> *nominalizer*), syntactic analysis: nominal, attested by IHTTC.

<**lhélqit ~ lhélqeyt**>, pcs //ɬə́l=q=i=T ~ ɬə́l=q=əy=T//, [ɬíqit ~ ɬɛ́lqit ~ ɬɛ́lqəyt ~ ɬɛ́lqeyt], WATR ['*soak it*'], semantic environment ['of smoked fish, salt fish, laundry, etc.'], FSH, FOOD, (<**=t**> *purposeful control transitivizer*), phonology: note the ey heard here in the lexical suffix, syntactic analysis: transitive verb, attested by Elders Group (5/26/76, 4/26/78), MH (Deming 1/4/79 prompted).

<**lhelelméxwtel**>, EB ['*wall lettuce*'], *see* lhél.

<**lhélest**>, WATR /'*splash s-o in the face, squirt s-o in the face*'/, *see* lhél.

<**lhellhélp'es**>, ANA ['*(have a) wrinkled face with many wrinkles*'], *see* lhél.

<**lhélp'**>, ANA /'*a wrinkle, (have a wrinkle?)*'/, *see* lhél.

<**lhélp'es**>, ANA ['*(have a) wrinkled face*'], *see* lhél.

<**lhélq**>, WATR /'*soaked, wet*'/, *see* lhél.

<**lhélqesem**>, WATR ['*wet one's face*'], *see* lhél.

<**lhélqi**>, FOOD /'*to soak (fish, beans, dried fruit, only food, not of cedar roots), rehydrate dried food, soak dried fish*'/, *see* lhél.

<**lhélqit ~ lhélqeyt**>, WATR ['*soak it*'], *see* lhél.

<**lhélqt**>, WATR ['*wet s-th*'], *see* lhél.

<**lhélqwelhem**>, WATR /'*wet one's head (sic?), (wet one's bed repeatedly)*'/, *see* lhél *sprinkle* for first meaning and lhéqw *wet* for second meaning.

<**lhélt**>, WATR ['*sprinkle it (usually by hand)*'], *see* lhél.

<**lhélt**>, WATR ['*splash*'], *see* lhél.

<**lheltálets**>, WATR /'*a channel that makes an island, inside channel*'/, *see* lhà:l.

<**Lheltá:lets ~ Lheltálets**>, PLN /'*a channel between an island and the main shore a) across Harrison River from where the Phillips smokehouse was at Chehalis village (slightly downriver from the mouth of Chehalis R. into Harrison R.),* also b) *at Harrison Lake where the hatchery was*'/, *see* lhà:l.

<**lheltáletsem**>, WATR ['*go through a channel*'], *see* lhà:l.

<**lhéltel**>, CAN /'*a bailer, canoe bailer*'/, *see* lhí:lt ~ lhílt.

<**lhéltes**>, WATR ['*splash on the face*'], *see* lhél.

<**lhéltest**>, WATR /'*splash s-o with water, spray s-o with water*'/, *see* lhél.

<**lhelhá:l**>, df //ɬəɬɛ́·l or C_1ə=ɬɛ́·l or ɬə[=C_1ɛ́(·)=]l//, [ɬəɬǽ·l (normal speed) ~ ɬæɬǽ·l (hyper-slow)], DIR /'*to the back (near the wall), on the inside (on a bed toward the wall)*'/, possibly root <**lhà:l**> /'*pull ashore in a canoe, land a canoe*'/ (since directions relative to house wall sides are related to toward the shore vs. toward the river and upriver vs. downriver)–if so this may be part of the metaphor HOUSE DIRECTIONS ARE RIVER DIRECTIONS, possibly <**R5=** or **=R9=**> meaning uncertain here, syntactic analysis: adverb/adverbial verb, attested by AC, example: <**lichxw li te s'eyí:ws q'a lichxw lhelhá:l?**>, //li-c-x^w li tə s=ʔɛy=í·ws q'ɛ li-c-x^w ɬəɬɛ́·l//, /'*Are you on the right side (outside, of a bed) or the other side (inside, toward the wall, of a bed)?*'/, attested by AC (10/13/71), <**lámchexw te lhelhá:l stetís te t'ómel.**>, //lɛ́=m-c-əx^w tə ɬəɬɛ́·l s=C_1ə=tə[=Aí=]s tə t'áməl//, /'*You'll go to the back near the wall.*'/, attested by AC.

<**lhelhewqí:m**>, EB /'*smallest gray swamp blueberries, smallest variety of Canada blueberry*'/, *see* lhewqí:m.

<**lhelhíxw ~ lhíxw**>, NUM ['*three things*'], *see* lhí:xw.

<**=lhelh ~ =lhál**>, da //=ɬəɬ ~ =ɬɛ́l//, ANA /'*on the front of the neck, in the windpipe, in the trachea*'/, syntactic analysis: lexical suffix, derivational suffix, also <**=lhál**>, //=ɬɛ́l//; found in <**sqwéllhelh**>, //s=q^wə́l=ɬəɬ or s=q^wɛ[=Aə́=]l=ɬəɬ//, /'*front of neck*'/, <**shxwehó:méllhelh**>, //sx^wəh=á·mə́l=ɬəɬ//, /'*adam's apple*'/, <**p'ith'lhált**>, //p'iθ'=ɬɛ́l=t//, /'*choke s-o*'/, literally /'squeeze front of neck purposely (+ 3rd person object))'/.

<**lhelhós**>, WATR /'*downriver, down that way*'/, *see* lhós.

<**lhelhq'etíwel**>, EZ ['*common bedbug*'], *see* lheq'át ~ lhq'á:t.

<**lhelhxwále**>, NUM ['*three little people*'], *see* lhí:xw.

<**Lhelhxwáyeleq**>, PLN ['*Three Creeks Mountain*'], *see* lhí:xw.

<**lhém**>, bound root //ɬə́m *drops of liquid, moisture*//.

<**lexwslhém ~ lexwslhám**>, ds //ləx^w=s=ɬə́m ~ ləx^w=s=ɬɛ́m//, [lʊx^wsɬɛ́m], ABDF /'*choke on water, choked on liquid*'/, WATR, (<**lexw=**> *always*, s= *nominalizer*?), phonology: [ɛ́] prob. rare allophone of /ə/, syntactic analysis: intransitive verb, attested by Elders Group, AC.

<**slhémxel**>, dnom //s=ɬə́m=x^yəl//, WETH ['*dew*'], WATR, literally /'something that's drops of liquid on the foot (or) something that's drops of liquid precipitation'/, (<**s=**> *nominalizer*), lx <**=xel**> *on the foot; precipitation*, syntactic analysis: nominal, attested by Elders Group, Deming.

<**slhémlhem**>, chrs //s=ɬə́m=C_1əC_2//, dnom, WETH ['*dew*'], WATR, literally /'something that's characteristically drops of liquid'/, (<**s=**> *nominalizer*), (<**=R2**> *characteristic*), syntactic analysis: nominal, dialects: possibly *Sumas, Deming*, attested by Elders Group (Sumas dial. esp.), Deming.

<**lhémtel**>, dnom //ɬə́m=təl//, WETH ['*dew*'], WATR, literally /'drops of liquid thing'/, lx <**=tel**> *thing to, device to*, syntactic analysis: nominal, attested by Elders Group.

<**lhéméxw**>, df //ɬə́m=ə́xʷ//, WETH ['*to rain*'], WATR, ASM ['if one hollers too much in the mountains it starts rain; if one is too rough with plants it starts rain; if one teases twins it makes it rain (Mary Lou Andrews did this with her twins in the 1970s) (twins are raised up in the mountains because bears usually have twins) (information from IHTTC)'], lx <**=éxw**> meaning uncertain, syntactic analysis: intransitive verb, attested by AC, BJ (5/64), AD; found in <**lhéméxwcha.**>, //ɬə́m=ə́xʷ-cɛ//, /'*It will rain.*'/, attested by AD.

<**lhémexw**>, cts //ɬə́m=əxʷ//, WETH /'*raining, ([having a] rainshower with light wind [BJ])*'/, WATR, (<**stress-shift**> *continuative*), syntactic analysis: intransitive verb, attested by AD, AC, Salish cognate: Clallam and Sooke /ɬə́mʔxʷ/ *it's raining* vs. /ɬə́məxʷ/ *it rains, to rain* (in G82a:37 set 175), and Samish /ɬə́m'xʷ/ *it's raining* vs. /ɬə́məxʷ/ *to rain, it rains* G86a:96 all with /-ʔ-/ (and vowel-loss?) *continuative*, also <**lhém:exw**>, //lə́m[-·-]=əxʷ//, also /'*[having a] rainshower with light wind*'/, (<**-:-**> *continuative*), phonology: lengthening, attested by BJ (5/64), example: <**ésta welh lhémexw.**>, //ʔə́stɛ wəɬ ɬə́m=əxʷ//, /'*It's started to rain.*'/, literally /'? already (is) raining'/, attested by Deming (3/31/77), <**yalh s'es me lhémexw.**>, //yɛɬ s-ʔəs mə ɬə́m=əxʷ//, /'*It just started to rain.*'/, attested by Deming, <**l sqwálewel kws més lhémexw tlówàyèl.**>, //l s=qʷɛ́l=əwəl kʷ-s mə-s ɬə́m=əxʷ tə=lá=wɛ̀yə̀l//, /'*I think it's going to rain today.*'/, literally /'it's my thought that it is coming to/start to be raining today'/, attested by EB.

<**slhém:exw ~ slhémexw**>, dnom //s=ɬə́m[=·=]=əxʷ ~ s=ɬə́m=əxʷ//, WETH ['*the rain*'], WATR, literally /'nominal= raining'/, (<**s=**> *nominalizer*), (<**=:=**> *continuative*), syntactic analysis: nominal, attested by AC, other sources: ES /sɬə́m·ə́xʷ/ (vs. MsCw /sɬə́məxʷ/), also <**slhém:éxw**>, //s=ɬə́m[=·=]=ə́xʷ//, attested by BJ (12/5/64), example: <**qé::x̲ te slhémexw.**>, //qə́[=··=]x̣ tə s=ɬə́m=əxʷ//, /'*There's A LOT OF rain.*'/, attested by AC.

<**lhémlhemexw**>, chrs //ɬə́m=C$_1$əC$_2$=əxʷ//, WETH ['*(be) rainy (off and on)*'], WATR, (<**=R2**> *characteristic*), phonology: reduplication, syntactic analysis: intransitive verb, attested by Elders Group.

<**lhémt**>, df //ɬə́m=t or ɬə́m=T//, WETH ['*a rainshower*'], WATR, (<**=t**> meaning uncertain or <**=T**> *purposeful control transitivizer*), syntactic analysis: nominal?, transitive verb?, attested by Elders Group (5/13/75).

<**lhémkiya ~ lhámkiya**>, df //ɬə́m(=)k(=)iyɛ//, [ɬɛ́mkiyɛ], HHG /'*pot to boil in, iron pot, smaller iron pot*'/, ACL, possibly <**=iya**> *little*, <**q → k**> *diminutive*, possibly sound symbolism, possibly root <**lhem**> *drops of liquid*, phonology: possible fronting, syntactic analysis: nominal, attested by Elders Group, JS, AC, comment: the /k/ could also indicate a borrowing from Thompson, see dialect form <**lhámkiya**>.

<**slhémoqel**>, strs //s=ɬə́m=ə[=Aa=]qəl//, ABDF /'*(have a) tooth missing, (have) teeth missing (any number), (be) toothless*'/, literally /'(have moisture/drops of liquid in the throat/inside mouth)'/, ANA, (<**s=**> *stative*), (<**á-ablaut**> *resultative* or *derivational*), lx <**=eqel**> *in the throat, inside mouth*, phonology: ablaut, syntactic analysis: adjective/adjectival verb, attested by Elders Group (1/21/76).

<**slhéms**>, ds //s=ɬə́m=s//, TIME ['*eleven o'clock*'], literally /'(?hour of the dew [when it forms])'/, lx <**s=...=s**> *hour, o'clock*, phonology: circumfix, syntactic analysis: nominal, attested by Elders Group (9/17/75, Fish Camp 7/19/78), Salish cognate: Squamish /s-ɬə́m-q/ *eleven o'clock* W73:98, K67:290, 327, example: <**alht'éqw' syiláws te slhéms**>, //ʔɛɬ=t'ə́q'ʷ s=yilɛ́w-s tə s=ɬə́m=s//, /'*(It's) half an hour past eleven o'clock., (It's) half past eleven., (It's) thirty minutes past eleven o'clock.*'/, attested by Elders Group at Fish Camp.

<**Lhemqwó:tel**>, rcps //ɬəm=qʷɛ́[=Aá=]·=T-əl or ɬəm=qʷ=á·T-əl//, PLN ['*mouth of Weaver Creek*'], ASM ['where Johnny Leon used to live'], ASM ['so called because of a story in which two people

did something and when they got up there were marks in the marshy ground where they sat (seems to imply some kind of sexual play)'], probably root <**lhém**> *moisture, drops of liquid*, possibly <**qwá:**> *hole*, (<**ó-ablaut**> on a-vowel required by control reciprocal), (<**=T**> *purposeful control transitivizer*), (<**-el**> *reciprocal, to each other*), phonology: ablaut, syntactic analysis: nominal, attested by DF, source: place names reference file #238, also /'*Morris Creek (*prob. error*)*'/, attested by EL.

<**Lhemqwótel Stótelō**>, cpds //ɬə́m=qʷɛ́=Aá=T-əl//, PLN /'*the first creek above Hemlock Valley road which also crosses the road to Morris Valley,* also *the name for Pretty Creek*'/, ASM ['both creeks go to the place called Lhemqwó:tel'], literally /'Lhemqwótel creek'/, syntactic analysis: simple nominal phrase, attested by EL, NP, EB (all on Chehalis Trip 9/27/77), source: place names reference file #303, #303a.

<**lhemét**>, HARV /'*pick s-th, (harvest s-th)*'/, *see* lhím.

<**lhéméxw**>, WETH ['*to rain*'], *see* lhém.

<**lhémexw**>, WETH /'*raining, ([having a] rainshower with light wind [BJ])*'/, *see* lhém.

<**lhémkiya ~ lhámkiya**>, HHG /'*pot to boil in, iron pot, smaller iron pot*'/, *see* lhém.

<**lhémlhemexw**>, WETH ['*(be) rainy (off and on)*'], *see* lhém.

<**lhemlhí:m**>, HARV ['*lots of people picking*'], *see* lhím.

<**Lhemqwó:tel**>, PLN ['*mouth of Weaver Creek*'], *see* lhém.

<**Lhemqwótel Stótelō**>, PLN /'*the first creek above Hemlock Valley road which also crosses the road to Morris Valley,* also *the name for Pretty Creek*'/, *see* lhém.

<**lhémt**>, WETH ['*a rainshower*'], *see* lhém.

<**lhémtel**>, WETH ['*dew*'], *see* lhém.

<**lhémth'**>, FOOD ['*picking food by the fingers before the meal*'], *see* lhím.

<**lhémxts'el**>, PE ['*fine comb*'], *see* méxts'el.

<**lhémxts'eltel**>, PE ['*real fine-tooth comb*'], *see* méxts'el.

<**lhép**>, bound root //ɬə́p *fold skin, close with skin*//.

<**lhéplexw**>, ncs //ɬə́p=l-əxʷ//, ABFC ['*blink*'], (<**=l**> *non-control transitivizer*), (<**-exw**> *third person object*), syntactic analysis: transitive verb, attested by AD, MP (both in IHTTC meeting).

<**lhép<u>x</u>lexw**>, ds //ɬə́p=x̣=l-əxʷ//, ABFC ['*blink one's eyes*'], (<**=<u>x</u>**> *distributive*), syntactic analysis: transitive verb, attested by AK, SP (both in IHTTC), Elders Group (2/8/78).

<**lhéplhep<u>x</u>lexw**>, chrs //ɬə́p=C_1əC_2=x̣=l-əxʷ//, its, ABDF ['*blinking one's eyes repeatedly*'], (<**=R2**> *characteristic* or *iterative*), syntactic analysis: transitive verb, attested by Elders Group.

<**lhéptel**>, dnom //ɬə́p=təl//, [ɬíptɪl ~ ɬíptəl], ANA /'*eyelid, eyelash*'/, lx <**=tel**> *device to, thing to*, syntactic analysis: nominal, attested by AD, Elders Group, AC, other sources: ES /ɬə́ptəl/ *eyelash*, H-T <tlúpEtEl> *eyelashes*.

<**lhepteló:ythel**>, ds //ɬəp=təl=á·yθəl//, ANA /'*red part of the lips, (both) lips*'/, lx <**=ó:ythel**> *on the lip, on the jaw, on the chin*, syntactic analysis: nominal, attested by IHTTC (8/4/77, 8/11/77).

<**lhéplexw**>, ABFC ['*blink*'], *see* lhép.

<**lhéplhep<u>x</u>lexw**>, ABDF ['*blinking one's eyes repeatedly*'], *see* lhép.

<**lhéptel**>, ANA /'*eyelid, eyelash*'/, *see* lhép.

<**lhepteló:ythel**>, ANA /'*red part of the lips, (both) lips*'/, *see* lhép.

<**lhépx̱lexw**>, ABFC ['*blink one's eyes*'], *see* lhép.

<**lhéq**>, free root //ɬə́q//, FSH possibly /'*catch a fish with hook and line (?)*'/, syntactic analysis: intransitive verb, attested by SP (compare root <**lhéq**> *join, fasten* as in *button*?).

<**lhéq**>, bound root //ɬə́q// *join, fasten*.

<**slheq(e)lí:s**>, stvi //s=ɬəq=əlí·s//, CLO ['*be buttoned*'], literally /'be fastened on a tooth'/, (<**s=**> *stative*), lx <**=elí:s**> *on the tooth, on the teeth*, phonology: the first vowel of the suffix is usually written in my field notes as a superscript barred i, a glide, and could be phonemically present or absent, (semological comment: possibly buttons were made out of teeth before contact, but even if they were only made of other bone the resemblance to teeth was noticeable before or after contact; early non-Indians had bone and perhaps tooth buttons as well as metal buttons), syntactic analysis: adjective/adjectival verb, attested by AC, example: <**lulh slheq(e)lí:s.**>, //lə=uɬ s=ɬəq=əlí·s//, /'*It's buttoned.*'/, literally /'third person past is buttoned'/, attested by AC.

<**lheq(e)lí:sem**>, mdls //ləq=əlí·s=əm//, CLO ['*button (up)*'], (<**=em**> *middle voice*), syntactic analysis: intransitive verb, attested by AC.

<**lheqlíst**>, pcs //ɬəq=əlís=T//, CLO ['*button it*'], (<**=t**> *purposeful control transitivizer*), syntactic analysis: transitive verb, attested by AD, example: <**lheqlíst ta' stl'epíwel.**>, //ɬəq=əlís=T t-ɛʔ s=ƛ'əp=íwəl//, /'*Button your shirt.*'/, syntactic comment: imperative through lack of subject pronoun and presence of second person possessed object, attested by AD.

<**lheq(e)léstel**>, dnom //ɬəq=əli[=Aə́=]s=təl//, [ɬəq(ə)lɪ́stəl], CLO ['*button*'], (<**é-ablaut**> *derivational*), lx <**=tel**> *device to, thing to*, phonology: ablaut, syntactic analysis: nominal, attested by AC, EB, example: <**me má tel lheqléstel.**>, //mə mɛ́ tə-l ɬəq=əli[=Aə́=]s=təl//, /'*My button came off.*'/, literally /'it becomes/became removed the -my button'/, attested by EB.

<**lhéqōwelh ~ lhéqwōwelh**>, ds //ɬə́q=owəɬ or ɬə́q=əwəɬ//, CAN ['*patch a canoe*'], lx <**=ōwelh**> *canoe, vessel*, phonology: the <**q**> may receive some rounding from the following <**ō**>, syntactic analysis: intransitive verb, attested by Elders Group.

<**lheqtó:léstexw**>, caus //ɬəq=tá·lə́=sT-əx^{w}//, MC ['*join s-th together*'], lx <**=tó:lé(s)**> meaning unclear, (<**=st**> *causative control transitivizer*), (<**-exw**> *third person object*), syntactic analysis: transitive verb, attested by JL (5/5/75); found in <**lheqtó:léstexwchxw**>, //ɬəq=tá·lə́=sT-əx^{w}-c-x^{w}//, /'*you join together*'/.

<**lheq**>, da //ɬəq//, MOOD /'*sometimes?, always?*'/, syntactic analysis: adverb/adverbial verb; found in <**lheq qwóqwel**>, //ɬəq q^{w}ɛ[=AáC$_{1}$ə=]l//, /'*speaker, master of ceremonies*'/.

<**lheqel ~ lhequl**>, df //ɬə́q=qəl or ɬə́q'=qəl//, WATR ['*head of a creek or island*'], <=qel> *at the head*, phonology: transcription by FM, syntactic analysis: nominal?, intransitive verb?, attested by Elders Group, Salish cognate: poss. Squamish /ɬə́q/ *get to the other side (of a body of water)* K69:70 (compare root <**lhéq**> *join* or root <**lhéq'**> *wide)*, compare/contrast <**lhéq'qel**> *end of a falling section of land, end of a level stretch of land*.

<**lheq(e)léstel**>, CLO ['*button*'], *see* lhéq.

<**lheq(e)lí:sem**>, CLO ['*button (up)*'], *see* lhéq.

<**lheqlíst**>, CLO ['*button it*'], *see* lhéq.

<**lhéqōwelh ~ lhéqwōwelh**>, CAN ['*patch a canoe*'], *see* lhéq.

<**lheqqwóqwel** or **lheq qwóqwel**>, SOC /'*speaker at a gathering, announcer at a gathering*'/, *see* qwà:l.

<**lheqtó:léstexw**>, MC [*'join s-th together'*], *see* lhéq.

<**lhéq' ~ lhíq'**>, free root //ɬə́q' ~ ɬíq'//, TIME /*'sometimes, (yes [RM])'*/, syntactic analysis: adverb/adverbial verb, attested by EB, LJ (Tait), also /*'yes'*/, dialects: *Chill.*, attested by RM, also <**lhíq'**>, //ɬíq'//, may be ultimately analyzable as <**lhí**>, free root //ɬí//, /*'when, (sometimes [EB])'*/ + <**=q'**> /*'on something else, within ssomething else'*/, dialects: *Cheh.*, attested by EB, RM reporting Cheh. form; found in <**lhéq'chel ~ lhíq'chel**>, //ɬə́q'-c-əl ~ ɬíq'-c-əl//, /*'Sometimes I do., Sometimes., Sometimes, yes.'*/, attested by EB, example: <**lhéq' st'á**>, //ɬə́q' s=t=(ɛ)ʔɛ́//, /*'Sometimes I do., Sometimes., Sometimes, yes.'*/, literally /'sometimes it's similar/alike'/, attested by EB, <**lhéq' me séltsʼtem tel sx̱óyes lhíl áx̱eth.**>, //ɬə́q' mə sə́l=lc'=T(=)əm tə-l s=x̣áy(=)əs ɬí-l ʔɛ́x̣əθ//, /*'Sometimes my head spins when I lay down.'*/, attested by LJ (Tait), Salish cognate: Nooksack <**lheq'**> *sometimes* (PA:SJ).

<**lhéq'e**>, if //ɬə́q'-ə//, TIME [*'is it sometimes?'*], (<**-e**> *yes/no-question*), syntactic analysis: verb phrase with yes/no interrogative, interrogative affix, attested by EB, example: <**lhéq'e t'ít'ets'em.**>, //ɬə́q'-ə t'í[-C_1ə-]c'=əm//, /*'Does he swim?'*/, attested by EB.

<**lhéq'elh**>, ds //ɬə́q'=əɬ//, TIME [*'used to'*], (<**=elh**> *past tense* used derivationally), syntactic analysis: adverb/adverbial verb, verb phrase with past tense, attested by EB, others, example: <**lhéq'elh x̱ét'e yé xwèlmèxw.**>, //ɬə́q'=əɬ x̣ə́t'ə yə x^{w}ə́lməx^w//, /*'The people used to say.'*/, phonology: downdrifting, updrifting, attested by EB, <**lhéq'elhchxw sex̱we'álex̱eth'.**>, //ɬə́q'=əɬ-c-x^w səx̣^{w}ə=ʔɛ́ləx̣əθ'//, /*'You used to wet your bed., You used to wet the bed.'*/, literally /'sometimes =past -subj. -you (sg.) urinate =in the bed'/, attested by EB, Salish cognate: Nooksack <lhéq'olh> *used to* (lit. "sometimes in past") (PA:SJ)

<**lhéq'es**>, ds //ɬə́q'=əs//, TIME [*'whenever'*], possibly <**=es**> *subjunctive* to form indefinite adv. or? <**=es**> *cyclic period*, syntactic analysis: indefinite adverb, attested by EB.

<**lhéq'**>, root meaning uncertain or possibly root <**lhoqw'**> *slap, spank* or <**lhaq'**> *wide*

<**welhéq'**>, ds //wə=ɬə́q' or wə=ɬa[=Aə́=]q'//, SD /*'(make the) sound of a spank on a bottom, (fall down with a bang [Elders Group 5/19/76])'*/, lx <**we=**> *suddenly*, possibly root <**lhaq'**> or <**lheq'á**> *wide*, possibly root <**lhóqw'**> *slap, spank*, (<**é-ablaut and unrounding**> *derivational*), phonology: labialization or delabialization (delabialization/unrounding), ablaut, syntactic analysis: intransitive verb, attested by AD (2/19/79), also /*'fall down with a bang'*/, attested by Elders Group (5/19/76).

<**welhéleq'**>, df //wə=ɬə́[=lə=]q'//, SD /*'fall splat, (make the) sound of a spank or slap'*/, possibly <**=le=**> *plural*, probably root <**lhóqw'**> *spank, slap*, (<**é-ablaut and unrounding**> *derivational*), phonology: labialization or delabialization (delabialization/unrounding), ablaut, syntactic analysis: intransitive verb, attested by Elders Group (10/27/76), EB (2/20/78), example: <**tsel mákwlh; tsel welhéleq' la te sth'í:qel.**>, //c-əl mɛ́k^{w}ɬ; c-əl wə=ɬə́ləq' lɛ tə s=θ'í·qəl//, /*'I got hurt; I fell splat in the mud.'*/, attested by EB.

<**lheq'á-**>, bound root //ɬəq'ɛ́=// *wide*

<**lheq'láts**>, dnom //ɬɛ́q'=lə[=M2=]c or ɬəq'ɛ́=lə[=M2=]c//, [ɬəq'lǽc], ANAH /*'hip, hips'*/, ANAA [*'hind leg'*], lx <**=lets**> *on the bottom, on the rump*, (<**metathesis type 2**> *derivational*), possibly root <**lheq'á-**> *wide* or <**lhéq'**> *across(?)*, phonology: metathesis, syntactic analysis: nominal, attested by AC, DM (12/4/64), Elders Group, other sources: ES /ɬə̀q'əlɛ́c/ *rump* (vs. /sc'ə́mləc/ *hip* [bone in rump]), example: <**tsel lekwlá:xw tel lheq'láts.**>, //c-əl lək^w=l-ə[=Aɛ́·=]x^w tə-l ɬəq'=lɛ́c//, /*'I broke my hip (break accidentally resultative).'*/, attested by AC.

<**lhílheq'làts**>, dmn //C_1í=ɬɛ́q'=lə[=M2=]c//, ANAH [*'small hips'*], ANAA [*'small hind quarters'*], (<**R4=**> *diminutive*), phonology: reduplication, syntactic analysis: nominal, attested by Elders

Group.

<**slheq'ó:lwelh**>, dnom //s=ɬɛq'=á·lwəɬ or s=ɬəq'ɛ́[=Aá=]·=əlwəlh//, ANAH [*'one side of the body (between arm and hip)'*], lx <**=ó:lwelh ~ =í:lwelh ~ =elwelh**> *on the side*, possibly <**ó-ablaut**> *derivational* or possibly triggered by suffix, possibly root <**lhéq'**> *across(?)*, phonology: ablaut?, vowel-reduction, syntactic analysis: nominal, dialects: *Cheh.*, attested by Elders Group (10/8/75), also <**s'í:lwelh**>, //s=ʔ=í·lwəɬ//, dialects: *Tait*, attested by Elders Group.

<**slhéq'ōwelh**>, dnom //s=ɬɛ[=Aə́=]q'=owəlh//, ANAH /*'the back (on the body), (lower back [Deming])'*/, (<**s=**> *nominalizer*), lx <**=ōwelh**> *canoe, vessel, canoe-shaped container*, (<**é-ablaut**> *derivational*), possibly root <**lhéq'**> *across(?)*, phonology: ablaut, syntactic analysis: nominal, attested by Elders Group (8/20/75), also /*'lower back'*/, attested by Deming, Salish cognate: in part, Squamish /ɬə́q'-č/ *have a broad back* with /-č/ *back (anat.)* W73:12, K67:328.

<**slháq'emex**>, df //s=ɬɛ́q'=aməxʸ or s=ɬəq'ɛ́=M2=aməxʸ//, LAND [*'a large portion of the earth'*], (<**s=**> *nominalizer*), possibly <**metathesis**> *derivational*, possibly <**=omex**> *in appearance*, possibly root <**lháq'**> *lay on the ground* or <**lheq'á-**> *wide*, phonology: metathesis perhaps, syntactic analysis: nominal?, attested by BJ (12/5/64) (compare <**lheq'át**> *be wide)*, Salish cognate: root perhaps cognate with Squamish root /ɬəq'/ *wide, broad, flat* as in /ɬq'-át/ *wide, broad, flat* and with Coeur d'Alene and Kalispel /ɬáq'/ *wide, be wide* K67:328.

<**lheq'át ~ lhq'á:t**>, df //ɬəq'ɛ́t ~ ɬəq'ɛ́·t or ɬɛ́q'=ə[=M2=]T or ɬəq'=ə[=Aɛ́(·)=]T//, DESC [*'be wide'*], possibly <**metathesis type 2**> *derivational* or possibly <**á-ablaut**> *durative* or possibly <**=et**> or <**=át**> *purposeful control transitivizer (crystallized with loss of meaning)?*, phonology: metathesis or ablaut or stressed transitivizer, syntactic analysis: adjective/adjectival verb, attested by AC, other sources: ES /ɬq'ɛ́·t/, JH /ɬəqé·t/ (compare <**lháq'**> in <**slháq'emey**> *large portion of the earth)*, also <**lhq'át**>, //ɬq'ɛ́t//, attested by EB, example: <**lheq'át te stó:lō.**>, //ɬəq'ɛ́t tə s=tá·lo//, /*'The river is wide.'*/, attested by AC, <**lalh lheq'át te xálh.**>, //lɛ-ɬ ɬəq'ɛ́t tə xʸɛ́ɬ//, /*'Widen the path.'*/, literally /'let the path be wide (imperative (2s), go, become, get)'/, attested by AC, <**xwel lheq'át**>, //xʷəl ɬəq'ɛ́t//, /*'wider'*/, literally /'still wide'/, semantic environment ['of a plank, etc.'], attested by AC, <**we'ól lheq'át**>, //wə=ʔál ɬəq'ɛ́t//, /*'wider'*/, literally /'more wide'/, semantic environment ['of a person'], attested by AC.

<**lhq'ó:tes**>, ds //ɬq'ɛ́[=Aá:]·t=əs//, [ɬq'á·tɪs], ANA [*'(have a) wide face'*], BPI, lx <**=es**> *on the face*, phonology: <**ó-ablaut**> triggered on all <**a**> vowels by addition of <**=es**>, syntactic analysis: adjective/adjectival verb, attested by BHTTC.

<**lheq'tíwél**>, ds //ɬəq'ɛt=íwə́l//, ANA /*'(have a) wide rump, (wide in the rectum)'*/, BPI, lx <**=íwel**> *in the insides, in the rump, in the rectum*, phonology: vowel-loss, updrifting, syntactic analysis: adjective/adjectival verb, attested by Elders Group.

<**lhelhq'etíwel**>, ds //C_1ə=ɬq'ɛt=íwəl or ɬə[=C_1ə=]q'ɛt=íwəl//, EZ [*'common bedbug'*], [*'Cimex lectularius* (order *Hemiptera*, family *Cimicidae)*'], literally /'(little?) wide in the rump'/, (semological comment: named from the fact that they are very wide in the rump with a tiny head), possibly <**R5=** or **=R1=**> *diminutive or derivational*, phonology: reduplication, vowel-change due to stress-shift, strong-valenced suffix, syntactic analysis: nominal, attested by Elders Group, also <**shxwelítemelh méxts'el**>, //s=xʷəlítəm=əɬ mə́xʸc'əl//, literally /'white man style louse'/.

<**lheq'tò:ls**>, ds //ɬəq'(ɛ)t=à·ls//, ANA [*'(have a) wide forehead'*], BPI, lx <**=ò:ls**> *spherical object, fruit, rock,* apparently also *forehead*, phonology: vowel-loss due to strong-valenced suffix, syntactic analysis: adjective/adjectival verb, attested by Elders Group.

<**lhálhq'etxel**>, ds //C_1ə=ɬq'ɛ́[=M2=]t=xʸəl//, [ɬǽɬq'ətxʸɪl], WETH [*'have wide snowflakes'*],

literally /'little wide precipitation'/, ANA ['*have wide feet*'], BPI, literally /'little wide in the foot'/, (<**R5=**> *diminutive*), (<**metathesis type 2**> *derivational*), lx <**=xel**> *precipitation; in the foot, in the leg*, phonology: reduplication, metathesis, syntactic analysis: adjective/adjectival verb, attested by ME (tape 11/21/72), IHTTC, ASM ['have wide snowflakes'], example: <**lhálhq'etxel te syíyeq.**>, //ɬɛ́ɬq'ət=xʸəl tə s=yí[-C₁ə-]q//, /'*The falling snow has wide snowflakes.*'/, attested by IHTTC, ASM ['have wide feet'], Elder's comment: "less frequent meaning", <**lhálhq'etxel tu spá:th.**>, //ɬɛ́ɬq'ət=xʸəl tu s=pɛ́·θ//, /'*(He/She has) wide feet [sort of like a] bear.*'/, attested by IHTTC, usage: insult.

<**lheq'á:tses ~ lheq'átses ~ lhq'á(:)tses**>, ds //ɬəq'ɛ́·(t)=cəs ~ ɬəq'ɛ́(t)=cəs ~ ɬq'ɛ́(·)(t)=cəs//, NUM ['*five*'], literally /'(wide on the hand)'/, lx <**=tses**> *on the hand*, phonology: consonant merger perhaps, ambi-valent stem, syntactic analysis: num, adjective/adjectival verb, attested by AC, BJ (5/64), CT (9/5/73), NP (12/6/73), Elders Group, other sources: ES /ɬəq'ɛ́·cəs/, JH /ɬqécəs/; found in <**lheq'á:tsestset. ~ í:tset lheq'á(:)tses.**>, //ɬəq'ɛ́·cəs-c-ət ~ ʔí·-c-ət ɬəq'ɛ́(·)cəs//, /'*(There's) five of us.*'/, attested by AC, example: <**ó:pel qas té lhq'à:tses**>, //ʔá·pəl qɛ-s tə ɬq'ɛ́·cəs//, /'*fifteen*'/, phonology: sentence-intonation gives optional higher tone to article and downstepping to the first high tone following, attested by CT, also <**ó:pel qas kw'e lheq'átses**>, //ʔá·pl qɛ-s k'ʷə ɬəq'ɛ́cəs//, attested by AC, <**ts'kw'éx qas té lhq'á:tses**>, //c'=k'ʷə́xʸ qɛ-s tə ɬq'ɛ́·cəs//, /'*twenty-five*'/, attested by CT (9/5/73), <**í:lhtset lheq'á(:)tses.**>, //ʔí·-ɬ-c-ət ɬəq'ɛ́(·)cəs//, /'*There were five of us., We were five in number.*'/, attested by AC, <**x̱élts't te pípe lám te lhq'á:tses**>, //x̣=əlc'=T tə pípə lɛ́=m tə ɬq'ɛ́·cəs//, /'*turn to page five, turn the page to page five*'/, literally /'turn it the paper go(ing) to the five'/, attested by Elders Group, <**ópel qas te lhq'átses qa('a) téxwswàyèl.**>, //ʔápəl qɛ-s tə ɬq'ɛ́cəs qɛ(ʔɛ) tə́xʷ=s=wɛ̀yə̀l//, /'*(It's) fifteen minutes to (until) noon.*'/, attested by Elders at Fish Camp (7/19/78), <**lhq'átses sméyeth**>, //ɬq'ɛ́cəs s=mɛ́yəθ//, /'*five animals*'/, attested by CT, HT, <**lhq'átses sléxwelh**>, //ɬq'ɛ́cəs s=lə́xʷəɬ//, /'*five canoes (counting them, belonging to various people)*'/, (semological comment: numeral classifier suffix is not used here when objects counted are separately owned, no classifier, distributive), attested by Elders Group (3/19/75) (compare <**lhq'atsesőwelh ~ lhq'atseséwelh**, //ɬq'ɛcəs=ówəɬ ~ ɬq'ɛcəs=ə́wəɬ//, /'*five canoes belonging to one person*'/), (semological comment: numeral classifier suffix is used here when objects counted are owned by one person, collective), attested by Elders Group (3/19/75).

<**lhq'átsále**>, ds //ɬq'ɛ́c(s)=ɛ́lə//, NUM ['*five people*'], SOCT, nca <**=ále**> *person, people*, phonology: consonant merger, syntactic analysis: num, attested by Elders Group.

<**lhq'atses'álh**>, ds //ɬq'ɛcəs=(ʔ)ɛ́ɬ//, NUM ['*five times*'], TIME, nca <**=álh ~ ='álh**> *times, occasions*, phonology: glottal-stop insertion, syntactic analysis: num, attested by Elders Group, also <**lheq'etslálh?**>, //ɬəq'əc=lɛ́ɬ?//, Elder's comment: "unsure", attested by AC.

<**lhq'atsesálhp**>, ds //ɬq'ɛcəs=ɛ́ɬp//, NUM ['*five trees*'], EB, nca <**=álhp**> *tree, trees, bush, plant*, syntactic analysis: num, attested by Elders Group.

<**lhq'átssámets'**>, ds //ɬq'ɛ́cs=ɛməc'//, NUM /'*five ropes, five threads, five sticks, five poles*'/, MC, EB, nca <**=ámets' ~ =ameth'**> *long slender object, as pole, stick, rope, thread*, syntactic analysis: num, attested by AD, Boas Scowlitz fields notes in APS library.

<**lhq'atsesáwtxw**>, ds //ɬq'ɛcəs=ɛ́wtxw//, NUM ['*five houses belonging to one person*'], BLDG, nca <**=áwtxw**> *house(s), building(s)*, syntactic analysis: num, attested by Elders Group.

<**lhéq'etselsxà**>, ds //ɬə[=´=]q'ɛc=əlsʸɛ̀//, NUM ['*fifty*'], nca <**=elsxá ~ =elsxà ~ =elhsxá**, phonology: stress-shift, vowel-reduction, consonant merger, syntactic analysis: num, attested by AC, also <**lheq'tselsxá**>, //ɬəq'c=əlsxʸɛ́//, phonology: vowel-loss, consonant merger, attested by BJ (12/5/64)(old p.336), example: <**lheq'atselsxá qas kw'e lhíxw**>, //ɬəq'ɛc=əlsxʸɛ́ qɛ-s

k'ʷə ɬíxʷ//, /'*fifty-three*'/, attested by AC.

<**lheq'etselsxále**>, ds //ɬəq'əc=əlsxʸɛ́=ɛlə//, NUM ['*fifty people*'], SOCT, nca <**=ále**> *people*, phonology: vowel-reduction, consonant merger, vowel merger, syntactic analysis: num, Elder's comment: "may be somewhat artificial since qéx̱ *many, lots of* would normally have been used instead of counting this high", attested by Elders Group.

<**lhèq'etselsxó:s ~ lhéq'etselsxó:s**>, ds //ɬə̀q'əc=əlsxʸɛ́=á·s ~ ɬə́q'əc=əlsxʸɛ́=á·s//, NUM ['*fifty dollars*'], TIME ['*(fifty cyclic periods [DM])*'], SOC, nca <**=ó:s**> *dollars, round things, cyclic periods, in the face*, phonology: stress-shift, vowel-reduction, consonant merger, vowel merger, downstepping, syntactic analysis: num, attested by AC, also /'*fifty (cyclic periods)*'/, attested by DM (12/4/64), example: <**lheq'etselsxó:s s=wà:yel**>, //ɬəq'əc=əlsxʸɛ=á·s swɛ̀·yəl//, /'*fifty days*'/, TIME, attested by DM (12/4/64).

<**lhq'atsesélwet**>, ds //ɬq'ɛcəs=ə́lwət//, NUM ['*five garments*'], CLO, nca <**=élwet**> *garments, clothes*, phonology: stress-shift, syntactic analysis: num, attested by Elders Group.

<**lhq'átseqel**>, ds //ɬq'ɛ́c=əqəl//, NUM ['*five containers*'], HHG, MC, nca <**=eqel**> *container(s)*, phonology: consonant merger, ambi-valent stem plus weak-valence suffix, syntactic analysis: num, attested by AD, CT, HT, example: <**lhq'átseqel shxwélwels**>, //ɬq'ɛ́c=əqəl s=xʷə́lwəls//, /'*five containers*'/, (semological comment: the nominal may mean more than just *container* since classified numerals are not followed by semantically redundant nominals), <**lhq'átseqel sí:tel**>, //ɬq'ɛ́c=əqəl sí·=təl//, /'*five baskets*'/, attested by CT, HT.

<**lhq'ó:tses**>, ds //ɬq'ɛ[=Aá=]·c=əs//, NUM ['*five dollars*'], SOC, ECON, PE, nca <**=es ~ =ó:s**> *dollar(s), round thing, cyclic period, on the face,* (and apparently also) *Indian blanket(s) (as a measure of wealth or payment which function was partly taken over by dollars),* (<**ó-ablaut triggered by =es suffix**>), phonology: ablaut, vowel-loss, consonant merger, syntactic analysis: num, attested by AC, other sources: Boas Scowlitz field notes in APS library <tlk·a'tcses> (macron over a, double underline under e) *five Indian blankets, five dollars.*

<**lhq'atseséyiws**>, ds //ɬq'ɛcəs=ɛ́y=iws//, NUM ['*five (pairs of) pants*'], CLO, nca <**=áy=iws ~ =éy=iws**> *pants*, nca <**from =áy ~ =éy**> *bark, wool, covering*, nca <**+ =íws ~ =ews**> *on the body*, phonology: stress-shift, ambi-valent stem, strong-valenced suffix, syntactic analysis: num, attested by Elders Group, AD.

<**lhq'atsesíqw**>, ds //ɬq'ɛcəs=íqʷ//, NUM ['*five fish*'], FSH, nca <**=íqw**> *fish (usually dead)*, phonology: stress-shift, ambi-valent stem, strong-valenced suffix, syntactic analysis: num, attested by BHTTC.

<**lhq'atssí:ws**>, ds //ɬq'ɛcs=í·ws//, NUM ['*five birds*'], HUNT, EZ, nca <**=í:ws**> *bird(s) (usu. already caught), on the body, on the skin*, phonology: stress-shift, strong-valenced suffix, syntactic analysis: num, attested by Elders Group, also <**lhq'atsí:ws**>, //ɬq'ɛc=í·ws//, phonology: consonant merger, vowel-loss, attested by EB, example: <**lhq'atsí:ws te mó:qwe xwe'í:lxwes.**>, //ɬq'ɛc=í·ws tə má·qʷ-ə xʷə=ʔí·=l-əxʷ-əs//, /'*He brought five mallards.*'/, literally /'it's five (caught) birds the mallard/duck he brings them'/, Elder's comment: "unsure", attested by EB.

<**lhq'átsesmó:t**>, ds //ɬq'ɛ́cəs=má·t//, NUM /'*five kinds, five piles* (perhaps a loose translation)'/, DESC, nca <**=mó:t**> *kinds,* (perhaps also) *piles*, phonology: ambi-valent stem can retain stress even before strong valenced suffix, syntactic analysis: num, attested by IHTTC, Elders Group.

<**lhq'atses'ó:llh**>, ds //ɬq'ɛcəs=ʔá·lɬ//, NUM /'*five little ones, five young (animal or human)*'/, nca <**='ó:llh ~ =ó:llh**> *young, offspring*, phonology: ambi-valent stem losing stress beore strong-valenced suffix, syntactic analysis: num, attested by Elders Group, also <**lhq'átsesó:llh**>, //ɬq'ɛ́cəs=á·lɬ//, also /'*five young in a litter*'/, EZ, phonology: ambi-valent stem retaining stress

even before strong valenced suffix, attested by AD.

<**lhq'atsesóls**>, ds //ɬq'ɛcəs=áls//, NUM /'*five spherical objects, five fruit, five rocks, five balls (five fruit in a group (as they grow on a plant) [AD])*'/, nca <**=òls ~ =óls**> *spherical objects, fruit, rocks, balls, etc.*, phonology: stress-shift before strong-valenced suffix, syntactic analysis: num, attested by Elders Group, also <**lhq'atsesòls**>, //ɬq'ɛcəs=àls//, also /'*five fruit in a group (as they grow on a plant)*'/, phonology: stress-shift before strong valenced suffix, attested by AD.

<**lhq'atsesō̃welh ~ lhq'atseséwelh**>, ds //ɬq'ɛcəs=ó̃wəɬ ~ ɬq'ɛcəs=ə́wəɬ//, NUM /'*five canoes belonging to one person, five boats*'/, nca <**=ōwelh ~ =éwelh ~ =ewelh**> *canoe, boat, vessel, canoe-shaped object*, phonology: stress-shift before ambi-valent suffix, syntactic analysis: num, attested by Elders Group, AD.

<**lhq'átsesō̃wes**>, ds //ɬq'ɛ́cəs=ó̃wəs//, NUM /'*five paddles, (by extension) five paddlers*'/, nca <**=ō̃wes**> *paddles, (by extension) paddlers*, phonology: ambi-valent stem retaining stress even before strong-valenced suffix, syntactic analysis: num, attested by Elders Group.

<**Slhq'átses**>, ds //s=ɬq'ɛ́cəs=s//, TIME /'*Friday; five o'clock*'/, NUM, nca <**s=...=s (circumfix)**> *day, hour, cyclic-period*, phonology: circumfix, syntactic analysis: nominal, num, attested by Elders Group, IHTTC, AC, ASM ['Friday'], <**Slhq'átses.**>, //s=ɬq'ɛ́cəs=s//, /'*Friday.*'/, semantic environment ['given in answer to the question, stám swàyèl tlówàyèl? *What day is today?*'], usage: , attested by IHTTC, example: <**wetéses te slheq'á:tses**>, //wə-tə́s-əs tə s=ɬəq'ɛ́·cəs//, /'*when it gets to five o'clock*'/, attested by AC.

<**lheq'á:tses ~ lheq'átses ~ lhq'á(:)tses**>, NUM ['*five*'], *see* lheq'á *wide*.

<**lhéq'e**>, TIME ['*is it sometimes?*'], *see* lhéq'.

<**lheq'él:exw ~ lhq'él:exw ~ lhq'élexw**>, EFAM /'*know s-th, know s-o*'/, *see* q'á:l.

<**lheq'elómet**>, EFAM /'*know oneself, be confident*'/, *see* q'á:l.

<**lhéq'elh**>, TIME ['*used to*'], *see* lhéq'.

<**lhéq'es**>, TIME ['*whenever*'], *see* lhéq'.

<**lhéq'etselsxà**>, NUM ['*fifty*'], *see* lheq'át ~ lhq'á:t.

<**lheq'etselsxále**>, NUM ['*fifty people*'], *see* lheq'át ~ lhq'á:t.

<**lhèq'etselsxó:s ~ lhéq'etselsxó:s**>, NUM ['*fifty dollars*'], *see* lheq'át ~ lhq'á:t.

<**lheq'ewílh**>, df //ɬəq'=əwíɬ//, DIR ['*opposite side of house on inside*'], BLDG, lx <**=ewílh**> perhaps ~ <**=ó:lwelh ~ =í(:)lwelh**> *on the side*, possibly root <**lhéq'**> *across(?)*, syntactic analysis: adverb/adverbial verb, attested by Elders Group.

<**lheq'láts**>, ANAH /'*hip, hips*'/, *see* lheq'át ~ lhq'á:t.

<**lheq'ó:les**>, df //ɬəq'=á·ləs//, ABFC ['*(have) one eye closed*'], possibly root <**lhéq'**> *across(?), opposite(?)*, lx <**=ó:les**> *in the eye, on the eye*, syntactic analysis: intransitive verb, attested by Elders Group.

<**lhéq'qel**>, df //ɬə́q'=qəl//, LAND /'*end of a falling section of land, end of a level stretch of land, (head of a creek or island [Elders Group])*'/, Elder's comment: "doesn't mean *way upriver*", possibly root <**lhéq'**> *across(?)*, possibly <**=qel**> *cliff, drop in land; in the throat*, syntactic analysis: adverb/adverbial verb?, nominal?, attested by AD (12/17/79), Salish cognate: poss. Squamish /ɬə́q/ *get to the other side (of a body of water)* K69:70, also <**slhéq'qel**>, //s=ɬə́q'=qəl//, also /'*way upriver*'/, attested by Elders Group (2/5/75), also <**lheqel ~ lhequl**>, //ɬəqəl or ɬə́q=əl or most likely

ɬə́q'=qəl//, also /'*head of a creek or island*'/, possibly <**=el**> *get, become, go, come*, phonology: transcription by FM, attested by Elders Group.

<**lheq'tíwél**>, ANA /'*(have a) wide rump, (wide in the rectum)*'/, *see* lheq'át ~ lhq'á:t.

<**lheq'tò:ls**>, ANA ['*(have a) wide forehead*'], *see* lheq'át ~ lhq'á:t.

<**lhéqw**>, free root //ɬə́q^{w}//, DESC /'*wet, be wet*'/, WATR, syntactic analysis: adjective/adjectival verb, attested by AC, BHTTC, EB, other sources: ES, JH /ɬə́q^{w}/ *wet*, example: <**lhéqw te swáyel.**>, //ɬə́q^{w} tə s=wɛ́yəl//, /'*It's a wet day.*'/, attested by AC, <**we'ólwe lhéqw**>, //wə=ʔál=wə ɬə́q^{w}//, /'*(It's) too wet., (It's) soaked.*'/, attested by EB.

<**lhóqwet**>, pcs //ɬə[=Aá=]q^{w}=əT//, WATR ['*wet s-th*'], (<**ó-ablaut**> *derivational*), (<**=et**> *purposeful control transitivizer*), phonology: ablaut, syntactic analysis: transitive verb, attested by EB.

<**lhóleqwet**>, plv //ɬə[=Aá=][-lə-]q^{w}=əT//, WATR ['*wetting many things*'], (<**-le-**> *plural*), phonology: ablaut, syntactic analysis: transitive verb, attested by EB.

<**lhélqwelhem**>, mdls //ɬə́l=əq^{w}=əɬ=əm or better ɬə[=lə=]q^{w}=əɬ=əm//, WATR /'*wet one's head (sic?), (wet one's bed repeatedly)*'/, if the meaning is *wet one's head* lx <**=eqw**> *on top of the head, on the hair* or if the meaning is *wet one's bed* the root is <**lhéqw**> *wet* as here, lx <**=elh**> *young, offspring; bed*, (<**=em**> *middle voice*), syntactic analysis: intransitive verb, attested by Elders Group (5/26/76).

<**lhéqw'**>, free root //ɬə́q'^{w} or ɬa[=Aə́=]q'^{w}//, BLDG /'*it peeled off, comes off*'/, semantic environment ['board off house, shingle in storm, bark, dandruff'], EZ, HARV, ABDF, possibly <**é-ablaut**> *resultative*, phonology: possible ablaut, syntactic analysis: intransitive verb, attested by EB, Elders Group (TM, others), Deming.

<**lheqw'ó:t**>, pcs //ɬá·q'^{w}=ə[=M2=]T or ɬəq'^{w}=ə[=Aá·=]T//, rsls, HARV /'*peel it (bark off a tree), bark it, (de-bark it), pull itdown (of bark, board, etc.), pull it up (of bark, board)*'/, probably <**ó:-ablaut**> *durative*, possibly <**metathesis**> *derivational*, (<**=et**> *purposeful control transitivizer*), phonology: ablaut, possible metathesis, syntactic analysis: transitive verb, attested by AD, NP, IHTTC.

<**lheqw'á:ls**>, sas //ɬəq'^{w}=ɛ́·ls or ɬaq'^{w}=ɛ́·ls//, HARV ['*peel bark (as structured activity)*'], (<**=á:ls**> *structured activity non-continuative*), phonology: possible vowel-reduction, syntactic analysis: intransitive verb, attested by AD, NP, example: <**atselcha lheqw'á:ls.**>, //ʔɛ-c-əl-cɛ ɬəq'^{w}=ɛ́·ls//, /'*I'm going to peel bark.*'/, syntactic analysis: ambiguous past, attested by AD, NP.

<**lhólheqw'els**>, cts //ɬá[-C$_1$ə-]q'^{w}=əls or C$_1$á-ɬəq'^{w}=əls//, HARV ['*peeling bark*'], probably <**-R1-**> *continuative*, possibly <**R10-**> *continuative*, (<**=els**> *structured activity continuative*), phonology: reduplication, syntactic analysis: intransitive verb, attested by IHTTC.

<**s'ó:lhqw'**>, strs //s=ɬá·[=M1=]q'^{w} or s=(ʔ)-ɬə[=Aá·=][=M1=]q'^{w}//, DESC ['*be ragged*'], probably <**metathesis type 1**> *resultative or derivational*, possibly <**ó:-ablaut**> *resultative*, phonology: ablaut, metathesis, epenthetic glottal-stop insertion, syntactic analysis: adjective/adjectival verb, attested by BHTTC.

<**lhqw'áy**>, dnom //ɬq'^{w}=ɛ́y//, CLO ['*cedar bark skirt*'], literally /'peeled bark =covering'/, lx <**=áy ~ =á:y ~ =ey**> *covering, bark, wool*, phonology: zero grade of root due to strong grade of suffix, syntactic analysis: nominal, attested by Elders Group (4/2/75).

<**slhqw'á:y**>, dnom //s=ɬq'^{w}=ɛ́·y//, HHG ['*cedar bark mat*'], literally /'peeled bark =bark/covering thing(=)'/, (<**s=**> *nominalizer*), lx <**=á:y ~ =áy ~ =ey**> *bark, covering, wool*, phonology: zero grade of root with strong grade of suffix, syntactic analysis: nominal, attested by Elders Group

(4/7/76).

<**lheqw'lhéqw'eqw**>, df //C_1əC_2=ɬə́q'^{w}=əq^w or ɬəq^w=C_1əC_2=´=əq^w//, ABDF ['*(have) dandruff*'], literally /'many peeled off in the hair (or) peel off over and over in the hair'/, probably <**R3=**> or <**=R2**> *plural or iterative* or <**=R2**> *characteristic* or <**=´= (stress-shift)**> *derivational*, lx <**=eqw**> *on top of the head, in the hair*, phonology: reduplication, perhaps stress-shift, syntactic analysis: intransitive verb, MED ['medicine for dandruff is a shampoo made from sth'élhp *mock orange* or from pipehomálews *plantain*; sth'élhp leaves foam up when rubbed in the hands briskly with water; willow root shampoo makes hair grow long [like the willow tree]'], attested by Elders Group (9/14/77).

<**lhoqw'esá:ls**>, sas //ɬə[=Aa=]q'^{w}=əs=ɛ́·ls or ɬəq'^{w}=a[=M2=]s=ɛ́·ls//, HARV ['*peel a tree*'], literally /'peel bark around as a structured activity (non-continuative, resultative)'/, ASM ['cedar bark is pulled off vertically by making incisions and pulling up and away, but most other peelable barks are peeled horizontally around the tree (for ex. bitter cherry bark)'], possibly <**ó:-ablaut**> or **metathesis type 2** *resultative*, lx <**=es**> *on the face, round/around*, (<**=á:ls**> *structured activity non-continuative*), syntactic analysis: intransitive verb, attested by IHTTC.

<**lhqw'íwst**>, pcs //ɬq'^{w}=íws=T//, HARV ['*peel it off (bark of a tree)*'], CLO ['*peel it off (clothes)*'], lx <**=íws ~ =ő́ws ~ =ews**> *on the skin, on the body*, (<**=t**> *purposeful control transitivizer*), phonology: zero grade of root with strong grade of suffix, syntactic analysis: transitive verb, attested by AD, NP.

<**lhéqw'ewsà:ls**>, sas //ɬa[=Aə́=]q'^{w}=əws=ɛ́·ls//, HARV ['*bark-peeler*'], ASM ['a stick curved at the end and sharpened'], (<**é-ablaut**> *derivational*), lx <**=ews**> *on the skin*, (<**=á:ls**> *structured activity non-continuative device*), phonology: stress-shift, syntactic analysis: nominal, attested by Elders Group.

<**lheqw'á:ls**>, HARV ['*peel bark (as structured activity)*'], *see* lhéqw'.

<**lhéqw'ewsà:ls**>, HARV ['*bark-peeler*'], *see* lhéqw'.

<**lheqw'lhéqw'eqw**>, ABDF ['*(have) dandruff*'], *see* lhéqw'.

<**lheqw'ó:t**>, HARV /'*peel it (bark off a tree), bark it, (de-bark it), pull itdown (of bark, board, etc.), pull it up (of bark, board)*'/, *see* lhéqw'.

<**lhéqw'tsesem**>, ABFC /'*clap one's hands, clap once with hands*'/, *see* lhóqw'et.

<**lhét**>, bound root, meaning unclear

<**lhétx̲tem**>, pcs //ɬə́t=x̣=T-əm or ɬə́t=x̣=təm//, ABDF ['*tremble*'], <**=x̲**> *distributive*, (=t *purposeful control transitivizer*, <**=em**> *passive* or <-tem> *stative*), probable syntactic analysis: transitive verb, passive, attested by EB, Salish cognate: Squamish /ɬə́tx̣m/ *tremble (from cold, fear)* K67:328, Musqueam /ɬə́tx̣t/ *shake it back and forth* Suttles ca1984:ch.7 [p.90].

<**lhátx̲tem**>, cts //ɬə[=Aɛ́=]t=x̣=T-əm//, ABDF /'*be trembling, shiver*'/, (<**á-ablaut**> *continuative* or perhaps *resultative*), phonology: ablaut, syntactic analysis: transitive verb, passive, attested by EB, Salish cognate: Musqueam /ɬɛ́tx̣t/ *be shaking it back and forth* Suttles ca1984: ch.7 [p.90], example: <**lhátx̲tem tel sx̲éle.**>, //ɬə[=Aɛ́=]t=x̣=T-əm tə-l s=x̣ə́lə//, /'*My leg is trembling.*'/, attested by EB; found in <**lhátx̲thá:lem.**>, //ɬə[=Aɛ́=]t=x̣=T-ɛ́·l(-)əm//, /'*I'm shivering.*'/, attested by EB, Elders Group with Deming Elders (trip to Mt. Baker).

<**lhétemet**>, df //ɬə́təmət//, possibly /'*stretched?? (said after giving another word meaning stretched)*'/, attested by CT, HT (6/21/76).

<**lhetqwá:ls**>, WATR ['*to boil*'], *see* lhot.

<**lhets'á:m**>, df //ɬəc'ɛ́·m//, EZ /'*weasel, one or both of the following which are in the area: short-tailed weasel and long-tailed weasel*'/, ['*Mustela erminea (fallenda and invicta) and Mustela frenata (altifrontalis and nevadensis)*'], ASM ['has a black tip on his tail because he got it burnt along with Marten and maybe Squirrel in a story (Elders Group 3/21/79)'], syntactic analysis: nominal, attested by Elders Group (3/1/72), other sources: ES /səɬc'ɛ́m/ and JH /sɬc'é·m ~ ɬc'é·m/ (JH66:5,8,24) *weasel*, H-T <cletsám> *weasel (Putorius erminea)*, also <**lhts'à:m**>, //ɬc'ɛ̀·m//, attested by Elders Group (2/11/76), also <**lhts'ám ~ slhets'ám**>, //ɬc'ɛ́m ~ s=ɬəc'ɛ́m//, (<**s=**> *nominalizer*), attested by ME (tape 11/21/72), also <**slhets'à:m**>, //s=ɬəc'ɛ̀·m//, (<**s=**> *nominalizer*), attested by AD (11/21/72 taped interview), also <**slhelhts'à:m**>, //s=ɬə[=C_1ə=]c'ɛ̀·m or s=C_1ə=ɬc'ɛ̀·m//, (<**s=**> *nominalizer*), possibly <**R5=** or **=R1=**> perhaps *diminutive*, attested by AK (11/21/72 taped interview).

<**lhéts'ches**>, ABDF /'*cut on one's hand, (cut one's finger [EB)*'/, *see* lhíts' ~ lhí:ts'.

<**lhets'elá:x̱el**>, ABDF ['*cut one's arm*'], *see* lhíts' ~ lhí:ts'.

<**lhéts'emel**>, MC /'*trimmings (of material), sawdust, shavings*'/, *see* lhíts' ~ lhí:ts'.

<**lhets'íméls te pítxel**>, EZ /'*centipede,* and poss. *millipede*'/, *see* lhts'íméls.

<**lhéts'xel**>, ABDF ['*cut one's foot*'], *see* lhíts' ~ lhí:ts'.

<**lhew**>, possible root, meaning unclear

<**slhewó:stel**>, df //s=ɬəw=á·s=təl//, CLO ['*mask*'], REL, literally /'nominal cure by shaman on the face device to '/ or /'nominal be inside s-th hollow on the face device to'/, (<**s=**> *nominalizer*), possibly root <**lhá:w ~ lháw ~ lhew**> *run away; cure by Indian doctoring* or root <**lew**> *be inside something hollow*, lx <**=ó:s**> *on the face*, lx <**=tel**> *device to*, syntactic analysis: nominal, attested by TG, also <**slhewómét** or **slewómét ~ sleqwómét**>, //s=ɬəw=ámət or s=ləw=ámət ~ sləqʷámə́t//, also /'*mask (any kind for dancing)*'/, attested by BJ (12/5/64, old pp.321 and 326).

<**Lhewálmel**>, PLN /'*an old course of the Chilliwack River, now Vedder River*'/, *see* lhá:w.

<**Lhewálh**>, df //ɬəw(=)ɛ́ɬ or ɬɛ́w=ə[=M2=]ɬ//, PLN ['*creek near Green Point on east side of Harrison Lake*'], ASM ['south of Sasquatch Park, there used to be a hatchery on the creek'], possibly root <**lháw**> *cure (of a shaman), heal (by Indian doctoring); run away*, possibly <**=elh**> *past tense*, phonology: possible metathesis, syntactic analysis: nominal, attested by EL (6/27/78 Boat trip).

<**lhewqí:m**>, df //ɬəw(=)q=í·m//, EB /'*short gray bog blueberries with berries in bunches,* probably *the Canada blueberry* also known as *velvet-leaf blueberry, this term is for both the fruit and the plant*'/, ['probably *Vaccinium myrtilloides*'], ASM ['the berries are said to be smaller than those of mó:lsem, the tall bog blueberry (Vaccinium uliginosum); the marsh on the northeast side of the Deas Is. tunnel used to have these blueberries as well as the tall variety (mó:lsem) and wild cranberries (qwemchó:ls); both blueberries were ripe in about Sept. (when the commercial ones come in); the cranberries grow under the blueberries and were ready and biggest just before Christmas though they could be picked any time after the first frost; the blueberries were blue with whitish dust, on average about 32 in. tall (short variety, lhewqí:m) and about 45 in. tall for the tall variety (mó:lsem), both sweet but sort of tart (more than the commercial varieties) and smaller than the store varieties (CC, MLS); blueberry combs were sometimes used for both varieties and Joe Lorenzetto made one one time (JL 8/8/79)'], root meaning unknown but possibly root <**lháw**> *cure (of a shaman), heal (by Indian doctoring); run away* if the plant was used for medicine, possibly <**=q**> *(closable container)*, possibly <**=í:m**> *repeatedly*, syntactic analysis: nominal, attested by Elders Group and Deming Elders (9/3/75 trip to Mt. Baker), Elders Group (4/23/80), AC, Clara Campbell and Mary Lou Sepass (5/7/79), other sources: ES /ɬəwqí·m/ *blueberry*, Salish cognate: Squamish /ɬəwqímʔ/ *small swamp blueberry* W73:40, K69:71, *Canada blueberry (V. myrtilloides)* Bouchard and Turner 1976 ms., and Thompson /ɬuʔqím'/ *velvet-*

leaf blueberry (V. myrtilloides) Turner and Thompson 1973 ms..

<**Lhewqí:m Tl'chás**>, cpds //ɬəwqí·m ƛ'cɛ́s//, PLN ['*Lulu Island*'], literally /'small marsh blueberry island'/, syntactic analysis: simple nominal phrase, attested by Elders Group (4/23/80).

<**lhelhewqí:m**>, dmpn //C_1ə=ɬəw(=)q=í·m//, EB /'*smallest gray swamp blueberries, smallest variety of Canada blueberry*'/, ['*Vaccinium myrtilloides*'], (<**R5=** (or **R4=Aə=)**> *diminutive plural*), phonology: reduplication, possibly ablaut, syntactic analysis: nominal, attested by Elders Group and Deming Elders (trip to Mt. Baker, 9/3/75).

<**Lhewqí:m Tl'chás**>, PLN ['*Lulu Island*'], *see* lhewqí:m.

<**lhexwáyiws**>, NUM ['*three pants*'], *see* lhí:xw.

<**lhèxwelsxá**>, NUM ['*thirty*'], *see* lhí:xw.

<**lhexwelsxáleqel**>, NUM ['*thirty containers*'], *see* lhí:xw.

<**lhexwelsxó:s**>, NUM ['*thirty dollars*'], *see* lhí:xw.

<**lhexwelhsxó:s**>, NUM ['*thirty cyclic periods*'], *see* lhí:xw.

<**lhexwòls**>, NUM ['*three fruit in a cluster (as they grow on a plant)*'], *see* lhí:xw.

<**lhéx̱**>, bound root //ɬə́x̣ *stiff*//, Salish cognate: Lushootseed /ɬəx̣/ *spread out; stiff* H76:299.

<**slhelháx̱**>, strs //s=ɬə[=C_1əAɛ́=]x̣//, ABDF ['*be stiff (of arm or foot)*'], DESC, (<**s=**> *stative*), (<**=R1=**> *resultative* or *continuative* and á-ablaut *resultative*), phonology: reduplication, ablaut, syntactic analysis: adjective/adjectival verb, attested by CT.

<**lhx̱étem**>, df //ɬx̣=ə́T=əm or ɬə́x̣=M1=T=əm or ɬə́x̣=M1=təm//, ABDF ['*stiff (of body)*'], possibly <**=ét** or **=t**> *purposeful control transitivizer* and <**=em**> *middle voice or intransitivizer* or <**=tem**> *participial/stative*, possibly <**metathesis**> *derivational*, phonology: possible metathesis, syntactic analysis: intransitive verb, attested by CT.

<**slhéx̱tses**>, stvi //s=ɬə́x̣=cəs//, ABDF /'*(have a) paralyzed hand, game hand*'/, literally /'be stiff on the hand'/, (<**s=**> *stative*), lx <**=tses**> *on the hand*, syntactic analysis: intransitive verb, attested by an elder from Deming or from Elders Group (5/78).

<**slhéx̱xel**>, stvi //s=ɬə́x̣=x^{y}əl//, ABDF /'*(have a) paralyzed leg, game leg*'/, literally /'be stiff on the leg'/, (<**s=**> *stative*), lx <**=xel**> *on the leg, on the foot*, syntactic analysis: intransitive verb, attested by an elder from Deming or from Elders Group)(5/78).

<**lhex̱éyléx**>, incs //ɬəx̣=íl=əx^y//, [ɬəx̣élíx^y], ABFC ['*stand up*'], literally /'stiff =get/become =upright'/, (<**=íl**> *get, become, go, come, inceptive*), lx <**=ex** or **=éx**> *upright*, phonology: possible updrifting on final syllable, syntactic analysis: intransitive verb, attested by AC, Elders Group (3/1/72), IHTTC, other sources: ES /ɬx̣ɛ́yləx^y/, JH /ɬə́x̣i·ləx/ *stand* (beside JH /ɬəx̣í·lə̀x̣/ *standing*; found in <**lhx̱eyléxlha.**>, //ɬx̣=íl=ə́x^y-ɬɛ//, /'*Stand up.*'/, attested by IHTTC, AC, example: <**lhx̱eyléxlha stetís te skw'echóstel.**>, //ɬx̣=íl=ə́x^y-ɬɛ s=tə[=C_1əAí=]s tə s=k'^{w}əc=ás=təl//, /'*Stand near the window.*'/, attested by IHTTC; found in <**lhx̱eyléxalha.**>, //ɬx̣=íl=ə́x^y-ɛɬɛ//, /'*Everybody stand up., (Stand up you guys.)*'/, syntactic comment: command imperative, attested by IHTTC, example: <**lhx̱éyléxlha x̱wém.**>, //ɬx̣=íl-ə́x^y-ɬɛx̣^{w}ə́m//, /'*Stand up, hurry., (Stand up fast.)*'/, attested by EB.

<**lhex̱é:ylex**>, cts //ɬəx̣=í[-·-]l=əx^y//, ABFC ['*standing up*'], (<**-:-**> *continuative*), phonology: lengthening, syntactic analysis: intransitive verb, attested by AC, other sources: JH /ɬəx̣í·lə̀x̣/.

<**Lhx̱é:ylex**>, ds //ɬx̣=í[-·-]l=əx^y//, PLN ['*Doctor's Point on northwest shore Harrison Lake*'], ASM ['opposite an area on east side about halfway between Mt. Douglas and a mountain with huge slides down to the water; a rock formation is here that looks like a standing Indian doctor/shaman; the rock was a shaman turned to stone by the Transformer after they had duelled

with their powers; the stone shaman is still painted with red and white Indian paint; Indian travellers left if food offerings so the weather would be calm for their return home; if food was not left, bad storms and winds could arise suddenly; this point is called Státelex in the Douglas dialect of Lillooet, also meaning *standing up*, and the fact it has names in both languages and that there are a number of Halkomelem names south of it, may show that this is the border between Stó:lō and Lillooet territories on the lake'], literally /'standing up'/, syntactic analysis: nominal, attested by EL (6/18/75 on boat trip to Port Douglas with Elders Group), source: place names reference file #118.

<**lhx̱eylexlómet**>, ncrs //ɬx=íl=əxʸ=l-ámət//, ABFC ['*stand up (by oneself)*'], (<**=l**> *non-control transitivizer (happen to, manage to, accidentally)),* (<**-ómet**> *reflexive*), syntactic analysis: intransitive verb, attested by Elders Group.

<**lhex̱eyléxstexw**>, caus //ɬəx=íl=áxʸ=sT-əxʷ//, CSTR ['*raise it (of a pole)*'], literally /'cause it to stand, make it stand'/, (<**=st**> *causative control transitivizer*), (<**-exw**> *third person object*), syntactic analysis: transitive verb, attested by EB.

<**lhex̱elwélhtel**>, CAN /'*crosspieces in a canoe, (thwarts)*'/, *see* lhá:x̱ ~ lháx̱.

<**lhex̱éyléptel**>, HHG /'*floor, floor mat, floor covering, linoleum, rug*'/, *see* lhá:x̱ ~ lháx̱.

<**lhex̱éyléx**>, ABFC ['*stand up*'], *see* lhéx̱.

<**lhex̱é:ylex**>, ABFC ['*standing up*'], *see* lhéx̱.

<**lhex̱eyléxstexw**>, CSTR ['*raise it (of a pole)*'], *see* lhéx̱.

<**lhex̱ōwéstel**>, CAN ['*boards in a canoe bottom*'], *see* lhá:x̱ ~ lháx̱.

<**lhex̱w**>, bound root //ɬəx̣ʷ *spit out*//.

<**lhex̱wót ~ lhx̱wó:t**>, pcrs //ɬəx̣ʷ=ə[=Aá(·)=]T//, ABFC /'*spit it out, spit it up*'/, (<**=et**> *purposeful control transitivizer*), (<**á-ablaut**> *resultative*), phonology: ablaut or stressed transitivizer, vowel-loss in zero-grade of root, syntactic analysis: transitive verb, attested by AC, JL, NP, Deming, other sources: ES /ɬx̣ʷá·t/ *spit* (but JH /ɬə̀x̣ə́t/ *to spit* and /ɬə́x̣ə̀t/ *spitting*); found in <**lhx̱wó:tlha.**>, //ɬəx̣ʷ=ə[=Aá·=]T-ɬɛ//, /'*Spit it out.*'/, attested by AC.

<**lhx̱wélhcha**>, ds //ɬx̣ʷ=ə́ɬcɛ//, ABFC ['*to spit*'], lx <**=élhcha**> *unclear liquid*, syntactic analysis: intransitive verb, attested by AC, CT, example: <**le lhex̱wélhcha te siyólexwe.**>, //lə ɬəx̣ʷ=əɬcɛ tə si=yáləxʷə//, /'*The old man spat., The old man spits.*'/, syntactic analysis: ambiguous past, attested by AC.

<**lhéx̱welhcha**>, cts //ɬə[-´-]x̣ʷ=əɬcɛ//, ABFC ['*spitting*'], (<-´-> *continuative*), phonology: stress-shift, syntactic analysis: intransitive verb, attested by AC, example: <**wiyóth kw'es lhéx̱welhchas**>, //wə=yáθ k'ʷə-s ɬə́x̣ʷ=əɬcɛ-s//, /'*He's always spitting.*'/, attested by AC, <**wiyóth kw'es lhéx̱welhchas te siyólexwe.**>, //wə=yáθ k'ʷə-s ɬə́x̣ʷ=əɬcɛ-s tə si=yáləxʷə//, /'*The old man is always spitting.*'/, attested by AC.

<**slhx̱wélhcha**>, dnom //s=ɬx̣ʷ=ə́ɬcɛ//, ANA /'*spit, saliva*'/, (<**s=**> *nominalizer*), syntactic analysis: nominal, attested by AC, LJ (History tape 34, 4/7/78), example: <**we'ólwe qéx̱ te slhex̱wélhchas.**>, //wə=ʔál=wə qə́x̣ tə s=ɬx̣ʷ=ə́ɬcɛ-s//, /'*(He's got) too much spit., (He's got) an awful lot of spit.*'/, attested by AC, <**éwechap lamáp hélem tel slhx̱wélhcha.**>, //ʔə́wə-c-ɛp lɛ=m-ɛ́p hə́-lɛ=m tə-l s=ɬxʷ=ə́ɬcɛ//, /'*Don't you people go to my spit.*'/, usage: pun on place name, attested by LJ (History tape 34, 4/7/78).

<**lhex̱wlhéx̱w**>, dnom //$C_1əC_2$=ɬə́x̣ʷ//, EB ['*choke cherry*'], ['*Prunus virginiana*'], ASM ['grow in the Tait-speaking area and were and are eaten there, somewhat puckery due to the tannin when eaten raw but one gets used to it'], <**R3=**> *iterative* or *plural*, semological comment: lit. "spit out

repeatedly", phonology: reduplication, syntactic analysis: nominal, dialects: *Tait*, attested by Elders Group.

<**lhx̲wélqsel**>, ds //ɬx̣ʷ=ə́lqs=əl//, incs, ABDF ['*(get/have a) runny nose*'], literally /'get spit out on the nose'/, lx <**=él(=)qs**> *on the nose*, (<**=el**> *get, become, go, come, inceptive*), syntactic analysis: intransitive verb, attested by Deming.

<**slholh(e)x̲wélqsel**>, stvi //s=ɬo[=C₁ə=]x̣ʷ=ə́lqs=əl or s=C₁á=ɬxʷ=ə́lqs=əl//, ABDF ['*(have) snot hanging from the nose*'], (<**s=**> *stative*), possibly <**=R1=** or **R10=**> *continuative or resultative*, phonology: reduplication, syntactic analysis: adjective/adjectival verb, attested by Elders Group.

<**slholh(e)x̲wélqsel mó:qw**>, cpds //s=C₁á=ɬ(ə)x̣ʷ=ə́lqs=əl má·qʷ//, dnom, EZ ['*wild turkey*'], ['*Meleagris gallopavo*'], literally /'snot hanging from its nose bird'/ after its snood (red fleshy skin flap growing from the base of the beak and hanging over it), ACL ['*(may have been introduced in small numbers in the Stó:lō area or neighboring areas), was introduced into Washington state for ex.*'], phonology: reduplication, syntactic analysis: simple nominal phrase, attested by Elders Group (6/4/75).

<**lhéx̲welòw**>, ds //ɬə[=´=]x̣ʷ=əlàw//, ANA /'*ruptured belly button, ruptured navel*'/, literally /'spit out on the belly'/, lx <**=elòw ~ =álwes ~ =élwes**> *on the belly*, (<-´-> *derivational*), phonology: stress-shift, syntactic analysis: intransitive verb?, nominal??, attested by BHTTC.

<**lhéx̲welòw**>, ANA /'*ruptured belly button, ruptured navel*'/, *see* lhex̲w.

<**lhéx̲welhcha**>, ABFC ['*spitting*'], *see* lhex̲w.

<**lhex̲wlhéx̲w**>, EB ['*choke cherry*'], *see* lhex̲w.

<**lhex̲wót ~ lhx̲wó:t**>, ABFC /'*spit it out, spit it up*'/, *see* lhex̲w.

<**lhe'á**>, df //ɬ(=)əʔɛ́//, TVMO /'*go through (somewhere), go via (somewhere), go by way of*'/, DIR, possibly <**lh=**> *use, extract, extract a portion*, possibly <**=e'á**> *comparative*, possibly a root, phonology: possible compound of prefix and suffix (which can require dummy roots), syntactic analysis: preposition/prepositional verb, attested by EB, Elders Group, example: <**ley lhe'á**>, //lə=yə= ɬəʔɛ́//, /'*he went through or via someplace*'/, literally /'third person past =travelling by/going along go through/via'/, dialects: *Cheh.*, attested by EB, <**lí lhe'á kw'eló?**>, //lí ɬəʔɛ́ k'ʷə=lá//, /'*Did he go through there?*'/, attested by Elders Group, <**tsel yelhe'á kw'e Sq'éwlets.**>, //c-əl yə=ɬ(=)əʔɛ́ k'ʷə s=q'ə́w=ləc//, /'*I went through (via) Scowlitz.*'/, attested by Elders Group, <**(ley, lay) lhe'á kw'e Sq'éwlets.**>, //(lə=yə=, lɛ=yə=) ɬəʔɛ́ k'ʷə s=q'ə́w=ləc//, /'*He went via Scowlitz (it was out of his way).*'/, (semological comment: le *third person past* and la *go* are both possible here), attested by Elders Group, also <**(ley, lay) lhe'á kw'e Sq'ówlets.**>, //(lə=yə=, lɛ=yə=) ɬəʔɛ́ k'ʷə s=q'aw=ləc//, attested by NP, DF, Johnny Williams Sr. (all 1/31/79).

<**lhí**>, free root //ɬí//, TIME /'*when, (sometimes [EB])*'/, CJ, syntactic analysis: conjunction, syntactic comment: not attested without subjunctive subject person markers, attested by EB, Elders Group, LJ (Tait), also /'*sometimes*'/, attested by EB, <**lhíl, lhíxw, lhís, lhít, lhíp**>, //ɬí-l, ɬí-xʷ, ɬí-s, ɬí-t, ɬí-p//, /'*when I, when you (sg.), when he/she/it/they (~ sometimes he/she/it/they), when we, when you folks*'/, attested by EB, example: <**lhíl lám**>, //ɬí-l lɛ́=m//, /'*when I go*'/, attested by Elders Group, <**lhíl yó:ys**>, //ɬí-l yá·ys//, /'*when I worked*'/, attested by Elders Group, <**le qelámthet tel th'ále lhíl ólew le kw'á:y.**>, //lə qəl=ɛ́m=θət tə-l θ'ɛ́lə ɬí-l ʔál=əw lə k'ʷɛ́·y//, /'*My heart gets weak when I get too hungry.*'/, attested by LJ (Tait, 6/28/78), <**x̲élh tel s'íles lhíl kw'á:y.**>, //x̣ə́ɬ tə-l s=ʔíləs ɬí-l k'ʷɛ́·y//, /'*My chest hurts when I get hungry.*'/, attested by LJ (Tait), <**wálh me x̲élh kw'a' sqwálewel lhíxw me p'élh?**>, //(ʔə)wə-ə-əɬ mə x̣ə́ɬ k'ʷ-ɛʔ s=qʷɛ́l=əwəl ɬí-xʷ mə p'ə́ɬ//, /'*Do you ever feel sorry when you sober up?*'/, literally /'does not -yes/no question -past become/get hurt the (abstract) -your

feelings when -you become sober/aware'/, attested by Elders Group, **<lhéq' me sélts'tem tel sx̲óyes lhíl áx̲eth.>**, //ɬə́q' mə səl=lc'=təm tə-l s=x̣áyəs ɬí-l ʔɛ́x̣əθ//, /'*Sometimes my head spins when I lay down.*'/, attested by LJ (Tait), **<lhíl ulh lám t'ókw'>**, //ɬí-l ʔuɬ lɛ́=m t'ák'ʷ//, /'*It's time for me to go home., when I'm going home*'/, literally /'when I already go homeward'/, (semological comment: lhí in combination with welh ~ ulh (already) appears to form an idiom), attested by Elders Group, **<lulh lhís kw'es me p'óp'etl'em.>**, //lə=uɬ ɬí-s k'ʷə-s mə p'á[-C_1ə-]ƛ'=əm//, /'*It was smoking quite a while ago.*'/, literally /'it was already when -it that -nominalizer start/become/get smoking'/, (semological comment: lhí in combination with welh ~ ulh (already) again), attested by Elders Group, **<lhíxw áxwest kw'e mő̄kw'ewátes>**, //ɬí-xʷ ʔɛ́xʷ=əs=T k'ʷə mok'ʷ=əwɛ́t=əs//, /'*give everyone equal amounts or equal share*'/, literally /'when you share (equally) with s-o the (abstract) everyone'/, attested by Elders Group (3/72).

<lhíkw' ~ lhí:kw'>, free root //ɬík'ʷ ~ ɬí·k'ʷ//, FSH /'*to hook, to catch (by horns or thorns), get hooked*'/, HUNT, HARV, ABFC, (semological comment: the subject of this verb is a semantic patient, thus the translation *to gore* was rejected as its subject is an agent), syntactic analysis: intransitive verb, attested by AC.

<lhekw'á:ls>, sas //ɬək'ʷ=ɛ́·ls//, FSH /'*hook fish, catch fish (by hook), to gaff-hook fish*'/, (semological comment: the subject of this verb is a semantic agent), (**<=á:ls>** *structured activity non-continuative*), syntactic analysis: intransitive verb, attested by AC, also **<lhkw'àls>**, //ɬk'ʷ=ɛ̀ls//, attested by Elders Group (3/15/72), example: **<le lhkw'àls.>**, //lə ɬk'ʷ=ɛ̀ls//, /'*He's gone gaff-hooking.*'/, attested by Elders Group (3/15/72).

<lhákw'els>, cts //ɬək'ʷ=ɛ́[-M2-]ls or ɬə[-Aɛ́-]k'ʷ=əls//, FSH /'*gaff-hooking (all the time, catching a lot)*'/, possibly **<metathesis type 2** or **á-ablaut>** *continuative*, possibly if the latter, then **<=els>** *structured activity continuative*, phonology: metathesis or ablaut, syntactic analysis: intransitive verb, attested by Elders Group (3/15/72).

<lhílhekw'els>, df //ɬí[-C_1ə-]k'ʷ=əls or C_1í=ɬək'ʷ=əls//, FSH ['*gaffing*'], possibly **<-R1->** *continuative*, or **<R4=>** *diminutive*, phonology: reduplication, syntactic analysis: intransitive verb, attested by Elders Group (3/15/72).

<lhílhekw'els>, df //C_1í=ɬək'ʷ=əls or ɬí[=C_1ə=]k'ʷ=əls//, WV ['*a hook for crocheting*'], possibly **<R4=>** *diminutive* or possibly **<=R1=>** *continuative* and probably **<=els>** *device for doing structured activity*, phonology: reduplication, syntactic analysis: nominal, attested by Elders Group (3/15/72).

<lhíkw'et>, pcs //ɬík'ʷ=əT//, FSH ['*gaff it (a fish)*'], ABFC ['*hook s-th (by horns)*'], (**<=et>** *purposeful control transitivizer*), syntactic analysis: transitive verb, attested by Elders Group, EB, AC, ASM ['gaff it (a fish)'], example: **<lhíkw'et te sth'óqwi>**, //ɬík'ʷ=əT tə s=θ'áqʷi(y)//, /'*gaff a fish*'/, *<**tsel lhkw'á:ls te sth'óqwi.**> *I gaffed a fish.* rejected by EB, ASM ['hook s-o, hook s-th (by horns)']; found in **<lhíkw'ethòm>**, //ɬík'ʷ=əT-àm//, /'*you got hooked (by its horns), hook you (by horns)*'/, syntactic analysis: passive, attested by AC.

<lhílhekw'et>, cts //ɬí[-C_1ə-]k'ʷ=əT//, FSH /'*catching a fish by hook, hooking s-th, gaffing a fish*'/, (**<-R1->** *continuative*), phonology: reduplication, syntactic analysis: transitive verb, attested by Elders Group, AC.

<Lhílhkw'eleqs ~ Lhílhkw'elqs>, ds //ɬí[=C_1ə=]k'ʷ=əl(ə)qs//, PLN /'*Hook-nose, Hook-nose Mountain, Hamersly Hopyard Hill*'/, ASM ['a mountain or rock shaped like a hook nose several miles west of Agassiz, the "nose" is a bluff right on the Fraser River just downriver from the old Hamersly Hopyards site; the rock was and is now a good dip-net and set-net site used by some Stólō people; near it is an ancient archeological village site (used so long ago no one knew anyone who ever lived there); unclear whether the word is also a body-part insult'], literally /'hook-nose, gaffing point'/, (<**=R1=**> *continuative*), lx <**=eleqs**> *on the nose, on the point, point of land*, phonology: reduplication, syntactic analysis: nominal, attested by EB, AK (History tape 34, 4/7/78), AC (1973), Harry Edwards (10/8/64), Elders Group (7/13/77), Wells 1965:23, source: place names reference file #68, also <**Lhílhkw'elqs Smámelt**>, //ɬí[=C_1ə=]k'ʷ=əlqs s=mɛ́[=C_1ə=]lt//, attested by AK (4/7/78).

<**lhékw'qsel**>, incs //ɬə́k'ʷ=qs=əl//, ABDF /'*get tripped, to trip*'/, lx <**=qs**> *on the nose, on the point,* (<**=el**> *get, become, inceptive*), syntactic analysis: intransitive verb, attested by EB, Elders Group.

<**lhékw'tel**>, dnom //ɬə́k'ʷ=təl//, FSH ['*gaff-hook (a large pole-mounted hook)*'], ASM ['used for sturgeon example'], lx <**=tel**> *device to*, syntactic analysis: nominal, attested by EB, Elders Group (3/15/72, 3/26/75), Deming, AC, BJ (5/64), DM (12/4/64), also /'*fish hook (any size)*'/, (semological comment: but later only translated as gaff-hook), attested by EB, other sources: ES /ɬə́k'ʷtəl/ *gaff, (*also*) hook on the line.*

<**lhékw'xel**>, ds //ɬə́k'ʷ=xʸəl//, ABDF ['*to trip*'], literally /'get hooked on the foot or leg'/, lx <**=xel**> *on the foot, on the leg*, syntactic analysis: intransitive verb, attested by Deming, Elders Group, AC, example: <**xwómxelem qetl'osésu lhékw'xel qetl'osésu (tselq, wets'étl') qetl'osésu lekwxál.**>, //xʷə[=Aá=]m=xʸəl=əm qə=ƛ'a-s-əs-u ɬə́k'ʷ-xʸəl qə=ƛ'a-s-əs-u (cə́l=q, wə=c'ə́ƛ') qə=ƛ'a-s-əs-u lək'ʷ=xʸə[=Aɛ́=]l//, /'*He was running and he tripped and he (fell, suddenly fell) and he broke his leg.*'/, attested by AC.

<**lhékw'xet**>, pcs //ɬə́k'ʷ=xʸə(l)=T//, ABDF ['*to trip s-o*'], (<**=t**> *purposeful control transitivizer*), phonology: consonant-loss (l before =t), syntactic analysis: transitive verb, attested by Deming; found in <**lhékw'xetes.**>, //ɬə́k'ʷ=xʸə(l)=T-əs//, /'*He tripped somebody.*'/, attested by Deming (4/10/80).

<**lhíkw'et**>, FSH ['*gaff it (a fish)*'], *see* lhíkw' ~ lhí:kw'.

<**lhí:l**>, bound root //ɬí·l// (or perhaps //ɬəl//, WV ['*weave*']

<**lhí:lt**>, pcs //ɬí·l=T// or perhaps //ɬəl=í·l=T//, WV ['*weave it*'], ASM ['of a blanket on a loom, of bullrush mat (with special needles), of cedarbark mat, of the bottom (coil) of a basket'], (<**=t**> *purposeful control transitivizer*), syntactic analysis: transitive verb, attested by Elders Group (4/7/76, 3/5/80), Salish cognate: Squamish root /ɬan ~ ɬən(ʔ)/ *weave* and especially /ɬə́nʔ-t/ *weave (tr.)*, probably also the root for *woman*, W73:286, K67:328-329; the second derivation in Halkomelem would show the cognate vowel with the Squamish cognate and account for the new apparent vowel (root-final el automatically drops before =í:l *inceptive*); the second derivation in Halkomelem also keeps distinct this root (as lhél) from lhí:l *bail* and lhá:l *pull onshore/land a canoe*, example: <**lichxw lhí:lt ta' skwéléts?**>, //li-c-xʷ ɬí·l=T t-ɛʔ s=kʷə́lə́c//, /'*Did you weave the bottom of the basket (the coil)?*'/, literally /'did you weave it your bottom coil of basket'/, attested by Elders Group (3/5/80).

<**slhá:lí**>, dnom //s=ɬɛ́·lí or s=ɬil=ɛ́·[=M2=]y or s=ɬí[=Aɛ=]·l=əy//, HUMC /'*woman, female*'/, HAT /'*(post-adolescent) woman, woman (15 yrs. or older)*'/, literally perhaps /'someone that weaves wool/bark'/, EZ ['*female*'], EB ['*female*'], (<**s=**> *nominalizer, someone to, someone that*), probably root <**lhí:l**> *weave*, comment: Kuipers 1967 proposes the same root for the word in Squamish, probably <**metathesis**> *derivational*, probably <**=á:y ~ =ey ~ =iy**> *bark, wool*, syntactic analysis: nominal, attested by NP, BJ (5/64), also <**slhá:li ~ slháli**>, //s=ɬɛ́·li ~ s=ɬɛ́li//, attested by AC, other sources: ES /sɬɛ́·li/ *woman*, H-T <sláli> (macrons on both vowels) *woman*, Salish cognate: Squamish /s=ɬán=əyʔ/ *woman* < root /ɬan ~ ɬən(ʔ)/ *weave* W73:291, K67:290, ASM ['woman'], example: <**iyómex slháli**>, //ʔɛy=áməxʸ s=ɬɛ́li//, /'*(She's a) beautiful woman.*'/, attested by AC, <**ló:s the slháli.**>, //lá·s θə s=ɬɛ́li//, /'*The woman is fat.*'/, attested by AC, ASM ['female'], <**slhá:li (the, kw'tha) mél:es**>, //s=ɬɛ́·li (θə, k'ʷ=θə) mə́l·ə-s//, /'*(his, her, their) daughter, (his, her, their)*

girl'/, attested by AC, ASM ['(post-adolescent) woman, woman (15 yrs. or older)'], <**xwe slhá:lí**>, //x^wə s=lɛ́·lí//, /'*become a woman*'/, attested by NP.

<**slheli'ál**>, df //s=ɬɛli=ʔɛ́l//, EB ['*female part of female plant*'], (<**=ál**> *part, component*), phonology: vowel-shift to schwa due to stress-shift, syntactic analysis: nominal, attested by IHTTC.

<**slhellhá:li**>, pln //s=C_1əC_2-lhɛ́·li//, HUMC ['*(a lot of) women*'], EZ, HAT, (<**R3-**> *plural*), phonology: reduplication, syntactic analysis: nominal, attested by AC, other sources: H-T <silsáli> (macrons over final i and a) *women (collect.)*, also <**slhellhálí**>, //s=C_1əC_2-lhɛ́lí//, attested by Elders Group.

<**slhálhli**>, dmn //s=ɬɛ́[=C_1ə=]li//, HUMC /'*little woman, small woman*'/, EZ, (<**=R1=**> *diminutive*), phonology: consonant-loss?, vowel-loss of e in reduplication due to speed, syntactic analysis: nominal, attested by EB.

<**slhelhlíli**>, dmpn //s=ɬə[=C_1ə=]líy=C2əC3//, HUMC ['*little ladies*'], (<**=C2əC3 irregular reduplication**> *plural* of *diminutive*), phonology: irregular reduplication (=C2əC3), reduplication, stress-shift, vowel-shift, syntactic analysis: nominal, attested by AD.

<**slhálhlí**>, ds //s=ɬɛ́[=C_1ə=]lí//, EZ /'*ladybug, ladybird beetle*'/, ['*order Coleoptera, family Coccinellidae)*'], (<**=R1=**> *diminutive*), phonology: reduplication, syntactic analysis: nominal, attested by AD, also <**slhálhi**>, //s=ɬɛ́l[=D=]i//, phonology: devoicing, attested by Elders Group (9/8/76).

<**slheliyó:llh**>, ds //s=lhəli(y)=á·lɬ//, HAT /'*girl child, girl (from 5 to 10 years or so)*'/, lx <**=ó:llh**> *child, offspring, young*, phonology: vowel initial suffix either shows a root-final y or triggers an allomorph with root-final y (consonant-loss in the unaffixed root, or consonant-addition in the allomorph); vowel-shift to <e> (schwa, /ə/) due to stress-shift, weak-valenced root, strong-valenced suffix, syntactic analysis: nominal, attested by AC, EB, other sources: H-T <sEliátl> (macron on i, umlaut over a) *girl (little)*, and <sisEliátl> (macron on second i, umlaut over a) *little girls (collect.)*, also <**q'áq'emi**>, //q'ɛ́[-C_1ə-]mi//, attested by EB.

<**slhelhliyó:llh**>, dmn //s=ɬə[=C_1ə=]li(y)=á·lɬ//, HAT ['*girl (from baby to 4 or 5 yrs.)*'], (<**=R1=**> *diminutive*), phonology: stress-shift, vowel-shift, consonant-addition?, reduplication, syntactic analysis: nominal, dialects: *Cheh.*, attested by EB, Elders Group.

<**lhílhló:ya**>, df //ɬí[=C_1ə=]l=á·yɛ or C_1í=ɬ(i)l=á·yɛ//, EZ ['*dragonfly*'], ['order *Odonata*'], (perhaps root <lhil> /'weave'/, semological comment: noting similar behavior of the creature we also call it "devil's darning needle" in English), <**R4=** or **=R1=**> *diminutive*, possibly <**=ó:ya**> probable variant of <**=íya**> *diminutive*, phonology: reduplication, stress-retention on root even with stressed suffix, syntactic analysis: nominal, attested by Elders Group (9/8/76), Salish cognate: Squamish /ɬə-ɬan-áya/ *dragonfly* W73:84, K67:328.

<**lhíl**>, bound root //ɬí(·)l//, CAN /'*bail*'/

<**lhí:lt ~ lhílt**>, df //ɬí(·)l=T//, CAN /'*bail, (bail s-th)*'/, WATR, semantic environment ['canoe, tub, sink, anything large filled with water'], (<**=t**> *purposeful control transitivizer* seems certain, yet the word is not attested in translation as *bail s-th*), syntactic analysis: transitive verb probably, attested by Elders Group (3/1/72, 1/25/78), EB.

<**lhalhí:lt**>, cts //C_1ɛ-ɬí·l=T//, CAN ['*bailing*'], (<**R8-**> *continuative*), phonology: reduplication, syntactic analysis: transitive verb prob., attested by EB.

<**lhí:lthet ~ lhílthet**>, pcrs //ɬí(·)l=T-ət//, CAN /'*bailing (a canoe, etc.), bail oneself*'/, (<**-et**> *reflexive*), syntactic analysis: intransitive verb, attested by Elders Group (3/1/72, 4/7/76, 1/25/78), AC; found in <**lhílthettsel.**>, //ɬíl=T-ət-c-əl//, /'*I am bailing.*'/, attested by Elders Group (3/1/72),

example: <**tsel lhílthet.**>, //c-əl ɬíl=T-ət//, /'*I bail myself.*'/, attested by Elders Group (3/1/72), comment: both examples can probably be glossed the same way.

<**lhéltel**>, dnom //ɬi[=Aə́=]l=təl//, CAN /'*a bailer, canoe bailer*'/, ASM ['made from a folded and tied piece of outer red cedar bark'], (<**é-ablaut**> *derivational*), lx <**=tel**> *device to*, phonology: ablaut, syntactic analysis: nominal, attested by Elders Group (3/1/72, 3/26/75).

<**Lhílheqey**>, df //ɬí[=C_1ə=]q=əy or C_1í=ɬəq=əy//, PLN ['*Mt. Cheam*'], ASM ['name of a woman in a story who was the wife of Mt. Baker and had three daughters and a dog; they quarrelled and she left him to come to the banks of the Fraser River with her daughters and her dog; all were transformed into mountains; this story is told with names for the daughters by CT, AC, DM, and others'], literally /'glacier '/ (according to CT 1973), possibly <**=R1=**> meaning uncertain or <R4=> *diminutive*, possibly <**=ey**> *covering (of snow* perhaps if *glacier* is correct literal meaning*)*, phonology: reduplication, syntactic analysis: nominal, attested by CT (1973), AC, DM (12/4/64), Elders Group, IHTTC, other sources: Wells 1965:11, 17, 1966 map, literally /'a folk etymology from lhélqi *soak fish or meat or berries* (because dried things could be soaked in the lake near the top of Mt. Cheam) is also quite possible but requires the name to originally have been <Lhilhleqey> because there is no plain l in Lhílheqey'/, attested by IHTTC, example: <**yeláwel p'éq' te Lhílheqey.**>, //yəlɛ́w=əl p'ə́q' tə ɬíɬəqəy//, /'*Mt. Cheam is the whitest.*'/, attested by Elders Group (3/9/77).

<**lhilhts'óltsep**>, HARV ['*sawing wood*'], *see* lhíts' ~ lhí:ts'.

<**lhím**>, free root //ɬím//, HARV /'*pick berries, pick off (leaves, fruit, vegetables, hops), (pluck off, harvest)*'/, EB, syntactic analysis: intransitive verb, attested by Elders Group (3/15/72,), AC, BHTTC, JL, EB, also <**lhí:m ~ lhím**>, //ɬí·m ~ ɬím//, attested by EB; found in <**lhímtsel.**>, //ɬím-c-əl//, /'*I'll pick (in just a second).*'/, (semological comment: present tense non-continuative often means imminently, in just a second, about to do something, immediate future), attested by BHTTC, example: <**lhímtselcha tlówàyèl.**>, //ɬím-c-əl-cɛ tlá=wɛ̀yə̀l//, /'*I will pick (later on) today.*'/, (semological comment: future tense usually means will (later on), not immediate future), attested by BHTTC, <**látselcha lhím.**>, //lɛ́-c-əl-cɛ ɬím//, /'*I will go pick.*'/, (semological comment: shows the displacement function of the auxiliary lá), attested by BHTTC, <**lámtsel lhím.**>, //lɛ́=m-c-əl ɬím//, /'*I am going to pick.*'/, (semological comment: shows the displacement and auxiliary near future function of auxiliary lám and gives a clue to the function of its =m suffix), attested by BHTTC, <**atselcha uw lhím.**>, //ʔɛ-c-əl-cɛ ʔuw ɬím//, /'*I will pick too.*'/, (semological comment: shows ambiguous past/present auxiliary can be used with future as well, also shows uw ~ ew ~ we contrastive function), syntactic comment: these five examples show minimal contrasts in present and future tenses and minimal contrasts in lá, lám and á auxiliaries, attested by BHTTC, <**lámtset te Alámex kwsetst lhím te hóps.**>, //lɛ́=m-c-ət tə ʔɛlɛ́məxʸ kʷ-sə-c-t ɬím tə háps//, /'*We're going to the Agassiz area to pick hops.*'/, syntactic comment: note the unusual use of -tst on the subordinate conjunction instead of on the following word; JL's aunt, AC, did this sometimes too, so it may show a family or microdialectal alternative, attested by JL (4/7/78), <**chelà:lqwlha kwa te slhíms.**>, //cəlɛ̀·l-qʷɬɛ kʷɛ tə s-ɬím-s//, /'*He was going to pick a lot.*'/, syntactic comment: shows emphatic/intensive use of -qwlha, attested by EB (6/23/78).

<**lhí:m**>, cts //ɬí[-·-]m//, HARV /'*picking (berries, etc.)*'/, (<**-:-**> *continuative*), phonology: lengthening, syntactic analysis: intransitive verb, attested by BHTTC, Elders Group, AC; found in <**lhí:mtsel.**>, //ɬí[-·-]m-c-əl//, /'*I will start picking.*'/, (semological comment: immediate future meaning of present tense), attested by BHTTC, also /'*I pick.*'/, attested by EB, example: <**tsel lhí:m.**>, //c-əl ɬí[-·-]m//, /'*I'm picking.*'/, syntactic comment: ambiguous past, attested by BHTTC, <**atsel lhí:m.**>, //ʔɛ-c-əl ɬí[-·-]m//, /'*I'm picking.*'/, semantic environment ['answer to question, achexw xwe'í:t *What are you doing?*'], syntactic analysis: ambiguous past with auxiliary verb, attested by BHTTC, <**tsel lhí:m te**

sth'í:m.>, //c-əl ɬí[-·-]m tə s=θ'í·m//, /'*I'm picking berries.*'/, semantic environment ['answer to question, chexw xwe'í:t *What are you doing?*'], attested by Elders Group, <**ílhtsel lhí:m.**>, //ʔí-ɬ-c-əl ɬí[-·-]m//, /'*I was picking.*'/, semantic environment ['answer to question, ílhchexw xwe'í:t *What were you doing?*'], attested by BHTTC; found in <**lhí:mtsel.**>, //ɬí[-·-]m-c-əl//, /'*I'm going to start picking.*'/, (semological comment: immediate future meaning of present tense), semantic environment ['answer to question, xwe'í:tchexw tlówàyèl *What are going to do today?*'], attested by Elders Group (10/20/76), example: <**li lhí:m ta swáqeth kw'e skw'ő:lmexw?**>, //li ɬí[-·-]m t-ɛ s=wɛ́q=əθ k'ʷə s=k'ʷó·lməxʷ//, /'*Is your husband picking blackberries?*'/, attested by AC, <**ewá:lhchexw lhì:m.**>, //ʔəwə-ə-ɬ-c-əxʷ ɬí[-·-]m//, /'*Weren't you going to pick?*'/, (semological comment: perhaps continuative shown in *going*), phonology: downstepping, attested by EB, <**ewétals lhí:m.**>, //ʔwə-´-tɛ-l-s ɬí[-·-]m//, /'*I didn't pick anything.*'/, literally /'it is nothing -my -nominalizer continuative picking'/, (semological comment: emphasizes the extended continuous nature of the picking with no results, even though this is not overtly translated), attested by EB, <**latst lhí:m.**>, //lɛ-c-t ɬí[-·-]m//, /'*We're going to pick (berries)., Let's pick (berries)., (Let's go picking.)*'/, syntactic comment: imperative 1p, attested by EB, AC.

<**lhemlhí:m**>, plv //C_1əC_2=ɬí[-·-]m//, cts, HARV ['*lots of people picking*'], (<**R3=**> *plural (agents)*), phonology: reduplication, lengthening, syntactic analysis: intransitive verb, attested by Elders Group.

<**lhilhím**>, dmv //C_1í=ɬím//, HARV /'*a small person (old or young) is picking or trying to pick, an inexperienced person is picking or trying to pick, picking a little bit, someone who can't pick well is picking*'/, (<**R4=**> *diminutive (of agent or action or both)*), (semological comment: note that a continuative meaning is also added), syntactic analysis: intransitive verb, attested by EB, SP, BHTTC, example: <**lhilhím, t'ót'.**>, //C_1í=ɬím, t'át'//, /'*She's picking, poor thing.*'/, attested by EB.

<**lhemét**>, pcs //ɬi[=Aə́=]m=əT//, [ɬə́mət], HARV /'*pick s-th, (harvest s-th)*'/, (<**é-ablaut**> *derivational*), (<**=et**> *purposeful control transitivizer*), phonology: ablaut, syntactic analysis: transitive verb, attested by BHTTC, example: <**txwém lhémetchexw.**>, //txʷ=x̣ʷə́m ɬi[=Aə́=]m=əT-c-əxʷ//, /'*Pick it right away.*'/, syntactic analysis: imperative, attested by BHTTC; found in <**lhemétchelcha.**>, //ɬi[=Aə́=]m=əT-c-əl-cɛ or ɬi[=Aə=]m=ə[=´=]T-c-əl-cɛ//, /'*I will pick it.*'/, phonology: stress-shift either *resultative* or merely phonological, (semological comment: possible resultative), attested by BHTTC.

<**lhémth'**>, df //ɬi[=Aə́=]m=θ'//, cts, FOOD ['*picking food by the fingers before the meal*'], (<**é-ablaut**> *continuative*), lx <**=th'**> probably *small portion* lx as also in <**sqwémth' ~ sqwómth'**> *lump* (beside <**sqwóm=ecel**> *hunchback)* and in <**ew=th'=át**> *tease s-o* (beside <**ew=ó(:)l=em**> *play)* and in <**lhílhàth'**> *making fun* and <**lhílhà(:)th't**> *making fun of s-o* beside Musqueam /**ɬiɬéθ'=t**/> *make fun of him (because of accident or bad luck)* and /**ɬéʔ=it**/> *insult him* (Suttles ca 1984:14.6.15**)**, phonology: ablaut, syntactic analysis: intransitive verb, attested by BHTTC.

<**lhámth't**>, df //ɬi[=Aɛ́=]m=θ'=T//, FOOD ['*pick food by one's fingers (before a meal)*'], (<**á-ablaut**> *derivational*, perhaps *resultative*?), lx <**=th'**> *small portion*, (<**=t**> *purposeful control transitivizer*), phonology: ablaut, syntactic analysis: transitive verb, attested by BHTTC; found in <**lhámth'tes.**>, //ɬi[=Aɛ́=]m=θ'=T-əs//, /'*He picked food by his fingers.*'/, attested by BHTTC.

<**lhí:m**>, HARV /'*picking (berries, etc.)*'/, *see* lhím.

<**lhímes**>, df //ɬím=əs//, CAN /'*pull in once with a canoe paddle wide or slow, pull in in turning (a canoe paddling stroke done by a bowman)*'/, lx <**=es**> *on the face, in the front or bow of a canoe*, possibly root <**lhím**> *pick off, (pull off as in harvesting, pluck)*, syntactic analysis: intransitive verb, attested by Deming, Elders Group.

<**lhímesem**>, mdls //ɬím=əs=əm//, CAN ['*pry (a canoe paddling stroke when the canoe is hard to*

turn)'], literally perhaps /'pull off on one's bow, pluck on one's bow'/, (<**=em**> *middle voice*), syntactic analysis: intransitive verb, attested by BHTTC (9/10/76).

<**lhímesem**>, CAN [*'pry (a canoe paddling stroke when the canoe is hard to turn)'*], *see* lhímes.

<**lhíq' ~ lhéq'**>, free root //ɬíq' ~ ɬə́q'//, TIME /*'sometimes, (yes [RM])'*/, syntactic analysis: adverb/adverbial verb, attested by EB, LJ (Tait), also /*'yes'*/, dialects: *Chill.*, attested by RM, may be ultimately analyzable as <**lhí**>, free root //ɬí//, /*'when, (sometimes [EB])'*/ + <**=q'**> /*'on something else, within ssomething else'*/, see <lhéq'>.

<**lhíqw**>, bound root, meaning unknown

<**slhíqw**>, dnom //s=ɬíq^w//, ANA /*'flesh (human, non-human), meat (of dried fish, animal, or bird)'*/, (<**s=**> *nominalizer*), phonology: ambi-valent root, syntactic analysis: nominal, attested by Elders Group (3/15/72, 7/27/75), AC, other sources: ES /sɬíyəq^w/ *meat*, H-T <sléuq> (macron over e) *flesh*, example: <**ewá:ta a slhíqw?**>, //ʔəwə= ´-ə=tɛ ʔɛ s=ɬíq^w//, /*'Have you got any meat?'*/, literally /'is it none your meat'/, attested by AC.

<**slheqwéla**>, ds //s=ɬiq^w=ə́lɛ or s=ɬi[=Aə=]q^w=ə́lɛ//, ANA [*'cheek'*], literally /'flesh on the side of the head/beside the ear'/, semantic environment ['of fish, human, animal'], lx <**=éla**> *on the side of the head, beside the ear*, possibly <**e-ablaut**> *derivational* or possibly merely valence triggered vowel reduction (before high toned/high stressed suffix), phonology: vowel-reduction due to stress-shift, possible ablaut, syntactic analysis: nominal, attested by Deming.

<**slheqwél:es**>, ds //s=ɬiq^w=ə́l·əs or s=ɬi[=Aə=]q^w=ə́l·əs//, ANA [*'gums'*], literally /'flesh on the teeth'/, lx <**=él:es ~ =elís**> *on the teeth*, phonology: vowel-reduction due to stress-shift, possible ablaut, syntactic analysis: nominal, attested by AC, also <**slheqwíl:es**>, //s=ɬíq^w=ə[=M2=]l·əs//, attested by Elders Group (10/8/75), also <**slhéqweles ~ slheqwíles**>, //s=ɬi[=Aə́=]q^w=ələs ~ s=ɬíq^w=ə[=M2=]ləs//, attested by BHTTC, other sources: ES /sɬq^{w}ə́lə́s/, JH /sɬə́q^{w}lə̀s/.

<**slhíqwetsel**>, ds //s=ɬíq^w=əcəl//, FSH [*'long thin slices of fish removed to dry from slhíts'es (wind-driedsalmon)'*], literally /'flesh on the back'/, lx <**=etsel ~ =ets ~ =(ew)íts**> *on the back*, phonology: weak-stress valenced suffix, syntactic analysis: nominal, attested by Elders at Fish Camp (7/11/78).

<**lhistélémét**>, EFAM /*'feel embarrassed and shy because ashamed, be ashamed'*/, *see* lháy.

<**lhístexw**>, EFAM [*'ashamed of s-th'*], *see* lháy.

<**lhít'**>, bound root //ɬít' *pass around to give out*//.

<**lhít'et**>, pcs //ɬít'=əT//, SOC /*'pass it around (papers, berries, anything)'*/, ECON, TVMO, (<**=et**> *purposeful control transitivizer*), syntactic analysis: transitive verb, attested by SJ, MV, Salish cognate: Squamish /ɬít'-it/ *give it around (esp. gifts at potlatch), distribute (tr.)* W73:116, K67:330.

<**lhít'es**>, ds //ɬít'=əs//, SOC [*'pass around to give away (at a dance example)'*], ECON, SPRD, lx <**=es**> *dollars, blankets, wealth, round objects, face*, syntactic analysis: intransitive verb, attested by Elders Group.

<**lhít'est**>, pcs //ɬít'=əs=T//, SOC [*'pass it around to s-o'*], ECON, SPRD, TVMO, (<**=t**> *purposeful control transitivizer*), syntactic analysis: transitive verb, attested by Elders Group.

<**lhít'es**>, SOC [*'pass around to give away (at a dance example)'*], *see* lhít'.

<**lhít'est**>, SOC [*'pass it around to s-o'*], *see* lhít'.

<**lhít'et**>, SOC /*'pass it around (papers, berries, anything)'*/, *see* lhít'.

<**lhíts' ~ lhí:ts'**>, free root //ɬíc' ~ ɬí·c'//, ABDF [*'get cut'*], HARV, FSH, HUNT, MC, phonology: ambi-valent or variable-stress root, syntactic analysis: intransitive verb, attested by Elders Group, BJ

(12/5/64), example: <**lhíts' te s'ó:thes**>, //ɬic' tə s=ʔá·θəs//, /'*cut on the face*'/, attested by Elders Group.

<**slhíts'**>, stvi //s=ɬíc'//, ABDF ['*be cut*'], HARV, FSH, HUNT, MC, (<**s=**> *stative*), syntactic analysis: intransitive verb, attested by AC.

<**Slhílhets'**>, ds //s=ɬí[=C_1ə=]c'//, PLN /'*old lake above Smith Falls, Smith Falls creek (which enters Cultus Lake at its northeast corner)*'/, literally /'place for cutting (of bulrushes for mats)'/, (<**s=**> *nominalizer*), (<**=R1=**> *continuative*), phonology: reduplication, syntactic analysis: nominal, source: <st"-LEET"-lihts> Wells 1965:11 (Smith Falls lake); place names reference file #259; <slah-LEET-lihts> Wells 1965:13 (the creek),

<**lhts'á:ls**>, sas //ɬ(i)c'=ɛ́·ls//, HARV /'*to cut wood (with a saw), saw wood, (to cut [as structured activity] [Deming)*'/, FIRE, (<**=á:ls**> *structured activity non-continuative*), phonology: zero-grade of variable stress root before strong-grade suffix, syntactic analysis: intransitive verb, attested by EB, also /'*to cut [as structured activity]*'/, attested by Deming.

<**lhílhets'els**>, cts //ɬí[-C_1ə-]c'=əls//, HARV /'*sawing wood, cutting wood with a saw*'/, FIRE, (<-**R1-**> *continuative*), (<**=els**> *structured activity continuative*), phonology: reduplication, syntactic analysis: intransitive verb, attested by EB, also /'*cutting*'/, attested by Deming, <**lhílhets'els te siyólh**>, //ɬí[-C_1ə-]c'=əls tə s=yáɬ//, /'*cutting wood (with a saw)*'/, attested by EB.

<**shxwlhílhets'els**>, dnom //sx^w=ɬí[=C_1ə=]c'=əls//, HARV ['*saw*'], FIRE, TOOL, (<**sxw=**> *nominalizer*), phonology: reduplication, syntactic analysis: nominal, attested by Elders Group.

<**lhí:ts'et**>, pcs //ɬí·c'=əT//, FSH /'*cut s-th (with anything: knife, saw, scythe, etc.), cut s-o*'/, HUNT, HARV, FOOD, MC, TOOL, ABDF, (<**=et**> *purposeful control transitivizer*), syntactic analysis: transitive verb, attested by AC, other sources: ES /ɬí·c'ət/ *cut*, also <**lhíts'et**>, //ɬíc'=əT//, attested by Deming, EB, <**léwe lhí:ts'et.**>, //lə́wə ɬí·c'=əT//, /'*YOU cut it.*'/, attested by AC, example: <**lhíts'et te máqel (?)**>, //ɬíc'=əT tə mɛ́qəl//, /'*cut the hair*'/, comment: speakers unsure if this is the right way to say it, attested by Deming, <**le lhíts'etes te qéx̱ smíyeth.**>, //lə ɬíc'=əT-əs tə qə́x̣ s=mə́yəθ//, /'*He cut off lots of meat.*'/, attested by EB, <**selchím kw'a' stl'í kw'es lhíts'et te sméyets? (?)**>, //səlcím k'^{w}-ɛʔ s=ƛ'í k'^{w}ə-s ɬíc'=əT tə s=mə́yəc//, /'*How do you want the meat cut?*'/, comment: speakers unsure, dialects: poss. *Matsqui or Downriver Halkomelem*, attested by Deming (2/22/79), <**lhíts'etes te kw'élőw.**>, //ɬíc'=əT-əs tə k'^{w}ə́lów//, /'*He cut the hide.*'/, attested by EB, <**le lhíts'etem.**>, //lə ɬíc'=əT-əm//, /'*They cut him., They cut her.*'/, syntactic analysis: passive, attested by EB.

<**lhíts'elhtset**>, bens //ɬíc'-əɬc-əT//, FOOD ['*cut something off for s-o*'], FSH, HUNT, HARV, MC, (<**-elhts**> *benefactive*), syntactic analysis: transitive verb, attested by EB, example: <**lhíts'elhtsetchelcha te smíyeth.**>, //ɬíc'-əɬc-əT-c-əl-cɛ tə s=mə́yəθ//, /'*I'll cut off some meat for someone.*'/, attested by EB, <**lhíts'elhthoméchelcha te sméyeth.**>, //ɬíc'-əɬc-T-ámə-c-əl-cɛ tə s=mə́yəθ//, /'*I'll cut off some meat for you.*'/, phonology: consonant merger, attested by EB, <**lhíts'elhthó:xchexw te sméyeth.**>, //ɬíc'-əɬc-T-á[=·=]x^y-c-əx^w tə s=mə́yəθ//, /'*Cut off some meat for me., (Cut off some meat for ME.)*'/, phonology: consonant merger, emphatic lengthening, attested by EB.

<**lhets'elá:x̱el**>, ds //ɬic'=əlɛ́·x̣əl or ɬi[=Aə=]c'=əlɛ́·x̣əl//, ABDF ['*cut one's arm*'], literally /'cut on the arm'/, lx <**=elá:x̱el ~ =eláx̱el**> *on the arm*, possibly <**e-ablaut**> *resultative*?, phonology: possible ablaut or vowel-reduction due to stress-shift, strong-valenced suffix, syntactic analysis: intransitive verb, attested by Elders Group.

<**lhéch'elechá:ls**>, sas //ɬic'=ələc=ɛ́·ls or ɬi[=Aə́=]c'=ələc=ɛ́·ls//, HARV /'*cut (grass, hay)*'/, lx <**=elets**> *on the bottom*, (<**=á:ls**> *structured activity non-continuative*), possibly <**é-ablaut**> *resultative*??, phonology: ablaut or perhaps vowel-reduction due to stress-shift to strong-valenced

final suffix, then epenthetic re-stressing of first syllable (since the first three syllable would be unstressed)--this would work something like sentence-stressing changes--it may in fact be sentence-stress since the form was only obtained in a sentence; additional evidence that this is not derivational ablaut may be provided by the continuative form which has the original root vowel unchanged (see below), syntactic analysis: intransitive verb, attested by Elders Group, example: <**lhéch'elechá:ls te só:x̱wel (.)**>, //ɬə́c'=ələc=ɛ́·ls tə sá·x̣ʷəl//, /'*to cut the hay, (He cuts the hay.)*'/, attested by Elders Group (5/5/75).

<**lhílhech'elchá:ls**>, cts //ɬí[-C_1ə-]c'=ələc=ɛ́·ls (sic for ɬí[-C_1ə-]c'=ələc=əls)//, HARV /'*cutting (grass, hay)*'/, (<**-R1-**> *continuative*), (<**=á:ls** (sic for **=els**> *structured activity continuative*)), phonology: reduplication, syntactic analysis: intransitive verb, attested by Elders Group, example: <**lhílhech'elchá:ls te só:x̱wel.**>, //ɬí[-C_1ə-]c'=ələc=əls tə sá·x̣ʷəl//, /'*(He's) now cutting the hay.*'/, literally /'he's cutting on the bottom as a structured activity the grass'/, attested by Elders Group.

<**lhts'élqsel**>, ds //ɬ(i)c'=ə́lqsəl//, ABDF ['*cut off the tip of one's nose*'], literally /'cut on the (tip of the?) nose'/, lx <**=élqsel**> *on the (tip of the) nose*, phonology: vowel-loss due to stress-shift to strong-valenced suffix, (semological comment: the form =élqsel seems to mean the tip of the nose rather than just the nose, this could be a feature of the initial =él or the final =el, or could just be due to the semantic environment), syntactic analysis: intransitive verb, attested by Elders Group.

<**lhéts'emel**>, ds //ɬi[=Aə́=]c'=əməl//, MC /'*trimmings (of material), sawdust, shavings*'/, literally /'cut-off part, cut-off portion'/, possibly <**é-ablaut**> *resultative*? or lhéts' allomorph, lx <**=emel ~ =ómél**> *part, portion, member*, phonology: possible ablaut, syntactic analysis: nominal, attested by IHTTC.

<**lhíts'eqwem**>, mdls //ɬíc'=əqʷ=əm//, ABFC ['*cut one's hair*'], lx <**=eqw**> *on the hair, on the top of the head*, (<**=em**> *middle voice*), syntactic analysis: intransitive verb, attested by Elders Group.

<**slhíts'es**>, dnom //s=ɬíc'=əs//, FSH ['*wind-dried opened and scored salmon*'], ASM ['left on skin, kept open with spreading sticks, hung by the sticks on roofed wind-drying racks in drier windy areas such as the Fraser River canyon; not all types of salmon can be wind-dried well, some are better smoked or salted'], literally /'something cut/sliced on the face'/, (<**s=**> *nominalizer*), lx <**=es**> *on the face*, syntactic analysis: nominal, attested by AC, MH (Deming), also <**shxwlhíts'es**>, //sxʷ=ɬíc'=əs//, attested by EB, example: <**lalh kwélem kw'e slhíts'es.**>, //lɛ-ɬ kʷə́l=əm k'ʷə s=ɬíc'=əs//, /'*Go get some wind-dried fish.*'/, attested by MH, <**tsel thá:yem te shxwlhíts'es.**>, //c-əl θi[=Aɛ́·=]y=əm tə sxʷ=ɬíc'=əs//, /'*I'm making [wind-]dried fish.*'/, attested by EB.

<**lhilhts'óltsep**>, cts //ɬi[-C_1ə-]c'=álcəp//, HARV ['*sawing wood*'], FIRE, (<**-R1-**> *continuative*), lx <**=óltsep**> *firewood, wood*, phonology: reduplication, vowel-loss due to stress-shift to strong-valenced suffix, syntactic analysis: intransitive verb, attested by Elders Group.

<**lhts'ó:ythel**>, ds //ɬ(i)c'=á·yθəl//, ABDF ['*cut on the mouth*'], ASM ['prob. about the lips, chin, or jaw'], lx <**=ó:ythel**> *on the lip, on the chin, on the jaw*, phonology: zero grade of root, vowel-loss due to stress-shift to strong-valenced suffix, syntactic analysis: intransitive verb, attested by Elders Group.

<**lhéts'ches**>, ds //ɬi[=Aə́=]c'=cəs//, [ɬíc'čɪs], ABDF /'*cut on one's hand, (cut one's finger [EB)*'/, literally /'cut on the hand'/, (<**é-ablaut**> *resultative*?), lx <**=tses ~ =ches**> *on the hand*, phonology: ablaut, syntactic analysis: intransitive verb, attested by BJ (12/5/64), Elders Group, also /'*cut one's finger*'/, attested by EB.

<**shxwlhéts'tses**>, dnom //sxʷ=ɬi[=Aə́=]c'=cəs//, [šxʷɬíc'cɪs], ABDF ['*a cut on the hand*'], (<**shxw=**> *nominalizer*), phonology: ablaut, syntactic analysis: nominal, attested by EB, example: <**mí iy'áyel tel shxwlhéts'tses.**>, //mí $C_1əC_2$=ʔɛ́y=əl tə-l sxʷ=ɬi[=Aə́=]c'=cəs//, /'*The cut on my*

hand got well.'/, literally /'get/become better my cut on the hand'/, attested by EB.

<**lhéts'xel**>, ds //ɬi[=Aə́=]c'=xʸəl//, ABDF ['*cut one's foot*'], literally /'cut on the foot, cut on the leg'/, (<**é-ablaut**> *resultative*?), lx <**=xel**> *on the foot, on the leg*, phonology: ablaut, syntactic analysis: intransitive verb, attested by Elders Group (4/16/75).

<**lhá:ts'tel**>, dnom //ɬi[=Aɛ́·=]c'=təl//, TOOL ['*knife*'], literally /'thing to cut with'/, (<**á:-ablaut**> *derivational*), lx <**=tel**> *device to, thing to*, phonology: ablaut, syntactic analysis: nominal, attested by AC, DM (12/4/64), AD, also <**lháts'tel**>, //ɬi[=Aɛ́=]c'=təl//, attested by BJ (5/64), Elders Group, example: <**s'eléqs te lhá:ts'tel**>, //s=ʔəl=ə́qs tə ɬi[=Aɛ́·=]c'=təl//, /'*point of a knife*'/, attested by DM (12/4/64), <**s'iyó:ths te lhá:ts'tel**>, //s=ʔɛy=á·θ-s tə ɬi[=Aɛ́·=]c'=təl//, /'*the sharp edge of a knife*'/, attested by DM (12/4/64), <**alétsa te lhá:ts'tel?**>, //ʔɛlə́cɛ tə ɬi[=Aɛ́·=]c'=təl//, /'*Where's the knife?*'/, attested by AD.

<**lhà:ts'telálá**>, ds //ɬi[=Aɛ̀·=]c'=təl=ɛ́lɛ́//, TOOL /'*handle of a knife, knife-handle*'/, (<**á:-ablaut**> *derivational*), lx <**=álá**> *container of*, phonology: ablaut, phonology: downstepping, syntactic analysis: nominal, attested by DM (12/4/64).

<**lhts'ímél**>, df //ɬic'=ə[=M2=]m(=)əl or ɬ(i)c'=ím=ə́l//, PE ['*comb (for hair)*'], HHG, possibly <**metathesis**> *derivational*, possibly <**=em**> *intransitivizer, verbalizer or middle voice*, possibly <**=ím**> *repeatedly*, possibly <**=el**> *get, become, come, go, inceptive*, possibly <**=els**> *device to*, (but <=els> would require an ad hoc loss of final s), possibly root <**lhíts'**> *cut*, phonology: possible metathesis, possible consonant-loss, syntactic analysis: nominal, attested by EB, Elders Group, DM (12/4/64).

<**lhets'íméls te pítxel**>, cpds //ɬəc'íməl-s tə pít=xʸəl//, EZ /'*centipede,* and poss. *millipede*'/, ['class *Chilopoda* and poss. class *Diplopoda*'], literally /'comb of the salamander'/, (<**-s**> *third person possessive pronoun*), syntactic analysis: nominal phrase with modifier(s), possessive, attested by Elders Group (9/1/76).

<**lhíts'elhtset**>, FOOD ['*cut something off for s-o*'], *see* lhíts' ~ lhí:ts'.

<**lhíts'eqwem**>, ABFC ['*cut one's hair*'], *see* lhíts' ~ lhí:ts'.

<**lhí:ts'et**>, FSH /'*cut s-th (with anything: knife, saw, scythe, etc.), cut s-o*'/, *see* lhíts' ~ lhí:ts'.

<**lhiwí:ws**>, df //ɬɛ[=Ai=]w=í·ws or ɬəw=í·ws//, CLO ['*petticoat*'], probably root <**lháw**> *run away* probably due to the fact that petticoats tend to swing in unauthorized directions and have to be pushed down often), lx <**=í:ws**> *on the body*, phonology: ablaut, syntactic analysis: nominal, attested by DM (12/4/64).

<**lhí:xw**>, free root //ɬí·xʷ//, NUM ['*three*'], syntactic analysis: num, attested by BJ (5/64), NP (12/6/73), CT (9/5/73), AC, also <**lhíxw**>, //ɬíxʷ//, attested by AC, other sources: ES and JH /ɬí·xʷ/, example: <**lhí:xw s(y)iló:lém**>, //ɬí·xʷ s=yilá·l=əm//, /'*three years*'/, phonology: updrifting, attested by AC, <**ó:pel qas kw'e lhí(:)xw**>, //ʔá·pəl qɛ-s k'ʷə ɬí(·)xʷ//, /'*thirteen*'/, literally /'ten and the (remote, abstract) three'/, attested by AC, also <**ó:pel qas te lhí:xw**>, //ʔá·pəl qɛ-s tə ɬí·xʷ//, literally /'ten and the (unmarked) three'/, attested by CT (9/5/73), <**ts'kw'éx qas té lhí:xw**>, //c'=k'ʷə́xʸ qɛ-s tə ɬí·xʷ//, /'*twenty-three*'/, literally /'twenty and the three'/, attested by CT (9/5/73).

<**lhelhíxw ~ lhíxw**>, ds //C_1ə=ɬíxʷ ~ ɬíxʷ//, NUM ['*three things*'], nca <**R5=**> *things,* nca possibly an old *distributive* (see <**x̲ex̲e'óthel**> *four to each* also with <**R5=**>), phonology: reduplication, syntactic analysis: num, attested by IHTTC.

<**lhxwá:le ~ lhxwále**>, ds //ɬixʷ=ɛ́·lə ~ ɬixʷ=ɛ́lə//, NUM ['*three people*'], SOCT, ASM ['includes sasquatches'], nca <**=á(:)le**> *people*, phonology: vowel-loss due to stress-shift to strong valenced suffix, syntactic analysis: num, attested by Elders Group, AC; found in <**lhxwáléchet**>, //ɬxʷ=ɛ́lə-

c-ət//, /'*(There's) three of us.*'/, literally /'we are three people'/, phonology: updrifting of stress/tone to last vowel before suffix of main verb subject suffix (also noted on object pronoun affixes in this position), attested by AC, example: <**lhxwá:le sásq'ets**>, //ɬxʷ=ɛ́·lə sɛ́sq'əc//, /'*three sasquatches*'/, Elder's comment: "EB's grandmother told a story of three sasquatches and another one about four sasquatches", attested by Elders Group (1/30/80).

<**lhelhxwále**>, dmpn //C_1ə=ɬxʷ=ɛ́lə//, NUM ['*three little people*'], SOCT, (<**R5=**> *diminutive plural*), phonology: reduplication, syntactic analysis: num, attested by IHTTC.

<**lhxwálews**>, ds //ɬxʷ=ɛ́ləws//, NUM ['*three leaves*'], EB, nca <**=álews**> *leaf, leaves*, phonology: zero-grade root, perhaps allomorph before strong-valenced suffix, perhaps vowel-loss due to stress-shift to suffix, syntactic analysis: num, attested by AD.

<**lhxwáléws**>, ds //ɬxʷ=ɛ́lə́ws//, EB ['*vanilla leaf*'], ['*Achlys triphylla*'], literally /'three leaves (since each leaf is trifoliate)'/, ASM ['leaves hung up to scent the house (with a vanilla-like scent)'], nca <**=áléws**> *leaf*, syntactic analysis: nominal, attested by Elders at Fish Camp (7/29/77), also <**lhxwálews**>, //ɬxʷ=ɛ́ləws//, attested by AD.

<**lhxwá:lth'ts**>, df //ɬxʷ=ɛ́·lθ'c//, NUM ['*third month since*'], TIME, nca <**=á:lth'ts**> meaning uncertain, affix not attested elsewhere, possibly *month/moon*, syntactic analysis: nominal?, num?, attested by AK (in IHTTC).

<**lhxwá:lh**>, ds //ɬxʷ=ɛ́·ɬ//, NUM /'*three times, thrice*'/, TIME, nca <**=á:lh**> *times, occasions*, phonology: zero-grade of root, either allomorph or phonological rule of vowel-loss due to stress-shift to strong-valenced suffix, syntactic analysis: num, adverb/adverbial verb, attested by AC, also <**lhxwálh**>, //ɬxʷ=ɛ́ɬ//, attested by Elders Group.

<**lhxwá:lhp**>, ds //ɬxʷ=ɛ́·ɬp//, NUM ['*three trees*'], EB, nca <**=á:lhp**> *tree, plant*, phonology: zero-grad of root, syntactic analysis: num, attested by Elders Group.

<**lhxwámeth'**>, ds //ɬxʷ=ɛ́məθ'//, NUM /'*three ropes, three threads, three sticks, three poles, (three long narrow objects)*'/, EB, MC, nca <**=ámeth'**> *long narrow object, pole, stick, rope, thread*, phonology: zero-grade of root, syntactic analysis: num, attested by AD.

<**lhxwá:wtxw**>, ds //ɬxʷ=ɛ́·wtxʷ//, NUM /'*three houses, (three buildings)*'/, nca <**=á:wtxw**> *building, house*, phonology: zero-grade of root, syntactic analysis: num, attested by Elders Group.

<**Lhelhxwáyeleq**>, df //C_1ə=ɬxʷ=ɛ́yələq//, PLN ['*Three Creeks Mountain*'], ASM ['mountain at east end of Seabird Island, i.e., Mt. Hicks or Bear Mt., probably Mt. Hicks since this is probably the mountain which Silhíxw flows down from Hick's Lake and Sílhíxw is a creek with three tributaries; the mountain in question can be seen heading east on Haig Highway where the last road with a stop sign joins Haig Hwy. from the north; if one stops there and faces north, the last mountain at the east end of Seabird Is. is Lhelhxwáyeleq'], literally /'three creeks'/, (<**R5=**> *derivational* possibly *diminutive plural*), lx <**=áyeleq ~ =áyeq ~ =oyeq**> *creeks* (compare <**St'ít'x̱oyeq**> (another place name, lit. little forks in a creek)), phonology: reduplication, zero-grade of root, syntactic analysis: nominal, attested by AK (8/30/77), source: place names reference file #253.

<**lhexwáyiws**>, ds //ɬəxʷ=ɛ́y=iws//, NUM ['*three pants*'], CLO, nca <**=éy=iws**> *pants*, phonology: schwa-grade of root, vowel-change due to stress-shift to strong-valenced suffix, syntactic analysis: num, attested by AD.

<**lhèxwelsxá**>, ds //ɬi[=Aə̀=]xʷ=əlsxʸɛ́//, NUM ['*thirty*'], probably <**è-ablaut**> *derivational*, nca <**=elsxá ~ =elhsxá**> *tens, times ten*, phonology: possible ablaut or schwa-grade of root + secondary stress returned to root, syntactic analysis: num, attested by AC, BJ (12/5/64), MC (9/5/73), also <**lhèxwelhsxá**>, //ɬi[=Aə̀=]xʷ=əɬsʸɛ́//, attested by DM (12/4/64), CT (9/5/73), others.

<**lhexwelhsxó:s**>, ds //ɬəxʷ=əɬsxʸɛ=á·s//, NUM ['*thirty cyclic periods*'], nca <**=ó:s**> *cyclic period, dollars, blankets, on the face*, phonology: ablaut, vowel merger, syntactic analysis: num, attested

by DM (12/4/64), example: <**lhexwelhsxó:s swà:yel**>, //ɬəxʷ=əɬsʸɛ́=á·s s=wɛ̀·yəl//, /'*thirty days*'/, attested by DM (12/4/64).

<**lhexwelsxó:s**>, ds //ɬi[=Aə=]xʷ=əlsxʸɛ́=á·s//, NUM ['*thirty dollars*'], ECON, nca <**=ó:s**> *dollars, cyclic periods, on the face*, phonology: ablaut, vowel merger, syntactic analysis: num, attested by Elders Group (7/27/75), AC (11/30/71).

<**lhxwelhsxále**>, ds //ɬxʷ=əɬsxʸɛ́=ɛ́lə//, NUM ['*thirty people*'], SOCT, nca <**=ále**> *people*, phonology: zero-grade of root, vowel merger, syntactic analysis: num, attested by Elders Group (3/19/75).

<**lhexwelsxáleqel**>, ds //ɬi[=Aə=]xʷ=əlsxʸɛ́=ɛ́ləqəl//, NUM ['*thirty containers*'], MC, nca <**=áleqel ~ =eqel**> *container*, phonology: ablaut, phonology: vowel merger, syntactic analysis: num, attested by AD.

<**lhíxweqel**>, ds //ɬíxʷ=əqəl//, NUM ['*three containers*'], MC, nca <**=eqel**> *containers*, phonology: strong-grade root with weak-valenced suffix, syntactic analysis: num, attested by AD.

<**lhíxweqw**>, ds //ɬíxʷ=əqʷ//, NUM ['*three fish*'], FSH, nca <**=eqw**> *fish; on top of the head, on the hair*, phonology: strong-grade root with weak-grade suffix, syntactic analysis: num, attested by BHTTC.

<**lhí:xwes**>, ds //ɬí·xʷ=əs//, NUM /'*three dollars, three tokens of wealth, three blankets (Boas), three cyclic periods*'/, ECON, nca <**=es ~ =ó:s**> *dollars, blankets, wealth, cyclic periods, on the face*, phonology: strong-grade root with weak-grade suffix, syntactic analysis: num, attested by AC, ASM ['three tokens of wealth'], example: <**lhíxwes kwóte ~ lhíxw kwóte**>, //ɬíxʷ=əs kʷátə ~ ɬíxʷ kʷátə//, /'*three quarters, seventy-five cents*'/, attested by Deming, <**lhíxwes mít ~ lhíxw mít**>, //ɬíxʷ=əs mít ~ ɬíxʷ mít//, /'*three bits, three dimes, thirty cents*'/, attested by Deming, ASM ['three cyclic periods'], <**lhíxes kwóte**>, //ɬíxʷ=əs kʷátə//, /'*third quarter moon, gibbous moon*'/, attested by Elders Group (3/12/75), ASM ['three Indian blankets, three dollars'], <**lhíxwes**>, //ɬíxʷ=əs//, /'*three Indian blankets, three dollars*'/, source: <tléqus> (macron over e) Boas Scowlitz field notes--APS Library.

<**lhxwíws**>, ds //ɬxʷ=íws//, NUM ['*three birds*'], HUNT, nca <**=íws**> *on the body; bird*, phonology: zero-grade of root with strong-grade suffix, syntactic analysis: num, attested by Elders Group (3/29/77).

<**lhixwmó:t**>, ds //ɬixʷ=má·t//, NUM /'*three kinds, three piles of things*'/, MC, nca <**=mó:t ~ =mò:t**> *kinds, piles of (different) things*, phonology: full-grade root plus full grade suffix., syntactic analysis: num, attested by IHTTC, Elders Group.

<**lhexwòls**>, ds //ɬi[=Aə=]xʷ=àls//, NUM ['*three fruit in a cluster (as they grow on a plant)*'], HARV, nca <**=òls ~ =ó:ls**> *fruit, spherical objects, rocks, balls*, phonology: ablaut, syntactic analysis: num, attested by AD.

<**lhxwó:lh**>, ds //ɬxʷ=á·ɬ//, NUM /'*three canoes, three wagons, three conveyances (any form of transportation), three boats*'/, CAN, TVMO, nca <**=ó:lh ~ =ő́welh ~ =áwelh**> *canoe, conveyance*, phonology: zero-grade of root with strong-grade of suffix, syntactic analysis: num, attested by Deming, also <**lhexwő́welh**>, //ɬi[=Aə=]xʷ=ówəɬ//, also /'*three canoes, three boats*'/, attested by AD.

<**lhxwő́:wes**>, ds //ɬxʷ=ó·wəs//, NUM /'*three paddles, three paddlers*'/, CAN, nca <**=ő́:wes**> *paddle, paddlers*, phonology: zero-grade of root with strong-grade of suffix, syntactic analysis: num, attested by Elders Group.

<**slhíxws**>, ds //s=ɬíxʷ=s//, NUM /'*three o'clock (< the third hour); Wednesday (< the third day)*'/, TIME, nca <**s=...=s**> (circumfix) *day of the week; o'clock* prob. related to <**=es ~ =ó:s**> *cyclic period*, phonology: circumfix, syntactic analysis: num, nominal, attested by Elders Group, Deming,

SJ, also <**slhí:xws**>, //s=ɬí·x^{w}=s//, attested by AC, <**wetéses te slhí:xws**>, //wə-tə́s-əs tə s=ɬí·x^{w}=s//, /'*when it gets three o'clock*'/, attested by AC, example: <**wets'ímél te slhíxws.**>, //wə=c'ím=ə́l tə s=ɬíx^{w}=s//, /'*(It's) nearly three o'clock.*'/, literally /'contrastive= nearly =get/become the third hour'/, attested by Deming, <**yíyelaw te shíxws.**>, //C$_1$í=yəlɛw tə s=ɬíx^{w}=s//, /'*(It's) past three o'clock.*'/, Elder's comment: "as close as the Stó:lō got to minutes", attested by SJ (1/20/77).

<**Sílhíxw**>, df //s(=)í=ɬíx^{w}//, PLN /'*creek from Hicks Lake [sic? from Deer Lake] that's actually three creeks all leaving from the lake,* probably *Mahood Creek, (*also *Hick's Mountain [LJ])*'/, ASM ['Mahood Creek enters and leaves Deer Lake (the only lake on Hicks Mountain in the right area) and also has a tributary after it leaves and before it joins Johnson Slough; the place name Qwōhóls is sometimes identified as Mahood Creek but from its meaning it could well be Johnson Slough instead'], probably <**s=**> *nominalizer*, probably <**ye=**> *travelling by*, syntactic analysis: nominal, attested by LJ (Tait)(visiting IHTTC), source: place names reference file #190, also /'also *Hick's Mountain*'/, attested by LJ (8/79 tape by AD).

<**lhíxweqel**>, NUM ['*three containers*'], *see* lhí:xw.

<**lhíxweqw**>, NUM ['*three fish*'], *see* lhí:xw.

<**lhí:xwes**>, NUM /'*three dollars, three tokens of wealth, three blankets (Boas), three cyclic periods*'/, *see* lhí:xw.

<**lhixwmó:t**>, NUM /'*three kinds, three piles of things*'/, *see* lhí:xw.

<**lhíx̱**>, ds //ɬɛ[=Aí=]x̣ or ɬíx̣//, REL /'*to paint red or black (spirit dancer, Indian doctor, etc.)*'/, SPRD, IDOC, ASM ['may include other colors (white is used rarely on spirit dancers), but red and black are the usual colors, they signify different powers or different quests, red is usually more powerful and is used by more ritualists'], semantic environment ['Indian religious participant or ceremony'], (<**í-ablaut**> *derivational*, perhaps *resultative*?), phonology: ablaut, probably not a separate root, (semological comment: probably a derived root since painting of the kind done here is done by spreading colored grease on the skin and root lháx̱ is *spread*), syntactic analysis: intransitive verb, attested by BHTTC.

<**lhíx̱esem**>, mdls //ɬɛ[=Aí=]x̣=əs=əm//, REL /'*paint one's face red or black (spirit dancer, Indian doctor, ritualist, etc.)*'/, SPRD, IDOC, lx <**=es**> *on the face*, (<**=em**> *middle voice*), phonology: ablaut, syntactic analysis: intransitive verb, attested by BHTTC.

<**lhíx̱et**>, pcs //ɬɛ[=Aí=]x̣=əT//, REL ['*spread red or black paint on s-th(?)/s-o*'], (<**=et**> *purposeful control transitivizer*), phonology: ablaut, syntactic analysis: transitive verb, attested by BHTTC.

<**lhíx̱**>, REL /'*to paint red or black (spirit dancer, Indian doctor, etc.)*'/, *see also* lhá:x̱ ~ lháx̱.

<**lhíx̱esem**>, REL /'*paint one's face red or black (spirit dancer, Indian doctor, ritualist, etc.)*'/, *see* lhá:**x̱** ~ lháx̱.

<**lhíx̱et**>, REL ['*spread red or black paint on s-th(?)/s-o*'], *see* lhá:**x̱** ~ lháx̱.

<**lhiyó:qwt**>, df //ɬiyá·q^{w}t//, TIME /'*be last, be behind, after*'/, TVMO, PLAY, syntactic analysis: adverb/adverbial verb, attested by Elders Group, AC, example: <**mí: lhiyó:qwt.**>, //mí· ɬiyá·q^{w}t//, /'*He came in after., He came in behind.*'/.

<**yelhyó:qwt**>, mos //yə=lhyá·q^{w}t//, TIME /'*be last (in travelling), be behind (in travelling)*'/, (<**ye=**> *in travelling, in motion, along*), syntactic analysis: adverb/adverbial verb, attested by EB, also <**ilhyóqwt**>, //yə=ɬyáq^{w}t//, also /'*hind, behind*'/, example: <**yelhyó:qwt te Bill.**>, //yə=ɬyá·q^{w}t tə Bill//, /'*Bill is behind., Bill is last.*'/, attested by EB, <**yelhyó:qwt kwes xwe'í.**>, //yə=ɬyá·q^{w}t k^{w}ə-s

xʷə=ʔí//, /'*He arrived last., He came in last.*'/, attested by EB, **<yelhyó:qwt te ts'q'éyx̲ músmes.>**, //yə=lyá·qʷt tə c'=q'íx̣ músməs//, /'*The black cow was behind., The black cow was last.*'/, attested by EB, **<ilhyóqwt te sx̲éles.>**, //yə=ɬyáqʷt tə s=x̣ə́lə-s//, /'*the hind leg*'/, literally /'is behind, hind the its leg'/, attested by EP, EB (both in BHTTC).

<**lhkw'ámő(w)s ~ lhkw'ámő:s**>, ANA ['*pulse*'], *see* slhákw'em.

<**lhkw'íwel:exw**>, EFAM /'*startled s-o, (excited s-o [Elders Group 3/2/77])*'/, *see* lhó:kw' ~ lhókw'.

<**lhlímelh**>, df //ɬ(=)líməɬ//, PRON /'*it is us, we are the ones, we ourselves*'/ (compare <**lh=wélep**> *it is you folks, you yourselves* and possibly **<ōwé=ta=lh>** *nobody*), syntactic analysis: pronominal verb/verbal pronoun, attested by AC, example: **<lhlímèlhcha o eyálewet.>**, //ɬlíməɬ-cɛ ʔa ʔəy=ɛ́ləw=əT//, /'*We'll do it ourselves.*'/, attested by AC, **<txwoye límelh á:lmelh.>**, //txʷ=áyə líməɬ ʔa[=Aɛ́·=]lm=əɬ//, /'*We're the babysitters.*'/, literally /'it's only us ourselves waiting for =children'/, attested by AD (1/19/79).

<**talhlímelh**>, ds //tɛ=ɬ=líməɬ//, PRON /'*we, us*'/, (<**ta=**> *nominalizer*), syntactic analysis: inp, syntactic comment: <**ta=**> *nominalizer* < <**te**> demonstrative article originally, attested by AC, BJ (12/5/64), others (compare <**ta=lh=wélep**> *you (pl.), you folks*, <**ōwé=ta**> *it's nothing, it's no-one,* and **<ōwé=ta=lh>** *it's nobody* **(<ő we>** *it's not*)), other sources: ES /tɛɬlíməɬ/ *we*, example: **<welóy talhlímelh>**, //wə=láy tɛ=ɬ=líməɬ//, /'*just us, only us*'/, attested by AC, **<lóy talhlímelh lám kw'e táwn.>**, //láy tɛ=ɬ=líməɬ lɛ́=m k'ʷə tɛ́wn//, /'*We (exclusive) are going to town., It's only us that's going to town.*'/, attested by AC.

<**tl'elhlímelh**>, ds //ƛ'ə=ɬ=líməɬ//, PRON /'*us (nominalized object of preposition), to us, with us*'/, (<**tl'e=**> *nominalized object of preposition*), syntactic analysis: independent object of prepositional verb, syntactic comment: tl'e= *nominalized object of preposition* derives originally from tl' a demonstrative article which is sometimes used before nominals as a generic preposition plus article, attested by AC, EB, Elders Group, example: **<stetís tl'elhlímelh.>**, //s=C_1ə=tə[=Aí=]s ƛ'ə=ɬ=líməɬ//, /'*She's close to us.*'/, attested by AC, **<ístexwchxw ó í tl'elhlímelh.>**, //ʔí=sT-əxʷ-c-xʷ ʔá ʔí ƛ'ə=ɬ=líməɬ//, /'*You leave it with us.*'/, attested by EB, **<óxwestchexw telí tl'elhlímelh.>**, //ʔáxʷəs=T-c-əxʷ təlí ƛ'ə=ɬ=líməɬ//, /'*Give it to him from us.*'/, attested by Elders Group.

<**lhók**>, free root //ɬák//, HHG ['*clock*'], TIME, syntactic analysis: nominal, borrowed from English [kɬák] clock, attested by Elders Group.

<**lhó:kw' ~ lhókw'**>, free root //ɬá·k'ʷ ~ ɬák'ʷ//, ABFC ['*to fly*'], TVMO, syntactic analysis: intransitive verb, attested by AC, BJ (12/5/64), EB, other sources: ES /ɬá·k'ʷ/, example: **<latsel lhókw'.>**, //lɛ-c-əl ɬák'ʷ//, /'*I'm going to fly.*'/, attested by AC, **<me lhókw' telí kw'e chókw tl'ésu íkw'elò kwses thiyéltxwem.>**, //mə ɬák'ʷ təlí k'ʷə cákʷ ƛ'ə=s=u ʔí=k'ʷə=là kʷ-s-əs θiy=ə́ltxʷ=əm//, /'*He flew from far away and he makes his home here.*'/, usage: used for literal flight but sometimes also metaphorical as when a person moved from a long distance away but didn't take a plane, attested by EB, Salish cognate: Nooksack //ɬok'ʷ//, **<lhokw'>** to fly.

<**lhólhekw'**>, cts //ɬá[-C_1ə-]k'ʷ//, ABDF ['*flying*'], TVMO, (<**-R1-**> *continuative*), phonology: reduplication, syntactic analysis: intransitive verb, attested by BJ (12/5/64), Elders Group.

<**lhólhekw' stim:őt**>, cpds //ɬá[-C_1ə-]k'ʷ stim·ót//, CAN ['*airplane*'], TVMO, literally /'flying steamboat, flying motor'/, phonology: reduplication, syntactic analysis: simple nominal phrase, attested by NP (9/30/75), also <**lhólhekw'**>, //ɬá[-C_1ə-]k'ʷ//, literally /'flying'/, syntactic comment: probably is relativized by the article required before all words used as nominals, attested by Elders Group (10/1/75), compare Nooksack [æy ɬoq'ʷ snʊ́xʷɪɬ] /ʔæy ɬók'ʷ snóxʷⁱɬ/ airplane (lit. "flying canoe")(PF:GS cards 2.177 has the phonetic transcription given).

<**Lhó:kw'elálexw ~ Lhó:kw'elàlèxw**>, df //ɬá·k'ʷ=əlɛ́ləxʷ ~ ɬá·k'ʷ=əlɛ̀lə̀xʷ//, N /'*name of Dan Milo's*

father, Milo'/, Elder's comment: "it means the one who flew here from the east and dropped pretty close to where we are", lx <**=elálexw ~ =álexw**> *male personal name ending* (compare <**hil=á:lxw**> *autumn*), syntactic analysis: nominal, attested by DM (12/4/64), DM (12/5/64), Salish cognate: Musqueam /=é·nxʷ ~ -é·nəxʷ ~ -énəxʷ/ *fish, fish run, (season?)* Suttles ca 1984:14.5.22.

<**lhekw'í:wel**>, ds //ɬok'ʷ=í·wəl//, EFAM ['*surprise*'], lx <**=í:wel**> *mind, insides, in the insides*, phonology: vowel-reduction due to stress-shift to strong-grade of suffix, in comparison with the following resultative form, it seems that the controlling environment of the vowel-reduction may be immediately adjacent to stressed affix; in the resultative form reduplication intervenes and allows the root vowel to stay unreduced, syntactic analysis: intransitive verb, attested by Elders Group (3/2/77).

<**lholhekw'íwel ~ lholhkw'íwel**>, rsls //ɬa[=C_1ə=]k'ʷ=íwəl//, EFAM /'*be startled, be dumbfounded, be shocked, be stupified, be speechless, be overwhelmed*'/, (<**=R1=**> *resultative*), phonology: reduplication, vowel-loss in one variant, syntactic analysis: intransitive verb, attested by Elders Group, HT.

<**slholhekw'íwel ~ slholhekw'í:wel**>, strs //s=ɬá[=C_1ə=]k'ʷ=í(·)wəl//, EFAM /'*be dumbfounded, be surprised, be stupified, be speechless*'/, (<**s=**> *stative*), phonology: reduplication, syntactic analysis: intransitive verb, attested by Elders Group, AC, example: <**alsu slholhekw'íwelò; ōwétal slhéq'elexw xwe'í:tes kw'els sqwà:l; alsu halq'emé:ylem.**>, //ʔɛl-s-u s=ɬa[=C_1ə=]k'ʷ=íwəl-à; ʔowə= ´=tɛ-l s=ɬə=q'əl=l-əxʷ xʷə=ʔí·t-əs k'ʷə-l-s s-qʷɛ̀·l; ʔɛl-s-u hɛ=lq'əm=íl=əm//, /'*And so, stupified, I didn't know what I was going to say; so I spoke Halkomelem.*'/, literally /'so I am dumbfounded -just; it is nothing -my knowledge of it where it is going -it the (abstract)/what -I -nominalizer speak; so I speak Halkomelem'/, attested by AC (text 11/10/71).

<**lhkw'íwel:exw**>, ncs //ɬak'ʷ=íwəl=l-əxʷ//, EFAM /'*startled s-o, (excited s-o [Elders Group 3/2/77])*'/, (<**=l**> *non-control transitivizer (accidental, happen to, manage to)*), (<**-exw**> *third person object*), phonology: consonant merger (l+l > l:), vowel-loss or zero-grade of root before strong-grade of suffix, syntactic analysis: transitive verb, attested by Elders Group (1/30/80), also /'*excited s-o*'/, attested by Elders Group (3/2/77).

<**Lhó:kw'elálexw ~ Lhó:kw'elàlèxw**>, N /'*name of Dan Milós father, Milo*'/, *see* lhó:kw' ~ lhókw'.

<**lhóleqwet**>, WATR ['*wetting many things*'], *see* lhéqw.

<**Lhó:leqwet**>, df //ɬá·[=lə=]qʷ(=)əT//, PLN /'*Bare Bluffs, a steep slope on the west side of Harrison Lake*'/, ASM ['steep 45-60 degree slope with comparatively few trees, high and massive, sliding right into the lake, from map comparison the location would be the slopes between a point opposite the north end of Long Island Bay and (north to) Mystery Creek; it's located west of Long Island in Harrison Lake'], literally /'bare bluffs'/, PLN ['*a nice place near Morris Creek on the (right?) side of Harrison River [IHTTC 8/25/77])*'], possibly root <**lheqw'**> *peel off* as in <**lheqw'ót ~ lheqw'ó:t**> *peel it off (for ex. bark)*, possibly <**=le=**> *plural*, possibly <**=et**> *purposeful control transitivizer*, possibly <**deglottalization**> *derivational*, phonology: possible infix, possible deglottalization, syntactic analysis: nominal, attested by EL (6/18/75), also /'*a nice place near Morris Creek on the (right?) side of Harrison River*'/, literally /'bare rock'/, ASM ['it was always windy there, people used to gather there when the mosquitoes were bad'], attested by IHTTC (8/25/77).

<**lholeqwót**>, df //ɬaləqʷát//, EZ /'*moth (esp, the grey one that comes out at night)*'/, ['order *Lepidoptera* (esp. incl. grey moths of families *Noctuidae, Geometridae,* and *Lymantriidae)*'], comment: most moths fly at night, they differ from butterflies in that moths keep their wings horizontal at night, have thick hairy bodies, and feathery antennae--this from scientific literature, not from interviews with elders, EZ ['*(butterfly (generic) [AC])*'], root meaning unknown unless <**lhal**> *weave* or <**lheqw'**> *peel off,*

possibly **<=le=>** *plural*, possibly **<=eqw>** *in the hair*, possibly **<=ót>** *female name ending*, syntactic analysis: nominal, attested by SJ, MC, MV, LG (all Deming), Elders Group (6/11/75), also **<lholiqwót>**, //ɬaliqʷát//, attested by Elders Group (1/15/75), also **<lholiqwót ~ lholiqwó:t>**, //ɬaliqʷát ~ ɬaliqʷá·t//, also /*'butterfly (generic)'*/, attested by AC, example: **<kw'óqwelexwes te (lholiqwó:t, sisemóye) te stl'eq'á:ls li te sp'áq'em.>**, //k'ʷáqʷ=l-əxʷ-əs tə (ɬaliqʷá·t, sisəm=áyɛ) tə s=ƛ'əq'=ɛ́·ls li tə s=p'ɛ́q'=əm//, /*'The (butterfly, bee) hit its wing on a flower.'*/, attested by AC.

<lhó:ltes>, WATR [*'spray'*], *see* lhél.

<lhólhekw'>, ABDF [*'flying'*], *see* lhó:kw' ~ lhókw'.

<lholhekw'íwel ~ lholhkw'íwel>, EFAM /*'be startled, be dumbfounded, be shocked, be stupified, be speechless, be overwhelmed'*/, *see* lhó:kw' ~ lhókw'.

<lhólhekw' stim:ő̋t>, CAN [*'airplane'*], *see* lhó:kw' ~ lhókw' or stim:ő:t.

<lhólheqw'els>, HARV [*'peeling bark'*], *see* lhéqw'.

<lhólheqw'et>, ABFC [*'slapping s-o'*], *see* lhóqw'et.

<lhólheqw'tsesem>, ABFC [*'clapping with (one's) hands'*], *see* lhóqw'et.

<lhólhes>, FSH [*'drifting (drift-netting)'*], *see* lhós.

<lholhetqsélem>, ABDF /*'sniffing (a person, like with a cold, etc.)'*/, *see* lhot.

<lholhistélemet>, EFAM [*'feeling embarrassed'*], *see* lháy.

<lhólho>, probably onomatopoeic root //ɬáɬa//

<slhólho>, df //s=ɬáɬa// or //s=C_1á=ɬa//, EZ /*'brown thrush* (could be *hermit thrush,* or possibly *gray-cheeked thrush)'*/, ['respectively *Hylocichla guttata* or *Catharus guttatus*, or possibly *Hylocichla minima* or *Catharus minimus*'], ASM ['typically these birds sit 20 or 30 in one bush (that eliminates Swainson's thrush as a possibility--it also already has a name, xwét)'], possibly **<s=>** *nominalizer*, possibly **<R10=>** meaning uncertain, perhaps imitative, phonology: possible reduplication, syntactic analysis: nominal, attested by Elders Group (3/1/72).

<lhóp>, free root //ɬáp//, TIME [*'late in the night'*], syntactic analysis: adverb/adverbial verb, attested by EB, AD, Salish cognate: Lushootseed /ɬúp/ *morning, early* H76:307, possibly Squamish /ɬúp/ *be way off, be out of reach, be away from the edge* K67:329, example: **<lámescha tu lhóp>**, //lɛ́=m-əs-cɛ tu ɬáp//, /*'later in the night (about 10 p.m. to midnight)'*/, literally /'when it will be going to a little late in the night'/, attested by AD, EB, **<lámtselcha ítet welámescha tu lhóp.>**, //lɛ́=m-c-əl-cɛ ʔítət wə-lɛ́=m-əs-cɛ tu ɬáp//, /*'I'm going to go to sleep later in the night.'*/, attested by AD.

<lhóp'>, free root not attested yet //ɬáp'// *eat soup.*

<slhóp'>, dnom //s=ɬáp'//, FOOD /*'soup, (stew)'*/, (**<s=>** *nominalizer*), syntactic analysis: nominal, attested by Wilfred Charlie (2/15/76), also **<slhóp>**, //s=ɬáp//, attested by EB, AC, other sources: JH /sɬáp'/, Duff 1952 /sɬáp/ *soup (using meat or fish, roots and berries)*, Salish cognate: Samish dial. of N. Straits /s=ɬáp'/ *soup, stew* and /ɬáp'/ *to eat soup/stew* as well as (VU) /ɬáɬəp'/ ~ (LD) /ɬáɬp'/ *eating soup/stew/Indian ice cream (whipped soapberry foam)* G86:88, poss. also Squamish /s-ɬumʔ/ *soup* and /ɬumʔ/ *eat soup* W73:243, K67:290,330, Northern Lushootseed /(s)ɬub ~ s-ɬuʔb/ *soup* H76:38,307, example: **<x̲ots'oyíqw slhóp>**, //x̣ac'ay=íqʷ s=ɬáp//, /*'fish-head soup'*/, literally /'barbecued fish head soup/stew'/, attested by MH (Deming).

<lhóq'ethet>, LAND [*'lie down'*], *see* lháq'.

<lhóqwet>, WATR [*'wet s-th'*], *see* lhéqw.

<**lhóqw'**>, root so far unattested free //ɬáq'^{w}//, ABFC *slap*.

<**lhóqw'et**>, pcs //ɬáq'^{w}=əT//, ABFC ['*slap s-o/s-th*'], SOC, (<**=et**> *purposeful control transitivizer*), syntactic analysis: transitive verb, attested by EB, IHTTC, also <**lhó:qw'et**>, //ɬá·q'^{w}=əT//, attested by AC; found in <**lhò:qw'ethóxes.**>, //ɬá·q'^{w}=əT-áx^{y}-əs//, /'*He slapped me.*'/, phonology: downstepping, attested by AC, <**lhóqw'etes.**>, //ɬáq'^{w}=əT-əs//, /'*He slapped s-o.*'/, attested by EB.

<**lhólheqw'et**>, cts //ɬá[-C_1ə-]q'^{w}=əT//, ABFC ['*slapping s-o*'], SOC, (<**-R1-**> *continuative*), phonology: reduplication, syntactic analysis: transitive verb, attested by IHTTC.

<**lhéqw'tsesem**>, mdls //ɬa[=Aə́=]q'^{w}=cəs=əm//, ABFC /'*clap one's hands, clap once with hands*'/, SOC, (<**é-ablaut**> *derivational* or *resultative*), lx <**=tses**> *on the hand(s)*, (<**=em**> *middle voice*), phonology: ablaut, syntactic analysis: intransitive verb, attested by Elders Group.

<**lhólheqw'tsesem**>, cts //ɬá[-C_1ə-]q'^{w}=cəs=əm//, ABFC ['*clapping with (one's) hands*'], SOC, (<**-R1-**> *continuative*), phonology: reduplication, syntactic analysis: Elders Group.

<**lhoqw'esá:ls**>, HARV ['*peel a tree*'], *see* lhéqw'.

<**lhós**>, free root //lás//, FSH /'*to drift-net, to fish with drift-net*'/, syntactic analysis: intransitive verb, attested by AC, Deming, Elders Group (3/15/72), also <**lhó:s**>, //ɬá·s//, Elder's comment: "unsure", attested by Elders Group (2/11/76), example: <**látsel lhós.**>, //lɛ́-c-əl ɬás//, /'*Let's drift-net., We're going to drift-net.*'/, attested by Elders Group (3/15/72), <**lámtset lhós te sth'óqwi.**>, //lɛ́=m-c-ət ɬás tə s=θ'áq^{w}i//, /'*We're going to drift-net (for) fish.*'/, attested by Deming.

<**lhólhes**>, cts //ɬá[-C_1ə-]s//, FSH ['*drifting (drift-netting)*'], (<**-R1-**> *continuative*), phonology: reduplication, syntactic analysis: intransitive verb, attested by Deming, Elders Group (3/15/72, 2/1/76), example: <**tsel lhólhes.**>, //c-əl ɬá[-C_1ə-]s//, /'*I'm drift-netting., I'm drifting.*'/, attested by Elders Group (3/15/72), <**tl'e lhólhes.**>, //ƛ'a ɬá[-C_1ə-]s//, /'*He's fishing (drift-netting).*'/, attested by Elders Group (2/11/76).

<**tellhó:s**>, ds //təl=ɬá·s//, WATR /'*downriver, (from downriver)*'/, DIR, lx <**tel=**> *from*, syntactic analysis: adverb/adverbial verb, attested by Elders Group.

<**Tellhós**>, ds //təl=ɬás//, SOCT ['*Squamish people*'], literally /'from downriver'/, lx <**tel=**> *from*, syntactic analysis: nominal, attested by BHTTC, also <**Sqwx̲wó:mex**>, //s(=)q^{w}x̣^{w}(=)á·məx^{y}//, attested by BHTTC.

<**lhelhós**>, df //C_1ə=ɬás//, WATR /'*downriver, down that way*'/, DIR, probably <**R5=**> *derivational or diminutive*?, phonology: reduplication, syntactic analysis: adverb/adverbial verb, attested by Elders Group.

<**tellhelhó:s**>, ds //təl=C_1ə=ɬá·s//, DIR ['*south wind*'], WETH, literally /'from downriver, from down that way'/, lx <**tel=**> *from*, phonology: reduplication, syntactic analysis: nominal, attested by Elders Group.

<**lhósex̲el**>, ds //ɬás=əx̣əl//, DIR /'*downriver, down that way, downriver below*'/, WATR, lx <**=ex̲el**> *side, direction*, syntactic analysis: adverb/adverbial verb, attested by Elders Group.

<**lhósem**>, mdls //ɬás=əm//, CLO ['*slide down (of clothes)*'], DIR, TVMO, (<**=em**> *middle voice*), syntactic analysis: intransitive verb, attested by BHTTC, Salish cognate: Squamish /ɬús, ɬús-m/ *slide down* W73:238, K67:330.

<**lhosemáyiws**>, ds //ɬas=əm=ɛ́y(=)iws//, CLO ['*(have) pants sliding down*'], TVMO, DIR, lx <**=áy=iws**> *pants*, syntactic analysis: intransitive verb, attested by BHTTC.

<**lhósem**>, CLO ['*slide down (of clothes)*'], *see* lhós.

<**lhosemáyiws**>, CLO ['*(have) pants sliding down*'], *see* lhós.

<**lhósex̲el**>, DIR /'*downriver, down that way, downriver below*'/, *see* lhós.

<**lhot**>, bound root //ɬat// *make sipping sound*

<**lhotqsélem**>, mdls //ɬat=qsə[=´=]l=əm//, ABDF /'*sniff (a person, like with a cold, etc.)*'/, SD, possibly root <**lhot**> *make sipping sound,* lx <**=qsel ~ =eqs ~ =qs**> *on the nose*, possibly <**=el**> *get, become, go, come, inceptive*, possibly <=´=> *derivational*, (<**=em**> *middle voice*), phonology: stress-shift, syntactic analysis: intransitive verb, attested by Elders Group, Salish cognate: Squamish perhaps /ɬút'-un/ *sip (a fluid)* K69:71.

<**lholhetqsélem**>, cts //ɬa[-C_1ə-]t=qsə[=´=]l=əm//, ABDF /'*sniffing (a person, like with a cold, etc.)*'/, SD, (<**-R1-**> *continuative*), phonology: reduplication, phonology: stress-shift, syntactic analysis: intransitive verb, attested by Elders Group.

<**lhótqwem**>, df //ɬát=qʷ=əm//, WATR ['*boil water*'], SD, FOOD, possibly root <**lhót**> *make sipping sound*, possibly <**=qw**> meaning unclear perhaps *around in circles*, (<**=em**> *middle voice*), syntactic analysis: intransitive verb, attested by BJ (5/64), Salish cognate: Lushootseed /ɬtqʷ/ (no gloss) found in /gʷə-ɬtqʷ-ád/ *a flock all takes to the air at one time (implies a lot of noise too)* H76:306 [note that the sound made by a flock all taking off from water at the same time is almost exactly like a sipping sound or sound of boiling water. BG]; perhaps also compare Sechelt /məɬqʷát/ *to boil (as water)* B77:67 and Sechelt /məɬuqʷ-úm/ *to boil (as water)* T77:26.

<**lhó:tqwem**>, cts //ɬá[-·-]t=qʷ=əm//, WATR ['*boiling (currently)*'], SD, FOOD, semantic environment ['of a pot, of potatoes, etc.'], (<**=:= (lengthening)**> *continuative*), phonology: lengthening, syntactic analysis: intransitive verb, attested by AC, Elders Group (3/1/72), also <**lhótqwem**>, //ɬát=qʷ=əm//, attested by MH, example: <**lhótqwem ta' sqá:wth.**>, //ɬát=qʷ=əm t-ɛʔ s=qɛ́·wθ//, /'*Your potatoes are boiling.*'/, attested by MH.

<**lhetqwá:ls**>, sas //ɬət=qʷ=ɛ́·ls//, WATR ['*to boil*'], SD, FOOD, (<**=á:ls**> *structured activity non-continuative*), phonology: vowel-shift to schwa-grade of root with strong grade of suffix, syntactic analysis: intransitive verb, attested by Elders Group (3/1/72).

<**lhotqsélem**>, ABDF /'*sniff (a person, like with a cold, etc.)*'/, *see* lhot.

<**lhótqwem**>, WATR ['*boil water*'], *see* lhot.

<**lhó:tqwem**>, WATR ['*boiling (currently)*'], *see* lhot.

<**lhóth'**>, free root //ɬáθ'//, ABDF /'*(have a) chronic skin disease marked by reddish skin and itching, have "seven-year itch"*'/, ASM ['said to often last for seven years'], comment: ("seven-year itch" is a nick-name for the disease but the disease is not the same as English "seven-year itch" which is really "a desire after seven years of marriage to commit adultery"), syntactic analysis: intransitive verb, attested by Elders Group (2/8/78), also <**lhóts'**>, //ɬác'//, attested by EB, Deming.

<**slhóth'**>, dnom //s=ɬáθ'//, ABDF /'*scabies (a skin disease), ("seven-year itch", itch lasting seven years [Deming 2/7/80])*'/, (<**s=**> *nominalizer*), syntactic analysis: nominal, attested by Elders Group (2/8/78), also /'*"seven-year itch", itch lasting seven years*'/, attested by Deming (2/7/80).

<**lhó:yel**>, df //ɬá·y=əl or ɬ=á·yəl//, WETH ['*getting dusk*'], TIME, literally /'extract a portion of =daylight'/, lx <**=ó:yel**> *daylight* (compare <**=úyel**> and <**s=wá:yel ~ s=wàyèl**> *day, sky*, possibly <**=el**> *get, become)*, syntactic analysis: intransitive verb, attested by IHTTC.

<**lhő:me**>, free root //ɬó·mə//, EB /'*clover*, prob. both *white clover* and *red clover*'/, ['prob. both *Trifolium repens* and *Trifolium pratense*'], ASM ['has white flowers, the leaf is clover, thin, shiny, can see through it; both white- and red-flowering varieties introduced by non-Indians; some Stó:lō now each the red flowers raw'], borrowed from English [kɬóvɚ] *clover*, phonology: lh from the allophone of English /l/, /v/ is usually borrowed as /m/ and final /r/ is just dropped in borrowings (perhaps after British and American r-less pronunciations), syntactic analysis: nominal, attested by Elders Group.

<**lhōwth'ám**>, CLO /'*take off one's clothes, undress*'/, *see* lhewíth'a.

<**lhp'ótl'em**>, PE ['*to smoke a pipe*'], *see* p'ótl'em.

<**lhqá:lts'**>, df //ɬqɛ́·lc' or ɬq=ɛ́·lc'//, WETH ['*moon* (possibly *one of the quarters)*'], root meaning unknown unless lheq *join together*, possibly <**=á:lts'**> *moon* as in <**lhxwá:lth'ts'**> *third month since*, syntactic analysis: nominal, attested by AC, DM (12/4/64), other sources: ES /ɬqɛ́·lc'/, JH /ɬqe·lc'/, Salish cognate: Squamish /ɬqáyc'/ *moon, month* W73:177, K67:327, example: <**les hó:ys te lhqá:lts'**>, //lɛ-s há·y-s tə ɬqɛ́·lc'//, /'*the old moon, the last quarter (moon)*'/, literally /'it's going to finish the moon (quarter)'/, attested by DM (12/4/64),

<**lhqéletel**>, CAN /'*anchor-line, mooring-line, bow-line, what is used to tie up a canoe*'/, *see* lhqé:ylt.

<**lhqé:ylt**>, pcs //ɬəq=í·l=T//, incs, CAN ['*tie it up (of a canoe)*'], probably root <**lheq**> *join together*, (<**=í:l**> *get, become, go, come, inceptive*, <**=t**> *purposeful control transitivizer*), phonology: zero grade of root with strong grade or *durative* of suffix, syntactic analysis: transitive verb, attested by Elders Group, Salish cognate: Squamish /ɬqə́nʔ-at/ *to anchor* W73:5, K69:70, example: <**lhqé:yltchxw ta' sléxwelh.**>, //ɬq=í·l=T-c-x^{w} t-ɛʔ s=ləx^{w}əɬ//, /'*Tie up your canoe.*'/, attested by Elders Group (3/5/80).

<**lhqéletel**>, df //ɬq=i[=Aə́=]l=təl//, CAN /'*anchor-line, mooring-line, bow-line, what is used to tie up a canoe*'/, literally /'device to tie up (a canoe) (get joined together (of a canoe))'/, probably <**é-ablaut**> *derivational or resultative*, lx <**=tel**> *device to*, syntactic analysis: nominal, attested by EB, Elders on raft trip (AK, AD, SP), also <**lhqé:yltel**>, //ɬq=í·l=təl//, attested by Elders Group (3/5/80), Salish cognate: Squamish /ɬqə́nʔ-tn/ *anchor* and /ɬəqnʔ-ə́wiɬ-tn/ *anchor-line* W73:5, K69:70, example: <**Alwís Lhqéletel**>, //ʔɛlwís-s ɬq=ə́lə=təl//, /'*Alwis's Bow-line, the name of the second creek south of Suka Creek on the east side of the Fraser River*'/, ASM ['named after Alwís, a man who tied his canoe to the mountain above this creek in the great Flood, the CN Railway has a bridge over it'] (compare <**Alwís**), attested by AK, AD, SP (all on raft trip 8/30/77).

<**lhqó:la ~ lhqó:le**>, ABFC ['*be thirsty*'], *see* qó:.

<**Lhq'á:lets**>, df //ɬq'ɛ́·=ləc or ɬɛ́·q'=M1=ləc or ɬəq'=ɛ́·ləc//, PLN /'*Vancouver, B.C.*'/, literally (perhaps) /'*wide on the bottom/end* (of the Fraser River)'/, or perhaps /'*other route across*'/, probably root <**lhá:q'** or **lhq'á:**> *wide*, possibly root <**lheq'**> *opposite, other side, across* (possibly root as in <**lheq'ewílh**> *opposite side of house on inside)*, or possibly root in <**lhéq'qel**> *end of a falling/level stretch of land*, lx <**=lets**> *on the bottom*, phonology: possible metathesis, syntactic analysis: nominal, attested by AC, EB, source: place names reference file #273, Salish cognate: possibly the root in Musqueam /ɬq'-ɛ́·n/ *other end* and /ɬəq'-əlíc/ *other side (as of hill)*, possibly also Musqueam /-ɛ́l'əc ~ -əlíc ~ɛ́ʔc ~ -əl'əc/ *route across* as in /t'q'^{w}-éʔləc/ *take a short cut (as a pass between islands)* Suttles ca1984: 14.5.66, also <**Lhqá:lets'**>, //ɬqɛ́·ləc'//, attested by AC (8/23/73), example: <**tl'olsuw tés kw'e Lhq'á:lets.**>, //ƛ'á-l-s-uw tə́s k'^{w}ə ɬq'ɛ́·=ləc//, /'*And I got there to (reached) Vancouver.*'/, attested by AC, <**lám kw'e Lhq'á:lets te qèlèmèx.**>, //lɛ́=m k'^{w}ə ɬq'ɛ́·=ləc tə qə̀l=əməx^{y}//, /'*He went to Vancouver, the lucky dog.*'/, attested by EB (1/20/78).

<**lhq'átsále**>, NUM ['*five people*'], *see* lheq'át ~ lhq'á:t.

<**lhq'átseqel**>, NUM ['*five containers*'], *see* lheq'át ~ lhq'á:t.

<**lhq'atsesálhp**>, NUM ['*five trees*'], *see* lheq'át ~ lhq'á:t.

<**lhq'atsesáwtxw**>, NUM ['*five houses belonging to one person*'], *see* lheq'át ~ lhq'á:t.

<**lhq'atsesélwet**>, NUM ['*five garments*'], *see* lheq'át ~ lhq'á:t.

<**lhq'atseséyiws**>, NUM [*'five (pairs of) pants'*], *see* lheq'át ~ lhq'á:t.

<**lhq'atsesíqw**>, NUM [*'five fish'*], *see* lheq'át ~ lhq'á:t.

<**lhq'átsesmó:t**>, NUM /*'five kinds, five piles* (perhaps a loose translation)'/, *see* lheq'át ~ lhq'á:t.

<**lhq'atsesóls**>, NUM /*'five spherical objects, five fruit, five rocks, five balls (five fruit in a group (as they grow on a plant) [AD])'*/, *see* lheq'át ~ lhq'á:t.

<**lhq'atsesố welh ~ lhq'atseséwelh**>, NUM /*'five canoes belonging to one person, five boats'*/, *see* lheq'át ~ lhq'á:t.

<**lhq'átsesốwes**>, NUM /*'five paddles, (by extension) five paddlers'*/, *see* lheq'át ~ lhq'á:t.

<**lhq'atses'álh**>, NUM [*'five times'*], *see* lheq'át ~ lhq'á:t.

<**lhq'atses'ó:llh**>, NUM /*'five little ones, five young (animal or human)'*/, *see* lheq'át ~ lhq'á:t.

<**lhq'átssámets'**>, NUM /*'five ropes, five threads, five sticks, five poles'*/, *see* lheq'át ~ lhq'á:t.

<**lhq'atssí:ws**>, NUM [*'five birds'*], *see* lheq'át ~ lhq'á:t.

<**lhq'ó:tes**>, ANA [*'(have a) wide face'*], *see* lheq'át ~ lhq'á:t.

<**lhq'ó:tses**>, NUM [*'five dollars'*], *see* lheq'át ~ lhq'á:t.

<**-lhqwe**>, (//**-ɬqʷə**//), MOOD [*'polite imperative'*], comment: now rare (its semantic place largely taken over by -chexw and -chap), syntactic analysis: is; found in <**emétlhqwe.**>, //ʔəmə́t-ɬqʷə//, /*'Sit down (polite command)., (Sit down please.)'*/.

<**lhqw'áy**>, CLO [*'cedar bark skirt'*], *see* lhéqw'.

<**lhqw'íwst**>, HARV [*'peel it off (bark of a tree)'*], *see* lhéqw'.

<**lhséq'**>, SH [*'half'*], *see* séq'.

<**lhth'óméls**>, TOOL [*'to file (abrasively)'*], *see* th'óméls.

<**-lhts**>, (//**-ɬc**//), TIB /*'benefactive, do for s-o, malefactive, do on s-o'*/, syntactic comment: purposeful control transitivizer normally follows, one example of causative control transitivizer following (perhaps), also <**-lh**>, //-ɬ//, attested by EB; found in <**thiyélhtset**>, //θiy-ə[-´-]ɬc=əT//, /*'make it for s-o'*/, attested by AC, <**tháyelhtset**>, //θi[-Aɛ́-]y-əɬc=əT//, /*'making it for s-o'*/, attested by AC, example: <**qó:lhchethóxes te qó:.**>, //qá·-ɬc=əT-áxʸ-əs or qá·=əɬcɛ=T-áxʸ-əs) tə qá·//, /*'He brought me the water. (fetch/pack water for s-o)'*/, syntactic comment: benefactive with direct object np, attested by AC; found in <**thiyélhchetlha.**>, //θiy=ə́ɬc=əT-ɬɛ//, /*'Make it for him., Fix it for him.'*/, attested by this and remaining examples by EB, <**thiyélhtsthóxchexw.**>, //θiy-ə[-´-]ɬc=əT-áxʸ-c-əxʷ//, /*'(You) make it for me.'*/, example: <**tl'es thiyélhtstes te sqwemá:y.**>, //ƛ'ə-s θiy-ə[-´-]ɬc=əT-əs tə s=qʷəm=ɛ́·y//, /*'He made it for the dog.'*/, syntactic comment: benefactive with indirect object np; found in <**iléqelhtstó:lxwlha.**>, //ʔiləq-əɬc=T-á·lxʷ-ɬɛ//, /*'Buy it for us.'*/, example: <**tl'es iléqelhtstes tl' Bill te sqwemá:y.**>, //ƛ'a-s ʔilə́q-əɬc=T-əsƛ' Bill tə s=qʷəm=ɛ́·y//, /*'Bill bought it for the dog.'*/, syntactic comment: benefactive with subject np and indirect object np, <**kwá:lxelhtsthóxes thútl'ò.**>, //kʷɛ́·l=xʸ=əɬc=T-áxʸ-əs θə=w=ƛ'á//, /*'She hid it for me. (hide s-th for s-o)'*/, syntactic comment: benefactive purposeful control inanimate object preferred, syntactic comment: benefactive with subject np (independent pronoun), <**kwá:lxelhtstem thútl'ò.**>, //kʷɛ́·l=xʸ=əɬc=T-əm θə=w=ƛ'á//, /*'It was hidden for her.'*/, syntactic comment: benefactive purposeful control inanimate object preferred, syntactic comment: benefactive with indirect object np (independent pronoun), syntactic comment: passive of benefactive; found in <**kwá:lxelhtsthométsel.**>, //kʷɛ́·l=xʸ=əɬc=T-ámə-c-əl//, /*'I hide it for you.'*/, syntactic comment: benefactive purposeful control inanimate object

preferred, <**ts'ekwx̱elhtsthóxchexw.**>, //c’əkʷ=x̣-əɬc=T-áxʸ-c-əxʷ//, /*'(You) fry it for me.'*/, syntactic comment: benefactive follows lexical suffixes, <**qw'emewselhtsthóxchexw.**>, //q’ʷəm=əws-əɬc=T-áxʸ-c-əxʷ//, /*'Pluck it for me.'*/, syntactic comment: benefactive follows lexical suffixes, <**qwélselhtstlha.**>, //qʷə́ls=əɬc=T-ɬɛ//, /*'Boil it for s-o (him/her/them).'*/, example: <**qwélselhtstes the slhálí te swáqeths.**>, //qʷə́ls=əɬc=T-əs θə s=ɬɛ́l=iy tə s=wɛ́q=əθ-s//, /*'The woman boiled it for her husband.'*/, syntactic comment: benefactive with subject np and indirect object np, <**píxwelhtstes te swíyeqe.**>, //píxʷ-əɬc=T-əs tə s=wɛ[=Aí=]q=ə//, /*'He/She/They brushed it for the man.'*/, syntactic comment: benefactive with indirect object np, <**lhíts'elhtsthométselcha te sméyeth.**>, //ɬíc’-əɬc=T-ámə-c-əl-cɛ tə s=mɛ́yəθ//, /*'I'll cut off the meat for you. (cut it off for s-o)'*/, syntactic comment: benefactive with direct object np; found in <**tsel yéqwelht.**>, //c-əl yə́qʷ-əɬ(c)=T//, /*'I burned it for him/her/them. (burn it for s-o)'*/, <**yeqwelhthóxchexw.**>, //yə́qʷ-əɬ(c)=T-áxʸ-c-əxʷ//, /*'Burn it for me. (urging imperative)'*/, example: <**p'ő̃wiyelhtsthóxchexw te(l) s(e)qíws.**>, //p’ów=iy-əɬ(c)=T-áxʸ-c-əxʷ tə(-l) s(ə)q=íws//, /*'Patch my pants for me.'*/, syntactic comment: benefactive with direct object np, <**petámelhtsthóxchexw we'ésulh xwe'í: tel s'ò:m.**>, //pətɛ́m-əɬ(c)=T-áxʸ-c-əxʷ wə-ʔə́-s-uɬ xʷə=ʔí· tə-l s=ʔà·m//, /*'Ask for me if my order is in.'*/, syntactic comment: benefactive with direct object subordinate clause; found in <**mà:lalhtsthóxchexw.**>, //mɛ́·lɛ-əɬ(c)=T-áxʸ-c-əxʷ//, /*'Bait it for me. (bait it for s-o)'*/, <**kwúlhtsthóxes.**>, //kʷú-əɬ(c)=T-áxʸ-əs//, /*'He took it for me. (take it for s-o)'*/, <**tseléqelhts**>, //cələ́q-əɬc//, /*'divide it in half with s-o (for s-o)'*/, example: <**qó:qelhtsthóxes tel tí.**>, //qá·=C_1ə-əɬ(c)=T-áxʸ-əs tə-l tí//, /*'He/She drank my tea on me. (drink it on s-o)'*/, (semological comment: malefactive), <**chexw lekwólhtsthóx tel sx̱éle.**>, //c-əxʷ ləkʷ-ə[=Aá=]ɬ(c)=T-áxʸ tə-l s=x̣ə́lə//, /*'You broke my leg for me. (break a bone/stick for s-o)'*/, (semological comment: malefactive), syntactic comment: benefactive with direct object np, syntactic comment: durative benefactive, <**ílhstexwchexwò te sqwemá:y.**>, //ʔí-ɬ(c)=sT-əxʷ-c-əxʷ-à tə s=qʷəm=ɛ́·y//, /*'Leave it here for the dog. (leave it here for s-o)'*/, syntactic comment: benefactive causative, <**tl'es ílhstexwes te sqwemá:y.**>, //ƛ’ə-s ʔí-ɬ(c)=sT-əxʷ-əs tə s=qʷəm=ɛ́·y//, /*'That's what he left here for the dog.'*/, contrast <**ístexw**> *leave s-th here*, syntactic comment: benefactive causative; found in <**q'áwelh**>, //q’ɛ́w-əɬ//, /*'pay for s-th'*/, contrast <**q'awét**> *pay s-o*, <**mamíyelhtel**>, //mɛ[-C_1ə-´-]y-əɬ(c)=T-əl//, /*'helping each other, helping one another'*/, syntactic comment: benefactive reciprocal.

<**lhts'á:ls**>, HARV /*'to cut wood (with a saw), saw wood, (to cut [as structured activity] [Deming)'*/, *see* lhíts' ~ lhí:ts'.

<**lhts'élqsel**>, ABDF [*'cut off the tip of one's nose'*], *see* lhíts' ~ lhí:ts'.

<**lhts'ó:ythel**>, ABDF [*'cut on the mouth'*], *see* lhíts' ~ lhí:ts'.

<**lhulhá**>, df //ɬi=wəɬ=ɛ́// or possibly free root, TIME /*'day before yesterday'*/, possibly <**lhi**> *when* or <**lhe= ~ lh=**> *use, extract, extract a portion*), possibly <**welh ~ ulh**> *already*, possibly <**-à**> *later* or <**á**> *recent past tense*, syntactic analysis: adverb, attested by AC, example: <**tsel má:ythome kw'e tseláqelhelh qe lhulhá.**>, //c-əl mɛ́·y=T-ámə k’ʷə cəlɛ́q=əɬ=əɬ qə ɬuɬɛ́//, /*'I helped you yesterday or the day before yesterday.'*/, attested by AC.

<**lhuwth'á:m**>, CLO [*'undressing'*], *see* lhewíth'a.

<**lhuwth'á:mestexw**>, CLO [*'undress s-o'*], *see* lhewíth'a.

<**lhuwth'ím**>, CLO /*'undress in front of someone, strip-tease'*/, *see* lhewíth'a.

<**lhwélep**>, df //ɬ=wə́l[=M2=]ə=p or ɬ=w=ə́l(=)əp//, [ɬwɪ́ləp], PRON /*'it is you (pl.), it is you folks, it is you people, it is you all'*/, possibly <**lh=**> meaning uncertain, perhaps *person*, possibly <**metathesis type 2 on the consonants**> *derivational*, possibly <**else =él(=)ep**> *second person plural*, probably with <**=él=**> *plural*, possibly <**=(e)p**> *second person plural subject*, possibly root <**léwe**> *you (sg.)* possibly root with metathesis or <**w**> (empty root, no meaning, holds affixes), syntactic analysis:

independent verbal pronoun, attested by AC, example: <**lhwélepcha o eyálewet**>, //ɬ=wə́ləp-cɛ ʔa ʔɛy=ɛ́ləw=əT//, /'*You people will do it yourselves.*'/, attested by AC, <**lhwélep l siyáya.** (or) **lhwélepel siyáya.**>, //ɬ=wə́ləp l s=iy=ɛ́yɛ (or) ɬ=w=ə́ləp-əl s-iy=ɛ́yɛ//, /'*You people are my friends., You all are my friends.*'/, attested by AC.

<**talhwélep**>, ds //tɛ=ɬ=wə́ləp//, PRON /'*you (pl.), you folks, you people*'/, (<**ta=**> *nominalizer*) (compare <**ta=lh=límelh**> *us* and <**ōwé=ta=lh**> *nobody, no-one)*, syntactic analysis: inp, attested by AC, Deming, others, also <**talhléwep**>, //ta=ɬ=lə́wə=p//, attested by BJ (12/5/64), other sources: ES /tɛlhləwə́p/ but Musqueam /tɛɬwə́ləp/ and Cowichan /θɛp'ɛɬwə́ləp/, example: <**talhwélepel siyáya**>, //tɛ=ɬ=wə́ləp-əl s=iy=ɛ́yɛ//, /'*you people my friends*'/, usage: used often in speeches, attested by AC, Deming, others, <**kw'í:lchap talhwélép?**>, //k'^{w}í·l-c-ɛp tɛ=ɬ=wə́ləp//, /'*How many are you?*'/, attested by AC, <**ts'áts'eltsel xwoyíwel tel sqwálewel kw'els me xwe'í sq'o talhluwep (ey l sí:yáye, l sí:yaye sí:yálm).**>, //c'ɛ́[=C_1ə=]l-c-əl x^{w}=ɛ[=Aá=]y=íwəl t-əl s=q^{w}ɛ̀l=əwəl k'^{w}-əl-s mə x^{w}ə=ʔí s=q'á tɛ=ɬ=lə́wə=p (ʔɛ́y l s=i[=´·=]yɛ́=yə, l s=i[=´·=]yɛ́yə s=i[=´·=]y=ɛ̀m)//, /'*I'm very happy to come here at this gathering my (good friends, dear friends).*'/, literally /'I am very happy the -my thoughts/feelings that -I come arrive/come here gathered together with you folks (good my friends, my friends dear (plural))'/, attested by Deming (5/18/78).

<**tl'alhwélep**>, ds //ƛ'ɛ=ɬ=wə́ləp//, PRON /'*you folks (object of preposition), to you folks, with you folks*'/, (<**tl'a=**> *object of preposition*) (compare <**tl'alhlímelh**> *us (obj. of prep.)*, <**tl'a'á('a)ltha**> *me (obj. of prep.), tl'eléwe> you (sg.)(obj. of prep.)*, and <**tl'**> *demonstrative article, sometimes generic preposition*), syntactic analysis: independent object of prepositional verb, attested by AC, also <**tl'alhléwep**>, //ƛ'ɛ=ɬ=lə́wə=p//, attested by EB, example: <**stetís tl'alhwélep.**>, //s=C_1ə=tə[=Aí=]sƛ'ɛ=ɬ=lə́wə=p//, /'*She's close to you all., She's near to you all.*'/, attested by AC, <**ístexwchel ó í tl'alhéwep.**>, //ʔí=sT-əx^{w}-c-əl ʔà ʔí ƛ'ɛ=ɬ=lə́wə=p//, /'*I leave it with you folks.*'/, attested by EB.

<**lhxwá:le ~ lhxwále**>, NUM ['*three people*'], *see* lhí:xw.

<**lhxwáléws**>, EB ['*vanilla leaf*'], *see* lhí:xw.

<**lhxwálews**>, NUM ['*three leaves*'], *see* lhí:xw.

<**lhxwá:lth'ts**>, NUM ['*third month since*'], *see* lhí:xw.

<**lhxwá:lh**>, NUM /'*three times, thrice*'/, *see* lhí:xw.

<**lhxwá:lhp**>, NUM ['*three trees*'], *see* lhí:xw.

<**lhxwámeth'**>, NUM /'*three ropes, three threads, three sticks, three poles, (three long narrow objects)*'/, *see* lhí:xw.

<**lhxwá:wtxw**>, NUM /'*three houses, (three buildings)*'/, *see* lhí:xw.

<**lhxwelhsxále**>, NUM ['*thirty people*'], *see* lhí:xw.

<**lhxwíws**>, NUM ['*three birds*'], *see* lhí:xw.

<**lhxwó:lh**>, NUM /'*three canoes, three wagons, three conveyances (any form of transportation), three boats*'/, *see* lhí:xw.

<**lhxwő:wes**>, NUM /'*three paddles, three paddlers*'/, *see* lhí:xw.

<**lhx̱étem**>, ABDF ['*stiff (of body)*'], *see* lhéx̱.

<**Lhx̱é:ylex**>, PLN ['*Doctor's Point on northwest shore Harrison Lake*'], *see* lhéx̱.

<**lhx̱eylexlómet**>, ABFC ['*stand up (by oneself)*'], *see* lhéx̱.

<**lhx̲wélqsel**>, ABDF ['*(get/have a) runny nose*'], *see* lhex̲w.

<**lhx̲wélhcha**>, ABFC ['*to spit*'], *see* lhex̲w.

M

<**mà**>, free root //mɛ̀//, EFAM /'*(meaning uncertain), (*perhaps *right, correct)*'/, syntactic analysis: particle?, attested by Elders Group, example: <**lí mà?**>, //lí mɛ̀//, /'*Is that right?*'/, attested by Elders Group, Salish cognate: perhaps Nooksack /mæ/ /'*(meaning uncertain), (*perhaps *then, until)*'/.

<**má ~ má'-**>, free root //mɛ́ ~ mɛ́ʔ=//, MC ['*come off*'], ANA, phonology: allomorph má' before vowels, syntactic analysis: intransitive verb, attested by Elders Group, example: <**lí mà?**>, //lí mɛ̀//, /'*Did it come off?*'/, phonology: downstepping, attested by Elders Group, <**me má te yélés.**>, //mə mɛ́ tə yə́lə́s//, /'*The tooth came out.*'/, attested by EB,

<**ma'álésem**>, mdls //mɛʔ=ə́lə́s=əm or mɛ́ʔ=ə[=M2=]lə́s=əm//, [mæʔɛ́lísm], ABDF /'*pulled out (of tooth or teeth), (have one's tooth pulled out)*'/, lx <**=élés ~ =elís**> *tooth, teeth, on the tooth/teeth,* (<**=em**> *middle voice*), phonology: assimilation of the first vowel of the suffix (<**é**>) to the final vowel of the root (<**á**>), glottal-stop insertion after vowel-final root; another explanation of the first stressed vowel could be metathesis (that is, //mɛ́ʔ=ə[=M2=]lə́s=əm//) which would account for the stress-shift from the root to the first syllable of a suffix which seldom (if ever) allows stress on the first syllable (only on the second) and which is not attested elsewhere with an initial <**a**> /ɛ/ vowel; or instead of processes one could say that <**má**> has allomorph <**má'**> before vowels (vowel-initial suffixes); a fourth possibility is that the root allomorph here is <**ma'á**> with an echo-vowel; historically the glottal stop is probably present in the root and lost except before vowels, syntactic analysis: intransitive verb.

<**ma'elétstem**>, pcs //mɛʔ=ələ́c(əl)=T-əm//, ABDF /'*castrated, he was castrated*'/, lx <**=elétsel ~ =átsel**> *on the testicles,* (<**=t**> *purposeful control transitivizer*), (<**=em**> *passive*), phonology: consonant-loss and vowel-loss of final <**el**> in any suffix or root by regular rule before <**=(e)t**> transitivizer and several other suffixes, syntactic analysis: transitive verb in passive > intransitive verb, attested by DF (on Banff trip 8/30/78), Salish cognate: Musqueam /-ələcən ~ -éləcən ~ -écən/ *testicles* (Suttles ca1984:14.5.68).

<**xwemá**>, incs //xʷə=mɛ́//, MC ['*open*'], semantic environment ['store, business, prob. box, door, etc.'], ECON, BLDG, SOC, (<**xwe=**> *become, get*), syntactic analysis: intransitive verb, attested by IHTTC, example: <**li xwels xwemá te shxwiymálé?**>, //li xʷəl-s xʷə=mɛ́ tə s=xʷiym=ɛ́lə́//, /'*Is the store still open?*'/, dialects: *Chill.*, attested by OW and AH (Deming).

<**shxwemá**>, stvi //s=xʷə=mɛ́//, MC ['*it's open*'], semantic environment ['box, store, business, building, door'], ECON, BLDG, HHG ['*be open (at the top)*'], SOC, DESC, (<**s=**> *stative*), syntactic analysis: intransitive verb, adjective/adjectival verb?, attested by IHTTC, EB.

<**xwema'à:ls**>, sas //xʷə=mɛʔ=ɛ̀·ls//, BLDG ['*open the door*'], (<**=á:ls ~ =à:ls**> *structured activity non-continuative*), phonology: possible downstepping in the suffix stress if =à:ls is not an allomorph, syntactic analysis: intransitive verb, attested by IHTTV.

<**xwéma'à:ls**>, dnom //xʷə=´=mɛʔ=ɛ̀·ls//, BLDG ['*doorman*'], SOCT, (<**=´=**> *nominalizer*), phonology: stress-shift, syntactic analysis: nominal, attested by IHTTC.

<**shxwema'ámel**>, dnom //s=xʷə=mɛʔ=ɛ́məl//, HHG ['*empty container (like bottles esp. if there's lots)*'], (<**s=**> *nominalizer*, xwe= *become, get*), lx <**=ámel ~ =ómel ~ =emel**> *part, portion, member*, syntactic analysis: nominal, attested by IHTTC.

<**xwmá:m or lexwmá:m**>, df //xʷə=mɛ́(ʔ)=əm or ləxʷ=xʷə=mɛ́(ʔ)=əm//, DESC /'*open (of a bottle, basket, etc.)*'/, MC, HHG, (<**=em**> *intransitivizer* or *middle voice*), possibly <**lexw=**> *always* or possibly the <**le**> may be a separate word (*past tense third person subject)*, phonology: the

speaker who gave this word here dropped the glottal-stop even before a vowel which allowed vowel merger, or if the suffix took the form of =m here the glottal stop would either be dropped or converted to length; either way the result would be the same; if there is the lexw= prefix then consonant merger takes place; vowel-loss of the e in xwe= also, syntactic analysis: intransitive verb, attested by CT.

<**shxwemám**>, stvi //s=xʷə=mɛ́=m//, DESC ['*be empty*'], (<**s=**> *stative*, xwe= *become, get*), (<**=m ~ =em**> *intransitivizer* or *middle voice*), phonology: these speakers here lose the glottal stop without vowel merger, and apparently have =m rather than =em (other derivations show either glottal stop or length from vowel merger) (compare <**shxwema'ám**> *an opener*, syntactic analysis: adjective/adjectival verb, attested by IHTTC.

<**shxwéma'ám**>, dnom //s=xʷə= ´=mɛʔ=ə[=Aɛ́=]m//, strs, HHG /'*an opener, can-opener, bottle-opener*'/, ACL, (<**á-ablaut**> *resultative*, <= ´=> *nominalizer*), (<**=em**> *intransitivizer*), phonology: ablaut, stress-shift, syntactic analysis: nominal, attested by IHTTC.

<**shxwémeqel**>, dnom //s=xʷə= ´=mɛ=qəl//, HHG /'*an opener, can-opener, bottle-opener*'/, ACL, (<**s=**> *stative* or *nominalizer*), (<= ´=> *nominalizer*), lx <**=eqel ~ =qel**> *container*, phonology: stress-shift, vowel-shift (of root vowel to schwa-grade), syntactic analysis: nominal, attested by AD.

<**shxwémeqèyls**>, sas //s=xʷə= ´=mɛ=qə(l)=í·ls//, HHG /'*an opener, can-opener, bottle-opener*'/, ACL, (<**=í:ls**> *structured activity (nominal?/resultative?)),* phonology: stress-shift, downstepping of stress on suffix, consonant-loss of l before -í:l, -í:ls, -(e)t, and some other suffixes, vowel merger, syntactic analysis: nominal, attested by AD.

<**xwemá:qet**>, pcs //xʷə=mɛ́=əqə(l)=əT//, HHG /'*take a cover off, take it off (a cover of a container), open it (bottle, box, kettle, book, etc.)*'/, (<**xwe=**> *become, get*), lx <**=eqel**> *container*, (<**=et**> *purposeful control transitivizer*), phonology: consonant-loss of l before =et, vowel merger (twice), (if =eqel has allomorph =qel here instead then length would have to be in an allomorph of root má', that is má: before consonants), compare <**xwemá:t**> *open it* for possible long allomorph also, syntactic analysis: transitive verb, attested by IHTTC, Deming, EB, Elders Group, example: <**xwmá:qet te kw'óxwe**>, //xʷə=mɛ́·=qə(l)=əT tə k'ʷáxʷə//, /'*open a box*'/, attested by EB, <**xwmá:qetlha ta' pékw.**>, //xʷə=mɛ́·=qə(l)=əT-ɬɛ t-ɛʔ pə́kʷ//, /'*Open your book.*'/, attested by Elders Group, <**xwmá:qet ta (skú:k, lhémkiya)**>, //x̣ʷə=mɛ́·=qə(l)=əT t-ɛ (s=kú·k, ɬə́m=k=iyɛ)//, /'*Open your (cooker, kettle).*'/, attested by EB.

<**xwemá:t**>, pcs //xʷə=mɛ́(·)=(ə)T//, MC ['*open it*'], (<**=(e)t**> *purposeful control transitivizer*), phonology: length either comes from vowel merger or from an allomorph of má' (//mɛ́ʔ// > /mɛ́·/ before consonants (glottal stop historically > length in Upriver Halkomelem before consonant; here the consonant is =t), syntactic analysis: transitive verb, attested by IHTTC.

<**xwmá:x**>, pcis //xʷə=mɛ́=əxʸ//, MC /'*open it (door, gate, anything)*'/, HHG, (<**=ex**> *purposeful control transtitivizer inanimate object preferred*), phonology: vowel merger, syntactic analysis: transitive verb, dialects: *Chill.*, attested by Deming, also <**xwemáx**>, //xʷə=mɛ́=(ə)xʸ//, attested by AC, also <**xwmá'x**>, //xʷ(ə)=mɛ́ʔ=xʸ//, dialects: *Sumas/Matsqui*, attested by Deming (5/20/76), example: <**xwemáx te xálh**>, //xʷə=mɛ́=(ə)xʸ tə xʸɛ́ɬ//, /'*open the door*'/, attested by AC.

<**máx**>, pcis //mɛ́=(ə)xʸ//, MC /'*take it off (of a table example), take it away (from something), take it off (of eyeglasses, of skin off an animal), take s-o off/away (from something), take s-th out (a tooth for ex.)*'/, (<**=(e)x**> *purposeful control transitivizer indefinite object preferred*), phonology: vowel-loss (in suffix), syntactic analysis: transitive verb, attested by Elders Group, AC, EB, CT, HT, example: <**máx kw'e léts'e**>, //mɛ́=xʸ k'ʷə lə́c'ə//, /'*take one off*'/, attested by Elders Group, <**máx ta st'óle'oléstel.**>, //mɛ́=xʸ t-ɛ s=t'álə=ʔalə́s=təl//, /'*Take off your eyeglasses.*'/, attested by AC, <**le**

máxes te yélés.>, //lə mɛ́=xʸ-əs tə yə́lə́s//, /'*He went (go) to take out the tooth.*'/, attested by EB, <**le máxem te yélés.**>, //lə mɛ́=xʸ-əm tə yə́lə́s//, /'*The tooth got taken out.*'/, syntactic analysis: passive of pcis, attested by EB.

<**hámex**>, cts //hɛ́-mɛ=xʸ//, MC ['*taking s-th off*'], HUNT, (<**há-**> *continuative* before resonants), phonology: vowel-reduction to schwa-grade of root after strong-grade stressed prefix, syntactic analysis: transitive verb, attested by EB, CT, HT, example: <**hámex te kw'eléws te sméyeth**>, //hɛ́=mɛ=xʸ tə k'ʷəl=ə́ws tə s=mɛ́yəθ//, /'*skin(ing) an animal, taking off the skin of an animal*'/, attested by CT, HT.

<**memáx**>, plv //C₁ə=mɛ́=xʸ//, SOC /'*to separate people fighting, to split up people fighting*'/, (<**R5=**> *plural object*), phonology: reduplication, syntactic analysis: intransitive verb, attested by EB, Salish cognate: Musqueam /məmɛ́ʔxʸ/ *remove it (plural perfective)* from /mɛ́ʔxʸ/ *remove it* Suttles ca1984: ch.7 [p.105].

<**mexlátst**>, pcs //mɛ́=xʸ=lə[=M2=]c=T or mɛ=xʸ=lɛ́c=T or mɛ=xʸ=lə[=Aɛ́=]c=T//, pcis, [mɪxʸlǽct], MC ['*take it off from the bottom of s-th (a pack for ex.)*'], lx <**=lets (~ =láts ?)**> *on the bottom*, possibly <**metathesis**> *derivational*, possibly <**á-ablaut**> *resultative*?, (<**=(e)x**> *purposeful control transitivizer inanimate object preferred*, and =t *purposeful control transitivizer*), phonology: possible metathesis, possible ablaut, syntactic analysis: transitive verb, syntactic comment: doubly transitivized stem with two purposeful control transitivizers, attested by Elders Group (3/16/77).

<**semáxel**>, strs //s=hə=mɛ́=xʸəl//, ANAH ['*(have a) bare foot*'], CLO, literally /'have taken off on the foot'/, (<**s=**> *stative*), (<**he=**> *resultative*), lx <**=xel**> *on the foot*, phonology: consonant merger, syntactic analysis: adjective/adjectival verb, attested by EB, also <**sebáxel**>, //s=hə=bɛ́=xʸəl//, phonology: b traces in DM's (and the Lorenzetto family's) speech, attested by DM (12/4/64).

<**máches**>, free root //mɛ́cəs//, [mǽč'ɪs], FIRE /'*match, matches*'/, syntactic analysis: nominal, attested by CT, HT, borrowed from English or from Chinook Jargon <matches> *match* itself of course from English <matches> Johnson 1978:363, example: <**éx̱qst te máches qesu yéqwt kw'e sísq'**>, //ʔə́x̣=qs=T tə mɛ́cəs qə-s-u yə́qʷ=T k'ʷə sí[=C₁ə=]q'//, /'*strike the match and light the kindling*'/, attested by CT, HT.

<**má:kwlh**>, possibly root //mɛ́·kʷɬ//, ABDF ['*get hurt*'], syntactic analysis: intransitive verb, attested by JL, Salish cognate: Squamish /máʔkʷɬ/ W73:147, K67:256, also <**má:kwlh ~ mákwlh**>, //mɛ́·kʷɬ ~ mɛ́kʷɬ//, attested by EB, example: <**tsel mákwlh; tsel welhéleq' la te sth'í:qel.**>, //c-əl mɛ́kʷɬ; c-əl wə=ɬə́ləq' lɛ tə s=θ'í·qəl//, /'*I got hurt; I fell splat in the mud.*'/, attested by EB.

<**mákw'a**>, bound root //mɛ́k'ʷɛ// *funeral?, to comfort?, corpse?*.

<**tsmákw'a**>, dnom //c=mɛ́k'ʷɛ//, REL ['*undertaker*'], SOCT, Elder's comment: "AK has heard this word, says it could have been originally the person who handled burials in the family grave houses", ASM ['there were also people who washed and prepared the body for the four-days mourning before burial in the grave house'], (<**ts=**> *have*), syntactic analysis: nominal, source: JH from DM, attested by AK (3/26/80), other sources: ES /cmɛ́mək'ʷɛ/ *funeral* and /šmɛ́k'ʷɛ/ *grave*.

<**smámekw'et**>, pcs //s=mɛ́[=C₁ə=]k'ʷə=T//, REL /'*comfort s-o, sympathize with s-o*'/, EFAM, (<**s=**> *stative*??), possibly <**=R1=**> *resultative*?, (<**=T**> *purposeful control transitivizer*), phonology: reduplication, syntactic analysis: transitive verb, attested by Elders Group; found in <**smámekw'ethóme**>, //s=mɛ́[=C₁ə=]k'ʷə=T-ámə//, /'*comfort you*'/.

<**smekw'e'ála**>, dnom //s=mək'ʷə=ʔɛ́lɛ//, REL ['*graveyard*'], (<**s=**> *nominalizer* or *stative*), lx <**=ála ~ =álá**> *container of*, phonology: vowel merger, syntactic analysis: nominal, attested by CT, also <**shmekw'álá**>, //š=mək'ʷə=ɛ́lɛ́//, attested by EB, other sources: ES /šmək'ʷɛ́·lɛ/ *graveyard*, Salish cognate: Squamish /smək'ʷəʔál/ *grave, dead man's cache* W73:123, K67:283.

<**má:l ~ mál**>, free root //mɛ́·l ~ mɛ́l//, KIN [*'father'*], syntactic analysis: nominal, attested by AC, BJ (5/64, 12/5/64), others, other sources: ES /mɛ́·l/, example: <**stsewó:t kwthel mál kw'es kwel:éxs lhelámes há:we.**>, //s=cəwá·t k^wθə-l mɛ́l k'^wə-s k^wəl·=əx^y-s ɬə-lɛ́=m-əs hɛ́·wə//, /*'My father knows how to shoot when he goes hunting.'*/, literally /'he knows how the (near but out of sight) -my father that -nominalizer shoot -he when- go to -subjunctive subj. 3 hunt(ing)'/, attested by AC, <**l má:l**>, //l mɛ́·l//, /*'my father'*/, attested by BJ (12/5/64).

<**smà:l**>, dmn //s=mɛ̀·l//, KIN [*'little father'*], usage: nickname, possibly <**s=**> here *diminutive/affectionate*, possibly related to <**s=**> in some terms for body parts *big*, elsewhere *nominalizer*, possibly <**stress-shift to mid-stress**> *derivational* (unless these speakers use <**mà:l**> *father*), phonology: stress-shift possibly, syntactic analysis: nominal, attested by IHTTC.

<**máma**>, dmn //C_1ɛ́=mɛ(l)//, KIN /*'grandfather (affectionate), (grampa)'*/, usage: affectionate, possibly <**R7=**> *diminutive*?, <final consonant-loss> *affectionate*?, phonology: consonant-loss, reduplication, syntactic analysis: nominal, Elder's comment: "some people say this", attested by EB.

<**mál ~ mél**>, bound root //mál ~ mə́l *be mixed up*//, Salish cognate: Squamish root /mil ~ mal/ *be mixed up* W73:177, K67:254, 256, 257, comment: possibly related is mí:l *submerge*, especially if memílets' *mixed up* were derived from it by R5= *resultative* + mí:l *submerge* + =(e)ts' *around in circles*, compare possibly root <**mí:l**> *submerge*.

<**mélmel**>, chrs //mə́l=C_1əC_2//, EFAM /*'make a mistake, blunder'*/, literally /'characteristically be mixed up'/, (<**=R2**> *characteristic),* phonology: reduplication, syntactic analysis: intransitive verb, attested by Elders Group (3/1/72), Deming (3/15/79)(SJ, MV, MC, LG), Salish cognate: Musqueam /mə́lməl/ *be confused, misidentify* under Suttles ca1984:14.6.37, Lushootseed /bálbal/ *confused, mistaken* H76:214.

<**melmeló:ythel**>, ds //məl=C_1əC_2=á·yθəl//, LANG [*'blunder in speaking'*], literally /'be mixed up in the mouth/lips'/, lx <**=ó:ythel**> *in the mouth, in the lips*, phonology: reduplication, syntactic analysis: intransitive verb, attested by Elders Group (3/1/72).

<**melmelṓws**>, ds //məl=C_1əC_2=ə́ws//, ABFC [*'get carried away and sleepy from eating too rich food'*], literally /'get mixed up in the body'/, lx <**=ṓws**> *in the body*, phonology: reduplication, syntactic analysis: intransitive verb, attested by Elders Group (3/2/77), also <**ló:metsel**>, //lá·m=əcəl//, attested by Elders Group (3/2/77).

<**melmílets'**>, df //məl=C_1əC_2=Aí=(l)əc' or C_1əC_2=mə[=Aí=]l=(l)əc'//, EFAM [*'confused'*], probably literally /'mixed up resultative in a circle'/, possibly <**=R2**> *characteristic or iterative*, or <**R3=**> *iterative*, possibly <**í-alaut**> *resultative*, possibly <**=(l)ets' ~ =(l)ts'**> *in a circle, around on itself*, phonology: reduplication, ablaut, consonant merger, syntactic analysis: intransitive verb, attested by Deming, Salish cognate: Squamish /məlmílč'/ *get mixed up (both about things and mentally)* W73:177, K67:254, 257.

<**memílets'**>, df //mə[=C_1əAí=]l=(l)əc'//, EFAM [*'mixed up'*], probably literally /'mixed up resultative in a circle'/, possibly <**=R1= and í-ablaut**> *resultative*, probably <**=(l)ets' ~ =(l)ts'**> *in a circle, around on itself*, phonology: reduplication, ablaut, consonant merger, syntactic analysis: intransitive verb, attested by Elders Group (3/1/72), comment: possibly mistranscribed for melmílets'.

<**mélets'methó:ythel**>, iecs //mə́l=(l)əc'=məT=á·yθəl//, LANG [*'mixed up in speaking'*], probably literally /' mixed up in a circle about s-th in the mouth/lips'/, possibly <**=(l)ets' ~ =(l)ts'**> *in a circle, around on itself*, possibly <**=met**> *indirect effect control transitivizer*, lx <**=ó:ythel**> *in the mouth, in the lips*, phonology: consonant merger, syntactic analysis: intransitive verb, attested by Elders Group (3/1/72) completive plus *on one occasion*).

<**malq**>, bound stem //mɛ́l=q// *forget*

<**shxwmelmálq**>, chrs //s(=)x^w=C_1əC_2=mə[=Aɛ́=]l=q or s(=)x^w=məl=C_1əC_2[=Aɛ́=]=q//, strs,

EFAM [*'forgetful'*], (<**s(=)xw=**> *stative*), possibly <**R3= or =R2**> *characteristic*, (<**á-ablaut**> *resultative*), lx <**=q ~ =élq**> *after* (as also in <**chél=q**> *fall,* <**chó:l=q=em**> *follow after,* <**tl'itl'ets'=élq=em**> *sneaking after*, and perhaps others like <**iyáq**> *change* and (with metathesis) <**ám=eq=t**> *bring s-o/s-th back);* Musqueam cognates of these and more in Suttles ca1984:14.6.37 all fit gloss *after*), phonology: reduplication, ablaut, possible consonant merger, syntactic analysis: adjective/adjectival verb, attested by BHTTC, Salish cognate: Squamish /may/ *forget*, /máy-nəxʷ/ *forgotten, have forgotten*, /s-miʔ-máyʔ ~ s-mə-miʔ-máyʔ/ *forgetful* W73:107, K67:256, 283, K69:45 and perhaps even Squamish /mál-qʷ/ *be mixed* W73:177, K67:256, Lushootseed /bálbal/ *confused, mistaken*, /báli/ *forget*, /báluqʷ/ *mixed up, entangled* H76:214.

<**málqeles**>, pncs //mə[=Aɛ́=]l=q=ələs//, rsls, EFAM /*'forgot s-th, have forgotten s-th, forgot s-o/s-th in one's mind'*/, literally /'mixed up resultative after happen to do psychological action toward s-o/s-th'/, (<**á-ablaut**> *resultative*), lx <**=q**> *after*, (<**=eles**> *psychological non-control transitivizer*), phonology: ablaut, syntactic analysis: transitive verb, attested by DC, Ben James, AD, AC, DF, Deming, example: <**tsel málqeles lis kw'í:l swáyel kwses skwetáxw li tethá yutl'ólem.**>, //c-əl mə[=Aɛ́=]l=q=ələs li-s k'ʷí·l s=wɛ́yəl kʷ-s-əs s=kʷətɛ́xʷ li tə=θɛ́ yə=uw=ƛ'á=lə=m//, /*'I've forgotten how many days they were inside there.'*/, usage: story of the flood, attested by AC.

<**málqlexw ~ málqelexw**>, ncs //mə[=Aɛ́=]l=q=l-əxʷ//, rsls, [mɛ́lqlʊxʷ ~ mɛ́lqəlʊxʷ], EFAM /*'forget s-th, forget s-o, forget s-th behind'*/, (<**á-ablaut**> *resultative or derivational*), lx <**=q**> *after*, (<**=l**> *non-control transitivizer*), (<**-exw**> *third person object*), phonology: ablaut or allomorph, syntactic analysis: transitive verb, attested by Deming, EB, DF, EK and DK (12/10/71), Elders Group, comment: DF (6/7/78) provided a nice minimal contrast between this form and málqeles; she translated málqlexw *forget s-th behind* and málqeles *forgot s-o/s-th in one's mind*, example: <**líyetsel málqlexw kw'e tewátes?**>, //lí-ə-c-əl mə[=Aɛ́=]l=q=l-əxʷ k'ʷə tə=wɛ́t=əs//, /*'Did I forget anybody?'*/, attested by Deming, <**wiyóth kw'elsu málqlexw.**>, //wə=yáθ k'ʷə-l-s-u mə[=Aɛ́=]l=q=l-əxʷ//, /*'I always forget.'*/, literally /'it's always that I contrastive forget him/her/them/it'/, attested by EB, <**málqlexw stámes**>, //mə[=Aɛ́=]l=q=l-əxʷ s=tɛ́m-əs//, /*'forget what it is'*/, attested by EB, <**látsel málqlexw.**>, //lɛ́-c-əl mə[=Aɛ́=]l=q=l-əxʷ//, /*'I forgot.'*/, literally /'I'm going to forget s-o/s-th.'/, attested by EK and DK, <**mícha xwe'í ewás lís máqelexwes.**>, //mí-cɛ xʷə=ʔí ʔəwə=ɛ́s lí-s mə[=Aɛ́=]l=q=l-əxʷ-əs//, /*'He's coming unless he forgets.'*/, literally /'he will be coming to get here if it's not that he forgets it.'/, attested by Elders Group.

<**mámelqlexw**>, cts //mə[=Aɛ́=][-C_1ə-]l=q=l-əxʷ//, rsls, EFAM [*'forgetting (s-th/s-o)'*], (<**-R1-**> *continuative*), phonology: ablaut, reduplication, syntactic analysis: transitive verb, attested by EB, example: <**wiyóth kw'elsu mámelqlexw.**>, //wə=yáθ k'ʷə-ɬ-s-u mə[=Aɛ́=][-C_1ə-]l=q=l-əxʷ//, /*'I'm always forgetting.'*/, literally /'it's always that I contrastive am forgetting s-o/s-th'/, attested by EB.

<**malqelómet**>, ncrs //mə[=Aɛ=]l=q=l-ámət//, EFAM [*'forget'*], (<**-ómet**> *reflexive*), phonology: ablaut, syntactic analysis: intransitive verb, attested by Deming.

<**lexwmálqewelh**>, ds //ləxʷ=mə[=Aɛ́=]l=q=əwəɬ or ləxʷ=mə[=Aɛ́=]l=q=əwəl=D//, EFAM [*'forgetful'*], ABDF [*'passed out (if drunk)'*], literally /'always forget on the inside/mind'/, lx <**lexw=**> *always*, lx <**=q**> *after*, lx <**=ewelh**> is from <**=ewel ~ =íwel**> *on the inside, mind,* (<**á-ablaut**> *resultative*), phonology: ablaut, devoicing of final consonant, syntactic analysis: intransitive verb, adjective/adjectival verb, attested by EB.

<**melqí:wsem**>, mdls //məl=q=í·ws=əm//, ABDF [*'to faint'*], literally /'forget one's body after/behind'/, lx <**=q**> *after, behind*, lx <**=í:ws**> *on the body, body,* (<**=em middle voice**>), syntactic analysis: intransitive verb, attested by EB, AC, example: <**lulh qwáyel te s'óthes**

yewá:lmels kwses melqí:wsem.>, //lə-u-ɬ qʷέy=əl tə s=ʔáθ=əs-s yəwέ·l=məls kʷ-s-əs məl=q=í·ws=əm//, /'*Her face is turning green before she faints.*'/, attested by AC.

<**mélqithílem**>, mdls //mə́l=q=(ə)yθ(əl)=íl=əm//, incs, LANG ['*blunder in speech*'], literally /'become mixed up after in one's speech/lips/mouth'/, lx <**=q**> *after, behind*, lx <**=ithel (< =eythel ~ =ó:ythel)**> *in the mouth, on the lips, in speech, music*, (<**=íl**> *get, become, go, come, inceptive*, <**=em**> *middle voice*), phonology: zero-grade of suffix =eythel drops e and y → i between consonants (vocalization), consonant-loss and vowel-loss (el lost automatically before =íl), syntactic analysis: intransitive verb, attested by Elders Group (3/1/72).

<**mélqeliythílem**>, mdls //mə́l=q=əl=iyθəl=íl=əm//, LANG /'*forget in speaking, forget one's words, forget a word*'/, lx <**=el=iythel**> *speaking, word, words*, (semological comment: shows minimal contrastive meaning of =el= *body-part affix-formative*), syntactic analysis: intransitive verb, attested by Elders Group (3/1/72).

<**smómeleqw**>, strs //s=mε[=AáC$_1$ə=]l=əqw//, DESC /'*mixed (of anything, vegetables, brains, etc.)*'/, ABDF ['*mixed (of brains)*'], (<**s=**> *stative*), (<**ó-ablaut**> *resultative*, <**=R1**=< *stative* or *resultative* or *continuative*), lx <**=eqw**> *on top of the head*, phonology: ablaut, reduplication, syntactic analysis: adjective/adjectival verb, attested by Deming, Salish cognate: Squamish /mál-qʷ/ *be mixed* W73:177, K67:256 Lushootseed /báluqʷ/ *mixed up, entangled* H76:214.

<**smómeleqw spíls s'élhtel sqe'óleqw**>, FOOD *V8 juice* (lit. mixed + planted + food + fruit juice), (attested by RG,EH 6/16/98 to SN, edited by BG with RG,EH 6/26/00)

<**melmóléqwet**>, plv //C$_1$əC$_2$=mə[=Aá=]l=əqʷ=əT//, pcs, MC ['*really mixed s-th up*'], FOOD, MED (<**R3=**> *plural*), (<**ó-ablaut**> *resultative*), (<**=et**> *purposeful control transitivizer*), phonology: ablaut, reduplication, updrifting, syntactic analysis: transitive verb, attested by Deming, Salish cognate: Squamish /mál-qʷ-t/ *mix (tr.)* W73:177, K67:256; found in <**melmóléqwetes.**>, //C$_1$əC$_2$=mə[=Aá=]l=əqw=əT-əs//, /'*He really mixed it up.*'/, attested by Deming.

<**melmelqwìwèl**>, chrs //məl=C$_1$əC$_2$=qʷ=ìwə̀l//, EFAM /'*forgetful, mixed up (mentally, emotionally)*'/, (<**=R2**> *characteristic*), lx <**=eqw**> *on top of the head*, lx <**=ìwèl**> *on the inside, in the mind*, phonology: reduplication, syntactic analysis: intransitive verb, attested by Deming.

<**má:la ~ má:le**>, free root //mέ·lε ~ mέ·lə//, FSH ['*bait (for fishing)*'], HUNT ['*bait (for trapline)*'], syntactic analysis: noun, attested by Elders Group (3/1/72, 6/11/75), Salish cognate: Lushootseed /bálbaliʔ/ *bait for fishing* H76:17.

<**shxwmálahá:lá**>, dnom //s(=)xʷ=mέlε=hέ·lέ//, FSH /'*fishing basket, bait basket*'/, ASM ['design very much the same as the White man's'], (<**shxw=**> *nominalizer, something that is*), lx <**=há:la (after vowel) ~ =á:la**> *container of*, syntactic analysis: nominal, attested by Elders Group.

<**má:lat**>, pcs //mέ·lε=T//, FSH /'*bait s-th (fish-line, fish-hook, fish-trap)*'/, HUNT ['*bait s-th (a trap for animals or birds)*'], (<**=t**> *purposeful control transitivizer*), syntactic analysis: transitive verb, attested by EB, Elders Group, example: <**má:latchexw tel (lhékw'tel, qwemó:thel).**>, //mέ·lε=T-c-əxʷ tə-l (ɬə́k'ʷ=təl, qʷəm=á·θəl)//, /'*You bait my (hook, fishing-line)., Bait my (hook, line).*'/, attested by EB.

<**mamá:lat**>, cts //C$_1$ε-mέ·lε=T//, FSH ['*baiting s-th (fish-line)*'], HUNT ['*baiting s-th (trap)*'], (<**R8-**> *continuative*), phonology: reduplication, syntactic analysis: transitive verb, attested by EB, Elders Group.

<**má:lalht**>, bens //mέ·lε=ɬc=T//, FSH ['*bait it for s-o*'], HUNT, (<**=lhts**> *benefactive*), phonology: consonant merger, syntactic analysis: transitive verb, attested by EB; found in <**mà:lalhthó:xchexw.**>, //mέ·lε=ɬc=T-á·xʸ-c-əxʷ//, /'*You bait it for me., Bait it for me.*'/, phonology: downstepping, consonant merger, attested by EB.

<**má:lalht**>, FSH ['*bait it for s-o*'], *see* má:la ~ má:le.

<**má:lat**>, FSH /'*bait s-th (fish-line, fish-hook, fish-trap)*'/, *see* má:la ~ má:le.

<**Máli ~ Málí**>, free root //mɛ́li ~ mɛ́lí//, N ['*Mary*'], syntactic analysis: nominal, attested by Elders Group.

<**Málí**>, df //mɛlí//, PLN ['*a village or place at Musqueam (now in Vancouver)*'], syntactic analysis: nominal, attested by Deming, borrowed from Musqueam /mɛ́l=i/, Salish cognate: Squamish /mámʔli/ *territory on which the Musqueam reserve is situated.*

<**málqeles**>, EFAM /'*forgot s-th, have forgotten s-th, forgot s-o/s-th in one's mind*'/, *see* mál ~ mél.

<**malqelómet**>, EFAM ['*forget*'], *see* mál ~ mél.

<**málqlexw ~ málqelexw**>, EFAM /'*forget s-th, forget s-o, forget s-th behind*'/, *see* mál ~ mél.

<**má:lt**>, bound root //mɛ́·lt//, meaning unknown

<**smá:lt**>, dnom //s=mɛ́·lt//, LAND /'*stone, rock (any size), mountain*'/, (<**s=**> *nominalizer*), syntactic analysis: nominal, attested by AC, BJ (5/64, 12/5/64)), DM (12/4/64), CT, HT, Deming, other sources: ES /smɛ́·lt/, also <**smált**>, //s=mɛ́lt//, attested by AC, EB, example: <**(híkw, tsítselh) smált**>, //(hík^w, cí[=C_1ə=]ɬ) s=mɛ́lt//, /'*(big, high) mountain*'/, attested by AC, <**latsel kw'íyeqel lá(m) te smált.**>, //lɛ-c-əl k'^{w}íy=əqəl lɛ́(=m) tə s=mɛ́lt//, /'*I'm going up the mountain.*'/, <**Skwím Smá:lt**>, //s=k^{w}ím s=mɛ́·lt//, PLN, /'*Twin Sisters Mountain*'/, literally /'red mountain'/, ASM ['so named because the mountain does often appear reddish'], attested by Deming (8/15/75), <**tl'osu tés te smá:lt.**>, //ƛ'a-s-u tə́s tə s=mɛ́·lt//, /'*and so they got to (get to, reach) the mountain.*'/, attested by AC, <**sqewós te smá:lt kws me p'éth' te syó:qwem telí tí tl'ó le qewétem.**>, //s=qəw=ás-s tə s=mɛ́·lt k^w-s mə p'ə́θ' tə s=yá·q^w=əm təlí tí ƛ'a lə qəw=ə́T-əm//, /'*It's the warm side of the mountain that the sun just comes out on from there so that is was warmed.*'/, attested by CT, HT, <**lám kw' smált kw' Máli.**>, //lɛ́=m k'^{w} s=mɛ́lt k'^{w} mɛ́li//, /'*Mary went to the mountain.*'/, attested by EB.

<**smámelet**>, dmn //s=mɛ́[=C_1ə=]][=ə=]t//, LAND /'*little stone, pebble, little rock hill, small rock mountain (like in the Fraser River in the canyon)*'/, (<**=R1=**> *diminutive*, <**=e=**> *derivational* unless epenthetic), phonology: reduplication, epenthesis perhaps, syntactic analysis: nominal, attested by Elders Group (3/15/72), AC.

<**smelmá:lt**>, pln //s=C_1əC_2=mɛ́·lt//, LAND ['*a lot of rocks*'], (<**R3=**> *plural (many)*), phonology: reduplication, syntactic analysis: nominal, attested by AC, Elders Group, example: <**qéx̱ te smelmá:lt.**>, //qə́x̣ tə s=C_1əC_2=mɛ́·lt//, /'*(There's) a lot of rocks.*'/, attested by AC, <**lhq'átses smelmá:lt**>, //ɬq'ɛ́=cəs s=C_1əC_2=mɛ́·lt//, /'*five rocks*'/, attested by Elders Group.

<**smemá:lt**>, dmpn //s=C_1ə=mɛ́·lt//, LAND ['*(many small rocks)*'], (<**R5=**> *diminutive plural*), phonology: reduplication, syntactic analysis: nominal, attested by AC (10/21/71).

<**smeltáléqel**>, df //s=mɛlt=ɛ́lə́=qəl//, ANA ['*kidneys*'], literally perhaps /'container of stones in the head/end of a river'/, lx <**=álá ~ =álé**> *container of*, lx <**=qel**> *in the head or end (of a river),* phonology: vowel-shift to schwa-grade of root before strong-grade suffix, syntactic analysis: nominal, attested by Elders Group (7/27/75), also <**meltáléqel**>, //mɛlt=ɛ́lə́=qəl//, attested by SJ (Deming 4/17/80).

<**malyí**>, free root //mɛlyí//, KIN /'*marry, get married*'/, SOC, syntactic analysis: intransitive verb, attested by AC, borrowed from Chinook Jargon /maliyé/ *to marry* itself from French <marier> *to marry, perform a marriage for* Johnson78:363 and <se marier> *to get married.*

<**smamalyí**>, strs //s=mɛ[=C_1ə=]lyí or s=C_1ɛ=mɛlyí//, KIN ['*be married*'], SOC, (<**s=**> *stative*),

possibly <**R8= or =R1=**> *resultative*, phonology: reduplication and (if doubling infix #1 with e) assimilation to preceding vowel or misrecording of vowel in the reduplication (a sic for e), syntactic analysis: adjective/adjectival verb, attested by AC, example: <**smamalyí te swíyeqe.**>, //s=C_1ɛ=mɛlyí tə s=wíqə//, /'*The man is married.*'/, attested by AC.

<**malyítses**>, ds //mɛlyí=cəs//, ANAH ['*third finger*'], literally /'get married on the hand'/, lx <**=tses**> *on the hand*, syntactic analysis: nominal, attested by Elders Group, AC.

<**malyítses**>, ANAH ['*third finger*'], *see* malyí.

<**máma**>, KIN /'*grandfather (affectionate), (grampa)*'/, *see* má:l ~ mál.

<**mamá:lat**>, FSH ['*baiting s-th (fish-line)*'], *see* má:la ~ má:le.

<**mamastiyexw** (or better) **mémestiyexw**>, HUMC ['*kids*'], *see* mestíyexw.

<**mameláselh**>, KIN /'*her deceased children, (his deceased children)*'/, *see* méle ~ mél:a.

<**mámele**>, KIN /'*children (kinterm, someone's), sons, daughters*'/, *see* méle ~ mél:a.

<**mámelehà:yèlhs te sisemóye**>, EZ ['*honeycomb*'], *see* méle ~ mél:a.

<**mámelehò:llh**>, ANA /'*egg (of bird, fowl)*'/, *see* méle ~ mél:a.

<**mámelqlexw**>, EFAM ['*forgetting (s-th/s-o)*'], *see* mál ~ mél.

<**mámeqe**>, WETH /'*it's snowing, (snow is accumulating)*'/, *see* máqa ~ máqe.

<**mámeq'em**>, ABFC ['*jumping (of fish)*'], *see* máq'em.

<**mameth'álem**>, EFAM /'*lying, telling a lie, (bluffing [BHTTC])*'/, *see* máth'el.

<**mameth'élexw**>, EFAM /'*doubting s-o/s-th, be not believing s-o/s-th*'/, *see* máth'el.

<**mámetsel**>, ANA ['*testicles*'], *see* mátsel.

<**mamíyet**>, SOC ['*helping*'], *see* máy.

<**mamts'ólthet**>, EFAM ['*think one(self) is smart*'], *see* máth'el.

<**máqa ~ máqe**>, free root //mɛ́qɛ ~ mɛ́qə//, WETH /'*fallen snow, (year)*'/, TIME ['*year*'], semantic environment ['numerals, counting, age'], phonology: máqa at hyper-slow speed, máqe at normal speed, syntactic analysis: nominal, attested by AC, Elders Group, Deming, EB, also <**má:qa**>, //mɛ́·qɛ//, attested by BJ (12/5/64), IHTTC, other sources: ES /mɛ̀qɛ/, ASM ['fallen snow'], example: <**qéx̲ te máqa li te smált. (HS) ~ qéx̲ te máqe li te smált. (N)**>, //qə́x̣ tə mɛ́qɛ li tə s=mɛ́lt (HS) ~ qə́x̣ tə mɛ́qə li tə s=mɛ́lt (N)//, /'*(There's) a lot of snow on the mountain.*'/, attested by AC, also /'*(There's) lots of snow on the mountain., (There's) thick snow on the mountain.*'/, attested by EB, <**spípew te syíq.**>, //s=pí[=C_1ə=]w tə s=yíq//, *<**spípew te máqe**> rejected, /'*The snow is frozen.*'/, literally /'is frozen the snow in the air'/, attested by AC, <**yélt te máqa.**>, //yə́lt tə mɛ́qɛ//, [yɪ́lt tə mǽqɛ], /'*(have a) snowslide, (have an avalanche)*'/, literally /'the fallen snow slides down'/, attested by Elders Group, <**máqa qetstu lóme xwlí te smá:lt.**>, //mɛ́qɛ qə-c-t-u lám=ə x^{w}=lí tə s=mɛ́·lt//, /'*(It was) (fallen) snow all the way until we reached the mountain.*'/, literally /'(it's) fallen snow until -we -contrastive hit -just get there the mountain'/, attested by EB, ASM ['years'], semantic environment ['numerals, counting, age'], <**achxw welh kw'í:l má:qa?**>, //ʔɛ-c-x^{w} wəɬ k'^{w}í·l mɛ́·qɛ//, /'*How old are you (already)?*'/, literally /'you are already how many fallen snow(s)'/, attested by IHTTC, <**t'x̲ém má:qa.**>, //t'x̣=ə́m mɛ́·qɛ//, /'*six years*'/, literally /'six fallen snows'/, usage: answer to achxw welh kw'í:l má:qa *How old are you?*, attested by IHTTC, <**t'x̲emelsxá qas te t'x̲ém máqa kwseselh kwó:l.**>, //t'x̣=əm=əlsx^{y}ɛ́ qɛ=s tə t'x̣=ə́m mɛ́qɛ k^{w}-s-əs-əɬ k^{w}á·l//, /'*She is sixty-six years old.*'/, literally /'it's sixty-six (sixty and the six) fallen snow(s) since -she/he -was born.'/, attested by Elders

Group.

<**mámeqe**>, cts //mɛ́[-C$_1$ə-]qə//, WETH /*'it's snowing, (snow is accumulating)'*/, (<**-R1-**> *continuative*), phonology: reduplication, syntactic analysis: intransitive verb, attested by AC, example: <**syíyeq te smált.**>, //s=yí[=C$_1$ə=]q tə smɛ́lt//, *<**mámeqe te smált**> rejected, /*'It's snowing on the mountain.'*/, attested by AC.

<**meqó:s**>, dnom //mɛqɛ=á·s//, TIME /*'about December, (January to February [Billy Sepass])'*/, WETH, literally /'fallen snow season'/, ASM ['each month name applies starting from the first sliver of moon visible after the black moon and lasts till the next first sliver roughly, but it is used about the time the event described usually happens, for meqó:s this is often in December but William (Billy) Sepass of Sardis, B.C. placed it January to February in Jenness's field notes; the English month it applied to probably depended on where one lived and what was the average month the year's major snowfalls occurred in in the past dozen or more years; it may have been that in Sepass's time (ca 1856-1936) before his interview (ca Jan.-Feb. 1936) the major snowfalls were more often in Jan. to Feb., or it may be that there was snow on the ground when he was interviewed; the more recent elders may also be reflecting more recent climatic changes to snow in December in their areas (it snows earlier in the Tait area than in the Sardis area example)'], lx <**=ó:s**> *cyclic period, round thing, on the face*, phonology: vowel-shift to schwa-grade of root before full-grade suffix, also vowel merger, syntactic analysis: nominal, attested by Elders Group, also <**moqó:s**>, //mɛ[-Aa-]qə=á·s//, also /*'about January to February'*/, phonology: ó-ablaut automatic on root vowel before =ó:s ~ =es suffix, there is also vowel merger of the final root vowel and suffix vowel, attested by Diamond Jenness's field notes, William Sepass calendar.

<**imqáxel ~ himqáxel**>, df //ʔi=mɛ́qə=M2=x^{y}əl ~ hi=mɛ́qə=M2=x^{y}əl//, [ʔimqǽx^{y}ɪl ~ himqǽx^{y}ɪl], WETH /*'(have) mixed snow and rain together that melts fast, to rain and snow mixed together'*/, possibly <**hi= ~ i=**> *continuative* possibly before resonants or <**yi= ~ i=**>*along, travelling by*, (<**metathesis**> *derivational*), lx <**=xel**> *precipitation; on the foot*, phonology: metathesis, vowel-loss of e in root prob. due to prefix, syntactic analysis: intransitive verb, attested by Elders Group (3/23/77), Deming (3/31/77), example: <**himqáxel kw'e tseláqelhelh.**>, //hi=mɛ́qə=M2=x^{y}əl k'^{w}ə cəlɛ́q=əɬ=əɬ//, /*'It rained and snowed together yesterday.'*/, attested by Deming (3/31/77).

<**má:qel**>, df //mɛ́·=qəl//, ANAH [*'hair (of the head)'*], literally /'comes off on the head'/, lx <**qel**> *on the head*, syntactic analysis: nominal, attested by AC, BJ (5/64), other sources: /mɛ́·qəl/ *hair (of head)*, H-T <mákEl> (umlaut on a), also <**máqel**>, //mɛ́=qəl//, attested by SJ, MV, example: <**télh tel máqel.**>, //tə́ɬ tə-l mɛ́=qəl//, /*'My hair got straight., My hair got straightened.'*/, attested by SJ and MV (Deming 2/9/79).

<**máqelhp**>, df //mɛ́qə(l)=(ə)ɬp//, EB [*'pretty white lacy moss'*], [*'unidentified so far'*], literally /'hair of head =plant/tree'/, lx <**=elhp**> *plant, tree*, phonology: consonant-loss with vowel merger or vowel-loss with consonant merger, syntactic analysis: nominal, attested by Deming (6/21/79), Salish cognate: Nooksack /mǽqən=əɬp/ *pretty white lacey moss* from Nooksack /mǽqən/ *hair (of head)* Deming (6/21/79).

<**máqelhp**>, EB [*'pretty white lacy moss'*], *see* má:qel.

<**máq'em**>, mdls //mɛ́q'=əm//, ABFC [*'to jump (of fish)'*], (<**=em**> *middle voice*), contrast root <**míq'**> *to sink*, phonology: possible ablaut if related to míq', syntactic analysis: intransitive verb, attested by AD.

<**mámeq'em**>, cts //mɛ́[-C$_1$ə-]q'=əm//, ABFC [*'jumping (of fish)'*], (<**-R1-**> *continuative*), phonology: reduplication, syntactic analysis: intransitive verb, attested by AD, EL, NP, EB (all on Chehalis place names trip 9/27/77), example: <**mámeq'em te hú:liya.**>, //mɛ́[-C$_1$ə-]q'=əm tə hú·l=iyɛ//, /*'The humpback salmon is jumping.'*/, attested by AD, EL, NP, EB (all 9/27/77).

<**mát**>, free root //mɛ́t//, ANAF [*'flat organ in sturgeon which was skinned off and boiled down for glue'*], syntactic analysis: nominal, attested by Elders Group, MED ['if you eat the gill of the sturgeon when you are pregnant you'll have a child with curly hair (Elders Group 9/21/77)'],

<**mátek**>, free root //mɛ́tək//, TOOL [*'mattock'*], LAND, syntactic analysis: nominal, attested by IHTTC, borrowed from English <mattock>.

<**mátexw**>, bound root //mɛ́təx^w//, meaning unknown

<**smátexwtel**>, df //s=mɛ́təx^w=təl//, rcps, KIN /*'husband's brother, wife's sister, spouse's sibling (cross-sex), brother-in-law, sister-in-law, sibling's spouse (cross-sex)'*/, ASM ['opposite sex from person from whose viewpoint this is being discussed (opposite sex from ego in anthropological terminology), the reason for this cross-sex pattern is probably the approved possibility of marriage--sororate or levirate marriage upon death of linking spouse or as co-wives without the death of linking spouse'], (<**s=**> *nominalizer*), (<**=tel**> *reciprocal*), root meaning unknown, syntactic analysis: nominal, attested by EB, NP, AC, CT, other sources: ES /smɛ́təx^{w}təl/ *spouse's sibling, sibling's spouse (cross-sex)*, H-T <smatúktil> (macron over a and u) *brother's wife*.

<**smetmátexwtel**>, pln //s=C_1əC_2=mɛ́təx^w=təl//, KIN /*'husband's brothers, (*perhaps also *wife's sisters?, spouse's siblings?, sibling's spouses?)'*/, (<**R3=**> *plural*), phonology: reduplication, syntactic analysis: nominal, attested by EB.

<**má:th**>, bound root //mɛ́·θ// possibly *flat opening*

<**Semá:th ~ Semáth ~Smá:th**>, df //s=hə=mɛ́·θ//, PLN /*'Sumas village and area from present-day Kilgard to Fraser River, Sumas village (on both sides of the Fraser at the east end of Sumas Mt.), (Devil's Run (below Láx̱ewey), the area between Sumas Mt. and Fraser River [Elders Group 7/13/77], Sumas River* (probably requires **Stó:lō** *river* or Stótelō *creek* to follow) [Wells 1965], *Sumas Lake* (probably requires X̱ótsa *lake* after Semáth for this meaning)'/ [Elders Group 7/13/77]), possibly <**s=**> *nominalizer or stative or big* possibly (as in <**s=méqsel**> *have a big nose),* possibly <**he=**> *resultative or continuative*, possibly root <**máth** or **má**> *flat opening*, possibly <**=eth**> *edge*, phonology: consonant merger, syntactic analysis: nominal, attested by Elders Group (7/13/77), BJ (5/64), Deming (8/15/74), Wells 1965:23 (lst ed.), compare <**Máthxwi**> /mɛ́θ(=)x^w=iy/ *Matsqui* said to mean *easy portage*, literally /'a big flat opening'/, source: Wells 1966, Wells tapes Kelleher interview, also /*'Devil's Run (below Láx̱ewey)'*/, ASM ['this is the area between Sumas Mt. and Fraser River'], attested by Elders Group (7/13/77), comment: two copies of my field notes disagree on whether the name applies to Sumas village at Devil's Run or to Devil's Run itself, also /*'Sumas River'*/, source: Wells 1965 (lst ed.):14, comment: probably requires Stó:lō *river* or Stótelō *creek* to follow Semáth (Semáth Stó:lō, etc.) for this gloss, also /*'Sumas Lake'*/, (semological comment: Sumas Lake was a huge shallow lake east of Sumas River and south of Sumas Mt. which was dyked and drained just after after World War I; it was home to many waterfowl and fish (incl. sturgeon) and plants such as wapato; it often dried up to only a few feet deep in dry seasons; but it was a mosquito breeding ground and potential farm-land and the area has been farmed extensively since), attested by Elders Group (7/13/77), comment: probably requires X̱ótsa *lake* after Semáth for this meaning, also <**Semáts X̱ótse**>, //səmɛ́c x̣ácə//, also /*'Sumas Lake'*/, dialects: *Matsqui*, attested by Deming (8/15/74), source: place names file reference #76.

<**Máthxwi**>, df //mɛ́θ(=)x^w=iy//, PLN /*'Matsqui village, (Matsqui Creek [Wells])'*/, possibly root <**máth**> *flat opening*, possibly <**=xw ~ =exw**> *lump-like, round* or <**=x̱w**> *round, around*, <**=iy**> *place; covering*, syntactic analysis: nominal, attested by IHTTC (8/17/77), source: place names reference file #220, also <**Máthx̱wi**>, //mɛ́θ(=)x̣^{w}=iy//, also /*'Matsqui village; Matsqui Creek'*/, literally /'easy portage'/, source: Wells 1965 (lst ed.):14-15, Duff 1952:27.

<**Máthedes**>, free root //mɛ́θədəs//, CH [*'Methodist'*], syntactic analysis: nominal, attested by Elders

Group (6/8/77), borrowed from English <Methodist>.

<**math'álem**>, EFAM /*'to bluff, pretend one knows something, (be) stuck up'*/, *see* máth'el.

<**máth'el**>, bound root //mɛ́θ'əl *pretend, deceive*//.

<**smáth'el**>, stvi //s=mɛ́θ'əl//, EFAM [*'(be) proud (pompous)'*], (<**s=**> *stative*), syntactic analysis: adjective/adjectival verb, attested by EB, Deming, Elders Group, EK and DK (12/10/71), Salish cognate: Squamish /smác'n/ W73:205, K67:283, also <**smá:th'el**>, //s=mɛ́·θ'əl//, attested by IHTTC, example: <**ő́wetsel smáth'el.**>, //ʔówə-c-əl s=mɛ́θ'əl//, /*'I'm not proud.'*/, attested by Elders Group; found in <**smáth'elchexw.**>, //s=mɛ́θ'əl-c-əxʷ//, /*'You're smart [smart-alec? therefore pompous and proud].'*/, dialects: *Matsqui*, attested by EK and DK (12/10/71).

<**smámth'el**>, dmv //s=mɛ́[=C_1ə=]θ'əl//, EFAM /*'(be a) little bit proud, [a little] proud'*/, (<**=R1=**> *diminutive action*), phonology: reduplication, syntactic analysis: adjective/adjectival verb, attested by Elders Group (3/1/72), Deming.

<**smá:leth'el ~ smá:lth'el**>, plv //s=mɛ́·[=lə=]θ'əl//, EFAM /*'(lots of people are) proud, (many are proud)'*/, (<**=le=**> *plural subject*), phonology: infixing, syntactic analysis: adjective/adjectival verb, attested by IHTTC.

<**smímts'el**>, dmv //s=C_1í=mɛθ'əl//, EFAM [*'acting smart'*], (<**R4=**> *diminutive*), phonology: reduplication, syntactic analysis: adjective/adjectival verb, attested by MV and EF (Deming 4/27/78).

<**math'álem**>, rsls //mɛθ'ə[=Aɛ́=]l=əm//, mdls, EFAM /*'to bluff, pretend one knows something, (be) stuck up'*/, LANG, (<**á-ablaut**> *resultative*), (<**=em**> *middle voice*), phonology: ablaut, syntactic analysis: intransitive verb, attested by Elders Group.

<**mameth'álem**>, cts //mɛ[-C_1ə-]θ'ə[=Aɛ́=]l=əm//, [mæməθ'æ̃ləm], EFAM /*'lying, telling a lie, (bluffing [BHTTC])'*/, LANG, (<**-R1-**> *continuative*), phonology: ablaut, reduplication, syntactic analysis: intransitive verb, attested by AC, Deming, also /*'bluffing'*/, attested by BHTTC, example: <**mameth'álem te qéyx̱es swíyeqe.**>, //mɛ[-C_1ə-]θ'ə[=Aɛ́=]l=əm//, /*'The blind man is bluffing.'*/, usage: answer in trying to see if there is a word for the game, blind man's bluff, attested by BHTTC.

<**meth'éléxw**>, ncs //mɛθ'ə[=´=]l=l-əxʷ//, EFAM /*'doubt s-o, not believe s-th/s-o'*/, (<**=´=**> *derivational*), (<**=l**> *non-control transitivizer*), (<**-exw**> *third person object*), phonology: vowel-reduction to schwa-grade of root with stress-shift, consonant merger, updrifting, syntactic analysis: transitive verb, attested by Elders Group, Deming; found in <**meth'éléxwtsel.**>, //mɛθ'ə[=´=]l=l-əxʷ-c-əl//, /*'I don't believe it.'*/, attested by Deming.

<**mameth'élexw**>, cts //mɛ[-C_1ə-]θ'ə[=´=]l=l-əxʷ//, [mæməθ'əlʊxʷ], EFAM /*'doubting s-o/s-th, be not believing s-o/s-th'*/, (<**-R1-**> *continuative*), phonology: reduplication, stress-shift, consonant merger, syntactic analysis: transitive verb, attested by Deming; found in <**mameth'élexwtsel.**>, //mɛ[-C_1ə-]θ'ə[=´=]l=l-əxʷ-c-əl//, /*'I don't believe it.'*/, attested by Deming.

<**shxwmáth'elqel**>, dnom //s=xʷ=mɛ́θ'əl=qəl//, EFAM [*'liar'*], LANG, SOC, (<**s=**> *nominalizer*, xw= *always* or *pertaining to the head or throat* or meaning uncertain), lx <**=qel ~ =eqel**> *in the throat, in speech, language*, syntactic analysis: nominal, attested by Elders Group, AC.

<**shxwmámth'elqel**>, dmn //s=xʷ=mɛ́[=C_1ə=]θ'əl=qəl//, EFAM [*'a little liar'*], LANG, SOC, (<**=R1=**> *diminutive (agent)*), phonology: reduplication, syntactic analysis: nominal, attested by EB.

<**smámth'eqel**>, dmn //s=mɛ́[=C_1ə=]θ'=əqəl//, EFAM [*'smart-alec'*], SOC, (<**s=**> *nominalizer*), (<**=R1=**> *diminutive*), lx <**=eqel ~ =qel**> *in the throat, in speech, language*, phonology: reduplication, syntactic analysis: nominal, dialects: *Matsqui*, attested by EK and DK (12/10/71).

<**math'elqéylem**>, mdls //mɛθ'əl=q(əl)=í·l=əm//, EFAM ['*to lie (prevaricate)*'], LANG, lx <**=eqel ~ =qel**> *in the throat, in speech, language*, (<**=í:l**> *go, get, become, come, inceptive*, <**=em**> *middle voice*), phonology: consonant merger, vowel-loss (both due to automatic loss of el before =í:l), syntactic analysis: intransitive verb, attested by Elders Group, Salish cognate: Squamish /(nə)xʷ-məc'nʔ-álqp-əm/ *to lie (itr.)* W73:162, K67:310 [-álqp *sound*].

<**xwmath'elqéylémt**>, pcs //xʷ=mɛθ'əl=qəl=í·l=əm=T//, EFAM ['*tell a lie for s-o*'], LANG, possibly <**xw=**> *always* or *derivational (relating to features of the head or neck)* or meaning uncertain, (<**=t**> *purposeful control transitivizer*), phonology: consonant merger, consonant-loss, updrifting, syntactic analysis: transitive verb, syntactic comment: transitivized middle, attested by EB; found in <**xwmath'elqéylémthóxchexw.**>, //xʷ=mɛθ'əl=qəl=í·l=əm=T-áxʸ-c-əxʷ//, [xʷmæθ'əlqéylə́mθáxʸčʊxʷ], /'*Tell a lie for me., You tell a lie for me.*'/, attested by EB.

<**mamts'ólthet**>, pcrs //mɛ[=C_1ə=]c'ə[=Aá=]l=T-ət//, rsls, dmv, EFAM ['*think one(self) is smart*'], (<**=R1=**> *diminutive*, ó-ablaut *resultative*), (<**=t**> *purposeful control transitivizer*), (<**-et**> *reflexive*), phonology: reduplication, ablaut, syntactic analysis: intransitive verb, attested by MV and EF (Deming 4/27/78).

<**math'elqéylem**>, EFAM ['*to lie (prevaricate)*'], *see* máth'el.

<**mátsel**>, df //m(=)ɛ́cəl//, ANA ['*testicle*'], lx <**=átsel ~ =elétsel**> *on the testicle(s)*, possibly root <**m**> meaning uncertain, syntactic analysis: nominal, attested by Elders Group (8/20/75), Salish cognate: Squamish /máč'n/ *testicle* W73:264, K69:45, Lushootseed /báčəd/ *testicles* and /=álačəd/ *testicles* H76:692, 689.

<**mámetsel**>, pln //m(=)ɛ́[=C_1ə=]cəl//, ANA ['*testicles*'], (<**=R1=**> *plural*), phonology: reduplication, syntactic analysis: nominal, attested by Elders Group (8/29/75).

<**máts'el**>, free root //mɛ́c'əl//, EB /'*black hawthorn berry, blackhaw berries*'/, ['*Crataegus douglasii*'], ASM ['berries ripe in August, eaten fresh and dried, easy to dry and keep, tree has long thorns which were picked and used for a comb when a carved comb was not available, black berries have large seed but meat is tasty if sucked, (AC says meat is okay if hungry and that the tree must be climbed usually to get the berries)'], syntactic analysis: nominal, attested by AC, others.

<**mats'íyelhp**>, ds //mɛ́c'əl=əɬp//, EB ['*black hawthorn tree*'], ['*Crataegus douglasii*'], lx <**=elhp**> *tree, plant*, phonology: vowel-shift, consonant-shift, el → íy before =elhp by regular rule, syntactic analysis: nominal, attested by AC, other sources: ES /mɛ́c'ələɬp/ *black haw*, Salish cognate: Samish /méč'ən'/ *black hawthorn berry* G86:71.

<**mats'íyelhp**>, EB ['*black hawthorn tree*'], *see* máts'el.

<**máx**>, MC /'*take it off (of a table example), take it away (from something), take it off (of eyeglasses, of skin off an animal), take s-o off/away (from something), take s-th out (a tooth for ex.)*'/, *see* má ~ má'-.

<**máxet**>, possibly root //mɛ́xʸət//, LAND ['*flint*'], TOOL, FIRE, syntactic analysis: nominal, attested by EL (on Stólō Sítel tape 1/22/79).

<**máy**>, bound root //mɛ́y *help*//.

<**má:yt ~ máyt**>, pcs //mɛ́·y=T ~ mɛ́y=T//, SOC /'*help s-o, defend s-o, protect s-o, aid s-o*'/, (<**=t**> *purposeful control transitivizer*), syntactic analysis: transitive verb, attested by AC, Elders Group (3/15/72, 3/1/76, 6/16/76), example: <**lalh má:yt.**>, //lɛ-ɬ mɛ́·y=T//, /'*Go and help him.*'/, attested by AC, <**máyt (the slháli, te swíyeqe, yithá, tàlèwe, talhwélep)**>, //mɛ́y=T (θə s=ɬɛ́li, tə s=wíqə, yi=θɛ́, tɛ=lə́wə, tɛ=ɬwə́ləp)//, /'*help (the woman, the man, them, you (sg.), you people)*'/, attested by AC; found in <**máytes.**>, //mɛ́y=T-əs//, /'*He helps him/her/them., She helps him/her/them.*'/, attested by AC, example: <**má:ytes te swíqe the (stóles, chá(:)xw).**>, //mɛ́·y=T-əs tə s=wíqə θə

(s=táləs-s, cɛ́(·)xʷ-s).//, /'*The man helped (his wife, his mistress).*'/, attested by AC, <**má:ytescha (tethá, yithá).**>, //mɛ́·y=T-əs-cɛ (tə=θɛ́, yi=θɛ́)//, /'*He will help (him, them).*'/, attested by AC, <**má:ytescha tethá yithá.**>, //mɛ·y=T-əs-cɛ tə=θɛ́ yi=θɛ́//, /'*They will help him.*'/, attested by AC, <**má:ytescha yithá tethá.**>, //mɛ́·y=T-əs-cɛ yi=θɛ́ tə=θɛ́//, /'*He will help them.*'/, attested by AC, <**(álthacha, lewécha) má:yt.**>, //(ʔɛlθɛ-cɛ, ləwə́-cɛ) mɛ́·y=T//, /'*(I'll, You'll) help him.*'/, attested by AC, <**álthacha la máyt.**>, //ʔɛ́lθɛ-cɛ lɛ mɛ́y=T//, /'*I'LL go and help him.*'/, attested by AC, <**tl'ocha tethá má:yt.**>, //ƛ'á-cɛ tə=θɛ́ mɛ́·y=T//, /'*He'll help him., (He's the one to help him.)*'/, literally /'that will be that one (male) help him'/, attested by AC, syntactic comment: máytes is not used when the subject of the subordinate clause is the subject of and focus of the main clause, <**tl'o (kwthe, te) swíqe le má:yt (the, te) (stóles, slháli).**>, //ƛ'a (kʷ=θə, tə) s=wíqə lɛ mɛ́·y=T (θə, tə) (s=táləs-s, s=ɬɛ́li)//, /'*The man helped (his wife, the woman).*'/, literally /'that's (the (near but out of sight), the (present/unmarked)) man past tense 3rd person subj. help -her (the (female), the (unmarked)) (his wife, woman)'/, attested by AC, <**tl'ocha yithá má:yt (yithá, tethá, teló).**>, //ƛ'a-cɛ yi=θɛ́ mɛ́·y=T (yi=θɛ́, tə=θɛ́, tə=lá)//, /'*They're the ones that will help (them, him (that one), this one/him (a person)).*'/, attested by AC, <**tl'ocha tethá má:yt yithá.**>, //ƛ'a-cɛ tə=θɛ́ mɛ́·y=T yi=θɛ́//, /'*He's the one to help them., He'll help them.*'/, attested by AC, <**tl'ocha Bill kw'e máyt ta siyáye.**>, //ƛ'a-cɛ Bill k'ʷə mɛ́y=T t-ɛ si=yɛ́yə//, /'*Bill will be the one to help your friend., Bill will help your friend.*'/, syntactic comment: many sentence examples of syntactic/semantic focus in this section, attested by AC, <**tl'ocha Bill kw'e máyt wexwe'í:s.**>, //ƛ'a-cɛ Bill k'ʷə mɛ́y=T wə-xʷə=ʔí·-s//, /'*Bill (is the one that) will help him when he arrives.*'/, attested by AC, <**maythóxalha.**>, //mɛy=T-áxʸ-ɛɬɛ//, /'*You (pl.) help me., (You folks help me.)*'/, syntactic comment: imperative 2p, attested by AC, <**maythóxescha yithá.**>, //mɛy=T-áxʸ-əs-cɛ yi=θɛ́//, /'*They will help me.*'/, attested by AC, <**maythóxescha tl'e Bill wexwe'í:s.**>, //mɛy=T-áxʸ-əs-cɛƛ'(ə) Bill wə-xʷə=ʔí·-s//, /'*Bill will help me when he gets here.*'/, attested by AC, <**métsa maythóxes.**>, //mə́-cɛ mɛy=T-áxʸ-əs//, /'*He'll come and help me.*'/, attested by AC; found in <**maythóxchexw.**>, //mɛy=T-áxʸ-c-əxʷ//, /'*You (sg.) will help me.*'/, example: <**maythóxchap.**>, //mɛy=T-áxʸ-c-ɛp//, /'*You (pl.) will help me.*'/, attested by AC, <**mítlh maythóx.**>, //mí-tɬ mɛy=T-áxʸ//, /'*Come and help me.*'/, syntactic comment: coaxing imperative, attested by AC, <**leweslha maythóx.**>, //lə́wə-s-ɬɛ mɛy=T-áxʸ//, /'*YOU help me.*'/, syntactic comment: imperative of independent verbal pronoun with 3rd person subject, attested by AC, <**(lichap me, lichap mi) maythóx?**>, //(li-c-ɛp mə, li-c-ɛp mi) mɛy=T-áxʸ?//, /'*Did you folks come to help me?*'/, attested by AC, <**(tl'ocha, tl'ocha yithá) maythóx.**>, //(ƛ'a-cɛ, ƛ'a-cɛ yi=θɛ́) mɛy=T-áxʸ//, /'*(He, They) will come help me.*'/, attested by AC; found in <**maythóme**>, //mɛy=T-ámə//, /'*help you*'/, attested by Elders Group (3/1/76), also <**máythòmè**>, //mɛ́y=T-àmə̀//, phonology: downstepping, updrifting, attested by Elders Group (3/15/72), <**maythométsel**>, //mɛy=T-ámə-c-əl//, /'*I'll help you right now., I'll help you (either now or tomorrow).*'/, phonology: stress-shift automatic on bisyllabic object suffixes before subject suffixes, (semological comment: note gloss for present tense (non-continuative) is immediate future (right now, now, or tomorrow)), attested by Elders Group (3/15/72), AC, example: <**maythométselcha.**>, //mɛy=T-amə́-c-əl-cɛ//, /'*I will help you.*'/, attested by Elders Group (3/1/76, 3/15/72), <**maythométsel wayeles.**>, //mɛy=T-amə́-c-əl wɛyəl=əs//, /'*I'll help you tomorrow.*'/, (semological comment: present non-continuative translates as immediate future), phonology: stress-shift, (stress omitted on last word), <**maythométsetcha.**>, //mɛy=T-amə́-c-ət-cɛ//, /'*We'll help you after a while.*'/, phonology: stress-shift automatic on bisyllabic object suffixes before subject suffixes, (semological comment: future tense translates as non-immediate future (after a while) or unspecified future), attested by AC, <**maythomécha yithá.**>, //mɛy=T-amə́-cɛ yi=θɛ́//, /'*They will help you.*'/, phonology: stress-shift automatic on bisyllabic object suffixes before future tense suffix (or any suffix?), syntactic comment: unusual solution to prohibition against third person subject with second person object: no subject suffix but independent demonstrative pronoun, attested by AC, <**tsel maythóme kw'e**

tseláqelhelh qe lhulhá.>, //c-əl mɛy=T-ámə k'ʷə cəlɛ́q=əɬ=əɬ qə ɬuɬɛ́//, /'*I helped you yesterday or day before yesterday.*'/, syntactic comment: ambiguous past, attested by AC, <**latsel maythóme.**>, //lɛ-c-əl mɛy=T-ámə//, /'*I'm going to help you., I'll go and help you., I will help you.*'/, attested by AC, <**látset/látst maythóme.**>, //lɛ́-c-ət/lɛ́-c-t mɛy=T-ámə//, /'*We'll go and help you., We're going to go and help you (willingly, good-natured, the person can say no).*'/, semantic environment ['with la auxiliary constructions like this the offer is made willingly, good-natured, the person can say no; these are also used as imperative 1s'], attested by AC, <**metsa maythóme wexwe'í:s.**>, //mə-cɛ mɛy=T-ámə wə-xʷə=ʔí·-s//, /'*He'll come help you when he gets here.*'/, phonology: subjunctive subject after í: (-es → -s as after auxiliary verb, thus showing that the environment is phonemic not morphemic), attested by AC, <**maythòmcha tl'e Bill wexwe'í:s.**>, //mɛy=T-àm-cɛ ƛ'ə Bill wə-xʷə=ʔí·-s//, /'*Bill will help you when he gets here., (You'll be helped by Bill when he gets here.)*'/, syntactic comment: passive replaces prohibited third-person subj. with second person obj., attested by AC, <**tl'otsa talhlí:melh má:ythóme.**>, //ƛ'a-cɛ tɛ=ɬlí·məɬ mɛ́·y=T-ámə//, /'*We'll be the ones to help you.*'/, literally /'that will be us help you'/, <**éy t'wa meythómes kw'e swótle.**>, //ʔɛ́y t'wɛ məy=T-ámə-əs k'ʷə s=wɛ[=Aá=]t=la//, /'*It would be good if someone helps you., (Someone should help you., Someone better help you.)*'/, literally /'it's good evidential/must be if he helps you the (remote) someone'/, phonology: unusual vowel merger (e + e → e not á), also schwa-grade of root optional, grammatical comment: note derivational make-up of swótle *someone*, syntactic comment: subjunctive subject pronoun 3 with object pronoun 2 not prohibited, attested by IHTTC, <**éy t'wa meythómet.**>, //ʔɛ́y t'wɛ məy=T-ámə=ət//, /'*It would be good if we help you., (We should help you., We'd better help you.)*'/, literally /'it's good evidential/must be/I guess if we help you'/, phonology: unusual vowel merger (e + e → e not á), schwa-grade of root optional, syntactic comment: subjunctive subject pronoun 1p with object pronoun 2, attested by IHTTC; found in <**maytólxwchexw.**>, //mɛy=T-álxʷ-c-əxʷ//, /'*Help us., You help us.*'/, syntactic analysis: mildly urging imperative, attested by AC, Elders Group (3/22/78 TM or DF or TG), example: <**milh maytólxwchexw**>, //mi-ɬ mɛy=T-álxʷ-c-əxʷ//, /'*You will help us.*'/, literally /'come -coaxing imperative you help us'/, attested by AC, <**éwe stl'íses meytóxwes welámet súwq'tòlè.**>, //ʔə́wə s=ƛ'í-s-əs məy=T-áxʷ-əs wə-lɛ́=m-ət súwq'=T-álə//, /'*He doesn't want to help us (when we) go find (look for, search for) you folks.*'/, phonology: downstepping and updrifting in súwq'tòlè, schwa-grade root in meytóxwes optional, syntactic analysis: vneg nominal=intransitive verb-possessive3-sjsb3 transitive verb-object pronoun1p-subject pronoun3 if/when-intransitive verb-sjsb1p transitive verb-object pronoun2p, dialects: *Tait*, attested by SP, AK, AD (IHTTC 8/22/77), dialects: *Tait and Cheh. -óxw second-person plural object* suffix is equivalent to Chill. -ólxw *second-person plural object* suffix, also <**éwe stlíses kws meytóxwes welámet súwq'tòlè.**>, //ʔə́wə s=ƛ'í-s-əs kʷ-s məy=T-áxʷ-əs wə-lɛ́=m-ət súwq'=T-álə//, dialects: *Cheh.*, attested by EB (IHTTC 8/22/77), also <**ewe stl'ís kw'es meytólxws welámet sṓwq'tòlè.**>, //ʔə́wə s=ƛ'í-s k'ʷə-s məy=T-álxʷ-s wə-lɛ́=m-ət sówq'=Tálə//, dialects: *Chill.*, attested by NP (IHTTC 8/22/77), <**maytólxwchapcha (tlowáyél, wáy:eles).**>, //mɛy=T-álxʷ-c-ɛp-cɛ (tə=la=wɛ́yə́l, wɛ́y·əl=əs)//, /'*You people help us (today, tomorrow).*'/, attested by AC, <**maytólxwescha yithá.**>, //mɛy=T-álxʷ-əs-cɛ yi=θɛ́//, /'*They will help us.*'/, attested by AC, <**maytó:lxwescha tl'e Bill wexwe'í:s.**>, //mɛy=T-á·lxʷ-əs-cɛ ƛ'ə Bill wə=xʷə=ʔí·-s//, /'*Bill will help us when he gets here.*'/, phonology: optional length on object pronoun suffix, attested by AC, <**(milh, michap, lachxw) maytó(:)lxw.**>, //(mi-ɬ, mi-c-ɛp, lɛ-c-xʷ) mɛy=T-á(·)lxʷ//, /'*(Come (coaxing imperative 2s), You folks come (mildly urging imperative 2p), You're going to (mildly urging imperative 2s)) help us.*'/, phonology: optional length on object pronoun suffix, attested by AC; found in <**maytolétsel.**>, //mɛy=T-álə-c-əl//, /'*I'll help you (pl.).*'/, phonology: stress-shift obligatory on bisyllabic object suffixes before subject suffixes, (semological comment: present tense as immediate future), attested by AC, <**maytolétsetcha.**>, //mɛy=T-álə-c-ət-cɛ//, /'*We'll help* *you (pl.)(after a while).*'/, phonology: stress-shift obligatory on bisyllabic object suffixes before subject suffixes, (semological comment: non-immediate future tense), attested by AC, example: <**(latsel, lats(e)t, lámtset) meytóle.**>, //(lɛ-c-əl, lɛ-c-(ə)t, lɛ́=m-c-ət) məy=T-álə//, /'*(I'll/I'll go, We'll/We'll go and, We'll/We're going to) help you.*'/, phonology: schwa-grade root optional, attested by AC, <**tl'ocha Bill kw'e maytóle wexwe'í:s.**>, //ƛ'a-cɛ Bill k'^{w}ə mɛy=T-álə wə-x^{w}ə=ʔí·-s//, /'*Bill's the one to help you (pl.) when he gets here.*'/, attested by AC, <**lámelhtsel maythóme.**>, //lɛ́=m-əɬ-c-əl mɛy=T-ámə//, /'*I was going to help you.*'/, syntactic comment: past affixed, attested by AC, <**tl'otsa yithá maythòm.**>, //ƛ'a-cɛ yi=θɛ́ mɛy=T-àm//, /'*They will help you.*'/, syntactic comment: passive due to prohibition of subject pronoun3 with object pronoun2, attested by AC, <**maytálemcha yithá.**>, //mɛy=T-áləm-cɛ yi=θɛ́//, /'*They will help you (pl.).*'/, phonology: optional stress-shift on bisyllabic object suffix before future suffix, syntactic comment: passive due to prohibition of subject pronoun3 with object pronoun2, attested by AC, <**maytolémcha tl'e Bill wexwe'í:s.**>, //mɛy=T-áləm-cɛ ƛ'ə Bill wə-x^{w}ə=ʔí·-s//, /'*Bill will help you (pl.) when he gets here.*'/, phonology: optional stress-shift on bisyllabic object suffix before future suffix, syntactic comment: note tl' ~ tl'e the (prepositional), by here and in earlier examples, passive due to prohibition of subject pronoun3 with object pronoun2, attested by AC.

<**mamíyet**>, cts //mɛ[-C_1ə ́-]y=əT//, (<**-R1- plus stress shift**> *continuative*), SOC ['*helping*'], phonology: reduplication, stress-shift, syntactic analysis: transitive verb, attested by AC, Elders Group, example: <**lílhechexw mayímet (kw'e, te) Ted?**>, //lí-ɬ-ə-c-əx^{w} mɛ[-C_1ə ́-]y=əT (k'^{w}ə, tə) Ted//, /'*Were you helping Ted?*'/, syntactic comment: interrogative past, past affixed, attested by AC, <**tl'o wiyóth mamíyet (~ maméyet)**>, //ƛ'a wə=yáθ mɛ[-C_1ə-´]y=əT//, /'*He [foregrounded] is always helping [s-o].*'/, literally /'that's him always helping s-o'/, syntactic comment: unusual lack of subject pronoun due to foregrounding as tl'o *that's him*, attested by AC; found in <**mamíythóxes.**>, //mɛ[-C_1ə ́-]y=T-áx^{y}-əs//, /'*He's helping me.*'/, attested by Elders Group (6/7/78), example: <**í:lhtsel mamíyethòme.**>, //ʔí·-ɬ-c-əl mɛ[-C_1ə ́-]y=əT-ámə//, /'*I was helping you.*'/, phonology: downstepping, attested by AC.

<**móylhtel**>, rcps //mɛ[-Aá-]y=ɬ(c)=T-əl//, bens, pcs, SOC /'*help out, go help, pitch in, help one another*'/, (<**=lh ~ =lhts ~ =elhts**> *benefactive*, <**=t**> *purposeful control transitivizer*), (<**-el**> *reciprocal*), phonology: ó-ablaut conditioned automatically on a-vowels in roots before reciprocal, syntactic analysis: intransitive verb, attested by IHTTC, also <**mó:ylhtel**>, //mɛ[-Aá·-]y=ɬ(c)=T-əl//, attested by AC, <**tl'esu mó:ylhtel qesésu lhém:exw kwses welh hóy te sléxwelhs.**>, //ƛ'ə-s-u mɛ[-Aá·-]y=ɬ=T-əl qə-s-əs-u ɬə́m·əx^{w} k^{w}-s-əs wəɬ háy tə s=lə́x^{w}əɬ-s//, /'*And so they helped one another and it rained when their canoe was already done/finished.*'/, usage: story of the Flood, attested by AC (12/7/71).

<**momíyelhtel**>, cts //mɛ[-Aa-][-C_1ə ́-]y=əɬ(c)=T-əl//, [mamíyɪɬtəl], SOC /'*helping one another, (helper [Elders Group])*'/, (<**-R1- plus stress-shift**> *continuative*), phonology: ablaut conditioned by reciprocal, reduplication, stress-shift, consonant-loss (of ts in benefactive), syntactic analysis: intransitive verb, attested by AC, also <**momíyelhtel ~ momíylhtel**>, //mɛ[-Aa-][-C_1ə ́-]y=əɬ(c)=T-əl ~ mɛ[-Aa-][-C_1ə ́-]y=ɬ(c)=T-əl//, also /'*helper*'/, attested by Elders Group (3/15/72).

<**míytel**>, dnom //mɛ[=Aí=]y=təl//, SOC ['*a helper*'], (<**í-ablaut**> *derivational*), lx <**=tel**> *device to, something to*, phonology: ablaut, syntactic analysis: nominal, attested by EB, example: <**thel míytel**>, //θə-l mɛ[=Aí=]y=təl//, /'*my (female) helper*'/, literally /'the (female) helper'/, attested by EB.

<**má:y-**>, bound root //mɛ́·y- or məy- or miy-//, WATR possibly *submerge*

<**smá:yeleq**>, df //s=mɛ́·y=ələq or s=məy=ɛ́·[=M2=]ləq//, WATR ['*waves*'], (<**s=**> *nominalizer* or *stative*), possibly <**metathesis**> *derivational*, lx <**=á:leq**> *waves, billows*, probably root as in

<**sméya**> *bay*, <**míq'**> *be underwater, sink to bottom* with <**miy-**> *submerge* + <=q'> *on something else* (and cognates such as Squamish /múy/ *submerge*, /mə́y/ *to sink* and /mí-mi/ *drown* K67:255, 257) and <**míliyel**> //míy=l=iyəl// *set a net (by canoe), set one's net, fish with a net, (submerge a net)* (Salish cognate: Squamish /múy-ʔayʔi/ *set one's net* and /múy/ *submerge* and /máyʔ-múy-unʔ/ *dip repeatedly in the water (tr.)* W73:227, K69:46, Sechelt /mə́l/ *to sink*), phonology: metathesis perhaps, syntactic analysis: nominal?, intransitive verb?, dialects: *Cheh.*, attested by Elders Group (3/26/75).

<**má:yt ~ máyt**>, SOC /'*help s-o, defend s-o, protect s-o, aid s-o*'/, *see* máy.

<**ma'álésem**>, ABDF /'*pulled out (of tooth or teeth), (have one's tooth pulled out)*'/, *see* má ~ má'-.

<**ma'elétstem**>, ABDF /'*castrated, he was castrated*'/, *see* má ~ má'-.

<**ma'eméstexw ~ máméstexw**>, TVMO /'*bring s-th, brought s-th*'/, *see* mí ~ mé ~ me.

<**ma'emét**>, ABFC /'*He sat., She sat.*'/, *see* emét.

<**ma'emí ~ ma'mí**>, TVMO /'*come, came, He came., She came.*'/, *see* mí ~ mé ~ me.

<**mechó:s**>, df //məcɛ=á·s//, EZ ['*lingcod*'], ['*Ophiodon elongatus*'], literally /'(prob.) lump/burl on the face'/, ASM ['the lingcod has three to five spines on each cheek which may account for its name in Halq'eméylem; some elders say it is black and looks something like a bullhead'], probably root <**mécha ~ metsa**> (as in <**smécha ~ smétsa**> *lump (on person, tree, etc.), burl, goiter*, lx <**=ó:s**> *on the face*, phonology: vowel merger, syntactic analysis: nominal, attested by Elders Group (3/1/72), also <**smechó:s**>, //s=məcɛ=á·s//, attested by Elders Group (3/26/75), also <**á:yt**>, //ʔɛ́·yt//, attested by Elders Group (3/26/75). Also see root <**metsa**>.

<**mékw**>, free root //mə́kʷ//, DESC /'*stout (of a person), thick (of a tree), thick around, coarse (of a rope), big (fat) (of a person). big (in girth)*'/, syntactic analysis: adjective/adjectival verb, attested by AC, BHTTC, Salish cognate: Lushootseed /s-bə́kʷ/ *ball* H76:26, also <**méqw**>, //mə́qʷ//, attested by AC, EB, JL, example: <**ts'ats'í:ts'etl' q'a mékw**>, //C₁ɛ=c'í·[=C₁ə=]ƛ' q'ɛ mə́kʷ//, /'*short and stout*'/, attested by AC, <**méqw mestíyexw**>, //mə́qʷ məstíyəxʷ//, /'*big person*'/, attested by AC, <**we'ólwe méqw ta x̱wé:ylem.**>, //wə=ʔál=wə mə́qʷ t-ɛx̣ʷí·(y)ləm//, /'*Your rope is too thick., Your rope is too coarse.*'/, attested by JL (7/13/79).

<**mekwélqel**>, ds //məkʷ=ə́lqəl//, ANA ['*(have) coarse hair*'], lx <**=álqel ~ =élqel ~ =elqel**> *hair, fur, fleece, wool*, syntactic analysis: intransitive verb, nominal?, attested by BHTTC.

<**mékweth ~ mékwethel**>, ds //mə́kʷ=əθ ~ mə́kʷ=əθəl//, ABFC /'*to kiss, kiss on the lips*'/, literally /'thick in the mouth'/, ASM ['subject is semantic agent'], lx <**=eth ~ =ethel ~ =óthel**> *in the mouth*, possibly <**=el**> *get, become*, syntactic analysis: intransitive verb, attested by Deming, Elders Group.

<**xwmékwàthel**>, ds //xʷ=mə́kʷ=ɛ̀θəl or xʷ=mə́kʷ=a[=Aɛ̀=]θ=əl//, ABDF ['*he got kissed*'], ASM ['subject is semantic patient'], lx <**xw=**> *pertaining to the face, head or throat or always*, possibly <**à-ablaut**> *resultative* or possibly <**=àthel**> (may be idiolectal variant of <**=óthel**>) *on the mouth*, <**=el**> *get, become*, phonology: ablaut possible, syntactic analysis: intransitive verb, attested by EB.

<**xwmékwàthem**>, mdls //xʷ=mə́kʷ=a[=Aɛ̀=]θ=əm//, ABDF ['*kiss*'], ASM ['subject is probably semantic agent'], (<**=em**> *middle voice*), phonology: ablaut, syntactic analysis: intransitive verb, attested by EB.

<**xwmékwàtht**>, pcs //xʷ=mə́kʷ=a[=Aɛ̀=]θ(əl)=T//, ABDF /'*kiss s-th, (kiss s-o [Deming, IHTTC])*'/, (<**=t**> *purposeful control transitivizer*), phonology: ablaut, affix could be =óthel with predictable consonant-loss and vowel-loss of el before =t, syntactic analysis: transitive verb, attested by EB, also <**xwmékwethet**>, //xʷ=mə́kʷ=əθ=əT//, also /'*kiss s-o*'/, attested by Deming, IHTTC; found

in <**xwmékwàthtes.**>, //xʷ=mә́kʷ=a[=Aὲ=]θ=T-әs//, /'*He kissed it.*'/, attested by EB, <**xwmékwethethóxlha.**>, //xʷ=mә́kʷ=әθ=әT-áxʸ-ɬɛ//, /'*Kiss me.*'/, attested by Deming, IHTTC.

<**mő́kweset**>, pcs //mә́kʷ=әs=әT//, ABDF ['*kiss s-o*'], lx <**=es**> *on the face*, (<**=et**> *purposeful control transitivizer*), syntactic analysis: transitive verb, attested by JL (5/5/75); found in <**mő́kwesetes.**>, //mә́kʷ=әs=әT-әs//, /'*He kisses her., She kissed him.*'/, attested by JL.

<**mekwó:méltses**>, dnom //mәk'ʷ=á·mә́l=cәs//, ANA ['*thumb*'], literally /'stout member/portion on/of the hand'/, lx <**=ó:mél**> *member, part, portion*, lx <**=tses**> *on the hand, of the hand*, (semological comment: somatic suffixes shift from locative to partitive in most body-part names), syntactic analysis: nominal, attested by AC, DM (12/4/64), Elders Group (8/20/75), other sources: H-T <mōkwā́multcis>, also <**kwoméltses**>, //(mә)kʷ=amә́l=cәs//, Elder's comment: "shortcut pronunciation", phonology: consonant-loss and vowel-loss in shortcut pronunciation, attested by Elders Group (5/3/78).

<**mekwó:mélxel**>, dnom //mәkʷ=á·mә́l=xʸәl//, ANA ['*(big) toe*'], literally /'stout member/portion on/of the foot'/, lx <**=ó:mél**> *member, portion*, lx <**=xel**> *on the foot, of the foot*, (semological comment: somatic suffixes shift from locative to partitive in most body-part names), syntactic analysis: nominal, attested by DM (12/4/64).

<**memekwóyetses**>, df //mә[=C_1ә=]kʷ=áyә=cәs//, ABDF ['*(have) fingers so cold they can't bend*'], possibly root <**mékw**> *thick, stout*, (<**=R1=**> *resultative* or *continuative*), lx <**=óye**> meaning uncertain, <**=tses**> *on the hand*, phonology: reduplication, syntactic analysis: adjective/adjectival verb, attested by IHTTC.

<**mékwmekw**>, ds //mә́kʷ=C_1әC_2//, EZ ['*bumblebee*'], ['family *Bombidae, Bombus spp.*'], literally probably /'stout characteristically'/, (<**=R2**> *characteristic*), phonology: reduplication, syntactic analysis: nominal, attested by Elders Group (9/3/75), other sources: JH /mә́kʷmә̀kʷ/, H-T <mókmok>.

<**mekwélqel**>, ANA ['*(have) coarse hair*'], *see* mékw.

<**mékweth ~ mékwethel**>, ABFC /'*to kiss, kiss on the lips*'/, *see* mékw.

<**mékwmekw**>, EZ ['*bumblebee*'], *see* mékw.

<**mekwó:méltses**>, ANA ['*thumb*'], *see* mékw.

<**mekwó:mélxel**>, ANA ['*(big) toe*'], *see* mékw.

<**mékw' ~ mő́kw'**>, free root //mә́k'ʷ (~ mók'ʷ)//, [mʊ́k'ʷ ~ mók'ʷ], NUM /'*all, every*'/, syntactic analysis: adjective/adjectival verb, attested by Elders Group (3/1/72, 3/29/77, etc.), TM, EB, AD, JL, Deming, BJ (12/5/64), other sources: ES /әwmә́k'ʷɛ/ (rej. by AC), Salish cognate: Lushootsedd /bә́k'ʷ/ *all* H76:26-27; found in <**mő́kw'chet**>, //mók'ʷ-c-әt//, /'*all of us*'/, attested by BJ (12/5/64), <**mōkw'elep**>, //mók'ʷ-әlәp//, /'*you all, all of you*'/, attested by AC, example: <**licHap mő́kw' álhtel?**>, //li-c-ɛp mók'ʷ ʔɛ́ɬ=tәl//, /'*Did you all eat?*'/, attested by AC, <**lemlémetchxw mékw' yel á:wkw'.**>, //C_1әC_2=lә́m=әT-c-xʷ mә́k'ʷ yә-l ʔɛ́·wk'ʷ//, /'*Fold all my clothes.*'/, attested by Elders Group, <**lemlémetchxw mékw' ye tskwí:m l á:wkw'.**>, //C_1әC_2=lә́m=әT-c-xʷ mә́k'ʷ yә c=kʷí·m l ʔɛ́·wk'ʷ//, /'*Fold all my red clothes.*'/, literally /'plural object= fold =them purposefully -main clause subj. -you all the (human plural) have= red my belongings'/, attested by Elders Group, <**mő́kw'tset lám.**>, //mók'ʷ-c-әt lɛ́=m//, /'*All of us are going.*'/, attested by AC, <**mōkw'tsapcha álhtel wáy:élés.**>, //mók'ʷ-c-ɛp-cɛ ʔɛ́ɬ=tәl wɛ́y·ә́l=ә́s//, /'*Both of you will eat tomorrow.*'/, literally /'it will be all you folks eat a meal tomorrow'/, attested by AC, <**mő́kw'tset éwelh teló:met welí:xw xwe'í:t.**>, //mók'ʷ-c-әt ʔә́wә-ɬ tәl=l-á·mәt wә-lí·-xʷ xʷәʔí·t//, /'*We don't (all) understand what you're saying.*'/, literally /'all -we don't -past know =happen/manage to -oneself if/when- (there) -you

subjunctive what is someone saying?'/, attested by AC, <**mékw'í tel mámele. ~ mékw'í l mámele.**>, //mə́k'ʷ ʔi təl C_1ɛ́=mələ ~ mə́k'ʷ ʔi l C_1ɛ́=mələ//, /'*My children are all here.*'/, phonology: consonant-loss of glottal-stop when í is pronounced as suffix (unusual), attested by Elders Group, <**mṓkw' swàyèl kws yóyes.**>, //mók'ʷ s=wɛ̀yə̀l kʷ-s yá[-C_1ə-](y)s.//, /'*She works every day.*'/, literally /'it's every day that she's working'/, attested by TM, EB, also /'*He works all day.*'/, attested by AD, <**mékw'cha swàyèl kw'els yóyes.**>, //mə́k'ʷ-cɛ s=wɛ̀yə̀l k'ʷə-l-s yá[-C_1ə-](y)s (or yáy[-ə-]s)//, /'*I'll be working every day.*'/, literally /'it will be every/all day that I am working'/, attested by AD, also <**chow mékw' swàyèl kw'els yóyes.**>, //cɛ-əw mə́k'ʷ s=wɛ̀yə̀l k'ʷ-əl-s yáy[-ə-]s//, literally /'future tense -contrastive every day that I am working'/, attested by AD, <**mṓkw' slát kw'es emís te lálemtset te isále spáth tl'osuw álhtels te qwe'óp.**>, //mók'ʷ s=lát k'ʷ-əs ʔəmí-s tə lɛ́ləm-c-ət tə ʔisɛ́lə s=pɛ́θ ƛ'a-s-uw ʔɛ́ɬ=təl-s tə qʷəʔáp//, /'*Every night two bears come to our house and eat apples.*'/, literally /'it's every night that -nom. they come to the our house the two bear that -so -contrastive eat a meal -they the apple'/, attested by AC, <**ōwe lís mékw'**>, //ʔówə lí-s mə́k'ʷ//, /'*some, not all*'/, literally /'is not aux (there?) -third person subj. all'/, attested by EB, <**esu mṓkw' ó:lh yutl'ólem.**>, //ʔə-s-u mók'ʷ ʔá·ɬ yə=u=ƛ'á=ləm//, /'*And so they all got in the canoe.*'/, literally /'ambig. past -third-person subj. -contrastive all get aboard (a canoe/conveyance) they'/, usage: story of the Flood, attested by AC (12/7/71), <**su eyémò kwsu mékw's.**>, //s-u ʔɛy=ə́m-à kʷ-s-u mə́k'ʷ-s//, /'*(They are all healthy.)*'/, literally /'nominalizer/third-person -contrastive is strong -just that-nominalizer-contrastive all -they -> so it's just strong that they all are'/, attested by JL, <**wemékw' su éysò á:lhtel.**>, //wə-mə́k'ʷ s-u ʔɛ́y-s-à ʔɛ́·ɬtəl//, /'*They are all well.*'/, literally /'contrastive- all nominalizer-contrastive be good -third-person subject -just they (known to hearer)'/, attested by JL, <**latset mekw' áyel tl'ekwtset t'át'iyeq'.**>, //lɛ-c-ət mə́k'ʷ ʔɛ́y=əl ƛ'ə=kʷ-c-ət t'ɛ́[-C_1ə-]yəq'//, /'*We all left because we were mad.*'/, attested by Deming, <**kw'étslexwes te swíyeqe mékw' yí slhellhálí.**>, //k'ʷə́c=l-əxʷ-əs tə s=wíqə mə́k'ʷ yə s=C_1əC_2=ɬɛ́lí//, /'*The man saw all the women.*'/, usage: double entendre, attested by Elders Group, <**éy tel sqwálewel kw'etslóle mṓkw' í(kw'elò).**>, //ʔɛ́y t-əl s=qʷɛ́l=əwəl k'ʷəc=l-álə mók'ʷ ʔí(=k'ʷə=là)//, /'*I'm glad to see you all here.*'/, attested by Deming, <**kw'e mṓkw'e st'á**>, //k'ʷə mók'ʷ-ə̀ s=t(ə)ʔɛ́//, /'*evenly*'/, literally /'what's (the (remote) as relativizer) all -just alike,similar, same'/, phonology: consonant merger with glottalization /tʔ/ → /t'/ or <t> + <'> -> <t'>, (semological comment: idiom), attested by EB, Elders Group (3/72), <**kw'e mṓkw'e sta'á kw'els kweléqlhtstòlè.**>, //k'ʷə mók'ʷ-ə̀ s=tɛʔɛ́ k'ʷ-əl-s kʷələ́q=ɬc=T-álə//, /'*I distribute it evenly.*'/, syntactic comment: bens, attested by Elders Group (3/72), <**mekw'(o) shxwlís.**>, //mək'ʷ(=à) sxʷ=lí-s//, /'*It's everywhere.*'/, literally /'it's every (=just) where it is'/, (semological comment: idiom), attested by EB, <**mekw'o shxwlís te qó: li te Semáth.**>, //mək'ʷ=à sxʷ=lí-s tə qá· li tə s=mɛ́θ//, /'*There's water everywhere at Sumas.*'/, literally /'it's everywhere the water at the Sumas'/, attested by EB, <**ye lí kw' mṓkw' shxwlís li te B.C.**>, //yə lí k'ʷ mók'ʷ sxʷ=lí-s li tə B.C.//, /'*many from all over B.C.*'/, literally /'the (plural human) at the (remote) everywhere in the (unmarked) B.C. (British Columbia)'/, usage: story of recent event, attested by AC (11/10/71), <**mékw'ó shxwélems**>, //mə́k'ʷ-à sxʷ=hə́-lɛ[=Aə́=]m-s//, /'*a person who is going from house to house or wandering from house to house, (an itinerant person, wanderer)*'/, literally /'every -jtst nominalizer= continuative/plural- going to -his'/, attested by EB (12/12/75).

<**semíkw'**>, strs //s=hə=mə[=Aí=]k'ʷ//, NUM ['*all of them (people)*'], (<**s=**> *stative*), (<**he=**> *resultative*), (<**í-ablaut**> *resultative*), phonology: ablaut, syntactic analysis: adjective/adjectival verb, attested by AC, example: <**semíkw' tel schápth**>, //s=mə[=Aí=]k'ʷ t-əl s=cɛ́pθ//, /'*all of my uncles' wives*'/, attested by AC (11/16/71).

<**mekw'stám ~ mōkw'rtám**>, cpds //mək'ʷ=s=tɛ́m (~ mok'ʷ=s=tɛ́m)//, NUM ['*everything*'], (<**=s(=)**> *nominalizer* (suffixed only in that the whole stem, stám, is compounded after the root mekw'; there it is s= *nominalizer* prefixed; but =s as a *nominalizer* is also found elsewhere phonetically suffixed, example on demonstrative articles that introduce subordinate clauses (kw'e-l-s *that I, that -my -*

nominalizer)), probably root <**mekw'**> *all, every* + root <**tám**> (bound form) *what,* (semological comment: diffictlt to fit into a semantic domain, could be the label for a super-ordinate domain, or it could have membership in all domains, it appears to include actions as well as things though it is nominal itself), syntactic analysis: indefinite nominal, adverb/adverbial verb?, syntactic comment: like mékw' *all, every*, it often appears at the beginning of a sentence for focus or emphasis since it has a categorical kind of meaning; in such positions, like a adverb/adverbial verb, it needs no subordinating demonstrative conjunction (kw'es, kwses, etc.), but can be followed immediately by its verb; yet it has the semantic function of a nominal subject or object; very unusual; it also can behave itself however and follow a demonstrative article like a regular nominal, attested by EB, AD, Elders Group, others, example: <**ch'íthométsel lám kw'e mōkw'stám.**>, //c'í=T-ámə-c-əl lɛ́=m k'ʷə mok'ʷ=s=tɛ́m//, /'*We thank you for everything.*'/, attested by AD, <**mekw'stám íl kw'étslexw.**>, //mək'ʷ=s=tɛ́m ʔí-l k'ʷə́c=l-əxʷ//, /'*I saw everything.*'/, literally /'if I see everything'/, attested by Elders Group, <**mekw'stám kw'étslexwes yi siwíyeqe.**>, //mək'ʷ=s=tɛ́m k'ʷə́c=l-əxʷ-əs yi s=i=wíqə//, /'*The men saw everything. (see)*'/, attested by Elders Group.

<**mekw'stám skw'xám ~ mekw'stám skw'áxem**>, cpds //mək'ʷ=s=tɛ́m s=k'ʷɛ́xʸ=M1=əm ~ mək'ʷ=s=tɛ́m s=k'ʷɛ́xʸ=əm//, NUM //'math, mathematics'//, morphosememic development (SMM), semantic comment: from lit. "everything (in) numbers"), attested by RG & EH (4/10/99 Ling332)

<**mekw'ewát**>, cpds //mək'ʷ=wɛ́t//, HUMC /'*everybody, everyone, (anybody [Elders Group 3/1/72])*'/, probably root <**mekw'**> *all, every* + root <**wát**> (bound form) *who*, phonology: epenthesis (e added before wát automatically to ease pronunciation of kw'w to kw'ew), (semological comment: this might be the label for the semantic domain HUMC (human categories)), syntactic analysis: indefinite nominal, adverb/adverbial verb?, syntactic comment: can appear as subject or object without a demonstrative article when sentence- or phrase-initial and does not then require a subordinating demonstrative conjunction for the verb which follows immediately after; highly unusual; appears sentence- or phrase-initial for focus or emphasis, but can appear after a demonstrative article also in the normal place of a nominal; when appearing without an article it still can have the semantic function of nominal subject or object;, syntactic comment: its positions of occurrence are more those of an adverbial verb but with nominal functions; sjsb 3 is used to derive some indefinite nominals but in examples below it is not certain yet whether there is derivation (=es) or still a verbal subjunctive function (-es) present (those preceded by an article could be nominal and thus derived with =es or they could be relativized and still verbal; those not preceded by an article are more likely still syntactically verbal and thus with -es), attested by Elders Group, Deming, EB, also <**mekw'át (prob. mekw'wát)**>, //mək'ʷ=wɛ́t//, also /'*anybody*'/, attested by Elders Group (3/1/72), also <**mékw' tewát**>, //mə́k'ʷ tə=wɛ́t//, attested by Elders Group, also <**mékw' tewát(es)**>, //mə́k'ʷ tə=wɛ́t(=əs/-əs)//, also /'*anybody*'/, comment: see minimal sentence contrast below, attested by Elders Group, example: <**mekw'ewát kw'étselexwes.**>, //mək'ʷ=wɛ́t k'ʷə́c=l-əxʷ-əs//, /'*He saw everybody.*'/, Elder's comment: "shortcut for mékw' tewát kw'étslexwes", attested by Elders Group, also <**mékw' tewát kw'étslexwes.**>, //mə́k'ʷ tə=wɛ́t k'ʷə́c=l-əxʷ-əs//, attested by Elders Group, <**lítsel kwéxelexw kw'e mekw'ewát.**>, //lí-c-əl kʷə́xʸ=l-əxʷ k'ʷə mək'ʷ=wɛ́t//, /'*Did I say everyone's name?*'/, literally /'do (yes/no-question) -subj. -I manage to name them/him/her/it the (remote) everyone'/, attested by Deming, <**mekw'ewát lám.**>, //mək'ʷ=wɛ́t lɛ́=m//, /'*Everybody went.*'/, attested by EB, also <**mṓkw'e lám.**>, //mók'ʷ=ə̀ lɛ́=m//, literally /'just all went'/, Elder's comment: "mekw'ewát lám is a better way to say it", attested by EB, <**éy mestíyexw; mekw'ewát tl'íls.**>, //ʔɛ́y məstíyəxʷ; mək'ʷ=wɛ́t ƛ'í=ls//, /'*He's a good person; everyone likes him., He's popular.*'/, attested by Elders Group, <**mekw'ewát kw'étslexwes te swíyeqe.**>, //mək'ʷ=wɛ́t k'ʷə́c=l-əxʷ-əs tə s=wíqə//, /'*The man saw everyone., The man saw everybody.*'/, usage: double entendre, attested by EB, Elders Group, <**kw'étslexwes te swíyeqe**

kw'e mekw'átes (mekw'wátes?).>, //k'ʷə́c=l-əxʷ-əs tə s=wíqə k'ʷə mək'ʷ=ɛ́t(-/=)əs (mək'ʷ=wɛ́t(-/=)əs?).//, /'*The man saw everyone.*'/, usage: double entendre, *<**kw'étslexw te swíyeqe kw'e mekw'ewátes.**> rejected by EB (4/24/78), <**mekw'ewát kw'étslexw te swíyeqe.**>, //mək'ʷ=wɛ́t k'ʷə́c=l-əxʷ tə s=wíqə//, /'*Everyone saw the man., Everybody saw the man.*'/, usage: double entendre, attested by EB, Elders Group, <**mekw'ewát lép'exes te xeytl'áls.**>, //mək'ʷ=wɛ́t lə́p'=əxʸ-əs tə xiƛ'=ɛ́ls//, /'*The grizzly ate everybody. (eat s-th/s-o)*'/, attested by Elders Group (3/29/77), also <**lép'exes te xeytl'áls mekw'ewátes.**>, //lə́p'=əxʸ-əs tə xiƛ'=ɛ́ls mək'ʷ=wɛ́t-əs//, attested by Elders Group (3/29/77), <**lép'exes te xeytl'áls mékw' tewátes.**>, //lə́p'=əxʸ-əs tə xiƛ'=ɛ́ls mə́k'ʷ tə=wɛ́t-əs//, /'*The grizzly ate anybody. (eat s-th/s-o)*'/, attested by Elders Group (3/29/77), <**stl'ís kw'e mṓkw'ewátes.**>, //s=ƛ'í-s k'ʷə mók'ʷ=wɛ́t(-/=)əs//, /'*He likes everyone.*'/, attested by EB, <**lhíxw áxwest kw'e mṓkw'ewátes**>, //ɬí-xʷ ʔɛ́xʷ=əs=T k'ʷə mók'ʷ=wɛ́t=əs//, /'*when you give equal amounts/an equal share to everyone*'/, attested by Elders Group (3/72).

<**mekw'ét ~ mōkw'ét ~ mōkw'ót**>, pcs //mək'ʷ=ə́T or mək'ʷ=ə[=´=]T ~ mok'ʷ=áT or mok'ʷ=ə[=Aá=]T//, ABFC /'*take it all, pick it all up*'/, possibly root <**mékw'**> *all, every* or possibly bound root <**mékw'**> *find, pick up, use second-hand*, possibly <**= ´= (stress-shift) or ó-ablaut**> *resultative* or possibly just *derivational*, (<**=et**> *purposeful control transitivizer*), phonology: ablaut or stress-shift or stressed transitivizer, syntactic analysis: transitive verb, attested by IHTTC, AC, Salish cognate: Lushootseed /bə́k'ʷ-əd/ (//bə́k'ʷ-ət//) *take it all* H76:28, also <**mékw'ét**>, //mə́k'ʷ=ə́T//, also /'*take it all*'/, attested by EB (12/15/75).

<**mōkw'éthet**>, pcrs //mok'ʷ=ə́T-ət or mok'ʷ=ə[=´=]T-ət//, ABFC /'*(take all of themselves, pick themselves all up)*'/, (<**-et**> *reflexive*), phonology: stress-shift or stressed transitivizer, syntactic analysis: intransitive verb, attested by AC, example: <**mōkw'éthetchàp emí.**>, //mok'ʷ=ə́T-ət-c-ɛ̀p ʔəmí//, /'*All of you come.*'/, literally perhaps /'take/pick up all of yourselves (and) come'/, attested by AC (11/17/71).

<**mékw' ~ mṓkw'**>, bound root //mə́k'ʷ ~ mók'ʷ *find, pick up, use second-hand* (may be secondary meanings from root of the same shape meaning *all, every*) or may be the same root//, Salish cognate: Lushootseed /bək'ʷ(u)/ *take what one finds (often referring to what can be eaten)* H76:28-29.

<**mékw'et ~ mṓkw'et**>, pcs //mə́k'ʷ=əT ~ mók'ʷ=əT//, MC /'*find it, pick it up*'/, HUNT, HARV, FSH, SOC, ABFC, (<**=et**> *purposeful control transitivizer*), syntactic analysis: transitive verb, attested by AC (9/8/71), EB (12/15/75), Salish cognate: Lushootseed /bək'ʷúd/ *pick up various eatable items from the ground (such as apples), gather up from the ground or floor* H76:29.

<**smṓkw'** or **semṓkw'**>, stvi //s=mók'ʷ or s=hə=mók'ʷ//, DESC ['*(be) found*'], (<**s=**> *stative*), possibly <**he=**> *resultative*, phonology: consonant merger, optional vowel-loss, syntactic analysis: adjective/adjectival verb, attested by AC (8/24/70).

<**Smímkw'**>, dmv //s=C_1í=mək'ʷ//, PLN ['*mountain in back of Restmore Lodge (or some say way back of Mt. Cheam)*'], ASM ['can't be seen from main Trans-Canada Highway, has large rocks there like bowling balls, thunder(bird) is there, this mountain threw rocks back and forth at Lhílheqey (Mt. Cheam) because she called Smímkw' an illegitimate half-sister, but Smímkw' said she was a full sister'], (<**R4=**> *diminutive*), phonology: reduplication, syntactic analysis: nominal, attested by SP and AK (at Fish Camp 8/2/77), MP (recorded in writing by SP and AD for Stalo Heritage Project on interview 1973-1974)(IHTTC 7/8/77), source: place names reference file #40.

<**chmékw'**>, izs //c=mék'ʷ//, [č=mʊ́k'ʷ], MC /'*find*'/, (<**ch= ~ ts=**> *intransitivizer*), attested by (EH,RG 7/23/99) (SU transcription, tape 2), example: <**tsel chmékw'**>, [čɪl čmʊ́k'ʷ], '*I found*', attested by (EH,RG 7/23/99) (SU transcription, tape 2).

<**chhémkw'**>, ctv //c=hə́-m ək'ʷ//, [č=hʌ́-mk'ʷ], MC /'*finding things*'/, attested by (EH,RG 7/23/99) (SU transcription, tape 2), example: <**tsel chhémkw'**>, [čɪl čhʌ́mk'ʷ], '*I'm finding things*', attested by (EH,RG 7/23/99) (SU transcription, tape 2).

<**mékw'em**>, df //mə́k’^{w}=əm//, MC ['*use second-hand*'], (<**=em**> *intransitivizer*), syntactic analysis: intransitive verb, attested by Elders Group, EB.

<**smékw'em**>, dnom //s=mə́k’^{w}=əm//, MC /'*something used that one picks up and uses, something second-hand*'/, (<**s=**> *nominalizer*), syntactic analysis: nominal, attested by EB, Salish cognate: Lushootseed /s-bə́k’^{w}-əb/ *plunder gotten in a raid* H76:29.

<**mékw'emáwtxw**>, ds //mə́k’^{w}=əm=ɛ́wtx^{w}//, BLDG ['*second-hand store*'], ECON, SOC, lx <**=áwtxw**> *building, house*, syntactic analysis: nominal, attested by Elders Group, EB.

<**mékw'em**>, MC ['*use second-hand*'], *see* mékw' ~ mőkw'.

<**mékw'emáwtxw**>, BLDG ['*second-hand store*'], *see* mékw' ~ mőkw'.

<**mékw'et ~ mőkw'et**>, MC /'*find it, pick it up*'/, *see* mékw' ~ mőkw'.

<**mekw'ét ~ mōkw'ét ~ mōkw'ót**>, ABFC /'*take it all, pick it all up*'/, *see* mékw' ~ mőkw'.

<**mekw'ewát**>, HUMC /'*everybody, everyone, (anybody [Elders Group 3/1/72])*'/, *see* mékw' ~ mőkw'.

<**mekw'ewátes ~ mekw'ewát**>, PRON /'*everybody, everyone*'/, *see* wát.

<**mekw'stám ~ mōkw'rtám**>, NUM ['*everything*'], *see* mékw' ~ mőkw'.

<**=mel**>, da //=məl//, DIR /'*location around a house, part*'/, syntactic analysis: lexical suffix, probably related to lx <**=ó:mél**> *member, part, portion*, derivational suffix; found in <**axélésmel**>, //ʔɛx^{y}ələ́s=məl//, /'*in front (of a house)*'/, <**tselkwáx̱elmel**>, //cəlk^{w}=ɛ́x̣əl=məl//, /'*behind or back of a house*'/, <**s'átl'qmel**>, //s=ʔɛ́ƛ’q=məl//, /'*outside (of a house)*'/, <**chélhmel**>, //cə́ɬ=məl//, /'*on top of a house*'/, <**s'aléts ~ s'alétsmel ~ alétsmel**>, //sʔɛlə́c ~ (s)ʔɛlə́c=məl//, /'*bottom of a tree (trunk) or house (foundation) (all examples occur without the =məl and correspondingly lack the meaning (of a house).*'/.

<**meláses**>, free root //məlɛ́səs//, FOOD ['*molasses*'], syntactic analysis: nominal, attested by Elders Group, borrowed from English /məlǽsəz/ prob. instead of Chinook Jargon [məlǽs ~ laməlǽs] *molasses* (latter Johnson 1978:367), Salish cognate: Squamish /mlášis/ *molasses* W73:177, K67:254 Lushootseed /blás/ *molasses* H76:40.

<**meláses te sisemóye**>, cpds //məlɛ́səs-s tə C_1í=səm=áyə//, FOOD ['*honey*'], literally /'molasses of the bee'/, (<**-s**> *his, her, its, their, third person possessive*), phonology: consonant merger, syntactic analysis: simple nominal phrase, attested by Elders Group 3/22/78.

<**meláses te sisemóye**>, FOOD ['*honey*'], *see* meláses.

<**méle ~ mél:a**>, free root //mə́lə ~ mə́l·ɛ//, KIN /'*child (of someone, kinterm), offspring, son, daughter*'/, ASM ['usually eight years or older, can even be adult'], (semological comment: sex (son vs. daughter) is shown by gender in the preceding article), syntactic analysis: nominal, Salish cognate: Samish /mə́n’ə/ [mə́nʔə] *child (of someone, kinterm), offspring, son, daughter* , N.Lushootseed /bədáʔ/ and S.Lushootseed /bə́dəʔ/ *offspring, (one's own) child* Hess1976:24, attested by AC, BJ (5/64, 12/5/64), EB, many others, other sources: ES /mə́lə/ *child (kinterm)*, also <**béle**>, //bə́lə//, dialects: *Squatits village or family therein, isolated other idiolects*, phonology: half-closed b, attested by JL, AL, Mrs. AJ (MJ); DM, example: <**tel méle**>, //tə-l mə́lə//, /'*my son*'/, literally /'the (male or gender unspecified)) offspring'/, attested by BJ (12/5/64), <**swíyeqe méle**>, //s=wíqə mə́lə//, /'*son*'/, literally /'male child (kin)'/, attested by AC, <**slhá:li (the, kw'the) mél:es**>, //s=ɬɛ́·li (θə, k’^{w}=θə) mə́l·ə-s//, /'*a daughter, her child is female*'/, literally /'is female (the (female present), the (female remote)) her/his child'/, semantic environment ['answer to question, *What (sex) is the child?*'], attested by AC, <**swí(y)eqe kw'e mél:es**>, //s=wíqə k’^{w}ə mə́l·ə-s//, /'*(his/her/its/their) child is a boy, a son*'/, literally /'is male the (remote, male or sex unmarked) his/her/its/their child'/, semantic environment ['answer to

question, *What (sex) is the child?*'], attested by AC, <**méles te tl'alqtéle**>, //mə́lə-s tə ƛ'á[=lə=]qt=ə́lə//, /'*the deer's baby*'/, literally /'its child/child of the deer'/, attested by AC, <**liye skwetáxw (the slháli, kwthe swíyeqe) a méle?**>, //li-ə s=kʷətɛ́xʷ (θə s=ɬɛ́li, kʷθə s=wíqə) ʔɛ mə́lə//, /'*Is your (daughter, son) home?*'/, literally /'is -yes/no question inside (the (female), the (male, near but out of sight)) your child/offspring'/, attested by AC, <**(e)wá tl'ós te chief qetl'osuw tl'ó te méles.**>, //ʔəwə-ɛ́ ƛ'á-s tə chief qə=ƛ'a=s=uw ƛ'á tə mə́lə-s//, /'*If it isn't the chief then it's his son.*'/, literally /'if not that's him the chief then -it's -contrastive that's the (male) his child'/, attested by AC, <**te swíyeqe al mél:a**>, //tə s=wíqə (ʔə)-l mə́l·ɛ//, /'*my son*'/, attested by EB, <**the slhá:li al mél:a**>, //θə s=ɬɛ́·li (ʔə)-l mə́l·ɛ//, /'*my daughter*'/, attested by EB, <**the slhálí mél:es**>, //θə s=ɬɛ́lí mə́l·ə-s//, /'*his daughter, her daughter*'/, attested by EB, <**átsele méle.**>, //ʔɛ́cələ mə́lə//, /'*Goodness child., Gee wiiz child.*'/, syntactic comment: vocative lacks article as iere, attested by EB.

<**mámele**>, pln //C_1ɛ́=mələ//, KIN /'*children (kinterm, someone's), sons, daughters*'/, (<**R7=**> *plural*), phonology: reduplication, syntactic analysis: nominal, attested by AC, BJ)5/64), other sources: H-T <mámela> (macron over first a) *children (collect.)*, example: <**l swál mámele**>, //l s=wɛ́-l C_1ɛ́=mələ//, /'*my (own) children*'/, attested by AC, <**tel mámele**>, //tə-l C_1ɛ́=mələ//, /'*my children, my family*'/, attested by BJ (12/5/64), also <**tel bábele**>, //tə-l C_1ɛ́=bə́lə//, dialects: *Squatits village, rare scattered other idiolects*, phonology: half-closed b, attested by JL, AL, Mrs. AJ (MJ), DM.

<**mameláselh**>, ds //C_1ɛ́=mələ-s=ɛ́[=M2=]ɬ//, KIN /'*her deceased children, (his deceased children)*'/, (<**-s**> *third-person possessive, his, her, their*), ds //=álh ~ =elh *past tense, deceased*//, (<**metathesis type 2**> *derivational*), phonology: reduplication, metathesis, syntactic analysis: nominal past.

<**mímele**>, dmn //C_1í=mələ//, KIN /'*baby (kin), child (kin) (up to about eigit years old)*'/, (<**R4=**> *diminutive*), phonology: reduplication, syntactic analysis: nominal, attested by Elders Group, EB; found in <**mímeles**>, //C_1í=mələ-s//, /'*her/his/their baby, her/his/their child (up to 8)*'/, attested by EB.

<**mímele**>, dmn //C_1í=mələ//, TIME ['*first month ?*'], literally /'little child'/, (<**R4=**> *diminutive*), phonology: reduplication, syntactic analysis: nominal, attested by Elders Group (3/12/75).

<**mémele**>, dmpl //C_1í[-Aə́-]=mələ// KIN /'*many little children*'/ (e-ablaut *plural* on C_1í- (<**R4=**> *diminutive*), phonology: reduplication, syntactic analysis: nominal, attested by RG,EH 6/16/98 to SN, edited by BG with RG,EH 6/26/00)

<**mémeles kápech**>, EB, FOOD *brussel sprouts,* FOOD (lit. many little children of + cabbage), (attested by RG,EH 6/16/98 to SN, edited by BG with RG,EH 6/26/00)

<**sémele**>, strs //s=hə́=mələ//, ABFC /'*have given birth, already had a child, had a baby, (delivered)*'/, (<**s=**> *stative*), (<**he=**> *resultative*), phonology: consonant merger, syntactic analysis: adjective/adjectival verb, attested by Elders Group, AC, example: <**lulh xwá sémela**>, //lə=uɬ xʷɛ́ s=hə́=mələ//, /'*"She's jtst born)e) a baby.", She's just had a baby.*'/, literally /'she =already get/becole have given birth/had a baby/delivdred'/, attested by AC.

<**semsémele**>, plv //C_1əC_2=sə́mələ//, ABFC ['*already had children*'], (<**R3=**> *plural*), phonology: reduplication, clearly the stative and resultative prefixed are felt as part of the root here as they are never elsewhere reduplicated, prefixes reduplicated, syntactic analysis: adjective/adjectival verb, attested by Elders Group.

<**smélàtel**>, dnom //s=mə́lɛ=təl//, ANA /'*womb, uterus*'/, literally /'something to have children'/, (<**s=**> *nominal* or *stative*), lx <**=tel**> *device to, something to*, phonology: updrifting, syntactic analysis: nominal, attested by NP.

<**tsméla**>, ds //c=mə́lɛ//, ABFC /'*giving birth, having a child, having a baby*'/, (<**ts=**> *have*), syntactic analysis: intransitive verb, attested by EB, also <**tsméle**>, //c=mə́lə//, attested by Elders Group,

example: <**xóxelhmet the tsméla**>, //x^{y}á[-C_1ə-]ɬ=məT θə c=mə́lɛ//, /'*looking after someone having a baby*'/, literally /'looking after s-o the (female) having a baby'/, attested by EB.

<**smelám**>, dnom //s=məlɛ=ɛ́m//, KIN ['*adopted child*'], SOCT, (<**s=**> *nominalizer*), (<**=ám**> *intransitivizer*), phonology: stressed intransitivizer, vowel merger, syntactic analysis: nominal, attested by Elders Group.

<**txwméla ~ texwméla**>, ds //təx^{w}=mə́lɛ//, KIN ['*adopt a child*'], lx <**texw=**> *mid-, half, step-*, syntactic analysis: intransitive verb, attested by Elders Group (3/1/72).

<**texwmélem**>, df //təx^{w}=mə́lə=m//, KIN ['*step-child*'], possibly <**=m**> *nominalizer?*, syntactic analysis: nominal, attested by AC, other sources: H-T <tutuqméla> (macron over u) *step-child.*

<**texwmámelem**>, pln //təx^{w}=C_1ɛ́=mələ=m//, KIN ['*step-children*'], (<**R7=**> *plural*), phonology: reduplication, syntactic analysis: nominal, attested by AC; found in <**texwmámelems**>, //təx^{w}=C_1ɛ́=mələ=m-s//, /'*his stepchildren*'/, attested by AC.

<**txwmelám**>, df //təx^{w}=məlɛ=ɛ́m or təx^{w}=mələ=Aɛ́=m//, KIN ['*adopt a child*'], SOCT, possibly <**=ám** or **=m**> *intransitivizer* or possibly <**á-ablaut**> *derivational*, phonology: stressed intransitivizer, vowel merger, syntactic analysis: intransitive verb, attested by Elders Group (3/1/76).

<**mámelehò:llh**>, ds //C_1ɛ́=mələ=há·lɬ//, ANA /'*egg (of bird, fowl)*'/, literally /'(many) young children'/, (<**R7=**> *plural*), lx <**=ó:llh ~ =(h)ó:lh ~ =ó:ylh ~ =ellh**> *young, child, offspring*, phonology: h-epenthesis (h inserted on some vowel-initial suffixes when added to vowel final stems), reduplication, syntactic analysis: nominal, attested by AC, also <**mamelehóllh**>, //C_1ɛ́=mələ=hálɬ//, also /'*bird egg*'/, attested by Elders Group (6/11/75).

<**mámelehà:yèlhs te sisemóye**>, cpds //C_1ɛ́=mələ=ha[=Aɛ́]·yɬ-s tə sisəmáyə//, EZ ['*honeycomb*'], literally /'many young offspring -of the bee'/, (<**á-ablaut**> *derivational*), phonology: reduplication, ablaut, syntactic analysis: nominal, attested by Elders Group (3/22/78).

<**mamelehá:yelh x̲éltel**>, cpds //C_1ɛ́=mələ=ha[=Aɛ́]·yɬ x̣ə́l=təl//, SCH /'crayon '/, literally /'young children writing-device'/, (<**á-ablaut**> *derivational*), phonology: reduplication, ablaut, syntactic analysis: nominal, attested by RG & EH (4/10/99 Ling332)

<**smìmeleholIháIa**>, ds //s=C_1í=(C_1ɛ́=)mələ=halɬ=ɛ́lɛ//, EZ ['*nest*'], literally /'little bird egg container of'/, (semological comment: Amy Cooper had forgotten the word for *little bird's nest* and a different word for *bigger nest (like a hawk's)*), (<**s=**> *nominalizer*, R4= *diminutive* (replaces R7= *plural*)), lx <**=hó:llh**> *young, offspring*, lx <**=ála**> *container of*, phonology: reduplication replacing reduplication, syntactic analysis: nominal, attested by Elders Group (6/11/75).

<**mimele'ó:ylha**>, df //C_1í=mələ=ʔá·yɬ(=)ɛ or C_1í=mələ=yá·[=M1=]ɬ(=)ɛ//, PE ['*doll*'], literally /'little child's young/offspring/child (or) little child's wood'/, PLAY, (<**R4=**> *diminutive*), possibly <**'ó:ylh(a)**> *young, offspring*, possibly <**=a?**> *derivational?*, or =yó:lh> *wood*, and possibly <**metathesis type 1**> *derivational*, phonology: reduplication, possible metathesis, syntactic analysis: nominal, attested by Elders Group (2/25/76).

<**mélemélhp**>, df //mə́lə(=)m=ə[=´=]ɬp//, EB /'*hemlock tree, Western hemlock*'/, ['*Tsuga heterophylla*'], ASM ['ground bark numbs the mouth, can be used to bring on vomiting, red bark "bleeds", the bark is also medicine for tuberculosis'], possibly root <**méle**> *child* or possibly root <**melám**> *adopted child* (could be called this due to its resemblance to red cedar?, application of kinterms in naming flora is well-attested in the Thompson language and some is found in Halkomelem elsewhere under th'á:ya), possibly <**=´=**> *derivational*, lx <**=elhp**> *tree,* phonology: stress-shift, syntactic analysis: nominal, attested by Elders Group (3/15/72)(except semantic info. from others below), other sources: JH /mə́ləmə́ɬp/, H-T <mElEmE´ltlp>, also <**melemélhp**>, //mələ(=)m=ə[=´=]ɬp//, attested by Deming, AC, also <**mélemelhp**>, //mə́lə(=)m=əɬp//, attested by Elders Group (1/29/75).

<**mél:eqw**>, possibly root //mə́l·əqʷ//, ANA [*'animal and bird gall-bladder'*], (semological comment: gloss could be reversed with that of mésel *fish gall-bladder*), syntactic analysis: nominal, attested by AC, other sources: JH /mə́ləqʷ/ *gall*, compare <**mélqw**> *fish heart; uvula.*

<**mélés**>, df //mə́l=ə[=´=]s//, EZ [*'racoon'*], [*'Procyon lotor pacificus'*], ASM ['there used to be lots of stories about him'], possibly root <**mel**> *get hit* (as in <xw=mél=kw'=es> *hit in the face)* after a story about why raccoon got the black mask across his eyes, lx <**=es**> *on the face*, possibly <=´=> *derivational*, phonology: possible stress-shift, syntactic analysis: nominal, attested by AK (11/21/72), JL, NP, Deming (at Fish Camp 7/19/79), Elders Group, AC (via Albert Cooper), BJ (12/5/64), other sources: ES and JH /mə́lə́s/.

<**Smelő'**>, df //s=məl(əs)=ó(w)ʔ//, N /*'Racoon (name in a story), (Lynx [JL])'*/, MYC, EZ, (<**s=**> *nominalizer/affectionate*), possibly <**=ó(w)'**> meaning uncertain, phonology: final glottal stop is unusual, perhaps shows a borrowing from downriver Halkomelem or another Salish language, syntactic analysis: nominal, attested by AK and ME (11/21/72 tape), also /*'Lynx'*/, ASM ['caught and jailed in a story, Qelóts'emes *Bobcat* escapes and feeds Smelő''], attested by JL (Fish Camp 7/19/79 with NP and Deming elders).

<**méléts'**>, root or stem //mə́lə́c'//, meaning uncertain

<**lheméléts'**>, df //ɬə(=)mə́lə́c' or ɬəm=ə́lə́c'//, EZ [*'deer fly'*], ['family *Tabanidae*, genus *Chrysops*'], ASM ['found in the mountains'], possibly <**lhe=**> *extract, extract a portion*, possibly <**=(el)ets'**> *around in circles* (as in <**sél=ts'**> *spin around in circles*, <**s=t'amx=á:lts'**> *a braid*, etc., cf. Suttles Musqueam suffix <**=ets'**> **14.6.29**), possibly root <**méléts'**> *mixed up* (perhaps because animals appear confused when bitten?), possibly root <**má(')**> *come off, take off*, syntactic analysis: nominal, attested by BJ (12/5/64, tape transcript old p.294), also <**lhmélets**>, //ɬ(=)mə́ləc or ɬm=ə́ləc//, literally perhaps /'pick/pluck on the bottom/rump'/, attested by Halkomelem Instructor's Association (10/26/77), also <**smémelets**>, //s=mə́məlec//, comment: many possible derivations for this (with R4Aə́=, with =R1=, with =elets, with root mel or mél or me or other vowels, with ts sic for ts', etc.), attested by Elders Group (6/11/75).

<**mélets'methó:ythel**>, LANG [*'mixed up in speaking'*], *see* mál ~ mél.

<**mélets'methó:ythel**>, LANG [*'mixed up in speaking'*], *see* mí:l ~ míl.

<**méleqw** (or) **leméleqw**>, df //mə́l=əqʷ or mə́=ləqʷ (or) ləm=ə́ləqʷ//, ABDF /*'fall on one's forehead, drop on one's forehead, fall onto one's head'*/, possibly root <**mél**> *hit*? or mé ~ (e)mí> *come* or possibly root <**lom**> *throw and hit*, lx <**=eqw ~ =éleqw**> *on top of the head*, phonology: possible vowel-reduction (if root lom), syntactic analysis: intransitive verb, attested by JL, EB, example: <**le méleqw te siyólh.**>, //lə mə́l(=)əqʷ tə s=yáɬ//, /*'Wood fell or dropped on one's forehead.'*/, attested by JL.

<**mélkw'**>, bound root or stem //mə́l(=)k'ʷ//, perhaps *get hit*

<**xwmélkw'es**>, df //xʷ=mə́l(=)k'ʷ=əs//, ABDF [*'get hit in the face'*], (<**xw=**> meaning uncertain or pertaining to the head), possibly <**=kw'**> *round*, lx <**=es**> *on the face*, syntactic analysis: intransitive verb, attested by JL, IHTTC.

<**melmélkw'es**>, df //$C_1əC_2$=mə́l(=)k'ʷ=əs//, ABDF [*'hit on the face (several times)'*], ASM ['and with the sqóyep *badger* the marks stayed'], compare <**mélés**> *racoon*, (<**R3=**> *plural*), lx <**=es**> *on the face*, phonology: reduplication, syntactic analysis: intransitive verb, attested by AK (11/21/72 tape).

<**mélmel**>, EFAM /*'make a mistake, blunder'*/, *see* mál ~ mél.

<**melmélkw'es**>, ABDF [*'hit on the face (several times)'*], *see* xwmélkw'es.

<**melmélkw'es sqoyép**>, EZ ['*badger or wolverine*'], *see* sqoyép.

<**melmeló:ythel**>, LANG ['*blunder in speaking*'], *see* mál ~ mél.

<**melmelő́ws**>, ABFC ['*get carried away and sleepy from eating too rich food*'], *see* mál ~ mél.

<**melmelqwìwèl**>, EFAM /'*forgetful, mixed up (mentally, emotionally)*'/, *see* mál ~ mél.

<**melmílets'**>, EFAM ['*confused*'], *see* mál ~ mél.

<**melmóléqwet**>, MC ['*really mixed s-th up*'], *see* mál ~ mél.

<**mélqeliythílem**>, LANG /'*forget in speaking, forget one's words, forget a word*'/, *see* mál ~ mél.

<**mélqithílem**>, LANG ['*blunder in speech*'], *see* mál ~ mél.

<**melqí:wsem**>, ABDF ['*to faint*'], *see* mál ~ mél.

<**mélqw**>, free root //mə́lqʷ//, ANAH ['*uvula (fleshy knob dangling down in throat)*'], ANAF ['*fish heart*'], syntactic analysis: nominal, attested by Deming, Elders Group, compare <**méleqw**> *animal and bird gall-bladder (or fish gall-bladder).*

<**mélqweqel ~ smélqweqel**>, ds //mə́lqʷ=əqəl ~ s=mə́lqʷ=əqəl//, ANAH /'*uvula, uvula down in the throat*'/, (<**s=**> *nominalizer*), lx <**=eqel**> *in the throat*, syntactic analysis: nominal, attested by Elders Group, example: <**híkw ta mélqweqel.**>, //híkʷ t-ɛ mə́lqʷ=əqəl//, /'*Your uvula is big.*'/, usage: said to you when you talk too much, attested by Elders Group (8/20/75).

<**mélqweqel ~ smélqweqel**>, ANAH /'*uvula, uvula down in the throat*'/, *see* mélqw.

<**melúmesmes**>, EZ /'*small adult cows, (small adult cattle)*'/, *see* músmes.

<**mélxw**>, bound root //mə́lxʷ *grease, oil*//.

<**mélxwt**>, pcs //mə́lxʷ=T//, MC /'*grease s-th/s-o, oil s-th/s-o, rub something on s-th/s-o*'/, semantic environment ['for ex. a newborn child with bear grease'], (<**=t**> *purposeful control transitivizer*), syntactic analysis: transitive verb, attested by EB, AC, BHTTC.

<**smólxw**>, strs //s=mə[=Aá=]lxʷ//, DESC ['*(be) oiled*'], (<**s=**> *stative*), (<**ó-ablaut**> *resultative*), phonology: ablaut, syntactic analysis: adjective/adjectival verb, attested by BHTTC, comment: smólxwt is an unlikely variant.

<**smelmólxw**>, chrs //s=C_1əC_2=mə[=Aá=]lxʷ//, strs, DESC ['*(be) oily (?)*'], (<**R3=**> *characteristic*), phonology: reduplication, ablaut, syntactic analysis: adjective/adjectival verb, attested by BHTTC.

<**mélxweqwem**>, mdls //mə́lxʷ=əqʷ=əm//, ABFC /'*oil one's hair, oil one's head*'/, CLO, PE, lx <**=eqw**> *on the hair, on top of the head*, (<**=em**> *middle voice*), syntactic analysis: intransitive verb, attested by EB.

<**melxwqwéylém**>, incs //məlxʷ=əqʷ=íl=əm//, mdls, ABFC /'*oil one's hair, oil one's head*'/, lx <**=eqw**> *on the hair, on top of the head*, (<**=íl**> *get, go, come, become, inceptive*, <**=em**> *middle voice*), phonology: updrifting, vowel-loss or zero-grade of suffix before strong-grade of suffix, syntactic analysis: intransitive verb, attested by EB.

<**mélxweqwt**>, pcs //mə́lxʷ=əqʷ=T//, ABFC ['*oil his/her/its head*'], lx <**=eqw**> *on the hair, on top of the head*, (<**=t**> *purposeful control transitivizer*), syntactic analysis: transitive verb, attested by EB.

<**melxwíwsem**>, mdls //məlxʷ=íws=əm//, ABFC ['*grease one's body*'], lx <**=íws**> *on the body, on the skin*, (<**=em**> *middle voice*), syntactic analysis: intransitive verb, attested by JL (Fish Camp 7/20/79).

<**mélxweqwem**>, ABFC /'*oil one's hair, oil one's head*'/, *see* mélxw.

<**mélxweqwt**>, ABFC ['*oil his/her/its head*'], *see* mélxw.

<**melxwíwsem**>, ABFC ['*grease one's body*'], *see* mélxw.

<**melxwqwéylém**>, ABFC /'*oil one's hair, oil one's head*'/, *see* mélxw.

<**mélxwt**>, MC /'*grease s-th/s-o, oil s-th/s-o, rub something on s-th/s-o*'/, *see* mélxw.

<**mélx̲weth'**>, bound stem //mə́lx̣ʷ(=)əθ'//, meaning uncertain

<**smélx̲weth'**>, df //s=mə́lx̣ʷ(=)əθ'//, EZ ['*dipper (bird)*'], ['*Cinclus mexicanus*'], ASM ['blue-grey bird found on little creeks'], (<**s=**> *nominalizer*), syntactic analysis: nominal, dialects: poss. *Tait*, attested by Elders Group (8/30/77), Salish cognate: Squamish /s-mə́l-mlx̣ʷ-ic'a/ *dipper (Cinclus mexicanus)* W73:79, K67:283, K69:56, Mainland Comox /smə́lx̣ʷ/ *dipper* B75:17prelim., also <**smélx̲wets'**>, //s=mə́lx̣ʷ(=)əc'//, dialects: poss. *Cheh. (for ex. HP)*, attested by Elders Group (6/4/75, 2/11/76, 2/18/76).

<**Mélx̲weth'**>, ds //mə́lx̣ʷ(=)əθ'//, PLN ['*a creek probably on the CPR side (west side) of the Fraser River between Yale and Strawberry Island*'], ASM ['probably below Shxw'ílemőwelh and above Alwís Lhqéletel (which is the second creek below Suka Creek on the CN (east) side); named from smélx̲weth' *dipper bird* because these birds abound on this creek'], grammatical comment: derived by removing the s= *nominalizer*, a process used in other place name derivation, syntactic analysis: nominal, attested by Elders Group (8/30/77), source: place names reference file #245.

<**mélhqw**>, bound root or stem //mə́ɬqʷ//, meaning uncertain.

<**smelhmélhqw**>, stvi //s=C_1əC_2=mə́ɬqʷ//, DESC /'*rough (of wood), lumpy (of ground, bark, etc.)*'/, semantic environment ['wood, ground, bark, etc.'], (<**s=**> *stative*, R3= *characteristic* or *plural*), phonology: reduplication, syntactic analysis: adjective/adjectival verb, attested by AC, BHTTC, Elders Group, other sources: H-T <smEtlmEtlkwélEp> (macron over e) *uneven, rough [of ground]*.

<**mélhx̲wel**>, df //mə́ɬx̣ʷəl or mə=ɬə́[=M2=]x̣ʷ=əl//, EB /'*Indian plum (the fruit),* (also called) *June plum*'/, ['*Osmaronia cerasiformis*'], ASM ['deep purple berry sized plum with a large pit or stone, the plum dries the mouth (has some tannin) but is tasty (somewhat watermelon-flavored), ripens in June, grows on a bush not a tree'], possibly <**me=**> *come, become, get*, possibly <**=el**> *go, come, get*, possibly **<metathesis>** *derivational*, possibly root <**lhx̲w ~ lhéx̲w**> *spit out*, comment: may have this root because, like lhéx̲wlhex̲w *choke cherry* with the same root, the fruit has tannin and a large pit which both promote spitting out of the pit, phonology: metathesis possible, syntactic analysis: nominal, noun, attested by AC, SP, AD, Elders Group, other sources: ES /mə́ɬx̣ʷəl/, Salish cognate: Squamish /smə́ɬx̣ʷl/ *Indian plum* W73:201, K69:56, example: <**ts'méth' te mélhx̲wel.**>, //c'=mə́θ' tə mə́ɬx̣ʷəl//, /'*The Indian plum is blue (or purple).*'/, attested by Elders Group.

<**mélhx̲welelhp**>, ds //mə́(=)ɬx̣ʷ=əl=əɬp//, EB ['*Indian plum bush*'], ['*Osmaronia cerasiformis*'], lx <**=elhp**> *plant, tree*, phonology: AC had some trouble pronouncing this word, this may indicate that it should be melhx̲wíyelhp, following the regular morphophonemic rule of consonant-change and vowel-change that el → íy before =elhp, instead of being irregular phonologically, syntactic analysis: nominal, attested by AC.

<**mélhx̲welelhp**>, EB ['*Indian plum bush*'], *see* mélhx̲wel.

<**memáx**>, SOC /'*to separate people fighting, to split up people fighting*'/, *see* má ~ má'-.

<**memekwóyetses**>, ABDF ['*(have) fingers so cold they can't bend*'], *see* mékw.

<**mémeleqel**>, HHG ['*small containers (a number of them)*'], *see* mímeleqel.

<**memílets'**>, EFAM ['*mixed up*'], *see* mál ~ mél.

<**memílets'**>, DESC ['*mixed up*'], *see* mí:l ~ míl.

<**memí:lt**>, EFAM /'*discriminate against s-o, not accept s-o*'/, *see* mí:lt.

<**memí:lt**>, SOC /'*not accept s-o, discriminate against s-o*'/, *see* mí:lt.

<**meqó:s**>, TIME /'*about December, (January to February [Billy Sepass])*'/, *see* máqa ~ máqe.

<**méqsel**>, possibly root //m(=)ə́qsəl//, ANA ['*nose*'], ASM ['young sprouts of tansy are used as medicine for nosebleed--they are stuck up the nose, tansy flowers are used for yellow dye also, but no halq'eméylem name has been learned for tansy, this info. from JL'][a good name for *tansy* might be *<**sthxwélqseltel**>, lit. 'nose-bleed medicine'-BG], possibly root <**m**> empty root or *nominalizer*, possibly <**=éqsel**> *on the nose*, syntactic analysis: nominal, perhaps noun, attested by AC, BJ (5/64), EB, JL, other sources: ES /mə́qsəl/, H-T <múksil>, example: <**í:x̱ te méqsel.**>, //ʔí·x̣ tə mə́qsəl//, /'*scratched on the nose, (The nose got scratched.)*'/, attested by JL.

<**Méqsel**>, df //m(=)ə́qsəl//, PLN ['*rock shaped like a man's nose on the north side of Harrison River*'], ASM ['formerly located halfway between the old Chehalis Indian cemetary (opp. side) or Morris Valley and the hot springs, located above (upriver or east here from) Dixon Point and below (west of) Venison Point, this rock was visible from half a mile away, it is now gone, dynamited by Dick Ward about the 1930's or earlier to find gold there; Dick Ward, a Whiteman, homesteaded there and was called Méqsel as a result (Edna Bobb remembers him with a white beard when she was 8 yrs. old [about 1921])'], phonology: zero-derivation, syntactic analysis: nominal, attested by EL, IHTTC, EB, NP, comment: the Nooksacks have a place also called Méqsel by some, prob. Méqsen is more correct (Nooksack and Downriver Halkomelem), it was a village on Bertrand Creek in Canada, near the border, see Nooksack Place Names articles and papers which document it; the two places were seldom if ever confused since in general the Deming elders didn't know of the Harrison River place and the Chehalis elders didn't know of the Nooksack place.

<**sméqsel**>, stvi //s=mə́qsəl//, BPI ['*(have a) big nose*'], ANA, (<**s=**> *stative* ? and with several body part words *big*), syntactic analysis: adjective/adjectival verb, attested by Elders Group, AC.

<**meqsélem**>, mdls //məqsə[=´=]l=əm//, ABFC ['*clean one's nose*'], PE, (<**=´=**> *derivational*), (<**=em**> *middle voice*), phonology: stress-shift, syntactic analysis: intransitive verb, attested by Deming (AH, LG).

<**Méqsel**>, PLN ['*rock shaped like a man's nose on the north side of Harrison River*'], *see* méqsel.

<**meqsélem**>, ABFC ['*clean one's nose*'], *see* méqsel.

<**méq'**>, free root //mə́q'//, ABFC /'*(be) full (from eating), (get filled (from eating) [AC])*'/, attested by AC, syntactic analysis: intransitive verb, attested by AC, MH, many others in Elders Group and Deming elders, other sources: JH /mə́q'/ *full from eating*, also /'*get filled (from eating)*'/, attested by AC, example: <**ítsel méq'.**> (or perhaps) <**étsel méq'.**>, //ʔí-c-əl mə́q' or ʔə́-c-əl mə́q'//, /'*I got filled.*'/, attested by AC, <**ítsel méq' te sthóqwi.**>, //ʔí-c-əl mə́q' tə s=θáqʷi//, /'*I got filled with fish.*'/, attested by AC; found in <**méq'tsel.**>, //mə́q'-c-əl//, /'*I'm full.*'/, attested by MH, example: <**lichap méq'?**>, //li-c-ɛp mə́q'//, /'*Are you (folks) full?*'/, attested by MH.

<**meq'lómet**>, ncrs //məq'=l-ámət//, ABFC ['*fill oneself up (by eating)*'], (<**=l**> *non-control transitivizer, happen to, manage to, accidentally*), (<**-ómet**> *reflexive*), syntactic analysis: intransitive verb, attested by Elders Group.

<**méq'et**>, pcs //mə́q'=əT//, ABFC /'*swallow s-th, swallow it*'/, (<**=et**> *purposeful control transitivizer*), syntactic analysis: transitive verb, attested by AC, others; found in <**méq'etlha.**>, //mə́q'=əT-ɬɛ//, /'*Swallow it.*'/, attested by AC, example: <**méq'et te st'élmexw**>, //mə́q'=əT tə s=t'ə́lməxʷ//, /'*swallow the medicine*'/, attested by AC, <**yalhs'es méq'etes.**>, //yɛɬ-s-ʔ-əs

mə́q’=əT-əs//, /'*He just swallowed it.*'/, attested by AC.

<**hémq'et**>, cts //hə́-mq’=əT//, ABFC ['*swallowing s-th*'], (<**hé-**> *continuative*), syntactic analysis: transitive verb, attested by AC, also <**hómq'et**>, //há-mq’=əT//, phonology: slow speech, attested by AC.

<**sméq'eth**>, dnom //s=mə́q’-əθ//, FOOD /'*feast left-overs, left-overs of food (which guests can take home)*'/, SOC, ASM ['at a gathering people used to put down cloth on floor for the food to sit on; guests could tear it at the end of the feast to wrap up their left-overs to take home (to help them while they travelled and when they got home); this custom is still practiced but often with paper napkins and paper plates and sometimes paper bags'], (<**s=**> *nominalizer*), lx <**=eth ~ =óth ~ =óthel**> *in the mouth*, syntactic analysis: nominal, attested by MH, AC, Deming, also <**smeq'óth**>, //s=məq’=áθ//, attested by AC.

<**méq'etsem**>, ds //mə́q’=əc=əm for mə́q’=əθ=əm//, FOOD ['*take left-over food*'], SOC, (<**=em**> *middle voice* or perhaps *intransitivizer*), phonology: ts is dialect variant for th here, dialects: *Deming* (AH has such variants, the Nooksack language would also show this form), attested by Deming (2/8/79), example: <**lámchxw méq'etsem.**>, //lɛ́=m-c-x^w mə́q’=əc=əm//, /'*Take what's left (of the food).*'/, literally /'you (mildly urging imperative) go take the left-overs'/, attested by Deming.

<**meq'ethále**>, ds //məq’=əθ=ɛ́lə//, FOOD /'*container for left-overs taken home from feast, doggie bag*'/, SOC, lx <**=álá ~ =ála ~ =ále**> *container for*, syntactic analysis: nominal, attested by Deming.

<**Hémq'eleq**>, ds //hə́=mq’=ələq//, PLN ['*large whirlpool in the Fraser River just above Hill's Bar and near the west (CPR) side*'], ASM ['located by where a rock was blasted out long time ago for riverboats, this whirlpool gets huge in high water, it may go into a hole in the bed of the river, huge logs and sometimes people get sucked up in it and sometimes are found far away (one belief about whirlpools is that they sometimes are connected by tunnels in the earth with other bodies of water)'], PLN /'maybe also *the whirlpool by Odlum on the same side but below Hope [AD, AK, SP (American Bar place names trip 6/26/78)]*'/, PLAY ['*pattern in cat's cradle designs*'], literally /'being swallowed in waves'/, (<**hé=**> *continuative*), lx <**=eleq ~ =áleq**> *waves, billows*, phonology: zero-grade of root after full-grade strong-stress-valenced prefix, syntactic analysis: nominal, attested by SP, AK, AD (all on raft trip 8/30/77), Elders Group (9/13/77), BHTTC, IHTTC (9/14/77), source: place names reference file #97, maybe also /'*the whirlpool by Odlum on the same side but below Hope*'/, attested by AD, AK, SP (American Bar place names trip 6/26/78).

<**méq'et**>, ABFC /'*swallow s-th, swallow it*'/, *see* méq'.

<**meq'ethále**>, FOOD /'*container for left-overs taken home from feast, doggie bag*'/, *see* méq'.

<**méq'etsem**>, FOOD ['*take left-over food*'], *see* méq'.

<**meq'lómet**>, ABFC ['*fill oneself up (by eating)*'], *see* méq'.

<**méqw' ~ mő̋qw'**>, free root //mə́q’^{w} ~ móq’^{w}//, [mə́q’^{w} ~ mʊ́q’^{w} ~ móq’^{w}], CST /'*burst, burst out, (get) smash(ed) (something round and filled)*'/, semantic environment ['balloon, spider, fruit, penis, etc.'], ABFC ['*ejaculate*'], syntactic analysis: intransitive verb, attested by AC, EB, Elders Group, JL, example: <**ő le méqw'.**>, //ʔó lə mə́q’^{w}//, /'*Oh it burst out.*'/, Elder's comment: "a woman might say this after a man climaxes", attested by JL (7/20/79 at Fish Camp).

<**meqw'méqw'**>, plv //C_1əC_2=mə́q’^{w}//, CST /'*many get crushed, get all crushed, many smashed (round and fill*ed)'/, (<**R3=**> *plural patients, plural subject*), phonology: reduplication, syntactic analysis: intransitive verb, attested by EB, example: <**meqw'méqw' te sth'í:ms.**>, //C_1əC_2=mə́q’^{w} tə s=θ’í·m-s//, /'*His berries got all crushed.*'/, attested by EB.

<**méqw'et**>, pcs //mə́q'ʷ=əT//, [mə́q'ʷət (preferred) ~ mʊ́q'ʷət ~ móq'ʷət], CST /'*squish s-th round and filled, smash s-th round and filled*'/, (<**=et**> *purposeful control transitivizer*), syntactic analysis: transitive verb, attested by EB.

<**méqw' ~ mṓqw'**>, root uncertain //mə́q'ʷ ~ móq'ʷ//, meaning uncertain

<**sméqw'o ~ smṓqw'o**>, df //s=mə́q'ʷ(=)a ~ s=móq'ʷ(=)a//, EZ /'*great blue heron, (often called) "crane"*'/, ['*Ardea herodias* especially subspecies *fannini*'], ASM ['big, tall, long legs, found by river, not sandhill crane which has separate name (<**slí:m**>) (except perhaps for DM, JH's elder)'], (<**s=**> *nominalizer*), possibly root <**méqw'**> *squash s-th round* perhaps after its tiny round body with long thin neck and legs, possibly <**=o**> meaning uncertain unless> *just*, syntactic analysis: nominal, attested by AC, BJ (12/5/64), other sources: ES /smə́q'ʷa/ *great blue heron*, JH /smə́k'ʷe/ *great blue heron, sandhill crane*, H-T <smṓk·wa> *crane (Grus canadensis)*, also <**smṓqw'a**>, //s=móq'ʷ(=)ɛ//, also /'*"crane"*'/, attested by Elders Group (2/18/76, 6/4/75).

<**Smémeqw'o**>, dmpn //s=C₁í=Aə́=məq'ʷ(=)a//, PLN /'*(heron nesting area which was the) upriver end of Herrling Island in Fraser River just below Popkum,* also *the name of the village or settlement on Herrling Island*'/, ASM ['just below Ed Nelson's place (his parents used to live on the island), the island was the home of "cranes", it is just across a channel of water from Popkum'], (<**s=**> *nominalizer*, R4= *diminutive*), (<**é-ablaut**> *plural of diminutive*), phonology: reduplication, ablaut, syntactic analysis: nominal, attested by JL and AK (Seabird Island trip 4/7/78, recorded on History tape #34, side one, part one), IHTTC (8/11/77), source: place names reference file #188, other sources: Wells 1965 (lst ed.):25.

<**méqw'et**>, CST /'*squish s-th round and filled, smash s-th round and filled*'/, *see* méqw' ~ mṓqw'.

<**meqw'méqw'**>, CST /'*many get crushed, get all crushed, many smashed (round and fill*ed)'/, *see* méqw' ~ mṓqw'.

<**mésel**>, possibly root //mə́səl//, ANAF /'*fish gall-bladder, (animal and bird gall-bladder [AC], gall-bladder (of fish, frog, animal, human) [Elders Group 2/27/80])*'/, syntactic analysis: nominal, noun, attested by AC, Elders Group (4/28/76), other sources: ES /mə́səl/ *gall*, Salish cognate: Squamish /mə́sn/ *gall* W73:110, K67:254, also <**mésel**>, //mə́səl//, [mɪ́sɪl], also /'*fish gall-bladder may be mistake for animal and bird gall-bladder*'/, attested by AC, also /'*gall-bladder (of fish, frog, animal, human)*'/, attested by Elders Group (2/27/80).

<**mesíyeltel ~ mesí:ltel**>, dnom //məs=íyəl=təl ~ məs=í·l-təl//, FSH ['*anchor*'], CAN, root probably cognate with the Lushootseed root meaning *stationary*, possibly <**=íyel**> *net* or more likely <**=í:l**> *get, become, go, come, inceptive*, lx <**=tel**> *device to, thing to*, syntactic analysis: nominal, attested by Elders Group (3/1/72), Salish cognate: Lushootseed /baʔs/ (root) *stationary* and /báʔs-təd/ *anchor (noun)* and /ʔəs-báʔs/ *child who won't move when told to* H76:21.

<**méstexw**>, TVMO /'*bring s-th, fetch s-th, get s-th (bring it), give it to s-o(as s-th fetched, not as a gift)*'/, *see* mí ~ mé ~ me.

<**mestíyexw**>, df //məstíyəxʷ//, HUMC ['*person*'], root meaning unknown, syntactic analysis: nominal, noun, attested by AC, EB, IHTTC, other sources: ES /məstí·yəxʷ/, H-T <miste'uq> (macrons on e and u), example: <**th'ó:kws mestíyexw**>, //θ'á·kʷs məstíyəxʷ//, /'*seven people*'/, attested by AC, <**qó::x̱ mestíyexw**>, //qə[-Aa-][=··=]x̱ məstíyəxʷ//, /'*MANY people.*'/, phonology: emphatic lengthening of e here ablauts e to o which can accept length, other cases of emphatic lengthening however ARE tolerated by e /ə/ (that is, é: /ə́·/is not allowed but some cases of é:: /ə́··/ are), attested by AC (8/4/70), <**li welh mímelha te** mestíyexw?>, //li wəɬ mí[-C₁ə-]ɬɛ tə məstíyəxʷ//, /'*Are the people winter-dancing (spirit-dancing) now?*'/, attested by AC, <**welh mestíyexw**>, //wəɬ məstíyəxʷ//, /'*a person who is never home, "a wild person"*'/, attested by IHTTC, <**tesós te mestíyexw.**>, //təs=ás tə məstíyəxʷ//, /'*The person is poor.*'/, usage: what rich people used to say, attested by IHTTC,

<**mestíyexw x̱élesem**>, //məstíyəxʷ x̣ə́l=əs=əm// 09or //məstíyəxʷ x̣i[=Aə́=]l=əs=əm//, //'picture of a person'//,lit. /'person pictured'/, attested by RG & EH (4/10/99 Ling332)

<**mímstiyexw**>, dmn //C_1í=məstiyəxʷ//, HUMC ['*kid*'], (<**R4=**> *diminutive*), phonology: reduplication, zero-grade of root after full-grade of prefix, syntactic analysis: nominal, noun, usage: informal (slang), attested by AC.

<**mamastiyexw** (or better) **mémestiyexw**>, dmpn //C_1íAə́=məstiyəxʷ//, HUMC ['*kids*'], (<**é-ablaut**> *plural of diminutive*), phonology: reduplication, ablaut, syntactic analysis: nominal, noun, usage: informal (slang), colloquial, attested by AC.

<**smestíyexw**>, dnom //s=məstíyəxʷ//, REL /'*conscience, spirit (which can be lost temporarily), soul, life-spirit, power of one's will*'/, ANA, ASM ['can get lost or be stolen from one's body and only be recovered by a shaman or a syewí:l, can also be lost if one is scared somewhere, will return to one if it is called to return'], (<**s=**> *big?* or *nominalizer/affectionate?*), syntactic analysis: nominal, attested by BHTTC, Elders Group, EB, AC.

<**smímstiyexw**>, dmn //s=C_1í=məstiyəxʷ//, REL ['*spirit*'], ASM ['which can be lost if you are scared somewhere, will return to you if you call to it to return'], (<**R4=**> *diminutive*), phonology: reduplication, syntactic analysis: nominal, attested by BHTTC.

<**Smimstiyexwálá ~ Smímstíyexwá:le**>, ds //s=C_1í=məstiyəxʷ=ɛ́lɛ́ ~ s=C_1í=məstíyəxʷ=ɛ́·lə//, PLN ['*place near mouth of Chehalis River where they had a mass burial during a smallpox epidemic*'], ASM ['too many died at the time of smallpox and some had to be buried there in a big communal grave about 150 yards above (in upriver direction parallel to Chehalis River from) the road from old Chehalis village to Chehalis River; there was always a flat grassy area there for years; now there's lots of brush and wet marsh, too much to walk there easily from the old Chehalis road; located at mouth of Chehalis River where Alec Joseph had his smokehouse'], literally /'container of small souls (or) container of small people'/, lx <**=álá ~ =á:la ~ =á:le**> *container of*, phonology: reduplication, zero grade of root, syntactic analysis: nominal, attested by EL (3/1/78 tape), EL and NP and EB (Chehalis trip 9/27/77), source: place names reference file #228, also <**Mimstiyexwála**>, //C_1í=məstiyəxʷ=ɛ́lɛ//, literally /'container of little people'/, ASM ['NP and MP say it means "container of (little) people" because it was where lots of people were buried together when they could keep up with the burials during the smallpox epidemic; DF says it means "container of a little person" because only one person (a short person or little (young) person) survived there from a smallpox epidemic'], attested by NP and MP and DF in Elders Group (8/24/77).

<**meshí:l**>, free root //məší·l//, TOOL ['*machine*'], syntactic analysis: nominal, attested by Elders Group (6/1/77), borrowed from English /məší·n/ *machine*.

<**=met**>, da //=məT//, TIB ['*indirect effect non-control transitivizer*'], phonology: the <**t**> //T// in <**=st**> //=sT// *causative* and in <**=t ~ =et**> //=T ~ =əT// *purposeful control transitivizer* and <**t**> in <**=met**> //=məT// here becomes <**th**> /θ/ before three inflections, <**-óme, -óx, -et**> (/-ámə, -áxʸ, -ət/) (*first person singular object, me, second person singular object, you,* and *purposeful control reflexive,* everywhere else it remains <**t**> /t/, (<**=met**> *indirectly affecting control transitivizer* may possibly be analyzed as an old middle <**=em**> + <**=et**> *purposeful control transitivizer*) syntactic analysis: derivational suffix; found in <**t'ílemethòxes.**>, //t'íl=əməT-áxʸ-əs//, /'*He sings it for me. (sing it for s-o)*'/, <**el'éliyemethométselcha.**>, //C_1əC_2=ʔə́l(=)iyɛ=məT-ámə-c-əl-cɛ//, /'*I'll be dreaming of you. (dreaming of s-o purposely)*'/.

<**mét ~ met**> or <**mat**>, bound root //mə́t ~ mət// meaning unknown or root <**mat**> *flat organ in sturgeon which was skinned off and boiled down for glue*

<**sméteqsel ~ smetóqsel**>, df //s=mə́t=əqsəl ~ s=mət=áqsəl//, ANA ['*snot*'], (<**s=**> *nominalizer*),

possibly root <**mát**>as in <**mát**> *flat organ in sturgeon which was skinned off and boiled down for glue* (because it is sticky?)(see **<smatmáteqsel>** below and **<ó-ablaut>** above poss. on metathesized root **vowel <á>?),** lx <**=éqsel**> *on the nose*, phonology: ablaut possible, metathesis remotely possible, syntactic analysis: nominal, attested by Elders Group, Salish cognate: Squamish /smə́tqsn/ *snot* W73:241, K67:283.

<**smetméteqsel ~ smatmáteqsel**>, chrs //s=C_1əC_2=mə́t=əqsəl ~ s=C_1əC_2=mɛ́t=əqsəl//, ANA ['*(be) snotty*'], (<**s=**> *stative*, R3= *characteristic*), lx <**=eqsel**> *on the nose*, phonology: reduplication, syntactic analysis: nominal, attested by Elders Group (3/3/76).

<**metú**>, free root //mətú//, EZ ['*domestic sheep*'], ['genus *Ovis*'], ACL, borrowed from French <mouton> *sheep* or reduced from Upriver Halkomelem <**lemetú**> *sheep* itself from Chinook Jargon <lemuto> *sheep* Johnson 1978:404, see main dialect form <**lemetú**>, phonology: possible consonant-loss and vowel-loss, syntactic analysis: nominal, noun, attested by BHTTC.

<**mímetú**>, dmn //C_1í=mətú//, EZ ['*little lamb*'], ['genus *Ovis*'], (<**R4=**> *diminutive*), phonology: reduplication, syntactic analysis: nominal, noun, attested by BHTTC, example: <**qí:qel te mímetú.**>, //C_1í=:=qəl tə C_1í=mətú//, /'*The little lamb is naughty.*'/, usage: lyrics to the Híltu song, attested by BHTTC, <**ts'ats'ats'tl'ím te mímetú.**>, //C_1ɛ=c'ɛ[=C_1ə=]ƛ'=əm=ím tə C_1í=mətú//, /'*The little lamb is hopping.*'/, syntactic comment: dmv, cts, its, dmn, attested by BHTTC.

<**metú:lqel ~ metú:'álqel**>, ds //mətú=əlqəl ~ mətú·=ʔɛ́lqəl//, WV ['*sheep wool*'], ANAA, lx <**=elqel ~ =álqel**> *wool*, phonology: vowel merger ~ epenthetic glottal stop, syntactic analysis: nominal, attested by BHTTC.

<**metú:lqel ~ metú:'álqel**>, WV ['*sheep wool*'], *see* metú.

<**mét'esemél**>, ANAH /'*first finger, index finger*'/, *see* mót'es.

<**met'mét'**>, df //C_1əC_2=mə́t'//, DESC /'*be supple, be easy to bend*'/, semantic environment ['never heard it used of people'], Elder's comment: "never heard it used of people", (<**R3=**> *iterative* or *plural* or *characteristic*), phonology: reduplication, syntactic analysis: adjective/adjectival verb, attested by EB, Salish cognate: Squamish /mə́t'/ *supple, pliable* W73:257, K69:45, example: <**met'mét' te kwémlexw.**>, //C_1əC_2=mə́t' tə k^{w}ə́mləx^w//, /'*The root is supple.*'/, attested by EB.

<**méthelh**>, free root //mə́θəɬ//, [mɪ́θəɬ], EB /'*grass or fibre for nets or twine, spreading dogbane, possibly also Indian hemp*'/, ['*Apocynum androsaemifolium,* possibly also *Apocynum cannabinum*'], ASM ['the bark was used to make strong twine, fish nets, and rope; the plant was identified as dogbane from samples picked near Laidlaw, B.C. with elders AK and SP; apparently Indian hemp is common in valleys and lower slopes in the southern Interior of B.C. while spreading dogbane grows from sea-level to moderate elevations in the mountains throughout much of B.C.; Indian hemp is said to be superior to dogbane for twine (Turner 1979:169) and probably was the plant obtained by trade in bundles as noted by AC; neither dogbane nor Indian hemp are true grasses and are bushes or shrubs though called a kind of grass by native speakers; showy milkweed *Asclepius speciosa* is used by Interior peoples as a poor substitute for Indian hemp but grows east of the Cascades (Turner 1979:175) and so probably only was obtained by the Stó:lō (if at all) in trade with Interior Salish peoples'], syntactic analysis: nominal, attested by Elders Group (2/11/76), DM (12/4/64), other sources: JH /mə́cəɬ/ *great milkweed*, H-T 1904 *great milkweed, Asclepius sp.*, also /'*a grass used for making fish nets*'/, EB /'*a grass which grows at a meadow above Duncan's place at Chehalis which was dried, twined, and used for making fish nets*'/, ASM ['it was gathered about May 24th; it also grows between Hope and Spuzzum'], attested by Elders Group (3/26/75), EB ['*a kind of marsh grass which grows near the foot of Agassiz Mountain may have also been called méthelh and used like it by the Chehalis people*'], attested by EL, comment: we stopped to pick some at a location EL knew of but could not find any, EB ['*a grass growing between Yale and Emory Creek used for fish-nets*'], attested

by Elders Group (2/29/75), EB ['*a special kind of grass used for making fish nets that grows at Hedley and was traded for in bundles*'], attested by AC.

<**=methet**>, //=məT-ət or better =məT=ət//, PRON ['*indirect effect non-control reflexive*'], see under stem <**-et** or **=et**> *reflexive.*

<**méthkw**>, bound stem //mə́θ(=)kʷ=iy//, root meaning perhaps same as for <math> *flat opening* (see above, or perhaps same as in <methelh> *dogbane, Indian hemp*, stem said in Musqueam to mean *a kind of plant no longer identifiable*

<**Xwméthkwiyem**>, df //xʷ=mə́θkʷ=iy=əm//, PLN ['*Musqueam village*'], probably <**xw=**> *always*, probably <**=iy**> *plant, bark*, probably <**=em**> *place to get*, syntactic analysis: nominal, attested by Elders Group (1/8/75), perhaps compare with <**Máthxwiy**> /mɛ́θ(=)xʷ=iy/ *Matsqui* which has a suspiciously similar form and may have the same root <**math**> *flat opening*, perhaps compare with <**méthelh**> *spreading dogbane, Indian hemp*, which could have the same root, source: place names reference file #127, other sources: Suttles ca1984:i.9 /xʷmə́θkʷəy'əm/ *village at the mouth of the North Arm of the Fraser River, just southeast of Point Grey, on the present Musqueam Indian Reserve*, literally *place of* /mə́θkʷəy'/ (a plant no longer identifiable).

<**méth'**>, bound root //mə́θ' *blue*//, comment: using derived forms of the root as a modifier of other color terms the following combinations were given by AK: semth'íl tsqwáy.

<**tsméth'**>, ds //c=mə́θ'//, LT /'*blue, be blue, have blue*'/, ASM ['squares circled on the color chart of Berlin and Kay (1969) (rows top to bottom = B-I, columns left to right = 1-40, side column of white to black = 0); individual speakers circled the following squares for ts(')méth', TM: B23, B24, B25, B26, B27, B28, B29, B30, B31, B32; EL: E26, F26, G26, E27, F27, G27, E28, F28, G28; Laurence James (color-blindness): C4; Evangeline Pete: F29; NP: G27, G28, G29; AK: E25, E26, E27, E28, E29, E30, F27, F28, F29, F30; TG (with RP)(after saying English "blue"): B23, B24, B25, B26, B27, B28, B29, B30, C23, C24, C25, C26, C27, C28, C29, C30, D22 (lower rt. diagonal), D23, D24, D25, D26, D27, D28, D29, D30, E22, E23, E24, E25, E26, E27, E28, E29, E30, F22, F23, F24, F25, F26, F27, F28, F29, F30, G22, G23, G24, G25, G26, G27, G28, G29, G30 (upper left diagonal)'], semantic environment ['shiny black mountain huckleberry (V. membranaceum), Alaska blueberry, bog blueberry, Cascade blueberry, blue elderberry, tall Oregon grape berry, plum, June plum, "bluejay" (Steller's jay), lake, river, water, sky, vein, eyes'], ASM ['the following color terms are used by AK before tsméth' to specify shades of the color: tsxwíkw', tsxwíxwekw', xwíxwekw', tsxwíxwekw'el, tsq'íx̲, tsqw'íx̲w, qw'íqw'ex̲wel, tsqw'íqw'ex̲wel, sqw'eqw'ex̲wel, stl'ítl'esel, p'(e)q'íl, sp'(e)q'íl'], (<**ts=**> *have, get, stative with colors*), syntactic analysis: adjective/adjectival verb, attested by AK, TG, EB, NP, AH, see charts by Rob MacLaury, attested by AC, BJ (12/5/64), Lawrence James, Evangeline Pete, NP, also AK (1987), TG (1987), EB (1987), NP (1987), AH (1987), also <**ts'méth'**>, //c'=mə́θ'//, phonology: glottalization, assimilation to final th', attested by Elders Group (3/1/72, 5/2/79, 5/16/79,), AC, Deming (SJ)(5/3/79), TM (2/14/79), EL (2/20/79), AK (1/24/79), TG and RP (1/24/79), JL (5/8/79), other sources: JH /cmə́θ'/ *blue*, Wells 1965 (2nd ed.):46 <shmets> *dark blue* (vs. <ch-WEH-ookw> (line through final w) *light blue*, prob. = tsxwíkw' *gray* in my material, thus perhaps also *blue-gray*), chart by Rob McLaury, example: **<ts'méth' te (kwxwómels, pléms, mélhx̲wel, swáyel).>**, //c'=mə́θ' tə (kʷxʷ=ámə=ls, plə́ms, mə́ɬx̣ʷəl, s=wɛ́yəl)//, /'*The (shiny black mountain huckleberry, plum, June plum, sky) is blue., The (shiny black mountain huckleberry, June plum) is purple.*'/, attested by Elders Group (5/2/79), **<ts'méth' te (léth'ilets, mólsem, xwíxwekw', th'íkwekw, th'ő̄lth'iy, kwá:y,, x̲ótsa, stó:lō, swáyél).>**, //c'=mə́θ' tə (lə́θ'iləc, málsəm, xʷí[=C₁ə=]k'ʷ, θ'íkʷəkʷ, kʷɛ́·y, x̣ácɛ, θ'ólθ'iy, s=tá·l=ow, s=wɛ́yə́l)//, /'*The (Alaska blueberry, bog blueberry, Cascade blueberry, blue/grey elderberry, tall Oregon grape berry, "bluejay" (Steller's jay), lake, river, sky) is blue.*'/, attested by Elders Group (5/16/79)i, **<ts'méth' te téteth.>**, //c'=mə́θ' tə tə́təθ//, /'*The vein is blue.*'/, attested by

PK (in Elders Group 5/16/79), also <**ts'méth' te tétets.**>, //c'=mə́θ' tə tə́təc//, attested by MP, <**ts'méth' te swáyél.**>, //c'=mə́θ' tə s=wɛ́yə́l//, /'*The sky is blue.*'/, attested by JL (5/8/79), also <**chméth' (te swáyél).**>, //c=mə́θ' (tə s=wɛ́yə́l)//, attested by BJ (12/5/64), <**ts'méth' te (mólsem, th'íkwekw, kwá:y).**>, //c'=mə́θ' tə (málsəm, θ'íkʷəkʷ, kʷɛ́·y)//, /'*The (swamp blueberry, blue/grey elderberry, "bluejay" (Steller's jay)) is blue.*'/, attested by Deming (5/3/79)(esp. SJ), <**ts'méth' te qó:.**>, //c'=mə́θ' tə qá·//, /'*The water is green., The water is blue.*'/, attested by Deming (5/3/79)(esp. SJ).

<**tsmeth'íl**>, stvi //c=məθ'=íl//, incs, LT ['*[be in a state of get blue]*'], (<**ts=**> *have, get, stative with colors*), (<**=el ~ =íl**> *go, come, get, become*), syntactic analysis: adjective/adjectival verb, attested by NP, see charts by Rob MacLaury.

<**ts'meth'ó:les**>, ds //c'=məθ'=á·ləs//, ANA ['*(have) blue eyes*'], LT, literally /'have blue on the eyes'/, lx <**=ó:les**> *on the eye(s)*, syntactic analysis: adjective/adjectival verb?, nominal?, attested by Elders Group (10/8/75, 5/16/79).

<**tsméth'òmèx**>, ds //c=mə́θ'=áməxʸ//, LT /'*[looks blue, blue-looking]*'/, (<**ts=**> *have, get, stative with colors*), (<**=ómex**> *looks, -looking, in color*), phonology: updrifting, downstepping, syntactic analysis: adjective/adjectival verb, attested by NP, see charts by Rob MacLaury.

<**tsmímeth'**>, dmv //c=C_1í=məθ'//, LT ['*[be a little blue]*'], (semological comment: the diminutive indicates all the lighter shades of blue here but also most of the greenish and lavender margins within blue as well; this extensive coverage is either cause or effect of the fact that the speaker uses no other modifiers with this root--no inceptive, continuative, etc.), (<**ts=**> *have, get, stative with colors*), (<**R4=**> *diminutive*), syntactic analysis: adjective/adjectival verb, attested by EB, see charts by Rob MacLaury.

<**meth'í:l**>, incs //məθ'=í·l//, LT /'*gone blue, (go blue, get blue, become blue)*'/, (<**=í:l**> *go, get, come, become*), syntactic analysis: intransitive verb, attested by AC, see charts by Rob MacLaury, also <**meth'íl**>, //məθ'=íl//, attested by NP, example: <**lulh meth'í:l.**>, //lə=uɬ məθ'=í·l//, /'*They've gone blue.*'/, literally /'he/she/it/they =already go/get/become blue'/, attested by AC.

<**smeth'íl**>, stvi //s=məθ'=íl//, incs, LT ['*[be in a state of get blue]*'], (<**s=**> *stative*), (<**=el ~ =íl**> *go, come, get, become*), syntactic analysis: adjective/adjectival verb, attested by NP, see charts by Rob MacLaury.

<**semth'íl**>, cts //s=hə=məθ'=íl//, incs, LT ['*[be in a state of getting blue]*'], (<**s=**> *stative*), (<**he=**> *continuative*), (<**=íl**> *come, go, get, become, inceptive*), ASM ['the following color terms are used by AK before semth'íl to specify shades of the color: tsxwíkw''], phonology: he- continuative before a set of verbs beginning in m, l, w, y, see charts by Rob MacLaury.

<**sméts'**>, dnom //s=mə́c'//, PE ['*rouge*'], (<**s=**> *nominalizer*), possibly root <**méth'**> *blue*, phonology: if related to méth' *blue* this form could be influenced by Nooksack which would have ts' for Halkomelem th', syntactic analysis: nominal, attested by Deming (2/22/79), example: <**ólewe qé<u>x</u> te sméts'**>, //ʔálə=wə qə́x̣ tə s=mə́c'//, /'*too much rouge*'/, attested by Deming.

<**sméth'qel**>, df //s=mə́θ'=qəl//, ANA ['*brain*'], (<**s=**> *nominalizer*), lx <**=qel**> *in the head*, probably root <**méth'**> *blue*, syntactic analysis: nominal, attested by AC, Elders Group, Deming, other sources: /smə́θ'qəl/, Salish cognate: Squamish /s-məc'-ál-qn/ *brain* W73:43, K67:283, Samish dial. of N. Straits /s-mə́θ'-qn ~ š-mə́θ'=qən'/ (LD), /s-mə́c'-qn ~ š-mə́c'-qən'/ *brains* G86:75, Sechelt /s-məc'-ála-qin/ T77:14, Lushootseed /s-c'əb-qíd/ *brain* H76:66, Thompson (Lytton dial.) /s-c'əm'-qín/ *brain* B74c:21 (metathesis?) Okanagan (Colville) /s-c'm-qín/ *brain* Bouchard & Kennedy75:17 Moses-Columbia /c'əm'qənálxʷ/ *brains* K81:57.

<**sméth'elheqw**>, df //s=mə́θ'=əl[=devoicing=]əqʷ//, ANA ['*brain*'], (<**s=**> *nominalizer*), lx <**=eleqw**> *on top of the head*, possibly <**=devoicing= (l → lh** > here**)** *derivational*, phonology: devoicing

possible, syntactic analysis: nominal, attested by Deming (3/4/76, 2/7/80), example: <**híkw te sméth'elheqws.**>, //híkʷ tə s=mə́θ'=əl[=devoicing=]əqʷ-s//, /'*His brain is big.*'/, attested by Deming (2/7/80).

<**Meth'á:lméxwem ~ Mth'á:lmexwem**>, ds //məθ'=ɛ́·lməxʷ=əm or mɛ́θ'=ə[=M2=]l=məxʷ=əm?//, PLN /'*slough called Billy Harris's Slough or Louie's Slough, the next slough east of Yálhxetel and west of Q'iq'ewetó:lthel*'/, possibly root <**méth'**> *blue* or possibly root <**máth'el**> *proud*, possibly <**=á:lmexw**> *on the breasts*, possibly <**=em**> *middle voice or place (to get)*, or <**=(el)mexw**> *people*, (perhaps) literally /'proud of her breasts (or) place to get proud people (or) place of proud people, (or) place to get blue breasts (or) place of blue breasts (or) get one's breasts blue'/ (putting a poultice for medicine with mud from this slough on the breasts could cause a blue color or a story about a woman or women proud of their breasts could provide possible explanations), phonology: metathesis possible, syntactic analysis: nominal, attested by EL (9/27/77, 3/1/78), source: place names reference file #296.

<**meth'éléxw**>, EFAM /'*doubt s-o, not believe s-th/s-o*'/, *see* máth'el.

<**méth'elh**>, possibly root //mə́θ'əɬ//, ANA ['*pus*'], possibly root <**méth'**> *blue*, possibly <**=elh**> *past*??, syntactic analysis: nominal, attested by AC, Elders Group, other sources: ES /mə́c'əɬ/.

<**méth'elhqìwèl**>, df //mə́θ'əɬ=q(əl)=ìwə̀l//, EZ /'*tick, woodtick,* probably *Pacific Coast tick* and *the wood tick*'/, ['class *Arachnida,* order *Acarina,* probably Ixodes pacificus and Dermacentor andersoni resp.'], ASM ['the Pacific Coast tick is the common coastal species, mainly in the wet season, Nov. to March; the wood tick is common in the Interior dry areas, found Apr. to June'], possibly <**=q**> *after* or possibly <**=eqel**> *container*, lx <**=ìwèl**> *in the insides*, phonology: possible consonant-loss and possible vowel-loss, syntactic analysis: nominal, attested by SP (6/4/75), Deming (2/7/80 prompted).

<**méth'elhqìwèl**>, EZ /'*tick, woodtick,* probably *Pacific Coast tick* and the *wood tick*'/, *see* méth'elh.

<**meth'í:l**>, LT /'*gone blue, (go blue, get blue, become blue)*'/, *see* méth'.

<**métsa**>, dnom //mə́cɛ// meaning uncertain, perhaps *lump.*

<**smétsa**>, dnom //s=mə́cɛ//, ANA /'*lump on person (or creature), goiter*'/, EB /'*lump on a tree, burl*'/, (<**s=**> *nominalizer*), syntactic analysis: nominal, attested by Elders Group, Salish cognate: Lushootseed /bəčú?(ə)b/ *lump* H76:24, compare <**mechó:s**> *ling cod.*

<**méwiya**>, df //mə́w(=)iyɛ//, ABFC ['*piggy-back*'], possibly <**=iya**> *affectionate diminutive*, syntactic analysis: intransitive verb, adjective/adjectival verb?, usage: possibly baby-talk, attested by EF (3/13/80).

<**mexlátst**>, MC ['*take it off from the bottom of s-th (a pack for ex.)*'], *see* má ~ má'-.

<**mexméxts'el**>, EZ ['*lots of lice*'], *see* méxts'el.

<**méxts'el**>, possibly root //mə́xʸc'əl or mɛ́(=Aə́=)xʸ(=)c'(=)əl//, [mɪ́xʸc'ɪl], EZ /'*human louse: head louse,* (secondarily) *body louse,* and possibly *crab louse,* (unclear if *animal lice* are included*)*'/, ['*Pediculus humanus: Pediculus capitis,* (secondarily) *Pediculus corporis,* and possibly *Pediculus pubis,* (unclear if others of the order *Phthiraptera)*'], ABDF, possibly root <**má=x**> *take it out, remove it*, possibly <**=ts'**> *around in circles*, possibly <**=el**> *get, go, come, become, inceptive*, possibly <**é-ablaut**> *derivational*, phonology: possible ablaut, homophonous with word for chickadee, syntactic analysis: nominal, attested by AC, Deming, SJ, MC, MV, LG, Elders Group, BHTTC, also <**méxth'el**>, //mə́xʸθ'əl//, attested by TM (3/29/78), other sources: ES /mɛ́xʸc'əl/ *louse*, Salish cognate: Lushootseed /bšč'ád/ *louse* H76:41, Squamish /mə́čn/ *black louse* W73:168, K67:254, Sechelt /məč'ə́n/ *louse* T77:10 N. Straits (Samish dial.) /ŋə́sən'/ (VU) *body louse, bedbug* G86:69,

Moses-Columbia /k’ə́sən’/ *head louse* and /k’əsən’ál’qs/ *body louse* K81:76 Mainland Comox /máʔč’in/ *louse* B75prelim:12, example: <**qéx̲ méxts'el**>, //qə́x̣ mə́xʸc’əl//, /'*a lot of lice*'/, attested by AC.

<**mexméxts'el**>, pln //C_1əC_2=mə́xʸc’əl//, EZ ['*lots of lice*'], ['*Pediculus humanus* and possibly others of order *Phthiraptera*'], ABDF, (<**R3=**> *plural*), phonology: reduplication, syntactic analysis: nominal, attested by Elders Group (4/7/76).

<**p'éq' méxts'el**>, cpds //p’ə́q’ mə́xʸ(=)c’(=)əl//, EZ /'*body louse, grayback*'/, ['*Pediculus capitis,* perhaps others of *Pediculus humanus*'], ABDF, literally /'white louse'/, syntactic analysis: adjective/adjectival verb nominal, attested by Deming (2/7/80).

<**shxwelítemelh méxts'el**>, cpds //s=xʷəlítəm=əɬ mə́xʸ(=)c’(=)əl//, EZ ['*common bedbug*'], ['*Cimex lectularius*'], ABDF, literally /'Whiteman style/kind of louse'/, (<**s=**> *stative*), lx <**=elh**> *style, kind of, in the fashion of,* syntactic analysis: adjective/adjectival verb nominal, attested by BHTTC, Elders Group, Deming.

<**lhémxts'el**>, ds //ɬə́=məxʸc’əl//, PE ['*fine comb*'], HHG, EZ ['*(louse-comb)*'], MED, ASM ['such combs were used for removing nits and lice'], literally /'extract louse'/, (<**lhé=**> *extract, extract a portion*), phonology: zero-grade of root after stressed full-grade of suffix, vowel-loss, syntactic analysis: nominal, attested by Elders Group (3/29/78).

<**lhémxts'eltel**>, dnom //ɬə́=məxʸc’əl=təl//, PE ['*real fine-tooth comb*'], HHG, EZ ['*(louse-comb)*'], MED, literally /'extract louse device to'/, lx <**=tel**> *device to,* phonology: zero-grade of root after stressed full-grade of prefix, vowel-loss, syntactic analysis: nominal, attested by EB.

<**ts'élxet**>, pcs //(mə)xʸc’əl=M4=əT or (mə=)xʸ(=)c’(=)əl=M4=əT//, [c’ɪ́lxʸɪt], MED ['*delouse s-o*'], (<**metathesis type 4**> *derivational,* <**=et**> *purposeful control transitivizer*), phonology: metathesis type 4 (moves consonant to follow two consonants later in stem, extremely rare), consonant-loss and vowel-loss of first syllable, stress-shift due to loss of stressed syllable in root, syntactic analysis: transitive verb, attested by Elders Group (3/29/78), also <**th'élxet**>, //(mə)xʸθ’əl=M4=əT or (mə=)xʸ(=)θ’(=)əl=M4=əT//, [θ’ɪ́lxʸɪt], attested by TM (3/29/78).

<**ts'álxet**>, cts //(mə)xʸc’ə[-Aɛ́-]l=M4=əT or (mə=)xʸ(=)c’(=)ə[-Aɛ́-]l=M4=əT//, MED ['*delousing s-o*'], (<**á-ablaut**> *continuative*), phonology: metathesis, ablaut, consonant-loss, vowel-loss, syntactic analysis: transitive verb, attested by Elders Group (3/29/78).

<**ts'élxetel**>, rcps //(mə)xʸc’əl=M4=əT-əl//, MED ['*delouse each other, looking for lice in each other's head*'], (<**-el**> *reciprocal*), phonology: metathesis, stress-shift due to loss of stressed syllable in root, syntactic analysis: intransitive verb, attested by Elders Group (3/29/78, 11/12/75).

<**méxts'el**>, free root //mə́xʸc’əl//, EZ /'*chickadee: black-capped chickadee,* prob. also *chestnut-backed chickadee,* poss. also *least bush-tit*'/, ['*Parus atricapillus occidentalis,* prob. *Parus rufescens,* poss. *Psaltriparus minimus*'], ASM ['when lots of them come you'll have visitors; if you listen to them they'll tell you how many children you'll have'], syntactic analysis: nominal, attested by Elders Group (6/4/75, 5/14/80), AC, Salish cognate: Lushootseed /c’əlc’əlkáyus ~ c’ìc’əlkáyus/ *chickadee* H76:68, also <**skíkek**>, //s=kíkək//, dialects: *Cheh.*, Salish cognate: Thompson /c’əskíkik/ *chickadee* B74c:13, *see* qá:q for this latter form.

<**=mexw**>, da //=məxʷ//, HUMC /'*people, person*'/, syntactic analysis: lexical suffix, derivational suffix; found in <**lets'ő:mexw**>, //ləc’=ó·=məxʷ//, /'*different people (used for different tribes or nationalities)*'/ (compare <**lá:ts'**> *be different),* <**xwélmexw**>, //xʷə́l=məxʷ//, /'*Indian*'/ (compare (perhaps) <**xwel**> *just, only),* <**s'ó:lmexw**>, //sʔá·l=məxʷ//, /'*water babies, water pygmies*'/, possibly <**st'élmexw**>, //st’ə́l=məxʷ//, /'*medicine*'/ (root <**t'el**> *stick on, adhere*)(lit. 's-th stuck on a person'), <**chí:tmexw**>, //cí·t=məxʷ//, /'*big horned owl*'/, <**syíwméxwtses ~ syő́wméxwtses**>,

//syíwmə́x^{w}=cəs//, /*'rattle used at spirit dance by some dancers'*/ (compare <**s=yíw=el**> *spirit song, spirit power*).

<**mex̲t'éles**>, df //məx̣t'(=)ə́ləs//, EB /*'gray or green tree "moss" (lichen) hanging on tree limbs,* possibly *wolf lichen or other species'*/, ['possibly *Letharia vulpina* or *Alectoria (Bryoria)* species or *Usnea* species'], possibly root <**x̲t'**> *shoot power*??, possibly <**=éles**> *on the tooth*??, syntactic analysis: nominal,

<**méyeth ~ méyéth**>, probably stem bound //mɛ́y(=)əθ ~ mɛy(=)ə́θ//, root meaning unknown unless <may> *help*, possibly has <=eth(el)> *on the mouth* since derived form <sméyeth> means *meat*.

<**sméyeth ~ sméyéth**>, df //s=mɛ́yəθ ~ s=mɛyə́θ//, [sméyɪθ ~ sméyɪ́θ], EZ /*'(game) animal, (meat)'*/, FOOD [*'meat'*], (<**s=**> *nominalizer*), syntactic analysis: nominal, attested by AC, BJ (5/64), DM (12/4/64), Elders Group (3/1/72), HT, CT, AD, EB, Deming, other sources: ES /smɛ́yəθ ~ ƛ'əlqtə́lə/ (also Musqueam and Cowichan dialects /smáyəθ/) *deer*, JH /smí·yəθ/ *meat, animal*, H-T <smíyEts> (macron over i) *deer, any of the larger quadrupeds*, also /*'(walking) animal'*/, attested by AC, also /*'cattle, meat'*/, attested by DM (12/4/64), ASM ['(game) animal'], example: <**ímex te sméyéth.**>, //ʔím=əx^{y} tə s=mɛyə́θ//, /*'The animal walks.'*/, attested by AC, <**lhq'átses sméyeth**>, //ɬq'ɛ́cəs s=mɛ́yəθ//, /*'five animals'*/, attested by CT, HT, <**háwe te sméyeth.**>, //hɛ́wə tə s=mɛ́yəθ//, /*'The animal is hunting.'*/, attested by AD, <**q'óq'ey te sméyeth.**>, //q'á[=C_1ə=]y tə s=mɛ́yəθ//, /*'The animal is sick.'*/, attested by EB, <**sq'óq'ey te sméyeth.**>, //s=q'á[=C_1ə=]y tə s=mɛ́yəθ//, /*'The animal is dead.'*/, attested by EB, <**táwelt te tl'elqtéle kw'es le kwélext te sméyéth**>, //tɛ́w=əl=T təƛ'ɛ[=lə=]qt=ə́lə k'^{w}ə-s lə k^{w}ə́l=əx^{y}=T tə s=mɛyə́θ//, /*'light up the deer and shoot the animal'*/, attested by CT, <**p'áth'et te kw'eléws te sméyeth li te st'elákw' siyólh**>, //p'ɛ́θ'=əT tə k'^{w}ələ́w-s tə s=mɛ́yəθ li tə s=t'əlɛ́k'^{w} si=yáɬ//, /*'sew the hide of an animal on a circular frame'*/, attested by HT, ASM ['meat'], <**wá:ta á sméyéth?**>, //(ʔə)wə-ɛ́·=tɛ ʔɛ s=mɛyə́θ//, /*'Have you got any meat?'*/, literally /'is it none your meat'/, attested by AC, <**sch'íyxw sméyeth**>, //s=c'ɛ[=Aí=]yx^{w} s=mɛ́yəθ//, /*'dried meat'*/, attested by Deming, <**spá:th sméyeth**>, //s=pɛ́·θ s=mɛ́yəθ//, /*'(might be) bear meat'*/, attested by AD, <**lhíts'etes té sméyeth.**>, //ɬíc'=əT-əs tə s=mɛ́yəθ//, /*'He cuts meat.'*/, phonology: sentence-stress on the article, attested by EB, <**tsétsmel sméyeth**>, FOOD *steak* (lit. cut off + meat), (attested by RG,EH 6/16/98 to SN, edited by BG with RG,EH 6/26/00)

<**smèyethálá**>, ds //s=mɛ̀yəθ=ɛ́lɛ́//, FOOD [*'tray for carrying meat'*], HHG, lx <**=álá**> *container of*, phonology: downstepping, syntactic analysis: nominal, attested by DM (12/4/64).

<**smímiyàth**>, dmn //s=C_1í=mɛyə[=M2=]θ//, EZ [*'little animal(s)'*], (<**R4=**> *diminutive*), (<**metathesis**> *derivational*), phonology: reduplication, metathesis, downstepping, syntactic analysis: nominal, attested by EB, example: <**lhq'átses smímiyàth**>, //ɬq'ɛ́cəs s=C_1í=mɛyə[=M2=]θ//, /*'five little animals'*/, attested by EB.

<**smímeyàth ~ smímoyàth**>, dmn //s=C_1í=mɛyə[=M2=]θ//, EZ [*'butterfly'*], ['order *Lepidoptera*'], literally perhaps /'little animal'/, ASM ['the scientific definition of butterfly notes that they fly in the daytime and rest with wings vertical rather than horizontal (both in contrast to moths)'], (<**s=**> *nominalizer*, R4= *diminutive*), (<**metathesis**> *derivational*), phonology: reduplication, metathesis, syntactic analysis: nominal, attested by Deming (3/15/79, SJ, MC, MV, LG), Elders Group (6/11/75, 2/11/76), also <**smimoyáts**>, //s=C_1í=mɛyə[=M2=]c//, attested by Elders Group (1/15/75).

<**míyethélwét**>, ds //míyəθ=ə́lwə́t//, CLO [*'buckskin clothes'*], lx <**=élwét**> *clothes*, (<**s=**> *nominalizer* dropped), phonology: consonant-loss of initial s=, syntactic analysis: nominal, attested by BHTTC.

<**mí ~ mé ~ me**>, free root //mí ~ mə́ ~ mə//, TVMO /*'come, coming, come to, coming to'*/, ASP

/'*begin(ning) to, start(ing) to, inceptive*'/, TIME, clearly a reduced form or root of <**emí**> *come*, phonology: vowel-reduction, stress-loss, syntactic analysis: auxiliary verb, preposition/prepositional verb, attested by Elders Group, EB, AC, MH, Deming, RP, AD, example: <**mí qelát**>, //mí qəlɛ́t//, /'*come again*'/, attested by Elders Group, <**míchel kw'e lò.**>, //mí-c-əl k'^{w}ə là//, /'*I'm coming here.*'/, attested by EB, <**mílha kw'e lò.**>, //mí-ɬɛ k'^{w}ə là//, /'*Come here.*'/, Elder's comment: "seldom use mílha all alone, usually one would add kw'e lò", attested by EB, <**míchelcha sq'eq'ó.**>, //mí-c-əl-cɛ s=C_1ə=q'á//, /'*I'll come along., (I will come along.)*'/, attested by EB, <**mítsel yó:ys.**>, //mí-c-əl yá·ys//, /'*I'm coming to work.*'/, attested by AC, <**míchxw oy'á:y.**>, //mí-c-x^{w} C_1əC_2=ʔɛ́·y//, /'*Come right in.*'/, literally /'come -mildly urging imperative keep on coming'/, attested by Elders Group, <**míchxw stetís tl'a'á'altha.**>, //mí-c-x^{w} s=tə[=C_1əAí=]sƛ'ɛ-C_1ɛ́=ʔɛlθɛ//, /'*Come close to me.*'/, attested by AC, <**míchxw q'ó:lthet kw'atsetólxw ōwe híthes.**>, //mí-c-x^{w} q'á·l=T-ət k'^{w}ɛc=əT-álx^{w} ʔówə híθ=əs//, /'*Come back and see us soon.*'/, literally /'come -mildly urging imperative return oneself see us not when it is a long time'/, attested by EB, <**méchxw maytó:lxw.**>, //mə́-c-x^{w} mɛy=T-á·lx^{w}//, /'*You're come to help us., (also: Come help us.)*'/, attested by AC, <**mechxw yikwelát kw'e s'álhtel.**>, //mə-c-x^{w} yi=k^{w}əl=ɛ́T k'^{w}ə s=ʔɛ́ɬ=Təl//, /'*(Come) Bring some food.*'/, attested by AC, <**míchap álhtel. ~ míyalha álhtel.**>, //mí-c-ɛp ʔɛ́ɬ=Təl ~ mí(y)-ɛɬɛ ʔɛ́ɬ=Təl//, /'*Come eat, you folks. ~ Come eat, you folks.*'/, attested by Deming, <**mechap maythóx.**>, //mə-c-ɛp mɛy=T-áx^{y}//, /'*Come help us.*'/, attested by AC, <**tewátesò kw'e tl'íls kws més yisq'ó.**>, //tə=wɛ́t=əs-à k'^{w}ə ƛ'í=ls k^{w}-s mə́-s yi=s=q'á//, /'*Anybody that want to can come along.*'/, literally /'it's anybody -just that wants -psychological non-control transitivizer that -he come -he travelling along= stative= together'/, attested by EB, <**mítlh kwetxwílem.**>, //mí-tɬ k^{w}ətx^{w}=íl=əm//, /'*Come inside.*'/, literally /'come -coaxing imperative inside =come/go/get =middle voice/oneself'/, attested by AC, also <**métlh kwetxwílem.**>, //mə́-tɬ k^{w}ətx^{w}=íl=əm//, attested by Elders Group (6/16/76), <**mítlh maythóx.**>, //mí-tɬ mɛy=T-áx^{y}//, /'*Come help me.*'/, (semological comment: coaxing imperative), attested by AC, <**mítlh álhtel.**>, //mí-tɬ ʔɛ́ɬ=Təl//, /'*Come eat.*'/, (semological comment: coaxing imperative), attested by MH, <**mítlh teséthet.**>, //mí-tɬ təs=ə́T-ət//, /'*Come and eat., Come near.*'/, literally /'come -coaxing imperative near =purposeful-control -reflexive'/, attested by RP, EB, <**míyalha maythóx.**>, //mí(y)-ɛɬɛ mɛy=T-áx^{y}//, /'*You (pl.) help me.*'/, literally /'come -command imperative 2p help =purposeful control -me'/, phonology: epenthesis (y added to ease pronunciation), attested by AC, <**míyalha álhtel (mámele, stá:xwelh).**>, //mí(y)-ɛɬɛ ʔɛ́ɬ=Təl (C_1ɛ́-mələ, stɛ́·x^{w}=əɬ)//, /'*Come eat children.*'/, literally /'come -command imperative 2p eat a meal (children (kinterm), children (age-term))'/, attested by AD, <**míyalha kwetxwílem emétchap íkw'elò.**>, //mí(y)-ɛɬɛ k^{w}ətx^{w}=íl=əm; ʔəmə́t-c-ɛp ʔi=k'^{w}ə=là//, /'*Come in and sit here (you folks).*'/, (semological comment: command imperative 2p), attested by RP, EB, <**míyalha teséthet.**>, //mí(y)-ɛɬɛ təs=ə́T-ət//, /'*Come near (you folks)., Come sit in (and eat) (you folks).*'/, attested by Elders Group (2/18/76), RP, EB, <**áscha ew me xwe'í látselcha ye sq'ó.**>, //ʔɛ́-s-cɛ ʔəw mə x^{w}ə=ʔí lɛ́-c-əl-cɛ yə=s=q'á//, /'*If he comes again, I'll go along.*'/, literally /'if he will again come to get here I will go along together'/, attested by EB, <**atselcha ew (me xw'í:lmethome, mi xw'í:lsòmè).**>, //ʔɛ-c-əl-cɛ ʔəw (mə x^{w}ə=ʔí·l=məT-amə, mí x^{w}ə=ʔí·=ls=ámə)//, /'*I'll come and see you again.*'/, literally /'I will again (come reach you here [indirect effect control transitivizer], come manage to get to you here [psychological non-control transitivizer])'/, phonology: vowel-loss in rapid speech, downstepping, updrifting, attested by EB, <**me pél:ékw**>, //mə pə́l·ək^{w}//, /'*come into view, come into sight*'/, semantic environment ['can be used of a person not seen in a long time, the sun, moon, etc.'], attested by EB, <**me pél:ékw tl'ésu lé me théxw.**>, //mə pə́l·ə́k^{w} ƛ'ə́-s-u lə mə θə́x^{w}//, /'*It came into sight and it disappeared.*'/, attested by EB, <**ts'áts'eltsel xwoyíwel tel sqwálewel kw'els me xwe'í sq'ó talhlúwep (éy l sí:yáye, l sí:yáye sí:yám).**>, //c'ɛ[=C_1ə=]l-c-əl x^{w}=ɛ[=Aa=]y=íwəl tə-l s=q^{w}ɛ́l=əwəl k'^{w}ə-l-s mə x^{w}ə=ʔí s=q'á tɛ=ɬ=lúwə=p (ʔɛ́y l s-í·-yɛ́yə, l s-í·-yɛ́yə s-í·-yɛ́m)//, /'*I'm very happy to come here at this gathering my (good friends, dear friends).*'/, usage: public speaking, attested by Deming (5/18/78), <**chelà:l yexw ye me xwe'í.**>, //cəlɛ̀·l yəx^{w} yə mə xʷə=ʔí//, /'*A lot of people came.*'/, literally /'it was sure lots the (plural human)/those that come get here/arrive'/, attested by EB, <**me lhókw' telí kw'e chókw.**>, //mə ɬák'ʷ təlí k'ʷə cákʷ//, /'*He came from (another country) far away.*'/, literally /'(he) came to fly from the (remote) far away'/, usage: saying used of a person who moves from another tribe; *he flew* is an idiom, comment: this explains Dan Milo's (and his ancestor's) name, Lhokw'elálexw, attested by EB (1/22/76), <**ewá:lhtsel mí:l alqá:ls (kw s'álhtel).**>, //ʔəwə-ɛ́·ɬ-c-əl mí-əl ʔɛlq=ɛ́·ls (s=ʔɛ́ɬ=Təl)//, /'*I wasn't going to buy (groceries) (but did).*'/, literally /'is not -past -subj. -I coming -subjunctive 1s buy -structured activity non-continuative (the (remote) food)'/, phonology: vowel merger (twice), syntactic comment: subordinate subjunctive on mí auxiliary, attested by EB, <**méchelcha me xwe'í.**>, //mə́-c-əl-cɛ mə xʷə=ʔí//, /'*I'm coming.*'/, Elder's comment: "unsure", attested by EB (12/11/75), <**mítlh latst ehá:we.**>, //mí-tɬ lɛ-c-t ʔəhɛ́·wə//, /'*Come let's go hunting.*'/, literally /'come -coaxing imperative 2s we('re) go(ing) hunting'/, attested by AC, <**metst á:ylexwstexw te sqwá:ltset.**>, //mə-c-t ʔɛ́·y=ləxʷ=sT-əxʷ tə s=qʷɛ́·l-c-ət//, /'*Let's keep our language alive.*'/, literally /'we come keep it alive the our talk/words'/, attested by EB, <**mís teló kwetxwílém.**>, //mí-s tə=lá kʷətxʷ=íl=əm//, /'*Let him come in.*'/, literally /'come -mildly urging imperative 3 this one (male) get inside'/, syntactic comment: third person imperative has same form after mí as subjunctive, attested by EB, ASM ['begin to, beginning to, start to, starting to'], <**me yíq.**>, //mə yíq//, /'*It's coming to snow., (It's beginning to snow.)*'/, attested by Deming, <**me tél:exw**>, //mə tə́l=l-əxʷ//, /'*beginning to understand, beginning to learn*'/, attested by Elders Group, <**tsel kwá welh me x̲à:m. ~ tsel kwá ulh me x̲à:m.**>, //c-əl kʷɛ́ wəɬ məx̣ɛ̀·m ~ c-əl kʷɛ́ ʔuɬ məx̣ɛ̀·m//, /'*I began to cry.*'/, attested by EB, <**ulh me lhalétem.**>, //ʔuɬ mə ɬɛlə́t=əm//, /'*It started to sprinkle.*'/, attested by Deming (3/31/77), <**ulh me pehá:ls.**>, //ʔuɬ mə pəh=ɛ́·ls//, /'*It started to blow.*'/, attested by Deming.

<**emí: ~ emí**>, possibly df //ʔə-mí· ~ ʔə-mí//, TVMO ['*come*'], possibly <**e-**> *non-auxiliary verb*, syntactic analysis: intransitive verb, attested by AC, Elders Group, AD, EB, other sources: ES /ʔəmí·/ *come*, example: <**l stl'í: kw'as emí:.**>, //l s=ƛ'í· k'ʷ-ɛ-s ʔə-mí·//, /'*I want you to come.*'/, literally /'it is my want that you come'/, attested by AC, <**mōkw'éthetchàp emí.**>, //mok'ʷ=ə́T-ət-c-ɛ̀p ʔə-mí//, /'*All of you come.*'/, phonology: downstepping, attested by AC, <**wás tl'ós te méles qe tl'ós te í:meths emí lis skw'áy kw'(e)s emís.**>, //(ʔə)wə-əs ƛ'á-s tə mə́lə-s qə ƛ'á-s tə ʔí·məθ-s ʔə-mí lí-s s=k'ʷɛ́y k'ʷ(ə)-s ʔə-mí-s//, /'*If it's not his son (then) it's his grandson that comes if he [the chief] can't come.*'/, syntactic analysis: vneg-subjunctive subject pronoun3 demonstrative pronoun-sbsp3 demonstrative article nominal-possessive3 conjunction demonstrative pronoun-sbsp3 demonstrative article nominal-possessive3 intransitive verb auxiliary verb-subjunctive subject pronoun3 adjective/adjectival verb demonstrative conjunction-sbsp3 intransitive verb-sbsp3, usage: recent event text, attested by AC, <**(s)taméxwelha q'a emí.**>, //(s)tɛmə́xʷ=ɬɛ q'ɛ ʔə-mí//, /'*I hope that he comes.*'/, literally /'(unclear) -imperative until come'/, Elder's comment: "unsure", attested by Elders Group (2/16/77), <**emí:lha**>, //ʔə-mí·-ɬɛ//, /'*Come.*'/, attested by AC, BJ (5/64).

<**ma'emí ~ ma'mí**>, df //mɛ=ʔə-mí//, TVMO /'*come, came, He came., She came.*'/, possibly <**ma=**> *resultative*? or poss. vaux *past 3rd person subject* like <**le**>, compare <**ma'emét**> *he/she sat* under <**emét**> *sit*, phonology: reduplication perhaps, syntactic analysis: auxiliary verb? intransitive verb, attested by EB, AD (9/25/78), example: <**chel má'mì.**>, //c-əl mɛ́ ʔmí//, /'*I come.*'/, phonology: downstepping, syntactic analysis: independent clause subject pronoun auxiliary verb intransitive verb, attested by EB (12/11/75), <**méchelcha ma'mì.**>, //mə́-c-əl-cɛ mɛ ʔmí//, /'*I'm coming.*'/, syntactic analysis: auxiliary verb-independent clause subject pronoun-future tense auxiliary verb intransitive verb, attested by EB (12/11/75).

<**ma'eméstexw ~ máméstexw**>, df //C_1ɛ=ʔə-mə́=sT-əxʷ or C_1ɛ́=mə́=sT-əxʷ//, TVMO /'*bring s-th, brought s-th*'/, SOC, (<**R8= ~ R7=**> *resultative*?, e- *non-auxiliary verb*?), phonology: vowel-loss possible, syntactic analysis: transitive verb, attested by EB, example: <**chel**

ma'eméstexw.>, //c-əl C₁ɛ=ʔə-mə́=sT-əxʷ//, /*I'll bring it to you.*'/, literally /'I present as immediate future resultative bring it'/, attested by EB, <**tsel máméstexw the ílh (stl'ís, a stl'í, a stl'íyelep).**>, //c-əl C₁ɛ́=mə́=sT-əxʷ (kʷ)θə ʔí-ɬ (s=ƛ'í-s, ʔɛ s=ƛ'í, ʔɛ s=ƛ'í(y)-ələp)//, /'*I brought what (he, you, you folks) wanted.*'/, literally /'I brought it the/what (near not visible) is (his want, your want, you folks' want)'/, attested by EB.

<**le'áméstexw**>, df //ləʔɛ́=mə́=sT-əxʷ//, TVMO ['*bring s-th to someone*'], SOC, (<**le'á=**> meaning uncertain), syntactic analysis: transitive verb, attested by Elders Group (1/25/78).

<**emíls**>, pncs //ʔə-mí=l(ə)s//, TVMO /'*come near s-o, (come to s-o)*'/, (<**e-**> *non-auxiliary verb*), (<**=ls ~ =les**> *psychological non-control transitivizer*), syntactic analysis: transitive verb, attested by AD, EB; found in <**emílsox**>, //ʔə-mí=ls-áxʸ//, /'*come near me*'/, phonology: downshifting, syntactic analysis: transitive verb, attested by AD, EB (9/22/78).

<**míthelh**>, if //mí-θəɬ//, TVMO ['*Come (urging one person).*'], semantic environment ['for ex. if one person stayed in the car after everyone else got off'], (<**-thelh**> *urging imperative 2s* (not attested elsewhere), syntactic analysis: intransitive verb, attested by EB (9/19/78).

<**xwmítsesem**>, mdls //xʷ=mí=cəs=əm//, ABFC ['*pass s-th (by hand)*'], TVMO, (<**xw=**> perhaps *move towards*), comment: cf. Musqueam /xʷ-2/ *move toward* in Suttles ca1984:13.2.6, but his examples are cognate with one's having my xw(e)= *go, get, become, come* which fit the meaning of xwmítsesem less well than does *move toward*, lx <**=tses**> *on the hand*, (<**=em**> *middle voice*), syntactic analysis: intransitive verb, attested by Elders Group.

<**méstexw**>, caus //mə́=sT-əxʷ//, [mɪ́stʊxʷ], TVMO /'*bring s-th, fetch s-th, get s-th (bring it), give it to s-o(as s-th fetched, not as a gift)*'/, ASM ['often translated *bring me s-th* or *fetch me s-th* in imperative'], (<**=st**> *causative control transitivizer*), (<**-exw**> *third person object*), syntactic analysis: transitive verb, attested by AC, EB, others, example: <**méstexw ta lopót.**>, //mə́=sT-əxʷ t-ɛ lapát//, /'*Bring me your cup.*'/, literally /'bring/fetch your cup'/, syntactic comment: mildly urging imperative shown by no subject marker and only a second person possessed object, attested by AC, <**méstexw tel yó:seqw.**>, //mə́=sT-əxʷ tə-l yá·s=əqʷ//, /'*Bring me my hat.*'/, literally /'bring/fetch my hat'/, syntactic comment: mildly urging imperative shown by lack of subject marker (this example proves that there needn't be a second person possessed object), attested by AC, <**méstexw te th'ále**>, //mə́=sT-əxʷ tə θ'ɛ́lə//, /'*Give me the heart.*'/, literally /'bring/fetch the heart'/, attested by AC, <**li iyó:lem kw'els méstexw kw'e (kópi, sth'í:m, kík, tí, póy, s'álhtel, slhóp)?**>, //li ʔiy=á·l=əm k'ʷ-əl-s mə́=sT-əxʷ k'ʷə (kápi, s=θ'í·m, kík, tí, páy, s=ʔɛ́ɬ=Təl, s=ɬáp)//, /'*Can I get you some (coffee, berries, cake, tea, pie, food, soup)?*'/, literally /'is it alright that I fetch/bring some (coffee, berries, cake, tea, pie, food, soup)'/, attested by EB (1977 during staff Halkomelem class); found in <**mesthóxchexw.**>, //mə=sT-áxʸ-c-əxʷ//, /'*Give it to me (as s-th fetched, not as a gift).*'/, attested by EB, example: <**mesthóxchexw te qó:.**>, //mə=sT-áxʸ-c-əxʷ tə qá·//, /'*Fetch me some water., Bring me some water.*'/, attested by EB.

<**mí:l ~ míl**>, bound root //mí·l ~ míl *submerge*//, comment: based on comparison with míq' *be underwater, sink to bottom* and =q' *on something else* and cognates such as Squamish /múy/ *submerge*, /mə́y/ *to sink* and /mí-mi/ *drown* K67:255, 257 it seems possible the Halkomelem root may be <mí(y)> /mí(y)/ *submerge*, from /m(ə)y ~ múy/; if that is the case, then the apparent root in Halkomelem has the inceptive =íl *come, go, get, become* and is really a stem, mí(y)=íl *become/go/get underwater* and míq' is really a stem also mí(y)=q' *underwater on something else*; since this is quite speculative I have conservatively shown both mí:l and míq' as separate roots until more cognates allow more certain reconstruction of their past histories, Salish cognate: Sechelt /mə́l/ *sink* T77:33.

<**míliyel**>, ds //míl=iyəl//, FSH /'*set a net (by canoe), set one's net, fish with a net, (submerge a net)*'/, CAN, literally /'submerge net'/, ASM ['done from a canoe by unrolling net into water keeping its floats and weights straight and keeping it from getting tangled'], lx <**=iyel**> *net*, syntactic analysis:

intransitive verb, attested by Elders Group (3/15/72, 3/26/75, 11/26/75, 2/11/76, 9/2/76, 5/16/79), EB, Salish cognate: Squamish /múy-ʔayʔi/ *set one's net* and /múy/ *submerge* and /máyʔ-múy-unʔ/ *dip repeatedly in the water (tr.)* W73:227, K69:46, Sechelt /mə́l/ *to sink* and /məl-mə́l-am ~ miy-may-šəliq/ *drown* G82:26, example: **<tsel la míliyel.>**, //c-əl lɛ míl=iyəl//, /'*I went to set a net.*'/, ***<tsel míliyel te swéltel.>** rejected by EB.

<semíliyel>, strs //s=hə=míl=iyəl//, FSH /'*a net is set, be set (of a net by canoe, not of a pole net)*'/, CAN, (**<s=>** *stative*), (**<he=>** *resultative*), phonology: consonant merger of s + h, syntactic analysis: intransitive verb, attested by EB, NP (5/16/79), also **<semláliyel>**, //s=hə=mil=ɛ́liyəl//, lx **<=áliyel ~ =iyel>** *net*, phonology: vowel-loss, attested by HT (5/16/79).

<semláliyel>, df //s=hə=mil=ɛ́liyəl//, FSH /'*a set net, a stationary net*'/, (**<s=>** *nominalizer* (or *stative*?)), syntactic analysis: nominal, poss. adjective/adjectival verb, attested by CT (6/8/76).

<mí:leqwem>, mdls //mí·l=$əq^w$=əm//, ABFC ['*soak one's head*'], PE, literally /'submerge one's hair or top of the head'/, PE, lx **<=eqw>** *on top of the head, on the hair*, (**<=em>** *middle voice*), syntactic analysis: intransitive verb, attested by Elders Group, example: **<lachxw mí:leqwem.>**, //lɛ-c-x^w mí·l=$əq^w$=əm//, /'*Go soak your head.*'/, attested by Elders Group (2/6/80).

<mí:leqwthet>, pcrs //mí·l=$əq^w$=T-ət//, ABFC ['*soak one's head*'], PE, literally /'submerge oneself purposely on the hair or top of the head'/, (**<=t>** *purposeful control transitivizer*), (**<-et>** *reflexive*), syntactic analysis: intransitive verb, attested by Elders Group (2/6/80).

<semlóthel>, df //s=(h)ə=mil=áθəl//, LAND /'*riverbank, bank of a river*'/, WATR, (**<s=>** *nominalizer*), (**<he=>** *resultative*), root **<míl>** *submerge/drop into the water*, lx **<=óthel>** *in the mouth, in the mouth of river/creek*, phonology: vowel-loss, epenthetic e before resonant, syntactic analysis: nominal, attested

<mí:lt>, pcs //mí·l=T//, ABFC ['*place s-th (prob. in water)*'], literally prob. /'submerge s-th purposely'/, (**<=t>** *purposeful control transitivizer*), syntactic analysis: intransitive verb, attested by AD; found in **<mí:ltes.>**, //mí·l=T-əs//, /'*He places it.*'/, attested by AD (4/27/79).

<hámelet>, cts //hɛ́-mil=əT//, ABFC ['*placing s-th (prob. in water)*'], literally prob. /'submerging s-th purposely'/, (**<há->** *continuative*), phonology: há- occurs only before resonants (m, l, y, w), weak-grade of root (schwa-grade) after strong-grade (stressed-grade) of prefix, syntactic analysis: transitive verb, attested by AD; found in **<hámeletes.>**, //hɛ́-mil=əT-əs//, /'*He is placing it.*'/, attested by AD (4/27/79).

<mí:lthet>, pcrs //mí·l=T-ət//, ABFC /'*go in the water, walk slowly into the water, (dip oneself in the water [HT]*'/, WATR, literally /'submerge oneself purposely'/, (**<=t>** *purposeful control transitivizer*), (**<-et>** *reflexive*), syntactic analysis: intransitive verb, attested by Elders Group (2/6/80), also /'*dip oneself in the water*'/, attested by HT (2/6/80).

<mí:leqwem>, ABFC ['*soak one's head*'], *see* mí:l ~ míl.

<mí:leqwthet>, ABFC ['*soak one's head*'], *see* mí:l ~ míl.

<míliyel>, FSH /'*set a net (by canoe), set one's net, fish with a net, (submerge a net)*'/, *see* mí:l ~ míl.

<mí:lt>, pcs //mí·l=T or mɛ=í·l=T//, SOC /'*not want s-o, not accept s-o, discriminate against s-o*'/, possibly root **<mí:l>** *submerge* (if so, a nice metaphor: DISCRIMINATING IS SUBMERGING), possibly root **<má'>** *take off, come off*, (**<=t>** *purposeful control transitivizer*), syntactic analysis: transitive verb, attested by Elders Group (6/7/78, 2/6/80), contrast with root **<mal ~ mel>** *mixed up*, example: **<mí:lthóxes.>**, //mí·l=T-áx^y-əs//, /'*He doesn't want me.*'/, attested by Elders Group (6/7/78), **<me mí:lthòm.>**, //mə mí·l=T-àm//, /'*(They) discriminate against you., (They) don't accept you.*'/, literally /'it comes to be you are discriminated against/not accepted (submerged)'/, syntactic comment: passive, attested by Elders Group (2/6/80).

<**memí:lt**>, df //C₁ə=mí·l=T or C₁ə-mí·l=T//, SOC /'*not accept s-o, discriminate against s-o*'/, literally /'(poss.) not wanting s-o'/, possibly root <**mí:l**> *submerge*, possibly <**R5=**> *resultative*? or R5-> *continuative*, phonology: reduplication, syntactic analysis: transitive verb, attested by Elders Group (2/6/80); found in <**memí:lthòm.**>, //C₁ə=mí·l=T-àm//, /'*(They) discriminate against you., (They) don't accept you., (You are discriminated against/not accepted).*'/, attested by Elders Group (2/6/80).

<**mí:lt**>, ABFC ['*place s-th (prob. in water)*'], *see* mí:l ~ míl.

<**mí:lthet**>, ABFC /'*go in the water, walk slowly into the water, (dip oneself in the water [HT]*'/, *see* mí:l ~ míl.

<**mílha**>, free root //míɬɛ//, SPRD /'*to spirit-dance, to spirit-dance (of a group), have aspirit-dance, to winter-dance*'/, ASM ['to dance and sing while possessed by one's guardian spirit'], syntactic analysis: intransitive verb, attested by Deming, EB, AC, BJ (12/5/64), RG & EH (4/10/99 Ling332), Salish cognate: Squamish /míɬaʔ/ *Indian dance, to dance* W73:74, K67:257, other sources: Duff 1952:109 reports that the term may be borrowed from Kwakiutl as Boas gave Kwakiutl <meiLa> (macron over e) for *winter-dancing season*, example: <**tl'otsasu qw'eyílex qa t'ílem tel siyáya welámet mílha.**>, //ƛ'a-cɛ-s-u q'ʷəy=íl=əxʸ qɛ t'íl=əm tə-l si=yɛ́yɛ wə-lɛ́=m-ət míɬɛ//, /'*My friends will sing and dance when we go to the pow-wow dance.*'/, literally /'it's them -future -subord. -contrastive dance and sing the -my friend when- go -we subjunctive to spirit dance'/, attested by AC.

<**mímelha**>, cts //mí[-C₁ə-]ɬɛ//, SPRD /'*(doing) spirit-dancing, winter-dancing (when they're in action)*'/, (<**-R1-**> *continuative*), phonology: reduplication, syntactic analysis: intransitive verb, attested by AC, BJ (12/5/64), Deming, EB, RG & EH (4/10/99 Ling332), example: <**éwelhtsel lám ye mímelha.**>, //ʔə́wə-ɬ-c-əl lɛ́=m yə mí[-C₁ə-]ɬɛ//, /'*I never go to spirit-dances.*'/, literally /'not -past -main verb -I go to the (plural human?) be spirit-dancing'/, attested by EB, <**éwetsel líl làm ye mímelha kw' spélwalh.**>, //ʔə́wə-c-əl lí-l lɛ́=m yə mí[-C₁ə-]ɬɛ k'ʷə s=pə́l(=)w(=)ɛɬ//, /'*I didn't go to spirit-dances last year.*'/, literally /'not -main verb -I vaux (there) -I subjunctive/subordinate go to the (plural human?) be spirit-dancing the (remote) last year (nominal- time- ? -past)'/, attested by EB, <**le q'ep'lóxes wiyothe kwsu háléms ye mímelha.**>, //lə q'əp'=l-áxʸ-əs wi=yáθ-ə kʷ-s-u hɛ́-lɛm-s yə mí[-C₁ə-]ɬɛ//, /'*He got me addicted/hooked on always going to spirit-dances.*'/, attested by EB.

<**smílha**>, dnom //s=míɬɛ//, SPRD /'*a spirit-dance, a winter-dance*'/, (<**s=**> *nominalizer*), syntactic analysis: nominal, attested by AC, BJ (12/5/64).

<**smímelha**>, cts //s=mí[=C₁ə=]ɬɛ//, SPRD ['*(the) spirit-dancing*'], (<**=R1=**> *continuative*), phonology: reduplication, syntactic analysis: nominal, attested by BJ (12/5/64).

<**smilha'áwtxw**>, ds //s=miɬɛ=ʔɛ́wtxʷ//, SPRD /'*Indian dance-house, "smoke-house", (spirit-dance building)*'/, BLDG, ASM ['these range today from smaller buildings to large plank longhouses, in Upriver (Upper Stó:lō) territory in the pre-contact era most of these were probably pithouses'], lx <**=áwtxw ~ ='áwtxw**> *house, building*, phonology: epenthetic glottal stop added at front of some suffixes after vowel, syntactic analysis: nominal, attested by Elders Group.

<**mímele**>, KIN /'*baby (kin), child (kin) (up to about eigit years old)*'/, *see* méle ~ mél:a.

<**mímele**>, TIME ['*first month ?*'], *see* méle ~ mél:a.

<**mímeleqel**>, ds //(ʔə=)C₁í=məl=əqəl//, dmn, HHG ['*small container*'], compare <**emímel**> *a little bit*, probably <**R4=**> *diminutive*, probably root <**mel**> *just*, lx <**=eqel**> *container*, phonology: reduplication, syntactic analysis: nominal, attested by CT, HT,

<**mémeleqel**>, pln //C₁í=Aə́=məl=əqəl//, HHG ['*small containers (a number of them)*'], (<**R4=**> *diminutive*, é-ablaut on R4 *plural*), phonology: reduplication, ablaut, syntactic analysis: nominal,

attested by CT, HT.

<**mimele'ó:ylha**>, PE [*'doll'*], *see* méle ~ mél:a.

<**mímelha**>, SPRD /*'(doing) spirit-dancing, winter-dancing (when they're in action)'*/, *see* mílha.

<**mí:meqw ~ mímeqw**>, EZ /*'small bird (any kind, generic)'*/, *see* mó:qw.

<**mímesem**>, MC [*'picking out'*], *see* mís.

<**mímetú**>, EZ [*'little lamb'*], *see* metú.

<**Mimexwílem**>, PLN [*'place in Fraser River where there's an underwater spring of cold water'*], *see* mímexwel.

<**Mímex̱wel** (or prob. better, **Mímexwel)**>, PLN /*'next slough on north side of Harrison River above (east of) Smímstíyexwá:le, a muddy slough where fish spawn, right across from Johnny Leon's place at Chehalis and about 100 yards downstream (west) of Yálhxetel'*/, *see* mímexwel.

<**mímstiyexw**>, HUMC [*'kid'*], *see* mestíyexw.

<**mímx̱woya**>, ANA [*'little belly-button'*], *see* mṓx̱woya ~ mṓx̱weya ~ méx̱weya.

<**míq'**>, possibly root //míq’ or mí(y)=q’//, WATR /*'be underwater, sink to the bottom'*/, semantic environment ['of people, canoes, boats, rocks'], possibly root <**mí(y)**> *submerge, be underwater, sink*, possibly <**=q'**> *on something else*, syntactic analysis: intransitive verb, attested by EB, Elders Group (3/72), Salish cognate: Nooksack /míq/ *sink* PA61, ASM ['be underwater'], example: <**welhíth kwses míq'.**>, //wəɬ=híθ kʷ-s-əs míq’//, /*'He was underwater a long time.'*/, attested by EB, ASM ['sink'], <**míq' te sléxwelh.**>, //míq’ tə s=lə́xʷəɬ//, /*'The canoe sank.'*/, attested by EB, <**ólewe xwétés tl'ésu míq'.**>, //ʔálə-wə xʷə́tə́s ƛ’ə́-s-u míq’//, /*'It was too heavy and sank.'*/, attested by EB.

<**smímeq'**>, strs //s=mí[=C_1ə=]q’ or s=mí=C_1ə=q’//, WATR [*'(be) sunk'*], (<**s=**> *stative*), (<**=R1=**> *resultative*), phonology: reduplication, syntactic analysis: adjective/adjectival verb, attested by EB.

<**míq'et**>, pcs //mí(=)q’=əT//, WATR /*'sink s-th, sink it'*/, (<**=et**> *purposeful control transitivizer*), syntactic analysis: transitive verb, attested by EB, Salish cognate: perhaps Lushootseed /bíq’-id/ *press down on it* and /ʔəs-bíq’-it-əb/ *pressed down (of a net for ex.)* H76:693.

<**míq'et**>, WATR /*'sink s-th, sink it'*/, *see* míq'.

<**mís**>, bound root //mís *pick out, sort, choose*//.

<**mísem**>, ds //mís=əm//, MC /*'pick out, sort'*/, (<**=em**> *intransitivizer*), syntactic analysis: intransitive verb, attested by EB.

<**mímesem**>, cts //mí[-C_1ə-]s=əm//, MC [*'picking out'*], (<**-R1-**> *continuative*), phonology: reduplication, syntactic analysis: intransitive verb, attested by EB.

<**míset**>, pcs //mís=əT//, MC /*'pick it, choose it, sort it, (choose s-o/s-th)'*/, (<**=et**> *purposeful control transitivizer*), syntactic analysis: transitive verb, attested by EB, also <**mí:set**>, //mí·s=əT//, attested by AC, <**mí:set te thíthe**>, //mí·s=əT tə θí=C_1ə//, /*'pick out the larger ones'*/, example: <**mí:set te thíthe qwe'óp**>, //mí·s=əT tə θí=C_1ə qʷəʔáp//, /*'pick out the larger apples'*/, attested by AC.

<**mísem**>, MC /*'pick out, sort'*/, *see* mís.

<**míset**>, MC /*'pick it, choose it, sort it, (choose s-o/s-th)'*/, *see* mís.

<**mí:t ~ mít**>, free root //mí·t ~ mít//, ECON /*'ten cents, dime'*/, syntactic analysis: nominal, attested by AC, many others, borrowed from Chinook Jargon <bit ~ mit> *shilling; dime* itself < English "bit" (as in "two bits") Johnson 1978:303, example: <**lhíxw mít**>, //ɬíxʷ mít//, /*'thirty cents'*/, literally /'three dimes'/, attested by AC, others, <**lhséq' mí:t**>, //ɬ=sə́q’ mí·t//, /*'five cents'*/, literally /'half dime'/, attested by AC (8/4/70), <**mí:t qas kw'e lhséq' mí:t**>, //mí·t qɛs k’ʷə ɬ=sə́q’ mí·t//, /*'fiften cents'*/,

literally /'dime and a half dime'/, attested by AC.

<**mí:t'**>, free root //mí·t'//, EZ /*'blue grouse, blue-billed grouse*'/, ['*Dendragapus obscurus fuliginosus*'], ASM ['eaten, tails used as fans'], syntactic analysis: nominal, attested by AC, JL, also <**mít'**>, //mít'//, attested by Elders Group (6/4/75, 2/18/76), other sources: ES /mí·t'/, JH /mít'/ both *blue grouse*, Salish cognate: Nooksack /mít'/ *blue grouse* PA61:6, N. Straits dialects (San., Sg., Sam. here): Saanich /ŋíʔit'/, Songish /ŋíʔet/, and Samish /ŋíʔit'/ *blue grouse* Squamish /múmʔtm/ *blue grouse* W73:124, K67:256, (PCS cognate set #56 in G82), Samish form G86:67.

<**míthelh**>, TVMO ['*Come (urging one person).*'], *see* mí ~ mé ~ me.

<**mítl'et**>, pcs //míƛ'=əT//, FOOD ['*squish it up*'], MED, MC, (<**=et**> *purposeful control transitivizer*), syntactic analysis: transitive verb, attested by Deming, Salish cognate: Lushootseed /bíƛ'-id/ *smash it, crush it* H76:36, Squamish /múƛ'-un/ *crush (by one-sided pressure)(tr.)* W73:71, K69:46, poss. Squamish /míƛ'-in-cut/ *to stoop* and /ʔəs-míʔ-miƛ'/ *to crouch* K69:46.

<**míxw**>, bound root //míxʷ//, root meaning unknown

<**mímexwel**>, df //mí[=C₁ə=]xʷ=əl//, WATR /*'(have/be) dirty water, (not clear, unclear, can't see the bottom (of water) [EL])*'/, possibly <**=R1=**> *continuative or resultative*, possibly <**=el**> *come, go, get, become*, phonology: reduplication, syntactic analysis: intransitive verb, attested by NP (8/24/77), Salish cognate: Samish dial. of N. Straits /xʷ=ŋíxʷ=əl' (qʷáʔ)/ *muddy (water)* G86:64, also <**mímex̱wel**>, //mí[=C₁ə=]x̣ʷ=əl//, also /*'not clear, can't see bottom (of water)*'/, attested by EL (3/1/78).

<**Mímex̱wel**> (or prob. better, <**Mímexwel**>)>, df //mí[=C₁ə=]x̣ʷ=əl (or prob. better, mí[=C₁ə=]xʷ=əl)//, PLN /*'next slough on north side of Harrison River above (east of) Smímstíyexwá:le, a muddy slough where fish spawn, right across from Johnny Leon's place at Chehalis and about 100 yards downstream (west) of Yálhxetel*'/, literally /'not clear, can't see bottom (of water)'/, phonology: reduplication, syntactic analysis: nominal, attested by EL (3/1/78, 9/27/77), source: place names reference file #227a, compare <**Mimexwílem**.

<**Mimexwílem**>, ds //mi[=C₁ə=]xʷ=íl=əm//, PLN ['*place in Fraser River where there's an underwater spring of cold water*'], ASM ['there's also one on Harrison River by the same name'], literally /'going/getting dirty water place'/, (<**=R1=**> *continuative* or *resultative*), (<**=íl**> *go, come, get, become*, <**=em**> *place, place to get*), phonology: reduplication, syntactic analysis: nominal, attested by Elders Group (incl. NP)(8/24/77), source: place names reference file #227.

<**míx̱**> or <**mex̱**>, root uncertain //míx̣// or //məx̣//, meaning uncertain but perhaps *butterfly*

<**smímex̱àlh**>, df //s=mí[=C₁ə=]x̣=ɛ́ɬ or s=C₁í=məx̣=ɛ́ɬ//, EZ ['*caterpillar*'], ['prob. most *Lepidoptera* (butterfly) larvae'], (<**s=**> *nominalizer*), possibly <**=R1=**> *continuative or resultative*, or possibly <**R4=**> *diminutive*, probably <**=álh**> *offspring* since they are the offspring of butterflies, phonology: reduplicatin, syntactic analysis: nominal, attested by Elders Group (2/11/76), also <**smímex̱álh**>, //s=C₁í=məx̣=ɛ́ɬ (or s=mí[=C₁ə=]x̣=ɛ́ɬ)//, attested by Deming (1/31/80), also <**smimex̱áth**>, //s=C₁í=məx̣=ɛ́θ or s=mí[=C₁ə=]x̣=ɛ́θ//, attested by Elders Group (1/15/75), Salish cognate: Samish dial. of N. Straits /məməx̣éɬ/ *caterpillar* G86:69, example: <**xwéqw'ethet te smímex̱álh.**>, //xʷə́q'ʷ=əT-ət tə s=míməx̣ɛ́ɬ//, /*'The caterpillar is crawling.*'/, attested by Deming (1/31/80).

<**míyethélwét**>, CLO ['*buckskin clothes*'], *see* sméyeth ~ sméyéth.

<**míytel**>, SOC ['*a helper*'], *see* máy.

<**miyúl**>, free root //miyúl//, EZ ['*mule*'], ['hybrid between a horse *Equus caballus* and an ass *Equus asinus*'], syntactic analysis: nominal, attested by Deming (3/29/79), borrowed from Chinook Jargon <mule>/myúl/ itself from English, Johnson 1978:371, or from English <mule> directly.

<**mó:l**> or <**xwma**>, bound root //má·l// root meaning unknown or //x^wmɛ// *open*

<**shxwmó:l**>, stvi //s=x^w(=)má·l or s=x^w(=)mɛ=Aá(·)=əl//, SOC ['*to beg*'], possibly <**s=**> *stative*, possibly <**xw=**> *become, get*, possibly <**ó(:)-ablaut on á**> *resultative*, possibly <**=el**> *come, go, get, become*, possibly root <**xw(=)má**> *open* possibly from <**má**> *take off*, phonology: possible ablaut, syntactic analysis: intransitive verb, attested by MP and TM (2/8/78), Elders Group (3/1/72), also <**xwmó:l**>, //x^w(=)mɛ=Aá(·)=əl//, attested by NP (2/8/78).

<**shxwmómel**>, cts //s=x^w(=)má[-C_1ə-]l or s=x^w=mɛ=Aá[-C_1ə-]l//, SOC ['*begging*'], (<**-R1-**> *continuative*), phonology: reduplication, poss. ablaut, syntactic analysis: intransitive verb, attested by Elders Group (4/16/75), also <**shxwmó:mel**>, //s=x^w(=)má·[-C_1ə-]l//, attested by TG (Elders Group 3/1/72).

<**lexwshxwmó:mel**>, dnom //ləx^w=s=x^w=má·[=C_1ə=]l or ləx^w=s=x^w=mɛ=Aá·[=C_1ə=]l//, SOCT ['*beggar*'], (<**lexw=s=**> *one who always*), phonology: reduplication, possible ablaut, syntactic analysis: nominal, attested by TG (Elders Group 3/1/72).

<**mólkw**>, bound root or stem //málk^w//, probably FOOD /'*spread* (verb)'/

<**smelmólkw**>, dnom *////*, probably FOOD /'*be spread*'/, <s-> *nominalizer*, <**R3= or C1eC2=**> *plural*, phonology: reduplication, syntax: probably nominal, (attested by RG,EH 6/16/98 to SN, edited by BG with RG,EH 6/26/00)

<**temíitō smelmólkw**>, FOOD *ketchup* (lit. tomato + spread), (attested by RG,EH 6/16/98 to SN, edited by BG with RG,EH 6/26/00)

<**mó:lsem ~ mólsem**>, df //má·ls=əm ~ máls=əm or mɛ=á·ls=əm//, EB /'*bog blueberry, tall swamp blueberry*'/, ['probably *Vaccinium uliginosum*'], ASM ['large berries, ripe about Sept., thicker skin, not shiny, grow esp. at the mouth of the Fraser River and near the coast, picked at Mission, Langley, Deas Island, and other spots downriver, used to be harvested with a blueberry comb such as Joe Lorenzetto made once; for a description of one place where they grew with wild cranberries and short marsh/bog blueberries (lhewqí:m) see under lhewqí:m; the berries were blue with whitish dust, averaged about 45" tall for the tall species (mó:lsem) and about 32" tall for the short species (lhewqí:m), sweet, sort of tart (more than commercial variety) and smaller than the store variety; but mó:sem has larger berries than lhewqí:m'], possibly root <**má**> *take off*, possibly <**=ó:ls**> *berry*, possibly <**=em**> *intransitivizer*, phonology: possible vowel merger, syntactic analysis: nominal, attested by AC, JL, Elders Group (4/23/80, 9/3/75, 3/1/72), Deming, others, other sources: ES /málsəm/ *swamp blueberry*, Salish cognate: cognate with terms for Vaccinium uliginosum in Cowichan Halkomelem, Saanich dial. of N. Straits, Squamish, and Thompson; thus: Cowichan /málʔsəm/ and Saanich /málsəŋ/ *bog blueberry, Vaccinium uliginosum* Turner and Bell 1971:83, Saanich /mál'səŋ/ *bog blueberry* B74a:17, Squamish /múlʔsm/ *large swamp blueberry* W73:40, K69:46 identified as *Vaccinium uliginosum* in Bouchard and Turner 1976, Thompson /mə́lsəm/ (dot underə́) *bog blueberry, Vaccinium uliginosum* (borrowed from Halkomelem) Turner and Thompson 1973ms, also Lushootseed /búl'cəb/ *swamp blueberry.*

<**mólsemelhp**>, ds //mólsəm=əɬp//, EB ['*bog blueberry bush*'], ['*Vaccinium uliginosum*'], lx <**=elhp**> *tree, plant*, syntactic analysis: nominal.

<**mólsemelhp**>, EB ['*bog blueberry bush*'], *see* mó:lsem ~ mólsem.

<**mómet'es**>, ABFC ['*pointing*'], *see* mót'es.

<**mómet'es**>, ANAH /'*index finger, pointing finger*'/, *see* mót'es.

<**Mómet'es**>, PLN ['*small sharp mountain high above X̲elhálh and across the Fraser River from Yale*'], *see* mót'es.

<**Momhiya?**>, df //ma[=C_1ə=]h=iyɛ?//, PLN ['*a place probably between Yale and Emory Creek*'], root meaning unknown, possibly <**=R1=**> *continuative or resultative or diminutive*, lx <**=iya**> *affectionate diminutive*, phonology: reduplication, syntactic analysis: nominal, attested by MP transcribed ca 1972-73 by SP and AD, pronounced by SP and AD 7/8/77 from their notes, source: place names reference file #49.

<**momíyelhtel**>, SOC /'*helping one another, (helper [Elders Group])*'/, *see* máy.

<**momí:yt**>, ABFC ['*aiming it*'], *see* mó:yt.

<**mopel**>, free root //mapəl// *marble* (borrowing from English)

<**mopeló:les**>, ds //mapəl=á·ləs//, ANA /'*(have) marble eyes, (have) blue eyes*'/, literally /'marble (in the) eyes'/, probably root <**mápel**> *marble*, lx <**=ó:les**> *in the eyes*, syntactic analysis: intransitive verb, nominal?, attested by Elders Group.

<**mó:qw**>, free root //má·qʷ//, EZ /'*larger bird (any kind, generic), waterfowl, duck, (mallard [Cheh. dial.])*'/, syntactic analysis: nominal, noun, dialects: *Chilliwack*, attested by AC, BJ (5/64, 12/5/64), Elders Group (3/1/72, 2/18/76), other sources: ES /má·qʷ/ *duck (generic)* (vs. ES /sq'ʷəlɛ́xʸ/ *bird*), H-T <mauq> *duck (Anas boschas)*, also <**xwé:yleqw**>, //xʷí·l=əqʷ//, dialects: *Chehalis*, attested by Elders Group, NP, also /'*mallard*'/, dialects: *Chehalis*, attested by EB, others, example: <**ōwéta mó:qw.**>, //ʔowə= ́=tɛ má·qʷ//, /'*There are no birds.*'/, attested by AC, <**qéx̱ te mó:qw.**>, //qə́x̣ tə má·qʷ//, /'*There are a lot of birds.*'/, attested by AC, <**lhq'atsesí:ws te mó:qwe xwe'í:lxwes.**>, //ɬq'ɛ(=)cəs=í·ws tə má·qʷ (kʷ)ə xʷə=ʔí·=l-əxʷ-əs//, /'*He brought five mallards (ducks).*'/, literally /'they are five birds the ducks that he brings s-th here'/, attested by EB.

<**mí:meqw ~ mímeqw**>, dmn //C_1í=maqʷ//, EZ /'*small bird (any kind, generic)*'/, ASM ['smaller than a duck example'], (<**R4=**> *diminutive*), phonology: reduplication, vowel reduction to schwa-grade of root after stressed full-grade prefix, syntactic analysis: nominal, attested by AC, Elders Group (3/1/72, 2/19/75, 6/4/75, 2/18/76, 12/15/76), also <**hemóqw**>, //hə=máqʷ//, (<**he=**> *diminutive*), attested by BJ (12/5/64) (old p.307 Wells tapes transcript), example: <**i'axwí::l mí:meqw**>, //C_1í=ʔɛxʷí·[=·=]l C_1í=maqʷ//, /'*(It's a) tiny bird.*'/, attested by AC, <**t'it'elem te mímeqw.**>, //t'í[-C_1ə-]l=əm tə C_1í=maqʷ//, /'*The little bird is singing.*'/, attested by Elders Group (12/15/76).

<**mó:qwem**>, ds //mə=qʷá·[=M2=]m//, LAND /'*(sphagnum) bog, marsh*'/, ASM ['not really a swamp because as AC notes a swamp would have puddles, more like moss on dirt'], EB /'*Labrador tea, "Indian tea", "swamp tea"*'/, ['*Ledum groenlandicum*'], ASM ['leaves gathered year-round, dried for an excellent tea (somewhat minty and herbal in flavor), starting to get very scarce in the Upper Stó:lō area as marshlands are in danger of disappearing forever to non-Indian drainage for "development"'], (<**me=**> *become, get, come*), probably root <**qwó:m**> *sphagnum moss, ground moss* (JL contrasts with < **mex̱t'éles**> *lichen, tree moss*), probably <**metathesis type 2**> *derivational*, phonology: metathesis, syntactic analysis: nominal, noun, attested by AC, Deming, others, other sources: ES /má·qʷəm/ *swamp*, H-T <mákwom> (macron over a) *marsh.*

<**móst'**>, bound root or stem //mást'// meaning uncertain

<**smóst'iyethel**>, df //s=mást'=əyəθəl//, ANAH ['*(have) pursed lips when pouting*'], (<**s=**> *stative*), lx <**=iyethel ~ =ó:ythel**> *on the lips*, root meaning unknown, syntactic analysis: adjective/adjectival verb?, nominal??, attested by IHTTC.

<**=mó:t**>, da //=má·t//, SH /'*piles, kinds*'/, semantic environment ['with numerals 1-5'], syntactic comment: obligatory, syntactic analysis: lexical suffix, derivational suffix; found in <**lhq'átsesmó:t**>, //ɬq'ɛ́cəs=má·t//, /'*five piles*'/.

<**mó:tx̱w ~ mótx̱w**>, bound root or stem //má·t(=)x̣ʷ// may mean *tattle (on someone)*, possible lx <**=x̱w**>

round, around

<**smó:tx̲w ~ smótx̲w**>, df //s=má·t(=)x̣ʷ ~ s=mát(=)x̣ʷ//, EZ /'*bullhead, (brown bullhead)*'/, ['*Ictalurus nebulosus*'], semantic environment ['fish, fishing, river, lake'], SOCT ['*tattletale*'], LANG, semantic environment ['used of children only if they are tattletales'], (<**s=**> *nominalizer*), root meaning unknown, possible lx <=**x̲w**> *round, around*, syntactic analysis: nominal, attested by Elders Group, AC.

<**mót'es**>, df //mát'=əs//, ABFC /'*point at, aim*'/, HUNT, FSH, semantic environment ['finger, gun, arrow, spear, other?'], possibly <=**es**> *on the face*, root meaning unknown, syntactic analysis: intransitive verb, attested by AC.

<**mómet'es**>, cts //má[-C_1ə-]t'=əs//, ABFC ['*pointing*'], (<-**R1-**> *continuative*), phonology: reduplication, syntactic analysis: intransitive verb, attested by AC.

<**mómet'es**>, ds //má[=C_1ə=]t'=əs//, ANAH /'*index finger, pointing finger*'/, (<=**R1=**> *continuative*), phonology: reduplication, zero-derivation, syntactic analysis: nominal, attested by AC, other sources: H-T <mutasémEl> *first finger (lit. pointer)* (see <**mét'esemél**> below).

<**Mómet'es**>, ds //má[=C_1ə=]t'=əs//, PLN ['*small sharp mountain high above X̲elhálh and across the Fraser River from Yale*'], ASM ['it resembles an index finger, it has a cave on its face to which a man can be lowered down on a rope, a group of Indians during the great Flood tied their canoe to this mountain and stayed in the cave till the water subsided, sometime perhaps 1890-1930 a group of men climbed the mountain and lowered one man to the cave with difficulty, when inside he found ancient pieces of rope and barbecue sticks from the people during the Flood, the rope just fell to dust when it was touched; most of this is from Amy Cooper's text the Story of the Flood; some is from Susan Peters who knew the man who climbed down to the cave (I believe he was her parent's generation, thus the date); more notes in place names files'], phonology: reduplication, zero-derivation, syntactic analysis: nominal, attested by AC, SP, P.D. Peters (10/5/76), MP (in notes taken by SP and AD and discussed in IHTTC 7/8/77), source: place names reference file #35.

<**mót'est**>, pcs //mát'=əs=T//, ANAH ['*point at s-th*'], (<=**t**> *purposeful control transitivizer*), syntactic analysis: transitive verb, attested by AC, Deming, example: <**mót'estchexw ta' méqsel.**>, //mát'=əs=T-c-əxʷ t-ɛʔ mə́qsəl//, /'*Point at your nose.*'/, attested by Deming.

<**mót'estel**>, dnom //mát'=əs=təl//, TVMO ['*a pointer (a stick)*'], DIR, SCH, lx <=**tel**> *device to, something to*, syntactic analysis: nominal, attested by Elders Group, AC, ANAH /'*first finger, index finger*'/, literally /'pointer'/, dialects: *Chill. and Cheh.*, attested by Elders Group (8/20/75).

<**shxwmót'estel**>, dnom //s(=)xʷ=mát'=əs=təl//, LAND ['*pointer to show direction (like in a trail) (could be an arrow or stick or mark in the ground)*'], DIR, TVMO, semantic environment ['arrow, stick, mark in the ground, on a trail, etc.'], (<**s(=)xw=**> *nominalizer*), syntactic analysis: nominal, attested by Elders Group.

<**mót'estses**>, ds //mát'=əs=cəs//, ANAH /'*first finger, index finger*'/, literally /'point on the hand'/, lx <=**tses**> *on the hand*, phonology: zero-derivation, syntactic analysis: nominal, attested by Elders Group (5/3/78).

<**mét'esemél**>, ds //ma[=Aə́=]t'=əs=əmə́l//, ANAH /'*first finger, index finger*'/, (<**é-ablaut**> *derivational*), lx <=**emél**> *member, part (often of body)*, phonology: ablaut, syntactic analysis: nominal, dialects: *Tait*, attested by Elders Group (8/20/75), other sources: H-T <mutasémEl> *first finger (lit. pointer)*, also <**met'esemél**>, //ma[=Aə=]t'=əs=əmə́l//, dialects: *Scowlitz*, source: reconstituted from Boas 1890 ms. field notes in APS Library Boas <metesemál> (all e's with double underline), attested by noted with Elders Group (5/3/78).

<**mót'est**>, ANAH ['*point at s-th*'], *see* mót'es.

<**mót'estel**>, TVMO ['*a pointer (a stick)*'], *see* mót'es.

<**mót'estses**>, ANAH /'*first finger, index finger*'/, *see* mót'es.

<**mótheqw**> or <**math**>, bound stem //máθ(=)əqʷ// *make/prepare fish oil* or root //mɛθ// *spread out*.

<**smótheqw**>, df //s=máθ=əqʷ or s=mɛ[=Aá=]θ=əqʷ//, FOOD ['*prepared fish oil (usually sockeye oil)*'], FSH, ASM ['prepared by leaving sockeye heads and parts out in hot sun all day then in rock holes by the river with water and hot rocks; this brings out the oil which floats on top and is skimmed off'], (<**s=**> *nominalizer*), (<**ó-ablaut (esp. on á)**> *resultative*), lx <**=eqw**> *fish*, probably root <**máth**> *spread out* due to the method of preparing fish oil, phonology: probable ablaut, syntactic analysis: nominal, attested by IHTTC, SP and AK (at Fish Camp 8/2/77).

<**hemhémetheqw**>, df //C_1əC_2=hə́-maθ=əqʷ or C_1əC_2=hə́-mɛθ=əqʷ//, FSH ['*a group making (fish) oil*'], FOOD, (<**R3=**> *plural agents*), (<**hé-**> *continuative* before resonants m, l, y, w), probably root <**máth**> *spread out*, lx <**=eqw**> *fish*, compare <**smótheqw**> *prepared fish oil*, phonology: reduplication of the prefix is very unusual, vowel-reduction to weak-grade (schwa-grade) of root after stressed full-grade of prefix, syntactic analysis: intransitive verb, possibly nominal, attested by IHTTC (9/2/77), also /'*place where they make smótheqw (prepared fish oil)*'/, comment: prob. corrected by IHTTC (9/2/77), prob. refers to the place name which could be said to mean something like this, attested by SP and AK at Fish Camp (8/2/77).

<**Hemhémetheqw**>, df //C_1əC_2=hə́=maθ=əqʷ or C_1əC_2=hə́=mɛθ=əqʷ//, PLN ['*flat rocks (bedrock) with holes at Hill's Bar where they used to make smótheqw (prepared fish oil) from sockeye heads*'], ASM ['Hill's Bar is on the east side of the Fraser River, the holes are a foot or more deep and several feet in diameter on average and there are a dozen or more'], literally /'many people making prepared fish oil'/, phonology: reduplication, vowel-reduction, syntactic analysis: nominal, attested by SP and AK at Fish Camp (8/2/77), on raft trip (8/30/77), and in Elders Group reviewing raft trip slides (9/13/77), source: place names file reference #140a.

<**mótl'**>, probably root //máƛ'//, EFAM ['*(be) stumped*'], syntactic analysis: adjective/adjectival verb, attested by Elders Group, example: <**mótl' te Hank.**>, //máƛ' tə Hank//, /'*Hank is stumped.*'/.

<**mótl'**>, probably root //máƛ' ~ mə́ƛ'//, WETH ['*be dirty*'], DESC, ASM ['(blowing dirt or dust?)'], syntactic analysis: adjective/adjectival verb, probably borrowed from Squamish /máƛ'/ *be dirty*, comment: since chmítl' shows the Halkomelem root is métl' (as in one Squamish alternant) and since Halkomelem would have inherited mátl', not mótl', corresponding to the Squamish form /máƛ'/, example: <**mótl' te swáyel.**>, //máƛ' tə s=wɛ́yəl//, /'*It's a dirty day.*'/, Salish cognate: Squamish root /maƛ' ~ məƛ'/ *be dirty* as in /mə́ƛ'/ *get stained, get dirty* and /máƛ'-n/ *make dirty (tr.)* W73:79,250, K69:45.

<**chmítl'**>, strs //c=mə[=Aí=]ƛ'//, BLDG ['*(be) dirty*'], DESC, (<**ch=**> *have, be*), (<**í-ablaut**> *resultative*), phonology: í-ablaut is the expected *resultative* on roots with e (schwa), syntactic analysis: adjective/adjectival verb, attested by EB (12/1/75), Salish cognate: Lushootseed /bíƛ'-il-dup/ *muddy, dirt* (derived from root /bíƛ'(i)/ *smash, crush* by Hess, H76:36-37 but may be a separate (or related) root as here and in Squamish, more cognates would be helpful.

<**móylhtel**>, SOC /'*help out, go help, pitch in, help one another*'/, *see* máy.

<**mó:yt**>, pcs //má·y=T//, ABFC ['*aim it*'], (semological comment: not clear whether it also is a member of domains of HUNT, FSH, GAM, CAN, etc.), (<**=t**> *purposeful control transitivizer*), syntactic analysis: transitive verb, attested by EB, AD.

<**momí:yt**>, df //ma[-C_1ə-´]y=T//, ABFC ['*aiming it*'], comment: one would expect mómiyt /má[-mə-]yt/ as a more regular continuative, (irregular)stress-shift onto infixed reduplication, phonology: reduplication, irregular stress-shift, syntactic analysis: transitive verb, attested by EB (4/12/78).

<**mṓkweset**>, ABDF ['*kiss s-o*'], *see* mékw.

<**mōkw'éthet**>, ABFC /'*(take all of themselves, pick themselves all up)*'/, *see* mékw' ~ mṓkw'.

<**mṓs**>, bound root //mós *four*//.

<**smṓs**>, df //s=mós=s//, TIME ['*Thursday (a less common name)*'], lx <**s=...=s**> *-th day, hour,* phonology: consonant merger, syntactic analysis: nominal, attested by AD and SP (both in BHTTC 11/9/76), usage: AD's parents and SP's father and stepmother used this form.

<**mṓx̱woya ~ mṓx̱weya ~ méx̱weya**>, df //móx̣ʷ=ayɛ ~ móx̣ʷ=əyɛ ~ məx̣ʷ=əyɛ//, ANA /'*belly-button, navel*'/, root meaning unknown, lx <**=oya ~ =eya ~ =iya**> *affectionate diminutive,* syntactic analysis: nominal, noun, attested by AC, BHTTC, others, other sources: ES /mə́x̣ʷəyɛ/ *navel,* Salish cognate: Squamish /mə́x̣ʷ-ya/ *navel* (and /s-məx̣ʷ-íws/ *small-pox*) from root /məx̣ʷ/ *dimple, mark (?)* W73:183, K67:255, Mainland Comox /mə́x̣ʷáju/ *belly-button* B75prelim:27, Sechelt /məx̣ʷə́yu/ *belly-button* T77:14, Samish dial. of N. Straits /mə́x̣ʷəyeʔ/ *belly-button, navel* G86:74, example: <**Híltu te mṓx̱woya.**>, //híltu tə móx̣ʷ=ayɛ//, /'*The belly-button is a Hindu.*'/, comment: comparison between the concentric wrapping of the turban and the concentric rings in some navels, usage: in the Híltu or Heel-toe song (sung to "Jimmy Crack Corn"), attested by BHTTC.

<**mímx̱woya**>, dmn //C_1í=məx̣ʷ=ayɛ//, ANA ['*little belly-button*'], (<**R4=**> *diminutive*), phonology: reduplication, syntactic analysis: nominal, attested by BHTTC, example: <**Híheltu te mímx̱woya.**>, //C_1í=həltu tə C_1í=məx̣ʷ=ayɛ//, /'*A little belly button is like a little Hindu.*'/, usage: in the Híltu or Heel-toe song, attested by BHTTC.

<**múmesmes**>, EZ ['*small adult cow*'], *see* músmes.

<**músmes**>, free root //músməs//, EZ /'*cow, bull, beef*'/, ['genus *Bovis*'], FOOD ['*beef*'], ACL, phonology: reduplication from the donor language, thus further reduplicating in derivations is tolerated, syntactic analysis: nominal, noun, attested by AC, Elders Group, Deming, EB, others, borrowed from Chinook Jargon <moos-moos> /músmus/ *cow, horned cattle, beef, buffalo* itself variously from Chinook Proper, Klickitat, Yakima or Cree Johnson 1978:287, example: <**te ts'q'éyx̱ músmes**>, //tə c'=q'íx̣ músməs//, /'*the black cow*'/, attested by EB, <**p'ip'eth'élmet te músmes**>, //p'i[-C_1ə-]θ'=ə́lməxʷ=əT tə músməs//, /'*milking the cow*'/, literally /'squeezing s-th/s-o on the breasts the cow'/, attested by Elders at Fish Camp (7/19/78).

<**múmesmes**>, dmn //mú[=C_1ə=]sməs//, EZ ['*small adult cow*'], (<**=R1=**> *diminutive*), phonology: double reduplication tolerated because the original reduplication was borrowed and not native, syntactic analysis: nominal, attested by IHTTC.

<**melúmesmes**>, dmpn //m[=əl=]ú[=C_1ə=]sməs//, EZ /'*small adult cows, (small adult cattle)*'/, (<**=el=**> *plural*), phonology: non-reduplicative infix, reduplication, syntactic analysis: nominal, attested by IHTTC (7/15/77).

<**músmesò:llh**>, dmn //músməs=á·ɬ//, EZ ['*calf*'], lx <**=ó:llh**> *offspring, young,* phonology: downstepping, syntactic analysis: nominal, attested by AC, CT, HT.

<**músmesò:llh**>, EZ ['*calf*'], *see* músmes.

N

<**n**>, comment: The sound /n/ appears only in borrowings, a few words of baby talk, and some very old place names. The place names may have been obtained by George Gibbs ca 1858-1863 through speakers of Downriver Halkomelem (thus Tzeachten and perhaps Skulkayn for places which all fluent Upriver speakers pronounce Ch'iyáqtel /č'iyɛ́q=təl/ and Sq'ewqéyl /s=q'əw=qíl/)., comment: Historically all Upriver Halkomelem n → l. It is so far not clear how recent that change was. There is a slight chance that it was still incomplete when Gibbs was gathering his information and that some of his Chilliwack and Tait word lists and place names may reflect real Upriver Halkomelem n's., comment: Until more work on comparative Halkomelem is done and records on Gibb's informants/speakers in the National Archives can be studied, the best guess is probably that Gibbs had a downriver speaker for some of the forms (possibly one from the Kwantlen dialect of Fort Langley). Words in baby talk are known to often tolerate sounds which are not phonemic in adult language. That seems the reason for the forms here..

<**nána**>, possibly root //nɛ́nɛ or R7=nɛ//, [nǽnæ], EFAM /'*hurt, sore*'/, ABDF, possibly <**R7=**> *diminutive*? or> meaning uncertain, possibly compare with <**lá:la**> *Well!*, phonology: possible reduplication, syntactic analysis: nominal?, intransitive verb?, usage: baby language, attested by AD, Elders Group (2/13/80), TG, example: <**Where's your nána?**>, //Where's your nɛ́nɛ//, /'*Where's your hurt?, Where's your sore?*'/, usage: language switching, attested by TG.

<**naníth**>, possible root or stem, bound //nɛní(=)əθ or /nɛ(=)níθ// root meaning unknown
<**Snaníth**>, df //s=nɛníθ//, PLN ['*a village at the south end of former Sumas Lake on the mountain*'], literally /'on the other side of the lake'/, possibly <**s=**> *stative or nominalizer*, possibly <**=eth**> *edge*, possibly root <**lóli(y)**> *be leaning*, comment: this may have been the village with houses built out over the water on stilts for protection from mosquitoes (described by Boundary Survey records), in which case a meaning of "leaning on the edge" might be appropriate; the literal meaning given above ("on the other side of the lake") is provided by the Elders Group, phonology: possible reduplication, syntactic analysis: nominal, dialects: *Sumas (thus the n's and the th - ts variation)*, attested by Elders Group (8/31/77), other sources: Wells 1965 (lst ed.):23 <nah-NEETS> in records as Saneats also, Wells 1966, source: place names reference file #258.

<**Nesókwech ~ Nasókwach**>, df //nə=sákʷ=əc or nə=sák'ʷ=əc//, PLN ['*Middle Creek*'], possibly <**le= ~ lexw=** (downriver **ne= ~ nexw=)**> *always*, possibly <**=ech**> *on the back*, possibly root <**sókw'**> *inner cedar bark*, possibly compare <**Sókw'ech**> *a creek between Hope and Yale*, syntactic analysis: nominal, source: Wells 1965 (lst ed.):13 <neh-SAK-wach.ch> , Wells 1966 <ne-SA-kwatch>, also <**Lóyeqw'e'áts** or **Lóyaqwe'áts'** or **Lóyaqwe'áth'**>, df //láyə=q'ʷəʔɛc or láyə=qʷəʔɛ·c' or láyə=qʷəʔɛ́θ'//, PLN ['*Middle Creek*'], possibly <**lóye**> *only*, possibly root <**qw'e'á:ts**> *little sucker-fish with big salmon-like mouth (prob. the largescale sucker, Catostomus macrocheilus),* syntactic analysis: nominal, source: Wells 1965 (lst ed.):13 <LIY-ah-quh-'AHT'z> from map by Billy Sepass where it is spelled <Lyaaquaatz>.

O

<**ókw'**>, bound root //ʔák'ʷ *hang on an arm or on something sticking out*//.

<**ókw'est**>, pcs //ʔák'ʷ=əs=T//, MC /'*hang s-th (on a nail or hat hanger), hook it back on (of a stitch lost in knitting)*'/, semantic environment ['on a nail, hat-hanger, or stitch in knitting, probably on anything sticking out'], lx <**=es**> *on the face*, (<**=t**> *purposeful control transitivizer*), syntactic analysis: transitive verb, attested by AD.

<**s'ókw'(e)stexw**>, caus //s=ʔák'ʷ(ə)=sT-əxʷ//, ABFC ['*carry s-th/s-o on one's arm*'], semantic environment ['of a purse, handbag, person, etc. as semantic patient'], (<**s=**> *stative*), (<**=st**> *causative control transitivizer*), syntactic analysis: transitive verb, attested by Elders Group, AD.

<**s'ókw'ches**>, stvi //s=ʔák'ʷ=cəs//, ABFC /'*to be arm in arm (like escorting someone), to take an arm (of someone)*'/, (<**s=**> *stative*), lx <**=ches**> *on the hand*, syntactic analysis: intransitive verb, attested by AD.

<**ókw'elexw**>, DIR ['*lose s-th*'], *see* íkw' ~ í:kw'.

<**ókw'est**>, MC /'*hang s-th (on a nail or hat hanger), hook it back on (of a stitch lost in knitting)*'/, *see* ókw'.

<**òl ~ -òl ~ -ò ~ el**>, free root //ʔàl ~ -àl ~ -à ~ ʔəl//, NUM /'*just (simply, merely)*'/, (semological comment: put into the NUM domain since it limits the number of items or the quantity of action, eliminates peripheral actions or items), phonology: independent word ~ phonological suffix, variants show vowel-reduction or consonant-loss in free-variation, syntactic analysis: adverb/adverbial verb ~ -adverb/adverbial verb, syntactic comment: can be suffixed to nominal, adverb/adverbial verb, adjective/adjectival verb, num, or conjunction and can precede -s-u, attested by Deming, EB, HT, Elders Group, EK and DK, example: <**l stl'í kw'els qwà:l kw'e axwí:l òl sqwà:l.**>, //l s=ƛ'í k'ʷə-l-s qʷɛ̀·l k'ʷə ʔɛxʷí·l ʔàl sqʷɛ̀·l//, /'*I would like to say just a few words.*'/, attested by Deming (5/18/78), usage: public speaking, <**yalholsú xwe'í.**>, //yɛɬ-al-s-u xʷə=ʔí//, /'*I just got here.*'/, attested by EB, <**iyólem kw'els kwú:t ò.**>, //ʔiy=ál=əm k'ʷə-l-s kʷú·=T ʔà//, /'*It's alright if I (just) take it.*'/, attested by HT; found in <**qá:ysò**>, //qɛ́·ys-à//, /'*just now, not long ago*'/, attested by EB, <**qá:ysò le ts'eqw'ō̃welh.**>, //qɛ́·ys-à lə c'əq'ʷ=ówəɬ//, /'*He just now made a basket.*'/, attested by EB, example: <**qá:ystsel (ò, le) yóys.**>, //qɛ́·ys-c-əl (ʔà, lə) yáys//, /'*I just now (started to, went to) work.*'/, attested by Elders Group, <**emímel el.**>, //ʔə=C_1í=məl ʔəl//, /'*Just a little bit.*'/, attested by AC, <**ō áy el te sqwóqwels.**>, //ʔəw-ʔɛ́·y ʔəl tə s=qʷɛ[-AáC$_1$ə-]l-s//, /'*He's talking without making any sense., He keeps on talking (in spite of the fact no one is listening).*'/, LANG, literally /'contrastive- keeps on just the his talking → His talking just keeps on and on.'/, attested by Elders Group.

<**we'ól ~ ól(e)we ~ ólew**>, ds //wə=ʔál ~ ʔál=(ə)wə ~ ʔál=əw//, NUM /'*too (overly), very much*'/, (<**we=**> *contrastive*), (<**=we ~ =ew**> *contrastive*), syntactic analysis: adverb/adverbial verb, syntactic comment: the contrastive affix can either be prefixed or suffixed, attested by AC, AD, Elders Group, EB, LJ (Tait), others, also /'*more*'/, attested by AC (8/6/70), also <**welól**>, //wə=lál//, attested by Deming, ASM ['too'], example: <**we'ól kw'ekw'ís**>, //wə=ʔál C_1ə=k'ʷís//, /'*(It's) too narrow*'/, attested by AC, <**ólew eyém**>, //ʔál=əw ʔɛy=ə́m//, /'*(It's/He's/She's) too strong*'/, semantic environment ['of medicine or strength of a person or thing'], attested by Elders Group, also <**wu'ól iyém**>, //wə=ʔál ʔɛy=ə́m//, attested by AD, <**ólew qé<u>x</u>**>, //ʔál=əw qə́x̣//, /'*(It's) too much.*'/, attested by EB, also <**wu'ól qé<u>x</u>**>, //wə=ʔál qə́x̣//, attested by AD, also <**we'ó(:)l weqé<u>x</u>**>, //wə=ʔá(·)l wə=qə́x̣//, attested by AC, syntactic comment: double contrastive, <**(we'ó:lew qé<u>x</u>, we'ó:l weqé<u>x</u>) te sts'ólha.**>, //(wə=ʔá·l=əw qə́x̣, wə=ʔá·l wə=qə́x̣) tə s=c'áɬɛ//, /'*(There are) too many leaves*'/,

attested by AC, <**we'ólwe siyólexwe**>, //wə=ʔál wə-siyáləxʷə//, /'*too old, very old*'/, attested by EB, <**chxw ólewe siyólexwe kw'as sexwe'álexeth'.**>, //c-xʷ ʔál=(ə)wə siyáləxʷə k'ʷ-ɛ-s səx̣ʷə=ʔɛ́ləx̣əθ'//, /'*You're too old to wet your bed.*'/, attested by EB (5/5/78), <**le qelámthet tel th'ále lhíl ólew le kw'á:y.**>, //lə qəl=ɛ́m=Tət tə-l θ'ɛ́lə ɬí-l ʔál=əw lə k'ʷɛ́·y//, /'*My heart gets weak when I get too hungry.*'/, attested by LJ (Tait)(6/28/78), <**we'ólwe sthethá:kw', líqwetlha.**>, //wə=ʔál wə=s=θə[=C₁ɛ́(·)=]k'ʷ, líqʷ=əT-ɬɛ//, /'*It's pulled too tight, loosen it.*'/, literally /'too contrastive= pulled tight, loosen it -command imperative 2s'/, attested by EB, ASM ['very much, too much'], <**ólewe totí:lt**>, //ʔál=əwə ta[=C₁ə]l=í·l=T//, /'*studying it very much*'/, attested by Elders Group, <**tsel we'ólwe ítet.**>, //c-əl wə=ʔál wə-ʔítət//, /'*I overslept., I slept too much.*'/, literally /'I ambiguous past too much contrastive- sleep'/, attested by EB, <**welól qéx̱ tále.**>, //wə=lál qə́x̣ tɛ́lə//, /'*That's too much money.*'/, attested by Deming (1/25/79).

<**=ò:l ~ =ól ~ =ò ~ ò ~ ó:l**>, da ~ free root //=à(·)l ~ =à ~ ʔà ~ ʔá·l//, MOOD /'*just, (exactly)*'/, either related to the previous root with the same shape (the meanings could be allosemes) or allomorphs converging with it, syntactic analysis: lexical suffix, derivational suffix, and postclitic; found in <**iyó:lem**>, //ʔiy=á·l=əm//, /'*okay, right, correct, alright*'/ (compare <**iy=**> bound form of <**éy**> *good)*, found in <**éy òl ~ éyòl ~ éyò**>, ds //ʔɛ́y ʔàl ~ ʔɛ́yàl ~ ʔɛ́yà//, VALJ /'*be alright, be well, be fine, be okay*'/, and its derivations or combinations such as <**we'éy òl ~ we'éyòl ~ we'éyò ~ u éyò ~ u'éyò**>, ds //wə=ʔɛ́y ʔàl ~ wə=ʔɛ́y=àl ~ wəʔɛ́yà ~ ʔu ʔɛ́yà ~ ʔu=ʔɛ́yà//, ABFC /'*be fine (in health), be alright (in health), be well*'/, for others (including <**iyó:lem**>, //ʔiy=á·l=əm//, /'*okay, right, correct, alright*'/) see <**éy**> *good.* (This last word, <**iyó:lem**> //ʔiy=á·l=ə=m//, may alternatively be derived from <**ó:le ~ óle**> (see following paragraph for <**ó:le ~ óle**> *true, right*).

<**ó:le ~ óle**>, df //ʔá·lə ~ ʔálə or ʔál=ə//, LANG /'*true, right*'/, possibly <**=e**> meaning uncertain, syntactic analysis: adjective/adjectival verb, attested by Elders Group, Andy Alex, Deming, example: <**li ó:le?**>, //li ʔá·lə//, /'*Is that right?*'/, attested by Elders Group (1/26/77), also <**lí òle?**>, //lí ʔàlə//, attested by AD (4/26/78), also <**liyóle?**>, //li(y)-álə//, attested by Andy Alex (HIA meeting, 10/26/77); found in <**ō'ó:le.**>, //ʔəw-ʔá·lə//, /'*That's right.*'/, attested by Elders Group, example: <**sta'á óle.**>, //s=t=əʔɛ́ ʔálə//, /'*Oh that's the way it is.*'/, literally /'is similar/alike/the same right'/, attested by Deming, <**éwe wel'óles éy te sqwéltels.**>, //ʔə́wə wəl-ʔálə-s ʔɛ́y tə s=qʷɛ[=Aə́=]l=təl-s//, /'*His talk isn't very good.*'/, LANG, literally /'is not very- right -it/he/she the his talk/language'/, attested by Deming.

<**lexws'ó:les**>, df //ləxʷ=s=ʔá·lə(=)s//, DESC /'*(be) willing to do one's work, (ambitious [BHTTC])*'/, (<**lexw=**> *always*, s= *stative*), possibly <**=s**> meaning uncertain, possibly root <**ó:le**> *right, true,* syntactic analysis: adjective/adjectival verb?, nominal?, attested by Elders Group (6/16/76), also /'*(be) ambitious*'/, attested by BHTTC.

<**-óle**>, (//**-álə**//), PRON /'*you (pl.), second person plural object*'/, phonology: attracts stress, stress-shift automatic to e before -tsel/-tset, syntactic analysis: is, syntactic comment: will not allow a third person subject -es suffix; found in <**imexstolétsel.**>, //ʔim=əxʸ=sT-álə-c-əl//, //ʔimɪxʸstalə́cɪl//, /'*I made you folks walk.*'/, <**kw'étslolétset.**>, //k'ʷə́c=l-álə-c-ət//, [k'ʷʊ́clalə́cɪt], /'*We see you folks.*'/.

<**-òlèm**>, (//**-àlə̀m** or **-àl(ə)=əm**//), PRON ['*first person plural patient or object of passive*'], VOIC, comment: historically may be connected with -óle *first person plural subject*, probably <**-em**> *passive*, phonology: possible vowel-loss, possible downdrifting, possible updrifting, syntactic analysis: is; found in <**ó:tòlèm.**>, //ʔá·=T-àlə̀m//, /'*You folks were called.*'/, <**kw'étslòlèm.**>, //k'ʷə́c=l-àlə̀m//, /'*You folks were seen., They/He/She saw you folks.*'/, <**éystòlem.**>, //ʔɛ́y=sT-àlə̀m//, /'*You folks were liked., He/She/They liked you folks.*'/, example: <**éwe lís yéthestòlèm.**>, //ʔə́wə lí-s yə́θə=sT-àlə̀m//, /'*You folks weren't told. (tell s-o)*'/, syntactic comment: note the third person subordinate subject/agent in lí-s.

<**ó:leqw'**>, MC ['*a lot got rubbed off*'], *see* íqw'.

<**=ó:les**>, da //=á·ləs//, ANA /'*on the eye(s), in the eye(s), on the eyelid(s)*'/, syntactic analysis: derivational suffix, lexical suffix; found in <**qe'ó:les**>, //qəʔ=á·ləs//, /'*tear*'/, <**kw'qwó:les**>, //k'ʷqʷ=á·ləs//, /'*hit on the eye(lid) (with a stick-like object)*'/, <**st'elmexwó:les**>, //st'əlməxʷ=á·ləs//, /'*eye medicine*'/, <**q'éyx̱ó:les**>, //q'ɛyx̣=á·ləs//, /'*pupil of eye, black of the eye*'/, <**skw'echó:steló:les**>, //s=k'ʷəc=á·s=təl=á·ləs//, /'*eyeglasses*'/, stem //skw'echó:stel *window, mirror*//, <**tsmeth'ó:les**>, //c=məθ'==á·ləs//, /'*blue eyes*'/.

<**=ó:lkwlh**>, da //=á·lkʷɬ//, SPRD /'*spirit power, spirit-dancer*'/, IDOC, syntactic analysis: lexical suffix; found in <**x̱awsó:lkwlh**>, //x̣ɛws=á·lkʷɬ//, /'*new spirit-dancer*'/ (compare <**x̱áws**> *new*), <**st'ó:lkwlh**>, //st'=á·lkʷɬ//, /'*a non-spirit-dancer*'/, Salish cognate: Samish (dial. of N. Straits) /x̣əw's=álkʷɬ/ *new spirit dancer, "baby", (lit. new spirit power?)* and /speʔes=álkʷɬ/ *bear spirit power* G86:81.

<**=ó:llh ~ =óllh ~ =elh ~ ='ó:llh**>, da //=á·lɬ ~ =álɬ ~ =əɬ ~ ʔá·ɬl//, HAT ['*young*'], EZ, semantic environment ['with numeral 5 so far/non-numerals'], phonology: glottal stop epenthetic after vowel, syntactic comment: optional, KIN ['*offspring*'], syntactic analysis: lexical suffix, derivational suffix, also <**=elh**>, //=əɬ//; found in <**swi(ye)qe'ó:llh**>, //s=wi(yə)q=ə=ʔ=á·lɬ//, /'*boy (3-4 years)*'/, <**siwí(ye)qe'ó:llh**>, //s=hi=wí(yə)q=ə=ʔ=á·lɬ//, /'*boys*'/, <**slheliyó:llh**>, //s=ɬɛl=iy=á·lɬ//, /'*girl child*'/, <**slhellheliyó:llh**>, //s=C_1əC_2=ɬɛl=iy=á·lɬ//, /'*little girls*'/ (compare <**slhá:li(y)**> *woman, female)*, <**màmelehó:llhá:lá**>, //mɛ̀məlɘ=h=á·lɬ=ɛ́·lɛ́//, /'*nest of a little bird*'/, <**stiqiwó:llh**>, //stiqiw=á·lɬ//, /'*colt, baby horse*'/, <**músmesò:llh**>, //músməs=à·lɬ//, /'*calf*'/, <**tepelhállh**>, //təpəɬ=ɛ́lɬ//, /'*board for stretching small hides (squirrel, etc.)*'/ (compare <**tpólh=t**> *prop it up)*, <**stl'ítl'eqelh**>, //s=ƛ'íƛ'əq=əɬ//, /'*child*'/ (<**R4=**> *diminutive*, root meaning unclear), <**stá:xwelh**>, //s=tɛ́·xʷ=əɬ//, /'*children*'/, (semological comment: this suppletive pair are age terms not kinterms), also see various words for frogs which have this suffix with <**ō-ablaut**> *derivational* (<<**pehó:mō̃:lh**> *big pretty frog, bullfrog with colors on his back,* <**sx̱ex̱ómō̃lh**> *huge pretty frog with supernatural powers,* <**wex̱ó:mō̃:lh**> *big frog (even bigger than pípehò:m and cries like a baby), (*probably *bullfrog,* possibly *green frog)*) as well as <**tl'elxálōllh**> *jack spring salmon with black nose*; comparative note: the <**ō-ablaut**> could be instead the original vowel from borrowings from Nooksack or other languages which have this corresponding to the Halkomelem <**o**> which changed after Central Salish separation.

<**ólmets**>, bound root //ʔálməc *wait*//.

<**ólmetsel**>, df //ʔálməc=əl or ʔá(·)[=lə=]mət=s=əl//, TVMO ['*wait*'], possibly root <**ó(:)met**> *sitting*, plus <**=le=**> *plural*, possibly <**=s**> *cyclic period* or <**=(i)ts**> *at the back*, (<**=el**> *get, become, go, come, inceptive*), syntactic analysis: intransitive verb, attested by Elders Group, EB, example: <**t'áyeq' kw'els ólmetsel**>, //t'ɛ́yəq' k'ʷə-l-s ʔálməc=əl//, /'*mad that I (have to) wait*'/, attested by Elders Group.

<**ó:lmetsel**>, cts //ʔá[-·-]lməc=əl//, TVMO ['*waiting*'], (<**-:-**> *continuative*), phonology: lengthening, syntactic analysis: intransitive verb, attested by EB, example: <**(chel, chu) ó:lmetsel (o kw'e yiláw, qew yiláwó) texwswáyel.**>, //(c-əl, c-əl-u) ʔá·lməc=əl (ʔà k'ʷə yilɛ́w, qə-w yilɛ́w-à) təxʷ=s=wɛ́yəl//, /'*I waited until after noon.*'/, literally /'(I, I -contrastive) ambiguous past waiting (just the (remote) past/after, until it's past/after -just) mid-day'/, attested by EB.

<**ólmetst**>, pcs //ʔálməc=T//, TVMO ['*wait for s-o*'], (<**=t**> *purposeful control transitivizer*), syntactic analysis: transitive verb, attested by Elders Group, AC, example: <**skw'áy kws ólmetst. ~ skw'áy kws ólmetstes.**>, //s=k'ʷɛ́y kʷ-s ʔálməc=T ~ s=k'ʷɛ́y kʷ-s ʔálməc=T-s//, /'*He can't wait., He's impatient.*'/, literally /'it's impossible that -he wait for s-o'/, attested by Elders Group.

<**ó:lmetst**>, cts //ʔá[-·-]lməc=T//, TVMO ['*waiting for s-o*'], (<**-:-**> *continuative*), phonology: lengthening, syntactic analysis: transitive verb, attested by Elders Group, AC; found in <**ó:lmetstes.**>, //ʔá·lməc=T-əs//, /'*He waits for someone., (He's waiting for s-o.)*'/, attested by Elders Group, example: <**tsel ó:lmetsthóme.**>, //c-əl ʔá·lməc=T-ámə//, /'*I'm waiting for you.*'/, attested by AC (8/27/73), <**ólew híth kw'elsu ó:lmethome.**>, //ʔál=əw híθ k'^{w}ə-l-s-u ʔá·lmə=T-amə//, /'*I waited for you too long.*'/, attested by EB, (irregular)ó:lmethome, comment: lack of ts here is probably an error.

<**ólmetsel**>, TVMO ['*wait*'], *see* ólmets.

<**ó:lmetsel**>, TVMO ['*waiting*'], *see* ólmets.

<**ólmetst**>, TVMO ['*wait for s-o*'], *see* ólmets.

<**ó:lmetst**>, TVMO ['*waiting for s-o*'], *see* ólmets.

<**ó:lmexw**> or <**ó:l**> or <ehó>, //ʔá·l(=)məx^{w}// root & stem meaning unclear or //ʔá·l// meaning unclear or //ʔəhá// *wrap up,* lx <**=mexw**> *people, person.*

<**s'ó:lmexw**>, df //s=ʔá·l=məx^{w} or s=ʔá=·lməx^{w} or s=ʔəhá=·lməx^{w}//, EZ /'*water pygmies, water baby*'/, ASM ['stl'áleqem creature, has dark skin, black hair, some lived in pools in the Coquihalla River and pulled fish spears from unfavored fishermen when they tried to spear fish in one pool; others lived in Chilliwack Lake and occasionally washed up on the shore crying; AC reported a man she knew (her age) had seen one, but when he went to bring his friends up the beach to show them it had returned to the water'], ABDF /'*midget, small people*'/, ASM ['if you eat fish heart you may become s'ó:lmexw'], possibly <**s=**> *nominalizer or stative,* possibly root <**ehó**>, bound root //ʔəhá//, MC ['*wrap up*']., probably <**=mexw**> *person, people* or <**=:l=mexw**> *people,* syntactic analysis: nominal, attested by TG (4/23/75), IHTTC (8/23/77), AK (1/30/80).

<**Oló:xwelwet**>, df //ʔalá·x^{w}=əlwət//, PLN /'*a mountain facing Chilliwack and adjacent to Mt. Cheam, the oldest sister of Lhilheqey (Mount Cheam)*'/, N, ASM ['other adjacent mountains and sister of Mt. Cheam or Lhílheqey are Ts'símtelot and X̲emóth'iye or X̲emóth'iyatel (a mountain without a view of the Fraser which therefore cries, i.e. has little streams all down it in winter); in some versions these mountains are daughters not sisters of Mt. Cheam; Smímkw' is a mountain also in back of the Cheam range perhaps that claimed to be a sister but whom Lhilheqey said was an illegitimate half-sister; Mt. Cheam's baby, Ó:yewòt or S'ó:yewòt, is a smaller and lower peak near the breast of Lhilheqey; Lhílheqey's dog is a mountain just to the southeast behind Mt. Cheam; Mt. Baker was Mt. Cheam's husband before they separated'], lx <**=elwet**> *female name ending; clothes,* syntactic analysis: nominal, attested by CT (1973), Elders Group, source: place names reference file #124.

<**Olóxwiyetel**>, ds //ʔaláx^{w}=iyə(=)təl//, N ['*male name version of Olóxwelwet*'], lx <**=iye(=)tel**> *male name ending,* syntactic analysis: nominal, attested by Elders Group.

<**Olóxwiyetel**>, N ['*male name version of Olóxwelwet*'], *see* Oló:xwelwet.

<**=ó:ls**>, da //=á·ls//, EB ['*fruit*'], SH /'*roughly spherical object(s), ball*'/, PLAY, EB ['*fruit*'], LAND ['*rocks*'], semantic environment ['with numeral 5 so far, non-numerals'], syntactic comment: optional?, syntactic analysis: lexical suffix, derivational suffix; found in <**lhq'atsesó:ls**>, //ɬq'ɛcəs=á·ls//, /'*five fruit, five spherical things (five rocks, five balls, etc.)*'/, <**sqe'ó:ls**>, //s=qəʔ=á·ls//, /'*juicy fruit*'/ (compare <**qó:**> *water*), <**xelkw'ó:ls**>, //x^{y}əlk'^{w}=á·ls//, /'*spherical*'/ (compare <**xeló:kw'**> *round* and <**xelékw'=t**> *roll s-th up),* <**xepó:lst**>, //x^{y}əp=á·ls=t//, /'*peel fruit or vegetable or vegetable root*'/ (compare <**xí:p=et**> *peel bark or tree root, peel it (of bark or root)*), <**kw'oqwiyó:ls**>, //k'^{w}aq^{w}=iy=á·ls//, /'*lacrosse*'/, literally /'club + bark + spherical object'/, <**ts'í:ts'qweló:l(s)**>, //c'í·c'q^{w}əl=á·l(s)//, /'*grass shinny*'/, <**Ts'qó:ls**>, //c'q=á·ls//, /'*Hope, B.C. (the Fraser River turns in a circle around the site)*'/ (however this etymology may be dubious), also see this suffix as numeral

classifier affix.

<**=ó:lthel**>, da //=á·lθəl//, ANA [*'on the knee'*], LAND [*'soft (knee-shaped) cliff on a beach'*], syntactic analysis: lexical suffix, derivational suffix; found in <**sq'ep'ó:lthetel**> *garter*, <**Peqwchō:lthel**> *American Bar*, <**Q'iq'ewetó:lthel**>, //C_1í=q'əw(=)ət=á·lθəl//, /*'a slough on Harrison River north side by the mouth of Chehalis River which has a knee-shaped sandbar at its mouth, this is the next slough above (upriver from) Meth'á:lmexwem'*/, literally /'little turn on the river like a knee'/, <**qep'ó:lthetel**>, //qəp'=á·lθəl=təl//, /*'knee (naming it, the name of it)'*/, literally /'something to close/cover on the knee'/.

<**ó:lthet**>, incs //ʔá·=əl=θət//, ABFC [*'to groan'*], (<**=el**> *go, get, become, inceptive*, <**=thet**> *go, get, become*), probably root <**ó:**> *call*, (compare <**ó:t**> *call s-o* with <**=t**> *purposeful control transitivizer)*, syntactic analysis: intransitive verb, attested by Elders Group (3/15/72, 5/19/76), also /*'groaning'*/, attested by EB (12/15/75), Salish cognate: Squamish /ʔíyn'-cut/ *groan* B78:80, possibly Sechelt /ʔánix̣t/ *groan* T77:29.

<**i'ó:lthet ò**>, df //C_1í-ʔá·l=θət ʔà or ʔi=ʔá·l=θət ʔà//, ABFC [*'keeps on groaning'*], possibly <**R4-**> *continuative or diminutive*? or i= ~ yi=> *travel along by, while moving along*, phonology: possible reduplication, syntactic analysis: intransitive verb, attested by Elders Group (5/19/76).

<**=ó:lwelh**>, da //=á·lwəɬ//, DIR /*'side, -ward'*/, syntactic analysis: lexical suffix, derivational suffix, compare <**í:lwelh**> *side*; found in <**stl'epó:lwelh**>, //s=ƛ'əp=á·lwəɬ//, /*'below, underneath'*/ (compare <**s=tl'ép**> *deep)*, <**stselhsó:lwelh (t'ó:mél)**>, //s=cəɬ(=)s=á·lwəɬ (t'á·mə́l)//, /*'carved post inside longhouse,* (possibly) *inside wall'*/ (compare <**t'ó:mél**> *wall)*, attested by DM, <**sle'ó:lwelh**>, //sləʔ=á·lwəɬ//, /*'on the other side'*/ (compare <**sle'óthel**> *across*, and <**sle'=ó:les**> *facing away, watchful*, though <**lhe'á**> *go via, by way of*, suggests the possibility that <**l**> in the root in <**sle'ó:lwelh**> and <**sle'óthel**> may be mistranscribed for <**lh**>), <**slheq'ó:lwelh**>, //sɬəq'=á·lwəɬ//, /*'one side of body (between arm and hip)'*/ (compare <**lheq'=á:t**> *wide)*, (examples of the free form of this suffix include <**s'eyí:ws í:lwelh**>, //s=ʔɛy=í·ws ʔí·lwəɬ//, /*'right side of the body'*/, and <**sth'íkwe í:lwelh**>, //s=θ'ík^{w}ə ʔí·lwəɬ//, /*'left side of the body'*/).

<**-ólxw ~ -óxw**>, (//**-álx^{w} ~ -áx^{w}**//), PRON /*'us, first person plural object'*/, phonology: attracts stress, allomorph without the l is Tait dialect, syntactic analysis: is; found in <**kwá:tálxwes.**>, //k^{w}ɛ́·=T-álx^{w}-əs//, /*'He lets us go. (let s-o go)'*/, also <**-óxw**>, //-áx^{w}//, <**tl'í:lsóxwes.**>, //ƛ'í·=ləs-áx^{w}-əs//, /*'He/She loves us.'*/.

<**ólh**>, bound root //ʔáɬ//, *respect*

<**ólhet**>, pcs //ʔáɬ=əT//, EFAM [*'respect s-o'*], SOC, (<**=et**> *purposeful control transitivizer*), syntactic analysis: transitive verb, attested by Elders Group.

<**s'ólh**>, df //s=ʔáɬ//, PRON /*'ours, our (emphatic), our respected'*/, <**s=**> *stative*, root <**ólh**> *respect* (this derivation from Rosaleen George through the research of Ethel Gardner, see Ethel's Ph.D. thesis), syntactic analysis: pronominal verb/verbal pronoun, attested by AC, example: <**tl'ó s'ólh tál.**>, //ƛ'á s=ʔáɬ tɛ́l//, /*'That's our mother.'*/, attested by AC, <**tl'o s'ólh sqwmáy.**>, //ƛ'a s=ʔáɬ s=q^{w}əm=ɛ́y//, /*'That's our dog.'*/, attested by AC, <**í:westólxwes te s'ólh má:l.**>, //ʔi[-·-]wəs=T-álx^{w}-əs tə s=ʔáɬ mɛ́·l//, /*'Our (own) father taught us.'*/, literally /'he was teaching us the our father'/, attested by AC, <**tl'ó s'ólh.**>, //ƛ'á s=ʔáɬ//, /*'That's ours.'*/, attested by AC.

<**=ólh**>, da //=áɬ//, CAN [*'canoe'*], syntactic analysis: lexical suffix, probably a doublet of <=ówelh> *canoe*, so also see that fuller form; found in <**yekw'ólhem**>, //yək'^{w}=áɬ=əm//, /*'"breaking one's canoe", last spirit dance of the season'*/ (root <**yékw'**> as in <**yékw'et**> *break s-th up)*, compare also with <**ó:lh**> *be aboard (a canoe)*.

<**ó:lh**>, free root //ʔá·ɬ//, CAN /'*get in a canoe, get aboard*'/, TVMO /'*get in a conveyance, get in a car, mount a horse*'/, syntactic analysis: intransitive verb, attested by AC, EB, others, example: <**t'x̱émele le ó:lh te sléxwelh.**>, //t'x̣=ém=alə lə ʔá·ɬ tə s=lə́xʷəɬ//, /'*Six people got in the canoe.*'/, literally /'it is six people past 3rd person get aboard the canoe'/, attested by AC, <**esu ó:tes te siyá:yes we'ó:lhes.**>, //ʔə-s-u ʔá·=T-əs tə si=yɛ́·yə-s wə-ʔá·ɬ-əs//, /'*Then he called his friends to get in the canoe.*'/, literally /'then -contrastive he calls him/her/them the his friend if/when he gets aboard'/, usage: story of the Flood, attested by AC, <**esu mők̲w' ó:lh yutl'ólem.**>, //ʔə-s-u mók'ʷ ʔá·ɬ yə=u=ƛ'á=lə=m//, /'*And so they all got in the canoe.*'/, usage: story of the Flood, attested by AC (12/7/71), also <**qetl'osésu ó:lh mők̲w' yutl'ólem.**>, //qə=ƛ'a-s-ə́s-u ʔá·ɬ mók'ʷ yə=u=ƛ'á=lə=m//, attested by AC.

<**ó:lhstexw**>, caus //ʔá·ɬ=sT-əxʷ//, TVMO /'*put s-th/s-o aboard, put it on-board*'/, CAN, (<**=st**> *causative control transitivizer*), (<**-exw**> *third person object*), syntactic analysis: transitive verb, attested by EB; found in <**ó:lhstexwlha.**>, //ʔá·ɬ=sT-əxʷ-ɬɛ//, /'*Put it on board.*'/, attested by EB.

<**eló:lh**>, df //ʔəl=á·ɬ or ʔ[=əl=]á·ɬ//, TVMO /'*be aboard, be in (a conveyance)*'/, CAN, possibly <**el=** or **=el=**> *prepositional*? or *adverbial*? or *stative*? or *resultative*? or *continuative*??, phonology: possible infix, syntactic analysis: intransitive verb, preposition/prepositional verb?, adverb/adverbial verb?, attested by AC, EB, example: <**líchxw mi eló:lh te (sléxwelh, kyó:, stiqíw)?**>, //lí-c-xʷ mi ʔəl=á·ɬ tə (s=lə́xʷəɬ, kʸá·, s=tiqíw)//, /'*Did you ride/come by (canoe, car, horse)?*'/, attested by EB, <**tsel mi eló:lh te sléxwelh.**>, //c-əl mi ʔəl=á·ɬ tə slə́xʷəɬ//, /'*I came down in a canoe.*'/, literally /'I ambiguous past come aboard/in the canoe'/, attested by AC, <**ímexósem eló:lh te xwóqw'eletsem.**>, //ʔím=əxʸ=ás=əm ʔəl=á·ɬ tə xʷáq'ʷ=ələc=əm//, /'*go for a ride in a streetcar, go for a ride in a high-bow canoe*'/, literally /'go for a walk aboard the streetcar/high-bow canoe'/, attested by EB.

<**yeló:lh**>, mos //yə=əl=á·ɬ//, TVMO /'*to travel by canoe,* (nowadays also) *travel by airplane, travel by train, travel by car*'/, CAN, (<**ye=**> *travel by, while moving*), phonology: vowel merger, syntactic analysis: intransitive verb, attested by EB, example: <**yeló:lh te sléxwelh.**>, //yə=əl=á·ɬ tə s=lə́xʷəɬ//, /'*He's riding a canoe.*'/, attested by EB, <**welh yeló:lh.**>, //wəɬ yə=əl=á·ɬ//, /'*He's already riding a canoe.*'/, attested by EB.

<**seló:lh**>, df //s=əl=á·ɬ//, TVMO ['*moving (one's residence)*'], (<**s=**> *stative*?), syntactic analysis: intransitive verb, attested by Elders Group (10/6/76).

<**eló:lhstexw**>, caus //ʔəl=á·ɬ=sT-əxʷ//, TVMO /'*get s-th aboard (a canoe, car, conveyance)*'/, (<**=st**> *causative control transitivizer*), syntactic analysis: transitive verb, attested by EB, AC; found in <**eló:lhstexwes.**>, //ʔəl=á·ɬ=sT-əxʷ-əs//, /'*He got s-th aboard (a canoe, car, etc.).*'/, attested by EB, example: <**esu eló:lhstexwes te pí:kwel.**>, //ʔə-s-u ʔəl=á·ɬ=sT-əxʷ-əs tə pí·kʷəl//, /'*And in the canoe was barbecue sticks.*'/, usage: story of the Flood, attested by AC.

<**ó:lhstexw**>, TVMO /'*put s-th/s-o aboard, put it on-board*'/, *see* ó:lh.

<**ò:m**>, ds //ʔà·=(ə)m//, ECON /'*to order (food, material, etc.)*'/, SOC, MC, probably root <**ó:**> *call* plus <**=em**> *intransitivizer*, compare <**ó:t**> *call s-o* with <**=t**> *transitivizer* and <**ó:lthet**> *groan* with <**=el**> and <**=thet**> *inceptives*, phonology: possible vowel merger, syntactic analysis: intransitive verb, attested by EB.

<**s'ò:m**>, ECON ['*an order (promise of goods/services)*'], SOC, MC, (<**s=**> *nominalizer*), syntactic analysis: nominal, attested by EB, example: <**petámelhthó:xchexw we'ésulh xwe'í thél s'ò:m.**>, //pətɛ́m-əɬ(c)=T-á·xʸ-c-əxʷ wə-ʔə́-s-uɬ xʷə=ʔí (kʷ)θə-l s=ʔà·m//, /'*Ask for me if my order is in.*'/, literally /'ask for s-o -benefactive -me -coaxing imperative 2s if it already get here the (near but out of sight) -my order'/, phonology: sentence-stress on article, syntactic comment: imperative of benefactive, subjunctive of adverbial particle by use of auxiliary, attested by EB (3/1/76).

<**-ò:m**>, (//**-à·m** or **-ám(ə)=(ə)m**//), PRON ['*second person singular patient or object of passive*'], VOIC, comment: historically may be connected with -óme *second person sing. object*, probably <**-em**> *passive*, phonology: possible vowel-loss, possible consonant merger (m + m → :m), syntactic analysis: is; found in <**ó:thò:m**>, //ʔá·=T-à·m//, /'*You were called.*'/, <**lhéts'là:mtsa.**>, //ɬi[=Aə́=]c'=l-à·m-cɛ//, /'*You'll get cut.*'/, <**x̱ét'esthò:m.**>, //x̣ə́t'ə=sT-à·m//, /'*You were told. (tell s-o)*'/, example: <**éwe lís yéthesthò:m.**>, //ʔə́wə lí-s yə́θə=sT-à·m//, /'*You weren't told. (tell s-o)*'/, syntactic comment: note the third person subordinate subject/agent in lí-s, <**le kw'exá:thò·m.**>, //lə k'ʷɛ́(·)xʸ[-M1-]=əT-à·m//, /'*You were counted., He counted you.*'/, <**kw'étslò·mcha te spá:th.**>, //k'ʷə́c=l-à·m-cɛ tə s=pɛ́·θ//, /'*The bear will see you.*'/, literally /'You'll be seen by the bear.'/.

<**=ó:me**>, da //=á·mə//, EB ['*berry*'], syntactic analysis: lexical suffix, derivational suffix; found in <**tselqó:me**>, //cəlq=á·mə//, /'*blackcap berry*'/, root <**tsélq**> *fall off, drop*, <**kwxwó:mels**>, //kʷxʷ=á·mə=ls//, /'*mountain black huckleberry (Vaccinium membranaceum)*'/, root <**kwóxw**> *knock, rap* (since they can be harvested by knocking them against the berry basket for ex.).

<**-óme**>, (//**-ámə**//), PRON /'*you (sg.), second person singular object*'/, phonology: attracts stress, stress-shift automatic to e before -tsel/-tset, syntactic analysis: is, syntactic comment: will not allow a third person subject -es suffix; found in <**imexsthométsel.**>, //ʔim=əxʸ=sT-ámə-c-əl//, [ʔimɪxʸsθamə́cɪl], /'*I made you walk.*'/, <**tl'í:lsométsel.**>, //ƛ'í·=ləs-ámə-c-əl//, [ƛ'í·lsamə́cɪl], /'*I love you.*'/.

<**omél:a**>, bound stem //ʔamə́l·ɛ// or //ʔam=ə́l·ɛ//, root or stem meaning unknown unless <**ò:m**>, ds //ʔà·=(ə)m//, ECON /'*to order (food, material, etc.)*'/, possibly itself from root <**ó:**> *call* plus <**=em**> *intransitivizer*, or unless from <**á:m (?)**>, free root //ʔɛ́·m (?)//, TIB ['*give*']

<**S'omél:a**>, df //s=ʔamə́l·ɛ or s=ʔam=ə́l·ɛ//, SOCT /'*Thompson Indian, Thompson person*'/, (<**s=**> *stative* or *nominalizer*), root meaning unknown, possibly <**=él:a**> *on the side of the head, around the ear/cheek* (1858 Boundary Survey meterials refer to a Thompson elder Teosaluk as from the Somena, showing that either in Thompson or Nooksack or both the final consonant is <**n**> and this fits the possible cognate affix <**=én(7)a**> *on the side of the head, around the ear/cheek* in those languages as well as Musqueam Halkomelem), syntactic analysis: nominal, attested by AC, BHTTC.

<**S'em'oméla**>, pln //s=C_1əC_2=ʔamə́lɛ//, SOCT ['*Thompson people*'], (<**s=**> *nominalizer* or *stative*, R3= *plural (collective)*), phonology: reduplication, syntactic analysis: nominal, attested by BHTTC, example: <**le thékw' xwlá te s'em'oméla.**>, //lə θə́k'ʷ xʷ=lɛ́ tə s=C_1əC_2=ʔam=ə́lɛ//, /'*She was pulled towards the Thompsons., She was influenced by the Thompsons.*'/, attested by BHTTC.

<**=ó:mél ~ =á:mel**>, da //=á·(=)mə́l ~ =ɛ́·(=)məl//, ANA ['*member or part (of the body)*'], LAND ['*part (of a place)*'], N ['*nick-*'], semantic environment ['name'], possibly <**=mel**> *part, portion*, syntactic analysis: lexical suffix, derivational suffix, also <**=á:mel**>, //=ɛ́·(=)məl//; found in <**mekwó:mélxel**>, //mək ʷ=á·məl=xʸəl//, /'*big toe*'/, literally /'stout member of foot'/, <**mekwó:méltses**>, //məkʷ=á·mə́l=cəs//, /'*thumb*'/, <**mét'esemél**>, //mə́t'əs=əmə́l//, /'*pointing finger, first finger, Index finger*'/, dialects: *Tait*, <**shxwehómél lhelh**>, //s=xʷəh=áməl=ɬəɬ//, /'*adam's apple*'/, literally /'upstream(?) member of front of neck'/.

<**óme léxw**>, ABFC ['*step on it accidentally*'], *see* ím.

<**omét**>, probably root //ʔəmə́t from ʔamə́t// *sit*

<**emét**>, probably root //ʔəmə́t from ʔamə́t//, ABFC /'*sit, sit down, sit up, arise (from lying or sitting), get up (from lying down, from bed or chair)*'/, phonology: vowel-reduction historically, syntactic analysis: intransitive verb, attested by AC, Elders Group (3/1/72, 4/2/75), EB, AD, MH, RP, IHTTC, Deming, RG & EH (4/9/99 Ling332), other sources: ES /ʔá·mət/ but Musqueam and Cowichan

/ʔémət/ *sit*, Salish cognate: Squamish root /mút/ *sit, seat* as in /mút-awʔi/ *sit down on someone's lap* and /ʔmʔút/ *be sitting down, be at home* W73:236, K67:257, K69:46; Samish (N. Straits)(all VU) /ʔémət/ *sit, sit down, sit up*, /ʔám'ət/ *sitting down/up*, /ʔəmát-txʷ/ *seat s-o*, and /ʔaʔám'ət/ *little child sitting (down/up), sitting by oneself lonely* G86:97; Clallam (S. Straits) /ʔémət/ *sit*, /ʔaʔáʔmət/ *sitting* Thompson & Thompson71:276, and from TTE74:189 (Cl = Clallam, Lm = Lummi, So = Sooke, San = Saanich, Sg = Songish): Cl /ʔa-ʔáʔmət/, LmSo /ʔóʔmət/ [ʔɔ́ʔmət] and SanSg /ʔáʔmət/ all *seated*, San /ʔəʔáʔmət/ *little child sitting down* beside Cl /ʔəmút-txʷ/, LmSo /ʔəmóttxʷ/ [ʔəmɔ́ttxʷ], and SanSg /ʔəmáttxʷ/ all *seat him*, also **<omét ~ émet>**, //ʔamə́t ~ ʔémət//, attested by AC, comment: rare alternants, emét is more common; found in **<emétchxw.>**, //ʔəmə́t-c-xʷ//, /'*You arise.*'/, attested by Elders Group (3/1/72), example: **<éy t'we kw'as emét.>**, //ʔɛ́y t'wə k'ʷ-ɛ-s ʔəmə́t//, /'*You better get up.*'/, attested by AD, **<emétchexw tl'esu la xó:kw'em.>**, //ʔəmə́t-c-əxʷ ƛ'ə-s-u lɛ xʸá·k'ʷ=əm//, /'*Get up and go bathe.*'/, attested by AD, (semological comment: coaxing imperative); found in **<emétlha.>**, //ʔəmə́t-ɬɛ//, /'*Sit down., Get up (from bed/chair).*'/, semantic environment ['said to a person'], (semological comment: command imperative 2s), attested by AC, Elders Group (3/1/72), contrast **<emét.>** *Sit. (said to a dog)*, attested by AC, **<emétalha.>**, //ʔəmə́t-ɛɬɛ//, /'*Sit down folks.*'/, (semological comment: command imperative 2p), attested by Deming, **<emétchap.>**, //ʔəmə́t-c-ɛp//, /'*Sit down folks.*'/, (semological comment: coaxing imperative 2p), attested by MH, example: **<omét li te sts'áletstel>**, //ʔamə́t li tə s=c'ɛ́=ləc=təl//, /'*sit down on the chair*'/, phonology: helps to prove the morphophonemic shape is //ʔamə́t//, attested by AC, **<emétlha lam te shxwch'áletstel.>**, //ʔəmə́t-ɬɛ lɛ=m tə sxʷ=c'ɛ́=ləc=təl//, /'*Go sit in the chair.*'/, attested by IHTTC, **<mílh kwetxwílem, emét íkw'elò.>**, //mí-ɬ kʷətxʷ=íl=əm, ʔəmə́t ʔí=k'ʷə=là//, /'*Come in and sit here.*'/, (semological comment: mildly urging imperative), attested by RP, EB.

<ma'emét>, df //mɛ=ʔəmə́t// or perhaps //mɛ ʔəmə́t//, ABFC /'*He sat., She sat.*'/, possibly **<ma=>** (prob. ~ **<me>)** *past (came) 3rd person*, syntactic analysis: intransitive verb or auxiliary verb intransitive verb, syntactic comment: seems to be analogous to le *past 3rd person subject* similarly from la *go*, attested by EB, AD,

<ó:met ~ ó'emet>, cts //ʔa[-´·-]mət ~ ʔa[-´C_1ə-]mət//, ABFC /'*sitting, sitting down, sitting up*'/, (**<-´:- ~ -´R1->** *continuative*), phonology: lengthening, reduplication, stress-shift, syntactic analysis: intransitive verb, attested by AC, EF, example: **<le ó:met.>**, //lə ʔa[-´·-]mət//, /'*He's sitting.*'/, attested by AC, **<ílh ó:met. ~ ílh ó'emet.>**, //ʔí-ɬ ʔa[-´·]mət ~ ʔí-ɬ ʔa[-´C_1ə-]mət//, /'*She was sitting down.*'/, attested by AC, **<sthethá:kw' kw'es ó:met.>**, //s=θə[=C_1əAɛ́·=]k'ʷ k'ʷ-əs ʔa[-´·-]mət//, /'*sit up straight*'/, attested by EF (Deming 4/26/79).

<shxw'ó:met>, dnom //s(=)xʷ=ʔa[=´·=]mət//, HHG /'*sofa, couch, chesterfield, place where one's sitting, (bed [AC, MC (Katzie)])*'/, (**<sxw=** or **s=xw=>** *nominalizer*), phonology: lengthening, stress-shift, syntactic analysis: nominal, attested by Elders Group (6/1/77), also **<shxw'émet>**, //s(=)xʷ=ʔa[=Aə́=]mət//, also /'*something to sit down on*'/, attested by DM (12/4/64), also /'*bed*'/, attested by AC (8/8/70), MC (Katzie)(in Elders Group 5/3/78), also /'*place where you sit down*'/, attested by Elders Group (3/1/72).

<ó:metáwtxw>, dnom //ʔa[=´·=]mət=ɛ́wtxʷ//, BLDG ['*(could be used for) living-room*'], literally /'sitting room'/, lx **<=áwtxw>** *building, room*, syntactic analysis: nominal, attested by RP (3/16/77).

<s'ú:met>, strs //s=ʔa[=Aú·=]mət//, EFAM /'*be always lazy, be a lazybones, be stupid, be a good-for-nothing*'/, (**<s=>** *stative*), (**<ú:-ablaut>** *resultative*), phonology: ú:-ablaut, comment: perhaps a borrowing from a language with /u/ in this root where Halkomelem has /a/, i.e., a doublet, syntactic analysis: adjective/adjectival verb, attested by AC, EK and DK (12/10/71), EB, Elders Group, AD, BHTTC, contrast **<í:ts'el>** *be temporarily lazy*, also **<s'ó:met>**, //s=ʔa[=´·=]mət//, attested by BHTTC, example: **<kwélh tu s'ú:met>**, //kʷə́ɬ tu s=ʔa[=Aú·=]mət//, /'*(he's/she's)* *very lazy*'/, attested by EB, <**ts'áts'el we s'ú:met (mestíyexw)**>, //c'ɛ́c'əl wə=s=ʔa[=Aú·=]mət (məstíyəxʷ)//, /'*really lazy (person)*'/, attested by Elders Group (1/19/77), also <**ts'áts'el ō s'ú:met**>, //c'ɛ́c'əl=əw s=ʔ=a[=Aú·=]mət//, dialects: *Chehalis*, attested by Elders Group (1/19/77), <**líchexw s'ú:met?**>, //lí-c-əxʷ s=ʔa[=Aú·=]mət//, /'*Are you a lazy-bones?*'/, syntactic comment: s= could be *nominalizer* here, attested by AD.

<**lexws'ú:met**>, dnom //ləxʷ=s=ʔa[=Aú·=]mət//, EFAM ['*a person that's always lazy*'], (<**lexw=s=**> *person that's always*, lexw= *always*, s= *nominalizer*), phonology: ú:-ablaut, syntactic analysis: nominal, attested by EB, also <**lexws'í:ts'el**>, //ləxʷ=s=ʔí·c'əl//, attested by EB (2/11/76).

<**s'i'omó:met**>, dmv //s=C_1í=C_1əC_2=ʔa[=´·=]mət//, EFAM ['*(be) kind of lazy*'], (<**s=**> *stative*, R4= *diminutive*, R3= meaning uncertain), (<= ´:=> *continuative*), phonology: double reduplication very unusual, stress-shift, lengthening, syntactic analysis: adjective/adjectival verb, attested by BHTTC.

<**=ómet**>?, da //=ámət//, CLO ['*(costume)*'], SPRD, syntactic analysis: lexical suffix, derivational suffix; found in <**Te Lewómet**>, *The Milky Way*, literally (probably) /'The Costume'/, (semological comment: some spirit-dancing costumes had mother of pearl shells attached which shone in the firelight, somewhat like stars in the dark), and found in <**slewómet**>, //s=ləw=ámət//, /'*entire costume of a dancer (spirit dancer--old or new, sx̱wóyx̱wey dancer, etc.) from head to toe*'/ (compare <**s=lew=íy**> *inner cedar bark)* and probable root <**lew=**> *put inside an opening*).

<**ó:metáwtxw**>, BLDG ['*(could be used for) living-room*'], *see* emét.

<**ó:met ~ ó'emet**>, ABFC /'*sitting, sitting down, sitting up*'/, *see* emét.

<**=ó:mex ~ =óméx ~ =òmèx ~ =ómex ~ =omex ~ =emex**>, da //=á(·)məxʸ//, DESC /'*in looks, -looking, in appearance*'/, LT ['*in color*'], syntactic analysis: derivational suffix, see charts by Rob MacLaury, also <**=emex**>, //=əməxʸ//; found in <**iyóméx ~ iyó:mex**>, //ʔɛy=ámə́xʸ ~ ʔɛy=á·məxʸ//, /'*good-looking, handsome, beautiful*'/ (compare <**éy**> *good)*, <**qeló:mex ~ qelelhó:mex**>, //qəl=á·məxʸ ~ qəl=əɬ=á·məxʸ//, /'*ugly*'/, (semological comment: some say qelelhó:mex means *clumsy* instead) (compare <**qél**> *bad*), <**elyó:mex**>, //ʔɛ[=l=]y=á·məxʸ//, /'*(plural/all) good-looking (-l- infix plural)*'/, <**te'ó:mex**>, //təʔ=á·məxʸ//, /'*(to) look like, resemble*'/ (compare <**s=ta'á ~ s=te'á**> *be like, be similar to)*, also <**st'at'=ó:mex**>, //s=t'ɛ=C_1ə=á·məxʸ//, dialects: *Cheh., Tait*, root <**s=t'á**> *be like, be similar to*, <**selchí:memex**>, //səlcí·m=əməxʸ//, /'*what color is it?, what does it look like?, how does it look?*'/ (compare <**selchí:m**> *how is it?*), <**sqw'íqw'ex̱welomex, tsqwáyòmèx, tsméth'òmèx, st'áwelòmèx, tskwimómex, p'eq'óméx, tsxwíkw'ómex, qálqomex**>, //s=q'ʷí[=C_1ə=]x̣ʷ=əl=aməxʸ, c=qʷɛ́y=àmə̀xʸ, c=mə́θ'=àmə̀xʸ, st'ɛ́wəl=àmə̀xʸ, c=kʷím=aməxʸ, p'əq'=ámə́xʸ, c=xʷík'ʷ=áməxʸ, qɛ́lq=aməxʸ//, /'*[be getting brown in looks], [black-looking, black in looks, looks black], [white-looking, white in looks, looks white], [gray-looking], [rose-looking, rose-colored]*'/, phonology: updrifting, downdrifting, attested by NP.

<**ómó:qw(es)**>, possible stem //ʔámá·qʷ(=)əs//, meaning unclear

<**s'ómó:qwes**>, df //s=ʔámá·qʷ(=)əs//, EB /'*bracket fungus, (*possibly also *some jelly fungi like yellow trembler)*'/, ['*Fomes* sp. including *Fomes applanatus* and probably others, possibly *Polyporus* sp., possibly *Ganoderma* sp., prob. also jelly fungi of *Tremella* and maybe *Auricularia* and *Dacrymyces* species, especially *Tremella mesenterica* (Yellow trembler) which is abundant only on the red alder and is reddish-orange matching the color, translucence and shape of those eaten by some of the Stó:lō elders, the jelly fungi could possibly have a differnet name from the bracket fungus'], ASM ['the fungus described by this name that grow on rotten alder or alder stumps were edible, should be washed and cooked, have a nice meaty taste; the bracket fungus is said by some to make rain if one

turns it upside down after picking it or if one scratches on it; the bracket fungus grows on tree trunks and roots especially, sticks out perpendicularly from the trunk in a half circle shape characteristically, and has a beige covering that scratches off leaving dark marks'], possibly <**s=**> *nominalizer*, possibly <**=es**> *on the face, round object*, root meaning unknown, syntactic analysis: nominal, attested by SP and a few others, Elders Group (1/28/76), also <**shxw'ómóqwes**>, //s(=)x^{w}=ʔámáq^{w}(=)əs//, ASM ['it makes rain if you scratch on it or if you turn it upside down soon after picking'], attested by SJ (Deming 5/24/79). other sources: JH /samá·q^{w}əs/ *toadstool.*

<**ó:pel**>, free root //ʔá·pəl//, NUM ['*ten*'], syntactic analysis: num, attested by AC, BJ (5/64, 12/5/64), CT (9/5/73), NP (12/6/73), DM (12/4/64), others, also <**ópel**>, //ʔápəl//, attested by AC, BJ, DM, BHTTC, other sources: ES /ʔá·pən/.

<**epále**>, (//**ʔa[=Aə=]p(əl)=ɛ́lə**//), [ʔəpǽlə], NUM ['*ten people*'], HUMC, possibly <**e-ablaut**> *derivational*, nca <**=ále**> *people*, phonology: ablaut or allomorphic variation in first vowel rather than vowel-reduction or weak/schwa-grade of root before stressed full-grade of suffix because such vowel-reduction does not occur before other stressed suffixes, similarly allomorphic loss of el possibly rather than el loss before =ále, syntactic analysis: num, nominal?, attested by AC, Elders Group; found in <**epálétset**>, //ʔəp=ɛ́lə-c-ət//, [ʔəpǽlə́cɪt], /'*There's ten of us.*'/, literally /'we're ten people'/, phonology: updrifting on third syllable predictable on tri-syllabic (or longer) words before -tsel and -tsel and perhaps other subject pronouns, attested by AC, example: <**epále qas te lólets'e**>, //ʔəp=ɛ́lə qɛ-s tə C_1á=ləc'ə//, /'*eleven people*'/, literally /'ten people and the one person'/, attested by Elders Group.

<**opeláleqel**>, (//**ʔapəl=ɛ́l(=)əqəl**//), NUM ['*ten containers*'], HHG, nca <**=ál(=)eqel**> *containers* nca (the connective <**=ál**> or infix <**=le=**> in this affix may be a lexical affix pluralizer), syntactic analysis: num, nominal?, adjective/adjectival verb?, attested by AD.

<**opelálh**>, (//**ʔapəl=ɛ́ɬ**//), NUM ['*ten times*'], TIME, nca <**=álh**> *times*, Elder's comment: "probably somewhat artificial as they didn't often count these beyond five", syntactic analysis: num, adverb/adverbial verb?, attested by Elders Group (3/19/75).

<**epálemets'**>, df //ʔəp=ɛ́l(=)əməc' or ʔəpɛ́l=əməc'//, NUM /'*ten ropes, ten threads, ten sticks, ten poles*'/, HHG, EB, MC, FSH, HUNT, HARV, nca <**=emets' ~ =emeth'**> *long thin objects*, nca either <**=ál**> or <**=el=**> *lexical affix pluralizer*, nca <**=emets' ~ =álemets'**> (allomorph), phonology: root allomorph /ʔəp/ or /ʔəpɛ́l/ (by analogy with *ten people*?) or vowel-reduction of first vowel and syllable-loss of final root syllable, syntactic analysis: num, nominal?, attested by AD (4/12/78) after Boas 1890 Scowlitz field notes (in APS library), Boas 1890 <apálemets'> (circumflex over first a, umlaut over second a, double-underline under both e's) *ten sticks*.

<**epóles**>, df //ʔəpɛ[=Aá=]l=əs//, NUM /'*ten dollars, (ten Indian blankets [Boas])*'/, ECON, (<**ó-ablaut**> *derivational* but phonologically automatic), nca <**=es**> *dollars, circular objects, on the face*, phonology: ó-ablaut on root a-vowel automatic before =es *dollars, circularobjects, on the face*, root allomorph /ʔəpɛ́l/ by analogy with form forten people, syntactic analysis: num, nominal?, attested by AC, AD, Rose Jones (5/19/76), RG & EH (4/10/99 Ling332), others, also /'*ten Indian blankets, ten dollars*'/, source: Boas 1890: Scowlitz field notes, example: <**epóles qas kw'e léts'e**>, //ʔəpɛ[=Aá=]l=əs qɛ-s k'^{w}ə lə́c'ə//, /'*eleven dollars*'/, literally /'ten dollar and the (remote) one (not one dollar)'/, attested by AC, <**epóles qas kw'e isá:le**>, //ʔəpɛ[=Aá=]l=əs qɛ-s k'^{w}ə ʔisɛ́·lə//, /'*twelve dollars*'/, literally /'ten dollar and the (remote) two (not two dollars)'/, attested by AC (11/30/71), <**epóles qas te isóles i ta' s'ehólets tl'esu sóles.**>, //ʔəpɛ[=Aá=]l=əs qɛ-s tə ʔisɛ[=Aá=]l=əs ʔi t-ɛʔ s=ʔəhá=ləc ƛ'ə-s-u sál=əs//, /'*Ten dollars and two dollars (twelve dollars) in your pocket and drunk.*'/, usage: humorous rhyme, attested by Rose Jones (5/19/76).

<**epoléstexw**>, caus //ʔəpɛ[=Aá=]l=əs=sT-əx^{w}//, NUM ['*cost ten dollars*'], ECON, (<**=st**> *causative control transitivizer*), (<**-exw**> *third person object*), lit. /“make it ten dollars”/, phonology: ó-

ablaut, consonant merger, stress-shift to penultimate syllable when some trisyllabic stems get suffixed, syntactic analysis: transitive verb, attested by Elders Group, also <epoléstexw>, //ʔəpɛ[=Aá=]l=əs=sT-əxʷ//, /'give him/her ten dollars'/, attested by RG & EH (4/10/99 Ling332); found in <**epoléstxwes.**>, //ʔəpɛ[=Aá=]l=əs=sT-əxʷ-əs//, [ʔəpaləstxʷɪs], /'*It costs ten dollars.*'/, attested by Elders Group (7/9/75).

<**epóléstel**>, ds //ʔəpɛ[=Aá=]l=əs=təl//, TIME /'*(first lunar month beginning in) July, (tenth month)*'/, NUM, literally /'tenth month'/, lx <**=tel**> *device for, something for*, phonology: ó-ablaut, stress-shift to or updrifing on penultimate syllable when some trisyllabic stems get suffixed, syntactic analysis: nominal, attested by Elders Group (3/12/75).

<**opelíws**>, (//**ʔapəl=íws**//), NUM ['*ten bodies*'], ANA, nca <**=íws**> *on the body, (here) bodies*, phonology: full root vowel retention in spite of stressed suffix, homophonous with *ten birds*, syntactic analysis: num. nominal?, attested by Elders Group (3/29/77), AK, Elder's comment: "AK has heard it for both meanings".

<**opelíws**>, (//**ʔapəl=íws**//), NUM ['*ten birds*'], HUNT, (semological comment: (probably used with birds killed rather than live birds)), nca <**=íws**> *birds*, phonology: full root vowel retention in spite of stressed suffix, homophonous with *ten bodies*, syntactic analysis: num, nominal?, attested by SP, AK, Elder's comment: "AK has heard it for both meanings".

<**opelòls**>, (//**ʔapəl=àls**//), NUM /'*ten fruit in a group (as they grow on a plant), (ten attached fruit)*'/, EB, HARV, nca <**=àls**> *fruit, (spherical objects)*, phonology: full root vowel retention in spite of stressed suffix, syntactic analysis: num, nominal?, attested by AD (4/12/78).

<**opelṓwelh**>, (//**ʔapəl=ówəɬ**//), NUM /'*ten canoes, ten boats*'/, CAN, ACL ['*ten boats*'], nca <**=ṓwelh**>, phonology: full root vowel retention in spite of stressed suffix, syntactic analysis: num, nominal?, attested by AD.

<**epálōwes**>, (//ʔəpɛ́l=owəs or ʔəpɛ́l=əwəs//), NUM ['*ten paddles*'], CAN, nca <**=ōwes ~ =ewes**> *paddles*, phonology: root allomorph <**epál**> perhaps by analogy to <**epále**> *ten people*, syntactic analysis: num, nominal?, attested by Elders Group, example: <**epálōwes qas te léts'e**>, //ʔəpɛ́l=owəs qɛ-s tə ləc'ə//, /'*eleven paddles*'/, literally /'ten paddles and the one (not: one paddle)'/, attested by Elders Group (7/27/75).

<**epálōws**>, (//ʔəp(əl)=ɛ́ləws//), NUM ['*ten leaves*'], EB, HARV, ASM ['(probably ten attached leaves)'], nca <**=álōws ~ =álews**> *leaves*, phonology: root allomorph <**ep**>, or <**epál**> with syllable loss of ál before ál of suffix, syntactic analysis: num, nominal?, attested by SP (3/29/77).

<**epálōws**>, (//ʔəpɛ́l=əws//), NUM ['*ten birds*'], HUNT, (semological comment: (probably used with birds killed rather than live birds)), nca <**=ews ~ =íws**> *birds*, phonology: root allomorph <**epál**> by analogy with epále *ten people*, syntactic analysis: num, nominal?, attested by Elders Group (3/29/77).

<**s'ó:pels**>, (//s=ʔápəl=s//), NUM /'*ten o'clock, (tenth hour)*'/, TIME, nca <**s=...=s**> *hour, day of the week, chronological period*, phonology: circumfix, syntactic analysis: num, nominal, attested by AC, example: <**wetéses te s'ó:pels**>, //wə-tə́s-əs tə s=ʔá·pəl=s//, /'*when it gets ten o'clock*'/, literally /'when it gets up to/approaches the tenth hour'/, attested by AC.

<**opeláleqel**>, NUM ['*ten containers*'], *see* ó:pel.

<**opelálh**>, NUM ['*ten times*'], *see* ó:pel.

<**opelíws**>, NUM ['*ten bodies*'], *see* ó:pel.

<**opelíws**>, NUM ['*ten birds*'], *see* ó:pel.

<**opelòls**>, NUM /'*ten fruit in a group (as they grow on a plant), (ten attached fruit)*'/, *see* ó:pel.

<**opelő̄welh**>, NUM /'*ten canoes, ten boats*'/, *see* ó:pel.

<**óp'esem**>, ABFC ['*wipe one's face*'], *see* áp'.

<**óq**>, possible bound root or stem //ʔá(=)q// *dung* but more likely root <**ó'**> *defecate*, possibly <**=q**> *after, behind*

<**s'óq**>, dnom //s=ʔá=q//, ANA /'*dung, excrement, feces*'/, (<**s=**> *nominalizer*), probably root <**ó'**> *defecate*, possibly <**=q**> *after*, *behind*, phonology: probable consonant-loss of root final glottal stop before consonant, syntactic analysis: nominal, dialects: *Matsqui*, attested by Deming, Salish cognate: Squamish /s-ʔáʔq/ *dung* and /ʔáʔq/ *defecate* W73:77,87, K69:94, probably with lexical suffix /=q/ *bottom, behind, trunk*, compare root <**ó'**> *to have a bowel movement, to defecate, to shit*, contrast <**sq'éth'**> *dung, shit.*

<**ó:qw**>, bound root //ʔá·qʷ//, root meaning possibly *pull out, unplug*

<**s'ó:qw**>, df //s=ʔá·qʷ//, ANA ['*after-birth*'], (<**s=**> *nominalizer*), syntactic analysis: nominal, attested by NP (9/19/75), Salish cognate: possibly Lushootseed root /ʔuq'ʷ ~ ʔəq'ʷ/ *pull out, unplug*? (H76:661-2,685) if deglottalization occured in Halq'eméylem, compare root <**óqw'**> as in <**s'óqw'**> *something that one hooks onto (like a trailer hitch)* and <**óqw'a**> *the last baby (youngest baby)*, and compare root in <**óqw=elets**> or <**óqw=el=ets**> *back of the body.*

<**óqwelets**>, df //ʔáqʷ=əl=əc or ʔáqʷ=ələc//, ANA /'*back of the body, the whole back*'/, possibly root <**óqw**> meaning uncertain, possibly <**=el**> *get, become, go, come*?, <**=ets ~ =íts ~ =ewíts**> *on the back*, prob. not <**=elets**> *on the rump/bottom*, syntactic analysis: nominal, attested by SJ (4/10/80), Elders Group (5/5/75, 5/26/76), AC, DM (12/4/64), also <**éqwelets**>, //ʔə́qʷ=əl=əts//, also /'*back (of a person)*'/, EB ['*back (of a tree) (the side away from the rising sun)*'], attested by CT, HT, also <**s'óqwelets**>, //s=ʔáqʷ=əl=əc//, also /'*back (of person, horse, other animal, etc.)*'/, also <**ő̄qwelets**>, //ʔóqʷ=əl=əc//, attested by MV (Deming 4/10/80), AC, Salish cognate: Nooksack /ʔóqʷəlæč/ *back* PA61, Lushootseed /s-ʔəqʷəlíč/ *back (of body)* H76:661, Songish (N. Straits) /ʔəqʷəléc/ *to be behind* M68:140, example: <**li ta ő̄qwelets.**>, //li t-ɛ ʔóqʷ=əl=əc//, /'*He's at your back.*'/, attested by AC, <**lí kw'el óqwelets**>, //lí k'ʷə-l ʔáqʷ=əl=əc//, /'*behind me, at my back*'/, attested by Elders Group (5/26/76), <**th'e<u>x</u>wót tel óqwelets**>, //θ'əx̣ʷ=áT tə-l ʔáqʷ=əl=əc//, [θ'əx̣ʷát tɪl ʔɔ́qʷələc], /'*wash my back*'/, attested by AC, <**qw'óqw'et te ő̄qwelets te siyólexwe**>, //q'ʷáqʷ=əT (k'ʷáqʷ=əT?) tə ʔóqʷ=əl=əts-s tə si=yáləxʷə//, /'*hit the old man's back*'/, literally /'whip s-o/s-th (club s-o/s-th) the back of the (male) old person'/, attested by AC, <**stamést'we eyó:th <u>x</u>eyp'et kw'el óqwelɛts.**>, //s=tɛm=ə́s-t'wə ʔɛy=á·θ x̣í=p'=əT k'ʷə-l ʔóqʷ=əl=əc//, /'*Something sharp scraped/scratched my back.*'/, attested by AC, <**éy, tl'ó yewál éy st'élmexw; welí kw'e li te éqwelets te thqát éwe lís eyém.**>, //ʔɛ́y, ƛ'á yəwɛ́l ʔɛ́y s=t'ə́lməxʷ; wə-lí k'ʷə li tə ʔə́qʷ=əl=əc-s tə θqɛ́t ʔə́wə lí-s ʔɛy=ə́m//, /'*It's good, it's the best medicine; if it's on the back)side away from the rising sun) of the tree it's not as strong.*'/, attested by CT, HT.

<**óqw'**>, bound root //ʔáq'ʷ *hooked onto*//, compare root <**ókw'**> *hang on an arm or on something sticking out* as in <**ókw'est**> *hang s-th (on a nail or hat hanger), hook it back on (of a stitch lost in knitting),* Salish cognate: perhaps Lushootseed root /ʔuq'ʷ ~ ʔə́q'ʷ/ *pull out, unplug* as in /ʔúq'ʷ-ud/ *pull it out* and /ʔəq'ʷ-úciid/ *open it* H76:661-2,685.

<**s'óqw'**>, dnom //s=ʔáq'ʷ//, MC ['*something that you hook onto (like a trailer hitch)*'], (<**s=**> *nominalizer*), syntactic analysis: nominal, attested by AD (AHTTC 2/27/80).

<**óqw'a**>, df //ʔáq'ʷ=ɛ//, KIN /'*last baby (youngest baby), the last-born, a child cranky and jealous of an expected brother or sister*'/, ASM ['the unborn child is pinching where the other one was in the womb, that's why the older child is cranky'], EFAM, lx <**=a**> *living thing*, syntactic analysis: nominal, attested by BHTTC (10/3/76), Elders Group (1/25/78), Salish cognate: Samish (dial. of N.

Straits) /šxʷ=áq'ʷaʔ/ *relative (any sex or age)* ~ TB /šxʷ=ʔáq'ʷəʔ/ *brother* and VU /ʔəq'ʷəy'təl'/ ~ LD /ʔəq'ʷíy'təl'/ *to be related together* G86:78.

<**oqw'exélem**>, mdls //ʔaq'ʷɛ=xʸə[=´=]l=əm//, KIN ['*to make a sign with its foot it wants a younger brother or younger sister*'], ASM ['an óqw'a or youngest baby does this by putting tie soles of its feet together or by putting its foot in its mouth; if the óqw'a is a boy and is well-behaved or talks early it wants a boy; if it is bad or slow to talk it wants a girl'], lx <**=xel**> *on the foot*, (<= ´=> *derivational*), (<**=em**> *middle voice*), phonology: stress-shift, rowel-reduction og final root vowel, syntactic analysis: intransitive verb, attested by Elders Group (1/25/78).

<**óqw'a**>, KIN /'*last baby (youngest baby), the last-born, a child cranky and jealous of an expected brother or sister*'/, *see* óqw'.

<**oqw'exélem**>, KIN ['*to make a sign with its foot it wants a younger brother or younger sister*'], *see* óqw'.

<**=ó:s ~ =ós ~ =es**>, da //=á·s ~ =ás ~ =əs//, ANA /'*on the face, face of the hand or foot, opened surface of a salmon*'/, LAND ['*face of a mountain*'], BSK /'*face of a basket, (design on a basket)*'/, CAN ['*bow of canoe or boat*'], WETH ['*face of the moon*'], TIME /'*cyclic period, moon, season*'/, ECON /'*money, dollar(s)*'/, semantic environment ['with numerals 3-99, kw'í:l, non-numerals'], (semological comment: obligatory), SH ['*circular objects*'], syntactic analysis: lexical suffix, derivational suffix; found in <**th'exwó:sem**>, //θ'əx̣ʷ=á·s=əm//, /'*wash one's face*'/, <**th'qw'ó:s**>, //θ'q'ʷ=á·s//, /'*punched in the face*'/, <**xwthó:s**>, //xʷ=θ=á·s//, /'*big face*'/, <**x̱éyp'es**>, //x̣ɛ́y=p'=əs//, /'*scraped on the face*'/, <**skw'echó:stel**>, //s=k'ʷəc=á·s=təl//, /'*window, mirror*'/, literally /'nominal see face device to'/, <**qéytes**>, //qɛ́yt=əs//, /'*headband*'/, <**qéyx̱es**>, //qɛ́yx̣=əs//, /'*blind*'/, <**íyes**>, //ʔíy=əs//, /'*fun, having fun*'/, literally /'good in the face'/, <**xwt'óx̱wesxel**>, //xʷ=t'áx̣ʷ=əs=xʸəl//, /'*arch of the foot*'/, literally /'pertaining to head go downriver on the face of the foot'/, (semological comment: references to head and face because *sole of the foot* < "pertaining to head face of the foot), <**xwt'óx̱westses**>, //xʷ=t'áx̣ʷ=əs=cəs//, /'*hollow of the hand*'/, <**Stíytó:s**>, //s=tiyt=á·s//, /'*Promontory Mountain*'/, literally /'something upriver on the face'/, <**sx̱éles**>, //s=x̣ə́l=əs//, /'*basket design*'/, literally /'nominal mark, design on face'/, <**slhíts'es ~ shxwlhíts'es**>, //s=ɬíc'=əs (Chill.) ~ sxʷ=ɬíc'=əs (Cheh.)//, /'*scored wind-dried salmon*'/, literally /'nominal cut on face'/, <**x̱éyqw'est ~ x̱íyqw'est**>, //x̣íy=q'ʷ=əs=t//, /'*hang s-o*'/, <**lhq'ó:tes**>, //ɬq'ɛ́[=Aá=]·t=əs//, /'*wide face*'/, <**lhq'ó:tses**>, //ɬq'ɛ[=Aá·=]c(ə)s=əs//, /'*five dollars*'/, <**teqó:tsó:s**>, //təqɛ[=Aá·=]cɛ=á·s//, /'*eight dollars*'/, also <**=es**>, //=əs//, <**Pelóqes**>, //pəláq=əs//, /'*torch moon (in January), (time to spear fish by torchlight)*'/ (compare <**pelóqel**> *torch*), <**Temtl'í:qes**>, //təm=ƛ'í·q=əs//, /'*moon (when one) gets jammed in (from snow) (in February)*'/, literally /'time + jammed in or stuck in a trap + moon or cyclic period'/, <**Welék'es**>, //wələ́k'=əs//, /'*little frog moon (in March)*'/, <**Lhemtóles ~ Lhemt'óles**>, //ɬəm=t=áləs=əs ~ ɬəm=t'=áləs=əs//, /'*spring showers moon (in April)*'/ (with either <**=es**> *cyclic period* or <**=ó:les**> *in the eyes* or both), <**Epóléstel**>, //ʔəpál=ə́s=təl//, /'*tenth moon (in July)*'/, <**Meqó:s**>, //məq=á·s//, /'*fallen snow moon (in December)*'/ (compare <**má:qa**> *fallen snow)*, <**skw'exó:s**>, //s=k'ʷəxʸ=á·s//, /'*moon, month*'/ (compare <**kw'ex=**> *count)*, <**wá:yélés**>, //wɛ́·yə́l=ə́s//, /'*tomorrow*'/ (compare <**wá:yel**> *come daylight*), <**imexó:sem**>, //ʔim=əxʸ=á·s=əm//, /'*go for a walk (walk in a circle without destination)*'/, <**lhokw'emó:les**>, //ɬak'ʷəm(=)á·l(=)əs//, /'*when the first fall storm comes*'/ (compare perhaps <**lhó:kw'**> *to fly*, and alternatively perhaps with <**=ó:les**> *eyes*).

<**ó:sem**>, mdls //ʔá·s=əm or ʔ=á·s=əm or ʔá·=əs=əm//, ABFC ['*turn one's face towards*'], possibly root <**ó:**> *call*, possibly root <**ó:s**> *face*, (compare suffix <**=ó:s**> *on the face* possibly used as root) or <**'**> **(/ʔ/)** empty root or *turn toward*?, possibly <**=em**> *middle voice*, phonology: if this is a case of a lexical suffix used as a root the initial glottal stop would be automatically inserted by phonological

rules preventing vowel initial words, syntactic analysis: intransitive verb, attested by IHTTC (9/16/77).

<**=òt ~ =ò:t**>, da //=àt ~ =á·t//, N ['*female name*'], syntactic analysis: lexical suffix, derivational suffix, comment: as in (compound) suffixes =elò:t ~ =eló:t, =elhót, =emòt, =ewòt all used in female names.

<**ó:t**>, pcs //ʔá·=T//, LANG ['*call s-o*'], (<**=t**> *purposeful control transitivizer*), probably root <**ó:**> *call*, compare <**ó:=l=thet**> *groan* and <**ó:=m**> *order*, syntactic analysis: transitive verb, attested by EB, AC, example: <**esu ó:tes te siyá:yes we'ó:lhes.**>, //ʔə-s-u ʔá·=T-əs tə si=yɛ́·yə-s wə-ʔá·ɬ-əs//, /'*Then he called his friends to get in the canoe.*'/, usage: story of the Flood1A AC, <**tl'osésu ó:tes te mestíyexw.**>, //ƛ'a-w-ə́s-u ʔá·=T-əs tə məstíyəxʷ//, /'*And so he called the people.*'/, usage: story of the Flood, attested by AC, <**ó:tes te mestíyeyw.welámes má:ytem thíyt te hí:kw q'ex̱wő́welh, sq'ém:el qas te sx̱wő́qwtel.**>, //ʔá·=T-əs tə məstíyəxʷ wə-lɛ́=m-əs mɛ́·y=T-əm θíy=T tə hí[=·=]kʷ q'əx̣ʷ=ówəɬ, s=q'ə́m·əl qɛ-s tə s=x̣ʷóq'ʷ=təl//, /'*He called the people when he goes, to help him make a big high-bow canoe, paddle, and a canoe pole.*'/, usage: story of the Flood, syntactic comment: awkward syntax here with no demb to conjoin má:ytem (passive) or thíyt, also no demonstrative article in second of three simple nominal phrase conjoined as object, attested by AC, <**esésu ó:tem te lólets'a chief.**>, //ʔə-s-ə́s-u ʔá·=T-əm tə C_1á=ləc'ə ciief//, /'*And so they called one chief.*'/, literally /'so tidn thdy he was called the one person chief'/, syntactic analysis: ambiguous past - subordinating nolinalizer -rbsp 3 -contrastive, usage: contemporary story, attested by AC, <**qetl'osésu ó:thálem welámàl qwà:l.**>, //qə=ƛ'a-s-ə́s-u ʔá·=T-ɛ́ləm wə-lɛ́=m-ɛ̀l qʷɛ̀·l//, /'*And they called me if I would go speak.*'/, literally /'and it's tiem I was called if I would go speak'/, usage: contemporary story, attested by AC (11/10/71).

<**ótsesem**>, mdls //ʔá=cəs=əm//, LANG /'*to signal with the hand to come, (call with the hand)*'/, lx <**=tses**> *on the hand*, (<**=em**> *middle voice*), syntactic analysis: intransitive verb, attested by Elders Group; found in <**ótsesémét**>, //ʔá=cəs-əm-ə́t//, /'*to signal with the hand to come*'/, phonology: updrifting, syntactic analysis: dependent passive?, attested by Elders Group (5/26/76).

<**ótqwt**>, SOC ['*caressing s-o*'], *see* etqwt.

<**ót'**>, free root //ʔát'//, MC ['*stretch*'], syntactic analysis: intransitive verb, attested by EB.

<**ó:t'**>, ds //ʔá[=·=]t'//, HUNT ['*slingshot (of the stretched kind)*'], (<**=:=**> *augmentative*), phonology: lengthening, syntactic analysis: nominal, attested by Elders Group (11/26/75).

<**ét''et'**>, chrs //ʔa[=Aə́=]t'=C_1əC_2//, DESC /'*(be) stretchy, (be) elastic*'/, (<**é-ablaut**> *derivational* perhaps *resultative*), (<**=R2**> *characteristic*), phonology: ablaut, reduplicatin, syntactic analysis: adjective/adjectival verb, attested by AHTTC (2/8/80).

<**ót'et**>, pcs //ʔát'=əT//, MC /'*stretch s-th out, stretch it*'/, semantic environment ['sweater, animal hide, accordion, person, etc.'], (<**=et**> *purposeful control transitivizer*), syntactic analysis: transitive verb, attested by EB, CT, HT, Elders Group, Salish cognate: Squamish /ʔút'-unʔ/ *stretch, lengthen, extend (tr.)* W73:255, K69:95, Lushootseed root in /ʔút'-əb/ *stretch* and /ʔəxʷ=ʔút'=ʔut'=alus/ *stretched eyes, slant eyes, sleepy eyes (an instlt for Bear)* H76:687, example: <**ót'et te kw'éléw**>, //ʔát'=əT tə k'ʷə́lə́w//, /'*stretch a hide*'/, attested by CT, HT; found in <**ót'etem**>, //ʔát'=əT-əm//, /'*it got stretched, they (indefinite)/romeone stretched it*'/, syntactic analysis: passive, attested by Elders Group, EB, example: <**ót'etem qweló:yethetel**>, //ʔát'=əT-əm qʷɛl=á·yəθ(əl)=təl//, /'*accordion*'/, literally /'stretched musibal instrument/wind instrument'/, usage: suggested in humor, attested by Elders Group (1/30/80); found in <**ot'etémét**>, //ʔat'=əT-əm-ə́t//, /'*stretched, something that somebody stretched*'/, syntactic analysis: dependent passive, attested by CT, HT, EB.

<**ót'ethet**>, pcrs //ʔát'=əT-ət//, ABFC ['*stretch oneself*'], (<**=et**> *purposeful control transitivizer*), (<**-et**> *reflexive*), syntactic analysis: intransitive verb, attested by Elders Group.

<**xwe'ít'et**>, ds //xʷə=ʔa[=Aí=]t'=əT//, incs, pcs, HUNT /'*draw a bow, cock a gun, (draw it (of a bow), cock it (of a gun))*'/, SOC, (<**xwe=**> *get, become, inceptive*), (<**í-ablaut**> *derivational* perhaps aspectual), root <**ót'**> *stretch*, phonology: ablaut, syntactic analysis: transitive verb, attested by Elders Group.

<**S'ót'o**>, df //s=ʔát'=a//, PLN ['*place just south of Doctor's Point on Harrison Lake northwest side*'], (<**s=**> *nominalizer* or *stative*), (<**=o**> meaning uncertain unless *just*), root <**ót'**> *stretch*, comment: said to mean *long breast* by Hill-Tout 1904:361 but appears to mean instead *something just stretched*, syntactic analysis: nominal, attested by EL (Nov. 1978).

<**ó:t'**>, HUNT ['*slingshot (of the stretched kind)*'], *see* ót'.

<**ót'et**>, MC /'*stretch s-th out, stretch it*'/, *see* ót'.

<**ót'etem qweló:ythetel**>, MUS ['*accordion*'], *see* qwà:l.

<**ót'ethet**>, ABFC ['*stretch oneself*'], *see* ót'.

<**=óth**>, da //=áθ//, SH ['*edge*'], syntactic analysis: lexical suffix, derivational suffix; found in <**iyóth**>, //ʔɛy=áθ//, /'*sharp(-edged)*'/ (<**iy**> is an unstressed allomorph of <**éy**> *good*), <**qelóth**>, //qəl=áθ//, /'*dull(-edged)*'/, <**qelótheqsel**>, //qəl=áθ=əqsəl//, /'*blunt (of a point or pole)*'/, <**semlóthel**>, //s=hə=mil=áθ=əl//, /'*riverbank*'/ (root <**mil**> *drop into water, submerge into water* as also in <**seml(=)ál=iyel**> *a set net, a stationary net* and <**míl=iyel**> *to set a net*), perhaps <**smeq'óth**>, //s=məq'=áθ//, /'*extra food which guests can take home*'/.

<**=ó:thel ~ =(e)thel**>, da //=á·θəl ~ =(ə)θəl//, ANA /'*on the mouth, in the mouth*'/, syntactic analysis: lexical suffix, derivational suffix, also <**=ethel**>, //=əθəl//, also <**=thel**>, //=θəl//; found in <**xwthó:thel**>, //xʷ=θ=á·θəl//, /'*big mouth*'/, <**thó:thel**>, //θá·θəl//, /'*mouth*'/, <**qw'iqw'emó:thel**>, //q'ʷiq'ʷəm=á·θəl//, /'*fishing with hook and line, trout-fishing*'/, <**sqép'ò:thel**>, //s=qə́p'=à·θəl//, /'*flying squirrel*'/, literally /'nominal cover on the mouth'/, (semological comment: so-called because of stories the animal will land against one's mouth when one is walking at night in the woods and smother one), <**sqwiqweyó:thel**>, //sqʷiqʷəy=á·θəl//, /'*jack-rabbit, big older rabbit*'/, comment: also see *harelip*.

<**ótheqw**>, free root //ʔáθəqʷ//, FOOD /'*to roast potatoes in hot sand or ashes, bake in ashes, bake in stove*'/, ACL ['*bake in stove*'], syntactic analysis: intransitive verb, attested by Elders Group.

<**ótheqwt**>, pcs //ʔáθəqʷ=T//, FOOD /'*bake s-th in ashes, bake s-th in a stove*'/, (<**=t**> *purposeful control transitivizer*), syntactic analysis: transitive verb, attested by Elders Group.

<**s'ótheqw**>, dnom //s=ʔáθəqʷ//, FOOD /'*roast potatoes, baked potatoes*'/, ASM ['made by covering in hot ashes'], (<**s=**> *nominalizer*), syntactic analysis: nominal, *baked potato* (lit. something + baked), (attested by RG,EH 6/16/98 to SN, edited by BG with RG,EH 6/26/00), attested by EB, example: <**lulh qw'élém ta' s'ótheqw.**>, //lə=uɬ q'ʷə́lə́m t-ɛʔ s=ʔáθəqʷ//, /'*Your roast potatoes are cooked.*'/, attested by MH.

<**s'ótheqw**>, stvi //s=ʔáθəqʷ//, FOOD /'*baked (in ashes), baked (in a stove)*'/, (<**s=**> *stative*), syntactic analysis: adjective/adjectival verb, attested by Elders Group, example: <**s'ótheqw seplí:l**>, //s=ʔáθəqʷ səplí·l//, /'*baked bread*'/, ASM ['in contrast to fried bread example'], <**s'ótheqw xáwéq**>, //s=ʔáθəqʷ xʸɛ́wə́q//, /'*baked carrots*'/, <**s'ótheqw sqá:wth**>, //s=ʔáθəqʷ s=qɛ́·wθ//, /'*baked potatoes*'/.

<**ó:th ~ óth**>, probably bound root //ʔá·θ//, meaning uncertain unless *edge, surface*

<**s'ó:thes ~ s'óthes**>, dnom //s=ʔá·θ=əs ~ s=ʔáθ=əs//, ANA ['*face*'], (<**s=**> *nominalizer*), possibly root <**ó:th**> *edge, surface* possibly root from <**=ó:th**> *edge*?, lx <**=es**> *on the face*, phonology: the long vowel probably only in careful/slow pronunciation, syntactic analysis: nominal, attested by AC, BJ

(5/64), Elders Group (3/1/72), many others, other sources: ES and JH /sʔá·θəs/ *face*, H-T <tsEátsus> (macron over á) *face*, Boas 1890 <s'átses> (macron over a, double underline under e) *face*, comment: Hill-Tout collected a lot of valuable information but his ear for phonetic detail was poor compared to that of Boas as the above and many other examples show, example: <**lí te s'óthes**>, //lí tə s=ʔáθəs-s//, /'*on his face*'/, phonology: consonant merger, attested by AC, <**kwímel ta' s'óthes.**>, //kʷím=əl t-ɛʔ s=ʔáθ=əs//, /'*Your face is red.*'/, attested by Elders Group (3/1/72), <**lulh qwáyel te s'óthes yewá:lmels kwses melqí:wsem.**>, //lə=uɬ qʷɛ́y=əl tə s=ʔáθ=əs-s yəwɛ́·l=məls kʷ-s-əs mɛlq=í·ws=əm//, /'*Her face is turning green before she faints.*'/, attested by AC.

<**shxw'óthestses ~ shxwe'óthestses**>, ds //s(=)xʷ=ʔáθəs=cəs//, ANA ['*palm (of the hand)*'], literally /'face on the hand, face of the hand'/, (<**sxw=**> *nominalizer*), lx <**=tses**> *on the hand*, syntactic analysis: nominal, attested by Elders Group.

<**shxw'óthesxel ~ shxwe'óthesxel**>, ds //s(=)xʷ=ʔáθəs=xʸəl//, ANA /'*sole (of the foot), (instep [AC, DM])*'/, literally /'face on the foot, face of the foot'/, (<**sxw=**> *nominalizer*), lx <**=xel**> *on the foot*, syntactic analysis: nominal, attested by Elders Group, AC, also /'*instep*'/, attested by AC, DM (12/4/64), other sources: ES /šxʷʔáθəsxʸəl/ *sole of foot*, H-T <cuátsecEl> (macrons over u and a) *sole*.

<**ótheqwt**>, FOOD /'*bake s-th in ashes, bake s-th in a stove*'/, *see* ótheqw.

<**ótsesem**>, LANG /'*to signal with the hand to come, (call with the hand)*'/, *see* ó:t.

<**ówelti:l**>, PLAY /'*racing, (a race (on foot/canoe/horse) (Elders Group))*'/, *see* ewelti:l.

<**òwelh ~ -òwèlh**>, (//ʔà=wəɬ ~ -à=wəɬ//), MOOD /'*(polite imperative?, (polite) certainly, (polite) of course)*'/, LANG, (semological comment: though never directly or unambiguously translated, a polite feeling is always added and the above translations fit all the uses seen so far), possibly root <**ò ~ -ò**> *just, merely, simply*??, possibly <**=welh**> *already*??, phonology: upstepping or updrifting, syntactic analysis: is or derivational suffix, dialects: *Chill.; Tait and Cheh. have àwelh ~ -àwèlh q.v.*, attested by AC, Elders Group, AD, Deming, others, example: <**lí òwèlh.**>, //lí ʔà=wəɬ//, /'*Is that right?*'/, literally /'is it certainly?, is it the case certainly?'/, attested by AD (4/26/78), <**hóy òwelh. ~ hóyòwèlh.**>, //háy ʔà=wəɬ ~ háy-à=wəɬ//, /'*Goodbye (leaver to stayer).*'/, literally /'it's finished certainly/of course (??), you (polite) finish (??), let's (polite) finish (??)'/, attested by AC, Elders Group, Deming, others, <**lám òwelh. ~ lámòwèlh.**>, //lɛ́=m ʔà=wəɬ ~ lɛ́=m-à=wəɬ//, /'*Goodbye (stayer to leaver).*'/, literally /'you (polite) go, you're (polite) going certainly/of course (??)'/, attested by AC, Elders Group, Deming, others, <**ő: òwelh.**>, //ʔó· ʔà=wəɬ//, /'*(I'm listening.)*'/, semantic environment ['said while listening to bedtime stories'], literally /'oh certainly, oh of course'/, attested by AC, <**á'á'òwèlh.**>, //ʔɛ́ʔɛ ʔà=wəɬ//, /'*You're welcome., Yes, (certainly).*'/, semantic environment ['said in reply to Yálh lixw kw'á'as hò:y. *Thank you.* and in reply to Qw'óqw'elex̱. *Excuse me.*'], (semological comment: here the translation (certainly) is strongly implied if not directly provided in translation), attested by AD.

<**ó:wqw'elmexw**> or <**ó:wkw'elmexw**>, df //ʔá·wq'ʷ=əl=məxʷ or ʔɛ[=Aá·=]wk'ʷ=əl=məxʷ//, SOCT /'*a group of people, a tribe of people, several tribes*'/, possibly root <**á:wkw'**> *belongings*, possibly <**=el=**> *plural*, lx <**=mexw**> *person*, phonology: probable ablaut, syntactic analysis: nominal, attested by BJ (5/10/64 new p.109, 12/5/64 new transcript old pp.334-335).

<**=ó(:)weqw**>, da //=ɛ[=Aá=](·)w=əqʷ//, CLO ['*hat*'], possibly <**=á:w**> *body*, possibly <**=eqw**> *on top of the head, on the hair* syntactic analysis: lexical suffix, derivational suffix; found in <**kawpōyóweq(w)**>, //kɛwpoy=áwəq(ʷ)//, /'*cowboy hat*'/, contrast <**yóseqw**> *hat*, Salish cognate: Musqueam /=áw'əqʷ/ *hat* Suttles ca1984:14.5.86.

<**ówthet**>, ABFC /'*to hurry, hurry up, move fast*'/, *see* áwth.

<**-óx**>, (//**-áxʸ**//), PRON /'*me, first person singular object*'/, phonology: attracts stress, syntactic analysis: is; found in <**imexsthóxes.**>, //ʔim=əxʸ=sT-áxʸ-əs//, /'*He made me walk.*'/, <**tl'í:lsóxes.**>, //ƛ'í·=ləs-áxʸ-əs//, /'*He/She loves me.*'/.

<**óxw**>, SOC ['*give it to me*'], *see* áxw.

<**óxwest**>, SOC /'*give it to s-o, give to s-o*'/, *see* áxw.

<**ó:xwest**>, SOC ['*giving it to s-o*'], *see* áxw.

<**ó<u>x</u>**>, free root //ʔáx̣//, EFAM ['*it's no good*'], semantic environment ['said of something disliked'], syntactic analysis: interjection, usage: slang, attested by AHTTC (2/15/80).

<**ó<u>x</u>we**>, possible root or stem //ʔáx̣ʷ(=)ə//, meaning unknown

<**s'ó<u>x</u>we**>, df //s=ʔáx̣ʷ(=)ə//, EZ /'*clam, butter clam, fresh-water clam, fresh-water mussel*'/, ['*Saxidomus giganteus*'], ASM ['the salt-water variety is said by some elders to be larger clams and butter clams are medium-sized and larger than the small-sized little neck clam *Protothaca staminea*; the fresh-water clams were found at Cultus Lake according to AC'], (<**s=**> *nominalizer*), root meaning unknown, possibly <**=e ~ =a**> *living thing*, probably borrowed from example Squamish or Ltshootseed since it has the same vowel as they do rather than the regtlar correspondence with Halkomelem <**á**> /ɛ́/, syntactic analysis: nominal, attested by Deming, LJ (Tait), others, other sources: JH /sʔá·x̣ʷe/ *clam*, Wayne Suttles (p.c. 10/9/79) /sʔáx̣ʷə/ *fresh-water mussel*, Salish cognate: Squamish /sʔáx̣ʷa/ *butter clam (Saxidomus gigantea)* Kennedy and Bouchard 1976, Samish dial. of N. Str<u>ai</u>ts /sʔáx̣ʷaʔ/ (VU) *butter clam* G86:68, Lushootsded /s-ʔáx̣ʷuʔ/ *butter clam, clam (generic)* and /ʔáx̣ʷuʔ/ *clamming* H76:649-650.

<**=óyaq**>, da //=áyɛq or =ɛ[=Aá=]y=ɛq//, EB ['*root? or trunk?*'], possibly <**=ɛ́y**> *bark*, possibly <**ó-ablaut**> *derivational*, possibly <**=aq**> *penis*?, syntactic analysis: lexical suffix, derivational suffix; found in <**st'it'<u>x</u>óyaq**>, //s=C₁í=t'əx̣=áyɛq//, /'*fork in a tree or root of a tree*'/ (compare <**s=t'é<u>x</u>**> *fork (in anything)*).

<**óyém**>, df //ʔáy=əm or ʔɛ[=Aá=]y=əm//, TIME /'*(be) slow, (be) late, go slow*'/, possibly root <**á:y**> *keep on, continue*, possibly <**ó-ablaut on root á**> *resultative*??, <**=em**> *middle voice*, phonology: possible ablaut, updrifting or allomorph oyém before suffixes, syntactic analysis: adverb/adverbial verb, adjective/adjectival verb?, attested by EB, Elders Group (6/16/76), also <**ó:yem**>, //ʔá·y=əm or ʔɛ[=Aá=]·y=əm//, attested by Elders Group (5/28/75), Salish cognate: Squamish /ʔúyumʔ/ *slow* W73:238, K67:396, Sechelt /ʔúyum/ *slow* T77:20, example: <**tu oyémchexw.**>, //tu ʔáy=ə́m-c-əxʷ//, /'*You go slow.*'/, literally /'a little more you go/are slow'/, attested by Elders Group (6/16/76), <**(tu) ó:yem kws mes qw'él te elíle.**>, //(tu) ʔá·y=əm kʷ-s mə-s q'ʷə́l tə ʔəlílə//, /'*The salmonberries are ripe late.*'/, attested by Elders Group (5/28/75).

<**i'oyóm**> or <**i'eyóm**>, mos //ʔi=ʔáy=ə[=M2=]m//, TVMO ['*to walk slow*'], (<**i= ~ ye=**> *travel by, while moving*), (<**metathesis**> *derivational*), phonology: metathesis, syntactic analysis: intransitive verb, attested by Elders Group (5/28/75).

<**íy'eyòm**>, dmv //C₁í=ʔáy=ə[=M2=]m//, TIME ['*(be) slower*'], TVMO, (<**R4=**> *diminutive* or *comparative*), (<**metathesis**> *derivational*), phonology: reduplication, metathesis, syntactic analysis: adverb/adverbial verb, adjective/adjectival verb?, attested by Elders Group (3/29/78).

<**oyémstexw**>, caus //ʔáy=ə́m=sT-əxʷ//, TIME /'*delay s-o, slow s-o down*'/, TVMO, (<**=st**> *causative control transitivizer*), phonology: possible allomorph oyém, syntactic analysis: transitive verb, attested by Deming, Elders Group (3/29/78), also <**éyómstexw ~ oyémstexw**>, //ʔáy=ə́[=M2=]m=sT-əxʷ ~ ʔáy=ə́m=sT-əxʷ//, attested by Elders Group (6/16/76); found in

<**oyémstexwlha.**>, //ʔáy=ə́m=sT-əx^{w}-ɬɛ//, /'*Slow him down.*'/, attested by Elders Group (6/16/76).

<**oyómt**>, pcs //ʔay=ə[=M2=]m=T//, TIME ['*delay s-o*'], TVMO, (<**metathesis**> *derivational*), (<**=t**> *purposeful control transitivizer*), phonology: metathesis, syntactic analysis: transitive verb, attested by Elders Group (3/29/78).

<**iy'eyómthet**>, pcrs //C$_1$əC$_2$=ʔáy=ə[=M2=]m=T-ət//, TIME ['*delay oneself*'], TVMO, (<**R3=**> *derivational*), (<**metathesis**> *derivational*), (<**=t**> *purposeful control transitivizer*), (<**-et**> *reflexive*), phonology: reduplication, metathesis, syntactic analysis: intransitive verb, attested by Elders Group (3/29/78).

<**oyémqel**>, ds //ʔáy=ə́m=qəl//, LANG ['*(have a) slow voice*'], ABFC, lx <**=qel**> *voice, in the throat, speech*, syntactic analysis: adjective/adjectival verb, attested by Elders Group.

<**oyémqel**>, LANG ['*(have a) slow voice*'], *see* óyém.

<**oyémstexw**>, TIME /'*delay s-o, slow s-o down*'/, *see* óyém.

<**=oyes**>, da //=ɛ[=Aa=]y=əs//, EB ['*flower*'], literally /'face of the plant'/, lx <**=á:y ~ =áy ~ =ay ~ =ey**> *plant, bark; wool, covering*, lx <**=es**> *on the face* (but here, as elsewhere in combination with other lexical suffixes, has alloseme *face*, phonology: <**o-ablaut**> on <**a**> in root or affix automatically conditioned by following <**=es**> suffix, syntactic analysis: lexical suffix, attested by SP, Elders Group (5/28/75); found in <**péth'oyes**>, //pɛ[=Aə́=]θ'=ɛ[=Aa=]y=əs//, /'*rice root*'/, EB, ['*Fritillaria camschatcensis*'], dialects: *Tait*, attested by SP, Elders Group (5/28/75), <**qwelíyes**>, //q^{w}íl=ə[=M2=]y=əs//, /'*flower of the red flowering currant*'/, EB, ['*Ribes sanguineum*'], literally /'body hair flower (due to the hairs all over the stem and branches)'/, probably root <**qwíl**> *body hair*, <**pepq'eyó:s**>, //C$_1$ə=p'[=D=]əq'=əy=á·s//, /'*snowberry, waxberry*'/, EB, ['*Symphoricarpos albus*'], literally /'many little white flowers, or many little white plant faces'/, (semological comment: the plant has both white flowers and white berries (that often remain on the bush all winter), thus the name could refer to the flowers or (as more literal *faces*) to the berries), (<**R5=**> *diminutive plural*), (<**D** or **deglottalization**> *derivational*), phonology: deglottalization, reduplication, syntactic analysis: nominal, attested by AC, others.

<**oyewílem**>, df //ʔɛy=íwə[=M2=]l=əm or ʔɛ[=Aa=]y=əw(əl)=íl=əm or ʔɛy=əw(əl)=íl=əm or ʔayəw=íl=əm//, EFAM ['*having fun at a non-spiritual dance*'], SOC, probably root <**éy**> *good*, probably <**=íwel ~ =ewel**> *in the mind, in the feelings*, probably <**=íl**> *go, come, get, become, inceptive*, possibly <**metathesis**> *derivational* or <**o-ablaut**> *derivational*, (<**=em**> *middle voice*), phonology: possible metathesis or possible ablaut, syntactic analysis: intransitive verb, attested by AD (4/28/78).

<**Óyewòt**>, df //ʔáyəw=àt or ʔáy=əwàt//, PLN /'*smallest peak just below Mount Cheam (on left of Mt. Cheam looking south), Lhílheqey's (Mt. Cheam's) baby (located about where her breast would be on the left hand side facing her)*'/, ASM ['Lhílheqey is holding this baby in her hand according to AC in an interview by Oliver Wells (2/8/62) (Wells 1970:12)'], N ['*Indian name of Mary Amy (Lorenzetto) (Commodore) Cooper*'], lx <**=òt**> or <**=ewòt**> *female name ending*, syntactic analysis: nominal, attested by AC, IHTTC, other sources: Wells 1965:11,17, source: place names reference file #173.

<**S'óyewòt**>, df //s=ʔáy=əwàt or s=ʔáyəw=àt//, PLN /'*another small peak just to the right of the Mount Cheam summit peak as one faces south, she is another daughter of Lhílheqey (Mt. Cheam)*'/, ASM ['Wells 1965:17 gives <say-oo-WAT> (our <S'óyewòt>) as a second daughter just on the right side of Mt. Cheam, the IHTTC recognized <Óyewòt>, probably this name <S'óyewòt> (less sure), and gave <X̲emóth'oya> as three small peaks around Mt. Cheam, her daughters'], syntactic analysis: nominal, attested by IHTTC, other sources: Wells 1965:17,

<**oyémstexw**>, TIME /'*delay s-o, slow s-o down*'/, *see* óyém.

<**=(')ó:ylha**> (normally written <**=ó:ylha**>), da //=(ʔ)á·yɬɛ//, EB ['*(wooden?)*'], perhaps originally a compound with root <yo:lh> *cut tree, log* plus metathesis yielding <=o:ylh> plus <=e ~ =a> *living entity*, could less plausibly be seen as <**=á:y**> *bark, plant, wool, covering*, possibly <**=lh**> *past tense*, syntactic analysis: lexical suffix, possibly compare <**=á(:)ylh ~ =á(:)lh ~ =elh (~ =iylh ~ =ó:llh**?)> *bed, (child, young)*; found in <**mimele'ó:ylha**>, //C_1í=mələ=ʔ=á·yɬɛ//, /'*doll*'/ (compare <**mímele**> *baby, tiny child* with <**R4=**> *diminutive* + <**méle**> *child*), <=**ó:ylh=a**> should be compared to <**s=yó:lh**> *firewood, wood* and <**s=yó:ylh**> *little firewood, little stick of wood* and <**=a**> *living thing*, contrast <**=iylh**> *child or young*. In my data the word for *doll* is the only example.

<**óyó:lwethet**>, SOC /'*be totally independent, doing the best one can*'/, *see* éy ~ éy:.

<**oyómt**>, TIME ['*delay s-o*'], *see* óyém.

<**ó:ytel**>, SOC ['*fighting*'], *see* iyó:tel.

<**=ó:ythel ~ =eyéthel ~ =eyth(íl)**>, da //=á·y(=)θəl ~ =əy(=)ə́θəl ~ =əy(=)θəl(=íl)//, ANA ['*on the lip or jaw*'], LANG ['*in speech*'], MUS ['*music*'], possibly <**=á:y ~ =ey**> *bark, covering*, possibly <**ó-ablaut of a**> *derivational*, possibly <**=thel**> *on the mouth*, syntactic analysis: lexical suffix, derivational suffix; found in <**ts'emxó:ythel**>, //c'əm=x^y=á·yθəl//, /'*jaw*'/, literally /'bite (upright?) on the jaw/lip'/, <**schelhó:ythel**>, //s=cəɬ=á·yθəl//, /'*upper lip*'/, <**stl'epó:ythel**>, //s=ƛ'əp=á·yθəl//, /'*lower lip*'/, <**lhts'ó:ythel**>, //ɬc'=á·yθəl//, /'*cut on the lip or jaw*'/, <**qwileyéthel**>, //q^wil=əyə́θəl//, /'*beard, mustache*'/, <**kw'esó:ythel**>, //k'^wɛ[=Aə=]s=á·yθəl//, /'*burned on the lip(s)*'/, <**melmeló:ythel**>, //məlməl=á·yθəl//, /'*blunder in speaking*'/, <**melqeleythílem**>, //məlq=əl=əyθíl=əm//, /'*forget in speaking, forget one's words*'/, <**mélets'methó:ythel**>, //mə́ləc'=məθ=á·yθəl//, /'*mixed up in speaking*'/, <**sqe'íyeqeló:ythel**>, //sqəʔíy=əqəl=á·yθəl//, /'*not fluent in speaking*'/, literally /'not know language in the lips'/, <**hó:ythel**>, //há·yθəl//, /'*finish eating*'/, phonology: blend of há·y and =á·yθəl, consonant-loss, <**qwelhoythí:lem** or **qweloythí:em**>, //q^wəl=ayθí·l=əm or q^wəl=ayθ=í·l=əm//, /'*making music*'/, <**qwelóythetel**>, //q^wɛ̀·l=á·yθəl=təl//, /'*musical instrument*'/, phonology: l → zero before =tel, <**qiqewótheló:ythel** or **qeyqewótheló:ythel**>, //qɛyqəwáθəl=á·yθəl//, /'*harelip, cleft palate*'/.

<**Ó:ywoses**>, df //ʔá·ywasəs or ʔɛ́·[=Aá·=]y=was=əs//, PLN /'*village or settlement on the west side of the Fraser River at Emory Creek by Frank Malloway's fish camp, Albert Flat (Yale Indian Reserve #5)*'/, ASM ['just north of the mouth of Emory Creek'], Elder's comment: "from <**s'ó:yelwelh**> /s=ʔá·y=əlwəɬ/ *on both sides*", comment: can't be from <**s'ó:yelwelh**> directly since <**Ó:ywoses**> has no trace of <**=elwelh**> *on the side* or of <**s=**> *stative*, but would have to be from the same root, <**ó:y**>, which could be <**á:y**> *keep on, continue* with <**ó(:)-ablaut**> *resultative* (or automatic when followed by lx <**=os ~ =es**> *on the face;* <**s'ó:yelwelh**> would literally be *be continued/kept on on the side(s)* and the root of <**Ó:ywoses**> would mean *kept on, continued*, possibly <**=es**> *on the face, circular object, cyclic period, dollar* or <**=wos**> meaning uncertain (affix not attested elsewhere), phonology: possible ablaut, syntactic analysis: nominal, attested by Elders Group (7/6/77), MP (1973-74) recorded in writing by SP and AD at interviews with MP (IHTTC 7/8/77), source: place names reference file #10, other sources: Wells 1965 (lst ed.):25.

<**ó'**>, free root //ʔáʔ//, ABFC /'*have a bowel movement, defecate, to shit*'/, perhaps compare with possible root in <**ó:=l=thet**> *groan*, and <**ó:=t**> *call s-o*?, phonology: rare final glottal stop, form may be imitative of a grunt, syntactic analysis: intransitive verb, attested by Elders Group, usage: the coarse translation *to shit* is given because that probably captures the same shock value of the term in Halq'eméylem, vulgar, taboo word as in English, Salish cognate: Squamish /ʔáʔ-q/ *defecate* W73:77, K69:94.

<**s'ó'**>, dnom //s=ʔáʔ//, ABFC /'*dung, feces, shit*'/, (<**s=**> *nominalizer*), syntactic analysis: nominal,

attested by Elders Group (5/14/80), usage: vulgar word with some shock value, taboo word like English *shit*, can be said for ex. when one loses a game and gets mad, Salish cognate: Squamish /s-ʔáʔ-q/ *dung* W73:87, K69:94.

<**ó'ayiwsem**>, mdls //ʔáʔ=ɛy(=)iws=əm//, ABDF ['*mess in one's pants (shit in one's pants)*'], lx <**=ay=iws**> *pants*, (<**=em**> *middle voice*), syntactic analysis: intransitive verb, attested by Elders Group (5/3/78).

<**s'óq**>, dnom //s=ʔá=q//, ANA /'*dung, excrement, feces*'/, (<**s=**> *nominalizer*), probably root <**ó'**> *defecate*, possibly <**=q**> *after, behind*, phonology: probable consonant-loss of root final glottal stop before consonant, syntactic analysis: nominal, dialects: *Matsqui*, attested by Deming, Salish cognate: Squamish /s-ʔáʔq/ *dung* and /ʔáʔq/ *defecate* W73:77,87, K69:94, probably with lexical suffix /=q/ *bottom, behind, trunk*, compare root <**ó'**> *to have a bowel movement, to defecate, to shit*, contrast <**sq'éth'**> *dung, shit.*

<**ó'ayiwsem**>, ABDF ['*mess in one's pants (shit in one's pants)*'], *see* ó'.

<**o(')el**>?, possible stem //ʔá(ʔ)əl//?, meaning uncertain.

<**s'o(')elexw**>?, df //s=ʔá(ʔ)əl=l-əx^{w}//?, WV ['*twined weave*'], possibly <**s=**> *stative or nominalizer*, probable <**=l**> *manage to/non-control transitivizer*, phonology: possible reduplication, syntactic analysis: adjective/adjectival verb?, nominal?, source: Wells 1969:16 <s'AH-uhl-'LOHq> is the only source.

Ō

<**ṓ ~ ō**>, free root //ʔó ~ ʔo//, LANG /'*oh, (yes, really [shows agreement with a public speaker]), (perhaps contrastive)*'/, EFAM, syntactic analysis: interjection, attested by Elders Group, many others at spirit dances, example: <**ṓ siyám.**>, //ʔó s=iy=ɛ́m//, /'*Yes, respected leader., (Really, respected leader.)*'/, usage: murmured during a public speech as audience reaction to show agreement with a public speaker, attested by Elders Group, RM, Deming, many others at spirit dances, <**ō kwo yálh.**>, //ʔo k^{w}a yɛ́ɬ//, /'*Oh yes (now I remember).*'/, literally /'oh yes anyway/consequential/then only now'/, comment: Suttles' translation for Musqueam /k^{w}ə/ *consequential (then)* (Suttles ca1984:15.1.17) seems like an improved translation for Upriver Halq'eméylem kwo ~ kwe also, beside translations given by Elders here, such as *anyway*; similarly Suttles' translation for Musqueam /yéɬ/ *only now, only thdn* (Suttles ca1984:4.3.1 and 18.4.14) also seems an improved translation for Upriver yálh which is cognate and is translated by EB as *now* in the example above, attested by EB, <**ō áy el te sqwóqwels.**>, //ʔo ʔɛ́y ʔəl tə s=q^{w}ɛ[=AáC$_1$ə=]l-s//, /'*He's talking without making any sense., He keeps on talking (in spite of the fact no one is listening).*'/, literally /'contrastive (or) oh keeps on just the his talking'/, comment: this example may belong under ō ~ u ~ ew ~ u- ~ -ow ~ -ew ~ we- *contrastive*, attested by Elders Group (3/13/80), <**le th'exwstélemet ō Siyám.**>, //lə θ'əx^w=sT-ə́ləmət ʔo s=iy=ɛ́m//, /'*Pity us, oh Lord.*'/, usage: part of prayer/words said before picking plants for medicine, attested by TM/DF/NP (Elders Group 3/22/78).

<**Ōhámél ~ Shxw'ōwhámél ~ Shxw'ōhámél**>, df //s(=)x^w=ʔə[=Ao=]ha=ɛ́mə́l//, PLN ['*village now called Ohamil Reserve or Laidlaw*'], (<**s(=)xw=**> *nominalizer*), probably root <**ehó**> *wrapped up*, lx <**=ámél ~ =ómél**> *part, portion (of body), member*, possibly <**ō-ablaut**> *derivational*, phonology: ō-ablaut (rare), vowel merger, syntactic analysis: nominal, last two pronunciations attested by IHTTC (8/5/77, 8/11/77), LJ (Tait)(in Elders Group 7/13/77), also <**Uhámél ~ Ōhámél**>, //ʔə[=Au=]ha=ɛ́məl ~ ʔə[=Ao=]ha=ɛ́məl//, phonology: clipped form, Elder's comment: "shortcut pronunciation", attested by IHTTC (8/11/77), other sources: Wells 1965 (lst ed.):25, source: place names reference file #57.

<**ṓwkw'**>, df //ʔówk'^{w} or ʔó·k'^{w} or ʔə́wk'^{w} or ʔi[=Aó·=]k'^{w}//, MC /'*ran out (of food, money, etc.), have no more, be finished (of food), (be empty (of container of supplies)* [EB: Cheh., Tait])'/, FOOD, ECON, probably <**ṓ:-ablaut**> *resultative*, probably root <**íkw'**> *be lost*, phonology: probable <**ṓ:-ablaut**> (rare), syntactic analysis: intransitive verb, dialects: *Chill.*, attested by Elders Group (3/72), AC, Deming, possibly compare <**á:wkw'**> *belongings*; also attested <**ú:kw'**> //ʔú·k^w ~ ʔúwk'^{w} or ʔi[=Aú·=]k'^{w}//, phonology: probable <**ú:-ablaut**> *resultative*, dialects: *Cheh., Tait*, attested by EB (12/16/75), Salish cognate: Saanich dial. of N. Straits /ʔəw'k'^{w}/ *give out, be all gone (as food)* B74a:64, Sechelt /ʔuk'^{w}-amiɬ/ *to give out (all gone), ("run out of food")* T77:28, Mainland Comox /ʔə́wk'^{w}-ə́miɬ/ *to give out, be all gone (as food)* B75prelim:76, example: <**latsel t'ó:kw' tl'okwses ṓ:kw' kwthel tále.**>, //lɛ-c-əl t'á·k'^{w} ƛ'a=k^w-s-əs ʔó·k'^{w} k'^{w}(=)θə-l tɛ́lə//, /'*I'm going home because my (near but not visible) money ran out.*'/, attested by AC, <**ulh tu ú:kw' te s'álhtel.**>, //ʔuɬ tu ʔú·k'^{w} tə s=ʔɛ́ɬ=təl//, /'*The food is nearly finished.*'/, literally /'already little more ran out the food'/, attested by EB, <**xwálqey ú:kw'**>, //x^{w}ɛ́lq=əy ʔú·k'^{w}//, /'*nearly empty*'/, attested by EB, <**ú:kw' tel tá:la**>, //ʔú·k'^{w} tə-l tɛ́·lɛ//, /'*My money ran out., I ran out of money.*'/, attested by EB, <**skw'áy kws ú:kw's.**>, //s=k'^{w}ɛ́y k^w-s ʔú·k'^{w}-s//, /'*It can't run out.*'/, attested by EB.

<**ú:kw'elets**>, ds //ʔi[=Aú·=]k'^{w}=ələc//, FOOD /'*run out of food, be out of food*'/, lx <**=elets**> *on the bottom*, phonology: ú:-ablaut, syntactic analysis: intransitive verb, syntactic comment: , Elder's comment: "don't use s'álhtel *food* with it (unlike ú:kw')", attested by EB, example: <**lámtsel kw'e**

tówel chulh le ú:kw'elets.>, //lɛ́=m-c-əl k'ʷə táwəl c-(əl)-uɬ lə ʔú·k'ʷ=ələc//, /*'I'm going to town because I'm out of food.'*/, literally /'I'm going to the (remote) town I already ambiguous past be out of food'/, attested by EB.

<**ú:kw't**>, pcs //ʔi[=Aú·=]k'ʷ=T//, FOOD [*'finish it (of food)'*], (<**=t**> *purposeful control transitivizer*), phonology: ú:-ablaut, syntactic analysis: transitive verb, attested by EB, example: <**ốwelh ú:kw'tes te s'álhtels.**>, //ʔówə=ɬ ʔú·k'ʷ=T-əs tə s=ʔɛ́ɬ=təl-s//, /*'He never finished his food.'*/, attested by EB, <**ú:kw'tlha ta'a s'álhtel.**>, //ʔú·k'ʷ=T-ɬɛ t-ɛʔɛ s=ʔɛ́ɬ=təl//, /*'Finish your food.'*/, syntactic comment: command imperative 2s, attested by EB.

<**ốkw'xatel**>, df //ʔók'ʷ=xʸə[=Aɛ=]l=təl//, HHG /*'mat, (foot mat)'*/, lx <**=xel**> *on the foot*, lx <**=tel**> *device to*, possibly <**a-ablaut**> *derivational* or perhaps phonological remainder from stress shifting, root meaning unknown, phonology: possible ablaut, regular rule of consonant-loss (of l on xel before =t...), syntactic analysis: nominal, attested by AC.

<**ố:leqw'**> or <**ố:l**> or <**o:l**> or <**éw**>, stem or root //ʔó·ləq'ʷ or ʔó·l or ʔa·l//, possible meanings of first two: *(be) suffering pain*, of the third *groan*, of the last <**éw**>, free root //ʔə́w//, DESC [*'too heavy to lift'*].

<**s'ố:leqw'**>, df //s=ʔó·ləq'ʷ or s=ʔa=Aó·=l=əq'ʷ or s=ʔa[=Aó=]·=əl=əq'ʷ//, ABDF [*'(be) suffering pain'*], (<**s=**> *stative*), possibly root <**ó:=l**> as in <**ó:=l=thet**> *groan*, possibly <**ó:-ablaut**> *resultative or continuative*, possibly <**=el**> *go, get, come, become*, possibly <**=eqw'**> meaning uncertain but perhaps *around in circles* (Galloway 1977:294) or *vigorously*, possibly compare Musqueam /**=q'ʷ**/ *vigorously?* in Suttles ca1984:14.6.41**)**, phonology: possible ó:-ablaut, syntactic analysis: intransitive verb, attested by Elders Group (10/6/76).

<**ốqwelets**>, //ʔóqʷ=əl=əc//, ANA /*'back of the body, the whole back'*/ attested by MV (Deming 4/10/80), AC, Salish cognate: Nooksack /ʔóqʷəlæ̀č/ *back* PA61, Lushootseed /s-ʔəqʷəlič/ *back (of body)* H76:661, Songish (N. Straits) /ʔəqʷəléc/ *to be behind* M68:140, example: <**li ta ốqwelets.**>, //li t-ɛ ʔóqʷ=əl=əc//, /*'He's at your back.'*/, attested by AC, see main dialect form <**óqwelets**>

<**ōqw'íles ~ ōqw'éyles**>, PLN /*'mouth of Hunter Creek, (Restmore Caves (Wells))'*/, *see* wốqw' ~ wéqw'.

<**ốts**>, free root //ʔóc//, EB /*'oats, both domestic oats and wild oats'*/, ['both *Avena sativa* and *Avena fatua*'], ACL [*'both introduced'*], syntactic analysis: nominal, attested by AC, borrowed from English <oats> or perhaps late Chinook Jargon <oats> *oats* Johnson 1978:378 (in Gibbs 1880), example: <**le pí:ltes te ốts.**>, //lə pí·l=T-əs tə ʔóc//, /*'He planted the oats.'*/, literally /'third person ambiguous past he plant s-th the oats'/, attested by AC.

< **ốwe ~ éwe**>, free root //ʔówə ~ ʔə́wə//, CJ /*'no, not be, be not'*/, ASM, LANG [*'say no'*], and its many derivations, see <**éwe ~ ốwe**> under the letter <**e**>

<**=ố:welh ~ =ốwelh ~ =ōwelh ~ =ewelh ~ =á:welh ~ =welh ~ =ewí:l**>, da //=ó·wəɬ ~ =owəɬ or =əwəɬ ~ =ɛ́·wəɬ ~ =wəɬ ~ =əwí·l//, CAN /*'canoe, boat'*/, semantic environment ['with *five* so far, kw'í:l *how many?*, and non-numerals'], SH /*'vessel, (container)'*/, HHG [*'dish'*], phonology: allomorph =ewí:l before =t *purposeful control transitivizer* as in Musqueam (Suttles p.c. 10/9/79), syntactic analysis: lexical suffix, derivational suffix, also <**=á:welh**>, //=ɛ́·wəɬ//, also <**=welh**>, //=wəɬ//, also <**=ewí:l**>, //=əwí·l//; found in <**lhq'atsesốwelh**>, //ɬq'ɛcəs=ówəɬ//, /*'five canoes (belonging to one person)'*/, contrast <**lhq'átses sléxwelh**> *five canoes (belonging to various people)*, <**q'e<u>x</u>wố:welh**>, //q'əx̣ʷ=ó·wəɬ//, /*'war canoe, largest canoe'*/, <**táyōwelh**>, //tɛ́y=owəɬ//, /*'racing canoe'*/, <**pōtốwelh**>, //pot=ówəɬ//, /*'row-boat'*/, <**xixepốwelh**>, //xʸixʸəp=ówəɬ//, /*'planing a canoe'*/, <**qep'ósōwelh**>, //qəp'=ás=owəɬ//, /*'canoe turned upside down (on land)'*/, <**t'ékwōwelh ~ t'éqwōwelh**>, //t'ə́kʷ=owəɬ (kʷ ~ qʷ)//, /*'"corking a canoe", caulking a canoe'*/, <**lhéqōwelh**>, //ɬə́q=owəɬ//, /*'patching a canoe'*/, <**t<u>x</u>wốwelh**>, //tx̣ʷ=ówəɬ//, /*'tow a canoe (through rough water)'*/,

<**xwekw'ṓwélh**>, //x^{w}ək'^{w}=ówə́l//, /'*drag a canoe*'/, <**ilemṓwelh**>, //ʔiləm=ówəɬ//, /'*carry a canoe on shoulders, portage a canoe*'/, <**élwélh**>, //ʔə́l=wə́ɬ//, /'*middle of a canoe (on inside), middle paddler(s)*'/, <**lhexelwélhtel**>, //ɬəx̣=əl=wə́ɬ=təl//, /'*cross-piece in canoe, thwart*'/, <**ts'eqw'ṓ:welh ~ ch'eqw'ṓ:welh**>, //c'əq'^{w}=ó·wəɬ//, /'*weave a cedar root basket*'/, root <**ts'éqw'**> *poke, pierce,* <**slhéq'ōwelh**>, //sɬə́q'=owəɬ//, /'*lower back*'/, literally /'(wide part? + canoe)'/, <**qwelhyṓwelh ~ qwelhyúwelh**>, //q^{w}əɬy=ówəɬ (ó ~ ú)//, /'*carved wooden spoon*'/, root <**qwelhá:y**> *driftwood,* <**xáwelh**>, //x^{y}ɛ́wəɬ//, /'*vulva, vagina*'/, (perhaps) < **t'emewí:lt**>, //t'əm=əwí·l=T//, /'*chop the inside of it out*'/, (semological comment: probably refers to a canoe),(perhaps) <**xepewí:lt**>, //x^{y}əp=əwí·l=T//, /'*plane it out inside*'/, (semological comment: probably refers to a canoe).

<**=ṓwes ~ =ṓ:wes ~ =á:wes ~ =ewes**>, da //=ówəs ~ =ó·wəs ~ =ɛ́·wəs ~ =əwəs//, CAN /'*canoe paddle, paddler(s)*'/, semantic environment ['with numbers 1-ll, kw'í:l, and non-numerals'], syntactic comment: optional?, syntactic analysis: lexical suffix, derivational suffix, also <**=á:wes**>, //=ɛ́·wəs//; found in <**lhq'átsesṓ:wes**>, //ɬq'ɛ́cəs=ó·wəs//, /'*five canoe paddles, five paddlers*'/, <**xets'ṓ:wes**>, //x^{y}əc'=ó·wəs//, /'*store canoe paddles away*'/; found in <**xets'=ét**> *store s-th away),* <**Xets'ṓ:westel**>, //x^{y}əc'=ó·wəs=təl//, /'*January moon, time to store canoe paddles away*'/, <**pōtṓwes**>, //pot=ówəs//, /'*oar*'/; found in <**pṓt**> *boat),* <**xwalxṓwes**>, //x^{w}ɛl=əx^{y}=ówəs//, /'*lift a paddle (while paddling)*'/; found in <**xwál=x**> *lift s-th),* <**ts'elts'elṓwsem ~ ts'élts'eltses**>, //c'əl=$C_1əC_2$=óws=əm ~ c'ə́l=$C_1əC_2$=cəs//, /'*repeatedly switching sides in paddling*'/, (compare <**ts'el=**> *switch* + <**=R2**> *characteristic* (or *plural*?) + <**=em**> *(middle voice), one's own* and for the second alternant: *characteristic (or plural?) + switch + in the hand),* <**yemáwéstel**>, //yəm=ɛ́wə́s=təl//, /'*wide cedar root strips for baskets*'/ (compare <**yem=**> *wide strip).*

<**ṓwestexw ~ éwestexw**>, LANG /'*deny it; say no; tell s-o to say no*'/, *see* éwe ~ ṓwe.

<**ōwéta xwlí:s**>, EFAM /'*it doesn't matter, it's useless*'/, *see* shxwlí.

<**ṓwethelh**>, CJ /'*never did, he/she/they never did*'/, *see* éwe ~ ṓwe.

<**=ṓwéx**>, da //=ówə́x̣ or =ə́w(=)əx̣//, ANA ['*on the rib(s)*'], BSK ['*slat(s)*'], possibly <**=ṓw**> *on the body*??, possibly <**=ex**> *distributive, all over*??, syntactic analysis: lexical suffix, derivational suffix; found in <**lṓwex** or **léwex**>, //l=ówəx̣ or l=ə́wəx// or possibly //lə́w=əx̣//, /'*ribs, (rib)*'/, <**th'ṓwéx**>, //θ'=ówəx̣//, /'*cedar slat basket*'/, phonology: updrifting, <**Th'ṓwxiya**>, //θ'=ówx̣=iyɛ//, /'*name of Cannibal Ogress who caught children in a cedar slat basket*'/.

<**ō'éy ~ ō éy ~ ōw'éy**>, ABFC ['*fine (in health)*'], *see* éy ~ éy:.

P

<**pákw'et**>, pcs //pɛ́k'^{w}=əT//, FIRE /'*heat it up, warm it up, smoke s-th over a fire*'/, semantic environment ['fish, buckskin, meat, hides, etc.'], FOOD, HUNT, FSH, (<**=et**> *purposeful control transitivizer*), syntactic analysis: transitive verb, Salish cognate: Lushootseed /p'ák'^{w}-ad/ *warm it* H76:350, attested by Elders Group (2/18/76), others, compare with <**pó(:)kw'**> *smoked fish* and less likely with <**pékw'**> *puff out (smoke, dust, powder)*?, contrast <**p'ákw'et**> *repair s-th, fix it up.*

<**pálchmel**>, free root //pɛ́lcməl//, [pǽlčməl], SOCT /'*Frenchman, French person*'/, phonology: by regular shifts for loan words /f/ → /p/, /r/ not C_V drops, /ɛ/ → /ɛ/, /n/ → /l/, /č/ → /c/[č], /m/ → /m/, /ə/ → /ə/, syntactic analysis: nominal, attested by BHTTC, borrowed from English <Frenchman>.

<**pálétst**>, df //pɛ́l(=)əc=T or pɛ́l=ə[=´=]c=T//, WATR ['*skim it off*'], FOOD, root meaning unknown but probably (as in Squamish) *to skin*, probably <**=ets**> *on the surface/top/back*, possibly <=´=> *derivational*, phonology: possible stress-shift, syntactic analysis: transitive verb, Salish cognate: Squamish /pál-t/ *to skim (tr.)* W73:237, K67:249, Saanich /p'é·lt/ *to skim [s-th] off* B74a:76.

<**Páléxel ~ Paléxel**>, ds //pɛ̀lə́=x^{y}əl//, [pælɪ́x^{y}ɪl], PLN ['*canyon area on Chehalis Creek just above (upriver or north from) the main highway bridge (esp. the first cliff on the east side) [means one-legged]*'], literally /'one-legged (refers to character in a legend about the place)'/, NUM, ANAH, probably root <**pálé**> *one* (survives only in this place name), lx <**=xel**> *on the foot, on the leg*, syntactic analysis: nominal, attested by Elders Group (8/24/77), Chehalis trip with EL and EB and NP (9/27/77), source: place names reference file #234, other sources: Boas 1895 (Bertz)(1980 version:33) for the story and character's name, Salish cognate: Sechelt /pála/ *one* T77:7, Thompson (Lytton dial.) /páyaʔ/ *one* B74c:1.

<**pá:pa**>, df //pɛ́·pɛ//, DESC /'*woolly, fluffy*'/, ANA, CLO, WV, possibly <**R7=** or **=C1V1**> reduplication of an old type, perhaps *characteristic*, phonology: reduplication, syntactic analysis: adjective/adjectival verb, attested by BHTTC, Elders Group, Salish cognate: Squamish /páʔpa/ *woolly, fuzzy* W73:292, K69:42.

<**pá:píth'a**>, ds //pɛ́·pɛ=íθ'ɛ//, CLO /'*flannelette, velvet, woolly material, fluffy material, soft material*'/, WV, semantic environment ['blanket (léxwtel), wool, etc.'], lx <**=íth'a**> *clothing, material, fabric*, phonology: vowel merger, reduplication, syntactic analysis: nominal, attested by Elders Group, also <**papíth'a**>, //pɛ́:pɛ=íθ'ɛ//, phonology: possible shortening in fast speech, possible stress-shift, attested by IHTTC.

<**xwpopó:s**>, ds //x^w=pɛ[=Aa=]pɛ=á·s or x^w=pɛ[=Aa=]pɛ=Aa=əs//, ANA /'*(have a) hairy face, (have) hair on the face, (have a woolly face)*'/, lx <**xw=**> *derivational* perhaps *have* perhaps required by <**=ó:s**> and some other suffixes, possibly *always*, (<**ó-ablaut on root á or a**> *derivational* but automatic with =ó:s), phonology: ó-ablaut on root á or a triggered by =ó:s, vowel merger, syntactic analysis: intransitive verb, adjective/adjectival verb?, attested by AC, Deming, IHTTC, also <**popó:s**>, //pɛ[=Aa=]pɛ=á·s//, attested by IHTTC.

<**pá:píth'a**>, CLO /'*flannelette, velvet, woolly material, fluffy material, soft material*'/, *see* pá:pa.

<**pas ~ pes**>, bound root //pɛs ~ pəs meaning uncertain//.

<**pespesó:ythílem**>, ds //C_1əC_2=pəs=á·yθ(əl)=íl=əm or pəs=C_1əC_2=á·yθ(əl)=íl=əm//, ABFC ['*make one's mouth like one's going to cry*'], probably <**=R2**> *characteristic*, lx <**=ó:ythel**> *on the lips, chin, jaw*, (<**=íl**> *go, come, get, become, inceptive*, <**=em**> *middle voice*), phonology: automatic syllable-loss (el before =íl), reduplication, syntactic analysis: intransitive verb, attested by IHTTC

(8/9/77).

<**paspesítsel ~ paspasyí:tsel ~ pespesí:tsel**>, df //pɛs=C_1əC_2=ícəl ~ pəs=C_1əC_2=í·cəl ~ pɛs=C_1əC_2=yí·cəl//, EZ /'*type of bird that begs for bones or food with the song: paspes(y)í(:)tsel kw'e sth'ò:m th'ò:m th'ò:m,* probably *a song sparrow*'/, ['probably *Melospiza melodia morphna*'], ASM ['the song is variously transcribed as paspesítsel kw'e sth'ò:m th'ò:m th'ò:m (IHTTC) and as paspasyí:tsel kw'e sthóm th'óm th'óm (SP) *begging for a bone bone bone*'], (probably <**=R2**> *characteristic*), possibly <**=í(:)tsel**> *on the back, on the surface, on the top* as in <**qw'es=í:tsel**> *swallow (bird)* lit. *go in the water on the surface?* referring to its flight skimming surfaces)(cf. also Suttles ca1984:14.5.67 where Musqueam /=ícən ~ =əcən/ is given this range of meanings**,** *surface, top, back* with convincing examples, phonology: reduplication, syntactic analysis: nominal, attested by SP, IHTTC (8/3/77, 8/9/77, 8/11/77).

<**paspesítsel ~ paspasyí:tsel ~ pespesí:tsel**>, EZ /'*type of bird that begs for bones or food with the song: paspes(y)í(:)tsel kw'e sth'ò:m th'ò:m th'ò:m,* probably *a song sparrow*'/, *see* pas ~ pes.

<**Pástel**>, free root //pɛ́stəl//, SOCT ['*American*'], PLN /'*America, United States*'/, syntactic analysis: nominal, attested by Deming (3/15/79)(SJ, MC, MV, LG), Elders Group, AC (1973), BHTTC, ME, SP, others, borrowed from Chinook Jargon <boston> /pástən/ *American* from English <Boston> Johnson 1978:258, borrowed into Lushootseed as /bástəd/ with same meaning (causing some jokes), source: place names reference file #283.

<**pá:th**>, bound root //pɛ́·θ// *bear* (original verb meaning unknown).

<**spá:th**>, dnom //s=pɛ́·θ//, EZ /'*bear (generic),* esp. *black bear,* also includes *brown bear, bear with a white breast, and grizzly bear* though these all have separate names'/, ['*Ursus spp.,* esp. *Ursus americanus altifrontalis*'], ASM ['black bears climb trees but grizzlies don't; when one talks to a bear, wolf or sasquatch, one can call it siyám *chief, respected leader*; when approaching a bear's den it is best to stand to the left of the entrance because a bear always turns right when it comes out; bear grease is best for cooking, doesn't taste strong either; some people refuse to kill or eat bears because they look human when skinned; the old people had a tradition that bears and other animals took off their skins when at home and looked more like people'], MED ['if you rub your feet (and usually also the rest of your body) every day with bear grease you will be a fast runner (EB 4/25/78)'], (<**s=**> *nominalizer*), syntactic analysis: nominal, attested by AC, Mrs. MJ and JL (Wells tapes), Elders Group, BJ (5/64, 12/5/64), EB, many others, contrast <**Sx̱éylmet**> *male brown/black bear with white spot on chest, proper name of such a bear if addressed*, contrast <**Sx̱éylmòt**> *female brown/black bear with white spot on chest, proper name of such a bear is addressed,* contrast <**Ts'aweyíles ~ Ts'áweyìlès**> *brown bear with a white chest,* other sources: ES /spɛ·θ/ (circumflex over ɛ) and JH /spé·θ/ *black bear*, H-T <spats> (macron over a) *bear (Ursus americanus)(black),* Salish cognate: Skagit dial. of Lushootseed /spáʔc/ *bear* H76:335, Saanich dial. of N. Straits /spéʔeθ/ *black bear* B74a:9, Samish dial. of N. Straits /spéʔes/ *black bear* G86:66, example: <**ts'q'éyx̱ spá:th**>, //c'=q'íx̣ s=pɛ́·θ//, /'*black bear*'/, <**tskwí:m spá:th ~ tskwímelqel spá:th**>, //c=kʷí·m s=pɛ́·θ ~ c=kʷím=əlqəl s=pɛ́·θ//, /'*brown bear*'/, literally /'red bear, reddish-brown bear'/, EZ ['*brown bear*'], ['*Ursus americanus cinnamomum,* also *Ursus americanus altifrontalis*'], <**kw'elốws te spá:th**>, //k'ʷəl=ów-s tə s=pɛ́·θ//, /'*bearskin, bear's hide*'/, <**kw'étslexwes te swíyeqe te spá:th.**>, //k'ʷə́c=l-əxʷ-əs tə s=wíq=ə tə s=pɛ́·θ//, /'*The man saw the bear.*'/, attested by IHTTC.

<**Spá:th**>, dnom //s=pɛ́·θ//, PLN ['*bear-shaped rock up on cliff on south side above Echo Point bay on Echo Island in Harrison Lake*'], ASM ['this rock is beside Chítmexw *an owl-shaped rock up the cliff on south side above Echo Point bay on Echo Island in Harrison Lake*'], syntactic analysis: nominal, attested by EL (6/27/78) on boat trip,

<**spathó:llh**>, ds //s=pɛθ=á·lɬ//, EZ ['*bear cub*'], ['*Ursus americanus*'], lx <**=ó:llh**> *young, offspring*, phonology: stress-shift without vowel-reduction before stressed suffix, syntactic analysis: nominal.

<**spàthélets**>, ds //s=pɛ́θ=ə́ləc//, [spæ̀θíləc], ABFC ['*bear dung*'], literally /'bear rump'/, lx <**=élets**> *on the rump, on the bottom*, phonology: downstepping, syntactic analysis: nominal, attested by SP, AK.

<**pathúyel**>, ds //pɛθ=úyəl//, HUNT ['*bear trap*'], lx <**=úyel**> *net, trap*, syntactic analysis: nominal, attested by Elders Group (11/26/75).

<**Pepá:thxetel**>, ds //C_1ə=pɛ́·θ=x^{y}ə(l)=təl//, SOCT ['*people from Semá:th (Sumas village)*'], ASM ['they were called this because it was said they all have feet shaped like a bear, (possibly also a play between Smá:th and spá:th)'], literally /'bear feet people'/, (<**R5=**> *diminutive plural*), lx <**=xel**> *(on the) foot*, lx <**=tel**> *thing to, device to*, phonology: reduplication, consonant-loss (l of xel automatically before =t...), syntactic analysis: nominal, attested by Elders Group.

<**páthet**>, pcs //pɛ́θ=əT//, TVMO ['*scatter s-th*'], (<**=et**> *purposeful control transitivizer*), syntactic analysis: transitive verb, attested by Elders Group, BHTTC.

<**pethíwet ~ pethíwét**>, ds //pɛθ=íwə(l)=T ~ pɛθ=íwə́(l)=T or pɛ[=Aə=]θ=íwə́(l)=T//, pcs, FSH ['*to take all the loose eggs out of s-th (a salmon)*'], FOOD ['*to strain s-th (for ex. fruit)*'], lx <**=íwel ~ =íwél**> *on the inside, in the bottom*, (<**=et**> *purposeful control transitivizer*), phonology: consonant-loss (automatic of l in =íwel before =t...), vowel-reduction to schwa-grade of root before stressed full-grade of suffix or possible ablaut, syntactic analysis: transitive verb, attested by NP.

<**pathúyel**>, HUNT ['*bear trap*'], *see* pá:th.

<**páth'**>, bound root //pɛ́θ'// *have animal odor/stink, have animal smell*

<**pápeth'em**>, mdls //pɛ́[=C_1ə=]θ'=əm//, SM /'*(have) animal smell (of bear, skunk, dog, etc.), (have) animal stink, (have) human smell (of underarm, body odor, etc.), (have) body odor*'/, ABFC, (<**=R1=**> *continuative*?), (<**=em**> *middle voice*), phonology: reduplication, syntactic analysis: intransitive verb, attested by Elders Group (11/10/76), Deming, also <**pápets'em**>, //pɛ́[=C_1ə=]c'=əm//, attested by Elders Group (11/10/76), compare with <**sth'épeq**> *skunk* for a metathesized version of this root, i.e., //s=pɛ[=Aə́=]θ'=M2=əq//, Salish cognate: Mainland Comox /p'áθ'm/ *body odor* G82:43 (cognate set 210), Samish dial. of N. Straits (VU) /pc'é=ŋ=sət/ (//péc'=M1=ŋ=sət//) *to get body odor* and (VU) /pəpəc'ín/ *skunk* G86:66, example: <**pápeth'em te sth'épeq.**>, //pɛ́[=C_1ə=]θ'=əm tə s=pɛ[=Aə́=]θ'=M2=əq//, [pǽpəθ'əm tə sθ'ə́pəq], /'*The skunk has animal-stink.*'/, attested by Deming.

<**sth'épeq**>, df //s=pɛ[=Aə́=]θ'=M2=əq//, EZ ['*striped skunk*'], ['*Mephitis mephitis spissigrada*'], ASM ['the skunk predicts "spring fever" because in December or so it lets out a different smell, baby striped skunks have a different name, they have white spots mixed with black (this may be the spotted skunk as well as baby striped skunk), they squeak'], MED ['skunk oil is medicine for earache (EF)'], (<**s=**> *nominalizer*), root <**páth'**> as in <**pápeth'em**> *have animal stink, have body odor*, <**é-ablaut**> *durative*, <**metathesis**> *derivational*, lx <**=eq**> *on the penis* (close to the location of the scent gland under the tail), phonology: ablaut, metathesis of consonants, syntactic analysis: nominal, attested by AC, BJ (5/10/64, 12/5/64), AK (11/21/72), Elders Group (3/29/79), EF (Deming 9/21/78), ME (11/21/72), other sources: ES /sθ'ə́pəq/ *striped skunk*, JH /sθə́pəq/ *skunk*, Salish cognate: Shuswap /s-c'ípəq/ *skunk* K74:177, for the root connection also suggestive are Samish dial. of NSt /pəpəc'ín/ *skunk* and /pc'é=ŋ=sət/ *get body odor* G86a:66, and possibly Sechelt /p'álac'/ *skunk* T77:9, contrast <**selíléx̲**> *spotted skunk (Spilogale gracilis latifrons), baby striped skunk (Mephitis mephitis spissigrada)*, example: <**emímel sth'épeq**>, //ʔəmíməl s=pɛ[=Aə́=]θ'=M2=əq//, /'*small skunk (with its stripes)*'/, attested by ME (11/21/72), <**slós te**

spú'amels te sth'épeq ?>, //s=lás-s tə s=púʔ=ɛməl-s tə s=pɛ[=Aə́=]θ'=M2=əq//, /'*skunk oil*'/, literally /'oil of the stink-sac of the skunk'/, attested by EF (Deming 9/21/78).

<**sth'íth'peq**>, dmn //s=C_1í=θ'əpəq//, EZ ['*little skunk*'], (<**R4=**> *diminutive*), phonology: reduplication, syntactic analysis: nominal, attested by AK (11/21/72).

<**S'épek ~ Í'pek ~ S'í'pek**>, dmn //s=Aʔ=θ'ə́p=əq=F ~ C_1í=Aʔ=θ'ə́p=əq=F ~ s=C_1í=Aʔ=θ'ə́p=əq=F//, [sʔÍʔpək ~ ʔíʔpək ~ sʔíʔpək], EZ ['*Skunk (name in story)*'], N, (//=Aʔ=// (consonant ablaut, replaces following consonant with glottal stop /ʔ/)> *derivational or diminutive*), (<**R4=**> *diminutive*), (<**=F**> (fronting of postvelars to velars, i.e., q → k, etc.) *diminutive*), phonology: ablaut, ablaut of consonants, metathesis of consonants, reduplication, fronting, syntactic analysis: nominal, attested by AK (11/21/72).

<**páwta**>, free root //pɛ́wtɛ//, MC ['*powder*'], phonology: by regular shifts for loan words: /d/ → /t/, final /r/ drops, syntactic analysis: nominal, attested by Elders Group, borrowed from English <powder> or Chinook Jargon <powder> *powder* itself from English Johnson 1978:390.

<**páx̲**>, bound root //pɛ́x̣ *spread apart*//.

<**páx̲et**>, pcs //pɛ́x̣=əT//, ABFC /'*spread the eyelids open with the fingers (done to oneself or to someone else), (*probably also *spread s-th apart)*'/, (<**=et**> *purposeful control transitivizer*), syntactic analysis: transitive verb, attested by IHTTC, Salish cognate: Lushootseed /páx̣/ *spread* H76:335.

<**spapx̲íwel**>, strs //s=pɛ[=C_1ə=]x̣=íwəl//, ABFC /'*spread one's legs (while sitting for example), (be spread in the bottom)*'/, literally /'be spread in the bottom'/, (<**s=**> *stative*), (<**=R1=**> *resultative*), lx <**=íwel**> *on the inside, insides, in the bottom, in the rump, in the rectum*, phonology: reduplication, vowel-loss of e in reduplication, syntactic analysis: adjective/adjectival verb, intransitive verb?, attested by Deming.

<**px̲íwét**>, pcs //pɛx̣=íwə́(l)=T//, ABFC ['*spread apart s-o's legs*'], literally /'purposely spread s-o apart on the inside/in the bottom/rectum'/, lx <**=íwel**> *on the inside, insides, in the bottom, in the rump, in the rectum*, (<**=t**> *purposeful control transitivizer*), phonology: consonant-loss (automatic of l in =íwel before =t), syntactic analysis: transitive verb, attested by Elders Group (1/25/78).

<**pex̲ó:lésem**>, mdls //pəx̣=á·ləs=əm//, ABFC ['*open both one's eyes real wide*'], lx <**=ó:les**> *in the eyes, in the eyelids*, (<**=em**> *middle voice*), phonology: vowel-reduction and stress-shift of root before stressed full-grade of suffix, updrifting on penultimate syllable, syntactic analysis: intransitive verb, attested by IHTTC, compare with <**píx̲eya**> *have a nightmare*?.

<**spex̲elís**>, stvi //s=pɛx̣=əlís//, CLO /'*(be) tight-fitting (of clothes, can't be quite buttoned)*'/, semantic environment ['of pants, shirt, etc.'], literally /'be spread apart on the buttons'/, (<**s=**> *stative*), lx <**=elís**> *on the teeth, on the buttons*, phonology: vowel-reduction in root before stressed full-grade of suffix, syntactic analysis: adjective/adjectival verb, attested by SJ (4/10/80).

<**spepíx̲**>, strs //s=pɛ[=C_1əAí=]x̣//, CLO /'*(be) tight-fitting (of clothes, can't be quite buttoned)*'/, literally /'be spread apart resultative'/, (<**s=**> *stative*), (<**=R1= and í-ablaut**> *resultative*), phonology: reduplication, ablaut, vowel-reduction of root to schwa-grade before stressed infix, syntactic analysis: adjective/adjectival verb, attested by AH, SJ, compare with <**píx̲=eya**> *have a nightmare* for perhaps the same root and ablaut.

<**páx̲et**>, ABFC /'*spread the eyelids open with the fingers (done to oneself or to someone else), (*probably also *spread s-th apart)*'/, *see* páx̲.

<**páyéts'em**>, df //pɛ́yə́c'=əm//, FIRE /'*(to spark), explode with sparks and make sparky noises*'/, (<**=em**> *middle voice* or *intransitive verbalizer, get, have*), syntactic analysis: intransitive verb, attested by Elders Group, Salish cognate: Squamish /píč'-m/ *to spark (cause sparks)* beside /pə́-pič'-

m/ *be emitting sparks* and /píč’-iʔn/ *to flash* W73:244,102, K67:250,248, K69:43, Sechelt /pič’-ím/ *spark* T77:8 beside /píč’ím/ *sparks flying* B83pc, Twana /p’áyč’əb/ *spark, sparkling* NT79 in G82:9 (cognate set 14b).

<**pá:yts'em**>, cts //pɛ́[-·-]yc’=əm//, FIRE /'*sparking, sparkling, exploding with sparks and making sparky noises, making sparky noises*'/, ASM ['a fire can do this or fireworks that shoot up and then burst with sparkles making little popping noises'], semantic environment ['fire, fireworks'], LT, SD, also <**pá:yth’em**>, //pɛ́[-·-]yθ’=əm//, /'*lots of sparks going up at the same time*'/, attested by RG & EH (4/10/99 Ling332), (<**-:-**> *continuative*), phonology: vowel-loss of e in root after lengthening of preceding syllable, prob. phonetically caused rather than morphologically caused, syntactic analysis: intransitive verb, attested by Elders Group (6/11/75, 4/23/80), also LT ['*sparkling (with reflections)*'], semantic environment ['ring, eyes, etc.'], attested by DF (4/23/80), also /'*lots of sparks*'/, attested by Elders Group (5/28/75), also /'*spark (of a fire), be sparking*'/, attested by Elders Group (6/11/75), example: <**pá:yts'em te héyeqw.**>, //pɛ́[-·-]yc’=əm tə hɛ́=yəqʷ//, /'*The fire is sparking.*'/.

<**pá:yewsem**>, CH /'*crossing oneself, (making the sign of the Cross)*'/, *see* pó:y.

<**pá:yts'em**>, FIRE /'*sparking, sparkling, exploding with sparks and making sparky noises, making sparky noises*'/, *see* páyéts'em.

<**peh** or **pó(:)h**>, bound root //pəh or pá(·)h *blow*//.

<**pehá:ls**>, sas //pəh=ɛ́·ls//, WETH ['*blow (wind)*'], (<**=á:ls**> *structured activity non-continuative*), syntactic analysis: intransitive verb, attested by IHTTC, Deming, example: <**ulh me pehá:ls.**>, //ʔuɬ mə pəh=ɛ́·ls//, /'*It started to blow.*'/, literally /'already start to/come to blow wind'/, attested by Deming.

<**spehá:ls**>, dnom //s=pəh=ɛ́·ls//, WETH ['*wind*'], (<**s=**> *nominalizer*), syntactic analysis: nominal, attested by AC, BJ (5/64, 12/5/64), Elders Group, Deming, other sources: ES /spəhɛ́·ls/ *wind*, JH /spəhé·ls/ *the wind*, example: <**híkw spehá:ls**>, //híkʷ s=pəh=ɛ́·ls//, /'*storm, heavy wind*'/, literally /'big wind'/, attested by BJ (12/5/64), <**hí:kw te spehá:ls li kw'e x̱ó:tsa.**>, //hí[=·=]kʷ tə s=pəh=ɛ́·ls li k’ʷə x̣á·cɛ//, /'*A big wind hit the lake.*'/, literally /'the wind is big at the (remote/distant) lake'/, attested by AC, <**timéthet te spehá:ls.**>, //tim=ə[=´=]T-ət tə s=pəh=ɛ́·ls//, /'*The wind is hard.*'/, attested by Deming, <**chémq te spehá ls.**>, //cə́mq tə s=pəh=ɛ́·ls//, [čímq tə spəhǽ·ls], /'*The wind has stopped.*'/, dialects: *Cheh.*, attested by Deming (3/31/77), also <**tsémq te spehá ls.**>, //cə́mq tə s=pəh=ɛ́·ls//, [címq tə spəhǽ·ls], also /'*The wind stopped blowing.*'/, attested by Elders Group (4/16/75), also <**líqwel te spehá ls.**>, //líqʷ=əl tə s=pəh=ɛ́·ls//, dialects: *Chill.*, attested by Deming (3/31/77), <**le chémq te spehá:ls.**>, //lə cə́mq tə s=pəh=ɛ́·ls//, /'*The wind stopped.*'/, attested by Elders Group (3/23/77).

<**pehó:mő:lh**>, df //pá·h=ə[=M2=]m=ó·ɬ or pá·h=ə[=M2=]m=ówəɬ or páh=ə[=M2=·=]m=ó·ɬ//, EZ /'*big pretty frog, bullfrog with colors on his back*'/, ['*Rana catesbeiana,* and prob. *Rana clamitans*'], ACL ['*both are introduced species*'], probably root <**pá(:)h ~ peh**> *blow* due to frogs’ apparent blowing of cheeks, (<**metathesis**> *derivational* perhaps *characteristic*), possibly <**=:=**> *continuative*, <**=óllh**> *young, offspring/child,* possibly <**ō-ablaut**> *derivational*, phonology: probable metathesis, syntactic analysis: nominal, attested by Elders Group (3/1/72).

<**pípehò:m**>, df //C_1í=pá·h=ə[=M2=]m or C_1í=páh=ə[=M2=·=]m//, [pípəhà·m], EZ /'*frog, (*esp. *Northwestern toad,* if generic also includes the *tree toad* and recent introductions the *bullfrog* and *green frog,* and the *tailed toad, red-legged frog,* and *western spotted frog),* (if generic may also include *water frog that lives in springs and keeps the water cold* [Halq'eméylem name unknown to Elders Group on 1/30/80], and a *huge pretty frog (bigger than pípehò:m) that has supernatural powers and cries like a baby [sx̱ex̱ómōlh ~ wex̱ó:mō:lh]), (big frog with warts* [AD])'/, ['family

Ranidae and family *Bufonidae*, esp. *Bufo boreas boreas* and recent introductions *Rana catesbeiana* and *Rana clamitans*, and *Ascaphus truei, Rana aurora aurora,* and *Rana pretiosa pretiosa*'], literally /'(prob.) little continuous blower/puffer'/, (<**R4=**> *diminutive*), (<**metathesis type 2**> *derivational* perhaps here *nominalizer*), possibly <=:=> *continuative*, phonology: reduplication, metathesis, perhaps lengthening, syntactic analysis: nominal, attested by Elders Group (3/1/72), AC, BJ (12/5/64),, other sources: H-T <pepahóm> (macron over e) *frog (Rana sp.)*, also /'*big frog with warts*'/, attested by AD (7/6/79), example: <**(qí:qel, ts'áts'ets'tl'ím) te pípehò:m.**>, //(C_1í=qəl, C_1ɛ́=C_1ə=c'ƛ'ɛ=m=ím) tə C_1í=páh=ə[=M2=·=]m//, /'*The frog (is naughty, is hopping).*'/, usage: lyrics to the Híltu or Heel-toe song, attested by BHTTC.

<**pepípehò:m**>, pln //C_1ə=C_1í=páh=ə[=M2=·=]m//, EZ ['*frogs*'], (<**R5=**> *diminutive plural*, R4= *diminutive* but crystallized since the stem is not glossed *little frog* thus the second reduplication is allowed), (<**metathesis**> *derivational* perhaps *nominalizer*, <=:=> *continuative* perhaps), phonology: double reduplication, metathesis, possible lengthening, syntactic analysis: nominal, attested by EB.

<**pipehó:mó:llh**>, dmn //C_1í=páh=ə[=M2=·=]m=á·ɬ//, EZ /'*baby frog,* probably also *tadpole*'/, lx <**=ó:llh**> *young, offspring*, phonology: reduplication, metathesis, possible lengthening, syntactic analysis: nominal, attested by Elders Group, AC, example: <**qé:x̱ te pipehó:mó:llh.**>, //qə́[=·=]x̣ tə C_1í=páh=ə[=M2=·=]m=á·ɬ//, /'*(There's) a LOT of baby frogs.*'/, phonology: emphatic lengthening of schwa (e), the only circumstance where e can appear long, attested by AC.

<**pipehomá:lews**>, ds //C_1í=páh=ə[=M2=·=]m=ɛ́·ləws//, EB /'*common plantain, ribbed plantain, called "frog leaf"*'/, ['*Plantago major, Plantago lanceolata*'], literally /'frog leaf'/, ASM ['so named because the frog likes to sit on the leaf'], MED ['leaves rumpled (yékw'et) and used as a poultice, also as an antiseptic applied to an open wound or blister, it can also draw out thorns or slivers, it is also used as medicine for rheumatism and the tea is good for stomach trouble'], lx <**=á:lews**> *leaf*, phonology: reduplication, metathesis, possible lengthening but then shortening and loss of stress on root before stressed full-grade suffix, syntactic analysis: nominal, attested by AC, LG, also <**slháwels te pípehò:m**>, //s=ɬɛ́w=əl-s tə C_1í=páh=ə[=M2=·=]m//, literally /'mat(tress) of the frog, frog's mat(tress)'/, attested by AC, others.

<**pó:t**>, pcs //páh=T//or //pə[=Aá=]h=T//or //pə[-Aá-]h=T//, ABFC /'*blow, blow s-th*'/, WETH, (<**=t ~ =et**> *purposeful control transitivizer*), comment: the transitive object is usually not expressed, thus showing this form is moving toward being a crystallized CVC root, phonology: possible vowel merger or consonant merger with h, syntactic analysis: transitive verb, attested by AC, Elders Group (3/1/72, 2/19/75, 2/27/80), AD, other sources: ES /pá·t/ *blow*, example: <**tsel pó:t. ~ chel pó:t.**>, //c-əl pá·=T//, /'*I blow.*'/, attested by Elders Group (3/1/72); found in <**pó:tes.**>, //pá·=T-əs//, /'*He blew it.*'/, attested by AC, example: <**pótlha ta' sméteqsel.**>, //pá·=T-ɬɛ t-ɛʔ s=mə́t=əqsəl//, /'*Blow your nose.*'/, literally /'blow =it -command imperative your snot'/, attested by AD (Aug. 1980).

<**pepó:tem**>, rsls //C_1ə=pá·=T-əm or C_1ə=pá·=təm//, ABFC ['*blown*'], MUS, WETH, (<**R5=**> *resultative*), probably <**=t**> *purposeful control transitivizer* and <**-em**> *passive* forming <**=tem**> *participial*, phonology: reduplication, syntactic analysis: adjective/adjectival verb, example: <**pepó:tem qwló:ythetel**>, //C_1ə=pá·=T-əm qʷɛl=á·yθə(l)=təl//, MUS /'*flute, wind instrument, blown musical instrument*'/, literally /'blown musical instrument (talk =in lips =device)'/, (semological comment: the root of *musical instrument* is *talk* which is something that birds and animals do in their own languages, thus the bird-song would be included in *talk*), attested by Elders Group (11/26/75).

<**pepepó:tem ~ pépepò:tem ~ pepepótem**>, df //C_1ə=C_1ə=pá·=T-əm or C_1ə=C_1ə=pá·=təm//, EB ['*rattlesnake plantain*'], ['*Goodyera oblongifolia*'], ASM ['grows under fir trees'], MED ['leaves used as a poultice and antiseptic after peeling the upper and lower surfaces apart (one can blow

into them then) and applying the moist inside part to the wound or open blister (a blister of mine healed in two days from such application); tea from the roots is good for stomach trouble as ulcer medicine, roots were chewed and the juice swallowed for coughs, especially whooping cough medicine'], possibly <**R5=**> *diminutive plural*, possibly <**second R5=**> *resultative*, possibly <**=tem**> *participial*, from <**=t**> *purposeful control transitivizer* plus <**-em**> *passive*, (semological comment: literally perhaps *many little blown things* after the fact that the leaves are small and can be blown into easily as was shown to me when SP did this and then applied it to a blister I got while we were digging cedar roots for baskets–the blister was healed the next morning), phonology: double reduplication (with same reduplication type), syntactic analysis: nominal, attested by SP, AD, JL (at Fish Camp 7/19/79).

<**pótel**>, dnom //pá(=T)=təl//, CAN ['*(a) sail*'], literally /'device to blow'/, lx <**=tel**> *device to*, phonology: possible consonant merger, syntactic analysis: nominal, attested by Elders Group.

<**spotelálá**>, dnom //s=pa=təl=ɛ́lɛ́//, CAN ['*mast on a canoe or boat*'], literally /'something that's a container of a sail'/, (<**s=**> *nominalizer*), lx <**=tel**> *device to*, lx <**=álá**> *container of*, phonology: stress-shift from root without vowel-reduction before stressed full-grade of suffix, syntactic analysis: nominal, attested by Elders Group.

<**Spópetes**>, df //s=pá[=C_1ə=]t=əs//, PLN /'*Katz river-bank, Ruby Creek settlement, village on north bank of Fraser River just below (west of) the mouth of Ruby Creek*'/, literally /'something that (where) it's blowing on the face (of riverbank)'/, Elder's comment: "so named because it's always windy there", (<**s=**> *nominalizer*), (<**=R1=**> *continuative*), lx <**=es**> *on the face*, phonology: reduplication, syntactic analysis: nominal, attested by SP (8/28/75), IHTTC, JL (4/3/78), source: place names reference file #44, other sources: Wells 1965 (lst ed.):25.

<**pehá:ls**>, WETH ['*blow (wind)*'], *see* peh or pó(:)h.

<**pehó:mő:lh**>, EZ /'*big pretty frog, bullfrog with colors on his back*'/, *see* peh or pó(:)h.

<**pékcha**>, free root //pə́kcɛ//, ACL /'*picture, photo, (drawing, etc.)*'/, PLAY ['*face card*'], syntactic analysis: nominal, attested by SJ, MV, Elders Group, borrowed from English <picture>/pɪ́kčɚ/, example: <**x̱álqem pékcha**>, //x̣ɛ́lq=əm pə́kcɛ//, /'*moving pictures, movies*'/, attested by SJ (Deming 8/10/78), also <**x̱álqem xwíthiya**>, //x̣ɛ́lq=əm xʷíθ=iya//, Elder's comment: "may be okay for *moving pictures*", attested by SJ, comment: xw may be sic for x̱w, <**wéte pékcha**>, //ʔəwə= ́tɛ pə́kcɛ//, /'*(There's) no face cards.*'/, attested by Elders Group (9/14/77).

<**pekchá:m**>, df //pəkcɛ=ɛ́m or pəkcɛ=ɛ́·m or pəkcɛ=əm or pəkcɛ= ́=əm//, ACL /'*take a picture, to photograph*'/, (<**=á(:)m** or **=em**> *intransitive verbalizer, get, make*), phonology: vowel merger (yields the non-schwa vowel of a pair of adjacent vowels and often adds length and stress), possible lengthening, syntactic analysis: intransitive verb, attested by SJ and MV (2/17/78).

<**pekchá:m**>, ACL /'*take a picture, to photograph*'/, *see* pékcha.

<**pékw' ~ péqw'**>, free root or stem //pə́k'ʷ ~ pə́q'ʷ or pəh=k'ʷ ~ pəh=q'ʷ//, LAND /'*smoke puffing out, (puff out (dust, powder, plant spores, seed fluff, light snow, smoke), form puffs of dust)*'/, EB, WETH, MC, possible connection with <**peh** or **pó(:)h**> *blow* + <**=kw' ~ =ekw'**> *round, around in circles* or <**=qw' ~ =eqw'**> *around in circles*, phonology: the root final h would drop before the suffix, also note the same variation of root vowel, syntactic analysis: intransitive verb, attested by AD and NP (4/11/80), Salish cognate: Squamish root /pə́k'ʷ/ *form puffs of dust, smoke or spray* W73:205, K67:249, Lushootseed root /p(a)q'ʷ (~ pə́q'ʷ)/ *smoke from fire* H76:334-335.

<**pekw'ém**>, mdls //pəkʷ=ə́m or pə́k'ʷ=ə[=M2=]m or pək'ʷ=ə[= ́=]m//, LAND /'*the dust flew, it's dusty*'/, EB ['*it burst (of spores or seed fluff)*'], possibly <**metathesis or = ́=**> *resultative or non-continuative*?, (<**=em**> *middle voice*), phonology: stress-shift unless the root is inherently

unstressed, stressed intransitivizer, possible metathesis, syntactic analysis: intransitive verb, attested by AC, example: <**la pekw'ém**>, //lɛ pək'ʷ=ə́m//, /'*It's dusty.*'/, attested by AC, <**lulh pekw'ém te sp'áq'em.**>, //lə=uɬ pək'ʷ=ə́m tə s=p'ɛ́q'=əm//, /'*The flower has burst (said of white stuff in fireweed, cottonwood or dandelion).*'/, attested by AC.

<**spekw'ém**>, dnom //s=pək'ʷ=ə́m or s=pə́k'ʷ=ə[=M2=]m or s=pək'ʷ=ə[=´=]m//, EB /'*bloom or (plant) fuzz (spore, pollen, seed fluff) after it bursts*'/, LAND, (<**s=**> *nominalizer*), phonology: stressed intransitivizer or metathesis or stress-shift, syntactic analysis: nominal, attested by AC, other sources: ES + JH /spk'ʷə́m/ *dust*, Salish cognate: Songish dial. of N. Straits /spkʷə́ŋ/ *dust, smoke* Mitchell 1968 (quoted in G82:45 set 233), Lummi dial. of N. Straits /spək'ʷəŋ/ (stress omitted) *dusty* (Demers 1982p.c.).

<**pékw'em**>, cts //pə[-´-]k'ʷ=əm or pək'ʷ=ə́[-M2-]m//, LAND ['*dust (is flying)*'], (<**-´- or metathesis**> *continuative*), phonology: stress-shift or metathesis, syntactic analysis: intransitive verb, attested by AC, Salish cognate: Straits: Lummi /pə́k'ʷəŋ/ *smoke, dust is spreading*, Saanich,Songish,Clallam /pə́k'ʷəŋ/ *smoking*, Sooke /pə́k'ʷəŋʔ/ *smoking* (all TTE74:192), Samish /pə́k'ʷəŋ'/ (where glottalized /ŋ/ is one marker of *continuative*) *dust/smoke is spreading, dust is flying* G86:65, Squamish /s-pə́k'ʷ-m/ *dust* W73:87, K67:249.

<**spólqw'**>, strs //s=pə[=Aá=lə=]q'ʷ//, DESC ['*be powdered*'], (<**s=**> *stative*), (<**ó-ablaut ~ ó:-ablaut**> *resultative*, <**=le=**> *plural*), phonology: ablaut, infixed plural, syntactic analysis: adjective/adjectival verb, attested by IHTTC, Deming (2/17/78), also <**spó:lqw'**>, //s=pə[=Aá·=lə=]q'ʷ//, attested by MH (Deming 1/4/79), example: <**spólqw' seplí:l**>, //s=pə[=Aá=lə=]q'ʷ səplí·l//, /'*flour*'/, literally /'powdered bread'/, attested by IHTTC, Deming (2/17/78), also <**spó:lqw' seplí:l**>, //s=pə[=Aá·=lə=]q'ʷ səplí·l//, attested by MH, <**léts'e lesák spólqw' seplí:l**>, //lə́c'ə ləsɛ́k s=pə[=Aá=lə=]q'ʷ səplí·l//, /'*a (one) sack of flour*'/, attested by Deming.

<**pókw'em**>, df //pə[=Aá=]k'ʷ=əm//, EB ['*when plant fuzz blows*'], LAND ['*when snow is so light it is blown by the wind like fuzz*'], probably <**ó-ablaut**> *resultative* or *derivational*, (<**=em**> *middle voice* or *intransitivizer*), phonology: ablaut, syntactic analysis: intransitive verb, attested by EB, Salish cognate: Shuswap /x-pq'ʷ-úm, c-x-pəq'ʷ-st-és/, root /puq'ʷ/ *to load (a gun)* and /(n-)pəq'ʷ-mín/ *gunpowder*, beside? Coeur d'Alene /p'aq'ʷ/ *powder* both in K74:143.

<**pó:lqw'em**>, pln //pə[=Aá·=lə=]q'ʷ=əm//, LAND ['*dust*'], EB, (<**=el=**> *plural*), probably <**ó:-ablaut**> *resultative* or *derivational*, phonology: ablaut, infixed plural, fronting/backing, vowel-loss in infix due to lengthened ablaut, syntactic analysis: nominal, intransitive verb?, attested by AC, Salish cognate: Sechelt /páɬuq'ʷ/ *dust* T77:8, Pentlatch <pálˇōkōm> (macron over a, underline under k, prob. /páɬuq'ʷum/) *wind whirls up dust* (Boas 1886 Pentlatch field notes), perhaps Thompson (Lytton dial.) /spiʔyukʷ/ *dust* (B74c:6), also <**spóléqwem**>, //s=pə[=Aá=lə=]qʷ=əm//, attested by BJ (12/5/64) checked, phonology: updrifting, glottalization perhaps missed?, example: <**spóléqwems te tèmèxw**>, //s=pə[=Aá=lə=]qʷ=əm-s tə tə̀mə̀xʷ//, /'*dust of the earth*'/, attested by BJ (12/5/64).

<**pópkw'em**>, df //pə[=Aá=C_1ə=]k'ʷ=əm//, EB /'*puffball,* probably *giant puffball* and *gemmed puffball,* and possibly *other species*'/, ['probably *Calvatia gigantea* and *Lycoperdon perlatum/gemmatum* and possibly other *Calvatia* or *Lycoperdon* spp.'], ASM ['those growing around Popkum were sometimes eaten and gave their name to that place, when they get old they burst and send out spores which can harm one's eyes'], MED ['spore powder was rubbed on a baby's navel to prevent bed-wetting'], (<**ó-ablaut**> *resultative*, <**=R1=**> *derivational*), (<**=em**> *middle voice*), phonology: ablaut, reduplication, syntactic analysis: nominal, attested by EP (IHTTC), also <**pópqw'em**>, //pə[=Aá=C_1ə=]q'ʷ=əm//, attested by AC.

<**Pópkw'em**>, df //pə[=Aá=C_1ə=]k'ʷ=əm//, PLN /'*village on east bank of Fraser River near the*

outlet from Cheam Lake, Popkum Indian village'/, phonology: ablaut, reduplication, syntactic analysis: nominal, attested by JL and AK (4/7/78), IHTTC, DM (12/4/64, Wells tapes transcript, new p.172), also <**Pópqw'em**>, //pə[=Aá=C_1ə=]q'^{w}=əm//, literally /'puffballs'/, attested by AC 8/29/70, source: place names reference file #59, other sources: Wells 1965 (lst ed.):25, Salish cognate: Squamish /pə́pk'^{w}-m/ *to smoke (form clouds or puffs of dust)* W73:240, K67:248.

<**pékw'em**>, LAND ['*dust (is flying)*'], *see* pékw' ~ péqw'.

<**pekw'ém**>, LAND /'*the dust flew, it's dusty*'/, *see* pékw' ~ péqw'.

<**pél** > **(~** <**pí:l** > by now**)**, bound root //pə́l (~ pə́[=Aí·=]l)// *planted, get buried*/, comment: <**í:-ablaut**> form with crystallized *resultative*.

<**pí:lt**>, pcs //pə[=Aí·=]l=T or pí·l=T//, LAND /'*bury s-th, plant s-th*'/, EB, HARV, CH, probably <**í:-ablaut**> *resultative* or probably now just *derivational*, <**=t**> *purposeful control transitivizer*, phonology: ablaut, syntactic analysis: transitive verb, attested by EB, AC, Salish cognates: Musqueam /pə́n/ *to get buried* WS82pc, Squamish root /pən/ *be buried, be in the soil or dirt* as in /pə́n-t/ *bury (tr.)*, Sechelt /pən-áš/ *to bury* T77, Mainland Comox /pə́nəš/ *to bury* and /pə́nʔəm/ *to plant* B75prelim., Island Comox /pə́naš/ *bury* and /pə́nʔəm/ *to plant* and [pənɪt] *It's buried* [sic for *bury it*] Harris77, Nooksack /pə́nət/ (SJ) *plant s-th* and /pənʔǽlik^{w}/ (SJ) *to plant [structured activity], planting* G84a, Saanich /čə́n-ət/ *to bury s-th/s-o* G82:40 cognate set 193, Lummi /čə́nət/ *bury s-th* Demers 1982p.c., Sooke root /čə́n-/ *to bury, plant* G84a, Clallam /čən-/ *bury*, Lushootseed root /pəd-/ *dirt, dust, soil, earth; bury* as in /pəd-ícəd/ *bury it* H76 and /pəd-íx^{w}/ *dirt* VH83pc, Twana root /pəd-/ *bury, plant* NT82pc, example: <**líchxw pí:lt?**>, //li-c-x^{w} pə[=Aí·=]l=T//, /'*Did you plant it?, Did you plant?*'/, attested by AC, <**le pí:ltes te ốts.**>, //lə pə[=Aí·=]l=T-əs tə ʔóc//, /'*He planted the oats.*'/, attested by AC, <**yalhs'es la pí:ltes te spí:ls.**>, //yɛɬ-s-ʔə-s lɛ pə[=Aí·=]l=T-əs tə s=pə[=Aí·=]l=ls-s//, /'*He's just gone to plant his grain.*'/, literally /'only now - nom. -aux. -he subj. go he plants it the his plantings'/, attested by AC; found in <**pí:ltem.**>, //pə[=Aí·=]l=T-əm//, /'*They buried him., He was buried.*'/, attested by EB.

<**spapí:l**>, strs //s=C_1ɛ=pə[=Aí·=]l//, LAND ['*(be) buried*'], CH, (<**s=**> *stative*, R8= *resultative*), (<**í:-ablaut**> *resultative*? (perhaps now just *derivational*)), phonology: reduplication, ablaut, syntactic analysis: adjective/adjectival verb, attested by EB.

<**spepíláwtxw**>, dnom //s=C_1ɛ=pə[=Aí·=]l=ɛ́wtx^{w}//, HARV /'*root cellar, (root house [AD]*'/, FOOD, BLDG, ASM ['covered with earth, separate from house, kept potatoes, apples, carrots, etc.'], literally /'buried house, buried room, buried building'/, lx <**=áwtxw**> *building, house, room*, phonology: reduplication, ablaut, syntactic analysis: nominal, attested by EB, also <**shxwpélmàlà**>, //s(=)x^{w}=pə́l=əm=ɛ̀lɛ̀//, also /'*root cellar, root house*'/, attested by AD.

<**spí:ls**>, dnom //s=pə[=Aí·=]l=ls//, sas, HARV /'*the planting, seeds to plant, what* is planted (sown), garden'/, FOOD, EB, (<**s=**> *nominalizer*), (<**í:-ablaut**> *resultative*?), lx <**=els**> *structured activity continuative*, phonology: ablaut, vowel-loss and consonant merger, syntactic analysis: nominal, attested by AC, other sources: H-T <spels> (macron over e) *seed*, example: <**li hóy ta spí:ls?**>, //li háy t-ɛ s=pə[=Aí·=]l=ls//, /'*Are you through planting?*'/, literally /'is it through/finished your planting'/, attested by AC, <**lulh hóy tel spí:ls.**>, //lə-uɬ háy tə-l s=pə[=Aí·=]l=ls//, /'*My planting is finished.*'/, attested by AC, <**lulh me (qwáqel, ts'í:sem) ta spí:ls.**>, //lə-uɬ mə (q^{w}ɛ́=qəl, c'í·s=əm) t-ɛ s=pə[=Aí·=]l=ls//, /'*Your garden (is sprouting up, is growing up).*'/, literally /'it past -already start to/coming to (sprout, grow) your planting'/, attested by AC.

<**spíls s'élhtel sqe'óleqw**>, FOOD *vegetable juice* (lit. planted + food + fruit juice), (attested by RG,EH 6/16/98 to SN, edited by BG with RG,EH 6/26/00)

<**smómeleqw spíls s'élhtel sqe'óleqw**>, FOOD *V8 juice* (lit. mixed + planted + food + fruit juice),

(attested by RG,EH 6/16/98 to SN, edited by BG with RG,EH 6/26/00)

<**spá:lxw**>, df //s=pi[=Aɛ́·=]l=x^{w}//, EB /'*blue camas, (any edible underground vegetable food [SP], vegetable root(s)* [MH])'/, ['*Camassia quamash and Camassia leichtlinii*'], ASM ['plant with bulbs about as big as garlic, two-inch diameter and about three-inches long, potato-like but with rings around it, looks like garlic, grows on long root, is a kind of lily (AC), formerly found in the water at Sumas Lake (the lake has been drained since ca 1919), bulbs are white with brown peel, when cooked in steam-pits tastes sweet with texture something like a potato, some were also obtained dried in trade from tribes both in the interior and on the coast; called Indian potato by some, only called camas by AC'], (<**s=**> *nominalizer*), root <**pil**> *bury*, <**á:-ablaut**> *derivational*, <**=xw**> *lump-like, round*, phonology: ablaut, syntactic analysis: nominal, attested by AC, Deming, also <**spá:lxw**>, //s=pə[=Aɛ́·=]l=x^{w}//, also /'*any edible underground food*'/, attested by SP, poss. other Tait speakers, also /'*vegetable roots (ground up for flour for ex.)*'/, attested by MH, other sources: ES /spɛ́·lx^{w}/ and Musqueam and Cowichan /spɛ́nx^{w}/ *camas*, Salish cognate: Squamish /s-pán-an-x^{w}/ *blue camas (Camassia quamash and Camassia leichtlinii)* (Louie Miranda felt the word was derived from /pə́nt/ *buried [bury s-th]* in Squamish) Bouchard and Turner 1976:50-51, K67:282,131.

<**pipelá:ls**>, sas //pi[-C$_1$ə-]l=ɛ́·ls or pə[=Ai=][-C$_1$ə-]l=ɛ́·ls//, cts, [pipəlǽ·ls], ABFC /'*making love, having intercourse*'/, literally /'planting (a seed) (structured activity)'/, possibly <**i-ablaut**> *resultative*?, (<**-R1-**> *continuative*), (<**=á:ls**> *structured activity continuative*), usage: metaphor, phonology: ablaut, reduplication, syntactic analysis: intransitive verb, attested by IHTTC (7/18/77)(SP).

<**pélemálá**>, dnom //pə́l=əm=ɛ́lɛ́//, BLDG ['*pantry*'], FOOD, HARV, literally /'got buried container, container of (what) got planted'/, (<**=em**> *intransitivizer, get, have*), lx <**=álá**> *container of*, syntactic analysis: nominal, attested by CT, HT.

<**spélmàlà**>, dnom //s=pə́l=əm=ɛ̀lɛ̀//, BLDG ['*root house*'], FOOD, HARV, (<**s=**> *nominalizer*), syntactic analysis: nominal, attested by Elders Group, also <**shxwpélmàlà**>, //s(=)x^{w}=pə́l=əm=ɛ̀lɛ̀//, attested by AD.

<**speláwél**>, df //s=pəl=ɛ́wə́l or s=pəl=i[=Aɛ́=]wəl//, EZ ['*mole*'], ['family *Talpidae*, especially *Scapanus orarius orarius*, also *Neurotrichus gibbsi*'], (<**s=**> *nominalizer*), root <**pel**> *plant, bury*, lx <**=áwél**> perhaps *head*, probably related to lx <=íwel ~ =ewel> *in the inside* perhaps by <**á-ablaut**> *durative* (compare <**=ewel**> in <**sqwálewel**> //s=q^{w}ɛ́l=əwəl// *thoughts, feelings, lit. words in the inside/in the mind/head*), Elder's comment: "the name means *planting head* (Deming 3/11/76)", phonology: possible ablaut, updrifting, syntactic analysis: nominal, attested by Deming, Elders Group, BJ (12/5/64), also <**kw'ókw'tel**>, //k'^{w}ák'^{w}təl or k'^{w}ɛ[=AáC$_1$ə=]t'[=D=]əl//, attested by CT, source: Galloway 1981:197, also <**kw'ókw't**>, //k'^{w}ák'^{w}t(əl)//, also /'*Mole*'/, usage: song, lullaby, attested by CT, source: Galloway 1981:197,

<**pel** or **pel=**>, bound root or prefix //pəl(=)// probably *season, time of* as in Salish cognate Lushootseed <pəd(=)> *time of* (Hess 1976:337.1).

<**spelwálh**>, df //s=pəl=wɛ́(=ə)ɬ//, TIME ['*last year*'], <**s=**> *stative* or *nominalizer*, <**pel=**> *season, time of*, possibly root <**wá**> meaning unknown or <**wálh**> as in <**wálhet**> //wɛ́ɬ=əT// /'*chase it away, (chase s-o/s-th away)*'/(<**=et**> *purposeful control transitivizer*; Salish cognate: Squamish /wáɬ-an/ *chase away, chase out (tr.)* K67:378), this would yield a lit. meaning of "season/time chased away", (possibly also <**=(e)lh**> *past tense*), phonology: possible vowel merger, syntactic analysis: intransitive verb?, nominal??, attested by EB, AC, Elders Group, example: <**híkw telí kw'e spelwálh.**>, //hík^{w} təlí k'^{w}ə s=pəl=wɛ́(=)ɬ//, /'*(It's) bigger than last year.*'/, literally /'it's big from/than the (remote) last year'/, attested by AC, <**spelwálh qwá:l**>, //s=pəl=wɛ́(=)ɬ q^{w}ɛ́·l//, /'*cranefly, "leatherjacket" (larvae of cranefly)*'/, EZ ['*cranefly*'], ['order *Diptera,* family *Tipulidae*'],

literally /'last year's mosquito'/, ASM ['insect resembling a mosquito but much larger, slow-flying'], attested by Elders Group.

<**pelále**>, free root //'pəlɛ́lə// , EB, FOOD //*'banana'*//, borrowed from English banana, syntactic analysis: noun, (attested by RG,EH 6/16/98 to SN, edited by BG with RG,EH 6/26/00)

<**pelále seplíl**>, FOOD *banana bread* (lit. banana + bread), (attested by RG,EH 6/16/98 to SN, edited by BG with RG,EH 6/26/00)

<**pél:ékw**>, free root //pə́l·ə́kʷ//, LT /*'appear, come into view, rise into view, emerge'*/, TVMO, syntactic analysis: intransitive verb, attested by EB, also <**pél:ekw**>, //pə́l·əkʷ//, attested by Deming, also <**pélekw**>, //pə́ləkʷ//, attested by IHTTC, and: <**pelékw**>, //pələ́kʷ//, attested by DM (12/4/64), <**pél:ékw te (skw'xó:s, syó:qwem, x̱áws skw'xó:s).**>, //pə́l·ə́kʷ tə (s=k'ʷxʸ=á·s, s=yə[=Aá·=]qʷ=əm,xɛ́ws s=k'ʷxʸ=á·s)//, /*'The (moon, sun, new (sliver of) moon) came into view/rose.'*/, attested by EB (4/28/76), comment: note that te *the (present and visible/unmarked)* can be used with heavenly bodies, also <**me pélekw te x̱áws skw'xós.**>, //mə pə́ləkʷ təxɛ́ws s=k'ʷxʸ=ás//, also /*'The new sliver of moon has appeared.'*/, attested by IHTTC, <**lulh me pél:ekw te syóqwem.**>, //lə=uɬ mə pə́l·əkʷ tə s=yə[=Aá=]qʷ=əm//, /*'The sun has come out.'*/, literally /'it ambiguous past =already comes appear the sun'/, attested by Deming, <**le me pelékw te syó:qwem.**>, //lə mə pələ́kʷ tə s=yə[=Aá·=]qʷ=əm//, /*'(It's) sunrise.'*/, literally /'it ambiguous past comes appear the sun'/, attested by DM (12/4/64), also <**me kwélekw [sic pélekw?] te syóqwem.**>, //mə pə́ləkʷ tə s=yáqʷ=əm//, also /*'The sun rises., The sun rose.'*/, attested by EB, <**stámcha skw'exós kw'e atse ōw me pélekw?**>, //s=tɛ́m-cɛ s=k'ʷəxʸ=ás k'ʷə ʔɛcə ʔəw mə pə́ləkʷ//, /*'What is the next moon to appear?'*/, literally /'is what? -future moon which is next contrastive coming to appear'/, attested by IHTTC, <**yálh o sés me pél:ékw.**>, //yɛ́ɬ ʔa-s-ə́s mə pə́l·ə́kʷ//, /*'(It's/He's/She's) just starting to show.'*/, literally /'only now just -dependent nominalizer -3subj. coming/starting to appear/come into view'/, attested by EB.

<**xwpelákw**>, df //xʷ=pələ[=Aɛ́=]kʷ//, CLO [*'peek under a woman's skirt'*], ABFC, literally /'peek on a woman's vulva/vagina'/, lx <**xw=**> *on the vulva, in the vagina*, (<**á-ablaut**> *durative or resultative* or *derivational*), phonology: ablaut, syntactic analysis: intransitive verb, attested by Elders Group (9/21/77).

<**pelókwes ~ peló:kwes**>, df //pələ[=Aɛ́=][=Aá(·)=]kʷ=əs//, ABFC [*'be peeking'*], (<**á-ablaut**> *continuative* or *derivational*, <ó-ablaut on stem á> automatic before <=es> *on the face*), possibly <-:-> *continuative*?, lx <**=es**> *on the face*, phonology: double ablaut, ó(:)-ablaut on stem á automatic before =es, syntactic analysis: intransitive verb, attested by Elders Group (3/12/75), example: <**peló:kwes te Rudy.**>, //pələ[=Aɛ́=][=Aá·=]kʷ=əs//, /*'Rudy is peeking.'*/.

<**pepélekwes**>, plv, dms //C1ə=pə́ləkʷ=əs//, //*'to bob'*//, lit. prob. /'much little peeking on the face'/, attested by RG & EH (4/9/99 Ling332)

<**spelékw**>, df //s=pələ́kʷ//, ABDF [*'(have) smallpox'*], literally /'something that appears'/, (<**s=**> *stative* or *nominalizer*), syntactic analysis: intransitive verb? or nominal?, attested by Deming (2/7/80), also <**spél:exw** (sic for **spél:ekw**)>, //s=pə́l:əkʷ//, attested by CT (10/15/73), comment: probably my transcription error.

<**pelkwí:ws**>, df //pələkʷ=í·ws//, ABDF /*'(have) smallpox, measles, chickenpox'*/, literally /'appear/emerge on the body/skin'/, lx <**=í:ws**> *on the body, on the skin*, syntactic analysis: intransitive verb, nominal??, attested by Deming (2/7/80), Salish cognate: Lushootseed though not having a cognate has a term with the same literal meaning, /s-ƛ'íq-abac/ *smallpox*, lit. *something that emerges on the body* H76:326,2.

<**pélel**>, df //pə́l(=)əl//, EB [*'blackened bitter cherry bark'*], [*'Prunus emarginata'*], ASM ['outer bark

peeled in May to use for basket decoration, some left red, some dyed black formerly by soaking underwater with bark of the red alder *Alnus rubra* but now by soaking underwater with rusted iron and other things, the bark when dried is stored in bundles, split, then rewet to weave into basketry imbrication'], possibly <**=el**> *get, become, go, come, inceptive*, root possibly <**pel**> *bury* if the bark was sometimes blackened by burying it with red alder bark in wet soil, syntactic analysis: nominal, dialects: *Tait*, attested by SP, perhaps others in Elders Group, also <**ts'q'éyx̲ st'elém** (or better) **ts'q'íx̲ st'elém**>, //c'=q'íx̣ s=t'əlә́m//, literally /'black bitter cherry bark'/, dialects: *Cheh.*, attested by Elders Group, Salish cognate: Lushootseed /plílaʔ(ac) ~ plálaʔ/ *wild cherry tree* H76:342-343.

<**pélemálá**>, BLDG ['*pantry*'], *see* pél (perhaps ~ pí:l by now).

<**pelkwí:ws**>, ABDF /'*(have) smallpox, measles, chickenpox*'/, *see* pél:ékw.

<**pelókwes ~ peló:kwes**>, ABFC ['*be peeking*'], *see* pél:ékw.

<**Pelólhxw**>, df //pəl(=)áɬxʷ//, SOCT /'*Pilalt tribe, Pilalt people, Pilalt dialect, (Pilalt, village at west end of Little Mountain by Agassiz [Wells, Duff])*'/, possibly root <**pel**> *bury, plant*, possibly <**=ólhxw**> meaning uncertain, syntactic analysis: nominal, attested by BJ (5/64) (= second transcription from tape too), source: place names reference file #63, also <**Peló:lhxw**>, //pəl(=)á·ɬxʷ//, ASM ['Laurence James says that the main Pilalt village was Qweqwe'ópelhp, now *Kwawkwawapilt Reserve*'], attested by Elders Group (7/13/77)(Laurence James), PLN /'*Pilalt, village at west end of Little Mountain by Agassiz*'/, source: Wells 1965:23, Duff 1952:35.

<**peló:qel**>, df //pəlá·qəl//, FIRE ['*torch*'], HHG, ASM ['torches were used to fish by at night (torchlighting, pit-lamping) example in February in Chehalis, among the Chilliwack bundles of cedar bark were lit to warm the hands in the morning in February'], possibly root <**pel**> *bury* (done to hold torch upright or to put it out?), possibly <**=eqel**> *container* or <=qel> *on the head*, syntactic analysis: nominal, attested by NP (2/5/75).

<**peló:qes**>, df //pəlá·q(=əl)=əs//, TIME /'*moon of February to March, (torch season)*'/, literally /'torch cyclic period/season'/, ASM ['so named because they fished with torches in February in Chehalis according to NP, so named because they used bundles of cedar bark for warming their hands in the morning in Feb. to March according to Billy Sepass (in Diamond Jenness's field notes)'], lx <**=es**> *cyclic period*, phonology: possible syllable-loss of el before =es, syntactic analysis: nominal, attested by NP, Elders Group (2/5/75, 3/28/79).

<**peló:qes**>, TIME /'*moon of February to March, (torch season)*'/, *see* peló:qel.

<**pelpólx̲wem**>, WETH /'*be steaming (in many places), be cloudy with rain-clouds*'/, *see* poléx̲wem.

<**pélh**>, free root //pә́ɬ//, SOC ['*get crowded*'], syntactic analysis: intransitive verb, attested by BHTTC.

<**pelhpélh**>, plv //C_1əC_2=pә́ɬ//, SOC ['*get crowded out*'], (<**R3=**> *plural*), phonology: reduplication, syntactic analysis: intransitive verb, attested by BHTTC.

<**plhét**>, pcs //pɬ=əT or p(ə)ɬ=ә́T or pә́ɬ=M1=T or pә́ɬ=ə[=M2=]T//, SOC ['*crowd s-o out*'], possibly <**metathesis type 1 or metathesis type 2**> *derivational*, (<**=t ~ =et ~ =ét**> *purposeful control transitivizer*), phonology: stressed transitivizer or metathesis, syntactic analysis: transitive verb, attested by BHTTC.

<**pelhpélh**>, SOC ['*get crowded out*'], *see* pélh.

<**pelhtó:ythel**>, ANA ['*(have) thick lips*'], *see* plhá:t.

<**pélhx̲el**>, bound root or bound derived stem //pә́ɬ(=)x̣(=)əl// or more likely //p'[=D=]]i[=Aә́=]ɬ(=)x̣(=)əl//, literal meaning possibly *get flat all around*, possibly from root <**p'ílh**> //p'íɬ// *get flat, flatten* (see that root for cognates and derived forms like <**sp'íp'elheqsel ~**

sp'élhqsel> //s=p'í[=C_1ə=]ɬ=əqsəl ~ s=p'i[=Aə́=]ɬ=qsəl// *(have a) flat nose*, [<**s=**> *stative*, <**=R1=** ~ **é-ablaut on root í**> *durative* (or *resultative*?)], plus <**=D=**> deglottalization *derivational*, <**é-ablaut**> *durative/resultative*, <**=x̱**> *all around*, <**=el**> *come, go, get, become*.

<**spélhx̱el**>, df //s=pə́ɬ(=)x̣(=)əl// or //p'[=D=]]i[=Aə́=]ɬ(=)x̣(=)əl////, LAND /'*prairie, grassy open land, (grassy valley [EB, Gibbs, Elders Group]*'/, (<**s=**> *nominalizer*), <**=x̱**> *distributive*, possibly <**=el**> *get, become*, possibly root <**p'élh**> *flat*, phonology: possible deglottalization *derivational* and <**é-ablaut**> *durative/resultative*, syntactic analysis: nominal, attested by AC, BJ (5/64), EB, Elders Group, Deming, other sources: ES /spə́ɬx̣əl/ *prairie*, also /'*prairie (like Sumas prairie, full of grass)*'/, attested by BJ (5/64), also /'*prairie, valley*'/, attested by EB after Gibbs, Elders Group (4/2/75), comment: but with the Elders Group 4/9/75 FM transcribed <xe xe xaut> for *valley* (perhaps <**sx̱ex̱ákw'**> *canyon* was meant here), perhaps as correction of the previous week; thus <**spélhx̱el**> is used for *valley* only when it is a flat grassy open valley, i.e., a prairie, example: <**li te spélhxel**>, //li tə s=pə́ɬ(=)x̣(=)əl//, /'*at the prairie*'/, attested by Deming. Salish cognate: Nooksack <**spálhx̱en**> /spǽɬx̣ən/ *prairie, meadow, open land*, Lushootseed /spáɬx̣əd/ *tide flats* (Hess 1976:334.4; these cognates point to Proto-Central-Salish final *n and *spáɬx̣ən which points to a different etymology (same prefix, different root or different ablaut, deglottalization if present would have had to be pre-PCS if Proto-Salish had *p' here, possibly *=x̣ən *foot* or *=x *all around* + *=ən meaning unclear instead of *=əl *come, go, become, inceptive*; <u>check with Kuipers 2002</u> comparative Salishan dictionary and with Squamish & add here; it is peculiar that such a perfect etymology for the word exists in Upriver Halkomelem but in no other Salishan language cognate I've found yet; if Halkomelem still occupies the original Proto-Salish homeland, could it be that it alone preserves the traces of this word's etymology and that Downriver and Island Halkomelem with final n show the route of diffusion into the other PCS languages or more likely is the Halkomelem etymology proposed a folk etymology, just a coincidence of formal resemblances?

<**spáplhx̱el**>, dmn //s=C_1ɛ́=pəɬ(=)x̣(=)əl//, LAND /'*meadow, (little prairie)*'/, (<**R7=**> *diminutive*), phonology: reduplication, syntactic analysis: nominal, Elder's comment: "unsure", attested by AC.

<**Pepá:thxetel**>, SOCT ['*people from Semá:th (Sumas village)*'], *see* pá:th.

<**pepélekwes**>, plv, dms //C1ə=pə́ləkʷ=əs//, **WATR** //'*to bob*'//, *see* pél:ékw.

<**pepepó:tem ~ pépepò:tem ~ pepepótem**>, EB ['*rattlesnake plantain*'], *see* pó:t.

<**pepípehò:m**>, EZ ['*frogs*'], *see* peh or pó(:)h.

<**pepíx̱eya**>, ABDF ['*having a nightmare*'], *see* píx̱eya.

<**pepó:l**>, PLAY ['*playing ball (playing with a ball)*'], *see* pó:l.

<**pepó:tem**>, ABFC ['*blown*'], *see* pó:t.

<**pepq'éyò:s**>, EB ['*snowberry*'], *see* p'éq'.

<**pepqw'ólh**>, EZ ['*small Chehalis spring salmon*'], *see* pó:qw' ~ póqw'.

<**Péps**>? or <**Píps**>?, df //pə́ps or píps//?, PLN ['*Hicks Creek*'], possibly <**=R1=**> *derivational* or possibly <**R4=**> *diminutive*, phonology: probable reduplication, syntactic analysis: nominal, source: Wells 1966 <PIHPS>.

<**pepx̱wíqsel**>, EZ /'*gnat*, probably includes *non-biting midges, biting midges, and (biting) black flies*'/, *see* píxw.

<**Pepx̱wíqsel**>, N ['*nickname for Nat Dickinson*'], *see* píxw.

<**peqá:s**>, possible root or stem <peq>.//pəq// or <páq>//pɛ́q//meaning unknown, or more likely //p'əq'// *white* + deglottalization

<**speqá:s**>, df //s=pəq=ɛ́·s or s=pəq=a[=Aɛ́=]·s or s=p'[=D=]əq'=D=á[=Aɛ́=]·s//, EZ /'*white Fraser River spring salmon that goes upriver with the red spring salmon, (white Fraser River chinook salmon)*'/, ['*Oncorhynchus tshawytscha*'], ASM ['white here I believe means white-fleshed salmon'], (<**s=**> *nominalizer*), possibly <**=D (deglottalization)**> *derivational*, possibly <**=ó:s**> *on the face*, (with <**á-ablaut**> *derivational*?) or <=á:s> meaning uncertain, probably root <**p'ə́q'**> *white*, phonology: possible deglottalization, possible ablaut, syntactic analysis: nominal, Elder's comment: "<speqá:s not speq'á:s>" (IHTTC 9/14/77), attested by Elders Group (3/26/75), IHTTC, also <**speq'á:s**>, //s=p'[=D=]əq'=a[=Aɛ́=]·s//, attested by Elders Group (3/1/72).

<**péqw**>, free root //pə́qʷ//, MC /'*split off, break off, break a piece off, break in two, split in two*'/, FOOD, LAND, semantic environment ['for ex. break bread with hands'], syntactic analysis: intransitive verb, attested by Deming, NP, AD,, Salish cognate: Lushootseed /pə́qʷ(u)/ *break/cut a piece off (leaving a larger piece)* H76:561, also <**péqw ~ póqw?**>, //pə́qʷ ~ páqʷ?//, [pʊ́qʷ ~ pɔ́qʷ], attested by AC, <**le péqw.**>, //lə pə́qʷ//, /'*It split in two., It's broken.*'/, attested by AC.

<**peqwpéqw**>, plv //C_1əC_2=pə́qʷ//, LAND ['*broken off in pieces (like a river-bank)*'], MC, (<**R3=**> *plural*), phonology: reduplication, syntactic analysis: intransitive verb, attested by EB.

<**peqwót**>, durs /pəqʷ=ə[=Aá=]T or pəqʷ=áT//, pcs, MC /'*break s-th in two (with one's hands), break it in half (with one's hands only), break off a piece of s-th*'/, FOOD, semantic environment ['apple, orange, other fruit, bread, possibly wood'], probably<**ó-ablaut**> *durative*, < **=et**> *purposeful control transitivizer*, phonology: possible stressed transitivizer or ablaut, syntactic analysis: transitive verb, attested by AC, NP, AD, EB, example: <**peqwót te qwe'óp**>, //pəqʷá=T tə qʷəʔáp//, /'*break the apple in two*'/, attested by AC.

<**peqwpéqwet**>, pcs //C_1əC_2=pə́qʷ=əT//, plv, FOOD ['*break it in pieces with one's hands*'], MC, (<**R3=**> *plural*), (<**=et**> *purposeful control transitivizer*), phonology: reduplication, syntactic analysis: transitive verb, attested by EB.

<**pqwá:ls**>, sas //pəqʷ=ɛ́·ls//, FOOD ['*break off*'], MC, semantic environment ['bread for ex.'], (<**=á:ls**> *structured activity non-continuative*), phonology: vowel-loss, zero-grade of root before stressed full-grade of suffix, syntactic analysis: intransitive verb, attested by IHTTC.

<**póqwels**>, cts //pə[=Aá=]qʷ=əls//, HARV ['*splitting wood (esp. blanks and bolts)*'], (<**ó-ablaut**> *continuative*), (<**=els**> *structured activity continuative*), phonology: ablaut, syntactic analysis: intransitive verb, attested by IHTTC.

<**Peqwchṓ:lthel ~ Peqwechṓ:lthel**>, df //pəqʷ=(ə)c=ó·lθəl//, PLN /'*village at American Bar, village on west bank of Fraser River at American Creek, American Bar Reserve*'/, literally /'river bar/bank caving in/off'/, lx <**=(e)ch=ṓ:lthel**> *riverbank, riverbar* itself possibly from <**=ó:lthel**> *on the knee/kneecap* with < **ṓ-ablaut**> *derivational* and <**=ech**> *on the back*?, phonology: possible ṓ-ablaut, syntactic analysis: nominal, attested by Elders Group, PDP, AD, AK, others, source: place names reference file #12, other sources: Wells 1965 (lst ed.):24, 25, also <**Peqwetsōwelthel**>, //pəqʷ=əc=ówəlθəl//, attested by Elders Group (4/2/75).

<**Peqwchṓ:lthel Stótelō**>, ds //pəqʷ=c=ó·lθəl s=tá[=C_1ə=]ləw//, PLN /'*Mill Creek (at American Bar), Puckat Creek* on map also'/, literally /'American Bar creek, riverbank caving off creek'/, (<**s=**> *nominalizer*), (<**=R1=**> *diminutive*), phonology: reduplication, syntactic analysis: simple nominal phrase, attested by AK, SP, AD (all on trip to American Bar).

<**Spōqwṓwelh ~ Speqwṓ:lh**>, df //s=pəqʷ=ówəɬ//, PLN /'*Chehalis River mouth (below the highway bridge, where land is breaking up into sand bars), (an opening one could get through in a canoe in high water near Chehalis IHTTC 8/25/77], small creek (branch of Chehalis River) several hundred yards up Chehalis River from where the road goes from old Chehalis village site to Chehalis River [EL 9/27/77])*'/, (<**s=**> *nominalizer*), lx <**=ṓwelh**> *canoe, vessel (container)*, syntactic analysis:

nominal, attested by DF, EB, source: place names reference file #103, #104, also /*'an opening one could get through in a canoe in high water near Chehalis'*/, attested by IHTTC (8/25/77), source: place names reference file #103, 104, also /*'small creek (branch of Chehalis River) several hundred yards up Chehalis River from where the road goes from old Chehalis village site to Chehalis River'*/, attested by EL (9/27/77), source: place names reference file #291.

<**péqweles**>, df //pə́qʷ=əl(=)əs//, LAND [*'a river bank caving in'*], possibly <**=el**> *go, come, get, become*, possibly <**=es**> *on the face*, syntactic analysis: nominal?, attested by Elders Group (4/2/75).

<**pqwíles**>, ds //pəqʷ=íləs//, ABDF [*'out of breath and over-tired and over-hungry'*], literally /'split in two in the chest'/, lx <**=íles**> *in the chest*, phonology: vowel-loss or zero-grade of root before stressed full-grade of suffix, syntactic analysis: adjective/adjectival verb, attested by Elders Group.

<**Peqwchő:lthel ~ Peqwechő:lthel**>, PLN /*'village at American Bar, village on west bank of Fraser River at American Creek, American Bar Reserve'*/, *see* péqw.

<**Peqwchő:lthel Stótelō**>, PLN /*'Mill Creek (at American Bar), Puckat Creek* on map also'/, *see* péqw.

<**péqweles**>, LAND [*'a river bank caving in'*], *see* péqw.

<**peqwót**>, MC /*'break s-th in two (with one's hands), break it in half (with one's hands only), break off a piece of s-th'*/, *see* péqw.

<**peqwpéqw**>, LAND [*'broken off in pieces (like a river-bank)'*], *see* péqw.

<**peqwpéqwet**>, FOOD [*'break it in pieces with one's hands'*], *see* péqw.

<**pésk'a**>, free root //pə́sk'ɛ//, [pɪ́sk'ʸɛ], EZ /*'hummingbird,* prob. including *rufous hummingbird, black-chinned hummingbird, and calliope hummingbird'*/, ['possibly *Trochilidae* family, probably including *Selasphorus rufus, Archilochus alexandri,* and *Stellula calliope*'], syntactic analysis: nominal, Elder's comment: "<pésk'a not p'ésk'a>" (BHTTC), attested by BHTTC (9/1/76), EB, also <**p'ésk'a**>, //p'ə́sk'ɛ//, attested by Elders Group (6/4/75, 2/18/76), also <**péska**>, //pə́skɛ//, attested by BJ (12/5/64) from Wells tape transcript old p.311 (a correction from my original transcription of the tape in 1973), other sources: ES /pɪ́sk'ʸɛ/ (footnote last p.) and JH /pə́sk'e/ both *hummingbird*, example: <**th'ó:kws te x̱wó:qw' qas te léts'e pésk'a.**>, //θ'á·kʷs təx̣ʷá·q'ʷ qɛ-s tə lə́c'ə pə́sk'ɛ//, /*'There are seven sawbill ducks and one hummingbird.'*/, comment: constructed by class member and approved by EB, attested by EB.

<**pespesó:ythílem**>, ABFC [*'make one's mouth like one's going to cry'*], *see* pas ~ pes.

<**pésqw**>, bound root //pə́sqʷ *to insult about the body*//.

<**pésqwt**>, pcs //pə́sqʷ=T//, LANG /*'insult s-o, calling s-o names referring to his anatomy or body part'*/, BPI, EFAM, SOC, (<**=t**> *purposeful control transitivizer*), (semological comment: one translation of this form is continuative which matches the metathesis pattern seen in Northern Straits for cognate terms; however, the translations obtained so far in Halq'eméylem are more often non-continuative for pésqwt), syntactic analysis: transitive verb, attested by Elders Group (3/3/76), Salish cognate: Nooksack /ps=pə́skʷ=ət-əm/ *he got cursed repeatedly by insults about his body* PA 1961 (in text), Lummi dial. of N. Straits /psə́kʷt/ *criticize [s-o]* Demers 1982pc, Samish dial. of N. Straits /psə́qwt/ *insult s-o regarding his body* beside /pə́sqʷt/ *insulting s-o regarding his body* G86:95; found in <**pesqwthò:m.**>, //pəsqʷ=T-à·m//, /*'I was insulted or called names.'*/, syntactic comment: passive, <**pésqwtem.**>, //pə́sqʷ=T-əm//, /*'He was insulted or called names.'*/, syntactic comment: passive.

<**pósqwet**>, cts //pə[-Aá-]sqʷ=əT//, LANG [*'insulting s-o'*], BPI, EFAM, SOC, (<**ó-ablaut**> *continuative*), phonology: ablaut, syntactic analysis: transitive verb, attested by Elders Group

(3/8/78); found in <**pósqwethò:m.**>, //pə[-Aá-]sq^{w}=əT-à·m//, /'*You're being insulted., He's/She's/They're insulting you.*'/.

<**popsíqwtel**>, durs //pə[-AaC$_{1}$ə-]s[=í=]q^{w}=T-əl//, rcps, cts, LANG /'*calling one another names (insults about their bodies), calling each other names*'/, BPI, EFAM, SOC, (<**o-ablaut plus -R1-**> *continuative*), (<**=í= infix**> *durative*), (<**=t**> *purposeful control transitivizer*), (<**-el**> *reciprocal, one another, each other*), phonology: ablaut, reduplication, í-infix, syntactic analysis: intransitive verb, attested by Elders Group (2/16/77).

<**pósqwtel**>, dnom //pə[=Aá=]sq^{w}=təl//, LANG ['*an insult*'], BPI, EFAM, SOC, (<**ó-ablaut**> *derivational*), lx <**=tel**> *something to, device to*, phonology: ablaut, syntactic analysis: nominal, attested by Elders Group (3/3/76).

<**lexwspésqw**>, dnom //ləx^{w}=s=pə́sq^{w}//, LANG ['*someone who always calls people names*'], BPI, EFAM, SOC, lx <**lexw=s=**> *someone who always*, syntactic analysis: nominal, attested by Elders Group (2/16/77).

<**pésqwt**>, LANG /'*insult s-o, calling s-o names referring to his anatomy or body part*'/, *see* pésqw.

<**petá:m**>, free root //pətɛ́·m//, LANG ['*ask*'], syntactic analysis: intransitive verb, attested by Elders Group, EB, other sources: JH /p'tém/ *inquire.*

<**pétem**>, cts //pə[-´-]tɛm//, LANG ['*asking*'], (<-´-> *continuative*), phonology: vowel-reduction and length-loss after stress-shift, syntactic analysis: intransitive verb, attested by Elders Group, EB, other sources: H-T <pE´tEm> *asking (unknown person).*

<**petá:met ~ ptámet**>, pcs //pətɛ́·m=əT ~ ptɛ́m=əT//, LANG ['*ask s-o*'], (<**=et**> *purposeful control transitivizer*), phonology: vowel-loss and length-loss in rapid speech, syntactic analysis: transitive verb, attested by Elders Group (3/1/72, 1/25/78), EB, AC, other sources: H-T <pEtámit> (umlaut over á) *ask (a known person)*; found in <**ptámetes.**>, //pətɛ́m=əT-əs//, /'*He asked (s-o) for it.*'/, attested by Elders Group, example: <**ptámet thel màl**>, //ptɛ́m=əT (k^{w})θə-l mɛ̀l//, /'*ask my father*'/, attested by AC, <**petá:methométsel.**>, //pətɛ́·m=əT-ámə-c-əl//, /'*I ask you.*'/, attested by Elders Group (3/1/72), <**petámettselcha wéyeles.**>, //pətɛ́m=əT-c-əl-cɛ wɛ́yəl=əs//, /'*I'll ask tomorrow.*'/, attested by Elders Group (3/1/72); found in <**ptámetem**>, //pətɛ́m=əT-əm//, /'*someone is asked (a question)*'/, syntactic comment: passive, attested by EB.

<**petámelht**>, bens //pətɛ́m=əɬ(c)=T//, LANG ['*ask something for s-o*'], (<**=elhts ~ (EB) =elh**> *benefactive*, <**=t**> *purposeful control transitivizer*), phonology: consonant-loss in benefactive suffix could be idiolectal, dialectal, or allomorphic, syntactic analysis: transitive verb, attested by EB, example: <**petámelhthó:xchexw we'ésulh xwe'í thel s'ò:m.**>, //pətɛ́m=əɬ=T-áx^{y}-c-əx^{w} wə-ʔə́s-uɬ x^{w}ə=ʔí (k^{w})θə-l s=ʔà·m//, /'*Ask for me if my order is in (get here).*'/, attested by EB (3/1/76).

<**pétemet**>, cts //pə[-´-]tɛm=əT//, LANG ['*asking s-o*'], (<-´-> *continuative*), phonology: vowel-reduction to schwa-grade with stress-shift, syntactic analysis: transitive verb, attested by Elders Group (3/1/72, 1/25/78), EB; found in <**pétemethò:me**>, //pə[-´-]tɛm=əT-à·mə//, /'*asking you*'/, attested by RP and Elders Group (3/1/72), also <**pétmethò:me**>, //pə[-´-]tɛm=əT-à·mə//, phonology: vowel-loss with stress-shift, attested by TG (3/1/72), <**pétemetem**>, //pə[-´-]tɛm=əT-əm//, /'*someone is being asked (a question), he was being asked*'/, syntactic comment: passive, attested by Elders Group (3/1/72), EB.

<**petá:mes**>, pncs //pətɛ́·m=(əl)əs//, LANG ['*ask for s-o*'], EFAM ['*ask about s-o*'], (<**=(e)les ~ =es**> *psychological non-control transitivizer*), phonology: =es is apparently an allomorph of =(e)les used with root petá:m, it may be in free variation with =eles (see variant below), syntactic analysis: transitive verb, attested by Elders Group (1/25/78), EB, also <**ptémeles**>, //pətɛ́[=Aə́=]m=ələs//, also /'*aske(d) about s-th*'/, (<**é-ablaut**> *resultative*?), phonology: ablaut, attested by Elders Group

(6/16/76); found in <**ptémeleses**>, //pətɛ́m=ələs-əs//, /'*He asked about it.*'/, syntactic comment: subject pronoun3 (-es) required after =(el)es as well as after =stative-exw and =n-exw, attested by Elders Group.

<**pétemes**>, cts //pə[-´-]tɛm=(əl)əs//, LANG ['*asking for s-o*'], EFAM /'*asking about s-o, asking after s-o*'/, (<-´-> *continuative*), phonology: stress-shift, vowel-reduction, syntactic analysis: transitive verb, attested by Elders Group, EB, also <**pétemles**>, //pə[-´-]tɛm-(ə)ləs//, phonology: free-variation with pétemes, attested by EB (6/7/78); found in <**pétemesò:m. ~ pétemlesò:m.**>, //pə[-´-]tɛm=(əl)əs-à·m ~ pə[-´-]tɛm=(ə)ləs-à·m//, /'*They/Someone was asking for you., They/Someone is asking about you., He's asking about you., (You are being asked about., You are being asked for.)*'/, syntactic comment: passive of psychological non-control stem, attested by Elders Group (1/25/78), EB (3/1/76, 4/14/78, 6/7/78), example: <**pétemesò:m tl' Lizzie.**>, //pə[-´-]tɛm=(əl)əs-à·mƛ' Lizzie.//, /'*Lizzie is asking about you.*'/, syntactic comment: passive as substitute for 3subj. with 2obj, attested by EB; found in <**pétemesoxes. ~ pétemlesóxes.**>, //pə[-´-]tɛm=(əl)əs-áxʸ-əs ~ pə[-´-]tɛm=(ə)ləs-áxʸ-əs//, /'*He/She's asking for me., He/She's asking after me.*'/, attested by EB (6/7/78).

<**petámelht**>, LANG ['*ask something for s-o*'], *see* petá:m.

<**petá:mes**>, LANG ['*ask for s-o*'], *see* petá:m.

<**petá:met ~ ptámet**>, LANG ['*ask s-o*'], *see* petá:m.

<**péte**>, free root //pə́tə//, FOOD ['*butter*'], ACL, phonology: uses regular sound-shift for loans: b → p, final r drops, syntactic analysis: nominal, attested by deduced from its derivative péte'àlà, borrowed from English.

<**péte'àlà**>, ds //pə́tə=ʔɛ̀lɛ̀//, HHG ['*butter dish*'], FOOD, ACL, lx <**=àlà ~ =álá**> *container for*, phonology: possible downstepping, syntactic analysis: nominal, attested by Deming Elders at Ft. Langley museum.

<**pétem**>, LANG ['*asking*'], *see* petá:m.

<**pétemes**>, LANG ['*asking for s-o*'], *see* petá:m.

<**pétemet**>, LANG ['*asking s-o*'], *see* petá:m.

<**Petéyn**>, df //pət=ɛ́yn ~ pətə́yn//, PLN /'*name of place right across from Bristol Island,* also called *Odlum*'/, root meaning unknown unless pét as in pét=l-exw *recognize s-o/s-th*, possibly <**=áyn**> (downriver dialect influence) ~ <**=áyel**> *net, trap* possibly since the place is on the Fraser River, perhaps a good fishing spot, phonology: <**n**> must be influence from downriver dialect or Thompson in the pronunciation of the person from whom AD heard this or by whom the place was named, syntactic analysis: nominal, attested by AD (5/1/79),

<**péte'àlà**>, HHG ['*butter dish*'], *see* péte.

<**pétlexw**>, df //pə́t=l-əxʷ//, ncs //'*recognize s-o*'//, (<**=l**> *non-control transitivizer*), (<**-exw**> *third person object*), syntactic analysis: transitive verb, attested by EB, AC, Salish cognate: Saanich dial. of N. Straits /pít=nəxʷ/ *recognize s-o* B74a:72, Lushootseed /pít-əb/ *notice; pay attention to; understand* H76:340, example: <**líchxw pételàx?**>, //lí-c-xʷ pə́t=l-áxʸ//, /'*Do you recognize me?, Do you know who I am now?*'/, phonology: epenthetic e separates t and l, i.e. syllabicizing l, attested by AC (8/27/73), <**líchxw peteló:lxw talhlímelh?**>, //lí-c-xʷ pət=l-á·lxʷ tɛ=ɬlíməɬ//, /'*Do you recognize US?*'/, syntactic comment: inp plus object pronoun shows emphasis on object, attested by AC (8/27/73).

<**pethíwet ~ pethíwét**>, FSH ['*to take all the loose eggs out of s-th (a salmon)*'], *see* páthet.

<**péth'oyes**>, ds //pɛ[=Aə́=]θ'=ɛ[=Aa=]y=əs//, EB /'*plant similar to stl'éleqw' (chocolate lily) but*

*different, (*probably *rice root)*'/, ['similar to *Fritillaria lanceolata* but different, probably *Fritillaria camschatcensis*'], probably root <**path'**> as in <**pápeth'em //pɛ́[=R1=]θ'=əm//** *(have) body odor, animal stink*, lx <**=oyes**> probably *flower* lx since it is from <**=áy ~ =ey**> *bark, covering, plant* and lx <**=es**> *face*, (<**é-ablaut**> *derivational*, <**o-ablaut**> on <**a**> not derivational but required by <=es>), comment: rice root is quite similar to chocolate lily in appearance and was used in the same way by all the coastal peoples of B.C. except the Halkomelem-speaking and Straits-speaking peoples who used the chocolate lily instead, one of the chief differences is in the disagreeable odor of the dark green-bronze to brown-purple flowers of the rice root (Turner 1974:84-90), phonology: é-ablaut, o-ablaut on a in suffix automatically conditioned by following =es *face* suffix, syntactic analysis: nominal, dialects: *Tait*, attested by SP, Elders Group (5/28/75).

<**pewá:ls**>, WATR ['*to freeze*'], *see* pí:w.

<**péxw**>, bound root //pə́xʷ//, root meaning unknown

<**spéxw**>, df //s=pə́xʷ//, ANA /'*animal tripe (stomach, upper and lower), bowel*'/, syntactic analysis: nominal, attested by AC, other sources: ES /spə́xʷ ~ sməq'tɛ́l/ *stomach*, Salish cognate: Squamish /s-pə́xʷ/ *tripe, animal stomach* W73:274, K67:282.

<**pexwlhálém**>, mdls //pəxʷ=ɬɛ́l=əm//, ABFC ['*to breathe (once)*'], possibly root <**peh**> *blow*, lx <**=lhál ~ =(él)lhelh**> *in the throat*, (<**=em**> *middle voice*), phonology: updrifting, syntactic analysis: intransitive verb, attested by EB (5/25/76), also <**spexwlhálém**>, //s=pəxʷ=ɬɛ́l=əm//, attested by Elders Group (5/26/76).

<**pexwelhálém**>, cts //pəxʷ[-ə-]=ɬɛ́l=əm//, ABFC ['*breathing*'], (<**-e-**> *continuative*), phonology: e-infix, updrifting on final syllable, syntactic analysis: intransitive verb, attested by EB (5/25/76), also <**spèxwelhá:lém**>, //s=pəxʷ[-ə-]ɬɛ́[-·-]l=əm//, also /'*breathe (when you breathe in and out), breathe air*'/, (<**-e- and -:-**> *continuative*), phonology: lengthening and e-infix, attested by BJ (12/5/64), Elders Group (3/1/72), also <**péxwelhàlèm**>, //pə́xʷ[-ə-]=ɬɛ́l=əm//, SPRD ['*breathe out*'], phonology: downstepping, updrifting (last vowel), attested by RG & EH (4/9/99 Ling332).

<**pexwelhálém**>, ABFC ['*breathing*'], *see* pexwlhálém.

<**pe<u>x</u>ó:lésem**>, ABFC ['*open both one's eyes real wide*'], *see* pá<u>x</u>.

<**pí:kwel**>, df //pí·kʷ(=)əl//, FSH /'*barbecue stick, cooking stick (split stick for barbecuing salmon),*'/, ASM ['made of cedar, hazelnut, or vine maple, about four feet long,split on one end, salmon held open with cross-piece sticks is inserted into this cooking stick and the ends are tied closed, the cooking stick is sharpened on the unsplit end which is stuck in the ground at a slant in front of a fire, the salmon roasts or barbecues in it while its fat drips onto the fire smoking it a little'], root meaning unknown, possibly <**=el**> *get, become, go, come*, syntactic analysis: nominal, attested by AC, DM (12/4/64), also <**píkwel**>, //píkʷ(=)əl//, attested by AD, NP, IHTTC, Salish cognate: Songish dial. of N. Straits /píʔkʷəl/ *forked stick for cooking fish over a fire* Raffo 1972 quoted in G82:44 cognate set 222, Lummi dial. of N. Straits /píʔkʷən/ *spit for roasting salmon* Demers 1982 p.c., Nooksack /píʔkʷən ~ pí·kʷən/ (LG) *barbecue stick (split kind)* G84a.

<**pí:lt**>, LAND /'*bury s-th, plant s-th*'/, *see* pél (perhaps ~ pí:l by now).

<**pípe**>, free root //pípə//, SCH ['*paper*'], ECON, LANG /'*letter, mail*'/, syntactic analysis: nominal, attested by EB, Elders Group, Deming, borrowed from Chinook Jargon <paper> /pépə/ *paper, writing, letter* itself from English <paper> Johnson 1978:382, example: <**pípe tálé**>, //pípə tɛ́lə́//, /'*paper money*'/, <**pípe qó:**>, //pípə qá·//, /'*Liquid Paper (typewriter correction fluid)*'/, Elder's comment: "just made up on the spot", literally /'paper water, paper liquid'/, attested by EB (11/7/78), <**pípe swíyeqe**>, //pípə s=wíq=ə//, /'*mailman, postman*'/, literally /'mail/letter man'/, attested by Elders Group.

<**pipeháwtxw**>, dnom //pipə=hɛ́wtx^{w}//, BLDG ['*post office*'], literally /'mail/letter building'/, lx <**=áwtxw** ~ (after vowel) **=háwtxw** ~ **='áwtxw**> *building, house, room*, phonology: epenthetic h, syntactic analysis: nominal, attested by Deming, Elder's comment: "unsure".

<**pipeháwtxw**>, BLDG ['*post office*'], *see* pípe.

<**pípehò:m**>, EZ /'*frog, (*esp. *Northwestern toad,* if generic also includes the *tree toad* and recent introductions the *bullfrog and green frog, and the tailed toad, red-legged frog, and western spotted frog),* (if generic may also include *water frog that lives in springs and keeps the water cold* [Halq'eméylem name unknown to Elders Group on 1/30/80], *and a huge pretty frog (bigger than pípehò:m) that has supernatural powers and cries like a baby [sx̲ex̲ómō̲lh ~ wex̲ó:mō̲:lh]), (big frog with warts [AD])*'/, *see* peh or pó(:)h.

<**pipehomá:lews**>, EB /'*common plantain, ribbed plantain, called "frog leaf"*'/, *see* peh or pó(:)h.

<**pipehó:mó:llh**>, EZ /'*baby frog,* probably also *tadpole*'/, *see* peh or pó(:)h.

<**pipelá:ls**>, ABFC /'*making love, having intercourse*'/, *see* pél (perhaps ~ pí:l by now).

<**pípewels**>, WATR /'*freezing, freezing cold*'/, *see* pí:w.

<**pípexwem**>, EB /'*to drop or blow plant fluff (like dandelions, fireweed, cottonwood, etc.), to blow (of dusty or flaky stuff like wood dust, dandruff, maybe seeds)*'/, *see* píxw.

<**pípexwem pó:l**>, MED /'*cotton balls*'/, PE, *see* píxw.

<**pí:q'**>, free root //pí·q'//, EZ /'*common nighthawk, (rain bird [Elders Group])*'/, ['*Chordeiles minor minor*'], ASM ['has a short body, longs wings, ugly, lays eggs in open gravel bars, says pí:q' as it zooms down in front of you or behind you, are heard early just before spring'], syntactic analysis: nominal, attested by AC, other sources: ES /q'^{w}ɛyθ'/ but Musqueam and Cowichan /píq'/ *nighthawk*, JH /pí·yəq'/ *night hawk*, also /'*nighthawk, rain bird*'/, ASM ['it asks for rain, comes when the sockeye come, grandparents got mad at it because it asked for rain'], attested by Elders Group (6/4/75).

<**pí:t**>, free root //pí·t//, HHG ['*bed*'], phonology: systematic sound shifts for loans include b → p and d → t, syntactic analysis: nominal, attested by LG (Deming 1/25/79), borrowed from Chinook Jargon <bed ~ pit> /pɛ́t ~ pít/ *bed* from English <bed> perhaps influenced by French <lit>? *bed* Johnson 1978:268.

<**pí:tawtxw**>, dnom //pí·t=ɛ́wtxw//, BLDG /'*bedroom, hotel*'/, literally /'bed building, bed house, bed room'/, lx <**=áwtxw**> *building, house, room*, phonology: possible stress-loss on affix after stressed full-grade root, syntactic analysis: nominal, attested by Deming (1/25/79).

<**pí:tawtxw**>, BLDG /'*bedroom, hotel*'/, *see* pí:t.

<**pí:txel**>, df //pí·t=x^{y}əl//, EZ /'*small red or brown "lizard", red salamander and western red-backed salamander,* and possibly also the following brown species attested in the area: *long-toed salamander, northwestern salamander,* and possibly the *British Columbia salamander*'/, ['*Ensatina eschscholtzi* and *Plethodon vehiculum* and possibly also: *Ambystoma macrodactylum macrodactylum, Ambystoma gracile gracile,* and possibly *Ambystoma gracile decorticatum*'], ASM ['no scales, smooth skin, red all over, loses tail easily (EB)'], but note possible cognate for the root in Mainland Comox below, lx <**=xel**> *on the foot*, syntactic analysis: nominal, attested by AC, other sources: ES /pítx^{y}əl/ *lizard*, JH /pí·txəl/ *lizard*, Salish cognate: Saanich dial. of N. Straits /píʔtšən/ *lizard* B74a:10, Samish dial. of N. Straits /pítšn'/ *lizard, salamander*, possibly Squamish /ʔə́pnʔ-šn/ *lizard* W73:164, K67:385, *western red-backed salamander (Plethodon vehiculum)* Kennedy and Bouchard 1976:118,133-134, a probable cognate with the root is Mainland Comox /pít/ *low* B75prelim:51, also <**pítxel**>, //pít=x^{y}əl//, attested by Elders Group (3/1/72), EB (12/12/75, 1/12/76), Deming, example: <**ímex te pítxel.**>, //ʔím=əx^{y} tə

pít=xʸəl//, /'*The salamander walks.*'/, attested by Deming.

<**pí:w**>, free root //pí·w// *freeze.*

<**spí:w**>, dnom //s=pí·w//, WATR ['*ice*'], WETH, (<**s=**> *nominalizer*), syntactic analysis: nominal, attested by AC, BJ (5/64, 12/5/64), Deming, others, also <**spíw**>, //s=píw//, attested by AC, other sources: ES /spìù/ and Musqueam /spíwʔ/ *ice*, example: <**qéx̱ te spí:w li te stó:lō.**>, //qə́x̣ tə s=pí·w li tə s=tá·l=əw//, /'*There's a lot of ice on the river.*'/, attested by AC.

<**spípew**>, strs //s=pí[=C$_1$ə=]w//, WATR ['*be frozen*'], WETH, (<**s=**> *stative*), (<**=R1=**> *resultative*), phonology: reduplication, syntactic analysis: adjective/adjectival verb, attested by AC, EB, example: <**spípew te stó:lō qetstu lóme xwlí te sle'ó:thel.**>, //s=pí[=C$_1$ə=]w tə s=tá·l=əw qə-c-t-u lám-ə xʷ=lí tə s=l=əʔɛ́=á·θ=əl//, /'*The river was frozen until we got across.*'/, literally /'was frozen the river until we hit -just get there at the across/opposite side'/, attested by EB (12/18/75), <**spípew te stó:lō qew lóme xwlí te sle'ó:thel.**>, //s=pí[=C$_1$ə=]w tə s=tá·l=əw qə-əw lám-ə xʷ=lí tə s=l=əʔɛ́=á·θ=əl//, /'*The river was frozen all the way across.*'/, literally /'was frozen the river until it hit get there to the opposite side/across'/, attested by EB, <**spípew te syíq.**>, //s=pí[=C$_1$ə=]w tə s=yíq//, /'*The snow [in the air] is frozen.*'/, attested by AC.

<**pewá:ls**>, sas //piw=ɛ́·ls//, WATR ['*to freeze*'], WETH, (<**=á:ls**> *structured activity non-continuative*), phonology: vowel-reduction to schwa-grade of root before stressed full-grade of suffix, syntactic analysis: intransitive verb, attested by EB, other sources: ES /pəwɛ́·ls/ (Musqueam /pəwɛ́ls/) *freeze.*

<**pípewels**>, cts //pí[-C$_1$ə-]w=əls//, WATR /'*freezing, freezing cold*'/, WETH, (<**-R1-**> *continuative*), (<**=els**> *structured activity continuative*), phonology: reduplication, syntactic analysis: intransitive verb, attested by Elders Group.

<**shxwpípewels**>, dnom //s(=)xʷ=pí[=C$_1$ə=]w=əls//, WATR ['*freezer*'], ACL, FOOD, (<**shxw=**> *nominalizer, something for*), phonology: reduplication, syntactic analysis: nominal, Elder's comment: "could say this though never heard it before", attested by Elders Group.

<**píwet**>, pcs //píw=əT//, WATR ['*freeze s-th/s-o*'], WETH, (<**=et**> *purposeful control transitivizer*), syntactic analysis: transitive verb, attested by AC, other sources: JH /pí·wət/ *freeze it*, example: <**le píwetem.**>, //lə píw=əT-əm//, /'*It got frozen.*'/, attested by AC, Elders Group.

<**pú:ches ~ púwches**>, df //pi[=Aú=]w=cəs or pi[=Aə́=]w=cəs//, WETH ['*fine needles of hoarfrost on a branch*'], WATR, EB, probably <**ú-ablaut** or **é-ablaut**> *resultative or derivational*, lx <**=ches ~ =tses**> *on the hand, on the branch (hand of a tree)*, phonology: possible ú-ablaut (unusual) or é-ablaut with éw → ú(w)/ú:, syntactic analysis: nominal, attested by IHTTC (7/26/77).

<**píwet**>, WATR ['*freeze s-th/s-o*'], *see* pí:w.

<**píxw**>, free root //píxʷ//, EB /'*fall off (of its own accord, of petals or seed fluff)*'/, syntactic analysis: intransitive verb, attested by EB, also <**píx̱w**>, //píx̣ʷ//, attested by EB.

<**píxwem**>, mdls //píxʷ=əm//, EB ['*fall off (of petals or seed fluff)*'], (<**=em**> *middle voice*), syntactic analysis: intransitive verb, attested by EB, also <**píx̱wem**>, //píx̣ʷ=əm//, attested by EB.

<**pípexwem**>, df //pí[=C$_1$ə=]xʷ=əm or pí[-C$_1$ə-]xʷ=əm//, EB /'*to drop or blow plant fluff (like dandelions, fireweed, cottonwood, etc.), to blow (of dusty or flaky stuff like wood dust, dandruff, maybe seeds)*'/, possibly <**=R1=**> *derivational or resultative* or possibly <**-R1-**> *continuative*, phonology: reduplication, syntactic analysis: intransitive verb, attested by Elders Group (5/21/75), AD (1/10/79), example: <**pípexwem te slà:y.**>, //pí[=C$_1$ə=]xʷ=əm tə s=lɛ̀·y//, /'*The fir bark is blowing.*'/, attested by AD.

<**pípexwem pó:l**>, cpds //pí[=C$_1$ə=]xʷ=əm pá·l//, MED /'*cotton balls*'/, PE, (constructed by students, lit. "blow plant fluff - ball"), attested by RG & EH (4/10/99 Ling332)

<**píxwet**>, pcs //píxʷ=əT//, ABFC /'*brush s-th off, brush it (by hand or with branches)*'/, MC, CLO, (<**=et**> *purposeful control transitivizer*), syntactic analysis: transitive verb, attested by Elders Group, AC, also <**píx̱wet**>, //píx̣=əT//, attested by EB, Salish cognate: Squamish /píxʷ-in/ *brush off (clothes)* K69:43, Lushootseed /ʔu-píxʷ-id/ *knock it off, shake it off* and /píxʷ-id/ *shake them down (for ex. of apples)* beside /ʔu-píxʷ-il/ *(a leaf, pine cone) fell*, /píxʷ-il-t/ *drop it/* H76:341-342, also Lushootseed /píxʷ=il/ *fall off, fall down (leaves, dust, etc.)* VH83pc, example: <**píxwet te léx̱wtel**>, //píxʷ=əT tə lə́x̣ʷ=təl//, /'*brush the blanket*'/.

<**spéxwqel ~ spéx̱wqel**>, df //s=pi[=Aə́=]xʷ=qəl ~ s=pi[=Aə́=]x̣ʷ=qəl//, EB /'*fine airborne seed(s)* (not used of plum or apple seed(s) or the hard seeds -- sth'emíwél is used for those) *(used for dandelion seeds, cottonwood seeds, etc., tail of a cat-tail reed, (plant fluff* (possibly including *tail of cat-tail rush)* [Elders Group 2/27/80])'/, (<**s=**> *nominalizer*), (<**é-ablaut of root í**> *resultative* or *derivational*), probably root <**=qel**> *in the head*?, phonology: é-ablaut of root í, fronting/backing variation, syntactic analysis: nominal, attested by AD (1/10/79), Elders Group (2/27/80), also <**spéx̱wqel**>, //s=pi[=Aə́=]x̣ʷ=qəl//, also /'*plant fluff* (possibly including *tail of cattail rush)*'/, attested by Elders Group (2/27/80), also <**spéx̱wqels**>, //s=pi[=Aə́=]x̣ʷ=qəl-s//, also /'*seed (of anything), bud (of cone of conifer)*'/, attested by Elders Group (3/22/78), example: <**spéx̱wqels te lá:yelhp**>, //s=pi[=Aə́=]x̣ʷ=qəl-s tə lɛ́·y=əɬp//, /'*bud (of cone) of Douglas fir*'/, attested by Elders Group (3/22/78).

<**tsqwá:y spéxwqel**>, EB, FOOD *alfalfa sprouts* (lit. green + fine airborne seed), (attested by RG,EH 6/16/98 to SN, edited by BG with RG,EH 6/26/00)

<**spéxwqels te syóqwem sp'áq'em**>, EB, FOOD *sunflower seeds* (lit. small airborne seed of + the + sun + flower), (attested by RG,EH 6/16/98 to SN, edited by BG with RG,EH 6/26/00)

<**pxwíqs**>, ds //píxʷ=M1=qs or píxʷ=ə[=M2=]qs//, EZ /'*sand-fly, no-see-um fly, biting midge*'/, ['family *Ceratopogonidae*'], (<**metathesis type 1** or **type 2**> *derivational* (perhaps *continuative* or *characteristic*)), root <**píxw ~ píx̱w**> *blow (of light seed/fluff/dust)*, lx <**=qs ~ =eqs**> *on the nose, in the nose*, phonology: metathesis, possible vowel-loss after metathesis, fronting/backing variation, syntactic analysis: nominal, attested by Elders Group (10/26/77), also <**px̱wíqs**>, //píx̣ʷ=M1=qs or píx̣ʷ=ə[=M2=]qs//, attested by Elders Group (6/11/75).

<**pepx̱wíqsel**>, ds //C₁ə=píx̣ʷ=M1=qsəl or C₁ə=píx̣ʷ=ə[=M2=]qsəl//, EZ /'*gnat,* probably includes *non-biting midges, biting midges, and (biting) black flies*'/, ['order *Diptera,* probably families *Chiromidae, Ceratopogonidae,* and *Simuliidae*'], (<**R5=**> *diminutive plural*), (<**metathesis type 1** or **2**> *derivational* perhaps *continuative* or *characteristic*), lx <**=eqsel ~ =qsel**> *on the nose, in the nose*, phonology: reduplication, metathesis, possible vowel-loss, syntactic analysis: nominal, dialects: *Sumas/Matsqui*, attested by Deming (6/11/75).

<**Pepx̱wíqsel**>, ds //C₁ə=píx̣ʷ=M1=qsəl or C₁ə=píx̣ʷ=ə[=M2=]qsəl//, N ['*nickname for Nat Dickinson*'], usage: pun of *gnat* on the name Nat, phonology: reduplication, metathesis, syntactic analysis: nominal, attested by Deming.

<**píxwem**>, EB ['*fall off (of petals or seed fluff)*'], *see* píxw.

<**píxwet**>, ABFC /'*brush s-th off, brush it (by hand or with branches)*'/, *see* píxw.

<**píx̱eya**>, df //píx̣=əyɛ or pɛ[=Aí=]x̣=əyɛ//, ABDF /'*have a nightmare, to sleep-walk*'/, MED ['medicine or cure for sleepwalking was putting a basket over the sleepwalker's head and scratching it'], possibly <**í-ablaut**> *resultative*?, <**=eya**> *affectionate diminutive* or possibly *male name ending*?, possibly root <**píx̱**> meaning uncertain or <**páx̱**> *spread apart* possibly root as in <**pex̱=ó:les=em**> *open both one's eyes real wide,* possibly yielding literally *be spread apart + resultative*, phonology: possible ablaut, syntactic analysis: intransitive verb, attested by BHTTC, IHTTC.

<**Píx̱eya**>, df //píx̣=əyɛ or pɛ[=Aí=]x̣=əyɛ//, N ['*nickname of Louie Punch*'], ASM ['he had that spirit

power (of the nightmare), got on his knees and scratched his head and shouted "**Á'althe píx̲eya.**" *I am a nightmare.* when starting his spirit song; Louie was from Leq'áme'l (Nicomen)'], lx <**=eya**> *male name ending or affectionate diminutive*, phonology: possible ablaut, syntactic analysis: nominal, attested by IHTTC (8/9/77).

<**pepíx̲eya**>, cts //C_1ə-píx̣=əyɛ or C_1ə-pɛ[=Aí=]x̣=əyɛ//, ABDF ['*having a nightmare*'], (<**R5-**> *continuative*), phonology: reduplication, possible ablaut, syntactic analysis: intransitive verb, attested by BHTTC.

<**Píx̲eya**>, N ['*nickname of Louie Punch*'], *see* píx̲eya.

<**píy**>, bound root //píy *braced or steadied with one's hand(s), supported by one's hands?*//.

<**píyet**>, pcs //píy=əT or pá·[=Aí=]y=əT//, ABFC /'*put one's hand on s-th to brace oneself, brace oneself on s-th/s-o*'/, (<**=et**> *purposeful control transitivizer*), probably root <**píy**> *braced/steadied/supported with one's hand(s),* possibly related to <**pó:y**> *bend*, possibly <**í-ablaut**> *resultative or derivational*?, phonology: possible ablaut, syntactic analysis: transitive verb, attested by IHTTC (7/13/77), example: <**píyethóxes.**>, //píy=əT-áx^y-əs//, /'*He braced himself on me.*'/, attested by IHTTC.

<**piypiyáleqálem**>, mdls //piy=C_1əC_2=ɛ́ləqə[=Aɛ́=]l=əm or C_1əC_2=piy=ɛ́ləqə[=Aɛ́=]l=əm//, durs, ABFC ['*lying on one side with one's head propped up on one hand*'], possibly <**=R2** or **R3=**> *characteristic or derivational* resp., lx <**=áléqel**> *on the side of the head*, (<**á-ablaut on affix**> *durative*), (<**=em**> *middle voice*), phonology: reduplication, á-ablaut on suffix, stress-shift would have reduced root vowel to schwa except before y, syntactic analysis: intransitive verb, attested by IHTTC (9/1/77).

<**piypiyólwelh**>, df //piy=C_1əC_2=álwəɬ or C_1əC_2=piy=álwəɬ//, ABFC ['*put a hand on one hip*'], literally /'put/brace a hand on a side'/, possibly <**=R2** or **R3=**> *characteristic or derivational* resp., lx <**=ólwelh ~ =ílwelh**> *on the side*, phonology: reduplication, syntactic analysis: intransitive verb, attested by IHTTC (9/1/77), also /'*put one's hands on one's hips*'/, attested by IHTTC (7/13/77).

<**piypiyólwelhem**>, mdls //piy=C_1əC_2=álwəɬ=əm or C_1əC_2=piy=álwəɬ=əm//, ABFC /'*put hands on both hips, (put hands akimbo)*'/, possibly <**=R2** or **R3=**> *characteristic or derivational* resp., lx <**=ólwelh ~ =ílwelh**> *on the side*, (<**=em**> *middle voice*), phonology: reduplication, syntactic analysis: intransitive verb, attested by IHTTC (9/1/77).

<**piyósem**>, mdls //piy=ás=əm//, ABDF ['*leaning the face on the hand with elbow propped*'], literally /'braced/supported/steadied with one's hands on one's face'/, lx <**=ós**> *on the face*, (<**=em**> *middle voice*), syntactic analysis: intransitive verb, attested by IHTTC (9/1/77).

<**Spíyem**>, df //s=píy=əm//, PLN /'*Spuzzum village (on south bank of Spuzzum Creek at its mouth onto the Fraser River),* also *Spuzzum Creek*'/, ASM ['this is the southern-most village in Thompson territory but may not be a borrowing of the Thompson name for the village'], possibly <**s=**> *nominalizer or stative*, possibly <**=em**> *place to get*, possibly root <**píy**> *braced/supported/steadied with one's hands*, comment: this etymology fits phonologically but is pure conjecture semantically for the site, possibly root <**pó:y**> *bend* with <**í-ablaut**> *durative*, comment: this is the Halkomelem name for the nearest Thompson settlement, the Thompson language has a different name for it, (semological comment: there is a big bend in the Fraser River here), syntactic analysis: nominal, attested by AD and AK (on trip to Five-Mile Creek 4/30/79).

<**píyet**>, ABFC /'*put one's hand on s-th to brace oneself, brace oneself on s-th/s-o*'/, *see* píy.

<**píyewsem ~ píwsem**>, CH /'*make the sign of the Cross, (cross oneself)*'/, *see* pó:y.

<**piyósem**>, ABDF ['*leaning the face on the hand with elbow propped*'], *see* píy.

<**piypiyáleqálem**>, ABFC ['*lying on one side with one's head propped up on one hand*'], *see* píy.

<**piypiyólwelh**>, ABFC ['*put a hand on one hip*'], *see* píy.

<**piypiyólwelhem**>, ABFC /'*put hands on both hips, (put hands akimbo)*'/, *see* píy.

<**piypó:yt**>, MC /'*bending lots of things, bending them (lots of things)*'/, *see* pó:y.

<**plems**>, free root //plə́ms//, EB /'*cultivated plum, plums*'/, ['*Prunus spp.*'], syntactic analysis: nominal, attested by Deming (SJ esp.), borrowed from English <plums>, example: <**tsqwá:y te pléms.**>, //c=qʷɛ́·y tə plə́ms//, /'*The plum is green., The plums are green.*'/, attested by Deming (SJ esp.).

<**plíst**>, pcs //plís=T//, CH ['*bless s-th/s-o*'], (<**=t**> *purposeful control transitivizer*), syntactic analysis: transitive verb, attested by AD, NP, borrowed from English <bless> or perhaps Chinook Jargon /plíst/ *priest* (Johnson 1978) which is not used for *priest* in Halkomelem (leplít is used for *priest* also from Chinook Jargon <leplate> from French <le pretre>), example: <**ō Síthikri, plíst te sq'éptset.**>, //ʔo síθikri, plís=T tə s=q'ə́p-c-ət//, /'*Oh Jesus, bless our meeting.*'/, attested by AD, <**plíst te s'álhtelchet**>, //plís=T tə s=ʔɛ́ɬ=təl-c-ət//, /'*bless our food*'/, attested by NP.

<**plhá:t**>, df //pəɬ[=M1=Aɛ́·=]t or pɬ=ə[=Aɛ́·=]T//, DESC ['*be thick*'], semantic environment ['of rope, of layer, of canoe, of lips, (not of tree)'], possibly <**á:-ablaut**> *durative*, crystallized =et> *purposeful control transitivizer*??, metathesis type 1> *derivational*, phonology: possible á:-ablaut, possible metathesis, syntactic analysis: adjective/adjectival verb, attested by AC, EB, others, other sources: ES /pɬɛ́·t/ *thick (in dimension)*, JH /pɬé·t/ *thick*, Salish cognate: Bella Coola /pɬt/ *thick* Nater 1977, Squamish root /pəɬ/ *thick* as in pɬ-uɬ *thick* and /pəɬ-c/ *thick-lipped* W73:264, K67:248-249, Mainland Comox, Pentlatch, Sechelt, Lushootseed /pə́ɬt/ *thick*, N. Straits,Clallam /čɬə́t/ *thick* (in G86a and G82a set 190), example: <**we'ó:lew plhá:t ta sléxwelh.**>, //wə=ʔá·l-əw pɬɛ́·t t-ɛ s=lə́xʷəɬ//, /'*Your canoe is too thick.*'/, attested by AC.

<**plhátstexw**>, caus //pɬɛ́·t=sT-əxʷ//, MC ['*make s-th thick*'], (<**=st**> *causative control transitivizer*), (<**-exw**> *third person object*), syntactic analysis: transitive verb, attested by EB, example: <**plhátstexw te frosting**>, //pɬɛ́t=sT-əxʷ tə frosting//, /'*make the frosting thick*'/, attested by EB.

<**pelhtó:ythel**>, df //pəɬt=á·yθəl or pɬt=á·yθəl//, ANA ['*(have) thick lips*'], BPI, lx <**=ó:ythel**> *on the lips*, phonology: possible vowel-loss on root with epenthetic schwa inserted before spirant, syntactic analysis: adjective/adjectival verb, attested by Deming (3/16/78).

<**plhátstexw**>, MC ['*make s-th thick*'], *see* plhá:t.

<**plhéqw'xel ~ p'lhéqw'xel**>, df //p'ɬə́q'ʷ=xʸəl or p'(i/ə)ɬ=əq'ʷ=xʸəl//, ABDF /'*(get a) sprained foot, leg got out of joint*'/, possibly root <**p'ílh ~ p'élh**> *flattened*, <**=éqw'**> *around in circles, in the joint*, <**=xel**> *on the foot/leg*, see main dialect form <**p'lhéqw'xel**>, phonology: possible vowel-loss in root before stressed suffix, syntactic analysis: intransitive verb, attested by Elders Group (1/30/80), Deming (1/31/80), Salish cognate: Squamish /p'áɬq'ʷ-šn/ *sprain one's ankle* W73:248, K67:252, Lushootseed /p'ə́ɬq'ʷ/ *sprain, get out of joint* and /p'əɬq'ʷ-šád/ *sprain ankle* (also /p'əɬq'ʷ-áčiʔ/ *sprain wrist* and /p'əɬq'ʷ-ùlágʷəp/ *hip out of joint* H76:355-356.

<**plhét**>, SOC ['*crowd s-o out*'], *see* pélh.

<**pókw'em**>, EB ['*when plant fuzz blows*'], *see* pékw' ~ péqw'.

<**pó:l**>, free root //pá·l//, PLAY ['*ball*'], syntactic analysis: nominal, borrowed from English <ball>, example <**pípexwem pó:l**>, cpds //pí[=C_1ə=]xʷ=əm pá·l//, MED /'*cotton balls*'/, PE, (constructed by students, lit. "blow plant fluff - ball"), attested by RG & EH (4/10/99 Ling332).

<**pepó:l**>, cts //C_1ə-pá·l//, PLAY ['*playing ball (playing with a ball)*'], (<**R5-**> *continuative*),

phonology: reduplication, syntactic analysis: intransitive verb, attested by Deming, example: <**la pepó:l á:lhtel.**>, //lɛ C_1ə-pá:l ʔɛ·ɬtəl//, /'*They are playing ball.*'/, attested by Deming.

<**pó:l**>, bound root //pá·l//, original root vowel may be different than this, root meaning unclear

<**spó:l**>, dnom //s=pá·l//, EZ /'*big crow, common crow,* also known as *western crow* or *American crow, (raven* [EF, some Deming elders]*)*'/, ['*Corvus brachyrhynchos,* (*Corvus corax* [EF, some Deming elders])'], ASM ['one difference between the crow and the raven is that the raven's cry is more noticeable (like a hoarse woman's voice) and less frequent, when a crow cries in a certain way it predicts bad news, it cried máw, máw ([mǽw mǽw], no gloss known) when it delivered good news in a story recorded by Boas 1895 (Bertz 1977 translation)'], (<**s=**> *nominalizer*), root meaning unknown (if not a root in <**p**> as above, only the root in <**sepsáp**> *(be) stubborn* [Salish cognate: Squamish /səp/ *stiff*] or <**pél**> *planted, get buried* are close in shape), syntactic analysis: nominal, attested by AC, BJ (12/5/64), Elders Group (3/1/72, 6/4/75, 2/18/76, 3/28/79, 1/16/80), EB, also <**spól'**>, //s=pálʔ//, dialects: prob. *Matsqui or Sumas*, attested by a speaker at Deming (AH?), also /'*raven*'/, attested by EF and some others at Deming (4/17/80), other sources: ES /spa·l/ (circumflex over a) *raven* beside /spəlál/ *crow*, JH /spá·l/ *crow, raven,* but H-T <skaúEks> *raven (Corvus corax principalis)* beside <spEpEtál> (macron over a) (t sic for l) *crow (Corvus caurinus)* (H-T's forms here correspond to terms and glosses I found most frequently).

<**spelól**>, dmn //s=p[=əC_2=]ál//, EZ /'*smaller crow, northwestern crow*'/, ['*Corvus caurinus*'], (<**=R6=**> *diminutive*), phonology: reduplication, syntactic analysis: nominal, attested by AC, other sources: ES /spəlál/ *crow*, H-T <spEpEtál> (macron over a)(t sic for l) *crow (Corvus caurinus)(cry resembles skak brother)..*

<**spopelál**>, df //s=pa[=C_1ə=C2ɛ́=]l or s=pa[=R[=əl=]9]l//, EZ ['*crow*'], ['prob. *Corvus caurinus*'], possibly <**=R1=** or **=R9=**> *diminutive or derivational*, possibly <**=C2ɛ́=**> meaning uncertain, <**=el=**> *plural*?, phonology: reduplication (unusual types), syntactic analysis: nominal, attested by Elders Group (5/3/78), other sources: H-T <spEpEtál> (macron over a)(t sic for l) *crow (Corvus caurinus)(cry resembles skak brother)*

<**spepelól ~ spepeló:l**>, dmpn //s=C_1ə=p[=əl=]á·l//, EZ /'*little crows, small crows, bunch of small crows, (bunch of northwestern crows)*'/, ['*Corvus caurinus*'], (<**R5=**> *diminutive*), (<**=el=**> *plural*), phonology: reduplication, infixed plural, syntactic analysis: nominal, attested by Elders Group (2/18/76, 6/4/75), AC, also <**spepelól'**>, //s=C_1ə=p[=əl=]álʔ//, also /'*small crow*'/, dialects: prob. *Matsqui or Sumas*, attested by Deming (prob. AH), other sources: H-T <spEpEtál> (macron over a)(t sic for l) *crow (Corvus caurinus).*

<**poleqwíth'a**>, bound stem //pal(=)əq$^{w(}$=)íθ'ɛ//; probably root <**póqw**> *to mould, rot (of wood),* probably <**=el=**> *plural*, lx <**=íth'a**> *clothing*, (semological comment: the possible literal meanings *thing that moulds/rots much clothing, thing that moulds/rots clothing many times*, feasible since the dead were put in wooden houses and rewrapped in new blankets every year or two.

<**spoleqwíth'a**>, df //s=paləq^w=íθ'ɛ or s=pa[=lə=]q^w=íθ'ɛ//, REL /'*ghost, corpse, dead body*'/, (<**s=**> *nominalizer*), probably root <**póqw**> *to mould, rot (of wood)*, probably <**=el=**> *plural*, lx <**=íth'a**> *clothing*, (semological comment: the possible literal meanings *thing that moulds/rots much clothing, thing that moulds/rots clothing many times* is especially appropriate because of the Stó:lō custom (different from the coast) of burying the dead in mortuary houses and yearly rewrapping the blankets of the dead (see Duff 1952 and elsewhere)), other possible roots may be <**pel**> *bury* or <**pél:ékw**> *appear, come into view, rise into view*, if <**pel**> *bury* then <=eqw> on top of the head would be needed as well as <**o-ablaut**>, if <**pél:ékw**> *appear, come into view, rise into view* were the root then a backing of <**kw**> to <**qw**> would be required and ablaut of the first vowel to <**o**>, phonology: perhaps infixed plural or <**o-ablaut**> or backing <**kw**> to <**qw**>, syntactic analysis: nominal, attested by Elders Group (3/15/72), EB, AC, BJ (12/5/64), other sources: ES /spələq^{w}íθ'ɛ/

ghost, corpse, example: <**me á:yelexw te spoleqwíth'a.**>, //mə ʔɛ́·yələx^{w} tə s=pa[=lə=]q^{w}=íθ'ɛ//, /'*The corpse came back to life.*'/, literally /'come alive the corpse'/, attested by EB.

<**spopeleqwíth'a ~ spopeleqwíth'e**>, dmn //s=pa[=C$_{1}$ə=lə=]q^{w}=íθ'ɛ//, EZ /'*screech owl* especially, probably *other small owls* as given below but only the *screech owl* is consistently mentioned by all speakers'/, ['*Otus asio kennicotti*'], literally /'little ghost'/, ASM ['spirits of recently deceased people can often appear as small owls, thus their name, meaning little ghost; AD notes that if you see an owl you can name all your family and if the owl drops dead after a name, that person will die; you can save that person by tearing the owl up in your hands; also if you kill an owl you should throw it over your shoulder and name someone [that you wish harm] for the spirit to go to (AD 9/21/78); EB noted that her mother talked to a little barn owl which came three times; she talked to it as if it was her deceased husband and said, "You've travelled to the other world. Don't come back and bother us. We've given everything away of yours." Then it flew away. (EB 9/21/78); Its cry can mean bad news like a crow's (Elders Group 3/21/79)'], (<**=R1=**> *diminutive*), phonology: reduplication, vowel-reduction on suffix, syntactic analysis: nominal, attested by Elders Group (3/1/72, 6/4/75), AC, EB, other sources: ES /spələq^{w}íθ'a/ beside Musqueam and Cowichan /spəpləq^{w}íθ'ɛ/ *screech owl*, also EZ ['*pygmy owl* and *saw-whet owl*'], ['*Glaucidium gnoma swarthi (or Glaucidium gnoma grinnelli)* and *Cryptoglaux acadia acadia (or Aegolius acadicus)*'], attested by Elders Group (9/8/76), also EZ /'*pygmy owl,* some also call *the moth (big ones or little ones)* by this name'/, ['*Glaucidium gnoma swarthi,* some also call order *Lepidoptera* by this name'], ASM ['BJ has never seen the pygmy owl because it comes out late in the evening'], attested by BJ (12/5/64), also EZ ['*barn owl*'], ['*Tyto alba*'], attested by EB (2/27/76, 9/21/78).

<**Popeleqwith'á:m ~ Lexwpopeleqwith'á:m**>, ds //(ləx^{w}=)pa[=C$_{1}$ə=lə=]q^{w}=iθ'ɛ=əm or pə[=C$_{1}$ə=lə]q^{w}=iθ'ɛ=ɛ́m//, PLN ['*rocky place between two CPR tunnels above and about half a mile east of Haig*'], literally /'place to get/have/find screech owl(s) (or pymy owls, etc.)'/, ASM ['Haig is a stop on CPR line on northwest side of the Fraser River,just northwest of and across from Hope; one can often see these "littleghosts" in the morning or early evening at this place'], (<**lexw=**> *always*), (<**=em ~ =ám**> *place to get/have/find*), phonology: vowel merger, possible stressed intransitivizer, syntactic analysis: nominal, attested by IHTTC, source: place names reference file #205.

<**poleqwíth'et**>, pcs //pa[=lə=]q^{w}=íθ'(ɛ)=əT or pa[=lə=]q^{w}=íθ'ə=T//, REL /'*to ghost s-o, (to haunt s-o)*'/, ASM ['typically a person ghosted will hear the voice of someone they were close to, will hear the ghost moving about the house, sometimes will see apparitions of the person, etc., they may also hear the ghosts spirit song; such ghosting can usually be cured by ritualists or Indian doctors or Indian shakers all of whom investigate what the ghost wants and try to provide it if possible (belongings or food not provided to the spirit at a funeral burning ceremony) or try to speak to the ghost to tell it to go away if the ghost wants a person;'], ASM ['ghosts usually wander about during dawn or dusk hours for various decreasing amounts of time after death; burning are held during those hours and the path between the ritual fire and the burial place is always left clear to avoid getting bumped by a ghost; someone bumped by a ghost can lose his spirit or become partially paralyzed or twisted-jawed or suffer other problems; ghosts eventually wind up going to the other side of the sky some believe, but they can become hungry and unhappy and return to earth if not fed and cared for by periodic burning ceremonies'], (<**=t ~ =et**> *purposeful control transitivizer*), phonology: vowel-loss or vowel-reduction to schwa in suffix, syntactic analysis: transitive verb, syntactic comment: note the dropping of the s= *nominalizer*, attested by Elders Group (1/7/76); found in <**poleqwith'ethométselcha.**>, //pa[=lə=]q^{w}=íθ'ə=T-ámə-c-əl-cɛ//, /'*I'm going to ghost you.*'/, phonology: stress-shift on object suffix automatic before subject suffix, downstepping on lexical suffix, <**poleqwíth'ethò:m.**>, //pa[=lə=]q^{w}=iθ'ə=T-à·m//, /'*I'm ghosted.*'/, syntactic comment: passive.

<**poleqwíth'et**>, REL /'*to ghost s-o, (to haunt s-o)*'/, *see* poleqwíth'a.

<**poléx̱wem**>, df //pa[=lə=][-´-]x̣ʷ=əm//, WATR /'*to steam, start to steam*'/, FIRE, LAND, WETH, possibly <**=le=**> *plural* but crystallized so the plurality is not realized anymore, (<-´-> to second syllable *non-continuative*), possibly root <**póx̱w**> *blow spray* or possibly root <**póxw ~ peh**> *blow*, (<**=em**> *middle voice*), phonology: stress-shift, infixed plural, syntactic analysis: intransitive verb, attested by CT (6/8/76), also <**poléxwem**>, //pa[=lə=][-´-]xʷ=əm//, attested by AD, also /'*steaming (sic)*'/, attested by Elders Group (5/26/76), Salish cognate: Songish dial. of N. Straits /pəláxʷəŋ/ *to steam, be steamed* Mitchell 1968, Samish dial. of N. Straits /spáləxʷŋ/ *steam (nominal)* and (VU) /pəláxʷŋ'/ *steam rising (like from moss in the morning sun or water on a fire)* G86:65, Squamish /spúxʷam/ *steam* B78:7, Sechelt /pəxʷə́m ~ pəxʷím/ *steam* T77:8, Mainland Comox /púxʷim/ *steam* B75prelim:6, comment: more speakers from a wider selection of areas use the forms with x̱w (including the derived forms) than use those with xw, so x̱w must be in the main dialect form; semantically a *plural blow spray itself* literal meaning seems more likely to account for *to steam* than does a literal meaning of *plural blow itself* where no water is implied; comparative evidence points to cognates for *steam* with only xw but with ample cognates to also establish a Proto-Central Salish root /pux̣ʷ/ *blow spray* as well; since Mitchell did not distinguish **x̱**w from xw in Songish the Songish cognate for *steam* is not clear evidence one way or the other;, comment: one possibility is the historical assimilation or confusion of **x̱**w to xw of root poxw ~ peh *blow* especially since **x̱**w is less common than xw and harder to hear and since the meanings are similar; clearly there is variation in Halq'eméylem with some speakers having a clear **x̱**w and others a clear xw, each legitimate and correct for the speaker that uses it, example: <**poléx̱wem te témexw.**>, //pa[=lə=][-´-]x̣ʷ=əm tə tə́məxʷ//, /'*The land steams (producing fog).*'/, attested by CT.

<**pó:lex̱wem**>, cts //pá[-·-][=lə=]x̣ʷ=əm//, WATR ['*steaming*'], LAND, FOOD, FIRE, WETH ['*shimmering (in heat)*'], (<-:-> *continuative*), phonology: infixed plural, lengthening, syntactic analysis: intransitive verb, attested by Elders Group (5/28/75, 6/1/77), also <**pó:lxwem**>, //pá[-·-][=lə=]xʷ=əm//, phonology: vowel-loss in infix after lengthening of previous vowel, attested by AD, also /'*to steam [sic for steaming]*'/, attested by Elders Group (5/26/76), example: <**pó:lex̱wem ta sqwéls.**>, //pá[-·-][=lə=]x̣ʷ=əm t-ɛ s=qʷəls//, /'*Your cooking/stew is steaming.*'/, attested by Elders Group (5/28/75), <**pólex̱wem te téméxw.**>, //pá[=lə=]x̣ʷ=əm tə tə́mə́xʷ//, /'*The ground is steaming., The ground is shimmering (in heat).*'/, attested by HP (Elders Group 6/1/77), <**pólex̱wem te síqetsel.**>, //pá[=lə=]x̣ʷ=əm tə síq=əcəl//, /'*The roof is steaming., The roof is shimmering (in heat).*'/, attested by HP (Elders Group 6/1/77).

<**pelpólx̱wem**>, plv //$C_1əC_2$=pá[=lə=]x̣ʷ=əm//, WETH /'*be steaming (in many places), be cloudy with rain-clouds*'/, LAND, WATR, (<**R3=**> *plural*), phonology: reduplication, infixed plural (crystallized), syntactic analysis: adjective/adjectival verb, attested by Deming (3/31/77), example: <**pelpólx̱wem te smá:lt.**>, //$C_1əC_2$=pá[=lə=]x̣ʷ=əm tə s=mɛ́·lt//, /'*The mountain is steaming., The mountain is cloudy with rainclouds.*'/.

<**poléxwt**>, pcs //po[=lə=][-´-]xʷ=T//, WATR ['*steam s-th*'], FOOD, (<-´-> *continuative*), (<**=t**> *purposeful control transitivizer*), phonology: stress-shift, infixed plural, syntactic analysis: transitive verb, attested by AD (3/14/79); found in <**poléxwtlha.**>, //pa[=lə=][-´-]xʷ=T-ɬɛ//, /'*Steam it.*'/, attested by AD.

<**pó:lxwt**>, cts //pá[-·-][=lə=]xʷ=T//, WATR ['*steaming it*'], FOOD, (<-:-> *continuative*), phonology: lengthening, infixed plural, vowel-loss in infix due to lengthening of preceding vowel, syntactic analysis: transitive verb, attested by AD, also /'*steam it*'/, attested by Elders Group (5/26/76).

<**pó:lex̱wem**>, WATR ['*steaming*'], *see* poléx̱wem.

<**poléxwt**>, WATR ['*steam s-th*'], *see* poléx̱wem.

<**pó:lqw'em**>, LAND [*'dust'*], *see* pékw' ~ péqw'.

<**pó:lxwt**>, WATR [*'steaming it'*], *see* poléx̲wem.

<**Popelehó:ys**>, df //pa[=C_1ə=]lə=há·ys or pɛ[=AaC_1ə=]lə=(h)á·y=əs//, PLN [*'Yale Mountain'*], ASM ['located above the new Yale graveyard; this mountain grew in the great Flood to save the people of the area, and some people were saved from starvation by finding spá:lx̲w *vegetable (root/bulb) food* there'], literally /'(said to mean) growing higher, rising up'/, (<**=R1=**> *continuative* (see literal translation)), possibly root <**pále**> *one*, possibly <**=ó:y=es**> *flower* **with epenthetic <h>** after vowel-final root, **<o-ablaut on root a>** automatic from <**=es**> suffix, (semological comment: the alternate literal meaning *being one flower* could account for the reported literal meaning if referring to one flower being or growing higher to show its vegetable food to starving people (??)), phonology: reduplication, possible ablaut automatic, syntactic analysis: nominal, attested by BHTTC, Elders Group (7/6/77, 9/13/77), SP (and AK) (at Fish Camp 8/2/77), source: place names reference file #8.

<**pópélem**> or <**xwpópélem**>, bound stem //pápə́l(=)əm or x$^{w(}$=)pɛ[=AáC_1ə=]l(ə)=əm//, meanings unclear

<**Shxwpópélem**>, df //s(=)x^w=pápə́ləm or s(=)x^w(=)pɛ[=AáC_1ə=]l(ə)=əm//, PLN /*'slough on west side of Harrison River, the first slough upriver from Q'iq'ewetó:lthel and first slough below Xemó:leqw'*/, (<**sxw=**> *nominalizer*), possibly <**ó-ablaut plus =R1=**> *continuative or derivational*, possibly <**=em**> *place to get/have/find or middle voice*?, root meaning unknown, phonology: reduplication, possible ablaut, possible vowel merger, syntactic analysis: nominal, attested by EL, source: place names reference file #298.

<**Popeleqwith'á:m ~ Lexwpopeleqwith'á:m**>, PLN [*'rocky place between two CPR tunnels above and about half a mile east of Haig'*], *see* poleqwíth'a.

<**pópeqwem**>, EB [*'getting mouldy in taste or smell'*], *see* póqw.

<**popeqwemáléqep**>, SM [*'(be) mouldy smelling'*], *see* póqw.

<**pópex̲wels**>, IDOC [*'blowing (of an Indian doctor on a patient)'*], *see* póx̲w.

<**pópeyt ~ pópiyt**>, MC [*'bending s-th'*], *see* pó:y.

<**pópkw'em**>, EB /*'puffball,* probably *giant puffball and gemmed puffball,* and possibly *other species'*/, *see* pékw' ~ péqw'.

<**Pópkw'em**>, PLN /*'village on east bank of Fraser River near the outlet from Cheam Lake, Popkum Indian village'*/, *see* pékw' ~ péqw'.

<**popsíqwtel**>, LANG /*'calling one another names (insults about their bodies), calling each other names'*/, *see* pésqw.

<**póqw**>, bound root //páq^w *to mould, rot (of wood)*//, Salish cognate: Squamish root /puq^w/ *be mouldy* W73:178, K69:43, Samish dial. of N. Straits /pápəq^w/ (VU) *get mouldy* G86:73.

<**spópeqw**>, df //s=pá[=C_1ə=]q^w//, EB /*'mould (on food, clothes, etc.)'*/, (<**s=**> *nominalizer* or possibly *stative*), (<**=R1=**> *resultative* or possibly *continuative*), phonology: reduplication, syntactic analysis: nominal, possibly adjective/adjectival verb?, attested by Elders Group.

<**pópeqwem**>, mdls //pá[-C_1ə-]q^w=əm//, cts, EB [*'getting mouldy in taste or smell'*], ASM ['can persist even after the mould has been thrown out'], (<**-R1-**> *continuative*), (<**=em**> *middle voice*), phonology: reduplication, syntactic analysis: adjective/adjectival verb, attested by Elders Group.

<**popeqwemáléqep**>, ds //pa[-C_1ə-]q^w=əm=ɛ́lə́qəp//, SM [*'(be) mouldy smelling'*], EB, lx <**=áléqep**> *in smell, fragrance, odor*, phonology: reduplication, syntactic analysis: intransitive verb, adjective/adjectival verb?, attested by Elders Group (5/25/77).

<**pqwá:y**>, ds //p(o)q^{w}=ɛ́·y//, EB [*'rotten wood'*], lx <**=á:y**> *bark, wood, covering*, phonology: vowel-loss in root or zero-grade in root before stressed full-grade suffix, syntactic analysis: nominal, attested by AC, other sources: ES and JH /pq^{w}áy/ *rotten wood.*

<**póqwthet**>, incs //páq^{w}=θət//, EB [*'get mouldy'*], (<**=thet**> *get, become, inceptive*), syntactic analysis: intransitive verb, attested by Deming, other sources: H-T <pákwEtsEt> (macron over a) *decayed*, also <**pó:qwthet**>, //pá·q^{w}=θət or pá[=·=]q^{w}=θət//, possibly <**=:=**> *emphatic*, attested by Elders Group, example: <**le pó:qwthet.**>, //lə pá[=·=]q^{w}=θət//, /*'It got mouldy.'*/, syntactic comment: ambiguous past, attested by Elders Group.

<**póqwels**>, HARV [*'splitting wood (esp. blanks and bolts)'*], *see* péqw.

<**póqwthet**>, EB [*'get mouldy'*], *see* póqw.

<**pó:qw' ~ póqw'**>, free root //pá·q'^{w} ~ páq'^{w}//, EZ /*'Harrison River spring salmon, Harrison River chinook salmon, big Chehalis River spring salmon, (preserved (smoked?) meat [AC: Tait dialect])'*/, [*'Oncorhynchus tschawytscha'*], ASM ['variety that runs up Harrison River and tributaries, has white meat not red meat, speckled skin'], comment: some variation with pó(:)kw' between speakers, this may indicate either the original form derived possibly from the root in pákw'=et smoke s-th (fish, hides, meat) over a fire or a competing form possibly derived from that root; it is unclear whether qw' or kw' was historically earlier; the qw' form is apparently the main dialect form since more speakers in more dialects have it and it appears in more derivations, phonology: possible backing from root pákw' *smoke over fire*, syntactic analysis: nominal, Elder's comment (AC): "Chehalis dialect word", dialects: *Cheh.*, attested by AC, Elders Group (3/1/72), others, other sources: ES /pá·q'^{w}/ *spring (tyee) salmon*, JH /pá·q'^{w}/ *Harrison River spring salmon*, see dialect form <**pókw' ~ pó:kw'**> (compare <**pákw'et**> *smoke s-th (fish, hides, meat) over a fire*), also /*'preserved (smoked?) meat'*/, dialects: *Tait (Yale to Rosedale)*, attested by AC, also <**pókw'**>, //pɛ[=Aá=]k'^{w}//, also /*'fall spring salmon, smoked salmon'*/, probably root <**pákw'**> *smoke over fire*, probably <**ó-ablaut**> *resultative or derivational*, Elder's comment: "MH's family used this mostly for *smoked salmon*" (compare <**póqw'**> *Harrison River spring salmon)*, attested by Deming (4/1/76), MH (1/4/79), example: <**pó:kw'**>, //pɛ[=Aá·=]k'^{w}//, also /*'Chehalis spring salmon'*/, attested by Elders Group (3/12/75), <**lalh kwélem kw'e pókw'.**>, //lɛ-ɬ k^{w}ə́l=əm k'^{w}ə pɛ[=Aá=]k'^{w}//, /*'Go get some big spring salmon.'*/, attested by MH (Deming 1/4/79).

<**pepqw'ólh**>, dmn //C$_1$ə=paq'^{w}=álɬ or C$_1$ə=páq'^{w}=ə[=M2=]ɬ//, EZ [*'small Chehalis spring salmon'*], (<**R5=**> *diminutive*), lx <**=ó(l)lh ~ =elh**> *young, offspring*, possibly <**metathesis**> *derivational*, phonology: reduplication, consonant-loss in suffix, possible metathesis, syntactic analysis: nominal, attested by NP (Fish Camp 7/11/78).

<**póqw'elh**>, (//**páq'^{w}=wəɬ**//), FSH [*'dry storage box in tree or on top of pole (for salmon and other dried provisions)'*], lx <**=welh**> *vessel, canoe*, phonology: consonant merger, syntactic analysis: nominal, attested by Elders Group (6/28/78), also <**p'óqw'elh**>, //páq'^{w}=wəɬ//, phonology: p' is almost certainly an error either by me or the speaker(s) on that occasion, attested by Elders Group (9/10/75).

<**tempó:kw'**>, ds //təm=pɛ[=Aá=]k'^{w}//, TIME /*'October moon, time to smoke Chehalis spring salmon'*/, FSH, literally /'time to smoke dry Chehalis spring salmon'/, lx <**tem=**> *time to, time for*, probably mistranscribed <**kw'**> for <**qw'**> rather than root <**pákw'**> *smoke over fire (fish, etc.)*, probably <**ó:-ablaut**> *resultative or derivational*, phonology: ó:-ablaut on root á, syntactic analysis: nominal or adverb/adverbial verb, attested by Elders Group (3/12/75).

<**póqw'elh**>, FSH [*'dry storage box in tree or on top of pole (for salmon and other dried provisions)'*], *see* pó:qw' ~ póqw'.

<**pósqwet**>, LANG [*'insulting s-o'*], *see* pésqw.

<**pósqwtel**>, LANG [*'an insult'*], *see* pésqw.

<**pó:t**>, pcs //páh=T//or //pə[=Aá=]h=T//or //pə[-Aá-]h=T//, ABFC /*'blow, blow s-th'*/, WETH, (<**=t ~ =et**> *purposeful control transitivizer*), comment: the transitive object is usually not expressed, thus showing this form is moving toward being a crystallized CVC root, phonology: possible vowel merger or consonant merger with h, syntactic analysis: transitive verb, attested by AC, Elders Group (3/1/72, 2/19/75, 2/27/80), AD, other sources: ES /pá·t/ *blow*, example: <**tsel pó:t. ~ chel pó:t.**>, //c-əl pá·=T//, /*'I blow.'*/, attested by Elders Group (3/1/72); found in <**pó:tes.**>, //pá·=T-əs//, /*'He blew it.'*/, attested by AC, example: <**pótlha ta' sméteqsel.**>, //pá·=T-ɬɛ t-ɛʔ s=mə́t=əqsəl//, /*'Blow your nose.'*/, literally /'blow =it -command imperative your snot'/, attested by AD (Aug. 1980).

<**pepó:tem**>, rsls //C_1ə=pá·=T-əm or C_1ə=pá·=təm//, ABFC [*'blown'*], MUS, WETH, (<**R5=**> *resultative*), probably <**=t**> *purposeful control transitivizer* and <**-em**> *passive* yielding <**=tem**> *participial*, phonology: reduplication, syntactic analysis: adjective/adjectival verb, example: <**pepó:tem qwló:ythetel**>, //C_1ə=pá·=T-əm q^wɛl=á·yθə(l)=təl//, MUS /*'flute, wind instrument, blown musical instrument'*/, literally /'blown musical instrument (talk =in lips =device)'/, (semological comment: the root of *musical instrument* is *talk* which is something that birds and animals do in their own languages, thus the bird-song would be included in *talk*), attested by Elders Group (11/26/75).

<**pepepó:tem ~ pépepò:tem ~ pepepótem**>, df //C_1ə=C_1ə=pá·=T-əm or C_1ə=C_1ə=pá·=təm//, EB [*'rattlesnake plantain'*], [*'Goodyera oblongifolia'*], ASM ['grows under fir trees'], MED ['leaves used as a poultice and antiseptic after peeling the upper and lower surfaces apart (one can blow into them then) and applying the moist inside part to the wound or open blister (a blister of mine healed in two days from such application); tea from the roots is good for stomach trouble as ulcer medicine, roots were chewed and the juice swallowed for coughs, especially whooping cough medicine'], possibly <**R5=**> *diminutive plural*, possibly second <**R5=**> *resultative*, possibly <**=tem**> *participial*, possibly <**=t**> *purposeful control transitivizer*, possibly plus <**-em**> *passive*, (semological comment: literally perhaps *many little blown things* after the fact that the leaves are small and can be blown into easily), phonology: double reduplication (with SAME reduplication type), syntactic analysis: nominal, attested by SP, AD, AD, JL (at Fish Camp 7/19/79).

<**pótel**>, dnom //pá(=T)=təl//, CAN [*'(a) sail'*], literally /'device to blow'/, lx <**=tel**> *device to*, phonology: possible consonant merger, syntactic analysis: nominal, attested by Elders Group.

<**spotelálá**>, dnom //s=pa=təl=ɛ́lɛ́//, CAN [*'mast on a canoe or boat'*], literally /'something that's a container of a sail'/, (<**s=**> *nominalizer*), lx <**=tel**> *device to*, lx <**=álá**> *container of*, phonology: stress-shift from root without vowel-reduction before stressed full-grade of suffix, syntactic analysis: nominal, attested by Elders Group.

<**Spópetes**>, df //s=pá[=C_1ə=]t=əs//, PLN /*'Katz river-bank, Ruby Creek settlement, village on north bank of Fraser River just below (west of) the mouth of Ruby Creek'*/, literally /'something that (where) it's blowing on the face (of riverbank)'/, Elder's comment: "so named because it's always windy there", (<**s=**> *nominalizer*), (<**=R1=**> *continuative*), lx <**=es**> *on the face*, phonology: reduplication, syntactic analysis: nominal, attested by SP (8/28/75), IHTTC, JL (4/3/78), source: place names reference file #44, other sources: Wells 1965 (lst ed.):25.

<**pótel**>, CAN [*'(a) sail'*], *see* pó:t.

<**pó:x**>, bound root //pá·x^y// *sharp*

<**pó:xeleqw**>, df //pá·x^y=ələq^w//, EB [*'yellow cedar'*], [*'Chamaecyparis nootkatensis'*], ASM ['used for canoes, carved utensils, now scarce; Turner 1979:68 notes that the needles are "prickly to the touch" and the branches are "more droopy and shaggy" than those of red cedar--thus the appearance of sharp hair'], literally /'sharp in the hair (or) sharp in the needles'/, probably root <**pó:x**> *sharp*, lx

<**=eleqw**> *on the hair, on top of the head, on the needles*, syntactic analysis: nominal, attested by Elders Group (1/29/75), Salish cognate: Samish dial. of N. Straits /páš=ələq^{w}/ *yellow cedar* G86:71.

<**pxá:y**>, df //pax^{y}=ɛ́·y//, EB /'*sharp grass, cut-grass*'/, ['*Scirpus microcarpus*'], ASM ['green all year round, cattle eat it year-round, some grows by the Old Chehalis Creek course at the end of the road to Chehalis village; blades of this grass can cut the skin'], probably root <**pox**> *sharp*, lx <**=á:y**> *bark, covering*, phonology: vowel-loss to zero-grade of root before stressed full-grade of suffix, syntactic analysis: nominal, attested by EL, AC, other sources: ES /px^{y}ɛ́·y/ *sharp grass*, JH /pxéy/ *sharp grass*, Salish cognate: Sooke dial. of N. Straits /pšéyʔ/ *sharp grass* E69, Turner and Bell 1971:74, Samish dial. of N. Straits /pšéy'/ *sharp grass (*prob. *Scirpus microcarpus)* G86:72.

<**pó:x̱ ~ péx̱**>, probable root //pá·x̣// meaning unknown or root //pɛx̣// *spread* or root //pə́x̣// meaning unknown

<**spó:x̱em ~ spéx̱em**>, df //s=pá·x̣=əm or s=pɛ[=Aá·=]x̣=əm ~ s=pə́x̣=əm//, EZ ['*early (March) spring salmon*'], ['*Oncorhynchus tschawytscha*'], (<**s=**> *nominalizer* or *stative*), possibly <**ó:-ablaut**> *resultative or continuative*, possibly <**=em**> *middle voice or intransitivizer, get, have*, possibly root <**páx̱**> *spread*??, phonology: possible ó:-ablaut on root a, syntactic analysis: nominal, attested by Elders Group (3/1/72), others.

<**póx̱w**>, bound root //páx̣^{w} *blow spray*, perhaps related to root <peh ~ poh>//pəh ~ pá(h)// *blow*.

<**póx̱wet**>, pcs //páx̣^{w}=əT//, IDOC /'*blow (spray) on a patient (of an Indian doctor or shaman), blow spray on s-o/s-th (of a shaman, a person ironing, a child teething)*'/, ABFC, CLO, ASM ['can be used if you put water in your mouth and blow on ironing, a child also does this while teething, an Indian doctor does it while working on some patients'], (<**=et**> *purposeful control transitivizer*), syntactic analysis: transitive verb, attested by BHTTC, Elders Group, AD, Salish cognate: Squamish /pə́x̣^{w}-n/ *to spit at s-o (e.g. with chewed medicinal herbs)(tr.) beside Coeur d'Alene /tə-pax̣^{w}/ (umlaut over a = /ɛ/) spit* both in K67:249, also Squamish /px̣^{w}-áys/ *to snort (about sea-lions, etc.)* K69:42, compare with <**poléx̱wem**> *steam*.

<**pópex̱wels**>, sas //pá[-C_1ə-]x̣^{w}=əls//, cts, IDOC ['*blowing (of an Indian doctor on a patient)*'], ABFC ['*blowing spray (humorously said of a child teething)*'], (<**-R1-**> *continuative*), (<**=els**> *structured activity continuative*), phonology: reduplication, syntactic analysis: intransitive verb, attested by AD (1/10/79), example: <**pópex̱wels te shxwlám.**>, //pá[-C_1ə-]x̣^{w}=əls tə s(=)x^{w}(=)lɛ́m//, /'*The Indian doctor is blowing (on a patient).*'/, usage: said seriously, also said humorously of a child teething.

<**spópex̱welsà:ls**>, dnom //s=pá[=C_1ə=]x̣^{w}=əls=ɛ̀·ls//, HHG ['*spray gun*'], EB, TOOL, (<**s=**> *nominalizer*), (<**=R1=**> *continuative*), (<**=els**> *structured activity continuative*), lx <**=à:ls**> *tool, device for*, (semological comment: this example proves the existence of two separate morphemes, <**=á:ls**> *structured activity non-continuative* (which varies with =els in the continuative aspect) and =à:ls (or =á:ls ~ =els) *tool, device for* (a nominalizer)), phonology: reduplication, syntactic analysis: nominal, dialects: *Chill. (Sardis)*, attested by BHTTC (9/2/76), also <**shxwpópex̱welsà:ls**>, //s(=)x^{w}=pá[=C_1ə=]x̣^{w}=əls=ɛ̀·ls//, dialects: *Tait*, attested by BHTTC (9/2/76).

<**póx̱wet**>, IDOC /'*blow (spray) on a patient (of an Indian doctor or shaman), blow spray on s-o/s-th (of a shaman, a person ironing, a child teething)*'/, *see* póx̱w.

<**pó:y**>, free root //pá·y//, FOOD ['*pie*'], syntactic analysis: nominal, attested by EB, borrowed from English <pie> /pá·y/.

<**pó:y**>, bound root //pá·y *bend*//, Salish cognate: Lushootseed /púy'/ *curve, bend* H76:348.

<**pó:yt**>, pcs //pá·y=T//, MC ['*bend s-th*'], (<**=t**> *purposeful control transitivizer*), syntactic analysis:

transitive verb, attested by Elders Group (3/1/72), also <**póyt**>, //páy=T//, attested by IHTTC, RG & EH (4/9/99 Ling332); found in <**pó:yttsel.**>, //pá·y=T-c-əl//, /'*I bend it.*'/, attested by Elders Group (3/1/72).

<**pópeyt ~ pópiyt**>, cts //pá[-C_1ə-]y=T//, MC ['*bending s-th*'], (<-**R1**-> *continuative*), phonology: reduplication, e → i before y, syntactic analysis: transitive verb, attested by Elders Group (2/8/78).

<**piypó:yt**>, plv //C_1əC_2=pá·y=T//, MC /'*bending lots of things, bending them (lots of things)*'/, (<**R3**=> *plural patients*), phonology: reduplication, e → i before y, syntactic analysis: transitive verb, attested by Elders Group (2/8/78).

<**spópiy**>, strs //s=pá·[=C_1ə=]y//, DESC /'*be bent, be crooked*'/, (<**s**=> *stative*), (<=**R1**=> *resultative*), phonology: length-loss automatic before reduplication type 1 in most dialects, e → i before y, syntactic analysis: adjective/adjectival verb, attested by AC, EB, also <**spó:piy**>, //s=pá·[=C_1ə=]y//, attested by Elders Group (3/1/72), example: <**spópiy te xáxlh.**>, //s=pá[=C_1ə=]y tə x^{y}ɛ́[=C_1ə=]ɬ//, /'*The trail is crooked.*'/, attested by AC, <**spópiy te q'ówes te siyólexwe.**>, //s=pá[=C_1ə=]y tə q'áwə-s tə si=yáləx^w=ə//, /'*The old person's cane is crooked.*'/, attested by AC, <**lets'ó te spópiys.**>, //ləc'ɛ=Aá tə s=pá[=C_1ə=]y-s//, /'*It has one bend., It has one crook.*'/, literally /'it's bent is one.'/, attested by AC.

<**spóypiy**>, chrs //s=páy=C_1əC_2//, stvi, DESC ['*be crooked [characteristically]*'], (<**s**=> *stative*), (<=**R2**> *characteristic*), phonology: reduplication, e → i before y, syntactic analysis: adjective/adjectival verb, attested by CT and HT (6/8/76), Salish cognate: Musqueam /spáy'pəy'/ *winding* Suttles ca1984: ch.7 [p.163], example: <**spóypiy te xálh.**>, //s=páy=C_1əC_2 tə x^{y}ɛɬ//, /'*The road is crooked.*'/, *<**xelts'íwélém te xálh**> rejected.

<**pó:yethel**>, ds //pá·y=əθəl or pá·y=(á·y)θəl//, ABDF /'*(have a) twisted mouth, twisted jaw*'/, BPI, Elder's comment: "you'll get this way if you eat anything growing in a graveyard and you won't be able to talk; also one of the symptoms of being hit by a ghost", lx <=**ethel**> *in the mouth* or lx <=**ó:yethel**> *in the jaw, in the lips*, phonology: possible syllable-loss, syntactic analysis: adjective/adjectival verb, attested by AD, others? (American Bar trip 6/26/78).

<**píyewsem ~ píwsem**>, df //pa[=Aí=]y=əws=əm//, CH /'*make the sign of the Cross, (cross oneself)*'/, (<**í-ablaut**> *derivational*), lx <=**ews**> *on the body*, (<=**em**> *middle voice*), phonology: ablaut, syntactic analysis: intransitive verb, attested by NP (9/19/75).

<**pá:yewsem**>, cts //pa[-Aɛ́-]·y=əws=əm//, CH /'*crossing oneself, (making the sign of the Cross)*'/, (<**á-ablaut**> *continuative*), phonology: ablaut, syntactic analysis: intransitive verb, attested by Elders Group, Deming.

<**póythet**>, incs //pá·y=θət//, DESC ['*went crooked*'], MC, lx <=**thet**> *go, get, inceptive*, syntactic analysis: intransitive verb, attested by EB.

<**spíytses**>, durs //s=pa[=Aí=]y=cəs//, stvi, ABDF ['*(have a) crooked hand*'], BPI, (<**s**=> *stative*), (<**í-ablaut**> *durative*), lx <=**tses**> *on the hand*, phonology: ablaut, syntactic analysis: adjective/adjectival verb, attested by EB.

<**spipíyxel**>, df //s=C_1əC_2=pa[=Aí=]y=x^{y}əl//, durs, stvi, ABDF /'*(have a) crooked leg, (be a) crooked-legged person*'/, BPI, (<**s**=> *stative*), possibly <**R3**=> *plural or derivational*, (<**í-ablaut**> *durative*), lx <=**xel**> *on the leg, on the foot*, phonology: reduplication, ablaut, e → i before y, syntactic analysis: adjective/adjectival verb, attested by Elders Group, example: <**ō telúwe spipíyxel.**>, //ʔo tɛ=lə́wə s=C_1əC_2=pa[=Aí=]y=x^{y}əl//, /'*(Oh) You crooked leg., You crooked-legged person.*'/, usage: insult, attested by Elders Group (3/3/76).

<**Spíyem**>, df //s=píy=əm//, PLN /'*Spuzzum village (on south bank of Spuzzum Creek at its mouth onto the Fraser River),* also *Spuzzum Creek*'/, ASM ['this is the southern-most village in Thompson

territory but may not be a borrowing of the Thompson name for the village'], possibly <**s=**> *nominalizer or stative*, possibly <**=em**> *place to get*, possibly root <**píy**> *braced/supported/steadied with one's hands*, comment: this etymology fits phonologically but is pure conjecture semantically for the site, possibly root <**pó:y**> *bend* with <**í-ablaut**> *durative*, comment: this is the Halkomelem name for the nearest Thompson settlement, the Thompson language has a different name for it, (semological comment: there is a big bend in the Fraser River here), syntactic analysis: nominal, attested by AD and AK (on trip to Five-Mile Creek 4/30/79).

<**pó:yethel**>, ABDF /*'(have a) twisted mouth, twisted jaw'*/, *see* pó:y.

<**Póylet**>, free root //páylət//, N [*'Violet'*], ACL, phonology: regular sound-shifts in loans include v → p or m, syntactic analysis: nominal, borrowed from English <Violet> /váylət/, attested by EB.

<**Poyőle**>, free root //payólə//, N [*'Viola'*], ACL, phonology: regular sound shifts in loans include v → p or m, syntactic analysis: nominal, borrowed from English <Viola> /vayólə/, attested by EB (3/22/78).

<**pó:yp**>, free root //pá·yp//, HHG [*'metal pipe'*], ACL, syntactic analysis: nominal, borrowed from English <pipe> /pá·yp/, attested by EB (8/10/76).

<**póysekel**>, free root //páysəkəl//, /'a bicycle '/, borrowed from English, syntactic analysis: noun, attested by RG & EH (4/9/99 Ling332)

<**xwpóysekel**>, ds //xʷ=páysəkəl//, <**xw=**> *on the vulva, in the vagina*, or possibly <**xw=**> *toward(s), for* or <**xw= ~ lexw= ~** (rarely) **le=**>, *always*, TVMO /*'to cycle, ride a bicycle'*/ (if the first prefix is correct the word really means /*'to bicycle (of a woman), ride a bicycle (of a woman)'*/, attested by RG & EH (4/9/99 Ling332)

<**pó:yt**>, MC [*'bend s-th'*], *see* pó:y.

<**póythet**>, DESC [*'went crooked'*], *see* pó:y.

<**pőt**>, free root //pót//, CAN [*'boat'*], ACL, phonology: regular sound-shift in loans include b → p, syntactic analysis: nominal, borrowed from English <boat>, attested by Elders Group, also <**pút**>, //pút//, attested by SJ.

<**púpt**>, df //pú[=C_1ə=]t//, CAN [*'double-ended canoe'*], (<**=R1=**> *plural*?), phonology: reduplication, vowel-loss in infix after stressed root, syntactic analysis: nominal, attested by SJ (Feb. 1978).

<**pőtőwelh**>, ds //pót=ówəɬ//, CAN [*'row-boat'*], ACL, lx <**=őwelh**> *canoe, vessel*, syntactic analysis: nominal, attested by Elders Group (1/28/76).

<**pōtőwes**>, ds //pot=ówəs//, CAN [*'oar'*], ACL, lx <**=őwes**> *paddle*, syntactic analysis: nominal, attested by Elders Group (1/28/76).

<**pőtőwelh**>, CAN [*'row-boat'*], *see* pőt.

<**pōtőwes**>, CAN [*'oar'*], *see* pőt.

<**pqwá:ls**>, FOOD [*'break off'*], *see* péqw.

<**pqwá:y**>, EB [*'rotten wood'*], *see* póqw.

<**pqwíles**>, ABDF [*'out of breath and over-tired and over-hungry'*], *see* péqw.

<**ptákwem**>, possibly root //ptɛ́kʷ(=)əm//, EB /*'bracken fern (top, part above ground)'*/, [*'Pteridum aquilinum'*], comment: by an interesting coincidence both the Latin and Halq'eméylem words begin with /pt/ and end with /əm/, ASM ['the roots and fiddleheads were cooked and eaten by the Chilliwacks'], possibly <**=em**> *intransitivizer, have, get*, syntactic analysis: nominal, attested by AC, CT (9/5/74 in Fern root text), Elders Group (3/15/72, 2/19/75), other sources: ES /ptɛ́kʷəm/ *fern*, JH

/pitékʷəm/ *fern,* H-T <piták·um> (macron over i and a) *fern (Pteris aquilina).*

<**pú:ches ~ púwches**>, WETH [*'fine needles of hoarfrost on a branch'*], *see* pí:w.

<**Puchí:l**>, free root //pucí·l//, PLN /*'Yale, Fort Yale'*/, ACL, phonology: regular sound-shifts in loans include f → p, syntactic analysis: nominal, borrowed from English <Fort Yale> /fɔčéyl/ in British English, attested by Elders Group (7/6/77), other sources: Wells 1965 (lst ed.):15, source: place names reference file #3.

<**pumí:l**>, free root //pum(=)í·l//, MUS [*'drumstick (for drum)'*], possibly <**=í:l**> *go, come, get, become,* syntactic analysis: nominal, attested by Elders Group (2/5/75), TG (4/23/75), Salish cognate: Thompson (Lytton dial.) /pumín/ *a drum* B74c:32, Columbian /puwmín/ *a drum* Kinkade 1981:33, Shuswap /pw-um/ *to beat a drum* and /pw-mín/ *drum* K74:143.

<**púpsò:llh**>, EZ [*'kitten'*], *see* pús.

<**púpt**>, CAN [*'double-ended canoe'*], *see* pŏt.

<**pús**>, free root //pús//, EZ [*'domestic cat'*], ACL, [*'Felis domestica'*], syntactic analysis: nominal, borrowed from Chinook Jargon <puss ~ poos-poos ~ pish-pish> *cat* itself partly from English <puss> Johnson 1978:286-287, attested by EB, AC, others.

<**púpsò:llh**>, dmn //pú[=C_1ə=]s=á·lɬ//, EZ [*'kitten'*], ACL, [*'Felis domestica'*], (<**=R1=**> *diminutive*), lx <**=ó:llh**> *young, offspring,* phonology: reduplication, vowel-loss in infix after stressed root and stressed suffix, downstepping on suffix with stressed full-grade root, syntactic analysis: nominal, attested by CT (6/8/76).

<**pú'**>, free root //púʔ//, ABFC /*'to pass gas, break wind, to fart'*/, phonology: final glottal stop is rare, rare u also, syntactic analysis: intransitive verb, see dialect form <**p'ehí ~ p'ehéy**>, Salish cognate: Squamish /púʔ-q/ *to fart* W73:96, K69:43, Lushootseed /p'úʔ/ *to pass gas* VH83pc, Shuswap /s-p'úʔ/ *to fart* and Kalispel /p'úʔ/ *to fart* both in K74:144.

<**spú'**>, dnom //s=púʔ//, ABFC [*'a fart'*], (<**s=**> *nominalizer*), phonology: final glottal stop is rare, rare u also, syntactic analysis: nominal, attested by EB and RP (1/29/76), also ANA [*'rump'*], usage: slang, attested by EB and RP (1/29/76).

<**pú'elets**>, ds //púʔ=ələc//, ABFC /*'fart on the rump, (a show-off)'*/, SOCT [*'show-off'*], EFAM, lx <**=elets**> *on the bottom, on the rump,* syntactic analysis: intransitive verb, nominal, usage: slang, attested by EB (5/12/78).

<**spú'amal ~ spú'emel**>, ds //s=púʔ=əməl//, ANAA /*'skunk's stink bag, skunk's stink sac'*/, literally /'fart part/member'/, (<**s=**> *nominalizer*), root <**pú'**> *fart,* lx <**=emel ~ =ómél**> *part (of body), member,* phonology: vowel-reduction or allomorph in suffix after stressed full-grade in root, syntactic analysis: nominal, attested by BHTTC (11/15/76), also <**skwukwtisláts**>, //skʷukʷ(=)tis=lɛ́c//, attested by BHTTC (1/15/76).

<**pú'elets**>, ABFC /*'fart on the rump, (a show-off)'*/, *see* pú'.

<**pxwíqs**>, EZ /*'sand-fly, no-see-um fly, biting midge'*/, *see* píxw.

<**px̲íwét**>, ABFC [*'spread apart s-o's legs'*], *see* páx̲.

P'

<**=p'**>, da //=p'//, TIB /'*on itself, within itself*'/, syntactic analysis: lexical suffix, derivational suffix; found in <**q'elq'élp'**>, //C_1əC_2=q'ə́l=p'//, /'*tangled on itself (for ex. a net in the water)*'/ (compare <**s=q'el=á:w**> *coiled (of a snake)* and <**=á:w ~ =í:w**> *(on top of itself, on the body))*, <**q'alq'elp'í:w**>, //q'ɛl=C_1əC_2=p'=í·w//, /'*inchworm (í:w is preferred to the version with =í:ws on the body* given as an example under the latter somatic suffix)'/, <**sq'elq'élp'eqw**>, //s=C_1əC_2=q'ə́l=p'=əq^w//, /'*curly hair*'/, <**x̱éyp'et**>, //x̣ɛ́y=p'=ət//, /'*scratch it (and leave a mark), scrape it, claw it*'/, <**slhellhelp'á:lí:ya**>, //s=C_1əC_2=ɬəl=p'=ɛ́·lí·yɛ//, /'*sloppy ears*'/ (compare <**s=lhél=lets**> *rump, buttocks* which must mean something like *(fold(ed) on the rump/bottom)* while <**s=lhel=p'**> means something like *(folded on itself))*.

<**p'ákw'**>, bound root //p'ɛ́k'^{w} *re-use, fix up something used, repair*//.

<**p'ákw'et**>, pcs //p'ɛ́k'^{w}=əT//, MC /'*repair s-th once discarded, make s-th better, fix s-th up, repair s-th*'/, (<**=et**> *purposeful control transitivizer*), syntactic analysis: transitive verb, attested by Elders Group, BHTTC, Salish cognate: Squamish /p'ák'^{w}-an/ *make do with, use for the lack of better (tr.)* K67:252, K69:44.

<**p'áp'ekw'et**>, cts //p'ɛ́[-C_1ə-]k'^{w}=əT//, MC /'*making s-th better, repairing s-th once discarded*'/, (<**-R1-**> *continuative*), phonology: reduplication, comment: ó-ablaut on root a is expected here before the reduplication, and since the continuative has it in the reflexive below it may be that this form is an error for p'óp'ekw'et, syntactic analysis: transitive verb, attested by Elders Group.

<**p'óp'ekw'ethet**>, pcrs //p'ɛ[-AáC_1ə-]k'^{w}=əT-ət//, cts, SOC ['*make oneself useful*'], EFAM, (<**ó-ablaut plus -R1-**> *continuative*), (<**-et**> *reflexive*), phonology: ó-ablaut of root á, reduplication, syntactic analysis: transitive verb, attested by BHTTC.

<**p'ekw'ethílem**>, mdls //p'ɛk'^{w}=əθ(əl)=íl=əm//, incs, FOOD /'*throw different leftovers together for a meal, throw a meal together, eat a snack*'/, literally /'go re-use one's food, go fix up one's food already used (leftovers)'/, lx <**=ethel**> *in the mouth,* (perhaps) *food*, (<**=íl**> *go, come, get, become, inceptive*, <**=em**> *middle voice*), phonology: syllable-loss (el before =íl), vowel-reduction to schwa grade in root before stressed full-grade suffix two syllables away, syntactic analysis: intransitive verb, attested by Elders Group.

<**p'ákw'et**>, MC /'*repair s-th once discarded, make s-th better, fix s-th up, repair s-th*'/, *see* p'ákw'.

<**p'álq'em**>, mdls //p'ɛ́l(=)q'=əm//, LT /'*shine like a reflection, reflect, glitter, sparkle*'/, semantic environment ['used of flashing leaves, spoon-hook lures in fishing, etc.'], (<**=em**> *middle voice*), possibly <**=q'**> *on s-th else*, syntactic analysis: intransitive verb, attested by Elders Group, SP and AD, Salish cognate: Lushootseed /p'ə́ləq'/ *flash, blinking light* as in /ʔalc'u-p'ə́ləq'-əb/ *blinking* and /p'ə́ləq'-əd/ *flash the light on s-o/s-th* H76:355.

<**p'elp'álq'em**>, plv //C_1əC_2=p'ɛ́lq'=əm//, LT /'*shining, (glittering, sparkling (with many reflections))*'/, (<**R3=**> *plural actions or agents*), phonology: reduplication, syntactic analysis: intransitive verb, adjective/adjectival verb, attested by Elders Group.

<**p'elp'álq'emá:lews ~ p'elp'àlq'emá:lews**>, ds //C_1əC_2=p'ɛ́lq'=əm=ɛ́·ləws//, EB /'*poplar, Lombardy poplar (intro.),* also *black cottonwood* and perhaps *trembling aspen* which may have rarely occurred on the eastern and northeastern edges of Stó:lō territory'/, ['*Populus spp.,* esp. *Populus nigra var. italica,* also *Populus balsamifera trichocarpa* and perhaps *Populus tremuloides*'], literally /'many glittering leaves'/, lx <**=á:lews**> *leaf*, phonology: downstepping

alternate high-stress syllables not uncommon, syntactic analysis: nominal, attested by Elders Group, SP and AD, also <**th'estíyelhp**>, //θ'əs=təl=əɬp//, literally /'(metal) nail tree'/, phonology: el → íy before =elhp by regular rule, (semological comment: so called because of its resemblance to a nail), also <**th'e<u>x</u>tíyelhp**>, //θ'əx̣=təl=əɬp//, literally /'rattlesnake tree2PC el → íy before =elhp by regular rule'/, (semological comment: so called because poplar bark was used as medicine for rattlesnake bite).

<**p'alyí:ws ~ p'alyíws ~ p'elyíws**>, df //p'ɛl=əy=í·ws ~ p'əl=əy=íws//, EB ['*bark (of any tree)*'], probably <**=ey**> *bark, covering, plant*, probably <**=í:ws**> *on the body, skin, covering*, root meaning unknown, phonology: vowel-loss in suffix before stressed suffix, possible vowel-reduction, possible length-loss, syntactic analysis: nominal, attested by Elders Group, AC, others, see dialect form <**p'elyíws ~ p'elyú:ws**>, other sources: ES /p'ələyə́w·s/ (Musqueam /p'ələyʔə́wʔs/ (~ /p'ə́ləyʔ/ Suttles 1965)) *bark*, Salish cognate: Squamish /p'ə́liʔ/ *thin bark* W73:14, K67:251, Sechelt /p'ə́l(ʔ)án/ B83pc, Mainland Comox /p'áʔayɛn/ Suttles 1965, Twana /p'əlʔád/, Songish dial. of N. Straits /č'əléʔ/ M68 ~ /č'ə́ləyʔ/ Suttles 1965, Samish dial. of N. Straits /č'ə́ləy'/ ~ /č'ə́ley'/, all *bark (of any tree)*, example: <**tsqwá:y te p'alyíws te q'á:y<u>x</u>elhp.**>, //c=qʷɛ́·y tə p'ɛl=y=íws-s tə q'ɛ́·yx̣=əɬp//, /'*The bark of cascara is yellow.*'/, attested by Elders Group.

<**p'áp'ekw'et**>, MC /'*making s-th better, repairing s-th once discarded*'/, *see* p'ákw'.

<**p'áp'eq'el**>, LT /'*[get whiter, getting white]*'/, *see* p'éq'.

<**p'áp'eq'em**>, EB /'*just starting to flower, blooming, (flowering)*'/, *see* p'áq'em.

<**p'áp'eth'**>, WV ['*sewing*'], *see* p'áth'.

<**p'áq'em**>, mdls //p'ɛ́q'=əm//, EB /'*to bloom, to flower*'/, (<**=em**> *middle voice*), syntactic analysis: intransitive verb, attested by EB, example: <**me p'áq'em**>, //mə p'ɛ́q'=əm//, /'*(start/come to) bloom*'/, attested by EB.

<**p'áp'eq'em**>, cts //p'ɛ́[-C₁ə-]q'=əm//, EB /'*just starting to flower, blooming, (flowering)*'/, (<**-R1-**> *continuative*), phonology: reduplication, syntactic analysis: intransitive verb, attested by Elders Group (3/15/72).

<**tsqwá:y p'áp'eq'em kápech**>, EB, FOOD *broccoli* (lit. green + flowering/flowered + cabbage), (attested by RG,EH 6/16/98 to SN, edited by BG with RG,EH 6/26/00)

<**sp'á:q'em**>, dnom //s=p'ɛ́[=·=]q'=əm//, EB ['*flower*'], (<**s=**> *nominalizer*), possibly <**=:=**> *derivational or resultative or durative*, phonology: possible lengthening, syntactic analysis: nominal, attested by AC, BJ (12/5/64), Elders Group (3/15/72, 5/16/79), EB, other sources: ES /sp'ɛ́·q'əm/ *flower*, example: <**qé<u>x</u> te sp'á:q'em.**>, //qə́x̣ tə s=p'ɛ́·q'=əm//, /'*(There's) a lot of flowers.*'/, attested by Elders Group (3/15/72), <**qé:<u>x</u> sp'á:q'em.**>, //qə́[=·=]x̣ s=p'ɛ́·q'=əm//, /'*(There's) a LOT of flowers.*'/, (semological comment: emphatic lengthening), phonology: emphatic lengthening of schwa (e /ə/), attested by AC, <**le thíyqwtes te sp'á:q'm.**>, //lə θíy=qʷ=T-əs tə s=p'ɛ́·q'=əm//, /'*He dug (up) flowers.*'/, literally /'he past he digs s-th the flower'/, attested by AC, <**th'ó:kws te sp'á:q'em.**>, //θ'á·kʷs tə s=p'ɛ́·q'=əm//, /'*There are seven flowers.*'/, attested by EB, <**tsqwá:y te sp'áq'ems te th'ő́lth'iyelhp.**>, //c=qʷɛ́·y tə s=p'ɛ́q'=əm-s tə θ'ól=C₁əC₂=əɬp//, /'*The flower of the tall Oregon grape is yellow.*'/, attested by Elders Group (5/16/79).

<**p'éq' sp'áq'em kápech**>, EB, FOOD *cauliflower* (lit. white + flower + cabbage), (attested by RG,EH 6/16/98 to SN, edited by BG with RG,EH 6/26/00)

<**spéxwqels te syóqwem sp'áq'em**>, EB, FOOD *sunflower seeds* (lit. small airborne seed of + the + sun + flower), (attested by RG,EH 6/16/98 to SN, edited by BG with RG,EH 6/26/00)

<**sp'eláp'q'em**>, dmpn //s=p'[=əl=]ɛ́[=C₁ə=]q'=əm//, EB ['*little flowers*'], (<**=el=**> *plural*, <**=R1=**> *diminutive*), phonology: infixed plural, reduplication, vowel-loss in infix after stressed root,

syntactic analysis: nominal, attested by Elders Group (5/16/79).

<p'áth'>, free root //p'ɛ́θ'//, WV [*'sew'*], CLO, HUNT, HHG, syntactic analysis: intransitive verb, attested by AC, other sources: ES /p'ɛ́·θ'/ but Musqueam and Cowichan /p'ɛ́θ'/ *sew*, compare with root **<p'íth'>** *squeeze* and with **<p'óth'es>** *basketry cradle, baby basket*, Salish cognate: Pentlatch /p'ác'-əm/ *to sew*, Sechelt /p'ác'-at/ *sew it*, Squamish /p'ác'-an/ *sew (tr.)*, Nooksack /ʔæy p'ǽʔθ'=xʸi=t-æs/ *someone is sewing for s-o* (GS, other speakers would have /p'ǽʔc'=ši=T-æs/), Saanich dial. of N. Straits /č'éθ'-/ *sew*, Lummi dial. of N. Straits /č'éʔy'əc'/ *to sew*, Songish dial. of N. Straits /č'éc'/ *to sew*, Clallam (S. Straits) /č'c'-íŋəɬ/ *to sew*, Lushootseed and Twana /p'ác'-ad/ *sew it* (all quoted in G86a, cognate set 197, sources there), example: **<p'áth'tsel. al:étsa kwthel x̲wéylem.>**, //p'ɛ́θ'-c-əl. ʔɛl·ə́cɛ kʷθə-lx̣ʷí·ləm//, /*'I'm going to sew. Where's my thread?'*/, literally /'I sew present → immediate future. where is the (near but not in sight) -my rope/string/thread'/, attested by AC.

<p'áp'eth'>, cts //p'ɛ́[-C_1ə-]θ'//, WV [*'sewing'*], (**<-R1->** *continuative*), phonology: reduplication, syntactic analysis: intransitive verb, attested by AC.

<shxwp'áp'eth'>, dnom //s(=)xʷ=p'ɛ́[=C_1ə=]θ'//, WV [*'sewing machine'*], CLO, ACL, TOOL, (**<shxw=>** *nominalizer, thing for*), phonology: reduplication, syntactic analysis: nominal, attested by Elders Group.

<p'áth'et>, pcs //p'ɛ́θ'=əT//, WV /*'sew s-th, sew it'*/, HUNT, CLO, (**<=et>** *purposeful control transitivizer*), syntactic analysis: transitive verb, attested by HT, CT, AD, also **<p'á:th'et>**, //p'ɛ́·θ'=əT//, attested by AC, example: **<le p'á:th'etes.>**, //lə p'ɛ́·θ'=əT-əs//, /*'She sewed it.'*/, attested by AC, **<p'áth'et te kw'eléws te sméyeth li te st'elákw' siyólh.>**, //p'ɛ́θ'=əT tə k'ʷəl=ə́w-s tə s=mɛ́yəθ li tə s=t'əlɛ́k'ʷ s=yáɬ//, /*'sew the hide of an animal on a circular frame'*/, attested by HT (6/21/76); found in **<p'áth'etemet ~ p'áth'etémét>**, //p'ɛ́θ'=əT-əm-ət ~ p'ɛ́θ'=əT-ə́m-ə́t//, /*'to be sewed'*/, syntactic comment: dependent passive -em-et, attested by CT, HT, AD, example: **<éy t'we kws p'áth'etemet.>**, //ʔɛ́y t'wə kʷ-s p'ɛ́θ'=əT-əm-ət//, /*'It better be sewed., It needs to be sewed.'*/, syntactic comment: dependent passive, attested by AD.

<sp'áp'eth'>, strs //s=p'ɛ́[=C_1ə=]θ'//, WV [*'(be) sewed (already)'*], HUNT, CLO, (**<s=>** *stative*), (**<=R1=>** *resultative*), phonology: reduplication, syntactic analysis: adjective/adjectival verb, attested by CT, HT (6/21/76).

<p'éth'tel>, dnom //p'ɛ[=Aə́=]θ'=təl//, [p'ɛ́θ'tl (AC), p'ɪ́θ'tl (BJ,DM,EB)], WV /*'needle (for sewing cloth, for mat-making)'*/, ASM ['sewing needles were made out of bone or wood, mat-making needles were made out of wood and were flat, about three feet long, for inserting through cat-tail rushes or bulrushes laid out flat in a row'], CLO, HUNT, HHG, TOOL, EB /*'needle of plant, (thorn)'*/, (**<é-ablaut>** *derivational*), lx **<=tel>** *device to*, phonology: ablaut, syntactic analysis: nominal, attested by AC, BJ (5/64), DM (12/4/64), other sources: ES /p'ə́θ'təl/ *sewing needle*, H-T <pétstEl> *needle*, example: **<siyólh p'éth'tel>**, //s(i)=yáɬ p'ɛ[=Aə́=]θ'=təl//, /*'wooden needle'*/, attested by DM (12/4/64).

<p'á:th'>, probably derived stem //p[=’=]ɛ́·θ'// from **<páth'>** *animal stink, body odor*

<sp'á:th'>, dnom //s=p'ɛ́·θ' or s=p[=G=]ɛ́[=·=]θ'//, EB /*'red-flowering currant berry, Indian currant berry,* probably also *stink currant berry* also called *skunk currant berry'*/, [*'Ribes sanguineum,* probably also *Ribes bracteosum'*], ASM ['the blue-colored berry was eaten but not sought out, the berry is said to drop into the water and develop into the speckled trout called sp'íp'ehàth' ~ spípehà:th' (note unglottalized p), AC describes the bush which she calls the Indian currant, as having red or pink blossoms which are one of the earliest flowers (about Easter) but blue berries which don't ripen till fall; botanists say the plant has "an aromatic smell" (Turner 1974) which may also point to an original root with plain p, i.e. root páth' *animal stink, body odor* which is also found (metathesized) in s=th'ép=eq *skunk*; these facts point to the possibility that the Halq'eméylem term applied also (or mainly) to the *skunk currant or stink currant (Ribes bracteosum)* which has a "characteristic musky odour" and had berries that were eaten more widely than the red-flowering currant berries by Coastal Indians (Turner 1975:171); comparative evidence confirms this (see cognates below)'], MED ['EF said that the roots of the red-flowered currant could be washed, pounded in cloth and put on the gums for toothache and could be used in an eyewash also'], probably root **<páth'>** *animal stink, body odor*, possibly **<=G= glottalization** and **=:= lengthening>** *derivational*, phonology: possible glottalization and lengthening, syntactic analysis: nominal, attested by AC, EF (921/78), others, other sources: ES /sp'ɛ̂·θ'/ *Indian currant*, Salish cognate: Squamish /sp'á·c'/ *stink currant berry (Ribes bracteosum)* Bouchard and Turner 1976:98 and /sp'ə́hc'/ *Indian currant* W73:72, K69:56, versus Squamish /q^{w}ílayus/ *red-flowering currant berry* (and /q^{w}ílayus-ay'/ *red-flowering currant bush*) Bouchard and Turner 1976:101 (/q^{w}ílayʔus/ *unidentified berry (is the first to flower and the last to ripen; the flowers are red, the berries purple* W73:36, K69:83) which is cognate with Halq'eméylem qwilíyes *flower of the red-flowering currant.*

<sp'á:th'elhp>, ds //s=p'ɛ̂·θ'=əɬp//, EB /'*Indian currant bush, red-flowering currant bush,* prob. also *stink currant bush*'/, ['*Ribes sanguineum,* prob. also *Ribes bracteosum*'], lx **<=elhp>** *plant, tree*, syntactic analysis: nominal, attested by AC.

<sp'íp'ehà:th' ~ sp'íp'ehàth'>, df //s=C_1í=p'[=əhɛ̀=]ɛ̂·θ'//, EZ /'*speckled trout, (*prob. *brook trout,* also called *speckled char)*'/, ['probably *Salvelinus fontinalis*'], ASM ['when the little blue berries that grow over creeks and streams (currants) drop into the water they come to life as a trout that has spots on it and is found in creeks in the mountains where no salmon can go up (BJ 12/5/64)'], (**<s=>** *nominalizer*, R4= *diminutive*), possibly **<=ehá=>** *similar to, compared to, comparative*, probably stem **<s=p'á:th'>** *red-flowering currant berry, (stink currant berry)* probably itself from root **<pá:th'>** *animal stink, animal odor, human body odor* probably root by derivational **<glottalization>**, phonology: reduplication, infixed =ehá=, glottalization, syntactic analysis: nominal, dialects: *Chill., Tait*, attested by BJ (12/5/64 old pp.306-307), Elders Group (2/13/80), AD, also **<spípehà:th'>**, //s=C_1í=p[=əhɛ̀=]ɛ̂·θ'//, attested by Elders Group (3/1/72), also EZ /'*small dog salmon*'/, attested by CT (6/8/76), also **<sp'íp'e'àth'>**, //s=C_1í-p'[=əʔɛ̀=]ɛ̂·θ'//, dialects: *Cheh.*, attested by TM (learned Halkomelem from Duncan and Chehalis ancestors).

<p'áth'et>, WV /'*sew s-th, sew it*'/, *see* p'áth'.

<p'átl'et>, pcs //p'ɛ́ƛ'=əT//, ABFC ['*feel it with fingertips*'], (**<=et>** *purposeful control transitivizer*), syntactic analysis: transitive verb, dialects: *Katzie (Downriver Halkomelem)*, attested by Evangeline Pete (Elders Group 2/13/80), Salish cognate: Lushootseed /p'əƛ'-(ə)d/ *feel it* H76:356.

<p'áts't>, free root //p'ɛ́c't//, FIRE /'*black coals, charcoal*'/, syntactic analysis: nominal, attested by Deming (1/31/80), Salish cognate: Squamish /p'íč't/ *ashes, charcoal, black paint* W73:9, K67:253, and Squamish /p'áč'/ *glowing hot, red hot (ab. fire, person in fever, not weather)* K69:44, Cowichan Halkomelem /p'ə́c't/ *charcoal* B74b, Nooksack /p'íčt/ *charcoal* PA61, Songish dial. of N. Straits /č'íc'ət/ *to char, turn to charcoal; to blacken with charcoal; black face paint* M68 (quoted in G82:9 cognate set 14a), Lummi dial. of N. Straits /č'íc'ət/ *coals* Demers 1982pc, Samish dial. of N. Straits (LD) /č'íθ'ət/ and (VU) /č'íc'ət/ *black ashes, charcoal*, Lushootseed /p'íč't/ *coals, embers* H76:358, *charcoal* Hilbert 1983pc.

<p'áxw>, probable root //p'ɛ́x^{w}//, root meaning uncertain

<p'áp'xwem>, df //p'ɛ́[=C_1ə=]x^{w}=əm//, mdls, EFAM /'*be shy, be not talkative, quiet (of a person)*'/, possibly **<=R1=>** *derivational*, (**<=em>** *middle voice*), phonology: reduplication, syntactic analysis: adjective/adjectival verb, attested by IHTTC, NP, example: **<p'áp'x̱wem>**, //p'ɛ́[=C_1ə=]x̣^{w}=əm//, attested by Elders Group (5/28/75), <**pápx̱wem**>, //pɛ́[=C_1ə=]x̣ʷ=əm//, attested by Elders Group (6/11/75).

<**p'ehí ~ p'ehéy**>, df //p'əhí//, ABFC [*'fart'*], EFAM [*'smarty'*], BPI, syntactic analysis: nominal?, intransitive verb??, attested by Deming (6/15/78), see main dialect form <**pú'**> *to pass gas, break wind, to fart.*

<**p'ékw**>, free root //p'ə́kʷ//, WATR /*'to float, come up to the surface, rise to the surface, to surface'*/, syntactic analysis: intransitive verb, attested by EB, Elders Group (3/15/72), AC, other sources: ES /p'əp'ɛ́kʷ/ *float*, JH /p'ə́kʷ/ *float*, Salish cognate: Squamish root /p'akʷ/ ~ /p'əkʷ/ *float* as in /p'áp'kʷ/ *float* and /p'ákʷ-mʔ/ *rise to surface of water*, /p'ákʷ-an-cut/ *come to surface of water (tr. reflex.)*, /p'ə́kʷ-wiɬ/ *bring down to the shore unfinished canoe-hull from the place where it was made*, /p'ə́kʷ-p'əkʷ/ *light in the water, floating easily* and /p'əkʷ-tín/ *float on net, cork* W73:258,103, K67:252, K69:44, also cognate set 246 in G82 shows cognates in N. Straits (Songish and Sooke /p'ekʷəŋ/ *to float*) and Clallam /p'ák'ʷəŋ/ *to float*, and see Nooksack /p'əkʷ-p'ǽkʷ-tæn/ *swimming log, cork float on gill nets* (PF:GS in G84b) and perhaps Lushootseed /p'ə́q'ʷ/ *to float* Hilbert 1983pc (compare Lushootseed root /p'əq'ʷ(u)/ *drift, throw into the water* as in /lə-p'ə́q'ʷ tə qʷɬáyʔ/ *The log is drifting.*, example: <**le p'ékw.**>, //lə p'ə́kʷ//, /*'He/She/It surfaced.'*/, literally /'third person subject past tense auxiliary'/, syntactic analysis: auxiliary past, attested by AC, <**me p'ékw**>, //mə p'ə́kʷ//, /*'to rise to the surface'*/, literally /'come rise to the surface'/, attested by EB.

<**p'ep'ákw ~ p'ap'ákw**>, cts //p'ə[-C_1ɛ́(·)-]kʷ or C_1ə-p'ɛ́kʷ ~ C_1ɛ-p'ɛ́kʷ or p'ɛ[-C_1ɛ́(·)-]kʷ//, WATR [*'be floating'*], root <**p'ékw ~ p'ákw**>, possibly <**-R9-** or **R5-** or **R8-**> *continuative*, phonology: reduplication, syntactic analysis: intransitive verb, attested by Elders Group (3/15/72, 2/26/75), AC, also <**p'áp'akw**>, //C_1ɛ́-p'ɛkʷ or p'é[-C_1ə-]kʷ//, attested by EB, example: <**p'ap'ákw te stsólha.**>, //C_1ɛ-p'ɛ́kʷ tə s=cáɬɛ//, /*'The leaf is floating.'*/, attested by AC, <**p'ep'ákw lí te qó:.**>, //p'ə[-C_1ɛ́(·)-]kʷ lí tə qá·//, /*'(He/She/It is) floating in the water.'*/, attested by Elders Group (2/26/75).

<**sp'ep'ákw'**>, df //s=C_1ə-p'ɛ́kʷ or s=p'ə[-C_1ɛ́(·)-]kʷ//, WATR [*'(be) floating'*], (<**s=**> *stative*), possibly <**R5-** or **-R9-**> *continuative or durative*, phonology: reduplication, syntactic analysis: adjective/adjectival verb, attested by AC, example: <**tl'osu á:y el sp'ep'ákw éwelh éxel sp'ep'ákw.**>, //ƛ'a-s-u ʔɛ́·y ʔəl s=C_1ə-p'ɛ́kʷ ʔə́wə-ɬ ʔə́xʸəl s=C_1ə-p'ɛ́kʷ//, /*'And they just went along (keep on), floating, not paddling, floating.'*/, attested by AC (story of the Flood).

<**p'ep'ákwem**>, df //p'ə[=C_1ɛ́(·)=]kʷ=əm or C_1ə=p'ɛ́kʷ=əm//, WATR /*'calm (of water), smooth (of water), (when the river is) quiet or calm'*/, possibly <**=R9=** or **R5=**> *durative or derivational*, possibly <**=em**> *middle voice or intransitivizer*, phonology: reduplication, syntactic analysis: adjective/adjectival verb, attested by CT, HT, Elders Group.

<**p'ekwtál**>, durs //p'əkʷ=tə[=Aɛ́=]l or p'ɛ́kʷ=tə[=M2=]l//, FSH [*'float (for fishing net)'*], WATR, lx <**=tel**> *device to, thing to*, probably <**á-ablaut in affix**> *durative*, phonology: á-ablaut in affix, syntactic analysis: nominal, attested by EB, other sources: ES /p'əkʷtɛ́l·/ *wood float.*

<**p'íp'ekwtà:l**>, df //C_1í=p'əkʷ=tə[=Aɛ́=]l or C_1í=p'ɛ́kʷ=tə[=M2=]l//, FSH [*'lots of floats'*], WATR, possibly <**R4=** or **=:=**> *plural*, (irregular), phonology: reduplication, ablaut or metathesis, downstepping, lengthening, syntactic analysis: nominal, attested by EB (2/6/76), also <**p'íp'ekw'tà:l**>, //C_1í=p'əkʷ=tə[=Aɛ́=]l or C_1í=p'ɛ́kʷ=tə[=M2=]l//, also FISH /*'big float'*/, phonology: kw' prob. error for kw, (semological comment: use of R4= (almost always *diminutive*) for *augmentative here is certainly unexpected),* attested by SP and AD (7/3/75), Salish cognate: Squamish /p'əkʷ-tín/ *float on net, cork* W73:103, K69:44, Sechelt /p'ə́kʷ-tn/ *cork- or floater-line* T77:19, Samish dial. of N. Straits /p'íp'kʷtən/ *a float* G86:85, Nooksack /p'əkʷ-p'ǽkʷ-tæn/ *swimming log, cork float on gill nets* (PF:GS in G84b).

<**p'ekwtál**>, FSH [*'float (for fishing net)'*], *see* p'ékw.

<**p'ekw'ethílem**>, FOOD /'*throw different leftovers together for a meal, throw a meal together, eat a snack*'/, *see* p'ákw'.

<**p'eléts'tem**>, WATR ['*overflows*'], *see* p'í:l or p'él.

<**p'elp'álq'em**>, LT /'*shining, (glittering, sparkling (with many reflections))*'/, *see* p'álq'em.

<**p'elp'álq'emá:lews ~ p'elp'àlq'emá:lews**>, EB /'*poplar, Lombardy poplar (intro.),* also *black cottonwood* and perhaps *trembling aspen* which may have rarely occurred on the eastern and northeastern edges of Stó:lō territory'/, *see* p'álq'em.

<**p'eltl'ómelh**>, FIRE ['*(be) choked with smoke*'], *see* p'ótl'em.

<**p'élxw**>, stem //p'ə́lxʷ//, root and stem meaning unclear

<**sp'élxwem**>, df //s=p'ə́lxʷ=əm//, ANA /'*lung, lungs (both)*'/, (<**s=**> *nominalizer*), (<**=em**> *middle voice*), root meaning unknown, syntactic analysis: nominal, attested by AC, Elders Group, Deming, other sources: ES /sp'ə́l·xʷəm/ *lung*, Salish cognate: Squamish /sp'ə́lʔxʷm/ *lung* W73:168, K67:282, Skagit dial. of Lushootseed /p'ə́l'xʷəb/ *lungs* H76:355, Samish dial. of N. Straits (LD) /sp'ə́l'xʷəŋ' ~ sp'ə́ləxʷəŋ'/ *lungs* G86:75, others (addable to G82:45 cognate set 238).

<**p'elyú:s ~ p'alyú:s** or **p'elyíws ~ p'alyíws**>, df //p'əl=əy=íws ~ p'ɛl=əy=íws//, EB /'*bark (of tree, bush, etc.)*'/, ASM ['words or prayer said to plant before picking bark, fruit, roots, etc. for medicine or other man-made things: Le th'exwstélemet ō siyám. *Pity us, oh Lord/high-class person.*, Maytólxwchexw. *Help us.*, Th'exwmetólxwchexw, lálh tstulh tsós. *Pity us, we're getting unfortunate.*, Qéx̱ te shxwhókwixtset. *We'll use it in many ways.*, Shxwemlólxwchxw. *You did us a favor.*, Yalh lixw kw'a's hóy. *Thank you.* (Elders Group (TM, DF, TG or NP) 3/22/78)'], probable root <p'al> *shine*, lx <**=ey ~ =áy**> *bark, covering, wool, plant?*, lx <**=íws**> *on the body, on the skin*, root meaning unknown, phonology: vowel-loss in suffix before stressed suffix, merger of vowel with semivowel, possible vocalization, syntactic analysis: nominal, noun, attested by AC, see main dialect form <**p'alyí:ws ~ p'alyíws**>.

<**p'élh**>, free root //p'ə́ɬ//, ABFC /'*become aware (said for ex. of a child about three years or so, or of realizing how something is done), come to one's senses, sober up*'/, EFAM, syntactic analysis: intransitive verb, attested by BHTTC, Elders Group, EB, Salish cognate: Squamish /p'ə́ɬ/ *be sober* and /p'ɬ-íws/ *sober up, come to after fainting* W73:242, K67:251, example: <**me p'élh**>, //mə p'ə́ɬ//, /'*to sober up*'/, literally /'become sober/aware'/, attested by EB, Elders Group, <**walh me x̱élh kw'a' sqwálewel lhíxw me p'élh?**>, //(ʔə́)wə-ə-əɬ mə x̣ə́ɬ k'ʷ-ɛʔ s=qʷɛ́l=əwəl ɬí-xʷ mə p'ə́ɬ//, /'*Do you ever feel sorry when you sober up?*'/, literally /'don't -yes/no question -past come/become hurt your thoughts/feelings when -you subjunctive come/become aware/sober'/, attested by Elders Group (6/28/78).

<**sp'ap'ílh**>, strs //s=C_1ɛ=p'ə[=Aí=]ɬ//, EFAM ['*(be) sober*'], ABFC, (<**s=**> *stative*), (<**í-ablaut**> *resultative*), phonology: reduplication, ablaut, syntactic analysis: adjective/adjectival verb, attested by EB.

<**p'elhéthet**>, pcrs //p'əɬ=ə[=´=]T-ət//, EFAM /'*smarten up, sober up*'/, (<**=´=**> *derivational or non-continuative*), (<**=et**> *purposeful control transitivizer*), (<**-et**> *reflexive*), phonology: stress-shift, syntactic analysis: intransitive verb, attested by Elders Group.

<**p'ílhat**>, pcs //p'ə[=Aí=]ɬ=əT//, SOC ['*sober s-o up*'], ABDF, EFAM, MC ['*flatten it*'], comment: *sober s-o up* is probably in error since the Elders Group on a number of occasions give only *flatten it* for this form; there may instead be a form p'elhét *sober s-o up* since the reflexive form p'elhéthet *smarten up; sober up* seems based on such a form, possibly <**í-ablaut**> *derivational or resultative?*, phonology: possible ablaut, syntactic analysis: transitive verb, attested by EB (5/26/76).

<**p'elhíws**>, ds //p'əɬ=íws//, ABFC /'*come to after fainting, (revive after fainting)*'/, lx <**=íws**> *on the*

body, syntactic analysis: intransitive verb, attested by BHTTC, Salish cognate: Squamish /p'ɬ-íws/ *sober up; come to after fainting* W73:242, K67:251.

<**p'elhéthet**>, EFAM /'*smarten up, sober up*'/, *see* p'élh.

<**p'elhíws**>, ABFC /'*come to after fainting, (revive after fainting)*'/, *see* p'élh.

<**p'ep'ákw ~ p'ap'ákw**>, WATR ['*be floating*'], *see* p'ékw.

<**p'ep'ákwem**>, WATR /'*calm (of water), smooth (of water), (when the river is) quiet or calm*'/, *see* p'ékw.

<**p'ép'eq'**>, LT ['*white ones*'], *see* p'éq'.

<**p'éq'**>, free root //p'ə́q'//, LT ['*be white*'], ASM ['on Berlin and Kay color chart (1969), rows top to bottom are B through I, columns left to right are 1 through 40 and the side column from white to black is 0, individual speakers of the Elders Group identified the following squares as p'éq', AK: B0 and C0, EL: B0 and pure white of uncolored border of chart, NP: B31, B32, B33, LJ (Chill.) (poss. color blind): D17 EP (Katzie living for many years in Tait area): B0'], ASM ['the following color terms are used by AK before p'éq' to specify shades of the color: stewő̈kw"], (semological comment: note also that Tait speaker TG uses ts'sás *ashes* to map the same color that Sumas speaker AH maps with stl'ítl'es, and others (Chilliwack speaker NP and Tait speaker AK) map largely with p'éq'. stl'ítl'es then probably could be glossed *dingy white, off-white* with inceptive form stl'ítl'esel elsewhere translated *dark (old clothes, complexion)*), comment: using derived forms of the root as a modifier of other color terms the following combinations were given by AK: p'éq' st'ewő̈kw'; sp(e)q'íl (tsqwáy, tsméth', tsxwíkw'); sp'q'íl ~ sp'eq'íl (tsqwáy, qálq, tsméth'), syntactic analysis: adjective/adjectival verb, attested by AC, BJ (5/64, 12/5/64), Lawrence James, EP, NP, EL, AK, EB, Elders Group, AK (1987), TG (1987), EB (1987), NP (1987), AH (1987), other sources: ES and JH /p'ə́q'/ *white*, see charts by Rob MacLaury, example: <**p'éq' te sx̱ámeth.**>, //p'ə́q' tə s=x̣ɛ́m(=)əθ//, /'*Cottonwood sap is white.*'/, attested by Elders Group, <**yeláwel p'éq' tel swéta.**>, //yəlɛ́w=əl p'ə́q' tə-l swə́tɛ//, /'*My sweater is whiter.*'/, literally /'is more white my sweater'/, attested by Elders Group, <**yeláwel p'éq' te Lhílheqey.**>, //yəlɛ́w=əl p'ə́q' tə ɬíɬəq=əy//, /'*Mt. Cheam is the whitest.*'/, literally /'is more white the Mt. Cheam'/, attested by Elders Group, <**isále p'éq' thqát**>, //ʔisɛ́lə p'ə́q' θqɛ́t//, /'*two white trees*'/, syntactic analysis: num adjective/adjectival verb nominal, attested by AC.

<**p'éq' q'áq'et'em kwó:l**>, EB, FOOD *white sweet corn* (lit. white + sweet + corn), (attested by RG,EH 6/16/98 to SN, edited by BG with RG,EH 6/26/00)

<**p'éq' sp'áq'em kápech**>, EB, FOOD *cauliflower* (lit. white + flower + cabbage), (attested by RG,EH 6/16/98 to SN, edited by BG with RG,EH 6/26/00)

<**p'éq' témelh**>, //p'ə́q' tə́məɬ//, SPRD //'white paint (for spirit dancers' faces)'//, lit. /'white red-ochre'/, attested by RG & EH (4/10/99 Ling332)

<**p'ép'eq'**>, df //p'ə́[=C_1ə=]q'//, LT ['*white ones*'], probably <**=R1=**> *plural*, phonology: reduplication, syntactic analysis: nominal?, adjective/adjectival verb??, attested by ME (tape 11/21/72).

<**sp'íq'**>, df //s=p'ə[=Aí=]q'//, ABDF ['*(have?) white spotted skin*'], (<**s=**> *stative* or possibly *nominalizer*), (<**í-ablaut on root é**> *resultative* or *durative*?), phonology: í-ablaut on root é, syntactic analysis: adjective/adjectival verb? or nominal?, attested by Deming.

<**sp'eq'p'íq'**>, df //s=C_1əC_2=p'ə[=Aí=]q'//, LT ['*(have?) white spots*'], ABDF, (<**s=**> *stative* or possibly *nominalizer*, R3= *plural*), (<**í-ablaut**> *resultative* or *durative*), phonology: reduplication, í-ablaut on root é, syntactic analysis: adjective/adjectival verb? or nominal?, attested by Deming.

<**p'íp'eq'**>, dmv //C_1í=p'əq'//, LT ['*[a little white]*'], ASM ['occurs almost alternately with p'áp'eq'el within the same areas (as shades of white tinged with orange, yellow or blue) so no difference in meaning can really be distinguished between the two forms, the second form has R7= *comparative*

or emphatic, (sometimes) continuative which was not attested in color term words by any of the others we interviewed'], (<**R4=**> *diminutive*), syntactic analysis: adjective/adjectival verb, attested by EB, see charts by Rob MacLaury.

<**p'íp'eq'el**>, dmv //C_1í=p'əq'=əl//, incs, LT ['*[get(ing)/go(ing)/becom(ing) a little white]*'], (semological comment: commonest for shades of white tinged with green or pink), (<**R4=**> *diminutive*), (<**=el ~ =íl**> *go, come, get, become*), syntactic analysis: adjective/adjectival verb, attested by EB, see charts by Rob MacLaury.

<**tsp'íp'eq'el**>, ds //c=C_1í=p'əq'=əl//, incs, LT ['*[be getting a little white]*'], (semological comment: occurs only once on EB's labelling of the Munsell chart as white tinged with lavender or light lavender (perhaps since nowhere else does the root p'éq' allow the prefix ts=)), (<**ts=**> *have, get, stative with colors*), (<**R4=**> *diminutive*), (<**=el ~ =íl**> *go, come, get, become*), syntactic analysis: adjective/adjectival verb, attested by EB, see charts by Rob MacLaury.

<**p'áp'eq'el**>, df //C_1ɛ́=p'əq'=əl//, incs, LT /'*[get whiter, getting white]*'/, ASM ['occurs almost alternately with p'áp'eq'el within the same areas (as shades of white tinged with orange, yellow or blue) so no difference in meaning between the two can really be distinguished'], (<**R7=**> *comparative or emphatic, (sometimes) continuative*), (<**=el ~ =íl**> *go, come, get, become*), syntactic analysis: adjective/adjectival verb, attested by EB, see charts by Rob MacLaury.

<**p'eq'í:l**>, incs //p'əq'=í·l//, [p'əq'é·l], LT ['*get white*'], ABDF, (<**=í:l ~ =el**> *get, become, go, come, inceptive*), phonology: vowel-loss, syntactic analysis: intransitive verb, adjective/adjectival verb, attested by AC, NP, see charts by Rob MacLaury, example: <**p'eq'í:l te s'ó:thes.**>, //p'əq'=í·l tə s=ʔáθ=əs-s//, /'*His face got white.*'/, attested by AC.

<**sp'q'í:l ~ sp'q'é:yl**>, stvi //s=p'əq'=í·l//, incs, LT ['*[be get/go/become white]*'], (<**s=**> *stative*), (<**=el ~ =íl ~ =í:l**> *go, come, get, become*), phonology: vowel-loss, syntactic analysis: adjective/adjectival verb, attested by NP, see charts by Rob MacLaury.

<**thós sp'eq'í:l tl'íkw'el**>, EB, FOOD *lima beans* (lit. big round + offwhite + bean), (attested by RG,EH 6/16/98 to SN, edited by BG with RG,EH 6/26/00)

<**p'eq'óméx**>, ds //p'əq'=áməx^y//, LT /'*[looks white, white-looking]*'/, (<**=ómex**> *looks, -looking, in color*), phonology: updrifting, syntactic analysis: adjective/adjectival verb, attested by NP, see charts by Rob MacLaury.

<**p'q'élqel**>, ds //p'q'=ə́lqəl//, EZ ['*mountain goat*'], ['*Oreamnos americanus americanus*'], literally /'white wool, white hair'/, ASM ['when one is going to hunt mountain goats, one is not supposed to tell anyone in advance where he will go to hunt; the people of the village of Cheam (Xwchí:yò:m) are said to descend from the mountain goat; the ancestor of the people from Pópkw'em village was also transformed to a mountain goat which is why there were so many goats on Mt. Cheam (Pópkw'em is at the very base of Mt. Cheam); mountain goat wool was gathered from killed goats but also from bushes in areas where they browsed when shedding; it was highly prized for spinning and weaving into patterned blankets (swṓqw'elh) that were a main item of wealth; mountain goat fat was also prized'], lx <**=élqel ~ =álqel**> *wool, fur, hair*, syntactic analysis: nominal, attested by AC, AK and ME (11/21/72 tape), Deming, Elders Group, BJ (12/5/64), DM (12/4/64), other sources: ES /p'q'ə́lqəl/ (Musqueam and Cowichan /p'q'ə́lʔqənʔ/) and JH /p'q'ə́lqə̀l/ *mountain goat*, Salish cognate: Nooksack /p'q'ǽlqin/ *mountain goat* (Suttles 1950, Galloway 1974-80 in G82:21, set 89a), Lummi dial. of N. Straits /p'əq'éləqən/ *mountain goat* Demers 1982pc, Samish dial. of N. Straits /p'q'ə́l'qən/ *mountain goat* G86:66 (poss. loan from Cowichan since goats do not occur in the N. Straits area), contrast with <**sí:lá:kw**> *male mountain goat* which is cognate with Squamish /**sínak**^w/ *old mountain goat* Kennedy and Bouchard 1976:44, example: <**tsel thíyt te swṓqw'elh telí te sáys te p'q'élqel.**>, //c-əl θíy=T tə s=wóq'^wəɬ təlí tə sɛ́·y-s tə p'q'=ə́lqəl//, /'*I made (make it) a blanket from the wool of the mountain goat.*'/, attested by AC.

<**sp'óq'es**>, dnom //s=p'əq'=á[=M2=]s//, EZ ['*bald eagle (mature with white head)*'], ['*Haliaeetus leucocephalus*'], (<**s=**> *nominalizer*), root <**p'eq'**> *white*, lx <**=ós ~ =ó:s ~ =es**> *on the face*, (<**metathesis**> *derivational*), phonology: metathesis, syntactic analysis: nominal, attested by Elders Group (3/1/72, 3/15/78, 2/13/80), also <**sp'óq'es ~ sp'ó:q'es**>, //s=p'əq'=á·[=M2=]s//, attested by AC, BJ (12/5/64), also <**p'óq'es**>, //p'əq'=á[=M2=]s//, attested by EB, other sources: ES /p'á·q'əs/ (Musqueam and Cowichan the same form) *bald eagle*, H-T <spákus> (macron over a) *eagle (Haliaetus leucocephalus)* (diaresis over e), Salish cognate: Squamish /s-p'áq'ʷ-us/ *bald eagle* W73:14, K69:56, contrast <**skw'á:lx̲**> *immature bald eagle (before the head turns white).*

<**Lexwp'ép'eq'es**>, df //ləx^w=C_1íAə́=p'əq'=əs or ləx^w=p'ə́[=C_1ə=]q'=əs//, PLN ['*unnamed mountain on the northwest side of the Fraser River between Hope and Yale which has white mineral deposits visible from the river*'], ASM ['the mineral deposits are and/or were mined by non-Indians'], lx <**lexw=**> *always*, lx <**=es**> *on the face*, probably <**R4=**> *diminutive* and <**é-ablaut on í in reduplication**> *plural* probably <**=R1=**> *plural*, phonology: reduplication, probable é-ablaut on í in reduplication, syntactic analysis: nominal, attested by SP (8/28/75, 8/30/77 on raft trip), source: place names reference file #99.

<**pepq'éyò:s**>, df //C_1ə=p[=D=]əq'=iy=á·s or C_1íAə=p'[=D=]əq'=iy=á·s//, EB ['*snowberry*'], ['*Symphoricarpos albus*'], probably <**R5=** or **R4=Aə=**> *diminutive plural*, probably <**=ey=ó:s**> *flower*, probably <(**lit.**> *plant face*) or =ey> *plant, bark, covering*, probably <**=ó:s**> *face, on the face*, probably <**=D= (deglottalization)**> *derivational*, phonology: reduplication, possible ablaut, deglottalization, syntactic analysis: nominal, attested by AC, Salish cognate: Cowichan dial. of Halkomelem [pə̀pq'eyá·siɬp] and Saanich dial. of N. Straits [pə́q'əya·s] *Symphoricarpos albus (waxberry, snowberry)* (Turner and Bell 1971:80).

<**p'ip'eq'eyós**>, df //C_1í=p'əq'=əy=ás//, EZ /'probably *butterfly with white spot, (*perhaps *white butterfly),* if the name applies to one or more predominantly white butterflies it could include the following which occur in the Stó:lō area*: Clodius parnassian butterfly, Phoebus' parnassian butterfly, pale tiger swallowtail butterfly, white pine butterfly, checkered white butterfly, veined white butterfly, albino females of alfalfa sulphur butterfly*'/, ['if the name applies to one or more predominantly white butterflies it could include the following which occur in the Stó:lō area: family *Papilionidae: Parnassius clodius, Parnassius phoebus, Papilio eurymedon*, family *Pieridae: Neophasia menapia, Pieris occidentalis, Pieris napi*, albino females of *Colias erytheme*'], ASM ['this information gleaned from Robert Michael Pyle: Watching Washington Butterflies 1974:32ff'], (<**R4=**> *diminutive*), root <**p'eq'**> *white*, probably <**=ey=ó:s**> *flower*, phonology: reduplication, syntactic analysis: nominal, attested by Deming (3/15/79)(SJ, MC, MV, LG), other sources: H-T <pepEk·aiása> (macron over e, umlaut over á) (could be <p'ip'eq'eq'oyáse or pipeq'oyáse or p'ip'eq'oyáthel or pipeq'oyáthel>), contrast <**ep'óyethel**> (reconstructed from H-T <apai´EsEl> (circumflex over first a) *butterfly (Papilio) (medium- and small-sized)*)(under <**á:p' ~ áp'**> *wipe*) and <**sesx̲á**> **(JH /səsx̣é/**> *butterfly*, (H-T <sEsqá>) *butterfly (Papilio spp.) (all large kinds)*, also <**pipq'oyó:s**>, //C_1í=p'[=D=]əq'=əy=á·s//, dialects: *Katzie (Downriver Halkomelem)*, attested by Mandy Charnley or Evangeline Pete (Elders Group 6/11/75), also <**p'ip'eq'oyáse?**>, //C_1í=p'əq'=ayɛ́sə?//, comment: prompted after Hill-Tout's form, also /'*(maybe) colored butterfly*'/, attested by AC, also <**p'ip'eq'oyáthe**>, //C_1í=p'əq'=ayɛ́θə//, comment: prompted after Hill-Tout's form, also /'*kind of butterfly (prob. white in part)*'/, attested by TG (2/6/80).

<**p'eq'ó:les**>, ds //p'əq'=á·ləs//, ABDF /'*(have a) white caste over the eye, (have a) cataract*'/, literally /'white on the eye'/, lx <**=ó:les**> *on the eye*, syntactic analysis: intransitive verb, poss. nominal, attested by BHTTC.

<**P'eq'ó:les**>, ds //p'əq'=á·ləs//, PLN ['*place across the Fraser River from Deroche*'], ASM ['Billy Hall used to talk of the place'], Elder's comment: "means *white eyebrow*", lx <**=ó:les**> *on the eye,*

on the eyelid/eyelash, on the eyebrow?, syntactic analysis: nominal, attested by Deming (10/14/77),

<**P'eq'ó:ls**>, ds //p'əq'=á·ls//, PLN /'*White Rock, B.C.*'/, literally /'white rock'/, ASM ['according to Akrigg and Akrigg 1986:335 White Rock was named after a large white rock on the beach, according to an Indian legend, "hurled across Georgia Strait by a young chief who had agreed with the girl whom he loved to make their home where the white rock landed"'], root <**p'eq'**> *white*, lx <**=ó:ls**> *rock; round object; fruit*, syntactic analysis: nominal, attested by Elders Group (6/8/77), contrast <**S(y)emyóme**> *White Rock, B.C., Blaine, Wash., Semiahmoo people*.

<**p'eq'í:l**>, LT ['*get white*'], *see* p'éq'.

<**p'éq' méxts'el**>, EZ /'*body louse, grayback*'/, *see* méxts'el.

<**p'eq'ó:les**>, ABDF /'*(have a) white caste over the eye, (have a) cataract*'/, *see* p'éq'.

<**P'eq'ó:les**>, PLN ['*place across the Fraser River from Deroche*'], *see* p'éq'.

<**P'eq'ó:ls**>, PLN /'*White Rock, B.C., Blaine, Wash.*'/, *see* p'éq'.

<**p'eq'óméx**>, LT /'*[looks white, white-looking]*'/, *see* p'éq'.

<**p'éq' tselqó:me**>, EB /'*whitecap berry, white blackcap berry*'/, *see* tsélq ~ chélq.

<**p'eth'**>, free root //p'ə́θ'//, WETH ['*just come out on (of sun)*'], syntactic analysis: intransitive verb, attested by CT and HT (6/27/76), compare with root <**p'íth'**> *squeeze*, example: <**sqewós te smá:lt kws me p'éth' te syó:qwem telí tí; tl'o le qewétem.**>, //s=qəw=ás-s tə s=mɛ́·lt kʷ-s mə p'ə́θ' tə s=yə[=Aá·=]qʷ=əm təlí tí; ƛ'a lə qəw=ə́T-əm//, /'*It's the warm side of a mountain that the sun just comes out on from there so that it was warmed*'/, attested by CT and HT.

<**wep'éth' ~ wep'áth'**>, ds //wə=p'ə́θ'//, [wʊp'ɛ́θ'], WETH /'*come out (of sun), come up (of sun)*'/, lx <**we=**> *suddenly*, phonology: stressed epsilon allophone probably of /ə/ rather than of /ɛ/, syntactic analysis: intransitive verb, attested by Elders Group, example: <**wep'áth' te syó:qwem.**>, //wə=p'ə́θ' tə s=yə[=Aá·=]qʷ=əm//, /'*The sun comes out., The sun comes up.*'/.

<**swep'áth'**>, dnom //s=wə=p'ə́θ'//, [swʊp'ɛ́θ'], WETH ['*place where the sun comes up*'], LAND, (<**s=**> *nominalizer*), syntactic analysis: nominal, attested by Elders Group (4/16/75).

<**p'éth'tel**>, WV /'*needle (for sewing cloth, for mat-making)*'/, *see* p'áth'.

<**p'ewíy ~ p'ōwíy**>, df //p'əw(=)íy//, MC ['*to patch*'], possibly <**=íy ~ =iy ~ =áy**> *covering, bark, wool*, syntactic analysis: intransitive verb, attested by EB.

<**p'éwiy ~ p'ṓwiy**>, df //p'ə[=´=]w(=)iy or p'ówiy//, EZ /'*halibut, flounder (*prob. *starry flounder)*'/, ['*Hippoglossus stenolepis,* prob. *Platichthys stellatus*'], literally /'patch'/, Elder's comment: "it means *patch*", possibly <**=iy**> *covering, bark*, syntactic analysis: nominal, attested by Elders at Fish Camp (8/2/77), Deming, other sources: JH /p'uwí·/ *halibut*, Salish cognate: cognate set 240 in G86a (Haas Conf.) includes: Proto-Central Salish */p'áwayʔ ~ *p'awáyʔ/ *flounder, (halibut)*. MCx /p'ágay/, MCx (B75) /p'áʔgəy ~ p'ə́gəy'/ *flounder, halibut*, ICx /p'əgáyʔ/ *halibut*, Sq /p'uáyʔ/ *black-dotted flounder*, Ms /p'áwəyʔ/ *flounder, halibut*, Lm /p'əwiʔ/ *flounder*, Smb (VU) /p'ə́wəy'/ *flounder* (*halibut* is unrelated /sá(ʔ)tx̣/), Sg /p'áwəyʔ/, Sg (M68) /p'áweʔ/, Cl /p'áwiʔ/, SLd /p'úwəyʔ/ (H83,H76:361) and NLd /p'uáyʔ/ (H76:361) *flounder*, Tw /p'əwáyʔ/ (abbreviations and sources in preface and bibliography to the present dictionary),

<**sp'ewéy**>, strs //s=p'əwi[=Aə́=]y//, MC ['*(be) patched*'], (<**s=**> *stative*), (<**é-ablaut on root í**> *resultative*), phonology: é-ablaut on root í, syntactic analysis: adjective/adjectival verb, attested by EB.

<**p'ōwíyt ~ p'ewíyt**>, pcs //p'owíy=T ~ p'əwíy=T//, WV /'*patch s-th (of clothes, nets), patch s-th up*'/,

CLO, (<**=t**> *purposeful control transitivizer*), syntactic analysis: transitive verb, attested by EB, CT, AC, example: <**p'ewíyt kw'e sqí:ws**>, //p'əwíy=T k'^{w}ə sq=íy=əws//, /'*patch some pants*'/, attested by CT, <**le p'ewíytes te swéltel.**>, //lə p'əwíy=T-əs tə s=wə́l=təl//, /'*He patched a net.*'/, literally /'third person past he patches it the net'/, attested by CT, <**le hó:kwixes thel tà:l te x̱wílem kwses p'éwíytes tel s'í:th'em.**>, //lə há·k^{w}=əx^{y}-əs θə-l tɛ̀·l təx̣^{w}íləm k^{w}-s-əs p'əwíy=T-əs tə-l s=ʔí·θ'ə=m//, /'*My mother used the thread to patch up my dress.*'/, attested by AC.

<**p'ő́wiyelhthóxchexw**>, bens //p'owiy=əɬ(c)=T-áx^{y}-c-əx^{w}//, WV ['*you patch it for me*'], (<**=elh(ts)**> *benefactive*), phonology: consonant-loss in benefactive suffix in EB's speech, syntactic analysis: transitive verb, attested by EB (3/1/76), example: <**p'ő́wiyelhthóxchexw te sqéyws.**>, //p'ówiy=əɬ(c)=T-áx^{y}-c-əx^{w} tə sq=ə́y=(ə)ws//, /'*Patch the/my pants for me.*'/, attested by EB.

<**p'e'ómthet**>, ABDF ['*be swollen*'], *see* p'ò:m.

<**p'í:**>, bound root //p'í· *put hand on, get hold of*//.

<**p'í:t**>, pcs //p'í·=T//, SPRD ['*bring it out for the first time (of a spirit-song)*'], ABFC, literally perhaps /'get hold of it'/, possibly root <**p'í:**> *put hand on, get hold of*, (<**=t**> *purposeful control transitivizer*), syntactic analysis: transitive verb, attested by CT (Elders Group 7/21/76), Salish cognate: Squamish root /p'iʔ/ *grab, get hold of, ravish* as in /p'iʔ-t/ *seize, grab (tr.)*, /p'iʔ-q^{w}-ánʔ/ *grab s-o by the head* W73:122,226, K67:252-253, K69:44, example: <**p'í:t te syúwel**>, //p'í·=T tə s=yə́w=əl//, /'*bring out a spirit song for the first time*'/, literally /'(prob.) get hold of/grab a spirit song'/, attested by CT.

<**p'í:qwt**>, pcs //p'í·(=)q^{w}=T or p'í·=(ə)q^{w}=T//, ABFC /'*pet s-th/s-o, stroke s-th/s-o*'/, possibly root <**p'í:**> *put hand on, get hold of*, possibly <**=qw**> *around in circles*, possibly <**=eqw**> *on top of the head, on the hair*, (<**=t**> *purposeful control transitivizer*), syntactic analysis: transitive verb, attested by Elders Group, Salish cognate: Squamish /p'iʔ-q^{w}-ánʔ/ *grab s-o by the head* W73:122, K67:252.

<**p'íth'**>, stem //p'í=θ' *squeeze in fingers or hands*//, possibly <**=th'**> perhaps *small portion* as in <**s=qwém=th'**> *lump* with root <**qwem**> *soft* and elsewhere, Salish cognate: Musqueam possible lexical suffix =th' (no gloss given but examples are consistent with gloss suggested above) Suttles ca1984:14.6.15.

<**p'íth'em**>, ds //p'í=θ'=əm//, ABFC ['*get squeezed (in hand or fingers)*'], (<**=em**> *intransitivizer, get, have*), syntactic analysis: Vi, attested by Elders Group, example: <**p'íth'em te qwíqwòyèls.**>, //p'í=θ'=əm tə C_1í=q^{w}ɛ́y=əls//, /'*The orange is squeezed.*'/.

<**p'íp'eth'em**>, cts //p'í[-C_1ə-]θ'=əm//, ABFC ['*squeezing out*'], semantic environment ['juice, clothes, etc.'], (<**-R1-**> *continuative*), phonology: reduplication, syntactic analysis: intransitive verb, attested by Elders Group.

<**p'íth'et**>, pcs //p'í=θ'=əT//, ABFC /'*squeeze s-th/s-o, wring s-th (of clothes), pinch s-th/s-o*'/, (<**=et**> *purposeful control transitivizer*), syntactic analysis: transitive verb, attested by AC, EB, Deming, Elders Group, other sources: ES /p'íθ'ət/ *squeeze*, compare with <**p'áth'**> *sew* and <**p'óth'=es**> *basketry cradle, baby basket*, example: <**p'íth'etchexw ta' méqsel.**>, //p'í=θ'=əT-c-əx^{w} t-ɛʔ mə́qsəl//, /'*Pinch your nose.*'/, attested by Deming.

<**p'íp'eth'et**>, cts //p'í[-C_1ə-]θ'=əT//, ABFC ['*squeezing s-th/s-o*'], (<**-R1-**> *continuative*), phonology: reduplication, syntactic analysis: transitive verb, attested by AC, EB, CT; found in <**p'íp'eth'tem**>, //p'í[-C_1ə-]θ'=əT-əm//, /'*being squeezed*'/, syntactic comment: passive, attested by EB, example: <**p'íp'eth'etem yéqwì:l**>, //p'í[-C_1ə-]θ'=əT-əm yə́q^{w}=í·l//, /'*flashlight*'/, literally /'being squeezed light (burn =go/come/get/become)'/, (semological comment: so named because one has to squeeze it before it lights), attested by CT.

<**p'ip'eth'élmet**>, ds //p'i[-C_1ə-]θ'=ə́lmə(x^{w})=T//, cts, ABFC /'*squeezing the breast of s-o/s-th,*

milking s-o/s-th'/, (<**-R1-**> *continuative*), lx <**=élmexw**> *on the breast (female)*, (<**=t**> *purposeful control transitivizer*), phonology: reduplication, consonant-loss of xw in =élmexw before =t, syntactic analysis: transitive verb, attested by Elders at Fish Camp (7/19/78), example: <**p'ip'eth'élmet te músmes**>, //p'i[-C₁ə-]θ'=ə́lmə(xʷ)=T tə músməs//, /'*milking the cow*'/.

<**p'ith'lhált**>, ds //p'i=θ'=ɬɛ́l=T//, pcs, ABFC ['*choke s-o/s-th*'], lx <**lhál**> *on the throat*, (<**=t**> *purposeful control transitivizer*), syntactic analysis: transitive verb, attested by Elders Group (5/26/76); found in <**p'ith'lhálthòmè**>, //p'i=θ'=ɬɛ́l=T-ámə//, /'*choke you*'/, phonology: downstepping, upshifting.

<**p'íp'eth'elà̱xel ~ p'ip'eth'elá̱xel**>, dnom //p'í[=C₁ə=]θ'=əlɛ́x̣əl//, EZ /'*bat,* may include any/all of the following which occur in the Stó:lō area: *western big-eared bat, big brown bat, silver-haired bat, hoary bat, California myotis, long-eared myotis, little brown myotis, long-legged myotis, Yuma myotis,* and possibly *the keen myotis*'/, ['order *Chiroptera,* family *Vespertilionidae*, may include any or all of the following: *Corynorhinus townsendi townsendi, Eptesicus fuscus bernardinus, Lasionycteris noctivagans, Lasiurus cinereus, Myotis californicus caurinus, Myotis evotis pacificus, Myotis lucifugus alascensis, Myotis volans longicrus, Myotis yumanensis saturatus,* and possibly *Myotis keeni keeni*'], (semological comment: classed as a kind of bird by some fluent elders), (<**=R1=**> *derivational* (perhaps from original *continuative* or *resultative* or *durative*)), lx <**=elá̱xel**> *on the arm*, phonology: reduplication, syntactic analysis: nominal, dialects: *Chill.*, attested by NP (9/19/75), Elders Group, other sources: H-T <petspasElakEl> (macron over e, umlaut over last a) *bat (Vespertilio subulatus)*, also <**skw'elyá̱xel**>, //s=k'ʷəly=ɛ́x̣əl//, dialects: *Cheh., Tait.*

<**p'íp'eth'tel**>, dnom //p'í[=C₁ə=]θ'=təl//, MED //'*tweezers* '//, PE, SMC lit. "device for pinching/squeezing" (elders gave limited support to this, word constructed by students–we moved on too fast for them to really refine it), attested by RG & EH (4/10/99 Ling332)

<**p'í:l** or **p'él**>, bound root //p'í·l or p'ə́l *overflow*//.

<**p'í:ltem**>, df //p'í·l=təm or p'ə[=Aí·=]l=təm//, WATR ['*overflowed*'], MC, possibly <**í:-ablaut**> *resultative*, possibly <**=tem**> *participial*, perhaps itself from <**=t**> *purposeful control transitivizer* plus <**=em**> *middle voice or intransitivizer, get, have*, phonology: possible í:-ablaut on root é, syntactic analysis: intransitive verb, attested by BHTTC, Salish cognate: Squamish /p'i-p'íam/ *overflow (verb)* W73:191, K69:44, Lushootseed /p'íl-əb-əxʷ/ *it flooded* beside /s-p'íl-əb/ *high tide* from root /p'il(i)/ *flat, broad* H76:358-359, Twana root /p'íl-/ *spread (of water only)* NT79.

<**p'eléts'tem**>, df //p'əl=ə́c'=təm or p'il=ə́c'=təm//, WATR ['*overflows*'], ABDF ['*(have an) upset stomach*'], probably <**=éts' ~ =ets' ~ =ts'**> *around in circles*, probably <**=tem**> *participial*, probably <**=t**> *purposeful control transitivizer* plus <**=em**> *middle voice or intransitivizer*, phonology: possible vowel-reduction before stressed suffix, syntactic analysis: intransitive verb, attested by BHTTC, Salish cognate: for =ets' ~ =ts' Musqueam possible lexical suffix /-əc' ~ -c'/ (gloss not speculated but all examples fit *around in circles* as for Halq'eméylem) Suttles ca1984:14.6.29.

<**p'í:ltem**>, WATR ['*overflowed*'], *see* p'í:l or p'él.

<**p'ílh**>, bound root //p'íɬ *get flat, flatten*//, Salish cognate: Sechelt /s-p'iɬ-ít/ *flat* T77:20, Squamish root /p'əlƛ̓'-/ *be crushed, squashed* as in /p'iƛ̓'-íʔ/ *be crushed* and /p'iƛ̓'-anʔ/ *crush, squish (tr.)* W73:71, K69:43, Nooksack /p'ílæ̀kʷs/ (kʷ sic? for q) *flat nosed* PA61, Lushootseed root /p'il(i)/ *flat, broad* as in /ʔəs-p'íl/ *it's flat*, /p'íl-id/ *flatten it*, and /p'íl-ilc/ *flat forehead* H76:358-359.

<**sp'íp'elh**>, strs //s=p'í[=C₁ə=]ɬ//, DESC ['*(be) flat*'], (<**s=**> *stative*), (<**=R1=**> *durative* (or *resultative*?)), phonology: reduplication, syntactic analysis: adjective/adjectival verb, attested by CT, Elders Group (3/15/72), example: <**alétse kw'as sp'íp'elh?**>, //ʔɛlə́cə k'ʷ-ɛ-s s=p'í[=C₁ə=]ɬ//,

/'*Where are you flat?*'/, usage: joking, attested by Elders Group (3/15/72).

<**st'elákw' sp'íp'elh seplíl**>, FOOD *pizza* (lit. round + flat + bread), (attested by RG,EH 6/16/98 to SN, edited by BG with RG,EH 6/26/00)

<**sp'íp'elheqw**>, strs //s=p'í[=C_1ə=]ɬ=əq^w//, ANA /'*(have a) flat head, (have cranial deformation by cradle-board)*'/, BPI, (<**s=**> *stative*), (<**=R1=**> *durative* (or *resultative*?)), lx <**=eqw**> *on top of the head*, phonology: reduplication, syntactic analysis: adjective/adjectival verb, attested by Elders Group (3/15/72), EB, example: <**sp'íp'elheqw st'a te Yéqwelhte.**>, //s=p'í[=C_1ə=]ɬ=əq^w s=tʔɛ tə yə́q^{w}əɬtə//, /'*(He/She has a) flat head like the Yuculta [Cape Mudge Kwakiutl].*'/, attested by EB.

<**sp'íp'elheqsel ~ sp'élhqsel**>, ds //s=p'í[=C_1ə=]ɬ=əqsəl ~ s=p'i[=Aə́=]ɬ=qsəl//, ANA ['*(have a) flat nose*'], BPI, (<**s=**> *stative*), (<**=R1= ~ é-ablaut on root í**> *durative* (or *resultative*?)), lx <**=eqsel ~ qsel**> *on the nose*, phonology: reduplication, é-ablaut on root í, syntactic analysis: adjective/adjectival verb, attested by EB.

<**sp'ap'ílh**>, df //s=C_1ɛ=p'íɬ//, DESC ['*(be) flattened*'], semantic environment ['of a tin can, bread loaf, etc.'], (<**s=**> *stative*, R8= *durative* or *resultative*), phonology: reduplication, syntactic analysis: adjective/adjectival verb, attested by EB.

<**p'ílhet**>, pcs //p'íɬ=əT//, MC /'*flatten s-th, flatten it*'/, (<**=et**> *purposeful control transitivizer*), syntactic analysis: transitive verb, attested by EB, Elders Group (3/15/72), BHTTC, also /'*sober s-o up*'/, attested by EB (5/26/76).

<**p'íp'elhet**>, cts //p'í[-C_1ə-]ɬ=əT//, MC ['*flattening it*'], (<**-R1-**> *continuative*), (<**=et**> *purposeful control transitivizer*), phonology: reduplication, syntactic analysis: transitive verb, attested by Elders Group (3/15/72).

<**p'ílhat**>, SOC ['*sober s-o up*'], *see* p'élh.

<**p'ílhet**>, MC /'*flatten s-th, flatten it*'/, *see* p'ílh.

<**p'íp'ekwtà:l**>, FSH ['*lots of floats*'], *see* p'ékw.

<**p'íp'elhet**>, MC ['*flattening it*'], *see* p'ílh.

<**p'íp'eq'**>, LT ['*[a little white]*'], *see* p'éq'.

<**p'íp'eq'el**>, LT ['*[get(ing)/go(ing)/becom(ing) a little white]*'], *see* p'éq'.

<**p'ip'eq'eyós**>, EZ /'probably *butterfly with white spot, (*perhaps *white butterfly),* if the name applies to one or more predominantly white butterflies it could include the following which occur in the Stó:lō area*: Clodius parnassian butterfly, Phoebus' parnassian butterfly, pale tiger swallowtail butterfly, white pine butterfly, checkered white butterfly, veined white butterfly, albino females of alfalfa sulphur butterfly*'/, *see* p'éq'.

<**p'íp'eth'elàx̲el ~ p'ip'eth'eláx̲el**>, EZ /'*bat,* may include any/all of the following which occur in the Stó:lō area: *western big-eared bat, big brown bat, silver-haired bat, hoary bat, California myotis, long-eared myotis, little brown myotis, long-legged myotis, Yuma myotis,* and possibly *the keen myotis*'/, *see* p'í:.

<**p'ip'eth'élmet**>, ABFC /'*squeezing the breast of s-o/s-th, milking s-o/s-th*'/, *see* p'í:.

<**p'íp'eth'em**>, ABFC ['*squeezing out*'], *see* p'í:.

<**p'íp'eth'et**>, ABFC ['*squeezing s-th/s-o*'], *see* p'í:.

<**p'íp'ex̲w**>, CAN ['*leaking*'], *see* p'íx̲w.

<**p'í:qwt**>, ABFC /'*pet s-th/s-o, stroke s-th/s-o*'/, *see* p'í:.

<**p'íqw'**>, probable root //s=p'i[=Aə́=]q'ʷ//

<**sp'éqw'**>, strs //s=p'i[=Aə́=]q'ʷ//, EFAM ['*(be) proud*'], (<**s=**> *stative*), (<**é-ablaut on root í**> *resultative*), phonology: é-ablaut on root í, syntactic analysis: adjective/adjectival verb, attested by IHTTC, Salish cognate: prob. Lushootseed /p'íq'ʷ/ *flatus, to break wind, (fart)* H76:359 (see other Halq'eméylem words for smarty/fart, i.e., spú'elets and p'ehí).

<**p'íqw'**>, bound root //p'íq'ʷ *purple*//, Salish cognate: Nooksack root in /p'əq'ʷ=p'íq'ʷ/ (attested once as *yellow?* (LT:GS), once as *green* with a comment that the same word [root?] means *dark blue* in Chilliwack Halkomelem), Nooksack /č=p'íq'ʷ/ *yellow* (PA:GS 1.26)(beside Upriver Halkomelem /s=p'iq'ʷ/ *yellow* from the same speaker 1.10), and Nooksack [pí·q'ʷəlæ̀·noxʷ] probably /p'íq'ʷ=əlænoxʷ/ *autumn, when leaves turn yellow* (PA:GS 1.10), root in Squamish /p'əq'ʷ=p'íq'ʷ/ *yellow, a kind of paint found in the mountains*'.

<**tsp'íqw'**>, ds //c=p'íq'ʷ//, LT ['*purple*'], (<**ts=**> *have, get, stative with colors*), syntactic analysis: adjective/adjectival verb, attested by NP, see charts by Rob MacLaury.

<**sp'íqw'**>, ds //s=p'íq'ʷ//, LT ['*purple*'], (<**s=**> *stative*), syntactic analysis: adjective/adjectival verb, attested by NP, see charts by Rob MacLaury.

<**sp'íp'eqw'el**>, cts //s=p'í[=C_1ə=]q'ʷ=əl//, incs, LT ['*[be getting/going purple]*'], (<**s=**> *stative*), (<**=R1=**> *continuative*), (<**=el ~ =íl**> *go, come, get, become*), syntactic analysis: adjective/adjectival verb, attested by NP, see charts by Rob MacLaury.

<**p'í:t**>, SPRD ['*bring it out for the first time (of a spirit-song)*'], *see* p'í:.

<**p'íth'**>, ABFC ['*(squeeze with hand)*'], *see* p'í:.

<**p'íth'em**>, ABFC ['*get squeezed (in hand or fingers)*'], *see* p'í:.

<**p'íth'et**>, ABFC /'*squeeze s-th/s-o, wring s-th (of clothes), pinch s-th/s-o*'/, *see* p'í:.

<**p'ith'lhált**>, ABFC ['*choke s-o/s-th*'], *see* p'í:.

<**p'íx̲w**>, free root //p'íx̣ʷ//, CAN ['*to leak*'], MC, WATR, syntactic analysis: intransitive verb, attested by EB, Salish cognate: Sooke dial. of N. Straits /p'íx̣ʷŋ/ *it is overflowing* E69 (quoted in G82:45 set 242), example: <**p'íx̲w te sléxwelh.**>, //p'íx̣ʷ tə s=lə́xʷəɬ//, /'*The canoe leaks.*'/, attested by EB.

<**p'íp'ex̲w**>, cts //p'í[-C_1ə-]x̣ʷ//, CAN ['*leaking*'], MC, WATR, (<**-R1-**> *continuative*), phonology: reduplication, syntactic analysis: intransitive verb, attested by Elders Group, EB, example: <**p'íp'ex̲w te sléxwelh.**>, //p'í[-C_1ə-]x̣ʷ tə s=lə́xʷəɬ//, /'*The canoe is leaking.*'/, attested by EB.

<**p'íx̲w**>, bound root //p'íx̣ʷ//, root meaning unknown

<**p'íp'ex̲wel**>, df //p'íp'əx̣ʷ=əl//, incs, LT /'*(tan, brownish)*'/, ASM ['p'íp'x̲wel is at F8, F10, G6 on the Munsell chart--contrasting with sp'íp'ex̲wel at I5, clearly the /s=/ provides a meaningful semantic addition, the /s=/ form seems to indicate a deeper type of brown than the tans represented by the unprefixed form'], possibly root <**p'íx̲w**> *to leak (as of a canoe)* which seems unrelated (but note its continuative **<p'íp'ex̲w>** *leaking*), possibly <**=R1=**> *continuative*, possibly <**R4=**> *diminutive*, (<**=el ~ =íl**> *go, come, get, become*), syntactic analysis: adjective/adjectival verb, attested by NP, see charts by Rob MacLaury.

<**sp'íp'ex̲wel**>, stvi //s=p'íp'əx̣ʷ=əl//, incs, LT /'*(tan, brownish)*'/, ASM ['on the Munsell color chart'], (<**s=**> *stative*), (<**=el ~ =íl**> *go, come, get, become*), syntactic analysis: adjective/adjectival verb, attested by NP, see charts by Rob MacLaury.

<**p'ò:m**>, df //p'à·m or p'áʔ=(ə)m//, ABDF /'*rise, swell*'/, possibly <**=em**> *middle voice or intransitivizer*, syntactic analysis: intransitive verb, attested by Deming Elders and JL and NP (at Fish Camp, 7/19/79), other sources: JH /p'á·m/ *swell, rise*, Salish cognate: Lummi dial. of N. Straits /p'oʔŋ/ *swell*

up, Saanich dial. of N. Straits /p'á·ŋ/ *swell up*, Songish dial. of N. Straits /p'á·ŋ/ *swell (as a river)*, Samish dial. of N. Straits /p'áŋ/ *to swell up (belly, tide, etc.)* G86:76, Nooksack /pòhóm-təm/ *swell* A61, Squamish root puh- ~ peh- *blow, swell* as in /púmʔ/ *to swell* and /pə́-pumʔ/ *be swelling* and /pú-pumʔ/ *swelling* W73:259, K67:248-249, all N. Straits forms but Samish and Nooksack and Squamish forms quoted in G82:28 set 130.

<**p'e'ómthet**>, rsls //p'áʔ=ə[=M2=]m=θət//, incs, ABDF ['*be swollen*'], (<**metathesis**> *resultative*), (<**=thet**> *get, become, inceptive*), phonology: metathesis, syntactic analysis: intransitive verb, adjective/adjectival verb?, attested by Deming Elders plus JL and NP (at Fish Camp 7/19/79), example: <**p'e'ómthet te s'ó:thes.**>, //p'áʔ=ə[=M2=]m=θət//, /'*The face is swollen.*'/.

<**p'óp'ekw'ethet**>, SOC ['*make oneself useful*'], *see* p'ákw'.

<**p'óp'eqw'em**>, WATR /'*foaming, bubbling, foamy*'/, *see* p'óqw'em.

<**p'óp'eqw'em**>, FOOD ['*beer*'], *see* p'óqw'em.

<**p'op'etl'á:leqem**>, SM ['*(have a) smoky smell*'], *see* p'ótl'em.

<**p'ó:p'etl'em ~ p'op'etl'em**>, FIRE ['*smoking*'], *see* p'ótl'em.

<**p'óqw'em**>, mdls //p'áq'ʷ=əm//, WATR ['*to foam*'], (<**=em**> *middle voice*), syntactic analysis: intransitive verb, attested by EB, AC, Salish cognate: Squamish /p'úq'ʷam/ *foam (verb)* W73:104, K67:252, Nooksack /púq'ʷum/ (p sic for p' ?) *to foam* (LG in G84a), Lummi dial. of N. Straits /s-p'óq'ʷəŋ/ *foam (nom.)* D82pc, Songish dial. of N. Straits /spáq'ʷəŋ/ *foam (noun), bubbles* M68 (quoted in G82:45 set 237), Samish (VU) /spáq'ʷəŋ/ *foam* G86:65, example: <**le p'óqw'em.**>, //lə p'áq'ʷ=əm//, /'*It foamed.*'/, literally /'past third person subject'/, attested by AC.

<**p'óp'eqw'em**>, cts //p'á[-C₁ə-]q'ʷ=əm//, WATR /'*foaming, bubbling, foamy*'/, (<**-R1-**> *continuative*), phonology: reduplication, syntactic analysis: intransitive verb, attested by Elders Group, EB, example: <**lóyéxwa p'op'eqw'émes kw sé<u>x</u>wes?**>, //láy=ə̀=xʷɛ p'á[-C₁ə-]q'ʷ=əm-əs kʷ sə́x̣ʷə-s//, /'*Does one have to have foamy urine?*'/, literally /'does one have to have (is only =yes/no question =become/get) if it's foamy (foamy =third person subject subjunctive) the (remote) urine'/, semantic environment ['a woman who drank beer was said by EB to have asked this'], usage: joking, phonology: stress-shift to penultimate syllable in four syllable word, attested by EB (5/25/76).

<**p'óp'eqw'em**>, dnom //p'á[=C₁ə=]q'ʷ=əm//, FOOD ['*beer*'], (<**=R1=**> *continuative* or *durative*, zero derivation *nominalizer*), phonology: reduplication, syntactic analysis: nominal, attested by Elders Group.

<**sp'óp'eqw'em**>, dnom //s=p'á[=C₁ə=]q'ʷ=əm//, HHG ['*soap*'], WATR ['*foam*'], (<**s=**> *nominalizer*), (<**=R1=**> *resultative* or *continuative* or just *derivational* to separate a word for *soap* from sp'óqw'em *foam*), phonology: reduplication, syntactic analysis: nominal, attested by Elders Group (6/1/77), example: <**sp'óp'eqw'ems te qó:**>, //s=p'á[=C₁ə=]q'ʷ=əm-s tə qá·//, /'*foam of the water*'/.

<**sp'óqw'em**>, dnom //s=p'áq'ʷ=əm//, WATR ['*foam*'], (<**s=**> *nominalizer*), syntactic analysis: nominal, attested by EB, AC, BJ (12/5/64), other sources: ES /sp'á·q'ʷəm/ *foam*.

<**p'ó:th'es ~ p'óth'es**>, df //p'i[=Aə́=](=)θ'=á(·)[=M2=]s or p'ɛ(=)θ'=á(·)[=M2=]s or p'ə(=)θ'=á(·)[=M2=]s or p'ɛ[=Aá=](·)θ'=əs or p'i[=Aá(·)=]θ'=əs//, [p'á·θ'ɪs ~ p'áθ'ɪs], HHG /'*baby basket, cradle basket, basketry cradle*'/, possibly root <**p'íth'**> *squeeze* + <**é-ablaut**> on root <**í**> *resultative*+ <**metathesis type 2**> derivational or root <**p'áth'**> *sew* + < **ó(:)-ablaut** on **á**> automatic before lx <**=ó:s ~ =ós ~ =es**> *on the face*, ASM ['baby baskets were usually woven out of cedar roots with cherry bark and scalded-white grass imbrication designs, rarely they were also made out of birch bark (Elders Group 4/5/78)'], comment: if the root is *squeeze* with *resultative* and =es *on the face* the

result is *squeezed on the face* which describes the look of a baby in the basket (not to mention the fact that where cranial deformation was practiced, as among some higher-class Downriver- and Island-Halkomelem- speaking peoples as well as other Coast Salish and Kwakiutlan peoples, a head-board was placed on the forehead while the baby was in the cradle basket to elongate the forehead; Capt. Wilson in 1858-1859 observed that cranial deformation was only practiced to Fort Langley [where the Kwantlen dialect of Downriver Halkomelem was spoken], Duff 1952:90-91 reports that the father from Nanaimo of one of the people he worked with from Yale had cranial deformation by headboards and was laughed at by the Yale people, but that it was widespread on the Coast), phonology: é-ablaut on root í, stress-shift to stressed suffix, then metathesis (these three processes seem most likely since this type of ablaut contributes a logical semantic element to the derivation and since the length variation is already well-recorded in the suffix =ó:s ~ =ós ~ =es *on the face*), or (less likely) vowel-reduction in root before stressed suffix and then metathesis, or metathesis first then vowel-reduction, or (least likely) ó(:)-ablaut, syntactic analysis: nominal, attested by Elders Group, AC, DM (12/4/64), other sources: ES /p'á·θ'əs/ *basketry cradle*, JH /p'á·θ'əs/ *cradle basket*.

<**Lexwp'oth'esála ~ Xwp'oth'esála**>, ds //(lə)xʷ=p'i[=Aə=](=)θ'=ás=ɛlɛ//, PLN /'*baby basket rock just below main bay and sand bar of Lexwtl'átl'ekw'em (Klaklacum, Indian Reserve #12, first village and reserve south of American Creek), on the west side of the Fraser River*'/, ASM ['the rock is about 20 or 30 feet high and hollowed out at its center where people put baby baskets when the baby outgrew them, they just left them and made a new one for the next child, this was done in memory of a story (sx̲wōx̲wiyám) in which a fish from salt water was sent a message to come upstream; she had a baby in a p'óth'es and it was heavy, so on the way up she and those travelling with her bathed the baby in medicines to make it grow fast so it could travel without the p'óth'es; at Xwp'oth'esála it finally got big enough and they left the p'óth'es at that rock (SP 8/24/77); this is similar to and probably part of the story of the sockeye baby told in Hill-Tout 1902 and Wells 1970:14-18 (in story told by DM July 1964); AD went to the rock with Reuben Ware and others from Coqualeetza and they took photos of the rock'], lx <**lexw= ~ xw=**> *always*, lx <**=ála**> *container, contains*, phonology: stress-shift from stem to stressed suffix, syntactic analysis: nominal, attested by SP, AD, source: place names reference file #207.

<**p'ótl'em**>, df //p'á·ƛ'=əm ~ p'áƛ'=əm//, FIRE ['*to smoke*'], semantic environment ['of a fire from a house for ex.'], probably <**=em**> *middle voice or intransitivizer, have, get*, syntactic analysis: intransitive verb, attested by EB, Salish cognate: Squamish /p'úƛ'am/ *smoke (about fire)* W73:240, K67:252.

<**p'ó:p'etl'em ~ p'op'etl'em**>, cts //p'á·[-C_1ə-]ƛ'=əm ~ p'á[-C_1ə-]ƛ'=əm//, FIRE ['*smoking*'], semantic environment ['of a person smoking a pipe, of tobacco, a house (from a fire inside), of a fire generally'], (<**-R1-**> *continuative*), phonology: reduplication, syntactic analysis: intransitive verb, attested by AC, Elders Group, EB, example: <**p'ó:p'etl'em te siyó:lexwe.**>, //p'á·[-C_1ə-]ƛ'=əm tə si=yó·ləxʷ=ə//, /'*The old man is smoking.*'/, attested by AC, <**p'óp'etl'em te láléms.**>, //p'á[-C_1ə-]ƛ'=əm tə lɛ́ləm-s//, /'*Smoke is coming from his house., (His house is smoking.)*'/, literally /'is smoking the house -his/her/their'/, attested by EB, <**lulh lhís kw'es me p'óp'etl'em.**>, //lə=uɬ ɬí-s k'ʷə-s mə p'á[-C_1ə-]ƛ'=əm//, /'*It was smoking quite a while ago.*'/, literally /'third person past =already when -third person subjunctive come to be smoking'/, attested by Elders Group.

<**p'op'etl'á:leqem**>, df //p'á[=C_1ə=]ƛ'=ɛ́·ləqəp=əm//, SM ['*(have a) smoky smell*'], FIRE, lx <**=á:leqep**> *smell, in smell, odor, fragrance*, probably <**=em**> *middle voice or intransitivizer, get, have*, phonology: reduplication, syllable-loss of final ep in suffix before =em, syntactic analysis: intransitive verb, attested by Elders Group (11/10/76), comment: note moving of =em from the root to follow the lexical suffix, compare with <**sp'otl'emáleqep**> *(have a) smoky smell*.

<**lhp'ótl'em**>, ds //ɬ=p'áƛ'=əm//, PE ['*to smoke a pipe*'], FIRE, literally /'extract smoke, extract a

portion of smoke'/, lx <**lh=**> *use, extract, extract a portion*, syntactic analysis: intransitive verb, attested by EB.

<**sp'ó:tl'em ~ sp'ótl'em**>, dnom //s=p'á·ƛ'=əm ~ s=p'áƛ'=əm//, FIRE ['*smoke*'], PE ['*tobacco*'], (<**s=**> *nominalizer*), syntactic analysis: nominal, attested by AC, BJ (5/64 [actually =5/10/64 discovered later]), DM (12/4/64), Elders Group, other sources: ES /sp'á·ƛ'əm/ *smoke*, example: <**xwelíl kwelhó thé sp'ó:tl'em**>, //xʷə=lílkʷəɬ=à (kʷ)θə s=p'á·ƛ'=əm//, /'*real thick smoke, real heavy smoke*'/, phonology: stressed article in sentence-intonation, attested by Elders Group (11/12/75).

<**sp'òtl'emálá ~ sp'ótl'emàlà**>, ds //s=p'áƛ'=əm=ɛ́lɛ́ ~ s=p'áƛ'=əm=ɛ̀lɛ̀//, PE ['*pipe (for smoking)*'], FIRE, literally /'container of smoke'/, lx <**=álá ~ =àlà**> *container of, contains*, phonology: downstepping on root or suffix, syntactic analysis: nominal, attested by BJ (5/10/64), DM (12/4/64).

<**sp'otl'emá:látel**>, ds //s=p'áƛ'=əm=ɛ́[=·=]lɛ́=təl//, BLDG ['*smokehole*'], FIRE, ASM ['a hole in a pit-house or communal-house, dance-house, or fish-smoking house through which the smoke of fires passed outside, sometimes had a raised plank cover to keep out rain, snow, etc.'], lx <**=álá**> *contain(s), container of*, lx <**=tel**> *device to, something to*, possibly <**=:=**> *derivational*, phonology: possible lengthening, syntactic analysis: nominal, attested by Elders Group.

<**sp'otl'emáleqep**>, ds //s=p'aƛ'=əm=ɛ́ləqəp//, SM ['*(have a) smoky smell*'], FIRE, lx <**=áleqep**> *smell, in smell, odor, fragrance*, phonology: stress-shift from root to stressed suffix, syntactic analysis: intransitive verb, prob. adjective/adjectival verb, attested by Deming (4/26/79), compare with <**p'op'etl'á:leqem**.

<**p'tl'ómt**>, pcs //p'áƛ'=ə[=M2=]m=T or p'áƛ'=M1=əm=T//, FIRE ['*to smudge (make smoke to get rid of mosquitoes)*'], EZ, ASM ['green bracken ferns were burned for this (EB 6/30/76)'], possibly <**metathesis type 1**> *non-continuative or derivational* or possibly <**metathesis type 2**> *durative or derivational*, (<**=t**> *purposeful control transitivizer*), phonology: metathesis, either vowel-loss or vowel merger, syntactic analysis: transitive verb, attested by EB, CT and HT.

<**p'eltl'ómelh**>, df //p'[=əl=]áƛ'=ə[=M2=]m=əɬ or p'[=əl=]áƛ'=M1=əm=əɬ//, FIRE ['*(be) choked with smoke*'], ABDF, possibly <**=el=**> *plural*, possibly <**metathesis**> *resultative or durative*, possibly <**=elh ~ =lhelh ~ =lhál**> *in the throat*, phonology: infixed =el=, metathesis, either vowel-loss or vowel merger, unusual allomorph of =lhelh, syntactic analysis: intransitive verb, attested by BHTTC.

<**p'ō̃wiy ~ p'éwiy**>, EZ /'*halibut, flounder (*prob. *starry flounder)*'/, *see* p'ewíy ~ p'ōwíy.

<**p'ō̃wiyelhthóxchexw**>, WV ['*you patch it for me*'], *see* p'ewíy ~ p'ōwíy.

<**p'ōwíyt ~ p'ewíyt**>, WV /'*patch s-th (of clothes, nets), patch s-th up*'/, *see* p'ewíy ~ p'ōwíy.

<**p'q'élqel**>, EZ ['*mountain goat*'], *see* p'éq'.

<**p'sákw'**>, df //p'sɛ́k'ʷ//, rsls, LANG /'*finished, done, the end, (*(possibly) *end of something (like twine, rope, etc.) [AD])*'/, semantic environment ['could be used at the end of a story'], root meaning unknown, syntactic analysis: intransitive verb?, nominal?, Elder's comment: "uncertain of form and meaning", attested by BHTTC (11/15/76), Salish cognate: perhaps Squamish root /p'ə́sk'ʷ/ *be squeezed* as in /p'əsk'ʷ-án/ *squeeze (tr.)* K67:251 or Squamish root /p'ə́s/ *to land, go to shore* as also in /p's-i(ʔ)/ *to land, go to shore* K67:251, also (possibly) /'*end of something (like twine, rope, etc.)*'/, attested by AD (3/5/79).

<**p'tl'ómt**>, FIRE ['*to smudge (make smoke to get rid of mosquitoes)*'], *see* p'ótl'em.

<**p'xwélhp**>, df //p'xʷ=ə[=´=]ɬp//, EB /'*oak tree, garry oak*'/, ['*Quercus garryana*'], ASM ['there are

stands of this tree on Vancouver Island and the Gulf Islands but on the mainland (in all of B.C.) the only stands reported are in the Upper Stó:lō area: on Sumas Mt. and 1.5 miles above Yale (at X̲elhálh or at Q'alelíktel)'], root meaning unknown, (<**stress shift**> *derivational*), lx <**=elhp**> *tree, plant*, phonology: stress-shift, syntactic analysis: nominal, source: ES and JH /p'x^{w}ə́ɬp/ *oak*.

Q

<**=q**>, da //=q//, MC ['*(closable container)*'], syntactic analysis: lexical suffix, derivational suffix, comment: probably a reduced form of =eqel *container* esp. before =et; found in <**qp'á:qet**>, //qp'ɛ́·=q=əT//, /'*cover it with a lid, close it (of a box, etc.)*'/ (compare <**qep'á=lets=tel**> *a cover or lid* and <**qep'=ó:yth=thò:m**> *you get covered on the mouth*), <**xwmá:qet**>, //x^{w}=mɛ́·=q=əT//, /'*open it (box, bottle, closable container)*'/ (compare <**xw=má:x**> *open it (door, gate, anything))*, <**meth'elhqí:wel**>, //məθ'əɬ=q=í·wəl//, /'*woodtick*'/, literally /'pus + inside container + on the insides'/.

<**=q ~ =élq**>, da //=q//, DIR *after, behind,* syntactic analysis: lexical suffix, derivational suffix; found in <**chél=q**> *fall,* <**chó:l=q=em**> *follow after*, <**tl'itl'ets'=élq=em**> *sneaking after*, <**málqlexw ~ málqelexw**>, *forget s-th, forget s-o, forget s-th behind* from <**mal=q**>, bound stem //mɛ́l=q// *forget* (compare <**mál ~ mél**>, bound root //mál ~ mə́l *be mixed up*//), and perhaps others like <**iyáq**> *change* and (with metathesis) <**ám=eq=t**> *bring s-o/s-th back);* Musqueam cognates of these and more in Suttles ca1984:14.6.37 all fit gloss *after*),

<**qa ~ qe ~ q'a**>, free root //qɛ ~ qə ~ q'ɛ//, CJ ['*or*'], syntactic analysis: conjunction, attested by AC, example: <**lí chòkw te lálems q'a lí stetís? ~ lí chòkw te lálems qa lí stetís?**>, //lí $cák^{w}$ tə lɛ́ləm-s q'ɛ/qɛ lí s=tə[=C_1əAí=]s//, /'*Is his house far or is it nearby?*'/, attested by AC, <**tsel má:ythome kw'e tseláqelhelh qe lhulhá.**>, //c-əl mɛ́·y=T-ámə k'^{w}ə cəlɛ́q=əɬ=əɬ qə ɬuɬɛ́//, /'*I helped you yesterday or the day before yesterday. (the (remote))*'/, attested by AC.

<**qá:l**>, free root //qɛ́·l//, SOC ['*steal*'], syntactic analysis: intransitive verb, attested by EB, also <**qál**>, //qɛ́l//, attested by AC, example: <**kwókwelxes te sqá:ls**>, //k^{w}ɛ[-AáC$_1$ə-]l=x^{y}-əs tə s-qɛ́·l-s//, /'*He's hiding what he stole.*'/, literally /'he's hiding the/what nom.-steal-his'/, syntactic analysis: relative clause, attested by EB, <**me qá:l te slhálí**>, //mə qɛ́·l tə s=ɬɛ́lí//, /'*They stole a woman.*'/, Elder's comment: "maybe you can say this", attested by EB.

<**qáqel**>, cts //qɛ́[-C_1ə-]l//, SOC ['*stealing*'], phonology: reduplication, syntactic analysis: intransitive verb, attested by Elders Group, EB, Deming, example: <**qél stl'ítl'qelh, qáqel**>, //qə́l s=C_1í=ƛ'q=əɬ, qɛ́[-C_1ə-]l//, /'*She's a bad child, (she's) stealing.*'/, attested by Deming.

<**qá:lt**>, pcs //qɛ́·l=T//, SOC /'*steal from s-o, rob s-o, short-change s-o*'/, (semological comment: the object is not what is stolen (as in European culture) but the victim, showing the social emphasis on people not objects here), (<**=t**> *purposeful control transitivizer*), syntactic analysis: transitive verb, attested by EB, example: <**tsel le qá:lt kw' Bill.**>, //c-əl lə qɛ́·l=T k'^{w}ə Bill//, /'*I robbed Bill.*'/, literally /'I past rob s-o the (remote) Bill'/, attested by EB; found in <**qá:lthóxes.**>, //qɛ́·l=T-áx^{y}-əs//, /'*He short-changed me., He stole from me.*'/, attested by Deming, <**qá:ltem.**>, //qɛ́·l=T-əm//, /'*to be robbed, Someone was robbed., They stole from him/her/them.*'/, syntactic comment: passive, attested by EB, example: <**le qá:ltem.**>, //lə qɛ́·l=T-əm//, /'*He was robbed.*'/, literally /'third person past someone was robbed'/, attested by EB, <**le qá:ltem kw' Bill.**>, //lə qɛ́·l=T-əm k'^{w}ə Bill//, /'*Bill was robbed.*'/, attested by EB.

<**qélqel**>, chrs //qɛ[=Aə́=]l=C_1əC_2//, SOCT ['*thief*'], (<**é-ablaut on root á**> *derivational*), (<**=R2**> *characteristic*), phonology: ablaut, reduplication, syntactic analysis: nominal, attested by AC, Elders Group.

<**qá:lá:lhp**>, EB ['*red huckleberry plant or bush*'], *see* sqá:le.

<**qá:le ~ qá:la**> possible stem or root //qa=ɛ́·lɛ or qɛ́·lə// meaning uncertain or more likely root is

//səq=ɛ́·lɛ// literally /'container hangs under'/, *see* seq.

<**sqá:la ~ sqá:le**>, df //s=qa=ɛ́·lɛ or s=qɛ́·lə// or more likely root is //səq=ɛ́·lɛ// literally /'container hangs under'/, EB ['*red huckleberry*'], ['*Vaccinium parvifolium*'], ASM ['berries ripe and edible in mid-July, harvested by clubbing branches on the hand and berries fell into baskets hanging underneath (see alternate name)'], possibly <**s=**> *nominalizer* or more likely root is //səq=ɛ́·lɛ// literally /'container hangs under'/, *see* seq, lx <**=á:la**> *container of*, phonology: possible vowel merger or more likely vowel loss or zero grade of root, syntactic analysis: nominal, attested by AC, Elders Group (3/1/72), others, other sources: ES /sqɛ́lə/ *red huckleberry*, H-T <skála> (macron over á) *huckleberry*.

<**qá:lá:lhp**>, ds //qa=ɛ́·lɛ́=əɬp//, EB ['*red huckleberry plant or bush*'], ['*Vaccinium parvifolium*'], lx <**=elhp**> (or perhaps after vowels <**=á:lhp**>) *tree, plant*, phonology: back formation allows dropping of root <**s**> under illusion it is <**s**> *nominalizer*, syntactic analysis: nominal, attested by IHTTC.

<**qálets'**>, df //qɛ́l=əc'//, WV ['*spin wool or twine*'], root meaning unknown (perhaps '*twist*'), lx <**=ets'**> *around in circles*, syntactic analysis: intransitive verb, attested by AC.

<**qáqelets'**>, cts //qɛ́[-C_1ə-]l=əc'//, WV ['*spinning wool*'], (<**-R1-**> *continuative*), phonology: reduplication, syntactic analysis: intransitive verb, attested by Elders Group.

<**shxwqáqelets'**>, dnom //sx^w=qɛ́[=C_1ə=]l=əc'//, WV /'*spindle for spinning wool, a hand spinner, a spinning machine*'/, literally /'thing for spinning wool'/, (<**sxw=**> *nominalizer, thing for*), phonology: reduplication, syntactic analysis: nominal, dialects: *Cheh.*, attested by Elders Group, also <**sélseltel**>, //si[=Aə́=]l=C_1əC_2=təl//, dialects: *Tait*, attested by Elders Group (3/24/76).

<**qá(:)l**> or less likely <**qwa**>, root uncertain, meaning unknown unless //qɛ́l// *twist* or less likely //q^{w}ɛ́// 'have a hole'.

<**sqá:le<u>x</u> ~ sqále<u>x</u>**>, df //s=q^w[=U=]ɛ́(·)=əl=əx̣ or s=qɛ́(·)l=əx̣//, [sqǽ·ləx̣ ~ sqǽləx̣], HARV ['*digging stick*'], ASM ['for digging roots, vegetables, clams, etc., often made of wild crabapple'], possibly <**s=**> *nominalizer*, possibly <**=el**> *get, become, go, come, inceptive*, possibly <**=e<u>x</u>**> *distributive, all around*, possibly <**=U= (unrounding, delabialization)**> *derivational?*, possibly root <**qwá:**> *have a hole* and the word thus would be literally *something to get a hole all around*, more likely is root <**qál**> and lit. meaning *something to twist all around*, phonology: possible delabialization/ unrounding, syntactic analysis: nominal, attested by Elders Group, Deming, BHTTC, other sources: ES /sqɛ́lə̀x̣/ (Cw and Ms /sqɛ́ləx̣/) *digging stick*, Salish cognate: Squamish /s-qálx̣/ *digging-stick, stick for digging clams* W73:252, K67:295, K69:79.

<**qá:lmílh**>, df //qɛ́·ɬ=əm=í(y)ɬ//, [qǽ·lmí(y)ɬ], KIN ['*reject someone as a spouse or partner for your child*'], SOC, probably root <**qá:lh**> *reject (a person)*, comment: qá:lh as root requires that the lh > l by assimilation or by derivational voicing and resonantizing which are rare but attested (=lhelh ~ lhál *on the throat*); lx <**=ílh ~ =iylh ~ =á:ylh ~ =ó:llh ~ =elh**> *child*, compare <**qá:lh**> *reject (a person)*, phonology: voicing and resonantizing, syntactic analysis: intransitive verb, attested by Elders Group (1/30/80), see qá:lh.

<**qá:lq**>, free root //qɛ́·lq//, EB /'*flower of wild rose, hip or bud of wild rose,* including: *Nootka rose, probably also dwarf or woodland rose and swamp rose,* possibly (from Hope east) *prickly rose*'/, ['including: *Rosa nutkana,* probably also *Rosa pisocarpa* and *Rosa gymnocarpa,* possibly (from Hope east) *Rosa acicularis*'], ASM ['flowers out in May and June, some parts of the plant are used for medicine, rose hips are eaten raw and dried to use for tea, BJ comments that qá:lq grows all through the Upper Stó:lō area (thus implying that it is primarily Nootka rose)'], MED ['*rose hip tea is taken for arthritis*'], LT ['*rose color*'], ASM ['on color chart from Berlin and Kay (1969) rows top to bottom are B through I, columns left to right are 1 through 40 and the side column from white to black is 0,

individual speakers from the Elders Group identified qá:lq as: EL (Cheh.): E1, E2, (but in fall): F39, F40; NP (Chill.): D38, D39, D40; Evangeline Pete (Katzie, living in Tait territory): C38; Lawrence James: E38; TM (Cheh.): C1, C2, C3, C4, C5, and as axwíl qá:lq *a little rose*: B1, B2, B3, B4, B5'], ASM ['the following color terms are used by AK before qálq to specify shades of the color: tsxwíkw', tsxwíxwekw', xwíxwekw'el, qw'íqw'e<u>x</u>wel, tsqw'íqw'e<u>x</u>wel, stl'ítl'esel, sp'(e)q'íl, kwíkwemel, skwíkwemel'], syntactic analysis: nominal, also adjective/adjectival verb, attested by EL, NP, Evangeline Pete, Lawrence James, TM, IHTTC, BJ (12/5/64), also AK (1987), EB (1987), NP (1987), AH (1987), see charts by Rob MacLaury, Salish cognate: Squamish /qálʔq/ *wild rose bud* K67:353.

<**qá:lqelhp**>, ds //qɛ́·lq=əɬp//, EB /'*wild rose bush,* including: *Nootka rose,* probably also *dwarf or woodland rose and swamp rose,* possibly (from Hope east) *prickly rose*'/, ['including: *Rosa nutkana,* probably also *Rosa pisocarpa* and *Rosa gymnocarpa*, possibly *Rosa acicularis*'], lx <**=elhp**> *tree, plant, bush*, syntactic analysis: nominal, attested by AC (prompted), other sources: ES /qɛ́lqəɬp/ *rose*, H-T <kalk·> (umlaut over a) *rose (wild).*

<**qálqomex**>, ds //qɛ́lq=áməxʸ//, LT /'*[looks rose, rose-looking*]'/, (<**=ómex**> *looks, -looking, in color*), syntactic analysis: adjective/adjectival verb, attested by NP, see charts by Rob MacLaury.

<**qelqósem**>, mdls //qɛ[=Aə=]lq=ás=əm//, SM ['*smell like a rose*'], EB, (<**e-ablaut**> *derivational*), lx <**=ós**> *in the face*, (<**=em**> *middle voice*), phonology: e-ablaut, syntactic analysis: intransitive verb, attested by Elders Group, example: <**le qelqósem.**>, //lə qɛ[=Aə=]lq=ás=əm//, /'*It smells like a rose.*'/, attested by Elders Group.

<**qá:lqelhp**>, EB /'*wild rose bush,* including: *Nootka rose,* probably also *dwarf or woodland rose and swamp rose,* possibly (from Hope east) *prickly rose*'/, *see* qá:lq.

<**qálqomex**>, LT /'*[looks rose, rose-looking*]'/, *see* qá:lq.

<**qá:lt**>, SOC /'*steal from s-o, rob s-o, short-change s-o*'/, *see* qá:l.

<**qá:lh**>, possibly root //qɛ́·ɬ//, SOC ['*reject (a person)*'], syntactic analysis: intransitive verb, attested by Elders Group (1/30/80), compare <**qá:lmílh**> *reject someone as a spouse or partner for your child.*

<**qá:lmílh**>, df //qɛ́·ɬ=əm=í(y)ɬ//, [qǽ·lmí(y)ɬ], KIN ['*reject someone as a spouse or partner for your child*'], SOC, probably root <**qá:lh**> *reject (a person)*, comment: qá:lh as root requires that the lh > l by assimilation or by derivational voicing and resonantizing which are rare but attested (=lhelh ~ lhál *on the throat*); lx <**=ílh ~ =iylh ~ =á:ylh ~ =ó:llh ~ =elh**> *child*, compare <**qá:lh**> *reject (a person)*, phonology: voicing and resonantizing, syntactic analysis: intransitive verb, attested by Elders Group (1/30/80).

<**qélh**>, possibly root //qə́ɬ or sic for x̣ə́ɬ *hurt*//, SOC ['*hurt inside*'], ABDF ['*hurt inside*'], possibly <**occlusion, <u>x</u> → q**> here (error or) *derivational*, phonology: possible occlusion, syntactic analysis: intransitive verb, attested by Elders Group (4/2/80).

<**qélhlexw**>, ncs //qə́ɬ=l-əxʷ or sic for x̣ə́ɬ=ləxʷ//, ABDF /'*accidentally hurt an old injury of s-o, (accidentally reinjure s-o)*'/, possibly <**occlusion**> *derivational*, (<**=l**> *non-control transitivizer*), (<-**exw**> *third person object*), phonology: possible occlusion, syntactic analysis: transitive verb, attested by Elders Group (4/2/80).

<**qám**>, free root //qɛ́m//, WATR /'*be calm (of water or wind), (get calm (wind/water), calm down (wind/water), be smooth (of water) [AC, LH])*'/, WETH, syntactic analysis: intransitive verb, attested by AD, Elders Group, Deming, also <**qó:m**>, //qɛ[=Aá·=]m//, also /'*be smooth (of water)*'/, (<**ó:-ablaut on root á**> *resultative*), phonology: ó:-ablaut on root á, attested by AC (from Lizzie Herrling via phone), also /'*water went down*'/, dialects: *Matsqui*, attested by Deming, example: <**qó:m te qó:.**>, //(probably) qɛ́·m tə qá·//, /'*smooth water [sic]*'/, literally /'The water is smooth.'/, attested by AC.

<**sqám**>, df //s=qɛ́m//, WATR /'*(have) quieter water, died down a little*'/, probably <**s=**> *stative* or

possibly *nominalizer*, syntactic analysis: intransitive verb, nominal?, attested by Elders Group.

<**Sqám ~ Sqà:m**>, df //s=qέm ~ s=qὲ·m//, PLN /'*Haig bay, a calm place on the west (C.P.R.) side of the Fraser River by the Haig railroad stop, below and across from Hope*'/, literally /'calm water'/, (<**s=**> *nominalizer*), syntactic analysis: nominal, attested by Elders Group, AD and SP and AK (trip to American Bar, 6/26/78), source: place names reference file #2.

<**Sqám**>, df //s=qέm//, PLN ['*Schkam Lake near Haig*'], literally /'slack water, calm water'/, (<**s=**> *nominalizer*), syntactic analysis: nominal, attested by PDP (Katz class 10/5/76).

<**sqáqem**>, strs //s=qέ[=C_1ə=]m//, WATR ['*calm water (calmer than sqám)*'], literally /'be calmed (of water)'/, (<**s=**> *stative*), (<**=R1=**> *resultative*), phonology: reduplication, syntactic analysis: adjective/adjectival verb?, nominal??, attested by Elders Group, also <**sqóqem**>, //sqε[=AáC_1ə=]m//, also /'*calm (water, wind)*'/, (<**s=**> *stative*), (<**ó-ablaut on root á and =R1=**> *resultative*), phonology: reduplication, ó-ablaut on root á, syntactic analysis: Deming.

<**Qémelets**>, ds //qε[=Aə́=]m=ələc//, PLN ['*bay at upper end of Íyém (Yale Indian Reserve #22)*'], (<**é-ablaut**> *derivational*), lx <**=elets**> *on the bottom*, phonology: ablaut, syntactic analysis: nominal, attested by AD and AK on trip to Five-Mile Creek (4/30/79),

<**Sqémelech**>, ds //s=qε[=Aə́=]m=ələc//, PLN /'*wide place in Maria Slough (just north of Lougheed Highway bridge), west mouth of Maria Slough*'/, literally /'calm water at bottom (of Seabird Island)'/, (<**s=**> *nominalizer*), (<**é-ablaut on root á**> *resultative*), lx <**=elets ~ =elech (rare)**> *on the bottom*, phonology: é-ablaut on root á, syntactic analysis: nominal, attested by LJ (Tait)(visiting in IHTTC 8/15/77), photo 6/20/78, source: place names reference file #194.

<**Sqemqémelets**>, ds //s=C_1əC_2=qε[=Aə́=]m=ələc//, PLN ['*bay at upper end of Yale Indian Reserve #2 (Four-and-a-half Mile Creek) (near the northern end of Stó:lō territory)*'], literally /'something that was calm many times on the bottom'/, (<**s=**> *nominalizer*, R3= *plural*), (<**é-ablaut**> *resultative*), lx <**=elets**> *on the bottom*, phonology: reduplication, é-ablaut on root á, syntactic analysis: nominal, attested by AD and AK (trip to Five-Mile Creek 4/30/79).

<**sqemélwélh ~ sqemélwelh**>, ds //s=qε[=Aə=]m=ə́lwəɬ//, PLN /'*place in Katz or Ruby Creek, may be name for Charlie Joe's place near Katz at the mouth of a creek where the water is always calm*'/, literally /'(calmed water on the side)'/, (<**s=**> *nominal*), (<**e-ablaut**> *resultative*), lx <**=élwelh**> *on the side*, phonology: e-ablaut on root á, probable updrifting, syntactic analysis: nominal, attested by SP, IHTTC, Elders Group, source: place names reference file #242.

<**qametólém ~ qametólem**>, rcps //qεm=əT=ál=əm//, pcs, WETH ['*get calm (of wind)*'], LANG /'*get calm (of people, when nobody says anything but just looks at each other), have a lull (in conversation, etc.), be in a lull*'/, SOC, (<**=et**> *purposeful control transitivizer*, <**=ól**> *reciprocal* (normally inflectional but here derivational), <**=em**> *get, have, intransitivizer*), phonology: updrifting, syntactic analysis: intransitive verb, attested by Elders Group (3/23/77).

<**qó:mthet**>, incs //qε[=Aá·=]m=θət//, WATR ['*still (of water)*'], literally /'got calm'/, (<**ó:-ablaut**> *derivational* but automatically triggered), (<**=thet**> *get, become, inceptive*), phonology: ó:-ablaut on root á automatically conditioned by =thet, syntactic analysis: intransitive verb, attested by Elders Group, example: <**qó:mthet te qó:.**>, //qε[=Aá·=]m=θət//, /'*still water*'/, literally /'The water is still.'/.

<**qémxel**>, rsls //qε[=Aə́=]m=xʸəl//, WETH /'*(the wind) is calm, calm (of wind)*'/, (<**é-ablaut on root á**> *resultative*), lx <**=xel**> *on the foot; precipitation*, phonology: é-ablaut on root á, syntactic analysis: adjective/adjectival verb, attested by Elders Group.

<**Welqémex**>, df //wəl=qε[=Aə́=]m=məxʸ//, PLN ['*Greenwood Island*'], ASM ['in the Fraser River just in front of and south of Hope, B.C., there used to be old tombs or gravehouses and a graveyard there, but in the 1894 high water people moved all the bodies to Union Bar, American Bar, Katz,

Squatits, and other Indian cemeteries so they wouldn't be washed away (Elders Group 7/6/77)'], literally /'really smooth flowing water'/, (<**wel=**> *really*), root <**qám**> *calm water, smooth water,* (<**é-ablaut**> *resultative*), possibly <**=(ó)mex**> *in appearance*, phonology: é-ablaut on root á, consonant merger, vowel-loss in suffix, syntactic analysis: nominal, attested by Katz Class (SP, TG, PDP, others)(10/5/76), Elders Group, elders on trip to American Bar (6/26/78), source: place names reference file #18.

<**qametólém ~ qametólem**>, WETH ['*get calm (of wind)*'], *see* qám.

<**qá:q**>, bound root //qɛ́q// *younger sibling* or more likely this is a reanalysis and the real root is <seq> *hang under* (see that root as well)

<**sqá:q**>, dnom //s=qɛ́q// or more likely //(s=)s(ə)q=ɛ́·q//, KIN /'*younger sibling, younger brother, younger sister, child of younger sibling of one's parent, "younger" cousin (could even be fourth cousin [through younger sibling of one's great great grandparent])*'/, ASM ['"younger cousins" can be older, younger or the same age as ego, it's their linking ancestor that must be younger, for the meanings younger brother or younger sister to be translated sqá:q must be preceded by a masculine or feminine article or the words swíyeqe *male* or slhálí *female* or otherwise cross-referenced semantically to a name or other item marked for sex gender; sqá:q by itself is ambiguous as to gender (as are most Halq'eméylem kinterms)'], (<**s=**> *nominalizer*) or more likely root <**séq**> or better <**seq**>, bound root //sə́q or səq *hang under*// + lx <**=á:q ~ =aq ~ =eq**> *male; penis*, thus literally *male that hangs under*, syntactic analysis: nominal, attested by AC, BJ (5/10/64), Deming (4/1/76), Elders Group, other sources: ES /sqɛ́·q/ and JH /sqé·q/ *younger sibling*, H-T 02:387 <skak·> (umlaut over a) *brother, sister, first cousin*, Salish cognate: Squamish /s-qáʔq/ *younger sibling* K67:353, example: <**tl'ól sqá:q.**>, //ƛ'á-l s=qɛ́·q//, /'*That's my younger sibling., He's my younger sibling., She's my younger sibling.*'/, attested by EB, <**tl'ól swal sqá:q.**>, //ƛ'á-l swɛ-l s=qɛ·q//, /'*That's my (own) younger sibling.*'/, attested by AC, <**lólets'e èl l swíyeqe sqá:q.**>, //C_1á=ləc'ə ʔə̀l l s=wíq=ə s=qɛ́·q//, /'*I have only one younger brother.*'/, literally /'is one person just/only my male younger sibling'/, attested by Deming, <**texqé:yltlha tá'a sqá:q.** (or better) **texqí:ltlha tá'a sqá:q.**>, //təxʸ=q(əl)=í·l=T-ɬɛ t-ɛ́ʔɛ s=qɛ́·q//, /'*Comb your little sister's hair. (sic for braid?)*'/, literally /'braid the hair of s-o -command imperative the -your (sg.) younger sibling'/, attested by EB (1/16/76), <**lólets'e èl l sqá:q.**>, //C_1á=ləc'ə ʔə̀l l s=qɛ́·q//, /'*I have only one younger sibling.*'/, attested by Deming.

<**ká:k ~ kyá:ky**>, dmn //q[=K=]ɛ́·q[=K=]//, [kʸǽ·kʸ], KIN ['*younger sibling (pet name)*'], (<**=K= (fronting to velar)**> *pet name, baby talk*), phonology: fronting, syntactic analysis: nominal, usage: pet name, baby talk, attested by AC, Elders Group, also /'*younger sister (pet name)*'/, attested by Elders Group (1/7/76).

<**sqiqáq**>, dmn //s=C_1í=qɛ́·q//, KIN ['*small younger sibling*'], (<**s=**> *nominalizer*, R4= *diminutive*), phonology: reduplication, length-loss after prefix, syntactic analysis: nominal, attested by ME (11/21/72 tape), EB, AD, example: <**skw'áy kws tu kwikwe'átes te sqiqáqs.**>, //s=k'ʷɛ́y kʷ-s tu C_1í=kʷ[=əʔɛ́]ɛ́=T-əs tə s=C_1í=qɛ́q-s//, /'*He never stops pestering his little brother., He never leaves his little brother alone.*'/, attested by EB, AD.

<**skíkek**>, dmn //s=C_1í=q[=K=]ɛ[=Aə=]q[=K=]//, [skʸíkʸɪkʸ], EZ /'*chickadee: black-capped chickadee,* probably also *chestnut-backed chickadee,* possibly also *the least bush-tit*'/, ['*Parus atricapillus occidentalis,* probably also *Parus rufescens,* possibly also *Psaltriparus minimus*'], (<**s=**> *nominalizer*, R4= *diminutive*, e-ablaut *derivational*), (<**=K=**> *pet name, baby talk*), phonology: reduplication, fronting to velar, syntactic analysis: nominal, dialects: *Cheh.*, attested by Elders Group (6/4/75), contrast <**méxts'el**> *chickadee, black-capped chickadee, etc.*.

<**sqelá:q**>, pln //s=q[=əl=]ɛ́·q//, KIN /'*younger siblings, "younger" cousins (first, second, or third*

cousins [whose connecting ancestor is younger than ego's])'/, (<**=el=**> *plural*), phonology: infixed plural, syntactic analysis: nominal, attested by BHTTC, AC, other sources: H-T <s'kElák·> *younger sibling (collective), younger cousin (child of younger sibling of parent)(coll.)*.

<**qeló:qtel**>, rcps //q[=əl=]ɛ[=Aá=]·q-təl//, [qəlá·qtəl], KIN /*'(be) brother and sister, (be siblings to each other), (be) first cousin to each other'*/, (<**=el=**> *plural*, ó-ablaut *derivational* but automatically triggered), (<**-tel**> *reciprocal*), phonology: infixed plural, ó-ablaut automatic before -tel, syntactic analysis: intransitive verb, attested by Elders Group (10/3/76, 6/9/76).

<**sqá:qele ~ sqáqele**>, df //s=qɛ́·q=əl(=)ə//, SOCT [*'baby'*], (<**s=**> *nominalizer*), root <**qá:q**> *younger sibling* or <**seq**> *hang under*, possibly <**=el**> *sort of, a little, -ish* as in < **tsqw'íqw'exwel**> *brownish-black* and <**sq'íq'exel**> *getting blackish* and <**sqwóqwiyel**> *yellowish* and <**stítethel**> *puny* from <**s=títh**> *skinny, thin*) and/or> *get, go, come, become, inceptive*, possibly <**=e**> *living thing*, possibly <**=ele**> *lacking* as in <**tsqó:le**> *thirsty*, syntactic analysis: nominal, attested by AC, BJ (5/10/64), other sources: ES /sqɛ̂qələ/ *baby (to about eight yrs.)*, H-T <skákEla> (umlaut over á) *infant* and <kákEla> (umlaut over á) *infants (coll.)*, Salish cognate: Squamish /s-qáql/ *baby, infant* W73:12, K67:295.

<**qáqel**>, root or stem //qɛ́qəl//, meaning *house-post, post*.

<**sqáqeltel**>, dnom //s=qɛ́qəl=təl//, BLDG /*'house-post, post'*/, (<**s=**> *nominalizer*), lx <**=tel**> *device to*, phonology: possible reduplication, syntactic analysis: nominal, attested by Elders Group, other sources: ES /qɛ́qəl/ (CwMs /qɛ́qən/) *housepost*, Salish cognate: Squamish /qáqn/ *housepost* W73:145, K69:80.

<**qáqel**>, SOC [*'stealing'*], *see* qá:l.

<**qáqelets'**>, WV [*'spinning wool'*], *see* qálets'.

<**qaqíw**>, ABDF /*'relaxing, resting'*/, *see* qá:w.

<**qas**>, CJ [*'and'*], *see* qe.

<**qás ~ q'as**>, bound root //qɛ́s ~ q'ɛ́s//, *tired*

<**qásel**>, df //qɛ́s=əl or q'[=D=]ə[=Aɛ́=]s=əl//, ABDF [*'tired'*], (<**=el ~ =í:l**> *get, become, go, come, inceptive*), possibly <**deglottalization**> *derivation*, syntactic analysis: intransitive verb, adjective/adjectival verb?, attested by BHTTC, compare UHk <**q'sém**> *tired of waiting* (see under q'), Salish cognate: Squamish root /q'əs/ *get tired (waiting)* as in /q's-íws/ *get tired waiting, get impatient* and /q'ə́s-šn/ *get tired feet* W73:269, K67:355, perhaps Lushootseed /q'ət'íl ~ k't'íl/ *grow tired, become impatient* as in /ʔu-q'ət'ís-əbš/ *tired of waiting for me* H76:239, 396-397, deglottalization perhaps influenced or related to Thompson (Lytton dial.) /qʔáz/ *tired* B74c:76 (which is cognate with Mainland Comox /qáʔyiws/ *to be tired* B75prelim:76).

<**qsí:l**>, df //qɛs=M1=í·l//, ABDF [*'tired out'*], possibly <**metathesis type 1**> *non-continuative or durative or resultative*, (<**=í:l ~ =el**> *get, become, go, come, inceptive*), phonology: possible metathesis type 1 with vowel merger or instead perhaps simply vowel-loss in root before stress affix, syntactic analysis: intransitive verb, attested by Elders Group.

<**qésqesí:l**>, df //qɛ[=Aə́=]s=$C_1əC_2$=í·l or $C_1əC_2$=qɛ[=Aə=]s=í·l//, ABDF [*'sobbing after crying'*], root <**qas**> *tired*, possibly root <**é-ablaut** or **e-ablaut**> *derivational*, possibly root <**=R2**> *characteristic?*, possibly root <**R3=**> *plural action*, (<**=í:l**> *get, become, go, come, inceptive*), phonology: é-ablaut, or e-ablaut with secondary re-stressing, reduplication, syntactic analysis: intransitive verb, attested by Elders Group.

<**qesqesí:lqel**>, df //$C_1əC_2$=qɛ[=Aə=]s=í·l=qəl//, ABDF [*'tired out from crying'*], lx <**=(e)qel**> *in the throat*, phonology: reduplication, e-ablaut, syntactic analysis: intransitive verb, attested by Elders Group (6/7/78).

<**qsí:lthet**>, pcrs //qɛs==M1=í·l=T-ət//, ABDF ['*tired out from crying*'], (<**=t**> *purposeful control transitivizer*), (<**-et**> *reflexive*), phonology: possible metathesis type 1 with vowel merger, syntactic analysis: intransitive verb, attested by Elders Group (6/7/78).

<**qsákw'**>, //qɛ́s[=M1=](=)k'ʷ or qɛ́s(=)ə[=M2=]k'ʷ//, ABFC /'*food settled (in the stomach), food is settled (in the stomach), (be settled (of food in the stomach), be comfortably digested (of food))*'/, root probably <qas ~ q'as> *tired*, <**metathesis type 1** or **2**> *resultative* <**=(e)kw'**> *round, around in circles* (Galloway 1993:234), phonology: metathesis, syntactic analysis: intransitive verb, attested by BHTTC (11/15/76), SP (Elders Group recopied 1/4/79).

<**qá:t**>, free root //qɛ́·t//, MED ['*put on a poultice, warm it [with steam esp.], (cook or heat with steam)*'], FOOD, syntactic analysis: prob. intransitive verb, attested by Deming and JL and NP (Fish Camp 7/19/79), Salish cognate: Squamish /qat-án/ *give a steambath, cause to take a steambath* W73:251, K67:353, k69:79, Lushootseed root /qaʔt(a)/ *get warm* as in /lə-qáʔt-əxʷ/ *(His body) is getting warm now (that you've given him blankets). (Said as you touch him.)* and /qáʔt-əd/ *warm it (as s-th on a stove, not an open fire)* H76:372, also <**qát**>, //qɛ́t//, attested by BHTTC.

<**qetás**>, df //qɛ́t=ə[=M2=]s//, FOOD /'*bake underground, (steam-cook underground, cook in a steam-pit)*'/, ASM ['steam-pits have not been used for about fifty years in the Stó:lō area, but were dug in sand or light soil and a fire was built in the bottom; when it was burned down to coals a few long sticks were stood upright in the pit and layers of skunk cabbage or similar leaves were piled in, alternating with the food to be cooked; dirt, sand or rocks were put on top and water was poured down the sticks to cause the steam; steaming was often done overnight; the followinf were some of the things steam-cooked: wild onions, bulbs of tiger lily, chocolate lily, rice root, wapato/arrowleaf, blue camas, wild caraway, spring gold, domestic carrot, black tree lichen (prob. Bryoria fremontii) often sweetened with berries (it cooked up into a licorice-flavored "moss-bread", and probably meats; many of these the vegetable bulbs and corms were roundish'], lx <**=es**> *round thing; on the face*, possibly <**metathesis**> *derivational or resultative or non-continuative*, phonology: metathesis, syntactic analysis: intransitive verb, attested by BHTTC, Elders Group.

<**qétes**>, cts //qɛ[=Aə́=]t=əs//, FOOD ['*baking underground*'], (<**é-ablaut**> *continuative*), phonology: é-ablaut on root á, syntactic analysis: intransitive verb, attested by BHTTC, also <**qáqetes**>, //qɛ́[-C_1ə-]t=əs//, Elder's comment: "probably", attested by Elders Group (1/25/78), example: <**ílhtsel qétes.**>, //ʔí-ɬ-c-əl qɛ[=Aə́=]t=əs//, /'*I was baking underground.*'/, attested by BHTTC.

<**sqetás**>, dnom //s=qɛ́t=ə[=M2=]s//, FOOD /'*stuff steam-cooked underground, what is baked underground*'/, (<**s=**> *nominalizer*), possibly <**metathesis**> *resultative*, lx <**=es**> *round thing*, phonology: metathesis, syntactic analysis: nominal, attested by Elders Group, BHTTC.

<**qetelméxwtel**>, ds //qɛt=əlmə[=´=]xʷ=təl or qɛ[=Aə=]t=əlmə[=´=]xʷ=təl//, EB ['*wall lettuce*'], ['*Lactuca muralis*'], ASM ['a plant almost exactly like alum root but used for medicine for the breasts to bring down swelling while nursing, some was gathered at Emory Creek'], MED ['medicine for the breasts to bring down swelling while nursing'], literally probably /'putting on as a poultice on the breast medicine, (or) something/device for putting on as a poultice/warming on the breast'/, root <**qát**> *put on as a poultice, warm it*, (<**e-ablaut**> *continuative*, <=´=> *derivational*), lx <**=elmexw ~ =álmexw**> *on the (female) breast*, lx <**=tel**> *device to, thing to, medicine*, phonology: stress-shift within suffix, probable e-ablaut, syntactic analysis: nominal, attested by SP, IHTTC, Elders at Fish Camp at Emory Creek.

<**Qétexem**>, ds //qɛ[=ə́=]t=əx̣=əm//, PLN /'*mountain on the west (C.P.R.) side of the Fraser River above American Bar which had a steaming pond at the top, (year-round village at mouth of American Creek on west bank of the Fraser River [Duff])*'/, root <**qát**> *cook or heat with steam,*

(<**é-ablaut**> *continuative*), lx <**=ex ~ =x**> *distributive*, (<**=em**> *place to get or have*), phonology: é-ablaut on root á, syntactic analysis: nominal, attested by IHTTC, source: place names reference file #29, also PLN [*'year-round village at mouth of American Creek on west bank of the Fraser River'*], other sources: Duff 1952:33, source: place names reference file #29a (p.42), attested by SP and AK (Fish Camp 8/2/77).

<**qatílésem**>, mdls //qɛt=íləs=əm//, FOOD /*'have a hot drink, warm one's chest inside'*/, lx <**=ílés**> *in the chest*, (<**=em**> *middle voice*), syntactic analysis: intransitive verb, attested by IHTTC.

<**qatíwsem**>, mdls //qɛt=íws=əm//, MED [*'take a sweat-bath, (take a steam bath), (sweat-house [Deming])'*], lx <**=íws**> *on the body, on the skin*, (<**=em**> *middle voice*), syntactic analysis: intransitive verb, attested by BHTTC, also <**qetíwsem**>, //qɛt=íws=əm or qɛ[=Aə=]t=íws=əm//, phonology: ablaut or vowel-reduction in root before stressed full-grade suffix, attested by EB, also <**qetí:wsem**>, //qɛt=í·ws=əm or qɛ[=Aə=]t=í·ws=əm//, phonology: ablaut or vowel-reduction in root before stressed full-grade suffix, attested by CT, HT, also /*'sweathouse'*/, attested by Deming (1/31/80).

<**qetíwstel**>, dnom //qɛt=íws=təl or qɛ[=Aə=]t=íws=təl//, BLDG [*'sweathouse'*], MED, root <**qát**> *cook or heat with steam*, possibly <**e-ablaut**> *continuative or derivational*, lx <**=íws**> *on the body, on the skin*, lx <**=tel**> *device to, thing to, medicine*, phonology: possible e-ablaut or vowel-reduction, syntactic analysis: nominal, attested by Elders Group.

<**qatílésem**>, FOOD /*'have a hot drink, warm one's chest inside'*/, *see* qá:t.

<**qatíwsem**>, MED [*'take a sweat-bath, (take a steam bath), (sweat-house [Deming])'*], *see* qá:t.

<**qátxels**>, TCH [*'feeling around'*], *see* qétxt.

<**qáthelhp**>, EB /*'oceanspray plant, "ironwood", "hardhack"'*/, *see* qáthexw.

<**qáthexw**>, free root //qɛ́θəxʷ//, FSH /*'prong of spear, prong of fish spear'*/, SOC, ASM ['made of oceanspray wood'], syntactic analysis: nominal, attested by EL, Elders Group (6/10/75).

<**qáthelhp**>, dnom //qɛ́θ(əxʷ)=əɬp//, EB /*'oceanspray plant, "ironwood", "hardhack"'*/, [*'Holodiscus discolor'*], ASM ['carved to make prongs of fish spears, also used to make needles for sewing bulrush/cattail mats, barbecue sticks, arrow shafts, and knitting needles; its white blooms are out in late June; wild crabapple is also usedto make mat needles'], literally /'spear-prong plant'/, root <**qáthexw**> *prong of fish spear*, lx <**=elhp**> *plant, bush, tree*, phonology: syllable-loss unless exw is an affix, syntactic analysis: nominal, attested by EL, Deming, Elders Group, other sources: ES /qɛ́θəɬp/ *hardhack, ironwood*, also <**qá:thelhp**>, //qɛ́·θ(əxʷ)=əɬp//, attested by AC, Salish cognate: Lushootseed /qcágʷ-ac/ *ironwood (oceanspray, spirea)* H76:372.

<**qá:w**>, free root //qɛ́·w//, ABFC [*'to rest'*], syntactic analysis: intransitive verb, attested by EB, Salish cognate: Lushootseed /qáʔkʷ/ *rest* H76:372, Saanich dial. of N. Straits /qékʷ-əŋ/ *rest* B74a:73, Samish dial. of N. Straits /qíkʷ-əŋ/ *rested* and /sqíʔqəw'/ *be resting* G86:96, also <**qáw**>, //qɛ́w//, attested by Elders Group.

<**qaqíw**>, cts //qɛ[-C_1əAí-]w//, ABDF /*'relaxing, resting'*/, (<**-R1- and í-ablaut**> *continuative*), phonology: reduplication, í-ablaut on e in reduplication, length-loss is normal before infixed reduplication, syntactic analysis: intransitive verb, attested by EB.

<**qáwlhelh**>, ds //qɛ́w=ɬəɬ//, ABFC [*'relaxed [in the throat]'*], lx <**=lhelh**> *in the throat*, syntactic analysis: intransitive verb, attested by Elders Group.

<**qá:wthet**>, pcrs //qɛ́·w=T-ət//, ABFC [*'rest oneself'*], (<**=t**> *purposeful control transitivizer*), (<**-et**> *reflexive*), syntactic analysis: intransitive verb, attested by TM.

<**qelá:wthet**>, plv //q[=əl=]ɛ́·w=T-ət//, pcrs, TVMO [*'camp and rest'*], literally /'rest oneself many

times'/, (<**=el=**> *plural action*), phonology: infixed plural, syntactic analysis: intransitive verb, attested by Elders Group.

<**qáwlhelh**>, ABFC [*'relaxed [in the throat]'*], *see* qá:w.

<**qáwth ~ qá:wth**>, bound root or stem //qɛ́wθ// meaning unknown or //qəw// *warm* or reanalysis of <**seq**> //səq// *hang under* + <**=á:w ~ =í:w ~ =ew**> *on the body, on top of itself* since all potatoes do hang under the plant and those growing in water were gathered by hanging one's body from a canoe and loosening it with one's toes in the mud till it floated up.

<**sqáwth ~ sqá:wth**>, df //s=qɛ́wθ or s=qə[=Aɛ́=]w=θ//, EB /*'potato (generic), including three or four kinds of wild potato: arrowleaf or wapato, Jerusalem artichoke, blue camas, and qíqemxel (so far unidentified plant), besides post-contact domestic potato'*/, ['including: *Sagittaria latifolia, Helianthus tuberosus, Camassia quamash* (and *Camassia leichtlinii*), and unidentified plant, besides *Solanum tuberosum*'], (<**s=**> *nominalizer*), possibly root <**qew**> *warm*, possibly <**á-ablaut**> *derivational*, possibly <**=th**> *in the mouth*, phonology: possible ablaut, syntactic analysis: nominal, attested by AC, other sources: ES /sqɛ́wθ/ *wapato, kows, potato*, also <**sqá:wth**>, //s=qə[=Aɛ́·=]w=θ//, attested by BJ (5/10/64)(p.120 new in transcript), Salish cognate: Squamish /sqáwc/ *potato* W73:203, K67:295, *domestic potato* in Bouchard and Turner 1976 where they report Suttles 1951 and Suttles 1955 view that the domestic potato and this term for it were diffused throughout a number of Salishan languages from an original term in Halkomelem, /sqɛ́wθ/ *wapato (Sagittaria latifolia)*, Lushootseed /s-qáwc/ *potato* H76:371, example: <**xepó:lst te sqá:wth**>, //x^yəp=á·ls=T tə s=qɛ́·w=θ//, /*'peel potatoes'*/, attested by AC, <**q'áq'et'em sqá:wth**>, //q'ɛ́[=C_1ə=]t'=əm s=qɛ́·w=θ//, EB, /*'blue camas'*/, [*'Camassia quamash, Camassia leichtlinii'*], literally /'sweet potato'/, <**sqáwth seplíl**>, FOOD *potato bread* (lit. potato + bread), (attested by RG,EH 6/16/98 to SN, edited by BG with RG,EH 6/26/00)

<**sqeqewíthelh**>, df //s=C_1ə=qɛw=ə[=Aí=]θ=əɬ//, EB [*'arrowleaf'*], [*'Sagittaria latifolia'*], Elder's comment: "", literally /'like little potatoes'/, (<**s=**> *nominalizer*, R5= *diminutive plural*), possibly <**í-ablaut on e in suffix**> *durative or resultative or derivational*, possibly <**=eth**> *in+the mouth*, lx <> *kind of, style, like*, phonology: ablaut, reduplication, vowel-reduction before stressed suffix, syntactic analysis: nominal, dialects: *Tait*, attested by Elders Group.

<**qá:wthet**>, ABFC [*'rest oneself'*], *see* qá:w.

<**qá:wx̲ ~ qáwx̲ ~ qí:wx̲ ~ qéywx̲**>, free root //qɛ́·wx̣ ~ qí·wx̣//, EZ [*'steelhead trout'*], [*'Salmo gairdneri'*], ASM ['ocean-going rainbow trout, classed as salmon by the Stó:lō because, for one reason, the river-ocean-river migration is like that of the salmon'], root meaning unknown unless qá:w *rest*??, possibly <**=x̲**> *distributive, all over*, syntactic analysis: nominal, attested by Elders Group (3/1/72, 3/15/72), also <**qéywx̲ ~ qí:wx̲**>, //qí·wx̣//, attested by BJ (12/5/64), also <**qáwx̲**>, //qɛ́wx̣//, attested by AC, other sources: ES /qɛ́wəx̣/ (Musqueam /qɛ́wʔx̣/) *steelhead*, H-T <kéuq> (macron over e) *steelhead salmon (Salmo gairdneri)*, Salish cognate: Squamish /sqíwʔx̣/ *steelhead* W73:251, K67:295, Sechelt /sqíwx̣/ *steelhead* T77:10, Lushootseed /qíw'x̣/ *steelhead (rainbow) trout* H76:387.

<**Qéywex̲em**>, ds //qí·w[=ə=]x̣=əm//, PLN /*'steelhead fishing place on the Fraser River below Lhílhkw'elqs, at Hogg Slough'*/, (<**=e=**> *derivational* but rare), (<**=em**> *place to get, place to have*), phonology: infixed e (rare), syntactic analysis: nominal, attested by Elders Group (7/13/77), source: place names reference file #69.

<**Qeywéx̲em**>, ds //qiw[=ə́=]x̣=əm//, PLN /*'Sakwi Creek, a stream that joins Weaver Creek about one-third mile above the salmon hatchery'*/, (<**=é=**> *derivational* but rare, stress may be to dissimilate from Qéywex̲em), (<**=em**> *place to get, place to have*), phonology: infixed é (rare), stress-shift, syntactic analysis: nominal, attested by EL (and perhaps NP and EB) on Chehalis place names trip (9/27/77), source: place names reference file #305.

<**qayéx̲**>, free root or stem for some speakers //qɛy(=)ə(´)x̣//, EZ ['*mink*'], attested by AK (11/21/72 tape)
<**sqáyéx̲ ~ sqayéx̲**>, df //s=qɛ́yə́x̣ ~ s=qɛyə́x̣ or s=qɛ́y=ə[=´=]x̣//, EZ ['*mink*'], ['*Mustela vison energumenos*'], N ['*Mink (name in some stories)*'], possibly <**s=**> *nominalizer*, possibly <**=ex̲**> *distributive*, possibly <=´=> *derivational*, possibly root <**qá:y(=)s**> *just now, at one recent moment, recently*, literally perhaps /'something that's everywhere at one instant'/ (perhaps thus the meaning of derived form <**sqoyéx̲iya**> *(be) bragging, extravagant in claims, bull-headed, claims he's the best*), Elder's comment: "it means he's foxy (BJ 12/5/64)", phonology: stress-shift, syntactic analysis: nominal, attested by AC, BJ (12/5/64), Elders Group, SP (11/21/72 tape), other sources: ES /sqáyə̀x̣/ (Ms Cw /cicíq'ən/) *mink*, JH /sqé·yə́x̣/ *mink*, also <**qayéx̲**>, //qɛy(=)ə(´)x̣//, attested by AK (11/21/72 tape), Salish cognate: Squamish /qáyix̣/ *name of a man who was changed into a mink, mink; "slippery" person (originally mink)* K67:353, K69:80, Sechelt /qáyx̣/ *mink* T77:9, also <**chachí:q'el**>, //cɛ(=)cí·q'(=)əl or C_1ɛ=cí·q'=əl or C_1ɛ=cə[=Aí·=]q'=əl//, also EZ ['*mink*'], ['*Mustela vison energumenos*'], attested by Elders Group, Salish cognate: Squamish /čičíq'n/ *mink* W73:176, K67:317, Samish dial. of N. Straits /č'eč'íq'ən/ *mink* G86:66.

<**Sqayéx̲iya ~ Sqáyèx̲iya**>, ds //s=qɛ́yə́x̣=iyɛ//, N /'*Mink (name in stories), pet name of Mink*'/, (<**s=**> *nominalizer*), (<**=iya**> *affectionate diminutive*), phonology: possible downstepping or stress-loss, syntactic analysis: nominal, attested by SP (11/21/72 tape), AC, JL (4/7/78), also <**Qayéx̲iya**>, //qɛyə́x̣=iyɛ//, attested by AK (11/21/72 tape), also <**Sqoyéx̲iya**>, //s=qɛ[=Aa=]yə́x̣=iyɛ//, attested by Elders Group (3/21/79).

<**Sqayéx̲iya Smált ~ Sqáqeyex̲iya Smált**>, ds //s=qɛyə́x̣=iyɛ s=mɛ́lt ~ s=qɛ[=´=C_1ə=]x̣=iyɛ s=mɛ́lt//, PLN ['*small shoreline ridge on the Fraser River and all along the river around the larger mountain across the Trans-Canada Highway from Jones Hill*'], literally /'Mink Mountain, Mink Rock'/, probably <=´=> *derivational*, probably <**=R1=**> *resultative or derivational*, phonology: stress-shift, reduplication, syntactic analysis: simple nominal phrase, attested by JL (4/7/78 on a trip), see drawing on file cards and in field notes.

<**sqoyéx̲iya**>, df //sqɛ[=Aa=]yə́x̣=iyɛ//, EFAM /'*(be) bragging, extravagant in claims, bull-headed, claims he's the best*'/, (semological comment: named from the name for Mink who has all these characteristics, this is probably what BJ means by "foxy" and Squamish has a cognate form (in part) for a "slippery" person), probably <**o-ablaut on root a**> *continuative*? or> *derivational*, phonology: o-ablaut on root a, syntactic analysis: adjective/adjectival verb?, nominal???, attested by Elders Group (7/27/75).

<**qá:ys**>, free root //qɛ́·y(=)s//, TIME /'*recently, just now, lately, (at one recent moment), not long ago*'/, possibly <=es> *cyclic period; face*, syntactic analysis: adverb/adverbial verb, attested by Elders Group, EB, AC (9/12/73), other sources: JH /qéys/ *now*, Salish cognate: Squamish /qáʔis ~ qaʔís/ *soon, not long* W73:243, K67:353, example: <**qá:ys me xwe'í.**>, //qɛ́·ys mə xʷə=ʔí//, /'*(He/She/They) recently got here., just got here*'/, attested by Elders Group, <**qá:ys syilólém**>, //qɛ́·ys s=yil(=)ál=əm//, /'*new year*'/, literally /'just now year, at one recent moment year'/, attested by Elders Group (4/23/80), <**qá:ys kwò:l**>, //qɛ́·ys kʷà·l//, /'*new born*'/, literally /'just now born, at one recent moment born'/, attested by Elders Group (4/23/80), <**te qá:ys tátsel**>, //tə qɛ́·ys tɛ́c=əl//, /'*the newcomer*'/, literally /'the one who just now gets here, comes here'/, syntactic analysis: relative clause, attested by EB (6/14/76), <**qá:ysò**>, //qɛ́·ys=à//, /'*not long ago, just now*'/, phonology: -à is neither derivational nor inflectional here, merely phonologically combined or suffixed onto the preceding adverb, attested by EB, <**qá:ysò le ts'eqw'ő́wélh.**>, //qɛ́·ys=à lə c'əqʼʷ=ówə́ɬ//, /'*He/She just now made a basket.*'/, literally /'just now third person past make a basket, weave a basket (lit. poke vessel)'/, attested by EB, <**qá:ystsel ò. ~ qá:ystsel ò yóys.**>, //qɛ́·ys-c-əl ʔà ~ qɛ́·ys-c-əl ʔà yáys//, /'*I just now started work.*'/, literally /'I just now ~ I just now work'/, (semological comment: present tense as

immediate past), syntactic comment: adverb/adverbial verb as main verb, attested by Elders Group (2/8/78), also <**qá:ystsel le.** (or **qá:ystselè.**) ~ **qá:ystsel le yóys.**>, //qɛ́·ys-c-əl lə (or qɛ́·ys-c-əl-ə̀) ~ qɛ́·ys-c-əl lə yáys//, /'*I just now started work (went to work).*'/, literally /'I just now go (or I just now) ~ I just now go to work'/, attested by EB (2/8/78).

<**tloqá:ys**>, ds //tə=la=qɛ́·y(=)s//, TIME /'*now, this moment, this instant, (right now)*'/, (<**te=**> *the (present visible or unmarked), lo= here, this*), phonology: te lo is usually a separate phrase as a demonstrative *this, the one here*, syntactic analysis: adverb/adverbial verb, attested by AC (9/12/73), also <**tleqá:ys**>, //təlo=qɛ́·ys//, also /'*right now*'/, attested by EB, example: <**lí kwthá tleqá:ys.**>, //lí k^{w}θ=ɛ́ tə=lo=qɛ́·ys//, /'*He's there now.*'/, literally /'he's there the (near, not visible) =place right now'/, semantic environment ['he's at Seabird Island, not visible from Sardis'], attested by EB.

<**qá:y(=)t**>, possible root or stem //qɛ́·y(=)t //, meaning unknown, or perhaps q'á:yt *send a message*

<**Qiqá:yt**>, df //C_1əC_2=qɛ́·y(=)t or C_1í=qɛ́·y(=)t or qi[=Aɛ́·C_1ə=]y=t or C_1í=q'[=D=]ɛ́·yt//, PLN /'*Reserve near New Westminster, B.C., (South Westminster [DF])*'/, possibly <**R3=**> *plural* or possibly <**R4=**> *diminutive* or possibly <**á:-ablaut plus =R1=**> *resultative or continuative or derivational*, or possibly, with <**=D= deglottalization**> *derivational*, q'á:yt *send a message*, phonology: reduplication, possible ablaut, possible deglottalization, syntactic analysis: nominal, attested by IHTTC, source: place names reference file #192a, also /'*South Westminster*'/, attested by DF (Elders Group 4/23/80).

<**qá:ytl'em**>, df //qɛ́·yƛ'=əm or qi[=Aɛ́·=]y(=)ƛ'=əm//, SD /'*(make/have a) squeaking sound (of a tree, of a chair, of shoes), squeaking (of shoes, trees), (creaking)*'/, possibly root <**qéytl'**> as in <**qéytl'=t**> *press it down (like yeast bread)* (but that could also be just <**qí(:)tl'=t**>), probably <**=em**> *intransitivizer, have, get or middle voice* probably from (*makes the sound on itself*), possibly <**á:-ablaut**> *durative*, possibly <**=tl'**> meaning unknown, phonology: possible ablaut, syntactic analysis: intransitive verb, attested by Elders Group (11/3/76, 5/14/80).

<**qe**>, free root //qə//, CJ /'*and, but, or*'/, syntactic analysis: conjunction, syntactic comment: conjoins verbs, phrases, sentences, and sometimes even nominals, attested by LJ (Tait), Elders Group, EB, MV, also <**qa**>, //qɛ//, [qæ], attested by AC, Elders Group, ASM ['and'], example: <**le lemélstexwes te Bill te sq'émél xwelám te Jim qe Bob.**>, //lə lom=ə[=´=]l=sT-əx^w-əs tə Bill tə s=q'ə́mə́l x^{w}ə=lɛ́=m tə Jim qə Bob//, /'*Bill threw (he throws it) the paddle to Jim and Bob.*'/, syntactic comment: omission of the article is allowed in the second conjoined np, <**tsel kw'etslóme qe Bob.**>, //c-əl k'^{w}əc=l-ámə qə Bob//, /'*I saw you and Bob. (see s-o)*'/, syntactic comment: conjoining an object suffix and a nominal/nominal phrase, attested by LJ (Tait), <**tl'otsasu qw'eyíléx qa t'í:lem tel siyá:ye.**>, //ƛ'a-cɛ s=u q'^{w}əy=íl=ə́x^y qɛ t'í·l=əm tə-l si=yɛ́·yə//, /'*(And then/so) my friends will sing and dance.*'/, syntactic comment: conjoining two verb phrases with the same simple nominal phrase subject gapped, attested by AC, ASM ['or'], <**líchxw lilíyem qa wáchxw líxw x̱àm?**>, //lí-c-x^w C_1əC_2=líy=əm qɛ wə-ə/ɛ́-c-x^w lí-x^{w}x̱ɛ̀m//, /'*Did you laugh or cry?*'/, literally /'did you laugh many times or if -yes/no question -you (aux. -you sg. subjuntive) cry'/, phonology: vowel merger, attested by Elders Group, <**lí lám kw'e Bill qe Bob?**>, //lí lɛ́=m k'^{w}ə Bill qə Bob//, /'*Did Bill or Bob go?*'/, attested by Elders Group, <**tl'ó t'we Bob qe tl'ó t'we Bill.**>, //ƛ'á t'wə Bob qə ƛ'á t'wə Bill//, /'*Maybe it's Bob or maybe it's Bill.*'/, attested by Elders Group, also <**yóswe tl'ós Bob yóswe tl'ós Bill.**>, //yáswə ƛ'á-s Bob yáswə ƛ'á-s Bill//, attested by Elders Group, <**tl'ó Bill qe tl'ó Bob.**>, //ƛ'á Bill qə ƛ'á Bob//, /'*It's Bill or Bob.*'/, attested by Elders Group, <**tl'ó: Bob qe tl'ó: Bill?**>, //ƛ'á=ə Bob qə ƛ'á-ə Bill//, /'*Is it Bob or it it Bill?*'/, phonology: vowel merger, attested by Elders Group, <**weswíyeqá:s qe weslhálíyes**>, //wə-s=wíqə-əs qə wə-s=ɬɛ́líy=əs//, /'*if it's a man or a woman*'/, literally /'if- man -subjunctive 3 or if- woman -subjunctive 3'/, phonology: vowel merger, attested by EB, <**wáslhálíyes**

qe wáswiyeqá:s?>, //wə-ə/ɛ-s=ɬɛ́líy-əs qə wə-ə/ɛ-s=wiqə=əs//, /'*Was it a woman or a man?*'/, literally /'if- yes/no question- woman -subjunctive 3 or if- yes/no question- man -subjunctive 3 (if is it a man?)'/, attested by EB (8/10/76), <**latsel alqá:ls kw sqá:wth qewas kw xáweq.**>, //lɛ-c-əl ʔɛlq=ɛ́·ls kʷ s=qɛ́·wθ qə-wə-ɛ́s kw xʸɛ́w=əq//, /'*I'm going to buy some potatoes or some carrots.*'/, literally /'I'm going to buy (structured activity) some potato or -if -subjunctive 3 some carrot'/, attested by EB, ASM ['but'], <**lí kw'e s'átl'q qe ő we ís chókw.**>, //lí k'ʷə s=ʔɛ́ƛ'q qə ʔówə ʔí-s cákʷ//, /'*It's outside but not far.*'/, literally /'it's at the (remote) outside but it's not aux. -subjunctive 3 far'/, attested by EB, <**qé<u>x</u> te tl'ikw'íyelhp qa ōwéte tl'íkw'el.**>, //qə́x̣ tə ƛ'ik'ʷəl=əɬp qɛ ʔowə= ́tɛ ƛ'ík'ʷəl//, /'*(There's) a lot of (bean) vines but (there's) no beans.*'/, attested by AC, <**lámelhtsel qe tsel ő we o.**>, //lɛ́=m-əɬ-c-əl qə c-əl ʔówə ʔà//, /'*I was going but I'm not now.*'/, literally /'going -past -subj. of main verb -I but subj. of main verb -I be not just'/, syntactic comment: vneg as main verb without subordinate, attested by Elders Group, <**lámtsel t'ó:kw' qechelew í ò.**>, //lɛ́=m-c-əl t'á·k'ʷ qə c-əl-əw ʔí ʔà//, /'*I was going home but instead I stayed.*'/, literally /'I am going homeward but I -contrastive be here just'/, attested by Elders Group, <**tsel wekw'ókw'etset qe lew lép'exes.**>, //c-əl wə-k'ʷɛ[-AáC$_1$ə-]c=əT qə lə-w lə́p'=əxʸ-əs//, /'*I was watching him but he ate it. (eat s-th)*'/, attested by Elders Group, <**ewálhtsel mí:l ámeq't qetsel (we) th'éxwmetò.**>, //ʔəwə=əɬ-c-əl mi·-l ʔɛməq'=T qə-c-əl əw θ'ə́xʷ=məT-à//, /'*I wasn't going to bring him/her back but I felt sorry for him.*'/, literally /'I wasn't coming to -subjunctive 1s bring s-o back but -I contrastive pity s-o/feel sorry for s-o -just'/, attested by EB, <**<u>x</u>í<u>x</u>ewetem qew le xókw'em.**>, //x̣í[-C$_1$ə-]w=əT-əm qə-w lə xʸák'ʷ=əm//, /'*He was warned but he bathed.*'/, literally /'he was warned but -contrastive third person past bathe'/, attested by Elders Group, <**ő wechxw swiyeqáxw qe xixpó:mchexw.**>, //ʔówə-c-xʷ s=wiqə-ɛ́xʷ qə xʸá·[-C$_1$ə-]p=ə[=M3/M2=]m-c-əxʷ (or C$_1$ə/C$_1$í=xʸá·p=ə[=M2=]m-c-əxʷ)//, /'*You're not a man but you're whistling.*'/, semantic environment ['a saying to a young girl around puberty to stop her from whistling'], usage: saying, attested by MV (Deming 5/4/78), <**qe ő we**>, //qə ʔówə ~ qə ʔə́wə//, /'*without, and not*'/, literally /'and not'/, attested by EB, AC, <**lám ò yelá:wxóxes qe ő we is yeqwelsthóxes.**>, //lɛ́=m ʔà yəlɛ́·w=xʸ-áxʸ-əs qə ʔówə ʔi-s yə=qʷɛ[=Aə=]l=sT-áxʸ-əs//, /'*He just passed by me without speaking to me.*'/, (semological comment: interesting motion stem (talk to s-o while moving)), syntactic comment: purposeful control inanimate object preferred stem with animate object personal pronoun suffix (rare),, attested by EB.

<**qew ~ qwō ~ qe ... u/ew**>, df //qə=w ~ qə ... u(w)//, TIME /'*until, till, while*'/, literally /'and -contrastive'/, syntactic analysis: conjunction, attested by EB, AC, example: <**<u>x</u>à:m ò qwō lame t'ókw'.**>, //x̣ɛ̀·m ʔà qə=w lɛ́=m-è t'ák'ʷ//, /'*He was crying until he went home.*'/, attested by EB, <**<u>x</u>à:m ò qwō mí e xwe'í te tá:ls.**>, //x̣ɛ̀·m ʔà qə=w mí ʔə xʷə=ʔí tə tɛ́·l-s//, /'*He was crying until his mother came.*'/, attested by EB, <**qetstu lám oy'á:y**>, //qə-c-t-u lɛ́=m C$_1$əC$_2$=ʔɛ́·y//, /'*while we are going*'/, literally /'while -we going to be keeping on'/, attested by EB (12/18/75), <**máqa qetstu lóme xwlí te smá:lt**>, //mɛ́qɛ qə-c-t-u lám-ə̀ xʷ=lí tə s=mɛ́·lt//, /'*(There was) snow (on the ground) all the way until we reached the mountain. (hit -just)*'/, attested by EB, <**hewth'átlha qetl'esu <u>x</u>à:ms.**>, //hə-wəθ'ɛ́=T-ɬɛ qə ƛ'a-s-ux̣ɛ̀·m-s//, /'*Tease him till he cries.*'/, attested by AC, <**ópel qas te lhq'átses qa('a) téxwswàyèl.**>, //ʔápəl qɛ=s tə ɬq'ɛ́cəs qɛ(ʔɛ) tə́xʷ=s=wɛ̀yə̀l//, /'*(It's) fifteen minutes to (till) noon.*'/, literally /'it's ten and the five until mid-day/noon'/, attested by Elders at Fish Camp (7/19/78).

<**qesu**>, df //qə=s=əw or qə s=u//, CJ /'*and so, and then*'/, (<**(=)s=u**> *so, then* (also occurs as free-form conjunction, itself composed of s= *conjunctive affix* and =ew *contrastive*)), phonology: u from ew, syntactic analysis: conjunction, attested by AC, CT, EB, others, example: <**qesu làm**>, //qə=s=u lɛ̀=m//, /'*and then he went*'/, attested by AC, <**qesu tótel:ò:met yutl'ó:lem**>, //qə=s=u tá[-C$_1$ə-]l=l-á·mət yə=w=ƛ'á·[=lə=]m//, /'*and (so) they understand*'/, attested by AC, <**é<u>x</u>qst te máches qesu yéqwt kw'e sísq'**>, //ʔə́x̣=qs=T tə mɛ́cəs qə=s=u yə́qʷ=T k'ʷə C$_1$í=səq'//, /'*strike the match and*

light (burn) the kindling'/, attested by CT, <**ts'qw'ét te sqá:wth qesu me lhá:x̱em í tel lóthel**>, //c'əq'^{w}=M1=T tə s=qɛ́·wθ qə=s=u mə ɬɛ́·x̣=əm ʔí tə-l láθəl//, /'*poke the potato and put it/serve it on my dish*'/, attested by EB.

<**qetl'osu ~ qetl'esu**>, df //qə=ƛ'a=s=u or qə ƛ'a s=u//, CJ /'*and so, and then*'/, (<**=tl'o=s=u ~ =tl'e=s=u**> *then, so* (also occurs independently, itself composed of tl'ó *that's him/her/it/them*, s=u *so, then*), syntactic analysis: conjunction, syntactic comment: sbsp occur within this form probably showing that su is an independent word (not affixed); the form also occurs without qe probably showing that tl'o is not affixed either; sbsp forms are added thus: (qe)tl'o-l-su *and so I, and then I*, (qe)tl'o-'a-su *and so you, and then you*, (qe)tl'o-(s'é)-s-su ~ (qe)tl'o-(sé)-s-su *and so/then he/she/it/they*, (qe)tl'o-s-'é-continuative aspect-u *and so we, and then we*, (probably) (qe)tl'o-'a-su ...-elép *and so you folks, and then you folks*; further suffixes are also found in this combination, i.e. th'a *reportative, it is said, they say, people say* is found thus: qe-tl'o-th'a-s-é-su *and then they say he, and so it is said he/she/it/they*, attested by AC, Elders Group, EB, others, example: <**máxlha ta st'ole'oléstel qetl'o'asu kw'étslexw.**>, //mɛ́=x^{y}-ɬɛ t-ɛ s=t'álə=alə[=´=]s=təl qə ƛ'a-ʔɛ s=u k'^{w}ə́c=l-əx^{w}//, /'*Take off your eyeglasses, and then you can see it. (take s-th off)*'/, <**qetlosésu qwà:l te lólets'e.**>, //qə=ƛ'a-s-ə́=s=u q^{w}ɛ̀·l tə C_1á=ləc'ə//, /'*And so the announcer/master of ceremonies speaks.*'/, literally /'and so/then he speak(s) the one person'/, usage: contemporary story, attested by AC, comment: many other examples in texts and in G77: Chapter 7ff.

<**qas**>, df //qɛ=s//, [qɛs], CJ ['*and*'], (<**=s**> *conjunctive affix*), syntactic analysis: conjunction, syntactic comment: conjoins numerals, independent pronouns, and nominals, precedes the demonstrative article of the second nominal/numeral/pronoun, attested by AC, Elders Group, EB, others, example: <**tl'ó swás isále sqwemáy qas te qéx̱ pús.**>, //ƛ'á swɛ́-s ʔisɛ́lə s=q^{w}əm=ɛ́y qɛ=s tə qə́x̣ pús//, /'*He has two dogs and lots of cats.*'/, <**tset ílhtel tloqá:ys te Bill qas ta'á'altha.**>, //c-ət ʔɛ[=Aí=]ɬ=təl tə=la=qɛ́·ys tə Bill qɛ=s tɛ=C_1ɛ́=ʔɛlθɛ//, /'*Bill and I are eating right now.*'/, <**ópel qas te léts'e ~ ópel qas kw'e léts'e**>, //ʔápəl qɛ=s tə lə́c'ə ~ ʔápəl qɛ=s k'^{w}ə lə́c'ə//, /'*eleven (present and visible or presence and visibility not specified) ~ eleven (remote or abstract)*'/, attested by AC, CT, many others, <**slháli qas kw'e swíqe**>, //s=ɬɛ́liy qɛ=s k'^{w}ə s=wíq=ə//, /'*a woman and a man*'/, attested by AC, <**th'ó:kws te x̱wó:qw' qas te léts'e pésk'a.**>, //θ'á·k^{w}s təx̣^{w}á·q'^{w} qɛ=s tə lə́c'ə pə́sk'ɛ//, /'*There are seven sawbill ducks and one hummingbird.*'/, attested by EB approved this sentence constructed by a class member, *<**th'ó:kws te x̱wó:qw' qas léts'e te pésk'a.**> rejected, *<**th'ó:kws te x̱wó:qw' qesu léts'e te pésk'a.**> rejected, <**kw'étslexwes te sléxwelh, sq'émel, qas te sx̱wõqw'tel.**>, //k'^{w}ə́c=l-əx^{w}-əs tə s=lə́x^{w}əɬ, s=q'ə́məl, qɛ=s tə s=x̣^{w}óq'^{w}=təl//, /'*He saw a canoe, a paddle and a canoe pole.*'/, syntactic comment: gapped article, attested by EB, <**qas kw'elhwát**>, //qɛ=s k'^{w}ə=ɬ=wɛ́t//, /'*and who? (of several), and who else?*'/, attested by EB.

<**=qel**>, da //=qəl//, ANA ['*in the head*'], WATR /'*at the head or source of a river, the inside head or inlet of a river*'/, LAND ['*head of an island*'], syntactic analysis: lexical suffix, derivational suffix; found in <**shxwétl'qel**>, //s=x^{w}ə́ƛ'=qəl//, /'*pillow (rolled bulrush mat)*'/, literally /'nominal rolled for the head'/, <**má:qel**>, //mɛ́·=qəl//, /'*hair*'/, literally probably /'comes out of in the head'/, <**sméth'qel**>, //s=mə́θ'=qəl//, /'*brain*'/, literally /'nominal blue in the head'/, <**Sx̱óchaqel**>, //s=x̣ácɛ=qəl//, /'*Chilliwack Lake (lake at the head (of the river)*'/, <**Sq'éwqel**>, //s=q'ə́w=qəl//, /'*Seabird Island*'/, literally /'turn in river at the head (a head-shaped mountain or head of the slough or head of the island)'/, <**skwetáxwqel**>, //s=k^{w}ətɛ́x^{w}=qəl//, /'*inlet*'/, literally /'the inside in the head'/, <**chélhqel ~ chelhqéyl** or **chelhqí:l**>, //(Tait) cə́ɬqəl ~ (Chill.) cəɬqɛ́yl//, /'*palate, roof of mouth and inside upper lip*'/.

<**qél**>, free root //qə́l//, VALJ /'*be bad (of water, person, anything), be dirty (of house, clothes, person, etc.)*'/, syntactic analysis: adjective/adjectival verb, attested by Elders Group (3/1/72, 2/26/75, 3/72, etc.), AC, BJ (5/10/64), other sources: ES /qə́l/ *bad*, ASM ['be dirty'], example: <**qél te lálems.**>, //qə́l

tə lɛ́ləm-s//, /'*Her house is dirty.*'/, attested by AC, <**le q'ó:y te qél.**>, //lə q'á·y tə qә́l//, /'*The dirty thing died.*'/, literally /'third person past die the/relativizer/one that's dirty'/, attested by Deming (2/7/80), ASM ['be bad'], <**qél te qó:.**>, //qә́l tə qá·//, /'*The water is bad.*'/, (semological comment: another word is used for dirty water), attested by AC, <**qél xwlá tl'eléwe. ~ qél xwlám tl'eléwe.**>, //qә́l x^w=lɛ́(=m) ƛ'ə=lә́wə//, /'*It's bad for you.*'/, attested by EB, <**yeláwel qél.**>, //yəlɛ́w=əl qә́l//, /'*(It's) worse.*'/, syntactic comment: comparative, attested by Elders Group (1/19/77), <**yeláwel qél telí tl'á'altha.**>, //yəlɛ́w=əl qә́l təlíƛ'=C_1ɛ́=ʔɛlθɛ//, /'*He's worse than me.*'/, attested by Elders Group (1/19/77), <**ts'áts'el qél.**>, //c'ɛ́=C_1ə=əl qә́l//, /'*(It's the) worst., (It's) real bad.*'/, literally /'very/extremely/really (on top of =derivational =get/go/become)'/, syntactic comment: superlative, attested by Elders Group (1/19/77), <**qél we'ól**>, //qә́l wə=ʔàl//, /'*(It's) worse., (It's) real worse.*'/, syntactic comment: comparative (or superlative), attested by Elders Group (1/19/77).

<**sqéls**>, dnom //s=qә́l=əls or s=qә́l=s//, HARV /'*part not used (like seeds of cantelope, core of apple, blood in fish, etc.), worst part*'/, FSH, HUNT, MC, (<**s=**> *nominalizer*), possibly <**=els**> *thing that's* perhaps from *structured activity continuative*, phonology: possible *syllable loss of el before =els,* syntactic analysis: nominal, attested by EB, Elders Group (1/19/77), example: <**tl'ó sqéls.**>, //ƛ'á s=qә́l=əls//, /'*That's the worst., That's the part not used (like seeds of canta- lope, core of apple, blood in fish, etc.).*'/, attested by Elders Group, EB.

<**qíqel**>, dmv //C_1í=qəl//, EFAM /'*be naughty, be bad (a menace) (but not quite as bad as qél)*'/, (<**R4=**> *diminutive*), phonology: reduplication, syntactic analysis: adjective/adjectival verb, attested by EB, BHTTC, example: <**qí:qel te (pípehò:m, mímetú, kwíkweshú).**>, //C_1í=:=qəl tə (C_1í=pəhà·m, C_1í=mətú, C_1í=k^wəšú)//, /'*The (frog, little lamb, little pig) is naughty.*'/, usage: lyrics to the Híltu song, attested by BHTTC, <**qíqel stl'ítl'qelh**>, //C_1í=qəl s=ƛ'íƛ'q=əɬ//, /'*bad child*'/, attested by EB.

<**sqelá:lh**>, ds //s=qəl=ɛ́·ɬ//, CLO ['*diaper*'], ASM ['made of inner cedar bark or nettle bark'], literally perhaps /'something for dirty (of) child'/, (<**s=**> *nominalizer*), lx <**=á:lh ~ =á:ylh ~ =ilh ~ =elh**> *child*, syntactic analysis: nominal, attested by AC, BJ (12/5/64).

<**qelá:m**>, df //qəl=ɛ́·m or qəl=ə[=Aɛ́·=]m//, ABDF ['*(be) weak*'], DESC, possibly <**=á:m ~ =ém**> *in strength* or possibly <**=em**> *middle voice or intransitivizer, become, get, have* or possibly <**á:-ablaut**> *durative*, phonology: possible á:-ablaut on suffix, syntactic analysis: adjective/adjectival verb, attested by BJ (5/64, 12/5/64), EB.

<**qiqelá:m ~ qiqelà:m**>, dmv //C_1í=qəl=ɛ́·m or C_1í=qəl=ə[=Aɛ́·=]m//, ABDF /'*(be) weak (in strength, also in taste [TM])*'/, (<**R4=**> *diminutive*), phonology: reduplication, possible ablaut, syntactic analysis: adjective/adjectival verb, attested by Elders Group (5/25/77), EB, also /'*(be) weak (in taste), (be) weak (in strength)*'/, attested by TM (in Elders Group 5/25/77).

<**qelámthet**>, incs //qəl=ɛ(·)m=θət//, ABDF ['*get weak*'], (<**=thet**> *get, become, inceptive*), phonology: length-loss probably in fast speech, syntactic analysis: intransitive verb, attested by LJ (Tait), example: <**le qelámthet tel th'ále lhíl ólew le kw'á:y.**>, //lə qəl=ɛm=θət tə-l θ'ɛ́lə ɬí-l ʔál=əw lə k'^wɛ́·y//, /'*My heart gets weak when I get too hungry. (get hungry)*'/, attested by LJ.

<**qiqelá:mthet**>, dmv //C_1í=qəl=ɛ́·m=θət//, incs, ABDF /'*get weak (from laughing, walking, working too long, sickness)*'/, semantic environment ['*from laughing, walking, working too long, sickness*'], (<**R4=**> *diminutive*), (<**=thet**> *get, become, inceptive*), phonology: reduplication, possible ablaut, syntactic analysis: intransitive verb, attested by AD.

<**qelélwes**>, ds //qəl=ә́lwəs//, [qəlɪ́lwəs], EFAM ['*afraid to try*'], literally /'bad in the stomach'/, lx <**=élwes**> *in the stomach*, syntactic analysis: adjective/adjectival verb, attested by Elders Group.

<**qélelhóméx**>, ds //qә́l=əɬ=áməx^y//, DESC /'*ugly, sloppy (in dress, walk, etc.)*'/, lx <**=elh**> *-style*, lx <**=ómex ~ =ó:mex**> *in looks, appearance, -looking*, phonology: updrifting, syntactic analysis:

adjective/adjectival verb, attested by EB, others, contrast <**qelóméx**> *look bad, look mean.*

<**qéqelelhó:mex**>, dmpv //C_1í=Aə́=qəl=əɬ=á·məxʸ//, DESC /'*scrubby little ones, (little ugly ones)*'/, semantic environment ['example of apples'], (<**R4=**> *diminutive*, é-ablaut plural (of diminutive)), (<**=elh**> *-style*, <**=ó:mex**> *in looks, appearance, -looking*), phonology: stress-shift, syntactic analysis: adjective/adjectival verb.

<**qél:em ~ qél:ém** or **leqél:em ~ leqél:ém**>, df //qə́l(=·)·=əm or lə=qə́l(=·)·=əm//, WETH /'*dirty (weather), bad weather, storm*'/, WATR ['*be dirty*'], root <**qél**> *bad, dirty*, possibly <**=em**> *intransitivizer, have, get*, possibly <**=:**> meaning uncertain (perhaps none if conditioned by updrifting after resonants), possibly <**le(xw)**> *always* or <**le**> *third person past tense*, phonology: updrifting, syntactic analysis: adjective/adjectival verb, attested by Elders Group (3/72, tape 33)(4/16/75), EB, example: <**me le qél:em te swáyel.**>, //mə lə qə́l(=·)·=əm tə s=wɛ́yəl//, /'*(There's a) storm coming., (There's) bad weather., (It's a) dirty day.*'/, attested by Elders Group (4/16/75), <**leqélém te stó:lō.**>, //ləqə́l(=·)·=əm tə s=tá·low//, /'*The river is dirty.*'/, attested by EB.

<**qéleqep**>, ds //qə́l=əqəp or qə́l=(əl)əqəp//, TAST ['*taste bad*'], SM /'*smell bad, (have a) bad fragrance, (have a) bad smell*'/, lx <**=áleqep ~ =eqep ~ =eleqep**> *smell, taste*, phonology: possible syllable-loss, syntactic analysis: adjective/adjectival verb or intransitive verb, attested by Elders Group (5/25/77), NP, also <**qeléqep**>, //qəl=ə́qəp//, attested by Deming (1/31/80), RG & EH (4/10/99 Ling332), example: <**qeléqep látelh slhákw'em**>, //qəl=ə́qəp lɛ́t=əɬ s=ɬɛ́k'ʷ=əm//, ABDF /bad morning breath/, attested by RG & EH (4/10/99 Ling332)

<**qelés**>, df //qə́l=ə[=M2=]s or qəl=ə[=´=]s//, DESC /'*dirty, (have a cross face [EB])*'/, lx <**=es**> *on the face*, possibly <**metathesis or stress-shift**> *derivational*, phonology: metathesis or stress-shift, syntactic analysis: adjective/adjectival verb, attested by Elders Group (3/72, tape 33, Lesson VII), example: <**qelés te lálwes.**>, //qə́l=ə[=M2=]s tə lɛ́lwəs//, /'*The floor is dirty.*'/, attested by JL (Elders Group 3/72), also /'*have a cross face*'/, attested by EB, <**kwélhtu qelés; skw'áy kw'es tu xwlíyémés.**>, //kʷə́ɬ(=)t=u qə́l=ə[=M2=]s; s=k'ʷɛ́y k'ʷə-s t=u xʷ=l=íy=əm=əs//, /'*She's got a cross face; she can't smile.*'/, attested by EB.

<**qelésem**>, mdls //qə́l=ə[=M2=]s=əm//, ABFC /'*turn away, turn one's face away*'/, (<**=em**> *middle voice*), phonology: metathesis, syntactic analysis: intransitive verb, attested by BHTTC, IHTTC.

<**qélsem**>, if //qə́l=s(T)-əm//, EFAM ['*be disliked*'], comment: prob. in error for qélstem (/qə́l=sT-əxʷ-əm/) *be disliked*, syntactic analysis: passive, attested by Elders Group (4/6/77).

<**qéletses**>, ds //qə́l=əcəs//, ABDF ['*(have) dirty hands*'], lx <**=etses**> *in the hand*, syntactic analysis: adjective/adjectival verb, attested by Elders Group (6/16/76).

<**qelétses**>, df //qə́l=ə[=M2=]cəs//, DESC /'*(be) dirty (in everything) (in one's clothes, house, person)*'/, ABDF, lx <**=tses ~ =etses**> *in the hand*, lx <**metathesis**> *derivational*, phonology: metathesis, syntactic analysis: adjective/adjectival verb, attested by Elders Group (6/16/76).

<**qelí:lt**>, pcs //qəl=í·l=T//, incs, VALJ ['*spoil s-th (purposely)*'], literally /'make s-th go/come/get/become bad'/, lx <**=í:l**> *get, become, go*, (<**=t**> *purposeful control transitivizer*), phonology: no syllable-loss (=í:l does not replace el of monosyllabic root here), syntactic analysis: transitive verb, attested by Elders Group (3/27/78).

<**qelqelí:lt**>, cts //C_1əC_2=qəl=í·l=T//, VALJ ['*spoiling s-th*'], (<**R3=**> *plural continuative* or just *continuative*), phonology: reduplication, no syllable-loss, syntactic analysis: transitive verb, attested by Elders Group.

<**qelqelí:lthet**>, pcrs //C_1əC_2=qəl=í·l=T-ət//, EFAM ['*get mad at oneself*'], (<**-et**> *reflexive*), phonology: reduplication, no syllable-loss, syntactic analysis: intransitive verb, attested by EB.

<**qelqéyl** or **qelqí:l**>, incs //qəl=qəl=í·l//, [qəlqéyl ~ qəlqé·l], VALJ /'*turn bad, (get) spoiled (of clothes for ex.), (get) dirty*'/, lx <**=qel**> *in the head*, lx <**=í:l**> *get, become, go*, phonology: syllable-loss of el

in suffix before =í:l, syntactic analysis: intransitive verb, attested by EB, AC, example: <**me qelqéyl tel sqwá:lewel.**>, //mə qəl=qəl=í·l tə-l s=qʷɛ̀·l=əwəl//, /'*I lost heart., I became disappointed., I became discouraged.*'/, EFAM /'*lose heart, become disappointed, become discouraged*'/, literally /'my thoughts/feelings started to turn bad/get spoiled'/, comment: idiom with sqwá:lewel, attested by CT, HT.

<**qelqé:ylt** or **qelqí:lt**>, pcs //qəl=qəl=í·l=T//, VALJ /'*spoil s-th, destroy s-th*'/, SOC, EFAM, MC, (<**=t**> *purposeful control transitivizer*), phonology: syllable-loss, syntactic analysis: transitive verb, attested by Elders Group; found in <**qelqé:yltes.**>, //qəl=qəl=í·l=T-əs//, /'*He destroyed something.*'/, attested by EB.

<**qelqéyláléqep**>, ds //qəl=qəl=í·l=ɛ́lə́qəp//, SM /'*turn bad in smell, smells like it's turned bad*'/, lx <**=qel**> *in the head*, lx <**=í:l**> *become, get, go, come*, lx <**=áléqep**> *in smell, smell, odor, fragrance*, phonology: syllable-loss, syntactic analysis: intransitive verb, attested by EB.

<**qéylés**>, df //qəl=í·ləs or qəl=í·l=əs//, EFAM ['*(be) gloomy*'], VALJ, possibly <**=í:l**> *get, become, go, come*, possibly <**=es**> *in the face*, possibly <**=í:les**> *in the chest*, phonology: syllable-loss of el in monosyllabic root before =í:l(es), syntactic analysis: adjective/adjectival verb, attested by Elders Group (3/15/72).

<**qelímó:les**>, ds //qəl=í·m=á·ləs//, VALJ /'*bad-looking (of log or board not of a person), rough*'/, LT, lx <**=í:m ~ =ím**> *repeatedly*, lx <**=ó:les**> *on the eyes, in appearance/looks*, phonology: length loss of one vowel before another long vowel, syntactic analysis: adjective/adjectival verb, attested by EB.

<**sqel:ép ~ sqél:ep**>, ds //s=qə́l=lə́p//, LAND ['*a lot of dirt*'], EB ['*weeds*'], VALJ /'*nuisance, something that's no good*'/, MC /'*garbage, trash*'/, literally /'something bad/dirty on the ground'/, lx <**s=**> *nominalizer*, lx <**=í:lep ~ =lep ~ =ep**> *ground, earth, dirt, on the ground*, phonology: consonant merger, possible updrifting, syntactic analysis: nominal, attested by Elders Group, AC, MH (Deming), other sources: H-T <sku'lEp> *weed*, example: <**íx̲wet ta' sqel:ép.**>, //ʔíx̣ʷ=əT t-ɛʔ s=qəl=lə́p//, /'*Sweep up your trash. (sweep s-th up)*'/, attested by MH, <**atl'qéyltchexw te sqel:ép.**>, //ʔɛƛ̓'qəl=í·l=T-c-əxʷ tə s=qəl=lə́p//, /'*Take out the garbage. (take s-th outside)*'/, attested by MH.

<**qelqélexw**>, ncs //C_1əC_2=qə́l=l-əxʷ//, EFAM ['*not like s-th any more*'], VALJ, (<**R3=**> *plural continuative* or *continuative*), (<**=l**> *non-control transitivizer*), (<**-exw**> *third person object*), phonology: reduplication, consonant merger, syntactic analysis: transitive verb, attested by Elders Group (4/6/77).

<**qelóméx**>, ds //qəl=ámə́xʸ//, VALJ /'*look bad, look mean*'/, EFAM, DESC, lx <**=óméx ~ =ó:mex**> *-looking, in looks, in appearance*, phonology: possible updrifting, syntactic analysis: adjective/adjectival verb, attested by EB, contrast <**qelelhóméx**> *ugly, sloppy (in dress, walk, etc.)*.

<**qelóth**>, ds //qəl=áθ//, DESC /'*(be) blunt (edge or point), dull (of edge/point)*'/, semantic environment ['knife, other tools, point, edge'], lx <**=óth**> *edge, point*, phonology: stress-shift from root to stressed full-grade suffix, syntactic analysis: adjective/adjectival verb, attested by EB, Elders Group (3/1/72, 3/3/76), AC.

<**qeló:ythel**>, ds //qəl=á·yθəl//, LANG ['*swear*'], literally /'bad speech, bad language'/, lx <**=ó:ythel**> *in the lips, chin, jaw, speech, language*, syntactic analysis: intransitive verb, attested by EB.

<**sqíqeló:ythel**>, stvi //s=C_1í=qəl=á·yθəl//, dmv, LANG ['*can't talk right*'], ABDF, literally /'be a little bad in speech/language'/, (<**s=**> *stative*, R4= *diminutive*), phonology: reduplication, syntactic analysis: adjective/adjectival verb, attested by Elders Group, contrast or compare <**sqe'íyeqel ~ sqe'í:qel**> *to not know, not know how* and esp. <**sqe'íyeqeló:ythel ~ sqe'íqeló:ythel**> *to be not fluent at speaking.*>.

<**qeliythílem ~ qeliythí:lem**>, mdls //qəl=əyθəl=í(·)l=əm//, LANG /'*swear, swearing, say bad*

words'/, lx <**=ó:ythel ~ =eythel**> *in the lips, chin, jaw, speech, language, words*, lx <**=í:l ~ =íl ~ =el**> *get, become, come, go*, (<**=em**> *middle voice*), phonology: syllable-loss of el before í(:)l, weak-grade (schwa-grade) of suffix or zero-grade with y vocalized, syntactic analysis: intransitive verb, attested by EB, Elders Group (3/1/72), AC, other sources: ES /qəlʔyəθíləm/ *curse at*, contrast H-T <kElE´tsil> *to swear (lit. 'evil mouth')*.

<**qeliythí:lmet**>, iecs //qəl=əyθəl=í·l=məT//, LANG ['*swear at s-o*'], literally /'get/go bad language/speech/words towards s-o'/, (<**=met**> *indirect effect control transitivizer*), phonology: syllable-loss, weak-grade or zero-grade with y vocalized, syntactic analysis: transitive verb, attested by AC.

<**qelqálém**>, df //qəl=C$_1$əC$_2$[=Aέ=]=əm//, EFAM ['*disgusted*'], probably <**=R2**> *characteristic*, probably <**á-ablaut**> *durative or resultative*, probably <**=em**> *middle voice or intransitivizer, get, have*, phonology: reduplication, ablaut on affixed reduplication, syntactic analysis: intransitive verb, attested by Elders Group (4/6/77).

<**qélqwlha**>, ds //qə́l=q^{w}ɬɛ//, VALJ ['*beautiful.*'], lx <**=qwlha**> perhaps *wonderfully.*, root <**qel**> *bad*, comment: note that éy=qwlha has the same meaning but with the root éy *good*, syntactic analysis: adjective/adjectival verb, attested by EB, example: <**qélqwlha te stl'píwels.**>, //qə́l=q^{w}ɬɛ tə s=ƛ'əp=íwəl-s//, /'*His shirt is beautiful.*'/, attested by EB.

<**qelsílém**>, mdls //qəl=(a)ləs=íl=əm//, ABDF /'*(be) partially blind, almost blind*'/, root <**qel**> *bad*, lx <**=óles**> *in the eye(s)*, (<**=íl**> *get, become, go, inceptive*), (<**=em**> *middle voice*), phonology: double vowel-loss, consonant merger, probable updrifting, syntactic analysis: intransitive verb, adjective/adjectival verb?, attested by Deming (3/9/78, 4/26/79).

<**qélstexw**>, caus //qə́l=sT-əx^w//, EFAM /'*dislike s-o/s-th, to not like s-o/s-th*'/, (<**=st**> *causative control transitivizer*), (<**-exw**> *third person object*), syntactic analysis: transitive verb, attested by EB, Elders Group (3/1/72, 1/30/80); found in <**qélstexwes.**>, //qə́l=sT-əx^w-əs//, /'*He doesn't like s-th., He doesn't like s-o.*'/, attested by Elders Group (3/1/72), <**qelsthométsel.**>, //qəl=sT-ámə-c-əl//, /'*I don't like you.*'/, phonology: stress-shift automatic on 2nd person object pronoun suffixes before first person subject suffixes, attested by Elders Group (3/1/72), <**qélstem.**>, //qə́l=sT-əm//, /'*Someone is not liked., (He is not liked., She is not liked., They are not liked., They (people) don't like him/her/it/them.)*'/, attested by Elders Group (1/30/80), example: <**qélstexwes kw'els th'e<u>x</u>wewíls.**>, //qə́l=sT-əx^w-əs k'^{w}ə-l-s θ'əx̣^{w}=əwíls//, /'*I hate to wash dishes.*'/, attested by AD (8/80).

<**sqeltí:l**>, rcps //s=qəl=T-əl=í·l or s=qəl=T-ə[=Aí·=]l//, EFAM ['*hate*'], literally possibly /'get bad to each other (or) durative bad to each other'/, possibly <**s=**> *nominalizer or stative*?, <**=í:l**> *get, become, inceptive, go, come* or more likely <**í:-ablaut**> *durative*, (<**=t**> *purposeful control transitivizer*), (<**-el**> *reciprocal*), phonology: possible syllable-loss or ablaut on suffix, syntactic analysis: prob. nominal, poss. intransitive verb, attested by Elders Group (3/15/72).

<**qélwelh**>, ds //qə́l=wəɬ//, EFAM ['*stingy*'], VALJ, lx <**=welh**> *in the mind, -minded, disposition*, syntactic analysis: adjective/adjectival verb, attested by Elders Group, also <**xwqélwelh ~ skw'íykw'iy**>, //x^w=qə́l=wəɬ ~ s=k'^{w}íy=C$_1$əC$_2$//, attested by EB.

<**lexwqélwelh**>, ds //lə(=)x^w=qə́l=wəɬ//, EFAM /'*(be) cranky, crabby, dirty-minded*'/, literally /'always be bad/dirty in the mind, always bad/dirty -minded, always have a bad/dirty disposition'/, lx <**lexw=**> *always, always have/be*, lx <**=welh**> *in the mind, -minded, disposition*, syntactic analysis: adjective/adjectival verb.

<**sqelwílh**>, durs //s=qəl=wə[=Aí=]ɬ//, EFAM /'*hold a grudge, hate*'/, (<**s=**> *stative*), lx <**=welh**> *in the mind, -minded, disposition*, (<**í-ablaut**> *durative*), phonology: stress-shift due to ablaut, syntactic analysis: intransitive verb, attested by Elders Group (3/23/77).

<**sqelwílhmet ~ qelwílhmet**>, iecs //s=qəl=wə[=Aí=]ɬ=məT//, EFAM [*'hate s-o'*], (<**s=**> *stative*), (<**=met**> *indirect effect control transitivizer*), syntactic analysis: intransitive verb, attested by Elders Group (3/15/72, 3/23/77), example: <**sqelwílhmethòmétsel. ~ tsel sqelwílhmethòmè. ~ atsel sqelwílhmethòmè.**>, //s=qəl=wə[=Aí=]ɬ=məT-ámə-c-əl ~ c-əl s=qəl=wə[=Aí=]ɬ=məT-ámə ~ ʔɛ-c-əl s=qəl=wə[=Aí=]ɬ=məT-ámə//, /*'I hate you.'*/, phonology: automatic stress-shift on object pronoun before subject suffix, updrifting, downstepping, syntactic comment: present, ambiguous past, auxiliary past, attested by Elders Group (3/15/72), <**tsel sqelwílhmethòmè tl'okw'els qíqel.**>, //c-əl s=qəl=wə[=Aí=]ɬ=məT-ámə ƛ'a=k'ʷə-l-s C_1í=qəl//, [cɪl sqəlwíɬməθàmə̀ ƛ'ak'ʷls qéqəl], /*'I hate you because I'm no good. (be naughty, a little bad)'*/, attested by Elders Group (3/15/72).

<**qelá:m**>, ABDF [*'(be) weak'*], *see* qél.

<**qelámthet**>, ABDF [*'get weak'*], *see* qél.

<**qelát**>, free root //qəlɛ́t//, NUM /*'again, another, more'*/, CJ, syntactic analysis: adverb/adverbial verb, attested by Elders Group (3/1/72, 3/1/76, 1/21/76), Deming, AD, AC, also <**qelá:t**>, //qəlɛ́·t//, attested by Elders Group (10/1/75), ASM ['again'], example: <**thétlha qelá:t.**>, //θə́t-ɬɛ qəlɛ́·t//, /*'Say it again.'*/, attested by Elders Group (10/1/75), <**mí qelát**>, //mí qəlɛ́t//, /*'come again'*/, attested by Elders Group (1/21/76); found in <**qelátscha**>, //qəlɛ́t-s-cɛ//, /*'do it again, do it over, try it again'*/, attested by Elders Group (3/1/72), ASM ['more'], example: <**l stl'í (kw'e) qelát kópi.**>, //l s=ƛ'í (k'ʷə) qəlɛ́t kápi//, /*'I'd like some more coffee., I want some more coffee.'*/, attested by Deming, <**te ō qelát**> or <**te ew qelát**>, //tə ʔo(w) qəlɛ́t (or) tə ʔəw qəlɛ́t//, /*'(something) more'*/, attested by AD.

<**qelátstexw**>, caus //qəlɛ́t=sT-əxʷ//, NUM /*'do it again, add more (to s-th)'*/, (<**=st**> *causative control transitivizer*), (<**-exw**> *third person object*), syntactic analysis: transitive verb, attested by AD, example: <**qelátstexwchexw esu las tu xwe xwétes.**>, //qəlɛ́t=sT-əxʷ-c-əxʷ ʔə-s-u lɛ-s t-u xʷə xʷə́təs//, /*'Add more and make it heavier.'*/, literally /'you add more to it and it goes a little to become heavy'/, attested by AD.

<**qelátstexw**>, NUM /*'do it again, add more (to s-th)'*/, *see* qelát.

<**Qelá:wiya**>, N [*'Beaver (name in a story)'*], *see* sqelá:w *under* seq.

<**qelá:wthet**>, TVMO [*'camp and rest'*], *see* qá:w.

<**qelélwes**>, EFAM [*'afraid to try'*], *see* qél.

<**qélelhóméx**>, DESC /*'ugly, sloppy (in dress, walk, etc.)'*/, *see* qél.

<**qélém ~ qél:ém**>, free root //qə́lə́m ~ qə́l·ə́m//, ANA /*'eye (of human, animal, fish, etc.)'*/, syntactic analysis: noun, nominal, attested by AC, BJ (5/64), Elders Group, Deming, other sources: ES /qə́lə́m/, H-T <kúlum>.

<**qeqéylém ~ qeqéylem ~ (qeqílém)**>, pln //C_1ə=qə[=Aí=]lə́m//, ANA [*'eyes'*], (<**R5= and í-ablaut**> *dual, plural (two)*), compare <**s=x̲ex̲éyle**> *both legs* for the same *dual*, phonology: reduplication, ablaut, syntactic analysis: nominal, attested by SJ (Deming 3/17/77).

<**qelqélem**>, pln //C_1əC_2=qə́lə́m//, ANA [*'lots of eyes'*], (<**R3=**> *plural (lots of/collective)*), phonology: reduplication, possibly downshifting, syntactic analysis: nominal, attested by BHTTC.

<**qelémes**>, ds //qə́lə́m=əs//, EB [*'roots (resembling eyes looking at you) of a kind of plant that's good for asthma'*], MED ['medicine for asthma, roots used by DF as medicine'], literally probably /'eyes on the face'/, lx <**=es**> *on the face*, phonology: probably downshifting, syntactic analysis: nominal, attested by DF (Elders Group 1/29/75), Salish cognate: possibly Lushootseed /qələ́b-us/ *bad face, ugly* from qələ́b *bad* H76:377.

<**qél:em ~ qél:ém** or **leqél:em ~ leqél:ém**>, WETH /*'dirty (weather), bad weather, storm'*/, *see* qél.

<**qelémes**>, EB [*'roots (resembling eyes looking at you) of a kind of plant that's good for asthma'*], *see* qélém ~ qél:ém.

<**qéléméx ~ ő qèlèmèx ~ ló qèlèmèx**>, df //qə́lə́mə́xʸ ~ ʔow qə̀ləmə̀xʸ ~ lá qə̀ləmə̀xʸ//, EFAM [*'oh my goodness.'*], possibly root <**qélém**> *eye*, possibly <**=ex**> *upright*, comment:ő *contrastive*, ló *here, this*, phonology: probable upshifting on final syllable, probable downstepping on second and third alternants, syntactic analysis: interjection, and pmod interjection, and dmadv interjection, attested by JL (Elders Group 10/27/76), NP and others (Elders Group 2/1/78), also <**qèlèmèx**>, //qə̀ləmə̀xʸ//, also /*'the lucky thing., the lucky dog.'*/, attested by EB (10/27/76), example: <**lám kw'e Lhq'á:lets te qèlèmèx.**>, //lɛ́=m k'ʷə ɬq'ɛ́·ləc tə qə̀ləmə̀xʸ//, /*'He went to Vancouver, the lucky dog. (go to)'*/, attested by EB (1/20/78).

<**qéleqep**>, TAST [*'taste bad'*], *see* qél.

<**qelés**>, DESC /*'dirty, (have a cross face [EB])'*/, *see* qél.

<**qelésem**>, ABFC /*'turn away, turn one's face away'*/, *see* qél.

<**qéletses**>, ABDF [*'(have) dirty hands'*], *see* qél.

<**qelétses**>, DESC /*'(be) dirty (in everything) (in one's clothes, house, person)'*/, *see* qél.

<**qél:éxw ~ qel(:)éxw**>, bound root //qə́l·ə́xʷ ~ qəl(·)ə́xʷ *throat*//, Salish cognate: Lushootseed /qə́dxʷ/ *mouth* H76:374, Squamish /qə́naxʷ/ *throat, (front part of) neck* W73:266, K67:352.

<**sqel:éxw**>, dnom //s=qəl·ə́xʷ//, BPI /*'someone who is greedy, someone who eats all the time, (glutton)'*/, EFAM, literally probably /'big throat'/, (<**s=**> *big* (as in sméqsel *big nose* beside méqsel *nose*)), syntactic analysis: nominal, attested by EB.

<**sqél:éxw**>, stvi //s=qə́l·ə́xʷ//, EFAM [*'be greedy'*], BPI, (<**s=**> *stative*), syntactic analysis: adjective/adjectival verb, attested by EB, Salish cognate: Squamish /ʔəs-qə́naxʷ/ *overeaten* lit. *throttled* W73:191, K67:352, also <**sqeléx̲w**>, //s=qələ́x̣ʷ//, phonology: x̲w prob. my error for xw, attested by Elders Group (3/15/72), example: <**sqél:éxw st'á te kweshú.**>, //s=qə́l·ə́xʷ s=t=(ə)ʔɛ́ tə kʷəšú//, /*'He's greedy like a pig.'*/, attested by EB.

<**sqelxwá:le ~ sqelxwále**>, dnom //s=qəl(ə́)xʷ=ɛ́(·)lə//, ANA /*'throat (inside part), gullet, voice'*/, (<**s=**> *nominalizer*), lx <**=á:la ~ =á:le ~ =ále**> *container of*, phonology: stress-shift from root to strong-valenced suffix, vowel-loss, syntactic analysis: nominal, attested by AC, DM (12/4/64), Elders Group, other sources: ES /qəlxʷɛ́lə/ (Cw,Ms /šqənxʷɛ́ylə/) *throat (gullet)*, ASM ['voice'], <**tl'epílestexw ta' sqelxwá:le.**>, //ƛ'əp=íl=sT-əxʷ t-ɛʔ s=qəlxʷ=ɛ́·lə//, /*'Lower your voice in pitch.'*/, literally /'lower s-th the -your nom.= throat =container'/, attested by Elders Group (12/15/76).

<**qéléx̲**>, free root //qə́lə́x̣//, ANAF /*'fish eggs, salmon eggs, roe, (cooked salmon eggs [JL])'*/, syntactic analysis: noun, nominal, attested by Deming, Elders Group, EB, AC, also /*'cooked salmon eggs'*/, attested by JL (Fish Camp 7/20/79).

<**qelí:lt**>, VALJ [*'spoil s-th (purposely)'*], *see* qél.

<**qelímó:les**>, VALJ /*'bad-looking (of log or board not of a person), rough'*/, *see* qél.

<**qeliythílem ~ qeliythí:lem**>, LANG /*'swear, swearing, say bad words'*/, *see* qél.

<**qeliythí:lmet**>, LANG [*'swear at s-o'*], *see* qél.

<**qelmí:lthel**>, FOOD /*'leftovers, scraps (not taken home as smeq'óth is)'*/, *see* qéylem ~ qé:ylem ~ qí(:)lem.

<**qeló:l**>, bound stem //qəlá·l//, root meaning unknown unless qel ~ qil *encircle.*
<**sqeló:líth'a**>, df //s=qəlá·l=íθɛ//, WETH ['*west wind*'], probably <**s=**> *nominalizer or stative*, lx <**=íth'a**> *clothes*, root meaning unknown, syntactic analysis: nominal, attested by Elders Group (2/5/75).

<**qelí:lt**>, VALJ ['*spoil s-th (purposely)*'], *see* qél.

<**qelímó:les**>, VALJ /'*bad-looking (of log or board not of a person), rough*'/, *see* qél.

<**qelíps**>, free root //qəlíps//, EB, FOOD /'*grape, grapes*'/, from English "grapes", (attested by RG,EH 6/16/98 to SN, edited by BG with RG,EH 6/26/00), example: <**qelíps sqe'óleqw**>, FOOD *grape juice* (lit. grape + fruit juice), (attested by RG,EH 6/16/98 to SN, edited by BG with RG,EH 6/26/00)

<**qeliythílem ~ qeliythí:lem**>, LANG /'*swear, swearing, say bad words*'/, *see* qél.

<**qeliythí:lmet**>, LANG ['*swear at s-o*'], *see* qél.

<**qelmí:lthel**>, FOOD /'*leftovers, scraps (not taken home as smeq'óth is)*'/, *see* qéylem ~ qé:ylem ~ qí(:)lem.

<**qélwelh**>, EFAM ['*stingy*'], *see* qél.

<**qelwíls**>, df //qəlw=íls or qəl=əw(s)=ə[=Aí=]ls//, ABFC ['*hug*'], possibly root <**qel**> *encircle*, possibly <**=els**> *structured activity continuative*, possibly <**=ews**> *on the body*, possibly <**metathesis**> *derivational*, possibly <**í-ablaut on suffix**> *durative*, phonology: possible ablaut, possible consonant-loss, syntactic analysis: intransitive verb, attested by Deming, Salish cognate: possibly?? Lushootseed /q^wul(u)/ as in /q^wúl-ud/ *hug s-o* H76:422.
<**qelwílst**>, pcs //qəl(=)w(=)íls=T//, ABFC ['*hug s-o*'], root meaning unknown, (<**=t**> *purposeful control transitivizer*), syntactic analysis: transitive verb, attested by Deming; found in <**qelwilsthométsel.**>, //qəl(=)w(=)ils=T-ámə-c-əl//, /'*I hug you.*'/, phonology: stress-shift automatic on object suffix.

<**qelwílst**>, ABFC ['*hug s-o*'], *see* qelwíls.

<**qélxel**>, bound stem //qə́l=x^yəl//, prob. *encircles the foot* from probable root < **qel**> *encircle*
<**sqélxel**>, dnom //s=qə́l=x^yəl//, CLO ['*moccasin*'], literally /'(poss.) something that encircles on the foot'/, (<**s=**> *nominalizer, something that*), root (possibly) < **qel**> *encircle* as in <**qel=wíls**> *hug*, lx <**=xel**> *on the foot*, syntactic analysis: nominal, attested by BJ (5/64), DM (12/4/64), others (Elders Group).

<**qélhlexw**>, ABDF /'*accidentally hurt an old injury of s-o, (accidentally reinjure s-o)*'/, *see* qélh.

<**qém**>, bound root //qə́m *bend*//.
<**sqóqem**>, strs //s=C_1á=qəm or s=qə[=Aá=C_1ə=]m or perhaps s=qá[=C_1ə=]m//, DESC /'*(be) bent, (*perhaps *bent round)*'/, (<**s=**> *stative*), possibly <**R10=** or **=R1=** or **ó-ablaut plus =R1=**> *resultative*, possibly root <**qém ~ qóm**, phonology: reduplication, possible ablaut, syntactic analysis: adjective/adjectival verb, attested by Elders Group.
<**sqémqsel**>, df //s=qə́m=qsəl//, ANA /'*(have a) hook nose, beak nose, Roman nose, (be bent-nosed)*'/, (<**s=**> *stative* or possibly *nominalizer*? or *big*?), lx <**=qsel**> *on the nose*, syntactic analysis: prob. adjective/adjectival verb, poss. nominal, attested by Elders Group.
<**qíqemxel ~ qéyqemxel**>, ds //C_1í=qəm=x^yəl//, EB /'*unidentified plant with round bulbs that look and taste like potatoes, round root like potatoes that used to be eaten and tastes like potatoes*'/, literally probably /'little bend (round) in the bulb/root/foot'/, (<**R4=**> *diminutive*), root <**qém**> *bend (round),* lx <**=xel**> *on the foot, (in the) root/bulb [of a plant],* phonology: reduplication, syntactic analysis: nominal, attested by Elders Group (9/22/76).

<**qém:el**>, df //qá[=Aə́=]·=m=M1=əl or qá·=Aə́=m=əl or qə́m·(=)əl//, [qə́m·əl], WATR /'*tide coming in, water coming in, water coming up (ocean tide or river)*'/, possibly root <**qó:**> *water* or stem <**qó:=m**> *fetch water, get water*, or root <**qém**> *bend*, possibly <**é-ablaut**> *continuative or derivational*, possibly <**metathesis type 1**> *continuative or derivational*, possibly <**=m**> *intransitivizer, get, have*, possibly <**=el**> *come, go, become, get*, phonology: possible ablaut, possible metathesis, syntactic analysis: intransitive verb, attested by CT (6/8/76), example: <**(me, le) qém:el**>, //(mə, lə) qá[=Aə́=]·=m=M1=əl//, /'*tide coming up (in ocean)*'/, attested by CT, <**le qém:el kwses mi xwe hahíkwthet te qó:.**>, //lə qá[=Aə́=]·=m=M1=əl k^w-s-əs mi x^wə C_1ɛ-hík^w=θət tə qá·//, /'*The tide comes in and the water rises.*'/, literally /'third person ambiguous past tide comes/coming in then it starts/comes to become getting big the water'/, attested by CT.

<**sqém:el**>, dnom //s=qaθ[=Aə́=]·=m=M1=əl//, WATR ['*(the) tide*'], (<**s=**> *nominalizer*), phonology: possible ablaut, possible metathesis type 1, syntactic analysis: nominal, attested by BJ (12/5/64), other sources: ES /sqə́məl/ *flood tide*, example: <**le th'á:m te sqém:el.**>, //lə θ'ɛ́·m tə s=qə́m·əl//, /'*The tide is going out.*'/.

<**Leqémél**>, df //lə=qə́m(·)əl//, PLN ['*Harrison Bay*'], literally /'(rough) tides'/, (<**le=**> *always? or derivational*), phonology: updrifting, downshifting after high stressed prefix, syntactic analysis: nominal, attested by Elders Group (7/13/77 incl. DF, SP, LJ, AG, others), EL with NP and EB on Chehalis field trip (9/27/77), source: place names reference file #70, also <**Qíqemqèmèl**>, //C_1í=C_1əC_2=qə́m(·)əl//, literally /'(rough) tides'/, (<**R4=**> *diminutive*, R3= *plural*), phonology: double reduplication, attested by Elders Group (7/13/77).

<**Qíqemqèmèl**>, dmpn //C_1í=C_1əC_2=qə́m(·)əl//, PLN /'*a little bay in the Fraser River a quarter mile east of Iwówes (Union Bar, Aywawwis)*'/, Elder's comment: "named because of pit-houses there (sqémél, sqemél) and because of tide washing in and out there ((s)qém:el)", (<**R4=**> *diminutive*, R3= *plural*), phonology: double reduplication, syntactic analysis: nominal, attested by MP (recorded in writing by SP and AD in 1973-74, pronounced from those records in IHTTC), source: place names reference file #39.

<**qemqémel ~ qemqémél**>, pln //C_1əC_2=qə́m(·)əl//, PLN ['*pool down from Tillie Gutierrez's grandfather's fish-drying rack at Íyém (Eayem)*'], literally /'many tides'/, (<**R3=**> *plural*), phonology: reduplication, updrifting, syntactic analysis: nominal, attested by TG (in IHTTC 8/5/77), IHTTC placenames meeting (8/23/77), source: place names reference file #189a.

<**qémél**>, bound root or stem //qə́mə́l or qə́m=ə[́]l//, meaning unknown, however, probably this is a reanalysis of the root, probably //səq=əm(=)əl//, with weak valence root <s(e)q> meaning *hang under* + lx <=ámel ~ =ómel ~ =emel> *part, portion, member*

<**sqémél**>, df //s=qə́mə́l or s=qə́m=ə[́]l or before reanalysis (s=)səq=əməl//, BLDG /'*pit-house, keekwillie house, semi-subterranean house*'/, ASM ['used as the regular winter family dwelling by the Upper Stṓ:lo from Yale down to about Nicomen Island, rarely built or used further downriver (Duff 1952:46-47), almost always circular from 15 to 35 feet in diameter and perhaps 4 to 6 feet deep in the ground, covered with beams, brush, then earth in a conical mound, up to 20 feet from floor to highest point of roof, smokehole for fire in center, a notched pole served as a ladder through the smokehole, inhabited from about January to March or the coldest months of the year, bed with partitions and tiered storage were around the perimeter inside'], last used in the Stó:lō area about 1870 (Mrs. August Jim was born in one in 1869 and never returned after she was a few months old; Duff's accounts of those who last lived in them were of the same generation); the rest of the year plank longhouses (or when camping, mat shelters) were used;, Elders (6/28/78) said pit-houses were aired and rebuilt every year and that a separate one was used for spirit dances from Iwówes (Union Bar) to Yale; this is confirmed by an account of the sx̱wolex̱wiyám *ancient people over a hundred years old (they can't move, just lay there in pit-house, take liquids, in spring the family dug out the*

roof to get them out into the sun) (BHTTC 9/9/76); the Interior Salish used pit-houses but perhaps only the Stó:lō among the Coast Salish used them, (<**s=**> *nominalizer*), possibly root <**qém**> *bend* as in <**s=qém=qsel**> *hook-nose, Roman nose, beak nose* and <**s=qóqem**> *bent* perhaps because people felt they had to go around bent over in the smaller ones, possibly <**=el**> *become, get, come, go*, possibly <**stress-insertion**> *derivational*, phonology: possible updrifting on second syllable or stress-insertion, syntactic analysis: nominal, attested by Elders Group (6/28/78, 1/21/76), BJ (12/5/64), DM (12/4/64), JL (5/5/75), also <**sqemél**>, //s=qə́m=ə[=M2=]l or s=qəm=ə[=´=]l//, phonology: metathesis or stress-shift, attested by AC, DM (12/4/64), CT (6/8/76), Elders Group (3/15/72).

<**sqíqemel**>, ds //s=C_1í=qəməl//, BLDG ['*puberty hut*'], literally /'little pit-house'/, ASM ['built for adolescent women to live in during their first menstruation, built much like a sweathouse according to Duff 1952:50'], (<**s=**> *nominalizer*, R4= *diminutive*), phonology: reduplication, syntactic analysis: nominal, attested by EB, other sources: H-T 1904.

<**sqemí:l**>, stvi //s=qəmə́l=í·l//, incs, BLDG ['*be inside a pit-house*'], (<**s=**> *stative*), (<**=í:l**> *come, go, get, become* or <**=el**> *come, go, get, become* + <=Aí:=> on 1st schwa <e> of suffix *durative*), phonology: syllable-loss, syntactic analysis: adjective/adjectival verb, attested by JL (5/5/75), example: <**le sqemí:l.**>, //lə s=qəməl=í·l//, /'*He was inside a pit-house.*'/, literally /'third person past be inside a pit-house'/.

<**Qémelets**>, PLN ['*bay at upper end of Íyém (Yale Indian Reserve #22)*'], *see* qám.

<**Qemlólhp**>, PLN ['*Queen's Island*'], *see* sq'émél.

<**qemó:**>, df //qá·=m=M1 or root qəmá·//, ABFC /'*suckle, suck milk from a breast*'/, possibly root <**qó:**> *water, liquid*, possibly <**??metathesis type 1**> *derivational*, possibly <**=(e)m**> *intransitivizer, get, have*, phonology: possible metathesis, syntactic analysis: intransitive verb, attested by AC.

<**qéqemó:**>, cts //qə[-C_1ə-]má·//, ABDF ['*suckling*'], probably <**-R1-**> *continuative*, phonology: probably epenthetic secondary stress, syntactic analysis: intransitive verb, attested by AC, example: <**qéqemó: te músmesò:llh.**>, //qə[-C_1ə-]má· tə mús=C_1əC_2=ó·ɬ//, /'*The calf is suckling.*'/, attested by AC.

<**qeqemótel**>, rcps //qə[-C_1ə-]má·=təl//, KIN ['*having the same parents*'], literally /'suckling with each other'/, (<**-R1-**> *continuative* or *resultative*), (<**=tel**> *reciprocal*), phonology: reduplication, syntactic analysis: intransitive verb, adjective/adjectival verb?, attested by BHTTC.

<**sqemó:**>, dnom //s=qəmá·//, ANAH /'*breast, nipple, milk*'/, ANAA, literally /'something that's suckled'/, (<**s=**> *nominalizer, something that*), syntactic analysis: nominal, attested by AC, MH, Elders Group, other sources: ES /sqə́má·/ *breast, (homonymous with) milk*, JH /sqəmá·/ *breast (of a woman), milk*, H-T <cumá> (macron over a) *teats*.

<**chí:s (or) tl'éxw ts'íyxw sqemó:**>, FOOD *cheese* (lit. cheese or hard + dry + milk), (attested by RG,EH 6/16/98 to SN, edited by BG with RG,EH 6/26/00)

<**thepth'epéy t'át'ets'em sqemó**>, FOOD *yogurt* (lit. curdled + sour + milk), (attested by RG,EH 6/16/98 to SN, edited by BG with RG,EH 6/26/00)

<**ts'áyxw sqemó**>, FOOD *powdered milk/coffee mate* (lit. dry + milk), (attested by RG,EH 6/16/98 to SN, edited by BG with RG,EH 6/26/00)

<**Qemqemó**>, ds //C_1əC_2=qəmá//, PLN ['*Mount Ogilvie*'], ASM ['so-named because it looks like breasts'], (<**R3=**> *plural*), comment: s= *nominalizer* and final length are probably dropped for derivational purposes, phonology: reduplication, length-loss, syntactic analysis: nominal, attested by SP and AG, source: place names reference file #13.

<**sqemálá**>, ds //s=qəma=ɛ́·lɛ//, CLO ['*bra*'], literally /'container of breast'/, HHG ['*nursing bottle*'], literally /'container of milk'/, lx <**=álá**> *container of*, phonology: ambivalent root plus strong

valenced suffix, vowel merger, syntactic analysis: nominal, attested by Elders Group.

<**sqemó'álá**>, ds //s=qəmá·=ʔɛ́lɛ́//, HHG ['*baby bottle*'], literally /'container of milk'/, lx <**='álá**> *container of*, phonology: ambivalent (or strong-valenced) root plus strong-valenced suffix with adjacent strong vowels requires suffix allomorph with epenthetic glottal-stop, syntactic analysis: nominal, attested by EB.

<**qemqémel ~ qemqémél**>, PLN ['*pool down from Tillie Gutierrez's grandfather's fish-drying rack at Íyem (Eayem)*'], *see* qém:el.

<**Qemqemó**>, PLN ['*Mount Ogilvie*'], *see* qemó:.

<**qémxel**>, WETH /'*(the wind) is calm, calm (of wind)*'/, *see* qám.

<**qépkwoya**>, df //qə́pk^w(=)ayɛ//, EZ /'*small owl, saw-whet owl*'/, ['*Cryptoglaux acadia acadia (or Aegolius acadicus)*'], possibly <**=oya**> *diminutive*, root meaning unknown, syntactic analysis: noun, nominal, attested by Elders Group (3/15/78), Salish cognate: Lushootseed /k'əp'k'^{w}əláʔ/ *some sort of small screech owl* H76:238.

<**qep'**>, bound root //qəp'// *to cover, to close*, Salish cognate: Squamish root /qəp'/ *close, shut* W73:61, K67:308,352, Lushootseed /qə́p'/ *cover; land, alight* as in /lə-qə́p'/ and /ʔu-qə́p'/ *landed (of birds for ex.)*, /ʔu-qə́p'-əd/ *smothered it (of a fire)*, /qp'-úcid/ *cover s-th like a pot or basket*, and /x̣-qp'-úcid/ *knee(-cap?)* H76:382.

<**qp'á:qet**>, pcs //qəp'=ɛ́·q(əl)=əT//, HHG /'*close s-th (for ex. a box), put a lid on s-th (for ex. a pot), cover it with a lid*'/, lx <**=á:qel ~ =eqel**> *container, in the throat*, (<**=et**> *purposeful control transitivizer*), phonology: vowel-loss or zero-grade of root before stressed full-grade suffix, syllable-loss of final el in lexical suffix before =et, syntactic analysis: transitive verb, attested by EB, Salish cognate: in part, Squamish /(n-)qp'ə-t/ *close, shut (tr.)* W73:61, K67:308,352, ASM ['put a lid on s-th'], example: <**qp'á:qet ta' skúk.**>, //qp'=ɛ́·q(əl)=əT t-ɛʔ s=kúk//, /'*Put a lid on your cooking.*'/, attested by EB, ASM ['close it (a box)'], <**qp'á:qet te kw'ó:xwe**>, //qp'=ɛ́·q(əl)=əT tə k'^{w}á·x^{w}ə//, /'*close a box*'/, attested by EB.

<**qp'á:letset**>, pcs //qəp'=ɛ́·ləc=əT//, HHG ['*cover it (s-th open)*'], MC, lx <**=á:lets**> *open space between two points?*, (<**=et**> *purposeful control transitivizer*), phonology: zero-grade of root before stressed full-grade of suffix, syntactic analysis: transitive verb, attested by EB, other sources: Musqueam /=él'əc ~ =əl'əc ~ =əlíc ~ =éʔc/ *route across* as in /t'q'^{w}-éʔlec/ *take a short cut (as a pass between islands)* (cf. /t'q'^{w}-át/ *cut it off*) and /ɬəq'-əlíc/ *other side (as of a hill)* (cf. /ɬq'-é·n/ *other end*) Suttles ca1984, (see Upriver Halq'eméylem t'qw'á:lets *short-ended cut-off canoe*).

<**qp'á:letstel**>, dnom //qəp'=ɛ́·ləc=təl//, HHG /'*a cover, lid*'/, lx <**=á:lets ~ =álets**> *open space between two points?*, lx <**=tel**> *device for, thing to*, phonology: zero-grade of root before stressed full grade of suffix, syntactic analysis: nominal, attested by EB, also <**qep'áletstel**>, //qəp'=ɛ́ləc=təl//, attested by Deming (3/11/76).

<**qiqep'eyósem**>, mdls //C$_1$í=qəp'=əyás=əm//, ABFC ['*lying on one's stomach with head down on one's arms*'], literally /'(prob.) covering/closing oneself in a little circle'/, (<**R4=**> *diminutive*), lx <**=eyós**> *in a circle*, (<**=em**> *middle voice*), phonology: reduplication, syntactic analysis: intransitive verb, attested by IHTTC.

<**qep'ó:lthetel**>, ds //qəp'=á·lθəl=təl//, ANA /'*knee (naming it, the name of it)*'/, literally /'something to close/cover on the knee'/, lx <**=ó:lthel**> *on the knee*, lx <**=tel**> *something to, device to*, phonology: consonant-loss (l of el before =tel), syntactic analysis: nominal, attested by IHTTC (9/19/77).

<**sqep'ó:lthetel**>, dnom //s=qəp'=á·lθəl=təl//, ANA ['*knee (someone's)*'], (<**s=**> *inalienable possession*), syntactic analysis: nominal, attested by IHTTC (9/19/77), AC, DM (12/4/64?), other sources: ES /šqp'á·lθətəl/, JH /sqp'á·lθətə̀l/, H-T <skEpálsitEl> (macron over a) all *knee*.

<**sq'epóleqwtelxel**> (perhaps error for <**sqep'óleqwtelxel**>), df //s=q'əp=áləqʷ=təl=xʸəl (perhaps error for //s=qəp'=áləqʷ=təl=xʸəl)//, ANA ['*kneecap*'], (<**s=**> *inalienable possession* or *nominalizer*), root <**qep'**> *cover, close* or root possibly <**q'ep**> *gather*, lx <**=óleqw**> *on top of the head, on top of a rounded surface? [in environment of another following body-part suffix]*, lx <**=tel**> *something to, device to*, lx <**=xel**> *on the leg*, syntactic analysis: nominal, attested by Elders Group (8/20/75), other sources: H-T <kepálokHitEl> (macron over a) *kneecap*, Salish cognate: Squamish /qp'-áls-tn ~ qp'-áyʔ-əqʷ-s-tn/ W73:154, K67:351.

<**qep'ós**>, ds //qəp'=ás//, ABFC /'*face down, (upside-down [Deming])*'/, literally /'close on the face'/, lx <**=ós ~ =ó:s ~ =es**> *on the face*, syntactic analysis: intransitive verb, adjective/adjectival verb?, attested by AC, also /'*upside down*'/, attested by Deming.

<**yeq'pó:s** (prob. error or variant for **yeqp'ó:s**)>, mos //yə=q'p=á·s (prob. error/variant for yə=qp'=á·s)//, ABFC ['*(travelling/moving) stooped over*'], (<**ye=**> *travelling along, moving*), phonology: zero-grade of root before long and stressed strong-grade of suffix, syntactic analysis: adverb/adverbial verb, attested by Deming, example: <**ye'í:mex yeq'pó:s**>, //yə=ʔí[-·-]m=əxʸ yə=q'p=á·s (yə=qp'=á·s)//, /'*walk(ing) stooped over*'/.

<**qep'ósem**>, mdls //qəp'=ás=əm//, ABFC /'*put one's head down, bend, bend over, bend over with one's head down, stoop down*'/, (<**=em**> *middle voice*), syntactic analysis: intransitive verb, attested by IHTTC, AC, Deming (3/11/76, 4/17/80), Elders Group.

<**qép'esem**>, cts //qə[-´-]p'=əs=əm//, ABFC ['*bending over*'], (<-´-> *continuative*), phonology: vowel-reduction to schwa-grade of suffix after stress-shift, syntactic analysis: intransitive verb, attested by Elders Group.

<**qep'óst**>, pcs //qəp'=ás=T//, DIR ['*turn s-th upside-down*'], literally /'turn someone's/something's head down (purposely)'/, (<**=t**> *purposeful control transitivizer*), syntactic analysis: transitive verb, attested by Deming.

<**sqép'ò:thèl**>, dnom //s=qə[=´=]p'=á·θəl//, EZ ['*flying squirrel*'], ['*Glaucomys sabrinus oregonensis* and from Hope north *Glaucomys sabrinus fuliginosus*'], literally /'something that's covering on the mouth'/, ASM ['so named because of the belief that the flying squirrel will drop on a person at night and cover his mouth'], (<**s=**> *nominalizer*), (<=´=> *continuative* or *derivational*), lx <**=ó:thel**> *on the mouth*, phonology: stress-shift, downshifting, updrifting on last syllable, syntactic analysis: nominal, attested by Deming, Elders Group (5/28/75), also <**sqép'óthel**>, //s=qə[=´=]p'=áθəl//, attested by Elders Group (2/11/76), also <**qép'othel**>, //qə[=´=]p'=aθəl//, Elder's comment: "an alternate way of saying it", attested by SP in BHTTC, also <**qép'iyethel**>, //qə[=´=]p'=əyəθəl//, lx <**=iyethel**> *on the lips, on the jaw/chin*, attested by Jimmy Peters (of Katz) at Elders Group (3/21/79).

<**qep'ó:ythòm**>, pcs //qəp'=á·yθ(əl)=T-àm → qəp'á·yθθàm//, if, ABFC ['*you get covered on the mouth (by a flying squirrel at night for ex.)*'], lx <**-ó:ythel**> *on the lips/jaw/chin*, (<**=t**> *purposeful control transitivizer*), (<**=òm**> *passive second person singular*), phonology: syllable-loss (el before =t), consonant merger, syntactic analysis: transitive verb in passive, attested by Deming.

<**qíqep'yó:lha ~ qéyqep'yó:lha**>, df //C_1í=qəp'=yá·ɬɛ or C_1í=qəp'=á·y[=M1=]ɬɛ//, [qéqəp'yá·ɬɛ], ABFC ['*lying down on one's stomach*'], (<**R4=**> *diminutive*), lx <**=yó:lha** or **=ó:ylha**> *on the stomach*, possibly <**metathesis type 1**> *derivational or continuative*, phonology: reduplication, possible metathesis, syntactic analysis: intransitive verb, attested by CT and HT (6/21/76), EB (6/30/76), also <**qiqep'ó:ylha**>, //C_1í=qəp'=á·yɬɛ or C_1í=qəp'=yá·[=M1=]ɬɛ//, attested by IHTTC, example: <**qéyqep'yó:lha tútl'ò.**>, //C_1í=qəp'=yá·ɬɛ t=ú=ƛ'à//, /'*He's laying on his stomach.*'/, attested by CT and HT.

<**qep'tá:lém**>, df //qəp'=tə[=Aɛ́·=]l=əm//, ANA ['*kneecap*'], possibly <**=tel**> *device to, something to,*

possibly <**á:-ablaut**> *derivational,* possibly <**=em**> *middle voice or intransitivizer, have, get or place to get***,** phonology: ablaut, syntactic analysis: nominal?, attested by IHTTC (8/4/77).

<**qép'esem**>, ABFC ['*bending over*'], *see* qep'.

<**qep'ó:lthetel**>, ANA /'*knee (naming it, the name of it)*'/, *see* qep'.

<**qep'ós**>, ABFC /'*face down, (upside-down [Deming])*'/, *see* qep'.

<**qep'ósem**>, ABFC /'*put one's head down, bend, bend over, bend over with one's head down, stoop down*'/, *see* qep'.

<**qep'óst**>, DIR ['*turn s-th upside-down*'], *see* qep'.

<**qep'ó:ythòm**>, ABFC ['*you get covered on the mouth (by a flying squirrel at night for ex.)*'], *see* qep'.

<**qep'tá:lém**>, ANA ['*kneecap*'], *see* qep'.

<**qéqelelhó:mex**>, DESC /'*scrubby little ones, (little ugly ones)*'/, *see* qél.

<**qéqemlò**>, EZ ['*lots of minnows*'], *see* sqíqemlò.

<**qéqemó:**>, ABDF ['*suckling*'], *see* qemó:.

<**qeqemótel**>, KIN ['*having the same parents*'], *see* qemó:.

<**qeqéylém ~ qeqéylem ~ (qeqílém)**>, ANA ['*eyes*'], *see* qélém ~ qél:ém.

<**qésqesí:l**>, ABDF ['*sobbing after crying*'], *see* qásel.

<**qesqesí:lqel**>, ABDF ['*tired out from crying*'], *see* qásel.

<**qesu**>, CJ /'*and so, and then*'/, *see* qe.

<**qetás**>, FOOD /'*bake underground, (steam-cook underground, cook in a steam-pit)*'/, *see* qá:t.

<**qetelméxwtel**>, EB ['*wall lettuce*'], *see* qá:t.

<**qétes**>, FOOD ['*baking underground*'], *see* qá:t.

<**Qétex̲em**>, PLN /'*mountain on the west (C.P.R.) side of the Fraser River above American Bar which had a steaming pond at the top, (year-round village at mouth of American Creek on west bank of the Fraser River [Duff])*'/, *see* qá:t.

<**qetíwstel**>, BLDG ['*sweathouse*'], *see* qá:t.

<**qéttel**>, CLO ['*waistband of a skirt*'], *see* qít.

<**qétx̲**>, bound stem //qə́t=x̣// *feel (around) with the fingers*

<**qétx̲t**>, pcs //qə́t=x̣=T or qɛ[=Aə́=]t=x̣=T//, TCH /'*feel s-th/s-o with fingers, feel s-th, feel s-o*'/, probably <**=x̲**> *distributive, all over,* possibly <**é-ablaut**> *derivational,* (<**=t**> *purposeful control transitivizer*), phonology: possible ablaut, syntactic analysis: transitive verb, attested by Elders Group (3/15/72 lesson VIII, 1/7/76, 4/28/76, 2/13/80), Deming; found in <**qétx̲tchexw.**>, //qə́t=x̣=T-c-əxʷ//, /'*Feel it.*'/, attested by Deming, <**qétx̲thòmè**>, //qə́t=x̣=T-ámə//, /'*feel you*'/, phonology: downstepping, updrifting, attested by Elders Group (4/28/76).

<**qátx̲els**>, sas //qə[=Aɛ́=]t=x̣=əls or qɛ́t=x̣=əls or qət=x̣=ɛ́[=M2=]ls//, cts, TCH ['*feeling around*'], possibly <**á-ablaut** or **metathesis**> *continuative,* possibly <**=els**> *structured activity continuative,* phonology: ablaut or metathesis, syntactic analysis: intransitive verb, attested by Elders Group (1/7/76), EB, also /'*to feel*'/, attested by Elders Group (3/15/72 tape, lesson VIII), example: <**tsel we qátx̲elsó.**>, //c-əl wə qɛ́t=x̣=əls-à//, /'*I'm just feeling around.*'/, attested by EB.

<**qetx̲éleqw**>, ds //qət=x̣=ə́ləqʷ//, TCH /'*feel one's head, (feel the head)*'/, lx <**=éleqw**> *on top of the*

head, on the hair, phonology: stress-shift to suffix, syntactic analysis: intransitive verb, attested by Elders Group.

<**qétx̲mel**>, ds //qə́t=x̣=məl//, TCH /'*the feeling, something's feel*'/, (<**=mel**> *part of, portion of*), syntactic analysis: nominal, attested by BHTTC, example: <**selchím te qétx̲mels?**>, //səlcím tə qə́t=x̣=məl-s//, /'*How does it feel?*'/, <**éy te qétx̲mels.**>, //ʔɛ́y tə qə́t=x̣=məl-s//, /'*It feels good.*'/.

<**qetx̲éleqw**>, TCH /'*feel one's head, (feel the head)*'/, *see* qétx̲t.

<**qétx̲mel**>, TCH /'*the feeling, something's feel*'/, *see* qétx̲t.

<**qethiyálh**>, df //qəθiy=ɛ́ɬ//, KIN /'*deceased uncle, deceased grand-uncle*'/, lx <**=álh**> *deceased; past tense* or possibly inflection <**-álh**> *past tense*, syntactic analysis: nominal, noun, attested by Elders Group (6/8/77), Salish cognate: Samish dial. of N. Straits LD /qsəčé·ɬ/ (VU /qsəčéləɬ/) *deceased parent's sibling* G86:79, Lushootseed /qəsíʔ/ *uncle, male sibling of either parent while that parent is living* H76:382, also /'*first cousins*'/, comment: probably error, attested by BHTTC, also <**(s)qeyá:lh?**>, also /'*uncle when your parents have died*'/, attested by BHTTC, contrast <**shxwemthiyà:lh**>, //sxʷəmθiy=ɛ̀·ɬ//, /'*deceased uncle or aunt or grandparent or someone responsible for you directly or indirectly*'/ (under xwemthiy).

<**qeth'ét**>, pcs //qəθ'=ə[=´=]T or qə́θ'=ə[=M2=]T//, MC /'*shake s-th down, pack s-th down, push s-th down, knead s-th (esp. of bread dough), press it down (like yeast bread)*'/, semantic environment ['like hops to fit more in, like rising yeast dough too'], possibly <= ´=> *non-continuative or derivational*, phonology: stressed transitivizer or stress-shift, syntactic analysis: transitive verb, attested by IHTTC, Elders Group (2/6/80), EB (6/15/78), CT and HT, also /'*kneading it (bread dough)*'/, attested by Elders Group (5/14/80), also <**qets'ét**>, //qəc'=ə́T or qəc'=ə[=´=]T//, also /'*kneading (bread dough), pushing down (like hops)*'/, attested by Deming (6/15/77), comment: corrected to knead (bread), push down (hops for ex.) by EB (4/19/78)i, also <**qéth't**>, //qə́θ'=T//, also /'*squish it (bread dough), press it (dough), knead it (dough)*'/, attested by Elders Group (5/14/80), also <**qáqets'et**>, //C_1ɛ́=qəc'=əT//, also /'*kneading (bread), pushing down (hops, etc.)*'/, attested by EB (4/19/78),

<**qetl'osésu ~ qetl'os'ésu**>, CJ /'*and so (he, she, it, they)*'/, *see* tl'ó ~ tl'o.

<**qetl'osu ~ qetl'esu**>, CJ /'*and so, and then*'/, *see* qe.

<**qets'óm(es)**>, bound root or stem //qəc'ám(=)əs// meaning unknown unless related to <**qó:tsó:m**> *blister*, thus lit. 'blisters on the face' describing its facial markings or perhaps origin from a story

<**sqets'ómes**>, df //s=qəc'ám(=)əs or s=qəc'(=)ɛ[=Aá=]m=əs or s=qəc'=əm=á[=M2=]s or s=qác'=ə[=M2=]m=əs//, EZ ['*bobcat*'], ['*Lynx rufus fasciatus*'], (<**s=**> *nominalizer*), possibly <**=es ~ =ós**> *on the face*, possibly <**=em**> *middle voice or intransitivizer, have, get*, possibly <**ó-ablaut**> **(automatic on stem a, conditioned by =es ~ =ós)** or <**metathesis**> *derivational*, phonology: probably metathesis or possibly ablaut, syntactic analysis: nominal, attested by AK and ME (tape 11/21/72), also /'*wildcat (prob. bobcat)*'/, attested by Elders Group (3/1/72).

<**Sqelóts'emes**>, ds //s=q[=əl=]əc'=á[=M2=]m=əs//, N ['*Bobcat*'], (<**=el=**> *plural*), possibly <**metathesis**> *derivational*, phonology: metathesis and infixing, syntactic analysis: nominal, usage: name in a story, attested by ME and AK (11/12/72 tape), also <**Qelóts'emes**>, //q[=əl=]əc'=á[=M2=]m=əs//, ASM ['escapes from jail [rather a place where he's emprisoned probably] in story and feeds Smelő' *Lynx*'], attested by JL (at Fish Camp 7/19/79).

<**qew**>, bound root //qəw *warm*//.

<**qewét**>, pcs //qəw=ə[-´-]T or qəw=ə́T//, MC /'*warm s-th, warm s-o*'/, TCH, HHG, WETH, FIRE, ABFC, (<**=et**> *purposeful control transitivizer*), probably <-´-> *non-continuative*, phonology: stressed transitivizer or stress-shift, syntactic analysis: transitive verb, attested by CT and HT; found

in <**qewétem.**>, //qəw=ə́T-əm//, syntactic analysis: passive, attested by CT and HT, example: <**sqewós te smá:lt kws me p'éth' te syó:qwem telí tí tl'ó le qewétem.**>, //s=qəw=ás tə s=mɛ́·lt k^{w}-s mə p'ə́θ' tə s=yá·q^{w}=əm təlí tí ƛ'á lə qəwə́təm.//, /'*It's the warm side of a mountain that the sun just comes out on from there so that it was warmed.*'/, attested by CT and HT, <**qewétlha ta' chálex.**>, //qəw=ə́T-ɬɛ t-ɛʔ cɛ́lə́x^{y}//, /'*Warm your hands.*'/, attested by CT and HT.

<**qewéthet**>, pcrs //qəw=ə[-´-]T-ət//, ABFC ['*warm up by a fire*'], FIRE, TCH, (<**-et**> *reflexive*), phonology: stressed transitivizer or stress-shift, syntactic analysis: intransitive verb, attested by BHTTC.

<**qéwethet**>, cts //qə́w=əT-ət//, ABFC ['*warming up by a fire*'], FIRE, TCH, syntactic analysis: intransitive verb, attested by BHTTC.

<**sqewá:meth'**>, df //s=qəw=ɛ́·məθ'//, EB /'*first warmed side of a tree, sunny side of a tree*'/, MED ['any medicine that uses bark uses the sunny side bark of a plant or tree'], (<**s=**> *nominalizer* or perhaps *stative*), lx <**=á:meth'**> *upright, in stature*, syntactic analysis: nominal or adjective/adjectival verb, attested by CT and HT, example: <**te sqewá:meth'[s] te thqát, tl'ó tl'émexw xípet.**>, //tə s=qəw=ɛ́·məθ'[-s] tə θqɛ́t, ƛ'á ƛ'ə́məx^{w} x^{y}íp=əT//, /'*The sunny side of a tree, that's the part you strip off (peel s-th).*'/, attested by CT and HT.

<**qewéletsem**>, mdls //qəw=ə[-´-]ləc=əm//, ABFC /'*warm one's rump, warm one's bottom*'/, (<**-´-**> *non-continuative*), lx <**=elets**> *on the bottom, on the rump*, (<**=em**> *middle voice*), phonology: stress-shift, syntactic analysis: intransitive verb, attested by IHTTC.

<**qówletst**>, pcs //qə[=Aá=]w=ləc=T or qə́w=ləc=T//, ABFC ['*warm it up (on the bottom)*'], lx <**=lets**> *on the bottom*, possibly <**ó-ablaut**> *derivational*, (<**=t**> *purposeful control transitivizer*), phonology: possible ablaut, syntactic analysis: transitive verb, attested by IHTTC.

<**sqewálets**>, cts //s=qəw=ɛ́ləc//, stvi, ABFC /'*warming your bum, (be warming the bottom or rump)*'/, (<**s=**> *stative*), lx <**=elets ~ =álets**> *on the bottom, on the rump*, phonology: stressed suffix allomorph attracts stress from ambivalent root, syntactic analysis: adjective/adjectival verb, attested by IHTTC.

<**qewletsá:ls**>, sas //qəw=ləc=ɛ́·ls//, FIRE /'*heat up (on fire, stove)*'/, FOOD, TCH, lx <**=lets**> *on the bottom*, (<**=á:ls**> *structured activity non-continuative*), phonology: stressed suffix attracts stress from ambivalent root, syntactic analysis: intransitive verb, attested by IHTTC, also <**qawletsá:ls**>, //qə[=Aɛ=]w=ləc=ɛ́·ls//, Elder's comment: "probably means "heating up food or water" (correction)", possibly <**a-ablaut**> *derivational*, phonology: possible ablaut, attested by EB (11/1/78), also /'*one that's heating up the food or water*'/, Elder's comment: "correction above", attested by IHTTC (9/2/77).

<**qowletsá:ls**>, dnom //qə[=Aa=]w=ləc=ɛ́·ls//, sas, HHG /'*water kettle, boiler pan (for canning, washing clothes or dishes)*'/, FOOD, CLO, HARV, FSH, ASM ['typically oval, two feet in length, usually enamelled metal, with a flat oval metal lid'], possibly <**o-ablaut**> *derivational*, lx <**=lets**> *on the bottom*, (<**=á:ls**> *structured activity nominalizer*), phonology: possible ablaut, syntactic analysis: nominal, attested by IHTTC.

<**sqewós**>, dnom //s=qəw=ás//, LAND ['*warm side*'], WETH, TCH, (<**s=**> *nominalizer*), lx <**=ós**> *on the face*, phonology: ambivalen root loses stress to stressed full-grade of suffix, syntactic analysis: nominal, attested by CT and HT, example: <**me pélekw te syó:qwem te sqewós te smá:lt.**>, //mə pə́lək^{w} tə s=yá·q^{w}=əm tə s=qəw=ás-s tə s=mɛ́·lt//, /'*The sun comes up on the warm side of/on the mountain.*'/, attested by CT and HT.

<**Qewítsel**>, dnom //qəw=ícəl//, SOCT /'*Cowichan (people, dialect, area)*'/, literally /'warmed on the back'/, ASM ['so called since they are headquartered by Mt. Tzouhalem which is said to be a frog warming its back (this information from Cowichan speakers)'], lx <**=ítsel**> *on the back*, phonology:

strong-stressed suffix, syntactic analysis: nominal, attested by EB, others.

<**qéw**> possible root //qə́w//, meaning unknown unless *warm* or more likely root <**qwá**> //qʷɛ́// *have a hole*, same entry under <**qwá**>

<**sqéweqs**>, df //s=qə́w=əqs// perhaps from //s=qʷ[-metathesis of vowel and labialization]ɛ́=əqs// as with the word for *rabbit* from same root, thus literally *something that has a hole in the nose*, due to the large holes in its beak, EZ ['*raven*'], ['*Corvus corax*'], ASM ['one cry resembles a hoarse woman's voice, ravens crowing in a certain way and going toward or by a house forecast a death in that family; a big bird (larger than a crow), lives to be about 100 yrs. old'], (<**s=**> *nominal*), root meaning unknown, lx <**=eqs**> *on the nose, point*, syntactic analysis: nominal, attested by AC, also <**skéweqs**>, //s=q[=K=]əw=əqs//, (<**=K=** or **fronting**> *diminutive*), attested by AC, SP and others, dialects: *Chill., Tait*, other sources: JH /sqáwəqs/ *raven*, H-T <skaúEks> *raven (Corvus corax principalis)* (but compare H-T <spEpEtál> (macron over a)(t sic for l) *crow (Corvus caurinus)(cry resembles skak brother)*–this last comment by H-T that its cry resembles skak *brother* and H-T's spelling of the term for raven may show a folk etymology of <**sqéweqs**> from <**sqá:q**> *younger sibling, younger brother, younger sister, child of younger sibling of one's parent, "younger" cousin (could even be fourth cousin [through younger sibling of one's great great grandparent])*), Salish cognate: Lushootseed /skáw'qs/ *raven; Brother of* /k'áʔk'aʔ/ *in myth age*, Lushootseed (Skagit dial.) /qə́wqs/ (Deming 4/17/80), also <**qéwqs**>, //qə́w=qs//, attested by SJ has heard this, also <**sqóweqs**>, //s=qáw=əqs//, attested by JH:DM; example: <**qéx̲ te sqéweqs. ~ qéx̲ te skéweqs.**>, //qə́x̣ tə s=qə́w=əqs ~ qə́x̣ tə s=q[=K=]ə́w=əqs//, /'*There's a lot of ravens.*'/, attested by AC.

<**skéweqs**>, dnom //s=q[=F=]ə́w=əqs//, [skə́wəqs], EZ ['*raven*'], ['*Corvus corax*'], ASM ['whichever way it goes and crows it predicts a death in that certain family'], (<**fronting q → k**> *affectionate diminutive*), phonology: fronting, syntactic analysis: nominal, attested by SP (and poss. all Tait speakers)(BHTTC), Elders Group 6/4/75 and 12/15/76, example: <**qwóqwel te skéweqs**>, //qʷɛ[-Aá-C_1ə-]l tə s=q[=F=]ə́w=əqs//, [qʷáqʷəl tə skə́wəqs], /'*The raven is talking (not necessarily warning)(a distinct call).*'/, (<**ó-ablaut and reduplication**> *continuative*), phonology: ó-ablaut, reduplication, fronting, attested by Elders Group 12/15/76, <**qwő̄lqwel te skéweqs**>, //qʷɛ[=Ao=]@l=C_1əC_2 tə s=q[=F=]ə́w=əqs//, [qʷólqʷəl tə skə́wəqs], /'*The raven is warning (a distinct call).*'/, (<**ō-ablaut**> *derivational*), (<**=reduplication**> *characteristic*?), phonology: ō-ablaut, reduplication, fronting, attested by Elders Group 12/15/76, ASM ['owls can warn like this too (using qwő̄lqwel)'], also <**skyéweqs**>, //s=q[=F=]ə́w=əqs//, [skʸɪ́wəqs], attested by Elders Group 5/3/78, Salish cognate: Lushootseed (Skagit) /kʸə́wqs/ (Deming 4/17/80).

<**Skwówéls**>, df //s=kʷáw=əls//or //s-qʷ[-K-]ɛ́[=Aa=]=wels//, N ['*Raven*'], (<**s=**> *nominalizer*), root meaning unknown unless <**qwa**> *have a hole*, possibly <**=els**> *structured activity continuative*, phonology: updrifting, possibly velarization/diminutive fronting if derived from root in <**sqéweqs**> (<**sqwa**> as in 'rabbit' above or <**sqew**>) (compare <**skéweqs**> above), syntactic analysis: nominal, usage: name in story.

<**qew ~ qwō ~ qe ... u/ew**>, TIME /'*until, till, while*'/, *see* qe.

<**qewáth**>, bound derived stem / //s=qʷɛ́=əθ// *hole in the mouth*, entry also under real root <**qwá**>

<**sqewáth**>, df /s=qʷɛ́=əθ//, EZ /'*(larger) rabbit: snowshoe or varying hare, now probably also eastern cottontail rabbit (introduced)*'/, ['*Lepus americanus cascadensis and Lepus americanus washingtoni,* now probably also *Sylvilagus floridanus mearnsi*'], <**s=**> *nominalizer*, root <**qwá**> *have a hole*, <**=eth**> *in the mouth*, compare <**sqweqwewáth**> *bunch of rabbits* and <**sqwiqweyóthel**> *rabbit* (lit. *little hole in the lip*), phonology: consonant merger, vowel merger, delabialization, syntactic analysis: nominal, attested by JL (5/5/75), AK (11/21/72 tape), also <**shxwóxw**>, //s(=)xʷáxʷ//, attested by AK (11/21/72 tape).

<**sqiqewóthel**>, dmn //s=C_1í=qəw=áθəl or s=C_1í=sq^{w}ɛ=áθəl//, EZ /'*big rabbit, older rabbit, big/older snowshoe/varying hare, now probably also big/older eastern cottontail rabbit (introduced)*'/, ['*Lepus americanus cascadensis and Lepus americanus washingtoni,* now probably also *Sylvilagus floridanus mearnsi*'], (<**s=**> *nominalizer*, R4= *diminutive*), possibly root <**s=qwá**> *hole*, lx <**=óthel**> *in the mouth*, phonology: delabialization, reduplication, consonant merger, vowel merger, syntactic analysis: nominal, attested by Adeline Lorenzetto (Elders Group 3/1/72), compare <**sqwiqweyóthel**> *big rabbit, older rabbit.*

<**qiqewótheló:ythel**>, ds //C_1í=q^{w}ɛ=áθəl=á·yθəl//, ABDF /'*cleft palate, harelip*'/, literally /'rabbit on the lip/jaw'/, stem //qiqewóthel *rabbit*//, lx <**=ó:ythel**> *on the lip, on the jaw*, phonology: reduplication, delabialization, vowel merger, syntactic analysis: nominal, attested by Elders Group (9/1/76).

<**sqíqewàth**>, dmn //s=C_1í=q^{w}ɛ́=əθ//, EZ /'*rabbit: snowshoe/varying hare, now probably also eastern cottontail rabbit (introduced), (baby rabbit, small rabbit or hare [Elders Group])*'/, ['*Lepus americanus cascadensis and Lepus americanus washingtoni,* now prob. also *Sylvilagus floridanus mearnsi*'], ASM ['rabbits were eaten and their fur used for blankets and baby shoes'], (<**s=**> *nominalizer*, R4= *diminutive*), probably root <**s=qwá**> *hole*, probably <**=eth**> *in the mouth*, phonology: reduplication, delabialization, vowel merger, syntactic analysis: nominal, attested by AC, BJ (12/5/64), AK (11/21/72 tape), also /'*baby rabbit, small rabbit*'/, attested by Elders Group (3/1/72 tape), also /'*small rabbit*'/, attested by Elders Group (5/5/75), also /'*rabbit (including snowshoe hare)*'/, attested by Elders Group (9/1/76), other sources: ES /sqiqəwɛc/ *rabbit*, JH /sqí·qəwèθ/ *rabbit*, H-T <skEkuwáts> (macron over u, umlaut over a) *rabbit ('jack') (Lepus americanus washingtoni).*

<**sqwíqweyóthel**>, dmn //s=C_1í=q^{w}ɛ=áy[=M1=]θəl//, EZ /'*big rabbit, older rabbit, big/older snowshoe/varying hare, now probably also big/older eastern cottontail rabbit (introduced)*'/, ['*Lepus americanus cascadensis and Lepus americanus washingtoni,* now probably also *Sylvilagus floridanus mearnsi*'], (<**s=**> *nominalizer*, R4= *diminutive*), root <**sqwá**> *hole*, lx <**=óythel**> *in the lip*, (<**metathesis type 1**> *derivational*), phonology: reduplication, metathesis, syntactic analysis: nominal, attested by SP (Elders Group 3/1/72).

<**qewéletsem**>, ABFC /'*warm one's rump, warm one's bottom*'/, *see* qew.

<**qewét**>, MC /'*warm s-th, warm s-o*'/, *see* qew.

<**qéwethet**>, ABFC ['*warming up by a fire*'], *see* qew.

<**qewéthet**>, ABFC ['*warm up by a fire*'], *see* qew.

<**Qewítsel**>, SOCT /'*Cowichan (people, dialect, area)*'/, *see* qew.

<**qewletsá:ls**>, FIRE /'*heat up (on fire, stove)*'/, *see* qew.

<**qewówelhp**>, df //qəwáw=əɬp//, EB ['*snowberry plant*'], ['*Symphoricarpos albus*'], root meaning unknown, lx <**=elhp**> *plant, tree*, phonology: has an Interior Salish style of reduplication, syntactic analysis: nominal, attested by Elders Group (4/7/76), also <**q'ewówelhp**>, //q'əwáw=əɬp//, also /'*a tree of some kind, must be a hardhack, used to make spoons*'/, possibly root <**q'éwe**> *cane*, attested by AC, other sources: JH /qəwá·wəɬp/ *hardhack (yew)*, Salish cognate: Thompson /sqəwáwɬp/ //s-qəwéw-ɬp// *snowberry bush (Symphoricarpos albus)* (Turner, Thompson, Thompson & York 1973 ms:30).

<**qéx̱**>, free root //qə́x̣//, NUM /'*be many, be a lot of, lots of, much*'/, syntactic analysis: adjective/adjectival verb, attested by AC, BJ (5/10/64, 12/5/64), Elders Group (3/72, many other times), Deming, EB, others, other sources: JH /qə́x̣/ *many, a lot*, ES /wəqə́x̣a/ (Ms /qáx̣/) *many,*

much; found in <**qéx̲tset.**>, //qə́x̣-c-ət//, /'*There's a lot of us.*'/, literally /'we are many'/, attested by AC, example: <**qéx̲ tel swá.**>, //qə́x̣ tə-l s=wɛ́//, /'*I have lots.*'/, literally /'my own is lots'/, attested by Elders Group (3/72), <**xwel qéx̲.**>, //xʷəl qə́x̣//, /'*There's still lots.*'/, attested by EB, <**qéx̲ te sléxwelh.**>, //qə́x̣ tə s=lə́xʷəɬ//, /'*There's lots of canoes.*'/, attested by Deming, <**qéx̲ ye qwá:l.**>, //qə́x̣ yə qʷɛ́·l//, /'*(There's) lots of mosquitoes.*'/, attested by EB, <**qéx̲ te qó:s.**>, //qə́x̣ tə qá·-s//, /'*(He/She/It has, They have) a lot of water.*'/, literally /'is a lot of the his/her/its/their water'/, attested by AC, <**tsel làm te stólō tl'òlsuw kw'ètslexw te qé::x̲ sthó:qwi.**>, //c-əl lɛ̀=m tə s=tá·low ƛ'a-l-s-uw k'ʷə̀c=l-əxʷ tə qə́[-:-]x̣ s=θá·qʷi//, /'*I went to the river and I saw a LOT of fish.*'/, literally /'non-subordinate subject I ambiguous past go to the river that's so I contrastive see them the lots -emphasis- fish'/, phonology: emphatic lengthening, attested by AC, <**qéx̲ te mestíyexw (lí te hí:kw lá:lem., skwetáxw kw'e xwelmexwáwtxw.)**>, //qə́x̣ tə məstíyəxʷ (lí tə hí·kʷ lɛ́·ləm., s=kʷətɛ́xʷ k'ʷə xʷəl=məxʷ=ɛ́wtxʷ.)//, /'*There's lots of people (in the big house., inside thesmokehouse/longhouse/Indian-house.)*'/, attested by AC, <**qéx̲ te shxwhókwextset.**>, //qə́x̣ tə sxʷ-hákʷ=əxʸ-c-ət//, /'*We'll use it in many ways.*'/, literally /'are many the our uses of it'/, syntactic comment: shxwhókwextset is a nominalized transitive verb with root hókw plus =ex purposeful control stem inanimate object preferred, attested by TM/DF/NP (Elders Group 3/22/78), usage: in prayer said to plant before harvest, <**líye qéx̲ te qwe'óp?**>, //lí-ə qə́x̣ tə qʷəʔáp//, [6li5yə 4qə́:x̣ 4tə 1qʷə2ʔáp], /'*Are there many apples?*'/, attested by AC, <**lí qéx̲ kw'e siyólh li kw'a lálem?**>, //lí qə́x̣ k'ʷə s=yáɬ li k'ʷ-ɛ lɛ́ləm//, /'*Have you got a lot of wood at your house?*'/, literally /'is it lots the (remote) wood at the (remote) -your house'/, attested by AC, <**qéx̲ táles telí tl'á'altha.**>, //qə́x̣ tɛ́lə-s təlíƛ'-C_1ɛ́=ʔɛ́lθɛ//, /'*(He has more money than me.*'/, literally /'is lots his money than/from obj. of prep.- emphasis- me'/, syntactic comment: comparative construction, attested by AD, <**yeláwel qéx̲ te swás telí tl'á'altha.**>, //yəlɛ́w=əl qə́x̣ tə s=wɛ́-s təlíƛ'-C_1ɛ́=ʔɛ́lθɛ//, /'*He has more than I do.*'/, literally /'is beyond/past much the his own than/from obj. of prep.- emphasis- me'/, syntactic comment: comparative construction, attested by AD, <**yeláwel qéx̲ te swás telí tel swá.**>, //yəlɛ́w=əl qə́x̣ tə s=wɛ́-s təlí tə-l s=wɛ́//, /'*He has more than I do.*'/, literally /'is beyond/past much the his own from/than the -my own'/, attested by AD, <**yeláwel qéx̲ tel swá.**>, //yəlɛ́w=əl qə́x̣ tə-l s=wɛ́//, /'*I've got the most.*'/, literally /'is beyond/past much the -my own'/, attested by Elders Group (3/9/77), <**ólew qéx̲.**>, //ʔál=əw qə́x̣//, /'*(It's) too much.*'/, literally /'just -contrastive much'/, attested by EB, <**we'ólwe qéx̲ te sthó:qwi.**>, //wə-ʔál wə qə́x̣ tə s=θá·qʷi//, /'*(It's) an awful lot of fish.*'/, attested by AC, <**we'ólew qéx̲ te stsá:xts ta qwe'ópelhp.**>, //wə-ʔál-əw qə́x̣ tə s=cɛ́·xʸt-s t-ɛ qʷəʔáp=əɬp//, /'*You've got too many branches on your apple tree.*'/, literally /'contrastive- just -contrastive are many the branch of the -your crab-apple tree'/, attested by AC, <**éwe ís qéx̲.**>, //ʔə́wə ʔí-s qə́x̣//, /'*It's not many., (It's) not much., (It's) a little., (It's) a few.*'/, attested by EB, also <**éwe lís qéx̲.**>, //ʔə́wə lí-s qə́x̣//, attested by BJ (12/5/64), AC, <**ōwe lís qéx̲ te spáth.**>, //ʔówə lí-s qə́x̣ tə s=pɛ́θ//, /'*There are not very many bears., There are few bears.*'/, attested by AC, <**qé::x̲ te q'á:lemey.**>, //qə́[-:-]x̣ tə q'ɛ́·[-lə-]məy//, /'*(There are) LOTS of girls.*'/, literally /'are lots -emphasis/augmentative the girls'/, attested by AC, <**li qé::x̲ te qwe'óp.**>, //li qə́[-:-]x̣ tə qʷəʔáp//, [3li2 5qə́:x̣ 4tə 2qʷə1ʔáp], /'*There are a LOT of apples.*'/, semantic environment ['answer to yes/no question'], attested by AC.

<**qx̲álets**>, ds //qəx̣=ɛ́ləc//, [qx̣ǽlɪc], NUM ['*a lot of people*'], numc //=álets *people*//, phonology: zero-grade of root before full-grade suffix, syntactic analysis: num, attested by Deming, Elders Group; found in <**qx̲áletschet.**>, //qəx̣=ɛ́ləc-c-ət//, [qx̣ǽlɪcčɪt], /'*There's a lot of us.*'/, literally /'we're a lot of people'/, attested by Elders Group.

<**qx̲álh**>, ds //qəx̣=ɛ́ɬ//, [qx̣ǽɬ], NUM ['*lots of times*'], numc //=álh *times, occasions*//, phonology: zero-grade of root before full-grade suffix, syntactic analysis: num, attested by Deming.

<**qx̲ó:s**>, ds //qəx̣=á·s//, [qx̣á·s], NUM /'*lots of money, (many dollars)*'/, numc //=ó:s *dollars, circular*

things, in the face//, phonology: zero-grade of root before full-grade of suffix, syntactic analysis: num, attested by Deming.

<**qéx̱stexw**>, caus //qə́x̱=sT-əxʷ//, NUM /'*make s-th lots, make lots of s-th*'/, (<**=st**> *causative control transitivizer*), (<**-exw**> *third-person object*), syntactic analysis: transitive verb, attested by EB.

<**qex̱óthet**>, ABFC ['*to slide (oneself)*'], *see* qíx̱em ~ (less good spelling) qéyx̱em.

<**qéx̱stexw**>, NUM /'*make s-th lots, make lots of s-th*'/, *see* qéx̱.

<**qéy**>, probably root //qə́y// or //qíy//, meaning unknown unless *encircle* as in <**qít**>, bound root //qít *encircle, to circle around completely//*.

<**Sqéyiya**>, df //s=qə́y-iyɛ or s=qíy=iyɛ//, N ['*Bluejay*'], semantic environment ['name only in a story'], (<**s=**> *nominalizer*), root meaning unknown, lx <**=iya**> *diminutive*, syntactic analysis: nominal, attested by BHTTC.

<**=qéyl ~ =qel**>, da //=qíl ~ =qəl//, ANA ['*in the head*'], EB ['*on top (for ex. of a tree)*'], MC ['*top*'], may have two allomorphs as here or the first may be <**=qel**> + <**=Aí=**> *durative* which often replaces the first schwa of a suffix, syntactic analysis: lexical suffix, attested by EB, many others; found in <**t'eqw'qéyl**>, //t'əq'ʷ=qíl//, /'*top cut off (for ex. like a tree top with an axe)*'/, attested by Elders Group.

<**qéylem ~ qé:ylem ~ qí(:)lem**>, bound stem //qí·l=əm *put away, save//*, root meaning unknown unless *encircle* as in <**qít**>, bound root //qít *encircle, to circle around completely//*.

<**qéylemt ~ qé:ylemt**>, pcs //qí·l=əm=T//, MC /'*put s-th away, save s-th (food for ex.)*'/, root meaning unknown unless related to =qéyl *on top (of tree for ex.)*, possibly <**=em**> *intransitivizer, have, get*, (<**=t**> *purposeful control transitivizer*), syntactic analysis: transitive verb, attested by EB, AD, Elders Group, Salish cognate: Lushootseed /qíl'il/ *lose one's child through death* H76:386, compare <**sq'é:yla ~ sq'é:yle**> *smoked meat/fish, dried provisions* which if related would have to have been derived with glottalization.

<**qéylemtem ~ qé:ylemtem**>, if //qí·l=əm=T-əm//, MC ['*s-o/s-th has been put away*'], REL /'*s-o has been put away (in grave-house or buried), he's/she's been buried*'/, Elder's comment: "not *funeral* unless it's already over", (<**-em**> *passive*), syntactic analysis: intransitive verb, attested by AD (2/26/80) correction on EB (5/25/76) entry, example: <**lulh qéylemtem.**>, //lə-uɬ qí·l=əm=T-əm//, /'*He's/She's already (past) been buried.*'/, attested by AD.

<**qeyqelémtem**>, rsls //qi(·)[=C₁ə=]l=ə[=´=]m=T-əm//, [qéyqələmtəm], MC /'*stored, in storage*'/, BLDG, (<**=R1=**> *resultative*, <=´=> *derivational*), phonology: reduplication, stress-shift, syntactic analysis: intransitive verb, adjective/adjectival verb?, attested by AD (11/19/79).

<**qéylemà:ls**>, sas //qí·l=əm=ɛ́·ls//, REL ['*have a funeral*'], (<**=á:ls**> *structured activity non-continuative*), phonology: downstepping, syntactic analysis: intransitive verb, attested by AD (2/16/80).

<**qelmí:lthel**>, df //qil=əm=í·l=(ə)θəl or qí·l=m=ə[=M2=]l=(ə)θəl or qí·l=əm=ə[=M3=]l=(ə)θəl//, FOOD /'*leftovers, scraps (not taken home as smeq'óth is)*'/, possibly <**=í:l**> *become, get*, possibly <**metathesis**> *derivational*, lx <**=ethel**> *in the mouth, food?*, phonology: possible metathesis, vowel-loss (two places), syntactic analysis: nominal, attested by Elders Group.

<**qéylemà:ls**>, REL ['*have a funeral*'], *see* qéylem ~ qé:ylem ~ qí(:)lem.

<**qéylemt ~ qé:ylemt**>, MC /'*put s-th away, save s-th (food for ex.)*'/, *see* qéylem ~ qé:ylem ~ qí(:)lem.

<**qéylemtem ~ qé:ylemtem**>, MC ['*s-o/s-th has been put away*'], *see* qéylem ~ qé:ylem ~ qí(:)lem.

<**qéylés**>, EFAM ['*(be) gloomy*'], *see* qél.

<**qeyqelémtem**>, MC /'*stored, in storage*'/, *see* qéylem ~ qé:ylem ~ qí(:)lem.

<**qéyqeyx̲elà**>, df //C_1í=q'[=D=]ix̣=əl=à or C_1í=q'[=D=]ix̣=ɛlɛ=Aà or qə́y=C_1əC_2=]x̣əlà//, LT ['*shadow*'], possibly literally /'just a characteristic/little container of darkness'/ if root <**q'íx̲**> *black*, possibly <**R4=**> *diminutive* or possibly <**=R2=**> *characteristic* or possibly <**=D= (deglottalization)**> *derivational* or possibly <**=el**> *get, become* or possibly <**=ò**> *just* or possibly <**=àla**> *container of* or possibly <**ò-ablaut**> *derivational*, phonology: reduplication, deglottalization, possible ablaut, poss. vowel-reduction, syntactic analysis: nominal, attested by AC, Elders Group (4/2/75), other sources: ES /qɛʔx̣əlɛ́təl/ *shadow.*

<**qeyqeyx̲elósem**>, df //C_1í=q'[=D=]ix̣=ɛlɛ(=à)=ás=əm//, WETH ['*(get a) ray of sun between clouds*'], lx <**=ós**> *on the face*, (<**=em**> *intransitivizer, have, get* or *middle voice*), phonology: reduplication, deglottalization, vowel merger, syntactic analysis: nominal?, intransitive verb?, attested by Elders Group (4/16/75).

<**qeyqeyx̲elósem**>, WETH ['*(get a) ray of sun between clouds*'], *see* qéyqeyx̲elà.

<**qéytl't ~ qí(y)tl't**>, pcs //qə́yƛ'=T or qɛ́yƛ'=T ~ qí(y)ƛ'=T//, ABFC ['*press s-th down (like yeast dough)*'], ASM ['as when one is making a loaf of bread and one is punching the dough down'], (<**=t**> *purposeful control transitivizer*), syntactic analysis: transitive verb, attested by CT, HT, EB, Deming, also <**qeth'ét**>, //qəθ'=ə[=´=]T//, with same meaning, attested by CT and HT, IHTTC, Elders Group, perhaps compare <**qá:ytl'em**> *creaking/squeaking (of shoes, trees, chair).*

<**Qéywex̲em**>, PLN /'*steelhead fishing place on the Fraser River below Lhílhkw'elqs, at Hogg Slough*'/, *see* qí:wx̲ ~ qéywx̲ ~ qá:wx̲ ~ qáwx̲.

<**Qeywéx̲em**>, PLN /'*Sakwi Creek, a stream that joins Weaver Creek about one-third mile above the salmon hatchery*'/, *see* qí:wx̲ ~ qéywx̲ ~ qá:wx̲ ~ qáwx̲.

<**qéyx̲es ~ qíx̲es**>, df //q'[=D=]íx̣=əs//, ABDF /'*(be) blind, (be) completely blind*'/, possibly root <**q'íx̲**> *black*, (<**deglottalization**> *derivational*), lx <**=es**> *in the face*, phonology: deglottalization (=D=), syntactic analysis: adjective/adjectival verb, attested by Elders Group (3/1/72, 1/8/75), Deming (4/26/79), BJ (12/5/64).

<**qe'álts ~ qiqe'álts**>, EFAM /'*easy to cry, (cries easily)*'/, *see* qó:.

<**qe'íy ~ qe'í:**>, probable root or stem //qəʔí(y) ~ qəʔí·//, meaning unknown

<**sqe'íyeqel ~ sqe'í:qel**>, df //s=qəʔí(y)=qəl ~ s=qəʔí·=qəl//, EFAM ['*not know how to*'], (<**s=**> *stative*), root meaning unknown, lx <**=qel**> *in the head*, syntactic analysis: adjective/adjectival verb, attested by AC, Deming (3/15/79 SJ, MC, MV, LG); found in <**sqe'íyeqeltsel.**>, //s=qəʔíy=qəl-c-əl//, /'*I don't know (how).*'/, attested by AC, example: <**sqe'í:qeltsel kw'els t'í:ts'em.**>, //s=qəʔíy=qəl-c-əl k'ʷə-l-s t'í·c'=əm//, /'*I don't know how to swim.*'/, literally /'I don't know how that -my -nom. swim'/, attested by Deming (SJ, MV, MC, LG).

<**sqe'iyeqeló:ythel ~ sqe'iqeló:ythel**>, df //s=qəʔi(y)=qəl=á·yθəl//, LANG ['*not fluent in speaking*'], EFAM, lx <**=ó:ythel**> *in the lips/jaw, in speech*, syntactic analysis: adjective/adjectival verb, attested by AC, Deming (1/18/79), Salish cognate: Lushootseed /(s)qəyíqəl' ~ qəʔíqəl'/ *not know how to* (a loan word from Halkomelem?) (LG) H76:383-384; found in <**sqe'iqeló:ytheltsel.**>, //s=qəʔi=qəl=á·yθəl//, /'*I'm not fluent in speaking., I'm not fluent at speaking.*'/, attested by AC, Deming.

<**qe'ó:les**>, ANA ['*tear (from eye)*'], *see* qó:.

<**qe'ó:ythel**>, WATR ['*liquid in the mouth*'], *see* qó:.

<**qí: ~ qí'**>, bound root //qí· ~ qíʔ// *soft.*

<**qí:qe ~ qéyqe ~ qíqe**>, df //qí·=C_1ə ~ qí=C_1ə//, [qéyqə ~ qíqə], TCH ['*soft*'], DESC, ASM ['of butter, snow, wool, cloth, easy to pull apart, easy to break, of soft top of baby's head'], (<**=R1**> *resultative or derivational*), phonology: crystallized reduplication, syntactic analysis: adjective/adjectival verb, attested by EB, Elders Group, Salish cognate: Squamish /qə́ʔqiʔ/ *soft* W73:242, K67:352, also <**qí'qe**>, //qíʔqə//, dialects: *Matsqui (Downriver Halkomelem)*, attested by AH (at Deming), example: <**qéyqe st'á te péte., qíqe st'á te péte.**>, //qí(·)qə s=t=(ə)ʔɛ́ tə pə́tə.//, [qé(y)qə/qé·qə st'ǽ tə pə́tə], /'*(It's) soft as butter.*'/, attested by EB.

<**sqe'éleqw**>, df //s=qiʔ=ə́ləqʷ//, ANAH /'*soft spot on (top of) a baby's head, fontanel*'/, (<**s=**> *nominalizer*), root <**qí: ~ qí'**> *soft*, lx <**=(')éleqw**> *on top of the head*, phonology: length varies with glottal stop, syntactic analysis: nominal, dialects: *Tait*, attested by Elders Group (8/20/75), also <**sqe'ó:ls**>, //s=qi·=á·ls//, dialects: *Cheh., Chill.*, attested by Elders Group (8/20/75), Salish cognate: Lushootseed /qʷúʔ-qid/ *crown, soft part of baby's head* H76:384.

<=qíl> possible alternate spelling for <**=qéyl ~ =qel**>, da //=qíl ~ =qəl//, ANA ['*in the head*'], EB ['*on top (for ex. of a tree)*'], MC ['*top*'], syntactic analysis: lexical suffix, attested by EB, many others; found in <**t'eqw'qéyl**>, //t'əq'ʷ=qíl//, /'*top cut off (for ex. like a tree top with an axe)*'/, attested by Elders Group, *see* =qéyl ~ =qel.

<**qí(:)lem ~ qéylem ~ qé:ylem**>, bound root //qí·l=əm *put away, save*//.

<**qéylemt ~ qé:ylemt**>, pcs //qí·l=əm=T//, MC /'*put s-th away, save s-th (food for ex.)*'/, root meaning unknown unless related to =qéyl *on top (of tree for ex.)*, possibly <**=em**> *intransitivizer, have, get*, (<**=t**> *purposeful control transitivizer*), syntactic analysis: transitive verb, attested by EB, AD, Elders Group, Salish cognate: Lushootseed /qíl'il/ *lose one's child through death* H76:386, compare <**sq'é:yla ~ sq'é:yle**> *smoked meat/fish, dried provisions* which if related would have to have been derived with glottalization.

<**qéylemtem ~ qé:ylemtem**>, if //qí·l=əm=T-əm//, MC ['*s-o/s-th has been put away*'], REL /'*s-o has been put away (in grave-house or buried), he's/she's been buried*'/, Elder's comment: "not *funeral* unless it's already over", (<**-em**> *passive*), syntactic analysis: intransitive verb, attested by AD (2/26/80) correction on EB (5/25/76) entry, example: <**lulh qéylemtem.**>, //lə-uɬ qí·l=əm=T-əm//, /'*He's/She's already (past) been buried.*'/, attested by AD.

<**qeyqelémtem**>, rsls //qi(·)[=C_1ə=]l=ə[=´=]m=T-əm//, [qéyqələmtəm], MC /'*stored, in storage*'/, BLDG, (<**=R1=**> *resultative*, <=´=> *derivational*), phonology: reduplication, stress-shift, syntactic analysis: intransitive verb, adjective/adjectival verb?, attested by AD (11/19/79).

<**qéylemà:ls**>, sas //qí·l=əm=ɛ̀·ls//, REL ['*have a funeral*'], (<**=á:ls**> *structured activity non-continuative*), phonology: downstepping, syntactic analysis: intransitive verb, attested by AD (2/16/80).

<**qelmí:lthel**>, df //qil=əm=í·l=(ə)θəl or qí·l=m=ə[=M2=]l=(ə)θəl or qí·l=əm=ə[=M3=]l=(ə)θəl//, FOOD /'*leftovers, scraps (not taken home as smeq'óth is)*'/, possibly <**=í:l**> *become, get*, possibly <**metathesis**> *derivational*, lx <**=ethel**> *in the mouth, food?*, phonology: possible metathesis, vowel-loss (two places), syntactic analysis: nominal, attested by Elders Group.

<**qá:lmílh**>, df //qi[=Aɛ́=]·l=əm=íyɬ or qɛ́·lm=íyɬ//, KIN ['*reject someone as a spouse or partner for one's child*'], possibly root <**qí:lem**> *put away, store away* possibly root <**with connotation of**> *scraps?*, lx <**=íylh ~ =ílh ~ =ó:llh**> *child, offspring*, possibly <**á-ablaut**> *derivational*, phonology: possible ablaut, syntactic analysis: intransitive verb, attested by Elders Group (1/30/80).

<**qí:qe ~ qéyqe ~ qíqe**>, TCH ['*soft*'], *see* qí: ~ qí'.

<**qíqel**>, EFAM /'*be naughty, be bad (a menace) (but not quite as bad as qél)*'/, *see* qél.

<**qiqelá:m ~ qiqelà:m**>, ABDF /*'(be) weak (in strength, also in taste [TM])'*/, *see* qél.

<**qiqelá:mthet**>, ABDF /*'get weak (from laughing, walking, working too long, sickness)'*/, *see* qél.

<**Qíqemqèmèl**>, PLN /*'a little bay in the Fraser River a quarter mile east of Iwówes (Union Bar, Aywawwis)'*/, *see* qém:el.

<**qíqemxel ~ qéyqemxel**>, EB /*'unidentified plant with round bulbs that look and taste like potatoes, round root like potatoes that used to be eaten and tastes like potatoes'*/, *see* qém.

<**qiqep'eyósem**>, ABFC [*'lying on one's stomach with head down on one's arms'*], *see* qep'.

<**qíqep'yó:lha ~ qéyqep'yó:lha**>, ABFC [*'lying down on one's stomach'*], *see* qep'.

<**qíqeq'els**>, SOCT [*'policeman'*], *see* qíq'.

<**qíqew**>, ABFC [*'menstruating'*], *see* qí:w.

<**qiqewótheló:ythel**>, ABDF /*'cleft palate, harelip'*/, *see* sqewáth.

<**qíqex̲életsem ~ qéyqex̲életsem**>, TVMO /*'slide on one's seat, (sliding on one's bottom)'*/, *see* qíx̲em ~ (less good spelling) qéyx̲em.

<**qíqex̲em**>, TCH /*'slippery, sliding'*/, *see* qíx̲em ~ (less good spelling) qéyx̲em.

<**qíq'**>, free root //qíq'//, SOC /*'(emprisoned), put in jail, grounded, restricted, caught, apprehended'*/, syntactic analysis: intransitive verb, attested by NP, EB, Elders Group, example: <**ílhtsel le qíq' kw'els e só:les.**>, //ʔí=ɬ-c-əl lə qíq' kʼʷə-l-s ʔə sá·l=əs//, /*'I went to jail when I was drunk.'*/, literally /'auxiliary past -non-subord. subject -I third person past (or la *go to*) put in jail when (simultaneous) -I just be drunk'/, attested by Elders Group.

<**qíq'et**>, pcs //qíq'=əT//, SOC [*'catch s-o'*], (<**=et**> *purposeful control transitivizer*), syntactic analysis: transitive verb, attested by NP.

<**qíq'áwtxw**>, dnom //qíq'=ɛ́wtxʷ//, BLDG [*'jail'*], literally /'apprehend/catch building'/, lx <**=áwtxw**> *building, house*, syntactic analysis: nominal, attested by EB, others.

<**qíqeq'els**>, dnom //qí[=C$_1$ə=]q'=əls//, sas, SOCT [*'policeman'*], (<**=R1=**> *continuative*), (<**=els**> *structured activity nominalizer/continuative*), phonology: reduplication, syntactic analysis: nominal, attested by NP, Elders Group, example: <**qíqeq'els te Bill.**>, //qí[=C$_1$ə=]q'=əls tə Bill//, /*'Bill is a policeman.'*/, attested by Elders Group.

<**qíq'áwtxw**>, BLDG [*'jail'*], *see* qíq'.

<**qíq'et**>, SOC [*'catch s-o'*], *see* qíq'.

<**qít**>, bound root //qít *encircle, to circle around completely*//, Salish cognate: Lushootseed /qít(i)/ *circle around something* as in /qít=id/ *circle around s-th* and /qit=úlč/ *go around the table (an expression used by Shakers for part of their ritual)* H76:387,212.

<**qítes ~ qéytes**>, ds //qít=əs//, [qétɪs], CLO /*'headband, headband made out of cedar bark woven by widow or widower when mourning'*/, lx <**=es**> *on the face*, syntactic analysis: nominal, noun, attested by BHTTC, Elders Group (8/20/75), also <**sqéytes**>, //s=qít=əs//, (<**s=**> *nominalizer*), attested by Elders Group (11/26/75), other sources: ES /sqítəstəl/ *headband*, Salish cognate: in part Squamish /qít-qʷ/ *headdress made of cedar bark* W73:138, K67:354, example: <**x̲awsólkwlh sqéytes**>, //x̣ɛws=álkʷɬ s=qít=əs//, CLO [*'new spirit dancer's headband'*], attested by Elders Group.

<**shxwékw'thelh sq'éytes**>, cpds //s=xʷəkʼʷ=θəɬ s=q'ít=əs// (sic for <**shxwékw'lhelh sqéytes**>, cpds //s=x ʷəkʼʷ=ɬəɬ s=q'ít=əs//), CLO /*'kerchief'*/, lit. /"dragged on the throat headband"/, <**s=**> nominalizer, <**xwekw'**> *drag*, <**=élhelh ~ =lhelh**> ~ poss. **=elhlelh**> *in the windpipe, throat*, <**s=**>

nominalizer, <**qít**> *tied*, <**=es**> *on the face*, attested by RG & EH (4/10/99 Ling332)

<**qéttel**>, df //qi[=Aə́=]t=təl//, CLO ['*waistband of a skirt*'], probably <**é-ablaut**> *resultative*, lx <**=tel**> *device to, something that*, phonology: probable ablaut, syntactic analysis: nominal.

<**qítes ~ qéytes**>, CLO /'*headband, headband made out of cedar bark woven by widow or widower when mourning*'/, *see* qít.

<**qí(y)tl't ~ qéytl't**>, pcs //qə́yƛ̕'=T or qɛ́yƛ̕'=T ~ qí(y)ƛ̕'=T//, ABFC ['*press s-th down (like yeast dough)*'], ASM ['as when one is making a loaf of bread and one is punching the dough down'], (<**=t**> *purposeful control transitivizer*), syntactic analysis: transitive verb, attested by CT, HT, EB, Deming, also <**qeth'ét**>, //qəθ'=ə[=´=]T//, with same meaning, attested by CT and HT, IHTTC, Elders Group, perhaps compare <**qá:ytl'em**> *creaking/squeaking (of shoes, trees, chair)*, .

<**qí:w**>, free root //qí·w//, ABFC ['*menstruate*'], syntactic analysis: intransitive verb, attested by NP.

<**qíqew**>, cts //qí[-C_1ə-]w//, ABFC ['*menstruating*'], (<**-R1-**> *continuative*), phonology: reduplication, syntactic analysis: intransitive verb, attested by NP.

<**qíx̲ ~ qéyx̲**>, bound stem //qíx̣//, *slip, slide*

<**qíx̲em** ~ (more phonetic spelling) **qéyx̲em**>, mdls //qíx̣=əm//, [qéx̣əm], TVMO /'*slip, slide, skid*'/, (<**=em**> *middle voice*), syntactic analysis: intransitive verb, attested by RG & EH (4/9/99 Ling332), others.

<**qíqex̲em**>, df //qí[=C_1ə=]x̣=əm or qí[-C_1ə-]x̣=əm//, TCH /'*slippery, sliding*'/, TVMO, probably <**=R1=**> *resultative or durative* or probably < **-R1-**> *continuative*, phonology: reduplication, syntactic analysis: adjective/adjectival verb, attested by EB, BHTTC, example: <**qíqex̲em pékcha ~ qéyqex̲em pékcha**>, //qí[-C_1ə-]x̣=əm pə́kcɛ//, /'*slides, sliding pictures*'/, attested by Deming (4/6/78).

<**qíqex̲életsem ~ qéyqex̲életsem**>, mdls //qí[-C_1ə-]x̣=ə́ləc=əm//, cts, TVMO /'*slide on one's seat, (sliding on one's bottom)*'/, (<**-R1-**> *continuative*), lx <**=élets**> *on the bottom, on the rump*, (<**=em**> *middle voice*), phonology: reduplication, syntactic analysis: intransitive verb.

<**shxwqeyqex̲elátsem ~ shxwqiqex̲elátsem**>, dnom //s(=)x^w=qi[=C_1ə=]x̣=ɛ́lə[=M2=]c=əm//, CAN ['*little sled*'], literally /'(prob.) something for sliding on one's rump on'/, (<**sxw=**> *nominalizer, something for*), (<**=R1=**> *continuative*, metathesis *derivational*), lx <**=álets**> *on the bottom* (perhaps with <=Aá=> *durative* ablaut on first schwa of suffix*)*, (<**=em**> *middle voice*), phonology: reduplication, metathesis, syntactic analysis: nominal, attested by Elders Group (11/10/76).

<**qéyx̲et**>, pcs //qix̣=əT//, /'*slide it*'/, (<**=əT**> *purposeful control transitivizer*), attested by RG & EH (4/9/99 Ling332)

<**qex̲óthet**>, durs //qix̣=ɛ[=Aá=]T-ət//, rfls, pcs, ABFC ['*to slide (oneself)*'], (<**ó-ablaut**> *derivational* triggered automatically on root a by =thet), (<**=əT**> *purposeful control transitivizer* + <**=Aá=**> *durative*), (<**-et**> *reflexive*), phonology: root vowel-reduction before stressed affix, stressed transitivizer, ablaut, syntactic analysis: intransitive verb, attested by EB.

<**qiqex̲óthet** (or less good spelling) **qeyqex̲óthet**>, cts //qí[-C_1ə-]x̣=ɛ[=Aá=]T-ət//, rfls, cts, PLAY ['*skating*'], TVMO, (<**-R1-**> *continuative*), phonology: reduplication, vowel-reduction, ablaut, syntactic analysis: intransitive verb, attested by Elders Group (12/10/75), also <**qíqex̲ethet**>, //qí[-C_1ə-]x̣=əT-ət//, dialects: *Cheh.*, attested by Elders Group (12/10/75).

<**shxwqiqex̲óthet**>, dnom //s(=)x^w=qi[=C_1ə=]x̣=ɛ[=Aá=]T=ət//, PLAY /'*ice skate, sled, toboggan*'/, (<**shxw=**> *something for, nominalizer*), phonology: reduplication, ablaut, syntactic analysis: nominal, attested by CT, RG & EH (4/9/99 Ling332)

<**xéletsem shxwqeyqex̲óthet**>, cpds //x^{y}ə́l=əc=əm /s(=)x^w=qi[=C_1ə=]x̣=ɛ[=Aá=]T=ət//, GAM

//'roller skates, roller blade skates'//, lit. "wheeled/rolling skate", attested by RG & EH (4/9/99 Ling332)

<**qíx̱es ~ qéyx̱es**>, df //q'[=D=]íx̣=əs//, ABDF */'(be) blind, (be) completely blind'/*, possibly root <**q'íx̱**> *black*, (<**deglottalization**> *derivational*), lx <**=es**> *in the face*, phonology: deglottalization (=D=), syntactic analysis: adjective/adjectival verb, attested by Elders Group (3/1/72, 1/8/75), Deming (4/26/79), BJ (12/5/64).

<**qíyqiyx̱elà** or **qíqiyx̱elà** or **qíqix̱elà**>, possible alternate spellings for <**qéyqeyx̱elà**>, df //C_1í=q'[=D=]ix̣=əl=à or C_1í=q'[=D=]ix̣=ɛlɛ=Aà or qə́y=C_1əC_2=]x̣əlà//, LT [*'shadow'*], possibly literally /'just a characteristic/little container of darkness'/ if root <**q'íx̱**> *black*, possibly <**R4=**> *diminutive* or possibly <**=R2=**> *characteristic* or possibly <**=D= (deglottalization)**> *derivational* or possibly <**=el**> *get, become* or possibly <**=ò**> *just* or possibly <**=ála**> *container of* or possibly <**ò-ablaut**> *derivational*, phonology: reduplication, deglottalization, possible ablaut, poss. vowel-reduction, syntactic analysis: nominal, attested by AC, Elders Group (4/2/75), other sources: ES /qɛʔx̣əlɛ́təl/ *shadow*, see main (more phonetic) spelling qéyqeyx̱elà.

<**qeyqeyx̱elósem**>, df //C_1í=q'[=D=]ix̣=ɛlɛ(=à)=ás=əm//, WETH [*'(get a) ray of sun between clouds'*], lx <**=ós**> *on the face*, (<**=em**> *intransitivizer, have, get* or *middle voice*), phonology: reduplication, deglottalization, vowel merger, syntactic analysis: nominal?, intransitive verb?, attested by Elders Group (4/16/75).

<**qó:**>, free root //qá·//, WATR [*'water'*], syntactic analysis: nominal, noun, attested by AC, BJ (5/10/64, 12/5/64), DM (12/4/64), EB, CT, Elders Group, other sources: ES and JH /qá·/ *water*, ES Ms and Cw /qáʔ/ *water*, Salish cognate: Squamish bound root /qʷu/, Lushootseed, Twana and Clallam /qʷuʔ/, San, Sg, So and Sam dials. of N. Straits /qʷáʔ/ all meaning *water* (Samish in G86:64, other citations in G82:33 cognate set 151b, example: <**éy qó:**>, //ʔɛ́y qá·//, */'good water'/*, attested by AC, <**lí: éy te qó:?**>, //lí-ə ʔɛ́y tə qá·//, */'Is the water good?'/*, attested by AC, <**stl'ís tl' Máli kw'e qó:.**>, //s=ƛ'í-sƛ' mɛ́li k'ʷə qá·//, */'Mary wants some water.'/*, literally /'her want the (human) Mary some water'/, attested by EB, <**su o'ó mí te qó:**>, //s=u ʔaʔá mí tə qá·//, WATR [*'spring tide (when a river first rises in May)'*], attested by CT (6/8/76), <**pípe qó:**>, //pípə qá·//, */'typewriter correction fluid'/*, literally /'paper water'/, comment: just made up after the trade name fluid, Liquid Paper, attested by EB (11/7/78).

<**qó:qe**>, ds //qá·=C_1ə//, ABFC [*'to drink'*], WATR, (<**=R1**> *derivational*), phonology: reduplication, syntactic analysis: intransitive verb, attested by MH (Deming 1/4/79), AC, EB, BJ (5/10/64), other sources: ES /qá·qa/ *drink*, also */'drinking, drink'/*, attested by AC; found in <**qó:qelha.**>, //qá·=C_1ə-ɬɛ//, */'Drink.'/*, attested by AC, example: <**ewá:lh qó:qe.**>, //ʔəwə=ɛ́ɬ qá·=C_1ə//, */'He never used to drink.'/*, attested by EB.

<**qó:qet**>, pcs //qá·=C_1ə=T//, ABFC [*'drink s-th'*], WATR, (<**=t**> *purposeful control transitivizer*), phonology: reduplication, syntactic analysis: transitive verb, attested by AC; found in <**qó:qetlha.**>, //qá·=C_1ə=T-lɛ//, */'Drink s-th., Drink it.'/*, attested by AC, example: <**qó:qet te st'élmexw**>, //qá·=C_1ə=T tə s=t'ə́lməxʷ//, */'drink the medicine'/*, attested by AC, <**qó:qetlha esu méq'et.**>, //qá·=C_1ə=T-ɬɛ ʔə=s=u mə́q'=əT//, */'Drink it and swallow it.'/*, attested by AC.

<**sqó:qe**>, dnom //s=qá·=C_1ə//, WATR [*'a drink'*], FOOD, (<**s=**> *nominalizer*), phonology: reduplication, syntactic analysis: nominal, attested by EB.

<**temqoqó: ~ temqó:**>, ds //təm=qá· ~ təm=C_1ə=qá· or təm=C1V1=qá·//, WATR */'high water time (yearly, usually in June), June'/*, lx <**tem=**> *time of/for, season of/for*, (<**R5=**> or a new type of reduplication (C1V1=, perhaps **<R11=)**> *augmentative* or *plural*), phonology: reduplication (perhaps doubling prefix #1 with same vowel), syntactic analysis: nominal?, adverb/adverbial verb?, Elder's comment: "prob. better name for June than another old name, temt'ámxw,

gooseberry time because there aren't many gooseberries around any more", attested by Elders Group (3/15/72, 3/12/75).

<**Qoqoláx̱el**>, df //qa=C1V1=l(=)ɛ́x̣əl or C1V1=qa=l(=)ɛ́x̣əl or C_1V_1=qa=l(=)ɛ́x̣əl//, PLN /'*Watery Eaves, a famous longhouse and early village on a flat area on Chilliwack River just a quarter mile upriver/east above Vedder Crossing*'/, literally /'watery eaves'/, ASM ['named for a famous and unique longhouse designed with a "V" in its roof which collected and held rain water, it could be accessed for drinking water or other water by pulling a rope connected to a raisable plank'], possibly <**C1V1= (i.e. R11=)**> *augmentative or plural* or possibly <**=C1V1**> *characteristic* or possibly <**=el**> *get, come, go, become*, lx <**=(l)áx̱el**> *part of a building, side of a building*, phonology: reduplication (perhaps doubling prefix #1 with same vowel= or =doubling suffix with same vowel), syntactic analysis: nominal, attested by BJ (Wells Tapes), Elders Group (8/24/77), other sources: Wells 1965 (1st ed.):19, Duff 1952, source: place names reference file #221.

<**qó:lem**>, ds //qá·=əl=əm//, WATR /'*to scoop, to dip, dip water*'/, FSH /'*to scoop (for ex. oolachens, eulachons)*'/, FOOD ['*to ladle*'], semantic environment ['to fetch/dip water, scoop oolachens, ladle out food'], (<**=el**> *get, become, go, come*, <**=em**> *intransitivizer, get, have*), phonology: vowel merger, syntactic analysis: intransitive verb, attested by Elders Group, Deming, example: <**latset qó:lem te swíwe.**>, //lɛ-c-ət qá·=əl=əm tə s=wíwə//, /'*Let's scoop oolachens.*'/, attested by Deming.

<**qóqelem**>, cts //qá·[-C_1ə-]=əl=əm//, WATR ['*dipping water*'], FSH, FOOD, (<**-R1-**> *continuative*), phonology: reduplication, length-loss automatic before -doubling infix #1 with e-, syntactic analysis: intransitive verb, attested by Elders Group.

<**sqíqemlò**>, df //s=C_1í=qəmlà// or possibly?? //s=C_1í=qá·lə[=M2=]m=M2=M1//, [sqíqəmlà], EZ ['*minnow*'], (<**s=**> *nominalizer*, R4= *diminutive*), stem <**qó:lem**> *scoop*, possibly <**triple metathesis**> *derivational*, Elder's comment: "from qó:lem *scoop* because during a famine minnows were scooped out of the river sometimes and boiled to make soup", phonology: reduplication, possibly triple metathesis, syntactic analysis: nominal, attested by EL (3/1/78).

<**Sqíqemlò**>, df //s=C_1í=qá·lə[=M2=]m=M2=M1//, PLN ['*point of land on Harrison River (somewhere between Lheltá:lets and Híqelem) where during a famine the old people scooped minnows and boiled them to make soup*'], literally /'minnow'/, phonology: reduplication, perhaps triple metathesis, syntactic analysis: nominal, attested by EL (3/1/78 Stó:lō Sítel tape),

<**qéqemlò**>, dmn //C_1í=Aə́=qəmlà// or perhaps //C_1í=Aə́=qá·lə[=M2=]m=M2=M1//, [qə́qəmlà], EZ ['*lots of minnows*'], phonology: reduplication, ablaut, perhaps triple metathesis, syntactic analysis: nominal, attested by Elders Group (1/28/76).

<**qó:lt**>, pcs //qá·=əl=T//, WATR ['*scoop s-th*'], FOOD, FSH, (<**=el**> *go, come, get, become*, <**=t**> *purposeful control transitivizer*), phonology: vowel merger, syntactic analysis: transitive verb.

<**qéltsesem**>, mdls //qá·[=Aə́=]=əl=cəs=əm//, ABFC /'*to cup water in one's hands, to cup berries in one's hands*'/, (<**é-ablaut**> *derivational*), (<**=el**> *have, get*), lx <**=tses**> *in the hand(s)*, (<**=em**> *middle voice*), phonology: ablaut, syntactic analysis: intransitive verb, attested by IHTTC.

<**lhqó:la ~ lhqó:le**>, df //ɬ=qá·=ɛlɛ or ɬ=qá·=ələ//, ABFC ['*be thirsty*'], (<**lh=**> *use, extract, extract a portion*), possibly <**=ála ~ =ále**> *container of* or possibly <**=ele**> *lacking*, phonology: vowel merger, syntactic analysis: intransitive verb, attested by EB, example: <**tsel lhqó:le.**>, //c-əl ɬ=qá·=ələ//, /'*I'm thirsty.*'/, attested by EB, <**me ts'íyxweqthàlèm; tsel me lhqó:la.**>, //mə c'íyx^w=əqəl=T-ɛ̀lə̀m; c-əl mə ɬ=qá·=ələ//, /'*My throat is dry; I'm thirsty.*'/, lx <**=eqel**> *in the throat*, (<**=t**> *purposeful control transitivizer*), (<**=àlèm**> *passive first person singular*), attested by EB.

<**tsqó:le**>, ds //c=qá·=ələ//, ABFC /'*be thirsty, get thirsty*'/, (<**ts=**> *have, get*), possibly <**=ele**> *lacking*,

syntactic analysis: adjective/adjectival verb, attested by AC, EB, also <**tsqóqele**>, //c=qá·[=C₁ə=]=ɛlə or c=qá·[=C₁ə=]=ələ//, (<**=R1=**> *resultative, durative, or continuative*), attested by AC, example: <**l stl'í kw'e qó:; tsqóqele tel sqwemáy.**>, //l s=ƛ'í k'ʷə qá·; c=qá·[=C₁ə=]=ələ//, /'*I want some water; my dog is thirsty.*'/.

<**qó:lets**>, df //qá·=əl=əc(əs) or qá·=ləc//, FSH /'*to dip-net, a dip-net*'/, root <**qó:**> *water*, possibly <**=el**> *go, come, get, become or intransitivizer, get, have,* possibly <**=əcəs**> *in the hand,* possibly <**=lets**> *on the bottom,* phonology: possible vowel merger, possible syllable-loss or loan from Nooksack since Nooksack /=əč ~ =əčəs/ *on the hand* corresponds to Halkomelem /=əcəs/ *in the hand* but Halkomelem variant /=əc/ *in the hand* is not attested elsewhere, syntactic analysis: intransitive verb; nominal, dialects: *Sumas, also Nooksack language,* attested by Deming (2/7/80), compare <**qéltsesem**> *to cup water/berries in one's hands;* also attested as <**qó'lets**>, //qáʔ=l(=)əc//, also /'*scoop fish, dip fish*'/, dialects: *Sumas,* attested by Deming (5/20/76), also <**qó'letstel**>, //qáʔ=l(=)əc=təl//, also /'*a dip net*'/, dialects: *Matsqui (Downriver Halkomelem),* attested by Deming (5/20/76), Salish cognate: Squamish /qʷú-lač-íʔm/ *scoop up water with hands* W73:224, K69:82.

<**qóqelets**>, df //qá·[-C₁ə-]=l(=)əc//, FSH /'*to dip a net, (dipping a net)*'/, probably <**-R1-**> *continuative or resultative or durative,* phonology: reduplication, length-loss automatic before doubling infix #1 with e, syntactic analysis: intransitive verb, attested by Deming (3/25/76).

<**qó:lhcha**>, ds //qá·=əɬcɛ//, FOOD ['*juice*'], WATR, EB, lx <**=elhcha**> *unclear liquid,* phonology: vowel merger, syntactic analysis: nominal, attested by AC, DM (12/4/64), EB, example: <**qéx̲ te qó:lhchas.**>, //qə́x̣ tə qá·=əɬcɛ-s//, /'*(There's) a lot of juice., It's real juicy.*'/, literally /'is lots the its juice'/, attested by AC.

<**qó:lhthet**>, pcrs //qá·=əɬ(cɛ)=T-ət//, EB ['*get juicy of its own accord*'], ABFC, FOOD, (<**=t**> *purposeful control transitivizer*), (<**-et**> *reflexive*), phonology: vowel merger, syllable-loss in suffix before =t, syntactic analysis: intransitive verb, attested by EB.

<**qó:m**>, ds //qá·=əm//, WATR /'*to dip water, get water, fetch water, pack water*'/, (<**=em**> *intransitivizer, get, have*), phonology: vowel merger, syntactic analysis: intransitive verb, attested by AC, Elders Group, EB, example: <**latst qó:m.**>, //lɛ-c-t qá·=əm//, /'*We're going to pack water.*'/, attested by EB, <**látsel qó:m.**>, //lɛ́-c-əl qá·=əm//, /'*I'm going to dip water., I'm going to get water.*'/, attested by AC, <**lalh qó:m.**>, //lɛ-ɬ qá·=əm//, /'*Go get water.*'/, literally /'go -imperative get water'/, attested by AC, <**la qó:m**>, //lɛ qá·=əm//, /'*fetch water*'/, *<**qó:m te qó:**> rejected by EB, <**lachxw tsesá:t kws lás (qó:m, kwél:em kw qó:).**>, //lɛ-c-xʷ cəs=ɛ́·T kʷ-s lɛ́-s (qá·=əm, kʷə́l=l=əm kʷ qá·)//, /'*Send him to get water.*'/, literally /'you go send s-o that-he go-he (get water, grab -non-control transitivizer =intransitivizer → get/fetch some water)'/, attested by EB.

<**sqó:m**>, dnom //s=qá·=əm//, WATR /'*water (someone) carried, (water fetched/gotten)*'/, (<**s=**> *nominalizer*), phonology: vowel merger, syntactic analysis: nominal, attested by Elders Group.

<**shxwqó:m**>, dnom //s(=)xʷ=qá·=əm//, BSK ['*water basket*'], WATR, (<**shxw=**> *nominalier, something to*), phonology: vowel merger, syntactic analysis: nominal, attested by TG (4/23/75).

<**Shxwqó:m**>, dnom //s(=)xʷ=qá·=əm//, PLN ['*Lake of the Woods*'], ASM ['a small lake across the Fraser River from Hope; a loon at the lake used to tell what kind of fish was there, it said "skwímeth, skwímeth" *little roundmouth sucker-fish (prob. longnose sucker Catostomus catostomus);* the people used dip-nets to catch lots, and thus the name (see qó:m *to dip water* or shxwqó:m *water basket)'],* literally /'something to dip (water) (or) water basket'/, phonology: vowel merger, syntactic analysis: nominal, attested by Elders on Trip to American Bar (6/26/78)(AD, AK, SP?), also <**Q'áleliktel**>, //q'ɛ́ləlík=təl//, attested by SP (6/26/78), comment: other speakers use Q'alelíktel for another place further upriver.

<**sqó:s**>, dnom //s=qá·=əs//, ANA [*'a tear (on the face)'*], (<**s=**> *nominalizer*), lx <**=es ~ =ó:s**> *on the face*, phonology: vowel merger, syntactic analysis: nominal, attested by BHTTC, example: <**me kw'élh ta' sqó:s.**>, //mə k'^{w}ə́ɬ t-ɛʔ s=qá·=əs//, /*'Tears streaming down your face.'*/, literally /'start(ing)/come/coming to flow/spill your tear on the face'/, attested by BHTTC.

<**sqeqó:qel**>, df //s=C_1ə=qá·=qəl//, WATR [*'(clean) pond (even if dry)'*], (<**s=**> *nominalizer*), possibly <**R5=**> *resultative, diminutive, or plural*, lx <**=qel**> *in the head, at the source (of a river/creek)*, phonology: reduplication, syntactic analysis: nominal, attested by AC.

<**qó:tsó:m**>, cpds //qá·=cá·m//, ANA [*'blister'*], literally /'water skin(ned)'/, root <**qó:**> *water*, root <**tsó:m**> *get skinned*, syntactic analysis: intransitive verb?, nominal?, attested by NP (10/26/75).

<**sqe'éleqw**>, df //s=qaʔ=ə́ləq^{w}//, EB [*'fruit juice'*], FOOD, (<**s=**> *nominalizer*), probably <**=éleqw**> *on top of the head*, perhaps here *on top of round thing/fruit*, phonology: vowel-reduction to schwa-grade of root before stressed suffix, glottal stop replaces length in allomorph of qó:, syntactic analysis: nominal, attested by IHTTC, also <**sqe'óleqw**> attested by RG,EH 6/16/98 to SN, edited by BG with RG,EH 6/26/00)

<**kwúkwewels sqe'óleqw** (or better: **qwemchó:ls sqe'óleqw**)>, FOOD *cranberry juice* (lit. highbush cranberry + fruit juice (or better:) bog cranberry + fruit juice), (attested by RG,EH 6/16/98 to SN, edited by BG with RG,EH 6/26/00)

<**q'éx̲q'ex̲el sqe'óleqw**>, FOOD *soda pop* (lit. perhaps: bubbling and fizzy/perhaps: metal can + fruit juice), (attested by RG,EH 6/16/98 to SN, edited by BG with RG,EH 6/26/00)

<**qelíps sqe'óleqw**>, FOOD *grape juice* (lit. grape + fruit juice), (attested by RG,EH 6/16/98 to SN, edited by BG with RG,EH 6/26/00)

<**qwe'óp sqe'óleqw**>, FOOD *apple juice* (lit. apple + fruit juice), (attested by RG,EH 6/16/98 to SN, edited by BG with RG,EH 6/26/00)

<**qwíyqwòyèls sqe'óleqw**>, FOOD *orange juice* (lit. orange + fruit juice), (attested by RG,EH 6/16/98 to SN, edited by BG with RG,EH 6/26/00)

<**s'óytheqw sqe'óleqw**>, FOOD *raspberry juice* (lit. raspberry + fruit juice), (attested by RG,EH 6/16/98 to SN, edited by BG with RG,EH 6/26/00)

<**sásex̲em qwíyqwòyèls sqe'óleqw**>, FOOD *grapefruit juice* (lit. grapefruit [itself bitter + yellow fruit] + fruit juice), (attested by RG,EH 6/16/98 to SN, edited by BG with RG,EH 6/26/00)

<**schíya sqe'óleqw**>, FOOD *strawberry juice* (lit. strawberry + fruit juice), (attested by RG,EH 6/16/98 to SN, edited by BG with RG,EH 6/26/00)

<**smómeleqw spíls s'élhtel sqe'óleqw**>, FOOD *V8 juice* (lit. mixed + planted + food + fruit juice), (attested by RG,EH 6/16/98 to SN, edited by BG with RG,EH 6/26/00)

<**spíls s'élhtel sqe'óleqw**>, FOOD *vegetable juice* (lit. planted + food + fruit juice), (attested by RG,EH 6/16/98 to SN, edited by BG with RG,EH 6/26/00)

<**sqw'ő:lmexw sqe'óleqw**>, FOOD *blackberry juice* (lit. blackberry + fruit juice), (attested by RG,EH 6/16/98 to SN, edited by BG with RG,EH 6/26/00)

<**st'elt'elíqw qwe'óp sqe'óleqw**>, FOOD *pineapple juice* (lit. pineapple [itself from bumpy and prickly + apple] + fruit juice), (attested by RG,EH 6/16/98 to SN, edited by BG with RG,EH 6/26/00)

<**sth'í:m sqe'óleqw**>, FOOD *berry juice* (lit. berry + fruit juice), (attested by RG,EH 6/16/98 to SN, edited by BG with RG,EH 6/26/00)

<**sx̲wő́sem sqe'óleqw**>, FOOD *soapberry juice* (lit. soapberry + fruit juice), (attested by RG,EH 6/16/98 to SN, edited by BG with RG,EH 6/26/00)

<**t'át'ets'em qwíyqwòyèls qas te t'át'ets'em tsqwáyqwòyèls sqe'óleqw**>, FOOD *lemonlime juice* (lit. lemon fruit [itself < sour little yellowish fruit] + and + the + lime fruit [itself < sour + greenish fruit]+ fruit juice), (attested by RG,EH 6/16/98 to SN, edited by BG with RG,EH 6/26/00)

<**t'át'ets'em qwíyqwòyèls sqe'óleqw**>, FOOD *lemonade* (lit. lemon [itself < sour little yellow fruit] + fruit juice), (attested by RG,EH 6/16/98 to SN, edited by BG with RG,EH 6/26/00)

<**temítō sqe'óleqw**>, FOOD *tomato juice* (lit. tomato + fruit juice), (attested by RG,EH 6/16/98 to SN, edited by BG with RG,EH 6/26/00)

<**xáweq sqe'óleqw**>, FOOD *carrot juice* (lit. carrot + fruit juice), (attested by RG,EH 6/16/98 to SN, edited by BG with RG,EH 6/26/00)

<**sqe'óleqw**>, df //s=qəʔ=áləqʷ or s=qáʔ=ə[=M2=]ləqʷ//, FOOD ['*soda pop*'], ACL, Elder's comment: "now used for *soda pop*", possibly <**=óleqw**> meaning unclear or metathesis> *derivational* possibly plus <**=eleqw**> *on top of the head*, phonology: possible metathesis or allomorph qe', syntactic analysis: nominal, attested by AD (1/15/79).

<**qe'ó:les**>, ds //qəʔ=á·ləs//, ANA ['*tear (from eye)*'], literally /'water in the eye'/, root <**qó: ~ qe'**> *water*, lx <**=ó:les**> *in the eye*, phonology: allomorph, syntactic analysis: nominal, noun, attested by AC.

<**qo'qo'ólésem**>, mdls //C1V1C2=qaʔ=áləs=əm//, ABFC ['*one's eyes are watering*'], (<**C1V1C2=**> perhaps //**R13=**// *plural continuative*), root <**qó'**> *water*, lx <**=óles**> *in the eye*, (<**=em**> *middle voice*), phonology: a downriver Halkomelem reduplication type and the downriver root form qó' instead of upriver qó:, updrifting on penultimate syllable, syntactic analysis: intransitive verb, dialects: *Matsqui*, attested by AH and LG (Deming 5/8/80); found in <**qo'qo'ólésemtsel.**>, //$C_1V_1C_2$=qaʔ=áləs=əm-c-əl//, /'*My eyes are watering.*'/, dialects: *Matsqui*.

<**sqe'ó:ls**>, ds //s=qəʔ=á·ls//, EB ['*juicy fruit*'], FOOD, (<**s=**> *nominalizer*), root <**qó: ~ qe'**> *water*, lx <**=ó:ls**> *fruit*, phonology: allomorph, syntactic analysis: nominal, attested by Elders Group (8/20/75).

<**qe'ó:ythel**>, ds //qəʔ=á·yθəl//, WATR ['*liquid in the mouth*'], ABFC, root <**qó: ~ qe'**> *water*, lx <**=ó:ythel**> *on the lips, on the jaw/chin*, phonology: allomorph, syntactic analysis: nominal?, intransitive verb?, attested by IHTTC.

<**qe'álts ~ qiqe'álts**>, df //qəʔ=ɛ́lc ~ C_1í=qəʔ=ɛ́lc//, EFAM /'*easy to cry, (cries easily)*'/, (<**R4=**> *diminutive*), possibly <**=álts**> meaning uncertain, Elder's comment: "not qiqe=álets (/qi=R1=ɛ́ləc/) which would be *soft rump*", phonology: reduplication, syntactic analysis: adjective/adjectival verb, attested by Elders Group (3/6/77).

<**qó:lem**>, WATR /'*to scoop, to dip, dip water*'/, *see* qó:.

<**qó:lets**>, FSH /'*to dip-net, a dip-net*'/, *see* qó:.

<**qó:lt**>, WATR ['*scoop s-th*'], *see* qó:.

<**qó:lhcha**>, FOOD ['*juice*'], *see* qó:.

<**qó:lhthet**>, EB ['*get juicy of its own accord*'], *see* qó:.

<**qó:m**>, WATR /'*to dip water, get water, fetch water, pack water*'/, *see* qó:.

<**qó:mthet**>, WATR ['*still (of water)*'], *see* qám.

<**qó:qe**>, ABFC ['*to drink*'], *see* qó:.

<**qóqelem**>, WATR ['*dipping water*'], *see* qó:.

<**qóqelets**>, FSH /'*to dip a net, (dipping a net)*'/, *see* qó:.

<**qó:qet**>, ABFC ['*drink s-th*'], *see* qó:.

<**Qoqoláx̲el**>, PLN /'*Watery Eaves, a famous longhouse and early village on a flat area on Chilliwack River just a quarter mile upriver/east above Vedder Crossing*'/, *see* qó:.

<**qot**>, bound root, meaning unknown

<**sqotemí:lep ~ sqoteméylep**>, df //s=qat(=)əm=í·ləp//, LAND /'*steep hill, sloping ground*'/, (<**s=**> *nominalizer*), root meaning unknown, lx <**=í:lep**> *ground, earth, dirt*, syntactic analysis: nominal, attested by Elders Group (4/2/75). also <**sqotemílep**>, df //s(=)qat(=)əm=íləp//, LAND ['*hill*'], possibly <**s=**> *nominalizer*, possibly <**=em**> *intransitivizer, get, have*, root meaning unknown, lx <**=ílep**> *dirt, earth, ground*, syntactic analysis: nominal, attested by Elders Group (3/15/72).

<**qó:tsó:m**>, ANA ['*blister*'], *see* qó:.

<**qowletsá:ls**>, HHG /'*water kettle, boiler pan (for canning, washing clothes or dishes)*'/, *see* qew.

<**qówletst**>, ABFC ['*warm it up (on the bottom)*'], *see* qew.

<**qoy**>, bound root, meaning unkonwn

<**sqoyép**>, df //s(=)qay(=)ə́p//, EZ /'EZ /'*yellow badger,* possibly *wolverine*'/, ['*Taxidea taxus taxus*, possibly *Gulo luscus luscus*'], ASM ['wolverine is probably in error here'], Elder's comment: "this animal got hit on the face in a story [of the Transformer age, time of X̲à:ls] and the marks stayed", possibly <**s=**> *nominalizer*, possibly <**=ép**> *on the ground, dirt, ground*, root meaning unknown, syntactic analysis: nominal, attested by AK and ME (11/21/72 tape), IHTTC.

<**melmélkw'es sqoyép**>, cpds //C_1əC_2=mə́lk'^{w}=əs s=qay(=)ə́p//, EZ ['*yellow badger or wolverine*'], ['*Taxidea taxus taxus* or *Gulo luscus luscus*'], literally /'hit repeatedly (by things falling) on the face'/, ASM ['this animal got it on the face in a story and the marks stayed'], (<**R3=**> *plural (action or agent)*), root <**mélkw'**> *hit (by s-th falling)*, lx <**=es**> *on the face*, compare <**xw=mélkw'=es**> *hit in the face*, phonology: reduplication, syntactic analysis: simple nominal phrase, attested by AK (11/21/72 tape), also <**skoyám**>, //s=kay(=)ɛ́m//, also /'*wolverine*'/, EZ, ['*Gulo luscus luscus*'], dialects: *Tait*.

<**sqoyép**>, df //s(=)qay(=)ə́p//, SPRD /'*a spirit power of a kw'ō̆xweqs dancer, (*perhaps *wolverine or badger spirit power)*'/, ASM ['this power caused a dancer to gash himself, eat small dogs, etc. (confirming that the power is ferocious, perhaps like the wolverine or badger) but has not been found in recent years (Hill-Tout, Duff, Jenness, Galloway 1979)'], literally probably /'badger or wolverine'/, syntactic analysis: nominal, attested by Elders Group (10/13/76), Salish cognate: Squamish /sqíəp/ *perform a dance characterized by the use of a rattle* W73:74, K69:59.

<**qo'qo'ólésem**>, ABFC ['*one's eyes are watering*'], *see* qó:.

<**qp'á:letset**>, HHG ['*cover it (s-th open)*'], *see* qep'.

<**qp'á:letstel**>, HHG /'*a cover, lid*'/, *see* qep'.

<**qp'á:qet**>, HHG /'*close s-th (for ex. a box), put a lid on s-th (for ex. a pot), cover it with a lid*'/, *see* qep'.

<**qsí:l**>, ABDF ['*tired out*'], *see* qásel.

<**qsí:lthet**>, ABDF ['*tired out from crying*'], *see* qásel.

<**qx̲álets**>, NUM ['*a lot of people*'], *see* qéx̲.

<**qx̲álh**>, NUM ['*lots of times*'], *see* qéx̲.

<**qx̲ó:s**>, NUM /'*lots of money, (many dollars)*'/, *see* qéx̲.

Q'

<**=q'**>, da //=q'//, DIR /'*on something else, within something else*'/, TIB; found in <**q'elq'élq'**>, //C_1əC_2=q'ə́l=q'//, /'*tangled on s-th else, snagged (as a net on a log or branch)*'/, <**q'elq'élq't**>, //C_1əC_2=q'ə́l=q'=t//, /'*coil it*'/, <**x̲éyq'et**>, //x̣ɛ́y=q'=ət//, /'*scratch it (to itch it)*'/ (compare with <**x̲éy=m=et**> *grab it*).

<**q'a ~ qa ~ qe**>, free root //q'ɛ ~ qɛ ~ qə//, CJ ['*or*'], syntactic analysis: conjunction, attested by AC, example: <**lí chòkw te lálems q'a lí stetís? ~ lí chòkw te lálems qa lí stetís?**>, //lí cákʷ tə lɛ́ləm-s q'ɛ/qɛ lí s=tə[=C_1əAí=]s//, /'*Is his house far or is it nearby?*'/, attested by AC, <**tsel má:ythome kw'e tseláqelhelh qe lhulhá.**>, //c-əl mɛ́·y=T-ámə k'ʷə cəlɛ́q=əɬ=əɬ qə ɬuɬɛ́//, /'*I helped you yesterday or the day before yesterday.*'/, attested by AC.

<**q'á:l**>, free root //q'ɛ·l//, EFAM ['*believe*'], syntactic analysis: intransitive verb, attested by Elders Group, AC, EB, example: <**skw'áy kw'els q'á:l kwes lúwes.**>, //s=k'ʷɛ́y k'ʷ-əl-s q'ɛ·l kʷə-s lúwə-s//, /'*I couldn't believe it was you.*'/, literally /'it can't be that -I -subordinate nominalizer believe thst -subordinate nominalizer is you -it (third person subord. subject)'/, attested by AC, <**ō̃welhtsellh q'à:l.**>, //ʔówə=ɬ-c-əl-ɬ q'ɛ̀·l//, /'*I don't/didn't believe.*'/, Elder's comment: "there's no word for doubt", attested by EB.

<**q'áq'el**>, cts //q'ɛ́[-C_1ə-]l//, EFAM ['*believing*'], (<**-R1-**> *continuative*), phonology: reduplication, syntactic analysis: intransitive verb, attested by Elders Group.

<**lheq'él:exw ~ lhq'él:exw ~ lhq'élexw**>, ncs //ɬ(ə)=q'ɛ[=Aə́=]l=l-əxʷ//, EFAM /'*know s-th, know s-o*'/, (<**lhe= ~ lh=**> *use, extract, extract a portion*), root <**q'á:l**> *believe*, (<**=l**> *non-control transitivizer, accidentally, happen to, manage to*, é-ablaut *resultative* or *durative*), (<**-exw**> *third person object*), phonology: consonant merger, ablaut, syntactic analysis: transitive verb, dialects: *Cheh., Tait*, attested by IHTTC, EB, AC, JL, other sources: ES /ɬəq'ə́l·əxʷ/ *know*, also <**slhéq'el:exw ~ lhéq'el:exw ~ slhéq'elexw**>, //s=ɬə=´=q'ɛl=l-əxʷ ~ ɬə=´=q'ɛl=l-əxʷ//, (<**s=**> *stative*, lhe= *use, extract, extrct a portion*), (<**= ´= (stress-shift)**> *derivational*), phonology: vowel-reduction to schwa-grade in root after stress-shift, dialects: *Chill.*, attested by IHTTC, AC, JL, also <**slhéq'awelh ~ slhéq'ewelh**>, //s=ɬə=´=q'ɛl=wəɬ//, dialects: *Pilalt (Chilliwack town) and Chill. (Sardis)*, prob. with <**=ulh ~ =welh**> *already*, attested by EB, AC; example: <**líchxw lheq'él:exw?**>, //lí-c-xʷ ɬə=q'ɛ[=Aə́=]l=l-əxʷ//, /'*Do you know?, (Do you know it?)*'/, attested by AC; found in <**lhéq'el:exwtsel.**>, //ɬə=´=q'ɛl=l-əxʷ-c-əl//, /'*I know.*'/, example: <**líchexw slhéq'awelh kw'as ch'eqw'ō̃welh?**>, //lí-c-əxʷ s=ɬə=´=q'ɛl=əwəɬ k'ʷ-ɛ-s c'əq'ʷ=ówəɬ//, /'*Do you know how to make a basket?*'/, attested by AC, <**qe ōwétal slhéq'elexw; tsel we xwlálá: el.**>, //qə ʔowə=´tɛ-l s-ɬə=´=q'ɛl=l-əxʷ; c-əl əw xʷlɛ́lɛ́· ʔəl//, /'*I didn't know/understand; I just listened.*'/, attested by AC, <**ōwétal slhéq'elexw.**>, //ʔowə=´tɛ-l s-ɬə=´=q'ɛl=l-əxʷ//, /'*I don't know.*'/, attested by AC, <**ōwéta slhéq'el:exwes.**>, //ʔowə=´tɛ s-ɬə=´=q'ɛl=l-əxʷ-əs//, /'*She doesn't know.*'/, attested by AC, <**tsel slhéq'elexw (kwses spá:th, kws spá:ths).**>, //c-əl s=ɬə=´=q'ɛl=l-əxʷ (kʷ-s-əs s=pɛ́·θ, kʷ-s s=pá·θ-s)//, /'*I know it was a bear.*'/, attested by AC, <**ōwéta slhéq'elexw wetemtámescha kw'es álhtelchet qelát.**>, //ʔowə=´tɛ s=ɬə=´=q'ɛl=l-əxʷ wə-təm=tɛ́m-əs-cɛ k'ʷə-s ʔi[=Aɛ́=]ɬ=təl-c-ət qəlɛ́t//, /'*No-one knows when we'll be able to eat again.*'/, literally /'nobody knows it when/if- time= is what -it (subjunctive) -will be/future that -subord.cl. eat meal -we again.'/, usage: story of the Flood, attested by AC, <**ōwéta slhéq'elexw te skwíxs te "cave".**>, //ʔowə=´tɛ s=ɬə=´=q'ɛl=l-əxʷ tə s=kʷíxʸ-s tə "cave"//, /'*Nobody knows the cave's name., (Nobody knows the name of the cave.)*'/, usage: story of the Flood, attested by AC, <**chel we lhq'élexw westámes kw'e le kwú:tes.**>, //c-əl wə

ɬ=q'ɛ[=Aə́=]l=l-əxʷ wə-s=tə́m-əs k'ʷə lə kʷú·=T-əs//, /'*I know what he took.*'/, literally /'non-subord.subj.- I contrastive know it if- is what -it (subjunct. subject) what (the (remote)) third person past he takes it'/, attested by EB, <**(chel we, chu) lhq'élexw wetewátes kw'e x̱t'ástxw tethá.**>, //(c-əl wə, c(-əl)-u) ɬ=q'ɛ[=Aə́=]l=l-əxʷ wə-tə=wə́t-əs k'ʷə x̣t'ɛ́=sT-əxʷ tə=θɛ́//, /'*I know who did it.*'/, literally /'I contrastive know it if/when- is who -3subj. that do s-th that'/, attested by EB, <**wétal slhéq'ewelh**>, //ʔowə= ́tɛ-l s=ɬə= ́=q'ɛl=wəɬ//, /'*I don't know.*'/, dialects: *Pilalt and Chill. (Chilliwack and Sardis)*, attested by EB (5/18/76), <**wétal lhq'élexw**>, //ʔəwə= ́tɛ-l ɬ=q'ə[=Aə́=]l=l-əxʷ//, /'*I don't know.*'/, dialects: *Cheh.*, attested by EB, <**líchxw lhq'él:àx?**>, //lí-c-xʷ ɬ=q'ɛ[=Aə́=]l=l-áxʸ//, /'*Do you know me?*'/, dialects: *Cheh., Tait*, attested by IHTTC, also <**líchxw slhéq'el:òx?**>, //lí-c-xʷ s=ɬə= ́=q'ɛl=l-áxʸ//, dialects: *Chill.*, attested by IHTTC (8/8/77).

<**lheq'elómet**>, ncrs //ɬə=q'ɛl=l-ámət//, EFAM /'*know oneself, be confident*'/, (<**-ómet**> *reflexive*), phonology: consonant merger, vowel-reduction to schwa-grade of root from stress-shift to affix, syntactic analysis: intransitive verb, attested by Elders Group (4/6/77), also <**slheq'el:ó:met**>, //s=ɬə=q'ɛl=l-á·mət//, also /'*understand*'/, phonology: consonant merger, dialects: *Chill.*, attested by AC (10/8/71), example: <**ŏwetsel líl slheq'el:ó:met**>, //ʔówə-c-əl lí-l s=ɬə=q'ɛl=l-á·mət//, /'*I don't understand.*'/, attested by AC.

<**q'élmet**>, iecs //q'ɛ[=Aə́=]l=məT//, EFAM /'*believe s-o, trust s-o*'/, (<**é-ablaut**> *non-continuative*), (<**=met**> *indirect effect control transitivizer*), phonology: ablaut, syntactic analysis: transitive verb, attested by Elders Group (2/16/77, 2/8/78), AC, example: <**ŏwetsellh q'élmethóme.**>, //ʔówə-c-əl-ɬ q'ɛ[=Aə́=]l=məT-ámə//, /'*I don't (didn't) believe you.*'/, attested by AC.

<**q'áq'elmet**>, cts //q'ɛ́[-C₁ə-]l=məT//, EFAM ['*believing s-o*'], (<**-R1-**> *continuative*), phonology: reduplication, syntactic analysis: transitive verb, attested by Elders Group (2/8/78).

<**q'elstá:xw**>, caus //q'ɛl=sT-ə[=Aɛ́·=]xʷ//, durs, EFAM /'*fool s-o, deceive s-o, (lie to s-o [SJ])*'/, (<**=st**> *causative control transitivizer*), probably <**á:-ablaut on suffix**> *durative* or possibly to dissimilate from <**q'élstexw**> *return it, bring it back, give it back* which has root <**q'ó:**> *together* or possibly <**q'ál**> *go over/around, go back on oneself, coil*, (<**-exw**> *third person object*), phonology: ablaut, syntactic analysis: transitive verb, attested by EB, Deming, also /'*lie to s-o*'/, attested by SJ (Deming 4/27/78), example: <**tsel q'elstá:xw.**>, //c-əl q'ɛl=sT-ə[=Aɛ́·=]xʷ//, /'*I fooled him.*'/, attested by EB; found in <**q'elstá:xwes.**>, //q'ɛl=sT-ə[=Aɛ́·=]xʷ-əs//, /'*He fooled someone.*'/, attested by EB, example: <**q'elstá:xwes qesu q'á:l.**>, //q'ɛl=sT-ə[=Aɛ́·=]xʷ-əs qə=s=u q'ɛ́·l//, /'*He fooled him and he believed.*'/, attested by EB, <**q'elstá:xwes á:lhtel te Lawéchten.**>, //q'ɛl=sT-ə[=Aɛ́·=]xʷ-əs ʔɛ́·ɬtəl tə lɛw(=)ə́c=tən//, /'*They fooled Lawéchten., They lied to Lawéchten.*'/, comment: Lawéchten is a Nooksack language proper name; Charlie Lewiston, an Indian doctor from the area of Nooksack, Wash., had that name till his death ca. 1920 (pronounced by non-Indians as Lewiston); the name was formally passed to Brent Galloway by Alice Hunt (AH) and Louisa George (LG) at a naming ceremony 10/9/77 at Chehalis, B.C.), attested by Deming (4/27/78); found in <**q'elstá:xwesthòx**>, //q'ɛl=sT-ə[=Aɛ́·=]xʷ=sT-áxʸ//, (irregular), comment: in this form =stá:xw is used as part of the root and a second causative =st is added, then the object pronoun suffix -òx *me*; it is not clear whether this is an error or is required and allowed to maintain the root vowel shifted into =stá:xw; normally the -exw is present only when a third person object is intended (even if it is reanalyzed and considered part of the causative and and non-control suffixes, as =stexw and =lexw, as do Suttles and Hukari in other dialects of Halkomelem); but here both the e (though moved) and the xw are retained with the third person object superceded by the -òx *second person singular object* suffix, phonology: the last vowel has stress downstepped to `, attested by Deming (4/27/78).

<**q'íq'elstá:xw**>, cts and dmv //C₁í=q'ɛl=sT-ə[=Aɛ́·=]xʷ//, EFAM /'*fooling s-o, (fool s-o as a joke, April-fool s-o [Deming])*'/, attested by Deming (2/7/80), (<**R4=**> *diminutive continuative*), phonology: reduplication, metathesis or ablaut plus vowel-reduction, morphological note:

causative durative and diminutive continuative, syntactic analysis: transitive verb, attested by Elders Group (3/29/78), also <**q'íq'elstaxw**>, //C_1í=q'ɛl=sT-ə[=Aɛ=]xʷ//, [q'éq'əlstʊxʷ], also /*'fool s-o as a joke, April-fool s-o'*/, (<**R4=**> *diminutive*), morphological note: causative durative diminutive, attested by Deming (2/7/80); found in <**q'éyq'elsthome**>, //C_1í=q'ɛl=sT-ámə//, /*'to April-fool you'*/, attested by Deming, <**q'íq'elsthòm.**>, //C_1í=q'ɛl=sT-àm//, /*'You're being fooled.'*/, attested by Elders Group (3/29/78).

<**q'ál**>, free root //q'ɛ́l//, TVMO /*'go over or around (hill, rock, river, etc.)'*/, syntactic analysis: intransitive verb, attested by SP and AK and perhaps AD (Elders on American Bar trip 6/26/78).

<**sq'elá:w**>, strs //s=q'ɛl=ə[=M2=]w or s=q'ɛl=ɛ́·w//, strs, ABFC [*'be coiled (ready to strike for ex. of a snake)'*], (<**s=**> *stative*), (possible <**metathesis**> *resultative* + <**=ew**> on the body, or lx <**=á:w**> variant of <**=í:ws ~ =ews**> *on the body*, see under <=**á:w**>, phonology: metathesis or vowel-reduction, lengthening, consonant-loss (another example of this loss of s on <=í:ws ~ =ews> *on the body* is shown in <q'álq'elp'í:w> *inchworm*), syntactic analysis: adjective/adjectival verb, attested by CT and HT (6/8/76), Elders Group (6/16/76), example: <**sq'elá:w te álhqey.**>, //s=q'ɛl=ə[=M2=]w tə ʔɛ́ɬqəy//, /*'The snake is coiled (ready to strike).'*/, attested by CT and HT.

<**sq'elq'elá:w**>, plv or chrs //s=C_1əC_2=q'ɛ́l=ə[=M2=]w or s=q'ɛl=C_1əC_2=ɛ́·w//, ABFC [*'(be) coiling (ready to strike) (of a snake)'*], (<**s=**> *stative*, R3= *plural (action)* or =R2 *characteristic*), phonology: reduplication, metathesis, consonant-loss, syntactic analysis: adjective/adjectival verb, attested by CT and HT.

<**q'alq'elő:wsem**>, chrs //q'ɛl=C_1əC_2=ó·ws=əm//, dnom, EZ /*'inchworm, (caterpillar of the geometrid moth family)'*/, ['order *Lepidoptera*, caterpillar of family *Geometridae*'], (<**=R3**> *characteristic*, <**=em**> *middle voice*), lx <**=ő:ws ~ =í:ws ~ =ews**> *on the body*, phonology: reduplication, syntactic analysis: nominal, attested by BHTTC (8/31/76), also <**q'alq'elp'í:w**>, //q'ɛl=C_1əC_2=p'=í·w//, attested by SP.

<**q'eléx̲el**>, rsls //q'ɛl=ɛ[=Aə́=]x̣əl or q'ɛ[=Aə=]l=ə́x̣əl//, dnom, CSTR [*'fence'*], literally probably /'go around/over side (construction)'/, lx <**=áx̲el**> *side (usu. of something on land, esp. buildings)*, (<**é-ablaut**> *resultative* or derivational), phonology: ablaut, vowel-reduction to schwa-grade of root before stressed affix, syntactic analysis: nominal, attested by EB, Salish cognate: Squamish /q'iáx̣an/ *fence, stockade, fortification* W73:98, K67:359, K69:82.

<**q'eléx̲elt**>, pcs //q'ɛl=ɛ[=Aə́=]x̣əl=T//, CSTR [*'fence s-th in'*], (<**=t**> *purposeful control transitivizer*), phonology: ablaut, vowel-reduction, syntactic analysis: transitive verb, attested by EB (4/25/78), Salish cognate: Squamish /q'iáx̣an-n/ *fence in (tr.)* may contain /=áx̣an/ *side* W73:98, K67:357, example: <**le q'eléx̲elt(es) te steliqíw.**>, //lə q'ɛl=ɛ[=Aə́=]x̣əl=T(-əs) tə s=t[=əl=]iqíw//, /*'He fenced the horses in.'*/.

<**q'elx̲á:lt**>, pcs //q'ɛl=ɛ́x̣[=M1=]əl=T//, CSTR [*'fence it'*], (<**metathesis type 1**> *non-continuative*), phonology: metathesis, vowel merger (á + e -> á:), syntactic analysis: transitive verb, attested by IHTTC, comment: may be a variant with q'eléx̲elt.

<**sq'eláx̲el**>, strs //s=q'ɛ[=Aə=]l=ɛ́x̣əl or s=q'ɛ́l=ə[=M2=]x̣əl//, CSTR [*'(be) fenced in'*], (<**s=**> *stative*), (<**e-ablaut** or **metathesis**> *resultative*), lx <**=áx̲el ~ =ex̲el**> *side*, phonology: ablaut or metathesis, syntactic analysis: adjective/adjectival verb, attested by EB.

<**Q'alelíktel**>, df //q'ɛl=əlík=təl or q'ɛl=əlíkʷ=U=təl or q'ɛl=əlíq=K=təl//, PLN /*'village on east bank of Fraser River below Siwash Creek (Aseláw), now Yale Indian Reserves 19 and 20, named because of a big rock in the area that the trail had to pass (go around), also the name of the rock'*/, Elder's comment: literally /'going up and over on a trail, going up and around on a trail'/, possibly <**=elík**> meaning uncertain unless cognate with Lushootseed /-alikʷ/> *creative activity* <(H76:9) or with Samish **/-ənəkʷ/** *ground* (G86:56), **<=U (unrounding)**> *derivational* possibly <**=K (fronting)**>

diminutive, lx <**=tel**> *something to, device to* or perhaps *reciprocal*, phonology: possibly unrounding (delabialization) or fronting, syntactic analysis: nominal, attested by AD or SP (6/26/78), SP and AK (8/2/77), IHTTC (8/11/77), other sources: Wells 1965 (lst ed.):25, source: place names reference file #141, also PLN /'*Lake of the Woods (small lake across the Fraser R. from Hope, B.C.)*'/, ASM ['perhaps so named ("go up and over on a trail") because from the river one had to go over the hill, past Q'ów (Mt.) and down onto the other side by the Fraser River again, probably a trail passed here between Haig and Hope Indian Reserve #12'], attested by Elders Group (7/6/77), SP and AK (8/2/77), source: place names reference file #1.

<**sq'álq'**>, stvi //s=q'ɛ́l=q'//, DESC ['*be tangled (on something)*'], (<**s=**> *stative*), lx <**=q'**> *on something else*, syntactic analysis: adjective/adjectival verb, attested by CT, example: <**sq'álq' te álhqey.**>, //s=q'ɛ́l=q' tə ʔɛ́ɬqəy//, /'*The snake is tangled.*'/, attested by CT (6/8/76).

<**sq'á:lq'**>, ds //s=q'ɛ́[=·=]l=q'//, DESC /'*be really tangled, it's really tangled*'/, semantic environment ['said when pulling to untangle a net stuck on something, for ex.'], (<**=:=**> *augmentative, emphatic*), phonology: lengthening, syntactic analysis: adjective/adjectival verb, attested by EB.

<**q'elq'élq'**>, plv //C_1əC_2=q'ɛ[=Aə́=]l=q'//, DESC /'*snagged, tangled on something, something gets tangled up (like a net)*'/, semantic environment ['of net, yarn, hair, or anything'], lx <**=q'**> *on something else*, (<**R3=**> *plural (action)*), possibly <**é-ablaut**> *resultative*, phonology: reduplication, possible ablaut, syntactic analysis: adjective/adjectival verb, attested by EB (5/21/76, 2/6/76), Salish cognate: Squamish /q'əl-q'lq'/ *get tangled up, get tangled around* W73:262, K69:80, example: <**q'elq'élq' te swéltel.**>, //C_1əC_2=q'ɛ[=Aə́=]l=q' tə s=wə́l=təl//, /'*The net got tangled.*'/, attested by EB.

<**q'élq't**>, pcs //q'ɛ[=Aə́=]l=q'=T//, TVMO /'*coil it, wind it up (of string, rope, yarn)*'/, semantic environment ['of something coilable, i.e. long and flexible'], lx <**=q'**> *on something else*, (<**=t**> *purposeful control transitivizer*), phonology: possible ablaut, syntactic analysis: transitive verb, attested by CT and HT, Elders Group, example: <**q'élq't te x̱wéylem**>, //q'ɛ[=Aə́=]l=q'=T tə x̣ʷíləm//, /'*wind up the rope, coil the rope*'/, attested by CT and HT, Elders Group, <**q'élq't te sá:y**>, //q'ɛ[=Aə́=]l=q'=T tə sɛ́·y//, /'*wind up the yarn*'/, attested by CT and HT.

<**q'élq'xetel**>, ds //q'ɛ[=Aə́=]l=q'=xʸə(l)=təl//, CLO /'*rags wound around the legs in the cold or to protect from mosquitoes, (leggings)*'/, possibly <**é-ablaut**> *resultative*, lx <**=q'**> *on something else*, lx <**=xel**> **(~** <**=xe**> before <**=t** or **=tel**>**)** *on the leg*, lx <**=tel**> *device to, thing to*, phonology: probably ablaut, consonant-loss (predictable, conditioned), syntactic analysis: nominal.

<**q'elq'élp'**>, plv //C_1əC_2=q'ɛ[=Aə́=]l=p'//, DESC ['*tangled on its own/itself*'], semantic environment ['of net, hair, yarn, anything'], (<**R3=**> *plural action*), (<**é-ablaut**> *resultative*), (<**=p'**> *on itself*), phonology: reduplication, probable ablaut, syntactic analysis: adjective/adjectival verb, attested by EB (5/25/76).

<**sq'elq'élp'eqw**>, df //s=C_1əC_2=q'ɛ[=Aə́=]l=p'=əqʷ//, ANA /'*curly hair, (be curly-haired(?), have curly hair(?))*'/, possibly <**s=**> *nominalizer or stative*, possibly <**é-ablaut**> *resultative*?, (<**R3=**> *plural (patient)*), lx <**=p'**> *on itself*, lx <**=eqw**> *on the hair, on top of the head*, phonology: reduplication, possible ablaut, attested by Deming, EB, Elders Group.

<**sq'ó:lp'eqw**>, ds //s=q'ɛ[=Aá·=]l=p'=əqʷ//, ANA /'*curly hair, (have curly hair(?))*'/, possibly <**s=**> *nominalizer or stative*, (<**ó:-ablaut on root a**> *durative*), lx <**=p'**> *on itself*, lx <**=eqw**> *on the hair, on top of the head*, phonology: ó:-ablaut on root a, syntactic analysis: nominal?, adjective/adjectival verb??, attested by EB (5/25/76).

<**sq'elq'élp'es**>, ds //s=C_1əC_2=q'ɛ[=Aə́=]l=p'=əs//, ANA /'*curly hair, (have curly hair(?))*'/, possibly <**s=**> *nominalizer or stative*, possibly <**é-ablaut**> *resultative*, (<**R3=**> *plural (patient)*), lx <**=p'**> *on itself*, lx <**=es**> *on the face*, phonology: reduplication, ablaut, syntactic analysis: nominal?,

adjective/adjectival verb?, attested by Deming.

<q'álq'elp'í:w>, chrs //q'ɛl=C_1əC_2=í·w(s)//, EZ /'*inchworm, (caterpillar of the geometrid moth family)*'/, ['order *Lepidoptera*, caterpillar of the family *Geometridae*'], literally /'characteristically tangling/going up and over on its own body'/, (**<=R2>** *characteristic*), lx **<=í:w(s)>** *on the body*, phonology: reduplication, consonant-loss, syntactic analysis: nominal, attested by Elders Group (9/1/76)(SP or AK?), also **<q'alq'elő:wsem>**, //q'ɛl=C_1əC_2=ó·ws=əm//, attested by BHTTC.

<q'eyq'elts'iyósem>, ds //C_1í=q'ɛl=(l)c'=iyás=əm//, TVMO ['*(whirling)*'], (**<R4=>** *diminutive*), probably root **<q'al>** *coil, go over and around*, lx **<=alts' ~ =(e)lts' ~ =ts'>** *twist, turn around*, lx **<=iyós>** *in a circle*, (**<=em>** *middle voice* or *intransitivizer, have, get*), phonology: reduplication, vowel-reduction, consonant merger, syntactic analysis: adjective/adjectival verb.

<q'eyq'elts'iyósem spehá:ls>, cpds //C_1í=q'ɛl=c'=iyás=əm s=pəh=ɛ́·ls// or /C_1í=q'ə=lc'=iyás=əm s=pəh=ɛ́·ls//, WETH ['*whirlwind*'], first possible derivation literally /'little= going over/around/up and down =twisting/turning around =in a circle =itself wind'/, second possible derivation literally /'little turning back around on itself wind'/, (**<R4=>** *diminutive*, *s= nominalizer*), lx **<=lts'>** *twisting, turning*, lx **<=iyós>** *in a circle*, (**<=em>** *middle voice*, <=á:ls> *structured activity*), phonology: reduplication, syntactic analysis: simple nominal phrase, attested by Elders Group (4/16/75), Deming (3/31/77), also **<skw'elkw'élxel>**, //s=C_1əC_2=k'ʷə́l=xʸəl//, ['*whirlwind*'], attested by Deming (3/31/77).

<Q'alelíktel>, PLN /'*village on east bank of Fraser River below Siwash Creek (Aseláw), now Yale Indian Reserves 19 and 20, named because of a big rock in the area that the trail had to pass (go around), also the name of the rock*'/, *see* q'ál.

<q'á:lemi ~ q'á:lemey>, HAT /'*(young) girls, lots of (adolescent) girls*'/, *see* q'á:mi ~ q'á:miy.

<q'á:lets>, df //q'ɛ́[=·=]l=əc or q'a[=Aɛ́=]·l=əc//, CAN /'*pry with paddle in stern to turn a canoe sharply, pry (canoe stroke done by a sternman)*'/, possibly root **<q'ál>** *go over/around/up and down* or possibly root **<q'ó:l>** *return*, lx **<=ets>** *on the back*, possibly **<=:=>** *derivational* or possibly **<á-ablaut>** *resultative*, phonology: ablaut or lengthening, syntactic analysis: intransitive verb, attested by Deming (2/7/80), also **<q'álets>**, //q'ɛ́l=əc or q'á·[=Aɛ́=]l=əc//, attested by Elders Group (3/26/75).**<q'á:lp'tem>**, ABDF ['*cramped*'], *see* q'élptem ~ q'élp'tem.

<q'alq'elő:wsem>, EZ /'*inchworm, (caterpillar of the geometrid moth family)*'/, *see* q'ál.

<q'álq'elp'í:w>, EZ /'*inchworm, (caterpillar of the geometrid moth family)*'/, *see* q'ál.

<q'á:mi ~ q'á:miy>, df //q'ɛ́·m=iy or q'ɛ́·m=əy// or perhaps better //q'i=m=ɛ́·[=M2=]y//, HAT /'*adolescent virgin girl, young girl (about ten to fifteen years), girl (from ten till she becomes a woman)*'/, possibly **<q'ey ~ q'i>**, bound root //q'əy ~ q'i *wound around, tied, knotted*// + **<=em>** *intransitive, have, get* + possibly **<=i(y) ~ =á:y>** *covering, bark, wool*? + poss. <metathesis> *derivational*, ssemantic note: this etymology is speculative but a similar etymology is confirmed for the word for *woman* **<slhá:lí>** (/'someone that weaves wool/bark'/, **<s=>** *nominalizer, someone to, someone that*), probably root **<lhí:l>** *weave* + **<=i(y) ~ =á:y>** *covering, bark, wool* + <metathesis> *derivational*, Kuipers 1967 proposes the same root for the word in Squamish), syntactic analysis: nominal, noun, attested by AC, CT, EB, Elders Group (3/15/72 and more recent), other sources: ES /q'ɛ́məy/ (MsCw /q'ɛ́məyʔ/) *adolescent virgin girl*, H-T <k·'ámi> (umlaut over a) *maid, maiden, young girl*, example: **<t'ít'elemetes the xwélmexw q'á:mi te pésk'a st'í:lem.>**, //t'í[-C_1ə-]l=əm=məT-əs θə xʷə́lməxʷ q'ɛ́·m=i tə pə́sk'ɛ s=t'íl=əm//, /'*The adolescent Indian girl sings the hummingbird song.*'/, literally /'sing s-th purposely -he/she the (female, present visible) Indian adolescent girl the hummingbird song'/, attested by EB approved this sentence made up by a staff class member.

<**q'á:lemi ~ q'á:lemey**>, pln //q'ɛ́·[=lə=]m=i(y)//, HAT /'*(young) girls, lots of (adolescent) girls*'/, (<**=le=**> *plural*), phonology: infixing, syntactic analysis: nominal, noun, attested by AC, other sources: H-T <k·'álami> (macron/umlaut over a) *maidens, young girls.*

<**q'áq'emi**>, dmn //q'ɛ́·[=C₁ə=]m=i(y)//, HAT /'*little girl (perhaps four years), young girl, (girl from five to ten years [EB])*'/, (<**=R1=**> *diminutive*), phonology: reduplication, syntactic analysis: nominal, noun, attested by AC, Elders Group (3/15/72), also /'*girl (from five to ten years)*'/, attested by EB, other sources: H-T:372, 375 <k·ák·ami> (macron/umlaut over a) *girl (dimin.).*

<**q'eq'elá:mi**>, dmpn //C₁ə=q'[=əl=]ɛ́·m=i(y)//, HAT ['*lots of little girls*'], (<**R5=**> *diminutive*), (<**=el=**> *plural*), phonology: reduplication, infixing, syntactic analysis: nominal, noun, attested by AC, other sources: H-T <k·ak·álami> (macron/umlaut over á) *little girls (collect., dimin.).*

<**q'ám**>, root //q'ɛ́m// meaning uncertain

<**sq'emq'ámth'**>, df //s=C₁əC₂=q'ɛ́m(=)θ'//, DESC ['*(be) wrinkled*'], (<**s=**> *stative*, R3= *plural* or *characteristic*), <**=th'**> *small portion*, phonology: reduplication, syntactic analysis: adjective/adjectival verb, Salish cognate: Lushootseed /q'ibq'ib/ *wrinkled* H76:398.

<**q'áp**>, SOC ['*gathering (of people)*'], *see* q'ép.

<**q'ápels**>, ECON ['*collecting*'], *see* q'ép.

<**q'ápt**> or <**q'ápet**>, HARV /'*collecting s-th, gathering s-th*'/, *see* q'ép.

<**q'áp'**>, free root //q'ɛ́p'//, ABDF /'*contract a disease, catch a disease, get addicted*'/, syntactic analysis: intransitive verb, attested by EB, corr. by AD (12/13/79), Salish cognate: Squamish root /q'ap' ~ q'əp'/ *be seized, catch a disease, included* as in /q'áp'/ *catch a disease*, /q'áp'-an/ *give s-o a disease (tr.)*, /q'áp'-ač-iʔn/ *seize s-o's hand (esp. with mouth or beak)*, and /q'áp'-nəwʔás-n/ *tie together (e.g. the ends of two ropes) (tr.)* K67:356, K69:81, example: <**le q'áp'.**>, //lə q'ɛ́p'//, /'*He contracted a disease., He caught a disease.*'/, attested by EB, corr. by AD.

<**q'ep'lóxes**>, ncs //q'ɛp'=l=áxʸ-əs//, if, ABDF /'*he passes on a disease to s-o, he gets s-o addicted*'/, (<**=l**> *non control transitivizer*), (<**-óx**> *me (object), first person object*, <**-es**> *third person subject*), phonology: vowel-reduction to schwa-grade of root before stressed suffix, syntactic analysis: transitive verb, attested by EB, example: <**le q'ep'lóxes te qél sq'óq'ey.**>, //lə q'ɛp'=l-áxʸ-əs tə qə́l s=q'á[=C₁ə=]y//, /'*He passed on a bad sickness to me.*'/, attested by EB, <**le q'ep'lóxes wiyóthe kwsu háléms ye mímelha.**>, //lə q'ɛp'=l-áxʸ-əs wə=yáθ-ə kʷ-s-u hɛ́-lɛm-s yə mí[-C₁ə-]ɬɛ//, /'*He got me addicted to/hooked on always going to spirit dances.*'/, literally /'third person past he gets me addicted always -just so that -contrastive going to -of the (plural) spirit-dancing'/, attested by EB.

<**q'áp'et ~ q'á:p'et**>, pcs //q'ɛ́p'=əT ~ q'ɛ́·p'=əT//, MC /'*tie it up, bind it, tie it (parcel, broken shovel handle, belt, two ropes together)*'/, MED ['*bandage it*'], (<**=et**> *purposeful control transitivizer*), syntactic analysis: transitive verb, attested by Elders Group (3/1/72, 3/24/76, 1/25/78), EB, AD, Salish cognate: Squamish root /q'ap' ~ q'əp'/ *be seized, catch a disease, included* as in /q'áp'/ *catch a disease*, /q'áp'-an/ *give s-o a disease (tr.)*, /q'áp'-ač-iʔn/ *seize s-o's hand (esp. with mouth or beak)*, and /q'áp'-nəwʔás-n/ *tie together (e.g. the ends of two ropes) (tr.)* K67:356, K69:81, example: <**q'á:p'et ta' yémxetel.**>, //q'ɛ́·p'=əT t-ɛʔ yə́m=xʸə(l)=təl.//, /'*Tie your shoelaces.*'/, attested by AD, also <**q'áp'et ta' yémxetel.**>, //q'ɛ́p'=əT t-ɛʔ yə́m=xʸə(l)=təl//, attested by EB, <**tsel q'á:p'et.**>, //c-əl q'ɛ́·p'=əT//, /'*I bound it up.*'/, attested by Elders Group (3/1/72).

<**q'áq'ep'et**>, cts //q'ɛ́[-C₁ə-]p'=əT//, MC ['*tying it up*'], (<**-R1-**> *continuative*), phonology: reduplication, syntactic analysis: transitive verb, attested by Elders Group (1/25/78).

<**q'áq'ep'els**>, sas //q'ɛ́[-C₁ə-]p'=əls//, cts, MC ['*tying up*'], (<**-R1-**> *continuative*), (<**=els**> *structured activity continuative*), phonology: reduplication, syntactic analysis: intransitive verb, attested by Elders Group (1/25/78).

<**q'ep'eláx̱tel**>, dnom //q'ɛp'=əlɛ́x̣(əl)=təl//, CLO ['*armband*'], literally /'device/something to tie on the arm'/, lx <**=eláx̱el**> *on the arm*, lx <**=tel**> *something to, device to*, phonology: syllable-loss of el before =tel predictably, vowel-reduction, syntactic analysis: nominal, attested by BHTTC.

<**sq'ep'ó:lthetel**>, dnom //s=q'ɛp'=á·lθə(l)=təl//, CLO ['*garter*'], literally /'nominal device/something to tie on the knee'/, (<**s=**> *nominalizer*), lx <**=ó:lthel**> *on the knee*, lx <**=tel**> *something to, device to*, phonology: syllable-loss of el before =tel predictably, vowel-reduction, syntactic analysis: nominal, attested by SP (in IHTTC 9/19/77), contrast <**sq'pólthetel**> *kneecap* (lit. device/something to gather together on the knee).

<**q'ép'xetel**> (unless <**q'épxetel**> is correct), df //q'ɛ[=Aə́=]p'=xʸə(l)=təl or q'ə́p=xʸə(l)=təl//, HUNT ['*something to tie the feet*'], SOC, root prob. <**q'áp'**> as in <**q'áp'et**> *tie s-th together* unless <**q'épxetel**> is correct, then <**q'ép**> *gather together* would be the root, possibly <**é-ablaut**> *derivational*, lx <**=xel**> *on the foot, on the leg*, lx <**=tel**> *something to, device to*, phonology: syllable-loss of el before =tel predictably, syntactic analysis: nominal, attested by Elders Group (6/8/77).

<**q'áp'et ~ q'á:p'et**>, MC /'*tie it up, bind it, tie it (parcel, broken shovel handle, belt, two ropes together)*'/, *see* q'áp'.

<**q'áq'el**>, EFAM ['*believing*'], *see* q'á:l.

<**q'áq'elmet**>, EFAM ['*believing s-o*'], *see* q'á:l.

<**q'áq'elptem**>, ABDF ['*cramping*'], *see* q'élptem ~ q'élp'tem.

<**q'áq'elqéyls**>, LANG ['*answering a letter*'], *see* q'ó:lthet.

<**q'áq'emi**>, HAT /'*little girl (perhaps four years), young girl, (girl from five to ten years [EB])*'/, *see* q'á:mi ~ q'á:miy.

<**q'áq'ep'els**>, MC ['*tying up*'], *see* q'áp'.

<**q'áq'ep'et**>, MC ['*tying it up*'], *see* q'áp'.

<**q'áq'et'em**>, TAST ['*(be) sweet*'], *see* q'át'em.

<**q'áq'et'emáléqep**>, SM ['*(have a) sweet smell*'], *see* q'át'em.

<**q'átx̱em**>, SD /'*scraping sound (like scraping food off dishes), rattling (of dishes, metal pots, wagon on gravel)*'/, *see* q'et.

<**q'átx̱(e)t**>, SD ['*rattling s-th*'], *see* q'et.

<**q'át'em**>, stem //q'ɛ́t'=əm *sweet*//, Salish cognate: Squamish /q'át'am/ *sweet* W73:259, K67:356.

<**q'áq'et'em**>, df //q'ɛ́[=C₁ə=]t'=əm//, TAST ['*(be) sweet*'], (<**=R1=**> *resultative* or *continuative* or *durative*), (<**=em**> *middle voice* or *intransitivizer, have, get*), phonology: reduplication, syntactic analysis: adjective/adjectival verb, attested by Elders Group, EB, AC, example: <**th'óqwetes te siyólexwe te q'áq'et'em.**>, //θ'áqʷ=əT-əs tə si=yáləxʷ=ə tə q'ɛ́[=C₁ə=]t'=əm//, /'*The old person sucked something sweet.*'/, syntactic comment: relative clause, syntactic analysis: transitive verb subject np object np, attested by AC.

<**q'áq'et'em sqá:wth**>, //q'ɛ́[=C₁ə=]t'=əm s=qɛ́·w=θ//, EB, FOOD /'*sweet potato,* prob. *blue camas,* prob. also now *domestic sweet potato*'/, /'prob. *Camassia quamash* and *Camassia leichtlinii*, prob. now also *Batatas edulis*'/, EB, attested by SJ (3/17/77)

<**p'éq' q'áq'et'em kwó:l**>, EB, FOOD /'*white sweet corn*'/ (lit. white + sweet + corn), (attested by RG,EH 6/16/98 to SN, edited by BG with RG,EH 6/26/00)

<**q'áq'et'emáléqep**>, ds //q'ɛ́[=C₁ə=]t'=əm=ɛ́lə́qəp//, SM ['*(have a) sweet smell*'], lx <**=áléqep**>

smell, phonology: reduplication, syntactic analysis: intransitive verb, attested by Deming.

<**q'et'emá:yelhp**>, ds //q'ɛt'=əm=ɛ́·y=əɬp//, EB /'*balsam fir* (has sweet sap or cambium, grows at higher altitudes, called larch by some, "balsam" is a popular name for trees of the genus Abies), from a sample taken prob. *subalpine fir (Abies lasiocarpa),* if sample is mistaken poss. *Pacific silver fir (Abies amabilis) or grand fir (Abies grandis),* if the term balsam is mistaken too, poss. *a variety of Douglas fir (Pseudotsuga menziesii)*'/, ['its bark has pockets of sweet pitch on it, the pitch was chewed, the needles are smaller and wider than those of a fir according to one elder, though the term "balsam" usu. refers to Abies firs; it is unclear to me which of the Abies firs might have sweet sap or sweet cambium; a higher altitude variety of Douglas fir is also a possibility as discussed in Turner, Bouchard and Kennedy 1977, "During the hottest part of the summer in certain localities the [Douglas] fir branches exude a white crystallizing sugar having a high concentration of a rare trisaccharide called melezitose....", They go on to say how the Okanagan Indians eat this whenever they can find it. J. Davidson: "Douglas Fir Sugar," in The Canadian Field Naturalist, 33:6-9 (April 1919) gives a full account of this sugar. The Stó:lō also mention a similar type of wild sugar as their only precontact sugar. Lots of q'et'emá:yelhp are said to be found at Hemlock Valley and in the U.S. on Mt. Baker, high up. (Larch is prob. in error as not found in Stó:lō areas but is quite similar to white fir)'], literally /'sweet bark tree'/, MED ['breathe steam from boiling boughs, inhaled to bring up tapeworm; tea is medicine for tuberculosis'], lx <**=á:y**> *bark, covering*, lx <**=elhp**> *tree, plant*, phonology: vowel-reduction of root before stressed suffix, syntactic analysis: nominal, attested by Elders Group, JL and NP and Deming (at Fish Camp 7/19/79).

<**q'et'ómthet**>, pcrs //q'ɛt'=ə[=M2=Aá=]m=T-ət//, SENS ['*sweeten oneself*'], (<**metathesis** and **ó-ablaut**> *derivational* or *durative*), (<**=t**> *purposeful control transitivizer*), (<**-et**> *reflexive*), phonology: metathesis, ó-ablaut of root á automatic before =thet, syntactic analysis: intransitive verb, attested by Elders Group (3/9/77).

<**q'et'ómthet**>, incs //q'ɛt'=ə[=M2=Aá=]m=θət//, SENS ['*get sweetened*'], (<**metathesis**> *resultative*, ó-ablaut *derivational* or *durative*), (<**=thet**> *get, become*), phonology: metathesis, ó-ablaut of root á automatic before =thet, syntactic analysis: intransitive verb, attested by Elders Group (3/9/77).

<**q'áth'**>, bound root //q'ɛ́θ' *be enfolded*//, Salish cognate: Squamish bound root /q'ac'/ *be enfolded, embraced* as in /q'ac'-č-ánʔ/ *hold one's arm around s-o's body (tr.)*, /q'ac'--íčn/ *hold one's arms on the back*, /q'əc'-q'ac'-č-s-tə́-namʔut/ *hug oneself, cross one's arms* K67:356.

<**sq'áq'eth'**>, strs //s=q'ɛ́[=C_1ə=]θ'//, DESC /'*(be) tight, (leaning backwards [EB])*'/, (<**s=**> *stative*), (<**=R1=**> *resultative*), phonology: reduplication, syntactic analysis: adjective/adjectival verb, attested by AD (1/4/79), also /'*leaning backwards*'/, attested by EB (12/4/75).

<**sq'éth'ep**>, df //s=q'ɛ[=Aə́=]θ'=əp//, ANA ['*(have the) hair in a bun*'], (<**s=**> *stative*), possibly root <**q'áth'**> *tight, enfolded*, possibly <**é-ablaut**> *durative*?, <**=ep**> *on the bottom*, phonology: ablaut, syntactic analysis: adjective/adjectival verb, attested by IHTTC.

<**sq'eth'ewíts ~ sq'eth'ōwíts**>, stvi //s=q'ɛθ'=əwíc//, ABFC ['*have one's hands behind one's back*'], (<**s=**> *stative*), lx <**=ewíts**> *on the back*, phonology: vowel-reduction before stressed suffix, syntactic analysis: adjective/adjectival verb, attested by IHTTC, SJ (Story of Mink and Miss Pitch), Salish cognate: Squamish /(n-)q'ac'-íčn/ *hold one's arms on the back* K67:356.

<**q'eth'ōwítsem**>, mdls //q'ɛθ'=əwíc=əm//, ABFC ['*put one's hands behind one's back*'], lx <**=ewíts**> *on the back*, (<**=em**> *middle voice*), phonology: vowel-reduction before stressed suffix, syntactic analysis: intransitive verb, attested by IHTTC.

<**q'átl'**>, possible root //q'ɛ́(·)ƛ'//, *have contortions*

<**q'áq'etl'**>, df //q'ɛ́[=R_1=]ƛ'//, ABDF /'*(have) fits, convulsions*'/, root meaning possibly related to that in q'átl'elxel *calf (of foot)* by a meaning like *stretch, extend*, possibly <**=R1=**> *continuative or*

resultative?, phonology: reduplication, syntactic analysis: intransitive verb, attested by SP and AK (7/13/75), Salish cognate: Samish dial. of N. Straits VU /sq'éq'əƛ'/ *to get fits* G86:76.

<**sq'á:tl'**>, dnom //s=q'ɛ́·ƛ'//, EZ /'*river otter,* perhaps also *sea otter*'/, ['*Lutra canadensis pacifica,* perhaps also *Enhydra lutris lutris*'], (semological comment: sea otters are unlikely to have been known about except through trade, since in B.C. they are found almost exclusively on the Pacific Coast (west coast of Vancouver Is. and further north on mainland) according to Cowan and Guiget (1965); the translation usually given by today's elders for sq'á:tl' is just "otter"), (<**s=**> *nominalizer*), possibly related to <**q'áq'etl'**> *fits, convulsions* due to the otter's frequent squirming contortions, syntactic analysis: nominal, attested by AC, also <**sq'átl'**>, //s=q'ɛ́ƛ'//, attested by AK and ME (11/21/72 tape), Elders Group (3/1/72 tape), other sources: JH /sq'é·ƛ'/ *sea otter* (vs. JH /sx^{w}əmə́cəl/ *river otter* (but my speakers say *fisher*)), ES /x̣á·qəl/ *otter* (=CwMs *otter* but my *marten*) ~ /sq'ɛ́·ƛ'/ (=CwMs *sea otter*), H-T <skat'> (umlaut over a) *otter (Lutra (Latax) canadensis) [i.e. river otter]),* Salish cognate: Squamish /sq'áƛ'/ *otter (land-, sea-)* W73:191, K69:59 but /sq'á·ƛ'/ *Canadian river otter (Lutracanadensispacifica)* in Kennedy and Bouchard 1976:27, Lushootseed /sq'áƛ'/ *land otter* H76:391.

<**q'átl'elxel**>, df //q'ɛ́ƛ'(=)əl=x^{y}əl//, ANA ['*calf (of the leg)*'], root meaning unknown unless related to q'áq'etl' *fits, convulsions* by a meaning like *stretch, extend,* possibly <**=el**> *get, have or go, come, get, become,* lx <**=xel**> *on the foot, on the leg,* syntactic analysis: nominal, attested by Elders Group (7/27/75).

<**q'á:w**>, free root or stem //q'ɛ́·w or q'a[=Aɛ́·=]w or q'ə[=Aɛ́·=]w//, ABFC ['*to howl*'], semantic environment ['of dog, wolf, coyote, cougar, rooster, loon, etc.'], possibly <**á:-ablaut**> *derivational,* phonology: possible ablaut, syntactic analysis: intransitive verb, attested by EB (2/11/76), Elders Group (7/6/77), AD and AK (American Bar trip 6/26/78), AC (all but EB report this meaning for this form used as a placename, Q'á:w), Salish cognate: Squamish /q'ə́w-m/ *howl, whistle (ab. animal, steamboat, etc.)* W73:145, K67:356, Lushootseed /q'^{w}əwá(h)əb/ *howl* H76:429, Saanich dial. of N. Straits /q'ə́w-əŋ/ *to howl (as a dog)* B74a:78, Mainland Comox /q'ə́gim/ *to howl (as coyote)* B75prelim:78.

<**Q'á:w**>, dnom //q'ɛ́·w or q'a[=Aɛ́·=]w or q'ə[=Aɛ́·=]w//, PLN ['*Dog Mountain above Katz Reserve*'], ASM ['above Al and Tillie Gutierrez's place at Katz, the mountain has a large rock shaped like a dog or coyote or wolf howling with its mouth open (photograph with telephoto lens confirms this) and was turned to stone during the time of X̲á:ls the Transformer'], literally /'howl'/, possibly <**á:-ablaut**> *derivational,* phonology: possible ablaut, syntactic analysis: nominal, attested by Elders Group, AK and AD (6/26/78), AC, source: place names reference file #28.

<**q'ó:w**>, cts //q'á·w or q'ɛ[-Aá-]·w//, ABFC ['*howling*'], semantic environment ['cougar, dog, wolf, coyote, anything'], phonology: possible ablaut, syntactic analysis: intransitive verb, attested by AC, Deming (2/7/80, 5/8/80), also <**q'aq'í:w**>, //q'ɛ[=C_1əAí=]·w//, ['*howling*'], [q'æq'é·w], <**í:-ablaut**> *durative,* attested by EB (2/11/76), example: <**q'ó:w te shxwéwe.**>, //q'á·w tə s=x^{w}ə́wə//, /'*The cougar is howling.*'/, attested by AC, <**qél te sqwóqwels te sqwemá:y q'aq'í:w.**>, //qə́l tə s=q^{w}ɛ[=AáC$_1$ə=]l-s tə s=q^{w}əm=ɛ́·y q'a[=Aɛ=][=C_1əAí=]·w//, /'*The sound of the dog howling is bad.*'/, literally /'is bad the its talking the dog howling'/, attested by EB.

<**q'ówem**>, mdls //q'áw=əm//, cts, ABFC /'*howling (of a dog), crowing (of a rooster)*'/, (<**=em**> *middle voice*), syntactic analysis: intransitive verb, attested by AH and LG (Deming 5/8/80).

<**q'ówel**>, incs //q'áw=əl or q'ɛ[-Aá-]=əl//, cts, ABFC ['*howling fast*'], literally /'get howling'/, (<**=el**> *get, go, come, become*), syntactic analysis: intransitive verb, attested by Deming (2/7/80), also <**q'ó:wel**>, //q'á·w=əl//, also /'*to howl*'/, attested by EB (12/16/75).

<**q'eq'ówel**>, dmpv //C_1í=Aə=q'áw=əl//, ABFC ['*many are howling*'], (<**R4=**> *diminutive,* e-ablaut

plural agents), phonology: reduplication, ablaut, syntactic analysis: intransitive verb, attested by EB (12/16/75), example: <**q'eq'ówel te sqwéqwemey.**>, //C_1í=Aə=q'áw=əl tə s=C_1í=Aə́=q^{w}əm=εy//, /'*The (little) dogs are howling.*'/.

<**Q'éwq'ewe**>, chrs //q'áw=C_1əC_2=ə//, PLN /'*Kawkawa Lake (near Hope, B.C.)*'/, ASM ['lake home of two loons, the male Q'ewq'ewelátsa and the female Q'ewq'eweló:t; also the original source of the first Sx̱wóyx̱wey mask'], (<**=R2**> *characteristic*), possibly <**=e**> *being, entity*?, phonology: reduplication, syntactic analysis: nominal, attested by Elders Group (7/9/75), ME/Maggie Pennier and Mary Peters and Lizzie Johnson and CT (Elders Meeting 7/6/77), also <**Q'áwq'ewe**>, //q'a[=Aέ=]w=C_1əC_2=ə//, attested by P.D. Peters (Katz), BJ (12/5/64 new transcr. old p.321), source: place names reference file #20, other sources: Wells 1965 (lst ed.).

<**Q'ewq'ewelátsa**>, df //C_1əC_2=q'aw=əlέcε or q'aw=C_1əC_2=əlέcε//, N ['*Male Loon*'], ASM ['lived at Kawkawa Lake in myth time'], possibly <**R3=**> *plural* or possibly <**=R2**> *characteristic*, lx <**=elátsa**> *male name ending*, phonology: reduplication, vowel-reduction, syntactic analysis: nominal, attested by Elders Group (7/9/75).

<**Q'ewq'eweló:t**>, df //C_1əC_2=q'aw=əlá·t or q'aw=C_1əC_2=əlá·t//, N ['*Female Loon*'], ASM ['lived at Kawkawa Lake in myth time'], possibly <**R3=**> *plural* or possibly <**=R2**> *characteristic*, lx <**=eló:t**> *female name ending*, phonology: reduplication, vowel-reduction, syntactic analysis: nominal, attested by Elders Group (7/9/75).

<**q'áw**>, bound root //q'έw// *pay*

<**q'áwet**>, pcs //q'έw=əT//, ECON ['*pay s-o*'], (<**=et**> *purposeful control transitivizer*), syntactic analysis: transitive verb, attested by Deming, EB; found in <**q'awétes.**>, //q'έw=əT-əs//, /'*He pays him or her.*'/, phonology: the stress-shift may be my error, attested by EB, example: <**líye q'áwethò:m.**>, //lí-ə q'έw=əT-à·m//, /'*Did he pay you?, (Were you payed?)*'/, syntactic analysis: intransitive verb passive, attested by EB.

<**q'áwelhs**>, bens //q'έw-əɬc//, ECON ['*pay for*'], (<**-elhts ~ (EB) -elhs**> *benefactive*), syntactic analysis: transitive verb, attested by EB (1/26/76), example: <**tl'éles q'áwelhs.**>, //ƛ'ə́=l-əs q'έw=əɬc or ƛ'ə́=l-əs q'έw=əɬc-s//, /'*That's what he paid for.*'/, attested by EB.

<**Q'á:w**>, PLN ['*Dog Mountain above Katz Reserve*'], *see* q'á:w.

<**q'áwelhs**>, ECON ['*pay for*'], *see* q'áwet.

<**q'áwetsel**>, df //q'έw=əcəl//, ANAF ['*dorsal fin (long fin in back)*'], root meaning unknown, lx <**=etsel**> *on the back*, syntactic analysis: nominal, attested by BHTTC, Salish cognate: Squamish /s=q'awʔ=íčn/ *back fin* with root /q'aw(ʔ)2/ *side* W73:99, K67:296, 357.

<**q'axí:l**>, TVMO /'*go with, come with, be partner with*'/, *see* q'ó.

<**q'á:yt**>, bound root, //q'έ·yt//, LANG perhaps /'bring a message'/ or as in cognate in Squamish /'holler '/.

<**sq'á:yt**>, dnom //s=q'έ·yt//, LANG /'*message, a messenger not left yet, Indian messenger*'/, (<**s=**> *nominalizer*), syntactic analysis: nominal, dialects: *Tait, Cheh., Chill.*, attested by BHTTC (11/15/76), IHTTC (9/7/77), Salish cognate: Nooksack sq'ó:yt /s=q'á·yt/ *message* (GC 9/7/77), Squamish /q'áyt/ *to holler* K67:357, example: <**lámtlh sq'á:yt.**>, //lέ=m-tɬ s=q'έ·yt//, /'*Go bring a message.*'/, literally /'go -coaxing imperative messenger not yet left'/, syntactic comment: vocative, attested by BHTTC.

<**sq'áq'eyt**>, cts //s=q'έ[=C_1ə=]yt//, LANG ['*a messenger on the run*'], (semological comment: a continuative nominal), (<**s=**> *nominalizer*), (<**=R1=**> *continuative*), phonology: reduplication, syntactic analysis: nominal, attested by BHTTC (11/15/76), IHTTC and Deming (9/8/77).

<**q'á:yx̱elhp**>, df //q'έ·yx̣=əɬp//, EB ['*cascara tree*'], ['*Rhamnus purshiana*'], MED ['bark chewed as

medicine for constipation, bark tea has the same effect and is used for a spring tonic; cascara bark and Oregon grape roots boiled a long time as medicine, then can be drunk cool as medicine for boils and pimples (latter from JL)'], root meaning unknown, lx <=**elhp**> *tree, plant*, syntactic analysis: nominal, attested by AC, Elders Group, JL (Fish Camp 7/19/79), Salish cognate: Skagit dial. of Lushootseed /q'áyx̣əc/ *cascara* H76:392, example: <**tsqwá:y te p'alyíws te q'á:yx̱elhp.**>, //c-qʷɛ·y tə p'əl=əy=í·ws-s tə q'ɛ́·yx̣=əɬp//, /'*The bark of cascara is yellow.*'/, attested by Elders Group.

<**q'el**>, bound root //q'əl *shelter*//.

<**q'élém**>, df //q'ə́l=ə́m//, TVMO /'*to camp, (camping [BHTTC])*'/, root <**q'él**> *shelter*, <**=em**> *middle voice* or <**=em**> *intransitivizer, get, have*, phonology: possible updrifting, syntactic analysis: intransitive verb, attested by EB, IHTTC, also <**k'élem**>, //q'[=K=]ə́l=əm//, usage: baby talk, attested by IHTTC, also <**q'élém**>, //q'ə́l=ə́m//, also /'*camping*'/, attested by BHTTC (8/20/76), Salish cognate: Squamish root /q'ay ~ q'əy/ *be high up* as in /q'i/ *be (camp) in the mountains* and /ʔəs-q'iʔ-ímʔ/ *camp* W73:51, K67:357, 387, Lushootseed /q'ə́l(ə)b/ *camp, stay overnight* H76:396, example: <**tsel q'élém kw cheláqelhelh.**>, //c-əl q'ə́l=ə́m kʷ cəlɛ́q=əɬ=əɬ//, /'*I camped yesterday.*'/, attested by EB, <**l stl'í kw'els q'élém.**>, //l s=ƛ'í k'ʷə-l-s q'ə́l=ə́m//, /'*I want to camp.*'/, attested by Deming, <**ícha kweló kws q'elémchet.**>, //ʔí-cɛ kʷə=là kʷ-s q'ə́l=ə́m-c-ət//, /'*This is where we'll make camp.*'/, literally /'is here -future the= this that we camp'/, attested by EB, <**plo plo plo q'élem.**>, //pla pla pla q'ə́l=əm//, PLAY, /'*the jump and camp game, words to the jump and camp game,*'/, ASM ['a game done poking a finger up a child's arm or down a child's leg while saying each pla syllable, then landing after saying q'élem, tickling when getting to the underarm or sole of foot'], usage: words to a game, root <**plo**> meaning uncertain, perhaps *jump*, dialects: *Chill.*, attested by IHTTC (9/15/77), also <**plo plo q'élem.**>, //pla pla q'ə́l=əm//, also /'*the plo plo game (tickle game, jump and camp game)*'/, ASM ['same description'], attested by EF (Deming 6/21/79), also <**plu plu plup q'élem.**>, //plu plu plup q'ə́l=əm//, dialects: *Tait*, attested by IHTTC (9/15/77).

<**q'élmel**>, dnom //q'ə́l=əm=məl or q'ə́l=məl//, TVMO ['*a camp*'], BLDG, lx <**=mel**> *part, portion*, phonology: possible consonant merger, syntactic analysis: nominal, attested by BHTTC.

<**q'eléts'**>, df //q'əl=ə[=´=]c'//, BLDG ['*rainshelter*'], WETH, possibly root <**q'el**> *shelter*, possibly <**=ets'**> *around in circles*, possibly <**=´=**> *derivational*, syntactic analysis: nominal, noun, attested by Elders Group (9/22/76).

<**q'eléts'éqwtel ~ q'eléts'eqwtel**>, ds //q'əl=ə́c'=əqʷ=təl//, HHG ['*umbrella*'], WETH, literally /'rainshelter on top of the head device to'/, lx <**=eqw**> *on top of the head*, lx <**=tel**> *device to*, phonology: optional updrifting on penultimate syllable, syntactic analysis: nominal, attested by Elders Group (9/22/76, 1/19/77), AC, Deming, example: <**tsel stl'epó:lwelh lí te q'eléts'eqwtel.**>, //c-əl s=ƛ'əp=á·lwəɬ lí tə q'əl=ə́c'=əqʷ=təl//, /'*I'm under the umbrella.*'/, literally /'I be underneath in the umbrella'/, attested by Elders Group (1/19/77).

<**sq'elóts'eqw**>, strs //s=q'əl=ə[=Aá=]c'=əqʷ//, HHG ['*be under an umbrella*'], WETH, (<**s=**> *stative*), (<**ó-ablaut**> *resultative*), phonology: ablaut, syntactic analysis: adjective/adjectival verb, attested by Elders Group (1/19/77); found in <**sq'elóts'eqwtsel.**>, //s=q'əl=ə[=Aá=]c'=əqʷ-c-əl//, /'*I'm under an umbrella.*'/.

<**q'eléts'tel**>, dnom //q'əl=ə́c'=təl//, REL ['*square dressing room or shelter of blankets where sx̱wóyx̱wey dancers change before doing the sx̱wóyx̱wey dance*'], literally /'shelter =around in circles =device to'/, root <**q'el**> *shelter*, lx <**=éts'**> *around in circles*, lx <**=tel**> *device to*, syntactic analysis: nominal, attested by DM (12/6/64).

<**q'eláq'a**>, df //q'[=əl=]ɛ́=C_1ɛ́(·)//, EZ /'*blackbird, Brewer's blackbird, or smaller crow, i.e., northwestern crow*'/, ['*Euphagus cyanocephalus,* or *Corvus caurinus*'], ASM ['found out in the fields, resembles a small crow, elders identified photo of Brewer's blackbird 6/4/75'], possibly <**=el=**> *plural*,

possibly <**=R9**> *characteristic*, probably onomatopoeic, phonology: reduplication, infixing, syntactic analysis: nominal, attested by Elders Group, BHTTC, Salish cognate: Squamish /q’lʔáq’a/ *crow* K67:355 and /q’ǝlá·q’a/ *common crow (Corvusbrachyrhynchos) and northwestern crow (Corvus caurinus)* Kennedy and Bouchard 1976:95-96, Lushootseed /k’áʔk’aʔ/ *crow* H76:238, also /'*small seagull*'/, attested by HP.

<**q'élém**>, TVMO /'*to camp, (camping [BHTTC])*'/, *see* q'el.

<**q'eléts'**>, BLDG ['*rainshelter*'], *see* q'el.

<**q'eléts'éqwtel ~ q'eléts'eqwtel**>, HHG ['*umbrella*'], *see* q'el.

<**q'eléts'tel**>, REL ['*square dressing room or shelter of blankets where sx̲wóyx̲wey dancers change before doing the sx̲wóyx̲wey dance*'], *see* q'el.

<**q'eléx̲el**>, CSTR ['*fence*'], *see* q'ál.

<**q'eléx̲elt**>, CSTR ['*fence s-th in*'], *see* q'ál.

<**q'ellhólemètsel**>, df //q’ǝl=ɬɛ[=Aá=]´l=ǝm=ǝ́cǝl or q’ól=ɬǝɬ=ǝm=ǝ́cǝl//, EZ /'*killer whale, blackfish*'/, ['*Grampus rectipinna* also known as *Orcinus rectipinna*'], possibly root <**q'el**> *fin*, lx <**=lhelh ~ =lhál**> *in the throat* [prob. refers to blowhole on back too], lx <**=étsel**> *on the back*, phonology: downstepping, syntactic analysis: nominal, attested by AC (prompted), other sources: ES /q’ǝlɬálǝmǝ̀cǝl/ *killer whale, blackfish*.

<**q'ellhomelétsel**>, df //q’ǝlɬamǝl=ǝ́cǝl or q’ǝl=ɬalǝm=M2=ǝ́cǝl//, EZ /'*shark, [*perhaps *basking shark, six-gill shark, thresher shark,* and/or others, probably *generic]*'/, ['perhaps *Cetorhinus maximus, Hexanchus griseus, Alopius vulpinus,* and/or others'], phonology: possible metathesis type 2 with consonants, syntactic analysis: nominal, attested by AK (11/21/72 tape).

<**q'élmel**>, TVMO ['*a camp*'], *see* q'el.

<**q'élmet**>, EFAM /'*believe s-o, trust s-o*'/, *see* q'á:l.

<**q'élptem ~ q'élp'tem**>, df //q’ǝ́lp=t(=)ǝm ~ q’ǝ́l=p’=t(=)ǝm//, ABDF /'*to have cramps, get a cramp, to be cramped*'/, root meaning unknown, possibly <**=p'**> *on itself*, possibly <**=tem**> *participial middle*, syntactic analysis: intransitive verb, attested by EB (12/11/75, 5/25/76), Salish cognate: Lushootseed /ʔǝs-q’ǝl-šád/ *cramp in the foot* and /q’ǝp-šád/ *cramp on the leg* versus /q’úp-šǝd/ *leg cramp* H76:395, 396, 407, the second form is derived from Lushootseed root /q’ǝp/ *gather* on p.396, compare <**q'élp'thet**> *to shrink* and <**q'élp't**> *shrink s-th*, example: <**q'élptem tel sx̲éle.**>, //q’ǝ́lp=tǝm tǝ-l s=x̣ǝ́lǝ//, /'*My leg cramped., My leg is cramped.*'/, attested by EB (12/11/75).

<**q'elq'élp'tem**>, plv //C_1ǝC_2=q’ǝ́l=p’=tǝm//, ABDF ['*getting a cramp*'], (<**R3=**> *plural* or perhaps here *continuative*?), phonology: reduplication, syntactic analysis: intransitive verb, attested by EB (5/25/76).

<**q'á:lp'tem**>, rsls //q’ǝ[=Aɛ́·=]l=p’=tǝm//, ABDF ['*cramped*'], (<**á:-ablaut**> *resultative*), phonology: ablaut, syntactic analysis: intransitive verb, attested by EB (4/28/76).

<**q'áq'elptem**>, cts //C_1ɛ́-q’ǝlp=tǝm//, ABDF ['*cramping*'], (<**R7-**> *continuative*), phonology: reduplication, syntactic analysis: intransitive verb, attested by EB (12/11/75).

<**q'élp't**>, pcs //q’ǝ́l=p’=T//, MC ['*shrink s-th*'], lx <**=p'**> *on itself*, (<**=t**> *purposeful control transitivizer*), syntactic analysis: transitive verb, attested by EB (4/28/76), Salish cognate: Lushootseed root /q’ʷup’/ *shrink, shrivel* as in /lǝq’ʷup’q’ʷup’-áčiʔ ʔǝ tiʔǝʔ scǝtxʷǝd/ *Bear's hands shrivelled up.*, /ʔǝs-q’ʷúp’-q’ʷup’/ *he was a cripple*, /q’ʷúp’-q’ʷup’-ǝči(ʔ)b/ *sleeves rolled up*, and /q’ʷúp’-q’ʷup’-šǝd-ǝb/ *roll up pantlegs* H76:432.

<**q'élp'thet**>, pcrs //q’ǝ́l=p’=T-ǝt//, ABDF ['*shrink*'], EB, WATR, FIRE, LAND, WETH, MC, SOCT,

(<**-et**> *reflexive*), syntactic analysis: intransitive verb, attested by EB (4/28/76).

<**q'élp'thet**>, ABDF [*'shrink'*], *see* q'élp't.

<**q'élqet**>, LANG /*'answer it (a letter, phone call, etc.), reply to s-th/s-o'*/, *see* q'ó:lthet.

<**q'elqéyls**>, LANG [*'answer a letter'*], *see* q'ó:lthet.

<**q'elq'élp'**>, DESC [*'tangled on its own/itself'*], *see* q'ál.

<**q'elq'élp'tem**>, ABDF [*'getting a cramp'*], *see* q'élptem ~ q'élp'tem.

<**q'elq'élq'**>, DESC /*'snagged, tangled on something, something gets tangled up (like a net)'*/, *see* q'ál.

<**q'elq'í:lthet ~ q'elq'éylthet**>, TVMO /*'back and forth, (go or come back and forth)'*/, *see* q'ó:lthet.

<**q'élq't**>, TVMO /*'coil it, wind it up (of string, rope, yarn)'*/, *see* q'ál.

<**q'élq'xetel**>, CLO /*'rags wound around the legs in the cold or to protect from mosquitoes, (leggings)'*/, *see* q'ál.

<**q'elsiyáqem** or **q'elts'yáqem**>, WETH [*'(have/get a) snowdrift'*], *see* yíq.

<**q'elstá:xw**>, EFAM /*'fool s-o, deceive s-o, (lie to s-o [SJ])'*/, *see* q'á:l.

<**q'élstexw**>, TVMO /*'give it back, bring it back, return s-th'*/, *see* q'ó:.

<**q'elx̱á:lt**>, CSTR [*'fence it'*], *see* q'ál.

<**q'élh**>, possible root //q'ə́ɬ//, meaning unknown

<**sq'élhq'elh**>, chrs //s=q'ə́ɬ=C_1əC_2//, EZ [*'muskrat'*], [*'Ondatra zibethica osoyoosensis'*], ASM ['muskrat was eaten as the meat has a good flavor (Elders Group 3/21/79), small muskrats were found in little lakes below X̱óx̱cha (ME)'], (<**s=**> *nominalizer*), root meaning unknown, (<**=R2**> *characteristic*), phonology: reduplication, syntactic analysis: nominal, attested by AC, AD, SP, ME (11/21/72 tape), also <**q'élhq'elh**>, //q'ə́ɬ=C_1əC_2//, attested by AK (11/21/72 tape), other sources: ES /sq'ə́ɬq'əɬ/, JH /sq'ə́ɬq'ə́ɬ/ both *muskrat*, Salish cognate: Lushootseed /q'ə́ɬq'əɬ ~ sq'ə́ɬq'əɬ/ *muskrat* H76:396, ??possibly related to the Squamish root /q'aɬ/ *obstruct passage* as in /n-q'áɬ/ *be in the way, bar passage, be hit* K67:356.

<**q'émél**>, perhaps root or stem //q'ə́mə́l// or //q'ə́m(=)əl// or //qo:(=)m// <qo:m> *dip up, scoop (water)* (as <**q'emós ~ q'emó:s**>, df //q[=G=]á·=m=ə[=M2=]s or q'əm=á(·)s//, *to dip-net* may be); this root with **glottalization** and **vowel change** *derivational* (as also in *to dip net*) would give a literal meaning of "come/go/get by dip[ing] up/scoop[ing] water (+ derivation)" for *to paddle* here

<**sq'émél**>, df //s=q'ə́mə́l or s=q'ə́m(=)əl//, CAN [*'canoe paddle'*], (<**s=**> *nominalizer*), root meaning unknown, probably <**=el**> *go, come, become, get*, phonology: possible updrifting, all the variants may be attributable to the form with two high stresses, syntactic analysis: nominal, attested by Elders Group (3/12/75), BJ (5/10/64), DM (12/4/64), also <**sq'émel**>, //s=q'ə́məl//, attested by Elders Group (1/28/76), EB, also <**sq'emél ~ sq'ém:el**>, //s=q'əmə́l ~ s=q'ə́m·əl//, attested by AC, also <**sq'emél**>, //s=q'əmə́l//, attested by Deming, other sources: ES /sq'ə́mə́l/ and JH /q'əmə́l/ *paddle*, example: <**kw'étslexwes te sléxwelh, sq'émel qas te sx̱wő́qw'tel.**>, //k'^{w}ə́c=l-əx^w-əs tə s=lə́x^{w}əɬ, s=q'ə́məl qɛ-s tə s=x̣^{w}óq'^{w}=təl//, /*'He saw a canoe, a paddle, and a canoe pole.'*/, attested by EB.

<**q'emő́:lhp ~ q'emő́welhp**>, df //q'ə́mə́[=Aó·=]l=ɬp//, EB [*'broad-leaf maple'*], [*'Acer macrophyllum'*], literally /'canoe-paddle tree'/, ASM ['wood used for canoe paddles, dishes, fish clubs'], MED ['six-inch to ten-inch sprouts used for tea to make medicine to make a person strong, maple also used perhaps for birth control medicine'], possibly <**ó:-ablaut**> *derivational*, lx <**=(e)lhp**> *tree*, phonology: ó:-ablaut, consonant merger, vowel-loss, syntactic analysis: nominal, attested by AC, BJ (12/5/64), SJ (Deming 5/24/79), AD, other sources: ES /q'əmə́w·ɬp/ (Ms

/q'ə́mələɬp/) *broadleaf maple* (both Chill. and Ms mean paddle tree), H-T <k·Emőetlp> *maple (white) (Acer macrophyllum).*

<**q'emő:lhpíwelh**>, ds //q'ə́mə́[=Aó·=]l=ɬp=í(y=)wəɬ//, HHG [*'maple dish'*], lx <**=í(y=)welh**> *dish* lx prob. from <**=áy ~ =ey**> (here ~ <**=í(y)**>) *bark, covering* plus lx <**=welh**> *vessel*, phonology: probably vowel-loss of the suffix =áy ~ =ey which leaves y which then is syllabicized to =i between consonants p and w and perhaps gets stress by updrifting on penultimate syllable, syntactic analysis: nominal, attested by Elders Group (3/72 tape), also <**q'emő:lhp lóthel**>, //q'ə́mə́[=Aó·=]l=ɬp láθəl//, literally /'maple dish/plate'/, Elder's comment: "less good way of saying it than q'emő:lhpíwelh", attested by Elders Group (3/72).

<**Qemlólhp**>, ds //q'[=D=]əməl=ə[=Aá=]ɬp//, PLN [*'Queen's Island'*], ASM ['west of the mouth of Harrison River; named after maple tree because there are so many maples there; the English name is after an Indian man named Skwí:l who lived there'], literally /'many maple trees'/, root <**q'émél**> *canoe paddle*, lx <**=elhp**> *tree*, (<**=D= (deglottalization)**> *derivational*, <**ó-ablaut**> *derivational*), phonology: deglottalization, ablaut, restoration of el before =elhp, syntactic analysis: nominal, attested by Elders Group (7/13/77), source: place names reference file #71.

<**q'ém:és ~ q'ém:es**>, df //q'ə́m·əs or q'ə́m·=ə[=´=]s//, EB [*'big all-white edible mushroom'*], ASM ['comes out from under moss, grows under fir trees, this mushroom (and any mushroom) is frog's umbrella'], root meaning unknown unless *dip water* or related to <**q'emós ~ q'emó:s**> *to dip-net*, possibly <**=es**> *on the face*, possibly <**= ´=**> *derivational*, phonology: possible updrifting or stress-shift, syntactic analysis: nominal, attested by JL (5/5/75), Elders Group (3/12/75, 1/28/76, 9/22/76), Salish cognate: Thompson /q'ə́m'as/ *wood mushroom, not identified botanically yet* and /q'əm'as-áyəq^w/ *unidentified mushroom (*possibly *Armillariaspecies)* (grows on roots of cottonwood tree, eaten by the Thompson people*)* Turner and Thompson 1973:2,4; Lillooet /qəm'sáləq^w/ (Turner and Bouchard: Pemberton Lillooet Ethnobotany (ms.)(1974)).

<**q'emós ~ q'emó:s**>, df //q[=G=]á·=m=ə[=M2=]s or q'əm=á(·)s//, FSH [*'to dip-net'*], possibly root <**qó:=m**> *dip up, scoop*, possibly <**=G= (glottalization)**> *derivational*, possibly <**metathesis**> *derivational*, possibly <**=ó:s ~ =es**> *on the face*, literally /'scoop/dip up on the face derivational'/, phonology: possible glottalization and metathesis, syntactic analysis: intransitive verb, attested by AC, Deming, example: <**latst q'emó:s.**>, //lɛ-c-t q'əmá·s//, /*'Let's go dip-net(ting).'*/, attested by AC.

<**q'íq'emó:s ~ q'éyq'emó:s**>, cts //C_1í-q'əmá·s//, FSH /*'dip-netting, fishing with a scoop net, (harpooning fish at night [DM 12/4/64])'*/, (<**R4-**> *continuative* from an original diminutive), phonology: reduplication, syntactic analysis: intransitive verb, attested by AC, Elders Group (3/15/72 tape), also /*'harpooning fish at night'*/, attested by DM (12/4/64), also <**q'éyq'emò:s**>, //C_1í-q'əmá·s//, phonology: downstepping, attested by Elders Group (3/26/75), also <**q'eq'mós**>, //q'ə[-C_1ə-]m=á·s//, attested by LJ (Tait) (4/7/78 History tape); found in <**q'íq'emó:s.**>, //C_1í-q'əmá·s//, /*'He's dip-netting.'*/, attested by AC, example: <**tsel q'éyq'emó:s.**>, //c-əl C_1í-q'əmá·s//, /*'I'm dip-netting.'*/.

<**q'emó:stel**>, dnom //q[=G=]á·=m=ə[=M2=]s=təl or q'əmá·s=təl//, FSH /*'a dip-net, (a scoop net [CT])'*/, ASM ['originally made of méthelh *dog-bane*, rings called x̱alwéla and made of horn or bone slid the net closed, it was mounted on a long pole perhaps four to six feet long'], lx <**=tel**> *device to, thing to*, phonology: possible glottalization and metathesis, syntactic analysis: nominal, attested by Deming, AC, Elders Group (2/11/76), TG (4/23/75), also /*'scoop net'*/, (semological comment: probably the same as a dip net), attested by CT (6/8/76), also <**q'emósthtel**>, //q'əm=á·s=θ=təl//, possibly <**=(e)th ~ =ó:th**> *on the mouth*, attested by Elders Group (3/26/75), also <**q'eq'mó:stel**>, //q'ə[=C_1ə=]m=á·s=təl//, (<**=R1=**> *continuative* or *derivational*), phonology: reduplication, attested by DM (12/4/64), TG (4/23/75), Deming, also <**sq'eq'mó:stel**>, //s=q'ə[=C_1ə=]m=á·s=təl//, (<**s=**> *nominalizer*), attested by DM (12/4/64).

<**q'emó:stel**>, FSH /'*a dip-net, (a scoop net [CT])*'/, *see* q'emós ~ q'emó:s.

<**q'emṓ:lhp ~ q'emṓwelhp**>, EB ['*broad-leaf maple*'], *see* q'émél.

<**q'emṓ:lhpíwelh**>, HHG ['*maple dish*'], *see* q'émél.

<**q'ép**>, free root //q'ə́p//, SOC /'*to gather (of people esp.), to collect*'/, phonology: usually a zero-grade root when derived, syntactic analysis: intransitive verb, attested by EB, AC, example: <**me q'ép**>, //mə q'ə́p//, /'*all gathered*'/, literally /'come to gather'/, attested by AC, <**látset q'ép.**>, //lɛ́-c-ət q'ə́p//, /'*We'll gather.*'/, literally /'we're going to gather'/, attested by AC.

<**q'áp**>, cts //q'ə[-Aɛ́-]p//, SOC ['*gathering (of people)*'], (<**á-ablaut**> *continuative*), phonology: ablaut, syntactic analysis: intransitive verb, attested by Elders Group (3/15/72).

<**sq'ép**>, dnom //s=q'ə́p//, SOC /'*a gathering, a meeting*'/, (<**s=**> *nominalizer*), syntactic analysis: nominal, attested by AC, AD, example: <**hí:kw te sq'ép li te ts'(a)héyelhá:wtxw.**>, //hí[=·=]k^w tə s=q'ə́p li tə c'ɛhɛ́yəɬ=ɛ́·wtx^w//, /'*(It's/There's) a BIG gathering at the church.*'/, attested by AC, <**tsel lám te sq'ép.**>, //c-əl lɛ́=m tə s=qə́p//, /'*I went to a gathering.*'/, attested by AC, <**ō Síthikri, plíst te sq'éptset.**>, //ʔo síθikri, plís=T tə s=q'ə́p-c-ət//, /'*Oh Jesus, bless our meeting.*'/, attested by AD.

<**sq'eq'íp**>, strs //s=q'ə[=C_1əAí=]p//, SOC ['*be gathered together*'], (<**s=**> *stative*), (<**=R1= with í-ablaut**> *resultative*), phonology: reduplication, ablaut, syntactic analysis: adjective/adjectival verb, attested by AC, example: <**xwélmexw sq'eq'íp li tethá.**>, //x^{w}ə́lməx^w s=q'ə[=C_1əAí=]p li tə θɛ́//, /'*Indians gathered over there.*'/, literally /'(it's/there's) Indian gathered at there ~ (it's/there's) Indian group at there'/, attested by AC.

<**sq'eq'íp**>, dnom //s=q'ə[=C_1əAí=]p//, SOC ['*a group*'], (<**s=**> *nominalizer*), (<**=R1= with í-ablaut**> *resultative*), phonology: reduplication, ablaut, syntactic analysis: nominal, attested by Elders Group (3/15/72), prob. AC.

<**q'pá:ls**>, sas //q'əp=ɛ́·ls//, ECON /'*collect, collect money, take a collection, gather*'/, MC, (<**=á:ls**> *structured activity non-continuative*), phonology: vowel-loss to zero-grade of root before stressed full-grade suffix, syntactic analysis: intransitive verb, attested by Elders Group (3/15/72, 3/8/78).

<**q'ápels**>, cts //q'ə[-Aɛ́-]p=əls//, sas, ECON ['*collecting*'], MC, (<**á-ablaut**> *continuative*), (<**=els**> *structured activity continuative*), phonology: ablaut, syntactic analysis: intransitive verb, attested by Elders Group (3/8/78).

<**q'pém**>, izs //q'p=əm or q'əp=ə[=´=]m//, MC /'*collect, gather*'/, possibly <**=´=**> (stress-shift) possibly *derivational or non-continuative*, (<**=em**> *intransitivizer, have, get*), phonology: stressed intransitivizer on zero-grade root or possibly stress-shift, syntactic analysis: intransitive verb, attested by Elders Group (3/8/78).

<**q'pét**>, pcs //q'p=əT or q'əp=ə[=´=]T//, HARV /'*gather s-th, pick up s-th (stuff that's scattered about), collect s-th, gather it up, pick them up (already gathered or not)*'/, MC, possibly <**=´=**> possibly *derivational or non-continuative*, (<**=et**> *purposeful control transitivizer*), phonology: stressed transitivizer on zero-grade root or possibly stress-shift, syntactic analysis: transitive verb, attested by EB, Elders Group (3/15/72), AD, RG & EH (4/9/99 Ling332), example: <**kw'élh te sth'í:ms, q'pétlha.**>, //k'^{w}ə́ɬ tə s=θ'í·m-s, q'p=ə́T-ɬɛ//, /'*His berries spilled, gather them [pick them up].*'/, attested by EB, <**q'pét te siyó:lh**>, //q'p=ə́T tə s=yá·ɬ//, /'*gather up firewood, pick up firewood (already gathered)*'/, attested by AD.

<**q'ápt** or **q'ápet**>, cts //q'ə[-Aɛ́-]p=(ə)T//, HARV /'*collecting s-th, gathering s-th*'/, MC, (<**á-ablaut**> *continuative*), (<**=t** or **=et**> *purposeful control transitivizer*), phonology: ablaut, syntactic analysis: transitive verb, attested by EB, Deming; found in <**q'áptes.**>, //q'ə[-Aɛ́-]p=(ə)T-əs//, /'*He's collecting something., He's gathering something., He's gathering it.*'/, attested by EB, Deming.

<**q'péthet**>, pcrs //q'p=ə́T-ət//, SOC /'*crowd together, gather together, people gather*'/, (<**=et**> *purposeful control transitivizer*), (<**-et**> *reflexive*), phonology: zero-grade root with stressed transitivizer, syntactic analysis: intransitive verb, attested by Elders Group (6/16/76, 3/15/72), Deming, EB, AC, also <**q'epéthet**>, //q'əp=ə́T-ət//, phonology: schwa-grade instead of zero-grade, attested by AC, example: <**q'epéthet ye xwélmexw.**>, //q'əp=ə́T-ət yə xʷə́lməxʷ//, /'*The Indians gathered.*'/, attested by AC.

<**q'ópthet**>, cts //q'ə[-Aɛ́-Aá-]p=T-ət//, pcrs, SOC ['*crowding together*'], (<**á-ablaut**> *continuative*, ó-ablaut of root á automatically triggered by =thet), (<**=t**> *purposeful control transitivizer*), (<**-et**> *reflexive*), phonology: á-ablaut and on top of that ó-ablaut of á automatically triggered by =thet (ablaut of ablaut), syntactic analysis: intransitive verb, attested by Deming (3/16/78).

<**sq'epláts**>, durs //s=q'ɛ́p=lə[=M2=]c or s=q'əp=lə[=Aɛ́=]c//, EB /'*thick crowded tight bushes, bushes growing wide from narrow roots or base*'/, (<**s=**> *nominalizer*), (<**á-ablaut** or **metathesis**> *durative*), lx <**=lets**> *on the bottom*, syntactic analysis: nominal, attested by AC, Elders Group, other sources: ES /šq'əplɛ́·c/ *bushes bunched up*.

<**sq'pólthetel**>, dnom //s=q'p=álθəl=təl//, CLO ['*garter*'], (<**s=**> *nominalizer*), root <**q'ep**> *gather, collect*, lx <**=ólthel**> *on the knee*, lx <**=tel**> *device to, thing to*, syntactic analysis: nominal, attested by BHTTC (10/21/76), comment: perhaps in error or perhaps legitimate alternate for sq'ep'ó:lthetel *garter* (SP in IHTTC 9/19/77 based on root q'ap' *tie, bandage*).

<**q'ep'eláx̲tel**>, CLO ['*armband*'], *see* q'áp'.

<**q'ep'lóxes**>, ABDF /'*he passes on a disease to me, he gets me addicted*'/, *see* q'áp'.

<**q'ép'xetel** (unless <**q'épxetel**> is correct), HUNT ['*something to tie the feet*'], *see* q'áp'.

<**q'eq'elá:mi**>, HAT ['*lots of little girls*'], *see* q'á:mi ~ q'á:miy.

<**q'éq'ewes**>, df //q'ə[=C_1ə=]w(=)əs//, EFAM ['*surprised*'], possibly root <**q'éw**> *turn around something*, possibly <**=R1=**> *resultative*?, <**=es**> *on the face*?, phonology: reduplication, syntactic analysis: intransitive verb, attested by Deming (6/15/78).

<**q'eq'exí:lt**>, TVMO ['*accompany s-o little or elderly*'], *see* q'ó.

<**q'eq'exí:lt**>, TVMO ['*accompanying s-o*'], *see* q'ó.

<**q'eq'éy**>, ANA /'*guts, intestines*'/, *see* q'ey ~ q'i.

<**q'eq'ótel**>, DIR ['*to meet (each other)*'], *see* q'ó.

<**q'eq'ówel**>, ABFC ['*many are howling*'], *see* q'á:w.

<**q'eq'x̲át**>, LANG ['*argue with s-o*'], *see* q'(e)x̲.

<**q'ésetsel**>, WV ['*tying a net*'], *see* q'ey ~ q'i.

<**q'ésq'esetsel**>, EZ ['*spider*'], *see* q'ey ~ q'i.

<**q'et**>, bound root //q'ət// *rattling sound, scraping sound.*

<**q'etx̲áls**>, sas //q'ət=x̣=ɛ́ls//, SOC /'*to rattle (cans, etc. to wake newlyweds), to shivaree (someone)*'/, SD, lx <**=x̲**> *distributive, all over*, (<**=áls ~ =á:ls**> *structured activity non-continuative*), syntactic analysis: intransitive verb, attested by Elders Group, Salish cognate: Squamish /q'ətx̣-ánʔ/ *rap, make clatter (tr.)* and /q'ətx̣-íʔuɬ-n/ *rap a dish (tr.)* W73:211, K69:80.

<**q'átx̲em**>, cts //q'ə[-Aɛ́-]t=x̣=əm//, SD /'*scraping sound (like scraping food off dishes), rattling (of dishes, metal pots, wagon on gravel)*'/, (<**á-ablaut**> *continuative*), lx <**=x̲**> *distributive*, (<**=em**> *intransitivizer, have, get*), phonology: ablaut, syntactic analysis: intransitive verb, attested by Elders

Group.

<**q'átx̱(e)t**>, pcs //q'ə[-Aɛ́-]t=x̣=(ə)T//, cts, SD [*'rattling s-th'*], (<**á-ablaut**> *continuative*), lx <**=x̱**> *distributive*, (<**=et ~ =t**> *purposeful control transitivizer*), phonology: ablaut, presence or absence of e here is uncertain since I so far have the word only without, in an inflected version, syntactic analysis: transitive verb, attested by Elders Group, example: <**le q'átx̱tes te lelóthel.**>, //lə q'ə[-Aɛ́-]t=x=T-əs tə C_1ə=láθəl (or C_1əC_2=láθəl)//, /*'She's rattling the dishes.'*/, (<**R5=**> *diminutive plural* or R3= *plural*).

<**q'étmel**>, df //q'ə́t=məl//, ANAF /*'fin, neck fin, i.e. pectoral fin'*/, possibly root <**q'et**> meaning uncertain *rattling sound, scraping sound* perhaps as made when taken out of water and thrown on deck or ground, lx <**=mel**> *portion, part*, syntactic analysis: nominal, attested by Elders Group, Deming.

<**q'etóléstexw**>, MC /*'mix s-th, put them together'*/, *see* q'ó.

<**q'etx̱áls**>, SOC /*'to rattle (cans, etc. to wake newlyweds), to shivaree (someone)'*/, *see* q'et.

<**q'et'emá:yelhp**>, EB /*'balsam fir* (has sweet sap or cambium, grows at higher altitudes, called larch by some, "balsam" is a popular name for trees of the genus Abies), from a sample taken prob. *subalpine fir (Abies lasiocarpa),* if sample is mistaken poss. *Pacific silver fir (Abies amabilis) or grand fir (Abies grandis),* if the term balsam is mistaken too, poss. *a variety of Douglas fir (Pseudotsuga menziesii)'*/, *see* q'át'em.

<**q'et'ómthet**>, SENS [*'sweeten oneself'*], *see* q'át'em.

<**q'et'ómthet**>, SENS [*'get sweetened'*], *see* q'át'em.

<**q'éth'**>, probable bound root //q'əθ'//, meaning uncertain if not *defecate*

<**sq'éth'**>, dnom //s=q'əθ'//, ABFC /*'dung, (excrement, feces), shit'*/, (<**s=**> *nominalizer*), syntactic analysis: nominal, usage: can be used as a cuss word when angry, attested by Deming (3/30/78), JL (3/31/78), Elders Group (5/14/80); found in <**sq'éth'.**>, //s=q'ə́θ'//, /*'Shit.'*/, usage: also said when one loses a game and is mad, attested by Elders Group (5/14/80).

<**sq'éth'x̱**>, ds //s=q'ə́θ'=x̣//, ABFC /*'dung, (scattered excrement?, fecal droppings?)'*/, (<**s=**> *nominalizer*), lx <**=x̱**> *distributive*, syntactic analysis: nominal, attested by EB (8/4/78), comment: the same speaker reports sq'éth' *policeman* as probably a Thompson word.

<**q'eth'ōwítsem**>, ABFC [*'put one's hands behind one's back'*], *see* q'áth'.

<**q'éw ~ q'ew**>, bound root //q'ə́w ~ q'əw// *turn around something.*

<**Sq'ewá:lxw**>, df //s=q'əw=ɛ́·lx^w//, PLN /*'a turn in the Fraser River between Ruby Creek and Katz (about a mile upriver from the mouth of Ruby Creek and Ruby Creek I.R. #9 (called Lukseetsis-sum on maps and D.I.A. records, see Lexwthíthesem)),* also the name of *a village at this spot, spelled Skawahlook, Indian Reserve #1, on topographical maps and D.I.A. records'*/, (<**s=**> *nominalizer*), lx <**=á:lxw**> meaning uncertain–perhaps *leaves* as in <**hil=á:lxw**>, or possibly <**=á:l**> *similar to, -like, or part/portion* plus lx <=xw> *lump-like, round* or <=x̱w> *round, around* , syntactic analysis: nominal, attested by Elders Group (7/6/77), IHTTC (7/8/77), also <**Sq'ewá:lx̱w**>, //s=q'əw=ɛ́·lx̣^{w}//, attested by SP (8/28/75), other sources: Wells 1965 (lst ed.):25 <sk'aw-EHL-kw> (bars through final kw show spirant), transliterable as /sk'owɛ́lx^w/, *village opposite Hunter Creek*, source: place names reference file #25 and #45.

<**q'ewílem**>, mdls //q'əw=íl=əm//, incs, CAN /*'go around a bend in the river, go around a turn, go around something in one's way'*/, TVMO, (<**=íl**> *come, go*, <**=em**> *middle voice*), syntactic analysis: intransitive verb, attested by Deming.

<**Sq'ewílem**>, ds //s=q'əw=íl=əm//, PLN /*'a turn in the Fraser River on the CPR (northwest) side two miles east of American Bar, Texas Bar bend in the Fraser River'*/, literally /'place to go around

a bend in the river'/, (<**s=**> *nominalizer*), (<**=íl**> *go, come*), lx <**=em**> *place to or middle voice*, syntactic analysis: nominal, attested by transcribed from MP by SP and AD 1973-4 (IHTTC 7/8/77), AD (6/26/78 on trip to American Bar), source: place names reference file #47.

<**Sq'iq'ewílem**>, ds //s=C_1í=q'əw=íl=əm//, PLN /'*beach in front of old Scowlitz village, the point the Harrison River goes around by Kilby's store*'/, literally /'(place to go around a) little turn in the river'/, (<**s=**> *nominalizer*, R4= *diminutive*), (<**=íl**> *go, come*, <**=em**> *place to* or *middle voice*), phonology: reduplication, syntactic analysis: nominal, attested by EL (with EB and NP on Chehalis trip 9/27/77), source: place names file reference #312.

<**q'ewí:lt**>, pcs //q'əw=í·l=T//, incs, CAN ['*come with s-o (in a canoe for ex.)*'], TVMO, (<**=í:l** ~ **=íl** ~ **=el**> *come, go*, <**=t**> *purposeful control transitivizer*), syntactic analysis: transitive verb, attested by Elders Group (11/9/77).

<**q'éwlets ~ q'ówlets**>, ds //q'ə́w=ləc ~ q'áw=ləc or q'ə[=Aá=]w=ləc//, CAN ['*go around a bend (in water)*'], literally /'go around on the bottom'/, possibly <**ó-ablaut**> *derivational or resultative*?, lx <**=lets**> *on the bottom*, phonology: possible ablaut, syntactic analysis: intransitive verb, attested by Elders Group (2/27/80).

<**q'ówletsem**>, mdls //q'áw=ləc=əm or q'ə[=Aá=]w=ləc=əm//, CAN /'*go around (a point, a bend, a curve, etc.) in the water, make a U-turn (in the water, could use today on land with a car)*'/, literally /'turn ones rump/bottom around in the water'/, lx <**=lets**> *on the bottom*, (<**=em**> *middle voice*), phonology: possible ablaut, syntactic analysis: intransitive verb, attested by Elders Group (2/27/80), example: <**le q'owletsem.**>, //lɛ q'áw=ləc=əm//, /'*go around (a point, a bend, a curve, etc.) in the water, make a U-turn (in the water, could use today with a car)*'/.

<**q'ówletst**>, pcs //q'áw=ləc=T or q'ə[=Aá=]w=ləc=T//, CAN ['*go around s-th in the water*'], lx <**=lets**> *on the bottom*, (<**=t**> *purposeful control transitivizer*), phonology: possible ablaut, syntactic analysis: transitive verb, attested by Elders Group (2/27/80).

<**Sq'éwlets ~ Sq'ówlets**>, dnom //s=q'ə́w=ləc ~ s=q'ə[=Aá=]w=ləc//, PLN ['*old Scowlitz village*'], ASM ['on the northeast bank of the mouth of Harrison River onto the Fraser River, about two miles east of present-day Scowlitz Reserve, old Scowlitz was near Kilby's store and on the opposite side of Harrison Bay from new Scowlitz, the river turns there around the bottom of a mountain, the new Scowlitz was named after the old village but is not on a turn'], literally /'turn of river at bottom (of mountain)'/, (<**s=**> *nominalizer*), lx <**=lets**> *on the bottom*, possibly <**ó-ablaut**> *derivational*, phonology: possible ablaut, syntactic analysis: nominal, attested by AC (1973), DF (Elders Group 7/13/77), EL (with NP and EB)(9/27/77), Elders Group, source: place names file reference #72, also <**Sq'ówlets (not Sq'éwlets)**>, //s=q'ə[=Aá=]w=ləc//, attested by NP and DF and Johnny Williams Sr. (1/31/79), <**tsel yelhe'á kw'e Sq'éwlets.**>, //c-əl yə=ɬ=əʔɛ́ k'ʷə s=q'ə́w=ləc//, /'*I went through (via) Scowlitz.*'/, attested by Elders Group (1/19/77), example: <**ley lhe'á kw'e Sq'éwlets.**>, //lə yə=ɬ=əʔɛ́ k'ʷə s=q'ə́w=ləc//, /'*He went via Scowlitz (it was out of his way).*'/, literally /'third person past travelling along =via (a place out of one's way) the (remote) Scowlitz'/, attested by Elders Group (1/19/77).

<**sq'ówqel**>, ds //s=q'ə[=Aá=]w=qəl//, WATR /'*a bend in a river, a curve of a lake*'/, LAND ['*a bend in a road*'], (<**s=**> *nominalizer*), possibly <**ó-ablaut**> *derivational*, lx <**=qel**> *in the head*, phonology: possible ablaut, syntactic analysis: nominal, attested by EB (1/30/76).

<**Sq'éwqel ~ Sq'ówqel**>, ds //s=q'ə́w=qəl ~ s=q'ə[=Aá=]w=qəl//, PLN /'*upper end of Seabird Island, village at the upper end of Seabird Island, Maria Slough separating Seabird Island from north shore of Fraser River, now used for Seabird Island as a whole*'/, ASM ['named after the turn on the upriver end of Seabird Island, now filled in by the CPR after the 1894 flood washed out the railroad bridge (4/3/78), we visited this spot'], literally /'turn in the river in the head (top of the island)'/, (<**s=**> *nominalizer*), lx <**=qel**> *in the head*, phonology: possible ablaut, syntactic

analysis: nominal, attested by AD and SP transcribed from MP in 1973-4 (IHTTC 7/8/77), Elders Group (7/13/77), IHTTC (8/5/77, 8/11/77, 8/23/77), EB and other elders on Seabird Is. trip (4/3/78), other sources: Wells 1965 (lst ed.):14, source: place names file reference #51.

<**Sq'ewqé(:)yl ~ Sq'ewqí:l**>, ds //s=q'əw=q(əl)=í·l//, PLN /'*Scowkale, sometimes misspelled Skulkayn, now Chilliwack Indian Reserves #10 and #11*'/, literally /'a turn/bend in the head go/come/get/become'/, comment: (contrary to the DIA name Skulkayn, the first syllable has "w" not "l", the last syllable end with "l" not "n"; only speakers from some distance downriver (30-40 miles downriver, speakers of Downriver or Island dialects) use "n" in native Halkomelem terms, and this place name is not a Downriver Halkomelem name; Thompson speakers have "n" and William Sepass, part Thompson and a fluent speaker of the Thompson language, was a prominent chief of the Reserve, so the "n" spelling may be his influence; he was reported as chief in Hill-Tout 1902 where his Thompson name is recorded as <Qateku'eta> (umlaut over first a, macron over next e and over u), (<**s=**> *nominalizer*), lx <**=qel**> *in the head,* (<**=í:l**> *go, come, get, become*), phonology: syllable-loss of el before =í:l, syntactic analysis: nominal, attested by AC (1973), Elders Group (1/15/75, 7/20/77), BJ (5/10/64), other sources: Wells 1965 (lst ed.):19, source: place names reference file #87.

<**q'ewqé:ylém ~ q'ewqéylém (better q'ewqí:lem)**>, mdls //q'əw=q(əl)=í·l=əm ~ q'əw=q(əl)=íl=əm//, CAN /'*turn around a bend, go around a bend, turn around (to go back), turn around a corner*'/, TVMO, literally /'go/get/become/come around a bend in a river/trail in one's head'/, lx <**=qel**> *in the head,* (<**=í:l**> *go, come, get, become,* <**=em**> *middle voice*), phonology: updrifting, syllable-loss of el before =í:l, syntactic analysis: intransitive verb, attested by EB (2/6/76, 5/5/76), example: <**tsel le q'ewqé:ylém.**>, //c-əl lə (or lɛ) q'əw=qəl=í·l=əm//, /'*I turned around a bend., I went around a bend., I turned around (to go back).*'/, attested by EB.

<**Q'iq'ewetó:lthel**>, df //C_1í=q'əw(=)ət=á·lθəl//, PLN /'*a slough on Harrison River north side by the mouth of Chehalis River which has a knee-shaped sandbar at its mouth, this is the next slough above (upriver from) Meth'á:lmexwem*'/, literally /'little turn on the river like a knee'/, (<**R4=**> *diminutive*), root <**q'ew**> *turn in the river*, possibly <**=et**> meaning uncertain here, lx <**=ó:lthel**> *on the knee*, phonology: reduplication, syntactic analysis: nominal, attested by EL (with NP and EB on Chehalis place names trip 9/27/77), EL (3/1/78 tape), source: place names reference file #295.

<**q'éwe**>, free root //q'ə́wə//, PE /'*cane, staff*'/, SPRD, syntactic analysis: noun, nominal, attested by Elders Group, EB, also <**q'ówe**>, //q'áwə//, attested by AC (8/6/70, 8/29/70, 1974), TG (4/23/75), SJ (1974), Salish cognate: Samish dial. of N. Straits /q'ə́kʷə/ *cane, dancer's staff* G86:84, (=Songish dial. form in M68:76), example: <**q'éwes te xawsólkwlh**>, //q'ə́wə-s təx̣ɛws=álkʷɬ//, /'*staff of a new spirit-dancer*'/, attested by Elders Group, <**kw'óqwethoxes te q'éwe.**>, //k'ʷáqʷ=əT-áxʸ-əs tə q'ə́wə//, /'*He hit me with a cane.*'/, literally /'he hit me with a stick-like object the cane'/, attested by Elders Group, <**tiyéléstchexw ta' q'éwe xwelám te t'ómél.**>, //tiy(=)əlśs=T-c-əxʷ t-ɛʔ q'ə́wə xʷə=lɛ́=m tə t'ám=əl//, /'*Lean your cane against the wall.*'/, literally /'you lean s-th the -your cane toward the wall'/, attested by EB.

<**q'ewú:w**>, dnom //q'ə́wə=úw or //, SPRD /'*new spirit dancer's cane*'/ (vs. <**q'éwe**> 'cane'), prob. <**=á:w ~ =í:w ~ =ew ~ =ú:w**> '*on the body, on top of itself*', attested by RG & EH (4/10/99 Ling332)

<**q'ewételhtst**>, MUS ['*drum for s-o*'], *see* q'ówet.

<**q'ewétem**>, MUS ['*drumming*'], *see* q'ówet.

<**q'ewétt**>, MUS ['*drum for s-o*'], *see* q'ówet.

<**q'ewílem**>, CAN /'*go around a bend in the river, go around a turn, go around something in one's way*'/, *see* q'éw ~ q'ew.

<**q'ewí:lestel**>, CLO ['*suspenders*'], *see* q'e:yw ~ q'í:w.

<**q'ewí:lt**>, CAN ['*come with s-o (in a canoe for ex.)*'], *see* q'éw ~ q'ew.

<**q'éwlets ~ q'ówlets**>, CAN ['*go around a bend (in water)*'], *see* q'éw ~ q'ew.

<**q'ewqé:ylém ~ q'ewqéylém (better q'ewqí:lem)**>, CAN /'*turn around a bend, go around a bend, turn around (to go back), turn around a corner*'/, *see* q'éw ~ q'ew.

<**Q'éwq'ewe**>, PLN /'*Kawkawa Lake (near Hope, B.C.)*'/, *see* q'á:w.

<**Q'ewq'ewelátsa**>, N ['*Male Loon*'], *see* q'á:w.

<**Q'ewq'eweló:t**>, N ['*Female Loon*'], *see* q'á:w.

<**q'exelám**>, df //q'əx^{y}=əl=ə[=Aɛ́=]m//, SD /'*(make) a whoop, a cowboy's whoop*'/, LANG, root poss. related (by fronting) to <**q'(e)x̲**> meaning *loud harsh noise*, <**=el**> *go, come, get, become*, <=em> *middle voice*, <**á-ablaut**> *durative*, syntactic analysis: prob. intransitive verb, attested by Elders Group (11/10/76).

<**q'exí:lt**>, TVMO /'*accompany s-o, go with s-o, go along with s-o*'/, *see* q'ó.

<**q'(e)x̲**>, bound root //q'əx̣ ~ q'x̣// perhaps *loud harsh noise.*

<**q'eq'x̲át**>, durs //q'ə[=C_1ə=]x̣=ə[=Aɛ́=]T//, LANG ['*argue with s-o*'], possibly <**=R1=**> *resultative or continuative*, comment: perhaps related to q'éx̲q'x̲el *metal can* which would have the same shaped root and is said to be named from its noise, thus the root of both could mean something like *loud harsh noise*, (<**á-ablaut**> *durative*), (<**=et**> *purposeful control transitivizer*), phonology: reduplication, ablaut, vowel-loss in reduplication, syntactic analysis: transitive verb, attested by IHTTC (9/14/77), Salish cognate: Squamish /q'ə-q'x̣-át-ayʔ/ *argue, debate (tr., recip.)* W73:7, K67:355; found in <**q'eq'x̲áthóxescha.**>, //q'ə[=C_1ə=]x̣=ə[=Aɛ́=]T-áx^{y}-əs-cɛ//, /'*He'll argue with me.*'/, attested by IHTTC (8/9/77).

<**q'eyq'x̲át** or **q'iq'x̲át**>, pcs //C_1í=q'əx̣=ə[=Aɛ́=]T//, durs, LANG ['*argue with s-o*'], (<**R4=**> *diminutive*? or here *continuative*?), phonology: reduplication, ablaut *durative*, vowel-loss in root, syntactic analysis: transitive verb, attested by IHTTC (8/9/77); found in <**q'iq'x̲áthóxes.**>, //C_1í=q'əx̣=ə[=Aɛ́=]T-áx^{y}-əs//, [q'eq'x̣ǽθáx^{y}ɪs], /'*He argued with me.*'/.

<**q'x̲ótel**>, rcps //q'(ə)x̣=ə[=Aɛ́=Aá=]T-əl//, durs, pcs, [q'x̣átəl], LANG /'*to argue, have an argument, [argue with each other], quarrelling, sassing back*'/, (<**á-ablaut**> *durative*, itself changed by ó-ablaut which is automatically triggered on preceding a-vowels by =(e)tel *reciprocal*, ablaut of ablaut), (<**=et**> *purposeful control transitivizer*), (<**-el**> *reciprocal*), phonology: double ablaut, vowel-loss in root to zero-grade, syntactic analysis: intransitive verb, attested by Elders Group.

<**q'eyq'x̲ótel**>, cts //C_1í=q'x̣=ə[=Aɛ́=Aá=]T-əl or q'ə[=Ai=C_1ə=]x̣=ə[=Aɛ́=Aá=]T-əl//, durs, rcps, LANG /'*arguing, arguing (back and forth)*'/, possibly <**R4=**> *continuative* (though *diminutive* in form) or <**i-ablaut**> *resultative* possibly plus <**=R1=**> *continuative*, (<**á-ablaut**> *durative*, itself changed to <**ó-ablaut**> triggered on preceding <**a**>-vowels by =tel *reciprocal*), phonology: double ablaut, vowel-loss, perhaps triple ablaut, reduplication, syntactic analysis: intransitive verb, attested by Elders Group, Salish cognate: Squamish /q'ə-q'x̣-át-ayʔ/ *argue, debate (tr., recip.)* W73:7, K67:355.

<**q'éx̲q'x̲el**>, chrs //q'ə́x̣=C_1əC_2=əl//, dnom, incs, [q'ə́x̣q'x̣əl], HHG /'*metal can (in U.S. English), a tin (in Canadian English)*'/, Elder's comment: "it's called this because it rattles and relates to q'etx̲áls *rattle* and q'átx̲els *rattling* (AK); named from noise q'átx̲em *bang cans together, etc.* (Elders Group 9/21/77)", comment: seems named for the noise but perhaps only by sound symbolism with q'etx̲áls, q'átx̲em since there is no =t= infix and no process which drops consonants in the middle of a root;

the root of q'etx̲áls and q'átx̲em is more likely q'et with =x̲ *distributive*, (<=**R2**> *characteristic*, <=**el**> *go, get, become*), phonology: reduplication, syntactic analysis: nominal, attested by SJ (3/17/77), AK, Elders Group, Salish cognate: Squamish /q'ə́-q'x̣l/ *tin can* W73:51, K69:81.

<**q'éx̲q'ex̲el sqe'óleqw**>, EB, FOOD *soda pop* (lit. perhaps: bubbling and fizzy/perhaps: metal can + fruit juice), (attested by RG,EH 6/16/98 to SN, edited by BG with RG,EH 6/26/00)

<**q'ex̲mí:l**>, possibly root //q'əx̣mí·l or q'əx̣=əm=í·l//, EB /'*hog fennel, Indian consumption plant*'/, ['*Lomatium nudicaule*'], MED ['medicine for tuberculosis'], possibly root <**q'ex̲**> *rattle* from sound of tubercular cough, possibly <**=em**> *intransitivizer, have, get*, possibly <**=í:l**> *go, come, get, become*, syntactic analysis: nominal, attested by AC (prompted), Elders Group, other sources: ES /qəx̣mí·l or q'əx̣mí·l/ *hog fennel.*

<**q'éxq'x̲el**>, HHG /'*metal can (in U.S. English), a tin (in Canadian English)*'/, *see* q'(e)x̲.

<**q'ex̲wő:welh ~ q'ex̲wőwelh**>, df //q'əx̣ʷ=ó(·)wəɬ//, CAN /'*big high-bowed canoe from the Coast, Nootka war canoe, huge canoe (Nootka type)*'/, ASM ['could seat up to 20, had four rows of four abreast plus two in front and two in back (Elders Group 1/28/76)'], possibly root <**q'ex̲**> as in <**q'x̲=ót=el**> *argue back and forth*, lx <**=ó:welh ~ =ówelh**> *canoe*, phonology: schwa-grade root varies with zero-grade, syntactic analysis: nominal, attested by AC, Deming, Elders Group, also <**q'x̲wő:welh**>, //q'x̣ʷó·wəɬ//, attested by DM (12/4/64), example: <**q'ex̲wő:welh ~ q'exwő:welh**>, //q'əx̣ʷ=ówəɬ ~ q'əxʷ=ó·wəɬ//, attested by AC, other sources: ES Cowichan /q'xʷə́wəɬ/ *Nootka-type canoe*, Salish cognate: Squamish /q'xʷə́wʔɬ/ *West Coast or Chinook canoe* W73:52, K67:355, K69:80, Samish dial. of N. Straits /q'x̣ʷə́w'ɬ/ *big canoe (but smaller than /ʔátx̣əs/)* word perhaps from Cowichan G86:86, <**tl'esu le tés kw'e Semáth te q'ex̲wówelh.**>, //ƛ'ə=s=u lə tə́s k'ʷə s(=)mɛ́θ tə q'əx̣ʷ=ówəɬ//, /'*Then the big canoe got to Sumas.*'/, usage: Story of the Flood, attested by AC, <**qe tl'o su máytemet tútl'o hí:kw te q'ex̲wówelhs.**>, //qə ƛ'a=s=u mɛ́y=T-əm-ət t=ú=ƛ'a hí[=·=]kʷ tə q'əx̣ʷ=ówəɬ-s//, /'*And so he was helped with his big canoe.*'/, usage: Story of the Flood, attested by AC.

<**q'ey, q'ey, q'ey**>, free root //q'əy, q'əy, q'əy//, EFAM ['*cry of a bluejay [Steller's jay] that means good news*'], EZ, root meaning unknown, probably onomatopoeia, phonology: transcribed with low pitch stress (unmarked), syntactic analysis: interjection, attested by Elders Group (3/21/79).

<**q'ey ~ q'i**>, bound root //q'əy ~ q'i *wound around, tied, knotted*//.

<**q'eq'éy**>, df //C_1ə=q'íy or C_1ə=q'ə́y//, [q'əq'éy], ANA /'*guts, intestines*'/, possibly <**R5= (if stress shifted to root)**> *diminutive plural*, probably root <**q'ey**> *tied, knotted, wound around* probably root as in <**q'eyós**> *barrel* probably root <**q'ís=et**> *tie s-th, knot s-th* probably root <**etc.**, phonology: reduplication, perhaps stress-shift, syntactic analysis: nominal, attested by AC, Elders Group (8/20/75), other sources: ES /q'əq'ɛ́y·/ *intestines*, H-T <k·uk·é> (macron over e) *bowels or guts*, Salish cognate: Squamish /q'iáx̣/ *intestines, guts* W73:151, K67:359, Lushootseed /q'əjáx̣/ *intestines* H76:395.

<**q'éyq'ey ~ q'íq'i**>, chrs //q'əy=C_1əC_2//, ABDF ['*(have/get) sore muscles*'], literally /'characteristically knotted/tied'/, root <**q'ey**> *knotted, tied, wound around*, (<=**R2**> *characteristic*), phonology: reduplication, syntactic analysis: adjective/adjectival verb?, attested by BHTTC (11/15/76).

<**q'eyós**>, df //q'əy=ás//, HHG /'*barrel,* probably also *tub*'/, possibly <**=ós**> *round thing, on the face*, syntactic analysis: nominal, attested by EB (1/9/76), (compare <**q'eq'éy**> *intestines*, <**q'ís**> *tied, knotted, wound around*, <**q'eyáweth'ches**> *cross one's hands*, and/or perhaps <**q'oyíyets ~ q'oyí:ts**> *elk*), Salish cognate: Squamish /q'ə=q'iʔás/ *barrel* (root /q'í/ *tie, knot (wind around?)* as in /q'ís/ *be tied, knotted*, /q'iáx̣/ *intestines*, and /q'iíʔč/ *moose* is suggested by Kuipers) W73:14, K67:356, 357, 358.

<**q'eyáweth'ches**>, df //q'əy=ɛ́wəθ'=cəs//, [q'eyǽwʊθ'čɪs], ABFC /'*cross one's hands* [prob. error], *(hands crossed)*'/, lx <**=áweth'**> meaning unknown, <**=tses ~ =ches**> *on the hand(s)*, syntactic analysis: intransitive verb, attested by IHTTC (9/1/77).

<**q'eyáweth'eláx̲el**>, df //q'əy=ɛ́w(=)əθ'=əlɛ́x̣əl//, ABFC /'*cross one's arms (but not fold one's arms across chest)* [prob. error], *(arms crossed [but not folded across chest)*'/, possibly <**=áweth'**> meaning unknown unless <**=áw ~ =ews**> *on the body* plus <**=eth'**> *small portion*, lx <**=eláx̲el**> *on the arm(s)*, syntactic analysis: intransitive verb, attested by IHTTC (9/1/77).

<**q'eyáweth'xel**>, df //q'əy=ɛ́w(=)əθ'=x^{y}əl//, ABFC /'*legs crossed, cross one's ankles (either sitting or standing)* [prob. error], *(ankles crossed (either sitting or standing))*'/, possibly <**=áweth'**> meaning unknown unless <**=áw ~ =ews**> *on the body* plus <**=eth'**> *small portion*, lx <**=xel**> *on the foot/feet, on the leg*, syntactic analysis: intransitive verb, attested by IHTTC (7/19/77, 9/1/77).

<**q'eyáweth'xelem**>, mdls //q'əy=ɛ́w(=)əθ'=x^{y}əl=əm//, ABFC ['*cross one's legs*'], possibly <**=áweth'**> meaning unknown unless <**=áw ~ =ews**> *on the body* plus <**=eth'**> *small portion*, lx <**=xel**> *on the foot, on the leg*, (<**=em**> *middle voice*), syntactic analysis: intransitive verb, attested by IHTTC (7/19/77).

<**q'oyéx̲ ~ q'eyéx̲**>, df //q'əy=ə́(=)x̣ or q'ə[=Ao=]y=ə= ́=x̣//, WATR ['*whirlpool*'], root <**q'ey**> *wound around, tied, knotted*, lx <**=x̲**> or perhaps here <**=éx̲**> (stressed allomorph/strong-grade after weak-grade root)> *distributive, all over, all around*, possibly <**o-ablaut**> *derivational*, possibly <**=e**> or <**=é**> meaning unknown if present unless> *living entity*, possibly <**= ́=**> *derivational*, phonology: possible stress-shift or stressed full-grade of suffix after weak-grade root, possible ablaut, syntactic analysis: nominal?, intransitive verb?, attested by AD (5/1/79), Salish cognate: Squamish /sq'iáx̣-atq^{w}ú-ʔm/ *whirlpool* W73:287, K69:59.

<**q'oyéx̲em**>, df //q'əy=ə́x̣=əm or q'ə[=Aa=]y=ə́x̣=əm//, WATR ['*whirlpool that suddenly starts from level water*'], (<**=em**> *middle voice* or *intransitivizer, have, get* or *place to get/have*), phonology: possible ablaut, syntactic analysis: intransitive verb or nominal, attested by AD (5/1/79).

<**q'éyex̲em**>, df //q'ə́y=(ə)x̣=əm//, WATR ['*whirlpool (large or small)*'], root <**q'ey**> *wound around, tied, knotted*, lx <**=x̲**> *distributive*, (<**=em**> *middle voice* or *intransitivizer, have, get* or *place to have/get*), phonology: strong-grade of root for these speakers, syntactic analysis: nominal? or intransitive verb?, attested by BJ (12/5/64), Elders Group (3/26/75).

<**Q'eyq'éyex̲em**>, df //$C_1əC_2$=q'ə́y=x̣=əm//, WATR ['*place on the Fraser River above Yale where there are whirlpools*'], literally /'many whirlpools'/, (<**R3=**> *plural*), lx <**=(e)x̲**> *distributive*, (<**=em**> *place to have/get*), phonology: reduplication, syntactic analysis: nominal, attested by SP (IHTTC 8/8/77, 8/23/77).

<**q'éyset ~ q'í(:)set**>, pcs //q'ə́y=s=əT ~ q'í(·)=s=əT//, WV /'*to fasten s-th by tying, tie up s-th (like canoe, horse, laces, nets, cow, shoelaces), tie it*'/, lx <**=s**> meaning uncertain or =es> *on the face*, (semological comment: =es *on the face* is plausible since the canoe bow is the face of a canoe in some words, the top of the foot (where shoelaces are tied) is the face of the foot, the cow and horse are tied around their faces, and *design, pattern* (s=x̲él=es) also uses the suffix =es *on the face*), (<**=et**> *purposeful control transitivizer*), syntactic analysis: transitive verb, attested by Elders Group (3/1/72, 3/72, 5/5/75, 5/26/76), EB, HT (6/21/76), AC, (compare <**q'í:=w=et**> *to hang s-th/s-o up*, <**s=q'éy(=)l(=)e**> *dried fish/meat (hung to smoke or wind-dry)*, or <**q'í(=)t'e**> *a swing)*, example: <**q'éyset kw'es selá ~ selá kw'es q'éyset**>, //q'ə́y=s=əT k'^{w}ə-s səlɛ́ ~ səlɛ́ k'^{w}ə-s q'ə́y=s=əT//, /'*tie it tightly*'/, attested by AC, <**selá kw'es q'éyset te x̲wéylem**>, //səlɛ́ k'^{w}ə-s q'ə́y=s=əT təx̣^{w}í·ləm//, /'*tie the rope tight*'/, attested by AC, EB, <**q'éyset te stiqíw.**>, //q'ə́y=s=əT tə s=tiqíw//, /'*tie the horse*'/, attested by Elders Group (5/26/76).

<**q'éyq'eset**>, cts //q'í[-C_1ə-]=s=əT//, WV ['*tying it*'], (<**-R1-**> *continuative*), phonology: reduplication, syntactic analysis: transitive verb, attested by EB, AC.

<**q'éysetsel**>, ds //q'í(·)=s=əcəl//, WV ['*to weave*'], lx <**=s**> meaning uncertain, <**=etsel**> *on the back*, (semological comment: most weaving was done on the back, i.e. side opposite the weaver so the weaver could see the patterns), syntactic analysis: intransitive verb, attested by JL (Elders Group 8/8/79).

<**q'éyq'esetsel**>, cts //q'í(·)[-C_1ə-]=s=əcəl//, WV /'*weaving (for ex. a tumpline), mending a net, making a net*'/, ASM ['fish nets were knotted and tied with square holes of different sizes depending on the fish to be caught, they were usually tied with méthelh twine (dogbane)'], (<**-R1-**> *continuative*), phonology: reduplication, syntactic analysis: intransitive verb, attested by JL (8/8/79), Lawrence James (Elders Group 1/7/76), EB, Elders Group, example: <**q'éyq'esetsel te q'sí:ltel**>, //q'í[-C_1ə-]=s=əcəl tə q'í·s=ə[=M2=]l=təl//, /'*weaving a packstrap/tumpline*'/, attested by JL, <**tsel q'éyq'esetsel.**>, //c-əl q'í[-C_1ə-]=s=əcəl//, /'*I'm making a net.*'/, attested by Elders Group (8/25/76).

<**shxwq'éyq'esetsel**>, dnom //sx^{w}=q'í[=C_1ə=]=s=əcəl//, WV /'*net shuttle, mesh-measure (usually part of the shuttle)*'/, ASM ['made with a place to wrap netting twine around it to weave it in and out'], (<**shxw=**> *something for, device for*), phonology: reduplication, syntactic analysis: nominal, attested by Elders Group, DM (12/4/64).

<**q'ésetsel**>, cts //q'i[-Aə́-]=s=əcəl//, WV ['*tying a net*'], (<**é-ablaut**> *continuative*), phonology: ablaut, syntactic analysis: intransitive verb, attested by JL (5/5/75).

<**q'ésq'esetsel**>, chrs //q'i[=Aə́=]=s=C_1əC_2=əcəl//, EZ ['*spider*'], ['*class Arachnida,* order *Araneida,* also order *Phalangida*'], literally /'little characteristic net makers'/, (<**é-ablaut**> *diminutive plural* or perhaps *resultative,* <**=R2**> *characteristic*), phonology: ablaut, reduplication, syntactic analysis: nominal, attested by Elders Group (3/1/72), AC, other sources: ES /q'ə́sq'əscəl/ *spider,* JH /q'ə́sq'ə́scəl/ *spider (the net maker),* H-T <kuskúsitsEl> *spider (Aranca sp.)(the weaver)* from <kaísitsEl> *to weave,* also <**q'esq'ésetsel**>, //C_1əC_2=q'i[=Aə́=]=s=əcəl//, (<**R3=**> *plural actions*), (<**é-ablaut on root i**> *diminutive*), phonology: reduplication, ablaut, attested by Elders Group (6/16/76).

<**tl'áleqtxel q'esq'ésetsel**>, cpds //ƛ'ɛ́[=lə=]qt=x^{y}əl C_1əC_2=q'i[=Aə́=]=s=əcəl//, EZ /'*daddy long-legs (spider), harvestman spider*'/, ['class *Arachnida,* order *Phalangida*'], literally /'long legs spider'/, (<**=le=**> *plural*), lx <**=xel**> *on the leg, leg*, phonology: infixed =el= plural, reduplication, ablaut, syntactic analysis: simple nominal phrase, attested by Elders Group (6/16/76).

<**q'sí:ltel**>, df //q'i=s=í·l=təl or q'í·=s=ə[=M2=]l=təl//, WV /'*woven headband of packstrap, tumpline*'/, PE, TVMO, HARV, HUNT, literally perhaps /'woven device to go/come'/, possibly <**metathesis**> *derivational,* (<**=í:l ~ =el**> *go, come, get, become*), lx <**=tel**> *device to*, phonology: perhaps metathesis, perhaps vowel-loss, syntactic analysis: nominal, attested by CT and HT, JL, Elders Group, AC, (contrast <**chématel ~ chámatel**> *packstrap, tumpline),* example: <**thá:yem te q'sí:ltel**>, //θi[=Aɛ́·=]y=əm tə q'í·=s=ə[=M2=]l=təl//, /'*weaving a packstrap*'/, literally /'making a packstrap'/, attested by JL (8/8/79).

<**sq'eyq'tóles**>, dnom //s=q'ey[=C_1ə=]=T=áləs//, CLO /'*mask (tied) over the eyes* '/, <**s=**> *nominalizer,* <**q'ey ~ q'i**>,*wound around, tied, knotted,* <=R1=> *resultative,* perhaps <**=T**> *purposeful control transitivizer,* <**=óles**> *on the eyes,* attested by RG & EH (4/10/99 Ling332)

<**q'eyáweth'ches**>, ABFC /'*cross one's hands* [prob. error], *(hands crossed)*'/, *see* q'ey ~ q'i.

<**q'eyáweth'elá<u>x</u>el**>, ABFC /'*cross one's arms (but not fold one's arms across chest)* [prob. error], *(arms crossed [but not folded across chest)*'/, *see* q'ey ~ q'i.

<**q'eyáweth'xel**>, ABFC /'*legs crossed, cross one's ankles (either sitting or standing)* [prob. error], *(ankles crossed (either sitting or standing))*'/, *see* q'ey ~ q'i.

<**q'eyáweth'xelem**>, ABFC ['*cross one's legs*'], *see* q'ey ~ q'i.

<**q'éyexem**>, WATR ['*whirlpool (large or small)*'], *see* q'ey ~ q'i.

<**q'éyq'ekw'et**>, ABFC /'*biting into s-th/s-o, biting s-o/s-th*'/, *see* q'éykw' or q'í:kw'.

<**q'éyq'eleq ~ (better) q'íq'eleq**>, SOCT /'*my dear, (little best friend, little dear friend, etc.)*'/, *see* q'ó.

<**q'éyq'elstexw**>, TVMO ['*bringing it back*'], *see* q'ó:lthet.

<**q'eyq'elts'iyósem spehá:ls**>, WETH ['*whirlwind*'], *see* q'eyq'elts'iyósem.

<**q'éyq'eset**>, WV ['*tying it*'], *see* q'ey ~ q'i.

<**q'éyq'esetsel**>, WV /'*weaving (for ex. a tumpline), mending a net, making a net*'/, *see* q'ey ~ q'i.

<**q'éyq'ete** or **q'íq'et'e**>, PLAY ['*swinging*'], *see* q'éyt'o ~ q'éyt'e.

<**q'éyq'ey ~ q'íq'i**>, ABDF ['*(have/get) sore muscles*'], *see* q'ey ~ q'i.

<**q'é:yq'ey**>, ABDF ['*be always sickly*'], *see* q'ó:y ~ q'óy.

<**Q'eyq'éyexem**>, WATR ['*place on the Fraser River above Yale where there are whirlpools*'], *see* q'ey ~ q'i.

<**q'eyq'xát** or **q'iq'xát**>, LANG ['*argue with s-o*'], *see* q'(e)x.

<**q'eyq'xótel**>, LANG /'*arguing, arguing (back and forth)*'/, *see* q'(e)x.

<**q'éyset ~ q'í(:)set**>, WV /'*to fasten s-th by tying, tie up s-th (like canoe, horse, laces, nets, cow, shoelaces), tie it*'/, *see* q'ey ~ q'i.

<**q'éysetsel**>, WV ['*to weave*'], *see* q'ey ~ q'i.

<**q'éyt'e**>, df //q'í·t'ə// or //q'ə́y=t'=ə//, PLAY ['*to swing*'], syntactic analysis: intransitive verb, attested by Elders Group (4/16/75), RG & EH (4/9/99 Ling332), example: <**q'éyt'e te q'á:mi.**>, //q'í·(=)t'(=)ə tə q'ɛ́·mi//, /'*A girl swings.*'/.

<**q'éyq'ete** or **q'íq'et'e**>, cts //q'í[-C_1ə-]t'ə//, PLAY ['*swinging*'], (<**-R1-**> *continuative*), phonology: reduplication, syntactic analysis: intransitive verb, attested by AC (8/24/70), RG & EH (4/9/99 Ling332).

<**q'éyt'o ~ q'éyt'e**>, df //q'í·(=)t'(=)a ~ q'í·(=)t'(=)ə or q'ə́y=t'=a ~ q'ə́y=t'=ə or q'í·t'a ~ q'í·t'ə//, HHG /'*a swing, a little treadle they swing the babies on*'/, PLAY, ASM ['a sturdy pole is lashed to the roof or ceiling and a baby basket is suspended from that by a rope, the rope is tied to another rope which is attached horizontally across the basket to provide for even suspension, a string/twine is attached to the bottom and runs to the mother's foot so she can jiggle and bounce the cradle while weaving or otherwise using both hands; now perhaps used for any modern swing as well'], literally perhaps /'something put up for a person/baby'/, (<**=t'**> meaning unknown, <**=a**> or <**=e**> *entity or person*), syntactic analysis: nominal, attested by AC, BJ (12/5/64), Elders Group, DM (12/4/64), AD (6/19/79), RG & EH (4/9/99 Ling332), other sources: ES /q'í·t'a/ *swing (noun)*, compare <**séqtel**> *swing for baby cradle* with same meaning.

<**q'éyt'o ~ q'í:t'o**>, df //q'ɛ[=Aí·=]t'=a or q'í·(=)t'(=)a//, EB ['*orange honeysuckle*'], ['*Lonicera ciliosa*'], ASM ['flowers can be sucked for sweet liquid nectar, berries are poison'], MED ['the plant part is medicine for "fits"'], literally perhaps /'sweetened entity (or perhaps) swing'/, possibly root <**q'at' ~ q'et'**> *sweet* or possibly root <**q'í·(=t'=ə)**> *swing* (after the vine part), possibly <**í:-ablaut**> *durative*,

possibly <**=o**> *entity, living thing*, phonology: ablaut, syntactic analysis: nominal, attested by Elders Group, other sources: ES /q'í·t'a/ *orange honeysuckle*.

<**q'eyth'**> bound root //q'iθ'// meaning unknown or root <**q'áth'**> //q'ɛ́θ'// *lean, slant*
<**sq'eyth'éleqw**>, df //s=q'iθ'=ə́ləqʷ or s=q'ɛ[=Ai=]θ'=ə́ləqʷ//, BLDG [*'peak of house'*], LAND [*'peak of mountain'*], (<**s=**> *nominalizer*), possibly root <**q'áth'**> as in <**sq'áq'eth'**> *leaning backwards*, possibly <**i-ablaut**> *durative*, lx <**=éleqw**> *on top of the head, on top*, phonology: possible ablaut, syntactic analysis: nominal, attested by Elders Group, Salish cognate: Squamish /q'íc'-iʔəqʷ/ *gabledroof* W73:110, K69:82.

<**q'éytl'**>, bound root //q'íƛ' *be healed, scarred over*//, Salish cognate: Squamish /q'íƛ'/ *be healed up (wound)* W73:139, K67:358.
<**sq'éytl'** or **sq'ítl'**>, dnom //s=q'íƛ'//, ABFC [*'a scar'*], (<**s=**> *nominalizer*), syntactic analysis: nominal, attested by NP.
<**q'éytl'thet**>, df //q'íƛ'=θət//, ABFC /*'it healed up, (to heal up)'*/, possibly root <**q'ey**> *tied, knotted*, (<**=thet**> *get, become* or *reflexive*), syntactic analysis: intransitive verb, attested by NP.

<**q'éytl'thet**>, ABFC /*'it healed up, (to heal up)'*/, *see* q'éytl'.

<**Q'éyts'i(y)**>, df //q'íc'=iy//, PLN [*'Katzie village'*], ASM ['a downriver-Halq'eméylem-speaking village'], literally [*'a multi-colored moss'*], comment: Upriver-speaking elders don't know this as a word for a kind of moss but know it as a place name, lx <**=iy**> *plant, bark, covering*, syntactic analysis: nominal, attested by Elders Group,

<**q'e:yw ~ q'í:w**>, bound root //q'í·w *hang over*//, contrast <**q'ew**> *turn in a river, bend in a road*
<**q'é:ywet** (or better) **q'í:wet**>, ABFC /*'hang s-th on a line, hang s-th on a nail, hang s-th up'*/, *see* q'e:yw ~ q'í:w.
<**q'éyxwet**>, pcs //q'í(=)xʷ=əT//, CLO /*'tighten it (a belt, a pack, etc.)'*/, MC, probably root <**q'i ~ q'ey**> see under <**q'íxwet**>.

<**q'éyx̲**>, bound root //q'íx̣ *black*//, see under <**q'íx̲**>.
<**q'ix̲ ~ q'eyx̲**>, bound root //q'ix̣// *tilt*
<**q'éyx̲eya**>, SOCT [*'Negro'*], *see* q'íx̲.

<**q'eyx̲óles**>, ANA [*'pupil of the eye'*], *see* q'íx̲.

<**q'e'í:lem ~ q'a'í:lem**>, mdls //q'əʔ=í·l=əm ~ q'ɛʔ=í·l=əm//, incs, DESC /*'very old, ancient, get ancient, be ancient'*/, HAT, semantic environment ['of a person, horse, house, etc.'], root meaning unknown, (<**=í:l**> *get, become*, <**=em**> *middle voice*), syntactic analysis: adjective/adjectival verb, attested by AC, other sources: ES /q'ɛʔí·ləm/ *old*, JH /q'eʔí·ləm/ *old person*, Salish cognate: Squamish /q'əʔílmiʔ/ *aged* as in /ʔán qəʔílmiʔ stélməxʷ/ *very old man* K69:81, example: <**lulh q'e'í:lem (te stiqíw, ta lálem).**>, //lə=uɬ q'əʔ=í·l=əm (tə s=tiqíw, t-ɛ lɛ́ləm)//, /*'(The horse, Your house) has gotten ancient/is ancient.'*/, attested by AC.

<**q'e'í:les ~ q'e'í:lés**>, df //q'əʔ=í·l=əs//, ABFC /*'sensible, wise, (get sensible, get wise)'*/, root meaning unknown unless the same as in <**q'e'=í:l=em**>, possibly <**=í:l**> *go, come, get, become*, possibly <**=es**> *on the face*, phonology: updrifting, syntactic analysis: adjective/adjectival verb, attested by Elders Group, Salish cognate: Squamish /n-q'íl-us/ *smart, clever, wise* W73:239, K67:309, example: <**chexw (le) q'e'í:lés.**>, //c-əxʷ (lə) q'ə=ʔí·l=əs//, /*'You're sensible.'*/.
<**q'e'ílésthet**>, pcrs //q'əʔ=í·l=əs=T-ət//, EFAM [*'smarten up'*], (<**-t**> *purposeful control transitivizer*), (<**-et**> *reflexive*), phonology: updrifting, syntactic analysis: intransitive verb, attested by IHTTC.

<**q'e'ó:leq**>, SOCT [*'dear friends'*], *see* q'ó.

<**q'í:kw' ~ q'éykw'**>, root //q'í·k'ʷ *bite*//.

<**sq'éykw'**>, dnom //s=q'í·k'ʷ//, ABFC ['*a bite*'], (<**s=**> *nominalizer*), syntactic analysis: nominal, attested by Elders Group (3/1/72), TG, example: <**tl'ó sq'éykw's telí te sqwmáy.**>, //ƛ'á s=q'í·k'ʷ-s təlí tə s=qʷm=ɛ́y//, /'*It's a bite from a dog.*'/, literally /'that's, it's his bite from the/a dog'/, attested by TG.

<**q'éykw'et ~ q'í:kw'et**>, pcs //q'í·k'ʷ=əT//, ABFC /'*bite into s-th/s-o, bite s-th, bite s-o*'/, (<**=et**> *purposeful control transitivizer*), syntactic analysis: transitive verb, attested by AC, Elders Group (3/1/72, 6/16/76), TG, other sources: ES and JH /q'í·k'ʷət/ *bite*; found in <**q'éykw'etes.**>, //q'í·k'ʷ=əT-əs//, /'*He bit it.*'/, attested by TG, example: <**tsel q'éykw'et.**>, //c-əl q'í·k'ʷ=əT//, /'*I bit something.*'/, attested by Elders Group (3/1/72); found in <**q'éykw'etem.**>, //q'í·k'ʷ=əT-əm//, /'*He was bitten.*'/, syntactic analysis: passive, attested by TG, <**q'éykw'ethò:m.**>, //q'í·k'ʷ=əT-à·m//, /'*You were bitten.*'/, syntactic analysis: passive, attested by TG, example: <**q'éykw'ethò:m te álhqey.**>, //q'í·k'ʷ=əT-à·m tə ʔɛ́ɬqəy//, /'*The snake bit you., You got bitten by the snake.*'/, attested by Elders Group (6/16/76), <**li q'éykw'ethò:m?**>, //li q'í·k'ʷ=əT-à·m//, /'*Have you been bitten?*'/, attested by TG.

<**q'éyq'ekw'et**>, cts //q'í·[-C$_1$ə-]k'ʷ=əT//, ABFC /'*biting into s-th/s-o, biting s-o/s-th*'/, (<**-R1-**> *continuative*), phonology: reduplication, syntactic analysis: transitive verb, attested by AC.

<**q'í:kw'et ~ q'éykw'et**>, ABFC /'*bite into s-th/s-o, bite s-th, bite s-o*'/, *see* q'éykw' or q'í:kw'.

<**q'í:l ~ q'éyl**>, bound root //q'í·l// *put away, store away*

<**sq'éyle**>, dnom //s=q'í·l=ə//, FOOD /'*preserved fish, preserved meat, dried fish, dried meat (usually fish), smoked salmon, wind-dried salmon (old word), what is stored away, what is put away*'/, (<**s=**> *nominalizer*), probably root <**q'éyl ~ q'í:l**> *put away, store away*, possibly <**=e**> *living thing*??, syntactic analysis: nominal, attested by IHTTC, AD (3/6/79), EB, also <**sq'é:yla**>, //s=q'í·lɛ//, attested by Deming (2/7/80), also <**sq'éylo**>, //s=q'í·l=a//, attested by AC, Salish cognate: Squamish /sq'íʔ/ *dried smoked salmon cut up thin* W73:86, K67:296, perhaps Lushootseed /k'áyayəʔ ~ k'ayáyəʔ/ *a very thoroughly smoke-dried fish* H76:237.

<**q'éylòm**>, df //q'í·l=à-m or q'í·l=àm//, HHG /'*put away, (it has been put away)*'/, (<**=ò**> meaning unclear here), (<**-m**> *passive*), syntactic analysis: intransitive verb, attested by AD (3/6/79), (compare <**qéylemt**> *store s-th away, store s-o away* (perhaps related by glottalization or deglottalization)), Salish cognate: perhaps Squamish /q'áy/ *e high up, be on top* and /q'áy-anʔ/ *put on top (tr.)* W73:209, K67:357.

<**sq'éylòm**>, df //s=q'í·l=à(-)m//, FOOD /'*leftover food, scraps*'/, literally /'something put away'/, (<**s=**> *nominalizer*), syntactic analysis: nominal, attested by Elders Group (3/15/72).

<**q'éylómstexw**>, caus //q'í·làm=sT-əxʷ//, TVMO ['*delay s-o (??)*'], (<**=st**> *causative control transitivizer*), syntactic analysis: transitive verb, Elder's comment: "unsure of meaning", attested by CT (6/16/76), Salish cognate: prob. not Lushootseed /q'əd/ *be slow* as in /q'əd-cut/ *slow down* H76:395.

<**q'eyléxw**>, ABFC /'*kill s-th/s-o accidentally, (happen to or manage to kill s-th/s-o)*'/, *see* q'ó:y ~ q'óy.

<**q'éylómstexw**>, TVMO ['*delay s-o (??)*'], *see* q'éylòm.

<**q'eyós**>, HHG /'*barrel,* probably also *tub*'/, *see* q'ey ~ q'i.

<**q'íp'**>, possible bound root //q'íp'//, meaning unknown

<**Sq'íp'e<u>x</u>w**>, df //s=q'íp'(=)əx̣ʷ or s=q'ə́y=p'=əx̣ʷ//, PLN /'*a real rough place in the Fraser River impassible in a canoe (in the Tait area, prob. between Spuzzum and Yale)*'/, Elder's comment: "ask

ME for location", <**s=**> *nominalizer*, root form and meaning uncertain, perhaps <**q'ey**> or <**q'áp'**> *tie together*, possibly <**=p'**> *on itself*, <**=ex̱w**> *round, around in circles*, syntactic analysis: nominal, attested by SP and AK (8/2/77), source: place names reference file #160.

<**Sq'ólep'ex̱w**>, df //s=q'ál=p'=əx̣^{w} or s=q'ɛ[=Aá=]l=p'=əx̣^{w} or s=q'í[=Aá=][=lə=]p'(=)əx̣^{w}//, PLN ['*another rough place in the Fraser River (Tait area)*'], Elder's comment: "ask ME for location", (<**s=**> *nominalizer*), root form & meaning uncertain, perhaps <**q'ál**> *go around/over/up and down* as in <**q'ál=p'**> *tangled on itself* or <**q'ó:l**> *return* as in <**q'ó:lthet**> *to return* and <**q'elq'ílthet**> *back and forth* or <**q'áp'**> *tie together*, possibly <**=p'**> *on itself*, possibly <**=le=**> *plural*, possibly <**=ex̱w**> *round, around in circles*, phonology: possible ablaut, possible infixing, syntactic analysis: nominal, attested by SP and AK (8/2/77), source: place names reference file #161.

<**q'íq'ekw'et ~ q'éyq'ekw'et**>, ABFC /'*biting into s-th/s-o, biting s-o/s-th*'/, *see* q'éykw' or q'í:kw'.

<**q'íq'eleq ~ q'éyq'eleq.**>, SOCT /'*my dear, (little best friend, little dear friend, etc.)*'/, *see* q'ó.

<**q'íq'elstá:xw**>, EFAM /'*fooling s-o, (fool s-o as a joke, April-fool s-o [Deming])*'/, *see* q'á:l.

<**q'íq'elstexw ~ q'éyq'elstexw**>, TVMO ['*bringing it back*'], *see* q'ó:lthet.

<**q'iq'elts'iyósem spehá:ls ~ q'eyq'elts'iyósem spehá:ls**>, WETH ['*whirlwind*'], *see* q'eyq'elts'iyósem.

<**q'íq'emó:s ~ q'éyq'emó:s**>, FSH /'*dip-netting, fishing with a scoop net, (harpooning fish at night [DM 12/4/64])*'/, *see* q'emós ~ q'emó:s.

<**q'íq'eset ~ q'éyq'eset**>, WV ['*tying it*'], *see* q'ey ~ q'i.

<**q'íq'esetsel ~ q'éyq'esetsel**>, WV /'*weaving (for ex. a tumpline), mending a net, making a net*'/, *see* q'ey ~ q'i.

<**q'íq'et'e ~ q'éyq'ete**>, PLAY ['*swinging*'], *see* q'éyt'o ~ q'éyt'e.

<**q'iq'ethá:m** or **q'eyq'ethá:m**>, EFAM ['*be short (in memory)*'], *see* q'thá:m.

<**Q'iq'ewetó:lthel**>, PLN /'*a slough on Harrison River north side by the mouth of Chehalis River which has a knee-shaped sandbar at its mouth, this is the next slough above (upriver from) Meth'á:lmexwem*'/, *see* q'éw ~ q'ew.

<**q'íq'ex̱el**>, LT ['*[getting black]*'], *see* q'íx̱.

<**Q'iq'éyex̱em ~ Q'eyq'éyex̱em**>, WATR ['*place on the Fraser River above Yale where there are whirlpools*'], *see* q'ey ~ q'i.

<**q'iq'x̱át ~ q'eyq'x̱át**>, LANG ['*argue with s-o*'], *see* q'(e)x̱.

<**q'iq'x̱ótel ~ q'eyq'x̱ótel** >, LANG /'*arguing, arguing (back and forth)*'/, *see* q'(e)x̱.

<**q'í(:)set ~ q'éyset**>, WV /'*to fasten s-th by tying, tie up s-th (like canoe, horse, laces, nets, cow, shoelaces), tie it*'/, *see* q'ey ~ q'i.

<**q'ísetsel ~ q'éysetsel**>, WV ['*to weave*'], *see* q'ey ~ q'i.

<**q'ít'e ~ q'éyt'e**>, df //q'í·t'ə// or //q'əy=t'=ə//, PLAY ['*to swing*'], syntactic analysis: intransitive verb, attested by Elders Group (4/16/75), example: <**q'éyt'e te q'á:mi.**>, //q'í·(=)t'(=)ə tə q'ɛ́·mi//, /'*A girl swings.*'/.

<**q'íq'et'e ~ q'éyq'ete**>, cts //q'í[-C_1ə-]t'ə//, PLAY ['*swinging*'], (<**-R1-**> *continuative*), phonology: reduplication, syntactic analysis: intransitive verb, attested by AC (8/24/70).

<**q'éyt'o ~ q'éyt'e**>, df //q'í·(=)t'(=)a ~ q'í·(=)t'(=)ə or q'əy=t'=a ~ q'əy=t'=ə or q'í·t'a ~ q'í·t'ə//, HHG /'*a swing, a little treadle they swing the babies on*'/, PLAY, ASM ['a sturdy pole is lashed to

the roof or ceiling and a baby basket is suspended from that by a rope, the rope is tied to another rope which is attached horizontally across the basket to provide for even suspension, a string/twine is attached to the bottom and runs to the mother's foot so she can jiggle and bounce the cradle while weaving or otherwise using both hands; now perhaps used for any modern swing as well'], literally perhaps /'something put up for a person/baby'/, (<**=t'**> meaning unknown, <**=a**> or <**=e**> *entity or person*), syntactic analysis: nominal, attested by AC, BJ (12/5/64), Elders Group, DM (12/4/64), AD (6/19/79), other sources: ES /q'í·t'a/ *swing (noun)*, compare <**séqtel**> *swing for baby cradle* with same meaning.

<**q'í:t'o ~ q'éyt'o**>, df //q'ɛ[=Aí·=]t'=a or q'í·(=)t'(=)a//, EB ['*orange honeysuckle*'], ['*Lonicera ciliosa*'], ASM ['flowers can be sucked for sweet liquid nectar, berries are poison'], MED ['the plant part is medicine for "fits"'], literally perhaps /'sweetened entity (or perhaps) swing'/, possibly root <**q'at' ~ q'et'**> *sweet* or possibly root <**q'í·(=t'=ə)**> *swing* (after the vine part), possibly <**í:-ablaut**> *durative*, possibly <**=o**> *entity, living thing*, phonology: ablaut, syntactic analysis: nominal, attested by Elders Group, other sources: ES /q'í·t'a/ *orange honeysuckle*.

<**q'ith' ~ q'eyth'**> bound root //q'iθ'// meaning unknown or root <**q'áth'**> //q'ɛ́θ'// *lean, slant*

<**sq'eyth'éleqw**>, df //s=q'iθ'=ə́ləqʷ or s=q'ɛ[=Ai=]θ'=ə́ləqʷ//, BLDG ['*peak of house*'], LAND ['*peak of mountain*'], (<**s=**> *nominalizer*), possibly root <**q'áth'**> as in <**sq'áq'eth'**> *leaning backwards*, possibly <**i-ablaut**> *durative*, lx <**=éleqw**> *on top of the head, on top*, phonology: possible ablaut, syntactic analysis: nominal, attested by Elders Group, Salish cognate: Squamish /q'íc'-iʔəqʷ/ *gabledroof* W73:110, K69:82.

<**q'ítl' ~ q'éytl'**>, bound root //q'íƛ' *be healed, scarred over*//, Salish cognate: Squamish /q'íƛ'/ *be healed up (wound)* W73:139, K67:358.

<**sq'éytl'** or **sq'ítl'**>, dnom //s=q'íƛ'//, ABFC ['*a scar*'], (<**s=**> *nominalizer*), syntactic analysis: nominal, attested by NP.

<**q'éytl'thet**>, df //q'íƛ'=θət//, ABFC /'*it healed up, (to heal up)*'/, possibly root <**q'ey**> *tied, knotted*, (<**=thet**> *get, become* or *reflexive*), syntactic analysis: intransitive verb, attested by NP.

<**q'ítl'thet ~ q'éytl'thet**>, ABFC /'*it healed up, (to heal up)*'/, *see* q'éytl'.

<**Q'íts'i(y) ~ Q'éyts'i(y)**>, df //q'íc'=iy//, PLN ['*Katzie village*'], ASM ['a downriver-Halq'eméylem-speaking village'], literally ['*a multi-colored moss*'], comment: Upriver-speaking elders don't know this as a word for a kind of moss but know it as a place name, lx <**=iy**> *plant, bark, covering*, syntactic analysis: nominal, attested by Elders Group,

<**q'í:w ~ q'e:yw**>, bound root //q'í·w *hang over*//, contrast <**q'ew**> *turn in a river, bend in a road*

<**q'é:ywet**> (or better) <**q'í:wet**>, pcs //q'í·w=əT//, [q'é·wət ~ q'í·wət], ABFC /'*hang s-th on a line, hang s-th on a nail, hang s-th up*'/, (<**=et**> *purposeful control transitivizer*), syntactic analysis: transitive verb, attested by EB, Elders Group, example: <**q'í:wetchexw ta' shxwelwétem.**>, //q'í·w=əT-c-əxʷ t-ɛʔ s=xʷ=əlwə́t=əm//, /'*Hang up your wash (to dry)., Hang your wash.*'/, attested by Elders Group (3/5/80), <**q'é:ywetlha ta' kopú.**>, //q'í·w=əT-ɬɛ t-ɛʔ kapú//, /'*Hang up your coat.*'/, attested by EB.

<**q'í:wethet**>, pcrs //q'í·w=əT-ət//, ABFC ['*leaning over (something)*'], literally /'hang oneself over on purpose'/, (<**-et**> *reflexive*), syntactic analysis: intransitive verb, attested by Elders Group (3/5/80).

<**sq'iwq'ewíles**>, chrs //s=q'iw=C$_1$əC$_2$=íləs//, stvi, ABFC ['*carry a packstrap or both packstraps over the shoulder(s) and under the arm(s)*'], TVMO, literally /'be hung characteristically over on the chest'/, (<**s=**> *stative*), lx <**=íles ~ =í:les**> *on the chest*, (<**=R2**> *characteristic*), phonology: stress-shift without vowel-reduction, syntactic analysis: adjective/adjectival verb, attested by IHTTC (8/10/77).

<**q'ewí:lestel**>, ds //q'iw=í·ləs=təl//, CLO ['*suspenders*'], literally /'device to hang over on the chest'/, lx <**=í:les ~ =íles**> *on the chest*, lx <**=tel**> *device to, thing to*, phonology: stress-shift with vowel-reduction, syntactic analysis: nominal, attested by BHTTC.

<**Sq'éywetselem ~ Sq'éywetsélém**>, ds //s=q'í·w=əcəl=əm ~ s=q'í·w=əcə́l=əm//, PLN ['*trail and steep slope on the west shore of Kawkawa Lake where the trail went up and over a steep hill and then down*'], root <**q'í:w**> *hang over*, (<**s=**> *nominalizer*), lx <**=etsel ~ =etsél**> *on the back*, (<**=em**> *middle voice* or *place to get/have*), phonology: updrifting, syntactic analysis: nominal, attested by BHTTC at Katz Class (10/5/76), Elders at place names meeting after IHTTC (8/23/77), source: place names reference file #209.

<**q'í:wethet**>, ABFC ['*leaning over (something)*'], *see* q'e:yw ~ q'í:w.

<**q'íxwet**>, pcs //q'í(=)xʷ=əT//, CLO /'*tighten it (a belt, a pack, etc.)*'/, MC, probably root <**q'i ~ q'ey**> *tied, knotted*, possibly <**=xw**> *lump-like, round, around*, (<**=et**> *purposeful control transitivizer*), syntactic analysis: transitive verb, attested by AD (4/17/80), example: <**q'íxwet ta' shxwyémtel.**>, //q'íxʷ=əT t-ɛʔ sxʷ=yə́m=təl//, /'*Tighten your belt.*'/.

<**q'íx̲**>, bound root //q'íx̣ *black*//, comment: using derived forms of the root as a modifier of other color terms the following combinations were given by AK: tsq'íx̣ (tsméth', tskwím, tsqwáy) and q'íq'ex̣el tsqwáy; Chilliwack dialect speaker NP also used one of these combinations ts=q'íq'ex=el ts=qwá:y following the same patterns.

<**tsq'éyx̲ ~ tsq'íx̲ ~ ts'q'éyx̲ ~ ts'q'íx̲**>, ds //c=q'íx̣ ~ c[=G]=q'íx̣//, LT ['*be black*'], (<**c=**> *stative with color terms*), phonology: optional =G (glottalization) is phonological assimilation to the following glottalized consonant, ASM ['squares circled on the color chart of Berlin and Kay (1969) (rows top to bottom = B-I, columns left to right = 1-40, side columns of white to black = 0); individual speakers circled the following squares for ts(')q'éyx̲, EL (2/20/79): H0 TG with RP (1/24/79): I20, I21, I22, I23, I24, I25, I26, I27, I28, I29, I30 NP (2/7/79): I22, I23, I24, I25 EP (Downriver Halkomelem) (2/7/79): I16 LJ (Pilalt) (2/7/79): F23 AK (1/24/79): I0, J0 TM (2/14/79): I14-I32 inclusive'], syntactic analysis: adjective/adjectival verb, attested by AC, BJ (5/10/64, 12/5/64), DM (12/4/64), EL, TG, RP, Deming, NP, LJ (Pilalt), AK, TM, EB, Elders Group (3/1/72, 5/16/79, etc.), Deming, SJ, EP (Downriver Halkomelem), AK (1987), TG (1987), EB (1987), NP (1987), AH (1987),, other sources: ES /c'q'íx̣/ *black*, chart by Rob McLaury, example: <**tsq'éyx̲ shxw=yáth'qels**>, //c=q'íx̣ sxʷ=yɛ́θ'=q=əls//, /'*black paint*'/, attested by DM (12/4/64 new p.181), <**tsq'éyx̲ spá:th**>, //c=q'íx̣ s=pɛ́·θ//, /'*black bear*'/, attested by AK (11/21/72 tape), <**ts'q'éyx̲ te (sq'ő:lmexw, tselqó:me, máts'el, spá:th, shxw'áthetel, músmes, spó:l, stiqíw, slát, sqéweqs, ts'esláts).**>, //c[=G]=q'íx̣ tə (s=qʷó·lməxʷ, cəlq=á·mə, mɛ́cəl, s=pɛ́·θ, sxʷ=ʔɛ́θə=təl, múm=C_1əC_2, s=pá·l, s=tiqíw, s=lɛ́t, s=qə́w=əqs, c'əslɛ́c)//, /'*The (blackberry, blackcap berry, black haw(thorn) berry, bear, cloud, cow, crow, horse, night, raven, saskatoon berry) is black.*'/, attested by Deming (esp. SJ) (5/3/79), <**ts'q'éyx̲ te ts'esláts.**>, //c'=q'íx̣ tə c'əslɛ́c//, /'*The saskatoon berry is black.*'/, attested by Elders Group (5/16/79), <**ts'q'éyx̲ te kwxwóméls.**>, //c'=q'íx̣ tə kʷaxʷ=ámə́=əls//, /'*The black huckleberry is black.*'/, attested by Elders Group (5/16/79).

<**ts'q'éyx̲em**>, ds //c[=G]=q'íx̣=əm//, TAST /'*vanilla, (vanilla extract)*'/, ACL, (semological comment: probably named for the dark color of vanilla extract), probably <**=em**> *have, get, intransitivizer or place to have/get or middle voice*?, phonology: glottalization, syntactic analysis: nominal, attested by Elders Group (6/16/76).

<**q'íx̲el**>, incs //q'íx̣=əl//, LT ['*get black*'], (<**=el**> *go, come, get, become*), syntactic analysis: intransitive verb, attested by AC, example: <**le q'íx̲el te shxw'áthetel.**>, //lə q'íx̣=əl tə sxʷ=ʔɛ́θə=təl//, /'*The clouds are black., (The clouds got black.)*'/, literally /'third person past get black the cloud'/, attested by AC.

<**q'íq'ex̲el**>, cts //q’í[=C$_1$ə=]x̣=əl//, incs, LT ['*[getting black]*'], (<**=R1=**> *continuative*), (<**=el ~ =íl**> *go, come, get, become*), syntactic analysis: adjective/adjectival verb, attested by EB, NP, see charts by Rob MacLaury in Galloway 1993.

<**tsq'íq'ex̲el**>, cts //c=q’í[=C$_1$ə=]x̣=əl//, incs, LT ['*[be getting black]*'], (<**ts=**> *have, get, stative with colors*), (<**=R1=**> *continuative*), (<**=el ~ =íl**> *go, come, get, become*), syntactic analysis: adjective/adjectival verb, attested by EB, NP, see charts by Rob MacLaury.

<**sq'íq'ex̲el**>, cts //s=q’í[=C$_1$ə=]x̣=əl//, incs, LT ['*[be getting black]*'], (<**s=**> *stative*), (<**=R1=**> *continuative*), (<**=el ~ =íl**> *go, come, get, become*), syntactic analysis: adjective/adjectival verb, attested by NP, see charts by Rob MacLaury.

<**q'éyx̲eya**>, dmn //q’íx̣=əyɛ//, SOCT ['*Negro*'], lx <**=iya ~ =eya**> *affectionate diminutive; name ending*, syntactic analysis: nominal, attested by IHTTC, also <**qw'íx̲wes ~ qw'éyx̲wes**>, //q’[=W]íx̣[=W]=əs or q’^{w}íx̣^{w}=əs//, (<**=W (labialization)**> *derivational*), phonology: double labialization, attested by IHTTC.

<**q'eyx̲óles**>, ds //q’ix̣=áləs//, ANA ['*pupil of the eye*'], literally /'black in the eye, black on the eye'/, lx <**=óles**> *in the eye, on the eye*, phonology: stress-shift without vowel-reduction, syntactic analysis: nominal, attested by EB.

<**q'ix̲ ~ q'eyx̲**>, bound root //q’ix̣// *tilt*

<**sq'eyx̲éleqw**>, ds //s=q’ix̣=ə́ləq^w//, ANA /'*crown of head, center of the top of the head where the hair starts*'/, BLDG /'*peak of house, gable or plank over smokehole*'/, (<**s=**> *nominalizer*), root meaning unknown unless q'íx̲ *black*??, lx <**=éleqw**> *on top of the head, on top, on the hair of the head*, (semological comment: the anatomical (alloseme) meaning uses the anatomical alloseme of the suffix (on top of the head, on the hair of the head) while the alloseme referring to a house part uses the non-anatomical alloseme of the suffix (on top)), phonology: stress-shift from root without vowel-reduction, syntactic analysis: nominal, attested by Elders Group, SP (IHTTC 8/4/77), also <**q'eyx̲éleqw**>, //q’ix̣=ə́ləq^w//, attested by AK (IHTTC 8/4/77).

<**q'óx̲esem**>, mdls //q’áx̣=əs=əm or q’ɛ[=Aá=]x̣=əs=əm//, ABFC ['*put one's head back (tilt one's face up)*'], lx <**=es**> *on the face*, (<**=em**> *middle voice*), syntactic analysis: intransitive verb, attested by IHTTC.

<**q'íx̲el**>, LT ['*get black*'], *see* q'íx̲.

<**q'íx̲eya ~ q'éyyx̲eya**>, SOCT ['*Negro*'], *see* q'íx̲.

<**q'íx̲óles ~ q'eyx̲óles**>, ANA ['*pupil of the eye*'], *see* q'íx̲.

<**q'lhól**>, possibly root //q’ɬál// or //q’ɬ=ɬɛ[=Aá=]l// or //q’áɬ=ə[=M2=]l//, CAN ['*bow of a canoe*'], possibly root <**q'ólh**> meaning unknown, if compound with <lhál> *land a canoe, pull onshore in canoe*, possibly <**q'=**> (if a variant of <**=q**> *on something else, within something else*) or <**q'lh=**> (or more likely root in compound) meaning unknown, <**=el**> *go, come, get, become*, possibly <**ó-ablaut**> *resultative or durative*, possibly <**metathesis**> *derivational*, phonology: possible compound or ablaut or metathesis, syntactic analysis: nominal, attested by Elders Group (3/26/75).

<**q'ó**>, free root //q’á//, DIR ['*with*'], syntactic analysis: preposition/prepositional verb, attested by Deming (2/7/80), example: <**mítlh q'ó tl'alhlímelh.**>, //mí-tɬ q’áƛ’ɛ-ɬlíməɬ//, /'*Come with us.*'/, literally /'come -coaxing imperative sg. with preposition object- us'/, attested by Deming (2/7/80).

<**q'ót**>, pcs //q’á=T//, DIR /'*put s-th with (something), add s-th (to something), include s-th*'/, (<**=t**> *purposeful control transitivizer*), syntactic analysis: transitive verb, attested by AD, DF, example: <**q'ótap te'íle.**>, //q’á=T-ɛp tə=ʔí=lə//, /'*Put this with it you folks., Include this you folks.*'/, attested by AD (5/5/80).

<**q'ó:thet**>, pcrs //q'á=əT-ət//, DIR /*'join, (include oneself purposely)'*/, TVMO, SOC, literally /'include oneself purposely'/, (<**=et ~ =(e)th**> *purposeful control transitivizer*), (<**-et**> *reflexive*), phonology: vowel merger, <**=th**> occurs before reflexives and singular object suffixes, syntactic analysis: intransitive verb, attested by Elders Group (1/30/80), example: <**lí iyólem kw'els q'ó:thet li talhléwep**>, //lí ʔəy=ál=əm k'ʷə-l-s q'á=əT-ət li tɛ=ɬ=lə́wə=p//, /*'Is is alright if I join you folks?'*/, literally /'is it alright that I include myself in you folks'/.

<**q'eq'ótel**>, rcps //C_1ə=q'á=T-əl//, DIR [*'to meet (each other)'*], TVMO, SOC, (<**R5=**> *resultative* or *continuative*), (<**=t**> *purposeful control transitivizer*), (<**-el**> *reciprocal*), phonology: reduplication, syntactic analysis: intransitive verb, attested by EB (4/2/76).

<**q'ótelt ~ q'ótòlt**>, df //q'á=T=əl=T ~ q'á=T=ə[=Aà=]l=T//, pcs, MC /*'put them together, (join them together)'*/, semantic environment ['of berries, of two pieces of cloth lined up, of yarn if knitted both together'], possibly <**=tel**> crystallized *purposeful reciprocal*, possibly <**ò-ablaut**> assimilation, (<**=t**> *purposeful control transitivizer*), phonology: assimilation to previous vowel, syntactic analysis: transitive verb, syntactic comment: perhaps doubly transitivized (crystallized transitivizer), attested by EB (6/30/76), CT and HT (6/21/76), example: <**q'ótelt kw'es p'íth'et**>, //q'á=T=əl=T k'ʷ-əs p'íθ'=əT//, /*'put it together to squeeze it'*/, attested by CT and HT.

<**q'etóléstexw**>, df //q'ó=Tə[=M2=]l=ə́=sT-əxʷ//, caus, MC /*'mix s-th, put them together'*/, possibly <**=tel**> *purposeful reciprocal* possibly crystallized, <**=é**> unknown, <**metathesis**> *derivational*, (<**=st**> *causative control transitivizer*), phonology: metathesis, perhaps updrifting, syntactic analysis: transitive verb, attested by EB (4/23/76).

<**sq'ó**>, dnom //s=q'á//, SOC /*'companion, other part'*/, (<**s=**> *nominalizer*), syntactic analysis: nominal, attested by AD, example: <**ta' sq'ó**>, //t-ɛʔ s=q'á//, /*'your companion'*/, attested by AD (5/5/80); found in <**sq'ós**>, //s=q'á-s//, /*'the other part of'*/, attested by AD (3/4/80).

<**sq'ó**>, stvi //s=q'á//, DIR /*'along, with, together with'*/, (<**s=**> *stative*), syntactic analysis: preposition/prepositional verb, attested by EB, Deming, others, example: <**ásche ew me xwe'í látselcha yesq'ó.**>, //ʔɛ-s-cɛ ʔəw mə xʷə=ʔí lɛ́-c-əl-cɛ yə-s=q'á//, /*'If he comes again, I'll go along.'*/, literally /'aux -if he (subjunctive third person) -future again come to come here go -I -future travelling along by- stative (being)- along/with'/, attested by EB, <**ts'áts'eltsel xwoyíwel tel sqwálewel kw'els me xwe'í sq'ó tl'alhluwep (éy l sí:yáye, l sí:yáye sí:yám).**>, //c'ɛ[=C_1ə=]l-c-əl xʷ=ɛ[=Aa=]y=íwəl tə-l s=qʷɛ́l=əwəl k'ʷə-l-s mə xʷə=ʔí s=q'á ƛ'ɛ=ɬ=luwə=p (ʔɛ́y l si[=´·=]yɛ́yə, l si[=´·=]yɛ́yə si[=´·=]yɛ́m//, /*'I'm very happy to come here (together with you folks) (my good friends, my dear friends).'*/, literally /'I'm very happy my thoughts/feelings that I come to come here together with preposition object- you folks (good my many friends, my plural friends plural dear)'/, usage: public speeches, attested by Deming (5/18/78).

<**sq'eq'ó**>, df //s=C_1ə=q'á//, DIR /*'along, together, be included, with'*/, (<**s=**> *stative*, R5= probably *resultative* or *continuative*), comment: for *continuative* compare sq'eq'ómet *coming with s-o* with sq'ómet *come with s-o* below, phonology: reduplication, syntactic analysis: preposition/prepositional verb, attested by EB, AC, Deming, ASM ['with'], example: <**michap wó:thel sq'eq'ó telhlímelh (or tl'elhlímelh)**>, //mi-c-ɛp w(=)á·θəl s=C_1ə=q'á ƛ'ə=ɬlíməɬ//, /*'Come (you folks) and share our meal with us.'*/, literally /'come -you folks share a meal with us'/, attested by Deming, ASM ['together'], <**lichxw ley sq'eq'ó?**>, //lí-c-xʷ lə yə-s=C_1ə=q'á//, /*'Did you go together?'*/, attested by AC, ASM ['be included'], <**ő we ís sq'eq'ó te s'álhtel.**>, //ʔówə ʔí-s s=C_1ə=q'á tə s=ʔɛ́ɬ=təl//, /*'The meal is not included.'*/, attested by Deming (1/25/79).

<**sq'ómet**>, iecs //s=q'á=məT//, DIR [*'come with s-o'*], TVMO, (<**s=**> *stative*), (<**=met**> *indirectly effecting control transitivizer*), syntactic analysis: transitive verb, attested by Elders Group; found in <**sq'ómethòx ~ sq'omethó:x**>, //s=q'á=məT-áxʸ//, /*'come with me'*/, attested by Elders Group (11/9/77, 3/24/76).

<**sq'eq'ómet**>, cts //s=C_1ə=q'á=məT//, iecs, DIR [*'coming with s-o'*], TVMO, (<**s=**> *stative*, R5= *continuative*), phonology: reduplication, syntactic analysis: transitive verb, attested by Elders Group (11/9/77).

<**sq'ó:t ~ sq'ót**>, pcs //s=q'á=əT ~ s=q'á=T//, DIR /*'accompany s-o, go with s-o'*/, TVMO, (<**=t ~ =et**> *purposeful control transitivizer*), phonology: vowel merger, syntactic analysis: transitive verb, attested by EB (Elders Group 9/27/78); found in <**sq'othóxes.**>, //s=q'a=T-áx^y-əs//, /*'She's going with me.'*/, attested by EB, <**sq'ótap**>, //s=q'á=T-ɛp//, /*'when you're all together'*/, literally /'if/when you're all going along with s-o'/, syntactic comment: subjunctive 2p without we-, attested by Elders Group (9/27/78), example: <**lámechap sq'ótàp?**>, //lɛ́=m-ə-c-ɛp s=q'á=T-ɛ́p//, /*'Are you all going with him?'*/, literally /'going -interrogative -you folks accompany/go with him -subjunctive2p'/, attested by EB.

<**sq'ó:xel ~ sq'óxel**>, dnom //s=q'á(·)=x^yəl//, SOCT [*'partner'*], literally /'something/(someone) to be with on foot'/, (<**s=**> *nominalizer*), lx <**=xel**> *on the foot*, syntactic analysis: nominal, attested by AC, DC.

<**sq'iq'exí:l ~ q'iq'exí:l**>, dmn //(s=)C_1í=q'a=x^yəl=í·l//, SOCT /*'little partner, little person who follows or goes with one'*/, (<**s=**> *nominalizer*, R4= *diminutive*), (<**=í:l**> *go, come, get, become*), phonology: reduplication, syllable-loss, vowel-reduction in root to schwa-grade before full-grade/strong-grade of suffix, syntactic analysis: nominal, attested by Elders Group.

<**sq'eq'axí:l**>, pln //s=C_1ə=q'a=Aɛ=x^yəl=í·l//, SOCT [*'partners'*], (<**s=**> *nominalizer*, R5= *plural*), possibly <**a-ablaut**> *durative or derivational*, lx <**=xel**> *on the foot*, (<**=í:l**> *go, come, get, become*), phonology: reduplication, possible ablaut, syllable-loss, syntactic analysis: nominal, attested by Elders Group.

<**q'axí:l**>, durs //q'a=Aɛ=x^yəl=í·l//, TVMO /*'go with, come with, be partner with'*/, DIR, SOC, (<**a-ablaut**> *durative*), lx <**=xel**> *on the foot*, (<**=í:l**> *go, come, become, get*), phonology: ablaut, syllable-loss, syntactic analysis: intransitive verb, attested by AC (8/23/73).

<**sq'exí:lmet**>, iecs //s=q'a=xəl=í·l=məT//, TVMO [*'follow s-o'*], (<**s=**> *stative*), (<**=met**> *indirectly effecting control transitivizer*), phonology: vowel-reduction, syllable-loss, syntactic analysis: transitive verb, attested by Elders Group.

<**q'exí:lt**>, pcs //q'a=x^yəl=í·l=T//, TVMO /*'accompany s-o, go with s-o, go along with s-o'*/, SOC, (<**=t**> *purposeful control transitivizer*), phonology: vowel-reduction, syllable-loss, syntactic analysis: transitive verb, attested by Elders Group, EB, also <**q'axí:lt**>, //q'a=Aɛ=x^yəl=í·l=T//, (<**a-ablaut**> *durative*), phonology: ablaut, attested by AC, example: <**látsel q'axí:lthòme.**>, //lɛ́-c-əl q'a=Aɛ=x^yəl=í·l=T-ámə//, /*'I'll go with you.'*/, phonology: downstepping, attested by AC, <**latsa q'axí:lthò:m (tl' Tom).**>, //lɛ-cɛ q'a=Aɛ=x^yəl=í·l=T-à·mƛ' Tom//, /*'Somebody (Tom) will go with you.'*/, literally /'go -future (third person subject zero) you are gone with (passive) (by Tom)'/, attested by AC (8/23/73), <**líchxw xwel la(m) q'exí:lt.**>, //lí-c-x^w x^wəl lɛ(=m) q'a=x^yəl=í·l=T//, /*'Are you still going along with him?'*/, attested by EB, <**lámtlh q'exí:lt.**>, //lɛ́=m-tɬ q'a=x^yəl=í·l=T//, /*'Go along with him.'*/, syntactic comment: coaxing imperative, attested by EB.

<**q'eq'exí:lt**>, dmv //C_1ə=q'a=x^yəl=í·l=T//, TVMO [*'accompany s-o little or elderly'*], SOC, (semological comment: diminutive verbs often imply small or elderly people as objects), (<**R5=**> *diminutive*), phonology: reduplication, vowel-reduction, syllable-loss, syntactic analysis: transitive verb, attested by EB; found in <**q'eq'exí:ltlha.**>, //C_1ə=q'a=x^yəl=í·l=T-ɬɛ//, /*'Accompany someone little or elderly.'*/, attested by EB.

<**q'eq'exí:lt**>, cts //C_1ə=q'a=x^yəl=í·l=T//, TVMO [*'accompanying s-o'*], SOC, (<**R5=**> *continuative*), phonology: reduplication, vowel-reduction, syllable-loss, syntactic analysis: transitive verb, attested by Elders Group; found in <**q'eq'exí:lthòx**>, //C_1ə=q'a=x^yəl=í·l=T-áx^y//,

/'accompanying me'/, phonology: downstepping.

<**q'óleq ~ q'e'óléq**>, ds //q'ó=ləq ~ q'ó=ʔə[=M2=]ləq//, SOCT */'pal, best friend, dear friend, chum'/*, literally /'someone who habitually accompanies/is together/is with'/, lx <**=eleq ~ =leq**> *someone who habitually*, (<**metathesis**> *derivational*), phonology: glottal-stop insertion (epenthetic), syntactic analysis: nominal, attested by EB, AD.

<**q'e'ó:leq**>, pln //q'ó[=·=]=ʔə[=M2=]ləq//, SOCT [*'dear friends'*], (<**=:=**> *plural*), phonology: lengthening, metathesis, epenthesis, syntactic analysis: nominal, attested by EB and AD (9/19/78).

<**q'éyq'eleq ~ (better) q'íq'eleq**>, dmn //C_1í=q'o=ləq//, SOCT */'my dear, (little best friend, little dear friend, etc.)'/*, (<**R4=**> *diminutive*), phonology: reduplication, vowel-reduction, syntactic analysis: nominal, attested by IHTTC, example: <**ō q'éyq'eleq.**>, //ʔo C_1í=q'o=ləq ~ ʔəw C_1í=q'o=ləq//, */'Oh my dear.'/*.

<**sq'eq'e'óleq**>, pln //s=C_1ə=q'ó=ʔə[=M2=]ləq//, SOCT */'pair of twins, pair of closest friends'/*, (<**s=**> *nominalizer inalienable possession*, R5= *dual*), lx <**=éleq**> *one who, -er, one who does as an occupation*, (<**=M2= (metathesis type 2)**> *derivational*), phonology: reduplication, metathesis, syntactic analysis: nominal, attested by IHTTC (8/23/77).

<**q'ó:lthet**>, incs //q'á·l=T=ət or q'á=əl=T-ət//, pcrs, TVMO */'return, come back, go back'/*, possibly root <**q'ó**> *together*, possibly <**=el**> *go, come, get, become*, (<**=t**> *purposeful control transitivizer*), (<**=et**> *reflexive*), phonology: possible vowel merger, syntactic analysis: intransitive verb, attested by EB, BJ (5/10/64), others, Salish cognate: Squamish /q'án-acut/ *to return* W73:216, K67:356, example: <**míchxw q'ó:lthet kw'atsetólxw ő́we híthes.**>, //mí-c-x^w q'á·l=T=ət k'^wɛ́c=əT-álx^w ʔówə híθ-əs//, */'Come back and see us soon.'/*, attested by EB, <**me q'ó:lthet**>, //mə q'á·l=T-ət//, */'to return, come back again'/*, attested by BJ (5/10/64), EB.

<**q'elq'í:lthet ~ q'elq'éylthet**>, plv //C_1əC_2=q'al=í·l=T-ət or C_1əC_2=q'á=í·l=T-ət//, incs, TVMO */'back and forth, (go or come back and forth)'/*, (<**R3=**> *plural*), (<**=í:l**> *go, come, get, become*, <**=t**> *purposeful control transitivizer*), (<**-et**> *reflexive*), phonology: possible syllable-loss or vowel merger, syntactic analysis: intransitive verb, attested by Elders Group.

<**q'élqet**>, pcs //q'a[=Aə́=]l=qəl=T//, LANG */'answer it (a letter, phone call, etc.), reply to s-th/s-o'/*, (<**é-ablaut**> *derivational*), lx <**=qel**> *in language, speech, in the throat*, (<**=t**> *purposeful control transitivizer*), phonology: ablaut, syntactic analysis: transitive verb, attested by Elders Group (11/9/77, 3/1/72), example: <**tsel le q'élqet.**>, //c-əl lə q'a[=Aə́=]l=qəl=T//, */'I answer., (I answered s-o/s-th.)'/*, attested by Elders Group (3/1/72).

<**q'elqéyls**>, sas //q'a[=Aə=]l=qəl=ɛ́·ls//, LANG [*'answer a letter'*], (<**e-ablaut**> *derivational*), lx <**=qel**> *in language*, (<**=á:ls** (here ~ allomorph **=éyls)**> *structured activity non-continuative*), phonology: ablaut, syllable-loss, allomorph =éyls replacing =á:ls after syllable-loss of preceding el, syntactic analysis: intransitive verb, attested by EB, Elders Group (3/1/72, 1/25/78), also */'answered'/*, (<**e-ablaut**> *resultative*), attested by Elders Group (11/9/77).

<**q'áq'elqéyls**>, cts //C_1ɛ́-q'əl=qəl=ɛ́·ls//, LANG [*'answering a letter'*], (<**R7-**> *continuative*), phonology: reduplication, syllable-loss, allomorph of =á:ls, syntactic analysis: intransitive verb, attested by EB, also <**q'éq'elqéyls**>, //C_1ɛAə́=q'əl=qəl=ɛ́·ls//, attested by Elders Group (1/25/78).

<**q'élstexw**>, caus //q'a[=Aə́=]l=sT-əx^w//, TVMO */'give it back, bring it back, return s-th'/*, SOC, possibly <**é-ablaut**> *derivational or resultative*, (<**=st**> *causative control transitivizer*), (<**-exw**> *third person object)*, phonology: ablaut, syntactic analysis: transitive verb, attested by Deming, EB, example: <**me q'élstexwes.**>, //mə q'o[=Aə́=]l=sT-əx^w-əs//, */'He brought it back.'/*, attested by EB.

<**q'éyq'elstexw**>, cts //C_1í=q'o[=Aə=]l=sT-əx^w//, TVMO [*'bringing it back'*], SOC, Elder's comment: "unsure of form", comment: perhaps <**q'áq'elstexw**> in light of <**q'áq'elqéyls**> *answering a letter*, (<**R4= usually**> *diminutive* but here *continuative*??), phonology: reduplication, ablaut,

syntactic analysis: transitive verb, attested by Deming.

<**q'óx̲el**>, possibly root //q'á=x̣əl//, EZ /'*sucker fish,* especially *big sucker or elephant sucker,* probably *largescale sucker*'/, ['probably *Catostomus macrocheilus*'], ASM ['these fish often fasten onto other fish as parasites'], <**=x̲el**> *on the foot, on the tail,* (lit. "together/with on the tail"), syntactic analysis: nominal, attested by Deming, Elders Group (7/9/75, 2/19/75), BJ (12/5/64 old p.305).

<**q'óleq ~ q'e'óléq**>, SOCT /'*pal, best friend, dear friend, chum*'/, *see* q'ó.

<**q'ópthet**>, SOC ['*crowding together*'], *see* q'ép.

<**q'óq'ey**>, ABDF ['*be sick*'], *see* q'ó:y ~ q'óy.

<**q'oq'eyá:wtxw**>, BLDG ['*hospital*'], *see* q'ó:y ~ q'óy.

<**q'óq'eystexw**>, ABDF ['*make s-o sick*'], *see* q'ó:y ~ q'óy.

<**q'óq'eyt**>, HUNT ['*killing s-th*'], *see* q'ó:y ~ q'óy.

<**q'óq'eytses**>, ABDF /'*(be) sick on the hand, (have) a sick hand, (have) a hurt hand*'/, *see* q'ó:y ~ q'óy.

<**q'óq'eyxel**>, ABDF /'*be lame, (be) sick on the foot, (have) a sick foot, (have) a hurt foot*'/, *see* q'ó:y ~ q'óy.

<**q'ót**>, DIR /'*put s-th with (something), add s-th (to something), include s-th*'/, *see* q'ó.

<**q'ótelt ~ q'ótòlt**>, MC /'*put them together, (join them together)*'/, *see* q'ó.

<**q'ó:thet**>, DIR /'*join, (include oneself purposely)*'/, *see* q'ó.

<**q'ó:w**>, ABFC ['*howling*'], *see* q'á:w.

<**q'ówel**>, ABFC ['*howling fast*'], *see* q'á:w.

<**q'ówem**>, ABFC /'*howling (of a dog), crowing (of a rooster)*'/, *see* q'á:w.

<**q'ówet**>, possibly root //q'áwət or q'əwá[=M2=]t or q'a[=´=]wə́t//, MUS /'*a drum, small stick used to drum or beat time to songs in slahal game*'/, PLAY, possibly <**metathesis** or =´=> *derivational,* phonology: possible metathesis or stress-shift, syntactic analysis: nominal, attested by TG, Elders Group (4/16/75), also <**q'éwet**>, //q'ə́wət//, attested by Elders Group (11/26/75), also /'*drumming*'/, attested by Elders Group (1/25/78), Salish cognate: Mainland Comox /q'ə́gətx̣/ *stick for beating rhythm; dancer's staff* B75prelim:44, Sechelt /q'ə́wa-t/ *drumstick* T77:18, Squamish /q'uát/ *drumstick* K67:357, N. Straits dialects: Samish /q'áwət/ *a drum, drumstick* and /q'aw'étŋ'/ *drumming* G86:93 beside Saanich /q'ə́wət/ *drumstick, stick for beating rhythm* B74a:35 and Songish /q'áwət/ *to drum, beat a drum* M68:75.

<**q'owét**>, possibly root //q'awə́t or q'áwə[=´=]t or q'əwá[=M2=]t//, MUS /'*to drum, a drum*'/, possibly <=´= or **metathesis**> *non-continuative or derivational,* phonology: possibly stress-shift or metathesis, syntactic analysis: intransitive verb, nominal, attested by Elders Group (3/72, 2/5/75), also <**q'ewét**>, //q'əwə́t or q'awə[=´=]t//, attested by Elders Group (3/72, 1/25/78).

<**q'ewétt**>, pcs //q'əwə́t=T//, MUS ['*drum for s-o*'], (<**=t**> *purposeful control transitivizer*), phonology: possible metathesis or stress-shift, syntactic analysis: transitive verb, attested by Elders Group (NP, EB, perhaps others 4/26/78); found in <**q'ewétthòx**>, //q'əwə́t=T-áx^{y}//, /'*drum for me*'/, phonology: downstepping, attested by NP and perhaps others (in Elders Group 4/26/78), <**q'ewétthòxes.**>, //q'əwə́t=T-áx^{y}-əs//, /'*He drummed for me.*'/, phonology: downstepping, attested by EB in Elders Group (4/26/78), <**q'ewétthòxlha.**>, //q'əwə́t=T-áx^{y}-ɬɛ//, /'*Drum for me.*'/, attested by Elders Group (4/26/78).

<**q'ewétem**>, izs //q'əwə́t=əm//, MUS ['*drumming*'], (<**=em**> *intransitivizer*), syntactic analysis: intransitive verb, attested by DF (4/26/78), Elders Group (3/72).

<**q'ewételhtst**>, bens //q'əwə́t=əɬc=T//, pcs, MUS ['*drum for s-o*'], (<**=elhts**> *benefactive*, <**=t**> *purposeful control transitivizer*), syntactic analysis: transitive verb, attested by Elders Group (4/26/78), example: <**q'ewetelhtsthóxes.**>, //q'əwət=əɬc=T-áx^y-əs//, /'*he drummed for me*'/, attested by Elders 4/26/78.

<**q'owét**>, MUS /'*to drum, a drum*'/, *see* q'ówet.

<**q'ówletsem**>, CAN /'*go around (a point, a bend, a curve, etc.) in the water, make a U-turn (in the water, could use today on land with a car)*'/, *see* q'éw ~ q'ew.

<**q'ówletst**>, CAN ['*go around s-th in the water*'], *see* q'éw ~ q'ew.

<**q'óx̱el**>, EZ /'*sucker fish,* especially *big sucker or elephant sucker,* probably *largescale sucker*'/, ['probably *Catostomus macrocheilus*'], *see* under root q'o

<**q'óx̱esem**>, mdls //q'áx̣=əs=əm or q'í[=Aá=]x̣=əs=əm//, ABFC ['*put one's head back (tilt one's face up)*'], lx <**=es**> *on the face*, (<**=em**> *middle voice*), syntactic analysis: intransitive verb, attested by IHTTC, see q'eyx̱ ~ q'ix̱.

<**q'óy**>, bound root perhaps //q'áy// meaning unknown

<**sq'óyes**>, df //s=q'áy=əs or s=q'ɛ[-Aá-]y=əs or s=q'əy=á[=M2=]s//, ANAB /'*down feathers, real fine feathers*'/, ASM ['sometimes worn over bear grease for warmth, then a shawl or blanket'], (<**s=**> *nominalizer*), root meaning uncertain, lx <**=es**> *on the face*, phonology: possible ablaut (automatic if root a precedes =es) or metathesis, syntactic analysis: nominal, attested by Elders Group (3/72 tape, 3/15/72 taped lesson VIII, 1/21/76).

<**sq'óyeseqw ~ sx̱óyeseqw**>, df //s=q'áy=əs=əq^w ~ s=x̣áy=əs=əq^w//, SPRD ['*soft (down) feathers put in oiled hair for dancing*'], for sq'óyeseqw but s=x̱óy(:)=es *head* is the stem of the alternate form, lx <**=eqw**> *on top of the head, on the hair*, syntactic analysis: nominal, attested by Elders Group.

<**q'ó:y ~ q'óy**>, free root //q'á·y ~ q'áy//, ABDF /'*die, be dead, be paralyzed*'/, syntactic analysis: intransitive verb, attested by AC, BJ (5/10/64), EB, Elders Group, other sources: ES /q'á·y/ *die*, ASM ['die'], example: <**le q'ó:y.**>, //lə q'á·y//, /'*He/She/It died.*'/, literally /'third person past die'/, attested by AC, ASM ['be dead'], <**mōkw' q'óy**>, //mók'^{w} q'áy//, /'*(They're) all dead.*'/, attested by AC, <**le q'óy te sméyeth.**>, //lə q'áy tə s=mɛ́yəθ//, /'*The animal is dead.*'/, attested by AC, <**lulh tu q'ó:y**>, //lə=uɬ tu q'á·y//, /'*dying*'/, literally /'third person past =already a little dead'/, attested by Elders Group (3/29/78), <**lhséq' q'ó:y**>, //ɬ=sə́q' q'á·y//, /'*half-dead*'/, attested by EB, ASM ['be paralyzed'], <**q'óy te lhq'í:ws**>, //q'áy tə ɬq'=í·ws//, /'*half of one's arm or body is paralyzed, had a stroke*'/, attested by Elders Group (9/24/75).

<**q'eyléxw**>, ncs //q'oy=l-ə[=´=]x^w//, ABFC /'*kill s-th/s-o accidentally, (happen to or manage to kill s-th/s-o)*'/, HUNT, FSH, (<**=l**> *non control transitivizer*), (<**=´= (stress-shift)**> *derivational*), phonology: vowel-reduction due to stress-shift, syntactic analysis: transitive verb, attested by AC, example: <**le q'eyléxwes te sméyeth.**>, //lə q'oy=l-ə[=´=]x^w-əs tə s=mɛ́yəθ//, /'*He killed the animal.*'/, literally /'third person past he (accidentally) kills s-th the animal'/, attested by AC.

<**q'ó:yt**>, pcs //q'á·y=T//, HUNT ['*kill s-th (purposely)*'], FSH, SOC ['*kill s-o (purposely)*'], (<**=t**> *purposeful control transitivizer*), syntactic analysis: transitive verb, attested by EB.

<**q'óq'eyt**>, cts //q'á[-C_1ə-]y=T//, HUNT ['*killing s-th*'], FSH, SOC, (<**-R1-**> *continuative*), phonology: reduplication, syntactic analysis: transitive verb, attested by AC, example: <**qóq'eyetes te x̱wiyx̱wiyáya.**>, //q'á[-C_1ə-]y=T-əs təx̣^{w}ɛy=C_1əC_2=ɛ́yɛ//, /'*They are killing flies.*'/, attested by AC.

<**q'óythet**>, pcrs //q'áy=T-ət//, SOC ['*kill oneself*'], (<**=t**> *purposeful control transitivizer*), (<**-et**> *reflexive*), syntactic analysis: intransitive verb, attested by AC, example: <**wetló'o le q'óythet.**>,

//wə-ƛ’á-ʔa lə q’áy=T-ət//, /'*He killed himself., She killed herself., It killed itself.*'/, literally /'contrastive- it's him/her/it third person past kill oneself'/, attested by AC.

<**sq'óq'ey**>, strs //s=q’á[=C_1ə=]y//, ABDF ['*be dead*'], (<**s=**> *stative*), (<**=R1=**> *resultative*), phonology: reduplication, syntactic analysis: adjective/adjectival verb, attested by EB, example: <**sq'óq'ey te sméyeth.**>, //s=q’á[=C_1ə=]y tə s=mɛ́yəθ//, /'*The animal is dead.*'/, attested by EB, <**sq'óq'ey te pús í kw'e xálh.**>, //s=q’á[=C_1ə=]y tə pús ʔí k’^{w}ə x^{y}ɛ́ɬ//, /'*There's a dead cat on the road.*'/, literally /'is dead the cat (here) on the (remote) road'/, attested by EB.

<**q'óq'ey**>, cts //q’á[=C_1ə=]y//, ABDF ['*be sick*'], literally probably /'dying'/, (<**=R1=**> *continuative* or *derivational*), phonology: reduplication, syntactic analysis: adjective/adjectival verb, attested by EB, AC, BJ (5/10/64, 12/5/64), Elders Group, Deming, other sources: ES /q’á·q’ɛy/ *sickness*, example: <**le q'áq'ey.**>, //lə q’á[=C_1ə=]y//, /'*He's sick.*'/, attested by BJ (12/5/64), <**q'óq'ey te sméyeth.**>, //q’á[=C_1ə=]y tə s=mɛ́yəθ//, /'*The animal is sick.*'/, attested by EB; found in <**q'óq'eytsel.**>, //q’á[=C_1ə=]y-c-əl//, /'*I'm sick.*'/, attested by Deming, also <**q'óq'eychel.**>, //q’á[=C_1ə=]y-c-əl//, attested by EB, also <**tsel q'óq'ey.**>, //c-əl q’á[=C_1ə=]y//, attested by Elders Group, <**q'óq'eycap.**>, //q’á[=C_1ə=]y-c-ɛp//, /'*You folks are sick.*'/, attested by EB, <**q'óq'eychet.**>, //q’á[=C_1ə=]y-c-ət//, /'*We're sick.*'/, attested by EB, <**q'óq'eychexw.**>, //q’á[=C_1ə=]y-c-əx^{w}//, /'*You're sick.*'/, attested by EB, example: <**q'óq'ey (theló, yethá, teló, tútl'ò).**>, //q’á[=C_1ə=]y (θə=lá, yə=θɛ́, tə=lá, tə=ú=ƛ’á)//, /'*(She is, They are, He is, He is) sick.*'/, Elder's comment: "teló means the same thing as tútl'ò *he*", attested by EB, <**tu q'óq'eytsel.**>, //tu q’á[=C_1ə=]y-c-əl//, /'*I'm a little sick.*'/, attested by Deming (1/18/79); found in <**q'óq'eychelcha.**>, //q’á[=C_1ə=]y-c-əl-cɛ//, /'*I will be sick.*'/, attested by EB, <**q'óq'eychexwcha.**>, //q’á[=C_1ə=]y-c-əx^{w}-cɛ//, /'*You will be sick.*'/, attested by EB, <**q'óq'eycha.**>, //q’á[=C_1ə=]y-cɛ//, /'*He/she/it will be sick.*'/, example: <**(lí:lhchexw, í:lhchexw) q'óq'ey.**>, //(lí·-ɬ-c-əx^{w}, ʔí·-ɬ-c-əx^{w}) q’á[=C_1ə=]y//, /'*You were sick.*'/, attested by EB, <**(lí:lhchel, í:lhchel) q'óq'ey.**>, //(lí·-ɬ-c-əl, ʔí·-ɬ-cəl) q’á[=C_1ə=]y//, /'*I was sick.*'/, attested by EB, <**lí:lhchap q'óq'ey.**>, //lí·-ɬ-c-ɛp q’á[=C_1ə=]y//, /'*You all were sick.*'/, attested by EB, <**lílhchet q'óq'ey.**>, //lí-ɬ-c-ət q’á[=C_1ə=]y//, /'*We were sick.*'/, attested by EB, <**lílh q'óq'ey yethá.**>, //lí-ɬ q’á[=C_1ə=]y yə=θɛ́//, /'*They were sick.*'/, attested by EB, <**(lílh, ílh) q'óq'ey thútl'ò.**>, //(lí-ɬ, ʔí-ɬ) q’á[=C_1ə=]y θ=ú=ƛ’á//, /'*She was sick.*'/, attested by EB, <**(lílh, ílh) q'óq'ey tútl'ò.**>, //(lí-ɬ, ʔí-ɬ) q’á[=C_1ə=]y t=ú=ƛ’á//, /'*He was sick.*'/, attested by EB (2/16/76).

<**sq'óq'ey**>, dnom //s=q’á[=C_1ə=]y//, ABDF ['*sickness*'], ASM, ANA ['*sperm*'], (<**s=**> *nominalizer*), phonology: reduplication, syntactic analysis: nominal, attested by BJ (12/5/64), Elders Group, ME (11/21/72), JL (7/20/79), ASM ['sickness'], example: <**stám ta' sq'óq'ey?**>, //s=tɛ́m t-ɛʔ s=q’á[=C_1ə=]y//, /'*What's your sickness?*'/, attested by Elders Group, <**eyém sq'óq'ey**>, //ʔɛy=ə́m s=q’á[=C_1ə=]y//, /'*real bad sickness*'/, literally /'strong sickness'/, attested by ME (11/21/72 tape), ASM ['sperm'], <**ta' sq'óq'ey**>, //t-ɛʔ s=q’á[=C_1ə=]y//, /'*your sperm, your sickness*'/, attested by JL (7/20/79 Fish Camp), <**le ő̃kw' tel sq'óq'ey.**>, //lə ʔók’^{w} tə-l s=q’á[=C_1ə=]y//, /'*My sperm has run out (emptied)., My come has run out (emptied)., I'm through coming/climaxing/ejaculating.*'/, literally /'third person past run out/be emptied my sickness'/, attested by JL (7/20/79 at Fish Camp).

<**q'óq'eystexw**>, caus //q’á[=C_1ə=]y=sT-əx^{w}//, ABDF ['*make s-o sick*'], EFAM, (<**=st**> *causative control transitivizer*), (<**-exw**> *third person object),* phonology: reduplication, syntactic analysis: transitive verb, attested by EB, example: <**me q'óq'eysthóxes yethá.**>, //mə q’á[=C_1ə=]y=sT-áx^{y}-əs yə=θɛ́//, /'*Those people make me sick.*'/, literally /'come to/start to they make me sick they/those plural'/, attested by EB.

<**q'óq'eytses**>, ds //q’á[=C_1ə=]y=cəs//, ABDF /'*(be) sick on the hand, (have) a sick hand, (have) a hurt hand*'/, lx <**=tses**> *on the hand*, phonology: reduplication, syntactic analysis: adjective/adjectival verb, attested by AC.

<q'óq'eyxel>, ds //q'á[=C_1ə=]y=x^{y}əl//, ABDF /'*be lame, (be) sick on the foot, (have) a sick foot, (have) a hurt foot*'/, lx **<=xel>** *on the foot,* phonology: reduplication, syntactic analysis: adjective/adjectival verb, attested by AC, other sources: H-T <kakaHyil> (macron over first a) *lame (lit. sore foot)*, example: **<skw'áy kw'es ímexs, q'óq'eyxel.>**, //s=k'^{w}ɛ́y k'^{w}-əs ʔím=əx^y-s q'á[=C_1ə=]y=x^{y}əl//, /'*He can't walk, he's lame.*'/, attested by AC.

<q'oq'eyá:wtxw>, ds //q'á[=C_1ə=]y=ɛ́·wtx^w//, BLDG ['*hospital*'], ABDF, lx **<=á:wtxw ~ =áwtxw>** *house, building*, phonology: reduplication, syntactic analysis: nominal, attested by Elders Group.

<q'é:yq'ey>, chrs //q'o[=Aí·=]y=C_1əC_2//, durs, ABDF ['*be always sickly*'], (**<í:-ablaut (realized after q' as é:y)>** *durative*), (**<=R2>** *characteristic*), phonology: í:/é:y-ablaut, reduplication, syntactic analysis: adjective/adjectival verb, attested by BHTTC.

<q'oyátl'iye>, df //q'ayɛ́ƛ'=iyɛ//, EZ /'*snail, slug*'/, ['probably most members of the class *Gastropoda*; also *Limax maximus* and *Arion aster*'], root meaning unknown, lx **<=iya>** *affectionate diminutive*, syntactic analysis: nominal, attested by BJ (12/5/64), EB (11/27/75), other sources: JH /q'á·yeƛ'íyé/ *snail*, Salish cognate: Squamish /q'iyáƛ'an/ *snail (pertains to most Gastropoda)* but not Squamish /ɬíx̣^{w}əm/ *slug (*probably *Limax maximus* or *Arion aster)* Kennedy and Bouchard 1976:110, W73:239, K67:331, and not Squamish /wəq'ə́q'/ *snail* W73:240, K67:377, Lushootseed /q'əyáƛ'əd/ *slug, snail* H76:397, Songish dial. of N. Straits /q'eyáƛ'ən/ *snail* M68:76, Samish dial. of N. Straits (VU) /q'əyáƛ'ən'/ *snail* G86:69.

<q'oyéx̲ ~ q'eyéx̲>, WATR ['*whirlpool*'], *see* q'ey ~ q'i.

<q'oyéx̲em>, WATR ['*whirlpool that suddenly starts from level water*'], *see* q'ey ~ q'i.

<q'oyíyets or **q'oyí:ts>**, df //q'ay=i[=´=]y=əc// or more likely //q'ay=í·c// or //q'əy=í·c//, EZ /'*elk, Roosevelt elk,* perhaps also *(introduced) Rocky Mountain elk*'/, ['*Cervus canadensis roosevelti,* perhaps also *Cervus canadensis nelsoni*'], elk up to about the 1860's were numerous in the Stó:lō area, being described as being like herds of cattle at times, coming down from Elk Mountain southeast of Chilliwack; they may have been the Roosevelt elk since Cowan and Guiget 1965 report, "This race is an inhabitant of the west coast rain forests. Here it formerly occupied the deciduous forest areas of the Fraser River delta and of the eastern coast of Vancouver Island. It was exterminated on the mainland by natural causes at least 100 years ago ....";, the date of their extinction in the area must have been post- contact due to the naming by non-Indians of Elk Mountain; it is unclear whether the Rocky Mountain elk also ranged within the Stó:lō area, but the oldest speakers seem to use q'oyí:ts for *elk* while the middle-aged Tait speakers in some cases now use the name for *moose* to reflect the absence of elk and presence of moose in the Stó:lō area;, according to Cowan and Guiget 1965, "Prior to 1920 there were virtually no moose south of the Hazelton-Prince George line. They have now moved to the International Boundary, and the most dense populations are in this newly invaded territory." They are shown on the map in that book as far west within the Stó:lō territory as the eastern shore of Harrison Lake, literally possibly /'knotted (horns) (covering) on the back?? (or possibly) fine down covering on the back??'/, possibly root **<q'ey ~ q'i>** *knotted, tied, wound around* or possibly root **<q'oy>** as in **<s=q'óy=es>** *down feathers*, lx **<=í:ts ~ =ets ~ =ewíts>** *on the back*, possibly **<=iy ~ =áy>** *covering, bark*, syntactic analysis: nominal, attested by AC, BJ (12/5/64), Elders Group (3/1/72, 9/1/76), other sources: ES /q'əyə́y·əc/ *elk*, H-T <kaiyéEtc> (macron on é) *elk (Cervus canadensis)*, JH /q'əyí·c/ *elk*, Salish cognate: Squamish /q'iíʔč/ *elk* possibly with root /q'il/ *knotted, tied, wound around* (Squamish /=(ʔ)=č/ *back*) W73:90, K67:359, 120, Sechelt /q'ə́yič/ *elk, moose* T77:9, Mainland Comox /q'íʔič/ *moose* (elk unknown) B75prelim:9, Saanich dial. of N. Straits /q'əyíʔč/ *elk* (vs. /k^{w}éwəʔeč/ *moose*) B74a:9, Samish dial. of N. Straits (VU) /q'ayé·č/ *elk* (vs. possibly /k^{w}íwič ~ k^{w}íwəyč/ *moose* perhaps from Cowichan) G86:66, (contrast Lushootseed /k^{w}ág^w=ičəd/ *elk, Big Dipper* H76:241 and note that all cognates of this word also have the lexical suffix for *back*), also /'*moose*'/, attested by EP and EB

(BHTTC 8/23/76), AK (11/21/72 tape), BHTTC (8/31/76 less sure), example: <**qéx̱ te q'ayíyets.**>, //qə́x̣ tə q'ay=íy=əc//, /'*(There's) lots of elk.*'/, attested by AC.

<**Q'oyíyets ~ Q'oyí:ts**>, df //q'ay=i[=´=]y=əc ~ q'ay=í·c//, WETH /'*Big Dipper, (the Elk)*'/, literally /'Elk'/, syntactic analysis: nominal, source: H-T 1902 reports that the Big Dipper is called the Elk, Salish cognate: Lushootseed also calls the Big Dipper *Elk* but uses the word cognate with *moose* in other languages, i.e. Lushootseed /k^{w}ág^{w}=ičəd/ *elk, Big Dipper* H76:241.

<**Q'oyíyets ~ Q'oyí:ts**>, df //q'ay=i[=´=]y=əc ~ q'ay=í·c//, PLN ['*elk (or) moose turned to stone in the Fraser River by Hill's Bar*'], ASM ['a hunter and his dog chased this elk into the river when they were all turned to stone, the elk is just below the dog (see Sqwmá:y) and is about two-thirds of the way over and away from the CN (east) side of the river; in low water it really looks like an elk; we passed the group of rocks (Hunter and Dog on the east shore and Elk in the river) on our raft trip with elders AD, SP and AK down the Fraser River; we took photos now in Coqualeetza's place name photo files'], syntactic analysis: nominal, attested by SP and AK (8/2/77 Fish Camp, 8/30/77 Raft trip), source: place names reference file #162, 272a.

<**q'oyíyetsó:llh**>, dmn //q'ay=íy=əc=á·ɬ//, EZ /'*baby elk, (young elk)*'/, lx <**=ó:llh**> *young, offspring*, syntactic analysis: nominal, attested by AC.

<**q'oyíyetsó:llh**>, EZ /'*baby elk, (young elk)*'/, *see* q'oyíyets or q'oyí:ts.

<**Q'oyíyets ~ Q'oyí:ts**>, WETH /'*Big Dipper, (the Elk)*'/, *see* q'oyíyets or q'oyí:ts.

<**Q'oyíyets ~ Q'oyí:ts**>, PLN ['*elk (or) moose turned to stone in the Fraser River by Hill's Bar*'], *see* q'oyíyets or q'oyí:ts.

<**q'ó:yt**>, HUNT ['*kill s-th (purposely)*'], *see* q'ó:y ~ q'óy.

<**q'óythet**>, SOC ['*kill oneself*'], *see* q'ó:y ~ q'óy.

<**q'pá:ls**>, ECON /'*collect, collect money, take a collection, gather*'/, *see* q'ép.

<**q'pém**>, MC /'*collect, gather*'/, *see* q'ép.

<**q'pét**>, HARV /'*gather s-th, pick up s-th (stuff that's scattered about), collect s-th, gather it up, pick them up (already gathered or not)*'/, *see* q'ép.

<**q'péthet**>, SOC /'*crowd together, gather together, people gather*'/, *see* q'ép.

<**q'sém**>, df //q'ɛs=ə́m or q'ə́s=ə[=M2=]m or q'ə́s=M1=(ə)m//, EFAM ['*tired of waiting*'], ABDF, possibly <**metathesis type 1**> *non-continuative* or possibly <**metathesis type 2**> *resultative or non-continuative*, (<**=em (or =ém)**> *intransitivizer, get, have*), phonology: possible metathesis type 1 or 2, possible vowel merger, syntactic analysis: intransitive verb, attested by Deming (3/31/77), compare UHk <**qás=el**> *tired* and the five words derived from it (see under letter q), Salish cognate: Squamish root /q'əs/ *get tired (waiting)* as in /q's-íws/ *get tired waiting, get impatient* and /q'ə́s-šn/ *get tired feet* W73:269, K67:355.

<**q'sí:ltel**>, WV /'*woven headband of packstrap, tumpline*'/, *see* q'ey ~ q'i.

<**q'thá:m**>, df //q'ɛ́·θ=M2=əm or q'iθ=ə[=Aɛ́·=]m//, EFAM ['*(have a) short memory*'], ABDF, root <**q'th** or **q'á:th** or **q'ith**> *short, not quite reaching, insufficient*, possibly <**metathesis**> *non-continuative*? or á:-ablaut> *derivational* or *durative*, lx <**=em**> *middle voice or intransitivizer, have, get*, phonology: possible metathesis or ablaut, syntactic analysis: intransitive verb, attested by Elders Group (3/3/76), Salish cognate: Squamish root /q'ic ~ q'əc/ *short, insufficient* as in /ʔəs-q'ə-q'íc/ *insufficient* and /(ʔə)s-q'c-ámʔ/ *too short, not quite reaching* K69:81-82.

<**sq'thà:m**>, stvi //s=q'θ=ɛ́·m//, ECON ['*be short (of money or other things)*'], SOC, EFAM, (<**s=**> *stative*), phonology: downshifting, syntactic analysis: adjective/adjectival verb, attested by EB,

example: <**tsel sq'thà:m.**>, //c-əl s=q'θ=ɛ́·m//, /'*I'm short (of money) [or other things].*'/.

<**q'iq'ethá:m** or **q'eyq'ethá:m**>, df //C_1í=q'əθ=ɛ́·m or C_1í=q'ɛ́·θ=M1=əm or q'i[=C_1ə=]θ=ɛ́·m//, EFAM ['*be short (in memory)*'], ABDF, possibly <**R4=**> *diminutive*, possibly <**=R1=**> *resultative or continuative or durative*, phonology: possible ablaut or metathesis, syntactic analysis: adjective/adjectival verb, attested by Elders Group (3/3/76), example: <**q'eyq'thá:m ta' télmel.**>, //q'i[=C_1ə=]θ=ɛ́·m t-εʔ tə́l=məl//, /'*Your memory is short.*'/, literally /'it is short (in memory) your mind'/.

<**q'thá:mtem**>, df //q'θ=ɛ́·m=təm//, EFAM /'*(be) absent-minded, forgetful*'/, ABDF, possibly <**=tem**> *stative or participial*, syntactic analysis: adjective/adjectival verb, attested by Elders Group (3/3/76).

<**q'thá:mtses**>, df //q'θ=ɛ́·m=cəs//, ABDF ['*can't reach (with hand)*'], lx <**=tses**> *on the hand*, syntactic analysis: adjective/adjectival verb, attested by Elders Group (4/28/76).

<**sq'thá:mtses**>, stvi //s=q'=ɛ́·m=cəs//, ABDF ['*can't reach*'], (<**s=**> *stative*), syntactic analysis: adjective/adjectival verb, attested by EB (4/27/76), example: <**sq'thá:mtses tútl'ò.**>, //s=q'θ=ɛ́·m=cəs t=ú=ƛ'á//, /'*He can't reach.*'/; found in <**sq'thá:mtsestsel.**>, //s=q'θ=ɛ́·m=cəs-t-əl//, /'*I can't reach.*'/.

<**q'thá:mtem**>, EFAM /'*(be) absent-minded, forgetful*'/, *see* q'thá:m.

<**q'thá:mtses**>, ABDF ['*can't reach (with hand)*'], *see* q'thá:m.

<**q'x̲ótel**>, LANG /'*to argue, have an argument, [argue with each other], quarrelling, sassing back*'/, *see* q'(e)x̲.

QW

<**qwá**>, free root //qʷɛ́//, DESC ['*get a hole*'], syntactic analysis: intransitive verb, attested by AC, example: <**le qwá te "tire".**>, //lə qʷɛ́ tə tire//, [lə qʷǽ tə táyər], /'*The tire got a hole.*'/, compare with <**sqweqwá ta "tire".**> *There's a hole in your tire.*, attested by AC.

<**sqwá**>, dnom //s=qʷɛ́//, WATR /'*tributary, small creek that goes into a bigger river*'/, (<**s=**> *nominalizer*), literally /'opening, outlet, hole, (tributary)'/, syntactic analysis: nominal, attested by TG, JS.

<**Sqwá**>, ds //s=qʷɛ́//, PLN /'*Skwah village, now Skwah Reserve,* also known as *Wellington Reserve*'/, ASM ['at the end of Wellington Avenue just outside of Chilliwack'], literally /'opening, outlet, hole, (tributary)'/, (semological comment: so named because one could enter Hope slough and come through quiet water parallel to the Fraser River and come out here), (<**s=**> *nominalizer*), syntactic analysis: nominal, attested by AC and CT (1973), Elders Group (7/20/77), compare with <**Sqwehá**, source: place names reference file #85, Wells 1965 (lst ed.):23.

<**sqweqwá**>, dnom //s=C_1ə=qʷɛ́//, DESC ['*a hole*'], ASM ['like a knothole, hole in a pail, cave, tunnel'], (<**s=**> *nominalizer* perhaps ~ *stative* here), possibly <**R5=**> *durative or resultative*, phonology: reduplication, syntactic analysis: nominal (perhaps ~ adjective/adjectival verb), attested by Elders Group (3/15/72), AC, example: <**sqweqwá ta "tire".**>, //s=C_1ə=qʷɛ́ t-ɛ tire//, /'*There's a hole in your tire.*'/, attested by AC, <**osesu kw'étslexwes te sqweqwá li te smált.**>, //ʔa-s-əs-u **k'ʷə́c=l-əxʷ**-əs tə s=C_1ə=qʷɛ́ li tə smɛ́lt//, /'*Then he saw the hole in the mountain.*'/, semantic environment ['it was a cave'], usage: Story of the Flood, attested by AC, <**sqweqwá tel skw'ówes.**>, //s=C_1ə=qʷɛ́ tə-l s=**k'ʷ**áwəs//, /'*(There's) a hole in my pail.*'/, attested by AC, <**tl'áqt sqweqwá**>, //ƛ'ɛ́qt s=C_1ə=qʷɛ́//, /'*long hole*'/, attested by Elders Group (3/15/72), <**te stl'eqtí:ms te sqweqwá**>, //tə s=ƛ'ɛqt=í·m-s tə s=C_1ə=qʷɛ́//, /'*the length of the tunnel*'/, literally /'the length of the hole'/, attested by Elders Group (3/15/72).

<**sqweqwá seplíl**>, EB, FOOD *donut, bagel* (lit. got a hole/with a hole + bread), (attested by RG,EH 6/16/98 to SN, edited by BG with RG,EH 6/26/00, also RG & EH (4/10/99 Ling332)

<**sqweqwá:ls ~ shxwqweqwá:ls**>, dnom //s=C_1ə=qʷɛ́=ɛ́(·)ls ~ sxʷ=C_1ə=qʷɛ́=ɛ́(·)ls//, TOOL /'*borer to make holes, auger*'/, (<**s= ~ shxw=**> *something to, something that,* R5= *resultative or durative* perhaps), (<**=á:ls ~ =áls**> *structured activity non-continuative*), phonology: reduplication, vowel merger, syntactic analysis: nominal, attested by DM (12/4/64, new p.184).

<**Sqwá:la**>, ds //s=qʷɛ́=ɛ́lɛ//, PLN /'*village at west end of Little Mountain (Mount Shannon) on Hope Slough,* also a name for *Hope Slough or Hope River*'/, ASM ['located a few miles east of Chilliwack, there is an Indian graveyard there at the base of Little Mountain (also known as Mt. Shannon)'], literally /'container of a hole/holes'/, (semological comment: if Wells 1966 is right (from an elder then) and the literal sense is *coming into the open* then this is explained by *container of a hole/opening*; if AC is right in noting the post-contact graveyard then the literal sense is *container of holes* and the name is post-contact), (<**s=**> *nominalizer*), root <**qwá**> *get a hole*, stem //s=qwá *hole*//, lx <**=ála ~ =á:la**> *container of*, phonology: vowel merger, syntactic analysis: nominal, attested by AC, Elders Group (6/20/78), source: place names reference file #287, also Wells 1965 (lst ed.):23, Wells 1966.

<**sqwahíwel**>, ds //s= *nominalizer*//, LAND /'*hole (in roof, tunnel, pants, mountain, at bottom of some lakes), tunnel*'/, DESC, stem //s=qwá *hole* ~ s=qwehá *go through*//, lx <**=íwel**> *on the inside, in the bottom*, phonology: epenthetic h (predictable between vowel-final root/stem and

vowel-initial suffix), syntactic analysis: nominal, attested by Elders Group (3/15/72, 1/21/76).

<**Sqwehíwel**>, ds //s=qʷɛ([=Aə=])=(h)íwəl//, PLN ['*Agassiz Mountain (or more likely Mount Woodside)*'], literally /'tunnel'/, ASM ['so named because there was a natural tunnel where one could crawl through from one side of the mountain to the other; the name was only reinforced when the railroad put another tunnel through the mountain'], stem //s=qwa=híwel *tunnel*//, possibly <**e=ablaut**> *derivational*, phonology: epenthetic h, possible ablaut, syntactic analysis: nominal, attested by Elders Group (8/24/77), source: place names reference file #240.

<**Sqweqwehíwel**>, dmpn //s=C_1ə=qʷɛ([=Aə=])=(h)íwəl//, [sqʷəqʷəhíwəl ~ sqʷʊqʷəhíwəl], PLN /'*beach on east side of Harrison Lake across from Long Island where there are lots of flat rocks, most of which have holes in them*'/, ASM ['such rocks used to be gathered long ago according to EL'], literally /'lots of holes inside'/, stem //s=qwá *hole*//, (<**R5=**> *diminutive plural*), possibly <**e-ablaut**> *derivational or durative*, lx <**=íwel**> *on the inside*, phonology: reduplication, epenthetic h, possible ablaut, syntactic analysis: nominal, attested by EL (9/27/77), source: place names reference file #300.

<**Sqwelíqwehíwel ~ Sqwelíqwehìwèl**>, dmpn //s=C_1ə[=əl=]=qʷɛ([=Aə=])=(h)íwəl//, [sqʷəlíqʷəhíwəl], PLN ['*natural holes or tunnels east of Iwówes and above Lhilheltálets that water came out of after rain*'], ASM ['since destroyed by the Canadian National railroad, this was the first hole or tunnel dug by Beaver to get the Sx̱wóyx̱wey mask to Lhilheltálets'], (<**s=**> *nominalizer*, R5= *diminutive plural*), (<**=el=**> *plural*), possibly <**e-ablaut**> *derivational or durative*, lx <**=íwel**> *on the inside*, phonology: reduplication, infixed plural, possible ablaut, epenthetic h, downstepping, updrifting, syntactic analysis: nominal, attested by Elders Group (7/6/77), SP and AD (transcribed during interview with MP in 1973-74), Elders at place names meeting after IHTTC (8/23/77), source: place names reference file #21.

<**sqwálats**>, ds //s=qʷɛ́=ləc//, DESC /'*hole in the bottom (of bucket, etc.)*'/, (<**s=**> *nominalizer* or *stative*), lx <**=lets ~ =lats**> *on the bottom*, phonology: vowel assimilation in suffix to root vowel, syntactic analysis: nominal, possibly adjective/adjectival verb, attested by Elders Group.

<**Sqwá:p**>, ds //s=qʷɛ́=ɛ́p//, PLN ['*the hole (lake) at the foot of Cheam Peak on the south side*'], ASM ['climbing the mountain one reaches a long ridge with meadows of blueberries before starting the final steep rocky ascent to the actual peak; from the meadow closest to the final ascent one can look down and see the little lake several hundred to a thousand feet below the meadow'], literally /'hole in the dirt'/, stem //s=qwá *hole*//, lx <**=áp**> *in the dirt*, phonology: vowel merger, syntactic analysis: nominal, attested by CT (1973), source: place names reference file #275.

<**sqwa'í:wel**>, ds //s=qʷɛ=ʔí·wəl//, DESC ['*(be) hollow*'], (<**s=**> *stative*), root <**qwá**> *hole*, lx <**=íwel ~ =íwel**> *on the inside, in the bottom*, ANA ['*rectum*'], phonology: epenthetic glottal stop (predictable between vowel-final root/stem and vowel-initial suffix), syntactic analysis: nominal, attested by JL (5/5/75).

<**qwát**>, pcs //qʷɛ́=T//, DESC /'*make a hole in s-th, drill a hole in s-th*'/, (<**=t**> *purposeful control transitivizer*), syntactic analysis: transitive verb, attested by BHTTC.

<**qwáth**>, bound derived stem //qʷɛ́=əθ// *hole in the mouth*, entry also under stem <**qewath**>

<**sqewáth**>, df /s=qʷɛ́=əθ//, EZ /'*(larger) rabbit: snowshoe or varying hare,* now probably also *eastern cottontail rabbit (introduced)*'/, ['*Lepus americanus cascadensis and Lepus americanus washingtoni,* now probably also *Sylvilagus floridanus mearnsi*'], <**s=**> *nominalizer*, root <**qwá**> *get a hole*, <**=eth**> *in the mouth*, compare <**sqweqwewáth**> *bunch of rabbits* and <**sqwiqweyóthel**> *rabbit* (lit. *little hole in the lip*), phonology: consonant merger, vowel merger, delabialization, syntactic analysis: nominal, attested by JL (5/5/75), AK (11/21/72 tape), also <**shxwóxw**>, //s(=)xʷáxʷ//, attested by AK (11/21/72 tape).

<**sqiqewóthel**>, dmn //s=C$_1$í=qəw=áθəl or s=C$_1$í=sq^{w}ɛ=áθəl//, EZ /'*big rabbit, older rabbit, big/older snowshoe/varying hare,* now probably also *big/older eastern cottontail rabbit (introduced)*'/, ['*Lepus americanus cascadensis and Lepus americanus washingtoni,* now probably also *Sylvilagus floridanus mearnsi*'], (<**s=**> *nominalizer,* R4= *diminutive*), possibly root <**s=qwá**> *hole,* lx <**=óthel**> *in the mouth,* phonology: reduplication, consonant merger, vowel merger, syntactic analysis: nominal, attested by Adeline Lorenzetto (Elders Group 3/1/72), compare with <**sqwiqweyóthel**> *big rabbit, older rabbit.*

<**qiqewótheló:ythel**>, ds //C$_1$í=q^{w}ɛ=áθəl=á·yθəl//, ABDF /'*cleft palate, harelip*'/, literally /'rabbit on the lip/jaw'/, stem //qiqewóthel *rabbit*//, lx <**=ó:ythel**> *on the lip, on the jaw,* phonology: reduplication, delabialization, vowel merger, syntactic analysis: nominal, attested by Elders Group (9/1/76).

<**sqíqewàth**>, dmn //s=C$_1$í=q^{w}ɛ́=əθ//, EZ /'*rabbit: snowshoe/varying hare,* now probably also *eastern cottontail rabbit (introduced), (baby rabbit, small rabbit or hare [Elders Group])*'/, ['*Lepus americanus cascadensis and Lepus americanus washingtoni,* now prob. also *Sylvilagus floridanus mearnsi*'], ASM ['rabbits were eaten and their fur used for blankets and baby shoes'], (<**s=**> *nominalizer,* R4= *diminutive*), probably root <**s=qwá**> *hole,* probably <**=eth**> *in the mouth,* phonology: reduplication, delabialization, vowel merger, syntactic analysis: nominal, attested by AC, BJ (12/5/64), AK (11/21/72 tape), also /'*baby rabbit, small rabbit*'/, attested by Elders Group (3/1/72 tape), also /'*small rabbit*'/, attested by Elders Group (5/5/75), also /'*rabbit (including snowshoe hare)*'/, attested by Elders Group (9/1/76), other sources: ES /sqiqəwɛc/ *rabbit,* JH /sqí·qəwèθ/ *rabbit,* H-T <skEkuwáts> (macron over u, umlaut over a) *rabbit ('jack') (Lepus americanus washingtoni).*

<**qwa(w)**> bound derived stem or <**qéw**> possible root //qə́w//, meaning unknown, or more likely root <**qwa**> //q^{w}ɛ́// *have a hole,* same entry under <**qew**>

<**sqéweqs**>, df //s=qə́w=əqs// perhaps from //s=q^w[-metathesis of vowel and labialization]ɛ́=əqs// as with the word for *rabbit* from same root, thus the raven is literally *something that has a hole in the nose,* due to the large holes in its beak, EZ ['*raven*'], ['*Corvus corax*'], ASM ['one cry resembles a hoarse woman's voice, ravens crowing in a certain way and going toward or by a house forecast a death in that family; a big bird (larger than a crow), lives to be about 100 yrs. old'], (<**s=**> *nominal*), root meaning unknown, lx <**=eqs**> *on the nose, point,* syntactic analysis: nominal, attested by AC, also <**skéweqs**>, //s=q[=K=]əw=əqs//, (<**=K=** or **fronting**> *diminutive*), attested by AC, SP and others, dialects: *Chill., Tait,* other sources: JH /sqáwəqs/ *raven,* H-T <skaúEks> *raven (Corvus corax principalis),* Salish cognate: Lushootseed /skáw'qs/ *raven; Brother of /k'á?k'a?/ in myth age,* example: <**qéx̱ te sqéweqs. ~ qéx̱ te skéweqs.**>, //qə́x̣ tə s=qə́w=əqs ~ qə́x̣ tə s=q[=K=]ə́w=əqs//, /'*There's a lot of ravens.*'/, attested by AC.

<**Skwówéls**>, df //s=k^{w}áw=əls//or //s-q^w[-K-]ɛ́[=Aa=]=wels//, N ['*Raven*'], (<**s=**> *nominalizer*), root meaning unknown unless <**qwa**> *have a hole,* possibly <**=els**> *structured activity continuative,* phonology: updrifting, possibly velarization/diminutive fronting if derived from root in <**sqéweqs**> (<**sqwa**> as in 'rabbit' above or <**sqew**>) (compare <**skéweqs**> above), syntactic analysis: nominal, usage: name in story.

<**qwehá**>, possibly root //q^{w}əhɛ́ or q^{w}ɛ́=(h)=ə=M2 or q^{w}ɛ=(h)ɛ́//, TVMO ['*go through*'], possibly root <**qwá**> *get a hole,* possibly <**=h**> epenthetic with no meaning, <**=e** or **=á**> meaning unclear, metathesis> *derivational,* phonology: possible metathesis or vowel-reduction, epenthetic h, syntactic analysis: intransitive verb, attested by Elders Group (7/20/77).

<**Sqwehá**>, ds //s=q^{w}ɛ́=(h)ə=M2//, PLN /'*Skwah village, now Skwah Reserve*'/, literally /'place to go through'/, ASM ['so named because people could canoe through Hope Slough in quieter water than

the Fraser River but parallel to the Fraser and then come out here again on the Fraser'], Elder's comment: "this is an older pronunciation than Sqwá", (<**s=**> *nominalizer, something to, place to*), stem //qwehá *go through*//, phonology: epenthetic h, metathesis or vowel-reduction, syntactic analysis: nominal, attested by Elders Group (7/20/77), compare with <**Sqwá**>, source: place names reference file #85, also <**Sqwá**>, //s=q^{w}ɛ́//, literally /'opening, outlet, hole'/, attested by Elders Group (7/20/77), CT (1973), AC (1973), source: Wells 1965 (lst ed.):23.

<**sqwehá:liya**>, df //s=q^{w}ɛ=(h)ɛ́líyɛ//, ANAH ['*pierced ear*'], SOC, (<**s=**> *stative* or *nominalizer*?), root <**qwá**> *get a hole,* lx <**=á(:)líya**> *on the ear*, phonology: epenthetic h, vowel-reduction, syntactic analysis: adjective/adjectival verb prob., poss. nominal, attested by IHTTC.

<**qwahéylém ~ qwahí:lém**>, mdls //q^{w}ɛ́=(h)í·l=əm//, ABFC ['*crawl through (like through a fence)*'], TVMO, (<**=í:l**> *come, go, get, become,* <**=em**> *middle voice*), phonology: epenthetic h, syntactic analysis: intransitive verb, attested by BHTTC.

<**qwōhóls** (or perhaps) **qwehóls**>, df //q^{w}ɛ=(h)áls or q^{w}ɛ=Ao=(h)áls//, DESC /'*sticking out through a hole (like a toe out of a sock, knee out of a hole in pants, a nail driven clear through the other side of a board), come out into the open*'/, possibly <**ō-ablaut**> *continuative or derivational,* lx <**=óls**> *spherical object*, phonology: vowel-reduction or rare ō-ablaut, epenthetic h, syntactic analysis: intransitive verb, attested by IHTTC.

<**Qwōhòls**>, ds //q^{w}ɛ=(h)áls or q^{w}ɛ=Ao=(h)áls//, PLN probably /'*Mahood Creek and Johnson Slough,* (possibly) *Wahleach River or Hicks Creek (creek at bridge on east end of Seabird Island [AK])*'/, literally /'come out into the open'/, phonology: vowel-reduction or rare ō-ablaut, epenthetic h, syntactic analysis: nominal, attested by Elders Group (7/13/77), IHTTC (8/5/77), source: place names reference file #64, also /'*creek at bridge on east end of Seabird Island*'/, attested by AK (8/30/77).

<**sqweqwewáth**>, dmpn //s=C$_1$ə=q^{w}ɛ́=w(=)ə[=M2=]**θ**//, EZ ['*bunch of rabbits*'], (<**s=**> *nominalizer,* R5= *diminutive plural*), lx <**=w**> meaning unknown, <**=eth**> *in the mouth, edge*, possibly metathesis *derivational*, phonology: reduplication, possible metathesis, syntactic analysis: nominal, attested by JL (5/5/75).

<**sqwíqweyóthel**>, ds //s=C$_1$í=q^{w}ɛ=áy[=M1=]θəl//, EZ /'*jackrabbit,* also *big or older rabbit (snowshoe/varying hare)*'/, ['*Lepus townsendi*, also big or older *Lepus americanus cascadensis* and *Lepus americanus washingtoni*', now probably also *Sylvilagus floridanus mearnsi*'], (<**s=**> *nominalizer,* R4= *diminutive* used here as *augmentative*), root <**qwá**> *get hole,* lx <**=eyóthel**> *on the lip, on the jaw,* (**metathesis type 1** *derivational*), phonology: reduplication, metathesis, syntactic analysis: nominal, attested by ME (11/21/72 tape), SP (Elders Group 3/1/72 tape), also <**sqiqewóthel**>, //s=C$_1$í=qəw=**áθ**əl//, attested by AL (Elders Group 3/1/72), also <**skwikweyóthel?**>, //s=C$_1$í=q^{w}[=K=]ɛ=əyáθəl//, attested by IHTTC (7/26/77).

<**sqwoqwtó:ythel**>, df //s=q^{w}ɛ=AaC$_1$ə=T=**á·y**θəl//, ABFC ['*(have the) mouth round and open with rounded lips*'], (<**s=**> *stative*), (<**ó-ablaut plus =R1=**> *continuative*), (<**=t**> *purposeful control transitivizer*), lx <**=ó:ythel**> *in the lips*, phonology: ablaut, reduplication, syntactic analysis: adjective/adjectival verb, attested by IHTTC (8/9/77).

<**slheqwe'álá**>, dnom //s=ɬə=q^{w}əʔ=ɛ́lɛ́//, CLO ['*pocket*'], (<**s=**> *nominalizer*), lx <**=álá**> *container of,* comment: root form and meaning unclear, possibly same as in <**sqwa'í:wel**> *(be) hollow*' (which has <**s=**> *stative*, root <**qwá(')**> *hole*, lx <**=íwel ~ =íwel**> *on the inside, in the bottom)*, possibly lx <lh(e)=> *use, extract, extract a portion of,* i.e. lit. perhaps *container of thing extracted from a hollow/hole* or *container to extract from something hollow*, syntactic analysis: nominal.

<**qwahéylém ~ qwahí:lém**>, ABFC ['*crawl through (like through a fence)*'], *see* qwá.

<**qwà:l**>, free root //q^{w}ɛ̀·l//, LANG /'*speak, talk, give a speech*'/, LANG /'*croak, etc.*'/, semantic

environment ['non-human creatures with cries are also said to qwà:l'], Elder's comment: "Stó:lō people never carry on talking at the same time as someone else; they are taught to stop right away if someone interrupts; it's more rude to continue talking than it is in English (AD 11/19/79)", syntactic analysis: intransitive verb, attested by AC, Elders Group, AD, EB, CT and HT, other sources: ES /q^{w}ɛ̀·l/ (Cw /q^{w}ál/, Ms /q^{w}ə́yl/) *say (speak)*, JH /q^{w}é·l/ *to speak*, contrast **<qwá:l>** *mosquito*; found in **<qwà:l.>**, //q^{w}ɛ̀·l//, /'*He speaks.*'/, attested by AC, **<qwà:llha.>**, //q^{w}ɛ̀·l-ɬɛ//, /'*Talk., Speak.*'/, attested by AC, example: **<le qwà:l.>**, //lə q^{w}ɛ̀·l//, /'*He talked., He spoke., He gave a speech.*'/, attested by AC, **<skw'áy kws qwà:ls.>**, //s=**k'**^{w}ɛ́y k^{w}-s q^{w}ɛ̀·l-s//, /'*He's/She's dumb (mute)., He can't talk.*'/, literally /'it can't be that talk/speak -he'/, attested by EB, **<qwà:l te siyá:m.>**, //q^{w}ɛ̀·l tə s=iy=ɛ́·m//, /'*The chief talks.*'/, attested by Elders Group (5/26/76), **<qwà:l li te qéx̲ xwémlexw>**, //q^{w}ɛ̀·l li tə qə́x̣ x^{w}ə́mləx^{w}//, /'*announce before lots of Indians*'/, attested by CT and HT (6/21/76), **<qwà:l li kw'e qéx̲ mestíyexw>**, //q^{w}ɛ̀·l li **k'**^{w}ə qə́x̣ məstíyəx^{w}//, /'*announce at a gathering, announce before lots of people*'/, attested by CT and HT (6/21/76), **<l stl'í kw'els qwà:l kw'e axwí:l òl sqwà:l.>**, //l s=ƛ'í **k'**^{w}ə-l-s q^{w}ɛ̀·l **k'**^{w}ə ʔɛx^{w}í·l ʔàl s=q^{w}ɛ̀·l//, /'*I would like to say just a few words.*'/, usage: public speaking, attested by Deming (5/18/78), **<qwà:l te welék'.>**, //q^{w}ɛ̀·l tə wələ́**k'**//, /'*The frog croaks., The frog talks.*'/, attested by Elders Group.

<qwà:ls>, sas //q^{w}ɛ̀·(l)=ɛ́·ls//, LANG /'*make a speech, talk*'/, possibly **<=á:ls>** *structured activity non-continuative*, phonology: consonant-loss of l, vowel merger, syntactic analysis: intransitive verb, attested by Elders Meeting (5/26/76), example: **<qwà:ls te siyá:m.>**, //q^{w}ɛ̀·l=ɛ́·ls tə s=iy=ɛ́·m//, /'*The chief makes a speech,, The chief talks.*'/.

<qwóqwel>, cts //q^{w}ɛ[-AáC$_{1}$ə-]l//, LANG /'*talking, speaking*'/, (**<ó-ablaut on root á plus -R1->** *continuative*), phonology: ablaut, reduplication, syntactic analysis: intransitive verb, attested by AC, Elders Group, AL (Elders Group 3/72), ME (11/21/72 tape), RG & EH (4/10/99 Ling332), example: **<le hóy kw'es qwóqwels.>**, //lə háy **k'**^{w}-əs q^{w}ɛ[-AáC$_{1}$ə-]l-s//, /'*They stopped talking.*'/, attested by AC, **<líchxw we'éy el qwóqwel kw'es me kwetxwílem (te xwelítem, kwthá siyáye)?>**, //lí-c-x^{w} wə=ʔɛ́y ʔəl q^{w}ɛ[-AáC$_{1}$ə-]l **k'**^{w}ə-s mə k^{w}ətx^{w}=íl=əm (tə x^{w}əlítəm, k^{w}=**θ**-ɛ s=iy=ɛ́yə)//, /'*Were you still talking when (your friend, the White man) came in? (come inside)*'/, attested by AC, **<x̲ét'estexwes yí o qwóqwel t'éqoya.>**, //x̣ə́**t'**ə=sT-əx^{w}-əs yə ʔa q^{w}ɛ[-AáC$_{1}$ə=]l **t'**ə́q=ayɛ//, /'*Some people say it "qwóqwel t'éqoya" (talking dirty).*'/, literally /'they say it those people just talking farty'/, attested by AL (Elders Group 3/72, Heritage Project tape 33), **<qwóqwel li te sxíxets.>**, //q^{w}ɛ[-AáC$_{1}$ə-]l li tə s=x^{y}í[=C$_{1}$ə=]c//, /'*(They're) talking in the bush/woods.*'/, semantic environment ['animals and birds are said to be doing this'], attested by ME (11/21/72 tape), **<qwóqwel te x̲wó:qw'.>**, //q^{w}ɛ[-AáC$_{1}$ə-]l təx̣^{w}**á·q'**^{w}//, /'*The sawbill (merganser) is talking.*'/, attested by AC, **<qwóqwel te tél:éqsel.>**, //q^{w}ɛ[-AáC$_{1}$ə-]l tə təl·=ə́qsəl//, /'*The mallard is talking.*'/, attested by AC (12/4/71), **<qwóqwel te skéweqs.>**, //q^{w}ɛ[-AáC$_{1}$ə-]l tə s=q[=K=]ə́w=əqs//, /'*The raven is talking (not necessarily warning).*'/, attested by Elders Group (12/15/76), contrast **<qwōlqwel te skéweqs.>** *The raven is warning (a different cry from talking).*>, **<ō áy el te sqwóqwels.>**, //ʔo ʔɛ́·y ʔəl tə s-q^{w}ɛ[-AáC$_{1}$ə-]l-s//, /'*He's talking without making any sense., He keeps on talking (in spite of the fact no one is listening).*'/, attested by Elders Group (3/13/80), **<qwóqwel>**, //q^{w}ɛ[-AáC$_{1}$ə-]l//, SPRD, //'*speaker* '//, attested by RG & EH (4/10/99 Ling332), **<ye qwóqwel>**, //yə q^{w}ɛ[-AáC$_{1}$ə-]l//, SPRD, /'*the speakers, officials at a spirit dance or other gathering, announcers, (master of ceremonies)*'/, ASM ['maybe one or two of them, they were masters of ceremony who conducted the work and introduced the other speakers'], attested by BJ (12/5/64), **<lhe qwóqwel li te (sq'ép, sq'eq'íp)>**, //ɬə q^{w}ɛ[-AáC$_{1}$ə-]l li tə (s=**q'**ə́p, s=**q'**ə[=C$_{1}$əAí=]p)//, /'*announcing at a gathering*'/, attested by CT and HT.

<lheqqwóqwel or **lheq qwóqwel>**, df //ɬəq=q^{w}ɛ[-AáC$_{1}$ə-]l or ɬəq q^{w}ɛ[-AáC$_{1}$ə-]l//, SOC /'*speaker at a gathering, announcer at a gathering*'/, SPRD, LANG, (**<lheq=>** or **<lheq>** meaning uncertain unless *sometimes* or *always*), phonology: reduplication, syntactic analysis: nominal, attested by EB, CT and HT, example: **<lheq qwóqwel li te sq'eq'íp>**, //ɬəq qʷɛ[-AáC_1ə-]l li tə s=**q'**ə[=C_1əAí=]p//, /'*speaker at a gathering*'/, attested by CT and HT.

<**qweqwà:l**>, durs //C_1ə=qʷɛ̀·l//, LANG /'*talking, (giving a speech)*'/, (<**R5=**> *durative*), phonology: reduplication, syntactic analysis: intransitive verb, attested by JL (Elders Meeting 8/29/79), Salish cognate: Musqueam /qʷəqʷ**ɛ́l'**/ *give a speech* durative of /qʷɛ́l/ *speak* Suttles 1984a: ch.7 [p.125], example: **<xwiy'éyelhs yé qweqwà:l>**, //x̣ʷ=C_1əC_2=ʔɛ́y=əɬ-s yə C_1ə=qʷɛ̀·l//, /'*(they're?) talking good*'/, literally /'plural clear/good voice -their/his/her the (plural human)/those giving a speech'/, phonology: high-pitch intonation on article, attested by JL.

<**sqwà:l**>, dnom //s=qʷɛ̀·l//, LANG /'*word, words*'/, LANG /'*subject, (topic)*'/, semantic environment ['to change s-th'], (<**s=**> *nominalizer*), syntactic analysis: nominal, attested by EB, AC, Elders Group, Deming, ASM ['word(s)'], example: **<eyém sqwà:l>**, //ʔɛy=ə́m s=qʷɛ̀·l//, /'*strong words*'/, ASM ['used by a chief or high councillor when he talked to his people, good words that were respected'], attested by Elders Group (5/3/78), **<sqwà:ls ta' syuwá:lelh>**, //s=qʷɛ̀·l-s t-ɛʔ s=yuwɛ́·l-əɬ//, /'*words of your ancestors*'/, literally /'word -of/his/her/their your ancestor -past tense/deceased'/, attested by EB, **<qetl'osésuw qwélqwel, yéthestes te mestíyexw te sqwà:ls te (sí:les, sx̱wewá:ys).>**, //qə=ƛ'a-s-ə́s-uw qʷɛ[=Aə́=]l=C_1əC_2 yə́θəs=T-əs tə məstíyəxʷ tə s=qʷɛ̀·l-s tə (sí·lə-s, s=x̣ʷəwɛ́·y-s)//, /'*And so, talking, he told the people the words of (his grandfather, his parent(s)).*'/, attested by AC, usage: recent story, **<l st'í kw'els qwà:l kw'e axwí:l òl sqwà:l.>**, //l s=ƛ'í **k'**ʷə-l-s qʷɛ̀·l **k'**ʷə ʔɛxʷí·l ʔàl s=qʷɛ̀·l//, /'*I would like to say just a few words.*'/, usage: public speaking, attested by Deming, **<stl'ítset kws me á:yelexwstexwtset te sqwá:ltset.>**, //s=ƛ'í-c-ət kʷ-s mə ʔɛ́·yələxʷ=sT-əxʷ-c-ət tə s=qʷɛ̀·l-c-ət//, /'*We want to keep our language alive. (keep s-th alive)*'/, literally /'it's our want that come to/become we keep it alive the our words'/, attested by EB, ASM ['subject'], **<iyáqtes te sqwà:ls.>**, //ʔiyɛ́q=T-əs tə s=qʷɛ̀·l-s//, /'*He changed the subject.*'/, literally /'change s-th -purposely it -he the word/subject -his'/, attested by Elders Group (3/3/76).

<**qwélqwel**>, chrs //qʷɛ[=Aə́=]l=C_1əC_2//, durs?, LANG /'*to tell something (news), talking something over (one at a time)*'/, (<**é-ablaut**> *durative*? or conditioned automatically before =R2), (<**=R2**> *characteristic*), phonology: reduplication, ablaut, syntactic analysis: intransitive verb, attested by AD, example: **<qwélqwel á:lhtel.>**, //qʷɛ[=Aə́=]l=C_1əC_2 ʔɛ́·ɬ=təl//, /'*They are talking something over (one at a time).*'/, attested by AD (12/17/79).

<**sqwélqwel**>, dnom //s=qʷɛ[=Aə́=]l=C_1əC_2//, LANG /'*news, a true story, what was told, message*'/, (<**s=**> *nominalizer*), stem //qwélqwel *talk over, tell news*//, phonology: reduplication, ablaut, syntactic analysis: nominal, attested by AC, Elders Group, EB, AD, example: **<éy sqwélqwel>**, //ʔɛ́y s=qʷɛ[=Aə́=]l=C_1əC_2//, /'*good news*'/, attested by Elders Group, **<qél sqwélqwel>**, //qə́l s=qʷɛ[=Aə́=]l=C_1əC_2//, /'*bad news*'/, attested by Elders Group, **<tsel kwelát te sqwélqwel.>**, //c-əl kʷəlɛ́T tə s=qʷɛ[=Aə́=]l=C_1əC_2//, /'*I've got news.*'/, attested by AD, **<welh xwe'í te sqwélqwel.>**, //wəɬ xʷə=ʔí tə s=qʷɛ[=Aə́=]l=C_1əC_2//, /'*The news is already here. (get here, arrive)*'/, attested by Elders Group, **<xwe'í te sqwélqwel.>**, //xʷə=ʔí tə s=qʷɛ[=Aə́=]l=C_1əC_2//, /'*The news has come.*'/, attested by EB, **<tl'osésu tl'ó sqwélqwels yutl'ólem swóweles kwses kw'iylómet qa skw'áy kw'es kw'iys welolets'á:s e kw'e thekw'ét.>**, //ƛ'a-s-ə́-s=u ƛ'á s=qʷɛ[=Aə́=]l=C_1əC_2 yə=u=ƛ'á[=lə=]m s=wi[=Aá=]wələs kʷ-s-əs **k'**ʷiy=l-ámət qɛ s=**k'**ʷɛ́y **k'**ʷə-s **k'**ʷíy-s wə-C_1á=lə**c'**ə-ɛ́s ʔə **k'**ʷə **θ**ə**k'**ʷ=ə[-´-]T//, /'*So then that's what the young men told, that they managed to get themselves/climb up but they couldn't get up (further) if it wasJust one person that pulled them.*'/, literally /'so then that's what they told/reported they young men that they manage to get themselves up but it's impossible/can't be that get up -they if it is one person just who pull s-th/s-o'/, usage: narrative of recent events after story of the Flood, attested by AC (12/7/71), **<esu tl'o sqwélqwels yutlólem.>**, //ʔə-s-u ƛ'a s=qʷɛ[=Aə́=]l=C_1əC_2

y=u=ƛ'a=lə=m//, /*'So that's what they told.'*/, usage: narrative of recent events after story of the Flood, attested by AC.

<**sqwelqweláwtxw**>, ds //s=q^{w}ɛ[=Aə́=]l=C_1əC_2=ɛ́wtxw//, LANG /*'language room, language house, (news room)'*/, literally /'news room, what is told room'/, lx <**=áwtxw**> *room, building, house*, syntactic analysis: nominal, comment: word made up on request, attested by Elders Group (1/15/75).

<**lexwsqwélqwel**>, ds //ləx^w=s=q^{w}ɛ[=Aə́=]l=C_1əC_2//, [lʊx^{w}sq^{w}ə́lq^{w}əl], LANG [*'tattletale'*], SOC, EFAM, literally /'one who always tells news'/, (<**lexw=s=**> *one who always*), phonology: ablaut, reduplication, syntactic analysis: nominal, attested by Elders Group, CT and HT.

<**qwelqweló:ythel**>, df //C_1əC_2=q^{w}ɛl=**á·yθəl**//, [q^{w}əlq^{w}əl**á·yθ**ɪl], LANG [*'(be) talkative'*], EFAM, literally probably /'talk lots in the lips/jaw'/, (<**R3=**> *plural*), lx <**=ó:ythel**> *in the lips*, phonology: reduplication, syntactic analysis: adjective/adjectival verb, attested by Elders Group.

<**qwélqwel**>, chrs //q^{w}ɛ[=Aə́=]l=C_1əC_2//, rsls or cts, EFAM /*'be rowdy, be a nuisance, be mischievious'*/, SOC, (<**é-ablaut**> *resultative*? or *continuative*), (<**=R2**> *characteristic*), phonology: ablaut, reduplication, syntactic analysis: adjective/adjectival verb, attested by EP and EB (BHTTC), Elders Group, Deming.

<**qwelqwálem ~ qwelqwá:lem**>, mdls //C_1əC_2=q^{w}ɛ̀·l=əm//, plv, LANG /*'grumble, grumbling, (muttering),* (prob. also) *mumbling'*/, SOC, EFAM, literally probably /'talk(ing) lots to oneself'/, (<**R3=**> *plural*), (<**=em**> *middle voice*), phonology: reduplication, length-loss optional, updrifting, syntactic analysis: intransitive verb, attested by EB, Elders Group (3/15/72, 5/14/80); found in <**qwelqwá:lemchexw.**>, //C_1əC_2=q^{w}ɛ̀·l=əm-c-əx^w//, /*'You are grumbling.'*/, attested by Elders Group (3/15/72), example: <**lachxw qwelqwá:lem.**>, //lɛ-c-x^w C_1əC_2=q^{w}ɛ̀·l=əm//, /*'You're going to be grumbling.'*/, attested by Elders Group (3/15/72), <**echxw qwelqwá:lem?**>, //ʔə-c-x^w C_1əC_2=q^{w}ɛ̀·l=əm//, /*'Are you grumbling?'*/, syntactic comment: unusual interrogative suffix as root, attested by Elders Group (3/15/72).

<**qwṓlqwel**>, plv //q^{w}ɛ[=Aó·=]l=C_1əC_2 or C_1əC_2[=Aó·=]=q^{w}ɛl//, [q^{w}ó·lq^{w}ʊl], LANG /*'talking together, all talking together, (telling news [EB], warning (birds and other creatures do this) [Elders Group])'*/, possibly <**ṓ:-ablaut**> *distributive or plural or continuative*?, probably <**R3=**> *plural*, phonology: rare ṓ:-ablaut, reduplication, possible vowel-reduction, syntactic analysis: intransitive verb, attested by AD, also /*'telling news'*/, attested by EB (4/29/76), also /*'reveal, announce'*/, attested by EB (1/30/76), also <**qwṓ:lqwel ~ qwṓlqwel**>, //C_1əC_2[=Aó(·)=]=q^{w}ɛl//, also /*'warning (of birds, other creatures)'*/, attested by Elders Group (12/15/76), also <**qwṓ:lqwel**>, //C_1əC_2[=Aó·=]=q^{w}ɛl//, SPRD /*'speaking to a lot of people/at a gathering'*//, attested by RG & EH (4/10/99 Ling332), also <**qwú:lqwel**>, //C_1əC_2[=Aú·=]=q^{w}ɛl//, [q^{w}ú·lq^{w}ʊl], attested by AC, example: <**qwṓ:lqwel á:lhtel.**>, //C_1əC_2[=Aó·=]=q^{w}ɛl ʔɛ́·ɬ=təl//, /*'They are all talking together.'*/, attested by AD, <**éwechexw qwú:lqwelexw.**>, //ʔə́wə-c-əx^w C_1əC_2[=Aú·=]=q^{w}ɛl-əx^w//, /*'Don't you ever tell.'*/, attested by AC, <**qwṓlqwel te skéweqs.**>, //C_1əC_2[=Aó=]=q^{w}ɛl tə s=q[=K=]ə́w=əqs//, /*'The raven is warning (a different cry from talking).'*/, attested by Elders Group (12/15/76).

<**qwṓ:lqweltel**>, rcps //C_1əC_2[=Aó·=]=q^{w}ɛl=T-əl//, pcs, plv, LANG /*'talking together, all talking at once (of a lot of people)'*/, (<**=t**> *purposeful control transitivizer*), (<**-el**> *reciprocal*), phonology: ó:-ablaut, reduplication, syntactic analysis: intransitive verb, attested by Elders Group (2/19/75), also <**qwélqweltel**>, //C_1əC_2[=Aə́=]=q^{w}ɛl=T-əl or q^{w}ɛ[=Aə́=]l=C_1əC_2=T-əl//, attested by EB (4/7/76), also <**qwú:lqweltel**>, //C_1əC_2[=Aú·=]=q^{w}ɛl=T-əl//, attested by AD (12/17/79), example: <**qwú:lqweltel á:lhtel.**>, //C_1əC_2[=Aú·=]=q^{w}ɛl=T-əl ʔɛ́·ɬ=təl//, /*'They are all talking (at once, a lot of people).'*/, attested by AD.

<**qwṓ:lqwelstem**>, caus //C_1əC_2[=Aó·=]=q^{w}ɛl=sT-əm//, pass, SPRD //*'being spoken to (of babies in*

spirit dancing [new dancers])'//, <=sT> *causative control transitivizer*, <-em> *passive*, attested by RG & EH (4/10/99 Ling332)

<qwíqweláts ~ qwíqwelà(:)c>, dmv //C_1í=qʷɛ̀·l=ə[=M2=]c//, LANG /*'gossip about someone, talk about someone behind his back'*/, EFAM, literally probably /'small talk on the back'/, (<**R4=**> *diminutive*), lx <**=ets ~ =íts**> *on the back*, phonology: reduplication, metathesis, optional length-loss, updrifting, syntactic analysis: intransitive verb, attested by Elders Group, EB, also /*'call someone down'*/, attested by EB, also /*'talking about someone, gossiping about someone'*/, attested by CT and HT, also /*'two of them gossiping'*/, attested by AC, example: <**lóy kws shxw'íys kws qwíqweláts.**>, //láy kʷ-s sxʷ=ʔɛ́y-s kʷ-s C_1í=qʷɛ̀·l=ə[=M2=]c//, /*'All he's good for is calling someone down.'*/, literally /'is only that what he's good for that calling down/gossiping'/, attested by EB.

<qwéqweláts>, dmpv //C_1í[=Aə́=]=qʷɛ̀·l=ə[=M2=]c//, [qʷə́qʷʊlǽc], LANG [*'to gossip'*], EFAM, (<**é-ablaut of i in reduplication**> *plural*), phonology: ablaut, metathesis, length-loss, updrifting, syntactic analysis: intransitive verb, attested by AC.

<qwélqwelàtstem>, pcs //C_1əC_2[=Aə́=]=qʷɛ̀·l=ə[=M2=]c=T=əm or C_1əC_2[=Aə́=]=qʷɛ̀·l=ə[=M2=]c=T-əm//, SOC [*'to squeal on someone'*], LANG, EFAM, (<**R3=**> *diminutive*), (<**é-ablaut**> *derivational*, metathesis *derivational* or *non-continuative*), (<**=t**> *purposeful control transitivizer*), possibly <**=em**> *middle voice* or possibly <**-em**> *passive*, phonology: ablaut, metathesis, syntactic analysis: intransitive verb (or transitive verb?-passive), attested by EB (1/30/76).

<qwelqwélés>, pncs //qʷɛl=C_1əC_2[=Aə́=]=ləs//, EFAM [*'telling on s-o'*], LANG, SOC, (<**é-ablaut**> *continuative*), (<**=R2**> *characteristic* or *derivational*, <**=(e)les**> *psychological non-control transitivizer*), phonology: reduplication, ablaut, updrifting on final vowel, syntactic analysis: transitive verb, attested by EB, CT and HT, comment: attested only in inflected form below; found in <**qwelqwéléses.**>, //qʷɛl=C_1əC_2[=Aə́=]=ləs-əs//, /*'He's telling on someone.'*/, attested by EB (6/30/76), example: <**le qwelqweléses tewátes.**>, //lə qʷɛl=C_1əC_2[=Aə́=]=ləs-əs tə=wɛ́t=əs//, /*'He's telling on somebody.'*/, attested by CT and HT (6/21/76); found in <**qwelqwéléső:xes**>, //qʷɛl=C_1əC_2[=Aə́=]=ləs-á·xʸ-əs.//, /*'He's telling on me.'*/, comment: prompted, attested by EB.

<qwoqwelíwel>, cts //qʷɛ[-AaC_1ə-]l=íwəl//, EFAM /*'thinking of something, (thinking)'*/, literally /'talking in the inside'/, (<**o-ablaut plus =R1=**> *continuative*), lx <**=íwel ~ =ewel**> *in the inside*, phonology: ablaut, reduplication, syntactic analysis: intransitive verb, attested by JL (6/19/79).

<sqwá:lewel ~ sqwálewel ~ sqwà(:)lewel>, dnom //s=qʷɛ̀·l=əwəl//, EFAM /*'thoughts, feelings'*/, literally /'words/talk in the inside,words/talk inside the head'/, (<**s=**> *nominalizer*), lx <**=ewel ~ =íwel**> *in the inside*, phonology: updrifting, syntactic analysis: nominal, syntactic comment: never attested without the nominalizer s= and always used in constructions as a nominal, i.e. it is my thought that = I think, attested by AC, EB, Elders Group (3/1/72, 2/16/77, 5/19/76, etc.), AD, DF, Deming, other sources: ES /skʷɛ́ləwəl/ *think (consider)*, example: <**xwe'í:t ta sqwàlewel?**>, //xʷəʔí·t t-ɛ s=qʷɛ̀·l=əwəl//, /*'What are you thinking about?'*/, literally /'what is it doing/saying/what's happening to/with it the (present and visible /unmarked) -your thoughts'/, (semological comment: contrast the unmarked/present visible thoughts here with the remote thoughts in the next example), attested by AC, <**xwe'í:t kw'a sqwàlewel?**>, //xʷəʔí·t **k'ʷ**-ɛ s=qʷɛ̀·l=əwəl//, /*'What are you thinking?'*/, literally /'what is it doing/saying/what's happening to/with it the (remote) -your thoughts'/, (semological comment: contrast the remote thoughts here with the unmarked/present visible thoughts in the previous sentence), attested by AC, <**li a sqwá:lewel kws xwe'í:s wáy:eles?**>, //li ʔɛ s=qʷɛ̀·l=əwəl kʷ-s xʷəʔí·-s wɛ́y·əl=əs//, /*'Do you think they will come tomorrow?'*/, attested by AC, <**li a sqwà:lewel kw'es mes xwathtálem wáy:eles?**>,

//li ʔɛ s=qʷɛ̀·ləwəl **k'ʷə**-s mə-s xʷɛ=θɛ́t=M1=əl=əm wɛ́y·əl=əs//, /*'Do you think it will be cloudy tomorrow?'*/, attested by AC, <**li a sqwá:lewel kw'es lhéméxws wày:èlès?**>, //li ʔɛ s=qʷɛ̀·l=əwəl **k'ʷə**-s ɬə́m=əxʷ-s wɛ́y·əl=əs//, /*'Do you think it will rain tomorrow?'*/, Elder's comment: "(said when she first had a hard time remembering *think*): Thinking would be the mind working, wouldn't it?", attested by AC, <**li a sqwá:lewel kw'es qéx̱ te sqwétxem wày:èlès?**>, //li ʔɛ s=qʷɛ̀·l=əwəl **k'ʷə**-s qə́x̣ tə s=qʷət=xʸ=əm wɛ́y·əl=əs//, /*'Do you think that there will be a lot of fog tomorrow?'*/, literally /'is it your thought that it is lots the fog tomorrow'/, attested by AC, <**l sqwálewel kw'els qw'él:émt te sth'ó:qwi tlówàyèl.**>, //l s=qʷɛ̀·l=əwəl **k'ʷə**-l-s **q'ʷə́l**·=əm=T tə s=**θ'á**·qʷi təlá=wɛ̀yə̀l//, /*'I think I'll barbecue the salmon today.'*/, attested by AC, <**welís thét ta sqwálewel**>, //wə-lí-s **θə́t** t-ɛ s=qʷɛ̀·l=əwəl//, /*'if you think that, if your mind (thoughts) says so'*/, attested by EB, <**lóy sqwálewels tl' Máli kw'e qó:.**>, //láy s=qʷɛ̀·l=əwəl-sƛ' mɛ́li **k'ʷə** qá·//, /*'Mary is only thinking of water.'*/, literally /'is only her thoughts by Mary some water'/, attested by EB, <**éy kw'el sqwá:lewel.**>, //ʔɛ́y **k'ʷə**-l s=qʷɛ̀·l=əwəl//, /*'I have good feelings., I'm glad.'*/, attested by Elders Group, <**wiyóth kwsu éys te sqwálewels te lólets'e.**>, //wə-yáθ kʷ-s-u ʔɛ́y-s tə s=qʷɛ̀·l=əwəl-s tə C_1á=lə**c'**ə//, /*'It's a person whose thoughts are always good., It's an optimist.'*/, literally /'it's always so that it's good the thoughts of the one person'/, attested by Elders Group (2/16/77), <**wiyóth kwsu qéls te sqwálewels te lólets'e.**>, //wə-yáθ kʷ-s-u qə́l-s tə s=qʷɛ̀·l=əwəl-s tə C_1á=lə**c'**ə//, /*'It's a person whose thoughts are always bad., It's a pessimist.'*/, attested by Elders Group (2/16/77), <**iyólem kw'els sqwálewel.**>, //ʔəy=ál=əm **k'ʷə**-l-s s=qʷɛ̀·l=əwəl//, /*'My thoughts are alright., I agree., My mind is alright., My mind is in the right place.'*/, attested by Elders Group (5/19/76), DF (Elders Group 4/26/78), <**st'átsa kw'els sqwálewel.**>, //s=təʔɛ́-cɛ **k'ʷə**-l-s s=qʷɛ̀·l=əwəl//, /*'My thoughts are similar., I agree.'*/, attested by Elders Group (5/19/76), <**ő éyeles sqwálewel.**>, //ʔo ʔɛ́y=ələs s=qʷɛ̀·l=əwəl//, /*'I agree with you.'*/, attested by Elders Group, <**x̱élh te sqwálewel**>, //x̣ə́ɬ tə s=qʷɛ̀·l=əwəl//, /*'feelings are hurt, be sorry'*/, attested by Deming, <**x̱élh tel sqwálewel.**>, //x̣ə́ɬ tə-l s=qʷɛ̀·l=əwəl//, /*'My feelings are hurt., I'm sorry.'*/, attested by Elders Group (3/1/72), others, also <**x̱élh kw'el sqwá:lewel.**>, //x̣ə́ɬ **k'ʷə**-l s=qʷɛ̀·l=əwəl//, attested by Elders Group (2/16/76), <**x̱élh kwe sqwálewels.**>, //x̣ə́ɬ kʷə s=qʷɛ̀·l=əwəl-s//, /*'He is sad., His feelings are hurt.'*/, attested by EB (12/19/75), <**wálh me x̱élh kw'a' sqwálewel lhíxw me p'élh?**>, //ʔəw-ə-əɬ mə x̣ə́ɬ **k'ʷ**-ɛʔ s=qʷɛ̀·l=əwəl ɬí-xʷ mə **p'**ə́ɬ//, /*'Do you ever feel sorry when you sober up?'*/, literally /'is not -yes/no question -past tense come to be hurt the (remote) -your feelings when -you become sober/aware (or) didn't your thoughts come to be hurt when you became aware/sober'/, attested by Elders Group (6/28/78), <**éy kw'ómwkw'emcha telí s'ólh sqwálewel xwlam kw'e ít totí:lt tlówàyèl.**>, //ʔɛ́y **k'ʷ**ám=C_1əC_2-cɛ təlí sʔáɬ s=qʷɛ̀·l=əwəl xʷ=lɛ́=m **k'ʷə** ʔí-t ta[-C_1ə-]l=í·l=T təlá=wɛ̀yə̀l//, /*'Let our thoughts be strong toward what we are studying today.'*/, usage: public speaking, prayer, attested by AD, <**híkw te sqwálewels.**>, //híkʷ tə s=qʷɛ̀·l=əwəl-s//, /*'He's got a lot of pride.'*/, literally /'his thoughts/feeling are big'/, attested by EB (7/8/76), <**léq' te sqwálewel**>, //lə́**q'** tə s=qʷɛ̀·l=əwəl//, /*'think alike'*/, literally /'the thoughts/feelings are level/even'/, attested by Elders Group (9/21/77), <**láts'ewtxw te sqwáléwéls.**>, //lɛ́**c'**=əwtxʷ tə s=qʷɛ̀·l=əwəl-s//, /*'His mind is somewhere else.'*/, literally /'is another building/room the his thoughts/feelings'/, attested by Deming (5/3/79).

<**qwélmet**>, iecs //qʷɛ[=Aə́=]l=məT//, LANG /*'scold s-o, bawl s-o out'*/, EFAM, SOC, (<**é-ablaut**> *non-continuative* or *derivational*), (<**=met**> *indirect effect control transitivizer*), phonology: ablaut, syntactic analysis: transitive verb, attested by Elders Group.

<**qwóqwelmet**>, cts //qʷɛ[-AáC_1ə-]l=məT//, LANG [*'scolding s-o'*], EFAM, SOC, Elder's comment: "does not mean *to argue*", (<**ó-ablaut plus -R1-**> *continuative*), phonology: ablaut, reduplication, syntactic analysis: transitive verb, attested by Elders Group, EB (3/8/76).

<**qwelqwélmét**>, df //C_1əC_2=qʷɛ[=Aə́=]l=məT//, LANG /*'to scold a child, (scold s-o (a child))'*/,

EFAM, SOC, literally possibly /'talk to s-o many times'/, (<**R3=**> *plural*), (semological comment: perhaps applied to a child because it is pluralized and an adult would be less likely to be *talked to/scolded many times*), phonology: reduplication, ablaut, updrifting, syntactic analysis: transitive verb, attested by EB, also <**qwélqwelmet**>, //qʷɛ[=Aə́=]l=C₁əC₂=məT//, (<**=R2**> *characteristic*, <**=met**> *indirect effect control transitivizer*), also /'*scold s-o*'/, attested by IHTTC (9/14/77), example: <**qwelqwélmétes te stl'ítl'qelh.**>, //C₁əC₂=qʷɛ[=Aə́=]l=məT-əs tə s=C₁í=ƛ'əq=əɬ//, /'*He scolds a child., She scholds a child.*'/, attested by EB, <**qwelqwélmétes tewátes.**>, //C₁əC₂=qʷɛ[=Aə́=]l=məT-əs tə=wɛ́t=əs//, /'*He scolds somebody.*'/, attested by EB.

<**qweloythí:lem**>, mdls //qʷɛl=ayθəl=í·l=əm//, incs, TIME /'*(month beginning in) March, ((birds) making music)*'/, literally /'speak =on the lips/jaw =go/come/get/become =one's own'/, Elder's comment: "it means (birds) making music", lx <**=óythel ~ =ó:ythel**> *on the lips*, (<**=í:l**> *come, go, get, become*, <**=em**> *middle voice*), phonology: syllable-loss of el before =í:l, vowel-reduction due to stress-shift to suffix, syntactic analysis: nominal, intransitive verb, attested by Elders Group (3/19/75).

<**qweló:ythetel ~ qwelóyethetel**>, ds //qʷɛl=á·yθə(l)=təl//, dnom, MUS /'*musical instrument, grammophone, phonograph, record player*'/, literally /'device to talk on the lips'/, lx <**-ó:ythel**> *on the lips*, lx <**=tel**> *device to, something to*, phonology: consonant-loss of l before =tel, syntactic analysis: nominal, attested by Elders Group, AC, EB.

<**qwő̃lqwel qweló:ythetel**>, cpds //qʷɛ[=Aó=]l=C₁əC₂ qʷɛl=á·yθə(l)=təl//, LANG ['*(maybe usable for) radio*'], ACL, literally /'news musical instrument/phonograph'/, phonology: ó-ablaut, reduplication, vowel-reduction, consonant-loss of l before =tel, syntactic analysis: simple nominal phrase, attested by Elders Group (6/1/77).

<**ót'etem qweló:ythetel**>, cpds //ʔát'=əT=əm qʷɛl=á·yθə(l)=təl//, MUS ['*accordion*'], ACL, literally /'squeezed on purpose musical instrument'/, (<**=et**> *purposeful control transitivizer*, <**=em**> *passive* or <**=tem**> *participle*), phonology: vowel=reduction, consonant-loss, syntactic analysis: simple nominal phrase, attested by Elders Group.

<**qwiqwelóythetel**>, df //C₁í=qʷɛl=áyθə(l)=təl//, cts, MUS ['*playing a musical instrument*'], (irregular), (<**R4=**> *continuative*), phonology: reduplication, vowel-reduction, consonant-loss, syntactic analysis: intransitive verb, attested by AC (8/24/70).

<**sqwéltel**>, dnom //s=qʷɛ[=Aə́=]l=təl//, LANG ['*language*'], literally /'something/device to speak/talk'/, (<**s=**> *nominalizer*), (<**é-ablaut**> *non-continuative* or *derivational*), lx <**=tel**> *something to, device to*, phonology: é-ablaut of root á, syntactic analysis: nominal, attested by Elders Group, AC, CT and HT, Salish cognate: Sechelt /qʷál-tən/ *language* Beaumont 1985:282, comment: apparently not reciprocal =tel /=T=əl/ since that is /-təl'/ Musqueam but Musqueam and Sechelt example have /=tən/ *instrument, device* and use the /=tən/ form in cognate for their word for *language*, example: <**íwesthòx te sqwéltel.**>, //ʔíwəs=T-áxʸ t-ɛ s=qʷɛ[=Aə́=]l=təl//, /'*Teach me your language.*'/, syntactic comment: no subject pronoun with 2s possessive pronoun (your) means imperative second-person sg. is understood, attested by AC, <**le xwel totí:ltes té sqwéltels.**>, //lə xʷəl ta[-C₁ə-]l=í·l=T-əs tə s=qʷɛ[=Aə́=]l=təl-s//, /'*He's still learning (his/her/their) language.*'/, attested by CT and HT.

<**qwó:ltel**>, rcps //qʷɛ̀[=Aá=]·l=T=əl//, LANG /'*argue, quarrel*'/, EFAM, SOC, literally /'talk purposefully to each other'/, (<**ó-ablaut**> automatic replacement on root <**a**> before <**=tel**> *reciprocal*), (<**=t**> *purposeful control transitivizer*, <**=el**> *reciprocal* (here derivational because the word means more than just *talk to each other*)), phonology: ablaut automatically conditioned, syntactic analysis: intransitive verb, attested by EB, Elders Group.

<**qwelqwó:ltel**>, plv //C₁əC₂=qʷɛ[=Aá=]·l=təl//, LANG /'*arguing, (everybody is) quarrelling*'/,

EFAM, SOC, (<**R3=**> *plural action and agents*), phonology: reduplication, ablaut, syntactic analysis: intransitive verb, attested by EB, Elders Group (4/26/78).

<**qwá:l**>, free root //qʷɛ́·l//, [qʷæ$_{51}$l], EZ /'*mosquito,* (also included as a type of "mosquito" is the *cranefly)*'/, ['family *Culicidae*, also included as a type of "mosquito" is family *Tipulidae*'], phonology: forms a minimal pair regarding pitch-stress or tone with qwà:l *talk*, proving both ´ and ` are phonemic, what ES and I write as a circumflex over long vowels is a high-falling tone 5 ➛ 1, allotone of /´/ on all vowels before length, syntactic analysis: noun, nominal, attested by Elders Group, AC, EB, BJ (5/10/64, 12/5/64), others, other sources: ES /qʷɛ̂·l/ *mosquito*, JH /kʷél/ *mosquito*, example: <**qéx̲ ye qwá:l.**>, //qə́x̣ yə qʷɛ́·l//, /'*(There's) lots of mosquitoes.*'/, literally /'is lots the (human/animate plural) mosquito'/, attested by EB, also <**qéx̲ te qwá:l.**>, //qə́x̣ tə qʷɛ́·l//, attested by AC.

<**spelwálh qwá:l**>, cpds //s=pəl=w=ɛ́ɬ qʷɛ́·l//, EZ /'*cranefly, leatherjacket (immature cranefly)*'/, ['family *Tipulidae*'], literally /'last year mosquito'/, (<**s=**> nominalizer), bound root //pel *time*//, lx <**=w**> meaning uncertain, (<**=álh**> *past tense*), syntactic analysis: simple nominal phrase, attested by Elders Group (9/8/76), compare <**tl'áleqtxel qwá:l**> *cranefly*.

<**tl'áleqtxel qwá:l**>, cpds //ƛ'ɛ́[=lə=]qt=xʸəl qʷɛ́·l//, EZ /'*cranefly, leatherjacket (immature cranefly)*'/, ['family *Tipulidae*'], literally /'long on the legs mosquito'/, (<**=le=**> *plural*), lx <**=xel**> *on the leg*, phonology: infixed plural, syntactic analysis: simple nominal phrase, attested by Elders Group (9/8/76), compare <**spelwálh qwá:l**> *cranefly*.

<**Qwá:l**>, ds //qʷɛ́·l//, N /'*name of a fierce old warrior from Sumas, an ancestor of the Commodore family*'/, literally /'mosquito'/, ASM ['stories about his exploits are on the Wells tapes interviews of BJ'], (semological comment: probably a nickname because he drew blood), syntactic analysis: noun, attested by BJ (12/5/64).

<**temqwá:l**>, ds //təm=qʷɛ́·l//, TIME ['*month or moon beginning in July*'], (semological comment: months/moons were counted as properly beginning with the first sliver after a black (new) moon), (<**tem=**> *time for, season of*), syntactic analysis: nominal, attested by Elders Group (3/12/75).

<**Qwá:l**>, N /'*name of a fierce old warrior from Sumas, an ancestor of the Commodore family*'/, *see* qwá:l.

<**qwà:ls**>, LANG /'*make a speech, talk*'/, *see* qwà:l.

<**qwálxtem**>, WETH ['*got stormy with lots of fine snow in the air*'], *see* qwélxel.

<**qwà:m ~ qwám**>, free root //qʷɛ̀·m ~ qʷɛ́m//, EB /'*moss (any kind, on rocks or trees)*'/, ['phylum *Bryophyta*'], ASM ['moss was put in the bottom of berry baskets to prevent staining'], syntactic analysis: noun, nominal, possibly related to <**qwém**> *soft*, dialects: *Cheh.*, attested by EL and EB, Elders Group (7/28/76), contrast <**mex̲t'éles**> *lichen,* <**sqwelíp**> *black tree lichen*, and <**q'íts'iy**> *multicolored moss that grew around Katzie, B.C.*, compare <**qwò:m**>, //qʷà·m//, dialects: *Chill.*, attested by Deming, also <**qwó:m**>, //qʷ**á**·m//, dialects: *Chill.*, attested by AC, also <**qwóm**>, //qʷám//, dialects: *Chill. and Tait*, attested by Elders Group, other sources: ES /qʷà·m/ and JH /qʷ**á**·m/ *moss*, Salish cognate: Lushootseed /qʷəjáb/ *moss* H76:414, Nooksack /qʷám/ *moss*, Sechelt /qʷáym/ *moss, lichen* T77:12, Mainland Comox /qʷáǰim/ *moss* B75prelim:23, Thompson /qʷəzém/ *moss* B74c:16.

<**qwomáléqep**>, ds //qʷam=ɛ́lə́qəp//, SM ['*have a mossy smell*'], EB, lx <**=áléqep**> *smell, fragrance*, phonology: full-vowel in root though stress shifts to suffix, syntactic analysis: intransitive verb, attested by Elders Group (5/25/77).

<**Qwómqwemels**>, chrs //qʷám=C$_1$əC$_2$=als//, PLN ['*place of moss-covered stones at upper end of Hope Slough not far from Harry Edwards' home (as of 1964)*'], literally /'place where stones are covered with moss'/, (<**=R2**> *characteristic*), lx <**=áls**> *stones, fruit, round objects*, phonology:

reduplication, vowel-reduction, syntactic analysis: nominal, attested by Elders Group (8/31/77), HE (10/8/64 Wells tapes), other sources: Wells 1965 (lst ed.):15, source: place names reference file #264.

<**qwemchó:ls**>, ds //qʷam=c=**á**·ls//, EB ['*bog cranberry*'], ['*Vaccinium oxycoccus, Vaccinium oxycoccus quadripetalus*'], literally /'moss fruit'/, ASM ['gathered from mid-September at bogs from Scowlitz and Harrison Bay west to the Katzie area and Deas Island, often grew beneath the marsh blueberries, mólsem and lhewqí:m, grew in sphagnum bogs, they were ready and biggest just before Christmas but were ready any time in the late fall, often picked after the first frost, ripe in mid-Sept. around Scowlitz river bank; probably endangered in the Fraser Valley so best to avoid frivolous picking'], lx <**=ch**> meaning unknown, <**=ó:ls**> *fruit*, phonology: root vowel-reduction, syntactic analysis: nominal, attested by AC, BJ (5/10/64, 12/5/64), Elders Group (9/3/75), Clara Campbell and Mary Lou Sepass (5/7/79), <**kwúkwewels sqe'óleqw** (or better: **qwemchó:ls sqe'óleqw**)>, EB, FOOD *cranberry juice* (lit. highbush cranberry + fruit juice (or better:) bog cranberry + fruit juice), (attested by RG,EH 6/16/98 to SN, edited by BG with RG,EH 6/26/00), other sources: ES /qʷɛmc**á**·ls/ *cranberry*.

<**qwáqel**>, df //qʷɛ́=qəl or qʷɛ́q=əl//, EB /'*sprouted up, sprouting up, (to sprout from a root)*'/, possibly root <**qwá**> *get a hole* or possibly root <**qwáq**> meaning uncertain, probably <**=qel**> *in the head* or probably <**=el**> *come, go, get, become*, syntactic analysis: intransitive verb, attested by AC, other sources: H-T <kwákEl> (macron over the a) *to sprout from a root*, example: <**lulh me qwáqel ta spí:ls.**>, //lə=uɬ mə qʷɛ́(=)q(=)əl t-ɛ s=pí·l-s.//, /'*Your garden is sprouting up., Your plantings (all that grows underground) is sprouted up.*'/, attested by AC, <**lulh me qwáqel te sqáweth.**>, //lə-uɬ mə qʷɛ́(=)q(=)əl tə s=qɛ́w(=)əθ//, /'*The potatoes are sprouted up.*'/, attested by AC.

<**qwáseliyel**>, FSH ['*drifting a net in different places*'], *see* qwés.

<**qwát**>, DESC /'*make a hole in s-th, drill a hole in s-th*'/, *see* qwá.

<**qwáts'et**>, pcs //qʷɛ́**c**'=əT//, ABFC /'*to belch, to burp*'/, (<**=et**> *purposeful control transitivizer*), syntactic analysis: transitive verb, attested by Elders Group, AC, MH (prompted)(Deming 1/4/79).

<**qwóqwets'et**>, cts //qʷɛ[-AáC$_1$ə-]**c**'=əT//, ABFC ['*belching*'], (<**ó-ablaut plus -R1-**> *continuative*), phonology: ablaut, reduplication, syntactic analysis: transitive verb, attested by Elders Group.

<**qwá:y**>, bound root //qʷɛ́·y *yellow with green*//, comment: using derived forms of the root as a modifier of other color terms the following combinations were given by AK: tsqwáy sts'óla, and sqwóqiyel sts'ólha.

<**tsqwá:y**>, stvi //c=qʷɛ́·y//, LT /'*be yellow, be green*'/, ASM ['the following color terms are used by AK before tsqwáy to specify shades of the color: tsxwíkw', tsxwíxwekw', sxwíxwekw', xwíxwekw'el, tsq'íx̱, q'íq'ex̱el, tsqw'íx̱w, tsqw'íqw'ex̱wel, qw'íqw'ex̱wel, tl'ítl'esel, stl'ítl'es, stl'ítl'esel, semth'íl, p'(e)q'íl, sp'(e)q'íl'], ASM ['individual elders and groups have translated *green* as follows: tsqwá:y AC, Elders Group (3/15/72 tape), SJ (Deming 5/3/79); sqwóqwiyel Lizzie Herrling via AC (12/1/71); same as *blue* BJ (12/5/64); and have translated *yellow* as follows: tsqwá:y AC, MP (via Oliver Wells on tape of BJ 12/5/64), Elders Group (5/16/79), AD (6/19/79); eyó:les (lit. good on the eyes, good color)(used with syáth'qels *paint* DM (12/4/64);'], squares circled on the color chart of Berlin and Kay (1969) (rows top to bottom = B-I, columns left to right = 1-40, side column of white to black = 0 (zero); individual speakers circled the following squares for tsqwá:y, tsqwáy TM (2/14/79): B10-O15 (inclusive), tsqwá:y Lawrence James (2/7/79): C0 (error), tsqwáy EP (2/7/79) (Katzie dial.): B11, tsqwáy NP (2/7/79): F16, F17, F18, B11, B12,, tsqwà:y TG and RP (1/24/79): B10, B11, B12, B13, B14, B15 (lower left diagonal), D10, D11, D12, D13, D14, D15, D16, D17 (lower left diagonal), E11 (upper right diagonal), E12, E13, E14, E15, E16, E17, E18, E19 (lower

left diagonal), F12 (upper right diagonal), F13, F14, F15, F16, F17, F18, F19, F13 (upper right corner), G14, G15, G16, G17, G18, G19 (upper left corner), tsqwà:y AK (1/24/79): B10, B11, B12, B13, C12, tsqwá:y EL (2/20/79): B10, B11, axwíl tsqwáy TM (2/14/79): B16-B22 inclusive, (on the 1969 chart rows A and J are lacking in comparison to the MacLaury charts here; the difference is unimportant since the later charts have row A with all pure white squares (=A0) and row B with all pure black squares (=J0) and the tests done with the later charts always tell the speakers to ignore rows A and J in mapping the colors; on results reported from early charts (as just below) I've adjusted row and column numbers so they refer to the same square and shade in both charts), (<**ts=**> *have, get, stative with colors*), syntactic analysis: adjective/adjectival verb, other sources: ES /cqʷ**á·**y/ (CwMs /cqʷáy/) *green* vs. /səl·**ə́**ləc'/ (CwMs /səlʔ**ə́**ləc'/) *yellow* (/səlʔə́ləc', səl·ə́ləc'/ may be related to the Upriver Halkomelem /lələ́c'/ '(have) jaundice, bile trouble' (perhaps with /s=/ 'stative' and /hə=/ 'continuative'?), JH /cqʷ**á·**y/ *green*, H-T <skwai> *green; yellow*, chart by Rob McLaury, example: <**tsqwá:y te (elíle., sp'áq'ems te th'ő lth'iyelhp., hilálxw sch'ó:lha., p'alyíws te q'á:yx̱elhp., sóx̱wel., qwe'óp.)**>, //c=qʷɛ́·y tə (ʔəlílə, s=**p'ɛ́q'**=əm-s tə **θ'**ól=C₁əC₂-əɬp, hil=ɛ́lxʷ s=**c'á·ɬɛ**, **p'**ɛl=əy=íws-s tə **q'**ɛ́·y(=)x̣=əɬp, sáx̣ʷəl, qʷəʔáp)//, /'*The (salmonberry (esp. those in the mountains), flower of the tall Oregon grape, fall leaves, bark of cascara, grass/hay (when over-ripe or dried), crabapple/apple) is yellow.*'/, <**tsqwá:y te (qwe'óp., sts'elxwíwels te st'élém., sóx̱wel., sts'ólha., tl'íkw'el., ts'esémelep., sí:ts'elhp.)**>, //c=qʷɛ́·y tə (qʷəʔáp, s=**c'**ələxʷ=íwəl-s tə s=**t'**ə́l(=)əm, sáx̣ʷəl, s=**c'áɬɛ**, **ƛ'**ík'ʷ=əl, **c'**əs=ə[=´=]m=ələp, sí·**c'**=əɬp)//, /'*The (crabapple/apple, inside cherry bark or inner cherry bark, grass, leaf, pea/bean/peas/beans, weeds, vine-maple) is/are green.*'/, attested by Deming (5/3/79) (SJ esp.), comment: SJ was the first to respond with most of these when I asked examples of things that are tsqwá:y; some others also responded and agreed, <**ts'áts'el tsqwá:y, (xw)ewás lép'ex.**>, //**c'**ɛ́[=C₁ə=]l c=qʷɛ́·y, (xʷ=)əwə=ɛ́s l**ə́p'**=əxʸ//, /'*(It's) very green, one does not eat it.*'/, attested by Deming (5/3/79, SJ esp.), <**xwel tsqwá:y**>, //xʷəl c=qʷɛ́·y//, /'*still green*'/, attested by Deming (5/3/79, SJ esp.), <**tsqwá:y te qwiqwáyels.**>, //c=qʷɛ́·y tə C₁í=qʷɛ́y=əls//, /'*The orange is yellow.*'/, attested by MP (Elders Group 5/16/79), <**tsqwá:y te st'émlexws te sth'épeq.**>, //c=qʷɛ́·y tə s=**t'**ə́lm[=M1=]əxʷ-s tə s=pə́**θ'**=M2=əq//, /'*The medicine of the skunk (skunk's spray) is yellow.*'/, attested by HT (Elders Group 5/16/79), <**sts'ólha tsqwáy**>, //s=**c'áɬɛ** c=qʷɛ́y//, /'*leaf green*'/, attested by AK (8/18/87).

<**tsqwá:y**>, ds //c=qʷɛ́·y//, EB ['*lemon (post-contact)*'], ['*Citrus limon*'], literally /'yellow ~ green'/, (**zero** *nominalizer*), phonology: zero-derivation, syntactic analysis: nominal, attested by Deming (2/79).

<**tsqwá:yem**>, df //c=qʷɛ́·y=əm//, FOOD ['*lemon extract*'], (<**=em**> *place to get/have*), syntactic analysis: nominal, attested by Elders Group (6/16/76).

<**tsqwayíws**>, ds //c=qʷɛy=íws//, ANA ['*yellow-bodied*'], DESC, literally /'yellow on the body'/, lx <**=í:ws**> *on the body*, phonology: no root vowel-reduction in spite of stressed suffix, syntactic analysis: adjective/adjectival verb, attested by Elders Group (5/16/79).

<**tsqwáyòmèx**>, ds //c=qʷɛ́y=áməxʸ//, LT /'*[looks yellow or green, yellow/green-looking]*'/, (<**ts=**> *have, get, stative with colors*), (<**=ómex**> *looks, -looking, in color*), phonology: downstepping, updrifting, syntactic analysis: adjective/adjectival verb, attested by NP, see charts by Rob MacLaury.

<**qwáyel**>, incs //qʷɛ́y=əl//, LT /'*turn yellow, got yellow*'/, ASM ['maybe lighter than qwáyewel (AD 6/19/79)'], (<**=el**> *go, come, get, become*), syntactic analysis: intransitive verb, attested by AD, AC.

<**qwóyel**>, cts //qʷɛ[-Aá-]y=əl//, LT /'*turning yellow, getting yellow, turning green*'/, (semological comment: perhaps a mistranslation for turn/get yellow/green since several speakers translate qwóqweyel as *turning yellow/green and since qwóqweyel has a normal continuative* inflection (ó-

ablaut on root á plus reduplication); further evidence of mistranslation is found in the examples below, all of which are in the past tense with le or lulh (*past* plus *already) where non-continuative is more likely; the examples are all translated in the present tense but should be translated in the past tense),* (<**ó-ablaut on root á**> *continuative*), phonology: ablaut, (semological comment: less often translated getting green since plants start out green and then get yellow), syntactic analysis: intransitive verb, attested by AC, example: <**lulh qwóyel te s'óthes yuwá:lmels kwses melqí:wsem.**>, //lə=uɬ qʷɛ[-Aá-]y=əl tə s=ʔáθ=əs-s yuwɛ́·l=məl=əls kʷ-s-əs mɛlq=í·ws=əm//, /'*Her face is turning green before she faints.*'/, attested by AC, (semological comment: (perhaps mistranslated, a better translation would be past tense and non-continuative)), <**lulh qwóyel teő:ts; lulh iyó:lem kw'as lhíts'et.**>, //lə=uɬ qʷɛ[-Aá-]y=əl tə ʔó·c; lə=uɬ ʔɛy=á·l=əm k'ʷ-ɛ-s ɬíc'=əT//, /'*The oats are getting yellow; it's alright (for you) to cut them.*'/, literally /'third-person past =already getting yellow the oats; third-person past =already alright that you cut it/them'/, attested by AC, (semological comment: (perhaps mistranslated, a better translation would be past tense and non-continuative)), <**lulh me qwóyel te só:x̲wel.**>, //lə=uɬ mə qʷɛ[-Aá-]y=əl tə sá·x̣ʷəl//, /'*The grass is turning yellow (already).*'/, attested by AC, (semological comment: (perhaps mistranslated, a better translation would be past tense and non-continuative)), <**le qwóyel te sóx̲wel.**>, //lə qʷɛ[-Aá-]y=əl tə sáx̣ʷəl//, /'*The grass is getting yellow.*'/, attested by AC, (semological comment: (perhaps mistranslated, a better translation would be past tense and non-continuative)), <**(le, lulh) qwóyel te swáyel.**>, //(lə, lə=uɬ) qʷɛ[-Aá-]y=əl tə s=wɛ́yəl//, /'*The sky is turning yellow (at sunset)., The day is getting yellow.*'/, attested by AC, (semological comment: (perhaps mistranslated, a better translation would be past tense and non-continuative)).

<**qwóqweyel ~ qwóqwiyel**>, cts //qʷɛ[-AáC$_1$ə-]y=əl//, LT /'*getting yellow, turning yellow, turning green*'/, (<**ó-ablaut plus -R1-**> *continuative*), (<**=el**> *go, come, get, become*), phonology: ablaut, reduplication, syntactic analysis: adjective/adjectival verb, attested by NP, AC, AD, see charts by Rob MacLaury.

<**sqwóqweyel ~ sqwóqwiyel**>, stvi //s=qʷɛ[=AáC$_1$ə=]y=əl//, cts, LT /'*be yellowish, be tan*'/, literally /'(stopped) in the state of becoming yellow'/, (<**s=**> *stative*), (<**ó-ablaut plus =R1=**> *continuative* (here derivational)), (<**=el**> *go, come, become, get*), phonology: reduplication, ablaut, syntactic analysis: adjective/adjectival verb, attested by AC (10/9/71 on trip to see Agnes Murphy in Laidlaw, AC's half-sister), MV (root-digging trip 4/10/78), AH (Deming 2/22/78, 1987), SJ esp. (Deming 5/3/79), NP (1987), TG (1987), see charts by Rob MacLaury, example: <**sqwóqwiyel te (músmes., stiqíw., sqwíqwemey., chékels.)**>, //s=qʷɛ[=AáC$_1$ə=]y=əl tə (mús=C$_1$əC$_2$, s=tiqíw, s=C$_1$í=qʷəm=ɛy, cə́kəls)//, /'*The (cow, horse, puppy, chicken) is tan.*, (also) *The chicken is yellow.*'/, attested by SJ esp. (Deming 5/3/79).

<**tsqwóqwiyel**>, incs //c=qʷɛ[=AáC$_1$ə=]y=əl//, LT /'*[stative/be getting yellow, stative/be getting green]*'/, (semological comment: the *get/have* meaning for ts= seems less likely than the stative meaning since =el already means *get/become/go/come*, also in most cases ts= terms with =el label shades intermingled with those labelled by s= stative terms with =el or label shades closer to the focus of color than those labelled with s= plus =el terms), (<**ts=**> *have, get, stative with colors*), (<**ó-ablaut plus =R1=**> *continuative*), (<**=el**> *go, come, get, become*), syntactic analysis: adjective/adjectival verb, attested by TG, NP, AH, see charts by Rob MacLaury.

<**tsqwóqwey**>, ds //c=qʷɛ́[=AáC$_1$ə=]y//, LT ['*[having/getting/being in a state of yellow or green]*'], ASM ['it can be a darker shade or if preceded by /tu/ it can be a lighter shade of yellow/green'], (<**ts=**> *have, get, stative with colors*), (<**=R1=**> *continuative*), syntactic analysis: adjective/adjectival verb, attested by TG, see charts by Rob MacLaury.

<**tsqwíqweyel**>, ds //c=C$_1$í=qʷɛy=əl//, LT ['*have/get/be in a state of going a little yellow or green*'],

(semological comment: this term labels almost all the margins of tsqwáy (from green's margins with blue, to yellow's margins with orange and pink and white), it also includes some moderately light green close to the focus of tsqwá:y, which, for EB of Chehalis, is green (as it is for AH of Sumas).), (<**ts=**> *have, get, stative with colors*), (<**R4=**> *diminutive*), (<**=el ~ =íl**> *go, come, get, become*), phonology: vowel-reduction to schwa following a stressed prefix, syntactic analysis: adjective/adjectival verb, attested by EB, see charts by Rob MacLaury.

<**qwiqwóyáls ~ qwiqwóyéls ~ qwiqwòyàls**>, dmn //C_1í=q^wɛy=á[=M2=]ls//, EB /'*orange (fruit), especially mandarin orange (the fruit),* also *domestic orange, (*also *orange (color))*'/, ['especially *Citrus sinensis,* also *Citrus aurantium*'], LT ['*orange (color)*'], literally /'little yellow fruit'/, ASM ['the mandarin orange may have been the first to reach the Stó:lō from the orient and especially from the Chinese who came in great numbers to work building the two railroads along the Fraser River in the 1860's and 1870's; the fruit was probably named before the color since =óls is *fruit* here rather than =els *structured activity verbalizer*'], ASM ['the following color terms are used by AK before qwiqwóyáls to specify shades of the color: xwíxwekw', tsqw'íx̲w, tsqw'íqw'ex̲wel, stl'ítl'esel'], (<**R4=**> *diminutive*), (metathesis *derivational*), lx <**=óls**> *fruit, spherical object*, phonology: metathesis, reduplication, updrifting, possible vowel-reduction, syntactic analysis: nominal, adjective/adjectival verb, attested by AC, LJ, EP, NP, AK, TG and RP, EL, AK (1987), EB (1987), NP (1987), AH (1987), charts by Rob McLaury, ASM ['squares circled on the color chart of Berlin and Kay (1969) (rows top to bottom = B-I, columns left to right = 1-40, side column of white to black = 0; individual speakers circled the following squares for qwiqwóyáls, NP (2/7/79): C7, C8, C9; AK (1/24/79): C6, C7, C8, C9; TG (with RP) (1/24/79): C6, C7, C8, C9, D6, D7, D8, D9; EL (2/20/79): D4, D5, D6; Lawrence James (2/7/79): D38; EP (2/7/79) (Katzie dial.): C9'].

<**qwíyqwòyèls sqe'óleqw**>, EB, FOOD *orange juice* (lit. orange + fruit juice), (attested by RG,EH 6/16/98 to SN, edited by BG with RG,EH 6/26/00)

<**qwíyqwòyèls seplíl**>, EB, FOOD *orange loaf* (lit. orange fruit + bread), (attested by RG,EH 6/16/98 to SN, edited by BG with RG,EH 6/26/00)

<**t'át'ets'em qwíyqwòyèls**>, EB, FOOD *lemon* (lit. sour + orange fruit/little yellowish fruit), (attested by RG,EH 6/16/98 to SN, edited by BG with RG,EH 6/26/00)

<**t'át'ets'em qwíqwòyèls kíks seplíl**>, EB, FOOD *lemon cake* (lit. lemon (itself from sour little yellowish fruit) + cake + bread), (attested by RG,EH 6/16/98 to SN, edited by BG with RG,EH 6/26/00)

<**t'át'ets'em qwíyqwòyèls sqe'óleqw**>, EB, FOOD *lemonade* (lit. lemon [itself < sour little yellow fruit] + fruit juice), (attested by RG,EH 6/16/98 to SN, edited by BG with RG,EH 6/26/00)

<**t'át'ets'em qwíyqwòyèls qas te t'át'ets'em tsqwáyqwòyèls sqe'óleqw**>, EB, FOOD *lemonlime juice* (lit. lemon fruit [itself < sour little yellowish fruit] + and + the + lime fruit [itself < sour + greenish fruit]+ fruit juice), (attested by RG,EH 6/16/98 to SN, edited by BG with RG,EH 6/26/00)

<**sásex̲em qwíyqwòyèls**>, EB, FOOD *grapefruit* (lit. bitter + orange fruit/little yellowish fruit), (attested by RG,EH 6/16/98 to SN, edited by BG with RG,EH 6/26/00)

<**sásex̲em qwíyqwòyèls sqe'óleqw**>, EB, FOOD *grapefruit juice* (lit. grapefruit [itself bitter + yellow fruit] + fruit juice), (attested by RG,EH 6/16/98 to SN, edited by BG with RG,EH 6/26/00)

<**tsqwáyqwòyèls**>, dnom //¢=q^wɛy=q^wəy=à[=M2=]ls//, EB /'*greenish fruit*'/, phonology: reduplication, metathesis, syntactic analysis: nominal, (attested by RG,EH 6/16/98 to SN, edited by BG with RG,EH 6/26/00)

<**t'át'ets'em tsqwáyqwòyèls**>, EB, FOOD *lime* (lit.sour + greenish fruit]), (attested by RG,EH 6/16/98 to SN, edited by BG with RG,EH 6/26/00), example: <**t'át'ets'em qwíyqwòyèls qas te t'át'ets'em tsqwáyqwòyèls sqe'óleqw**>, EB, FOOD *lemonlime juice* (lit. lemon fruit [itself < sour little yellowish fruit] + and + the + lime fruit [itself < sour + greenish fruit]+ fruit juice), (attested by RG,EH 6/16/98 to SN, edited by BG with RG,EH 6/26/00)

<**qwel'qwóyes**>, dmpv //C_1í[=əl'=]=qʷɛ[=Aá=]y=əs//, LT ['*orange*'], possibly EB, FOOD /'*oranges*'/, literally perhaps /'little yellow round things'/, (<**R4=**> *diminutive*), (<**=el'=**> *plural*), lx <**=es**> *round objects, face, dollar, cyclic period*, phonology: infixed plural, ó-ablaut of root a triggered automatically by =es, phonology: glottalized resonants allowed in Sumas/Matsqui and Downriver dialects, syntactic analysis: adjective/adjectival verb, dialects: *Sumas/Matsqui*, attested by AH, see charts by Rob MacLaury.

<**qwáyewel**>, ds //qʷɛ́y=əw=əl//, LT ['*turning to real yellow*'], possibly <**=ew ~ =uw**> *contrastive*, possibly <**=el**> *go, come, become, get*, syntactic analysis: intransitive verb, attested by AD (6/19/79).

<**qwáyúwél**>, df //qʷɛ́y=u[=´=]w=əl//, EB ['*dandelion*'], ['*Taraxacum officinale*'], ASM ['perhaps post-contact, AC did not know the Halq'eméylem name but said that the Stó:lō made strings from the roots, used the root also as a tonic, and used the greens for lettuce'], (<**=´=**> *derivational*), phonology: stress-shift, updrifting, syntactic analysis: nominal, attested by JL (6/19/79), AC.

<**qwíqwi ~ qwíyqwiy**>, df //qʷíy=C_1əC_2 or qʷɛ[=Aí=]y=C_1əC_2 or qʷɛ[=Aə́=]y=C_1əC_2//, LAND ['*copper*'], probably root <**qwá:y**> *yellow, green*, possibly <**é-ablaut** or **í-ablaut**> *derivational*, probably <**=R2**> *characteristic*, phonology: reduplication, ablaut, syntactic analysis: nominal, attested by JS (Elders Group 3/26/80), AK and SP (Elders Group 9/21/77), Elders Group (5/28/75, 7/23/75), Elder's comment: "SP says it may mean *brass* too, AK thinks there's another word for brass", Salish cognate: Squamish /qʷə́y-qʷi ~ sqʷaʔíls/ *copper* K67:361, also <**sqw'él**>, //s(=)**q'ʷ**əl//, attested by Elders Group (3/72), (semological comment: elsewhere translated as *metal from mines that resembles gold*), Salish cognate: Musqueam /**sq'ʷ**əl/ *copper* quoted in K67:361.

<**qwáyel**>, LT /'*turn yellow, got yellow*'/, *see* qwá:y.

<**qwáyewel**>, LT ['*turning to real yellow*'], *see* qwá:y.

<**qwáylhechàls**>, FOOD /'*to stir (a liquid), stir (mixing ingredients)*'/, *see* qwá:y.

<**qwáyúwél**>, EB ['*dandelion*'], *see* qwá:y.

<**qwayx̱élechem**>, ANAH ['*swivel one's hips (as in the Hawaiian hula for ex.) (shake one's bottom around)*'], *see* qwá:y.

<**qwá:yx̱(e)t**>, TVMO ['*(shake s-th)*'], *see* qwá:y.

<**qwá:yx̱thet**>, TVMO /'*it shook (shakes itself), shaking, bobbing around*'/, *see* qwá:y.

<**qwechíwiya**>, df //qʷəc(=)íw=iyɛ or qʷəc=íw(əl)=iyɛ//, EZ /'*late fall Harrison River and Chehalis River sockeye salmon (last run, kind of red)*'/, ['late fall Harrison/Chehalis River run of *Oncorhynchus nerka*'], stem meaning unknown but possibly <**qwá**> get a hole + <**=ewíts ~ =íts ~ =ích ~ =ech**>*on the back*, possibly <**=á:w ~ =í:w ~ =ew**>, da //=ɛ́·w ~ =í·w ~ =əw//, ANA /'*on the body, on top of itself*'/, rare variant of =í:ws ~ =ews *on the body*, (<**=iya**> *affectionate diminutive; personal name ending*), phonology: probable loss of <s> on first suffix, syntactic analysis: nominal, attested by BHTTC, EL (Chehalis trip 9/27/77).

<**qwehá**>, TVMO ['*go through*'], *see* qwá.

<**qwélatses**>, df //qʷi[=Aə́=]l=ɛcəs or qʷə[=´=]l=ɛcəs//, EB /'*fir boughs, needle of any other conifer*

than spruce'/, literally probably /'body-hair on the hand/bough'/, possibly root <**qwíl**> *any hair but that on the scalp*, possibly <**é-ablaut** or **stress-shift**> *derivational*, lx <**=tses ~ =átses**> *on the hand, on the bough (of a tree)*, phonology: ablaut or vowel-reduction plus stress-shift, syntactic analysis: nominal, attested by IHTTC, Elders Group (3/22/78).

<**qwél:és ~ qwélés**>, df //q^{w}ə́l·ə́s or q^{w}i(l)=ə́l·ə́s q^{w}i[=Aə́=]l=(ə́)l·ə́s//, EZ /'*whale (*perhaps *generic),* could include the following *balleen whales: common finback whale, humpback whale,* possibly *gray whale, Sei/Pollack whale, Minke whale, blue whale, Pacific right whale,* could include the following *toothed whales: sperm whale,* poss. *Baird beaked whale, Stejneger beaked whale, Cuvier whale*'/, ASM ['probably excluding killer whale and dolphin, probably including the balleen whales since they are distinguished by hair on the balleen in the mouth to strain food rather than teeth (see literal meaning of qwél:és), especially common finback whale and humpback whale which are both found in the Strait of Georgia, the others seldom are; if including the toothed whales, the sperm whale is more common of these; the Stó:lō elders reported stories of whales coming up the Fraser River and even the Harrison River as far as Harrison Lake'], ['perhaps generic, most likely includes all local balleen whales, i.e., suborder *Mysticeti*, especially *Balaenoptera physalus* and *Megaptera novaeangliae,* possibly *Eschrichtius glaucus, Balaenoptera borealis, Balaenoptera acutorostrata, Sibbaldus musculus, Eubalaena sieboldi*, could include the following toothed whales (suborder *Odontoceti): Physeter catodon*, possibly *Berardius bairdi, Mesoplodon stejnegeri, Ziphius cavirostrus*'], literally possibly /'hair on the teeth'/, (semological comment: possibly so named due to the hair on the balleen of balleen whales used to strain their food), possibly root <**qwil**> *any hair but that on the scalp*, probably <**=él:és ~ =elís**> *(on the) tooth, teeth*, phonology: vowel-loss, possible ablaut, consonant-loss or consonant merger, syntactic analysis: noun, nominal, attested by BJ (12/5/64), AC (prompted), EL (3/1/78 Stó:lō Sitel tape, 6/27/78 Chehalis boat trip, 9/27/77 Chehalis land trip with EB and NP), other sources: ES /q^{w}ə́l·ə́s/ *whale* and JH /q^{w}ə́ləs/ *whale*, Salish cognate: Squamish /q^{w}ənís/ (/q^{w}anís/ *whale* W73:287, K67:361) *any whale, e.g. common finback [Balaenoptera physalus (Linnaeus)]* Kennedy and Bouchard 1976:119.

<**Qwél:és**>, df //q^{w}i(l)=ə́l·ə́s//, PLN ['*Whale Point at the southwest end of Harrison Lake*'], literally /'whale'/, ASM ['the point consists largely of a rock shaped like a whale perhaps twenty feet long when we saw and photographed it, partly submerged on thenorthwest shore just above the outlet of Harrison River'], phonology: consonant-loss or consonant merger, vowel-loss or ablaut, syntactic analysis: nominal, attested by EL (9/27/77, 3/1/78 Stó:lō Sitel tape, 6/27/78), source: place names reference file #293.

<**qwelíyes**>, df //q^{w}íl=ə[=M2=]y(=)əs//, EB ['*flower of the red-flowering currant*'], ['flower of *Ribes sanguineum*'], literally probably /'hair flower'/, (semological comment: possibly so named after the hairy character of most currant and gooseberry stems and/or berries), possibly root <**qwíl**> *hair except of the scalp*, possibly <**=ey=es**> *flower* possibly from <**=ey**> *plant, bark* plus <**=es**> *face* possibly metathesis *derivational*, phonology: metathesis, syntactic analysis: noun, nominal.

<**qwélmet**>, LANG /'*scold s-o, bawl s-o out*'/, *see* qwà:l.

<**qweló:ythetel ~ qwelóyethetel**>, MUS /'*musical instrument, grammophone, phonograph, record player*'/, *see* qwà:l.

<**qweloythí:lem**>, TIME /'*(month beginning in) March, ((birds) making music)*'/, *see* qwà:l.

<**qwelqwálem ~ qwelqwá:lem**>, LANG /'*grumble, grumbling, (muttering),* (prob. also) *mumbling*'/, *see* qwà:l.

<**qwélqwel**>, LANG /'*to tell something (news), talking something over (one at a time)*'/, *see* qwà:l.

<**qwélqwel**>, EFAM /'*be rowdy, be a nuisance, be mischievious*'/, *see* qwà:l.

<**qwélqwelàtstem**>, SOC ['*to squeal on someone*'], *see* qwà:l.

<**qwelqwélés**>, EFAM ['*telling on s-o*'], *see* qwà:l.

<**qwelqwélmét**>, LANG /'*to scold a child, (scold s-o (a child))*'/, *see* qwà:l.

<**qwelqweló:ythel**>, LANG ['*(be) talkative*'], *see* qwà:l.

<**qwelqwélxel**>, WETH /'*fog appearing on the water, (fine snow [AK])*'/, *see* qwélxel.

<**qwelqwélxel**>, ANAH /'*bushy hair on horses' legs (tufts like on Clydesdale breed), tufts of fur on horse's feet*'/, *see* qwíl ~ qwel.

<**qwelqwó:ltel**>, LANG /'*arguing, (everybody is) quarrelling*'/, *see* qwà:l.

<**qwéls**>, FOOD /'*to boil, make boil*'/, *see* qwó:ls.

<**qwelselhtsthó:x**>, FOOD ['*boil it for me*'], *see* qwó:ls.

<**qwélst**>, FOOD ['*boil s-th*'], *see* qwó:ls.

<**qwelxómé**>, WETH ['*real fine snow*'], *see* qwélxel.

<**qwélxel**>, df //qʷə́ɬ=V=xʸəl or qʷə́lxʸ=əl or qʷə́l=xʸ(əl)=əl//, WETH /'*get fog on the water, (get steam (of the ground) [DC])*'/, possibly root <**qwélh**> *drift ashore* or possibly root <**qwélx**> *fine low drifting precipitation*, possibly <**=V (voicing, here lh to l)**> *derivational* now but probably originally only phonological**,** <**=xel**> *on the foot/feet, precipitation* possibly <**=el**> *get, go, come, become*, (semological comment: the element that this stem and all the meanings of the forms derived from it seem to share is *drifting precipitation/at foot level),* phonology: possible syllable-loss of el before =el, syntactic analysis: intransitive verb, attested by EB (IHTTC 7/26/77), also /'*get steam (of the ground)*'/, attested by DC (IHTTC 7/26/77), example: <**me qwélxel**>, //mə qʷə́ɬ=V=xʸəl//, /'*get fog on the water*'/, attested by EB, also /'*get steam (of the ground)*'/, attested by DC.

<**qwelqwélxel**>, df //C_1əC_2=qʷə́l=xʸəl or C_1ə=qʷə́l(=)xʸ=əl//, WETH /'*fog appearing on the water, (fine snow [AK])*'/, (<**R3=**> *plural*), phonology: reduplication shows how old the voicing is, attested by AK (11/21/72 tape), JS (IHTTC 7/26/77), also WETH ['*fine snow*'], attested by AK (11/21/72 tape, IHTTC 7/26/77), also WETH ['*small balls of snow on one's feet*'], attested by AK and NP (IHTTC 7/26/77), contrast <**qwelqwélxel**> *tufts of fur [hair] on horse's feet* from root <**qwil**> *hair not on the scalp.*

<**qwelxómé**>, df //qʷəɬ=V=xʸ(əl)=ámə́ or qʷəlxʸ=ámə́//, WETH ['*real fine snow*'], possibly <**=xel**> *precipitation; on the foot/feet*, possibly <**=ómé**> *berry*, phonology: syllable-loss of el before =ómé, possible vowel-reduction on root, voicing, syntactic analysis: intransitive verb?, attested by IHTTC (7/26/77).

<**sqwelxómé ~ sqwelxóme**>, dnom //s=qʷəɬ=V=xʸ(əl)=ámə́ or s=qʷəlxʸ=ámə́//, WETH /'*dry snow coming in (drifting), fine snow that leaks into a house*'/, (<**s=**> *nominalizer*), lx <**=xel**> *precipitation, on the foot/feet*, lx <**=ómé**> *berry*, phonology: possible root vowel-reduction, possible syllable-loss, voicing, syntactic analysis: nominal, attested by Elders Group (3/1/76, 4/16/75).

<**sqwélxem**>, df //s=qʷə́ɬ=V=xʸ(əl)=əm or s=qʷə́lxʸ=əm//, WETH ['*dry snow (that can drift)*'], (<**s=**> *nominalizer*), possibly <**é-ablaut**> *derivational,* (perhaps) *similar to*, possibly <**=xel**> *on the foot/feet*, possibly <**=em**> *middle voice or intransitivizer, have, get*, phonology: possible ablaut, possible syllable-loss, voicing, syntactic analysis: nominal, attested by Elders Group (3/1/76).

<**qwálxtem**>, df //qʷə[=Aɛ́=]lxʸ=təm or qʷə[=Aɛ́=]ɬ=V=xʸ(əl)=təm//, WETH ['*got stormy with lots of fine snow in the air*'], possibly <**á-ablaut**> *resultative*, possibly <**=tem**> *participial*, phonology:

possible ablaut, possible syllable-loss, possible voicing, syntactic analysis: adjective/adjectival verb, attested by NP (IHTTC 7/26/77).

<**qwelxw**>, bound root or possibly stem //qʷəlxʷ//

<**sqwelxwó:lés**>, df //s=qʷəlxʷ=á·ləs//, ABDF /'*(have) one white eye, (have a cataract on one eye)*'/, (<**s=**> *stative* or *nominalizer*), root meaning unknown, lx <**=ó:les**> *on the eye*, phonology: updrifting on final syllable, syntactic analysis: adjective/adjectival verb?, attested by Elders Group.

<**qwélh**>, free root //qʷə́ɬ//, WATR ['*drift ashore*'], LAND ['*to fall on something (of a drunk)*'], syntactic analysis: intransitive verb, attested by AD, NP, also CAN ['*tip over (of a canoe)*'], attested by Elders Group (3/26/75), comment: this may be an error for kw'élh *spill, capsize* but it could be a variant meaning of qwélh *drift ashore, fall on something (of a drunk)* if it means *tip over after running over something near shore (of a canoe).*

<**qwlhá:y**>, ds //qʷəɬ=ɛ́·y//, EB ['*driftwood, (log (in the water))*'], WATR, ASM ['often thick bark of firs'], literally /'drift ashore bark/wood'/, lx <**=á:y**> *bark, wood, covering*, phonology: zero-grade of root before stressed suffix, syntactic analysis: nominal, attested by EB, Elders Group, other sources: ES /qʷɬɛ́·i/ *log*, H-T <kwEtlái> (umlaut over a) *log (in the water)* in contrast to H-T <s'yáuk> (umlaut over a)(/syɛ́yəq'/) *log (in the forest)*, also /'*plank (more than a log)*'/, attested by AC, also <**qwlhà:y**>, //qʷəɬ=ɛ̀·y//, also /'*a snag*'/, phonology: downdrifting, attested by CT.

<**qwéqwelhi(y)**>, dmpn //C_1í[=Aə́]=qʷəɬ=əy//, EB ['*lots of little pieces of driftwood*'], WATR, (<**R4=**> *diminutive*), (<**é-ablaut**> *plural of diminutive*), phonology: reduplication, ablaut, vowel-reduction in suffix then vocalization, syntactic analysis: nominal, attested by Elders Group.

<**qwelhyő̂welh ~ qwelhliyő̂welh ~ qwelhlyúwelh**>, ds //qʷəɬ=ɛy=ówəɬ//, HHG /'*big wooden dish (often two feet long), feast dish, wooden platter, (big stirring spoon [LJ], carved wooden spoon, big wooden spoon [AC, BJ, DM])*'/, FOOD, literally /'driftwood vessel/canoe/dish'/, lx <**=ő̂welh**> *canoe, vessel, bowl*, phonology: zero-grade of suffix before a stressed suffix, optional vocalizationn, syntactic analysis: nominal, attested by Elders Group, Maggie Pennier, JL, DM (12/4/64), also /'*big stirring spoon*'/, attested by Lawrence James (Elders Group 4/5/78), also /'*carved wooden spoon, big wooden spoon*'/, attested by AC, BJ (5/10/64), DM (12/4/64), also <**qwelhyúwelh ~ qwelhlíywelh ~ qwelhiyúwelh ~ qwelhlí:welh**>, //qʷəɬ=ɛy=ówəɬ//, attested by Elders Group, Maggie Pennier, JL, DM (12/4/64).

<**qwlhí:xel ~ qwelhí:xel**>, ds //qʷəɬ=(ə)y=´=xʸəl//, CLO ['*shoe*'], literally /'drift ashore bark/covering/driftwood on the foot'/, root <**qwelh**> *drift ashore*, lx <**=á:y ~ =ey ~ =y ~ =i**> *bark, covering*, lx <**=xel**> *on the foot*, (<=´:=> *derivational*), phonology: zero-grade of root, zero-grade of suffix, vocalization of suffix consonant with stress-shift to it, lengthening, syntactic analysis: nominal, attested by AC, Salish cognate: Squamish /qʷɬíʔ-šn/ *shoe* W73:229, K67:360.

<**qwelhlixélem ~ qwelhixélem**>, mdls //qʷəɬ=(ə)y=xʸə[=´=]l=əm//, CLO ['*put on one's shoes*'], (<=´=> *derivational*), (<**=em**> *middle voice*), phonology: zero-grade/vowel-loss then vocalization of y, stress-shift, syntactic analysis: intransitive verb, attested by AD.

<**qwelhlixélem ~ qwelhixélem**>, CLO ['*put on one's shoes*'], *see* qwélh.

<**qwelhyő̂welh ~ qwelhliyő̂welh ~ qwelhlyúwelh**>, HHG /'*big wooden dish (often two feet long), feast dish, wooden platter, (big stirring spoon [LJ], carved wooden spoon, big wooden spoon [AC, BJ, DM])*'/, *see* qwélh.

<**qwem**>, bound root //qʷəm *soft*//.

<**sqwemá:y ~ sqwmá:y ~ sqwemáy**>, ds //s=qʷəm=ɛ́·y//, EZ ['*dog*'], ['*Canis familiaris*'], ASM ['there were two native breeds, one used for hunting, and another bred and sheered for its wool for

blankets; the woolly dogs appear in an illustration by Paul Kane and are described as having white very soft wool, almost like a Pomeranian poodle; there are no known photos and the pure breed died out perhaps in the 1860's; the word has since been applied to all breeds'], literally /'something with soft wool/covering'/, (<**s=**> *nominalizer*), lx <**=á:y**> *wool, covering*, syntactic analysis: nominal, attested by AC, Elders Group (3/1/72 tape, 3/3/76), BJ (5/10/64, 12/5/64), other sources: ES /sq^{w}əmɛ́·y/ *dog*, example: <**sá:ys te sqwemáy**>, //sɛ́·y-s tə s=q^{w}əm=ɛ́·y//, /'*wool of the dog*'/, attested by AC, <**t'át'eyeq' te sqwmáy**>, //t'ɛ́[-C$_1$ə-]yəq' tə s=q^{w}əm=ɛ́·y//, /'*The dog is mad.*'/, attested by AC, <**tl'ó: tethá le á:ystexw tel sqwmáy?**>, //ƛ'á-ə tə=θɛ́ lə ʔɛ́·y=sT-əx^w tə-l s=q^{w}əm=ɛ́·y//, /'*Is that the one that was chasing my dog?*'/, attested by AC, <**sta'á kw'e sqwmáy**>, //s=t=ɛʔɛ́ k'^{w}ə s=q^{w}əm=ɛ́·y//, /'*like a dog*'/, attested by AC, <**ta sqwemáy**>, //t-ɛ s=q^{w}əm=ɛ́·y//, /'*your dog*'/, attested by AC, <**ló:s te sqwmáy.**>, //lá·s tə s=q^{w}əm=ɛ́·y//, /'*The dog is fat.*'/, attested by AC, <**ō telúwe sqwmá:y.**>, //ʔo tə=lúwə s=q^{w}əm=ɛ́·y//, /'*Oh you dog.*'/, attested by Elders Group.

<**Sqwemá:y (?)**>, ds //s=q^{w}əm=ɛ́·y//, PLN ['*a rock shaped like a dog on the east shore of the Fraser River near Hill's Bar and below Tewít (a rock shaped like a human hunter)*'], ASM ['this dog had chased an elk into the Fraser River and was followed closely by his master when all three were changed to stone by the Transformer; when we passed the rocks on a raft with elders SP, AD, and AK on a place name survey from Hope to Strawberry Island, the elders said that the dog rock had been blasted to clear a way for sternwheelers many years ago, so it no longer resembles a dog'], syntactic analysis: nominal, attested by SP and AK and AD (8/30/77, 9/13/77), source: place names reference file #272.

<**sqwíqwemay**>, ds //s=C$_1$í=q^{w}əm=ɛy//, EZ ['*puppy*'], (<**s=**> *nominalizer*, R4= *diminutive*), phonology: reduplication, syntactic analysis: nominal, attested by AC, others.

<**sqwíqwemeyò:llh**>, ds //s=C$_1$í=q^{w}əm=ɛy=á·lɬ//, EZ ['*small puppy*'], lx <**=ó:llh**> *young, offspring*, phonology: downstepping, syntactic analysis: nominal, attested by CT.

<**sqwéqwemay**>, dmpn //s=C$_1$í=Aə́=q^{w}əm=ɛy//, EZ /'*a lot of (small) dogs, puppies*'/, (<**s=**> *nominalizer*, R4= *diminutive*, é-ablaut *plural diminutive*), phonology: reduplication, ablaut, stress-shift, syntactic analysis: nominal, attested by AC, others.

<**sqweqweméytses**>, ds //s=C$_1$í=Aə=q^{w}əm=ɛ́y=cəs or s=C$_1$ə=q^{w}əm=ɛ́y=cəs//, EB ['*pussy willow*'], ['*Salix* species, possibly *Salix hookeriana* or *Salix sitchensis* or any *Salix?*'], literally /'puppies in/on the hand'/, (<**s=**> *nominalizer*, R4= plus e-ablaut or R5= *diminutive plural*), lx <**=tses**> *on the hand*, phonology: reduplication, perhaps ablaut, syntactic analysis: nominal, attested by CT (6/8/76), IHTTC (7/8/77).

<**Qweqwemeytá:ye**>, df //C$_1$ə=q^{w}əm=ɛ́·y=t=ə[=M2=]yɛ//, N ['*Pussy Willow (name in stories)*'], possibly <**=t**> meaning unknown, R5=> *diminutive plural*, lx <**=eya ~ =iya**> *affectionate diminutive; name ending,* phonology: reduplication, metathesis, syntactic analysis: nominal, attested by IHTTC (7/8/77).

<**sqwemá:yalqel**>, ds //s=q^{w}əm=ɛ́·y=ɛlqəl//, ANAA ['*dog wool*'], WV, ASM ['sometimes whitened with st'ewő̄kw' *diatomaceous earth* which also helped it to be spun, sometimes mixed with seed fluff from fireweed or cottonwood'], lx <**=alqel**> *wool*, syntactic analysis: nominal, attested by BHTTC.

<**qweqwemeylíth'e**>, df //q^{w}ə[=C$_1$ə=]m=ɛy=əl=íθ'ɛ or C$_1$ə=q^{w}əm=ɛy=əl=íθ'ɛ//, WV ['*dog wool fibre*'], Elder's comment: "sometimes mixed with cedar fibre or perhaps nettle fibre to make the latter soft and warm for clothes", possibly <**R5=**> *diminutive plural* or possibly <**=R1=**> *continuative*? or> *derivational* or possibly <**=el**> *come, go, get, become*, lx <**=íth'a**> *clothes, blanket*, phonology: reduplication, syntactic analysis: nominal, attested by AD (7/4/79).

<**sqwemayáwtxw**>, ds //s=q^{w}əm=ɛy=ɛ́wtxw//, BLDG ['*dog house*'], EZ, lx <**=áwtxw**> *building, house*, syntactic analysis: nominal, attested by Elders Group, also <**láléms te sqwemáy**>, //lɛ́lə́m-s tə s=q^{w}əm=ɛ́·y//, literally /'house -his/her/its the dog'/.

<**qwemchíwet**>, pcs //q^{w}əm=cəs=íws=əT//, ABFC ['*hug s-o around*'], probably root <**qwem**> *soft, round?*, possibly lx <**=tses**> *(on the) hand* or more likely <**=ewíts ~ =íts ~ =ích ~ =ech**> *on the back*, lx <**=íws**> *on the body*, (<**=et**> *purposeful control transitivizer*), phonology: consonant-loss of s on =tses or more likely vowel-loss on =ech ~ =ich, consonant-loss of s on =íws, syntactic analysis: transitive verb, attested by MV (Deming 5/4/78).

<**qwémxel**>, ds //q^{w}ə́m=x^{y}əl//, EZ /'*chipmunk, i.e., Northwestern chipmunk and Townsend chipmunk*'/, ['*Eutamias amoenus felix, Eutamias amoenus affinis?, Eutamias townsendi*'], literally /'soft on the foot/feet'/, Elder's comment: "means *soft feet*", root <**qwém**> *soft*, lx <**=xel**> *on the foot/feet*, syntactic analysis: nominal, attested by ME (11/21/72 tape), IHTTC (8/10/77).

<**Qwémxel**>, ds //q^{w}ə́m=x^{y}əl//, TIME ['*month or moon that begins in February*'], literally /'chipmunk (soft feet)'/, Elder's comment: "so named because chipmunks come out of their house then and take out their mattress and shake it outside (EB:ME)", ASM ['named after the chipmunk because that's when the chipmunk shakes out his mattress and blankets (IHTTC)'], phonology: zero derivation, syntactic analysis: nominal, attested by ME (11/21/72 tape), IHTTC (8/10/77).

<**qwemchíwet**>, ABFC ['*hug s-o around*'], *see* qwem.

<**qwemchó:ls**>, EB ['*bog cranberry*'], *see* qwà:m ~ qwám.

<**qwémélép ~ qwemélep**>, df //q^{w}ə́m=ə́lə́p//, EB /'*cottonwood bark driftwood (it was used to carve toy canoes), cottonwood driftwood used for carving toy canoes*'/, possibly root <**qwém**> *soft*, possibly <**=élép**> *in the dirt*, phonology: three high stresses, possible updrifting, syntactic analysis: nominal, attested by BHTTC, AK or SP or AD (on raft trip 8/30/77).

<**Qwemí(:)líts**>, df //q^{w}əm=í·l=íc//, PLN /'*Chilliwack Mountain, village of Cameleats on west end of Chilliwack Mountain*'/, possibly root <**qwem**> *soft*, possibly <**=í:l**> *go, come, get, become*, possibly <**=íts**> *on the back*, syntactic analysis: nominal, attested by BJ (5/10/64), other sources: Wells 1965 (lst ed.):11, 19, Wells 1966, source: place names reference file #316.

<**qwemqwémx̲wtses**>, ANAH ['*knuckles (all the joints of the hand and fingers)*'], *see* qwó:m ~ qwóm ~ qwem.

<**qwemqwémx̲wxel**>, ANAH ['*all the joints of the foot and toes*'], *see* qwó:m ~ qwóm ~ qwem.

<**qwemqwó:mth'**>, LAND ['*lots of anthills*'], *see* qwó:m ~ qwóm ~ qwem.

<**Qwemth'í:les**>, PLN /'*Mount Ogilvie or a round peak or bluff on Mt. Ogilvie where mountain goats live, the mountain or peak or bluff resembles big breasts*'/, *see* qwó:m ~ qwóm ~ qwem.

<**qwémxel**>, EZ /'*chipmunk, i.e., Northwestern chipmunk and Townsend chipmunk*'/, *see* qwem.

<**Qwémxel**>, TIME ['*month or moon that begins in February*'], *see* qwem.

<**qwémx̲wtses**>, ANAH /'*wrist, wrist bone (on outer side of wrist, little finger side, lump of wrist)*'/, *see* qwó:m ~ qwóm ~ qwem.

<**qwémx̲wxel**>, ANAH ['*ankle (the lump part)*'], *see* qwó:m ~ qwóm ~ qwem.

<**qweqwà:l**>, LANG /'*talking, (giving a speech)*'/, *see* qwà:l.

<**qweqwá:l ~ qwōqwá:l**>, df //C$_1$ə=q^{w}ɛ́·l or C$_1$ə=q^{w}ɛ́=əl//, FSH ['*small float for nets (made from singed cedar)*'], possibly <**R5=**> *diminutive plural?*, <**=el**> *get, come, become, go*, possibly root <**qwá**> *hole*

or possibly root <**qwá:l**> meaning uncertain, (semological comment: if the root is <**qwá**> perhaps the meaning *get many little holes* refers to the fact that such floats need such holes to float whether made of singed cedar (or now) of cork), phonology: reduplication, syntactic analysis: nominal, attested by SP and AK (7/13/75), also <**qwelqwà:lt**>, //C$_1$əC$_2$=q^{w}ɛ̀·lt or C$_1$əC$_2$=q^{w}ɛ̀=əlt//, also FSH /'*float line, cork line*'/, ASM ['a line of net suspended by floats (originally made of singed cedar, now made of cork or even plastic bleach bottles)'], attested by CT (6/8/76).

<**qwéqweláts**>, LANG ['*to gossip*'], *see* qwà:l.

<**qwéqwelhi(y)**>, EB ['*lots of little pieces of driftwood*'], *see* qwélh.

<**qweqwemeylíth'e**>, WV ['*dog wool fibre*'], *see* qwem.

<**Qweqwemeytá:ye**>, N ['*Pussy Willow (name in stories)*'], *see* qwem.

<**qweqweqwtí:mxel**>, WETH /'*(maybe) fine mist of fog or rain,* ((perhaps) *getting foggy* [EB])'/, *see* qwétxem.

<**Qweqwe'ópelhp**>, PLN ['*Kwakwawapilt village and reserve (Chilliwack Indian Reserve #6)*'], *see* qwe'óp.

<**qwés**>, possibly root //q^{w}ə́s or q^{w}ɛ[=Aə́=]s//, WATR /'*fall in the water, fall overboard (of one person)*'/, possibly <**é-ablaut**> *resultative*, phonology: possible ablaut, syntactic analysis: intransitive verb, attested by Elders Group (3/72, 3/26/75).

<**qwsá:yel**>, ds //q^{w}ɛ́·s[-M1-]=əyəl//, FSH /'*throw a net into water (to drift, not to set), throw a net out, (gill net [TG])*'/, literally /'fall overboard net'/, (<**metathesis type 1**> *non-continuative*), lx <**=eyel ~ =iyel**> *net*, phonology: metathesis, vowel merger, syntactic analysis: nominal, attested by Elders Group (5/16/79, 3/15/72), also FSH ['*gill net*'], attested by TG (4/23/75), example: <**lámtsel qwsá:yel.**>, //lɛ́=m-c-əl q^{w}ɛ́·s[-M1-]=əyəl//, /'*I'm going to throw a net into the water (to drift).*'/, attested by Elders Group (5/16/79).

<**qwsá:wiyel**>, df //q^{w}ɛ́·s[-M1-]=əws=iyəl or q^{w}ɛ́·s[-M1-]=w=iyəl or q^{w}ɛ́·s=ə[=M2=]w(s)=iyəl//, FSH ['*set a net and drift with it*'], (<**metathesis type 1**> *non-continuative*), possibly <**=ews**> *(on the) body* or possibly <**=a:w**> allomorph *on the body, on top of itself*, lx <**=iyel**> *net*, phonology: metathesis, vowel merger, consonant-loss of s on suffix before =iyel, syntactic analysis: intransitive verb, attested by Elders Group (3/15/72 tape).

<**qwesú:yel**>, df //q^{w}ɛs=ə́w(s)=iyəl//, FSH ['*drop a net into water*'], possibly <**=éws**> *on the body* or possibly <**=ew**> allomorph *on the body, on top of itself*, lx <**=iyel**> *net*, phonology: consonant-loss of s on suffix before =iyel, vowel-reduction in root, vocalization perhaps after possible vowel-loss and stress-shift, syntactic analysis: intransitive verb, attested by BHTTC.

<**qwáseliyel**>, ds //q^{w}ɛ́s=əl=iyəl//, FSH ['*drifting a net in different places*'], (lack of metathesis 1 means *continuative* here), possibly <**=el**> *plural of suffix* or possibly more likely *come, go, get, become*, lx <**=iyel**> *net*, syntactic analysis: intransitive verb, attested by BHTTC.

<**qwsét**>, pcs //q^{w}ə́s=M1=T or q^{w}sə́=T or q^{w}s=ə́T//, WATR /'*launch s-th/s-o into the water, push s-o/s-th into the water, throw it in the water*'/, CAN, possibly root <**qwés** or **qwsé** or **qw(e)s**> *fall in the water*, probably metathesis *non-continuative*, probably <**=t** (or **=ét)**> *purposeful control transitivizer*, phonology: probable metathesis or possible stressed transitivizer, syntactic analysis: transitive verb, attested by EB, AD, NP (4/11/80), example: <**le qwsétes te sléxwelh.**>, //lə q^{w}ə́s=M1=T-əs tə s=lə́x^{w}əɬ//, /'*Someone launched a canoe.*'/, attested by EB.

<**qwesú:yel**>, FSH ['*drop a net into water*'], *see* qwés.

<**qwétxem**>, mdls //q^{w}ə́tx^y=əm//, WETH ['*getting foggy*'], possibly <**=x(el)**> *precipitation*, (<**=em**>

middle voice), syntactic analysis: intransitive verb, attested by Deming.

<**sqwétxem**>, dnom //s=q^{w}ə́tx^{y}=əm//, WETH /'*fog, mist*'/, (<**s=**> *nominalizer*), syntactic analysis: nominal, attested by Elders Group (3/15/72 tape), Deming, AC, BJ (12/5/64), AD, NP, other sources: ES /sqwə́tx^{y}əm/ *fog*, example: <**li a sqwá:lewel kw'es qé<u>x</u> te sqwétxem wày:èlès?**>, //li ʔɛ s=q^{w}ɛ̀·l=əwəl **k'**^{w}ə-s qə́x̣ tə s=q^{w}ə́tx^{y}=əm wɛ̀y·əl=əs//, /'*Do you think there will be a lot of fog tomorrow?*'/, attested by AC, <**qé<u>x</u> te sqwétxem.**>, //qə́x̣ tə s=q^{w}ə́tx^{y}=əm//, /'*There's a lot of fog., There's thick fog.*'/, attested by AC (8/4/70), <**shxwóxwel te sqwétxem.**>, //s=x^{w}á=C$_{1}$ə=əl tə s=q^{w}ə́tx^{y}=əm//, /'*The fog lifted.*'/, attested by AD and NP (1/23/80).

<**qweqweqwtí:mxel**>, df //C$_{1}$ə=q^{w}ə[=C$_{1}$ə=]t=í·m=x^{y}əl//, WETH /'*(maybe) fine mist of fog or rain,* ((perhaps) *getting foggy* [EB])'/, possibly <**R5=**> *plural diminutive*, possibly <**=R1=**> *resultative*, (<**=í:m**> *repeatedly*), lx <**=xel**> *precipitation*, phonology: double reduplication may show ritual form, syntactic analysis: intransitive verb, usage: in a (ritual?) song to change the weather (CT), attested by Elders Group (9/27/78), CT (in a song)(on Stó:lō Sitel tape made by Albert Friesen of songs sung by various elders), also /'*getting foggy*'/, attested by EB (prompted 9/18/78).

<**qweth**>, bound root //q^{w}**əθ**// meaning unknown.

<**sqwéthem**>, df //s=q^{w}**ə́θ**=əm//, CAN /'*canoe with shovel-nose at both ends, same as tl'elá:y*'/, (<**s=**> *nominalizer*), root meaning unknown, possibly <**=em**> *intransitivizer, get, have*, syntactic analysis: nominal, attested by Elders Group, Deming.

<**qwethíles**>, df //q^{w}**əθ**=íl(=)əs//, FOOD ['*long feast dish*'], HHG, possibly <**=íles**> *on the chest* or possibly <**=íl**> *go, come, get, become* and <**=es**> *on the face, circular object*?, root meaning unknown, syntactic analysis: nominal, dialects: *Cowichan* and prob. also *Cheh.*, attested by HP (5/30/78).

<**qwethíles**>, FOOD ['*long feast dish*'], *see* qweth.

<**qwéth'**> or <**qwíth'**>, probably bound root or stem //q^{w}**ə́θ'** or qwɛ́y=θ'//, meaning uncertain, prob. a characteristic action or description of the grouse & squirrel in some way, poss. onomatopoeic imitation of sounds both make, also perhaps compare <**qwíth'** or **qwéth'**>, df //qwɛ́y=θ'// *yellow + small portion* (which may reflect one of their colors: the ruffed grouse is reddish-brown & spotted on top and & yellowish barred with dark on bottom; the Douglas squirrel has an orangish buff belly in the summer, an orangish line of fur between the fur on its back and that on the belly, and its tail hairs are tipped with yellow).

<**sqwéth'**>, df //s=q^{w}**ə́θ'**//, EZ /'*ruffed grouse,* (also known as) *willow grouse*'/, ['*Bonasa umbellus sabini*'], (<**s=**> *nominalizer*), root meaning unknown, syntactic analysis: nominal, dialects: JL reports this as the *Chill.* form, BHTTC reports this as the *Cheh.* form and also *an alternate for the other dialects, ME gives it for Tait*, attested by JL, ME (11/21/72 tape), BHTTC, Salish cognate: Squamish /sk^{w}**ə́c'**/ *willow grouse* (W73:124, K67:293) ~ /sq^{w}**ə́c'**/ *ruffed grouse (Bonasa umbellus)* Kennedy and Bouchard 1976:75, also <**sqwéth'qweth'**>, //s=q^{w}**ə́θ'**=C$_{1}$əC$_{2}$//, (<**=R2**> *characteristic*), dialects: *JL gives this as the Tait form*, attested by SP (11/21/72 taped interview of ME), BHTTC, JL (Tait), Elders Group (2/18/76), also <**skwéts'kwets'**>, //s=k^{w}**ə́c'**=C$_{1}$əC$_{2}$//, attested by Elders Group (6/4/75).

<**shxwelítemelh sqwéth'**>, df //s=x^{w}əlítəm=əɬ s=q^{w}**ə́θ'**//, (probably) EZ ['*(ring-necked) pheasant*'], ['*Phasianus colchicus*'], literally /'White-man style/kind of ruffed grouse'/, (<**s=**> *stative*, <**=elh**> *style, kind*), syntactic analysis: simple nominal phrase, attested by ME (11/21/72 tape).

<**sqwéth'elh**>, df //s=q^{w}**ə́θ'**(=)əɬ//, EZ ['*Douglas squirrel*'], ['*Tamiasciurus douglasi mollipilosus*'], (<**s=**> *nominalizer*), root meaning unknown, possibly <**=elh**> meaning unknown here unless *child* (that might make squirrel lit. *grouse's child)*, Elder's comment: "qwóqwel lí te sxíxets; ōwéta

tl'oqá:ys. (ME) *They used to always talk in the bush; now there's no more.*", (semological comment: may have gotten its dark marks from being burnt in a story along with marten and weasel (AD)), syntactic analysis: nominal, attested by AC, BJ (12/5/64), AD (Elders Group 3/21/79), Elders Group (2/11/76), BHTTC (11/15/76), ME (11/21/72 tape), other sources: ES /sqʷə́cə̀ɬ/ and JH /sqʷə́θəɬ/ *squirrel*, contrast <**Skwóya**> *Squirrel*, also <**qwéth'elh**>, //qʷə́θ'(=)əɬ//, attested by AK (11/21/72 tape).

<**qwéx̱em**>, bound root //qʷə́x̣(=)əm//, meaning uncertain

<**sqwéx̱em**>, df //s=qʷə́x̣(=)əm//, EZ /'*silver spring salmon that came up Harrison River and Chehalis Creek, (first spring salmon [Deming])*'/, ['*Oncorhynchus tshawytscha*'], (<**s=**> *nominalizer*), root meaning unknown, possibly <**=em**> *intransitivizer or middle voice*, syntactic analysis: nominal, attested by Elders Group, also /'*first spring salmon*'/, attested by Deming (4/1/76).

<**Qwíqwex̱em**>, dmn //C_1í=qʷəx̣(=)əm//, PLN ['*Lake Errock*'], (<**R4=**> *diminutive*), ASM ['so named because many sqwéx̱em could be gotten there; sqwéx̱em is the origin of "Squawkum" in the "Squawkum Park" campground and development of the Scowlitz Reserve at Lake Errock'], syntactic analysis: nominal by zero derivation, attested by EL (with NP and EB on Chehalis Trip 9/27/77), source: place names reference file #306.

<**qwéyleq ~ qwíleq**>, ANA ['*pubic hair*'], *see* qwíl ~ qwel.

<**qwe'íqw**>, bound root //qʷəʔíqʷ *thin, scrawny*//.

<**qwe'íqws**>, df //qʷəʔíqʷ=(ə)s//, DESC ['*thin (of tree or pole)*'], syntactic analysis: adjective/adjectival verb, attested by CT (6/8/76).

<**qwe'íqwepsem**>, ds //qʷəʔíqʷ=əpsəm//, BPI /'*(have a) small neck, (have a) scrawny neck*'/, lx <**=epsem**> *on the neck*, syntactic analysis: adjective/adjectival verb, attested by Elders Group.

<**qwe'íqweqs**>, ds //qʷəʔíqʷ=əqs//, DESC ['*(have a) thin (point or nose)*'], lx <**=eqs**> *on the point, on the nose*, syntactic analysis: adjective/adjectival verb, attested by CT (6/8/76).

<**qwe'íqweqw**>, ds //qʷəʔíqʷ=əqʷ//, DESC /'*be scrawny, be thin*'/, lx <**=eqw**> *on top of the head, on the hair of the head*, syntactic analysis: adjective/adjectival verb, attested by EB, example: <**qwe'íqweqw te thqá:t.**>, //qʷəʔíqʷ=əqʷ tə θqɛ́·t//, /'*The tree is scrawny (or thin).*'/, (semological comment: possibly referring to the branches (as its head hair)), attested by EB, <**we'ólwe qwe'íqweqws ta (x̱wé:ylem, x̱éltel, pő:l).**>, //wə=ʔál=wə qʷəʔíqʷ=əqʷ-s t-ɛ (x̣ʷí·ləm, x̣ə́l=təl, pó·l)//, /'*Your (rope, pen/pencil, pole) is too thin/narrow.*'/, attested by JL (7/13/79).

<**qwe'íqwepsem**>, BPI /'*(have a) small neck, (have a) scrawny neck*'/, *see* qwe'íqw.

<**qwe'íqweqs**>, DESC ['*(have a) thin (point or nose)*'], *see* qwe'íqw.

<**qwe'íqweqw**>, DESC /'*be scrawny, be thin*'/, *see* qwe'íqw.

<**qwe'íqws**>, DESC ['*thin (of tree or pole)*'], *see* qwe'íqw.

<**qwe'óp**>, free root //qʷəʔáp//, EB /'*crabapple, (now) domesticated apple*'/, ['*Pyrus fusca, Pyrus malus (= Malus malus)*'], ASM ['green crabapples were ready to be picked in fall, Oct. and Nov., lots grew by Chehalis, picked and stored, eaten when brown and soft, could be eaten when green but sour, good jelly is made from them when green, some grow way back of Seabird Island, some on Dave Pat's Reserve on Ashwell Rd., the Kwawkwawapilt Reserve, which was named for them (Elders Group 9/22/76)'], syntactic analysis: noun, nominal, attested by AC, BJ (12/5/64), Elders Group (3/1/72 tape, 9/22/76, 5/16/79), NP (9/30/75), Deming (esp. SJ)(5/3/79), other sources: ES /qʷəʔáp/ *crabapple*, example: <**xepólst te qwe'óp**>, //xʸip=áls=T tə qʷəʔáp//, /'*peel apples*'/, attested by AC, <**tsqwá:y te**

qwe'óp.>, //c-qʷɛ́·y tə qʷəʔáp//, /'*The crabapple/apple is yellow.*'/, attested by Elders Group (5/16/79), also /'*The crabapple/apple is green.*'/, attested by Deming (esp. SJ) (5/3/79).

<**qwe'óp sqe'óleqw**>, EB, FOOD *apple juice* (lit. apple + fruit juice), (attested by RG,EH 6/16/98 to SN, edited by BG with RG,EH 6/26/00)

<**st'elt'elíqw qwe'óp**>, EB, FOOD *pineapple* (lit. bumpy and prickly + apple), (attested by RG,EH 6/16/98 to SN, edited by BG with RG,EH 6/26/00), example: <**st'elt'elíqw qwe'óp sqe'óleqw**>, *pineapple juice* (lit. pineapple [itself from bumpy and prickly + apple] + fruit juice), (attested by RG,EH 6/16/98 to SN, edited by BG with RG,EH 6/26/00)

<**qwe'ó:pelhp**>, ds //qʷəʔá[=·=]p=əɬp//, EB /'*crabapple tree, domestic apple tree*'/, ['*Pyrus fusca, Pyrus malus*'], lx <**=elhp**> *tree*, (<**=:=**> meaning uncertain here, perhaps to dissimilate from the place name <**Qweqwe'ópelhp**>), ASM ['wood used (as was oceanspray wood) to make bulrush mat needles'], MED ['crabapple bark is good medicine for afterbirth in pregnancy; take the second bark from the sunny side, cut in pieces, boil in water a few minutes, drink half a cup before and after afterbirth, also makes children spaced two years apart instead of every year (birth control) (CT and HT 6/21/76 tape), tea from crabapple bark spaces children every four years, just take small patch of bark from the side the sun first hits (AD 6/19/79)'], syntactic analysis: nominal, attested by AC, BJ (12/5/64), Elders Group (3/1/72 tape), other sources: JH /qʷəʔá·pəɬp/ *crabapple tree*, example: <**ì:'axwí:l qwe'ó:pelhp**>, //C_1í=ʔɛxʷ(=)í·l qʷəʔa[=·=]p=əɬp//, /'*small crabapple tree*'/, attested by AC.

<**Qweqwe'ópelhp**>, dmpn //C_1í=Aə=qʷəʔáp=əɬp//, PLN ['*Kwakwawapilt village and reserve (Chilliwack Indian Reserve #6)*'], literally /'lots of small crabapple trees'/, (<**R5=**> *plural* or <**R4=**> *diminutive* and <**e-ablaut**> *plural of diminutive*), phonology: reduplication, ablaut, syntactic analysis: nominal, attested by Elders Group, BJ (5/10/64), other sources: Wells 1965 (lst ed.):23 gives it as a village between Koquapilt slough and Skwah with lit. meaning *place of crabapple grove* and on p.14 gives it as Kwawkwawapilt Slough with lit. meaning *where crabapples grow* (Duff 1952:37 has [ʔəwaθáy] as the name for the slough, source: place names reference file #83.

<**Sqwe'óp (?)**>, df //s=qʷəʔáp (?)//, PLN ['*Cheam Creek on north side below Ford Creek*'], (<**s=**> *nominalizer*), root meaning unknown but prob. *crabapple*, syntactic analysis: nominal, source: Wells 1965 (lst ed.):13 gives <skwuh-AWP>,

<**qwíl ~ qwel**>, bound root //qʷíl ~ qʷəl *any hair but that on the scalp*//.

<**qwilṓws**>, ds //qʷil=óws ~ qʷil=ə́ws//, ANA /'*hair anywhere on the body (arms, legs, chest, underarms, etc.)*'/, lx <**=ṓws**> *on the body*, syntactic analysis: nominal, attested by EB.

<**sqwelqwílōws ~ sqwelqwéylōws**>, pln //s=C_1əC_2=qʷíl=əws//, ANA ['*hair on the body*'], (<**s=**> *nominalizer*, R3= *plural*), lx <**=ōws ~ =ews ~ =ṓws**> *on the body*, phonology: reduplication, syntactic analysis: nominal, attested by Elders Group.

<**sqwelqwelá:lí:ya**>, pln //s=C_1əC_2=qʷil=ɛ́·lí·yɛ//, ANA ['*hair in the ears*'], (<**s=**> *nominalizer*, R3= *plural*), lx <**=á:lí:ya**> *in the ear*, phonology: reduplication, vowel-reduction, syntactic analysis: nominal, attested by Elders Group.

<**qwéyleq ~ qwíleq**>, ds //qʷíl=əq//, ANA ['*pubic hair*'], lx <**=eq ~ =áq**> *on the penis, in the pubic region*, syntactic analysis: nominal, attested by Elders Group (8/20/75).

<**qwiliyéthel**>, ds //qʷil=əyə[=´=]yəθəl//, ANA /'*hair on the chin or jaw, beard, mustache*'/, ASM ['rare with Stó:lō people who had a tendency toward sparse facial hair'], lx <**=eyethel ~ =ó:ythel**> *on the chin, on the jaw*, probably <**=´=**> *derivational*, phonology: stress-shift, syntactic analysis: nominal, attested by Elders Group, AC, DM (12/4/64), other sources: ES /qʷíliyə̀θəl/ *beard,*

mustache, H-T <kweliétsEl> (macron over both e's) *hair of face*, contrast JH /sxʷqwí·ləs/ *hair on the face*.

<**sqwelqwélqsel**>, pln //s=C₁əC₂=qʷi[=Aə́=]l=qsəl//, ANA ['*hair in the nose*'], (<**s=**> *nominalizer*, R3= *plural*), possibly <**é-ablaut**> *diminutive plural*, lx <**=qsel**> *in the nose*, phonology: ablaut, reduplication, syntactic analysis: nominal, attested by Elders Group.

<**qwelqwélxel**>, pln //C₁əC₂=qʷi[=Aə́=]l=xʸəl//, ANAH /'*bushy hair on horses' legs (tufts like on Clydesdale breed), tufts of fur on horse's feet*'/, (<**R3=**> *plural*), possibly <**é-ablaut**> *diminutive plural*, lx <**=xel**> *on the leg, on the foot*, phonology: reduplication, ablaut, syntactic analysis: nominal, attested by NP (IHTTC 7/26/77)), Elders Group, contrast <**qwelqwélxel**> *fog appearing on the water, fine snow, small balls of snow on one's feet* from root <**qwélxel**> *get fog on the water*>.

<**sqwelíp**>, df //s=qʷíl=ə[=M2=]p//, FOOD ['*moss bread*'], EB /'*black tree lichen, black tree "moss"*'/, ['*Alectoria fremontii*'], ASM ['black tree lichen was gathered from conifers, esp. spruce trees, and cooked in underground steaming pits overnight till it formed a licorice-flavored loaf of "moss bread"; Madeline Charlie and Agnes Kelly recall that both the Thompsons and the Stó:lō fixed it the same way;'], Madeline's description: dig a pit several feet deep (depending on how much you have to cook), make fire in it to get hot rocks, when fire is out put green boughs on it then rice sacks (something study and not burnable) the moss and whatever vegetables you might want to cook at the same time, then more sacks, boughs, dirt and another fire, leaving a hole in the side, next pour water in the hole inside and let steam overnight, dig up next day;, EB saw the Thompsons also put in boughs, mat or sacking, moss and onions or whatever (they don't flavor each other), mat, boughs, then roll in hot rocks into holes in the sides maybe one or two feet across, pour water into holes and cover fast with boughs and boards; on another occasion EB described this process: dig a hole six feet deep, put 4 or 5 inches of boughs on the bottom then sqwelíp (lots), then boughs, then boards, then a little dirt, left overnight after pouring boiling water on it; in my experience it cooks way down so lots is required to make a loaf, also if not done properly it can be bitter, (<**s=**> *nominalizer*), probably root <**qwíl**> *body or face hair*, (**metathesis** *derivational*), lx <**=ep**> *in the dirt*, phonology: metathesis, syntactic analysis: nominal, attested by Elders Group (7/21/76), AK, EB, contrast <**Thompson /wiʔé/ with the same meaning**>.

<**qwiliyéthel**>, ANA /'*hair on the chin or jaw, beard, mustache*'/, *see* qwíl ~ qwel.

<**qwilṓws**>, ANA /'*hair anywhere on the body (arms, legs, chest, underarms, etc.)*'/, *see* qwíl ~ qwel.

<**qwíqw**>, probable root //qʷíqʷ//, meaning uncertain but perhaps imitative (onomatopoeic), or poss. //qwɛ́y-qw// *yellow on top of head*

<**sqwíqw**>, df //s(=)qʷíqʷ//, EZ /'*hoary marmot,* (also known as) *"mountain groundhog", "groundhog", or "whistler",* poss. also *yellow-bellied marmot*'/, ['*Marmota caligata cascadensis,* poss. also *Marmota flaviventris avara*'], (The hoary marmot is a member of the rodent family. Hoary marmots have grizzled gray underparts, which gives them their name \"hoary,\" with a light tan rump and lower back and black feet. Hoary marmots have black on their faces that shades to a whiter area in front between their eyes. Their underside is light colored and their tail has a light tan tip with brown on the top and dark brown below), possibly <**s=**> *nominalizer*, root meaning unknown unless <**qwi(y)**> from root <**qwá:y**> *yellow, green* perhaps after the *yellow-bellied marmot*, syntactic analysis: nominal, attested by Elders Group (3/1/72 tape, 2/5/75, 2/11/76, 9/1/76), AK and ME (11/21/72 tape), also <**sqwí:qw**>, //s(=)qʷí·qʷ//, attested by Elders Group (2/5/75).

<**qwíqweláts ~ qwíqwelà(:)c**>, LANG /'*gossip about someone, talk about someone behind his back*'/, *see* qwà:l.

<**qwiqwelóythetel**>, MUS ['*playing a musical instrument*'], *see* qwà:l.

<**qwíqwelh**>, df //qʷíqʷəɬ or qʷɛ[=Aí=]y=C_1əC_2=əɬ(p) or C_1í=qʷəɬ or qʷí[=C_1ə=]ɬ//, EB /'*mountain ash berries,* (perhaps also) *mountain ash tree*'/, ['*Sorbus sitchensis*'], ASM ['the brilliant orange-red berries are sour but were mixed one-third with two-thirds blueberries or blue huckleberries, smashed and eated with sugar, the berries were bigger and sweeter at high elevations; they were helpful especially to make the blueberries or huckleberries go further'], possibly root <**qwíqwi**> *copper* or possibly root <**qwá:y**> *yellow, green* (a Basic Color Term which includes orange), possibly <**=elhp**> *tree* but loss of final p would be unexplained/unlikely, possible but also unlikely are R4= *diminutive* possibly <-**R1-**> *continuative or resultative or derivational*, phonology: possible ablaut, possible reduplication, syntactic analysis: nominal, attested by Elders Group (7/23/75, 9/3/75).

<**Qwíqwexem**>, PLN ['*Lake Errock*'], *see* qwéx̱em.

<**qwíqwi ~ qwíyqwiy**>, df //qʷíy=C_1əC_2 or qʷɛ[=Aí=]y=C_1əC_2 or qʷɛ[=Aə́=]y=C_1əC_2//, LAND ['*copper*'], probably root <**qwá:y**> *yellow, green*, possibly <**é-ablaut** or **í-ablaut**> *derivational,* probably <**=R2**> *characteristic*, phonology: reduplication, ablaut, syntactic analysis: nominal, attested by JS (Elders Group 3/26/80), AK and SP (Elders Group 9/21/77), Elders Group (5/28/75, 7/23/75), Elder's comment: "SP says it may mean *brass* too, AK thinks there's another word for brass", Salish cognate: Squamish /qʷə́y-qʷi ~ sqʷaʔíls/ *copper* K67:361, also <**sqw'él**>, //s(=)**q**'ʷə́l//, attested by Elders Group (3/72), (semological comment: elsewhere translated as *metal from mines that resembles gold*), Salish cognate: Musqueam /s**q**'ʷə́l/ *copper* quoted in K67:361.

<**qwiqwóyáls ~ qwiqwóyéls ~ qwiqwòyàls**>, EB /'*orange (fruit), especially mandarin orange (the fruit),* also *domestic orange, (*also *orange (color))*'/, *see* qwá:y.

<**qwís**>, probably bound root //qʷís//, *narrow*

<**qweqwís**>, df //C_1ə=qʷís//, DESC ['*(be) narrow*'], possibly <**R5=**> probably aspectual, meaning uncertain, phonology: reduplication, syntactic analysis: adjective/adjectival verb, attested by SJ (Deming 4/10/80), AC, JL, Salish cognate: Squamish /ʔəqʷís-us/ *narrow-faced* W73:183, K69:93, Lushootseed /qʷəqʷqʷíʔs/ *thin, slender* H76:415, also <**qwqwís**>, //C_1ə=qʷís//, [qʷqʷís], attested by SJ (Deming 4/10/80), also <**sqwqwís**>, //s=C_1ə=qʷís//, attested by MV (Deming 4/10/80), example: <**we'ól qweqwís**>, //wə=ʔál C_1ə=qʷís//, /'*too narrow*'/, attested by AC, <**ólewe qweqwís**>, //ʔálə=wə C_1ə=qʷís//, /'*too narrow*'/, attested by JL (7/13/79).

<**qwítx̱**>, df //qʷít=x̣//, EB /'*Pacific dogwood flower, flowering dogwood flower*'/, ['*Cornus nuttallii*'], root meaning unknown, probably <**=x̱**> *distributive*, syntactic analysis: nominal.

<**qwítx̱elhp**>, ds //qʷít=x̣=əɬp//, EB /'*Pacific dogwood, flowering dogwood*'/, ['*Cornus nuttallii*'], lx <**=elhp**> *tree*, syntactic analysis: nominal, attested by AC, Elders Group, other sources: JH /kʷítx̣ə̀ɬp/ *dogwood.*

<**qwíth'** or **qwéth'**>, df //qwɛ́y=θ'// *yellow + small portion*, LT ['*a yellowish glow at night given off by old birch and alder*'], EB, comment: mentioned as root of place name Qwíth'qweth'iyósem, an alternative name for *Hill's Bar*; since there is no CíC= reduplication it seems likely that the root is qwíth' with =R2 *characteristic* suffix, possibly <**é-ablaut**> *durative or derivational*, syntactic analysis: intransitive verb, attested by Elders Group member (on or soon after 9/13/77).

<**Qwíth'qweth'iyósem**>, df //qʷíθ'=C_1əC_2=iyás=əm//, PLN ['*Hill's Bar*'], root <**qwíth'**> *yellowish glow at night from old birch or alder trees*, (<**=R2**> *characteristic*, <**=iyós**> *around in a circle*, <**=em**> *place that has, place to get*), Elder's comment: "named from the fact that the old alder here glowed in the past", (semological comment: an alternate name for Hill's Bar), phonology: reduplication, syntactic analysis: nominal, attested by Elders Group member (on or after 9/18/77),

source: noted on place names card of Qw'álets *Fraser River where it goes over Hill's Bar on the CN (east) side of the river*, place names reference file #147.

<**qwiwílh**>, df //q^{w}iwíɬ//, EZ ['*wood duck (makes nest in tree)*'], ['*Aix sponsa*'], root meaning unknown, syntactic analysis: nominal, attested by Lawrence James (Elders Group 9/8/76), Elders Group (2/11/76), also /'*duck that builds nest on stumps, wood-duck?*'/, attested by Elders Group (2/11/76).

<**qwíx̱w**>, probably root //q^{w}íx̣^{w} or q^{w}íy=x̣^{w}//, HUNT /'*to miss a shot (an arrow, spear or gun)*'/, possibly root <**qwíy**> *shake, move*, possibly <**=x̱w**> *around, round*, syntactic analysis: intransitive verb, attested by EB.

<**qwíx̱wet**>, pcs //q^{w}íx̣^{w}=əT or q^{w}íy=x̣^{w}=əT//, HUNT /'*miss s-th (in shooting at it with arrow, spear or gun)*'/, (<**=et**> *purposeful control transitivizer*), syntactic analysis: transitive verb, attested by EB; found in <**qwíx̱wetes.**>, //q^{w}íy=x̣^{w}=əT-əs//, /'*He missed it.*'/, attested by EB.

<**qwiy**> or <**qwey**> or perhaps <**qwá:y**>, bound root //q^{w}iy or q^{w}əy// or possibly //q^{w}ɛ́·y// *shake, move around*, (semological comment: there may be some confusion as to aspect throughout with this root, some speakers vary in translating qwá:y as *continuative* with qwíy as *non-continuative*), Salish cognate: Saanich dial. of N. Straits /q^{w}íyəx̣əŋ tθə téŋəx^w/ *earthquake* B74a:2, Samish dial. of N. Straits /q^w**ə́**y'əx̣əŋ' tə téŋəx^w/ *earthquake, the earth is shaking* and /q^{w}ə́yəx̣sət tə sx^{w}əx^w**á**ʔas/ *have a thunderstorm, thunderbird is shaking himself* G86:63.

<**qwá:yx̱(e)t**>, pcs //q^{w}ɛ́·y=x̣=(ə)T//, TVMO ['*(shake s-th)*'], lx <**=x̱**> *distributive*, (<**=t ~ =et**> *purposeful control transitivizer*), syntactic analysis: transitive verb, attested by Deming, example: <**qwá:yx̱tem te téméxw.**>, //q^{w}ɛ́·y=x̣=T-əm//, LAND, /'*There's an earthquake.*, (The earth shook.)'/, attested by Deming.

<**qwá:yx̱thet**>, pcrs //q^{w}ɛ́·y=x̣=T-ət//, TVMO /'*it shook (shakes itself), shaking, bobbing around*'/, (<**-et**> *reflexive*), (semological comment: the *continuative* translations here may be errors or may be taking qwá:y as a continuative form of qwíy with á:-ablaut), syntactic analysis: intransitive verb, attested by EB, AC; found in <**qwá:yx̱thetes**>, //q^{w}i[-Aɛ́·-]y=x̣=T-ət-əs//, /'*it was bobbing around*'/, usage: story of the flood, syntactic comment: -es *third person subject* cannot follow reflexive =thet so the -es must here be *third person subjunctive subject* or -s *third person subordinate subject*, attested by AC, also /'*he is shaking it*'/, attested by EB, example: <**qetl'osésu qwá:ythetes te sléxwelhs slát qas te swàyèl.**>, //qə=ƛ'a-s-əs-əw q^{w}i[-Aɛ́·-]y=T-ət-s tə slə́x^{w}əɬ-s s=lɛ̂t qɛs tə s=wɛ̀yə̀l//, /'*And so the canoe was just bobbing around night and day.*'/, usage: story of the flood, attested by AC (12/7/71), <**qwá:yx̱thetes te sléxwelh te swíyeqe.**>, //q^{w}i[-Aɛ́·-]y=x̣=T-ət-əs tə slə́x^{w}əɬ tə s=wí(yə)q=ə//, /'*A man is shaking the canoe.*'/, syntactic comment: =thet *reflexive* is surely an error for =t here, attested by EB.

<**qwíyx̱(e)t**>, cts //q^{w}ɛ[-Aí-]y=x̣=(ə)T//, TVMO ['*shaking s-th*'], (<**í-ablaut**> *continuative*), lx <**=x̱**> *distributive*, (<**=t ~ =et**> *purposeful control transitivizer*), syntactic analysis: transitive verb; found in <**qwíyx̱tes.**>, //q^{w}ɛ[-Aí-]y=x̣=T-əs//, /'*(He's shaking them.)*'/, example: <**qwíyx̱tes te lhéptels te shxwexwó:s.**>, //q^{w}ɛ[-Aí-]y=x̣=T-əs tə ɬə́p=təl-s tə s=x^{w}əx^w(=)**á**·s//, /'*The Thunderbird is shaking his eyelashes.*'/, (morphosememic development: //'It's lightning., There's lightning.'//), attested by IHTTC, <**qwíyx̱tes te tl'qá:ls te shxwexwó:s.**>, //q^{w}ɛ[-Aí-]y=x̣=T-əs tə ƛ'q=ɛ́·l-s tə s=x^{w}əx^w(=)**á**·s.//, /'*The Thunderbird is shaking his wings.*'/, (morphosememic development: //'There's thunder., It's thundering.'//), attested by IHTTC.

<**qwíyx̱thet**>, pcrs //q^{w}ɛ[-Aí-]y=x̣=T-ət//, cts, TVMO /'*(shaking, quaking, moving oneself)*'/, lx <**=x̱**> *distributive*, (<**=t**> *purposeful control transitivizer*), (<**-et**> *reflexive*), syntactic analysis: intransitive verb, attested by AC, BJ (12/5/64), example: <**qwíyx̱thet te téméxw.**>, //q^{w}ɛ[-Aí-

]y=x̣=T-ət tə tə́məxʷ.//, LAND, /'*There's an earthquake.*'/, literally /'The earth shook.'/, attested by BJ (12/5/64), others.

<**qwayx̱élechem**>, mdls //qʷɛy=x̣=ə́ləc=əm//, ANAH ['*swivel one's hips (as in the Hawaiian hula for ex.) (shake one's bottom around)*'], literally /'(shake one's bottom around)'/, lx <**=x̱**> *distributive*, lx <**=elets**> *on the bottom/rump*, (<**=em**> *middle voice*), phonology: stress-shift to suffix, syntactic analysis: intransitive verb, attested by Elders Group (4/2/75).

<**qwáylhechàls**>, sas //qʷɛ́y=ɬcə=M1=ɛ̀ls//, FOOD /'*to stir (a liquid), stir (mixing ingredients)*'/, WATR, literally /'move liquid in structured activity'/, lx <**=lhche**> *unclear liquid*, (metathesis *derivational*, <=àls ~ =á:ls> *structured activity non-continuative*), phonology: metathesis type 1, syntactic analysis: intransitive verb, attested by Elders Group (4/2/75), MH (Deming 1/4/79)(prompted).

<**shxwqwáylhechàls**>, dnom //sxʷ=qʷɛ́y=ɬcə=M1=ɛ̀ls//, FOOD ['*long-handled stirring spoon*'], HHG, (<**shxw=**> *something to, something that, nominalizer*), phonology: metathesis, syntactic analysis: nominal, attested by Elders Group (4/2/75).

<**qwíyx̱(e)t**>, TVMO ['*(shaking s-th)*'], *see* qwá:y.

<**qwíyx̱thet**>, TVMO /'*(shaking, quaking, moving oneself)*'/, *see* qwá:y.

<**qwló**> or <qwol>, possible root //qʷlá or qʷál//, root meaning uncertain

<**sqwló**>, df //s=qʷlá or s=qʷál=M1//, ANAA /'*seal fat, seal blubber*'/, probably <**s=**> *nominalizer*, root meaning unknown unless related to qwó:ls *boil* by metathesis and esp. if qwó:ls consists of qwó:=l=ls so that the =(e)ls can be segmented, syntactic analysis: nominal, attested by EL (Chehalis boat trip 6/27/78), also <**skwló**>, //s=kʷlá//, attested by EL (3/1/78 tape).

<**Skwló ~ Sqwló**>, dnom //s=kʷlá ~ s=qʷlá//, PLN /'*Seal Fat Rock on Harrison River just upriver from Th'éqwela (place by Morris Lake where Indian people used to play Indian badminton), this rock has what resembles seal fat all around it*'/, photo taken on place names trip, phonology: zero derivation, syntactic analysis: nominal, attested by EL (3/1/78, 6/27/78),

<**=qwlha**>, da //*(emphatic admiration), wonderfully, how (emphatically)., really.*//, syntactic analysis: derivational suffix; found in <**éyqwlha.**>, //ʔɛ́y=qʷɬɛ//, /'*beautiful.*'/, syntactic analysis: adjective/adjectival verb, interjection, attested by EB (1/19/76), <**qélqwlha.**>, //qə́l=qʷɬɛ//, /'*beautiful.*'/, root <**qél**> *bad*, literally perhaps /'wonderfully bad'/, comment: note that éy=qwlha has the same meaning but with the root éy *good*, syntactic analysis: adjective/adjectival verb, attested by EB, example: <**qélqwlha te stl'píwels.**>, //qə́l=qʷɬɛ tə s=ƛ̓əp=íwəl-s//, /'*His shirt is beautiful.*'/, attested by EB; found in <**yú:wqwlha.**>, //yə́w·=qʷɬɛ//, /'*how beautiful, be really beautiful*'/, syntactic analysis: interjection, attested by EB (5/18/76), contrast <**yú:w**> *(said when praising something beautiful)* and <**yó:wthet**> *bragging*, example: <**yú:wqwlha ta' qwlhíxel.**>, //yə́w·=qʷɬɛ t-ɛʔ qʷəɬ=ə[=´=]y=xʸəl//, /'*You've got really beautiful shoes.*'/, literally /'is really beautiful your shoe'/, attested by EB.

<**qwlhá:y**>, EB ['*driftwood*'], *see* qwélh.

<**qwlhí:xel ~ qwelhí:xel**>, CLO ['*shoe*'], *see* qwélh.

<**Qwolíwiya** or **X̱wolíwiya**>, df //qʷalíw=iyɛ orx̣ʷalíw=iyɛ//, PLN /'*village at east end of Little Mountain on Hope Slough, upper end of Mount Shannon [DM]*'/, Elder's comment: "could be from Qwolíwiya *Seagull* in a story", (semological comment: another version has it as a transformed shaman on Hope Slough), probably <**=iya**> *affectionate diminutive, esp. in personal names*, syntactic analysis: nominal, attested by IHTTC, other sources: Wells 1965 (lst ed.):23 (from DM), source: place names reference file #243.

<**qwó:ls**>, cts //qʷ**á·**=əls//, sas, FOOD /'*boiling, making boil, (cooking in boiling liquid)*'/, WATR, comment: root retains old Central Salish labialization (from PCS */qʷúʔ/ *water*) which elsewhere was lost in Upriver Halkomelem when *u > a (as in Upriver Halkomelem /**qá·**/ *water*), from this it is also clear that the continuative form here preserves the root vowel and it is the non-continuative that is ablauted or inflected, (<**=els**> *structured activity continuative*), phonology: vowel merger, syntactic analysis: nominal, attested by AC, DM (12/4/64), EL, example: <**le qwó:ls.**>, //lə qʷ**á·**=əls//, /'*It's boiling.*'/, attested by AC.

<**Qwó:ls**>, dnom //qʷ**á·**=əls//, PLN ['*Harrison Hot Springs*'], literally /'boiling'/, ASM ['Indian people used to sometimes cook food in the hot springs there'], phonology: zero derivation, syntactic analysis: nominal, attested by EL (3/1/78), DM (12/4/64), AC, other sources: Wells 1965 (1st ed.):15, source: place names file reference #167.

<**sqwóls**>, stvi //s=qʷ**á·**=əls//, WATR ['*be boiled*'], (<**s=**> *stative*), (<**=els**> *structured activity continuative*), phonology: vowel merger, syntactic analysis: adjective/adjectival verb, attested by EB, example: <**sqwóls qó:**>, //s=qʷ**á·**=əls qá·//, /'*boiled water*'/, attested by EB.

<**slós (s)qwóls sqá:wth**>, EB, FOOD *French fries* (lit. fat + boiled + potato), (attested by RG,EH 6/16/98 to SN, edited by BG with RG,EH 6/26/00)

<**sh(xw)qwó:ls**>, dnom //sxʷ=qwá·=əls//, FOOD ['*something to boil in*'], HHG, (<**sxw=**> *something to*), phonology: vowel merger, syntactic analysis: nominal, attested by AC (10/23/71).

<**qwéls**>, (//**qʷa[-Aə́-]=ɛls**//), sas, FOOD /'*to boil, make boil*'/, WATR, (<**é-ablaut**> *non-continuative*), phonology: vowel merger, ablaut, syntactic analysis: intransitive verb, comment: metathesis type one and rare ablauts like this are the only non-continuative inflections found so far, usually the base forms are non-continuative, attested by DM, CT (6/8/76), example: <**qwéls te sth'óqwi**>, //qʷa[-Aə́-]=ɛls tə s=**θ'**áqʷi//, /'*(make/boil) salmon stew, (make/boil) fish stew*'/, attested by CT.

<**sqwéls**>, dnom //s=qʷa[=Aə́=]=ɛls//, FOOD /'*(the) cooking, (soup, stew [DM, CT])*'/, HUNT, FSH, HARV, (<**s=**> *nominalizer*), (<**é-ablaut**> *non-continuative*), phonology: ablaut, vowel merger, syntactic analysis: nominal, attested by AC, also /'*soup, stew*'/, attested by DM (12/4/64), CT (6/8/76), example: <**lulh hóy te sqwéls.**>, //lə=uɬ háy tə s=qʷa[=Aə́=]=ɛls//, /'*It has finished cooking.*'/, attested by AC.

<**qwélst**>, pcs //qʷa[-Aə́-]=ɛls=T//, FOOD ['*boil s-th*'], HUNT, FSH, HARV, (<**=t**> *purposeful control transitivizer*), phonology: ablaut, vowel merger, syntactic analysis: transitive verb, attested by AC, EB, MH, example: <**qwélstes te qó:.**>, //qʷa[-Aə́-]=ɛls=T-əs tə **qá·**//, /'*He boiled the water.*'/, attested by EB, <**qwélst te sqá:wth**>, //qʷa[-Aə́-]=ɛls=T tə s=q**ɛ́**·w=**θ**//, /'*boil the potatoes*'/, attested by MH (Deming 1/4/79), <**qwélst te skw'ő:lmexw**>, //qʷa[-Aə́-]=ɛls=T tə sk'ʷó·lməxʷ//, /'*boil the blackberries*'/, attested by AC.

<**qwelselhtsthó:x**>, bens, //qʷa[-Aə́-]=ɛls=əɬc=T-**á**·xʸ//, FOOD ['*boil it for me*'], (<**=elhts**> *benefactive*, <**=t**> *purposeful control transitivizer*), syntactic analysis: transitive verb, attested by Elders Group (3/24/76); found in <**qwelslhthó:xchexw.**>, //qʷa[-Aə́-]=ɛls=əɬc=T-**á**·xʸ-c-əxʷ//, /'*Boil it for me.*'/, attested by EB (3/1/76).

<**qwó:lst**>, pcs //qʷ**á·**=əls=T//, cts, FOOD ['*boiling s-th*'], HUNT, HARV, FSH, (<**=t**> *purposeful control transitivizer*), phonology: vowel merger, syntactic analysis: transitive verb, attested by AC, example: <**tsel héqwlexw te s'álhtels; le qwó:lstes.**>, //c-əl hə́qʷ=l-əxʷ tə s=ʔɛ́ɬ=təl-s; lə qʷ**á·**=əls=T-əs//, /'*I smelled her food boiling.*'/, literally /'I smelled her food; she was boiling it.'/, attested by AC.

<**Qwó:ls**>, PLN ['*Harrison Hot Springs*'], *see* qwó:ls.

<**qwó:lst**>, FOOD ['*boiling s-th*'], *see* qwó:ls.

<**qwó:ltel**>, LANG /'*argue, quarrel*'/, *see* qwà:l.

<**qwó:m ~ qwóm ~ qwem**>, bound root //q^{w}**á**·m ~ q^{w}ám ~ q^{w}əm *lump*//.

<**sqwómetsel**>, stvi //s=q^{w}ám=əcəl//, ABDF ['*get hunchbacked*'], (<**s=**> *stative*), lx <**=etsel**> *on the back*, syntactic analysis: adjective/adjectival verb, attested by EF, MC, SJ (all Deming 4/26/79), example: <**sqwómetselchexwcha kw'e'asu ewás ó:metexw (thékw', sthethá:kw').**>, //s=q^{w}ám=əcəl-c-əx^{w}-cɛ **k'**^{w}ə-ʔɛ-s-əw ʔəwə-ɛ́s ʔ**á**·mət-əx^{w} (s=C$_1$ə=θə[=Aɛ́·=]**k'**^{w}, **θ**ə́**k'**^{w})//, /'*You'll get hunchbacked if you don't sit up straight.*'/, attested by (MC and SJ, vs. EF resp. gave the versions in parentheses).

<**skwómàtsel (sqwómàtsel)**>, dnom //s=q^{w}ám=ɛ̀cəl//, ABDF /'*hunchback, humpback, lump on the back*'/, (<**s=**> *nominalizer*), lx <**=àtsel ~ =etsel**> *on the back*, phonology: kw is probably an error for qw, syntactic analysis: nominal, attested by EB.

<**qwó:mth'**>, df //q^{w}**á**·m=**θ**'//, ANA ['*lump*'], LAND, lx <**=th'**> *small portion*, syntactic analysis: noun, nominal, attested by SP and AK (7/13/75).

<**qwemqwó:mth'**>, pln //C$_1$əC$_2$=q^{w}**á**·m=**θ**'//, LAND ['*lots of anthills*'], EZ, literally /'many lumps'/, (<**R3=**> *plural*), lx <**=th'**> meaning uncertain, phonology: reduplication, syntactic analysis: nominal, attested by SP and AK (7/13/75).

<**Qwemth'í:les**>, ds //q^{w}am=**θ**'=í·ləs//, PLN /'*Mount Ogilvie or a round peak or bluff on Mt. Ogilvie where mountain goats live, the mountain or peak or bluff resembles big breasts*'/, Elder's comment: "the name means *big breasts*", literally /'lump on the chest'/, lx <**=í:les**> *on the chest*, syntactic analysis: nominal, attested by SP and AK (7/13/75), Elders Group (7/13/77), source: place names reference file #53.

<**sqwemqwó:mx̱w**>, df //s=C$_1$əC$_2$=q^{w}**á**·m=x̣^{w}//, pln, ANA ['*lots of lumps (any size)*'], LAND, (<**s=**> *nominalizer*, R3= *plural*), lx <**=x̱w**> *round, around*, phonology: reduplication, syntactic analysis: nominal, attested by EB (1/12/76).

<**Sqwemqwómx̱w**>, dnom //s=C$_1$əC$_2$=q^{w}**á**·m=x̣^{w}//, PLN ['*a lumpy mountain back of Seabird Island*'], literally /'lots of lumps'/, (<**s=**> *nominalizer*, R3= *plural*), lx <**=x̱w**> *round, around*, phonology: reduplication, syntactic analysis: nominal, attested by AK (8/30/77), source: place names reference file #251.

<**qwóméx̱weth'**>, df //q^{w}ám=ə́x̣^{w}(=)ə**θ**'//, LAND ['*lumpy clay*'], possibly <**=éx̱w (? ~ =x̱w)**> *round, around*, possibly <**=eth' (~ =th'**> *small portion*), root meaning uncertain, or <=**é**x̱weth'> meaning uncertain, syntactic analysis: nominal, attested by IHTTC (8/15/77).

<**Qwoméx̱weth'**>, df //q^{w}am=ə́x̣^{w}(=)ə**θ**'//, PLN /'*a place just past the west end of Seabird Island, towards Agassiz, AK's grandfather only translated it as Hamersley's (see Hamersley's hopyards), it was located at the west end of Seabird Island i.e. property between Dan Thomas's and Uncle Dave Charles's places, across from* ***Sqémelets*** *[*Elders on Seabird Is. trip 6/20/78])'/, literally /'lumpy clay'/, phonology: zero derivation, syntactic analysis: nominal, attested by AK and Lizzie Johnson (History tape 34, 4/7/78), AK (8/30/77), Elders on Seabird Is. trip 6/20/78 (EB, NP, AD, AK prob.), source: place names reference file #255.

<**S'áqwemx̱weth'**>, df //s=ʔɛ́=q^{w}am=x̣^{w}=ə**θ**'//, PLN ['*name of place with clay at the edge of the river at some location*'], (<**s=**> *nominalizer*), possibly <**'á=**> meaning uncertain, comment: this may be a more correct name for place name #255 than Qwoméx̱weth' which is not modified from the word for *lumpy ground*, syntactic analysis: nominal, attested by IHTTC place names at Seabird Island from Lizzie Johnson (8/15/77), source: place names reference file #199.

<**qwémx̱wtses**>, ds //q^{w}a[=Aə́=]m=x̣^{w}=cəs//, ANAH /'*wrist, wrist bone (on outer side of wrist, little finger side, lump of wrist)*'/, (<**é-ablaut**> *derivational*), lx <**=x̱w**> *round, around*, lx <**=tses**> *on the*

hand, phonology: ablaut, syntactic analysis: nominal, attested by Elders Group (7/27/75), other sources: ES /qʷə́mx̣ʷcəs/ (MsCw /qʷə́mʔx̣ʷcəs/) *wrist*.

<**qwemqwémx̲wtses**>, pln //C_1əC_2=qʷa[=Aə́=]m=x̣ʷ=cəs//, ANAH ['*knuckles (all the joints of the hand and fingers)*'], (<**R3=**> *plural*), phonology: reduplication, ablaut, syntactic analysis: nominal, dialects: *Cheh.*, attested by Elders Group (7/27/75).

<**qwémx̲wxel**>, ds //qʷa[=Aə́=]m=x̣ʷ=xʸəl//, ANAH ['*ankle (the lump part)*'], (<**é-ablaut**> *derivational*), lx <**=x̲w**> *round, around*, lx <**=xel**> *on the leg/foot*, phonology: ablaut, syntactic analysis: nominal, attested by Elders Group (7/27/75), other sources: ES /qʷə́mx̣ʷxʸəl/ (Ms /qʷə́mʔx̣ʷxʸən/, Cw /qʷə́mʔx̣ʷšən/) *ankle*, Salish cognate: Squamish /qʷə́mʔx̣ʷ-šn/ *ankle* W73:6, K67:360, Lushootseed /qʷə́px̣ʷ(šəd)/ *ankle* H76:358.

<**qwemqwémx̲wxel**>, pln //C_1əC_2=qʷa[=Aə́=]m=x̣ʷ=xʸəl//, ANAH ['*all the joints of the foot and toes*'], (<**R3=**> *plural*), phonology: reduplication, ablaut, syntactic analysis: nominal, dialects: *Cheh.*, attested by Elders Group (7/27/75).

<**sqwemqwemóx̲w**>, plv //s=C_1əC_2=qʷám=ə[=M2=]x̣ʷ//, stvi, ABFC ['*all doubled up*'], (<**s=**> *stative*, R3= *plural*), (metathesis *derivational*), phonology: reduplication, metathesis, syntactic analysis: adjective/adjectival verb, attested by IHTTC (7/13/77), comment: this form is probably in error for sqw'emqw'emóx̲w, but the latter form and its relatives below could possibly be derived from the root above by derivational glottalization (though this doesn't seem likely), see main dialect form <**sqw'emqw'emóx̲w**> *all doubled up*, also <**sqw'emóx̲w**> *doubled up in bed on side with knees drawn up*, <**sqw'eqw'emóx̲w**> *U-shaped or horseshoe-shaped knife for scraping out canoe*, <**sqw'ómx̲wes**> *rolled up in a ball (of twine,yarn, etc.)*, and <**qw'ómx̲west**> *roll s-th up in a ball*.

<**qwomáléqep**>, SM ['*have a mossy smell*'], *see* qwà:m ~ qwám.

<**qwóméx̲weth'**>, LAND ['*lumpy clay*'], *see* qwó:m ~ qwóm ~ qwem.

<**Qwoméx̲weth'**>, PLN /'*a place just past the west end of Seabird Island, towards Agassiz, AK's grandfather only translated it as Hamersley's (see Hamersley's hopyards), it was located at the west end of Seabird Island i.e. property between Dan Thomas's and Uncle Dave Charles's places, across from Sqémelets* [Elders on Seabird Is. trip 6/20/78])'/, *see* qwó:m ~ qwóm ~ qwem.

<**Qwómqwemels**>, PLN ['*place of moss-covered stones at upper end of Hope Slough not far from Harry Edwards' home (as of 1964)*'], *see* qwà:m ~ qwám.

<**qwó:mth'**>, ANA ['*lump*'], *see* qwó:m ~ qwóm ~ qwem.

<**qwó:pelhp**>, df //qʷ**á·**p=əɬp//, EB ['*devil's club plant*'], ['*Oplopanax horridum*'], ASM ['has many large infectious thorn all along stems, branches, and under leaves'], MED ['medicine for arthritis and protection from spirits, esp. charred stems are burnt and mixed with grease to make face paint for spirit-dancers, by one account this black paint is not used for dancers who have powers of a ritualist, shaman, or person who has given themselves up voluntarily to seek power, those dancers normally have powers that require red paint, or long ago even white paint'], root meaning unknown, lx <**=elhp**> *tree, plant*, syntactic analysis: nominal, attested by Elders Group, other sources: ES /qʷ**á·**pəɬp/ *devil's club*, also <**qwópelhp**>, //qʷáp=əɬp//, attested by AD (7/23/79).

<**qwóqwel**>, LANG /'*talking, speaking*'/, *see* qwà:l.

<**qwóqwelem**>, df //qʷá[=C_1ə=](=)l=əm//, SM /'*smelling damp, rank*'/, WATR, possibly root <**qwó**> *water* with survival of labialization (from PCS */qʷúʔ/ *water*) (insulated from delabialization by suffix unlike Upriver Halkomelem <**qó:**> /qá·/ which is the free form for *water*), possibly <**=R1=**> *continuative or resultative*, possibly <**=el**> *go, come, get, become*, possibly <**=em**> *middle voice or*

intransitivizer, have, get, phonology: reduplication, vowel merger, syntactic analysis: intransitive verb, attested by Elders Group (5/25/77).

<**qwoqwelíwel**>, EFAM /'*thinking of something, (thinking)*'/, *see* qwà:l.

<**qwóqwelmet**>, LANG ['*scolding s-o*'], *see* qwà:l.

<**qwóqwets'et**>, ABFC ['*belching*'], *see* qwáts'et.

<**qwóqweyel ~ qwóqwiyel**>, LT /'*getting yellow, turning yellow, turning green*'/, *see* qwá:y.

<**qwósem**>, df //q^{w}ɛ=ás=əm//, mdls, EB ['*just coming out of the earth (of plants for ex.)*'], probably root <**qwá**> *get a hole*, possibly <**=ós**> *on the face, (*also *flower of a plant)*, (<**=em**> *middle voice*), phonology: vowel merger, syntactic analysis: intransitive verb, attested by IHTTC, example: <**qwósem tel spí:ls.**>, //q^{w}ɛ=ás=əm t-əl s=pí·l=ls//, /'*My plants are just coming out (of the earth).*'/, attested by IHTTC.

<**qwó:tl'**> or <**qwá:tl'**>, probable bound root //q^w**á·**ƛ'// or //q^w**ɛ́·**ƛ'//, meaning uncertain

<**sqwó:qwetl'í:wèl**>, df //s=q^w**á·**[=C$_1$ə=]ƛ'=í·wəl// or //s=q^w**ɛ́·**[=Aa:C$_1$ə=]ƛ'=í·wəl//, EZ ['*tapeworm*'], ['order *Cestoidea*, esp. *Taenia solium*'], (<**s=**> *nominalizer*), root meaning unknown, possibly <**=R1=**> and automatic root <**a**>→ <**o**> before the infix *continuative or resultative*, lx <**=í:wel**> *on the insides, in the gut/rectum*, phonology: reduplication, syntactic analysis: nominal, attested by JL and NP and Deming elders (7/19/79) said this is probably right when this form was pronounced from JH, other sources: JH /sq^w**á·**q^{w}əƛ'í·wə̀l/ *tapeworm*.

<**qwóx̱wlexw**>, ncs //q^{w}áx̣^{w}=l-əx^w//, SOC ['*offend s-o*'], root meaning unknown, (<**=l**> *non-control transitivizer, accidentally, manage to, happen to do to s-o*), (<**-exw**> *third person object*), syntactic analysis: transitive verb, attested by Elders Group (4/6/77).

<**qwox̱wlómét**>, ncrs //q^{w}áx̣^{w}=l-ámə́t//, SOC /'*get offended, get irritated*'/, root meaning unknown, (<**=l**> *non-control transitivizer*), (<**-ómét**> *reflexive*), syntactic analysis: intransitive verb, attested by Elders Group (4/6/77).

<**qwox̱wlómét**>, SOC /'*get offended, get irritated*'/, *see* qwóx̱wlexw.

<**qwóyel**>, LT /'*turning yellow, getting yellow, turning green*'/, *see* qwá:y.

<**qwó:yxw**> or <**qwó:y**>, bound root or stem //q^w**á·**y(=)x^w//, meaning unknown.

<**sqwó:yxw**>, df //s=q^w**á·**yx^w//, EZ /'*late fall sockeye salmon (last run on Harrison River and Chehalis River, kind of red)*'/, ['*Oncorhynchus nerka*'], (<**s=**> *nominalizer*), root meaning unknown, syntactic analysis: nominal, attested by EL (9/27/77), also <**qwechíwiya**>, //q^{w}əc(=)íw=iyɛ//, attested by EL (9/27/77).

<**qwōhóls**> (or perhaps) <**qwehóls**>, DESC /'*sticking out through a hole (like a toe out of a sock, knee out of a hole in pants, a nail driven clear through the other side of a board), come out into the open*'/, *see* qwá.

<**Qwōhòls**>, PLN probably /'*Mahood Creek and Johnson Slough,* (possibly) *Wahleach River or Hicks Creek (creek at bridge on east end of Seabird Island [AK])*'/, *see* qwá.

<**qwṓlqwel**>, LANG /'*talking together, all talking together, (telling news [EB], warning (birds and other creatures do this) [Elders Group])*'/, *see* qwà:l.

<**qwṓlqwel qweló:ythetel**>, LANG ['*(maybe usable for) radio*'], *see* qwà:l.

<**qwṓ:lqweltel**>, LANG /'*talking together, all talking at once (of a lot of people)*'/, *see* qwà:l.

<**qwőqw** or **qwéqw**>, possibly bound root //q^{w}óq^w or q^{w}əq^w// *white*

<**sqwőqweqw**>, df //s=q^{w}óq^w=əq^w//, EZ /'*snowy owl, white owl*'/, ['*Nyctea scandiaca*'], (<**s=**> *nominalizer*), possibly root <**qwőqw** or **qwéqw**> *white*, comment: poss. survival of same root as in Lushootseed root /q^w**ə́q'**^{w} / *white*, lx <**=eqw**> *on top of the head, hair*, syntactic analysis: nominal, attested by BJ (12/5/64, old p.314 in transcript), Elders Group (3/1/72), EL (9/15/78), also <**sqwéqweqw**>, //s=q^{w}ə́q^w=əq^w//, attested by Elders Group (6/4/75, 2/18/76), also <**skwőkweqw**>, //s=k^{w}ók^w=əq^w//, attested by Elders Group (9/8/76), comment: kw prob. error for qw.

<**qwsá:wiyel**>, FSH ['*set a net and drift with it*'], *see* qwés.

<**qwsá:yel**>, FSH /'*throw a net into water (to drift, not to set), throw a net out, (gill net [TG])*'/, *see* qwés.

<**qwsét**>, WATR /'*launch s-th/s-o into the water, push s-o/s-th into the water, throw it in the water*'/, *see* qwés.

<**qwsó:les**>, df //q^{w}s(=)**á·**ləs//, HHG ['*long china platter*'], root meaning unknown, possibly <**=ó:les**> *on the eyes*, Elder's comment: "TG's grandfather used this word", syntactic analysis: nominal, attested by TG (Elders Group 1/23/80).

QW'

<**=qw' ~ =eqw'**>, da //=q'ʷ ~ =əq'ʷ//, SH (perhaps) ['*around in circles*'], syntactic analysis: lexical suffix, also <**=eqw'**>, //=əq'ʷ//; found in <**sqéymeqw'**>, //s=qím=əq'ʷ//, /'*octopus*'/, <**xweth'éqw'tses**>, //xʷɛθ'=ə[=´=]q'ʷ=cəs//, /'*sprained wrist*'/, <**yet'qw'íwsem**>, //yi[=Aə́=]t'=q'ʷ=íws=əm//, /'*lather one's body*'/, literally /'melt around in circles on one's body'/, root <**yít'**> as in <**yít'em**> *melt, thaw*, <**yélqw't**>, //yə́l=q'ʷ=T//, /'*upset s-th (like a bed), mess s-th up*'/, root <**yél**> *turn*, <**yó:lqw'**>, //yə[=Aá·=]l=q'ʷ//, /'*make a mess, mess up*'/.

<**Qw'áléts**>, possibly root //q'ʷɛ́lə́c or q'ʷə[=Aɛ́=]l=əc//, PLN /'*Hill's Bar (between Yale and Hope), Fraser River where it goes over Hill's Bar on the CN (east) side*'/, Elder's comment: "means *piled up rocks*", root meaning unknown unless qw'él *cooked, barbecued* (see alternate name for this place, Qw'elóqw', lit. *barbecued fish heads*, after the way they cooked fish at that place), possibly <**=ets**> *on the back* or possibly <**=lets**> *on the bottom* or possibly also <**á-ablaut**> *derivational*, phonology: possibly ablaut, syntactic analysis: nominal, attested by BHTTC (10/21/76), SP and AK (Fish Camp 8/2/77), Elders Group (9/13/77), source: place names reference file #147.

<**qw'át'ts'em**>, df //q'ʷɛ́t'c'=əm//, SD /'*(have) sound of water sloshing around inside (a bottle, etc.) or gurgling*'/, WATR, root meaning unknown, possibly <**=em**> *intransitivizer, have, get or middle voice*, syntactic analysis: intransitive verb, attested by Elders Group (11/3/76).

<**qw'á:ts**>, free root //q'ʷɛ́·c//, EZ /'*little suckerfish with big salmon-like mouth,* prob. *largescale sucker*'/, ['prob. *Catostomus macrocheilus*'], syntactic analysis: noun, nominal, attested by Elders Group (7/9/75), also <**qw'e'áts**>, //q'ʷəʔɛ́c//, attested by AD (2/16/79).

<**qw'á:y**>, bound root //q'ʷɛ́·y *scorch, blacken near fire*//.

<**qw'á:ychep**>, ds //q'ʷɛ́·y=cəp//, FIRE /'*sparks, red hot ashes thrown out*'/, lx <**=chep ~ =tsep**> *firewood*, syntactic analysis: nominal, attested by Elders Group (4/23/80).

<**qw'á:yt**>, pcs //q'ʷɛ́·y=T//, FIRE /'*scorch s-th, blacken s-th with fire, heat it up (near a fire), burning a canoe with pitchwood to remove splinters and burn on black pitch)*'/, (<**=t**> *purposeful control transitivizer*), syntactic analysis: transitive verb, attested by Elders Group (Fish Camp 8/2/77, 3/26/75), BHTTC (8/25/76).

<**qw'óqw'iy**>, rsls //q'ʷɛ[=AáC$_1$ə=]y//, FIRE /'*burned (of rocks), scorched (of rocks)*'/, (<**ó-ablaut plus =R1=**> *resultative*), phonology: ablaut, reduplication, syntactic analysis: adjective/adjectival verb, attested by Elders Group (Fish Camp 8/2/77).

<**qw'á:ychep**>, FIRE /'*sparks, red hot ashes thrown out*'/, *see* qw'á:y.

<**qw'á:yt**>, FIRE /'*scorch s-th, blacken s-th with fire, heat it up (near a fire), burning a canoe with pitchwood to remove splinters and burn on black pitch)*'/, *see* qw'á:y.

<**qw'ech**>, probable bound root f //q'ʷəc//, meaning uncertain

<**sqw'echém**>, df //s=q'ʷəc(=)ə[=´=]m//, ABDF ['*a boil*'], (<**s=**> *nominalizer* or *stative*), root meaning unknown, possibly <**stress-shift**> *derivational*, possibly <**=em**> *middle voice or intransitivizer, have, get*, phonology: poss. stress-shift, syntactic analysis: nominal, attested by BJ (12/5/64), TG (Elders Group 3/1/72).

<**qw'él**>, free root //q'ʷə́l//, FOOD ['*cooked (over fire)*'], EB /'*ripe, ripened*'/, HARV, syntactic analysis: adjective/adjectival verb, attested by AC, Elders Group, EB, other sources: H-T <kwEl> *ripe, cooked*, example: <**yalhs'es qw'el.**>, //yɛɬ-s-ʔəs q'ʷə́l//, /'*They're just ripe.*'/, attested by AC, <**lúlh qw'èl.**>,

//lə=uɬ q'ʷə́l//, /'*They're ripe., They've gotten ripe., They've become ripe.*'/, literally /'third person past =already ripe'/, attested by AC, <**xwōwá ís me qw'él.**>, //xʷ=(ʔ)əwə=Aɛ́ ʔí-s mə q'ʷə́l//, /'*They're not ripe.*'/, literally /'be not yet aux (here) -they/it come to/start to be ripe'/, attested by AC, <**xwōwá: is me qw'él te sth'ì:m?**>, //xʷ=(ʔ)əwə=Aɛ́-ə ʔí-s mə q'ʷə́l//, /'*Is the fruit ripened yet?*'/, literally /'be not yet -yes/no question aux (here) -they/it start to ripen'/, attested by AC, <**li welh qw'él te skw'ố́lmexw?**>, //li wəɬ q'ʷə́l tə s=k'ʷólməxʷ//, /'*Are the blackberries ripe?*'/, literally /'yes/no question already ripe the blackberry'/, attested by AC, ASM ['cooked'], <**lulh qw'él te sqáwth.**>, //lə-uɬ q'ʷə́l tə s=qɛ́w(=)θ//, /'*The potatoes are cooked.*'/, literally /'third person past -already cooked the potato'/, attested by AC, <**ốwe lís qw'él.**>, //ʔə́wə lí-s q'ʷə́l//, /'*It's not cooked., It's raw.*'/, attested by EB, <**li welh qw'él?**>, //li wəɬ q'ʷə́l//, /'*Is it cooked?*'/, literally /'yes/no question already cooked'/, attested by AC, <**lulh qw'él. ~ lí lulh qw'él.**>, //lə-uɬ q'ʷə́l ~ lí lə-uɬ q'ʷə́l//, /'*It's cooked. ~ Yes, it's cooked.*'/, attested by AC.

<**sqw'él**>, dnom //s=q'ʷə́l//, FOOD ['*(the) cooking*'], (<**s=**> *nominalizer*), syntactic analysis: nominal, attested by Elders Group (3/5/80), example: <**xwel x̱éyth' te sqw'él.**>, //xʷəl x̣í(·)θ' tə s=q'ʷə́l//, /'*The cooking is still raw., Your cooking is not done.*'/.

<**qw'eqwél**>, cts //C_1ə-q'ʷə́l//, FOOD ['*getting cooked*'], EB ['*getting ripe*'], (<**R5-**> *continuative*), phonology: reduplication, syntactic analysis: intransitive verb, attested by BHTTC.

<**sqw'eqw'í:l**>, strs //s=C_1ə=q'ʷə[=Aí·=]l//, FOOD /'*(be) cooked, (be) already cooked*'/, (<**s=**> *stative*, R5= *stative or resultative*), (<**í:-ablaut**> *resultative*), phonology: reduplication, ablaut, syntactic analysis: adjective/adjectival verb, attested by EB (12/19/75, 4/14/78), example: <**ulh sqw'eqw'í:l te skwúkws.**>, //ʔuɬ s=C_1ə=q'ʷə[=Aí·=]l tə s=kʷúk'ʷ-s//, /'*Her cooking is already cooked.*'/, attested by EB.

<**qw'èlqw'èl**>, df //C_1əC_2=q'ʷə́l or q'ʷə́l=C_1əC_2//, EB ['*overripe*'], probably <**R3=**> *plural action or completive*, or <**=R2**> *characteristic*, phonology: reduplication, syntactic analysis: adjective/adjectival verb, attested by AC, example: <**lúlh qw'èlqw'èl.**>, //lə-uɬ C_1əC_2=q'ʷə́l (or) lə-uɬ q'ʷə́l=C_1əC_2//, /'*They've gone overripe.*'/, attested by AC.

<**qw'élt**>, pcs //qʷə́l=T//, FOOD ['*cook s-th*'], (<**=t**> *purposeful control transitivizer*), syntactic analysis: transitive verb, attested by AC, example: <**lalh qw'élt.**>, //lɛ-ɬ q'ʷə́l=T//, /'*Go cook it.*'/, attested by AC.

<**sqw'éls**>, dnom //s=q'ʷə́l=ls//, FOOD ['*something that's cooked*'], contrast <**sqwéls**> *(the) cooking* under root <**qwó:ls**> *boil*, (<**s=**> *nominalizer*), (<**=(e)ls**> *structured activity nominalizer*), phonology: consonant merger, syntactic analysis: nominal, attested by EB (1/20/76).

<**qw'élém**>, izs //q'ʷə́l=ə[=´=]m//, FOOD /'*barbecue, bake (meat, vegetables, etc.) in open fire, bake over fire, roast over open fire, bake under hot sand, bake in oven, cook in oven, (boiled down (as jam) [CT, HT])*'/, (<**=em**> *intransitivizer, have, get*), (<**=´=**> *derivational*), phonology: stress-shift, syntactic analysis: intransitive verb, attested by EB (12/19/75, etc.), Elders Group, AC, MH, other sources: ES /q'ʷəl·ə́m/ *cook (roast)*, JH /q'ʷələ́m/ *to cook, bake*, also <**qw'él:ém**>, //qʷə́l=·=ə[=´=]m//, also /'*bake over fire or under hot sand (Deming), barbecue (AC)*'/, attested by Deming (6/21/79), AC, phonology: lengthening and stress-shift (perhaps phonological conditioned in environment ə́lə, rather than *derivational*), also /'*boiled down (as jam)*'/, attested by CT and HT (6/8/76), also <**qw'elém**>, //qʷə́l=ə[=M2=]m//, attested by EB (3/8/76), also /'*bake underground*'/, attested by HT and some other elders (Elders Group 1/25/78), example: <**qw'élém te sth'óqwi**>, //q'ʷə́l=ə[´=]m tə s=θ'áqʷ(=)i//, /'*barbecue the salmon, the salmon is barbecued*'/, attested by EB (5/4/76), also /'*barbecue fish, bake the fish*'/, attested by MH (Deming 1/4/78), <**lachxw qw'élém te sth'óqwi.**>, //lɛ-c-xʷ q'ʷə́l=ə[=´=]m tə s=θ'áqʷi//, /'*Go and barbecue the fish (salmon).*'/, attested by AC, <**l (stl'í, sqwálewel) kw'els qw'él:ém(t) te sth'ó:qwi tlówàyèl.**>, //l (s=ƛ'í, sqʷɛ́l=əwəl)

k'ʷə-l-s q'ʷə́l=·=ə[=´=]m(=T) tə s=θ'ákʷi tlá=wɛ̀yə̀l//, /'*I (want to, think I'll) barbecue the salmon today.*'/, attested by AC, comment: possible =t *purposeful control transitivizer*, <**qw'elémchetcha kw sth'óqwi.**>, //q'ʷə́l=ə[=M2=]m-c-ət-cɛ kʷ s=θ'áqʷ(=)i//, /'*We'll barbecue salmon.*'/, attested by EB (5/4/76), <**le qw'él:ém.**>, //lə q'ʷə́l=·=ə[=´=]m//, /'*boiled down (as jam for ex.)*'/, attested by CT and HT (6/8/7), <**qw'él:em chékel**>, *roast chicken* (lit. roasted/barbecued + chicken), (attested by RG,EH 6/16/98 to SN, edited by BG with RG,EH 6/26/00)

<**sqw'él:ém**>, dnom //s=qʷə́l=·=ə[=´=]m//, FOOD /'*barbecued food, (salmon bake [Deming])*'/, (<**s=**> *nominalizer*), phonology: lengthening, stress-shift, syntactic analysis: nominal, attested by AC (10/15/71), EB (3/15/76), also <**sqw'elém**>, //s=q'ʷə́l=ə[=M2=]m//, also /'*bake, boil*'/, attested by Elders Group (3/1/72), also /'*barbecue*'/, attested by Elders Group (2/8/78), example: <**yalhtsel sqw'él:ém**>, //yɛɬ-c-əl s=q'ʷə́l=·=ə[=´=]m//, /'*the first time I barbecued*'/, also <**sqw'élém**>, //s=q'ʷə́l=ə[=´=]m//, also /'*salmon bake*'/, attested by Deming (3/25/76).

<**sqw'elém**>, stvi //s=q'ʷə́l=ə[=M2=]m//, FOOD /'*barbecued, roasted, (baked (in an oven) [DC])*'/, (<**s=**> *stative*), (<**metathesis**> *derivational*), phonology: metathesis, syntactic analysis: adjective/adjectival verb, attested by AC, DM (12/4/64), also /'*baked (in an oven, etc.), (oven-baked)*'/, attested by DC (12/19/78), example: <**sqw'élém seplíl**>, //s=qʷə́l=ə[=´=]m səplíl//, /'*oven(-baked) bread*'/.

<**qw'eqw'élém**>, cts //C₁ə-q'ʷə́l=ə[=´=]m//, FOOD /'*baking over an open fire, roasting over an open fire, barbecuing, cooking in an oven*'/, (<**R5-**> *continuative*), phonology: reduplication, syntactic analysis: intransitive verb, attested by EB, Elders Group (1/25/78), example: <**qw'eqw'élém te sth'óqwi**>, //C₁ə-q'ʷə́l=ə[=´=]m tə s=θ'áqʷ=i//, /'*barbecuing the salmon*'/, attested by EB.

<**qw'elemáwtxw**>, ds //q'ʷəl=əm=ɛ́wtxʷ//, FOOD ['*bakery*'], BLDG, literally /'bake in an oven building for'/, lx <**=áwtxw**> *building, house, building for,* syntactic analysis: nominal, attested by Elders Group (6/1/77).

<**Qw'elóqw'**>, df //q'ʷəl=áq'ʷ or q'ʷəl=i[=Aá=]qʷ=[G]//, PLN /'*Hill's Bar (a stretch of shoreline between Yale and Hope, on the east side of the Fraser river)*'/, literally /'barbecue (salmon) heads'/, ASM ['so named because Hill's Bar was a good place to do that'], possibly <**=óqw'**> glottalized from <**=íqw**> *on top of the head, fish head,* perhaps **ó-ablaut** and glottalization ([G])> *derivational*, phonology: possible ablaut and glottalization, syntactic analysis: nominal, attested by IHTTC, SP and AK and AD on Raft Trip (8/30/77), source: place names reference file #11a and prob. #148.

<**qw'éltel**>, dnom //q'ʷə́l=təl//, FOOD /'*barbecue sticks, (split roasting stick)*'/, lx <**=tel**> *device to, something to*, syntactic analysis: nominal, attested by TM's late mother used this (reported by TM at Fish Camp 7/11/78), contrast <**pí:kwel**> *barbecue sticks, split roasting stick.*

<**qw'él**>, possibly bound root //q'ʷə́l// or more likely related to or same as free root above <**qw'él**> '*cooked (over fire)*' since metal is "cooked over a fire" to purify and shape it.

<**sqw'él**>, df //sq'ʷə́l//, LAND perhaps /'*copper, (hard metal that looks like gold but isn't, maybe copper [Elders at Katz Class 10/5/76], metal found in mines and used for arrowheads [Elders Group 5/28/75], gold [EB])*'/, possibly <**s=**> *nominalizer*, syntactic analysis: nominal, attested by Elders Group (3/72), also /'*hard metal that looks like gold but isn't, maybe copper*'/, attested by Elders at Katz Class (10/5/76, TG or PDP or EP?), also /'*metal found in mines and used for arrowheads*'/, attested by Elders Group (5/28/75), also /'*gold*'/, attested by EB (1/20/76), also <**sqw'ôl**>, //s=q'ʷól//, also /'*native copper or brass (made thin as paper)*'/, attested by BJ (12/5/64, Wells transcripts old p. 328), other sources: ES Musqueam dial. of Downriver Halkomelem /sq'ʷə́l/ *copper*, Salish cognate: ?Squamish /sqʷəʔíls ~ qʷə́y-qʷi/ *copper* W73:67, K67:296 and 361,

K69:59, Lushootseed /q'ʷúlalatxʷ/ *copper?* H76:431 and compare Lushootseed /=alatxʷ/ *part of a building* H76:689.

<**qw'elá:m**>, ANAH ['*to change (of a boy's voice at puberty)*'], *see* qw'íl.

<**qw'élém**>, FOOD /'*barbecue, bake (meat, vegetables, etc.) in open fire, bake over fire, roast over open fire, bake under hot sand, bake in oven, cook in oven, (boiled down (as jam) [CT, HT])*'/, *see* qw'él.

<**qw'elemáwtxw**>, FOOD ['*bakery*'], *see* qw'él.

<**qw'eléqel**>, df //q'ʷəl(=)ə́qəl or q'ʷil=ə́qəl or q'ʷi[=Aə=]l=ə́qəl//, LAND /'*cliff, vertical rock face*'/, probably root <**qw'íl**> *uncover*, possibly <**=éqel**> *on the throat, throat (of land),* syntactic analysis: nominal, attested by Elders Group (5/28/75).

<**qw'eléqel**>, df //q'ʷə́l=ə́qəl//, ABDF ['*(have) trench mouth*'], possibly root <**qw'él**> *cooked, roasted,* possibly literally /'roasted/cooked in the throat'/, lx <**=éqel**> *in the throat*, syntactic analysis: intransitive verb?, attested by Elders Group (4/7/76).

<**qw'eléqetel**>, df //q'ʷəl=ə́qə(l)=təl//, EB /'*small-flowered alumroot,* and possibly *smooth Heuchera*'/, ['*Heuchera micrantha* and possibly *Heuchera glabra or hybrid*'], MED ['used as medicine for: hangover, trench mouth, and thrush (white coating on a baby's mouth)'], literally /'something for trenchmouth'/, lx <**=éqel**> *on the throat*, lx <**=tel**> *something for*, phonology: consonant-loss (l before =tel, predictable), syntactic analysis: nominal, attested by EL (9/27/77), also <**xweqw'éle'áltel ~ xweqw'ele'á:ltel**>, //xʷə(=)q'ʷə́lə=ʔɛ́ltəl//, literally /'hangover medicine'/, attested by EL (9/27/77).

<**qw'elíteq**>, df //q'ʷəlítəq//, EZ /'*seagull (possibly generic),* certainly including *the glaucus-winged gull,* and possibly including any or all of the following which occur in the Upriver Halkomelem-speaking area*: Bonaparte's gull, short-billed gull, ring-billed gull, California gull, herring gull*'/, ['possibly genus *Larus*, certainly including *Larus glaucescens* and possibly any/all of the following: *Larus philadelphia, Larus canus, Larus delawarensis, Larus californicus, Larus argentatus*'], syntactic analysis: nominal, dialects: *Chill., Deming, Katzie,* attested by Deming, Elders Group (2/18/76), BJ (12/5/64), also <**slí:lōwya**>, //s=lí[=C_1ə=]w=iya//, attested by Elders Group (2/18/76), also <**á:we**>, //ʔɛ́·wə//, attested by Elders Group (2/18/76), BJ (12/5/64).

<**Qw'elóqw'**>, PLN /'*Hill's Bar (a stretch of shoreline between Yale and Hope, on the east side of the Fraser river)*'/, *see* qw'él.

<**qw'èlqw'èl**>, EB ['*overripe*'], *see* qw'él.

<**qw'élt**>, FOOD ['*cook s-th*'], *see* qw'él.

<**qw'éltel**>, FOOD /'*barbecue sticks, (split roasting stick)*'/, *see* qw'él.

<**qw'ém**>, free root //q'ʷə́m//, ABFC ['*come out (of hair) (like hair in a comb)*'], syntactic analysis: intransitive verb.

<**qw'eméqel**>, cts //q'ʷə́m=ə[-M2-]qəl or q'ʷəm=ə[-´-]qəl//, ABFC /'*hair is falling out, losing one's hair*'/, lx <**=qel ~ =eqel**> *in the head*, possibly <**metathesis** or **stress-shift**> *continuative,* comment: later examples show the apparent metathesis or stress-shift without any continuative translation; if they are correct the translations here perhaps should be *hair falls out, lose one's hair* and the root may just be a weak grade which only accepts stress when there is no affix to take it, phonology: metathesis or stress-shift, syntactic analysis: intransitive verb.

<**qw'emét**>, pcs //q'ʷə́m=ə[=M2=]T or q'ʷəm=ə́T//, ABDF ['*pull out (hair)*'], HARV ['*pull up by the roots*'], HUNT, (<**=et** or **=ét**> *purposeful control transitivizer*), possibly <**metathesis**>

continuative? or derivational?, phonology: weak grade root or metathesis, syntactic analysis: transitive verb, attested by Elders Group (7/23/75, 1/7/76).

<**qw'emṓwst** or **qw'eméwst**>, pcs //q'ʷəm=óws=T or q'ʷəm=ə́ws=T//, HUNT ['*pluck it (a bird/fowl)*'], lx <**=óws ~ =éws**> *on the body*, (<**=T**> *purposeful control transitivizer*), phonology: possibly weak grade root, syntactic analysis: transitive verb, attested by Elders Group (1/7/76).

<**qw'emōwselhtsthó:x**>, bens //q'ʷəm=ows=əɬc=T-á·xʸ//, if, HUNT ['*pluck it for me*'], lx <**=ōws**> *on the body*, (<**=elhts**> *benefactive*, <=t> *purposeful control transitivizer*), (<**-ó:x**> *second person singular object*), syntactic analysis: transitive verb, attested by Elders Group (3/24/76), also <**qw'emṓwslhthó:x**>, //q'ʷəm=óws=ɬ=T-á·xʸ//, attested by EB (3/1/76); found in <**qw'emṓwslhthó:xchexw.**>, //q'ʷəm=óws=ɬ=T-á·xʸ-c-əxʷ//, /'*Pluck it for me., You pluck it for me.*'/, attested by EB.

<**sqw'éméls**>, dnom //s=q'ʷə́m=məls//, ANAH ['*forehead*'], literally (perhaps) /' part the hair comes out of'/, (<**s=**> *nominalizer*), probably root <**qw'em**> *come out (of hair), come out by the roots*, lx <**=mels**> *part, portion*, phonology: consonant merger resulting in updrifting instead of length, syntactic analysis: nominal, attested by BJ (5/10/64), EB, others, example: <**tsel tós tel sqw'éméls.**>, //c-əl tás t-əl s=q'ʷə́m=məls//, /'*I got bumped on my forehead.*'/, attested by EB.

<**qw'eméqel**>, ABFC /'*hair is falling out, losing one's hair*'/, *see* qw'ém.

<**qw'emét**>, ABDF ['*pull out (hair)*'], *see* qw'ém.

<**qw'emétx̲w**>, df //q'ʷə́m=ə[=M2=]t(=)x̣ʷ//, EB /'*water-lily, yellow pond lily*'/, ['*Nuphar polysepalum*'], MED ['the roots were used for medicine to soak in for rheumatism or arthritis (EF)'], BLDG ['*door-knob*'], Elder's comment: "so named because it's round", possibly root <**qw'em**> *come out by the roots*, possibly <**=et**> *purposeful control transitivizer* possibly crystallized, <**=x̲w**> *around, round*, phonology: possible metathesis, syntactic analysis: nominal, attested by IHTTC, Elders Group, EF (Deming 9/21/78).

<**qw'emó**> or <**qw'óm**>, possible root or stem //q'ʷəm(=)á// or //q'ʷám// *make a U-shape,* prob. the root of <**qw'ómx̲w**>, bound stem //q'ʷám=x̣ʷ *double up, roll up in a ball*//, clearly related by metathesis, *see also* <**qw'óm**>.

<**qw'emó:thel**>, df //q'ʷəmá=áθəl//, FSH /'*to fish with a pole or rod, to fish by a line*'/, lx <**=ó:thel**> *in the mouth*, semantic comment: prob. so-named due to catching fish this way with a bent u-shape hook in the mouth, syntactic analysis: intransitive verb, attested by Elders Group (3/15/72), EB, also <**qw'emóthel**>, //q'ʷəmá=áθəl//, also /'*fishing by line*'/, attested by Deming (3/25/76).

<**qw'iqw'emó:thel ~ qw'íqw'emó:thel**>, dmv //C_1í=q'ʷəmá=áθəl//, FSH /'*fishing by a line, line-fishing, trout-fishing, fishing with a pole (for trout)*'/, (<**R4=**> *diminutive*), phonology: reduplication, syntactic analysis: intransitive verb, attested by AC, EB (3/9/76), Elders Group (3/15/72), example: <**tsel qw'íqw'emó:thel.**>, //c-əl C_1í=q'ʷəmá=áθəl//, /'*I'm fishing with a pole (for trout).*'/, attested by Elders Group (3/15/72 tape).

<**qw'emóthetel**>, dnom //q'ʷəmá=áθə(l)=təl//, FSH ['*fishing line*'], lx <**=tel**> *device to, something to*, phonology: consonant-loss (l predictably before =tel), length-loss, syntactic analysis: nominal, dialects: *Tait, Chill.*, attested by Deming, AC, Elders Group (2/11/76), also <**qw'emóthtel**>, //q'ʷəmá=áθ(əl)=təl//, phonology: syllable-loss (el before =tel), dialects: *Cheh.*, attested by Elders Group (2/11/76), EB (3/9/76).

<**qw'emóx̲w**>, bound stem //q'ʷəmá=x̣ʷ//, *bend in a u-shape* clearly related to <**qw'ómx̲w**>, bound stem //q'ʷám=x̣ʷ *double up, roll up in a ball*//.

<**sqw'emóx̲w sxíxep**>, cpds //s=q'ʷəm=ə[=Aá=]x̣ʷ s=xʸí[=C_1ə=]p//, CAN ['*bent U-shaped plane with handle on each end for canoe-making*'], TOOL, (<**s=**> *stative*), (<**ó-ablaut**> *resultative*),

probably root <**qw'emó**> *bend in u-shape*, probably <**=x̲w**> *round, around*, (<**s=**> *nominalizer*), (<**=R1=**> *continuative*), phonology: ablaut, reduplication, syntactic analysis: nominal phrase with modifier(s), attested by Elders Group (early fall 1976).

<**sqw'emóx̲w xíxepels**>, cpds //s=q'ʷəm=ə[=Aá=]x̣ʷ xʸí[=C_1ə=]p=əls//, sas, CAN [*'bent U-shaped plane with handle on each end for canoe-making'*], TOOL, (<**s=**> *stative*), (<**ó-ablaut**> *resultative*), probably root <**qw'emó**> *bend in u-shape*, probably <**=x̲w**> *round, around*, (<**=R1=**> *continuative*), (<**=els**> *structured activity continuative device for*), phonology: ablaut, reduplication, syntactic analysis: nominal phrase with modifier(s), attested by Elders Group (early fall 1976).

<**qw'emó:thel**>, df //q'ʷəmá=áθəl//, FSH /*'to fish with a pole or rod, to fish by a line'*/, *see* qw'emó or qw'óm

<**qw'emóthetel**>, FSH [*'fishing line'*], *see* qw'emó or qw'óm.

<**qw'emōwselhtsthó:x**>, HUNT [*'pluck it for me'*], *see* qw'ém.

<**qw'emṓwst** or **qw'eméwst**>, HUNT [*'pluck it (a bird/fowl)'*], *see* qw'ém.

<**qw'eqwél**>, FOOD [*'getting cooked'*], *see* qw'él.

<**qw'eqw'élém**>, FOOD /*'baking over an open fire, roasting over an open fire, barbecuing, cooking in an oven'*/, *see* qw'él.

<**qw'ex̲w**> bound stem, //q'ʷi[=Aə=]x̣ʷ// either from <**qw'íx̲w**> *miss (in throwing a spear)* or *homonym* <**qw'íx̲w**> *brown*

<**Sqw'ex̲wáq**>, df //s=q'ʷix̣ʷ=ɛ́q//, PLN [*'pool where Kawkawa Creek comes into the Coquihalla River'*], ASM ['on the Coquihalla River just below the wooden bridge going across the Coquihalla River to Kawkawa Lake, this pool was where the dark-skinned (dark brown) water pygmies lived that kept people from being able to spear sucker-fish that lived there'], (<**s=**> *nominalizer*), possibly root <**qw'íx̲w**> *miss (in throwing a spear)* or possibly root <**qw'íx̲w**> *brown* as in <**qw'íx̲w=es**> *negro, (lit. brown face)* and in <**ts=qw'íx̲w**> *brown*), possibly <**=áq**> *penis; male* (or perhaps a durataive ablaut variant of <**=eq ~ =eleq**> *one who habitually*), syntactic analysis: nominal, attested by IHTTC (8/17/77), AD and SP (Field trip with Reuben Ware 8/18/77), IHTTC and others (place names meeting 8/23/77), source: place names reference file #204, also <**Skw'ex̲wáq**>, //s=k'ʷəx̣ʷ=ɛ́q//, attested by IHTTC (8/23/77), AD and SP (8/18/77).

<**Skw'íkw'x̲weq**> (or better, <**Sqw'íqw'x̲weq**>), df //s=q'ʷí[=C_1ə=]x̣ʷ=əq or s=C_1í=q'ʷəx̣ʷ=ɛq//, PLN [*'maybe the same place as Sqw'ex̲wáq (pool where Kawkawa Creek comes into the Coquihalla River and where the water pygmies lived)'*], possibly <**=R1=**> *diminutive* or possibly <**R4=**> *diminutive*, comment: this form may confirm the root is qw'íx̲w, phonology: reduplication, vowel-loss, possibly vowel-reduction, syntactic analysis: nominal, attested by SP (8/18/77), IHTTC (8/23/77).

<**qw'ex̲wéltses**>, df //q'ʷix̣ʷ=ə[= ´=]l=cəs or q'ʷə́x̣ʷ=ə[=M2=]l=cəs//, ANA /*'fingernail, nail of finger, claw'*/, possibly root <**qw'ix̲w**> *dark brown*, possibly <**=el**> (perhaps) *plural* (of lexical suffixes) or merely connective, <**stress-shift**> *derivational*, lx <**=tses**> *on the hand*, phonology: possible vowel-reduction, stress-shift, syntactic analysis: nominal, attested by AC, others, other sources: ES /q'ʷx̣ʷál·cəs/ *claw*, JH /sq'ʷx̣ʷá·lcəs/ *claw*, H-T <k·wōquoltcis> (macron over u) *fingernail.*

<**s(i)yátl'qels te qw'x̲wéltses**>, cpds ///s=yə[-Aɛ́-]ƛ'=q'=əls-s tə q'ʷix̣ʷ=ə[= ´=]l=cəs//, PE /*'nail polish'*/ (lit. "paint for (of) the fingernail"), attested by RG & EH (4/10/99 Ling332)

<**shxwth'ámqels qw'x̲wéltses/qw'x̲wélches**>, cpds //s=xʷɛ́θ'=ə[=M2=]m=q=əls q'ʷix̣ʷ=ə[= ´=]l=cəs or q'ʷə́x̣ʷ=ə[=M2=]l=cəs//, PE /*'fingernail clippers'*/, lit. "scissors for the fingernails",

<**shxw=**> *nominalizer*), root <**xwáth'**> *teeter, rock,* <**=em**> *intransitivizer/have/get or middle voice*, possibly <**metathesis**> *continuative*, lx <**=q**> *closable container*, (<**=els**> *structured activity continuative device for*),. <**qw'íx̲w**> *dark brown*, <**=el=**> *plural*, <**=tses**> *on the hand*, attested by RG & EH (4/10/99 Ling332)

<**qw'x̲wélxel**>, df //q'ʷix̣ʷ=ə[=´=]l=xʸəl or q'ʷə́x̣ʷ=ə[=M2=]l=xʸəl//, ANA ['*toenail*'], possibly root <**qw'ix̲w**> *dark brown*, possibly <**=el**> (perhaps) *plural* or connective, <**stress-shift**> *derivational*, lx <**=xel**> *on the foot*, phonology: possible vowel-reduction, stress-shift, syntactic analysis: nominal, attested by Elders Group, other sources: ES /q'ʷx̣ʷə́lxʸəl/ *toenail*, H-T <k·wōQúlHyil> *toenail*.

<**qw'éx̲weqs**>, df //q'ʷə́x̣ʷ=əqs or q'ʷi[=Aə́=]x̣ʷ=əqs//, SPRD ['*a kind of spirit-dance done after the syúwel (spirit power) has left a dancer but the dancer still needs to dance*'], ASM ['anybody can dance along and sing without harm, the dancer is still under a trance but is not possessed, just a few such songs exist, everybody sings along'], root meaning uncertain, possibly <**qw'íx̲w**> *dark brown* with <**e- ablaut**>, possibly <**=eqs**> *on the nose, point*, perhaps the dancer's face paint includes brown on the nose, phonology: possible ablaut, syntactic analysis: nominal, attested by EB (1/26/76), Elders Group (10/13/76), Salish cognate: Squamish /q'ʷə́x̣ʷaʔqs/ *to perform a dance characterized by shaking of the head* W73:74, K69:83, also <**kw'ő̃xweqs**>, //k'ʷóxʷ=əqs//, comment: this last is probably mistranscribed (in light of the cognate), attested by Elders Group (10/13/76).

<**qw'eyél:ex ~ qw'eyél:éx**>, PLAY ['*dancing*'], *see* **qw'eyílex ~ qw'eyíléx**.

<**qw'eyílex ~ qw'eyíléx**>, df //q'ʷəy=íl=əxʸ or qʷ[=G=]əy=íl=əxʸ//, PLAY ['*to dance (any kind)*'], SPRD, possibly root <**qwey**> *shake, move*, possibly <**=G= (glottalization)**> *derivational*, (<**=íl**> *go, come, get, become*), lx <**=ex**> *upright*, phonology: possible glottalization, possible updrifting, syntactic analysis: intransitive verb, attested by AC, Deming, EB, other sources: ES /q'ʷəyʔílíxʸ/ *dance*, Salish cognate: Sechelt /q'ʷəyílš/, Squamish /q'ʷyílš/, Nooksack (A61) /q'ʷyíliš/ A61 beside /q'ʷəyílixʸ/ (G84a:GS) and /q'ʷəʔyíləš/ (G84a:LG), Sn Lm(D82pc) Smb /q'ʷəyíləš/, Sg /q'ʷəyélʔəš/ and (S65) /q'ʷəyíʔləš/, So /q'ʷiʔíš/, Cl /q'ʷəyíyəš/ all *to dance* (G82a cognate set 170, G88a set 11), example: <**tl'otsasew qw'eyílex/qw'eyíléx qa t'ílem tel siyáya.**>, //ƛ'á-cɛ-s-əw q'ʷəy=íl=əxʸ qɛ t'íl=əm t-əl s=iy(=)ɛ́y(=)ɛ//, /'*My friends will sing and dance.*'/, attested by AC, <**lets'áxw kw'els e qw'eyíléx.**>, //ləc'ə=ɛxʷ k'ʷ-əl-s ʔə q'ʷəy=íl=əxʸ//, /'*I danced once.*'/, attested by EB, <**schewót kw'es qw'eyílexs.**>, //s=cəwát k'ʷə-s q'ʷəy=íl=əxʸ-s//, /'*He's good at dancing.*'/, literally /'He knows how that he dance'/, attested by AC.

<**skwetóxwes sqw'eyílex**>, cpds //s=kʷətɛ́[=Aá=]xʷ=əs s=q'ʷəy=íl=əxʸ//, SPRD /'*mask dance*'/, semantic comment: the only mask in Stó:lō area was <**sx̲wó:yx̲wey**>, attested by RG & EH (4/10/99 Ling332)

<**qw'eyél:ex ~ qw'eyél:éx**>, cts //q'ʷəy=i[-Aə́-]l[-·-]=əxʸ//, PLAY ['*dancing*'], (<**é-ablaut plus -:-**> *continuative*), phonology: ablaut, lengthening perhaps with automatic metathesis type 1 in environment after schwa and before resonant, syntactic analysis: intransitive verb, dialects: *Chill.*, attested by AC, BJ (12/5/64), Deming, also <**qw'eyél'lex**>, //q'ʷəy=i[-Aə́-]l[-ʔ-]=əxʸ//, dialects: *Matsqui-Sumas*, attested by AH (Deming 3/23/78).

<**sqw'eyílex**>, dnom //s=q'ʷəy=íl=əxʸ//, PLAY ['*a dance (social event for ex.), a dance (of someone's spirit dance)*'], (<**s=**> *nominalizer*), syntactic analysis: nominal, attested by AC, example: <**étset lám te sqw'eyílex.**>, //ʔə́-c-ət lɛ́=m tə s=q'ʷəy=íl=əxʸ//, /'*We went to the dance.*'/, literally /'ambiguous past go to the dance'/, attested by AC, as in <**sqw'eyílexs**>, //s=q'ʷəy=íl=əxʸ-s//, SPRD /'his/her dance'/, attested by RG & EH (4/10/99 Ling332)

<**lexwsqw'eyíléx**>, dnom //ləx^{w}s=q'^{w}əy=íl=əx^y//, PLAY /'*a person that likes to dance, a person that always dances*'/, SOCT, (<**lexws=**> *a person who always*), comment: the translation shows that lexws= functions as a separate prefix rather than two (lexw= *always* and s= *nominalizer*) since it's not the dancing that is nominalized but the person who does it, syntactic analysis: nominal, attested by EB (2/11/76).

<**qw'eyilexáwtxw**>, dnom //q'^{w}əy=il=əx^y=ɛ́wtx^w//, BLDG ['*dance-hall*'], PLAY, lx <**=áwtxw**> *building, house*, phonology: stress-shift to suffix, syntactic analysis: nominal, attested by Elders Group.

<**qw'eyíléxelhp**>, dnom //q'^{w}əy=íl=ə[=´=]x^y=əɬp//, EB /'*pine, "yellow" pine, western white pine*'/, ['*Pinus monticola*'], literally /'dance tree'/, lx <**=elhp**> *tree*, possibly <=´=> *continuative or durative*, phonology: stress-shift, syntactic analysis: nominal, attested by Elders Group (1/29/75, 3/22/78), AC, also <**qw'iqw'iyíléxelhp**>, //q'^{w}(ə)y=C_1əC_2=íl=əx^y=əɬp//, (<**=R2=**> *characteristic*), attested by EB (5/26/76), other sources: ES /q'^{w}əq'^{w}əyíləx^{y}əɬp/ *white pine (Pinus monticola) (lit. dancing tree)*, H-T <k·ok·wáiyeliHyEtlp> (macrons over a and e) *fir (Douglas)*.

<**qw'eyilexáwtxw**>, BLDG ['*dance-hall*'], *see* qw'eyílex ~ qw'eyíléx.

<**qw'eyíléxelhp**>, EB /'*pine, "yellow" pine, western white pine*'/, *see* qw'eyílex ~ qw'eyíléx.

<**qw'íl**>, bound root //q'^{w}íl *uncover*//.

<**sqw'íqw'el**>, strs //s=q'^{w}í[=C_1ə=]l//, DESC ['*(be) uncovered*'], (<**s=**> *stative*), (<**=R1=**> *resultative*), phonology: reduplication, syntactic analysis: adjective/adjectival verb, attested by BHTTC.

<**qw'í:lt**>, pcs //q'^{w}í[=·=]l=T//, DESC ['*uncover it*'], ABFC, (<**=t**> *purposeful control transitivizer*), possibly <**=:=**> *derivational*, phonology: lengthening, syntactic analysis: transitive verb, attested by BHTTC.

<**qw'elá:m**>, mdls //q'^{w}il=ə[=Aɛ́·=]m//, durs, ANAH ['*to change (of a boy's voice at puberty)*'], (<**á:-ablaut**> *durative*), (<**=em**> *middle voice*), phonology: ablaut, syntactic analysis: intransitive verb, attested by Elders Group (4/23/80).

<**qw'iqw'elá:mqel ~ qw'iqw'elámqel**>, cts //q'^{w}i[-C_1ə-]l=ə[=Aɛ́·=]m=qəl//, durs, ANAH ['*changing in voice (of a boy)*'], (<**-R1-**> *continuative*), (<**á:-ablaut**> *durative*), lx <**=(e)qel**> *in the throat*, phonology: reduplication, ablaut, syntactic analysis: intransitive verb, attested by Elders Group (10/26/75, 11/10/76), example: <**qw'íqw'elámqel te swíweles.**>, //q'^{w}i[-C_1ə-]l=ə[=Aɛ́·=]m=qəl tə s=wí[=C_1ə=]ləs-s//, /'*The boy's voice is changing.*'/, phonology: consonant merger, attested by NP (10/26/75).

<**qw'íles**>, ds //q'^{w}íl=əs//, EB /'*sprout(ing) up, stick(ing) its head out of the ground (of a plant)*'/, literally /'uncover on the face'/, lx <**=es**> *on the face*, syntactic analysis: intransitive verb, attested by EB, EL, contrast <**qwáqel**> *sprouted up*, example: <**me qw'íles te spí:ls.**>, //mə q'^{w}íl=əs tə s=pí·l=ls//, /'*The plant is sticking its head out of the ground., The plant is sprouting up.*'/, attested by EL (3/1/78), <**lulh qw'íles te spí:ls.**>, //lə-uɬ q'^{w}íl=əs tə s=pí·l=ls//, /'*My planting has (already) sprouted up.*'/, attested by EB (2/16/76), <**me qw'íles**>, //mə q'^{w}íl=əs//, /'*spring (season), come spring-time*'/, TIME, literally /'start to sprout/uncover the face'/, attested by EB (2/16/76), ME (11/21/72), other sources: Gibbs (1859-1863).

<**temqw'íles ~ temqw'éyles**>, ds //təm=q'^{w}íl=əs//, TIME /'*spring (season), (time to sprout up)*'/, (<**tem=**> *time for, season for*), syntactic analysis: nominal, attested by Elders Group (3/12/75).

<**qw'íles**>, EB /'*sprout(ing) up, stick(ing) its head out of the ground (of a plant)*'/, *see* qw'íl.

<**qw'í:lt**>, DESC ['*uncover it*'], *see* qw'íl.

<**qw'í:m**>, df //q'ʷí(·)=əm or q'ʷiy=(ə)m//, CAN /'*get off (a canoe or conveyance), get out of a canoe, (disembark)*'/, (<**=em**> *middle voice*), phonology: vowel merger or vocalization, syntactic analysis: intransitive verb, attested by AC, example: <**esu qw'í:m yutl'ó:lem.**>, //ʔə-s-u q'ʷí·=m y=u=ƛ'á·=lə=m//, /'*Then they got off.*'/, attested by AC.

<**qw'íméls**>, sas //q'ʷím=əls//, cts, CAN /'*unloading a canoe, taking things out of a canoe*'/, (<**=els**> *structured activitiy continuative*), phonology: updrifting (only on e in last syllable?), syntactic analysis: intransitive verb, attested by EB and RM (4/23/76).

<**qw'ímét**>, pcs //q'ʷí=m=əT//, CAN ['*take it out of water*'], (<**=et**> *purposeful control transitivizer*), phonology: updrifting, syntactic analysis: transitive verb, attested by Elders Group (5/26/76).

<**qw'íméls**>, sas //q'ʷím=əls//, ECON /'*get credit, borrow (money for ex.), (getting credit, borrowing)*'/, root meaning unknown, (<**=els**> *structured activity continuative*), phonology: updrifting, syntactic analysis: intransitive verb, dialects: *Pilalt (Chilliwack Landing)*, attested by RM (4/23/76), also /'*borrow (money)*'/, attested by Deming (1/25/79), example: <**látsel qw'íméls.**>, //lɛ́-c-əl q'ʷím=əls//, /'*I'm going to get credit.*'/, attested by RM, <**l stl'í kw'els qw'íméls te (axwíl, qéx̱) tále.**>, //l s=ƛ'í k'ʷ-əl-s q'ʷím=əls tə (ʔɛxʷíl, qə́x̣) tɛ́lə//, /'*I want to borrow (a little, a lot of) money.*'/, attested by Deming.

<**qw'íméls**>, CAN /'*unloading a canoe, taking things out of a canoe*'/, *see* qw'í:m.

<**qw'ímét**>, CAN ['*take it out of water*'], *see* qw'í:m.

<**qw'iqw'elá:mqel ~ qw'iqw'elámqel**>, ANAH ['*changing in voice (of a boy)*'], *see* qw'íl.

<**qw'iqw'emó:thel ~ qw'íqw'emó:thel**>, FSH /'*fishing by a line, line-fishing, trout-fishing, fishing with a pole (for trout)*'/, *see* qw'emó or qw'óm.

<**qw'íqw'ex̱w**>, LT ['*(brownish)*'], *see* qw'íx̱w.

<**qw'íqw'ex̱wel**>, LT ['*[getting brown]*'], *see* qw'íx̱w.

<**qw'íqw'x̱wes**>, SOCT ['*small Negro*'], *see* qw'íx̱w.

<**qw'íwelh**>, df //q'ʷí(y)=wəɬ or qʷ[=G=]ə́y=wəɬ or q'ʷíw=(w)əɬ//, WATR ['*rough (of a river or creek)*'], possibly root <**qwey**> *shake, move*, possibly <**=G= (glottalization)**> *derivational*, possibly <**=welh**> *canoe, vessel*, phonology: possible glottalization, syntactic analysis: adjective/adjectival verb, attested by Elders at Fish Camp (8/2/77).

<**Qw'íywelh** or **Qw'éywelh**>, df //q'ʷíy=wəɬ or qʷ[=G=]ə́y=wəɬ//, PLN ['*mountain across the Fraser River from American Bar*'], ASM ['a berry-picking place on the CN (east) side of the Fraser'], (semological comment: possibly derived from qw'i(y)welh *rough (of river or creek)*), phonology: possible glottalization, syntactic analysis: nominal, attested by Mary Peters (recorded in writing 1973-4 by AD and SP)(IHTTC), source: place names reference file #30.

<**qw'íwelh**>, df //q'ʷí(y)(=)wəɬ//, HUNT ['*outside brisket of meat*'], root meaning unknown, syntactic analysis: nominal, attested by Elders Group (2/76).

<**qw'íx̱w**>, bound root //q'ʷíx̣ʷ *brown*//, comment: using derived forms of the root as a modifier of other color terms the following combinations were given by AK: tsqw'íx̣w (tsqwáy "dark yellow", qwiqwóyáls, tsméth', tskwím, sts'ólha); tsqw'íqw'ex̣wel (qálq "dark dark ...", tsméth', tsqwáy, qwiqwóyáls); qw'íqw'ex̣wel (qálq once "dark rose", tsméth', tsqwáy, tskwím); sqw'éqw'ex̣wel tsméth'.

<**tsqw'íx̱w**>, ds //c=q'ʷíx̣ʷ//, LT ['*be brown*'], ASM ['the following color terms are used by AK before tsqw'íx̱w to specify shades of the color: tsxwíxwekw'el ("like dark brown"), stl'ítl'esel'], (<**ts=**> *have, get, stative with colors*), syntactic analysis: adjective/adjectival verb, attested by AK, TG, NP,

AH (all 1987), see charts by Rob MacLaury, also <**tsqw'íx̲w ~ ts'qw'íx̲w**>, //c=q'ʷíx̣ʷ ~ c=G=q'ʷíx̣ʷ//, phonology: possible glottalization assimilation, attested by AC (8/4/70).

<**qw'íqw'ex̲w**>, dmv //q'ʷi[=C_1ə=]x̣ʷ//, LT ['*(brownish)*'], ASM ['circled the following colors on the Berlin and Kay (1969) color chart (where rows are B-I top-bottom, columns left-right are 1-40): H7, H8, H9'], (<**=R1=**> *diminutive*), phonology: reduplication, syntactic analysis: adjective/adjectival verb, attested by AK (1/24/79).

<**tsqw'íqw'ex̲w**>, stvi //c=q'ʷi[=C_1ə=]x̣ʷ//, LT ['*brown*'], ASM ['it can be a darker shade or if preceded by /tu/ it can be a lighter shade of gray/[brown] (TG also uses this root for brown; the other speakers use the root for brown and label gray with forms from /xʷík'ʷ/)'], (<**ts=**> *stative with color terms*), (<**=R1=**> *diminutive or continuative*), phonology: reduplication, syntactic analysis: adjective/adjectival verb, attested by EB (mentioned while digging for cedar roots 4/10/78), TG (1987), see charts by Rob MacLaury.

<**qw'íqw'ex̲wel**>, cts //q'ʷí[=C_1ə=]x̣ʷ=əl//, incs, LT ['*[getting brown]*'], (<**=R1=**> *continuative*), (<**=el ~ =íl**> *go, come, get, become*), syntactic analysis: adjective/adjectival verb, attested by AK, NP, see charts by Rob MacLaury.

<**tsqw'íqw'ex̲wel**>, cts //c=q'ʷí[=C_1ə=]x̣ʷ=əl//, incs, LT ['*[be getting brown]*'], (<**ts=**> *have, get, stative with colors*), (<**=R1=**> *continuative*), (<**=el ~ =íl**> *go, come, get, become*), syntactic analysis: adjective/adjectival verb, attested by NP, see charts by Rob MacLaury.

<**sqw'íqw'ex̲wel**>, cts //s=q'ʷí[=C_1ə=]x̣ʷ=əl//, incs, LT ['*[be getting brown]*'], (<**s=**> *stative*), (<**=R1=**> *continuative*), (<**=el ~ =íl**> *go, come, get, become*), syntactic analysis: adjective/adjectival verb, attested by NP, see charts by Rob MacLaury.

<**sqw'íqw'ex̲welomex**>, ds //s=q'ʷí[=C_1ə=]x̣ʷ=əl=áməxʸ//, cts, incs, LT /'*[looks a state of going brown, be getting brown-looking]*'/, (<**s=**> *stative*), (<**=R1=**> *continuative*), (<**=el ~ =íl**> *go, come, get, become*), (<**=ómex**> *looks, -looking, in color*), syntactic analysis: adjective/adjectival verb, attested by NP, see charts by Rob MacLaury.

<**qw'íx̲wes**>, ds //q'ʷíx̣ʷ=əs//, SOCT ['*Negro*'], lx <**=es**> *on the face*, syntactic analysis: nominal, attested by BHTTC, IHTTC.

<**qw'íqw'x̲wes**>, dmn //q'ʷí[=C_1ə=]x̣ʷ=əs or C_1í=q'ʷix̣ʷ=əs//, SOCT ['*small Negro*'], probably <**=R1=** or **R4=**> *diminutive*, phonology: reduplication, syntactic analysis: nominal, attested by IHTTC.

<**qw'lhòlèm** or **qw'lhlòlèm**>, mdls //q'ʷáɬ=ə[=M2=]l=əm//, incs, ABFC /'*to climax, come (sexually), ejaculate*'/, root meaning unknown unless <**qw'ólh** or **qw'álh**>, bound root //q'ʷáɬ or q'ʷɛ́ɬ// *watch, notice*, probably <**=el**> *get, come, go, become*, probably <**=em**> *middle voice*, possibly <**metathesis**> *derivational*, (semological comment: another possible analysis of this word would relate it to the root qw'ólh or qw'alh with =l non-control transitivizer and -àlèm *passive first person singular* thus literally *get myself noticed*; but the trouble with that is that the metathesis never extends into the passive and the meaning of the verb is really more likely to need the middle voice and an inceptive =el), syntactic analysis: intransitive verb, attested by JL, example: <**tsellh me ts'ímél kw'els qw'lhòlèm.**>, //c-əl-ɬ mə c'ím-əl k'ʷ-əl-s q'ʷáɬ-ə[=M2=]l=əm//, /'*I'm going to come (climax).*'/, attested by JL (reporting 7/20/79 at Fish Camp how this would be said).

<**qw'ó:leqwet**>, SOC ['*whipping s-o/s-th many times*'], *see* qw'óqw.

<**Qw'ó:ltl'el**>, df //q'ʷá·lƛ'(=)əl//, PLN /'*Kwantlen, Langley, B.C.*'/, SOC /'*Kwantlen people, Kwantlen dialect of Downriver Halkomelem*'/, root meaning unknown, syntactic analysis: nominal, attested by EB, BJ (5/10/64), source: place names reference file #112, #112a, other sources: Wells (1965 1st

ed):15, also <**Qw'ó:ntl'an**>, //q'ʷá·nƛ'(=)ɛn//, dialects: *Kwantlen dial. of Downriver Halkomelem,* attested by EB.

<**qw'ólh** or **qw'álh**>, bound root //q'ʷáɬ or q'ʷɛ́ɬ// *watch, notice,* contrast <**qw'óqw'elex̲**> *watch out, excuse me.*

<**qw'óqw'elhlexw**>, ncs //q'ʷɛ[=AáC_1ə=]ɬ=l-əxʷ or q'ʷá[=C_1ə=]ɬ=l-əxʷ//, ABFC ['*notice s-o/s-th*'], SOC, EFAM, probably <**=(Aá)R1=**> *resultative,* (<**=l**> *non-control transitivizer, happen to/accidentally/manage to do to s-o/s-th*), (<**-exw**> *third-person object*), phonology: reduplication, probably ablaut, compare <**qw'óqw'elex̲**> *watch out, excuse me,* syntactic analysis: transitive verb, attested by AD (3/6/80), Salish cognate: possibly Lushootseed /ʔəs-q'ʷú-q'ʷuɬ/ *be prepared, ready* as in /čn ʔəs-q'ʷú-q'ʷuɬ/ *I am ready (e.g. at the start of a race)* H76:387; found in <**qw'óqw'elhlexwes.**>, //q'ʷɛ[=AáC_1ə=]ɬ=l-əxʷ-əs//, /'*They notice them.*'/, attested by AD, example: <**qw'óqw'elhlexwes te mekw'stám.**>, //q'ʷɛ[=AáC_1ə=]ɬ=l-əxʷ-əs tə mək'ʷ=stɛ́m//, /'*He always notices everything.*'/, attested by AD.

<**qw'óqw'elhmet**>, iecs //q'ʷɛ[=AáC_1ə=]ɬ=məT//, ABFC /'*watch for s-o to come, be on the watch for s-o*'/, SOC, possibly <**=(Aá)R1=**> *resultative,* (<**=met**> *indirect effect control transitivizer*), phonology: reduplication, possible ablaut, syntactic analysis: transitive verb, attested by AD, example: <**tu qw'óqw'elhmetchexw.**>, //t=u q'ʷɛ[=AáC_1ə=]ɬ=məT-c-əxʷ//, /'*Sort of watch for someone to come., Be on the watch for him.*'/, attested by AD (3/6/80).

<**qw'ólhla**>, possibly root //q'ʷáɬlɛ//, ANAF /'*spinal rope inside sturgeon, (sturgeon spinal cord)*'/, ASM ['this was pulled out and cut up and eaten as a treat'], syntactic analysis: nominal, attested by BHTTC.

<**qw'óm**> or <**qw'emó**>, possible bound root //q'ʷəm(=)á// or //q'ʷám// *make a U-shape,* prob. the root of <**qw'ómx̲w**>, bound stem //q'ʷám=x̣ʷ *double up, roll up in a ball//,* clearly related by metathesis, *see also* <**qw'emó**>.

<**sqw'emóx̲w**>, df //s=q'ʷám=M1=x̣ʷ or s=q'ʷám=ə[=M2=]x̣ʷ//, ABFC ['*(be) doubled up in bed on one's side with knees drawn up*'], CAN ['*bent U-shaped plane with handle on each end for canoe-making*'], (<**s=**> *stative*), possibly <**metathesis type 1** or **2**> *resultative?,* (<**=x̲w**> *around in a circle, round*), phonology: metathesis, possibly epenthetic e before m after metathesis 1, syntactic analysis: adjective/adjectival verb, attested by IHTTC.

<**sqw'emóx̲w sxíxep**>, cpds //s=q'ʷám=M1=x̣ʷ s=xʸí[=C_1ə=]p//, CAN ['*bent U-shaped plane with handle on each end for canoe-making*'], TOOL,(<**s=**> *nominalizer*), (<**=R1=**> *continuative*), phonology: metathesis, reduplication, syntactic analysis: nominal phrase with modifier(s), attested by Elders Group (early fall 1976).

<**sqw'emóx̲w xíxepels**>, cpds //s=q'ʷám=M1=x̣ʷ xʸí[=C_1ə=]p=əls//, sas, CAN ['*bent U-shaped plane with handle on each end for canoe-making*'], TOOL,(<**=R1=**> *continuative*), (<**=els**> *structured activity continuative device for*), phonology: metathesis, reduplication, syntactic analysis: nominal phrase with modifier(s), attested by Elders Group (early fall 1976).

<**sqw'emqw'emóx̲w**>, stvi //s=q'ʷəm[=C_1əC_2=]=á=x̣ʷ or s=C_1əC_2=q'ʷám=M1=x̣ʷ//, ABFC /'*(be) doubled up (a person with knees up to his chest), all doubled over*'/, (<**s=**> *stative*), possibly <**=R2=**> *characteristic* or <**R3=**> *plural,* phonology: reduplication, metathesis, syntactic analysis: adjective/adjectival verb, attested by Elders Group (2/27/80), SJ (Story of the Mink and Miss Pitch, toldon tape 5/3/78).

<**sqw'emqw'emóx̲w**>, dnom //s=q'ʷəm[=C_1əC_2=]=á=x̣ʷ or s=C_1əC_2=q'ʷám=M1=x̣ʷ//, CAN ['*U-shaped or horseshoe-shaped knife for scraping out an adzed canoe*'], TOOL, (<**s=**> *nominalizer*), possibly <**=R2=**> *characteristic* or possibly <**R3=**> *plural* or possibly <**metathesis**> *resultative or derivational,* phonology: reduplication, metathesis, syntactic analysis: nominal, attested by

Elders Group (2/27/80), also <**sqwemqwemóx̲w**>, //s=q’^{w}əm[=C$_1$əC$_2$=]áx̣^{w} or s=C$_1$əC$_2$=q’^{w}ám=M1=x̣^{w}//, /'*all doubled up*'/, comment: this last probably mistranscribed, attested by IHTTC (7/13/77).

<**sqw'ómx̲wes**>, stvi //s=q’^{w}ám=x̣^{w}=əs//, DESC /'*(be) rolled up in a ball (twine, yarn, etc.)*'/, (<**s=**> *stative*), lx <**=x̲w**> *around in a circle,* lx <**=es**> *on the face, round object*, syntactic analysis: adjective/adjectival verb, attested by IHTTC (8/22/77).

<**qw'ómx̲west**>, pcs //q’^{w}ám=x̣^{w}=əs=T//, DESC ['*roll s-th up in a ball*'], lx <**=x̲w**> *around in a circle,* lx <**=es**> *round object*, (<**=t**> *purposeful control transitivizer*), syntactic analysis: transitive verb, attested by IHTTC (8/22/77).

<**qw'ómx̲west**>, DESC ['*roll s-th up in a ball*'], *see* qw'óm.

<**qw'ópx̲w**>, bound root or stem //q’^{w}áp(=)x̣^{w} *rapid repeated sound made on wood*//.

<**qw'ópx̲wem**>, df //q’^{w}áp(=)x̣^{w}=əm//, SD ['*(make a) rapid repeated sound usually on wood*'], ANAB, ASM ['made on trees, floors, etc., like noises when a new house is built or someone is working and tapping something on wood or a woodpecker is working'], possibly <**=x̲w**> *around in a circle,* (<**=em**> *intransitivizer, get, have or middle voice*), syntactic analysis: intransitive verb, attested by AD and NP (AHTTC 4/21/80, 4/25/80).

<**qw'opx̲wiqsélem**>, dnom //q’^{w}ap(=)x̣^{w}=iqs=ə[=´=]l=əm//, EZ /'*small red-headed woodpecker,* probably *red-breasted sapsucker,* and/or possibly *the hairy woodpecker or downy woodpecker*'/, ['probably *Sphyrapicus (varius) ruber* and/or possibly *Dryobates villosus harrisi* and *Dryobates villosus orius* or (downy woodpecker) *Dryobates pubescens (gairdneri esp.)*, for Munro and Cowan's *Dryobates* genus Peterson uses *Dendrocopos* and Udvardy uses *Picoides*'], literally /'come/go make a rapidly repeated noise on wood on one's nose'/, lx <**=x̲w**> *around in a circle,* lx <**=iqs**> *on the nose,* (<**=el**> *come, go, get, become,* <**=em**> *middle voice*), possibly <**=´=**> *derivational*, phonology: stress-shift, zero-derivation to nominal, syntactic analysis: nominal, attested by AHTTC (4/25/80) correcting my transcription of EL (9/15/78), also <**qw'opxwiqsélem**>, //q’^{w}ap(=)x^{w}=iqs=ə[=´=]l=əm//, also /'*ordinary small woodpecker*'/, Elder's comment: "this woodpecker is also called t'ót'ep'els", contrast <**t'ót'ep'els**> *ordinary small woodpecker; pecking*, attested by EL (9/15/78).

<**qw'ópx̲wem**>, SD ['*(make a) rapid repeated sound usually on wood*'], *see* qw'ópx̲w.

<**qw'opx̲wiqsélem**>, EZ /'*small red-headed woodpecker,* probably *red-breasted sapsucker,* and/or possibly *the hairy woodpecker or downy woodpecker*'/, *see* qw'ópx̲w.

<**qw'óqw**>, free root //q’^{w}áq^{w}//, ABFC /'*whip once (with stick), got hit*'/, SOC, comment: probably mispronounced for kw'óqw *clubbed, hit with a stick-like object* but since this and derivatives are glossed *whip* more than once itcould be a separate root; there is also some comparative evidence for sucha second root meaning *whip* in contrast to kw'óqw *club, hit withstick-like object* (though I can't find it at present), syntactic analysis: intransitive verb, attested by EB.

<**qw'óqwet**>, pcs //q’^{w}áq^{w}=əT//, ABFC ['*whip it*'], SOC, (<**=et**> *purposeful control transitivizer*), syntactic analysis: transitive verb, attested by EB, AC, example: <**qw'óqwet te stiqíw**>, //q’^{w}áq^{w}=əT tə s=tiqíw//, /'*whip the horse*'/, attested by AC.

<**qw'óqw'eqwet**>, cts //q’^{w}á[-C$_1$ə-]q^{w}=əT//, ABFC /'*beating (s-o/s-th), thrashing (s-o/s-th)*'/, SOC, (<**-R1-**> *continuative*), phonology: reduplication, syntactic analysis: transitive verb, attested by Elders Group (3/1/72).

<**qw'ó:leqwet**>, plv //q’^{w}á·[=lə=]q^{w}=əT//, SOC ['*whipping s-o/s-th many times*'], semantic environment ['as of a horse, a child, etc.'], (<**=le=**> *plural action*), phonology: infixed plural,

syntactic analysis: transitive verb, attested by EB (4/11/78 correcting 2/6/76); found in <**qw'ó:leqwetes.**>, //q’ʷá·[=lə=]qʷ=əT-əs//, /'*He's whipping it many times (a horse, a child)., He whips it (a horse).*'/, attested by EB, <**qw'ó:leqwetem.**>, //q’ʷá·[=lə=]qʷ=əT-əm//, /'*(He/She/It/They) got whipped (with a stick)(many times).*'/, attested by EB.

<**kw'óqwtel**> or better <**qw'óqwtel**>, dnom //q’ʷáqʷ=təl or k’ʷáq=təl//, SOC ['*a whip*'], lx <**=tel**> *device to*, syntactic analysis: nominal, attested by BHTTC.

<**qw'oqw'qwiyóls**>, dnom //q’ʷa[=C_1ə=]qʷ=iyáls//, PLAY ['*lacrosse*'], literally /'whipping/clubbing a ball'/, lx <**=iyáls**> *spherical object, ball*, phonology: zero derivation to nominal, syntactic analysis: nominal, attested by SJ (Deming 3/15/79), also <**qw'íqw'qwiyóls**>, //C_1í=q’ʷaqʷ=iyáls//, attested by SJ (Deming 3/15/79), also <**qw'oqw'kwiyóls**>, //q’ʷá[=C_1ə=]qʷ=iyáls//, comment: <**kw**> probable error or mistranscription, attested by Deming (7/27/78).

<**qw'óqwet**>, ABFC ['*whip it*'], *see* qw'óqw.

<**qw'óqw'el**>, df //q’ʷá[=C_1ə=]l or q’ʷɛ́[=AáC_1ə=]l//, EZ ['*(be) tame*'], SOC, probably <**=AáR1=**> *resultative or continuative*, phonology: reduplication, probable ablaut, syntactic analysis: adjective/adjectival verb, attested by CT (6/8/76), Salish cognate: Squamish /q’ʷalʔ/ *tame (ab. person), reserved, distant* and /q’ʷá-q’ʷayʔ/ *very tame, friendly* and /q’ʷáyʔ-at/ *tame (tr. verb)* W73:262, K69:83; Lushootseed root /q’ʷal(a) *tame* as in /ʔəs-q’ʷál/ *it is tame* and /lə-q’ʷál-əxʷ/ *it is getting tame* H76:425, Samish dial. of N. Straits /q’ʷél’q’ʷəl’/ *tame* G86:91; these cognates show that Halkomelem may have either borrowed the word from a language with /a/ or may have ablaut since the Halkomelem cognate should have /ɛ/, example: <**qw'óqw'el (smíyeth, spá:th, sqwemáy).**>, //q’ʷɛ́[=AáC_1ə=]l (s=mə́yəθ, s=pɛ́·θ, s=qʷəm=ɛ́y)//, /'*(It's a) tame (animal, bear, dog).*'/, attested by CT.

<**qw'óqw'ele<u>x</u>**>, df //q’ʷá[=C_1ə=]l(=)əx̣ or q’ʷɛ́[=AáC_1ə=]l(=)əx̣ or q’ʷá[=C_1ə=]ɬ[=L=]=əx̣ //, LANG /'*excuse me, Excuse me., Watch out.*'/, semantic environment ['used when passing closely to someone, polite'], root meaning prob. <**qw'ólh** or **qw'álh**>, bound root //q’ʷáɬ or q’ʷɛ́ɬ// *watch, notice* as in <qw'óqw'elhmet> *be on the watch for s-o* and <qw'óqw'elhlexw> *notice s-o/s-th* or poss.? <qw'óqw'el> *tame*, possibly <**=(e)<u>x</u>**> *distributive*, possibly <**=R1=** or **=AáR1=**> *resultative or continuative*, (semological comment: there is no inflection for *me* present in the word), phonology: reduplication, voicing, liquidization ablaut, syntactic analysis: intransitive verb, interjection?, syntactic comment: can be used all by itself as an utterance, attested by Deming, RP and EB, AC, Salish cognate: Squamish /q’ʷá-q’ʷayʔáx̣/ *excuse me* as in /q’ʷá-q’ʷayʔáx̣-čxʷ qʷəqʷtqáncut-čn/ *excuse me, I am going to pass by (a phrase of politeness when inconveniencing someone in a narrow passage) cf.? /q’ʷayʔq’ʷáyʔəx̣/ shy, nervous, wild (ab. animals)* W73:92, K69:83 (where one is directed to K67:364); found in <**qw'óqw'ele<u>x</u>lha.**>, //q’ʷɛ[=AáC_1ə=]l(=)əx̣-ɬɛ//, /'*Excuse me., Watch out.*'/, attested by AC, <**qw'óqw'ele<u>x</u>chap.**>, //q’ʷɛ[=AáC_1ə=]l(=)əx̣-c-ɛp//, /'*Excuse me folks., Watch out you folks.*'/, attested by AC, <**qw’óqw’ele<u>x</u>thòx**>, ///q’ʷɛ[=AáC_1ə=]l(=)əx̣=T-áxʸ//, /'Excuse me.'/, attested by RG & EH (4/10/99 Ling332), <**qw’óqw’ele<u>x</u>tòlè**>, ///q’ʷɛ[=AáC_1ə=]l(=)əx̣=T-álə//, /'Excuse us.'/, phonology: downstepping, updrifting, attested by RG & EH (4/10/99 Ling332)

<**qw'óqw'elhlexw**>, ABFC ['*notice s-o/s-th*'], *see* qw'ólh or qw'álh.

<**qw'óqw'elhmet**>, ABFC /'*watch for s-o to come, be on the watch for s-o*'/, *see* qw'ólh or qw'álh.

<**qw'óqw'eqwet**>, ABFC /'*beating (s-o/s-th), thrashing (s-o/s-th)*'/, *see* qw'óqw.

<**qw'óqw'iy**>, FIRE /'*burned (of rocks), scorched (of rocks)*'/, *see* qw'á:y.

<**qw'óqw'iy**>, df //q'ʷá[=C_1ə=]y//, FSH [*'fishing pole'*], (<**=R1=**> *continuative* or *derivational*), phonology: reduplication, syntactic analysis: nominal, attested by Elders Group (2/11/76, Fish Camp 8/2/77), Deming (3/25/76).

<**Qw'oqw'íyets** or **Qw'óqw'iyets**>, df //q'ʷa[=C_1ə=]y=í[=M2=]c or q'ʷɛ[=AaC$_1$ə=]y=í[=M2=]c or q'ʷa[=C_1ə= ´=]y=əc//, PLN [*'location closest to & southwest of <Sqw'á:lets> Hill's Bar on same side of river'*][prob. same as Qw'oqw'iy in Stó:lō Coast Salish HIstorical Atlas (2001), i.e. location closest to & southwest of <**Sqw'á:lets**> *Hill's Bar* on same side of river], root prob. *scorched*, possibly <**=íts ~ =ets**> *on the back*, phonology: possible reduplication or ablaut or metathesis, syntactic analysis: nominal, attested by CT (1973), source: place names reference file #281.

<**qw'oqw'qwiyóls**>, PLAY [*'lacrosse'*], *see* qw'óqw.

<**qw'ót**>, probable bound root //q'ʷát//, meaning uncertain

<**sqw'óteleqw**>, df //s=q'ʷát=ələqʷ//, ANA [*'crown of head'*], (<**s=**> *nominalizer*), root meaning unknown, lx <**=eleqw**> *on top of the head*, syntactic analysis: nominal, attested by IHTTC, compare <**sqwóteleqw**> *crown of the head, top of the head*, Salish cognate: Samish dial. of N. Straits VU /q'təlíʔqʷ/, LD /šq'ətəlíʔqʷ/ *crown, top of head* (VU says may be slang term, is the same as the word for *roof* G86:73, (Songish dial. of N. Straits /sq'tələ́qʷ/ *roof* M68:97), maybe Squamish /q'ət-iʔəqʷ-ánʔ/ *go around the head* W73:138, K69:80 beside Squamish /n-q'áy-c-iʔəqʷ/ *top of the head* W73:137, K67:309, also <**sqwóteleqw**>, //s=qʷá(=)t=ələqʷ//, possibly root <**sqwá**> *hole*, (semological comment: this root may have been suggested by EB after the hole or soft spot in a baby's crown), attested by BJ (5/10/64, new transcript p.118), EB (5/25/76), Elders Group (9/17/75).

<**qw'oxwemáléqep**>, df //q'ʷax̣ʷ=əm=ɛ́lə́qəp//, ABFC [*'(have an) underarm smell'*], root meaning unknown unless *dirty* as perhaps in qw'exw=él=tses *fingernail, claw* lit. perhaps *gray/brown/dirty =part =on the hand* and ts=qw'íxw *brown, brownish-black*, possibly <**=em**> *middle voice or intransitivizer*, lx <**=áléqep**> *smell, odor*, syntactic analysis: intransitive verb, attested by Elders Group (5/25/77), Salish cognate: Lushootseed /q'ʷáx̣ʷəb/ *strong and unpleasant odor* H76:426.

<**qw'ő:l**>, (formerly spelled) <**q'ő:l** >, free root //q'ʷó·l//, ANA [*'ear'*], HHG [*'handle of a cup'*], (semological comment: named after the similarity of shape of the handle to an ear), usage: somewhat humorous as cup handle, phonology: the perception of labialization (the <**w**>/ʷ/) is weakened by the rounding of the following vowel, syntactic analysis: noun, nominal, attested by Elders Group (2/25/76, elsewhere), BJ (5/10/64), AC, other sources: ES /q'ʷə́wəl/ [q'ʷó·l] (Cw /q'ʷí·n/), JH /q'ʷú·l/, H-T <k·wōl>, also <**qw'í:n**>, //q'ʷí·n//, [q'ʷéyn], dialects: *Katzie dial. of Downriver Halkomelem*, attested by Mandy Charnley (Elders Group 5/3/78), ASM ['ear'], example: <**tós tel qw'ő:l**>, //tás t-əl q'ʷó·l//, /*'bump my ear'*/, attested by AC, <**lí: sáyem ta qw'ő:l?**>, //lí-ə sɛ́y=əm t-ɛ q'ʷó·l//, /*'Have you got an earache?'*/, literally /'does your ear ache'/, attested by AC, <**th'átsem kw'el q'ő:l.**>, //θ'ɛ́c=əm k'ʷ-əl q'ʷó·l//, /*'My ears are ringing.'*/, attested by Elders Group (11/10/76), <**tám kw'el q'ő:l.**>, //tɛ́m k'ʷ-əl q'ʷó·l//, /*'My ears are ringing.'*/, literally /'my ear(s) is/are call/ring (of a telephone)'/, attested by Elders Group (11/10/76), ASM ['handle of a cup'], <**wéte q'ő:ls.**>, //ʔəwə= ´tɛ q'ʷó·l-s//, /*'It has no handle., It has no ear.'*/, literally /'it is none its ear'/, usage: humorous, attested by Elders Group (2/25/76).

<**qw'ő:l ~ kw'ő:l**>, bound root or stem //q'ʷó·l or k'ʷól or q'ʷów=l or k'ʷów=l//, root meaning unknown

<**sqw'ő:lmexw ~ skw'ő:lmexw**>, df //s=q'ʷó·l(=)mexw or s=k'ʷów=lməxʷ//, EB /*'blackberry (fruit),* (before contact, only) *wild trailing blackberry,* (now also) *evergreen blackberry,* (now also) *Himalaya blackberry'*/, ['before contact, only *Rubus ursinus,* now also *Rubus laciniatus,* and *Rubus procerus*'], ASM ['the berries of the trailing variety are ready as early as July, those of the evergreen

somewhat later, those of the Himalaya in late August and even later'], MED ['a tea made from boiled roots is diarrhea medicine, a tea from the leaves is medicine for stomach ache'], (<**s=**> *nominalizer*), root meaning unknown, possibly <**=mexw**> *people* or possibly <**=lmexw**> *medicine??* or *on the breast??*, perhaps related to root //in kw'ew=ítsel// *grizzly bear* (where =ítsel may be *on the back),* phonology: labialization is sometimes less noticeable before ō here almost sk'ő:lmexw, syntactic analysis: nominal, attested by AC, other sources: ES /sk'ʷə́w·lməxʷ/ (CwMs /sk'ʷí·lməxʷ/) *blackberries*, H-T <skő̄lmoq> *blackberry (trailing) (Rubus sp.)*, also <**sqw'ő:lmexw**>, //s=q'ʷów=lməxʷ//, attested by BJ (5/10/64, 12/5/64), example: EB, FOOD <**sqw'ő:lmexw sqe'óleqw**>, *blackberry juice* (lit. blackberry + fruit juice), (attested by RG,EH 6/16/98 to SN, edited by BG with RG,EH 6/26/00)

<**skw'ő:lmexwelhp**>, ds //s=k'ʷó·lməxʷ=əɬp//, EB /'*blackberry vine, blackberry bush*'/, ['*Rubus ursinus, Rubus laciniatus, Rubus procerus*'], lx <**=elhp**> *plant, tree*, syntactic analysis: nominal, attested by AC, Elders Group.

<**shxwelméxwelh skw'ő:lmexwelhp**>, ds //s=xʷəl=mə[=´=]xʷ=əɬ s=k'ʷó·lməxʷ=əɬp//, EB ['*trailing blackberry vine*'], ['*Rubus ursinus*'], literally /'Indian kind of blackberry'/, ASM ['this was the pre-contact blackberry in the area'], (<**s=**> *stative*), lx <**=elh**> *style, kind of*, syntactic analysis: simple nominal phrase.

<**xwelítemelh skw'ő:lmexwelhp**>, ds //xʷəlítəm=əɬ s=k'ʷó·lməxʷ=əɬp//, EB /'*Himalaya blackberry bush, evergreen blackberry bush*'/, ['*Rubus procerus, Rubus laciniatus*'], literally /'White-man kind of blackberry'/, ASM ['both introduced by non-Indians'], lx <**=elh**> *kind of, style*, syntactic analysis: simple nominal phrase.

<**qw'ő:m**>, df //q'ʷó·m or q'ʷə́w=əm//, ABDF /'*(get) a disease gotten by contacting a frog, a skin eruption,* also *the same disease as the man got in Kawkawa Lake in the Sx̱wó:yx̱wey story,* (perhaps also) *leprosy*'/, possibly <**=em**> *middle voice*, root meaning unknown, syntactic analysis: prob. intransitive verb, attested by HP (Elders Group 9/22/76).

<**qw'sí:tsel**>, df //q'ʷəs=í·cəl//, EZ /'*swallow,* especially *tree swallow* and *bank swallow,* poss. *others found in the area* such as *violet-green swallow?, barn swallow?, cliff swallow?* and *rough-winged swallow?*'/, ['especially *Iridoprocne bicolor* and *Riparia riparia*'], root meaning unknown, possibly <**=í:tsel**> *on the back*, syntactic analysis: nominal, attested by AC (prompted), other sources: ES /q'ʷsí·səl/, JH /q'ʷəq'ʷsí·cəl/ both *swallow.*

R (reduplication)

<**-R1-** or **-C1e-**>, (//**-R1-** or **-C1ə-**//), ASP /'*continuative, be -ing*'/, (semological comment: means the action is still continuing to happen), phonology: infixed reduplication, a type of doubling in Halkomelem lessons and classes, takes the first consonant of the root then adds e (schwa) and inserts or infixes the two sounds after the first vowel of the root, grammatical comment: as discovered by Wayne Suttles in his Musqueam Grammar (consonant alternation 1984) all affixes and ablauts used to express continuative can also be used to express resultative aspect (a different meaning) for the same words, another way to say this is the plain continuative form of a given word is the same as the plain resultative form, they are homophonous, so if a given word takes a particular kind of reduplication or ablaut to express continuative it will use the same means to express resultative aspect (if it has a resultative aspect form), this is true also of Upriver Halkomelem, though a few roots have been found for which this is not true, i.e., the continuative aspect has one type of reduplication or ablaut while the resultative aspect of the same root has another type of ablaut or reduplication, syntactic analysis: ii (inflectional infix); found in <**cháchelh**>, cts //cɛ́[-C$_1$ə-]ɬ//, ABDF ['*it's aching of arthritis*'], <**kw'íkw'ets'**>, cts //k'^{w}í[-C$_1$ə-]c'//, FSH ['*butchering*'], <**kwíkwemel**>, cts //k^{w}í[-C$_1$ə-]m=əl//, LT ['*it's getting red*'], <**tskwíkwem**>, cts //c=k^{w}í[=C$_1$ə=]m//, LT ['*[being red]*'], <**kwókwexwels**>, cts //k^{w}ó[-C$_1$ə-]x^w=əls//, ABFC /'*knocking, rapping*'/, <**kw'okw'etl'élmel**>, cts //k'^{w}ɛ[=AaC$_1$ə=]ƛ'=ə́lməl//, ABFC ['*thinking about having intercourse*'], <**làlets'éwtxwem**>, cts //lɛ́[-C$_1$ə-]c'=ə[-´-]wtx^w=əm//, SOC ['*be visiting*'], <**lhálheqem**>, cts //ɬɛ́[-C$_1$ə-]q=əm//, ABFC ['*whispering*'], <**mámelqlexw**>, cts //mə[=Aɛ́=][-C$_1$ə-]l=q=l-əx^w//, rsls, EFAM ['*forgetting (s-th/s-o)*'], <**mímesem**>, cts //mí[-C$_1$ə-]s=əm//, MC ['*picking out*'], <**q'áq'el**>, cts //q'ɛ́[-C$_1$ə-]l//, EFAM ['*believing*'].

<**=R1=** or **=C1e=**>, da //=C$_1$ə= or =C1ə=//, ASP /'*resultative, -ed, have -en (usually results in a past tense or past participle translation in English)*'/, (semological comment: means the action has been completed with some results, inflectional hyphens should probably be used instead of derivational equal signs but the result is often an adjective, thus changing the syntactic subclass of the word and that makes it somewhat derivational too, in Galloway 1977 this was translated as verbal adjective or participle and usually involves the stative prefix s= added onto the same word), phonology: infixed reduplication, a type of doubling in Halkomelem lessons and classes, takes the first consonant of the root then adds e (schwa) and inserts or infixes the two sounds after the first vowel of the root,, syntactic analysis: derivational infix, syntactic comment: usually used along with s= *stative*; found in <**sq'áq'eth'**>, strs //s=q'ɛ́[=C$_1$ə=]θ'//, DESC /'*(be) tight, (leaning backwards [EB])*'/, <**smímeq'**>, strs //s=mí[=C$_1$ə=]q' or s=mí=C$_1$ə=q'//, WATR ['*(be) sunk*'], <**lholhekw'íwel ~ lholhkw'íwel**>, rsls //ɬa[=C$_1$ə=]k'^{w}=íwəl//, EFAM /'*be startled, be dumbfounded, be shocked, be stupified, be speechless, be overwhelmed*'/, <**slhálhe<u>x</u>**>, strs //s=ɬɛ́[=C$_1$ə=]x̣//, FOOD ['*be served*'], literally /'(be spread)'/, <**slí:leqw**>, stvi //s=lí·[=C$_1$ə=]q^w//, DESC /'*be slack, loose, too loose, hanging loose (of a slackened rope)*'/, <**kw'íkw'ets'**>, rsls //k'^{w}í[=C$_1$ə=]c'//, FSH ['*sides of butchered salmon with knife marks in them*'], (<**=R1=**> *resultative*).

<**=R1=** or **=C1e=**>, da //=C$_1$ə= or =C1ə=//, DESC /'*diminutive, little (of subject, object, agent, patient or action)*'/, EFAM ['*pet name*'], phonology: infixed reduplication, a type of doubling in Halkomelem lessons and classes, takes the first consonant of the root then adds e (schwa) and inserts or infixes the two sounds after the first vowel of the root,, syntactic analysis: derivational infix; found in

<**cháchket**>, dms //cɛ́[=C_1ə=]kət//, CLO [*'small jacket'*],<**kw'elókw't'el**>, ds //k'^{w}[-əl-]ɛ[=AáC_1ə=]t'əl//, EZ [*'a few mice'*], (<**-el- infix**> *plural*), (<**á-ablaut** and **R1**> *diminutive*), <**kw'íkw'exwelhp**>, dmn //k'^{w}í[=C_1ə=]x^w=əɬp//, EB /*'"jack pine", lodgepole pine'*/, [*'Pinus contorta'*], (<**=R1=**> *diminutive*), <**smámelet**>, dmn //s=mɛ́[=C_1ə=]l[=ə=]t//, LAND /*'little stone, pebble, little rock hill, small rock mountain (like in the Fraser River in the canyon)'*/, <**múmesmes**>, dmn //mú[=C_1ə=]sməs//, EZ [*'small adult cow'*], <**q'áq'emi**>, dmn //q'ɛ́·[=C_1ə=]m=i(y)//, HAT /*'little girl (perhaps four years), young girl, (girl from five to ten years [EB])'*/, <**húheliya**>, dmn //hú[=C_1ə=]l=iyɛ//, EZ [*'small-sized humpback salmon'*], [*'Oncorhynchus gorbuscha'*], <**á'iy ~ 'á'iy** >, dmn //ʔɛ́[=C_1ə=]y or C_1ɛ́=ʔɛy//, VALJ [*'cute little one'*], probably <**-R1-**> *diminutive*, possibly <**R7=**> *diminutive*.

<**=R1=** or **=C1e=**>, da //=C_1ə= or =C1ə=//, ASP [*'comparative or augmentative'*], phonology: infixed reduplication, a type of doubling in Halkomelem lessons and classes, takes the first consonant of the root then adds e (schwa) and inserts or infixes the two sounds after the first vowel of the root,, syntactic analysis: derivational infix; found in <**sóseqwt** ~ (rarely) **só:seqwt**>, df //sá[=C_1ə=]q^{w}t//, KIN /*'younger, younger sibling, cousin of a junior line (cousin by an ancestor younger than the speaker's), junior cousin (child of a younger sibling of one's parent, (great) grandchild of a younger sibling of one's(great) grandparent), younger brother, younger sister'*/, possibly <**=R1=**> *comparative*, <**thíthe**>, augs //θí=C_1ə//, plv, DESC /*'(be) larger, bigger'*/, (<**=R1**> *augmentative*.

<**=R2** or **=C1eC2**>, da //=C_1əC_2 or =C1əC2//, ASP /*'characteristic, inherent continuative'*/, (semological comment: called inherent continuative in Galloway 1977, this suffix means that the action is done continuously or many times so that it becomes characteristic of the thing doing the action, it is often converts the word to a nominal or noun in English, such as *thief* (characteristically steals, steals many times, steals continuously) or *stinging nettle* (characteristically stings or poisons, stings many times, stings continuously) but also creates verbal adjectives too like *rowdy, talkative* (characteristically talks, talks many times, talks continuously)), phonology: suffixed reduplication which copies the first consonant of the root adds an e (schwa) and then adds a copy of the second consonant of the root, and adds the sequence of three sounds to the end of the root, called a type of doubling in Halkomelem classes and lessons, this suffix usually is also accompanied by ablaut or change of the root vowel to é (schwa), syntactic analysis: derivational suffix; found in <**qélqel**>, chrs //qɛ[=Aə́=]l=C_1əC_2//, SOCT [*'thief'*], (<**é-ablaut on root á**> *derivational*), (<**=R2**> *characteristic*), <**th'é<u>x</u>th'e<u>x</u>**>, chrs //θ'ə́x̣=C_1əC_2//, EB [*'stinging nettle'*], [*'Urtica dioica'*], literally /'sting/poison =characteristically'/, <**qwélqwel**>, chrs //q^{w}ɛ[=Aə́=]l=C_1əC_2//, EFAM /*'be rowdy, be a nuisance, be mischievious'*/, SOC, (<**é-ablaut**> *resultative*? or *continuative*), (<**=R2**> *characteristic*), <**spóypiy**>, chrs //s=páy=C_1əC_2//, stvi, DESC [*'be crooked [characteristically]'*], (<**s=**> *stative*), (<**=R2**> *characteristic*), <**sélseltel**>, chrs //səl=C_1əC_2=təl//, WV /*'spindle for spinning wool, a hand spinner'*/, TOOL, (<**=R2**> *characteristic*), <**sí:si**>, chrs //síy=C_1əC_2//, EFAM /*'be afraid, be scared, be nervous'*/, (<**=R2**> *characteristic*)(<**síy**>, bound root //síy or sə́y *nervous, afraid*//, Salish cognate: Lushootseed /sáy/ *nervous, fidgety, at loose ends, excited* H76:703), <**s'éts-'ets**>, chrs //s=ʔə́c=C_1əC_2//, [sʔɪ́cʔɪc (normal speed), sʔɛ́cʔɛc (hyper-slow speed)], LANG /*'stuttering, to stutter'*/, (<**s=**> *stative*), possibly root <**áts**> as in <**átslexw**> *hear about it*?, (<**=R2**> *characteristic*), <**lésleseqw**>, chrs //lo[=Aə́=]s=C_1əC_2=əq^w//, DESC [*'greasy-headed'*], ANA [*'fatty salmon head'*], FOOD, (<**é-ablaut**> *derivational*), (<**=R2**> *characteristic*), <**yélyelesem**>, chrs //yə́l[=C_1əC_2=]əs=əm//, ABDF /*'(have) a steady toothache, have a toothache'*/, (<**=R2=**> *characteristic*).

<**=R2** or **=C1eC2**>, da //=C_1əC_2 or =C1əC2//, NUM /*'plural, inherent plural'*/, (semological comment: inherent plural and plural in Galloway 1977, this suffix means that an action is done many times so that it becomes characteristic of the thing doing the action, it is often converts the word to a nominal

or noun in English, such as *thief* (characteristically steals, steals many times, steals continuously) or *stinging nettle* (characteristically stings or poisons, stings many times, stings continuously) but also can create some simple plurals as in syáq'yeq' *a lot of logs*), phonology: suffixed reduplication which copies the first consonant of the root adds an e (schwa) and then adds a copy of the second consonant of the root, and adds the sequence of three sounds to the end of the root, called a type of doubling in Halkomelem classes and lessons, this suffix usually is also accompanied by ablaut or change of the root vowel to **é** (schwa), syntactic analysis: derivational suffix; found in <**syáq'yeq'**>, pln //s=yɛq'=C_1əC_2//, EB ['*a lot of logs*'], (<**=R2**> *plural*), <**tewtewá:la ~ tutuwále**>, chrs //təw[=C_1əC_2=](=)ɛ́·lɛ//, LAND /'*side hills, tilted hills, slopes*'/, <**s'éts-'ets**>, chrs //s=ʔə́c=C_1əC_2//, [sʔɪ́cʔɪc (normal speed), sʔɛ́cʔɛc (hyper-slow speed)], LANG /'*stuttering, to stutter*'/, (<**s=**> *stative*), possibly root <**áts**> as in <**átslexw**> *hear about it*?.

<**R3=** or **C1eC2=**>, da //C_1əC_2= or C1əC2=//, NUM /'*plural, (usually) many in a group, collective*'/, (semological comment: plural in Upriver Halkomelem is seldom used for just a few objects or actions, usually it means many in a group), phonology: prefixed reduplication which copies the first consonant of the root adds an e (schwa) and then adds a copy of the second consonant of the root, and adds the sequence of three sounds to the front of the root, called a type of doubling in Halkomelem classes and lessons, added only to the beginning of the root, never before a prefix (such as s=, lexw=, shxw=, etc.), syntactic analysis: derivational prefix, syntactic comment: because it doesn't change the syntactic class of a word it should probably be shown with an inflectional hyphen rather than derivational equal sign, I started to use the equal sign because as a plural marker it seemed to be largely optional semantically and syntactically--unlike inflections, which are normally obligatory as required by the syntax and morphology; found in <**lets'ló:ts'tel**>, plv //C_1əC_2=lɛ́[=Aá=]·c'=T-əl//, rcps, LT ['*(many) different colors*'], <**lemlemá:t**>, its //C_1əC_2=ləmɛ́·=T//, ABFC ['*kick s-th around*'], (<**R3=**> *iterative*), <**steqtéq**>, pln //s=C_1əC_2=tə́q or s=C_1əC_2=tɛ[=Aə́=]q//, WATR /'*jampile, log-jam*'/, EB, (<**s=**> *nominalizer*, R3= *plural*), <**xwiyxwiyáye**>, pln //C_1əC_2=x̣ʷɛ́y=i[=M2=]yɛ//, EZ /'*a lot of flies, big blow-flies*'/, ['order *Diptera*, family *Calliphoridae*'], (<**R3=**> *plural*), <**yelyelísem**>, ds //C_1əC_2=y=əlís=əm or C_1əC_2=yə́lə[=Aí=]s=əm//, WETH ['*(have/get) many icicles*'], <**S'em'oméla**>, pln //s=C_1əC_2=ʔaməlɛ//, SOCT ['*Thompson people*'], (<**s=**> *nominalizer* or *stative*, R3= *plural (collective)*), <**p'elp'álq'em**>, plv //C_1əC_2=p'ɛlq'=əm//, LT /'*shining, (glittering, sparkling (with many reflections))*'/, (<**R3=**> *plural actions or agents*).

<**R4=** or **C1í=**>, da //C_1í= or C1í=//, DESC /'*diminutive, little (of subject, object, agent, patient or action), small, (*all *diminutive* verbs are also *continuative)*'/, (semological comment: as Suttles noticed in his Musqueam Grammar manuscript, diminutives of verbs are semantically also continuative, as in *a little person is/was picking* rather than *a little person picks or picked*), phonology: prefixed reduplication which copies the first consonant of the root adds **í** and adds the two sounds to the front of the root, called a type of doubling in Halkomelem classes and lessons, added only to the beginning of the root, never before a prefix (such as s=, lexw=, shxw=, etc.), to make a plural of such diminutives the **í** is normally ablauted or changed to **é** (schwa) in the reduplication, since this ablaut clearly has a separate semantic function, it is not necessary to set up a new reduplication C1**é**=, syntactic analysis: derivational prefix, syntactic comment: because it doesn't change the syntactic class of a word it should probably be shown with an inflectional hyphen rather than derivational equal sign, I started to use the equal sign because it seemed to be often optional semantically (unlike inflections, which are normally obligatory as required by the syntax and morphology) and seemed to add a more derivation meaning, but it now seems to have been used more by the eldest speakers as a semi-obligatory prefix with verbs; found in <**híhòkwexes**>, dmv //C_1í=hákʷ=əxʸ-əs//, if, CLO ['*he (a small child) is wearing it.*'], (<**R4=**> *diminutive*), <**siseqíws ~ síseqíws**>, dmn //C_1í=səq=íws//, CLO /'*short pants, little pants, underpants*'/, (<**R4=**> *diminutive*), <**qwíqweláts ~ qwíqwelà(:)c**>, dmv

//C_1í=qʷɛ̀·l=ə[=M2=]c//, LANG /*'gossip about someone, talk about someone behind his back'*/, EFAM, literally probably /'small talk on the back'/, (<**R4=**> *diminutive*), <**p'íp'eq'**>, dmv //C_1í=p'əq'//, LT ['*[a little white]*'], ASM ['occurs almost alternately with p'áp'eq'el within the same areas (as shades of white tinged with orange, yellow or blue) so no difference in meaning can really be distinguished between the two forms, the second form has R7= *comparative or emphatic, (sometimes) continuative* which was not attested in color term words by any of the others we interviewed'], (<**R4=**> *diminutive*), <**tsqwíqweyel**>, ds //c=C_1í=qʷɛy=əl//, LT ['*[have/get/be in a state of going a little yellow or green]*'], (semological comment: this term labels almost all the margins of tsqwáy (from green's margins with blue, to yellow's margins with orange and pink and white), it also includes some moderately light green close to the focus of tsqwá:y, which, for EB of Chehalis, is green (as it is for AH of Sumas).), (<**ts=**> *have, get, stative with colors*), (<**R4=**> *diminutive*), (<**=el ~ =íl**> *go, come, get, become*).

<**R5-** or **C1e-**>, (//**R5-** or **C1ə-**//), ASP /*'continuative, be -ing'*/, (semological comment: means the action is still continuing to happen), phonology: prefixed reduplication which copies the first consonant of the root adds e (schwa) and adds the two sounds to the front of the root, called a type of doubling in Halkomelem classes and lessons, added only to the beginning of the root, never before a prefix (such as s=, lexw=, shxw=, etc.),, syntactic analysis: ip (inflectional prefix); found in <**ch'ech'émels**>, cts //C_1ə=c'ə́m=əls//, sas, dnom, ABFC /*'a biter (animal, fish, etc.), a thing that is (always) biting'*/, (<**R5=**> *continuative*), (<**=els**> *structured activity continuative nominal*), <**th'eth'ám**>, cts //C_1ə-θ'ɛ́=m//, ABFC ['*chewing (gum)*'], (<**R5-**> *continuative*), comment: this seems the regular *continuative* for this verb, not th'á:m, see th'eth'át *chewing s-th*, <**tl'etl'áxel**>, df //C_1ə-ƛ'(ʔ)ɛ́=xʸəl or C_1ə=ƛ'(ʔ)ɛ́=xʸəl//, SOC /*'inviting (to come eat, dance), to give a potlatch, (give a feast or gathering), to invite to a feast, invite to a potlatch'*/, possibly <**R5-**> *continuative*, possibly <**R5=**> *derivational*,<**kwekwó:thet**>, cts //C_1ə-kʷɛ[=Aa=]´·=T-ət//, [kʷʊkʷá·θət], ABFC ['*galloping*'], (<**R5-**> *continuative*),

<**R5=** or **C1e=**>, da //C_1ə= or C1ə=//, ASP /*'resultative, -ed, have -en (usually results in a past tense or past participle translation in English)'*/, (semological comment: means the action has been completed with some results, inflectional hyphens should probably be used instead of derivational equal signs but the result is often an adjective, thus changing the syntactic subclass of the word and that makes it somewhat derivational too, in Galloway 1977 this was translated as inherent continuative, often syntactically a verbal adjective/adjectival verb or participle, it may also involve the stative prefix s= added onto the same word), phonology: prefixed reduplication which copies the first consonant of the root adds e (schwa) and adds the two sounds to the front of the root, called a type of doubling in Halkomelem classes and lessons, added only to the beginning of the root, never before a prefix (such as s=, lexw=, shxw=, etc.),, syntactic analysis: derivational prefix; found in <**stl'etl'íq'**>, strs //s=C_1ə=ƛ'íq'//, TCH /*'(be) too tight (of shoes, clothes, trap, box), tight (of a dress one can't get into), too tight to get into (of dress, car, box of cards, etc.)'*/, (<**s=**> *stative*), (<**R5=**> *resultative*), <**sqweqwá**>, dnom //s=C_1ə=qʷɛ́//, DESC ['*a hole*'], ASM ['like a knothole, hole in a pail, cave, tunnel'], (<**s=**> *nominalizer* perhaps ~ *stative* here), possibly <**R5=**> *durative or resultative,*

<**R5=** or **C1e=**>, (//**R5=** or **C1ə=**//), NUM /*'(rare) plural, (usually) many in a group, collective'*/, also alloseme (ASM) NUM /diminutive plural/ is an alternative to usually stressed schwa ablaut on R4 *diminutive*, (semological comment: plural in Upriver Halkomelem is seldom used for just a few objects or actions, usually it means many in a group (as in *legs, feet*)), phonology: prefixed reduplication which copies the first consonant of the root adds e (schwa) and adds the two sounds to the front of the root, called a type of doubling in Halkomelem classes and lessons, added only to the beginning of the root, never before a prefix (such as s=, lexw=, shxw=, etc.), more often found added to a form also pluralized by =el= infix; found in sts'eló:meqw ~ sts'ets'eló:meqw *great grandparents/-*

children, syntactic analysis: derivational prefix; found in <**sx̱ex̱éyle** or **sx̱ex̱íle**>, //s=C₁ə=x̣ə[=Aí=]lə//, /'*legs, feet*'/. Other examples are: <**sqweqweméytses**>, ds //s=C₁í=Aə=qʷəm=ɛ́y=cəs or s=C₁ə=qʷəm=ɛ́y=cəs//, EB ['*pussy willow*'], ['*Salix* species, possibly *Salix hookeriana* or *Salix sitchensis* or any *Salix?*'], literally /'puppies on the hand'/, (<**s=**> *nominalizer*, R4= plus e-ablaut or R5= *diminutive plural*), <**sqweqwewáth**>, dmpn //s=C₁ə=qʷɛ́=w(=)ə[=M2=]θ//, EZ ['*bunch of rabbits*'], (<**s=**> *nominalizer*, R5= *diminutive plural*), <**th'eth'elá:ykwem**>, dmpv //C₁ə=θ'[-əl-]ɛ́·ykʷ=əm//, SD ['*squeaking (of lots of mice)*'], ABFC, (<**R5=**> *diminutive*), (<**-el-**> *plural*), <**yutl'étl'elòm**>, df //y=əw=C₁əAə́=ƛ'[=əl=]à=m//, PRON /'*(that's) them (lots of little ones), they (many small ones)*'/, DEM, (<**R5= with é-ablaut**> *diminutive plural*), (<**=el=**> *plural*), <**lhelhewqí:m**>, dmpn //C₁ə=ɬəw(=)q=í·m//, EB /'*smallest gray swamp blueberries, smallest variety of Canada blueberry*'/, ['*Vaccinium myrtilloides*'], (<**R5= (or R4=Aə=)**> *diminutive plural*), <**memáx**>, plv //C₁ə=mɛ́=xʸ//, SOC /'*to separate people fighting, to split up people fighting*'/, (<**R5=**> *plural object*). Some of the diminutive plural forms could also be cited under the diminutive alloseme below.

<**R5=** or **C1e=**>, (//**R5=** or **C1ə=**//), NUM /'*distributive, to each*'/, (semological comment: so far only found with one word, a numeral), phonology: prefixed reduplication which copies the first consonant of the root adds e (schwa) and adds the two sounds to the front of the root, called a type of doubling in Halkomelem classes and lessons, added only to the beginning of the root, never before a prefix (such as s=, lexw=, shxw=, etc.),, syntactic analysis: derivational prefix; found in <**x̱ex̱e'ó:thel**>, //C₁ə=x̣=əʔɛ=á·θəl//, /'*four to each*'/, attested by AC, <**lhelhíxw ~ lhíxw**>, ds //C₁ə=ɬíxʷ ~ ɬíxʷ//, NUM ['*three things*'], nca <**R5=**> *things* nca (possibly an old *distributive* nca, see <**x̱ex̱e'óthel**> *four to each* also with <**R5=**). <**memáx**>, plv //C₁ə=mɛ́=xʸ//, SOC /'*to separate people fighting, to split up people fighting*'/, (<**R5=**> *plural object*).

<**R5=** or **C1e=**>, da //C₁ə= or C1ə=//, DESC /'*diminutive, small, little*'/, phonology: prefixed reduplication which copies the first consonant of the root adds e (schwa) and adds the two sounds to the front of the root, called a type of doubling in Halkomelem classes and lessons, added only to the beginning of the root, never before a prefix (such as s=, lexw=, shxw=, etc.),, syntactic analysis: derivational prefix; found in <**sx̱wex̱wiyá:m**>, //s=C₁ə=x̣ʷiyɛ́·m//, /'*story, fable, fairy tale*'/, compare <**sx̱wiyá:m ~ sx̱weyá:m**> *myth, legend*,

<**=R6=** or **=eC2=**>, da //=əC₂= or =əC2=//, NUM /'*(rare) plural, (usually) many in a group, collective*'/, (semological comment: plural in Upriver Halkomelem is seldom used for just a few objects or actions, usually it means many in a group), syntactic analysis: derivational infix; found in <**ts'tl'étl'xel**>, df //c'[=əC₂=]i[=Aə́=]ƛ'=xʸəl//, ABFC ['*takes short steps*'], (<**=R6=**> *plural or diminutive or out-of-control*), <**sts'iyáye**>, df //s=c'iyáyə or s=c'[=əC₂=]áyə or s=c'iy=áyə//, KIN ['*twins*'], ASM ['twins were sometimes taken up into the mountains to be raised since they were said to have great power, for example over the weather, even today if twins are teased it will cause rain'], (<**s=**> *nominalizer*), possibly root <**ts'iy**> *near, close by* as in Squamish, possibly <**=R6=**> *plural*, possibly <**=óye**> *affectionate diminutive*, <**chewő:lhp**>, dnom //c[=əC₂=]ə́w=(ə)ɬp//, EB ['*black cottonwood tree*'], ['*Populus balsamifera trichocarpa*'], ASM ['the sweet cambium, sx̱á:meth or ts'its'emá:welh, was scraped or licked off of the peeled bark and eaten fresh; the cotton from the catkins was gathered and mixed with dog and goat wool to whiten it and make it go further'], literally /'many shores tree or little shore tree (so named since it grows mainly on the shores of rivers or lakes)'/, (<**=R6= (here =ew=)**> either *plural* or *diminutive*),

<**=R6=** or **=eC2=**>, da //=əC₂= or =əC2=//, DESC /'*diminutive, little (of subject, object, agent, patient or action), small, (*all *diminutive* verbs are also *continuative)*'/, syntactic analysis: derivational infix; found in <**spelól**>, dmn //s=p[=əC₂=]ál//, EZ /'*smaller crow, northwestern crow*'/, ['*Corvus caurinus*'],

(<**=R6=**> *diminutive*), <**sá:yt'em ~ sayít'em**>, cts //si[-Aɛ́·-]y=t'=əm ~ s[-əC_2-]íy=t'=əm or less likely si[-Aɛ-]y[=í=]=t'=əm//, izs, ABFC /'*being tickled, (having tickling, getting tickling), tickley*'/, (<**á(:)-ablaut ~ -R6-**> *continuative*).

<**R7=** or **C1á=**>, da //C_1ɛ́= or C1ɛ́=//, NUM /'*(rare) plural, (usually) many in a group, collective*'/, (semological comment: plural in Upriver Halkomelem is seldom used for just a few objects or actions, usually it means many in a group), syntactic analysis: derivational prefix; found in <**mámele**>, pln //C_1ɛ́=mələ//, KIN /'*children (kinterm, someone's), sons, daughters*'/, (<**R7=**> *plural*), phonology: reduplication, syntactic analysis: nominal, attested by AC, BJ)5/64), other sources: H-T <mámela> (macron over a) *children (collect.)*,

<**R7=** or **C1á=**>, da //C_1ɛ́= or C1ɛ́=//, DESC /'*diminutive, little (of subject, object, agent, patient or action), small, (*all *diminutive* verbs are also *continuative)*'/, syntactic analysis: derivational prefix; found in <**ts'áts'ets'tl'ím te kwíkweshú**>, //C_1ɛ́=C_1ə=c'ƛ'ɛ́=m=ím tə C_1í=k^{w}əšú//, /'*The little pig is hopping.*'/, (<**R7=**> *continuative* or *emphatic*, R5= *diminutive*), <**máma**>, dmn //C_1ɛ́=mɛ(l)//, KIN /'*grandfather (affectionate), (grampa)*'/, usage: affectionate, possibly <**R7=**> *diminutive*?, consonant-loss> *affectionate*?,

<**R7=** or **C1á=**>, da //C_1ɛ́= or C1ɛ́=//, EFAM ['*emphatic*'], syntactic analysis: derivational prefix; found in <**á'altha**>, ds //C_1ɛ́=ʔɛ́lθɛ//, PRON /'*it's me., that's me., I* do, *I* am (ls emphatic)'/, (<**R7=**> *emphatic*), <**á:'a**>, us //possibly C_1ɛ́[=·=]=ʔɛ//, CJ ['*yes*'], possibly <**R7=**> *emphatic*, probably <**=:=**> *emphatic*, possibly root <**á**> *yes* as in Cheh. <**li á**> or <**li'á**> *yes*, <**sásq'ets**>, df //C_1ɛ́=səq'=əc or sɛ́[=C_1ə=]q'=əc//, EZ ['*sasquatch*'], ASM ['a stl'**á**leqem creature resembling a huge (six- to nine-foot tall) wild hairy man, the name was first borrowed into English apparently after being spelled by J.W. Burns, a teacher at Chehalis Indian school on Harrison River where sasquatches were sighted fairly often (John Green: On the Track of The Sasquatch, etc.)'], possibly root <**séq'**> *split, crack*, possibly <**R7=**> *augmentative*, possibly <**=ets**> *on the back*,

<**R8=** or **C1a=**>, da //C_1ɛ= or C1ɛ=//, ASP /'*continuative, be -ing*'/, (semological comment: means the action is still continuing to happen), syntactic analysis: derivational prefix; found in <**mamá:lat**>, cts //C_1ɛ-mɛ́·lɛ=T//, FSH ['*baiting s-th (fish-line)*'], HUNT ['*baiting s-th (trap)*'], (<**R8-**> *continuative*), <**lhalhí:lt**>, cts //C_1ɛ-ɬí·l=T//, CAN ['*bailing*'], (<**R8-**> *continuative*).

<**R8=** or **C1a=**>, da //C_1ɛ= or C1ɛ=//, ASP /'*resultative, -ed, have -en (usually results in a past tense or past participle translation in English)*'/, (semological comment: means the action has been completed with some results, inflectional hyphens should probably be used instead of derivational equal signs but the result is often an adjective, thus changing the syntactic subclass of the word and that makes it somewhat derivational too, in Galloway 1977 this was translated as verbal adjective or participle and usually involves the stative prefix s= added onto the same word), syntactic analysis: derivational prefix; found in <**smamalyí**>, strs //s=mɛ[=C_1ə=]lyí or s=C_1ɛ=mɛlyí//, KIN ['*be married*'], SOC, (<**s=**> *stative*), possibly <**R8=** or **=R1=**> *resultative*, <**ma'eméstexw ~ máméstexw**>, df //C_1ɛ=ʔə-mə́=sT-əx^w or C_1ɛ́=mə́=sT-əx^w//, TVMO /'*bring s-th, brought s-th*'/, SOC, (<**R8= ~ R7=**> *resultative*?, e- *non-auxiliary verb*?), <**spapí:l**>, strs //s=C_1ɛ=pə[=Aí·=]l//, LAND ['*(be) buried*'], CH, (<**s=**> *stative*, R8= *resultative*),

<**R8=** or **C1a=**>, da //C_1ɛ= or C1ɛ=//, NUM /'*(rare) plural, (usually) many in a group, collective*'/, (semological comment: plural in Upriver Halkomelem is seldom used for just a few objects or actions, usually it means many in a group), syntactic analysis: derivational prefix; found in <**chachí:q'el**>, dnom //C_1ɛ=cí·q'əl//, EZ ['*mink*'], ['*Mustela vison energumenos*'], ASM ['The story-character Mink is known from many stories in which he tries to marry or have sex with all manner of creatures (and

plants, etc.) before and during the time of the Transformers; he usually fails for comic reasons.'], (<**R8=**> *derivational*).

<**=R9=** or **=C1á(:)=**>, da //=C_1έ(·)= or =C1έ(:)=//, ASP /'*continuative, be -ing*'/, (semological comment: means the action is still continuing to happen), syntactic analysis: derivational infix; found in <**t'ot'á**>, df //t'a-C_1έ(·)//, ABDF /'*sprain, (getting sprained?)*'/, possibly <**-R9**> *continuative or resultative.*

<**=R9=** or **=C1á(:)=**>, da //=C_1έ(·)= or =C1έ(:)=//, ASP /'*resultative, -ed, have -en (usually results in a past tense or past participle translation in English)*'/, (semological comment: means the action has been completed with some results, inflectional hyphens should probably be used instead of derivational equal signs but the result is often an adjective, thus changing the syntactic subclass of the word and that makes it somewhat derivational too, in Galloway 1977 this was translated as verbal adjective or participle and usually involves the stative prefix s= added onto the same word), syntactic analysis: derivational infix; found in <**sx̱ex̱ákw'**>, strs //s=xə[=C_1έ(·)=]k'^{w}//, SH /'*(be) squeezed in, jammed up, tight*'/, (<**s=**> *stative*), (<**=R9=**> *resultative*), <**xwtetáq**>, df //x^w(ə)=C_1ə=tέq or x^w(ə)=C_1ə=tə[=Aέ=]q or x^w(ə)=tə[=C_1έ(·)=]q//, BLDG ['*be closed*'], ECON, (<**xw(e)=**> *become, get*), possibly <**R5=** or **=R9=**> *resultative*, possibly <**á-ablaut**> *durative*,

<**R10=** or **C1ó=**>, da //C_1á= or C1á=//, HUMC ['*person*'], syntactic analysis: derivational prefix; found in <**lólets'e**>, //C_1á=ləc'ə//, /'*one person, alone*'/. There are a few examples which may show this type indicating *continuative*: <**kwekwí:l ~ kwokwí:l**>, cts //C_1ə-k^{w}ε[-Aí-]·l ~ C_1á-k^{w}ε[-Aí-]·l//, [k^{w}ʊk^{w}í·l ~ k^{w}ɔk^{w}í·l], SOC /'*hiding, hiding oneself*'/, (<**R5-** or **R10-**> *continuative*), (<**í-ablaut**> *durative*), <**kwókwelōws ~ kwókwelews**>, rsls //C_1á-k^{w}ε[=Aə=]l=əws or C_1á=k^{w}ε[-Aə-]l=əws//, cts, SOC /'*murdering, murderer (of more than one)*'/, (<**R10-**> *continuative*).

<**R11=** or **C1V1=**>, da //C_1V_1= or C1V1=//, NUM ['*plural or augmentative*'], syntactic analysis: derivational prefix, dialects: *Chilliwack, Sumas, Matsqui (and downriver and island Halkomelem)*; found in <**temqoqó: ~ temqó:**>, ds //təm=qá· ~ təm=C_1ə=qá· or təm=C1V1=qá·//, WATR /'*high water time (yearly, usually in June), June*'/, lx <**tem=**> *time of/for, season of/for*, (<**R5=**> or a new type of reduplication **(**<**C1V1=**>**,** perhaps <**R11=**>**)** *augmentative* or *plural*), <**Qoqoláx̱el**>, df //qa=C1V1=l(=)έx̣əl or C1V1=qa=l(=)έx̣əl or C_1V_1=qa=l(=)έx̣əl//, PLN /'*Watery Eaves, a famous longhouse and early village on a flat area on Chilliwack River just a quarter mile upriver/east above Vedder Crossing*'/, literally /'watery eaves'/, ASM ['named for a famous and unique longhouse designed with a "V" in its roof which collected and held rain water, it could be accessed for drinking water or other water by pulling a rope connected to a raisable plank'], possibly <**C1V1= (i.e. R11=)**> *augmentative or plural* or possibly <**=C1V1**> (i.e. R12) *characteristic* or possibly <**=el**> *get, come, go, become*, lx <**=(l)áx̱el**> *part of a building, side of a building*, <**yáysele ~ yéysele**>, dnom //ʔi=ʔisέ[=M2=]lə//, [yǽysələ ~ yéysələ], HUMC ['*two people*'], EZ ['*two supernatural creatures*'], NUM, lx <**metathesis**> and irregular type of reduplication *people (classifier)*.

<**=R12** or **=C1V1**>, da //=C_1V_1 or =C1V1//, ASP ['*characteristic*'], syntactic analysis: derivational suffix, dialects: probably only *Sumas, Matsqui (and downriver and island Halkomelem)*; found in <**Qoqoláx̱el**>, df //qa=C1V1=l(=)έx̣əl or C1V1=qa=l(=)έx̣əl or C_1V_1=qa=l(=)έx̣əl//, PLN /'*Watery Eaves, a famous longhouse and early village on a flat area on Chilliwack River just a quarter mile upriver/east above Vedder Crossing*'/, literally /'watery eaves'/, ASM ['named for a famous and unique longhouse designed with a "V" in its roof which collected and held rain water, it could be accessed for drinking water or other water by pulling a rope connected to a raisable plank'], possibly <**C1V1= (i.e. R11=)**> *augmentative or plural* or possibly <**=C1V1**> (i.e. R12) *characteristic* or possibly <**=el**> *get, come, go, become*, lx <**=(l)áx̱el**> *part of a building, side of a building*, phonology: reduplication (perhaps doubling prefix #1 with same vowel= or =doubling suffix with same vowel), syntactic

analysis: nominal, attested by BJ (Wells Tapes), Elders Group (8/24/77), other sources: Wells 1965`(1st`ed.):19, Duff 1952, source: place names reference file #221.

<**R13=** or **C1V1C2=**>, da //$C_1V_1C_2$= or C1V1C2=//, NUM ['*plural continuative*'], syntactic analysis: derivational prefix, dialects: probably only *Sumas, Matsqui (and downriver and island Halkomelem)*; found in <**qo'qo'ólésem**>, mdls //C1V1C2=qaʔ=áləs=əm//, ABFC ['*one's eyes are watering*'], (<**C1V1C2=** perhaps **R13=**> *plural continuative*), root <**qó'**> *water*, lx <**=óles**> *in the eye*, (<**=em**> *middle voice*).

S

<**s, s, s, s, s. s**>, free root //s, s, s, s, s, s//, LANG ['*shhh. (said to babies for ex.)*'], syntactic analysis: interjection, attested by Deming (7/27/78).

<**s=**>, da //s=//, CJ /'*nominalizer, something to, something that, someone to/that*'/, (semological comment: more often used with non-continuative stems than is <shxw=> *nominalizer, something for, something that* which is almost always used with continuative stems (a surprising discovery)), syntactic analysis: derivational suffix, syntactic comment: also nominalizes (subordinates) verbs and verb phrases and sentences, in such functions it is phonologically suffixed to the abstract demonstrative article <**kw'e**> or <**kw**> or to possessive pronoun suffixes attached to the article (only <**-el**> or <**-a**> precede the possessed nominal), sometimes the first verb in a relative clause is also nominalized (it needn't be, it only needs to be preceded by a demonstrative article), in all these syntactic functions the prefix is usually shown as <**s-**> or <**-s**> since it is required by the syntax not by the semantics; found in <**sp'ótl'em**>, //s=p'áƛ'=əm//, /'*smoke*'/, *see* under stem <**p'ótl'em**> *to smoke*, <**st'í:lem**>, //s=t'í·l=əm//, /'*a song*'/, literally /'something to sing'/, *see* under stem <**t'í:lem**> *sing*, <**sq'ép**>, //s=q'ə́p//, /'*a gathering*'/, literally /'something to gather'/, *see* under stem <**q'ép**> *gather*, <**smékw'em**>, //s=mə́k'ʷ=əm//, /'*something second-hand*'/, *see* under stem <**mékw'em**> *use second-hand*, literally /'something to use second-hand'/, <**skwexá:m**>, //s=kʷɛ́·xʸ=M1=əm//, /'*a number*'/, literally /'something to count'/, *see* under stem <**kwexá:m**> *count*, <**swótle**>, //s=wɛ[=Aá=]t=əl=ə//, /'*somebody*'/, example: <**éy kw'els lám.**>, //ʔɛ́y k'ʷ-əl-s lɛ́m//, /'*It's good that I go., I'd better go.*'/, <**tel s'í:kw'**>, //te-l s-ʔí·k'ʷ//, /'*what I lost*'/, contrast <**te q'áq'et'em**> *something sweet*. ASM: *inalienable possession nominalizer*-- with body parts beginning with s=, the s= is present when someone's part is mentioned, but can be omitted when talking about body parts in general; <**th'emxweláx̱el te'íle**>, //θ'əm=xʷ=əlɛ́x̣əl tə ʔí=lə//, /'*This is an elbow.*'/, syntactic comment: when naming a number of body parts like this the s= *nominalizer* is left off; the s= is present when the body part is possessed (inalienable possession); the following body parts are attested working this way: (s=)th'emxweláx̱el *elbow*, Cheh. (s=)th'emeláx̱el *arm bone, point of elbow*,(s=)qep'ó:lthetel *knee*, (sh-)xw'ílàmàlà ~ (sh-)xw'ílámálá*shoulder*, and perhaps others, attested by IHTTC.

<**s=**>, da //s=//, ASP /'*stative, be*'/, CJ, syntactic analysis: derivational suffix; found in <**spópiy**>, //s=pá[=C_1ə=]y//, /'*be crooked*'/, *see* under stem <**pó:y**> *bend*, <**spípew**>, //s=pí[=C_1ə=]w//, /'*be frozen*'/, *see* under stem <**pí:w**> *freeze*, <**sthethá:kw'**>, //s=θə[=C_1ɛ́(·)=]k'ʷ//, /'*be stretched, straight, be pulled*'/, *see* under stem <**thékw'**> *pull*, <**syémyem**>, //s=yə́m=C_1əC_2//, /'*be pregnant*'/, *see* under stem <**yem=**> *around the middle*, <**st'ápi**>, //s=t'ɛ́p=iy//, /'*be dead (of tree)*'/, *see* under stem <**t'ápi(y)**> *die (of tree)*, <**selá ~ slá**>, //s=hə=lɛ́ ~ s=lɛ́//, /'*be tight, tightly*'/, <**schewót**>, //s=cəwát//, /'*be smart, be good at, know how to*'/. <**(e)sél:és ~ (e)sèl:ès**>, //(ʔəs=)sə́l=ə[=´=]s//, (<**es= ~ s=**> *stative* **shows a survival of an almost completely vanished allomorph** /ʔəs=/ *stative* in Upriver Halkomelem (preposed /ʔə/ *just* seems very unlikely since Galloway 1993:438 lists that adverb as only attested <u>after</u> the main verb), attested by JL (5/5/75), similarly in <**ílhtsel le q'íq kw'els esó:les.**>, //ʔí=ɬ-c-əl lə q'íq k'ʷ-əl-s ʔəsə[=Aá·=]l=əs//, /'*I went to jail when I was drunk.*'/, attested by Elders Group, (semological comment: Sumas speaker AH has minimal contrasts between forms with s= and with c=; tsqwóqwiyel and sqwóqwiyel don't seem semantically distinct, but there are a number of colors labelled by tskwíkwemel and a number by skwíkwemel; on the Munsell charts she did with us these two are are fairly evenly mixed with each other, though the forms with ts= are found mostly close to the focus, while the s= forms occur close to the focus but also as the farthest away

from the focus (C4, E6, I2, C35, etc.). NP's charted forms also show such a contrast: under tsqw'í<u>x</u>w ts= forms are more focal, while s= forms are more distant from focus, blackest;), under tsqwá:y ts= forms are at intense margins, while s= forms are at light margins or blackest; under tsméth' ts= forms are at light margins, some dark, while s= forms are one ex. next to focus; under tskwím ts= forms are at intense margins, while s= forms are at light margins or near focus; under tskwím + R5= ts= forms are more focal, while s= forms are more distant from focus; under tsq'í<u>x</u> ts= forms are (one ex.) browner, while s= forms are one ex., bluer, darker?; under p'éq' ts= forms are not found, while s= forms are closer to /p'ə́q'/ than non=statives;, under tsp'íqw' ts= forms are at I35, H34, D32, darker or lighter, while s= forms are at F34 but focused at H32, and sp'íp'eqw'el at I36; ("intense margins" refers to margins between colors other than white or black.). Chehalis speaker EB has no /s=/ forms to contrast. Tait speaker TG has one contrast, tsqwóqwiyel vs. sqwóqwiyel, where the ts= form is more focal than most of the examples of the s= form., syntactic analysis: derivational prefix, *see* charts by Rob MacLaury.

<**-s**>, (//**-s**//), PRON /'*his, her, its, their, third person possessive pronoun, third person subordinate subject*'/, syntactic analysis: is, syntactic comment: also used as subordinate subject by possessing a nominalized clause, example: <**te má:ls**>, //tə mɛ́·l-s//, /'*his/her/its/their father*'/, <**stl'í:s kw'es lám.**>, //s=ƛ'í·-s k'ʷə-s lɛ́=m//, /'*He/She/It wants to go., They want to go.*'/, literally /'(it) is his/her/its/their want that he/she/it/they go'/, <**te lálém s te má:ls**>, //tə lɛ́ləm-s tə mɛ́·l-s//, /'*the house of his father, his father's house*'/, literally /'the his house the his father'/.

<**s=...=s**>, da //s=...=s//, TIME /'*hour, o'clock, day of week*'/, semantic environment ['with numerals 1-12, kw'í:l'], TIME ['*-th day of the week*'], semantic environment ['with numerals 2-5'], (semological comment: as an hour marker thie circumfix is found with numbers one to 12, as a day of the week marker it occurs only with numbers themá *second*, lhíxw *three*, <u>x</u>e'óthel *four* and lhq'á:tses *five*, it appears to be made up from s= *nominalizer* for the days and perhaps s= *stative* for the hours, both plus a form derived from =es *cyclic period*), ASM ['Old Louie from Skw'átets (grandfather of Mrs. Steven Kelly -- AK's mother) could tell time by the sun (with a stick sun-dial or without; he also had knotted rags to tell days and months; he was first cousin to Joe Lorenzetto's grandmother (MJ)'], syntactic analysis: circumfix, compare <**=es**> *cyclic period*; attested by Elders at Fish Camp (7/19/78); found in <**steqá:tsas**>, //s=təqɛ́·cɛ=s//, /'*eight o'clock*'/, *see* under stem <**teqá:tsa**> *eight*, <**slhq'á:tses**>, //s=ɬq'ɛ́·cəs=s//, /'*five o'clock; Friday*'/, *see* under stem <**lhq'á:tses**> *five*, <**slhíxws**>, //s=ɬíxʷ=s//, /'*three o'clock; Wednesday*'/, *see* under stem <**lhíxw**> *three*.

<**sakweláx ~ sekwelá<u>x</u>**>, HUNT /'*arrow, gun*'/, *see* kwél.

<**sá:lch'ōwelh**>, TVMO ['*go in full circle with the current*'], *see* sél or sí(:)l.

<**Sáléch**>, free root //sɛ́ləc//, SOCT ['*Saanich people*'], PLN ['*Saanich reserves area*'], comment: borrowed from Northern Straits language, syntactic analysis: nominal, attested by Elders Group (6/8/77).

<**Sálesh**>, free root //sɛ́ləš//, SOCT ['*Salish people*'], comment: borrowing, syntactic analysis: nominal, attested by AC, also <**Syálex**>, [s(=)yɛ́ləxʸ], attested by Stanley Jones (Elders Group 1975).

<**sá:letel ~ sá:ltel**>, BSK ['*a lot of baskets*'], *see* sí:tel ~ sítel.

<**Salq'íwel**>, PLN /'*Salkaywul, an area with big cracked cedar trees on Hope Slough above Schelowat (Chilliwack I.R. #1) (S<u>x</u>eláwtxw)*'/, *see* séq'.

<**sá:lts'tem**>, ABDF ['*(be) dizzy*'], *see* sél or sí(:)l.

<**sá:q**>, free root //sɛ́·q//, EB /'*bracken fern root, rhizome of bracken fern*'/, ['*Pteridum aquilinum*'], ASM ['in times of little food bracken fern roots (rhizomes) were dug up, roasted in coals, then peeled and

eaten except for the core, best dug in the fall'], MED ['pound bracken roots and use in a wash as medicine for thinning hair'], syntactic analysis: noun, nominal, attested by AC, Elders Group (3/15/72 lesson VIII tape, 2/19/75), MC (Deming 2/10/77), Salish cognate: Nooksack /sǽʔæq/ *bracken fern root* (Deming).

<**Lexwsá:q**>, ds //ləx^w=sɛ́·q//, SOCT ['*Nooksack people*'], PLN /'*place in Whatcom County, Washington, (Nooksack River [AC or CT])*'/, ASM ['so named because bracken ferns were always there for emergency food, the people were named after this place'], comment: see Galloway and Richardson 1983, (<**lexw=**> *always*), syntactic analysis: nominal, attested by BHTTC, Elders Group, also /'*Nooksack River in Washington*'/, attested by AC and CT (1973), source: place names reference file #115, also <**Xwsá:q**>, //x^w=sɛ́·q//, attested by AC (11/24/71); found in <**xwsá:qtsel.**>, //x^w=sɛ́·q-c-əl//, /'*I'm from the Nooksack (people).*'/, literally /'I'm Nooksack.'/, also <**Nexwsá:q**>, //nəx^w=sɛ́·q//, also /'*Nooksack River, Nooksack people*'/, attested by Deming (3/25/76).

<**sasetáleqep**>, SD ['*keep on hearing a distant sound*'], *see* sát.

<**sásewel**>, FOOD ['*a small lunch*'], *see* sáwel.

<**sásex̲em ~ sá:sex̲em**>, TAST ['*be bitter (like of cascara bark or medicine or rancid peanuts)*'], *see* sáx̲em.

<**sásq'ets**>, df //C_1ɛ́=səq'=əc or sɛ́[=C_1ə=]q'=əc//, EZ ['*sasquatch*'], POW, ASM ['a stl'áleqem creature resembling a huge (six- to nine-foot tall) wild hairy man, the name was first borrowed into English apparently after being spelled by J.W. Burns, a teacher at Chehalis Indian school on Harrison River where sasquatches were sighted fairly often (John Green: On the Track of The Sasquatch, etc.)'], possibly root <**séq'**> *split, crack*, possibly <**R7=**> *augmentative*, possibly <**=ets**> *on the back*, phonology: reduplication, syntactic analysis: nominal, attested by AC, BJ (12/5/64), Elders Group, EB, example: <**(lhxwá:le, x̲ethíle) sásq'ets**>, //(ɬix^w=ɛ́·lə, x̣ə(ʔa)θ=ílə) C_1ɛ́=səq'=əc//, /'*(three, four) sasquatches*'/, (semological comment: the people classifier (=á:le ~ =íle) is here used for sasquatches, EB's grandmother used these forms in telling a story about sasquatches), attested by Elders Group, EB.

<**Sásq'ets** > (probably), df //C_1ɛ́=səq'=əc//, PLN ['*Sasquatch rock on Harrison River or Harrison Lake*'], phonology: reduplication, syntactic analysis: nominal, attested by EL and EB and NP (on Chehalis place names trip 9/27/77).

<**Sásq'etstel**>, ds //C_1ɛ́=səq'=əc=təl//, PLN ['*Pretty's Bay on Harrison River*'], literally /'sasquatch place'/, (<**=tel**> *something for, trap, (here) place?*), phonology: reduplication, syntactic analysis: nominal, attested by Elders Group (7/13/77), source: place names file reference #74.

<**sát**>, bound root //sɛ́t// *reach, pass on, pass along*.

<**sátet**>, pcs //sɛ́t=əT//, TVMO ['*pass s-th (at a meal for ex.)*'], FOOD, ABFC, (<**=et**> *purposeful control transitivizer*), syntactic analysis: transitive verb, attested by AD (8/80), Salish cognate: Squamish root /sat/ as in /sát-anʔ/ *give(tr.)* K69:302, also <**s'átet**>, //sʔɛ́t=ət//, attested by AD (8/80), example: <**sátetchexw te péte.**>, //sɛ́t=ət-c-əx^w tə pə́tə//, /'*Pass the butter.*'/, <**s'átetchexw te seplí:l.**>, //sʔɛ́t=əT-c-əx^w tə səplí·l//, /'*Pass the bread.*'/.

<**sóstem**>, df //sɛ[=AáC$_1$ə=]t=əm//, ABDF ['*lost (deceased)*'], possibly <**ó-ablaut**> *durative*, possibly <**=R1=**> *resultative*, possibly <**=em**> *intranstivizer*, phonology: ablaut, reduplication, syntactic analysis: intransitive verb, attested by Elders Group (6/8/77), example: <**sóstem te shxwewálíselh.**>, //sɛ[=AáC$_1$ə=]t=əm tə s=x^w=wɛ́líy-s-əɬ//, /'*(He) lost his (late/deceased) parents.*'/, attested by Elders Group, comment: EB questions this.

<**stáléqep**>, df //sɛt=(M1=)ɛ́lə́qəp//, SD ['*(make) a distant sound*'], literally (probably) /'passed on along sound'/, possibly <**metathesis**> *derivational*, lx <**=áléqep**> *sound*, phonology: possible metathesis, syntactic analysis: intransitive verb, attested by Elders Group (11/3/76), example: <**me stáléqep.**>, //mə sɛ́t=(M1=)ɛ́lə́qəp//, /'*A distant sound comes.*'/.

<**sasetáleqep**>, cts //sɛ[-C_1ə-]t=ɛ́lə́qəp//, SD ['*keep on hearing a distant sound*'], (<**-R1-**> *continuative*), lx <**=áléqep**> *sound*, phonology: reduplication, syntactic analysis: intransitive verb, attested by BHTTC (11/3/76).

<**stewéqel**>, df //sɛ́[=M1=]t[=Aə]=əw(=)ə́qəl//, REL ['*deceased one*'], prob. root <**sát**> //sɛ́t// *reach, pass on, pass along*, lx <**=ew**> *on the body* or <**=ew**> *contrastive*, <**=eqel**> *in the throat, in the esophagus, in the voice*, lit. "passed along contrastive/in body in voice" if this derivation is correct; alternatively poss. <**s-**> *nominalizer*, <**tew**> *tilted*? or <**tewéqel**> meaning unknown, phonology: metathesis, ablaut, syntactic analysis: nominal, attested by AD and EB (9/22/78), Salish cognate: Squamish /tə́waqin/ *be in mourning* K69:48.

<**stáweqel**>, pln //sɛ́[=M1=]t=əw(=)əqəl or s=tə[=Aɛ́=]w(=)əqəl//, REL /'*deceased ones, late ones*'/, prob. root <**sát**> //sɛ́t// *reach, pass on, pass along*, lx <**=ew**> *on the body* or <**=ew**> *contrastive*, <**=eqel**> *in the throat, in the esophagus, in the voice*, alternatively poss. <**s-**> *nominalizer*, <**tew**> *tilted*?, possibly <**á**-ablaut> *plural*, phonology: metathesis, ablaut, syntactic analysis: nominal, attested by AD and EB (9/22/78).

<**stá:xwelh**>, df //s=tɛ́·xʷ=əɬ//, [stǽ·xʷəɬ ~ (hyper-slow) stǽʔæxʷəɬ], HAT /'*children (not one's own necessarily, generic)*'/, ASM ['age term not kinship'], possibly <**s=**> *nominalizer, (*perhaps *alienable possession)*, root meaning uncertain but probably <**sát**>, bound root //sɛ́t// *reach, pass on, pass along*, or possibly <ta'á> *alike, similar*, or <**tá:xw**> meaning unknown, if one of the first two is root possibly <**=xw**> *round, around*, lx <**=elh ~ =íylh ~ =ó:llh**> *child, young*, if the first root is root here the literal meaning may be something like "pass along/around child/young"; phonology: possible =M1= metathesis of V1 and C2, grammatical comment: suppletive plural for <**stl'ítl'eqelh**> *child (generic)*, syntactic analysis: nominal, attested by AC, EB, DF, many others, other sources: ES /stɛ́·xʷəɬ/ *children (preadolescent)*, Salish cognate: Squamish /s-táwʔxʷɬ/ *child* W73:58, K67:284, Skagit dial. of Lushootseed /s-táwixʷəʔɬ/ *children* H76:484, examples: <**éyes te stá:xwelh.**>, //ʔɛ́y=əs tə s=tɛ́·xʷ=əɬ//, /'*The children had a lot of fun.*'/, attested by AC, <**líyleyem te stá:xwelh.**>, //líy=C_1əC_2=əm tə s=tɛ́·xʷ=əɬ//, /'*The children are laughing.*'/, attested by AC, <**sisistáxwes te stá:xwelh.**>, //siy=C_1əC_2=sT-ə[=Aɛ́=]xʷ-əs tə s=tɛ́·xʷ=əɬ//, /'*He's scaring the children.*'/, attested by EB, <**wiyóths kw'es í:wolems te stá:xwelh, t'ít'elem kw'es í:wólems.**>, //wə=yáθ-s k'ʷə-s ʔi[-´·-]wal=əm-s tə s=tɛ́·xʷ=əɬ, t'í[-C_1ə-]l=əm k'ʷə-s ʔi[-´·-]wal=əm-s//, /'*The children are playing all the time, singing as they're playing.*'/, attested by AC (10/15/71), <**qéx̱ te stá:xwelh.**>, //qə́x̣ tə s=tɛ́·xʷ=əɬ//, /'*(There's) lots of children.*'/, attested by AC.

<**sátet**>, TVMO ['*pass s-th (at a meal for ex.)*'], *see* sát.

<**sá:tl'atel**>, KIN /'*older siblings, elder cousins (first/second/third cousins by an older sibling of one's ancestor)*'/, *see* sétl'a ~ sétl'o.

<**sáwel**>, df //s=sɛ́w=əl or sɛ́wəl//, FOOD /'*(food) provisions for a trip, box lunch*'/, possibly <**s=**> *nominalizer*, possibly <**=el**> *go, come, get, become*, syntactic analysis: nominal, attested by EB, Elders Group, Salish cognate: Squamish /sə-sawʔán/ *take food along on trip* W73:260, K69:62.

<**sáwel**>, dnom //(s=)sɛ́wəl//, EZ /'*whiskey jack, Canada jay*'/, ['*Perisoreus canadensis griseus*'], literally /'trip provisions, trip food'/, ASM ['so named because he always tries to steal one's provisions'], syntactic analysis: nominal, attested by Elders Group (2/11/76).

<**sásewel**>, dmn //sɛ́[=C_1ə=]wəl//, FOOD [*'a small lunch'*], (<**=R1=**> *diminutive*), phonology: reduplication, syntactic analysis: nominal, attested by EB.

<**sawéts'em**>, df //sɛw(=)ə́c'=əm//, SD /*'(have/get) a rustling noise (not continuous) (of paper, silk, or other material), (to rustle)'*/, root meaning unknown, possibly <**=ts' ~ =elts' ~ =á:lts'**> *twist, turn around, around in circles*, (<**=em**> *intransitivizer, have, get* or *middle voice*), syntactic analysis: intransitive verb, attested by BHTTC (9/15/76).

<**sá:wts'em**>, cts //sɛ[-´·-]w(=)c'=əm//, SD /*'(making a) continuous rustling noise (of paper or silk or material), rustling (of leaves, paper, a sharp sound)'*/, (<**-´:-**> *continuative*), phonology: stress-shift, syntactic analysis: intransitive verb, attested by BHTTC (9/15/76), Elders Group (10/27/76), example: <**sá:wts'em te pípe.**>, //sɛ[-´·-]wc'=əm tə pípə//, /*'rustling paper, (Paper is rustling.)'*/, attested by Elders Group.

<**sá:wts'em**>, SD /*'(making a) continuous rustling noise (of paper or silk or material), rustling (of leaves, paper, a sharp sound)'*/, *see* sawéts'em.

<**sá<u>x</u>em**>, stem //sɛx̣=əm *bitter*//.

<**sáse<u>x</u>em ~ sá:se<u>x</u>em**>, stvi //sɛ́[=C_1ə=]x̣=əm ~ sɛ́·[=C_1ə=]x̣=əm//, TAST [*'be bitter (like of cascara bark or medicine or rancid peanuts)'*], (<**=R1=**> *stative*), (<**=em**> *middle voice* or *intransitivizer, have, get*), phonology: reduplication, syntactic analysis: adjective/adjectival verb, attested by Elders Group (3/1/72, 6/16/75, 5/25/77), EB, AC, example: <**sáse<u>x</u>em te s<u>x</u>ameléxwthelh.**>, //sɛ́[=C_1ə=]x̣=əm tə sɛx̣=M1=əm=əl=ə́xʷθəɬ//, /*'The tiger lily is bitter.'*/, attested by Elders Group (5/25/77).

<**sáse<u>x</u>em qwíyqwòyèls**>, EB, FOOD *grapefruit* (lit. bitter + orange fruit/little yellowish fruit), (attested by RG,EH 6/16/98 to SN, edited by BG with RG,EH 6/26/00), example: <**sáse<u>x</u>em qwíyqwòyèls sqe'óleqw**>, *grapefruit juice* (lit. grapefruit [itself bitter + yellow fruit] + fruit juice), (attested by RG,EH 6/16/98 to SN, edited by BG with RG,EH 6/26/00)

<**s<u>x</u>ameléxwthelh**>, ds //sɛx̣=M1=əm=əl=ə́xʷθəɬ//, EB [*'tiger lily'*], [*'Lilium columbianum'*], ASM ['now scarce, blooms in June, bulbs were dug up and cooked in steam pit,has bitter but good taste, often dried, often mixed with other things,nowadays with a gravy of flour, sugar, and water by one recipe'], (<**metathesis type 1**> *derivational*, <**=em**> *middle voice* or *intransitivizer, have, get*, <**=el**> connective with lexical suffixes (possibly plural?), <**=éxwthelh**> *on the tongue*), phonology: metathesis, syntactic analysis: nominal, attested by Elders Group (9/22/76, 5/25/77), example: <**sáse<u>x</u>em te s<u>x</u>ameléxwthelh**>, //sɛ́[=C_1ə=]x̣=əm tə sɛx̣=M1=əm=əl=ə́xʷθəɬ//, /*'The tiger lily is bitter.'*/.

<**sá:y**>, free root //sɛ́·y//, ANAA /*'wool, fur, animal hair'*/, syntactic analysis: noun, nominal, attested by AC, other sources: ES /sɛ́·y/ *fur, wool*, H-T <sáe> (umlaut on a, macron on e) *wool, yarn (of mt. goat)*, <tsái> (macron over a) *hair of animals*, example: <**sá:ys te (p'q'élqel, sqwmáy, lemetú)**>, //sɛ́·y-s tə (p'q'=ə́lqəl, s=qʷəm=ɛ́y, ləmətú)//, /*'wool of the (mountain goat, dog, domestic sheep)'*/, attested by AC.

<**siysá:yiws**>, plv //C_1əC_2=sɛ́·y=iws//, ANAA [*'furry on the whole body (of an animal)'*], TCH, (<**R3=**> *plural*), lx <**=iws**> *on the body*, phonology: reduplication, syntactic analysis: adjective/adjectival verb, attested by Elders Group (3/9/77).

<**sáyem**>, ds //sɛ́y=əm//, ABDF /*'have pain, to hurt'*/, (<**=em**> *middle voice* or *have, get, intransitivizer*), syntactic analysis: intransitive verb, attested by Elders Group (3/1/72, 1/24/79, 4/23/80), AC, example: <**sáyem tel s<u>x</u>él:e.**>, //sɛ́y=əm t-əl s=x̣ə́l·ə//, /*'My foot hurts.'*/, attested by Elders Group, <**sáyem tépsem**>, //sɛ́y=əm tə́psəm//, /*'(have a) stiff neck'*/, literally /'(have a) sore neck'/, attested by Elders Group, <**sáyem tel kw'él:a.**>, //sɛ́y=əm t-əl k'ʷə́l·ɛ//, /*'My stomach hurts., I have a pain in the*

stomach.'/, attested by Elders Group, <**lí: sáyem ta cháléx?**>, //lí-ə sɛ́y=əm t-ɛ cɛ́lə́x^{y}//, /'*Does your hand hurt?*'/, attested by AC, <**li, le sáyem tel cháléx.**>, //li, lə sɛ́y=əm t-əl cɛ́lə́x^{y}//, /'*Yes, my hand hurts.*'/, usage: answer to previous sentence, attested by AC, <**liye sá:yem ta yél:és?**>, //lí-ə sɛ́[=:=]y=ɛm t-ɛ yə́l·ə́s//, /'*Does your tooth hurt?, Have you got a toothache?*'/, attested by AC.

<**sáyém**>, cts //sɛ́y=ə[-´-]m//, ABDF /'*(be) sore, (be) hurting all the time, painful, aching*'/, semantic environment ['of body part'], DESC ['*strong*'], semantic environment ['of medicine'], (<-´-> *continuative*), phonology: stress-shift, syntactic analysis: adjective/adjectival verb, attested by AD, BHTTC.

<**sá:yt'els**>, ABFC ['*tickling*'], *see* síyt'.

<**sá:yt'em ~ sayít'em**>, ABFC /'*being tickled, (having tickling, getting tickling), tickley*'/, *see* síyt'.

<**sá:yt't**>, ABFC ['*tickling s-o*'], *see* síyt'.

<**sá'eltel**>, BSK ['*baskets*'], *see* sí:tel ~ sítel.

<**Scháchewxel ~ Cháchewxel**>, PLN ['*a village of the Pilalt people*'], *see* cháchew ~ cháchu.

<**schácheхw**>, SOC ['*got married to a wife*'], *see* chá:xw.

<**scháchxwelmel**>, SOC /'*want to get a wife, He wants to get a wife.*'/, *see* chá:xw.

<**schákwel**>, MOOD ['*how is s-o/s-th?*'], *see* chákw.

<**schá:lhtel ~ stsá:lhtel**>, FSH ['*dried fish*'], *see* =chílh ~ chílh=.

<**schéchewòt**>, DESC ['*little smart one*'], *see* chewót.

<**schechwétiyethel**>, LANG ['*fluent (at speaking)*'], *see* chewót.

<**scheláka**>, df //s(=)cəlɛ́kɛ//, EZ ['*carp*'], ['*Cyprinus carpio*'], (semological comment: introduced post-contact), phonology: from the /k/ and /č/ and final vowel with no recognizable suffixes this form could be borrowed from an Interior Salish language such as Thompson, Lillooet or Okanagan, syntactic analysis: nominal, attested by IHTTC (9/14/77).

<**schelá:w**>, MC ['*be turned inside out*'], *see* chaléwt.

<**schewíts**>, df //s=cəw=(w)íc or sc=əwíc//, ABFC ['*(be) with one's back towards something or someone*'], DIR, possibly <**s=**> *stative*, root meaning unknown, lx <**=ewíts ~ =íts**> *on the back*, syntactic analysis: adjective/adjectival verb, attested by Elders Group (8/31/77), comment: may or may not be the literal version of the place name from Wells 1965 (lst ed.):11 and the Sepass n.d. map, Wells has <s'ch-WEETZ> *Lindeman Lake or Post Lake.*

<**Schewíts**>, PLN ['*Lindeman Lake or Post Lake*'], *see* cháchew ~ cháchu *beach.*

<**schéxwem**>, dnom //s=cə́x^{w}=əm//, WETH ['*west wind*'], syntactic analysis: nominal, attested by BJ, numerous other elders, WETH /'*south wind, warm wind*'/, attested by Deming.

<**sch'á:yxw**>, strs //s=c'i[=Aɛ́·=]yx^{w}//, DESC ['*(be) dried*'], *see* ts'íyxw ~ ts'éyxw ~ ch'íyxw.

<**sch'á:yxwels**>, dnom //s=c'i[=Aɛ́·=]yx^{w}=əls//, sas, FOOD ['*dried meat*'], *see* ts'íyxw ~ ts'éyxw ~ ch'íyxw.

<**secheláts**>, df //səc=əlɛ́c or səc=ələ[=Aɛ́=]c//, EFAM /'*(be) eager, enthused*'/, possibly root <**sech**> as in <**sích**> *proud*, possibly <**á-ablaut**> *durative*, possibly <**=elets**> *on the bottom*, syntactic analysis: adjective/adjectival verb, dialects: *Tait*, attested by Elders Group (3/2/77).

<**sékwelàxs te té<u>x</u>wets**>, //s[=ə́=]=kʷəl=ə[=Aɛ́=]xʸ-s tə tə́xʷəc//, /'*arrow of a bow*'/, *see* té<u>x</u>wets, **kwélex**.

<**sél** or **sí(:)l**>, bound root //sə́l or sí(·)l *spin*//.

<**sélsel**>, chrs //sə́l=C_1əC_2 or sí[=Aə́=]l=C_1əC_2//, WV /'*wool spinner, spindle for spinning wool, spinning stick*'/, TOOL, possibly <**é-ablaut**> *derivational* but automatic before =R2 (as in Musqueam), possibly <**é-ablaut on root i**> *continuative or resultative*, (<**=R2**> *characteristic*), phonology: reduplication, syntactic analysis: nominal, attested by SJ (Deming 9/21/78), Elders Group (9/10/75), compare <**sélseltel**> *spindle for spinning wool.*

<**sélseltel**>, chrs //səl=C_1əC_2=təl//, WV /'*spindle for spinning wool, a hand spinner*'/, TOOL, (<**=R2**> *characteristic*), lx <**=tel**> *device to*, phonology: reduplication, syntactic analysis: nominal, dialects: *Chill.*, *Tait*, attested by DM (12/4/64), Elders Group (3/24/76 Tait dialect), also <**qáqelets'**>, //qɛ́[=C_1ə=]ləc'//, dialects: *Cheh.*, attested by Elders Group (3/24/76), Salish cognate: Squamish /sə́lsəltən/ *(Indian) spinning wheel* W73:245, K67:301.

<**séles**>, ds //sə́l=əs or si[=Aə́=]l=əs//, ABDF /'*(get) dizzy, get drunk*'/, ACL, literally /'spin on the face'/, lx <**=es**> *on the face*, syntactic analysis: intransitive verb, adjective/adjectival verb?, attested by Elders Group (3/72), EB, Salish cognate: Squamish /syáy-ʔus/ *dizzy* as in /na kʷ syáyʔus/ *he's getting dizzy, he's getting high (while drinking)* W73:81, K69:60, also <**sél:és**>, //sə́l=ə[=´=]s//, phonology: lengthening (automatic with resonants between stressed schwas), derivational stress-shift, attested by Elders Group (6/16/76), also <**(e)sél:és ~ (e)sèl:ès**>, //(ʔəs=)sə́l=ə[=´=]s//, (<**es= ~ s=**> *stative*), attested by JL (5/5/75), example: <**mé séles**>, //mə sə́l=əs//, /'*getting drunk*'/, (me *come, become*), attested by EB (12/19/75).

<**só:les**>, strs //(s=)sə[=Aá·=]l=əs//, ABDF /'*be drunk, got drunk*'/, possibly <**s=**> *stative*, (<**ó-ablaut**> *resultative*), phonology: ablaut, syntactic analysis: intransitive verb, attested by EB, Elders Group (6/28/78), RJ (5/19/76), example: <**welh só:les**>, //wəɬ sə[=Aá·=]l=əs//, /'*(already) drunk*'/, attested by EB (12/19/75), <**ílhtsel le q'íq kw'els e só:les.**>, //ʔí=ɬ-c-əl lə q'íq k'ʷ-əl-s ʔə sə[=Aá·=]l=əs//, /'*I went to jail when I was drunk.*'/, literally /'I past got incarcerated/ emprisoned when I was drunk'/, attested by Elders Group, <**epóles qas te isóles i ta' s'ehólets tl'esu só:les.**>, //ʔápə[=M2=]l=əs qɛ-s tə ʔisɛ[=Aá=]l=əs ʔi t-ɛʔ s=ʔəhá=ləc ƛ'ə-s-u sə[=Aá·=]l=əs//, /'*Ten dollars and two dollar in your pocket and you're drunk.*'/, usage: rhyme, attested by Rose Jones (5/19/76).

<**séleslexw**>, ncs //sə́l=əs=l-əxʷ//, ABDF ['*get s-o drunk*'], SOC, (<**=l**> *non-control transitivizer*), (<**-exw**> *third person object*), syntactic analysis: transitive verb, attested by Elders Group (6/7/8); found in <**seleslóxes.**>, //səl=əs=l-áxʸ-əs//, /'*He got me drunk.*'/.

<**sélts'**>, ds //sə́l=c'//, SPRD /'*(circle) around the fire once and return to the start, make one circle in longhouse*'/, TVMO, lx <**=ts'**> *around in a circle or in an arc*, syntactic analysis: intransitive verb, attested by Elders Group (8/25/76), example: <**lá:m sélts'**>, //lɛ́·=m sə́l=c'//, /'*go around fire once and return to start, make one circle in longhouse*'/.

<**sá:lch'ōwelh**>, df //sə[=Aɛ́·=]l=c'=owəɬ//, TVMO ['*go in full circle with the current*'], semantic environment ['of a canoe, driftwood, anything in the river'], CAN, WATR, (<**á**:-ablaut> *durative or resultative*), lx <**=ōwelh**> *canoe, vessel*, phonology: ablaut, syntactic analysis: intransitive verb, attested by IHTTC (8/31/77).

<**selch'éle**>, df //səl=c'=ə́lə//, TVMO ['*go in a semi-circle (or part of a circle) with the current*'], CAN, lx <**=éle**> meaning uncertain here, syntactic analysis: intransitive verb, attested by IHTTC.

<**Selch'éle**>, df //səl=c'=ə́lə//, PLN ['*the whole riverbank on the CPR (west) side of the Fraser River just south of Strawberry Island and just north of Peqwchō:lthel*'], literally /'go in a semi-

circle with the current'/, syntactic analysis: nominal, attested by SP and AK and AD (Raft trip 8/30/77), IHTTC (8/31/77), Elders on American Bar trip (AD, AK? 6/26/78), source: place names reference file #247.

<**selts'elwílem**>, df //səl=c'=əlwəɬ=íl=əm//, mdls, incs, BLDG ['*go around inside the longhouse counter-clockwise*'], TVMO, SPRD, lx <**=ts'**> *around in a circle*, possibly <**=elwelh**> (only if <**elh**> can be dropped before <**=íl**>) *side*, (<**=íl**> *go, come, become, get*, <**=em**> *middle voice*), phonology: possible syllable-loss of elh before -íl, syntactic analysis: intransitive verb, attested by Elders Group (8/25/76).

<**séltsʼe<u>x</u>el**>, ds //sə́l=c'=əx̣əl//, BLDG ['*around the outside of the house*'], lx <**=e<u>x</u>el**> *(outside) side of a building*, syntactic analysis: intransitive verb?, nominal?, attested by Elders Group (8/25/76).

<**séltsʼtem**>, ds //sə́l=c'=təm//, ABDF ['*(be) dizzy*'], (<**=tem**> *participial or stative*), syntactic analysis: adjective/adjectival verb, attested by Elders Group (8/25/76), Lizzie Johnson (Elders Group 6/28/78), example: <**lhéq' me séltsʼtem tel s<u>x</u>óyes lhíl á<u>x</u>eth.**>, //ɬə́q' mə sə́l=c'=təm t-əl s=x̣áyəs ɬí-l ʔɛ́x̣əθ//, /'*Sometimes my head spins when I lay down.*'/, attested by Lizzie Johnson.

<**sá:ltsʼtem**>, df //sə[=Aɛ·=]l=c'=təm//, ABDF ['*(be) dizzy*'], (<**á**:-ablaut> *durative or resultative*), phonology: ablaut, syntactic analysis: adjective/adjectival verb, attested by TB (Elders Group 3/72), also <**sá:lth'tem**>, //sə[=Aɛ́·=]l=θ'=təm//, attested by Elders Group (3/72).

<**siseltsʼiyósem**>, mdls //C_1í=səl=c'=iyás=əm//, dmv, TVMO /'*spinning, whirling*'/, (<**R4=**> *diminutive*), lx <**=ts'**> *around in a circle*, lx <**=iyós**> *in a circle*, (<**=em**> *middle voice*), phonology: reduplication, syntactic analysis: intransitive verb, attested by Elders Group (8/25/76), example: <**siseltsʼiyósem spehá:ls**>, //C_1í=səl=c'=iyás=əm s=pəh=ɛ́·ls//, WETH ['*whirlwind*'], attested by Elders Group.

<**siseltsʼiyósem spehá:ls**>, //C_1í=səl=c'=iyás=əm s=pəh=ɛ́·ls//, WETH ['*whirlwind*'], attested by Elders Group.

<**sí:lcheptel**>, ds //sə[=Aí·=]l=lcəp=təl or sí·l=lcəp=təl//, FIRE /'*fire-drill, stick spun to start fire*'/, TOOL, possibly <**í:-ablaut**> *derivational*, lx <**=(él)chep**> *firewood, fire*, lx <**=tel**> *device to*, phonology: ablaut, possible consonant merger, syntactic analysis: nominal, attested by DM (12/4/64), Salish cognate: Squamish /ší-čəp/ *fire-drill* W73:101, K69:69 is cognate with an alternate version of this, UHk /s=x^yə́l=cəp/, compare <**sxélchep**> *firedrill*.

<**sí:ltem**>, rsls //sə[=Aí·=]l=əT-əm//, pcs, WV /'*it's twined (like rolled on thigh and twisted, spun)*'/, (<**í:-ablaut**> *resultative*), (<**=et**> *purposeful control transitivizer*), (<**-em**> *passive*), phonology: ablaut, syntactic analysis: intransitive verb, attested by AD (11/16/79).

<**schelhá:liya**>, ANA ['*top of the ear*'], *see* =chílh ~ chílh=.

<**schelhó:les**>, ANA /'*upper circle over the eye,* probably *upper eyelid*'/, *see* =chílh ~ chílh=.

<**schelhóyethel**>, ANA ['*upper lip*'], *see* =chílh ~ chílh=.

<**schewétmet**>, DESC ['*be good at s-th*'], *see* schewót.

<**schewót**>, stvi //s=cəwát//, DESC /'*smart, know how, good at it*'/, *see* chewót.

<**schéxwmet**>, SOC ['*to propose to someone*'], *see* chá:xw.

<**schichí'**>, dnom //s=C_1í=ciʔ//, EZ /'*something scary, monster*'/, *see* chí'.

<**schí:lh**>, SOC ['*first-born*'], *see* =chílh ~ chílh=.

<**schí:m**>, TVMO ['*a pack*'], *see* chám.

<**schí:wetálh**>, KIN /'*sons-in-law, daughters-in-law, children's spouses*'/, *see* schiwtálh.

<**schiwtálh**>, dnom //s=ciwt=ɛ́ɬ//, KIN /'*child's spouse, son-in-law, daughter-in-law, (man's) sister's husband*'/, *see* chiwt.

<**schí:ya**>, dnom //s=cí·yɛ//, EB ['*wild strawberry*'], ACL ['also *domestic strawberry*'], ['*Fragaria vesca, Fragaria virginiana*'], *see* chí:ya.

<**schí:yà:lhp**>, EB /'*strawberry vine, strawberry plant, strawberry patch*'/, *see* schí:ya.

<**schíyeláxel**>, ANAH ['*strawberry birthmark on the arm*'], *see* schí:ya.

<**schókwelelh**>, strs //s=cá[-kʷə-]l=əɬ//, SOC ['*be borrowed*'], (<**s=**> *stative*), root <**chélhta**> *lend, let s-o borrow* with <-R1-> reduplication *continuative* except with <**kw**> replacing the <**ch**> (consonant ablaut (-Akw-), final consonant in root revoices before <**=elh**> *resultative* probably either a rare survival from PCS or borrowed with the form from another Salish language, the root of this word may be related (or identical) to that in chó(:)(=)kw *be far away, distant,* syntactic analysis: adjective/adjectival verb, example: <**tl'ól schókwelelh**>, //ƛ'á-l s=cákʷ=əl=əɬ//, /'*That's what I borrowed.*'/, attested by EB, <**schókwelelh ò te skwí:xs**>, //s=cákʷ=əl=əɬ ʔà tə s=kʷí·xʸ-s//, /'*He's borrowed his name.*'/, attested by EB, *see* chélhta.

<**scholéxwem**>, ANA ['*blood*'], *see* choléxwem.

<**schxwó:les**>, ABDF /'*(be) swollen on the eye, (have a) swollen eye*'/, *see* chxw= ~ =chíxw.

<**sch'ákwxels**>, //s=c'ə[=Aɛ́=]kʷx̣=əls//, FOOD ['*frying pan*'], *see* <**ts'ákwxels**> under ch'ékwx ~ ts'ékwx

<**sch'á(:)letstel ~ ch'áletstel ~ shxwch'áletstel**>, dnom //c'ɛ́=ləc=təl ~ s=c'ɛ́(·)=ləc=təl ~ sxʷ=c'ɛ́=ləc=təl//, HHG /'*chair, bench, seat, something to sit on*'/, literally /'device to put the rump on top of ~ something to put the rump on top of device'/, *see* ts'á:.

<**sch'á:yxw**>, DESC ['*(be) dried*'], *see* ts'íyxw ~ ts'éyxw ~ ch'íyxw.

<**sch'á:yxwels**>, FOOD ['*dried meat*'], *see* ts'íyxw ~ ts'éyxw ~ ch'íyxw.

<**sch'eqw'ő welh**>, BSK ['*basket-weaving*'], *see* ts'éqw'.

<**Sch'iyáq**>, PLN ['*creek with its mouth on the south side of Chilliwack River and above the mouth of Middle Creek*'], *see* ts'iyáq ~ ch'iyáq.

<**sch'ó:lha ~ sts'ó:lha ~ sts'ólha**>, df //s=c'á·ɬ(=)ɛ ~ s=c'áɬ(=)ɛ//, EB ['*leaf*'], LT ['*leaf-green*'], see ch'ó:lh ~ ts'ó:lh (poss. lit. 'material for on top of (plants)').

<**secheláts**>, df //səc=əlɛ́c or səc=ələ[=Aɛ́=]c//, EFAM /'*(be) eager, enthused*'/, possibly root <**sech**> as in <**sích**> *proud*, possibly <**á-ablaut**> *durative*, possibly <**=elets**> *on the bottom*, syntactic analysis: adjective/adjectival verb, dialects: *Tait*, attested by Elders Group (3/2/77).

<**sékwluwi**>, us //sə́kʷluwi//, TCH /'*soft smooth texture*'/, (attested by RG,EH 6/16/98 to SN, edited by BG with RG,EH 6/26/00)

<**thós sth'emíwel sékwluwi**>, EB, FOOD *avocado* (lit. big round + pit + soft smooth texture), (attested by RG,EH 6/16/98 to SN, edited by BG with RG,EH 6/26/00)

<**sékw'emiy**>, EB /'*birch, western white birch*'/, *see* síkw'.

<**Sekw'sekw'emá:y**>, PLN /'*place where a grove of birches stood/stand near the Kickbush place on Chilliwack River Road in Sardis, (village at junction of Semmihault Creek and Chilliwack River [Wells 1965 (lst ed.):19])*'/, *see* síkw'.

<**selá ~ slá ~ slá:**>, DESC /*'be tight, be secured tightly; be tucked away, put away so well you can't find it, be solid*'/, *see* <**lá:**> *tight, put away,*

<**Seláq'oyatel**>, df //səlɛ́=q'=iyɛ=təl or s[=əl=]ɛ́q'=iyɛ=təl//, N ['*(Indian name of) David (of Cultus Lake)*'], ASM ['husband of Mrs. Matilda David who retaught Amy (Lorenzetto)(Commodore) Cooper the Halkomelem language'], possibly root <**selá**> *tight* or possibly root <**sáq'**> meaning uncertain, possibly <**=q'**> *on something else*, possibly <**=el=**> *plural?*, lx <**=iya**> *endearing diminutive, personal name ending*, lx <**=tel**> *device to, male name ending*, syntactic analysis: nominal, attested by AC.

<**selá:ts'**>, DESC ['*be different*'], *see* láts'.

<**selá:wa**>, strs //s=hə=lɛ́·wɛ//, EFAM /*'pitiful, (bereft, poor)*'/, (<**s=**> *stative*), (<**he=**> *resultative*), syntactic analysis: adjective/adjectival verb, attested by Elders Group (9/8/76).

<**selchí:m ~ selchím**>, df //s=ɛləcɛ=í·m//, MOOD /*'how is it?, be how?*'/, possibly <**s=**> *nominalizer or stative*, possibly <**=í:m**> *repeatedly*, possibly root <**alétsa**> *where to?*, phonology: possible vowel-reduction, possible vowel merger, syntactic analysis: interrogative verb, attested by EB, BJ (5/10/64), AD, DC, Ben James, Deming, Elders Group, BHTTC, AC, Salish cognate: Squamish /txʷ-nčə-ʔámʔ/ *how?, be how, be how much* W73:145, K67:260, also <**chím**>, //cím//, Elder's comment: "short for selchím", attested by EB (9/18/78), example: <**selchímchexw tlówàyèl?**>, //səlcím-c-əxʷ təlá=wɛ̀yə̀l//, /*'How are you today?*'/, semantic environment ['used for someone who has been sick'], attested by AD, <**selchím (tha/ta mà:l, ta sí:le, tha tà:l)?**>, //səlcím ((kʷ)θ-ɛ ~ t-ɛ mɛ̀·l, t-ɛ sí·lə, θ-ɛ tɛ̀·l)//, /*'How's your (father, grandparent, mother)?*'/, attested by BJ, DC and AD (12/19/79), <**selchím kw'a's lhíts'et te sméyets?**>, //səlcím k'ʷ-ɛʔ-s ɬíc'=əT tə s=mɛ́yəc//, /*'How do you cut the meat?*'/, dialects: *(Sumas/Matsqui)*, attested by Deming (2/22/79), <**selchím kw'a' sq'óq'ey?**>, //səlcím k'ʷ-ɛʔ s=q'á[=C₁ə=]y//, /*'How are you sick., What's your sickness.*'/, attested by Elders Group, <**selchím te t'ás?**>, //səlcím tə t'ɛ́-s//, /*'How does it taste?*'/, literally /'How is it's taste.'/, attested by BHTTC, <**le selchí:m kw'as lé thìyt?**>, //lə səlcí·m k'ʷ-ɛ-s lə θíy=T//, /*'How did you make it?*'/, attested by AC (1973 p.121), also <**le selchí:m kw'asé thìyt?**>, //lə səlcí·m k'ʷ-ɛ-s-ə́ θíy=T//, comment: apparently EB's -é is *past tense*, attested by EB (1/9/76), <**lachexw selchí:m welámexw t'ó:kw'?**>, //lɛ-c-əxʷ səlcí·m wə-lɛ́=m-əxʷ t'á·k'ʷ//, /*'How are you going home?*'/, literally /'you are going how? when you go home'/, attested by AC, <**lé selchí:m?**>, //lə səlcí·m//, /*'How much is it?*'/, attested by BJ (5/10/64).

<**selchímáléqep**>, ds //səlcím=ɛ́lə́qəp//, SM /*'how does it smell?, How does it smell?*'/, MOOD, lx <**=áléqep**> *smell, odor, fragrance*, syntactic analysis: interrogative verb, attested by EB (5/18/76).

<**selchí:meleqel**>, ds //səlcí·m=ələqəl//, SD /*'what does it sound like?, What does it sound like?, (how does it sound?)*'/, MOOD, lx <**=eleqel**> *sound; in the throat; language*, syntactic analysis: interrogative verb, attested by Elders Group (11/3/76).

<**selchímomex**>, ds //səlcím=aməxʸ//, DESC /*'what does it look like?, what does he/she look like?, (how is he/she/it in appearance or looks?), (what color is it? [NP])*'/, LT, MOOD, lx <**=amex ~ =ámex**> *looks, in appearance*, syntactic analysis: interrogative verb, attested by Deming (2/22/79), also /*'what color is it?*'/, attested by NP (1/30/76), example: <**selchímomex te kyó:s?**>, //səlcím=aməxʸ tə kʸá·-s//, /*'What color is his car?*'/, attested by NP (1/20/76).

<**tl'ekwselchíms ~ tl'ekwselchí:ms**>, ds //ƛ'a=kʷ=səlcí(·)m-s or ƛ'a kʷ(s) səlcí(·)m-s//, MOOD ['*why?*'], literally /'if that's how it is?'/, usage: used for ex. if someone didn't do what they were supposed to, if they stood you up, etc. (EB), (<**tl'ó(=)**> *it's that, that's it, kw(=) which*), (<**=s**> *third person subjunctive* used to derive indefinites), syntactic analysis: interrogative verb, possibly simple nominal phrase, attested by Elders Group (10/6/76), EB, example: <**tl'ekwselchí:ms tl'o'ese**

x̱tá tethá?>, //ƛ'a=k^{w}=səlcí·m=s ƛ'a-ʔɛ-s-ə x̣tɛ́ tə=θɛ́//, /'*Why did you do this to yourself?*'/, attested by EB (1/9/76).

<**selchímáléqep**>, SM /'*how does it smell?, How does it smell?*'/, *see* selchí:m ~ selchím.

<**selchí:meleqel**>, SD /'*what does it sound like?, What does it sound like?, (how does it sound?)*'/, *see* selchí:m ~ selchím.

<**selchímomex**>, DESC /'*what does it look like?, what does he/she look like?, (how is he/she/it in appearance or looks?), (what color is it? [NP])*'/, *see* selchí:m ~ selchím.

<**selch'éle**>, TVMO ['*go in a semi-circle (or part of a circle) with the current*'], *see* sél or sí(:)l.

<**Selch'éle**>, PLN ['*the whole riverbank on the CPR (west) side of the Fraser River just south of Strawberry Island and just north of Peqwchō̸:lthel*'], *see* sél or sí(:)l.

<**selélets'**>, DESC ['*two different things*'], *see* láts'.

<**séles**>, ABDF /'*(get) dizzy, get drunk*'/, *see* sél or sí(:)l.

<**séleslexw**>, ABDF ['*get s-o drunk*'], *see* sél or sí(:)l.

<**selí:kw**>, ABDF ['*be broken (of stick-like object)*'], *see* lékw.

<**seliléx̱**>, df //s(ə)=C_1í=ləx̣ or s=(h)ə=lílə́x̣//, EZ /'*baby striped skunk (before it gets stripes),* possibly *spotted skunk*'/, ['baby *Mephitis mephitis spissigrada,* possibly *Spilogale gracilis latifrons*'], probably <**s=**> *nominalizer*, probably <**R4=**> *diminutive*, probably <**he=**> *resultative or continuative*, root meaning unknown, phonology: reduplication, epenthetic e before resonant or consonant merger, syntactic analysis: nominal, attested by AK (11/21/72 tape).

<**Selísi**>, PLN /'*Mt. Slesse; village at mouth of Slesse Creek onto Chilliwack R.*'/, *see* éy ~ éy:.

<**Selísi (Stótelō)**>, PLN ['*Slesse Creek*'], *see* éy ~ éy:.

<**selístel**>, BSK ['*little baskets*'], *see* sí:tel ~ sítel.

<**seléts' ~ sléts'**>, MC ['*be full*'], *see* léts'.

<**selíy**>, free root or stem //səl(=)íy//, EB ['*short Oregon grape berry*'], ['*Berberis nervosa*'], ASM ['the blue berry is edible but not popular raw (too tart/sour), it is good for jelly or jam, AC's grandfather made wine from the berries'], possibly <**=iy**> *bark, covering*, syntactic analysis: nominal, attested by AC.

<**selíyelhp**>, ds //səl(=)íy=əɬp//, EB ['*short Oregon grape bush*'], ['*Berberis nervosa*'], ASM ['the bush is usually about one foot tall (always under two feet) (in contrast to the tall Oregon grape which is often three to five feet tall)'], MED ['a spring tonic can be made from the roots (and leaves) (AC), the roots are also good for other medicines such as when boiled a long time with cascara bark and drunk cool as medicine for boils and pimples (tall Oregon grape may also work here) (JL at Fish Camp 7/19/79)'], lx <**=elhp**> *plant, tree*, syntactic analysis: nominal, attested by AC, others.

<**selíyelhp**>, EB ['*short Oregon grape bush*'], *see* selíy.

<**selkwá:tses**>, ABDF /'*her hand is broken, his hand is broken*'/, *see* lékw.

<**seló:lh**>, TVMO ['*moving (one's residence)*'], *see* ó:lh.

<**sélsel**>, WV /'*wool spinner, spindle for spinning wool, spinning stick*'/, *see* sél or sí(:)l.

<**sélseltel**>, WV /'*spindle for spinning wool, a hand spinner*'/, *see* sél or sí(:)l.

<**selsí:le**>, KIN ['*grandparents*'], *see* sí:le.

<**séltl'o**>, KIN ['*oldest (sibling)*'], *see* sétl'a ~ sétl'o.

<**sélts'**>, SPRD /'*(circle) around the fire once and return to the start, make one circle in longhouse*'/, *see* sél or sí(:)l.

<**selts'elwílem**>, BLDG ['*go around inside the longhouse counter-clockwise*'], *see* sél or sí(:)l.

<**sélts'e<u>x</u>el**>, BLDG ['*around the outside of the house*'], *see* sél or sí(:)l.

<**sélts'tem**>, ABDF ['*(be) dizzy*'], *see* sél or sí(:)l.

<**Semá:th ~ Semáth ~Smá:th**>, df //s=hə=mɛ́·θ//, PLN /'*Sumas village and area from present-day Kilgard to Fraser River, Sumas village (on both sides of the Fraser at the east end of Sumas Mt.), (Devil's Run (below Lá<u>x</u>ewey), the area between Sumas Mt. and Fraser River [Elders Group 7/13/77], Sumas River* (probably requires **Stó:lō** *river* or Stótelō *creek* to follow) [Wells 1965], *Sumas Lake* (probably requires <u>X</u>ótsa *lake* after Semáth for this meaning)'/, *see* má:th possibly *flat opening*

<**semáxel**>, ANAH ['*(have a) bare foot*'], *see* má ~ má'-.

<**semelá:lh**>, SOCT ['*high class people*'], *see* smelá:lh.

<**sémele**>, ABFC /'*have given birth, already had a child, had a baby, (delivered)*'/, *see* méle ~ mél:a.

<**semíkw'**>, NUM ['*all of them (people)*'], *see* mékw' ~ mṓkw'.

<**semíliyel**>, FSH /'*a net is set, be set (of a net by canoe, not of a pole net)*'/, *see* mí:l ~ míl.

<**semláliyel**>, FSH /'*a set net, a stationary net*'/, *see* mí:l ~ míl.

<**semlóthel**>, df //s=(h)ə=mil=áθəl//, LAND /'*riverbank, bank of a river*'/, WATR, (<**s=**> *nominalizer*), (<**he=**> *resultative*), root <**míl**> *submerge/drop into the water*, lx <**=óthel**> *in the mouth, in the mouth of river/creek,* phonology: vowel-loss, epenthetic e before resonant, syntactic analysis: nominal, attested by Lizzie Johnson (3/26/76), *see* mí:l ~ míl.

<**semsémele**>, ABFC ['*already had children*'], *see* méle ~ mél:a.

<**semth'íl**>, LT ['*[be in a state of getting blue]*'], *see* méth'.

<**semyó: ~ semyó**>, strs //s=hə=myá·//, [sɪmyá· ~ sɪmyá], ECON ['*be cheap*'], (<**s=**> *stative*), (<**he=**> *resultative*), root shape uncertain, phonology: he= ~ ha= is a resultative/continuative prefix before some roots beginning in l, m, y, w upriver (also n downriver), s + h > s by consonant merger, syntactic analysis: adjective/adjectival verb, attested by EB (12/19/75), AD (11/19/79), comment: I sometimes mistakenly wrote this word as syemyó, Salish cognate: Musqueam root and prefix as in /məyáʔt/ *come down in price* and /hə́m'yaʔt/ *be coming down in price* Suttles ca1984: ch.7 [p.133], also <**semyó ~ semyó'**>, //s=hə=myá ~ s=hə=myáʔ//, dialects: *Matsqui/Sumas*, attested by AH (Deming 1/25/79), example: <**tu semyó**>, //tu s=hə=myá//, /'*cheaper*'/, literally /'a little cheap'/, attested by AD, <**u semyó'.**>, //ʔu(w) s=hə=myáʔ//, /'*It's cheap.*'/, attested by AH.

<**Semyó:me ~ Sam(i)yó:me**>, df //s=hə=myá·=á·mə ~ s=hɛ=məyá=á·mə//, PLN /'*Semiahmoo, White Rock, B.C.*'/, literally (probably) /'cheap berries'/, (semological comment: there were many bog blueberry patches near here, known to Indians and whites alike, some may have been domesticated, some introduced, but they have now been harvested commercially in the area by non-Indians for nearly a century and probably were sold to whites cheaply before that), (<**s=**> *stative*), (<**he= ~ ha=**> *resultative*), root <**m(i)yó:**> *get cheap, (come down in price)*, lx <**=ó:me**> *berry*, comment: the place is in Downriver Halkomelem territory and therefore may well simply be a borrowed name, phonology: consonant merger or consonant-loss, vowel merger, syntactic analysis: nominal, attested

by AC (1973), source: place names file reference #285, Elders Group (6/8/77), contrast <**P'eq'ó:ls**> *White Rock.*

<**Semyó:me ~ Sam(i)yó:me**>, PLN /'*Semiahmoo, White Rock, B.C.*'/, *see* semyó: ~ semyó.

<**sépelets**>, df //sə́p=ələc or sɛ[=Aə́=]p=ələc//, ABDF /'*missed the chair in sitting down, missed one's chair*'/, HHG, N ['*nickname of Freddie Joe*'], root meaning unknown, possibly <**é-ablaut**> *resultative,* lx <**=elets**> *on the bottom, on the rump,* phonology: possible ablaut, syntactic analysis: intransitive verb, attested by Elders Group (8/3/77, 4/5/78), Salish cognate: possibly Squamish /sə́p/ *stiff* K67:301, possibly Sechelt /səp'-náč-t/ *spank s-o* T77:33 and Mainland Comox /sáp'-nəč-t/ *to spank s-o* B75prelim:91.

<**seplíl ~ seplí:l**>, free root //səplíl ~ səplí·l//, FOOD /'*bread, flour*'/, ACL, syntactic analysis: nominal, attested by AC, MH, EB, others, borrowed from Chinook Jargon <sapolil ~ saplil> *wheat, bread, flour* itself perhaps from French <la farine>?? (the sound shifts work for Upriver Halkomelem alone among Salishan languages, with s= *nominalizer* added) (Gibbs 1863) but also reported by Gibbs to be from Chinook Proper (Johnson 1978:450), example: <**xwélmexw seplí:l**>, //x^{w}ə́lməx^{w} səplí·l//, /'*Indian bread*'/, attested by MH (Deming 1/4/79), <**xwelítem seplí:l**>, //x^{w}əlítəm səplí·l//, /'*white man's bread*'/, attested by MH (Deming 1/4/79), <**spó:lqw' seplí:l**>, //s=pá·lq'^{w} səplí·l//, /'*flour*'/, literally /'powder bread'/, <**tl'éx̱w te seplíl.**>, //ƛ'ə́x̣^{w} tə səplíl//, /'*The bread is hard.*'/, attested by EB.

<**pelále seplíl**>, FOOD *banana bread* (lit. banana + bread), (attested by RG,EH 6/16/98 to SN, edited by BG with RG,EH 6/26/00)

<**qwíyqwòyèls seplíl**>, FOOD *orange loaf* (lit. orange fruit + bread), (attested by RG,EH 6/16/98 to SN, edited by BG with RG,EH 6/26/00)

<**sqáwth seplíl**>, FOOD *potato bread* (lit. potato + bread), (attested by RG,EH 6/16/98 to SN, edited by BG with RG,EH 6/26/00)

<**sqweqwá seplíl**>, EB, FOOD *donut, bagel* (lit. got a hole/with a hole + bread), (attested by RG,EH 6/16/98 to SN, edited by BG with RG,EH 6/26/00, also RG & EH (4/10/99 Ling332)

<**st'elákw' sp'íp'elh seplíl**>, FOOD *pizza* (lit. round + flat + bread), (attested by RG,EH 6/16/98 to SN, edited by BG with RG,EH 6/26/00)

<**st'elt'elákw' seplíl**>, FOOD *waffle* (lit. many squares + bread), (attested by RG,EH 6/16/98 to SN, edited by BG with RG,EH 6/26/00)

<**t'át'ets'em qwíqwòyèls kíks seplíl**>, FOOD *lemon cake* (lit. lemon (itself from sour little yellowish fruit) + cake + bread), (attested by RG,EH 6/16/98 to SN, edited by BG with RG,EH 6/26/00)

<**t'át'ets'em seplíl**>, FOOD *sourdough bread* (lit. sour + bread), (attested by RG,EH 6/16/98 to SN, edited by BG with RG,EH 6/26/00)

<**tl'áqt ts'íyxw seplíl**>, FOOD *spaghetti* (lit. long + dry + bread), (attested by RG,EH 6/16/98 to SN, edited by BG with RG,EH 6/26/00)

<**ts'íyxw stotekwtíqw seplíl**>, FOOD *noodles* (lit. dry + stringy hair + bread), (attested by RG,EH 6/16/98 to SN, edited by BG with RG,EH 6/26/00)

<**xáweq kíks seplíl**>, FOOD *carrot cake* (lit. carrot + cake + bread), (attested by RG,EH 6/16/98 to SN, edited by BG with RG,EH 6/26/00)

<**sepsáp**>, df //C_1əC_2=sɛ́p//, EFAM ['*(be) stubborn*'], possibly <**R3=**> *plural or characteristic,* root meaning unknown, phonology: reduplication, syntactic analysis: adjective/adjectival verb, attested by EB (4/26/76), Salish cognate: Squamish /səp/ *stiff* as in /sə-sp-íʔ/ *become stiff* K69:301.

<**séq**> or better <**seq**>, bound root //sə́q or səq *hang under*//.

<**seqíws ~ seqí:ws**>, df //səq=íws ~ səq=í·ws//, CLO /'*pants, trousers*'/, literally /'hang under on the body'/, lx <**=íws ~ =í:ws**> *on the body, on the skin,* syntactic analysis: nominal, attested by AC, BJ

(5/10/64), example: <**isále te seqíws.**>, //ʔisɛ́lə tə səq=íws//, /'*(There's) two pants., There's two pairs of pants.*'/, attested by Elders Group.

<**siseqíws ~ síseqíws**>, dmn //C_1í=səq=íws//, CLO /'*short pants, little pants, underpants*'/, (<**R4=**> *diminutive*), phonology: reduplication, syntactic analysis: nominal, attested by Elders Group, AD, example: <**Alétsa tel síseqíws?**>, //ʔɛlɛ́cɛ t-əl C_1í=səq=íws//, /'*Where's my underpants?*'/, attested by AD (8/80 Lesson #16).

<**seqí:wsem**>, mdls //səq=íws=əm//, CLO ['*put on one's pants*'], (<**=em**> *middle voice*), syntactic analysis: intransitive verb, attested by Elders Group (2/26/75), AD, also <**haqí:wsem**>, //hɛq=íws=əm or hɛ-(s)q=íws=əm//, attested by Elders Group (2/26/75), also <**heqíwsem**>, //həq=íws=əm or hə=(s)=íws=əm//, attested by AD (4/17/80), example: <**seqíwsemchexw.**>, //səq=íws=əm-c-əx^w//, /'*Put on your pants.*'/, syntactic analysis: urging imperative, attested by AD (8/80), <**seqíwsemlha.**>, //səq=íws=əm-ɬɛ//, /'*Put on your pants.*'/, syntactic analysis: command imperative, attested by AD (8/80).

<**séqtel**>, dnom //sə́q=təl//, CSTR ['*swing for baby cradle*'], PLAY, ASM ['made from a bent vine maple pole tied to roof in the middle, the vine maple about five inches wide is first cut in half-lengthwise, then tied in the middle to the roof (flat side down), one end ended at a wall, the other end was hung with a rope (about as big as a little finger) tied on, the other end of the rope had two ropes which were tied to straps on the baby cradle (one at each end), a string was tied from where the two ropes met to the mother's foot so she could bounce the baby, the baby's head was usually covered'], on file card, literally /'device to hang under, something to hang under'/, lx <**=tel**> *device to, something to*, syntactic analysis: nominal, contrast <**q'ít'o**> *swing for baby cradle*, attested by Elders Group (2/25/76), AD (6/19/79).

<**sqá:la**>, df //(s=)sq(=)ɛ́·lɛ//, EB ['*red huckleberry*'], ['*Vaccinium parvifolium*'], ASM ['berries ripe and edible mid-July, they were harvested by clubbing the branches on the hand and the berries fell into the basket which was hung under them'], (possibly <**s=**> *nominalizer*), root probabnly seq *hang under*, possibly <**=á:la**> *container of*, thus lit. /'*s-th to hang a container under* '/, syntactic analysis: nominal, attested by Elders Group, AC, contrast <**skw'éqwtses**> *red huckleberry.*

<**sqá:lá:lhp ~ qá:lá:lhp**>, ds //s=qɛ́lɛ=ɛ́ɬp ~ qɛ́·lɛ=ɛ́ɬp or qɛ́·lɛ=əɬp//, EB ['*red huckleberry bush*'], ['*Vaccinium parvifolium*'], lx <**=álhp ~ =elhp**> *plant, tree*, phonology: vowel merger, syntactic analysis: nominal, attested by Elders Group, SP, others.

<**sqelá:w**>, dnom //s=səq=əl=ɛ́·w//, EZ ['*beaver*'], ['*Castor canadensis leucodontus*'], ASM ['beavers holler to warn when falling a tree'], (<**s=**> *nominalizer*), root probably <seq> *hang under*, <=el> *come, go, get*, lx.<**=á:w ~ =í:w ~ =ew**> *on the body, on top of itself* (rare variant of =í:ws ~ =ews *on the body)*, thus lit. '*something that gets/goes its body hung under*', syntactic analysis: nominal, attested by AC, BJ (12/5/64), ME and AK (11/21/72 tape), Elders Group (2/19/75, 3/21/79), other sources: ES /sqəláw/ (MsCw /sqəlɛ́wʔ/), H-T <s'kElaú> *beaver (Castor canadensis).*

<**Sqelá:w (Stótelō)**>, dnom //s=qəlɛ́·w (stá[=C_1ə=]lo)//, PLN ['*Beaver Creek (at U.S.-Canada boundary line)*'], literally /'beaver creek'/, syntactic analysis: simple nominal phrase, source: Wells 1965 (1st ed.):13,

<**Sqelá:w (X̱óx̱tsa)**>, dnom //s=qəlɛ·w (x̣á[=C_1ə=]cɛ)//, PLN ['*Beaver Lake or Hanging Lake*'], literally /'beaver (little lake)'/, syntactic analysis: simple nominal phrase, source: Wells 1965 (lst ed.):11,

<**sqiqelá:w**>, dmn //s=C_1í=qəlɛ́·w//, EZ ['*little beaver*'], ['*Castor canadensis leucodontus*'], (<**s=**> *nominalizer*, R4= *diminutive*), phonology: reduplication, syntactic analysis: nominal, attested by Deming.

<**Qelá:wiya**>, ds //qəlɛ́·w=iyɛ//, N ['*Beaver (name in a story)*'], comment: note dropping of s= nominalizer, lx <**=iya**> *affectionate diminutive, personal name ending*, syntactic analysis: nominal, attested by AK (11/21/72 tape interview).

<**sqémél**>, df //(s=)səq=əməl//, BLDG /'*pit-house, keekwillie house, semi-subterranean house*'/, ASM ['used as the regular winter family dwelling by the Upper Stő:lo from Yale down to about Nicomen Island, rarely built or used further downriver (Duff 1952:46-47), almost always circular from 15 to 35 feet in diameter and perhaps 4 to 6 feet deep in the ground, covered with beams, brush, then earth in a conical mound, up to 20 feet from floor to highest point of roof, smokehole for fire in center, a notched pole served as a ladder through the smokehole, inhabited from about January to March or the coldest months of the year, bed with partitions and tiered storage were around the perimeter inside'], last used in the Stó:lō area about 1870 (Mrs. August Jim was born in one in 1869 and never returned after she was a few months old; Duff's accounts of those who last lived in them were of the same generation); the rest of the year plank longhouses (or when camping, mat shelters) were used;, Elders (6/28/78) said pit-houses were aired and rebuilt every year and that a separate one was used for spirit dances from Iwówes (Union Bar) to Yale; this is confirmed by an account of the sx̱wolex̱wiyám *ancient people over a hundred years old (they can't move, just lay there in pit-house, take liquids, in spring the family dug out the roof to get them out into the sun)* (BHTTC 9/9/76); the Interior Salish used pit-houses but perhaps only the Stó:lō among the Coast Salish used them, (<**s=**> *nominalizer*), probably //s=səq=əm(=)əl//, with weak valence root <**seq**> meaning *hang under* + lx <**=ámel ~ =ómel ~ =emel**> *part, portion, member*, possibly <**=el**> *become, get, come, go*, with weak valence root which loses its only vowel a suffix must get stress, possibly <**stress-insertion**> *derivational*, phonology: possible updrifting on last syllable or stress-insertion, morphological comment: reanalyzed as having <**s=**> and root <**qémél**> for forms derived from it, syntactic analysis: nominal, attested by Elders Group (6/28/78, 1/21/76), BJ (12/5/64), DM (12/4/64), JL (5/5/75), also <**sqemél**>, ///s=səq=əməl or s=səq=əmə[=´=]l//, phonology: s + s →s, vowel loss of weak-valenced root vowel, updrifting, attested by AC, DM (12/4/64), CT (6/8/76), Elders Group (3/15/72).

<**sqíqemel**>, ds //s=C$_1$í=qəməl//, BLDG ['*puberty hut*'], literally /'little pit-house'/, ASM ['built for adolescent women to live in during their first menstruation, built much like a sweathouse according to Duff 1952:50'], (<**s=**> *nominalizer*, R4= *diminutive*), phonology: reduplication, syntactic analysis: nominal, attested by EB, other sources: H-T 1904.

<**sqemí:l**>, stvi //s=qəmə́l=í·l//, incs, BLDG ['*be inside a pit-house*'], (<**s=**> *stative*), (<**=í:l**> *come, go, get, become*), phonology: syllable-loss, syntactic analysis: adjective/adjectival verb, attested by JL (5/5/75), example: <**le sqemí:l.**>, //lə s=qəməl=í·l//, /'*He was inside a pit-house.*'/, literally /'third person past be inside a pit-house'/.

<**sqéymeqw'**>, df //s=qí·m(=)əq'ʷ or sq=í·m=əq'ʷ?//, EZ ['*octopus*'], ['probably genus *Octopus*, the Squamish cognate is identified as *Octopus apollyon*'], possibly <**s=**> *nominalizer* or more likely <**seq**> *hang under*, possibly <**=í:m**> *repeatedly*, <**=eqw'**>*around in circles* (see Galloway 1993:234), lit. *something that hangs under repeatedly around in circles* (which could describe the tentacles going around in circles hanging under), syntactic analysis: nominal, attested by SP with others agreeing from Deming (7/7/77), Salish cognate: Lushootseed /s-qíbk'ʷ/ *octopus and squid* H76:384, Samish dial. of N. Straits VU /sqé·ymək'ʷ/ *octopus* versus VU /píl·əwəs ~ qəm'k'ʷá·ɬ/ *large octopus* G86:68.

<**síq**>, df //sə[=Aí=]q//, DIR ['*(hung) under*'], (<**í-ablaut on root e**> *resultative or durative*), phonology: í-ablaut on root e, syntactic analysis: preposition/prepositional verb?, attested by Elders Group (2/16/77), example: <**síq te shxw'áx̱eth**>, //síq tə sxʷ=ʔɛ́x̣əθ//, /'*under the bed*'/.

<**síqetsel**>, df //sə[=Aí=]q=əcəl//, BLDG /*'roof, shake(s) on roof, shingle(s) on roof, ceiling*'/, literally /'hung under on the back'/, ASM ['roof planks/shakes in the old days were made like shallow troughs and set on the roof side by side first convex side up, then where each two planks adjoined another plank was set convex side down to cover the join;'], some planks were put on the roof with upward overlapping: some were put on the roof with no upward overlapping (AD), (semological comment: the literal meaning probably refers to the fact that aboriginal (and modern) shakes or shingles hang under each other on the back of a roof), lx <**=etsel**> *on the back*, syntactic analysis: nominal, attested by Elders Group (11/12/75, 8/25/76, 5/3/78), AD (Elders Group 4/23/80), DM (12/4/64), Salish cognate: Squamish /síqč/ *shingles* K67:305, Lushootseed root /šə́q/ *high, up* as in /šə́q-əd/ *lift it up* and especially /šəq-álatxʷ/ *roof, upstairs, ceiling; above the whole house* H76:459-460.

<**síqetseláwtxw**>, ds //sə[=Aí=]q=əcəl=ɛ́wtxʷ//, BLDG /*'shakes on house, roof*'/, lx <**=áwtxw**> *house, building*, syntactic analysis: nominal, attested by Elders Group (11/12/75).

<**síqes**>, df //síq=əs//, LANG ['*whistle with finger*'], HUNT, literally perhaps /'hung under on the face'/, probably root <**seq**> *hang under*, probably <**í-ablaut on root é**> *resultative* or *durative*, possibly <**=es**> *on the face*, syntactic analysis: intransitive verb, attested by MV (Deming 5/4/78), Deming (7/27/78).

<**sisqelísem**>, mdls //si[-C_1ə-]q=əlís=əm//, LANG /*'whistling on one's teeth, whistling through the teeth*'/, Elder's comment: "not *humming*", (<**-R1-**> *continuative*), lx <**=elís**> *on the teeth*, (<**=em**> *middle voice*), phonology: reduplication, syntactic analysis: intransitive verb, attested by Elders Group (6/1/77), Deming (7/27/78), also /*'humming*'/, attested by Elders Group (12/15/76).

<**sqá:q**>, dnom //s=qɛ́q// prob. a reanalysis from //(s=)s(ə)q=ɛ́·q//, KIN /*'younger sibling, younger brother, younger sister, child of younger sibling of one's parent, "younger" cousin (could even be fourth cousin [through younger sibling of one's great great grandparent])*'/, ASM ['"younger cousins" can be older, younger or the same age as ego, it's their linking ancestor that must be younger, for the meanings younger brother or younger sister to be translated sqá:q must be preceded by a masculine or feminine article or the words swíyeqe *male* or slhálí *female* or otherwise cross-referenced semantically to a name or other item marked for sex gender; sqá:q by itself is ambiguous as to gender (as are most Halq'eméylem kinterms)'], (<**s=**> *nominalizer*) or more likely root <**séq**> or better <**seq**>, bound root //sə́q or səq *hang under*// + lx <**=á:q ~ =aq ~ =eq**> *male; penis*, thus literally *male that hangs under*, syntactic analysis: nominal, attested by AC, BJ (5/10/64), Deming (4/1/76), Elders Group, other sources: ES /sqɛ́·q/ and JH /sqé·q/ *younger sibling*, H-T 02:387 <skak·> (umlaut over a) *brother, sister, first cousin*, Salish cognate: Squamish /s-qáʔq/ *younger sibling* K67:353, example: <**tl'ól sqá:q.**>, //ƛ'á-l s=qɛ́·q//, /*'That's my younger sibling., He's my younger sibling., She's my younger sibling.*'/, attested by EB, <**tl'ól swal sqá:q.**>, //ƛ'á-l swɛ-l s=qɛ·q//, /*'That's my (own) younger sibling.*'/, attested by AC, <**lólets'e èl l swíyeqe sqá:q.**>, //C_1á=ləc'ə ʔə̀l l s=wíq=ə s=qɛ́·q//, /*'I have only one younger brother.*'/, literally /'is one person just/only my male younger sibling'/, attested by Deming, <**texqé:yltlha tá'a sqá:q.** (or better) **texqí:ltlha tá'a sqá:q.**>, //təxʸ=q(əl)=í·l=T-ɬɛ t-ɛ́ʔɛ s=qɛ́·q//, /*'Comb your little sister's hair. (sic for braid?)*'/, literally /'braid the hair of s-o -command imperative the -your (sg.) younger sibling'/, attested by EB (1/16/76), <**lólets'e èl l sqá:q.**>, //C_1á=ləc'ə ʔə̀l l s=qɛ́·q//, /*'I have only one younger sibling.*'/, attested by Deming.

<**ká:k ~ kyá:ky**>, dmn //q[=K=]ɛ́·q[=K=]//, [kʸǽ·kʸ], KIN ['*younger sibling (pet name)*'], (<**=K= (fronting to velar)**> *pet name, baby talk*), phonology: fronting, syntactic analysis: nominal,

usage: pet name, baby talk, attested by AC, Elders Group, also */'younger sister (pet name)'/*, attested by Elders Group (1/7/76).

<**sqiqáq**>, dmn //s=C_1í=qɛ́·q//, KIN [*'small younger sibling'*], (<**s=**> *nominalizer*, R4= *diminutive*), phonology: reduplication, length-loss after prefix, syntactic analysis: nominal, attested by ME (11/21/72 tape), EB, AD, example: <**skw'áy kws tu kwikwe'átes te sqiqáqs.**>, //s=k’^{w}ɛ́y k^w-s tu C_1í=k^w[=əʔɛ́]ɛ́=T-əs tə s=C_1í=qɛ́q-s//, */'He never stops pestering his little brother., He never leaves his little brother alone.'/*, attested by EB, AD.

<**skíkek**>, dmn //s=C_1í=q[=K=]ɛ[=Aə=]q[=K=]//, [sk^{y}ík^{y}ɪk^y], EZ */'chickadee: black-capped chickadee,* probably also *chestnut-backed chickadee,* possibly also *the least bush-tit'/*, [*'Parus atricapillus occidentalis,* probably also *Parus rufescens,* possibly also *Psaltriparus minimus'*], (<**s=**> *nominalizer*, R4= *diminutive*, e-ablaut *derivational*), (<**=K=**> *pet name, baby talk*), phonology: reduplication, fronting to velar, syntactic analysis: nominal, dialects: *Cheh.*, attested by Elders Group (6/4/75), contrast <**méxts'el**> *chickadee, black-capped chickadee, etc.*.

<**sqelá:q**>, pln //s=q[=əl=]ɛ́·q//, KIN */'younger siblings, "younger" cousins (first, second, or third cousins [whose connecting ancestor is younger than ego's])'/*, (<**=el=**> *plural*), phonology: infixed plural, syntactic analysis: nominal, attested by BHTTC, AC, other sources: H-T <s'kEläk·> *younger sibling (collective), younger cousin (child of younger sibling of parent)(coll.)*.

<**qeló:qtel**>, rcps //q[=əl=]ɛ[=Aá=]·q-təl//, [qəlá·qtəl], KIN */'(be) brother and sister, (be siblings to each other), (be) first cousin to each other'/*, (<**=el=**> *plural*, ó-ablaut *derivational* but automatically triggered), (<**-tel**> *reciprocal*), phonology: infixed plural, ó-ablaut automatic before -tel, syntactic analysis: intransitive verb, attested by Elders Group (10/3/76, 6/9/76).

<**sqá:qele ~ sqáqele**>, df //s=qɛ́·q=əl(=)ə//, SOCT [*'baby'*], (<**s=**> *nominalizer*), root or stem <(s)**qá:q**> *younger sibling* or <**seq**> *hang under*, possibly <**=el**> *sort of, a little, -ish* as in < **tsqw'íqw'exwel**> *brownish-black* and <**sq'íq'exel**> *getting blackish* and <**sqwóqwiyel**> *yellowish* and <**stítethel**> *puny* from <**s=títh**> *skinny, thin*) and/or> *get, go, come, become, inceptive*, possibly <**=e**> *living thing*, possibly <**=ele**> *lacking* as in <**tsqó:le**> *thirsty*, syntactic analysis: nominal, attested by AC, BJ (5/10/64), other sources: ES /sqɛ̂qələ/ *baby (to about eight yrs.)*, H-T <skákEla> (umlaut over á) *infant* and <kákEla> (umlaut over á) *infants (coll.)*, Salish cognate: Squamish /s-qáql/ *baby, infant* W73:12, K67:295.

<**seqí:wsem**>, CLO [*'put on one's pants'*], *see* seqíws ~ seqí:ws *under* <**séq**> or better <**seq**>.

<**séqsel**>, df //sə́q=əs=əl//, TIME [*'has come around (of a cyclic period of time)'*], root meaning unknown unless *around*, lx <**=es**> *cyclic period of time*, (<**=el**> *go, come, get, become*), phonology: vowel-loss, syntactic analysis: intransitive verb, attested by Elders Group (4/16/75), example: <**séqsel te skwó:ls.**>, //sə́q=əs=əl tə s=k^{w}á·l-s//, */'Her birthday has come around.'/*, <**le séqsel te syilólem.**>, //lə sə́q=əs=əl tə s=yilál=əm//, */'A year has come around.'/*.

<**séqtel**>, CSTR [*'swing for baby cradle'*], *see* <**séq**> or better <**seq**>.

<**séq'**>, free root //sə́q’//, SH */'to crack, to split (of its own accord), ((*also*) cracked, a crack [*AC*])'/*, semantic environment ['(of log, wooden dish, ceramic dish, canoe, rock, flat plank, etc., the object doesn't have to be round)'], syntactic analysis: intransitive verb, attested by Deming, EB, also */'split, cracked, a crack'/*, attested by AC, example: <**le séq'.**>, //lə sə́q’//, */'It split (of poles or any kind of wood).'/*, attested by AC.

<**seq'síq'**>, durs //C_1əC_2=sə[=Aí=]q’//, SH [*'lots of cracks'*], (<**R3=**> *plural*), phonology: reduplication, ablaut, syntactic analysis: nominal? (s= nominizer + s on root would merge), intransitive verb?, attested by Elders Group.

<**sisíq'**>, durs //s=C_1í=sə[=Aí=]q'//, dmn, SH ['*a crack*'], (<s=> *nominizer*), (<**R4=**> *diminutive*), (<**í-ablaut**> *durative*), phonology: reduplication, ablaut, s+s →s, syntactic analysis: nominal, attested by EB.

<**Sisíq'**>, dmn //s=C_1í=sə[=Aí=]q'//, PLN ['*a cracked mountain where the pipeline crosses the Fraser River between Hope and Agassiz*'], (semological comment: so named because the mountain is split or cracked near the crossing), (<**R4=**> *diminutive*), (<**í-ablaut**> *durative*), phonology: reduplication, ablaut, syntactic analysis: nominal, attested by P.D. Peters (Katz class 10/5/76).

<**Sesíq'**>, durs //s=C_1ə=sə[=Aí=]q'//, PLN ['*a mountain above Evangeline Pete's place at Katz*'], (<**R3=**>perhaps *diminutive plural*), (<**í-ablaut**> *durative*), phonology: reduplication, s+s →s, ablaut, syntactic analysis: nominal, attested by Elders Group (7/6/77), IHTTC (AD and SP wrote name down from MP in 1973-74)(7/8/77), Elders on trip to American Bar (6/26/78), source: place names reference file #27.

<**sísq'**>, dnom //s=sə[=Aí=C_1ə=]q'//, FIRE ['*kindling*'], ASM ['dry fir or cedar sticks'], (<**í-ablaut**> *durative*, <=**R1**=> *resultative*), phonology: ablaut, reduplication, s+s →s, syntactic analysis: nominal, attested by Elders Group (3/15/72), EB, CT, example: <**éx̲qst te máches qesu yéqwt kw'e sísq' or kw'estámés**>, //ʔəx̣=qs=T tə mɛ́cəs qə-s-u yə́qʷ=T k'ʷə sə[=Aí=C_1ə=]q' or k'ʷə=s=tɛ́m=əs//, /'*strike the match and light the kindling or something*'/, attested by CT and HT (6/21/76).

<**séq'et**>, pcs //sə́q'=əT//, HARV /'*chop wood, split wood, (chop/split s-th wood)*'/, semantic environment ['for ex. in splitting planks, shakes, etc.'], SH, BLDG, (<**=et**> *purposeful control transitivizer*), syntactic analysis: transitive verb, attested by EB.

<**seq'séq'et**>, plv //C_1əC_2=sə́q'=əT//, HARV /'*splitting wood, (splitting it (a lot of wood)*'/, BLDG, SH, (<**R3=**> *plural object/action*), phonology: reduplication, syntactic analysis: transitive verb, attested by EB.

<**seq'át ~ sq'át**>, pcs //səq'=ə[=Aɛ́=]T//, durs, SH /'*split s-th, crack s-th*'/, (<**=et**> *purposeful control transitivizer*), (<**á**-ablaut> *durative*), phonology: ablaut, vowel-loss, syntactic analysis: transitive verb, attested by AC, EB, Deming, other sources: ES /sq'ɛ́t/ *split*.

<**seq'á:lí:ya**>, ds //səq'=ɛ́·lí·yɛ//, SD ['*ear-splitting*'], probably root <**séq'**> *split, crack*, lx <**=á:lí:ya**> *in the ear, on the ear*, phonology: originally mis-transcribed as seqá:lí:ya, syntactic analysis: adjective/adjectival verb, attested by Elders Group (12/15/76).

<**lhséq'**>, ds //ɬ=sə́q'//, SH ['*half*'], NUM, SOCT ['*half-breed*'], ECON /'*a half dollar, fifty cents*'/, (<**lh=**> *extract a portion*), syntactic analysis: adjective/adjectival verb, nominal, num, attested by AC, BJ (12/5/64), DM (12/4/64), ER (Deming 1/20/77), Deming (8/4/77), Elders Group, SJ, other sources: ES and JH /ɬsə́q'/ *half*, example: <**lhséq' skw'xó:s**>, //ɬ=sə́q' s=k'ʷəxʸ=á·s//, /'*a half moon*'/, attested by DM, <**lhséq' swàyel**>, //ɬ=sə́q' s=wɛ̀yəl//, /'*mid-morning, middle of the forenoon, halfway till dinnertime*'/, attested by DM, <**slhíxws qas te lhséq'**>, //s=ɬíxʷ=s qɛ-s tə ɬ=sə́q'//, /'*three-thirty (time, 3:30)*'/, literally /'third hour and the half, three o'clock and the half'/, Elder's comment: "ER's mother used this (SJ didn't hear it used)", attested by ER, <**lhséq' xwelítem**>, //ɬ=sə́q' xʷəlítəm//, /'*half white-man*'/, attested by Deming (esp. SJ) (5/3/79), <**kwthe lhséq'chap**>, //kʷθə ɬ=sə́q'-c-ɛp//, /'*half of the crowd, (half of you folks)*'/, attested by AC.

<**Salq'íwel**>, pln //s[=əl=]əq'=íwəl//, PLN /'*Salkaywul, an area with big cracked cedar trees on Hope Slough above Schelowat (Chilliwack I.R. #1) (Sx̲eláwtxw)*'/, ASM ['so named because there were many big cedar trees cracked by lightning there, one was still there in 1964'], literally /'many cracked on the insides'/, (<**=el=**> *plural (many patients)*), lx <**=íwel**> *on the insides, in the rectum,*

phonology: infixed plural, syntactic analysis: nominal, attested by HE (10/8/64 tape), other sources: Wells 1965 (lst ed.):23,

<**sq'x̲áp**>, dnom //s=sq'=x̣=ɛ́p//, EB ['*stump (of a tree [still rooted])*'], literally (probably) /'something split all around in the dirt'/, (<**s=**> *nominalizer*), root <**seq'**> *split*, lx <**=x̲**> *distributive*, lx <**=áp**> *in the dirt*, phonology: consonant merger (s= + s → s), syntactic analysis: nominal, attested by AC, EB, other sources: ES /sq'x̣ɛ́·p/ *stump*, H-T /sk·Ehá̈p/ (umlaut over a) *stump*, Salish cognate: Lushootseed /s-q'ʷuháp/ *stump still rooted* H76:431.

<**seq'á:lí:ya**>, SD ['*ear-splitting*'], *see* séq'.

<**seq'át ~ sq'át**>, SH /'*split s-th, crack s-th*'/, *see* séq'.

<**séq'et**>, HARV /'*chop wood, split wood, (chop/split s-th wood)*'/, *see* séq'.

<**seq'séq'et**>, HARV /'*splitting wood, (splitting it (a lot of wood)*'/, *see* séq'.

<**seq'síq'**>, SH ['*lots of cracks*'], *see* séq'.

<**séqw'emí:ws**>, HARV /'*inner cedar bark (maybe error), (birch bark [AHTTC])*'/, *see* síqw'em *under* <**síkw'**>.

<**sése**>, free root //sə́sə//, EZ /'*widgeon (duck), American widgeon or baldpate,* probably also the *European widgeon, (pintail duck [BJ])*'/, ['*Anas americana (~ Mareca americana),* prob. also *Anas penelope (~ Mareca penelope), (Anas acuta [BJ])*'], ASM ['the name may imitate the distinctive two-syllable call which sounds a lot like a rubber squeaky toy with stress and high pitch on the first syllable'], phonology: probable reduplication, syntactic analysis: nominal, attested by EL and JL (9/15/78), also <**sása**>, //sɛ́sɛ//, attested by HP (Elders Group 3/3/76), Elders Group (2/18/76), also /'*pintail duck*'/, attested by BJ (12/5/64).

<**Sése**>, ds //C_1ə= ́=sɛ//, cts, PLN /'*Mary Ann Creek, village at mouth of Mary Ann Creek into the Fraser (in Yale, B.C., Yale Town Indian Reserve #1)*'/, Elder's comment: "said to mean *where the river washes up and over the rocks* after what happens in high water time", (semological comment: said in Wells 1965 (lst ed.):14,25 to mean *coming in waves*, possibly derived from a form meaning *be rising*), (<**R5=**> *continuative* (here derivational)), (<= ́=> *derivational*), p9ossibe root <**sá:**> *rise* not attested yet Upriver but in Musqueam, phonology: reduplication, stress-shift, syntactic analysis: nominal, attested by Elders at Fish Camp (8/2/77), IHTTC (8/11/77), Elders Group (9/13/77)(slide identification from raft trip), source: place names file reference #98, other sources: Wells 1965 (lst ed.):14, 25, Salish cognate: Musqueam root and prefix in /sɛ́ʔ/ *rise* and /səsɛ́ʔ/ *be rising* Suttles ca1984: ch.7 [p.44].

<**seséx̲we**>, ABFC ['*urinating*'], *see* séx̲we.

<**Sesíq'**>, PLN ['*a mountain above Evangeline Pete's place at Katz*'], *see* séq'.

<**sesí:si**>, EFAM ['*scared a little*'], *see* síy.

<**seswá:yél**>, TIME ['*days*'], *see* wáyel.

<**sesx̲á**>, df //səsx̣ɛ́//, EZ ['*butterfly*'], ['order *Lepidoptera*'], phonology: probable reduplication, possible metathesis, syntactic analysis: nominal, dialects: *Chill.*, source: DM (in JH), other sources: H-T <sEsqá> *butterfly (Papilio) (all large kinds)*.

<**sétqtstes**> or perhaps better <**sétqstes**>, pcs //sə́t(=)qc=T-əs or sɛ[=Aə́=]t=qs=T-əs//, if, FIRE /'*(he) light(s) s-th on fire, (he) set s-th on fire*'/, root probably <**sát**> *reach, pass along, pass on*, possibly <**=qc**> meaning unknown or (more likely) <**=qs**> *on the nose, point, tip*, (<**=t**> *purposeful control transitivizer*), phonology: possible epenthetic ts for s, syntactic analysis: transitive verb, attested by

CT and HT (6/21/76), EB, example: <**sétqtstes kw'e pípe or wood.**>, //sə́t(=)qc=T-əs k'ʷə pípə or wood//, /*'He lights paper or wood (on fire).'*/, attested by CT and HT, <**sétqtstes kw'estámés.**>, //sə́t(=)qc=T-əs k'ʷə=s=tɛ́m=əs//, /*'He lights something., He sets something on fire.'*/, attested by CT and HT.

<**séttsesem**>, mdls or vis //sə́t=cəs=əm or sɛ́[=Aə́=]t=cəs=əm//, ABFC /*'reach'*/, lit. /'reach with one's hand'/, root prob. <**sát**> *reach, pass on, pass along,* <=**tses**> *hand, with the hand,* <=**em**> *middle voice*, attested by RG & EH (4/9/99 Ling332)

<**sétsetets**>, chrs //sə́t=C_1əC_2=əc//, EZ [*'northwest jumping mouse'*], [*'Zapus trinotatus trinotatus'*], root prob. <**sát**> *reach, pass on, pass along*, (<=**R2**> *characteristic*), lx <=**ets**> *on the back*, phonology: reduplication, syntactic analysis: nominal, attested by Elders Group (9/1/76), other sources: JH /sə́tsətə̀c/ *meadow jumping mouse.*

<**sét'xt**>, ABFC (probably) /*'tickle the bottom of someone's feet, (tickle s-o on the foot)'*/, *see* síyt'.

<**sétl'a ~ sétl'o**>, bound root //sə́ƛ'ɛ ~ sə́ƛ'a *older sibling*//.

<**sétl'atel**>, rcps //sə́ƛ'ɛ=təl or sə́ƛ'a=Aɛ=təl//, KIN /*'older sibling, elder cousin (child of older sibling of one's parent, grandchild of older sibling of one's grandparent, great grandchild of older sibling of one's great grandparent), cousin of senior line, older brother, older sister'*/, possibly <**a-ablaut**> *derivational*, (<=**tel**> *reciprocal*), phonology: possible ablaut, syntactic analysis: nominal, attested by AC, BJ (5/10/64), Deming, BHTTC, CT, other sources: H-T <sitlátEl> (macron over a) *elder sibling, elder cousin (child of elder sibling of parent)*, example: <**tl'ó sétl'atels.**>, //ƛ'á sə́ƛ'ɛ=təl-s//, /*'That's her older sister.'*/, attested by AC; found in <**sétl'atels**>, //sə́ƛ'ɛ=təl-s//, /*'his older sister'*/, attested by CT (6/8/76), example: <**tl'ól sétl'atel.**>, //ƛ'á-l sə́ƛ'ɛ=təl//, /*'He's/She's olders than me.'*/, literally /'That's my older sibling.'/, attested by AC, <**tl'ól swál sétl'atel.**>, //ƛ'á-l s=wɛ́-l sə́ƛ'ɛ=təl//, /*'That's my older sibling.'*/, syntactic comment: note double possessive is allowed with swá *own*, attested by AC.

<**sá:tl'atel**>, pln //sə[=Aɛ́·=]ƛ'ɛ=təl//, KIN /*'older siblings, elder cousins (first/second/third cousins by an older sibling of one's ancestor)'*/, (<**á**:-ablaut> *plural*), phonology: ablaut, syntactic analysis: nominal, attested by AC, Deming (2/22/79), other sources: H-T <sátlEtEl> (umlaut over a) *elder siblings/cousins (collect.) (a cousin is elder if a child of an elder sibling of ego's parent)*; found in <**sá:tl'atels**>, //sə[=Aɛ́·=]ƛ'ɛ=təl-s//, /*'(his/her/their) older sisters (or brothers/cousins)'*/, attested by AC, <**ōwá'ata'a slhellhálí sátl'atel?**>, //ʔowə=ɛ́=tɛ-ʔɛ s=C_1əC_2=ɬɛ́lí sə[=Aɛ́=]ƛ'ɛ=təl//, /*'Do you have any other sisters?'*/, dialects: *Matsqui/Sumas*, attested by Deming (prob. AH).

<**séltl'o**>, plv //sə́[=lə=]ƛ'ɛ=Aa or sə́[=lə=]ƛ'a//, KIN [*'oldest (sibling)'*], (<=**le**=> *plural*), possibly <**o-ablaut**> *derivational*, phonology: infixed plural, possible ablaut, syntactic analysis: adjective/adjectival verb, attested by Deming, AC, other sources: H-T <súltla (me'la)> (macron over e) *first (oldest) child*, Salish cognate: Squamish /sinƛ'/ *senior-line children or cousins, older children* W73:68, W67:305, example: <**tl'ó séltl'o.**>, //ƛ'á sə́[=lə=]ƛ'a//, /*'That's/He's/She's the older (oldest).'*/, attested by AC, <**áltha séltl'o.**>, //ʔɛ́lθɛ sə́[=lə=]ƛ'a//, /*'I am the oldest.'*/, attested by Deming (2/22/79), <**tsen welól séltl'o.**>, //cən wəl=ál sə́[=lə=]ƛ'a//, /*'I am the oldest (sibling).'*/, dialects: *Downriver Halkomelem*, attested by Deming (2/22/79).

<**sétl'atel**>, KIN /*'older sibling, elder cousin (child of older sibling of one's parent, grandchild of older sibling of one's grandparent, great grandchild of older sibling of one's great grandparent), cousin of senior line, older brother, older sister'*/, *see* sétl'a ~ sétl'o.

<**sewólem**>, PLAY [*'a game'*], *see* ewólem.

<**sewsewólem**>, PLAY ['*games*'], *see* ewólem.

<**sexw=**>, da //səxʷ=//, KIN ['*-in-law*'], syntactic analysis: derivational prefix; found in <**sexwsí:le**>, //səxʷ=síˑlə//, /'*grandparent-in-law*'/.

<**sex̲éylem** or **sex̲ílem**>, TVMO ['*move over*'], *see* síx̲.

<**séx̲w**>, free root //sə́x̣ʷ//, BSK ['*to split roots from the wrong end (small end)*'], syntactic analysis: intransitive verb, attested by Elders Group (5/28/75).

<**séx̲watel ~ séx̲wàtel**>, ANA ['*bladder*'], *see* séx̲we.

<**séx̲we**>, free root //sə́x̣ʷə ~ sə́x̣ʷɛ//, ABFC ['*urinate*'], ASM ['used for males but also when gender is unspecified'], syntactic analysis: intransitive verb, attested by BHTTC, AD, many others, Salish cognate: Squamish /sə́x̣ʷaʔ/ *urinate, urine* K67:302, K69:61, Lushootseed /sʔəx̣ʷáʔ ~ sx̣ʷáʔ/ *urinate(male)* versus Lushootseed /tiwáʔ/ *urinate (female)* H76:452, comment: the word séx̲watel ~ séx̲wàtel *bladder* preserves the cognate final vowel.

<**seséx̲we**>, cts //C_1ə-sə́x̣ʷə//, ABFC ['*urinating*'], (<**R5-**> *continuative*), phonology: reduplication, syntactic analysis: intransitive verb, attested by DF (Banff trip 8/30/78).

<**séx̲we**>, dnom //s=sə́x̣ʷə//, ANA ['*urine*'], (<**s=**> *nominalizer*), phonology: consonant merger, syntactic analysis: nominal, attested by Elders Group, other sources: ES /sə́x̣ʷa/ *urine*.

<**séx̲watel ~ séx̲wàtel**>, dnom //s=sə́x̣ʷɛ=təl//, ANA ['*bladder*'], literally /'something for urine'/, lx <**=tel**> *device for, something for*, phonology: upshifting to à, syntactic analysis: nominal, attested by Elders Group (10/8/75).

<**sex̲we'álá**>, dnom //s=səx̣ʷə=ʔɛ́lɛ́ or s=səx̣ʷəʔ=ɛ́lɛ́//, ANA ['*bladder*'], literally /'container of urine'/, lx <**=álá ~ ='álá (after vowel)**> *container of*, phonology: historically the glottal stop is part of the root (as in Squamish and Lushootseed) which only survives before vowel-initial suffixes, but =álá has allomorphs ='álá and =hálá after other vowel-final stems too, some of which may have cognates without final glottal stop, syntactic analysis: nominal, attested by Deming (3/4/76).

<**sex̲we'áléx̲eth'**>, ds //səx̣ʷəʔ=ɛ́lə́x̣əθ'//, ABDF /'*wet the bed, (urinate in the bed)*'/, lx <**=áléx̲eth'**> *bed*, syntactic analysis: intransitive verb, attested by Elders Group (5/3/78), AD (1/15/79), also <**sex̲we'álex̲eth'**>, //səx̣ʷəʔ=ɛ́ləx̣əθ'//, attested by EB (5/5/78), example: <**lhéq'elhchxw sex̲we'álex̲eth'.**>, //ɬə́q'=əɬ-c-xʷ səx̣ʷəʔ=ɛ́ləx̣əθ'//, /'*You used to wet your bed.*'/, attested by EB, <**chxw ólewe siyólexwe kw'as sex̲we'álex̲eth'.**>, //c-xʷ ʔálə-wə si=yáləxʷ=ə k'ʷ-ɛ-s səx̣ʷəʔ=ɛ́ləx̣əθ'//, /'*You're too old to wet your bed.*'/, attested by EB.

<**sex̲we'ayíwsem**>, mdls //səx̣ʷəʔ=ɛy=íws=əm//, ABDF /'*wet one's pants, (urinate in one's pants)*'/, lx <**=ay=íws**> *pants* itself from lx <**=ay**> *bark, wool, covering* plus lx <**=íws**> *on the body, on the skin*, (<**=em**> *middle voice*), syntactic analysis: intransitive verb, attested by AD (1/15/79).

<**séx̲we**>, ANA ['*urine*'], *see* séx̲we.

<**sex̲we'álá**>, ANA ['*bladder*'], *see* séx̲we.

<**sex̲we'áléx̲eth'**>, ABDF /'*wet the bed, (urinate in the bed)*'/, *see* séx̲we.

<**sex̲we'ayíwsem**>, ABDF /'*wet one's pants, (urinate in one's pants)*'/, *see* séx̲we

<**séyem éliyels**>, EB /'*garlic*'/ (lit. strong + [domestic] onion), *see* eyém

<**séyí:m**>, EFAM ['*be haunted*'], *see* síy.

<**seyíyex̱**>, df //səyíyəx̣ or s=hə=yí[=C₁ə=]x̣ or sə=C₁í=yəx̣//, EZ /'*big gray rock lizard,* probably *Pacific giant salamander* which is cognate in Squamish, possibly also *the Pacific coast newt* which is commonest in B.C. and also is found in this area, prob. also *the northern alligator lizard*'/, ['prob. *Dicamptodon ensatus*, poss. also *Taricha granulosa granulosa*, prob. also *Gerrhonotis coeruleus principis*'], possibly <**s= (epenthetic e)**> *nominalizer*, possibly <**he=**> *resultative or continuative =R1=*> *continuative or resultative*, possibly <**R1=**> *diminutive*, root meaning unknown, phonology: probable reduplication, syntactic analysis: nominal, attested by Elders Group (3/1/72, 6/9/76), other sources: H-T <sEyia'H> (macron over i) *lizard (Lacertilia)*, Salish cognate: Squamish /s-i-ʔíx̣-ix̣as/ *big lizard* W73:164, K67:306 from /s-ix̣ás ~ s-yəx̣ás/ *large rock* K67:300, 306, attested as /sʔəy'íx̣yix̣əs/ and identified as *Pacific giant salamander* in Kennedy and Bouchard 1976:118, also <**tseyí:yex̱**>, //(prob. tə səyíyəx̣)//, attested by Elders Group (3/1/72).

<**se'ó:seqwt**>, KIN ['*youngest (sibling)*'], *see* sóseqwt ~ (rarely) só:seqwt.

<**s-há:y**>, dnom //s=hɛ̀[=´=]·y// [shǽ ·y] (not *[šǽ ·y]), CAN /'*canoe-work, canoe-making*'/, phonology: stress shift, orthographic hyphen here is to separate graphemes s and h from the grapheme sh, it does not mean inflection rather than derivation in this case, syntactic analysis: nominal, example: <**tel s=há:y**>, //t-əl s=hɛ̀·y//, /'*my canoe-work*'/, *see* hà:y.

<**s-hí:lekw ~ s-hílekw**>, stvi //s=hi[-´·-]lək^w ~ s=hi[-´-]lək^w//, TVMO ['*be ready*'], syntactic analysis: stvi, phonology: stress shift?, lengthening, syntactic comment: statives are usually built on a continuative stem; example: <**líchap welh s-hí:lekw**>, //lí-c-ɛp wəɬ s=hi[-´·-]lək^w//, /'*Are you folks ready?*'/, attested by BHTTC, <**líchxw xwel s-hílekw**>, //lí-c-x^w x^{w}əl s=hi[-´-]lək^w//, /'*Are you still ready?*'/, attested by EB, *see* hilékw.

<**s-hómkw**>, stvi //s=hámk^w//, WETH /'*sultry, humid*'/, (<**s=**> *stative*), syntactic analysis: adjective/adjectival verb, comment: this is one of the few words requiring a hyphen in the Stó:lō writing system to show that both s and h are pronounced separately (as in English "misheard"), not together as a digraph for a single sound ([š]) as it usually is (as in English "mush"), attested by IHTTC, *see* hómkw.

<**s-hómkwstem**>, stca //s=hámk^w=sT=əm//, SOC ['*(someone) standing in the middle of a crowd*'], (<**s=**> *stative*), probably <**=st**> *causative*, probably <**=em**> *middle voice*, or possibly <**=em**> *intransitivizer*, or <**=tem ~ =em**> *participial*, possibly root as in <**s-hómkw**> *sultry, humid*??, syntactic analysis: intransitive verb, comment: another rare word requiring a hyphen in the Stó:lō writing system to show s and h are pronounced separately (not as in English "mush"), attested by IHTTC, *see* hómkw.

<**s-hóqwem**>, dnom //s=háq^w=əm//, SM ['*a smell*'], syntactic analysis: nominal, attested by NP, Elders, example: <**ewéta s-hóqwems**>, //ʔəwə=´=tɛ s=háq^w=əm-s//, /'*It has no smell.*'/, *see* hóqw.

<**s-hótl'eqw**>, dnom //s=háƛ'=əq^w//, HUNT ['*blunt-headed arrow*'], PLAY, ASM ['the head is made of cloth or hide, etc.; the shaft may be feathered or not'], lx <**=eqw**> *on the head*, syntactic analysis: nominal, attested by Deming, *see* hótl'.

<**s-hóyiws**>, dnom //s=háy=iws//, SPRD /'*spirit-dancing costume, wool hat for spirit-dancer (Deming)*'/, (<**s=**> *nominalizer*), lx <**=iws**> *on the body, on the skin*, phonology: one of the few words requiring a hyphen in the Stó:lō writing system to show that s and h are here pronounced separately as in English "misheard" and not together as in English "mush", syntactic analysis: nominal, attested by Elders, CLO /'*dancer's uniform, (any) coordinated outfit*'/, attested by RG & EH (4/10/99 Ling332) example: SPRD <**s-hó:yiws te x̱awsólkwlh**>, //s=há·y=iws-s təx̣ɛws=álk^{w}ɬ//, /'*whole costume of a new spirit-dancer*'/, syntactic analysis: nominal phrase with modifier(s), attested by Elders 11/26/75, also /'*wool hat for spirit-dancer*'/, attested by Deming, SPRD <**s-hóyiws máqel**>, //s=háy=iws-s mɛ́=qəl//, /'*hair*

hat for experienced spirit-dancer'/, lit. “it’s costume - hair” or “hair of the costume”, syntactic analysis: nominal phrase with modifier(s), attested by Deming, *see* hóyiws.

<**sí:**>, free root //sí·//, FSH [*'fish drying rack (for wind-drying)*'], CSTR, syntactic analysis: noun, nominal, attested by Elders Group (5/19/76).

<**sích ~ síts**>, free root //síc or sə[=Aí=]c//, EFAM [*'proud*'], possibly <**í-ablaut**> *durative or resultative*, syntactic analysis: adjective/adjectival verb, attested by Elders Group, example: <**síts ta' sqwálewel.**>, //síc t-ɛʔ s=q^{w}ɛ̀l=əwəl//, /*'(You have) pride.*'/, literally /'are proud your thoughts/feelings'/, attested by Elders Group (3/15/72), <**sích te sqwálewel**>, //síc tə s=q^{w}ɛ̀l=əwəl//, /*'think big of oneself*'/, attested by Elders Group (9/21/77).

<**sikelít**>, free root //sikəlít//, FIRE [*'cigarette*'], PE, syntactic analysis: nominal, attested by Deming (3/29/79), borrowed from English /sɪgərɛ́t/.

<**sikó**>, free root //siká//, FIRE [*'cigar*'], PE, syntactic analysis: nominal, attested by Deming (3/29/79), borrowed from English /sigár/.

<**síkw'**>, free root //sík’^{w}//, HUNT [*'get skinned, debarked*'], syntactic analysis: intransitive verb, attested by Elders Group, Salish cognate: Lushootseed root /sík’^{w}(i)/ *tear, take apart, rip apart* as in /ʔə(s)sík’^{w}/ *it's torn* H76:445.

<**síkw'et**>, pcs //sík’^{w}=əT//, HUNT [*'pull skin off s-th (like a bird that's easy to skin)*'], (<**=et**> *purposeful control transitivizer*), syntactic analysis: transitive verb, attested by Elders Group, Salish cognate: Lushootseed /sík’^{w}-id/ *tear it, take it apart, take down; rip it apart* H76:445.

<**síkw'em**>, izs //sík’^{w}=əm//, HUNT [*'skin or bark pulls off*'], (<**=em**> *intransitivizer*), syntactic analysis: intransitive verb, attested by Elders Group, compare with <**sókw'**> *inner core of cow parsnip (yó:le) with bark peeled off,* [perhaps also *of some other plants with barked peeled off]* and as in <**sókw'em**> *outer cedar bark* and <**Sókw'ech**> *winter village at mouth of Gordon Creek (lit. peeled off bark in the back).*

<**sékw'emiy**>, ds //si[=Aə́=]k’^{w}=əm=iy//, EB /*'birch, western white birch*'/, [*'Betula papyriforma commutata*'], literally /'bark always peeled off tree'/, (<**é=ablaut**> *durative*), lx <**=iy**> here *tree* or perhaps its usual meaning *bark*, phonology: ablaut, syntactic analysis: nominal, attested by Elders Group (3/1/72), Deming, CT, AC, BJ (5/10/64), also <**súkw'emiy**>, //súk’^{w}=əm=iy//, attested by EB, example: <**p'elyí:ws te sékw'emi**>, //p’əl=əy=í·ws-s tə si[=Aə́=]k’^{w}=əm=iy//, /*'birch bark*'/, attested by CT.

<**Sekw'sekw'emá:y**>, df //C_1əC_2=sək’^{w}=əm=i[=Aɛ́·=]y or C_1əC_2=sək’^{w}=əm=ɛ́·y//, PLN /*'place where a grove of birches stood/stand near the Kickbush place on Chilliwack River Road in Sardis, (village at junction of Semmihault Creek and Chilliwack River [Wells 1965 (lst ed.):19])*'/, ASM ['the old Kickbush house is now the next house north of Don Kickbush's house (the latter is at 7915 Chilliwack River Road), the Kickbush farm was on the southwest corner of Luckakuck Way and Chilliwack River Road'], literally /'birch grove place, many birch place'/, (<**R3=**> *plural (many, always collective)*), possibly <**á**:-ablaut> *derivational* or possibly <**=á:y**> *place* as in Nooksack language, phonology: reduplication, possible ablaut, syntactic analysis: nominal, attested by BJ (12/5/64 old p.319), source: place names file reference #86 and #265, also <**Sekw'sékw'emiy**>, //C_1əC_2=sək’^{w}=əm=iy//, attested by Elders Group (8/31/77), also /*'village at junction of Semiault Creek and Chilliwack River*'/, attested by Wells 1965 (lst ed.):19.

<**síqw'em**>, izs //síq'ʷ=əm or sík'ʷ=əm//, HARV [*'peel cedar bark'*], (<**=em**> *intransitivizer*), phonology: may have been mispronounced for síkw'em, but poss. also a separate root, syntactic analysis: intransitive verb, attested by AC (12/1/71).

<**sèqw'emí:ws**>, df //si[=Aə́=]q'ʷ=əm=í·ws//, HARV /*'inner cedar bark (maybe error), (birch bark [AHTTC])'*/, CLO [*'cedar bark skirt'*], (<**é-ablaut**> *resultative or durative*), (<**=em**> *intransitivizer*), lx <**=í:ws**> *on the skin, on the body*, phonology: ablaut, syntactic analysis: nominal, attested by AC (from Lizzie Herrling by phone) (12/1/71), also /*'birch bark'*/, attested by AHTTC (2/15/80).

<**skw'álx̱**>, df //s=k'ʷɛ́l(=)x̣// or more likely //sik'ʷ=ɛ́l(=)x̣//, EZ [*'immature bald eagle'*], ASM ['before the head feathers turn white, age one to three years'], [*'Haliaeetus leucocephalus'*], possibly <**s=**> *nominalizer*) or <**síkw'**>, //sík'ʷ//, [*'get skinned'*], possibly <**=x̱**> *distributive, all around*, syntactic analysis: nominal, attested by Elders Group 2/13/80, 3/15/78, also <**skw'àlx̱**>, attested by Elders Group 2/18/76, also <**skw'á:lx̱**>, attested by Elders Group 6/4/75, also <**sqw'á:lx̱**>, attested by Elders Group 3/1/72, also <**skw'álx̱ ~ sqw'álx̱**>, also /*'golden eagle'*/.

<**síkw'em**>, HUNT [*'skin or bark pulls off'*], *see* síkw'.

<**síkw'et**>, HUNT [*'pull skin off s-th (like a bird that's easy to skin)'*], *see* síkw'.

<**sí:l**>, free root //sí·l//, CLO [*'cloth'*], WV, syntactic analysis: noun, nominal, attested by Elders Group (prob. EL, 7/10/75), borrowed from Chinook Jargon <sail> *cloth, cotton, linen goods, sail* Johnson 1978:398.

<**siláwtxw ~ sí:láwtxw**>, ds //sil=ɛ́wtxʷ ~ sí·l=ɛ́wtxʷ//, BLDG [*'tent'*], literally /'cloth house'/, lx <**=áwtxw**> *house, building*, syntactic analysis: nominal, attested by Elders Group (prob. EL, 7/10/75), SP (1975), also <**sí:tálxw**>, //sí·tɛ́lxʷ//, comment: probably my mistranscription, attested by AC.

<**sí:lá:kw**>, ds //sí·l(=)ɛ́·kʷ//, EZ /*'male mountain goat'*/, ZOO [*'Oreamnos americanus americanus'*], attested by Elders Group, Salish cognate: Squamish /**sínakʷ**/ *old mountain goat* Kennedy and Bouchard 1976:44.

<**siláwtxw ~ sí:láwtxw**>, BLDG [*'tent'*], *see* sí:l.

<**sí:lcheptel**>, FIRE /*'fire-drill, stick spun to start fire'*/, *see* sél or sí(:)l.

<**sí:le**>, free root //sí·lə or sí·l=ə//, KIN /*'grandparent, grandparent's sibling, grandparent's first cousin'*/, possibly <**=e**> *living being*, perhaps compare with <**siyó:lexw=e**> *old person*, syntactic analysis: noun or nominal, attested by Deming, Elders Group, AC, DC and Ben James and AD, BJ (12/5/65), NP, many others, other sources: ES /sí·lə/ *grandparent*, Salish cognate: Squamish /síʔl/ *grandparent* W73:122, K67:305, example: <**l sí:le**>, //l sí·lə//, /*'my grandfather, my father's father'*/, attested by BJ, <**le t'ít'elem te syéwels te sí:les.**>, //lə t'í[-C_1ə-]l=əm tə s=yə́w=əl-s tə sí·lə-s//, /*'She's singing her grandmother's (spirit-)song.'*/, attested by AC (10/15/71), <**éy swàyèl, sí:le.**>, //ʔɛ́y s=wɛ̀yə̀l, sí·lə//, /*'Good day, grandmother., Good day grandfather.'*/, attested by Deming, <**selchím ta sí:le?**>, //s(=)əlc=ím t-ɛ sí·lə//, /*'How's your grandparent?'*/, attested by DC and Ben James and AD.

<**selsí:le**>, pln //C_1əC_2=sí·l(=)ə//, KIN [*'grandparents'*], (<**R3=**> *plural*), phonology: reduplication, syntactic analysis: noun, nominal, attested by AC.

<**sísele**>, dmn //sí[=C_1ə=]l(=)ə//, KIN /*'grandmother (pet name), grandfather (pet name), granny, grandpa'*/, (<**=R1=**> *pet name, diminutive*), phonology: reduplication, syntactic analysis: noun, nominal, attested by AC.

<**sísi**>, dmn //C_1í=si(lə)//, KIN [*'grampa'*], (<**R4=**> *diminutive*), phonology: syllable-loss or clipping, syntactic analysis: nominal, usage: baby talk, attested by AC, Salish cognate: Squamish /sí-siʔ/ *uncle (brother of father or mother)* K67:304.

<**silílh**>, possibly root //silíɬ// or more likely stem //s=hi=líɬ//, ABFC [*'sitting cross-legged'*], possibly <**s=**> *stative*, possibly <**hi=**> *continuative or resultative*, syntactic analysis: adjective/adjectival verb, attested by IHTTC (9/1/77).

<**silís**>, ANA /*'(have) sharp teeth, (have) fangs'*/, *see* éy ~ éy:.

<**silíxw**>, free root //silíx^w// or more likely stcs //s-hi-líx^w//, TVMO /*'slow down, go slow'*/, most likely the structure is //s-hi-líx^w// with continuative prefix <hi->, stative prefix <s-> which causes the <h> to drop, and root <líxw> syntactic analysis: intransitive verb, attested by Elders Group (3/29/78); see main entry under root <líxw>

<**silíxwstexw**>, caus //silíx^w=sT-əx^w// or //s=hi=líx^w=sT-əx^w//, TVMO [*'making s-o slow'*], (<**=st**> *causative control transitivizer*), (<**-exw**> *third person object*), the continuative translation here makes it most likely the stem structure is //s-hi-líx^w// with continuative prefix <hi->, stative prefix <s-> which causes the <h> to drop, and root <líxw> as in <**slílexwelh**>, stvi //s=lí[=C_1ə=]x^w(=)əɬ//, EFAM [*'be calm'*], syntactic analysis: transitive verb, attested by Elders Group; found in <**silíxwsthométsel.**>, //silíx^w=sT-ámə-c-əl//, /*'I'm making you slow.'*/; see main entry under root <líxw>

<**sí:ltem**>, WV /*'it's twined (like rolled on thigh and twisted, spun)'*/, *see* sél or sí(:)l.

<**Sílhixw**>, PLN /*'creek from Hicks Lake* [sic? *from Deer Lake] that's actually three creeks all leaving from the lake,* probably *Mahood Creek, (*also *Hick's Mountain [LJ])'*/, *see* lhí:xw.

<**sílhqey**>, EZ [*'two-headed supernatural snake'*], POW, *see*álhqey ~ álhqay.

<**sílhqey**>, EZ [*'supernatural double-headed snake'*], POW, . *see* isá:le ~ isále ~ isá:la.

<**simáléqep**>, df //s=ʔiy=ə́m=ɛ́ləqəp//, SM /*'smell that one cannot locate, strong stink'*/, probably root <**eyém**> *strong*, lx <**=áléqep**> *smell, odor, fragrance*, syntactic analysis: nominal, attested by Elders Group (5/25/77); see under root <**ey**> and stem <**ey=em**> 'strong'.

<**simíwél**>, EFAM /*'strong feelings, mad all the time but won't fight'*/, *see* éy ~ éy:.

<**síq**>, df //sə[=Aí=]q//, DIR [*'(hung) under'*], (<**í-ablaut on root e**> *resultative or durative*), phonology: í-ablaut on root e, syntactic analysis: preposition/prepositional verb?, attested by Elders Group (2/16/77), example: <**síq te shxw'á<u>x</u>eth**>, //síq tə sx^w=ʔɛ́x̣əθ//, /*'under the bed'*/, also *see under* séq.

<**síqetsel**>, df //sə[=Aí=]q=əcəl//, BLDG /*'roof, shake(s) on roof, shingle(s) on roof, ceiling'*/, literally /'hung under on the back'/, ASM ['roof planks/shakes in the old days were made like shallow troughs and set on the roof side by side first convex side up, then where each two planks adjoined another plank was set convex side down to cover the join;'], some planks were put on the roof with upward overlapping: some were put on the roof with no upward overlapping (AD), (semological comment: the literal meaning probably refers to the fact that aboriginal (and modern) shakes or shingles hang under each other on the back of a roof), lx <**=etsel**> *on the back*, syntactic analysis: nominal, attested by Elders Group (11/12/75, 8/25/76, 5/3/78), AD (Elders Group 4/23/80), DM (12/4/64), RG & EH (4/10/99 Ling332), Salish cognate: Squamish /síqč/ *shingles* K67:305, Lushootseed root /šəq/ *high, up* as in /šə́q-əd/ *lift it up* and especially /šəq-álatx^w/ *roof, upstairs, ceiling; above the whole house* H76:459-460.

<**síqetseláwtxw**>, ds //sə[=Aí=]q=əcəl=ɛ́wtx^w//, BLDG /*'shakes on house, roof'*/, lx <**=áwtxw**> *house, building*, syntactic analysis: nominal, attested by Elders Group (11/12/75).

<**síqes**>, df //síq=əs//, LANG ['*whistle with finger*'], HUNT, literally perhaps /'hung under on the face'/, probably root <**seq**> *hang under*, probably <**í-ablaut on root é**> *resultative*, possibly <**=es**> *on the face*, syntactic analysis: intransitive verb, attested by MV (Deming 5/4/78), Deming (7/27/78).

<**sisqelísem**>, mdls //si[-C_1ə-]q=əlís=əm//, LANG /'*whistling on one's teeth, whistling through the teeth*'/, Elder's comment: "not *humming*", (<**-R1-**> *continuative*), lx <**=elís**> *on the teeth*, (<**=em**> *middle voice*), phonology: reduplication, syntactic analysis: intransitive verb, attested by Elders Group (6/1/77), Deming (7/27/78), also /'*humming*'/, attested by Elders Group (12/15/76).

<**síq'**>, free root or stem //síq' or s-hí-yq'//, LAND /'*hard clay, hard earth, smooth (hard) earth*'/, possible root <**yéq'**> *file, abrade*, syntactic analysis: noun, nominal, attested by Elders Group, IHTTC, Salish cognate: Squamish /səyq'/ *clay, hard pan* W73:60, K69:61.

<**síqw'em**>, izs //síq'^{w}=əm or sík'^{w}=əm//, HARV ['*peel cedar bark*'], (<**=em**> *intransitivizer*), phonology: may have been mispronounced for síkw'em, but poss. also a separate root, syntactic analysis: intransitive verb, attested by AC (12/1/71).

<**sèqw'emí:ws**>, df //si[=Aə́=]q'^{w}=əm=í·ws//, HARV /'*inner cedar bark (maybe error), (birch bark [AHTTC])*'/, CLO ['*cedar bark skirt*'], (<**é-ablaut**> *resultative or durative*), (<**=em**> *intransitivizer*), lx <**=í:ws**> *on the skin, on the body*, phonology: ablaut, syntactic analysis: nominal, attested by AC (from Lizzie Herrling by phone) (12/1/71), also /'*birch bark*'/, attested by AHTTC (2/15/80).

<**sísele**>, KIN /'*grandmother (pet name), grandfather (pet name), granny, grandpa*'/, *see* sí:le.

<**siselts'iyósem**>, TVMO /'*spinning, whirling*'/, *see* sél or sí(:)l.

<**sísem**>, EFAM /'*feel creepy, fear something behind one*'/, *see* síy.

<**sisemó:ya ~ sisemóya ~ sisemóye ~ sísemòye**>, dmn //C_1í=səm=á·yɛ//, EZ /'*bee, honeybee, hornet, wasp*'/, ['order *Hymenoptera*, superfamily *Apoidea*, family *Apidae*, including *Apis mellifera* (introduced), also family *Bombidae* and family *Vespidae* and possibly bee-like members of family *Syrphidae* (order *Diptera*)'], ASM ['DC's grandfather, Frank Dan of Chehalis had the spirit song and spirit power) of a bee (EB, NP, AC)'], possibly root <**sísem**> *feel creepy, fear something behind one*, (<**R4=**> *diminutive*), lx <**=iya ~ =ó:ya**> *affectionate diminutive, personal name ending*, phonology: reduplication, syntactic analysis: nominal, attested by AC, BJ (12/5/64), EB, NP, Elders Group, other sources: ES /səsəmá·yə/ (CwMs /səmáʔyə/) *bumblebee*, JH /sí·məmá·ye/ *bee* vs. JH /mə́k^{w}mək^{w}/ *bumblebee*, H-T <sisEmaía> (macron over i) *bee (Apis sp.)* vs. H-T <mókmok> *bumblebee (Apis sp.)*, contrast <**mékwmekw**> *bumblebee (family Bombidae, Bombus spp.)*, Salish cognate: Squamish /sə-smáyʔ/ *bee, bumblebee* W73:34, K67:301, Lushootseed /x^{w}=sə́bəd/ *bee*, example: <**híkw sisemóya**>, //hík^{w} C_1í=səm=áyɛ//, /'*big bees*'/, Elder's comment: "there may be another word for *bumblebees*", attested by AC, <**sisemóyetsel, sisemóyetsel.**>, //C_1í=səm=áyə-c-əl, C_1í=səm=áyə-c-əl//, /'*I am a bee, I am a bee.*'/, usage: words to Frank Dan's spirit song, attested by AC, <**x̲ex̲p'ítsel sisemó:ye**>, //x̣ə[=C_1ə=]p'=ícəl C_1í=səm=á·yə//, /'*yellow-jacket bee*'/, attested by Elders Group (9/8/76), <**meláses te sisemóye**>, //məlɛ́səs-s tə C_1í=səm=áyə//, /'*honey*'/, literally /'molasses of the bee'/, attested by Elders Group (3/22/78).

<**meláses te sisemóye**>, //məlɛ́səs-s tə C_1í=səm=áyə//, FOOD /'*honey*'/, literally /'molasses of the bee'/, attested by Elders Group (3/22/78).

<**x̲ex̲p'ítsel sisemó:ye**>, ds //x̣ə[=C_1ə=]p'=ícəl C_1í=səm=á·yə//, EZ ['*yellow-jacket bee*'], ['family *Vespidae,* genus *Vespula, i.e. Vespula spp.*'], literally /'striped on the back bee'/, phonology: reduplication, syntactic analysis: simple nominal phrase, attested by Elders Group (9/8/76).

<**siseqíws ~ síseqíws**>, CLO /*'short pants, little pants, underpants'*/, *see* seqíws ~ seqí:ws *under* seq..

<**sísesem**>, EFAM /*'feeling creepy, fearing something behind one'*/, *see* síy.

<**sísewel**>, ABFC [*'hearing (about)'*], *see* síw.

<**síse<u>x</u>wem**>, ABFC [*'wading in shallow water'*], *see* sí<u>x</u>wem.

<**sísi**>, KIN [*'grampa'*], *see* sí:le.

<**sí:si**>, EFAM /*'be afraid, be scared, be nervous'*/, *see* síy.

<**sí:silexw**>, EFAM [*'scare s-o accidentally'*], *see* síy.

<**sí:silómet ~ sí:silòmét**>, EFAM /*'scare oneself (in being reckless), scare oneself (do something one knows is dangerous and get scared even more than expected)'*/, *see* síy.

<**sí:simet**>, EFAM [*'be afraid of s-th/s-o'*], *see* síy.

<**sisíq'**>, SH [*'a crack'*], *see* séq'.

<**Sisíq'**>, PLN [*'a cracked mountain where the pipeline crosses the Fraser River between Hope and Agassiz'*], *see* séq'.

<**sisistáxwes.**>, EFAM [*'He's scaring them.'*], *see* síy.

<**sisqelísem**>, LANG /*'whistling on one's teeth, whistling through the teeth'*/, *see* síqes *under* seq.

<**sísq'**>, FIRE [*'kindling'*], *see* séq'.

<**sí:stel**>, BSK [*'little basket'*], *see* sí:tel ~ sítel.

<**sí:tel ~ sítel**>, df //sí·=təl//, BSK [*'basket (any kind)'*], root meaning unknown unless sí: *drying rack (for wind-drying fish)* or sá: *rise*, lx <**=tel**> *device for*, syntactic analysis: nominal, attested by AC, DM (12/4/64), BJ (5/10/64), Elders Group (3/1/72, 6/11/75), CT and HT, other sources: ES and JH /sí·təl/ *basket (generic)*, example: <**lhq'átseseqel sí:tel**>, //ɬq'ɛ́t=cəs=əqəl sí·=təl//, /*'five baskets'*/, literally /'five containers basket'/, attested by CT and HT (6/21/76).

<**sí:stel**>, dmn //sí·[=C_1ə=]=təl//, BSK [*'little basket'*], possibly <**=R1=**> *diminutive*, phonology: reduplication, vowel-loss, syntactic analysis: nominal, attested by EB, also <**sístel**>, //sí[=C_1ə=]=təl//, attested by Elders Group (6/11/75).

<**selístel**>, dmpn //s[=əl=]í[=C_1ə=]=təl//, BSK [*'little baskets'*], (<**=el=**> *plural*), phonology: reduplication, infixed plural, syntactic analysis: nominal, attested by EB, also <**siseltel**>, //si[=C_1ə=əl=]=təl//, attested by SJ.

<**sá:letel ~ sá:ltel**>, pln //si[=Aɛ́]·[=lə=]=təl//, BSK [*'a lot of baskets'*], (<**á-ablaut**> *plural*, <**=le=**> *plural*), phonology: ablaut, infixed plural, syntactic analysis: nominal, attested by EB.

<**sá'eltel**>, pln //si[=Aɛ́=]ʔ[=əl=]=təl//, BSK [*'baskets'*], (<**á-ablaut**> *plural*, <**=le=**> *plural*), phonology: ablaut, infixed plural, dialects: *Sumas/Matsqui*, comment: this most downriver of the Upriver Halkomelem dialects shows glottal stop <'>/ʔ/ corresponding to Upriver length before consonants in some cases, a more consistent feature in Downriver Halkomelem, attested by ER and AH (sisters) (Deming 3/17/77).

<**Síthikwi**>, free root //síðik^{w}i//, CH [*'Jesus Christ'*], N, phonology: <th> is actually voiced here, in this borrowed word only in the whole language, phonetically a thorn ([ð]), syntactic analysis: nominal, attested by AC, EB (12/18/75), borrowed from Chinook Jargon /cesukli/ *Jesus Christ* Johnson 1978:350 itself from French <Jésus Christ>/žésu krí/, also <**Síthikri**>, //síðikri//, attested by SP (IHTTC 9/15/77), AD (1/11/80), also <**Sísikri**>, //sísikri//, attested by NP (IHTTC 9/15/77), example:

<**ō Síthikri, plíst te sq'éptset.**>, //o síðikri, plís=T tə s=q'ə́p-c-ət//, /'*Oh Jesus, bless our meeting.*'/, attested by AD.

<**síts**>, free root //síts//, HHG ['*sheets*'], syntactic analysis: noun, nominal, attested by CT (6/8/76), borrowed from Chinook Jargon /sít/ <sheet> itself from English <sheet> Johnson 1978:404, example: <**a'axwíl síts ~ emémel síts**>, //C_1ε=ʔεxʷíl síts ~ ʔəmə́məl síts//, /'*small sheets*'/.

<**sí:ts'**>, probable bound root //sí·c'//, meaning unclear

<**sí:ts'elhp**>, df //sí·c'=əɬp//, EB /'*vine maple, Douglas maple*'/, ['*Acer circinatum, Acer glabrum var. douglasii* or *Acer douglasii*'], ASM ['vine maple was heated over the fire and used for switches to whip children lazy in getting up to go bathe in the river each morning (the pitch would stick and burn a bit), also heated and used to switch runners' legs to make them tough, a vine maple pole was tied to the ceiling or used in the bush to make a swing (séqtel or q'éyt'o) for a baby in a cradle, with the cradle suspended from the pole by a rope a woman could even work at a loom, etc. and bounce the cradle by a string tied to her foot, vine maple wa also used in other things required strong flexible wood; Douglas maple leaves (considered a variety of Rocky Mountain maple by some botanists) were used to separate food in underground steam-pit cooking'], MED ['vine maple bark was used in a hot bath to reduce swelling on the body (AD), black ashes from vine maple was mixed with grease to make a medicine for swelling (Deming), leaves from last year were used for ulcer medicine--washed, put in clear water and boiled, then the tea is drunk as medicine (JL)'], root meaning unknown unless the same as in sts'á(:)s *fine white ashes* (as speculated by the Deming elders), lx <**=elhp**> *tree, plant*, syntactic analysis: nominal, attested by AC, BJ (12/5/64), JL (Fish Camp 7/19/79), AD (6/19/79), SJ, other sources: JH /sí·səɬp/ *vine maple*, H-T <sítsElp> (macron over i) *vine maple (Acer circinatum)*, example: <**tsqwá:y te sí:ts'elhp.**>, //c=qʷέ·y tə sí·c'=əɬp//, /'*The vine maple is green.*'/, attested by Deming (esp. SJ)(5/3/79).

<**síw**>, bound root //síw *to sense the future, to hear about*//, Salish cognate: Squamish root /siw ~ səw/ as in /síw-i/ *become attentive, prick one's ears* K69:62.

<**síwe ~ syéwe**>, dnom //(s=)síw=ə or s=yə́w=ə//, POW /'*seer, fortune-teller, person that senses the future*'/, (<**s=**> *nominalizer*), probably root <**síw**> *to sense (the future), hear about*, possibly instead root <**yéw**> *spirit power*, lx <**=e**> *person*, syntactic analysis: nominal, compare with root <**yew**> *spirit power*.

<**síwél**>, stem //síw=əl *sense, hear about*//, Salish cognate: Squamish /síw-i/ *become attentive, prick one's ears* K69:62.

<**sísewel**>, cts //sí[-C_1ə-]w=əl//, incs, ABFC ['*hearing (about)*'], (<**-R1-**> *continuative*), (<**=el**> *get, become, go, come*), phonology: reduplication, syntactic analysis: intransitive verb, attested by Deming (6/15/78).

<**síwélmét ~ síwélmet**>, iecs //síw=əl=məT//, POW ['*sense something (that will happen)*'], ABFC ['*hear about it*'], (<**=el**> *get, become, go, come*, <**=met**> *indirect effect control transitivizer*), phonology: updrifting, syntactic analysis: transitive verb, attested by Elders Group (1/7/76), Deming (6/15/78).

<**síwél**>, SENS /'*(sense, hear about)*'/, *see* síw.

<**síwélmét ~ síwélmet**>, ABFC /'*sense something (that will happen), hear about it*'/, *see* síw.

<**síwe ~ syéwe**>, POW /'*seer, fortune-teller, person that senses the future*'/, *see* síw *and* yew.

<**sí:wí:qe**>, HAT /'*men, males*'/, *see* wíyeqe ~ wíyqe ~ wí:qe.

<**siwíqe'ó:llh** or **siwí:qe'ó:llh**>, HAT ['*boys*'], *see* wíyeqe ~ wíyqe ~ wí:qe.

<**síx̱**>, bound root //síx̣ *move over*//.

<**síx̱et**>, pcs //síx̣=əT//, TVMO ['*move s-th over*'], (<**=et**> *purposeful control transitivizer*), syntactic analysis: transitive verb, attested by NP (10/7/75).

<**sex̱éylem** or **sex̱ílem**>, mdls //sìx̣=íl=əm//, TVMO ['*move over*'], ABFC, (<**=íl ~ =el**> *go, come, get, become*, <**=em**> *middle voice*), phonology: vowel-reduction in root due to stressed suffix, syntactic analysis: intransitive verb, attested by Elders Group, NP.

<**síx̱et**>, TVMO ['*move s-th over*'], *see* síx̱.

<**síx̱wem**>, mdls //síx̣ʷ=əm//, ABFC ['*to wade*'], WATR, (<**=em**> *middle voice*), syntactic analysis: intransitive verb, attested by Elders Group, EB, Salish cognate: Squamish /síx̣ʷ-im/ *walk into water* K69:62, Saanich dial. of N. Straits /síx̣ʷ-əŋ/ *wade* B73:82.

<**sísex̱wem**>, cts //sí[-C_1ə-]x̣ʷ=əm//, ABFC ['*wading in shallow water*'], WATR, (<**-R1-**> *continuative*), (<**=em**> *middle voice*), phonology: reduplication, syntactic analysis: intransitive verb, attested by LJ (Tait) (Elders Group 4/26/78), contrast <**x̱élhchem**> *wading in deep water*, Salish cognate: Squamish /sí-six̣ʷ-im/ *wade (itr.)* W73:280, K69:62.

<**síy**>, bound root //síy or sə́y *nervous, afraid*//, Salish cognate: Lushootseed /sáy/ *nervous, fidgety, at loose ends, excited* H76:703.

<**sí:si**>, chrs //síy=C_1əC_2//, EFAM /'*be afraid, be scared, be nervous*'/, (<**=R2**> *characteristic*), phonology: reduplication, syntactic analysis: intransitive verb, attested by Elders Group (3/15/72), TG, Deming, AC, BJ (12/5/64), also <**sí'si**>, //síʔsi//, dialects: *Matsqui/Sumas*, attested by AH (Deming 6/15/78), other sources: ES /sí·sì·/ *fear, be afraid*; found in <**sí:sitsel.**>, //síy=C_1əC_2-c-əl//, /'*I'm scared., I'm afraid.*'/, attested by AC, Elders Group (3/15/72), example: <**atsel sí:si.**>, //ʔɛ-c-əl síy=C_1əC_2//, /'*I'm afraid.*'/, syntactic analysis: auxiliary past, attested by AC, <**ts'áts'eltsel sí:si.**>, //c'ɛ́[=C_1ə=]l-c-əl síy=C_1əC_2//, /'*I'm very afraid., I'm really afraid.*'/, syntactic analysis: adverb/adverbial verb-non-subordinate subject marker-subject pronoun intransitive verb, attested by AC, Elders Group (3/15/72), <**tsel me sí:si.**>, //c-əl mə síy=C_1əC_2//, /'*I got scared.*'/, attested by Elders Group (3/15/72), <**tsel wel sí:si.**>, //c-əl wəl síy=C_1əC_2//, /'*I'm very scared.*'/, attested by TG (4/75), <**ts'áts'el wel sí:si.**>, //c'ɛ́[=C_1ə=]l wəl síy=C_1əC_2//, /'*I'm really very scared.*'/, attested by TG (4/75), <**híkwtsel sí:si.**>, //híkʷ-c-əl síy=C_1əC_2//, /'*I'm really scared.*'/, literally /'I'm big scared.'/, syntactic analysis: adjective/adjectival verb-non-subordinate subject marker-subject pronoun intransitive verb, attested by AC, Salish cognate: Nooksack (BG:GS) //síyʔsiyʔ '*be afraid*' and //sə́yʔsəyʔ// '*be afrai*d'--pl. //sələ́yʔsəyʔ// (ə́ -í here), and (PA:SJ 7/20/56) //ówa-čæxw æy sísæyʔ-nít-æxʷ// *don't be afraid of it.*

<**sesí:si**>, dmv //C_1ə=síy=C_1əC_2//, EFAM ['*scared a little*'], (<**R5=**> *diminutive*), (<**=R2**> *characteristic*), phonology: double reduplication, syntactic analysis: intransitive verb, attested by EB (2/12/76), Elders Group (3/15/72), example: <**(átset, ítset) sesí:si.**>, //(ʔɛ-c-ət, ʔí-c-ət) C_1ə=síy=C_1əC_2//, /'*We got scared.*'/, syntactic analysis: auxiliary past, attested by Elders Group, <**líchxw sesí:si?**>, //lí-c-xʷ C_1ə=síy=C_1əC_2//, /'*Are you scared?*'/, attested by Elders Group, <**sesí:si yé mestíyexw.**>, //C_1ə=síy=C_1əC_2 yə məstíyəxʷ//, /'*The people are scared.*'/, syntactic comment: plural demonstrative article, attested by Elders Group, <**ő́wetsel (sesí:si, sí:si).**>, //ʔówə-c-əl (C_1ə=síy=C_1əC_2, síy=C_1əC_2)//, /'*I'm not afraid.*'/, (irregular), syntactic comment: missing subjunctive subject pronoun, attested by Elders Group.

<**sí:silexw**>, ncs //síy=C_1əC_2=l-əxʷ//, EFAM ['*scare s-o accidentally*'], (<**=l**> *non-control transitivizer*), phonology: reduplication, syntactic analysis: transitive verb, attested by IHTTC, Deming, AC (8/29/73); found in <**sí:silòx ~ sisilóx**>, //síy=C_1əC_2=l-áxʸ//, /'*scared me*

accidentally'/, attested by IHTTC, <**sí:silómxes.**>, //síy=C_1əC_2=l-ámx^y-əs//, /'*He/It scared me.*'/, dialects: *(Matsqui/Sumas)*, attested by AH (Deming 6/15/78), example: <**sí:silóxes te spá:th.**>, //síy=C_1əC_2=l-áx^y-əs tə s=pɛ́·θ//, /'*The bear scared me.*'/, attested by AC; found in <**sí:silométsel.**>, //síy=C_1əC_2=l-ámə-c-əl//, /'*I scared you accidentally.*'/, phonology: automatic stress-shift, attested by IHTTC (8/9/77), contrast <**sí:silómettsel.**> *I scared myself (in being reckless).*

<**sí:silómet ~ sí:silòmèt**>, ncrs //síy=C_1əC_2=l-ámət//, EFAM /'*scare oneself (in being reckless), scare oneself (do something one knows is dangerous and get scared even more than expected)*'/, (<**-ómet**> *reflexive*), phonology: reduplication, optional downstepping and upshifting, syntactic analysis: intransitive verb, attested by IHTTC, EB, Elders Group (3/15/72); found in <**sí:silómettsel.**>, //síy=C_1əC_2=l-ámət-c-əl//, /'*I scared myself (in being reckless).*'/, attested by IHTTC (8/9/77), example: <**tsel me sí:silòmèt.**>, //c-əl mə síy=C_1əC_2=l-ámət//, /'*I got myself scared (doing something I knew was dangerous that scared me even more than expected)., I got scared.*'/, attested by EB (3/19/76), Elders Group (3/15/72), <**atset me sí:silòmèt.**>, //ʔɛ-c-ət mə síy=C_1əC_2=l-ámət.//, /'*We got scared.*'/, attested by Elders Group.

<**sí:simet**>, iecs //síy=C_1əC_2=məT//, EFAM ['*be afraid of s-th/s-o*'], (<**=met**> *indirect effect control transitivizer*), phonology: reduplication, syntactic analysis: transitive verb, attested by AC, example: <**líchxw sí:simet?**>, //lí-c-x^w síy=C_1əC_2=məT//, /'*Are you afraid of something?*'/, <**sí:simetes te sqwétxem.**>, //síy=C_1əC_2=məT-əs tə s=q^{w}ə́tx^{y}əm//, /'*He's afraid of the fog.*'/, <**(le) sí:simetes te álhqey.**>, //(lə) síy=C_1əC_2=məT-əs tə ʔɛ́ɬqəy//, /'*He's afraid of snakes.*'/, <**sí:simettsel te híkw spáth.**>, //síC$_1$əC_2=məT-c-əl tə hík^w s=pɛ́·θ//, /'*I'm scared of big bears.*'/, <**ő wetsel sí:simet te spáth.**>, //ʔówə-c-əl síy=C_1əC_2=məT tə s=pɛ́·θ//, /'*I'm not scared of bears.*'/.

<**sisistáxwes.**>, caus //siy=C_1əC_2=sT-ə[=Aɛ́=]x^w-əs//, durs, EFAM ['*He's scaring them.*'], (<**=st**> *causative control transitivizer*), (<**-exw**> *third person object*, <**-es**> *third person subject*), (<**á-**ablaut> *durative*), phonology: reduplication, ablaut, syntactic analysis: transitive verb, attested by EB (12/12/75).

<**lexwsí:si ~ xwsí:si**>, ds //(lə)x^w=síy=C_1əC_2//, EFAM ['*(be) always scared*'], (<**lexw= ~ xw=**> *always*), phonology: reduplication, syntactic analysis: adjective/adjectival verb, attested by Elders Group (4/15/75), EB, example: <**ōwéta kw' xwsí:sis.**>, //ʔowə= ´tɛ k'^{w} x^w=síy=C_1əC_2-s//, /'*He's/She's never afraid.*'/, attested by EB (12/19/75).

<**lexwsí:si**>, dnom //ləx^{w}s=síy=C_1əC_2//, EFAM /'*coward, person that's always afraid*'/, (<**lexws=**> *a person that always*), phonology: consonant merger, reduplication, syntactic analysis: nominal, attested by Elders Group (1/15/75), EB.

<**sísem**>, df //sí(y)=s=əm//, EFAM /'*feel creepy, fear something behind one*'/, possibly <**=s**> meaning uncertain, <**=em**> *middle voice*, phonology: reduplication =doubling infix #1 with e= is ruled out here because of the continuative form below which adds -doubling infix #1 with e- and no case has yet been found of two occurrences of the same type of reduplication within the same word, where that would occur ablaut or another type of reduplication is substituted for one of the original reduplications, syntactic analysis: intransitive verb, attested by Elders Group (4/16/75); found in <**sísemtsel.**>, //síy=s=əm-c-əl//, /'*I feel creepy.*'/.

<**sísesem**>, cts //sí[-C$_1$ə-]s=əm//, EFAM /'*feeling creepy, fearing something behind one*'/, (<**-R1-**> *continuative*), phonology: the lack of a /y/ after the reduplication here shows that the root has been reanalyzed as /sí/ rather than /síy/, syntactic analysis: intransitive verb, attested by Elders Group (4/16/75).

<**séyí:m**>, rpts //si[=Aə́=]y=í·m//, durs, EFAM ['*be haunted*'], literally /'fear durative repeatedly'/, (<**é-ablaut on root i**> *durative*), (<**=í:m**> *repeatedly*), phonology: é-ablaut on root i, syntactic analysis: adjective/adjectival verb, attested by Elders Group (4/16/75), example: <**séyí:m te lálem.**>, //si[=Aə́=]y=í·m tə lɛ́[=C_1ə=]m//, /'*The house is haunted.*'/.

<**siyachís**>, ANAH ['*right arm*'], *see* éy ~ éy:.

<**siyálémtses**>, df //s=yɛ́lə́m=cəs or s=yi[=Aɛ́=]l=əm=cəs//, CLO ['*finger ring*'], PE, possibly root <**yíl**> *turn over, go around* possibly root as in <**s(y)ilólem**> *year*, (<**s=**> *nominalizer*), possibly <**=em**> *intransitivizer, have, get*, lx <**=tses**> *on the hand, on the finger*, phonology: epenthetic i between s= and y or ablaut, updrifting, syntactic analysis: nominal, attested by Elders Group (9/24/75), Salish cognate: Samish dial. of N. Straits VU /šxʷ=yə́ləm=čis/, LD /š=yə́ləm=čis/ *finger ring* G86:85, Squamish /slmčís/ *ring* W73:217, K67:291, possibly Lushootseed /s-yay'lúp-qs-ačiʔ/ *ring for finger* H76:628.

<**siyám ~ siyá:m**>, df //s=ʔiy=ɛ́(·)m//, SOC /'*respected leader, chief, upper-class person, boss, master, your highness*'/, ASM ['this term is used when a Stó:lō person talks to a wolf, bear, or sasquatch'], ECON /'*rich, wealthy*'/, SOC ['*dear*'], possibly <**s=**> *nominalizer*, probably root <**éy ~ iy**> *good*, possibly <**=ém ~ =á(:)m**> *in strength* (if so compare <eyém> *strong)*, phonology: consonant-loss of root-initial glottal stop, syntactic analysis: nominal, attested by AC, BJ (5/10/64, 12/5/64), EB, AD, Elders Group (3/21/79), RM (Elders Group 11/9/77), Deming, other sources: ES /siyɛ́·m/ *upper-class person* (homonymous with *'rich')*, H-T <siám> (macron over i, umlaut over a) *chief*, ASM ['respected leader'], example: <**ő siyám.**>, //ó s=iy=ɛ́m//, /'*Oh respected leader.*'/, usage: said while listening to a speaker at a gathering, indicates agreement and respect, attested by Elders Group, many others at spirit dances, ASM ['chief']; found in <**siyáms**>, //s=iy=ɛ́m-s//, /'*his chief, her chief, their chief*'/, attested by AC, ASM ['upper-class person'], example: <**telí te siyáms**>, //təlí tə s=iy=ɛ́m-s//, /'*She's from the upper class.*'/, attested by AC, ASM ['master'], semantic environment ['no special name for a young man becoming or training to become a chief, just might call him this'], attested by BJ (12/5/64), ASM ['rich, wealthy'], <**siyám mestíyexw**>, //s=iy=ɛ́m məstíyəxʷ//, /'*wealthy person*'/, attested by AC, ASM ['dear'], <**siyám éy siyáye,**>, //s=iy=ɛ́m ʔɛ́y si=yɛyə//, /'*Dear good friends,*'/, usage: vocative, used in speeches, syntactic comment: a term of address or vocative since there is no article (te, etc.), attested by Deming (12/15/77), <**siyám l siyáye,**>, //s=iy=ɛ́m l si=yɛ́yə//, /'*My dear friends,*'/, usage: vocative, used in speeches, attested by Deming (5/18/78), <**Chíchelh Siyá:m ~ Chíchelh Siyám**>, //cí[=C_1ə=]ɬ s=iy=ɛ́·m//, /'*High Master, God, Lord, supreme being, Chief above, Master above, Lord above*'/, attested by BJ (12/5/64, 5/10/64), AC (8/25/70), many others. Also see short entry under <ey> 'good' under the letter e.

<**sí:yá:m**>, pln //s=i[=´·=]y=ɛ́·m or s=hə́=iy=ɛ́·m//, SOC /'*respected leaders, chiefs, upper-class people*'/, possibly <**hé=**> *plural*, possibly <**= ´:=**> *plural*, phonology: stress-shift or consonant merger, possible lengthening, syntactic analysis: nominal, attested by Deming, others, example: <**ts'áts'eltsel xwoyíwel tel sqwálewel kw'els me xwe'í sq'ó talhlúwep l sí:yáye sí:yám.**>, //c'ɛ́[=C_1ə=]l-c-əl xʷ=ɛ[=Aa=]y=íwəl t-əl s=qʷɛ̀l=əwəl k'ʷə-l-s mə xʷə=ʔí s=q'á tɛ=ɬ=lúwə=p l s=i[=´·=]y=C_1əC_2[=Aɛ́=]=ə s=i[=´·=]y=ɛ́m (or better, s-ʔɛ́y=M2=C_1əC_2 s=i[=´·=]y=ɛ́m)//, /'*I'm very happy to come here at this gathering my dear friends.*'/, usage: speech, attested by Deming (5/18/78).

<**shxwsiyám**>, dnom //sxʷ=s=iy=ɛ́m//, SOC ['*boss*'], (<**shxw=**> *something/someone that*), syntactic analysis: nominal, attested by EB (Elders Group 11/9/77).

<**siyómelh**>, ds //s=iy=ɛ[=Aá=]m=əɬ//, SOC /'*chief's, (belonging to a chief, in the style of a chief)*'/, (<**ó-ablaut**> *derivational*), lx <**=elh**> *in the style of, as if belonging to*, phonology: ablaut, syntactic

analysis: adjective/adjectival verb, attested by TG (4/23/75), example: <**siyómelh yó:seqw**>, //s=iy=ɛ[=Aá=]m=əɬ yá·s=əqʷ//, /'*chief's hat*'/.

<**sí:yá:met**>, ds //s=i[-´·-]y=ɛ́m=məT//, SOC ['*flirting with s-o*'], literally /'being a high-class person toward/with s-o'/, (<-´:-> *continuative*), (<**=met**> *indirect effect control transitivizer*), phonology: stress-shift, lengthening, syntactic analysis: transitive verb, attested by Elders Group; found in <**sí:yá:methòxes.**>, //s=i[=´·=]y=ɛ́m=məT-áxʸ-əs//, /'*He's flirting with me.*'/, attested by Elders Group (4/28/76).

<**sí:yá:m**>, SOC /'*respected leaders, chiefs, upper-class people*'/, *see* siyám ~ (rare) siyá:m.

<**siyá:m**>, SOC /'*chief, leader, respected person, boss, rich, dear*'/, *see* éy ~ éy:.

<**sí:yá:met**>, SOC ['*flirting with s-o*'], *see* siyám ~ (rare) siyá:m.

<**siyá:ya ~ siyáya ~ syá:ya ~ siyá(:)ye**>, df //s=ʔɛ́y=M2=C₁əC₂ (or poss.) s=ʔiy=C₁əC₂[=Aɛ́·=]=ə//, SOCT ['*friend*'], *see* yá:ya.

<**sí:yá:ye**>, pln //s=ʔi[=´·=]y=C₁əC₂[=Aɛ́·=]=ə//, SOCT ['*lots of friends*'], *see* yá:ya.

<**siyelyólexwa**>, HAT ['*elders (many collective)*'], *see* siyólexwe or *see* yó:lexw.

<**Siyét'e**>, df //s=yi[=Aə́=]t'=ə//, PLN /'*village now at north end of Agassiz-Rosedale bridge, now Tseatah Indian Reserve #2 (of Cheam band)*'/, *see* yét'.

<**siyolexwálh**>, HAT /'*elders past, deceased old people*'/, *see* siyólexwe or *see* yó:lexw.

<**siyólexwe**>, df //s=yáləxʷ(=)ə//, HAT ['*old*'], (<**s=**> *stative*), syntactic analysis: adjective/adjectival verb, also *see* yó:lexw.

<**siyólexwe**>, dnom //s=yáləxʷ=ə//, HAT /'*old person, an elder*'/, (<**s=**> *nominalizer*), lx <**=e**> *person, animate being*, syntactic analysis: nominal, attested by AC, AD, EB, Elders Group, many others, example: <**ŏwechexw lámexwcha xwa siyólexwe a'áchewlh x̲áp'kw'tem ta' sth'eth'elòm.**>, //ʔówə-c-əxʷ lɛ́=m-əxʷ-cɛ xʷɛ s=yáləxʷ=ə ʔɛʔɛ́-cɛ-wɬ x̣ɛ́p'k'ʷ=təm t-ɛʔ s=C₁ə=θ'[=əl=]àm//, /'*You're not going to get (become) old until (root meaning unknown unless) your bones are aching.*'/, usage: saying or proverb, attested by AD, <**chxw ólewe siyólexwe kw'as sex̲we'álex̲eth'.**>, //c-xʷ ʔálə-wə s=yáləxʷ=ə k'ʷ-ɛ-s səx̣ʷəʔ=ɛ́ləx̣əθ'//, /'*You're too old to wet your bed.*'/, attested by EB (5/5/78).

<**siyolexwálh**>, ds //s=yaləxʷ=ə=əɬ or s=yaləxʷ=ə=ɛ́ɬ//, HAT /'*elders past, deceased old people*'/, (<**=elh ~ =álh**> *past tense, deceased*), phonology: vowel merger (e + e → á), syntactic analysis: nominal past, attested by AD, example: <**éy kws hákw'eleschet te s'í:wes te siyolexwálh.**>, //ʔɛ́y kʷ-s hɛ́k'ʷ=ələs-c-ət tə s=ʔí·wəs-s tə s=yaləxʷ=ə=əɬ//, /'*Let us remember the teachings of the elders past.*'/, attested by AD.

<**sí:yólexwe**>, pln //s(i)[=´·=]yáləxʷ=ə//, HAT /'*old people, elders*'/, (<=´**:**=> *plural (many)*), phonology: stress-shift, lengthening, syntactic analysis: nominal, attested by AC, Elders Group.

<**siyelyólexwa**>, pln //s=C₁əC₂=yáləxʷ=ə//, HAT ['*elders (many collective)*'], (<**R3=**> *plural (many collective)*), phonology: reduplication, syntactic analysis: nominal, attested by AD, Elders Group, example: <**tó:lmels ye siyelyólexwa**>, //tá·l=məls-s yə s=C₁əC₂=yáləxʷ=ə//, /'*wisdom of the elders*'/, usage: used as title of the Classified Word List for Upriver Halq'eméylem (Galloway and Elders' Groups 1980).

<**sí:yólexwe**>, HAT /'*old people, elders*'/, *see* siyólexwe or *see* yó:lexw.

<**sí:yólexwe**>, HAT ['*old people*'], *see* siyólexwe or *see* yó:lexw.

<**siyólexwe**>, HAT /'*old person, an elder*'/, *see* siyólexwe or *see* yó:lexw.

<**siyó:lexwe ~ syó:lexwe ~siyólexwe**>, DESC ['*old person*'], *see* siyólexwe or *see* yó:lexw.

<**siyólh ~ siyó:lh ~ syólh**>, HARV /'*wood, firewood*'/, *see* yólh.

<**siyólhá:wtxw**>, BLDG ['*wood-shed*'], *see* yólh.

<**siyómelh**>, SOC /'*chief's, (belonging to a chief, in the style of a chief)*'/, *see* siyám ~ (rare) siyá:m.

<**siyóqelhtsthet**>, SOC ['*change (money)*'], *see* iyá:q.

<**siyót**>, SOC ['*beware*'], *see* yó:t ~ yót.

<**siyó:ylexwe**>, HAT ['*little old person*'], *see* siyólexwe or *see* yó:lexw.

<**Siyó:ylexwe Smá:lt**>, PLN /'*Bear Mountain,* also called *Lhóy's Mountain*'/, *see* siyólexwe or *see* yó:lexw.

<**siyó:yseqw**>, CLO ['*be wearing a hat*'], *see* yó:seqw ~ yóseqw.

<**siysá:yiws**>, ANAA ['*furry on the whole body (of an animal)*'], *see* sá:y.

<**síyt'**>, root //síyt' // *tickle* or possibly stem //síy=t'// *tickle* with root <**síy**> *nervous, afraid* and possible <**=t'**> *tactile sensation*?.

<**síyt't ~ sí:t't**>, pcs //síy=t'=T//, ABFC ['*tickle s-o*'], possibly <**=t'**> *tactile sensation*?, (<**=t**> *purposeful control transitivizer*), syntactic analysis: transitive verb, attested by BHTTC, EB (1/30/76), Elders Group (12/15/76); found in <**síyt'tem.**>, //síy=t'=T-əm//, /'*He's tickled.*'/, attested by Elders Group.

<**sá:yt't**>, cts //si[-Aέ·-]y=t'=T//, ABFC ['*tickling s-o*'], (<**á**:-ablaut> *continuative*), phonology: ablaut, syntactic analysis: transitive verb, attested by Elders Group (12/15/76), example: <**tsel sá:yt'thòmè.**>, //c-əl si[-Aέ·-]y=t'=T-ámə//, /'*I'm tickling you.*'/, phonology: downstepping, updrifting.

<**sá:yt'em ~ sayít'em**>, cts //si[-Aέ·-]y=t'=əm ~ s[-əC$_2$-]íy=t'=əm or less likely si[-Aε-]y[=í=]=t'=əm//, izs, ABFC /'*being tickled, (having tickling, getting tickling), tickley*'/, (<**á**(:)-ablaut ~ -R6-> *continuative*), possibly <**=í=**> *derivational or continuative*?, (<**=em**> *intrantivizer, get, have*), phonology: ablaut, reduplication, syntactic analysis: intransitive verb, attested by Elders Group (12/15/76), BHTTC (late Oct. 1976).

<**sá:yt'els**>, sas //si[-Aέ·-]y=t'=əls//, cts, ABFC ['*tickling*'], (<**á**:-ablaut> *continuative*), (<**=els**> *structured activity continuative*), phonology: ablaut, syntactic analysis: intransitive verb, attested by Elders Group (12/15/76).

<**síyt'eqem**>, mdls //síy=t'=εq=əm//, ABFC /'*want to pee, (want to urinate, feel like one has to urinate)*'/, literally /'tickle on/in one's penis/genitals'/, lx <**=áq ~ =eq**> *on/in the penis, on/in the genitals*, (<**=em**> *middle voice, one's*), phonology: possible vowel-reduction, syntactic analysis: intransitive verb, attested by JL (Tait) (Fish Camp 7/20/79).

<**sét'xt**>, pcs //sí(y)=Aə́=t'=x^y(əl)=T//, ABFC (probably) /'*tickle the bottom of someone's feet, (tickle s-o on the foot)*'/, possibly <**é-ablaut**> *derivational*, lx <**=xel ~ =x** (before **=t**)> *on the foot*, (<**=t**> *purposeful control transitivizer*), comment: EB was unsure of the translation she offered so it may be possible that the vowel is wrong (though the translation seems right)--one would expect *<**síyt'xt**> here, phonology: possible ablaut, syllable-loss of el before =t, syntactic analysis: transitive verb, attested by EB (3/1/76).

<**sá:yx̱wem**>, df //si[=Aέ·=]y=x̣^{w}=əm//, ABFC /'*tickled (by a hair, by a light touch)*'/, probably root <**síy**> *nervous, afraid*, (<**á**:-ablaut> *resultative*), lx <**=x̱w**> *around, around in a circle*, (<**=em**>

intransitivizer, get, have), phonology: ablaut, syntactic analysis: intransitive verb, attested by BHTTC (late Oct. 1976).

<**síyt'eqem**>, ABFC /*'want to pee, (want to urinate, feel like one has to urinate)'*/, *see* síyt'.

<**síyt't ~ sí:t't**>, ABFC [*'tickle s-o'*], *see* síyt'.

<**skáslekem**>, us //skɛ́sləkəm//, [skǽslɪkəm], KIN [*'illegitimate child'*], borrowed from French <se casse le commun> *break up the common-law relationship*, syntactic analysis: nominal, Salish cognate: Squamish /s-kásnəkm/ *illegitimate child* (Kuipers 1967:293), attested by Elders Group 8/25/76.

<**skemí'iya**>, dnom //s=kəmíʔ=iyɛ//, EZ /*'a white-headed duck, [could be bufflehead, snow goose, emperor goose,* poss. *oldsquaw,* or *hooded merganser,* other duck-like birds with white heads do not occur in the Stó:lō area and *the emperor goose* would be only an occasional visitor*]'*/, (<**s=**> *nominalizer*), (<**=iya**> *diminutive*), (possibly <**fronting**>, i.e., **q → k** *diminutive*), phonology: possibly fronting, syntactic analysis: nominal, source: JH:DM.

<**skéweqs**>, dnom //s=q[=F=]ə́w=əqs//, [skə́wəqs], EZ [*'raven'*], [*'Corvus corax'*], ASM ['whichever way it goes and crows it predicts a death in that certain family'], (fronting **q → k** *affectionate diminutive*), phonology: fronting, syntactic analysis: nominal, attested by SP (and poss. all Tait speakers)(BHTTC), Elders Group 6/4/75 and 12/15/76, example: <**qwóqwel te skéweqs**>, //q^{w}ɛ[-Aá-C_1ə-]l tə s=q[=F=]ə́w=əqs//, [q^{w}áq^{w}əl tə skə́wəqs], /*'The raven is talking (not necessarily warning)(a distinct call).'*/, (<**ó-ablaut** and **reduplication**> *continuative*), phonology: ó-ablaut, reduplication, fronting, attested by Elders Group 12/15/76, <**qwṓlqwel te skéweqs**>, //q^{w}ɛ[=Ao=]´l=C_1əC_2 tə s=q[=F=]ə́w=əqs//, [q^{w}ólq^{w}əl tə skə́wəqs], /*'The raven is warning (a distinct call).'*/, (<**ō-ablaut**> *derivational*), (<**=reduplication**> *characteristic*?), phonology: ō-ablaut, reduplication, fronting, attested by Elders Group 12/15/76, ASM ['owls can warn like this too (using qwṓlqwel)'], also <**skyéweqs**> and <**sqéweqs**>, //s=q[=F=]ə́w=əqs//, [sk^{y}ɪ́wəqs], attested by Elders Group 5/3/78, Salish cognate: Lushootseed (Skagit) /k^{y}ə́wqs/ (Deming 4/17/80); Salish cognate: Squamish /sqəwq'/ (Kuipers 1967), Salish cognate: Lushootseed (Skagit dial.) /qə́wqs/ (Deming 4/17/80), *see* sqéweqs and qéw and qwá (possible roots).

<**skíkek**>, EZ /*'chickadee: black-capped chickadee,* probably also *chestnut-backed chickadee,* possibly also *the least bush-tit'*/, *see* qá:q or seq.

<**sklú**>, free root //sklú//, TOOL [*'a screw'*], syntactic analysis: nominal, attested by Elders Group (9/21/77), borrowed from English /skrúw/ *screw.*

<**Skoyá:m ~ Skeyá:m**>, df //s=kay(=)ɛ́·m//, PLN /*'a stone like a statue at Harrison Lake,* probably *Doctor's Point'*/, ASM ['formerly a man turned to stone by X̲á:ls the Transformer who took the man's arms and threw them away, the stone has no nose or ears either, even now it is said that if one talks bad to it heavy winds are going to come up on the Lake (BJ 12/5/64 old p.331)'], contrast <**Lhx̲é:ylex**> *Doctor's Point*, possibly <**s=**> *nominalizer*, phonology: plain k may show a borrowing from Lillooet or fronting *diminutive*, syntactic analysis: nominal, attested by BJ (12/5/64), source: place names file reference #180, comment: H-T 1904:342 has a main character in a story told by Francois of Chehalis, this character is called <Kai'am> [H-T] *Wolverine*, which is very close to the form of this place name; could the stone have been named for a wolverine turned to stone in another story?.

<**skyéweqs**>, EZ [*'raven'*], [*'Corvus corax'*], *see* sqéweqs and skeweqs *(under q and s)*

<**sk'ak'áxwe**>, df //s=C_1ɛ=k'ɛ́x^{w}ə//, EB [*'dried saskatoon berries'*], [*'Amelanchier alnifolia'*], ASM ['ripe in July, the best ones are found north of Hope, B.C.; fresh berries are eaten and have a separate name;

the dried berries are obtained in cakes or sheets from the Thompson and other Interior Salish Indians; saskatoons can be mixed with bulbs of the sxameléxwthelh *tiger lily* and kw'épan [k'ʷʊ́pɛn] (a Thompson word, a white root, like a sweet potato in taste) and then either with sugar or with fish eggs'], borrowed from Thompson /s=k'ɛ́x=əm/ *dried berries* (Thompson /x/ is velar and corresponds to Upriver Halkomelem velar /xʷ/ in this word), (<**R8=**> *diminutive or resultative or derivational*), possibly <**=e ~ =a**>, da //=ə ~ =ɛ//, EZ ['*living thing*'], phonology: reduplication, syntactic analysis: nominal, attested by Elders Group, Deming (M.H.), AC, DM 12/4/64; unclear whether borrowed with the reduplication and s= nominalizer from Thompson or borrowed as the root <k'axwe> or stem <k'axw> and then these were added from UHk.

<**sk'ámets ~ sk'ámeth**>, dnom //s=k'ɛ́məc ~ s=k'ɛ́məθ//, EB /'*blue camas, yellow dog-tooth violet = yellow avalanche lily*'/, ['resp. *Camassia leichtlinii and Camassia quamash, Erythronium grandiflorum*'], semantic environment ['wild sweet potatoes, obtained in trade, don't grow here; camas, like sweet potatoes with little sausage-shaped potatoes on root; dried bulbs of both camas and avalanche lily were obtained in trade probably both from the Interior and the Coast Indian peoples'], borrowed from Thompson /sk'ém'ec/ *dog-tooth violet, blue camas, white easter lily, Indian potato*, syntactic analysis: nominal, attested by Elders Group, also <**sk'ámeth'**>, //sk'ɛ́məθ'//, attested by Deming; may have been borrowed with or without the **s=** nominalizer of Thompson.

<**sk'ek'iyáp ~ slek'iyáp**>, df //s=k'ək'iyɛ́p ~ s=lək'iyɛ́p//, [sk'ɪk'iyǽp ~ slɪk'iyǽp], EZ ['*coyote*'], ['*Canis latrans lestes*'], borrowed from Thompson /snk'y'ép/ *coyote* (Thompson and Thompson 1980:58), syntactic analysis: nominal, attested by AC, DM, other sources: JH:DM /skəkiyé·p/, also <**snek'iyáp ~ snek'eyáp**>, //snək'iyɛ́p ~ snək'əyɛ́p//, [snɪk'iyǽp ~ snɪk'əyǽp], attested by BJ 5/64 and 12/5/64; probably borrowed with the Thompson <s=> and reduplication, rather than as the root in the Thompson word then with UHk s= and reduplicated prefix added.

<**sk'í:l**>, dnom //s=k'í·l//, EZ /'*Rocky Mountain pika, hoary marmot, rock-rabbit*'/, ['*Ochotona princeps brunnescens*'], ASM ['named for their sound; when Susan Peters (SP) was young she chased a pika at Maggie Emery's house at Yale, and it started to rain real heavy; when you chase them it rains; they live from Hope, B.C. north (and in the high mountains)'], WETH, SD, borrowed from Thompson /sk'íl'/ [sk'í·l'] *marmot* (Thompson and Thompson 1980:41), syntactic analysis: nominal, attested by ME, SP, Elders Group, also <**sk'ì:l**>, //s=k'ì·l//, attested by AK; probably borrowed with the Thompson s= nominalizer rather than as the k' initial root then an UHk s= added.

<**skwálepel**>, SOC ['*something hidden away*'], *see* kwà:l.

<**Skwálepel**>, PLN ['*Skwellepil Creek*'], *see* kwà:l.

<**Skwáli**>, df //s=kʷɛ́l=i or skʷ=ɛ́li//, PLN /'*Skwali, a village north of Hope Slough and Skwah*'/, possibly <**s=**> *nominalizer*, possibly <**kwà:l**.> *hide*, possibly <**=iy**> *covering or place*, phonology: kw could be qw instead, comment: only attested in Wells's transcription <SKWAH-lee>, syntactic analysis: nominal, source: Wells 1965 (lst ed.):23.

<**skwálóws**>, SOC ['*got murdered*'], *see* kwà:l.

<**skwá:m ~ skwám**>, BSK /'*storage basket (for oil, fruit, clothes), burial basket for twins, round basket (any size, smaller at top), clay jug (to store oil or fruit)*'/, *see* kwá:m ~ kwám.

<**skwátsem ~ skwáchem**>, ABFC ['*a scream*'], *see* kwátsem ~ kwáchem.

<**skwekwelím shxw'ólewù**>, EB ['*radishes*'] (lit. little red ones + turnip), *see* kwím *or* **shxw'ólewù**

<**skwekwíkwemel**>, LT ['*[be getting/going a little red]*'], *see* kwí:m.

<**skwekwó:tel**>, KIN ['*separated in marriage*'], *see* kwá:.

<**skwél**>, dnom //s=kʷə́l//, [skʷíl], WATR /'*waterfall, falls*'/, LAND, *see* kwél.

<**skwelálhchiyelh**>, SOC ['*what he owes*'], *see* kwél.

<**skwélemel**>, HHG ['*handle of a spoon*'], *see* kwél.

<**skwélets**>, BSK ['*coiled bottom of a basket before the sides are on*'], *see* kwél.

<**skwetáxw**>, BLDG /'*be inside a house, be inside an enclosure*'/, *see* kwetáxw.

<**skwetáxwstexw**>, BLDG ['*leave s-o/s-th inside*'], *see* kwetáxw.

<**skwetóxwes**>, SPRD /'*mask covering the face*'/, *see* kwetáxw.

<**skwetóxwes sqw'eyílex**>, SPRD /'*mask dance*'/, *see* kwetáxw.

<**skwetxwewílh**>, MC ['*the inside (of a container)*'], *see* kwetáxw.

<**skwetxwó:lwelh**>, BLDG /'*inner lining, inner side*'/, *see* kwetáxw.

<**skwetxwós**>, BLDG ['*ceiling*'], *see* kwetáxw.

<**skwéthqsel**>, df //s-kʷə́θ=qsəl//, stvi, BPI ['*(have) a big nose*'], *see* kwéth.

<**skwéth' ~ skwéth'kweth'**>, dnom //s=kʷə́θ' ~ s=kʷə́θ'=C_1əC_2//, EZ /'*willow grouse, ruffed grouse*'/, ['*Bonasa umbellus sabini*'], *see* kwéth'.

<**skwíkwel**>, WATR ['*small waterfall*'], *see* skwél.

<**skwíkwemel**>, LT /'*[be getting red, be going red]*'/, *see* kwí:m.

<**skwíkwexel**>, dnom //s=C_1í=kʷɛ=xʸəl or s=C_1í=kʷɛ=Aə=xʸəl//, EZ ['*baby sockeye salmon*'], ['*Oncorhynchus nerka*'], (<**s=**> *nominalizer*, R4= *diminutive*), see possible root <**kwá**> *let go*.

<**skwíkwexetem**>, dnom //s=kʷí[-C_1ə=]]xʸ=əT-əm//, pass., cts, SPRD /'*a naming ceremony*'/, *see* kwí:x ~ kwíx.

<**skwímeth**>, EZ /'*little roundmouth suckerfish,* probably *longnose sucker*'/, *see* kwí:m.

<**skwí:x ~ skwíx**>, N ['*personal name*'], *see* kwí:x ~ kwíx.

<**Skwíyò**>, df //s=kʷíyà//, PLN /'*village just below (on the south side of) Suka Creek, on the CN side (east side) of the Fraser River across from Dogwood Valley*'/, possibly <**s=**> *nominalizer*, perhaps related to root //Skwóyá// *Squirrel* by metathesis??, Elder's comment: "possibly a Thompson name? or from skwél *waterfall* since there are waterfalls there on the creek?", syntactic analysis: nominal, attested by SP and AD transcribed from MP 1973-4 (IHTTC 7/8/77), SP and AK (Fish Camp 8/2/77, Raft Trip 8/30/77), source: place names file reference #50, other sources: Wells 1965 (lst ed.):25 (but bank or side of Fraser River misidentified there).

<**Skwíyò Smált**>, ds //s=kʷíyà s=mɛ́lt//, PLN ['*the mountain above Suka Creek*'], literally /'Skwíyò mountain'/, syntactic analysis: simple nominal phrase, attested by AK and SP (Fish Camp 8/2/77).

<**Skwíyò Stó:lō**>, ds //s=kʷíyà s=tá·l=ow//, PLN ['*Suka Creek (on east side of Fraser River above Hope)*'], literally /'Skwíyò river'/, syntactic analysis: simple nominal phrase, attested by AK and SP (Fish Camp 8/2/77).

<**Skwiyó:m**>, ds //s=kʷiyà=əm//, PLN /'*a place near Deroche, B.C., just east of Lakahahmen Indian Reserve #10 (which is registered with D.I.A. as Skweam)*'/, ASM ['to get there turn left after crossing the bridge heading south at the upriver end of Nicomen Island, the place was owned by Joe Punch and Louie Punch for years, named after Skwíyò because Louie Punch came from Skwíyò *Suka Creek village*'], probably <**=em**> *place to have/get*, phonology: vowel merger, stress-shift,

syntactic analysis: nominal, attested by Elders Group (7/13/77), source: place names file reference #66.

<**Skwiyó:m**>, PLN /'*a place near Deroche, B.C., just east of Lakahahmen Indian Reserve #10 (which is registered with D.I.A. as Skweam)*'/, *see* Skwíyò.

<**Skwíyò Smált**>, PLN ['*the mountain above Suka Creek*'], *see* Skwíyò.

<**Skwíyò Stó:lō**>, PLN ['*Suka Creek (on east side of Fraser River above Hope)*'], *see* Skwíyò.

<**skwló ~ sqwló**>, df //s=kʷlá ~ s=qʷlá//, ANAA ['*seal fat*'], *see* kwló ~ qwló.

<**Skwló ~ Sqwló**>, PLN /'*Seal Fat Rock on Harrison River just upriver from Th'éqwela (place by Morris Lake where Indian people used to play Indian badminton), this rock has what resembles layers of seal fat all around it along its bottom* '/, ['located above (upstream from) Th'éqwela ~ Ts'éqwela and below (downstream from) Híkw Sméya; the seal fat layers are usually underwater in June (as they were when we visited the site by boat 6/27/78)'], *see* sqwló or kwló ~ qwló.

<**skwókwep ~ skwokwepílep**>, df //s=kʷá[=C_1ə=]p ~ s=kʷá[=C_1ə=]p=íl=əp//, LAND /'*hill (dirt, includes both sides of hill), little hill*'/, possibly <**s=**> *nominalizer*, root meaning unknown, possibly <**=R1=**> *resultative or derivational*, (<**=íl**> *get, become, come, go*), lx <**=ep**> *dirt, ground*, phonology: reduplication, syntactic analysis: nominal, attested by AD (3/7/78), Elders Group (3/8/78).

<**Skwokwílàla**>, PLN ['*several places where there were pit-houses in which to hide from enemy raids (place to hide)*'], *see* kwà:l.

<**skwómàtsel (sqwómàtsel)**>, ABDF /'*hunchback, humpback, lump on the back*'/, *see* qwó:m ~ qwóm ~ qwem.

<**skwó:wech ~ skwówech**>, df //s=kʷá·w(=)əč or s=kʷáw=wəč//, EZ /'*sturgeon, white sturgeon*'/, ['*Acipenser transmontanus*'], ASM ['these grow very large and very old, often live in quiet sloughs, when Sumas Lake was drained some survived for several years in the mud; glue was made from an organ on the backbone of the sturgeon; the bones of the sturgeon (if examined closely) contain the patterns for most of the Stó:lō tools made'], (<**s=**> *nominalizer*), root meaning unknown unless kwów *bone*??, lx <**=wech ~ =ech ~ =ōwíts**> *on the back*, phonology: possible consonant merger, syntactic analysis: nominal, attested by AC, BJ (12/5/64), Elders Group (3/1/72), EL (6/27/78), other sources: H-T <skwáwitc> (macron over a) *sturgeon (Acipenser transmontanus)*, Salish cognate: Squamish /skʷáʔwač/ *sturgeon* W73:256, K67:253.

<**Tsólqthet te Skwówech**>, pcrs //cɛ[=Aá=]lq=T-ət tə s=kʷáw=wəch//, PLN ['*Rainbow Falls (on Harrison Lake's southeast side)*'], literally /'the sturgeon dropped himself'/, ASM ['so named because a sturgeon was found at the bottom that had fallen down the falls and no one knew how he had gotten to the top'], (<**ó-ablaut**> *resultative*), (<**=T**> *purposeful control transitivizer*), (<**-et**> *reflexive*), phonology: ablaut, possible consonant merger, syntactic analysis: intransitive verb simple nominal phrase, attested by EL (Chehalis boat trip 6/27/78).

<**Skwówéls**>, df //s=kʷáw=əls//, N /'*Raven, (Mister Raven or Mister Crow?* [AK 1/16/80]*)*'/, (<**s=**> *nominalizer*), root meaning unknown, possibly <**=els**> *structured activity continuative*, syntactic analysis: nominal, attested by Elders Group (3/1/72), also <**Skwówel**>, //s=kʷáw=əl//, also /'*Mister Raven or Mister Crow?*'/, (<**=el**> *go, come, get, become*), attested by AK (Elders Group 1/16/80), *also see* qéw and qwá.

<**skwóye**>, df //skʷ=áyə or s=kʷáy(=)ə//, EZ /'*squirrel, Douglas squirrel*'/, ['*Tamiasciurus douglasi mollipilosus*'], possibly <**s=**> *nominalizer*, possibly <**=e**> *animate being, person*, root meaning

unknown, syntactic analysis: nominal, attested by IHTTC, Elders Group (2/11/76), also <**skwóyá**>, //s=kʷáyɛ́//, attested by Deming (3/11/76).

<**skwó:yex̱thet ~ skwó:yx̱thet**>, TVMO ['*a doing*'], *see* kwíyx̱.

<**Skwtéxwqel**>, PLN /'*point on west side of Harrison River on which or across from which Sx̱wó:yx̱wey is located (the rock formation resembling a sx̱wó:yx̱wey mask); the first point on Harrison River after it leaves Harrison Lake*'/, *see* kwetáxw.

<**skwthá**>, MC ['*piled up*'], *see* kwthá.

<**skwúkw**>, FOOD /'*cooking, (cooking) food*'/, *see* kwúkw.

<**skwúkwelstéleq**>, SCH ['*teacher*'], *see* skwú:l.

<**skwukwtisláts**>, df //skʷukʷ=tis=lɛ́c//, ANAA ['*skunk's stink bag (stink sac)*'], probably root <**skwukw**> *skunk*, borrowed from English *skunk*, lx <**=tis(=)láts**> *odor gland?* with lx <**=láts**> *on the rump/bottom*, syntactic analysis: nominal, attested by BHTTC (11/15/76), contrast <**spú'amal**> *skunk's stink bag.*

<**skwú:l**>, free root //skʷú·l//, SCH ['*school*'], borrowed from English /skúl/ *school*, grammatical comment: may have been reanalyzed as having s= *nominalizer*, syntactic analysis: nominal, example: <**skwúl letám**>, //s=kʷúl lətɛ́m//, /'*school desk*'/.

<**skwuláwtxw**>, dnom //skʷul=ɛ́wtxw//, BLDG ['*schoolhouse*'], SCH, lx <**=áwtxw**> *building, room*, phonology: stress-shift due to strong-grade suffix, syntactic analysis: nominal, attested by Deming.

<**skwúkwelstèleq**>, dnom //s=kʷú[=C$_1$ə=]l=sT=ə̀ləq//, SCH ['*teacher*'], (<**s=**> *nominalizer*), (<**=R1=**> *continuative*?), (<**=st**> *causative*?), lx <**=éleq**> *one who does as occupation*, phonology: reduplication, syntactic analysis: nominal, attested by Elders Group.

<**skwuláwtxw**>, BLDG ['*schoolhouse*'], *see* skwú:l.

<**skw'álx̱**>, df //s=k'ʷɛ́l(=)x̣// or more likely //sik'ʷ=ɛ́l(=)x̣//, EZ ['*immature bald eagle*'], ASM ['before the head feathers turn white, age one to three years'], ['*Haliaeetus leucocephalus*'], possibly <**s=**> *nominalizer*) or more likely <**síkw'**>, //sík'ʷ//, ['*get skinned*'], with vowel loss before <**=á:l**> *similar to, -like, or part/portion* and <**=x̱**> *distributive, all around* with the idea of the white feathers "skinned off like" or "skinned off part/portion" or "similar to skinned off", syntactic analysis: nominal, attested by Elders Group 2/13/80, 3/15/78, also <**skw'àlx̱**>, attested by Elders Group 2/18/76, also <**skw'á:lx̱**>, attested by Elders Group 6/4/75, also <**sqw'á:lx̱**>, attested by Elders Group 3/1/72, also <**skw'álx̱ ~ sqw'álx̱**>, also /'*golden eagle*'/.

<**Skw'á:lx̱w**>, df //s=k'ʷɛ́·lx̣ʷ//, PLN ['*a little bay or eddy on Harrison River about two miles downriverfrom Chehalis*'], syntactic analysis: nominal, attested by Elders Group 9/7/77, other sources: H-T04:315 skwa^ltuq (macron over u, ^ over the a) *a camp about two miles below Chehalis village in a sunny bay, abandoned before 1904 butmarked by an old logging camp of the early white settlers*, said to mean literally *sheltered* (the latter points to a form Skwáltxw perhaps (root <**kwá:l**> *hide*, <**=altxw**> *house*).

<**skw'álhem**>, BSK ['*little berry basket*'], *see* kw'élh.

<**skw'álhew**>, KIN /'*in-laws (?), parents-in-law, spouse's parents*'/, *see* skw'ílhew.

<**Skw'átets**>, PLN /'*Squatits village on east bank of Fraser river across from the north end of Seabird Island, Peters Indian Reserves #1, 1a, and 2 on site*'/, *see* kw'át.

<**skw'áts**>, ABFC /'*eyesight, sight*'/, *see* kw'áts ~ kw'éts.

<**skw'á:y**>, EFAM /'*it is impossible, it can't be, it never is*'/, *see* kw'á:y ~ kw'áy.

<**skw'echó:stel**>, BLDG ['*window*'], *see* kw'áts ~ kw'éts.

<**skw'echó:steló:les**>, CLO ['*eyeglasses*'], *see* kw'áts ~ kw'éts.

<**skw'ékw'ewes**>, HHG ['*small pot*'], *see* skw'ó:wes ~ skw'ówes.

<**skw'ekw'ílwes**>, KIN ['*children's in-laws*'], *see* skw'élwés.

<**skw'ékw'ith**>, SOC /'*pitiful person, helpless person, person unable to do anythingfor himself*'/, *see* skw'iyéth.

<**skw'ekw'íx**>, NUM ['*be counted*'], *see* kw'áx.

<**Skw'ékw'qwòs**>, PLN /'*Coqualeetza stream esp. where it joins Luckakuck Creek, later Coqualeetza (residential school, then hospital, then Indian cultural centre and Education Training Centre)*'/, see under main dialect form <**Kw'eqwálíth'a**> under root kw 'eqw.

<**skw'ekw'xwós**>, WETH ['*the hail*'], *see* kw'xwós.

<**skw'él:a**>, BPI /'*have a big belly, big-bellied person*'/, *see* kw'él:a ~ kw'éla.

<**skw'élewōqws**>, //s-k'ʷələw=əqʷ-s//, /'*his scalp*'/, (<**s-**> *inalienable possession*), (<**-s**> *third person possessive*), *see* kw'eléw ~ kw'elṓw.

<**skw'elkw'élxel**>, df //s=C_1əC_2=k'ʷə́l=xʸəl//, WETH ['*whirlwind*'], *see* kw'él.

<**skw'élwés**>, df //s=k'ʷə́lwə́s//, KIN /'*child's spouse's parent, child's spouse's sibling, child's in-laws*'/, *see* kw'élwés.

<**skw'elyáx̱el**>, dnom //s=k'ʷəly=ɛ́x̣əl//, EZ ['*bat*'], ['order *Chiroptera,* family *Vespertilionidae*'], EZ /'may include any or all of the following (all of which occur in the area): *western big-eared bat, big brown bat, silver-haired bat, hoary bat, California myotis, long-eared myotis, little brown myotis, long-legged myotis, Yuma myotis,* and possibly *the keen myotis, respectively*'/, *see* kw'ely.

<**skw'éqwtses**>, EB ['*red huckleberry*'], literally /'clubbed on the hand'/, *see* kw'oqw.

<**skw'éstel**>, df //s=k'ʷə́s=təl//, CAN /'*homemade anchor, kilik, calik, (killick)*'/, *see* kw'és.

<**skw'éts'eles**>, ANAH /'*(have a) part in the hair, to part (hair)*'/, *see* probable root kw'íts'.

<**skw'exá:m**>, NUM ['*number*'], *see* kw'áx.

<**skw'exó:s ~ skw'xó:s**>, dnom //s=k'ʷəxʸ=á·s ~ s=k'ʷxʸ=á·s//, WETH ['*moon*'], semantic environment ['used when pointing or describing'], TIME ['*month*'], semantic environment ['used when counting'], (<**s=**> *nominalizer*), probably root <**kw'ax**> *count*, also see under that root, lx <**=ó:s**> *on the face, round thing*, syntactic analysis: nominal, attested by AC, DM (12/4/64), BJ (12/5/64, 5/64), EB, Elders Group, IHTTC, NP, other sources: JH /sk'ʷxá·s/ ~ /ɬqé·lc'/ *moon*, (semological comment: many interesting morphosememic shifts can be seen in the expressions for the phases of the moon below), ASM ['moon'], example: <**lulh xelo:kw' te skw'exó:s**>, //lə=uɬ xʸəlá·k'ʷ tə s=k'ʷəxʸ=á·s//, /'*The moon is full.*'/, literally /'the moon past already is circular'/, attested by AC, <**selíts' te skw'exó:s**>, //s=(ə)lə[=Aí=]c' tə s=k'ʷəxʸ=á·s//, /'*It's full moon, The moon is full.*'/, ASM ['about the middle of the Stó:lō month'], attested by Elders Group 3/12/75, <**léts' skw'exó:s ~ slíts' skw'exó:s**>, //lə́c' s=k'ʷəxʸ=á·s ~ s=lə[=Aí=]c' s=k'ʷəxʸ=á·s//, /'*full moon*'/, attested by IHTTC, <**léts'e(s) skw'xó:s**>, //lə́c'ə(s) s=k'ʷxʸ=á·s//, /'*first quarter of the moon, new moon; one month*'/, ASM ['this is the beginning of the Stó:lō month'], attested by DM 12/5/65, <**x̱áws te skw'exó:s**>, //x̣ɛ́ws tə s=k'ʷəxʸ=á·s//, /'*It's first quarter moon.*'/, literally /'The moon is new.'/, (semological comment: this

differs from the English "new moon" which is all dark; a drawing of this moon shows it as a crescent with horns facing left), attested by Elders Group 3/12/75, <**me pélekw te x̱áws skw'exós**>, //mə pə́ləkʷ təx̣ɛ́ws s=k'ʷəxʸ=ás//, /'*The new sliver of moon has appeared., The new crescent moon has appeared.*'/, literally /'the new moon has come to appear, come up on the horizon, come out from behind something'/, attested by IHTTC, <**lhséq' skw'xó:s**>, //ɬ=sə́q' s=k'ʷxʸ=á·s//, /'*a half-moon*'/, attested by DM 12/4/64, <**yuwál lhséq' te skw'exó:s**>, //yuwɛ́l ɬ=sə́q' tə s=k'ʷəxʸ=á·s//, /'*It's the first half-moon.*'/, literally /'The moon is first half.'/, ASM ['a drawing of this moon shows the right half visible'], attested by Elders Group, <**lhséq' te skw'exó:s**>, //ɬ=sə́q' tə s=k'ʷəxʸ=á·s//, /'*second half-moon, The moon is in second half., The moon is half.*'/, literally /'The moon is half.'/, ASM ['a drawing of this moon shows the left half visible, the expression is said to be the only way to refer to the second half-moon in contrast to the expression for the first half-moon, but it can also be used for any half-moon'], attested by Elders Group, <**th'éx̱ te skw'exó:s**>, //θ'ə́x̣ tə s=k'ʷəxʸ=á·s//, /'*It's a new moon (dark).*'/, literally /'The moon is burnt out.'/, attested by Elders Group, <**th'éth'ex̱ te skw'exó:s**>, //θ'ə́[-C_1ə-]x̣ tə s=k'ʷəxʸ=á·s//, /'*It's the last quarter moon.*'/, literally /'The moon is burning out.'/, attested by Elders Group 3/12/75, <**kw'e'ós skw'exó:s**>, //k'ʷəʔ=ás s=k'ʷəxʸ=á·s//, /'*It's a quarter moon with horns up.*'/, literally /'it's a face-up moon'/, attested by IHTTC, <**kw'élh skw'exó:s**>, //k'ʷə́ɬ s=k'ʷəxʸ=á·s//, /'*It's a quarter moon with horns down (straight down or down left or down right).*'/, literally /'it's a spilled moon'/, attested by IHTTC, <**lhékw'qsel te skw'exós**>, //ɬə́k'ʷ=qsəl tə s=k'ʷəxʸ=ás//, /'*The moon is in the day-time sky (when the sun is out too).*'/, literally /'The moon tripped., The moon hooked its nose.'/, attested by IHTTC, <**stámcha skw'exós kw'e atse ōw me pélekw**>, //s=tɛ́m-cɛ s=k'ʷəxʸ=ás k'ʷə ʔɛcɛ ʔəw mə pə́ləkʷ//, /'*What is the next moon to appear?*'/, literally /'what will be the moon that next comes to appear'/, attested by IHTTC, <**lálems te skw'exó:s**>, //lɛ́ləm-s tə s=k'ʷəxʸ=á·s//, /'*halo around the moon*'/, literally /'the house of the moon'/, attested by Elders Group, <**q'elóts'eqw(em te skw'exó:s)**>, //q'əlác'=əqʷ(=əm tə s=k'ʷəxʸ=á·s)//, /'*(the moon has a) halo*'/, literally /'(the moon has a) rainshelter'/, attested by Elders Group, ASM ['month'], ASM ['each month began with the first sliver of moon after the burnt out moon; Old Louie from Skw'átets (grandfather of Mrs. Steven Kelly, Agnes Kelly's grandmother) could tell time by the sun with a stick sun-dial or without; he also had knotted rags to tell days and months; he was first cousin to Joe Lorenzetto's grandmother (Fish Camp 7/19/78)'], <**kw'í:l skw'xó:s**>, //k'ʷí·l s=k'ʷxʸ=á·s//, /'*how many months*'/, semantic environment ['how many months (old) is that child?'], attested by AC, <**stám te skw'exó:s**>, //s=tɛ́m tə s=k'ʷəxʸ=á·s//, /'*What month is it?, What moon is it?*'/, (semological comment: a typical answer might be: Tem'elíle (May, salmonberry time)), attested by IHTTC (Calendar Lesson), <**kw'e les hó:ys te skw'xó:s**>, //k'ʷə lɛ-s há·y-s tə s=k'ʷəxʸ=á·s//, /'*the last day of the month*'/, literally /'what has-gone finished of the month'/, attested by EB, <**skw'exó:s sq'óq'ey**>, //s=k'ʷəxʸ=á·s s=q'ó[=C_1ə=]y//, /'*menstruation*'/, ABDF, literally /'moon sickness'/, attested by NP.

<**skw'ikw'echó:sem**>, HHG /'*mirror, (*probably *small mirror)*'/, *see* kw'áts ~ kw'éts.

<**skw'íkw'elyàx̱el**>, EZ ['*young bat*'], *see* skw'elyáx̱el.

<**Skw'íkw'ets'tel**>, df //s=k'ʷí[=C_1ə=]c'=təl or s=C_1í=k'ʷəc'=təl//, PLN ['*Elk Creek falls*'], (<**s=**> *nominalizer*), probably root <**kw'íts'**> *butcher*, probably <**=R1=**> *continuative*, (<**=tel**> *device, thing for*), Elder's comment: "that's *spawning ground*" (which is more like *skw'ikw'etl'tel), phonology: reduplication, syntactic analysis: nominal, attested by CT (1973), source: place names reference file #282.

<**skw'íkw'iy ~ skw'íkw'i**>, EFAM ['*be stingy*'], *see* kw'íy.

<**Skw'íkw'x̲weq** (or better, **Sqw'íqw'x̲weq**)>, PLN ['*maybe the same place as Sqw'ex̲wáq (pool where Kawkawa Creek comes into the Coquihalla River and where the water pygmies lived)*'], *see* Sqw'ex̲wáq.

<**skw'íles**>, NUM ['*be what day?*'], *see* kw'í:l ~ kw'íl.

<**skw'í:lets**>, ABDF /'*be lame (in hip, esp. from birth)*'/, *see* kw'í ~ kw'íy.

<**skw'í:ls**>, NUM /'*be what hour?, be what time?*'/, *see* kw'í:l ~ kw'íl.

<**skw'ílhew**>, df //s=k'ʷíɬəw//, KIN /'*mother-in-law, father-in-law, spouse's parent, parent-in-law*'/, probably <**s=**> *nominalizer*, syntactic analysis: nominal, attested by AC, CT, other sources: ES /sk'ʷíɬəw/ *spouse's parent, wife's brother*, *see* also under probable root/stem <**kw'ílhew**>

<**skw'íts'òlès**>, stvi //s=k'ʷíc'=áləs//, ANAH /'*cross-eyed,* prob. also *cock-eyed*'/, probably root <**kw'íts'**> *butchered, cut open*, (<**s=**> *stative*), lx <**=óles**> *in the eye(s)*, phonology: downdrifting, syntactic analysis: intransitive verb, attested by AH, LG.

<**skw'iyéth**>, dnom //s=k'ʷiy=ə́θ or s=k'ʷɛ[=Aí=]y=ə́θ//, SOC ['*slave*'], (<**s=**> *nominalizer*), possibly root <**kw'áy**> *hungry*, possibly <**í-ablaut**> *derivational* or *durative*, lx <**=eth**> *mouth, edge*, phonology: possible ablaut, syntactic analysis: nominal, attested by NP, other sources: ES /sk'ʷəyə́θ/ (CwMs /sk'ʷə́yəθ/), JH /sk'ʷiyə́θ/, H-T skweíts (macron over e), Salish cognate: Squamish /sk'ʷiúc/ *slave* W73:238, K67:294, also <**skw'íyeth**>, //s=k'ʷíy=əθ or s=k'ʷə́y=əθ//, attested by AC, Elders Group (Mar. 1972), also <**skw'íyéth**>, //s=k'ʷíy=ə́θ//, attested by EB, example: <**kwólòmet te skw'íyeth**>, //kʷɛ=Aá=l-àmət tə s=k'ʷíy=əθ//, /'*The slave escaped.*'/, attested by Elders Group (Mar. 1972), <**kw'íkw'ets'em ta' skw'íyéth**>, //k'ʷí[-C_1ə-]c'=əm t-ɛʔ s=k'ʷíy=ə́θ//, /'*butchering your slave*'/, phonology: reduplication, usage: a saying used humorously of one's spouse or child, etc., attested by EB, not known to other members of the Elders Group.

<**skw'ékw'ith**>, df //s=k'ʷə́[=C_1ə=]y=(ə)θ//, [sk'ʷʊ́k'ʷiθ], SOC /'*pitiful person, helpless person, person unable to do anythingfor himself*'/, literally /'little slave'/, (<**=R1=**> *diminutive*), phonology: reduplication, syntactic analysis: nominal, attested by Elders Group, EB, example: <**ő: te skw'ékw'ith**>, //ʔó· tə s=k'ʷə́[=C_1ə=]y=θ//, /'*Oh, the helpless person.*'/, semantic environment ['said when someone did something wrong unintentionally'], attested by EB, <**melh áyeles ta' skw'ékw'ith**>, //mə-ɬ ʔɛ́y=ələs t-ɛʔ s=k'ʷə́[=C_1ə=]y=θ//, /'*Leave your skw'ékw'ith [helpless/pitiful person] alone.*'/, literally /'come-imperative go away from s-o your little slave'/, attested by EB.

<**Skw'iykw'íylets**>, PLN ['*village at the confluence of Sweltzer and Soowahlie creeks with Chilliwack River*'], *see* kw'í ~ kw'íy.

<**skw'íytel**>, HHG /'*ladder, notched cedar pole ladder, rope ladder (pre-contact or later), modern ladder*'/, *see* kw'í ~ kw'íy.

<**skw'ókw'es**>, WETH ['*heat*'], *see* kw'ás.

<**skw'ókw'exwe**>, MC /'*It's boxed., It's in a box.*'/, *see* kw'óxwe.

<**skw'okw'qá:q ~ skw'okw'qáq ~ skw'ōkw'qáq**>, dnom //s=k'ʷak'ʷqɛ́·q ~ s=k'ʷak'ʷqɛ́q ~ sk'ʷək'ʷqɛ́q, probably s=k'ʷɛ[=AaC_1ə=]q=V1´C2//, EZ ['*American*'], ['*Turdus migratorius caurinus*'], ASM ['migrates south in winter unlike the varied thrush (sx̲wík')'], (<**s=**> *nominalizer*), probably root <**kw'aq**> *lie on one's back*, possibly <**o-ablaut plus =R1=**> *continuative or derivational*, possibly <**=áq**> *on the penis, male* or possibly an otherwise very rare =V1C2 reduplication perhaps cognate with *out-of-control* in other languages, phonology: possible ablaut, possible reduplication, syntactic analysis: nominal, attested by AC, BJ, EL, Elders Group (3/1/72, 2/18/76, 6/4/75, 3/19/75), other

sources: ES /sk'ʷqɛ́q/ *robin, varied thrush,* H-T s'kukōkáq (macron over the u) *robin (Merula migratoria),* Salish cognate: Squamish /s-k'ʷq-áq/ *robin* (derived from root /k'ʷəq/ *be split (ab. tree)(for ex. of a branch hanging from a tree) W73:218, K67:294, Lushootseed /s-k'ʷəqíq/ robin* (< root /k'ʷəq/ *fall/lie on back* so named because it tilts it head back when singing) H76:256, example: <**qweloythí:lem te skw'okw'qáq**>, //qʷɛl=ayθ(əl)=í·l=əm tə s=k'ʷak'ʷqɛ́q//, /*'Robins are singing (making music).'*/, attested by Elders Group, *see* kw'aq.

<**skw'óqwtses**> ~ <**skw'éqwtses**>, EB [*'red huckleberry'*], [*'Vaccinium parvifolium'*], literally /'clubbed on the hand'/, see under main dialect form <**kw'óqwtses**> under root kw'eqw.

<**skw'ó:wes ~ skw'ówes**>, dnom //s=k'ʷá·wəs ~ s=k'ʷáwəs//, HHG /*'pail, bucket, kettle (BJ, Gibbs)'*/, (possibly <**s=**> *nominalizer*), root form and meaning uncertain unless <sikw'> *get debarked, skinned,* in case the first liquid containers were made of peeled off bark, syntactic analysis: nominal, attested by AC, EB, other sources: ES /sk'ʷá·wəs/ *bucket,* also /*'kettle'*/, attested by BJ, Gibbs, example: <**stám kw'es lí:w í te skw'ó:wes**>, //s=tɛ́m k'ʷə-s lí·w ʔí tə s=k'ʷá·wəs//, /*'What's in the pail? (inside)'*/, attested by EB, <**sqweqwá tel skw'ówes**>, //s=C_1ə=qʷɛ́ tə-l s=k'ʷáwəs//, /*'hole in my pail'*/, attested by AC, *also see* kw'ó:wes ~ kw'ówes.

<**skw'ékw'ewes**>, dmn //s=k'ʷa[=Aə́C_1ə=]wəs//, [sk'ʷʊ́k'ʷʊwəs], HHG [*'small pot'*], (<**é-ablaut**> and <**=R1=**> *diminutive*), phonology: ablaut, reduplication, syntactic analysis: nominal, attested by EB.

<**skw'ókw'exwe**>, stvi //s=k'ʷá[=C_1ə=]xʷə//, MC /*'It's boxed., It's in a box.'*/, (<**s=**> *stative*), (<**=R1=**> *stative* or *resultative*), phonology: reduplication, syntactic analysis: intransitive verb, attested by Elders Group (5/26/76), *see* kw'óxwe

<**skw'ő:lmexw ~ sqw'ő:lmexw**>, df //s=k'ʷó·l(=)mexw or s=q'ʷé[=Aó=]l(=)mexw or sik'ʷ=ó·(=)lmexw or s=k'ʷów=lməxʷ//, EB /*'blackberry (fruit), (before contact, only) wild trailing blackberry, (now also) evergreen blackberry, (*now also*) Himalaya blackberry'*/, ['before contact, only *Rubus ursinus,* now also *Rubus laciniatus,* and *Rubus procerus*'], ASM ['the berries of the trailing variety are ready as early as July, those of the evergreen somewhat later, those of the Himalaya in late August and even later'], MED ['a tea made from boiled roots is diarrhea medicine, a tea from the leaves is medicine for stomach ache'], (<**s=**> *nominalizer*), root meaning unknown root meaning unknown unless related to <**qw'él**> *ripe, cooked,* possibly <**=mexw**> *people* or possibly <**=lmexw**> *medicine?? or on the breast??,* perhaps related to root //in kw'ew=ítsel// *grizzly bear* (where =ítsel may be *on the back),* phonology: labialization is sometimes less noticeable before ō here almost sk'ő:lmexw, syntactic analysis: nominal, attested by AC, other sources: ES /sk'ʷə́w·lməxʷ/ (CwMs /sk'ʷí·lməxʷ/) *blackberries,* H-T <skőlmoq> *blackberry (trailing) (Rubus sp.),* also <**sqw'ő:lmexw**>, //s=q'ʷów=lməxʷ//, attested by BJ (5/10/64, 12/5/64), example: <**sqw'ő:lmexw sqe'óleqw**>, FOOD *blackberry juice* (lit. blackberry + fruit juice), (attested by RG,EH 6/16/98 to SN, edited by BG with RG,EH 6/26/00), also see under kw'ő:l ~ qw'ő:l or kw'ő:w ~ qw'ő:w

<**skw'ő:lmexwelhp**>, ds //s=k'ʷó·lməxʷ=əɬp//, EB /*'blackberry vine, blackberry bush'*/, [*'Rubus ursinus, Rubus laciniatus, Rubus procerus'*], lx <**=elhp**> *plant, tree,* syntactic analysis: nominal, attested by AC, Elders Group.

<**shxwelméxwelh skw'ő:lmexwelhp**>, ds //s=xʷəl=mə[=´=]xʷ=əɬ s=k'ʷó·lməxʷ=əɬp//, EB [*'trailing blackberry vine'*], [*'Rubus ursinus'*], literally /'Indian kind of blackberry'/, ASM ['this was the pre-contact blackberry in the area'], (<**s=**> *stative*), lx <**=elh**> *style, kind of,* syntactic analysis: simple nominal phrase.

<**xwelítemelh skw'ő:lmexwelhp**>, ds //xʷəlítəm=əɬ s=k'ʷó·lməxʷ=əɬp//, EB /*'Himalaya blackberry bush, evergreen blackberry bush'*/, [*'Rubus procerus, Rubus laciniatus'*], literally /'White-man kind

of blackberry'/, ASM ['both introduced by non-Indians'], lx <**=elh**> *kind of, style*, syntactic analysis: simple nominal phrase.

<**skw'ő:lmexwelhp**>, EB /'*blackberry vine, blackberry bush*'/, *see* skw'ő:lmexw.

<**skw'qwém**>, also /'*axe*'/, //s=k'ʷqʷ=ə́m//, see main dialect form <**kw'qwém**>, dnom //k'ʷqʷ=əm//, [k'ʷqʷʊ́m ~ k'ʷqʷm], TOOL /'*little hatchet, little axe*'/, under kw 'eqw.

<**slá ~ selá ~ slá:**>, DESC /'*be tight, be secured tightly; be tucked away, put away so well you can't find it, be solid*'/, *see* <**lá ~ lá: ~ lah**> *tight, put away*,

<**Slahích ~ Lohíts ~ Lahíts ~ Lahích**>, df //s=lɛ=híc ~ la=híc ~ lɛ=híc ~//, PLN ['*Five-Mile Creek*'], *see* <**lá ~ lá: ~ lah**> *tight, put away*

<**slálem álhqey**>, cpds //s=lɛ́·[=C_1ə=]m ʔɛ́ɬqəy//, EZ //'*turtle*'//, lit. /"snake with a house, housed snake"/, *see* lá:lém.

<**slálets**>, DESC ['*firmly planted in ground (can't be pulled out)*'], *see* slá ~ selá ~ slá: (probably).

<**slá:m**>, IDOC ['*spirit power of an Indian doctor or shaman*'], *see* lá:m.

<**slá:meth**>, df //s(=)lɛ́·m(=)əθ//, FSH /'*sturgeon club, fish club (for salmon, sturgeon, etc.)*'/, ASM ['a long club'], possibly <**s=**> *nominalizer*, possibly <**=eth**> *on the mouth*, syntactic analysis: nominal, attested by BHTTC, Elders Group, TG, DM (12/4/64).

<**slá:t ~ slát**>, TIME ['*night*'], *see* lá:t.

<**sláx̲et**>, LT /'*any kind of light that one carries, torch (made from pitch), lantern, lamp, flashlight*'/, *see* láx̲et.

<**slá:y**>, EB ['*fir bark*'], *see* lá:y.

<**Slá:yli**>, PLN ['*Cheam View*'], *see* yóle ~ yóla ~ yó:le.

<**slehà:l**>, PLAY /'*the slahal game, the bone-game, (slahal sticks, gambling sticks [BJ])*'/, *see* lehà:l.

<**slék'**>, EFAM ['*nickname for someone who is proud*'], *see* lék'.

<**slek'iyáp**>, EZ ['*coyote*'], ['*Canis latrans lestes*'], *see* lek'iyáp ~ **k'iyáp**.

<**slékwlets ~ slékwelets**>, ABDF /'*be lame (esp. if deformed), be a cripple, to limp, have a limp*'/, *see* lékw.

<**slépets**>, TVMO ['*something sent*'], *see* lépets.

<**slésxel**>, ANA ['*bone marrow*'], *see* ló:s ~ lós.

<**slets'éleq**>, KIN /'*brother-in-law's wife, (spouse's sibling's spouse), (step-sibling, step-brother, step-sister [AC])*'/, *see* láts'.

<**sléts'elhp**>, NUM ['*one tree*'], *see* léts'a ~ léts'e.

<**slets'őweyelh ~ lets'őw(e)yelh**>, KIN /'*half-sibling, half-brother, half-sister*'/, *see* láts'> *different*

<**slewí**>, EB ['*inner cedar bark*'], *see* léw.

<**slewíws**>, CLO /'*a dress, woman's dress*'/, *see* léw.

<**slewómet ~ lewómet**>, CLO ['*dancing costume*'], *see* léw.

<**sléxwelh**>, CAN /'*canoe (any kind), car, vehicle (any kind)*'/, *see* léxwelh.

<**slexwelháwtxw**>, CAN ['*canoe shed*'], *see* léxwelh.

<**sléxwelhmet**>, CAN ['*raid s-o in canoes*'], *see* léxwelh.

<**slexwíws**>, df //s=ləx^w=íws//, ANA ['*body (while alive)*'], *see* lexw(=)íws

<**slé<u>x</u>tses**>, ANA ['*finger*'], *see* lé<u>x</u>.

<**slé<u>x</u>xel**>, ANA ['*toe*'], *see* lé<u>x</u>.

<**sle'álets**>, DIR ['*be with behind facing toward something (like a fire)*'], *see* le'á.

<**sle'ó:les**>, DIR /'*be watchful, be facing away*'/, *see* le'á.

<**sle'ólwelh**>, DIR /'*be on the other side of, be on the side facing away*'/, *see* le'á.

<**sle'ó:thel**>, DIR /'*be across, be on the other side of*'/, *see* le'á.

<**slí**>, free root //slí//, CAN ['*sleigh*'], syntactic analysis: nominal, attested by Elders Group (11/10/76), borrowed from English or Chinook Jargon /sléy/ *sleigh* Johnson 1978:414.

<**slí:leqw**>, DESC /'*be slack, loose, too loose, hanging loose (of a slackened rope)*'/, *see* líqw.

<**slílexwelh**>, stvi //s=lí[=C_1ə=]x^w=əɬ//, EFAM ['*be calm*'], *see* líxw.

<**slílōwya**>, df //s=lí[=C_1ə=]w=iyɛ or s=C_1í=ləwyɛ//, EZ /'*seagull (generic), gull,* certainly including *the glaucous-winged gull,* and possibly including any or all of the following species which occur in the Stó:lō area*: Bonaparte's gull, short-billed gull, ring-billed gull, California gull, herring gull*'/, ['possibly genus *Larus*, certainly including *Larus glaucescens*, possibly including any/all of the following (respectively): *Larus philadelphia, Larus canus, Larus delawarensis, Larus californicus, Larus argentatus*'], ASM ['after studying drawings of all the types found in the Stó:lō area, EL said he uses slílōwya for all gulls'], possibly <**s=**> *nominalizer*, possibly <**=R1=**> *resultative or continuative or stative*, possibly <**R4=**> *diminutive*, possibly <**=iya**> *diminutive*, possibly root <**líw**> *inside something hollow*, syntactic analysis: nominal, dialects: *Cheh.*, attested by EL (9/15/78), Elders Group (2/18/76), contrast <**á:we** (Tait dial.)> *seagull, gull*, contrast <**qw'elíteq (Katzie, Chill.)**> *seagull, gull*, also /'*big seagull*'/, attested by Elders Group (6/4/75).

<**slílxwelh**>, CAN ['*small canoe*'], *see* léxwelh.

<**slí:m**>, df //s=lí·m or səl=í·m or sí·l=ə[=M2=]m//, EZ ['*sandhill crane*'], ['*Grus canadensis tabida*'], Elder's comment: "they make a peculiar sound when flying, taller than the blue heron, there used to be a few on Sumas Lake, also called locally "wild turkey"", possibly <**s=**> *nominalizer*, possibly <**=í:m**> *repeatedly*, <**=em**> *intransitivizer, have, get*, possibly <**metathesis**> *derivational*, root meaning unknown, syntactic analysis: nominal, dialects: *Cheh., Chill., Katzie,* prob. also *Tait*, attested by EL (9/15/78), BJ (12/5/64), Elders Group (6/4/75).

<**slímiyeqwxel**>, df //slím=iyəq^w=x^{y}əl or slím=iq^w=x^{y}əl//, ABDF /'*(be) pigeon-toed, (sandhill crane toed*'/, literally perhaps /'sandhill crane on the toes (on top of the head of foot)'/, possibly <**=iqw**> *on top of the head* possibly used with <**=xel**> *on the foot* possibly makes up *on the toes*, (semological comment: this seems reasonable since the *sole of the foot* is literally *face of the foot*, etc.), syntactic analysis: adjective/adjectival verb, attested by Deming (esp. SJ) (4/26/79).

<**slímiyeqwxel**>, ABDF /'*(be) pigeon-toed, (sandhill crane toed*'/, *see* slí:m.

<**slíq'**>, DESC ['*to be even*'], *see* léq'.

<**slíw**>, DIR /'*be inside (a hollow object), be in (a hollow object)*'/, *see* léw.

<**slíx**>, DIR ['*lying on its side*'], *see* lex.

<**slókwech**>, df //s=lák^w=əc//, EZ /'*white trout, (if not rainbow or cutthroat trout,* probably *lake trout* also called *grey trout)*'/, ['*Salvelinus namaycush*'], possibly <**s=**> *nominalizer*, possibly <**=ech**> *on the back*, root meaning unknown, syntactic analysis: nominal, attested by Elders Group (3/1/72).

<**slóli**>, stvi //s=láli(y) or s=lá[=C_1ə=]y//, DESC ['*be leaning*'], (<**s=**> *stative*), possibly <**=R1=**> *continuative or durative*, phonology: reduplication?, syntactic analysis: adjective/adjectival verb, attested by NP, *see* lóli(y) ~ lóy.

<**slóliyes ~ slólí:s**>, df //s=lá[=C_1ə=]y(=/-)əs//, DESC ['*be leaning*'], possibly <**=es**> *on the face* or possibly <**-es**> *third person subject subjunctive*? or -s> *third person possessive*, syntactic analysis: adjective/adjectival verb, attested by Elders Group, SP (and AK, AD)(Raft trip), example: <**slóliyes te thqát.**>, //s=lá[=C_1ə=]yəs tə θqɛ́t//, /'*The tree is leaning.*'/, attested by Elders Group, also <**slólí:s te thqá:t.**>, //s=lálí·s tə θqɛ́·t//, attested by SP (and AK, AD).

<**sló:litses**>, df //s=lá·[=C_1ə=]y=cəs//, DESC ['*leaning to one side*'], literally /'leaning on the hand'/, lx <**=tses**> *on the hand*, syntactic analysis: adjective/adjectival verb?, intransitive verb, attested by Elders Group, also <**slólitses**>, //s=lá[=C_1ə=]y=cəs//, also /'*leaning a board or pole*'/, attested by TM, example: <**ye'í:mex te sló:litses.**>, //yə=ʔí[-·-]m=əx^y tə s=lá[=C_1ə=]y=cəs//, /'*He's walking leaning to one side.*'/, attested by Elders Group.

<**sló:litses**>, DESC ['*leaning to one side*'], *see* slóli.

<**slóliyes ~ slólí:s**>, DESC ['*be leaning*'], *see* slóli.

<**sló:ltes**>, df //s=lá·lt=əs or s=lɛ[=Aá·C_1ə=]t=əs//, EFAM /'*looking sad, (making a sour face [MV, EF])*'/, *see* lo:lt.

<**sló:s ~ slós**>, ANA /'*fat, grease, lard, (oil [EB], shortening [MH])*'/, *see* ló:s ~ lós.

<**slós qwóls sqá:wth**>, FOOD /'*French fries*'/ (lit. fat + boiled + potato), *see* ló:s ~ lós or **qwó:ls**

<**Sloyámén**>, free root //slayɛ́mə́n//, SOCT /'*Sliammon people, Sliammon dialect (of the Comox language, Mainland Comox)*'/, comment: probably Anglicized since this is exactly how it is pronounced in English (by non-Indians) and since the Sliammon name for the place and dialect is /ɬáʔamən/ (Davis 1970:90), syntactic analysis: nominal, attested by NP (2/22/80).

<**slhákw'em**>, dnom //s=ɬɛ́k'^{w}=əm//, mdls, ABFC ['*breath (noun)*'], also <**slháqwem**>, *see* lhákw'.

<**slhá:lí**>, dnom //s=ɬɛ́·lí or s=ɬil=ɛ́·[=M2=]y or s=ɬí[=Aɛ=]·l=əy//, HUMC /'*woman, female*'/, HAT /'*(post-adolescent) woman, woman (15 yrs. or older)*'/, literally perhaps /'someone that weaves wool/bark'/, EZ ['*female*'], EB ['*female*'], *see* lhí:l.

<**slhálqi**>, stcs //s-ɬə[-Aɛ́-]l=q=i//, FOOD ['*is soaking (dried fish)*'], *see* lhél *sprinkle, splash, spray.*

<**slhálqi**>, dnom //s=ɬə[-Aɛ́-]l=q=i//, FOOD ['*what is soaking (dried fish)*'], *see* lhél *sprinkle, splash, spray.*

<**slhálqi**>, strs //s-ɬə[-Aɛ́-]l=q=i//, FOOD ['*already soaked dried fish*'], *see* lhél *sprinkle, splash, spray.*

<**Slhálqi**>, PLN /'*village on west bank of old course of Chilliwack River near Tzeachton,* also *the place nearby where the Stó:lō used to soak dried fish*'/, *see* lhél.

<**slhálheq'**>, LAND ['*be lying on the ground*'], *see* lháq'.

<**slhálhex̱**>, FOOD ['*be served*'], *see* lhá:x̱ ~ lháx̱.

<**slhálhlí**>, EZ /'*ladybug, ladybird beetle*'/, *see* slhá:lí.

<**slhálhli**>, HUMC /'*little woman, small woman*'/, *see* slhá:lí.

<**slháq'emex**>, df //s=ɬɛ́q'=oməx^y or s=ɬəq'ɛ́=M2=oməx^y//, LAND ['*a large portion of the earth*'], *see* lheq'á- *wide* or less likely lháq' *lay (flat?), put down.*

<**Slhélets**>, PLN ['*four rocks in the Fraser River by Peqwchō:lthel (American Bar) that are shaped like rumps*'], *see* lhél.

<**slhél:éts ~ slhél:ets ~ slhéléts ~ slhélets**>, ANAH /'*butt, ass, rump, buttocks*'/, *see* lhél.

<**slheliyó:llh**>, HAT /'*girl child, girl (from 5 to 10 years or so)*'/, *see* slhá:lí.

<**slheli'ál**>, EB ['*female part of female plant*'], *see* slhá:lí.

<**slhellhá:li**>, HUMC ['*(a lot of) women*'], *see* slhá:lí.

<**slhellhelp'á:lí:ya**>, ANA /'*(have) sloppy ears, big ears*'/, *see* lhél.

<**slhellhélp'elets**>, HARV ['*sloppy pack*'], *see* lhél.

<**slhellhelp'élets**>, ANA ['*(have a) sloppy rump*'], *see* lhél.

<**slhelp'íwel**>, ANA ['*(have a) sloppy ass*'], *see* lhél.

<**slhelp'ó:ythel**>, ANA /'*(have) flabby lips, (have) sloppy lips*'/, *see* lhél.

<**slhélqi**>, FSH ['*dried fish that's been soaked (rehydrated)*'], *see* lhél.

<**slhelhá<u>x</u>**>, ABDF ['*be stiff (of arm or foot)*'], *see* lhé<u>x</u>.

<**slhelhlíli**>, HUMC ['*little ladies*'], *see* slhá:lí.

<**slhelhliyó:llh**>, HAT ['*girl (from baby to 4 or 5 yrs.)*'], *see* slhá:lí.

<**slhelhts'à:m**>. see main dialect form <**lhets'á:m**>, df //ɬəc'ɛ́·m//, EZ /'*weasel, one or both of the following which are in the area: short-tailed weasel and long-tailed weasel*'/, ['*Mustela erminea (fallenda and invicta) and Mustela frenata (altifrontalis and nevadensis)*'],

<**slhém:exw ~ slhémexw**>, WETH ['*the rain*'], *see* lhém.

<**slhémlhem**>, WETH ['*dew*'], *see* lhém.

<**slhémoqel**>, ABDF /'*(have a) tooth missing, (have) teeth missing (any number), (be) toothless*'/, *see* lhém.

<**slhéms**>, TIME ['*eleven o'clock*'], *see* lhém.

<**slhémxel**>, WETH ['*dew*'], *see* lhém.

<**slheq(e)lí:s**>, CLO ['*be buttoned*'], *see* lhéq.

<**slheq'ó:lwelh**>, ANAH ['*one side of the body (between arm and hip)*'], *see* lheq'á-.

<**slhéq'el:exw ~ lhéq'el:exw ~ slhéq'elexw ~ slhéq'ewelh ~ slhéq'awelh**>, EFAM /'*know s-th, know s-o*'/, *see* q'á:l.

<**slheq'el:ó:met**>, //s=ɬə=q'ɛl=l-á·mət//, EFAM /'*know oneself, be confident,understand*'/, *see* q'á:l.

<**slhéq'ōwelh**>, ANAH /'*the back (on the body), (lower back [Deming])*'/, *see* lheq'á-.

<**slhéq'qel**>, see main dialect form <**lhéq'qel**>, df //ɬə́q'=qəl//, LAND /'*end of a falling section of land, end of a level stretch of land, (head of a creek or island [Elders Group])*'/

<**slheqwéla**>, ANA ['*cheek*'], *see* slhíqw.

<**slheqwél:es**>, ANA ['*gums*'], *see* slhíqw.

<**slheqwe'álá**>, dnom //s=ɬə=q^wəʔ=ɛlɛ́//, CLO [*'pocket'*], *see* qwá

<**slhets'ám ~ slhets'à:m**>, see main dialect form <**lhets'á:m**>, df //ɬəc'ɛ́·m//, EZ /*'weasel, one or both of the following which are in the area: short-tailed weasel and long-tailed weasel'*/, [*'Mustela erminea (fallenda and invicta) and Mustela frenata (altifrontalis and nevadensis)'*].

<**slhewómét** or **slewómét ~ sleqwómét**>, //s=ɬəw=ámət or s=ləw=ámət ~ sləq^wámə́t//, also /*'mask (any kind for dancing)'*/, *see* lhew.

<**slhewó:stel**>, df //s=ɬəw=á·s=təl//, CLO [*'mask'*], *see* lhew.

<**slhéxtses**>, ABDF /*'(have a) paralyzed hand, game hand'*/, *see* lhéx *stiff*.

<**slhéxxel**>, ABDF /*'(have a) paralyzed leg, game leg'*/, *see* lhéx *stiff*.

<**Slhílhets'**>, PLN /*'old lake above Smith Falls, Smith Falls creek (which enters Cultus Lake at its northeast corner)'*/, *see* lhíts' ~ lhí:ts'.

<**slhílhexes**>, dnom //s=ɬɛ[=Aí=][=C_1ə=]]x̣=əs=əm or s=ɬí[=C_1ə=]x̣=əs=əm//, SPRD /*'the painted people (spirit-dancers)'*/, *see* **lhá:x ~ lháx**.

<**slhíqw**>, dnom //s=ɬíq^w//, ANA /*'flesh (human, non-human), meat (of dried fish, animal, or bird)'*/, *see* lhíqw.

<**slhíqwetsel**>, FSH [*'long thin slices of fish removed to dry from slhíts'es (wind-driedsalmon)'*], *see* slhíqw.

<**slhíts'**>, ABDF [*'be cut'*], *see* lhíts' ~ lhí:ts'.

<**slhíts'es**>, FSH [*'wind-dried opened and scored salmon'*], *see* lhíts' ~ lhí:ts'.

<**slhíxws**>, NUM /*'three o'clock (< the third hour); Wednesday (< the third day)'*/, *see* lhí:xw.

<**slholhekw'íwel ~ slholhekw'í:wel**>, EFAM /*'be dumbfounded, be surprised, be stupified, be speechless'*/, *see* lhó:kw' ~ lhókw'.

<**slholh(e)xwélqsel**>, ABDF [*'(have) snot hanging from the nose'*], *see* lhexw.

<**slholh(e)xwélqsel mó:qw**>, EZ [*'wild turkey'*], *see* lhexw.

<**slhólho**>, df //s=ɬáɬa// or //s=C_1á=ɬa//, EZ /*'brown thrush* (could be *hermit thrush,* or possibly *gray-cheeked thrush)'*/, *see* lhólho.

<**slhóp'**>, dnom //s=ɬáp'//, FOOD /*'soup, (stew)'*/, *see* lhóp' *eat soup.*

<**slhóth'**>, ABDF /*'scabies (a skin disease), ("seven-year itch", itch lasting seven years [Deming 2/7/80])'*/, *see* lhóth'.

<**Slhq'átses**>, TIME /*'Friday, five o'clock'*/, *see* lheq'át ~ lhq'á:t.

<**slhqw'á:y**>, HHG [*'cedar bark mat'*], *see* lhéqw'.

<**slhxwélhcha**>, ANA /*'spit, saliva'*/, *see* lhexw.

<**smà:l**>, KIN [*'little father'*], *see* má:l ~ mál.

<**smá:leth'el ~ smá:lth'el**>, EFAM /*'(lots of people are) proud, (many are proud)'*/, *see* máth'el.

<**smá:lt**>, dnom //s=mɛ́·lt//, LAND /*'stone, rock (any size), mountain'*/, *see* má:lt.

<**smamalyí**>, KIN [*'be married'*], *see* malyí.

<**smámekw'et**>, REL /*'comfort s-o, sympathize with s-o'*/, *see* mákw'a.

<**smámelet**>, LAND /*'little stone, pebble, little rock hill, small rock mountain (like in the Fraser River in the canyon)'*/, *see* smá:lt.

<**smámth'el**>, EFAM /*'(be a) little bit proud, [a little] proud'*/, *see* máth'el.

<**smámth'eqel**>, EFAM [*'smart-alec'*], *see* máth'el.

<**smátexwtel**>, probably df //s(=)mɛ́təx^{w}=təl//, KIN /*'spouse's sibling, sibling's spouse (cross sex), for ex., husband's brother, (wife's sister, woman's sister's husband, man's brother's wife)'*/, ASM ['cross-sex means that the two people being related are of the opposite sex from each other, a woman's smátexwtel will be male and a man's smátexwtel will be female, the word probably developed to label a potential spouse for widows or widowers (levirate and sororate marriage, resp.)'], (probably <**s=**> *nominalizer*), root meaning unknown, (<**=tel**> *reciprocal or something to*), syntactic analysis: nominal, attested by Elders Group, other sources: ES /smɛ́təx^{w}təl/ *spouse's sibling, sibling's spouse (cross-sex)*, also filed under <**mátexw**>, bound root //mɛ́təx^{w}//, meaning unknown.

<**smáth'el**>, EFAM ['*(be) proud (pompous)*'], *see* máth'el.

<**smá:yeleq**>, df //s=mɛ́·y=ələq or s=məy=ɛ́·[=M2=]ləq//, WATR ['*waves*'], *see root* <**má:y**.

<**smékw'em**>, MC /*'something used that one picks up and uses, something second-hand'*/, *see* mékw' ~ mő́kw'.

<**smekw'e'ála**>, REL ['*graveyard*'], *see* mákw'a.

<**smelá:lh**>, df //s(=)məlɛ́·ɬ//, SOCT /*'respected person, (high class person [EB])'*/, possibly <**s=**> *nominalizer*, root meaning unknown, syntactic analysis: nominal, attested by SP and AK (7/13/75), BHTTC (9/9/76), also /*'high class person'*/, attested by EB (9/18/78).

<**semelá:lh**>, pln //s=hə=məlɛ́·ɬ//, SOCT ['*high class people*'], (<**he=**> *plural*), phonology: consonant merger, syntactic analysis: nominal, attested by EB (9/18/78).

<**smelám**>, KIN ['*adopted child*'], *see* méle ~ mél:a.

<**smélàtel**>, ANA /*'womb, uterus'*/, *see* méle ~ mél:a.

<**smelmá:lt**>, LAND ['*a lot of rocks*'], *see* smá:lt.

<**smelmólkw**>, FOOD ['*spread*'] as in <**temítō smelmólkw**>, *ketchup* (lit. tomato + spread), *see* molkw

<**smelmólxw**>, DESC ['*(be) oily (?)*'], *see* mélxw

<**Smelő'**>, N /*'Racoon (name in a story), (Lynx* [JL]*)'*/, *see* mélés.

<**smélqweqel**>, ds //məlq^{w}=əqəl ~ s=məlq^{w}=əqəl//, ANAH /*'uvula, uvula down in the throat'*/, see under mélqweqel.

<**smeltáléqel**>, ANA ['*kidneys*'], *see* smá:lt.

<**smél<u>x</u>weth'**>, df //s=mə́lx̣^{w}(=)əθ'//, EZ ['*dipper (bird)*'], ['*Cinclus mexicanus*'], ASM ['blue-grey bird found on little creeks'], *see* mél<u>x</u>weth'.

<**smelhmélhqw**>, stvi //s=C$_1$əC$_2$=mə́ɬq^{w}//, DESC /*'rough (of wood), lumpy (of ground, bark, etc.)'*/, *see* mélhqw.

<**smemá:lt**>, LAND ['*(many small rocks)*'], *see* smá:lt.

<**Smémeqw'o**>, PLN /*'(heron nesting area which was the) upriver end of Herrling Island in Fraser River just below Popkum,* also *the name of the village or settlement on Herrling Island'*/, *see* sméqw'o ~ smő́qw'o.

<**sméqsel**>, BPI ['*(have a) big nose*'], *see* méqsel.

<**sméq'eth**>, FOOD /'*feast left-overs, left-overs of food (which guests can take home)*'/, *see* méq'.

<**smeq'óth**>, FOOD /'*feast left-overs, left-overs of food (which guests can take home)*'/, *see* méq'.

<**sméqw'o ~ smő̄qw'o**>, df //s=mə́q'ʷ(=)a ~ s=móq'ʷ(=)a//, EZ /'*great blue heron, (often called) "crane"*'/, ['*Ardea herodias* especially subspecies *fannini*'], *see* méqw' ~ mő̄qw'.

<**smestíyexw**>, REL /'*conscience, spirit (which can be lost temporarily), soul, life-spirit, power of one's will*'/, *see* mestíyexw.

<**sméteqsel ~ smetóqsel**>, df //s=mə́t=əqsəl ~ s=mət=áqsəl//, ANA ['*snot*'], (<**s=**> *nominalizer*), possibly root <**mét ~ met**> or <**mat**> *flat organ in sturgeon which was skinned off and boiled down for glue* (because it is sticky?), see under <**mét ~ met**>.

<**smetmátexwtel**>, KIN /'*husband's brothers, (*perhaps also *wife's sisters?, spouse's siblings?, sibling's spouses?)*'/, *see* smátexwtel.

<**smetméteqsel ~ smatmáteqsel**>, ANA ['*(be) snotty*'], *see* sméteqsel ~ smetóqsel.

<**sméth'elheqw**>, df //s=mə́θ'=əl[=devoicing=]əqʷ//, ANA ['*brain*'], *see* méth' *blue.*

<**smeth'íl**>, LT ['*[be in a state of get blue]*'], *see* méth'.

<**sméth'qel**>, df //s=mə́θ'=qəl//, ANA ['*brain*'], *see* méth' *blue.*

<**smétsa**>, dnom //s=mə́cɛ//, ANA /'*lump on person (or creature), goiter*'/, EB /'*lump on a tree, burl*'/, *see* **métsa** meaning uncertain, perhaps *lump*.

<**sméts'**>, df //s=mə́c'//, PE ['*rouge*'], LT, possibly <**s=**> *nominalizer*, root meaning unknown unless related to root méth' *blue*, syntactic analysis: nominal, attested by Deming (2/22/79), example: <**ólewe qé<u>x</u> te sméts'.**>, //ʔálə-wə qə́x̣ tə s=mə́c'//, /'*(There's) too much rouge.*'/, attested by Deming.

<**sméya**>, probably df //s=mɛ́yɛ or sm=ə́yɛ//, WATR ['*bay*'], LAND, possibly <**s=**> *nominalizer*, root meaning unknown, syntactic analysis: nominal, attested by Elders Group (4/2/75).

<**sméyeth ~ sméyéth**>, df //s=mɛ́yəθ ~ s=mɛ́yə́θ//, [sméyɪθ ~ sméyɪ́θ], EZ /'*(game) animal, (meat)*'/, FOOD ['*meat*'], *see* méyeth ~ méyéth.

<**sméyethálá**>, FOOD ['*tray for carrying meat*'], *see* sméyeth ~ sméyéth.

<**smílha**>, SPRD /'*a spirit-dance, a winter-dance*'/, *see* mílha.

<**smilha'áwtxw**>, SPRD /'*Indian dance-house, "smoke-house", (spirit-dance building)*'/, *see* mílha.

<**smìmelehollhála**>, EZ ['*nest*'], *see* méle ~ mél:a.

<**smímelha**>, SPRD ['*(the) spirit-dancing*'], *see* mílha.

<**smímeq'**>, WATR ['*(be) sunk*'], *see* míq'.

<**smíme<u>x</u>àlh**>, df //s=mí[=C_1ə=]x̣=ɛ́ɬ or s=C_1í=məx̣=ɛ́ɬ//, EZ ['*caterpillar*'], ['prob. most *Lepidoptera* (butterfly) larvae'], *see* mí<u>x</u> perhaps *butterfly.*

<**smímeyàth ~ smímoyàth**>, dmn //s=C_1í=mɛyə[=M2=]θ//, EZ ['*butterfly*'], ['order *Lepidoptera*'], literally perhaps /'little animal'/, *see* méyeth ~ méyéth

<**smímiyàth**>, EZ ['*little animal(s)*'], *see* méyeth ~ méyéth.

<**Smímkw'**>, PLN [*'mountain in back of Restmore Lodge (or some say way back of Mt. Cheam)'*], *see* mékw' ~ mőkw'.

<**smímstiyexw**>, REL [*'spirit'*], *see* mestíyexw.

<**Smimstiyexwálá ~ Smímstíyexwá:le**>, PLN [*'place near mouth of Chehalis River where they had a mass burial during a smallpox epidemic'*], *see* mestíyexw.

<**smímts'el**>, EFAM [*'acting smart'*], *see* máth'el.

<**Smiyó:lh**>, df //s=miyá·=aɬ?//, PLN /*'Semmihault Creek, a stream from the east joining the old Chilliwack River near the Chilliwack airport'*/, root meaning unknown unless root <**m(i)yó:**> *get cheap, (come down in price)*, <**s=**> *nominalizer*, probably <**=ólh**> *canoe* (allomorph of <=ówelh> *canoe)*, syntactic analysis: nominal, attested by Bob Joe (1/16/64), other sources: Wells 1965 (lst ed.):13 <smee-AWLTH> (line through L), Wells (Maud, Galloway and Weeden) 1987:80.

<**smólxw**>, DESC [*'(be) oiled'*], *see* mélxw.

<**smómeleqw**>, DESC /*'mixed (of anything, vegetables, brains, etc.)'*/, *see* mál ~ mél.

<**smómeleqw spíls s'élhtel sqe'óleqw**>, *V8 juice* (lit. mixed + planted + food + fruit juice), *see* mál ~ mél

<**smóst'iyethel**>, df //s=mást'=əyəθəl//, ANAH [*'(have) pursed lips when pouting'*], *see* móst'.

<**smó:tx̱w ~ smótx̱w**>, df //s=má·t(=)x̣ʷ//, EZ /*'stickleback,* possibly *threespine stickleback'*/, possibly [*'Gasterosteus aculeatus'*], ASM ['this fish is said to be a tattletale on fishermen--when it sees a fisherman it goes to warn the other fish'], possibly <**s=**> *nominalizer*, possibly <**=x̱w**> *around in a circle*, root meaning unknown, syntactic analysis: nominal, attested by AC, BJ (12/5/64), other sources: ES /smátx̣ʷ/ *small bullhead*, also see mó:tx̱w ~ mótx̱w.

<**smótheqw**>, FOOD [*'prepared fish oil (usually sockeye oil)'*], *see* mótheqw or metheqw.

<**smőkw'** or **semőkw'**>, DESC [*'(be) found'*], *see* mékw' ~ mőkw'.

<**smőqw'o**>, dnom //s=móq'ʷa//, EZ [*'great blue heron'*], compare <**sméqw'o**.

<**smős**>, TIME [*'Thursday (a less common name)'*], *see* mős.

<**Snaníth**>, df //s=nɛníθ//, PLN [*'a village at the south end of former Sumas Lake on the mountain'*], literally /'on the other side of the lake'/, possibly <**s=**> *stative or nominalizer*, possibly <**=eth**> *edge*, possibly root <**lóli(y)**> *be leaning*, comment: this may have been the village with houses built out over the water on stilts for protection from mosquitoes (described by Boundary Survey records), in which case a meaning of "leaning on the edge" might be appropriate; the literal meaning given above ("on the other side of the lake") is provided by the Elders Group, phonology: possible reduplication, syntactic analysis: nominal, dialects: *Sumas (thus the n's and the th - ts variation)*, attested by Elders Group (8/31/77), other sources: Wells 1965 (lst ed.):23 <nah-NEETS> in records as Saneats also, Wells 1966, source: place names reference file #258, *see* naníth.

<**sókw'**>, free root or free stem //sák'ʷ// or //si[=Aá=]k'ʷ//, EB /*'inner core of cow parsnip (yó:le) with bark peeled off, [*perhaps also *of some other plants with barked peeled off]'*/, possibly root <**síkw'**> *peel off, skin off*, possibly <**ó-ablaut**> *resultative or durative*, (attested by RG,EH 6/16/98 to SN, edited by BG with RG,EH 6/26/00)

<**xwelítemelh sókw'**>, EB, FOOD *celery* (lit. white man style inner core of cow parsnip (i.e., yó:le), (attested by RG,EH 6/16/98 to SN, edited by BG with RG,EH 6/26/00)

<**Sókw'ech ~ Sókw'ets**>, df //sák'^{w}=əc or si[=Aá=]k'^{w}=əc//, PLN ['*winter village on flat at mouth of Gordon Creek*'], ASM ['two miles below Yale on west bank of Fraser River and north side of the creek mouth, an area just past Hémq'eleq, named Sókw'ets because the driftwood logs pile up there and get peeled and there is lots of peeled bark'], possibly root <**síkw'**> *peel off, skin off*, possibly <**ó-ablaut**> *resultative or durative*, lx <**=ech ~ =ets**> *on the back*, compare with <**sókw'em**> *outer (cedar) bark; bark splint*, compare with Tait <**súsekw'**> *young cedar*, compare with root <**síkw'**> as in <**síkw'em**> *skin or bark peels off*, phonology: possible ablaut, syntactic analysis: nominal, attested by SP and AK (Fish Camp 8/2/77, Raft Trip 8/30/77, Slide identifications 9/13/77), Elders Group (8/31/77), AD and AK (Trip to Five-Mile Creek 4/30/79), other sources: Wells 1965 (lst ed.):25, source: place names file reference #145.

<**Sókw'ech Stó:lō**>, df //sák'^{w}=əc s=tá·l=ow//, PLN ['*Gordon Creek*'], literally /'bark peeled off in the back river'/, syntactic analysis: simple nominal phrase, attested by AK and SP (Fish Camp 8/2/77), source: place names file reference #146 and #268.

<**sókw'em**>, df //s=sák'^{w}=əm or s=si[=Aá=]k'^{w}=əm//, EB ['*outer cedar bark*'], ['*Thuja plicata*'], MED ['*splint (made of outer cedar bark)*'], (<**s=**> *nominalizer*), possibly root <**síkw'**> *peel off, skin off*, possibly <**ó-ablaut**> *resultative or durative*, (<**=em**> *intransitivizer, have, get*), phonology: consonant merger, possible ablaut, syntactic analysis: nominal, attested by CT and HT (6/21/76), Elders Group (4/2/75), Salish cognate: Squamish /súk'^{w}am/ *[outer] cedar bark* W73:14, K67:304, Lushootseed /súk'^{w}əb/ *cedar bark still on tree* ~ (one speaker's) *not the bark but the act of removing it, remove [peel off] cedar bark* H76:448.

<**sókw'émelhp**>, ds //sák'^{w}=əm=əɬp or si[=Aá=]k'^{w}=əm=əɬp//, EB ['*cedar pole*'], ASM ['to be a pole it must have been from a young cedar tree'], compare with Tait <**súsekw'**> *young cedar*, lx <**=elhp**> *tree, plant*, phonology: possible ablaut, syntactic analysis: nominal, attested by CT and HT (6/21/76).

<**sóskw'em**>, dmn //sá[=C_1ə=]k'^{w}=əm or si[=Aá=C_1ə=]k'^{w}=əm//, BLDG ['*pole ?*'], (<**=R1=**> *diminutive*), phonology: reduplication, possible ablaut, syntactic analysis: nominal, attested by CT and HT (6/21/76).

<**sokw'emáwtxw**>, ds //sak'^{w}=əm=ɛ́wtx^{w} or si[=Aa=]k'^{w}=əm=ɛ́wtx^{w}//, BLDG ['*bark house*'], lx <**=áwtxw**> *building, house*, phonology: possible ablaut, syntactic analysis: nominal, attested by Elders Group (1/21/76), Salish cognate: Squamish /suk'^{w}am-áwʔtx^{w}/ *lodging made of cedar bark* W73:14, K67:304.

<**súsekw'**>, df //sú[=C_1ə=]k'^{w} or sa[=Aú=C_1ə=]k'^{w} or si[=Aú=C_1ə=]k'^{w}//, EB ['*young cedar*'], ['*Thuja plicata*'], possibly root <**síkw'**> *peel off*, possibly <**ú-ablaut**> *derivational*, (<**=R1=**> *diminutive*), phonology: reduplication, probable ablaut, syntactic analysis: nominal, attested by Elders Group (6/11/75), probably borrowed from a neighboring Salish language (all but N. Straits have u in cognate forms), compare <**sókw'em**> *outer cedar bark*, and <**síkw'em**> *bark or skin peels off*, Salish cognate: Squamish /súk'^{w}am/ *[outer] cedar bark* K67:304, Lushootseed /súk'^{w}əb/ *cedar bark still on the tree ~ remove cedar bark from tree* H76:448, Thompson [šíšək'^{w}] /sísək'^{w}/ *young cedar* (Elders Group 6/11/75).

<**Sókw'ech ~ Sókw'ets**>, PLN ['*winter village on flat at mouth of Gordon Creek*'], *see* sókw'.

<**Sókw'ech Stó:lō**>, PLN ['*Gordon Creek*'], *see* sókw'.

<**sókw'em**>, EB ['*outer cedar bark*'], *see* sókw'.

<**sokw'emáwtxw**>, BLDG ['*bark house*'], *see* sókw'.

<**sókw'émelhp**>, EB ['*cedar pole*'], *see* sókw'.

<**solá:ts**>, possibly root //salɛ́·c//, HHG [*'cattail mat (large or small)'*], syntactic analysis: nominal, attested by Deming (4/17/80), other sources: JH /salé·c/ *large mat,* also <**selá:ts**>, //səlɛ́·c//, attested by SJ (Deming 4/23/80), Salish cognate: Skagit dial. of Lushootseed /súlič/ *cattail mat (large or small)* (Deming 4/17/80 prob. LG), prob. itself from /s=wúl=ič/ *nominalizer= bulrush/cattailreed =ontheback.*

<**só:les**>, ABDF /*'be drunk, got drunk'*/, *see* sél or sí(:)l.

<**Sólkweyem??** or **Solkw'í:m??**>, df //sálk^{w}(=)əy=əm or sa[=lə=]k'^{w}=í·m//, PLN [*'monument at Saddle Rock at Five Mile Creek'*], possibly root <**sokw'**> *peel bark,* possibly <**=le=**> *plural,* possibly <**=ey**> *bark,* possibly <**=í:m**> *repeatedly,* phonology: possible infixed plural, syntactic analysis: nominal, source: only found in Wells 1965 (lst ed.):15.

<**sóqw'**>, free root //sáq'^{w}//, EB [*'cow parsnip sprout (especially the edible inside part)'*], [*'Heracleum lanatum'*], ASM ['once peeled the sprout can be eaten raw or cooked, is a bit slimy but has a good flavor, eaten in the spring when tender'], probably a mistranscription or doublet of <**sókw'**>, syntactic analysis: noun, nominal, attested by CT, Elders Group, see **sókw'**.

<**sóseqwt ~ (rarely) só:seqwt**>, df //sá[=C_1ə=]q^{w}t//, KIN /*'younger, younger sibling, cousin of a junior line (cousin by an ancestor younger than the speaker's), junior cousin (child of a younger sibling of one's parent, (great) grandchild of a younger sibling of one's(great) grandparent), younger brother, younger sister'*/, possibly <**=R1=**> *comparative* or *diminutive or stative,* root meaning unknown, phonology: reduplication, syntactic analysis: adjective/adjectival verb, also nominal perhaps, attested by AC, EB, Elders Group, other sources: ES /sásəq^{w}t/ *junior sibling, cousin of junior line,* JH /sá·səq^{w}t/ *younger sibling,* example: <**tl'ó sóseqwt.**>, //ƛ'á sá[=C_1ə=]q^{w}t//, /*'He's younger., She's younger.'*/, contrast <**tl'ól sóseqwt.**> *That my younger sibling., He's/She's my younger sibling.*, *<**tl'ól sóseqwt.**> *That's/He's my younger.* rejected, Elder's comment: "can't say tl'ól sóseqwt.", attested by EB, also <**tl'ó só:seqwt.**>, //ƛ'á sá·[=C_1ə=]q^{w}t//, also /*'He/She/That's the younger., That's her younger sister.'*/, attested by AC, <**ts'áts'el sóseqwt**>, //c'ɛ́[=C_1ə=]l sá[=C_1ə=]q^{w}t//, /*'the very youngest'*/, attested by EB (5/5/78), <**ólewe sóseqwt**>, //ʔálə-wə sá[=C_1ə=]q^{w}t//, /*'youngest (sibling)'*/, attested by EB, <**we'ól sáseqwt**>, //wə-ʔál sá[=C_1ə=]q^{w}t//, /*'the youngest'*/, literally /'very younger'/, attested by AC.

<**se'ó:seqwt**>, cpvs //s[=əʔɛ]á(·)[=C_1ə=]q^{w}t//, KIN [*'youngest (sibling)'*], (<**=e'á=**> *comparative, superlative*), phonology: infixed comparative, reduplication, syntactic analysis: adjective/adjectival verb, attested by AC, other sources: H-T <tsEásuk·t> (macrons on a and u) *last [youngest] child,* example: <**áltha se'ó:seqwt.**>, //ʔɛ́lθɛ s[=əʔɛ́=]á·[=C_1ə=]q^{w}t//, /*'I'm the youngest one.'*/, attested by AC, <**we'ól tl'ó se'ó:seqwt.**>, //wə-ʔál ƛ'á s[=əʔɛ́=]á·[=C_1ə=]q^{w}t//, /*'That's the youngest.'*/, attested by AC, <**we'ólewe se'óseqwt**>, //wə-ʔálə-wə s[=əʔɛ́=]á[=C_1ə=]q^{w}t//, /*'youngest one'*/, attested by AC.

<**soseqwtóletses**>, df //sa[=C_1ə=]q^{w}t=álə(=)cəs//, ANAH /*'little finger, fourth finger'*/, literally /'youngest (sibling) finger'/, probably <**=óletses**> *finger* probably <**with =tses**> *on the hand,* phonology: reduplication, syntactic analysis: nominal, dialects: *Tait, Chill.*, attested by Elders Group (8/20/75, 5/3/78), other sources: H-T 1902 <tsasuk·tálatcis> (macrons over first 3 vowels) *little finger (lit. youngest),* also <**sóseqwtses**>, //sá[=C_1ə=]q^{w}=cəs//, literally /'youngest on the hand'/, dialects: *Chehalis,* attested by Elders Group (8/20/75).

<**soseqwtóletses**>, ANAH /*'little finger, fourth finger'*/, *see* sóseqwt ~ (rarely) só:seqwt.

<**sósetel é<u>x</u>wtel**> or perhaps better <**sóset'el é<u>x</u>wtel**> , cpds //só[=C_1ə=]t'=təl ʔi[=Aə=] ´x̣^{w}=təl// or ///sɛ́[=C_1ə=](t)=təl ʔi[=Aə=] ´x̣^{w}=təl//, HHG /*'vaccuum cleaner'*/ (lit. "sucking broom"), root form

uncertain but compare <**sot'elhàlèm**>, *breathe in*, root form and meaning uncertain but perhaps *to suction* or *to suck in)*, possibly <**ó-ablaut**> *durative* or automatic on root vowel <a> with <**=R1=**> *continuative*, <**=tel**> *device, thing to*, phonology: possible ablaut, possible consonant merger <**t't**> → <**t'**> or <**t**>, reduplication attested by RG & EH (4/10/99 Ling332)

<**sóskw'em**>, BLDG ['*pole ?*'], *see* sókw'.

<**sóstem**>, ABDF ['*lost (deceased)*'], *see* sát.

<**só:tets**>, free stem or root //sá·t(=)əc//, WETH /'*north-east wind, north wind, east wind, cold wind*'/, ASM ['spirit dancers begin to feel their spirit powers wanting them to sing and dance when this wind first starts to blow in the winter (about December), the first to feel it are those furthest east as the wind and the spirit power stirring moves gradually westward'], possibly <**sót ~ sót'**> *suck in air*, possibly <**=ets**> *on the back*, syntactic analysis: noun, nominal, attested by AC, BJ (5/10/64, 12/5/64), Deming, Elders Group (2/5/75, 3/1/76), other sources: ES /sá·təc/ *northeast wind*, JH /sá·təc/ *north or east wind*, Salish cognate: Squamish /sútič/ *Squamish wind, cold north wind* W73:290, K67:304.

<**sot'elhàlèm**>, mdls //sát'=//, ABFC /'*breathe in*'/, root form and meaning uncertain but perhaps *to suction* or *to suck in air* (compare <**sósetel éx̲wtel**> *vaccuum cleaner* (lit. "sucking broom"), root form uncertain), <**=lhelh ~ =lhál**> *on the front of the neck, in the windpipe, in the trachea*, <=em> *middle voice*, phonology: downstepping and updrifting, attested by RG & EH (4/9/99 Ling332)

<**só:x̲wel ~ sóx̲wel**>, df //sá·x̣ʷ(=)əl//, EB /'*grass (every kind) (wild and now domestic types), hay*'/, ['family *Gramineae* and possibly family *Cyperaceae* (sedges)'], possibly <**=el**> *get, become, come, go*, root meaning unknown, syntactic analysis: nominal, noun?, attested by AC, BJ (5/10/64, 12/5/64), Elders Group (3/15/72, 5/16/79), Deming (esp. SJ) (5/3/79), other sources: ES /sá·x̣ʷəl/ *grass*, H-T <sáQEl> (macron over a) *grass*, Salish cognate: Squamish /sáx̣ʷiʔ/ *grass, hay, straw* W73:122, K67:303, Lushootseed /sáx̣ʷil/ *grass, hay*, example: <**tsqwá:y te sóx̲wel.**>, //c=qʷɛ́·y tə sáx̣ʷ(=)əl//, /'*The grass (or hay) (when overripe or dried) is yellow.*'/, attested by Elders Group, also /'*The grass is green.*'/, attested by Deming (esp. SJ).

<**temsóx̲wel**>, ds //təm=sáx̣ʷ(=)əl//, HARV ['*haying time*'], lx <**tem=**> *time for, season for*, syntactic analysis: nominal, attested by AC.

<**sox̲weláwtxw**>, ds //sáx̣ʷ(=)əl=ɛ́wtxʷ//, BLDG /'*barn, (hay house, grass building)*'/, HARV, literally /'hay house, hay building'/, lx <**=áwtxw**> *house, building*, syntactic analysis: nominal, attested by IHTTC.

<**sox̲wí:les**>, ds //sax̣ʷ(=əl)=í·l=əs//, TIME /'*month or moon of March to April, grass moon*'/, literally /'grass =comes =cyclic period, when the grass comes'/, (<**=í:l**> *come, go, get, become*), lx <**=es**> *cyclic period, round thing, on the face*, phonology: possible syllable-loss (if el is part of the root only), syntactic analysis: nominal, attested by AC, other sources: Jenness's field notes on interviews of William Sepass of Sardis.

<**sox̲weláwtxw**>, BLDG /'*barn, (hay house, grass building)*'/, *see* só:x̲wel ~ sóx̲wel.

<**sox̲wí:les**>, TIME /'*month or moon of March to April, grass moon*'/, *see* só:x̲wel ~ sóx̲wel.

<**sóy**>, bound root //sáy *dim*//.

<**sóyt**>, pcs //sáy=T//, LT ['*dim it*'], (<**=t**> *purposeful control transitivizer*), syntactic analysis: transitive verb, attested by IHTTC, example: <**sóytlha ta yeqwí:l.**>, //sáy=T-ɬɛ t-ɛ yəqʷ=í·l//, /'*Dim your lamp.*'/, attested by IHTTC.

<**só:yel**>, incs //sá·y=əl//, [sá·y=ɪl], LT /'*(get) dusk, (get dim)*'/, literally /'get dim'/, (<**=í:l**> *go, come, get, become*), syntactic analysis: intransitive verb, attested by DM (12/4/64).

<**sóyéx̱el**>, ds //sáy=ə́x̣əl//, LAND ['*edge of the world*'], LT ['*sunset*'], literally /'dim portion/part'/, lx <**=éx̱el**> *part, portion*, syntactic analysis: nominal, attested by Deming (3/15/79) (SJ, MC, MV, LG), ASM ['sunset'], example: <**kwímel te sóyéx̱el.**>, //kʷím=əl tə sáy=ə́x̣əl//, /'*The sunset is getting red.*'/.

<**súyéx̱el**>, ds //sa[=Aú=]y=ə́x̣əl or súy=ə́x̣əl//, LAND ['*on the other side of the world*'], ASM ['when Black Bear's children wandered over to the other side of the world, beyond the sunset/horizon they returned as the Transformers, spirits of the deceased sometimes wander on this side before they reach their proper place on the other side of the world'], possibly <**ú-ablaut**> *derivational*, phonology: possible ablaut (or this may be Nooksack or Lushootseed influence in using cognate /u/ instead of /a/), syntactic analysis: nominal, attested by Deming (3/15/79) (SJ, MC, MV, LG); found in <**lílhtsel kw'e súyéx̱el.**>, //lí-ɬ-c-əl k'ʷə súy=ə́x̣əl//, phonology: sung to the rhythm of (half note, dotted quarter, eighth, quarter, quarter, half) and the melody (so, mi, so, mi, mi, re), usage: Ida Ensley's spirit song, attested by Deming (3/15/79)(SJ, MC, MV, LG).

<**só:yel**>, LT /'*(get) dusk, (get dim)*'/, *see* sóy.

<**sóyéx̱el**>, LAND ['*edge of the world*'], *see* sóy.

<**sóyt**>, LT ['*dim it*'], *see* sóy.

<**sṓp**>, free root //sóp//, PE ['*soap*'], syntactic analysis: noun, nominal, dialects: *Chill.*, attested by Elders Group (6/1/77), also <**súp**>, //súp//, dialects: *Cheh., Tait*, attested by Elders Group (6/1/77).

<**sṓ:q't ~ séwq't ~ sú:q't ~ súwq't**>, pcs //só·q'=T ~ sú·q'=T ~ sə́w(=)q'=T ~ súw(=)q'=T//, TVMO ['*search for s-o*'], possibly <**=q'**> *on s-th else*, (<**=t**> *purposeful control transitivizer*), phonology: vocalization, syntactic analysis: transitive verb, attested by Adeline Lorenzerro (Elders Group 3/72, tape 33), EB (2/9/76), IHTTC (SP, AK, AD, EB), example: <**kw'as sṓ:q't li te qó**>, //k'ʷ-ɛ-s só·q'=T li tə qá//, /'*that you drag the water for s-o, that you search for s-o in the water*'/, attested by AL (Elders Group 3/72), <**sú:q't lí te qó**>, //sú·q'=T lí tə qá//, /'*search for s-o in the water (dragging for them)*'/, attested by EB, <**éwe stlíses meytóxwes welámet súwq'tòlè.**>, //ʔə́wə s=ƛ'í-s-əs mɛy=T-áxʷ-əs wə-lɛ́=m-ət súw=q'=T-álə//, /'*He doesn't want to help us (when we) go find you folks.*'/, dialects: *Tait*, attested by SP and AK and AD (IHTTC 8/22/77), also <**éwe stl'íses kws meytóxwes welámet súwq'tòlè.**>, //ʔə́wə s=ƛ'í-s-əs kʷ-s mɛy=T-áxʷ-əs wə-lɛ́=m-ət súw=q'=t-álə//, dialects: *Cheh.*, attested by EB (IHTTC 8/22/77), also <**éwe stlís kw'es meytólxws welámet séwq'tòlè.**>, //ʔə́wə s=ƛ'í-s k'ʷə-s mɛy=T-álxʷ-s wə-lɛ́=m-ət sə́w=q'=T-álə//, dialects: *Chill.*, attested by NP (IHTTC 8/22/77).

<**sōqw'áx̱el**>, BLDG ['*lower [downriver] end of house (inside or outside)*'], *see* wṓqw' ~ wéqw'.

<**sōqw'ólwelh**>, DIR ['*(be) downstream below something*'], *see* wṓqw' ~ wéqw'.

<**spá:lxw**>, df //s=pi[=Aɛ́·=]l=xʷ//, EB /'*blue camas, (any edible underground vegetable food [SP], vegetable root(s)* [MH])'/, *see* pél > **(~ <pí:l** > by now**)**, *planted, get buried*

<**spapí:l**>, LAND ['*(be) buried*'], *see* pél (perhaps ~ pí:l by now).

<**spáplhx̱el**>, LAND /'*meadow, (little prairie)*'/, *see* spélhx̱el.

<**spapx̱íwel**>, ABFC /'*spread one's legs (while sitting for example), (be spread in the bottom)*'/, *see* páx̱.

<**spatálép ~ spatálep**>, df //s=pɛt=ɛ́ləp//, ANAH /'*thigh, leg above the knee*'/, (<**s=**> *nominalizer*), root meaning unknown, lx <**=álep**> *on the upper leg*, phonology: updrifting, syntactic analysis: nominal, attested by DM (12/4/64), JL (5/5/75).

<**spá:th**>, EZ /'*bear (generic),* esp. *black bear,* also includes *brown bear, bear with a white breast, and grizzly bear* though these all have separate names'/, *see* pá:th.

<**Spá:th**>, PLN ['*bear-shaped rock up on cliff on south side above Echo Point bay on Echo Island in Harrison Lake*'], *see* pá:th.

<**spàthélets**>, ABFC ['*bear dung*'], *see* pá:th.

<**spathó:llh**>, EZ ['*bear cub*'], *see* pá:th.

<**spayő:l**>, free root //spɛyó·l//, SOCT ['*Spaniard*'], syntactic analysis: nominal, attested by BHTTC (11/19/76), borrowed from Spanish <Español>/ʔɛspænyól/ *Spanish.*

<**spehá:ls**>, WETH ['*wind*'], *see* peh or pó(:)h.

<**spekw'ém**>, EB /'*bloom or (plant) fuzz (spore, pollen, seed fluff) after it bursts*'/, *see* pékw' ~ péqw'.

<**speláwél**>, EZ ['*mole*'], *see* pél (perhaps ~ pí:l by now).

<**spelékw**>, ABDF ['*(have) smallpox*'], *see* pél:ékw.

<**spélmàlà**>, BLDG ['*root house*'], *see* pél (perhaps ~ pí:l by now).

<**spelól**>, EZ /'*smaller crow, northwestern crow*'/, *see* spó:l.

<**spelwálh**>, df //s=pəl=wɛ́(=ə)ɬ//, TIME ['*last year*'], *see* pel or **pel=**> probably *season, time of*

<**spelwálh qwá:l**>, EZ /'*cranefly, leatherjacket (immature cranefly)*'/, *see* qwá:l.

<**spélhx̲el**>, df //s=pə́ɬ(=)x̣(=)əl//, LAND /'*prairie, grassy open land, (grassy valley [EB, Gibbs, Elders Group]*'/, *see* pélhx̲el> meaning possibly *get flat all around*

<**spepelól ~ spepeló:l**>, EZ /'*little crows, small crows, bunch of small crows, (bunch of northwestern crows)*'/, *see* spó:l.

<**spepíláwtxw**>, HARV /'*root cellar, (root house [AD]*'/, *see* pél (perhaps ~ pí:l by now).

<**spepíx̲**>, CLO /'*(be) tight-fitting (of clothes, can't be quite buttoned)*'/, *see* páx̲.

<**speqá:s**>, EZ /'*white Fraser River spring salmon that goes upriver with the red spring salmon, (white Fraser River chinook salmon)*'/, *see* peqá:s, possible root or stem

<**Speqwő:lh ~ Spōqwőwelh**>, PLN /'*Chehalis River mouth (below the highway bridge, where land is breaking up into sand bars), (an opening one could get through in a canoe in high water near Chehalis IHTTC 8/25/77], small creek (branch of Chehalis River) several hundred yards up Chehalis River from where the road goes from old Chehalis village site to Chehalis River [EL 9/27/77])*'/, *see* péqw.

<**spéxw**>, df //s=pə́x^w//, ANA ['*tripe*'], *see* péxw.

<**spexwlhálém**> *to breathe (once), see* under dialect variant <**pexwlhálém**>

<**spèxwelhá:lém**>, *breathing,* also /'*breathe (when you breathe in and out), breathe air*'/, *see* under dialect variant <**pexwelhálém**>.

<**spéxwqel ~ spéx̲wqel**>, EB /'*fine airborne seed(s) (not used of plum or apple seed(s) or the hard seeds -- sth'emíwél is used for those) (used for dandelion seeds, cottonwood seeds, etc., tail of a cat-tail reed, (plant fluff* (possibly including *tail of cat-tail rush)* [Elders Group 2/27/80])'/, *see* píxw.

<**spéxwqels te syóqwem sp'áq'em**>, EB ['*sunflower seeds*'] (lit. small airborne seed of + the + sun + flower), *see* píxw.

<**spex̲elís**>, CLO /*'(be) tight-fitting (of clothes, can't be quite buttoned)'*/, *see* páx̲.

<**spéx̲em ~ spó:x̲em**>, EZ [*'early (March) spring salmon'*], *see* pó:x̲ ~ péx̲

<**spéx̲wqel ~ spéxwqel**>, EB /*'fine airborne seed(s) (not used of plum or apple seed(s) or the hard seeds -- sth'emíwél is used for those) (used for dandelion seeds, cottonwood seeds, etc., tail of a cat-tail reed, (plant fluff (*possibly including *tail of cat-tail rush)* [Elders Group 2/27/80])'/, *see* píxw.

<**spí:ls**>, HARV /*'the planting, seeds to plant, what* is planted (sown), garden'/, *see* pél (perhaps ~ pí:l by now).

<**spíls s'élhtel sqe'óleqw**>, *vegetable juice* (lit. planted + food + fruit juice), *see* pél (perhaps ~ pí:l by now).

<**spípew**>, WATR [*'be frozen'*], *see* pí:w.

<**spipíyxel**>, ABDF /*'(have a) crooked leg, (be a) crooked-legged person'*/, *see* pó:y.

<**spít**>, free root //spít//, PLAY [*'spade (suit in cards)'*], syntactic analysis: nominal, attested by Elders Group (9/14/77), borrowed from English /spéyd/ *spade*.

<**spí:w**>, WATR [*'ice'*], *see* pí:w.

<**Spíyem**>, df //s=píy=əm//, PLN /*'Spuzzum village (on south bank of Spuzzum Creek at its mouth onto the Fraser River),* also *Spuzzum Creek'*/, ASM ['this is the southern-most village in Thompson territory but may not be a borrowing of the Thompson name for the village'], possibly <**s=**> *nominalizer or stative*, possibly <**=em**> *place to get*, possibly root <**píy**> *braced/supported/steadied with one's hands*, comment: this etymology fits phonologically but is pure conjecture semantically for the site, possibly root <**pó:y**> *bend* with <**í-ablaut**> *durative*, comment: this is the Halkomelem name for the nearest Thompson settlement, the Thompson language has a different name for it, (semological comment: there is a big bend in the Fraser River here), syntactic analysis: nominal, attested by AD and AK (on trip to Five-Mile Creek 4/30/79), *also see* <**píy**> *braced/supported/steadied with one's hands* and <**pó:y**> *bend*.

<**spíytses**>, ABDF [*'(have a) crooked hand'*], *see* pó:y.

<**spó:l**>, dnom //s=pá·l//, EZ /*'big crow, common crow,* also known as *western crow or American crow, (raven [EF, some Deming elders])'*/, [*'Corvus brachyrhynchos,* (*Corvus corax* [EF, some Deming elders])'], ASM ['one difference between the crow and the raven is that the raven's cry is more noticeable (like a hoarse woman's voice) and less frequent, when a crow cries in a certain way it predicts bad news, it cried máw, máw ([mǽw mǽw], no gloss known) when it delivered good news in a story recorded by Boas 1895 (Bertz 1977 translation)'], (<**s=**> *nominalizer*), root meaning unknown, syntactic analysis: nominal, attested by AC, BJ (12/5/64), Elders Group (3/1/72, 6/4/75, 2/18/76, 3/28/79, 1/16/80), EB, also <**spól'**>, //s=pálʔ//, dialects: prob. *Matsqui or Sumas*, attested by a speaker at Deming (AH?), also /*'raven'*/, attested by EF and some others at Deming (4/17/80), other sources: ES /spa·l/ (circumflex over a) *raven* beside /spəlál/ *crow*, JH /spá·l/ *crow, raven*, but H-T <skaúEks> *raven (Corvus corax principalis)* beside <spEpEtál> (macron over a) (t sic for l) *crow (Corvus caurinus)* (H-T's forms correspond to terms and glosses I found most frequently), same entry found under possible root pó:l.

<**speló̲l**>, dmn //s=p[=əC_2=]ál//, EZ /*'smaller crow, northwestern crow'*/, [*'Corvus caurinus'*], (<**=R6=**> *diminutive*), phonology: reduplication, syntactic analysis: nominal, attested by AC, other sources: ES /spəlál/ *crow*, H-T <spEpEtál> (macron over a) *crow (Corvus caurinus)(cry resembles skak brother)*.

<**spopelál**>, df //s=pa[=C_1ə=C2ɛ́=]l or s=pa[=R[=əl=]9]l//, EZ ['*crow*'], ['prob. *Corvus caurinus*'], possibly <=**R1**= or =**R9**=> *diminutive or derivational*, possibly <=**C2ɛ́**=> meaning uncertain, <=**el**=> *plural*?, phonology: reduplication (unusual types), syntactic analysis: nominal, attested by Elders Group (5/3/78).

<**spepelól ~ spepeló:l**>, dmpn //s=C_1ə=p[=əl=]á·l//, EZ /'*little crows, small crows, bunch of small crows, (bunch of northwestern crows)*'/, ['*Corvus caurinus*'], (<**R5**=> *diminutive*), (<=**el**=> *plural*), phonology: reduplication, infixed plural, syntactic analysis: nominal, attested by Elders Group (2/18/76, 6/4/75), AC, also <**spepelól'**>, //s=C_1ə=p[=əl=]álʔ//, also /'*small crow*'/, dialects: prob. *Matsqui or Sumas*, attested by Deming (prob. AH), other sources: H-T <spEpEtál> (macron over a)(t sic for l) *crow (Corvuscaurinus)*.

<**spóléqwem**>//s=pə[=Aá=lə=]q^w=əm//, LAND ['*dust*'], *see* main variant <**pó:lqw'em**> under <**pékw' ~ péqw'**> /'*smoke puffing out, (puff out (dust, powder, plant spores, seed fluff, light snow, smoke), form puffs of dust)*'/.

<**spoleqwíth'a**>, REL /'*ghost, corpse, dead body*'/, *see* poleqwíth'a, possibly lit. *thing that moulds/rots much clothing* if root is póqw *to mould, to rot*.

<**spólqw'**>, DESC ['*be powdered*'], *see* pékw' ~ péqw'.

<**spólqw' seplí:l**>, //s=pə[=Aá=lə=]q'^{w} səplí·l//, /'*flour*'/, *see* pékw' ~ péqw'.

<**spó:ltsep**>, df //s=pá·lcəp//, EZ /'*"grayling"*, probably *mountain whitefish*'/, probably ['*Prosopium williamsoni*'], (<**s**=> *nominalizer*), root meaning unknown, syntactic analysis: nominal, attested by Elders Group (7/9/75), EZ /'*cut-throat trout, coastal cut-troat trout*'/, ['*Salmo clarki clarki*'], attested by MJ and JL and AC (10/62 tape by Oliver Wells) (copied with Elders Group 3/28/79).

<**spopelál**>, EZ ['*crow*'], *see* spó:l.

<**spopeleqwíth'a ~ spopeleqwíth'e**>, EZ /'*screech owl especially,* probably *other small owls,* but only *the screech owl* is consistently mentioned by all speakers'/, *see* poleqwíth'a.

<**spópeqw**>, EB /'*mould (on food, clothes, etc.)*'/, *see* póqw.

<**Spópetes**>, PLN /'*Katz river-bank, Ruby Creek settlement, village on north bank of Fraser River just below (west of) the mouth of Ruby Creek*'/, *see* pó:t.

<**spópe<u>x</u>welsà:ls**>, HHG ['*spray gun*'], *see* pó<u>x</u>w.

<**spópiy**>, DESC /'*be bent, be crooked*'/, *see* pó:y.

<**spotelálá**>, CAN ['*mast on a canoe or boat*'], *see* pó:t.

<**spó:<u>x</u>em ~ spé<u>x</u>em**>, EZ ['*early (March) spring salmon*'], *see* pó:<u>x</u> ~ pé<u>x</u>

<**spóypiy**>, DESC ['*be crooked [characteristically]*'], *see* pó:y.

<**Spōqwṓwelh ~ Speqwṓ:lh**>, PLN /'*Chehalis River mouth (below the highway bridge, where land is breaking up into sand bars), (an opening one could get through in a canoe in high water near Chehalis IHTTC 8/25/77], small creek (branch of Chehalis River) several hundred yards up Chehalis River from where the road goes from old Chehalis village site to Chehalis River [EL 9/27/77])*'/, *see* péqw.

<**spú:l**>, free root //spú·l//, FOOD ['*(metal) spoon*'], PE, HHG, ASM ['this word is just for non-Indian spoons, there are several words for different types of Indian spoons carved from wood or animal horn'], syntactic analysis: nominal, attested by AD, borrowed from English /spú:n/ *spoon*, example: <**alétsa te spú:l?**>, //ʔɛlə́cɛ tə spú·l//, /'*Where is the spoon?*'/.

<**spú'**>, ABFC ['*a fart*'], *see* pú'.

<**spú'amal ~ spú'emel**>, ANAA /'*skunk's stink bag, skunk's stink sac*'/, *see* pú'.

<**sp'áp'eth'**>, WV ['*(be) sewed (already)*'], *see* p'áth'.

<**sp'ap'ílh**>, EFAM ['*(be) sober*'], *see* p'élh.

<**sp'ap'ílh**>, DESC ['*(be) flattened*'], *see* p'ílh.

<**sp'á:q'em**>, EB ['*flower*'], *see* p'áq'em.

<**sp'áq'ems te álhqey**>, EB /'"*snake's flower*", prob. *same plant as "snakeberry", q.v.*'/, *see* álhqey ~ álhqay.

<**sp'á:th'**>, EB /'*red-flowering currant berry, Indian currant berry,* probably also *stink currant berry* also called *skunk currant berry*'/, *see* p'á:th'>, probably derived stem //p[='=]ɛ́·θ'// from <**páth'**> *animal stink, body odor*

<**sp'á:th'elhp**>, EB /'*Indian currant bush, red-flowering currant bush,* prob. also *stink currant bush*'/, <**p'á:th'**>, probably derived stem //p[='=]ɛ́·θ'// from <**páth'**> *animal stink, body odor.*

<**sp'eláp'q'em**>, EB ['*little flowers*'], *see* p'áq'em.

<**sp'élxwem**>, df //s=p'ə́lxʷ=əm//, ANA /'*lung, lungs (both)*'/, *see* p'élxwem

<**sp'élhqsel ~ sp'íp'elheqsel**>, ANA ['*(have a) flat nose*'], *see* p'ílh.

<**sp'ep'ákw'**>, WATR ['*(be) floating*'], *see* p'ékw.

<**sp'eq'p'íq'**>, LT ['*(have?) white spots*'], *see* p'éq'.

<**sp'éqw'**>, strs //s=p'i[=Aə́=]q'ʷ//, EFAM ['*(be) proud*'], *see* p'íqw'

<**sp'ewéy**>, MC ['*(be) patched*'], *see* p'ewíy ~ p'ōwíy.

<**sp'íp'ehà:th' ~ sp'íp'ehàth'**>, EZ /'*speckled trout, (*prob. *brook trout,* also called *speckled char)*'/, *see* sp'á:th', under p'á:th'.

<**sp'íp'elh**>, DESC ['*(be) flat*'], *see* p'ílh.

<**sp'íp'elheqsel ~ sp'élhqsel**>, ANA ['*(have a) flat nose*'], *see* p'ílh.

<**sp'íp'elheqw**>, ANA /'*(have a) flat head, (have cranial deformation by cradle-board)*'/, *see* p'ílh.

<**sp'íp'eqw'el**>, LT ['*[be getting/going purple]*'], *see* p'íqw'.

<**sp'íp'e<u>x</u>wel**>, LT /'*(tan, brownish)*'/, *see* p'íp'e<u>x</u>wel.

<**sp'íp'e'àth'**>, *see* main dialect form <**sp'íp'ehà:th' ~ sp'íp'ehàth'**>, EZ /'*speckled trout, (*prob. *brook trout,* also called *speckled char)*'/, *see* sp'á:th'.

<**sp'íq'**>, ABDF ['*(have?) white spotted skin*'], *see* p'éq'.

<**sp'íqw'**>, LT ['*purple*'], *see* p'íqw'.

<**sp'óp'eqw'em**>, HHG ['*soap*'], *see* p'óqw'em.

<**sp'óq'es**>, EZ ['*bald eagle (mature with white head)*'], *see* p'éq'.

<**sp'óqw'em**>, WATR ['*foam*'], *see* p'óqw'em.

<**sp'ó:tl'em ~ sp'ótl'em**>, FIRE ['*smoke*'], *see* p'ótl'em.

<**sp'òtl'emálá ~ sp'ótl'emàlà**>, PE ['*pipe (for smoking)*'], *see* p'ótl'em.

<**sp'otl'emá:látel**>, BLDG ['*smokehole*'], *see* p'ótl'em.

<**sp'otl'emáleqep**>, SM ['*(have a) smoky smell*'], *see* p'ótl'em.

<**sp'q'í:l ~ sp'q'é:yl**>, LT ['*[be get/go/become white]*'], *see* p'éq'.

<**sqá:la**>, df //(s=)sq(=)ɛ́·lɛ//, EB ['*red huckleberry*'], ['*Vaccinium parvifolium*'], ASM ['berries ripe and edible mid-July, they were harvested by clubbing the branches on the hand and the berries fell into the basket which was hung under them'], (possibly <**s=**> *nominalizer*), root probabnly seq *hang under*, possibly <**=á:la**> *container of*, thus lit. /'*s-th to hang a container under* '/, syntactic analysis: nominal, attested by Elders Group, AC, *see* seq, contrast <**skw'éqwtses**> *red huckleberry*.

<**sqá:lá:lhp ~ qá:lá:lhp**>, ds //s=qɛ́lɛ=ɛ́ɬp ~ qɛ́·lɛ=ɛ́ɬp or qɛ́·lɛ=əɬp//, EB ['*red huckleberry bush*'], ['*Vaccinium parvifolium*'], lx <**=álhp ~ =elhp**> *plant, tree*, phonology: vowel merger, syntactic analysis: nominal, attested by Elders Group, SP, others.

<**sqá:lá:lhp ~ qá:lá:lhp**>, EB ['*red huckleberry bush*'], *see* sqá:la.

<**sqá:lex̲ ~ sqálex̲**>, df //s=qʷ[=U=]ɛ́(·)=əl=əx̣ or s=qɛ́(·)l=əx̣//, [sqǽ·ləx̣ ~ sqǽləx̣], HARV ['*digging stick*'], *see* **qá(:)l** *twist.*

<**sqám**>, WATR /'*(have) quieter water, died down a little*'/, *see* qám.

<**Sqám**>, PLN ['*Schkam Lake near Haig*'], *see* qám.

<**Sqám ~ Sqà:m**>, PLN /'*Haig bay, a calm place on the west (C.P.R.) side of the Fraser River by the Haig railroad stop, below and across from Hope*'/, *see* qám.

<**sqá:q**>, dnom //s=qɛ́q//, KIN /'*younger sibling, younger brother, younger sister, child of younger sibling of one's parent, "younger" cousin (could even be fourth cousin [through younger sibling of one's great great grandparent])*'/, *see* qá:q or seq.

<**sqá:qele ~ sqáqele**>, SOCT ['*baby*'], *see* qá:q or seq.

<**sqáqem**>, WATR ['*calm water (calmer than sqám)*'], *see* qám.

<**sqáwth ~ sqá:wth**>, df //s=qɛ́wθ or s=qə[=Aɛ́=]w=θ//, EB /'*potato (generic), including three or four kinds of wild potato: arrowleaf or wapato, Jerusalem artichoke, blue camas, and qíqemxel (so far unidentified plant), besides post-contact domestic potato*'/, ['including: *Sagittaria latifolia, Helianthus tuberosus, Camassia quamash* (and *Camassia leichtlinii*), and unidentified plant, besides *Solanum tuberosum*'], *see* qáwth ~ qá:wth.

<**sqáyéx̲ ~ sqayéx̲**>, df //s=qɛ́yə́x̣ ~ s=qɛyə́x̣ or s=qɛ́y=ə[=´=]x̣//, EZ ['*mink*'], ['*Mustela vison energumenos*'], N ['*Mink (name in some stories)*'], *see* qayéx̲.

<**Sqayéx̲iya ~ Sqáyéx̲iya**>, N /'*Mink (name in stories), pet name of Mink*'/, *see* qayéx̲.

<**Sqayéx̲iya Smált ~ Sqáqeyex̲iya Smált**>, PLN ['*small shoreline ridge on the Fraser River and all along the river around the larger mountain across the Trans-Canada Highway from Jones Hill*'], *see* qayéx̲.

<**sqelá:lh**>, CLO ['*diaper*'], *see* qél.

<**sqelá:q**>, KIN /'*younger siblings, "younger" cousins (first, second, or third cousins [whose connecting ancestor is younger than ego's])*'/, *see* qá:q or seq.

<**Sqelá:w (Stótelō)**>, PLN ['*Beaver Creek (at U.S.-Canada boundary line)*'], *see* sqelá:w *under* seq..

<**Sqelá:w (X̲óx̲tsa)**>, PLN ['*Beaver Lake or Hanging Lake*'], *see* sqelá:w *under* seq.

<**sqel:ép ~ sqél:ep**>, LAND ['*a lot of dirt*'], EB ['*weeds*'], VALJ /'*nuisance, something that's no good*'/, MC /'*garbage, trash*'/, literally /'something bad/dirty on the ground'/, *see* qél.

<**sqél:éxw**>, EFAM ['*be greedy*'], *see* qél:éxw ~ qel(:)éxw.

<**sqel:éxw**>, BPI /'*someone who is greedy, someone who eats all the time, (glutton)*'/, *see* qél:éxw ~ qel(:)éxw.

<**sqeló:líth'a**>, df //s=qəlá·l=íθɛ//, WETH ['*west wind*'], probably <**s=**> *nominalizer or stative*, lx <**=íth'a**> *clothes*, root meaning unknown, syntactic analysis: nominal, attested by Elders Group (2/5/75), *see* qeló:l.

<**Sqelóts'emes**>, N ['*Bobcat*'], *see* sqets'ómes.

<**sqéls**>, HARV /'*part not used (like seeds of cantelope, core of apple, blood in fish, etc.), worst part*'/, *see* qél.

<**sqeltí:l**>, EFAM ['*hate*'], *see* qél.

<**sqelwílh**>, EFAM /'*hold a grudge, hate*'/, *see* qél.

<**sqelwílhmet ~ qelwílhmet**>, EFAM ['*hate s-o*'], *see* qél.

<**sqélxel**>, dnom //s=qə́l=x^yəl//, CLO ['*moccasin*'], literally /'(poss.) something that encircles on the foot'/, (<**s=**> *nominalizer, something that*), root (possibly) < **qel**> *encircle* as in <**qel=wíls**> *hug*, lx <**=xel**> *on the foot*, syntactic analysis: nominal, attested by BJ (5/64), DM (12/4/64), others (Elders Group), *see* qélxel.

<**sqelxwá:le ~ sqelxwále**>, ANA /'*throat (inside part), gullet, voice*'/, *see* qél:éxw ~ qel(:)éxw.

<**sqelyíqem (**or **sq'elyíqem)**>, WETH ['*a snowdrift*'], *see* yíq.

<**sqemálá**>, CLO ['*bra*'], *see* qemó:.

<**sqémél**>, df //s=qə́mə́l or s=qə́m=ə[´]l//, BLDG /'*pit-house, keekwillie house, semi-subterranean house*'/, *see* qémél *and* seq.

<**sqém:el**>, WATR ['*(the) tide*'], *see* qém:el.

<**Sqémelech**>, PLN /'*wide place in Maria Slough (just north of Lougheed Highway bridge), west mouth of Maria Slough*'/, *see* qám.

<**sqemélwélh ~ sqemélwelh**>, PLN /'*place in Katz or Ruby Creek, may be name for Charlie Joe's place near Katz at the mouth of a creek where the water is always calm*'/, *see* qám.

<**sqemí:l**>, BLDG ['*be inside a pit-house*'], *see* sqémél.

<**sqemó:**>, ANAH /'*breast, nipple, milk*'/, *see* qemó: *suckle*.

<**sqemó'álá**>, HHG ['*baby bottle*'], *see* qemó:.

<**Sqemqémelets**>, PLN ['*bay at upper end of Yale Indian Reserve #2 (Four-and-a-half Mile Creek) (near the northern end of Stó:lō territory)*'], *see* qám.

<**sqémqsel**>, ANA /'*(have a) hook nose, beak nose, Roman nose, (be bent-nosed)*'/, *see* qém.

<**sqépò:thél**>, EZ ['*flying squirrel*'], *see* qep'.

<**sqep'óleqwtelxel**>, df //s=q'əp=áləq^w=təl=x^yəl (perhaps error for //s=qəp'=áləq^w=təl=x^yəl)//, ANA ['*kneecap*'], *see* qep'.

<**sqep'ó:lthetel**>, ANA ['*knee (someone's)*'], *see* qep'.

<**sqeqewíthelh**>, EB ['*arrowleaf*'], *see* qáwth ~ qá:wth.

<**sqeqó:qel**>, WATR ['*(clean) pond (even if dry)*'], *see* qó:.

<**sqetás**>, FOOD /'*stuff steam-cooked underground, what is baked underground*'/, *see* qá:t.

<**sqets'ómes**>, df //s=qəc'ám(=)əs or s=qəc'(=)ɛ[=Aá=]m=əs or s=qəc'=əm=á[=M2=]s or s=qác'=ə[=M2=]m=əs//, EZ ['*bobcat*'], ['*Lynx rufus fasciatus*'], *see* qets'ómes.

<**sqewálets**>, ABFC /'*warming your bum, (be warming the bottom or rump)*'/, *see* qew.

<**sqewá:meth'**>, EB /'*first warmed side of a tree, sunny side of a tree*'/, *see* qew.

<**sqewáth**>, df /s=qʷɛ́=əθ//, EZ /'*(larger) rabbit: snowshoe or varying hare,* now probably also *eastern cottontail rabbit (*introduced*)*'/, ['*Lepus americanus cascadensis and Lepus americanus washingtoni,* now probably also *Sylvilagus floridanus mearnsi*'], *see* qewáth *and* qwá.

<**sqéweqs**>, df //s=qə́w=əqs// perhaps from //s=qʷ[-metathesis of vowel and labialization]ɛ́=əqs// as with the word for *rabbit* from same root, thus the raven is literally *something that has a hole in the nose*, due to the large holes in its beak, otherwise poss. root <qew> *warm* would yield lit. *something that warms his nose*, EZ ['*raven*'], ['*Corvus corax*'], ASM ['one cry resembles a hoarse woman's voice, ravens crowing in a certain way and going toward or by a house forecast a death in that family; a big bird (larger than a crow), lives to be about 100 yrs. old'], (<**s=**> *nominal*), root meaning unknown, lx <**=eqs**> *on the nose, point*, syntactic analysis: nominal, attested by AC, also <**skéweqs**>, //s=q[=K=]əw=əqs//, (<**=K=** or **fronting**> *diminutive*), attested by AC, SP and others, dialects: *Chill., Tait*, other sources: JH /sqáwəqs/ *raven*, H-T <skaúEks> *raven (Corvus corax principalis)*, Salish cognate: Lushootseed /skáw'qs/ *raven; Brother of* /k'áʔk'aʔ/ *in myth age*, example: <**qéx̲ te sqéweqs. ~ qéx̲ te skéweqs.**>, //qə́x̣ tə s=qə́w=əqs ~ qə́x̣ tə s=q[=K=]ə́w=əqs//, /'*There's a lot of ravens.*'/, attested by AC, *see* qwá *and* qéw.

<**sqewós**>, LAND ['*warm side*'], *see* qew.

<**Sqéyiya**>, df //s=qə́y-iyɛ or s=qíy=iyɛ//, N ['*Bluejay*'], semantic environment ['name only in a story'], (<**s=**> *nominalizer*), root <**qéy**> meaning unknown unless *encircle*, lx <**=iya**> *diminutive*, syntactic analysis: nominal, attested by BHTTC, *see* qéy.

<**sqéymeqw'**>, df //s=qí·məq'ʷ or sq=í·m=əq'ʷʔ//, EZ ['*octopus*'], ['probably genus *Octopus*, the Squamish cognate is identified as *Octopus apollyon*'], possibly <**s=**> *nominalizer* or more likely <**seq**> *hang under*, possibly <**=í:m**> *repeatedly*, <**=eqw'**>*around in circles* (see Galloway 1993:234), lit. *something that hangs under repeatedly around in circles* (which could describe the tentacles going around in circles hanging under), syntactic analysis: nominal, attested by SP with others agreeing from Deming (7/7/77), Salish cognate: Lushootseed /s-qíbk'ʷ/ *octopus and squid* H76:384, Samish dial. of N. Straits VU /sqé·ymək'ʷ/ *octopus* versus VU /píl·əwəs ~ qəm'k'ʷá·ɬ/ *large octopus* G86:68.

<**sqéytes**>ds //qít=əs//, [qétɪs], CLO /'*headband, headband made out of cedar bark woven by widow or widower when mourning*'/, see main dialect form <**qítes ~ qéytes**>, under qít.

<**sqe'éleqw**>, ANAH /'*soft spot on (top of) a baby's head, fontanel*'/, *see* qí: ~ qí'.

<**sqe'éleqw ~ sqe'óleqw**>, EB ['*fruit juice*'], *see* qó:.

<**sqe'íyeqel ~ sqe'í:qel**>, df //s=qəʔí(y)=qəl ~ s=qəʔí·=qəl//, EFAM ['*not know how to*'], *see* qe'íy ~ qe'í:.

<**sqe'iyeqeló:ythel ~ sqe'iqeló:ythel**>, LANG ['*not fluent in speaking*'], *see* sqe'íyeqel ~ sqe'í:qel under qe'íy ~ qe'í:..

<**sqe'óleqw**>, FOOD ['*soda pop*'], *see* qó:.

<**sqe'ó:ls**>, EB [*'juicy fruit'*], *see* qó:.

<**sqiqáq**>, KIN [*'small younger sibling'*], *see* qá:q or seq.

<**sqiqelá:w**>, EZ [*'little beaver'*], *see* sqelá:w *under* seq.

<**sqíqeló:ythel**>, LANG [*'can't talk right'*], *see* qél.

<**sqíqemel**>, BLDG [*'puberty hut'*], *see* sqémél.

<**sqíqemlò**>, df //s=C_1í=qəmlà or possibly?? s=C_1í=qá·lə[=M2=]m=M2=M1//, [sqíqəmlà], EZ [*'minnow'*], *see* <**qó:lem**> *scoop* under <**qó:**> *water*.

<**Sqíqemlò**>, PLN [*'point of land on Harrison River (somewhere between Lheltá:lets and Híqelem) where during a famine the old people scooped minnows and boiled them to make soup'*], *see* sqíqemlò.

<**sqíqewàth**>, EZ /*'rabbit: snowshoe/varying hare,* now probably also *eastern cottontail rabbit (*introduced*), (baby rabbit, small rabbit or hare [Elders Group])'*/, *see* sqewáth and qwá.

<**sqiqewóthel**>, EZ /*'big rabbit, older rabbit, big/older snowshoe/varying hare,* now probably also *big/older eastern cottontail rabbit (*introduced*)'*/, *see* sqewáth and qwá.

<**sqó:m**>, WATR /*'water (someone) carried, (water fetched/gotten)'*/, *see* qó:.

<**sqó:qe**>, WATR [*'a drink'*], *see* qó:.

<**sqóqem**>, DESC /*'(be) bent, (*perhaps *bent round)'*/, *see* qém.

<**sqó:s**>, ANA [*'a tear (on the face)'*], *see* qó:.

<**sqotemí:lep ~ sqoteméylep**>, df //s=qat(=)əm=í·ləp//, LAND /*'steep hill, sloping ground'*/, (<**s=**> *nominalizer*), root meaning unknown, lx <**=í:lep**> *ground, earth, dirt*, syntactic analysis: nominal, attested by Elders Group (4/2/75), also <**sqotemílep**>, df //s(=)qat(=)əm=íləp//, LAND [*'hill'*], possibly <**s=**> *nominalizer*, possibly <**=em**> *intransitivizer, get, have*, root meaning unknown, lx <**=ílep**> *dirt, earth, ground*, syntactic analysis: nominal, attested by Elders Group (3/15/72), *see* qot-.

<**sqoyép ~ melmélkw'es sqoyép**>, df //s=qay(=)ə́p ~ C_1əC_2=mə́lk'^{w}=əs s=qay=ə́p//, EZ /*'yellow badger, possibly wolverine'*/, [*'Taxidea taxus taxus,* possibly *Gulo luscus luscus'*], ASM ['wolverine is probably in error here'], literally <**melmélkw'es**> is /*'hit many times on the face by something falling '*/ due to the stripes on the face (Elder's comment: "this animal got hit on the face in a story [of the Transformer age, time of X̲à:ls] and the marks stayed", from an origin story like raccoon), (<**s=**> *nominalizer*, R3= *plural agent or action*, <**=es**> *on the face*), root <**mélkw'**> *hit by something falling*, for <qoy or qoyép>, possibly <**=ép**> *on the ground, dirt, ground*, phonology: reduplication, syntactic analysis: nominal ~ simple nominal phrase, attested by AK and ME (11/21/72 tape), IHTTC, contrast Tait <skoyám> *wolverine (Gulo luscus luscus)*; *see* mélkw' *and* qoy.

<**sqoyép**>, SPRD /*'a spirit power of a kw'ōxweqs dancer, (*perhaps *wolverine or badger spirit power)'*/, *see* sqoyép *yellow badger,* possibly *wolverine*, *see* qoy.

<**sqoyéx̲iya**>, EFAM /*'(be) bragging, extravagant in claims, bull-headed, claims he's the best'*/, *see* sqáyéx̲ ~ sqayéx̲ or qáyéx̲ ~ qayéx̲.

<**sq'á:lq'**>, DESC /*'be really tangled, it's really tangled'*/, *see* q'ál.

<**sq'álq'**>, DESC [*'be tangled (on something)'*], *see* q'ál.

<**sq'áq'eth'**>, DESC /*'(be) tight, (leaning backwards [EB])'*/, *see* q'áth'.

<**sq'áq'eyt**>, LANG [*'a messenger on the run'*], *see* sq'á:yt.

<sq'á:tl'>, EZ /'*river otter,* perhaps also *sea otter*'/, *see* q'átl'.

<sq'á:yt>, LANG /'*message, a messenger not left yet, Indian messenger*'/, *see* q'á:yt

<sq'elá:w>, ABFC ['*be coiled (ready to strike for ex. of a snake)*'], *see* q'ál.

<sq'eláx̲el>, CSTR ['*(be) fenced in*'], *see* q'ál.

<sq'elóts'eqw>, HHG ['*be under an umbrella*'], *see* q'el.

<sq'elq'elá:w>, ABFC ['*(be) coiling (ready to strike) (of a snake)*'], *see* q'ál.

<sq'elq'élp'eqw>, ANA /'*curly hair, (be curly-haired(?), have curly hair(?))*'/, *see* q'ál.

<sq'elq'élp'es>, ANA /'*curly hair, (have curly hair(?))*'/, *see* q'ál.

<sq'élhq'elh>, chrs //s=q'ə́ɬ=C_1əC_2//, EZ ['*muskrat*'], *see* q'élh.

<sq'émél>, df //s=q'ə́mə́l or s=q'ə́m(=)əl//, CAN ['*canoe paddle*'], *see* q'émél

<sq'emq'ámth'>, DESC ['*(be) wrinkled*'], *see* q'ám

<sq'ép>, SOC /'*a gathering, a meeting*'/, *see* q'ép.

<sq'epláts>, EB /'*thick crowded tight bushes, bushes growing wide from narrow roots or base*'/, *see* q'ép.

<sq'ep'ó:lthetel>, CLO ['*garter*'], *see* q'áp'.

<sq'eq'axí:l>, SOCT ['*partners*'], *see* q'ó.

<sq'eq'mó:stel>, //s=q'ə[=C_1ə=]m=á·s=təl//, FSH /'*a dip-net, (a scoop net [CT])*'/, ASM ['originally made of méthelh *dog-bane*, attested by DM (12/4/64), see main dialect form **<q'emó:stel>** under q'emós ~ q'emó:s.

<sq'eq'e'óleq>, SOCT /'*pair of twins, pair of closest friends*'/, *see* q'ó.

<sq'eq'íp>, SOC ['*be gathered together*'], *see* q'ép.

<sq'eq'íp>, SOC ['*a group*'], *see* q'ép.

<sq'eq'ó>, DIR /'*along, together, be included, with*'/, *see* q'ó.

<sq'eq'ómet>, DIR ['*coming with s-o*'], *see* q'ó.

<sq'éth'>, dnom //s=q'əθ'//, ABFC /'*dung, (excrement, feces), shit*'/, *see* q'éth'.

<sq'éth'ep>, ANA ['*(have the) hair in a bun*'], *see* q'áth'.

<sq'eth'ewíts ~ sq'eth'ōwíts>, ABFC ['*have one's hands behind one's back*'], *see* q'áth'.

<sq'éth'x̲>, ABFC /'*dung, (scattered excrement?, fecal droppings?)*'/, *see* sq'éth'.

<Sq'ewá:lxw>, PLN /'*a turn in the Fraser River between Ruby Creek and Katz (about a mile upriver from the mouth of Ruby Creek and Ruby Creek I.R. #9 (called Lukseetsis-sum on maps and D.I.A. records, see Lexwthíthesem)),* also *the name of a village at this spot, spelled Skawahlook, Indian Reserve #1, on topographical maps and D.I.A. records*'/, *see* q'éw ~ q'ew.

<Sq'ewílem>, PLN /'*a turn in the Fraser River on the CPR (northwest) side two miles east of American Bar, Texas Bar bend in the Fraser River*'/, *see* q'éw ~ q'ew.

<Sq'éwlets ~ Sq'ówlets>, PLN ['*old Scowlitz village*'], *see* q'éw ~ q'ew.

<**Sq'éwqel ~ Sq'ówqel**>, PLN /'*upper end of Seabird Island, village at the upper end of Seabird Island, Maria Slough separating Seabird Island from north shore of Fraser River, now used for Seabird Island as a whole*'/, *see* q'éw ~ q'ew.

<**Sq'ewqé(:)yl ~ Sq'ewqí:l**>, PLN /'*Scowkale, sometimes misspelled Skulkayn, now Chilliwack Indian Reserves #10 and #11*'/, *see* q'éw ~ q'ew.

<**sq'exí:lmet**>, TVMO ['*follow s-o*'], *see* q'ó.

<**sq'éykw'**>, ABFC ['*a bite*'], *see* q'éykw' or q'í:kw'.

<**sq'éyle**>, FOOD /'*preserved fish, preserved meat, dried fish, dried meat (usually fish), smoked salmon, wind-dried salmon (old word), what is stored away, what is put away*'/, *see* q'éyl ~ q'í:l

<**sq'éylòm**>, FOOD /'*leftover food, scraps*'/, *see* q'éylòm.

<**sq'eyq'tóles**>, dnom //s=q'ey[=C_1ə=]=T=áləs//, CLO /'*mask (tied) over the eyes* '/, <**s=**> *nominalizer*, <**q'ey ~ q'i**>,*wound around, tied, knotted*, <=R1=> *resultative*, perhaps <**=T**> *purposeful control transitivizer*, <**=óles**> *on the eyes*, attested by RG & EH (4/10/99 Ling332)

<**sq'eyth'éleqw**>, BLDG ['*peak of house*'], *see* q'eyth'

<**sq'éytl'** or **sq'ítl'**>, ABFC ['*a scar*'], *see* q'éytl'.

<**Sq'éywetselem ~ Sq'éywetsélém**>, PLN ['*trail and steep slope on the west shore of Kawkawa Lake where the trail went up and over a steep hill and then down*'], *see* q'e:yw ~ q'í:w.

<**sq'eyx̲éleqw**>, ANA /'*crown of head, center of the top of the head where the hair starts*'/, BLDG /'*peak of house, gable or plank over smokehole*'/, *see* q'eyx̲

<**Sq'íp'ex̲w**>, PLN /'*a real rough place in the Fraser River impassible in a canoe (in the Tait area, prob. between Spuzzum and Yale)*'/, *see* q'íp'

<**Sq'iq'ewílem**>, PLN /'*beach in front of old Scowlitz village, the point the Harrison River goes around by Kilby's store*'/, *see* q'éw ~ q'ew.

<**sq'iq'exí:l ~ q'iq'exí:l**>, SOCT /'*little partner, little person who follows or goes with one*'/, *see* q'ó.

<**sq'íq'ex̲el**>, LT ['*[be getting black]*'], *see* q'íx̲.

<**sq'iwq'ewíles**>, ABFC ['*carry a packstrap or both packstraps over the shoulder(s) and under the arm(s)*'], *see* q'e:yw ~ q'í:w.

<**sq'ó**>, SOC /'*companion, other part*'/, *see* q'ó.

<**sq'ó**>, DIR /'*along, with, together with*'/, *see* q'ó.

<**Sq'ólep'ex̲w**>, PLN ['*another rough place in the Fraser River (Tait area)*'], *see* Sq'íp'ex̲w.

<**sq'ó:lp'eqw**>, ANA /'*curly hair, (have curly hair(?))*'/, *see* q'ál.

<**sq'ómet**>, DIR ['*come with s-o*'], *see* q'ó.

<**sq'óq'ey**>, ABDF ['*be dead*'], *see* q'ó:y ~ q'óy.

<**sq'óq'ey**>, ABDF ['*sickness*'], *see* q'ó:y ~ q'óy.

<**sq'ó:t ~ sq'ót**>, DIR /'*accompany s-o, go with s-o*'/, *see* q'ó.

<**sq'ówqel**>, WATR /'*a bend in a river, a curve of a lake*'/, *see* q'éw ~ q'ew.

<**sq'ó:xel ~ sq'óxel**>, SOCT ['*partner*'], *see* q'ó.

<**sq'óyes**>, df //s=q'áy=əs or s=q'ɛ[-Aá-]y=əs or s=q'əy=á[=M2=]s//, ANAB /'*down feathers, real fine feathers*'/, *see* q'óy

<**sq'óyeseqw ~ sx̱óyeseqw**>, SPRD ['*soft (down) feathers put in oiled hair for dancing*'], *see* q'óyes.

<**sq'pólthetel**>, CLO ['*garter*'], *see* q'ép.

<**sq'thà:m**>, ECON ['*be short (of money or other things)*'], *see* q'thá:m.

<**sq'thá:mtses**>, ABDF ['*can't reach*'], *see* q'thá:m.

<**sq'x̱áp**>, dnom //s=sq'=x̣=ɛ́p//, EB ['*stump (of a tree [still rooted])*'], literally (probably) /'something split all around in the dirt'/, *see* **seq'** *split*.

<**sqwá**>, WATR /'*tributary, small creek that goes into a bigger river*'/, *see* qwá.

<**Sqwá**>, PLN /'*Skwah village, now Skwah Reserve,* also known as *Wellington Reserve*'/, *see* qwá.

<**sqwahíwel**>, LAND /'*hole (in roof, tunnel, pants, mountain, at bottom of some lakes), tunnel*'/, *see* qwá.

<**sqwà:l**>, LANG /'*word, words*'/, *see* qwà:l.

<**Sqwá:la**>, PLN /'*village at west end of Little Mountain (Mount Shannon) on Hope Slough,* also *a name for Hope Slough or Hope River*'/, *see* qwá.

<**sqwálats**>, DESC /'*hole in the bottom (of bucket, etc.)*'/, *see* qwá.

<**sqwá:lewel ~ sqwálewel ~ sqwà(:)lewel**>, EFAM /'*thoughts, feelings*'/, *lit.* /'*words/talk in the inside, words/talk inside the head', see* qwà:l.

<**Sqwá:p**>, PLN ['*the hole (lake) at the foot of Cheam Peak on the south side*'], *see* qwá.

<**sqwátem**>, WATR /'*trickling, running under*'/, attested by LJ (in Elders Group 7/13/77), *see* kw'át.

<**sqwa'í:wel**>, DESC ['*(be) hollow*'], *see* qwá.

<**Sqwehá**>, PLN /'*Skwah village, now Skwah Reserve*'/, *see* qwá.

<**sqwehá:liya**>, ANAH ['*pierced ear*'], *see* qwá.

<**Sqwehíwel**>, PLN ['*Agassiz Mountain (or more likely Mount Woodside)*'], *see* qwá.

<**sqwelíp**>, FOOD ['*moss bread*'], EB /'*black tree lichen, black tree "moss"*'/, *see* qwíl ~ qwel

<**Sqwelíqwehíwel ~ Sqwelíqwehìwél**>, PLN ['*natural holes or tunnels east of Iwówes and above Lhilheltálets that water came out of after rain*'], *see* qwá.

<**sqwélqwel**>, LANG /'*news, a true story, what was told, message*'/, *see* qwà:l.

<**sqwelqwelá:lí:ya**>, ANA ['*hair in the ears*'], *see* qwíl ~ qwel.

<**sqwelqweláwtxw**>, LANG /'*language room, language house, (news room)*'/, *see* qwà:l.

<**sqwelqwélqsel**>, ANA ['*hair in the nose*'], *see* qwíl ~ qwel.

<**sqwelqwílōws ~ sqwelqwéylōws**>, ANA ['*hair on the body*'], *see* qwíl ~ qwel.

<**sqwéls**>, FOOD /'*(the) cooking, (soup, stew [DM, CT])*'/, *see* qwó:ls.

<**sqwéltel**>, LANG ['*language*'], *see* qwà:l.

<**sqwélxem**>, WETH ['*dry snow (that can drift)*'], *see* qwélxel.

<**sqwelxómé ~ sqwelxóme**>, WETH /'*dry snow coming in (drifting), fine snow that leaks into a house*'/, *see* qwélxel.

<**sqwelxwó:lés**>, df //s=q^{w}əlx^{w}=á·ləs//, ABDF /*'(have) one white eye, (have a cataract on one eye)'*/, *see* qwelxw.

<**sqwemá:y ~ sqwmá:y ~ sqwemáy**>, EZ ['*dog*'], *see* qwem.

<**Sqwemá:y (?)**>, PLN ['*a rock shaped like a hunting dog on the east shore of the Fraser River near Hill's Bar and below Tewít (a rock shaped like a human hunter)*'], *see* qwem.

<**sqwemá:yalqel**>, ANAA ['*dog wool*'], *see* qwem.

<**sqwemayáwtxw**>, BLDG ['*dog house*'], *see* qwem.

<**sqwemqwemó<u>x</u>w**>, plv //s=C$_{1}$əC$_{2}$=q^{w}ám=ə[=M2=]x̣^{w}//, stvi, ABFC ['*all doubled up*'], *see* qwó:m ~ qwóm ~ qwem.

<**sqwemqwó:m<u>x</u>w**>, ANA ['*lots of lumps (any size)*'], *see* qwó:m ~ qwóm ~ qwem.

<**Sqwemqwóm<u>x</u>w**>, PLN ['*a lumpy mountain back of Seabird Island*'], *see* qwó:m ~ qwóm ~ qwem.

<**sqweqwá**>, DESC ['*a hole*'], *see* qwá.

<**sqweqwá seplíl**>, ['*donut*'] (lit. be got a hole/with a hole + bread), *see* qwá.

<**sqweqwá:ls ~ shxwqweqwá:ls**>, TOOL /*'borer to make holes, auger'*/, *see* qwá.

<**Sqweqwehíwel**>, PLN /*'beach on east side of Harrison Lake across from Long Island where there are lots of flat rocks, most of which have holes in them'*/, *see* qwá.

<**sqwéqwemay**>, EZ /*'a lot of (small) dogs, puppies'*/, *see* qwem.

<**sqweqweméytses**>, EB ['*pussy willow*'], literally /'puppies in/on the hand'/, *see* qwem.

<**sqwéqweqw**>, //s=q^{w}ə́q^{w}=əq^{w}//, EZ /*'snowy owl, white owl'*/, ['*Nyctea scandiaca*'], attested by Elders Group (6/4/75, 2/18/76), see main dialect form <**sqwő́qweqw**> under qwő́qw ~ qwéqw.

<**sqweqwewáth**>, EZ ['*bunch of rabbits*'], *see* qwá.

<**sqwétxem**>, WETH /*'fog, mist'*/, *see* qwétxem.

<**sqwéthem**>, CAN /*'canoe with shovel-nose at both ends, same as tl'elá:y'*/, *see* qweth.

<**sqwéth'**>, EZ /*'ruffed grouse, (*also known as*) willow grouse'*/, *see* qwéth'

<**sqwéth'elh**>, df //s=q^{w}ə́θ'(=)əɬ//, EZ ['*Douglas squirrel*'], *see* qwéth'

<**sqwéth'qweth'**>, EZ /*'ruffed grouse, (*also known as*) willow grouse'*/, *see* qwéth'

<**sqwé<u>x</u>em**>, EZ /*'silver spring salmon that came up Harrison River and Chehalis Creek, (first spring salmon [Deming])'*/, *see* qwé<u>x</u>em.

<**Sqwe'óp (?)**>, PLN ['*Cheam Creek on north side below Ford Creek*'], *see* qwe'óp.

<**sqwíqw**>, df //s(=)q^{w}íq^{w}//, EZ /*'hoary marmot, (*also known as*) "mountain groundhog", "groundhog", or "whistler",* poss. also *yellow-bellied marmot'*/, *see* qwíqw

<**sqwíqwemay**>, EZ ['*puppy*'], *see* qwem.

<**sqwíqwemeyò:llh**>, EZ ['*small puppy*'], *see* qwem.

<**sqwíqweyóthel**>, EZ /*'jackrabbit,* also *big or older rabbit (snowshoe/varying hare)'*/, *see* qwá.

<**sqwló**>, ANAA /*'seal fat, seal blubber'*/, *see* qwló.

<**Sqwló ~ Skwló**>, dnom //s=qʷlá ~ s=kʷlá//, PLN /'*Seal Fat Rock on Harrison River just upriver from Th'éqwela (place by Morris Lake where Indian people used to play Indian badminton), this rock has what resembles seal fat all around it*'/, *see* qwló.

<**sqwóls**>, WATR ['*be boiled*'], *see* qwó:ls.

<**sqwómetsel**>, ABDF ['*get hunchbacked*'], *see* qwó:m ~ qwóm ~ qwem.

<**sqwó:qwetl'í:wèl**>, df //s=qʷá·[=C_1ə=]ƛ'=í·wəl//, EZ ['*tapeworm*'], *see* qwó:tl'.

<**sqwóqweyel ~ sqwóqwiyel**>, LT /'*be yellowish, be tan*'/, *see* qwá:y.

<**sqwoqwtó:ythel**>, ABFC ['*(have the) mouth round and open with rounded lips*'], *see* qwá.

<**sqwóteleqw**>, ANAH [' *crown of the head, top of the head* '], *see* qw'ót.

<**sqwó:yxw**>, df //s=qʷá·yxʷ//, EZ /'*late fall sockeye salmon (last run on Harrison River and Chehalis River, kind of red)*'/, *see* qwó:yxw

<**sqw'ő:lmexw ~ skw'ő:lmexw**>, df //s=k'ʷó·l(=)mexw or s=k'ʷów=lməxʷ//, EB /'*blackberry (fruit), (before contact, only) wild trailing blackberry, (*now also*) evergreen blackberry, (*now also*) Himalaya blackberry*'/, *see* **qw'ő:l ~ kw'ő:l**.

<**sqwőqweqw**>, df //s=qʷóqʷ=əqʷ//, EZ /'*snowy owl, white owl*'/, ['*Nyctea scandiaca*'], *see* qwőqw.

<**sqwqwís**>, strs //s=C_1ə=qʷís//, DESC ['*(be) narrow*'], attested by MV (Deming 4/10/80), see main dialect form <**qweqwís**>, under qwís.

<**Sqwx̲wó:mex**>, df //s=qʷx̣ʷ=á·məxʸ//, SOCT ['*Squamish people*'], (<**s=**> *nominalizer*), root meaning unknown unless related to qw'íx̲w ~ qw'x̲w *dark, brown* by deglottalization, lx <**=ó:mex**> *in looks, appearance, -looking*, syntactic analysis: nominal, attested by BHTTC (11/19/76), Salish cognate: Squamish /s-qʷx̣ʷúʔ-miš/ *Squamish (village, tribe, language)* K67:295.

<**sqw'echém**>, df //s=q'ʷəc(=)ə[=´=]m//, ABDF ['*a boil*'], *see* qw'ech.

<**sqw'él**>, FOOD ['*(the) cooking*'], *see* qw'él.

<**sqw'él**>, df //sq'ʷəl//, LAND perhaps /'*copper, (hard metal that looks like gold but isn't, maybe copper [Elders at Katz Class 10/5/76], metal found in mines and used for arrowheads [Elders Group 5/28/75], gold [EB])*'/, *see* qw'él (#2, prob. same as #1).

<**sqw'él:ém**>, FOOD /'*barbecued food, (salmon bake [Deming])*'/, *see* qw'él.

<**sqw'elém**>, FOOD /'*barbecued, roasted, (baked (in an oven) [DC])*'/, *see* qw'él.

<**sqw'éls**>, FOOD ['*something that's cooked*'], *see* qw'él.

<**sqw'éméls**>, ANAH ['*forehead*'], *see* qw'em

<**sqw'emóx̲w**>, ABFC ['*(be) doubled up in bed on one's side with knees drawn up*'], CAN ['*bent U-shaped plane with handle on each end for canoe-making*'], *see* qw'emó or qw'óm.

<**sqw'emóx̲w sxíxep**>, CAN ['*bent U-shaped plane with handle on each end for canoe-making*'], *see* xíp.

<**sqw'emóx̲w xíxepels**>, CAN ['*bent U-shaped plane with handle on each end for canoe-making*'], *see* xíp.

<**sqw'emqw'emóx̲w**>, ABFC /'*(be) doubled up (a person with knees up to his chest), all doubled over*'/, *see* qw'emó or qw'óm.

<**sqw'emqw'emóx̲w**>, CAN ['*U-shaped or horseshoe-shaped knife for scraping out an adzed canoe*'], *see* qw'emó or qw'óm.

<**sqw'eqw'í:l**>, FOOD /'*(be) cooked, (be) already cooked*'/, *see* qw'él.

<**Sqw'ex̲wáq**>, PLN ['*pool where Kawkawa Creek comes into the Coquihalla River*'], *see* qw'ex̲w ~ qw'ix̲w.

<**sqw'eyílex**>, PLAY ['*a dance (social event for ex. or someone's individual spirit dance)*'], *see* qw'eyílex ~ qw'eyíléx.

<**sqw'íqw'el**>, DESC ['*(be) uncovered*'], *see* qw'íl.

<**sqw'íqw'ex̲wel**>, LT ['*[be getting brown]*'], *see* qw'íx̲w.

<**sqw'íqw'ex̲welomex**>, LT /'*[looks a state of going brown, be getting brown-looking]*'/, *see* qw'íx̲w.

<**Sqw'íqw'x̲weq**>, PLN ['*maybe the same place as Sqw'ex̲wáq (pool where Kawkawa Creek comes into the Coquihalla River and where the water pygmies lived)*'], *see* qw'ex̲w ~ **qw'ix̲w**.

<**sqw'ómx̲wes**>, DESC /'*(be) rolled up in a ball (twine, yarn, etc.)*'/, *see* qw'emó or qw'óm.

<**sqw'óteleqw**>, ANA ['*crown of head*'], *see* qw'ót.

<**sqw'ōl**>, LAND /'*native copper or brass (made thin as paper)*'/, *see* qw'él (#2, prob. same as #1).

<**=st**>, da //=sT//, TIB ['*causative control transitivizer*'], comment: this suffix could also be shown as =stexw (/=sTəx^{w}/), cognate with Musqueam and Cowichan dialects /=stəx^{w}/ (as in work of Suttles, Hukari, etc.), however -exw can just as well be segmented as *third person object* here and from =lexw (/=l-əx^{w}/, leaving /=l// *non-control transitivizer*), besides setting up object suffixes for all persons this also eliminates the need for a rule deleting the exw in all other persons (though such a rule may be historically motivated, it is synchronically uneconomical and unmotivated), phonology: the <t>//T// in causative <=st>//=sT// and in <=t ~ =et> //=T ~ =əT// and in <=met> //=məT// becomes <th>/θ/ before three inflections, <-óme, -óx, -et> (/-ámə, -áx^{y}, -ət/) (*first person singular object, me, second person singular object, you*, and *purposeful control reflexive*, everywhere else it remains <t>/t/, syntactic analysis: derivational suffix.

<**Stehiyáq??**> or more likely <**Sch'iyáq**>, df //s=tɛhiyɛ́q?? or s=ch'iyɛ́q//, PLN ['*Centre Creek*'], (<**s=**> *nominalizer*), Carlson, McHalsie, & Perrier (2001:149) give the <Stehiyáq> and literal meaning as *place of the fish trap*, so probably root <**sts'iyáq**> *fish trap, weir* (for that *see* **<ch'iyáq ~ ts'iyáq>**), phonology: phonemic shape unusual perhaps due to Wells mistranscription (perhaps his first <e> is typo for <c> giving <s'tchee-AHK> (which would be <**Sch'iyáq** ~ **Sts'iyáq**> *fish trap, weir*, syntactic analysis: nominal, source: Wells 1966 <s'tehee-AHK> *Centre Creek*.

<**stáléqep**>, SD ['*(make) a distant sound*'], *see* sát.

<**stà:m**>, ABFC /'*a holler, (a yell, a shout)*'/, *see* tà:m.

<**stám**>, MOOD /'*what is it?, be what?*'/, *see* tám.

<**stámel**>, MOOD /'*what use is it?, what use have you got for it?*'/, *see* tám.

<**stámés**>, PRON /'*whatever it is, what it is, it is anything, it is something*'/, *see* tám.

<**staméxw** ~ **taméxw**>, possibly root //tɛməx^{w} ~ stɛməx^{w}//, EFAM ['*hope*'], *see* taméxw.

<**staqí:l**>, SD ['*sound like (in voice)*'], *see* ta'á ~ te'á ~ t'á.

<**státew** ~ **státōw**>, LT /'*be light, (be lit up), be illuminated*'/, *see* táw.

<**státewel**>, LT ['*be light (illuminated)*'], *see* táw.

<**statiqíwò:llh**>, EZ ['*colt*'], *see* stiqíw.

<**statí:wel**>, KIN /'*nephews, nieces, sibling's children*'/, *see* stí:wel.

<**stáweqel**>, REL /'*deceased ones, late ones*'/, *see* sát.

<**stá:xwelh**>, df //s=tɛ́·xʷ=əɬ//, [stǽ·xʷəɬ ~ (hyper-slow) stǽʔæxʷəɬ], HAT /'*children (not one's own necessarily, generic)*'/, ASM ['age term not kinship'], possibly <**s=**> *nominalizer, (*perhaps *alienable possession)*, root meaning uncertain but probably <**sát**>, bound root //sɛ́t// *reach, pass on, pass along*, or possibly <ta'á> *alike, similar*, or <**tá:xw**> meaning unknown, if one of the first two is root possibly <**=xw**> *round, around*, lx <**=elh ~ =íylh ~ =ó:llh**> *child, young*, if the first root is root here the literal meaning may be something like **"pass along/around child/young"**; phonology: possible =M1= metathesis of V1 and C2, grammatical comment: suppletive plural for <**stl'ítl'eqelh**> *child (generic)*, syntactic analysis: nominal, attested by AC, EB, DF, many others, other sources: ES /stɛ·xʷəɬ/ *children (preadolescent)*, Salish cognate: Squamish /s-táwʔxʷɬ/ *child* W73:58, K67:284, Skagit dial. of Lushootseed /s-táwixʷəʔɬ/ *children* H76:484, examples: <**éyes te stá:xwelh.**>, //ʔɛ́y=əs tə s=tɛ́·xʷ=əɬ//, /'*The children had a lot of fun.*'/, attested by AC, <**líyleyem te stá:xwelh.**>, //líy=C_1əC_2=əm tə s=tɛ́·xʷ=əɬ//, /'*The children are laughing.*'/, attested by AC, <**sisistáxwes te stá:xwelh.**>, //siy=C_1əC_2=sT-ə[=Aɛ́=]xʷ-əs tə s=tɛ́·xʷ=əɬ//, /'*He's scaring the children.*'/, attested by EB, <**wiyóths kw'es í:wolems te stá:xwelh, t'ít'elem kw'es í:wólems.**>, //wə=yáθ-s k'ʷə-s ʔi[-´·-]wal=əm-s tə s=tɛ́·xʷ=əɬ, t'í[-C_1ə-]l=əm k'ʷə-s ʔi[-´·-]wal=əm-s//, /'*The children are playing all the time, singing as they're playing.*'/, attested by AC (10/15/71), <**qéx̱ te stá:xwelh.**>, //qə́x̣ tə s=tɛ́·xʷ=əɬ//, /'*(There's) lots of children.*'/, attested by AC.

<**sta'á ~ ste'á**>, CJ /'*be like, be similar to, be the same as, be a kind of*'/, *see* ta'á ~ te'á ~ t'á.

<**sta'á:wel**>, EFAM ['*think*'], *see* ta'á ~ te'á ~ t'á.

<**stekták**>, df //s=C_1əC_2=tɛ́k//, EFAM /'*(be) in a daze, day-dreaming*'/, *see* tákw.

<**stekwtákw**>, df //s=C_1əC_2=tɛ́kʷ//, [stʊkʷtǽkʷ], EFAM /'*(be) in a daze, day-dreaming*'/, *see* tákw.

<**=st=élémét** or **=st-élémét ~ =st-elómet**>, da //=sT=ə̀lə̀mə̀t or =sT-ə̀lə̀mə̀t ~ =sT-əlámət//, PRON /'*non-control reflexive, make oneself do something, keep oneself doing something*'/, phonology: =élémét ~ =elómet is clearly related to the non-control reflexive =l=ó:met, perhaps with the latter being historically from =l=lómet > =l:ómet > =ló·met, and the former having downstepping, updrifting, and vowel-reduction, syntactic analysis: derivational suffix, or derivational suffix plus is, syntactic comment: the reflexive part of this combination has been shown as an inflection thoughout most of the dictionary, but could probably better be counted as derivational since it changes a transitive verb to an intransitive syntactically, Salish cognate: Musqueam /-st-ənámət/ and (after unstressed roots) /-st-ə́nəmət/ are shown in Suttles ca1984 as *causative reflexive*, the vowel /á/ there confirms the connection with the *non-control reflexive* /=l-ámət/; found in <**lhistélémét**>, //ɬiy=sT-ə́lə́mə́t//, /'*feel embarrassed and shy because ashamed, be ashamed*'/, literally /'cause oneself to be ashamed, be ashamed of oneself'/, phonology: updrifting, <**th'ex̱wstélémét**>, //θ'əx̣ʷ=sT-ə́lə́mə́t//, /'*feel sorry for oneself*'/, literally /'cause oneself to be pitied/helped'/, <**tesestélemet**>, //təsas=sT-ə́ləmət//, /'*feel sorry for oneself*'/, literally /'cause oneself to be unfortunate/poor/bereft'/, root <**tesós ~ t-sós**> *be unfortunate, poor, bereft*, phonology: vowel-reduction, <**éystelómet ~ éy:stelómet**>, //ʔɛ́y=sT-əlámət//, /'*pretending to be good; want to be accepted*'/, literally /'cause oneself to be good, cause oneself to be liked'/, attested by Elders Group, <**tl'emstélemet ~ tl'ostélmet**>, //ƛ'əm=sT-ə́ləmət ~ ƛ'a=sT-ə́ləmət//, /'*thing s-o is talking/laughing about oneself*'/.

<**steliqíw**>, EZ ['*herd of horses*'], *see* stiqíw.

<**stélmel**>, EFAM /'*someone's own knowledge, someone's own idea*'/, *see* tól.

<**stelqóye**>, EZ ['*wolves*'], *see* stqó:ya ~ stqó:ye ~ stqó:yá.

<**stélwél**>, df //s=tə́l(=ə)wəl//, EB ['*cedar limb rope (slitted)*'], *see* télwél.

<**steqá:tsas**>, NUM ['*eight o'clock*'], *see* tqá:tsa.

<**steqiwó:llh**>, EZ ['*baby horse*'], *see* stiqíw.

<**steqtá:l**>, BLDG /'*door, doorway, door of a big (communal) house or longhouse*'/, *see* téq.

<**steqtéq**>, WATR /'*jampile, log-jam*'/, *see* téq.

<**stesó:s**>, ECON ['*be broke [financially]*'], *see* t-sós ~ tesós.

<**stételes**>, KIN ['*little wives*'], *see* tó:les.

<**stételō**>, WATR ['*lots of little creeks*'], *see* tó:l ~ tò:l.

<**stetís**>, DIR /'*be near, be close to, be beside, be next to*'/, *see* tés.

<**stetísmels**>, DIR ['*person next to one*'], *see* tés.

<**stetisthóx ~ stetísthó:x**>, DIR ['*(be) near me*'], *see* tés.

<**stewéqel**>, REL ['*deceased one*'], *see* sát

<**Stkwóthel**>, *see* main entry <**Tekwóthel ~ Tkwóthel**>, df //tək^{w}=áθəl//, PLN ['*a mountain just south of Yale Mountain (Popelehó:ys) with a big hole like a tunnel in it above the highway at Yale*'],

<**stim:ő:t**>, free root //stim·ó·t//, CAN ['*steamboat*'], syntactic analysis: noun, nominal, attested by Elders Group (10/1/75), borrowed from English /stímbot/ *steamboat* or from late Chinook Jargon /stimpot/ *steamboat* Johnson 1978:423, also <**stimőt**>, //stimót//, attested by NP (9/30/75).

<**lhólhekw' stimőt**>, cpds //ɬá[-C_1ə-]k'^{w} stimót//, CAN ['*airplane*'], literally /'flying steamboat'/, (<-**R1**-> *continuative*), phonology: reduplication, syntactic analysis: simple nominal phrase, attested by NP.

<**stiqíw ~ stiqí:w**>, df //s=tiq=íw ~ s=tiq=í·w//, [stiqí(·)w ~ stiqé(·)w], EZ ['*horse*'], ['*Equus caballus*'], (<**s=**> *nominalizer*), prob. root <**tiq**> *take in motion* as in <**tiqxálém**> (/tiq=x^{y}ə[=Aɛ́=]l=əm/) *take a step* (where =xál=ém means *on one's leg/foot*), lx. <**=á:w ~ =í:w ~ =ew ~ =ú:w**> *on the body, on top of itself*, thus *horse* is literally /"something that takes a body in motion" or "something that takes in motion on top of itself"/,, syntactic analysis: nominal, attested by AC, EB, others, other sources: H-T <stEkéyu> (macrons over e and u) *horse (Equus sp.)(introduced since the advent of whites)*, also <**steqíw**>, //s=təqíw//, [stəqíw ~ stɪqíw], attested by AC, Elders Group (3/1/72), also <**stiqí:w ~ steqí:w ~ stiqíw**>, //s=tiqí·w ~ s=təqí·w ~ s=tiqíw//, attested by EB, example: <**x̲wéylems te stiqíw**>, //x̣^{w}í·ləm-s tə s=tiqíw//, /'*the horse's rope*'/, literally /'rope of the horse'/, attested by AC, <**qéx̲ steqíw**>, //qə́x̣ s=təqíw//, /'*a lot of horses.*'/, attested by AC, <**qéx̲ ti stiqíw.**>, //qə́x̣ tə yi-s=tiqíw//, /'*There's lots of horses.*'/, attested by AC, <**qéx̲ ta stiqíw.**>, //qə́x̣ t-ɛ s=tiqíw//, /'*There's a lot of horses (all belonging to you)., (You have a lot of horses.)*'/, attested by AC, <**xwel sts'ets'á te stiqí:w.**>, //x^{w}əl s=C_1ə=c'ɛ́ tə s=tiqí·w//, /'*He's still astride the horse.*'/, attested by EB (3/1/76), <**tsel me sts'ets'á te steqí:w.**>, //c-əl mə s=C_1ə=c'ɛ́ tə s=təqí·w//, /'*I rode the horse.*'/, attested by EB, <**sts'ets'á te stiqí:w**>, //s=C_1ə=c'ɛ́ tə s=tiqí·w//, /'*ride a horse*'/, attested by EB, <**léts'e stiqíw**>, //lə́c'ə s=tiqíw//, /'*one horse*'/, attested by EB, also *see* tiq.

<**stiteqíw**>, dmn //s=ti[=C_1ə=]qíw//, EZ ['*little horse*'], (<**=R1=**> *diminutive*), phonology: reduplication, syntactic analysis: nominal, attested by Deming (6/15/77).

<**statiqíwò:llh**>, dmn //s=C_1ɛ=tiqíw=**à·lɬ**//, EZ ['*colt*'], (<**R8=**> *diminutive*), lx <**=ó:llh**> *young, offspring*, phonology: downstepping, reduplication, syntactic analysis: nominal, attested by HT and CT (6/8/76).

<**steqiwó:llh**>, ds //s=təqiw=á·lɬ//, EZ ['*baby horse*'], lx <**=ó:llh**> *young, offspring*, syntactic analysis: nominal, attested by AC.

<**steliqíw**>, pln //s=t[=əl=]iqíw//, EZ ['*herd of horses*'], (<**=el=**> *plural (collective)*), phonology: infixed plural, syntactic analysis: nominal, attested by AC, example: <**qéx̱ ti steliqíw**>, //qə́x̣ tə yi-s=t[=əl=]iqíw//, /'*a lot of horses, herd of horses*'/, attested by AC.

<**stíqw'teqw'**>, BLDG /'*beams (of longhouse, all of them), houseposts*'/, *see* tíqw'.

<**stiteqíw**>, EZ ['*little horse*'], *see* stiqíw.

<**stí:tethel**>, ABDF ['*(be) puny*'], *see* títh ~ tí:th.

<**Stitó:s ~ Stitó:s**>, dnom //s=C_1í=təs=á·s//, PLN ['*Promontory Mountain by Vedder Crossing*'], *see* titó:s ~ titó:s.

<**stíth ~ stí:th**>, DESC /'*be skinny, be thin*'/, *see* títh ~ tí:th.

<**stít-sòs** or **stítesòs**>, SOCT /'*low class person, [person on the lowest economic class]*'/, *see* t-sós ~ tesós.

<**stí:wel**>, dnom //s=tí·wəl//, KIN /'*nephew, niece, sibling's child (child of sister or brother or cousin (up to and including fourth cousin), see* tí:wel.

<**stíxem**>, ANA /'*fish slime, slime (of any kind, from fish, algae, etc.)*'/, *see* tíxem.

<**stíxwem**>, dnom //s=tíx^w(=)əm or s=tə[=Aí=]x^w(=)əm//, EZ /'*willow grouse (a local name for ruffed grouse), ruffed grouse*'/, ['*Bonasa umbellus sabini*'], *see* téxwem.

<**stíx̱eqw ~ stí:x̱eqw**>, df //s=tíx̣=əq^w ~ s=tí·x̣=əq^w//, ANA ['*bushy hair*'], *see* tíx̱.

<**stiytáx̱el** or **stitáx̱el**>, BLDG ['*upper end of house (inside or outside)*'], *see* tiyt.

<**stí'àlà**>, PE ['*teapot*'], *see* tí.

<**stókel**>, CLO /'*stocking, socks*'/, *see* tókel.

<**stó:les**>, dnom //s=tá·ləs//, KIN ['*wife*'], *see* tó:les.

<**stó:lō**>, WATR ['*river*'], *see* tó:l ~ tò:l.

<**Stó:lō**>, PLN /'*Fraser River, (Chehalis Creek, Chehalis River [Elders Group, EL/EB/NP])*'/, *see* tó:l ~ tò:l.

<**stolōwálá**>, WATR ['*riverbed*'], *see* tó:l ~ tò:l.

<**stómchele**>, PRON /'*someplace, somewhere*'/, *see* tám.

<**stó:méx**>, dnom //s=tá·méx^y//, SOC /'*warrior, (leader of a raiding party, see* tó:méx prob. from tám *holler*.

<**stó:qw'em**>, ABDF /'*a cough, a cold with a cough*'/, *see* tó:qw'em.

<**stósem temítō**>, FOOD /'*ketchup/stewed tomatoes*'/, (lit. smashed + tomato), *see* tós, temítō

<**stotekwtíqw**>, ABDF /'stringy hair'/, *see* tokwt

<**Stótelō**>, PLN /'*Statlu Creek, one of the main tributaries of Chehalis Creek*'/, *see* tó:l ~ tò:l.

<**stótelō ~ stó:telō**>, WATR /'*creek, little river, small creek, small river*'/, *see* tó:l ~ tò:l.

<**Stótlōtel**>, PLN ['*Little Matsqui Creek*'], *see* tó:l ~ tò:l.

<**stqó:ya ~ stqó:ye ~ stqó:yá**>, df //s=tq(=)á·yɛ ~ s=tqá·yə ~ stqá·yɛ́//, EZ ['*wolf*'], ['*Canis lupus fuscus q/[tentative], Canis lupus columbianus*'], see <**tq(=)ó:ya**>, poss. itself from <tíq> *take a step, take in motion.*

<**st'ó'o ~ st'á ò**>, ds //s=**t'**ɛ[=Aá=] **ʔà** ~ s=**t'ɛ ʔà**//, CJ ['*just like*'], literally /'like just'/, *see* ta'á ~ te'á ~ t'á.

<**Stṓtelō**>, PLN /'*Hatchery Creek, tributary of Sweltzer Creek (which drains Cultus Lake)*'/, *see* tó:l ~ tò:l.

<**stpólh**>, CSTR ['*propped up*'], *see* tpólh.

<**stqá:qel**>, ABDF ['*lost one's voice*'], *see* téq.

<**stú:p**>, free root //stú·p//, HHG ['*stove*'], syntactic analysis: noun, nominal, attested by Elders Group (11/12/75), borrowed from English /stó·v/ *stove* or late Chinook Jargon /stov/ *stove* Johnson 1978:427.

<**kwúkwstú:p**>, cpds //k^{w}úk^{w}stú·p//, HHG /'*pot-bellied stove, cook-stove*'/, root <**kwúkw**> *cook*, root <**stú:p**> *stove*, syntactic analysis: nominal, attested by Deming (at Fort Langley museum 3/9/78), borrowed from English /kʊ́kstó·v/ *cook-stove*, contrast Skagit dialect of Lushootseed /**x^{w}údali**/ *pot-bellied stove, cook-stove* given the same time by LG (Deming 3/9/78).

<**stútlō**>, WATR ['*smaller creek*'], *see* tó:l ~ tò:l.

<**stutuwóthel ~ stewtewóthel**>, df //s=təw=C_1əC_2=áθəl//, WATR ['"*a little below*"'], *see* tew.

<**stú:xws**>, NUM ['*nine o'clock*'], *see* tú:xw.

<**st'ál**>, dnom //s=t'ɛ́l//, FSH /'*fish cut real thin for wind-drying but without cross cuts, dried fish cut differently than slhíts'es*'/, *see* t'ál.

<**st'á:lq**>, strs //s=t'ɛ́·lq or s=t'ə[=Aɛ́·=]lq//, DESC /'*spotted with irregular shaped blobs (like if mud-spattered, used of dogs, deer, and other animals so marked)*'/, *see* t'á:lq or **t'élq**.

<**st'ált'exw**>, LT ['*a shade*'], *see* t'á:l.

<**st'ált'exw**>, LT ['*sheltered*'], *see* t'á:l.

<**st'álh**>, BLDG ['*cross-beam (in a house)*'], *see* t'álh.

<**st'ám**>, LANG ['*(be a) guess*'], *see* t'ám.

<**St'ámiya**>, PLN ['*Hope Mountain*'], *see* t'ámiya.

<**st'amt'í:m** (or better) **st'emt'í:m**>, TOOL ['*chopped in different places*'], *see* t'ém.

<**st'amxá:lts'**>, PE ['*a braid*'], *see* t'ámex.

<**st'ápiy**>, EB ['*dead and broken [of a plant]*'], *see* t'ápiy.

<**st'áqsel**>, df //st'ɛ́=qsəl or s=t'ɛ́=qsəl//, SH /'*stick out (of something), protrude*'/, possibly <**s=**> *stative*?, root uncertain, possibly root <**t'á ~ t=e'á**> *same, alike, similar*?, lx <**=qsel**> *on the nose, point*, syntactic analysis: intransitive verb, attested by Elders Group (5/26/76).

<**st'at'á**>, CJ ['*being similar*'], *see* ta'á ~ te'á ~ t'á.

<**st'á:t'el**>, LT /'*(the) shade (of a tree for ex.), something that's not showing*'/, *see* t'á:l.

<**st'át'elh**>, DIR ['*across*'], *see* t'álh.

<**st'át'elhíles**>, HARV ['*carry a packstrap slung across the chest (over one shoulder and under one arm)*'], *see* t'álh.

<**st'át'em**>, LANG ['*(be) guessing*'], *see* t'ám.

<**st'at'ó:mex**>, DESC /'*to resemble, look like, (similar-looking)*'/, *see* ta'á ~ te'á ~ t'á.

<**st'áwel**>, df //s(=)t'ɛ́w=əl//, LT ['*purple*'], *see* t'áw.

<**st'awélmet**>, ABFC ['*thinking about s-th*'], *see* ta'á ~ te'á ~ t'á.

<**st'áwelòméx**>, LT /'*[looks purple, purple-looking]*'/, *see* st'áwel.

<**st'áxet**>, df //s=t'ɛ́(=)x^yə(=)t//, EB /'*wild nodding onion,* prob. also *Hooker's onion*'/, ['*Allium cernuum,* prob. also *Allium acuminatum*'], ASM ['does not include domestic onion, éniyels'], *see* t'áx.

<**st'á:yx̱w**>, EFAM /'*worried, sad, looking sad*'/, *see* t'ay.

<**st'a'áleqep**>, TAST ['*(the) taste*'], *see* t'á *and* **ta'á ~ te'á ~ t'á**.

<**st'ekwíwel**>, ABDF /'*(stuck in the rectum), stuck in the ass*'/, *see* t'ékw.

<**st'ekwt'ékw**>, LAND ['*mud*'], *see* t'ékw.

<**st'elákw'**>, SH /'*circular, round and flat*'/, *see* t'el.

<**st'elákw'**>, SH ['*a circle*'], *see* t'el.

<**st'elákw' siyólh**>, HUNT ['*circular frame (for tanning hides)*'], *see* yólh.

<**st'elákw' sp'íp'elh seplíl**>, FOOD ['*pizza*'] (lit. round + flat + bread), *see* t'el, **p'ílh, seplíl**.

<**st'eláx̱el**>, dnom //s=t'əl(=)ɛ́x̣əl or s=t'əl=(əl)ɛ́x̣əl or s=t'əlɛ́=ɛ́x̣əl//, SH /'*square, corner, arm with elbow out*'/, *see* t'el.

<**st'él'e**>, dnom //s=t'ə́lʔ=ə//, EZ /'*younger deer, baby horse, younger cow, fawn, colt, calf*'/, *see* t'el'.

<**st'elém**>, BSK ['*cherry bark (for baskets)*'], *see* t'elém.

<**st'élmexw**>, df //s=t'ə́lməx^w or s=t'ə́l(=)məx^w or s=t'(=)ə́lməx^w//, MED ['*medicine*'], *see* t'élmexw and its probable root t'él *stuck on.*

<**st'elmexwíwel**>, MED ['*love medicine*'], *see* t'élmexw.

<**st'elmexwó:les**>, MED ['*eye medicine*'], *see* t'élmexw.

<**st'élt'el**>, MUS /'*a person that sings all the time (any song), a singer*'/, *see* t'íl.

<**st'elt'elákw' seplíl**>, FOOD ['*waffle*'] (lit. many squares + bread), *see* t'el *and* **seplíl**.

<**st'elt'eláx̱el**>, SH ['*lots of squares*'], *see* st'eláx̱el under t'él.

<**st'elt'elíqw**>, plv //st'əlt'əlíq^w//, DESC /'*bumpy and prickly*'/, *see* t'ál.

<**st'elt'elíqw qwe'óp**>, EB ['*pineapple*'] (lit. bumpy and prickly + apple), *see* t'ál.

<**st'elt'elíqw qwe'óp sqe'óleqw**>, *pineapple juice* (lit. pineapple [itself from bumpy and prickly + apple] + fruit juice), *see* t'ál.

<**st'elt'élq**>, DESC ['*spotted with lots of [irregular] spots*'], *see* t'á:lq.

<**st'elt'ílém**>, pln //s=C_1əC_2=t'íl=əm//, MUS ['*songs*'], *see* t'íl.

<**st'elt'ólkwlh**>, pln //s=C_1əC_2=t'ál=(ál)k^wɬ//, SPRD ['*non-spirit-dancers (lots of them)*'], *see* t'ól.

<**St'élxweth'**>, df //s=t'ə́l=x^w=əθ'//, PLN /'*village near the mouth of Choate Creek, (Choate Creek [AK, SP/AD], (Stullawheets village on a hill on the east bank of the Fraser River near the mouth of Suka Creek [elders on American Bar Trip (AD/AK/?)])*'/, *see* t'élxweth'.

<**St'élxweth' Stótelō**>, cpds //s=t'ə́lx^{w}əθ' s=tá[=C_1ə=]ləw//, PLN /'*Choate Creek on the west (C.P.R,) side of the Fraser River*'/, *see* t'élxweth'.

<**St'élxweth' X̲ótsa**>, cpds //s=t'ə́lx^{w}əθ' x̣ácɛ//, PLN probably ['*Texas Lake*'], *see* t'élxweth'.

<**st'emíywelh**>, df //s=t'ɛ́[=Aə=]m=íy=wəɬ//, WV ['*warp (vertical threads of weaving)*'], *see* t'am.

<**st'émt'em**>, chrs //s=t'ɛ[=Aə́=]m=C_1əC_2//, stvi, EFAM ['*(be) cautious*'], literally /'be durative characteristically guess'/, *see* t'ám.

<**st'éps ~ st'epsóye**>, df //s=t'ə́ps ~ s=t'əps=áyə//, BPI ['*midget*'], *see* t'éps.

<**st'et'eméls ~ st'et'ebéls**>, dnom //s=C_1ə=t'əm=ə́ls ~ s=C_1ə=t'əb=ə́ls//, TOOL ['*adze*'], *see* t'ém.

<**st'ewṓkw'**>, df //s=t'əwók'^{w}//, LAND /'*diatomaceous earth (could be mixed with things to whiten them--for ex. dog and goat wool), white clay for white face paint (for pure person spirit-dancers), white powder from mountains, white clay they make powder from to lighten goat and dog wool for blankets, powder, talc, white face paint*'/, SPRD, PE, LT /'*(powder white, purplish white?)*'/, *see* t'ewṓkw' ~ **t'ewṓqw'**.

<**st'ewíqw'es**>, strs //s=t'əwo[=Aí=]q'^{w}=əs//, PE ['*powdered on the face*'], *see* t'ewṓkw' ~ **t'ewṓqw'**.

<**st'éx̲**>, dnom //s=t'ə́x̣//, EB ['*a fork in a tree*'], LAND ['*a fork in a road (or trail)*'], WATR ['*a fork in a creek*'], *see* t'éx̲.

<**st'ex̲láts**>, ds //s=t'əx̣=lɛ́c or s=t'əx̣=lə[=Aɛ́=]c//, possibly /'*fork in a tree?*'/, *see* t'éx̲.

<**st'e'áwel ~ st'áwel**>, EFAM /'*to guess, make a guess*'/, *see* ta'á ~ te'á ~ t'á.

<**st'ílém**>, MUS ['*song (non-religious)*'], *see* t'íl.

<**st'ít'ele**>, dmn //s=C_1í=t'ələ//, EZ /'*fawn, baby deer*'/, *see* t'el'.

<**st'ít'eqel**>, dnom //s=t'í[=C_1ə=]q=əl//, ABDF ['*a bruise*'], *see* t'íqel.

<**st'it'eqó:les**>, strs //s=t'i[=C_1ə=]q=á·ləs//, ABDF /'*black eye, bruised eye*'/, *see* t'íqel.

<**St'ít'x̲oya**>, dmn //s=C_1í=t'əx̣=ayɛ//, PLN ['*Ruby Creek (the creek not the village)*'], *see* t'éx̲.

<**st'it'x̲óyaq**>, df //s=C_1í=t'əx̣=a[=´=]yɛ=q or s=C_1í=t'əx̣=áyɛq//, EB /'*fork in tree, fork in tree roots*'/, *see* t'éx̲.

<**st'íwiyelh**>, df //s=t'íw=iyəɬ//, REL ['*prayer*'], *see* t'íw ~ t'i:w, MUS ['*slow beat*'].

<**(s)t'lhíléstel ~ (s)tl'lhíléstel**>, dnom //(s=)t'ɬ=íləs=təl//, ANA ['*collarbone*'], *see* t'álh.

<**st'ó(:)lkwlh**>, SPRD ['*a non-spirit-dancer*'], *see* t'ól.

<**st'óle'oléstel**>, PE /'*eyeglasses, (probably dark glasses)*'/, *see* t'á:l.

<**st'ót'ep**>, strs //s=t'á[=C_1ə=]p//, EB /'*(be) blazed (of a mark in a tree), chipped (of mark in tree)*'/, *see* t'óp.

<**st'uslóye**>, df //s=t'usl=áyə//, EB ['*licorice fern*'], ['*Polypodium glycyrrhiza*'], ASM ['grows from trees (on trunks as well as roots) and perhaps less often from soil and soil on rocks, the root is chewed year-round for its licorice flavor and sweetness'], MED ['the root is also chewed as medication for colds,

asthma and coughs'], (<**s=**> *nominalizer*), root meaning unknown, possibly <**=óye**> *affectionate diminutive; name ending*, syntactic analysis: nominal, dialects: *Tait*, attested by Elders Group, contrast <**tl'asíp**> *licorice fern* **(Chill., Cheh. dialects)**.

<**st'x̲éms**>, nums //s=t'x̣=ə́m=s//, numc, TIME ['*six o'clock*'], *see* t'éx̲.

<**sthá:lhp**>, stvi //s=θi=ɛ́ɬp or s=θɛ=ɛ́ɬp//, EB /'*big tree, (be big of a tree or plant)*'/, *see* thi ~ tha ~ the ~ thah ~ theh.

<**Sthamí:l**>, df //s=θəmɛ=M2=í·l//, PLN /'*creek between Popkum and Cheam,* also *a location near Popkum, (must be second of two creeks above Popkum that cross Highway #1 [JL 4/7/78])*'/, possibly <**s=**> *nominalizer*, possibly <**metathesis type 2**> *derivational*, possibly <**=í:l**> *go, come, get, become*, possibly root <**themá**> *second, twice*, phonology: metathesis, vowel merger, syntactic analysis: nominal, attested by AC (1973), source: place names reference file #276 and #277, also /'*must be one of two creeks above Popkum that cross Highway #1*'/, attested by JL (4/7/78), also <**semí:l**>, //s=(h)ə=mí·l or səm=í·l//, also /'*creek near Popkum*'/, possibly <**s=**> *stative or nominalizer*, possibly <**he=**> *resultative*, possibly root <**míl**> *submerge/drop into the water*, attested by CT (1973).

<**stháthiyel**>, df //s=θɛ́[=C_1ə=]y(=)əl//, ANA ['*blood*'], *see* tháthiyel.

<**stháthqiy**>, df //s=θɛ́[=C_1ə=]q=iy or s=θ'[=D=]ɛ́[=C_1ə=]q=iy or s=θ'[=D=]ə[=Aɛ́C_1ə=]q=iy//, EB /'*a sprout or shoot (esp. of the kinds peeled and eaten in spring), sweet green inner shoots, green berry shoots, salmonberry shoots, wild raspberry shoots and greens, salmonberry sprouts, blackcap shoots, thimbleberry shoots, wild rhubarb shoots, fern shoots*'/, *see* tháq.

<**stháwtxw**>, ds //s=θ(ə)=ɛ́wtx^w//, BLDG /'*longhouse for spirit-dancers, the big house, smokehouse (for spirit-dancing)*'/, *see* thi ~ tha ~ the ~ thah ~ theh.

<**sthehíthet**>, df //s=θəh=ə[=Aí=]T or s=θəhiy=T//, possibly /'*hook onto s-th*'/, *see* theh.

<**sthémelts ~ sthemélts**>, ds //s=θə[=´=]m(ɛ)=əlc-s ~ s=θəm(ɛ́)=ə́lc-s//, TIME ['*Tuesday*'], literally /'second day'/, *see* themá.

<**stheqelxél:ém ~ stheqelxélém**>, dnom //s=θəq(=)əl=x^{y}ə[=´=]l=əm//, WETH ['*a rainbow*'], *see* theqelxélém.

<**sthéqeytel**>, dnom //s=θə́qəy=təl//, FSH ['*sockeye net*'], *see* théqi ~ théqey.

<**sthéqi ~ sthéqey**>, df //s=θə́q(=)i ~ s=θə́q(=)əy//, [sθə́qi(y) ~ sθə́qəy], EZ ['*sockeye salmon*'], ['*Oncorhynchus nerka*'], *see* théqi ~ théqey.

<**sthethá:kw'**>, strs //s=θə[=C_1əAɛ́·=]k'^{w}//, DESC /'*be straight (of rope but not tree), pulled tight (of rope), stretched tight, tight*'/, *see* thékw'.

<**sthethíy**>, strs //s=C_1ə=θíy//, MC /'*be fixed, be fixed up properly*'/, *see* thíy.

<**sthí:qel**>, stvi //s=θí=əqəl//, SD ['*loud (of a voice)*'], literally /'be big voice/speech'/, *see* thi ~ tha ~ the ~ thah ~ theh.

<**sthí:qel**>, dnom //s=θí=əqəl//, SD ['*a loud voice*'], *see* thi ~ tha ~ the ~ thah ~ theh.

<**sthiyáp**>, stvi //s=θiy=ə[=Aɛ́=]p//, CLO ['*be wearing a loincloth*'], *see* thíy.

<**sthíyep**>, df //s=θíy=əp//, CLO /'*loincloth, dog-hair apron, dog-hair mat*'/, *see* thíy.

<**sthí:ystexw**>, caus //s=θí[=·=]y=sT-əx^w//, augs, SOC ['*do s-th well*'], *see* thíy.

<**sthqálem**>, dnom //s=θqɛ́l=əm//, FSH /'*place where one fishes by waiting with a dip-net, dip-net fishing place, place where one still-dips*'/, *see* thqá:lem.

<sthxwélqsel>, df //s=θax^{w}=ə́lqsəl//, ABDF /'*bleeding nose, (be/have bleeding in the nose)*'/, *see* thóxw or théxw.

<sthx̲á:lem>, df //s=θx̣ɛ́·l=əm or s=θx̣=ə[=Aɛ́·=]l=əm or s=θɛ́·x̣=ə[=M2=]l=əm//, EB ['*sword fern*'], ['*Polystichum munitum*'], *see* thx̲á:l.

<sth'á:qel>, df //s=θ'ɛ́·q=əl or s=θ'ɛ́·=qəl or sɛ́·θ'=M1=qəl//, EB /'*cat-tail, cattail reed*'/, ['*Typha latifolia*'], ASM ['a reed ready for harvest in July, used for mats sewn with special long flat needles, also used for pillows (often a rolled-up mat)'], possibly **<s=>** *nominalizer*, possibly **<=qel>** *in the head*??, root poss. **<sá:th' or th'á:q>** meaning unknown or **<th'áq>** *skinned*, syntactic analysis: nominal, attested by AC, Elders Group.

<sth'áth'elh>, strs //s=θ'ɛ́[=C_1ə=]ɬ//, WETH /'*it is cool [of weather], (be) cool (of a place)*'/, *see* th'álh.

<sth'ékw'>, ds //s=θ'ə́k'^{w}//, EZ /'*worm, bug*'/, ['probably class *Arthropoda*'], *see* th'ékw'.

<sth'ekwe'í:ws>, dnom //s=θ'ik^{w}ə=ʔí·ws or s=θ'i[=Aə=]k^{w}əʔ=í·ws or s=θ'ik^{w}ə=í·ws//, ANA ['*left side of the body*'], *see* th'íkwe.

<sth'ékw'oye>, dmn //s=θ'ə́k'^{w}=ayə//, EZ ['*little bug*'], *see* th'ékw'.

<sth'ékw's te téméxw>, cpds //s=θ'ə́k'^{w}-s tə tə́mə́x^{w}//, EZ ['*earthworm (esp. the most common introduced in B.C.)*'], ['esp. *Lumbricus terrestris*'], literally /'its worm the earth, worm -of the earth'/, *see* th'ékw'.

<sth'ekw'th'ékw'>, pln //s=C_1əC_2=θ'ə́k'^{w}//, ABDF /'*lots of sores,* (possibly) *rash*'/, *see* th'ekw' ~ th'íkw.

<sth'élhp>, df //sθ'=əɬp//, EB ['*mock orange*'], ['*Philadelphus gordianus*'], ASM ['leaves foam if rubbed with water on the body and are used for soap and hair rinse, the hard wood was used for cooking sticks (píkwel) and needles for making cattail or bulrush mats or needles for knitting wool (introduced), the wood was also used for spears'], MED ['medicine for dandruff, used in many medicines including eyewash and a wash after one touches a rotting corpse, the deep purple berries are said to be poison (though a girl ate them by AC's house and nothing happened) but the white flowers are good for diarrhea medicine'], root meaning unknown, lx **<=elhp ~ =álhp>** *plant*, phonology: zero grade of root forces stress to fall on usually unstressed allomorph =elhp, syntactic analysis: nominal, attested by AC, Elders Group (6/1/77), also /'*little orange*'/, attested by SP (Elders Group 6/1/77).

<sth'eméxwelets>, df //s=θ'əmə́x^{w}=ələc or s=θ'ɛm=ə́x^{w}=ələc//, LAND ['*point of land at the end of an island*'], *see* th'à:m ~ th'ám.

<Sth'eméxwelets>, df //s=θ'ɛm(=)ə́x^{w}=ələc//, PLN ['*west or downriver end of Seabird Island*'], *see* th'à:m ~ th'ám.

<sth'emí:wel ~ sth'emíwel ~ sth'emíwél>, ds //s=θ'am=í·wəl or s=θ'a[=Aə=]m=í·wəl//, EB /'*heart of a root, seed, nut (kernel), core of plant or seedling, core (of tree, branch, any growing thing), pith (of bush), seed or pit [U.S.] or pip [Cdn.] of a fruit*'/, LAND /'*core of a rock, center of a rock, core of anything, heart of anything inanimate*'/, *see* th'ó:m.

<sth'émlets>, stvi //s=θ'a[=Aə́=]m=ləc//, BPI /'*(have a) skinny butt, (be skinny on the rump or bottom)*'/, ANA, *see* th'ó:m.

<sth'émqsel>, ds //s=θ'a[=Aə́=]m=qsəl//, ANA ['*bridge of nose*'], literally /'bone in the nose'/, *see* th'ó:m.

<sth'emth'ó:m>, pln //s=C_1əC_2=θ'á·m//, ANA ['*bones*'], *see* th'ó:m.

<sth'émxel>, dnom //s=θ'a[=Aə́=]m=xʸəl//, ANA ['*shin*'], literally /'bone in the leg'/, *see* th'ó:m.

<sth'emxweláx̱el>, dnom //s=θ'am=xʷ=əlɛ́x̣əl or s=θ'a[=Aə=]m=xʷ=əlɛ́x̣əl//, ANA ['*(someone's) elbow*'], *see* th'ó:m.

<sth'épeq>, df //s=pɛ[=Aə́=]θ'=M2=əq//, EZ ['*striped skunk*'], ['*Mephitis mephitis spissigrada*'], *see* th'ép and its source páth' *have animal odor/stink, have animal smell.*

<Sth'éqwela>, dnom //s=θ'ə́qʷ=əlɛ//, PLN ['*Morris Lake Mountain*'], *see* ts'éqw ~ th'éqw.

<sth'eth'eló:m>, dmpn //s=C_1ə=θ'[=əl=]á·m//, ANA ['*small bones*'], *see* th'ó:m.

<sth'eth'íkw'>, dnom //s=θ'ə[=C_1ə=Aí=]k'ʷ//, ABDF /'*a sore, open sore(s)*'/, *see* th'ekw' ~ th'íkw.

<sth'íkwe>, dnom //s=θ'íkʷə//, DIR /'*the left, the left side*'/, *see* th'íkwe.

<sth'íkwechís>, dnom //s=θ'íkʷə=cə[=Aí=]s//, ANA ['*left arm*'], *see* th'íkwe.

<sth'ikweláx̱el>, dnom //s=θ'ikʷ(ə)=əlɛ́x̣əl//, ANAA ['*[left] front leg quarter of deer or other animal*'], *see* th'íkwe.

<sth'íkwem>, ds //s=θ'íkʷ=əm//, EB /'*tiny slivers of fir bark, fir bark powder*'/, *see* th'íkw.

<sth'ím ~ sth'í:m>, EB /'berry'/, *see bound root* **th'ím ~ th'í:m** *lick.*

<sth'í:m sqe'óleqw>, *berry juice* (lit. berry + fruit juice), *see* th'ím ~ th'í:m.

<sth'íms te álhqey>, cpds //s=θ'ím-s tə ʔɛ́ɬqəy//, EB /'*"snakeberry", includes false Solomon's seal, star-flowered Solomon's seal,* and probably *twisted-stalk (2 spp.)* and *Hooker's fairy bells*'/, ['*Smilacina racemosa, Smilacina stellata,* and probably *Streptopus amplexifolius, Streptopus roseus*, and *Disporum hookerii*'], literally /'berry of the snake'/, *see* th'ím ~ th'í:m.

<sth'ímàlà ~ sth'ímà:la>, ds //s=θ'ím=ɛ̀lɛ̀ ~ s=θ'ím=ɛ̀·lɛ//, HARV ['*berry-basket*'], literally /'berry container'/, *see* th'ím ~ th'í:m.

<sth'ímiya>, ds //s=θ'ím=iyɛ//, dmn, EZ /'*small (fully grown) coho salmon, [kokanee]*'/, ['small fully grown *Oncorhynchus kisutch*'], literally /'dear little berry'/, *see* th'ím ~ th'í:m.

<sth'í:qel>, df //s=θ'í ·q=əl//, LAND /'*mud, wet mud*'/, *see* th'í:q.

<sth'íth'eqel>, dnom //s=θ'í[=C_1ə=]q=əl//, LAND ['*mud*'], *see* th'í:q.

<sth'íth'eqw kúkumels>, *relish* (lit. chopped + cucumber), *see* th'íyeqw'~ th'íqw'.

<sth'íth'peq>, dmn //s=C_1í=θ'əpəq//, EZ ['*little skunk*'], *see* th'ép and páth'.

<sth'í:tsem>, df //s=θ'í·c=əm// or more likely //s=θ'ə[=Aí·=]c=əm//, EB /'*hazelnut (the nut), any nut*'/, ['*Corylus cornuta*', etc.], FOOD, possibly **<s=>** *nominalizer*, root **<th'ets>** (lit. something to get hardened, since the shell of nuts has to harden before they are edible, RG,EH 6/16/98 to SN, edited by BG with RG,EH 6/26/00), syntactic analysis: nominal, attested by AC, Elders Group, *see* th'ets.

<sth'í:tsemelhp>, ds //s=θ'í·c=əm=əɬp//, EB ['*hazelnut bush or tree*'], ['*Corylus cornuta*'], lx **<=elhp>** *tree, plant*, syntactic analysis: nominal, attested by AC, Elders Group.

<sth'íwéq'>, df //s=θ'íwə́q'//, EB ['*red elderberry (the berry)*'], ['*Sambucus racemosa*'], ASM ['the berries ripen about June and last several months, they are cooked and sweetened before eating (the small seeds can be eaten)'], MED ['cooked and sweetened they can be taken as medicine for constipation, laxative'], possibly **<s=>** *nominalizer*, root meaning unknown, syntactic analysis: nominal, attested by AC, Elders Group, *see* th'íwéq'.

<**sth'íwéq'elhp**>, ds //s=θ'íwə́q'=əɬp//, EB ['*red elderberry bush*'], ['*Sambucus racemosa*'], *see* th'íwéq'.

<**sth'kwólh**>, df //s(=)θ'k^w(=)áɬ//, SOCT /'*Lillooet people, Port Douglas (*also *Lillooet) people*'/, root meaning unknown, (<**s=**> *nominalizer*), syntactic analysis: nominal, attested by BHTTC (11/19/76).

<**sth'ó:kws**>, ds //s=θ'á·k^{w}s=s//, numc, nums, NUM ['*seven o'clock*'], *see* th'ó:kws.

<**sth'olólh**>, df //s=θ'aláɬ//, EZ ['*spring salmon which goes to Chehalis Lake in May then returns to salt water*'], ['*Oncorhynchus tshawytscha*'], *see* th'olólh.

<**sth'ó:m**>, ds //s=θ'á·m//, ANA ['*bone*'], *see* th'ó:m.

<**Sth'ó:mes**>, free root //sθ'á·məs//, PLN /'*Victoria, B.C., city of Victoria area, Fort Victoria*'/, syntactic analysis: nominal, attested by AC and CT (1973), others, borrowed from Songish dial. of N. Straits /sc'á·ŋəs/ *former village in the Fort Victoria area, Albert Head* M68:84, [Albert Head is a rocky point east of Victoria and s.w. of Equimalt and just south of present Rodd Point and Royal Roads Military Academy]. source: place names file reference #278, other sources: Wells 1965 (lst ed.):15 where he says it means *place of the gathering of ts'AW-mihs (camas)* (however both the Halkomelem and N. Straits words for camas are different than the word he cites).

<**sth'ó:qweleqw**>, stvi //s=θ'á·q^w=ələq^w//, ABDF ['*(be) bald-headed*'], *see* th'óqweleqw.

<**sth'ó:qwi ~ sth'óqwi**>, df //s=θ'á(·)q^w(=)i//, EZ /'*fish (any kind), (salmon (any kind, not trout or sturgeon) [AC])*'/, *see* th'ó:qwi ~ th'óqwi.

<**sth'óqwes**>, ds //s=θ'áq^{w}i=ə[=Aə=]s//, FSH ['*cooked fish head*'], FOOD, literally /'fish face'/, *see* th'ó:qwi ~ th'óqwi.

<**sth'óth'elh**>, strs //s=θ'ɛ[=AáC$_1$ə=]ɬ//, LT ['*(be) transparent*'], *see* th'ál.

<**sth'óth'eqwi**>, dmn //s=θ'á[=C$_1$ə=]q^{w}i//, EZ ['*small salmon (generic)*'], (<**=R1=**> *diminutive*), phonology: reduplication, syntactic analysis: nominal, attested by CT (6/8/76).

<**sth'óth'eqwi**>, dnom //s=θ'á[=C$_1$ə=]q^{w}i//, FSH /'*a fisherman, a man that goes out fishing*'/, literally /'something/someone that is fishing'/,

<**sth'ő̄wsem** or **sth'éwsem**>, df //s=θ'ə́w(=)əs=əm//, WATR ['*fine little marble-sized pieces of ice*'], ASM ['found on the river in high water at winter, they form around little burls'], *see* th'éw.

<**stl'á:leqem**>, df //s=ƛ'ɛ́·ləq(=)əm//, EZ /'*animal or bird one is afraid of and can't see, powerful creature, supernatural creature*'/, POW, ASM ['includes the sasquatch, Cannibal Ogress (Th'ő̄wx̱iya), sí:lhqey (two-headed snake), thunderbird (shxwexwó:s), water pygmies (s'ó:lmexw), schichí' (monster), underwater bear (Halkomelem name unknown), sx̱ex̱omő̄:lh (huge pretty frog with supernatural powers), X̱éylx̱elemós (chief of the river monsters), Spótpeteláx̱el (Thunderwind), and creatures (Halkomelem name unknown) seen in small muddy swirls of water which then gave the person seeing them xó:lís, *see* tl'á:leq.

<**Stl'áleqem Smált**>, cpds //s=ƛ'ɛ́ləqəm s=mɛ́lt//, PLN (probably) ['*Slollicum Peak*'], ASM ['near Chehalis, B.C.'], literally /'stl'áleqem mountain'/, *see* tl'á:leq.

<**Stl'áleqem Stótelō**>, cpds //s=ƛ'ɛ́ləqəm s=tá[=C$_1$ə=]l=əw//, PLN (probably) ['*Slollicum Creek*'], ASM ['near Chehalis, B.C.'], literally /'stl'áleqem creek'/, *see* tl'á:leq.

<**Stl'áleqem X̱ótsa**>, cpds //s=ƛ'ɛ́ləqəm x̣ácɛ//, PLN (probably) ['*Slollicum Lake*'], ASM ['near Chehalis, B.C.'], literally /'stl'áleqem lake'/, *see* tl'á:leq.

<**stl'ápx̱**>, strs //s=ƛ'ə[=Aɛ́=]p=x̣//, HARV ['*(be) scattered all over*'], DIR, MC, *see* tl'ép.

<stl'átl'el>, strs //s=ƛ'έ[=C_1ə=]l//, CLO /'*to be attached, to be fixed or fastened, be put on*'/, *see* tl'ál.

<stl'éleqw'>, df //s=ƛ'ə́l(=)əq'^{w}//, EB ['*chocolate lily*'], ['*Fritillaria lanceolata*'], *see* **<tl'éleqw'>** *a pop, a shot*, and *see* tl'ál ~ tl'á:l.

<stl'eltl'áléqem>, pln //s=C_1əC_2=ƛ'έləq=əm//, EZ /'*lots of stl'áleqems, (lots of supernatural creatures)*'/, *see* tl'á:leq.

<stl'ép>, stvi //s=ƛ'ə́p//, DIR ['*be deep*'], *see* tl'ép.

<stl'epá:leq>, ds //s=ƛ'əp=έ·ləq//, CLO /'*underskirt, petticoat*'/, *see* tl'ép.

<stl'epá:lí:ya ~ stl'epá:liya>, ds //s=ƛ'əp=έ·lí·yε//, ANA ['*ear lobe*'], *see* tl'ép.

<stl'epláts>, durs //s=ƛ'əp=lə[=Aέ=]c//, dnom, WATR /'*deep bottom (of a river, lake, water, canoe, anything)*'/, *see* tl'ép.

<stl'epó:lemelh ~ stl'epó:les>, dnom //s=ƛ'əp=á·ləməɬ ~ s=ƛ'əp=á·ləs//, ANA ['*lower circle under eye*'], *see* tl'ép.

<stl'epólwelh ~ stl'pólwelh>, stvi //s=ƛ'əp=álwəɬ//, DIR /'*(be) below, (be) underneath, (be) at the bottom of a pile or stack*'/, literally /'be on the side below'/, *see* tl'ép.

<stl'epóyethel>, dnom //s=ƛ'əp=áyθəl//, ANA ['*lower lip*'], *see* tl'ép.

<stl'ep'él:ets ~ stl'ep'élets>, df //s=ƛ'əp=G=ə́ləc or s=ƛ'əp'=ə́ləc//, ANA /'*tail (of animal, bird)*'/, ANAH ['*rump (slang)*'], *see* tl'ép'.

<stl'eqówtel>, df //s=ƛ'əq(=)áw=təl//, BSK ['*awl (any kind)*'], TOOL, *see* tl'eqów.

<stl'eqtí:m>, df //s=ƛ'εqt=í·m//, DIR ['*length*'], *see* **tl'áqt**.

<stl'eqtóletses>, ds //s=ƛ'εqt=álə(=)cəs//, ANAH /'*second finger, index finger*'/, literally /'long finger'/, *see* **tl'áqt**.

<stl'eqtl'éq>, stvi //s=C_1əC_2=ƛ'ə́q//, plv, DESC ['*spotted*'], *see* tl'eq.

<stl'éqxel>, df //s=ƛ'i[=Aə́=]q=x^{y}əl or s=ƛ'ə́q=x^{y}əl//, CLO ['*deer-skin moccasin*'], literally (probably) /'something to be stuck on on the foot'/, *see* tl'íq.

<stl'etl'íq'>, strs //s=C_1ə=ƛ'íq'//, TCH /'*(be) too tight (of shoes, clothes, trap, box), tight (of a dress one can't get into), too tight to get into (of dress, car, box of cards, etc.)*'/, *see* tl'iq'.

<stl'etl'íqw'>, strs //s=C_1ə=ƛ'íq'^{w} or s=ƛ'ə[=C_1əAí=]q'^{w}//, CLO ['*(be) all bundled up*'], *see* tl'íqw'.

<stl'ítl'eqelh ~ stl'í:tl'eqelh>, df //s=ƛ'í[=C_1ə=]q=əɬ ~ s=ƛ'í[=C_1ə=]q=əɬ or s=C_1í=ƛ'əq=əɬ//, HAT /'*child (post-baby to pre-adolescent), child (under 12), (young* [BJ])'/, *see* tl'íq.

<stl'ítl'es>, df //s=ƛ'í[=C_1ə=]s//, LT /'*(dingy white, off-white)*'/, *see* tl'ís.

<stl'ítl'esel>, strs //s=ƛ'í[=C_1ə=]s=əl//, LT /'*(be) a dark color (of clothes, complexions, etc.), (dark gray, dark brown)*'/, *see* tl'ís.

<stl'ítl'ets>, dnom //s=ƛ'í[=C_1ə=]c//, WV /'*embroidery, trimming (stitches on an edge)*'/, SPRD /'*trimmings on uniform (paddles, etc.)*'/, *see* tl'íts ~ tl'ích

<stl'ítl'leqem>, dmn //s=C_1í=ƛ'(ε)ləq=əm//, EZ /'*(little supernatural creature), little stl'áleqem*'/, *see* tl'á:leq.

<stl'lhíléstel ~ tl'lhíléstel ~ (s)t'lhíléstel>, dnom //(s=)t'ɬ=íləs=təl//, ANA ['*collarbone*'], *see* t'álh.

<**stl'óqtes**>, ds //s=ƛ'ɛ[-Aá-]qt=əs//, ANA ['*long face*'], BPI, *see* **tl'áqt**.

<**stl'pí:wel ~ tl'pí:wel**>, dnom //s=ƛ'əp=í·wəl ~ ƛ'əp=í·wəl//, CLO ['*shirt*'], literally /'something down below in the inside(s)'/, *see* tl'ép.

<**stl'p'álqel**>, df //s=ƛ'əp=G=ɛ́lqəl or s=ƛ'p'=ɛ́lqəl//, ANAB ['*long feather (from wing)*'], ASM ['used by some people to clear ears'], (semological comment: from the cognates and the meaning of the root (prob. deep) this seems more likely to mean (or have meant) *down feathers*), *see* tl'ép'.

<**stl'qáwtel**>, //s=ƛ'q(=)ɛ́w=təl//, BSK ['*awl (any kind)*'], TOOL, *see* tl'qáw or **tl'qew**.

<**stl'q'á:l**>, df //s=ƛ'q'ɛ́·l//, ANAB /'*wing, (big feather* [IHTTC]*)*'/, *see* tl'q'á:l.

<**stselá:l**>, df //s=cəlɛ́·l//, ABDF ['*be fading (of eyesight)*'], (<**s=**> *stative*), root meaning unknown root meaning unknown unless related to <**chá:l** or **chó:l**> *follow behind, go a distance*// with el-inflex *plural*, not semantically related to <**chelà:l**>, us //cəlɛ̀·l//, EFAM /'*what a lot., it's sure a lot*'/., syntactic analysis: adjective/adjectival verb, attested by AC, example: <**stselá:l te skw'áts.**>, //s=cəlɛ́·l tə s=k'^{w}ɛ́c-s//, /'*Her eyesight is fading., "Her eyes are fading."*'/, attested by AC.

<**stsél:ém**>, df //s(=)cə́l·(=)ə[=´=]m//, ANA ['*liver*'], possibly <**s=**> *nominalizer*, possibly <**=em**> *intransitivizer, have, get* or *middle voice,* perhaps <=´=> *derivational*, root meaning unknown, phonology: possible stress-shift or updrifting, syntactic analysis: nominal, attested by AC, DM (12/4/64), Deming (4/17/80), Elders Group, also <**schél:ém**>, //s=cə́l·(=)ə[=´=]m//, attested by SJ (Deming 4/17/80), other sources: ES /scə́l·ə̀m/ (CwMs /scə́ləm/) *liver*, H-T <tsúlEm> *liver.*

<**stselqwá:ls**>, ds //s=cá(=)l=əq^{w}=ɛ́·ls//, REL (possibly) ['*clean out brush from a graveyard or the ceremony of graveyard cleaning*', *see* chá:l or chó:l.

<**stselqwá<u>x</u>el**>, dnom //s=cá(=)l=əq^{w}=ɛ́x̣əl//, BLDG /'*back end of a house (inside or outside), back part of a house*'/, *see* chá:l or chó:l.

<**stselqwóthel**>, dnom //s=cá(=)l=əq^{w}=áθəl//, DIR (maybe) ['*the backwoods side*'], *see* chá:l or chó:l.

<**stselhsó:lwelh**>, ds //s=cíɬ=s=á·lwəɬ//, DIR /'*over, in the air over, above*'/, *see* chílh.

<**sts'ákw<u>x</u> ~ sch'ákw<u>x</u>**>, strs //s=c'ə[=Aɛ́=]k^{w}x̣//, FOOD ['*(already) fried*'], *see* ts'ékw<u>x</u> ~ ch'**ékw<u>x</u>**.

<**sts'á:ltexw**>, ds //s=c'ɛ́=ɛ́ltəx^{w}//, BLDG /'*top of roof, roof planks*'/, literally /'something to put/go on top of the building'/, *see* ts'á:.

<**sts'álts'**>, df //s=c'ɛ́lc'//, ANAF ['*fish scales*'], *see* ts'álts'.

<**sts'ámex**>, df //s=c'ɛ́m(=)əx^{y}//, [sc'ɛ́mɪx^{y}], FOOD ['*dry herring eggs*'], *see* ts'ám ~ ch'ám ~ **ts'ém**.

<**sts'ápe<u>x</u>el**>, strs //s=c'ə[=Aɛ́=]p=əx̣=əl//, LAND ['*(be) rusty*'], *see* ts'ápe<u>x</u>el.

<**sts'á:s ~ sts'ás**>, df //sic'=ɛ́·s or s=c'ɛ́·s//, FIRE ['*fine white ashes*'], ASM ['those from vine maple mixed with grease are medicine for swelling'], root meaning unknown unless the same as in sí:ts'elhp *vine maple* (as speculated by the Deming elders), possibly <**=á:s ~ =ás**> meaning uncertain, possibly <**s=**> *nominalizer*, phonology: possible vowel-loss, syntactic analysis: nominal, attested by Elders Group (3/1/72), TG (8/19/87), also /'*black ashes*'/, attested by Deming (1/31/80), also <**ts'sás ~ ch'sás**>, //s=c'[=M1=ɛ́s or c'sɛ́s//, LT ['*ash color*'], (semological comment: note that Tait speaker TG uses ts'sás *ashes* to map the same color that Sumas speaker AH maps with stl'ítl'es, and others (Chilliwack speaker NP and Tait speaker AK) map largely with p'éq'. stl'ítl'es then probably could be glossed *dingy white, off-white* with inceptive form stl'ítl'esel elsewhere translated *dark (old clothes,*

complexion)), phonology: probable metathesis *derivational*, syntactic analysis: adjective/adjectival verb, attested by TG, *see* charts by Rob MacLaury.

<**sts'áts'elstexw**>, caus //s=c'ɛ́[=C_1ə=]=əl=sT-əxʷ//, TVMO /'*carry it carefully, handle it with care*'/, ABFC, literally /'make/cause it to be going/coming on top'/, *see* ts'á:.

<**sts'áts'exw ~ sch'ách'exw**>, strs //s=c'ɛ́[=C_1ə=]xʷ//, LANG /'*(be) silent, quiet, keep quiet*'/, *see* ts'áxw.

<**sts'ats'íts'etl'tses**>, ds //s=C_1ɛ=c'í[=C_1ə=]ƛ'=cəs//, ANAH ['*third finger*'], literally /'shorter finger'/, *see* ts'í:tl' ~ ts'ítl'.

<**sts'á:xt**>, dnom //s=c'ɛ́·xʸt//, EB /'*tree limb, branch (of tree), (knot on a tree* [CT]*)*'/, *see* ts'á:xt.

<**sts'axtálá**>, ds //s=c'ɛxʸt=ɛ́lɛ́//, EB ['*knothole*'], literally /'container of a tree branch/limb'/, *see* ts'á:xt.

<**sts'áxw**>, stvi //s=c'ɛ́xʷ//, LANG /'*quiet or silent (after noise) (used of people), (be/have) a lull in conversation*'/, *see* ts'áxw.

<**sts'ék'**>, poss. dnom //s(=)c'ə́k'//, EB ['*pine-cone*'], (perhaps <**s=**> *nominalizer*), syntactic analysis: nominal, probably borrowed from Thompson /sc'ə́k'/ *pine nut* beside /sc'ək'-qín'-kaʔ/ *pine cone* T73:9.

<**sts'eláxwem**>, df //s=c'əl(=)ə[=Aɛ́=]xʷ=əm//, SPRD ['*an experienced spirit dancer*'], ASM ['a dancer for four years or more'], literally (possibly) /'something (or someone) that has gotten into quieter water'/, *see* ts'eláxw>, possible strs stem //c'əl(=)ə[=Aɛ́=]xʷ//, prob. from stem <**ts'élexw**>, df //c'ə́l=əxʷ//, TVMO /'*turn back into a quiet slough from the river*.

<**sts'élexw**>, dnom //s=c'ə́l=əxʷ//, WATR /'*slough, backwater, ((*also*) eddy [AC])*'/, literally /'something to go into quieter water'/, *see* ts'el *turn, turn around*.

<**sts'élqes**>, ds //s=c'ə́l=q=əs or s=c'ə́l=q'=D=əs//, HUNT ['*whirled slingshot*'], *see* root <ch'el= ~ ts'el=>

<**Sts'elxwíqw ~ Ts'elxwíqw ~ Ts'elxwéyeqw**>, ds //s=c'əl=(ə)xʷ=íqʷ ~ c'əl=(ə)xʷ=íqʷ//, PLN ['*Chilliwack River*'], SOCT ['*Chilliwack Indian people*'], *see* ts'el *turn, turn around*.

<**sts'elxwíwel**>, ds //s=c'əl=(ə)xʷ=íwəl//, ANA /'*insides (animal or human or other?), (internal organs, guts, etc.), (stomach [inside]* [DM]*)*'/, *see* ts'el *turn, turn around*.

<**sts'émlets**>, dnom //s=c'ə́m=ləc//, ANA ['*hip*'], literally (probably) /'bone on the rump'/, (<**s=**> *nominalizer*), *see* th'ó:m.

<**sts'épxwel ~ sch'épxwel**>, ds //s=c'ə́p=xʷ=əl//, ABDF ['*wart*'], *see* ts'ép.

<**sts'épx̲**>, stvi //s=c'ə́p=x̣//, DESC ['*be dirty*'], *see* ts'épx̲.

<**sts'éqw' ~ sch'éqw'**>, dnom //s=c'ə́q'ʷ//, BSK /'*fine cedar root weaving, fine cedar root work*'/, literally /'something that got pierced/poked'/, *see* ts'éqw'.

<**sts'ets'á**>, strs //s=C_1ə=c'ɛ́//, DIR ['*be on top of*'], ABFC /'*be astride, be sitting on*'/, TVMO ['*ride (on)*'], *see* ts'á:.

<**sts'éts'esem**>, dnom //s=c'i[=Aə́C_1ə=]s=əm//, EB ['*small little plants*'], literally /'something that is many little growing'/, *see* ts'ísem.

<**sts'ets'íx̲**>, strs //s=c'ə[=C_1əAí=]x̣ or s=C_1ə=c'ə[=Aí=]x̣//, BLDG ['(perhaps*) (be) clean (of a house)*'], *see* ts'ex̲ ~ **th'ex̲**.

<**sts'éxttses**>, dnom //s=c'ɛ[=Aə́=]x^{y}t=cəs//, variant of <**sts'á:xt**>, EB /*'tree limb, branch (of tree), (knot on a tree* [CT]*)'*/, *see* ts'á:xt.

<**sts'íts'exw**>, strs //s=c'í[=C$_1$ə=]x^w//, EFAM [*'(be) considerate'*], *see* **th'íxw ~ th'éxw**.

<**sts'íts'exwtel**>, rcps //s=c'í[=C$_1$ə=]x^w-təl//, EFAM [*'(be) considerate of each other'*], *see* **th'íxw ~ th'éxw**.

<**sts'iyáq**>, dnom //s=c'iyɛ́q//, FSH /*'fish trap, weir'*/, *see* **ts'iyáq ~ ch'iyáq**.

<**Sch'iyáq**>, dnom //s=c'iyɛ́q//, PLN [*'creek with its mouth on the south side of Chilliwack River and above the mouth of Middle Creek'*], *see* **ts'iyáq ~ ch'iyáq**.

<**sts'iyáye**>, df //s=c'iyáyə or s=c'[=əC$_2$=]áyə or s=c'iy=áyə//, KIN [*'twins'*], *see* ts'iyáye.

<**sts'ó:**>, dnom //s=c'á·//, KIN [*'relative (of any kind)'*], *see* ts'ó: ~ **ts'ó'**.

<**sts'ókw'elxel**>, plv //s=c'ák'^{w}=əl=x^{y}əl//, CLO [*'got (both) shoes on wrong feet'*], *see* ts'ó:kw'.

<**sts'ó:kw'xel**>, df //s=c'á·k'^{w}=x^{y}əl//, CLO [*'get a shoe on the wrong foot'*], *see* ts'ó:kw'.

<**sts'ólemeqw**>, pln //s=c'á[=lə=]m(=)əq^w//, KIN /*'great grandchildren, great grandparents'*/, *see* ts'ó:meqw.

<**sts'ó:ltsep**>, dnom //s=c'ɛ́[=Aá=]·=eltsep//, FIRE /*'flame'*/, *see* ts'á: ~ ch'á:.

<**sts'ó:lha ~ sch'ó:lha ~ sts'ólha**>, df //s=c'á·ɬ(=)ɛ ~ s=c'áɬ(=)ɛ//, EB [*'leaf'*], LT [*'leaf-green'*], *see* ts'ó:lha ~ ch'ó:lha ~ ts'ólha.

<**sts'ó:meqw**>, df //s=c'á·m(=)əq^w//, KIN /*'great grandparent, great grandchild, sibling or (up to fourth) cousin of great grandparent, great grandchild of brother or sister or (up to fourth) cousin'*/, *see* ts'ó:meqw.

<**sts'ó:qw'els**>, dnom //s=c'ə[=Aá·=]q'^{w}=əls//, sas, HHG [*'fork'*], *see* ts'éqw' *be hit (with arrow, bullet, anything shot that you've aimed), got shot, (got pierced), got poked into, got wounded (with gun or arrow)*.

<**su**>, df //s=əw ~ s=u//, CJ /*'then (action following a previous action, contrastive), so (contrastive)'*/, possibly <**s=**> *nominalizer*??, <**=ew ~ =u**> *contrastive*, phonology: always unstressed, vowel-deletion (of e), vocalization (of w after e is lost in rapid speech), syntactic analysis: conjunction, syntactic comment: connects/conjoins main verb sentences, appears attached at the end of many other particles and conjunctions, such as e *auxiliary*, ó(l) *just*, qe *and*, tl'ó ~ tl'é *that*, etc., attested by AC, Elders Group, Deming, BJ, DM, many others; found in <**sésu**>, //s-əs=u//, /*'then he, then she, then it, then they'*/, attested by Elders Group (10/27/76, etc.).

<**súkwe ~ súkwa ~ shúkwe**>, free root //súk^{w}ə ~ súk^{w}ɛ//, [súk^{w}ə ~ šúk^{w}ə], FOOD [*'sugar'*], phonology: allophone sh normally only appears before xw but also appears elsewhere in some borrowings, syntactic analysis: noun, nominal, attested by AC, MH (Deming 1/4/79), EB, Ed and Delphine Kelly (12/10/71), borrowed from Chinook Jargon /súk^{w}a ~ šúk^{w}a/ *sugar* itself from French <sucre> Johnson 1978:428, example: <**lí welí kw súkwa?**>, //lí-ə wə-lí k^w súk^{w}ɛ//, /*'Is there any sugar?'*/, attested by EB (2/2/76).

<**súkwet ~ shúkwet**>, pcs //súk^{w}ə=T//, FOOD [*'sugar it'*], (<**=t**> *purposeful control transitivizer*), syntactic analysis: transitive verb, attested by Elders Group (3/8/78).

<**shúkwe'àlà**>, ds //súk^{w}ə=ʔɛ̀lɛ̀//, FOOD [*'sugar bowl'*], HHG, lx <**='àlà ~ =álá ~ =hàlà**> *container of*, syntactic analysis: nominal, attested by Deming (at Fort Langley museum 3/9/78).

<**súp ~ sőp**>, free root //sóp//, PE ['*soap*'], syntactic analysis: noun, nominal, dialects: *Chill.*, attested by Elders Group (6/1/77), also <**súp**>, //súp//, dialects: *Cheh., Tait*, attested by Elders Group (6/1/77).

<**swá**>, ds //s=wɛ́//, PRON /'*(one's) own, belongs to (one)*'/, (<**s=**> *nominalizer*), syntactic analysis: inp, syntactic comment: is given person by possessive pronoun affixes, attested by EB, AC, AD, Elders Group, IHTTC, Salish cognate: PCS */swáʔ/ *one's own*, Pentlatch /s-wá/, Lummi and Samish dials. of N. Straits /sk^{w}éʔ/, Lushootseed /sg^{w}áʔ/ (cognate set 22 in G88a); found in <**l swá, aswá, swás, swátset, aswá'elep**>, //l s=wɛ́, ʔɛ-s=wɛ́, s=wɛ́-s, s=wɛ́-c-ət, ʔɛ-s=wɛ́-ʔələp//, /'*is mine/my own, yours/your own, his/hers/its/theirs/his own/her own/its own/their own, ours/our own, you folks'/your (pl.) own*'/, attested by EB, others, example: <**tel swá, ta' aswá, te swás, te swátset, te swáelep ~ ta' swá'elep**>, //tə-l s=wɛ́, t-ɛʔ ʔɛ-s=wɛ́, tə s=wɛ́-s, tə s=wɛ́-c-ət, tə s=wɛ́-ələp ~ t-ɛʔ s=wɛ́-ələp//, /'*my (male) own, thy (male) own, his own, our (male) own, your (male) own, their (male) own*'/, attested by EB (2/11/76), <**thel swá, tha' aswá, the swás, the swátset, the swá'elep**>, //θəl s=wɛ́, θ-ɛʔ ʔɛ-s=wɛ́, θə s=wɛ́-s, θə s=wɛ́-c-ət, θə s=wɛ́-ʔələp//, /'*my (female) own, thy (female) own, her own, our (female) own, your (pl. female) own, their (female) own*'/, attested by EB (2/11/76), <**l swátsa.**>, //l s=wɛ́-cɛ//, /'*It will be mine.*'/, attested by AC, <**l swál (sqwemáy, mámele)**>, //l s=wɛ́-l (s=q^{w}əm=ɛ́y, C$_1$ɛ́=mələ)//, /'*my (own) (dog, children)*'/, attested by AC, <**tl'ó átlh l swá tethá.**>, //ƛ'á ʔɛ-tɬ l s=wɛ́ tə=θɛ́//, /'*That's mine.*'/, attested by AD (3/6/80), <**yeláwel qé<u>x</u> tel swá.**>, //yəlɛ́w=əl qə́x̣ tə-l s=wɛ́//, /'*I've got the most.*'/, attested by Elders Group (3/9/77), <**aswát.a**>, //ʔɛ-s=wɛ́-cɛ//, /'*This is yours.*'/, attested by AC, <**tl'ó aswá.**>, //ƛ'á ʔɛ-s=wɛ́//, /'*That's yours.*'/, attested by AC, <**tl'o aswá (tál, sqwemá:y).**>, //ƛ'a ʔɛ-s+wɛ́ (tɛ́l, s=q^{w}əm=ɛ́·y)//, /'*That's your (mother, dog).*'/, attested by AC, <**tl'ó: aswá sqwmá:y?**>, //ƛ'á-ə ʔɛ-s=wɛ́ s=q^{w}əm=ɛ́·y//, /'*Is that your dog?*'/, attested by AC, <**yeláwel tl'áqt tel <u>x</u>éltel telí ta swá.**>, //yəlɛ́w=əlƛ'ɛ́qt tə-l x̣ə́l=təl təlí tɛ s=wɛ́//, /'*My pencil is longer than yours.*'/, literally /'is past/more long my writing=device from your own'/, attested by Elders Group (1/19/77), <**tl'ó swás.**>, //ƛ'á s=wɛ́-s//, /'*That's his.*'/, attested by AC, <**tl'ó swás sqwemá:y.**>, //ƛ'á s=wɛ́-s s=q^{w}əm=ɛ́·y//, /'*That's his dog.*'/, attested by AC, <**te swátset sqwemáy**>, //tə s=wɛ́-c-ət s=q^{w}əm=ɛ́y//, /'*our dog*'/, attested by AC, <**tl'ó aswá'elép tál.**>, //ƛ'á ʔɛ-s=wɛ́-ʔələ́p tɛ́l//, /'*That's your (pl.) mother.*'/, attested by AC, <**ta swá'elép sqwmá:y**>, //t-ɛ swɛ́-ʔələ́p s=q^{w}əm=ɛ́·y//, /'*your (pl.) dog, (you folks' dog)*'/, attested by AC.

<**swástexw**>, caus //s=wɛ́=sT-əx^{w}//, SOC ['*make it especially for s-o*'], (<**=st**> *causative control transitivizer*), syntactic analysis: transitive verb, attested by AD (11/19/79); found in <**swasthóxes.**>, //s=wɛ=sT-áx^{y}-əs//, /'*He made it especially for me.*'/, attested by AD (11/19/79).

<**swálém**>, df //s=wɛ́l=əm or s=wɛ́l=ə[=´=]m//, KIN ['*orphan*'], *see* wál.

<**swá:ls**>, dnom //s=wɛ́(l)=ɛ́ls//, ECON /'*scramble-giving, a scramble*'/, *see* wál or wá:l.

<**swà:m**>, df //s=wɛ̀·m//, FOOD ['*dried big clams threaded onto a string of inner cedar bark (obtained in trade)*'], EZ ['*(horse clam)*'], ['*Tersus capax ~ Schizothaerus capax*'], *see* wà:m.

<**swáqeth**>, df //s=wɛ́q(=)əθ or s=wi[=Aɛ́=]q=ə(=)θ//, KIN ['*husband*'], literally (possibly) /'someone that's a male spouse'/, *see* wáq ~ **wiq**.

<**swatíya**>, df //s(=)wɛt=íyɛ//, EZ ['*porcupine*'], ['*Erethizon dorsatum nigrescens*'], ASM ['they were a main survival food when a person was lost, you could get close and club them, they are good eating (WC)'], possibly <**s=**> *nominalizer*, possibly <**=íya**> *affectionate diminutive, little*, syntactic analysis: nominal, attested by AD (BHTTC 11/3/76, Elders Group 10/27/76), WC (Elders Group 3/21/79), Salish cognate: Lytton dial. of Thompson /swetíyeʔ/ *porcupine* B74c:9, also <**swetíya**>, //s=wət=íyɛ//, attested by Elders Group (10/27/76), also <**swet'íyá**>, //s=wət'=íyɛ//, attested by BJ (12/5/64 old p.312.

<**swáts'et**>, df //s=wɛ́c'ət//, FIRE /'*torch (made from pitch) (SJ and MV), (bark shield for fire* (Elders Group 3/6/78))'/, *see* wáts'et.

<**swáweth'**>, strs //s=wɛ́[=C_1ə=]θ'//, MC ['*(be) locked with a stick*'], *see* **wáth'**.

<**swáyel ~ swáyél ~ swàyèl**>, dnom //s=wɛ́y=əl//, WETH /'*day, daytime, sky, weather, (horizon (BJ))*'/, TIME ['*day*'], *see* wáy.

<**swáyels te Chíchelh Siyám**>, npc //s=wɛ́yəl-s tə cí[=C_1ə=]ɬ siyɛ́m//, CH ['*Christmas day*'], TIME, literally /'the day of the Lord'/, *see* chílh.

<**swék'**>, df //s=wə́k' or s=wə́q'=K//, SOCT /'*a dandy, someone who overdresses, a show-off, comedian, someone who always cracks jokes, smart-alec; proud*'/, *see* wék'.

<**Swék'ten**>, ds //s=wə́k'=tən//, N ['*Hank Pennier's nickname*'], *see* wék'.

<**swelmáylh ~ swelméylh**>, df //s=wal=əm=ɛ́yɬ//, KIN /'*child of deceased sibling, child of deceased brother/sister*'/, *see* wál.

<**swéltel**>, df //s=wɛ[=Aə́=]l=təl//, FSH /'*net (any kind, for any purpose), fish net, gill-net (Elders Group 11/26/75))*'/, HUNT /'*net (for ducks, fish)*'/, EZ ['*web (of spider)*'], literally /'something to throw device'/, *see* wál or wá:l.

<**sweltì:l**>, dnom //s=ʔəw=əl=T-ə[=Aí·=]l//, PLAY ['*a race*'], *see* eweltì:l.

<**swélwelàm**>, dnom //s=wə́l=C_1əC_2=ə[=Aɛ́=]m or s=wɛ́l=C_1əC_2=ə[=M3=]m//, SD ['*an echo*'], *see* wélwelàm ~ wélwelà:m, poss. itself from **wál** or **wá:l** *throw.*.

<**swélweleq**>, df //s=wə́l=C_1əC_2=ələq//, WATR ['*a kind of ice*'], *see* wélweleq, poss. itself from **wál** or **wá:l** *throw.*

<**swepwíp**>, plv //s=C_1əC_2=wíp//, TVMO ['*each had a heavy pack*'], HUNT, literally /'many have heavy load, many are loaded heavily'/, *see* wíp ~ wép.

<**swep'áth'**>, dnom //s=wə=p'ə́θ'//, [swʊp'ɛ́θ'], WETH ['*place where the sun comes up*'], LAND, *see* p'eth'.

<**swéta**>, free root //swə́tɛ//, [swʊ́tɛ], CLO ['*sweater*'], syntactic analysis: noun, nominal, attested by EB (12/18/75).

<**swétexel**>, df //s=wə́tə=xʸəl or s=wə́t=əxʸ=əl//, WETH ['*rainbow*'], *see* wétexel.

<**swets'a'á**>, dnom //s=wə=c'ɛʔɛ́//, LAND ['*the summit (of a mountain)*'], *see* ts'á:.

<**swewíp**>, df //s=C_1ə=wíp//, TVMO ['*more than one person heavily loaded with packs*'], HUNT, *see* wíp ~ wép.

<**Swílth'**>, df //s=wíl=θ' or s=wə[=Aí=]l=θ' or s=wɛ[=Aí=]l=θ'//, PLN ['*wide place at the mouth of the east (upriver) branch of Jones Creek*'], ASM ['just downriver from Ohamil (branch now bulldozed over) where peoplefished with nets for qw'áts' (elephant sucker fish)'], probably root <**wel ~ wál**> *throw*, compare <**s=wél=tel**> *net* and <**wá:l=x**> *throw s-th*, (<**s=**> *nominalizer*), (<**í-ablaut**> *durative*?), lx <**=th'**> *small portion*, phonology: probable ablaut, syntactic analysis: nominal, attested by AK and JL (Seabird Is. place names trip 4/7/78), IHTTC (AK esp., SP absent 8/5/77), AK and SP and AD (8/30/77), source: place names file reference #185.

<**Swílhcha**>, df //s=wíy=ɬcɛ//, PLN /'*Cultus Lake, (*also *village at Cultus Lake near Hatchery Creek [Wells (lst ed.):19])*'/, ASM ['the name Cultus is just Chinook Jargon for *bad* because the lake was avoided by many people because of stl'áleqem creatures in its waters, if one looked into the water and

saw circular stirrings of murk in the lake these were stl'áleqem creatures and one could get xó:lís (*sick from seeing supernatural/stl'áleqem creatures*) and vomit until one died; Boas, Hill-Tout and Wells give stories of these creatures which were said to strip the flesh from human divers into the lake, people training for power sometimes used the lake because of its danger, it was also said to have an outlet in its bottom that lead underground out to the ocean; the stl'áleqem creatures have been gone for years now and annual canoe races are held on the lake, which is a provincial park; before contact there was a settlement of Nooksack people on the lake'], possibly <**s=**> *nominalizer*, possibly root <**wíy ~ wáy**> *warning*, lx <**=(e)lhcha**> *dirty water, unclear liquid*, syntactic analysis: nominal, attested by AC (8/14/70), source: place names file reference #166, other sources: Wells 1965 (lst ed.):11, Wells 1966, also /'*village at Cultus Lake near Hatchery Creek*'/, source: Wells (lst ed.):19.

<**Swílhcha Stótelō**>, cpds //s=wíy=ɬcɛ s=tá[=C_1ə=]l=ow//, PLN ['*Sweltzer Creek (the stream from Cultus Lake to Chilliwack River at Soowahlie)*'], ASM ['Sweltzer is a poorly-spelled effort to spell Swílhcha'], literally /'warning dirty water creek/little river'/, (<=**R1**=> *diminutive*), phonology: reduplication, syntactic analysis: simple nominal phrase, source: Wells 1965 (lst ed.):13.

<**Swílhcha Smá:lt**>, cpds //s=wíy=ɬcɛ s=mɛ́·lt//, PLN /'*Cultus Lake Mountain, actually Mount Amadis or International Ridge*'/, ASM ['see 1858 map'], literally /'warning dirty water mountain'/, syntactic analysis: simple nominal phrase, source: Wells 1965 (lst ed.):11, source: place names file reference #317.

<**swí:qe ~ swíyeqe ~ swíyqe**>, df //s=wí·q=ə//, HAT ['*man (15 years and up)*'], EZ ['*male (creature)*'], EB ['*male (plant)*'], *see* wíyeq ~ wíyq ~ wí:q.

<**swiqe'ál** or **swiyeqe'ál**>, df //s=wiq=ə=ʔɛ́l//, EB ['*male part of male plant*'], *see* wíyeq ~ wíyq ~ wí:q.

<**swíp**>, strs //s=wə[=Aí=]p//, TVMO ['*(be) loaded with a heavy pack*'], HUNT, *see* wíp ~ wép.

<**swí:tì**>, free root //swí·tì//, SD ['*call of the chickadee*'], ASM ['another call is English "swéet-hèart"'], syntactic analysis: interjection, attested by TM (Elders Group 5/14/80), borrowed from possibly English <sweetie>?? or perhaps a pre-contact form.

<**swí:we ~ swíwe**>, df //s=wí(·)wə or s=wí(·)w=ə or s=C_1í=wə or s=wí(·)=C_1ə//, EZ /'*eulachon, oolachen, candle-fish*'/, ['*Thaleichthys pacificus*'], ASM ['small oily fish that run in great numbers up the Fraser River in spring], *see* wí:we ~ wíwe.

<**swíweles ~ swíwles**>, df //s=C_1í=wələs or s=wí[=C_1ə=]ləs//, HAT /'*adolescent boy (about 10 to 15 yrs. old), teenaged boy, young man (teenager)*'/, *see* wíweles.

<**swíwíqe**>, dmn //s=C_1í=wíq=ə//, HAT /'*little man, small man*'/, *see* wíyeq ~ wíyq ~ wí:q.

<**swiwiqe'ó:llh**>, dmn //s=C_1í=wiq=ə=ʔá·lɬ//, HAT ['*boy (from baby to 4 or 5 years)*'], *see* wíyeq ~ wíyq ~ wí:q.

<**swíyeqe ~ swíyqe ~ swí:qe**>, df //s=wí·q=ə//, HAT ['*man (15 years and up)*'], EZ ['*male (creature)*'], EB ['*male (plant)*'], *see* wíyeq ~ wíyq ~ wí:q.

<**swiyeqe'ó:llh**>, ds //s=wí·q=ə=ʔá·lɬ//, HAT ['*boy (from 5 to 10 yrs.)*'], *see* wíyeq ~ wíyq ~ wí:q.

<**swókwel**>, df //s=wákʷ=əl//, EZ /'*common loon,* possibly also *red-throated loon* (though that has a separate name in Squamish), possibly also *arctic loon*'/, ['*Gavia immer,* possibly also *Gavia stellata*, possibly also *Gavia arctica*'], possibly <**s=**> *nominalizer*, possibly <**=el**> *intransitivizer, have, get or come, go, get, become*, root meaning unknown, syntactic analysis: nominal, attested by Elders Group (3/1/72, 6/4/75), AC, BJ (12/5/64), other sources: ES and JH /swákʷəl/ *loon*, Salish cognate:

Squamish /swákʷl/ *common loon* W73:167, K69:60 and Squamish /swákʷəl/ *common loon (Gavia immer)* Kennedy and Bouchard 1976:65.

<**Swókwel**>, df //s=wákʷ=əl//, PLN ['*Sowaqua Creek*'], literally /'loon'/, syntactic analysis: nominal, attested by Elders Group (3/1/72), source: place names file reference #113.

<**swóqeweqeweth** (or better) **swóq-weqeth**>, plv //s=wɛ[=Aá=]q=C_1əC_2=ə(=)θ//, strs, KIN /'*married women, ((plural) got husbands)*'/, *see* wáq ~ **wiq**.

<**swótle**>, df //s=wɛ[=Aá=]t=lə//, PRON /'*somebody, someone*'/, *see* wát.

<**swóweles**>, pln //s=wi[=Aá=][=C_1ə=]ləs//, HAT ['*lots of adolescent/teenaged boys*'], *see* wíweles.

<**swóweqeth**>, dnom //s=wɛ[=AáC_1ə=]q=ə(=)θ//, KIN /'*hubby, dear husband, pet term for husband*'/, *see* wáq ~ **wiq**.

<**swóweqeth**>, stvi //s=wɛ[=AáC_1ə=]q=ə(=)θ//, KIN /'*married woman, got a husband, got married to a husband*'/, literally /'be having a male spouse, got a male spouse'/, *see* wáq ~ **wiq**.

<**Swóyel**>, df //s=wɛ[=Aá=]y=əl//, PLN ['*village across from or a little above the mouth of Centre Creek into Chilliwack River*'], possibly <**s=**>*nominalizer*, possibly <**=el**> *come, go, get, become or intransitivizer, have, get*, possibly <**ó-ablaut**> *derivational*, possibly root <**wáy**> *warn(ing)*, (semological comment: this root is possible because all the villages on the Chilliwack River were wiped out by avalanches at one point or other, including presumably this one; there was a story of a boy who detected a widening crack in rocks above his village (not necessarily this one) and tried to warn the village, only his grandfather believed him and they alone were saved when they moved out in time), phonology: possible ablaut, syntactic analysis: nominal, source: Wells 1966 <SWIY-ihl>.

<**swő̃qw'elh**>, df //s=wóq'ʷ=əɬ//, WV /'*woven goat-wool blanket, (twilled weave (JL))*'/, *see* wő̃qw'elh.

<**sxáwelh**>, //s=xʸɛ́(=ə)wəɬ//, *see* main entry <**xá:welh**>, //xʸ=ɛ́·wəɬ or xʸɛ́=ɛ́wəɬ//, ANA /'*woman's genitals, vulva, vagina*'/.

<**sxáxem**>, strs //s=xʸɛ́[=C_1ə=]m//, WATR ['*shallow*'], *see* xá:m.

<**sxáxem**>, dnom //s=xʸɛ́[=C_1ə=]m//, WATR ['*shallow water*'], *see* xá:m.

<**sxáye**>, df //s=xʸɛ́(=i)yə//, KIN /'*a husband's younger wives, co-wife*'/, (<**s=**> *nominalizer*), possibly root <**xá**> *genital*, possibly <**=iye**> *affectionate diminutive*, phonology: possible vowel merger, syntactic analysis: nominal, attested by AC (8/15/70), other sources: ES /sxʸá·yɛ/ *co-wife*, Salish cognate: Squamish /šáʔyu/ *co-wife; screech owl; corpse; lie dead* W73:289, K67:323, Samish dial. of NSt /sáyeʔ/ *two wives, co-wives, husband of ex-wife, wife of ex-husband* G86:79.

<**sxélcha ~ sxélche**>, dnom //s=xʸə́lcɛ ~ s=xʸə́lcə//, FSH /'*one's catch (fish, game, etc.)*'/, HUNT, *see* xélcha ~ xélche.

<**sxéle**>, df //s=xʸə́lə or s=xʸɛ[=Aə́=](=)lə//, ANA ['*penis*'], *see* x= and **xéle**.

<**Sxéle**>, df //s=xʸə́lə//, PLN ['*Penis Rock near Cheam View*'], *see* x= and **xéle**.

<**sxelmá:l**>, pln //s=xʸə[=lə=]mɛ́·l//, SOC ['*enemies*'], *see* xemá:l.

<**sxéltsep**>, ds //s=xʸə́l=(ə́l)cəp//, FIRE ['*firedrill*'], TOOL, *see* xél>, bound root //xʸə́l *roll, rotate*//.

<**sxélts' ~ sxél:ts'**>, ds //s=xʸə́l=lc'//, ANAB /'*feather (any kind), (fine feathers [EB], small feathers [IHTTC], lots of feathers [EB])*'/, literally /'something to rotate around in circles'/, *see* xél> *roll, rotate*.

<**sxemá:l**>, df //s=xʸəmɛ́·l//, SOC ['*enemy*'], *see* xemá:l.

<**Sxixálh**>, df //sx^{y}ix^{y}έɬ or s=C$_1$í=x^{y}έɬ//, SOCT /'*Sechelt people, Sechelt person*'/, (<**s=**> *nominalizer*), possibly <**R4=**> *diminutive*, comment: words for non-Halkomelem-speaking Indian people are easily assumed to be borrowed into Halkomelem when the words are related in shape, but it is also possible that the form is cognate in the two languages, not just borrowed, or even that the term used for a people came first from another language; since these are possibilities, if a derivation of a name is seems possible in Halkomelem, I have given that analysis as a possibility even if it seems less likely than just being a borrowing; here it is clear that at least the s= *nominalizer* prefix is Halkomelem and not part of a borrowing since the Sechelt word for the Sechelt people is Shishálh with no s= prefix, syntactic analysis: nominal, attested by NP (2/22/80), also <**Sixálh**>, //six^{y}έɬ//, attested by AD (2/22/80), Salish cognate: Sechelt /šišέɬ/ AD and NP 2/22/80, Beaumont 1985:xvii.

<**sxíxeles**>, stvi //s=x^{y}í[=C$_1$ə=]l(=)əs//, EFAM /'*insistant, persistant (like a child pressing to go along), bull-headed, doesn't mind, does just the opposite, (stubborn, contrary)*'/, *see* xíxeles.

<**sxíxep**>, dnom //s=x^{y}í[=C$_1$ə=]p//, TOOL ['*a planer*'], *see* xíp.

<**sxíxeq?** or **sxíxeq'?**>, df //s=x^{y}í[=C$_1$ə=]q or s=C$_1$í=x^{y}εq'//, EB ['*a kind of blueberry*'], *see* xíq.

<**sxí:xets' ~ sxíxets'**>, df //s=xí·[=C$_1$ə=]c'//, EB /'*(be in the) woods, (amidst bush or vegetation, be tucked away?)*'/, *see* xí:ts' ~ xíts' ~ xets'.

<**sxiyí:ws**>, ds //s=x^{y}εy=í·ws or s=x^{y}ε[=Aə=]y=í·ws or s=x^{y}ε[=Ai=]y=í·ws//, ABDF ['*smallpox*'], literally (probably) /'like fish scales on the skin/body'/, *see* xá:y ~ xà:y.

<**sxókw'**>, dnom //s=x^{y}ák'^{w}//, TIME ['*fourth day after a death (when everyone washes up (bathes))*'], REL, SOC, *see* xókw' ~ xó:kw'.

<**Sxowál??** or **Xowál??**>, df //s=x^{y}aw(=)έl or x^{y}aw(=)έl//, PLN ['*village above Ruby Creek*'], possibly <**s=**> *nominalizer*, possibly root <**xow**> *bone* (an old root), possibly <**=á:l**> *similar to, -like, or part/portion*, syntactic analysis: nominal, source: Wells 1965 (lst ed.):25 <shah-WEHL>.

<**sxóxep**>, strs //s=x^{y}á[=C$_1$ə=]p'//, ABFC ['*(be) squatting*'], *see* xóp'.

<**sxoxwí:ls**>, dnom //s=x^{y}a[=C$_1$ə=]l=əls//, sas, TOOL /'*a borer, an auger*'/, *see* xó:l.

<**sxoxwő:ls**>, sas //s=x^{y}a[-C$_1$ə-]l=əls//, cts, TOOL /'*boring a hole*'/, *see* xó:l.

<**sxtl'í:qw**>, ds //s=x^y(ε)ƛ'=í·q^w//, ANA ['*head of the penis*'], literally /'the top of the head of an erection'/, *see* xátl'.

<**sxwehóthes**>, dnom //s(=)x^w=əhá=aθəs//, CLO ['*a veil*'], literally /'something wrapped on the face'/, phonology: TG's idiolect consistently has [sx^w] where other speakers have [šx^w]; also in this citation the initial glottal stop of the root has been dropped, *see* ehó.

<**sx̱á:lts'**>, strs //s=x̣ə[=Aέ·=]l=(əl)c'//, DIR /'*(be) turned around, turned the wrong way*'/, *see* x̱élts'.

<**sx̱á:lts'emeth'**>, strs //s=x̣ə[=Aέ·=]l=c'=əməθ'//, ds, EB ['*grown twisted (of a tree)*'], *see* x̱élts'.

<**sx̱álts'ewel**>, ds //s=x̣ə[=Aέ=]l=c'=iwəl//, ABFC ['*be twisted*'], literally /'be twisted in the insides'/, *see* x̱élts'.

<**sx̱álts'xel**>, ds //s=x̣ə[=Aέ=]l=c'=x^{y}əl//, ABFC ['*(have the) legs crossed*'], *see* x̱élts'.

<**sx̱á:meth**>, df //s=x̣έ·m=əθ or sέ·x̣=M1=əθ//, EB ['*black cottonwood cambium (soft matter between the bark and the wood)*'], ['cambium from *Populus balsamifera trichocarpa*'], ASM ['the sweet cambium was scraped or licked off of the peeled bark and eaten fresh, it was not bitter but (according to Turner 1975:226) soured or fermented very quickly when exposed to air'], possibly <**s=**> *nominalizer*,

possibly <**metathesis**> *derivational*, possibly root <**x̲á:m**> *weep* (perhaps *tears on the tongue* since the sap looks like tears on the bark) or possibly root <**sá:x̲**> as in <**sásex̲=em**> *bitter* and as in <**sx̲ámeléxwthelh**> *tiger lily*, lx <**=eth**> *in the mouth or edge*, syntactic analysis: nominal, contrast <**ts'its'emá:welh**> *cottonwood cambium*, contrast <**chewő welhp ~ chewő:lhp**> *black cottonwood.*

<**sx̲áx̲as**>, strs //s=x̣ɛ́[=C_1ə=]s//, EFAM /'*(be) determined, got your mind made up*'/, *see* x̲ás.

<**sx̲áx̲e**>, strs //s=x̣ɛ́=C_1ə//, REL /'*(be) sacred, holy*'/, *see* x̲áx̲e.

<**Sx̲áx̲e**>, dnom //s=x̣ɛ́=C_1ə//, PLN /'*Morris Creek (near Chehalis, B.C.), Morris Lake (near Chehalis)*'/, literally /'something to be sacred/taboo'/, *see* x̲áx̲e.

<**sx̲ax̲elh(l)át ~ sx̲ex̲elh(l)at**>, REL ['*Sunday (sacred day)*'], *see* x̲áx̲e.

<**sx̲ax̲esélmet**>, EFAM ['*determination*'], *see* x̲ás.

<**Sx̲áx̲e Smá:lt**>, PLN ['*Morris Mountain (near Chehalis)*'], *see* x̲áx̲e.

<**sx̲ax̲e'áylh**>, HUMC ['*deformed baby*'], *see* x̲áx̲e.

<**Sx̲elálets??**>, df //s=x̣əl=ɛ́ləc??//, PLN ['*Sumas Prairie west (on the west side of Sumas Lake)*'], possibly <**s=**> *nominalizer*, possibly <**=álets**> *on the bottom*, possibly root <**x̲el**> *marked, painted*, syntactic analysis: nominal, source: Wells 1965 (lst ed.):15 <S'Q-lah-lehts> (hyphen through Q) *Sumas Prairie west (on west side of Sumas Lake).*

<**sx̲elá:ls**>, SCH ['*writings*'], *see* x̲él ~ **x̲é**:yl (or better) x̲í:l.

<**Sx̲elá:wtxw**>, PLN /'*Schelowat, a village at the bend in Hope Slough at Annis Rd. where there was a painted or marked house*'/, *see* x̲él ~ **x̲é**:yl (or better) x̲í:l.

<**sx̲él:e**>, ANA /'leg'/, *see* x̲él:e

<**sx̲éles**>, BSK ['*picture, design, design on basket*'], *see* x̲él ~ **x̲é**:yl (or better) x̲í:l.

<**sx̲éles te chékel**>, FOOD /'*chicken drumstick*'/, (lit. leg of + the + chicken),*see* x̲éle

<**sx̲elpéla**>, ANAH ['*sideburn(s)*'], *see* x̲él ~ **x̲é**:yl (or better) x̲í:l.

<**sx̲élqs**>, DESC ['*a stripe (on the nose or point)*'], *see* x̲él ~ **x̲é**:yl (or better) x̲í:l.

<**sx̲elx̲éles**>, BSK /'*designs on basket, basket designs*'/, *see* x̲él ~ **x̲é**:yl (or better) x̲í:l.

<**sx̲elx̲éles te syó:qwem**>, WETH ['*rays of light, sunbeams*'], *see* x̲él ~ **x̲é**:yl (or better) x̲í:l *or* yéqw.

<**sx̲élx̲elqs**>, DESC ['*stripes (on the nose or point)*'], *see* x̲él ~ **x̲é**:yl (or better) x̲í:l.

<**sx̲elx̲éyle**>, ANA /'*legs (more than two, for ex. non-human)*'/, *see* s**x̲é**l:e.

<**sx̲élh**>, ABDF /'*a wound, (a hurt?)*'/, *see* x̲élh.

<**sx̲élhx̲elh**>, ANAF /'*tiny fin above tail of fish, (*perhaps *spines above tail of some fish)*'/, *see* x̲élh.

<**sx̲épeqw** (or **sx̲ép'eqw?** or **sx̲ép'ekw'?)**>, dnom //s=x̣ə́p=əq^{w} or s=x̣ə́p'=D=əq^{w} (or s=x̣ə́p'=əq^{w} or s=x̣ə[=´=]p'ək'^{w})//, ANAF ['*edible gristle inside fish head (nose gristle)*'], literally (perhaps) /'something crispy/to chew with a crunch in the top of the head'/, *see* x̲épeqw (or x̲ép'eqw? or x̲ép'ekw'?)

<**sx̲épxel** (or **sx̲ép'xel)**>, dnom //s=x̣ə́p=x^{y}əl or s=x̣ə́p'=D=x^{y}əl (or s=x̣ə́p'=x^{y}əl)//, ANAF ['*fish tail*'], literally perhaps /'something to chew with a crunch on the foot (tail)'/, *see* x̲épxel (or x̲ép'xel).

<**sx̲eq'x̲éq'et**>, LAND ['*a little bluff (of rock)*'], *see* x̲eq'.

<**sx̲éwe**>, dnom //s=x̣ə́wə//, FOOD ['*dried fish backbone (with meat left on it)*'], *see* x̲éwe.

<**sx̲ex̲ákw'**>, SH /'*(be) squeezed in, jammed up, tight*'/, *see* x̲ékw'.

<**sx̲ex̲ákw'**>, LAND /'*canyon (narrow, walled in with rock)*'/, *see* x̲ékw'.

<**sx̲ex̲é:yl**>, SCH ['*already written*'], *see* x̲él ~ **x̲é**:yl (or better) x̲í:l.

<**sx̲ex̲é:yle** or **sx̲ex̲í:le**>, ANAH /'*whole leg, (whole of both legs)*'/, *see* s**x̲é**l:e.

<**sx̲ex̲éyle** or **sx̲ex̲íle**>, ANAH /'*(both human) legs, (both) feet*'/, *see* s**x̲é**l:e.

<**sx̲ex̲é:yls**>, SCH /'*something one writes with, (writing implement)*'/, *see* x̲él ~ **x̲é**:yl (or better) x̲í:l.

<**sx̲ex̲óm̋ōlh**>, df //s=x̣ɛ=C_1ə=phám=ówɬ or s=x̣ə[=C_1əAá=]m=óɬ//, EZ ['*huge pretty frog with supernatural powers*'], *see* x̲áx̲e> *sacred, holy, taboo*

<**sx̲éyeltel ~ sx̲í:ltel**>, ABFC /'*footprint, tracks*'/, *see* s**x̲é**l:e.

<**Sx̲éyeltels Te Sqoyéx̲iya**>, PLN /'*the Tracks of Mink, holes shaped like a mink's tracks toward the base of the rock-face called Xwyélés or Lexwyélés*'/, *see* s**x̲é**l:e.

<**sx̲éyes ~ sx̲éy:es**>, df //s=x̣éy(·)=əs//, ANA ['*head (of any living thing)*'], *see* x̲éyes ~ x̲éy:es.

<**Sx̲éyes te Sx̲wó:yx̲wey**>, PLN ['*rock that was a sx̲wó:yx̲wey head (mask) turned to stone at X̲elhlálh*'], *see* sx̲éyes ~ sx̲éy:es.

<**Sx̲éyes te Sx̲wó:yx̲wey**>, PLN ['*a sx̲wó:yx̲wey head turned to stone on land at X̲elhlálh somewhere*'], *see* sx̲wó:yx̲wey ~ sx̲wóyx̲wey under x̲wóy.

<**sx̲éykwel**> ~ <**sx̲íkwel**>, df //s=x̣ík^w=əl or s=x̣ə́yk^w=əl//, EB /'*wild red potato (grew at American Bar in the 1920's),* possibly *Jerusalem artichoke*'/, ['possibly *Helianthus tuberosus*'], ASM ['a tall plant with big leaves, pigs later ate these potatoes'], *see* x̲íkwel.

<**sx̲éykwel**> ~ <**sx̲íkwel**>, df //s=x̣í(y)k^w=əl//, ANA ['*gizzards*'], *see* x̲íkwel.

<**Sx̲é:ylmet** or **sx̲é:ylmet**>, EZ ['*male black bear with white spot [or mark] on the chest*'], *see* x̲él ~ **x̲é**:yl (or better) x̲í:l.

<**Sx̲éylmòt** or **sx̲éylmòt**>, EZ ['*female black bear with white spot [or mark] on the chest*'], *see* x̲él ~ **x̲é**:yl (or better) x̲í:l.

<**sx̲éylstexw**>, SCH ['*got s-th written down*'], *see* x̲él ~ **x̲é**:yl (or better) x̲í:l.

<**sx̲éyp**> ~ <**sx̲íp**>, df //s=x̣í(=)p or s=x̣í=p'=D//, LT ['*a line*'], *see* x̲íp ~ **x̲éyp**.

<**sx̲éypx̲ep**>, LT ['*lots of lines*'], *see* x̲íp ~ **x̲éyp**.

<**sx̲éytl'**>, TIME ['*winter*'], *see* x̲éytl' ~ x̲í:tl'.

<**sx̲éyx̲ep**>, LT ['*lines*'], *see* x̲íp ~ **x̲éyp**.

<**sx̲éyx̲ep'**>, LT ['*a stripe*'], *see* x̲íp' ~ x̲éyp'.

<**sx̲eyx̲ep'ewíts ~ sx̲eyx̲ep'ōwíts**>, LT ['*striped on back*'], *see* x̲íp' ~ x̲éyp'.

<**sx̲éyx̲eth'**>, EFAM ['*disappointed and angry-looking without talking*'], *see* x̲íth' ~ **x̲é**yth'.

<**sx̲eyx̲eth'ó:ythel**>, ABDF /'*ugly expression in mouth, ugly grin*'/, *see* x̲íth' ~ **x̲é**yth'.

<**sx̲éyx̲ewes**>, EFAM /'*(be) scowling (if mad or ate something sour), ((made a) funny (strange) face [Elders Group 1/21/76])*'/, *see* x̲éywel.

<**sx̲e'áth'**>, DESC /'*a measure, a true mark*'/, *see* x̲áth' ~ x̲e'áth'.

<**sx̲e'áth'**>, HARV ['*spotted (marked and located)*'], *see* x̲áth' ~ x̲e'áth'.

<**sx̲e'áth'tel**>, dnom //s=x̣[=əʔɛ́=]θ'=təl//, DESC /*'measuring device'*/, prob. also /*'ruler, tape measure'*/, *see* x̲áth' ~ x̲e'áth'.

<**sx̲e'áth'tels té tèmèxw**>, cpds //s=x̣[=əʔɛ́=]θ'=təl-s tə́ tə̀mə̀xʷ//, PLN /*'map'*/, *see* x̲áth' ~ x̲e'áth'.

<**sx̲e'óthels**>, TIME /*'Thursday, four o'clock, (fourth cyclic period)'*/, *see* x̲e'ó:thel ~ x̲e'óthel.

<**sx̲íkwel**> ~ <**sx̲éykwel**>, df //s=x̣íkʷ=əl or s=x̣ə́ykʷ=əl//, EB /*'wild red potato (grew at American Bar in the 1920's),* possibly *Jerusalem artichoke'*/, ['possibly *Helianthus tuberosus*'], ASM ['a tall plant with big leaves, pigs later ate these potatoes'], *see* x̲íkwel.

<**sx̲íkwel**> ~ <**sx̲éykwel**>, df //s=x̣í(y)kʷ=əl//, ANA [*'gizzards'*], *see* x̲íkwel.

<**sx̲íp**> ~ <**sx̲éyp**>, df //s=x̣í(=)p or s=x̣í=p'=D//, LT [*'a line'*], *see* x̲íp> ~ <**x̲éyp**.

<**Sx̲óchaqel**>, PLN [*'Chilliwack Lake'*], *see* x̲ó:tsa ~ x̲ó:cha.

<**sx̲ó:lem**>, LT /*'(be) real gray (of hair), (grey hair)'*/, *see* x̲ólem.

<**sx̲ó:lts'iyethel**>, ABDF [*'to have a crooked jaw'*], *see* x̲élts'.

<**sx̲ómes**>, dnom //s=x̣ɛ́[=Aá=]m=əs//, SOC //'a gift in memory from someone gone'//, PE, SPRD, lit./ "something - wept - on the face"/, *see* **x̲à:m ~ x̲á:m**.

<**sx̲óyeseqw ~ sq'óyeseqw**>, df //s=x̣áyəs=əqʷ ~ s=q'áyəs=əqʷ//, CLO [*'soft feathers put in oiled hair for dancing'*], *see* x̲óyes.

<**sx̲óytl'thet ~ sx̲ó:ytl'thet**>, stvi //s=x̣á(·)yƛ'=T-ət or s=x̣á(·)yƛ'=θət or s=x̣ɛ[=Aá=y=]ƛ'=T-ət or s=x̣ɛ[=Aá=y=]ƛ'=θət//, EFAM /*'(be) aggressive, cranky, ready to fight, (be) violent, hot-headed'*/, *see* x̲óytl' ~ x̲ó:yt.

<**sx̲tá(:)**>, QUAL /*'the same kind, the same'*/, *see* x̲ét'e.

<**sx̲tá(:)stexw**>, TIB [*'do it this way'*], *see* x̲ét'e.

<**sx̲wéqw'ellhelh**>, CLO [*'necklace'*], *see* x̲wíqw'.

<**sx̲wéqw'lhelh**>, CLO /*'scarf, neckerchief'*/, *see* x̲wíqw'.

<**Sx̲wesálh**>, PLN /*'place above Yale where the Fraser River splits around a rock, island above Steamboat Island (latter just below Five-Mile Creek)'*/, *see* x̲wés.

<**sx̲wétexel** or **sx̲wét'exel**>, df //s=x̣ʷə́tə=xʸəl or s=x̣ʷə́t'=əxʸəl//, [sx̣ʷɪ́tɪxʸɪl or sx̣ʷɪ́t'ɪxʸɪl], WETH [*'rainbow'*], LT, possibly <**s=**> *nominalizer*, possibly <**=xel**> *precipitation*, root meaning unknown, phonology: I recall transcribing t' in one variant but no longer have that transcription, t' and x̲w both seem most likely since they are both present in N. Straits and Lushootseed cognates, syntactic analysis: nominal, dialects: *Cheh.*, attested by HP via NP (Elders Group 5/16/79), contrast <**stheqelxélém ~ stheqelxél:ém ~ thelqxálém**> *rainbow*, Salish cognate: Songish dial. of N. Straits /xʷətáʔšən/ *rainbow* M68:131 (but she also transcribes /x̣ʷ/ as /xʷ/ throughout, so this could also be /x̣ʷətáʔšən/), Samish dial. of N. Straits /xʷə́t'ašən/ *rainbow* G86:64, Lushootseed /s-t'əx̣ʷšád/ *rainbow* (LG) beside /s-t'əx̣ʷšád/ *root* (LG and another speaker) ~ /s-t'ə́x̣ʷšəd/ *root (esp. cedar), ancestors (fig.)* (other speakers) H76:531, also <**swétexel ~ swét'exel**>, //s=wə́tə=xʸəl ~ s=wə́t'=əxʸəl//, [swɪ́tɪxʸɪl ~ swɪ́t'ɪxʸɪl], attested by Elders Group, Deming.

<**sx̲wétl'qel**>, df //s=x̣ʷə́ƛ'=qəl//, HHG /*'pillow, rolled bulrush mat'*/, *see* x̲wétl' probably *rolled.*

<**sx̲wetl'qelá:la**>, HHG /*'pillow slip, pillow-case'*/, *see* sx̲wétl'qel.

<**sx̲wewál**>, df //s=x̣ʷəwɛ́l or s=x̣ʷɛ́w=ə[=M2=]l or more likely x̣ʷ[=F=]əw(=)ə=ɛ́l//, EZ [*'fox'*], [*'Vulpes fulva cascadensis'*], *see* x̲wewe.

<**sx̱wéxixeq ~ sx̱w'éxixeq**>, df //s=x̣ʷə́xʸixʸəq ~ s=x̣ʷʔə́xʸixʸəq or s=x̣ʷ(ʔ)ə́=C_1í=xʸəq or s=x̣ʷ(ʔ)ə́=xʸi[=C_1ə=]q or s=x̣ʷ(ʔ)ə́xʸ=əC_2=əq//, EB /'*small gray mountain blueberry on a low plant, dwarf blueberry*'/, ['*Vaccinium caespitosum*'], *see* xíq.

<**sx̱wex̱wéyt** or **sx̱wex̱wít**>, SH ['*torn*'], *see* x̱wét.

<**sx̱wex̱wiyám ~ sx̱wōx̱wiyá:m**>, LANG /'*child's fable, story, fairy tale, child's story*'/, *see* x̱wiyám.

<**sx̱wéythiyes ~ sx̱wíythiyes**>, CLO /'*headdress, face costume, mask*'/, *see* x̱wíyth.

<**sx̱wík'**>, df //s=x̣ʷík' or s=x̣ʷiq'=F//, EZ /'*winter robin, bush robin, varied thrush*'/, ['*Ixoreus naevius naevius*'], SD ['*call of the winter robin or varied thrush*'], *see* x̱wík'.

<**sx̱wíqel**>, df //s=x̣ʷíq(=)əl or s=x̣ʷə[=Aí=]q=əl//, WETH ['*tree bent to ground with ice and frozen*'], EB, *see* x̱wíqel.

<**sx̱wítl'**>, df //s(=)x̣ʷíƛ'//, EZ /'*catbird (has black head), rufous-sided towhee*'/, ['*Pipilo erythrophthalmus*'], *see* x̱wítl'.

<**sx̱wíx̱weqw'**>, FSH ['*(hung up in a fish net)*'], *see* x̱wíqw'.

<**sx̱wiyám**>, LANG /'*story, (myth, legend)*'/, *see* x̱wiyám.

<**sx̱wíythi ~ sx̱wéythi**>, PE /'*likeness, portrait, photograph, photo, statue*'/, *see* x̱wíyth.

<**sx̱wíythiyes ~ sx̱wéythiyes**>, CLO /'*headdress, face costume, mask*'/, *see* x̱wíyth.

<**sx̱wolex̱wiyám**>, HAT ['*ancient people over a hundred years old*'], *see* x̱wiyám.

<**sx̱wotíx**>, df //s=x̣ʷatíxʸ//, EZ /'*hell-diver, pied-billed grebe*'/, ['*Podilymbus podiceps*'], *see* x̱wotíx.

<**Sx̱wótl'aqwem**>, df //s=x̣ʷáƛ'ɛqʷ=əm//, PLN /'*Emory Creek,* also *village at mouth of Emory Creek on both sides of the creek*'/, Elder's comment: literally /'water always boiling up rough'/, *see* x̱wótl'aqw.

<**Sx̱wóx̱wiymelh**>, PLN ['*village near and above [upriver from] Katz where 36 pit-houses were wiped out in an epidemic*'], *see* x̱wà:y ~ x̱wá:y.

<**Sx̱woyehá:lá**>, PLN ['*Squia-ala (now Chilliwack Indian Reserve #7)*'], *see* x̱wà:y ~ x̱wá:y.

<**sx̱wóyéleqw**>, df //s=x̣ʷáy=ələqʷ or s=x̣ʷɛ[=Aá=]y=ələqʷ//, CLO ['*(special head-dress)*'], SPRD, *see* x̱wóy.

<**sx̱wóyéleqws te x̱awsólkwlh**>, CLO ['*new spirit-dancer's head-dress or [cedar-bark] hat*'], *see* sx̱wóyéleqw.

<**Sx̱woyímelh**>, PLN ['*New Westminster*'], *see* x̱wà:y ~ x̱wá:y.

<**sx̱wó:yx̱wey ~ sx̱wóyx̱wey**>, df //s=x̣ʷá(·)y=C_1əC_2 or s=x̣ʷɛ[=Aá=]·y=C_1əC_2//, REL /'*sx̱wóyx̱wey ceremony featuring a masked dance, the sx̱wóyx̱wey mask and dance*'/, *see* x̱wóy.

<**Sx̱wó:yx̱wey ~ Sx̱wóyx̱wey**>, PLN /'*rock shaped like a man's head with a sx̱wó:yx̱wey mask on a point near the head of Harrison River,* the point also called *Spook's Point*'/, *see* x̱wóy.

<**Sx̱wó:yx̱weyla ~ Sx̱wóyx̱weyla**>, PLN ['*village above Yakweakwioose on both sides of the Chilliwack River*'], *see* x̱wóy.

<**sx̱wōqw'tel**>, CAN ['*canoe pole*'], *see* x̱wóqw'.

<**sx̱wōsem ~ sx̱wō:sem ~ sx̱ō(:)sem**>, ds //s=x̣ʷó(·)s(=)əm//, EB ['*soapberry*'], ['*Shepherdia canadensis*'], FOOD /'*Indian ice-cream, whipped soapberry foam*'/, *see* x̱wōs.

<**sx̱wő sem sqe'óleqw**>, FOOD /*'soapberry juice'*/, (lit. soapberry + fruit juice), *see* sx̱wősem ~ sx̱wő:sem ~ sx̱ő(:)sem *under* **x̱w**.

<**sx̱wōsemálá**>, ds //s=x̣^{w}osəm=ɛ́lɛ́//, BSK /*'soapberry basket, Indian ice-cream basket'*/, *see* x̱wős.

<**sx̱wőx̱wtha**>, df //s=x̣^{w}ə́[=C$_1$ə=]θ=ɛ//, EZ /*'song sparrow,* also *brown sparrow,* (could include any or all of the following which occur in the Stó:lō area: *Savannah sparrow, vesper sparrow, lark sparrow, tree sparrow, chipping sparrow, Harris sparrow, fox sparrow, white-crowned sparrow, golden-crowned sparrow, and song sparrow) (type of brown wren [BHTTC 11/15/76], larger wren (but smaller than robin) [Elders Group 2/18/76])'*/, *see* x̱wőx̱wtha.

<**Syálex**>, probably root //syɛ́ləx^{y}//, SOCT [*'Salish people'*], syntactic analysis: nominal, attested by Stanley Jones (7/2/75), compare with <**Sálex**> *Salish people*.

<**syalyelísem**>, WETH [*'icicles'*], *see* yél:és.

<**syáq'yeq'**>, EB [*'a lot of logs'*], *see* yáq'.

<**syá:tel**>, dnom //s=yɛ́·t(=)əl or s=yɛ́·=təl//, SOCT /*'widow, widower'*/, *see* yá:tel.

<**syá:ttel**>, MED [*'throw-up medicine'*], *see* yá:t.

<**syátl'q'els**>, MC [*'paint (nominal)'*], *see* yétl'.

<**syátl'qels te qw'x̱wéltses**>, MC [*'nail polish'*], (lit' "paint for the fingernail"), *see* yétl'.

<**syáyeq'**>, EB [*'log'*], literally /'something that has fallen (of a tree)'/, *see* yáq'.

<**syélt**>, LAND [*'large rock slide that includes trees and other debris'*], *see* yélt.

<**syémyem**>, ABFC [*'to be pregnant'*], *see* yém ~ yem.

<**Syéqw**>, PLN [*'village site (burned) on Atchelitz Creek'*], *see* yéqw.

<**syeqwá:ls**>, REL /*'clothing, food, and possessions burned and given away when a person dies, (possessions and food burned and given away at a burning)'*/, *see* yéqw.

<**syéqwlhàlà**>, FIRE /*'firepit, fireplace'*/, *see* yéqw.

<**syeqwlhá:ltel**>, FIRE /*'tinder, material used to start a fire with (fine dried cedar bark)'*/, *see* yéqw.

<**syeqwyíqw**>, LT [*'burnt color'*], *see* yéqw.

<**syesyewálelh**>, KIN /*'ancestors past, (all one's ancestors)'*/, *see* yewá:l.

<**syewá:lelh ~ syewálelh**>, KIN [*'departed ancestors'*], *see* yewá:l.

<**syewá:l ~ syewál**>, KIN [*'ancestors'*], *see* yewá:l.

<**syéw:e ~ syéwe ~ syő:we ~ syú:we**>, REL /*'fortune-teller, seer, person who can see things in the future, female witch'*/, *see* yéw: ~ yéw.

<**syéw:el ~ syúwél**>, SPRD /*'an Indian dancer's spirit power; spirit power song'*/, *see* yéw: ~ yéw.

<**syewí:l ~ syiwí:l**>, REL /*'a sung spell, power to help or harm people or to do [ritual] burning, power to do witchcraft and predict the future, an evil spell, (magic spell) (someone who has power to take things out of a person or put things in [by magic] [Elders Group 2/25/76], ritualist [Elders Group 1/21/76], witch [EB 4/25/78])'*/, *see* yéw: ~ yéw.

<**syéx̱cha ~ syéx̱tsa**>, dnom //s=yə́x̣cɛ//, SOC /*'a gift'*/, *see* yéx̱ch ~ yéx̱ts ~ yéx̱cha ~ yéx̱tsa.

<**syéx̱w**>, LAND [*'rockslide (that already happened)'*], *see* yíx̱w.

<**syéx̱w**>, SH [*'unravelled'*], *see* yíx̱w.

<**syéyelh**>, HARV [*'lots of little sticks of firewood'*], *see* yólh.

<**syílòlèm ~ siló:lém ~ sílòlèm**>, TIME [*'year'*], *see* yelòlèm.

<**syíq**>, WETH /*'a snow, a snowfall'*/, *see* yíq.

<**syí:ts'em**>, df //s=yí·c'=əm//, LAND [*'sand'*], *see* yí:ts'em.

<**syí:ts'emílep**>, LAND [*'sand bar'*], *see* yí:ts'em.

<**syiwí:leqw**>, REL /*'war-whoop,* ((probably) *a sung spell before battle)'*/, *see* yéw: ~ yéw.

<**syiwí:l ~ syewí:l**>, REL /*'a sung spell, power to help or harm people or to do [ritual] burning, power to do witchcraft and predict the future, an evil spell, (magic spell) (someone who has power to take things out of a person or put things in [by magic] [Elders Group 2/25/76], ritualist [Elders Group 1/21/76], witch [EB 4/25/78])'*/, *see* yéw: ~ yéw.

<**syíyeq**>, WETH /*'falling snow, be snowing'*/, *see* yíq.

<**Syíyeqw**>, PLN [*'burnt mountain across from American Bar'*], *see* yéqw.

<**syíyex̱w**>, SH [*'be unwrapped'*], *see* yíx̱w.

<**syó:letsep**>, df //s=yá·ləcəp or s=yá·l=cəp//, WATR [*'a wave'*], *see* yó:letsep, itself prob. from **yó:l** *turn over*.

<**syó:qwem**>, WETH [*'sun'*], *see* yéqw.

<**syó:qw'em**>, ANA [*'sweat [noun]'*], *see* yóqw'em.

<**syóyelh**>, HARV [*'little stick of firewood'*], *see* yólh.

<**syó:ys**>, SOC [*'work'*], *see* yó:ys.

<**syúwél ~ syéw:el**>, SPRD /*'an Indian dancer's spirit power; spirit power song'*/, *see* yéw: ~ yéw.

<**s'álem**>, dnom //s=ʔɛ́ləm//, [sʔɛ́ləm], FSH /*'spear, shaft (of spear/harpoon/gaff-hook), gaff-hook pole'*/, HUNT /*'spear, shaft of spear'*/, (<**s= nominalizer**>), probably root <**'ál**> *pole/shaft/length*?, possibly <**=em**> *place to have/get*, syntactic analysis: nominal, attested by BHTTC, compare <**s'aléts**> *bottom of a tree, trunk of a tree* with same possible root, also <**s'álém**>, //s=ʔɛ́lə́m//, [sʔɛ́lə́m], dialects: *Cheh.*, attested by EL.

<**s'aléqs ~ s'eléqs**>, dnom //s=ʔɛl=ə[=´=]qs//, MC [*'point'*], (<**s= nominalizer**>), probably root <**'al**> *pole/shaft/length*?, lx <**=eqs**> *on the nose, on the point*, probably <**=´=**> *derivational*, phonology: vowel-reduction, stress-shift, geminate consonant (unusual word finallly), syntactic analysis: nominal, attested by DM (Chill.), example: <**s'eléqs: te lháts'tel**>, //s=ʔəl=ə́qs-s tə ɬɛ́c'=təl//, [sʔələ́qs· tə ɬǽc'təl], /*'point of a knife'*/, attested by DM.

<**s'aléts**> dnom //s=ʔɛ(l)=lə́c//, EB [*'bottom of a tree, trunk of a tree'*], (<**s= nominalizer**>, probably root <**'al**> *pole/shaft/length*?, <**=lets**> *on the bottom*), syntactic analysis: nominal, attested by BHTTC

<**s'alétsmel**>, dnom //s=ʔɛlə́c=məl//, BLDG /*'foundation of a house, bottom of a tree'*/, EB [*'bottom of a tree'*], (<**s= nominalizer**>), (<**=mel**> *part, portion*; prob. also =lets *on the bottom*), syntactic analysis: nominal, attested by BHTTC, also <**alétsmel**>, //ʔɛlə́c=məl//, phonology: free variant.

<**s'álqsel**>, dnom //s=ʔɛ́l=qsəl//, [sʔɛ́lqsəl], ANA [*'tip or point of one's nose'*], LAND [*'point of land'*], semantic environment ['semantic environments determine which alloseme is selected (those with components of ['land'] select the second, those with ['animate'] select the first listed'], (<**s=**

nominalizer>), probably root <**'ál**> *pole, shaft, length*?, lx <**=qsel**> *on the nose, on the point*, syntactic analysis: nominal.<**S'alxwítsel**>, PLN /'*Camp Slough, Camp River*'/, *see* alxwítsel.

<**S'alxwítsel**>, dnom //s=ʔɛlxʷ=íc(=)əl//, PLN /'*Camp Slough, Camp River*'/, literally /'middle (stream), the center (stream)'/, *see* alxwítsel.

<**s'álhtel**>, FOOD ['*food*'], *see* álhtel.

<**S'áqwemx̲weth'**>, PLN ['*name of place with clay at the edge of the river at some location*'], *see* qwó:m ~ qwóm ~ qwem.

<**s'átl'q**>, DIR ['*the outside*'], *see* átl'q.

<**s'átl'qmel**>, BLDG ['*the outside part of a house*'], *see* átl'q.

<**s'áxwem**>, FOOD ['*(food) given*'], *see* áxw.

<**S'áx̲etxel**>, //s=ʔɛ́x̣ə=t(əl?)=xʸəl//, PLN /'*where B.C. Hopyard used to be at Agassiz, (*probably *the same place as Áx̲etel)*'/, *see* Áx̲etel *under* áx̲e.

<**s'ehó**>, MC ['*wrapped up*'], *see* ehó.

<**s'ehólets**>, CLO ['*pocket*'], *see* ehó.

<**s'ekw''í:kw'**>, ABDF ['*to perish (of a lot of people)*'], *see* íkw' ~ í:kw'.

<**s'élíyá**>, REL /'*spirit dream, vision, (any) dream*'/, *see* élíyá.

<**s'élhtel**>, FOOD /'*food, meal*'/, *see* álhtel

<**s'émqsel**>, stvi //s=ʔə́m=qsəl//, LANG ['*nasal-sounding*'], posr <em> *sit*, lx <**=qsel**> *in the nose*, syntactic analysis: participle, attested by BHTTC.

<**S'em'oméla**>, SOCT ['*Thompson people*'], *see* S'omél:a.

<**S'épek ~ Í'pek ~ S'í'pek**>, EZ ['*Skunk (name in story)*'], *see* sth'épeq under path' and th'ep.

<**s'ep'ó:s**>, dnom //ʔɛ[=Aə=]p'=á·s=əm//, SPRD /'*people without paint on face (non-dancers)*'/, *see* á:p' ~ áp'.

<**s'éts-'ets**>, chrs //s=ʔə́c=C$_1$əC$_2$//, [sʔícʔɪc (normal speed), sʔɛ́cʔɛc (hyper-slow speed)], LANG /'*stuttering, to stutter*'/, (<**s=**> *stative*), possibly root <**áts**> as in <**átslexw**> *hear about it*?, (<**=R2**> *characteristic*), phonology: reduplication, syntactic analysis: intransitive verb, attested by AC, compare <**átslexw**> *hear about it*, example: <**s'éts-'ets swíyeqe**>, //s=ʔə́c=ʔəc s=wíyəqə//, /'*stuttering man*'/, attested by AC.

<**s'eweltá:l**>, HUNT /'*snare, snare trap*'/, *see* íwel.

<**s'eyí:ws**>, ANAH ['*right side*'], *see* éy ~ éy:.

<**s'eyí:wtses**>, ANAH ['*right hand*'], *see* éy ~ éy:.

<**s'í:kw'**>, DIR /'*lost and presumed dead, perish*'/, *see* íkw' ~ í:kw'.

<**s'í:les ~ s'í:lés**>, dnom //s=ʔ=í·ləs ~ s=ʔ=í·lə́s//, ANA ['*chest (human or animal thorax)*'], (<**s=**> *nominalizer*), lx <**=í:les**> *(on the) chest*, root <**'**> *(empty root for lexical affixes)*, syntactic analysis: nominal, attested by AC, DM, MH, LJ (Tait), other sources: ES /sʔí·ləs/ *chest (animal or human thorax), JH /sʔí·ləs/, HT <se'lis> (macron over e)*; example: <**th'ex̲wót tel s'í:lés**>, //θ'əx̣ʷ=áT t-əl s=ʔ=í·lə́s//, /'*wash my chest*'/, attested by AC, <**x̲élh tel s'í:les**>, //x̣ə́ɬ t-əl s=ʔ=í·ləs//, /'*I have heartburn.*'/, literally /'I hurt in my chest.'/, attested by MH (Deming), <**x̲élh tel s'íles lhíl kw'à:y**>,

//x̣ə́ɬ t-əl s=ʔ=í·ləs ɬi-l k'ʷɛ̀·y//, /'*My chest hurts when I get hungry.*'/, syntactic comment: note auxiliary lhí *when* which takes subjunctive subject pronoun, attested by LJ (Tait).

<**s'í:ltexw**>, dnom //s=ʔí·ltəxʷ//, BLDG /'*thick plank for side of house, thick shake for longhouse roof, covering over hole in roof of pit-house*'/, *see* í:ltexw

<**s'iltexwáwtxw ~ iltexwáwtxw**>, BLDG ['*plank house*'], *see* í:ltexw.

<**s'iltexwím**>, BLDG ['*plank building*'], *see* s'í:ltexw.

<**s'í:lwelh**>, ANA ['*one side of the body (*probably *someone's)*'], *see* í:lwelh.

<**s'ímex**>, ABFC /'*gait, a walk*'/, *see* ím.

<**s'íteyí:les**>, stvi //s=ʔítəy=í·ləs//, BSK ['*carry a packstrap around the shoulders and across the chest at the collarbone*'], CLO, FSH, HARV, HUNT, SOC, TVMO, *see* ítey.

<**s'íth'em**>, CLO /'*clothes, clothing (esp. Indian clothing, men's or women's), something to wear, dress, gown*'/, *see* íth'a.

<**s'í:wes**>, SOC /'*training, teaching, upbringing*'/, *see* íwes.

<**s'iwesá:ylhem**>, SOC /'*teachings for children, what is taught to one's children*'/, *see* íwes.

<**s'íx̱w**>, BLDG ['*be swept*'], *see* íx̱w.

<**s'iyláx̱el**>, ANAH ['*right arm*'], *see* éy ~ éy:.

<**s'i'á:ytses**>, ABFC ['*he's holding s-th in each hand*'], *see* á:y.

<**s'i'hó**>, EFAM ['*wrapped up (in stupidity)*'], *see* ehó.

<**s'i'omó:met**>, EFAM ['*(be) kind of lazy*'], *see* emét.

<**S'í'pek ~ S'épek ~ Í'pek**>, EZ ['*Skunk (name in story)*'], *see* sth'épeq under path' and th'ep.

<**s'ókw'ches**>, ABFC /'*to be arm in arm (like escorting someone), to take an arm (of someone)*'/, *see* ókw'.

<**s'ókw'(e)stexw**>, ABFC ['*carry s-th/s-o on one's arm*'], *see* ókw'.

<**s'ó:lmexw**>, df //s=ʔá·l=məxʷ or s=ʔá=·lməxʷ or s=ʔəhá=·lməxʷ//, EZ /'*water pygmies, water baby*'/, ASM ['stl'áleqem creature, has dark skin, black hair, some lived in pools in the Coquihalla River and pulled fish spears from unfavored fishermen when they tried to spear fish in one pool; others lived in Chilliwack Lake and occasionally washed up on the shore crying; AC reported a man she knew (her age) had seen one, but when he went to bring his friends up the beach to show them it had returned to the water'], ABDF /'*midget, small people*'/, ASM ['if you eat fish heart you may become s'ó:lmexw'], possibly <**s=**> *nominalizer or stative*, possibly root <**ehó**>, bound root //ʔəhá//, MC ['*wrap up*']., probably <**=mexw**> *person, people* or <**=:l=mexw**> *people*, syntactic analysis: nominal, attested by TG (4/23/75), IHTTC (8/23/77), AK (1/30/80), *see under possible roots* <**ó:lmexw**> or <**ó:l**> or <ehó>, //ʔá·l(=)məxʷ// meaning unclear or //ʔá·l// meaning unclear or //ʔəhá// *wrap up (since water pygmies are hidden and seldom seen?)*.

<**s'ólh**>, df //s=ʔáɬ//, PRON /'*ours, our (emphatic)*'/, <**s=**> *stative*, root <**olh**> *respect*, *see* under <**olh**> *respect*, syntactic analysis: pronominal verb/verbal pronoun, attested by AC, example: <**tl'ó s'ólh tál.**>, //ƛ'á s=ʔáɬ tɛ́l//, /'*That's our mother.*'/, attested by AC, <**tl'o s'ólh sqwmáy.**>, //ƛ'a s=ʔáɬ s=qʷəm=ɛ́y//, /'*That's our dog.*'/, attested by AC, <**í:westólxwes te s'ólh má:l.**>, //ʔi[-·-]wəs=T-álxʷ-əs tə s=ʔáɬ mɛ́·l//, /'*Our (own) father taught us.*'/, literally /'he was teaching us the our father'/, attested by AC, <**tl'ó s'ólh.**>, //ƛ'á s=ʔáɬ//, /'*That's ours.*'/, attested by AC.

<**s'ó:lhqw'**>, DESC ['*be ragged*'], *see* lhéqw'.

<**s'ò:m**>, ECON ['*an order (promise of goods/services)*'], *see* ò:m.

<**S'omél:a**>, df //s=ʔamə́l·ɛ or s=ʔam=ə́l·ɛ//, SOCT /'*Thompson Indian, Thompson person*'/, *see* omél:a>, bound stem //ʔamə́l·ɛ// or //ʔam=ə́l·ɛ//, root or stem meaning unknown unless <**ò:m**>, ds //ʔà·=(ə)m//, ECON /'*to order (food, material, etc.)*'/ or <**s'ò:m**> *an order (promise of goods/services)*, probably themselves from root <**ó:**> *call* plus <**=em**> *intransitivizer*, or root meaning unknown unless from <**á:m** (?)>, free root //ʔɛ́·m (?)//, TIB ['*give*'], both roots could refer to the well-known practice of the Thompson people trading interior goods for coastal goods with the Stó:lō people, speakers of Upriver Halkomelem, possibly <**=él:a**> *on the side of the head, around the ear/cheek*, syntactic analysis: nominal, attested by AC, BHTTC.

<**s'ó:met**>, //s=ʔa[=´·=]mət//, EFAM /'*be always lazy, be a lazybones, be stupid, be a good-for-nothing*'/,attested by BHTTC , see main dialect form <**s'ú:met**> under bound root omét *sit*

<**s'ómó:qwes**>, df //s=ʔámá·q^{w}(=)əs//, EB /'*bracket fungus, (*possibly also *some jelly fungi like yellow trembler)*'/, ['*Fomes* sp. including *Fomes applanatus* and probably others, possibly *Polyporus* sp., possibly *Ganoderma* sp., prob. also jelly fungi of *Tremella* and maybe *Auricularia* and *Dacrymyces* species, especially *Tremella mesenterica* (Yellow trembler) which is abundant only on the red alder and is reddish-orange matching the color, translucence and shape of those eaten by some of the Stó:lō elders, the jelly fungi could possibly have a differnet name from the bracket fungus'], ASM ['the fungus described by this name that grow on rotten alder or alder stumps were edible, should be washed and cooked, have a nice meaty taste; the bracket fungus is said by some to make rain if one turns it upside down after picking it or if one scratches on it; the bracket fungus grows on tree trunks and roots especially, sticks out perpendicularly from the trunk in a half circle shape characteristically, and has a beige covering that scratches off leaving dark marks'], possibly <**s=**> *nominalizer*, possibly <**=es**> *on the face, round object*, root meaning unknown, syntactic analysis: nominal, attested by SP and a few others, Elders Group (1/28/76), also <**shxw'ómóqwes**>, //s(=)x^{w}=ʔámáq^{w}(=)əs//, ASM ['it makes rain if you scratch on it or if you turn it upside down soon after picking'], attested by SJ (Deming 5/24/79). other sources: JH /samá·q^{w}əs/ *toadstool.*

<**s'ó:pels**>, NUM /'*ten o'clock, (tenth hour)*'/, *see* ó:pel.

<**s'óq**>, dnom //s=ʔá=q//, ANA /'*dung, excrement, feces*'/, *see* óq>, possible bound root or stem //ʔá(=)q// *dung*, the word is cognate with Squamish /s-ʔáʔq/ *dung* and /ʔáʔq/ *defecate* W73:77,87, K69:94, probably with lexical suffix /=q/ *bottom, behind, trunk*, compare with root <**ó'**> *to have a bowel movement, to defecate, to shit*

<**s'ó:qw**>, df //s=ʔá·q^{w}//, ANA ['*after-birth*'], *see* ó:qw, bound root //ʔá·q^{w}//, root meaning possibly *pullout, unplug*

<**s'óqwelets**>, //s=ʔáq^{w}=əl=əc//, also /'*back (of person, horse, other animal, etc.)*'/, *see* more common variant <**óqwelets**>, df //ʔáq^{w}=əl=əc or ʔáq^{w}=ələc//, ANA /'*back of the body, the whole back*'/

<**s'óqw'**>, MC ['*something that you hook onto (like a trailer hitch)*'], *see* óqw'.

<**S'ót'o**>, PLN ['*place just south of Doctor's Point on Harrison Lake northwest*']. *see* root <**ót'**> *stretch*, comment: said to mean *long breast* by Hill-Tout 1904:361 but appears to mean instead *something just stretched*

<**s'ótheqw**>, FOOD /'*baked potato*'/, (lit. something baked), *see* ótheqw

<**s'ótheqw**>, stvi //s=ʔáθəq^{w}//, FOOD /'*baked (in ashes), baked (in a stove)*'/, (<**s=**> *stative*), *see* ótheqw

<**s'ó:thes ~ s'óthes**>, dnom //s=ʔá·θ=əs ~ s=ʔáθ=əs//, ANA [*'face'*], (<**s=**> *nominalizer*), possibly root <**ó:th**> *edge, surface* possibly root from <**=ó:th**> *edge*?, lx <**=es**> *on the face*, phonology: the long vowel probably only in careful/slow pronunciation, syntactic analysis: nominal, attested by AC, BJ (5/64), Elders Group (3/1/72), many others, other sources: ES and JH /sʔá·θəs/ *face*, H-T <tsEátsus> (macron over á) *face*, Boas 1890 <s'átses> (macron over a, double underline under e) *face*, comment: Hill-Tout collected a lot of valuable information but his ear for phonetic detail was poor compared to that of Boas as the above and many other examples show, example: <**lí te s'óthes**>, //lí tə s=ʔáθəs-s//, /*'on his face'*/, phonology: consonant merger, attested by AC, <**kwímel ta' s'óthes.**>, //kʷím=əl t-ɛʔ s=ʔáθ=əs//, /*'Your face is red.'*/, attested by Elders Group (3/1/72), <**lulh qwáyel te s'óthes yewá:lmels kwses melqí:wsem.**>, //lə=uɬ qʷɛ́y=əl tə s=ʔáθ=əs-s yəwɛ́·l=məls kʷ-s-əs mɛlq=í·ws=əm//, /*'Her face is turning green before she faints.'*/, attested by AC, *see under possible root* <**ó:th ~ óth**>, probably bound root //ʔá·θ//, meaning uncertain root meaning unknown unless *edge, surface*

<**s'oth'ó:mes**>, dnom //s=ʔi[=Aa=]θ'ɛ[=Aá·=]m=əs or s=ʔi[=Aa=]θ'ɛ=m=á·[=M2=]s//, CLO [*'big shawl'*], *see* íth'a.

<**s'oth'ó:mősem**>, mdls //s=ʔi[=Aa=]θ'ɛ[=Aá·=]m=ə́ws=əm or s=ʔi[=Aa=]θ'ɛ[=Aá·=]m=ə[=Aó=]s=əm//, CLO [*'put on a shawl'*], *see* íth'a.

<**s'ówth**>, strs //s=ʔɛ[=Aá=]wθ//, ABFC [*'be in a hurry'*], *see* áwth.

<**s'óx̲we**>, df //s=ʔáx̣ʷ(=)ə//, EZ /*'clam, butter clam, fresh-water clam, fresh-water mussel'*/, *see* óx̲we, possible root //ʔáx̣ʷə//, meaning unknown

<**S'óyewòt**>, df //s=ʔáy=əwàt or s=ʔáyəw=àt//, PLN /*'another small peak just to the right of the Mount Cheam summit peak as one faces south, she is another daughter of Lhílheqey (Mt. Cheam)'*/, *see* **Óyewòt**>, df //ʔáyəw=àt or ʔáy=əwàt//, PLN /*'smallest peak just below Mount Cheam (on left of Mt. Cheam looking south), Lhílheqey's (Mt. Cheam's) baby (located about where her breast would be on the left hand side facing her)'*/

<**s'ó:ytheqw**>, EB /*'raspberry'*/, *see* eyóth *under* éy

<**s'ó:ytheqwelhp**>, dnom //s=ʔ(ɛ)y=á·[=M2=]θ=əqʷ=əɬp//, EB /*'wild red raspberry plant, domestic red raspberry plant'*/, *see* eyóth *under* éy

<**s'ó'**>, dnom //s=ʔáʔ//, ABFC /*'dung, feces, shit'*/, *see* ó', free root //ʔáʔ//, ABFC /*'have a bowel movement, defecate, to shit'*/, *see* o' *defecate*

<**s'o(')elexw**>?, df //s=ʔá(ʔ)əl=l-əxʷ?//, WV [*'twined weave'*], *see* o(')el, possible stem //ʔá(ʔ)əl//?, meaning uncertain

<**s'ő:leqw'**>, df //s=ʔó·ləq'ʷ or s=ʔa=Aó·=l=əq'ʷ or s=ʔa[=Aó=]·=əl=əq'ʷ//, ABDF [*'(be) suffering pain'*], *see* ő:leqw'

<**s'ú:met**>, strs //s=ʔa[=Aú·=]mət//, EFAM /*'be always lazy, be a lazybones, be stupid, be a good-for-nothing'*/, *see* omét (probably root //ʔəmə́t from ʔamə́t// *sit*)

SH

<**sh**> . This represents the same sound as in English, but the sound is an allophone of /s/ in Upriver Halq'eméylem. It occurs only before /x^{w}/ (<**xw**>) in native words; it also occurs in a few interjections (which may be native or borrowed) and a few borrowed words. Its occurrence is so limited that it does not appear before /x̣^{w}/ <**x̱w**> in native words; however, since it has a clear distinct sound and is found in borrowings not before <**xw**>, it is written <**sh**> in the Stó:lō writing system wherever it occurs.

<**sh**>, free root //š//, EFAM ['*shoo*'], semantic environment ['said while waving off a pesky animal, etc.'], syntactic analysis: interjection, attested by Elders Group (5/14/80), AH and LG (Deming 5/8/80).

<**Shéykes**>, free root //šɛ́ykəs//, REL ['*Shakers*'], ASM ['members of the Indian Shaker church'], syntactic analysis: nominal, dialects: *Chilliwack Landing (Pilalt?)*, attested by Elders Group (6/8/77), borrowed from English /šéykrz/ *Shakers*.

<**shíka leplít**>, //šíkɛ ləplít//, REL /'*Shaker minister*'/, attested by AH, *also see* leplít.

<**sht ~ sh:t**>, free root //št ~ š·t//, EFAM ['*shh*'], semantic environment ['said to quiet kids, etc.'], syntactic analysis: interjection, attested by Elders Group (5/14/80).

<**shúkwe ~ súkwe ~ súkwa**>, free root //súk^{w}ə ~ súk^{w}ɛ//, [súk^{w}ə ~ šúk^{w}ə], FOOD ['*sugar*'], phonology: allophone sh normally only appears before xw but also appears elsewhere in some borrowings, syntactic analysis: noun, nominal, attested by AC, MH (Deming 1/4/79), EB, Ed and Delphine Kelly (12/10/71), borrowed from Chinook Jargon /súk^{w}a ~ šúk^{w}a/ *sugar* itself from French <sucre> *sugar* Johnson 1978:428, example: <**lí welí kw súkwa?**>, //lí-ə wə-lí k^{w} súk^{w}ɛ//, /'*Is there any sugar?*'/, attested by EB (2/2/76).

<**shúkwet ~ súkwet**>, pcs //súk^{w}ə=T//, FOOD ['*sugar it*'], (<**=t**> *purposeful control transitivizer*), syntactic analysis: transitive verb, attested by Elders Group (3/8/78).

<**shúkwe'àlà**>, ds //súk^{w}ə=ʔɛ̀lɛ̀//, FOOD ['*sugar bowl*'], HHG, lx <**='àlà ~ =álá ~ =hàlà**> *container of*, syntactic analysis: nominal, attested by Deming (at Fort Langley museum 3/9/78).

<**Shushxwáp**>, free root //šušx^{w}ɛ́p//, SOCT ['*Shuswap people*'], syntactic analysis: nominal, attested by DM (1/8/62 or July 64 or 12/4/64), also <**Shúshwop**>, //šúšwap//, attested by BHTTC, Salish cognate: Shuswap /səx^{w}ép-mx ~ səx^{w}ép-məx/ *Shuswap Indian(s)* Kuipers 1974:187.

<**shxw=**>, da //sx^{w}= or s=x^{w}=//, [šx^{w}=], CJ /'*nominalizer, something for, someone for, something that*'/, <s(h)=> *nominalizer*, <xw=> *towards*, (semological comment: almost always used with *continuative* stems, thus the translation *something for [doing X]* in contrast to the translation for s= used mostly with non-continuatives *something to [do X]*, occasionally both suffixes violate this semantic distinction and then they have the literal translation *something that [does/is doing X]*, discovering this semantic principle has allowed the derivations of a number of words from their proper roots). Rather than cross referencing every word with this suffix under the <**sh**> here, the reader should look up the forms under the consonant following the <**shxw**> as such words will be found under the root beginning with that consonant. A few sample words only are listed here under <**sh**>, along with those whose roots are unclear or the few words that begin with borrowed or sound symbolic <**sh**>.

<**Shxwá:y**>, //sx^{w}ɛ́·y//, less correct variant of <**Shxwhá:y**>, dnom //sx^{w}=hɛ̀[=´=]·y//, PLN /'*village at outlet of old Chilliwack River on Fraser River, now known as Skway reserve (Chilliwack Indian*

Reserve #5)'/, literally /'place to make canoes'/, *see* **hà**:y *make a canoe*

<**shxwá:ye**>, stvi //s=xʷɛ́·yə//, DIR /'*be in the middle, be in the center*'/, *see* xwá:ye.

<**shxwá:ytses**>, dnom //s=xʷɛ́·yə=cəs//, ANA /'*second finger, middle finger*'/, literally /'something to be in the middle on the hand'/, *see* xwá:ye.

<**Shxwchí:yò:m**>, //s=xʷ=cí·yɛ=əm//, literally /'place to pick strawberries'/, attested by SP, variant of **Xwchí:yò:m**>, dnom //xʷ=chí·yɛ=əm//, PLN /'*Cheam Island (my name for an island in the Fraser River across from Cheam Indian Reserve #2), Cheam village, Cheam Indian Reserve #1*'/, *see* chí:ya.

<**shxwch'áletstel ~ ch'áletstel ~ sch'á(:)letstel**>, dnom //c'ɛ́=ləc=təl ~ s=c'ɛ́(·)=ləc=təl ~ sxʷ=c'ɛ́=ləc=təl//, HHG /'*chair, bench, seat, something to sit on*'/, literally /'device to put the rump on top of ~ something to put the rump on top of device ~ something that put the rump on top of device'/, *see* ch'á: ~ ts'á: *on top of.*

<**shxwch'á:yxwels**>, dnom //sxʷ=c'i[=Aɛ́·=]yxʷ=əls//, sas, FSH ['*fish-drying rack*'], literally /'something for drying fish as a structured activity continuative'/, *see* ts'íyxw ~ ts'éyxw ~ ch'íyxw.

<**shxwch'ech'áls**>, dnom //s(=)xʷ=$C_1əC_2$=c'ɛ́=əls//, sas, cts, HHG ['*shelf*'], literally /'something for putting on top of in a structured activity'/, *see* ch'á: ~ ts'á: *on top of.*

<**shxwehóméllhelh**>, df //sxʷ=qʷəhɛ́=ámə́l=ɬəɬ or s=xʷəh=ámə́l=ɬəɬ//, ANA ['*adam's apple*'], literally perhaps /'something that goes through a tunnel/hole part of in the windpipe/throat'/, *see* xwehó.

<**shxwékw'thelh sq'éytes**>, cpds //s=xʷək'ʷ=θəɬ s=q'ít=əs// (sic for <**shxwékw'lhelh sqéytes**>, cpds //s=x ʷək'ʷ=ɬəɬ s=q'ít=əs//), CLO /'*kerchief*'/, lit. /"dragged on the throat headband"/, <**s=**> nominalizer, <**xwekw'**> *drag*, <**=élhelh ~ =lhelh** ~ poss. **=elhlelh**> *in the windpipe, throat*, <**s=**> nominalizer, <**qít**> *tied*, <**=es**> *on the face*, attested by RG & EH (4/10/99 Ling332)

<**shxwélchep**>, df //s=xʷ(=)ə́lcəp//, FIRE /'*home-made lantern (using candle in a can with a hole in it, etc.), jack-o-lantern*'/, LT, HHG, *see* xwélchep.

<**shxwélem ~ shxwélém**>, dnom //sxʷ=hə́=lɛm ~ sxʷ=hə́=lɛ́[=Aə́=]=m//, TVMO /'*wandering, where someone goes*'/, *see* lám *go*, under la.

<**shxwelí**> *life spirit, soul), see* éliya *dream, vision*, also xwelí.

<**shxwelítemelh**>, //s=xʷəlítəm=əɬ//, /'*in the white man's way, according to the ways of the white man*'/, *see* xwelítem *white man.*

<**shxwelítemelh méxts'el**>, cpds //s=xʷəlítəm=əɬ mə́xʸ(=)c'(=)əl//, EZ ['*common bedbug*'], ['*Cimex lectularius*'], ABDF, literally /'Whiteman style/kind of louse'/, *see* <méxts'el>, possibly root //mə́xʸc'əl or mɛ́(=Aə́=)xʸ(=)c'(=)əl//, [mɪ́xʸc'ɪl], EZ /'*human louse: head louse, (secondarily) body louse,* and possibly *crab louse,* (unclear if *animal lice* are included)'/.

<**shxwelítemelh sqwéth'**>, df //s=xʷəlítəm=əɬ s=qʷə́θ'//, EZ (probably) ['*(ring-necked) pheasant*'], *see* qwéth'

<**shxwelméxwelh skw'ő:lmexwelhp**>, EB ['*trailing blackberry vine*'], ['*Rubus ursinus*'], literally /'Indian kind of blackberry'/, *see* xwélmexw, skw'ő:lmexw (under kw'ő:l ~ qw'ő:l).

<**shxwelókw'**>, strs //s=xʷələ[=Aá=]k'ʷ//, SH ['*(be) wrapped*'], *see* xwélekw'.

<**shxwélwels**>, df //s=xʷə́lw(=)əls//, sas, HHG ['*container*'], *see* xwélwels.

<**shxwemá**>, stvi //s=xʷə=mɛ́//, MC ['*it's open*'], *see* <má ~ má'->, free root //mɛ́ ~ mɛ́ʔ=//, MC ['*come*

off']

<**shxwématsel ~ shxwémetsel**>, df //s=x^{w}ə́m=əcəl//or //shxw=qwómetsel//, EZ /'*fisher, an animal close to a mink, animal like an otter*'/, ['*Martes pennanti pennanti*'], also EZ ['*wolverine*'], ['*Gulo luscus luscus*'], *see* xwématsel ~ xwémetsel.

<**shxwemám**>, stvi //s=x^{w}ə=mɛ́=m//, DESC ['*be empty*'], *see* <má ~ má'->, free root //mɛ́ ~ mɛ́ʔ=//, MC ['*come off*'].

<**shxwéma'ám**>, dnom //s=x^{w}ə= ´=mɛʔ=ə[=Aɛ́=]m//, strs, HHG /'*an opener, can-opener, bottle-opener*'/, *see* <má ~ má'->, free root //mɛ́ ~ mɛ́ʔ=//, MC ['*come off*'].

<**shxwema'ámel**>, dnom //s=x^{w}ə=mɛʔ=ɛ́məl//, HHG ['*empty container (like bottles esp. if there's lots)*'], *see* <má ~ má'->, free root //mɛ́ ~ mɛ́ʔ=//, MC ['*come off*']

<**shxwémeqel**>, dnom //s=x^{w}ə= ´=mɛ=qəl//, HHG /'*an opener, can-opener, bottle-opener*'/, *see* <má ~ má'->, free root //mɛ́ ~ mɛ́ʔ=//, MC ['*come off*']

<**shxwémeqèyls**>, sas //s=x^{w}ə= ´=mɛ=qə(l)=í·ls//, HHG /'*an opener, can-opener, bottle-opener*'/, *see* <má ~ má'->, free root //mɛ́ ~ mɛ́ʔ=//, MC ['*come off*'].

<**shxwémlexw**>, stvi //s=x^{w}ə́m=l-əx^w//, SOC ['*did s-o a favor*'], *see* xwémlexw.

<**shxwemlá:lekw**>, pln //s=x^{w}əmli[=Aɛ́·=lə=]k^w//, KIN /'*uncles (all of them), aunts (all of them)*'/, *see* xwemlí:kw.

<**shxwemlí:kw**>, df //s=x^{w}əmlí·k^w//, KIN /'*parent's cousin, parent's sibling, uncle, aunt*'/, *see* xwemlí:kw.

<**shxwemthiyà:lh**>, //sx^{w}əmθiy=ɛ̀·ɬ//, /'*deceased uncle or aunt or grandparent or someone responsible for you directly or indirectly*'/, *see* xwemthiy.

<**shxwemxwemthiyá:lh**>, //s=C$_1$əC$_2$=x^{w}əmθiy=ɛ́·ɬ//, /'*deceased uncles or aunts or grandparents responsible for someone*'/.

<**shxwep'életstel ~ shxwp'életstel**>, ds //s(=)x^w=(ə)p'=ə́ləc=təl or s(=)x^w=ʔɛp'=ə́ləc=təl//, [šx^{w}ʊp'ə́lɪctəl ~ šx^{w}p'ə́lɪctəl], HHG ['*toilet paper*'], PE, literally /'device/thing to wipe on the rump/bottom'/, *see* á:p' ~ áp' *wipe*.

<**shxweqw'eléqstel**>, //s=x^{w}əq'^{w}=ələ́qs=təl//, /'*nose-ring*'/, *see* xwókw' ~ xwekw'ó *drag*.

<**shxwéth'tel** or **shxwwéth'tel**>, dnom //sx^w=wɛ[=Aə́=]θ'=təl//, MC /'*a latch, Indian lock*'/, BLDG, ASM ['a latch fastened in the middle or on one end, or loose which slides through'], *see* wáth'.

<**shxw(x̱w)etl'qelá:lá**>, //sx^w=x̣^{w}ə́ƛ̓'=qəl=ɛ́·lɛ́//, /'*pillow case, container for pillow, pillow*'/, literally /'container for rolled thing under head'/, *see* x̱wétl', probably *rolled*.

<**shxwewá(:)y**>, df //sx^w=wɛ́(·)y//, KIN ['*parent*'], *see* wá(:)y.

<**shxwéwe**>, df //sx^w=wə́wə or s=x^{w}əw=ə or sx^w=wə́=C$_1$ə or sx^w=wə́w=ə//, EZ ['*cougar*'], ['*Felis concolor oregonensis*'], *see* wéwe.

<**Shxwewéwe**>, dnom //sx^w=wə́w(=)ə or sx^w=wə́=C$_1$ə//, PLN ['*next slough entering Harrison River above Xemó:leqw*'], *see* wéwe.

<**shxwexwí**>, strs //s=C$_1$ə=x^{w}íy//, ABFC ['*be awake*'], *see* xwíy ~ x^{w}í.

<**shxwexwó:s**>, df //s=x^{w}əx^w(=)á·s or sxw=xwí[=Aó:=]s//, EZ ['*thunderbird*'], WETH ['*thunder*'], *see* xwexwó:s, itself perhaps from xwís- as in xwíset *shake s-th*.

<**shxweyó:yes** or better **shxwyó:yes**>, ds //sx^w=yá[= ·=C$_1$ə=](y)s//, TOOL ['*tool*'], literally /'something for really working'/, *see* yó:ys.

<**Shxwhá:y**>, dnom //sx^w=hɛ̀[=´=]·y//, PLN /'*village at outlet of old Chilliwack River on Fraser River, now known as Skway reserve (Chilliwack Indian Reserve #5)*'/, literally /'place to make canoes'/, *see* hà:y *make a canoe.*

<**shxwhéyqwala**>, //sx^w=hɛ́=yəq^w=ɛlɛ//, /'*firepit*'/, literally /'container for burning'/, *see* yeqw.

<**shxwhő:wtewelh**>, df //sx^{w}hó·wtəwəɬ or s=x^{w}hó=əwtx^w=əɬ or sx^w=ʔəhá=əwtx^w=əɬ//, BLDG ['*plank house*'], possibly <**shxw=**> *nominalizer, something for*, possibly root <**ehó**> *wrap*, possibly <**=áwtxw ~ =ewtxw**> *building, house*, possibly <**=elh**> *past or according to/in the manner/style of*, phonology: vowel merger, consonant-loss, syntactic analysis: nominal, attested by DM.

<**shxwítel**>, dnom //s=x^{w}íy=təl//, HHG /'*chamberpot, potty-chair, urinal*'/, *see* xwítel.

<**shxwíxweqwels**>, dnom //sx^w=x^{w}í[=C$_1$ə=]q^w=əls//, sas, cts, HHG ['*an iron*'], CLO, literally /'something for pressing and rubbing hard as a structured activity device'/, *see* xwíqw.

<**shxwixwóxwth'**>, dmv //s=C$_1$í=x^{w}ɛ[=AáC$_1$ə=]θ'//, EFAM /'*(be) stupid, not all there (mentally), (be) a little crazy*'/, literally /'a little bit teetered/rocked'/, *see* xwáth'.

<**shxwiyáxkel**>, df //s=x^{w}iyɛ́x^{y}k^{y}əl//, EZ /'*(moose, British Columbia moose), elk*'/, ['*(Alces alces andersoni)*'], *see* xwiyáxkel.

<**shxwiymálá ~ shxwimá:le ~ shxwiymála ~ shxwímàlà**>, //s=x^{w}iy=əm=ɛ́lɛ́//, /'*store*'/, literally /'nominal + sell + container for'/, *see* xwóyem.

<**shxwiyòtqw'ewí:ls** or better **shxwyòt'qw'ewí:ls**>, df //sx^w=yát=q'^{w}=əwí·ls or sx^w=yát'=q'^{w}=əwí·ls//, HHG ['*dishcloth*'], literally perhaps /'something for rubbing around in circles on dishes'/, *see* yot'.

<**shxwíyq'el** or **shxwíq'el**>, ds //sx^w=hí-yəq'=əl//, TOOL ['*a file*'], literally /'something for going to file'/, *see* yéq'.

<**shxwíyxwiy ~ shxwíxwiy**>, chrs //s=x^{w}íy=C$_1$əC$_2$//, stvi, ABFC ['*(be) easy to wake up*'], *see* xwíy ~ x^w**í**.

<**shxwiyxwiyós** or **shxwixwiyós**>, chrs //s=x^{w}iy=C$_1$əC$_2$=ás//, stvi, EFAM ['*wide-awake*'], literally /'be characteristically alert/awake in the face'/, *see* xwíy ~ x^w**í**.

<**shxwiyxwiyós**>, dnom //s=x^{w}iy=C$_1$əC$_2$=ás//, chrs, EFAM ['*early-bird*'], ABFC, literally /'someone that is characteristically alert/wakes up in the face'/, *see* xwíy ~ x^w**í**.

<**shxwkwál**>, dnom //s(=)x^w=k^{w}ɛ́l//, SOC ['*a hiding*'], *see* kwà:l.

<**sh(xw)kw'ekw'í**>, dnom //sx^w=C$_1$ə=k'^{w}í//, BLDG ['*main rafters of longhouse*'], ASM ['poles going across the top of a longhouse'], *see* kw'íy ~ kw'í *climb, rise.*

<**shxwlàm**>, dnom //sx^w=lɛ́=m//, TVMO ['*place to go to*'], *see* lám *go*, under la.

<**shxwlá:m**>, df //sx^w=lɛ́·m//, IDOC /'*Indian doctor, shaman, medicine man, Indian doctor's spirit power (Elders Group 11/19/75)*'/, *see* lá:m possibly *function as shaman.*

<**shxwlámá:lá**> ~ <**shxwlámálá**>, //sx^{w}lɛ́m=ɛ́:lɛ́//, /'*bottle*'/, *see* lám *rum, liquor.*

<**shxwlathílé**>, dnom //s(=)x^w=lo[=Aɛ=]θ(əl)=ɛ[=Aí=]lə́ or sx^w=lo[=Aí=]θ(əl)=ɛ[=M2/M3=]lə́//, [šx^{w}læθílə́], HHG ['*any kind of cupboard*'], literally /'device to contain dish/plate/tray'/, *see* ló:thel.

<**shxwlemóthetále**>, dnom //sx^w=ləmɛ=Aá=T-ət=ɛ́lə//, IDOC ['*place of training to become an Indian doctor (pit made from repeated jumping every year on the same spot)*'], *see* lá:m (possibly *function as shaman).*

<**shxwlí**>, ds //sx^{w}=lí//, DIR /*'where it's at, where it's from'*/, *see* lí ~ li *at, in, be at, be* .

<**shxwlístexw**>, caus //sx^{w}=lí=sT-əx^{w}//, EFAM [*'care about s-o/s-th'*], *see* lí ~ li *at, in, be at, be in* or perhaps from <**shxwelí**> *life, soul, see* under <**élíyá**> *dream.*

<**shxwlósàlà**>, dnom //s(=)x^{w}=lás=ɛ̀lɛ̀//, HHG [*'grease bowl'*], *see* ló:s ~ lós *be fat.*

<**shxwlhílhets'els**>, dnom //sx^{w}=ɬí[=C$_{1}$ə=]c'=əls//, HARV [*'saw'*], *see* lhíts' ~ lhí:ts' *cut.*

<**shxwlhíts'es**>, ds //sx^{w}=ɬíc'=əs//, FSH [*'wind-dried opened and scored salmon'*], *see* lhíts' ~ lhí:ts' *cut.*

<**shxwlhéts'tses**>, dnom //sx^{w}=ɬi[=Aə́=]c'=cəs//, [šx^{w}ɬɪ́c'cɪs], ABDF [*'a cut on the hand'*], *see* lhíts' ~ lhí:ts' *cut.*

<**shxwmálahá:lá**>, //sx^{w}=mɛ́lɛ=hɛ́·lɛ́//, /*'fishing basket, bait basket'*/, literally /'nominal + bait + container for'/, *see* má:la ~ má:le *bait.*

<**shxwmámth'elqel**>, dmn //s=x^{w}=mɛ́[=C$_{1}$ə=]θ'əl=qəl//, EFAM [*'a little liar'*], *see* máth'el.

<**shxwmáth'elqel**>, //s=x^{w}=mɛ́θ'əl=qəl//, /*'liar'*/, *see* máth'el.

<**shxwmelmálq**>, chrs //s(=)x^{w}=C$_{1}$əC$_{2}$=mə[=Aɛ́=]l=q or s(=)x^{w}=məl=C$_{1}$əC$_{2}$[=Aɛ́=]=q//, strs, EFAM [*'forgetful'*], *see* <malq>, bound stem //mɛ́l=q// *forget*, under root <mál ~ mél>, bound root //mál ~ mə́l *be mixed up*//.

<**shxwmó:l**>, stvi //s=x^{w}(=)má·l or s=x^{w}(=)mɛ=Aá(·)=əl//, SOC [*'to beg'*], *see* <mó:l> or <**xwma**>, bound root //má·l// root meaning unknown or //x^{w}mɛ// *open.*

<**shxwmómel**>, cts //s=x^{w}(=)má[-C$_{1}$ə-]l or s=x^{w}=mɛ=Aá[-C$_{1}$ə-]l//, SOC [*'begging'*], *see* <mó:l> or <**xwma**>, bound root //má·l// root meaning unknown or //x^{w}mɛ// *open.*

<**shxwmót'estel**>, dnom //s(=)x^{w}=mát'=əs=təl//, LAND [*'pointer to show direction (like in a trail) (could be an arrow or stick or mark in the ground)'*], *see* <mót'es>, df //mát'=əs//, ABFC /*'point at, aim'*/

<**shxwóxwekw'**>, strs //s=x^{w}á[=C$_{1}$ə=]k'^{w}//, ABDF [*'numb (can also be used joking of a drunk)'*], *see* xwókw' *numb.*

<**shxwótkw**>, strs //s=x^{w}ɛ[=Aá=]t(=)k^{w}//, SH /*'(be) dug out, (be hollowed out)'*/, *see* xwótkw ~ xwótqw.

<**shxwótkwewel**>, stvi //s=x^{w}át(=)k^{w}=iwəl or s=x^{w}ɛ[=Aá=]t(=)k^{w}=əwəl//, SH [*'hollow (of tree or log)'*], *see* xwótkw ~ xwótqw.

<**shxwótqwelwetem**>, //s=x^{w}átq^{w}=əlwət=əm//, /*'washboard'*/, *see* xwótqwem *rumble.*

<**shxwoweth'ílep** or **shxwwoweth'ílep**>, dnom //sx^{w}=wɛ[=AaC$_{1}$ə=]θ'=íləp//, TOOL [*'shovel'*], LAND, literally /'something for prying earth'/, *see* wáth'.

<**shxwóxw**>, df //s=x^{w}áx^{w}//, EB /*'rabbit, (varying hare,* perhaps now also the introduced *eastern cottontail)'*/, [*'Lepus americanus cascadensis and Lepus americanus washingtoni,* now perhaps *Sylvilagus floridanus mearnsi'*], *see* xwóxw.

<**shxwóxwel**>, incs //s=x^{w}ɛ=AáC$_{1}$ə=əl//, ABFC /*'to lift, raise'*/, literally /'go/get to be lightweight'/, *see* xwá.

<**shxwóxwelstexw**>, caus //s=x^{w}ɛ[=AáC$_{1}$ə=]=əl=sT-əx^{w}//, ABFC /*'keep it in the air, lift s-th/s-o off the floor'*/, SPRD [*'lift s-o (of a spirit dancer being initiated)'*], *see* xwá.

<**shxwóxwth'**>, strs //s=x^{w}ɛ[=AaC$_{1}$ə=]θ'//, EFAM /*'be crazy, be insane'*/, literally /'be teetered/rocked'/,

see xwáth.

<**shxwő:qel ~ shxwőwqel ~ shxwéwqel**>, df //s=xʷów=qəl ~ s=xʷə́w=qəl or s=x̣ʷ[=F=]i[=Aə́=]w=qəl//, EZ /'*whistling swan,* probably also *trumpeter swan*'/, ['*Olor columbianus,* probably also *Olor buccinator*'], literally perhaps /'something that's whistling in the throat'/, *see* xwő:qel ~ xwőwqel ~ xwéwqel.

<**shxwōqw'ő:lh**>, df //s=xʷe=wq'ʷ=ó·ɬ//, EZ ['*August run spring salmon that go up Silver Creek (near Hope)*'], ['August Silver Creek run of *Oncorhynchus tshawytscha*'], lit. *something that's drifting back downriver (like spawned-out salmon), see* xwōqw'ő:lh.

<**shxwpélmàlà**>, //s(=)xʷ=pə́l=əm=ɛ̀lɛ̀//, /'*root cellar, root house (covered with earth, separate from house, kept potatoes, apples, carrots, etc)*.'/, *see* main variant <**spepíláwtxw**> under root <**pél** > (~<**pí:l** > by now) *planted, get buried* and variant <**spélmàlà**> *root house* under root <**pél** > also.

<**shxwpípewels**>, dnom //s(=)xʷ=pí[=C_1ə=]w=əls//, WATR ['*freezer*'], *see* <pí:w> //pí·w// *freeze.*

<**Shxwpópélem**>, df //s(=)xʷ=pápə́ləm or s(=)xʷ(=)pɛ[=AáC$_1$ə=]l(ə)=əm//, PLN /'*slough on west side of Harrison River, the first slough upriver from Q'iq'ewetó:lthel and first slough below Xemó:leqw'*'/, *see* pópélem.

<**shxwpópex̱welsà·ls ~ spópex̱welá:ls**>, //Tait dial.sxʷ=pá[=C_1ə=]x̣ʷ=əlsɛ́·ls ~ Chwk. dialect s=pá[=C_1ə=]x̣ʷ=əlsɛ́·ls//, /'*spray-gun (for plants)*'/ (compare <**póx̱w=et**> *blow spray on patient (done by Indian doctor)), see* <póx̱w>, bound root //páx̣ʷ// *blow spray.*

<**shxwp'áp'eth'**>, dnom //s(=)xʷ=p'ɛ́[=C_1ə=]θ'//, WV ['*sewing machine*'], *see* p'áth' *sew.*

<**shxwp'életstel ~ shxwep'életstel ~**>, ds //s(=)xʷ=(ə)p'=ə́ləc=təl or s(=)xʷ=ʔɛp'=ə́ləc=təl//, [šxʷʊp'ə́lɪctəl ~ šxʷp'ə́lɪctəl], HHG ['*toilet paper*'], PE, literally /'device/thing to wipe on the rump/bottom'/, *see* á:p' ~ áp' *wipe.*

<**shxwqáqelets'**>, dnom //sxʷ=qɛ́[=C_1ə=]l=əc'//, WV /'*spindle for spinning wool, a hand spinner, a spinning machine*'/, literally /'thing for spinning wool'/, *see* qálets' *spin wool or twine*

<**shxwqeyqex̱elátsem ~ shxwqiqex̱elátsem**>, dnom //s(=)xʷ=qi[=C_1ə=]x̣=ɛ́lə[=M2=]c=əm//, CAN ['*little sled*'], literally /'(prob.) something for sliding on one's rump on'/, *see* qíx̱ ~ qéyx̱ *slip, slide.*

<**shxwqiqex̱óthet**>, dnom //s(=)xʷ=qi[=C_1ə=]x̣=ɛ[=Aá=]T=ət//, PLAY /'*ice skate, sled, toboggan*'/, *see* qíx̱ ~ qéyx̱ *slip, slide.*

<**shxwqó:m**>, dnom //s(=)xʷ=qá·=əm//, BSK ['*water basket*'], *see* qó:.

<**Shxwqó:m**>, dnom //s(=)xʷ=qá·=əm//, PLN ['*Lake of the Woods*'], *see* qó:.

<**shxwq'éyq'esetsel**>, WV /'*net shuttle, mesh-measure (usually part of the shuttle)*'/, *see* q'ey ~ q'i *wound around, tied, knotted.*

<**shxwqwáylhechàls**>, dnom //sxʷ=qʷɛ́y=ɬcə=M1=ɛ̀ls//, FOOD ['*long-handled stirring spoon*'], *see* qwiy.

<**sh(xw)qwó:ls**>, dnom //sxʷ=qwá·=əls//, FOOD ['*something to boil in*'], *see* qwó:ls.

<**shxwqwó:lthels**>, df //s=xʷqʷ=á·lθ(=əl)=əls//, MC ['*a wood carving*'], literally perhaps /'something being exposed/uncovered by structured activity on the knee'/, ASM ['Joe Lorenzetto, one of the last traditional elder carvers, did most of his carving of wood and bone spoons, etc. on his knees while sitting, Stó:lō carvers and other elders talk about selecting wood so that the figure to be carved can emerge from the wood as it is carved'], (<**s=**> *nominalizer*), possibly root <**xwíqw**> *be uncovered,*

exposed?? (see Squamish possible cognate), lx <**=ó:lth(el)**> *on the knee*, (<**=els**> *structured activity continuative*), phonology: possible syllable-loss of el before =els, syntactic analysis: nominal, attested by DM (12/4/64), TG (4/23/75), Salish cognate: possibly Squamish /xʷiʔ-qʷ/ *be uncovered, exposed* as in /xʷiʔ-qʷ-ánʔ/ *uncover, expose (tr.)* K67:349, 350, also *see* xwqwó:lthels.

<**shxwtále'álá**>, ds //sxʷ=tɛ́lə=ʔɛ́lɛ́//, ECON /'*wallet, purse*'/, *see* tá:le ~ tále

<**shxwtatí:m**>, //sxʷ=tɛtí·m//, /'*telephone*'/, *see* tà:m *holler, yell,*

<**shxwtelí**>, dnom //sxʷ=təl=lí//, DIR ['*where s-o came from*'], *see* tel=.

<**shxwtélhtses**>, ds //sxʷ=tə́ɬ=cəs//, TOOL /'*hammer, stone hand hammer, sledge hammer*'/, *see* télhches.

<**Shxwtépsem**>, ds //sxʷ=t(=)ə́psəm//, PLN ['*a neck of land on the west side of Harrison Lake just north of Twenty-Mile Creek and across from the north tip of Long Island*'], *see* tépsem.

<**shxwtéxelqèyls**>, dnom //sxʷ=tə[=´=]xʸ=əlq(əl)=í·l=(əl)s//, [šxʷtɪ́xʸɪlqèyls], WV ['*a carder (for carding wool)*'], *see* tex, perhaps *insert comb between.*

<**shxwtitós** or **shxwtiytós**>, df //s(=)xʷ=C_1í=təs=ás//, DIR ['*the only safe place to cross a river*'], *see* tiytós or titós.

<**shxwt'álh**>, dnom //sxʷ=t'ɛ́ɬ//, CSTR ['*bridge*'], *see* t'álh.

<**shxwt'ám:etsel**>, df //sxʷ=t'ɛ́m·=əcəl or sxʷ=t'ə[=Aɛ́=]m=əcəl//, EB ['*young (red) cedar*'], *see* t'am: .

<**shxwt'át'ekwels**>, dnom //sxʷ=t'ɛ́[=C_1ə=]kʷ=əls//, CAN /'*a ferry (canoe, boat, ferryboat)*'/, *see* t'ákwel.

<**shxwt'elémels**>, dnom //sxʷ=t'ələ́m=əls//, sas, MC ['*glue*'], literally /'something for sticking as a structured activity'/, *see* t'elém.

<**shxwt'et'emélep**>, dnom //sxʷ=C_1ə=t'əm=ə́ləp//, TOOL ['*hoe*'], HARV, literally /'something for chopping the ground'/, *see* t'ém.

<**shxwt'ólhestel**>, dnom //sxʷ=t'ɛ[-Aá-]ɬ=əs=təl//, BLDG ['*beam*'], literally /'device for stretching across on the face (of a building)'/, *see* t'álh.

<**shxwt'ót'ep'els**>, dnom //s=xʷ=t'á[=C_1ə=]p'=əls//, TOOL ['*a pick*'], *see* **t'óp'**.

<**shxwtháyelets**>, ds //sxʷ=θi[=Aɛ́=]y=ələc//, CAN ['*rudder*'], literally /'something for steering a canoe'/, *see* tháyelets.

<**shxwthéletstel**>, df //sxʷ=θə́l=ləc=təl//, HHG ['*cushion*'], *see* thél.

<**shxwthí:lestel**>, df //sxʷ=θə́l=í·ləs=təl//, CLO ['*fancy lining*'], lit. "something for cover/pad under on the chest", *see* thél.

<**shxwthó:yeltsep**>, ds //sxʷ=θi[=Aá·=]y=əlcəp or sxʷ=θi[=Aɛ[=Aá=]·=]y=əlcəp//, FIRE ['*fire poker*'], literally /'something for fixing/straightening up fire'/, *see* thíy.

<**shxwthóyeqwels**>, dnom //sxʷ=θi[=Aá=]y=qʷ(ɛ)=əls//, HARV ['*digging stick*'], LAND, literally /'something for digging, something for fixing/making get hole as structured activity'/, *see* thíy.

<**shxwthó:yqw**>, cpds //sxʷ=θi[=Aá·=]y=qʷ(ɛ) or sxʷ=θi[=Aɛ́[=Aá=]·=]y=qʷ(ɛ)//, LAND /'*hole in the ground, trench (if discussing length)*'/, *see* thíy.

<**shxwth'á:lhtel**>, df //sxʷ=θ'ɛ́·ɬ=təl or s=xʷθ'ɛ́·ɬ=təl or sxʷ=wáθ'[=M1=]=əɬ=təl//, BSK ['*fine cedar*

root strips for baskets'], ASM ['these are bundled and wrapped with wider strips called yemáwéstel'], possibly **<shxw=>** *something that, nominalizer,* root meaning unknown unless wáth' as in wáth'et *pry s-th*, lx **<=tel>** *device for, something for,* syntactic analysis: nominal, attested by Elders Group (6/11/75).

<shxwth'ámqels>, //s=xʷɛ́θ'ə[=M2=]m(=)q=əls//, /'*scissors*'/, *see* xwath' *teeter*

<shxwth'ámqels qw'x̱wéltses/qw'x̱wélches>, cpds //s=xʷɛ́θ'=ə[=M2=]m=q=əls q'ʷix̣ʷ=ə[=´=]l=cəs or q'ʷə́x̣ʷ=ə[=M2=]l=cəs//, PE /'*fingernail clippers*'/, lit. "scissors for the fingernails", *see* **xwáth'** *teeter, rock,* & **qw'íx̱w** *dark brown.*

<shxwth'éx̱welwetem>, //sxʷ=θ'ə́x̣ʷ=əlwət=əm//, /'*washtub, washing machine*'/, *see* th'éx̱w or th'óx̱w *wash*

<shxwth'ox̱wewí:ls (or **shxwth'ex̱wewí:ls)>**, //sxʷ=θ'ax̣ʷ=əwí·ls (a probably sic forə)//, /'*sink, dishpan*'/, *see* th'éx̱w or th'óx̱w *wash*

<shxwtl'ép>, ds //s=xʷ=ƛ'ə́p//, DIR /'*be deep, be very deep, be deep water*'/, *see* tl'ép.

<shxwtl'éxelep>, //sxʷ=ƛ'ə́xʸ=ələp//, /'*a plow*'/ (compare root **<tl'éx>** *rip or break apart)*

<shxwtl'ó:s>, df //s=xʷƛ'=á·s or s=xʷ=ƛ'á·s//, SD ['*(be) loud*'], *see* tl'ó:s.

<Shxwúwélem>, //sxʷ=wú=C_1ə=´=əl=əm or sxʷ=wə́=C_1ə=´=əl=əm//, *see* main entry **<Shxwewéwe>**.

<shxwúxwe>, stvi //s=xʷi[=Aə́=]=C_1ə or s=xʷi[=Aú=]=C_1ə//, EFAM /'*(be) ambitious, (be) willing*'/, *see* xwúxwe.

<shxwwáli>, pln //sxʷ=wɛ́l=əy// or //sxʷ=wɛ́[=lə=]y//, KIN /'*parents, relations (ancestors?)*'/, *see* wál..

<shxwwéth'tel or **shxwéth'tel>**, dnom //sxʷ=wɛ[=Aə́=]θ'=təl//, MC /'*a latch, Indian lock*'/, BLDG, ASM ['a latch fastened in the middle or on one end, or loose which slides through'], *see* wáth'.

<shxwwoweth'ílep or **shxwoweth'ílep>**, dnom //sxʷ=wɛ[=AaC$_1$ə=]θ'=íləp//, TOOL ['*shovel*'], LAND, literally /'something for prying earth'/, *see* wáth'.

<shxwxóxekw'em>, dnom //sxʷ=xʸá[=C_1ə=]k'ʷ=əm//, BLDG ['*bathtub*'], literally /'something for bathing oneself'/, *see* **xókw' ~ xó:kw'.**

<shxwyáx̱q'els ~ shxwiyáx̱q'els>, dnom //sxʷ=yɛ́x̣q'=əls//, sas, HUNT ['*pouch (like for gunpowder)*'], PE, *see* yáx̱q' ~ iyáx̱q'.

<shxwyélhtel ~ shxwiyélhtel>, rsls //sxʷ=yo[=Aə́=]ɬ=təl//, dnom, FIRE /'*ashes (cinder-like), cinders (heavy and dirty), embers*'/, *see* yólh.

<shxwyémtel ~ shxwiyémtel>, df //sxʷ=yə́m=təl//, CLO /'*belt, (necklace?? [DM])*'/, literally perhaps /'device that stretches around the middle'/, *see* yém ~ yem.

<shxwyó:yes ~ shxweyó:yes>, ds //sxʷ=yá[= ·=C_1ə=](y)s//, TOOL ['*tool*'], literally /'something for really working'/, *see* yó:ys.

<shxw'álex>, dnom //sxʷ=ʔɛ́ləxʸ//, HUMC, KIN /'*sister-in-law, husband's sister, brother's wife, wife's sister*; *see* álex *sibling, brother, sister*

<shxw'állhelh>, dnom //sxʷ=ʔɛ́l=ɬəɬ//, [šxʷʔɛ́lɬəɬ], ANA ['*front of the neck*'], (**<sxw=>** *nominalizer*), probably root **<'ál>** *pole/shaft/length*, lx **<=lhelh>** (or poss. **<=llhelh)>**) *on the throat, on the front of the neck*, syntactic analysis: nominal.

<**shxw'áp'ewí:ls**> dnom //s=x^{w}=ʔɛ́p'=əwí·ls//, HHG ['*dish towel*'],, *see* á:p' ~ áp' *wipe*

<**shxw'á:q'**> dnom ///s=x^{w}=ʔɛ́[==˙]q'//, ANA /'*foreskin*'/. prob. <shxw=> *nominalizer*, perhaps same root as in <**áq'elh**>, us //ʔɛ́q'(=)əɬ//, ABDF ['*choke on bone or s-th solid*'], with attested <=:=> *continuative*, attested by DM, sourc: JH66:11.

<**shxw'áthelets**>, //sx^{w}=ʔɛ́θ=ələc//, /'*bottom of anything*'/, *see* áthelets.

<**shxw'áthtel**>, dnom /s=x^{w}ə=θɛ́[=M1=]t=əl//, WETH ['*cloud*'], literally probably /'something for going dark or something to become getting dark'/, *see* thá:t.

<**shxw'átl'q**>, ds //s=ʔɛ́ƛ'q//, DIR ['*the outside*'], (<**s=**> *nominalizer*), syntactic analysis: nominal, also <**shxw'átl'q**>, *see* s'átl'q under átl'q.

<**shxw'awkw'ála**>, dnom //sx^{w}=ʔɛwk'^{w}=ɛ́lɛ//, HHG ['*clothes basket*'], CLO, BSK, *see* á:wkw'.

<**shxw'áwkw'emálá**>, //sx^{w}=ʔɛ́wk'^{w}=əm=ɛ́lɛ́//, HHG ['*suitcase*'], also <**shxw'á:wkw'emálá ~ shxw'á:wkw'álá**>, //sx^{w}=ʔɛ́·wk'^{w}=əm=ɛ́lɛ́ ~ sx^{w}=ʔɛ́·wk'^{w}=ɛ́lɛ́//, HHG /'*clothes container, suitcase, clothes case*'/, *see* á:wkw'.

<**shxw'á<u>x</u>eth**>, dnom //s<u>x</u>^{w}=ʔɛ́<u>x</u>əθ//, HHG ['*bed*'], literally /'what one lies down on'/, *see* á<u>x</u>eth.

<**shxw'el'álex**>, pln //sx^{w}=C$_1$əC$_2$-ʔɛ́ləx^{y}//, HUMC, KIN ['*sisters-in-law*'], *see* álex *sibling, brother, sister.*

<**shxw'émet**>//s(=)x^{w}=ʔa[=Aə́=]mət//, also /'*something to sit down on*'/, attested by DM (12/4/64), *see* <omét>, probably root //ʔəmə́t from ʔamə́t// *sit.*

<**shxw'étselets**>, //sx^{w}=ʔɛ[=Aə́=]c=(ə)ləc//, [šx^{w}ʔɪ́cɪlɪc], LAND ['*base of mountain or something high*'], EB ['*base of a tree*'], *see* áthelets.

<**shxw'éy**>, dnom //sx^{w}=ʔɛ́y//, VALJ ['*what s-o/s-th is good for*'], *see* éy ~ éy: *good*

<**shxw'éyelh**>, stvi //s=x^{w}=ʔɛ́y=əɬ//, ABFC /'*be in clear voice, be in good voice, be in good health, healthy*'/, *see* éy ~ éy: *good*

<**shxw'éywelh**>, //s=x^{w}=ʔɛ́y=wəɬ//, variant of <**xw'éywelh ~ xwe'éywelh ~ xwe'éy:welh**>, ds //x^{w}=ʔɛ́y=wəɬ ~ x^{w}ə=ʔɛ́y=wəɬ ~ x^{w}ə=ʔɛ́y·=wəɬ//, EFAM /'*good-hearted, kind-hearted, kind, generous, helpful, easy-going, good-natured*'/, *see* éy ~ éy: *good*

<**shxw'ílámálá ~ shxw'ílàmàlà**>, dnom //s=x^{w}=ʔílɛ́m=ɛ́lɛ́ ~ s=x^{w}=ʔílɛ̀m=ɛ̀lɛ̀//, ANA /'*shoulder (especially the top), shoulder (someone's, possessed)*'/, HARV ['*yoke*'], (<**s=**> *nominalizer*), syntactic analysis: nominal, attested by BHTTC, IHTTC, also <**shxw'í:lá:má:lá:**>, attested by DM (12/4/64), Elders Group 7/27/75, *see* ílàm.

<**Shxw'ílamṓwelh**>, dnom //s=x^{w}=ʔílɛm=ówəɬ//, PLN /'*rocky place across from and just above Emory Creek, on east/CN side of Fraser River*'/, *see* ilàm.

<**shxw'ílá<u>x</u>el**>, dnom //s=x^{w}=ʔí=lɛ́x̣əl or s=x^{w}=ʔíl=ɛ́x̣əl or s=x^{w}=ʔílɛ́=ɛ́x̣əl//, ANA ['*armpit*'], (<**s=**> *nominalizer*), lx <**xw=**> *(meaning unclear)*, lx <**=(e)lá<u>x</u>el**> *on the arm*, root <**í** or **íl** or **ílá**>, syntactic analysis: nominal, *see* ílá<u>x</u>el.

<**shxw'íle ~ shxw'í:le**>, dnom //s=x^{w}=ʔ=ílə ~ s=x^{w}=ʔi=ílə//, ANA /'*cheek, cheek-bone*'/, (<**s=**> *nominalizer*), lx <**xw=**> *(meaning unclear, toward the face?)*, lx <**=íle**> *on the side of the head, on the cheek*, root <**'i** or **'**> *(empty root for lexical suffixes, place-holder root)*, syntactic analysis: nominal, attested by Elders Group, IHTTC.

<**shxw'el'íle**>, pln //s=xʷ=C_1əC_2-ʔ=ílə//, ANA [*'both cheeks'*], (<**R3=**> *plural*), phonology: reduplication, syntactic analysis: nominal.

<**shxw'ímex**>, dnom //s=xʷ=ʔím=əxʸ or sxʷ=ʔím=əxʸ//, TVMO /*'what one walks on (trail, board sidewalk, cement sidewalk, etc.)'*/, MC, ACL /*'board sidewalk, cement sidewalk'*/, *see* .

<**shxw'íqw'els**>, sas //s=xʷ=ʔíq'ʷ=əls//, SCH [*'eraser (for pencil or blackboard)'*], *see* íqw' *rub.*

<**shxwíqw'estel**>, dnom //s=xʷ=ʔiq'ʷ=əs=təl//, HHG [*'face-cloth'*], *see* íqw' *rub.*

<**shxwiqw'ewí:ls**>, dnom //s=xʷ=ʔiq'ʷ=əwí·ls//, HHG [*'dish towel'*], *see* íqw' *rub.*

<**shxw'í'àlh**>, stvi //s=xʷ=ʔɛ́y=ʔɛ̀ɬ//, LANG /*'soft voice, have a soft voice'*/, *see* éy ~ éy: *good.*

<**shxw'iy'éyelh**>, stvi //s=xʷ=C_1əC_2=ʔɛ́y=əɬ//, LANG [*'be in clear voice'*], *see* éy ~ éy: *good.*

<**shxw'ólewù**>, free root //sxʷ=ʔáləwù//, EB [*'domestic turnip'*], [*'Brassica campestris'*], ASM ['introduced by non-Indians'], possibly <**shxw=**> *something that, nominalizer*, root meaning unknown, syntactic analysis: nominal, attested by IHTTC, borrowed from Chinook Jargon /lətowó/ <ledowo> *turnip* Johnson 1978:413, Salish cognate: Squamish /sx̣ʷlawə́ʔ/ *Swedish turnip* from French <chou-navet> *turnip* W73:275, K67:297.

<**skwekwelím shxw'ólewù**>, EB, FOOD *radishes* (lit. little red ones + turnip), (attested by RG,EH 6/16/98 to SN, edited by BG with RG,EH 6/26/00)

<**tskwím shxw'ólewù**>, EB, FOOD *beets* (lit. red + turnip), (attested by RG,EH 6/16/98 to SN, edited by BG with RG,EH 6/26/00)

<**shxw'ó:met**>, dnom //s(=)xʷ=ʔa[=´·=]mət//, HHG /*'sofa, couch, chesterfield, place where one's sitting, (bed [AC, MC (Katzie)])'*/, *see* <omét>, probably root //ʔəmə́t from ʔamə́t// .

<**shxw'ómóqwes**>, //s(=)xʷ=ʔámáqʷ(=)əs//, [*'bracket fungus'*], *see* <s'ómó:qwes> //s=ʔámá·qʷ(=)əs//, EB [*'bracket fungus'*], since it is a variant of the latter more common form, under possible root or stem <**ómó:qw**>.

<**shxw'óp'estel**>, dnom //s(=)xʷ=ʔɛ[=Aá=]p'=əs=təl//, HHG [*'large towel'*], literally /'device/thing to wipe on the face'/, *see* á:p' ~ áp' *wipe.*

<**shxw'óthestses ~ shxwe'óthestses**>, ds //s(=)xʷ=ʔáθəs=cəs//, ANA [*'palm (of the hand)'*], literally /'face on the hand, face of the hand'/, (<**sxw=**> *nominalizer*), lx <**=tses**> *on the hand*, syntactic analysis: nominal, attested by Elders Group, *see* <s'ó:thes ~ s'óthes>, dnom //s=ʔá·θ=əs ~ s=ʔáθ=əs//, ANA [*'face'*], (<**s=**> *nominalizer*), possibly root <**óth**> *edge, surface* possibly root from <**=ó:th**> *edge?*, *see* under <**ó:th ~ óth**>, probably bound root //ʔá·θ//, meaning uncertain unless *edge, surface*

<**shxw'óthesxel ~ shxwe'óthesxel**>, ds //s(=)xʷ=ʔáθəs=xʸəl//, ANA /*'sole (of the foot), (instep [AC, DM])'*/, literally /'face on the foot, face of the foot'/, (<**sxw=**> *nominalizer*), lx <**=xel**> *on the foot*, syntactic analysis: nominal, attested by Elders Group, AC, also /*'instep'*/, attested by AC, DM (12/4/64), other sources: ES /šxʷʔáθəsxʸəl/ *sole of foot*, H-T <cuátsecEl> (macrons over u and a) *sole, see* <s'ó:thes ~ s'óthes>, dnom //s=ʔá·θ=əs ~ s=ʔáθ=əs//, ANA [*'face'*], (<**s=**> *nominalizer*), possibly root <**ó:th**> *edge, surface* possibly root from <**=óth**> *edge?*, *see* also under <**ó:th ~ óth**>, probably bound root //ʔá·θ//, meaning uncertain unless *edge, surface*

<**Shxw'ōhámél ~ Ōhámél ~ Shxw'ōwhámél**>, df //s(=)xʷ=ʔə[=Ao=]ha=ɛ́məl//, PLN [*'village now called Ohamil Reserve or Laidlaw'*], (<**s(=)xw=**> *nominalizer*), probably root <**ehó**> *wrapped up*, lx <**=ámél ~ =ómél**> *part, portion (of body), member*, possibly <**ō-ablaut**> *derivational*, phonology: ō-ablaut (rare), vowel merger, syntactic analysis: nominal, last two pronunciations attested by IHTTC

(8/5/77, 8/11/77), LJ (Tait)(in Elders Group 7/13/77), also <**Uhámél ~ Ōhámél**>, //ʔə[=Au=]ha=ɛ́mə́l ~ ʔə[=Ao=]ha=ɛ́mə́l//, phonology: clipped form, Elder's comment: "shortcut pronunciation", attested by IHTTC (8/11/77), other sources: Wells 1965 (lst ed.):25, source: place names reference file #57.

T

<**t**>, bound root //t// meaning unclear, examples: <**ta'á ~ te'á ~ t'á**>, //t=ɛʔɛ́ ~ t=əʔɛ́ ~ t=ʔɛ > t'ɛ́ *similar, alike, same*//, if stem probably root <t> meaning unknown plus lx <**=a'á ~ =e'á**> *comparative*, <**tépsem**>, root or stem //tə́psəm or t=ə́psəm//, ANA /'*neck, (back of head and back of neck* [EB], *nape of the neck* [Elders Group 5/3/78]*)*'/, <**=épsem**> *on the neck, on the back of the neck, on the back of the head*; perhaps related to <**te=**>, da //tə=//, DEM /'*nominalizer (male or gender unspecified, present and visible or presence or proximity unspecified), demonstrative article*'/.

<**=t ~ =et**>, da //=T ~ =əT//, TIB /'*purposeful control transitivizer, do purposely to s-o/s-th*'/, phonology: the //T// in =stative //=sT// and in =t ~ =et //=T ~ =əT// and in =met //=məT// becomes /θ/ before three inflections, (/-ámə, -áxʸ, -ət/) (*first person singular object, me, second person singular object, you*, and *purposeful control reflexive*, everywhere else it remains /t/, syntactic analysis: derivational suffix, also <**=et**>, //=əT//; found in <**maythóxchexw.**>, //mɛy=T-áxʸ-c-əxʷ//, /'*You help me., Help me.*'/, <**máytes.**>, //mɛ́y=T-əs//, /'*He/She/It helps him/her/it/them., They help him/her/it/them.*'/, <**kw'átsetes.**>, //k'ʷɛ́c=əT-əs//, /'*He looked at him.*'/, <**kw'eqwethóxes.**>, //k'ʷəqʷ=əT-áxʸ-əs//, /'*He hit me intentionally.*'/, <**píxwethòxes.**>, //píxʷ=əT-áxʸ-əs//, /'*He brushes me off. (brush s-o off)*'/.

<**ta=**>, da //tɛ=//, DEM /'*nominalizer (male or gender unspecified, present and visible or presence or proximity unspecified), demonstrative article*'/, phonology: variant (allomorph) of te= which occurs only with personal pronouns, syntactic analysis: derivational prefix, syntactic comment: a number of verbs (demonstrative, interrogative, pronominal) can serve a nominal or pronominal function when phonologically prefixed with te= ~ ta=; found in <**ta'á'altha**>, //tɛ=C_1ɛ́=ʔɛlθɛ//, /'*it's me, I am the one*'/, <**talhlímelh**>, //tɛ=ɬlím=əɬ//, /'*it's us, we are the ones*'/.

<**=´ta**>, da //=´tɛ//, PRON ['*thing*'], syntactic analysis: lexical suffix, derivational suffix, compare with <**te**> demonstrative article '*the*'; found in <**ō̸wéta ~ wéta**>, //ʔowə́=tɛ ~ wə́=tɛ//, /'*nothing*'/, compare with <**ő̸we ~ éwe**> *(be) no, not*.

<**tákw**>, possible bound root //tɛ́kʷ//, meaning unknown.

<**stekwtákw**>, df //s=C_1əC_2=tɛ́kʷ//, [stʊkʷtǽkʷ], EFAM /'*(be) in a daze, day-dreaming*'/, (<**s=**> *stative*), probably <**R3=**> *plural or characteristic*, phonology: reduplication, syntactic analysis: adjective/adjectival verb, attested by NP (Elders Group 3/23/77), also <**stekták**>, //s=C_1əC_2=tɛ́k//, attested by Elders Group (3/23/77).

<**tá:l ~ tà:l ~ tál**>, free root //tɛ́·l ~ tɛ̀·l ~ tɛ́l//, KIN ['*mother*'], syntactic analysis: noun, nominal, attested by AC, BJ (5/10/64, 12/15/64), Elders Group, Deming, other sources: ES /tɛ́·l/ *mother*, example: <**thel tá:l ~ thel tál ~ l tá:l**>, //**θ**ə-l tɛ́·l ~ **θ**ə-l tɛ́l ~ l tɛ́·l//, /'*my mother*'/, literally /'the (female, present or distance unspecified)'/, attested by AC, BJ, <**tsel lépetst tha tà:l te sthóqwi.**>, //c-əl lə́pəc=T **θ**-ɛ tɛ̀·l tə s=**θ**áqʷ(=)i//, /'*I sent your mother the salmon.*'/, attested by AC (12/8/71).

<**tátel**>, dmn //tɛ́[=C_1ə=]l//, KIN /'*Mother (the speaker's), Mom, Mum*'/, (<**=R1=**> *diminutive or vocative*), phonology: reduplication, syntactic analysis: noun, nominal.

<**tà:t, tát** or **tàt**>, dmn //tɛ̀(·)[=C_1ə=](l)//, KIN /'*Mother (the speaker's), Mom, Mum*'/, <**clipping**> or <**syllable loss**> *affectionate*, phonology: syllable-loss or clipping, syntactic analysis: noun, nominal, attested by AC, other sources: H-T <tat> (umlaut over a) *mother (speaker's own)*.

<**táta**>, df //C_1ɛ́=tɛ(l)//, KIN /'*Grandma, Father's Mother (nickname)*'/, (<**R7=**> *derivational/nickname* perhaps from *diminutive*), <**clipping**> *affectionate nickname*, phonology: reduplication, clipping,

syntactic analysis: noun, nominal, attested by AC.

<**tá:le ~ tále**>, free root //tɛ́·lə ~ tɛ́lə//, ECON ['*money*'], syntactic analysis: noun, nominal, attested by Elders Group (1/7/76, 3/2/77), AC, EB, Deming, borrowed from Chinook Jargon /tála/ *money; dollar* Johnson 1978:304 itself from English /dálr/ ~ (r-less British dialect) roughly /dálə/ *dollar*, example: <**ílhchel x̲ethós tel tá:le.**>, //ʔí=ɬ-c-əl x̣əθ=ás tə-l tɛ́·lə//, /'*I bet my money.*'/, attested by EB (3/8/76), also <**théx̲estel tel tá:le**>, //θə́x̣=əs=T-əl tə-l tɛ́·lə//, also /'*bet my money*'/, attested by Elders Group (1/7/76), <**léts'es pípe tále**>, //lə́c'ə=əs pípə tɛ́lə//, /'*one paper dollar*'/, literally /'one dollar paper money'/, attested by Elders Group (3/2/77).

<**tále te syó:qwem**>, cpds //tɛ́lə(-s) tə s=yə[=Aá·=]qʷ=əm//, EZ /'*metallic blue-green beetle, "June bug", probably metallic wood-boring beetle,* or possibly *some types of long-horn beetle which aremetallic green with reddish legs*'/, ['probably order *Coleoptera*, family *Buprestidae*, genus *Buprestis*, or possibly family *Cerambycidae*, genus *Gaurotes*'], literally /'money (of) the sun'/, ASM ['it's good luck to find and keep one'], (irregular)dropping of -s *possessive* may be *derivational* here to separate the idiom from the literal phrase, phonology: ablaut, consonant-loss, syntactic analysis: nominal phrase with modifier(s), attested by SP or AK or AD (Raft Trip from X̲elhálh to Alhqá:yem 8/30/77).

<**shxwtále'álá**>, ds //sxʷ=tɛ́lə=ʔɛ́lɛ́//, ECON /'*wallet, purse*'/, PE, (<**shxw=**> *something to, something for*), lx <**='álá ~ =álá ~ =àlà ~ =ále**> *container of*, phonology: possible epenthetic glottal stop, syntactic analysis: nominal, attested by Elders Group (11/26/75), also <**shxwtále'ále**>, //sxʷ=tɛ́lə=ʔɛ́lə//, also /'*wallet, purse, money-bag, money-container*'/, attested by EB (12/15/75, 12/15/76), example: <**tsel kwá:lx tel shxwtále'ále.**>, //c-əl kʷɛ́·l=əxʸ tə-l sxʷ=tɛ́lə=ʔɛ́lə//, /'*I hid my money-bag (purse, wallet, etc.).*'/, attested by EB (12/16/76).

<**tale'áwtxw**>, ds //tɛlə=ʔɛ́wtxʷ//, ECON /'*bank (money house, money building)*'/, BLDG, literally /'money house/building'/, lx <**=áwtxw**> *house, building*, phonology: epenthetic glottal stop ('), syntactic analysis: nominal, attested by Elders Group (1/15/75).

<**tále te syó:qwem**>, EZ /'*metallic blue-green beetle, "June bug",* probably *metallic wood-boring beetle,* or possibly *some types of long-horn beetle which aremetallic green with reddish legs*'/, *see* tá:le ~ tále, *see* yéqw.

<**taléwe**>, PRON ['*you (sg.)*'], *see* léwe.

<**tale'áwtxw**>, ECON /'*bank (money house, money building)*'/, *see* tá:le ~ tále.

<**tá:lstem**>, ABDF ['*staggering (after you trip for ex.)*'], *see* tél ~ tá:l ~ tiy.

<**tá:lxel**>, df //tɛ́·l=xʸəl//, HUNT ['*follow tracks*'], possibly root <**tel ~ tá:l**> *repeat, respond*, lx <**=xel**> *on the foot*, syntactic analysis: intransitive verb, attested by IHTTC.

<**tátelxel**>, cts //tɛ́[-C_1ə-]l=xʸəl//, HUNT ['*following tracks*'], (<**-R1-**> *continuative*), phonology: reduplication, syntactic analysis: intransitive verb, attested by IHTTC.

<**tá:lh**>, free root //tɛ́·ɬ//, FSH /'*spear (any kind), spear (for fish or war), fish-spear, telescopic spear for sturgeon, harpoon, detachable harpoon points*'/, SOC ['*war spear*'], ASM ['the fish spear was typically 12 to 14 feet in length, had two prongs (qáthexw) made of oceanspray wood (hardhack) (qá:thelhp) on one end with places to attach the detachable (stone) harpoon points, the points were attached to strong twine (toléptel *string attached to fish spear point)* which ran up the sides of the pole *(*s'álém *shaft of fish spear, fish spear itself*) and were used for hauling in the fish (EL)'], on Elders Group (EL 1/26/77 card and field notes), syntactic analysis: noun, nominal, attested by Elders Group (11/10/76, 2/19/75, 6/11/75, 11/26/75), EL (Elders Group 1/26/77), CT (6/8/76), Deming (3/25/76), AK or SP or AD (Raft Trip 8/30/77, 9/13/77), also <**tá'alh**>, //tɛ́ʔɛɬ//, dialects: *Sumas*, attested by

Deming (3/25/76), also <**s'álém**>, //s=ʔɛ́l(=)ə[=´=]m//, also /'*shaft of fish spear, whole fish spear*'/, example: <**x̱éyx̱elex̱ tá:lh or x̱íx̱elex̱ tá:lh**>, //x̣í[=C₁ə=]l(=)əx̣ tɛ́·ɬ//, /'*war spear*'/, attested by Elders Group (11/26/75).

<**Tá:lh**>, free root //tɛ́·ɬ//, PLN ['*spear-shaped rock on beach on the Fraser near Hill's Bar*'], ASM ['it is next to a larger rock, the Hunter, Tewít, who was hunting an Elk in the middle of the river when he, the spear and the elk were all turned to stone by the Transformer'], literally /'spear'/, syntactic analysis: nominal, attested by AK or SP or AD (Raft Trip 8/30/77, Elders Group 9/13/77), source: place names file reference #271.

<**Tá:lh**>, PLN ['*spear-shaped rock on beach on the Fraser near Hill's Bar*'], *see* tá:lh.

<**=´talh**>, da //=´tɛ(=)ɬ//, HUMC ['*person*'], syntactic analysis: lexical suffix, derivational suffix; found in <**ōwétalh**>, //ʔowə=´tɛɬ//, /'*nobody*'/.

<**talhlímelh**>, PRON /'*we, us*'/, *see* lhlímelh.

<**talhwélep**>, PRON /'*you (pl.), you folks, you people*'/, *see* lhwélep.

<**tám**>, bound root //tɛ́m *what?*//.

<**stám**>, stvi //s=tɛ́m//, MOOD /'*what is it?, be what?*'/, (<**s=**> *stative*), syntactic analysis: interrogative verb, attested by AC, BJ (5/10/64), BHTTC, AC, NP, Deming, IHTTC, EB, LJ (4/7/78), other sources: ES /stɛ́m/ *what*, example: <**stám kw'e stl'í?**>, //s=tɛ́m k'ʷ-ɛ s=ƛ'í//, /'*What do you want?*'/, literally /'your want is what?'/, attested by AC, <**stám kw'a skwíx?**>, //s=tɛ́m k'ʷ-ɛ s=kʷíxʸ//, /'*What is your name?*'/, attested by AC, BHTTC, others, also <**(wát, tewát) (kw'a, ta') skwíx?**>, //(wɛ́t, tə=wɛ́t) (k'ʷ-ɛ, t-ɛʔ) s=kʷíxʸ//, attested by BHTTC, others, <**stám kw'a syó:ys?**>, //s=tɛ́m k'ʷ-ɛ s=yá·ys//, /'*What's your work?*'/, attested by AC, <**stám te í?**>, //s=tɛ́m tə ʔí//, /'*What is this?, What's this?*'/, literally /'is what? that is here'/, attested by NP, <**stám te hó:y?**>, //s=tɛ́m tə há·y//, /'*What did you get done?*'/, usage: sarcastic, attested by Deming (5/18/78); found in <**stámcha?**>, //s=tɛ́m-cɛ//, /'*What will it be?*'/, attested by AC, example: <**stám swàyèl tlówàyèl?**>, //s=tɛ́m s=wɛ̀yə̀l təlá=wɛ̀yə̀l//, /'*What day is today?*'/, usage: answers might include any of the days of the week, attested by IHTTC, <**stámcha swàyèl wàyèlès?**>, //s=tɛ́m-cɛ s=wɛ̀yə̀l wɛ̀yə̀l=əs//, /'*What day is tomorrow?*'/, attested by IHTTC, <**stám te skw'exó:s?**>, //s=tɛ́m tə s=k'ʷəxʸ=á·s//, /'*What moon is it?*'/, usage: answers might include any of the names for months/moons, attested by IHTTC, <**stámcha skw'exós kw'e atse ōw me pélekw?**>, //s=tɛ́m-cɛ s=k'ʷəxʸ=ás k'ʷə ʔɛ-cɛ ʔəw mə pə́ləkʷ//, /'*What is the next moon to appear?*'/, attested by IHTTC, <**stám kw'e mél:es?**>, //s=tɛ́m k'ʷə mə́l·ə-s//, /'*What is (her/his/their) child?, What sex is her/his child?*'/, attested by AC (10/23/71), <**stám kw'a sth'óqwi i kwélexw?**>, //s=tɛ́m k'ʷ-ɛ s=θ'áqʷ=i ʔi kʷə́l=l-əxʷ//, /'*What kind of fish do you have?*'/, attested by EB, <**stám kw'e íxw kw'e sí:simet li kw'e s'átl'q?**>, //s=tɛ́m k'ʷə ʔi-xʷ k'ʷə síy=C₁əC₂=məT li k'ʷə s=ʔɛ́ƛ'q//, /'*What are you afraid of outside?*'/, literally /'is what? that here -you subjunctive which (the remote) afraid of s-th at the (remote) outside'/, attested by AC, <**esésu tl'ó x̱ét'estem, stám kw'e yalh ...?**>, //ʔə-s-əs-u ƛ'á x̣ə́t'ə=sT-əm, s=tɛ́m k'ʷə yɛɬ ...//, /'*And they said "That's-," now what was it? ...*'/, usage: speech editing, indirect quote, attested by Lizzie Johnson (4/7/78 History Tape #34), <**stámelh swàyèl kw'e cheláqelhelh?**>, //s=tɛ́m-əɬ s=wɛ̀yə̀l k'ʷə cəlɛ́q=əɬ-əɬ//, /'*What day was yesterday?*'/, literally /'it was what? day the remote yesterday'/, attested by IHTTC, <**kw'e stám?**>, //k'ʷə s=tɛ́m//, /'*What do you mean?*'/, attested by AC, <**tl'e kwésu stáms te x̱elóx̱cha.**>, //ƛ'a kʷ-ə-s-u s=tɛ́m-s təx̣[-əl-]á[=C₁ə=]cɛ//, /'*(That's what are little lakes.)*'/, attested by JL (4/7/78 History tape 34), <**stámèscha o kw'es álhtelchet?**>, //s=tɛ́m-əs-cɛ ʔà k'ʷə-s ʔɛ́ɬ=təl-c-ət//, /'*Whatever will we eat?*'/, literally /'what will it be just that-subordator we eat (as a meal)'/, attested by AD (about 3/12/80).

<**stámel**>, incs //s=tɛ́m=əl//, MOOD /'*what use is it?, what use have you got for it?*'/, literally

/'becomes what?, goes/comes/gets to what?'/, (<**=el**> *go, come, get, become*), syntactic analysis: interrogative verb, Elder's comment: "my late mother used to use this", attested by AD (2/20/80), example: <**tl'ó kwá stámel te'ílé?**>, //ƛ'á kʷɛ́ s=tɛ́m=əl tə=ʔí=la//, /'*What use have you got for this?*'/, attested by AD, <**é kwe ò stámelò te'ílé?**>, //ʔə́ kʷɛ ʔà s=tɛ́m=əl-à tə=ʔí=la//, /'*Just what use have you got for this?*'/, attested by AD.

<**stámés**>, df //s=tɛ́m-ə[=´=]s → s=tɛ́m=ə́s//, PRON /'*whatever it is, what it is, it is anything, it is something*'/, probably <**-es**> *subjunctive/subordinate subject third person* plus < = ´=> *derivational* is developing to <**=es**> *indefinite pronoun*, syntactic analysis: indefinite pronoun, vpron, attested by EB, AD, AC, example: <**chel ō lhq'élexw westámes.**>, //c-əl (ʔ)əw-ɬ=**q**'ə́l=l-əxʷ wə=s=tɛ́m=əs//, /'*I know what it is.*'/, attested by EB (1/12/76), <**westámes kw'e wetl'ós te shxwelítemelh s<u>x</u>etá <u>x</u>wílem "rope"**>, //wə=s=tɛ́m=əs k'ʷə wə-ƛ'á-əs tə s=xʷəlítəm=əɬ s=x̣tɛ́x̣ʷíləm "rope"//, /'*what it was, if it was the same thing as white people's "rope"*'/, literally perhaps /'if it was anything/something that when/if it was that the white man style same as rope "rope"'/, usage: story of the Flood, attested by AC (12/7/71), <**westámescha kw'es álhteltset**>, //wə=s=tɛ́m=əs-cɛ k'ʷə-s ʔɛ́l=təl-c-ət//, /'*what(ever) we'll eat*'/, literally perhaps /'when/if it will be anything that we eat (as a meal)'/, usage: story of the Flood, attested by AC, <**westámescha kw'e syó:ys**>, //wə-s=stɛ́m=əs-cɛ k'ʷə s=yá·ys//, /'*if/when he will work at anything*'/, attested by AD (about 3/12/80), <**kw stámés ~ kwstámés**>, //kʷ s=tɛ́m-ə[=´=]s//, /'*something, anything*'/, attested by EB (1/9/76), <**ewe isí kw'étslexwes kw stámés tl' Bill.**>, //ʔə́wə ʔi-s (y)ə=k'ʷə́c=l-əxʷ-əs kʷ s=tɛ́m-ə[=´=]sƛ' Bill//, /'*Bill didn't see anything.*'/, attested by EB, <**íleqels te stámes**>, //ʔɛ[-Aí-]l[=ə=]q=əls tə s=tɛ́m=əs//, /'*buying something*'/, attested by EB (2/2/76), <**é<u>x</u>qst te máches qesu yéqwt kw'e stámés**>, //ʔə́x̣=qs=T tə mɛ́cəs qə-s-u yə́qʷ=T k'ʷə s=tɛ́m-ə[=´=]s//, /'*strike the match and light something*'/, attested by CT and HT (6/21/76), <**stámés t'wo eyó:th <u>x</u>éyp'et kw'el óqwelets.**>, //s=tɛ́m-ə[=´=]s **t'**wa ʔɛy=á·θ x̣íy=**p**'=əT k'ʷə-l ʔáqʷ=ələc//, /'*Something sharp scratched my back.*'/, attested by AC, <**lachxw kwát te stámés t'wo.**>, //lɛ-c-xʷ kʷɛ́=T tə s=tɛ́m-ə[=´=]s **t'**wa//, /'*Let go of something.*'/, literally /'you're going to let go of s-th the something evidently/must be'/, attested by EB (12/16/75).

<**stómchele**>, cpds //s=tɛ[=Aá=]m=(ʔɛ)ləc[=M2=]ə//, [stámčɪlə], PRON /'*someplace, somewhere*'/, DIR, (<**s=**> *nominalizer or stative*), root <**tam**> *what, something*, root <**alétse**> *where is it?*, <**ó-ablaut**> *derivational*, <**metathesis**> *derivational*, phonology: ablaut, metathesis type 2 of consonants (unusual), syllable-loss, syntactic analysis: indefinite nominal, attested by BHTTC (8/30/76), example: <**lámtsel kw'e stómchele.**>, //lɛ́=m-c-əl k'ʷə s=tɛ[=Aá=]m=(ʔɛ)ləc[=M2=]ə//, /'*I'm going someplace., I'm going somewhere.*'/.

<**temtám**>, ds //təm=tɛ́m//, TIME /'*when?, when is it?*'/, MOOD, lx <**tem=**> *time, season*, root <**tám**> *when?*, syntactic analysis: interrogative verb, attested by AC, EB, Elders Group, others; found in <**temtámcha?**>, //təm=tɛ́m-cɛ//, /'*When will it be?, What day will it be?*'/, attested by Elders Group (10/6/76), AC, example: <**temtámtsa welámál yó:ys?**>, //təm=tɛ́m-cɛ wə-lɛ́m-ɛ́l yá·ys//, /'*When am I going to work?*'/, attested by AC, <**temtámtsa welámexw t'ó:kw'?**>, //təm=tɛ́m-cɛ wə-lɛ́m-əxʷ **t'á·k'**ʷ//, /'*When are you going home?*'/, attested by AC, <**temtám kw'as lé thíyt?**>, //təm=tɛ́m k'ʷ-ɛ-s lə **θ**íy=T//, /'*When did you make it?*'/, literally /'when is it? that -you -subord. past tense make s-th'/, attested by AC, also <**temtám kw'asé thìyt?**>, //təm=tɛ́m k'ʷ-ɛ-s-ə́ **θ**íy=T//, attested by EB (1/9/76).

<**temtámes**>, ds //təm=tɛ́m=əs//, TIME /'*whenever, whenever it is*'/, MOOD, (<**=es**> *indefinite pronoun* (probably from -es *subjunctive third person*)), syntactic analysis: vpron, attested by Elders Group (10/6/76), AC; found in <**temtámescha**>, //təm=tɛ́m=əs-cɛ//, /'*whenever it will be*'/, attested by Elders Group, example: <**wetemtámescha kwe wátescha kw'e kw'étslexw.**>,

//wə-təm=tɛ́m=əs-cɛ kʷə wɛ́t=əs-cɛ k'ʷə k'ʷə́c=l-əxʷ//, /'*(Whenever it will be, there will be somebody that will see it.)*'/, usage: story of the Flood, attested by AC (12/7/71).

<**tà:m**>, free root //tɛ̀·m//, ABFC /'*call (by voice), shout, yell, holler*'/, ACL, LANG ['*call (by phone)*'], syntactic analysis: intransitive verb, attested by EB (2/11/76, 5/4/76), Elders Group (11/10/76, 3/14/79), also <**tá:m**>, //tɛ́·m//, attested by Deming (6/22/78), example: <**tàm kw'el qw'ő:l.**>, //tɛ̀·m k'ʷə-l **q'ʷő·l**//, ABDF, /'*My ears are ringing.*'/, literally /'my ears shout'/, attested by Elders Group, compare with <**th'átsem kw'el qw'ő:l.**> *My ears are ringing.*.

<**stà:m**>, dnom //s=tɛ̀·m//, ABFC /'*a holler, (a yell, a shout)*'/, (<**s=**> *nominalizer*), syntactic analysis: nominal, attested by AC.

<**tà:met ~ tàmet**>, pcs //tɛ̀·m=əT//, ABFC /'*call s-o (by voice), holler at s-o, shout at s-o, shout at s-o*'/, ACL, LANG /'*call s-o (by phone), phone s-o*'/, (<**=et**> *purposeful control transitivizer*), phonology: length-loss optional, syntactic analysis: transitive verb, attested by Elders Group (3/14/79), EB (5/4/76), also <**támet**>, //tɛ́m=əT//, attested by Deming (6/22/78), AC, example: <**támethòm wáyeles.**>, //tɛ́m=əT-àm wɛ́yəl=əs//, /'*I'll call you tomorrow., (You'll be called tomorrow.)*'/, usage: said to me on the phone, attested by AC (11/29/71).

<**tatí:m**>, rpts //tɛ[-C_1ə-]m=í·m//, cts, ABFC /'*shouting repeatedly, hollering repeatedly, yelling (repeatedly)*'/, (<**-R1-**> *continuative*), (<**=í:m**> *repeatedly, over and over*), phonology: reduplication, consonant-loss of m before =í:m, syntactic analysis: intransitive verb, attested by EB, Elders Group, Deming, other sources: JH /tetím/ *shouting*, example: <**tatí:m stl'ís kws mes má:ytem.**>, //tɛ[-C_1ə-]m=í·m s=ƛ'í-s kʷ-s mə-s mɛ́·y=T-əm//, /'*He's shouting for help.*'/, literally /'he's shouting repeatedly his want that he be helped'/, attested by EB (5/4/76).

<**(kw)the tátí:m**>, dnom //(kʷ)θə tɛ́[=C_1ə=]m=í·m//, SOC ['*the messenger*'], phonology: consonant-loss in article, reduplication, consonant-loss of m before =í;m, syntactic analysis: nominal, attested by Elders Group, example: <**le á:y the tátí:m.**>, //lə ʔɛ́·y (kʷ)θə tɛ́[=C_1ə=]m=í·m//, /'*The messenger is on his way.*'/, literally /'past third person subj. keep on going the one (near but out of view) shouting repeatedly'/, attested by Elders Group (11/19/75).

<**shxwtátì:m**>, dnom //sxʷ=tɛ́[=C_1ə=]m=ì·m//, LANG ['*telephone*'], literally /'something that shouts/hollers/calls repeatedly'/, (<**shxw=**> *something that*), phonology: reduplication, consonant-loss, downstepping, syntactic analysis: nominal, attested by Elders Group (4/21/76).

<**tá:mstexw**>, caus //tɛ́·m=sT-əxʷ//, LANG /'*repeat the call, repeat the holler*'/, (<**=st**> *causative control transitivizer*), (<**-exw**> *third person object*), syntactic analysis: transitive verb, attested by Deming (6/22/78).

<**Lexwtamílem?**>, df //ləxʷ=tɛm=íl=əm?//, PLN ['*Promontory Point above Vedder Crossing*'], literally /'always= holler =go/come/become =place for'/, lx <**lexw=**> *always*, root <**tà:m**> *shout, holler, call*, (<**=íl**> *go, come, get, become*, <**=em**> *place for*), syntactic analysis: nominal, source: Wells 1965 (lst ed.):15 <law-HOOT-oh-meh-lum> *Promontory Point above Vedder Crossing (lit. place of calling)*.

<**tà:met ~ tàmet**>, ABFC /'*call s-o (by voice), holler at s-o, shout at s-o, shout at s-o*'/, *see* tà:m.

<**taméxw ~ staméxw**>, possibly root //tɛmə́xʷ ~ stɛmə́xʷ//, EFAM ['*hope*'], syntactic analysis: intransitive verb, attested by Elders Group (2/16/77), Salish cognate: perhaps Squamish /tm-ʔáyʔ/ *get hungry for something* with /-ayʔ/ *to want* K67:259, prob. not Lushootseed /tágʷəxʷ/ *hunger* as in /ʔəs-tágʷəxʷ-čəd/ *I'm hungry.* H76:473, compare with <**tém=ex**> *wish for it* and <**tám=ex**> *wishing for it*, example: <**(s)taméxwelha q'a emí(?).**>, //(s=)tɛm=ə́xʷ(=)əɬə **q'ɛ** ʔəmí//, (irregular)=éxw is unknown, -alha *plural command imperative* wouldn't seem to fit here but =elha is unknown, q'a *but* doesn't fit here semantically or syntactically it would seem, Elder's comment: "unsure of form", /'*I*

hope that he comes.'/, attested by Elders Group (2/16/77).

<**tá:mstexw**>, LANG /*'repeat the call, repeat the holler'*/, *see* tà:m.

<**tà:t ~ tát ~ tàt**>, KIN /*'Mother (the speaker's), Mom, Mum'*/, *see* tá:l ~ tà:l ~ tál.

<**táta**>, KIN /*'Grandma, Father's Mother (nickname)'*/, *see* tá:l ~ tà:l ~ tál.

<**tátel**>, KIN /*'Mother (the speaker's), Mom, Mum'*/, *see* tá:l ~ tà:l ~ tál.

<**Tátelín??**>, df //tɛ́[=C_1ə=]l(=)ín??//, PLN [*'Upper Sumas Creek'*], root meaning unknown unless related to tó:l *go to the (center) of a river*, possibly <**=R1=**> *diminutive or resultative*, phonology: reduplication, dialects: /n/ signals that this is Downriver Halkomelem or Nooksack, syntactic analysis: nominal, source: attested only in Wells 1966 and Wells 1965 (lst ed.):14.

<**tátelxel**>, HUNT [*'following tracks'*], *see* tá:lxel.

<**táteqlexw**>, ABDF /*'hurting, feeling sore, (feel[ing] pain [BJ])'*/, *see* téqlexw.

<**tátey**>, CAN /*'racing in a canoe, canoe-racing (while you're doing it)'*/, *see* tá:y.

<**tatí:m**>, ABFC /*'shouting repeatedly, hollering repeatedly, yelling (repeatedly)'*/, *see* tà:m.

<**tátsel**>, incs //tɛ́c=əl//, TVMO /*'just came, (just arrived)'*/, root meaning unknown, (<**=el**> *go, come, get, become*), syntactic analysis: intransitive verb, attested by EB (6/14/76), Salish cognate: Samish dial. of N. Straits /**téč'əl**/ *just got here, just arrived* G85: field notes, example: <**yálhs'es tátsel.**>, //yɛ́ɬ-s-ʔə-s tɛ́c=əl//, /*'Now he comes., (Now he's just arrived.)'*/, attested by EB, <**te qá:ys tátsel**>, //tə qɛ́·ys tɛ́c=əl//, /*'the newcomer'*/, literally /'the one who now just came'/, attested by EB (6/14/76).

<**táw**>, bound root //tɛ́w *light up, illuminate*//.

<**státew ~ státōw**>, strs //s=tɛ́[=C_1ə=]w//, LT /*'be light, (be lit up), be illuminated'*/, (<**s=**> *stative*), (<**=R1=**> *resultative*), phonology: reduplication, syntactic analysis: adjective/adjectival verb, attested by AC, example: <**li státew?**>, //li-ə s=tɛ́[=C_1ə=]w//, /*'Is it light?'*/, attested by AC.

<**táwel**>, incs //tɛ́w=əl//, LT [*'get light'*], WETH, (<**=el**> *get, become, go, come*), syntactic analysis: intransitive verb, attested by AC, DM (12/4/64), BJ (12/5/64), example: <**me táwel te swáyel.**>, //mə tɛ́w=əl tə s=wɛ́yəl//, /*'It's getting daylight.'*/, literally /'(It's) starting/coming to get light the day/sky'/, attested by AC, <**me táwel**>, //mə tɛ́w=əl//, /*'(get) daylight'*/, attested by DM, also <**swá:yél (su) me táwél.**>, //s=wɛ́yə́l (s-u) mə tɛ́w=əl//, attested by BJ, <**we'ó me táwél**>, //wə-ʔá mə tɛ́w=əl//, /*'dawn, before the sun rises'*/, literally /'if/when it's just become get light'/, attested by DM (12/4/64).

<**státewel**>, incs //s=tɛ́[=C_1ə=]w=əl//, strs, LT [*'be light (illuminated)'*], (<**s=**> *stative*), (<**=R1=**> *resultative*), (<**=el**> *go, come, get, become*), phonology: reduplication, syntactic analysis: adjective/adjectival verb, attested by EB (12/19/75).

<**táwelt**>, pcs //tɛ́w=əl=T//, LT /*'light s-th, make a light (of s-th), turn it on (a light)'*/, (<**=t**> *purposeful control transitivizer*), syntactic analysis: transitive verb, attested by Elders Group, EB, contrast <**yeqwí:ls**> *make a light*, example: <**táwéltlha ta' yeqwíl.**>, //tɛ́w=əl=T-ɬɛ t-ɛʔ yəq^w=íl//, /*'Light your lamp., Turn on your lamp.'*/, phonology: updrifting, attested by EB (12/15/75).

<**tstáwél ~ táwél**>, ds //c=tɛ́w=əl or c=tɛ́w=ə[=´=]l ~ tɛ́w=ə[=´=]l//, LT [*'bright (in color)'*], (<**ts=**> *have, stative with color terms*), (<**=el**> *get, become, go, come*), possibly <=´=> *derivational*, phonology: updrifting or stress-shift, syntactic analysis: adjective/adjectival verb, attested by EB (12/17/75), example: <**kwelh tu tstáwél te s'íth'ems.**>, //k^wəɬ t-u c=tɛ́w=ə[=´=]l tə s=ʔíθ'=əm-s//, /*'Her dress is bright.'*/, literally /'too a little bright the dress -her'/, attested by EB.

<**táwet**>, pcs //tɛ́w=əT//, LT /*'light up s-th/s-o, shine a light on s-th/s-o'*/, (<**=et**> *purposeful control transitivizer*), syntactic analysis: transitive verb, attested by CT and HT (6/21/76), also <**táwelt**>, //tɛ́w=əl=T//, attested by EB or AD correcting táwet, comment: since the meanings *make a light of s-th, turn it on (a light)* of EB and *shine a light on s-th/s-o* of CT are different, it is possible that CT and HT use different forms for these and that EB (and/or AD) uses one form for both meanings (i.e. táwelt for them has a broader meaning), example: <**táwet te tl'elqtéle kw'es le kwélext te (sméyéth, tl'elqtéle)**>, //tɛ́w=ət təƛ̓'ɛ[=lə=]qt=ə́lə k'ʷə-s lə kʷə́l=əxʸ=T tə (s=mə́y(=)əθ,ƛ̓'ɛ[=lə=]qt=ə́lə)//, /*'light up the deer and shoot the (animal, deer)'*/, attested by CT and HT (6/21/76), also <**táwelt te tl'elqtéle kw'es le kwélext te (sméyéth, tl'elqtéle)**>, //tɛ́w=əl=T təƛ̓'ɛ[=lə=]qt=ə́lə k'ʷə-s lə kʷə́l=əxʸ=T tə (smə́y(=)əθ,ƛ̓'ɛ[=lə=]qt=ə́lə)//, attested by EB or AD, <**le táwet te sméyeth qesu kwélext**>, //lə tɛ́w=əT tə s=mə́y(=)əθ qə-s-u kʷə́l=əxʸ=T//, /*'light up the animal and shoot it'*/, attested by CT and HT (6/21/76), also <**le táwelt te sméyeth qesu kwélext**>, //lə tɛ́w=əl=T tə s=mə́y(=)əθ qə-s-u kʷə́l=əxʸ=T//, attested by EB or AD, <**mi táwetes te sméyeth qesu kwéléxtes tutl'o su mi kweléxwes.**>, //mi tɛ́w=əT-əs tə s=mə́y=əθ qə-s-u kʷə́l=əxʸ=T-əs t=u=ƛ̓'a s-u mi kʷə́l=l-əxʷ-əs//, /*'He lit up an animal and shot it and caught it., He shone a light on an animal and shot it and caught it.'*/, attested by CT and HT (6/21/76), also <**mi táweltes te sméyeth qesu kwéléxtes tutl'o su mi kweléxwes.**>, //mi tɛ́w=əl=T-əs tə s=mə́y=əθ' qə-s-u kʷə́l=əxʸ=T-əs t=u=ƛ̓'a s-u mi kʷə́l=l-əxʷ-əs//, attested by AD or EB.

<**táwel**>, LT ['*get light*'], *see* táw.

<**táwelt**>, LT /*'light s-th, make a light (of s-th), turn it on (a light)'*/, *see* táw.

<**táwet**>, LT /*'light up s-th/s-o, shine a light on s-th/s-o'*/, *see* táw.

<**táwsel**>, free root //tɛ́wsəl//, NUM ['*thousand*'], syntactic analysis: num, attested by JL (7/13/79), example: <**isále kws táwsels**>, //ʔisɛ́lə kʷ-s tɛ́wsəl-s//, /*'two thousand'*/, attested by JL.

<**tá:xw**>, possible root meaning unknown, but more likely root is <**sát**> *reach, pass on, pass along*, or possibly <ta'á> *alike, similar.*

<**stá:xwelh**>, df //s=tɛ́·xʷ=əɬ//, [stǽ·xʷəɬ ~ (hyper-slow) stǽʔæxʷəɬ], HAT /*'children (not one's own necessarily, generic)'*/, ASM ['age term not kinship'], possibly <**s=**> *nominalizer, (*perhaps *alienable possession)*, root meaning uncertain but possibly <**sát**>, bound root //sɛ́t// *reach, pass on, pass along*, or possibly <ta'á> *alike, similar*, or <**tá:xw**> meaning unknown, if one of the first two is root possibly <**=xw**> *round, around*, lx <**=elh ~ =íylh ~ =ó:llh**> *child, young*, if the first root is root here the literal meaning may be something like **"pass along/around child/young"**; phonology: possible =M1= metathesis of V1 and C2, grammatical comment: suppletive plural for <**stl'ítl'eqelh**> *child (generic)*, syntactic analysis: nominal, attested by AC, EB, DF, many others, other sources: ES /stɛ́·xʷəɬ/ *children (preadolescent)*, Salish cognate: Squamish /s-táwʔxʷɬ/ *child* W73:58, K67:284, Skagit dial. of Lushootseed /s-táwixʷəʔɬ/ *children* H76:484, examples: <**éyes te stá:xwelh.**>, //ʔɛ́y=əs tə s=tɛ́·xʷ=əɬ//, /*'The children had a lot of fun.'*/, attested by AC, <**líyleyem te stá:xwelh.**>, //líy=C_1əC_2=əm tə s=tɛ́·xʷ=əɬ//, /*'The children are laughing.'*/, attested by AC, <**sisistáxwes te stá:xwelh.**>, //siy=C_1əC_2=sT-ə[=Aɛ́=]xʷ-əs tə s=tɛ́·xʷ=əɬ//, /*'He's scaring the children.'*/, attested by EB, <**wiyóths kw'es í:wolems te stá:xwelh, t'ít'elem kw'es í:wólems.**>, //wə=yáθ-s k'ʷə-s ʔi[-´·-]wal=əm-s tə s=tɛ́·xʷ=əɬ, t'í[-C_1ə-]l=əm k'ʷə-s ʔi[-´·-]wal=əm-s//, /*'The children are playing all the time, singing as they're playing.'*/, attested by AC (10/15/71), <**qéx̱ te stá:xwelh.**>, //qə́x̣ tə s=tɛ́·xʷ=əɬ//, /*'(There's) lots of children.'*/, attested by AC.

<**tá:y**>, free root //tɛ́·y//, CAN ['*to race in a canoe*'], PLAY, syntactic analysis: intransitive verb, attested by Elders Group (3/26/75), Salish cognate: Squamish /táy/ *race (in canoe), canoe-race* W73:210,

K67:254, Lushootseed root /táy/ as in /lə-táy/ *coming to raid* H76:484 where /lə-/ is *progressive* (since raiding was done in a group of fast canoes), example: <**létset tá:y.**>, //lɛ́-c-ət tɛ́·y//, /'*Let's go canoe-racing.*'/.

<**tátey**>, cts //tɛ́·[-C_1ə-]y//, CAN /'*racing in a canoe, canoe-racing (while you're doing it)*'/, PLAY, (<-**R1**> *continuative*), phonology: reduplication, length-loss before -doubling infix #1 with e- is the rule, syntactic analysis: Vi, attested by Elders Group (3/26/75).

<**táyewelh**>, ds //tɛ́y=əwəɬ//, CAN ['*racing-canoe*'], PLAY, ASM ['these come in different sizes: one-person, two-person, six-person, and eleven-person'], syntactic analysis: nominal, attested by Elders Group, Deming, Salish cognate: Squamish /tayə́-wiɬ/ *race canoe* W73:210, K67:263.

<**istéytiyel**>, df //ʔi=s=tɛ́y=C_1əC_2=əl or yi=s=tə́yt=í·l//, mos, tlcs, CAN ['*group of canoes travelling upstream (moving to camp for fish-drying for ex.)*'], TVMO, possibly <**i- ~ ye=**> *travelling while, along*, possibly <**s=**> *nominal or stative*, possibly <**=R2**> *characteristic or plural*, possibly <**=el ~ =í:l**> *go, come, get, become*, possibly root <**tá:y**> *race in a canoe, move in water*, possibly root <**tíyt**> *upstream*, phonology: possible reduplication, syntactic analysis: intransitive verb, possibly nominal, attested by Elders Group (3/26/75), Salish cognate: (possibly related) Squamish /táyaq-i(y)/ *to move (from one place to another)* K67:265.

<**táyéqel**>, df //tɛ́y(=)ə́q=əl or tɛ́y=əqəl//, WATR ['*change course (of a river)*'], possibly root <**tá:y**> *race in a canoe, move in water* or possibly root <**táyeq**> meaning uncertain, possibly <**=eqel**> *in the throat, on a cliff (of land)* or perhaps more likely <**=el**> *go, come, get, become*, syntactic analysis: intransitive verb, attested by Elders Group (8/31/77), Salish cognate: Squamish /táyaq-i(y)/ *to move (from one place to another)* K67:265 with /=i(y)/ *become, assume a state, be in a state, [and from glosses of exx. in section 186:34 clearly also] go, get* K67:129.

<**táyewelh**>, CAN ['*racing-canoe*'], *see* tá:y.

<**ta'á ~ te'á ~ t'á**>, probably stem but perhaps root //t=ɛʔɛ́ ~ t=əʔɛ́ ~ t=ʔɛ > **t'ɛ** *similar, alike, same*//, if stem probably root <t> meaning unknown plus lx <**=a'á ~ =e'á**> *comparative*

<**sta'á ~ ste'á**>, cpvs //s=t=ɛʔɛ́ ~ s=t=əʔɛ́//, [stɛʔǽ ~ stəʔɛ], stvi, CJ /'*be like, be similar to, be the same as, be a kind of*'/, (<**s=**> *stative*), lx <**=a'á ~ =e'á**> *comparative*, phonology: consonant merger and glottalization, syntactic analysis: adjective/adjectival verb, attested by AC, AD (11/19/79), Elders Group, Deming, AHTTC, also <**st'á**>, //s=**t'ɛ** (from s=t=(ə)ʔɛ́)//, attested by EB (4/12/78), Elders Group (3/15/72), example: <**sta'á kw'e sthó:qwi.**>, //s=t=ɛʔɛ́ k'^{w}ə s=**θá·**q^w-i//, /'*It's like a fish., It's a kind of fish.*'/, attested by AC (11/17/71), <**sta'á kw'e sqwmáy.**>, //s=t=ɛʔɛ́ k'^{w}ə s=q^{w}əm=ɛ́y//, /'*like a dog*'/, attested by AC, <**stá kw'e spá:th te Bob.**>, //s=t=(əʔ)ɛ́ k'^{w}ə s=pɛ́·θ tə Bob//, /'*Bob is like a bear.*'/, attested by Elders Group (3/23/77), <**st'átsa kw'els sqwálewel.**>, //s=**t'**ɛ́-cɛ k'^{w}ə-l-s s=q^{w}ɛ̀l=əwəl//, EFAM, /'*My thoughts are similar., I agree.*'/, attested by Elders Group, <**sta'á kwthá**>, //s=t=ɛʔɛ́ k^w **θ**ɛ́//, /'*(It's) like that., Right on.*'/, attested by AD, <**st'á t(e) thá, siyám, st'á t(e) thá.**>, //s=**t'**ɛ tə **θ**ɛ́, s=iy=ɛ́m, s=**t'**ɛ tə **θ**ɛ́//, /'*Right on, chief, right on.*'/, literally /'like that, chief, like that'/, usage: said by TM and others to speakers when agreeing with the speaker's words, audience response to public speaking, attested by Elders Group (3/15/72), TM, others, <**sta'á óle.**>, //s=t=ɛʔɛ́ ʔálə//, /'*Oh that's the way it is.*'/, literally /'it's similar too'/, attested by Deming (5/4/78), <**lhéq' sta'á (kwthá, tethá).**>, //ɬə́q' s=t=ɛʔɛ́ (k^w **θ**ɛ́, tə **θ**ɛ́)//, /'*(He/She/It/They) used to be like that.*'/, attested by AD (11/19/79), <**íxwōw sta'á**>, //ʔíx^w-əw s=t=ɛʔɛ́//, /'*if it's right, if it's the same, if it's similar*'/, literally /'I wonder if contrastive it's the same/similar'/, attested by AHTTC (2/15/80), <**éy kws ste'ás.**>, //ʔɛ́y k^w-s s=t=əʔɛ́-s//, /'*Amen.*'/, literally /'it's good that it is alike/the same/similar'/, usage: blessing a meeting, public speaking,

attested by AD (1/17/80), NP, others.

<**st'ó'o ~ st'á ò**>, ds //s=**t'**ɛ[=Aá=] **ʔà** ~ s=**t'ɛ ʔà**//, CJ [*'just like'*], literally /'like just'/, possibly <**ó-ablaut**> meaning unclear, phonology: ablaut or assimilation at fast speed, consonant merger, glottalization, syntactic analysis: adjective/adjectival verb, attested by EB (8/23/76), AD (11/19/79), example: <**st'ó'o tl'eléwe (fast) ~ st'á ò tl'eléwe**>, //s=**t'**ɛ **ʔà** ƛ'ə=lə́wə//, /*'just like you are'*/, attested by EB.

<**st'at'á**>, cts //s=C_1ɛ-**t'**ɛ́//, CJ [*'being similar'*], (<**s=**> *stative*), (<**R8-**> *continuative*), phonology: reduplication, consonant merger, glottalization, syntactic analysis: adjective/adjectival verb, attested by EB (4/12/78).

<**st'at'ó:mex**>, ds //s=C_1ɛ=**t'**ɛ́=á·məx^y//, DESC /*'to resemble, look like, (similar-looking)'*/, lx <**=ó:mex**> *in looks, appearance, -looking*, phonology: reduplication, consonant merger, glottalization, syntactic analysis: adjective/adjectival verb, attested by EB (1/30/76).

<**st'e'áwel ~ st'áwel**>, df //s=**t'**əʔɛ́=əwəl ~ s=**t'**ɛ́=əwəl or s=**t'**ɛw=əl//, EFAM /*'to guess, make a guess'*/, LANG, possibly <**s=**> *stative?*, lx <**=ewel ~ =íwel**> *in the insides*, phonology: vowel merger, syntactic analysis: intransitive verb, attested by EB (12/16/75), compare with <**t'wa ~ t'we**> *must be (evidently), I guess*, example: <**tsel st'áwel kwses thét kws lámtset.**>, //**c'**-**əl' š**=**t'**ɛ́=əwəl k^w-s-əs **θ**ə́t k^w-s lɛ́=m-c-ət//, /*'I guess that she said that we're going.'*/, syntactic comment: double embedding, attested by EB.

<**st'a'áleqep**>, dnom //s=t'ɛʔɛ́=ɛləqəp//, TAST [*'(the) taste, taste like'*], (<**s=**> *nominalizer*), lx <**=áleqep**> *smell, taste*, phonology: glottal stop insertion between vowel-final root and vowel-initial suffix, or preservation of root-final glottal stop before vowel-initial suffix (root-final glottal stops are normally dropped in Upriver Halkomelem), an alternate possibility for the root is <**t'á**> *taste*, so the word is also given there, syntactic analysis: nominal, dialects: *Chill.*, attested by NP, also <**st'áleqep**>, //s=t'ɛ=ɛ́ləqəp//, dialects: *Cheh.*, attested by DF, example: <**ōwéta st'a'áleqeps.**>, //ʔowə= ́tɛ s=t'ɛʔɛ́=ɛləqəp-s//, /*'It has no taste.'*/, attested by NP (Elders Group 5/25/77), <**ōwéta st'áleqeps.**>, //ʔowə= ́tɛ s=t'ɛ=ɛ́ləqəp-s//, attested by DF (Elders Group 5/25/77).

<**staqí:l**>, ds //s=t=(əʔ)ɛ=(ə)q(əl)=í·l//, SD [*'sound like (in voice)'*], ABFC, lx <**=eqel**> *in the throat, speech, talk, language*, (<**=í:l**> *get, become, go, come*), phonology: syllable-loss of el before =í:l, syntactic analysis: intransitive verb, attested by Elders Group (11/3/76), also <**st'aqí:l ~ st'aqéyl**>, //s=**t'**ɛ=əqəl=í·l//, LANG, also /*'talk alike'*/, attested by BHTTC, example: <**staqí:l te má:ls.**>, //s=t=(əʔ)ɛ́=əq(əl)=í·l tə mɛ́·l-s//, /*'He sounds like his father.'*/, attested by Elders Group (11/3/76), <**tsel staqí:l tel mà:l. (?) or tsel st'e'áqel tel mà:l. (?)**>, //c-əl s=t=əʔɛ́=əqəl=í·l tə-l mɛ̀·l ~ c-əl s=t=əʔɛ́=əqəl tə-l mɛ̀·l//, /*'I sound like my father.'*/, Elder's comment: "unsure which is correct", attested by Elders Group (11/3/76).

<**sta'á:wel**>, ds //s=t=ɛʔɛ́=əwəl//, EFAM [*'think'*], ABFC, lx <**=íwel ~ =ewel**> *in the insides, in the mind*, phonology: vowel merger, syntactic analysis: intransitive verb, attested by AC, also <**ste'áwel**>, //s=t=əʔɛ́=(ə)wəl//, also /*'be thinking'*/, attested by AD (3/6/79), Salish cognate: Squamish /(n-)tə-**ʔ**áwʔn/ *think, expect, consider* W73:265, K67:307, example: <**líchxw sta'á:wel wespá:thes?**>, //lí-c-x^w s=t=ɛʔɛ́=əwəl wə-s=pɛ́·θ-əs//, /*'Do you think it is/was a bear?'*/, literally /'do you think if it is a bear'/, syntactic comment: subjunctive of a nominal used as verb, attested by AC (8/23/73), <**ílhchel ste'áwel kw'els la t'ókw'.**>, //ʔí-ɬ-c-əl s=t=əʔɛ́=(ə)wəl k'^{w}ə-l-s lɛ **t'ák'**^{w}//, /*'I was thinking I'll go home.'*/, attested by AD (3/6/79).

<**st'awélmet**>, iecs //s=**t'**ɛ=wə[- ́-]l=məT//, cts, ABFC [*'thinking about s-th'*], (<= ́=> *continuative*), (<**=met**> *indirect effect control transitivizer*), phonology: stress-shift, consonant merger, glottalization, syntactic analysis: transitive verb, attested by Elders Group (1/7/76).

<**ta'áltha**>, PRON /'*me, I*'/, *see* áltha ~ álthe.

<**ta'á'altha**>, PRON /'*me myself, I myself (emphatic)*'/, *see* áltha ~ álthe.

<**ta'elólets'e**>, NUM ['*each (person)*'], *see* léts'a ~ léts'e.

<**te=**>, da //tə=//, DEM /'*nominalizer (male or gender unspecified, present and visible or presence or proximity unspecified), demonstrative article*'/, phonology: probably phonologically prefixed because in some cases the merges with a following consonant (for ex. =w) to form a new vowel (as in tú:tlò *it's him*), syntactic analysis: derivational prefix, syntactic comment: a number of verbs (demonstrative, interrogative, pronominal) can serve a nominal or pronominal function when phonologically prefixed with te= ~ ta=, it is prefixed syntactically too since in some cases the resultant form can be preceded by another demonstrative article (kw'e tewátes for ex., *somebody (out of sight)*); found in <**te'íle**>, //tə=ʔílə//, /'*this one*'/, <**tethá ~ te thá**>, //tə=θɛ́ ~ tə θɛ́//, /'*that one*'/, <**tewát**>, //tə=wɛ́t//, /'*who is it?*'/, <**tú·ƛ'à**>, //tə́=w=ƛ'á//, /'*he is the one, it's him*'/, <**tewátes**>, //tə=wɛ́t=əs//, /'*someone, somebody (unknown)*'/.

<**te**>, free root //tə//, CJ /'*the (male, present, visible), the (gender or presence and visibility unspecified), a (male, present and visible), a (gender or presence and visibility unspecified)*'/, (semological comment: *the* and *a* are not translated in English before proper names nor before possessive pronouns (see example below)), CJ /'*what, which, that which, the one that/who*'/, semantic environment ['before verbs'], phonology: e is merged or dropped before -a *your*, syntactic analysis: demonstrative article, syntactic comment: this or another demonstrative article precedes any nominal except those used as a term of address (vocatives) or those in a list, if the speaker saw all the items in a list at once the article can be left out except before the first and last item, no articles can be left out if the speaker saw the items separately (Deming 5/25/78, EB 4/13/78), attested by AC, Elders Group, Deming, EB, many others, ASM ['the (male, present and visible or presence and visibilityunspecified)'], <**máytchexw te swíyeqe.**>, //mɛ́y=T-c-əxʷ tə s=wí·q=ə//, /'*Help the man.*'/, attested by AC, comment: see many examples throughout dictionary, especially with kinterms and animals where sex is only specified by the article here, ASM ['the (present and visible or unspecified)'], comment: see many examples throughout dictionary, ASM ['what, which'], example: <**te kwíkwexetem "chiefs"**>, //tə kʷí[-C_1ə-]xʸ=əT-əm "chiefs"//, /'*what they call chiefs, (what are being called chiefs)*'/, attested by AC, <**kwókwelxes te sqá:ls.**>, //kʷɛ[-AáC_1ə-]l=əxʸ-əs tə s-qɛ́·l-s//, /'*He's hiding what he stole .*'/, attested by EB (2/6/76), ASM ['a (gender and visibility and presence unspecified)'], <**kw'étslexwes te músmes, stiqíw, chékel, pípehò:m, qas te sqelá:w.**>, //k'ʷə́c=l-əxʷ-əs tə mús=C_1əC_2, s=tiqíw, cə́kəl, C_1í=pəhà·m, qɛ=s tə s=qəlɛ́·w//, /'*He saw a cow, a horse, a chicken, a frog, and a beaver.*'/, attested by EB (4/13/78), <**ta skwí:x**>, //t-ɛ s=kʷə[=Aí·=]xʸ//, /'*your name*'/, attested by AC, <**tel skw'ówes**>, //tə-l s=k'ʷáw(=)əs//, /'*my pail*'/, attested by AC, <**tel sqwemáy**>, //tə-l s=qʷəm=ɛ́y//, /'*my dog*'/, attested by AC.

<**te í ~ te'í**>, DIR ['*this (speaker is not holding it but is close enough to touch it)*'], *see* í.

<**tehí:lewel**>, df //təh(=)í·l=əwəl//, EFAM ['*depending on someone*'], root meaning unknown, possibly <**=í:l**> *go, come, become, get*, lx <**=ewel**> *in the insides, in the mind*, syntactic analysis: intransitive verb, attested by Deming, example: <**tehí:lewel ol.**>, //təh(=)í·l=əwəl ʔàl//, /'*(He's/She's/They're) just depending on someone.*'/, attested by Deming (11/30/78).

<**Tekwóthel ~ Tkwóthel**>, df //təkʷ=áθəl//, PLN ['*a mountain just south of Yale Mountain (Popelehó:ys) with a big hole like a tunnel in it above the highway at Yale*'], ASM ['the hole used to come down near the Fraser River but after the white people came it caved in (perhaps as result of the CPR construction), the remnants of the hole used to be seen frequently from the train, they can't be seen from the highway however'], root meaning unknown unless same in <**stekwtákw**>, df

//s=C₁əC₂=tɛ́kʷ//, [stʊkʷtǽkʷ], EFAM /'(be) in a daze, day-dreaming'/, see **tákw**., lx <**=óthel**> *in the mouth*, phonology: vowel-loss optional, syntactic analysis: nominal, attested by Elders Group (7/6/77, 9/13/77 esp. AK, SP, AD), also <**Stkwóthel**>, //s=təkʷ=áθəl//, attested by JL (12/14/77), source: place names file reference #26.

<**tel=**>, da //təl=//, DIR ['*from*'], syntactic analysis: derivational prefix, lexical affix, attested by IHTTC, Elders Group, Deming, others, compare <**telí**> *be from*, comment: could be shortened from telí or telí could be derived tel=í, Salish cognate: Squamish /ti-/ *from* W73:108, K67:265, Lushootseed /**tul'**-/ *from* H76:510; found in <**telchó:kw**>, //təl=cá·kʷ//, DIR, /'*(be) from far away*'/, Salish cognate: Lushootseed /**tul'-čaʔkʷ**/ *south wind (lit. "from the sea") H76:510,* <**tellhó:s**>, //təl=ɬá·s//, DIR, /'*(be) from downriver*'/, WATR, <**teltíyt**>, //təl=tíy(=)t//, WATR, DIR, /'*(be) from upriver, Tait dialect, Tait-dialect-speaking people*'/, LANG, SOCT, <**tel'alétse ~ tel:étse**>, //təl=ʔɛlə́cə ~ təl=(ʔɛ)lə́cə//, /'*be from where?*'/, attested by IHTTC (8/10/77), others, Salish cognate: Squamish /ti-ʔə́nča/ *be from where?* K67:117, Lushootseed /**tul'-čád**/ *be from where* H76:510.

<**telí**>, ds //təl=lí or təl=ʔí//, DIR ['*be from*'], semantic environment ['location'], CJ ['*than*'], semantic environment ['after adjectival word, esp. comparative/superlative'], CJ ['*of (partitive)*'], semantic environment ['after numeral'], (<**tel=**> *from*), possibly root <**lí**> *there, at*, possibly root <**í**> *here*, phonology: consonant merger, syntactic analysis: preposition/prepositional verb, attested by IHTTC, Elders Group, CT and HT, AD, AC, Salish cognate: Nooksack /tulí/ *be from* G83b,G84a, in part Squamish /ti-náʔ/ *be from* from /náʔ/ *be at, be there* K67:117, and Lushootseed //**tul'-ʔál**// usually /tuʔlə́l/ *be from* H76:511, ASM ['be from'], example: <**telítsel kw'e Ts'a'íles.**>, //təlí-c-əl k'ʷə **c'ɛʔ**=íləs//, /'*I am from Chehalis, B.C.*'/, literally /'I am from the (remote) Chehalis'/, attested by IHTTC (8/10/77), <**sqewós te smá:lt kws me p'éth' te syó:qwem telí tí tl'o le qewétem.**>, //s=qəw=ás-s tə s=mɛ́·lt kʷ-s mə **p'ə́θ'** tə s=yə[=Aá·=]qʷ=əm təl=lí tí ƛ'a lə qəw=ə[=´=]T-əm//, /'*It's the warm side of the mountain that the sun just comes out (squeezes out) on from (over) there, so that it was warmed.*'/, attested by CT and HT (6/21/76), <**óxwestchexw telí tl'elhlímelh.**>, //**ʔáx**ʷəs=T-c-əxʷ təl=lí ƛ'ə=ɬlíməɬ//, /'*Give it to him from us.*'/, syntactic comment: independent object of prepositional verb, attested by Elders Group (1/19/77), <**éy kw'ómkw'emcha telí s'ólh sqwálewel xwlam kw'e ít totí:lt tlówàyèl.**>, //ʔɛ́y k'ʷám=C₁əC₂-cɛ təl=lí s=**ʔáɬ** s=qʷàl=əwəl xʷ=lɛ́=m k'ʷə ʔí-t tá[-C₁ə-]l=í·l=T təlá=wɛ̀yə̀l//, /'*Let our thoughts be strong toward what we are studying today.*'/, literally /'it's good will be strong from our thoughts toward the (remote) here (aux.) -we (subjunct. subj.) studying s-th this day'/, syntactic comment: note subjunctive pronoun is used as subject of subordinate vp whose object is promoted to object of the main vp's previous preposition/prepositional verb, usage: blessing a meeting, public speaking, attested by AD (1/17/80), <**lólets'e mestíyexw telí kw'e "north"**>, //C₁á=lə**c'**ə məstíyəxʷ təl=lí k'ʷə "north"//, /'*one person from the north*'/, attested by AC, ASM ['of (partitive)'], <**lólts'e telí tl'alhlímelh kw'e lám.**>, //C₁á=ləc'ə təl=líƛ'ɛ=ɬlíməɬ k'ʷə lɛ́=m//, /'*One of us could go.*'/, attested by AC, ASM ['than'], <**yeláwel x̲éytl' tlówàyèl telí kw'e cheláqelh(elh).**>, //yəlɛ́w=əl x̣íƛ' təlá=wɛ̀yə̀l təl=lí k'ʷə cəlɛ́q=əɬ(=əɬ)//, /'*Today is colder than yesterday.*'/, attested by Elders Group (1/19/77), <**yeláwel lós telí tl'á'altha.**>, //yəlɛ́w=əl lás təl=lí ƛ'ɛ=C₁ɛ́=ʔɛlθɛ//, /'*He's fatter than me.*'/, syntactic comment: independent object of prepositional verb, attested by Elders Group (1/19/77), <**yeláwel éy telí tl'á'altha.**>, //yəlɛ́w=əl ʔɛ́y təl=líƛ'ɛ=C₁ɛ́=ʔɛlθɛ//, /'*(He's/She's) better than me.*'/, syntactic comment: independent object of prepositional verb, attested by Elders Group (3/9/77), <**yeláwel tl'áqt tel x̲éltel telí ta swá.**>, //yəlɛ́w=əl ƛ'ɛ́qt tə-l x̣i[=Aə́=]l=təl təl=lí t-ɛ s=wɛ́//, /'*My pencil is longer than yours.*'/, attested by Elders Group (1/19/77).

<**shxwtelí**>, dnom //sxʷ=təl=lí//, DIR ['*where s-o came from*'], PLN, (<**shxw=**> *something to, nominalizer*), syntactic analysis: nominal, attested by AC, Elders Group; found in <**shxwtelís**>, //sxʷ=təl=lí-s//, /'*where they (/he/she/it) came from*'/, attested by Elders Group (3/29/78),

example: <**shxwtelís te syewálelh**>, //sxʷ=təl=lí-s tə s=yəwɛ́l=əɬ//, /'*where the deceased ancestors came from*'/, attested by Elders Group (3/29/78), <**tl'ól shxwtelí (+ article + place name or proper name).**>, //ƛ'á-l sxʷ=təl=lí ...//, /'*I'm descended from* ...'/, attested by AC (9/29/71).

<**tel'alétse ~ tel:étse**>, ds //təl=ʔɛlə́cə ~ təl=(ʔɛ)lə́cə//, DIR ['*be from where?*'], PLN, lx <**tel=**> *from*, root <**alétse**> *be where?*, phonology: syllable-loss optional, syntactic analysis: interrogative verb, attested by IHTTC, others; found in <**tel'alétsechexw? ~ tel:étsechexw?**>, //təl=(ʔɛ)lə́cə-c-əxʷ//, /'*Where are you from?*'/, attested by IHTTC.

<**=tel**>, da //=təl//, MC /'*device, implement, thing used for*'/, comment: over 100 examples have been found to date, phonology: =tel sometimes conditions the dropping of the last l in the preceding suffixes =ó:ythel *in the lips*, =xel *in the foot, leg*, =eláx̱el *in the arm*, maybe others, syntactic analysis: lexical suffix, derivational suffix; found in <**éx̱wtel**>, //ʔə́x̣ʷ=təl//, /'*broom*'/, compare with <**íx̱wet**> *sweep it*, <**x̱éltel**>, //x̣ə́l=təl//, /'*pen, pencil, writing instrument*'/, compare with <**x̱éyl=t**> *write s-th*, <**lhá:ts'tel**>, //ɬɛ́·c'=təl//, /'*knife*'/, compare with <**lhí:ts'=et**> *cut s-th or s-o*, compare with <**lhéts'-**> *cut*, <**skw'íytel**>, //s=k'ʷíy=təl//, /'*ladder (native notched pole or any modern kind)*'/, compare with <**kw'íy**> *climb*, <**shxwch'á:letstel ~ sch'á:letstel**>, //s(xʷ)=c'ɛ́·=ləc=təl//, /'*chair, bench*'/, literally /'nom. + on top, astride + rump + device'/, <**sx̱wōqw'tel**>, //s=x̣óq'ʷ=təl//, /'*canoe pole*'/, compare with <**x̱wóqw'=et**> *pole it (of a canoe)*, <**sí:tel**>, //sí·=təl//, /'*basket (generic)*'/, <**q'eléts'eqwtel**>, //q'ələ́c'=əqʷ=təl//, /'*umbrella*'/, <**q'oléts'tel**>, //q'alə́c'=təl//, /'*square dressing room of blankets for sx̱wóyx̱wey dancers*'/, compare with <**q'eléts'**> *rainshelter, protection*, <**shxwyémtel**>, //sxʷ=yə́m=təl//, /'*belt, sling, strap*'/, literally /'nom. + wide strip + device'/, <**sthéqitel**>, //sθə́qi=təl//, /'*sockeye net*'/, <**kwōxwethtel**>, //kʷóxʷəθ=təl//, /'*coho net*'/, <**tl'élx̱xeltel**>, //ƛ'əlx̣xʸəl=təl//, /'*spring salmon net*'/, <**swéltel**>, //s=wə́l=təl//, /'*net, web*'/, <**th'éstel**>, //θ'ə́s=təl//, /'*(metal) nail*'/, <**th'esélatel**>, //θ'əs=ə́lɛ=təl//, /'*arrow pouch, quiver*'/, compare with perhaps <**th'ís=et**> *nail it*, compare with <**=éla ~ =á:la**> *container*, <**shxwth'á:lhtel**>, //sxʷθ'ɛ́·ɬ=təl//, /'*fine cedar root strips for baskets*'/, root meaning unknown, <**shxwt'álhtel**>, //sxʷ=t'ɛ́ɬ=təl//, /'*bridge made of big log, big bridge*'/, compare with <**sxw=t'álh**> *bridge made of small log*, comment: root probably means *span, go across*, <**(s)t'lhíléstel**>, //(s=)t'ɬ=íləs=təl//, /'*collarbone*'/, comment: root probably means *span, go across*, <**mót'estel**>, //mát'əs=təl//, /'*first finger, pointer finger*'/, literally /'point, aim + device'/, <**séx̱watel ~ séx̱wetel ~ sex̱we'á:lá**>, //sə́x̣ʷɛ=təl (ɛ ~ ə) ~ səx̣ʷə=ʔɛ́·lɛ́//, /'*bladder*'/, compare with <**séx̱we (e ~ a)**> *urine*, <**smélàtel**>, //s=mə́lɛ̀=təl//, /'*womb, uterus*'/, compare with <**mélà ~ méle**> *child (kinterm)*, <**th'áx̱tel ~ ts'áx̱tel**>, //θ'ɛ́x̣=təl (θ' ~ c')//, /'*rattlesnake*'/, <**sqwéltel**>, //s=qʷə́l=təl//, /'*word, language*'/, compare with <**qwá:l**> *talk, speak*, <**sp'otl'emá:látel**>, //sp'aƛ'əm=ɛ́·lɛ́=təl//, /'*smokehole*'/, literally /'smoke + container + device'/, <**qweló:ythetel**>, //qʷəl=á·yθə(l)=təl//, /'*musical instrument*'/, <**lháx̱xetel**>, //ɬɛ́x̣=xʸə(l)=təl//, /'*rug*'/, <**q'epeláx̱tel**>, //q'əp=əlɛ́x̣(əl)=təl//, /'*armband*'/.

<**=t=el**>, da //=T=əl (or perhaps just =təl)//, PRON /'*purposeful control reciprocal,* (perhaps just) *reciprocal, (do purposely to) each other, (do purposely to) one another*'/, (semological comment: found crystallized in some nominals too), syntactic analysis: derivational suffix, syntactic comment: the reciprocal part of this combination has been shown as an inflection thoughout most of the dictionary, but could probably better be counted as derivational since it changes a transitive verb to an intransitive syntactically; found in <**qwōlqweltel ~ qwélqweltel**>, //qʷɛ[=Aó=]l=C_1əC_2=T=əl//, /'*(a lot of people) talking together*'/, <**q'eq'ótel**>, //C_1ə=q'á·=T=əl//, /'*to meet*'/, literally /'be together with each other purposely'/, <**thethkw'í:tel**>, //θə[=C_1ə=]k'ʷ=ə[=Aí·=]T=əl//, /'*(have) a tug-of-war*'/, literally /'pulling each other purposely for a long time [durative'/, <**kweltó:l**>, //kʷəl=T=ə[=Aá·=]l//, /'*to wrestle*'/, literally /'grab each other for a long time (durative)'/, <**skwekwótel**>,

//s=C_1ə=k^{w}ɛ́=T=əl//, /'*to separate in marriage*'/, literally /'be letting each other loose purposely'/, <**tl'ítl'ex̱wtò:l**>, //C_1í=ƛ’əx̣^{w}=T=ə[=Aá·=]l//, /'*beating one another (in contest), competing*'/, <**q'iq'x̱ótel**>, //q’i[=C_1ə=]x̣=ə[=Aá=]T=əl//, /'*contradicting each other*'/, <**iyó:tel**>, //ʔiyá·=T=əl//, /'*to fight*'/, <**yáyetel**>, //yɛ́yə=T=əl//, /'*making friends*'/, <**st'eló:stel**>, //s=t’əl(=)ə[=Aá·=]s=T=əl//, /'*be sitting side by side*'/, literally /'be sitting beside each other'/, <**á**:xwí:tel>, //ʔɛ́·x^w=ə[=Aí·=]T=əl//, /'*they're sharing*'/, literally /'giving gifts/food purposely to each other'/, <**mamíyelhtel**>, //mɛ[=C_1ə=´]y=əɬ(c)=T=əl//, /'*helping one another*'/, literally /'helping benefactive each other, helping for each other purposely'/, <**qeqemótel**>, //qə[=C_1ə=]má·=T=əl//, /'*having the same parents*'/, literally /'suckling purposely with each other'/, <**sétl'atel**>, //sə́ƛ’ɛ=T=əl//, /'*elder sibling*'/, compare with <**séltl'o**> *oldest (of children)*, <**x̱éyeslótel**>, //x̣íy=əs=əl=ə[=Aá=]T=əl//, /'*wild ginger (Asarum caudatum)*'/, literally /'facing one another'/, (semological comment: referring to the paired facing leaves).<**telál**>, possibly root //təlɛ́l//, DIR ['*by way of*'], syntactic analysis: preposition/prepositional verb, attested by EB (6/14/78), example: <**ley telál kw'e Agassiz.**>, //lɛ yə=təlɛ́l k’^{w}ə Agassiz//, /'*Someone is going by way of Agassiz.*'/, attested by EB.

<**tél ~ tá:l ~ tiy**>, bound root //tə́l ~ tɛ́·l ~ tiy *respond, repeat*//.

<**xwtélqet**>, pcs //x^w(=)tə́l=(ə)q(əl)=əT//, LANG ['*repeat s-th (verbally)*'], possibly <**xw=**> *always*? or xwe=> *become*?, root <**tel**> perhaps *respond*, lx <**=qel ~ =eqel**> *in the throat, in talk, verbally*, (<**=et**> *purposeful control transitivizer*), phonology: syllable-loss of el before =et, syntactic analysis: transitive verb, attested by Elders Group (3/14/79), compare with <**xwetiyéqel ~ xweteyéqel**> *to answer, reply* **(AC)**, other sources: Suttles ca1984:ch.7 p.28 Musqueam /x^{w}tə́lqət/ *answer him* and /x^{w}tétəl’qət/ *be answering him* are derived from root /tél/ *copy, follow suit* plus /-qən/ *voice* plus transitivizer, Salish cognate: Squamish /n-tə́lq-t/ *answer (a person) (tr.)* W73:6, K67:307, Lushootseed /təj-úcid/ *answer* with /-úcid/ *(in the) mouth* H76:488, example: <**xwtélqet ta' sqwà:l.**>, //x^w=tə́l=qəl=T t-ɛʔ s=q^{w}ɛ̀·l//, /'*Repeat your words.*'/, attested by Elders Group.

<**télstem**>, caus //tə́l=sT-əm or tɛ[=Aə́=]l=sT-əm//, ABDF /'*to stumble, get staggered*'/, possibly <**é-ablaut on root á:**> *resultative*, (<**=st**> *causative control transitivizer*), (<**-em**> *passive*), phonology: possible ablaut, syntactic analysis: intransitive verb, attested by CT and HT (6/21/76), Elders Group (5/26/76), Salish cognate: possibly Lushootseed /t’álx̣/ *lose balance backwards but not quite fall* H76:562,519-520 (vs. unrelated root /tálx̣/ as in /ʔəs-tálx̣/ *able, capable* and causative habitual /ƛ’u-tálx̣-dx^w/ *use s-th to do something* H76:480-481,704), possibly Sechelt /tantínim ~ tntínim/ *to stagger* T77:34; found in <**le telsthòm.**>, //lə tɛ[=Aə=]l=sT-àm//, /'*You get staggered.*'/, syntactic analysis: passive of causative, attested by Elders Group, example: <**le télstem kw tewátes wels yi'í:mexs.**>, //lə tɛ[=Aə́=]l=sT-əm k^w tə=wɛ́t=əs wəl-s yi=ʔí[-·-]m=əx^y-s//, /'*Somebody stumbled while he was walking.*'/, literally /'past third person got staggered the (remote) somebody really -s travelling along= walking -he/she'/, attested by CT and HT.

<**tá:lstem**>, caus //tə[-Aɛ́·-]l=sT-əm or tɛ́·l=sT-əm//, ABDF ['*staggering (after you trip for ex.)*'], possibly <**á**:-ablaut> *continuative*, (<**=st**> *causative control transitivizer*), (<**-em**> *passive*), phonology: possible ablaut, syntactic analysis: intransitive verb, attested by Elders Group (5/26/76).

<**yitá:lstem**>, mos //yi=tɛ́·l=sT-əm or yi=tə[=Aɛ́·=]l=sT-əm//, ABDF ['*staggering around*'], lx <> *along, travelling along, while in motion*, phonology: possible ablaut, syntactic analysis: intransitive verb, attested by Elders Group (5/26/76).

<**telchókw**>, DIR ['*from far away*'], *see* chó:kw.

<**telchó:leqwtel**>, DIR ['*from away from the river*'], *see* chá:l or chó:l.

<**Te Lewómet**>, WETH ['*The Milky Way*'], *see* slewómet ~ lewómet *dancing costume*.

<**tél:exw** ~ (in rapid speech) **télexw**>, EFAM /'*find s-th out, understand s-th, learn s-th, realize s-th, now*

know what s-th is like, read (and comprehend) s-th, understand s-o'/, *see* tól.

<**telí**>, DIR [*'be from'*], *see* tel=.

<**telkwó:lésem**>, df //təlk^{w}=á·ləs=əm//, ABDF /*'poke oneself in the eye (with finger, stick, etc.)'*/, root meaning unknown, lx <**=ó:les**> *in the eye*, (<**=em**> *middle voice*), phonology: updrifting (not stress-shift since it moves again before inflection), syntactic analysis: intransitive verb, attested by EB (9/18/78), CT (6/15/76 Stó:lō Sítel Friesen tape), example: <**telkwó:lesémlha chítmexw uwthe'ítexwcha kwa chítmexw.**>, //təlk^{w}=á·ləs=əm-ɬɛ cít(=)məx^{w} wə-θəʔít-əx^{w}-cɛ k^{w}ɛ cít(=)məx^{w}//, /*'Poke your eyes, horned owl, if you're really a true horned owl.'*/, usage: song of an old lady climbing Mt. Cheam who sees a horned owl which isn't a real owl (is a spirit or ghost), attested by CT (6/15/76 tape).

<**tellhelhó:s**>, DIR [*'south wind'*], *see* lhós.

<**tellhó:s**>, WATR /*'downriver, (from downriver)'*/, *see* lhós.

<**Tellhós**>, SOCT [*'Squamish people'*], *see* lhós.

<**télmel**>, EFAM /*'the mind, someone's own knowledge'*/, *see* tól.

<**telómelthet**>, EFAM [*'acknowledge oneself'*], *see* tól.

<**teló:met ~ tel:ómet**>, EFAM [*'understand'*], *see* tól.

<**teló= ~ tló=**>, da //tə=lá= tlá=//, DEM [*'this'*], syntactic analysis: derivational prefix; found in <**tlowáyél ~ tlówàyèl**>, //tlawɛ́yə́l ~ tláwɛ̀yə̀l//, /*'today'*/, literally /'this day'/, <**tloqá:ys**>, //tlaqɛ́·ys//, /*'now'*/, literally /'this instant'/, <**tlo xwelá:lt**>, //tla x^{w}ə=lɛ́·[=C$_1$ə=]t//, /*'tonight (maybe tla=)'*/, literally /'this evening'/.

<**télstem**>, ABDF /*'to stumble, get staggered'*/, *see* tél ~ tá:l ~ tiy.

<**teltelewá:m**>, WATR [*'lots of little streams (like the kind coming down a hill after a rain)'*], *see* tó:l ~ tò:l.

<**teltíyt**>, DIR [*'from upriver'*], *see* tiyt.

<**telxwítsel**>, TIME [*'toward November'*], *see* xwís.

<**télwél**>, possible root //tə́l(=ə)wəl//, root meaning uncertain

<**stélwél**>, df //s=tə́l(=ə)wəl//, EB [*'cedar limb rope (slitted)'*], MC, ASM ['made by taking a pliable red cedar limb, slitting it with a knife, then twisting it around to make it still more pliable, used to haul animals caught or other things obtained away from one's canoe, camp, or home'], probably <**s=**> *nominalizer*, root meaning unknown unless <**t'álew**> *arm* or <**tel**> *repeat,* possibly <**=ewel**> *in the insides*, phonology: possible vowel-loss, syntactic analysis: nominal, attested by EL (Elders Group 7/23/75).

<**telxwíts**>, df //təlx^{w}ít=əs or təlx^{w}íc//, TIME [*'month or moon in November'*], Elder's comment: "means *when leaves are falling*", root meaning unknown, possibly <**=es**> *cyclic period*??, syntactic analysis: nominal?, attested by Elders Group (3/19/75), also <**telxwít??**>, //təlx^{w}ít//, also /*'moon in October'*/, Elder's comment: "means *when leaves fall*", attested by Elders Group (3/12/75).

<**tel'alétsa**>, DIR /*'where is he/she/it from?, from where?'*/, *see* alétsa.

<**tel'alétse ~ tel:étse**>, DIR [*'be from where?'*], *see* tel=.

<**télh**>, probably root //tə́ɬ//, SH /*'straightened out, got straight(ened)'*/, possibly <**é-ablaut**> *resultative*, syntactic analysis: intransitive verb, attested by MV and SJ (Deming 2/9/78), example: <**télh tel máqel.**>, //tə́ɬ tə-l mɛ́=qəl//, /*'My hair got straight., My hair got straightened.'*/, attested by MV and

SJ.

<**tlhét ~ tlhát ~ telhét**>, pcs //tə́ɬ[-M1-]=əT//, SH /'*spread it out (of blanket, net, book, etc.)*'/, MC, (<**metathesis type 1**> *non-continuative*), (<**=et**> *purposeful control transitivizer*), phonology: metathesis, vowel merger (**é** + e → á as usual), syntactic analysis: transitive verb, attested by Elders Group (5/26/76, 3/14/79), example: <**tlhát ta' pékw.**>, //tə́ɬ[-M1-]=əT t-ɛʔ pə́kʷ//, /'*Spread out your book.*'/, attested by Elders Group (3/14/79).

<**tlhéthet**>, pcrs //tə́ɬ-M1=əT-ət//, ABFC ['*straighten oneself out*'], EFAM, (<**-et**> *reflexive*), phonology: metathesis, syntactic analysis: intransitive verb, attested by Elders Group (3/14/79).

<**télhches**>, df //tə́ɬ=cəs//, TOOL ['*hit on the hand with a hammer*'], ABDF, probably root <**télh**> *get straightened out*, lx <**=tses ~ =ches**> *on the hand*, syntactic analysis: intransitive verb, attested by EB (5/19/76).

<**shxwtélhtses**>, ds //sxʷ=tə́ɬ=cəs//, TOOL /'*hammer, stone hand hammer, sledge hammer*'/, ASM ['sledge hammers were made with vine maple for the handle and a block of wood for the sledge, used often with wedges made from crabapple wood or stone'], (<**shxw=**> *something to, nominalizer*), syntactic analysis: nominal, attested by Elders Group (4/5/78), CT (6/8/76), also <**shxwtélhches**>, //sxʷ=tə́ɬ=cəs//, attested by EB (5/19/76).

<**tem=**>, da //təm=//, TIME /'*time for, time to, season of*'/, syntactic analysis: lexical prefix, attested by AC, Elders Group, Deming, others; found in <**temqw'íles**>, //təm=**q**'ʷíl=əs//, /'*spring-time*'/, literally /'time for things to come up'/, <**temkw'ókw'es**>, //təm=k'ʷɛ[=AáC₁ə=]s//, /'*summer*'/, literally /'season of hot'/, <**temx̱éytl'**>, //təm=x̣íƛ'//, /'*winter*'/, literally /'season of cold'/, <**temhilálxw**>, //təm=hil=ɛ́lxʷ//, /'*autumn, fall*'/, literally /'season of falling leaves'/, <**tempó:kw'**>, //təm=pá·k'ʷ//, /'*moon of October, time for Chehalis River spring salmon*'/, <**temtl'í:q'es**>, //təm=ƛ'í·q'=əs//, /'*moon of February, time one gets stuck or trapped (in pithouses by the snow)*'/, <**temtám**>, //təm=tɛ́m//, /'*be when?, when is it?*'/, literally /'season of what?'/, <**temt'elémtses**> *moon of February, time things get stuck on the hand (with cold)*, <**temkwíkwexel**> *moon of April, time for baby sockeye salmon*, <**tem'elíle**> *moon of May, time for salmonberries*, <**temt'ámxw**> *moon of June, time for gooseberries*, <**temqoqó:**> *moon of June, time of high water*, <**temqwá:l**> *moon of July, time for mosquitoes*, <**temthéqi**> *moon of August, time for sockeye salmon*, <**temkw'ó:lexw**> *moon of September, time for dog salmon*.

<**=tem**>, da //=təm//, ASP ['*be in a state of -ness*'], (semological comment: distinguished only from the homophonous =t-em /=T-əm/ passive by meaning, may be segmentable into =t=em with =t /=t/ cognate with Musqueam /=t/ *state(?)* which Suttles proposes as a possible lexical suffix (Suttles ca1984:14.6.5): "(identical with the -t *subordinate passive* and the -t that appears in a few resultative forms of the verb?)", if segmentable in Upriver Halkomelem, the =em would be the *intransitivizer, have, get*), syntactic analysis: derivational suffix, Salish cognate: in part Musqueam /-t/ *state?* as in /ɬq'ét/ *wide* (cf. /lq'-/ *across, other side*, /ɬéq'əməxʸ/ *flat country*, /ɬq'écəs/ *five [hand spread out?]*, /ɬéq'ət/ *lay it down*), /pɬét/ *thick* (root?), /ƛ'éqt/ *long* (root?), /θqét/ *standing upright, tree* (cf. root /θqén-/ of /θqénxʸ/ *stand it up*), /tə́ywət/ *the "North" (i.e., Johnstone Strait and beyond)* (cf. /xʷtə́yəwəl/ *the "Northern" tribes*), and /sx̣ə́ləc't/ *place where strong currents meet* (cf. /sx̣ə́ləc'/ *current*, /x̣ə́lc't/ *turn it*) [Suttles ca1984 uses /e/ in place of his earlier /ɛ/ for ease of typing rather than from any fundamental change in analysis]; these are cognate to Upriver Halkomelem forms <lhq'át> /ɬq'ɛ́t/ *wide*, <plhát> /pɬɛ́t/ *thick*, <tl'áqt> /ƛ'ɛ́qt/ *long*, <thqát> /θqɛ́t/ *tree*.; found in <**x̱á:p'qwtem**>, //x̣ɛ́·p'qʷ=təm//, /'*be aching, rheumatism*'/, <**xwókweltem**>, //xʷákʷ=əl=təm//, /'*(be) numb*'/, compare <**xwókwel**> *get numb*, <**xwó:xwth'tem**>, //xʷɛ[=Aá·=C₁ə=]θ'=təm//, /'*(be) sexy*'/, compare <**shxwó:xwth'**> *be crazy*, compare root <**xwáth'**> *teeter*, <**ót'tem**>, //ʔát'=təm//, /'*(be) stretched*'/, compare <**ó:t'**> *stretch*, <**sá:lts'tem ~ sá:lth'tem**>, //sə[=Aɛ́·=]l=c'=təm//, /'*(be) dizzy*'/,

compare (perhaps) <**sel**> *spin*, <**q'thá:mtem**>, //q'θɛ́·m=təm//, /'*(be) absent-minded*'/, compare <**q'thá:m**> *have a short memory*, <**lhx̱étem**>, //ɬə́x̣=M1=təm//, /'*(be) stiff (in body, as of arm, leg, etc.)*'/, compare <**slhelháx̱**> *(be) stiff (in body, as of arm, leg, etc.)*, <**q'á:lptem**>, //q'ɛ́·l(=)p=təm or q'ə[=Aɛ́·=]l=p'=D=təm//, /'*be cramped*'/, compare root <**q'él**> *tangle*?, <**q'élptem**>, //q'əl=p'=D=təm//, /'*to cramp, have cramps*'/, compare root <**q'él**> *tangle*?, <**q'áq'elptem**>, //q'ɛ́[=C_1ə=]l=p'=D=təm//, /'*be cramping*'/, compare root <**q'él**> *tangle*?, <**syélthtem**>, //s=yə́lθ=təm//, /'*(be) poisoned*'/, compare <**yélth**> *to poison*, <**chxwétem**>, //cə́xʷ=M1=təm//, /'*(be) swelling (of infected sore, balloon, etc.)*'/, compare <**tsetsíxw**> *swollen*, <**télstem**>, //tə́l=s=təm//, /'*get staggered*'/, <**tá:lstem**>, //tə[=Aɛ́·=]l=s=təm//, /'*(be) staggering*'/, <**x̱wex̱weló:stem**>, //x̣ʷə[=C_1ə=]l=á·s=təm//, /'*(be) staggering*'/, <**tl'áxtem**>, //ƛ'ə[=Aɛ́=]xʸ=təm//, /'*(have) diarrhea*'/, compare root <**tl'éx**> *ripped apart*, <**tl'xátem**>, //ƛ'ɛ́xʸ=M1=təm//, /'*(have) continuing diarrhea*'/, <**lhétx̱tem**>, //ɬə́t=x̣=təm//, /'*to tremble*'/, comment: but lhátx̱tem *trembling, shiver, shivering* beside lhátx̱thá:lem *I'm trembling* seems to point to a passive in =t-em /=T-əm/, <**toteqw'ó:mestem**>, //ta[=C_1ə=]q'ʷ=əm=á·[=M2=]s=təm//, /'*tuberculosis*'/, compare <**tóteqw'em**> *coughing*.

<**temchálhtel**>, TIME /'*time to dry fish, first of July (at Yale), October (at Chehalis)*'/, *see* =chílh ~ chílh=.

<**témélh**>, free root //təmə́ɬ//, LAND /'*red ochre, (clay colored reddish by oxides of iron)*'/, EB perhaps /'*red rock fungus used for Indian paint, (*perhaps*) Indian paint fungus*'/, (perhaps) ['*Echinodontium tinctorium*'], REL /'*Indian red paint (used by spirit dancers, ritualists, and Indian doctors or shamans)*'/, ASM ['red Indian paint was made by mixing grease with powder from clay colored reddish by oxides of iron and/or reddish soot from baked red rock fungus, it was and is used as face paint by powerful Stó:lō (and other) spirit dancers, by ritualists, and shamans or Indian doctors, and was (and still may be) painted on certain sacred rocks such as the stone shaman at Doctor's Point in Harrison Lake, Indian spirit dancers with red paint are said to have different spirit powers than those with black paint,'], a sample of Stó:lō Indian red face paint (for spirit dancers) was obtained from Mrs. Amy Cooper by Oliver Wells, kept by the Wells family after his death, and chemically analyzed from Oct. to Nov. 1981 at Simon Fraser University for Dr. Ralph Maud, Marie Weeden and Dr. Brent Galloway in their project to transcribe the Oliver Wells tapes and inventory his Indian research materials, the analysis by Keith Slessor of S.F.U. together with graphs of three tests (see illustrations) follows:, "Face Paint Analysis. X-ray analysis (Prof. John D. Auria): sample contained about 10 percent iron Fe, also contained other minor components so we suspect an iron-containing clay rather than a pure iron oxide, Microanalysis (Ms. S.A. Black): showed about 70 percent organic consistent with a grease or fat added to and mixed in with the iron-bearing clay, Fat analysis (Ms. S. A. Black and Mr. B. D. Johnston): capillary gas chromatography of the methyl ester of the fatty material showed a highly saturated fat typically of animal origin, plant and fish oil (fats) are reasonably unsaturated and I believe can be ruled out in this case,, [Summary]: The face paint is probably an iron-containing clay that would be dark brown (or red brown) ground up finely in the presence of four times the volume of animal fat. [from another note dated 27/11/81]: In discussion here about the face paint, the suggestion that the animal fat origin is very likely to be black bear arose. I think that's a very sensible suggestion, which you might find useful." (Keith Slessor), PE ['*lipstick*'], LT /'*red ochre color, color of red clay of iron oxide used for religious paint and face paint*'/, ASM ['used as a secondary color term by a number of elders, identified on the color chart in Berlin and Kay 1969 (rows top to bottom B-I, columns left to right 1-40) as follows: EL (2/20/79): G4, H4; AK (1/24/79): H1, H2, H3, H4; in Aug. 1987 NP and AH also mapped **témélh** using Munsell color chips with MacLaury and Galloway, NP at H2, AH at G3, G4 (focused at G4)'], charts by Rob MacLaury, X-ray and gas chromatography graphs and printouts, syntactic analysis: noun, nominal, attested by CT and

HT (6/21/76), Deming (2/22/79), Elders Group (6/4/75), EL (2/20/79), AK (1/24/79), AD (7/23/79), AC, other sources: ES /təmə́ɬ/ *ochre*, also <**témelh**>, //təməɬ//, attested by Deming, ASM ['red ochre face paint'], <**thíyt te témélh**>, //θíy=T tə təmə́ɬ//, /'*make paint*'/, literally /'make s-th the red ochre paint'/, attested by AC, ASM ['lipstick'], <**ólewe qéx̱ te témelh.**>, //ʔólə-wə qə́x̣ tə təməɬ//, /'*(There's) too much lipstick.*'/, attested by Deming (2/22/79), ASM ['dancer's paint'] (attested by RG & EH (4/10/99 Ling332)), ASM ['face paint'], <**p'éq' témelh**>, //p'ə́q' təməɬ//, SPRD //'white paint (for spirit dancers' faces)'//, lit. /'white red-ochre'/, attested by RG & EH (4/10/99 Ling332), <**tskwí:m témelh**>, //c=kwí·m təməɬ//, SPRD /'*red paint (for spiritual purposes)*'/, attested by RG & EH (4/10/99 Ling332), <ts'q'éyx̱ témelh>, //c'=q'í·x̣ təməɬ//, SPRD /'*black paint (for spiritual purposes)*'/, attested by RG & EH (4/10/99 Ling332).

<**Temélhem**>, ds //təmə́ɬ=əm//, PLN ['*a spring-water stream south of Skowkale*'], literally /'place for getting red paint'/, lx <**=em**> *place to get* from <**=em**> *intransitivizer, get, have*, syntactic analysis: nominal, source: Wells 1965 (lst ed.):13 <tih-MIH.TH-luhm> *a spring-water stream, south Skowkale (place for getting red paint),*

<**temélhépsem**>, ds //təmə́ɬ=ə́psəm//, EZ /'*large red-necked woodpecker, large red-headed woodpecker, rain crow (black with red comb on head) (AC), pileated woodpecker*'/, ['*Dryocopus pileatus*'], ASM ['called a rain crow by AC (who had forgotten its Halkomelem name), the bird of this name predicts rain according to EL (we heard its cry on the Harrison River one day on a place names trip, and EL said, "Did you hear that call of the temélhépsem? When it calls like that there will be a change of weather within 24 hours. You see nothing but blue sky now, but it will be pouring rain in less than a day." He was right.), EL however says the temélhepsem is a small regular woodpecker and that the pileated woodpecker (in photo in Udvardy 1977) has another name, if a woodpecker pecks on your house a few times it means bad news according to Elders on 3/21/79'], lx <**=épsem**> *on the back of the head and neck*, syntactic analysis: nominal, attested by Elders Group (3/1/72, 6/4/75, 3/21/79), EL (9/15/78), AC, BJ (12/5/64 old p.315), other sources: ES /təm·ə́ɬəpsəm/ *pileated woodpecker*, H-T <tEmétlepseEm> *woodpecker (Picus) (large red-headed).*

<**Temélhem**>, PLN ['*a spring-water stream south of Skowkale*'], *see* témélh.

<**temélhépsem**>, EZ /'*large red-necked woodpecker, large red-headed woodpecker, rain crow (black with red comb on head) (AC), pileated woodpecker*'/, *see* témélh.

<**témés**>, free root //tə́məs//, CLO ['*velvet*'], syntactic analysis: noun, nominal, attested by BHTTC, Elders Group (4/7/76), Deming (1/31/80), AC, Salish cognate: Squamish /tə́mus/ *velvet* W73:279, K69:47.

<**témex**>, pcis //tə́m=əxʸ//, [tɪ́mɪxʸ], EFAM /'*desire s-th, desire s-o, wish for s-th/s-o*'/, (<**=ex**> *purposeful control transitive inanimate object preferred*), syntactic analysis: transitive verb, attested by Elders Group (3/29/78), EB (3/22/76), Deming (3/25/76), also <**témex ~ támex**>, //tə́m=əxʸ ~ tɛ́m=əxʸ//, [tɪ́mɪxʸ ~ tɛ́mɪxʸ], also /'*wishing for it*'/, attested by Elders Group (3/23/77), AC, ABFC ['*turned on sexually*'], literally /'wishing for it, desiring it'/, attested by Elders Group (3/23/77); found in <**témextsel.**>, //tə́m=əxʸ-c-əl//, /'*I wish (for s-th).*'/, attested by Deming, also <**támextsel.**>, //tɛ́m=əxʸ-c-əl//, /'*I'm wishing.*'/, attested by AC, example: <**lichxw támex te qwe'óp?**>, //li-c-xʷ tɛ́m=əxʸ tə qʷəʔáp//, /'*Are you wishing for that apple?*'/, attested by AC.

<**téméx**>, cts //tə́m=ə[-´-]xʸ//, EFAM ['*desiring s-th*'], (<-´-> *continuative*), phonology: stress-shift, syntactic analysis: transitive verb, attested by Elders Group (3/29/78), also <**támex ~ témex**>, //tɛ́m=əxʸ ~ tə́m=əxʸ//, [tɛ́mɪxʸ ~ tɪ́mɪxʸ], also /'*wishing for it*'/, attested by Elders Group (3/23/77), AC, also /'*be turned on sexually, (desiring s-th/s-o sexually)*'/, attested by Elders Group (3/23/77), example: <**lichxw támex te qwe'óp?**>, //li-c-xʷ tɛ́m=əxʸ tə qʷəʔáp//, /'*Are you wishing for that*

apple?'/, attested by AC.

<**téméx**>, EFAM ['*desiring s-th*'], *see* témex.

<**tém:éxw ~ tem:éxw ~ ~ tèm:èxw ~ témexw**>, free root //tə́m·ə́xʷ ~ təm·ə́xʷ ~ tə̀m·ə̀xʷ ~ tə́məxʷ//, LAND /'*earth, ground, land, the earth, the world*'/, phonology: lengthening of resonant between stressed vowels or updrifting adjacent to long resonant, syntactic analysis: noun, nominal, attested by AC, BJ (5/10/64, 12/5/64), Elders Group (3/72, 4/2/75), other sources: ES /təm·ə̀xʷ/ CwMs /tə́məxʷ/ *earth*, Salish cognate: Squamish /tmíxʷ/ *earth, land, dirt* W73:88, K67:259, Nooksack /təmíxʷ/ A61, Twana /təbíxʷ/ *earth, land, country*, LmSanSo /tə́ŋəxʷ/ *earth, land, ground* G82 (cognate set 37), example: <**spóléqwems té tèm:èxw**>, //s=pá[=lə=]qʷ=əm-s tə tə̀m·ə̀xʷ//, [(pitch transcription of vowels): 4 4 1 4 3 3], /'*dust of the earth*'/, attested by BJ (12/5/64), <**x̱éytl' te témexw.**>, //x̣íƛ' tə tə tə́məxʷ//, /'*The ground is cold.*'/, attested by AC.

<**temhilálxw**>, TIME /'*autumn, fall (season)*'/, *see* híl.

<**temí:lt**>, pcs //təm=í·l=T//, FOOD ['*cool it (of food)*'], DESC, root meaning unknown, probably <**=í:l**> *go, come, get, become*, (<**=t**> *purposeful control transitivizer*), syntactic analysis: transitive verb, attested by Elders Group (3/22/78).

<**títemí:lt**>, cts //C_1í-təm=í·l=T//, FOOD ['*cooling it (of food)*'], DESC, (irregular), (<**R4-**> *continuative*), phonology: reduplication, syntactic analysis: transitive verb, attested by Elders Group (3/22/78).

<**temí:lthet**>, pcrs //təm=í·l=T-ət//, FOOD ['*cool off (of food)*'], DESC, (<**-et**> *reflexive*), syntactic analysis: intransitive verb, attested by Elders Group (5/19/76).

<**titemí:lthet**>, cts //C_1í-təm=í·l=T-ət//, FOOD ['*cooling off (of food)*'], DESC, (irregular), (<**R4-**> *continuative*), phonology: reduplication, syntactic analysis: intransitive verb, attested by Elders Group (3/22/78).

<**temí:lthet**>, FOOD ['*cool off (of food)*'], *see* temí:lt

<**temítō**>, free root //təmíto//, EB, FOOD /'tomato'/, borrowed from English "tomato", syntactic analysis: noun, (attested by RG,EH 6/16/98 to SN, edited by BG with RG,EH 6/26/00)

<**temítō smelmólkw**>, FOOD *ketchup* (lit. tomato + spread), (attested by RG,EH 6/16/98 to SN, edited by BG with RG,EH 6/26/00)

<**temítō sqe'óleqw**>, FOOD *tomato juice* (lit. tomato + fruit juice), (attested by RG,EH 6/16/98 to SN, edited by BG with RG,EH 6/26/00)

<**stósem temítō**>, FOOD *ketchup/stewed tomatoes* (lit. smashed + tomato), (attested by RG,EH 6/16/98 to SN, edited by BG with RG,EH 6/26/00).

<**témkwes**>, df //tə́mkʷ=əs//, SH ['*blunt (end of canoe pole)*'], CAN, root meaning unknown unless related to mékw *stout*, possibly lx <=kw> *round, around in circles*, probably <**=es**> *on the face*, syntactic analysis: adjective/adjectival verb, attested by Elders Group (3/1/72), compare <**témqweqsel**> *blunt (of poles)*.

<**temkwō̃xweth**>, TIME /'*coho salmon time, August to September*'/, *see* kwō̃xweth.

<**temkw'à:y**>, TIME /'*hungry time (about mid-April to mid-May), famine (Elders 3/72)*'/, *see* kw'à:y.

<**temkw'éyles**>, TIME /'*(be) Spring, [time or season] when everything comes up*'/, *see* kw'í ~ kw'íy.

<**temkw'ókw'es**>, TIME ['*summer*'], *see* kw'ás.

<**temkw'ó:lexw**>, TIME /'*September to October, dog salmon time*'/, *see* kw'ó:lexw.

<**tempó:kw'**>, TIME /'*October moon, time to smoke Chehalis spring salmon*'/, *see* pó:qw' ~ póqw'.

<**temqó: ~ temqoqó:**>, WATR /'*high water time (yearly, usually in June), June*'/, *see* qó:.

<**temqwá:l**>, TIME ['*month or moon beginning in July*'], *see* qwá:l.

<**témqweqsel**>, df //tə́mqʷ=əqsəl//, SH ['*blunt (of poles)*'], root meaning unknown unless related to t'em *chop off*, lx <**=eqsel**> *on the nose, point*, syntactic analysis: adjective/adjectival verb, attested by Elders Group (3/1/72), compare <**témkwes**> *blunt (end of canoe pole)*.

<**temqw'íles ~ temqw'éyles**>, TIME /'*spring (season), (time to sprout up)*'/, *see* qw'íl.

<**temsóx̲wel**>, HARV ['*haying time*'], *see* só:x̲wel ~ sóx̲wel.

<**temtám**>, TIME /'*when?, when is it?*'/, *see* tám.

<**temtámes**>, TIME /'*whenever, whenever it is*'/, *see* tám.

<**temt'á:mxw**>, TIME /'*gooseberry time, the month or moon (first sliver) that starts in June*'/, *see* t'á:mxw.

<**temt'elémtses**>, TIME /'*month beginning with first sliver of moon in February, (time things stick to the hand (in cold))*'/, *see* t'elém.

<**temthéqi**>, TIME /'*sockeye moon, month to get sockeye salmon (begins with first quarter after black moon in July, lasts into August), July to August, (June to July [Jenness: WS])*'/, *see* sthéqi ~ sthéqey.

<**temth'oló:lh**>, TIME /'*July to August, (big spring salmon time)*'/, *see* sth'olólh.

<**temth'ó:qwi**>, TIME /'*November, time to catch salmon*'/, *see* sth'ó:qwi ~ sth'óqwi.

<**temtl'í:q'es**>, TIME /'*moon or month beginning in February, (November to December, time when ice forms [and sticks] [Billy Sepass in Jenness])*'/, *see* tl'íq'.

<**temwíwe**> (or possibly) <**temswíwe**>, TIME /'*month beginning in April at the mouth of the Fraser, May-June (Jenness:Sepass), oolachen moon*'/, *see* swí:we ~ swíwe.

<**temxwá**>, TIME ['*famine*'], *see* xwá.

<**temx̲éytl'**>, TIME ['*winter*'], *see* x̲éytl' ~ x̲í:tl'.

<**temx̲é:ytl'thet**>, TIME ['*winter*'], *see* x̲éytl' ~ x̲í:tl'.

<**tem'elíle**>, TIME /'*salmonberry time, (usually) May*'/, *see* elíle.

<**tépelhállh**>, HUNT /'*board for stretching squirrel or skunk hides, etc.*'/, *see* tpólh.

<**tépsem**>, possibly root //tə́psəm or t=ə́psəm//, ANA /'*neck, (back of head and back of neck [EB], nape of the neck [Elders Group 5/3/78])*'/, (irregular), possibly root <**t**> meaning unknown, possibly <**=épsem**> *on the neck, on the back of the neck, on the back of the head*, grammatical comment: may be empty root, syntactic analysis: noun or nominal, attested by AC, BJ (5/10/64), Elders Group, IHTTC (9/21/77), other sources: ES /tɛ́psəm/ (CwMs /tə́psəm/) *neck*, H-T <tE´psum> *back of head; neck (back part), Boas Scowlitz field notes nape of neck*, also /'*back of head and neck*'/, attested by EB (IHTTC 9/21/77), also /'*nape of the neck*'/, attested by Elders Group (5/3/78), example: <**tsel kw'óqw í tel tépsem.**>, //c-əl k'ʷáqʷ ʔí tə-l tə́psəm//, /'*I was hit on my neck.*'/, attested by EB (1/12/76).

<**Shxwtépsem**>, ds //sxʷ=t(=)ə́psəm//, PLN ['*a neck of land on the west side of Harrison Lake just north of Twenty-Mile Creek and across from the north tip of Long Island*'], ASM ['this neck-shape extension of land (past Twenty-Mile Bay) narrows the lake so that deer can swim from the neck to ten-mile long Long Island'], (<**shxw=**> *nominalizer, something that*), syntactic analysis: nominal, attested by EL (Elders Group boat trip to Port Douglas 6/18/75), see file card or map.

<**téq**>, free root //tə́q or tɛ[=Aə́=]q//, SH ['*close by itself*'], TVMO, BLDG, possibly root <**táq**> or <**tqá**>, possibly <**é-ablaut**> *resultative*, syntactic analysis: intransitive verb, attested by EB (2/6/76), example: <**le téq té xàlh.**>, //lə tə́q tə x^{y}ɛ̀ɬ//, /'*The door closed by itself.*'/, phonology: sentence-intonation raises pitch on article to 6 and lowers following pitch, attested by EB.

<**tqát**>, pcs //təq=M1=əT or təq=ə[=Aɛ́=]T or tɛ́q=M1=(ə)T//, SH ['*close s-th*'], TVMO, BLDG, possibly <**metathesis**> *non-continuative* or possibly <**á**-ablaut> *durative*, (<**=et**> *purposeful control transitivizer*), phonology: metathesis with vowel merger or ablaut and vowel-loss, syntactic analysis: transitive verb, attested by AD, AC, Salish cognate: Lushootseed root /təq(á)/ *close, block* as in /dx^w-tq-ád tə šə̀g^{w}ɬ/ *Shut the door.* H76:491, example: <**tqát te skw'echóstel**>, //təq=ə[=Aɛ́=]T tə s=k'^{w}əc=ás=təl//, /'*close the window*'/, attested by AD (3/13/80), <**tqát te pékw**>, //təq=ə[=Aɛ́=]T tə pə́k^w//, /'*close the book*'/, attested by AD, <**tqát te steqtá:l**>, //təq=ə[=Aɛ́=]T tə s=təq=tə[=Aɛ́·=]l or tɛ́q=M1=əT tə s=tɛ́·q=tə[=M2=]l//, /'*close the door*'/, attested by AC.

<**xwtáq**>, df //x^{w}ə=tɛ́q or x^{w}ə=tə[=Aɛ́=]q//, SH /'*(get closed, become closed)*'/, BLDG, (<**xw(e)=**> *become, get*), possibly <**á**-ablaut> *resultative/durative*, phonology: possible ablaut, syntactic analysis: intransitive verb, Elder's comment: "unsatisfied with translation as *close it*", attested by DC (Elders Group 3/26/80).

<**xwtetáq**>, df //x^w(ə)=C$_1$ə=tɛ́q or x^w(ə)=C$_1$ə=tə[=Aɛ́=]q or x^w(ə)=tə[=C$_1$ɛ́(·)=]q//, BLDG ['*be closed*'], ECON, (<**xw(e)=**> *become, get*), possibly <**R5= or =R9=**> *resultative*, possibly <**á**-ablaut> *durative*, phonology: reduplication or ablaut, syntactic analysis: intransitive verb, attested by AH (Deming 1/18/79), example: <**le xwtetáq te shxwiymálé.**>, //lə x^w=C$_1$ə=tɛ́q tə s=x^{w}iyəm=ɛ́lə́//, /'*The store is closed.*'/, attested by AH.

<**steqtéq**>, pln //s=C$_1$əC$_2$=tə́q or s=C$_1$əC$_2$=tɛ[=Aə́=]q//, WATR /'*jampile, log-jam*'/, EB, (<**s=**> *nominalizer*, R3= *plural*), possibly <**é-ablaut**> *resultative/durative*, phonology: reduplication, possible ablaut, syntactic analysis: nominal, attested by Elders Group, AC, other sources: H-T <s'tuk·tuk·> *logs (a jam of)*.

<**teqáp** or **teqíp**>, df //təq=ɛ́p or tɛ́q=ə[=M2=]p or təq=ə[=Aɛ́=]p or təq=ə[=Aí=]p//, EZ ['*beaver dam*'], BLDG, literally /'closed off/blocked in the dirt/on the bottom'/, probably root <**teq or táq**> *closed off/blocked*, possibly <**=áp or =ep**> *dirt or on the bottom*, possibly <**metathesis or í-ablaut**> *derivational*, possibly <**á**-ablaut> *durative/resultative*, phonology: possible ablaut or metathesis, syntactic analysis: nominal, attested by JL and NP (Fish Camp 7/19/79), other sources: JH /təqép/ *beaver dam*,

<**steqtá:l**>, df //s=təq=tə[=Aɛ́·=]l or s=tɛ́·q=tə[=M2=]l//, BLDG /'*door, doorway, door of a big (communal) house or longhouse*'/, (<**s=**> *nominalizer*), lx <**=tel**> *device to*, <**á**:-ablaut> *durative* or possibly root <**metathesis**> *derivational*, phonology: possible ablaut or metathesis, syntactic analysis: nominal, attested by AC, DM (12/4/64), Elders Group (3/72), also <**shxwteqtá:l ~ shteqtá:l**>, //sx^w=təq=tə[=Aɛ́·=]l//, attested by DM (12/4/64 new p.175), also <**steqtál**>, //s=təq=tə[=Aɛ́=]l//, attested by IHTTC (9/15/77), example: <**xwemxálemlha la(m) te steqtál.**>, //x^{w}əm=x^{y}ə[=Aɛ́=]l=əm-ɬɛ lɛ́=m tə s=təq=tə[=Aɛ́=]l//, /'*Run to the door.*'/, attested by IHTTC.

<**stqá:qel**>, df //s=tɛ́(·)q=M1=əqəl or s=tə́q=M1=əqəl or s=təq=ə[=Aɛ́·=]qəl//, ABDF ['*lost one's voice*'], literally /'blocked/closed off in the voice'/, (<**s=**> *stative*), possibly <**metathesis**> *non-continuative* or possibly <**á**:-ablaut> *resultative/durative*, lx <**=eqel**> *in the throat, speech, voice*, phonology: possible metathesis or ablaut, syntactic analysis: adjective/adjectival verb, attested by Elders Group (11/16/76).

<**táqalh**>, df //tɛ́q=ɛɬ or tə[=Aɛ́=]q=(ɬ)ɛɬ//, EB /'*a grass that grows with berries in fields and*

everywhere and has seeds that stick in one's throat when eaten with berries, probably *a type of brome grass,* likely *California brome grass,* possibly *sweet cicely'*/, ['probably a *Bromus* sp., likely *Bromus carinatus,* possibly *Osmorhiza chilensis* and *Osmorhiza purpurea,*'], ASM ['if you get the seeds in with your berries they stick in your throat and only go one way--one can't get them up or out (LJ, AD), the grass looks like oats or rye and has sharp seeds that choke you if eaten with berries (Deming), drawing of California brome grass in book on grasses of B.C. identified as likely by AD and Deming, sweet cicely has seeds described like this but has leaves that are not very grass-like'], possibly root <**táq ~ tqá ~ tə[=Aɛ́=]q**> *close off, shut off,* possibly <**=(lh)alh ~ =lhelh**> *in the windpipe, in the throat,* syntactic analysis: nominal, attested by LJ (6/18/79) via AD (6/19/79), Deming (6/21/79), also <**táqelh**>, //tɛ́qəɬ//, attested by LJ, Salish cognate: Squamish /táqaʔɬ/ *California brome grass (Bromus carinatus) and sweet cicely (Osmorhiza chilensis and Osmorhiza purpurea), the Squamish found this species [sweet cicely] particularly annoying when they were picking salmonberries because it often got into their berry baskets and could cause gagging if it was swallowed* Kennedy and Bouchard 1976:46,66.

<**teqáp or teqíp**>, EZ ['*beaver dam*'], *see* téq.

<**tqá:tsa**>, df //tqɛ́·=cɛ or tɛ́·q=M1=cɛ or tə[=Aɛ́·=]q=M1=cɛ//, NUM ['*eight*'], possibly root <**tqá:**> or <**tá:q**> *close,* ASM ['plausible because holding up four fingers of each hand to show eight closes the hands with the thumbs and because four is the ritual number done to complete things and thus a multiple of four could be seen as closing an action'], lx <**=tsa (uncommon) ~ =tses**> *on the hand,* possibly <**metathesis type 1**> *non-continuative or derivational,* possibly <**ablaut**> *resultative,* phonology: possible metathesis, possible ablaut, syntactic analysis: adjective/adjectival verb, nominal, attested by AC, BJ (5/10/64), NP (12/6/73), CT (9/5/73), DM (12/4/64), Elders Group, Deming, others, other sources: ES /tqɛ́·cɛ/ *eight*; found in <**teqá:tsatset.**>, //tqɛ́·=cɛ-c-ət//, /'*There's eight of us.*'/, literally /'were are eight'/, attested by AC, example: <**ópel qas te tqá:tsa**>, //ʔápəl qɛ-s tə tqɛ́·=cɛ//, /'*eighteen*'/, attested by AC, DM (12/4/64), CT (9/5/73), <**tskw'éx qas te tqá:tsa**>, //c=k'ʷə́xʸ qɛ-s tə tqɛ́·=cɛ//, /'*twenty-eight*'/, attested by CT (9/5/73).

<**tqátsáleqel**>, ds //tqɛ́=cɛ=ɛ́ləqəl//, NUM ['*eight containers*'], lx <**=áleqel**> *container(s),* phonology: vowel merger, syntactic analysis: nominal, adjective/adjectival verb, attested by AD (4/12/78).

<**tqatsálh**>, ds //tqɛ=cɛ́=ɛ́ɬ//, NUM ['*eight times*'], lx <**=álh**> *times,* phonology: vowel merger, syntactic analysis: adverb/adverbial verb, Elder's comment: "not used often since they didn't count these often beyond five", attested by Elders Group (3/19/75).

<**tqátsámets'**>, ds //tqɛ́=cɛ=ɛ́məc' or tqɛ́=cɛ=əməc'//, NUM /'*eight ropes, eight threads, eight sticks, eight poles*'/, lx <**=ámets' ~ =emets' ~ =ámeth' ~ =emeth'**> *long stick-like object(s); standing, upright,* phonology: vowel merger, syntactic analysis: nominal, adjective/adjectival verb, attested by AD (4/12/78), other sources: Boas Scowlitz field notes ms..

<**teqátsa'ále**>, ds //tqɛ́=cɛ=ʔɛ́lə//, NUM ['*eight people*'], lx <**=ále**> *people,* phonology: vowel merger, syntactic analysis: nominal, adjective/adjectival verb, attested by Elders Group (3/19/75).

<**teqtselhsxá**>, ds //t[=ə=]q=c=əɬ(=)sxʸɛ́ or tɛq=c(ɛ)=əɬ(=)sxʸɛ́//, NUM ['*eighty*'], lx <**=elhsxá ~ =elsxá**> *ten times* itself containing <**=elh ~ =álh**> *times,* phonology: vowel-loss, vowel-reduction or epenthetic infixation of e, syntactic analysis: nominal, adjective/adjectival verb, attested by BJ (12/5/64 Wells transcript old p. 336), others, also <**téqetselsxà**>, //tə[=ə́=]qɛ=c(ɛ)=əl(=)sxʸɛ́ or tɛ[=Aə́=]q=c(ɛ)=əl(=)sxʸɛ́//, phonology: downstepping, epenthesis or ablaut, vowel-loss, attested by AC, CT (9/5/73), others.

<**teqetselsxá:le**>, ds //təqɛ=c(ɛ)=əl=sxʸɛ́=ɛ́lə//, NUM ['*eighty people*'], lx <**=ále**> *people,* phonology: vowel merger, syntactic analysis: nominal, adjective/adjectival verb, comment:

probably somewhat artificial since **qéx̲** *many* would usually be used instead of counting this high, attested by Elders Group (3/19/75).

<**téqetselsx̲ós**>, ds //t[=ə́=]qɛ=c(ɛ)=əl=sxʸɛ=ás//, NUM ['*eighty dollars*'], ECON, lx <**=ós ~ =es**> *dollar, round objects, on the face*, phonology: vowel merger, syntactic analysis: nominal, attested by AC (11/30/71).

<**steqá:tsas**>, ds //s=tqɛ́·=cɛ=s//, NUM ['*eight o'clock*'], TIME, lx <**s=...=s**> *o'clock* lx which could have been derived from <**s=**> *nominalizer* and lx <**=es**> *cyclic period*, phonology: circumfix, syntactic analysis: nominal, attested by AC.

<**teqatsíqw**>, ds //tqɛ=cɛ=íqʷ//, NUM ['*eight fish*'], FSH, EZ, lx <**=íqw**> *fish, on top of the head*, phonology: vowel merger, syntactic analysis: nominal, adjective/adjectival verb, attested by BHTTC (8/24/76).

<**tqatsíws**>, ds //tqɛ=cɛ=íws//, NUM ['*eight birds*'], EZ, lx <**=íws**> *on the skin, on the body; birds*, phonology: vowel merger, syntactic analysis: nominal, adjective/adjectival verb, attested by Elders Group (3/29/77), also <**tqatse'íws**>, //tqɛ=cɛ=ʔíws//, attested by TM (Elders Group 3/29/77).

<**tqòtsòls**>, ds //tqɛ[=Aa=]´=cɛ=áls//, NUM ['*eight fruit in a group [or cluster] (as they grow on a plant)*'], EB, possibly <**o-ablaut**> *derivational* unless automatically conditioned, lx <**=óls**> *fruit, rocks, spherical objects*, phonology: o-ablaut on a automatic before =óls, vowel merger, updrifting, downstepping, syntactic analysis: nominal, adjective/adjectival verb, attested by AD (4/12/78).

<**tqó:tsó:s**>, ds //tqɛ[=Aa=]´·=cɛ=á·s//, NUM ['*eight dollars*'], ECON, possibly <**o-ablaut**> *derivational*, lx <**=ó:s**> *dollars, round things*, phonology: o-ablaut on a automatic before =ó:s, vowel merger, syntactic analysis: nominal, adjective/adjectival verb, attested by AC, ECON /'*eight Indian blankets [Boas], eight dollars*'/, attested by Boas Scowlitz field notes.

<**tqátsa'ő́welh ?**>, ds //tqɛ́=cɛ=ʔówəɬ ?//, NUM /'*eight canoes, eight boats*'/, CAN, lx <**=ő́welh**> *canoe(s), boat(s)*, phonology: epenthetic glottal stop, syntactic analysis: nominal, adjective/adjectival verb, Elder's comment: "(uncertain)", attested by AD (4/12/78).

<**teqátsa'ále**>, NUM ['*eight people*'], *see* tqá:tsa.

<**teqatsíqw**>, NUM ['*eight fish*'], *see* tqá:tsa.

<**teqetselsxá:le**>, NUM ['*eighty people*'], *see* tqá:tsa.

<**téqetselsx̲ós**>, NUM ['*eighty dollars*'], *see* tqá:tsa.

<**téqlexw**>, ncs //tə́q=l-əxʷ or tɛ[=Aə́=]q=l-əxʷ//, ABDF /'*to hurt again (as when a painful place is bumped and hurts again or as when a pain inside one's body returns again), (to ache [SJ])*'/, possibly <**é-ablaut**> *resultative*, (<**=l**> *non-control transitivizer*), (<**-exw**> *third person object*), phonology: possible ablaut, syntactic analysis: transitive verb, attested by AD (2/28/79), also /'*to ache*'/, attested by SJ (3/17/77), example: <**téqlexw tel sx̲éle.**>, //tə́q=l-əxʷ tə-; s=x̣ələ//, /'*My foot aches.*'/, attested by SJ.

<**táteqlexw**>, cts //tə[-Aɛ́C₁ə-]q=l-əxʷ or tɛ́[-C₁ə-]q=l-əxʷ//, ABDF /'*hurting, feeling sore, (feel[ing] pain [BJ])*'/, (<**-R1- or á-ablaut and -R1-**> *continuative*), (<**=l**> *non-control transitivizer*), (<**-exw**> *third person object*), phonology: reduplicatiion, possible ablaut, syntactic analysis: transitive verb, attested by Elders Group (10/6/76), also /'*feel a pain*'/, attested by BJ (12/5/64 new transcript old p. 333).

<**teqtselhsxá**>, NUM ['*eighty*'], *see* tqá:tsa.

<**téq'**>, free root //tə́q'//, ABFC /'*to fart, pass gas*'/, syntactic analysis: intransitive verb, attested by Elders Group (5/14/80), others, Salish cognate: Squamish /**tə́q'**/ *to fart* and /**təq'**-númut/ *fart*

inadvertently and /st**ə́q'**/ *fart (noun)* K69:48, example: <**ō téq'.**>, //ʔo tə́**q**'//, /'*Oh fart.*'/, EFAM, usage: said when one loses a game and get mad, attested by Elders Group (5/14/80).

<**tés**>, free root //tə́s//, [tís], TVMO /'*approach, get near, get closer, reach, go up to, get up to*'/, syntactic analysis: intransitive verb, attested by EB, Elders Group, AC, example: <**lámchexw te théqet (qe)tl'o(se)su tés te theqát.**>, //lɛ́=m-c-əx^{w} tə **θ**[=Aə́=]qɛt (qə-)ƛ'a(-sə)-s-u tə́s tə **θ**əqɛ́t//, /'*Go through the thicket and get to the (big) tree.*'/, attested by AC, <**esu tés te theqát.**>, //ʔə-s-u tə́s tə θəqɛ́t//, /'*And it got up to the tree(s).*'/, semantic environment ['talking about flood waters'], attested by AC, <**qesu tés stetís kw'e Fort Yale.**>, //qə-s-u tə́s s=C_1ə=tə[=Aí=]s k'^{w}ə Fort Yale//, /'*And they got up to near Fort Yale.*'/, semantic environment ['people in a canoe'], usage: story of the Flood, attested by AC, <**wetésescha kw'e/kws tés**>, //wə-tə́s-əs-cɛ k'^{w}ə/k^{w}-s tə́s//, /'*until*'/, semantic environment ['this phrase can be used before an hour, day (tomorrow for ex.) or before something that will happen (we go, etc.)'], attested by Elders Group (10/6/76), AD (1/15/79).

<**tetés**>, cts //C_1ə-tə́s//, TVMO /'*approaching, getting near, getting closer*'/, (<**R5-**> *continuative*), phonology: reduplication, syntactic analysis: intransitive verb, attested by Elders Group (11/9/77, 12/7/77), EB (4/12/78).

<**teséstexw**>, caus //tə́s=M1=sT-əx^{w}//, TVMO /'*make s-o get near, bring s-o near*'/, probably <**metathesis type 1**> *non-continuative*, (<**=st**> *causative control transitivizer*), phonology: probably metathesis, syntactic analysis: transitive verb, <**tesésthòx**>, //tə́s=M1=sT-áx^{y}//, /'*come near me,* (sic? for *make me get near)*'/, comment: probably mistranslation, attested by Elders Group (2/26/75).

<**teséthet ~ tséthet**>, pcrs //tə́s[-M1-]=T-ət or tə́s=ə[-M2-]T-ət//, TVMO /'*come close, come near, come sit in (with a group)*'/, (<**metathesis type 1 or 2**> *non-continuative*), (<**=t**> *purposeful control transitivizer*), (<**-et**> *reflexive*), phonology: metathesis, syntactic analysis: intransitive verb, attested by Elders Group (2/18/76), EB and AD (9/19/78), MH (Deming 1/4/79); found in <**teséthetalha.**>, //tə́s[-M1-]=T-ət-ɛɬɛ//, /'*Come near (you folks)., Come sit in (and eat), you folks.*'/, syntactic comment: plural command imperative, attested by Elders Group, example: <**míthelh tséthet.**>, //mí=**θ**ə-ɬ tə́s[-M1-]=T-ət//, /'*Come join in (eating).*'/, semantic environment ['said to someone hanging back'], literally /'come eat -coaxing imperative come near'/, syntactic comment: short imperative, attested by EB and AD, <**míchap teséthet.**>, //mí-c-ɛp tə́s[-M1-]=T-ət//, /'*Come sit in folks., Come join us at the table folks.*'/, attested by MH, <**míyalha teséthet.**>, //míy-ɛɬɛ tə́s[-M1-]=T-ət//, /'*Come near (you folks)., Come sit in (and eat) you folks.*'/, syntactic comment: plural command imperative, attested by Elders Group.

<**stetís**>, durs //s=C_1ə=tə[=Aí=]s//, strs, DIR /'*be near, be close to, be beside, be next to*'/, (<**s=**> *stative,* R5= *resultative*), (<**í-ablaut**> *durative*), phonology: reduplication, metathesis, syntactic analysis: preposition/prepositional verb, attested by AC, EB, Elders Group, IHTTC, BJ (5/10/64), other sources: ES /stətɛ́·s/ *near*, example: <**líye chòkw te lálems q'a líye stetís?**>, //lí-ə cák^{w} tə lɛ́ləm-s **q'**ɛ lí-ə s=C_1ə=tə[=Aí=]s//, /'*Is his house far or is it nearby?*'/, attested by AC, <**stetís te t'ómel.**>, //s=C_1ə=tə[=Aí=]s tə **t'**áməl//, /'*(It's/He's/She's) near the wall.*'/, attested by AC, <**stetís yithá.**>, //s=C_1ə=tə[=Aí=]s yə=**θ**ɛ́//, /'*She's close to them., She's near them.*'/, attested by AC, <**stetís tl'alőwe. ~ stetís tl'lőwe.**>, //s=C_1ə=tə[=Aí=]s ƛ'ɛ=lə́wə//, /'*She's close to you., She's near you.*'/, phonology: the first pronunciation is at slow tempo, the second is at normal speed, attested by AC, <**stetís (tl'elhlímelh, tl'a'á'eltha, tl'alhwélep).**>, //s=C_1ə=tə[=Aí=]s (ƛ'ɛ=ɬlíməɬ,ƛ'ɛ=C_1ɛ́=ʔɛlθɛ,ƛ'ɛ=ɬw=ə́ləp)//, /'*She close to (us, me, you folks)., She's near (us, me, you folks).*'/, attested by AC (8/25/70), <**á**'altha stetís taléwe.>, //C_1ɛ́=ʔɛlθɛ s=C_1ə=tə[=Aí=]s tɛ=lə́wə (orƛ'ɛ=lə́wə ?)//, /'*I'm next to you.*'/, attested by Elders Group (7/9/75), <**lhx̱eyléxlha stetís te skw'echóstel.**>, //ɬx̣=í·l=əx^{y}-ɬɛ s=C_1ə=tə[=Aí=]s tə s=k'^{w}əc=ás=təl//, /'*Stand near the*

window.'/, attested by IHTTC.

<**stetisthóx ~ stetísthó:x**>, df //s=C_1ə=tə[=Aí=]s=(s)T-áx^y//, if, DIR ['*(be) near me*'], possibly <**=st**> *causative control transitivizer* or (less likely semantically) <**=t**> *purposeful control transitivizer*, (<**-óx**> *me, first person object*), phonology: reduplication, ablaut, syntactic analysis: transitive verb, attested by Elders Group (2/19/75, 3/24/76).

<**stetísmels**>, dnom //s=C_1ə=tə[=Aí=]s=məls//, DIR ['*person next to one*'], lx <**=mels**> *part, portion, area*, phonology: reduplication, ablaut, syntactic analysis: nominal, attested by AD (2/16/79), example: <**ptámetlha ta' stetísmels te skwíxs.**>, //ptɛ́m=əT-ɬɛ t-ɛʔ s=C_1ə=tə[=Aí=]s=məls tə s=k^{w}íx^y-s//, /'*Ask the person next to you his name.*'/, literally /'ask s-o -command imperative your nearby part person the his name'/.

<**tesálèqel**>, TCH ['*bump the head*'], *see* tós.

<**teséleqw**>, TCH ['*bumped on the head*'], *see* tós.

<**tesestélemet**>, EFAM ['*feeling sorry for oneself*'], *see* t-sós ~ tesós.

<**tesésthòx**>, TVMO /'*come near me, (sic? for make me get near)*'/, *see* tés.

<**teséthet ~ tséthet**>, TVMO /'*come close, come near, come sit in (with a group)*'/, *see* tés.

<**tesláts**>, TCH ['*touching bottom (of a canoe or a person)*'], *see* tós.

<**téslatstem**>, TCH ['*it got smashed in the back end or rear end*'], *see* tós.

<**téslexw**>, TCH /'*touch s-o accidentally, bump s-o, bumped s-o*'/, *see* tós.

<**testéstexw**>, TCH ['*bump them together*'], *see* tós.

<**tétath**>, possibly root //tə́tɛθ or R4=Aə́=tɛθ//, [tɪ́tɛθ], ANA /'*vein, veins*'/, possibly <**R4=**> *diminutive*, possibly <**é-ablaut on R4**> *plural*, root meaning unknown unless related to títh as in s=títh *be skinny*, phonology: possible reduplication, possible ablaut, syntactic analysis: noun, nominal, attested by Elders Group (7/27/75), Salish cognate: Lushootseed /tətíʔc/ *vein* H76:496.

<**tétemest**>, df //tə́[-C_1ə-]məs=T//, pcs, MUS ['*sing a lullaby to s-o*'], possibly root <**témés**> *velvet*, possibly <**-R1-**> *continuative*, (<**=t**> *purposeful control transitivizer*), phonology: reduplication, syntactic analysis: transitive verb, attested by CT and HT (6/21/76 tape).

<**tetés**>, TVMO /'*approaching, getting near, getting closer*'/, *see* tés.

<**tétesxel**>, df //tə́[=C_1ə=]s=x^{y}əl//, ANA ['*marrow*'], possibly <**=R1=**> meaning uncertain here, lx <**=xel**> *on the leg/foot* lx as in <**slósxel**>, contrast <**slósxel**> *marrow*, phonology: possible reduplication, syntactic analysis: nominal, attested by Deming (3/4/76).

<**tew**>, bound root //təw//, *slope, tilt or backward*

<**tewále**>, possibly root //təwɛ́lə or təw=ɛ́lɛ//, SH /'*sloping floor, (tilted)*'/, possibly <**=ála**> *container of*, syntactic analysis: nominal??, adjective/adjectival verb??, attested by Elders Group (4/2/75), Salish cognate: Squamish /təw-ánʔ/ *tilt (tr.)* W73:268, K69:48 (the suffix is a transitivizer, probably not cognate with Upriver Halkomelem =ále (since =ál is never a transitivizer and =e *animate entity* is unlikely).

<**tewtewá:la ~ tutuwále**>, chrs //təw[=C_1əC_2=](=)ɛ́·lɛ//, LAND /'*side hills, tilted hills, slopes*'/, (<**=R2=**> *characteristic*), phonology: reduplication, syntactic analysis: nominal, attested by SP and AK (Fish Camp 8/2/77), Elders Group (4/2/75).

<**Tewtewá:la ~ Tutuwále**>, df //təw[=C_1əC_2=](=)ɛ́·lɛ ~ təw[=C_1əC_2=](=)ɛ́lə//, PLN ['*side hills or tilted hills northwest of X̱ó:letsa near Yale*'], literally /'tilted hills'/, phonology: reduplication,

syntactic analysis: nominal, attested by SP and AK (Fish Camp 8/2/77), Elders Group (4/2/75), source: place names file reference #122.

<**tewá:let**>, pcs //təw(=)ɛ́·lə=T//, TVMO /*'tilt s-th, lift s-th up at one end or one side, tilt s-th sideways'*/, (<**=t**> *purposeful control transitivizer*), syntactic analysis: transitive verb, attested by EB (4/29/76), example: <**tewá:let te sléxwelh**>, //təw(=)ɛ·lə=T tə s=lə́x^{w}əɬ//, /*'tilt the canoe sideways (to dump out water)'*/, attested by EB.

<**tewélehàm**>, df //təw(=)ɛ́lə(h)=ə[=Aɛ́=]m//, LAND ['*a slope*'], possibly <**á**-ablaut> *durative*, possibly <**=em**> *place to have/get*, phonology: ablaut, epenthetic h, vowel-reduction, downstepping, syntactic analysis: nominal, attested by AD (about 1/79).

<**tewálehélets**>, ds //təw(=)ɛ́ləh=ə́ləc//, ABFC ['*sitting on one cheek of the rump*'], literally /'tilted on the rump'/, lx <**=élets**> *on the bottom, on the rump*, phonology: epenthetic h, syntactic analysis: adjective/adjectival verb, attested by AD (about 1/79).

<**tewálehílép**>, ds //təw(=)ɛ́ləh=ílə́p//, LAND ['*sloping ground*'], lx <**=ílép ~ =ílep**> *ground, dirt*, phonology: epenthetic h, syntactic analysis: nominal, attested by CT (6/8/76), also <**tewàléhilep**>, //təw(=)ɛ́lə[=´=]h=iləp//, attested by Elders Group (4/2/75).

<**stutuwóthel ~ stewtewóthel**>, df //s=təw=C$_1$əC$_2$=áθəl//, WATR ['*"a little below"*'], (<**s=**> *stative or nominalizer*), probably root <**tew**> *tilt or backward*, possibly <**=R2**> *characteristic*, lx <**=óthel**> *in the mouth (of river)*, phonology: reduplication, u-formation from ew, syntactic analysis: adverb/adverbial verb? or nominal?, attested by Elders Group (9/7/77).

<**tewálehélets**>, ABFC ['*sitting on one cheek of the rump*'], *see* tewále.

<**tewálehílép**>, LAND ['*sloping ground*'], *see* tewále.

<**tewá:let**>, TVMO /*'tilt s-th, lift s-th up at one end or one side, tilt s-th sideways'*/, *see* tewále.

<**tewát**>, PRON ['*be who?*'], *see* wát.

<**tewátes**>, PRON /*'somebody, anybody'*/, *see* wát.

<**tewélehàm**>, LAND ['*a slope*'], *see* tewále.

<**tewít**>, free root //təwít//, HUNT /*'expert hunter (who comes back with game every time he hunts), good hunter'*/, compare perhaps <**s=chewót**> *be good at, know how to*?, syntactic analysis: noun, nominal, attested by AD and NP (1/23/80), EB (12/12/75), AC, others, also <**tewì:t**>, //təwì·t//, attested by JL (5/5/75), example: <**le há:we té tewì:t.**>, //lə hɛ́·wə tə təwì·t//, /*'A good hunter (went hunting).'*/, phonology: sentence intonation on article, attested by JL, <**íkw'elò kwses iyóthet te tewít.**>, //ʔí=k'^{w}ə=là k^w-s-əs ʔiyá=T-ət tə təwít//, /*'The expert hunter starts here.'*/, attested by AD and NP (1/23/80).

<**Tewít**>, free root //təwít//, PLN ['*a hunter turned to stone now located below Hemhémetheqw near Hill's Bar on the east bank of the Fraser River*'], ASM ['there is also the sharp spear rock next to it and the dog rock downriver and the elk rock in the river downriver still further, all turned to stone by the Transformer'], literally /'expert hunter'/, syntactic analysis: noun, nominal, attested by Elders on Raft Trip (8/30/77), Elders Group (9/13/77), source: place names file reference #270.

<**tewláts**>, df //təw(=ə)l(=)ɛ́c or tɛ́w(=)l(=)ə[=M2=]c or təw(=)l(=)ə[=Aɛ́=]c//, CAN /*'drifting backwards in two canoes with net between to catch sturgeon, (drift-netting), backing up (of canoe, train)'*/, FSH, possibly root <**taw ~ tew**> *tilt*, possibly <**=el**> *go, come, get, become* and <**=ets**> *on the back*, possibly <**=lets**> *on the bottom* possibly <**metathesis**> *derivational* possibly <**á**-ablaut> *resultative*, phonology: possible metathesis or ablaut, syntactic analysis: intransitive verb, attested by IHTTC.

<**Titáwlechem**>, dmn //C_1í=tɛ́w=əl=əc=əm or C_1í=tɛ́w=ləc=əm//, PLN [*'slough where people used to drift-net by Martin Harris's place at Seabird Island'*], ASM ['people used to driftnet for sturgeon there when the slough was the main river (Martin Harris's place is like an island now)'], literally /'place to have/get a little driftnetting'/, (<**R4=**> *diminutive*, <=**em**> *place to have or get*), phonology: reduplication, syntactic analysis: nominal, attested by LJ via IHTTC (8/15/77), source: place names file reference #193.

<**tewtewá:la ~ tutuwále**>, LAND /*'side hills, tilted hills, slopes'*/, *see* tewále.

<**Tewtewá:la ~ Tutuwále**>, PLN [*'side hills or tilted hills northwest of X̱ó:letsa near Yale'*], *see* tewále.

<**tex**>, bound root //təx^{y} perhaps *insert comb between*//.

<**texqéylem**>, mdls //təx^{y}=qəl=í·l=əm//, PE /*'comb one's hair, comb one's own hair'*/, lx <**=qel**> *in the head*, (<**=í:l**> *go, come, get, become*, <**=em**> *middle voice*), phonology: syllable-loss of el before =í:l, syntactic analysis: intransitive verb, attested by Elders Group, EB, also <**texqéylém**>, //təx^{y}=qəl=í·l=əm//, phonology: updrifting optional, attested by EB, AD, example: <**tsel texqéylem.**>, //c-əl təx^{y}=qəl=í·l=əm//, /*'I combed my hair.'*/, attested by EB, <**texqéylémlha ta' máqel**>, //təx^{y}=qəl=í·l=əm-ɬɛ t-ɛʔ mɛ́=qəl//, /*'Comb your hair.'*/, attested by AD (Lesson 16, 8/80).

<**texqé:ylt**>, pcs //təx^{y}=qəl=í·l=T//, PE [*'comb s-o's hair'*], (<**=t**> *purposeful control transitivizer*), phonology: syllable-loss, syntactic analysis: transitive verb, attested by EB, example: <**texqé:yltlha ta'a sqá:q.**>, //təx^{y}=qəl=í·l=T-ɬɛ t-ɛʔɛ s=qɛ́·q//, /*'Comb your (younger) sister's hair.'*/, attested by EB (1/16/76).

<**téxelqéylem**>, cts //tə[-´-]x^{y}=əlqəl=í·l=əm//, [tɪ́x^{y}ɪlqéyləm], PE [*'combing one's hair'*], (<-´-> *continuative*), lx <**=alqel ~ =elqel**> *hair, wool*, (<**=í:l**> *go, come, get, become*, <**=em**> *middle voice*), phonology: stress-shift, syllable-loss of el before =í:l, syntactic analysis: intransitive verb, attested by Elders Group (3/8/78); found in <**téxelqéylem.**>, //tə[-´-]x^{y}=əlqəl=í·l=əm//, /*'She's combing her hair.'*/, example: <**líchxw téxelqéylem?**>, //lí-c-x^{w} tə[-´-]x^{y}=əlqəl=í·l=əm//, /*'Are you combing your hair?'*/, <**ílhtsel téxelqéylem.**>, //ʔí-ɬ-c-əl tə[-´-]x^{y}=əlqəl=í·l=əm//, /*'I was combing my hair.'*/.

<**téxelqèylt**>, pcs //tə[-´-]x^{y}=əlqəl=í·l=T//, WV /*'card wool, comb s-th, (carding/combing s-th (wool/hair))'*/, (semological comment: probably should be translated continuative), lx <**=elqel**> *wool, hair*, possibly <-´-> *continuative or less likely derivational?*, (<**=í:l**> *go, come, get, become*, <**=t**> *purposeful control transitivizer*), phonology: possible stress-shift, syllable-loss, downstepping, syntactic analysis: transitive verb, attested by Elders Group (3/24/76).

<**shxwtéxelqèyls**>, dnom //sx^{w}=tə[=´=]x^{y}=əlq(əl)=í·l=(əl)s//, [šx^{w}tɪ́x^{y}ɪlqèyls], WV [*'a carder (for carding wool)'*], literally /'something for combing/carding wool/hair as a structured activity'/, (<**shxw=**> *something for*), (<=´=> *continuative*), lx <**=els**> *structured activity continuative*, phonology: stress-shift, syllable-loss of el before and after =í:l, syntactic analysis: nominal, attested by Elders Group (3/24/76).

<**téxelqéylem**>, PE [*'combing one's hair'*], *see* tex.

<**téxelqèylt**>, WV /*'card wool, comb s-th, (carding/combing s-th (wool/hair))'*/, *see* tex.

<**texqéylem**>, PE /*'comb one's hair, comb one's own hair'*/, *see* tex.

<**texqé:ylt**>, PE [*'comb s-o's hair'*], *see* tex.

<**texw=**>, da //təx^{w}=//, KIN [*'step-'*], DIR, TIME [*'mid-'*], syntactic analysis: derivational prefix, lexical affix; found in <**texwméle ~ texwmélem**>, //təx^{w}mélə(m)//, /*'stepchild'*/, <**texwmámele**>, //təx^{w}=mɛ́mələ//, /*'step-children'*/, <**texwmelám**>, //təx^{w}=məlɛ́=m//, /*'adopt a child'*/, <**texwswá:yel**

~ **téxwswàyèl**>, //təxʷ=swɛ́·yəl//, /'*noon, mid-day*'/, <**téxwslá:t**>, //tə́xʷ=slɛ́·t//, /'*midnight*'/, <**téxw=xwthelh or t=éxwthelh**>, //tə́xʷθəɬ//, /'*tongue*'/, comment: alternate analysis to t= empty root + =éxwthelh *on the tongue.*

<**téxwem**>, izs //tə́xʷ=əm//, ABF /'*to beat (of the heart)*'/, ABDF ['*(have/get) throbbing pain*'], (<**=em**> *intranstivizer, have, get*), syntactic analysis: intransitive verb, attested by BHTTC.

<**stíxwem**>, dnom //s=tíxʷ(=)əm or s=tə[=Aí=]xʷ(=)əm//, EZ /'*willow grouse (a local name for ruffed grouse), ruffed grouse*'/, ['*Bonasa umbellus sabini*'], Elder's comment: "so mamed because of their "pum-pum-pum" call", (<**s=**> *nominalizer*), root <**téxwem**> *to beat (of the heart)*, possibly <**í-ablaut**> *derivational*?, possibly <**=em**> *middle voice*, phonology: possible ablaut, syntactic analysis: nominal, attested by EL (9/27/77).

<**Títxwemqsel**>, df //tí[=C_1əC_2=]xʷ(=)əm=qsəl//, PLN /'*Wilson's Point (on Harrison River), (also called) Grouse Point*'/, ASM ['a point on the downriver end of Lhá:lt, so named because willow grouse or ruffed grouse abound here'], possibly <**=R2=**> *diminutive or derivational*, lx <**=qsel**> *point (of land, etc.)*, phonology: reduplication, syntactic analysis: nominal, attested by EL (9/27/77, 3/1/78).

<**texwmámelem**>, KIN ['*step-children*'], *see* méle ~ mél:a.

<**texwmélem**>, KIN ['*step-child*'], *see* méle ~ mél:a.

<**téxwswàyel ~ texwswàyèl ~ texwswáyél**>, TIME /'*midday, noon*'/, *see* wáyel.

<**téxwthelh**>, df //t=əxʷ**θəɬ** or tə́xʷ=**əθ**əl=D//, ANA ['*tongue*'], possibly root <**t=**> meaning unknown or empty or téxw(=) ~ **téx̱**w(=)> *mid-, middle,later*, lx <**=éxwthelh**> *on the tongue* or lx <**=(e)thel**> *in the mouth*, possibly <**=D (devoicing)**> *derivational*, phonology: possible devoicing, syntactic analysis: nominal, attested by AC, BJ (5/10/64), EB, others, other sources: ES and JH /tə́xʷ**θ**əɬ/ *tongue*, H-T <tõqtcitl> *tongue*, example: <**kw'ás te téxwthelh**>, //k'ʷɛ́s tə t(=)ə́xʷ(=)**θ**əɬ//, /'*burn the tongue*'/, attested by EB.

<**tex̱**>, bound root //təx̣ *stretch out, extend*//.

<**tex̱eláx̱el**>, ds //təx̣=əlɛ́x̣əl//, ABFC /'*stretch out the wings, stretch out the arm(s)*'/, lx <**=eláx̱el**> *on the arm, on the wing*, syntactic analysis: intransitive verb, attested by IHTTC.

<**tex̱eláx̱elem**>, mdls //təx̣=əlɛ́x̣əl=əm//, ABFC /'*hold both arms (or wings) outstretched, (stretch out one's arms/wings)*'/, (<**=em**> *middle voice*), syntactic analysis: intransitive verb, attested by IHTTC (9/1/77).

<**tx̱ét**>, pcs //tə́x̣=M1=T//, SH ['*stretch it (stretch out someone's arms or wings)*'], possibly <**metathesis**> *non-continuative*, (<**=t**> *purposeful control transitivizer*), phonology: possible stressed transitivizer or metathesis, syntactic analysis: transitive verb, attested by IHTTC (9/1/77), EB (6/7/78), Salish cognate: Lushootseed /təx̣/ as in /s-tə-tx̣-əb-šád/ *toes spread out* and /ʔəs-təx̣-t(ə)x̣-áb-šəd/ *chapped feet* (where the skin is characteristically spread beyond its normal bounds) H76:497.

<**xwtóx̱esem**>, df //xʷ=tə́[=Aá=]x̣=əs=əm//, mdls, ANAH ['*shading one's eyes from the sun with the hand (looking into the sun)*'], WETH, probably <**xw=**> meaning uncertain (used with suffixes of face and head), probably root <**téx̱**> *straighten out, extend, stretch out*, <**á-ablaut**> durative, lx <**=es**> *on the face*, (<**=em**> *middle voice*), lit. /'extend for a long time on one's face '/, phonology: á-ablaut changed automatically to ó before <**=es**> *on the face*, syntactic analysis: intransitive verb, attested by SP or AK or AD (Raft trip 8/30/77).

<**tex̱eláx̱el**>, ABFC /'*stretch out the wings, stretch out the arm(s)*'/, *see* tex̱.

<**tex̲elάx̲elem**>, ABFC */'hold both arms (or wings) outstretched, (stretch out one's arms/wings)'/*, *see* tex̲.

<**téx̲w**>, free root //tə́x̣ʷ//, TIME */'later, after a while, later on, wait a while; mid-'/*, syntactic analysis: adverb/adverbial verb, attested by Elders Group (10/6/76), EB (3/11/76, 1/9/76), RP and EB (2/12/76), DM (12/4/64?), BJ (5/10/64?), ASM ['later, after a while']; found in <**téx̲wcha.**>, //tə́x̣ʷ-cɛ//, */'(It will be) later on, after a while., Wait a while.'/*, attested by Elders Group, EB, <**téx̲wchàp.**>, //tə́x̣ʷ-c-ɛp//, */'You people wait.'/*, literally /'be after a while, you folks'/, attested by EB, example: <**téx̲wchelcha là:m.**>, //tə́x̣ʷ-c-əl-cɛ lɛ́=(ə)m//, */'I'll go later.'/*, literally /'I will later go'/, attested by EB, <**téx̲wchelcha hó:yt te thá.**>, //tə́x̣ʷ-c-əl-cɛ há·y=T tə θɛ́//, */'I'll finish that later.'/*, literally /'I will later finish it the that'/, attested by EB, <**téx̲wchelcha kw'etslóme.**>, //tə́x̣ʷ-c-əl-cɛ k'ʷəc=l-ámə//, */'I'll see you later.'/*, attested by RP and EB (2/12/76), ASM ['mid- (probably lit. *later*)'], <**téx̲w swàyèl**>, //tə́x̣ʷ s=wɛ̀yə̀l//, */'mid-day, noon, noon-time'/*, literally /'later day'/, attested by AC, BJ (5/10/64?), DM (12/4/64?), Salish cognate: Squamish /tə́x̣ʷ skʷáyl/ *noontime* K67:263, <**téx̲w slát**>, //tə́x̣ʷ s=lɛ́t//, */'midnight'/*, literally /'later night'/, attested by AC, DM (12/4/64?).

<**téx̲wets**>, possibly root //tə́x̣ʷəc or possibly tə́x̣=əwəc//, HUNT [*'bow (weapon)'*], possibly root <**téx̲**> *stretch out, extend*, possibly <**=ewíts ~ =ewets ~ =íts ~ =ets**> *on the back*, phonology: possible consonant merger (**x̲** + w > **x̲**w), syntactic analysis: nominal, attested by AC, DM (12/4/64), Elders Group, TG, JL and his grandmother MJ, other sources: ES /tə́x̣ʷá·c/ *bow*, JH /tə́x̣ʷec/ *bow (weapon)*, Salish cognate: Squamish /tə́x̣ʷaʔč/ *bow (for shooting)* W73:42, K67:263, also <**tőx̲wets**>, //tə́x̣ʷəc//, attested by BJ (5/10/64), also <**téx̲wots**>, //tə́x̣ʷac//, attested by DM (12/4/64), example: <**sékwelàxs te téx̲wets**>, //s[=ə́=]=kʷəl=ə[=Aɛ́=]xʸ-s tə tə́x̣ʷəc//, */'arrow of a bow'/*, attested by JL and his grandmother MJ (Elders Group).

<**téx̲wetselhp**>, ds //tə́x̣ʷəc=əɬp or tə́x̣=wəc=əɬp//, EB */'yew tree, Pacific yew'/*, [*'Taxus brevifolia'*], ASM ['wood used for bows'], literally /'bow tree'/, lx <**=elhp**> *tree, plant*, syntactic analysis: nominal, attested by AC, BJ (12/5/64), Elders Group, other sources: ES /páxʸələqʷ ~ tə́x̣ʷacəɬp/ *yellow cedar*.

<**téx̲wetselhp**>, EB */'yew tree, Pacific yew'/*, *see* téx̲wets.

<**té:yqxálem**>, ABFC [*'taking a step'*], *see* tiqxálém ~ tiyqxálém.

<**te'íle ~ te'í:le**>, DIR */'this (speaker is holding it), this one, this thing here'/*, *see* í.

<**tí**>, free or bound root //tí//, meaning probably *over there, yonder*

<**lí(:) tí or lí(:)tí**>, df //lí(·) tí or lí(·)=tí or lí=y tí(y)//, DIR */'(be) over there, (be) yonder'/*, possibly root <**lí**> *(be) there*, phonology: usually said with word-boundary between the syllables, length is optional (usually heard with help of high falling pitch allotone), syntactic analysis: adverb/adverbial verb, dem, attested by AC, EB, MJ, ME, others, Salish cognate: perhaps in part Lushootseed /túdiʔ/ *over there* H76:507, example: <**le lí(:) tí.**>, //lə lí(·) tí//, */'It's over there.'/*, attested by AC, <**te lí(:) tí**>, //tə lí(·) tí//, */'that's the one, that one'/*, literally /'the one that's over there, that which is over there'/, attested by AC, <**lí tí te sts'áletstel.**>, //lí(:) tí tə s=cɛ́=ləc=təl//, */'The chair is over there.'/*, attested by AC (10/23/71), <**stám te lí tí ts'íts'esem?**>, //s=tɛ́m tə lí tí **c**'í[-C$_1$ə-]s=əm//, */'What is that (over there) growing?'/*, attested by AC (11/17/71), <**t(e) thá lí tí**>, //tə θɛ́ lí tí//, */'that thing yonder'/*, attested by EB (1/9/76).

<**tí**>, free root //tí//, FOOD [*'tea'*], ACL, syntactic analysis: noun, nominal, attested by EB, many others, borrowed from English or Chinook Jargon, both /tí/ <tea> Johnson 1978:434, example: <**axwethóxchexw kw' tí.**>, //ʔɛxʷ=əT-áxʸ-c-əxʷ k'ʷə tí//, */'Give me some tea.'/*, attested by EB.

<**tí'àlà**>, ds //tí=ʔɛ̀lɛ̀//, PE [*'teapot'*], HHG, ACL, literally /'container for tea, container of tea'/, lx

<**='àlà**> *container for, container of*, syntactic analysis: nominal, attested by Deming (at Fort Langley museum 3/9/78), also <**stí'àlà**>, //s=tí=ʔɛ̀lɛ̀//, attested by AD, example: <**alétsa te stí'àlà?**>, //ʔɛlə́cɛ tə s=tí=ʔɛ̀lɛ̀//, /'*Where's the tea-pot?*'/, attested by AD (8/80).

<**tí:lt**>, pcs //tí·l=T//, HARV ['*clear it (of land)*'], HHG /'*clean it (of table, land, etc.)*'/, (<**=t**> *purposeful control transitivizer*), syntactic analysis: transitive verb, attested by Elders Group (6/16/76), CT (1973 story), example: <**tí:lt te letá:m**>, //tí·l=T tə lətɛ́·m//, /'*clear the table*'/, attested by Elders Group.

<**tí:lthet**>, pcrs //tí·l=T-ət or tí·l=θət//, HARV ['*to clear land*'], (<**-et**> *reflexive* or), (<**=thet**> *get, become*), syntactic analysis: intransitive verb, attested by Elders Group, EB.

<**tí:ltel**>, free root //tí·ltəl//, MUS ['*to ring a bell*'], syntactic analysis: intransitive verb, attested by EB, Elders Group, NP, borrowed from Chinook Jargon /tíntin/ <tin-tin> *bell, music, musical instrument, hour* itself from English <ding-ding> or onomatopoetic Johnson 1978:268-269, example: <**la ts'ímel kws tí:tels.**>, //lɛ c'íməl kʷ-s tí·ltəl-s//, /'*The bell is going to ring.*'/, literally /'going to nearly that it ring a bell -3rd person subj.'/, attested by Elders Group (3/14/79).

<**tíltel mál**>, cpds //tíltəl mɛ́l//, REL ['*bellringer*'], literally /'ring a bell father'/, syntactic analysis: simple nominal phrase, attested by Elders Group (1/7/76).

<**tíltel mál**>, REL ['*bellringer*'], *see* tí:ltel.

<**tí:lthet**>, HARV ['*to clear land*'], *see* tí:lt.

<**tímet**>, pcs //tím=əT//, QUAL ['*do it harder*'], ABFC, (<**=et**> *purposeful control transitivizer*), syntactic analysis: transitive verb, attested by AC, EB, Salish cognate: Squamish /tím-it/ *perform with all one's might (tr.)* as in /... q n ʔat tímit ta sʔísun-čət/ *...when we paddle with all our might* and also /tímicut/ *exert oneself (as hard as one can)* W73:196, K67:266, Lushootseed /tíb/ *strong, hard* as in /tíb tə dsu-yáyus/ *I work hard* and /tíbicut/ *try hard (to do something physical), Try your best (what is said to someone who is trying to lift something very heavy)* and /stíbtib/ *strong person* H76:499.

<**tíméthet**>, pcrs //tím=ə[=´=]T-ət//, ABFC /'*exert oneself, make a big effort, do with all one's might, [do] as hard as possible, do it harder (used if already paddling for ex.)*'/, (<**-et**> *reflexive*), possibly <=´=> *derivational*, phonology: possible stress-shift, syntactic analysis: intransitive verb, attested by AC, AD (12/18/78), Elders Group (1/30/80), EB (4/26/76), Deming (3/31/77), example: <**timéthet te spehá:ls.**>, //tim=ə[=´=]T-ət tə s=pəh=ɛ́·ls//, /'*The wind is hard.*'/, literally /'exerts itself as hard as possible the wind'/, attested by Deming (3/31/77).

<**tíméthet**>, ABFC /'*exert oneself, make a big effort, do with all one's might, [do] as hard as possible, do it harder (used if already paddling for ex.)*'/, *see* tímet.

<**tiq**>, bound root //tiq// *take in motion*.

<**stiqíw ~ stiqí:w**>, df //s=tiq=íw ~ s=tiq=í·w//, [stiqí(·)w ~ stiqé(·)w], EZ ['*horse*'], ['*Equus caballus*'], (<**s=**> *nominalizer*), prob. connected with root <**tiq**> in <**tiqxálém**> (/tiq=xʸə[=Aɛ́=]l=əm/) *take a step* (where =xál=ém means *on one's leg/foot*), lx. <**=á:w ~ =í:w ~ =ew ~ =ú:w**> *on the body, on top of itself*, thus horse is literally /"something that takes a body in motion" or "something that takes in motion on top of itself"/, syntactic analysis: nominal, attested by AC, EB, others, other sources: H-T <stEkéyu> (macrons over e and u) *horse (Equus sp.)(introduced since the advent of whites)*, also <**steqíw**>, //s=təqíw//, [stəqíw ~ stɪqíw], attested by AC, Elders Group (3/1/72), also <**stiqí:w ~ steqí:w ~ stiqíw**>, //s=tiqí·w ~ s=təqí·w ~ s=tiqíw//, attested by EB, example: <**x̲wéylems te stiqíw**>, //x̌ʷí·ləm-s tə s=tiqíw//, /'*the horse's rope*'/, literally /'rope of the horse'/, attested by AC, <**qéx̲ steqíw**>, //qə́x̌ s=təqíw//, /'*a lot of horses.*'/, attested by AC, <**qéx̲ ti stiqíw.**>, //qə́x̌ tə yi-s=tiqíw//, /'*There's lots of horses.*'/, attested by AC, <**qéx̲ ta stiqíw.**>, //qə́x̌ t-ɛ s=tiqíw//, /'*There's a*

lot of horses (all belonging to you)., (You have a lot of horses.)'/, attested by AC, <**xwel sts'ets'á te stiqí:w.**>, //xʷəl s=C_1ə=**c'**ɛ́ tə s=tiqí·w//, /*'He's still astride the horse.'*/, attested by EB (3/1/76), <**tsel me sts'ets'á te steqí:w.**>, //c-əl mə s=C_1ə=**c'**ɛ́ tə s=təqí·w//, /*'I rode the horse.'*/, attested by EB, <**sts'ets'á te stiqí:w**>, //s=C_1ə=**c'**ɛ́ tə s=tiqí·w//, /*'ride a horse'*/, attested by EB, <**léts'e stiqíw**>, //lə́c'ə s=tiqíw//, /*'one horse'*/, attested by EB.

<**stiteqíw**>, dmn //s=ti[=C_1ə=]qíw//, EZ [*'little horse'*], (<**=R1=**> *diminutive*), phonology: reduplication, syntactic analysis: nominal, attested by Deming (6/15/77).

<**steqiwó:llh**>, ds //s=təqiw=á·ɬ//, EZ [*'baby horse'*], lx <**=ó:llh**> *young, offspring*, syntactic analysis: nominal, attested by AC.

<**statiqíwò:llh**>, dmn //s=C_1ɛ=tiqíw=**à**·ɬ//, EZ [*'colt'*], (<**R8=**> *diminutive*), lx <**=ó:llh**> *young, offspring*, phonology: downstepping, reduplication, syntactic analysis: nominal, attested by HT and CT (6/8/76).

<**steliqíw**>, pln //s=t[=əl=]iqíw//, EZ [*'herd of horses'*], (<**=el=**> *plural (collective)*), phonology: infixed plural, syntactic analysis: nominal, attested by AC, example: <**qé<u>x</u> ti steliqíw**>, //qə́x̣ tə yi-s=t[=əl=]iqíw//, /*'a lot of horses, herd of horses'*/, attested by AC.

<**tiqxálém ~ tiyqxálém**>, mdls //təyq=xʸɛ́l=əm//, ABFC [*'take one step'*], root meaning unknown, lx <**=xál ~ =xel**> *on the foot*, (<**=em**> *middle voice*), phonology: weak root and stressed suffix gets á-vowel, syntactic analysis: intransitive verb, attested by EB, AD.

<**té:yqxálem**>, cts //tə[-Aɛ́·-]yq=xʸɛ́l=əm or tə[-´·-]yq=xʸɛ́l=əm//, ABFC [*'taking a step'*], (<**-´:- or á:-ablaut**> *continuative*), phonology: lengthening and stress-shift or less likely ablaut, syntactic analysis: intransitive verb, attested by AD.

<**tíqw'**>, bound root //tíq'ʷ//, meaning uncertain

<**stíqw'teqw'**>, chrs //s=tíq'ʷ=C_1əC_2//, dnom, BLDG /*'beams (of longhouse, all of them), houseposts'*/, <**s=**> *nominalizer*, <**=R2**> *characteristic aspect*, attested by RG & EH (4/10/99 Ling332).

<**Titáwlechem**>, PLN [*'slough where people used to drift-net by Martin Harris's place at Seabird Island'*], *see* tewláts.

<**títemí:lt**>, FOOD [*'cooling it (of food)'*], *see* temí:lt.

<**titemí:lthet**>, FOOD [*'cooling off (of food)'*], *see* temí:lt.

<**títexem**>, TCH [*'slimy'*], *see* tíxem.

<**títe<u>x</u>el or tíyte<u>x</u>el**>, DIR /*'upriver, up that way, (way upriver [RP, EB])'*/, *see* tiyt.

<**títe<u>x</u>em**>, df //tí[=C_1əC_2=]x̣=əm//, TAST [*'bitter'*], possibly <**=R2=**> *resultative*, possibly <**=em**> *middle voice or intransitivizer*, compare <**tsítse<u>x</u>em ~ chíche<u>x</u>em**> *bitter*, comment: could títe<u>x</u>em be mistranscribed for tsítse<u>x</u>em?, phonology: reduplication, syntactic analysis: adjective/adjectival verb, attested by EB (5/28/76).

<**titím**> or <**tiytím**>, possible stem //tiyt=ím//

<**xwtitím or xwtiytím**>, df //xʷ=tiyt=ím//, WATR /*'eddy water (where you set nets), [to eddy repeatedly?]'*/, (<**xw=**> *always*), possibly root <**tiyt**> *upriver*, or <**tiy**> *back, against*, lx <**=ím**> *repeatedly*, syntactic analysis: intransitive verb?, nominal?.

<**títiye<u>x</u>w**>, EFAM [*'carried away'*], *see* tíye<u>x</u>w.

<**titómelest**>, us //titáməlǝst//, SD [*'(make a) rumbling noise'*], possibly root <**tím**> *do it harder?*, syntactic analysis: intransitive verb, attested by Elders Group (about 7/2/75).

<**Títxwemqsel**>, PLN /'*Wilson's Point (on Harrison River), (also called) Grouse Point*'/, *see* stíxwem.

<**títh ~ tí:th**>, bound root //tí**θ** ~ tí·θ//.

<**stíth ~ stí:th**>, stvi //s=tí**θ** ~ s=tí·θ//, DESC /'*be skinny, be thin*'/, ABDF, (<**s=**> *stative*), syntactic analysis: adjective/adjectival verb, attested by AC, example: <**stíth mestíyexw**>, //s=tí**θ** məstíyəx^w//, /'*skinny person*'/, <**stí:th, westh'ò:m el.**>, //s=tí·θ, wə-s=**θ'à·**m ʔəl//, /'*He's skinny, all bones/boney.*'/, literally /'(he/she/it) is skinny when/if bone just'/.

<**chtíth**>, ds //c=tí**θ**//, DESC ['*be skinny*'], ABDF, (<**ch=**> *have, get*), syntactic analysis: adjective/adjectival verb, attested by EB, example: <**chtíth the Málí.**>, //c=tí**θ θ**ə mɛ́lí//, /'*Mary is skinny.*'/.

<**títhel**>, incs //tí**θ**=əl//, ABDF ['*get skinny*'], lx <**=el**> *get, become, go, come*, syntactic analysis: intransitive verb, attested by EB, example: <**me títhel**>, //mə tí**θ**=əl//, /'*getting skinny*'/, literally /'start to get skinny'/.

<**stí:tethel**>, df //s=tí·[=C_1əC_2=]**θ**=əl or s=C_1í=ti**θ**=əl or s=tí·[-C_1əC_2-]**θ**=əl//, ABDF ['*(be) puny*'], DESC, (<**s=**> *stative*), possibly <**=R2= or R2=**> *diminutive* or possibly <**-R2-**> *resultative*, phonology: length retained even before reduplication, syntactic analysis: adjective/adjectival verb, attested by AC.

<**títhel**>, ABDF ['*get skinny*'], *see* títh ~ tí:th.

<**tí:wel**>, prob. free form //tí·wəl//, *uncle's wife's sister's/brother's child (male), aunt's husband's sister's/brother's child (male)* if H-T 1902 <téwEl> (macron over e) is right or merely *nephew, niece, sibling's child (child of sister or brother or cousin (up to and including fourth cousin)* as below.

<**stí:wel**>, dnom //s=tí·wəl//, KIN /'*nephew, niece, sibling's child (child of sister or brother or cousin (up to and including fourth cousin) [Elders Group])*'/, (<**s=**> *nominalizer*), syntactic analysis: nominal, attested by AC, also <**stí:wél**>, //s=tí·wə́l//, also /'*child of sister/brother/cousin (up to and including fourth cousin)*'/, attested by Elders Group, other sources: ES /stí·wəl/ *sibling's child*, H-T 1902 <téwEl> (macron over e) *uncle's wife's sister's/brother's child (male), aunt's husband's sister's/brother's child (male)'*, <stétwEl> (macron over e) *uncle's wife's sister's/brother's child (feminine), aunt's husband's sister's/brother's child (feminine)'*, <stEtéwEl> (macron over e) *uncle's wife's sister's/brother's children (collective), aunt's husband's sister's/brother's children (collective)'*, example: <**a stí:wel**>, //ʔɛ s=tí·wəl//, /'*your niece/nephew*'/, attested by AC.

<**statí:wel**>, pln //s=C_1ɛ=tí·wəl or s=C_1ɛ-tí·wəl//, KIN /'*nephews, nieces, sibling's children*'/, (<**R8= or R8-**> *plural*), phonology: reduplication, syntactic analysis: nominal, attested by AC, other sources: H-T 1902 <stEtéwEl> (macron over e) *uncle's wife's sister's/brother's children (collective), aunt's husband's sister's/brother's children (collective)*.

<**tíxem**>, stem //tíx^y=əm *get slime*//.

<**títexem**>, rsls //tí[=C_1ə=]x^y=əm//, TCH ['*slimy*'], (<**=R1=**> *resultative*), probably <**=em**> *intransitivizer or middle*, phonology: reduplication, syntactic analysis: adjective/adjectival verb, attested by Elders Group, BHTTC.

<**stíxem**>, dnom //s=tíx^y=əm//, ANA /'*fish slime, slime (of any kind, from fish, algae, etc.)*'/, EB /'*green pond slime or river slime, algae*'/, ['*Spirogyra spp.*'], probably <**=em**> *intransitivizer or middle*, syntactic analysis: nominal, attested by Elders Group, Deming, example: <**stíxems te stótelō**>, //s=tíx^y=əm-s tə s=tá[=C_1əC_2=]lo//, /'*slime of a creek*'/, attested by Deming (5/24/79).

<**tíx̱**>, bound root //tíx̣//, *bushy*

<**stíx̱eqw ~ stí:x̱eqw**>, df //s=tíx̣=əq^w ~ s=tí·x̣=əq^w//, ANA ['*bushy hair*'], (<**s=**> *stative or nominalizer*), root meaning unknown, lx <**=eqw**> *on top of the head, in the hair*, syntactic analysis:

adjective/adjectival verb?, nominal?, attested by Deming (3/4/76, 4/26/79), Salish cognate: Ld. /əs-tíq(=)il/ *bushy* (Hess:1976:502).

<**tiy**>, bound root //tiy *against*//.

<**xwtíyches**>, df //x^w(ə)=tíy=cəs//, SOC [*'fight back'*], probably <**xw(e)=**> *become*, lx <**=ches ~ =tses**> *on the hand*, syntactic analysis: intransitive verb, attested by BHTTC.

<**xwtí:chest ~ xwtí(:)ychest**>, pcs //x^w=tíy=cəs=T or x^w=tí[=·=]y=cəs=T//, SOC [*'got even with s-o'*], (<**=t**> *purposeful control transitivizer*), possibly <**=:=**> *durative or resultative*?, phonology: possible lengthening, syntactic analysis: transitive verb, attested by Elders Group (4/28/7); found in <**xwtí:chesthométsel.**>, //x^w=tí(·)y=cəs=T-ámə-c-əl//, /*'I got even with you.'*/, phonology: automatic stress-shift.

<**tiyó:les**>, df //tiy=á·ləs//, DIR [*'leaning'*], comment: the suffix or suffixes are not clear in form or meaning here, <**=ó:les**> *on the eye(s), in the eye(s), on the eyelid(s)* is unlikely, but root seems to be <**tiy**> *against*, syntactic analysis: transitive verb or adjective/adjectival verb?, attested by EB (4/23/76), Salish cognate: Saanich dial. of NSt. /tə**č**á**l**əst/ *lean something against something* (B74a:67).

<**tiyélést**>, pcs //tiy=əl=əs=T or tiy=ə́lə́s=T//, DIR [*'lean s-th against something'*], comment: =el *go, come, get, become* and =es *on the face* are semantically possible but tiyó:les *leaning* makes that analysis seem unlikely, (=**élés** *on the teeth* is very unlikely semantically but fits phonologically), (<**=t**> *purposeful control transitivizer*), syntactic analysis: transitive verb, attested by EB, example: <**tiyéléstchexw ta' q'éwe xwelám te t'ómél.**>, //tiy=ə́lə́s=T-c-əx^w t-ɛʔ **q'**ə́wə x^wə(=)lɛ́=m tə **t'**ámə́l//, /*'Lean your cane against (toward) the wall.'*/, attested by EB.

<**xwetiyéqel**>, ds //x^wə=tiy=ə́qəl//, LANG /*'answer, reply, (answer back [BHTTC])'*/, (<**xwe=**> *become*), lx <**=éqel**> *in the throat, in speech*, syntactic analysis: intransitive verb, attested by AC, Elders Group (1/25/78), also <**xwtíyéqel**>, //x^wə=tíy=ə́qəl//, also /*'answer back'*/, attested by BHTTC, Salish cognate: Lushootseed has the same root with the suffix for *mouth; language* instead, /təj-úcid/ [tədzúcid] *answer* (H76:488).

<**xwetá:yeqel**>, cts //x^wə=ti[-Aɛ́·-]y=əqəl//, LANG /*'answering, replying, answering back'*/, (<**á:**-ablaut> *continuative*), phonology: ablaut, syntactic analysis: intransitive verb, attested by Elders Group (1/25/78, 4/26/78), also <**xwtatíyeqel**>, //x^wə=C_1ɛ-tíy=əqəl//, dialects: *some Cheh.*, attested by EB, example: <**wiyóth kws xwtatíyeqels.**>, //wə=yáθ k^w-s x^wə=C_1ɛ-tíy=əqəl-s//, /*'He's always answering back.'*/, attested by EB.

<**lexwtitityeqel or lexwtitiytíyeqel**>, chrs //lə(=)x^w=C_1í=C_1əC_2=tíy=əqəl//, LANG [*'a person always answering back'*], (<**lexw=**> *always*, R4= *continuative or diminutive*?, R3= *characteristic*), phonology: double reduplication, comment: compare dispositional progressives or diminutives in Suttles ca 1984 (p.7-142 and preceding) Musqueam Grammar, syntactic analysis: nominal, intransitive verb, attested by BHTTC.

<**tiyélést**>, DIR [*'lean s-th against something'*], *see* tiy.

<**tíyexw**>, uf //tíyəx̣^{w}//, EFAM [*'carried away'*], possibly root <**tíy**> *against*, possibly <**=xw**> *around in circles, round*??, syntactic analysis: adjective/adjectival verb, attested by Elders Group (3/2/77), Salish cognate: Squamish /tíʔax̣^{w}/ *get excited, get busy* K69:49.

<**títiyexw**>, rsls //tí[=C_1əC_2=]yəx̣^{w}//, EFAM [*'carried away'*], ASM ['for ex. keeping on walking further than intended, keep doing work in a hurry to finish'], (<**=R2=**> *resultative*), phonology: reduplication, syntactic analysis: adjective/adjectival verb, attested by Elders Group (3/2/77).

<**tiyó:les**>, DIR [*'leaning'*], *see* tiy.

<**tiyt**>, bound root //tiyt *upriver*//.

<**teltíyt**>, tlcs //təl=tíyt//, DIR [*'from upriver'*], LANG [*'Tait dialect of Halkomelem'*], (<**tel=**> *from*), syntactic analysis: adverb/adverbial verb, nominal, attested by AC, others.

<**stiytá<u>x</u>el or stitá<u>x</u>el**>, dnom //s=tiyt=ɛ́x̣əl//, BLDG [*'upper end of house (inside or outside)'*], DIR, literally /'nominal upriver section/side/arm'/, (<**s=**> *nominalizer*), lx <**=á<u>x</u>el**> *section, side, arm*, syntactic analysis: nominal, attested by Elders Group.

<**títe<u>x</u>el or tíyte<u>x</u>el**>, ds //tíyt=əx̣əl//, DIR /*'upriver, up that way, (way upriver [RP, EB])'*/, literally /'upriver section/side'/, lx <**=e<u>x</u>el**> *section, side*, syntactic analysis: adverb/adverbial verb, attested by Elders Group (2/18/76), also /*'way upriver'*/, attested by RP and EB.

<**tiytós or titós**>, possible root or stem //tí(y)tás// or //tíyt=ás// or //C_1í=təs=ás//, root meaning unknown

<**shxwtitós or shxwtiytós**>, df //s(=)x^w=C_1í=təs=ás//, DIR [*'the only safe place to cross a river'*], CAN, (<**sxw=**> *nominalizer, something that's*), possibly <**R4=**> *diminutive*, possibly <**=ós**> *on the face*, probably root <**tés**> *approach, come near*, phonology: syllable-loss of es before =ós, syntactic analysis: nominal, attested by JL and EB (5/12/78).

<**Stitó:s ~ Stitó:s**>, dnom //s=C_1í=təs=á·s//, PLN [*'Promontory Mountain by Vedder Crossing'*], ASM ['used as a look-out point by the Chilliwacks during eras of raiding, one tradition has it that a tower was even built for the person posted there to warn of war canoes coming up the river'], (semological comment: possibly named because it is a place where the mountains get close on the Chilliwack River and one of the best crossings as well as one of the best ambush points for war canoes), (<**s=**> *nominalizer*), possibly <**R4=**> *diminutive*, possibly <**=ó:s**> *on the face*, probably root <**tés**> *approach, come near*, phonology: syllable-loss of es before =ós, syntactic analysis: nominal, attested by AC, source: place names file reference #279, other sources: Wells 1965 (lst ed.) Promontory (at Vedder Crossing), point on Promontory Bluffs.

<**tí'àlà**>, PE [*'teapot'*], *see* tí.

<**tloqá:ys**>, TIME /*'now, this moment, this instant, (right now)'*/, *see* ló and *see* qá:ys.

<**tlówàyèl ~ tlowáyél**>, TIME [*'today'*], *see* ló and *see* wáyel.

<**tlhét ~ tlhát ~ telhét**>, SH /*'spread it out (of blanket, net, book, etc.)'*/, *see* télh.

<**tlhéthet**>, ABFC [*'straighten oneself out'*], *see* télh.

<**-tlh ~ -lh**>, (//**-tɬ ~ -ɬ**//), MOOD [*'coaxing imperative singular'*], syntactic analysis: is, syntactic comment: used mainly with auxiliary verbs, dialects: *AC prefers -lh, EB prefers -tlh*, contrast <**-lhqwe**> *polite imperative*, contrast <**-chexw**> and <**-chap**> *mildly urging imperative*, contrast <**-lha**> and <**-alha**> *command imperative*, also <**-lh**>, //-ɬ//; found in <**mílh kwetxwílem.**>, //mí-ɬ k^wətɛx^w=íl=əm//, /*'Come inside.'*/, <**lalh á:yel.**>, //lɛ-ɬ ʔɛ́·y=əl//, /*'Go away.'*/, attested by AC, also <**lámtlh á:yel.**>, //lɛ́=m-tɬ ʔɛ́·y=əl//, attested by EB, <**melh q'ó:lthet.**>, //mə-ɬ q'á·l=T-ət//, /*'Come back.'*/, attested by AC, <**metlh yesq'ó. ~ mítlh yesq'ó.**>, //mə-tɬ yə-s=q'á ~ mí-tɬ yə-s=q'á//, /*'Come along.'*/, attested by EB, <**emétlh.**>, //ʔəmə́t-tɬ//, /*'Sit (down/up) (coaxing).'*/, <**héytlh**>, //hɛ́y-tɬ//, /*'Let's (coaxing one person)'*/, <**<u>x</u>wémtlh.**>, //$x̣^w$ə́m-tɬ//, /*'Hurry up (coaxing one person)'*/.

<**tó**>, free root //tá//, LANG /*'thank you (in baby talk), please (in baby talk)'*/, EFAM, syntactic analysis: interjection, usage: baby talk, attested by IHTTC (9/14/77).

<**tókel**>, backformation root //tákəl// from Chinook Jargon and ultimately English

<**stókel**>, free root //stákəl//, [sták^yɪl], CLO /*'stocking, socks'*/, comment: reanalyzed as s=tákəl, borrowed from Chinook Jargon /stákɪn/ <stocken ~ stoken> *stockings, socks* Johnson 1978:425,

syntactic analysis: nominal, attested by AC, others, example: <**alétsa tel stókel?**>, //ʔɛlə́cɛ t-əl s=tákəl//, /'*Where's my stockings?*'/, attested by AD.

<**tókelem**>, mdls //tákəl=əm//, CLO /'*put on one's socks, (put on one's stockings)*'/, (<**=em**> *middle voice*), phonology: back-formation: the s in stókel is reanalyzed as s= *nominalizer* and then dropped for the verb form, syntactic analysis: intransitive verb, attested by AD; found in <**tókelemtsel.**>, //tákəl=əm-t-əl//, /'*I put on my socks.*'/, attested by Halkomelem lesson #16 checked with AD (8/80).

<**tókelem**>, CLO /'*put on one's socks, (put on one's stockings)*'/, *see* stókel.

<**tókwt**> or <**tákwt**>, possible root or stem //tákʷt// or //tɛ́kʷt//, root meaning unknown but related to DESC *stringy*

<**stotekwtíqw**>, strs //s-tá[-C₁ə-]kʷt=íqʷ//, ABDF /'*stringy hair*'/, (<**s-**> *stative*, <-**R1**-> *resultative*, <**=íqw**> *hair*)(attested by RG,EH 6/16/98 to SN, edited by BG with RG,EH 6/26/00)

<**ts'íyxw stotekwtíqw seplíl**>, FOOD /'*noodles*'/ (lit. dry + stringy hair + bread), (attested by RG,EH 6/16/98 to SN, edited by BG with RG,EH 6/26/00)

<**tó:l ~ tò:l**>, free root //tá·l ~ tà·l//, WATR /'*go out into the river, go down to the river, walk down to the river*'/, CAN ['*go out from the beach (if in a canoe)*'], syntactic analysis: intransitive verb, attested by Elders Group (6/4/75), BHTTC (9/2/76), also <**tò:l**>, //tà·l//, attested by BHTTC (9/10/76), Salish cognate: Squamish /túy/ *to cross a body of water* K67:265, example: <**le tó:l.**>, //lə tá·l//, /'*Someone walked down to the river or went away from the shore (in a canoe).*'/, attested by Elders Group (6/4/75), <**xwémlha tó:l.**>, //xʷə́m-ɬɛ tá·l//, /'*Hurry down to the river.*'/, attested by Elders Group (6/4/75).

<**tó:lxel**>, ds //tá·l=xʸəl//, HUNT ['*tracks going down to the river*'], LAND, WATR, lx <**=xel**> *on the feet, tracks*, syntactic analysis: nominal?, attested by IHTTC.

<**stó:lō**>, df //s=tá·l=əw//, WATR ['*river*'], (<**s=**> *nominalizer*), (<**=ō(w) meaning unknown unless =ōw ~ =áw ~ =ōws**> *body, covering*), syntactic analysis: nominal, attested by AC, BJ (12/5/64), Elders Group (4/16/75), many others, other sources: . ES /stá·lə̀w/ *river*, JH /stá·lù·/ *river*, example: <**lheq'át te stó:lō.**>, //ɬəq'ɛ́t tə s=tá·l=əw//, /'*The river is wide.*'/, attested by AC, <**hí:kw te stó:lō.**>, //hí[=·=]kʷ tə s=tá·l=əw//, /'*The river is big.*'/, attested by AC, <**tsel sle'óthel te stó:lō.**>, //c-əl s=ləʔɛ́=áθəl tə s=tá·l=əw//, /'*I'm on the other side of the river.*'/, literally /'I'm across the river'/, *<**tsel sle'ólwelh te stó:lō.**> rejected by Elders Group, <**lam kw'e sle'óthels te stó:lō.**>, //lɛ=m k'ʷə s=ləʔɛ́=áθəl-s tə s=tá·l=əw//, /'*He went across the river.*'/, literally /'(he) go to the (remote) other side -of the river'/, attested by EB.

<**Stó:lō**>, df //s=tá·l=əw//, PLN /'*Fraser River, (Chehalis Creek, Chehalis River [*Elders Group, EL/EB/NP])'/, SOCT /'*Stó:lō people, Halkomelem-speaking people living along the Fraser River or its tributaries from Five Mile Creek above Yale downriver to the mouth of the Fraser*'/, ASM ['including the Katzie and Kwantlen people, not apparently including the Musqueam or Tsawwassen people--though they did speak downriver Halkomelem--perhaps because the main mouth of the Fraser was in Kwantlen territory not in Musqueam territory, and the Tsawwassen didn't live on a tributary of the Fraser at all; some Musqueams have told me they do not consider themselves Stó:lō (or Stó'lō' as they would pronounce it)'], literally /'river'/, (<**s=**> *nominalizer*), (<**=ō(w) meaning unknown**>), syntactic analysis: nominal, attested by Elders Group, AC (8/4/70), others, source: place names file reference #179, also /'*Chehalis Creek/River*'/, attested by Elders Group (8/24/77), Placenames trip to Chehalis (EL, EB, NP) (9/27/77), source: place names file reference #233, example: <**stó:lō syesyewálelh**>, //s=tá·l=əw s=C₁əC₂-yəwɛ́l-əɬ//, /'*Stó:lō (or Stalo) ancestors*'/, attested by Elders Group (3/29/78).

<**stótelō ~ stó:telō**>, dmn //s=tá·[=C_1ə=]l=əw//, WATR /'*creek, little river, small creek, small river*'/, (<**=R1=**> *diminutive*), phonology: reduplication, syntactic analysis: nominal, attested by AC, Elders Group, other sources: ES /stá·tləw/ *creek*.

<**Stótelō**>, dmn //s=tá[=C_1ə=]l=əw//, PLN /'*Statlu Creek, one of the main tributaries of Chehalis Creek*'/, Elder's comment: "not a proper name, just means *creek*", phonology: reduplication, syntactic analysis: nominal, attested by Elders Group (8/24/77), source: place names file reference #235.

<**Stótlōtel**>, ds //s=tá[=C_1ə=]l=əw=təl//, PLN ['*Little Matsqui Creek*'], ASM ['a small creek running into Matsqui slough and thence to the Fraser'], lx <**=tel**> *device to, something to*, phonology: reduplication, syntactic analysis: nominal, dialects: *probably Matsqui (downriver Halkomelem)*, source: Wells 1965 (lst ed.):14.

<**stételō**>, dmpn //s=ta[=Aə́=C_1ə=]l=əw//, WATR ['*lots of little creeks*'], (<**=R1=**> *diminutive*, **é**-ablaut *(diminutive) plural*), phonology: reduplication, ablaut, syntactic analysis: nominal, attested by AD.

<**stútlō**>, dmn //s=tú[=C_1ə=]l=əw//, WATR ['*smaller creek*'], Elder's comment: "perhaps a Lhéchelesem [Nooksack language] word", comment: certainly the Nooksack cognate for stótelō; at one time there was a small settlement on Cultus Lake bilingual in Nooksack and Chilliwack Halkomelem, so this word may have been borrowed only by speakers in the area of Soowahlie and Cultus Lake; the Nooksack word for *river* is stú'lōw', phonology: reduplication, syntactic analysis: nominal, attested by AC (10/23/71).

<**Stōtelō**>, dmn //s=tú[=C_1ə=]l=əw//, PLN /'*Hatchery Creek, tributary of Sweltzer Creek (which drains Cultus Lake)*'/, comment: a Nooksack language place name in what is now Chilliwack Halkomelem territory (see Galloway 1985c), phonology: reduplication, syntactic analysis: nominal, source: Wells 1965 (1st ed.): 13.

<**stolōwálá**>, ds //s=tal=əw=ɛ́lɛ́//, WATR ['*riverbed*'], LAND, literally /'river container of'/, lx <**=álá**> *container of*, syntactic analysis: nominal, attested by Elders Group (4/2/75).

<**teltelewá:m**>, df //C_1əC_2=ta([=Aə=]?)l=əw=ɛ·m//, WATR ['*lots of little streams (like the kind coming down a hill after a rain)*'], (<**R3=**> *plural*), possibly <**e-ablaut**> *diminutive plural*, possibly <**=á:m**> meaning uncertain, phonology: reduplication, possible ablaut, syntactic analysis: nominal, attested by Elders Group (4/16/75).

<**tó:lthíwa**>, df //tá·l=θ(=)íwɛ//, EZ ['*cricket*'], ['probably mostly family *Gryllidae*, but perhaps family *Prophalanopsidae*, also perhaps singing groups such as family *Tettigoniidae* (order *Orthoptera*) or Cicadidae (order *Hemiptera)*'], ASM ['can be heard around Yale and above, not many downriver'], Elder's comment: "the name means *calling you to go down to the river*", possibly <**=th**> meaning unknown, <**=íwa**> possibly *cord, rope* (see <**thelí:wá:xel**> *snowshoe*, <**xixweláwa**> *swim bladder of fish*, possibly some others?), syntactic analysis: nominal, attested by Elders Group (6/4/75), comment: AC knew there was a word for this but had forgotten it.

<**teléqsel ~ tel:éqsel**>, df //tal=ə́qsəl or tal=(ə)lə́qsəl//, EZ /'*mallard, duck*'/, ['*Anas platyrhynchos*, perhaps generic for duck'], possibly root <**tál**> *river*, lx <**=(el)éqsel**> *on the nose, point*, syntactic analysis: nominal, attested by AC, BJ (12/5/64), Elders Group, other sources: ES /təl·ə́qsəl/ *mallard*, example: <**qwóqwel te tél:éqsel.**>, //q^wɛ[-AáC_1ə-]l tə tal=lə́qsəl//, /'*The mallard is talking.*'/, attested by AC (12/4/71).

<**tól**>, bound root //tál *know, learn*//.

<**tél:exw ~ (in rapid speech) télexw**>, ncs //ta[=Aə́=]l=l-əx^w//, rsls, EFAM /'*find s-th out, understand*

s-th, learn s-th, realize s-th, now know what s-th is like, read (and comprehend) s-th, understand s-o'/, (<**é-ablaut**> *resultative*), (<**=l**> *non-control transitivizer (manage to, happen to, accidentally do)*), (<**-exw**> *third person object*), phonology: consonant merger, ablaut, syntactic analysis: transitive verb, attested by Elders Group, AC, EB, AD, SJ, Salish cognate: Squamish /tə́lʔ-nəxʷ/ *have found out, learnt, understood; know* W73:159, K67:263, compare also Lushootseed /túl-ud/ *interpret s-th, translate it* H76:509, ASM ['find s-th out'], example: <**tsel télexw.**>, //c-əl ta[=Aə́=]l=l-əxʷ//, /'*I found out.*'/, attested by EB, <**télexwtsel kw'e lech'áxw.**>, //ta[=Aə́=]l=l-əxʷ-c-əl k'ʷə ləc'ə=ɛ́xʷ//, /'*I found it out once.*'/, attested by AD, <**líchxw kwe tél:exw?**>, //lí-c-xʷ kʷə ta[=Aə́=]l=l-əxʷ//, /'*Did you find out?*'/, attested by AC (8/8/70), ASM ['understand s-th, learn s-th'], <**me tél:exw**>, //mə ta[=Aə́=]l=l-əxʷ//, /'*beginning to understand, beginning to learn*'/, attested by Elders Group (5/3/78), <**úwlh me tél:exwes kws p'áth's.**>, //ʔu=wɬ mə ta[=Aə́=]l=l-əxʷ-əs kʷ-s **p'ɛθ'**-s//, /'*She's learned how to sew.*'/, literally /'She/he already come to learn/understand that she/he sew'/, attested by EB (5/23/76), ASM ['realize s-th'], <**tsel me tél:exw.**>, //c-əl mə ta[=Aə́=]l=l-əxʷ//, /'*I realized something.*'/, attested by Elders Group (4/28/76), ASM ['read and comprehend s-th'], <**(s)kw'áy kw'els tél:exw te pípe.**>, //(s=)k'ʷɛ́y k'ʷ-əl-s ta[=Aə́=]l=l-əxʷ tə pípə//, /'*I can't read the paper., I don't understand the paper.*'/, attested by SJ (Deming 3/15/79), ASM ['understand s-o'], <**líchxw tél:òx?**>, //lí-c-xʷ ta[=Aə́=]l=l-áxʸ//, /'*Did you understand me?*'/, attested by AC (8/27/73), <**líchxw tel:ó:lxw?**>, //lí-c-xʷ təl=l-á·lxʷ//, /'*Do you understand us?*'/, attested by AC (8/27/73), ASM ['know how it is, know what it's like, know how it feels, understand it'], <**tél:exwes.**>, //ta[=Aə́=]l=l-əʷ-əs//, /'*Now he knows how it is., Now he understands it., Now he knows what it's like., Now we're even., Now you know how it feels., There you are.*'/, semantic environment ['said after getting even with someone or showing him how to do something, or what one kid says to another after he has returned a beating or slapped someone back (can be said to the person beaten or slapped even though it uses third person--perhaps this makes it more insulting)'], attested by AC (8/24/70), TG (8/22/72), AD (12/17/79), <**lí kwe télexwes. ~ kwe télexwes.**>, //(lí) kʷə ta[=Aə́=]l=l-əxʷ-əs//, /'*Now he knows what it's like (you got even with him).*'/, attested by EB (12/15/75).

<**tótel:exw**>, cts //tá[-C_1ə-]l=l-əxʷ//, EFAM ['*understanding (s-th/s-o)*'], (<**-R1-**> *continuative*), (<**=l**> *non-control transitivizer*), phonology: reduplication, syntactic analysis: transitive verb, attested by Elders Group (5/3/78).

<**teló:met ~ tel:ómet**>, ncrs //ta[=Aə=]l=l-ámət//, rsls, EFAM ['*understand*'], (<**e-ablaut**> *resultative*), (<**=l**> *non-control transitivizer*), (<**-ómet**> *reflexive*), phonology: ablaut, consonant merger with length transferred to next vowel, syntactic analysis: intransitive verb, attested by AC, EB, example: <**mōkw'tset ōwelh teló:met welí:xw xwe'í:t.**>, //mók'ʷ-c-ət ʔówə-ɬ ta[=Aə=]l=l-ámət wə-lí·-xʷ xʷəʔí·t//, /'*We don't understand what you're saying.*'/, literally /'all of us not-past understand if/when -there -you what is s-o saying?'/, attested by AC, <**ṓwetsellh teló:met.**>, //ʔówə-c-əl-ɬ ta[=Aə=]l=l-ámət//, /'*I don't understand.*'/, attested by AC, <**ōwétalh tèló:mét.**>, //ʔəwə= ´tɛ-ɬ ta[=Aə́=]l=l-ámət//, /'*Nobody understands.*'/, phonology: sentence-stress, updrifting, syntactic comment: past habitual added to negative nominal, attested by AC, <**éw:etàlh teló:mét.**>, //ʔə́w[=·=]ə=tɛ=ɬ ta[=Aə=]l=l-ámət//, /'*Nobody understands (said feeling sorry for oneself).*'/, Elder's comment: "drag **éw:e**... if you feel sorry for yourself", phonology: emphatic lengthening of schwa here shows on following consonant, attested by AC (10/6/71), <**ewá:chxwlh teló:met. ~ ewá:chxw teló:met.**>, //ʔəwə=ə-c-xʷ(-ɬ) ta[=Aə=]l=l-ámət//, /'*You don't understand. (sic? for Didn't you understand?)*'/, phonology: vowel merger, syntactic comment: past interrogative of negative verb, attested by AC.

<**toteló:met**>, cts //ta[-C_1ə-]l=l-ámət//, EFAM ['*understand(ing)*'], (<**-R1-**> *continuative*), (<**=l**> *non-control transitive*), (<**-ómet**> *reflexive*), phonology: reduplication, consonant merger with

transferred lengthening, syntactic analysis: intransitive verb, attested by AC, example: **<líchxw toteló:met?>**, //lí-c-xʷ ta[-C_1ə-]l=l-ámət//, /'*Do you understand?*'/, attested by AC, **<ōwá:chxw í:xw toteló:met.>**, //ʔəwə-ə-c-xʷ ʔí·-xʷ ta[-C_1ə-]l=l-ámət//, /'*You yourself don't understand. (sic? for Don't you yourself understand?)*'/, literally /'Don't you (here)-you understand - yourself'/, attested by AC, **<ōwetsel í:l toteló:met.>**, //ʔówə-c-əl ʔí·-l ta[-C_1ə-]l=l-ámət//, /'*I myself don't understand.*'/, attested by AC.

<télmel>, df //ta[=Aə́=]l=(əl)məl//, [tə́lməl], rsls, EFAM /'*the mind, someone's own knowledge*'/, (**<é-ablaut>** *resultative*), lx **<=mel>** *part, portion* or lx **<=élmel>** *in the mind*, comment: or instead of root tól this could be an empty root t= *nominalizer*? before the lexical suffix =élmel (as with t=épsem *back of the neck and back of the head),* phonology: ablaut, if tol is the root and =élmel is the suffix, possible syllable-loss, syntactic analysis: nominal, attested by Elders Group (3/3/76, 1/23/80).

<x̱wéylemt te télmels>, cpds //x̣ʷí·l(=)əm=T tə ta[=Aə́=]l=(əl)məl-s//, SCH /'*measure his/her knowledge, give s-o a test*'/, **<x̱wéylémt>** *weigh s-th, measure s-th*; <-s> *3rd person possessive*, attested by RG & EH (4/10/99 Ling332)

<stélmel>, dnom //s=ta[=Aə́=]l=(əl)məl//, [stə́lməl], EFAM /'*someone's own knowledge, someone's own idea*'/, (**<s=>** *nominalizer*), (**<é-ablaut>** *resultative*), lx **<=mel>** *part, portion* or lx **<=élmel>** *in the mind*, phonology: ablaut, possible syllable-loss or empty root, syntactic analysis: nominal, attested by Elders Group (1/23/80), example: **<tl'ó: a swá stélmel?>**, //ƛ'á-ə ʔɛ s=wɛ s=ta[=Aə́=]l=məl//, /'*Is that your own idea (or knowledge)?*'/, **<tl'ó stélmelchet.>**, //ƛ'á s=ta[=Aə́=]l=məl-c-ət//, /'*That's our idea.*'/.

<telómelthet>, pcrs //ta[=Aə=]l=áməl=T-ət or tál=ə[=M2=]məl=T-ət//, EFAM ['*acknowledge oneself*'], possibly **<e-ablaut>** *resultative*, possibly **<=ómel ~ =(e)mel>** *part, portion* or **<metathesis>** *derivational*, (**<=t>** *purposeful control transitivizer*), (**<-et>** *reflexive*), phonology: possible ablaut or metathesis, syntactic analysis: intransitive verb, attested by AD and NP (1/23/80).

<tó:lt>, pcs //tá·l=T//, EFAM ['*study it*'], (**<=t>** *purposeful control transitivizer*), phonology: possible lengthening if length is not in the root and lost in all the other derivations, syntactic analysis: transitive verb, attested by Elders Group (3/16/77, 1/23/80), CT and HT, Salish cognate: Lushootseed /túlu-d/ *interpret it, translate it* H76:509, Squamish /təlʔ-t/ *learn, study (tr.)* W73:159, K67:263; found in **<tó:ltchexw.>**, //tá·l=T-c-əxʷ//, /'*Study it.*'/, attested by Elders Group (3/16/77), example: **<tó:lt te sqwéltels>**, //tá·l=T tə s=qʷɛ[=Aə́=]l=təl-s//, /'*learn (his/her/its/their) language*'/, attested by CT and HT (6/21/76).

<totí:lt>, cts //ta[-C_1əAí-]·l=T//, [tatí·lt ~ tatíylt], EFAM /'*studying s-th, thinking about s-th, learning s-th, training for s-th, trying to do s-th*'/, (**<-R1- plus í-ablaut>** *continuative* for certain roots), phonology: reduplication, ablaut, syntactic analysis: transitive verb, attested by AC, CT, HT, EB, Elders Group, Deming, also /'*study, studying it*'/, attested by EB (4/23/76), Elders Group (3/16/77), ASM ['studying s-th']; found in **<totí:ltes.>**, //ta[-C_1əAí-]·l=T//, /'*He's studying it.*'/, attested by Elders Group (3/16/77), also /'*He's thinking.*'/, attested by AC (8/28/70), example: **<í:lhtsel totí:lt.>**, //ʔí·-ɬ-c-əl ta[-C_1əAí-]·l=T//, /'*I was studying it.*'/, attested by Elders Group (3/16/77), ASM ['thinking about s-th'], **<itsel totí:lt.>**, //ʔi-c-əl ta[-C_1əAí-]·l=T//, /'*I'm thinking.*'/, attested by AC, **<tsel totí:lt ta sqwà:l.>**, //c-əl ta[-C_1əAí-]·l=T t-ɛ s=qʷɛ̀·l//, /'*I'm thinking of what you said.*'/, literally /'I'm thinking about it the/what -your words'/, attested by AC, **<líchxw totí:lt?>**, //lí-c-xʷ ta[-C_1əAí-]·l=T//, /'*Are you thinking [about s-o/s-th]?*'/, attested by AC, **<ilh totí:ltes.>**, //ʔí-ɬ ta[-C_1əAí-]·l=T-əs//, /'*He used to think [about s-o/s-th]., He was thinking [about it/s-o].*'/, attested by AC, **<ōwéta kw totí:ltá:l.>**, //ʔowə= ́tɛ kʷ ta[-C_1əAí-]·l=T-ɛ́·l//, /'*I've got* *nothing to think about.'*/, literally /'there's nothing that my thinking about'/, attested by Deming (6/15/78), <**stám kw'e totí:ltexw. ~ stám kw'e íxw totí:lt.**>, //s=tɛ́m k'ʷə ta[-C_1əAí-]·l=T-əxʷ ~ s=tɛ́m k'ʷə ʔí-xʷ ta[-C_1əAí-]·l=T//, /'*What are you thinking?*'/, attested by Deming (4/13/78), ASM ['learning s-th'], <**le xwel totí:ltes te sqwéltels.**>, //lə xʷəl ta[-C_1əAí-]·l=T-əs tə s=qʷɛ[=Aə́=]l=təl-s//, /'*He's still learning a language.*'/, literally /'He was still learning it the his/her/its/their language'/, attested by CT and HT, <**á**tsel totí:lt te halq'eméylem sqwà:l.>, //ʔɛ́-cəl ta[-C_1əAí-]·l=T tə hɛ=ləq'ɛməl=í·l=əm s=qʷɛ̀·l//, /'*[I (am/was) learning Halkomelem words., I (am/was) studying the Halkomelem language.]*'/, attested by AC, <**tsel totí:lt te halq'eméylem sqwéltel.**>, //c-əl ta[-C_1əAí-]·l=T tə hɛ=ləq'ɛməl=í·l=əm s=qʷɛ[=Aə́=]l=təl//, /'*[I (am/was) learning/studying the Halkomelem language.]*'/, attested by AC, <**totí:ltes kws p'áp'eth's.**>, //ta[-C_1əAí-]·l=T-əs kʷ-s **p'ɛ́[-C_1ə-]θ'**-s//, /'*She's learning to sew.*'/, literally /'He/she is studying it the his/her sewing'/, attested by EB (4/23/76), <**totí:ltes te syó:ys te ts'qw'ő:welhs.**>, //ta[-C_1əAí-]·l=T-əs tə s=yá·ys-s tə **c'q'**=ó·wəɬ-s//, /'*She's/He's learning basket work.*'/, attested by Elders Group (3/16/77), also <**totí:ltes kws thíytes te ts'qw'ő:welh.**>, //ta[-C_1əAí-]·l=T-əs kʷ-s θíy=T-əs tə **c'q'**=ó·wəɬ//, dialects: *Cheh.*, attested by EB (3/16/77), also /'*trying to do s-th (thinking about doing s-th)*'/, <**tsel totí:lt kw'els là:m.**>, //c-əl ta[-C_1əAí-]·l=T k'ʷ-əl-s lɛ̀·=m//, /'*I'm trying to go.*'/, literally /'I'm thinking about that I go'/, attested by AC (11/30/71), <**tsel totí:lt kw'els là:m áyel.**>, //c-əl ta[-C_1əAí-]·l=T k'ʷ-əl-s lɛ̀·=m ʔɛ́y=əl//, /'*I'm trying to go away.*'/, literally /'I'm thinking about that I go away'/, attested by AC, ASM ['training to do s-th, training for s-th'], <**totí:ltes kw'es s'ewólem.**>, //ta[-C_1əAí-]·l=T-əs k'ʷ-əs s=ʔi[=Aə=]wál=əm//, /'*He's training for a game., He's training for a sport.*'/, attested by CT and HT (6/21/76), <**totí:ltes kw'es x̱wómxelem.**>, //ta[-C_1əAí-]·l=T-əs k'ʷ-əs x̣ʷə[=Aá=]m=xʸəl=əm//, /'*He's training to run.*'/, literally /'He's studying/training that he is running'/, attested by CT and HT (6/21/76).

<**tó:lthet**>, pcrs //tá·l=T-ət//, EFAM /'*think, ponder, study, decide*'/, (<**=t**> *purposeful control transitivizer*), (<**-et**> *reflexive*), syntactic analysis: intransitive verb, attested by EB (4/23/76), Elders Group (1/23/80, 1/26/77).

<**totí:lthet**>, cts //ta[-C_1əAí-]·l=T-ət//, EFAM /'*thinking, pondering, studying, be studying*'/, (<**-R1-plus i-ablaut**> *continuative*), phonology: reduplication, ablaut, syntactic analysis: intransitive verb, attested by EB, Elders Group, TG (at Elders Group 1/23/80), example: <**totí:lthetchexw kw'a's li á:y.**>, //ta[-C_1əAí-]·l=T-ət-c-əxʷ k'ʷ-ɛʔ-s lə-yə-ʔɛ́·y//, /'*Study as you go along (look at everything, plants, etc., as you walk along).*'/, usage: TG's grandfather always told her this on trips, attested by TG (in Elders Group 1/23/80).

<**tóltí:lqel**>, dnom //tá·l=C_1əC_2=í·l=(ə)qəl//, LANG //'*dictionary*'//, <**=R2**> *plural*, <**=í:l**> *get, go, come*, <**=(e)qel**> *language*, lit. /"get plural knowledges/understandings of a language"/, attested by RG & EH (4/10/99 Ling332).

<**toléptel**>, df //tol(=)ə́p=təl//, FSH ['*string attached to detachable point on harpoon or spear*'], possibly root <**tol**> *go out into the river*, possibly <**=ép**> *in the dirt*, lx <**=tel**> *device to*, syntactic analysis: nominal, attested by EL (Elders Group 1/26/77), NP (Elders Group 2/1/78).

<**tó:les**>, poss. bound root or stem //tá·l(=)əs//, prob. *wife*

<**stó:les**>, dnom //s=tá·ləs//, KIN ['*wife*'], (<**s=**> *nominalizer*), syntactic analysis: nominal, attested by AC, BJ (12/5/64), EL, EB, LJ (Tait), IHTTC, others, contrast <swáqeth> *husband*, other sources: ES /stá·ləs/ *husband, wife*, H-T <stálEs ~ stálus> (each a with macron) *wife*, example: <**tl'el stó:les.**>, //ƛ'a-l s=tá·ləs//, /'*That's my wife.*'/, attested by AC, <**l stó:les**>, //l s=tá·ləs//, /'*my wife*'/, attested by BJ (12/5/64), <**wéta stó:les.**>, //ʔəwə= ́tɛ s=tá·ləs//, /'*He has no wife.*'/, attested by EL (Elders Group 3/26/80), <**le xwchém:éstes te stó:les.**>, //lə xʷ=co[=Aə́=]m=əs=T-əs tə s=tá·ləs-s//, /'*He met his wife. (meet s-o)*'/, attested by EB (5/4/76), <**x̱ét'estxwes te stó:les te Paul Webster**

...>, //x̣**ə́t**'ə=sT-əxʷ-əs tə s=tá·ləs-s tə Paul Webster ...//, /'*Paul Webster's wife said ...*'/, attested by LJ (Tait) (History tape 34, 4/7/78), <**kw'étslexwes te swíyeqe the stó:les.**>, //k'ʷə́c=l-əxʷ-əs tə s=wíqə **θ**ə s=tá·ləs//, /'*The man saw his wife.*'/, semantic environment ['often implies the wife is partially undressed as whenever kw'**é**tslexw *see s-o, catch sight of s-o* is used with human subject and human object with no other explanation of context'], attested by IHTTC (8/5/77).

<**stételes**>, dmpn //s=C_1í=[=Aə́=]taləs//, KIN ['*little wives*'], (<**R4=**> *diminutive*), (<**é-ablaut**> *plural (of dim.)*), phonology: ablaut, reduplication, syntactic analysis: nominal, attested by AD (about Jan. 1979).

<**tó:lt**>, EFAM ['*study it*'], *see* tól.

<**tó:lthet**>, EFAM /'*think, ponder, study, decide*'/, *see* tól.

<**tó:lthíwa**>, EZ ['*cricket*'], *see* tó:l ~ tò:l.

<**tó:lxel**>, HUNT ['*tracks going down to the river*'], *see* tó:l ~ tò:l.

<**tó:méx**>, bound root or stem //tá·m=ə́xʸ//, poss from root <tám> *shout* + <=ex> *upright*.

<**stó:méx**>, dnom //s=tá·mə́xʸ//, SOC /'*warrior, (leader of a raiding party [CT])*'/, (<**s=**> *nominalizer*), syntactic analysis: nominal, attested by BJ (12/5/64), also <**stóméx**>, //s=támə́xʸ//, also /'*leader of a raiding party*'/, attested by CT (6/8/76).

<**tómiyeqw**>, df //tám(=)iyəqʷ or tám(=)iqʷ//, KIN /'*great great great great grandparent, great great great great grandchild, sibling or cousin (up to fourth) of great great great great grandparent or -child*'/, root meaning unknown, possibly <**=iyeqw or =iqw**> perhaps now *great grandparent/-child,* prob. not related to <**=iqw ~ =eqw**> *on top of the head*, syntactic analysis: nominal, attested by AC, Deming (4/1/76), other sources: H-T <támiyuk·> (macrons over a and i) *great great great great grandparent* (H-T 1902:387), Salish cognate: Squamish /təmíxʷiy'iqʷ/ *great great great great grandparent and beyond* B78:31.

<**Tómtomiyeqw**>, df //tɛ[=Aá=]m=C_1əC_2=iyəqʷ or tám[=C1V1C2=]iyəqʷ or tám[=C_1əC_2=]iyəqʷ//, PLN ['*mountain with caves that is behind Hunter Creek (in 1976-1977 they blasted this mountain where it was beside Trans-Canada Highway #1 to shorten the highway past it)*'], probably root <**tam**> *shout, holler, yell*, possibly root <**tómiyeqw**> *great great great great grandparent/-child,* possibly <**=R2=**> *characteristic* or possibly <**=C1V1C2=**> an old or borrowed *plural*, possibly <**=iqw**> *on top of the head*, phonology: reduplication, syntactic analysis: nominal, attested by SP and AK (Fish Camp 8/2/77), source: place names file reference #164.

<**tóqweltsep**>, df //táqʷ=əlcəp//, FIRE ['*cool down enough to touch (or handle or work with)*'], DESC, root meaning unknown, lx <**=eltsep**> *firewood*, syntactic analysis: intransitive verb, attested by NP (4/11/80), example: <**tóqweltsep te shxwyélhtel.**>, //táqʷ=əlcəp tə sxʷ=ya[=Aə́=]ɬ=təl//, /'*The ashes have cooled enough (to handle).*'/, attested by NP.

<**tqwó:chep**>, df //tá·qʷ=M1=cəp//, FIRE ['*fine ashes floating up from a fire*'], possibly <**metathesis type 1**> *derivational* apparently not *non-continuative* which one would expect from this type of metathesis, lx <**=chep ~ =eltsep ~ =elchep**> *firewood*, phonology: metathesis, syntactic analysis: nominal, attested by Elders Group (4/23/80).

<**tó:qw'em**>, mdls //tá·q'ʷ=əm//, ABDF ['*to cough*'], (<**=em**> *middle voice*), syntactic analysis: intransitive verb, attested by NP, AC, BJ (12/5/64).

<**tóteqw'em**>, cts //tá[-C_1ə-]**q'**ʷ=əm//, ABDF ['*coughing*'], (<**-R1-**> *continuative*), phonology: reduplication, syntactic analysis: intransitive verb, attested by NP, AC.

<**stó:qw'em**>, dnom //s=tá·q'ʷ=əm//, ABDF /'*a cough, a cold with a cough*'/, (<**s=**> *nominalizer*),

syntactic analysis: nominal, attested by EB, example: <**kweléxwes te stó:qw'em.**>, //kʷəl=l-ə[= ´=]xʷ-əs tə s=tá·q'ʷ=əm//, /'*He caught a cough., He caught a cold. (catch s-th)*'/, attested by EB (1/16/76).

<**toteqw'ó:mestem**>, df //ta[=C_1ə=]**q'**ʷ=ə[=Aá·=]m=əs=təm//, ABDF ['*(have) tuberculosis*'], possibly /' <**=R1=**> *continuative or resultative*, <**ó:-ablaut**> *durative*, possibly <**=em**> *intransitivizer or middle voice*, possibly <**=st**> *causative* plus <**=em**> *middle voice or middle voice*, comment: <**=es**> *in the face* plus <**=tem**> *participial, stative* are less likely semantically, phonology: reduplication, ablaut, syntactic analysis: intransitive verb, attested by NP (9/19/75).

<**tós**>, free root //tás//, TCH /'*bump, get hit by something moving (for ex. by a car)*'/, syntactic analysis: intransitive verb, attested by EB, AC, example: <**xwá:lq yi-tós te kyó.**>, //xʷɛ́·lq yə-tás tə kʸá//, /'*He almost got hit by a car.*'/, attested by EB, <**tós tel qw'ő:l.**>, //tás t-əl **q'**ʷó·l//, /'*?My ear got bumped.*'/, Elder's comment: "unsure of translation", attested by AC.

<**tesálèqel**>, rsls //ta[=Aə=]s=ɛ́lə̀qəl//, TCH ['*bump the head*'], (<**e-ablaut**> *resultative*), lx <**=áleqel**> *on the head*, phonology: ablaut, syntactic analysis: intransitive verb, attested by AC (11/11/71).

<**tesláts**>, rsls //ta[=Aə=]s=lɛ́c//, TCH ['*touching bottom (of a canoe or a person)*'], (<**e-ablaut**> *resultative*), lx <**=lets ~ =láts**> *on the bottom*, phonology: ablaut, syntactic analysis: intransitive verb, attested by Elders Group.

<**téslatstem**>, pcs //ta[=Aə́=]s=lɛc=T-əm//, rsls, TCH ['*it got smashed in the back end or rear end*'], (<**é-ablaut**> *resultative*), lx <**=lats**> *on the bottom*, (<**=t**> *purposeful control transitivizer*), (<-**em**> *passive*), phonology: ablaut, syntactic analysis: transitive verb, attested by EB from LJ (6/30/78).

<**teséleqw**>, rsls //ta[=Aə=]s=ə́ləqʷ//, TCH ['*bumped on the head*'], (<**e-ablaut**> *resultative*), lx <**=éleqw**> *on top of the head*, phonology: ablaut, syntactic analysis: intransitive verb, attested by Elders Group (5/14/80).

<**tósem**>, ds //tás=əm//, HARV /'*crush (of berries), smash (of berries), squish (of berries, etc.), to mash*'/, (<**=em**> *intransitivizer*), syntactic analysis: intransitive verb, attested by Elders Group, EB.

<**stósem temítō**>, FOOD *ketchup/stewed tomatoes* (lit. smashed + tomato), (attested by RG,EH 6/16/98 to SN, edited by BG with RG,EH 6/26/00)

<**tótesem**>, cts //tá[-C_1ə-]s=əm//, HARV /'*mashing, grinding (stones, something hard)*'/, (<**-R1-**> *continuative*), phonology: reduplication, syntactic analysis: intransitive verb, attested by EB, Elders Group.

<**téslexw**>, ncs //ta[=Aə́=]s=l-əxʷ//, rsls, TCH /'*touch s-o accidentally, bump s-o, bumped s-o*'/, (<**é-ablaut**> *resultative*), (<**=l**> *non-control transitivizer*), (<**-exw**> *third person object*), phonology: ablaut, syntactic analysis: transitive verb, attested by Elders Group, EB, IHTTC; found in <**téslòmè**>, //ta[=Aə́=]s=l-ámə//, /'*bumped you*'/, phonology: downstepping, updrifting, attested by EB, example: <**téslexwes thú:tl'ò te swíyeqe.**>, //ta[=Aə́=]s=l-əxʷ-əs **θ**=ú·=ƛ'**à** tə s=wíqə//, /'*She bumped the man.*'/, attested by IHTTC, <**téslexwes te swíyeqe thútl'ò.**>, //ta[=Aə́=]s=l-əxʷ-əs tə s=wíqə **θ**=ú=ƛ'**à**//, /'*She bumped the man.*'/, syntactic comment: in contrast with the last sentence this shows that thútl'ò and pronouns in that class cannot be object nominal phrases, attested by IHTTC.

<**tóset**>, pcs //tás=əT//, TCH /'*touch s-o purposely, squish it (of berries, etc.), smash s-th, mash it (berries, potatoes, carrots, etc.), bump it*'/, HARV, FOOD, ABFC, (<**=et**> *purposeful control transitivizer*), syntactic analysis: transitive verb, attested by Elders Group (4/28/76, 9/21/77, 5/14/80), EB (12/12/75, 1/16/76), AD (2/80).

<**tóteset**>, cts //ta[-C_1ə-]s=əT//, TCH /'*tapping it (with something), mashing s-th, grinding s-th, be*

bumping s-o'/, HARV, FOOD, ABFC, (<**-R1-**> *continuative*), phonology: reduplication, syntactic analysis: transitive verb, attested by Elders Group (2/13/80, 5/19/76), EB (1/16/76), AD (2/80), example: <**ő́wechxw tótesetexw.**>, //ʔówə-c-xʷ ta[-C_1ə-]s=əT-əxʷ//, /'*Don't bump him.*'/, usage: esp. said around an Indian doctor or a spirit dancer as this could set off the doctor or dancer at a wrong moment and bumper could suffer harm from the spirit or the doctor or dancer or at least have to throw a dance to pay off the person bumped and the witnesses present, attested by AD (2/80), also /'*Don't touch it.*'/, usage: used in many circumstances, attested by Elders Group (4/28/76).

<**testéstexw**>, plv //C_1əC_2=ta[=Aə́=]s=sT-əxʷ//, caus, rsls, TCH ['*bump them together*'], (<**R3=**> *plural object (with transitive verbs)*), (<**é-ablaut**> perhaps *resultative* unless allomorphic), (<**=st**> *causative control transitivizer*), (<**-exw**> *third person object*), phonology: reduplication, ablaut or allomorph, syntactic analysis: transitive verb, attested by EB (1/20/78).

<**tósem**>, HARV /'*crush (of berries), smash (of berries), squish (of berries, etc.), to mash*'/, *see* tós.

<**tóset**>, TCH /'*touch s-o purposely, squish it (of berries, etc.), smash s-th, mash it (berries, potatoes, carrots, etc.), bump it*'/, *see* tós.

<**tótel:exw**>, EFAM ['*understanding (s-th/s-o)*'], *see* tól.

<**toteló:met**>, EFAM ['*understand(ing)*'], *see* tól.

<**tóteqw'em**>, ABDF ['*coughing*'], *see* tó:qw'em.

<**toteqw'ó:mestem**>, ABDF ['*(have) tuberculosis*'], *see* tó:qw'em.

<**tótesem**>, HARV /'*mashing, grinding (stones, something hard)*'/, *see* tós.

<**tóteset**>, TCH /'*tapping it (with something), mashing s-th, grinding s-th, be bumping s-o*'/, *see* tós.

<**totí:lt**>, EFAM /'*studying s-th, thinking about s-th, learning s-th, training for s-th, trying to do s-th*'/, *see* tól.

<**totí:lthet**>, EFAM /'*thinking, pondering, studying, be studying*'/, *see* tól.

<**tówel**>, free root //táwəl//, PLN ['*town*'], borrowed from Chinook Jargon /táwn/ itself from English, Johnson 1978:441, syntactic analysis: nominal, attested by EB, RP, also <**táwn**>, //tɛ́wn//, attested by AC, borrowed from English /tǽwn/ *town*, example: <**lámechap tówel?**>, //lɛ́=m-ə-c-ɛp tówəl//, /'*Are you folks going to town?*'/, syntactic comment: interrogative affix, attested by RP and EB (2/12/76), <**lílhechap lám kw'e tówel?**>, //lí-ɬ-ə-c-ɛp lɛ́=m k'ʷə táwəl//, /'*Did you folks go to town.*'/, syntactic comment: interrogative affix, past affixed, attested by RP and EB (2/12/76), <**lámtsel kw'e tówel chulh le ú:kw'elets.**>, //lɛ́=m-t-əl k'ʷə táwəl c(-əl)-w(ə)ɬ lə ʔówk'ʷ=ələc//, /'*I'm going to town because I'm out of food.*'/, attested by EB (12/15/75), <**lámtset kw'e táwn.**>, //lɛ́=m-c-ət k'ʷə tɛ́wn//, /'*We're going to town.*'/, attested by AC (8/6/70).

<**tó<u>x</u>w**>, bound root //táx̣ʷ *drag behind*//.

<**tó<u>x</u>wem**>, mdls //táx̣ʷ=əm//, TVMO ['*drag out behind*'], (<**=em**> *middle voice*), syntactic analysis: intransitive verb, attested by IHTTC.

<**to<u>x</u>wemíwel**>, ds //tax̣ʷ=əm=íwəl//, CAN /'*automobile, car*'/, literally /'trailing out the behind'/, Elder's comment: "so named because of its gas/smoke "trailing behind"", lx <**=íwel**> *in the insides, in the rectum*, syntactic analysis: nominal, attested by RM (6/13/77), IHTTC, Elders Group (4/26/78).

<**tó<u>x</u>welh**>, df //táx̣ʷ=əɬ or táx̣ʷ=wəɬ//, FSH ['*to set a line for sturgeon*'], ASM ['a line set with hooks is lowered to the bottom with weights'], literally /'drag behind canoe?'/, possibly <**=welh**> *canoe*,

phonology: possible consonant merger, syntactic analysis: intransitive verb, attested by Elders Group.

<**tóx̱wesem**>, mdls //táx̣ʷ=əs=əm//, CAN /'*pulling a canoe through rough water by a rope in the front, pulling a canoe with a rope*'/, ASM ['at least one paddler stays in to push the canoe away from banks'], lx <**=es**> *on the face, on the prow (of canoe)*, (<**=em**> *middle voice*), literally /'drag behind on one's prow'/, syntactic analysis: intransitive verb, attested by Elders Group (3/3/76, 3/26/75).

<**tx̱wṓwelh**>, ds //tax̣ʷ=M1=ówəɬ//, CAN ['*pulling a canoe through rough water by a rope in the front*'], possibly <**metathesis**> *derivational*?, lx <**=ṓwelh**> *canoe*, literally /'drag a canoe behind'/, phonology: metathesis or zero-grade of full-grade root, syntactic analysis: intransitive verb, attested by Elders Group (3/3/76).

<**tóx̱weth**>, ds //táx̣ʷ=əθ//, FSH ['*rope for sturgeon fishing*'], lx <**=eth ~ =óthel**> *in the mouth*, literally /'drag behind in the mouth'/, syntactic analysis: nominal, attested by BHTTC.

<**tóx̱wethem**>, df //táx̣ʷ=əθ=əm//, FSH ['*fish for sturgeon from shore with a single line*'], ASM ['only one to three hooks on the end, anchored, line fastened on a stick which is in piled-up rocks'], probably <**=em**> *intransivizer, have, get*, literally prob. /'get dragged behind in the mouth'/, syntactic analysis: intransitive verb, attested by BHTTC (11/10/76), also <**tóxweth**>, //táxʷ=əθ//, also /'*fish for sturgeon with baited hook*'/, comment: probably xw should be **x̱**w, attested by AK (Elders Group 3/26/80).

<**tóx̱welh**>, FSH ['*to set a line for sturgeon*'], *see* tóx̱w.

<**tóx̱wem**>, TVMO ['*drag out behind*'], *see* tóx̱w.

<**tox̱wemíwel**>, CAN /'*automobile, car*'/, *see* tóx̱w.

<**tóx̱wesem**>, CAN /'*pulling a canoe through rough water by a rope in the front, pulling a canoe with a rope*'/, *see* tóx̱w.

<**tóx̱weth**>, FSH ['*rope for sturgeon fishing*'], *see* tóx̱w.

<**tóx̱wethem**>, FSH ['*fish for sturgeon from shore with a single line*'], *see* tóx̱w.

<**tpélhtel ~ tepélhtel**>, HUNT /'*frame for stretching hides, frame (for drying hides, etc.), frame for a drum*'/, *see* tpólh.

<**tpólh**>, bound root //tpáɬ *prop up*//.

<**stpólh**>, strs //s=tpáɬ//, CSTR ['*propped up*'], semantic environment ['like a building or a tree limb'], (<**s=**> *stative*), comment: the unusual shape of the root may be due in part to metathesis or ablaut or -elh of some kind used as *resultative*, syntactic analysis: adjective/adjectival verb, attested by CT (6/21/76).

<**tpólht**>, pcs //tpáɬ=T//, HARV ['*prop it up*'], CSTR, semantic environment ['like the limb of a tree heavy with fruit'], (<**=t**> *purposeful control transitivizer*), syntactic analysis: transitive verb, attested by CT (6/21/76), EB (6/30/76).

<**tpólhtel**>, dnom //tpáɬ=təl//, CSTR ['*a prop*'], HUNT ['*a prop used to trip a deadfall trap*'], lx <**=tel**> *device for*, syntactic analysis: nominal, attested by NP (Elders Group 2/8/78), also <**tpélhtel**>, //tpa[=Aə́=]ɬ=təl//, attested by Lawrence James (Elders Group 2/8/78), Salish cognate: Squamish /tpúɬ-tn/ *frame on which blankets are woven, stretching board* W73:107, K67:259, K69:46.

<**tpélhtel ~ tepélhtel**>, dnom //tpa[=Aə́=]ɬ=təl//, HUNT /'*frame for stretching hides, frame (for drying hides, etc.), frame for a drum*'/, MUS, (<**é-ablaut**> *durative or resultative or derivational*), lx <**=tel**> *device for*, phonology: ablaut, syntactic analysis: nominal, attested by Elders Group (3/24/76, 10/20/76, 9/1/76).

<**tépelhállh**>, df //t[=ə́=]paɬ=ɛ́lɬ or t[=ə́=]paɬ=a[=Aɛ́=]lɬ//, HUNT /'*board for stretching squirrel or skunk hides, etc.*'/, possibly <**=é=**> *derivational*, possibly <**á**-ablaut> *derivational*?, <**=óllh**> *young*, (semological comment: probably meaning *board for stretching small hides*, small hides could probably be done on a board, while larger hides would require more circulation provided by a large open frame), phonology: infixed vowel, possible ablaut, syntactic analysis: nominal, attested by Elders Group (11/26/75).

<**tpólht**>, HARV ['*prop it up*'], *see* tpólh.

<**tpólhtel**>, CSTR ['*a prop*'], *see* tpólh.

<**tqát**>, SH ['*close s-th*'], *see* téq.

<**tqátsáleqel**>, NUM ['*eight containers*'], *see* tqá:tsa.

<**tqatsálh**>, NUM ['*eight times*'], *see* tqá:tsa.

<**tqátsámets'**>, NUM /'*eight ropes, eight threads, eight sticks, eight poles*'/, *see* tqá:tsa.

<**tqátsa'ő̃welh ?**>, NUM /'*eight canoes, eight boats*'/, *see* tqá:tsa.

<**tqatsíws**>, NUM ['*eight birds*'], *see* tqá:tsa.

<**tqòtsòls**>, NUM ['*eight fruit in a group [or cluster] (as they grow on a plant)*'], *see* tqá:tsa.

<**tqó:tsó:s**>, NUM ['*eight dollars*'], *see* tqá:tsa.

<**tq(=)ó:ya**>, prob. stem //tq(=)á·yɛ//, poss. itself from <tíq> *take a step, take in motion*

<**stqó:ya ~ stqó:ye ~ stqó:yá**>, df //s=tq(=)á·yɛ ~ s=tqá·yə ~ stqá·yɛ́//, EZ ['*wolf*'], ['*Canis lupus fuscus q/[tentative], Canis lupus columbianus*'], (<**s=**> *nominalizer*), root meaning unknown unless <tiq> *take a step, take in motion*, possibly <**=ó:ya**> *name ending*? or *diminutive*, thus poss. "name of s-th that takes little steps", syntactic analysis: nominal, attested by BJ (5/64, 12/5/64), AC, DM (12/4/64), also <**stqóye**>, //s=tq(=)áyə//, attested by AK (11/21/72), ME (tape 11/21/72), also <**steqóye ~ steqóyé**>, //s=təq(=)áyə ~ s=təq(=)áyə́//, attested by Elders Group (3/1/72), other sources: ES /stəqàyɛ́/ *wolf*, H-T <tEkaíya> *wolf (Canis lupus occidentalis)*, Salish cognate: Squamish /stqáya/ *wolf* W73:291, K67:284, K69:57, Lushootseed /s-tiqáyuʔ/ *wolf* (and possibly /tíq-/ as in /ʔəs-tiq-il/ *bushy*) H76:502.

<**stelqóye**>, pln //s=t[=əl=]q(=)áyə//, EZ ['*wolves*'], (<**=el=**> *plural*), phonology: infixed plural, syntactic analysis: nominal.

<**tqwó:chep**>, FIRE ['*fine ashes floating up from a fire*'], *see* tóqweltsep.

<**t-sós ~ tesós**>, uf //tsás or tás=M1=əs or ta[=Aə=]s=ás//, ECON /'*poor, unfortunate*'/, possibly root <**tás**> *smash, squish, mash, bump, touch*, possibly <**e-ablaut**> *durative or resultative*, possibly <**=es ~ =ós**> *in the face; money*, possibly <**metathesis**> *derivational or non-continuative*, phonology: possible ablaut or metathesis, hyphen shows the initial t (aspirated) and s are pronounced separately (not like ts in tsel), syntactic analysis: adjective/adjectival verb, attested by EB, IHTTC, TM or DF or TG (3/22/78), example: <**tesós te mestíyexw.**>, //təsás tə məstíyəx^w//, /'*The person is poor.*'/, usage: what rich people used to say, attested by IHTTC, <**th'exwmetólxwchexw, lálh tstulh t-sós.**>, //θ'əx^w=məT-álx^w-c-əx^w, lɛ́-ɬ cət-uɬ tsás//, /'*Pity us, we're getting unfortunate.*'/, usage: in a prayer to plants before picking them for medicine, etc., attested by TM or DF or NP (Elders Group 3/22/78).

<**stesó:s**>, strs //s=ta[=Aə=]s=á·s//, ECON ['*be broke [financially]*'], (<**s=**> *stative*), (<**e-ablaut**> *resultative*), phonology: ablaut, syntactic analysis: adjective/adjectival verb, attested by AC (11/17/71); found in <**stesó:stsel**>, //s=ta[=Aə=]s=á·s-c-əl//, /'*I'm broke.*'/, attested by AC.

<**stít-sòs**>, dmn //s=C_1í=ta[=Aə=]s=ás//, SOCT /'*low class person, [person on the lowest economic*

class]'/, ECON, (<**s=**> *nominalizer*), (<**R4=**> *diminutive*), (<**e-ablaut**> *durative or resultative*), phonology: reduplication, ablaut, downstepping, syntactic analysis: nominal, attested by EB (11/28/75).

<**tesestélemet**>, rfls //ta[=Aə=]s=əs=sT-ə́ləmət//, caus, EFAM [*'feeling sorry for oneself'*], literally /'cause oneself to be unfortunate/poor'/, (<**e-ablaut**> *durative or resultative*), (<**=st**> *causative*), (<-**élemet**> *reflexive of causative*), contrast <**lhistélémét and lholhistélémét**> *feel sorry for oneself*, phonology: ablaut, syntactic analysis: transitive verb, attested by EP (IHTTC 8/8/77).

<**tu**>, df //t=əw//, MOOD /*'a little, a little like, slightly'*/, ASM ['also used before color terms to distinguish lighter shades and shades between colors other than black or white'], (<**=u ~ =ew**> *contrastive*), phonology: u from ew, syntactic analysis: particle, attested by Elders Group, BHTTC, EB, IHTTC (7/26/77), others, see charts by Rob MacLaury, example: <**welh tu ítet**>, //wəɬ t=u ʔítət//, /*'nearly asleep'*/, literally /'already a little (like) go to sleep'/, attested by EB, <**tu iyólem.**>, //t=u ʔəy=ál=əm//, /*'It's alright.'*/, literally /'a little (like) alright'/, attested by Elders Group, <**lhálhq'etxel tu spá:th**>, //**ɬá**[=C$_{1}$ə=]**q'**ət=x^{y}əl t=u s=pá·θ//, /*'(have) wide feet like a bear'*/, literally /'have wide feet a little like bear'/, Elder's comment: "tu may mean "a little like"", attested by IHTTC (7/26/77), <**tú s'ólh kw'elhá.**>, //t=u s=ʔ**áɬ** k'^{w}əɬ(=)ɛ́//, /*'That's terrible. (of someone's actions)'*/, comment: this idiomatic phrase is currently unanalyzable, attested by BHTTC (10/14/76).

<**tumiyáth'**>, uf //tumiyɛ́θ'//, HAT /*'adolescent male (before he changes to a man, about 13, when his voice changes, etc.)'*/, syntactic analysis: nominal, attested by EL (Shirley Leon's tape about 3/14/80).

<**tu s'éy ~ u s'éyò**>, EFAM [*'be careful'*], *see* éy ~ éy:.

<**tutl'étl'elò:m**>, PRON [*'that's them (little ones) (male?)'*], *see* tl'ó ~ tl'o.

<**tutl'ó:lem**>, PRON /*'that's them (male), they (male), them (male)'*/, *see* tl'ó ~ tl'o.

<**tú:tl'ò ~ tútl'ò ~ tútl'o**>, DEM /*'he (present or presence unspecified), he's the one that, it's him that, she or it (present or presence unspecified), that or this (immediately before nominal)'*/, *see* tl'ó ~ tl'o.

<**tú:tl'òtl'èm**>, PRON /*'that's a little one (male, about one to five years old), he (little)'*/, *see* tl'ó ~ tl'o.

<**tú:xw**>, free root //tú·x^{w}//, NUM [*'nine'*], syntactic analysis: num, attested by AC, CT (9/5/73), BJ (5/64), DM (12/4/64), Elders Group, others, other sources: ES /tú·x^{w}/ *nine*, Salish cognate: PCS *tə́wəx^{w} *nine* Galloway 1982a: cognate set 218, including: CwMsCh /tú·x^{w}/, Se /tə́wix^{w}/, MCx /tə́gəx^{w}/, LmSoCl /tə́k^{w}x^{w}/, San /tə́k^{w}əx^{w}/, Sg (S65) /tə́k^{w}əx^{w}/, Sam-b VU + TB /tə́k^{w}əx^{w}/ and LD /tə́k^{w}x^{w}/, example: <**ó:pel qas te tú:xw ~ ópel qas te tú:xw**>, //ʔá·pəl qɛ-s tə tú·x^{w} ~ ʔ**ápəl** qɛ-s tə tú·x^{w}//, /*'nineteen'*/, attested by DM (12/4/64), CT (9/5/73), also <**ó:pel qas kw'e tú:xw**>, //ʔ**á·**pəl qɛ-s k'^{w}ə tú·x^{w}//, attested by AC (8/24/70), <**ts'kw'éx qas te tú:xw**>, //**c'**=k'^{w}ə́x^{y} qɛ-s tə tú·x^{w}//, /*'twenty-nine'*/, attested by CT (9/5/73).

<**tuxwále**>, numc //tux^{w}=álə//, NUM [*'nine people'*], lx <**=ále**> *people*, syntactic analysis: num, attested by Elders Group (3/19/75).

<**tuxwáleqel**>, numc //tux^{w}=ɛ́ləqəl//, NUM [*'nine containers'*], lx <**=áleqel**> *containers; on the head*, syntactic analysis: num, attested by AD (4/12/78).

<**tú:xwà:lh**>, numc //tú·x^{w}=ɛ̀·ɬ//, NUM [*'nine times'*], Elder's comment: "they didn't often count these beyond five", lx <**=à:lh**> *times*, syntactic analysis: adverb/adverbial verb, attested by Elders Group (3/19/75), other sources: JH /tú·x^{w}**è·ɬ**/ *nine times*, Salish cognate: Pentlatch /təwix^{w}áɬ/ (cited in Galloway 1982a), Nooksack LG [tú·x^{w}**hæ·ɬ**] and SJ [tú·x^{w}ɛɬ] all glossed *nine times*.

<**tuxwámets'**>, numc //tux^{w}=ɛ́məc'//, NUM /*'nine ropes, nine threads, nine sticks, nine poles'*/, lx <**=ámets' ~ =ámeth'**> *objects much longer than wide*, syntactic analysis: num, attested by AD after Boas 1890 Scowlitz Halkomelem ms..

<**tú:xwelsxá ~ tù:xwelsxá**>, numc //tú·xʷ=əlsxʸɛ́ ~ tù·xʷ=əlsxʸɛ́//, NUM ['*ninety*'], lx <**=elsxá ~ =elhsxá**> *times ten*, phonology: downshifting, syntactic analysis: num, attested by AC, BJ (12/5/64), CT (9/5/73), also <**tú:xwelhsxá**>, //tú·xʷ=əɬsxʸɛ́//, attested by DM, others.

<**tuxwelsxá:le**>, numc //tuxʷ=əlsxʸɛ́=ɛ́lə//, NUM ['*ninety people*'], (semological comment: probably somewhat artificial as **qéx̲** *many* would most likely have been used instead of counting this high), lx <**=ále**> *people*, phonology: vowel merger, syntactic analysis: num, attested by Elders Group (3/19/75).

<**tú:xwelsxó:s**>, numc //tú·xʷ=əlsxʸɛ=á(·)s//, NUM ['*ninety dollars*'], lx <**=ó:s ~ =ós ~ =es**> *dollars*, phonology: vowel merger, syntactic analysis: num, attested by AC (11/30/71).

<**tú:xwes**>, numc //tú·xʷ=əs//, NUM /'*nine dollars, (nine Indian blankets* [Boas]*)*'/, lx <**=es ~ =ós ~ =ó:s**> *dollars*, syntactic analysis: num, attested by AC, other sources: Boas 1890 Scowlitz Halkomelem ms. word list in APS library <tō'uques> *nine Indian blankets, nine dollars*, also /'*nine Indian blankets or dollars*'/, source: Boas 1890 ms.

<**tuxwíqw**>, numc //tuxʷ=íqʷ//, NUM ['*nine fish*'], lx <**=íqw**> *fish; on top of the head*, syntactic analysis: num, attested by BHTTC.

<**tuxwíws**>, numc //tuxʷ=íws//, NUM ['*nine birds*'], lx <**=íws**> *birds; on the skin*, syntactic analysis: num, attested by Elders Group (3/29/77).

<**tuxwòls**>, numc //tuxʷ=áls//, NUM ['*nine fruit in a group or cluster (as they grow on a plant)*'], lx <**=óls ~ =ó:ls**> *fruit, rocks, spherical objects*, phonology: downstepping, syntactic analysis: num, attested by AD (4/12/78).

<**tuxwő̂welh**>, numc //tuxʷ=ówəɬ//, NUM /'*nine canoes, nine boats*'/, lx <**=ówelh**> *canoes, vessels, boats*, syntactic analysis: num, attested by AD (4/12/78).

<**stú:xws**>, numc //s=tú·xʷ=s//, NUM ['*nine o'clock*'], lx <**s=...=s**> *o'clock, hours*, phonology: circumfix, syntactic analysis: num, attested by AC (10/6/71), example: <**wetéses te stú:xws**>, //wə-tə́s-əs tə s=tú·xʷ=s//, /'*when it gets (approaches) nine o'clock*'/, attested by AC.

<**tuxwále**>, NUM ['*nine people*'], *see* tú:xw.

<**tuxwáleqel**>, NUM ['*nine containers*'], *see* tú:xw.

<**tú:xwà:lh**>, NUM ['*nine times*'], *see* tú:xw.

<**tuxwámets'**>, NUM /'*nine ropes, nine threads, nine sticks, nine poles*'/, *see* tú:xw.

<**tuxwelsxá:le**>, NUM ['*ninety people*'], *see* tú:xw.

<**tú:xwelsxá ~ tù:xwelsxá**>, NUM ['*ninety*'], *see* tú:xw.

<**tú:xwelsxó:s**>, NUM ['*ninety dollars*'], *see* tú:xw.

<**tú:xwes**>, NUM /'*nine dollars, (nine Indian blankets [Boas])*'/, *see* tú:xw.

<**tuxwíqw**>, NUM ['*nine fish*'], *see* tú:xw.

<**tuxwíws**>, NUM ['*nine birds*'], *see* tú:xw.

<**tuxwòls**>, NUM ['*nine fruit in a group or cluster (as they grow on a plant)*'], *see* tú:xw.

<**tuxwő̂welh**>, NUM /'*nine canoes, nine boats*'/, *see* tú:xw.

<**txwéltsep**>, df //txʷ=ə́lcəp or to[=Aə=]xʷ=ə́lcəp//, FIRE ['*keep the fire at a constant temperature*'], literally (perhaps) /'firewood dragged behind'/, possibly root <**tóxw**> *drag behind*, possibly <**e-ablaut**> *durative or resultative*, lx <**=éltsep**> *firewood*, phonology: possibly ablaut, syntactic

analysis: intransitive verb, attested by NP (AHTTC 2/15/80).

<**txwém**>, df //t=xʷə́m or txʷ=xʷə́m//, TIME /'*early, right away*'/, probably <**txw=**> *toward*, probably root <**xwém ~ x̲wém**> *hurry, be fast*, phonology: possible consonant merger, syntactic analysis: adverb/adverbial verb, attested by Elders Group (5/28/75, 9/17/75), BHTTC (10/21/76), example: <**(tsel, tset, me) txwém xwe'í.**>, //(c-əl, c-ət, mə) txʷ=xʷə́m xʷə=ʔí//, /'*(I, We, He) got here early.*'/, <**me txwém qw'él te elíle.**>, //mə txʷ=xʷə́m **q'ʷə́l** tə ʔəlílə//, /'*The salmonberries are ripe early.*'/, <**txwém lhémetchexw.**>, //txʷ=xʷə́m ɬə́m=əT-c-əxʷ (or ɬi[=Aə́=]m=əT-c-əxʷ)//, /'*Pick it right away.*'/, attested by BHTTC.

<**txwméla ~ texwméla**>, KIN ['*adopt a child*'], *see* méle ~ mél:a.

<**txwmelám**>, KIN ['*adopt a child*'], *see* méle ~ mél:a.

<**txwó:ye**>, df //txʷ=á·yə or tá·xʷ=M1=yə//, TIME ['*be only remaining*'], probably root <**tó:xw**> *drag behind* or probably root <**téx̲w**> *later on, after a while*, possibly <**=ó:ye**> meaning uncertain unless related to (we)=ló:y> *only*, possibly <**metathesis**> *derivational*??, phonology: possible metathesis, syntactic analysis: adverb/adverbial verb?, attested by EB and AD (9/25/78), example: <**txwó:ye lúwe.**>, //txʷ=á·yə lúwə//, /'*Only you were remaining.*'/, <**txwó:ye lhwélep.**>, //txʷ=á·yə ɬwə́ləp//, /'*Only you folks were remaining.*'/, <**txwó:ye talhlímelh álwem.**>, //txʷ=á·yə tɛ=ɬlíməɬ ʔɛ́lw=əm//, /'*Only we were (remaining) left behind.*'/.

<**tx̲ét**>, SH ['*stretch it (stretch out someone's arms or wings)*'], *see* tex̲.

<**tx̲wṓwelh**>, CAN ['*pulling a canoe through rough water by a rope in the front*'], *see* tóx̲w.

T'

<**t'á**>, free root //t'ɛ́//, TAST ['*taste*'], syntactic analysis: intransitive verb, attested by BHTTC, example: <**selchím te t'ás?**>, //səlcím tə t'ɛ́-s//, /'*How does it taste?*'/, attested by BHTTC (11/26/76).

<**t'át ~ t'á:t**>, pcs //t'ɛ́=T ~ t'ɛ́·=T//, TAST /'*taste s-th, try s-th*'/, MC /'*try it, attempt it, test it*'/, SOC, SCH /'*test s-o*'/, SPRD /'*test s-o*'/, (<**=t**> *purposeful control transitivizer*), syntactic analysis: transitive verb, attested by AC, EB (12/12/75, 4/14/78), RG & EH (4/10/99 Ling332) other sources: H-T <t'at> (umlaut over a) *taste*, ASM ['taste s-th'], example: <**etsel t'át.**>, //ʔə-c-əl t'ɛ́=T//, /'*I tasted it.*'/, attested by AC (11/30/71), <**t'átlha kw'e axwí:l.**>, //t'ɛ́=T-ɬɛ k'ʷə ʔɛxʷí·l//, /'*Try a little.*'/, attested by EB (4/14/78), ASM ['try s-th, attempt s-th'], <**tsel le t'á:t.**>, //c-əl lə t'ɛ́·=T//, /'*I tried.*'/, attested by EB (12/12/75), <**tsel t'á:t kw'els xwemxálém kw'e la me t'éqw' te slhákw'em.**>, //c-əl t'ɛ́·=T k'ʷ-əl-s xʷəm=xʸə[=Aɛ́=]l=əm k'ʷə lə mə t'ə́q'ʷ tə s=ɬɛ́k'ʷ=əm//, /'*I tried to run but I ran out of breath.*'/, literally /'I tried it that I run that past come/begin to break my breath'/, attested by EB (12/12/75), <**t'át ew esu éyem**>, //t'ɛ́=T əw əsu éy=em//, SPRD /'test him/her if he/she is strong'/, attested by RG & EH (4/10/99 Ling332)

<**t'et'át**>, cts //C_1ə-t'ɛ́=T//, MC ['*trying it*'], TAST, SOC, (<**R5-**> *continuative*), phonology: reduplication, syntactic analysis: transitive verb, attested by EB (3/22/76); found in <**t'et'átes.**>, //C_1ə-t'ɛ́=T-əs//, /'*He's trying it.*'/.

<**t'óthet**>, pcrs //t'ɛ[-Aá-]=T-ət//, TIB /'*make an attempt (to do something difficult, like running rapids in a canoe, mountain-climbing, winning a game, etc.), give it a try*'/, (<**=t**> *purposeful control transitivizer*), (<**-et**> *reflexive*), phonology: ó-ablaut of root á automatic when -et reflexive is added, syntactic analysis: intransitive verb, attested by AD; found in <**t'óthetchelcha.**>, //t'ɛ[-Aá-]=T-ət-c-əl-cɛ//, /'*I'll make an attempt.*'/, usage: sometimes said under their breath by grandparents of today's elders before trying something hard, attested by AD (11/22/79).

<**t'át'emet te syőwels**>, iecs //t'ɛ́=C_1ə-=məT tə s=yúw=əl-s//, SPRD /'*singer for someone (at spirit dance)*'/, lit. /"trying-conserning-it/s-o the spirit-song-his/her"/, attested by RG & EH (4/10/99 Ling332)

<**st'a'áleqep**>, dnom //s=t'ɛ=ʔɛ́ləqəp//, TAST ['*(the) taste*'], (<**s=**> *nominalizer*), lx <**=áleqep**> *smell, taste*, phonology: glottal stop insertion between vowel-final root and vowel-initial suffix, or preservation of root-final glottal stop before vowel-initial suffix (root-final glottal stops are normally dropped in Upriver Halkomelem), an alternate possibility for the root is <**ta'á ~ te'á ~ t'á**> *similar, alike, same*, so the word is also given there, syntactic analysis: nominal, dialects: *Chill.*, attested by NP, also <**st'áleqep**>, //s=t'ɛ=ɛ́ləqəp//, dialects: *Cheh.*, attested by DF, example: <**ōwéta st'a'áleqeps.**>, //ʔowə= ´tɛ s=t'ɛ=ʔɛ́ləqəp-s//, /'*It has no taste.*'/, attested by NP (Elders Group 5/25/77), <**ōwéta st'áleqeps.**>, //ʔowə= ´tɛ s=t'ɛ=ɛ́ləqəp-s//, attested by DF (Elders Group 5/25/77).

<**t'ets'élmel**>, comment: probably mistranscribed for t'et'élmel, df //C_1ə=t'ɛ=ə́lməl//, TAST ['*taste*'], (<**R5=**> *continuative or resultative*), lx <**=élmel**> *in the mind*, phonology: vowel merger, syntactic analysis: nominal?, attested by Elders Group (5/25/77), example: <**ōwéta t'ets'élmels.**>, //ʔowə= ´tɛ C_1ə=t'ɛ=ə́lməl-s//, /'*It has no taste., It's tasteless.*'/.

<**t'ákwel**>, incs //t'ɛ́kʷ=əl//, CAN /'*cross a river, cross a road, cross over*'/, (<**=el**> *come, go, get, become*), syntactic analysis: intransitive verb, attested by IHTTC, Deming (3/16/78), Elders Group

(6/9/76).

<**t'át'ekwel**>, cts //t'ɛ́[-C₁ə-]kʷ=əl//, CAN ['*crossing over*'], (<**-R1-**> *continuative*), phonology: reduplication, syntactic analysis: intransitive verb, attested by Deming, Elders Group.

<**xwt'át'ekwel**>, dnom //xʷ=t'ɛ́[=C₁ə=]kʷ=əl//, CSTR /'*bridge, cable crossing*'/, CAN /'*something used to cross over a river, ferry, place good for crossing*'/, (<**xw=**> *always, [here something used for]*), (<**=R1=**> *continuative*), phonology: reduplication, syntactic analysis: nominal, attested by Deming (3/16/78), Elders Group (3/22/78).

<**t'át'ekwels**>, sas //t'ɛ́[=C₁ə=]kʷ=əls//, CAN ['*a ferryman*'], (<**=R1=**> *continuative*), lx <**=els**> *structured activity continuative*, phonology: reduplication, syntactic analysis: nominal, attested by IHTTC (9/2/77).

<**shxwt'át'ekwels**>, dnom //sxʷ=t'ɛ́[=C₁ə=]kʷ=əls//, CAN /'*a ferry (canoe, boat, ferryboat)*'/, (<**shxw=**> *something for*), (<**=R1=**> *continuative*), lx <**=els**> *structured activity continuative*, phonology: reduplication, syntactic analysis: nominal, attested by IHTTC (9/2/77).

<**t'kwíléstexw**>, caus //t'ɛkʷ=íl=əsT-əxʷ//, CAN /'*bring s-th/s-o across a river, (ferry s-o/s-th over)*'/, (<**=íl ~ =el**> *come, go, get, become*), (<**=(e)st**> *causative control transitivizer*), (<**-exw**> *third person object*), phonology: vowel-loss or zero-grade of root, updrifting, syntactic analysis: transitive verb, attested by Elders Group (3/22/78).

<**t'ál**>, probable root //t'ɛ́l//, perhaps meaning 'slice/split open' as in Lushootseed, or perhaps the entire word is borrowed from Lushootseed, with the s- prefix; if not borrowing it is cognate.

<**st'ál**>, dnom //s=t'ɛ́l//, FSH /'*fish cut real thin for wind-drying but without cross cuts, dried fish cut differently than slhíts'es*'/, (<**s=**> *nominalizer*), syntactic analysis: nominal, dialects: *Chill., Cheh.*, attested by IHTTC (8/5/77), contrast <**slhíts'es ~ shxwlhíts'es**> *wind-dried salmon with cross cuts*, also <**st'á:l**>, //s=t'ɛ́·l//, attested by Deming (2/7/80), Salish cognate: Lushootseed root /t'al(a)/ *slice, split open* as in /s-t'ál/ *sliced (fish) and /t'álad/ slice it* H76:518, also <**sit'ólh**>, //sit'áɬ or s=i=t'ɛ[=Aá=]ɬ//, also /'*fish cut real thin for wind-drying but without cross cuts*'/, possibly root <**t'álh**> *stretched across*, dialects: *Tait*, attested by IHTTC (8/5/77).

<**st'elt'elíqw**>, plv //st'əlt'əlíqʷ//, DESC /'*bumpy and prickly*'/ (perhaps lit. "sliced/split open everywhere"), (<**s-**> stative, <**R3=** or **C1eC2=**>, *plural, (usually) many in a group,* <=íqʷ > *on top of the head, hair* (attested by RG,EH 6/16/98 to SN, edited by BG with RG,EH 6/26/00)

<**st'elt'elíqw qwe'óp**>, EB, FOOD *pineapple* (lit. bumpy and prickly + apple), (attested by RG,EH 6/16/98 to SN, edited by BG with RG,EH 6/26/00)

<**st'elt'elíqw qwe'óp sqe'óleqw**>, FOOD *pineapple juice* (lit. pineapple [itself from bumpy and prickly + apple] + fruit juice), (attested by RG,EH 6/16/98 to SN, edited by BG with RG,EH 6/26/00)

<**t'á:l**>, free root //t'ɛ́·l//, LT /'*go out of sight (behind something), disappear [behind something], [get in shade]*'/, WETH, syntactic analysis: intransitive verb, attested by Elders Group (4/2/75, 5/19/76, 3/29/78), also <**t'ál**>, //t'ɛ́l//, attested by EB (5/18/76), Salish cognate: Squamish /t'ánʔuʔ/ *disappear, get out of sight, stand in the shade* W73:80, K67:270, example: <**lé t'à:l.**>, //lə t'ɛ̀·l//, /'*It went out of sight (like behind a cloud).*'/, attested by Elders Group (3/29/78), <**le t'á:l te syóqwem.**>, //lə t'ɛ́·l tə s=yə[=Aá=]qʷ=əm//, /'*The sun went out of sight., The sun disappeared.*'/, attested by Elders Group (4/2/75, 5/19/76), <**le t'á:l te mestí:yexw.**>, //lə t'ɛ́·l tə məstí·yəxʷ//, /'*A person went out of sight.*'/, attested by Elders Group (4/2/75).

<**t'á(:)lt**>, pcs //t'ɛ́·l=T//, WETH ['*eclipse s-th*'], LT, (<**=t**> *purposeful control transitivizer*), syntactic analysis: transitive verb, attested by Elders Group (5/19/76), example: <**t'áltes te skw'exós te syóqwem.**>, //t'ɛ́·l=T-əs tə s=k'ʷəxʸ=ás tə s=yə[=Aá=]qʷ=əm//, /'*The moon eclipses the sun.*'/.

<**t'ó:ltel ~ t'óltel**>, dnom //t'ɛ[-Aá-]·l=təl or t'ɛ[=Aá=]·l=təl//, WETH [*'an eclipse (of sun or moon)'*], LT, lx <**=tel**> *something to*, possibly <**ó-ablaut**> *durative or derivational*, phonology: ó-ablaut may instead be automatic root á → ó before =tel, syntactic analysis: nominal, attested by Elders Group (3/29/78, 5/19/76), also <**t'óltel ~ t'áltel**>, //t'ɛ[-Aá-]l=təl ~ t'ɛ́l=təl//, attested by IHTTC (8/10/77).

<**st'á:t'el**>, dnom //s=t'ɛ́·[=C_1ə=]l//, LT /*'(the) shade (of a tree for ex.), something that's not showing'*/, (<**s=**> *nominalizer*), (<**=R1=**> *continuative or resultative*), phonology: reduplication, syntactic analysis: nominal, attested by JL (5/5/75), also <**st'át'el**>, //s=t'ɛ́[=C_1ə=]l//, attested by Elders Group (4/2/75), EB (1/9/76).

<**st'ált'exw**>, comment: prob. mistranscribed for st'áltexw, df //s=t'ɛ́l=ltəx^w//, LT [*'a shade'*], BLDG [*'a shelter'*], (<**s=**> *nominal*), probably <**=eltexw ~ =áwtxw**> *building*, phonology: possible consonant merger, syntactic analysis: nominal, attested by Elders Group (9/7/77).

<**st'ált'exw**>, comment: prob. mistranscribed for st'áltexw, df //s=t'ɛ́l=ltəx^w//, LT [*'sheltered'*], (<**s=**> *stative*), probably <**=eltexw ~ =áwtxw**> *building*, phonology: possible consonant merger, syntactic analysis: adjective/adjectival verb, attested by Elders Group (9/7/77).

<**t'oléstel**>, df //t'ɛ[=Aa=]l=ə[=´=]s=təl//, HHG /*'window shades, blinds, blinders (on a horse, etc.)'*/, literally /'device to keep shade on the face'/, (<**o=ablaut**> *durative or derivational*, <=´=> *derivational*), lx <**=es**> *on the face*, lx <**=tel**> *device for*, phonology: stress-shift, ablaut or automatic root a → o before =tel, syntactic analysis: nominal, attested by Elders Group (7/9/75), also <**shxwt'oléstel**>, //sx^w=t'ɛ[=Aa=]l=ə[=´=]s=təl//, also /*'curtain, window shades, blinders on a horse'*/, attested by EB (5/25/76).

<**st'óle'oléstel**>, dnom //s=t'ɛ[=Aá=]l=ə=ʔalə[=´=]s=təl//, PE /*'eyeglasses, (probably dark glasses)'*/, literally /'device for shade on the eyes'/, (<**s=**> *nominalizer*), (<**o-ablaut**> *durative or derivational*), possibly <**=e=**> meaning uncertain, <=´=> *derivational*, lx <**=óles**> *on the eyes*, lx <**=tel**> *device for*, phonology: ablaut or automatic root a → o before =tel, stress-shift, syntactic analysis: nominal, attested by AC (11/11/71), also <**st'ole'ólestel**>, //s=t'ɛ[=Aa=]l=ə=ʔáləs=təl//, attested by Elders Group (7/9/75), example: <**máx ta st'óle'oléstel qe tl'o'asu kw'étslexw.**>, //mɛ́=x^y t-ɛ s=t'ɛ[=Aá=]l=ə=alə[=´=]s=təl qə ƛ'a-ʔɛ-s-u k'^{w}ə́c=l-əx^w//, /*'Take off your eyeglasses, then you can see it.'*/, attested by AC.

<**t'á:lew ~ t'álew**>, free root //t'ɛ́·ləw ~ t'ɛ́ləw//, ANAH [*'arm'*], ASM ['from wrist up'], ANA [*'front leg'*], syntactic analysis: noun, nominal, attested by Elders Group, AC, BJ (5/64), other sources: ES /t'ɛ́lə̀w·/ (CwMs /t'ɛ́ləwʔ/) *arm*, JH /t'elú·/ *arm*, H-T <tálu> (macrons over a and u) *arm*, <tEltálu> (macrons over a and u) *arms*.

<**t'álkw'els**>, FOOD [*'warming up food'*], *see* t'álqw' or t'élqw'.

<**t'á:lq**> or <**t'élq**>, possible root or stem //t'ɛ́·lq or t'ə[=Aɛ́·=]lq//, meaning uncertain

<**st'á:lq**>, strs //s=t'ɛ́·lq or s=t'ə[=Aɛ́·=]lq//, DESC /*'spotted with irregular shaped blobs (like if mud-spattered, used of dogs, deer, and other animals so marked)'*/, possibly <**á:-ablaut**> *resultative or durative*, phonology: possible ablaut, syntactic analysis: adjective/adjectival verb, attested by AD (10/15/79), CT (6/8/76), contrast <**tl'eltl'él<u>x</u>**> *spotted with circles (or round dots)*; compare <**st'elákw'**>, stvi //s=t'əlɛ́k'^{w}//, SH /*'circular, round and flat'*/

<**st'elt'élq**>, plv //s=C_1əC_2=t'ɛ[=Aə́=]lq or s=C_1əC_2=t'ə́lq//, DESC [*'spotted with lots of [irregular] spots'*], possibly <**é-ablaut**> *resultative or durative*, phonology: reduplication, possible ablaut, syntactic analysis: adjective/adjectival verb, attested by CT (6/8/76), Salish cognate: Squamish /ʔəs-t'ə́-t'lq^w/ *form a spot on* K69:50.

<**t'álqw' or t'élqw'**>, bound root //t'ɛ́lq'^{w} or t'ə́lq'^{w} *warm*//.

<**t'álqw'em**>, izs //t'ɛ́lq'^{w}=əm or t'ə[=Aɛ́=]lq'^{w}=əm//, FOOD /'*warm, luke-warm*'/, FIRE, DESC, (<**=em**> *intransitivizer, get, have*), syntactic analysis: adjective/adjectival verb, attested by AC (8/7/70, 10/1/71), MH (Deming 1/4/79), Salish cognate: Squamish /t'íʔq^{w}m/ *spark, flame, throw off large sparks or chips of glowing (cedar) wood* W73:244, K67:271, K69:51, example: <**t'álqw'em qó:**>, //t'ɛ́q'^{w}=əm qá·//, /'*warm water*'/, attested by MH.

<**t'elkw'á:ls**>, comment: prob. mistranscribed for t'elqw'á:ls, sas //t'əlq'^{w}=ɛ́·ls or t'ɛlq'^{w}=ɛ́·ls//, FOOD /'*warm up (food, tea, etc.)*'/, FIRE, lx <**=á:ls**> *structured activity non-continuative*, syntactic analysis: intransitive verb, attested by IHTTC (8/22/77, 9/2/77).

<**t'álkw'els**>, comment: prob. mistranscribed for t'álqw'els, cts //t'ɛ́lq'^{w}=əls//, sas, FOOD ['*warming up food*'], FIRE, lx <**=els**> *structured activity continuative*, syntactic analysis: intransitive verb, attested by IHTTC (9/2/77).

<**t'élqw't**>, pcs //t'ə́lq'^{w}=T or t'ɛ[=Aə́=]lq'^{w}=T//, FOOD ['*warm it up*'], (<**=t**> *purposeful control transitivizer*), syntactic analysis: transitive verb, attested by Elders Group (5/19/76), also <**t'élkw't**>, //t'ə́lk'^{w}=T//, also /'*warm it up (food, tea, etc.)*'/, attested by IHTTC (8/22/77).

<**T'eláqw'tel**>, df //t'ɛ́l[=M1=]q'^{w}=təl//, N ['*Indian name of Old Jack (of Yakweakwioose or perhaps Scowkale)*'], Elder's comment: "that means "something that would be hot"", literally /'something to warm'/, possibly <**metathesis**> *derivational*, lx <**=tel**> *device to, something to*, phonology: metathesis, syntactic analysis: nominal, attested by DM (12/4/64).

<**t'álqw'em**>, FOOD /'*warm, luke-warm*'/, *see* t'álqw' or t'élqw'.

<**t'á(:)lt**>, WETH ['*eclipse s-th*'], *see* t'á:l.

<**t'álh**>, bound root //t'ɛ́ɬ *stretch across*//.

<**st'álh**>, dnom //s=t'ɛ́ɬ//, BLDG ['*cross-beam (in a house)*'], (<**s=**> *nominalizer*), syntactic analysis: nominal, source: Boas summer 1890 Scowlitz word list, "Sk·'au ́lits. Harrison mouth. (Dialect of Snanaimuq)", discussed in Elders Group 5/3/78, contrast <**shxwt'ólhestel**> (EB) *beam*, contrast <**t'élhmel**> (TG) *cross beam (in house)*.

<**shxwt'álh**>, dnom //sx^{w}=t'ɛ́ɬ//, CSTR ['*bridge*'], (<**shxw=**> *something that*), syntactic analysis: nominal, attested by Elders Group (3/15/72), EB (2/6/76).

<**st'át'elh**>, strs //s=t'ɛ́[=C_1ə=]ɬ//, DIR ['*across*'], (<**s=**> *stative*), (<**=R1=**> *resultative*), phonology: reduplication, syntactic analysis: adjective/adjectival verb, attested by Elders Group (5/3/78).

<**st'át'elhíles**>, strs //s=t'ɛ́[=C_1ə=]ɬ=íləs//, HARV ['*carry a packstrap slung across the chest (over one shoulder and under one arm)*'], (<**s=**> *stative*), (<**=R1=**> *resultative*), lx <**=íles**> *on the chest*, phonology: reduplication, syntactic analysis: intransitive verb, attested by IHTTC (8/10/77).

<**(s)tl'lhíléstel**>, comment: prob. mistranscribed for (s)t'lhíléstel, dnom //(s=)t'ɬ=íləs=təl//, ANA ['*collarbone*'], literally prob./'something that stretches across on the chest'/, (<**s=**> *nominalizer*), probably root <**t'alh**> *stretch across*, probably <**vowel-loss**> *derivational*, lx <**=íles**> *on the chest*, lx <**=tel**> *something that*, phonology: vowel-loss, updrifting, syntactic analysis: nominal, attested by Elders Group (8/20/75).

<**t'élhmel**>, dnom //t'ɛ[=Aə́=]ɬ=məl//, BLDG ['*cross-beam (in a house)*'], (<**é-ablaut**> *durative or derivational*), lx <**=mel**> *part, portion*, phonology: ablaut, syntactic analysis: nominal, attested by TG (Elders Group 5/3/78).

<**t'élhtel**>, dnom //t'ɛ[=Aə́=]ɬ=təl//, WV ['*loom*'], literally /'device that something is stretched across'/, (<**é-ablaut**> *durative or derivational*), lx <**=tel**> *device that, something that*, phonology: ablaut,

syntactic analysis: nominal, attested by JL (Elders Group 8/8/79).

<t'lhéses>, dnom //t'ɬ=ə́s(=)əs//, WV ['*a loom*'], literally poss. /'stretched design on the face??'/, possibly **<vowel-loss>** *derivational*, possibly **<=es>** *design*, possibly **<=es>** *on the face*, possibly **<=éses>** meaning unknown, phonology: vowel-loss, syntactic analysis: nominal, attested by AK (5/27/76).

<t'élhtsestel>, dnom //t'ɛ[=Aə́=]ɬ=cəs=təl//, WV /'*net shuttle and net-measure, gill-net measure, (loom [Elders Group])*'/, FSH, literally /'device that is stretched across in the hand'/, (**<é-ablaut>** *durative or derivational*), lx **<=tses>** *in/on the hand*, lx **<=tel>** *device that*, phonology: ablaut, syntactic analysis: nominal, attested by JL (8/8/79), Deming (4/17/80), also /'*loom, net shuttle and net-measure*'/, attested by Elders Group (8/25/76), also **<shxwt'élhtsestel>**, //sxʷ=t'ɛ[=Aə́=]ɬ=cəs=təl//, also /'*net-measure*'/, attested by JL (Elders Group 4/5/78).

<shxwt'ólhestel>, dnom //sxʷ=t'ɛ[-Aá-]ɬ=əs=təl//, BLDG ['*beam*'], literally /'device for stretching across on the face (of a building)'/, (**<shxw=>** *something that*), lx **<=es>** *on the face*, lx **<=tel>** *something for, device for*, phonology: root á becomes ó automatically before =es, syntactic analysis: nominal, attested by EB (5/25/76).

<t'ót'elhem>, df //t'á[=C₁ə=]ɬ=əm//, EZ ['*jumping flea*'], ['order *Siphonaptera*'], PLAY ['*name of a cat's cradle design or pattern*'], probably literally *stretching across*, having to do with their jumps stretching across or their long legs (**<=R1=>** *continuative*), **<=em>** *have, get, intransitive*, possibly **<-em>** *middle voice*, phonology: reduplication, syntactic analysis: nominal, attested by AC, BJ (12/5/64), Deming (2/7/80), Elders Group (3/1/72), IHTTC (9/14/77), other sources: ES /t'át'əɬəm/ *flea*, H-T <ta'tetlEm> (macron over a) *flea (Pulex irritans)*.

<t'am>, bound root, //t'ɛ́m//, *braid, weave*

<t'ámex>, pcis //t'ɛ́m=əxʸ//, [t'ɛ́mɪxʸ], PE ['*to braid (hair)*'], WV, (**<=ex>** *purposeful control inanimate object preferred*), root meaning unknown, syntactic analysis: transitive verb, attested by AC, AD (8/80), example: **<t'ámex ta máqel>**, //t'ɛ́m=əxʸ t-ɛ mɛ́=qəl//, /'*braid your hair*'/, attested by AC, **<t'ámexchexw ta' máqel.>**, //t'ɛ́m=əxʸ-c-əxʷ t-ɛʔ mɛ́=qəl//, /'*Braid your hair.*'/, attested by AD.

<st'amxá:lts'>, df //s=t'ɛm=əxʸ=ɛ́·lc'//, PE ['*a braid*'], WV, literally /'something braid-twisted'/, (**<s=>** *nominalizer*), lx **<=á:lts'>** *twisted*, phonology: vowel-loss, syntactic analysis: nominal, attested by Deming (3/11/76), also **<st'emxá:lts' ~ st'amxá:lts>**, //s=t'ɛm=xʸ=ɛ́·lc' ~ s=t'ɛm=xʸ=ɛ́·lc//, attested by Elders Group (10/8/75).

<T'ít'emt'ámex>, df //C₁í=C₁əC₂=t'ɛ́m=əxʸ//, PLN ['*railway tunnel just past (east of) Ruby Creek*'], (semological comment: possibly so called because one trail twisted around (like a braid, st'ámex) to get by where the tunnel is; SP on the other hand said that the place is the real home of T'ámiya as explained in a story and is derived from that word (but why was =iya replaced by =ex, which makes the end of the word look exactly like it derives from t'ámex?)), (**<R4=>** *diminutive*), probably **<R3=>** *plural*, phonology: double reduplication, syntactic analysis: nominal, attested by SP, perhaps others (IHTTC 8/11/77, Raft trip 8/30/77, American Bar trip 6/26/78), source: place names file reference #190a.

<st'emíywelh>, df //s=t'ɛ[=Aə=]m=íy=wəɬ//, WV ['*warp (vertical threads of weaving)*'], Elder's comment: "ask AK for these words since her grandmother used to wear a swő̄qw'elh (woven goat wool blanket) when she danced; JL saw it when AK was only 4 or 5 yrs. old", (**<s=>** *nominalizer*), root **<t'am>** *braid, weave*, derivational ablaut or stress shift and downgrading to schwa before stressed suffix **<=iy>** *bark, covering, wool*, possibly **<=welh>** *vessel, canoe* (perhaps since the loom is a long vessel for the weaving), syntactic analysis: nominal, source: Wells 1969:13

<st'MAY-wuhlth> *the warp*, attested by JL (8/8/79) only discusses the gloss, comment: Wells 1969 also gives other weaving terms, some not attested elsewhere: <THASS-eh-tuh-tel> *the loom*, <s'AH-uhl-'LOHq> *twined weave, ceremonial blanket* (pp.6 and 16), as well as <SWOH-kwah-'tl> (Stó:lō orthog. <swṓqw'elh>) *twilled weave*, and <KIY-siht-sel> (Stó:lō orthog. <q'ísetsel>) *to weave*; however it should be mentioned that the words cited in Wells 1969 (others as well as those repeated here) are among his brother Casey's worst transcriptions--deviating from his own system and more inaccurate (esp. pp.6-7) than his transcriptions elsewhere.

<**t'ám**>, possibly root //t'ɛ́m *guess* or t'ɛ́ *try*//.

<**st'ám**>, stvi //s=t'ɛ́m or s=t'ɛ́=əm//, LANG ['*(be a) guess*'], (<**s=**> *stative*), possibly <**=em**> *intransitivizer, have, get*, syntactic analysis: adjective/adjectival verb, attested by BHTTC (10/2/76), example: <**st'ám s'ewólem**>, //s=t'ɛ́m s=ʔi[=Aə=]wál=əm//, /'*a guess game*'/, PLAY.

<**st'át'em**>, cts //s=t'ɛ́[-C_1ə-]m//, LANG ['*(be) guessing*'], (<**-R1-**> *continuative*), phonology: reduplication, syntactic analysis: adjective/adjectival verb, attested by BHTTC (10/2/76), example: <**st'át'em s'ewólem**>, //s=t'ɛ́[-C_1ə-]m s=ʔi[=Aə=]wál=əm//, /'*a guessing game*'/, PLAY.

<**t'ámet**>, pcs //t'ɛ́m=əT//, LANG ['*guess it*'], PLAY ['*[make] a point in slahal*'], (<**=et**> *purposeful control transitivizer*), syntactic analysis: transitive verb, attested by Elders Group (9/8/76), also <**t'e'ámet**>, //t'əʔɛ́m=əT//, also /'*guess it*'/, attested by BHTTC (10/2/76).

<**t'ót'emethet**>, pcrs //t'ɛ[-Aa-]´[=C_1ə=]m=əT-ət//, rsls, EFAM /'*suspect, be suspicious*'/, literally /'have guessed purposely oneself'/, (<**=R1=**> *resultative*), phonology: reduplication, o-ablaut on root á automatic with =thet reflexive, syntactic analysis: intransitive verb, attested by Deming (5/6/76).

<**st'émt'em**>, chrs //s=t'ɛ[=Aə́=]m=C_1əC_2//, stvi, EFAM ['*(be) cautious*'], literally /'be durative characteristically guess'/, (<**s=**> *stative*), (<**é-ablaut**> *resultative or durative* or automatic with *characteristic*), (<**=R2**> *characteristic*), phonology: reduplication, ablaut, syntactic analysis: adjective/adjectival verb, attested by BHTTC (10/2/76).

<**t'át'emes**>, dnom //t'ɛ́[=C_1ə=]m=əs//, PLAY ['*guesser (in slahal)*'], (<**=R1=**> *continuative or durative*), possibly <**=es**> *in the face; dollars, money*, phonology: reduplication, syntactic analysis: nominal, attested by Elders Group (3/14/79).

<**st'e'áwel ~ st'áwel**>, df //s=t'əʔɛ́=əwəl ~ s=t'ɛ́=əwəl//, EFAM /'*to guess, make a guess*'/, LANG, possibly <**s=**> *stative*?, lx <**=ewel ~ =íwel**> *in the insides*, phonology: vowel merger, syntactic analysis: intransitive verb, attested by EB (12/16/75), compare <**t'wa ~ t'we**> *must be (evidently), I guess*, example: <**tsel st'áwel kwses thét kws lámtset.**>, //c'-əl' š=t'ɛ́=əwəl k^w-s-əs θə́t k^w-s lɛ́=m-c-ət//, /'*I guess that she said that we're going.*'/, syntactic comment: double embedding, attested by EB.

<**t'à:m**>, free root //t'ɛ̀·m//, SPRD ['*to sing along or follow in singing a spirit song*'], syntactic analysis: intransitive verb, attested by Elders Group (9/1/76), also <**t'ám ?**>, //t'ɛ́m ?//, also /'*song of an Indian doctor or shaman*'/, attested by BHTTC (8/31/76).

<**t'am:**> or <***t'amʔ**> or <**t'em**>, possible root //t'ɛ́m· or t'amʔ or t'ə[=Aɛ́=]m//, meaning unknown

<**shxwt'ám:etsel**>, df //sx^w=t'ɛ́m·=əcəl or sx^w=t'ə[=Aɛ́=]m=əcəl//, EB ['*young (red) cedar*'], (<**shxw=**> *something that*), root meaning unknown unless t'ém *chop*, possibly <**á-ablaut**> *derivational*, lx <**=etsel**> *on the back*, syntactic analysis: nominal, dialects: *Cheh.*, attested by Elders Group (6/11/75).

<**t'ámel (or) t'ém:el**>, MC ['*wood chips*'], *see* t'ém.

<**t'ámet**>, LANG [*'guess it'*], *see* t'ám.

<**t'ámiya**>, df //t'ɛ́m=iyɛ//, HUMC /*'hermaphrodite (person with organs of both sexes), hermaphrodite baby'*/, ABDF [*'deformed baby'*], ASM ['called "morphodite" by several elders; couldn't tell its sex till about three years old; they didn't let them live unles found out only after grown, i.e. about three year old; the Chilliwacks left them to die up the mountain they called T'amiyahó:y (McGuire Mt., the Whites confused the mountain with one next to it which they now call Mt. Tamihi, according to AC)'], probably root <**t'ám**> *guess*, lx <**=iya**> *affectionate diminutive; personal name ending*, syntactic analysis: nominal, attested by AC, others, other sources: ES /st'ə́məyə/ *berdache* (a person of one sex who assumes a role of the other sex, sometimes transvestite, the word berdache is Chinook Jargon), JH /t'əmihé·y/ *hermaphrodite*, comment: the place name for Hope Mt., St'ámiya, also translated as *hermaphrodite* and resembling such a person lying on its back, besides the form given by Elmendorf and Suttles (ES), points to a possible alternate form of this word, i.e., st'ámiya; that would keep the word clear from another word, t'ámiya *winter wren*.

<**St'ámiya**>, df //s=t'ɛ́m=iyɛ//, PLN [*'Hope Mountain'*], ASM ['resembles a person lying on its back with head, breasts, and lump for male genitals at hips, when viewed from the north side, as on the Fraser River several miles above Hope, looking south'], literally /'hermaphrodite'/, (<**s=**> *nominalizer*), syntactic analysis: nominal, attested by Elders Group (7/13/77), AK/AD/SP/NP/EB (Trip to American Bar 6/26/78), source: place names file reference #55.

<**T'amiyahó:y**>, cpds //t'ɛm=iyɛ=há·y//, PLN /*'Mount McGuire, (Tamihi Mountain [BJ])'*/, probably root <**t'ámiya**> *hermaphrodite* and probably root <**hó:y**> *finish, end*, syntactic analysis: nominal, attested by AC, SP (Elders Group 8/24/77), source: place names file reference #168, #231, also /*'Tamihi Mountain'*/, attested by BJ (12/5/64).

<**T'ami(ye)hóy (Stótelō)**>, cpds //t'ɛm=i(yə)=háy s=tá[=C_1ə=]low//, PLN [*'Tamihi Creek'*], ASM ['tributary of Chilliwack River entering from the south'], literally /'hermaphrodite finish creek'/, (<**=R1=**> *diminutive*), phonology: reduplication, syntactic analysis: nominal phrase with modifier(s), attested by (photo identification 6/19/78), source: Wells 1965 (lst ed.):13, source: place names file reference #169.

<**T'ami(ye)hóy (X̱ótsa)**>, cpds //t'ɛm=i(yə)=háy x̣ácɛ//, PLN [*'Tamihi Lake'*], literally /'hermaphrodite finish lake'/, syntactic analysis: nominal phrase with modifier(s), source: Wells 1965 (lst ed.):11.

<**T'emiyéq(w) ??**>, df //t'ɛm=iyɛ=ə́q(ʷ)//, PLN [*'Tamihi village at the mouth of Tamihi Creek'*], probably root <**t'amiya**> *hermaphrodite*, possibly <=eqw> *top of head* or <=aq ~ =eq> *penis, genitals*, phonology: known only from Wells 1965, syntactic analysis: nominal, source: Wells 1965 (lst ed.):19.

<**t'ámiya**>, df //t'ɛ́m=iyɛ//, EZ /*'little winter wren (a real little bird), wren (likes dense woods and woodpiles), may also include (esp.) Bewick's wren, long-billed marsh wren, house wren, and rock wren (all five possible in the area)'*/, [*'Troglodytes troglodytes pacificus*, may also include (esp.)*Thryomanes bewickii, Telmatodytes palustris paludicola, Troglodytes aedon,*and *Salpinctes obsoletus'*], root meaning unknown, lx <**=iya**> *affectionate diminutive; personal name ending*, syntactic analysis: nominal, attested by BJ (12/5/64), AC, Elders Group (3/1/72, 2/18/76).

<**t'át'emiya**>, dmn //t'ɛ́[=C_1ə=]m=iyɛ//, EZ /*'baby wren, little or young wren'*/, (<**=R1=**> *diminutive*), phonology: reduplication, if doubling infix #1 with e is right rather than doubling prefix with á then it proves that the root vowel is á rather than é (as in Elmendorf and Suttles), syntactic analysis: nominal, attested by Elders Group (3/1/72, 2/18/76).

<**T'amiyahó:y**>, PLN /*'Mount McGuire, (Tamihi Mountain [BJ])'*/, *see* t'ámiya.

<**T'ami(ye)hóy (Stótelō)**>, PLN ['*Tamihi Creek*'], *see* t'ámiya.

<**T'ami(ye)hóy (X̲ótsa)**>, PLN ['*Tamihi Lake*'], *see* t'ámiya.

<**t'á:mxw**>, uf //t'ɛ́·mxʷ//, EB ['*gooseberry*'], ['*Ribes* spp., *Ribes divaricatum, Ribes lobbii*, possibly others'], possibly <**=mexw**> meaning unclear (as in skw'ő:lmexw ~ sqw'ő:lmexw> *blackberry*), syntactic analysis: noun, nominal, attested by AC, other sources: ES /t'ɛ́·məxʷ/ *gooseberry*.

<**t'á:mxwelhp**>, ds //t'ɛ́·mxʷ=əɬp//, EB ['*gooseberry bush*'], Elder's comment: "sour, see how many you can chew", lx <**=elhp**> *plant, tree*, syntactic analysis: nominal, attested by AC.

<**temt'á:mxw**>, ds //təm=t'ɛ́·mxʷ//, TIME /'*gooseberry time, the month or moon (first sliver) that starts in June*'/, (<**tem=**> *time for, season for*), syntactic analysis: nominal, attested by Elders Group (3/12/75).

<**t'á:mxwelhp**>, EB ['*gooseberry bush*'], *see* t'á:mxw.

<**t'ápiy**>, stem //t'ɛ́p=iy *dead (of flora)*//, possibly related to root in <**t'ópet**> *to chip it (like wood), peck s-th/s-o, chisel s-th* with <**=á:y ~ =ey ~ =iy**> *bark, wood, plant.*

<**st'ápiy**>, strs //s=t'ɛ́p=iy or s=t'ə[=Aɛ́=]p=iy//, EB ['*dead and broken [of a plant]*'], (<**s=**> *stative*), possibly <**á-ablaut**> *resultative or durative*, lx <**=iy**> *plant*, phonology: possible ablaut, syntactic analysis: adjective/adjectival verb, attested by AC, other sources: ES /st'ɛ́pəy/ (though with s= *nominalizer*) *snag (dead tree standing)*, Salish cognate: perhaps Squamish root /t'ap/ *free from water, watertight* W73:284, K69:50, example: <**st'ápiy theqá:t**>, //s=t'ɛ́p=iy θəqɛ́·t//, /'*dead and broken tree*'/, attested by AC.

<**t'ápiythet**>, incs //t'ɛ́p=iy=θət//, EB ['*it's dead (of a tree)*'], (<**=thet**> *inceptive, get, become*), syntactic analysis: intransitive verb, attested by AC (11/22/71).

<**t'ópiythet**>, cts //t'ɛ[-Aá-]p=iy=θət//, EB ['*it's going dead (of a tree)*'], (<**ó-ablaut**> *continuative*), phonology: ablaut, syntactic analysis: intransitive verb, attested by AC (11/22/71), example: <**le t'ópiythet te theqá:t.**>, //lə t'ɛ[-Aá-]p=iy=θət tə θəqɛ́·t//, /'*The tree went dead.*'/, comment: the English translation is inconsistent with the expected continuative; --either the gloss of the sentence is wrong or the vowel should be á not ó or the glosses of both t'ápiythet and t'ópiythet are reversed above, attested by AC (11/22/71).

<**t'ápiythet**>, EB ['*it's dead (of a tree)*'], *see* t'ápiy.

<**t'áqà:lhp**>, EB ['*salal bush*'], *see* t'áqe.

<**t'áqe**>, free root //t'ɛ́qə//, EB ['*salal berry*'], ['*Gaultheria shallon*'], ASM ['black berry is at peak in August, eaten whenever ripe, can be dried and stored'], may be derived from or related to <**t'íq**>, possibly root //t'íq or t'ə[=Aí=]q *discolored, bruised*//, as in Squamish cognate, syntactic analysis: noun, nominal, attested by BJ (12/5/64 old p.302), also <**t'á:qa**>, //t'ɛ́·qɛ//, attested by AC, other sources: ES /t'ɛ́qə/ and JH /t'éqə/ *salal berry*, Salish cognate: Squamish /t'áqaʔ/ *be bruised (so that the skin has the color of a salalberry), salalberry* W73:46, K67:270, Samish dial. of N. Straits /t'áqaʔ/ *to get bruised* and /št'əqaʔáləs/ *(get) a black eye* G86c:76

<**t'áqà:lhp**>, ds //t'ɛ́qə=ɛ́ɬp//, EB ['*salal bush*'], lx <**=álhp ~ =elhp**> *plant, tree*, phonology: vowel merger, syntactic analysis: nominal, attested by AC.

<**t'ás**>, free root //t'ɛ́s//, SD ['*quiet (in movement)*'], TVMO, syntactic analysis: adjective/adjectival verb, attested by IHTTC (7/18/77), example: <**t'ás mestíyexw**>, //t'ɛ́s məstíyəxʷ//, /'*quiet person (in movement)*'/, attested by IHTTC.

<**t'et'ás**>, cts //C_1ə-t'ɛ́s//, SD ['*be stealthy*'], TVMO, literally /'being quiet in movement'/, (<**R5-**> *continuative*), phonology: reduplication, syntactic analysis: intransitive verb, attested by Elders

Group (3/23/77); found in <**t'et'áschap.**>, //C_1ə-t'ɛ́s-c-ɛp//, /'*You folks be stealthy.*'/.

<**t'esí:l**>, incs //t'ɛs=í·l//, ABFC ['*go down (of swelling)*'], literally /'become quiet (in movement)'/, lx <**=í:l**> *go, come, get, become*, phonology: vowel-reduction, syntactic analysis: intransitive verb, attested by BHTTC (9/14/76), ABFC /'*stop burning (of a burn), go down (of swelling)*'/, attested by EB (BHTTC 9/14/76).

<**t'ásxel**>, ds //t'ɛ́s=x^{y}əl//, TVMO /'*walk silently, walk quietly*'/, ABFC, lx <**=xel**> *on the foot*, syntactic analysis: intransitive verb, attested by IHTTC (7/18/77).

<**t'et'ásxel or t'at'ásxel**>, cts //C_1ə-t'ɛ́s=x^{y}əl or C_1ɛ-t'ɛ́x^{y}əl//, TVMO ['*walk*[ing] silently or quietly'], ABFC, (<**R5- or R8-**> *continuative*), phonology: reduplication, syntactic analysis: intransitive verb, attested by IHTTC (7/18/77).

<**t'ásxelem**>, mdls //t'ɛ́s=x^{y}əl=əm//, TVMO /'*walk lightly, sneak*'/, ABFC, (<**=em**> *middle voice*), syntactic analysis: intransitive verb, attested by Elders Group (12/15/76).

<**t'et'ásxelem**>, cts //C_1ə-t'ɛ́s=x^{y}əl=əm//, TVMO /'*tip-toeing, (walking lightly, sneaking)*'/, ABFC, (<**R5-**> *continuative*), phonology: reduplication, syntactic analysis: intransitive verb, attested by IHTTC (7/18/77).

<**t'esítsmels**>, df //t'ɛs=íc=əm=əls or t'ɛ[=Aə=]s=íc=məl=əls//, FSH ['*hide-away that a fish makes*'], lx <**=íts**> *on the back*, possibly <**=em**> *middle voice or intransitivizer*, possibly <**=mel**> *part of, portion of*, possibly <**=els**> *structured activity continuative/nominalizer*, phonology: possible syllable-loss, possible ablaut, syntactic analysis: nominal, attested by TG (Elders Group 2/6/80).

<**t'ásxel**>, TVMO /'*walk silently, walk quietly*'/, *see* t'ás.

<**t'ásxelem**>, TVMO /'*walk lightly, sneak*'/, *see* t'ás.

<**t'át ~ t'á:t**>, TAST /'*taste s-th, try s-th*'/, *see* t'á.

<**t'át'ekwel**>, CAN ['*crossing over*'], *see* t'ákwel.

<**t'át'ekwels**>, CAN ['*a ferryman*'], *see* t'ákwel.

<**t'át'emes**>, PLAY ['*guesser (in slahal)*'], *see* t'ám.

<**t'át'emiya**>, EZ /'*baby wren, little or young wren*'/, *see* t'ámiya.

<**t'át'eth'em**>, TAST /'*sour (unripe or half-ripe fruit, lemon, Oregon grape, fermenting fruit)*'/, *see* t'áth'.

<**t'át'eyeq' ~ t'át'iyeq'**>, EFAM /'*being angry, continue to be angry, angry, mad, roused, stirred up*'/, *see* t'ay.

<**t'at'íyelt**>, SOC ['*entertaining s-o*'], *see* t'íyelt or t'í:lt.

<**t'áth'**>, bound root //t'ɛ́θ' *to ferment, to sour*//.

<**t'át'eth'em**>, df //t'ɛ́[=C_1ə=]θ'=əm//, TAST /'*sour (unripe or half-ripe fruit, lemon, Oregon grape, fermenting fruit)*'/, (<**=R1=**> *continuative or resultative*), (<**=em**> *middle voice or intransitive, have, get*), phonology: reduplication, syntactic analysis: adjective/adjectival verb, attested by AHTTC, TG (4/75, Elders Group 3/26/80), AD, AC, Elders Group (6/16/75), also <**t'át'ets'em**>, //t'ɛ́[=C_1ə=]c'=əm//, attested by Elders Group (6/16/75), TM (AD 12/17/79), EB (1/7/76), AK/SP (Raft Trip 8/30/77), Salish cognate: Lushootseed /t'ác'əb/ *bitter (taste), sour (as sour milk); spoil* H76:516, example: <**t'át'eth'em te'íle léth'ilets.**>, //t'ɛ́[=C_1ə=]θ'=əm tə=í=lə lə́θ'=iy=ləc//, /'*These blueberries are [sour].*'/, attested by EB (4/14/78), <**t'át'ets'em ts'esémelep**>, //t'ɛ́[=C_1ə=]c'=əm c'is=ə[=´=]m=ələp//, EB /'*sourgrass, (sheep sorrel)*'/, ['*Rumex acetosella*'], literally /'sour weeds'/, ASM ['introduced post-contact, leaves eaten raw for their lemony flavor'], attested by AK/SP (Raft Trip 8/30/77).

<**t'át'ets'em kúkumels**>, FOOD *pickles* (lit. sour + cucumber), (attested by RG,EH 6/16/98 to SN, edited by BG with RG,EH 6/26/00)

<**t'át'ets'em qwíyqwòyèls**>, EB, FOOD *lemon* (lit. sour + orange fruit/little yellowish fruit), (attested by RG,EH 6/16/98 to SN, edited by BG with RG,EH 6/26/00)

<**t'át'ets'em qwíyqwòyèls sqe'óleqw**>, FOOD *lemonade* (lit. lemon [itself < sour little yellow fruit] + fruit juice), (attested by RG,EH 6/16/98 to SN, edited by BG with RG,EH 6/26/00)

<**t'át'ets'em qwíqwòyèls kíks seplíl**>, FOOD *lemon cake* (lit. lemon (itself from sour little yellowish fruit) + cake + bread), (attested by RG,EH 6/16/98 to SN, edited by BG with RG,EH 6/26/00)

<**t'át'ets'em tsqwáyqwòyèls**>, EB, FOOD *lime* (lit. sour + greenish fruit), (attested by RG,EH 6/16/98 to SN, edited by BG with RG,EH 6/26/00)

<**t'át'ets'em qwíyqwòyèls qas te t'át'ets'em tsqwáyqwòyèls sqe'óleqw**>, FOOD *lemonlime juice* (lit. lemon fruit [itself < sour little yellowish fruit] + and + the + lime fruit [itself < sour + greenish fruit]+ fruit juice), (attested by RG,EH 6/16/98 to SN, edited by BG with RG,EH 6/26/00)

<**t'át'ets'em seplíl**>, FOOD *sourdough bread* (lit. sour + bread), (attested by RG,EH 6/16/98 to SN, edited by BG with RG,EH 6/26/00)

<**thepth'epéy t'át'ets'em sqemó**>, FOOD *yogurt* (lit. curdled + sour + milk), (attested by RG,EH 6/16/98 to SN, edited by BG with RG,EH 6/26/00)

<**t'eth'ó:mthet**>, incs //t'εθ'=ə[=Aá·=]m=θət//, durs, TAST [*'fermenting'*], EB, probably <**ó:-ablaut**> *durative*, (<**=thet**> *get, become*), phonology: ablaut, syntactic analysis: intransitive verb, attested by AHTTC (2/15/80).

<**t'á:ts'**>, free root //t'ɛ́·c'//, FSH /*'fish-spreader for drying fish, cross-piece for drying fish, salmon stretcher'*/, ASM ['best made from pink spirea wood, from about 5 to 10 inches long, a number of these are used on each scored salmon to keep the flesh open when being wind-dried or smoked'], (semological comment: an original meaning something like *split stick* is implied by derived form t'ats'e<u>x</u>elí:m *mistake in splitting roots by making them uneven*), syntactic analysis: nominal, attested by SP and AD (6/27/75).

<**t'áts'elhp**>, ds //t'ɛ́c'=əɬp//, EB /*'pink spirea, "hardhack"'*/, [*'Spiraea douglasii'*], ASM ['hard wood used for making fish-spreaders and also for mat-making needles, spoons, and spears'], lx <**=elhp**> *plant, tree*, phonology: length-loss perhaps optional, syntactic analysis: nominal, attested by SP and AD (6/27/75), AC (prompted), other sources: ES /t'ɛ́·c'əɬp/ *pink spirea.*

<**t'ats'e<u>x</u>elí:m**>, df //t'εc'=əx̣əl=í·m or t'εc'=əx̣əl=ə[=Aí·=]m//, BSK [*'mistake in splitting roots by making them uneven'*], lx <**=e<u>x</u>el**> *part, portion, arm*, probably <**=í:m**> *repeatedly*, possibly <**í:-ablaut**> *durative* with <**=em**> *middle voice or intransitivizer, have, get*, phonology: possible ablaut, syntactic analysis: intransitive verb, attested by Elders Group (5/28/75).

<**t'ats'e<u>x</u>elí:m**>, BSK [*'mistake in splitting roots by making them uneven'*], *see* t'á:ts'.

<**t'áw**>, possible bound root //t'ɛ́w//, meaning unknown

<**st'áwel**>, df //s(=)t'ɛ́w=əl//, LT [*'purple'*], (<**s=**> *stative*), (<**=el ~ =íl**> *go, come, get, become*), compare <**st'ewő kw'**> *diatomaceous earth, whitish powder for whitening wool,* syntactic analysis: adjective/adjectival verb, attested by NP, see charts by Rob MacLaury.

<**st'áwelòmèx**>, ds //s=t'ɛ́w=əl=áməx^{y}//, LT /*'[looks purple, purple-looking]'*/, (<**s=**> *stative*), (<**=el ~ =íl**> *go, come, get, become*), (<**=ómex**> *looks, -looking, in color*), phonology: updrifting, downstepping, syntactic analysis: adjective/adjectival verb, attested by NP, see charts by Rob MacLaury.

<**t'áwleqw**>, df //t'ɛw=l(=)əq^{w}//, FSH ['*skin of fish head without gristle*'], ASM ['used in fish soup'], root meaning unknown unless same stem as in <**st'áwel**>, df //s(=)t'ɛw=əl//, LT ['*purple*'], lx <**=(l)eqw**> *on the head; fish,* syntactic analysis: nominal, attested by Deming (4/1/76).

<**t'áx**>, possible root or stem //t'ɛ́(=)x^{y}//, meaning unknown

<**st'áxet**>, df //s=t'ɛ́(=)x^{y}ə(=)t//, EB /'*wild nodding onion, prob. also Hooker's onion*'/, ['*Allium cernuum*, prob. also *Allium acuminatum*'], ASM ['does not include domestic onion, éniyels'], (<**s=**> *nominalizer*), possibly root <**t'á**> *taste*, possibly <**=xel**> *on the foot,* possibly <**=t**> meaning unclear here, phonology: possible consonant-loss of l before =t, syntactic analysis: nominal, attested by AD, SP, others.

<**t'áxwqem**>, izs //t'ɛ́x^{w}(=)q=əm//, SD ['*suction sound of feet pulling out of mud*'], root meaning unknown, (<**=em**> *intransitivizer, have, get*), syntactic analysis: intransitive verb, attested by Elders Group (11/3/76).

<**t'ay**>, bound root //t'ɛ́y *emotionally upset*//.

<**t'áyeq'**>, df //t'ɛ́y=əq'//, EFAM /'*get angry, get mad, be angry*'/, probably root <**t'áy**> *emotionally upset*, possibly <**=(e)q'**> *on something else*, syntactic analysis: adjective/adjectival verb, attested by Elders Group (3/1/72, 3/16/77), EB (1/9/76), Salish cognate: Squamish /t'áyaq'/ *get angry* W73:5, K67:271, also /'*(have/feel) anger*'/, attested by BJ (5/10/64), example: <**t'áyeq' tútl'ó.**>, //t'ɛ́y=əq' t=ú=ƛ'á//, /'*He's angry.*'/, attested by Elders Group (3/1/72), also <**t'áyeq' tutl'ó.**>, //t'ɛ́y=əq' t=u=ƛ'á//, also /'*He got mad.*'/, attested by EB, <**tsel t'áyeq'.**>, //c-əl t'ɛ́y=əq'//, /'*I'm mad.*'/, attested by Elders Group (3/1/72), <**t'áyeq' kw'els ólmetsel**>, //t'ɛ́y=əq' k'^{w}-əl-s ʔálməc=əl//, /'*made that I (have to) wait*'/, attested by Elders Group (3/16/77).

<**t'át'eyeq' ~ t'át'iyeq'**>, cts //t'ɛ́[-C_1ə-]y=əq'//, rsls //t'ɛ́[=C_1ə=]y=əq'//, EFAM /'*being angry, continue to be angry, angry, mad, roused, stirred up*'/, (<**-R1-**> *continuative*), (<**=R1=**> *resultative*), phonology: reduplication, syntactic analysis: adjective/adjectival verb, attested by Elders Group (3/1/72), EB, AC, BJ (5/10/64), Deming (2/10/77), Salish cognate: Squamish /t'á-t'ayaq'/ *be angry* W73:5, K67:270, example: <**t'át'eyeq' te sqwmáy.**>, //t'ɛ́[-C_1ə-]y=əq' tə s=q^{w}m=ɛ́y//, /'*The dog is mad [angry].*'/, attested by AC; found in <**t'át'eyeq'chexw.**>, //t'ɛ́[-C_1ə-]y=əq'-c-əx^{w}//, /'*You're angry.*'/, attested by Elders Group (3/1/72), example: <**latset mekw' áyel tl'ekwtset t'át'iyeq'.**>, //lɛ-c-ət mə́k'^{w} ʔɛ́y=əl ƛ'ə=k^{w}-c-ət t'ɛ́[-C_1ə-]y=əq'//, /'*We all left because we were mad. (leave)*'/, attested by Deming.

<**t'it'á:yeq'**>, dmv //C_1í=t'ɛ́[=·=]y=əq'//, EFAM ['*cranky*'], (<**R4=**> *diminutive*), (<**=:=**> *diminutive or continuative*), phonology: lengthening diminutive (rare) corresponding to glottal stop insertion downriver, reduplication, syntactic analysis: adjective/adjectival verb, attested by NP (10/26/75).

<**t'ayéq'psem**>, ds //t'ɛy=q'=ə́[=M1=]psəm//, ANA ['*cleft in back of the neck*'], ASM ['if the cleft is deep in a baby, the baby will be cranky'], literally /'angry thing in the back of the neck'/, lx <**=épsem**> *in the back of the neck, in the back of the head,* (<**metathesis type 1**> *derivational, (here) nominalizer*), phonology: metathesis, syntactic analysis: nominal, attested by Elders Group (5/3/78).

<**t'áyx̱**>, ds //t'ɛ́y=x̣//, EFAM ['*be envious*'], probably root <**t'áy**> *emotionally upset,* possibly <**=x̱**> *distributive, all over,* syntactic analysis: intransitive verb, attested by EB (4/27/76).

<**st'á:yx̱w**>, stvi //s=t'ɛ́[=·=]y=x̣^{w}//, EFAM /'*worried, sad, looking sad*'/, probably root <**t'áy**> *emotionally upset*, possibly <**=x̱w**> *around in circles*, possibly <**=:=**> *derivational*?, phonology: possible lengthening, syntactic analysis: adjective/adjectival verb, attested by Elders Group (10/1/75), also <**st'ó:yx̱w**>, //s=t'ɛ[=Aá·=]y=x̣^{w}//, also /'*sad*'/, (<**ó:-ablaut**> *derivational or*

continuative), phonology: ablaut, attested by BHTTC (10/14/76), also <**st'óyx̱w**>, //s=t'ɛ[=Aá=]y=x̣ʷ//, also EFAM ['*brooding*'], (<**ó-ablaut**> *derivational or continuative*), phonology: ablaut, attested by NP (1/20/76), EB (4/27/76), example: <**st'á:yx̱w te Frank.**>, //s=t'ɛ́·y=x̣ʷ tə Frank//, /'*Frank is sad.*'/, attested by Elders Group (10/1/75), <**xwe'ít asu st'á:yx̱w ó?**>, //xʷəʔít ʔɛ-s=u s=t'ɛ́·y=x̣ʷ ʔá//, /'*Why are you looking sad?*'/, literally /'why is it your thus looking sad just'/, attested by Elders Group (10/1/75).

<**t'áyeq'**>, EFAM /'*get angry, get mad, be angry*'/, *see* t'ay.

<**t'ayéq'psem**>, ANA ['*cleft in back of the neck*'], *see* t'ay.

<**t'ayíts'em**>, izs //t'ɛyíc'=əm//, SD ['*fizzing*'], semantic environment ['of soda pop, etc. but also of something dropped in the water (thus the original meaning perhaps, before contact)'], (<**=em**> *intransitivizer, get, have*), syntactic analysis: intransitive verb, adjective/adjectival verb?, attested by Elders Group (12/15/76).

<**t'áyx̱**>, EFAM ['*be envious*'], *see* t'ay.

<**t'ékw**>, free root //t'ə́kʷ//, LAND /'*get stuck in the mud, get mired, be mired, get muddy*'/, syntactic analysis: intransitive verb, attested by AC (8/14/70, 10/31/73), EB (12/15/75), Salish cognate: Squamish /t'ə́k'ʷ/ *get mired, get stuck in the mud, be soggy* W73:176, K67:269, K69:50, example: <**tsel t'ékw.**>, //c-əl t'ə́kʷ//, /'*I got stuck in the mud., I got muddy.*'/, syntactic comment: ambiguous past, attested by AC (8/14/70), <**t'ékw te stiqíw.**>, //t'ə́kʷ tə s=tiqíw//, /'*The horse is mired in the mud.*'/, attested by AC (10/31/73), <**tsel t'ékw lí te st'ekwt'ékw.**>, //c-əl t'ə́kʷ lí tə s=C_1əC_2=t'ə́kʷ//, /'*I got stuck in the mud.*'/, attested by EB.

<**t'ékwt'ekw**>, chrs //t'ə́kʷ=C_1əC_2//, LAND ['*muddy*'], (<**=R2**> *characteristic*), phonology: reduplication, syntactic analysis: adjective/adjectival verb, attested by AC (8/14/70. 10/31/73), other sources: ES /t'ə́qʷt'əqʷ/, Salish cognate: Squamish /t'ə́kʷt'əkʷ/ *very muddy* K69:80.

<**st'ekwt'ékw**>, dnom //s=C_1əC_2=t'ə́kʷ//, pln, LAND ['*mud*'], (<**s=**> *nominalizer*), (<**R3=**> *plural or derivational*), phonology: reduplication, syntactic analysis: nominal, attested by EB, example: <**tsel t'ékw lí te st'ekwt'ékw.**>, //c-əl t'ə́kʷ lí tə s=C_1əC_2=t'ə́kʷ//, /'*I got stuck in the mud.*'/, attested by EB (12/15/75).

<**t'ekwót**>, pcs //t'(ə)kʷá=T or t'əkʷ=áT or t'ə[-Aá-]kʷ-M1=T or t'əkʷ=ə[=Aá=]T//, MC /'*plug it (a hole, leak)*'/, semantic environment ['in a canoe, wall, or anything'], (<**=t or =et**> *purposeful control transitivizer*), possibly <**metathesis type 1**> *non-continuative* or possibly <**ó-ablaut**> *durative*, phonology: BəCʷ roots → BCʷá before =T in non-continuative (as in Suttles consonant alternation1984:7.58)(B = Suttles T = obstruent) or alternatively BəCʷ roots get á-ablaut before (in)transitivizers (=T, =l, =əm, etc.) or =əls (structured activity) plus metathesis *non-continuative* or alternatively derivational ablaut, syntactic analysis: transitive verb, attested by IHTTC, example: <**t'ekwót ta' thóthel.**>, //t'əkʷá=T t-ɛʔ θ(=)áθəl//, /'*Plug your mouth.*'/, attested by IHTTC.

<**t'ót'ekwels**>, sas //t'ə[-Aá-C_1ə-]kʷ=əls//, cts, MC ['*plugging a hole or leak or crack in anything*'], (<-**R1-**> *continuative*), (<**=els**> *structured activity continuative*), phonology: BəCʷ roots get á-ablaut before =els or (in)transitivizers or alternatively BəCʷ, syntactic analysis: intransitive verb, attested by IHTTC.

<**t'ekwá:lí:ya**>, ds //t'əkʷ=ɛ́·lí·yɛ//, ABFC /'*put something in the ear (to block hearing), (plug the ear)*'/, lx <**=á:lí:ya**> *in the ear*, syntactic analysis: intransitive verb, attested by Elders Group (10/13/76).

<**t'kwíles ~ t'ekwíles**>, ds //t'(ə)kʷ=íləs//, ABDF /'*choke on food, get choked on food*'/, FOOD, literally /'get mired in the chest'/, lx <**=íles**> *in the chest*, phonology: BəCʷ root → BCʷ non-continuative before lexical suffixes, optional vowel-loss, syntactic analysis: intransitive verb,

attested by Elders Group (3/22/78), IHTTC, AC, also <**t'kwí:lés**>, //t'kʷ=í·lə́s//, attested by Elders Group (10/8/75), Salish cognate: Squamish /t'kʷ-inas/ *get choked (by food)* W73:176, K69:50.

<**t'ékweles**>, cts //t'ə[-´-]kʷ=iləs//, ABDF ['*getting choked on food*'], (<-´-> *continuative*), phonology: stress-shift or BəCʷ root → Bə́Cʷ continuative before lexical suffixes, vowel-reduction in suffix, syntactic analysis: intransitive verb, attested by IHTTC.

<**t'kwíwel**>, ds //t'(ə)kʷ=íwəl//, ABDF ['*constipated*'], literally /'mired in the rectum/insides'/, lx <**=íwel**> *in the insides, in the rectum*, phonology: BəCʷ root → BCʷ non-continuative/non-resultative before lexical suffixes, syntactic analysis: adjective/adjectival verb, attested by JL (3/31/78), also <**t'ekwíwel**>, //t'əkʷ=íwəl//, phonology: vowel-loss optional, attested by EB (6/7/76).

<**st'ekwíwel**>, strs //s=t'əkʷ=íwəl//, ABDF /'*(stuck in the rectum), stuck in the ass*'/, (semological comment: the translation preserves the same shock value as in Halkomelem), (<**s=**> *stative*), syntactic analysis: adjective/adjectival verb, attested by Deming (6/4/76).

<**t'ekwíwet**>, pcs //t'əkʷ=íwə(l)=T//, ABDF ['*stick it up someone's rump*'], (<**=t**> *purposeful control transitivizer*), phonology: consonant-loss of l before =t, syntactic analysis: transitive verb, attested by Deming (4/27/78).

<**t'ekwó:ythí:lem**>, mdls //t'əkʷ=á·yθ(əl)=í·l=əm//, incs, ABFC /'*shut your mouth, (shut one's mouth)*'/, literally /'go get mired in one's own jaw/mouth'/, lx <**=ó:ythel**> *in the chin/jaw/mouth*, (<**=í:l**> *go, come, get, become, inceptive*), (<**=em**> *middle voice*), phonology: syllable-loss, syntactic analysis: intransitive verb, attested by IHTTC.

<**t'ékwōwelh**>, cts //t'ə[-´-]k'ʷ=owəɬ//, CAN /'*caulking a canoe, plugging a canoe*'/, (<-´-> *continuative*), lx <**=ōwelh**> *canoe*, phonology: stress-shift, syntactic analysis: intransitive verb, attested by IHTTC, Elders Group (3/26/75), other sources: Musqueam Halkomelem /t'ə́kʷəwəɬ/ *be caulking a canoe* beside /t'kʷɛ́wəɬ/ *caulk a canoe* Suttles ca 1984:7.66.

<**t'ekwá:lí:ya**>, ABFC /'*put something in the ear (to block hearing), (plug the ear)*'/, *see* t'ékw.

<**t'ékweles**>, ABDF ['*getting choked on food*'], *see* t'ékw.

<**t'ekwíwet**>, ABDF ['*stick it up someone's rump*'], *see* t'ékw.

<**t'ekwót**>, MC /'*plug it (a hole, leak)*'/, *see* t'ékw.

<**t'ekwó:ythí:lem**>, ABFC /'*shut your mouth, (shut one's mouth)*'/, *see* t'ékw.

<**t'ékwōwelh**>, CAN /'*caulking a canoe, plugging a canoe*'/, *see* t'ékw.

<**t'ékwt'ekw**>, LAND ['*muddy*'], *see* t'ékw.

<**t'ekw'élmél**>, EFAM ['*(be) homesick*'], *see* t'ó:kw'.

<**t'ékw'stexw ~ t'ókw'stexw**>, TVMO ['*take s-o home*'], *see* t'ó:kw'.

<**t'el**>, possible bound root //t'əl// perhaps *stuck together, shape.*

<**st'elákw'**>, stvi //s=t'əlɛ́k'ʷ//, SH /'*circular, round and flat*'/, (<**s=**> *stative*), root meaning unknown unless t'el *stuck together, shape*?, possibly <**=(á)kw'**> *around in a circle*, compare <**st'eláx̱el**> *corner, arm with elbow out, square*, <**t'elém**> *get stuck* and <**st'á:lq**>, //s=t'ɛ́·lq or s=t'ə[=Aɛ́·=]lq//, *spotted with irregular shaped blobs*, syntactic analysis: adjective/adjectival verb, attested by HT and CT (6/8/76), AC, Elders Group (3/15/72), example: <**p'áth'et te kw'eléws te sméyeth li te st'elákw' siyolh.**>, //p'ɛ́θ'=əT tə k'ʷələ́w-s tə s=mɛ́yəθ li tə s=t'əlɛ́k'ʷ s=yáɬ//, /'*sew the hide of an animal on a circular frame*'/, attested by HT (6/21/76), <**st'elákw' skw'echóstel**>, //s=t'əlɛ́k'ʷ s=k'ʷɛc=ás=təl//, /'*round window*'/, attested by Elders Group (3/15/72),

<**st'elákw' sqweqwá**>, //s=t'əlɛ́k'^{w} s=C_1ə=q^{w}ɛ́//, /'*round hole*'/, attested by Elders Group (3/15/72), <**st'elákw' qesu sp'íp'elh**>, //s=t'əlɛ́k'^{w} qə-s=u s=p'í[=C_1ə=]ɬ//, /'*round and flat*'/, attested by CT (6/8/76).

<**st'elákw'**>, dnom //s=t'əlɛ́k'^{w}//, SH ['*a circle*'], Elder's comment: "probably", (<**s=**> *nominalizer*), syntactic analysis: nominal, attested by EB (2/9/76), other sources: H-T <stEla'k·u> (umlaut over a) *a circle*.

<**st'elákw' sp'íp'elh seplíl**>, FOOD *pizza* (lit. round + flat + bread), (attested by RG,EH 6/16/98 to SN, edited by BG with RG,EH 6/26/00)

<**st'eláx̱el**>, dnom //s=t'əl(=)ɛ́x̣əl or s=t'əl=(əl)ɛ́x̣əl or s=t'əlɛ́=ɛ́x̣əl//, SH /'*square, corner, arm with elbow out*'/, (<**s=**> *nominalizer*), root meaning unknown unless t'el *stuck together, shape*, lx <**=eláx̱el**> *on the arm, (long angular object)*, phonology: possible syllable-loss, syntactic analysis: nominal, attested by Elders Group (6/1/77), IHTTC (7/28/77), compare <**st'elákw'**> *a circle*, compare with <**t'elém**> *get stuck*.

<**st'elt'eláx̱el**>, pln //s=C_1əC_2=t'əl=(əl)ɛ́x̣əl//, SH ['*lots of squares*'], (<**R3=**> *plural*), phonology: reduplication, syntactic analysis: nominal, attested by Elders Group (6/1/77), also /'*a square*'/, attested by Elders Group (5/21/75).

<**st'elt'elákw' seplíl**>, (probably in error for <**st'elt'eláx̱el seplíl**> FOOD *waffle* (lit. many squares + bread), (attested by RG,EH 6/16/98 to SN, edited by BG with RG,EH 6/26/00)

<**T'eláqw'tel**>, N ['*Indian name of Old Jack (of Yakweakwioose or perhaps Scowkale)*'], *see* t'álqw' or t'élqw'.

<**t'él'**>, possible root //t'əlʔ// possibly Sumas dial. var. of <**t'el**> *stuck together*, as above.

<**st'él'e**>, dnom //s=t'əlʔ=ə//, EZ /'*younger deer, baby horse, younger cow, fawn, colt, calf*'/, (<**s=**> *nominalizer*), possibly <**t'el**> *stuck together* + <**=e ~ =a**> *living thing* perhaps since such young are stuck to their mothers, phonology: l' occurs in Sumas/Matsqui dialect and Downriver and Island dialects, syntactic analysis: nominal, dialects: *Sumas/Matsqui*, attested by Deming (6/15/77).

<**st'ít'ele**>, dmn //s=C_1í=t'ələ//, EZ /'*fawn, baby deer*'/, (<**R4=**> *diminutive*), phonology: reduplication, syntactic analysis: nominal, attested by Elders Group (3/29/77), also <**t'ít'ele**>, //T4=t'ə́lə//, attested by Deming (6/15/77).

<**t'elém**>, possibly root or stem //t'ələ́m or t'əl=ə[=´=]m//, MC ['*get stuck*'], most likely root <**t'el**>, possible bound root //t'əl// perhaps *stuck together, shape*, plus <**=em**> *have, get, intransitivizer*, possibly <=´=> *derivational*, phonology: possible stress-shift, syntactic analysis: intransitive verb, attested by EB (5/4/76).

<**t'elémt**>, pcs //t'ələ́m=T//, MC /'*stick it on, paste it on (of stamps or anything)*'/, (<**=t**> *purposeful control transitivizer*), syntactic analysis: transitive verb, attested by EB (4/29/76, 5/4/76), example: <**t'elémtes te stámp li te envelope.**>, //t'ələ́m=T-əs tə stɛ́mp li tə envelope.//, /'*He stuck the stamp on the envelope., He stuck the stamp to the envelope.*'/, attested by EB (5/4/76), <**t'elémtes tutl'o te stámp.**>, //t'ələ́m=T-əs t=u=ƛ'a tə stɛ́mp//, /'*He stuck on the stamp.*'/, attested by EB (5/4/76).

<**st'elém**>, dnom //s=t'ələ́m//, BSK ['*cherry bark (for baskets)*'], (<**s=**> *nominalizer*), syntactic analysis: nominal, attested by Elders Group (3/12/75, 6/11/75), also <**pélel**>, //pə́ləl//, dialects: *Tait*, attested by Elders Group (6/11/75), example: <**tsqwá:y te sts'elxwíwels te st'élém.**>, //c=q^{w}ɛ́·y tə s=c'əl-əx^w=íwəl-s tə s=t'ə́lə́m//, /'*The inner/inside cherry bark is green.*'/, attested by Deming (SJ esp. 5/3/79), <**ts'q'éyx̱ st'elém**>, //c'=q'íx̣ s=t'ələ́m//, /'*blackened cherry bark*'/, ASM ['blackened by immersion with alder bark and now metal objects, used plain and blackened for basketry imbrication or designs'], dialects: *Chehalis*, attested by Elders Group (6/11/75).

<**shxwt'elémels**>, dnom //sx^w=t'ələ́m=əls//, sas, MC ['*glue*'], literally /'something for sticking as a

structured activity'/, (<**shxw=**> *something for*), (<**=əls**> *structured activity continuative/nominal*), syntactic analysis: nominal, attested by Elders Group (9/21/77).

<**t'elémelhp**>, dnom //t'ələ́m=əɬp//, EB /'*wild cherry tree, bitter cherry tree*'/, ['*Prunus emarginata*'], literally /'stick on tree'/, ASM ['outer bark is peeled in May to use for basket decoration, some is left red, some dyed black, the cherries are not eaten but are now used for pectin in jams or jellies'], MED ['inner bark is used for diarrhea medicine'], lx <**=elhp**> *tree, plant*, syntactic analysis: nominal, attested by Elders Group (3/12/75), other sources: ES /t'ələ́məɬp/ *wild cherry tree.*

<**t'elémtses**>, ds //t'ələ́m=cəs//, ABFC /'*one's hand sticks to something (in cold, to honey, to glue, etc.)*'/, lx <**=tses**> *on the hand*, syntactic analysis: intransitive verb, attested by Elders Group (3/12/75).

<**temt'elémtses**>, ds //təm=t'ələ́m=cəs//, TIME /'*month beginning with first sliver of moon in February, (time things stick to the hand (in cold))*'/, literally /'time things stick to the hand (in cold)'/, lx <**tem=**> *time for*, syntactic analysis: nominal?, intransitive verb?, contrast <**temtl'í:q'es**> *month beginning with first sliver of moon in February*, lit. */'time to get jammed in or stuck (as in pit-houses under snow)'/*), attested by Elders Group.

<**st'élmexw**>, df //s=t'ə́lməx^w or s=t'ə́l(=)məx^w or s=t'(=)ə́lməx^w//, MED ['*medicine*'], (<**s=**> *nominalizer*), probably <**t'él**> *stick, stick on, adhere*, probably <**=mexw**> *person*, thus lit. "something stuck on a person" as poultices & other medicines often were, syntactic analysis: nominal, attested by AC, Elders Group (5/16/79), EB, CT (6/21/76), SJ (8/25/78), also <**st'élméxw**>, //s=t'ə́lmə́x^w//, attested by BJ (12/5/64), also <**st'émlexw**>, //s=t'ə́mləx^w//, attested by HT (in Elders Group 5/16/79), other sources: ES /st'ə́lmə́x^w/ *charm, medicine*, for full entry with derivations *see below under* t'élmexw

<**t'elémelhp**>, EB /'*wild cherry tree, bitter cherry tree*'/, *see* t'elém.

<**t'elémt**>, MC /'*stick it on, paste it on (of stamps or anything)*'/, *see* t'elém.

<**t'elémtses**>, ABFC /'*one's hand sticks to something (in cold, to honey, to glue, etc.)*'/, *see* t'elém.

<**t'éleq**>, possible stem or root //t'ə́ləq//, meaning uncertain

<**wet'éleq**>, df //wə(=)t'ə́ləq//, SD /'*splat, sound of something wet and soft dropped, to splatter*'/, semantic environment ['for ex. jello, mush, wet mud, wet cloth, wet fish'], possibly <**we=**> *sudden*, possibly root <**t'el(ém)**> *stick on, adhere*, possibly <**=eq**> meaning unclear, syntactic analysis: intransitive verb, attested by Elders Group (5/14/80), BHTTC (11/3/76), EB correction, also <**wet'éleq'**>, //wə=t'ə́ləq'//, also /'*to splatter*'/, attested by Elders Group (10/27/76), comment: corrected to wet'éleq by EB.

<**t'éléth'**>, possible root or stem //t'ə́l(=)əθ'//, meaning uncertain

<**wet'éléth'**>, possibly root //wə(=)t'ə́l(=)əθ'//, WATR ['*to squirt*'], ABFC, possibly <**we=**> *sudden*, possibly root <**t'el(ém)**> *stick on, adhere*, possibly <**=eth'**> *small portion*, syntactic analysis: intransitive verb, attested by CT and HT (6/21/76), Salish cognate: Squamish /t'lc'-ánʔ/ *squirt (tr.)* K69:50.

<**t'éléx̱**>, bound root //t'ə́lə́x̣ *hew (stone, wood, anything), carve stone*//.

<**t'élex̱è:yls**>, sas //t'ə́lə́x̣=ɛ[=Aí=]·ls//, CARV /'*hew (stone, wood, anything)*'/, (<**=á:ls**> *structured activity non-continuative*), (<**í-ablaut**> *derivational*, prob. *durative*), phonology: ablaut, syntactic analysis: intransitive verb, attested by JL (5/5/75).

<**t'eléx̱ot**>, pcs //t'ələ[=´=]x̣=ə[=Aa=]T or t'ələ[=M2=]x̣=ə[=Aa=]T//, durs, CARV /'*carve stone, work in stone*'/, (<**=et**> *purposeful control transitivizer*), (<**o-ablaut on suffix**> *durative*), possibly <**=´=**> *derivational*, possibly <**metathesis**> *derivational*, phonology: ablaut, stress-shift or

metathesis, syntactic analysis: transitive verb, attested by JL (5/5/75), example: <**t'eléx̱ot te smà:lt**>, //t'ələ́x̣=aT tə s=mɛ̀·lt//, /'*carve stone, work in stone*'/, attested by JL (5/5/76).

<**t'élex̱è:yls**>, CARV /'*hew (stone, wood, anything)*'/, *see* t'éléx̱.

<**t'eléx̱ot**>, CARV /'*carve stone, work in stone*'/, *see* t'éléx̱.

<**t'elkw'á:ls**>, FOOD /'*warm up (food, tea, etc.)*'/, *see* t'álqw' or t'élqw'.

<**t'élmexw**>, bound stem //t'əl=məxʷ//, probably *stick on a person.*

<**st'élmexw**>, df //s=t'əlməxʷ or s=t'əl(=)məxʷ or s=t'(=)əlməxʷ//, MED ['*medicine*'], (<**s=**> *nominalizer*), probably <**t'él**> *stick, stick on, adhere*??, probably <**=mexw**> *person*, thus lit. "something stuck on a person" as poultices & other medicines often were, syntactic analysis: nominal, attested by AC, Elders Group (5/16/79), EB, CT (6/21/76), SJ (8/25/78), also <**st'élméxw**>, //s=t'əlmə́xʷ//, attested by BJ (12/5/64), also <**st'émlexw**>, //s=t'ə́mləxʷ//, attested by HT (in Elders Group 5/16/79), other sources: ES /st'əlmə́xʷ/ *charm, medicine*, example: <**qó:qet te st'élmexw**>, //qá·=C₁ə=T tə s=t'əlməxʷ//, /'*drink the medicine*'/, literally /'drink it the medicine'/, attested by AC, <**méq'et te st'élmexw**>, //mə́q'=əT tə s=t'əlməxʷ//, /'*swallow the medicine*'/, literally /'swallow s-th the medicine'/, attested by AC, <**qél st'élmexw**>, //qə́l s=t'əlməxʷ//, /'*bad medicine*'/, attested by AC, EB (11/28/75), <**éy xwlá(m) tl'eléwe te st'élmexw.**>, //ʔɛ́y xʷ(=)lɛ́(=m) ƛ'ə=lə́wə tə s=t'əlməxʷ//, /'*The medicine is good for you.*'/, attested by EB (5/12/78), <**xó:lxwem te st'élmexw.**>, //xʸá·lxʷ=əm tə s=t'əlməxʷ//, /'*The medicine has a menthol taste.*'/, attested by SJ (on Elders' Banff Trip 8/25/78), <**éy, tl'ó yewál éy st'élmexw; welí kw'e li te éqwelets te thqát éwe lis eyém.**>, //ʔɛ́y, ƛ'á yəwɛ́l ʔɛ́y s=t'əlməxʷ; wə-lí k'ʷə li tə ʔə́qʷ=ələc-s tə θqɛ́t ʔə́wə li-s ʔɛy=ə́m//, /'*It's good, it's the best medicine; if it's on the back of the tree (the side away from the rising sun) it's not as strong.*'/, attested by CT (6/21/76), <**tsqwá:y te st'émlexws te sth'épeq.**>, //c=qʷɛ́·y tə s=t'ə́mləxʷ-s tə s=θ'ə́pəq//, /'*The medicine of the skunk [i.e., it's spray] is yellow.*'/, attested by HT (Elders Group 5/16/79).

<**t'elmexwáwtxw**>, ds //t'əlməxʷ=ɛ́wtxʷ//, MED ['*drug store*'], BLDG, literally /'medicine building'/, lx <**=áwtxw**> *building*, grammatical comment: s= *nominalizer* is dropped, syntactic analysis: nominal, attested by Elders Group (6/1/77).

<**st'elmexwíwel**>, ds //s=t'əlməxʷ=íwəl//, MED ['*love medicine*'], ASM ['aphrodisiac medicine to make someone irresistable or to restore sexual functioning to someone, medicine to make a given person desire someone in particular, the latter type usually used (uses?) hair (or something else) from the person to be bewitched and this is wrapped around a power object of some kind with certain spells and left in some place to "work"--the bewitched person then goes mad with lust for the person who commissioned the shaman or ritualist or witch to do the love medicine; such magic can be done by a knowledgable person in his/her own behalf but can easily go wrong and backfire on that person, making the person casting the spell go crazy him/herself'], lx <**=íwel**> *in the insides, in the rectum*, syntactic analysis: nominal, attested by Elders Group (1/22/75), also <**t'elmexwíws**>, //t'əlməxʷ=íws//, lx <**=íws**> *on the body, on the skin*, attested by GC (Deming 2/10/77).

<**st'elmexwó:les**>, ds //s=t'əlməxʷ=á·ləs//, MED ['*eye medicine*'], lx <**=ó:les**> *in the eye*, syntactic analysis: nominal, attested by Elders Group (7/9/75).

<**t'elmexwáwtxw**>, MED ['*drug store*'], *see* st'élmexw.

<**t'élqw't**>, FOOD ['*warm it up*'], *see* t'álqw' or t'élqw'.

<**t'élt'elem**>, MUS ['*continuing on singing*'], *see* t'íl.

<**t'élxweth'**>, probable stem //t'əl=xʷ=(ə)θ'//, root meaning unknown but perhaps from t'el *stick on* +

=xw *lump-like, round* + =eth' *small portion*, perhaps referring to small village stuck on small hill

<St'élxweth'>, df //s=t'ə́l=x^{w}=əθ'//, PLN /'*village near the mouth of Choate Creek, (Choate Creek [AK, SP/AD], (Stullawheets village on a hill on the east bank of the Fraser River near the mouth of Suka Creek [elders on American Bar Trip (AD/AK/?)])*'/, ASM ['on the west (CPR) side of the Fraser River, on top of hill near the mouth of the creek'], root meaning unknown, syntactic analysis: nominal, attested by SP and AK (at Fish Camp 8/2/77), also /'*Choate Creek*'/, attested by AK and SP or AD (Raft Trip 8/30/77), also /'*Stullawheets village on a hill on the east bank of the Fraser R. near the mouth of Suka Creek*'/, attested by elders on American Bar Trip (AD/AK/?)(6/26/78), other sources: Wells (1965 lst ed.:25), source: place names reference file #13 and #150, Salish cognate: possibly?? Squamish /st'əlx̣^{w}c'/ *octopus* W73:188, K69:50.

<St'élxweth' Stótelō>, cpds //s=t'ə́lx^{w}əθ' s=tá[=C_1ə=]ləw//, PLN /'*Choate Creek on the west (C.P.R,) side of the Fraser River*'/, comment: stótelō *creek*, phonology: reduplication, syntactic analysis: nominal phrase with modifier(s), attested by AK and SP (at Fish Camp 8/2/77, American Bar Trip 6/26/78), source: place names reference file #151.

<St'élxweth' X̲ótsa>, cpds //s=t'ə́lx^{w}əθ' x̣ácɛ//, PLN ['*probably Texas Lake*'], comment: **x̲**ótsa *lake*, Elder's comment: "ask Joe Lorenzetto", syntactic analysis: nominal phrase with modifier(s), attested by AK and SP (Fish Camp 8/2/77, American Bar Trip 6/26/78), source: place names reference file #37.

<t'élheqw' ~ t'lhóqw'>, bound root or stem //t'ə́ɬəq'^{w} ~ t'ɬáq'^{w} *scratch to pry open*//.

<t'élheqw'et>, pcs //t'ə́ɬəq'^{w}=əT//, ABFC ['*scratch on s-th*'], (**<=t>** *purposeful control transitivizer*), comment: this base form could be *continuative* if some of the forms below and in Musqueam are correct, syntactic analysis: transitive verb, attested by Elders Group (10/27/76), other sources: Suttles (ca1984:7.2.6.2, p.69) Musqueam root /t'ɬáq'^{w}/ *get twisted* and /t'ɬáq'^{w}-t/ *pry it off* versus /t'ə́ləq'^{w}-t/ *prying it off*--Suttles gives C1ə́C2əC3 as the regular continuative pattern for his TTVC roots, comment: an alternative account of these patterns is shown here, that is, a non-continuative inflection (as in metathesis type one for some roots) with a continuative base form, example: **<le t'élheqw'tes te xálh.>**, //lə t'ə́ɬəq'^{w}=T-əs tə x^{y}ɛ́ɬ//, /'*He scratched on the door.*'/.

<t'elht'élheqw'et>, plv //C_1əC_2=t'ə́ɬəq'^{w}=əT-əs//, ABFC ['*scratch s-th up*'], (**<R3=>** *plural*), phonology: reduplication, syntactic analysis: transitive verb, attested by Elders Group; found in **<t'elht'élheqw'etes.>**, //C_1əC_2=t'ə́ɬəq'^{w}=əT-əs//, /'*It has scratched up something.*'/.

<t'élheqw'els>, sas //t'ə́ɬəq'^{w}=əls//, cts, ABFC ['*scratching to get in (?)*'], (**<=els>** *structured activity continuative*), syntactic analysis: intransitive verb, attested by Elders Group.

<t'elht'élheqw'els>, plv //C_1əC_2=t'ə́ɬəq'^{w}=əls//, ABFC ['*scratching repeatedly to get in*'], (**<R3=>** *plural*), phonology: reduplication, syntactic analysis: intransitive verb, attested by Elders Group (10/27/76).

<t'lhóqw'els>, sas //t'əɬə[-Aá-]q'^{w}=əls//, df, SD ['*(make/have a) scratching noise*'], possibly **<ó-ablaut>** *non-continuative*, phonology: ablaut, vowel-loss, syntactic analysis: intransitive verb, attested by TM and others (Elders Group 2/1/78).

<t'lhóqw'est>, ds //t'əɬə[-Aá-]q'^{w}=əs=T//, pcs, ABFC ['*scratch s-o on the face*'], possibly **<ó-ablaut>** *non-continuative*, lx **<=es>** *on the cface*, (**<=t>** *purposeful control transitivizer*), phonology: ablaut, vowel-loss, syntactic analysis: transitive verb, attested by Elders Group (11/3/76).

<t'élheqw'els>, ABFC ['*scratching to get in (?)*'], *see* t'élheqw' ~ t'lhóqw'.

<t'élheqw'et>, ABFC ['*scratch on s-th*'], *see* t'élheqw' ~ t'lhóqw'.

<t'élhmel>, BLDG ['*cross-beam (in a house)*'], *see* t'álh.

<**t'élhtel**>, WV [*'loom'*], *see* t'álh.

<**t'elht'élheqw'els**>, ABFC [*'scratching repeatedly to get in'*], *see* t'élheqw' ~ t'lhóqw'.

<**t'elht'élheqw'et**>, ABFC [*'scratch s-th up'*], *see* t'élheqw' ~ t'lhóqw'.

<**t'élhtsestel**>, WV /*'net shuttle and net-measure, gill-net measure, (loom [Elders Group])'*/, *see* t'álh.

<**t'ém**>, bound root //t'ə́m *chop*//.

<**t'eméls**>, sas //t'əm=ɛ[-Aə́-]ls or t'ə́m-ɛ[-M2-]ls or t'əm=ə́ls//, TOOL /*'to chop with an adze, to chop, to adze, an adze'*/, (<**=als or =éls**> *structured activity non-continuative*), possibly <**é-ablaut or metathesis**> *derivational*, phonology: =éls may be an allomorphic variant of =áls, possible ablaut or metathesis, syntactic analysis: intransitive verb, also nominal, syntactic comment: =els and =éls *structured activity* suffixes are often used to form tool nominals, attested by Elders Group.

<**t'et'éméls**>, cts //C_1ə-t'ə́m=əls//, sas, TOOL /*'adzing, chopping, chopping with an adze'*/, (<**R5-**> *continuative*), (<**=els**> *structured activity continuative*), phonology: reduplication, updrifting on final syllable, syntactic analysis: intransitive verb, attested by Elders Group.

<**t'et'émels**>, dnom //C_1ə=t'ə́m=əls//, TOOL [*'a chisel'*], (<**=els**> *structured activity tool-nominalizer*), phonology: reduplication, syntactic analysis: nominal, attested by Elders Group (3/26/75).

<**st'et'eméls ~ st'et'ebéls**>, dnom //s=C_1ə=t'əm=ə́ls ~ s=C_1ə=t'əb=ə́ls//, TOOL [*'adze'*], (<**s=**> *nominalizer*), phonology: b with half-closure for /m/, reduplication, syntactic analysis: nominal, attested by DM (12/4/64 new transcript p. 183 Wells tapes), other sources: ES /st'ət'əmə́ls/ *D-adze*.

<**t'emt'émet**>, plv //C_1əC_2=t'ə́m=əT//, pcs, TOOL [*'chop s-th in different places'*], (<**R3=**> *plural action*), (<**=et**> *purposeful control transitivizer*), phonology: reduplication, syntactic analysis: transitive verb, attested by IHTTC; found in <**t'emt'émetem**>, //C_1əC_2=t'ə́m=əT-əm//, /*'it's been chopped in different places'*/, syntactic comment: passive pl..

<**st'amt'í:m** (or better) **st'emt'í:m**>, plv //s=C_1əC_2=t'əm=í·m or s=C_1əC_2=t'ə[=Aí·=]m//, strs, TOOL [*'chopped in different places'*], (<**s=**> *stative*), (<**R3=**> *plural action*), probably <**í:-ablaut**> *resultative*, possibly <**=í:m**> *repeatedly*, phonology: reduplication, probably ablaut, possibly syllable-loss, syntactic analysis: adjective/adjectival verb, attested by IHTTC.

<**t'émches**>, ds //t'ə́m=cəs//, ABDF /*'chop one's hand, [get chopped on the hand]'*/, lx <**=ches ~ =tses**> *on the hand*, syntactic analysis: intransitive verb, attested by Elders Group.

<**t'émxel**>, ds //t'ə́m=x^yəl//, ABDF /*'chop one's foot (with axe), [get chopped on the foot (with axe)]'*/, lx <**=xel**> *on the foot/leg*, syntactic analysis: intransitive verb, attested by Elders Group.

<**t'ámel (or) t'ém:el**>, ds //t'ə́m=məl//, MC [*'wood chips'*], lx <**=mel**> *part, portion*, phonology: consonant merger, syntactic analysis: nominal, attested by IHTTC.

<**t'et'émélep**>, cts //C_1ə-t'ə́m=ə́ləp//, HARV [*'chopping the ground (with hoe or mattock)'*], (<**R5-**> *continuative*), lx <**=élep**> *ground, dirt*, phonology: reduplication, syntactic analysis: intransitive verb, attested by Elders Group.

<**shxwt'et'emélep**>, dnom //sx^w=C_1ə=t'əm=ə́ləp//, TOOL [*'hoe'*], HARV, literally /'something for chopping the ground'/, (<**shxw=**> *something for*), phonology: reduplication, syntactic analysis: nominal, attested by IHTTC.

<**t'mí:ws**>, ds //t'əm=í·ws//, HARV [*'smooth a log by chopping'*], TOOL, literally /'chop on the skin'/, lx <**=í:ws**> *on the skin, on the body*, phonology: vowel-loss, syntactic analysis: intransitive verb, attested by Elders Group.

<t'mí:wsà:ls>, sas //t'əm=í·ws=ɛ̀·ls//, BLDG ['*log cabin*'], HARV, literally /'logs made smooth by structured chopping'/, lx **<=í:ws>** *on the skin*, (**<=á:ls>** *structured activity non-continuative nominalizer*), phonology: donwstepping, vowel-loss, syntactic analysis: nominal, attested by Elders Group (1/7/76).

<t'émleqw>, ds //t'ə́m=ləqʷ//, FSH ['*split dried fish head with gristle removed*'], ANA /'*top of the head, scalp*'/, (semological comment: prob. top of the head or scalp when chopped off--a scalp; this was sometimes done by warriors during raids), literally /'chopped on top of the head'/, lx **<=(e)leqw ~ =eqw>** *on top of the head*, syntactic analysis: nominal, attested by AK (IHTTC 8/4/77), IHTTC (8/3/77), Elders Group (8/20/75).

<t'émches>, ABDF /'*chop one's hand, [get chopped on the hand]*'/, *see* t'ém.

<t'eméls>, TOOL /'*to chop with an adze, to chop, to adze, an adze*'/, *see* t'ém.

<t'émeqw'>, probably root //t'ə́m(=)əq'ʷ//, SD ['*splash (the noise and the action)*'], semantic environment ['of a rock for ex.'], possibly root **<t'ém>** *chop*, possibly **<=eqw'>** meaning uncertain unless *around in circles*?, syntactic analysis: intransitive verb, attested by Elders Group (8/25/76), also **<t'eméqw'>**, //t'əmə́q'ʷ//, attested by Deming (6/17/76), example: **<le t'émeqw'.>**, //lə t'ə́məq'ʷ//, /'*He splashed.*'/, attested by Elders Group.

<wet'émeqw'>, ds //wə=t'ə́m(=)əq'ʷ//, SD /'*splash (the sound and the action), [splash suddenly], splash once*'/, lx **<we=>** *suddenly*, syntactic analysis: intransitive verb, attested by Elders Group (8/25/76, 10/27/76), example: **<le wet'émeqw'.>**, //lə wə=t'ə́m(=)əq'ʷ//, /'*He splashed.*'/, attested by Elders Group.

<t'ó:mqw'em>, cts //t'ə[-Aá·-]m(=)əq'ʷ=əm//, mdls, SD /'*splashing, splashing (lots of times)*'/, (**<ó:-ablaut>** *continuative*), (**<=em>** *middle voice*), phonology: ablaut, vowel-loss, syntactic analysis: intransitive verb, attested by Elders Group (8/25/76, 10/27/76, 11/3/76).

<t'emt'émqw'xel>, plv //$C_1əC_2$=t'ə́m(=)əq'ʷ=xʸəl//, WETH /'*(get) lots of water all over since it's raining so hard, really getting rainy*'/, SD, literally /'many splashing precipitation'/, (**<R3=>** *plural action*), lx **<=xel>** *precipitation; on the foot*, phonology: reduplication, vowel-loss, syntactic analysis: intransitive verb, attested by Elders Group (9/27/78), EB (9/18/78), CT (in a song).

<T'emiyéq(w) ??>, PLN ['*Tamihi village at the mouth of Tamihi Creek*'], *see* t'ámiya.

<t'émleqw>, ANA /'*top of the head, scalp*'/, *see* t'ém.

<t'emó:sa>, us //t'əmá·sɛ//, EB /'*wild rhubarb, western dock, common yellow dock, domestic rhubarb*'/, ['*Rumex occidentalis, Rheum hybridum*'], ASM ['wild rhubarb grew on Sumas prairie, near creeks; domestic rhubarb was introduced and cultivated first by non-Indians; western dock stems are steamed or boiled like regular rhubarb but the leaves can also be eaten--either cooked with the stems or fried with water and meat (unlike domestic rhubarb's which are poisonous); dock was eaten in the spring till about June; domestic rhubarb stems are steamed or boiled or made into jam like use by non-Indians'], syntactic analysis: nominal, attested by AC, others.

<t'émq'ethel>, df //t'ə́m=q'=əθ=əl//, LAND /'*jade (nephrite) (used for sharpening [chopping] stones), any agate (can be used as flint to strike a spark)*'/, literally probably /'get chop edge on something else'/, probably root **<t'ém>** *chop*, probably **<=q'>** *on something else*, lx **<=eth ~ =óth>** *edge*, (**<=el>** *come, go, get, become*), syntactic analysis: nominal, attested by Elders Group (5/28/75, 2/19/75, 1/16/80).

<t'emt'émet>, TOOL ['*chop s-th in different places*'], *see* t'ém.

<t'emt'émqw'xel>, WETH /'*(get) lots of water all over since it's raining so hard, really getting rainy*'/, *see* t'émeqw'.

<**t'émxel**>, ABDF /*'chop one's foot (with axe), [get chopped on the foot (with axe)]'*/, *see* t'ém.

<**t'éps**>, probable root or stem //t'ə́p(=)s//, meaning uncertain but perhaps related to <**t'ő̄p**> the root in <**T'ept'ő̄p**> *Ryder Lake* (lit. "sand fleas (ridge)", so the word for *midget* might be related to *flea* or at least have the same root.

<**st'éps ~ st'epsóye**>, df //s=t'ə́ps ~ s=t'əps=áyə//, BPI ['*midget*'], (<**s=**> *nominalizer*), root meaning unknown, possibly <**=óye**> *affectionate diminutive*, syntactic analysis: nominal, attested by IHTTC (8/23/77).

<**t'it'epsó:ye**>, dmn //C_1í=t'əps=á[=·=]yə//, BPI ['*(probably) tiny midget*'], (<**R4=**> *diminutive*), probably <**=:=**> *augmentative (more so)*, phonology: reduplication, lengthening, syntactic analysis: nominal, attested by IHTTC (8/23/77).

<**T'ept'ő̄p Stótelō̄**>, PLN ['*Ryder Lake Creek*'], *see* t'ő̄p.

<**T'ept'ő̄p (X̲ótsa)**>, PLN ['*Ryder Lake*'], *see* t'ő̄p.

<**t'éqoya**>, DESC ['*dirty*'], *see* t'íq.

<**t'éqw'**>, free root //t'ə́q'ʷ//, MC /*'break (of a flexible object like a rope, string or breath), it broke'*/, ABDF ['*run out (of breath)*'], syntactic analysis: intransitive verb, attested by AD, AC, EB, Salish cognate: Lushootseed root /t'əq'ʷ(u)/ *snap flexible object (break rope/string/, etc.)* in contrast to /čəx̣/ *crack, split (break a plate); half*, /jix̣(i)/ 'collapse, break off and fall; break down, be out of order, /pəqʷ(u)/ 'break/cut a piece off (leaving a larger piece), and /xʷəƛ'/ *break rigid object in two* H76:561, Squamish /t'əq'ʷ/ *break (itr.), be bruised* beside /t'áq'ʷ-an/ *break, cut in two (ropes)(tr.)* W73:44, K67:269, 271, Sechelt /t'ə́q'ʷ/ *break (line, rope, etc.)(itr.)* B85:253, ASM ['break (of rope)'], <**le t'éqw' te x̲wéylem.**>, //lə t'ə́q'ʷ tə x̣ʷí·l=əm//, /*'The rope broke.'*/, attested by AC, ASM ['run out (of breath)'], <**tsel t'á:t kw'els xwemxálém kw'e la me t'éqw' tel slhákw'em.**>, //c-əl t'ɛ́·=T k'ʷ-əl-s xʷəm=xʸə[=Aɛ́=]l=əm k'ʷə lə mə t'ə́q'ʷ t-əl s=ɬɛ́k'ʷ=əm//, /*'I tried to run but I ran out of breath.'*/, attested by EB (12/12/75).

<**t'eqw'ót**>, pcs //t'əq'ʷ=áT or t'əq'ʷá=T or t'əq'ʷ=ə[=Aá=]T//, HARV /*'cut it (wood, lawn, etc.)'*/, (<**=et or =t or =ót**> *purposeful control transitivizer*), possibly <**ó-ablaut**> *durative*, phonology: stressed transitivizer with á in environment C1əCʷ where C1 is obstruent, syntactic analysis: transitive verb, attested by Deming (4/17/80), other sources: Suttles ca1984:14.5.66 Musqueam /t'q'ʷát/ *cut it off.*

<**t'óqw'tem**>, df //t'əq'ʷ=á[=M2=]T=əm//, TIME ['*Saturday*'], literally perhaps /'(place to) have/get cut on purpose (of flexible object) or it got cut on purpose (of string, flexible object)'/, (semological comment: note the use below of this root with time in alht'éqw' *half an hour*, it may be that time is regarded as a flexible object or a string of days/hours), (<**metathesis**> *derivational*), possibly <**=em**> *intransitivizer, have, get* or possibly <**=em**> *place to have/get* or possibly <**-em**> *passive*, phonology: metathesis, syntactic analysis: nominal, attested by Elders Group, IHTTC, example: <**Q: stám swàyèl tlówàyèl?, A: t'óqw'tem.**>, //s=tɛ́m s=wɛ̀yəl tlá=wɛ̀yəl, təq'ʷ=a[=M2=]T=əm//, /*'Q: What day is today?, A: Saturday.'*/, attested by IHTTC (8/10/77).

<**t'eqw't'éqw'et**>, plv //C_1əC_2=t'ə́q'ʷ=əT//, HARV ['*cut it all up*'], (<**R3=**> *plural objects*), phonology: reduplication, syntactic analysis: transitive verb, attested by Deming (4/17/80).

<**t'qw'á:lats**>, df //t'əq'ʷ=ɛ́·lɛc//, CAN ['*a canoe or boat cut off short in the rear (because the stern couldn't be repaired)*'], possibly <**=á:lats**> ~ <**=elets**> *on the bottom, on the rear*, phonology: possible ablaut?, irregular vowels?, syntactic analysis: nominal, attested by EB (5/18/76), other

sources: Suttles ca1984:14.5.66 Musqueam /t'q'ʷéʔlec/ *take a short cut* with /-él'ec ~ -eʔc ~ -əl'əc ~ -líc/ *route across.*

<**alht'éqw'**>, df //ʔɛɬ=t'ə́q'ʷ or ʔɛ-ɬ=t'ə́q'ʷ//, NUM ['*half*'], possibly /'*your half*'/, possibly <**alh= ~ lh=**> *use a portion*, possibly <**a-**> *your*, syntactic analysis: nominal, attested by Elders at Fish Camp (7/19/78), Salish cognate: Squamish /ʔəs-t'ə́q'ʷ/ *half (broken-off)* W73:44, K67:385, example: <**alht'éqw' syiláws te slhéms**>, //ʔɛɬ=t'ə́q'ʷ s=yilɛ́w-s tə s=ɬə́m=s//, /'*half an hour past eleven o'clock, thirty minutes after eleven*'/, literally /'half past the eleventh hour'/.

<**t'eqw'élhelh**>, ds //t'əq'ʷ=ə́ɬəɬ//, ABDF /'*pass out, faint*'/, literally /'break (flexible obj.)/run out of breath/cut off in the windpipe'/, lx <**=élhelh**> *in the windpipe, throat*, syntactic analysis: intransitive verb, attested by Deming (3/11/76), Salish cognate, Nooksack //t'k'ʷ=ə́ɬniɬ// *faint* (PA:SJ, Ghost Catching story, notebook 2).

<**t'eqw'lhálém**>, mdls //t'əq'ʷ=ɬɛ́l=əm//, ABDF ['*cut off one's breath*'], literally /'cut off/break (flexible obj.) in the windpipe/throat one's own'/, lx <**=lhál**> *in the windpipe, in the throat*, (<**=em**> *middle voice*), syntactic analysis: intransitive verb, attested by AHTTC (2/15/80).

<**t'eqw'qéyl or t'eqw'qí:l**>, ds //t'əq'ʷ=qəl=í·l//, HARV ['*(get the) top cut off*'], semantic environment ['for ex. of a tree with an axe'], lx <**=qel**> *on top of the head*, (<**=í:l**> *go, come, get, become*), phonology: syllable-loss, syntactic analysis: intransitive verb, attested by Elders Group (12/12/77).

<**t'ot'qw'íth'et**>, pcs //t'ə[-AaC$_1$ə-]q'ʷ=íθ'ə=T//, df, HARV ['*cutting them up (of logs)*'], (<**o-ablaut plus -R1-**> *continuative*), possibly <**í-ablaut**> *durative*, <**=eth'**> *small portion*, (<**=rt**> *purposeful control transitivizer*), phonology: ablaut, reduplication, vowel-reduction, syntactic analysis: transitive verb, attested by HT (Elders Group 2/6/80).

<**t'eqw'élhelh**>, ABDF /'*pass out, faint*'/, *see* t'éqw'.

<**t'eqw'lhálém**>, ABDF ['*cut off one's breath*'], *see* t'éqw'.

<**t'eqw'ót**>, HARV /'*cut it (wood, lawn, etc.)*'/, *see* t'éqw'.

<**t'eqw'qéyl or t'eqw'qí:l**>, HARV ['*(get the) top cut off*'], *see* t'éqw'.

<**t'eqw't'éqw'et**>, HARV ['*cut it all up*'], *see* t'éqw'.

<**t'esí:l**>, ABFC ['*go down (of swelling)*'], *see* t'ás.

<**t'esítsmels**>, FSH ['*hide-away that a fish makes*'], *see* t'ás.

<**t'etí:l**>, EFAM ['*(being) lonesome (refers to someone else)*'], *see* t'í:l.

<**t'et'ás**>, SD ['*be stealthy*'], *see* t'ás.

<**t'et'ásxelem**>, TVMO /'*tip-toeing, (walking lightly, sneaking)*'/, *see* t'ás.

<**t'et'ásxel or t'at'ásxel**>, TVMO ['*walk*[ing] silently or quietly'], *see* t'ás.

<**t'et'át**>, TIB ['*trying it*'], *see* t'á.

<**t'et'émélep**>, HARV ['*chopping the ground (with hoe or mattock)*'], *see* t'ém.

<**t'et'éméls**>, TOOL /'*adzing, chopping, chopping with an adze*'/, *see* t'ém.

<**t'et'émels**>, TOOL ['*a chisel*'], *see* t'ém.

<**t'eth'ó:mthet**>, TAST ['*fermenting*'], *see* t'áth'.

<**t'ets'élmel**>, TAST ['*taste*'], *see* t'á.

<**t'ewő́kw' ~ t'ewő́qw'**>, root or stem //t'əwók'ʷ ~ t'əwóq'ʷ or /t'ɛ̃[=Aə=]wók'ʷ ~ t'ɛ̃[=Aə=]wóq'ʷ//, meaning uncertain unless same root as in <**st'áwel**>, df //s(=)t'ɛ̃w=əl//, LT ['*purple*'], the Squamish

cognate and derived form <**st'ewíqw'es**> point to a <**qw'**>, while the first two derived forms point to <**kw'**>.

<**st'ewṓkw'**>, df //s=t'əwók'ʷ//, LAND /'*diatomaceous earth (could be mixed with things to whiten them--for ex. dog and goat wool), white clay for white face paint (for pure person spirit-dancers), white powder from mountains, white clay they make powder from to lighten goat and dog wool for blankets, powder, talc, white face paint*'/, SPRD, PE, LT /'*(powder white, purplish white?)*'/, ASM ['the following color terms are used by AK before st'ewṓkw' to specify shades of the st'ewṓkw': p'éq'. '], (semological comment: identified as diatomaceous earth in an exhibit by the B.C. Provincial Museum which had the word and a sample of the substance and explanation of its use, could perhaps be other white clays as well), (<**s=**> *nominalizer*), (<**s=**> *stative*), poss. the same root (meaning uncertain) as in <**s=t'áw=el**> *purple*, comment: using derived forms of the root as a modifier of other color terms the following combinations were given by AK: st'ewṓkw' p'éq', and p'éq' st'ewṓkw', see charts by Rob MacLaury, phonology: the /o/ cannot be //əw// here as seen by the resultative form which seems to be /st'əwíq'ʷəsəm/ rather than /st'əwíwq'ʷəsəm/ and as seen by the Squamish form /st'ə́waq'ʷ/ with only one /w/--but the /o/ could be /ə/ with an unusually lowered allophone [ʊ˘] /w_Cʷ, syntactic analysis: nominal (with nominalizer), adjective/adjectival verb (with stative), attested by SJ and EF (Deming 9/21/78), BHTTC, AD (7/23/79), IHTTC (7/18/77), AC, BJ (12/5/64)(new transcript, old p.293), AK (1987), Salish cognate: Squamish /st'ə́waq'ʷ/ *kind of mud which was burnt and used as white paint, both on the body and as dye for animal hair, etc. of which blankets were woven* W73:181, K67:284-285, example: <**hó:kwexlha te st'ewṓkw'.**>, //há·kʷ=əxʸ-ɬɛ tə s=t'əwók'ʷ//, /'*Use the white paint.*'/, attested by AC.

<**t'ewṓkw'esem**>, mdls //t'əwók'ʷ=əs=əm//, SPRD ['*put (white) paint on one's face*'], PE /'*to powder one's face, put powder on one's face*'/, lx <**=es**> *on the face*, (<**=em**> *middle voice*), syntactic analysis: intransitive verb, attested by AC, BHTTC, IHTTC, also <**t'ewṓqw'esem**>, //t'əwóq'ʷ=əs=əm//, attested by IHTTC (7/18/77), Salish cognate: Squamish /st'ə́waq'ʷ/ above shows qw' but only the IHTTC on 7/18/77 show Upriver Halkomelem with qw'--all other attestations show kw', example: <**lalh t'ewṓkw'esem.**>, //lɛ=ɬ t'əwók'ʷ=əs=əm//, /'*Go paint yourself.*'/, attested by AC (8/29/70).

<**st'ewíqw'es**>, strs //s=t'əwo[=Aí=]q'ʷ=əs//, PE ['*powdered on the face*'], (<**s=**> *stative*), (<**í-ablaut**> *resultative*), lx <**=es**> *on the face*, phonology: ablaut, syntactic analysis: adjective/adjectival verb, attested by IHTTC (7/18/77), Salish cognate: for qw' see Squamish /st'ə́waq'ʷ/ above.

<**t'ewṓkw'esem**>, SPRD ['*put (white) paint on one's face*'], *see* st'ewṓkw'.

<**t'exelá**>, us //t'əxʸəlɛ́//, HUNT ['*arrowhead*'], syntactic analysis: noun, nominal, attested by EL (Elders Group 2/19/75).

<**t'éx̱**>, bound root //t'ə́x̣ *to fork or branch, split unevenly*//.

<**st'éx̱**>, dnom //s=t'ə́x̣//, EB ['*a fork in a tree*'], LAND ['*a fork in a road (or trail)*'], WATR ['*a fork in a creek*'], (<**s=**> *nominalizer*), syntactic analysis: nominal, attested by Elders Group (5/28/75), other sources: JH /st'ə́x̣/ *tree fork*.

<**st'ex̱láts**>, ds //s=t'əx̣=lɛ́c or s=t'əx̣=lə[=Aɛ́=]c//, possibly /'*fork in a tree?*'/, Elder's comment: "unsure of meaning of this word", (<**s=**> *nominalizer*), lx <**=lets or =láts**> *on the bottom*, possibly <**á-ablaut on suffix**> *durative*, syntactic analysis: nominal, attested by AC (11/26/71).

<**t'x̱éthet**>, df //t'ə́x̣=M1=θət//, WATR ['*forks in stream*'], (<**metathesis**> *derivational*), (<**=thet**> *get, become*), phonology: metathesis, syntactic analysis: nominal, source: ES Ch and Cw dialects, compare Ms /st'əx̣ə́θət/.

<**T'ít'x̱elhchò:m**>, dmn //C_1í=t'əx̣=əɬcə=ə[=Aá·=]m//, PLN ['*place where Yale Creek divides (forks)*

above the highway bridge over the creek'], literally /'little forked dirty water place'/, (<**R4=**> *diminutive*), lx <**=elhcha**> *unclear liquid*, possibly <**ó:-ablaut**> *derivational*, possibly <**=em**> *place to get/have*, phonology: reduplication, vowel-loss, ablaut, syntactic analysis: nominal, attested by SP and AK (Fish Camp 8/2/77), source: place names reference file #154.

<**St'ít'x̲oya**>, dmn //s=C₁í=t'əx̣=ayɛ//, PLN ['*Ruby Creek (the creek not the village)*'], literally /'small little forks'/, (<**s=**> *nominalizer*), (<**R4=**> *diminutive*), lx <**=oya ~ =iya**> *affectionate diminutive*, phonology: reduplication, vowel-loss, syntactic analysis: nominal, attested by AD and SP from MP (IHTTC 7/8/77), AK (8/5/77), LJ (4/7/78, History tape #34), source: place names reference file #43, also <**St'it'x̲ó:ye**>, //s=C₁í=t'əx̣=á·yə//, attested by AK (History tape #34, 4/7/78), also <**St'ít'ex̲eya**>, //s=C₁í=t'əx̣=iyɛ//, attested by Elders Group (5/28/75).

<**st'it'x̲óyaq**>, df //s=C₁í=t'əx̣=a[=´=]yɛ=q or s=C₁í=t'əx̣=áyɛq//, EB /'*fork in tree, fork in tree roots*'/, (<**s=**> *nominalizer*), (<**R4=**> *diminutive*), possibly <**=oya**> *diminutive*, possibly <**=´=**> *derivational*, possibly <**=óyaq**> meaning unknown, possibly <**=aq**> *genitals, crotch*, phonology: reduplication, possible stress-shift, syntactic analysis: nominal, attested by Elders Group (5/28/75).

<**t'x̲ém**>, df //t'ə́x̣=M1=əm or t'əx̣=ə[=´=]m//, NUM ['*six*'], possibly <**metathesis or stress-shift**> *derivational*, probably root <**t'éx̲**> *to fork, to branch*, (<**=em**> *have, get, intransitivizer*), (semological comment: the semantic development of 'six' from 'have/get branch/fork' is plausible due to the need in counting on the fingers to use another branch of the body to count six), phonology: possible metathesis or stress-shift, syntactic analysis: num, attested by AC, NP (12/6/73), BJ (5/10/64), CT (9/5/73), many others, other sources: ES /t'x̣ə́m·/, JH /t'x̣ə́m/; found in <**t'x̲émtset.**>, //t'x̣=ə́m-c-ət//, /'*There's six of us.*'/, literally /'We're six.'/, attested by AC, example: <**ó:pel qas kw'e t'x̲ém**>, //ʔá·pəl qɛ-s k'ʷə t'x̣=ə́m//, /'*sixteen*'/, attested by AC, also <**ó:pel qas te t'x̲ém**>, //ʔá·pəl qɛ-s tə t'x̣=ə́m//, attested by CT (9/5/73), <**ts'kw'éx qas te t'x̲ém**>, //c'=k'ʷə́xʸ qɛ-s tə t'x̣=ə́m//, /'*twenty-six*'/, attested by CT (9/5/73).

<**t'x̲emálh**>, nums //t'x̣=əm=ɛ́ɬ//, numc, NUM ['*six times*'], TIME, Elder's comment: "perhaps somewhat artificial as they didn't often count these beyond five", lx <**=álh**> *times, occasions*, syntactic analysis: adverb/adverbial verb, attested by Elders Group (3/19/75), also <**t'x̲ém:elh**>, //t'x̣=ə́m(·)=əɬ//, attested by AC (10/8/71).

<**t'x̲émele**>, nums //t'x̣=ə́m=ələ//, numc, NUM ['*six people*'], HUMC, lx <**=ele**> *people*, syntactic analysis: nominal, adjective/adjectival verb, attested by AC, Elders Group (3/19/75, 7/27/75); found in <**t'x̲émelétset**>, //t'x̣=ə́m=ələ-c-ət//, /'*There's six of us.*'/, phonology: automatic stress-insertion (on schwa before subj. pron.?), attested by AC, example: <**t'x̲émele le ó:lh te sléxwelh.**>, //t'x̣=ə́m=ələ lə ʔá·ɬ tə s=lə́xʷ=wəɬ//, /'*Six people got in the canoe. (get aboard)*'/, syntactic comment: this may be two sentences or may have irregular word order-- one would expect: le ó:lh te sléxwelh te tx̲émele, attested by AC.

<**t'x̲emelsxá**>, nums //t'x̣=əm=əlsxʸɛ́//, numc, NUM ['*sixty*'], lx <**=elsxá**> *times ten*, syntactic analysis: num, attested by DM (12/4/64 new transcript old p.262), BJ (12/5/64 new transcript old p.336), AC (8/4/70), also <**t'x̲èmelhsxá**>, //t'x̣=ə́m=əɬsxʸɛ́//, phonology: downdrifting, attested by CT (9/5/73), AC (8/24/70), example: <**t'x̲emelhsxá qas kw'e lheq'átses**>, //t'x̣=əm=əɬsxʸɛ́ qɛ-s k'ʷə ɬəq'ɛ́t=cəs//, /'*sixty-five*'/, attested by AC (8/24/70).

<**t'x̲emelsxá:le**>, nums //t'x̣=əm=əlsxʸɛ́=ɛ́lə or t'x̣=əm=əlsxʸɛ=ələ//, numc, NUM ['*sixty people*'], HUMC, Elder's comment: "prob. somewhat artificial since qéx̲ *many, lots* would be used instead of counting this high", lx <**=ále**> *people*, phonology: vowel merger, syntactic analysis: nominal, adjective/adjectival verb, attested by Elders Group (3/19/75).

<**t'x̲émelsxós**>, nums //t'x̣=ə́m=əlsxʸɛ=ás//, numc, ECON ['*sixty dollars*'], NUM, lx <**=ós**> *dollars; on the face*, phonology: vowel merger, syntactic analysis: nominal, attested by AC

(11/30/71).

<**t'x̱émemets'**>, nums //t'x̣=ə́m=əməc'//, numc, MC /'*(six long objects), six ropes, six threads, six sticks, six poles*'/, NUM, lx <**=emets' ~ =emeth'**> *long objects*, syntactic analysis: nominal, adjective/adjectival verb, attested by AD (4/12/78 after Boas 1890 Scowlitz ms.).

<**t'x̱émeqel**>, nums //t'x̣=ə́m=əqəl//, numc, MC ['*six containers*'], lx <**=eqel**> *container, in the throat*, syntactic analysis: nominal, adjective/adjectival verb, attested by AD (4/12/78).

<**t'x̱ém:es ~ t'x̱émés**>, nums //t'x̣=ə́m(·)=əs//, numc, ECON /'*six dollars, (six Indian blankets [Boas])*'/, NUM, lx <**=es**> *dollars, faces*, phonology: length optional, updrifting, syntactic analysis: nominal, attested by AC (10/6/71, 10/8/71), also /'*six Indian blankets, six dollars*'/, attested by AD (4/12/78 after Boas 1890 Scowlitz ms.).

<**t'x̱emíqw**>, nums //t'x̣=əm=íq^w//, numc, FSH ['*six fish*'], NUM, lx <**=íqw**> *fish, heads*, syntactic analysis: nominal, adjective/adjectival verb, attested by BHTTC (8/24/76).

<**t'x̱emòls**>, nums //t'x̣=əm=áls//, numc, EB ['*six fruit in a group (as they grow on a plant)*'], HARV, NUM, lx <**=óls**> *fruit, rocks, spherical things*, syntactic analysis: nominal, adjective/adjectival verb, attested by AD (4/12/78).

<**t'x̱emő́welh**>, nums //t'x̣=əm=ówəɬ//, numc, CAN /'*six canoes, six boats*'/, NUM, lx <**=ő́welh**> *canoe, boat, vessel*, syntactic analysis: nominal, adjective/adjectival verb, attested by AD (4/12/78).

<**t'x̱emő́wes**>, nums //t'x̣=əm=ówəs//, numc, CAN /'*six paddles, six paddlers*'/, NUM, lx <**=ő́wes**> *canoe paddles*, syntactic analysis: nominal, adjective/adjectival verb, attested by Elders Group (7/27/75).

<**t'x̱emő́ws**>, nums //t'x̣=əm=óws//, numc, EZ ['*six birds (dead or alive)*'], HUNT, lx <**=ő́ws**> *birds, skins*, syntactic analysis: nominal, adjective/adjectival verb, attested by Elders Group (3/29/77).

<**st'x̱éms**>, nums //s=t'x̣=ə́m=s//, numc, TIME ['*six o'clock*'], NUM, lx <**s=...=s**> *o'clock, hours*, phonology: circumfix, syntactic analysis: nominal, attested by AC (10/6/71), example: <**wetéses te st'x̱éms**>, //wə-tə́s-əs tə s=t'x̣=ə́m=s//, /'*when it gets to six o'clock, at six o'clock*'/, attested by AC.

<**T'ex̱qé:yl or T'ex̱qí:l**>, dnom //t'əx̣=qəl=í·l//, PLN /'*Sumas Mountain (also Tuckquail, a village on both sides of Lower Sumas River [Wells])*'/, ASM ['east of Abbotsford, not the U.S. Sumas Mt. east of Everson, Wash.'], literally /'come/go/get fork/branch in the head'/, (semological comment: for a key to the literal meaning see that given in Wells below, combined with the appearance of the mountain which has a number of large ravines as if the mountain broke apart in chunks; it figures in a story of the Flood as a mountain which grew to stay above the flood water to save some of the Indian people; Jenness relates a story of Billy Sepass hunting for the cave of thunderbird on Sumas Mountain), lx <**=qel**> *in the head*, (<**=í:l**> *come, go, get, become*), phonology: syllable-loss, syntactic analysis: nominal, attested by BJ (1/16/64 tape), other sources: Wells 1966 <tuk-QAYL> (line through k) ~ <t'uh-KAY-oh> ~ <tuhk-KAY-uhq>, (semological comment: said by Wells to mean literally "gap left when chunk broke off"), also /'*also Tuckquail, a village on both sides of Lower Sumas River*'/, attested by Wells 1965 (lst ed.):23, source: place names reference file #315.

<**T'ex̱qé:yl or T'ex̱qí:l**>, PLN /'*Sumas Mountain (also Tuckquail, a village on both sides of Lower Sumas River [Wells])*'/, *see* t'éx̱.

<**t'í:l**>, free root //t'í·l//, EFAM ['*(be) lonesome (referring to oneself)*'], syntactic analysis: adjective/adjectival verb, attested by NP (Elders Group 3/5/80), EB (12/17/75), example: <**tsel me t'í:l.**>, //c-əl mə t'í·l//, /'*I'm lonesome.*'/, attested by EB.

<**t'etí:l**>, df //C_1ə-t'í·l//, EFAM ['*(being) lonesome (refers to someone else)*'], probably <**R5-**> *continuative*, phonology: reduplication, syntactic analysis: adjective/adjectival verb, attested by NP (Elders Group 3/5/80).

<**t'í:lmet ~ t'ílmet**>, iecs //t'í·l=məT ~ t'íl=məT//, EFAM /*'be lonesome for s-o, miss s-o'*/, (<**=met**> *indirect effect non-control transitivizer*), syntactic analysis: transitive verb, attested by EB (12/17/75, 8/14/78); found in <**t'ílmethométsetcha.**>, //t'íl=məT-amə-c-ət-cɛ//, /*'We'll be lonesome for you., We'll miss you.'*/, phonology: automatic stress-shift, attested by EB, example: <**tsel me t'í:lmet kw'e Mary**>, //c-əl mə t'í·l=məT k'ʷə mɛ́riy//, /*'I'm lonesome for Mary.'*/, attested by EB (12/17/75).

<**t'íl**>, bound root //t'íl *sing*//.

<**st'élt'el**>, chrs //s=t'i[=Aə́=]l=C_1əC_2//, MUS /*'a person that sings all the time (any song), a singer'*/, (<**s=**> *nominalizer*), (<**=R2**> *characteristic*), phonology: é-ablaut triggered automatically by reduplication type 2, syntactic analysis: nominal, attested by BHTTC (11/1/76).

<**t'ílém ~ t'ílem**>, df //t'íl=əm//, MUS [*'sing'*], ABFC [*'buzz (of insects)'*], (<**=em**> *middle voice or intransitive/have/get*), phonology: optional updrifting, syntactic analysis: intransitive verb, attested by AC, BJ (12/5/64), BHTTC, IHTTC, MC (Deming 1/6/76), other sources: ES /tiʔíləm/, MsCw /t'íləm/ *sing*; found in <**t'ilémtsel.**>, //t'íl=ə́m-c-əl//, /*'I'm going to sing (now).'*/, (semological comment: present tense as immediate future), attested by BHTTC (10/21/76), example: <**tsel t'ílem.**>, //c-əl t'íləm//, /*'I sang.'*/, (semological comment: ambiguous past), attested by BHTTC (10/21/76); found in <**t'ilémlha.**>, //t'íl=ə́m-ɬɛ//, /*'Sing., You sing it.'*/, attested by IHTTC, AC, <**t'ilémalha.**>, //t'íl=ə́m-ɛɬɛ//, /*'Sing you guys.'*/, attested by IHTTC (9/15/77), example: <**tl'ótsa sew qw'eyíléx qa t'ílém tel siyáya welámet mílha.**>, //ƛ'á-cɛ s-əw q'ʷəy=íl=əxʸ qɛ t'íl=ə́m t-əl s=yɛ́yɛ wə-lɛ́=m-ət míɬɛ//, /*'My friends will sing and dance when we go to spirit-dance.'*/, attested by AC, <**ōwáchxw t'ílemexw?**>, //ʔowə-ə-c-xʷ t'íl=əm-əxʷ//, /*'Will you sing?'*/, literally /'are you not? sing'/, syntactic comment: interrogative negative with subjunctive dependent verb, attested by MC (Deming 1/6/76).

<**t'ít'elem**>, cts //t'í[-C_1ə-]l=əm//, MUS [*'singing'*], ABFC [*'buzzing (of insects)'*], (<**-R1-**> *continuative*), phonology: reduplication, syntactic analysis: intransitive verb, attested by AC, BJ (12/5/64), BHTTC, Elders Group, example: <**le t'ít'elem te syéw:els te sí:le.**>, //lə t'í[-C_1ə-]l=əm tə s=yə́w=əl-s tə sí·lə//, /*'She's singing her grandmother's (spirit) song.'*/, (semological comment: shows that third person endings can refer to females as well as males), attested by AC, <**wiyóths kw'es í:wólems te stá:xwelh, t'ít'elem kw'es í:wólems.**>, //wə=yáθ-s k'ʷə-s ʔi[-´·-]wál=əm-s tə s=tɛ́·xʷ=əɬ t'í[-C_1ə-]l=əm k'ʷə-s ʔi[-´·-]wál=əm-s//, /*'The children are playing all the time, singing as they're playing.'*/, attested by AC (10/15/71), <**schewót kw'es t'ít'elem.**>, //s=cəwát k'ʷə-s t'í[-C_1ə-]l=əm//, /*'(He/She) knows how to sing.'*/, (semological comment: as Suttles points out (ca1984 ch.7 p.7 (7.2)) continuative is sometimes used for habitual action and not translated with -ing), attested by AC (11/10/71), <**schewót kw'es (s)t'ít'elems.**>, //s=cəwát k'ʷə-s (s=)t'í[-C_1ə-]l=əm-s//, /*'He's good at singing.'*/, possibly /*'he's good at his singing'*/, attested by AC (11/11/71), <**tsel t'ít'elem.**>, //c-əl t'í[-C_1ə-]l=əm//, /*'I am singing.'*/, attested by BHTTC, <**t'ít'elem te mímeqw.**>, //t'í[-C_1ə-]l=əm tə C_1í=maqʷ//, /*'The little bird is singing.'*/, attested by Elders Group (12/15/76), <**t'ít'elem te sisemó:ye**>, //t'í[-C_1ə-]l=əm tə C_1í=səm=á·yə//, /*'The bee is buzzing.'*/, literally /'the bee is singing'/, attested by AC.

<**t'élt'elem**>, chrs //t'i[=Aə́=]l=C_1əC_2=əm//, MUS [*'continuing on singing'*], (<**=R2**> *characteristic*), (<**=em**> *middle voice*), phonology: é-ablaut triggerdd by reduplication type 2 (also see Suttles consonant alternation1984 for this in Mtsqueam), syntactic analysis: intransitive verb, attested by BHTTC (11/1/76).

<**st'ílém**>, dnom //s=t'íl=əm//, MUS [*'song (non-religious)'*], (<**s=**> *nominalizer*), phonology: updrifting, syntactic analysis: nominal, attested by AC, BJ (12/5/64), others, other sources: ES /st'íl ə́m/ *secular song*.

<**st'elt'ílém**>, pln //s=C_1əC_2=t'íl=əm//, MUS ['*songs*'], (<**R3=**> *plural*), phonology: updrifting, syntactic analysis: nominal, attested by BHTTC (11/1/76).

<**lexwst'í:lem**>, chrs //ləxʷ=s=t'í·l=əm//, MUS ['*a person that always sings*'], (<**lexw=s=**> *person that always*), syntactic analysis: nominal, attested by EB (2/11/76).

<**t'ílemet**>, iecs //t'íl=əm=məT//, MUS ['*sing about s-o/s-th*'], (<**=met**> *indirect effect control transitivizer*), phonology: consonant merger, syntactic analysis: transitive verb, attested by IHTTC (8/9/77), EB (2/13/78); found in <**t'ílemethòxes**>, //t'íl=əm=məT-áxʸ-əs//, /'*He sings about me.*'/, Elder's comment: "not 'he sings it for me', that would be t'ílemelhtsthóxes", attested by IHTTC, example: <**tsel t'í:lemet xwoxweyíwel te ílh á skwól.**>, //c-əl t'í·l=əm=məT xʷa[-C_1ə-]y=íwəl tə ʔí-ɬ ʔɛ s=kʷál//, /'*I sang happy birthday to you.*'/, literally /'I sang about being happy the past your birth'/, attested by EB (2/13/78) approved this sentence constructed by staff class member.

<**t'ít'elemet**>, cts //t'í[-C_1ə-]l=əm=məT//, iecs, MUS ['*be singing about s-o/s-th*'], (<**-R1-**> *continuative*), phonology: reduplication, consonant merger, syntactic analysis: transitive verb, attested by EB (2/15/78), example: <**t'ít'elemetes the xwélmexw q'á:mi te pésk'a st'í:lem.**>, //t'í[-C_1ə-]l=əm=məT-əs θə xʷə́lməxʷ q'ɛ́·m=iy tə pə́sk'ɛ s=t'í·l=əm//, /'*The Indian adolescent girl is singing the hummingbird song.*'/, syntactic comment: two cases of nouns used as adjectives, attested by EB (2/13/78) approved this sentence constructed by a staff class member.

<**t'ílemelhtst**>, bens //t'íl=əm=əɬc=T//, pcs, MUS ['*sing it for s-o*'], (<**=elhts**> *benefactive*), (<**=t**> *purposeful control transitivizer*), syntactic analysis: transitive verb, attested by IHTTC (8/9/77).

<**t'ílemestexw**>, caus //t'íl=əm=sT-əxʷ//, MUS /'*sing for s-o, (cause s-o to sing?)*'/, (<**=st**> *causative control transitivizer*), (<**-exw**> *third person object*), syntactic analysis: transitive verb, attested by EB (3/31/78), AD (3/31/78), example: <**ewá:lh t'ílemesthòm té syùwèls?**>, //ʔəwə-ə-ɛ́ɬ t'íl=əm=sT-àm tə s=yə́w=əl-s//, /'*Does he ever sing you his spirit song?*'/, literally /'is not -interrogative -past habitual you are sung for the spirit song -his'/, literally /'weren't you ever sung his spirit song'/, phonology: vowel merger, downdrifting and updrifting, attested by EB, <**éwelh t'ílemesthò:m té syùwèls.**>, //ʔə́wə-ɬ t'íl=əm=sT-à·m tə s=yə́w=əls//, /'*He never sang you his spirit song.*'/, literally /'is not -past you are sung for the spirit song -his'/, phonology: downdrifting and updrifting, attested by AD (3/31/78).

<**t'ílém ~ t'ílem**>, MUS ['*sing*'], *see* t'íl.

<**t'ílemelhtst**>, MUS ['*sing it for s-o*'], *see* t'íl.

<**t'ílemestexw**>, MUS /'*sing for s-o, (cause s-o to sing?)*'/, *see* t'íl.

<**t'ílemet**>, MUS ['*sing about s-o/s-th*'], *see* t'íl.

<**t'iléqel**>, df //t'il(=)ə́q(=)əl//, ABFC ['*salmon after spawning when its eggs are loose*'], root meaning unknown unless <**t'í:l**> *(be) lonesome (referring to oneself)*, possibly <=eq> *genitals, penis*, <=el> *get, come, go*, syntactic analysis: nominal, attested by Elders Group (4/28/76).

<**t'í:lmet ~ t'ílmet**>, EFAM /'*be lonesome for s-o, miss s-o*'/, *see* t'í:l.

<**t'íq**>, possibly root //t'íq or t'ə[=Aí=]q *discolored, bruised*//, possibly <**í-ablaut**> *resultative.*

<**t'íqel**>, df //t'ə[=Aí=]q=əl or t'íq=əl//, ABDF ['*be bruised*'], possibly <**í-ablaut**> *resultative*, (<**=el**> *go, come, get, become*), phonology: possible ablaut, syntactic analysis: intransitive verb, attested by EB (1/7/76), Salish cognate: Squamish /t'áqaʔ/ *be bruised (so that the skin has the color of a salalberry), salalberry* W73:46, K67:270, Samish dial. of N. Straits /t'áqaʔ/ *to get bruised* and /št'əqaʔáləs/ *(get) a black eye* G86a:76, compare <**t'áqa**> *salalberry*, example: <**t'íqel te qélems.**>, //t'ə[=Aí=]q=əl tə qə́ləm-s//, /'*His eye is bruised.*'/, attested by EB.

<**st'ít'eqel**>, dnom //s=t'í[=C$_1$ə=]q=əl//, ABDF ['*a bruise*'], (<**s=**> *nominalizer*), possibly <**=R1=**> *resultative*?, phonology: reduplication, syntactic analysis: nominal, attested by EB (1/7/76), NP (10/26/75).

<**st'it'eqó:les**>, strs //s=t'i[=C$_1$ə=]q=á·ləs//, ABDF /'*black eye, bruised eye*'/, (<**s=**> *stative*), possibly <**=R1=**> *resultative*, lx <**=ó:les**> *on the eye*, phonology: reduplication, syntactic analysis: adjective/adjectival verb, attested by NP (10/26/75), Elders Group (3/3/76).

<**t'íqqwlha**>, augs //t'íq=q^{w}ɬɛ//, DESC /'*dirty, filthy*'/, semantic environment ['said of someone who is (or has clothes that are) filthy/dirty'], lx <**=qwlha**> *augmentative, very*, syntactic analysis: adjective/adjectival verb, attested by EB (1/19/76), example: <**t'íqqwlha te s'íth'ems te slhálí.**>, //t'íq=q^{w}ɬɛ tə s=ʔíθ'əm-s tə s=ɬɛ́l=íy//, /'*The woman's dress is dirty.*'/, attested by EB.

<**t'éqoya**>, df //t'ə́q=ayɛ or t'i[=Aə́=]q=ayɛ//, DESC ['*dirty*'], possibly <**é-ablaut**> *derivational*, lx <**=oya**> *diminutive*, phonology: possible ablaut, syntactic analysis: adjective/adjectival verb, attested by Elders Group (3/72, tape 33, lesson 7), example: <**x̲ét'estexwes yí o qwóqwel t'éqoya.**>, //x̣ə́t'ə=sT-əx^w-əs yi ʔa q^{w}ɛ[-AáC$_1$ə-]l t'ə́q=ayɛ//, /'*Some people say (just) qwóqwel t'éqoya (talking dirty).*'/, attested by Adaline Lorenzetto (Elders Group 3/72 tape 33).

<**t'íqel**>, ABDF ['*be bruised*'], *see* t'íq.

<**t'íqqwlha**>, DESC /'*dirty, filthy*'/, *see* t'íq.

<**t'it'á:yeq'**>, EFAM ['*cranky*'], *see* t'ay.

<**t'ít'elem**>, MUS ['*singing*'], *see* t'íl.

<**t'ít'elemet**>, MUS ['*be singing about s-o/s-th*'], *see* t'íl.

<**t'it'epsó:ye**>, BPI ['*(probably) tiny midget*'], *see* st'éps ~ st'epsóye.

<**t'ít'etsem ~ t'ít'echem**>, ABFC /'*swimming, (swimming under the water after diving (Cheh.) [Elders Group], swimming with crawl strokes, etc. [Deming])*'/, *see* t'ítsem.

<**T'ít'x̲elhchò:m**>, PLN ['*place where Yale Creek divides (forks) above the highway bridge over the creek*'], *see* t'éx̲.

<**t'í:tsel**>, df //t'í·c(=)əl//, HUNT ['*spring snare*'], root meaning unknown, possibly <**=el**> *go, come, get, become*, syntactic analysis: nominal, attested by Deming (4/13/78), contrast <**weltá:lt**> *spring snare.*

<**t'ítsem**>, mdls //t'íc=əm//, ABFC /'*swim (of a person), swim (with crawl strokes, etc.)*'/, semantic environment ['of a person, can't be used with fish or animals'], (<**=em**> *middle voice*), syntactic analysis: intransitive verb, attested by RM (4/23/76), BJ (12/5/64, new transcript old p.306), other sources: Suttles (ca1984:ch.7) Musqueam /t'ícəm/ *swim on the surface*, Salish cognate: Lushootseed /t'íčib/ *wade out, swim* H7676:531, Squamish /t'íč-im/ *swim* W73:259, K67:271, also <**t'í:ts'em**>, //t'í·c'=əm//, comment: probably my mistranscription, attested by AC, Elders Group (1/26/77), Deming (3/15/79) (SJ, MC, MV, LG), also <**x̲élhchem**>, //x(=)ə́ɬc=əm//, dialects: *Cheh.*, attested by RM (4/23/76), Elders Group (4/5/78), example: <**le t'íts'em.**>, //lə t'íc'=əm//, /'*He swam.*'/, attested by Elders Group (1/26/77), <**skw'áy kw'els t'í:ts'em.**>, //s=k'^{w}ɛ́y k'^{w}-əl-s t'í·c'=əm//, /'*I can't swim.*'/, attested by Deming (3/15/79)(SJ, MC, MV, LG).

<**t'ít'etsem ~ t'ít'echem**>, cts //t'í[-C$_1$ə-]c=əm//, ABFC /'*swimming, (swimming under the water after diving (Cheh.) [Elders Group], swimming with crawl strokes, etc. [Deming])*'/, (<**-R1-**> *continuative*), phonology: reduplication, syntactic analysis: intransitive verb, attested by BJ (12/5/64), DF and MP (Elders Group 4/26/78), also <**t'ít'ets'em**>, //t'í[-C$_1$ə-]c'=əm//, comment: probably mistranscribed, also /'*swimming under the water when diving*'/, dialects: *Cheh.*, attested by Elders Group (4/5/78), also /'*swimming (with crawl strokes, etc.)*'/, attested by Deming (8/4/77),

example: <**mőkw' t'ít'ets'em**>, //mók'^{w} t'í[-C_1ə-]c'=əm//, /'*all swimming*'/, attested by AC, <**lhéq'e t'ít'ets'em?**>, //ɬə́q'-ə t'í[-C_1ə-]c'=əm//, /'*Does he swim?*'/, literally /'sometimes -yes/no question swimming'/, attested by EB (3/31/78).

<**t'íw ~ t'ì:w**>, free root //t'íw ~ t'ì·w//, MUS ['*slow beat*'], ABDF ['*overstretch one's legs when walking with too big a step*'], syntactic analysis: intransitive verb, attested by Elders Group (12/15/76), AD (AHTTC 2/27/80).

<**t'í:wqel**>, ds //t'í·w=əqəl//, LANG /'*high-pitched words, slow-talking words, high-pitched and slow-talking words*'/, lx <**=eqel**> *in voice, in speech*, phonology: vowel-loss, syntactic analysis: adjective/adjectival verb, attested by Elders Group (11/10/76).

<**st'íwiyelh**>, df //s=t'íw=iyəɬ//, REL ['*prayer*'], (<**s=**> *nominalizer*), possibly <**=iyelh**> meaning unknown, syntactic analysis: nominal, attested by NP (9/19/75), others, Salish cognate: Lushootseed /t'ig^w(i) ~ t'íwiɬ/ *thank, pray* and /t'íwiɬ/ *pray* and /st'íwiɬ/ *religion* and /ʔu-t'íg^w-id čəd/ *Thank you.* H76:532, example: <**s'ólh má:l st'íwiyelh**>, //sʔáɬ mɛ́·l s=t'íw=iyəɬ//, /'*the Our Father prayer, the Lord's Prayer*'/, attested by NP (9/19/75), <**ō Máli st'íwiyelh**>, //ʔo(w) mɛ́li s=t'íw=iyəɬ//, /'*the Hail Mary Prayer*'/, attested by NP (9/19/75).

<**t'í:wqel**>, LANG /'*high-pitched words, slow-talking words, high-pitched and slow-talking words*'/, *see* t'íw ~ t'ì:w.

<**T'íxwelátse ~ Tíxwelátsa**>, df //t'íx^w=əlɛ́cɛ ~ tíx^w=əlɛ́cɛ//, N ['*name of Chief Albert Louie's father*'], root meaning unknown, lx <**=elátsa**> *male name*, syntactic analysis: nominal, attested by BJ (12/5/64), AL (7/28/65).

<**t'íyelt or t'í:lt**>, pcs //t'íy(=)əl=T or t'í·l=T//, SOC ['*entertain s-o*'], root meaning unknown unless t'í:l *sing*, possibly <**=el**> *go, come, get, become*, (<**=t**> *purposeful control transitivizer*), syntactic analysis: transitive verb, attested by NP (10/10/75).

<**t'at'íyelt**>, cts //C_1ɛ-t'íy(=)əl=T//, SOC ['*entertaining s-o*'], (<**R8-**> *continuative*), phonology: reduplication, syntactic analysis: transitive verb, attested by NP (10/10/75).

<**t'kwíléstexw**>, CAN /'*bring s-th/s-o across a river, (ferry s-o/s-th over)*'/, *see* t'ákwel.

<**t'kwíles ~ t'ekwíles**>, ABDF /'*choke on food, get choked on food*'/, *see* t'ékw.

<**t'kwíwel**>, ABDF ['*constipated*'], *see* t'ékw.

<**t'lhéses**>, WV ['*a loom*'], *see* t'álh.

<**t'lhóqw'els**>, SD ['*(make/have a) scratching noise*'], *see* t'élheqw' ~ t'lhóqw'.

<**t'lhóqw'est**>, ABFC ['*scratch s-o on the face*'], *see* t'élheqw' ~ t'lhóqw'.

<**t'mí:ws**>, HARV ['*smooth a log by chopping*'], *see* t'ém.

<**t'mí:wsà:ls**>, BLDG ['*log cabin*'], *see* t'ém.

<**t'ó**>, free root //t'á//, ABDF ['*to sprain*'], syntactic analysis: intransitive verb, attested by NP (10/26/75), also <**t'ó:**>, //t'á·//, also /'*(get/be) sprained*'/, attested by Deming (1/31/80), example: <**t'ó tel sx̱éle**>, //t'á t-əl s=x̣ə́lə//, /'*sprain my leg*'/, attested by NP.

<**t'ot'á**>, df //t'a-C_1ɛ́(·)//, ABDF /'*sprain, (getting sprained?)*'/, possibly <**-R9**> *continuative or resultative*, phonology: reduplication, syntactic analysis: intransitive verb, attested by NP (10/26/75), example: <**t'ot'á tel s'í:lwelh**>, //t'a-C_1ɛ́(·) t-əl s=ʔí·lwəɬ//, /'*sprain my side*'/, attested by NP.

<**xwt'ó:welh**>, df //x^w=t'á·=wəɬ//, ABDF ['*your back is sprained*'], possibly <**xw=**> meaning uncertain, possibly <**=welh**> *on the back*, syntactic analysis: intransitive verb, attested by Deming

(1/31/80).

<**t'ó:kw'**>, free root //t'á·k'ʷ//, DIR ['*(get/go) home*'], syntactic analysis: adverb/adverbial verb, intransitive verb, attested by AC, EB, EF, NP, Elders Group, example: <**lámechexw t'ò:kw'?**>, //lɛ́=m-ə-c-əxʷ t'á·k'ʷ//, /'*You're going home?, Are you going home?*'/, phonology: sentential downstepping, syntactic comment: interrogative affix, attested by AC, also <**lámechexw t'ó:kw'?**>, //lɛ́=m-ə-c-əxʷ t'á·k'ʷ//, attested by NP (10/26/75), <**látsel t'ò:kw'. ~ lámtsel t'ò:kw'.**>, //lɛ́(=m)-c-əl t'á·k'ʷ//, /'*I'm going home.*'/, phonology: sentential downstepping, attested by AC, <**lalh t'ó:kw'.**>, //lɛ-ɬ t'á·k'ʷ//, /'*Go home.*'/, syntactic comment: short imperative, attested by AC, <**lílhtsel la t'ò:kw'.**>, //lí-ɬ-c-əl lɛ t'á·k'ʷ//, /'*I went home.*'/, attested by AC, <**látset t'ó:kw'.**>, //lɛ́-c-ət t'á·k'ʷ//, /'*Let's go home.*'/, attested by EB (11/26/75), <**tsel me t'ókw'.**>, //c-əl mə t'ák'ʷ//, /'*I came home.*'/, attested by EB (3/8/76), <**tsel la t'ókw'**>, //c-əl lɛ t'ák'ʷ//, /'*I went home.*'/, *<**tsel t'ókw'.**> rejected by EB (3/8/76), <**héylha t'ó:kw'.**>, //hɛ́y-ɬɛ t'á·k'ʷ//, /'*Let's go home.*'/, attested by EF (Deming 5/4/78), <**lhíl ulh lám t'ókw'.**>, //ɬí-l ʔuɬ lɛ́=m t'ák'ʷ//, /'*It's time for me to go home.*'/, literally /'when I already am going to (get/go) home'/, attested by Elders Group (6/28/78), <**tl'élsuwlh lá:m t'ó:kw'.**>, //ƛ'ə́-l-s-u-wɬ lɛ́=m t'á·k'ʷ//, /'*I have to go home.*'/, literally /'it's that/because -I -already am going home'/, attested by EB (11/26/75), <**tl'o kwá sulh látset t'ó:kw'.**>, //ƛ'a kʷɛ s-u-u-ɬ lɛ́-c-ət t'á·k'ʷ//, /'*We have to go home.*'/, literally /'it's that anyway so -already we're going home'/, attested by EB (11/26/75), <**lámtsel t'ó:kw' qechelew í ò.**>, //lɛ́=m-c-əl t'á·k'ʷ qə-c-əl-əw ʔí ʔà//, /'*I was going home but instead I stayed.*'/, attested by Elders Group (3/16/77).

<**t'ekw'élmél**>, ds //t'ak'ʷ=ə́lməl or t'a[=Aə=]k'ʷ=ə́lməl//, EFAM ['*(be) homesick*'], literally /'be/get home -in the mind'/, possibly <**e-ablaut**> *resultative*?, lx <**=élmél**> *in the mind*, phonology: updrifting, syntactic analysis: vowel-reduction or ablaut, attested by Elders Group (3/15/72).

<**t'ót'ekw'élmel**>, cts //t'á[-C_1ə-]k'ʷ=ə́lməl//, EFAM ['*being homesick*'], (<**-R1-**> *continuative*), phonology: reduplication, syntactic analysis: intransitive verb, attested by Elders Group (3/15/72).

<**t'ékw'stexw ~ t'ókw'stexw**>, caus //t'a[=Aə́=]k'ʷ=sT-əxʷ ~ t'ák'ʷ=sT-əxʷ//, TVMO ['*take s-o home*'], DIR, literally /'cause s-o to get/be home'/, (<**é-ablaut**> *derivational* optional), (<**=st**> *causative control transitivizer*), (<**-exw**> *third person object*), phonology: ablaut, syntactic analysis: transitive verb, attested by Elders Group (3/24/76), EB, example: <**le t'ékw'stexwes.**>, //lə t'a[=Aə́=]k'ʷ=sT-əxʷ-əs//, /'*He took someone home.*'/, attested by Elders Group, <**skw'áy kw'es les t'ókw'sthóxes.**>, //s=k'ʷɛ́y k'ʷə-s lɛ-s t'ák'ʷ=sT-áxʸ-əs//, /'*He can't take me home.*'/, attested by Elders Group.

<**t'oléstel**>, HHG /'*window shades, blinds, blinders (on a horse, etc.)*'/, *see* t'á:l.

<**t'ól**>, possible root or more likely stem //t'í[=Aá=]l// prob. *sing a non-spirit song* or //s=t'ɛ́[=Aá=]l// prob. *out of sight behind something* or //t'ál// meaning unknown

<**st'ó(:)lkwlh**>, df //s=/t'í[=Aá=]l=á(:)lkʷɬ or s=t'ɛ́[=Aá=]l=á(:)lkʷɬ or s=t'á(:)l=(ál)kʷɬ//, SPRD ['*a non-spirit-dancer*'], possibly <**s=**> *nominalizer*, root probably <**t'íl**> *sing (non-spirit song)* or <**t'á:l**> *go out of sight (behind something), disappear [behind something], [get in shade]*, , lx <**=ólkwlh**> *spirit-dancer, spirit-power*, phonology: probable **ó**-ablaut, possible syllable-loss, phonology: ó:?, syntactic analysis: nominal, attested by IHTTC (8/22/77).

<**st'elt'ólkwlh**>, pln //s=C_1əC_2=t'ál=(ál)kʷɬ//, SPRD ['*non-spirit-dancers (lots of them)*'], (<**R3=**> *plural*), phonology: reduplication, syntactic analysis: nominal, attested by IHTTC (8/22/77).

<**t'ómel ~ t'ómél**>, df //t'ám(=)əl//, BLDG ['*wall (inside or outside)*'], root meaning unknown unless <**t'em**> *chop*, possibly <**=el**> *come, go, get, become*, phonology: optional updrifting, syntactic analysis: nominal, attested by AC, DM (12/4/64), Elders Group (8/25/76), EB, example:

<**tiyéléstchexw ta' q'éwe xwelám te t'ómél.**>, //tiy=ə́lə́s=T-c-əxʷ t-ɛʔ q'ə́wə xʷə(=)lɛ́(=)m tə t'ám(=)əl//, /'*Lean your cane against the wall.*'/, literally /'you lean it your cane towards the wall'/, attested by EB, <**lámchexw te lhelhá:l stetís te t'ómel.**>, //lɛ́=m-c-əxʷ tə C_1ə=ɬɛ́·l s=C_1ə=tə[=Aí=]s tə t'ám(=)əl//, /'*You'll go to the back [of inside of building] near the wall.*'/, attested by AC (10/13/71), <**skwetxwólwelh t'ómel**>, //s=kʷətɛxʷ=álwəɬ t'ám(=)əl//, /'*inside wall*'/, literally /'stative- inside -side wall'/, dialects: *Chill., Cheh.*, attested by IHTTC (8/29/77).

<**t'omeliwétel**>, ds //t'am(=)əl=íwə́l=təl//, BLDG /'*a partition, wall inside*'/, ASM ['as example in a longhouse to separate families'], lx <**=íwél**> *in the inside(s)*, lx <**=tel**> *device to, something to*, phonology: consonant-loss of l before =tel, possible stress-shift, syntactic analysis: nominal, dialects: *Tait*, attested by IHTTC (8/29/77).

<**t'óp**>, bound root //t'áp *to chip*//, also compare <**t'ápiy**>, stem //t'ɛ́p=iy *dead (of flora)*//

<**st'ót'ep**>, strs //s=t'á[=C_1ə=]p//, EB /'*(be) blazed (of a mark in a tree), chipped (of mark in tree)*'/, TVMO, (<**s=**> *stative*), (<**=R1=**> *resultative*), phonology: reduplication, syntactic analysis: adjective/adjectival verb, attested by Elders Group (2/6/80).

<**t'ópet**>, pcs //t'áp=əT//, HARV ['*to chip it (like wood)*'], EB, ABFC ['*peck s-th/s-o*'], (<**=et**> *purposeful control transitivizer*), syntactic analysis: transitive verb, attested by TG and NP (Elders Group 2/6/80), IHTTC (7/18/77), other sources: JH /t'á·pət ~ t'ápət/ *to chisel*.

<**xwt'ót'epels ~ shxwt'ót'epels**>, dnom //xʷ=t'á[=C_1ə=]p=əls ~ s=xʷ=t'á[=C_1ə=]p=əls//, sas, TOOL ['*adze (for making canoes and pit-house ladders)*'], CAN, BLDG, literally /'something for structured activity chipping'/, (<**xw= ~ shxw=**> *something for*), (<**=R1=**> *continuative*), (<**=els**> *structured activity continuative*), phonology: reduplication, syntactic analysis: nominal, attested by IHTTC (7/18/77).

<**t'óp'**>, bound root //t'áp' *peck*//, comment: this root may be the same as t'óp *chip* if the former was mistranscribed or if the two are in variation (I've not found cognate yet to help sort this out), but since the two may be separate or related roots, I've kept them separate to be cautious; it may be possible later to connect them.

<**t'óp'els**>, sas //t'áp'=ɛls//, ABFC ['*to peck*'], (<**=als**> *structured activity non-continuative*), phonology: vowel-reduction on suffix, syntactic analysis: intransitive verb, attested by Elders Group (4/28/76).

<**t'ót'ep'els**>, cts //t'á[-C_1ə-]p'=əls//, ABFC ['*pecking*'], (<**-R1-**> *continuative*), (<**=els**> *structured activity continuative*), phonology: reduplication, syntactic analysis: intransitive verb, attested by Elders Group (4/28/76).

<**shxwt'ót'ep'els**>, dnom //s=xʷ=t'á[=C_1ə=]p'=əls//, TOOL ['*a pick*'], (<**shxw=**> *something for*), (<**=R1=**> *continuative or resultative*), (<**=els**> *structured activity nominal/tool*), phonology: reduplication, syntactic analysis: nominal, attested by IHTTC (8/25/77).

<**t'ót'ep'els**>, dnom //t'á[=C_1ə=]p'=əls//, ANAB ['*bird's bill*'], (<**=R1=**> *continuative*), (<**=els**> *structured activity nominal/tool*), phonology: reduplication, syntactic analysis: nominal, attested by Elders Group (4/28/76), also EZ ['*ordinary small woodpecker*'], attested by EL and JL (9/15/78), contrast <**qw'opxwiqsélem**> *ordinary small woodpecker*.

<**t'óp'els**>, dnom //t'áp'=əls//, ANAB ['*bird's bill*'], (<**=els**> *structured activity nominalizer/tool*), syntactic analysis: nominal, attested by Elders Group (4/28/76).

<**t'ot'ep'íqselem**>, dnom //t'a[=C_1ə=]p'=íy=qs=əl=əm//, EZ /'*red-headed woodpecker, (pileated woodpecker)*'/, ['*Dryocopus pileatus*'], literally /'come/go pecking its own nose on bark'/, (<**=R1=**> *continuative*), lx <**=íy**> *bark*, lx <**=qs**> *nose, on the nose*, (<**=el**> *go, come*), (<**=em**> *middle voice*), phonology: reduplication, syntactic analysis: nominal, attested by Elders Group (4/28/76), contrast

<**temélhepsem**> *red-headed woodpecker.*

<**t'óqwel**>, incs //t'áq^w=əl//, WATR /'*to drain (of a pond), (get) dried up (of creek, empty cup, etc.)*'/, root meaning unknown, (<**=el**> *go, come, get, become*), syntactic analysis: intransitive verb, attested by BHTTC (8/24/76), IHTTC (8/31/77), Salish cognate: Squamish /t'áq^w-alʔ/ *dry* K67:270, Lushootseed /t'ák^w-il/ *gone dry* H76:518, historical/comparative detail: historically the Halkomelem form should have an /ɛ́/ <á> vowel if cognate with Squamish and Lushootseed, the Halkomelem /á/ <ó> may show that the form is borrowed or influenced from a Salish language other than Nooksack or Northern Straits (since they too have PCS /*a/ > /ɛ/).

<**t'ó:t'**>, df //t'á[=·=]t'//, EFAM /'*poor little one, you poor thing (said to a child)*'/, possibly <**=:=**> *emphasis (or here) diminutive*, phonology: possible lengthening, syntactic analysis: interjection, attested by Elders Group (3/2/77, 1/28/76), EB (1/9/78), example: <**lhilhím, t'ót'.**>, //C_1í=ɬím t'át'//, /'*She's picking, poor thing.*'/, literally /'someone little is picking, poor thing (or) she/he is picking a little bit, poor thing'/, attested by EB (1/9/78).

<**t'ót'**>, possible root t'át'// or root or stem //ʔát' or wət'át'//, root meaning uncertain

<**wet'ót'**>, df //wə=C_1əC_2=ʔát' or wə-C_1əC_2=ʔát' or wə=t'át' or wə-t'át'//, TIME ['*long ago*'], possibly <**we=**> (*emphasis), really*, possibly <**we-**> *when/if/subjunctive*, possibly <**R3=**> *plural*, possibly root <**ót'**> *stretch*, possibly root <**t'ót'**> meaning unknown (not> *poor little thing*), phonology: possible reduplication, syntactic analysis: adverb/adverbial verb, attested by AD (2/28/80).

<**t'ót'elhem**>, EZ ['*jumping flea*'], see t'alh

<**t'ót'emethet**>, EFAM /'*suspect, be suspicious*'/, *see* t'ám.

<**t'ót'ep'els**>, ABFC ['*pecking*'], *see* t'óp'.

<**t'ót'ep'els**>, ANAB ['*bird's bill*'], *see* t'óp'.

<**t'ot'ep'íqselem**>, EZ /'*red-headed woodpecker, (pileated woodpecker)*'/, *see* t'óp'.

<**t'ót'exw**>, DIR ['*going towards the river or water*'], *see* t'óxw.

<**t'ot'qw'íth'et**>, HARV ['*cutting them up (of logs)*'], *see* t'éqw'.

<**t'óthet**>, TIB /'*make an attempt (to do something difficult, like running rapids in a canoe, mountain-climbing, winning a game, etc.), give it a try*'/, *see* t'á.

<**t'óxw**>, free root //t'áx^w//, DIR /'*go down(hill) to the water, go towards the river*'/, WATR, syntactic analysis: adverb/adverbial verb, attested by Deming (4/17/80), EB (5/25/76), other sources: ES /t'áx^w/ *downhill, toward water*, example: <**le t'óxw.**>, //lə t'áx^w//, /'*He went towards the river.*'/, attested by EB.

<**t'ót'exw**>, cts //t'a[-C_1ə-]x^w//, DIR ['*going towards the river or water*'], WATR, (<**-R1-**> *continuative*), phonology: reduplication, syntactic analysis: adverb/adverbial verb, attested by EB (5/25/76), example: <**ley t'ót'exw.**>, //lə yə(-) t'á[-C_1ə-]x^w//, /'*He's going towards the river.*'/, attested by EB.

<**xwt'óxwestses**>, ds //x^w=t'áx^w=əs=cəs//, ANA ['*hollow of hand*'], literally /'go downhill (toward the water) on the face of the hand'/, (<**xw=**> meaning uncertain), lx <**=es**> *on the face*, lx <**=tses**> *on the hand*, syntactic analysis: nominal, attested by Elders Group (8/20/75).

<**xwt'óxwesxel**>, ds //x^w=t'áx^w=əs=x^{y}əl//, ANA ['*arch of foot*'], literally /'go downhill on the face of the foot'/, (<**xw=**> meaning uncertain), lx <**=es**> *on the face*, lx <**=xel**> *on the foot*, syntactic analysis: nominal, attested by Elders Group (8/20/75), also <**xwt'óqwesxel**>, //x^w=t'áq^w=əs=x^{y}əl//, comment: probably mispronounced or mistranscribed, attested by SP (BHTTC 8/24/76).

<**t'ó:xw ~ t'óxw ~ t'óx̲w**>, free root //t'á·xʷ ~ t'áxʷ ~ t'áx̣ʷ//, EB /'*white fir, probably grand fir*'/, ['probably *Abies grandis*'], syntactic analysis: noun, nominal, historical/comparative detail: t'ó:xw appears to be the original form, with length lost through fast pronunciation or mistranscription, and with x̲w evolving through dissimilation with t'óxw *go down(hill) to the water*, attested by Elders Group (5/28/75, 3/22/78), Deming (2/17/78), SJ (Deming 4/17/80), other sources: ES /t'à·xʷ/ *white fir*, JH /t'áx̣ʷ/ *white fir*, H-T <talQ> (macron over a) *fir (white)*, Salish cognate: Squamish /t'úʔxʷ-ay/ *white fir* W73:100, K69:51, but *grand or "balsam" fir, Abies grandis* Bouchard and Turner 1976:32, Lushootseed /t'úxʷ(əc)/ *white fir (tree)* H76:540, Sechelt /t'úʔxʷ-ay/ *balsam fir* T77:11, Saanich dial. of NSt /t'áʔxʷ/ *balsam tree* B74a:15, also <**t'óxwelhp ~ t'óx̲welhp**>, //t'áxʷ=əlp ~ t'áx̣ʷ=əɬp//, attested by Elders Group (5/28/75, 3/22/78), also <**t'ó:xwelhp**>, //t'á·xʷ=əɬp//, also /'*Douglas fir [sic]*'/, attested by Elders Group (3/15/72), also <**t'óqwelhp**>, //t'áqʷ=əɬp//, comment: probably mistranscribed, attested by Elders Group (1/29/75), also <**t'ó'x̲w**>, //t'áʔx̣ʷ//, attested by LG (Deming 4/17/80), also <**t'óxwtses**>, //t'áxʷ=cəs//, also EB /'*grand fir, white fir*'/, ['*Abies grandis*'], MED ['heart medicine'], ASM ['grows at Harrison Lake'], attested by Elders Group (4/2/80).

<**t'óx̲wtses**>, df //t'áx̣ʷ=cəs//, EB ['*white fir branch*'], ['branch of probably *Abies grandis*'], lx <**=tses**> *hand, branch (of tree)*, syntactic analysis: nominal, attested by Elders Group (3/22/78).

<**t'óx̲wtses**>, EB ['*white fir branch*'], *see* t'ó:xw ~ t'óxw ~ t'óx̲w.

<**t'ōp**>, possible root //t'óp//, meaning uncertain but see first entry immediately below

<**T'ept'ōp**>, df //C₁əC₂=t'óp//, PLN ['*village at junction of Ryder Lake Creek and Chilliwack River*'], (<**R3=**> *plural*), root meaning unknown unless <**t'áp**> *dead (of tree)* or <**t'óp**> *to chip* or a survival of the root in Nooksack ch'ōt'ep' /č'ót'əp'/ *flea*, literally /'sand-flea ridge (AC) (recently I also found Nooksack //k'ʷót'æp// *flea* in Fetzer's notes) or *where vine maples grow* (Wells) (or perhaps *many dead trees*)'/ (Nooksack has <st'ápey> *dead (of standing tree)*, <**R3-**> *plural (many)*, phonology: reduplication, syntactic analysis: nominal, attested by AC, source: Wells (lst ed.):19, Galloway 1985, source: place names reference file #230.

<**T'ept'ōp (X̲ótsa)**>, cpds //C₁əC₂=t'óp (x̣ácɛ)//, PLN ['*Ryder Lake*'], (<**R3=**> *plural*), except x̲ótsa *lake*, phonology: reduplication, syntactic analysis: nominal phrase with modifier(s), source: Wells (lst ed.), also <**St'ept'ōp**>, //s=C₁əC₂=t'óp//, Elder's comment: "may be a lhéchelesem [Nooksack language] word", comment: possible due to the root /o/ found here, source: Galloway 1985c, attested by AC.

<**T'ept'ōp Stótelō**>, cpds //C₁əC₂=t'óp s=tá[=C₁ə=]l=əw//, PLN ['*Ryder Lake Creek*'], literally /'Ryder Lake creek'/, phonology: reduplication, syntactic analysis: nominal phrase with modifier(s), attested by Wells (lst ed.):13, Duff 1952.

<**t'pí**>, df //t'(ɛ)p(=)i[=´=](y)//, EZ /'*tick, wood tick, and probably Pacific Coast tick*'/, ['class *Arachnida*, order *Acarina*, Dermacentor andersoni, and probably *Ixodes pacificus*'], ASM ['the wood tick is common in the Interior dry areas (and thus also Tait area) and is found April to June, the Pacific Coast tick is the common coastal species mainly in the wet season, November through March'], possibly root <**t'ap**> *dead (of tree)* or <**t'ōp**> as in *flea*, possibly <**=iy**> *covering, bark*, possibly <= ´=> *derivational*, (semological comment: wood ticks frequent dead bark), phonology: vowel-loss, stress-shift, syntactic analysis: nominal, attested by CT (Elders Group 6/4/75), Deming (2/7/80), contrast <**meth'elhqíwel**> *tick, wood tick.*

<**t'qwém**>, df //t'qʷ(=)ə[=´=]m//, EB ['*thimbleberry*'], ['*Rubus parviflorus*'], ASM ['tender sweet shoots peeled and eaten raw in spring, berries ripe in July and eaten fresh, large leaves used to clean slime from fish when butchering'], root meaning unknown, possibly <= ´=> *derivational*, possibly <**=em**> *middle voice or intransitivizer/have/get*, phonology: possible stress-shift, syntactic analysis: nominal,

attested by AC, Elders Group (2/19/75, 7/9//75).

<**t'qwémelhp**>, ds //t'q^{w}(=)ə́m=əɬp//, EB [*'thimbleberry plant or bush'*], lx <**=elhp**> *plant, tree,* syntactic analysis: nominal, attested by Elders Group (2/19/75).

<**t'qwíqst**>, pcs //t'q^{w}=i[=´=]y=qs=T//, HARV /*'join two poles together, splice it together (of a rope), (join together on the ends)*'/, root meaning unknown, possibly <**=iy**> *bark, covering,* lx <**=qs**> *on the nose, on the point,* (<**=t**> *purposeful control transitivizer*), phonology: possible stress-shift, possible vowel-loss, syntactic analysis: transitive verb, attested by CT and HT (6/21/76), Elders Group (5/26/76), example: <**t'qwíqst te sókw'emelhp**>, //t'q^{w}=íy=qs=T tə sák'^{w}=əm=əɬp//, /*'join poles'*/, attested by CT and HT, <**t'qwíqst te xwéylem**>, //t'q^{w}=íy=qs=T təx̣^{w}í(y)l(=)əm//, /*'splice a rope'*/, attested by Elders Group (5/26/7).

<**t'qw'á:lats**>, CAN [*'a canoe or boat cut off short in the rear (because the stern couldn't be repaired)'*], *see* t'éqw'.

<**t'ú'**>, free root //t'úʔ//, EZ [*'gray or brown-gray chichadee-sized bird which calls t'ú' or tsk tsk in maple woods near American Bar'*], ['unidentified bird'], phonology: final glottal stop and /u/ may indicate a borrowed word, probably borrowed from Thompson?, syntactic analysis: noun, nominal, source: Galloway (5/29/79): Index to Upriver Halkomelem Fauna,

<**t'usló:ye**>, df //t'us(=ə)l=á·yə//, EB [*'licorice fern'*], [*'Polypodium glycyrrhiza'*], ASM ['small fern that grows out from trunks and roots of trees and also from rocks sometimes, the roots are chewed year-round for their sweetness and licorice flavor, they can keep a hungry person sustained while walking in the woods'], MED ['roots are chewed year-round for colds, asthma, and cough medicine'], root meaning unknown, possibly <**=el**> *go, come, get, become,* lx <**=ó:ye**> *affectinate diminutive,* phonology: vowel-loss, syntactic analysis: nominal, dialects: *Tait,* attested by AK and MP and others (IHTTC 9/19/77), also <**st'usló:ye**>, //s=t'us(=ə)l=á·yə//, dialects: *Tait,* attested by SP (IHTTC 9/19/77), also <**tl'asíp**>, //ƛ'ɛs(=)íp//, dialects: *Cheh. and Chill.*, attested by IHTTC (9/19/77).

<**t'wa ~ t'we**>, free root //t'wɛ ~ t'wə or t'ɛ́w=M1//, MOOD /*'maybe, I guess, I'm uncertain, must be (evidently), (evidential), have to (I guess)'*/, phonology: unstressed word, syntactic analysis: particle, attested by Elders Group (10/6/77, 1/26/77), EB, AD, Deming, AC, IHTTC, prob. <**t'áw**> as in <**st'áwel**> *guess,* example: <**lí t'wa.**>, //lí t'wɛ//, /*'Maybe., I guess., I'm uncertain.'*/, semantic environment ['answer to a question'], attested by Elders Group (10/6/76), EB (4/23/76), also <**lí t'we 'á.**>, //lí t'wə ʔɛ́//, literally /'it is (answer to yes/no question) evidently yes'/, attested by EB (4/23/76), <**yóswe t'wá.**>, //yáswə t'wə-ɛ́//, /*'Maybe it was.'*/, literally possibly/perhaps /'it evidently must be yes'/, attested by Elders Group (1/26/77), <**lílh t'we.**>, //lí-ɬ t'wə//, /*'It must have been.'*/, attested by Elders Group (1/26/77), <**Lí t'we à.**>, //lí t'wə ʔɛ́//, /*'such and such, so and so, Maybe yes, maybe no., I don't know.'*/, literally /'it is (answer to a yes/no question) evidently yes'/, attested by AD (3/13/80), <**t'we kw'els kwú:t.**>, //t'wə k'^{w}-əl-s k^{w}ú·=T//, /*'I'll have to take it.'*/, literally /'it must (evidently)' that I take it'/, attested by Deming (1/25/79), also <**kwú:ttsel t'we.**>, //k^{w}ú·=T-c-əl t'wə//, attested by Deming (1/25/79), <**tl'ó t'we stóles te spáth the í'axwil spáth tl'ó sq'óxels.**>, //ƛ'á t'wə s=táləs-s tə s=pɛ́θ θə C$_{1}$í=ʔɛx^{w}=íl s=pɛ́θ ƛ'á s=q'á=x̣^{y}əl-s//, /*'The little bear must be the bear's wife; that's his partner.'*/, attested by AC (11/30/71), <**éy t'wa meythómet.**>, //ʔɛ́y t'wɛ mɛy=T-ámə-t//, /*'It would be good if we help you., (We'd should/better help you.)'*/, attested by IHTTC (8/8/77), <**éy t'wa meythómes kw'e swótle.**>, //ʔɛ́y t'wɛ mɛy=T-ámə-s k'^{w}ə s=wa=Aá=tla//, /*'It would be good if someone helps you., (Someone should/better help you.)'*/, attested by IHTTC (8/8/77), <**ét'wōwlh le lhélq thel slhálqi.**>, //ʔə-t'wə-wəɬ lə ɬə́lq (k^{w})θə-l s=ɬə[=Aɛ́=]lq=i//, /*'It must be already soaked, what I'm soaking.'*/, attested by EB (IHTTC 8/17/77).

<**t'x̱ém**>, NUM ['*six*'], *see* t'éx̱.

<**t'x̱emálh**>, NUM ['*six times*'], *see* t'éx̱.

<**t'x̱émele**>, NUM ['*six people*'], *see* t'éx̱.

<**t'x̱emelsxá**>, NUM ['*sixty*'], *see* t'éx̱.

<**t'x̱emelsxá:le**>, NUM ['*sixty people*'], *see* t'éx̱.

<**t'x̱émelsxós**>, ECON ['*sixty dollars*'], *see* t'éx̱.

<**t'x̱émemets'**>, MC /'*(six long objects), six ropes, six threads, six sticks, six poles*'/, *see* t'éx̱.

<**t'x̱émeqel**>, MC ['*six containers*'], *see* t'éx̱.

<**t'x̱ém:es ~ t'x̱émés**>, ECON /'*six dollars, (six Indian blankets [Boas])*'/, *see* t'éx̱.

<**t'x̱emíqw**>, FSH ['*six fish*'], *see* t'éx̱.

<**t'x̱emòls**>, EB ['*six fruit in a group (as they grow on a plant)*'], *see* t'éx̱.

<**t'x̱emőwelh**>, CAN /'*six canoes, six boats*'/, *see* t'éx̱.

<**t'x̱emőwes**>, CAN /'*six paddles, six paddlers*'/, *see* t'éx̱.

<**t'x̱emőws**>, EZ ['*six birds (dead or alive)*'], *see* t'éx̱.

<**t'x̱éthet**>, WATR ['*forks in stream*'], *see* t'éx̱.

TH

<**thá**>, free root //θɛ́//, DEM ['*there (nearby)*'], (semological comment: when preceded by te *the (present and visible or unspecified)* the combination means *there (close and visible), that (close and visible)*, when preceded by kwe or kwthe, both *the (near but out of sight)*, that combination means *there/that (near but not visible)*, for some like EB who use kwe rather than kw'e for *the (remote)* kwe thá seems to mean *there/that (remote)*), phonology: te thá is often pronounced tethá or even tthá, kwe thá is often pronounced and written kwethá or kwthá, kwthe thá is only pronounced and written kwthá, showing vowel-loss and consonant merger, syntactic analysis: demonstrative article, attested by EB, BJ (12/5/64), AC, JL (4/7/78), AD, others, example: <**te thá ~ tethá ~ tthá**>, //tə θɛ́ ~ təθɛ́ ~ tθɛ́//, /'*that thing there, that one, he/she/him/her/they/them, there*'/, attested by EB (1/9/76), BJ (12/5/64), AC, many others, <**tethá lí tí ~ tthá lí tí**>, //tə θɛ́ lí tí//, /'*that thing yonder*'/, attested by EB (1/9/76), <**st'á tethá.**>, //s=t=əʔɛ́ tə θɛ́//, /'*(It's) like that.*'/, attested by EB (1/9/76), <**lhéltel tethá.**>, //ɬi[=Aə́=]l=təl tə θɛ́//, /'*That's a bailer.*'/, attested by EB (11/24/75), <**lí te thá**>, //lí tə θɛ́//, /'*over there, there (close by)*'/, attested by AC, EB (1/9/76), <**lí kwthá tleqá:ys.**>, //lí k^{w} θɛ́ təla=qɛ́·ys//, /'*He's there now.*'/, semantic environment ['speaking at Sardis of someone at Seabird Island (about 20 miles away, could be remote or (relative to more distant locations) near, not visible)'], attested by EB (1/9/76), <**tewát kw'e lí kwethá?**>, //tə=wɛ́t k'^{w}ə lí k^{w}ə θɛ́//, /'*Who's there? (is who?)*'/, attested by EB (1/12/76), <**tl'ó te thá. ~ tl'ó tthá.**>, //ƛ'á tə θɛ́ ~ ƛ'á t θɛ́//, /'*It's that one.*'/, attested by AC, other sources: ES /ƛ'á·tθɛ́·/ *it's that one*, <**wulí t(e)thá.**>, //wə-lí t(ə) θɛ́//, /'*He's there.*'/, attested by EB (2/2/76), <**lhíq'elh sta'á kwthá. ~ lhíq'elh sta'á tethá.**>, //ɬíq'-əɬ s=t=ɛʔɛ́ k^{w} θɛ́ ~ ɬíq'-əɬ s=t=ɛʔɛ́ tə θɛ́//, /'*(He/She/It/They) used to be like that.*'/, attested by AD (11/19/79), <**tl'e kwses x̱ét'e á:lhtel, tl'óts'a Siyó:ylexwe Smált tethá.**>, //ƛ'ə k^{w}-s-əs x̣ə́t'ə ʔɛ́·ɬtəl, ƛ'á-θ'ɛ s=yá·[=C_1ə=]ləx^{w}=ə s=mɛ́lt tə θɛ́//, /'*That's what they said, that's Siyó:lexwe Smált (mountain just of Seabird Island) there.*'/, attested by JL (4/7/78 History Dept. tape 34).

<**thahápsem**>, ANA ['*(have a) big neck*'], *see* thi ~ tha ~ the ~ thah ~ theh.

<**thahélets**>, ANA /'*(have a) big rump, (have a) big "bum" (bottom)*'/, *see* thi ~ tha ~ the ~ thah ~ theh.

<**tháq**>, bound root or stem ///θɛ́q//, probably from <**th'áq ~ th'eq**> from //θ'ɛ́q ~ c'ɛ́q// *skinned off, bare*

<**stháthqiy**>, df //s=θɛ́[=C_1ə=]q=iy or s=θ'[=D=]ɛ́[=C_1ə=]q=iy or s=θ'[=D=]ə[=Aɛ́C_1ə=]q=iy//, EB /'*a sprout or shoot (esp. of the kinds peeled and eaten in spring), sweet green inner shoots, green berry shoots, salmonberry shoots, wild raspberry shoots and greens, salmonberry sprouts, blackcap shoots, thimbleberry shoots, wild rhubarb shoots, fern shoots*'/, ASM ['those especially eaten include those of the blackcap, salmonberry, thimbleberry, wild raspberry, wild rhubarb or western dock shoots, fern shoots, perhaps also cow parsnip and fireweed (which are eaten like this too in spring)'], (<**s=**> *nominalizer*), possibly root <**th'áq ~ th'eq**> *skinned off, bare*, possibly <**=D= (deglottalization)**> *derivational*, possibly <**=R1=**> *resultative*, possibly <**á-ablaut**> *resultative* or *durative*, lx <**=iy**> *bark, covering*, phonology: reduplication, possible deglottalization, possible ablaut, syntactic analysis: nominal, attested by AC, DM (12/4/64), Elders Group (2/19/75, 7/9/75), others, other sources: ES /sθɛ́θqəy/ *sprout*, JH /sé·θqi/ *sprouts (of plant)*.

<**thá:q**>, ANA /'*big penis, (have a big penis)*'/, *see* thi ~ tha ~ the ~ thah ~ theh.

<**thá:q'els**>, FSH /'*spearing fish, spearing (fish)*'/, *see* théq'.

<**tháq't**>, FSH ['*spearing s-th*'], *see* théq'.

<**thá:t**>, free root //θɛ́·t//, WETH ['*(be) dark (as at night)*'], LT, syntactic analysis: adjective/adjectival verb, attested by AC, EB (12/19/75), others, other sources: ES /θɛ́·t/ *dark (as night)*, also <**chát**>, //cɛ́t//, attested by TM (Elders Group 2/14/79), example: <**kwélhtu thá:t**>, //kʷə́ɬ=t=əw θɛ́·t//, /'*very dark*'/, attested by EB, <**chát tskwí:m**>, //cɛ́t c=kʷí·m//, /'*dark red*'/, ASM ['on the Berlin and Kay color chart Teresa mapped this color as g8 through n8, (also perhaps including f7-n7, i6-n6, f5-n5, g4-n4, i3-n3, i2-n2, g1-n1 ?)(see main color terms like tskwí:m, tsqwá:y, etc. for explanation of the letter-number locations on the color chart)'], historical/comparative detail: ch is what Salish languages not undergoing PS *č > θ would have, for ex. Thompson, Lillooet, Squamish, Nooksack, attested by TM (Elders Group 2/14/79).

<**thetí:l**>, incs //θɛt=í·l//, WETH ['*get dark*'], LT, (<**=í:l**> *get, become, go, come*), phonology: vowel-reduction, syntactic analysis: intransitive verb, attested by AC, DM (12/4/64), Elders Group (1/24/79), also <**thatìl**>, //θɛt=íl//, phonology: downdrifting, attested by EB (12/19/75), example: <**lá thetí:l.**>, //lɛ́ θɛt=í·l//, /'*It's gone dark.*'/, attested by AC, <**le thetí:l te swàyèl.**>, //lə θɛt=í·l tə swɛ̀yə̀l//, /'*The sky is dark.*'/, attested by AC, <**kwses welh ebí: te swá:yel, lát, ch'ímel thetí:l.**>, //kʷ-s-əs wəɬ ʔəmí· tə swɛ́·yəl lɛ́t c'ím=əl θɛt=í·l//, /'*just before it gets dark, evening*'/, literally /'when the day has already come, it's night, nearly gone dark'/, phonology: b is half-closed allophone of /m/ in idiolects of some families like DM, Mrs. MJ, JL, attested by DM (12/4/64), <**látelh kws le yóyes qew láme thetì:l.**>, //lɛ́t=əɬ kʷ-s lə yáy[-ə-]s qə-əw lɛ́m-ə θɛt=í·l//, /'*She works all day until it gets dark.*'/, literally /'it's morning (night -past) when past third person subj. is working until it's going -just get dark'/, phonology: sentence-stress on last syllable, attested by Elders Group (1/24/79).

<**xwathtálém**>, cts //xʷɛ=θɛ́t=ə[-M2-]l=əm or xʷɛ=θɛ́t=M1=əl=əm//, incs, WETH /'*getting cloudy, clouding up*'/, literally perhaps /'get itself becoming dark'/, (<**xwe= ~ xwa**> *get, become*), root <**thá(:)t**> *dark (of daylight or night)*, (<**=el ~ =íl**> *go, come, get, become*), possibly <**metathesis type 2**> *continuative or derivational*, possibly <**metathesis type 1**> *derivational*, (<**=em**> *have/get/intransitivizer or middle voice* (weather acting on itself)), phonology: metathesis, possible vowel merger, possible vowel-loss, updrifting, syntactic analysis: intransitive verb, attested by AC, Deming, example: <**me xwathtálém**>, //mə xʷɛ=θɛ́t=ə[-M2-]l=əm//, grammatical comment: me *inceptive, come to, start to*, /'*It's getting cloudy.*'/, attested by Deming: SJ, MC, MV, LG, <**melh xwathtálem.**>, //mə-ɬ xʷə=θɛ́t=M1=əl=əm//, /'*It's coming clouds., It's clouding.*'/, attested by AC (8/14/70), <**li a sqwá:lewel kw'es mes xwathtálem wáy:eles?**>, //li ʔɛ s=qʷɛ̀·l=əwəl k'ʷ-əs mə-s xʷɛ=θɛ́t=M1=əl=əm wɛ́y·əl=əs//, /'*Do you think it will be cloudy tomorrow?*'/, attested by AC (10/6/71).

<**shxw'áthtel**>, dnom //sxʷ=(ʔ)θɛ́[=M1=]t=əl or s=xʷə=θɛ́[=M2=]t=əl or s=xʷə=θɛ́[=M1=]t=əl//, WETH ['*cloud*'], literally probably /'something for going dark or something to become getting dark'/, (<**shxw=**> *something for*), possibly <**s=**> *nominalizer, something to*, possibly <**xwe=**> *get, become*, probably <**metathesis**> *derivational or continuative*, (<**=el**> *go, come, get, become*), phonology: metathesis, insertion of epenthetic glottal-stop, possible vowel-loss, syntactic analysis: nominal, other sources: ES /šxʷɛ̀θətəl/ (MsCw /šxʷʔɛ́θtən/) *cloud*, Salish cognate: Saanich dial. of NSt /šxʷʔəθítən/ *cloud* B74a (San.):3, Songish dial. of NSt /šxʷéʔsətən/ *cloud* M68:110, Samish dial. of NSt (VU) /ʔesítŋ/ *cloud* G86:63, also <**shxw'áthetel**>, //s=xʷə=θɛ́[=M2=]t=əl//, dialects: *Chill.*, attested by AC, SJ, MV, LG, MC, BJ (5/10/64, 12/5/64), example: <**ts'q'íx̱ shxw'áthetel**>, //c'=q'íx̣ s=xʷə=θɛ́[=M2=]t=əl//, /'*black cloud*'/, attested by SJ, MC, MV, LG, <**lulh me q'íx̱el te shxw'áthetel**>, //lə=wɬ mə q'íx̣=əl tə s=xʷə=θɛ́[=M2=]t=əl//, grammatical analysis: past=already inceptive black=get/go/(be)come

demonstrative article(the) nominal(cloud), /'*The cloud is getting black. ~ The clouds are getting black.*'/, attested by SJ, MC, MV, LG, <**le q'íx̲el te shxw'áthetel.**>, //lə q'íx̣=əl tə sx^{w}=θɛ́[=M1=]t=əl//, /'*The clouds got black.*'/, attested by AC (10/13/71).

<**thátkwem**>, izs //θɛ́tk^{w}=əm//, TCH /'*to tingle (like arm waking up from numbness), (have/get a) stinging feeling*'/, (<**=em**> *have, get, intransitivizer*), syntactic analysis: intransitive verb, attested by BHTTC.

<**háthelmet**>, EFAM ['*admiring s-o/s-th*'], *see* thélmet.

<**tháthiyel**> or <**thath**> or <**thay**>, possible bound root or stem //θɛ́θ(=)iy(=)əl or θɛ́[=C_1ə=]y(=)əl//, root meaning uncertain

<**sttháthiyel**>, df //s=θɛ́[=C_1ə=]y(=)əl//, ANA ['*blood*'], (<**s=**> *nominalizer*), probably <**=R1=**> *resultative or continuative*, probably <**=el**> *go, come, get, become*, phonology: reduplication, e →i before y, syntactic analysis: nominal, attested by AC, BJ (12/5/64), DM (12/4/64), Elders Group (3/1/72), other sources: ES /sθɛ́θiyəl/ *blood*, example: <**tháthiyels te sth'óqwi**>, //θɛ́[=C_1ə=]y=əl-s tə s=θ'áq^{w}(=)i//, /'*fish's blood*'/, syntactic comment: the dropping of the nominalizer is part of the same inalienable possession construction found with other body parts, that is, the nominalizer is dropped when the body part is inflected with a possessive affix, attested by Elders Group (4/28/76).

<**tháx̲t**>, ABFC ['*pushing s-o/s-th*'], *see* théx̲.

<**tháyelets**>, df //θɛ́y=ələc or θi[=Aɛ́=]y=ələc//, CAN ['*steer a canoe*'], literally (possibly)/'fixing the stern'/, probably root <**thiy**> *fix, make*, probably <**á-ablaut**> *continuative*, probably <**=elets**> *on the bottom, stern (of canoe/boat)*, phonology: probable ablaut, syntactic analysis: intransitive verb, attested by Elders Group (3/26/75).

<**tháyeletstel**>, ds //θi[=Aɛ́=]y=ələc=təl//, CAN ['*rudder*'], literally /'device to steer a canoe'/, lx <**=tel**> *device to, something to*, phonology: probable ablaut, syntactic analysis: nominal, dialects: *Cheh.*, attested by Elders Group (4/28/76).

<**shxwtháyelets**>, ds //sx^{w}=θi[=Aɛ́=]y=ələc//, CAN ['*rudder*'], literally /'something for steering a canoe'/, (<**shxw=**> *something for*), phonology: probable ablaut, syntactic analysis: nomo, dialects: *Tait*, attested by Elders Group (4/28/76).

<**tháyeletstel**>, CAN ['*rudder*'], *see* tháyelets.

<**tháyelhtset**>, MC /'*making it for s-o, fixing it for s-o*'/, *see* thíy.

<**thá:yém**>, FOOD ['*baking (bread esp.)*'], *see* thíy.

<**thá:yt**>, MC /'*fixing s-th, making s-th*'/, *see* thíy.

<**the**>, free root //θə//, DEM /'*the (female, present and visible), the (female, unspecified presence and/or unspecified visibility)*'/, syntactic analysis: demonstrative article, attested by AC, Deming (5/25/78), Elders Group, others, example: <**máyt the slháli**>, //mɛ́y=T θə s=ɬɛ́l(=)i//, /'*help the woman*'/, attested by AC, <**thel tàl**>, //θə-l tɛ̀l//, /'*my mother*'/, attested by AC, <**tha tàl**>, //θ-ɛ tɛ̀l//, /'*your mother*'/, attested by AC, <**theló slháli**>, //θə=lá s=ɬɛ́l(=)i//, /'*this woman*'/, attested by AC, <**the (sí:le, sts'ó:meqw, méla, álex, slets'ő́wiyelh, sétl'àtel, skw'ílhew, syá:tel)**>, //θə (sí·lə, s=c'á·m(=)əq^{w}, mə́l(=)ɛ, ʔɛ́ləx^{y}, s=lɛc'=ə́wiyəɬ, sə́ƛ'ɛ=təl, s=k'^{w}íɬəw, s=yɛ́·təl)//, /'*the (grandmother/sister or female cousin of grandparent, great-grandmother or sister/female cousin of great grandparent), daughter, sister, half-sister, elder sister/daughter of parent's elder sister, mother-in-law, widow)*'/, attested by Elders Group.

<**the=**>, da //θə=//, DEM /'*nominalizer (female present and visible or presence or proximity unspecified), demonstrative article*'/, phonology: probably phonologically prefixed because in some cases <**the**>

merges with a following consonant (for ex. =**w**) to form a new vowel (as in thú:tlò *it's her*), syntactic analysis: derivational prefix; found in <**thú:tl'ò ~ thútl'o**>, //θə́=w=ƛ'á//, /'*it's her, she is the one*'/, <**thutl'ólem**>, //θə́=w=ƛ'á[=lə=]=m//, /'*that's them (female), they (female), them (female)*'/.

<**theh**>, probably root //θəh//, probably *hook onto*

<**thehímélh**>, df //θəh=ím=əɬ or θəh=ə[=Aí=]m=əɬ//, FSH /'*(gaff) hook fisherman, a hooker*'/, possibly root <**theh**> perhaps *to hook*, possibly <**=ím**> *repeatedly* or possibly <**í-ablaut**> *durative* plus <**=em**> *have/get/intransitive*, <**=elh**> probably *according to the ways of the, in the way of the*, syntactic analysis: nominal, attested by Elders Group (3/15/72).

<**thehít**>, df //θəh=ə[=Aí=]T or θəhiy=T//, possibly /'*hook onto s-th*'/, possibly root <**theh**> perhaps *to hook*, probably <**í-ablaut**> *durative*, (<**=et**> *purposeful control transitivizer*), phonology: probable ablaut, syntactic analysis: transitive verb, attested by Elders Group (2/16/76), example: <**thehítchexw ta' sqwálewel.**>, //θəh=ə[=Aí=]T-c-əx^{w} t-ɛʔ s=q^{w}ɛ̀l=əwəl//, /'*Keep your mind on what you're doing., (Concentrate.)*'/, literally possibly /'you hook onto it your thoughts/feelings'/.

<**thehíthet**>, pcrs //θəh=ə[=Aí=]T-ət//, EFAM ['*be careful*'], (<**-et**> *reflexive*), phonology: possible ablaut, syntactic analysis: intransitive verb, attested by Elders Group (2/16/77), also <**sthehíthet**>, //s=θəh=ə[=Aí=]T-ət//, attested by EB (1/12/76), example: <**thehíthetchxw.**>, //θəh=ə[=Aí=]T-ət-c-x^{w}//, /'*Be careful.*'/, attested by Elders Group, <**sthehíthetchxwò.**>, //s=θəh=ə[=Aí=]T-ət-c-x^{w}-à//, /'*Just you be careful.*'/, attested by EB.

<**thehíthet**>, EFAM ['*be careful*'], *see* thehít.

<**thehíwel**>, ANA ['*(have a) big rump*'], *see* thi ~ tha ~ the ~ thah ~ theh.

<**thehíws**>, EZ ['*big bird*'], *see* thi ~ tha ~ the ~ thah ~ theh.

<**thehó:ythel**>, ANA ['*(have a) big mouth*'], *see* thi ~ tha ~ the ~ thah ~ theh.

<**thékwàl**>, df //θə́k^{w}ɛ̀l//, ANAH /'*big person (of females), big lady*'/, root meaning unknown unless thí ~ tha ~ the ~ thah ~ theh *big*, possibly <**=ekw ~ =íkw**> (perhaps) *round*, <**ál**> possibly *length/pole/shaft*, syntactic analysis: nominal, attested by IHTTC (8/11/77), SP esp. (IHTTC 8/11/77).

<**thékw'**>, free root //θə́k'^{w}//, DESC ['*straight*'], semantic environment ['of road, stick, root, line, tree, canoe'], EFAM /'*pulled, influenced*'/, semantic environment ['towards, (perhaps other words)'], syntactic analysis: adjective/adjectival verb, attested by Elders Group (6/1/77, 4/28/76), Deming (MC, SJ, etc. 4/26/79), AC, BHTTC, other sources: JH /sθə́k'^{w}/ *straight*, ASM ['straight'], example: <**thékw' sx̱éyp**> or <**thékw' sx̱íp**>, //θə́k'^{w} s=x̣íp//, /'*straight line*'/, attested by Elders Group (6/1/77), <**liye thékw'?**>, //li-ə θə́k'^{w}//, /'*Is it straight?*'/, attested by AC, ASM ['influenced, pulled'], <**le thékw' xwlá s'em'oméla.**>, //lə θə́k'^{w} x^{w}lɛ́ s=C_1əC_2=ʔamə́lɛ//, /'*She was pulled towards the Thompsons., She was influenced by the Thompsons.*'/, attested by BHTTC (10/23/76).

<**sthethá:kw'**>, strs //s=θə[=C_1əAɛ́·=]k'^{w}//, DESC /'*be straight (of rope but not tree), pulled tight (of rope), stretched tight, tight*'/, (<**s=**> *stative*), probably <**=R1= plus á:-ablaut**> *resultative*, phonology: reduplication, ablaut, syntactic analysis: adjective/adjectival verb, attested by AC, EB (Elders Group 4/26/78), Deming (incl. EF)(4/26/79), also /'*straight (of root, pole, rope, etc.), pulled tight (of rope)*'/, attested by EB, other sources: ES /sθəθɛ́·k'^{w}/ *straight*, example: <**sthethá:kw' kw'as lhx̱éyléx.**>, //s=θə[=C_1əAɛ́·=]k'^{w} k'^{w}-ɛ-s ɬx̣(=)íl=əx^{y}//, /'*Stand up straight.*'/, attested by EF (Deming 4/26/79), <**we'ólwe sthethá:kw'; líqwetlha.**>, //wə-ʔál wə-s=θə[=C_1əAɛ́·=]k'^{w}; líq^{w}=əT-ɬɛ//, /'*It's pulled too tight; loosen it.*'/, attested by EB.

<**thekw'ét ~ thkw'ét**>, pcs //θə́k'^{w}-M1=T//, ABFC ['*pull s-th/s-o*'], (<**metathesis type 1**> *non-continuative*), (<**=t**> *purposeful control transitivizer*), phonology: metathesis, syntactic analysis:

transitive verb, attested by AC, Elders Group (7/9/75, 4/26/78), Deming (2/14/80), RG & EH (4/9/99 Ling332), other sources: ES and JH /θk'ʷə́t/ *pull*, and JH /θé·k'ʷt/ *pulling*, example: <**thekw'ét te máqels**>, //θə́k'ʷ=M1=T tə mɛ́=qəl-s//, /'*pull his hair*'/, attested by Deming, <**thkw'ét ta sx̱él:e**>, //θə́k'ʷ=M1=T t-ɛ s=x̣ə́l·ə//, /'*pull your leg*'/, attested by Elders Group, <**thekw'ét te méqsels**>, //θə́k'ʷ=M1=T tə mə́qsəl-s//, /'*pull his nose*'/, attested by Deming, <**thekw'étchexw ta' qw'ő:l.**>, //θə́k'ʷ=M1=T-c-əxʷ t-ɛʔ q'ʷó·l//, /'*Pull your ear.*'/, attested by Deming, <**tímet thekw'ét**>, //tímət θə́k'ʷ=M1=T//, /'*pull harder*'/, attested by AC, <**le thekw'étes (qetl')osésu x̱eth'étes (qetl')osésu tselq.**>, //lə θə́k'ʷ=M1=T-əs (qə=ƛ'a,ʔa)-s-əs-əw x̣ə́θ'=M1=T-əs (qə=ƛ'a,ʔa)-s-əs-əw cə́lq//, /'*He pulled it (and) then he pushed it and it fell. (push s-th) (to fall)*'/, attested by AC (10/13/71).

<**thkw'éthet**>, pcrs //θə́k'ʷ=M1=T-ət//, ABFC /'*pull oneself up, straighten (oneself) up*'/, (<**-et**> *reflexive*), phonology: metathesis, syntactic analysis: intransitive verb, attested by EB (4/29/76), AD (July/Aug. 1979).

<**thethkw'í:tel**>, rcps //θə[=C_1ə=]k'ʷ=ə[=Aí·=]T-əl//, durs, PLAY ['*tug-of-war*'], literally /'pulling each other for a long time'/, (<**=R1=**> *continuative*), (<**í:-ablaut**> *durative*), (<**-el**> *reciprocal* (or =t-el *purposeful control reciprocal*)), phonology: ablaut, reduplication, syntactic analysis: intransitive verb, attested by NP (10/10/75), Elders Group (11/26/75).

<**thekw'ét ~ thkw'ét**>, ABFC ['*pull s-th/s-o*'], *see* thékw'.

<**thél**>, bound root //θə́l *cover under, pad under*//.

<**shxwthéletstel**>, df //sxʷ=θə́l=ləc=təl//, HHG ['*cushion*'], (<**shxw=**> *nominalizer, something for*), probably root <**thél**> *cover under or pad under*, Elder's comment: "root the- is related to thíy *fix*", lx <**=élets ~ =lets**> *on the bottom/rump*, lx <**=tel**> *device, thing for*, syntactic analysis: nominal, attested by AD (1/21/80).

<**shxwthí:lestel**>, df //sxʷ=θə́l=í·ləs=təl//, CLO ['*fancy lining*'], lit. "something for cover/pad under on the chest", <**shxw=**> *nominalizer, something for*, <**=í:les**> *on the chest*, lx <**=tel**> *device, something for*, syntactic analysis: nominal, attested by IHTTC (8/9/77).

<**thelí:wá:xel**>, df //θəlí·wɛ́·=xʸəl//, HHG ['*snowshoes*'], possibly root <**thél**> *cover under/pad under*, possibly <**=í:wá:**> *cord, rope*, lx <**=xel**> *on the foot*, syntactic analysis: nominal, attested by Elders Group (9/1/76), also <**tselíwáxel**>, //cəl=íwɛ=xʸəl//, attested by Elders Group (2/5/75), comment: my recollection is that either or both forms are from Ed Leon.

<**thélxetel**>, df //θə́l=xʸəl=təl//, HHG /'*floor mat, rug*'/, probably root <**thél**> *cover under/pad under*, lx <**=xel**> *on the foot*, lx <**=tel**> *device to*, phonology: consonant-loss, syntactic analysis: nominal, attested by Elders Group (11/12/75), Salish cognate: Sechelt root in /cil-úl-mixʷ-tn/ *floor mat* T77:17.

<**thelí:wá:xel**>, HHG ['*snowshoes*'], *see* thél.

<**thélmet**>, iecs //θə́l=məT//, EFAM ['*admire s-th/s-o*'], possible root <**thél**> *cover under or pad under* or possibly <**thál**> with deglottalization from <**th'ála**> *heart*, (<**=met**> *indirect effect non-control transitivizer*), syntactic analysis: transitive verb, attested by Elders Group (12/7/77), EB (12/18/75).

<**tháthelmet**>, cts //C_1ɛ́-θəl=məT or θɛ́[-C_1ə-ll=məT//, EFAM ['*admiring s-o/s-th*'], (<**R7-**> or <**-R1-**> *continuative*), phonology: reduplication, syntactic analysis: transitive verb, attested by Elders Group (3/1/72, 11/9/77, 12/7/77), EB (12/18/75).

<**thelqxálém**>, WETH ['*rainbow*'], *see* theqelxélém.

<**thélxetel**>, HHG /'*floor mat, rug*'/, *see* thél.

<**themá**>, free root //θəmɛ́//, NUM /'*twice, two times*'/, syntactic analysis: adverb/adverbial verb, attested by AC (8/8/70, 10/8/71), Elders Group (3/19/75).

<**sthémelts ~ sthemélts**>, ds //s=θə[=´=]m(ɛ)=əlc-s ~ s=θəm(ɛ́)=ə́lc-s//, TIME ['*Tuesday*'], literally /'second day'/, (<**s=...=s**> *cyclic period, day, hour*), lx <**=elc ~ =élc ~ =álth'ts**> *day*, possibly <**stress-shift**> *derivational*, phonology: stress-shift, vowel-loss, syntactic analysis: nominal, attested by Elders Group (3/19/75), IHTTC (8/10/77), example: **Q:** <**stám swàyèl tlówàyèl?**> **A:** <**(yiláwelhàt, sthemélts, slhíxws, sx̱e'óthels, slhq'átses, t'óqw'tem, sx̱ax̱elhát).**>, //s=tɛ́m s=wɛ̀yə̀l təlá=wɛ̀yə̀l? (yiɬɛ́w=əɬ(=l)ɛ́t, s=θəm=ə́lc=s, s=ɬíxʷ=s, s=x̱əʔáθəl=s, s=ɬq'ɛ́t=cəs=s, t'áq'ʷ=T=əm, s=x̱ɛ́x̱ə=ɬ(=l)ɛ́t)//, /'*Q: What day is today? A: (Monday, Tuesday, Wednesday, Thursday, Friday, Saturday, Sunday).*'/, attested by IHTTC (8/10/77).

<**Sthamí:l**>, ds //s=θəmɛ=M2=í·l//, PLN /'*one (second) of two creeks just above Popkum which cross Highway #1, (creek between Popkum and Cheam, also a place near Popkum [AC])*'/, possibly <**metathesis**> *derivational*, (<**=í:l**> *come, go, get, become*), phonology: metathesis, vowel merger, syntactic analysis: nominal, attested by JL (Seabird Is. trip #2, 4/7/78), also /'*creek near Popkum*'/, attested by CT (1973), also /'*creek between Popkum and Cheam; also a location near Popkum*'/, attested by AC (1973).

<**themthómél**>, ANA ['*both eyebrows*'], *see* thómél.

<**thepth'epéy**> (probably sic for either <**thepthepéy**> or <**th'epth'epéy**>), DESC /'*curdled*'/, FOOD, root meaning uncertain unless related to root in <**th'ép-lexw ~ th'ép'-lexw**> *shut eyes*, <**=R2**> or <**=C1eC2**> *characteristic, inherent continuative*, possible lexical suffix =**éy**, phonology: reduplication, syntactic analysis: adjectival verb, (attested by RG,EH 6/16/98 to SN, edited by BG with RG,EH 6/26/00)

<**thepth'epéy t'át'ets'em sqemó**>, FOOD *yogurt* (lit. curdled + sour + milk), (attested by RG,EH 6/16/98 to SN, edited by BG with RG,EH 6/26/00)

<**théq**>, free root //θə́q//, LAND /'*steep (of road, hill, etc.), (very steep slope* [Elders Group]*)*'/, may also mean something like *upright* in derivations as in <**thqá:t**> *tree* and <**thqá:lem**> *to still dip* (after the fact that one must stand upright with the net upright unlike other methods of fishing), syntactic analysis: adjective/adjectival verb, attested by Elders Group (3/15/72), CT (6/8/7), also /'*very steep slope*'/, attested by Elders Group (3/8/78).

<**theqílep**>, dnom //θəq=íləp//, LAND ['*steep slope (but less steep than théq)*'], literally /'steep dirt/land'/, lx <**=ílep**> *dirt, land*, syntactic analysis: nominal, attested by Elders Group (3/8/78).

<**theqát ~ thqá:t**>, free root //θəqɛ́t ~ θqɛ́·t//, EB ['*tree*'], root may mean something like *upright* in this and forms such as <**théq**> *steep* and <**thqá:lem**> *to still dip* (after the fact that one must stand upright with the net upright unlike other methods of fishing),, syntactic analysis: noun, nominal, attested by AC, BJ (12/5/64), CT and HT (6/21/76), others, other sources: ES /θqɛ́·t/ and JH /θqé·t/ *tree*, example: <**i'axwí:l thqá:t**>, //C_1í=ʔɛxʷ(=)í·l θqɛ́·t//, /'*a small tree*'/, attested by AC, <**híkw thqá:t**>, //híkʷ θqɛ́·t//, /'*big tree*'/, attested by AC, <**híkw te theqát.**>, //híkʷ tə θəqɛ́t//, /'*The tree is big.*'/, attested by AC, <**weli kw'e li te éqwelets te thqát, éwe lís eyém.**>, //wə-li k'ʷə lí tə ʔə́qʷə=ləc-s tə θqɛ́t, ʔə́wə lí-s ʔɛy=ə́m//, /'*If it's on the back of the tree it's not as strong.*'/, attested by CT and HT (6/21/7), <**te sqewá:meth' te thqát, tl'ó tl'émexw xípet.**>, //tə s=qəw=ɛ́·məθ'-s tə θqɛ́t, ƛ'á ƛ'ə́məxʷ (or ƛ'á=C_1ə=əm-əxʷ) xʸíp=əT//, /'*The sunny side of a tree, that's the part you strip off.*'/, attested by CT and HT (6/21/76).

<**théqet**>, pln //θə[=´=]qɛt//, EB /'*a lot of trees close together (young), thicket*'/, (<**=´= (stress-shift)**> *plural*), phonology: stress-shift, vowel-reduction of second vowel, syntactic analysis: nominal,

attested by AC, example: <**lámchexw te théqet (qetl'osésu, tl'ó:su) tés te theqát.**>, //lɛ́=m-c-əxʷ tə θə[= ´=]qɛt (qə-ƛ'a-s-ə́s-əw, ƛ'á-ɛ-s-əw) tə́s tə θəqɛ́t//, /'*Go to the thicket (and he, then you) get to the tree.*'/, attested by AC (11/22/71).

<**theqthéqet**>, pln //C_1əC_2=θə[= ´=]qɛt//, EB /'*trees, thicket, timber, woods, forest*'/, (<**R3=**> *plural (many)*), (<**stress-shift**> *plural or derivational*), phonology: reduplication, stress-shift, vowel-reduction, syntactic analysis: nominal, attested by AC (11/16/71, 11/22/71), EB (2/6/76), Deming (1/31/80), other sources: H-T <tsuk·su'k·Et> *wood*, example: <**qéx te theqthéqet.**>, //qə́x tə C_1əC_2=θə[= ´=]qɛt//, /'*[There's a] lot of trees.*'/, attested by Deming.

<**thí:thqet**>, dmn //C_1í=θəqɛt//, EB ['*little tree*'], (<**R4=**> *diminutive*), phonology: reduplication, vowel-reduction, vowel-loss, syntactic analysis: nominal, attested by AC (10/13/71).

<**thétheqet**>, dmpn //C_1í[=Aə́=]=θəqɛt//, EB ['*little tree*[s]'], (<**é-ablaut**> *plural (of diminutive)*), phonology: reduplication, ablaut, vowel-reduction, syntactic analysis: nominal, attested by Elders Group (7/9/75).

<**théqelem**>, FSH /'*holding on to a thqá:lem, waiting dip-netting, still-dipping*'/, *see* thqá:lem.

<**theqelxélém**>, mdls //θəq(=)əl=xʸə[= ´=]l=əm//, [θəqəlxʸɪ́l·ə́m], WETH ['*(have/get a) rainbow*'], root meaning unknown unless <**théq**> *steep*, possibly <**=el**> *have/get/intransitivizer*, lx <**=xel**> *on the leg/foot, precipitation*, possibly <**= ´=**> *derivational*, (<**=em**> *middle voice*), phonology: updrifting, lengthening (phonetic option for resonants before updrifted schwa), syntactic analysis: intransitive verb, dialects: *Chill.*, attested by BJ (5/10/64), Elders Group (NP, RM)(5/16/79).

<**thelqxálém**>, df //θəq(=)l[=M1=]=xʸə[=Aɛ́=]l=əm//, [θəlqxʸǽlə́m], WETH ['*rainbow*'], possibly <**metathesis**> *derivational*, possibly <**á-ablaut**> *derivational* perhaps *durative* or *continuative*, phonology: metathesis, ablaut, updrifting, syntactic analysis: intransitive verb, attested by Deming (3/31/77).

<**stheqelxél:ém ~ stheqelxélém**>, dnom //s=θəq(=)əl=xʸə[= ´=]l=əm//, WETH ['*a rainbow*'], (<**s=**> *nominalizer*), phonology: stress-shift, updrifting, lengthening, syntactic analysis: nominal, attested by BJ (12/5/64), Elders Group (4/2/75), Deming (3/31/77), other sources: ES /sθəqəlxʸə́ləm/ *rainbow*, also <**stheqelsxél:ém**>, //s=θəq(=)əls=xʸə[= ´=]l=əm//, attested by AC (prompted from ES) (9/1/70), comment: perhaps the internal s is an error since AC did not remember the word independently, also <**swétexel**>, //s(=)wə́təxʸəl//, Elder's comment: "Deming elders report this is Tait or Cheh. dialect", attested by Elders Group (4/2/75), Deming (3/31/77).

<**théqet**>, EB /'*a lot of trees close together (young), thicket*'/, *see* theqát ~ thqá:t.

<**théqi ~ théqey**>, root or stem //θə́q(=)i ~ θə́q(=)əy// *sockeye salmon*

<**sthéqi ~ sthéqey**>, df //s=θə́q(=)i ~ s=θə́q(=)əy//, [sθə́qi(y) ~ sθə́qəy], EZ ['*sockeye salmon*'], ['*Oncorhynchus nerka*'], (<**s=**> *nominalizer*), root meaning unknown, syntactic analysis: nominal, attested by AC, BJ (12/5/64), Elders Group (3/1/72, 3/15/72), others, other sources: ES /sθə́qəy/ *sockeye salmon*, contrast <**swá:ychel**> *Chilliwack River sockeye salmon*, contrast <**qwechíwiya ~ sqwó:yxw**> *late fall Harrison River and Chehalis River sockeye salmon (kind of red)*, example: <**thí:the te sthéqi tloqáys.**>, //θí·=C_1ə tə s=θə́qi tla=qɛ́ys//, /'*The sockeye are bigger now.*'/, attested by AC (8/23/73).

<**thíthqey**>, dmn //C_1í=θəqəy//, EZ ['*small sockeye salmon*'], (<**R4=**> *diminutive*), phonology: reduplication, syntactic analysis: nominal, attested by RB (Elders Group 3/1/72), also <**tsésqey**>, //cə́sqəy//, attested by SP (Elders Group 3/1/72), also <**kwíkwexel**>, //C_1í=kʷə(=)xʸəl or C_1í=kʷəxʸ=əl//, attested by AC.

<**sthéqeytel**>, dnom //s=θə́qəy=təl//, FSH ['*sockeye net*'], lx <**=tel**> *device for*, syntactic analysis:

nominal, attested by Elders Group (3/26/75).

<**temthéqi**>, ds //təm=θə́qi//, TIME /'*sockeye moon, month to get sockeye salmon (begins with first quarter after black moon in July, lasts into August), July to August, (June to July [Jenness: WS])*'/, FSH, lx <**tem=**> *time, time/season to*, probably root <**théqi**> *get sockeye salmon*, comment: with s= removed the root is usually a verb, syntactic analysis: nominal, attested by Elders Group (3/12/75), also /'*June-July, sockeye moon*'/, source: Diamond Jenness's field notes of interviews with Billy Sepass of Sardis (filed under Elders Group 3/28/79), also <**temhóps**>, //təm=háps//, also /'*August*'/, literally /'time for hops, hops time'/, usage: said jokingly, attested by Elders Group (3/12/75).

<**theqílep**>, LAND ['*steep slope (but less steep than théq)*'], *see* théq.

<**theqthéqet**>, EB /'*trees, thicket, timber, woods, forest*'/, *see* theqát ~ thqá:t.

<**théq'**>, bound root //θə́q' *stab, pierce, spear*//.

<**thq'á:ls**>, sas //θəq'=ɛ́·ls or θəq'-M1=ɛ́·ls//, FSH ['*to spear fish*'], (<**=á:ls**> *structured activity non-continuative*), possibly <**metathesis type 1**> *non-continuative*, phonology: possible metathesis and vowel merger, syntactic analysis: intransitive verb, attested by EB (5/3/76), example: <**la thq'á:ls te sth'óqwi**>, //lɛ θəq'-M1=ɛ́·ls tə s=θ'áq^{w}=i//, /'*going to spear fish*'/, attested by EB.

<**thá:q'els**>, cts //θə[-Aɛ́·-]q'=əls//, sas, FSH /'*spearing fish, spearing (fish)*'/, (<**á:-ablaut**> *continuative*), (<**=els**> *structured activity continuative*), phonology: ablaut, syntactic analysis: intransitive verb, attested by Elders Group (3/26/75), EB (5/3/76).

<**thq'ét**>, pcs //θə́q'-M1=T//, FSH, HUNT, SOC /'*spear it (a fish), stab s-o/s-th with something sharp, pierce s-o/s-th, prick s-o (with a pin, for ex.), poke s-o (with a pin, etc.)*'/, (<**metathesis type 1**> *non-continuative*), (<**=t**> *purposeful control transitivizer*), phonology: metathesis, syntactic analysis: transitive verb, attested by EB (4/23/76, 5/3/76), Elders Group (3/26/75); found in <**thq'éthóxes**>, //θə́q'=M1=T-áx^{y}-əs//, /'*He poked me or pricked me with a pin.*'/, attested by EB (5/3/76).

<**tháq't**>, cts //θə[-Aɛ́-]q'=T//, FSH ['*spearing s-th*'], HUNT, SOC, (<**á-ablaut**> *continuative*), (<**=t**> *purposeful control transitivizer*), phonology: ablaut, syntactic analysis: transitive verb, attested by EB (4/23/76); found in <**tháq'tes.**>, //θə[-Aɛ́-]q'=T-əs//, /'*He's spearing it.*'/.

<**thithq'eyóls**>, df //C_1í=θəq'=əy(=)áls//, PLAY ['*pool (the game)*'], (<**R4=**> *diminutive*), root <**théq'**> *poke, stab, spear, pierce*, lx <**=óls ~? =eyóls**> *spherical object*, phonology: reduplication, syntactic analysis: nominal?, intransitive verb?, attested by SP (IHTTC and Deming 9/8/77), Elders Group (9/14/77), compare <**ts'its'kwiyóls**> *playing pool*.

<**thq'ó:les**>, df //θəq'=á·ləs//, ABDF ['*get dust or bark in one eye*'], literally perhaps /'pricked in the eye'/, lx <**=ó:les**> *in the eye*, syntactic analysis: intransitive verb, attested by EB and AD (9/25/78).

<**thq'elq'ó:les**>, plv //θ[=C_1əC_2=]q'=á·ləs//, ABDF ['*get dust or bark in both eyes*'], (irregular)=R3= applied (in error?) to stem as if initial th was prefix and ó: of =ó:les was part of root (no other exx. of this in the language, and th- or th= is not a prefix), phonology: reduplication, syntactic analysis: intransitive verb, attested by EB and AD (9/25/78), DM (7/64 new p.61 tape transcription of Story of Black Bear and Grizzly Bear and Their Children).

<**théqw'**>, free root //θə́q'^{w}//, EFAM ['*get carried away (emotionally)*'], syntactic analysis: intransitive verb, dialects: *Tait, not known in Cheh.*, attested by SP (Elders Group 10/6/76), example: <**le théqw' kw'es lóy t'ít'elem.**>, //lə θə́q'^{w} k'^{w}-əs láy t'í[-C_1ə-]l=əm//, /'*He got carried away singing.*'/, literally /'he/she (past) get carried away that/when -he only is singing'/, attested by SP.

<**thét**>, free root //θə́t//, LANG ['*say*'], syntactic analysis: intransitive verb, attested by AC, EB (4/28/78), Elders Group, example: <**le thét**>, //lə θə́t//, /'*he said*'/, attested by AC, <**ôwelh le thét welóyes te**

slhéméxw.>, //ʔowə-ɬ lə θə́t wə-láy-əs tə s=ɬəmə́xʷ//, /'*They never said if it was only the rain.*'/, usage: Story of the Flood, attested by AC (12/7/71), <**welís thét ta sqwálewel**>, //wə-lí-s θə́t t-ɛ s=qʷɛ́l=əwəl//, /'*if your mind says so, if you think that*'/, attested by EB (4/28/78), <**thétlha qelát.**>, //θə́t-ɬɛ qəlɛ́t//, /'*Say it again.*'/, literally /'say again'/, attested by Elders Group.

<**thtíwél**>, ds //θət=íwəl//, LANG ['*say to oneself*'], EFAM, lx <**=íwel**> *in the insides, in the mind*, phonology: updrifting, vowel-loss, syntactic analysis: intransitive verb, dialects: *Chill.*, attested by SJ (in Story of Mink and Miss Pitch), EB and AD (11/10/78), also <**xwthetíwél**>, //xʷ=θət=íwəl//, dialects: *Cheh., Tait*, attested by AD and EB (11/10/78).

<**=thet**>, //=T-ət or better =T=ət//, PRON /'*purposeful control reflexive, do purposely to oneself*'/, see under stem <**-et**> or <**=et**> *reflexive*.

<**=thet**>, da //=θət//, ASP /'*get, (become), turn, go*'/, (semological comment: there is no element of purposeful control by animate agent here, unlike with the reflexive <**=th=et**> /=T=ət/), phonology: triggers <**o-ablaut**> of root <**a**>, syntactic analysis: derivational suffix; found in <**xó:mthet**>, /'*got shallow*'/ (compare <**xám**> *shallow)*, <**hí:kwthet**>, //hí[=·=]kʷ=θət//, /'*get big*'/ (compare <**híkw**> *be big)*, <**x̱é:ytl'thet**>, //x̣í[-·-]ƛ'=θət//, /'*getting colder*'/ (compare <**x̱éytl'**> *be cold)*, <**kw'ósthet**>, /'*get warm, get warmer*'/ (compare <**root kw'ás**> *scald, burn)*, <**póythet**>, /'*went crooked*'/ (compare <**póy**> *bend*), <**x̱olémthet**>, /'*getting gray (of hair), turning gray (of hair)*'/ (compare <**x̱ólem**> *gray (of hair))*, <**x̱óytl'thet ~ sx̱óytl'thet**>, /'*aggressive, ready to fight*'/ (compare <**x̱éy**> *against)*, <**th'qw'ó:mthet**>, /'*getting rotten*'/ (compare <**th'ó(:)qw'em**> *rotten, to rot)*, <**x̱ótl'thet**>, /'*(get) windy, (get turbulent)*'/ (compare <**x̱átl'**> *turbulent, rough (wind/water))*.

<**=thet**>, da //=θət//, N ['*male name*'], comment: prob. related to <**=thet**> *get* or <**=th-et**> *do purposely to oneself*, syntactic analysis: lexical suffix, derivational suffix; found in <**Hó:ytl'thet**>, //há·yƛ'=θət//, /'*Indian name of Peter Williams of Chahalis (died about 1921, great grandfather of Tillie Phillips)*'/, <**Siyólewethet**>, //siyáləwə=θət//, /'*Indian name of Roy Point from Scowkale*'/.

<**thetí:l**>, WETH ['*get dark*'], *see* thá:t.

<**thétheqet**>, EB ['*little tree*[s]'], *see* theqát ~ thqá:t.

<**The Théthex̱w**> or <**Thethéthex̱w**>, PLN ['*a rock in the creek at the upriver end of Seabird Island that was a girl washing after her first period*'], *see* thox̱w.

<**thethéx̱w**>, TVMO ['*disappearing*'], *see* théxw ~ théx̱w.

<**thethíx̱w**>, durs //C_1ə=θa[=Aí=]x̣ʷ or θə[=C_1ə=Aí=]x̣ʷ//, HAT /'*girl at puberty, (girl's first period)*'/, SOCT, root <**thox̱w**> *bleeding*, see that root and also compare <**s=thxw=élqsel**> *bleeding nose*, possibly <**R5=** or **=R1=**> *continuative or resultative*, (<**í-ablaut**> *durative*), phonology: reduplication, ablaut, syntactic analysis: nominal, attested by Elders Group (1/21/76), Salish cognate: Squamish /cə-cíx̣ʷ/ *girl's puberty* K69:52.

<**théwelhem**>, ABFC ['*spawning (in action when you see them)*'], *see* cháchew ~ cháchu.

<**théxw ~ théx̱w**>, free root //θə́xʷ ~ θə́x̣ʷ//, TVMO /'*disappear, drop out of sight, (to fade* [Elders Group 3/72]*)*'/, LT, ASM ['disappear is used when someone is just about out of sight, also used for someone who was always in the area--then suddenly disappeared or dropped out of sight'], syntactic analysis: intransitive verb, attested by AC (8/6/70, 12/7/71), Elders Group (3/72, 3/29/78), EB (1/15/76, 12/15/75, 4/28/76), other sources: H-T <suQ> ([səxʷ]) *to disappear* as in <le suQ> *he's gone*, Salish cognate: Squamish /cə́xʷ/ *disappear* W73:80, K67:274, K69:52; Saanich dial. of NSt /θələ́xʷ/ *disappear* B74a:60, also /'*to fade*'/, attested by Elders Group (3/72), example: <**le théx̱w te Louie; lí xwchá:l?**>, //lə θə́x̣ʷ tə Louie; lí xʷcɛ́·l//, /'*Louie disappeared; where did he go?*'/, attested

by EB (1/15/76), <**welh le théx̲w; skw'áy kw'els kw'étslexw.**>, //wəɬ lə θə́x̣ʷ; s=k'ʷɛ́y k'ʷ-əl-s k'ʷə́c=l-əxʷ//, /*'It has disappeared; I can't see it.'*/, literally /'already it past disappear; it can't be that -I see it'/, attested by EB (1/15/76), <**le théxw.** (or) **la théxw.**>, //lə θə́xʷ (or) lɛ θə́xʷ//, /*'It disappeared.'*/, attested by AC (8/6/70), <**chexw lám e théxw.**>, //c-əxʷ lɛ́=m ʔə θə́xʷ//, /*'You disappeared.'*/, literally /'you (ambiguous past) go just disappear'/, attested by Elders Group (3/72), <**lachexw le théxw.**>, //lɛ-c-əxʷ lə θə́xʷ//, /*'You disappear.'*/, attested by Elders Group (3/72), <**latsel le théxw.**>, //lɛ-c-əl lə θə́xʷ//, /*'I disappeared.'*/, attested by Elders Group (3/72), <**tsel kw'étslexw te spá:th tl'ésu lé me théxw.**>, //c-əl k'ʷə́c=l-əxʷ tə s=pɛ́·θ ƛ'ə́-s-əw lə mə θə́xʷ//, /*'I caught sight of a bear and it disappeared. (catch sight of s-th/s-o)'*/, attested by EB (4/28/76), <**théx̲w te témexw.**>, //θə́x̣ʷ tə tə́məxʷ//, /*'The earth disappeared.'*/, semantic environment ['under flood waters in the Story of the Flood'], attested by AC (12/7/71), <**la th'éxw te syóqwem.**>, //lɛ θ'ə́xʷ tə s=yə[=Aá=]qʷ=əm//, comment: th' probably error for th, /*'sunset'*/, literally /'it goes to/it's going to disappear the sun'/, attested by DM (12/4/64 new tape transcript old p.261).

<**thethéx̲w**>, cts //C_1ə-θə́x̣ʷ//, TVMO ['*disappearing*'], LT, (<**R5-**> *continuative*), phonology: reduplication, syntactic analysis: intransitive verb, attested by Elders Group (3/29/78).

<**thexwó:thet**>, pcrs //θəxʷ=ə[=Aá·=]T-ət//, TVMO ['*disappear (purposely)*'], possibly <**ó:-ablaut**> *derivational*, (<**=et**> *purposeful control transitivizer*), (<**-et**> *reflexive*), phonology: possible ablaut or allomorph, syntactic analysis: intransitive verb, attested by Elders Group (3/72), example: <**latsel thexwó:thet.**>, //lɛ-c-əl θəxʷ=ə[=Aá·=]T-ət//, /*'I disappeared (on purpose).'*/, attested by Elders Group.

<**thxwáléqep**>, ds //θəxʷ=ɛ́lə́qəp//, SD ['*(have a) steady sound that's been stopped for a while*'], literally /'disappeared sound'/, lx <**=áléqep**> *sound*, syntactic analysis: intransitive verb, attested by Elders Group (11/3/76).

<**théxweleqep**>, cts //θə[=´=]xʷ=ɛləqəp//, SD ['*(make/have a) sound getting softer*'], literally /'disappearing sound'/, possibly <**stress-shift**> *continuative*, lx <**=áléqep**> *sound*, phonology: stress-shift, vowel-reduction, syntactic analysis: intransitive verb, attested by Elders Group (11/3/76), example: <**lóy théxweleqep**>, //láy θə[=´=]xʷ=ɛləqəp//, /*'sound getting softer'*/, literally /'only sound getting softer'/, attested by Elders Group.

<**théxwlexw**>, ncs //θə́xʷ=l-əxʷ//, possibly /*'lose s-th/s-o'*/, literally /'manage to/happen to/accidentally disappear s-o/s-th/drop s-o/s-th out of sight'/, (<**=l**> *non-control transitivizer, manage to/happen to/accidentally do to s-o/s-th*), (<**-exw**> *third person object*), syntactic analysis: transitive verb, attested by Deming (4/27/78); found in <**théxwlexwes.**>, //θə́xʷ=l-əxʷ-əs//, possibly /*'he lost something'*/, Elder's comment: "could this mean *he discoveered it*?", dialects: *Deming*.

<**théxweleqep**>, SD ['*(make/have a) sound getting softer*'], *see* théxw ~ théx̲w.

<**théxwlexw**>, possibly /*'lose s-th/s-o'*/, *see* théxw ~ théx̲w.

<**thexwó:thet**>, TVMO ['*disappear (purposely)*'], *see* théxw ~ théx̲w.

<**théx̲**>, free root //θə́x̣//, ABFC /*'push, (got pushed [EB])'*/, syntactic analysis: intransitive verb, attested by NP (1/20/76), also /*'got pushed'*/, attested by EB (2/27/76).

<**thx̲ét ~ thex̲ét**>, ds //θə́x̣-M1=T//, ABFC ['*push s-o/s-th*'], (<**metathesis type 1 or 2**> *non-continuative*), (<**=t ~ =et**> *purposeful control transitivizer*), phonology: metathesis, epenthetic schwa optional, syntactic analysis: transitive verb, attested by CT and HT (6/21/76), EB (2/27/76), NP (1/20/76), AC, RG & EH (4/9/99 Ling332), other sources: ES /θx̣ə́t/ *push*; found in <**thex̲éthoxes.**>, //θə́x̣-M1=T-axʸ-əs//, /*'He pushed me.'*/, attested by AC.

<**tháx̲t**>, cts //θə[-Aɛ́-]x̣=T//, ABFC ['*pushing s-o/s-th*'], (<**á-ablaut**> *continuative*), phonology:

ablaut, syntactic analysis: transitive verb, attested by EB (2/27/76).

<**thex̲ósem**>, mdls //θəx̣=ás=əm//, CAN [*'push out from shore (in canoe)'*], lx <**=ós**> *on the face, on the bow (with canoe),* (<**=em**> *middle voice*), syntactic analysis: intransitive verb, attested by BHTTC.

<**théx̲es**>, cts //θə́x̣=əs//, PLAY /*'betting, (bet* [Elders Group 1/7/76])'/, ECON, semantic environment ['usually in slahal (the bone game)'], ASM ['you can state what you bet if you want, can have an object or not'], literally /'pushing money'/, comment: lack of *non-continuative* metathesis indicates this is *continnuative*, lx <**=es**> *money, on the face*, syntactic analysis: intransitive verb, attested by EB (3/8/76), also /*'bet'*/, attested by Elders Group (1/7/76), also <**x̲ethós**>, //xəθ=ás or θəx̣=M2=ás//, also /*'bet'*/, attested by EB (3/8/76), example: <**ílhchel théx̲es.**>, //ʔí-ɬ-c-əl θə́x̣=əs//, /*'I was betting.'*/, attested by EB.

<**théx̲estel**>, rcps //θə́x̣=əs=təl//, PLAY /*'betting (each other), (bet (each other)* [Elders Group 1/7/76])'/, (<**=tel**> *reciprocal*), syntactic analysis: intransitive verb, attested by EB (3/8/76), also /*'bet (each other)'*/, attested by Elders Group (1/7/76), example: <**théx̲estel tel tá:le**>, //θə́x̣=əs=təl t-əl tɛ́·lə//, /*'bet my money'*/, attested by Elders Group (1/7/76).

<**thithx̲óstel**>, dmv //C_1í=θəx̣=ás=təl//, PLAY [*'betting each other'*], (<**R4=**> *diminutive (and continuative)),* phonology: reduplication, syntactic analysis: intransitive verb, attested by Elders Group (2/11/76).

<**théx̲es**>, PLAY /*'betting, (bet [Elders Group 1/7/76])'*/, *see* théx̲.

<**théx̲estel**>, PLAY /*'betting (each other), (bet (each other) [Elders Group 1/7/76])'*/, *see* théx̲.

<**thex̲láxw**>, ncs //θəx̣=l-ə[=Aɛ́=]xʷ//, durs, SOC /*'discover s-th, find s-th'*/, possibly root <**théx̲**> *push, got pushed*, (<**=l**> *non-control transitivizer, manage to/happen to/accidentally*), (<**-exw**> *third person object*), (<**á-ablaut**> *durative*), phonology: ablaut, syntactic analysis: transitive verb, attested by Elders Group (3/15/72, "Lesson VIII"), AC, example: <**skw'áy kw'es thex̲láxws te sléxwelh.**>, //s=k'ʷɛ́y k'ʷ-əs θəx̣=l-ə[=Aɛ́=]xʷ-s tə s=lə́xʷ=wəɬ//, /*'They can't find the canoe.'*/, attested by AC (12/7/71 Story of the Flood).

<**thex̲ósem**>, CAN [*'push out from shore (in canoe)'*], *see* théx̲.

<**thex̲ó:th**>, df //θəx̣(=)á·θ//, EZ [*'dolly varden trout'*], [*'Salvelinus malma'*], (<**s=**> *nominalizer*), root meaning unknown unless <**théx̲**> *got pushed*, possibly <**=ó:th**> *on the mouth*, possibly <**=ó:th**> *edge*, syntactic analysis: nominal, attested by BJ (12/5/64)(new transcript, old p.306), other sources: JH /sθx̣á·θ/ *mountain trout*, H-T <stEqa'tc ~ sEHa'ts> (macrons over each a) *speckled trout (Salmo sp.)*, Salish cognate: not Lushootseed /čk'ʷac ~ p'šač ~ p'sač/ *dolly varden trout* H76:257, 360, also <**sthex̲óts**>, //s=θəx̣(=)ác//, attested by Elders Group (7/9/75), also <**sth'ex̲óts**> or <**sth'x̲óts**>, //s=θ'əx̣=ác//, attested by Elders Group (2/5/75).

<**thex̲we'í:ls**>, df //θəx̣ʷ=əʔ=ɛ[=Aí=]·ls//, durs, REL [*'it went into him/her (of spirit power)'*], probably root <**thex̲w**> *disappear*, possibly <**=e'**> *being, entity, living thing,* (<**í-ablaut**> *durative*), possibly <**=á:ls**> *structured activity non-continuative*, phonology: ablaut, syntactic analysis: intransitive verb, attested by AD (7/23/79).

<**the'í:t**>, df //θəʔə[=Aí·=]t or θ=əʔɛ[=Aí·=]=t//, VALJ /*'be true, it's true, be truly'*/, root meaning unknown unless <**thet**> *say*, possibly <**=e'á**> *comparative*, possibly <**í:-ablaut**> *durative*, possibly <**=t**> meaning unclear, phonology: probable ablaut, syntactic analysis: adjective/adjectival verb, attested by Elders Group (2/5/75), AC, JL, example: <**wel the'í:t.**>, //w=əl θ=əʔɛ[=Aí·=]=t//, /*'It's really true.'*/, attested by Elders Group, <**ōwe lis the'í:t ste'á kw'e sx̲wōx̲wiyám.**>, //ʔə́wə li-s θ=əʔɛ[=Aí·=]=t s=t=əʔɛ́ k'ʷə s=x̣ʷə[=C_1ə=]yɛ́m//, /*'It's not true, it's like a fable.'*/, attested by AC

(11/11/71), <**ts'áts'el wel the'í:t s'ú:met.**>, //c'ɛ́[=C_1ə=]l w=əl θ=əʔɛ[=Aí·=]=t s=ʔə[=Aú·=]mət//, /'*He's really truly lazy.*'/, literally /'is very contrastive =just (i.e. really) truly lazy'/, attested by Elders Group, <**esesu x̱óx̱cha the'ít tethá lí te chóleqwmels.**>, //ʔə-s-əs-u x̣á[=C_1ə=]cɛ θ=əʔɛ[=Aí=]=t tə θɛ́ lí tə cál=əqʷ=məl-s//, /'*It's really a lake there on the side away from the river.*'/, attested by JL (History Tape 34, 4/7/78).

<**the'íttel**>, rcps //θ=əʔɛ[=Aí=]=t=təl//, EFAM ['*(be) true to one another*'], (<**=tel**> *reciprocal*), phonology: each t is pronounced, syntactic analysis: intransitive verb, attested by Elders Group (9/21/77).

<**the'ó:thel**>, df //θ=əʔɛ=á·θəl//, LANG /'*talk like that, talk like somebody*'/, root meaning unknown, possibly <**=e'á**> *comparative*, lx <**=ó:thel**> *in the mouth*, phonology: vowel merger, syntactic analysis: intransitive verb, attested by BHTTC (9/14/76).

<**the'íttel**>, EFAM ['*(be) true to one another*'], *see* the'í:t.

<**the'ó:thel**>, LANG /'*talk like that, talk like somebody*'/, *see* the'í:t.

<**thi ~ tha ~ the ~ thah ~ theh**>, bound root //θi ~ θɛ ~ θə ~ θɛh ~ θəh *big*//.

<**sthá:lhp**>, stvi //s=θi=ɛ́ɬp or s=θɛ=ɛ́ɬp//, EB /'*big tree, (be big of a tree or plant)*'/, (<**s=**> *stative*), lx <**=elhp ~ =álhp**> *tree, plant*, phonology: vowel merger, syntactic analysis: adjective/adjectival verb, attested by BHTTC (9/3/76).

<**thá:q**>, ds //θɛ=ɛ́q or θi=ɛ́q//, ANA /'*big penis, (have a big penis)*'/, lx <**=áq**> *penis*, phonology: vowel merger, syntactic analysis: adjective/adjectival verb, nominal?, syntactic comment: a word derived in the same way, thó:qw *have a big head*, is used in a sentence as a adjective/adjectival verb not a nominal, attested by Elders Group (7/9/75).

<**stháwtxw**>, ds //s=θ(ə)=ɛ́wtxʷ//, BLDG /'*longhouse for spirit-dancers, the big house, smokehouse (for spirit-dancing)*'/, SPRD, literally /'big house'/, (<**s=**> *nominalizer*), lx <**=áwtxw**> *building, house*, phonology: vowel merger, syntactic analysis: nominal, attested by IHTTC (8/25/77).

<**sthí:qel**>, stvi //s=θí=əqəl//, SD ['*loud (of a voice)*'], literally /'be big voice/speech'/, (<**s=**> *stative*), lx <**=eqel**> *throat, voice, speech*, phonology: vowel merger, syntactic analysis: adjective/adjectival verb, attested by Elders Group (11/3/76, 7/27/75), also <**shxwtl'ó:s**>, //s=xʷ(=)ƛ'=á·s//, dialects: *Cheh.*, comment: sth'í:qel is more Chilliwack dialect, attested by Elders Group.

<**sthí:qel**>, dnom //s=θí=əqəl//, SD ['*a loud voice*'], ANA, literally /'a big voice'/, (<**s=**> *nominalizer*), lx <**=eqel**> *throat, voice, speech*, phonology: vowel merger, syntactic analysis: nominal, attested by Elders Group (11/3/76).

<**thíwelh**>, df //θí=wəɬ//, SD ['*big voice (usually deep)*'], ANA, possibly <**=welh**> *vessel, canoe*?, syntactic analysis: nominal?, adjective/adjectival verb?, attested by Elders Group (12/15/76).

<**thó:lchep ~ thó:ltsep**>, df //θi=ə[=Aá=]lcəp//, FIRE /'*be big (of a fire), the fire is big, the fire is going strong, big fire*'/, lx <**=élchep ~ =éltsep**> *fire*, possibly <**ó(:)-ablaut**> *durative*, phonology: vowel merger, possible ablaut, syntactic analysis: adjective/adjectival verb, nominal?, attested by NP and AD (AHTTC 2/22/80), NP (4/11/80), example: <**thó:lchep ta' híyeqw.**>, //θi=álcəp t-ɛʔ hə́=yəqʷ//, /'*Your fire is big.*'/, attested by NP and AD (AHTTC 2/22/80).

<**thó:qw**>, ds //θi=áqʷ or θi=ə[=Aá·=]qʷ//, ANA ['*have a big head*'], BPI, lx <**=eqw**> *top of the head*, possibly <**ó(:)-ablaut**> *durative*, phonology: vowel merger, possible ablaut, syntactic analysis: adjective/adjectival verb, attested by Elders Group (3/3/76, 2/5/75), also <**xwthó:qw**>, //xʷ=θi=ə[=Aá(·)=]qʷ//, attested by AC (11/11/71), example: <**thó:qw te Wilfred.**>, //θi=áqʷ tə Wilfred//, /'*Wilfred has a big head.*'/, attested by Elders Group (3/3/76).

<**thítheqw**>, plv //θí=C_1ə=əqʷ//, ANA ['*(have) big heads (of a bunch of fish for ex.)*'], (<**=R1=**>

plural), lx <**=áqw ~ =eqw**> *top of the head; fish*, phonology: reduplication, syntactic analysis: adjective/adjectival verb, nominal?, attested by Elders Group (2/5/75).

<**thó:s ~ thós**>, ds //θi=á·s//, DESC /'big round'/, (attested by RG,EH 6/16/98 to SN, edited by BG with RG,EH 6/26/00)

<**thós sth'emíwel sékwluwi**>, EB, FOOD *avocado* (lit. big round + pit + soft smooth texture), (attested by RG,EH 6/16/98 to SN, edited by BG with RG,EH 6/26/00)

<**thós sp'eq'í:l tl'íkw'el**>,EB, FOOD *lima beans* (lit. big round + offwhite + bean), (attested by RG,EH 6/16/98 to SN, edited by BG with RG,EH 6/26/00)

<**xwthó:s**>, ds //x^w=θi=á·s//, ANA ['*(have) a big face*'], BPI, (<**xw=**> meaning uncertain or pertains *to the face*), lx <**=ó:s ~ =es**> *face*, phonology: vowel merger, syntactic analysis: adjective/adjectival verb, nominal?, attested by AC (11/11/71).

<**xwthó:thel**>, ds //x^w=θi=á·θəl//, ANA ['*(have) a big mouth*'], BPI, (<**xw=**> *pertains to the face* or meaning uncertain), lx <**=ó:thel**> *mouth*, phonology: vowel merger, syntactic analysis: adjective/adjectival verb, nominal?, attested by AC (11/11/71).

<**thahápsem**>, df //θɛh=ə[=Aɛ́=]psəm//, ANA ['*(have a) big neck*'], BPI, lx <**=épsem**> *neck*, possibly <**á-ablaut**> *durative*, phonology: ablaut, syntactic analysis: adjective/adjectival verb, nominal?, attested by Elders Group (3/3/76).

<**thahélets**>, ds //θɛh=ə́ləc//, ANA /'*(have a) big rump, (have a) big "bum" (bottom)*'/, BPI, lx <**=élets**> *rump, bottom*, syntactic analysis: adjective/adjectival verb, nominal?, attested by Elders Group (3/3/76).

<**thehíwel**>, ds //θəh=íwəl//, ANA ['*(have a) big rump*'], literally /'big insides/rectum'/, lx <**=íwel**> *insides, rectum, (some use for) rump*, syntactic analysis: adjective/adjectival verb, attested by Elders Group (3/3/76), example: <**thehíwel sta'á te kweshú.**>, //θəh=íwəl s=t=ɛʔɛ́ tə k^{w}əšú//, /'*(He/She has a) big rump like a pig.*'/, attested by Elders Group (3/3/76).

<**thehíws**>, ds //θəh=íws//, EZ ['*big bird*'], lx <**=íws**> *body; bird*, syntactic analysis: nominal?, adjective/adjectival verb?, attested by Elders Group (8/11/77).

<**thehó:ythel**>, ds //θəh=á·yθəl//, ANA ['*(have a) big mouth*'], BPI, literally /'(have a) big jaw/lips'/, lx <**=ó:ythel**> *jaw, lips*, syntactic analysis: adjective/adjectival verb?, nominal?, attested by Elders Group (10/1/75), MV and EF (Deming Evening Class 4/27/78), also <**thithehóythel**>, //θi[=C_1ə=]h=áyθəl or C_1í=θəh=áyθəl//, attested by MV and EF (Deming Evening Class 4/27/78).

<**thíthe**>, augs //θí=C_1ə//, plv, DESC /'*(be) larger, bigger*'/, (<**=R1**> *augmentative* or *augmentative plural*), phonology: reduplication, syntactic analysis: adjective/adjectival verb, attested by AC, example: <**thíthe tl'íkw'el**>, //θí=C_1ə ƛ'ík'^{w}(=)əl//, /'*larger beans*'/, attested by AC (11/24/71), <**mí:set te thíthe**>, //mí·s=əT tə θí=C_1ə//, /'*pick out the larger ones (pick s-th out)*'/, attested by AC (11/24/71), <**mí:set te thíthe qwe'óp**>, //mí·s=əT tə θí=C_1ə q^{w}əʔáp//, /'*pick out the larger apples*'/, attested by AC (11/24/71), <**thí:the te sthéqi tloqáys**>, //θí[=·=]=C_1ə tə s=θə́qi tə=lá=qɛ́ys//, /'*The sockeye are bigger now.*'/, attested by AC (8/23/73), <**thíthe te theqthéqet**>, //θí=C_1ə tə C_1əC_2=thə[=´=]qɛt//, /'*The trees are big.*'/, attested by Deming (1/31/80), <**thí:the te sthó:qwi.**>, //θí[=·=]=C_1ə tə s=θá·q^{w}i//, /'*bigger fish, (The fish are bigger.)*'/, attested by AC (8/23/73), <**thí:the te qwe'ops.**>, //θí[=·=]=C_1ə tə q^{w}əʔáp-s//, /'*bigger apple, (His/Her/Their apples are bigger.)*'/, attested by AC (8/23/73).

<**thitheháleq**>, ds //θí[=C_1ə=]h=ɛ́ləq//, WATR /'*big waves, (have big waves)*'/, lx <**=áleq**> *wave*, phonology: reduplication, syntactic analysis: nominal?, adjective/adjectival verb?, attested by Elders Group (5/26/76).

<**thithehá:lí:ya**>, ds //θi[=C_1ə=]h=ɛ́·lí·yɛ//, ANA /'*big ears, (have big ears)*'/, BPI, lx <**=á:lí:ya**>

ear, phonology: reduplication, syntactic analysis: nominal?, adjective/adjectival verb?, attested by Elders Group (5/26/76).

<**thíthes**>, ds //θí=C_1ə=əs//, DESC /'*something big (and round) (for ex. big fruit, big rocks, etc.)*'/, possibly <**=es**> *face, round object*, phonology: reduplication, syntactic analysis: nominal?, adjective/adjectival verb?, attested by Elders Group (8/11/77).

<**Thíthesem**>, ds //θí[=C_1ə=]=əs=əm//, PLN ['*place on mountain above Ruby Creek where there's lots of boulders all over the mountain lined up in rows*'], literally /'place to have/get lots of big(ger) rocks'/, (<**=em**> *place to have/get*), phonology: reduplication, syntactic analysis: nominal, attested by SP (IHTTC 8/11/77), AK (IHTTC 8/5/77), source: place names reference file #182a, source: Wells 1965 (lst ed.):14, also <**Lexwthíthesem**>, //ləx^w=θí[=C_1ə=]=əs=əm//, literally /'always a place to have/get lots of big(ger) rocks'/, attested by AK (IHTTC 8/5/77), SP (IHTTC 8/11/77).

<**thíthehí:ws**>, ds //θí[=C_1ə=]h=í·ws//, ANAH /'*big-bodied people, (have big bodies)*'/, DESC, BPI, lx <**=í:ws**> *body*, phonology: reduplication, syntactic analysis: nominal?, adjective/adjectival verb?, attested by Elders Group (3/15/72).

<**thithehó:les**>, ds //θí[=C_1ə=]h=á·ləs//, ANA ['*(have) big eyes*'], BPI, lx <**=ó:les**> *eye*, phonology: reduplication, syntactic analysis: adjective/adjectival verb, nominal?, attested by Elders Group (3/3/76).

<**thíthetses**>, ds //θí=C_1ə=cəs//, ANA ['*(have) big hand(s)*'], BPI, lx <**=tses**> *hand*, phonology: reduplication, syntactic analysis: adjective/adjectival verb, nominal?, attested by Elders Group (3/3/76).

<**thíthexel**>, ds //θí=C_1ə=x^yəl//, ANA ['*(have) big feet*'], BPI, lx <**=xel**> *foot*, phonology: reduplication, syntactic analysis: adjective/adjectival verb, nominal?, attested by Elders Group (3/3/76), also <**thíthaxel**>, //θí=C_1ɛ́(·)=x^yəl//, also /'*(have a) big foot*'/, (semological comment: when you wear size 10's or 12's in shoes), attested by AC (11/11/71).

<**thí:thaxel**>, augs //θí=·=C_1ɛ́(·)=x^yəl//, ANA /'*(have a) real big foot, (have a) huge foot*'/, (<**=:=**> *augmentative*), phonology: reduplication, lengthening, syntactic analysis: adjective/adjectival verb, nominal?, attested by AC (11/11/71).

<**thipéle,** possibly **th'ipéle**>, df //θip=ə́lə or θ'ip=ə́lə//, ANAF ['*fish cheeks*'], root meaning unknown, lx <**=éle**> *on the side of the face, cheek*, syntactic analysis: nominal, attested by Elders Group (4/28/76).

<**thí:thaxel**>, ANA /'*(have a) real big foot, (have a) huge foot*'/, *see* thi ~ tha ~ the ~ thah ~ theh.

<**thíthe**>, DESC /'*(be) larger, bigger*'/, *see* thi ~ tha ~ the ~ thah ~ theh.

<**thitheháleq**>, WATR /'*big waves, (have big waves)*'/, *see* thi ~ tha ~ the ~ thah ~ theh.

<**thithehá:lí:ya**>, ANA /'*big ears, (have big ears)*'/, *see* thi ~ tha ~ the ~ thah ~ theh.

<**thíthehí:ws**>, ANAH /'*big-bodied people, (have big bodies)*'/, *see* thi ~ tha ~ the ~ thah ~ theh.

<**thithehó:les**>, ANA ['*(have) big eyes*'], *see* thi ~ tha ~ the ~ thah ~ theh.

<**thítheqw**>, ANA ['*(have) big heads (of a bunch of fish for ex.)*'], *see* thi ~ tha ~ the ~ thah ~ theh.

<**thíthes**>, DESC /'*something big (and round) (for ex. big fruit, big rocks, etc.)*'/, *see* thi ~ tha ~ the ~ thah ~ theh.

<**Thíthesem**>, PLN ['*place on mountain above Ruby Creek where there's lots of boulders all over the mountain lined up in rows*'], *see* thi ~ tha ~ the ~ thah ~ theh.

<**thíthetses**>, ANA ['*(have) big hand(s)*'], *see* thi ~ tha ~ the ~ thah ~ theh.

<**thíthexel**>, ANA ['*(have) big feet*'], *see* thi ~ tha ~ the ~ thah ~ theh.

<**thí:thqet**>, EB ['*little tree*'], *see* theqát ~ thqá:t.

<**thíthqey**>, EZ ['*small sockeye salmon*'], *see* sthéqi ~ sthéqey.

<**thithq'eyóls**>, df //C₁í=θəq'=əy(=)áls//, PLAY ['*pool (the game)*'], (<**R4=**> *diminutive*), see under root <**théq'**> *poke, stab, spear, pierce*.

<**Thíthx̱**>, PLN ['*a spring water stream near Yakweakwioose*'], *see* thíx̱.

<**thithx̱óstel**>, PLAY ['*betting each other*'], *see* théx̱.

<**thíts'et**>, pcs //θíc'=əT//, BSK ['*split s-th open (with fingernail)*'], ASM ['the thin inside bulrush or white grass (blue-joint reed-grass), the bulrush part split off can be rolled on thigh and used for string'], (<**=et**> *purposeful control transitivizer*), syntactic analysis: transitive verb, attested by Elders Group (10/13/76).

<**thíwelh**>, SD ['*big voice (usually deep)*'], *see* thi ~ tha ~ the ~ thah ~ theh.

<**thíx̱**>, free root //θíx̣//, WATR ['*spring (water source)*'], LAND, syntactic analysis: noun, nominal, attested by AC (11/24/71), DM (12/4/64), other sources: ES /θíx̣/ *spring*, example: <**thíx̱ qó:**>, //θíx̣ qá·//, /'*spring water*'/, attested by AC.

<**Thíthx̱**>, dmn //θí[=C₁ə=]x̣//, PLN ['*a spring water stream near Yakweakwioose*'], literally /'little spring'/, (<**=R1=**> *diminutive*), phonology: reduplication, syntactic analysis: noun, nominal, source: Wells 1965 (lst ed.):13,

<**thíy**>, free root //θíy or θə[=Aí=]y//, MC /'*made, fixed, repaired*'/, Elder's comment: "not *make, fix*", possibly <**í-ablaut**> *resultative or durative*, phonology: possible ablaut, syntactic analysis: intransitive verb, attested by AD (12/17/79), Salish cognate: root in Sechelt /ci-cəy-ím/ *to work* T77:36.

<**thíyt**>, pcs //θíy=T//, MC /'*make s-th, fix s-th, do s-th*'/, (<**=t**> *purposeful control transitivizer*), syntactic analysis: transitive verb, attested by Elders Group, AC, BJ, EB; found in <**thíytlha.**>, //θíy=T-ɬɛ//, /'*Make it., Fix it., Do it., Fix s-th.*'/, attested by BJ (5/10/64), EB (12/15/75), example: <**thíytchexw kw'e sléxwelh, sq'émel, qas kw'e sx̱wő̄qw'tel.**>, //θíy=T-c-əxʷ k'ʷə s=lə́xʷ=wəɬ, s=q'ə́m=əl, qɛ-s k'ʷə s=x̣ʷóq'ʷ=təl//, /'*Make a canoe, a paddle, and a canoe pole.*'/, attested by EB (4/13/78), <**thíyt te syúwel**>, //θíy=T tə s=yə́w=əl//, /'*fix a spirit song, straighten out a spirit song*'/, attested by Elders Group (7/21/76), <**welóyè léwe le thíyt.**>, //wə-láy-ə̀ lə́wə lə θíy=T//, /'*You did something by yourself.*'/, literally /'contrastive- only -just it's you past do it/make it/fix it'/, attested by AC (8/8/70), <**líchxw lólets'è kw'es le thíyt?**>, //lí-c-xʷ C₁á=ləc'ə-ə̀ k'ʷ-əs lə θíy=T//, /'*Were you alone when you fixed it?*'/, attested by AC (8/8/70), <**tsel thíyt kw'e (léts'e, isále, sléxwelh).**>, //c-əl θíy=T k'ʷə (lə́c'ə, ʔisɛ́lə, s=ləxʷ=wəɬ)//, /'*I made (one, two, a canoe).*'/, attested by AC (8/28/70), <**esu thíytes te lólets'e; kwú:tes te siyólh qetl'os'esu thíytes te chí:tmexw.**>, //ʔə-s-u θíy=T-əs tə C₁á=ləc'ə; kʷú·=T-əs tə s=yáɬ qə-ƛ'a-s-ʔəs-əw θíy=T-əs tə cí·t=məxʷ//, /'*So one man made it; he got some wood (get/fetch s-th) and made an owl.*'/, ASM ['a man carved a wooden owl on the canoe of the Flood to mark it when the water had gone down and the people were dispersing'], usage: Story of the Flood, attested by AC (12/7/71).

<**thá:yt**>, cts //θi[-Aɛ́·-]y=T//, MC /'*fixing s-th, making s-th*'/, (<**á:-ablaut**> *continuative*), phonology: ablaut, syntactic analysis: transitive verb, attested by Elders Group (1/7/76), AC, BJ, example: <**líchxw thá:yt kw'e p'ó:th'es?**>, //lí-c-xʷ θi[=Aɛ́·=]y=T k'ʷə p'ɛ[=Aá=]θ'=əs//, /'*Are you making a baby basket?*'/, attested by AC (11/17/71); found in <**thá:ytes.**>, //θi[=Aɛ́·=]y=T-əs//, /'*He's making it.*'/, attested by BJ (5/10/64), example: <**stám te í:xw thá:yt?**>, //s=tɛ́m tə ʔí·-

x^w θi[=Aɛ́·=]y=T//, /'*What are you making?*'/, attested by AC (11/17/71).

<**thíythet**>, pcrs //θíy=T-ət//, PE ['*fix oneself up*'], EFAM ['*straighten oneself out*'], (<**-et**> *reflexive*), syntactic analysis: intransitive verb, attested by EB (1/30/76), IHTTC; found in <**thíythetlha.**>, //θíy=T-ət-ɬɛ//, /'*Fix yourself., Fix yourself up., Straighten yourself out.*'/, attested by IHTTC (9/15/77), <**thíythetalha.**>, //θíy=T-ət-ɛɬɛ//, /'*Fix yourselves., Fix yourselves up., Straighten yourselves out.*'/, attested by IHTTC (9/15/77).

<**thiyélhtset ~ thiyélhchet**>, bens //θiy-ə́ɬc=əT//, MC /'*make it for s-o, fix it for s-o*'/, (<**-elhts**> *benefactive*), (<**=et**> *purposeful control transitivizer*), syntactic analysis: transitive verb, attested by EB (3/1/76), Elders Group, also <**thiyélht**>, //θiy-ə́ɬ=T//, attested by EB (3/1/76); found in <**thiyélhtlha.** ~ (prompted) **thiyélhchetlha.**>, //θiy-ə́ɬ=T-ɬɛ ~ θiy=ə́ɬc=əT-ɬɛ//, /'*Make it for him.*'/, attested by EB (3/1/76), <**thiyélhtsthó:x**>, //θiy=ə́ɬc=T-áx^y//, /'*make it for me*'/, attested by Elders Group (3/24/76), <**thiyélhthóxchexw.**>, //θiy-ə́ɬ=T-áx^y-c-əx^w//, /'*Make it for me., You make it for me.*'/, attested by EB (3/1/76).

<**tháyelhtset**>, cts //θi[-Aɛ́-]y=əɬc-əT//, bens, MC /'*making it for s-o, fixing it for s-o*'/, (<**á-ablaut**> *continuative*), phonology: ablaut, syntactic analysis: transitive verb, attested by AC (11/11/71), example: <**tewát kw'e íxw tháyelhtset te sweltel?**>, //tə=wɛ́t k'^wə ʔí-x^w θi[-Aɛ́-]y=əɬc-əT tə s=wə́l=təl//, /'*who are you making the fishnet for?*'/, attested by AC (11/11/71).

<**sthethíy**>, strs //s=C_1ə=θíy//, MC /'*be fixed, be fixed up properly*'/, (<**s=**> *stative*), (<**R5=**> *resultative*), phonology: reduplication, comment: note that the *resultative* here has a different form than the *continuative* (which above has ablaut); this is true for several other roots, though for Musqueam (Suttles ca1984:ch.7) it is never thought to be the case, syntactic analysis: intransitive verb, attested by IHTTC (9/15/77), example: <**le xwe sthethíy.**>, //lə x^wə s=C_1ə=θíy//, /'*It's fixed.*'/, literally /'it past get/become fixed'/, <**sthethíy kw'as lhx̱é:ylexélep.**>, //s=C_1ə=θíy k'^w-ɛ-s ɬx̣=í·l=əx^y-ə́ləp//, /'*Stand properly everyone.*'/, literally /'be fixed properly that -you -subord. you folks' standing'/, <**sthethíy kw'as lhx̱é:ylex.**>, //s=C_1ə=θíy k'^w-ɛ-s ɬx̣=í·l=əx^y//, /'*Stand properly.*'/, <**tu sthethíylha kw'as ó:metélep.**>, //təw s=C_1ə=θíy-ɬɛ k'^w-ɛ-s ʔə[-Aá·-]mət-ə́ləp//, /'*Sit properly everyone.*'/, literally /'sort of get fixed up properly -imperative that/when -you -subord. you folks' sitting'/, syntactic comment: -alha *plural imperative* would be more expected here, but may be optional since -elep *your (pl.), you folks'* appears just two words later, <**tu sthethíylha kw'as ó:met.**>, //təw s=C_1ə=θíy-ɬɛ k'^w-ɛ-s ʔə[-Aá·-]mət//, /'*Sit properly (ordering one person).*'/.

<**thiyá:lhem ~ thiyálhem**>, df //θiy=ɛ́·ɬ=əm ~ θiy=ɛ́ɬ=əm//, HHG /'*make a bed, make (straighten up) a bed, make one's bed*'/, lx <**=á:lh ~ =álh**> *bed*, (<**=em**> *middle voice or intransitivizer/have/get*), syntactic analysis: intransitive verb, attested by EB (4/28/76), Elders Group (6/1/77), example: <**thiyá:lhemchxw lí te lhx̱éyléptel.**>, //θiy=ɛ́·ɬ=əm-c-x^w lí tə ɬx̣=ílə́p=təl//, /'*Make your bed on the floor., You make the bed on the floor.*'/, attested by EB.

<**thiyéltxwem**>, df //θiy=ə́ltx^w=əm//, BLDG ['*build a house (make a house)*'], lx <**=éltxw ~ =áwtxw**> *building, house*, (<**=em**> *middle voice or intransitivizer*), syntactic analysis: intransitive verb, attested by EB (1/7/76).

<**thiyéltsep**>, ds //θiy=ə́lcəp//, FIRE /'*fix a fire, straighten the fire up, stoke the fire*'/, lx <**=éltsep ~ =élchep**> *fire*, syntactic analysis: intransitive verb, attested by NP (AHTTC 2/15/80), also <**thiyélchep**>, //θiy=ə́lcəp//, attested by AD (AHTTC 2/15/80).

<**shxwthó:yeltsep**>, ds //sx^w=θi[=Aá·=]y=əlcəp or sx^w=θi[=Aɛ[=Aá=]·=]y=əlcəp//, FIRE ['*fire poker*'], literally /'something for fixing/straightening up fire'/, (<**shxw=**> *something for*), possibly <**á:-ablaut**> *continuative*, (<**ó-ablaut**> or <**ó:-ablaut**> *derivational*), phonology: ablaut, perhaps ablaut on ablaut, syntactic analysis: nominal, attested by CT and HT (6/21/76).

<**thíyém**>, izs //θíy=ə[=´=]m//, FOOD /'*to bake (bread, other food)*'/, (<**=em**> *intransitivizer, have, get*), possibly <=´=> *derivational*, phonology: stress-shifting, syntactic analysis: intransitive verb, attested by EB (12/19/75, 4/14/78), Elders Group (1/25/78), Deming (1/4/79), also <**thíyem**>, //θíy=əm//, attested by EB (12/15/75, 12/19/75 or 1/12/76), example: <**mőkw'a stám éy kw'as thíyem.**>, //mə́k'ʷ-ɛ s=tɛ́m ʔɛ́y k'ʷ-ɛ-s θíy=əm//, /'*You cook everything nice.*'/, attested by EB (12/19/75 or 1/12/76), <**thíyém te seplí:l**>, //θíy=ə[=´=]m tə səplí·l//, /'*bake bread*'/, literally /'bake the bread (or) the bread bakes'/, attested by EB (12/19/75), <**tewátesò kw'e thíyem.**>, //tə=wɛ́t=əs-à k'ʷə θíy=əm//, /'*Anybody can do the baking.*'/, literally /'it's anybody -just that bakes'/, attested by EB (1/12/76), <**yálhòlse thíyém te seplí:l.**>, //yɛ́ɬ-àl-s-ə θíy=ə[=´=]m tə səplí·l//, /'*begin to bake bread*'/, attested by EB (12/19/75).

<**thá:yém**>, cts //θi[-Aɛ́·-]y=ə[=´=]m//, FOOD ['*baking (bread esp.)*'], (<**á:-ablaut**> *continuative*), phonology: ablaut, syntactic analysis: intransitive verb, attested by Elders Group (1/25/78, 3/14/79), also <**thá:yem**>, //θi[-Aɛ́·-]y=əm//, attested by EB (4/14/78), also <**thá:yem**>, //θi[-Aɛ́·-]y=əm//, also /'*making (knitting)*'/, attested by Elders Group (3/14/79), example: <**thá:yem te swéta**>, //θi[-Aɛ́·-]y=əm tə swə́tɛ//, /'*making a sweater*'/.

<**thiyeqwá:ls ~ thiyqwá:ls**>, cpds //θiy=qʷ(ɛ)=ɛ́(·)ls//, sas, HARV ['*dig*'], LAND, semantic environment ['for dig potatoes, vegetables, etc.'], literally /'fix/make= get hole =structured activity'/, root <**thiy**> *fix, make*, root <**qwá**> *get a hole*, (<**=áls ~ =á:ls**> *structured activity non-continuative*), phonology: vowel merger, syntactic analysis: intransitive verb, semantic content: one of the few compounds found in the language, attested by AC, IHTTC (9/2/77), others, other sources: ES /θiqʷɛ́·ls/ *dig*, *<**thiyqwá:ls te témexw**> rejected, /'*dig the ground*'/, attested by EB (5/3/76).

<**thóyeqwels**>, cts //θi[-Aá-]y=qʷ(ɛ)=əls//, sas, LAND ['*digging*'], HARV, (<**ó-ablaut**> *continuative*), (<**=els**> *structured activity continuative*), phonology: ablaut, vowel-loss or irregular vowel merger, syntactic analysis: intransitive verb, attested by AC, IHTTC (9/2/77).

<**shxwthóyeqwels**>, dnom //sxʷ=θi[=Aá=]y=qʷ(ɛ)=əls//, HARV ['*digging stick*'], LAND, literally /'something for digging, something for fixing/making get hole as structured activity'/, (<**shxw=**> *something for*), phonology: ablaut, vowel-loss, syntactic analysis: nominal, attested by EB (5/25/76), DM (12/4/64), also HARV ['*hoe*'], attested by EB (2/6/76).

<**thíyeqwt or thíyqwt**>, pcs //θíy=qʷ(ɛ)=T//, cpds, HARV /'*dig it, dig s-th, dig for s-th*'/, LAND, root <**thíy**> *fix, make*, root <**qwá**> *get a hole*, (<**=t**> *purposeful control transitivizer*), phonology: vowel-loss, syntactic analysis: transitive verb, attested by CT (6/8/76), AC, EB (5/3/76), example: <**thíyqwt te témexw**>, //θíy=qʷ(ɛ)=T tə tə́məxʷ//, /'*dig a hole in the ground*'/, attested by AC (8/28/70), <**thíyqwtes kw stáméstwo.**>, //θíy=qʷ(ɛ)=T-əs kʷ s=tɛ́m=ə́s=t'wɛ-ò//, /'*He dug for something.*'/, attested by EB (5/3/76), <**le thíyqwtes kw'e (sth'ékw., thí:thqet., theqát.)**>, //lə θíy=qʷ(ɛ)=T-əs k'ʷə (s=θ'ə́kʷ, C_1í=θqɛt, θəqɛ́t)//, /'*He dug (for worms., a little tree., a tree.)*'/, attested by AC (10/13/71), <**le thíyqwtes te (sp'á:q'em., spí:w.)**>, //lə θíy=qʷ(ɛ)=T-əs tə (s=p'ɛ́·q'=əm, s=pí·w)//, /'*He dug (flowers., the ice.)*'/, attested by AC (10/13/71).

<**thiyeqwewí:lt**>, ds //θiy=qʷ(ɛ)=í·wə[=M2=]l=T or θiy=qʷ(ɛ)=əwəl=í·l=T//, CAN /'*make it hollow (of canoe, log, etc.)*'/, MC, literally /'make s-th get a hole in the inside on purpose'/, lx <**=í:wel ~ =ewel**> *in the insides*, possibly <**=í:l**> *go, come, get, become*, (<**=t**> *purposeful control transitivizer*), phonology: vowel-loss, metathesis, possible syllable-loss, syntactic analysis: transitive verb, attested by Elders Group (6/16/76).

<**shxwthó:yqw**>, cpds //sxʷ=θi[=Aá·=]y=qʷ(ɛ) or sxʷ=θi[=Aɛ́[=Aá=]·=]y=qʷ(ɛ)//, LAND /'*hole in the ground, trench (if discussing length)*'/, (<**shxw=**> *something for*), root <**thiy**> *make, fix*, possibly <**ó:-ablaut**> *durative or derivational*, possibly <**á:-ablaut**> *continuative*, phonology: ablaut,

vowel-loss, syntactic analysis: nominal, attested by Elders Group (3/15/72), also <**sthó:yqw**>, //s=θi[=Aá·=]y=qʷ(ɛ)//, attested by Elders Group (3/15/72), example: <**tl'ép te shxwthó:yqw.**>, //ƛ'ə́p tə sxʷ=θi[=Aá·=]y=qʷ(ɛ)//, /'*The hole in the ground is deep.*'/, <**tl'áqt te shxwthó:yqw.**>, //ƛ'ɛ́qt tə sxʷ=θi[=Aá·=]y=qʷ(ɛ)//, /'*The hole in the ground/trench is long.*'/, <**te stl'eqtí:ms te shxwthó:yqw**>, //tə s=ƛ'ɛqt=í·m-s tə sxʷ=θi[=Aá·=]y=qʷ(ɛ)//, /'*the length of the trench*'/, attested by Elders Group (3/15/72), <**le xwe tl'ép te shxwthó:yqw.**>, //lə xʷə ƛ'ə́p tə sxʷ=θi[=Aá·=]y=qʷ(ɛ)//, /'*The hole is getting deeper (said of grave).*'/, literally /'it past become/get deep the hole in the ground'/, attested by Elders Group (3/15/72).

<**sthí:ystexw**>, caus //s=θí[=·=]y=sT-əxʷ//, augs, SOC ['*do s-th well*'], VALJ, TIB, literally /'cause it to be really fixed/made'/, possibly <**s=**> *stative*?, (<**=:=**> *augmentative*), (<**=st**> *causative control transitivizer*), (<**-exw**> *third person object*), phonology: lengthening, syntactic analysis: transitive verb, attested by Elders Group (6/16/76), example: <**sthí:ystxwes te syó:ys.**>, //s=θí[=·=]y=sT-əxʷ-əs tə s=yá·ys-s//, /'*He does his work well.*'/, phonology: consonant merger.

<**sthíyep**>, df //s=θíy=əp//, CLO /'*loincloth, dog-hair apron, dog-hair mat*'/, (<**s=**> *nominalizer*), root <**thíy**> *fixed, made*, <**=ep ~ =ép**> *on the rump*, or possibly <**=ep ~ =ép ~ =ílep**> *dirt*, syntactic analysis: nominal, attested by AC (10/23/71), other sources: JH /sθí·yəp/ *a girdle*, Salish cognate: perhaps Lushootseed /sč'ájəp ~ sč'áyəp/ *cedar bark skirt, skirt* H76:106, 696, also <**sthíyép**>, //s=θíy=ə́p//, attested by Elders Group (10/1/75).

<**sthiyáp**>, stvi //s=θiy=ə[=Aɛ́=]p//, CLO ['*be wearing a loincloth*'], (<**s=**> *stative*), possibly <**á-ablaut**> *continuative*, phonology: ablaut, syntactic analysis: intransitive verb, attested by AC (10/23/71), example: <**sthiyáp te swótle.**>, //s=θiy=ə[=Aɛ́=]p//, /'*Somebody is wearing a loincloth.*'/, attested by AC (10/23/71).

<**thiyá:lhem ~ thiyálhem**>, HHG /'*make a bed, make (straighten up) a bed, make one's bed*'/, *see* thíy.

<**thiyéltxwem**>, BLDG ['*build a house (make a house)*'], *see* thíy.

<**thiyéltsep**>, FIRE /'*fix a fire, straighten the fire up, stoke the fire*'/, *see* thíy.

<**thiyélhtset ~ thiyélhchet**>, MC /'*make it for s-o, fix it for s-o*'/, *see* thíy.

<**thíyém**>, FOOD /'*to bake (bread, other food)*'/, *see* thíy.

<**thíyéqel**>, df //θíy(=)ə́(=)qəl//, EZ /'*hooded merganser, smaller sawbill*'/, ['*Lophodytes cucullatus*'], root meaning unknown, possibly <**=qel**> *in the head*, syntactic analysis: nominal, attested by EL (9/15/78).

<**thiyeqwá:ls ~ thiyqwá:ls**>, HARV ['*dig*'], *see* thíy.

<**thiyeqwewí:lt**>, CAN /'*make it hollow (of canoe, log, etc.)*'/, *see* thíy.

<**thíyeqwt** or **thíyqwt**>, HARV /'*dig it, dig s-th, dig for s-th*'/, *see* thíy.

<**thíyt**>, MC /'*make s-th, fix s-th, do s-th*'/, *see* thíy.

<**thíythet**>, PE ['*fix oneself up*'], *see* thíy.

<**thkw'éthet**>, ABFC /'*pull oneself up, straighten (oneself) up*'/, *see* thékw'.

<**thó:lchep ~ thó:ltsep**>, FIRE /'*be big (of a fire), the fire is big, the fire is going strong, big fire*'/, *see* thi ~ tha ~ the ~ thah ~ theh.

<**thómél**>, free root //θámə́l (or)//, df //θám=məl//, ANA ['*eyebrow*'], root meaning unknown, possibly <**=mel**> *part of, portion*, phonology: possible updrifting, syntactic analysis: noun, nominal, attested by BJ (5/10/64), Elders Group (8/20/75), AD (2/20/80), other sources: ES /θá·mə̀l/ *eyebrow*, H-T

<tsa'mEl> (macron over a) *eyebrow*, Salish cognate: Squamish /cúmn/ *eyebrow* W73:94, K67:274, Lushootseed /cúbəd/ *eyebrow* H76:55, example: **<lhíts' tel thómél.>**, //ɬíc' t-əl θáməl//, /'*My eyebrow got cut.*'/, attested by AD.

<**themthómél**>, pln //C_1əC_2=θáməl//, ANA ['*both eyebrows*'], (semological comment: one of the few cases where plural doesn't mean *many*), (<**R3=**> *plural*), phonology: reduplication, syntactic analysis: noun, nominal, attested by Elders Group (8/20/75).

<**thó:qw**>, ANA ['*have a big head*'], *see* thi ~ tha ~ the ~ thah ~ theh.

<**thó:s** ~ **thós**>, ds //θi=á·s//, DESC /'big round'/, (attested by RG,EH 6/16/98 to SN, edited by BG with RG,EH 6/26/00), *see* **thi**

<**thós sth'emíwel sékwluwi**>,FOOD, EB ['*avocado*'] (lit. big round + pit + soft smooth texture), *see* **thi**

<**thós sp'eq'í:l tl'íkw'el**>,FOOD, EB ['*lima beans*'] (lit. big round + offwhite + bean), *see* **thi**

<**thó:thel** ~ **thóthel**>, possibly root //θá(·)θəl or θ=á(·)θəl//, ANA ['*mouth*'], probably <**=ó(:)thel**> *(in the) mouth*, phonology: possible empty root (meaningless consonant for the lexical suffix to attach to), syntactic analysis: noun, nominal, attested by AC, BJ (5/10/64), others, other sources: ES and JH /θá·θəl/ *mouth*, Salish cognate: MCx /θóθən or θúθən or θúθin/, ICx /sósin/, Pt /θúθin or θúθən/, Se and Sq /cúcin/, CwMs /θáθən/, Nk /cócæn ~ cócin/, Sn /θáθən ~ sásən/, LmSo /sósən/, SmbSg /sásən/, Cl /núcən/, Tw /cucíd/ all *mouth* (G86a and G88a:cognate set 12), example: <**hí:kw te thó:thels te stiqíw.**>, //hí[=·=]k^w tə θ=á·θəl-s tə s=tiqíw//, /'*The horse has a big mouth.*'/, attested by AC (9/18/71).

<**thóxw** or **théxw**>, bound root //θáx^w or θəx^w *bleed*//

<**thethíx̱w**>, durs //C_1ə=θə[=Aí=]x̣^{w} or θə[=C_1ə=Aí=]x̣^{w}//, HAT /'*girl at puberty, (girl's first period)*'/, SOCT, possibly root <**thex̱w**> *bleeding*, compare <**s=thxw=élqsel**> *bleeding nose*, possibly <**R5=** or **=R1=**> *continuative or resultative*, (<**í-ablaut**> *durative*), phonology: reduplication, ablaut, syntactic analysis: nominal, attested by Elders Group (1/21/76), Salish cognate: Squamish /cə-cíx^w/ *girl's puberty* K69:52.

<**The Théthex̱w** or **Thethéthex̱w**>, df //θə θə́[=C_1ə=]x̣^{w} or C_1ə=θə́[=C_1ə=]x̣^{w}//, PLN ['*a rock in the creek at the upriver end of Seabird Island that was a girl washing after her first period*'], ASM ['the rock was a girl washing in the river after having her first period when she was changed to rock by the X̱ex̱éyls (the Transformers); the rock can't be seen from Haig Highway'], literally /'the one (female) menstruating for the first time'/, possibly <**R5=**> *diminutive*, probably <**=R1=**> *continuative*, phonology: reduplication, syntactic analysis: simple nominal phrase or nominal, attested by AK (8/30/77), source: place names reference file #250.

<**sthxwélqsel**>, df //s=θax^w=ə́lqsəl//, ABDF /'*bleeding nose, (be/have bleeding in the nose)*'/, (<**s=**> *nominalizer* (or s= *stative*)), lx <**=élqsel**> *in the nose*, ASM ['young sprouts of tansy are used as medicine for nosebleed--they are stuck up the nose, tansy flowers are used for yellow dye also, but no Halq'eméylem name has been learned for tansy, this info. from JL'][a good name for *tansy* might be *<**sthxwélqseltel**>, lit. 'nose-bleed medicine'-BG], syntactic analysis: nominal, intransitive verb??, attested by AH (Deming 2/14/80).

<**thxwómélqsel**>, ds //θáx^w-M1=əm=ə́lqsəl//, ABDF ['*have a nose bleed*'], (<**metathesis type 1**> *non-continuative*), (<**=em**> *intransitivizer, have, get*), comment: not =em *middle voice* since that would have to follow =élqsel, phonology: metathesis, syntactic analysis: intransitive verb, attested by NP and AD (AHTTC 2/15/80).

<**thóxwemélqsel**>, cts //θáx^w=əm=ə́lqsəl//, ABDF ['*having a nose bleed*'], comment: lack of metathesis (or of initial consonant cluster) *continuative*, syntactic analysis: intransitive verb,

attested by NP and AD (AHTTC 2/15/80).

<**thóxwemélqsel**>, ABDF ['*having a nose bleed*'], *see* thóxw or théxw.

<**thóyeqwels**>, LAND ['*digging*'], *see* thíy.

<**thqá:lem**>, df //θqɛ́·l=əm or θəq=ə[=Aɛ́·=]l=əm//, FSH /'*to still-dip, rest dip-net on bottom (of river)*'/, ASM ['hold the net end planted on the bottom of the river'], FSH /'*to bag net, to sack net, to still-dip with two canoes*'/, ASM ['the net drags on the bottom, two men in two canoes hold net poles in the prows while two men steer in the stern; EL identified this meaning of the word from drawings by Hillary Stewart and Peter Lindley; EL thinks it probably is the same thing named by DM as xíxemal'], root meaning unknown unless something like *upright* as in <**thqá:t**> *tree* and <**théq**> *steep* after the fact that one must stand upright with the net upright unlike other methods of fishing, possibly <**á:-ablaut**> *non-continuative or durative*, possibly <**=el**> *go, come, get, become*, possibly <**=em**> *intransitivizer, have, get*, possibly <**=em**> *middle voice*, syntactic analysis: intransitive verb, attested by Elders Group (3/15/72, 2/11/76), Deming (5/20/76), EL (2/20/79), example: <**tsel theqá:lem.**>, //c-əl θəqɛ́·l=əm//, /'*I still-dip.*'/, attested by Elders Group (3/15/72).

<**thqálem**>, dnom //θqɛ́l=əm//, FSH ['*a waiting dip-net with frame and string trap*'], syntactic analysis: nominal, attested by Elders Group (3/26/75).

<**théqelem**>, cts //θə[-´-]q=ɛl=əm//, FSH /'*holding on to a thqá:lem, waiting dip-netting, still-dipping*'/, (<**-´- (stress-shift)**> *continuative*), phonology: stress-shift, vowel-reduction, syntactic analysis: intransitive verb, attested by Elders Group (3/26/75, 11/26/75).

<**sthqálem**>, dnom //s=θqɛ́l=əm//, FSH /'*place where one fishes by waiting with a dip-net, dip-net fishing place, place where one still-dips*'/, (<**s=**> *nominalizer*), possibly <**=em**> *place to have/get*, syntactic analysis: nominal, attested by Elders Group (3/26/75), also <**sthqá:lem**>, //s=θqɛ́·l=əm//, also /'*fishing platform (used upriver in the Fraser Canyon)*'/, (semological comment: this too is a place where one fishes by waiting with a dip net), attested by DM (12/4/64).

<**thq'á:ls**>, sas //θəq'=ɛ́·ls or θəq'-M1=ɛ́·ls//, FSH ['*to spear fish*'], see under <**théq'**>, bound root //θə́q' *stab, pierce, spear*//.

<**thá:q'els**>, cts //θə[-Aɛ́·-]q'=əls//, sas, FSH /'*spearing fish, spearing (fish)*'/, (<**á:-ablaut**> *continuative*), (<**=els**> *structured activity continuative*), phonology: ablaut, syntactic analysis: intransitive verb, attested by Elders Group (3/26/75), EB (5/3/76).

<**thq'elq'ó:les**>, ABDF ['*get dust or bark in both eyes*'], *see* théq'.

<**thq'ét**>, pcs //θə́q'-M1=T//, FSH, HUNT, SOC /'*spear it (a fish), stab s-o/s-th with something sharp, pierce s-o/s-th, prick s-o (with a pin, for ex.), poke s-o (with a pin, etc.)*'/, see under <**théq'**>, bound root //θə́q'// *stab, pierce, spear.*

<**tháq't**>, cts //θə[-Aɛ́-]q'=T//, FSH ['*spearing s-th*'], HUNT, SOC, (<**á-ablaut**> *continuative*), (<**=t**> *purposeful control transitivizer*), phonology: ablaut, syntactic analysis: transitive verb, attested by EB (4/23/76); found in <**tháq'tes.**>, //θə[-Aɛ́-]q'=T-əs//, /'*He's spearing it.*'/.

<**thq'ó:les**>, df //θəq'=á·ləs//, ABDF ['*get dust or bark in one eye*'], literally perhaps /'pricked in the eye'/, see also under root <**théq'**> *poke, stab, spear, pierce*, lx <**=ó:les**> *in the eye*, syntactic analysis: intransitive verb, attested by EB and AD (9/25/78).

<**thq'elq'ó:les**>, plv //θ[=C_1əC_2=]q'=á·ləs//, ABDF ['*get dust or bark in both eyes*'], (irregular)=R3= applied (in error?) to stem as if initial th was prefix and ó: of =ó:les was part of root (no other exx. of this in the language, and th- or th= is not a prefix), phonology: reduplication, syntactic analysis: intransitive verb, attested by EB and AD (9/25/78), DM (7/64 new p.61 tape transcription of Story of Black Bear and Grizzly Bear and Their Children).

<**thswál**>, us //θswɛ́l//, EZ [*'fisher (mink-like animal)'*], [*'Martes pennanti pennanti'*], contrast <**shxwémetsel**> *fisher (animal)*, compare <**sx̱ewál**> *fox*??, comment: could this be an erroneous citation of <**the sx̱(e)wál**> *female fox*?, phonology: unusual consonant cluster, syntactic analysis: nominal, attested by HP (3/3/76).

<**thtíwél**>, LANG [*'say to oneself'*], *see* thét.

<**thú:tl'ò**>, PRON /*'that's her, she (present or presence unspecified), her (present or presence unspefified), that (female)'*/, *see* tl'ó ~ tl'o.

<**thutl'ó:lem**>, PRON /*'that's them (female), they (female), them (female)'*/, *see* tl'ó ~ tl'o.

<**thxwáléqep**>, SD [*'(have a) steady sound that's been stopped for a while'*], *see* théxw ~ théx̱w.

<**thxwómélqsel**>, ABDF [<**thx̱ét ~ thex̱ét**>, ABFC [*'push s-o/s-th'*] *have a nose bleed*'], *see* thóxw or théxw.

<**thxwót**>, pcs //θxw=ə[=Aá=]T//, ABFC /*'to thrust something'*/, root uncertain but perhaps related to <**théx̱**> *push* as in <**thx̱ét ~ thex̱ét**> *push s-o/s-th*, attested by RG & EH (4/9/99 Ling332)

<**thx̱á:l**> possible stem //θx̣ɛ́·l// or <**thx̱**> possible root //θx// or <thá:x̱> //θɛ́·x//, meaning uncertain

<**sthx̱á:lem**>, df //s=θx̣ɛ́·l=əm or s=θx̣=ə[=Aɛ́·=]l=əm or s=θɛ́·x̣=ə[=M2=]l=əm//, EB [*'sword fern'*], [*'Polystichum munitum'*], ASM ['roots edible when roasted on hot coals or baked in hot ashes and peeled'], MED ['part of the root near the base of the leaves is used as medicine to bring on childbirth, pregnant bears also lay on it and eat the root-stock, thus the alternate name, slháwels te spá:th bear's mattress'], (<**s=**> *nominalizer*), root meaning unknown unless <**théx̱**> *push* as in <**thx̱ét ~ thex̱ét**> *push s-o/s-th* due to the plant being medicine to push out the baby, possibly <**=el**> *come, go, get, become*, possibly <**=em**> *intransitivizer, have, get*, possibly <**=em**> *middle voice*, possibly <**á:-ablaut** or **metathesis**> *durative*, phonology: possible ablaut or metathesis, syntactic analysis: nominal, attested by AC (11/22/71), other sources: ES /sθx̣ɛ̀ləm/ *sword fern*, JH /sθqéləm/ *sword fern*, also <**thx̱álem**>, //θx̣ɛ́l=əm//, attested by Elders Group (2/26/75).

<**thx̱ét ~ thex̱ét**>, ABFC [*'push s-o/s-th'*], *see* théx̱.

TH'

<**=th'**>, da //=θ'//, DESC (probably) ['*small portion*'], syntactic analysis: lexical suffix; found in <**lhémth'**>, //ɬi[=Aə́=]m=θ'//, /'*picking food by the fingers before the meal*'/, <**sqwémth' ~ sqwómth'**>, //s=q^{w}ə́m=θ' ~ s=q^{w}ám=θ'//, /'*lump*'/, compare <**sqwóm=ecel**> *hunchback*, Salish cognate: Musqueam /sk^{w}ə́mθ'/ *lump (as on body)* contrasted with /sk^{w}ám'əcən/ *hump-backed* and /sk^{w}ə́mƛ'/ *bulge, ridge* Suttles ca1984: 14.6.15, <**ew=th'=át**>, //ʔəw=θ'=ə[=Aɛ́=]T or ʔə=wɛ́θ'=ə[-M2-]T//, /'*tease s-o*'/, compare <**ew=ó(:)l=em**> *play*, comment: however if the root is wáth' *pry* this form does not have =th', Salish cognate: Musqueam /həw'θ'ɛ́ʔt/ *tease him* contrasted with /həw'áləm/ *play* Suttles ca 1984:14.6.15), <**lhílhàth'**>, //ɬíɬɛ̀θ'//, /'*making fun*'/, <**lhílhà(:)th't**>, //ɬíɬɛ̀(·)=θ'=T//, /'*making fun of s-o*'/, Salish cognate: Musqueam /ɬiɬéθ'=t/ *make fun of him (because of accident or bad luck)* and /ɬéʔ=it/ *insult him* Suttles ca 1984:14.6.15), <**p'íth'et**>, //p'í(·)=θ'=əT//, /'*squeeze s-o/s-th (with fingers/hands)*'/, compare root <**p'í:**> *put hand on, get hold of*, <**sq'emq'ámth'**>, //s=C_1əC_2=q'ɛ́m=θ'//, /'*(be) wrinkled*'/.

<**th'a**>, bound root //θ'ɛ *chew*//.

<**th'ám**>, ds //θ'ɛ́=m//, ABFC ['*chew*'], (<**=(e)m**> *middle voice* or *intransitive*), phonology: vowel-loss, syntactic analysis: intransitive verb, attested by AC (8/15/70), EB (12/10/75, 5/4/76), prob. not Squamish /č'ə́mʔ/ *bite (itr.)(dog, fish, fly, etc.)* and /č'əmʔ-t/ *bite (tr.)* K67:319, Salish cognate: Sechelt /c'əʔ-ə́m/ and /c'əʔ-át/ *to chew* T77:26, contrast <**ts'ámet**> *put s-th between one's teeth,bite on s-th (but not into)*, historical/comparative detail: it's unclear whether the words th'ám and ts'ámet are doublets or unrelated, example: <**th'ám te kw'íxw**>, //θ'ɛ́=m tə k'^{w}íx^w//, /'*chew the gum*'/, attested by EB (5/4/76), AC (8/15/70).

<**th'á:m ~ ts'á:m**>, cts //θ'ɛ́[-·-]=m ~ c'ɛ́[-·-]=m//, ABFC ['*chewing*'], (<**-:- (lengthening)**> *continuative*), phonology: lengthening, syntactic analysis: intransitive verb, attested by EB (3/22/76).

<**th'eth'ám**>, cts //C_1ə-θɛ́=m//, ABFC ['*chewing (gum)*'], (<**R5-**> *continuative*), comment: this seems the regular *continuative* for this verb, not th'á:m, see th'eth'át *chewing s-th*, phonology: reduplication, syntactic analysis: intransitive verb, attested by EB (5/3/76).

<**th'át**>, pcs //θ'ɛ́=T//, ABFC ['*chew s-th*'], (<**=t**> *purposeful control transitivizer*), syntactic analysis: transitive verb, attested by AC (8/27/73), Salish cognate: Cw /θ'eʔ-t/ *chew [s-th]* B74b:58, Sechelt /c'əʔ-át/ *chew [s-th]* T77:26, example: <**th'át te kw'íxw**>, //θ'ɛ́=T tə k'^{w}íx^w//, /'*chew the gum*'/, literally /'chew the pitch'/, attested by AC (8/27/73).

<**th'eth'át**>, cts //C_1ə-θ'ɛ́=T//, ABFC ['*chewing s-th*'], (<**R5-**> *continuative*), phonology: reduplication, syntactic analysis: transitive verb, attested by AC, example: <**th'eth'á:tes te smíyeth.**>, //C_1ə-θ'ɛ́·=T-əs tə s=míyəθ//, /'*He's chewing the meat.*'/, attested by AC (8/27/73).

<**th'akw'ó:y**>, EZ ['*smallest of a litter or family*'], *see* sth'ékw'.

<**th'á:lá ~ th'ála ~ th'á:le ~ th'ále**>, free root //θ'ɛ́·lɛ́ ~ θ'ɛ́lɛ ~ θ'ɛ́·lə ~ θ'ɛ́lə//, ANA ['*heart*'], semantic environment ['of animate being'], possibly root <**th'**> meaning unknown, possibly <**=á:lá**> *container (of)*, syntactic analysis: noun, nominal, attested by AC, Elders Group (7/27/75), LJ (Elders Group 6/28/78), Elders Group (incl. SP, AG, LJ, DF, and others)(7/13/77), EL (with EB and NP)(Chehalis place names trip 9/27/77), other sources: ES /θ'ɛ́·lɛ̀·/ *heart*, H-T <tsa'la> (umlaut over first a) *heart*, example: <**óxwesthóxlha te th'áles te músmes.**>, //ʔáx^{w}əs=T-áx^y-ɬɛ tə θ'ɛ́lə-s tə mús=C_1əC_2//, /'*Give me the cow's heart.*'/, attested by AC, <**le qelámthet tel th'ále lhíl ólew le kw'á:y.**>, //lə

qəl=ɛ́m=θət t-əl θ'ɛ́lə ɬí-l ʔál=əw lə k'ʷɛ́·y//, /'*My heart gets weak when I get too hungry.*'/, attested by LJ (Elders Group 6/28/78).

<**Th'áth'ele**>, df //θ'ɛ́[=C₁ə=]lə//, PLN ['*heart-shaped mountain on the CN (south) side of the Fraser River east of Mt. Cheam*'], ASM ['third mountain west of Tl'ítl'xeleqw, as seen from Silver Creek Road looking south, it looks like a heart from across the Fraser River or from Highway #1 from below its first major bend east of Silver Creek, the resemblance comes from two rounded slopes that angle together and join at the bottom with a shallow gully down the middle, this heart-shaped feature is part way down a larger mountain and faces north'], (<**=R1=**> *diminutive*?), phonology: reduplication, syntactic analysis: nominal, attested by SP and AK (Fish Camp 8/2/77), photos 6/21/78 and 6/26/78, source: place names reference file #163.

<**Th'álátel ~ Th'á:lá ~ Th'ála**>, ds //θ'ɛlɛ́=təl ~ θ'ɛ́·lɛ́ ~ θ'ɛ́lɛ//, PLN ['*heart-shaped island near the mouth of Chehalis River that beat like a heart*'], ASM ['this rock was supported by tree roots whose dirt had washed out below, thus the rock could move up and down beating with the waves, the rock was washed out by backwash from logging tugs about the 1940's-1950's, the rock's name is the reason for the naming of Chehalis, /s=c'ɛʔ-í·ləs/, literally *on top of the chest* according to EL (9/27/77) who provided all this information'], lx <**=tel**> *something, device*, syntactic analysis: nominal, attested by Elders Group (incl. SP, AG, LJ, DF)(7/13/77), EL (+ NP, EB)(9/27/77),Elders (6/20/78), source: place names reference file #75.

<**th'alátel**>, ds //θ'ɛlɛ́=təl//, EB ['*wild ginger*'], ['*Asarum caudatum*'], Elder's comment: "means heart medicine", literally /'something for the heart'/, ASM ['a few people also used it to flavor meats'], MED ['*heart medicine, also medicine to prevent colic or gas in babies, to make it pour hot water over the whole plant, then cool it some and bathe the baby*'], lx <**=tel**> *something for,* (perhaps) *medicine*, syntactic analysis: nominal, attested by (not recorded), contrast <**x̱éyeslótel**> *wild ginger.*

<**th'el'á:ltel**>, df //θ'ɛl=ʔɛ́·ltəl or θ'ɛ[=Aə=]lɛ́=ʔə[=M2=]l(=)təl//, MED ['*heart medicine (of any kind)*'], ASM ['usually made from juniper'], EB ['(possibly the name for) *common juniper or creeping juniper*'], ['*Juniperus communis*'], possibly <**='á:ltel or ='eltel**> *medicine*, possibly <**e-ablaut**> *derivational*, possibly <**metathesis**> *derivational*, phonology: possible ablaut or vowel-reduction, possible metathesis, syntactic analysis: nominal, attested by SP and AK (7/13/75).

<**th'alátel**>, EB ['*wild ginger*'], *see* th'á:lá ~ th'ála ~ th'á:le ~ th'ále.

<**Th'álátel ~ Th'á:lá ~ Th'ála**>, PLN ['*heart-shaped island near the mouth of Chehalis River that beat like a heart*'], *see* th'á:lá ~ th'ála ~ th'á:le ~ th'ále.

<**th'ál**>, possible bound root //θ'ɛl//, *transparent*

<**th'álx̱em**>, izs //θ'ɛl(=)x̣=əm//, LT /'*transparent, can be seen through (skin, curtain, etc.), translucent*'/, possibly root <**th'ál or th'álx̱**> meaning uncertain unless *transparent*, possibly <**=x̱**> *distributive*, (<**=em**> *intransitivizer, have, get*), syntactic analysis: adjective/adjectival verb, attested by Elders Group (3/2/77), compare <**th'áth'elh**> *crystal* which may have same root.

<**th'áth'elh**>, df //θ'ɛ[=C₁ə=]ɬ or θ'ɛ[=C₁ə=]l=UV//, LAND ['*crystal*'], HHG, root meaning unknown unless< **th'ál**> *transparent*, probably <**=R1=**> *resultative or continuative*, possibly <**UV (devoicing) l → lh**> word finally *derivational*, phonology: reduplication, possible devoicing, syntactic analysis: adjective/adjectival verb?, nominal?, attested by Elders Group (5/28/75).

<**sth'óth'elh**>, strs //s=θ'ɛ[=AáC₁ə=]ɬ//, LT ['*(be) transparent*'], (<**s=**> *stative*), (<**ó-ablaut and =R1=**> *resultative*), phonology: ablaut, reduplication, syntactic analysis: adjective/adjectival verb, attested by IHTTC (9/19/77).

<**th'álh**>, free root //θ'ɛ́ɬ//, ABFC ['*cool down (of a person)*'], syntactic analysis: intransitive verb,

attested by IHTTC (9/1/77), Salish cognate: Colville-Okanagan /c'áɬ-t/ *cold (weather)* and /c'ʔáɬ/ *get cold* besides /c'áɬ-ɬ-t/ *cold, frozen* and /(s-)c'áɬ-t/ *cold weather* M87:14-17, 302; Shuswap /(x-)c'éɬ/ *to get cold* and /c'éɬ-t/ *cold* K74:177.

<**sth'áth'elh**>, strs //s=θ'ɛ́[=C_1ə=]ɬ//, WETH /'*it is cool [of weather], (be) cool (of a place)*'/, (<**s=**> *stative*), (<**=R1=**> *resultative*), phonology: reduplication, syntactic analysis: adjective/adjectival verb, attested by Elders Group (6/28/78), IHTTC (9/1/77, 9/19/77), example: <**sth'áth'elh te íkw'elò.**>, //s=θ'ɛ́[=C_1ə=]ɬ tə ʔí=k'ʷə=là//, /'*It's cool here.*'/, attested by Elders Group.

<**th'ólhem**>, mdls //θ'ɛ[=Aá=]ɬ=əm//, ABDF /'*(cold (of a person) or get cooled down, get cold)*'/, (<**ó-ablaut**> *resultative or durative*), possibly <**=em**> *get, have, intransitivizer*, possibly <**=em**> *middle voice*, phonology: ablaut, syntactic analysis: intransitive verb, attested by Elders Group (7/23/75), Salish cognate: Samish dial. of NSt (VU) /c'áɬəŋ/ and (LD) /θ'áɬŋ/ *cold (of weather)* G84a:89 and (VU) /s-c'áɬ-ŋ/ *a cold* G84a:76, Squamish /c'úɬ-um/ *be cold, feel cold* W73:63, K67:280, 277.

<**th'ólhem sq'óq'ey**>, cpds //θ'ɛ[=Aá=]ɬ=əm s=q'á[=C_1ə=]y//, ABDF ['*(have/get) a head cold*'], literally /'get durative cold sickness'/, (<**s=**> *nominalizer*), (<**=R1=**> *continuative*), phonology: ablaut, reduplication, syntactic analysis: nominal phrase with modifier(s), attested by Elders Group (7/23/75).

<**th'óth'elhem**>, rsls //θ'ɛ[=Aá=C_1ə=]ɬ=əm//, ABDF /'*be chilled (of a person), got cold (of a person)*'/, (<**ó-ablaut**> *durative*), (<**=R1=**> *resultative*), phonology: ablaut, reduplication, syntactic analysis: intransitive verb, adjective/adjectival verb?, attested by AC (8/4/70, 8/13/70. 10/1/71), Salish cognate: Squamish /c'ú-c'uɬ-um/ *be cold, feel cold* W73:63, K67:280; found in <**th'óth'elhemtsel.**>, //θ'ɛ[=Aá=C_1ə=]ɬ=əm-c-əl//, /'*I'm chilled.*'/, attested by AC (10/1/71).

<**th'álhethet**>, pcrs //θ'ɛ́ɬ=əT-ət//, ABFC ['*cool oneself off*'], (<**=et**> *purposeful control transitivizer*), (<**-et**> *reflexive, oneself*), syntactic analysis: intransitive verb, attested by IHTTC (9/19/77).

<**th'ólhethet**>, durs //θ'ɛ[=Aá=]ɬ=əT-ət//, pcrs, ABFC ['*cool oneself*'], (<**ó-ablaut**> *durative*), (<**=et**> *purposeful control transitivizer*), (<**-et**> *reflexive*), phonology: ablaut, syntactic analysis: intransitive verb, attested by IHTTC (7/8/77).

<**th'elhílésem**>, mdls //θ'ɛɬ=íləs=əm or θ'ɛ[=Aə=]ɬ=íləs=əm//, ABFC ['*cools one's chest inside*'], FOOD ['*(have?) a cool drink*'], possibly <**e-ablaut**> *derivational*, lx <**=íles**> *in the chest*, (<**=em**> *middle voice*), phonology: possible vowel-reduction, possible ablaut, updrifting on penultimate syllable maybe automatic before <**=em**> *middle voice*, syntactic analysis: intransitive verb, nominal??, attested by IHTTC (7/8/77).

<**th'elhqéylem or th'elhqílem ~ th'elhqílém**>, mdls //θ'ɛɬ=qəl=íl=əm or θ'ɛ[=Aə=]ɬ=qəl=íl=əm//, FOOD ['*have a cool drink*'], literally /'get oneself cool in the throat'/, possibly <**e-ablaut**> *derivational*, lx <**=eqel ~ =qel**> *in the throat*, (<**=íl**> *come, go, get, become*), (<**=em**> *middle voice*), phonology: syllable-loss (el before =íl), optional updrifting, syntactic analysis: intransitive verb, attested by IHTTC (9/1/77, 9/19/77).

<**th'álhethet**>, ABFC ['*cool oneself off*'], *see* th'álh.

<**th'ám**>, ABFC ['*chew*'], *see* th'a.

<**th'à:m ~ th'ám**>, free root //θɛ̀·m ~ θ'ɛ́m or θ'ɛ́=m//, WATR /'*to go down (of water), subside (of water), the tide goes out or down, (be going out (of tide)* [BJ])'/, possibly <**=m**> *intransitivizer, have, get*, syntactic analysis: intransitive verb, attested by CT, AC (12/7/71 Story of the Flood), EB, also <**ts'ám**>, //c'ɛ́m//, also /'*tide went out*'/, attested by Deming (5/6/76), also /'*be going out (of tide)*'/, attested by BJ (12/5/64), example: <**le th'ám.**>, //lə θ'ɛ́m//, /'*The tide went down.*'/, attested by EB (3/9/76), <**qe yálhs'es le th'à:m.**>, //qə yɛ́ɬ-s-ʔ-əs lə θ'ɛ̀·m//, /'*Then the water goes down (low water*

after June)'/, attested by CT (6/8/76), <**tl'esésu le th'ám te qó:.**>, //ƛ'ə-s-əs-əw lə θ'ɛ́m tə qá·//, /'*And so the water went down (of flood water)*'/, attested by AC (12/7/71 Story of the Flood), <**esésu le th'à:m.**>, //ʔə-s-əs-əw lə θ'ɛ̀·m//, /'*Then it went down (the flood water subsided).*'/, attested by AC (12/7/71), <**le th'à:m te sq'ém:el.**>, //lə θ'ɛ̀·m tə s=q'ə́m=məl//, [4lə 4θ'ɛ̀·m 5tə 4sq'ə́m:1əl], /'*The tide is going out.*'/, phonology: typical intonation pattern is shown by the numbers before each syllable, attested by BJ (12/5/64 checked in new transcript, old p.290).

<**Th'ámxwelqs**>, df //θ'ɛ́m=xʷ=əlqs//, PLN ['*west fork of stream which goes into Chehalis River above Páléxel*'], possibly root <**th'ám**> *go out (of water)*, possibly <**=xw**> meaning uncertain, lx <**=elqs**> *on the point, on the nose*, syntactic analysis: nominal, attested by EL (with NP and EB)(Chehalis place names trip 9/27/77), source: place names reference file #302.

<**sth'eméxwelets**>, df //s=θ'əmə́xʷ=ələc or s=θ'ɛm=ə́xʷ=ələc//, LAND ['*point of land at the end of an island*'], WATR, (<**s=**> *nominalizer*), possibly root <**th'am**> *water goes down or subsides*, possibly <**=xw ~ =éxw**> meaning uncertain, lx <**=elets**> *on the bottom, on the end (of an island), stern (of canoe)*, phonology: vowel-reduction, syntactic analysis: nominal, attested by Elders Group (4/2/75).

<**Sth'eméxwelets**>, df //s=θ'ɛm(=)ə́xʷ=ələc//, PLN ['*west or downriver end of Seabird Island*'], literally /'point of land at the end of an island'/, syntactic analysis: nominal, attested by AK (8/30/77), source: place names reference file #254, also <**Th'émexwlats**>, //θ'ɛ[=Aə́=]m=əxʷ=lɛc//, also /'*tail of Seabird Island where Dan Thomas used to live*'/, attested by CT (10/15/73).

<**th'á:m ~ ts'á:m**>, ABFC ['*chewing*'], *see* th'a.

<**th'amawéstel or th'emawéstel**>, HHG /'*soapberry beater, stick for whipping up soapberries or Indian ice cream*'/, *see* th'ím ~ th'í:m.

<**th'áq ~ ts'áq**> **or** <**ts'éq ~ th'éq**>, bound root //θ'ɛ́q ~ c'ɛ́q or c'ə́q ~ θ'ə́q// *skinned, bare, scraped*, comment: there might ultimately be two roots here which with time have become confused with each other, more comparative evidence is needed to prove whether one or two exist.

<**ts'áq**>, possibly root //c'ɛ́q or c'ə[=Aɛ́=]q//, ABDF /'*scrape where skin comes off, skinned*'/, possibly <**á-ablaut**> *resultative or durative*, phonology: possible ablaut, syntactic analysis: intransitive verb, attested by BHTTC (10/21/76), Salish cognate: Squamish /c'áq/ *become bald, lose all fur*, comment: the Squamish form would lead us to expect Halkomelem th'áq, contrast <**th'óqw-eleqw**> *bald-headed*, also <**ts'éq**>, //c'ə́q or c'ɛ[=Aə́=]q//, also /'*bare, skinned off*'/, possibly <**é-ablaut**> *resultative or durative*, phonology: possible ablaut, attested by Elders Group (7/6/77).

<**th'eqeláx̱el**>, ds //θ'əq=əlɛ́x̣əl or θ'ɛq=əlɛ́x̣əl//, ABDF ['*skinned elbow*'], literally /'skinned on the arm'/, lx <**=eláx̱el**> *on the arm*, phonology: possible vowel-reduction, syntactic analysis: adjective/adjectival verb, nominal??, attested by BHTTC (10/21/76).

<**th'qó:lthel**>, ds //θ'əq=á·lθəl or θ'ɛq=á·lθəl//, ABDF ['*skinned knee(s)*'], literally /'skinned on the knee'/, lx <**=ó:lthel**> *on the knee*, phonology: vowel-loss, syntactic analysis: adjective/adjectival verb, nominal??, attested by BHTTC (10/21/76).

<**ts'qó:ls**>, df //c'q=á·ls//, LAND /'*bald rock, bare rock*'/, possibly root <**θ'ə́q ~ c'ə́q**> *bald, bare, skinned*, lx <**=ó:ls**> *spherical object, rock, fruit*, phonology: vowel-loss, syntactic analysis: nominal?, adjective/adjectival verb?, attested by HP visiting in BHTTC (10/21/76).

<**Ts'qó:ls**>, df //c'(ə)q=á·ls//, PLN /'*village on the site of Hope, modern Hope, B.C.*'/, literally /'bare rock'/, ASM ['so named because most rocks in the Fraser River by Hope are bare of moss, there were pit-houses where now Tel-teyit Park and campground are'], syntactic analysis: nominal,

attested by SP and AK (7/13/75), PDP (Katz Class 10/5/76), Elders Group (7/6/77), AD and AK (American Bar Trip 6/26/78), source: place names reference file #17, source: Wells 1965 (lst ed.):25.

<**th'á:q**>, possible root //θ'ɛ·q// or stem <**th'á:**> //θ'ɛ·// meaning uncertain

<**sth'á:qel**>, df //s=θ'ɛ·q=əl or s=θ'ɛ·=qəl//, EB /'*cattail, cattail rush or reed, (bulrush [AC, BJ])*'/, ['*Typha latifolia*'], ASM ['ready to harvest in July, used for mats sewn with special long wooden needles and mat-creasers, flat reeds in contrast to wṓ:l *bulrush* which was used for the same purpose but less commonly, the mats were used as mattresses, rolled and used as pillows, put on walls as insulation, and hung between families in the longhouse for privacy, they were also carried and used for roof and walls of mat shelters for camping in summer'], (<**s=**> *nominalizer*), root meaning unknown unless th'áq *skinned*, possibly <**=el**> *go, come, get, become*, possibly <**=qel**> *on the head*, syntactic analysis: nominal, attested by AC, BJ (5/10/64, 12/5/64), Deming (4/10/80), also /'*bulrush*'/, attested by AC, BJ (12/5/64).

<**th'áq'em**>, WATR /'*be dripping, (have) continuous dripping, water dropping*'/, *see* th'q'ém ~ th'eq'ém.

<**th'át**>, ABFC ['*chew s-th*'], *see* th'a.

<**th'átx̲em ~ ts'átx̲em**>, df //θ'ɛt=x̣=əm ~ c'ɛt=x̣=əm//, SD /'*(have) clinking (of glass or dishes or metal), (have) tinkling sound (of glass, ice in glass, glasses together)*'/, semantic environment ['of glass, dishes, metal, ice, probably stone'], (semological comment: pre-contact work with stone and stone tools would have provided occasions for use besides use with ice (if the sound applies to stone), stone tools have been unused for so long that this application of the word may not readily come to mind), root meaning unknown unless related to th'ó:t *pull out a nail*, probably <**=x̲**> *distributive*, (<**=em**> *have, get, intransitivizer*), phonology: sound symbolism of initial th'-?, syntactic analysis: intransitive verb, attested by Elders Group (12/15/76), compare <**th'á:tsem**> *rattle, jingle, toll, peal.*

<**Th'áth'ele**>, PLN ['*heart-shaped mountain on the CN (south) side of the Fraser River east of Mt. Cheam*'], *see* th'á:lá ~ th'ála ~ th'á:le ~ th'ále.

<**th'áth'ewem**>, TAST ['*to be tasteless*'], *see* th'áwém ~ th'áwem.

<**th'áth'iyekw**>, df //θ'ɛ[=C_1ə=]y(=)əkʷ or C_1ɛ=θ'iyəkʷ//, EFAM ['*(be/get) really worried*'], possibly <**=R1=**> *resultative*, possibly <**R7=**> *augmentative or resultative*, phonology: reduplication, syntactic analysis: intransitive verb, attested by Deming (6/15/78), contrast <**th'ó:yx̲wem**> *nervous, excited*, compare (perhaps) <**th'eth'íkw'thet**> *get frightened*, compare <**th'á:ykwem**> *squeak (of a mouse)*, contrast <**sth'íkwem**> *tiny slivers of fir bark* which seems unrelated, contrast <**th'íth'ekwem**> *prickly (from fir bark), have an allergic reaction (to fir bark for ex.), irritant* which seems unrelated, Salish cognate: perhaps Squamish root /cík'ʷ ~ cək'ʷ/ *be frightened, startled* as in /cík'ʷ-iʔn/ *be frightened, startled* and /cəck'ʷ-ít/ *frighten (tr.)* W73:108, K69:275, 273.

<**th'áth'iyekwémet**>, iecs //θ'ɛ[=C_1ə=]y(=)əkʷ=əməT//, EFAM ['*(be/get) worried about s-o*'], (<**=(e)met**> *indirect effect non-control transitivizer*), phonology: reduplication, secondary stress, syntactic analysis: transitive verb, attested by Deming (6/15/78), example: <**atsel th'áth'iyekwémethome.**>, //ʔɛ-c-əl θ'ɛ[=C_1ə=]y(=)əkʷ=əməT-amə//, /'*I was worried about you.*'/, attested by Deming.

<**th'áth'iyekwémet**>, EFAM ['*(be/get) worried about s-o*'], *see* th'áth'iyekw.

<**th'á(:)ts or th'éts**>, bound root //θ'ɛ(·)c or θ'ə́c *rattle, jingle, ring, peal*//.

<**th'á:tsem**>, izs //θ'ɛ·c=əm ~ θ'ɛc=əm or θ'ə[-Aɛ(·)-]c=əm//, SD /'*to rattle (of dishes or anything else loose), jingle (of money or any metal shaken), peal or toll (of a bell), make the sound of a bell, to ring (of a bell, telephone, in the ears)*'/, comment: another way of giving the meanings is:, SD ['*to*

rattle'], semantic environment ['of dishes or anything else loose'], SD ['*to jingle*'], semantic environment ['of money or any metal shaken'], SD /'*to peal, to toll, make the sound of a bell*'/, semantic environment ['of a bell'], SD ['*to ring*'], semantic environment ['of a bell or phone, or in the ears'], (semological comment: it may be that these should all be *continuative*, i.e., *rattling, jingling, pealing, tolling, making the sound of a bell, ringing* since based on the Squamish cognate with root schwa and Upriver Halkomelem th'étst *ring s-o up*, th'á(:)tsem may have á(:)-ablaut *continuative* and just have been mistranslated above without -ings), (**<=em>** *intransitivizer, have, get*), comment: =em not *middle voice* since it can precede body-part suffixes; found in th'atsemá:lí:ya *ringing in the ear*, phonology: sound symbolist of initial th'-?, possible ablaut, syntactic analysis: intransitive verb, attested by Elders Group (7/27/75, 11/10/76), EB (2/9/76), Salish cognate: Squamish /c'ə́c'-iʔn/ *jingle, tinkle* W73:153, K69:54, example: **<th'átsem kw'el q'ő:l.>**, //θ'ə[-Aɛ́-]c=əm k'ʷ-əl q'ʷó·l//, /'*My ears are ringing.*'/, literally /'my ear rings'/, attested by Elders Group (11/10/76), comment: the example sentence shows a continuative translation, but the alternate way of saying the same thing using **<tám>** *shout* also does and is not a continuative form, also **<tám kw'el q'ő:l.>**, //tɛ́m k'ʷ-əl q'ʷó·l//, also /'*My ears are ringing.*'/, literally /'my ear shouts/yells/hollers'/, attested by Elders Group (11/10/76), **<th'átsem tí:ltel>**, //θ'ə[-Aɛ́-]c=əm tí·l=C_1əC_2//, /'*Jingle Bells (name of song)*'/, attested by Elders Group, DF, EB.

<th'atsemá:lí:ya>, ds //θ'ə[-Aɛ-]c=əm=ɛ́·lí·yɛ//, SD ['*(have) ringing in the ear*'], ABDF, lx **<=á:lí:ya>** *in the ear*, syntactic analysis: intransitive verb, attested by Elders Group (11/10/76).

<th'étsàls>, sas //θ'ə́c=ɛ̀ls//, SD /'*ringing, phoning*'/, (semological comment: -ing here is probably not continuative here and may reflect the structured activity part of the activity, both the root and suffix seem to be clearly *non-continuative*, also see the non-continuative th'étst just below), (**<=áls>** *structured activity non-continuative*), phonology: downstepping, syntactic analysis: intransitive verb, attested by Elders Group (6/1/77).

<th'étst>, pcs //θ'ə́c=T//, SD /'*ring s-o up, phone s-o*'/, (**<=t>** *purposeful control transitivizer*), syntactic analysis: transitive verb, attested by Elders Group (6/1/77).

<th'á:tsem>, SD /'*to rattle (of dishes or anything else loose), jingle (of money or any metal shaken), peal or toll (of a bell), make the sound of a bell, to ring (of a bell, telephone, in the ears)*'/, *see* th'éts or th'á(:)ts.

<th'atsemá:lí:ya>, SD ['*(have) ringing in the ear*'], *see* th'éts or th'á(:)ts.

<th'áwém ~ th'áwem>, izs //θ'ɛ́w=əm//, WATR /'*be fresh (of water), be tasteless*'/, TAST, (**<=em>** *intransitivizer, have, get*), phonology: possible updrifting, syntactic analysis: adjective/adjectival verb, attested by DC (Elders Group 3/26/80), Salish cognate: Squamish /c'áwam/ *fresh (about water)* W73:108, K67:279, also **<th'á:wem>**, //θ'ɛ́·w=əm//, also /'*clear (of water), fresh (of water)*'/, attested by EB (5/25/76), example: **<th'á:wem qó:>**, //θ'ɛ́·w=əm qá·//, /'*fresh water*'/, attested by EB, others.

<th'áth'ewem>, df //θ'ɛ́[=C_1ə=]w=əm//, TAST ['*to be tasteless*'], (**<=R1=>** *resultative or continuative*), phonology: reduplication, syntactic analysis: adjective/adjectival verb, attested by DC and others (Elders Group 3/26/80).

<th'áx̱>, bound root //θ'ɛ́x̣ *scald*//.

<th'áx̱et>, pcs //θ'ɛ́x̣=əT//, WATR /'*to scald s-th/s-o, burn s-th/s-o [with hot liquid]*'/, ABDF, FOOD, HARV, (**<=et>** *purposeful control transitivizer*), syntactic analysis: transitive verb, attested by EB (2/27/76).

<th'á:x̱ey ~ th'áx̱ey>, ds //θ'ɛ́(·)x̣=əy//, EB /'*grass scalded and bleached white for basketry imbrication (designs), sometimes called white straw grass, probably blue-joint reed-grass*'/, ['probably *Calamagrostis canadensis*'], ASM ['used for cedar-root basket designs, ready for harvest in May and early June even before it flowers, grows in the river, is cut when pliable and green, soaked in boiling water (scalded) then dried on the roof (or elsewhere) for several days in the sun which bleaches it white, the stems when split and re-wet are woven into patterns on the outside of cedar root baskets, reddish-brown and black parts of the design are made by (resp.) plain and dyed/stained bitter cherry bark, Susan Peters with Agnes Kelly, Amelia Douglas and I went to a location by Hatzic Lake to harvest some, we scalded and bleached it at Coqualeetza and it was later used in basketry classes, identified from a sample by graduate students in the University of Victoria herbarium, this identification also seeming likely to Nancy Turner (the sample lacked the flower which would have made identification easier)'], literally /'scald bark'/, lx <**=ey ~ =á:y**> *bark, covering*, syntactic analysis: nominal, attested by AC, Deming (6/21/79), SP, AK, AD, others, other sources: ES /θ'ɛ́·x̣əy/ *white grass for basketry imbrication*, Salish cognate: Squamish /c'áx̣iʔ/ *white grass* W73:288, K69:55 and more specifically *blue-joint reed-grass (Calamagrostis canadensis)* Turner and Bouchard 1976:46-47 where a Sechelt cognate is also quoted, /c'áx̣i/.

<**ts'á:yas te th'á:x̲ey**>, cpds //c'ɛ́·yɛ-s tə θ'ɛ́·x̣=əy//, EB ['*reed canary-grass*'], ['*Phalaris arundinacea*'], literally /'relative of deceased spouse of scald-bark (blue-joint reed-grass)'/, ASM ['sample identified by Nancy Turner who noted it is hard to tell from reed-grass and used a magnifying glass to do so, the same sample was identified in Halkomelem by an elder who also called it (unprompted) "grass of canaries", the grass was apparently introduced after contact from Eurasia, at first glossed by elders as "grass that looks like th'á:x̲ey"'], (<**-s**> *third person possessive*), syntactic analysis: nominal phrase with modifier(s), attested by LJ via AD (6/18/79).

<**th'áx̲et**>, WATR /'*to scald s-th/s-o, burn s-th/s-o [with hot liquid]*'/, *see* th'áx̲.

<**th'á:x̲ey ~ th'áx̲ey**>, EB /'*grass scalded and bleached white for basketry imbrication (designs), sometimes called white straw grass, probably blue-joint reed-grass*'/, *see* th'áx̲.

<**th'á:ya**>, //θ'ɛ́·yɛ//, KIN ['*relative of deceased spouse*'], see also duplicate entry under stem **ts'á:ya**.

<**ts'á:ya**>, possibly root //c'ɛ́·yɛ or c'ɛ́·y=ɛ or c'ɛ́·=iyɛ//, KIN /'*relative of deceased spouse, mother/brother/sister/cousin/relative of deceased husband, dead spouse's relative or sibling, daughter-in-law if son dies*'/, possibly root <**ts'á:**> *on top of*?, possibly <**=iya**> *affectionate diminutive*, possibly <**=a**> *living thing*, phonology: possible vrmg, syntactic analysis: noun, nominal, attested by AC (11/16/71), LJ via AD (6/16/79), IHTTC (7/25/77), other sources: ES /c'ɛ́·yɛ/ *deceased spouse's relative*, Salish cognate: Squamish /č'áyayʔ/ *deceased spouse's sibling or cousin* K67:321, Samish dial. of NSt /č'é·y'ə/ *spouse of deceased sibling* G86a:79, also <**th'á:ya**>, //θ'ɛ́·yɛ//, attested by CT (6/8/76), example: <**ts'á:yas te th'áx̲ey**>, //c'ɛ́·yɛ-s tə θ'ɛ́x̣=əy//, /'*reed canary grass*'/, attested by LJ via AD (6/18/79).

<**ts'its'á:ya**>, pln //C_1í=c'ɛ́·=iyɛ//, KIN ['*in-laws or relatives when the connecting link dies*'], (<**R4=**> *plural*), (irregular), phonology: reduplication, syntactic analysis: noun, nominal, attested by AC (11/16/71), also <**th'ith'á:ya**>, //C_1í=θ'ɛ́·yɛ//, also /'*all the relatives (in-laws) of one's deceased husband*'/, attested by EB (6/9/76).

<**th'áyá:m**>, ds //θ'ɛ́yɛ=əm//, KIN ['*to marry a sibling of one's deceased spouse*'], (<**=em**> *middle voice or intransitivizer/have/get*), phonology: vowel merger, syntactic analysis: intransitive verb, attested by EB (12/18/75), Salish cognate: Squamish /č'áyayʔ-m/ *marry deceased spouse's sibling or cousin* K67:321, Lushootseed /č'ájajəb/ *inherit* H76:106, Samish dial. of NSt /č'éy'eŋ/ *to marry spouse of deceased sibling* G86a:79.

<**th'áyá:m**>, KIN ['*to marry a sibling of one's deceased spouse*'], *see* ts'á:ya.

<**th'á:ykwem**>, mdls //θ'ɛ́·ykʷ=əm//, SD ['*squeak (of a mouse)*'], ABFC, (<**=em**> *middle voice*),

syntactic analysis: intransitive verb, attested by Elders Group (5/14/80), compare **<th'áth'iyekw>** *really worried*, compare (perhaps) **<th'eth'íkw'thet>** *get frightened*, compare (perhaps) **<th'ó:yx̲wem>** *nervous, excited.*

<th'eth'elá:ykwem>, dmpv //C_1ə=θ'[-əl-]ɛ·ykʷ=əm//, SD ['*squeaking (of lots of mice)*'], ABFC, (**<R5=>** *diminutive*), (**<-el->** *plural*), phonology: reduplication, infixed plural, syntactic analysis: intransitive verb, attested by Elders Group (5/14/80).

<th'á:ykw'em>, ABFC ['*twitching*'], *see* th'iykw'.

<th'ékwa>, us //θ'ə́kʷɛ//, EB /'*mountain fern with a wide top (used by flower shops), probably spiny wood-fern*'/, ['probably *Dryopteris austriaca*'], possibly **<=a ~ =e>** *living thing*, syntactic analysis: noun?, nominal, attested by Elders Group (2/19/75), Salish cognate: Klallam <tsáqwa> and Lushootseed (Green River or Muckleshoot dial.) <tsṓkwi> and Cowlitz <ts'kwai> *Dryopteris dilatata* (Hoffm.) Gunther 73:14, Squamish /c'ə́kʷaʔ/ *spiny wood-fern (Dryopteris austriaca)* Turner and Bouchard 1976:16-17 where they also report Mainland Comox /θ'ə́kʷu/ *Athyrium filix-femina* and Mt. Currie Lillooet /c'ə́kʷa/ *Dryopteris austriaca* from their earlier work.

<th'èkwetselsxó:s>, NUM ['*seventy dollars*'], *see* th'ó:kws.

<th'èkwetselhsxá>, NUM ['*seventy*'], *see* th'ó:kws.

<th'ekwòls>, NUM ['*seven fruit in a group or cluster (as they grow on a plant)*'], *see* th'ó:kws.

<th'ekwsále>, NUM ['*seven people*'], *see* th'ó:kws.

<th'ekwsáleqel>, NUM ['*seven containers*'], *see* th'ó:kws.

<th'ekwsálh>, NUM ['*seven times*'], *see* th'ó:kws.

<th'ekwselsxá:le>, NUM ['*seventy people*'], *see* th'ó:kws.

<th'ekwsíws>, NUM ['*seven birds*'], *see* th'ó:kws.

<th'ekw' ~ th'íkw'>, possibly root //θ'ək'ʷ ~ θ'ík'ʷ *sore (pain as in an open sore)*//, comment: perhaps related to or confused with th'ekw *to prickle*?.

<sth'eth'íkw'>, dnom //s=θ'ə[=C_1ə=Aí=]k'ʷ//, ABDF /'*a sore, open sore(s)*'/, (**<s=>** *nominalizer*), possibly **<=R1=>** *resultative*, (**<í-ablaut>** *durative*), phonology: reduplication, ablaut, syntactic analysis: nominal, attested by EB (6/14/76), Elders Group (9/10/75), Salish cognate: probably Lushootseed (Skagit) /ʔəs-č'əq'ʷ-il/ *open sore, filth* and (non-Skagit) /č'íq'ʷil/ *filth, infection, dirt, dirty* derived from root /č'(i)q'ʷ/ as in /č'q'ʷíl/ *become rotten, decay* H76:111, 115, possibly Squamish /č'íʔx̣/ *sore, sensitive, tender* W73:243, K69:68, historical/comparative detail: historically ts' /c'/ and qw' /q'ʷ/ would be expected in Halkomelem or /c'/ and /k'ʷ/ in Lushootseed but neither is attested, except by some Chilliwack speakers in a derived word, ts'qw'í:wíyelhp *swamp gooseberry, prickly swamp current*--see below under th'kw'íwíyelhp; but also notice the variation in the Squamish form (if related) which may be due to the cognate of Halkomelem =**x̲** *distributive*; (if that is so, the root in Proto-Central Salish may have been *č'iy or *č'iʔ).

<sth'ekw'th'ékw'>, pln //s=C_1əC_2=θ'ə́k'ʷ//, ABDF /'*lots of sores,* (possibly) *rash*'/, (**<R3=>** *plural*), phonology: reduplication, syntactic analysis: nominal, attested by NP (10/26/75), EB (6/14/76).

<Xwth'kw'ém>, ds //xʷ=θ'ə́k'ʷ=ə[=M2=]m//, PLN ['*medicine spring on the Fraser River beach about a half mile above (north) of the American Bar beach*'], ASM ['the distance from American Bar is also given as a quarter mile and a mile or two, but we hiked to it along the beach and half a mile seems more correct, in 1977 there was reported to be a sandbar there, so beach conditions change, probably it was usually reached by canoe'], literally /'place for sore in the vagina'/, Elder's comment:

"so named because bathing in the creek cured sores", (<**xw=**> *in the vagina*), root <**th'ékw'**> *sore (pain from an open sore)*, (<**=em**> *place for*), (<**metathesis**> *derivational*), phonology: metathesis, syntactic analysis: nominal, attested by AD and AK (Trip to Five-Mile Creek 4/30/79), IHTTC (7/8/77 prob. from MP via AD and SP), SP and AK (Fish Camp 8/2/77), AK and AD (Trip to American Bar 6/26/78 water too high to reach the spring), source: place names reference file #36.

<**th'kw'íwel**>, ds //θ'ək'ʷ=íwəl//, ABDF /'*(have) hemorrhoids, (have) open sores on genitals or rump*'/, lx <**=íwel**> *on the inside, in the anus, in the rump*, syntactic analysis: intransitive verb?, nominal??, attested by Elders Group (9/10/75).

<**th'kw'íwíyelhp**>, ds //θ'ək'ʷ=íwəl=əɬp//, EB /'*prickly swamp currant, swamp gooseberry*'/, ['*Ribes lacustre*'], literally /'hemorrhoid plant'/, MED ['*the bush is used in a tea as hemorrhoid medicine*'], ASM ['the berries are tasty and can be dried, the thorns are poisonous like devil's club thorns'], lx <**=elhp**> *plant*, phonology: el→íy before =elhp automatically, syntactic analysis: nominal, attested by Elders Group (9/10/75), also <**th'qw'í:wíyelhp**>, //θ'əq'ʷ=í·wəl=əɬp//, attested by Elders Group (date unrecorded), also <**ts'qw'í:wíyelhp**>, //c'əq'ʷ=í·wəl=əɬp//, dialects: *some Chill.*, attested by Elders Group (same unrecorded date), also <**th'qw'ó:wú:lhp**>, //θ'əq'ʷ=i[=Aá·=]w(əl)=ə[=Aú·=]ɬp//, phonology: ú:-ablaut and ó:-ablaut unusual together, dialects: *some Tait*, attested by Elders Group (same unrecorded date), also <**th'kw'ó:wú:lhp**>, //θ'ək'ʷ=i[=Aá·=]w9(əl)=ə[=Aú·=]ɬp//, (<**ó:-ablaut and ú:-ablaut**> meaning uncertain), phonology: ú:-ablaut and ó:-ablaut unusual together, attested by CT (Elders Trip to Mt. Baker 9/3/75).

<**th'ékw'**>, probable bound root //θ'ə́k'ʷ//, meaning unknown

<**sth'ékw'**>, ds //s=θ'ə́k'ʷ//, EZ /'*worm, bug*'/, ['probably class *Arthropoda*'], (<**s=**> *nominalizer*), root meaning unknown, syntactic analysis: nominal, attested by AC, Elders Group (6/11/75, 8/25/76), Deming, other sources: ES /sθ'ə́kʷ/ *worm*, Salish cognate: Squamish /s-c'ə́k'ʷ/ *worm* W73:293, K67:286, Lushootseed /s-c'ə́k'ʷ/ *worm (generic), bug* H76:67, example: <**le thíyqwtes kw'e sth'ékw'.**>, //lə θíy=qʷ=T-əs k'ʷə s=θ'ə́k'ʷ//, /'*He dug for worms.*'/, attested by AC, <**qéx̱ te sth'ékw'.**>, //qə́x̣ tə s=θ'ə́k'ʷ//, /'*(There's) a lot of worms.*'/, attested by AC.

<**sth'ékw's te téméxw**>, cpds //s=θ'ə́k'ʷ-s tə tə́mə́xʷ//, EZ ['*earthworm (esp. the most common introduced in B.C.)*'], ['esp. *Lumbricus terrestris*'], literally /'its worm the earth, worm -of the earth'/, (<**-s**> *third person possessive; of*), syntactic analysis: nominal phrase with modifier(s), attested by Deming (2/7/80).

<**sth'ékw'oye**>, dmn //s=θ'ə́k'ʷ=ayə//, EZ ['*little bug*'], (<**s=**> *nominalizer*), lx <**=oye ~ =ó:ya ~ =iya**> *affectionate diminutive*, syntactic analysis: nominal, attested by Deming Evening Class (5/18/78).

<**th'íth'kw'**>, dmn //C_1í=θ'(ə)k'ʷ//, EZ /'*runt of litter, smallest pup or kitten or animal in litter*'/, literally /'little worm'/, (<**R4=**> *diminutive*), phonology: reduplication, vowel-loss, syntactic analysis: noun, nominal, dialects: *Chill.*, attested by IHTTC (8/23/77).

<**th'íth'kw'oya**>, dmn //C_1í=θ'ək'ʷ=ayɛ//, EZ /'*runt of litter, smallest pup or kitten or animal in litter*'/, literally /'dear little tiny worm'/, lx <**=oya**> *diminutive*, phonology: reduplication, vowel-loss, syntactic analysis: noun, nominal, dialects: *Cheh.*, attested by IHTTC (8/23/77).

<**th'ith'kw'ó:y**>, dmn //C_1í=θ'(ə)k'ʷ=á·y(ə)//, EZ ['*smallest of a litter or family*'], HAT, (<**R4=**> *diminutive*), lx <**=ó:ye**> *affectionate diminutive*, phonology: reduplication, vowel-loss (twice), syntactic analysis: noun, nominal, attested by IHTTC (8/23/77).

<**th'akw'ó:y**>, dmn //θ'ə[=Aɛ=]k'ʷ=á·y(ə)//, EZ ['*smallest of a litter or family*'], HAT, possibly <**a-ablaut**> *diminutive or derivational*, lx <**=ó:ye**> *affectionate diminutive*, phonology: ablaut,

syntactic analysis: noun, nominal, attested by IHTTC (8/23/77).

<th'eth'ekw'íwetem>, df //C_1ə=θ’ək’^{w}=íwəl=əT=əm//, ABDF /'*have worms, he got worms*'/, possibly **<R5=>** *resultative*, lx **<=íwel>** *in the insides*, possibly **<=t>** *purposeful control transitivizer*, possibly **<=em>** *intransitivizer, have, get*, phonology: reduplication, syllable-loss of el before =et, syntactic analysis: intransitive verb, attested by JL (with NP and Deming, Fish Camp 7/19/79), example: **<th'eth'ekw'íwetem te (stl'ítl'eqelh, siyóylexwelh).>**, //C_1ə=θ’ək’^{w}=íw(əl)=əT=əm tə (s=C_1í=ƛ’əq=əɬ, s=yá[=C_1ə=]ləx^w=əɬ).//, /'*The (child, old person) has worms.*'/, attested by JL.

<th'elétsxel>, ANA /'*heel, (both heels)*'/, *see* th'éts.

<th'el'á:ltel>, MED ['*heart medicine (of any kind)*'], *see* th'á:lá ~ th'ála ~ th'á:le ~ th'ále.

<th'elhílésem>, ABFC ['*cools one's chest inside*'], *see* th'álh.

<th'elhqéylem or th'elhqílem ~ th'elhqílém>, FOOD ['*have a cool drink*'], *see* th'álh.

<th'em>, perhaps from <th'om> //θ’am// *bone*

<th'eth'emí:l>, df //θ’a[=C_1ə=]m=í·l or θ’ə[=C_1ə=]m=í·l or C_1ə=θ’əm=í·l//, DESC /'*thin (of material like a dress, also of a string)*'/, CLO, WV, root meaning unknown unless <th'om> *bone*, possibly **<=R1= or R5=>** *resultative or continuative*, (**<=í:l>** *come, go, get, become*), phonology: reduplication, syntactic analysis: adjective/adjectival verb, attested by EB (2/9/76).

<th'eth'emí:lstexw>, caus //θ’ə[=C_1ə=]m=í·l=sT-əx^w//, DESC /'*make it thin (of dough, etc.)*'/, FOOD, (**<=st>** *causative control transitivizer*), (**<-exw>** *third person object*), phonology: reduplication, syntactic analysis: transitive verb, attested by EB (2/9/76).

<th'emeláx̲el>, ANA /'*point of elbow, arm bone*'/, *see* hth'b.txt.

<th'émtel>, PE /'*soapberry spoon, soapberry paddle, short-handled spoon, flat spoon for sx̲wõsem*'/, *see* th'ím ~ th'í:m.

<Th'emth'ómels>, PLN /'*Granite Mountain, the second mountain back of X̲óletsa, northwest of Kwelkwelqéylem*'/, *see* th'óméls.

<th'emxweláx̲el>, ANA /'*an elbow, elbow (the name of it)*'/, *see* hth'b.txt.

<th'ép> from <path'> //pɛ[=Aə́=]θ’=M2// from //pɛθ’// *have animal odor/stink*

<sth'épeq>, df //s=pɛ[=Aə́=]θ’=M2=əq//, EZ ['*striped skunk*'], ['*Mephitis mephitis spissigrada*'], ASM ['the skunk predicts "spring fever" because in December or so it lets out a different smell, baby striped skunks have a different name, they have white spots mixed with black (this may be the spotted skunk as well as baby striped skunk), they squeak'], MED ['*skunk oil is medicine for earache (EF)*'], (**<s=>** *nominalizer*), probably root **<páth'>** as in **<pápeth'em>** *have animal stink, have body odor*, possibly **<é-ablaut>** *durative*, possibly **<metathesis>** *derivational*, lx **<=eq>** *on the penis, male*, phonology: ablaut, metathesis of consonants, syntactic analysis: nominal, attested by AC, BJ (5/10/64, 12/5/64), AK (11/21/72), Elders Group (3/29/79), EF (Deming 9/21/78), ME (11/21/72), other sources: ES /sθ’ə́pəq/ *striped skunk*, JH /sθə́pəq/ *skunk*, Salish cognate: Shuswap /s-c’ípəq/ *skunk* K74:177, for the root connection also suggestive are Samish dial. of NSt /pəpəc’ín/ *skunk* and /pc’é=ŋ=sət/ *get body odor* G86a:66, and possibly Sechelt /p’álac’/ *skunk* T77:9, contrast **<selíléx̲>** *spotted skunk (Spilogale gracilis latifrons), baby striped skunk (Mephitis mephitis spissigrada)*, example: **<emímel sth'épeq>**, //ʔəmíməl s=pɛ[=Aə́=]θ’=M2=əq//, /'*small skunk (with its stripes)*'/, attested by ME (11/21/72), **<slós te spú'amels te sth'épeq ?>**, //s=lás-s tə s=púʔ=ɛməl-s tə s=pɛ[=Aə́=]θ’=M2=əq//, /'*skunk oil*'/, literally /'oil of the stink-sac of the skunk'/, attested by EF (Deming 9/21/78).

<sth'íth'peq>, dmn //s=C_1í=θ’əpəq//, EZ ['*little skunk*'], (**<R4=>** *diminutive*), phonology:

reduplication, syntactic analysis: nominal, attested by AK (11/21/72).

<**S'épek ~ Í'pek ~ S'í'pek**>, dmn //s=Aʔ=θ'ə́p=əq=F ~ C_1í=Aʔ=θ'ə́p=əq=F ~ s=C_1í=Aʔ=θ'ə́p=əq=F//, [sʔípək ~ ʔíʔpək ~ sʔíʔpək], EZ ['*Skunk (name in story)*'], N, (<**Aʔ=**> (consonant ablaut, replaces following consonant with glottal stop <'>/ʔ/) *derivational or diminutive*), (<**R4=**> *diminutive*), (<**=F**> (fronting of postvelars to velars, i.e., <**q**> → <**k**>, etc.) *diminutive*), phonology: ablaut, ablaut of consonants, metathesis of consonants, reduplication, fronting, syntactic analysis: nominal, attested by AK (11/21/72).

<**th'ép**> or <**th'ip**> or perhaps <**th'ip'**>, root //θ'ə́p// or //θ'ip// or perhaps //θ'ip'// all meaning *shut eyes*

<**th'éplexw**> (or perhaps <**th'ép'lexw**>**)**, ncs //θ'ə́p=l-əxʷ or θ'i[=Aə́=]p=l-əxʷ// or perhaps //θ'i[=Aə́=]p'=l-əxʷ//, ABFC /'*shut one's eyes, close one's eyes, (blink [EB])*'/, possibly <**=l**> *non-control transitivizer, happen/manage to, accidentally*, possibly <**-exw**> *third person object*, (semological comment: the transitivizer is petrified and probably not functional-- see th'eplexwlóxes below *he snaps eyes at me [in anger]*), phonology: /p/ is attested here and in all derivations but cognates in the Cowichan dialect of Halkomelem (Island Halkomelem) and in two related languages show /p'/, since /p'/ might be exceptionally hard to hear in this position (/θ'/ being more fortis before it and glottalization being somewhat swallowed before the l) it is possible I have mistranscribed all the attestations, if true th'éplexw and all its derivations should be spelled th'ép'lexw, etc., however it is also possible that Upriver dialects have lost the glottalization of p' here, perhaps influenced by lhép<u>x</u>lexw *blink* which is semantically and phonologically very very similar, syntactic analysis: transitive verb??, attested by Elders Group (2/8/78), Deming (4/13/78), other sources: Cowichan /θ'ə́p'nəxʷ/ *close one's eyes* versus /ɬə́px̣nəxʷ/ blink B74b:58, 55, Salish cognate: Squamish /c'ip'q-áyʔus-m/ *blink eyes, wink* W73:39, K69:55, Lushootseed /c'íp'əl-il/ *close eyes* H76:72, also /'*blink*'/, attested by EB (1/8/76), example: <**éy kw'els totí:lt weth'éplexwàl.**>, //ʔɛ́y k'ʷ-əl-s ta[-C_1ə-]l=í:l=T wə-θ'ə́p=ləxʷ-ɛ̀l//, /'*It's good that I think when I close my eyes., (I'd better be thinking/studying s-th when I close my eyes.)*'/, attested by Deming (4/13/78).

<**th'íth'eplexw**> (or perhaps <**th'íth'ep'lexw**>**)**, cts //θ'í[-C_1ə-]p=ləxʷ// or perhaps //θ'í[-C_1ə-]p'=ləxʷ//, ABFC /'*closing one's eyes, shutting one's eyes*'/, (<**-R1-**> *continuative*), phonology: reduplication, possible deglottalization, syntactic analysis: transitive verb??, attested by Elders Group (2/8/78), EB (1/8/76), *<**th'íth'eplóxes**> rejected, */'he managed to close my eyes'/ rejected by EB, *<**th'íth'eplexw te qélém**> rejected, */'close the eyes'/ rejected by EB, example: <**t'wá í:tet; th'íth'eplexw.**>, //t'wɛ́ ʔí[-·-]tət θ'í[-C_1ə-]p=ləxʷ (or θ'í[-C_1ə-]p'=ləxʷ)//, /'*He must be sleeping; his eyes are closed/he's closed his eyes.*'/, also <**ts'íts'eplexw**>, //c'í[-C_1ə-]p=ləxʷ//(or perhaps //c'í[-C_1ə-]p'=ləxʷ//, also /'*one eye being closed*'/, attested by Elders Group (8/5/76), <**éy kw'els totí:lt weth'íth'eplexwàl.**>, //ʔɛ́y k'ʷ-əl-s ta[-C_1ə-]l=í·l=T wə-θ'í[-C_1ə-]p=ləxʷ-ɛ̀l//, /'*It's good that I think when I close my eyes.*'/, attested by Deming (4/13/78).

<**th'elíth'eplexw ~ ts'elíts'eplexw**> (or perhaps <**ts'elíts'ep'lexw**>**)**, plv //θ'[=əl=]í[-C_1ə-]p=ləxʷ or θ'[=əl=]í[-C_1ə-]p'=ləxʷ ~ c'[=əl=]í[-C_1ə-]p'=ləxʷ//, ABFC ['*lots of eyes being closed*'], EB ['*Japanese wineberry*'], ['*Rubus phoenicolasius*'], ASM ['delicious sticky red berries resembling red blackcaps, rare, prob. gone wild from gardens, the leaves are twisted closed till just before the berries ripen, then they open, thus the Halq'eméylem name, species introduced by non-Indians, some grow near Laidlaw, they are called Japanese wineberries in English because the flowers before opening look like Japanese eyes'], (<**=el=**> *plural*), phonology: reduplication, infixed plural, syntactic analysis: transitive verb??, attested by Elders Group (8/25/76, 3/24/76), AK, Vaughn Jones.

<**th'épth'eplexw**> (or perhaps <**th'ép'th'ep'lexw**>, plv //θ'ə́p=C_1əC_2=ləxʷ or

θ'i[=Aə́=]p'=C₁əC₂=ləxʷ//, ABFC /'*shutting one's eyes repeatedly, (blinking [EB])*'/, (<**=R2**> *plural or characteristic*), phonology: reduplication, possible ablaut, syntactic analysis: transitive verb??, attested by Elders Group (7/8/78), also /'*blinking*'/, attested by EB (1/8/76).

<**th'éplexwlexw**> (or perhaps <**th'ép'lexwlexw**>), ncs //θ'ə́p=ləxʷ=l-əxʷ or θ'i[=Aə́=]p'=ləxʷ=l-əxʷ//, ABFC ['*snap one's eyes at s-o [in anger or disgust]*'], EFAM, (<**=l**> *non-control transitivizer*), (<**-exw**> *third person object*), phonology: possible ablaut, syntactic analysis: transitive verb, attested by MV and EF (Deming Evening Class 4/27/78); found in <**th'eplexwlóxes.**>, //θ'əp=ləxʷ=l-áxʸ-əs//, /'*He snaps eyes at me.*'/, attested by MV, EF.

<**th'ép'oyeqw ~ th'épeyeqw**>, df //θ'ə́p'=ay(=)əqʷ ~ θ'ə́p=əy(=)əqʷ//, EB /'*hull of berry (inside left after the berry is picked), "stem" or base of berry left after the berry is picked*'/, probably root <**th'ép' ~ th'ép**> *close/shut an eye*?, possibly <**=ey**> *bark*, possibly <**=eqw**> *on top of the head*, syntactic analysis: nominal, attested by Elders Group (7/9/75, 3/1/76).

<**th'éplexwlexw**> (or perhaps <**th'ép'lexwlexw**>), ABFC ['*snap one's eyes at s-o [in anger or disgust]*'], *see* th'éplexw (or perhaps th'ép'lexw).

<**thepth'epéy**> (probably sic for either <**thepthepéy**> or <**th'epth'epéy**>), DESC /'*curdled*'/, FOOD, root meaning uncertain, <**=R2 or =C1eC2**> *characteristic, inherent continuative*, possible lexical suffix =**éy**, phonology: reduplication, syntactic analysis: adjectival verb, (attested by RG,EH 6/16/98 to SN, edited by BG with RG,EH 6/26/00)

<**thepth'epéy t'át'ets'em sqemó**>, FOOD *yogurt* (lit. curdled + sour + milk), (attested by RG,EH 6/16/98 to SN, edited by BG with RG,EH 6/26/00)<**th'épth'eplexw**> (or perhaps <**th'ép'th'ep'lexw**>), ABFC /'*shutting one's eyes repeatedly, (blinking [EB])*'/, *see* th'éplexw (or perhaps th'ép'lexw).

<**th'ép'ayeqw ~ th'épayeqw**>, df //θ'ə́p'(=)ay(=)əqʷ ~ θ'ə́p(=)ay(=)əqʷ//, KIN /'*great great grandparent, great great grandchild, sibling or cousin (up to fourth) of great great grandparent/-child*'/, root meaning unknown, possibly <**=oy(=)eq ~ =iy(=)eqw ~ =ey(=)eqw**> meaning uncertain but used with ancestors and descendants beyond three generations, syntactic analysis: nominal, attested by Elders Group (7/9/75), AC (8/15/70, 9/29/71), other sources: ES /θ'ə́p'ayàqʷ/ (CwMs /θ'ə́p'ayəqʷ/) *great great great grandparent or -grandchild* beside /ʔə́kʷəyəqʷ/ (=CwMs) *great great grandparent or -grandchild*, H-T <tsō'piyuk·> (macron over i) *great great grandparent or -child* beside <ō'kwiuk·> (macron over i) *great great great grandparent or -child*, Salish cognate: Squamish (LM) /c'əp'-iʔə́qʷ/ *great great grandparent or -child* beside /həkʷ-iʔə́qʷ/ *great great great grandparent or -child* K67:277, 373, these glosses are reversed as corrections in K69:54, 87, but B78:39 (Bouchard's corrected Classified Word List (largely with LM) has the glosses as in K67, Samish dial. of NSt also has speaker differences, i.e. VU /c'ə́p'ayəqʷ/ and LD /ʔə́kʷiyəqʷ/ for *great great grandparent/-child* beside VU /ʔə́kʷiyəqʷ/ and LD /θ'ə́p'ayəqʷ/ *great great great grandparent/-child* G86a:79, Lushootseed has /ʔəkʷyíqʷ/ *great great grandparent/-child* and /c'əp'yíqʷ/ *great great great grandparent/-child* H76:656, 69; apparently there was instability at least in Proto-Central Salish.

<**th'eth'í:payeqw**>, pln //C₁ə=θ'ə[=Aí·=]p=ayəqʷ or C₁ə=θ'í·p=ayəqʷ//, KIN ['*great great grandchildren*'], (<**R5=**> *plural*), possibly <**í:-ablaut**> *plural*, phonology: reduplication, possible ablaut, syntactic analysis: nominal, attested by AC, example: <**ta th'eth'í:payeqw**>, //t-ɛ C₁ə=θ'ə[=Aí·=]p=ayəqʷ//, /'*your great great grandchildren*'/, attested by AC (11/16/71).

<**th'eqeláxel**>, ABDF ['*skinned elbow*'], *see* th'áq ~ ts'áq or ts'éq ~ th'éq.

<**th'eq'**>, bound root //θ'əq'// *to drip*

<**th'q'ém ~ th'eq'ém**>, izs //θ’ə́q’-M1=(ə)m//, WATR /'*to drip (once), water drops once, a drop of water, a drip*'/, (<**metathesis type 1**> *non-continuative*), (<**=em**> *have, get, intransitivizer*), phonology: metathesis, possible vowel-loss, syntactic analysis: intransitive verb, nominal?, attested by Elders Group (5/28/75), AC, EB (12/15/75), example: <**le th'eq'ém.**>, //lə θ’ə́q’-M1=əm//, /'*It dripped.*'/, attested by AC.

<**th'áq'em**>, cts //θ’ə[-Aɛ́-]q’=əm//, WATR /'*be dripping, (have) continuous dripping, water dropping*'/, (<**á-ablaut**> *continuative*), phonology: ablaut, syntactic analysis: intransitive verb, attested by EB (12/15/75, 4/23/76), AC (8/14/70), IHTTC (9/7/77), also <**th'á:q'em**>, //θ’ə[-Aɛ́·-]q’=əm//, attested by Elders Group (5/28/75), Deming (4/17/80), example: <**th'áq'em te síqetsel.**>, //θ’ə[-Aɛ́-]q’=əm tə síq=əcəl//, /'*The shingles are dripping., The shingles are leaking., (The roof is dripping/leaking.)*'/, attested by EB (4/23/76).

<**th'q'émelets ~ ts'q'émelets**>, ds //θ’ə́q’=M1=əm=ələc//, WATR ['*collected rain-water from a drip*'], literally /'drip on the bottom'/, lx <**=elets**> *on the bottom*, phonology: metathesis, syntactic analysis: nominal, attested by AD (about 1/79).

<**th'q'emelétsem**>, df //θ’əq’=əm=ələ[=´=]c=əm//, WATR ['*collected rain-water drops in a bucket*'], possibly <**=´=**> *derivational*, probably <**=em**> *have, get, intransitivizer*, possibly <**=em**> *place to have/get*, phonology: stress-shift, syntactic analysis: intransitive verb, nominal?, attested by Elders Group (5/28/75).

<**th'eq'mítem**>, durs //θ’əq’=əm=ə[=Aí=]T-əm or θ’əq’=əm=ə[=Aí=]T=əm//, pcs, WATR ['*soaked (right through)*'], (<**=et**> *purposeful control transitivizer*), (<**í-ablaut**> *durative*), probably <**-em**> *passive*, possibly <**=em**> *have/get/intransitivizer*, phonology: ablaut, syntactic analysis: intransitive verb, adjective/adjectival verb?, attested by Elders Group (3/9/77).

<**sth'eqwá:y**>, df //s=θ’əq^{w}(=)ɛ́·y//, EZ /'*trout (any kind), trout (generic)*'/, ['genera *Salvelinus* and *Salmo*'], (<**s=**> *nominalizer*), root meaning unknown unless th'óqw *suck* or th'eqw as in th'eqwélhcha *dirty pond, stagnant water*, possibly <**=á:y**> *bark, covering*, syntactic analysis: nominal, attested by AC (9/10/71).

<**th'eq'mítem**>, WATR ['*soaked (right through)*'], *see* th'q'ém ~ th'eq'ém.

<**th'eqw**>, probable root //θ’əq^{w}//, meaning uncertain unless *dirty, mottled*

<**th'eth'qwá:y**>, pln //C_1ə=θ’əq^{w}=ɛ́·y//, EZ ['*[lot of] trout*'], possible root <**th'eqw**>, meaning uncertain unless *dirty, mottled,* possibly <**=á:y**> *covering,* (<**R5=**> *plural*), phonology: reduplication, syntactic analysis: nominal, attested by Elders Group (3/15/72).

<**th'qwélhcha**>, df //θ’q^{w}=ə́ɬcɛ//, WATR /'*puddle that's always dirty, dirty pond, stagnant pool of water, (it never dries out [AK])*'/, root meaning unknown, lx <**=élhcha**> *unclear liquid*, phonology: vowel-loss in root, syntactic analysis: nominal, attested by AC (11/24/71), also /'*it never dries out*'/, attested by AK (4/7/78 on History Dept. tape 34).

<**Th'qwélhcha**>, df //θ’q^{w}=ə́ɬcɛ//, PLN ['*lake in back of Paul Webster's old place on Hicks Rd. near Jones Creek*'], literally /'dirty pool, stagnant pond'/, syntactic analysis: nominal, attested by LJ and JL (4/7/78 on History Dept. tape #34), comment: note on my file slip says this is a different place than the location given next by Squatets but that it has the same name.

<**Th'qwélhcha**>, df //θ’q^{w}=ə́ɬcɛ//, PLN ['*stagnant water lake or ponds at the downriver end of Skw'átets or Peters Reserve near Laidlaw*'], ASM ['a channel (where the water gets stagnant in dry times) between the island off of the west end of Skw'átets and Skw'átets or Peters Reserve, it exists at low water time, otherwise the Fraser River runs through at high water'], literally /'stagnant pond/pool, dirty pond'/, syntactic analysis: nominal, attested by LJ (in IHTTC 8/15/77), AK (8/30/77 en route home from Raft Trip), source: place names reference file #197, #257,

comment: one of these numbers should be reassigned to the Paul Webster pond also called Th'qwélhcha.

<**th'éqw'ōwelh** ~ (probably **ts'éqw'ōwelh**)>, BSK /*'making a basket, (weaving a cedar root basket)'*/, *see* ts'éqw'.

<**th'és**>, bound root //θ'ə́s *fall down hard*//.

<**th'esét** ~ **th'sét**>, pcs //θ'ə́s-M1=T or θ'ə́s=ə[-M2-]T//, ABFC /*'throw s-o down hard (like a wrestler), tap s-th (a container's bottom) [hard] on something to make the contents settle (like berry basket)'*/, PLAY, SOC, HARV, MC, (<**metathesis type 1**> *non-continuative*), possibly <**metathesis type 2 (less likely)**> *non-continuative*, comment: though shown sometimes as a suffix by placement after the root, metathesis is always an infix since it rearranges sounds within the root, (<**=t**> *purposeful control transitivizer*), phonology: metathesis, possible epenthesis, syntactic analysis: transitive verb, attested by IHTTC, Elders Group (2/6/80).

<**th'esáp**>, ds //θ'əs=ɛ́p//, ABDF [*'slip and fall hard (either a person or something he's carrying)'*], ASM ['like on ice'], lx <**=áp**> *on the thigh(s), (secondarily) on the rump*, syntactic analysis: intransitive verb, attested by IHTTC (8/15/77), AD (3/5/79).

<**th'esth'esélets**>, plv //C_1əC_2=θ'əs=ə́ləc//, ABDF [*'bumping or bouncing hard on the rump'*], semantic environment ['used example of people being driven in a car over a pot-holed road (in getting to a Fraser canyon fish-drying camp)'], (<**R3=**> *plural action*), lx <**=élets**> *on the bottom, on the rump*, phonology: reduplication, syntactic analysis: intransitive verb, attested by Elders Group (Fish Camp 8/2/77), IHTTC (8/15/77).

<**th'eséletst**>, pcs //θ'əs=ə́ləc=T//, ABFC [*'throw s-o down [hard] on the rump'*], SOC, PLAY, lx <**=élets**> *on the bottom*, (<**=t**> *purposeful control transitivizer*), syntactic comment: transitive verb, attested by Elders Group (2/6/80).

<**th'esáp**>, ABDF [*'slip and fall hard (either a person or something he's carrying)'*], *see* th'és.

<**th'esélatel**>, df //θ'əs(=)ə́lɛ=təl//, [θ'ɪsílætəl], HUNT /*'arrow pouch, (a quiver for arrows)'*/, SOC, possibly root <**th'és** ~ **th'is**> *nail, horn, antler*, compare <**th'éstel**> *metal nail*, compare <**th'íset**> *nail it*, compare <**th'ístel**> *animal horn*, possibly <**=éla**> *on the side of the head, on the cheek*, (semological comment: perhaps because arrows in a pouch on the back would brush the cheek or side of the head when carried), comment: =álá *container of* is not likely since it does not have an variant (allomorph) =éla, lx <**=tel**> *something to, device to*, phonology: vowel-reduction, syntactic analysis: nominal, attested by Elders Group (2/19/75).

<**th'eséletst**>, ABFC [*'throw s-o down [hard] on the rump'*], *see* th'és.

<**th'esét** ~ **th'sét**>, ABFC /*'throw s-o down hard (like a wrestler), tap s-th (a container's bottom) [hard] on something to make the contents settle (like berry basket)'*/, *see* th'és.

<**th'éstel**>, BLDG [*'a metal nail'*], *see* th'ís.

<**th'estíyelhp**>, EB [*'poplar'*], *see* th'ís.

<**th'esth'esélets**>, ABDF [*'bumping or bouncing hard on the rump'*], *see* th'és.

<**th'étmel**>, df //θ'ə́t=məl//, ANAF [*'belly fin'*], root meaning unknown unless <**th'át**>*chew s-th* (see root th'a), lx <**=mel**> *part, portion*, syntactic analysis: nominal, attested by Elders Group (4/28/76).

<**th'eth'ám**>, ABFC [*'chewing (gum)'*], *see* th'a.

<**th'eth'át**>, ABFC [*'chewing s-th'*], *see* th'a.

<**th'eth'ekw'íwetem**>, ABDF /*'have worms, he got worms'*/, *see* sth'ékw'.

<**th'eth'elá:ykwem**>, SD ['*squeaking (of lots of mice)*'], *see* th'á:ykwem.

<**th'eth'emí:lstexw**>, DESC /'*make it thin (of dough, etc.)*'/, *see* th'eth'emí:l.

<**th'eth'íkw'thet**>, EFAM ['*get frightened*'], *see* th'íkw' or th'ekw'.

<**th'eth'í:payeqw**>, KIN ['*great great grandchildren*'], *see* th'ép'ayeqw ~ th'épayeqw.

<**th'eth'qwá:y**>, EZ ['*[lot of] trout*'], *see* sth'eqwá:y.

<**th'eth'x̲éyt or th'eth'x̲ít**>, CLO ['*bead*'], *see* th'ex̲ét.

<**th'éts**>, free root //θ'ə́c//, DESC /'*stiff, hard*'/, FOOD ['*too hard to eat*'], ASM ['of bread, biscuit, dried out or undercooked meat'], Elder's comment: "(JL) this word is seldom used", syntactic analysis: adjective/adjectival verb, attested by BHTTC (8/31/76), JL (7/13/79), Elders Group (2/6/80).

<**th'etsét**>, pcs //θ'ə́c-M1=T// or perhaps //θ'ə́c=ə[-M2-]T//, CST /'*to harden (of pitch, wax, etc.), (harden s-th)*'/, (<**metathesis type 1**> *non-continuative*), possibly <**metathesis type 2**> (less likely) *non-continuative*, (<**=t**> *purposeful control transitivizer*), phonology: metathesis, possible epenthesis, syntactic analysis: transitive verb, attested by Elders Group (2/6/80).

<**th'etselétsxel**>, ds //θ'əc=ələ[=´=]c=x^{y}əl or θ'əc=ə́lə[=M2=]c=x^{y}əl//, ANA /'*both heels, two heels, (heel)*'/, literally /'hardened on the bottom of the foot'/, (semological comment: there is nothing to show *plural* in this form so it may just mean *heel*, the translations may have been switched with the next term which has an =el= *plural* infix), lx <**=élets**> *on the bottom*, (<**stress-shift or metathesis**> *derivational*), lx <**=xel**> *on the foot, (after another body part suffix) of the foot*, phonology: stress-shift or metathesis, syntactic analysis: nominal, attested by Elders Group (7/27/75, 10/8/75), other sources: ES /sθ'əclə́cx^{y}əl/ (Ms /sθ'əcnə́cx^{y}ən/, Cw /sθ'əcnə́cšən/) *heel*.

<**th'elétsxel**>, df //θ'[=əl=]ə́c=x^{y}əl//, ANA /'*heel, (both heels)*'/, literally /'hardened plural on the foot'/, (semological comment: the translations probably were switched with the previous term, both of which were obtained at the same meetings, another difference is that this forms lacks the =eléts *on the bottom* suffix), (<**=el=**> *plural*), lx <**=xel**> *on the foot*, phonology: infixed plural, syntactic analysis: nominal, attested by Elders Group (7/27/75, 10/8/75).

<**sth'í:tsem**>, df //s=θ'ə[=Aí·=]c=əm//, EB, FOOD /'*nut of hazelnut bush, acorn, any nut, walnut, peanut, etc.*'/, literally /'something to get hardened'/, (semological comment: the only edible nut in the Stó:lō area was hazelnut but there were (are?) a few rare stands of garry oak in the area too (on Sumas Mt. and 1.5 mi. north of Yale--at X̲elhálh or Q'alelíktel), the only stands in B.C. except on the Gulf Islands and Vancouver Island (see p'xwélhp garry oak), since sth'í:tsem was extended to any nut, it must have aboriginally applied to garry oak acorns as well, the literal meaning of sth'í:tsem probably refers to the fact that the shell has to harden before the nut is edible), (<**s=**> *nominalizer*), root <**th'éts**> *hardened* (lit. *something to get hardened*, since the shell of nuts has to harden before they are edible; root th'ets, explaination by RG,EH 6/16/98 to SN, edited by BG with RG,EH 6/26/00), probably <**í:=ablaut**> *durative or resultative*, (<**=em**> *have, get, intransitivizer*), phonology: probable ablaut, syntactic analysis: nominal, attested by AC, BJ (12/5/64), AD (6/19/79), other sources: ES /θ'í·cəm/ (CwMs /sθ'ícəm/) *hazel(nut)*.

<**sth'í:tsemelhp**>, ds //s=θ'ə[=Aí·=]c=əm=əɬp//, EB ['*hazelnut tree or bush*'], ['*Corylus cornuta*'], ASM ['the nut is edible by the end of August or early Sept., the wood was sometimes used for crosspieces for wind-drying fish (t'á:ts')--example by AD's parents'], lx <**=elhp**> *tree, plant*, phonology: ablaut, syntactic analysis: nominal, attested by AD (6/19/79).

<**th'etséla**>, df //θ'əc=ə́lɛ//, EZ /'*kingfisher, belted kingfisher*'/, ['*Megaceryle alcyon*'], literally /'(stiff on the side of the head)'/, probably root <**th'éts**> *stiff, hardened*, lx <**=éla**> *on the side of the head*,

(semological comment: referring to the peculiar stiff feathers on the side of its head), syntactic analysis: nominal, other sources: ES /θ’əcə́lə́/ and JH /θ’əcə̀lé·/ and H-T <th'tcila'> (umlaut on a) *kingfisher (Ceryle alcyon)*, Salish cognate: Squamish /c’čəl/ *belted kingfisher (Megaceryle alcyon)* Kennedy and Bouchard 1976:86, W73:154, K67:277, also <**ts'él:e**>, //c’ə́l·ə//, comment: probably mistranscribed from tape for th'tsél:a, attested by Elders Group (3/1/72).

<**th'étsàls**>, SD /*'ringing, phoning'*/, *see* th'éts or th'á(:)ts.

<**th'etséla**>, EZ /*'kingfisher, belted kingfisher'*/, *see* th'éts.

<**th'etselétsxel**>, ANA /*'both heels, two heels, (heel)'*/, *see* th'éts.

<**th'etsét**>, CST /*'to harden (of pitch, wax, etc.), (harden s-th)'*/, *see* th'éts.

<**th'étst**>, SD /*'ring s-o up, phone s-o'*/, *see* th'éts or th'á(:)ts.

<**th'éw**>, free root //θ’ə́w//, DESC /*'be worn out (of clothes for ex.), be old (of clothes), smashed up when dropped, dissolved'*/, possibly <**é-ablaut**> *resultative*, phonology: possible ablaut, syntactic analysis: adjective/adjectival verb, attested by AC (10/23/71), CT (6/8/76), example: <**le th'éw.**>, //lə θ’ə́w//, /*'It's old (of clothes example, in sense of worn out).'*/, attested by AC, <**le th'éw te qwlhíyxel. ~ le th'éx̱ te qwlhíyxel.**>, //lə θ’ə́w tə qʷəɬ=ɛ[=Aí=]y=xʸəl ~ lə θ’ə́x̣ tə qʷəɬ=ɛ[=Aí=]y=xʸəl//, /*'The shoe is worn out.'*/, attested by CT.

<**Th'ewá:lí**>, ds //θ’ə́w=ɛ́·lí//, PLN /*'Soowahlie village (where Sweltzer Creek met Chilliwack River), Soowahlie Reserve near Vedder Crossing'*/, literally /'dissolved people'/, ASM ['so named because the people "dissolved" in a great famine one time and died off'], lx <**=á:lí**> *people*, comment: the suffix seems to be in the Nooksack or Chillawhockwem language (a substratum language comparatively between Nooksack and Halkomelem, spoken until about 1790 in the Chilliwack River valley above Vedder Crossing), Salish cognate to the suffix is Nooksack <=áli> *people, container, (in) a bundle*, perhaps several homophonous suffixes, syntactic analysis: nominal, attested by AC, BJ (12/5/64), Elders Group (1/15/75, 8/24/77), other sources: Wells 1965 (lst ed.):19 <soo-WAH-lihl>, source: place names reference file #178.

<**(Th'ewálí:l)**>, df //θ’əw=ɛ́lí=í·l//, PLN /*'a spring water stream with source at present-day Sardis Park, Soowahlihl'*/, comment: Wells reports it means *large stream that disappeared",* literally perhaps /'go/come to the dissolved people/Soowahlie village'/, possibly <**=í:l**> *go, come, get, become*, phonology: vowel merger, syntactic analysis: nominal, source: Wells (lst ed.):13, <soo-WAH-lihl>.

<**sth'ő̃wsem or sth'éwsem**>, df //s=θ’ə́w(=)əs=əm//, WATR [*'fine little marble-sized pieces of ice'*], ASM ['found on the river in high water at winter, they form around little burls'], (<**s=**> *nominalizer*), root probably <**th'éw**> *dissolve*, possibly <**=es**> *on the face, round object*, possibly <**=em**> *have, get, intransitivizer*, phonology: vowel-loss, syntactic analysis: nominal, attested by IHTTC (9/13/77).

<**th'éxwmet**>, EFAM /*'to pity s-o, feel sorry for s-o'*/, *see* th'íxw ~ th'éxw.

<**th'exwstélémét**>, EFAM /*'ask a favor, ask pity, beseech'*/, *see* th'íxw ~ th'éxw.

<**th'exwstí:lmet**>, possibly /*'(ask for a favor or pity for s-o)'*/, *see* th'íxw ~ th'éxw.

<**th'éxwth'exw**>, EZ /*'osprey, fishhawk'*/, *see* th'íxw ~ th'éxw.

<**th'éx̱**>, free root //θ’ə́x̣//, FIRE [*'go out completely (of fire)'*], WETH /*'worn out (used when quarter moon is nearly invisible), (set (of the sun))'*/, syntactic analysis: intransitive verb, attested by EB (12/15/75), NP (1/20/76), Salish cognate: Squamish /c’ə́x̣/ *be gone (for ex. of moon), consumed*

(burnt, worn out, etc.) K67:278, example: **<th'éx̲w te syó:qwem. ~ ts'éx̲w te syó:qwem.>**, //θ'ə́x̣ʷ tə s=yə[=Aá·=]qʷ=əm. ~ c'ə́x̣ʷ tə s=yə[=Aá·=]qʷ=əm//, */'The sun sets.'/*, comment: probably misspoken or mistranscribed for th'éx̲, attested by Elders Group (4/16/75).

<th'ex̲míl>, df //θ'əx̣=mə[=Aí=]l or θ'əx̣=məl=íl//, FIRE */'(portion not burnt up, burnt or gone out completely portion)'/*, literally /'worn out/gone out/consumed =durative=/become/get =part/portion'/, (**<=mel>** *part, portion*), possibly **<í-ablaut>** *durative*, possibly **<=íl>** *go, come, get, become,* phonology: ablaut or syllable-loss, syntactic analysis: nominal, attested by Deming (3/15/79 incl. SJ, MC, MV, LG).

<th'ex̲míls te sp'ótl'em>, cpds //θ'əx̣=mə[=Aí=]l-s tə s=p'áƛ'=əm//, FIRE [*'cigarette butt'*], literally /'burnt/gone out completely portion of the cigarette/smoke (or) the cigarette/smoke its burnt/gone out completely portion'/, (**<-s>** *third person possessive, its, (his/her/their), of*), attested by Deming.

<th'éx̲>, bound root //θ'ə́x̣ *to sting, to poison*//, comment: possibly related to <th'áx̲et> *scald s-o/s-th*?.

<th'éx̲th'ex̲>, chrs //θ'ə́x̣=C_1əC_2//, EB [*'stinging nettle'*], [*'Urtica dioica'*], literally /'sting/poison =characteristically'/, ASM ['young shoots are snipped in April, boiled usually with one water change and often cooked with bacon now as "Indian spinach" (tastes much much better than spinach cooked this way), the first water is thrown out and the shoots reboiled to get rid of any of the stinging portions, thread, rope and diapers were made from the boiled and dried stem fiber'], (**<=R2>** *characteristic*), phonology: reduplication, syntactic analysis: nominal, attested by AC, others, other sources: ES /θ'ə́x̣θ'əx̣/ *stinging nettle.*

<th'éx̲tel>, ds //θ'ə́x̣=təl//, EZ */'Pacific rattlesnake, (a poison [LG: Chill.])'/*, [*'Crotalus viridus oreganus'*], literally /'something that stings/poisons, device that stings/poisons'/, lx **<=tel>** *something that, device that*, syntactic analysis: nominal, dialects: *some Tait speakers*, attested by Elders Group (8/25/76), AD (Elders Group 6/7/78), Salish cognate: Squamish /c'ə́x̣-tn/ *rattlesnake, poison* W73:211, K67:278, also **<ts'éx̲tel>**, //c'ə́x̣=təl//, dialects: *some Cheh. and Tait speakers*, attested by Elders Group (8/25/76), TG (Elders Group 6/7/78), also **<ts'éx̲tel>**, //c'ə́x̣=təl//, also */'a poison'/*, dialects: *Chill.*, attested by LG (Deming 6/21/79).

<th'ex̲tíyelhp>, ds //θ'əx̣=təl=əɬp//, EB */'"poplar", probably includes black cottonwood and trembling aspen (though trembling aspen is rare in Upriver Halq'eméylem territory)'/*, ASM ['could include white balsam poplar but it apparently does not occur in the Stó:lō area, term could possibly have been extended to include non-native poplars introduced by non-Indians, such as Lombardy poplar'], ['probably genus *Populus*, probably includes Populus trichocarpa and *Populus tremuloides*, could include *Populus balsamifera* but it apparently isn't found in the area, possibly includes non-native *Populus nigra*'], literally /'rattlesnake tree'/, MED [*'so named because its bark was used as medicine for bite of rattlesnake'*], lx **<=elhp>** *tree, plant*, phonology: el → íy before =elhp (regular morphophonemic rule), syntactic analysis: nominal, attested by IHTTC (9/13/77).

<th'ex̲elís>, df //θ'əx̣=əlís//, ABFC [*'showing his/her teeth'*], ASM ['in anger or exertion or when smiling'], root meaning unknown unless metaphorical *poison*, lx **<=elís>** *on the teeth*, syntactic analysis: intransitive verb, attested by Elders Group (8/31/77, 9/13/77), example: **<th'ex̲elís kwses xwlíliyem(s).>**, //θ'əx̣=əlís kʷ-s-əs xʷ=lí[-C_1ə-]y=əm(-s)//, */'(He's) showing his teeth when/as he smiles.'/*, attested by Elders Group (8/31/77), **<th'ex̲elís kwses t'á:yeq'.>**, //θ'əx̣=əlís kʷ-s-əs t'ɛ́·yəq'//, */'(He's) showing his teeth when/as he is mad.'/*, attested by Elders Group (8/31/77), **<th'ex̲elís the Téli.>**, //θ'əx̣=əlís θə tə́li//, */'Tillie is showing her teeth.'/*, attested by Elders Group (8/31/77).

<Th'ex̲elís>, df //θ'əx̣=əlís//, PLN [*'rock above Yale where X̲á:ls gritted his teeth and scratched rocks* *as he duelled with a medicine man across the Fraser*'], ASM ['rock on the west side of the Fraser River near the second railroad tunnel above Yale where the Transformer, X̲á:ls, sat, grimaced, and raked the stone with his nails as he duelled in power with a powerful medicine man sitting across the river at the southern end of X̲elhálh, the marks of the nails of both men can still be seen on both sides of the river'], literally /'showing his teeth, angry with mouth open'/, syntactic analysis: nominal, attested by BHTTC (11/24/76), Elders Group (8/31/77, 9/13/77), source: place names reference file #267.

<**th'ex̲ét**>, possibly root //θ'əx̣ə́t//, LAND /'*gravel, sand smaller than pebbles*'/, syntactic analysis: nominal, attested by AC (10/21/71), Salish cognate: MCx /θáθx̣áy's/ *pebbles*, Pt /θá(ʔa)sx̣ənš or θá(ʔa)sx̣inš/ *stones on beach*, Se /cacx̣íls/ *pebbles* ~ /cácx̣íls/ *gravel*, Sq /c'ə́x̣t/ *gravel beach*, Cw /θ'x̣ə́t/ and Ms /θ'əx̣ə́t/ *fine gravel*, Nk /c'ə́x̣ət/ *fine gravel*, Lm /c'x̣ít/ *beach gravel - sand*, Smb (LD) /θ'x̣ét/ and (VU) /c'x̣ét/ *gravel, pebbles*, Sg /cx̣ét/ (sic for /c'x̣ét/) *to be stony, covered with pebbles, to be in a stony place/beach*, Tw /c'ə́x̣at/ *sand, sand sole (fish)* G88a:cognate set 15, Proto-Central Salish */c'ə́x̣at/ *fine gravel, pebbles, gravelly beach* G82a cognate set 43, G88a cognate set 15.

<**th'eth'x̲éyt or th'eth'x̲ít**>, durs //θ'ə[=C_1ə=]xə[=Aí=]t or C_1ə=θ'əxə[=Aí=]t//, dmn, CLO ['*bead*'], possibly <**=R1=**> *diminutive*, (<**í-ablaut**> *durative*), phonology: reduplication, ablaut, syntactic analysis: nominal, attested by Elders Group (10/1/75), also <**th'ith'x̲éyt or th'ith'x̲ít**>, //C_1í=θ'əxə[=Aí=]t//, (<**R4=**> *diminutive*), attested by EB (1/6/76).

<**th'ex̲míl**>, FIRE /'*(portion not burnt up, burnt or gone out completely portion)*'/, *see* th'éx̲.

<**th'ex̲míls te sp'ótl'em**>, FIRE ['*cigarette butt*'], *see* th'éx̲.

<**th'éx̲tel**>, EZ /'*Pacific rattlesnake, (a poison [LG: Chill.])*'/, *see* th'éx̲.

<**th'ex̲tíyelhp**>, EB /'*"poplar", probably includes black cottonwood and trembling aspen (though trembling aspen is rare in Upriver Halq'eméylem territory)*'/, *see* th'éx̲.

<**th'éx̲th'ex̲**>, EB ['*stinging nettle*'], *see* th'éx̲.

<**th'éx̲w ~ th'óx̲w**>, bound root //θ'ə́x̣ʷ or θ'áx̣ʷ *wash*//, phonology: this root has non-continuative forms with stress on a vowel after the x̲w of the root, Suttles (consonant alternation1984) finds this for a group of roots in Musqueam with shape CəCʷ and assigns the vowels to the suffix (as I did first here), Thompson and Thompson for other Salish languages have found a type of metathesis indicates *non-continuative* (as I have with metathesis type one in this dictionary), the present root could be accounted for in either way but not both, a third alternative would have ablaut indicating *non-continuative* (unlike elsewhere in the dictionary), and a fourth would have CVCV́ root allomorphs (unlike elsewhere in the dictionary).

<**th'ex̲wót**>, pcs //θ'əx̣ʷ=áT or θ'áx̣ʷ-M1=T or θ'əx̣ʷ=ə[=Aá(·)=]T//, PE ['*wash s-th*'], ABFC, possibly <**metathesis**> *non-continuative*, possibly <**ó-ablaut**> *durative*, possibly <**=et or =ót or =t**> *purposeful control transitivizer*, phonology: possible metathesis or allomorph or ablaut, syntactic analysis: transitive verb, attested by AC, other sources: ES and JH /θ'x̣ʷá·t/ *wash*, example: <**th'ex̲wót tel (óqwelets, s'í:les)**>, //θ'əx̣ʷ=ót t-əl (ʔáqʷəlɛc, s=ʔ=í·ləs)//, /'*wash my (back, chest)*'/, attested by AC (11/11/71), <**th'ex̲wót ta lő́wex̲**>, //θ'əx̣ʷ=áT t-ɛ lə́wəx̣//, /'*wash your ribs*'/, attested by AC, <**th'ex̲wót ta sqelxwále**>, //θ'əx̣ʷ=áT t-ɛ s=qəlxʷ=ɛ́lə//, /'*wash your throat, gargle*'/, attested by AC, <**th'ex̲wót q'e éwechxw ts'áyxwtexw.**>, //θ'əx̣ʷ=áT q'ə ʔə́wə-c-xʷ c'ɛ́yxʷ=T-əxʷ//, /'*Wash it but don't dry it.*'/, attested by AC.

<**th'ex̲wá:tsesem**>, mdls //θ'əx̣ʷ=ɛ́·cəs=əm or θ'áx̣ʷ-M1Aɛ́·=cəs=əm//, PE ['*wash one's hands*'], ABFC, possibly <**metathesis type 1 plus á:-ablaut**> *non-continuative*, lx <**=tses**> (or stressed

allomorph? **<=á:tses>** *on the hand*, possibly **<á:-ablaut>** *durative*, (**<=em>** *middle voice*), phonology: metathesis, possible allomorphs, syntactic analysis: intransitive verb, attested by AC (11/11/71), AD (8/80), example: **<tsel th'ex̲wátsesem.>**, //c-əl θ'əx̣ʷ=ɛ́cəs=əm//, /'*I washed my hands.*'/, attested by AD.

<**th'ex̲wélesem**>, mdls //θ'əx̣ʷ=ə́ləs=əm//, PE ['*brush one's teeth*'], ABFC, literally /'wash on one's teeth'/, lx **<=éles>** *on the tooth/teeth*, (**<=em>** *middle voice*), syntactic analysis: intransitive verb, attested by Elders Group (6/1/77), example: **<líchxw th'ex̲wélesem?>**, //lí-c-xʷ θ'əx̣=ə́ləs=əm//, /'*Did you brush your teeth?*'/, checked with AD (8/80), **<th'ex̲wélesemchap tloqá:ys.>**, //θ'əx̣ʷ=ə́ləs=əm-c-ɛp tə=la=qɛ́·ys//, /'*Brush your teeth now (you pl.).*'/, attested by checked with AD (8/80), also PE ['*mouthwash*'] **<alétsa te th'ex̲wílésem>** /'*Where is the mouthwash*?'/, attested by RG & EH (4/10/99 Ling332)(**<í>** sic for **<é>**).

<**th'x̲welwétem**>, mdls //θ'əx̣ʷ=əlwə[-´-]t=əm//, PE ['*wash one's clothes*'], CLO, lx **<=élwet>** *clothes*, (**<stress-shift off of root>** *non-continuative*), (**<=em>** *middle voice*), phonology: stress-shift off root, syntactic analysis: intransitive verb, attested by EB (12/12/75), also **<th'x̲wélwetem>**, //θ'əx̣ʷ=ə́lwət=əm//, also /'*laundry*'/, CLO, attested by EB (12/16/75), example: **<q'é:ywet tel th'x̲wélwetem ~ q'í:(y)wet tel th'x̲wélwetem.>**, //q'í·w=əT t-əl θ'əx̣ʷ=ə́lwət=əm//, /'*hang up my laundry (hang s-th up)*'/, attested by EB (12/16/75).

<**th'éx̲welwetem**>, cts //θ'ə[-´-]x̣ʷ=əlwət=əm or θ'ə́x̣ʷ=əlwət=əm//, PE ['*washing one's clothes*'], CLO, (**<stress-shift onto root or lack of stress-shift>** *continuative*), phonology: possible stress-shift to root, syntactic analysis: intransitive verb, attested by AC (8/24/70), EB (12/12/75).

<**shxwth'éx̲welwetem**>, dnom //sxʷ=θ'ə[=´=]x̣ʷ=əlwət=əm or sxʷ=θ'ə́x̣ʷ=əlwət=əm//, HHG /'*washtub, washing machine*'/, CLO, literally /'something for washing one's clothes'/, (**<shxw=>** *something for*), comment: shxw= with continuative stems again, phonology: possible stress-shift to root, syntactic analysis: nominal, attested by BHTTC (9/1/76).

<**th'ex̲wewíls ~ th'ex̲wwí:ls ~ th'x̲wwí:ls ~ th'x̲wí:ls**>, ds //θ'əx̣ʷ=əwí·ls//, HHG ['*wash the dishes*'], lx **<=ewí:ls>** *dishes*, phonology: optional vowel-loss (in root and suffix), more vowel-loss before long syllables than short ones is a rule frequently applied, optional consonant merger, syntactic analysis: intransitive verb, attested by AD (8/80), EB (12/12/75), MH (Deming 1/4/79); found in **<th'ex̲wewílschexw.>**, //θ'əx̣ʷ=əwíls-c-əxʷ//, /'*Wash the dishes.*'/, attested by AD, **<th'ex̲wí:lslha.>**, //θ'əx̣ʷ=(ə)wí·ls-ɬɛ//, /'*Wash the dishes.*'/, attested by EB, example: **<lí a stl'í kw'as th'ex̲wewíls?>**, //lí ʔɛ s=ƛ'í k'ʷ-ɛ-s θ'əx̣ʷ=əwíls//, /'*Do you want to wash the dishes?*'/, literally /'is it? your want that you subord.nom. wash the dishes'/, attested by AD (8/80).

<**th'óx̲wí:ls**>, cts //θ'ə[-Aá-]x̣ʷ=(ə)wí·ls or θ'ə[-´-]x̣ʷ=(ə)wí·ls//, HHG ['*washing dishes*'], (**<ó-ablaut or stress-shift to root>** *continuative*), phonology: ablaut or stress-shift to root, syntactic analysis: intransitive verb, attested by EB (12/12/75).

<**shxwth'ox̲wewí:ls**>, dnom //sxʷ=θ'ə[=Aa=]x̣ʷ=əwí·ls//, HHG /'*sink, dish-pan*'/, literally /'something for washing dishes'/, (**<shxw=>** *something for*), (**<ó-ablaut>** *continuative*), phonology: ablaut, syntactic analysis: nominal, attested by Elders Group (6/1/77), also **<shxwth'ox̲wewíls>**, //sxʷ=θ'ə[=Aa=]x̣ʷ=əwíls//, attested by BHTTC (9/1/76), AD (8/80), also **<shxwth'ex̲wí:ls>**, //sxʷ=θ'əx̣ʷ=(ə)wí·ls//, also /'*dish-pan*'/, phonology: vowel-loss, consonant merger, attested by MH (Elders Group 1/4/79), also **<shxwth'óx̲wìls>**, //sxʷ=θ'ə[=Aá=]x̣ʷ=(ə)wíls//, also /'*dish-pan*'/, phonology: vowel-loss, consonant merger, downstepping, attested by EB (2/6/76), example: **<alétsa te shxwth'ox̲wewíls?>**, //ʔɛlə́cɛ tə sxʷ=θ'ə[=Aa=]x̣ʷ=əwíls//, /'*Where is the sink/dishpan?*'/, attested by checked with AD (8/80).

<**th'ex̲wíqwem**>, mdls //θ'əx̣ʷ=íqʷ=əm//, PE /'*wash one's hair, wash one's head*'/, ABFC, lx **<=íqw>**

on the hair, on top of the head, (<**=em**> *middle voice*), syntactic analysis: intransitive verb, attested by IHTTC (7/19/77), AD (8/80), EB (3/29/76), example: <**tsel th'ex̲wíqwem.**>, //c-əl θ'əxʷ=íqʷ=əm//, /'*I washed my hair.*'/, attested by checked with AD (8/80).

<**th'ex̲wíwsem**>, mdls //θ'əx̣ʷ=íws=əm//, PE ['*wash one's body*'], ABFC, lx <**=íws**> *on the body,* (<**=em**> *middle voice*), syntactic analysis: intransitive verb, attested by AD (8/80), example: <**tsel th'ex̲wíwsem.**>, //c-əl θ'əxʷ=íws=əm//, /'*I washed my body.*'/, attested by checked with AD (8/80).

<**th'ex̲wó:sem ~ th'ex̲wósem**>, mdls //θ'əx̣ʷ=á(·)s=əm//, PE ['*wash one's face*'], ABFC, lx <**=ó:s ~ =ós ~ =es**> *on the face?,* (<**=em**> *middle voice*), syntactic analysis: intransitive verb, attested by AC (8/24/70, 11/11/71), AD (8/80), example: <**tsel th'ex̲wósem.**>, //c-əl θ'əx̣ʷ=ás=əm//, /'*I washed my face.*'/, attested by checked with AD (8/80).

<**th'éx̲wesèm**>, cts //θ'ə[-´-]x̣ʷ=əs=əm or θ'ə[-´-]x̣ʷ=as=əm//, PE /'*washing one's face, washing his/her face*'/, ABFC, (semological comment: middle voice forms can be used as a third person form without further inflection, thus AC's translation here "washing his face" could even be "He's washing his face.", the subject could also be "she", "it" or "they"), (<**stress shift to root**> *continuative*), lx <**=ó:s ~ =ós ~ =es**> *on the face,* (<**=em**> *middle voice*), phonology: stress-shift, suffix allomorph or vowel-reduction, updrifting, syntactic analysis: intransitive verb, attested by AC (8/24/70), example: <**le th'éx̲wesèm.**>, //lə θ'ə[-´-]x̣ʷ=əs=əm//, /'*He is/was washing his face.*'/, attested by AC.

<**th'x̲woythílem**>, mdls //θ'əx̣ʷ=ayθəl=íl=əm//, incs, PE ['*(go) wash one's mouth out*'], literally /'wash on the lips/jaw go/come/get middle voice (one's own)'/, lx <**=óythel**> *on the lips/jaw,* (<**=íl**> *go, come, get, become, inceptive*), (<**=em**> *middle voice*), phonology: syllable-loss, syntactic analysis: intransitive verb, attested by AD (8/80), example: <**th'x̲woythílemchap.**>, //θ'əx̣ʷ=ayθəl=íl=əm-c-ɛp//, /'*(Go) wash your mouths out (you pl.).*'/, attested by checked with AD (8/80).

<**th'ex̲wqéylem or th'ex̲wqílem**>, mdls //θ'əx̣ʷ=əqəl=íl=əm//, incs, PE ['*(go) wash one's mouth out*'], literally /'wash in the throat/speech go/come/get middle voice (one's own)'/, lx <**=eqel**> *in the throat/speech,* (<**=íl**> *go, come, get, become*), (<**=em**> *middle voice*), phonology: syllable-loss, syntactic analysis: intransitive verb, attested by AD, example: <**th'ex̲wqéylemchap.**>, //θ'əxʷ=əqəl=íl=əm-c-ɛp//, /'*Wash your mouths out (you pl.).*'/, attested by checked with AD (8/80).

<**th'èxwxél:ém**>, mdls //θ'əx̣ʷ=xʸə[-´-]l=əm//, PE ['*wash one's feet*'], ABFC, (<**stress-shift to first syllable after root**> *non-continuative*), lx <**=xel**> *on the foot/feet, on the leg/legs,* (<**=em**> *middle voice*), phonology: stress-shift, updrifting, syntactic analysis: intransitive verb, attested by AC (11/11/71).

<**th'ex̲wá:tsesem**>, PE ['*wash one's hands*'], *see* th'éx̲w or th'óx̲w.

<**th'ex̲wélesem**>, PE ['*brush one's teeth*'], *see* th'éx̲w or th'óx̲w.

<**th'éx̲welwetem**>, PE ['*washing one's clothes*'], *see* th'éx̲w or th'óx̲w.

<**th'éx̲wesèm**>, PE /'*washing one's face, washing his/her face*'/, *see* th'éx̲w or th'óx̲w.

<**th'ex̲wewíls ~ th'ex̲wwí:ls ~ th'x̲wwí:ls ~ th'x̲wí:ls**>, HHG ['*wash the dishes*'], *see* th'éx̲w or th'óx̲w.

<**th'ex̲wíqwem**>, PE /'*wash one's hair, wash one's head*'/, *see* th'éx̲w or th'óx̲w.

<**th'ex̲wíwsem**>, PE ['*wash one's body*'], *see* th'éx̲w or th'óx̲w.

<**th'ex̲wíyelhp**>, df //θ'əx̣ʷ=əl=əɬp or θ'əx̣ʷ=i[=´=]y=əɬp//, EB /'*red-osier dogwood, (also called "red willow" [SJ, EL])*'/, ['*Cornus stolonifera*'], ASM ['has red bark, its white berries are ripe in July'], MED ['*berries or bark tea used to cause vomiting to clean one out (AD), also used for bile trouble (AD) or when training for something athletic or spiritual, for purification and power, also boil the*

bark and drink the tea for eye wash (not applied to the eye?)(JL), red osier dogwood and cascara and Oregon grape roots and spruce roots and a few other things are V.D. medicine (LG)'], possibly root <**th'ex̲w**> *wash, cleanse*, (semological comment: perhaps since the tea washes one out as a purgative), possibly <**=el**> *go, come, get, become*, possibly <**=iy ~ =á:y (normally the stressed allomorph)**> *bark*, possibly <**=´=**> *derivational*?, lx <**=elhp**> *tree, plant*, phonology: el→íy before =elhp (a regular rule) or stress-shift, syntactic analysis: nominal, attested by AD (6/19/79), SJ (Deming 9/21/78), JL (Fish Camp 7/19/79), EL (9/27/77 Chehalis trip), LG (Deming 9/21/78), also /*"red willow"*'/, Elder's comment: "the same plant", attested by SJ, EL.

<**th'ex̲wó:sem ~ th'ex̲wósem**>, PE ['*wash one's face*'], *see* th'éx̲w or th'óx̲w.

<**th'ex̲wót**>, PE ['*wash s-th*'], *see* th'éx̲w or th'óx̲w.

<**th'ex̲wqéylem or th'ex̲wqílem**>, PE ['*(go) wash one's mouth out*'], *see* th'éx̲w or th'óx̲w.

<**th'èx̲wxél:ém**>, PE ['*wash one's feet*'], *see* th'éx̲w or th'óx̲w.

<**th'éyx̲westem**>, caus //c'íyx^{w}=əs=sT=əm//, /θ'íyx^{w}əstəm/, [θ'éyx^{w}əstəm], pass., REL /'*his/her face/their faces are made dry*'/, *see* ts'íyxw ~ ts'éyxw ~ ch'íyxw.

<**th'íkw**>, possibly root //θ'ík^{w} *to prickle*//.

<**sth'íkwem**>, ds //s=θ'ík^{w}=əm//, EB /'*tiny slivers of fir bark, fir bark powder*'/, ASM ['the most salient feature of these in stories and elsewhere is the painful prickly irritating feeling they cause on the skin and especially in the eyes'], literally /'something to have/get prickles'/, (<**s=**> *nominalizer, something to, something that*), (<**=em**> *have, get, intransitivizer* or *middle voice*), syntactic analysis: nominal, attested by BHTTC.

<**th'íth'ekwem**>, rsls //θ'í[=C_1ə=]k^{w}=əm//, TCH /'*prickly (from fir bark, wool, or something one is allergic to), irritant, have an allergic reaction (to fir powder or cedar bark)*'/, (<**=R1=**> *resultative*), (<**=em**> *have/get/intransitivizer/middle voice*), phonology: reduplication, syntactic analysis: adjective/adjectival verb, attested by BHTTC (late Oct. 1976).

<**th'ith'kwimelálews**>, df //θ'i[=C_1ə=]k^{w}=ə[=Ai=]m=əl=ɛ́ləws//, EB ['*big-leaved avens*'], ['*Geum macrophyllum*'], ASM ['plant identified by botanists from a sample, said to be a favorite food of the ruffed grouse'], MED ['*part is rubbed on as a numbing medicine*'], Elder's comment: "called "grouse leaf" by some in English", (semological comment: derivation from skwéth' *ruffed grouse* is possible but circuitous, involving consonant metathesis then diminutive reduplication of the metathesized result which is not attested elsewhere, then application of the remaining suffixes), probably <**=R1=**> *resultative*, probably <**=em**> *have/get/intransitivizer/middle voice*, possibly <**i-ablaut**> *durative*, possibly <**=el**> *go, come, get, become*, lx <**=álews**> *leaf*, phonology: reduplication, ablaut, syntactic analysis: nominal, attested by SJ (Deming (2/10/77), others.

<**th'íkwe**>, free root //θ'ík^{w}ə//, DIR ['*left (of a side)*'], ANA, syntactic analysis: adjective/adjectival verb, attested by AC (8/25/70), other sources: ES /θ'ík^{w}a/ *left (side)*.

<**th'íkwetses**>, ds //θ'ík^{w}ə=cəs//, ANA ['*left-handed*'], lx <**=tses**> *on the hand*, syntactic analysis: adjective/adjectival verb, attested by AC (8/25/70).

<**sth'íkwetses**>, stvi //s=θ'ík^{w}ə=cəs//, ANA ['*(be) left-handed*'], (<**s=**> *stative*), lx <**=tses**> *on the hand*, syntactic analysis: adjective/adjectival verb, attested by AC (10/13/71).

<**sth'íkwe**>, dnom //s=θ'ík^{w}ə//, DIR /'*the left, the left side*'/, ANA, (<**s=**> *nominalizer*), syntactic analysis: nominal, attested by AC (10/13/71), EB (1/6/76), Elders Group, also <**shxwth'íkwa**>, //sx^{w}=θ'ík^{w}ɛ//, also /'*left arm*'/, comment: (perhaps questionable since there is no affix for arm here), attested by DM (12/4/64), <**ta sth'íkwe**>, //t-ɛ s=θ'ík^{w}ə//, /'*your left*'/, attested by AC, example: <**li te sth'íkwes**>, //li tə s=θ'ík^{w}ə-s//, /'*on his left*'/, attested by AC, <**lámchxw ta' sth'íkwe.**>, //lɛ́=m-

c-xʷ t-ɛʔ s=θ'íkʷə//, /'*You go (to your) left.*'/, attested by EB, <**sth'íkwe í:lwelh**>, //s=θ'íkʷə ʔí·lwəɬ//, /'*left side of the body*'/, literally /'left side'/, attested by Elders Group (5/5/75).

<**sth'íkwechís**>, dnom //s=θ'íkʷə=cə[=Aí=]s//, ANA ['*left arm*'], lx <**=ches ~ =tses**> *of the hand*, possibly <**í-ablaut**> *derivational*, phonology: ablaut, syntactic analysis: nominal, attested by Elders Group (9/1/76).

<**sth'ikweláx̲el**>, dnom //s=θ'ikʷ(ə)=əlɛ́x̣əl//, ANAA ['*[left] front leg quarter of deer or other animal*'], lx <**=eláx̲el**> *of the arm*, phonology: vowel-loss in root, syntactic analysis: nominal, attested by Elders Group (9/1/76).

<**sth'ekwe'í:ws**>, dnom //s=θ'ikʷə=ʔí·ws or s=θ'i[=Aə=]kʷəʔ=í·ws or s=θ'ikʷə=í·ws//, ANA ['*left side of the body*'], lx <**=í:ws or ='í:ws**> *of the body*, phonology: epenthetic glottal stop or allomorph of root/suffix, syntactic analysis: nominal, attested by BHTTC (8/30/76).

<**th'í:kwekw ~ th'í:qweqw**>, df //θ'í·kʷ(=)əkʷ ~ θ'í·qʷəqw//, EB ['*blue elderberry*'], ['*Sambucus cerulea*'], ASM ['the berries ripen about August and are cooked and sweetened before eating nowadays'], MED ['*cooked berries are medicine also for constipation*'], possibly root <**th'íkw**> *to prickle* possibly referring to taste, possibly <**=ekw ~ =íkw**> *round*, phonology: possible reduplication, syntactic analysis: noun, nominal, attested by SP and AD (6/27/75), other sources: ES /sθ'ə́kʷəkʷ/ *blue elderberry*, Salish cognate: Lushootseed /c'íkʷikʷ/ *blue elderberry* H76:72, Thompson /c'íkʷukʷ/ *blue elderberry* Turner and Bouchard 1973ms:30, Okanagan /c'kʷíkʷ/ *blue elderberry* from root /c'ákʷt/ *a type of sour taste* Turner, Bouchard and Kennedy 1980:94, also <**sth'ékwekw**>, //s=θ'ə́kʷəkʷ//, attested by AC (11/19/71).

<**th'íkwekwelhp**>, ds //θ'íkʷəkʷ=əɬp//, ['*blue elderberry bush, blue elderberry tree*'], ASM ['often as large as a tree'], lx <**=elhp**> *tree, plant*, syntactic analysis: nominal, attested by Elders Group (3/72), Salish cognate: Okanagan /c'kʷəkʷíɬp/ *blue elderberry tree/bush* Turner, Bouchard and Kennedy 1980:94.

<**th'íkwekwelhp**>, ['*blue elderberry bush, blue elderberry tree*'], *see* th'í:kwekw ~ th'í:qweqw.

<**th'íkwetses**>, ANA ['*left-handed*'], *see* th'íkwe.

<**th'ikwóstel**>, ABFC /'*wink at each other, ((maybe) squint [EB])*'/, *see* th'iykw'.

<**th'íkw' or th'ekw'**>, possibly root //θ'íkʷ or θ'əkʷ *to frighten*//.

<**th'eth'íkw'thet**>, df //θ'ə[=C_1ə=Aí=]k'ʷ=θət or C_1ə=θ'ə[=Aí=]k'ʷ=θət or C_1ə=θ'ík'ʷ=θət//, EFAM ['*get frightened*'], possibly <**=R1= or R5=**> *resultative*, possibly <**í-ablaut**> *durative or resultative*, (<**=thet**> *get, become*), comment: perhaps related to th'ékw *to prickle*??, phonology: reduplication, possible ablaut, syntactic analysis: intransitive verb, attested by Elders Group (3/16/77), compare <**th'áth'iyekw**> *really worried*, Salish cognate: Squamish root /cik'ʷ ~ cək'ʷ/ *be frightened, startled* as in /cík'ʷ-iʔn/ *be frightened, startled* and /cəck'ʷ-ít/ *frighten (tr.)* W73:108, K67:275, 273, historical/comparative detail: irregular correspondence of Sq /c/ to UHk /θ'/, perhaps explained by Halkomelem confusion with similar root th'ékw ~ th'ikw *to prickle*, or glottalization by assimilation, otherwise one would expect UHk /θ/ or Sq /c'/, also note the probably related or confused th'áth'iyekw with a plain kw, more cognates are needed to tell the tale.

<**th'ith'íkw'elexw**>, ncs //C_1í=θ'ík'ʷ=l-əxʷ or C_1í=θ'ə[=Aí=]k'ʷ=l-əxʷ//, EFAM /'*frightened s-o [accidentally], [happened/managed to] frighten s-o*'/, possibly <**R4=**> *diminutive*, possibly <**í-ablaut**> *resultative*, (<**=l**> *non-control transitivizer*), (<**-exw**> *third person object*), phonology: reduplication, possible ablaut, syntactic analysis: transitive verb, attested by IHTTC; found in <**th'ith'íkw'elòx**>, //C_1í=θ'ík'ʷ=l-áxʸ//, /'*frightened me (and made me jump)*'/, attested by IHTTC.

<**th'ikw'ólésem**>, ABFC ['*to wink*'], *see* th'iykw'.

<**th'ikw'ósem**>, ABFC [*'to wink'*], *see* th'iykw'.

<**th'ím ~ th'í:m**>, bound root //θ'ím ~ θ'í·m *lick*//.

<**th'ímet ~ ts'í:met**>, pcs //θ'ím=əT ~ c'í·m=əT//, ABFC [*'lick s-th (with tongue)'*], (<**=et**> *purposeful control transitivizer*), phonology: the ts' may be Thompson influence on the speaker, syntactic analysis: transitive verb, attested by EB (2/27/76, 12/17/75, 3/22/76), Salish cognate: Squamish /c'imʔ-ínʔ/ *lick (tr.)* W73:161, K67:279, K69:54, historical/comparative detail: from the cognate Squamish form Halkomelem should have th'í:met not ts'í:met.

<**th'íth'emet**>, cts //θ'í[-C_1ə-]m=əT//, ABFC [*'licking it'*], (<**-R1-**> *continuative*), phonology: reduplication, syntactic analysis: transitive verb, attested by EB (2/27/76).

<**th'émtel**>, durs //θ'i[=Aə́=]m=təl//, dnom, PE /*'soapberry spoon, soapberry paddle, short-handled spoon, flat spoon for sx̱wṓsem'*/, FOOD, literally /'lick a long time device'/, ASM ['short-handled, flat wooden spoon for licking soapberry froth also known as Indian ice cream, resembles a miniature paddle, each person owned his own and brought it when travelling to likely gatherings, so they were personal effects rather than household goods'], (<**é-ablaut**> *durative*), lx <**=tel**> *device, something to*, phonology: ablaut, syntactic analysis: nominal, attested by Elders Group (4/5/78), IHTTC (9/19/77), TG (4/23/75), also /*'wooden spoon'*/, comment: probably meaning *wooden soapberry spoon* not just any wooden spoon, attested by Elders Group (4/2/75).

<**th'amawéstel or th'emawéstel**>, df //θ'im=ɛwə[=´=]s=təl or θ'i[=Aɛ=]m=ɛwə[=´=]s=təl//, HHG /*'soapberry beater, stick for whipping up soapberries or Indian ice cream'*/, FOOD, ASM ['a stick with fine coiled cedar tied on'], literally /'lick paddle device (or) berry paddle device'/, possibly root <**th'í:m**> *lick* or *berry*?, possibly <**á-ablaut**> *derivational*?, (<**stress-shift**> *derivational*), lx <**=áwes ~ =ṓwes ~ =ōwes**> *paddle* or perhaps <**=áwés**> *basket* (as in <**yemáwéstel**>, //yəm=ɛ́wə́s=təl//, /*'wide cedar root strips for baskets'*/ (compare with <**yem=**> *wide strip)*., lx <**=tel**> *device, something for)*, phonology: stress-shift, possible ablaut, syntactic analysis: nominal, Elder's comment: "unsure of form", attested by IHTTC (9/19/77).

<**ts'its'emá:welh**>, df //c'i[=C_1ə=]m=ɛ́·wəɬ//, EB /*'cottonwood sap, cottonwood cambium'*/, ['sap or cambium of *Populus balsamifera trichocarpa*'], ASM ['licked in the spring as a treat, cambium is a sap-like substance from the inside of peeled bark, it was licked or scraped and eaten fresh'], literally probably /'licking on the dish/vessel/canoe'/, possibly root <**th'í:m**> *lick*, (<**=R1=**> *resultative or continuative*), possibly <**=á:welh ~ =ōwelh**> *canoe, vessel (like feast dish, etc.)*, phonology: reduplication, syntactic analysis: nominal, attested by Elders Group (5/21/75), contrast <**sx̱á:meth**> *cottonwood sap/cambium*.

<**sth'í:m ~ sth'ì:m**>, dnom //s=θ'í·m ~ s=θ'ì·m//, EB /*'berry, berries, (fruit [AC, AD])'*/, (<**s=**> *nominalizer, something to*), probably root <**th'í:m**> *lick*, syntactic analysis: nominal, attested by AC (8/11/70, 10/15/71), BJ (5/10/64 new p.120), DM (12/4/64 new p.191), Elders Group (3/1/72), other sources: ES /sθ'ì·m/ *berry*, also /*'fruit'*/, attested by AC (11/19/71), AD (8/80), also <**sth'ím**>, //s=θ'ím//, attested by MH (Deming 1/4/79), AD (8/80), example: <**sch'á:yxw sth'ì:m**>, //s=c'i[=Aɛ́·=]yxʷ s=θ'ì·m//, /*'dried berries'*/, attested by DM, <**sth'ím sí:tel**>, //s=θ'ím sí·(=)təl//, /*'berry basket'*/, Elder's comment: "unsure, perhaps <**sth'ímàlà**> is better", attested by Elders Group (6/11/75), <**lí a stl'í kw'e sth'ím?**>, //lí ʔɛ s=ƛ'í k'ʷə s=θ'ím//, /*'Do you want some fruit?'*/, attested by AD (8/80).

<**sth'íms te álhqey**>, cpds //s=θ'ím-s tə ʔɛ́ɬqəy//, EB /*'"snakeberry", includes False Solomon's seal, star-flowered Solomon's seal,* and probably *Twisted-stalk (2 spp.)* and *Hooker's fairy bells'*/, ['*Smilacina racemosa, Smilacina stellata,* and probably *Streptopus amplexifolius, Streptopus roseus*, and *Disporum hookerii*'], literally /'berry of the snake'/, ASM ['so named because it is said

that snakes eat the berries'], MED ['*star-flowered Solomon's seal is good for dandruff (AC 11/19/71)*'], (**<-s>** *of* (before following nominal phrase), *third person possessive*), syntactic analysis: nominal phrase with modifier(s), attested by Elders Group (SP, AK esp.), AC (forgot name), contrast **<x̲ex̲q'elá:lhp>** *False Solomon's seal, Twisted-stalk, rosy-flowered twisted stalk, star-flowered Solomon's seal* (lit. "scratching on the side of the head (dandruff) plant").

<sth'ímàlà ~ sth'ímà:la>, ds //s=θ'ím=ɛ̀lɛ̀ ~ s=θ'ím=ɛ̀·lɛ̀//, HARV ['*berry-basket*'], literally /'berry container'/, lx **<=àlà ~ =à:là>** *container, container of*, phonology: possible downstepping, syntactic analysis: nominal, attested by Elders Group (6/11/75 unsure), TG (4/23/75), Elders Group (3/24/76).

<th'í:melhp>, ds //θ'í·m=əɬp//, EB ['*berry plant*'], lx **<=elhp>** *plant*, comment: notice the dropping of the s= *nominalizer*, syntactic analysis: nominal, attested by Elders Group (4/7/76).

<sth'ímiya>, ds //s=θ'ím=iyɛ//, dmn, EZ /'*small (fully grown) coho salmon, [kokanee]*'/, ['small fully grown *Oncorhynchus kisutch*'], literally /'dear little berry'/, ASM ['so named because of the belief that land-locked salmon are in mountain lakes because they develop from a berry that drops into the lake'], lx **<=iya>** *affectionate diminutive*, syntactic analysis: nominal, attested by Elders Group (3/1/72, 9/3/76), also **<th'ímiya>**, //θ'ím=iyɛ//, also /'*baby coho salmon*'/, attested by AG (Elders Group 10/26/77), example: **<x̲à:m te th'ímiya.>**, //x̲ɛ̀·m tə θ'ím=iyɛ//, /'*The baby coho is crying.*'/, Elder's comment: "that's what they say when it rains; the coho is crying because he wants the river higher so he can go upriver to spawn", attested by AG.

<th'í:melhp>, EB ['*berry plant*'], *see* sth'í:m ~ sth'i:m.

<th'ímet ~ ts'í:met>, ABFC ['*lick s-th (with tongue)*'], *see* th'ím ~ th'í:m.

<th'íq>, possibly root //θ'íq//, ABDF ['*(get/have) white spots on the skin*'], ASM ['this happens if one eats sx̲wō̃sem (soapberries) when a widow'], syntactic analysis: intransitive verb, attested by BHTTC (late Oct. 1976).

<th'íq>, possibly root //θ'íq//, EZ /'*red-shafted flicker (woodpecker), medium-sized woodpecker with red under the wing, (pileated woodpecker* [AK] (but this is a large bird), *small red-headed woodpecker [*probably *red-breasted sapsucker,* possibly *hairy woodpecker or downy woodpecker] [Elders Group 3/1/72)*'/, ['*Colaptes cafer cafer* and rarely *Colaptes cafer collaris,* (if large is correct *Dryocopus pileatus* [AK], if small is correct, probably *Sphyrapicus (varius) ruber* or possibly *Dryobates villosus harrisi* and *Dryobates villosus orius* or *Dryobates pubescens* (esp.) *gairdneri* some zoologists replace the genus *Dryobates* with *Dendrocopos*, others with *Picoides*)'], syntactic analysis: noun, nominal, attested by EL (9/15/78), BJ (12/5/64 old p.315), other sources: H-T <tsek·t> (macron over e) *woodpecker (Picus)(medium-sized)* beside <sHak> (umlaut over a) *woodpecker (Picus)(small red-headed)* and <tsu'tEm> *woodpecker (Picus)(small)*, Salish cognate: Squamish /c'íqt/ *common flicker (Colaptes auratus)* Kennedy and Bouchard 1976:86, this ethnozoology is thought to correct /c'íqt/ *black-chested woodpecker, hairy or downy woodpecker* W73:292, K67:281, K69:56, probably related is Shuswap /c'əqʔ-ím/ *to peck* K74:180, also **<th'íq'>**, //θ'íq'//, also /'*pileated woodpecker*'/, (semological comment: identified from photo and description, but pileated woodpecker is a large woodpecker), contrast **<temélhépsem>** *pileated woodpecker*, contrast **<t'ot'epíqselem>** *pileated woodpecker*, attested by AK (Elders Group 9/8/76), also **<th'í:q ~ ts'í:q>**, //θ'í·q ~ c'í·q//, also /'*small red-headed woodpecker* [probably *red-breasted sapsucker,* possibly *hairy woodpecker or downy woodpecker]*'/, contrast **<t'ót'ep'els>** *small red-headed woodpecker, etc.*, contrast **<qw'opxwiqsélem>** *small red-headed woodpecker, etc.*, contrast **<(sxáq')>** *small red-headed woodpecker*, attested by Elders Group (3/1/72), also **<ts'íq ~ ts'íqtàl>**, //c'íq ~ c'íq(=)t(=)ə[=Aɛ́=]l//, also /'*a kind of woodpecker*'/, attested by EL (taped at home by Shirley Leon 3/14/80).

<**th'í:q**>, possibly bound root //θ’í·q//, meaning unknown

<**sth'í:qel**>, df //s=θ’í ·q=əl//, LAND /'*mud, wet mud*'/, (<**s=**> *nominalizer*), root meaning unknown, possibly <**=el**> *go, come, get, become*, syntactic analysis: nominal, attested by BJ (12/5/64), EB (2/20/78), also <**sth'íqel**>, //s=θ’íq=əl//, attested by Elders Group (3/9/77), example: <**tsel mákwlh. tsel welhéleq' la te sth'í:qel.**>, //c-əl mɛ́k^{w}ɬ. c-əl wə=ɬə́l(=)əq’ lɛ tə s=θ’í·q=əl//, /'*I got hurt. I fell splat in the mud.*'/, attested by EB.

<**th'íth'eqel**>, rsls //θ’í[=C_1ə=]q=əl//, LAND ['*muddy*'], FSH ['*gone soft and spoiled (of dried fish)*'], semantic environment ['of fish'], (<**=R1=**> *resultative*), phonology: reduplication, syntactic analysis: adjective/adjectival verb, attested by Elders Group (3/9/77), BHTTC (late Oct. 1976).

<**sth'íth'eqel**>, dnom //s=θ’í[=C_1ə=]q=əl//, LAND ['*mud*'], (<**s=**> *nominalizer*), phonology: reduplication, syntactic analysis: nominal, attested by Elders Group (11/3/76), example: <**lí te sth'íth'eqel**>, //lí tə s=θ’í[=C_1ə=]q=əl//, /'*in the mud*'/.

<**Th'elíth'eqes**>, df //θ’[=əl=]í[=C_1ə=]q=əs//, PLN ['*rock figure near the rocks shaped like a family underwater*'], literally /'many mud faces'/, root probably <**th'íq**> *mud*, possibly <**=el=**> *plural*, possibly <**=R1=**> *continuative or resultative*, possibly <**=es**> *on the face*, phonology: possible reduplication, possible infixed plural, syntactic analysis: nominal, attested by BHTTC (10/21/76).

<**th'í:qw'**>, root, perhaps bound, //θ’í·q’^{w}//, *punch*

<**th'í:qw'et**>, pcs //θ’í·q’^{w}=əT//, SOC /'*punch s-o/s-th, hit s-o/s-th with fist*'/, ABFC, (<**=et**> *purposeful control transitivizer*), syntactic analysis: transitive verb, attested by AC, other sources: ES /θ’íq’^{w}ət/ *hit*; found in <**th'í:qw'etes**>, //θ’í·q’^{w}=əT-əs//, /'*He hits someone (with his fist)., He punches someone.*'/, attested by EB (12/16/75).

<**th'qw'á:lí:ye**>, rsls //θ’(i)q’^{w}=ɛ́·lí·yɛ//, SOC ['*punched on the ear*'], possibly <**stress-shift or vowel-loss in root**> *resultative*, lx <**=á:lí:ya**> *on the ear*, phonology: vowel-loss in root, stress-shift,vowel-reduction by speed on final vowel, syntactic analysis: intransitive verb, attested by Elders Group (3/3/76).

<**th'qw'álewest**>, pcs //θ’(i)q’^{w}=ɛ́lwəs=T//, rsls, SOC ['*punched s-o on the stomach*'], (<**vowel-loss in root or stress-shift**> *resultative*), lx <**=álwes**> *on the stomach*, (<**=t**> *purposeful control transitivizer*), phonology: vowel-loss on root, stress-shift, syntactic analysis: transitive verb, attested by Elders Group (3/3/76); found in <**th'qw'álewestem**>, //θ’q’^{w}=ɛ́lwəs=T-əm//, /'*(he/she got) punched on the stomach*'/.

<**th'qw'élqsel**>, rsls //θ’(i)q’^{w}=ə́lqsəl or θ’q’^{w}=ə́lqs=əl//, SOC ['*punched on the nose*'], (<**vowel-loss in root or stress-shift**> *resultative*), lx <**=élqsel ~ =eqs ~ =elqs ~ =eqsel**> *on the nose*, possibly <**=el**> *go, come, get, become*, phonology: vowel-loss, stress-shift, syntactic analysis: intransitive verb, attested by Elders Group (6/24/76).

<**th'qw'íwet**>, pcs //θ’(i)q’^{w}=íw(əl)=əT//, rsls, SOC ['*punched s-o on the rump*'], (<**vowel-loss in root or stress-shift**> *resultative*), lx <**=íwel**> *in the inside(s), in the rump*, (<**=et**> *purposeful control transitivizer*), phonology: vowel-loss, stress-shift, syllable-loss of el before =et, syntactic analysis: transitive verb, attested by Elders Group (3/3/76).

<**th'qw'ó:s**>, rsls //θ’(i)q’^{w}=á·s//, SOC ['*punched in the face*'], (<**vowel-loss in root or stress=shift**> *resultative*), lx <**=ó:s**> *on the face*, phonology: vowel-loss, stress-shift, syntactic analysis: intransitive verb, attested by Elders Group (6/24/76), EB (3/3/76).

<**th'í:qw'est**>, pcs //θ’í·q’^{w}=əs=T//, SOC /'*hit s-o in the face, punch s-o in the face*'/, lx <**=es**> *on the face*, (<**=t**> *purposeful control transitivizer*), syntactic analysis: transitive verb, attested by EB (12/16/75), also <**th'íqw'est**>, //θ’íq’^{w}=əs=T//, attested by Elders Group (4/16/75); found in <**th'íqw'esthòm.**>, //θ’íq’^{w}=əs=T-àm//, /'*You are punched in the face.*'/, attested by Elders Group.

<**th'ith'qw'óstel**>, rcps //θ’i[=C_1ə=]q’^{w}=ás=T-əl//, cts, pcs, PLAY [*'boxing (the game)'*], literally /'punching each other in the face'/, (<**=R1=**> *continuative*), lx <**=ós**> *on the face*, (<**=t**> *purposeful control transitivizer*), (<**-el**> *reciprocal*), phonology: reduplication, syntactic analysis: intransitive verb, attested by Elders Group (9/14/77), also <**th'ith'qw'iyós**>, //θ’i[=C_1ə=]=iyás//, also /*'boxing*'/, literally /'punching around in a circle'/, lx <**=iyós**> *around in a circle*, attested by SP (IHTTC 9/6/77).

<**th'óleqw'esthòm**>, plv //θ’i[=Aá=lə]q’^{w}=əs=T-àm or θ’i[=Aá=lə=]q’^{w}=sT-àm//, if, SOC [*'you'll get punched all over*'], (semological comment: *on the face* should be added if the suffix is =es, if not this word means all over the whole body), possibly <**ó-ablaut**> *resultative*, (<**=le=**> *plural action*), possibly <**=es**> *on the face*?, possibly <**=sT**> *causative control transitivizer*, (<**-òm**> *passive second person singular*), phonology: ablaut, infixed plural, syntactic analysis: intransitive verb, attested by Deming (5/3/79, SJ esp.).

<**th'ith'qw'iyóls**>, df //C_1í=θ’əq’^{w}=iy(=)áls//, PLAY [*'pool (the game)'*], literally /'little poking spherical object/ball'/, possibly root <**ts'eqw'**> *poke, stab*, (<**R4=**> *diminutive*), lx <**=iyóls ~ =óls**> *spherical object, ball, fruit, rock*, probably <**=iy**> *bark, wool, covering*, probably <**=óls**> *spherical object, fruit, rock, ball*, phonology: reduplication, syntactic analysis: nominal?, intransitive verb?, attested by MH (Deming 9/6/77), compare <**ts'its'kwiyóls**> *playing pool*.

<**th'iqw'élchep or th'iyqw'éltsep**>, HARV /*'chop wood (with an axe), split wood*'/, *see* th'íyeqw' ~ th'íqw'.

<**th'í:qw'est**>, SOC /*'hit s-o in the face, punch s-o in the face*'/, *see* th'í:qw'et.

<**th'ís**>, bound root, //θ’ís// ís perhaps *to tack, to nail*, Salish cognate: Squamish root /c’is/ *be nailed up* as in /c’ís-inʔ/ *nail up (tr.)* and /c’ís-tn/ *horn, antler, nail* W73:182, 144, K67:280, K69:55, Lushootseed root /c’is(i)/ *nailing* as in /c’ísi-d ~ c’ə́s-əd/ *nail it* and /c’ə́s-təd/ *a nail* H76:73.

<**th'íset**>, pcs //θ’ís=əT//, BLDG [*'nail it*'], CSTR, (<**=et**> *purposeful control transitivizer*), syntactic analysis: transitive verb, attested by EB (4/2/76), Salish cognate: Lushootseed /c’ísi-d ~ c’ə́s-əd/ *nail it* H76:73, Squamish /c’ís-inʔ/ *nail up (tr.)* W73:182, K69:55.

<**th'ístel**>, dnom //θ’ís=təl//, ANAH [*'horn of an animal*'], literally perhaps /'something to tack/nail'/, lx <**=tel**> *something to, device*, syntactic analysis: nominal, attested by IHTTC (8/15/77), Elders Group (7/9/75), BJ (12/5/64), Salish cognate: Squamish /c’ís-tn/ *horn, antler, nail* W73:144, K67:280, also <**th'í:stel**>, //θ’í·s=təl//, attested by Elders Group (11/26/75).

<**Ts'ístel**>, dnom //c’ís=təl//, PLN [*'Saddle Rock above Yale*'], literally /'antler'/, ASM ['(in the story of Beaver and Frog) the frog and her four daughters started out (in high water) from Spuzzum; one landed at Ts'ístel (Saddle Rock), one at Ts'ókw'á:m (Five-Mile Creek), one at Q'alelíktel (rock on east side one mile above Yale), one at Peqwchṓ:lthel (American Bar), and the mother landed at We<u>x</u>ésem (Bill Bristol Island, lit. "frog place")', this may be the conclusion of the same story told in Nooksack where Miss Frog rejects the sincere proposal of marriage from Mr. Beaver and insults his body; Beaver or his sons sing a rain song and make the water rise to a flood; Frog is later seen floating down the river calling “Help I'll marry you”, and Beaver says to his sons “Just push her out further in the river”], phonology: perhaps <ts'> from Thompson influence since the place is between Thompson and Stó:lō territory (it has Upriver Halkomelem =tel though not Thompson =ten), syntactic analysis: nominal, attested by AK (Trip to Five-Mile Creek 4/30/79).

<**Xwth'ístel**>, df //x^w=θ’ís=təl//, PLN [*'a place across the Fraser River from the rock named Q'alelíktel*'], ASM ['above Yale'], literally /'always horn (or) horn in the vagina'/, possibly <**xw=**> *always* or possibly <**xw=**> *in the vagina*, syntactic analysis: nominal, attested by TG (IHTTC 8/5/77, 8/8/77), IHTTC (8/23/77), source: place names reference file #188a, 216.

<**Lexwts'ístel**>, ds //ləxʷ=c'ís=təl//, PLN ['*north and south sides of the mouth of Five-Mile Creek*'], Elder's comment: "the name means *always antlers*", ASM ['the mountain above Lexwts'ístel used to have an Indian name (probably a Halkomelem name but possibly Thompson)'], (<**lexw=**> *always*), phonology: ts' instead of th' is irregular unless Thompson influence, syntactic analysis: nominal, attested by AD and AK (Trip to Five-Mile Creek 4/30/79).

<**th'éstel**>, durs //θ'i[=Aə́=]s=təl//, dnom, BLDG ['*a metal nail*'], CSTR, TOOL, literally /'durative horn'/, (<**é-ablaut on root i**> *durative*), phonology: ablaut, syntactic analysis: nominal, attested by IHTTC (8/15/77), Elders Group (7/9/75, 7/27/75).

<**th'estíyelhp**>, ds //θ'i[=Aə́=]s=təl=əɬp//, EB ['*poplar*'], EB /'*"poplar", probably includes black cottonwood and trembling aspen (though trembling aspen is rare in Upriver Halq'eméylem territory)*'/, ASM ['could include white balsam poplar but it apparently does not occur in the Stó:lō area, term could possibly have been extended to include non-native poplars introduced by non-Indians, such as Lombardy poplar'], ['probably genus *Populus*, probably includes Populus trichocarpa and *Populus tremuloides*, could include *Populus balsamifera* but it apparently isn't found in the area, possibly includes non-native *Populus nigra*'], literally /'(metal) nail tree'/ (or perhaps formerly /'horn/antler tree'/, ASM ['probably so named because of its appearance (esp. Lombardy poplar)'], lx <**=elhp**> *tree*, phonology: ablaut, el→íy before =elhp automatically, syntactic analysis: nominal, attested by Elders Group (7/2/75, 7/9/75), contrast <**p'elp'àlq'emá:lews**> *poplar* and <**th'ex̱tíyelhp**> *poplar.*

<**th'íset**>, BLDG ['*nail it*'], *see* th'ís.

<**th'ístel**>, ANAH ['*horn of an animal*'], *see* th'ís.

<**th'íth'ekwem**>, TCH /'*prickly (from fir bark, wool, or something one is allergic to), irritant, have an allergic reaction (to fir powder or cedar bark)*'/, *see* th'íkw.

<**th'íth'emet**>, ABFC ['*licking it*'], *see* th'ím ~ th'í:m.

<**th'íth'eplexw**> (or perhaps **<th'íth'ep'lexw>)**, ABFC /'*closing one's eyes, shutting one's eyes*'/, *see* th'éplexw (or perhaps th'ép'lexw).

<**th'íth'eqel**>, LAND ['*muddy*'], *see* sth'í:qel.

<**th'íth'eqw kúkumels**>, FOOD *relish* (lit. chopped + cucumber), (attested by RG,EH 6/16/98 to SN, edited by BG with RG,EH 6/26/00), *see* th'íyeqw'~ th'íqw'.

<**th'íth'ewel**>, EFAM ['*being annoyed*'], *see* th'íwél.

<**th'íth'exwstélémét**>, SOC /'*begging for a favor, asking for help*'/, *see* th'íxw ~ th'éxw.

<**th'ith'ikwóstel**>, ABFC ['*winking at each other*'], *see* th'iykw'.

<**th'ith'íkw'elexw**>, EFAM /'*frightened s-o [accidentally], [happened/managed to] frighten s-o*'/, *see* th'íkw' or th'ekw'.

<**th'ith'ikw'ósem**>, ABFC ['*winking*'], *see* th'iykw'.

<**th'ith'kwimelálews**>, EB ['*big-leaved avens*'], *see* th'íkw.

<**th'íth'kw'**>, EZ /'*runt of litter, smallest pup or kitten or animal in litter*'/, *see* sth'ékw'.

<**th'ith'kw'ó:y**>, EZ ['*smallest of a litter or family*'], *see* sth'ékw'.

<**th'íth'kw'oya**>, EZ /'*runt of litter, smallest pup or kitten or animal in litter*'/, *see* sth'ékw'.

<**th'ith'lhákw'etem**>, ABFC ['*someone is being pinched*'], *see* th'lhákw'.

<**th'ith'qw'óstel**>, PLAY [*'boxing (the game)'*], *see* th'í:qw'et.

<**th'iwél**>, df //θ'íw=əl or θ'íy=əwəl//, EFAM [*'annoyed'*], see under stem <**ts'íw**> *annoyed, fed up, bored.*

<**th'íth'ewel**>, cts //θ'í[-C_1ə-]w=əl//, EFAM [*'being annoyed'*], see under stem <**ts'íts'ewel**> *bored.*

<**th'íwélmét**>, iecs //θ'íw(=)əl=məT//, EFAM /*'to be fed up [with s-o/s-th], (annoyed with s-o/s-th)'*/, see under stem <**ts'íwélmet**> *annoyed with s-th, annoyed by s-o, tired of s-o.*

<**th'íwélstexw**>, caus //θ'íw(=)əl=sT-əxʷ//, EFAM /*'annoyed s-o, bothered s-o, pestered s-o'*/, see under stem <**ts'íw**> *annoyed, fed up, bored.*

<**th'íwélmét**>, EFAM /*'to be fed up [with s-o/s-th], (annoyed with s-o/s-th)'*/, *see* th'íwél.

<**th'íwélstexw**>, EFAM /*'annoyed s-o, bothered s-o, pestered s-o'*/, *see* th'íwél or ts'íw.

<**th'íwéq'**>, root //θ'íwə́q'//, *red elderberry*

<**sth'íwéq'**>, df //s=θ'íwə́q'//, EB [*'red elderberry'*], [*'Sambucus racemosa'*], ASM ['berries ripen about June and last several months, they are cooked and sweetened before eating'], MED [*'also medicine for constipation'*], (<**s=**> *nominalizer*), syntactic analysis: nominal, attested by AC, BJ (12/5/64), SP and AD (6/27/75), other sources: ES /sθ'íwə́q'/ *red elderberry*, also <**th'íwéq'**>, //θ'íwə́q'//, attested by CT (6/8/76), example: <**lulh me qw'él te sth'íwéq'.**>, //lə=wɬ mə q'ʷə́l tə s=θ'íwə́q'//, /*'The red elderberries are ripe.'*/, literally /'past =already start to/come to be ripe the red elderberry'/, attested by AC, <**le qw'éltem te sth'íwéq'.**>, //lə q'ʷə́l=T-əm tə s=θ'íwə́q'//, /*'The red elderberries are cooked.'*/, attested by AC.

<**sth'íwéq'elhp**>, ds //s=θ'íwə́q'=əɬp//, EB [*'red elderberry bush'*], [*'Sambucus racemosa'*], ASM ['usually about ten feet high'], lx <**=elhp**> *plant, tree*, syntactic analysis: nominal, attested by AC.

<**th'íxw ~ th'éxw**>, bound root //θ'íxʷ ~ θ'ə́xʷ//, comment: historically only the first alternant is correct, th'íxw.

<**th'éxwmet**>, iecs //θ'i[=Aə́=]xʷ=məT//, EFAM /*'to pity s-o, feel sorry for s-o'*/, possibly <**é-ablaut**> *durative or non-continuative*??, (<**=met**> *indirect effect non-control transitivizer*), phonology: possible ablaut, syntactic analysis: transitive verb, attested by Elders Group (2/1/78), TM/DF/TG (Elders Group 3/22/78), EB (3/31/78), Salish cognate: Squamish /c'íxʷ-n/ *help out of trouble (tr.)* K69:55, also <**th'éx̱wmet**>, //θ'i[=Aə́=]x̣ʷ=məT//, attested by NP (9/19/75), also <**ts'éx̱wmet**>, //c'i[=Aə́]x̣ʷ=məT//, attested by Elders Group (2/16/77), also <**ts'éx̱wmet**>, //c'i[=Aə́=]x̣ʷ=məT//, also /*'help s-o'*/, attested by Elders Group (6/4/75); found in <**ts'éx̱wmethòmè**>, //c'ə́x̣ʷ=məT-ámə//, /*'pity you'*/, phonology: downstepping, updrifting, attested by Elders Group (2/16/77), <**ts'ex̱wmethométsel.**>, //c'əx̣ʷ=məT-ámə-c-əl//, /*'I help you.'*/, phonology: automatic stress-shift, attested by Elders Group (6/4/75), example: <**th'exwmetólxwchexw, lálh tstulh tesós.**>, //θ'i[=Aə=]xʷ=məT-álxʷ-c-əxʷ lɛ́-ɬ ct-uɬ tsás//, /*'Pity us, we're getting unfortunate.'*/, usage: prayer to plants, attested by TM/DF/NP (Elders Group 3/22/78), <**ewálhtsel mí:l ámeq't, qetsel (we?) th'éxwmetò.**>, //ʔəwə=əɬ-c-əl mí·l ʔɛ́məq'=T qə-c-əl (wə-)θ'ə́xʷ=məT-à//, /*'I wasn't going to bring him/her back, but I felt sorry for him/her.'*/, attested by EB.

<**th'exwstélémét**>, //θ'ixʷ=sT-ə́lə́mə́t or θ'i[=Aə=]xʷ=sT-ə́lə́mə́t//, EFAM /*'ask a favor, ask pity, beseech'*/, SOC, ASM ['some people would go out in the woods and do this before white religion was introduced, it was the closest pre-contact thing to prayer'], (<**=st**> *causative control transitivizer*), (<**-élémét ~ -lómet**> *reflexive*), syntactic analysis: intransitive verb, attested by Elders Group (2/1/78), NP (9/19/75), TM/DF/TG (Elders Group 3/22/78), example: <**le th'exwstélémét ō siyám.**>, //lə θ'əxʷ=sT-ə́lə́mə́t ʔo s=iy(=)ɛ́m//, /*'Pity us, oh Lord.'*/, usage: prayer for plants, attested by TM/DF/NP, <**lámtsel th'exwstélémét.**>, //lɛ́=m-c-əl θ'əxʷ=sT-ə́lə́mə́t//,

/'*I'm going to ask a favor.*'/, attested by Elders Group (2/1/78).

<**th'íth'exwstélémét**>, cts //θ'í[-C₁ə-]xʷ=sT-ə́lə́mə́t//, SOC /'*begging for a favor, asking for help*'/, EFAM, (<-**R1**-> *continuative*), phonology: reduplication, syntactic analysis: intransitive verb, attested by Elders Group (2/1/78), Salish cognate: closely related is Squamish /c'í-c'ixʷ-numʔ-ut/ *pitiful, to be pitied* W73:199, K69:55, also <**ts'its'exwstélmét**>, //c'i[-C₁ə-]xʷ=sT-ə́lə́mə́t//, attested by Deming (11/11/76).

<**sts'íts'exw**>, strs //s=c'í[=C₁ə=]xʷ//, EFAM ['*(be) considerate*'], (<**s=**> *stative*), (<**=R1=**> *resultative*), phonology: reduplication, either the **ts' > th'** sound change missed this or it was borrowed as a doublet from a neighbor which did not undergo the sound change to th' (Nooksack, Squamish for ex.), syntactic analysis: adjective/adjectival verb, attested by Deming (11/11/76), Salish cognate: Squamish /c'í-c'ixʷ/ *helpful* K69:55.

<**sts'íts'exwtel**>, rcps //s=c'í[=C₁ə=]xʷ-təl//, EFAM ['*(be) considerate of each other*'], (<**-tel**> *reciprocal*), phonology: reduplication, also see comments on stem of this word, above, syntactic analysis: intransitive verb, attested by Deming (11/11/76).

<**th'exwstí:lmet**>, df //θ'əxʷ=sT=ə[=Aí·=]ləmət?//, possibly /'*(ask for a favor or pity for s-o)*'/, possibly <**í:-ablaut**> meaning unclear here, phonology: possible ablaut, syntactic analysis: transitive verb??, intransitive verb?, Elder's comment: "this is a word, EB will check to find out meaning", attested by EB (2/1/78).

<**ts'éx̲wts'ex̲w** (or more correct) **th'éxwth'exw**>, chrs //c'ə́x̣ʷ=C₁əC₂ or θ'ə́xʷ=C₁əC₂//, EFAM ['*pity*'], (<**=R2**> *characteristic*), phonology: reduplication, syntactic analysis: intransitive verb?, nominal??, attested by Elders Group (2/16/77).

<**th'éxwth'exw**>, chrs //θ'ə́xʷ=C₁əC₂//, EZ /'*osprey, fishhawk*'/, ['*Pandion haliaetus*'], literally /'helpful (according to one tradition)'/, (<**=R2**> *characteristic*), phonology: reduplication, syntactic analysis: nominal, attested by AC (11/17/71, 11/26/71), Salish cognate: Squamish /c'íxʷc'əxʷ/ *osprey, fishhawk* derived from root /c'íxʷ/ *help* W73:191, K69:56, Sechelt /sc'íxʷc'ixʷ/ *fishhawk* T77:10, also <**th'éx̲wth'ex̲w ~ ts'éx̲wts'ex̲w**>, //θ'ə́x̣ʷ=C₁əC₂ ~ c'ə́x̣ʷ=C₁əC₂//, attested by Elders Group (2/18/76, 6/4/75).

<**th'iyaméle or th'iyaméla**>, df //θ'iyɛm=ə́lɛ//, ANAH ['*temples (on head)*'], root meaning unknown, lx <**=éla**> *on the side of the head*, syntactic analysis: nominal, attested by IHTTC (8/4/77).

<**th'iykw'**>, bound root //θ'iy(=)k'ʷ *twitch*//.

<**th'á:ykw'em**>, cts //θ'i[-Aɛ́·-]yk'ʷ=əm//, mdls, ABFC ['*twitching*'], (<**á:-ablaut**> *continuative*), (<**=em**> *middle voice*), phonology: ablaut, syntactic analysis: intransitive verb, attested by IHTTC (7/19/77), Salish cognate: possibly Lushootseed /ləcu-cíkʷi-cut/ *twitching* based on root /cíkʷ(i)/ *move, jerk, tug* as also in /cíkʷitəb/ *(a fish) jerked (on the line)* H76:51.

<**th'ikw'ólésem**>, mdls //θ'i(y)k'ʷ=áləs=əm//, ABFC ['*to wink*'], literally /'twitch on one's eye'/, lx <**=óles**> *on the eye*, (<**=em**> *middle voice*), phonology: updrifting, consonant-loss (iyC→iC), syntactic analysis: intransitive verb, attested by EB (12/12/75), LG (Deming 5/8/80), Salish cognate: Squamish /c'íyk'ʷ-in/ *squeeze, pinch (with two fingers)(tr.)* W73:249, K67:281, Sechelt /c'ayk'ʷ-ús-m/ *to wink* T77:36, also <**ts'iykw'ólésem**>, //c'iyk'ʷ=áləs=əm//, dialects: *Sumas/Matsqui*, attested by AH (Deming 5/8/80).

<**th'ikw'ósem**>, mdls //θ'i(y)k'ʷ=ás=əm//, ABFC ['*to wink*'], lx <**=ós**> *on the face*, (<**=em**> *middle voice*), phonology: consonant-loss (iyC→iC), syntactic analysis: intransitive verb, attested by Elders Group (8/25/76).

<**th'ith'ikw'ósem**>, cts //θ'i[-C₁ə-]yk'ʷ=ás=əm//, ABFC ['*winking*'], (<-**R1**-> *continuative*), phonology: reduplication, vowel-raising (əyC→iC), syntactic analysis: intransitive verb, attested

by Elders Group (8/25/76), also <**th'íth'kw'ó:sem**>, //θ'i[-C_1ə-]k'^{w}=á·s=əm//, phonology: vowel-loss more frequent before long syllable, attested by EB (1/8/76), also <**th'ith'ikwósem**>, //θ'i[-C_1ə-]k^{w}=ás=əm//, attested by Elders Group (2/8/78).

<**th'ikwóstel**>, rcps //θ'i(y)k^{w}=ás=T-əl//, ABFC /'*wink at each other, ((maybe) squint [EB])*'/, literally /'twitch on the face at each other on purpose'/, lx <**=ós**> *on the face*, (<**=t**> *purposeful control transitivizer*), (<**-el**> *reciprocal*), phonology: deglottalized form may be variant or error, syntactic analysis: intransitive verb, attested by AC (8/14/70), also /'*(maybe) squint*'/, attested by EB (12/12/75).

<**th'ith'ikwóstel**>, cts //θ'i[-C_1ə-]yk^{w}=ás=T-əl//, rcps, ABFC ['*winking at each other*'], (<**-R1-**> *continuative*), phonology: reduplication, syntactic analysis: intransitive verb, attested by AC (8/14/70).

<**th'íyeqw'**> ~ <th'íqw'>, //θ'íyəq'^{w} ~ θ'íq'^{w}// *to chop.*

<**th'íth'eqw kúkumels**>, FOOD *relish* (lit. chopped + cucumber), (attested by RG,EH 6/16/98 to SN, edited by BG with RG,EH 6/26/00), *see* th'íyeqw'~ th'íqw'.

<**th'íyeqw't**>, pcs //θ'íyəq'^{w}=T//, HARV ['*split it (firewood)*'], FIRE, (<**=t**> *purposeful control transitivizer*), syntactic analysis: transitive verb, attested by IHTTC.

<**th'iyeqw'á:ls**>, sas //θ'iyəq'^{w}=ɛ́·ls//, HARV ['*split firewood*'], FIRE, (<**=á:ls**> *structured activity non-continuative*), syntactic analysis: intransitive verb, attested by IHTTC.

<**th'óyeqw'els**>, cts //θ'i[-Aá-]yəq'^{w}=əls//, HARV ['*splitting firewood*'], FIRE, (<**ó-ablaut**> *continuative*), (<**=els**> *structured activity continuative*), phonology: ablaut, syntactic analysis: intransitive verb, attested by IHTTC.

<**th'iqw'élchep or th'iyqw'éltsep**>, ds //θ'iyq'^{w}=ə́lcəp//, HARV /'*chop wood (with an axe), split wood*'/, lx <**=élchep ~ =éltsep**> *firewood*, phonology: vowel-loss, syntactic analysis: intransitive verb, attested by AC (8/6/70), EB (12/11/75), example: <**lalh th'iqw'éltsep.**>, //lɛ-ɬ θ'iyq'^{w}=ə́lcəp//, /'*Go and split wood.*'/, syntactic analysis: imperative with go, attested by AC.

<**th'iyeqw'á:ls**>, HARV ['*split firewood*'], *see* th'íyeqw'.

<**th'íyeqw't**>, HARV ['*split it (firewood)*'], *see* th'íyeqw'.

<**th'íyx̲westem**>, caus //c'íyx^{w}=əs=sT=əm//, /θ'íyx^{w}əstəm/, [θ'éyx^{w}əstəm], pass., REL /'*his/her face/their faces are made dry*'/, *see* ts'íyxw ~ ts'éyxw ~ ch'íyxw.

<**th'kw'íwel**>, ABDF /'*(have) hemorrhoids, (have) open sores on genitals or rump*'/, *see* th'ekw' or th'íkw'.

<**th'kw'íwíyelhp**>, EB /'*prickly swamp currant, swamp gooseberry*'/, *see* th'ekw' or th'íkw'.

<**th'lhákw'**>, free root //θ'ɬɛ́k'^{w}//, ABFC ['*to pinch*'], syntactic analysis: intransitive verb, attested by EB (2/5/76).

<**th'lhákw't**>, pcs //θ'ɬɛ́k'^{w}=T//, ABFC /'*pinch s-th, pinch s-o (and pull the skin)*'/, (<**=t**> *purposeful control transitivizer*), syntactic analysis: transitive verb, attested by Elders Group (5/26/76), IHTTC (9/2/77), EB (2/5/76); found in <**th'lhákw'etlha.**>, //θ'ɬɛ́k'^{w}=T-ɬɛ//, /'*Pinch him., Pinch her.*'/, phonology: epenthesis, attested by EB, <**th'lhákw'etem.**>, //θ'ɬɛ́k'^{w}=T-əm//, /'*Someone got pinched.*'/, phonology: epenthesis, attested by EB.

<**th'ith'lhákw'etem**>, cts //C_1í-θ'ɬɛ́k'^{w}=T-əm//, if, ABFC ['*someone is being pinched*'], (<**R4-**> *continuative*), phonology: reduplication, epenthesis, syntactic analysis: intransitive verb, passive, attested by EB.

<**ts'elhkw'á:ls**>, sas //c'ɬɛ́k'^{w}-M1=ɛ́·ls//, ABFC ['*pinch*'], (<**metathesis**> *non-continuative*), (<**=á:ls**>

structured activity non-continuative), phonology: metathesis, epenthesis, historical/comparative detail: in most cases of th' ~ ts' in Upriver Halkomelem the th' proves to be historically correct and the ts' either archaic or borrowed, syntactic analysis: intransitive verb, attested by IHTTC (9/2/77).

<**ts'álhkw'els**>, cts //c'ɬɛ[-M1-]k'ʷ=əls//, sas, ABFC ['*pinching*'], (<**metathesis**> *continuative*), (<**=els**> *structured activity continuative*), phonology: metathesis, syntactic analysis: intransitive verb, attested by IHTTC (9/2/77).

<**th'lhákw't**>, ABFC /'*pinch s-th, pinch s-o (and pull the skin)*'/, *see* th'lhákw'.

<**th'ó:kws**>, free root //θ'á·kʷs//, NUM /'*seven, to be seven*'/, syntactic analysis: num, adjective/adjectival verb, attested by AC, BJ (5/10/64), NP (12/6/73), CT (9/5/73), EB (2/13/78), others, other sources: ES /θ'á·kʷs/ *seven*; found in <**th'ó:kwstset.**>, //θ'á·kʷ-c-ət//, /'*There's seven of us.*'/, literally /'we are seven'/, attested by AC (10/8/71), example: <**ó:pel qas kw'e th'ó:kws**>, //ʔá·pəl qɛ-s k'ʷə θ'á·kʷs//, /'*seventeen*'/, attested by AC, also <**ó:pel qas té th'ò:kws**>, //ʔá·pəl qɛ-s tə θ'á·kʷs//, attested by CT (9/5/73), <**ts'kw'éx qas té th'ó:kws**>, //c'k'ʷə́xʸ qɛ-s tə θ'á·kʷs//, /'*twenty-seven*'/, attested by CT (9/5/73), <**th'ó:kws te sp'á:q'em.**>, //θ'á·kʷs tə s=p'ɛ́·q'=əm//, /'*There are seven flowers.*'/, attested by EB, <**th'ó:kws te x̲wó:qw' qas te léts'e pésk'a.**>, //θ'á·kʷs təx̣ʷá·q'ʷ qɛ-s thɛ lə́c'ə pə́sk'ɛ//, /'*There are seven sawbill ducks (mergansers) and one hummingbird.*'/, attested by EB approved this sentence constructed by a staff class member, *<**th'ó:kws te x̲wó:qw' qas léts'e te pésk'a.**> rejected, *<**th'ó:kws te x̲wó:qw' qesu léts'e te pésk'a.**> rejected.

<**th'ekwsále**>, ds //θ'akʷs=ɛ́lə//, numc, nums, NUM ['*seven people*'], HUMC, CAN /'*seven paddlers, seven "pullers"*'/, lx <**=ále ~ =á:le**> *persons, people*, phonology: vowel-reduction, syntactic analysis: adjective/adjectival verb, num, attested by Elders Group (3/19/75, 7/27/75), example: <**th'akwsá:le**>, //θ'akʷs=ɛ́·lə//, attested by AC.

<**th'ekwsáleqel**>, ds //θ'akʷs=[-ɛ́l-]əqəl//, numc, nums, NUM ['*seven containers*'], HHG, (<**-ál-**> *plural*), lx <**=eqel**> *container*, phonology: vowel-reduction, infixed plural in affix, affix pluralizer, syntactic analysis: adjective/adjectival verb, num, syntactic comment: shows -ál- *plural* infix required in the lexical suffix when the number reaches seven, since from numbers one to six only =eqel *container* is used, there are also other cases where the -el- added to lexical suffixes (for ex. with body part suffixes) seems to pluralize the affix as well, attested by AD (4/12/78).

<**th'ekwsálh**>, ds //θ'akʷs=ɛ́ɬ//, numc, nums, NUM ['*seven times*'], TIME, (semological comment: probably somewhat artificial as they didn't often count these past five), lx <**=álh**> *times*, phonology: vowel-reduction, syntactic analysis: adverb/adverbial verb, num, attested by Elders Group (3/19/75).

<**th'èkwetselhsxá**>, ds //θ'əkʷəc=ɛɬ=sxʸɛ́ or θ'əkʷəc=əɬsxʸɛ́//, numc, nums, NUM ['*seventy*'], literally /'seven =times =ten'/, possibly <**=sxá**> *ten*, possibly <**=elhsxá ~ =elsxá**> *times ten*, phonology: root allomorph th'ekwets, epenthetic stress (here added on fourth syllable before final stress), syntactic analysis: adjective/adjectival verb, num, attested by CT (9/5/73), also <**th'èkwetselsxá**>, //θ'əkʷəc=əl=sxʸɛ́//, attested by AC (8/4/70), also <**th'ekwtselsxá ~ th'èkwselsxá**>, //θ'əkʷc=əl=sxʸɛ ~ θ'akʷs=əl=sxʸɛ́//, attested by BJ (12/5/64 old p.336 of new transcript), also <**th'ekwselsxá**>, //θ'akʷs=əl=sxʸɛ́//, attested by DM (12/4/64 old p.262 of new transcript), example: <**th'ekwselsxá swà:yèl**>, //θ'akʷs=əl=sxʸɛ́ s=wɛ̀·yə̀l//, /'*seventy days*'/, attested by DM (12/4/64).

<**th'ekwselsxá:le**>, ds //θ'akʷs=əl=sxʸɛ́=ɛ́(·)lə//, numc, nums, NUM ['*seventy people*'], HUMC, (semological comment: probably somewhat artifical as qéx̲ *many* would be used more often instead of manually counting this high), lx <**=ále ~ =á:le**> *persons, people*, phonology: vowel merger, voicing of l from lh (allomorph), syntactic analysis: adjective/adjectival verb, num,

attested by Elders Group (3/19/75).

<**th'èkwetselsxó:s**>, ds //θ'əkʷəc=əl=sxʸɛ́=á(·)s or θ'əkʷəc=əl=sxʸɛ́=əs//, numc, nums, NUM ['*seventy dollars*'], ECON, lx <**=ó:s ~ =es**> *dollars*, phonology: vowel merger, perhaps also a→o before =es/=ó:s, syntactic analysis: nominal, num, attested by AC (11/30/71).

<**th'okwsámets'**>, ds //θ'akʷs=ɛ́məc'//, numc, nums, NUM /'*(seven long objects), seven ropes, seven threads, seven sticks, seven poles*'/, lx <**-ámeth' ~ =ámets'**> *long objects, rope/thread/stick/pole, standing, height*, comment: prompted by Boas' 1890 Scowlitz manuscript, syntactic analysis: adjective/adjectival verb, num, attested by AD (4/12/78).

<**th'ókwses**>, ds //θ'ákʷs=əs//, numc, nums, NUM /'*seven dollars, (seven Indian blankets or dollars [Boas])*'/, ECON, lx <**=es**> *dollar(s), round thing(s), face(s)*, syntactic analysis: nominal, num, attested by AC (10/8/71), AD (4/12/78), also /'*seven Indian blankets or dollars*'/, source: Boas 1890 Scowlitz manuscript.

<**th'okwsíqw ~ th'okwsesíqw**>, ds //θ'akʷs=íqʷ//, numc, nums, NUM ['*seven fish*'], EZ, FSH, lx <**=íqw**> *fish*, syntactic analysis: adjective/adjectival verb, num, nominal?, attested by BHTTC (8/24/76).

<**th'ekwsíws**>, ds //θ'akʷs=íws//, numc, nums, NUM ['*seven birds*'], EZ, HUNT, lx <**=íws**> *bird*, phonology: vowel-reduction, syntactic analysis: adjective/adjectival verb, num, nominal?, attested by Elders Group (3/29/77).

<**th'ekwòls**>, ds //θ'akʷs=áls//, numc, nums, NUM, EB ['*seven fruit in a group or cluster (as they grow on a plant)*'], HARV, lx <**=óls**> *fruit, spherical objects*, phonology: vowel-reduction, consonant loss, downstepping, syntactic analysis: adjective/adjectival verb, num, nominal?, attested by AD (4/12/78).

<**th'okwső́welh**>, ds //θ'akʷs=ówəɬ//, numc, nums, NUM /'*seven canoes, seven boats*'/, CAN, lx <**=ő́welh**> *canoe, boat*, syntactic analysis: adjective/adjectival verb, num, nominal?, attested by AD (4/12/78).

<**sth'ó:kws**>, ds //s=θ'á·kʷs=s//, numc, nums, NUM ['*seven o'clock*'], lx <**s=...=s**> *hour, o'clock*, phonology: consonant merger, syntactic analysis: nominal, attested by AC, others, example: <**wetéses te sth'ó:kws**>, //wə-tə́s-əs tə s=θ'á·kʷs=s//, /'*at seven o'clock, when it gets (to) seven o'clock*'/, attested by AC (10/6/71).

<**th'okwsámets'**>, NUM /'*(seven long objects), seven ropes, seven threads, seven sticks, seven poles*'/, *see* th'ó:kws.

<**th'ókwses**>, NUM /'*seven dollars, (seven Indian blankets or dollars [Boas])*'/, *see* th'ó:kws.

<**th'okwsíqw ~ th'okwsesíqw**>, NUM ['*seven fish*'], *see* th'ó:kws.

<**th'okwső́welh**>, NUM /'*seven canoes, seven boats*'/, *see* th'ó:kws.

<**th'óleqw'esthòm**>, SOC ['*you'll get punched all over*'], *see* th'í:qw'et.

<**th'olólh**>, bound stem //θ'aláɬ//, EZ ['*spring salmon*'], root meaning unknown

<**sth'olólh**>, df //s=θ'aláɬ//, EZ ['*spring salmon which goes to Chehalis Lake in May then returns to salt water*'], ['*Oncorhynchus tshawytscha*'], (<**s=**> *nominalizer*), root meaning unknown, syntactic analysis: nominal, attested by Elders Group (3/26/75).

<**temth'oló:lh**>, ds //təm=θ'alá·ɬ//, TIME /'*July to August, (big spring salmon time)*'/, literally /'big spring salmon time (Jenness)'/, (<**tem=**> *season (for), time (for)*), syntactic analysis: nominal, attested by Elders Group (3/28/79), comment: prompted by, source: Diamond Jenness' field notes of interviews with Wm. Sepass of Sardis.

<**th'ólhem**>, ABDF /'*(cold (of a person) or get cooled down, get cold)*'/, *see* th'álh.

<**th'ólhem sq'óq'ey**>, ABDF ['*(have/get) a head cold*'], *see* th'álh.

<**th'ólhethet**>, ABFC ['*cool oneself*'], *see* th'álh.

<**th'ó:m**>, root (not attested as free form) //θ'á·m// *bone*

<**sth'ó:m**>, ds //s=θ'á·m//, ANA ['*bone*'], (<**s=**> *nominalizer*), syntactic analysis: nominal, attested by AC, DM (12/4/64), Elders Group (3/15/72), NP, other sources: ES and JH /sθ'á·m/ *bone*, example: <**sth'ó:ms te sméyeth**>, //s=θ'á·m-s tə s=mɛ́yəθ//, /'*the animal's bone*'/, attested by AC, <**le texw sth'ó:m el.**>, //lə təx^{w} s=θ'á·m ʔəl//, /'*He's/She's all bone left.*'/, literally /'past 3rd person half bone just'/, attested by AC (8/6/70), <**westh'ó:m el.**>, //wə-sθ'á·m ʔəl or əw s=θ'á·m ʔəl//, /'*He's all boney., He's all bones.*'/, attested by AC (9/30/71), <**x̲á:p'qwtem tel sth'ó:m.**>, //x̣ɛ́·p'q^{w}=təm t-əl s=θ'á·m//, /'*My bones are aching.*'/, attested by NP.

<**sth'emth'ó:m**>, pln //s=C_1əC_2=θ'á·m//, ANA ['*bones*'], (<**R3=**> *plural*), phonology: reduplication, syntactic analysis: nominal, attested by EB (6/76).

<**sth'eth'eló:m**>, dmpn //s=C_1ə=θ'[=əl=]á·m//, ANA ['*small bones*'], (<**R5=**> *diminutive*), (<**=el=**> *plural*), phonology: infixed plural, reduplication, syntactic analysis: nominal, attested by Elders Group (3/15/72), also <**sth'éth'elòm**>, //s=C_1í[=Aə́=]=θ'[=əl=]m//, attested by AD (4/27/79), example: <**te ōw qelát sth'éth'elòm**>, //tə ʔəw-qəlɛ́t s=C_1í[=Aə́=]=θ'[=əl=]m//, /'*more small bones*'/, attested by AD, <**ṓwechexw lámexwcha xwa siyólexwe a'áchewlh x̲áp'kw'tem ta' sth'éth'elòm.**>, //ʔówə-c-əx^{w} lɛ́=m-əx^{w}-cɛ x^{w}ɛ s=yáləx^{w}=ə ʔɛʔɛ́-cɛ-wɬ-x̣ɛ́p'k'^{w}=təm t-ɛʔ s=C_1í[=Aə́=]=θ'[=əl=]m//, /'*You're not going to get/become old until/unless your bones are aching.*'/, usage: a saying/proverb, attested by AD.

<**th'ómetsel**>, df //θ'ám=əcəl//, CLO ['*bracelet*'], PE, literally /'bone on the back'/, lx <**on the back**, syntactic analysis: nominal, attested by Elders Group (9/24/75).

<**sth'emí:wel ~ sth'emíwel ~ sth'emíwél**>, ds //s=θ'am=í·wəl or s=θ'a[=Aə=]m=í·wəl//, EB /'*heart of a root, seed, nut (kernel), core of plant or seedling, core (of tree, branch, any growing thing), pith (of bush), seed or pit [U.S.] or pip [Cdn.] of a fruit*'/, LAND /'*core of a rock, center of a rock, core of anything, heart of anything inanimate*'/, possibly <**e-ablaut**> *derivational*, lx <**=í:wel ~ =íwel**> *in the insides*, phonology: probable vowel-reduction, possible ablaut, optional updrifting, syntactic analysis: nominal, attested by AC (8/29/70. 11/19/71), Elders Group (5/28/75), JL (3/31/78), example: <**sth'emíwels te plum/apple**>, //s=θ'əm=íwəl-s tə plə́m/ʔɛ́pəl//, /'*seeds/pits of plum/apple*'/, attested by JL, <**sth'emíwels té sth'ì:m**>, //s=θ'əm=íwəl-s tə s=θ'í·m//, /'*seeds on berries*'/, literally /'seed -of the berry'/, attested by JL (3/31/78).

<**sth'émlets**>, stvi //s=θ'a[=Aə́=]m=ləc//, BPI /'*(have a) skinny butt, (be skinny on the rump or bottom)*'/, ANA, (<**s=**> *stative*), possibly <**é-ablaut**> *durative*, lx <**=lets**> *on the rump*, phonology: ablaut, syntactic analysis: adjective/adjectival verb, attested by AC (11/11/71).

<**sts'émlets**>, dnom //s=c'ə́m=ləc//, ANA ['*hip*'], literally probably /'bone on the rump'/, (<**s=**> *nominalizer*), probably root <**th'óm**> *bone*, lx <**=lets**> *on the rump*, phonology: ts' may be misrecorded for th' or if ts' is correct the root is not th'óm, syntactic analysis: nominal, source: ES /sc'ə́mləc/ *hip*.

<**sth'émqsel**>, ds //s=θ'a[=Aə́=]m=qsəl//, ANA ['*bridge of nose*'], literally /'bone in the nose'/, possibly <**é-ablaut**> *derivational or durative*, lx <**=qsel**> *in the nose*, phonology: possible ablaut, syntactic analysis: nominal, attested by Elders Group (8/20/75).

<**sth'émxel**>, dnom //s=θ'a[=Aə́=]m=x^{y}əl//, ANA ['*shin*'], literally /'bone in the leg'/, possibly <**é-ablaut**> *derivational or durative*, lx <**=xel**> *in the leg*, phonology: ablaut, syntactic analysis:

nominal, attested by Elders Group (7/27/75).

<th'omewích ~ th'ó:bewíts>, ds //θ'am=əwíc ~ θ'á·m=əwíc//, ANA /*'(someone's) spine, (someone's) backbone*'/, literally /'bone on the back'/, (semological comment: inalienable, used without nominalizer only as someone's body part, never as just the word or without being possessed, for that see shxwth'omewíts), lx **<=ewích ~ =ewíts>** *on the back*, phonology: b (with half-closed velum) for m, syntactic analysis: nominal, attested by DM (12/4/64 new transcript old p.260), example: **<ta th'ó:bewích ~ ta th'omewíts>**, //t-ɛ θ'á(·)m=əwíc//, /*'your spine, your backbone*'/, attested by DM.

<shxwth'omewíts>, ds //sx^w=θ'am=əwíc//, ANA /*'the spine, the backbone*'/, (**<shxw=>** *nominalizer (alienable), something for*), syntactic analysis: nominal, attested by DM (12/4/64 p.260).

<th'ómtsestel>, ds //θ'ám=cəs=təl//, PLAY [*'slahal bone(s)*'], ASM ['thumb-sized bone or bones from a set of four (two marked ones are called "the man", two unmarked ones are called "the lady"), the set is hidden in two players hands and the other team guesses which hands hold the marked bone in the gambling game called slehal, slahal, or the bone game'], literally /'bone on the hand device'/, lx **<=tses>** *on the hand*, lx **<=tel>** *device, something to/that*, syntactic analysis: nominal, attested by JL (Fish Camp 7/17/78), Deming (7/27/78), see also **<slehà:l>** *slahal game, the bone game.*

<th'emeláx̲el>, dnom //θ'am=əlɛ́x̣əl or θ'a[=Aə=]m=əlɛ́x̣əl//, ANA /*'point of elbow, arm bone*'/, literally /'bone in the arm'/, possibly **<e-ablaut>** *derivational or durative*, lx **<=eláx̲el>** *in the arm*, phonology: possible ablaut, syntactic analysis: nominal, dialects: *Cheh.*, attested by IHTTC (9/19/77).

<th'emxweláx̲el>, dnom //θ'am=x^w=əlɛ́x̣əl or θ'a[=Aə=]m=x^w=əlɛ́x̣əl//, ANA /*'an elbow, elbow (the name of it)*'/, possibly **<e-ablaut>** *derivational or durative*, lx **<=xw>** *round or (better) lump-like*, lx **<=eláx̲el>** *on the arm*, phonology: possible ablaut, grammatical comment: with no s= prefix (*inalienable nominalizer* with body parts) this word is only used to name the part, the s= is required when someone's body part is being discussed, sqep'ó:lthetel *knee*, shxw'ílàmàlà *shoulder* (and others) work this way also, syntactic analysis: noun, nominal, attested by IHTTC (9/19/77), also **<th'emxwiláx̲el>**, //θ'əm=x^w=i(=)lɛ́x̣əl//, possibly **<=iy>** *covering*??, attested by DM (12/4/64 new transcript old p.259), example: **<th'emxweláx̲el te'íle.>**, //θ'əm=x^w=əlɛ́x̣əl tə=ʔí=lə//, /*'This is an elbow.*'/, attested by IHTTC (9/19/77).

<sth'emxweláx̲el>, dnom //s=θ'am=x^w=əlɛ́x̣əl or s=θ'a[=Aə=]m=x^w=əlɛ́x̣əl//, ANA [*'(someone's) elbow*'], (**<s=>** *inalienable nominalizer*), possibly **<e-ablaut>** *derivational or durative*, lx **<=eláx̲el>** *on the arm*, phonology: possible ablaut, grammatical comment: see under th'emxweláx̲el, syntactic analysis: nominal, attested by IHTTC (9/19/77), Elders Group (8/20/75, 10/8/75), example: **<séyem tel sth'emxweláx̲el.>**, //sɛ́y=əm t-əl s=θ'əm=x^w=əlɛ́x̣əl//, /*'My elbow is hurt., My elbow is sore.*'/, attested by IHTTC (9/19/77).

<ts'ets'emíkw>, df //C_1ə=c'əm(=)ík^w//, dmpn, CLO [*'little tiny beads*'], (**<R5=>** *diminutive plural*), possibly root **<th'óm ~ th'em>** *bone*, possibly **<=íkw>** *round*, phonology: reduplication, syntactic analysis: nominal, attested by AK (Elders Group 3/26/80).

<th'óméls>, df //θ'ám=ə[=´=]ls//, sas, TOOL /*'whetstone, a file, sandstone*'/, root meaning unknown, (**<=əls>** *structured activity continuative/nominalizer*), possibly **<=´= (stress-shift)>** *derivational*, phonology: stress-shift, syntactic analysis: nominal, attested by EB (3/2/76), Elders Group (3/15/72, 4/2/80), also **<xth'óméls>**, //x^y=θ'ám=ə[=´=]ls//, (**<x=>** meaning unknown), comment: could x= be error for sh= *something for* or xw= *always*, attested by EB (3/2/76).

<lhth'óméls>, ds //ɬ=θ'ám=ə[=´=]ls//, sas, TOOL [*'to file (abrasively)*'], (**<lh=>** *use (a portion of)*), phonology: stress-shift, syntactic analysis: intransitive verb, attested by EB (3/22/76).

<Th'óth'emels>, ds //θ'á[=C_1ə=]m=əls//, PLN /*'village on a small flat a little above Vedder Crossing,* *on the north side of Chilliwack River*'/, probably <**=R1=**> *continuative or resultative*, phonology: reduplication, syntactic analysis: nominal, source: Duff 1952, Wells 1965 (lst ed.):19 where he says it means *steep*, source: place names reference file #223.

<**Th'emth'ómels**>, pln //C₁əC₂=θ'ám=əls//, PLN /'*Granite Mountain, the second mountain back of X̲óletsa, northwest of Kwelkwelqéylem*'/, ASM ['X̲óletsa is the mountain above Yale Creek and Yale Reserve'], literally /'many files'/, ASM ['so named because it wears out the shoes'], (<**R3=**> *plural*), phonology: reduplication, syntactic analysis: nominal, attested by SP and AK (Fish Camp 8/2/77), source: place names reference file #158.

<**th'ómetsel**>, CLO ['*bracelet*'], *see* sth'ó:m.

<**th'omewích ~ th'ó:bewíts**>, ANA /'*(someone's) spine, (someone's) backbone*'/, *see* sth'ó:m.

<**th'ómtsestel**>, PLAY ['*slahal bone(s)*'], *see* sth'ó:m.

<**th'óqw**>, root //θ'áqʷ// *suck*

<**th'óqwet**>, pcs //θ'áqʷ=əT//, ABFC ['*suck s-th*'], (<**=et**> *purposeful control transitivizer*), syntactic analysis: transitive verb, attested by EB (3/22/76), AK (Elders Group 1/30/80), AC, other sources: ES /θ'á·qʷət/ *suck*, Salish cognate: Squamish /c'úqʷ-unʔ/ *suck (act.-itr.)* W73:257, K69:55, also <**ts'óqwet**>, //c'áqʷ=əT//, attested by NP (Elders Group 1/30/80), example: <**th'óqwetes te siyólexwe te q'áq'et'em.**>, //θ'áqʷ=əT-əs tə s=yáləxʷ-ə tə q'ɛ́[=C₁ə=]t'(=)əm//, /'*The old person sucked something sweet.*'/, attested by AC (10/15/71).

<**th'óth'eqwet**>, cts //θ'á[-C₁ə-]qʷ=əT//, ABFC ['*be sucking s-th*'], (<**-R1-**> *continuative*), phonology: reduplication, syntactic analysis: transitive verb, attested by AC, example: <**th'óth'eqwetes te q'áq'et'em.**>, //θ'á[-C₁ə-]qʷ=əT-əs tə q'ɛ́[=C₁ə=]t'(=)əm//, /'*He's sucking something sweet.*'/, attested by AC (10/15/71).

<**th'óqweleqw**>, df //θ'áqʷ=ələqʷ//, ABDF ['*bald-headed*'], root meaning uncertain, lx <**=eleqw**> *on top of the head, on the hair*, syntactic analysis: adjective/adjectival verb, attested by BHTTC (10/21/76), also <**ts'qó:leqw**>, //c'á·q=M1=ələqʷ//, attested by BHTTC (10/21/76), compare root <**th'áq ~ th'eq**> *skinned*, Salish cognate: Squamish root /c'aq/ *bald* K67:279 as in /n-c'áq-iʔəqʷ/ *bald* W73:14, K67:307, also /'*skinned on the head*'/, attested by EB (1/10/78).

<**sth'ó:qweleqw**>, stvi //s=θ'á·qʷ=ələqʷ//, ABDF ['*(be) bald-headed*'], (<**s=**> *stative*), syntactic analysis: adjective/adjectival verb, attested by AC (11/11/71), also <**sthóqweleqw**>, //s=θ'áqʷ=ələqʷ//, also /'*bald*'/, comment: th probably my error for th', attested by Elders Group (3/26/75), also <**sts'óqweleqw**>, //s=c'áqʷ=ələqʷ//, (<**s=**> *stative*), attested by BHTTC (10/21/76).

<**th'ó:qwi ~ th'óqwi**>, bound root or stem //θ'á(·)qʷ(=)i//, EZ /'*fish (any kind), (salmon (any kind, not trout or sturgeon) [AC])*'/, (<**s=**> *nominalizer*), root meaning unknown

<**sth'ó:qwi ~ sth'óqwi**>, df //s=θ'á(·)qʷ(=)i//, EZ /'*fish (any kind), (salmon (any kind, not trout or sturgeon) [AC])*'/, (<**s=**> *nominalizer*), root meaning unknown, syntactic analysis: nominal, attested by AC, NP (12/6/73), Elders Grop (3/15/72), BJ (5/10/64, 12/5/64), Salish cognate: Squamish /sc'úqʷiʔ/ *fish (generic)* W73:101, K67:286, K69:58, also /'*salmon (any kind, not trout or sturgeon)*'/, attested by AC, example: <**lachxw qw'élem ta sth'óqwi.**>, //lɛ-c-xʷ q'ʷə́l=əm t-ɛ s=θ'áqʷi//, /'*Go and barbecue your fish.*'/, attested by AC (8/13/70), <**l sqwálewel kw'els qw'él:em te sth'ó:qwi tláwàyèl.**>, //l s=qʷɛ́l=əwəl k'ʷ-əl-s q'ʷə́l=əm tə s=θ'á·qʷi tə=lá=wɛ̀yə̀l//, /'*I think I'll barbecue the salmon today.*'/, attested by AC (10/15/71), <**thí:the te sth'ó:qwi.**>, //θí[=·=]=C₁ə tə s=θ'áqʷi//, /'*Fish is bigger.*'/, (<**=:=**> *augmentative*), attested by AC (8/23/73), <**hí:kw te sth'ó:qwi.**>, //hí[=·=]kʷ tə s=θ'á·qʷi//, /'*The fish is big.*'/, (<**=:=**> *augmentative*), attested by AC (8/23/73), <**chel chxélcha te sth'óqwi.**>, //c-əl c=xʸə́lcɛ tə s=θ'áqʷi//, /'*I caught a fish.*'/, attested

by EB (1/8/76), <**qéx̱ te sth'óqwi.**>, //qə́x̣ tə s=θ'áqʷi//, /'*There's lots of fish.*'/, attested by AC, Deming (5/20/76), <**qwéls te sth'óqwi**>, //qʷə́ls tə s=θ'áqʷi//, /'*salmon stew, fish stew*'/, literally /'boil the fish/salmon'/, attested by CT (6/8/76), <**tl'álhem sth'óqwi**>, //ƛ'ɛ́ɬ=əm s=θ'áqʷi//, /'*salt fish*'/, ASM ['fish preserved in brine then dried'], attested by Elders Group (5/16/79), <**sth'ó:ms te sth'óqwi**>, //s=θ'á·m-s tə s=θáqʷi//, /'*fish bone*'/, literally /'bone of the fish'/, attested by Elders Group (3/15/72), <**sth'eth'eló:ms te sth'óqwi**>, //s=C_1ə=θ'[=əl=]á·m-s tə s=θ'áqʷi//, /'*small fish bones*'/, literally /'many small bones -of the fish'/, attested by Elders Group (3/15/72), <**stám kw'es sth'óqwi i kwélexw?**>, //s=tɛ́m k'ʷ-əs s=θ'áqʷi ʔi kʷə́l=l-əxʷ//, /'*What kind of fish do you have?*'/, attested by EB (12/15/75), <**qw'élém te sth'óqwi.**>, //q'ʷə́lə́m tə s=θ'áqʷi//, /'*The salmon is barbecued., barbecue the salmon*'/, attested by EB (5.4.76), also /'*bake the fish, barbecue fish*'/, attested by MH (Deming 1/4/78).

<**sth'óqwes**>, ds //s=θ'áqʷi=ə[=Aə=]s//, FSH ['*cooked fish head*'], FOOD, literally /'fish face'/, (<**e-ablaut**> *derivational*), lx <**=es**> *face*, phonology: vowel merger, ablaut, syntactic analysis: nominal, attested by AC (8/13/70).

<**sth'óth'eqwi**>, dmn //s=θ'á[=C_1ə=]qʷi//, EZ ['*small salmon (generic)*'], (<**=R1=**> *diminutive*), phonology: reduplication, syntactic analysis: nominal, attested by CT (6/8/76).

<**tsth'óqwi**>, ds //c=θ'áqʷi//, FSH ['*to fish*'], (<**ts= ~ ch=**> *have, get, verbalizer*), syntactic analysis: intransitive verb, attested by Elders Group (3/15/72), also <**chth'óqwi**>, //c=θ'áqʷi//, attested by Deming (5/20/76), EB (3/1/76), example: <**látset chth'óqwi.**>, //lɛ́-c-ət c=θ'áqʷi//, /'*We're going fishing.*'/, literally /'we're going to fish'/, attested by EB.

<**sth'óth'eqwi**>, dnom //s=θ'á[=C_1ə=]qʷi//, FSH /'*a fisherman, a man that goes out fishing*'/, literally /'something/someone that is fishing'/, (<**s=**> *nominalizer, someone that*), (<**=R1=**> *continuative*), phonology: reduplication, syntactic analysis: nominal, attested by Elders Group (3/15/72, 2/11/76, 2/18/76), example: <**sth'óth'eqwi te swíyeqe.**>, //s=θ'á[=C_1ə=]qʷi tə s=wíq=ə//, /'*The man is a fisherman.*'/, attested by Elders Group (2/18/76).

<**temth'ó:qwi**>, ds //təm=θ'á·qʷi//, TIME /'*November, time to catch salmon*'/, literally /'time to fish or get fish/salmon'/, lx <**tem=**> *time to, time, season*, syntactic analysis: nominal, attested by DM (12/4/64).

<**th'óqw'em ~ th'ó:qw'em**>, df //θ'á(·)q'ʷ=əm//, EB /'*to rot, rotten (of fruit, animal, flora, fauna, food)*'/, ABDF, FOOD, (<**=em**> *have/get/intransitivizer or middle voice*), syntactic analysis: intransitive verb, attested by AC, EB (3/22/76), Deming (3/23/78), other sources: ES /θ'á·q'ʷəm/ *rotten*.

<**th'óth'eqw'em**>, cts //θ'á[-C_1ə-]q'ʷ=əm//, EB ['*rotting*'], ABDF, FOOD, (<**-R1-**> *continuative*), phonology: reduplication, syntactic analysis: intransitive verb, attested by EB (1/22/76), Deminmg (3/23/78).

<**th'óth'eqw'em**>, rsls //θ'á[=C_1ə=]q'ʷ=əm//, EB ['*rotten*'], FOOD, ABDF, (<**=R1=**> *resultative*), (semological comment: good semantic contrast between *continuative* in previous word and *resultative* here), phonology: reduplication, syntactic analysis: adjective/adjectival verb, attested by EB (1/7/76).

<**th'óth'eqw'emáléqep**>, ds //θ'á[=C_1ə=]q'ʷ=əm=ɛ́ləqəp//, TAST ['*(have) a rotten taste*'], SM ['*(have) a rotten smell*'], (<**=R1=**> *resultative*), lx <**=áléqep**> *(in) taste, (in) smell*, phonology: reduplication, syntactic analysis: adjective/adjectival verb, attested by Elders Group (5/25/77).

<**th'qw'ó:mthet**>, incs //θ'á·q'ʷ=M1=θət//, FOOD ['*rotted*'], EB, ABDF, possibly <**metathesis type 1**> *durative*, (<**=thet**> *get, become*), phonology: metathesis, phonology: proves that EB has a long vowel in the root, syntactic analysis: adjective/adjectival verb, attested by EB (3/22/76).

<**th'ót**>, pcs //θ'á=T//, BLDG /'*pull out a nail, (pull it out (a metal nail))*'/, CSTR, (<**=t**> *purposeful*

control transitivizer), syntactic analysis: transitive verb, attested by Elders Group (4/28/76), Salish cognate: Squamish /c'uʔ/ *pulled (being pulled), come out* W73:206, K67:279.

<**th'óth'elhem**>, ABDF /'*be chilled (of a person), got cold (of a person)*'/, *see* th'álh.

<**Th'óth'emels**>, PLN /'*village on a small flat a little above Vedder Crossing, on the north side of Chilliwack River*'/, *see* th'ómels.

<**th'óth'eqwet**>, ABFC ['*be sucking s-th*'], *see* th'óqwet.

<**th'óth'eqw'em**>, EB ['*rotting*'], *see* th'óqw'em ~ th'ó:qw'em.

<**th'óth'eqw'em**>, EB ['*rotten*'], *see* th'óqw'em ~ th'ó:qw'em.

<**th'óth'eqw'emáléqep**>, TAST ['*(have) a rotten taste*'], *see* th'óqw'em ~ th'ó:qw'em.

<**th'óx̲wí:ls**>, HHG ['*washing dishes*'], *see* th'éx̲w or th'óx̲w.

<**th'óyeqw'els**>, HARV ['*splitting firewood*'], *see* th'íyeqw'.

<**th'óyéx̲wem**>, EFAM /'*being nervous, being excited, (getting nervous/excited)*'/, *see* th'ó:yx̲wem.

<**th'ó:yx̲wem**>, ds //θ'á·y=x̣^{w}=əm or θ'ɛ[=Aá·=]y=x̣^{w}=əm//, EFAM /'*(get/become) nervous, (get/become) excited*'/, possibly <**ó:-ablaut**> *derivational*, lx <**=x̲w**> *around in circles*, (<**=em**> *have/get/intransitivizer or middle voice*), phonology: possible ablaut, syntactic analysis: intransitive verb, attested by Deming (6/15/78), compare <**th'áth'iyekw**> *really worried*, compare **(perhaps)** <**th'eth'íkw'thet**> *get frightened*, compare (perhaps) <**th'eth'elá:ykwem**> *squeaking (of lots of mice)*.

<**th'óyéx̲wem**>, cts //θ'áy=ə[-´-]x̣^{w}=əm or θ'ɛ[=Aá=]y=[-ə́-]x̣^{w}=əm//, EFAM /'*being nervous, being excited, (getting nervous/excited)*'/, (<**-´- (stress-shift) or -é- infix**> *continuative*), phonology: possible ablaut, probable stress-shift, possible infix of é, syntactic analysis: intransitive verb, attested by Deming (6/15/78).

<**th'ő:lth'iyelhp**>, chrs //θ'ó·l=$C_1əC_2$=əɬp//, EB ['*tall Oregon grape bush*'], ['*Berberis aquifolium*'], ASM ['berries are edible but not popular raw, good for jelly or jam, the bush is about four feet high'], MED ['*root tea is medicine for many things, including diabetes and leukemia, roots (of tall/short?) plus cascara bark boiled a long time then drunk cool is medicine for boils and pimples*'], root meaning unknown unless th'ő:l *sour* as in the Thompson cognate, (<**=R2**> *characteristic*), lx <**=elhp**> *tree, plant*, phonology: el→íy before =elhp automatically, reduplication, syntactic analysis: nominal, attested by AC, JL (Fish Camp 7/19/79), others, other sources: ES /θ'ə́w·lθ'əyəɬp/ *Oregon grape (long)*, Salish cognate: Thompson /sc'əl'-seʔ-éɬp/ *tall Oregon grape bush (Berberis aquifolium)* from Thompson /s-c'ul'cul'/ [sc'ól'c'ol'] *sour* Turner and Bouchard ms. 1973:26, example: <**tsqwá:y te sp'áq'ems te th'őlth'iyelhp.**>, //c=q^{w}ɛ́·y tə sp'ɛ́q'=əm-s tə θ'ól=$C_1əC_2$=əɬp//, /'*The flower of the tall Oregon grape is yellow.*'/, attested by Elders Group (5/16/79).

<**th'ő:lth'iyelhp sth'í:m ~ sth'í:ms te th'ő:lth'iyelhp**>, cpds //θ'ó·l=$C_1əC_2$=əɬp s=θ'í·m ~ s=θ'í·m-s tə θ'ó·l=$C_1əC_2$=əɬp//, EB ['*tall Oregon grape berry*'], literally /'tall Oregon grape bush berry ~ berry of the tall Oregon grape plant'/, syntactic analysis: nominal phrase with modifier(s), attested by AC (11/24/71), also <**th'ő:lth'iy**>, //θ'ó·l=θ'iy//, comment: form produced reluctantly and surely a back-formation, perhaps not really used since AC avoided it and used the phrase with sth'í:m *berry* (unlike for all other berries where the =elhp is dropped), attested by Elders Group (Fish Camp 7/29/77).

<**th'ő:lth'iyelhp sth'í:m ~ sth'í:ms te th'ő:lth'iyelhp**>, EB ['*tall Oregon grape berry*'], *see* th'ő:lth'iyelhp.

<**th'ṓwex̲ ~ th'ṓwéx̲**>, possibly root //θ'ówəx̣ ~ θ'ówə́x̣ or θ'ów=əx̣//, BSK /'*cedar slat basket, cedar sapling basket*'/, ASM ['open spaces between slats, these were used for picking hops and some precontact items too, woven from just shxwt'ámetsel or súsekw' (strips of young cedar trunk), this is the kind of basket the cannibal ogress, Th'ṓwx̲iya, used (thus her name)'], possibly root <**th'ṓw**> as in <**th'ṓwt**> *beat s-th/s-o to a pulp, smash it to pieces*, possibly <**=ex̲**> *distributive*, syntactic analysis: nominal, noun?, attested by JL (8/8/79), Elders Group (6/11/75), others

<**Th'ṓwx̲iya**>, ds //θ'ów(=)x̣=iyɛ//, N /'*Cannibal Ogress, Wild Cannibal Woman*'/, literally /'dear little cedar slat basket'/, ASM ['so named because she kidnapped small children in such a basket and took them home to her cave to eat, children were told not to stay out too late or Th'ṓwx̲iya would get them'], Elder's comment: "she was captured by railroad men and taken to Vancouver where she died, she didn't last long there (JL)[there's a similar report of a sasquatch captured in the late 19th century by railroad men which appeared in the newpapers at the time], someone told JL they saw her kick fish out of water then hit on rock and put in basket", lx <**=iya**> *affectionate diminutive*, syntactic analysis: nominal, attested by Elders Group (10/1/75, 1/20/80), JL (Elders Group 8/8/79), AC, CT, many others, example: <**isále Th'ṓwx̲iya**>, //ʔisɛ́lə θ'ów(=)x̣=iya//, /'*two Cannibal Ogresses (if talking about them)*'/, Elder's comment: "maybe", (semological comment: this tests whether Cannibal Ogress needs the human numeral classifier, yéysele, and she may not), attested by AK (Elders Group 1/30/80).

<**th'ṓ:wt**>, pcs //θ'ó·w=T//, ABFC /'*smash s-th to pieces (hard pitch, splintery wood, a glass), break s-th to pieces, beat s-th/s-o to a pulp*'/, SOC ['*beat s-o to a pulp*'], (<**=t**> *purposeful control transitivizer*), syntactic analysis: transitive verb, attested by SJ (Story of Mink and Miss Pitch), EB and AD (11/10/78), AD (12/18/78).

<**Th'ṓwx̲iya**>, N /'*Cannibal Ogress, Wild Cannibal Woman*'/, *see* th'ṓwex̲ ~ th'ṓwéx̲.

<**th'qó:lthel**>, ABDF ['*skinned knee(s)*'], *see* th'áq ~ ts'áq or ts'éq ~ th'éq.

<**th'q'elhx̲á:m**>, df //θ'q'(=)əɬx̣ɛ́=əm or θ'q'=ɛ́·ɬ(=)x̣=ə[-M1-]m or θ'q'(=)əɬ=x̣=ə[=Aɛ́·=]m//, ABFC /'*to kneel, kneel down*'/, root meaning unknown, possibly <**=elhx̲á or =á:lh or =elh**> meaning unclear, possibly <**metathesis type one**> *non-continuative or derivational*, possibly <**á:-ablaut**> *derivational or durative*?, probably <**=em**> *middle voice*, phonology: possible metathesis, possible ablaut, syntactic analysis: intransitive verb, attested by AC (9/18/71, 11/16/71), EB (12/17/75), Salish cognate: Cowichan /θq'əɬx̣éʔem/ *to kneel* B74b:66, Saanich dial. of NSt. /θq'əɬx̣éʔeŋ/ *to kneel* B74a:66, perhaps Sechelt /č'əq'-íqʷ-ɬa-m/ *kneel* T77:30 and Mainland Comox /č'íq'iqʷɬa/ *to kneel* B75prelim.:79, also <**th'q'elhx̲ám**>, /θ'q'əɬx̣ɛ́m/, attested by IHTTC (9/1/77), RG & EH (4/9/99 Ling332)

<**th'q'álhx̲e [or th'q'álhx̲em]**>, cts //θ'q'(=)əɬ(=)x̣ɛ́-M2=əm or θ'q'(=)ɛ́ɬ(=)x̣=əm or θ'q'(=)ə[-Aɛ́-]ɬx̣=əm//, ABFC ['*kneeling*'], possibly <**metathesis type 2 or á-ablaut**> *continuative*, possibly <**lack of metathesis**> *continuative*, phonology: possible metathesis or ablaut, syntactic analysis: intransitive verb, attested by IHTTC (9/1/77).

<**th'q'elhx̲oméstexw**>, caus //θ'q'əɬx̣(=)ɛ[=Aa=]m[=ə́=]=sT-əxʷ//, ABFC ['*make s-o kneel*'], REL, SOC, possibly <**o-ablaut**> meaning uncertain, possibly <**=é=**> meaning uncertain, (<**=st**> *causative control transitivizer),* phonology: possible ablaut, possible infixed schwa, syntactic analysis: transitive verb, attested by EB; found in <**th'q'elhx̲oméstem**>, //θ'q'əɬx̣(=)ɛ[=Aa=]m[=ə́=]=sT-əm//, [θ'q'əɬx̣amə́stəm], /'*They made him kneel.*'/, syntactic comment: passive, attested by EB (12/17/75).

<th'eq'elhsx̲á:m>, caus ///θ'əq'(=)əɬ=sT=x̣=ə[=Aɛ́=]m//, ABFC /they made them/him/her kneel down/, REL, passive, odd to have <**=st**> *causative* precede other derivational suffixes and lose the

<t> but prob. as a cluster simplification, prob. <=x̲> *all around*, <=em> is passive here rather than middle voice, <=Aá:> may be *durative* throughout as the only ablaut that can replace schwa <e> in suffixes, attested by RG & EH (4/9/99 Ling332)

<**th'q'álhx̲e [or th'q'álhx̲em]**>, ABFC ['*kneeling*'], *see* th'q'elhx̲á:m.

<**th'q'elhx̲oméstexw**>, ABFC ['*make s-o kneel*'], *see* th'q'elhx̲á:m.

<**th'q'émelets ~ ts'q'émelets**>, WATR ['*collected rain-water from a drip*'], *see* th'q'ém ~ th'eq'ém.

<**th'q'emelétsem**>, WATR ['*collected rain-water drops in a bucket*'], *see* th'q'ém ~ th'eq'ém.

<**Th'qwélhcha**>, PLN ['*lake in back of Paul Webster's old place on Hicks Rd. near Jones Creek*'], *see* th'qwélhcha.

<**Th'qwélhcha**>, PLN ['*stagnant water lake or ponds at the downriver end of Skw'átets or Peters Reserve near Laidlaw*'], *see* th'qwélhcha.

<**th'qwó:lecha ~ th'qwó:letse**>, df //θ'qʷá·lə(=)cɛ or θ'á·qʷ=M1=ɛ́lɛ=cɛ//, CLO ['*glove*'], root meaning unknown unless th'óqw or th'ó:qw (ES) *suck*, possibly <**=ála**> *container*, possibly <**metathesis**> *derivational*, possibly <**=cha rare variant of =ches ~ =tses**> *on the hand*, phonology: possible metathesis, possible vowel merger, syntactic analysis: nominal, attested by Elders Group (3/15/72), NP (9/19/75), EB (11/27/75), Salish cognate: Squamish /c'qʷúʔl-ač/ *gloves* W73:117, K67:277, compare possibly related <**th'óqwet**> *suck s-th*.

<**th'qwó:letses**>, pln //θ'á·qʷ=M1=álə=cəs//, CLO /'*mittens, gloves*'/, lx <**=tses**> *on the hand*, comment: the use of the full suffix =tses ~ =ches (in contrast to the shortened allomorph =cha) seems inadequate to indicate *plural* here, attested by EB (11/27/75).<**th'táme**>, us //θ'tɛ́mə//, CAN ['*raft*'], syntactic analysis: nominal, attested by Elders Group (2/11/76).

<**th'qwó:letses**>, CLO /'*mittens, gloves*'/, *see* th'qwó:lecha ~ th'qwó:letse.

<**th'qw'álewest**>, SOC ['*punched s-o on the stomach*'], *see* th'í:qw'et.

<**th'qw'á:lí:ye**>, SOC ['*punched on the ear*'], *see* th'í:qw'et.

<**th'qw'élqsel**>, SOC ['*punched on the nose*'], *see* th'í:qw'et.

<**th'qw'íwet**>, SOC ['*punched s-o on the rump*'], *see* th'í:qw'et.

<**th'qw'ó:mthet**>, FOOD ['*rotted*'], *see* th'óqw'em ~ th'ó:qw'em.

<**th'qw'ó:s**>, SOC ['*punched in the face*'], *see* th'í:qw'et.

<**th'x̲**>, possible bound root //θ'x̣//, meaning uncertain

\<**th'x̲ámél**>, df //θ'x̣ɛ́=məl or θ'ə[=Aɛ́=]x̣=M1=məl//, ANA /'*breast bone, part of human body between breast bone and ribs*'/, root meaning unknown unless th'éx̲ *disappear*, possibly <**metathesis**> *derivational*, lx <**=mel**> *part, portion*, phonology: possible metathesis, updrifting, syntactic analysis: nominal, attested by EB (2/6/76, 3/20/78).

<**th'x̲éyles**> or <**th'x̲íles**>, df //θ'x̣=íləs or θ'ɛx̣=íləs or θ'x̣ɛ=íləs//, ANAA /'*inside brisket of meat (deer, etc.)*'/, root meaning unknown unless th'éx̲ *disappear*, lx <**=íles**> *on the chest*, phonology: possible vowel merger, syntactic analysis: nominal, attested by Elders Group (2/76).

<**th'x̲ámél**>, ANA /'*breast bone, part of human body between breast bone and ribs*'/, *see* th'x̲.

<**th'x̲ét**>, df //θ'əx̣-M1=T or θ'əx̣ʷ=[delab]-M1=T//, pcs, HHG (possibly) ['*to clean s-th*'], (<**metathesis**> *non-continuative*), possibly <**delabialization**> *derivational*, (<**=t**> *purposeful control transitivizer*), phonology: possible delabialization, metathesis, syntactic analysis: transitive verb, attested by EB (1/16/76), compare root <**th'éx̲w**> *wash*, compare <**sts'ets'íx̲**> (perhaps) *clean (of a*

house), Salish cognate: Sechelt /c'ə́x̣ʷ-t/ *to clean* T77:26.

<th'x̲éyles> or **<th'x̲íles>**, ANAA /'*inside brisket of meat (deer, etc.)*'/, *see* th'x̲.

<th'x̲welwétem>, PE ['*wash one's clothes*'], *see* th'éx̲w or th'óx̲w.

<th'x̲woythílem>, PE ['*(go) wash one's mouth out*'], *see* th'éx̲w or th'óx̲w.

TL’

<**tl'**>, free root //ƛ’//, DEM /'*agent (human, gender unspecified, absent)*'/, semantic environment ['before proper names only (so far)'], DEM /'*by (agent. human, gender unspecified, absent)*'/, semantic environment ['after passive verb'], syntactic analysis: demonstrative article, attested by AC, EB, example: <**(maythóxescha, maytólxwescha, maythòmcha, maytòlèmcha) tl' Bill wexwe'í:s.**>, ////, /'*Bill will help (me, us, you, you folks) when he gets here.*'/, attested by AC, <**le emét kw'e Albert stetís tl' Amy.**>, //lə ʔəmə́t k’^{w}ə Albert s=C$_1$ə=tə[=Aí=]sƛ’ Amy//, /'*Albert sat beside (near) Amy.*'/, attested by AC, <**le thíytes tl' Oliver Wells qe Casey Wells te sqwéltels tl' Daniel Milo qe Bob Joe lí te machines te xwelítem.**>, //lə θ’íy=T-əsƛ’ Oliver Wells qə Casey Wells tə s=q^{w}ɛ[=Aə́=]l=təl-sƛ’ Daniel Milo qə Bob Joe lí tə məšín-s tə x^{w}əlítəm//, /'*Oliver Wells and Casey Wells made the voices of Daniel Milo and Bob Joe on the white man's machine.*'/, attested by AC, <**tl'o tethá les iléqelhtstes tl' Bill te sqwemá:y.**>, //ƛ’a tə=θɛ́ lə-s ʔilə́q-əɬc=T-əsƛ’ Bill tə s=q^{w}əm=ɛ́·y//, /'*That's what Bill bought for the dog.*'/, attested by EB, <**maythóxes tl' Bill.**>, //mɛy=T-áx^{y}-əs ƛ’ Bill//, /'*Bill (absent, even if in next room) helped me.*'/, attested by EB, <**maythóxes tl' Málí.**>, //mɛy=T-áx^{y}-əsƛ’ mɛ́lí//, /'*Mary (absent, even if in next room) helped me.*'/, attested by EB, <**máythò:m tl' Málí.**>, //mɛ́y=T-à·mƛ’ mɛ́lí//, /'*Mary (absent) helped you.*'/, attested by EB, <**pétemesò:m tl' Lizzie.**>, //pə[-´-]tɛm=əs-à·mƛ’ Lizzie//, /'*Lizzie is asking about you.*'/, attested by EB.

<**tl'a- ~ tl'e- ~ tl'-**>, ia //ƛ’ɛ- ~ ƛ’ə- ~ƛ’-//, TIB ['*independent object of preposition*'], PRON, syntactic analysis: ip, syntactic comment: prefixed to independent pronouns, attested by AC, EB, AD, NP, others, example: <**stetís (tl'lốwe, tl'elhlímelh, tl'a'á'altha, tl'alhwélep).**>, //s=C$_1$ə=tə[=Aí=]s (ƛ’-lə́wə, ƛ’ə-ɬlíməɬ,ƛ’ɛ-C$_1$ɛ́=ʔɛlθɛ,ƛ’ɛ-ɬw(=)ə́ləp)//, /'*She's close to (you, us, me, you folks).*'/, attested by AC (8/25/70), <**míchxw stetís tl'a'á'altha.**>, //mí-c-x^{w} s=C$_1$ə=tə[=Aí=]sƛ’ɛ-C$_1$ɛ́=ʔɛlθɛ//, /'*Come close to me.*'/, attested by AC; found in <**tl'á'altha**>, //ƛ’-C$_1$ɛ́=ʔɛlθɛ//, /'*me (obj. of prep.)*'/, dialects: *Cheh.*, attested by EB, <**tl'alhléwep**>, //ƛ’ɛ-ɬ=lə́wə=p//, /'*you folks (obj. of prep.)*'/, dialects: *Cheh.*, attested by EB, example: <**le wálxes te sq'émél stetís tl'e'álthe.**>, //lə wɛ́l=x^{y}-əs tə s=q’ə́məl s=C$_1$ə=tə[=Aí=]s ƛ’ə-ʔɛ́lθə//, /'*He threw the paddle near me.*'/, attested by AC, <**le x̲eth'étes te sq'émél telí tl'e'áltha.**>, //lə x̣əθ’=ə[-M2-]T-əs tə s=q’ə́məl təlí ƛ’ə-ʔɛ́lθɛ//, /'*He pushed the paddle away from me.*'/, attested by AC, <**kwútes t(e)lí (tl'a'altha, tl'léwe, tl'alhlímelh, tútl'ò).**>, //k^{w}ú=T-əs t(ə)lí (ƛ’-C$_1$ɛ́=ʔɛlθɛ,ƛ’-lə́wə,ƛ’ɛ-ɬlíməɬ, tə́w=ƛ’á)//, /'*He took it from (me, you, us, him).*'/, attested by EB, <**óxwestchexw xwelá(m) tl'á'altha.**>, //ʔáx^{w}əs=T-c-əx^{w} x^{w}ə=lɛ́(=m)ƛ’-C$_1$ɛ́=ʔɛlθɛ//, /'*Give it to him from me.*'/, attested by EB, <**óxwestchexw thútl'ò xwelá(m) tl'(e)léwe.**>, //ʔáx^{w}əs=T-c-əx^{w} θə́w=ƛ’á x^{w}ə=lɛ́(=m)ƛ’(ə)-lə́wə//, /'*Give it to her from you.*'/, attested by EB, <**mís sq'ó tl'á'altha.**>, //mí-s s=q’áƛ’-C$_1$ɛ́=ʔɛlθɛ//, /'*He came with me.*'/, attested by EB, <**melh yesq'ó tl'á'altha.**>, //mə-ɬ yə-s=q’áƛ’-C$_1$ɛ́=ʔɛlθɛ//, /'*Come along with me.*'/, attested by EB, <**ístexwchexw ó tl'á'altha. ~ ístexwchxwò tl'á'eltha.**>, //ʔí=sT-əx^{w}-x-əx^{w} ʔáƛ’-C$_1$ɛ́=ʔɛlθɛ//, /'*Leave it here with me.*'/, attested by EB.

<**tl'ákw'**>, probable root //ƛ’ɛ́k’^{w}//, perhaps meaning *peaks in water*

<**Tl'átl'ekw'em ~ Lexwtl'átl'ekw'em**>, dnom //ƛ’ɛ́[=C$_1$ə=]k’^{w}=əm ~ ləx^{w}=ƛ’ɛ́[=C$_1$ə=]k’^{w}=əm//, PLN ['*Hope Indian Reserve #12 (Klaklacum)*'], ASM ['on east bank of Fraser River not far south of American Creek'], literally /'place of rough water getting peaks ~ place of water always making(getting/having) peaks'/, ASM ['so named because the rocks under the Fraser River here are all in peaks and cause the water to be rough and make peaks'], (<**lexw=**> *always*), probably root <**tl'ákw'**> *peak?*, probably <**=R1=**> *continuative*, (<**=em**> *place to have/get*), phonology:

reduplication, syntactic analysis: nominal, attested by place names meeting after IHTTC (8/23/77), Elders Group (8/24/77), also <**Lexwtl'átl'ekw'em**>, //ləxʷ=ƛ'ɛ[=C₁ə=]k'ʷ=əm//, attested by SP (Elders Group 8/24/77), AK and/or AD (American Bar Trip 6/26/78), source: place names file reference #208, compare <**S<u>x</u>wótl'akw'em**> *Emory Creek* said to mean *water boils up*.

<**tl'ákw'<u>x</u>el**>, df //ƛ'ɛk'ʷ=ɛ́x̣əl or ƛ'k'ʷ=ɛ́[=M1=]x̣əl//, EZ /'*smaller goose, brant, (black brant), for the smaller goose* possibly also *the cackling goose* and *lesser Canada goose*'/, ['*Branta bernicla, (Branta nigricans)*, possibly also *Branta canadensis minima* and *Branta canadensis (leucopareia or parvipes)*'], ASM ['(largely a salt-water bird)'], root meaning unknown unless tl'ákw' *water peak, rough water*??, possibly <**=á<u>x</u>el**> *on the arm, on the wing, on the side appendage*, possibly <**metathesis**> *derivational*, syntactic analysis: nominal, attested by BJ (5/10/64, 12/5/64), Salish cognate: Squamish /ƛ'ák'ʷx̣n/ *snow goose (Chen hyperborea)* Kennedy and Bouchard 1976b:68-69, W73:122, K69:73 in contrast to /ʔəx̣/ *wild goose, Canada goose (Branta canadensis)* Kennedy and Bouchard 1976:68, W73:122, K67:389, K69:93, Lushootseed /ƛ'k'ʷáx̣ad/ *unidentified goose* H76:327 (perhaps with /-ax̣ad/ *edge, side appendage* H76:12??) in contrast to /ʔəx̣áʔ/ *snow goose* H76:662, Samish dial. of NSt /ƛ'ék'ʷ-əx̣ən/ *goose* vs. /x̣ə́l'x̣əl'c'/ *brant* B84a:67, not cognate with Sechelt /x̣á/ *any goose* T77:11 which is cognate with Upriver Halkomelem /ʔɛ́x̣ə/, Squamish /ʔəx̣/ and Lushootseed ʔax̣áʔ/.

<**tl'ál**>, bound root //ƛ'ɛl *attach, fasten, put on*//.

<**tl'álx**>, pcis //ƛ'ɛl=xʸ//, CLO /'*put s-th on (of a design on a dress, of a shirt, shoes, etc.), attach it, stick it on, fasten it*'/, MC, (<**=x**> *purposeful control transitivizer inanimate object preferred*), syntactic analysis: transitive verb, attested by AD (4/21/80), Salish cognate: Lushootseed root /ƛ'al/ *put clothing on; encase; be stranded* as in /ʔu-ƛ'ál-š/ *put clothing on* H76:312-315; found in <**tl'álxes**>, //ƛ'ɛl=xʸ-əs//, /'*She put it on (of a design on a dress, etc.), attaches it, sticks it on, fastens it*'/, attested by AD (4/21/80), example: <**tl'álxes te "zipper".**>, //ƛ'ɛl=xʸ-əs tə zipper//, /'*He/She put on the zipper (attached it).*'/, attested by AD (4/21/80), <**tl'álxes te "rivets".**>, //ƛ'ɛl=xʸ-əs tə rivets//, /'*She put the rivets on (on a leather purse for ex.)*'/, attested by AD, <**tl'álxchxw te s<u>x</u>el<u>x</u>éyles te letàm.**>, //ƛ'ɛl=xʸ-c-xʷ tə s=C₁əC₂=x̣ə[=Aí=]lə-s tə (lətɛ́m, sch'áletstel).//, /'*Put the legs (back) on the (table, chair).*'/, literally /'you put it/them on the legs -of the (table, chair)'/, attested by AD, <**tl'álxchxw ta' "pocket".**>, //ƛ'ɛl=xʸ-c-xʷ t-ɛʔ pocket//, /'*You put on a pocket.*'/, attested by AD, <**tl'álxes te stl'epíwels.**>, //ƛ'ɛl=xʸ-əs tə s=ƛ'əp=íwəl-s//, /'*He put on his shirt.*'/, attested by AD.

<**stl'átl'el**>, strs //s=ƛ'ɛ[=C₁ə=]l//, CLO /'*to be attached, to be fixed or fastened, be put on*'/, MC, (<**s=**> *stative*), (<**=R1=**> *resultative*), phonology: reduplication, syntactic analysis: adjective/adjectival verb, attested by AD (4/21/80), example: <**lulh stl'átl'el te qwlhíxels.**>, //lə=uɬ s=ƛ'ɛ[=C₁ə=]l tə qʷɬ=íy=xʸəl-s//, /'*His shoes are already put on.*'/, attested by AD (4/21/80).

<**tl'ál ~ tl'á:l**>, bound root //ƛ'ɛl ~ƛ'ɛ·l *sharp sound*//.

<**tl'á:l<u>x</u>em**>, ds //ƛ'ɛ·l=x̣=əm orƛ'ɛ[=·=]l=x̣=əm//, SD ['*(have/get a) crackle and pop (sound of a log in a fire or of firecrackers)*'], FIRE ['*to spark (with a pop)*'] (attested by RG & EH (4/10/99 Ling332)), possibly <**=:=**> *non-continuative*, lx <**=<u>x</u>**> *distributive, all over, all around,* probably <**=em**> *have/get or middle voice*, phonology: possible lengthening, syntactic analysis: intransitive verb, attested by Elders Group (11/3/76), EB (3/12/76), Salish cognate: Lushootseed /ƛ'álx̣/ *pop, crack* beside /ƛ'əlx̣-cút/ *crackling noise* and /xʷul' ʔəlc'u-ƛ'àləx̣əb/ *Your fire is just crackling.* all from root /ƛ'al/ *sound* H76:317, also <**tl'á:y<u>x</u>em**>, //ƛ'ɛ·y=x̣=əm//, also /'*crackling (less than tl'áyé<u>x</u>em), crackle (of wood in fire)*'/, attested by EB (2/6/76, 12/19/75), historical/comparative detail: considering the Halkomelem /l/-Thompson /y/ sound correspondence and the fact that EB

lived in Thompson territory, married a Thompson and speaks some Thompson, the y here could be Thompson influence.

<**tl'áléx̲em**>, cts //ƛ’ɛ́l=[=ə́=]x̣=əm orƛ’ɛ́l=ə[=´=]x̣=əm//, SD [*'crackling and popping (of a log in fire or firecrackers)'*], possibly <**=é=** or **=´=**> *continuative*, phonology: possible stress-shift, possible infixed schwa, syntactic analysis: intransitive verb, attested by Elders Group (11/3/76), also <**tl'á:léx̲em**>, //ƛ’ɛ́·l=[=ə́=]x̣=əm or ƛ’ɛ́·l=ə[=´=]x̣=əm//, attested by EB (3/12/76), also <**tl'áyéx̲em**>, //ƛ’ɛ́y=[=ə́=]x̣=əm orƛ’ɛ́y=ə[=´=]x̣=əm//, also /*'crackling a lot (of fire, firecrackers)'*/, attested by EB (2/6/76).

<**tl'eléqw**>, df //ƛ’ɛl=ə[=´=]qʷ orƛ’ɛ[=Aə=]l=ə[=´]qʷ//, SD [*'explode'*], FIRE, possibly <**=eqw**> *on top of the head*, possibly <**=é=** or **=´=**> *continuative or derivational*, phonology: infixed schwa or stress-shift, syntactic analysis: intransitive verb, attested by Elders Group (1/7/76).

<**wetl'éleqw**>, df //wə=ƛ’ɛ́[=Aə́=]l=əqʷ//, SD /*'a shot, explosion'*/, (<**we=**> *suddenly*), possibly <**é-ablaut**> *non-continuative or resultative or nominalizer or derivational*, phonology: ablaut, syntactic analysis: nominal?, intransitive verb?, attested by Elders Group (10/27/76).

<**tl'eltl'ó:lqwem**>, plv //C_1əC_2=ƛ’ɛ́[-Aá·-]l=əqʷ=əm//, cts, SD [*'popping (of firecrackers)'*], (<**R3=**> *plural*), (<**ó:-ablaut**> *continuative*), phonology: ablaut, reduplication, syntactic analysis: intransitive verb, attested by Elders Group (11/3/76), comment: possibly <**qw**> is error for <**qw'**>.

<**tl'éleqw'**>, df //ƛ’ɛ[=Aə́=]l=əq’ʷ//, SD /*'a pop, a shot'*/, possibly <**é-ablaut**> *nominalizer or derivational*, possibly <**=eqw'**> *around in circles*, phonology: possible ablaut, syntactic analysis: nominal?, intransitive verb?, attested by Elders Group (11/3/76).

<**tl'éltl'eleqw'**>, chrs //ƛ’ə́l=C_1əC_2=əq’ʷ//, SD [*'continuous shooting or popping sounds'*], (<**=R2**> *characteristic or continuative*), phonology: reduplication, syntactic analysis: intransitive verb, attested by Elders Group (11/3/76).

<**tl'á:leq**>, probable stem //ƛ’ɛ́·ləq//, stem meaning unknown

<**stl'á:leqem**>, df //s=ƛ’ɛ́·ləq(=)əm//, EZ /*'animal or bird one is afraid of and can't see, powerful creature, supernatural creature'*/, ASM ['includes the sasquatch, Cannibal Ogress (Th'ṓwx̲iya), sí:lhqey (two-headed snake), thunderbird (shxwexwó:s), water pygmies (s'ó:lmexw), schichí' (monster), underwater bear (Halkomelem name unknown), sx̲ex̲omṓ:lh (huge pretty frog with supernatural powers), X̲éylx̲elemós (chief of the river monsters), Spótpeteláx̲el (Thunderwind), and perhaps some creatures without supernatural powers such as grizzly bear; if one sees a stl'áleqem one can get a special sickness called xo:lí:s which cause one to either vomit till one dies or twist up till one dies or go crazy with soul-loss, medicine-men in training often seek them to grab them and possess their power'], (<**s=**> *nominalizer*), root meaning unknown, possibly <**=em**> *have/get*, syntactic analysis: nominal, attested by AC (12/4/71), BJ (12/5/64), other sources: ES /sƛ’ɛʔɛ́ləqəm/ *animal* (later corrected to *powerful creature*), also <**stl'áleqem**>, //s=ƛ’ɛ́ləqəm//, attested by EB (2/11/76), Salish cognate: Squamish /sƛ’álqm/ *monster* and perhaps related is /sƛ’əɬálm/ *grizzly bear* W73:177, K67:291, Lushootseed /s-ƛ’álqəb/ *monster, anything you are afraid of, a fierce power (incl. Basket Ogress)* H76:317, Samish dial. of NSt /sƛ’éləqəm/ *powerful monster, creature with power to do harm (incl. any fierce water or land creatures like grizzly, snake, bear, killer whale, wolf, etc., and creatures like giants, wild small people, thunderbird, giant lizard-like creature, two-headed snake, sea monster).*

<**Stl'áleqem Smált**>, cpds //s=ƛ’ɛ́ləqəm s=mɛ́lt//, PLN probably [*'Slollicum Peak'*], ASM ['near Chehalis, B.C.'], literally /'stl'áleqem mountain'/, syntactic analysis: nominal phrase with modifier(s), attested by EB (2/11/76).

<**Stl'áleqem Stótelō**>, cpds //s=ƛ’ɛ́ləqəm s=tá[=C_1ə=]l=əw//, PLN probably [*'Slollicum Creek'], ASM ['near Chehalis, B.C.'], literally /'stl'áleqem creek'/, syntactic analysis: nominal phrase with*

modifier(s), attested by EB (2/11/76).

<**Stl'áleqem X̱ótsa**>, cpds //s=ƛ'ɛ́ləqəm x̣ácɛ//, PLN probably ['*Slollicum Lake*'], ASM ['near Chehalis, B.C.'], literally /'stl'áleqem lake'/, syntactic analysis: nominal phrase with modifier(s), attested by EB (2/11/76).

<**stl'ítl'leqem**>, dmn //s=C_1í=ƛ'(ɛ)ləq=əm//, EZ /'*(little supernatural creature), little stl'áleqem*'/, (<**R4=**> *diminutive*), phonology: reduplication, syntactic analysis: nominal, attested by Elders Group (1/30/80).

<**stl'eltl'áléqem**>, pln //s=C_1əC_2=ƛ'ɛ́ləq=əm//, EZ /'*lots of stl'áleqems, (lots of supernatural creatures)*'/, (<**R3=**> *plural*), phonology: reduplication, updrifting on penultimate syllable, syntactic analysis: nominal, attested by Elders Grop (1/30/80).

<**tl'áleqtxel**>, ANA ['*long legs*'], *see* tl'áqt.

<**tl'áleqtxel q'ésq'esetsel**>, EZ /'*daddy long-legs, harvestman spider*'/, *see* tl'áqt , *see* q'ey ~ q'i.

<**tl'áleqtxel qwá:l**>, EZ /'*cranefly, leatherjacket (immature cranefly)*'/, *see* qwá:l , *see* tl'áqt.

<**tl'áléx̱em**>, SD ['*crackling and popping (of a log in fire or firecrackers)*'], *see* tl'ál ~ tl'á:l.

<**tl'alqtéle ~ tl'elqtéle**>, EZ /'*deer (Columbia blacktail or Coast), mule deer*'/, *see* tl'áqt.

<**tl'alqtélets ~ tl'alqtélech**>, EZ ['*ring-necked pheasant*'], *see* tl'áqt.

<**tl'álx**>, CLO /'*put s-th on (of a design on a dress, of a shirt, shoes, etc.), attach it, stick it on, fasten it*'/, *see* tl'ál.

<**tl'á:lx̱em**>, SD ['*(have/get a) crackle and pop (sound of a log in a fire or of firecrackers)*'], *see* tl'ál ~ tl'á:l.

<**tl'álhem**>, df //ƛ'ɛ́ɬ=əm//, LAND ['*salt*'], root meaning unknown, possibly <**=em**> *have/get*, syntactic analysis: nominal, attested by AC, MH (Deming 1/4/79), NP (9/30/75), Elders Group (5/16/79), other sources: ES /ƛ'ɛ́·ɬəm/ *salt*, JH /ƛ'é·ɬəm/ *salt*, Salish cognate: Squamish /ƛ'áɬm/ *salt, salt water* W73:222, K67:333, Sechelt /ƛ'áɬm/ *salt* T77:21, MCx /ƛ'áɬəm/ *salt*, Lushootseed /ƛ'áɬəb/ *salt, salty* H76:318, Nk /ƛ'ǽɬæm/ *salt* Amoss 1961, LmSanSg /ƛ'éɬəŋ/ *salt, salty* TTE74, Clallam /ƛ'áɬəŋ/ *salt, be salty* TTE74, all in cognate set 107 G82, also <**tl'á:lhem**>, //ƛ'ɛ́·ɬ=əm//, attested by BJ (12/5/64 new transcript old p.292), example: <**tl'álhem sth'óqwi**>, //ƛ'ɛ́ɬəm s=θ'áq^{w}i//, /'*salt fish*'/, attested by Elders Group (5/16/79).

<**chólmelelh tl'álhem**>, FOOD /'*soy sauce*'/, (lit. Chinese style + salt), (attested by RG,EH 6/16/98 to SN, edited by BG with RG,EH 6/26/00)

<**tl'átl'elhem**>, ds //ƛ'ɛ[=C_1ə=]ɬ=əm//, TAST ['*salty*'], (<**=R1=**> *continuative or resultative*), phonology: reduplication, syntactic analysis: adjective/adjectival verb, attested by AC, others.

<**tl'alhémáleqep**>, ds //ƛ'ɛɬə[=´=]m=ɛ́ləqəp//, SM /'*smells like salt, (have/get a salt smell)*'/, (<=´=> *derivational*), lx <**=áleqep ~ =áléqep**> *in smell*, phonology: stress-shift, syntactic analysis: intransitive verb, attested by Elders Group (5/25/77).

<**tl'alhémáleqep**>, SM /'*smells like salt, (have/get a salt smell)*'/, *see* tl'álhem.

<**tl'alhwélep**>, PRON /'*you folks (object of preposition), to you folks, with you folks*'/, *see* lhwélep.

<**tl'ám**> or <**tl'em**>, probable bound root //ƛ'ɛ́m// or //ƛ'əm// *sound of crackle or crunch*

<**tl'ámkw'em**>, cts //ƛ'ə[=Aɛ́=]m(=)k'^{w}=əm//, SD /'*(have) sound of popping small round things (snowberries, herring eggs as when eating them, rice krispies, crabapples, cranberries, etc.), (have a crunching sound (as of grasshopper, rice krispies))*'/, possibly stem <**tl'émkw'**> //**ƛ'əm(=)k'**^{w}// *crunch when biting, pop small round things*, possibly <**á-ablaut**> *continuative*, <**=kw'**> *round things*, probably <**=em**> *have/get/intransitivizer*, syntactic analysis: intransitive verb, attested by

Elders Group (11/3/76), RM (4/23/76), Salish cognate: Squamish /ƛ'mk'ʷ-ánʔ/ *crack louse or nit between teeth (tr.)* W73:70, K69:72.

<**tl'ámqw'els**>, sas //ƛ'ə[=Aέ=]m=q'ʷ=əls//, SD /'*crunchy (loud when eating), crackling (sound or noise when eating)*'/, possibly <**=qw'**> *around in circles*, (<**=els**> *structured activity continuative*), phonology: ablaut, syntactic analysis: intransitive verb, adjective/adjectival verb?, attested by Elders Group (12/10/75), *<**tsel tl'ámqw'els te qwe'óp.**> rejected, */'I crunched the apple.'/ rejected by EB (5/3/76).

<**tl'emékw'**>, dnom //ƛ'əm=[=ə́=]k'ʷ//, EZ /'*grasshopper, (*possibly *the longhorned grasshopper)*'/, ['order *Orthoptera* family *Acrididae* or perhaps family *Tettigoniidae*'], probably <**=é=**> *nominalizer*, phonology: infixed schwa, syntactic analysis: nominal, Elder's comment: "from tl'ámkw'em", attested by RM (4/23/76), also <**tl'émqwxel**>, //ƛ'ə́m=qʷ=xʸəl//, Elder's comment: "from tl'émqw- the noise it makes", lx <**=xel**> *on the legs*, attested by RM (6/13/77), contrast <**ts'tl'ám ~ ts'tl'ém**> *jump* for another derivation of a similar word for grasshopper.

<**tl'ámkw'em**>, SD /'*(have) sound of popping small round things (snowberries, herring eggs as when eating them, rice krispies, crabapples, cranberries, etc.), (have a crunching sound (as of grasshopper, rice krispies))*'/, *see* tl'ém.

<**tl'ámqw'els**>, SD /'*crunchy (loud when eating), crackling (sound or noise when eating)*'/, *see* tl'ém.

<**tl'ápe<u>x</u>em**>, HARV /'*to fall down and scatter, drop and scatter*'/, *see* tl'ép.

<**tl'ap'élatsem**>, ABFC ['*to wag its tail*'], *see* stl'ep'él:ets ~ stl'ep'élets.

<**tl'áqt**>, free root //ƛ'έqt//, DESC /'*(be) long, tall (of tree, anything)*'/, syntactic analysis: adjective/adjectival verb, attested by AC, EB (5/12/76), Elders Group (1/19/77), other sources: ES /ƛ'έ·qt/ *long*, JH /ƛ'é·qt/ *long*, Salish cognate: Squamish /ƛ'áqt/ *long (space, time)* W73:165, K67:333, Sechelt /ƛ'áqt/ *long* T77:20, example: <**tl'áqt te máqels.**>, //ƛ'έqt tə mέ=qəl-s//, /'*Her hair is long.*'/, attested by AC, <**tl'áqt (sts'ó:lha, <u>x</u>wéylem)**>, //ƛ'έqt (s=c'á·ɬε,x̣ʷí·ləm)//, /'*long (leaf, rope)*'/, attested by AC, <**tl'áqt theqá:t**>, //ƛ'έqt θəqέ·t//, /'*tall tree*'/, attested by AC, <**yeláwel tl'áqt tel <u>x</u>éltel telí ta swá.**>, //yəlέw=əlƛ'έqt t-əl x̣i[=Aə́=]l=təl təlí t-ε s=wέ//, /'*My pencil is longer than yours.*'/, attested by Elders Group.

<**tl'áqt ts'íyxw seplíl**>, FOOD /'*spaghetti*'/, (lit. long + dry + bread), (attested by RG,EH 6/16/98 to SN, edited by BG with RG,EH 6/26/00)

<**tl'eqtámeth' ~ tl'eqtáméth'**>, ds //ƛ'εqt=έməθ'//, DESC ['*tall (of a person)*'], lx <**=ámeth'**> *height, upright*, phonology: vowel-reduction, syntactic analysis: adjective/adjectival verb, attested by AC, EB (12/1/75), also <**tl'eqtómeth'**>, //ƛ'εqt=ε[=Aá]məθ'//, also /'*tall person*'/, attested by AC (11/11/71, 10/13/71).

<**tl'alqtéle ~ tl'elqtéle**>, ds //ƛ'ε[=lə=]qt=ə́lε//, pln, EZ /'*deer (Columbia blacktail or Coast), mule deer*'/, ['*Odocoileus hemionis columbianus, Odocoileus hemionis hemionis*'], (semological comment: said to mean lit. *long ears*, perhaps so named after the ears of the mule deer, which are much longer (8.75 in. from notch) than those of the Coast (7.5 in. from notch), the mule deer also is larger than the Coast deer (3 typical adult males 68-74 in. long and 180-400 lbs. vs. 56-66 in. long and 110-250 lbs.), the Coast deer occurred widely with the largest specimens in the Fraser Valley, but the mule deer also occurred regularly in the Upper Fraser Valley (measurments and distribution from Cowan and Guiguet 1965), the mule deer then may have been prototypical and more prized and this name probably originated in Upriver Halkomelem because the area was one of the few Salish language areas where both types of deer existed), (<**=le=**> *plural*), lx <**=éla**> *on the side of the head, on the cheek/temple*, phonology: vowel-loss (in infix), optional vowel-reduction (in root andsuffix), infixed plural, syntactic analysis: nominal, attested by AC, BJ (5/10/64, 12/5/64),

Deming (6/15/77), AK (11/21/72), MJ with JL and AC (Wells tape), Elders Group (1/30/80), CT and HT (6/21/76), other sources: ES /ƛ’əlqtə́lə ~ smɛ́yəθ/ *deer*, example: **<latsel kw'í(y)qel la(m) te smált; latsel háwe kw'e tl'alqtéle.>**, //lɛ-c-əl k’ʷíy=əqəl lɛ(=m) tə s=mɛ́lt; lɛ-c-əl hɛ́wə k’ʷəƛ’ɛ[=lə=]qt=ə́lɛ//, /'*I'm going up (climbing) the mountain to hunt deer.*'/, literally /'I'm going to climb (going) to the mountain; I'm going to hunt the (remote)/some deer'/, attested by AC (10/23/71), **<isále tl'elqtéle tel kw'étslexw>**, //ʔisɛ́lə ƛ’ə[=lə=]qt=ə́lə t-əl k’ʷə́c=l-əxʷ//, /'*two deer that I saw (see s-th)*'/, attested by HT (Elders Group 1/30/80), **<táwet te tl'elqtéle kw'es le kwélext te (sméyéth, tl'elqtéle)>**, //tɛ́w=əT təƛ’ɛ[=lə=]qt=ə́lɛ k’ʷə-s lə kʷə́l(=)əxʸ=T tə (s=mɛ́yəθ,ƛ’ɛ[=lə=]qt=ə́lɛ)//, /'*light up the deer and shoot the (animal, deer) (light s-th up, shoot s-th)*'/, attested by CT and HT (6/21/76), **<p'éq' te stl'ep'élets tl'elqtéle>**, //p’ə́q’ tə s=ƛ’əp=ə́ləc ƛ’ɛ[=lə=]qt=ə́lɛ//, EZ ['*white-tailed deer*'], ['*Odocoilus virginianus*'], literally /'the tail is-white deer'/, (semological comment: (not reported from the Fraser Valley but found now in the Kootenays and eastern central B.C.)), Elder's comment: "there's a shorter name", attested by CT and HT (6/21/76), **<ts'q'éyx̱ te éqwelets tl'elqtéle>**, //c’=q’íx̣ tə ʔə́qʷ=ələcƛ’ɛ[=lə=]qt=ə́lɛ//, EZ ['*black-tailed deer*'], ['*Odocoilus hemionis*'], literally /'the lower back is-black deer'/, Elder's comment: "there's a shorter name, found way up in the mountains", attested by CT and HT (6/21/76).

<tl'alqtélets ~ tl'alqtélech>, ds //ƛ’ɛ[=lə=]qt=ə́ləc//, pln, EZ ['*ring-necked pheasant*'], ['*Phasianus colchicus*'], ASM ['(introduced to Vancouver Island and then the mainland in the 1890's)'], literally /'long tail, long on the rump'/, ASM ['so named because of long tail'], (**<=le=>** *plural*), lx **<=élets>** *on the rump*, phonology: vowel-reduction, infixed plural, syntactic analysis: nominal, attested by AC (8/4/70, 9/18/71).

<tl'éqtepsem>, ds //ƛ’ɛ[=Aə́=]qt=əpsəm//, ANA ['*(have a) long neck*'], BPI, literally /'long on the back of the neck and head'/, (**<é-ablaut>** *derivational*), lx **<=épsem>** *on the back of the neck and head*, phonology: ablaut, syntactic analysis: adjective/adjectival verb, attested by Elders Group (3/3/76).

<Tl'éqteqsel>, ds //ƛ’ɛ[=Aə́=]qt=əqsəl//, PLN ['*longest dirt point sticking out on Harrison River about a quarter mile above Harrison Bay bridge*'], (semological comment: outside of Charlie Pretty's place, has crabapple trees, etc., growing on it), literally /'long point, long nose'/, (**<é-ablaut>** *derivational*), lx **<=eqsel>** *on the nose, point*, phonology: ablaut, syntactic analysis: nominal, attested by EL (with EB and NP)(Chehalis place names trip 9/27/77), source: place names reference file #309.

<xwtl'óqtes>, ds //xʷ=ƛ’ɛ[-Aá-]qt=əs//, ANA ['*(have a) long face*'], BPI, EFAM ['*(be) morose*'], (**<xw=>** meaning uncertain unless from **<xwe=>** *become*), lx **<=es>** *on the face*, phonology: ó-ablaut on root á automatic before =es ~ =ó(:)s, syntactic analysis: adjective/adjectival verb, attested by AC (9/18/71, 9/18/71), example: **<tl'ó kwthá xwtl'óqtes.>**, //ƛ’á kʷ=θɛ́ xʷ=ƛ’ɛ[-Aá-]qt=əs//, /'*That's the one with the long face.*'/, attested by AC.

<stl'óqtes>, ds //s=ƛ’ɛ[-Aá-]qt=əs//, ANA ['*long face*'], BPI, (**<s=>** *nominalizer or stative*), lx **<=es>** *on the face*, phonology: ablaut, syntactic analysis: nominal?, intransitive verb??, attested by MV and EF (Deming Evening Class 4/27/78).

<stl'eqtí:m>, df //s=ƛ’ɛqt=ə[-Aí:-]m//, DIR ['*length*'], (**<s=>** *nominalizer*), **<í:-ablaut>** *durative*, phonology: ablaut, vowel-reduction, syntactic analysis: nominal, attested by Elders Group (3/15/72), example: **<te stl'eqtí:ms>**, //tə s=ƛ’ɛqt=í·m-s//, /'*its/his/her length*'/.

<tl'eqtíwél>, ds //ƛ’ɛqt=íwəl//, DESC ['*tall (of tree)*'], lx **<=íwel>** *in the insides*, (semological comment: perhaps referring to the trunk), phonology: updrifting, syntactic analysis: adjective/adjectival verb, attested by CT (6/8/76), example: **<tl'eqtíwél thqát>**, //ƛ’ɛqt=íwəl θqɛ́t//, /'*tall tree*'/, attested by CT.

<**stl'eqtóletses**>, ds //s=ƛ'ɛqt=álə(=)cəs//, ANAH /'*second finger, index finger*'/, literally /'long finger'/, (<**s=**> *nominalizer*), lx <**=óletses**> *(on the) finger* (with lx <**=tses**> *on the hand)*, phonology: vowel-reduction, syntactic analysis: nominal, attested by Elders Group (5/3/78).

<**tl'áleqtxel**>, pln //ƛ'ɛ́[=lə=]qt=x^{y}əl//, ANA //'*long legs, long-legged*'//, ds, ANA ['*ƛ'ɛ́[=lə=]qt=x^{y}əl*'], (<**=le=**> *plural*), lx <**=xel**> *(on the) leg*, phonology: infixed plural, syntactic analysis: adjective/adjectival verb, attested by Elders Group (6/16/76).

<**tl'áleqtxel q'ésq'esetsel**>, cpds //ƛ'ɛ́[=lə=]qt=x^{y}əl q'i[=Aə́=]s=C_1əC_2=əcəl//, EZ /'*daddy long-legs, harvestman spider*'/, ['class *Arachnida*, order *Phalangida*'], literally /'long legs spider, long-legged spider'/, phonology: infixed plural, ablaut, reduplication, syntactic analysis: nominal phrase with modifier(s), attested by Elders Group (6/16/76).

<**tl'áleqtxel qwá:l**>, cpds //ƛ'ɛ́[=lə=]qt=x^{y}əl q^{w}ɛ́·l//, EZ /'*cranefly, "leatherjacket" (immature cranefly)*'/, ['order Diptera, family *Tipulidae*'], literally /'long-legged mosquito'/, phonology: infixed plural, syntactic analysis: nominal phrase with modifier(s), attested by Elders Group (6/16/76, 9/8/76), contrast <**spelwálh qwá:l**> *cranefly, "leatherjacket"* (lit. *last year's mosquito)*.

<**Tl'aqewólem??** or **Tl'iq'ewólem??** or more likely **Tl'ikw'ólem**>, df //ƛ'ɛq'əwál=əm or ƛ'iq'əwál=əm or ƛ'ík'^{w}ə[=Aá=]l=əm//, PLN ['*Lindeman Lake*'], root meaning unknown unless <**tl'aq' ~ tl'q'**>, bound root //ƛ'ɛq' ~ ƛ'q' *shorten?* or more likely <**tl'íkw'el**>, ds //ƛ'ík'^{w}əl// *kinnikinnick berries*, (<**=em**> *place to have/get*), compare <**Tl'íkw'elem**>, ds //ƛ'ík'^{w}əl=əm// *Silver Creek, Silver Hope Creek*, literally /'place to have/get kinnikinnick berries'/, syntactic analysis: nominal, source: Wells <kleh-kah-WA-lum> *Lindeman Lake* Wells 1966.

<**tl'aq' ~ tl'q'**>, bound root //ƛ'ɛq' ~ ƛ'q' *shorten?*//.

<**tl'atl'eq'xélém**>, df //ƛ'ɛ[-C_1ə-]q'=x^{y}ə[=´=]l=əm//, TVMO ['*shortcut*'], possibly <**-R1-**> *continuative* or *resultative*, possibly <**=´=**> *derivational*, <**=xel**> *on the foot*, possibly <**=em**> *place to have/get*, phonology: reduplication, stress=shift, updrifting, syntactic analysis: nominal, attested by SP (Elders Group 9/13/77).

<**Tl'átl'eq'xélém**>, df //ƛ'ɛ́[=C_1ə=]q'=x^{y}ə[=´=]l=əm//, PLN /'*mountain west of X̱ó:letsa, (mountain north of Sése (Mary Ann Creek), shortcut to X̱ó:letsa [Elders Group (Fish Camp 9/29-31/77)])*'/, ASM ['X̱ó:letsa is the mountain above Yale Creek near Yale, B.C.'], literally /'shortcut'/, syntactic analysis: nominal, attested by SP and AK (Fish Camp 8/2/77), source: place names reference file #157, also <**Lexwtl'átl'eq'xélem**>, //ləx^{w}=ƛ'ɛ́[=C_1ə=]q'=x^{y}ə[=´=]l=əm//, also /'*mountain north of Sése (Mary Ann Creek), shortcut to X̱ó:letsa*'/, literally /'always a shortcut'/, ASM ['it was a shortcut to X̱ó:letsa (a mountain with lots of lakes on it)'], (<**lexw=**> *always*), attested by Elders Group (Fish Camp 9/29-31/77), source: place names reference file #101.

<**tl'ítl'q'ey**>, df //C_1í=ƛ'(ɛ)q'=əy//, TVMO ['*a shortcut*'], possibly <**R4=**> *diminutive*, possibly <**=ey**> meaning uncertain unless *place* as in Nooksack, phonology: reduplication, vowel-loss, syntactic analysis: nominal, attested by IHTTC/Elders Group/NP (9/13/77).

<**tl'itl'q'oyám**>, durs //C_1í=ƛ'(ɛ)q'=əy=ə[=Aɛ́=]m//, TVMO ['*take a shortcut*'], possibly <**=em**> *have, get, intransitivizer*, possibly *middle voice*, (<**á-ablaut**> *durative*), phonology: reduplication, vowel-loss, ablaut, syntactic analysis: intransitive verb, attested by NP (Elders Group 9/13/77).

<**tl'asíp**>, df //ƛ'ɛs=ə[=Aí=]p//, EB ['*licorice fern*'], ['*Polypodium glycyrrhiza*'], ASM ['this fern grows especially on maple trees, its root is peeled andchewed year-round for its sweet long-lasting licorice flavor and temporarysustenance'], MED ['the root is chewed as medicine for colds, coughs, and asthma'], possibly root <**tl'as-**> *sweet*??, possibly <**í-ablaut**> *durative*, (semological comment: perhaps *durative* because of the long-lasting flavor), possibly <**=ep**> *in the dirt*, phonology: possible ablaut, syntactic analysis: nominal, dialects: *Chill., Cheh.*, attested by Elders Group (2/26/75),

IHTTC, Salish cognate: Squamish /ƛ'asíp/ *sweet substance obtained from maple trees (maple syrup or sugar)* W73:173, K67:333, but identified as *licorice fern (Polypodium glycyrrhiza)* in Bouchard and Turner 1976:18-19 with the same uses as above, Clallam (SSt) <klasip> (macron over i) and Lummi <klasíp> (macron over i) both *licorice fern (Polypodium vulgare)* Gunther 1973:13, Samish dial. of NSt /ƛ'əsíp/ *licorice fern (added to any medicine to kill the taste of other ingredients)* G84a:72-73, also <**st'uslóye**>, //s=t'usl(=)áyə//, dialects: *Tait*, attested by SP, others?.

<**Tl'átl'elh ?**>, df //ƛ'ɛ́ƛ'əɬ ?//, PLN ['*burial grove of Scowkale*'], (HT?, Boas?, Sepass map?, Wells?, Gibbs?) <Claclelth>.

<**tl'átl'elhem**>, TAST ['*salty*'], *see* tl'álhem.

<**tl'atl'eq'xélém**>, TVMO ['*shortcut*'], *see* tl'aq' ~ tl'q'.

<**Tl'átl'eq'xélém**>, PLN /'*mountain west of X̲ó:letsa, (mountain north of Sése (Mary Ann Creek), shortcut to X̲ó:letsa [Elders Group (Fish Camp 9/29-31/77)])*'/, *see* tl'aq' ~ tl'q'.

<**tl'áts'eq**>, possibly root or stem //ƛ'ɛ́c'əq//, FIRE ['*fire box or fire platform and fire shield for torch-lighting or pit-lamping fire*'], CAN, HUNT, FSH, ASM ['made of metal for many years now but probably platform was made of flat rocks in the old days'], syntactic analysis: noun?, nominal, attested by EL (Elders Group 1/26/77).

<**tl'áwels**>, ABFC ['*barking*'], *see* tl'éw.

<**tl'á:wq'em**>, df //ƛ'ɛ́·wq'=əm//, LT ['*to glitter*'], root meaning unknown, probably <**=em**> *have/get/intransitivizer or middle voice*, syntactic analysis: intransitive verb, attested by EB (2/9/76).

<**tl'áxweleq**>, PLAY /'*be winning, he was winning*'/, *see* tl'éxw.

<**tl'áxwt**>, PLAY ['*taking advantage of s-o*'], *see* tl'éxw.

<**tl'á'altha**>, PRON /'*me (after prepositional verbs), I (after prepositional verbs)*'/, *see* áltha ~ álthe.

<**tl'chá:s ~ tl'tsá:s**>, free root //ƛ'cɛ́·s//, LAND ['*island*'], syntactic analysis: noun, nominal, attested by BJ (12/5/64), also <**tl'chás ~ tl'tsás**>, //ƛ'cɛ́s//, attested by AD (7/23/79), Elders Group (7/9/75, 4/2/75).

<**tl'ékwálsulh**>, CJ /'*now I, (now I'm already)*'/, *see* tl'ó ~ tl'o.

<**tl'ekwselchíms ~ tl'ekwselchí:ms**>, MOOD ['*why?*'], *see* selchí:m ~ selchím.

<**tl'ékwela**>, df //ƛ'ə́kʷ=əlɛ or ƛ'ə́k'ʷ[=D=]=əlɛ//, ABDF /'*deaf, deaf (but can hear a little)*'/, Elder's comment: "stone deaf is another word (IHTTC)", probably root as in tl'ékw'=el *go out (of fire)* where =el is *go, come, get, become*, possibly <**=D= (deglottalization)**> *derivational*, lx <**=ela**> *on the side of the head, on the temple, on the ear*, phonology: possible deglottalization, syntactic analysis: intransitive verb, attested by EB (1/7/76), JL and NP with Deming Elders (Fish Camp 7/19/79), IHTTC (7/18/77), other sources: JH /ƛ'kʷə́lɛ̀/ *deaf*, Salish cognate: Squamish /ƛ'kʷə́ni/ *deaf* W73:76, K67:332 (corr. on W73), Cowichan /ƛ'ə́kʷənə/ *deaf* B74b:45, perhaps Lushootseed /t(ə)kʷ-adiʔ/ *deaf* H76:493, MCx /tə́kʷan'a/ *deaf* B75prelim:55, Sechelt /təkʷə́na/ *deaf* T77:22, Thompson /sən-təkʷán'i/ *deaf* B74c:41, historical/comparative detail: from the distribution of cognates it appears Squamish and Halkomelem tl' /ƛ'/ is secondary here historically, whether it indicates a separate root (innovation) or not is unclear, also <**tl'ékw'el:a**>, //ƛ'ə́k'ʷ=əlɛ//, attested by Elders Group (1/21/76), example: <**ō li kwetlh wetl'ékwela.**>, //ʔəw-li kʷəɬ wə-ƛ'ə́kʷəlɛ//, /'*Oh he's so deaf.*'/, (<**we-**> *contrastive*), attested by JL and NP with Deming Elders (Fish Camp 7/19/79).

<**tl'ekwselchíms ~ tl'ekwselchí:ms**>, MOOD ['*why?*'], *see* selchí:m ~ selchím.

<**tl'ékw'**>, probably bound root //ƛ'ə́kʷ// *out (of fire, flame or lamp)*

<**tl'ékw'el**>, incs //ƛ'ə́kʷ=əl//, FIRE /'*go out (of fire, flame or lamp)*'/, (<**=el**> *go, come, get, become*), syntactic analysis: intransitive verb, attested by EB (11/27/75, 12/15/75), DM (12/4/64), example: <**la tl'ékw'el.** or **le tl'ékw'el.**>, //lɛ ƛ'ə́k'ʷ=əl or lə ƛ'ə́k'ʷ=əl//, /'*It went out (a fire).*'/, attested by DM, <**tl'ékw'el te yeqwí:ls.**>, //ƛ'ə́k'ʷ=əl tə yəqʷ=í·ls//, /'*The lamp goes out.*'/, attested by EB (12/15/75).

<**tl'ékw'elt**>, pcs //ƛ'ə́k'ʷ=əl=T//, FIRE /'*to extinguish it, put it out (a fire)*'/, (<**=t**> *purposeful control transitivizer*), syntactic analysis: transitive verb, attested by Elders Group (3/72, 1/7/76).

<**tl'ékw'elt**>, FIRE /'*to extinguish it, put it out (a fire)*'/, *see* tl'ékw'el.

<**tl'él**>, bound root //ƛ'ə́l *spotted, speckled*//.

<**tl'eltl'éli̱x**>, plv //C_1əC_2=ƛ'ə́l=x̣//, DESC ['*spotted with circles or round dots*'], (<**R3=**> *plural*), lx <**=x̱**> *distributive, all over, all around*, phonology: reduplication, syntactic analysis: adjective/adjectival verb, attested by AD (10/15/79).

<**tl'eltl'élx̱os**>, ds //C_1əC_2=ƛ'ə́l=x̣=as//, ANA /'*(have a) speckled face, (have) freckles*'/, literally /'many spotted with circles/dots all around on the face'/, lx <**=os**> *on the face*, phonology: unusual unstressed allophone (for =ós ~ =es), reduplication, syntactic analysis: prob. adjective/adjectival verb, poss. nominal??, attested by NP (10/26/75).

<**tl'élx̱xel ~ tl'álx̱xel**>, ds //ƛ'ə́lx̣=xʸəl ~ƛ'ɛ́l=x̣=xʸəl//, [ƛ'ə́lx̣xʸɪl ~ƛ'ɛ́lx̣xʸɪl], EZ /'*spring salmon (generic), (Chinook salmon)*'/, ['*Oncorhynchus tshawytscha*'], literally /'spotted all over on the foot/fish-tail'/, lx <**=xel**> *on the foot, (here) on the fish tail*, Elder's comment: "speckled spring salmon, has red flesh, runs in June (AC), year-round spring salmon (Elders 3/1/72)", (semological comment: salmon use their tails somewhat like feet to move themselves along and jump, since =xel also means *on the foot, on the leg* perhaps it more basically means *on the body-part that moves a creature along on land/water*), (semological comment: the Stó:lō prize spring salmon and have nine names for them, depending on what streams they spawn in, their size, etc., see under these names for information additional to the general word <**tl'élx̱xel**>: <**tl'elxálōwelh ~ tl'elxálōllh, pó:qw', pepqw'ólh, speq'á:s ~ sp'eq'á:s, spá:x̱em ~ spéx̱em, sqwéx̱em, sth'olólh, shxwōqw'ő:lh or shxwōqw'őllh or shxwōqw'őwelh**>), phonology: the phonetic [ɛ́] is /ɛ́/ if more fronted, and /ə́/ if more medial, comment: if the root can be shown to have <**á**>/ɛ́/ then the stem may have <**é-ablaut**> *durative* or *resultative*, syntactic analysis: nominal, attested by Elders Group (3/1/72, 3/15/72), AC (8/29/70), BJ (12/5/64), Deming (4/1/76, 2/2/80), Salish cognate: Squamish stem in /ƛ'í-ƛ'lx̣-íws/ *speckled trout* W73:245, K67:334 (lit. *littled speckled all over on the skin/body*).

<**tl'elxéltel (**or **tl'elx̱xéltel)**>, df //ƛ'əl(=x̣)=xʸə[=´=]l=təl//, FSH ['*spring salmon net*'], literally /'spring salmon device'/, possibly <**=´=**> *derivational*, lx <**=tel**> *device*, phonology: possible consonant-loss, stress-shift, syntactic analysis: nominal, attested by Elders Group (3/26/75).

<**tl'elxálōwelh** or better **tl'elxálōllh**>, df //ƛ'əl=xʸə[=Aɛ́=]l=a[=Ao=]wəɬ or more likely ƛ'ɛ́l=xʸə[=M2=]l=a[=Ao=]lɬ//, EZ ['*jack spring salmon with black nose*'], ['*Oncorhynchus tshawytscha*'], ASM ['"jack" varieties are smaller varieties'], possibly root <**tl'él**> *spotted, speckled*, possibly root <**tl'ál**> meaning uncertain, possibly <**á-ablaut**> *durative or derivational* unless <**á**> is original in root, possibly <**ō-ablaut**> *derivational*, possibly <**metathesis**> *derivational*, <**=óllh**> *young, offspring/child*, phonology: possible ablaut, possible metathesis, syntactic analysis: nominal, attested by Elders Group (3/1/72).

<**tl'eláxwelets**>, TVMO ['*stay in one place*'], *see* tl'élexw.

<**tl'eláxwstexw**>, TVMO /'*hold it steady, (hold s-th steady)*'/, *see* tl'élexw.

<**tl'eláxw ~ tl'láxw**>, TVMO ['*stopped*'], *see* tl'élexw.

<**tl'elá:y**>, possibly root //ƛ'əlɛ́·y or ƛ'əl=ɛ́·y//, CAN ['*shovel-nose canoe*'], ASM ['this was the canoe for short trips by one or two individuals, a small canoe, with shovel-nose sometimes at both ends, the shovel-shape was good for landing, the canoe was also good for rapids and for fishing too'], perhaps a "home canoe" if root is <**tl'el-**> *stop, be at home*, possibly <**=á:y**> *bark,* perhaps reinforced by há:y *make a canoe, tá:y race a canoe*?, syntactic analysis: nominal, attested by Deming (1/31/80), Elders Group (1/28/76), DM (12/4/64), Salish cognate: Lushootseed /ƛ'əláyʔ/ *shovel-nose canoe* H76:322-323.

<**tl'eléqw**>, SD ['*explode*'], *see* tl'ál ~ tl'á:l.

<**tl'éleqw'**>, SD /'*a pop, a shot*'/, *see* tl'ál ~ tl'á:l.

<**stl'éleqw'**>, df //s=ƛ'ə́l(=)əq'ʷ//, EB ['*chocolate lily*'], ['*Fritillaria lanceolata*'], ASM ['now scarce, the bulbs were dug up in July and cooked in a steam pit, they looked like clusters of rice, nowadays they are cooked by boiling'], (<**s=**> *nominalizer*), possibly root <**tl'ál-**> *sharp sound* possibly root as in <**tl'eléqw**> *explode* and <**tl'éleqw'**> *a pop, a shot*,, (semological comment: I have a note that the chocolate lily's seeds are launched when the seed capsule explodes or pops open but I cannot confirm this now from the books at hand), possibly <**=eqw' ~ =qw'**> *around in circles*, syntactic analysis: nominal, attested by Elders Group (5/28/75, 7/21/76).

<**tl'eléwe ~ tl'léwe**>, PRON ['*you (sg.) (object of preposition)*'], *see* léwe.

<**tl'élexw**>, df //ƛ'ə́l(=)əxʷ//, TVMO ['*stop*'], possibly <**=exw**> meaning unknown, syntactic analysis: intransitive verb, attested by AC (8/25/70, 9/29/71), EB (4/29/76), CT and HT (6/21/76), Salish cognate: Lushootseed root /ƛ'ə́l/ as in /gʷə-ƛ'əl-ád(-əxʷ)/ *stop!, keep still!, behave!* and /ƛ'ə́l-d/ *don't touch it, leave it alone, forget it, pay no attention to it, never mind it* and /ʔəs-ƛ'ə́l/ *silent, esp. the stillness of the deep forest* H76:321-322, example: <**etset tl'élexw li ta shxwlís kwtha màl.**>, //ʔə-c-ət ƛ'ə́ləxʷ li t-ɛ sxʷ=lís kwth-ɛ mɛ̀l//, /'*We stopped at the place where your father is at.*'/, attested by AC, <**tl'élexw kw'a's í:mex.**>, //ƛ'ə́ləxʷ k'ʷ-ɛʔ-s ʔí[-·-]m=əxʸ//, /'*Stop your walking.*'/, attested by EB, <**tl'élexw kw'es ye'í:mex**>, //ƛ'ə́ləxʷ k'ʷə-s yə=ʔí[-·-]m=əxʸ//, /'*to stop walking*'/, attested by CT and HT; found in <**tl'eléxwlha.**>, //ƛ'ə́ləxʷ-ɬɛ//, /'*Stop.*'/, phonology: possible stress-shift to penultimate syllable before -lha, comment: possibly an alternative pronunciation of the word is tl'eléxw or the word is pronounced by all as tl'éléxw and mistranscribed above, attested by Elders Group (3/16/77).

<**tl'eléxwstexw**>, caus //ƛ'ələ[=´=]xʷ=sT-əxʷ//, TVMO ['*stop s-th*'], possibly <**= ´=**> *derivational* if not an allomorph or automatically conditioned, (<**=st**> *causative control transitivizer*), (<**-exw**> *third person object*), phonology: stress-shift, syntactic analysis: transitive verb, comment: this form proves that the lexw is not the *non-control transitivizer* plus *third person object*, attested by EB (3/29/76).

<**tl'elxwí:wsem**>, mdls //ƛ'ələxʷ=í·ws=əm//, TVMO ['*quiet down (of a person), relax*'], LANG, EFAM, literally /'stop one's body'/, lx <**=í:ws**> *on the body*, (<**=em**> *middle voice*), phonology: vowel-loss, syntactic analysis: intransitive verb, attested by Elders Group (3/23/77), RG & EH (4/9/99 Ling332).

<**tl'eláxw ~ tl'láxw**>, durs //ƛ'ələ[=Aɛ́=]xʷ//, TVMO ['*stopped*'], BLDG /'*at home, be living (somewhere), stay*'/, SOC, (<**á-ablaut**> *durative*), phonology: ablaut, syntactic analysis: intransitive verb, attested by EB (1/9/76), AC (8/28/70), Elders Group (5/26/76), example: <**li tl'eláxw.**>, //li ƛ'ələ[=Aɛ́=]xʷ//, /'*He's at home.*'/, attested by AC, <**li tl'láxw kw'el màl?**>, //li ƛ'ələ[=Aɛ́=]xʷ k'ʷ-əl mɛ̀l//, /'*Is my father home [distant]?*'/, attested by AC, <**li tl'láxw sel tàl?**>, //li ƛ'ələ[=Aɛ́=]xʷ s-əl tɛ̀l//, /'*Is my mother home?*'/, attested by AC; found in <**tl'eláxwchxwò.**>, //ƛ'ələ[=Aɛ́=]xʷ-c-xʷ-à//, /'*Stay where you are.*'/, literally /'stay -you -just'/, attested by Elders Group, <**tl'eláxwò.**>,

//ƛ'əl'ə[=Aέ=]x^w-à//, /*'keep still (where you are)'*/, attested by Elders Group.

<**tl'eláxwelets**>, ds //ƛ'ələ[=Aέ=]x^w=ələc//, durs, TVMO [*'stay in one place'*], semantic environment ['said to someone who is always on the go'], literally /'stop/stay/at home on the rump'/, lx <**=elets**> *on the bottom, on the rump*, syntactic analysis: intransitive verb, attested by MV (Deming 5/4/78).

<**tl'eláxwstexw**>, caus //ƛ'ələ[=Aέ=]x^w=sT-əx^w//, TVMO /*'hold it steady, (hold s-th steady)'*/, (<**á-ablaut**> *durative*), (<**=st**> *causative control transitivizer*), (<**-exw**> *third person object*), phonology: ablaut, syntactic analysis: transitive verb, attested by Elders Group (6/16/76).

<**tl'éltl'elmet**>, chrs //ƛ'ə́l=C_1əC_2=məT//, iecs, EFAM [*'get used to s-th/s-o'*], (<**=R2**> *characteristic*), (<**=met**> *indirect effect non-control transitivizer*), phonology: reduplication, syntactic analysis: transitive verb, attested by Elders Group (1/7/76), EB (1/8/76), Salish cognate: Lushootseed root /ƛ'al'/ as in /ʔəs-ƛ'ál'-əb čəd/ *I'm used to doing it; I have a habit.* and /ʔəs-ƛ'ál'-b-id/ *used to doing or saying that* and /ƛ'ál'/ *too* H76:315, example: <**ewéta kw stámes láme tl'éltl'elmet, étlh?**>, //ʔəwə=´tɛ k^w(=)s=tέm=əs lέ=m-ə̀ ƛ'ə́l=C_1əC_2=məT, ʔə́tɬ//, /*'You never get used to it, do you?'*/, syntactic comment: tag-question, attested by EB (1/8/76).

<**tl'eléxwstexw**>, TVMO [*'stop s-th'*], *see* tl'élexw.

<**tl'éltl'eleqw'**>, SD [*'continuous shooting or popping sounds'*], *see* tl'ál ~ tl'á:l.

<**tl'éltl'elmet**>, EFAM [*'get used to s-th/s-o'*], *see* tl'élexw.

<**tl'eltl'él<u>x</u>**>, DESC [*'spotted with circles or round dots'*], *see* tl'él.

<**tl'eltl'él<u>x</u>os**>, ANA /*'(have a) speckled face, (have) freckles'*/, *see* tl'él.

<**tl'eltl'ó:lqwem**>, SD [*'popping (of firecrackers)'*], *see* tl'ál ~ tl'á:l.

<**tl'elxálōwelh** or **tl'elxálōllh**>, EZ [*'jack spring salmon with black nose'*], *see* tl'él.

<**tl'elxéltel (**or **tl'el<u>x</u>xéltel)**>, FSH [*'spring salmon net'*], *see* tl'él.

<**tl'elxwí:wsem**>, TVMO [*'quiet down (of a person)'*], *see* tl'élexw.

<**tl'él<u>x</u>xel ~ tl'ál<u>x</u>xel**>, EZ /*'spring salmon (generic), (Chinook salmon)'*/, *see* tl'él.

<**tl'elhlímelh**>, PRON /*'us (nominalized object of preposition), to us, with us'*/, *see* lhlímelh.

<**tl'ém**>, possibly root //ƛ'ə́m *short hard loud noise of some kind (like something hard being snapped or bitten)*//.

<**tl'eméqw**>, possibly root //ƛ'əmə́q^w or ƛ'əm=ə[=´=]q^w//, SD /*'to snap (one's fingers, a louse when one bites it, etc.)'*/, ABFC, possibly root <**tl'em**> *short loud noise of some kind*?, comment: such a root could also be in tl'em=<u>x</u>w=<u>x</u>íl=em *hail*, possibly <**=eqw**> *on top of the head, on the hair*, syntactic analysis: intransitive verb, attested by Elders Group (11/3/76), Salish cognate: Squamish /ƛ'ə́mk'^{w}-anʔ/ *crack louse or nit between teeth (tr.)* W73:70, K69:72, historical/comparative detail: UHk /q^w/ doesn't correspond to Squamish /k'^{w}/, more cognates are needed.

<**tl'eméqwtses**>, ds //ƛ'əmə́q^w=cəs//, SD [*'snap one's fingers'*], ABFC, lx <**=tses**> *on the hand*, syntactic analysis: intransitive verb, attested by Elders Group (11/3/76).

<**tl'em<u>x</u>wxéylem** or **tl'em<u>x</u>wxílem**>, df //ƛ'əm=x̣^{w}=x̣=íl=əm//, WETH /*'to hail, be hailing'*/, literally /'get/have go/come short hard crack noise lump/spherical all over'/, probably root <**tl'ém**> *(make) short hard crack/snap noise*, lx <**=<u>x</u>w**> *lump, spherical/round object*, lx <**=<u>x</u>**> *distributive, all over, all around*, (<**=íl**> *come, go, get, become*), (<**=em**> *have/get/intransitivizer*), syntactic analysis: intransitive verb, dialects: *Chill.*, attested by Deming (3/31/77), example: <**tl'em<u>x</u>w<u>x</u>ílem te swáyel.**>, //ƛ'əm=x̣^{w}=x̣=íl=əm tə s=wέyəl//, /*'The day is hailing.'*/, dialects: *Chill.*, attested by

Deming (3/31/77).

<tl'emx̱wéyle>, df //ƛ'əm=x̣ʷ=íl=ə//, WETH ['*the hail*'], possibly **<=e>** *entity*??, phonology: consonant-loss, syntactic analysis: nominal, dialects: *Sumas*, attested by Deming (3/31/77), Salish cognate: Lushootseed /ƛ'əbx̣ʷílaʔ/ *hail* H76:700, example: **<ōwéta tl'emx̱wéyle tlowáyél.>**, //ʔowə= ́tɛ ƛ'əm=x̣ʷ=íl=ə təla=wɛ́yə́l//, /'*There's no hail today.*'/, dialects: *Sumas*, attested by Deming (3/31/77).

<tl'ámkw'em>, cts //ƛ'ə[=Aɛ́=]m(=)k'ʷ=əm//, SD /'*(have) sound of popping small round things (snowberries, herring eggs as when eating them, rice krispies, crabapples, cranberries, etc.), (have a crunching sound (as of grasshopper, rice krispies))*'/, root or stem **<ƛ'əm(=)k'ʷ>** *crunch when biting, pop small round things*, possibly **<á-ablaut>** *continuative*, possibly **<=kw'>** *round things*, probably **<=em>** *have/get/intransitivizer*, syntactic analysis: intransitive verb, attested by Elders Group (11/3/76), RM (4/23/76), Salish cognate: Squamish /ƛ'mk'ʷ-ánʔ/ *crack louse or nit between teeth (tr.)* W73:70, K69:72.

<tl'ámqw'els>, sas //ƛ'ə[=Aɛ́=]m=q'ʷ=əls//, SD /'*crunchy (loud when eating), crackling (noise when eating)*'/, possibly **<=qw'>** *around in circles*, (**<=els>** *structured activity continuative*), phonology: ablaut, syntactic analysis: intransitive verb, adjective/adjectival verb?, attested by Elders Group (12/10/75), ***<tsel tl'ámqw'els te qwe'óp.>** rejected, */'I crunched the apple.'/ rejected by EB (5/3/76).

<tl'emékw'>, dnom //ƛ'əm=[=ə́=]k'ʷ//, EZ /'*grasshopper, (*possibly *the longhorned grasshopper)*'/, ['order *Orthoptera* family *Acrididae* or perhaps family *Tettigoniidae*'], probably **<=é=>** *derivational*, phonology: infixed schwa, syntactic analysis: nominal, Elder's comment: "from tl'ámkw'em", attested by RM (4/23/76), also **<tl'émqwxel>**, //ƛ'ə́m=qʷ=xʸəl//, Elder's comment: "from tl'émqw- the noise it makes", lx **<=xel>** *on the legs*, attested by RM (6/13/77), see **<ts'tl'ám ~ ts'tl'ém>** *jump* for another derivation of a similar word for grasshopper.

<tl'emtl'émxel>, df //$C_1əC_2$=ƛ'ə́m=xʸəl//, EZ ['*grasshopper*'], ['order *Orthoptera*, family *Acrididae* or perhaps family *Tettigoniidae*'], Elder's comment: "from ts'tl'ém *jump* (AC)", Elder's comment: "named from the noise it makes (RM)", possibly root **<ts'tl'ém>** *jump*, comment: unusual loss of initial stem consonant if correct, (**<R3=>** *plural*), possibly root **<tl'ém>** *make hard loud noise (as if snapping or cracking hard object),* comment: perhaps from the sound it make in biting and eating, lx **<=xel>** *on the leg*, phonology: reduplication, possible consonant-loss, syntactic analysis: nominal, attested by HP (Elders Group 4/16/75).

<tl'emékw'>, EZ /'*grasshopper, (*possibly *the longhorned grasshopper)*'/, *see* tl'ém.

<tl'eméqw>, SD /'*to snap (one's fingers, a louse when one bites it, etc.)*'/, *see* tl'ém.

<tl'eméqwtses>, SD ['*snap one's fingers*'], *see* tl'ém.

<tl'émexw>, possibly root //ƛ'ə́məxʷ//, NUM /'*part, (portion)*'/, syntactic analysis: noun, nominal, attested by CT and HT (6/21/76), example: **<te sqewá:meth' te thqát, tl'ó tl'émexw xípet.>**, //tə s=qəw=ɛ́·məθ' tə θqɛ́t ƛ'á ƛ'ə́məxʷ xʸíp=əT//, /'*The sunny side of a tree, that's the part you strip off (peel s-th)*'/, attested by CT and HT.

<tl'émstexw>, caus //ƛ'ə́m=sT-əxʷ//, EFAM ['*think someone is talking about s-o*'], LANG, root meaning unknown, (**<=st>** *causative control transitivizer*), (**<-exw>** *third person object*), syntactic analysis: transitive verb, attested by Elders Group (2/16/77).

<tl'emstélemet ~ tl'emstélémét>, //ƛ'əm=sT-ə́ləmət//, caus, EFAM ['*think someone is talking or laughing about oneself*'], (**<-élemet>** *reflexive (for causative)*), phonology: optional updrifting, syntactic analysis: intransitive verb, attested by Elders Group (10/6/76, 2/16/77), contrast

<**tl'ostélmet**> *think someone is talkiing or laughing about oneself,* example: <**tsel tl'emstélemet. ~ tsel tl'emstélémét.**>, //c-əl ƛ'əm=sT=ə́l(-)əmət//, /'*I think someone is talking or laughing about me.*'/, attested by Elders Group (10/6/76, 2/16/77).

<**tl'emstélemet ~ tl'emstélémét**>, EFAM ['*think someone is talking or laughing about oneself*'], *see* tl'émstexw.

<**tl'emtl'émxel**>, df //C_1əC_2=ƛ'ə́m=x^{y}əl//, EZ ['*grasshopper*'], ['order *Orthoptera*, family *Acrididae* or perhaps family *Tettigoniidae*'], Elder's comment: "from ts'tl'ém *jump* (AC)", Elder's comment: "named from the noise it makes (RM)", possibly root <**ts'tl'ém**> *jump*, comment: unusual loss of initial stem consonant if correct, (<**R3=**> *plural*), possibly root <**tl'ém**> *make hard loud noise (as if snapping or cracking hard object),* comment: perhaps from the sound it make in biting and eating, lx <**=xel**> *on the leg,* phonology: reduplication, possible consonant-loss, syntactic analysis: nominal, attested by HP (Elders Group 4/16/75).

<**tl'emx̲wéyle**>, WETH ['*the hail*'], *see* tl'ém.

<**tl'emx̲wxéylem** or **tl'emx̲wxílem**>, WETH /'*to hail, be hailing*'/, *see* tl'ém.

<**tl'ép**>, free root //ƛ'ə́p//, DIR /'*deep down, below, down below, low*'/, syntactic analysis: adverb/adverbial verb, attested by EB (3/9/76, 12/1/75), Elders Group (3/1/72), BJ (12/5/64), example: <**tl'ép te sqweqwá li te témexw.**>, //ƛ'ə́p tə s=C_1ə=q^{w}ɛ́ li tə tə́məx^w//, /'*(It's a) deep pit. (There's a) deep hole in the ground.*'/, attested by EB, <**li kw'e tl'ép**>, //li k'^{w}ə ƛ'ə́p//, /'*downstairs*'/, literally /'in/on the (remote/abstract) down below'/, attested by EB (3/9/76).

<**stl'ép**>, stvi //s=ƛ'ə́p//, DIR ['*be deep*'], (<**s=**> *stative*), syntactic analysis: adjective/adjectival verb, attested by AC, BJ (12/5/64).

<**lexwstl'ép**>, ds //ləx^w=s=ƛ'ə́p//, DIR /'*deeper, always deep*'/, (<**lexw=**> *always*), syntactic analysis: adjective/adjectival verb, attested by Elders Group (4/2/75), example: <**lexwstl'ép telí tethá.**>, //ləx^w=s=ƛ'ə́p təlí tə=θɛ́//, /'*(It's) deeper than that.*'/, <**we'ólwe lexwstl'ép**>, //wə=ʔál=wə ləx^w=s=ƛ'ə́p//, /'*(It's) too deep., (It's) always deep.*'/.

<**shxwtl'ép**>, ds //s=x^w=ƛ'ə́p//, DIR /'*be deep, be very deep, be deep water*'/, (<**s=**> *stative*), (<**xw=**> *intensifier*), contrast <**stl'ép**> *be deep,* syntactic analysis: adjective/adjectival verb, attested by EB (12/1/75, 3/9/76), Elders Group (3/26/75), example: <**te shxwtl'ép qó:**>, //tə s=x^w=ƛ'ə́p qá·//, /'*the deep water*'/, attested by EB, <**shxwtl'ép te qó:.**>, //s=x^w=ƛ'ə́p tə qá·//, /'*The water is very deep.*'/, attested by EB, <**shxwtl'épcha te qó:.**>, //s=x^w=ƛ'ə́p-cɛ tə qá·//, /'*It will be deep water.*'/, literally /'the water will be deep'/, attested by EB, <**ŏwe ís shxwtl'ép.**>, //ʔə́wə ʔí-s s=x^w=ƛ'ə́p//, /'*(It is) shallow., (It's) not deep.*'/, attested by EB.

<**tl'épt**>, pcs //ƛ'ə́p=T//, DIR ['*lower s-th down*'], (<**=t**> *purposeful control transitivizer*), syntactic analysis: transitive verb, attested by Deming (2/7/80), Salish cognate: Squamish /ƛ'áp-at/ *lower, diminish, slow down (tr.)* W73:168, K69:73.

<**tl'ípethet**>, pcrs //ƛ'ə́[=Aí=]p=əT-et//, ABFC //'*crouch down*'//, <=Aí=> *durative,* <-et> *reflexive,* lit. /"lower oneself down purposely for a while"/, attested by RG & EH (4/9/99 Ling332).

<**stl'epá:leq**>, ds //s=ƛ'əp=ɛ́·ləq//, CLO /'*underskirt, petticoat*'/, (<**s=**> *nominalizer*), lx <**=á:leq**> *waves, skirt,* syntactic analysis: nominal, attested by AC (9/10/71), Elders Group (11/26/75), also <**tl'páleq**>, //ƛ'əp=ɛ́ləq//, also /'*underskirt*'/, attested by Deming (1/25/79).

<**stl'epá:lí:ya ~ stl'epá:liya**>, ds //s=ƛ'əp=ɛ́·lí·yɛ//, ANA ['*ear lobe*'], (<**s=**> *nominalizer, something that*), lx <**=á:líya**> *on the ear,* phonology: optional downdrifting, optional length-loss, syntactic analysis: nominal, attested by IHTTC (8/4/77, 8/11/77).

<**tl'pí:l ~ tl'epí:l**>, incs //ƛ'əp=í·l ~ ƛ'əp=í·l//, DIR /'*go down, go down below, get low*'/, (<**=í:l**> *come,*

go, get, become), syntactic analysis: intransitive verb, attested by EB (12/15/75, 2/6/76), AC (8/25/70, 9/30/71, 12/7/71), example: <**le tl'pí:l.**>, //lə ƛ'əp=í·l//, /'*(He/She/It) went down.*'/, attested by EB (12/15/75), <**lalh tl'epíl.**>, //lɛ-ɬ ƛ'əp=íl//, /'*Go down below.*'/, grammatical comment: imperative with la, attested by AC, <**tl'osesu le tl'epí:l kw'ilést'wa yutl'ólem swóweles.**>, //ƛ'a-s-əs-u lə ƛ'əp=í·l k'ʷil=əs-t'wɛ y=u=ƛ'á=l=əm s=wi[=Aá=]wələs//, /'*And then they went down, it doesn't say how many, those young men.*'/, literally /'and then they past go down how many people - evidential/must be they/those young men'/, usage: Story of the Flood, attested by AC (12/7/71), <**wulh le tl'epí:l te stó:lō.**>, //wəɬ lə ƛ'əp=í·l tə s=tá·l=əw//, /'*The river is getting low.*'/, literally /'already past go down, get low the river'/, attested by EB (2/6/76).

<**tl'pílém**>, mdls //ƛ'əp=íl=əm//, TVMO /'*go down hill, go down from anything*'/, DIR, literally /'get oneself down below'/, (<**=em**> *middle voice*), phonology: updrifting, syntactic analysis: intransitive verb, attested by BHTTC.

<**tl'pí:lstexw**>, caus //ƛ'əp=í·l=sT-əxʷ//, TVMO ['*lower s-th down*'], DIR, literally /'cause it to get/go/come down below'/, (<**=st**> *causative control transitivizer*), (<**-exw**> *third person object*), syntactic analysis: transitive verb, attested by Deming (2/7/80), also <**tl'epílestexw**>, //ƛ'əp=íl=sT-əxʷ//, attested by Elders Group (12/15/76), example: <**tl'epílestexw ta' sqelxwá:le.**>, //ƛ'əp=íl=sT-əxʷ t-ɛʔ s=qəlxʷ=ɛ́·lə//, /'*lower your voice in pitch*'/, literally /'cause it to lower your throat/gullet'/, attested by Elders Group (12/15/76).

<**tl'pí:lt ~ tl'épelt**>, pcs //ƛ'əp=í·l=T ~ ƛ'ə[-´-]p=əl=T//, TVMO /'*lower it down, (lower s-th down)*'/, DIR, (semological comment: though these were given with the same non-continuative meaning, I suspect that tl'épelt may be *lowering it down* with *continuative* stress-shift), possibly <**-´-**> *continuative*??, (<**=t**> *purposeful control transitivizer*), phonology: stress-shift, vowel-reduction, syntactic analysis: transitive verb, attested by Deming (2/7/80).

<**tl'pí:lx ~ tl'pì:lx**>, pcis //ƛ'əp=í·l=xʸ//, TVMO /'*bring it down (from upstairs or from upper shelf, etc.)*'/, (<**=x**> *purposeful control inanimate object preferred*), phonology: optional downdrifting, syntactic analysis: transitive verb, attested by EB (6/21/76, 6/30/76).

<**stl'pí:wel ~ tl'pí:wel**>, dnom //s=ƛ'əp=í·wəl ~ ƛ'əp=í·wəl//, CLO ['*shirt*'], literally probably now /'something down below in the inside(s)'/, perhaps from an older root of same shape as in Squamish /s-ƛ'p-íwʔn/ *shirt* from root /ƛ'əp/ *cover, clothing (?)* W73:14, K67:332 (but H76:324 derives the Lushootseed cognates of undershirt (/ƛ'iƛ'pikʷ/) and underpants (/ƛ'iƛ'pəq/) from root /ƛ'əp/ *deep, beneath (surface)*), (semological comment: perhaps so named because shirts were worn inside blankets or were tucked in pants or were first urged on people to cover themselves), (<**s=**> *nominalizer*), lx <**=í:wel**> *in the inside(s),* syntactic analysis: nominal, attested by BJ (5/10/64).

<**stl'epláts**>, durs //s=ƛ'əp=lə[=Aɛ́=]c//, dnom, WATR /'*deep bottom (of a river, lake, water, canoe, anything)*'/, MC, (<**s=**> *nominalizer*), lx <**=lets**> *on the bottom*, possibly <**á-ablaut**> *durative*, phonology: ablaut, syntactic analysis: nominal, attested by Elders Group (4/2/75).

<**stl'epó:lemelh ~ stl'epó:les**>, dnom //s=ƛ'əp=á·ləməɬ ~ s=ƛ'əp=á·ləs//, ANA ['*lower circle under eye*'], (<**s=**> *nominalizer*), lx <**=ó:lemelh**> *on the eyelid*?, lx <**=ó:les**> *on the eye*, syntactic analysis: nominal, attested by IHTTC (8/4/77).

<**stl'epólwelh ~ stl'pólwelh**>, stvi //s=ƛ'əp=álwəɬ//, DIR /'*(be) below, (be) underneath, (be) at the bottom of a pile or stack*'/, literally /'be on the side below'/, (<**s=**> *stative*), lx <**=ólwelh**> *on the side*, phonology: vowel-loss, syntactic analysis: adverb/adverbial verb, attested by AC, Elders Group (2/16/77).

<**stl'epóyethel**>, dnom //s=ƛ'əp=áyθəl//, ANA ['*lower lip*'], (<**s=**> *nominalizer*), lx <**=óy(e)thel**> *on the lip. on the jaw*, syntactic analysis: nominal, attested by AC, other sources: ES and JH /sƛ'páyθəl/ *lower lip*.

<**tl'épstexw**>, caus //ƛ'ə́p=sT-əx^{w}//, DIR ['*(make s-th deep or low)*'], (<**=st**> *causative control transitivizer*), (<**-exw**> *third person object*), syntactic analysis: transitive verb, attested by Elders Group (4/6/77).

<**tl'épstexw ta' sqwálewel.**>, cpds //ƛ'ə́p=sT-əx^{w} t-ɛʔ s=q^{w}ɛ̀l=əwəl//, EFAM /'*be patient, Be patient.*'/, literally /'make them deep/low your feelings/thoughts'/, syntactic analysis: imperative sentence: transitive verb demonstrative article -possessive pronoun affix nominal, attested by Elders Group (4/6/77).

<**tl'ítl'eptel**>, dmn //C_1í=ƛ'əp=təl//, CLO ['*skirt*'], literally /'little something to be below, little below device'/, (<**R4=**> *diminutive*), lx <**=tel**> *device, something to*, phonology: reduplication, syntactic analysis: nominal, attested by EB (12/1/75, 3/1/76), Deming (1/25/79).

<**tl'ép<u>x</u>t**>, pcs //ƛ'ə́p=x̣=T//, HARV /'*sow s-th, drop or spread seed in rills, scatter s-th, (sowing s-th [AC])*'/, literally /'do low/deep down to s-th all over'/, lx <**=<u>x</u>**> *distributive, all around, all over*, (<**=t**> *purposeful control transitivizer*), syntactic analysis: transitive verb, attested by AC (11/24/71), EB (2/6/76), also /'*sowing s-th*'/, attested by AC (11/24/71), example: <**tl'ép<u>x</u>t te spí:ls**>, //ƛ'ə́p=x̣=T tə s=pí·l=əls//, /'*sowing the seed*'/, attested by AC (11/24/71).

<**stl'áp<u>x</u>**>, strs //s=ƛ'ə[=Aɛ́=]p=x̣//, HARV ['*(be) scattered all over*'], DIR, MC, (<**s=**> *stative*), (<**á-ablaut**> *resultative*), lx <**=<u>x</u>**> *distributive, all over*, phonology: ablaut, syntactic analysis: adjective/adjectival verb, attested by EB (1/30/76).

<**tl'ápe<u>x</u>em**>, izs //ƛ'ə[=Aɛ́=]p=x̣=əm//, rsls, HARV /'*to fall down and scatter, drop and scatter*'/, DIR, MC, semantic environment ['example of apples from a tree one has shaken'], (<**á-ablaut**> *resultative*), lx <**=<u>x</u> ~ =e<u>x</u>**> *distributive, all over*, (<**=em**> *have/get/intransitivizer*), phonology: ablaut, syntactic analysis: intransitive verb, attested by Elders Group (1/7/76).

<**tl'épstexw**>, DIR ['*(make s-th deep or low)*'], *see* tl'ép.

<**tl'épstexw ta' sqwálewel.**>, EFAM /'*be patient, Be patient.*'/, *see* tl'ép.

<**tl'épt**>, DIR ['*lower s-th down*'], *see* tl'ép.

<**tl'ép<u>x</u>t**>, HARV /'*sow s-th, drop or spread seed in rills, scatter s-th, (sowing s-th [AC])*'/, *see* tl'ép.

<**tl'ep' ~ tl'p'**>, probable root or stem //ƛ'əp=G// or //ƛ'əp'//, meaning uncertain

<**stl'p'álqel**>, df //s=ƛ'əp=G=ɛ́lqəl or s=ƛ'p'=ɛ́lqəl//, ANAB ['*long feather (from wing)*'], ASM ['used by some people to clear ears'], (semological comment: from the cognates and the meaning of the root (poss. *deep*) this seems more likely to mean (or have meant) *down feathers*), (<**s=**> *nominalizer*), possibly root <**tl'ep**> *deep, low, below*, possibly <**=G (glottalization)**> *derivational*, lx <**=álqel**> *feather*, phonology: possible glottalization, syntactic analysis: nominal, attested by EB (5/25/76), other sources: ES /sƛ'p'ɛ́·lqəl ~ sx^{y}ə́lc'/ (MsCw /sƛ'p'ɛ́lʔqən/) *feather*, Salish cognate: Squamish /s-ƛ'p-álʔqn/ *feathers, down* W73:97, K67:291, Samish VU /sƛ'p-él'qən'/ and LD /ƛ'p-él'qən'/ *fine down feathers (like ducks', used for pillows, etc.)* G86:77.

<**stl'ep'él:ets ~ stl'ep'élets**>, df //s=ƛ'əp=G=ə́ləc or s=ƛ'əp'=ə́ləc//, ANA /'*tail (of animal, bird)*'/, ANAH ['*rump (slang)*'], (<**s=**> *nominalizer*), possibly root <**tl'ep**> *deep, low, below*, possibly <**=G (glottalization)**> *derivational*, lx <**=élets**> *on the rump*, phonology: possible glottalization, optional lengthening, syntactic analysis: nominal, attested by AC, Elders Group (3/15/72), EB and RP (1/29/76), other sources: ES /sƛ'əp'ə́l·əc/ (Cw /sƛ'ə́p'əysnəc/) *tail*, Salish cognate: Sooke dial. of NSt /sƛ'əp'íʔsnəč/, Saanich dial. of NSt /šƛ'ə́pisnəč/, Songish dial. of NSt /sƛ'ə́peʔnəč/ (G82:28 cognate set 132b), also <**tl'p'élets**>, //ƛ'əp=G=ə́ləc//, attested by BJ (12/5/64), example: <**tl'áqt ta stl'ep'él:ets.**>, //ƛ'ɛ́qt t-ɛ s=ƛ'əp=G=ə́ləc//, /'*Your tail is long.*'/, attested by AC (9/10/71).

<**tl'ap'élatsem**>, mdls //ƛ'ə[=Aɛ́=]p'=ə́ləc=əm//, ABFC ['*to wag its tail*'], possibly <**á-ablaut**>

derivational, (<**=em**> *middle voice*), phonology: ablaut, syntactic analysis: intransitive verb, attested by AC (10/17/73).

<**tl'eq**>, possible root //ƛ’ə́q//, meaning uncertain,

<**stl'eqtl'éq**>, stvi //s=C_1əC_2=ƛ’ə́q//, plv, DESC ['*spotted*'], Elder's comment: "may be Thompson language?", comment: but Thompson (Lytton dial.) /sɬɛɬə́q/ *spotted* B74c:42, (<**s=**> *stative*), (<**R3=**> *plural*), root meaning unknown, phonology: reduplication, syntactic analysis: adjective/adjectival verb, attested by EB (5/12/76).

<**tl'eqtámeth' ~ tl'eqtáméth'**>, DESC ['*tall (of a person)*'], *see* tl'áqt.

<**tl'éqtepsem**>, ANA ['*(have a) long neck*'], *see* tl'áqt.

<**Tl'éqteqsel**>, PLN ['*longest dirt point sticking out on Harrison River about a quarter mile above Harrison Bay bridge*'], *see* tl'áqt.

<**tl'eqtíwél**>, DESC ['*tall (of tree)*'], *see* tl'áqt.

<**tl'esu**>, DEM /'*and then (he, she, it)*'/, *see* tl'ó ~ tl'o.

<**tl'etl'áxel**>, SOC /'*inviting (to come eat, dance), to give a potlatch, (give a feast or gathering), to invite to a feast, invite to a potlatch*'/, *see* tl'e'á ~ tl'á'.

<**tl'étl'elò:m**>, PRON /'*that's them (little kids), they (little kids)*'/, *see* tl'ó ~ tl'o.

<**tl'éts'**>, DIR /'*close together, (narrow? [MV])*'/, *see* tl'í:ts'.

<**tl'éw**>, bound root //ƛ’ə́w *bark*//.

<**tl'éwt**>, pcs //ƛ’ə́w=T//, ABFC ['*bark at s-o/s-th*'], semantic environment ['dogs, wolves, coyotes'], (<**=t**> *purposeful control transitivizer*), syntactic analysis: transitive verb, attested by IHTTC (7/12/77).

<**tl'ewéls**>, sas //ƛ’əw=ə́ls//, ABFC ['*to bark*'], (<**=éls ~ =áls ~ =á:ls**> *structured activity non-continuative*), syntactic analysis: intransitive verb, attested by AC (8/25/70), Elders Group (1/25/78), also <**tl'éwéls**>, //ƛ’ə́w=ə́ls//, attested by Elders Group (7/12/77).

<**tl'áwels**>, cts //ƛ’ə[-Aɛ́-]w=əls//, sas, ABFC ['*barking*'], (<**á-ablaut**> *continuative*), (<**=els**> *structured activity continuative*), phonology: ablaut, syntactic analysis: intransitive verb, attested by AC (8/25/70), IHTTC (7/12/77), Elders Group (1/25/78, 3/21/79).

<**tl'éwtl'ewels**>, plv //ƛ’ə́w=C_1əC_2=əls//, sas, cts, ABFC /'*barking a lot, lots of barking*'/, ds //=C_1əC_2 *plural or plural continuative*//, (<**=els**> *structured activity continuative*), phonology: reduplication, syntactic analysis: intransitive verb, attested by IHTTC (7/12/77), Elders Group (1/25/78, 3/1/72).

<**tl'ewéls**>, ABFC ['*to bark*'], *see* tl'éw.

<**tl'ewlómét ~ tl'ōwlómét**>, TVMO /'*to escape (as an animal from a trap), got away from something that trapped a person or animal*'/, *see* tl'í:w.

<**tl'éwt**>, ABFC ['*bark at s-o/s-th*'], *see* tl'éw.

<**tl'éwtl'ewels**>, ABFC /'*barking a lot, lots of barking*'/, *see* tl'éw.

<**tl'éx**>, possibly root //ƛ’ə́x^y or ƛ’ɛ[=Aə́=]x^y//, LAND /'*break (of ground), crack apart (of its own accord) (of ground), rip*'/, CST, possibly <**é-ablaut**> *durative*, phonology: possible ablaut, syntactic analysis: intransitive verb, attested by Elders Group (5/26/76), EB (3/15/76), Salish cognate: Squamish /ƛ’ə́š/ *rip off (itr.), be released because hooked-up part rips* W73:217, K69:72.

<**tl'xát**>, pcs //ƛ’ɛ́x^y-M1=T or ƛ’əx^y=ə[-Aɛ́-]T//, CST ['*rip it apart*'], possibly <**metathesis type 1**>

non-continuative, possibly <**á-ablaut**> *durative*, (<**=t**> *purposeful control transitivizer*), phonology: metathesis or ablaut, syntactic analysis: transitive verb, attested by SP and AK (Fish Camp 8/2/77).

<**tl'xátem**>, df //ƛ'ɛ́xʸ=M1=T=əm or ƛ'əxʸ=ə[=Aɛ́=]T=əm//, ABDF ['*get diarrhea*'], literally /'it got someone ripped apart'/, MED ['tea of mullein leaves is medicine for diarrhea (MC (Deming 2/10/77))'], probably <**=em**> *passive*, comment: the example shows this is used (at least by JL) as a passive, though semantically no purposeful control is involved and *have/get/intransitivizer* or *middle voice* fit better semantically, the example seems unlikely to show a conjugated middle but see tl'**x̱**wòlèm *I got hard* under tl'éx̱w which seems similar but with no transitivizer, possibly <**=em**> *have/get/intransitivizer or middle voice*, phonology: metathesis or ablaut, syntactic analysis: intransitive verb, attested by Elders Group, JL, Salish cognate: Squamish /ƛ'ə-ƛ'š-íʔqʷ/ *defecate (itr.)* from root /ƛ'əš/ *rip off (itr.), be released because hooked-up part rips* W73:77, K69:72, example: <**me tl'xáthàlèm.**>, //mə ƛ'ɛ́xʸ=M1=T=ɛ̀lə̀m//, /'*I got diarrhea.*'/, syntactic analysis: auxiliary verb transitive verb-1s passive, attested by JL (3/31/78).

<**tl'xáx̱el**>, df //ƛ'ɛ́xʸ-M1=x̣=əl orƛ'ɛ́xʸ-M1=ɛ́x̣əl//, CST /'*burst open, split open of its own accord (like a dropped watermelon)*'/, possibly <**metathesis type 1**> *non-continuative*, probably <**=x̱**> *distributive, all over*, probably <**=el**> *go/come/get/become*, possibly <**=áx̱el**> *side portion*, phonology: probable metathesis, possible vowel merger, syntactic analysis: intransitive verb, attested by Elders Group (1/7/76).

<**tl'xáx̱et**>, pcs //ƛ'ɛ́xʸ-M1=x̣=əT//, HUNT ['*to split s-th open (like deer or fish)*'], CST, possibly <**metathesis type 1**> *non-continuative*, probably <**=x̱**> *distributive, all over*, (<**=et**> *purposeful control transitivizer*), phonology: metathesis or ablaut, syntactic analysis: transitive verb, attested by Elders Group (1/7/76).

<**Tl'ítl'xeleqw**>, dmn //C_1í=ƛ'ɛ́xʸ=ələqʷ//, PLN ['*Isolillock Mountain (near Silver Creek)*'], ASM ['the double-peaked mountain by Silver Creek on the CN (south) side of the Fraser River, it can even be seen from Hope bridge and further north looking south, some Indians call it Holy Cross Mountain because of a glacier resembling an X or cross on it, it can also be seen from the north side of Highway 1 by the Husky Station at Silver Creek'], literally /'little ripped on top of the head'/, Elder's comment: "from tl'xát *ripped apart* because an iceberg came through years ago and ripped it apart, it was one mountain before that", (<**R4=**> *diminutive*), lx <**=eleqw**> *on top of the head*, phonology: reduplication, vowel-loss, syntactic analysis: nominal, contrast <**Isléleqw**> *Isolillock Mountain* under <**isále** *two* (Mary Peters' name for it), attested by AK and ME, IHTTC (7/8/77), AK/SP/AD (Raft trip 8/30/77), AK and SP (Fish Camp 8/2/77), source: place names reference file #33.

<**shxwtl'éxelep**>, dnom //sxʷ=ƛ'ə́xʸ=ələp//, LAND ['*a plow*'], TOOL, HARV, literally /'something that rips/breaks apart ground'/, dnom //shxw= *nominalizer, something for/that*//, lx <**=elep**> *ground, earth*, syntactic analysis: nominal, attested by Deming (3/11/76).

<**stl'éxs**>, ds //s=ƛ'ə́xʸ=əs//, LAND ['*ravine*'], literally /'something that's ripped apart on the face'/, (<**s=**> *nominalizer, something that's*), lx <**=es**> *on the face*, syntactic analysis: nominal, attested by Elders Group (9/17/75).

<**tl'éxw**>, free root //ƛ'ə́xʷ//, PLAY /'*lose (a contest or fight), (lost (a fight/contest), loser* [BHTTC])'/, SOC, literally perhaps /'beaten'/, syntactic analysis: intransitive verb, attested by Elders Group (3/16/77), Salish cognate: Squamish root in /s-ƛ'ə́xʷ ~ ʔəs-ƛ'ə́xʷ/ *loser (in game, fight)* W73:167, K67:291, K69:58,92, Sechelt /ƛ'ə́xʷ/ *lose* T77:30 (vs. /ƛ'əxʷ-ílq/ *win* T77:36, also /'*lost (a fight/contest)*'/, attested by BHTTC (11/10/76), also /'*loser*'/, attested by BHTTC (11/10/76), also <**tl'éx̱w**>, //ƛ'ə́x̣ʷ//, comment: **x̱**w is an error for xw since tl'éx̱w has a different meaning, attested by Elders Group (7/9/75), example: <**tsel tl'éx̱w.**>, //c-əl ƛ'ə́xʷ//, comment: **x̱**w is error for xw, /'*I lost.*'/,

attested by Elders Group (7/9/75).

<**tl'xwé**>, bound stem //ƛ'ə́xʷ=M1 *win*//, (<**metathesis type 1**> *not, un-, antonym*), phonology: metathesis, comment: an alternative analysis would be to set up root tl'xwé *win* (with shape unlike almost all other roots in this dictionary) and have tl'éxw *lose* derive from it by metathesis: //ƛ'xʷə́=M1//, this seems backwards since metathesis type one always operates on VC of a root and usually produces a *non-continuative* form (as in *win*); another alternative is to merely set up two separate roots, tl'éxw *lose* and tl'xwé *win* and not worry about the obvious fact that they are related.

<**tl'xwéleq**>, df //ƛ'ə́xʷ=M1=ləq//, PLAY /'*win, win (a prize, money, etc.), come in first (in contest)*'/, SOC, lx <**=leq**> meaning uncertain unless related to lx <**=élq**> *after*, contrast <**=éleq**> usually means *someone who* but does not here, phonology: metathesis, syntactic analysis: intransitive verb, attested by Elders Group (3/16/77), BHTTC (11/10/76), AD (3/10/80), Salish cognate: Squamish /ƛ'xʷə-nq/ *win* W73:290, K67:332, Sechelt /ƛ'əxʷ-ílq/ *win* T77:36, also <**tl'xwél:eq**>, //ƛ'ə́xʷ=M1=ləq//, phonology: phonetic lengthening, attested by Elders Group (7/9/75), also <**tl'xwéléq**>, //ƛ'ə́xʷ=M1=ləq//, phonology: updrifting, attested by Elders Group (2/16/77), example: <**tsel tl'xwél:eq.**>, //c-əl ƛ'ə́xʷ=M1=ləq//, /'*I won., I came in first (in race or contest).*'/, attested by Elders Group (7/9/75), <**chel lhq'él:exw kw'els tl'xwéléqcha.**>, //c-əl ɬ=q'ɛ[=Aə́=]l=l-əxʷ k'ʷ-əl-s ƛ'ə́xʷ=M1=ləq-cɛ//, /'*I know I'm going to win.*'/, attested by Elders Group (2/16/77).

<**tl'áxweleq**>, cts //ƛ'ə[-Aɛ́-]xʷ=ələq//, PLAY /'*be winning, he was winning*'/, SOC, (<**á-ablaut**> *continuative*), phonology: ablaut, syntactic analysis: intransitive verb, attested by AD (3/10/80).

<**tl'xwém**>, izs //ƛ'ə́xʷ=M1=m//, PLAY ['*to win a contest*'], SOC, (<**=(e)m**> *intransitivizer*), phonology: metathesis, syntactic analysis: intransitive verb, attested by EB (1/30/76).

<**tl'xwét**>, pcs //ƛ'ə́xʷ=M1=T//, PLAY /'*beat s-o in a contest, win over s-o (in a contest), beat s-o out of something*'/, SOC, (<**=t**> *purposeful control transitivizer*), phonology: metathesis, syntactic analysis: transitive verb, attested by Elders Group (1/25/78), EB (3/22/76), Salish cognate: Squamish /ƛ'xʷə-t/ *win, master (tr.)* W73:290, K67:332, example: <**tsel tl'xwét.**>, //c=əl ƛ'ə́xʷ=M1-T//, /'*I won (a race, slahal game, etc.).*'/, literally /'I beat them.'/, attested by EB (3/22/76); found in <**tl'e<u>x</u>wéthò:mcha.**>, //ƛ'ə́xʷ=M1=T-à·m-cɛ//, /'*He'll cheat you., He'll beat you out of something.*'/, literally /'You will be beaten out of something/beaten in a contest (by him/her/them)'/, phonology: mistranscription of xw as <u>x</u>w, attested by AC (8/8/70), <**tl'xwéthométselcha.**>, //ƛ'ə́xʷ=M1=T-amə-c-əl-cɛ//, /'*I'll beat you (in a contest).*'/, phonology: automatic stres-shift, attested by Elders Group (6/16/76), example: <**tl'xwétes.**>, //ƛ'ə́xʷ=M1=T-əs//, /'*He won over s-o., He beat s-o.*'/, attested by AD (3/10/80).

<**tl'éxwet**>, cts //ƛ'ə[-´-]xʷ=ət//, PLAY ['*beating s-o in a contest*'], (<**-´-**> *continuative*), (<**=et**> *purposeful control transitivizer*), phonology: stress-shift, syntactic analysis: transitive verb, attested by Elders Group (1/25/78).

<**tl'áxwt**>, cts //ƛ'ə[-Aɛ́-]xʷ=T//, PLAY ['*taking advantage of s-o*'], (<**á:-ablaut**> *continuative*), phonology: ablaut, possible emphatic lengthening, syntactic analysis: transitive verb, attested by Elders Group (2/25/76), also <**tl'á:xwt**>, //ƛ'ə[-Aɛ́·-]xʷ=T//, also /'*beating s-o (many times)*'/, attested by AD (3/10/80), example: <**ő̋wechexw ol tl'áxwt ta' siyáye.**>, //ʔə́wə-c-əxʷ ʔal ƛ'ə[-Aɛ́-]xʷ=T t-ɛʔ s=yɛ́yə//, /'*Don't take advantage of your friends.*'/, literally /'don't you just be taking advantage of them your friend'/, attested by Elders Group (2/25/76).

<**tl'exwtl'éxwtem**>, plv //C_1əC_2=ƛ'ə[=´=]xʷ=T-əm//, PLAY /'*(be) badly beaten, really lost (a contest)*'/, (<**R3=**> *plural action/plural subject*), (<**=´=**> *derivational with plural*), (<**-em**> *passive*), phonology: stress-shift, reduplication, syntactic analysis: intransitive verb, attested by BHTTC (11/10/76).

<**tl'ítl'ex̱wtò:l** (or better) **tl'ítl'exwtò:l**>, rcps //C_1í=ƛ'əx^{w}=T-ə[=Aà·=]l//, dmv, durs, PLAY /'*beating one another at a game (gambling, racing, etc.)*'/, literally /'beating one another a little on purpose (in a game) for a long time'/, (<**R4=**> *diminutive action (continuative implied as usual)*), (<**=t**> *purposeful control transitivizer*), (<**-el**> *reciprocal*), (<**ó:-ablaut**> *durative*), phonology: reduplication, ablaut, **x̱**w mistranscribed for xw, grammatical comment: transitive, syntactic analysis: intransitive verb since it can't take an np object, attested by Elders Group (1/7/76).

<**tl'éxwet**>, PLAY ['*beating s-o in a contest*'], *see* tl'éxw.

<**tl'exwewítstel**>, CLO ['*blanket robe*'], *see* tl'xw ~ tl'exw.

<**tl'exwló:st**>, df //ƛ'əx^{w}(=)əl=á·s=T or ƛ'əx̣^{w}=F=əl=á·s=T//, pcs, EFAM ['*take s-o for granted*'], root meaning unknown unless tl'éxw *lose (in contest)* or tl'éx̱w *stiff, hard*, possibly <**=F (fronting)**> *derivational*, possibly <**=el**> *come, go, get, become*, probably <**=ó:s**> *in the face*, (<**=t**> *purposeful control transitivizer*), phonology: possible fronting, possible vowel-loss, syntactic analysis: transitive verb, attested by Elders Group (2/25/76), also <**tl'exwló:ltes**>, //ƛ'əx^{w}=lá·l=T-əs//, also /'*He takes someone for granted.*'/, possibly <**=ló:l**> affix meaning unknown, (<**-es**> *third person subject),* attested by (not recorded on cards).

<**tl'exwtl'éxwtem**>, PLAY /'*(be) badly beaten, really lost (a contest)*'/, *see* tl'éxw.

<**tl'éx̱w**>, free root //ƛ'ə́x̣^{w}//, DESC /'*(be) hard, stiff (material), strong (of rope, material, not of a person), tough*'/, syntactic analysis: adjective/adjectival verb, attested by EB (12/1/75, 1/6/76, 1/7/76), BHTTC (10/76), Elders Group (3/15/72, 6/16/76), Salish cognate: Squamish /ƛ'ə́x̣^{w}/ *hard, strong (of materials)* W73:130, K67:333, ASM ['hard'], example: <**tl'éx̱w te (seplíl, qwe'óp).**>, //ƛ'ə́x̣^{w} tə (səplíl, q^{w}əʔáp)//, /'*The (bread, apple) is hard.*'/, attested by EB, ASM ['strong'], <**tl'éx̱w x̱wéylem.**>, //ƛ'ə́x̣^{w} x̣^{w}í·ləm//, /'*strong rope*'/, attested by Elders Group (6/16/76).

<**tl'éxw ts'íyxw sqemó**:> (or) <**chí:s**>, FOOD /'*cheese*'/, (lit. cheese or hard + dry + milk), (attested by RG,EH 6/16/98 to SN, edited by BG with RG,EH 6/26/00)

<**tl'ex̱wéthet**>, incs //ƛ'ə́x̣^{w}=M1=θət//, CST ['*to harden*'], (<**metathesis type 1**> *non-continuative*), (<**=thet**> *get, become*), phonology: metathesis, syntactic analysis: intransitive verb, attested by Elders Group (3/15/72).

<**tl'x̱wòlèm**>, df //ƛ'x̣^{w}-ɛ[=Aa=] `ləm or ƛ'x̣^{w}=ə[=Aà=]l=əm//, ABFC /'*I got hard (of arm, leg, penis, etc.)*'/, possibly <**=àlèm**> *passive or conjugated middle??*, possibly <**a-ablaut**> *resultative or durative*, possibly <**=el**> *go, come, get, become*, possibly <**=em**> *middle voice*, phonology: ablaut, possible updrifting, vowel-loss in root, syntactic analysis: intransitive verb, syntactic comment: possible conjugated middle or passive with transitive, attested by JL (Fish Camp 7/20/79), Salish cognate: perhaps in part Squamish /ƛ'x̣^{w}-íʔ/ *harden, congeal* W73:130, K69:72.

<**tl'x̱wéylep** or **tl'x̱wílep**>, ds //ƛ'əx̣^{w}=íləp//, LAND ['*hard ground*'], lx <**=ílep**> *ground, earth, dirt*, syntactic analysis: nominal or adjective/adjectival verb?, attested by Elders Group (6/16/76).

<**tl'x̱wíth'a**>, ds //ƛ'əx̣^{w}=íθ'ɛ//, CLO ['*strong (of material)*'], lx <**=íth'a**> *clothing*, syntactic analysis: adjective/adjectival verb, attested by EB (1/13/76).

<**tl'x̱wíws**>, ds //ƛ'əx̣^{w}=íws//, ANA ['*tough skin*'], lx <**=íws**> *on the skin, on the body*, syntactic analysis: nominal or adjective/adjectival verb?, attested by BHTTC (10/20/76).

<**tl'ex̱wéthet**>, CST ['*to harden*'], *see* tl'éx̱w.

<**tl'e'á ~ tl'á'**>, bound root //ƛ'(=)əʔɛ́ ~ƛ'ɛ́ʔ *invite to a feast*//.

<**tl'etl'áxel**>, df //C_1ə-ƛ'(ʔ)ɛ́=x^{y}əl or C_1ə=ƛ'(ʔ)ɛ́=x^{y}əl//, SOC /'*inviting (to come eat, dance), to give a potlatch, (give a feast or gathering), to invite to a feast, invite to a potlatch*'/, possibly <**R5-**> *continuative*, possibly <**R5=**> *derivational*, possibly <**=e'á**> *comparative*??, possibly <**=xel**> *on the*

foot, phonology: reduplication, possible consonant-loss, syntactic analysis: intransitive verb, attested by EB (12/16/75, 1/30/76), Salish cognate: Squamish /ƛ'əʔášn/ *invite to a feast (itr.), feast (not potlatch), party, dance* W73:152, W67:333.

<**stl'etl'áxel**>, dnom //s=C_1ə=ƛ'(ʔ)ɛ́=xʸəl//, SOC ['*a feast*'], (<**s=**> *nominalizer*), phonology: reduplication, syntactic analysis: nominal, attested by EB (12/16/75), example: <**híkw stl'etl'áxel**>, //hík'ʷ s=C_1ə=ƛ'(ʔ)ɛ́=xʸəl//, /'*a big feast*'/, attested by EB.

<**tl'e'áxet**>, pcs //ƛ'(=)əʔɛ́=xʸ(əl)=əT//, SOC /'*invite s-o (to come eat, dance etc.) (any number), invite s-o to a feast*'/, possibly <**=e'á**> *comparative*?, possibly <**=xel**> *on the foot*, (semological comment: perhaps *on foot* because invitations had to be personally delivered), (<**=et**> *purposeful control transitivizer*), phonology: automatic syllable-loss (el before =et), syntactic analysis: transitive verb, attested by Elders Group (6/16/76), also <**tl'etl'áxet**>, //C_1ə=ƛ'(ʔ)ɛ́=xʸ(əl)=əT//, phonology: reduplication, syllable-loss, consonant-loss, attested by EB (12/16/75); found in <**tl'etl'áxethóxes.**>, //C_1ə=ƛ'ɛ́=xʸ(əl)=əT-áxʸ-əs//, /'*She invited me to a feast.*'/, attested by EB, example: <**mőkw'ewátes tl'etl'áxetes.**>, //mók'ʷ=ə=wɛ́t=əs C_1ə=ƛ'ɛ́=xʸ(əl)=əT-əs//, /'*He/She invited everybody.*'/, attested by EB.

<**stl'e'áleq**>, dnom //s=ƛ'(=)əʔɛ́=ləq//, SOC ['*a potlatch*'], (<**s=**> *nominalizer, something to*), lx <**=leq**> meaning uncertain unless related to/same as lx <**=élq**> *after*, syntactic analysis: nominal, attested by BJ (12/5/64, new transcript old p.335), other sources: ES /ƛ'əʔəléq/ (CwMs /ƛ'ə́nəq/) *potlatch*, Salish cognate: Squamish /ƛ'əʔə́nq/ *potlatch* W73:303, K67:333.

<**tl'e'áxet**>, SOC /'*invite s-o (to come eat, dance etc.) (any number), invite s-o to a feast*'/, *see* tl'e'á ~ tl'á'.

<**tl'e'ímél ~ tl'e'í:mel**>, df //ƛ'əʔí(=)məl ~ ƛ'əʔí·(=)məl//, ANA /'*cord, muscle, tendon, nerve cord by backbone*'/, ASM ['the nerve cord (of deer, etc.) was cleaned and used for bowstring, very strong'], root meaning unknown, possibly <**=mel**> *part, portion (of body esp.)*, syntactic analysis: nominal, attested by Elders Group (2/5/75, 7/27/75, 8/20/75), other sources: ES /ƛ'əʔíməl/ (CwMs /ƛ'ímən/) *tendon*, Salish cognate: Squamish /ƛ'əʔímin/ *sinew* (vs. Squamish /tímin/ *muscle*) K67:333, W73:235 error, (also vs. Lushootseed /tíǰ/ *muscle, sinew* H76:5 Samish dial. of NSt /ƛ'íʔiŋən/ *muscle* G86a:75.

<**tl'í ~ tl'í:**>, free root //ƛ'í ~ ƛ'í·//, VALJ /'*(be) difficult, hard (of work, etc.)*'/, ECON ['*expensive*'], syntactic analysis: adjective/adjectival verb, attested by AC (8/29/70), AD (11/19/79), EB, Salish cognate: Squamish /ƛ'íʔ/ *difficult, dangerous, excessive, dear* K67:334, ASM ['difficult, hard'], example: <**tl'í syó:ys**>, //ƛ'í s=yá·ys//, /'*hard (difficult) work*'/, attested by AC, <**tl'í te syó:ys teló.**>, //ƛ'í ɬə s=yá·ys tə=lá//, /'*(That work is difficult.)*'/, attested by AC, <**tl'í syó:ys qe y xwa ets xwét:es.**>, //ƛ'í s=yá·ys qə yə-xʷɛ ʔəc xʷə́t·əs//, /'*It's hard and heavy work.*'/, attested by AC, ASM ['expensive'], <**tu tl'í(.)**>, //təw ƛ'í//, /'*(It's) more expensive*'/, attested by AD, <**we'ólew tl'í**>, //wə=ʔál=əw ƛ'í//, /'*(It's) too expensive*'/, attested by AD, also <**we'ólewe tl'í**>, //wə=ʔálə=wə ƛ'í//, also /'*expensive*'/, attested by EB, <**éwe lís u ólewe tl'í.**>, //ʔə́wə lí-s ʔəw ʔálə=wə ƛ'í//, /'*It's not too expensive.*'/, attested by AD.

<**tl'ístexw**>, caus //ƛ'í=sT-əxʷ//, ECON ['*make s-th expensive*'], (<**=st**> *causative control transitivizer*), (<**-exw**> *third person object*), syntactic analysis: transitive verb, attested by AD (11/19/79); found in <**tl'ístem**>, //ƛ'í=sT-əm//, /'*It's expensive.*'/, probably <**-em**> *passive*, attested by AD.

<**stl'í ~ stl'í:**>, dnom //s=ƛ'í ~ s=ƛ'í·//, EFAM /'*want, desire, like, need*'/, (<**s=**> *nominalizer*), syntactic analysis: nominal, syntactic comment: usually possessed with possessive pronouns and first in sentence, then followed by a nominal phrase (grammatically the subject but semantically the object), then translated as *to want, to desire, like*, thus literally "is my want the water" → "the water is my want" → "I want the water.", Salish cognate: Squamish /s-ƛ'íʔ/ *desire, object desired* from root /ƛ'íʔ/ *dear, difficult, dangerous, excessive* K67:334, historical/comparative detail: most of the

Central Coast Salish languages share this syntactic peculiarity of a grammatical nominal--semantic verb, attested by AC, Deming, AD, NP, EB, SP, AK, others, example: <**l stl'í kw'els qwà:l kw'e axwí:l òl sqwà:l.**>, //l s=ƛ'í k'ʷ-əl-s qʷɛ̀·l k'ʷə ʔɛxʷ(=)í·l ʔàl s=qʷɛ̀·l//, /'*I would like to say just a few words.*'/, attested by Deming (5/18/78), <**l stl'í**>, //l s=ƛ'í//, /'*I want*'/, attested by AC, BJ (5/10/64), <**l stl'í ta sqwówes.**>, //l s=ƛ'í t-ɛ s=qʷáwəs//, /'*I want your pail.*'/, attested by AC (9/1/71), <**l stl'í kw'e qó:; tsqóqele tel sqwemáy.**>, //l s=ƛ'í k'ʷə qá·; c=qá=C_1ə=lə t-əl s=qʷəm=ɛ́y//, /'*I want some water; my dog is thirsty.*'/, attested by AC (ca10/13/71), <**lámtsel welí:sl stl'í kw'els lám.**>, //lɛ́=m-c-əl wə-lí·-s-l s=ƛ'í k'ʷ-əl-s lɛ́=m//, /'*I'm going when I want to go.*'/, attested by AC (10/6/71), <**lí l stl'í?**>, //lí l s=ƛ'í//, /'*Do I want?*'/, Elder's comment: "uncommon", attested by AD (3/19/80), <**lí stl'ítset.**>, //lí s=ƛ'í-c-ət//, /'*Do we want?*'/, Elder's comment: "uncommon", attested by AD (3/19/80), <**l stl'í tel yóseqw.**>, //l s=ƛ'í t-əl yás=əqʷ//, /'*I need my hat., I want my hat.*'/, attested by Deming (2/22/79), <**li a stl'í kw'as lép'ex te skw'ōlmexw?**>, //li ʔɛ s=ƛ'í k'ʷ-ɛ-s lə́p'=əxʸ tə s=k'ʷólməxʷ//, /'*Do you want to eat blackberries?*'/, attested by NP (10/26/75), <**lí a stl'í kw'e tí?**>, //lí ʔɛ s=ƛ'í k'ʷə tí//, /'*Do you want some tea?*'/, attested by EB (1977 during staff class), <**wetl'ó: te th'áles te músmes a stl'í?**>, //wə-ƛ'á-ə tə θ'ɛ́lɛ-s tə mús=C_1əC_2 ʔɛ s=ƛ'í//, /'*Is that the heart of the cow you want?*'/, attested by AC (9/18/71), <**lí a stl'í kw'e qó:?**>, //lí ʔɛ s=ƛ'í k'ʷə qá·//, /'*Do you want some water?*'/, attested by AC (9/10/71), <**li a stl'í kw'as yó:ys?**>, //lí ʔɛ s=ƛ'í k'ʷ-ɛ-s yá·ys//, /'*Do you want to work?*'/, literally /'is it your want that you work'/, attested by AC (10/6/71), <**a stl'íye kw'as emí:?**>, //ʔɛ s=ƛ'í(y)=ə k'ʷ-ɛ-s ʔəmí·//, /'*Do you want to come?*'/, attested by AC, <**lí a stl'íyelep ~ a stl'íya'elep**>, //lí ʔɛ s=ƛ'í(y)-ələp ~ ʔɛ s=ƛ'í(y)-ə-ələp//, /'*do you folks want?*'/, syntactic analysis: interrogative verb possessive nominal-intransitive verb-possessive ~ possessive nominal=intransitive verb-interrogative affix-possessive, syntactic comment: interrogative affix, *<**l stl'íya**> rejected, */'do I want?'/ rejected, *<**stlíyatset**> rejected, */'do we want?'/ rejected by AD (3/19/80), <**eses stl'ís te lólets'e xwélmexw kws tél:exwes westámes kw'e li skwetáxw li te thá.**>, //ʔə-s-əs s=ƛ'í-s tə C_1á=ləc'ə xʷə́l(=)məxʷ kʷ-s tə́l=l-əxʷ-əs wə-stɛ́m=əs k'ʷə li s=kʷətɛ́xʷ li tə θɛ́//, /'*And one Indian wanted to find out what(ever) was inside there.*'/, literally /'so it is his want the one person Indian that he find s-th out if it's what(ever) that is inside in there'/, usage: Story of the Flood, attested by AC (12/7/71), <**tl'ó me stl'ís.**>, //ƛ'á mə s=ƛ'í-s//, /'*That's what he wants.*'/, literally /'that's come to be his want'/, attested by Deming (SJ, MC, MV, LG) (3/15/79), <**lí a stl'í ~ a stlíya**>, //lí ʔɛ s=ƛ'í ~ ʔɛ s=ƛ'í(y)=ə//, /'*do you want?*'/, attested by AD (3/19/80), <**éwe stl'ís kw'es meytólxws welámet séwq'tòlè.**>, //ʔə́wə s=ƛ'í-s k'ʷə-s mɛy=T-álxʷ-s wə-lɛ́=m-ət sə́wq'=T-álə//, /'*He doesn't want to help us (when we) go find you folks (search for you folks).*'/, dialects: *Chill.*, attested by IHTTC (8/22/77), also <**éwe stl'íses meytóxwes welámet súwq'tòlè.**>, //ʔə́wə s=ƛ'í-s-əs mɛy=T-áxʷ-əs wə-lɛ́=m-ət sówq'=T-álə//, dialects: *Tait*, attested by SP and AK and AD (IHTTC 8/22/77), also <**éwe stl'íses kws meytóxwes welámet súwq'tòlè.**>, //ʔə́wə s=ƛ'í-s-əs kʷ-s mɛy=T-áxʷ-əs wə-lɛ́=m-ət sówq'=T-álə//, dialects: *Cheh.*, attested by EB (IHTTC 8/22/77).

<**stl'ítl'el**>, dnom //s=ƛ'í=C_1ə=(ə)l//, EFAM /'*love, like*'/, literally (probably) /'something to get a little want/desire'/, (<**s=**> *nominalizer, something to*), probably <**=R1=**> *diminutive*, possibly <**=R1=**> *continuative or resultative*, probably <**=el**> *go, come, get, become*, phonology: reduplication, vowel-loss in suffix, syntactic analysis: nominal, attested by Elders Group (3/23/77), compare stem <**tl'íls**> *to love s-o, like s-o*, example: <**l stl'ítl'el tel ímeth.**>, //l s=ƛ'í=C_1ə=(ə)l t-əl ʔíməθ//, /'*I love my grandchild.*'/, attested by Elders Group.

<**tl'íls ~ tl'í:ls**>, pncs //ƛ'í=ləs ~ ƛ'í=ələs//, EFAM /'*to love s-o, like s-o*'/, (<**=eles ~ =les ~ =ls**> *psychological non-control transitivizer*), phonology: vowel-loss or vowel merger, syntactic analysis: transitive verb, attested by Elders Group (3/3/76, 3/23/77, 4/6/77), example: <**éy**

mestíyexw; mekw'ewát tl'íls.>, //ʔɛ́y məstíyəxʷ; mək'ʷ=ə=wɛ́t ƛ'í=ls//, /'*He's a good person; everyone likes him.*'/, attested by Elders Group (4/6/77), <**tsel tl'í:lsome kw'a'sa thíthaxel.**>, //c-əl ƛ'í=əls-ámə k'ʷ-ɛʔ-s-ɛ θí=C_1ə=xʸəl//, /'*I like you because you've got big feet.*'/, attested by Elders Group (3/3/76), <**tl'í:lsomé**tsel> *I love you* IHHTC; found in <**tl'ílsem**>, //ƛ'í=ls-əm//, /'*be liked*'/, possibly <**-em**> *passive*, syntactic comment: passive of psychological non-control transitivizer, attested by Elders Group (4/6/77).

<**tl'íchet**>, WV /'*embroider it, embroider s-th*'/, *see* tl'íts ~ tl'ích.

<**tl'íkw'el**>, free root //ƛ'ík'ʷəl//, EB /'*kinnikinnick berry, bearberry, Indian tobacco, domestic pea, domestic green bean, and probably giant vetch berry*'/, ['*Arctostaphylos uva-ursi*, (intro.) *Pisum sativum*, (intro.) *Phaseolus vulgaris*, and probably *Vicea gigantea*'], ASM ['kinnikinnick is a low creeping mat-like bush, its red berry is ripe in August and is eaten, tasting like a pea or bean, has a stone, the leaves were dried and smoked as tobacco or with tobacco (after contact), the kinnikinnick leaves when smoked have a mild relaxant effect, the domestic pea and green bean were of course introduced after contact and were planted by a number of Indians'], MED ['the leaves and roots were also used as medicine to prevent bed-wetting'], (semological comment: perhaps related to the word tl'ékw'el *go out (of fire)* since the kinnikinnick leaves were smoked and had a mild relaxant effect, the word has diffused however perhaps from/to Wakashan since Nitinat has /ƛ'i·k'ʷid/ *peas*), syntactic analysis: noun, nominal, attested by , other sources: ES /ƛ'ík'ʷəl/ (CwMs /ƛ'ík'ʷənʔ/) *bearberry, pea, bean*, Salish cognate: Saanich /ƛ'ík'ʷənʔ/ and Cowichan /ƛ'ík'ʷənʔ/ both *giant vetch, kinnikinnick, garden pea, garden bean* Turner and Bell 1971:82,85, example: <**thíthe tl'íkw'el**>, //θí=C_1ə ƛ'ík'ʷəl//, /'*larger beans*'/, attested by AC (11/24/71), <**tsqwá:y te tl'íkw'el.**>, //c=qʷɛ́·y tə ƛ'ík'ʷəl//, /'*The pea/bean is green., The peas/beans are green.*'/, attested by Deming (esp. SJ 5/3/79).

<**thós sp'eq'í:l tl'íkw'el**>, FOOD, EB /'*lima beans*'/, (lit. big round + off-white + bean), (attested by RG,EH 6/16/98 to SN, edited by BG with RG,EH 6/26/00)

<**tskwimómex tl'íkw'el**>, FOOD, EB /'*kidney beans*'/, (lit. dark red in appearance + bean), (attested by RG,EH 6/16/98 to SN, edited by BG with RG,EH 6/26/00)

<**ts'íts'esem tl'íkw'el**>, FOOD, EB /'*bean sprouts*'/, (lit. growing up + bean), (attested by RG,EH 6/16/98 to SN, edited by BG with RG,EH 6/26/00)

<**tl'ikw'íyelhp**>, ds //ƛ'ik'ʷəl=əɬp//, EB /'*kinnikinnick plant, domestic pea-vine, domestic bean-vine, giant vetch vine*'/, lx <**=elhp**> *plant*, phonology: automatic el→íy before =elhp, syntactic analysis: nominal, attested by AC, SP and AK (7/13/75), example: <**qéx̱ te tl'ikw'íyelhp qa ōwéta tl'íkw'el.**>, //qə́x̱ tə ƛ'ik'ʷəl=əɬp qɛ ʔowə= ́tɛ ƛ'ík'ʷəl//, /'*There's a lot of vines but no beans.*'/, attested by AC (11/24/71).

<**Tl'íkw'elem**>, ds //ƛ'ík'ʷəl=əm//, PLN /'*Silver Creek, Silver Hope Creek*'/, literally /'place to have/get kinnikinnick berry'/, ASM ['so named because lots of kinnikinnick berries were always found here'], lx <**=em**> *place to have/get*, syntactic analysis: nominal, attested by JL (3/8/78), other sources: Wells (1966) <KLEH-kwun-num> *Silver Creek, Silver Hope Creek*, also <**Xwtl'íkw'elem**>, //xʷ=ƛ'ík'ʷəl=əm//, literally /'place to always have/get kinnikinnick berry'/, attested by JL (3/8/78).

<**Lexwtl'íkw'elem**>, ds //ləxʷ=ƛ'ík'ʷəl=əm//, PLN ['*village at mouth of Stulkawhits Creek on Fraser River*'], literally /'place to always have/get kinnikinnick berry'/, ASM ['between Suka Creek and Strawberry Island'], (<**lexw=**> *always*), lx <**=em**> *place to have/get*, syntactic analysis: nominal, attested by SP and AK (Fish Camp 8/2/77), source: place names reference file #152, other sources: Duff 1952, Wells 1965 (lst ed.):25 village #17.

<**Tl'ikw'ólem** or less likely **Tl'aqewólem??** or **Tl'iq'ewólem??**>, df //ƛ'ík'ʷə[=Aá=]l=əm or less

likely ƛ'ɛq'əwál=əm or ƛ'iq'əwál=əm//, PLN [*'Lindeman Lake'*], root meaning unknown unless **<tl'aq' ~ tl'q'>**, bound root //ƛ'ɛq' ~ ƛ'q' *shorten?* or more likely **<tl'íkw'el>**, ds //ƛ'ík'ʷəl// *kinnikinnick berries*, (**<=em>** *place to have/get*), compare **<Tl'íkw'elem>**, ds //ƛ'ík'ʷəl=əm// *Silver Creek, Silver Hope Creek*, literally /'place to have/get kinnikinnick berries'/, syntactic analysis: nominal, source: Wells <kleh-kah-WA-lum> *Lindeman Lake* Wells 1966.

<**Tl'íkw'elem**>, PLN /*'Silver Creek, Silver Hope Creek'*/, *see* tl'íkw'el.

<**tl'ikw'íyelhp**>, EB /*'kinnikinnick plant, domestic pea-vine, domestic bean-vine, giant vetch vine'*/, *see* tl'íkw'el.

<**tl'íls ~ tl'í:ls**>, EFAM /*'to love s-o, like s-o'*/, *see* tl'í ~ tl'í:.

<**tl'ím**>, probable room //ƛ'ím//, meaning unknown

<**stl'ítl'em**>, strs //s=ƛ'í[=C_1ə=]m//, DESC [*'bent over?'*], (<**s=**> *stative*), (<**=R1=**> *resultative*), Elder's comment: "slightly unsure of translation", phonology: reduplication, syntactic analysis: adjective/adjectival verb, attested by Elders Group (3/23/77).

<**tl'í:na**>, free root //ƛ'í·nɛ//, FOOD [*'eulachon oil'*], syntactic analysis: noun, Elder's comment: "this word is from the Kwakiutl language", attested by Rudy Leon (3/12/75)(son of EL), Salish cognate: Squamish /ƛ'íʔna/ *eulachon oil* K67:334.

<**tl'íq**>, probable root //ƛ'iq//, meaning uncertain unless related to <**tl'íq'**> *adhere, stick on* as in <**stl'éqxel**>, CLO [*'deer-skin moccasin'*], lit. "something stuck on the foot", possible D (deglottalization).

<**tl'ítl'eqel**>, rsls //ƛ'í[=C_1ə=]q=əl//, FOOD [*'(go/get/become) soggy'*], DESC, root meaning unknown, probably <**=R1=**> *resultative*, probably <**=el**> *go, come, get, become*, phonology: reduplication, syntactic analysis: adjective/adjectival verb, attested by BHTTC (10/76), Elders Group (3/9/77), example: <**tl'ítl'eqel seplí:l**>, //ƛ'í[=C_1ə=]q=əl səplí·l//, /*'soggy bread'*/, attested by Elders Group.

<**tl'íq**> or <**tl'eq**>, probable root //ƛ'iq// or //ƛ'əq//, meaning uncertain unless related to <**tl'íq'**> *adhere, stick on* as in <**stl'éqxel**>, CLO [*'deer-skin moccasin'*], lit. "something stuck on the foot", possible D (deglottalization)..

<**stl'ítl'eqelh ~ stl'í:tl'eqelh**>, df //s=ƛ'í[=C_1ə=]q=əɬ ~ s=ƛ'í[=C_1ə=]q=əɬ or s=C_1í=ƛ'əq=əɬ//, HAT /*'child (post-baby to pre-adolescent), child (under 12), (young* [BJ]*)'*/, literally possibly /'nominal soggy offspring/young'/ or /stuck on offspring/young (since they adhere to their parents or otherchildren), (<**s=**> *nominalizer*), possibly <**=R1=**> *resultative or diminutive*, possibly <**R3=**> *diminutive*, root meaning unknown unless as in stem tl'ítl'eq=el *soggy or* , lx <**=elh ~ =óllh**> *offspring, young, child*, phonology: reduplication, syntactic analysis: nominal, attested by AC, BJ (12/5/64), other sources: ES /sƛ'í·ƛ'qəɬ/ *child (preadolescent)*, also /*'young'*/, attested by BJ (12/5/64), also <**stl'ítl'qelh**>, //s=ƛ'í[=C_1ə=]q=əɬ or s=C_1í=ƛ'əq=əɬ//, attested by CT and HT (6/8/76), Deming, EB, example: <**í:'axwì:l stl'í:tl'eqelh**>, //C_1í=ʔɛxʷ(=)í·l s=ƛ'í·[=C_1ə=]q=əɬ//, /*'small child'*/, attested by AC, <**qél stlítl'qelh, qáqel.**>, //qə́l s=ƛ'í[=C_1ə=]q=əɬ, qɛ́[=C_1ə=]l//, /*'He's/She's a bad child, (he/she is) stealing.'*/, attested by Deming (SJ, MC, MV, LG on 3/15/79), <**ewálhchxw kwáxw stl'ítl'qelh?**>, //ʔəwə-ə-əɬ-c-xʷ kʷɛ́-xʷ s=ƛ'í[=C_1ə=]q=əɬ//, /*'Weren't you ever a child?'*/, syntactic comment: vneg -interrogative affix -interrogative past -non-subordinate subject marker -subject pronoun adverb/adverbial verb -sbsp nominal as verb, syntactic comment: shows dependent subjunctive -xw attached to kwá *anyway* an adverbial verb, usually the dependent subjunctive is attached to auxiliary verbs ending in i, that is í, lí, mí, or to the main verb, this may show that the auxiliaries really have an adverbial function, attested by EB (3/31/78), <**stl'í:tl'eqelh te le kw'óqwet te éqwelets te siyólexwe.**>, //s=ƛ'í·[=C_1ə=]q=əɬ tə lə k'ʷáqʷ=T tə ʔə́qʷ=ələc-s tə s=yáləxʷ=ə//, /*'(It was this) child that hit the back of the old man.'*/, attested by AC (10/13/71).

<**stl'éqxel**>, df //s=ƛ'i[=Aə́=]q=x^{y}əl or s=ƛ'ə́q=x^{y}əl//, CLO ['*deer-skin moccasin*'], literally (probably) /'something to be stuck on on the foot'/, (<**s=**> *nominalizer, something to, something that*), probably <**é-ablaut**> *resultative or durative*, probably root <**tl'iq**> *stick on*, lx <**=xel**> *on the foot*, phonology: probable ablaut, syntactic analysis: nominal, attested by Deming (6/15/77).

<**tl'íq'**>, possibly root //ƛ'íq' or ƛ'ə[=Aí=]q'//, TCH /'*get wedged (by falling tree, for ex.), got run over (by car, train, etc.)*'/, possibly <**í-ablaut**> *resultative*, phonology: possible ablaut, syntactic analysis: intransitive verb, attested by EB (4/29/76), Salish cognate: Squamish /ƛ'ə́yq'/ *get trapped, caught* and also /ƛ'əyq'-ánʔ/ *grip, pinch (tr.)* K67:333, Lushootseed (Snohomish dial.) root /ƛ'íq'(i)/ and (Skagit dial.) root /ƛ'ík'(i)/ both *adhere* (Skagit as in /ƛ'ík'id/ *stick it on*) H76:327,324.

<**tl'íq't**>, pcs //ƛ'íq'=T//, TCH /'*run over it (with car), spread it (for ex. on bread with knife), put it up (of wallpaper), (stick it on), stick s-th closed (with pitch for ex.)*'/, (<**=t**> *purposeful control transitivizer*), syntactic analysis: transitive verb, attested by EP and EB (BHTTC 8/23/76), EB (4/23/76), Deming (1/31/80), Salish cognate: Lushootseed (Skagit dial.) stem /ƛ'ík'id/ *stick it on* and related (Skagit) /ɬu-ƛ'í-ƛ'ik'-alùs-cid/ *she'll stick your eyes (shut with pitch)* H76:324, example: <**tl'íq'etestsa ta' qélém.**>, //ƛ'íq'=əT-əs-cɛ t-ɛʔ qə́lə́m//, /'*She'll stick your eyes closed (with pitch).*'/, attested by Deming.

<**stl'etl'íq'**>, strs //s=C_1ə=ƛ'íq'//, TCH /'*(be) too tight (of shoes, clothes, trap, box), tight (of a dress one can't get into), too tight to get into (of dress, car, box of cards, etc.)*'/, (<**s=**> *stative*), (<**R5=**> *resultative*), phonology: reduplication, syntactic analysis: adjective/adjectival verb, attested by EB (4/23/76, 4/29/76).

<**tl'iq'áwtxw**>, ds //ƛ'iq'=ɛ́wtx^w//, HUNT ['*deadfall trap*'], lx <**=áwtxw**> *building, house*, syntactic analysis: nominal, attested by Elders Group (10/20/76).

<**tl'ítl'eq'el**>, incs //ƛ'í[=C_1ə=]q'=əl//, TCH ['*gummy (sticky)*'], possibly <**=R1=**> *continuative*, (<**=el**> *go, come, get, become*), phonology: reduplication, syntactic analysis: adjective/adjectival verb, attested by BHTTC (10/76), Salish cognate: related Lushootseed /ʔəs-ƛ'íq'/ *it's sticky* H76:327.

<**temtl'í:q'es**>, ds //təm=ƛ'í[=·=]q'=əs//, TIME /'*moon or month beginning in February, (November to December, time when ice forms [and sticks] [Billy Sepass in Jenness])*'/, literally /'time to really stick cyclic period'/, Elder's comment: "time when you stick to things cold (when you touch them)", lx <**tem=**> *time to, season to*, possibly <**=:=**> *emphatic*, lx <**=es**> *cyclic period*, phonology: lengthening, syntactic analysis: nominal, attested by Elders Group (3/12/75), also <**tl'íq'es**>, //ƛ'íq'=əs//, also /'*November to December*'/, Elder's comment: "ice forms", literally /'stick on cyclic period'/, source: Diamond Jenness' field notes interview of Wm. Sepass of Sardis, attested by reconstructed by Elders Group (3/28/79).

<**tl'í:q'etses**>, ds //ƛ'í[=·=]q'=əcəs//, TCH /'*one's hand jammed (in a trap, under a box, etc.)*'/, possibly <**=:=**> *emphatic*?, lx <**=etses**> *on the hand*, phonology: possible lengthening, syntactic analysis: adjective/adjectival verb, attested by Elders Group (3/12/75).

<**tl'iq'áwtxw**>, HUNT ['*deadfall trap*'], *see* tl'íq'.

<**tl'í:q'etses**>, TCH /'*one's hand jammed (in a trap, under a box, etc.)*'/, *see* tl'íq'.

<**tl'íq't**>, TCH /'*run over it (with car), spread it (for ex. on bread with knife), put it up (of wallpaper), (stick it on), stick s-th closed (with pitch for ex.)*'/, *see* tl'íq'.

<**tl'íqw'**> or <**tl'eqw'**>, probable root //ƛ'íq'^{w} or ƛ'əq'^{w}//, meaning uncertain

<**stl'etl'íqw'**>, strs //s=C_1ə=ƛ'íq'^{w} or s=ƛ'ə[=C_1əAí=]q'^{w}//, CLO ['*(be) all bundled up*'], (<**s=**> *stative*), possibly <**R5= or =R1= plus í-ablaut**> *resultative*, phonology: reduplication, possible ablaut, syntactic analysis: adjective/adjectival verb, attested by AD (3/6/80), Salish cognate: possibly

Lushootseed root /ƛ'úq'^{w}(u)/ *stuff into, plug in* H76:331?.

<**tl'ís**> or <**tl'es**>, bound root //ƛ'ís// or //ƛ'əs//, meaning uncertain

<**stl'ítl'es**>, df //s=ƛ'í[=C_1ə=]s//, LT /'*(dingy white, off-white)*'/, (<**s=**> *stative*), root meaning unknown, probably <**=R1=**> *continuative or resultative*, (semological comment: note that Tait speaker TG uses ts'sás *ashes* to map the same color that Sumas speaker AH maps with stl'ítl'es, and others (Chilliwack speaker NP and Tait speaker AK) map largely with p'éq'. stl'ítl'es then probably could be glossed *dingy white, off-white* with inceptive form stl'ítl'esel elsewhere translated *dark (old clothes, complexion)*), comment: using derived forms of the root as a modifier of other color terms the following combinations were given by AK: stl'ítl'esel (qálq, tskwím, tsméth', tsqwáy, tskwím "really dark ...", tsqw'íx̣w, qwiqwóyáls, sts'óla); tl'ítl'esel (tsqwáy once "two times tsqwáy"); stl'ítl'es(el) tsqwáy, see charts by Rob MacLaury.

<**stl'ítl'esel**>, strs //s=ƛ'í[=C_1ə=]s=əl//, LT /'*(be) a dark color (of clothes, complexions, etc.), (dark gray, dark brown)*'/, ASM ['squares circled on the color chart of Berlin and Kay 1969 (rows top to bottom = B-I, columns left to right = 1-40, side column of white to black = 0); individual speakers circled the following squares at the Elders Group 2/7/79: NP: D0-E0 EP: C0 Lawrence James: G0, B32'], see charts by Rob MacLaury, (<**s=**> *stative*), (<**=R1=**> *resultative*), (<**=el**> *go, come, get, become*), phonology: reduplication, syntactic analysis: adjective/adjectival verb, attested by Elders Group (9/8/76), Deming (esp. SJ 5/3/79), Salish cognate: Squamish /ƛ'í-ƛ'is-iʔ/ *jaundice* from /ƛ'ís/ *green* besides /ƛ'əs-ƛ'ís/ *green, pale (color of grass)* K67:334,332, Sechelt stem /ƛ'əs-ím/ *green* and /ƛ'əs-im-ús/ *pale [prob. of a person, lit. green in the face]* T77:21-22, historical/comparative detail: note antonymic reversal from pale to dark (or vice versa), example: <**stl'ítl'esel te s'óthes te xwélmexw.**>, //s=ƛ'í[=C_1ə=]s=əl tə s=ʔáθ=əs-s tə x^{w}ə́l=məx^{w}//, /'*The Indian's face is dark (in complexion).*'/, Elder's comment: "not all Indians are like this", phonology: consonant merger, attested by Deming (esp. SJ 5/3/79).

<**tl'ístexw**>, ECON ['*make s-th expensive*'], *see* tl'í ~ tl'í:.

<**tl'ítl'echels**>, WV ['*embroidering*'], *see* tl'íts ~ tl'ích.

<**tl'ítl'eptel**>, CLO ['*skirt*'], *see* tl'ép.

<**tl'ítl'eq'el**>, TCH ['*gummy (sticky)*'], *see* tl'íq'.

<**tl'ítl'ets'**>, TVMO /'*to sneak along, (sneaking along)*'/, *see* tl'í:ts'.

<**tl'ítl'ets'élqem**>, HUNT ['*sneaking after an animal*'], *see* tl'í:ts'.

<**tl'í:tl'ets'et**>, TVMO ['*sneaking up to s-o*'], *see* tl'í:ts'.

<**tl'ítl'ew**>, TVMO ['*running away*'], *see* tl'í:w.

<**tl'ítl'ex̱wtò:l** (or better) **tl'ítl'exwtò:l**>, PLAY /'*beating one another at a game (gambling, racing, etc.)*'/, *see* tl'éxw.

<**tl'ítl'q'ey**>, TVMO ['*a shortcut*'], *see* tl'aq' ~ tl'q'.

<**tl'itl'q'oyám**>, TVMO ['*take a shortcut*'], *see* tl'aq' ~ tl'q'.

<**tl'íts ~ tl'ích**>, bound root //ƛ'íc *embroider, trim (stitch an edge)*//.

<**tl'íchet**>, pcs //ƛ'íc=əT//, WV /'*embroider it, embroider s-th*'/, (<**=et**> *purposeful control transitivizer*), syntactic analysis: transitive verb, attested by IHTTC (7/12/77).

<**tl'ítl'echels**>, sas //ƛ'í[-C_1ə-]c=əls//, cts, WV ['*embroidering*'], (<**-R1-**> *continuative*), (<**=els**> *structured activity continuative*), phonology: reduplication, syntactic analysis: intransitive verb, attested by IHTTC (7/12/77).

<**stl'ítl'ets**>, dnom //s=ƛ'í[=C_1ə=]c//, WV /'*embroidery, trimming (stitches on an edge)*'/, SPRD /'*trimmings on uniform (paddles, etc.)*'/, (<**s=**> *nominalizer*), (<**=R1=**> *resultative*), phonology: reduplication, syntactic analysis: nominal, attested by Elders Group (8/31/77), attested by RG & EH (4/10/99 Ling332).

<**tl'í:ts'**>, bound root //ƛ'í·c' *sneak up to*//.

<**tl'ítl'ets'**>, cts //ƛ'í[-C_1ə-]c'//, TVMO /'*to sneak along, (sneaking along)*'/, HUNT, (<**-R1-**> *continuative*), phonology: reduplication, syntactic analysis: intransitive verb, attested by EB (1/30/76).

<**tl'í:ts'et**>, pcs //ƛ'í·c'=əT//, TVMO ['*sneak up to s-o/s-th*'], HUNT, (<**=et**> *purposeful control transitivizer*), syntactic analysis: transitive verb, attested by AC (8/7/70), Elders Group (12/10/75), Salish cognate: Squamish /ƛ'íč'-it/ *to stalk (tr.)* beside /ƛ'i-ƛ'ič'-it-sut/ *sneak along* W73:241, K67:334, probably not (by metathesis) Sechelt /č'áƛ'-am/ *to sneak up, stalk* and /č'áƛ'-at/ *to sneak up [to s-th/s-o], stalk [s-o/s-th]* T77:13 (which appears to be more cognate with Upriver Halkomelem /c'ɛƛ'-əm/ *jumping*) but see the variant Upriver Halkomelem form <**ts'its'etl'álqem ~ ts'its'etl'éqem**> *sneaking* under <**tl'itl'ets'élqem**> below.

<**tl'í:tl'ets'et**>, pcs //ƛ'í·[-C_1ə-]c'=əT//, TVMO ['*sneaking up to s-o*'], HUNT, (<**-R1-**> *continuative*), phonology: reduplication, syntactic analysis: transitive verb, attested by AC (8/7/70), also <**tl'ítl'ets'et**>, //ƛ'í[-C_1ə-]c'=əT//, attested by Elders Group (12/10/75); found in <**tl'í:tl'ets'ethòm**>, //ƛ'í·[-C_1ə-]c'=əT-àm//, /'*(someone/they are) sneaking up to you*'/, literally /'you are being sneaked up to'/, syntactic analysis: passive, attested by AC.

<**tl'ítl'ets'élqem**>, df //ƛ'í[-C_1ə-]c'=ə́lq=əm//, cts, HUNT ['*sneaking after an animal*'], TVMO ['*sneaking in*'], (<**-R1-**> *continuative*), lx <**=élq**> *after*, contrast <**chókwelélqem**> under <**chó:l**> *follow*, (<**=em**> *intransitive/have/get or middle voice*), phonology: reduplication, syntactic analysis: intransitive verb, attested by Elders Group (12/10/75), Deming (4/17/80), Salish cognate: Squamish /ƛ'i-ƛ'č'-álʔq=m/ *sneak up (itr.)* W73:241, K69:73, also <**ts'its'etl'álqem ~ ts'its'etl'élqem**>, //c'i[-C_1ə-]ƛ'=ɛ́lq=əm ~ c'i[-C_1ə-]ƛ'=ə́lq=əm//, [c'ic'əƛ'ɛ́lqəm ~ c'ic'əƛ'ílqəm], phonology: note metathesis which may relate to the Sechelt cognate above, attested by IHTTC (7/18/77), example: <**chexw tl'itl'ets'élqem.**>, //c-əx^w ƛ'i[-C_1ə-]c'=ə́lq=əm//, /'*(You're sneaking in after.)*'/, usage: said to someone arriving late, attested by Deming (4/17/80).

<**tl'éts'**>, durs //ƛ'i[=Aə́=]c'//, DIR /'*close together, (narrow? [MV])*'/, (<**é-ablaut**> *durative*), phonology: ablaut, syntactic analysis: adjective/adjectival verb?, dialects: *Cheh.*, attested by EB/NP and SJ (Deming 4/10/80), also /'*narrow?*'/, attested by MV (Deming (4/10/80).

<**tl'í:ts'et**>, TVMO ['*sneak up to s-o/s-th*'], *see* tl'í:ts'.

<**tl'í:w**>, free root //ƛ'í·w//, TVMO /'*to escape (of a man or a slave), run away*'/, syntactic analysis: intransitive verb, attested by Elders Group (1/7/76), EB (1/8/76, 1/20/76), Salish cognate: Squamish /ƛ'íwʔ/ *run away (about a captive)* K67:335, example: <**qíq'et te ílh le tl'í:w**>, //qíq'=əT tə ʔí-ɬ lə ƛ'í·w//, /'*caught the one who escaped (catch/apprehend s-o)*'/, Elder's comment: "<**qíq'et**> is better than <**kwélém**> here", attested by EB (1/8/76).

<**tl'ítl'ew**>, cts //ƛ'í[-C_1ə-]w//, TVMO ['*running away*'], (<**-R1-**> *continuative*), phonology: reduplication, syntactic analysis: Elders Group (1/7/76).

<**yitl'ítl'ew**>, mos //yi=ƛ'í[-C_1ə-]w//, TVMO ['*[travelling along] running away*'], (<**ye- ~ yi-**> *travelling along, along, while moving*), phonology: reduplication, syntactic analysis: adverb/adverbial verb?, attested by Elders Group (1/7/76).

<**tl'ewlómét ~ tl'ōwlómét**>, ncrs //ƛ'iw=l-ámə́t or ƛ'i[=Aə=]w=l-ámət//, TVMO /'*to escape (as an animal from a trap), got away from something that trapped a person or animal*'/, possibly <**e-**

ablaut> *resultative*, (<**=l**> *non-control transitivizer, happen to/manage to/accidentally do*), (<**-ómét ~ -ómet**> *reflexive*), phonology: possible vowel-reduction, possible ablaut, probable updrifting, syntactic analysis: intransitive verb, attested by Elders Group (3/72), AD (3/5/79), Salish cognate: Squamish /ƛ'íwʔ-numut/ *manage to escape* K69:73.

<**tl'ő́wstexw**>, caus //ƛ'i[=Aə́=]w=sT-əxʷ//, SOC /'*kidnap s-o, run away with s-o*'/, TVMO, (<**é-ablaut**> *resultative*), (<**=st**> *causative control transitivizer*), (<**-exw**> *third person object*), phonology: ablaut, syntactic analysis: transitive verb, attested by Elders Group (1/16/80); found in <**tl'ő́wstem te slhálí.**>, //ƛ'ə́w=sT-əm tə s=ɬɛ́l(=)í//, /'*They kidnapped the woman., They ran away with the woman.*'/, attested by Elders Group (1/16/80).

<**tl'kwót**>, pcs ///ƛ'ákw=M1=T (or) ƛ'əkw=ə[=Aá=]T (or) ƛ'ikw=ə[=Aá=]T//, ABFC /to grasp/, root form and meaning uncertain, possibly <**metathesis type 1**> *non-continuative* or <**ó-ablaut**> *durative*, <**=et**> *purposeful control transitivizer*, attested by RG & EH (4/9/99 Ling332)

<**tl'ó ~ tl'o**>, free root or stem //ƛ'á ~ ƛ'a or ƛ'=a//, DEM /'*that's (an animate being), it's (usually animate)*'/, possibly root <**tl'**> *agent (human, gender unspecified, absent)*, possibly <**=ò**> *just?*, syntactic analysis: demonstrative pronoun, syntactic comment: always first in sentence, usually requires the following np to delete its article, attested by EB (11/24/75 esp.), AC, MV, Elders Group, Deming, JL, example: <**tl'o te (Bill, músmes, x̲wex̲áye).**>, //ƛ'a tə (Bill, mús=C_1əC_2, C_1ə=x̣ʷɛ́y=ə)//, /'*That's (Bill, the cow, the fly).*'/, attested by EB (11/24/75), <**tl'ó: a sts'ó:meqw?**>, //ƛ'á-ə ʔɛ s=c'á·m(=)əqʷ//, /'*Is that your great grandchild?*'/, phonology: vowel merger, attested by AC (9/29/71), <**tl'ó yewá:lelh ts'lhimexóstels.**>, //ƛ'á yəwɛ́·l-əɬ c'əɬ=ʔim=əxʸ=ás=təl-s//, /'*That's the first one he was going with (romantically)/going for a walk with.*'/, attested by MV (Deming 5/4/78), <**tl'ó yeláwel éy.**>, //ƛ'á yəlɛ́w=əl ʔɛ́y//, /'*That's the best., That's better.*'/, attested by Elders Group (3/9/77), <**tl'o ilh mamíyet.**>, //ƛ'a ʔi-ɬ mɛ[-C_1ə-]y=əT//, /'*That's the one that was helping him.*'/, attested by AC (10/23/71), <**tl'ól texwmélem.**>, //ƛ'á-l təxʷ=mə́lə=m//, /'*That's my step-child.*'/, attested by AC (11/16/71), <**tl'el stó:les.**>, //ƛ'a-l s=tá·ləs//, /'*That's my wife.*'/, phonology: fast pronunciation, attested by AC (10/21/71), <**tl'ol lálem.**>, //ƛ'a-l lɛ́ləm//, /'*That's my house.*'/, attested by AC (10/21/71), <**tl'ól siyá:ya.**>, //ƛ'á-l s=yɛ́·yɛ//, /'*It's my friend.*'/, attested by AC (9/29/71), <**tl'ó te thá. ~ tl'ó tethá.**>, //ƛ'á tə θɛ́ ~ ƛ'á tə=θɛ́//, /'*That's the one., It's that one.*'/, attested by AC (8/25/70), other sources: ES /ƛ'á·tθɛ́·/ *that (it's that one)*, <**tl'ó: te thá?**>, //ƛ'á-ə tə θɛ́//, /'*Is that the one?*'/, attested by AC (8/25/70), <**tl'ó te thá l stl'í.**>, //ƛ'á tə θɛ́ l s=ƛ'í//, /'*I want that., I'd like that.*'/, attested by Deming (2/8/79), <**tl'e kwses x̲ét'e á:lhtel, tl'óts'a Siyó:ylexwe Smált tethá.**>, //ƛ'ə kʷ-s-əs x̣ə́t'ə ʔɛ́·ɬ=təl, ƛ'á-c'ɛ s=yá·[=C_1ə=]ləxʷ=ə s=mɛ́lt tə=θɛ́//, /'*That's what they said, that's Siyá:ylexwe (Old Person) Mountain there.*'/, attested by JL (4/7/78 History Dept. tape #34), <**tl'e kwésu stáms te x̲elóx̲cha.**>, //ƛ'ə kʷ=ʔə́s-əw s=tɛ́m-s təx̣[-əl-]á[=C_1ə=]cɛ//, /'*(That's what are little lakes.)*'/, phonology: vowel=-reduction: in rapid speech tl'o can become tl'e, attested by JL (4/7/78 History Dept. tape #34).

<**tl'esu**>, if //ƛ'ə-s-əw//, DEM /'*and then (he, she, it)*'/, (<**-s**> meaning unclear), (<**-ew**> *contrastive*), syntactic analysis: demonstrative conjunction, attested by EB, Elders Group, many others, example: <**tsel kw'étslexw te spá:th tl'ésu le me théxw.**>, //c-əl k'ʷə́c=l-əxʷ tə s=pɛ́·θ ƛ'ə-s-əw lə mə θə́xʷ//, /'*I caught sight of (it) a bear and it disappeared.*'/, attested by EB (4/28/76), <**kwútes te lepál tl'esu kw'oqwethóxes.**>, //kʷú=T-əs tə ləpɛ́l ƛ'ə-s-əw k'ʷaqʷ=əT-áxʸ-əs//, /'*He took the shovel and hit me. (take s-th, hit/club s-o)*'/, attested by Elders Group (10/6/76).

<**tl'osésu ~ tl'os'ésu**>, if //ƛ'a-s-(ʔ)ə́s=əw//, CJ /'*and so (he, she, it, they)*'/, DEM, (<**-es**> *third person dependent subject*), syntactic analysis: demonstrative conjunction, attested by AC, many others.

<**qetl'osésu ~ qetl'os'ésu**>, if //qə=ƛ'a-s-ə́s=əw ~ qə=ƛ'a-s-ʔə́s=əw//, CJ /'*and so (he, she, it, they)*'/,

DEM, (<**qe=** ~ **qe**> *and*), syntactic analysis: demonstrative conjunction, attested by AC, many others.

<**tl'o'asu**>, if //ƛ'a-ʔ-ɛ-s-əw//, CJ ['*so then you*'], DEM, (<**-a**> *you (possessive pron., dependent subject)*), syntactic analysis: demonstrative conjunction, attested by AC, many others.

<**tl'olsu**>, if //ƛ'a-l-s-əw//, CJ ['*so then I*'], DEM, (<**-l**> *I (possessive pron., dependent subject)*), syntactic analysis: demonstrative conjunction, attested by AC, many others.

<**tl'okw'es ~ tl'okwses ~ tl'ekwses**>, ds //ƛ'a=k'ʷ-əs ~ ƛ'a=kʷ-s-əs//, CJ /'*because (he, she, it, they)*'/, DEM, (<**-es**> *he/she/it/they (dependent subject)*), comment: other inflections are also shown below with -c-et *we*, -elep *you folks*, -el *I*, and -a *you*, syntactic analysis: demonstrative conjunction, attested by AC (11/17/71, etc.), Elders Group (10/6/76), Deming, others, example: <**latsel áyel tl'ekwses e t'át'iyeq'.**>, //lɛ-c-əl ʔɛ́y=əl ƛ'ə=kʷ-s-əs ʔə t'ɛ́[-C_1ə-]yəq'//, /'*I left because he was mad.*'/, attested by Deming (esp. MC) (2/10/77), <**la áyel alhtel tl'ekwses t'át'iyeq'.**>, //lɛ ʔɛ́y=əl ʔɛɬ=təl ƛ'ə=kʷ-s-əs t'ɛ́[-C_1ə-]yəq'//, /'*They left because they were mad.*'/, attested by Deming (2/16/77), <**latset mékw' áyel tl'ekwtset t'át'iyeq'.**>, //lɛ-c-ət mə́k'ʷ ʔɛ́y=əl ƛ'ə=kʷ-c-ət t'ɛ́[-C_1ə-]yəq'//, /'*We all left because we were mad.*'/, attested by Deming (2/16/77), <**tset la áyel tl'ekwtset t'át'iyeq'.**>, //c-ət lɛ ʔɛ́y=əl ƛ'ə=kʷ-c-ət t'ɛ́[-C_1ə-]yəq'//, /'*We left because we were mad.*'/, attested by Deming (2/10/77), <**chap la áyel tl'ekwselep t'át'iyeq'.**>, //c-ɛp lɛ ʔɛ́y=əl ƛ'ə=kʷ-s-ələp t'ɛ́[-C_1ə-]yəq'//, /'*You folks left because you all were mad.*'/, attested by Deming (2/10/77), <**latsel áyel tl'é kw'as e t'át'iyeq'.**>, //lɛ-c-l ʔɛ́y=əl ƛ'ə́=k'ʷ-ɛ-s ʔə t'ɛ́[-C_1ə-]yəq'//, /'*I left because you were mad.*'/, attested by Deming (2/10/77), <**latsel áyel tl'é kw'els e t'át'iyeq'.**>, //lɛ-c-əl ʔɛ́y=əl ƛ'ə́ k'ʷ-əl-s ʔə t'ɛ́[-C_1ə-]yəq'//, /'*I left because I was mad.*'/, attested by Deming (2/10/77).

<**tl'ékwálsulh**>, if //ƛ'ə́=kʷ-ɛ́l-s=uɬ//, CJ /'*now I, (now I'm already)*'/, DEM, (<**=ulh ~ welh**> *already, (contrastive past)*), syntactic analysis: demonstrative conjunction, attested by EB, example: <**tl'ékwálsulh lám.**>, //ƛ'ə́=kʷ-ɛ́l-s=uɬ lɛ́=m//, /'*Now I'll be going.*'/, attested by EB (12/19/75).

<**tl'ostélmet**>, caus //ƛ'a=sT-ə́lməl-T//, rfls, EFAM ['*think someone is talking or laughing about oneself*'], root <**tl'o**> *it's him/her/it/that*, (<**=st**> *causative control transitivizer*), (<**-élmel**> *in the mind, thinking about*, <-t> *purposeful control*, phonology: loss of l in <**=-élmel**> before <-t> is regular process, syntactic analysis: attested by Elders Group (10/6/76).

<**tú:tl'ò ~ tútl'ò ~ tútl'o**>, ds //t=əw=ƛ'a//, DEM /'*he (present or presence unspecified), he's the one that, it's him that, she or it (present or presence unspecified), that or this (immediately before nominal)*'/, PRON, (<**t=**> *the (male, present and visible, or gender unspecified, or presence and visibility unspecified))*, (<**ew=**> *contrastive*), probably root <**tl'ó**> *that's, it's*, phonology: vowel-upgrading or vocalization, syntactic analysis: demonstrative pronoun, syntactic comment: like the others in this set, can be used as subject or object of a verb but not as object where another member of the same set is subject of the same verb, attested by IHTTC (8/5/77), EB (12/15/75, 1/9/76), AC, other sources: ES /tú·ƛ'a/ *he (visible)*, example: <**lám tútl'ò.**>, //lɛ́=m t=ə́w=ƛ'à//, /'*He goes., He is going.*'/, attested by AC, <**welís stl'ís kw'es áyelexw yutl'ólem qetl'esu méytemet tútl'o.**>, //wə-lí-s s=ƛ'í-s k'ʷ-əs ʔɛ́yələxʷ y=əw=ƛ'á=lə=m qə=ƛ'ə=s=əw mɛ́y=T-əm-ət t=ə́w=ƛ'a//, /'*If they want to live then they (must) help him.*'/, literally /'if it is their want that they live they and so he is helped he'/, usage: Story of the Flood, attested by AC (12/71), <**le x̲éyetem tútl'o te x̲eytl'àls.**>, //ləx̣ɛ́y=əT-əm t=ə́w=ƛ'a tə x̣iƛ'=ɛ̀ls//, /'*He was beaten up/mauled by the grizzly.*'/, syntactic comment: when two np's follow a passive the first is the patient and the second is the agent, "by" is required by English but not by Upriver Halkomelem, (semological comment: MJ at the time she was recorded was a monolingual speaker of the Tait dialect in her 90's and born in a pithouse, JL's grandmother, recorded by Oliver Wells 10/30/62 and 2/24/65), attested by MJ (10/30/62 or 2/24/65), <**welóy tútl'o**>, //wə=láy t=ə́w=ƛ'a//, /'*only him*'/, attested by AC, <**ístexwchelcha ò í**

tútl'ò.>, //ʔí=sT-əxʷ-c-əl-cɛ ʔà ʔí t=ə́w=ƛ'a//, /*'I'll leave it with him.*'/, attested by EB (12/16/75), <**kwútes telí tútl'o.**>, //kʷú=T-əs təlí t=ə́w=ƛ'a//, /*'He took it from him.*'/, attested by EB, <**óxwestchexw tútl'ò xwelá thútl'ò.**>, //ʔáxʷ=əs=T-c-əxʷ t=ə́w=ƛ'à xʷə=lɛ́ θ=ə́w=ƛ'à//, /*'Give it to him from her.*'/, attested by EB (3/5/76).

<**tutl'ó:lem**>, df //t=əw=ƛ'á·=lə=m//, PRON /*'that's them (male), they (male), them (male)*'/, DEM, (<**t=**> *the (male/gender unspecified, present/presence unspecified))*, (<**=le=**> *plural*), (<**=m**> meaning unclear), phonology: vocalization, syntactic analysis: demonstrative pronoun, attested by IHTTC (8/5/77), AC, other sources: Galloway 1977:415-416.

<**tú:tl'òtl'èm**>, df //t=əw=ƛ'à=C_1ə=m//, PRON /*'that's a little one (male, about one to five years old), he (little)*'/, DEM, (<**=R1=**> *diminutive*), (<**=m**> meaning unclear), phonology: vocalization, exclude first syllable for reduplication, updrifting, syntactic analysis: demonstrative pronoun, usage: insulting to use for an old person, attested by AC, other sources: Galloway 1977:415-416.

<**tutl'étl'elò:m**>, df //t=əw=C_1əAə́=ƛ'[=əl=]à·=m//, PRON [*'that's them (little ones) (male?)*'], DEM, (<**R5= with é-ablaut**> *diminutive plural*), (<**=le=**> *plural*), (<**=m**> meaning unclear), phonology: vocalization, reduplication, ablaut, infixed plural, syntactic analysis: demonstrative pronoun, attested by AC, other sources: Galloway 1977:415-416.

<**thú:tl'ò**>, df //θ=ə́w=ƛ'à//, PRON /*'that's her, she (present or presence unspecified), her (present or presence unspefified), that (female)*'/, DEM, (<**th=**> *the (female, present and visible or presence/visibility unspecified)*), phonology: vocalization, syntactic analysis: demonstrative pronoun, attested by IHTTC (8/5/77), AC, other sources: Galloway 1977:415-416, example: <**lám thútl'ò.**>, //lɛ́=m θ=ə́w=ƛ'à//, /*'She goes., She's going.*'/, attested by AC, <**óxwestchexw thútl'ò.**>, //ʔáxʷ=əs=T-c-əxʷ θ=ə́w=ƛ'à//, /*'Give it to her., You give it to her.*'/, attested by EB, <**tl'otsalsu qwemchíwet thútl'o q'á:mi.**>, //ƛ'a-cɛ-əl-s-əw qʷəm(=)c=íw(əl)=əT θ=ə́w=ƛ'a q'ɛ́·mi//, /*'Then I'm going to hug that girl. (hug s-o)*'/, usage: Story of Mink and Miss Pitch, attested by SJ, <**kwá:lxelhtstem thútl'ò.**>, //kʷɛ́·l=xʸ-əɬc=T-əm θ=ə́w=ƛ'à//, /*'It was hidden for her.*'/, attested by EB, <**téslem thútl'ò te swíyeqe.**>, //tə́s=l-əm θ=ə́w=ƛ'à tə s=wíq=ə//, /*'She was bumped by the man., The man bumped her.*'/, syntactic comment: transitive verb-passive patient agent, "by" need not be expressed in Upriver Halkomelem (on the very rare occasion when it is expressed with passives it is expressed by tl'), attested by EB, <**téslexwes thútl'ò te swíyeqe. ~ téslexwes te swíyeqe thútl'ò.**>, //tə́s=l-əxʷ-əs θ=ə́w=ƛ'à tə s=wíq=ə ~ tə́s=l-əxʷ-əs tə s=wíq=ə θ=ə́w=ƛ'à//, /*'She bumped the man.*'/, syntactic comment: when a transitive verb with third person subject and third person object is followed by two np's, one a demonstrative pronoun and the other article + nominal, the demonstrative pronoun can only serve as subject so it can either precede or follow the other np; found in the two alternate sentences just above, both translated the same way, attested by EB.

<**thutl'ó:lem**>, df //θ=əw=ƛ'á·=lə=m//, PRON /*'that's them (female), they (female), them (female)*'/, DEM, (<**=le=**> *plural*), (<**=m**> meaning unclear), phonology: vocalization, infixed plural, syntactic analysis: demonstrative pronoun, attested by IHTTC (8/5/77), AC, other sources: Galloway 1977:415-416.

<**yutl'ó:lem**>, df //y=əw=ƛ'á·=lə=m//, PRON /*'that's them (gender unspecified), they, them*'/, DEM, (<**y=**> *the (human plural)*), (<**=le=**> *plural*), (<**=m**> meaning unclear), phonology: vocalization, infixed plural, syntactic analysis: demonstrative pronoun, attested by IHTTC (8/5/77), AC, other sources: Galloway 1977:415-416, example: <**tl'ó sqwélqwels yutl'ólem.**>, //ƛ'á s=qʷɛ[=Aə́=]l=C_1əC_2-s y=əw=ƛ'á=lə=m//, /*'That's their story.*'/, <**kw'étslexwes yutl'ó:lem.**>, //k'ʷə́c=l-əxʷ-əs y=əw=ƛ'á=əl=əm//, /*'They saw it.*'/, */'He saw them.'/ rejected by IHTTC (8/5/77), <**wetl'ó o yutl'ólem.**>, //wə-ƛ'á ʔa y=əw=ƛ'á=lə=m//, /*'They did it themselves.*'/, literally /'if it's

just them.'/, attested by AC (8/8/70), <**tl'o siyáms yutl'ólem.**>, //ƛ'a s=iy=Ɛ́m-s y=ə́w=ƛ'á=lə=m//, /'*That's their chief.*'/, usage: News of a gathering of chiefs., attested by AC (11/10/71), <**le t'kwíléstem yútl'òlèm.**>, //lə t'k^w=íl=ə́=sT-əm y=ə́w=ƛ'à=lə=m//, /'*They were brought across (the river).*'/, usage: Story of Black Bear and Grizzly Bear, attested by DM.

<**yutl'étl'elòm**>, df //y=əw=C_1əAə́=ƛ'[=əl=]à=m//, PRON /'*(that's) them (lots of little ones), they (many small ones)*'/, DEM, (<**R5= with é-ablaut**> *diminutive plural*), (<**=el=**> *plural*), phonology: reduplication, ablaut, infixed plural, vocalization, syntactic analysis: demonstrative pronoun, attested by ME (from tape 11/72), example: <**tskwékwelìm yutl'étl'elòm.**>, //c=C_1əAə́=k^w[=əl=]ím y=əw=C_1əAə́=ƛ'[=əl=]à=m//, /'*There's lots of little small red ones.*'/, literally /'are many small red that's them (many small)'/, phonology: reduplication, ablaut, infixed plural, both the stative verb (red) and the pronoun subject (them) are inflected in the same way, both have reduplication type 5 plus é-ablaut prefixed and =el= plural infixed, attested by ME (11/72).

<**kwthú:tl'ò**>, df //k^{w}θ=ə́w=ƛ'à//, PRON /'*that's him (absent), that's her (absent), it's him/her (absent), he (absent), she (absent)*'/, DEM, (<**kwth=**> *the (near but absent/not visible)*), phonology: vocalization, syntactic analysis: demonstrative pronoun, attested by AC, other sources: Galloway 1977:415-416.

<**kwthú:tl'òlem**>, df //k^{w}θ=ə́w=ƛ'à=lə=m//, PRON /'*that's them (absent, not present), they (absent)*'/, DEM, (<**=le=**> *plural*), (<**=m**> meaning unclear), phonology: vocalization, syntactic analysis: demonstrative pronoun, attested by AC, other sources: Galloway 1977:415-416.

<**kwthú:tl'ò:lèmèlh**>, df //k^{w}θ=ə́w=ƛ'à=lə=m=əɬ//, PRON /'*that was them (deceased), they (deceased)*'/, DEM, (<**=le=**> *plural*), (<**=m**> meaning unclear), (<**=elh**> *past tense, deceased*), phonology: vocalization, infixed plural, updrifting, syntactic analysis: demonstrative pronoun, attested by AC, other sources: Galloway 1977:415-416.

<**kwsú:tl'ò**>, df //k^{w}s=ə́w=ƛ'à//, PRON /'*that's her (absent), she (absent)*'/, DEM, (<**kws=**> *the (female, near but absent)),* phonology: vocalization, syntactic analysis: demonstrative pronoun, attested by AC, DM, other sources: Galloway 1977:415-416, example: <**welís ó:thò:m kw'as le t'kwíléstexw kwsú:tl'ò kw'í:tsel qesu t'át kw'as wő̄qw'et.**>, //wə-lí-s ʔá·=T-à·m k'^{w}-Ɛ-s lə t'ək^w=íl=ə́=sT-əx^w k^{w}s=ə́w=ƛ'à k'^{w}(w)=í·cəl qə-s=əw t'Ɛ́=T k'^{w}-Ɛ-s wóq'^{w}=əT//, /'*If she calls you to go bring her, that grizzly, across, then try to drown her. (you are called, bring s-o across)*'/.

<**kwsú:tl'ò:lh**>, df //k^{w}s=ə́w=ƛ'à=əɬ//, PRON /'*that was her (deceased), she (deceased)*'/, DEM, (<**=elh**> *past tense, deceased*), phonology: vocalization, vowel merger, syntactic analysis: demonstrative pronoun, attested by AC, other sources: Galloway 1977:415-416.

<**kw'ú:tl'ò:lh**>, df //k'^{w}=ə́w=ƛ'à=əɬ//, PRON /'*that was him (deceased), he (deceased)*'/, DEM, (<**kw'=**> *the (remote)*), (<**=elh**> *past tense, deceased*), phonology: vocalization, vowel merger, syntactic analysis: demonstrative pronoun, attested by AC, other sources: Galloway 1977:415-416.

<**tl'étl'elò:m**>, df //C_1əAə́=ƛ'[=əl=]à·=m//, PRON /'*that's them (little kids), they (little kids)*'/, DEM, Elder's comment: "not used much", (<**R5= with é-ablaut**> *diminutive plural*), (<**=el=**> *plural*), (<**=m**> meaning unclear), phonology: vocalization, syntactic analysis: demonstrative pronoun, attested by AC, compare <**yutl'étl'elòm**> *that's them (many small ones)*, other sources: Galloway 1977:415-416.

<**tl'okw'es ~ tl'okwses ~ tl'ekwses**>, CJ /'*because (he, she, it, they)*'/, *see* tl'ó ~ tl'o.

<**tl'olsu**>, CJ ['*so then I*'], *see* tl'ó ~ tl'o.

<**tl'óm**>, probable bound root //ƛ'ám//, meaning uncertain

<**tl'ótl'em**>, df //ƛ'á[=C_1ə=]m//, VALJ ['*okay*'], root meaning unknown, (<**=R1=**> *resultative or*

continuative?), phonology: reduplication, syntactic analysis: adjective/adjectival verb, attested by GC (Deming 6/24/76), Salish cognate: Lushootseed /ƛ’úb/ *okay, all right* H76:328, also Squamish /ƛ’ám/ *be enough* K69:72 and Squamish /ʔəs-ƛ’á-ƛ’m/ *fitting, sufficient* K67:386, Samish dial. of N.St. /sƛ’áƛ’əm’ ~ sƛ’áʔƛ’əm’/ *it's right, okay* G86:90, historical/comparative detail: one would expect Squamish /ú/ not /á/ from the cognates.

<**tl'ó:s**> or <**xwtl'**>, possible root /ƛ’á·s// or //xʷƛ’//, meaning uncertain

<**shxwtl'ó:s**>, df //s=xʷƛ’=á·s or s=xʷ=ƛ’á·s//, SD ['*(be) loud*'], possibly <**s=**> *stative*, possibly <**xw=**> meaning uncertain but used with features of the head, root meaning unknown, possibly <**=ó:s**> *on the face*?, syntactic analysis: adjective/adjectival verb, dialects: *Cheh.*, attested by Elders Group (4/16/75), contrast <**sth'í:qel**> *be loud*, example: <**le shxwtl'ó:s.**>, //lə s=xʷƛ’=á·s//, /'*(It/He/She was) loud.*'/, attested by Elders Group.

<**tl'osésu ~ tl'os'ésu**>, CJ /'*and so (he, she, it, they)*'/, *see* tl'ó ~ tl'o.

<**tl'óst** or **tl'óstexw**>, probable stem //ƛ’ás=T or ƛ’á=sT-əxʷ//, EFAM /'*(make that s-th (instead), cause that to be s-th (instead))*'/, EFAM /'*I'd rather have (s-th), I'd prefer (s-th) (make that s-th instead)*'/, semantic environment ['before an imperative'], possibly root <**tl'ó**> *that's*, possibly <**=t**> *purposeful control transitivizer* or <**=st**> *causative control transitivizer*, syntactic analysis: possibly transitive verb, comment: this form is reconstructed from the only two example sentences (both of which lack -exw), syntactic comment: unusual syntax if dropped third person object -exw before imperative -lha, possibly polite imperative -tlha (if the latter form could be merely tl’o-s, attested by Deming (SJ, MC, MV, LG 3/15/79), example: <**l stl'í te sth'óqwi, tl'óstlha te sth'óqwi.**>, //l s=ƛ’í tə s=θ’áqʷi, ƛ’á=sT-ɬɛ tə s=θ’áqʷi//, /'*I'd like fish; I'd rather have fish. (I'd prefer s-th)*'/, literally /'is my want the fish; make that s-th -imperative the fish'/, attested by Deming (SJ, MC, MV, LG 3/15/79), <**tl'óstlha te slhóp'.**>, //ƛ’á=sT-ɬɛ tə s=ɬáp’//, /'*I'd rather have soup.*'/, literally /'make that -imperative the soup'/, attested by Deming (SJ, MC, MV, LG 3/15/79).

<**tl'ostélmét**>, rfls //ƛ’a=sT-ələmət//, EFAM ['*think s-o is talking or laughing about one*'], literally perhaps /'make that oneself instead'/, root <**tl'óst**> *make that instead*, (<**=sT**> *causative control transitivizer*), (<**-èlèmèt**> *reflexive (of causative)*), possibly <**=élmel**> *in the mind, thinking about*, phonology: possible syllable-loss of el before =et or =met, possible consonant merger, possible vowel-loss, updrifting, syntactic analysis: transitive verb or intransitive verb, attested by EB (Elders Group 10/6/76), contrast <**tl'émstexw**> *think s-o is talking or laughing about s-o.*

<**tl'ostélmét**>, EFAM ['*think s-o is talking or laughing about one*'], *see* tl'óst or tl'óstexw.

<**tl'ó:t**>, pcs //ƛ’á·=T//, EFAM /'*pacify a baby, pacify it (a baby), sing or hum to a baby to quiet it, sing to it (a zaby), (sing a lullaby to it)*'/, SOC, (<**=t**> *purposeful control transitivizer*), syntactic analysis: transitive verb, attested by EB, Salish cognate: Cowichan /ƛ’áʔt/ *to pacify a child* B74b:70 (Cowichan), Saanich dial. of NSt /ƛ’áʔət/ *to pacify a child* B74a:70 (Saanich); found in <**tl'ó:tlha.**>, //ƛ’á·=T-ɬɛ//, /'*Pacify it., Sing to it.*'/, attested by EB (4/2/76).

<**tl'ó:thet**>, pcrs //ƛ’á·=T-ət//, EFAM ['*fix oneself in bed*'], literally /'pacify oneself'/, (<**-et**> *reflexive*), syntactic analysis: intransitive verb, attested by BHTTC (9/3/76).

<**tl'ó:thet**>, EFAM ['*fix oneself in bed*'], *see* tl'ó:t.

<**tl'óth'et**>, pcs //ƛ’áθ’=əT//, MC /'*tighten it up, wind it up*'/, (<**=et**> *purposeful control transitivizer*), syntactic analysis: transitive verb, attested by Elders Group (4/23/80), Salish cognate: Squamish /ƛ’úc’-un/ *pack close together (tr.)* from root /ƛ’uc’ ~ ƛ’əc’/ *be packed tightly* as well as /ƛ’əc’-úy-n/ *cram, stuff, force full (tr.)* K69:73, perhaps Lushootseed /ƛ’úcud/ *tie it (knot for a net), wrap up a package* from root /ƛ’úc(u)/ *tie, knot, wrap up package* H76:330.

<**tl’ótl’ethet**>, pcrs //ƛ’á[=C1ə=]θ’=T-et//, ABFC /'*to tighten up (tense one’s muscles, for ex.)*'/,

<**=R1=**> *continuative* or *resultative* or *durative*, <**-et**> *reflexive*, phonological comment: consonant cluster simplification of <**th'th**> → <**th**>, attested by RG & EH (4/9/99 Ling332)

<**tl'o'asu**>, CJ ['*so then you*'], *see* tl'ó ~ tl'o.

<**tl'ő̃wstexw**>, SOC /'*kidnap s-o, run away with s-o*'/, *see* tl'í:w.

<**tl'pát**>, possibly root //ƛ'pɛ́t//, BSK ['*cedar sapling basket*'], ASM ['open weave for carrying larger objects'], synonym <**th'ő̃wex̱**>, syntactic analysis: noun?, nominal, attested by Elders Group (2/25/76), Salish cognate: Squamish /ƛ'p-at/ *cedarbark basket* from root /ƛ'əp/ *cover, clothing (?)* as in /s-ƛ'p-iwʔn/ *shirt*, /s-ƛ'p-álʔqn/ *feather*, /ƛ'i-ƛ'p-tn-áyʔc'a/ *undershirt* and /ƛ'i-ƛ'p-tn-áyʔq/ *underpants* W73:14, K67:332 (but H76:324 derives the Lushootseed cognates of undershirt (/ƛ'iƛ'pikʷ/) and underpants (/ƛ'iƛ'pəq/) from root /ƛ'əp/ *deep, beneath (surface)*), Sechelt /ƛ'ə́pəɬ/ *cedarbark basket* T77:19.

<**tl'pí:l ~ tl'epí:l**>, DIR /'*go down, go down below, get low*'/, *see* tl'ép.

<**tl'pílém**>, TVMO /'*go down hill, go down from anything*'/, *see* tl'ép.

<**tl'pí:lstexw**>, TVMO ['*lower s-th down*'], *see* tl'ép.

<**tl'pí:lt ~ tl'épelt**>, TVMO /'*lower it down, (lower s-th down)*'/, *see* tl'ép.

<**tl'pí:lx ~ tl'pì:lx**>, TVMO /'*bring it down (from upstairs or from upper shelf, etc.)*'/, *see* tl'ép.

<**tl'qáw** or **tl'qew**>, possibly stem //ƛ'q(=)ɛ́w// or //ƛ'q(=)əw/, meaning uncertain unless related to <**tl'iq**> *stuck on.*

<**stl'eqówtel**>, df //s=ƛ'əq(=)ɛ́w=təl//, BSK ['*awl (any kind)*'], TOOL, (<**s=**> *nominalizer*), root meaning unknown, possibly <**=á:w ~ =í:w ~ =ew**>, /'*on the body, on top of itself*'/, lx <**=tel**> *device to*, syntactic analysis: nominal, attested by AC (8/24/70), other sources: ES /sƛ'qáw·təl/ *awl*, JH /sƛ'qáwətəl/ *awl*, also <**stl'qáwtel**>, //s=ƛ'q(=)ɛ́w=təl//, attested by Elders Group (3/1/72), also <**stl'qéwtel**>, //s=ƛ'q(=)ə́w=təl//, attested by BJ (5/10/64), AC (10/21/71), also <**tl'qówtel**>, //ƛ'qáw=təl//, attested by BJ (5/10/64).

<**tl'q'á:l**>, probably stem //ƛ'q'ɛ́·l//, meaning uncertain unless related to <**tl'iq'**> /'*get wedged (by falling tree, for ex.), got run over, stuck on*'/.

<**stl'q'á:l**>, df //s=ƛ'q'ɛ́·l//, ANAB /'*wing, (big feather* [IHTTC]*)*'/, (<**s=**> *nominalizer*), root meaning unknown, syntactic analysis: nominal, attested by BJ (12/5/64), EB (5/25/76), other sources: ES /sƛ'q'ɛ́·l/ *wing*, H-T <stluka'l> (umlaut over a) *wing*, also <**stl'eq'á:l**>, //s=ƛ'əq'ɛ́·l//, attested by AC (8/13/70, 10/13/71), Elders Group (3/15/72), also <**stl'q'ál**>, //s=ƛ'q'ɛ́l//, also /'*big feather*'/, attested by IHTTC (9/19/77), example: <**kw'óqwelexwes te (sisemóye, lholiqwó:t) te stl'eq'á:ls li te sp'áq'em.**>, //k'ʷáqʷ=l-əxʷ-əs tə (C_1í=səm=áyə, ɬal=iqʷ=á·t) tə s=ƛ'əq'ɛ́·l-s li tə s=p'ɛ́q'=əm//, /'*The (bee, butterfly) hit it's wing on a flower.*'/, attested by AC (10/13/71).

<**tl'q'áláx̱el**>, ds //ƛ'q'ɛ́l=(əl)ɛ́x̣əl//, ANAB /'*wing, whole wing*'/, root <**tl'q'ál**> *big feather*, lx <**=(el)áx̱el**> *on the appendage, on the wing, on the arm*, phonology: possible syllable-loss, syntactic analysis: nominal, attested by IHTTC (9/19/77).

<**tl'q'áláx̱el**>, ANAB /'*wing, whole wing*'/, *see* stl'q'á:l.

<**tl'qw'á:y**>, root or stem //ƛ'q'ʷ(=)ɛ́·y//, ABFC /'*milt, salmon milt*'/, if stem, root meaning unknown unless same as in <**tl'qw'ót**> *cut s-th (string or rope)*, possibly <**=á:y ~ =ey ~ =iy**> *bark, wood, wool, fur* (and thus perhaps *covering*), syntactic analysis: noun, nominal, attested by Deming (4/1/76), Elders Group (4/28/76), Salish cognate: Squamish /ƛ'q'ʷáyʔ/ *milt, soft roe (of salmon)* W73:176, K69:72, Mainland Comox /ƛ'áq'ʷəy/ *salmon milt* B75prelim.:30, Samish dial. of NSt /ƛ'k'ʷíʔ/ *milt* beside /ƛ'q'ʷə́y'/ *fish liver* G84a:77.

<**tl'qw'ót**>, pcs //ƛ'áq'ʷ[-M1-]=T or ƛ'q'ʷ=ə[=Aá=]T//, MC [*'cut s-th (string or rope)'*], CST, semantic environment ['for ex. if it is too long'], possibly <**metathesis type 1**> *non-continuative*, possibly <**ó-ablaut**> *durative*??, (<**=t ~ =et**> *purposeful control transitivizer*), phonology: metathesis, syntactic analysis: transitive verb, attested by EB (4/29/76), compare <**t'qw'ót**> *cut s-th (string/rope),* historical/comparative detail: perhaps a doublet?.

<**tl'xát**>, CST [*'rip it apart'*], *see* tl'éx.

<**tl'xátem**>, ABDF [*'get diarrhea'*], *see* tl'éx.

<**tl'xá<u>x</u>el**>, CST /*'burst open, split open of its own accord (like a dropped watermelon)'*/, *see* tl'éx.

<**tl'xá<u>x</u>et**>, HUNT [*'to split s-th open (like deer or fish)'*], *see* tl'éx.

<**tl'xw ~ tl'exw**>, bound root //ƛ'xʷ ~ ƛ'əxʷ *cover*//.

<**tl'<u>x</u>wét** (or probably **tl'xwét)**>, pcs //ƛ'xʷ=əT or ƛ'ə́xʷ=M1=T//, MC /*'cover s-o, cover s-th (like yeast bread)'*/, possibly <**metathesis type 1**> *non-continuative*, (<**=et** or **=t**> *purposeful control transitivizer*), phonology: possible metathesis, syntactic analysis: transitive verb, attested by EB (1/9/76).

<**tl'xwá:ylhem**>, mdls //ƛ'xʷ=ɛ́·yɬ=əm//, ABFC /*'sit on eggs, to hatch eggs, to brood eggs'*/, literally /'cover one's children'/, lx <**=á:ylh**> *child, children*, (<**=em**> *middle voice, one's own*), syntactic analysis: intransitive verb, attested by Elders Group (1/7/76).

<**tl'exwewítstel**>, ds //ƛ'əxʷ=əwíc=təl//, CLO [*'blanket robe'*], literally /'device/something to cover on the back'/, lx <**=ewíts**> *on the back (of a creature)*, lx <**=tel**> *device to, something to*, syntactic analysis: nominal, attested by EB (5/25/76).

<**tl'xwíqwtel**>, ds //ƛ'xʷ=íqʷ=təl//, CLO [*'kerchief'*], literally /'device/something to cover on the hair/top of the head'/, lx <**=íqw**> *on the hair, on top of the head*, lx <**=tel**> *device to, something to*, syntactic analysis: nominal, attested by Elders Group (1/8/75).

<**tl'xwá:ylhem**>, ABFC /*'sit on eggs, to hatch eggs, to brood eggs'*/, *see* tl'xw ~ tl'exw.

<**tl'xwéleq**>, PLAY /*'win, win (a prize, money, etc.), come in first (in contest)'*/, *see* tl'éxw.

<**tl'xwém**>, PLAY [*'to win a contest'*], *see* tl'éxw.

<**tl'xwét**>, PLAY /*'beat s-o in a contest, win over s-o (in a contest), beat s-o out of something'*/, *see* tl'éxw.

<**tl'xwíqwtel**>, CLO [*'kerchief'*], *see* tl'xw ~ tl'exw.

<**tl'<u>x</u>wét** (or probably **tl'xwét)**>, MC /*'cover s-o, cover s-th (like yeast bread)'*/, *see* tl'xw ~ tl'exw.

<**tl'<u>x</u>wéylep** or **tl'<u>x</u>wílep**>, LAND [*'hard ground'*], *see* tl'é<u>x</u>w.

<**tl'<u>x</u>wíth'a**>, CLO [*'strong (of material)'*], *see* tl'é<u>x</u>w.

<**tl'<u>x</u>wíws**>, ANA [*'tough skin'*], *see* tl'é<u>x</u>w.

<**tl'<u>x</u>wòlèm**>, ABFC /*'I got hard (of arm, leg, penis, etc.)'*/, *see* tl'é<u>x</u>w.

<**tl'<u>x</u>wõmálqel ~ tl'a<u>x</u>wõmálqel**>, df //ƛ'x̣ʷóm=ɛ́lqəl ~ ƛ'ɛx̣ʷóm=ɛ́lqəl//, EZ /*'big Canada goose, big honker'*/, [*'Branta canadensis canadensis'*], root meaning unknown, lx <**=álqel ~ =élqel**> *wool, (feather/down)*, (semological comment: perhaps the name refers to some feature of the well-known goose down if not to the other feathers), syntactic analysis: nominal, attested by BJ (5/10/64 new transcript, new p.121), also <**t'<u>x</u>wõmélqel**>, //t'x̣ʷom=ə́lqəl//, root meaning unknown, attested by BJ (12/5/64 new transcript old p.309).

Dictionary of Upriver Halkomelem

Volume II

Dictionary of Upriver Halkomelem
Volume II

Brent D. Galloway

UNIVERSITY OF CALIFORNIA PRESS
Berkeley • Los Angeles • London

University of California Press, one of the most distinguished university presses in the United States, enriches lives around the world by advancing scholarship in the humanities, social sciences, and natural sciences. Its activities are supported by the UC Press Foundation and by philanthropic contributions from individuals and institutions. For more information, visit www.ucpress.edu.

University of California Publications in Linguistics, Volume 141

University of California Press
Berkeley and Los Angeles, California

University of California Press, Ltd.
London, England

Printed in the United States of America

Cataloging-in-Publication data for this title is on file with the Library of Congress.

ISBN 978-0-520-09872-5 (pbk. : alk. paper)

The paper used in this publication meets the minimum requirements of ANSI/NISO Z39.48-1992 (R 1997) (Permanence of Paper).

TS

<**ts**>, comment: The Stó:lō orthography uses both <**ch**> ([č]) and <**ts**> ([¢]), for two allophones of a single Halkomelem phoneme, /c/. This has the advantage of showing phonetic preferences of the speakers which are difficult to predict purely from environments; in linguistic terms [č] and [¢] are evolving from a state of free variation to conditioned variation (or vice versa)(see Galloway 1977:5-7 for a statement of the environments, dialects, and idiolects conditioning these two sounds). As it happens, comparatively few cases of initial <**ts**> [¢] occur. Therefore if a reader is looking up a word spelled or sounded with an initial ts, he should be sure to check under <**ch**> as well, as more speakers may pronounce it with <**ch**>..

<**ts= ~ ch= ~ ts'=**>, da //c= ~ c'=//, TIB /*'stative (with color terms), have, get (elsewhere)*'/, phonology: since most roots begin with a consonant and there is a phonemic rule that /c/ → [¢] <**ts**>etween word boundary and a consonant, this prefix is only rarely found as [č] <**ch**>; there is also an allomorphic rule that {c-} → /c'/ <**ts'**> before glottalized consonant, syntactic analysis: derivational prefix; found in <**tschá:xw**>, //c=cɛ́·xʷ//, /*'get a wife*'/, <**tskwí:m**>, //c=kʷí·m//, /*'be red, (have red)*'/, */'get red'/ rejected, <**tsqwá:y**>, //c=qʷɛ́·y//, /*'be yellow, be green, (have yellow/green)*'/; for EB there are two cases of minimal contrast, forms with ts= vs. without (p'íp'eq'el with diminutive vs. tsp'íp'eq'el, and q'íq'e<u>x</u>el with continuative vs. tsq'íq'e<u>x</u>el); the ts= forms may be a little more intense, deeper in the color, than the forms without. This would fit with the literal meanings for each set ("going a little white" vs. "have/get/be in a state of going a little white", "going a little black" vs. "have/get/be in a state of going a little black"; or if one uses the -ish meaning, "a little whitish" vs. "have/get/be in a state of a little whitish", etc.)., For Chilliwack speaker NP there are quite a few such contrasts, in fact with inceptives based on all the roots but xwíkw', *gray*, qálq *rose*,and st'áwel *purple*. Sumas speaker AH has minimal contrasts between forms with s= and with c=; tsqwóqwiyel and sqwóqwiyel don't seem semantically distinct, but there are a number of colors labelled by tskwíkwemel and a number by skwíkwemel; on the Munsell charts she did with us these two are are fairly evenly mixed with each other, though the forms with ts= are found mostly close to the focus, while the s= forms occur close to the focus but also as the farthest away from the focus (C4, E6, I2, C35, etc.)., NP's charted forms also show such a contrast: under tsqw'í<u>x</u>w ts= forms are more focal, while s= forms are more distant from focus, blackest; under tsqwá:y ts= forms are at intense margins, while s= forms are at light margins or blackest; under tsméth' ts= forms are at light margins, some dark, while s= forms are one ex. next to focus; under tskwím ts= forms are at intense margins, while s= forms are at light margins or near focus; under tskwím + R5= ts= forms are more focal, while s= forms are more distant from focus; under tsq'í<u>x</u> ts= forms are (one ex.) browner, while s= forms are one ex., bluer, darker?; under p'éq' ts= forms are not found, while, s= forms are closer to /p'ə́q'/ than non=statives; under tsp'íqw' ts= forms are at I35, H34, D32, darker or lighter, while s= forms are at F34 but focused at H32, and sp'íp'eqw'el at I36; ("Intense margins" refers to margins between colors other than white or black.). Chehalis speaker EB has no /s=/ forms to contrast. Tait speaker TG has one contrast, tsqwóqwiyel vs. sqwóqwiyel, where the ts= form is more focal than most of the examples of the s= form., syntactic analysis: derivational prefix, see charts by Rob MacLaury, see dialect form <**ch=**>; found in <**ts'q'éy<u>x</u>**>, //c'=q'ɛ́yx̣//, /*'black, be black*'/, <**tsqwáy**>, //c=qʷɛ́y//, /*'green, yellow, be yellow or green*'/, <**tsméth' ~ (rarely) ts'méth'**>, //c=mə́θ' (sometimes c'=mə́θ')//, /*'blue, be blue*'/, <**tskwí:m**>, //c=kʷí·m//, /*'red, be red*'/, <**tskwí:meqw**>, //c=kʷí·m=əqʷ//, /*'red-head(ed)*'/, <**ts'meth'ó:les**>, //c'=məθ'=á·ləs//, /*'blue eyes*'/, <**tsqw'í<u>x</u>w ~ ts'qw'í<u>x</u>w**>, //c=q'ʷíx̣ʷ ~ c'=q'ʷí<u>x</u>w//,

/'*be brown*'/, <**tskwíkwemel(=í:wel)**>, //c=k^{w}ík^{w}əm=əl(=í·wəl)//, /'*reddish-brown, be reddish-brown*'/, (<**=el**> *-ish*), <**tsxwíkw'**>, //c=x^{w}ík'^{w}//, /'*gray, be gray*'/, <**ts'qw'íqw'e<u>x</u>wel**>, //c'=q'^{w}íq'^{w}əx̣^{w}=əl//, /'*brownish-black, be brownish-black*'/, (<**=el**> *-ish*), <**tstáwél**>, //c=tɛ́wə́l//, /'*bright-colored*'/, root <**táwel**> *bright, light*, comment: note that not all colors have this prefix for ex. p'éq' *white, be white*, qwiqwóyáls *orange, be orange; an orange*, and stl'ítl'esel *dark gray, dark color*, <**tsqw'íqw'e<u>x</u>w**>, //c=q'^{w}í[=C$_1$ə=]x̣^{w}//, /'*brown*'/, <**tskwíkwemel**>, //c=k^{w}í:[=C$_1$ə=]m=əl//, /'*pink*'/, <**chmítl'**>, //c=míƛ' or c=má[=Aí=]ƛ'//, /'*dirty*'/, phonology: ch= rather than ts= here may be Thompson influence on EB who speaks Thompson as well as Chehalis Halkomelem, attested by EB, ASM ['derivational'], <**tsmékw'**>, //c=mə́k'^{w}//, /'*discover, find*'/, also <**chmékw'**>, phonology: ch= rather than ts= here may be Thompson influence, attested by EB, ASM ['have, get'], <**tschá:xw**>, //c=cɛ́·x^w//, /'*get a wife*'/, <**tsth'óqwi**>, //c=θ'áq^{w}i//, /'*to fish*'/, literally /'to get fish'/.

<**ts- ~ ch-**>, ia //c-//, CJ /'*subject of independent clause, non-subordinate subject*'/, (semological comment: with -tset *we (non-subordinate subject), our* and -chap *you folks (non-subordinate subject), you folks's* the prefix is apparently petrified in those pronouns when used as possessive pronoun inflections--they are possessive pronouns without being non-subordinate subjects simultaneously), syntactic analysis: non-subordinate subject marker, compare <**-tsel**> *I (non-subordinate subject)*, with <**-chexw**> *you (non-subordinate subject)*, <**-chap**> *you folks (non-subordinate subject), you folks's*, and <**-tset**> *we (non-subordinate subject), our*.

<**tsálmalqel**>, LANG ['*Chinese language*'], *see* chá:lmel.

<**tscháxw**>, KIN ['*get a wife*'], *see* chá:xw.

<**-tsel ~ (very rarely) -chel**>, ia //-c-əl//, PRON ['*I (non-subordinate subject)*'], phonology: phonologically a suffix except where it precedes the verb in the ambiguous past construction, phonologically it is shown to be a suffix (rather than a postposed enclitic or postclitic) by the fact that it causes a stress shift to schwa in object suffixes attached to any verb stem; found in <**tsel maythóme ~ tsel máythòmè**> *I helped you* vs. <**maythométsel**> *I help you* and <**maythométselcha**> *I'll help you*, there is also no word boundary before <**-tsel, -tset, -chexw** or **-chap**>, syntactic analysis: subject pronoun, attested by all speakers, comment: see many examples throughout the dictionary, also in Galloway 1977.

<**tselá:l**>, probable root or stem //cəlɛ́·l//, root meaning uncertain unless related to <**chá:l** or **chó:l**> *follow behind, go a distance//* with **el**-inflex *plural*, not semantically related to <**chelà:l**>, us //cəlɛ̀·l//, EFAM /'*what a lot., it's sure a lot*'/.

<**stselá:l**>, df //s=cəlɛ́·l//, ABDF ['*be fading (of eyesight)*'], (<**s=**> *stative*), root meaning unknown, syntactic analysis: adjective/adjectival verb, attested by AC, example: <**stselá:l te skw'áts.**>, //s=cəlɛ́·l tə s=k'^{w}ɛ́c-s//, /'*Her eyesight is fading., "Her eyes are fading."*'/, attested by AC.

<**tsélcheptel?**>, df //c=ə́lcəp=təl?//, TIME /'*October to November, (wood gathering time)*'/, Elder's comment: "it means *wood-gathering time*", possibly <**ts=**> *get*, lx <**=élchep**> *firewood*, lx <**=tel**> *something to*, syntactic analysis: nominal, attested by Elders Group (3/28/79) after Wm. Sepass as recorded by Jenness, source: Diamond Jenness field notes on Wm. Sepass of Sardis.

<**tsél:ém**>, possible root or stem //cə́l·(=)ə[=´=]m//, probably ANA ['*liver*']

<**stsél:ém**>, df //s(=)cə́l·(=)ə[=´=]m//, ANA ['*liver*'], possibly <**s=**> *nominalizer*, possibly <**=em**> *intransitivizer, have, get* or *middle voice*, perhaps <=´=> *derivational*, root meaning unknown, phonology: possible stress-shift or updrifting, syntactic analysis: nominal, attested by AC, DM (12/4/64), Deming (4/17/80), Elders Group, also <**schél:ém**>, //s=cə́l·(=)ə[=´=]m//, attested by SJ (Deming 4/17/80), other sources: ES /scə́l·əm/ (CwMs /scə́ləm/) *liver*, H-T <tsúlEm> *liver*.

<**tseléqelhtst**>, bens //cələ́q=əɬc=T//, SOC ['*divide something in half with s-o*'], NUM, (<**=elhts**> *benefactive*), (<**=t**> *purposeful control transitivizer*), syntactic analysis: transitive verb, attested by Elders Group (3/72), Salish cognate: Squamish /cíaq-n/ [//cíyaq-n//] *divide off (a part from a whole) (tr.)* W73:81, K69:53, Lushootseed root /cəlq/ *halve, divide into equal parts* as in /cə́lq-əd/ *share it equally with s-o* and /cə́lq-c/ *give me half, divide it in two* H76:48, historical/comparative detail: Upriver Halkomelem <**th**> is expected from normal sound correspondences; found in <**tseléqelhtsthòmè**>, //cələ́q=əɬc=T-ámə//, /'*divide (in half) with you*'/, attested by Elders Group (3/72 tape 33).

<**tsélq ~ chélq**>, free root //cə́lq//, TVMO /'*fall, fall off, drop, drop off, drop or fall down (of person)*'/, semantic environment ['for ex.: from a shelf, from a mountain, into a hole'], syntactic analysis: intransitive verb, attested by AC (8/6/70, 10/13/71), EB (12/15/75, 4/29/76), Elders Group (8/25/76, 3/72), CT (6/8/76), RG & EH (4/9/99 Ling332), other sources: ES /c'ə́lq/ *fall*, contrast <**wets'étl' ~ wech'étl'**> *fall off, drop down, fall (from a shelf example)* (with <**we=**> *suddenly*), example: <**le tsélq.**>, //lə cə́lq//, /'*He fell in (caught his foot and fell in a hole).*'/, attested by AC, <**me tsélq te mestíyexw.**>, //mə cə́lq tə məstíyəx^w//, /'*The person fell down.*'/, attested by EB (12/15/75).

<**tsélqlexw**>, ncs //cə́lq=l-əx^w//, ABFC ['*drop s-th (accidentally)*'], (<**=l**> *non-control transitivizer*), (<**-exw**> *third person object*), syntactic analysis: transitive verb, attested by AD (3/5/79), EB (1/20/76).

<**tsélqt**>, pcs //cə́lq=T//, ABFC ['*drop it on purpose*'], (<**=t**> *purposeful control transitivizer*), syntactic analysis: transitive verb, attested by AD (3/5/79).

<**chólqthet**>, pcrs //cə[=Aá=]lq=T-ət//, ABFC /'*let oneself fall, drop oneself down (by parachute, rope, etc., said of little birds trying to fly out of nest, little animals trying to get down and let themselves fall)*'/, (<**-et**> *reflexive*), phonology: ó-ablaut (usually of root á) conditioned by =thet, syntactic analysis: intransitive verb, attested by AD (3/5/79).

<**Tsólqthet te Skwówech**>, cpds //cə[=Aá=]lq=T-ət tə s=k^{w}áw=əc//, PLN /'*Rainbow Falls on Harrison Lake, (Sturgeon's Drop)*'/, literally /'the sturgeon dropped himself on purpose, sturgeon's drop'/, ASM ['so named because a sturgeon was found at the base of the falls that had dropped from the top of the falls'], syntactic analysis: sentence, attested by EL (Chehalis boat trip 6/27/78).

<**tsélqòlèm**>, df //cə́lq=àl(=)əm or cə́lq=ə[=Aà=]l-əm//, ABDF /'*drop s-th (of a bunch of apples, etc. that one is carrying)*'/, possibly <**=òlèm**> meaning uncertain, possibly <**=(e)l**> *non-control transitivizer* or <**-el-**> *plural*, possibly <**ò-ablaut**> *durative*, possibly <**=em**> *intransitivizer/get/become* or <**-em**> *passive*, phonology: possible ablaut, possible updrifting, syntactic analysis: intransitive verb, attested by AD (3/5/79), example: <**líchxw tsélqòlèm?**>, //lí-c-x^w cə́lq=ə[=Aà=]l=əm//, /'*Did you drop something?*'/, attested by AD.

<**tselqó:me ~ tselqómo**>, ds //cəlq=á·mə//, EB ['*blackcap berry or berries*'], ['*Rubus leucodermis*'], literally /'drop berry'/, (semological comment: so named because they fall off very easily), lx <**=ó:me**> *berry*, syntactic analysis: nominal, attested by AC (8/11/70, 11/24/71), AK and SP (7/13/75), other sources: ES /cəlqá·mà/ *blackcap*, H-T <tsilka'ma> (macron on first a) *raspberry (black)*, also <**tselqómé**>, //cəlq=ámə//, attested by EB (5/12/78), example: <**éy xwlá(m) tl'eléwe te tselqómé.**>, //ʔɛ́y x^w=lɛ́(=m) ƛ'ə-lə́wə tə cəlq=ámə//, /'*Blackcaps are good for you.*'/, attested by EB (5/12/78).

<**tselqó:má:lhp**>, ds //cəlq=á·mə=əɬp or cəlq=á·mə=ɛ́ɬp//, EB ['*blackcap bush*'], ['*Rubus leucodermis*'], lx <**=elhp** or **=álhp**> *plant*, phonology: vowel merger, possible allomorph of =elhp, syntactic analysis: nominal, attested by AC.

<**p'éq' tselqó:me**>, cpds //p'ə́q' cəlq=á·mə//, EB /'*whitecap berry, white blackcap berry*'/, ASM ['a kind of blackcap, grows by blackcaps at Lexwyó:qwem by Yale, quite rare, the berry is totally white when ripe but is sweet, the leaves are those of blackcaps, sample of fruit and leaves pressed in collection and verified by botanists as blackcap'], ['*Rubus leucodermis*, albino variety'], literally /'white blackcap berry'/, syntactic analysis: nominal phrase with modifier(s), attested by AK and SP (7/13/75).

<**tsélqlexw**>, ABFC ['*drop s-th (accidentally)*'], *see* tsélq ~ chélq.

<**tsélqòlèm**>, ABDF /'*drop s-th (of a bunch of apples, etc. that one is carrying)*'/, *see* tsélq ~ chélq.

<**tselqó:má:lhp**>, EB ['*blackcap plant or bush*'], *see* tsélq ~ chélq.

<**tselqó:me ~ tselqómo ~tselqó:mé**>, EB ['*blackcap berry or berries*'], *see* tsélq ~ chélq.

<**tsélqt**>, ABFC ['*drop it on purpose*'], *see* tsélq ~ chélq.

<**tselqwáx̲el**>, DIR ['*(in) back of a house*'], *see* chá:l or chó:l.

<**tselqwáx̲elmel**>, DIR /'*in back of a house, behind a house*'/, *see* chá:l or chó:l.

<**=tses ~ =ches**>, da //=cəs//, ANA /'*on the hand or finger, in the hand or finger*'/, EB ['*limb or bough of tree*'], syntactic analysis: lexical suffix, derivational suffix, also <**=ches**>, //=cəs//; found in <**kw'éstses**>, //k'^{w}ɛ[=Aə́=]s=cəs//, /'*burned on the hand or finger*'/, <**lhéts'tses**>, //ɬi[=Aə́=]c'=cəs//, /'*cut on the hand*'/, <**th'ex̲wá:tsesem**>, //θ'əx̣^{w}ɛ́·=cəs=əm//, /'*wash one's hands*'/, <**sléx̲tses**>, //s=lə́x̣=cəs//, /'*finger*'/, <**qw'x̲wéltses**>, //q'^{w}x̣^{w}ə́l=cəs//, /'*fingernails*'/, <**qwémxwtses**>, //q^{w}ə́m=x^{w}=cəs//, /'*wrist bone*'/, literally /'lump of hand'/, <**tl'í:q'(e)tses**>, //ƛ'í·q'=(ə)cəs//, /'*one's hand jammed or stuck*'/, <**sth'íkwetses**>, //sθ'ík^{w}ə=cəs//, /'*left hand, left-handed*'/, <**lí:letses**>, //ʔəlí·lə=cəs//, /'*little berry basket attached to waist (it holds what the hand picks and when full is dumped into a large berry basket on one's back)*'/, root <**elí:le**> *salmonberries*, also <**lí:latses**>, //ʔəlí·lɛ=cəs//, <**x̲pá:ytses**>, //x̣pɛ́·y=cəs//, /'*cedar limb*'/, <**Siyémches**>, //s=ʔɛy=ə́m=cəs//, /'*proper name of the youngest Wealick brother in a legend; now the name of Frank Malloway*'/, literally /'said to mean *chiefly hand* or *rich hand*'/, <**lheq'átses ~ lhq'á:tses**>, //ɬəq'ɛ́cəs ~ ɬq'ɛ́·cəs//, /'*five*'/, literally /'wide on the hand or fingers'/.

<**tsesá ~ tssá** or **tsás**>, bound root //c(ə)sɛ́ or cɛ́s *send for something*//.

<**tsesá:t ~ tssá:t ~ tsesát ~ tssát**>, pcs //c(ə)sɛ́=(ə)T or cɛ́s=M1=(ə)T//, SOC /'*send s-o to do/get something, send s-o for something, (send s-o on an errand)*'/, ECON, possibly <**metathesis type 1**> *non-continuative*, (<**=et ~ =t**> *purposeful control transitivizer*), phonology: optional vowel-loss in root or metathesis, possible vowel merger, syntactic analysis: transitive verb, attested by EB (1/16/76, 3/2/76, 1/30/76), AD (1/10/79), Salish cognate: Lushootseed root /č(ə)s(a)/ *send s-o on an errand* as in /čsá-d/ *send him; send him away* and /ʔu-čsá-t-əb čəd dx^{w}ʔal x^{w}uyubàlʔtx^{w}/ *They sent me to the store.* H76:97, Squamish /čə́š-n/ *send (a person)(tr.)* W73:226, K67:316, example: <**lachxw tsesá:t kws láms kw' shxwiymálá.**>, //lɛ-c-x^{w} cəsɛ́=əT k^{w}-s lɛ́=m-s k'^{w}ə s=x^{w}iyəm=ɛ́lɛ́//, /'*Send him (to go to) the store.*'/, attested by EB (1/16/76), <**lachxw tsesá:t kws las kwél:em kw qó:.**>, //lɛ-c-x^{w} cəsɛ́=əT k^{w}-s lɛ-s k^{w}ə́l=l=əm k^{w} qá·//, /'*Send him to get water.*'/, attested by EB (1/16/76), <**lichxw tsesá:t kws las kwél:em kw s'álhtel?**>, //lí-c-x^{w} cəsɛ́=əT k^{w}-s lɛ-s k^{w}ə́l=l=əm k^{w} s=ʔɛ́ɬ=təl//, /'*Did you send him to get food?*'/, attested by EB (1/16/76).

<**tsésetem**>, cts //cə[-´-]sɛ=T-əm//, if, SOC ['*s-o was being sent [on errands]*'], (<-´-> *continuative*), (<**-em**> *passive*), phonology: stress-shift, vowel-reduction, syntactic analysis: intransitive verb, attested by IHTTC, example: <**wiyóth tsésetem.**>, //wə=yáθ cə[-´-]sɛ=T-əm//, /'*He was always [being] sent.*'/, attested by IHTTC (8/9/77).

<**tssálem**>, ncs //csɛ́=l-əm or csɛ́=l=əm//, SOC ['*send somebody off with a message*'], LANG, (<**=l**> *non-control transitivizer, manage to/happen to*), possibly <**-em**> *passive* or possibly <**=em**> *intransitivizer, get, become*, syntactic analysis: intransitive verb, attested by Elders Group, example: <**le tssálem.**>, //lə csɛ́=l-əm//, /'*send somebody off with a message, (Somebody was sent off with a message.)*'/, attested by Elders Group (2/76).

<**tssàlèm**>, ncs //csɛ́=l=əm//, izs, SOC ['*send (a person) for something*'], (<**=l**> *non-control transitivizer*), (<**=em**> *intransitivizer*), phonology: downdrifting, updrifting, syntactic analysis: intransitive verb, attested by EB (3/2/76, 3/8/76), example: <**tsel la tssàlèm.**>, //c-əl lɛ csɛ́=l=əm//, /'*I went and sent for something.*'/, attested by EB (3/8/76).

<**tssátses**>, ds //csɛ́=cəs//, SOC ['*reach*'], ABFC, lx <**=tses**> *on the hand*, syntactic analysis: intransitive verb, attested by Elders Group (4/28/76).

<**tsesá:t ~ tssá:t ~ tsesát ~ tssát**>, SOC /'*send s-o to do/get something, send s-o for something, (send s-o on an errand)*'/, *see* tsesá ~ tssá or tsás.

<**tsésetem**>, SOC ['*s-o was being sent [on errands]*'], *see* tsesá ~ tssá or tsás.

<**tsésqey**>, us //cə́sqəy//, EZ ['*small sockeye salmon*'], ['*Oncorhynchus nerka*'], syntactic analysis: nominal, noun?, attested by SP (Elders Group 3/1/72), compare <**thíthqey**> *small sockeye salmon* **(RB)**.

<**-tset ~ -chet**>, ia //-c-ət//, PRON /'*we (non-subordinate subject), our*'/, syntactic analysis: subject pronoun, possessive, attested by all speakers; found in <**qéx̱tset.**>, //qə́x̣-c-ət//, /'*(There's) a lot of us.*'/, literally /'we are many'/, attested by AC, <**mõkw'chet**>, //mɛ́k'ʷ-c-ət//, /'*all of us*'/, literally /'we are all'/, attested by BJ (12/5/64), example: <**lálhtstulh tsós.**>, //lɛ́-ɬ-c-t-wəɬ tsás//, /'*We're getting unfortunate.*'/, attested by TM/DF/TG (Elders Group 3/22/78), <**qéx̱ te shxwhókwextset.**>, //qə́x̣ tə sxʷ=hákʷ=əxʸ-c-ət//, /'*We'll use it in many ways.*'/, literally /'are many the our use s-th'/, attested by TM/DF/TG (Elders Group 3/22/78), <**ts'áts'el éy te kópitset.**>, //c'ɛ́[=C_1ə=]l ʔɛ́y tə kápi-c-ət//, /'*Our coffee is very good., We have very good coffee.*'/, attested by Deming (2/8/79), <**éy kw's lámtset.**>, //ʔɛ́y k'ʷ-s lɛ́=m-c-ət//, /'*It's good that we go., We'd better go.*'/, literally /'our go(ing) is good'/.

<**tsétsmel**>, stem //cə́c=məl//, root meaning & form uncertain, probably *cut off*, lx <=mel> *portion, part.*

<**tsétsmel sméyeth**>, dnom cpd //cə́c=məl s=méy əth//, FOOD /'*steak*'/, root meaning & form uncertain, probably *cut off*, lx <=mel> *portion, part* (lit. cut off portion + meat), (attested by RG,EH 6/16/98 to SN, edited by BG with RG,EH 6/26/00)

<**tseyí:yex̱**>, us //cəyí·yəx̣//, EZ /'*big gray lizard, (Pacific giant salamander)*'/, ['*Dicamptodon ensatus*'], syntactic analysis: nominal, attested by Elders Group (3/1/72), other sources: H-T <sEyia'H> (macron over i) *lizard (Lacertilia)*, Salish cognate: Squamish /s-iʔ-íx̣-ix̣as/ *big lizard* from root /s-ix̣ás ~ s-yəx̣ás/ *large rock* W73:164, K67:306,300, identified as *Pacific giant salamander (Dicamptodon ensatus)* in Bouchard and Kennedy 1976:118, see main dialect form <**seyíyex̱** > *gray rock lizard (Dicamptodon ensatus)*.

<**ts-hélàk**>, CSTR ['*logging*'], *see* lók ~ làk.

<**tsitsepyóthel**>, df //C_1í=cəp=əy(=)áθəl//, EZ ['*chipmunk*'], ['*Eutamias amoenus, Eutamias townsendi*'], root meaning unknown, possibly <**=ey**> *bark*, possibly <**=óthel**> *in the mouth*, or possibly <**=eyóthel ~ =óyethel**> *in the jaw*, phonology: reduplication, syntactic analysis: nominal, attested by AC (prompted), other sources: ES /cicəpyáθəl/ *chipmunk*, Salish cognate: possibly related is Songish dial. of NSt /c'əpsiyásən/ *squirrel (Tamiasciurus spp.)* M68:32.

<**Tsítsqem**>, df //C_1í=cq=əm or cí[=C_1ə=]q=əm//, PLN ['*village on north bank of the Fraser River*

above Agassiz Mountain'], ASM ['the village was founded by freed slaves who were formerly kept on Greenwood Island near Hope, B.C.'], Elder's comment: "means *freedom village*", root meaning unknown, possibly <**=R1=**> *resultative* or <**R4=**> *diminutive*, (<**=em**> *place to have/get*), phonology: reduplication, syntactic analysis: nominal, attested by AK and DC (IHTTC 8/11/77), other sources: Wells 1965 (lst ed.):25, source: place names reference file #189.

<**tskwékwelim**>, LT ['*lots of little red*'], *see* kwí:m.

<**tskwekwíkwemel**>, LT ['*[be getting/going a little red]*'], *see* kwí:m.

<**tskwíkwem**>, LT ['*[being red]*'], *see* kwí:m.

<**tskwíkwemel**>, LT ['*reddish*'], *see* kwí:m.

<**tskwí:m**>, LT /'*be red, red, reddish-brown, copper-colored*'/, *see* kwí:m.

<**tskwí::m**>, LT ['*[be extra specially red]*'], *see* kwí:m.

<**Tskwím Smált**>, PLN ['*third mountain behind X̱ó:letsa and northwest of Th'emth'ómels*'], *see* kwí:m.

<**tskwím shxw'ólewù**>, EB /'*beets* '/, (lit. red + turnip), *see* kwí:m.

<**tskwímel**>, LT ['*[be get/go/become red]*'], *see* kwí:m.

<**tskwímelqel**>, ANAA /'*have reddish-brown fur, have reddish-brown animal hair*'/, *see* kwí:m.

<**tskwí:meqw**>, ANAH /'*have red hair, have reddish-brown hair*'/, *see* kwí:m.

<**tskwimó:les**>, ANA ['*have red eyes*'], *see* kwí:m.

<**tskwimómex**>, LT /'*[looks red, red-looking]*'/, *see* kwí:m.

<**tskwimómex tl'íkw'el**>, EB /'*kidney beans* '/, (lit. dark red in appearance + bean), *see* kwí:m.

<**tslháltxw**>, BLDG /'*upper part or top of a house, upper part or top of a pit-house*'/, *see* =chílh ~ chílh=.

<**tslhilá:m**>, df //cɬ=ilɛ́·m//, KIN ['*step-parent*'], possibly <**tselh=**> *close to, near to*, possibly root <**ilá:m**> *carry on shoulder*, syntactic analysis: nominal, attested by AC (1/16/71), other sources: ES /cɬilɛ́·m/ *step-parent*, H-T <tstli'am> (macron over i, umlaut over a) *step-parent*, Salish cognate: Lushootseed root /čəɬ/ *make, build* which derives terms for step- relations as in /čəɬ-bádəb/ *step-father*, /čəɬ-tádəb/ *step-mother*, and /čəɬ-ʔíbacəb/ *step-grandchild*, Squamish uses /səxʷ=/ prefix instead as does Upriver Halkomelem for some terms.

<**tslhítselxel**>, ANA ['*top of the foot*'], *see* =chílh ~ chílh=.

<**tsmákw'a**>, REL ['*undertaker*'], *see* mákw'a.

<**tsméla**>, ABFC /'*giving birth, having a child, having a baby*'/, *see* méle ~ mél:a.

<**tsméth'**>, LT /'*blue, be blue, have blue*'/, *see* méth'.

<**tsmeth'íl**>, LT ['*[be in a state of get blue]*'], *see* méth'.

<**tsméth'òmèx**>, LT /'*[looks blue, blue-looking]*'/, *see* méth'.

<**tsmímeth'**>, LT ['*[be a little blue]*'], *see* méth'.

<**Tsólqthet te Skwówech**>, PLN ['*Rainbow Falls (on Harrison Lake's southeast side), (Sturgeon's Drop)*'], *see* tsélq ~ chélq. *and* skwó:wech ~ skwówech..

<**tsp'íp'eq'el**>, LT ['*[be getting a little white]*'], *see* p'éq'.

<**tsp'íqw'**>, LT ['*purple*'], *see* p'íqw'.

<**tsqó:le**>, ABFC /'*be thirsty, get thirsty*'/, *see* qó:.

<**tsq'éyx̲ ~ tsq'íx̲ ~ ts'q'éyx̲ ~ ts'q'íx̲**>, LT ['*be black*'], *see* q'íx̲.

<**tsq'iq'ex̲el**>, LT ['*[be getting black]*'], *see* q'íx̲.

<**tsqwá:y**>, LT /'*be yellow, be green*'/, *see* qwá:y.

<**tsqwá:y**>, EB ['*lemon (post-contact)*'], *see* qwá:y.

<**tsqwá:y p'áp'eq'em kápech**>, EB ['*broccoli* '], (lit. green + flowering/flowered + cabbage), *see* qwá:y.

<**tsqwá:y spéxwqel**>, EB /'*alfalfa sprouts* '/, (lit. green + fine airborne seed), *see* qwá:y.

<**tsqwá:yem**>, FOOD /'*lemon extract*'/, *see* qwá:y.

<**tsqwayíws**>, ANA ['*yellow-bodied*'], *see* qwá:y.

<**tsqwáyòmèx**>, LT /'*[looks yellow or green, yellow/green-looking]*'/, *see* qwá:y.

<**tsqwáyqwòyèls**>, EB /'*greenish fruit*'/, *see* qwá:y.

<**tsqwíqweyel**>, LT ['*[have/get/be in a state of going a little yellow or green]*'], *see* qwá:y.

<**tsqwóqwey**>, LT ['*[having/getting/being in a state of yellow or green]*'], *see* qwá:y.

<**tsqwóqwiyel**>, LT /'*[stative/be getting yellow, stative/be getting green]*'/, *see* qwá:y.

<**tsqw'iqw'ex̲w**>, LT ['*brown*'], *see* qw'íx̲w.

<**tsqw'íqw'ex̲wel**>, LT ['*[be getting brown]*'], *see* qw'íx̲w.

<**tsqw'íx̲w**>, LT ['*be brown*'], *see* qw'íx̲w.

<**tssálem**>, SOC ['*send somebody off with a message*'], *see* tsesá ~ tssá or tsás.

<**tssàlèm**>, SOC ['*send (a person) for something*'], *see* tsesá ~ tssá or tsás.

<**tssátses**>, SOC ['*reach*'], *see* tsesá ~ tssá or tsás.

<**tstáwél ~ táwél**>, LT ['*bright (in color)*'], *see* táw.

<**tsth'óqwi**>, FSH ['*to fish*'], *see* sth'ó:qwi ~ sth'óqwi.

<**tsxwíkw'**>, LT /'*(have/be) gray, (have/be) grey*'/, *see* xwíkw'.

<**tsxwíkw'ómex**>, LT /'*[looks gray, gray-looking]*'/, *see* xwíkw'.

<**tsxwíxwekw'**>, LT ['*[be getting gray]*'], *see* xwíkw'.

<**tsxwíxwekw'el**>, LT ['*grayish*'], *see* xwíkw'.

<**tsx̲éylém** or **tsx̲ílém**>, df //cx̣=íl=əm//, incs, mdls, TVMO ['*go away (as away from the fire)*'], (<**=íl**> *go, come, get, become*), (<**=em**> *middle voice*), phonology: vowel-loss in root, updrifting, syntactic analysis: intransitive verb, attested by EF (8/10/79 at Salish Conference), example: <**tsx̲éylémchxw telí te híyeqw.**>, //cx̣=íl=əm-c-x^w təlí tə hə́=yəq^w//, /'*Go away from the fire.*'/, attested by EF.

TS'

<**=ts' ~ =elts' ~ =á:lts'**>, da //=c' ~ =əl=c' ~ =ɛ́·l=c'//, TVMO /'*twist, turn around, around in circles*'/, syntactic analysis: lexical suffix, derivational suffix, also <**=elts'**>, //=əl=c'//, also <**=á:lts'**>, //=ɛ́·l=c'//; found in <**x̱élts't**>, //x̣ə́l(=)c'=T or x̣ə́l=(əl)c'=T orx̣=ə́lc'=T//, /'*turn or twist s-o or s-th*'/, <**x̱élts'thet**>, //x̣ə́l=c'=T-ət//, /'*turn oneself over or around*'/, <**sx̱á:lts'**>, //s=x̣ə[=Aɛ́·=]l=c'//, /'*turned around, turned the wrong way*'/, <**sx̱á:lts'emeth'**>, //s=x̣=ɛ́·lc'=əməθ'//, /'*grown twisted*'/, <**st'amxá:lts'**>, //s=t'ɛmxʸ=ɛ́·lc' or s=t'ɛm=xʸə[=Aɛ́·=]l=c'//, /'*a braid*'/ (from <**t'áméx**> *to braid)*, <**q'eyq'elts'iyósem spehá:ls**>, //q'i[=C₁ə=]l=c'=iyás=əm s=pəh=ɛ́·ls (or) q'ɛyq'=əlc'=iyás=əm spəhɛ́·ls//, /'*whirlwind*'/, <**siselts'iyósem**>, //si[=C₁ə=]l=c'=iyás=əm or C₁í=səl=c'=iyás=əm//, /'*turn around in a circle*'/ (from <**sísel=**> *spinning* (<**síl**> *spin* + **R2)** + <**=ts'**> *twist or turn around* + <**=iyós**> *in a circle* + <**=em**> *middle voice (by or for itself)).*

<**-ts'á**>, is //-c'ɛ́//, MOOD /'*so they say, (reportedly, reportative, evidential?)*'/, syntactic analysis: is, attested by BHTTC (9/9/76), JL (4/7/78 History Tape 34), see dialect form <**-th'á**>, Salish cognate: Saanich dial. of NSt /-č'əʔ/ *evidential* (variously translated as *apparently, I hear, so they say, they say, it is said)* M86:294-206, Samish dial. of NSt /-č'ə/ *evidential/ G86:60, Squamish /-č'/ apparently, known from indirect evidence/hearsay* K67:164, example: <**tl'e kwses x̱ét'e á:lhtel, tl'ots'a Siyó:ylexwe Smált tethá.**>, //ƛ'ə kʷ-s-əs x̣ə́t'ə ʔɛ́·ɬ=təl ƛ'a-c'ɛ s=yá·[=C₁ə=]ləxʷ=ə s=mɛ́·lt tə=θɛ́//, /'*That's what they said, that's Siyó:ylexwe Smált (Old person mountain) there.*'/, attested by JL (4/7/78).

<**ts'á: ~ ch'á:** >, bound root //c'ɛ́· *on top of*//.

<**wets'á:**>, ds //wə=c'ɛ́·//, DIR ['*get to the top or summit of a mountain*'], LAND, (<**we=**> *suddenly or emphatic*), syntactic analysis: intransitive verb, attested by EB (4/5/76), Elders Group (9/17/75), example: <**le wets'á:.**>, //lə wə=c'ɛ́·//, /'*He got to the top/summit of a mountain.*'/, attested by EB, <**le ts'ímél kws wets'á:s.**>, //lə c'ím(=)ə́l kʷ-s wə=c'ɛ́·-s//, /'*He's nearly got to the top.*'/, attested by EB, <**te wets'á:s te smá:lt**>, //tə wə=c'ɛ́·-s tə s=mɛ́·lt//, /'*the summit of a mountain*'/, attested by Elders Group.

<**hewts'á:**>, cts //hə-wə=c'ɛ́·//, DIR ['*getting to the summit of a mountain*'], LAND, (<**he-**> *continuative*), syntactic analysis: intransitive verb, attested by EB (4/5/76).

<**swets'a'á**>, dnom //s=wə=c'ɛʔɛ́//, LAND ['*the summit (of a mountain)*'], (<**s=**> *nominalizer*), phonology: echo vowel, glottal stop for length, syntactic analysis: nominal, attested by Elders Group (4/2/75, 9/17/75).

<**wets'á:lómet**>, ncrs //wə=c'ɛ́·=l-ámət//, TVMO ['*bring oneself to a summit (of a mountain)*'], LAND, ABFC /'*bring oneself to a climax, to climax, to orgasm, masturbate*'/, (<**we=**> *suddenly* or *emphatic*), (<**=l**> *non-control transitivizer, happen to/manage to/accidentally*), (<**-ómet**> *reflexive*), syntactic analysis: intransitive verb, attested by Elders Group (9/17/75), EB (3/22/76).

<**sts'ets'á**>, strs //s=C₁ə=c'ɛ́//, DIR ['*be on top of*'], ABFC /'*be astride, be sitting on*'/, TVMO ['*ride (on)*'], semantic environment ['a horse, for ex.'], (<**s=**> *stative*), (<**R2=**> *resultative*), phonology: reduplication, syntactic analysis: preposition/prepositional verb, attested by EB (4/2/76), AC (8/28/70), Elders Group (4/28/76), example: <**sts'ets'á te stiqíw**>, //s=C₁əC₂=c'ɛ tə s=tiqíw//, /'*ride a horse*'/, attested by Elders Group, also /'*sitting on a horse*'/, attested by AC, <**xwel sts'ets'á te stiqí:w.**>, //xʷəl s=C₁əC₂=c'ɛ tə s=tiqí·w//, /'*He's still astride the horse.*'/, attested by EB (3/1/76).

<**yets'ets'á**>, mos //yə=C₁əC₂=c'ɛ́//, TVMO /'*to travel by horse, already riding a horse*'/, (<**ye=**>

travel by means of, moving along), phonology: reduplication, syntactic analysis: intransitive verb, attested by EB (4/29/76).

<**ch'alech'á (~ ts'alets'á)**>, plv //C_1ɛ[=lə=]=c'ɛ́//, TVMO ['*they came on (top of)*'], (<**R8=**> *resultative*), (<**=le=**> *plural*), phonology: reduplication, infixed plural, syntactic analysis: intransitive verb, attested by AC, example: <**ch'alech'á te stiqíw.**>, //C_1ɛ[=lə=]=c'ɛ́ tə s=tiqíw//, /'*They came on a horse.*'/, attested by AC (8/28/70).

<**xwch'alech'á:ls**>, sas //xʷ=C_1ɛ[=lə=]=c'ɛ́=ɛ́ls//, FOOD ['*put on the stove (water/food)*'], HHG, literally /'(unclear +) many things put on top of in a structured activity'/, possibly <**xw=**> meaning unclear, (<**=á:ls**> *structured activity non-continuative*), phonology: reduplication, infixed plural, vowel merger, syntactic analysis: intransitive verb, attested by IHTTC (9/2/77).

<**shxwch'ech'áls**>, dnom //s(=)xʷ=C_1əC_2=c'ɛ́=əls//, sas, cts, HHG ['*shelf*'], literally /'something for putting on top of in a structured activity'/, (<**shxw=**> *something for*), (<**R2=**> *continuative*), lx <**=els**> *structured activity continuative nominal/tool*, phonology: reduplication, vowel merger, syntactic analysis: nominal, attested by Elders Group (6/1/77), AD (8/80), example: <**lí te shxwch'ech'áls.**>, //lí tə sxʷ=C_1əC_2=c'ɛ́=əls//, /'*It's on the shelf.*'/, attested by AD.

<**sts'á:ltexw**>, ds //s=c'ɛ́=ɛ́ltəxʷ//, BLDG /'*top of roof, roof planks*'/, literally /'something to put/go on top of the building'/, (<**s=**> *nominalizer, something to*), lx <**=áltexw ~ =áwtxw**> *building, house*, phonology: vowel merger, syntactic analysis: nominal, attested by Elders Group (9/17/75).

<**ts'ech'ó:lwelh**>, ds //C_1əC_2=c'ɛ́=á·lwəɬ//, HHG ['*(being/put) on the top shelf*'], BLDG, literally /'(being/put) on the top side'/, (<**R2=**> *continuative or resultative*), lx <**=ó:lwelh**> *side*, phonology: reduplication, vowel merger, syntactic analysis: adverb/adverbial verb, attested by EB (12/18/75).

<**ts'ílem**>, mdls //c'ɛ=íl=əm//, TVMO ['*get on top of something*'], literally /'go/come/get oneself on top'/, (<**=íl**> *go, come, get, become*), (<**=em**> *middle voice*), phonology: vowel merger, syntactic analysis: intransitive verb, attested by EB (4/2/76), example: <**ts'ílem te stiqíw**>, //c'ɛ=íl=əm tə s=tiqíw//, /'*mount a horse*'/, attested by EB, <**ts'ílemchxw í te sch'áletstel.**>, //c'ɛ=íl=əm-c-xʷ ʔí tə s=c'ɛ́=ləc=təl//, /'*You get on top of the chair.*'/, attested by EB.

<**ts'ílém**>, cts //c'ɛ=íl=ə[-´-]m//, TVMO /'*mounting a horse, mounting a person*'/, (<**-´-**> *continuative*), phonology: vowel merger, stress-shift, syntactic analysis: intransitive verb, attested by Elders Group (3/5/80).

<**ch'áletstel ~ sch'á(:)letstel ~ shxwch'áletstel**>, dnom //c'ɛ́=ləc=təl ~ s=c'ɛ́(·)=ləc=təl ~ sxʷ=c'ɛ́=ləc=təl//, HHG /'*chair, bench, seat, something to sit on*'/, literally /'device to put the rump on top of ~ something to put the rump on top of device ~ something that put the rump on top of device'/, (<**s=**> *something to, nominalizer*), (<**shx=**> *something for/that, nominalizer*), lx <**=lets**> *rump, bottom*, (semological comment: here the body part is the subject/object and not locative), lx <**=tel**> *device to, thing to*, syntactic analysis: nominal, attested by AC (1023/71, 12/8/71), AD and NP (1/23/80), TG (Elders Group 3/1/72), Elders Group (3/1/72, 1/7/76), EB (4/2/76, 2/11/76), IHTTC (9/15/77), example: <**emét li te sts'áletstel**>, //ʔəmə́t li tə s=c'ɛ́=ləc=təl//, /'*sit down on the chair*'/, attested by AC, <**lí tí te sts'áletstel.**>, //lí tí tə s=c'ɛ́=ləc=təl//, /'*The chair is over there.*'/, attested by AC, <**emétlha lam te shxwch'áletstel.**>, //ʔəmə́t-ɬɛ lɛ=m tə sxʷ=c'ɛ́=ləc=təl//, /'*Go sit in the chair.*'/, attested by IHTTC.

<**ch'álechem**>, mdls //c'ɛ́=ləc=əm//, ABFC /'*find a seat, have a seat, sit down*'/, SOC, usage: more polite than emét, lx <**=lets ~ =lech**> *rump, bottom*, (<**=em**> *middle voice*), syntactic analysis: intransitive verb, attested by Elders Group (3/1/72, 2/26/75), Deming (12/15/77), example: <**ch'álechemchap.**>, //c'ɛ́=ləc=əm-c-ɛp//, /'*You folks have a seat.*'/, attested by Deming.

<**xwch'áletsem**>, mdls //xʷ=c'ɛ́=ləc=əm//, ABFC ['*have a seat*'], SOC, (<**xw=**> meaning unclear

(perhaps *towards*)), syntactic analysis: intransitive verb, attested by IHTTC (9/15/77).

<**Ts'a'í:les**>, ds //c'ɛʔ=í·ləs//, PLN /'*Chehalis village on Harrison River, the Heart Rock for which Chehalis, B.C. was named (at the mouth of Chehalis River)*'/, ASM ['the Heart Rock was about 14 ft. around, was shaped like a heart, was supported by a great root probably a willow (possibly a cottonwood) with lots of solid earth and grasses, it went up and down with the river's rise and fall (beating like a heart), the wash from the logging tugs washed it out about 4 or 5 years ago [i.e. 1973-1974], it was probably a little upstream [north][on Harrison River] from the Chehalis River mouth and close to the village, Ed Leon knew the location, his son Rudy knows it also (EL with Ken McRae, November 1978)'], (semological comment: the word and place name is not related at all to Chehalis, Washington, that is in another language and has a totally different meaning), literally /'on top on the chest'/, lx <**=í:les**> *on the chest*, phonology: glottal stop final in root or epenthetic, such glottal stops vary rarely with h in the speech of some of the oldest elders and so //) is possible that an alternate old pronunciation was accurately reflected in the English spelling Chehalis, such a pronunciation also might have had the older historical features of <**ch'**> instead of <**ts'**> and <**éy**> allophone of /**i**/ after [**h**], thus ***Ch'ahéyles** /č'ɛh=í·ləs/ [č'ɛhɛ́ylɪs], syntactic analysis: nominal, attested by EL with Ken McRae (11/78), AC (1973 for the form), John Williams said it means literally /'over the top (when canoeing)'/ (less likely than the former etymology since it doesn't reflect the meaning of the suffix), ASM ['so named after the place of rough water past Chehalis on the way to Harrison Lake'], attested by John Williams of Scowlitz (1/29/79), also /'*Chehalis River*'/, source: Wells 1965 (lst ed.):14.

<**sts'áts'elstexw**>, caus //s=c'ɛ́[=C₁ə=]=əl=sT-əxʷ//, TVMO /'*carry it carefully, handle it with care*'/, ABFC, literally /'make/cause it to be going/coming on top'/, (<**s=**> *stative*), probably root <**ts'á**> *on top*, (<**=R1=**> *continuative or derivational*), possibly <**=el**> *go, come, get, become*, (<**=st**> *causative control transitivizer*), (<**-exw**> *third person object*), phonology: reduplication, syntactic analysis: transitive verb, attested by IHTTC (9/9/77).

<**sts'ó:ltsep**>, dnom //s=c'ɛ́[=Aá=]·=eltsep//, FIRE /'*flame*'/, <s=> *nominalizer*, <=Aó=> *durative* or *derivational*, <=éltsep> *firewood*, lit. /"something on top of firewood"/, attested by RG & EH (4/10/99 Ling332).

<**ts'ahéyelh**>, df //c'ɛh=ə́yəɬ or c'ɛ(h)=íyəɬ//, REL /'*to pray, have a church service, (a Church (organization, not building) [Elders Group])*'/, possibly root <**ts'á:** ~ **ch'á:** > with allomorph <**ts'ah**> *on top of*, possibly <**=íyelh** ~ **=iylh**> meaning unknown, possibly *child* possibly after Jesus the child of God?, phonology: h in root or epenthetic, syntactic analysis: intransitive verb, attested by Deming (12/15/77), AC (9/18/71, 10/23/71), EB (3/30/76), compare <**st'íwiyelh**> *prayer, hymn* with the same suffix and root <**t'íw**> that means *slow beat (in music), slow words*, contrast <**ts'ít**> *to praise*, phonology: note the same archaic feature of h in root or epenthesis, Salish cognate: Lushootseed root /č'íɬ(i)/ *praise* H76:696, also /'*a church (organization, not building)*'/, attested by Elders Group (11/9/77)

<**Kyelchóch Ts'ahéyelh**>, //kʸəlcác c'ɛh=íyəɬ//, REL /'*Anglican Church*'/, attested by Elders Group (11/9/77).

<**ts'í:yelh**>, cts //c'ɛ(h)=í[-·-]yəɬ//, REL /'*(be) praying, (pray [Elders Group])*'/, (<**-:-**> *continuative*), phonology: lengthening, syntactic analysis: intransitive verb, attested by EB (3/30/76), also /'*pray*'/, attested by Elders Group (2/6/80), example: <**lhéq'elh yóth ts'í:yelh yé xwèlmèxw kw'ulhíthelh.**>, //ɬə́q'-əɬ yáθ c'ɛ(h)=í[-·-]yəɬ yə xʷə́l=məxʷ k'ʷ=əw=ɬíθ-əɬ//, /'*The people used to pray all the time, long ago.*'/, literally /'sometimes -past always be praying the (plural human) Indian(s) the (remote)= contrastive= long time =past'/, attested by EB (1/9/76).

<**ts'ahéyelhá:wtxw**>, dnom //c'ɛh=íyəɬ=ɛ́·wtxʷ//, REL /'*church house, the church (building)*'/, BLDG,

lx <**=á:wtxw**> *house, building*, syntactic analysis: nominal, attested by AC (9/18/71, 10/23/71).

<**ts'ahéyelhá:wtxw**>, REL /'*church house, the church (building)*'/, *see* ts'ahéyelh.

<**ts'ákwxels**>, FOOD ['*frying*'], *see* ts'ékwxt.

<**ts'ákwxels**>, FOOD ['*frying pan*'], *see* ts'ékwxt.

<**ts'ákwxt**>, FOOD ['*(be) frying s-th*'], *see* ts'ékwxt.

<**ts'ál**>, probably bound root //c'ɛ́l// *very, extremely, painfully*

<**ts'áts'el**>, df //c'ɛ́[=C_1ə=]l or C_1ɛ́=c'əl or c'ɛ́=C_1ə=əl//, MOOD /'*(be) very, (extremely), really*'/, possibly root <**ts'ál**> *very, extremely, painfully*, possibly root <**ts'á**> *on top of*, probably <**=R1=**> *resultative/continuative or derivational*, possibly <**R7=**> *derivational*, possibly <**=el**> *go, come, get, become*, phonology: reduplication, syntactic analysis: adverb/adverbial verb, syntactic comment: only found preceding main verb or adjective/adjectival verb or adverb/adverbial verb, attested by AC, Deming (5/4/78, 5/18/78, 2/8/79, 5/3/79 esp. SJ), Elders Group (1/19/77), RP and EB (2/12/76), also <**ts'éts'el**>, //c'ə́[=C_1ə=]l//, attested by MV (Deming 5/4/78), example: <**ts'áts'el kw'ókw'es tlòwáyél.**>, //c'ɛ́[=C_1ə=]l k'ʷɛ[-AáC$_1$ə-]s təla=wɛ̀yə́l//, /'*It's very hot today., It's really hot today.*'/, dialects: *Chill.*, attested by AC, RP (2/12/76), also <**ts'áts'elew kw'ókw'es tlòwáyél.**>, //c'ɛ́[=C_1ə=θ']l=əw k'ʷɛ[-AáC$_1$ə-]s təla=wɛ́yə́l//, dialects: *Cheh.*, attested by EB (2/12/76), <**ts'áts'elew sthewót**>, //c'é[=T1=]l'=əw' s=θəwát//, /'*(He's/She's/They're) very smart*'/, dialects: *idiolectal th for ch here*, attested by EB, <**ts'áts'eltsel méq'.**>, //c'ɛ́[=C_1ə=]l-c-əl mə́q'//, /'*I'm very full.*'/, attested by AC, <**ts'áts'el wel the'í:t s'ú:met.**>, //c'ɛ́[=C_1ə=]l wəl θəʔí·t s=ʔú·mət//, /'*He's really truly lazy.*'/, syntactic analysis: adverb/adverbial verb adverb/adverbial verb adverb/adverbial verb adjective/adjectival verb, <**ts'áts'el éy**>, //c'ɛ́[=C_1ə=]l ʔɛ́y//, EFAM, /'*(he's/she's/it's) very good., (He/She) is polite.*'/, attested by Deming (2/8/79), <**ts'áts'el spópiy**>, //c'ɛ́[=C_1ə=]l s=pá[=C_1ə=]y//, /'*very crooked*'/, attested by AC, <**ts'áts'eltsel sí:si.**>, //c'ɛ́[=C_1ə=]l-c-əl síy=C_1əC_2//, /'*I'm really afraid.*'/, attested by Elders Group, <**ts'áts'el tsqwá:y, (xw)ewás lép'ex.**>, //c'ɛ́[=C_1ə=]l c=qʷɛ́·y (x̣ʷ=ʔəwə=Aɛ́=əs, ʔəwə=əs) lə́p'=əxʸ//, /'*It's very green, one doesn't eat it.*'/, literally /'(it) is very green, one doesn't (yet) eat it'/, attested by Deming (5/3/79, SJ esp.), <**ts'áts'eltsel xwoyíwel tel sqwálewel kw'els me xwe'í sq'ó talhlúwep (éy l sí:yáye, l sí:yáye sí:yám).**>, //c'ɛ́[=C_1ə=]l-c-əl xʷ=ɛ[=Aá=]y=íwəl t-əl s=qʷɛ̀l=əwəl k'ʷ-əl-s mə xʷə=ʔí s=q'á tɛ=ɬ=ləẃə=p (ʔɛ́y l s=i[=´·=]yɛ́=yə, l s=i[=´·=]yɛ́yə s=i[=´·=]y=ɛ́m)//, /'*I'm very happy to come here at this gathering my (good friends, dear friends).*'/, literally /'I am very happy the -my thoughts/feelings that -I come arrive/come here gathered together with you folks (good my friends, my friends dear (plural))'/, attested by Demiong (5/18/78), <**ts'áts'el we s'ú:met (mestíyexw)**>, //c'ɛ́[=C_1ə=]l wə=s=ʔə[=Aú·=]mət (məstíyəxʷ)//, /'*(He's/She's a) really lazy (person)*'/, attested by Elders Group (1/19/77), also <**ts'áts'el ō s'ú:met**>, //c'ɛ́[=C_1ə=]l ʔəw s=ʔə[=Aú·=]mət//, dialects: *Cheh.*, attested by Elders Group (1/19/77).

<**ts'áts'elem**>, mdls //c'ɛ́[-C_1ə-]l=əm//, ABFC /'*having labor pains, being in labor in childbirth*'/, possibly root <**ts'ál**> *very, extremely, painfully* as in <**ts'áts'el**> and <**ts'áléqel**> (<**-R1-**> *continuative*), (<**=em**> *middle voice*), phonology: reduplication, syntactic analysis: intransitive verb, attested by AK (Elders Group 3/26/80), Salish cognate: Squamish /č'á-č'l-m/ *give birth* K67:320, also <**th'áth'elem**>, //θ'ɛ́[-C_1ə-]l=əm//, attested by Elders Group (2/8/78).

<**ts'áléqel**>, df //c'ɛ́l=ə[=´=]q=əl//, ABFC /'*going to piss right away, almost piss oneself, (have an urgent or extreme or painful need to urinate)*'/, literally /'very/extremely/painfully in the penis/genitals go/come/get/become'/, probably root <**ts'ál**> *very, (extremely, painfully)*, lx <**=áq ~ =eq**> *on/in the penis, on the genitals*, probably <**=´=**> *derivational*, (<**=el**> *go, come, get, become*), phonology: stress-shift, syntactic analysis: intransitive verb, attested by JL (Fish Camp 7/20/79),

example: <**etsel tsellh mel ts'áléqel.**>, //ʔə-c-əl cəlɬ məl c'ɛ́l=ə[=´=]q=əl//, /'*I'm going to piss right away., I'm going to piss myself.*'/, literally /'ambig.past -I almost a bit almost pissed myself'/, attested by JL.

<**ts'á:lq'em**>, TVMO /'*spinning (while hanging), (twirling)*'/, *see* ts'el.

<**ts'álts'**>, probably root or stem //c'ɛ́lc'//, perhaps *shiny*

<**sts'álts'**>, df //s=c'ɛ́lc'//, ANAF ['*fish scales*'], (<**s=**> *nominalizer*), probably root as in ts'á:lts'em *shiny*, syntactic analysis: nominal, attested by Elders Group (11/19/75), Deming (4/1/76), Salish cognate: Cowichan /θ'ə́l'c'/ *scales* B74b:24 (Cow.), Saanich dial. of NSt /θ'ə́ləc'/ *scale of fish* B74a:24 (Saan.), also <**sts'élts'**>, //s=c'ə́lc'//, attested by SP (BHTTC 10/2/76).

<**ts'á:lts'em**>, izs //c'ɛ́·lc'=əm//, LT ['*shiny*'], (<**=em**> *intransitivizer/have/get*), syntactic analysis: adjective/adjectival verb, attested by Elders Group (10/13/76).

<**ts'álxet**>, MED ['*delousing s-o*'], *see* méxts'el.

<**ts'álhkw'els**>, ABFC ['*pinching*'], *see* th'lhákw'.

<**ts'ám ~ ch'ám ~ ts'ém**>, bound root //c'ɛ́m ~ c'ə́m// *bite*

<**ts'ámet ~ ch'ámet ~ ts'émet**>, pcs //c'ɛ́m=əT ~ c'ə́m=əT//, [c'ɛ́mət ~ c'ə́mət], ABFC /'*put s-th between the teeth, put it in one's mouth, bite on s-th (not into it)*'/, related to th'ám *chew*, (<**=et**> *purposeful control transitivizer*), syntactic analysis: transitive verb, attested by AC (8/15/70, 9/30/71), EB (3/22/76), Salish cognate: Squamish /č'ə́mʔ/ *bite (itr.)(dog, fish, fly, etc.)* and /č'ə́mʔ-t/ *bite (tr.)* W73:38, K67:319, perhaps not Shuswap /c'm-em/ and /c'm-nt-es/ and /s-c'm-st-es/ *to bite and suck blood (of mosquito, sand fly, etc.)* K74:177, nor Shuswap root /k'em/ *surface* in many body parts K74 (but the latter may be cognate with Upriver Halkomelem /c'əmx^{y}á·yθəl/ *jaw*, contrast <**th'ám**> *chew*.

<**ch'mát**>, cts //c'ɛ́m=M1=T//, ABFC ['*biting on s-th*'], (<**metathesis type 1**> *continuative* (irregular)), phonology: metathesis, syntactic analysis: transitive verb, attested by Elders Group (2/8/78).

<**ch'emá:ls**>, sas //c'əm=ɛ́·ls//, dnom, ABFC ['*a thing that bites*'], (<> *structured activity non-continuative nominal*), syntactic analysis: nominal, attested by IHTTC (9/2/77).

<**ch'ech'émels**>, cts //C_1ə=c'ə́m=əls//, sas, dnom, ABFC /'*a biter (animal, fish, etc.), a thing that is (always) biting*'/, (<**R5=**> *continuative*), (<**=els**> *structured activity continuative nominal*), phonology: reduplication, syntactic analysis: nominal, attested by IHTTC (9/2/77), example: <**ch'ech'émels te sqwemáy.**>, //C_1ə=c'ə́m=əls//, /'*The dog is a biter.*'/, attested by IHTTC.

<**sts'ámex**>, df //s=c'ɛ́m(=)əx^{y}//, [sc'ɛ́mɪx^{y}], FOOD ['*dry herring eggs*'], FSH, Elder's comment: "a Stó:lō word though the eggs are brought from the coast", (<**s=**> *nominalizer*), root meaning uncertain but probably <**ts'ám ~ ch'ám ~ ts'ém**> *bite*, poss. <**=ex**> *upright*, syntactic analysis: nominal, attested by Elders Group (3/12/75), Salish cognate: Lushootseed /č'ə́bs/ *dried herring eggs (ready for eating)* H76:110.

<**ts'ápe<u>x</u>el**>, rsls //c'ə[=Aɛ́=]p=əx̣=əl//, LAND ['*it got rusty*'], probably root <**ts'ép**> *dirty*, compare <**s=ts'ép=<u>x</u>**> *be dirty*, (<**á-ablaut**> *resultative*), possibly <**=e<u>x</u> ~ =<u>x</u>**> *distributive, all over*, (<**=el**> *go, come, get, become*), phonology: ablaut, syntactic analysis: intransitive verb, attested by EB (5/5/78), compare with <**sts'ép<u>x</u>**> *be dirty*, Elder's comment: "ts'áp<u>x</u>el may also be a word but EB is unsure of its meaning".

<**sts'ápe<u>x</u>el**>, strs //s=c'ə[=Aɛ́=]p=əx̣=əl//, LAND ['*(be) rusty*'], (<**s=**> *stative*), phonology: ablaut, syntactic analysis: adjective/adjectival verb, attested by MV (Deming 5/4/78).

<ts'áq>, ABDF /*'scrape where skin comes off, skinned'*/, *see* th'áq ~ ts'áq or ts'éq ~ th'éq.

<ts'átem>, ABFC [*'crawling'*], *see* ts'tá:m.

<ts'átem stim:ốt>, //c'ɛ́t=əm stim=mót//, CAN, /*'train'*/, literally /'crawling steamboat'/, attested by IHTTC (7/28/77), also **<ts'étem stim:ốt ~ ch'étem stim:ōt>**, //c'ə́t=əm stim=mót//, attested by NP (9/30/75), see ts'tá:m.

<ts'áṯxem ~ th'áṯxem>, izs //cɛ́t=x̱=əm ~ θ'ɛ́t=x̱=əm or θ'a[=Aɛ́=]t=x̱=əm//, SD /*'clinking, tinkling (of glass, ice in glass, glasses together, dishes together, metal together)'*/, root meaning unknown unless th'ót *pull out a nail*, possibly **<á-ablaut>** *continuative or resultative*, lx **<=x̱>** *distributive, all over*, (**<=em>** *intransitivizer, have/get/become*), phonology: probable ablaut, syntactic analysis: intransitive verb, attested by Elders Group (12/15/76).

<ts'átxwels ~ ch'átxwels>, df //c'ɛ́t(=)x^w=əls//, sas, ABFC /*'(mice) chewing (a wall, box, etc.)'*/, possibly root **<ts'á:(t)>** *chew (s-th)*, **<=xw>** *lump-like, round*, (**<=els>** *structured activity continuative*), syntactic analysis: intransitive verb, attested by Elders Group (10/27/76), Salish cognate: possibly Squamish /č'ít-inʔ/ *gnaw* W73:117, K69:68, possibly Lushootseed /č'ít'-id/ *chewed it up, destroyed it as would an insect* H76:118, Sechelt /c'əʔ-át/ *chew [s-th]* T77:26.

<ts'á:txwels>, dnom //c'ɛ́·t=x^w=əls//, sas, EZ /*'a big rat* (prob. the introduced *Norway rat,* probably *native species of large vole* which may include any or all of the following that are found in the area: *creeping vole, long-tail vole, mountain heather vole, boreal redback vole),* possibly also the introduced *roof rat*'/, ['prob. the introduced *Rattus norvegius,* native species possiblyincluding any/all of these four: *Microtus oregoni serpens, Microtus longicaudus macrurus, Phenacomys intermedius oramontis*, and *Clethrionomys gapperi cascadensis*, possibly also the introduced *Rattus rattus*'], literally /'something chewing (as a structured activity like a mouse on a wall or box)'/, **<=xw>** *lump-like, round*, (**<=els>** *structured activity continuative nominal*), syntactic analysis: nominal, attested by Elders Group (7/27/75).

<ts'á:txwels>, EZ /*'a big rat* (prob. the introduced *Norway rat,* probably *native species of large vole* which may include any or all of the following that are found in the area: *creeping vole, long-tail vole, mountain heather vole, boreal redback vole),* possibly also the introduced *roof rat*'/, *see* ts'átxwels ~ ch'átxwels.

<ts'á:tl'em ~ ch'á:tl'em ~ ts'átl'em>, ABFC /*'jumping, hopping'*/, *see* ts'tl'ám ~ ts'tl'ém.

<ts'áts'el>, df //c'ɛ́[=C_1ə=]l or C_1ɛ́=c'əl or c'ɛ́=C_1ə=əl//, MOOD /*'(be) very, (extremely), really'*/, probably root **<ts'ál>** *very, extremely, painfully*, see under **<ts'ál>**, possibly root **<ts'á>** *on top of*, probably **<=R1=>** *resultative/continuative or derivational*, possibly **<R7=>** *derivational*, possibly **<=el>** *go, come, get, become*, phonology: reduplication, syntactic analysis: adverb/adverbial verb, syntactic comment: only found preceding main verb or adjective/adjectival verb or adverb/adverbial verb, attested by AC, Deming (5/4/78, 5/18/78, 2/8/79, 5/3/79 esp. SJ), Elders Group (1/19/77), RP and EB (2/12/76), also **<ts'éts'el>**, //c'ə́[=C_1ə=]l//, attested by MV (Deming 5/4/78), example: **<ts'áts'el kw'ókw'es tlòwáyél.>**, //c'ɛ́[=C_1ə=]l k'^wɛ[-AáC_1ə-]s təla=wɛ́yə́l//, /*'It's very hot today., It's really hot today.'*/, dialects: *Chill.*, attested by AC, RP (2/12/76), also **<ts'áts'elew kw'ókw'es tlòwáyél.>**, //c'ɛ́[=C_1ə=θ'l=əw k'^wɛ[-AáC_1ə-]s təla=wɛ́yə́l//, dialects: *Cheh.*, attested by EB (2/12/76), **<ts'áts'elew sthewót>**, //c'é[=T1=]l'=əw' s=θəwát//, /*'(He's/She's/They're) very smart'*/, dialects: *idiolectal th for ch here*, attested by EB, **<ts'áts'eltsel méq'.>**, //c'ɛ́[=C_1ə=]l-c-əl mə́q'//, /*'I'm very full.'*/, attested by AC, **<ts'áts'el wel the'í:t s'ú:met.>**, //c'ɛ́[=C_1ə=]l wəl θəʔí·t s=ʔú·mət//, /*'He's really truly lazy.'*/, syntactic analysis: adverb/adverbial verb adverb/adverbial verb adverb/adverbial verb adjective/adjectival verb, **<ts'áts'el éy>**, //c'ɛ́[=C_1ə=]l ʔɛ́y//, EFAM,

/'(he's/she's/it's) very good., (He/She) is polite.'/, attested by Deming (2/8/79), <**ts'áts'el spópiy**>, //c'ɛ́[=C_1ə=]l s=pá[=C_1ə=]y//, */'very crooked'/*, attested by AC, <**ts'áts'eltsel sí:si.**>, //c'ɛ́[=C_1ə=]l-c-əl síy=C_1əC_2//, */'I'm really afraid.'/*, attested by Elders Group, <**ts'áts'el tsqwá:y, (xw)ewás lép'ex.**>, //c'ɛ́[=C_1ə=]l c=q^{w}ɛ́·y (x̣^{w}=ʔəwə=Aɛ́=əs, ʔəwə=əs) lə́p'=əx^y//, */'It's very green, one doesn't eat it.'/*, literally /'(it) is very green, one doesn't (yet) eat it'/, attested by Deming (5/3/79, SJ esp.), <**ts'áts'eltsel xwoyíwel tel sqwálewel kw'els me xwe'í sq'ó talhlúwep (éy l sí:yáye, l sí:yáye sí:yám).**>, //c'ɛ́[=C_1ə=]l-c-əl x^w=ɛ[=Aá=]y=íwəl t-əl s=q^{w}ɛ̀l=əwəl k'^{w}-əl-s mə x^{w}ə=ʔí s=q'á tɛ=ɬ=lə́wə=p (ʔɛ́y l s=i[=´·=]yɛ́=yə, l s=i[=´·=]yɛ́yə s=i[=´·=]y=ɛ́m)//, */'I'm very happy to come here at this gathering my (good friends, dear friends).'/*, literally /'I am very happy the -my thoughts/feelings that -I come arrive/come here gathered together with you folks (good my friends, my friends dear (plural))'/, attested by Demiong (5/18/78), <**ts'áts'el we s'ú:met (mestíyexw)**>, //c'ɛ́[=C_1ə=]l wə=s=ʔə[=Aú·=]mət (məstíyəx^w)//, */'(He's/She's a) really lazy (person)'/*, attested by Elders Group (1/19/77), also <**ts'áts'el ō s'ú:met**>, //c'ɛ́[=C_1ə=]l ʔəw s=ʔə[=Aú·=]mət//, dialects: *Cheh.*, attested by Elders Group (1/19/77).

<**ts'áts'esem**>, izs //c'ɛ́[=C_1ə=]s=əm//, TAST */'good tasting (savory, not sweet), tasty'/*, semantic environment ['used with meat, nuts, some other things, but not a sweet flavor'], (<**=R1=**> *continuative or resultative*), (<**=em**> *have/get/intransitivizer*), phonology: reduplication, syntactic analysis: adjective/adjectival verb, attested by Elders Group (6/16/75, 7/9/75), Salish cognate: Lushootseed /č'ásəb/ *It has a good taste.* and /ʔu-č'ásəb/ *delicious* H76:106.

<**ts'áts'etl'em**>, ABFC ['*jumping*'], *see* ts'tl'ám ~ ts'tl'ém.

<**ts'áts'etl'em**>, EZ */'grasshopper (ordinary),* perhaps *longhorned grasshopper'/*, *see* ts'tl'ám ~ ts'tl'ém.

<**ts'ats'etl'í:m**>, ABFC */'jumping along, jumping up and down'/*, *see* ts'tl'ám ~ ts'tl'ém.

<**ts'ats'etl'í:m**>, EZ */'grasshopper (ordinary),* perhaps *longhorned grasshopper'/*, *see* ts'tl'ám ~ ts'tl'ém.

<**ts'áts'ets'tl'ím**>, ABFC ['*be hopping*'], *see* ts'tl'ám ~ ts'tl'ém.

<**ts'ats'í:ts'etl' ~ ts'ats'íts'etl'**>, DESC ['*shorter*'], *see* ts'í:tl' ~ ts'ítl'.

<**ts'aweyí:les**>, EZ */'white-breasted bear, a bear with white on the breast, (brown bear with a white chest [AK])'/*, *see* ts'áwi or ts'áwiy.

<**ts'áwi** or **ts'áwiy**>, probably root //c'ɛ́wi or c'ɛ́w=iy//, ANA ['*shell (shiny part)*'], HHG ['*glass*'], possibly <**=iy**> *bark, covering*?, syntactic analysis: noun?, nominal, attested by Elders Group (6/1/77, 5/28/75), AK and SP (Elders Group 6/1/77), example: <**ts'áwis te (s'óx̱we, q'oyátl'iya, á:yx̱, mimelehó:llh)**>, //c'ɛ́w(=)iy-s tə (s=ʔáx̣^{w}ə, q'ayɛ́ƛ'=iyɛ, ʔɛ́·yx̣, C_1í=mələ=há·lɬ)//, */'shell of a (clam, snail, crab, egg)'/*, Elder's comment: "both AK and SP heard this", attested by AK and SP (Elders Group 6/1/77).

<**ts'aweyí:les**>, ds //c'ɛw(=)əy=í·ləs//, EZ */'white-breasted bear, a bear with white on the breast, (brown bear with a white chest [AK])'/*, ['variety of *Ursus americanus altifrontalis* or *Ursus americanus cinnamomum*'], literally /'glass/shiny shell =on the chest'/, (semological comment: so named because the white fur is shiny like glass), lx <**=í:les**> *on the chest*, syntactic analysis: nominal, attested by Elders Group (10/13/76), IHTTC (7/25/77), also <**ts'áweyìlès**>, //c'ɛ́w(=)əy=íləs//, also */'brown bear with white chest'/*, phonology: downstepping, updrifting, attested by AK (11/21/72).

<**ch'áwq'em**>, df //c'ɛ́w(=)q'=əm//, SD ['*sizzling*'], FOOD, semantic environment ['of grease in a frying pan or in roasting meat'], root meaning unknown, possibly <**=q'**> *on something else*?, (<**=em**> *have/get/intransitivizer*), syntactic analysis: intransitive verb, attested by Elders Group (12/15/76).

<ts'á:xt>, bound root or stem //c’Ɛ·x^{y}t//, meaning uncertain

<sts'á:xt>, dnom //s=c’Ɛ·x^{y}t//, EB /*'tree limb, branch (of tree), (knot on a tree* [CT])'/, (**<s=>** *nominalizer*), syntactic analysis: nominal, attested by AC, BJ (12/5/64),, other sources: ES /sc’Ɛ·x^{y}t/ *stick (of wood)*, JH /sc’é·xt/ *limb (of a tree)*, H-T <tsai'qt> (macrons over both vowels) *branch (a)*, Salish cognate: Lushootseed /s-č’ást/ *branch, limb* H76:106, Samish dial. of NSt (VU) /sc’ə́yst ~ sc’éyst/ *limb oɬ a tree, knot in a tree or wood, knothole* G86a:73, also <**sts'éxttses**>, //s=c’ɛ[=Aə́=]x^{y}t=cəs//, attested by CT (6/8/76), also /*'knot on a tree'*/, attested by CT (6/8/76), example: <**qéx̱ te sts'á:xts ta qwe'ópelhp.**>, //qə́x̣ tə s=c’Ɛ·x^{y}t-s t-ɛ q^{w}əʔáp=əɬp//, /*'You've got a lot of branches on your apple tree.*'/, literally /'there's lots the branches of your apple tree'/, attested by AC (11/24/71).

<**sts'axtálá**>, ds //s=c’ɛx^{y}t=ɛ́lɛ́//, EB ['*knothole*'], literally /'container of a tree branch/limb'/, lx <**=álá**> *container of, container*, syntactic analysis: nominal, attested by EB (7/8/76), Elders Group (3/15/72).

<**sts'éxttses**>, ds //s=c’ɛ[=Aə́=]x^{y}t=cəs//, EB ['*limb (of tree)*'], (<**é-ablaut**> *derivational*), lx <**=tses**> *on the hand, bough (of tree)*, phonology: ablaut, syntactic analysis: nominal, attested by CT (6/8/76).

<**ts'áxw**>, bound root //c’Ɛx^{w} *quiet/silent (after noise)*//.

<**ts'áxws**>, if //c’Ɛx^{w}-s//, LANG ['*everyone got quiet*'], SD, (<**-s**> *third person possessive/subordinate*), syntactic analysis: intransitive verb, attested by Elders Group (3/23/77).

<**sts'áxw**>, stvi //s=c’Ɛx^{w}//, LANG /*'quiet or silent (after noise) (used of people), (be/have) a lull in conversation*'/, SD, (<**s=**> *stative*), syntactic analysis: adjective/adjectival verb, attested by AD (12/7/79).

<**sts'áts'exw ~ sch'ách'exw**>, strs //s=c’Ɛ́[=C$_{1}$ə=]x^{w}//, LANG /*'(be) silent, quiet, keep quiet*'/, SD, (<**=R1=**> *resultative*), phonology: reduplication, syntactic analysis: adjective/adjectival verb, attested by AD (12/9/79), EB (12/18/75), Elders Group (3/3/76); found in <**sch'ách'exwchexwo.**>, //s=c’Ɛ́[=C$_{1}$ə=]x^{w}-c-əx^{w}-a//, /*'You keep quiet.*'/, attested by Elders Group.

<**ch'áxwel ~ ts'áxwel**>, incs //c’Ɛ́x^{w}=əl//, LANG /*'shut up, (go or get or become quiet)*'/, SD, (<**=el**> *go, come, get, become*), syntactic analysis: intransitive verb, usage: not polite, attested by Elders Group (2/19/75), EB (5/3/76); found in <**ch'áxwellha.**>, //c’Ɛ́x^{w}=əl-ɬɛ//, /*'Shut up.*'/, attested by Elders Group, *<**ts'áxwellha ta' thóthel.**> rejected by EB.

<**ch'exweló:ythel ~ ts'exweló:ythel**>, ds //c’ɛx^{w}=əl=á·yθəl or c’ɛ[=Aə=]x^{w}=əl=á·yθəl//, LANG /*'stop talking, shut up (the lips or jaw)*'/, literally /'go/get silent on the lips/jaw'/, possibly <**e-ablaut**> *derivational/resultative/durative*, lx <**=ó:ythel**> *on the jaw, on the lips*, phonology: vowel-reduction or ablaut, syntactic analysis: intransitive verb, attested by IHTTC, Elders Group; found in <**ch'exweló:ythellha.**>, //c’ɛx^{w}=əl=á·yθəl-ɬɛ//, /*'Stop talking.*'/, attested by IHTTC (9/15/77), example: <**skw'áy kw'es ts'exweló:ythels.**>, //s=k’^{w}Ɛ́y k’^{w}-əs c’ɛx^{w}=əl=á·yθəl-s//, /*'(He/She/They) can't shut up.*'/, attested by Elders Group (2/25/75); found in <**ch'exweló:ythelalha.**>, //c’ɛx^{w}=əl=á·yθəl-ɛɬɛ//, /*'Stop talking you guys., Stop talking you folks.*'/, attested by IHTTC.

<**ch'exwí:lt**>, pcs //c’ɛx^{w}=í·l=T//, KIN /*'hush a baby from crying, (hush s-o (a baby) from crying)*'/, LANG, (<**=el ~ =í:l**> *go, come, get, become*), (<**=t**> *purposeful control transitivizer*), phonology: vowel-reduction, syntactic analysis: transitive verb, attested by IHTTC (9/15/77).

<**ts'exwí:lthet**>, pcrs //c’ɛx^{w}=í·l=T-ət//, LANG ['*one gets silent*'], literally /'hush oneself, get oneself quiet'/, (<**-et**> *reflexive*), phonology: vowel-reduction, syntactic analysis: transitive verb, attested by Elders Group (3/23/77).

<**ts'xwó:ythel**>, ds //c'(ɛ)xʷ=á·yθəl//, LANG /'*silence the mouth, keep the mouth quiet*'/, literally /'quiet the jaw/lips'/, lx <**=ó:ythel**> *(on the) jaw, lips*, phonology: vowel-loss, syntactic analysis: intransitive verb, attested by EB (5/3/76); found in <**ts'xwó:ythellha.**>, //c'(ɛ)xʷ=á·yθəl-ɬɛ//, /'*Silence your mouth., Keep your mouth quiet.*'/, *<**ts'xwó:ythellha ta' thóthel.**> rejected by EB.

<**ts'áxws**>, LANG ['*everyone got quiet*'], *see* ts'áxw.

<**ts'á:ya**>, possibly root //c'ɛ́·yɛ or c'ɛ́·y=ɛ or c'ɛ́·=iyɛ//, KIN /'*relative of deceased spouse, mother/brother/sister/cousin/relative of deceased husband, dead spouse's relative or sibling, daughter-in-law if son dies*'/, possibly root <**ts'á:**> *on top of*?, possibly <**=iya**> *affectionate diminutive*, possibly <**=a**> *living thing*, phonology: possible vrmg, syntactic analysis: noun, nominal, attested by AC (11/16/71), LJ via AD (6/16/79), IHTTC (7/25/77), other sources: ES /c'ɛ́·yɛ/ *deceased spouse's relative*, Salish cognate: Squamish /č'áyayʔ/ *deceased spouse's sibling or cousin* K67:321, Samish dial. of NSt /č'é·y'ə/ *spouse of deceased sibling* G84a:79, also <**th'á:ya**>, //θ'ɛ́·yɛ//, attested by CT (6/8/76), example: <**ts'á:yas te th'áx̲ey**>, //c'ɛ́·yɛ-s tə θ'ɛ́x̣=əy//, /'*reed canary grass*'/, lit. /'relative of deceased spouse of grass scalded and bleached white for basketry imbrication (designs), relative of deceased spouse of white straw grass, relative of deceased spouse of blue-joint reed-grass'/ (prob. since the scalded grass is dead/deceased; the Thompson language has a number of plants named as relatives of other plants), attested by LJ via AD (6/18/79, see also duplicate entry under stem <**th'á:ya**>

<**ts'its'á:ya**>, pln //C_1í=c'ɛ́·=iyɛ//, KIN ['*in-laws or relatives when the connecting link dies*'], (<**R4=**> *plural*), (irregular), phonology: reduplication, syntactic analysis: noun, nominal, attested by AC (11/16/71), also <**th'ith'á:ya**>, //C_1í=θ'ɛ́·yɛ//, also /'*all the relatives (in-laws) of one's deceased husband*'/, attested by EB (6/9/76).

<**th'áyá:m**>, ds //θ'ɛ́yɛ=əm//, KIN ['*to marry a sibling of one's deceased spouse*'], (<**=em**> *middle voice or intransitivizer/have/get*), phonology: vowel merger, syntactic analysis: intransitive verb, attested by EB (12/18/75), Salish cognate: Squamish /č'áyayʔ-m/ *marry deceased spouse's sibling or cousin* K67:321, Lushootseed /č'ájajəb/ *inherit* H76:106, Samish dial. of NSt /č'éy'eŋ/ *to marry spouse of deceased sibling* G84a:79.

<**ts'á:yas te th'á:x̲ey**>, EB ['*reed canary-grass*'], *see* ts'á:ya, th'á:ya, *and* th'áx̲.

<**ts'áyxw**>, DESC ['*drying*'], *see* ts'íyxw ~ ts'éyxw ~ ch'íyxw.

<**Ts'a'í:les**>, PLN /'*Chehalis village on Harrison River, the Heart Rock for which Chehalis, B.C. was named (at the mouth of Chehalis River)*'/, *see* ts'á:.

<**ts'ech'ó:lwelh**>, HHG ['*(being/put) on the top shelf*'], *see* ts'á:.

<**ts'ék'**>, possibly bound root //c'ə́k'//, meaning unknown

<**sts'ék'**>, dnom //s(=)c'ə́k'//, EB ['*pine-cone*'], (perhaps <**s=**> *nominalizer*), syntactic analysis: nominal, probably borrowed from Thompson /sc'ə́k'/ *pine nut* beside /sc'ək'-qín'-kaʔ/ *pine cone* T73:9.

<**ts'ékwx̲** ~ **ch'ékwx̲**>, probable bound stem //c'ə́kʷ(=)x̣//, root meaning uncertain

<**ts'ékwx̲t**>, pcs //c'ə́kʷ(=)x̣=T//, FOOD ['*fry s-th*'], possibly <**=x̲**> *distributive*, (<**=t**> *purposeful control transitivizer*), syntactic analysis: transitive verb, attested by , Salish cognate: Squamish /čəkʷx̣-án/ *fry (tr.)* beside /čəkʷx̣-ímʔ/ *fry (act. itr.)* W73:109, K67:316, Songish dial. of NSt /č'kʷə́x̣t/ *to fry (tr.)* M68:39, also <**ts'éqwx̲wt**>, //c'ə́qʷx̣ʷ=T//, comment: probably mistranscribed for ts'ékwx̲t, attested by AC (9/18/71), EB (12/15/75), example: <**ts'eqwx̲wt te stsél:èm**>, //c'ə́qʷx̣ʷ=T tə s=cə́l·əm//, /'*fry the liver*'/, comment:<**ts'eqwx̲wt**> prob. mistranscribed, attested by AC; found in <**ts'ékwx̲tchexw. ~ ts'ékwx̲tlha.**>, //c'ə́kʷx̣=T-c-əxʷ ~ c'ə́kʷx̣=T-ɬɛ//, /'*Fry it.*'/,

attested by EB (3/1/76).

<**ts'ákwx̲t**>, cts //c'ə[-Aɛ́-]kʷ(=)x̣=T//, FOOD ['*(be) frying s-th*'], (<**á-ablaut**> *continuative*), phonology: ablaut, syntactic analysis: transitive verb, attested by EB (5/3/76), example: <**ílhtsel ts'ákwx̲t.**>, //ʔí-ɬ-c-əl c'ə[-Aɛ́-]kʷx̣=T//, /'*I was frying it.*'/, attested by EB, <**ts'ákwx̲tes te chékel.**>, //c'ə[-Aɛ́-]kʷx̣=T-əs tə cə́kəl//, [c'ǽkʷx̣tɪs tə čɪ́kʸɪl], /'*She's frying the chicken.*'/, attested by EB (3/1/76).

<**sts'ákwx̲ ~ sch'ákwx̲**>, strs //s=c'ə[=Aɛ́=]kʷx̣//, FOOD ['*(already) fried*'], (<**s=**> *stative*), (<**á-ablaut**> *resultative*), phonology: ablaut, syntactic analysis: adjective/adjectival verb, attested by IHTTC (8/24/77), AD (12/19/78), also <**sch'ékwx̲**>, //s=c'ə́kʷx̣//, attested by Danny Charlie Sr. (12/19/78), <**sch'ákwx̲ seplíl**>, //s=c'ə[=Aɛ́=]kʷx̣ səplíl//, /'*fried bread*'/, attested by AD, also <**sch'ékwx̲ seplíl**>, //s=c'ə́kʷx̣ səplíl//, attested by DC.

<**ts'ekwx̲á:ls ~ ts'ekwx̲áls**>, sas //c'əkʷx̣=ɛ́·ls//, FOOD ['*to fry (as a structured activity)*'], (<**=áls**> *structured activity non-continuative*), syntactic analysis: intransitive verb, attested by EB (3/1/76, 5/3/76), example: <**ílhtsel ts'ekwx̲áls te seplí:l.**>, //ʔí-ɬ-c-əl c'əkʷx̣=ɛ́ls tə səplí·l//, /'*I fried bread.*'/, attested by EB; found in <**ts'ekwx̲á:lslha.**>, //c'əkʷx̣=ɛ́·ls-ɬɛ//, /'*Fry some.*'/, ASM ['meaning do the work for awhile'], attested by EB, example: <**ts'ekwx̲á:lslha kw seplí:l. ~ ts'ekwx̲álschexw kw seplì:l.**>, //c'əkʷx̣=ɛ́·ls-ɬɛ kʷ səplí·l ~ c'əkʷx̣=ɛ́ls-c-əxʷ kʷ səplí·l//, /'*Fry some bread.*'/, attested by EB (3/1/76, 5/3/76).

<**ts'ákwx̲els**>, cts //c'ə[-Aɛ́-]kʷx̣=əls//, sas, FOOD ['*frying*'], (<**á-ablaut**> *continuative*), (<**=els**> *structured activity continuative*), phonology: ablaut, syntactic analysis: intransitive verb, attested by EB (5/3/76 corrects 12/15/75), example: <**ílhtsel ts'ákwx̲els te seplí:l**>, //ʔí-ɬ-c-əl c'ə[-Aɛ́-]kʷx̣=əls tə səplí·l//, /'*I was frying bread.*'/, attested by EB (5/3/76).

<**ts'ákwx̲els**>, dnom //c'ə[=Aɛ́=]kʷx̣=əls//, FOOD ['*frying pan*'], TOOL, HHG, (<**á-ablaut**> *continuative*), (<**=els**> *structured activity continuative nominal*), phonology: ablaut, syntactic analysis: nominal, attested by Deming Elders at Ft. Langley, B.C. museum (3/9/78), also <**sch'ákwx̲els**>, //s=c'ə[=Aɛ́=]kʷx̣=əls//, attested by Elders Group (6/1/77), AD (8/80), example: <**alétsa te sch'ákwx̲els?**>, //ʔɛlə́cɛ tə s=c'ə[=Aɛ́=]kʷx̣=əls//, /'*Where's the frying pan?*'/, attested by AD.

<**ts'ékwx̲elhtst**>, bens //c'ə́kʷx̣-əɬc=T//, pcs, FOOD ['*fry it for s-o*'], (<**-elhts**> *benefactive*), (<**=t**> *purposeful control transitivizer*), syntactic analysis: transitive verb, attested by Elders Group (3/24/76), also <**ts'ékwx̲elht**>, //c'ə́kʷx̣=əɬ=T//, attested by EB (3/1/76); found in <**ts'ekwx̲elhtsthó:x**>, //c'əkʷx̣-əɬc=T-áxʸ//, /'*fry it for me*'/, attested by Elders Group, example: <**ts'ekwx̲elhthó:xchexw.**>, //c'əkʷx̣-əɬ=T-áxʸ-c-əxʷ//, /'*Fry it for me.*'/, attested by EB.

<**ts'ekwx̲á:ls ~ ts'ekwx̲áls**>, FOOD ['*to fry (as a structured activity)*'], *see* ts'ékwx̲t.

<**ts'ékwx̲elhtst**>, FOOD ['*fry it for s-o*'], *see* ts'ékwx̲t.

<**ts'ékw'iya**>, df //c'ə́k'ʷ-iyɛ//, dmn, BPI ['*midget*'], root meaning unknown unless <**th'ékw'**> *worm*, lx <**=iya**> *affectionate diminutive*, syntactic analysis: nominal, attested by Deming (1/31/80), compare with <**ts'ókw**> *minnow*?.

<**ts'ekw'xále**>, NUM ['*twenty people*'], *see* ts'kw'éx.

<**ts'el**>, bound root //c'əl *turn, turn around*//, Salish cognate: Lushootseed root /č'ə́lp/ *twist, turn, sprain* [perhaps with /=p/ *on itself* as in Upriver Halkomelem /=p'/ *on itself* but with loss of glottalization] as in Lushootseed /ʔəs-č'ə́lp/ *it's turned*, /č'ə́lp-əd/ *turn it, twist it*, /č'əlp-ús-əd/ *turn the head (of a horse when riding)* H76:110-111.

<**ts'eláltxw**>, ds //c'əl=ɛ́ltxʷ//, SOC ['*steal someone's spouse*'], literally /'turn/turn around the

spouse/home'/, lx <**=áltxw**> *spouse, home*, comment: this use contrasts with that of <**=áwtxw**> *house, building*, clearly a related suffix, syntactic analysis: intransitive verb, attested by Deming (4/26/79).

<**ts'ólesem ~ ts'ólésem**>, mdls //c'ə[=Aá=]l=əs=əm ~ c'ə[=Aá=]l=ə[=´=]s=əm//, ABFC /'*turn one's face, (turn one's body away [IHTTC])*'/, DIR, probably <**ó-ablaut**> *derivational*, lx <**=es**> *on the face*, possibly <=´=> *derivational*, (<**=em**> *middle voice*), phonology: probable ablaut, possible updrifting, syntactic analysis: intransitive verb, attested by EF (9/21/78), also /'*turn one's body away*'/, attested by IHTTC (9/16/77), example: <**ts'ólésem, ts'ólésem telúwe q'ámi. I stl'í kw'els kw'atsethóme. Pshaw, it's only my cousin.**>, //c'ə[=Aá=]l=əs=əm, c'ə[=Aá=]l=əs=əm, tɛ=lúwə q'ɛ́miy. I s=ƛ'í k'ʷ-əl-s k'ʷɛc=əT-ámə.//, /'*Turn your face, turn your face, you, girl. I want to see you. Pshaw, it's only my cousin.*'/, usage: love song, attested by EF (9/21/78).

<**ts'ó:lex̱eth'**>, df //c'ə[=Aá=]l=ləx̣əθ' or c'ə[=Aá=](l)=ɛ́ləx̣əθ'//, ABFC /'*roll over in bed, turn over in bed*'/, DIR, (<**ó-ablaut**> *derivational*), lx <**=(a)lex̱eth'**> *in bed*, phonology: possible vowel-loss in suffix and consonant merger (l+l→:l), or possible consonant-loss in root and vowel merger, (semological comment: the non-body-part suffix here seems clearly locative and has the <**=el=** ~ **=ál=**> like many body-part suffixes, could this indicate that the <**=el=** ~ **=ál=**> element was originally *locative*? and then that meaning element spread to the other body part suffixes by analogy even when <**=el=/=ál=**> was not added?), syntactic analysis: intransitive verb, attested by NP (Elders Group 3/5/80), also <**ch'ó:lex̱eth'**>, //c'ə[=Aá=]l=ləx̣əθ'//, attested by HT (Elders Group 3/5/80).

<**ts'elqéylt** or **ts'elqí:lt**>, pcs //c'əl=q=í·l=T//, DIR ['*turn s-th around*'], possibly <**=q ~ =q'**> *(on) something else* or perhaps <**=qel**> *(in) the head* with <**i:-ablaut**> *durative* or <**=í:l**> *go, come, get, become*), (<**=t**> *purposeful control transitivizer*), phonology: allomorph or deglottalization of =q', syntactic analysis: transitive verb, attested by Deming (4/17/80).

<**ts'elqéylém**>, mdls //c'əl=q=í·l=əm//, DIR /'*turn (oneself) around, make a U-turn*'/, TVMO, literally /'turn oneself around (on) something else'/ or /'turn one's head around durative'/, possibly lx <**=q ~ =q'**> *(on) something else* or perhaps <**=qel**> *(in) the head* with <**i:-ablaut**> *durative* or <**=í:l**> *go, come, get, become*), (<**=em**> *middle voice*), phonology: syllable-loss, updrifting, allomorph or deglottalization of =q', syntactic analysis: intransitive verb, attested by Deming (4/17/80), example: <**ts'elqéylém ta' (wákel, stiqíw, kyó, péki).**>, //c'əl=q=í·l=əm t-ɛʔ (wɛ́kəl, s=tiqíw, kʸá, pə́ki)//, /'*Turn your (wagon, horse, car, buggy) around.*'/, attested by Deming (4/17/80).

<**sts'élqes**>, ds //s=c'ə́l=q=əs or s=c'ə́l=q'=D=əs//, HUNT ['*whirled slingshot*'], ASM ['whirled from one end'], literally /'something to turn around something else on the face (or) something round to turn around something else'/, (<**s=**> *nominalizer, something to*), lx <**=q ~ =q'**> *(on) something else*, lx <**=es**> *on the face, round object*, phonology: allomorph or deglottalization of =q', syntactic analysis: nominal, attested by Deming (7/27/78), also <**tsélqes**>, //c'ə́l=q=əs or c'[=D=]ə́l=q=əs//, comment: ts probably mistranscribed for ts', phonology: possible deglottalization, attested by Elders Group (2/11/76), also <**th'élqos**>, //θ'ə́=q=as//, attested by Elders Group (11/26/75).

<**ts'á:lq'em**>, cts //c'ə[-Aɛ́·-]l=q'=əm//, TVMO /'*spinning (while hanging), (twirling)*'/, DIR, literally /'go/come/get turning around on something else (or) turning itself around on something else'/, (<**á:-ablaut**> *continuative*), lx <**=q'**> *on something else*, (<**=em**> *go/come/get/become or middle voice*), phonology: ablaut, syntactic analysis: intransitive verb, attested by Elders Group (10/13/76), also perhaps <**s'álq'em**> *hanging*, (which I strongly suspect is a computer typo for <ts'**álq'em**>), attested by RG & EH (4/9/99 Ling332).

<**ts'élexw**>, df //c'ə́l=əxʷ//, TVMO /'*turn back into a quiet slough from the river, be going into a slough from the river*'/, CAN, DIR, possibly <**=exw**> *round, around*, syntactic analysis: intransitive

verb, attested by Elders Group (2/26/75), also <**ts'éléxw**>, //c'ə́l=əxʷ//, also /*'(a fish) going into a quieter stream'*/, attested by Elders Group (7/20/77), example: <**ts'élexw te sthóqwi.**>, //c'ə́l=əxʷ tə s=θáqʷi//, /*'The fish is going into a slough from the river.'*/, attested by Elders Group (2/26/75).

<**sts'élexw**>, dnom //s=c'ə́l=əxʷ//, WATR /*'slough, backwater, ((also) eddy [AC])'*/, literally /'something to go into quieter water'/, (<**s=**> *nominalizer, something to*), syntactic analysis: nominal, attested by EB (6/14/78), also <**sts'èlèxw**>, //s=c'ə̀lə̀xʷ//, also /*'eddy, backwater'*/, attested by AC (9/1/71).

<**Sts'elxwíqw ~ Ts'elxwíqw ~ Ts'elxwéyeqw**>, ds //s=c'əl=(ə)xʷ=íqʷ ~ c'əl=(ə)xʷ=íqʷ//, PLN [*'Chilliwack River'*], SOCT [*'Chilliwack Indian people'*], ASM ['there are traditions that these people lived on the Chilliwack River from Chilliwack Lake to Soowahlie (the headquarters) and spoke a language closer to the Nooksack language than to Halkomelem, a language DM called <**Ch'élexwoqwem**> (Wells tapes, new transcript), sometime about the 1790's they began to mix with and adopt Upriver Halkomelem, a few placenames only survived (Th'ewálí, St'ept'ō̸p, Stútelō) and these are discussed in Galloway 1985c'], literally /'slough/backwater/quieter water at the top of the head (or) something to go into slough/quieter water from the river at the top of the head'/, (semological comment: perhaps so named because of the many (named) sloughs at the mouth of (top of the head of) the Chilliwack river where it formerly hit the Fraser River), lx <**=íqw**> *on the top of the head*, phonology: vowel-loss, phonology: this name is the source of the modern names of Chilliwack, B.C. and the former municipality of Chilliwhack nearby, syntactic analysis: nominal, attested by AC (8/4/70, 10/31/73), Elders Group (7/20/77), other sources: JH /c'ilxʷí·qʷ/ *slough, Chilliwack*, source: place names reference file #79, also <**Ch'elxwíqw ~ Ch'elxwí:qw ~ Ch'elxwéyeqw**>, //c'əl=xʷ=í(·)qʷ//, (semological comment: Wells glosses it as *Chilliwack River* and says it literally means *going back upstream, a backwater*, but on the same page is also gives it as the names for Dolly Varden Creek as well as Chilliwack Creek (= Chilliwack River), later he also says it was the name for a village below Centre Creek, an old village destroyed by a slide), attested by Wells 1965 (lst ed.):13, 19.

<**Ch'élexwoqwem**>, ds //c'ə́l=əxʷ=aqʷ=əm or c'ə́l=əxʷ=i[=Aa=]qʷ=əm//, LANG /*'the old Chilliwack language,* ([also prob.] *to speak the old Chilliwack language'*/, SOCT, (semological comment: this language was either midway between Halkomelem and Nooksack languages or was a dialect of lhéchelesem, the Nooksack language), possibly <**=íqw ~ =aqw ~ =eqw**> *on top of the head*, possibly <**o-ablaut**> *derivational*, (<**=em**> *intransitivizer/have/get, speak*), phonology: possible ablaut, syntactic analysis: nominal, (also prob. intransitive verb), attested by DM (Wells tapes, new transcripts),

<**sts'elxwíwel**>, ds //s=c'əl=(ə)xʷ=íwəl//, ANA /*'insides (animal or human or other?), (internal organs, guts, etc.), (stomach [inside]* [DM])'/, ASM ['(includes the guts, stomach, heart, liver, etc.)'], literally /'backwater/slough in the insides'/, lx <**=íwel**> *in the insides*, syntactic analysis: nominal, attested by AC (11/11/71), Deming (esp. SJ 5/3/79), other sources: ES /šc'əlxʷíwəl/ *guts*, also /*'stomach [inside]'*/, attested by DM (12/4/64), example: <**tsqwá:y te sts'elxwíwels te st'élém.**>, //c=qʷɛ́·y tə s=c'əl=əxʷ=íwəl-s tə s=t'ə́l=əm//, /*'The inside/inner cherry bark is green.'*/, attested by Deming (esp. SJ).

<**ts'elxwí:wsem**>, mdls //c'əl=(ə)xʷ=í·ws=əm//, ABFC [*'relieved (in one's body)'*], literally /'turn into quieter water on (in?) one's body'/, lx <**=í:w**> *on the body*, (<**=em**> *middle voice*), syntactic analysis: intransitive verb, attested by Elders Group (3/23/77).

<**ts'eláltxw**>, SOC [*'steal someone's spouse'*], *see* ts'el.

<**tsʼeláxw**>, possible strs stem //c'əl(=)ə[=Aɛ́=]xʷ//, prob. from stem <**ts'élexw**>, df //c'ə́l=əxʷ//, TVMO

/'*turn back into a quiet slough from the river*, *see* ts'el.

<**sts'eláxwem**>, df //s=c'əl(=)ə[=Aɛ́=]xʷ=əm//, SPRD ['*an experienced spirit dancer*'], ASM ['a dancer for four years or more'], literally possibly /'something (or someone) that has gotten into quieter water'/, (<**s=**> *nominalizer, something that, (rarely) someone that*), possibly <**á-ablaut**> *resultative or durative*, (<**=em**> *intransitivizer/get/become or middle voice*), phonology: possible ablaut, syntactic analysis: nominal, attested by IHTTC (8/22/77), AC (11/10/71), Salish cognate: Samish dial. of NSt /sč'ə́xʷəŋ'/ *a spirit dancer (old or new), Indian dancer* G86a:81, possibly same root as Squamish /č'i(y)ʔ/ *to fast* (K67:321).

<**ts'eléletl'xel**>, BPI ['*has short legs*'], *see* ts'í:tl' ~ ts'ítl'.

<**ts'élexw**>, TVMO /'*turn back into a quiet slough from the river, be going into a slough from the river*'/, *see* ts'el.

<**ts'elqéylém**>, DIR /'*turn (oneself) around, make a U-turn*'/, *see* ts'el.

<**ts'elqéylt** or **ts'elqí:lt**>, DIR ['*turn s-th around*'], *see* ts'el.

<**ts'élxet**>, MED ['*delouse s-o*'], *see* méxts'el.

<**ts'élxetel**>, MED ['*delouse each other, looking for lice in each other's head*'], *see* méxts'el.

<**ts'elxwí:wsem**>, ABFC ['*relieved (in one's body)*'], *see* ts'el.

<**ts'elh=**>, dp //c'əɬ= *(person) next to, close to*//.

<**ts'elh'á:y**>, ds //c'əɬ=ʔɛ́·y//, SOCT /'*sweetheart, person of the opposite sex that one is running around with, girl-friend, boy-friend*'/, literally /'a person one keeps next to/close to, a person one keeps going next to/close to'/, (<**ts'elh=**> *person next to, person close to*), root <**á:y**> *keep on, keep on going*, syntactic analysis: nominal, attested by Elders Group (10/1/75), EB (12/12/75), example: <**the ts'elh'á:y**>, //θə c'əɬ=ʔɛ́·y//, /'*the girl-friend, the (female) sweetheart*'/, attested by EB, <**tl'é ts'elh'á:ys**>, //ƛ'á c'əɬ=ʔɛ́·y-s//, /'*That's his sweetheart.*'/, attested by Elders Group, <**the ts'elh'á:ys te Brent**>, //θə c'əɬ=ʔɛ́·y-s tə Brent//, /'*Brent's sweetheart, the (female) one Brent is running around with*'/, attested by Elders Group.

<**ts'lhimexóstel**>, rcps //c'əɬ=(ʔ)im=əxʸ=ás=təl//, SOCT /'*going with each other [romantically], going for a walk with each other*'/, literally /'go for a walk close/next to each other'/, (<**ts'elh=**> *next to, close to*), root <**ím**> *step*, lx <**=ex**> *upright*, lx <**=ós**> *round object, cyclic period*, (<**=tel**> *reciprocal, each other*), phonology: consonant-loss in root, syntactic analysis: intransitive verb, attested by MV (Deming 5/4/78), example: <**tl'ó yewá:lelh ts'lhimexóstels.**>, //ƛ'á yəwɛ́·l-əɬ c'əɬ=(ʔ)im=əxʸ=ás=təl-s//, /'*That's the first one (past) he was going with., That's the first one he was going for a walk with.*'/, attested by MV.

<**ts'élhxwélmexw**>, ds //c'ə[=´=]ɬ=xʷə́l(=)məxʷ//, SOCT ['*neighbor*'], literally /'next/close-to Indian person'/, possibly <**=´=**> *derivational*, root <**xwélmexw**> *Indian, (Indian) person*, phonology: stress-shift, syntactic analysis: nominal, attested by Elders Group (11/12/75).

<**ts'elhxwílmexw**>, pln //cə(l)ɬ=xʷə[=Aí=]l(=)məxʷ//, SOCT ['*near neighbors*'], possibly <**í-ablaut**> *plural*, phonology: ablaut, the <**l**> before <**lh**> is unexplained, syntactic analysis: nominal, attested by EB and AD (9/26/78).

<**ts'elhkw'á:ls**>, ABFC ['*pinch*'], *see* th'lhákw'.

<**ts'élhxwélmexw**>, SOCT ['*neighbor*'], *see* ts'elh=.

<**ts'elhxwílmexw**>, SOCT ['*near neighbors*'], *see* ts'elh=.

<**ts'elhx̱à:m**>, SOC /'*cry with someone, a person one cries with (related or not), unrelated grandparents*

of a deceased grandchild, etc.'/, *see* x̲à:m ~ x̲á:m.

<**ts'elh'á:y**>, SOCT /*'sweetheart, person of the opposite sex that one is running around with, girl-friend, boy-friend'*/, *see* ts'elh=.

<**ts'emxó:ythel**>, df //c'əm(=ə)xʸ=á·yθəl//, ANA /*'chin, jaw (of fish, human, etc.), (lips (both), cheek, side of the face [DM])'*/, probable root <**ts'ém**> *bite*, possibly <**=ex**> *upright, vertical?*, lx <**=ó:ythel**> *of the jaw*, syntactic analysis: nominal, attested by AC, BJ (5/10/64), DM (12/4/64), Deming (4/1/76), contrast Cowichan /sθ'əmʔáyθən/ *jaw* B74b:20, other sources: JH /c'əmxáyθəl *chin*, H-T <sumqai'EtsEl, sumkai'Etsum> *jaw*, Salish cognate: possibly Shuswap root /k'em/ *surface* as in many body part words such as /t-k'm-épeʔs-qn/ *chin* and /t-k'm-cín'/ *lip, edge* K74:213, also /*'lips (both), chin, cheek, side of the face'*/, attested by DM (12/4/64).

<**ts'ep**>, probable root //c'ə́p// *dirty (esp. of skin, also of house).*

<**ts'epí:wel**>, ds //c'əp=í·wəl//, BPI /*'(have a) dirty behind, (dirty in the rump, dirty in the rectum)'*/, lx <**=í:wel**> *in the insides, in the rump*, syntactic analysis: adjective/adjectival verb, attested by Elders Group (5/13/75).

<**ts'épxel**>, ds //c'ə́p=xʸəl//, BPI [*'(have) dirty feet'*], lx <**=xel**> *on the foot*, syntactic analysis: adjective/adjectival verb, attested by Elders Group (5/13/75).

<**sts'épxwel ~ sch'épxwel**>, ds //s=c'ə́p=xʷ=əl//, ABDF [*'wart'*], (<**s=**> *nominalizer*), possibly <**=xw**> *around in circle, lump?*, possibly <**=el**> *come/go/get/become*, syntactic analysis: nominal, attested by NP (10/26/75), Salish cognate: Squamish /sč'ə́pxʷəlʔ/ *wart* W73:282, K67:288.

<**ts'épx̲**>, probably stem //c'ə́p=x̣ *dirty (esp. of body parts, also of house)*//. <**=x̲**> *distributive, all over.*

<**sts'épx̲**>, stvi //s=c'ə́p=x̣//, DESC [*'be dirty'*], (<**s=**> *stative*), possibly <**=x̲**> *distributive, all over*, syntactic analysis: adjective/adjectival verb, attested by EB (1/19/76), compare with <**ts'ápex̲el**> *it got rusty*, Salish cognate: Sechelt /č'ə́px̣/ *dirty* T77:21, example: <**sts'épx̲ te láléms.**>, //s=c'ə́p=x̣ tə lɛ́[=C₁ə=]m-s//, /*'Her house is dirty.'*/, attested by EB, <**kwélhtu sts'épx̲ te láléms.**>, //kʷə́ɬ=t=əw s=c'ə́p=x̣ tə lɛ́[=C₁ə=]m-s//, /*'She's got a (really) dirty house.'*/, attested by EB.

<**ts'epx̲élqsel**>, ds //c'əp=x̣=ə́l(=)qs(=)əl//, BPI [*'(have a) dirty nose'*], lx <**=x̲**> *distributive, all over*, lx <**=élqsel ~ =eqs ~ =élqs ~ =éqsel ~ =eqsel**> *on the nose*, possibly <**=el**> *go/come/get/become*, syntactic analysis: adjective/adjectival verb, attested by Deming (3/4/76).

<**ts'épx̲es**>, ds //c'ə́p=x̣=əs//, BPI [*'(have a) dirty face'*], lx <**=x̲**> *distributive, all over*, lx <**=es**> *on the face*, syntactic analysis: adjective/adjectival verb, attested by Elders Group (3/72, 5/13/75).

<**ts'epx̲tses**>, ds //c'ə́p=x̣=cəs//, BPI [*'(have) dirty hands'*], lx <**=x̲**> *distributive, all over*, lx <**=tses**> *on the hand*, syntactic analysis: adjective/adjectival verb, attested by Elders Group (6/16/76).

<**ts'épx̲el**>, BPI [*'(have) dirty feet'*], *see* ts'épx̲.

<**ts'epx̲élqsel**>, BPI [*'(have a) dirty nose'*], *see* ts'épx̲.

<**ts'épx̲es**>, BPI [*'(have a) dirty face'*], *see* ts'épx̲.

<**ts'epx̲tses**>, BPI [*'(have) dirty hands'*], *see* ts'épx̲.

<**ts'ep'ét**>, pcs //c'əp'=M1=T//, MC [*'dab it on'*], root meaning unknown, probably <**metathesis type 1**> *non-continuative*, (<**=t**> *purposeful control transitivizer*), phonology: probable metathesis, syntactic analysis: transitive verb, attested by Elders Group (5/26/76).

<**ts'éq'**>, free root //c'ə́q'//, EFAM [*'be surprised'*], syntactic analysis: intransitive verb, Elder's comment: "Adaline says this is in the old language her husband [Ed Lorenzetto] learned from the old lady [MJ?]", attested by Elders Group (2/16/77), AL (Elders Group 3/1/72), Salish cognate: Squamish

/č'ə́q'/ *be surprised* W73:258, K69:68, also /'*I'm surprised.*'/, attested by Elders Group (2/16/77), example: <**le ts'éq'.**>, //lə c'ə́q'//, /'*(He/She was) astonished, surprised*'/, attested by AL (Elders Group 3/1/72), <**ts'áts'eltsel ts'éq'.**>, //c'ɛ́[=C_1ə=]l-c-əl c'ə́q'//, /'*I'm really surprised.*'/, attested by AL (Elders Group 3/1/72).

<**ts'éqw ~ th'éqw**>, bound root //c'ə́qʷ ~ θ'ə́qʷ//, root meaning unknown.

<**Ts'éqwela ~ Th'éqwela**>, df //c'ə́qʷ=əlɛ ~ θ'ə́qʷ=əlɛ//, PLN ['*a fairly flat clearing on a mountain in Morris Valley where they used to play ts'its'eqweló:l or Indian badminton*'], ASM ['the game was played with cedar things that have wings (winged cedar seeds?), the place was located on the Harrison River side of Morris Lake Mountain'], root meaning unknown unless related to th'í:qw' *punch, hit with fist*, probably <**=ela**> meaning uncertain unless> *on the side of the head, cheek*, comment: the suffix seems cognate with that in Squamish and in Northern Straits (Samish /-əláʔ/ *structured activity (non-continuative)* (G84a:38)), syntactic analysis: nominal, dialects: *Cheh.*, attested by EL (Chehalis Place Names trip 9/27/77), EL (3/1/78 tape), source: place names reference file #292, 292a, Salish cognate: Squamish /č'qʷə́laʔ/ *hockey-like game* W73:111, K69:67.

<**Sth'éqwela**>, dnom //s=θ'ə́qʷ=əlɛ//, PLN ['*Morris Lake Mountain*'], (<**s=**> *nominalizer*), syntactic analysis: nominal, attested by EL (Chehalis Place Names trip 9/27/77), source: place names reference file #304, Salish cognate: Squamish /s-č'qʷə́laʔ/ *the puck (for a hockey-like game)* W73:111, K69:67.

<**ts'íts'qweló:l**>, df //C_1í=c'əqʷ=əlɛ=á·l or C_1í=c'əqʷ=əlá·=əl//, PLAY /'*Indian badminton (played with cedar things that have wings), (grass shinny (a game like grass hockey, uses a big round ball) [BJ])*'/, (<**R4=**> *diminutive*), root meaning unknown, possibly <**=ela** or **=elá:**> meaning uncertain, possibly <**=el**> *go/come/get/become*, phonology: reduplication, vowel merger, syntactic analysis: nominal?, attested by EL (Chehalis place names trip 9/27/77), also /'*grass shinny (a game like grass hockey, uses a big round ball)*'/, attested by BJ (12/5/64)(Wells tapes, new transcript old p.397), other sources: ES /k'ʷɛ́yk'ʷqʷəyáls/ (CwMs /k'ʷək'ʷqʷəyáls/) *shinny (game)*, historical/comparative detail: the forms in Elmendorf and Suttles (and Upriver Halkomelem <kw'ekw'iyó:ls> in this dictionary) mean literally *clubbing a spherical object with a stick-like object* and seem more likely to refer to *shinny*, the game played with a round ball, the form just above does not seem to have the same suffix and so seems more likely to refer to *Indian badminton*, which was not played with a spherical ball but with winged cedar seeds.

<**Ts'éqwela ~ Th'éqwela**>, PLN ['*a fairly flat clearing on a mountain in Morris Valley where they used to play ts'its'eqweló:l or Indian badminton*'], *see* ts'éqw ~ th'éqw.

<**ts'éqw'**>, rsls //c'ə́q'ʷ//, HUNT /'*be hit (with arrow, bullet, anything shot that you've aimed), got shot, (got pierced), got poked into, got wounded (with gun or arrow)*'/, EFAM ['*be overcome with pleasurable feelings after eating great salmon or a great meal*'], phonology: possible ablaut, syntactic analysis: intransitive verb, attested by Elders Group (2/19/75, 3/2/77), EB (11/28/75, 4/23/76, 5/12/76), Salish cognate: Musqueam /c'ə́q'ʷ/ *get pierced* Suttles ca1984ms:ch.7, p.106, example: <**le ts'éqw'.**>, //lə c'ə́q'ʷ//, /'*He got shot (arrow, bullet, etc.).*'/, attested by EB (11/28/75).

<**ts'qw'ét**>, pcs //c'ə́q'ʷ-M1=T//, MC /'*poke it, pin s-th, pick it up (on sharp pointed object), pick s-th up on a fork (or other sharp object)*'/, (<**metathesis type 1**> *non-continuative*), (<**=t**> *purposeful control transitivizer*), phonology: metathesis, syntactic analysis: transitive verb, attested by CT and HT (6/21/76), EB (5/3/76, 4/23/76, 5/25/76, 5/26//76), example: <**ts'qw'ét te sqá:wth qesu me lhá:x̱em í tel lóthel**>, //c'ə́q'ʷ=M1=T tə s=qɛ́·w(=)θ qə-s-u mə ɬɛ́·x̣=əm ʔí t-əl láθəl//, /'*poke/pick up the potato (with a fork) and put it (serve yourself) on my dish*'/, attested by CT and HT, <**ts'qw'ét kwthéstàmès li kw'e sts'óqw'els qesu lhá:x̱em**>, //c'ə́q'ʷ=M1=T kʷθə s=tɛ́m=əs li k'ʷə

s=c'áq'ʷ=əls qə-s-u ɬɛ́·x̣=əm//, */'pick something up on a fork and serve yourself (on a dish)'/*, attested by CT and HT (6/21/76), <**qesu mí ts'qw'ét te sqá:wth**>, //qə-s-u mí c'ə́q'ʷ=M1=T tə s=qɛ́·w(=)θ//, */'and come poke the potato'/*, attested by CT and HT; found in <**ts'qw'étem**>, //c'ə́q'ʷ=M1=T-əm//, */'He got shot., (Somebody shot him.)'/*, syntactic analysis: passive, attested by EB (4/23/76).

<**ts'eqw'ts'eqw'thóxes**>, plv //C_1əC_2=c'ə́q'ʷ=T-áxʸ-əs//, cts, if, ABDF [*'he/she/it is poking me [purposely]'*], (<**R3=**> *plural (subject/action)*), (<**-óx**> *me (object)*), (<**-es**> *third person subject*), phonology: reduplication, syntactic analysis: transitive verb, attested by AC (11/19/71).

<**ts'eqw'eláxw**>, ncs //c'əq'ʷ=l-ɛ́xʷ//, HUNT [*'hit with an arrow accidentally'*], (<**=l**> *non-control transitivizer, accidentally/managed to*), (<**-exw ~ -áxw (after CəC roots where C is obstruent)**> *third person object*), phonology: allomorph (as noted in Suttles consonant alternation1984 ms. ch.7), syntactic analysis: transitive verb, attested by Elders Group (2/19/75).

<**ts'eqw'ts'éqw' ~ ts'éqw'ts'eqw'**>, dnom //C_1əC_2=c'ə́q'ʷ or c'ə́q'ʷ=C_1əC_2//, EB */'Scotch thistle,* (includes two introduced thistles and probably two native ones, from samples gathered, pressed and examined: *Scotch thistle, Canada thistle,* probably *montane edible thistle* and *Indian thistle)'/*, [*'Cirseum vulgare, Cirseum arvense,* and probably *Cirseum edule, Cirseum brevistylum'*], Elder's comment: "a made-up name that means *poke-poke*, made-up since they had no Scotch thistles before the Whites came (AC)", MED ['EF (Deming 9/21/78) noted that bull thistle roots could be chewed in thumbnail sized bit for insomnia, but noted it was poison in big quantities, she did not remember the Halkomelem word for this thistle and it may or may not be the same word given here'], possibly <**=R2**> *characteristic*, possibly <**R3=**> *plural*, phonology: stress omitted in field notes, reduplication, syntactic analysis: nominal, attested by AC (11/19/71), other sources: ES /c'əq'ʷc'ə́q'ʷ/ *Scotch thistle*, also <**ts'eqw'ts'éqw'**>, //C_1əC_2=c'ə́q'ʷ//, */'thorn'/*, attested by Elders Group (5/21/75).

<**ts'ets'éqw'**>, df //C_1ə=c'ə́q'ʷ//, EB [*'needle of spruce'*], (<**R5=**> *diminutive or derivational*), phonology: reduplication, syntactic analysis: nominal, attested by Elders Group (3/22/78).

<**ts'qw'élhp**>, ds //c'ə́q'ʷ=ə[=M2=]ɬp//, EB */'spruce tree, Sitka spruce'/*, [*'Picea sitchensis'*], literally /'pierce/poke tree'/, lx <**=elhp**> *tree, plant*, (<**metathesis**> *derivational*), phonology: metathesis, vowel-loss, syntactic analysis: nominal, attested by Elders Group (1/29/75), AC, others, other sources: ES and JH /c'q'ʷə́ɬp/ *spruce*, example: <**ts'qw'élhp kwémléxw**>, //c'ə́q'ʷ=ə[=M2=]ɬp kʷə́mlə́xʷ//, */'spruce root(s)'/*, attested by AC.

<**ts'qw'élá**>, ds //c'ə́q'ʷ=ə[=M2=]lɛ or c'əq'ʷ=ə́lɛ//, CLO [*'ear-ring'*], PE, literally /'pierce/poke on the ear/side of the head'/, lx <**=éla ~ =ela**> *on the side of the head, on the ear*, possibly <**metathesis**> *derivational*, phonology: possible metathesis, updrifting, syntactic analysis: nominal, attested by Elders Group (9/24/75).

<**ts'eqw'eláx**>, df //c'əq'ʷ=əl=ə[=Aɛ́=]xʸ//, HUNT [*'arrow'*], probably root <**ts'eqw'**> *pierce, hit with something shot*, possibly <**=el**> *go/come/get/become*, possibly <**=ex**> *upright?*, possibly <**á-ablaut**> *durative or derivational*, phonology: possible ablaut, syntactic analysis: nominal, comment: possibly a back-formation after <**sákw'elàx**> *arrow* which has cognates but has a different root and stem, <**kw'él=ex**> *shoot (an arrow/gun)* with root <**kw'él**> *hold*, contrast <**sákw'elàx**> *arrow*, attested by RP (BHTTC 10/18/76), not recognized by others in Elders Group (10/20/76).

<**ts'eqw'eléstel**>, ds //c'əq'ʷ=ilə[= ́=]s=təl//, CLO */'brooch, pin (ornament pinned to clothing)'/*, PE, literally /'device/something to pin on the chest'/, lx <**=iles**> *on the chest*, probably <**= ́=**> *derivational*, lx <**=tel**> *device, something to*, phonology: probable stress-shift, vowel-reduction, syntactic analysis: nominal, attested by Elders Group (9/24/75), Elders at Fish Camp (JL, NP, Deming)(7/19/79).

<**ts'eqw'élqsel**>, ds //c'əq'ʷ=ə́lqsəl//, ABDF ['*(have a) scabby nose*'], literally /'got pierced/poked into on the nose'/, lx <**=élqsel**> *on the nose*, syntactic analysis: intransitive verb, attested by Elders Group (1/30/80).

<**sts'ó:qw'els**>, dnom //s=c'ə[=Aá·=]q'ʷ=əls//, sas, HHG ['*fork*'], FOOD, literally /'something for piercing/poking into as a structured activity'/, (<**s=**> *nominalizer*), root <**ts'eqw'**> *pierce, poke into*, (<**ó:-ablaut**> *derivational or durative*), (<**=els**> *structured activity continuative nominal*), phonology: ablaut, syntactic analysis: nominal, attested by EB (11/28/75), AD (8/80), CT (6/21/76), NP (1026/75), example: <**alétsa te sts'ó:qw'els?**>, //ʔɛlə́cɛ tə s=c'ə[=Aá·=]q'ʷ=əls//, /'*Where's the fork?*'/, attested by AD, <**ts'qw'ét kwthéstàmès li kw'e sts'óqw'els qesu lhá:x̱em**>, //c'ə́q'ʷ=M1=T kʷθə s=tɛ́m=əs li k'ʷə s=c'áq'ʷ=əls qə-s-u ɬɛ́·x̣=əm//, /'*pick something up on a fork and serve yourself (on a dish)*'/, attested by CT and HT, <**íkw'elò te sts'ó:qw'els.**>, //ʔí=k'ʷə=là tə s=c'ə[=Aá·=]q'ʷ=əls//, /'*This+is a fork.*'/, attested by NP.

<**sts'éqw' ~ sch'éqw'**>, dnom //s=c'ə́q'ʷ//, BSK /'*fine cedar root weaving, fine cedar root work*'/, literally /'something that got pierced/poked'/, (semological comment: prob. so named because one uses an awl to poke holes in the roots in the basket as one weaves, and the roots are poked through each other in places), (<**s=**> *nominalizer*), syntactic analysis: nominal, attested by Elders Group (6/11/75, 3/24/76), example: <**sts'éqw' syó:ys**>, //s=c'ə́q'ʷ s=yá·ys//, /'*fine cedar root work (only roots used)*'/, attested by Elders Group (6/11/75).

<**ts'eqw'ő:welh ~ ts'eqw'ő́welh ~ ch'eqw'ő́welh**>, ds //c'əq'ʷ=ó·wəɬ ~ c'əq'ʷ=ówəɬ//, BSK ['*to weave a cedar root basket*'], literally /'pierce/poke into vessel/canoe/?basket'/, lx <**=ő:welh ~ =ő́welh ~ =ewelh**> *canoe, vessel, basket?*, syntactic analysis: intransitive verb, attested by Elders Group (6/11/75), AC (8/13/70), also <**ts'qw'ő́welh ~ ts'qw'ő́wélh ~ th'qw'ő́welh**>, //c'əq'ʷ=ówəɬ ~ θ'əq'ʷ=ówəɬ//, attested by EB (IHTTC 9/2/77, 12/19/75), example: <**líchexw slhéq'alexw kw'as ch'eqw'ő́welh?**>, //lí-c-əxʷ s=ɬə́=q'ɛl=l-əxʷ k'ʷ-ɛ-s c'əq'ʷ=ówəɬ//, /'*Do you know how to make a basket?*'/, literally /'do you have knowledge of it that you weave a basket'/, attested by AC, <**yalhòlse ts'qw'ő́wélh.**>, //yɛɬ=à-l-s-ə c'əq'ʷ=ówəɬ//, /'*I started to make a basket.*'/, attested by EB (12/19/75), <**yálho'ó kw'a'sé ts'qw'ő́welh.**>, //yɛ́ɬ=a à k'ʷ-ɛʔ-s-ə c'əq'ʷ=ówəɬ//, /'*You just start to make a basket.*'/, attested by EB (12/19/75), <**qá:ysò le ts'eqwő́wélh.**>, //qɛ́·ys-à lə c'əq'ʷ=ówəɬ//, /'*He just now made a basket.*'/, attested by EB (12/19/75), <**totí:ltes te syó:ys te ts'qw'ő:welhs.**>, //ta[-C_1ə-]l=í·l=T-əs tə s=yá·ys-s tə c'əq'ʷ=ó·wəɬ-s//, /'*He/She is learning basketwork.*'/, literally /'he/she is learning s-th the work -of the his/her make a basket'/, attested by Elders Group (3/16/77), also <**totí:ltes kws thíytes te ts'qw'ő:welh.**>, //ta[-C_1ə-]l=í·l=T-əs kʷ-s θíy=T-s tə c'əq'ʷ=ó·wəɬ//, attested by EB (Elders Group 3/16/77).

<**th'éqw'ōwelh ~** (probably **ts'éqw'ōwelh)**>, cts //θ'ə[-´-]q'ʷ=owəɬ ~ c'ə[-´-]q'ʷ=əwəɬ//, BSK /'*making a basket, (weaving a cedar root basket)*'/, (<**-´-**> *continuative*), phonology: stress-shift, syntactic analysis: intransitive verb, attested by EB (IHTTC 9/27/77).

<**sch'eqw'ő́welh**>, dnom //s=c'əq'ʷ=ówəɬ//, BSK ['*basket-weaving*'], (<**s=**> *nominalizer*), syntactic analysis: nominal, attested by AC (11/17/71), example: <**hókwixtsel li tel sch'eqw'ő́welh.**>, //hákʷ=əxʸ-c-əl li t-əl s=c'əq'ʷ=ówəɬ//, /'*I'm using it on my basket-weaving.*'/, attested by AC.

<**ts'eqw'eláx**>, HUNT ['*arrow*'], *see* ts'éqw'.

<**ts'eqw'eláxw**>, HUNT ['*hit with an arrow accidentally*'], *see* ts'éqw'.

<**ts'eqw'eléstel**>, CLO /'*brooch, pin (ornament pinned to clothing)*'/, *see* ts'éqw'.

<**ts'eqw'elítsetel**>, df //c'əq'ʷ=əlíc=təl//, CAN ['*a boom on a boat*'], possibly root <**ts'qw'**> as in <**ts'qw'ét**> *prop it up on a Y-like object*, lx <**=elíts**> *on the back*, lx <**=tel**> *device to, something to,*

syntactic analysis: nominal, attested by AK (Elders Group 1/23/80).

<**ts'eqw'élqsel**>, ABDF ['*(have a) scabby nose*'], *see* ts'éqw'.

<**ts'eqw'ő:welh ~ ts'eqw'ő́welh ~ ch'eqw'ő́welh**>, BSK ['*to weave a cedar root basket*'], *see* ts'éqw'.

<**ts'eqw'ts'éqw'**>, EB /'*Scotch thistle,* (includes two *introduced thistles* and probably two *native ones,* from samples gathered, pressed and examined: *Scotch thistle, Canada thistle,* probably *montane edible thistle and Indian thistle)*'/, *see* ts'éqw'.

<**ts'eqw'ts'eqw'thóxes**>, ABDF ['*he/she/it is poking me [purposely]*'], *see* ts'éqw'.

<**ts'esémelep ~ ts'esémelép**>, EB ['*weeds in a garden*'], *see* ts'ísem.

<**ts'esláts**>, df //c'əs=lɛ́c or c'is=lɛ́c or c'əs=əl=ɛ́c//, EB /'*fresh saskatoon berry, service-berry, June berry*'/, ['*Amelanchier alnifolia*'], ASM ['ripen in July, best ones are above Hope, fresh berries are eaten when available but dried berries were obtained pressed into cakes from the Thompson and other Interior groups where more berries grow, the berries are black in color'], possibly root <**ts'es**> *black* as in <**ts'ésqsel**>*"black-nose" or "smut" (a card game),* possibly root <**ts'is**> *grow*, possibly <**=láts ~ =lets**> *on the bottom*, possibly <**=el**> *go/come/get/become*, possibly <**=áts**> a rare variant of <**=tses**> *on the hand*, phonology: possible vowel-reduction, syntactic analysis: nominal, attested by Elders Group (7/2/75, 7/9/75).

<**ts'eslátselhp**>, ds //c'əs=lɛ́c=əɬp//, EB /'*saskatoon bush, service-berry bush*'/, ['*Amelanchier alnifolia*'], lx <**=elhp**> *plant, tree*, syntactic analysis: nominal.

<**ts'eslátselhp**>, EB /'*saskatoon bush, service-berry bush*'/, *see* ts'esláts.

<**ts'ésqel**>, ds //c'ə́s=qəl//, EZ ['*golden eagle*'], ['*Aquila chrysaetos*'], literally perhaps /'black in the head'/, ASM ['had a dark brown head (and body) with a golden nape visible only at close range'], possibly root <**ts'és**> *dark brown, black* possibly root as in <**ts'ésqsel**> *"black-nose" or "smut" (a card game in which the nose is colored black on the loser)*, lx <**=qel**> *in the head*, syntactic analysis: nominal, attested by Elders Group (6/4/75, 7/9/75, 2/18/76, 2/23/80), other sources: ES and JH /c'ə́sqəl/ (CwMs /c'ə́sqən/) *golden eagle*, Salish cognate: Squamish /č'ə́sqn/ *snow eagle, golden eagle* W73:87, K69:67, but only *golden eagle (Aquila chrysaetos)* in Bouchard and Kennedy 1976:72, Saanich /č'ə́sqən/ *golden eagle*.

<**ts'ésqsel**>, ds //c'ə́s=qsəl//, PLAY ['*"black-nose" or "smut" card game*'], ASM ['a card game like Old Maid (hide one odd extra card, pair off during the game, whoever gets stuck with the hidden card after all other cards are paired off loses and gets painted black on the tip of his nose, as more games are played, if the same player loses again he gets more of his nose blackened, then his cheeks or forehead are started on (Elders Group 2/13/80)'], literally /'black on the nose'/, root <**ts'és**> *black* root <**a rare bound root clearly glossed only in this stem**, lx <**=qsel**> *on the nose*, syntactic analysis: nominal, attested by Elders Group (11/12/75, 2/18/76, 2/13/80).

<**ts'étl' ~ ch'étl'**> or <**wets'étl' ~ wech'étl'**>, possibly root or stem //c'ə́ƛ' or wəc'ə́ƛ' or wə=c'ə́ƛ' or wə=c'i[=Aə́=]ƛ'//

<**wets'étl' ~ wech'étl'**>, possibly root //wəc'ə́ƛ' or wə=c'ə́ƛ' or wə=c'i[=Aə́=]ƛ'//, TVMO /'*fell of its own accord (of an object from a height or from upright), drop down (object/person, from a shelf, bridge, cliff, etc.), fall off*'/, possibly <**we=**> *suddenly*, possibly root <**ts'étl'** or **ts'ítl'**> *short*, possibly <**é-ablaut on root i**> *resultative or derivational*, phonology: possible ablaut, syntactic analysis: intransitive verb, attested by EB (12/15/75), AC, Elders Group (3/72), HT (6/8/76), CT (6/8/76), example: <**le wech'étl'.**>, //lə wə(=)c'ə́ƛ'//, /'*He dropped down., He fell off.*'/, attested by AC (10/13/71), <**me wets'étl'.**>, //mə wə(=)c'ə́ƛ'//, /'*It dropped (from a shelf, for ex.).*'/, attested by

EB, <**le wets'étl' te stl'ítl'qelh li te shxwt'álh.**>, //lə wə(=)c'ə́ƛ' tə s=C₁í=ƛ'əq=əɬ li tə sxʷ=t'ɛ́ɬ//, /'*A child drops off a bridge.*'/, attested by HT, <**le wets'étl' te qó: li te qw'eléqel.**>, //lə wə(=)c'ə́ƛ' tə qá· li tə q'ʷələ́qəl//, /'*a drop-off, The water drops off a cliff.*'/, attested by CT.

<**wets'étl'lexw**>, ncs //wə(=)c'ə́ƛ'=l-əxʷ//, ABDF ['*drop s-th by accident*'], (<**=l**> *non-control transitivizer, accidentally, happen to, manage to*), (<**-exw**> *third person object*), syntactic analysis: transitive verb, attested by EB (2/9/76).

<**ts'ets'éqw'**>, EB ['*needle of spruce*'], *see* ts'éqw'.

<**ts'exwí:lthet**>, LANG ['*one gets silent*'], *see* ts'áxw.

<**ts'ex̱ ~ th'ex̱**>, root //c'əx̣ or θ'əx̣//, probably *wash* or *clean*

<**sts'ets'íx̱**>, strs //s=c'ə[=C₁əAí=]x̣ or s=C₁ə=c'ə[=Aí=]x̣//, BLDG (perhaps) ['*(be) clean (of a house)*'], DESC, (<**s=**> *stative*), possibly <**í-ablaut**> *resultative*, possibly <**R5=** or **=R1=**> *resultative*, phonology: reduplication, ablaut, possible delabialization, syntactic analysis: adjective/adjectival verb, attested by EB (1/16/76), compare <**th'x̱ét**> *(*possibly*) clean s-th*, contrast root <**th'éx̱w**> *wash*.

<**ts'éx̱wts'ex̱w** (or more correct) **th'éxwth'exw**>, EFAM ['*pity*'], *see* th'íxw ~ th'éxw.

<**ts'ílém**>, TVMO /'*mounting a horse, mounting a person*'/, *see* ts'á:.

<**ts'ílem**>, TVMO ['*get on top of something*'], *see* ts'á:.

<**ts'ímél ~ ts'ímel**>, ds //c'ím=əl//, DIR /'*get close, approach, get near, nearly, (go close, come close)*'/, probably <**=el**> *go, come, get, become*, phonology: optional updrifting, syntactic analysis: adverb/adverbial verb, attested by AC (11/17/71), EB (12/15/75, 4/5/76, 4/12/78), Elders Group (3/1/72), Deming (1/20/77), Salish cognate: Squamish /č'ím-i/ *approach* K67:321, example: <**me ts'ímel**>, //mə c'ím=əl//, /'*approach (your nets for ex.), get close, (come close)*'/, literally /'come get close'/, attested by Elders Group, <**le ts'ímél**>, //lə c'ím=əl//, /'*approach (your nets for ex.), get close, (go close)*'/, attested by Elders Group, <**welh ts'ímel tl'ékw'el.**>, //wəɬ c'ím=əl ƛ'ə́k'ʷ=əl//, /'*It's nearly going out (of fire).*'/, literally /'already nearly go out (of fire)'/, attested by EB, <**wets'ímél te slhíxws**>, //wə-c'ím=əl tə s=ɬíxʷ=s//, /'*nearly three o'clock*'/, literally /'if/when nearly the three o'clock'/, attested by Deming, <**le ts'ímél kws wets'á:s.**>, //lə c'ím=əl kʷ-s wə-c'ɛ́·-əs//, /'*He's nearly got to the top.*'/, attested by EB (4/5/76), <**látsel t'ókw' wets'ímeles te Christmas.**>, //lɛ́-c-əl t'ák'ʷ wə-c'ím=əl-əs tə Christmas//, /'*I'm going home near Christmas.*'/, literally /'I'm going home when it gets near the Christmas'/, attested by AC.

<**ts'íts'emel**>, cts //c'í[-C₁ə-]m=əl//, DIR ['*getting close*'], (<**-R1-**> *continuative*), phonology: reduplication, syntactic analysis: adverb/adverbial verb, attested by EB (4/12/78).

<**ts'ímélmet**>, iecs //c'ím=əl=məT//, TVMO /'*get close to s-o/s-th, approach s-th/s-o*'/, DIR, (<**=met**> *indirect effect non-control transitivizer*), phonology: updrifting, syntactic analysis: transitive verb, attested by Elders Group (3/1/72), EB (4/12/78), example: <**le ts'imélmet. ~ me ts'imélmet. ~ le ts'ímele kw'e stetís.**>, //lə c'ím=əl=məT ~ mə c'ím=əl=məT ~ lə c'ím=əl-ə k'ʷə s=C₁ə=tə[Aí=]s//, /'*approach it*'/, literally /'go get close to s-th ~ come get close to s-th ~ go just get close to s-th which is nearby'/, attested by Elders Group (3/1/72).

<**ts'ímélthet**>, pcrs //c'ím=əl=T-ət//, TVMO ['*approach (your nets for ex.)*'], (<**=t**> *purposeful control transitivizer*), (<**-et**> *reflexive*), phonology: updrifting, syntactic analysis: intransitive verb, attested by Elders Group (3/1/72).

<**ts'ímélmet**>, TVMO /'*get close to s-o/s-th, approach s-th/s-o*'/, *see* ts'ímél ~ ts'ímel.

<**ts'ímélthet**>, TVMO ['*approach (your nets for ex.)*'], *see* ts'ímél ~ ts'ímel.

<**ts'ísem**>, mdls //c'ís=əm//, ABFC ['*to grow*'], EB, (<**=em**> *middle voice*), syntactic analysis: intransitive verb, attested by Elders Group (3/15/72), EB (12/15/75, 2/6/76), <**ch'ísem ~ ts'ísem**>, [č'ísɪm] EH, [¢'ísɪm] RG, '*grow*', attested by RG,EH 8/27/99 (SU transcription, tape 6), compare <**ts'ístel ~ th'ístel**> *horn, antler*??, other sources: possibly related to H-T <tse'Em> (macron over e) *to sprout (from stem of tree)* and <tse'lEm> (macron over e) *to sprout (said of buds)*, also <**ts'í:sem**>, //c'í·s=əm//, attested by AC (11/24/71), example: <**lulh me ts'í:sem ta spí:ls.**>, //lə-uɬ mə c'í·s=əm t-ɛ s=pí·ls//, /'*Your garden is growing up.*'/, literally /'past -already come/coming to/start to grow your plantings'/, attested by AC, <**lulh me ts'í:sem ta méle.**>, //lə-uɬ mə c'í·s=əm t-ɛ mélɛ//, /'*Your child is growing.*'/, attested by AC (11/24/71).

<**ts'íts'esem**>, cts //c'í[-C_1ə-]s=əm//, ABFC /'*growing (of animals, children, etc.)*'/, EB, (<**-R1-**> *continuative*), phonology: reduplication, syntactic analysis: intransitive verb, attested by Elders Group (3/15/72), <**ch'ích'esem ~ ts'íts'esem**>, [č'íč'ɪsɪm] EH, [¢'í¢ɪsɪm] RG, '*growing*', attested by RG,EH 8/27/99 (SU transcription, tape 6), also <**ts'í:ts'esem**>, //c'í·[-C_1ə-]s=əm//, attested by AC (11/24/71).

<**ts'íts'esem tl'íkw'els**>, FOOD *bean sprouts*, EB, (lit. growing up + bean), (attested by RG,EH 6/16/98 to SN, edited by BG with RG,EH 6/26/00)

<**sts'éts'esem**>, dnom //s=c'i[=AéC_1ə=]s=əm//, EB ['*small little plants*'], literally /'something that is many little growing'/, (<**s=**> *nominalizer*), (<**é-ablaut** and **=R1=**> *plural diminutive*), phonology: reduplication, ablaut, syntactic analysis: nominal, attested by Elders Group (4/7/76).

<**ts'símt**>, df //c'ís=M1=T or c'ís=ə[=M2=]m=T or c'is=əm=ím=T or c'ís=M1=məT//, KIN /'*growing [s-o] up, (raising s-o)*'/, (<**metathesis type**> *continuative*? or *derivational*), possibly <**=ím**> *repeatedly*, (<**=t**> *purposeful control transitivizer*), possibly <**=met**> *indirect effect non-control transitivizer*, phonology: possible metathesis, possible syllable-loss, syntactic analysis: transitive verb?, attested by Elders Group (1/29/75).

<**Ts'símteló:t**>, df //c'ís=M1=T=əlà·t or c'ís=M2=təl=à·t//, PLN ['*other sister of Lhílheqey or Mount Cheam*'], N ['*(also name of the late) Mrs. Cecilia Thomas of Seabird Island*'], ASM ['the other sisters of Mt. Cheam (all turned to stone with her) are Olóxwelwet and X̲emóth'iyetel'], possibly <**=tel**> *name ending*, lx <**=elò:t ~ =ò:t**> *female name ending*, phonology: possible metathesis, syntactic analysis: nominal, attested by CT (1973), Elders Group (1/29/75), source: place names reference file #125.

<**ts'esémelep ~ ts'esémelép**>, ds //c'is=ə[=´=]m=iləp//, EB ['*weeds in a garden*'], EB /'*marijuana, "pot", "weed"*'/, semantic environment ['smoking'], (<**=´=**> *derivational*), lx <**=ílep**> *dirt*, phonology: stress-shift, vowel-reduction, optional updrifting, syntactic analysis: nominal, attested by Elders Group (3/15/72, 4/7/76), Deming (3/8/79, 3/15/79 (SJ, MC, MV, LG), 5/3/79), example: <**tsqwá:y te ts'esémelep.**>, //c=q^wɛ́·y tə c'is=ə[=´=]m=iləp//, /'*The weeds are green.*'/, attested by Deming (esp. SJ 5/3/79), <**p'óp'etl'em te ts'esémelep**>, //p'á[-C_1ə-]ƛ'=əm tə c'is=ə[=´=]m=ələp//, /'*smoking pot (marijuana)*'/, literally /'smoking the weed'/, attested by Deming (3/8/79, 3/15/79).

<**Ts'ístel**>, PLN ['*Saddle Rock above Yale*'], *see* th'ís.

<**ts'ít ~ ch'í:t**>, pcs //c'íy=T//, SOC /'*greet s-o, thank s-o*'/, (<**=t**> *purposeful control transitivizer*), phonology: vocalization, syntactic analysis: transitive verb, attested by Elders Group (5/19/76, 7/21/76), Elder's comment: "the root may be ts'á *on top of* especially considering ts'itóléstexw *pile it up* (EB (4/23/76)", comment: EB may be right or the two roots may be unconnected, Salish cognate: Sechelt /č'íy-it/ *to thank* T77:35, B85:296, also <**th'í:t**>, //θ'íy=T or θ'í[=·=]y=T//, also /'*praise s-o (with words), thank s-o*'/, attested by EB (4/23/76), also <**th'ít ~ ch'ít**>, //θ'íy=T ~ c'íy=T//, attested

by Deming (4/20/78), example: **<ch'í:t te syúwel>**, //c'íy=T tə s=yə́w=əl//, SPRD, /'*thank a spirit song, ((also) thank a spirit power)*'/, ASM ['done before you sing it'], attested by Elders Group (7/21/76), **<lúwe ts'ít te Chíchelh Siyám.>**, //lúwə c'íy=T tə cí[=C_1ə=]ɬ s=iy=ɛ́m//, /'*It's you to thank the Lord.*'/, attested by Deming (12/15/77), **<ts'ítchxw ta' siyáye.>**, //c'íy=T-c-əxʷ t-ɛʔ s=yɛ́yə//, /'*Thank your friend.*'/, attested by AD (12/17/79), **<ts'í:tchexw ta' siyáye.>**, //c'í[=·=]y=T-c-əxʷ t-ɛʔ s=yɛ́yə//, /'*Really thank your friend.*'/, attested by AD (12/17/79), **<tsel th'í:thòmè.>**, //c-əl θ'íy=T-ámə//, /'*I praised you (with words)., I thanked you.*'/, attested by EB; found in **<ch'ítolétsel. ~ th'ítolétsel.>**, //c'íy=T-álə-c-əl ~ θ'íy=T-álə-c-əl//, /'*I thank you folks., I thank you all very much., I praise you folks.*'/, attested by Deming (12/15/77, 4/20/78), example: **<ch'íthométset lám kw's mōkw'stám.>**, //c'íy=T-amə-c-ət lɛ́=m k'ʷ-s mok'ʷ=s=tɛ́m//, /'*We thank you for everything.*'/, usage: blessing a meeting, attested by AD (1/17/80), **<ts'ítolètsel kws mṓkw'elep>**, //c'íy=T-alə-c-əl kʷ-s mok'ʷ-ələp//, /'*I thank you everyone.*'/, attested by RG & EH (4/10/99 Ling332), **<ts'ithométsel>**, ///c'íy=T-ámə-c-əl//, /'*I thank you; I praise you.*'/, attested by RG & EH (4/10/99 Ling332).

<xwth'í:t>, df //xʷ=θ'íy=T//, SOC /'*thank s-o (for a cure, for pall-bearing, a ceremony, being a witness)*'/, REL, ASM ['one thanks a witness with a token wrapped in a colored scarf, the token is often a quarter'], (**<xw=>** meaning uncertain unless perhaps *towards*), syntactic analysis: transitive verb, usage: it is an insult to translate this word as *pay s-o (for a cure, for pall-bearing, etc.)*, attested by EB (4/23/76); found in **<xwth'í:tes.>**, //xʷ=θ'íy=T-əs//, /'*He thanked him (for a cure, pall-bearing, etc.)*'/, attested by EB, **<xwth'í:thóxes.>**, //xʷ=θ'íy=T-áxʸ-əs//, /'*He thanked me (for a cure, pall-bearing, a ceremony).*'/, attested by EB, example: **<á:xwesthoxes te tále tl'óles shxwth'í:thóxes.>**, //ʔɛ́·xʷəs=T-áxʸ-əs tə tɛ́lə ƛ'á lə-s sxʷ=θ'íy=T-áxʸ-əs//, /'*He gave me money, that's how he thanked me. (give it to s-o)*'/, attested by EB; found in **<shxwth'í:tèmèt.>**, //sxʷ=θ'íy=T-ə̀m-ə̀t//, /'*They thanked someone (for a cure, pall-bearing, being a witness).*'/, attested by EB.

<ts'itóléstexw>, df //c'iy=tálə́=sT-əxʷ//, caus, SOC /'*pile it up (blankets, rocks, anything)*'/, possibly **<=tólé>** meaning unknown, (**<=st>** *causative control transitivizer*), (**<-exw>** *third person object*), Elder's comment: "derived from ts'á *on top*", syntactic analysis: transitive verb, attested by EB (4/23/76).

<ts'í:tl' ~ ts'ítl'>, bound root //c'í·ƛ' ~ c'íƛ' *short*//.

<ts'í:ts'etl'>, df //c'í·[=C_1ə=]ƛ'//, DESC ['*short*'], probably **<=R1=>** *resultative*, phonology: reduplication, syntactic analysis: adjective/adjectival verb, attested by AC (8/6/70), other sources: ES /c'í·c'əƛ'/ *short*.

<ts'ats'í:ts'etl' ~ ts'ats'íts'etl'>, df //C_1ɛ=c'í(·)[=C_1ə=]ƛ'//, DESC ['*shorter*'], probably **<R8=>** *comparative or augmentative/diminutive*, phonology: double reduplication, syntactic analysis: adjective/adjectival verb, attested by AC (8/6/70, 10/15/71), example: **<l stl'í te we'ól ts'ats'its'etl' xwéylem.>**, //l s=ƛ'í tə wə-ʔál C_1ɛ=c'í[=C_1ə=]ƛ'x̣ʷí·l=əm//, /'*I want the shortest rope.*'/, literally /'is my want the more shorter rope'/, attested by AC (8/6/70).

<sts'ats'íts'etl'tses>, ds //s=C_1ɛ=c'í[=C_1ə=]ƛ'=cəs//, ANAH ['*third finger*'], literally /'shorter finger'/, (**<s=>** *nominalizer*), lx **<=tses>** *on the hand*, phonology: double reduplication, syntactic analysis: nominal, attested by NP (Elders Group 5/3/78), other sources: Boas 1890 (Scowlitz field notes).

<ch'í:tl'emeth'>, ds //c'í·ƛ'=əməθ'//, BPI /'*short person, short (in stature)*'/, DESC, lx **<=emeth'>** *in height, stature*, syntactic analysis: nominal?, adjective/adjectival verb?, attested by AC (11/11/71).

<ts'í:ts'tl'emeth'>, dmv //c'í·[=C_1ə=]ƛ'=əməθ'//, BPI /'*short (of a person), shorty*'/, DESC, ABFC ['*call of a little bird (chickadee?)*'], Elder's comment: "probably of the chickadee (AD)", (**<=R1=>**

diminutive or resultative), phonology: reduplication, syntactic analysis: nominal?, adjective/adjectival verb?, attested by EB (12/1/75), IHTTC (8/23/77), AD (IHTTC 8/23/77).

<**ts'ítl'ewelh**>, ds //c'íƛ'=əwəɬ//, CAN ['*short canoe*'], lx <**=ewelh ~ =ő welh**> *canoe, vessel*, syntactic analysis: nominal?, adjective/adjectival verb?, attested by EB and AD (9/19/78).

<**ts'ítl'ōwes** or **ts'ítl'ewes**>, ds //c'íƛ'=owəs or c'íƛ'=əwəs//, CAN ['*short paddle*'], lx <**=ő wes ~ =ōwes ~ =ewes**> *paddle*, syntactic analysis: nominal?, adjective/adjectival verb?, attested by EB and AD (9/19/78).

<**ts'íts'etl'thet**>, incs //c'í[-C_1ə-]ƛ'=θət//, cts, DESC ['*be getting shorter*'], (<**-R1-**> *continuative*), (<**=thet**> *get, become*), phonology: reduplication, syntactic analysis: intransitive verb, attested by Elders Group (3/14/79), example: <**ts'íts'etl'thet te swàyèl.**>, //c'í[-C_1ə-]ƛ'=θət tə s=wɛ̀yə̀l//, TIME, /'*The days are getting shorter.*'/, attested by Elders Group.

<**ts'tl'étl'xel**>, df //c'[=əC_2=]i[=Aə́=]ƛ'=x^yəl//, ABFC ['*takes short steps*'], (<**=R6=**> *plural or diminutive or out-of-control*), comment: a rare type of reduplication, probably <**é-ablaut**> *durative or derivational*, lx <**=xel**> *on the foot*, phonology: reduplication, ablaut, syntactic analysis: intransitive verb, attested by EB (9/18/78).

<**ts'eléletl'xel**>, df //c'[=əl=]i[=Aə́=lə=]ƛ'=x^yəl//, BPI ['*has short legs*'], possibly <**=el=**> *plural*, possibly <**é-ablaut**> *durative or derivational*, possibly <**=le=**> *plural*, phonology: double infixed plural?, ablaut, syntactic analysis: adjective/adjectival verb, attested by EB (9/18/78), also <**ch'áléléth'xel**>, //c'ɛ́lə́ləθ'=x^yəl//, also /'*short-legged runt*'/, Elder's comment: "a swear-word", attested by AC (11/11/71).

<**ts'ítl'ewelh**>, CAN ['*short canoe*'], *see* ts'í:tl' ~ ts'ítl'.

<**ts'ítl'ōwes** or **ts'ítl'ewes**>, CAN ['*short paddle*'], *see* ts'í:tl' ~ ts'ítl'.

<**ts'í:ts'á:tl'em**>, EZ /'*grasshopper (ordinary),* perhaps *longhorned grasshopper*'/, *see* ts'tl'ám ~ ts'tl'ém.

<**ts'its'á:ya**>, KIN ['*in-laws or relatives when the connecting link dies*'], *see* ts'á:ya.

<**ts'íts'emel**>, DIR ['*getting close*'], *see* ts'ímél ~ ts'ímel.

<**ts'íts'esem**>, ABFC /'*growing (of animals, children, etc.)*'/, *see* ts'ísem.

<**ts'íts'esem tl'íkw'els**>, EB /'*bean sprouts*'/ (lit. growing up + bean), *see* ts'ísem.

<**ts'í:ts'etl'**>, DESC ['*short*'], *see* ts'í:tl' ~ ts'ítl'.

<**ts'íts'etl'thet**>, DESC ['*be getting shorter*'], *see* ts'í:tl' ~ ts'ítl'.

<**ts'íts'ewel**>, EFAM ['*bored*'], *see* ts'íw.

<**ch'ich'ewós**>, df //c'i[-C_1ə-]w=ás//, cts, ABFC ['*sunning oneself*'], root meaning unknown, (<**-R1-**> *continuative*), lx <**=ós**> *on the face*, phonology: reduplication, syntactic analysis: intransitive verb, attested by IHTTC (8/4/77), comment: translation omitted in original notes.

<**sts'íts'exw**>, strs //s=c'í[=C_1ə=]x^w//, EFAM ['*be considerate*'], see under stem <**th'íxw**> *help*.

<**sts'its'exwtel**>, pcrs //s=c'í[=C_1ə=]x^w=T-əl//, EFAM ['*(be) considerate of each other*'], see under stem <**th'íxw**> *help*.

<**ts'its'kwiyóls**>, df //C_1í=c'əq'ʷ=iy(=)áls//, PLAY ['*playing pool*'], literally possibly /'little poking spherical object/ball'/, (<**R4=**> *diminutive*), possibly root <**ts'eqw'**> *poke into, pierce*, lx <**=iyóls**> *ball*, probably <**=iy ~ =ey ~ =á:y**> *bark, wool, covering*, probably <**=óls**> *spherical object*, phonology: reduplication, kw probably mistranscribed for qw', syntactic analysis: intransitive verb, attested by Deming (7/27/78), also <**thíthq'eyóls**>, //C_1í=θq'=əy(=)áls or θí[=C_1ə=]q'=əy(=)áls//,

PLAY, also /*'pool (the game)'*/, attested by IHTTC (with Deming), also <**th'ith'qw'iyóls**>, //C_1í=θ'əq'^{w}=iy(=)áls//, PLAY, also /*'pool (the game)'*/, attested by MH (Deming 9/6/77), example: <**ts'its'kwiyóls á:lhtel.**>, //C_1í=c'ək^{w}=iy(=)áls ʔɛ·ɬtəl//, /*'They are playing pool.'*/, attested by Deming (7/27/78).

<**ts'íts'lhà:m ~ ts'its'lhá:m ~ ts'ets'lhà:m**>, ABFC /*'hearing, (hear [Elders Group, EB])'*/, *see* ts'lhà:m.

<**ts'its'lhá:met ~ ts'íts'lhámet**>, ABFC [*'hearing s-th/s-o'*], *see* ts'lhà:m.

<**ts'íts'qweló:l**>, PLAY /*'Indian badminton (played with cedar things that have wings), (grass shinny (a game like grass hockey, uses a big round ball) [BJ])'*/, *see* ts'éqw ~ th'éqw.

<**ts'í:ts'tl'emeth'**>, BPI /*'short (of a person), shorty'*/, *see* ts'í:tl' ~ ts'ítl'.

<**ts'íw**>, bound root //c'íw *annoyed, bothered, fed up, bored*//.

<**th'íwél**>, df //θ'íw=əl or θ'íy=əwəl//, EFAM [*'annoyed'*], possibly <**í-ablaut**> *resultative or durative*, possibly <**=ewel**> *in the mind*, possibly <**=el**> *go, come, get, become*, phonology: <**th'**> for <**ts'**> possibly idiolectal, this form is only attested by EB, <**ch'íwelmet**>, [č'íwɪlmɪt], *'be fed up'*, attested by EH 6/6/00 (SU transcription, tape 7), derived forms with **ts'** are attested by Elders Group and the Deming Elders and are cognate with forms in Squamish and Lushootseed by the regular sound correspondences (**ts'** here is regular, **th'** is unexpected and irregular), phonology: probable updrifting, possible ablaut, syntactic analysis: intransitive verb, attested by EB (12/15/75, 4/27/76), Salish cognate: Lushootseed /č'ig^{w}il/ *impatient, disgusted, irritated* H76:114, Squamish /č'íwiʔ/ *feel annoyed, feel bothered, get fed up* W73:6, K69:68.

<**ts'íts'ewel**>, cts or rsls //c'í[-C_1ə-]w=əl//, EFAM [*'bored'*], (<**-R1-**> *continuative* or *resultative*), phonology: reduplication, syntactic analysis: intransitive verb, attested by Deming (6/15/78), <**ch'ích'iwélmet**>, [č'íč'iwílmɪt], *'really fed up'*, attested by EH 6/6/00 (SU transcription, tape 7), also <**th'íth'ewel**>, //θ'í[-C_1ə-]w=əl//, also /*'being annoyed'*/, attested by EB (4/27/76).

<**ts'íwélmét**>, iecs //c'íw(=)əl=məT//, EFAM /*'annoyed with s-th, annoyed by s-o, tired of s-o'*/, (<**=met**> *indirect effect non-control transitivizer*), phonology: updrifting, syntactic analysis: transitive verb, attested by Elders Group (4/6/77), Deming (6/15/78), also <**th'íwélmet**>, //θ'íw(=)əl=məT//, also /*'to be fed up [with s-o/s-th]'*/, attested by EB (12/15/75, 4/27/76).

<**th'íwélstexw**>, caus //θ'íw(=)əl=sT-əx^{w}//, EFAM /*'annoyed s-o, bothered s-o, pestered s-o'*/, possibly <**í-ablaut**> *durative or resultative*, (<**=st**> *causative control transitivizer*), (<**-exw**> *third person object*), phonology: th' is perhaps idiolectal for more widespread ts' here, phonology: possible ablaut, updrifting, syntactic analysis: transitive verb, attested by EB (4/27/76); found in <**th'íwélstxwes.**>, //θ'íw=əl=sT-əx^{w}-əs//, /*'He annoyed her., He bothered her., He pestered her.'*/, attested by EB.

<**ts'íwélmét**>, EFAM /*'annoyed with s-th, annoyed by s-o, tired of s-o'*/, *see* ts'íw.

<**ts'iyáq ~ ch'iyáq**>, root or stem //c'iyɛ́q//, FSH /*'fish trap, weir'*/.

<**sts'iyáq**>, dnom //s=c'iyɛ́q//, FSH /*'fish trap, weir'*/, (<**s=**> *nominalizer*), syntactic analysis: nominal, attested by Deming (3/25/76), Salish cognate: Squamish /č'iáq/ *salmon weir* W73:286, K67:322, also /*'trapping animals'*/, attested by AC (8/28/70).

<**Sch'iyáq**>, dnom //s=c'iyɛ́q//, PLN [*'creek with its mouth on the south side of Chilliwack River and above the mouth of Middle Creek'*], (semological comment: Wells says it means *place of fish weir*), syntactic analysis: nominal, source: Wells 1965 (lst ed.):13.

<**ch'iyáqtel**>, ds //c'iyɛ́q=təl//, FSH /*'salmon weir, fish trap'*/, root <**ch'iyáq**> *to trap fish*, lx <**=tel**> *device to*, syntactic analysis: nominal, attested by DM (12/4/64).

<**Ch'iyáqtel**>, dnom //c'iyɛ́q=təl//, PLN /'*Tzeachten, a (recent) settlement on the upper reaches of the lower Chilliwack River, now Chilliwack Indian Reserve #13 near Sardis*'/, literally /'device to trap fish'/, (semological comment: Wells says it means *place of the fish weir*), lx <**=tel**> *device to, something to*, phonology: the <n> in the Anglicized spelling of the name either reflects the pronunciation at first recording by whites (Gibbs) in which case the sound change of Downriver /n/ to Upriver /l/ was not complete consonant alternation 1858, or /n/ reflects a recording of this name by Downriver speakers to Gibbs about the same time, none of the Elders from the 1890's to the present pronounce /l/ with /n/, syntactic analysis: nominal, attested by AC, BJ (5/10/64), DM (12/4/64), other sources: Wells 1965 (lst ed.):19, Wells 1966, H-T <TciáktEl>, source: place names reference file #181.

<**ts'iyáye**>, bound root or stem //c'iyáyə or c'[=əC_2=]áyə or s=c'iy=áyə//, root or stem meaning uncertain, lx <**=iya ~ =óya**> *affectionate diminutive.*

<**sts'iyáye**>, df //s=c'iyáyə or s=c'[=əC_2=]áyə or s=c'iy=áyə//, KIN ['*twins*'], ASM ['twins were sometimes taken up into the mountains to be raised since they were said to have great power, example over the weather, even today if twins are teased it will cause rain'], (<**s=**> *nominalizer*), possibly root <**ts'íy**> *near, close by* as in Squamish (otherwise not attested in UHk), or possibly <**ts'íy**> *greet, thank, praise* (which is found in UHk), possibly <**=R6=**> *plural* or more likely <**=óya ~ =íya**> *affectionate diminutive*, phonology: possible reduplication, syntactic analysis: nominal, attested by AC, other sources: ES /sc'iyíləm/ (CwMs /sc'iyáyə/) *twins*, Salish cognate: Squamish /č'iúy/ [should be //č'iy=úy//] ~ /sč'iúy/ *twins* from root /č'i/ *near, close by* W73:275, K67:289,321, K69:69, Lushootseed /č'íyùyaʔ/ *twins* H76:118.

<**ts'í:yelh**>, REL /'*(be) praying, (pray [Elders Group])*'/, *see* ts'ahéyelh.

<**ts'íyxw ~ ts'éyxw ~ ch'íyxw**>, free root //c'íyx^w ~ c'ə́yx^w//, DESC /'*be dry, get dry, to dry*'/, possibly <**í-ablaut** or **é-ablaut**> *resultative*, syntactic analysis: intransitive verb, attested by AC, BHTTC (10/76), EB (12/1/75, 2/6/76), Deming (1/31/80), Salish cognate: Squamish root /č'iʔ ~ č'ayʔ/ *dry out, wither* K69:68 as in /č'iʔx^w/ *dry* K67:322, K69:68 and /č'áyʔ-i/ *dry out (ab. living things), die (ab. tree)* K69:68, all W73:86, example: <**lulh ts'éyxw.**>, //lə=uɬ c'ə́yx^w//, /'*It's dry.*'/, literally /'past - already is dry'/, attested by AC, <**ts'íyxw tel thóthel.**>, //c'íyx^w t-əl θ=áθəl//, /'*My mouth is dry.*'/, attested by Deming, <**lulh le ts'íyxw te stó:lō.**>, //lə=uɬ lə c'íyx^w tə s=tá·l=əw//, /'*The river is getting dry.*'/, literally /'past -already past 3rd person subject get dry the river'/, attested by EB.

<**ts'íyxw stotekwtíqw seplíl**>, FOOD *noodles* (lit. dry + stringy hair + bread), (attested by RG,EH 6/16/98 to SN, edited by BG with RG,EH 6/26/00)

<**chí:s** (or) **tl'éxw ts'íyxw sqemó:**>, FOOD *cheese* (lit. cheese or hard + dry + milk), (attested by RG,EH 6/16/98 to SN, edited by BG with RG,EH 6/26/00)

<**tl'áqt ts'íyxw seplíl**>, FOOD *spaghetti* (lit. long + dry + bread), (attested by RG,EH 6/16/98 to SN, edited by BG with RG,EH 6/26/00)

<**ts'áyxw**>, cts //c'i[-Aɛ́-]yx^w//, DESC ['*drying*'], (<**á-ablaut**> *continuative*), phonology: ablaut, syntactic analysis: intransitive verb, attested by Deming (1/31/80), other sources: ES and JH /c'ɛ́·yx^w/ *dry.*

<**ts'áyxw kúkumels** (could be **ts'íyxw kwúkwemels**)>, FOOD *zucchini*, EB, (lit. dried + cucumber), (attested by RG,EH 6/16/98 to SN, edited by BG with RG,EH 6/26/00)

<**ts'áyxw sqemó**>, FOOD *powdered milk/coffee mate* (lit. dry + milk), (attested by RG,EH 6/16/98 to SN, edited by BG with RG,EH 6/26/00)

<**shxwch'á:yxwels**>, dnom //sx^w=c'i[=Aɛ́·=]yx^w=əls//, sas, FSH ['*fish-drying rack*'], literally /'something for drying fish as a structured activity continuative'/, (<**shxw=**> *something for*),

(<**=els**> *structured activity continuative nominal*), phonology: ablaut, syntactic analysis: nominal, attested by DM (12/4/64 new transcript new p. 187).

<**sch'á:yxw**>, strs //s=c'i[=Aɛ́·=]yxʷ//, DESC ['*(be) dried*'], FOOD, (<**s=**> *stative*), (<**á:-ablaut**> *resultative*), phonology: ablaut, syntactic analysis: adjective/adjectival verb, attested by DM (12/4/64 new transcript new p.191), example: <**sch'á:yxw (swí:wa, sth'í:m)**>, //s=c'i[=Aɛ́·=]yxʷ (s=wí·wɛ, s=θ'í·m)//, /'*dried (eulachons, berries)*'/, attested by DM.

<**sch'á:yxwels**>, dnom //s=c'i[=Aɛ́·=]yxʷ=əls//, sas, FOOD ['*dried meat*'], (<**s=**> *nominalizer*), (<**ó:-ablaut**> *resultative*), (<**=els**> *structured activity continuative*), phonology: ablaut, syntactic analysis: nominal, attested by DM (12/4/64 new transcript new p.190).

<**ts'íyxwt ~ ts'éyxwt**>, pcs //c'íyxʷ=T ~ c'ə́yxʷ=T//, FSH ['*dry s-th*'], HUNT, HARV /'*spread them out to dry (berries, bulrushes, etc.)*'/, MC, (<**=t**> *purposeful control transitivizer*), syntactic analysis: transitive verb, attested by AC (10/1/71, 10/13/71), EB (4/28/76), example: <**éwechexw ts'íyxwtexw.**>, //ʔə́wə-c-əxʷ c'íyxʷ=T-əxʷ//, /'*Don't dry it.*'/, attested by AC, <**lachxw ch'éyxwt te qwe'óp.**>, //lɛ-c-xʷ c'ə́yxʷ=T tə qʷəʔáp//, /'*You go dry the apple.*'/, attested by AC, <**léwe ts'éyxwt ta s'óthes.**>, //lə́wə c'ə́yxʷ=T t-ɛ s=ʔáθ=əs//, /'*You dry your face.*'/, attested by AC, <**th'ex̲wót q'e éwechxw ts'éyxwtexw.**>, //θ'əx̣ʷ=áT q'ə ʔə́wə-c-xʷ c'ə́yxʷ=T-əxʷ//, /'*Wash it but don't dry it.*'/, attested by AC.

<**ch'áyxwt**>, cts //c'i[-Aɛ́-]yxʷ=T//, HARV ['*drying s-th*'], HUNT, FSH, MC, (<**á-ablaut**> *continuative*), phonology: ablaut, syntactic analysis: transitive verb, attested by AC (8/24/70, 10/13/71); found in <**ch'áyxwtes.**>, //c'i[-Aɛ́-]yxʷ=T-əs//, /'*He/She is drying it (clothes, fruit, dishes, etc.).*'/, attested by AC, example: <**tsel ts'áyxwt.**>, //c-əl c'i[-Aɛ-]yxʷ=T//, /'*I'm drying it.*'/, attested by AC (8/24/70).

<**ch'íyxweqel**>, ds //c'íyxʷ=əqəl//, ABDF ['*dry in the throat*'], lx <**=eqel**> *in the throat*, syntactic analysis: adjective/adjectival verb, attested by Deming (1/31/80).

<**ts'iyxweqthàlèm**>, df //c'iyxʷ=əq(əl)=T-ɛ̀lə̀m//, if, ABDF ['*my throat is dry*'], literally possibly /'something dried out my throat on purpose'/, possibly <**=t**> *purposeful control transitivizer*, (<**-àlèm**> *first person singular passive*), phonology: syllable-loss predictable, syntactic analysis: transitive verb -passive, attested by EB (12/19/75), example: <**me ts'íyxweqthàlèm, tsel me lhqó:le.**>, //mə c'íyxʷ=əq(əl)=T-ɛ̀lə̀m, c-əl mə ɬ=qá·-lə//, /'*My throat is dry, I'm thirsty.*'/, attested by EB.

<**ch'iyxwíwel**>, ds //c'iyxʷ=íwəl//, ABDF ['*really constipated*'], literally /'dry in the rectum, dry in the insides'/, lx <**=íwel**> *in the rectum, in the insides, in the bottom*, syntactic analysis: adjective/adjectival verb, attested by JL (3/31/78).

<**th'éyx̲westem**>, caus //c'íyxʷ=əs=sT=əm//, /θ'íyxʷəstəm/, [θ'éyxʷəstəm], pass., REL /'*his/her face/their faces are made dry*'/, semantic environment: ['a word used when showing a picture of the deceased at a memorial ceremony, and telling the family to dry their tears'], phonological comment: related to <**ts'íyxw**> *dry*, <**ts'íyxwt**> *dry it*, some say <**ch'íyxw**> and <**ch'íyxwt**>, apparently <**th'eyx̲w**> is the correct way in some dialects (Cheh. has this kind of variation with /c'/); <**=es**> *face*, <**=t**> *do purposely to s-o/s-th* or <**=st**> *cause/make someone do something*, <**-em**> *passive*, RG & EH (4/9/99 Ling332).

<**ts'iyxweqthàlèm**>, ABDF ['*my throat is dry*'], *see* ts'íyxw ~ ts'éyxw ~ ch'íyxw.

<**ts'íyxwt ~ ts'éyxwt**>, FSH ['*dry s-th*'], *see* ts'íyxw ~ ts'éyxw ~ ch'íyxw.

<**ts'kw'éx**>, possibly root //c'k'ʷə́xʸ or c[=G=]=k'ʷɛ[=Aə́=]xʸ//, [c'k'ʷɪ́xʸ], NUM ['*twenty*'], probably root <**kw'ɛ́x**> *count*, possibly <**ts=**> *have, get*, possibly <**=G= (glottalization)**> *derivational,*

possibly <**é-ablaut**> *derivational*, phonology: possible glottalization, possible ablaut, syntactic analysis: num, adjective/adjectival verb, attested by AC, DM, BJ, CT, others, other sources: ES /c'k'ʷɛ́xʸ/, JH /c'k'ʷéx/, also <**tskw'éx ~ ts'kw'éx**>, //ck'ʷə́xʸ ~ c'k'ʷə́xʸ//, attested by AC; found in <**ts'kw'éxtset**>, //c'k'ʷə́xʸ-c-ət//, /'*We're twenty., There's twenty of us.*'/, attested by AC, example: <**ts'kw'éx qas kw'e léts'e**>, //c'k'ʷə́xʸ qɛs k'ʷə lə́c'ə//, /'*twenty-one*'/, attested by AC, BJ, also <**ts'kw'éx qas te léts'e**>, //c'k'ʷə́xʸ qɛs tə lə́c'ə//, attested by CT 9/5/73, *see* <**kw'áx**>

<**ts'ekw'xále**>, ds //c'k'ʷə[=M1=]xʸ=ɛ́lə//, NUM ['*twenty people*'], lx <**=óle**> *people*, syntactic analysis: nominal, attested by Elders Group, also <**ts'kw'éx mestíyexw**>, //c'k'ʷə́xʸ məstíyəxʷ//, attested by AC.

<**ts'kw'exáleqel**>, ds //c'k'ʷəxʸ=ɛ́ləqəl//, NUM ['*twenty containers*'], lx <**=áleqel**> *containers*, syntactic analysis: nominal, attested by AD.

<**ts'kw'xó:s**>, ds //c'k'ʷxʸ=á·s//, NUM ['*twenty dollars*'], lx <**=ó:s**> *on the face, round thing, dollar*, syntactic analysis: nominal, attested by Elders Group, also <**ts'ekw'xó:s**>, //c'k'ʷə[=M1=]xʸ=á·s//, attested by AC (11/30/71).

<**ts'kw'exáleqel**>, NUM ['*twenty containers*'], *see* ts'kw'éx.

<**ts'kw'xó:s**>, NUM ['*twenty dollars*'], *see* ts'kw'éx.

<**ts'lhà:m**>, df //c'ɬɛ́=əm or c'ɛ́ɬ=M1=əm or c'ɛɬ=ə[=M2=]m or c'ɬ=ɛ́·m//, ABFC ['*to hear*'], root meaning unknown, possibly <**metathesis**> *derivational*, possibly <**=em**> *middle voice*, possibly <**=em**> *have/get/intransitivizer*, phonology: possible stressed intransitivizer, possible metathesis, downdrifting, syntactic analysis: intransitive verb, attested by EB (12/16/75), other sources: JH /c'ɬé·m/ *to hear*.

<**ts'íts'lhà:m ~ ts'its'lhá:m ~ ts'ets'lhà:m**>, cts //C_1í-c'ɬɛ́=əm ~ C_1ə-c'ɬɛ́=əm//, ABFC /'*hearing, (hear [Elders Group, EB])*'/, (<**R4-** or **R5-**> *continuative*), phonology: reduplication, syntactic analysis: intransitive verb, Elder's comment: "ts'ets'lhá:m is lower Fraser (downriver Halkomelem)(AC)", attested by EB (12/16/65, 5/4/76), AC (8/14/70, 9/18/71), other sources: ES /c'əc'ɬɛ́·m/ *hear*, also /'*hear*'/, attested by Elders Group (3/15/72), attested by EB (5/4/76).

<**ts'lhá:met**>, iecs //c'ɬɛ́·=məT//, ABFC ['*hear s-o/s-th*'], (<**=met**> *indirect effect non-control transitivizer*), syntactic analysis: transitive verb, attested by BJ (12/15/64), AC (11/10/71, 12/4/71), JL (5/5/75), EB (12/16/75), example: <**tsel ts'lhámet.**>, //c-əl c'ɬɛ́=məT//, /'*I heard it.*'/, attested by AC (12/4/71), <**tsel ts'lhá:met kw'e'ase q'óq'ey.**>, //c-əl c'ɬɛ́·=məT k'ʷ-ɛʔ-s-ə q'á[=C_1ə=]y//, /'*I heard that you were sick.*'/, attested by EB, <**tl'olsuw ts'lhá:met tel skwí:x.**>, //ƛ'a-l-s-uw c'ɬɛ́·=məT t-əl s=kʷí·xʸ//, /'*Then I heard my name.*'/, usage: contemporary story, attested by AC (11/10/71).

<**ts'its'lhá:met ~ ts'íts'lhámet**>, cts //C_1í-c'ɬɛ́·=məT//, ABFC ['*hearing s-th/s-o*'], (<**R4-**> *continuative*), phonology: reduplication, syntactic analysis: transitive verb, attested by JL (5/5/75), AC (9/18/71, 12/4/71), Elders Group (3/15/72), EB (5/4/76), example: <**lichxw ts'its'lhá:methóx?**>, //lí-c-xʷ C_1í-c'ɬɛ́·=məT-áxʸ//, /'*Can you hear me?*'/, attested by AC (9/18/71); found in <**ts'its'lhámethòmè**>, //C_1í-c'ɬɛ́=məT-ámə//, /'*hear(ing) you*'/, phonology: downstepping, updrifting, attested by Elders Group, example: <**ts'its'lhá:metes ye t'ít'elem.**>, //C_1í-c'ɬɛ́·=məT-əs yə t'í[-C_1ə-]l=əm//, /'*He's hearing the singing.*'/, *<**ts'its'lhá:m ye t'ít'elem.**> rejected, */'hearing the singing'/ rejected, Elder's comment: "broken Indian, would mean the ones hearing would be doing the singing too", attested by EB (5/4/76), <**lí: ts'its'lhá:methò:m?**>, //lí-ə C_1í-c'ɬɛ́·=məT-à·m//, /'*Can he hear you?*'/, literally /'is he hearing you, are you being heard'/, syntactic analysis: passive, attested by AC (9/18/71), <**lí. tsel ts'its'lhà:metháme.**>, //lí. c-əl C_1í-c'ɬɛ́·=məT-ámə//, /'*Yes. I hear you.*'/, attested by AC

(9/18/71).

<**ts'lhá:met**>, ABFC [*'hear s-o/s-th'*], *see* ts'lhà:m.

<**ts'lhéqw'ewíts**>, ABDF [*'sprain the back'*], *see* ts'lhóqw'.

<**ts'lhéqw'xel**>, ABDF */'leg got sprained, (sprain one's ankle [JL])'/*, *see* ts'lhóqw'.

<**ts'lhimexóstel**>, SOC */'go with each other (romantically), go for a walk with each other (romantically)'/*, *see* ím *or* ts'elh=.

<**ts'lhóqw'**>, possibly root //c'ɬáq'ʷ//, ABDF */'(get or develop a) sprain, to sprain'/*, syntactic analysis: intransitive verb, attested by Deming, Salish cognate: either a suffix or sound symbolism is involved in this root; found in p'lhéqw'xel *get a sprained foot, leg got out of joint*, root t'lhóqw' **pry*, Musqueam /t'ɬáq'ʷ *get twisted* Suttles ca1984:ch.7, Squamish /p'álq'ʷ-šn/ *sprain one's ankle* W73:248, K67:252, Colville Okanagan root /mɬq'ʷ/ in /k'ɬ-mɬq'ʷ-cin-xn/ *sprain one's ankle* and /k'ɬ-mɬq'ʷ-cn-ikst/ *sprain one's wrist* M87:342,100, example: <**ts'lhóqw' te (shxw'ílàmàlà, slhéq'ōwelh, sth'emxweláx̱el)**>, //c'ɬáq'ʷ tə (sxʷ=ʔílɛ̀m=ɛ̀lɛ̀, s=ɬə́q'=owəɬ, s=θ'am=xʷ=əlɛx̣əl)//, */'sprain the (shoulder, back, elbow)'/*, attested by Deming (1/31/80), <**ts'lhóqw' tel (tépsem, t'álō̸w)**>, //c'ɬáq'ʷ t-əl (t=ə́psəm, t'ɛ́lów)//, */'sprain my (neck, arm)'/*, attested by Deming (1/31/80).

<**ts'lhéqw'ewíts**>, df //c'ɬa[=Aə́=]q'ʷ=əwíc//, ABDF [*'sprain the back'*], literally /'sprained on the back'/, possibly <**é-ablaut**> *durative or resultative or derivational*, lx <**=ewíts**> *on the back*, phonology: possible ablaut, syntactic analysis: intransitive verb, attested by Deming (1/31/80).

<**ts'lhéqw'xel**>, df //c'ɬa[=Aə́=]q'ʷ=xʸəl//, ABDF */'leg got sprained, (sprain one's ankle [JL])'/*, literally /'sprained on the leg/foot'/, possibly <**é-ablaut**> *resultative/durative/derivational*, lx <**=xel**> *on the leg, on the foot*, phonology: possible ablaut, syntactic analysis: intransitive verb, attested by Deming (1/31/80), also */'sprain one's ankle'/*, attested by JL (5/5/75).

<**ts'meth'ó:les**>, ANA [*'(have) blue eyes'*], *see* méth'.

<**ts'ó: ~ ts'ó'** (Sumas dial.)>, free root //c'á· ~ c'áʔ// *relative*

<**sts'ó:**>, dnom //s=c'á·//, KIN [*'relative (of any kind)'*], (<**s=**> *nominalizer*), syntactic analysis: nominal, dialects: *Cheh.*, attested by Deming (4/1/76), also <**ts'ó'**>, //c'áʔ//, dialects: *Sumas*, attested by Deming (4/1/76).

<**ts'ókw**>, free root or stem //c'ákʷ//, EZ [*'minnow'*], syntactic analysis: noun, nominal, attested by Elders Group (1/28/76).

<**Ts'okw'á:m ~ Lexwts'okw'á:m ~ Lexwch'okw'á:m**>, PLN */'village at Five-Mile Creek (five miles above Yale), (village about half a mile above mouth of Sawmill Creek* [SP and AK (Fish Camp 8/2/77)], *Five-Mile Creek, Saddle Rock* [Halkomelem Instructors Association 10/26/77], *area of skunk cabbages right across the Fraser River from Five-Mile Creek, a low area at the swampy south end of Q'aleliktel* [AK (Trip to Five-Mile Creek 4/30/79)], *area along the banks of Five-Mile Creek, the original area is a quarter mile north from SLAHEECH CEMETERY No. 3 (marked by sign and white picket fence of west side of highway) and a quarter mile west* [Albert Phillips (Trip to Five-Mile Creek 4/30/79)])'/, *see* ts'ó:kw'e ~ ch'ó:kw'e ~ ts'ó:kw'a.

<**ts'ó:kw'e ~ ch'ó:kw'e ~ ts'ó:kw'a**>, possibly root //c'á·k'ʷə ~ c'á·k'ʷɛ or c'á·k'ʷ=ɛ//, EZ [*'skunk cabbage'*], [*'Lysichitum americanum'*], ASM ['leaves used to wrap food for cooking and as waxed paper'], MED ['roots used for spring tonic (AC), leaf put on head for antidote for baldness, roots used as medicine for rheumatism (wash limbs in it) (EF), leaves are medicine for swelling and arthritis and put on the chest for emphysema (EF)'], possibly <**=a ~ =e**> *living thing*, syntactic analysis: noun, nominal, attested by AC, EF (Deming 9/21/78), other sources: ES /c'ák'ʷa/ *skunk cabbage*, JH

/c'á·k'ʷe/ *skunk cabbage*, Salish cognate: Northern Lushootseed /č'ú(ʔ)k'ʷ/ *skunk cabbage* H76:119, Squamish /č'úk'ʷa/ *skunk cabbage* W73:237, K67:321, K69:68, also <**ts'ókw'elets**>, //c'ák'ʷ=ələc//, lx <**=elets**> *on the bottom*, attested by Deming (4/12/79).

<**Ts'okw'á:m ~ Lexwts'okw'á:m ~ Lexwch'okw'á:m**>, ds //c'ak'ʷ(=)ɛ=əm ~ ləxʷ=c'ak'ʷ(=)ɛ=əm//, PLN /'*village at Five-Mile Creek (five miles above Yale), (village about half a mile above mouth of Sawmill Creek* [SP and AK (Fish Camp 8/2/77)], *Five-Mile Creek, Saddle Rock* [Halkomelem Instructors Association 10/26/77], *area of skunk cabbages right across the Fraser River from Five-Mile Creek, a low area at the swampy south end of Q'aleliktel* [AK (Trip to Five-Mile Creek 4/30/79)], *area along the banks of Five-Mile Creek, the original area is a quarter mile north from SLAHEECH CEMETERY No. 3 (marked by sign and white picket fence of west side of highway) and a quarter mile west* [Albert Phillips (Trip to Five-Mile Creek 4/30/79)])'/, lx <**=em**> *place to have/get*, lx <**lexw=**> *always*, phonology: vowel merger, syntactic analysis: nominal, attested by AK (Trip to Five-Mile Creek 4/30/79), other sources: Wells 1965 (lst ed.):25, source: place names reference file #133, also /'*village about half a mile aove mouth of Sawmill Creek*'/, attested by SP and AK (Fish Camp 8/2/77), also /'*Five-Mile Creek, Saddle Rock*'/, attested by Halkomelem Instructors Association (10/26/77), also /'*area of skunk cabbages right across the Fraser River from Five-Mile Creek, a low area at the swampy south end of Q'aleliktel*'/, attested by AK (Trip to Five-Mile Creek 4/30/79), also /'*area along the banks of Five-Mile Creek, the original area is a quarter mile north from SLAHEECH CEMETERY No. 3 (marked by sign and white picket fence of west side of highway) and a quarter mile west*'/, attested by Albert Phillips (Trip to Five-Mile Creek 4/30/79).

<**ts'ó:kw'**>, probable root or stem //c'á·k'ʷ//, root meaning unknown unless distantly related to **th'íkwe** *left side*, perhaps *left, wrong* as in many languages.

<**sts'ó:kw'xel**>, df //s=c'á·k'ʷ=xʸəl//, CLO ['*get a shoe on the wrong foot*'], (<**s=**> *stative*), root meaning unknown, lx <**=xel**> *on the foot*, syntactic analysis: intransitive verb, attested by EB (9/21/76).

<**sts'ókw'elxel**>, plv //s=c'ák'ʷ=əl=xʸəl//, CLO ['*got (both) shoes on wrong feet*'], (<**=el=**> *plural lexical suffix*), grammatical comment: clear example of =el= infix pluralizing the lexical suffix, phonology: infixed plural, syntactic analysis: intransitive verb, attested by EB (9/22/76).

<**ts'ó:l**>, probablyfree root //c'á·l//, ABDF /'*to get skinned, peel the skin off*'/, syntactic analysis: intransitive verb, attested by Elders Group (4/16/75), example: <**ts'ó:l tel chálex**>, //c'á·l t-əl cɛ́ləxʸ//, /'*skin my hand, peel the skin on my hand*'/, attested by Elders Group.

<**ts'óls** or **ts'ó:ls**>, sas //c'á·(l)=ɛ́ls//, FOOD /'*peel (as a structured activity, for ex. in fixing vegetables)*'/, HARV, (<**=áls**> *structured activity non-continuative*), phonology: probable syllable-loss (of el before =áls), syntactic analysis: intransitive verb, attested by MH (Deming 1/4/79), example: <**ts'óls te (xáwéq, sqá:wth)**>, //c'á·(l)=ɛ́ls tə (xʸɛ́w(=)əq, s=qɛ́·w(=)θ)//, /'*peel the (carrots, potatoes)*'/, attested by MH.

<**ts'ólesem ~ ts'ólésem**>, ABFC /'*turn one's face, (turn one's body away [IHTTC])*'/, *see* ts'el.

<**ts'ó:lexeth'**>, ABFC /'*roll over in bed, turn over in bed*'/, *see* ts'el.

<**ts'óls** or **ts'ó:ls**>, FOOD /'*peel (as a structured activity, for ex. in fixing vegetables)*'/, *see* ts'ó:l.

<**ts'ó:lha ~ ch'ó:lha ~ ts'ólha**>, probable bound root or stem //c'á·ɬ(=)ɛ ~ c'áɬ(=)ɛ//, meaning unknown.

<**sts'ó:lha ~ sch'ó:lha ~ sts'ólha**>, df //s=c'á·ɬ(=)ɛ ~ s=c'áɬ(=)ɛ//, EB ['*leaf*'], LT ['*leaf-green*'], ASM ['the following color terms are used by AK before sts'ólha to specify shades of the color: tsxwíkw', xwíxwekw'el, tsqw'í**x**w, tsqwáy, sqwóqwiyel, stl'ítl'esel'], (<**s=**> *nominalizer*), root meaning unknown, possibly <**=a**> *living thing*, syntactic analysis: nominal, attested by AC, BJ (5/10/64, 12/5/64), EB (2/16/76), Elders Group (5/16/79), other sources: ES /sc'áɬa/ (Cw /sc'áɬɛʔ/, Ms

/sc'áɬaʔ/) *leaf,* Salish cognate: Squamish /sč'úɬaʔ/ *leaf (of any tree)* W73:158, K67:288, Lushootseed /s-č'úɬəyʔ/ *leaf (in general)* H76:119, see charts by Rob MacLaury, example: <**ts'ats'í:ts'etl' sts'ó:lha x̱wá:lá:lhp**>, //C_1ɛ=c'í·ƛ'[=C_1ə=]ƛ' s=c'ɛ́·ɬɛ x̣ʷɛ́·lɛ=ɛ́ɬp//, EB, /'*short leaf willow, short-leaf willow, Sitka willow*'/, /'*Salix sitchensis*'/ (<**x̱wá:lá:lhp**> *short-leaf willow, Sitka willow),* attested by AC (11/26/71), <**tl'áqt sts'ó:lha x̱wá:lá:lhp**>, //ƛ'ɛ́qt s=c'á·ɬɛx̣ʷɛ́·lɛ=ɛ́ɬp//, EB, /'*long leaf willow, Pacific willow*'/, /'*Salix lasiandra*'/, contrast <**xélts'epelhp**> *Pacific willow, long-leaf willow,* attested by AC (11/26/71), <**tsqwá:y te hilálxw sch'ó:lha.**>, //c=qʷɛ́·y tə hil=álxʷ s=c'á·ɬɛ//, /'*The Fall leaves are yellow.*'/, attested by Elders Group (5/16/79), <**tsqwá:y te sts'ólha.**>, //c=qʷɛ́·y tə s=c'áɬɛ//, /'*The leaf is green.*'/, attested by Deming (5/3/79, SJ esp.).

<**ts'ó:meqw**>, probable stem or root //s=c'á·m(=)əqʷ//, root meaning unknown.

<**sts'ó:meqw**>, df //s=c'á·m(=)əqʷ//, KIN /'*great grandparent, great grandchild, sibling or (up to fourth) cousin of great grandparent, great grandchild of brother or sister or (up to fourth) cousin*'/, (<**s=**> *nominalizer*), root meaning unknown, possibly <**=eqw**> *on top of the head, on the hair,* syntactic analysis: nominal, attested by AC (9/29/71, 8/15/70), Elders Group (6/8/77, 7/9/75), other sources: ES /sc'á·məqʷ/ *great grandparent, great grandchild,* example: <**tl'ó: a sts'ó:meqw.**>, //ƛ'á-ə ʔɛ s=c'á·məqʷ//, /'*Is that your great grandchild?*'/, attested by AC.

<**sts'ólemeqw**>, pln //s=c'á[=lə=]m(=)əqʷ//, KIN /'*great grandchildren, great grandparents*'/, (<**=le=**> *plural*), phonology: infixed plural, syntactic analysis: nominal, attested by AC (11/16/71).

<**Ts'qó:ls**>, PLN /'*village on the site of Hope, modern Hope, B.C.*'/, *see* ts'qó:ls.

<**ts'q'éyx̱em**>, TAST /'*vanilla, (vanilla extract)*'/, *see* q'íx̱.

<**ts'qw'élá**>, CLO ['*ear-ring*'], *see* ts'éqw'.

<**ts'qw'élhp**>, EB /'*spruce tree, Sitka spruce*'/, *see* ts'éqw'.

<**ts'qw'ét**>, MC /'*poke it, pin s-th, pick it up (on sharp pointed object), pick s-th up on a fork (or other sharp object)*'/, *see* ts'éqw'.

<**ts'qw'ít** or **th'qw'it**>, pcs //c'q'ʷ=ə[=Aí=]T or θ'q'ʷ=ə[=Aí=]T//, durs, EB /'*prop up a limb with a Y-shaped stick, (prop s-th up (of a limb, with a Y-shaped stick))*'/, root meaning unknown, (<**=et**> *purposeful control transitivizer*), (<**í-ablaut**> *durative*), phonology: ablaut, vowel-loss in root, syntactic analysis: transitive verb, attested by EB (6/30/76), also <**ts'qw'ít** or **ts'qw'át**> or something else?, //c'q'ʷ=ə[=Aí=]T or c'ɛ́q'ʷ=M1=T//, also /'*prop up a limb*'/, attested by HT (6/21/76).

<**ts'qw'ő̄stel ~ ts'qw'ő̄wstel**>, df //c'q'ʷ=ə́ws=təl//, HHG ['*big copper pot*'], FOOD, root meaning unknown unless ts'qw' as in ts'qw'ít *prop it up on a Y-shaped stick,* possibly <**=ó̄ws**> *on the body, on the skin,* lx <**=tel**> *device to,* Elder's comment: "borrowed from the Thompson language (BHTTC)", syntactic analysis: nominal, attested by BHTTC (8/24/76), Salish cognate: perhaps Squamish /n-qʷíʔs-tn/ *cooking pot* W73:203, K67:309, (the Squamish root is cognate with Upriver Halkomelem qwéls *boil,* as are Samish /šqʷə́l's/ *cooking pot* G86a:83 and Cowichan /šqʷál's/ *cooking pot* B74b:32), but contrast Squamish /sqʷʔíls ~ qʷə́y=qʷi/ *copper* W73:67, K67:296, K69:59, and Lushootseed /q'ʷúlalatxʷ/ *copper* H76:431 and Upriver Halkomelem /qʷíqʷi/ *copper* and /sq'ʷə́l/ *a metal found in mines and used for arrowheads,* also <**tsqw'ő̄:stel**>, //cq'ʷ=ó·s=təl//, attested by Elders Group (1/21/76), also <**ts'qwő̄:stel**>, //c'qʷ=ó·s=təl//, also /'*big metal pot*'/, attested by Elders Group (1/22/75).

<**ts'qw'í:wíyelhp**>, ds //c'q'ʷ=í·wəl=əɬp//, EB /'*swamp gooseberry, prickly swamp currant*'/, dialects: *some Chill.*, compare <**th'kw'íwíyelhp**> *swamp gooseberry, prickly swamp currant,* with root

<th'ekw' ~ th'ikw'> *sore.*

<ts'sá:y>, df //c'sʹ=Ɛ́·y or c'Ɛ́s=M1=əy//, EB [*'Douglas fir log or wood'*], [*'Pseudotsuga menziesii'*], ASM ['the bark ranges from gray in young trees to black to reddish-brown or grayish-brown in older trees, it is excellent firewood'], root meaning unknown unless ts'es *black, brown-gray* or ts'á:s in sts'á:s *fine whitish ash* or ts'ís *grow*, lx **<=á:y ~ =ey>** *bark, covering*, possibly **<metathesis>** *derivational*, phonology: possible metathesis and vowel merger, possible vowel-loss, syntactic analysis: nominal, attested by BJ (12/5/64), Salish cognate: Squamish /č'š-áyʔ/ *Douglas fir* W73:100, K67:319, possibly Northern Lushootseed /č'əsáyʔ/ *straight spear for crabs and bottom fish* (E.K.) ~ *two-pronged pole for spearing (usu. of fir)* (D.M.) ~ *a stick of firewood* (Louisa George), H76:112.

<ts'sá:yelhp>, ds //c's=Ɛ́·y=əɬp//, EB [*'(Douglas) fir tree'*], [*'Pseudotsuga menziesii'*], lx **<=elhp>** *tree*, syntactic analysis: nominal, attested by BJ (12/5/64), others.

<ts'sá:yelhp>, EB [*'(Douglas) fir tree'*], *see* ts'sá:y.

<ts'símt>, KIN /*'growing [s-o] up, (raising s-o)'*/, *see* ts'ísem.

<Ts'símteló:t>, PLN [*'other sister of Lhilheqey or Mount Cheam'*], *see* ts'ísem.

<ts'sítsim>, df //c'is=ic=im or c'ís=M1=əc=im//, FSH /*'spear pole knot hitch (two half-hitches), clove-hitch knot'*/, MC, ASM ['this knot is handy to know if one keeps a gaff hook in cork in a pocket, and if he sees a fish he can cut a pole fast and attach the hook with this knot (EL)'], literally possibly /'grow in back repeatedly'/, (semological comment: possibly so named due to the way a clove hitch is tied: right over and back around left, then new left over and back around new right), possibly root **<ts'is>** *grow*?, possibly **<=íts ~ =ets ~ =ewíts>** *on the back*, possibly **<metathesis>** *derivational*, possibly **<=ím>** *repeatedly*, phonology: possible metathesis, possible vowel-loss in root, syntactic analysis: nominal?, intransitive verb?, attested by EL (Elders Group 1/26/77).

<ts'tá:m>, ds //c'Ɛ́t-M1=əm//, ABFC [*'crawl'*], (**<metathesis type 1>** *non-continuative*), (**<=em>** *middle voice*), phonology: metathesis, vowel merger, syntactic analysis: intransitive verb, attested by EB (12/11/75), AC (8/6/70), RG & EH (4/9/99 Ling332), Salish cognate: Samish dial. of NSt /č'tə́ŋ/ *crawl* (beside /č'ə́tŋ'/ *crawling*) G86a:93, Cowichan dial. of Halkomelem /c'tém/ *crawl* B74b:59, possibly Squamish /č'ít-n/ *bring close (tr.)* W73:61, K67:321, also **<ts'tám>**, //c'Ɛ́t=M1=(ə)m//, attested by Deming (3/16/78), example: **<lulh ts'tá:m tel mímele.>**, //lə=uɬ c'Ɛ́t=M1=əm t-əl C_1í=məlƐ//, /*'My baby is already crawling.'*/, literally /'my little child has already crawled'/, attested by EB.

<ts'átem>, cts //c'Ɛ́t=əm//, [c'Ɛ́təm], ABFC [*'crawling'*], (**<lack of metathesis means>** *continuative*), syntactic analysis: intransitive verb, attested by AC (8/6/70), EB (12/11/75), RG & EH (4/9/99 Ling332), Deming (3/16/78), IHTTC (7/28/77), Salish cognate: Samish dial. of NSt /č'ə́tŋ'/ *crawling* G86a:93, also **<ts'étem ~ ch'étem>**, //c'ə́t=əm//, attested by NP (9/30/75), example: **<ts'átem stim:ốt>**, //c'Ɛ́t=əm stim=mót//, CAN, /*'train'*/, literally /'crawling steamboat'/, attested by IHTTC (7/28/77), also **<ts'étem stim:ốt ~ ch'étem stim:ōt>**, //c'ə́t=əm stim=mót//, attested by NP (9/30/75).

<ts'tés>, df //c'tə́s//, SD /*'(make a) ringing sound when something drops (spoon, metal ashtray or something heavy)'*/, semantic environment ['for ex. of a spoon, metal ashtray, or something heavy'], root perhaps same as in th'átsem *ringing, jingling*, comment: th'átsem if related would be /θ'ə[-AƐ́-]ts=əm/ and ts'tés would be really th'tés /θ'ə́t[=M1=]s/, phonology: possible metathesis or vowel-loss, syntactic analysis: intransitive verb, attested by Elders Group (11/3/76).

<ts'tíxem>, df //c'tíxʸ=əm//, FSH [*'coiled up méthelh rope for fishing (for sturgeon and spring salmon)'*], root meaning unknown, possibly **<=em>** *have/get/intransitivizer*, syntactic analysis: nominal, attested by Elders Group (3/26/75), Salish cognate: Squamish /s-č’tíšm/ *harpoon-line of cedar-bark* W73:130, K67:288.

<**ts'tl'ám ~ ts'tl'ém**>, mdls //c’ɛƛ’-M1=m ~ c’ə́ƛ’-M1=m or c’ɛƛ’=ə[-´-]m//, [c’ƛ’ɛ́m ~ c’ƛ’ə́m], ABFC /'*jump, hop (once)*'/, TVMO, (<**metathesis type 1**> *non-continuative*), (<**=em**> *middle voice*), phonology: metathesis, vowel-loss or vowel merger, syntactic analysis: intransitive verb, attested by AC (8/7/70), Elders Group (3/1/72, 3/15/72), EB (12/12/75), JL (5/5/75), RG & EH (4/9/99 Ling332), example: <**le ts'tl'ám.**>, //lə c’ɛƛ’=M1=m//, /'*He jumped.*'/, attested by AC, JL.

<**ts'á:tl'em ~ ch'á:tl'em ~ ts'átl'em**>, cts //c’ɛ́[-·-]ƛ’=əm//, ABFC /'*jumping, hopping*'/, TVMO, (<**-:-** and **lack of metathesis**> *continuative*), phonology: lengthening, syntactic analysis: intransitive verb, attested by AC (8/7/70), Elders Group (3/15/72), JL (5/5/75), example: <**le ts'átl'em.**>, //lə c’ɛ́ƛ’=əm//, /'*He's jumping.*'/, attested by AC.

<**ts'í:ts'á:tl'em**>, dmn //C_1í=c’ɛ́·ƛ’=əm//, EZ /'*grasshopper (ordinary),* perhaps *longhorned grasshopper*'/, ['order *Orthoptera*, family *Acrididae* or perhaps family *Tettigoniidae*'], literally /'little jumping/hopping'/, (<**R4=**> *diminutive*), phonology: reduplication, syntactic analysis: nominal, attested by AC (12/4/71).

<**ts'áts'etl'em**>, cts //c’ɛ́[-C_1ə-]ƛ’=əm//, ABFC ['*jumping*'], TVMO, (<**-R1-**> *continuative*), phonology: reduplication, syntactic analysis: intransitive verb, attested by Elders Group (3/1/72).

<**ts'áts'etl'em**>, dnom //c’ɛ́[=C_1ə=]ƛ’=əm//, EZ /'*grasshopper (ordinary),* perhaps *longhorned grasshopper*'/, ['order *Orthoptera*, family *Acrididae* or perhaps family *Tettigoniidae*'], literally /'jumping, hopping'/, phonology: reduplication, syntactic analysis: nominal, attested by Elders Group (3/1/72).

<**ts'ats'etl'í:m**>, durs //c’ɛ́[-C_1ə-]ƛ’=ə[=Aí·=]m or c’ɛ́[-C_1ə-]ƛ’=əm=í·m//, rpts, cts, ABFC /'*jumping along, jumping up and down*'/, TVMO, probably <**í:-ablaut**> *durative*, possibly <**=í:m**> *repetitive*, phonology: reduplication, ablaut or syllable-loss (em before =ím), syntactic analysis: intransitive verb, attested by Elders Group (3/1/72, 3/15/72).

<**ts'ats'etl'í:m**>, dnom //c’ɛ́[=C_1ə=]ƛ’=ə[=Aí·=]m or c’ɛ́[=C_1ə=]ƛ’=əm=í·m//, EZ /'*grasshopper (ordinary),* perhaps *longhorned grasshopper*'/, ['order *Orthoptera*, family *Acrididae* or perhaps family *Tettigoniidae*'], literally /'jumping along/jumping up and down'/, syntactic analysis: nominal, source: H-T <tastaskle'm> (macron over e) ~ <kakawate'lE> (umlaut over first <a> and macron over e) *grasshopper (Caloptenus sp.)*(first named from <tsa'klEm> *to jump, hop*, the second name refers to the strident noise the insect makes–that name may be <q’aq’awetxíle> or <q’ikw’etxíle> or something similar in Stó:lō orthography).

<**ts'áts'ets'tl'ím**>, dmv //c’ɛ́[-C_1ə-][=C_1ə=]ƛ’=ə[=Aí=]m or c’ɛ́[-C_1ə-][=C_1ə=]ƛ’=əm=ím//, durs, rpts, cts, ABFC ['*be hopping*'], TVMO, (<**=R1=**> *diminutive*), phonology: double reduplication, ablaut or syllable-loss, syntactic analysis: intransitive verb, attested by BHTTC (10/21/76), example: <**ts'áts'ets'tl'ím te (pípehò:m, mímetú, kwíkweshú).**>, //c’ɛ́[-C_1ə-][=C_1ə=]ƛ’=ə[=Aí=]m tə (C_1í=pəhà·m, C_1í=mətú, C_1í=kʷəšú)//, /'*The (frog, little lamb, little pig) is hopping.*'/, attested by BHTTC.

<**ts'tl'émet**>, iecs //c’ə́ƛ’-M1=məT//, ABFC ['*jump at s-o*'], ABFC ['*strike (of a snake) at s-o*'], semantic environment ['snake'], (<**metathesis type 1**> *non-continuative*), (<**=met**> *indirect effect non-control transitivizer*), phonology: metathesis, syntactic analysis: transitive verb, attested by Elders Group (6/16/76), example: <**ts'tl'émethò:m te álhqey.**>, //c’ə́ƛ’=M1=məT-à·m tə ʔɛ́ɬqəy//, /'*The snake strikes at you., The snake jumps at you.*'/, syntactic comment: passive, attested by Elders Group.

<**ts’tl’émetst**>. pcs //c’ə́ƛ’-M1=m=əcəl=T (or poss.) c’ə́ƛ’-M1=m=əc=T//, GAM /to skip rope/, <**=T**> *purposeful control transitivizer*, <**=ewíts ~ =íts ~ =ích ~ =ech**> *on the back, on the back of*

something (those allomorphs without <=ew> also have extended allosemes/meanings DIR ['*on the surface, on top*'], for ex. **<=í:tsel ~ =etsel>** *on the back, on the surface, on the top*, attested by RG & EH (4/9/99 Ling332).

<tl'emtl'émxel>, df //(c'=)C_1əC_2=ƛ'ə́m=x^{y}əl//, EZ /'*grasshopper (ordinary), perhaps longhorned grasshopper*'/, ['order *Orthoptera*, family *Acrididae* or perhaps family *Tettigoniidae*'], literally possibly /'many jump on the foot'/, (semological comment: if so named, perhaps after grasshopper plagues), (**<R3=>** *plural subject or? action*), lx **<=xel>** *on the foot*, phonology: reduplication, consonant-loss (first consonant of root, very odd), syntactic analysis: nominal, attested by HP (4/16/75).

<ts'tl'émet>, ABFC ['*jump at s-o*'], *see* ts'tl'ám ~ ts'tl'ém.

<ts'tl'étl'xel>, ABFC ['*takes short steps*'], *see* ts'í:tl' ~ ts'ítl'.

<ts'xwélmexw ~ ts'xwílmexw>, SOCT ['*friends*'], *see* xwélmexw.

<ts'xwót>, pcs //c'x^{w}á=T or c'áx^w=M1=T or c'x^w=áT//, TIB /'*add some, add it, (do it again [AD])*'/, possibly **<metathesis type 1>** *non-continuative*, (**<=t>** *purposeful control transitivizer*), phonology: metathesis or allomorph of suffix, syntactic analysis: transitive verb, attested by Elders Group (3/16/77), Salish cognate: Lushootseed /č'x^w-úd/ *add it to something* H76:696, Squamish root /č'ix^w ~ č'əx^w/ *increase* as in /č'x^w-ut/ *increase (tr.)* W73:149, K67:319,320, K69:68, also /'*do it again*'/, attested by AD (11/19/79).

<ch'exwélhchat>, ds //c'əx^w=ə́ɬcɛ=T//, WATR ['*add some water [to s-th]*'], TIB, FOOD, lx **<=élhcha>** *water, unclear liquid*, syntactic analysis: transitive verb, attested by IHTTC (8/17/77).

<ts'xwó:ythel>, LANG /'*silence the mouth, keep the mouth quiet*'/, *see* ts'áxw.

U

<**Uhámél ~ Ōhámél**> //ʔə[=Au=]ha=ɛ́məl ~ ʔə[=Ao=]ha=ɛ́məl//, PLN [*'village now called Ohamil Reserve or Laidlaw'*], see under more common variants <**Ōhámél**> and <**Shxw'ōhámél**>.

<**ú:kw'elets**>, FOOD /*'run out of food, be out of food'*/, *see* ṓwkw'.

<**ú:kw't**>, FOOD [*'finish it (of food)'*], *see* ṓwkw'.

<**Uqw'íles**>, df //wq'ʷ=íl=əs or ʔə=wq'ʷ=íl=əs//, PLN /*'Restmore Caves* [Wells]*), (mouth of Hunter Creek [IHTTC])'*/, literally /'go drift downriver on the face'/, (semological comment: so named after an Indian murderer who lived there and killed people coming upriver till he was killed by an organized group of Indian people (Duff 1952)), phonology: vocalization of w to u, possibly <**e= ~ hé=**> *continuative*?, root <**wṓqw'**> *drift downriver*, possibly <**=íl**> *go, come, get, become*, probably <**=es**> *on the face*, (<**zero**> *nominalizer*), comment: i.e. a verb used over time as place name becoming a nominal/noun, syntactic analysis: nominal, source: Wells 1965 (lst ed.):15, source: place names reference file #184, also <**ōqw'íles ~ ōqw'éyles**>, //wq'ʷ=íl=əs//, also /*'mouth of Hunter Creek'*/, phonology: vocalization of w to ō or e → ō, attested by IHTTC (8/5/77 incl. AK, TG, AD but not SP on that day).

<**úx̲**>, possibly root //ʔúx̣//, EFAM [*'it smells (said to child)'*], phonology: sound symbolism with other interjections, syntactic analysis: interjection, usage: baby talk, attested by AHTTC (2/15/80).

<**unknown**>, WETH [*'four days of northeast wind'*], Elder's comment: "there is a word for this", attested by EB.

<**unknown**>, WETH [*'eight days of northeast wind'*], Elder's comment: "there is a word for this", attested by EB.

W

<**wá:ch ~ wá:ts**>, bound root //wɛ́·c//, *dung, shit, excrement.*

<**wá:cháwtxw**>, ds //wɛ́·c=ɛ́wtx^w//, BLDG /*'outhouse (for solid waste), (shit-house)'*/, literally /'shit house, dung building'/, (semological comment: this term is coarser than <**átl'qeláwtxw**> *outhouse* (lit. *outside house*) or lílem *outhouse* (lit. *little house*) and so a coarse term in English, like *shit-house* gives a more accurate sense of when the term would be used in Halq'eméylem), lx <**=áwtxw**> *house, building*, syntactic analysis: nominal, attested by Elders Group (1/21/76), Salish cognate: Sechelt /wáč/ *excrements* T77:15.

<**wákel ~ wákyel**>, free root //wɛ́kəl or wɛ́k^{y}əl//, [wǽk^{y}ɪl], CAN [*'wagon'*], syntactic analysis: noun, nominal, attested by EB (12/18/75), Elders Group (3/2/77), example: <**wákyel xàlh**>, //wɛ́k^{y}əl x^{y}ɛ̀ɬ//, /*'wagon road'*/, phonology: sentence-stress, attested by Elders Group.

<**wál**>, bound root //wɛ́l// meaning uncertain

<**swálém**>, df //s=wɛ́l=əm or s=wɛ́l=ə[=´=]m//, KIN [*'orphan'*], (<**s=**> *nominalizer, something to, (here) someone that*), root meaning unknown unless <**wál** or **wá:l**>, bound root //wɛ́l or wɛ́·l *throw*//., comment: it is tempting to connect the root in shxw=wáli *parents* here but Downriver and Island Halkomelem and Squamish cognates show that the word for orphan originally had a root with wán and the word for parents originally had a root with wál, possibly <**=em**> *have/get/intransitivizer or middle voice*, possibly <= ´=> *derivational*, phonology: possible *stress-shift*, syntactic analysis: nominal, attested by Elders Group (8/25/76), Salish cognate: Squamish /wánim/ *orphan* W73:191, K67:378.

<**swelmáylh ~ swelméylh**>, df //s=wal=əm=ɛ́yɬ//, KIN /*'child of deceased sibling, child of deceased brother/sister'*/, (<**s=**> *nominalizer, someone that*), probably root <**wálém**> *orphan*, possibly <**=áylh**> *child*, possibly <**=lh**> *past tense, deceased*, phonology: vowel-loss in suffix, syntactic analysis: nominal, attested by AC (11/16/71), other sources: ES /swəlmɛ́yɬ/ (CwMs /swənmɛ́yɬ/) *deceased sibling's child*, H-T <swilmai'tl> *cousin after parent's death*, also <**swelmá:ylh**>, //s=wal=əm=ɛ́·yɬ//, attested by Elders Group (6/8/77).

<**wál** or **wá:l**>, bound root //wɛ́l or wɛ́·l *throw*//.

<**wá:ls**>, sas //wɛ́(l)=ɛ́ls//, ECON /*'to scramble-give, throw money/blankets/poles to a crowd, give away at a big (winter) dance [by throwing]'*/, ASM ['sometimes these things were thrown from the roof or platform at roof level connected to the longhouse/dance house, when blankets were thrown people would try to hang on to the largest portion if they couldn't get away with a whole blanket, then a person would come around and cut the blanket apart in each portion, when poles were thrown the portion of pole that a person could hang onto was redeemed by a proportionate amount of money or other gifts, when coins were thrown people just scrambled for them, this type of giving was done besides the formal presentations within the longhouse to particular named people'], probably root <**wál**> *throw*, (<**=á:ls ~ =áls**> *structured activity non-continuative*), phonology: consonant-loss (l before =áls), syntactic analysis: intransitive verb, attested by Elders Group (6/16/76), Salish cognate: Squamish /wáls/ *throw away as a "scramble-gift", give away (itr.)* W73:224, K69:89.

<**wówí:ls**>, cts //wɛ[-AáC$_1$ə-](l)=ə[=Aí·=]ls//, [wáwí·ls], ECON [*'(be scramble-giving)'*], (<**ó-ablaut plus -R1-**> *continuative*), probably <**í:-ablaut on e in a suffix**> *durative*, (<**=els**> *structured activity continuative*), phonology: double ablaut, reduplication, consonant-loss,

syntactic analysis: intransitive verb, attested by BJ (12/5/64 new transcript old p.324).

<**swá:ls**>, dnom //s=wɛ́(l)=ɛ́ls//, ECON /'*scramble-giving, a scramble*'/, (<**s=**> *nominalizer, something to*), phonology: consonant-loss, syntactic analysis: nominal, attested by AC (9/15/71), BJ (12/5/64), other sources: ES /swɛ̂·ls/ *scramble-giving*, Salish cognate: Squamish /swáls/ *scatter (tr.?), throw away; scramble-gift* W73:224, K67:299, K69:60,75.

<**wá:lx**>, pcis //wɛ́·l=x^{y}//, ABFC /'*throw s-th (a rock, etc.), throw it (to someone)*'/, (<**=x**> *purposeful control inanimate object preferred*), syntactic analysis: transitive verb, attested by AC, RG & EH (4/9/99 Ling332), other sources: ES /wɛ́·lx^{y}/ *throw*, also <**wálx**>, //wɛ́l=x^{y}//, attested by EB (4/29/76); found in <**wá:lxchexw yewá:lmels kw'as wets'étl'.**>, //wɛ́·l=x^{y}-c-əx^{w} yəwɛ́·l=məls k'^{w}-ɛ-s wə=c'ə́ƛ'//, /'*Throw it before you fall.*'/, attested by AC (10/13/71), example: <**tsel le wá:lx te í:'axwìl smàlt.**>, //c-əl lə wɛ́·l=x^{y} tə C_1í=ʔɛx^{w}íl s=mɛ́lt//, /'*I threw a little rock.*'/, attested by AC (10/21/71), <**wálxlha te qweqwáyels lam tl' Bill.**>, //wɛ́l=x^{y}-ɬɛ tə C_1ə=q^{w}ɛ́y=əls lɛ=mƛ' Bill//, /'*Throw the orange to Bill.*'/, attested by EB (4/29/76), <**wálx té smà:lt**>, //wɛ́l=x^{y} tə s=mɛ̀·lt//, /'*to throw a rock*'/, attested by EB (1/30/76), <**tsel wá:lxòlèm.**>, //c-əl wɛ́·l=x^{y}-àlə̀m//, /'*I fell down.*'/, literally /'I was thrown (?)'/, syntactic analysis: passive?, attested by EB (12/10/75).

<**swéltel**>, df //s=wɛ[=Aə́=]l=təl//, FSH /'*net (any kind, for any purpose), fish net, gill-net (Elders Group 11/26/75))*'/, HUNT /'*net (for ducks, fish)*'/, EZ ['*web (of spider)*'], literally /'something to throw device'/, (<**s=**> *nominalizer*), probably root <**wál**> *throw*, probably <**é-ablaut**> *derivational*, lx <**=tel**> *device to*, phonology: probable ablaut, syntactic analysis: nominal, attested by Elders Group (3/26/75, 6/14/75), EB (2/11/75), TG (4/23/75), Deming (3/25/76), AC (10/23/70), EL (2/20/79), Salish cognate: Squamish /swítn/ *net; spider web* W73:184, K67:299, also /'*gill-net*'/, attested by Elders Group (11/26/75), example: <**tewát kw'e íxw tháyelhtset ta swéltel?**>, //tə=wɛ́t k'^{w}ə ʔí-x^{w} θi[-Aɛ́-]y=əɬc=əT t-ɛ s=wɛ[=Aə́=]l=təl//, /'*Who are you making the fish-net for?*'/, attested by AC (11/11/71).

<**lesák swéltel**>, cpds //ləsɛ́k s=wɛ[=Aə́=]l=təl//, FSH /'*bag net, sack net*'/, literally /'sack/bag net'/, (semological comment: lesák is borrowed from Chinook Jargon), ASM ['this term used later by EL as he's not sure of the real term, he saw it done: other men threw spears at the fish to drive them into the net, it was done at Páléxel, and EL saw them get 50 steelhead'], syntactic analysis: nominal phrase with modifier(s), attested by EL (2/20/79),

<**weltá:lt**>, df //wɛ́·l=tə[=M2=]l=T or wəl=ti[=Aɛ́·=]l=t//, HUNT /'*spring snare [s-th], [a?] spring snare*'/, possibly root <**wá:l**> *throw* and stem <**wá:ltel**> lit. "*throw device*" as in *net* , probably <**=tel**> *device to*, possibly <**metathesis**> *derivational*, possibly <**á:-ablaut**> *derivational or durative*, possibly <**=t**> *purposeful control transitivizer*, phonology: metathesis or ablaut, syntactic analysis: transitive verb? or nominal??, attested by Deming (4/11/78), contrast with <**t'í:tsel**> *spring snare*, also <**íweltàlt**>, //ʔíwəl=tɛ̀l=t//, HUNT ['*spring snare trap*'], (semological comment: no derivational affix =t is known elsewhere; it may be that the suffix is -t *purposeful control transitivizer* and that the translation of íweltàlt should be *set it (snare trap), set a snare),* attested by Elders Group 10/20/76, for this latter form and alternated etymology and related words *see* íwel.

<**wá:ls**>, ECON /'*to scramble-give, throw money/blankets/poles to a crowd, give away at a big (winter) dance [by throwing]*'/, *see* wál or wá:l.

<**wá:lx**>, ABFC /'*throw s-th (a rock, etc.), throw it (to someone)*'/, *see* wál or wá:l.

<**wálhet**>, pcs //wɛ́ɬ=əT//, ABFC /'*chase it away, (chase s-o/s-th away)*'/, TVMO, (<**=et**> *purposeful control transitivizer*), syntactic analysis: transitive verb, attested by EB (1/16/76), Salish cognate: Squamish /wáɬ-an/ *chase away, chase out (tr.)* K67:378.

<**wà:m**>, possibly root //wɛ̀·m// meaning unknown

<swà:m>, df //s=wɛ̀·m//, FOOD [*'dried big clams threaded onto a string of inner cedar bark (obtained in trade)'*], EZ [*'(horse clam)'*], [*'Tersus capax ~ Schizothaerus capax'*], (**<s=>** *nominalizer*), root meaning unknown, syntactic analysis: nominal, attested by Elders Group (7/21/76), Salish cognate: Squamish /swám/ *horse clam* W73:60, K67:299 and /swaám/ *horse clam (Tersus capax)* Kennedy and Bouchard 1976b:104.

<wáq ~ wiq>, bound root //wɛ́q ~ wiq// *male*; found in **<swíqe>** *man*, see below under **<wíyeq ~ wíyq ~ wí:q>**, since the vowel of the root is variable.

<swáqeth>, df //s=wɛ́q(=)əθ or s=wi[=Aɛ́=]q=ə(=)θ//, KIN [*'husband'*], literally (possibly) /'someone that's a male spouse'/, (**<s=>** *nominalizer, someone that*), possibly root **<wíq>** *male*, possibly **<á-ablaut>** *derivational*, possibly **<=e>** *living entity*, lx **<=th ~ =eth>** *spouse*, phonology: possible ablaut, syntactic analysis: nominal, attested by AC, others, other sources: H-T <swa'kuts> (umlaut over a) *husband*, Salish cognate: Nooksack /šwǽqəc/ *husband* Amoss 1961, Sechelt /s-wáqac/ *husband* T77:16, MCx /gáqaθ/ *married woman* and MCx /gáwqaqaθ/ *married women* all quoted in G82:36 (cognate set 171) where the PCS *-c *spouse* is confirmed by Lushootseed //s-q'ʷúyʔ-c// /s-q'ʷíc'/ *widow(er)* and /ʔu-q'ʷíc'-il/ *just lost a spouse* H76:431 with an apparent root /q'ʷúyʔ/ *die* cognate with Halq'eméylem /q'á·y/ *die*.

<swóweqeth>, dnom //s=wɛ[=AáC_1ə=]q=ə(=)θ//, KIN /*'hubby, dear husband, pet term for husband'*/, (**<s=>** *nominalizer*), (**<ó-ablaut plus -R1->** *affectionate diminutive*), phonology: ablaut, reduplication, syntactic analysis: nominal, attested by AD (11/19/79).

<swóweqeth>, strs //s=wɛ[=AáC_1ə=]q=ə(=)θ//, KIN /*'married woman, got a husband, got married to a husband'*/, literally /'got a male spouse'/, (**<s=>** *stative*), (**<ó-ablaut on root á plus =R1=>** *resultative*), phonology: ablaut, reduplication, syntactic analysis: adjective/adjectival verb, attested by AC (10/23/71), JS (Elders Group 3/26/80), EB and AD (9/25/78), example: **<éwe ís swóweqeth.>**, //ʔə́wə ʔí-s s=wɛ[=Aá·C_1ə=]q=ə(=)θ//, /*'She's got no husband.'*/, attested by JS.

<swóqeweqeweth (or better) **swóq-weqeth>**, plv //s=wɛ[=Aá=]q=C_1əC_2=ə(=)θ//, strs, KIN /*'married women, ((plural) got husbands)'*/, (**<=R2>** *plural*), phonology: ablaut, reduplication, extra ew apparently mistranscribed, syntactic analysis: adjective/adjectival verb, attested by Elders Group (3/72), example: **<ŏwelh le t'ókw' ye swóqeweqeweth.>**, //ʔə́wə=ɬ lə t'ák'ʷ yə s=wɛ́[=Aá=]q=C_1əC_2=ə(=)θ//, /*'The married women never went home.'*/, usage: conversation, attested by Elders Group (3/72).

<wásewey>, df //wɛ́səw=ɛy or wɛ́səw=əy//, EB [*'small mountain alder'*], [*'Alnus tenuifolia'*], ASM ['botanically identified from a sample'], root meaning unknown, lx **<=ay ~ =ey>** *bark*, syntactic analysis: nominal, attested by SP, Salish cognate: Squamish /yásawʔi/ *tree similar to the alder but small (grows high up in the mountains)* W73:4, K67:382 and /yásaw'ay/ *mountain alder (Alnus sinuata) (Regel) Rydb.* Bouchard and Turner 1976:75, Fraser R. dial. of Lillooet /zásaw-az'/ *mountain alder (Alnus incana), Sitka alder (Alnus crispa (ssp. sinuata))* Turner 1974:49,101, Lushootseed /yəsáwi/ *alder* H76:632, historical/comparative detail: Upriver Halkomelem has apparently assimilated the initial consonant to the third consonant.

<wát>, free root //wɛ́t//, PRON /*'who?, who'*/, syntactic analysis: interrogative verb, attested by BHTTC (10/3/76), other sources: ES /wɛ́t/ and JH /wét/ *who*, example: **<wát kw'a skwíx?>**, //wɛ́t k'ʷ-ɛ s=kʷíxʸ//, /*'What's your name?'*/, attested by BHTTC (10/3/76).

<tewát>, ds //tə=wɛ́t//, PRON [*'be who?'*], (**<te=>** *the (gender and proximity/visibility unspecified)*), phonology: te= is phonologically, syntactically, and semantically a prefix here, syntactic analysis: interrogative verb, syntactic comment: te= is not functioning here as a demonstrative article (which cannot occur sentence initially), attested by AC, EB (1/12/7), AD (5/5/80), BHTTC (10/3/76), example: **<tewát kw'e lí kwethá?>**, //tə=wɛ́t k'ʷə lí kʷə=θɛ́//, /*'Who is there?'*/, attested by EB,

<**tewát kw'e tl'íls kws láms?**>, //tə=wɛ́t k'ʷə ƛ'í=ls kʷ-s lɛ́=m-s//, /'*Who wants to go?*'/, attested by EB, <**tewát kw'e tl'íls kws més ísq'ó?**>, //tə=wɛ́t k'ʷə ƛ'í=ls kʷ-s mə́-s yə=s=q'á//, /'*Who wants to come along?*'/, attested by EB, <**tewát kw'a's sq'ó?**>, //tə=wɛ́t k'ʷ-ɛʔ-s s=q'á//, /'*Who is with you?*'/, literally /'who is? your someone with'/, attested by AD, <**tewát kw'e thíyt te'íle?**>, //tə=wɛ́t k'ʷə θíy=T tə=ʔí=lə//, /'*Who made this?*'/, attested by EB, <**tewát kw'e íxw tháyelhtset ta swéltel?**>, //tə=wɛ́t k'ʷə ʔí-xʷ θi[-Aɛ́-]y=əɬc=əT t-ɛ s=wə́l=təl//, /'*Who are you making the fish-net for?*'/, literally /'who is? that aux -you are making for s-o your net'/, attested by AC (11/11/71), <**tewát te lhexéylex?**>, //tə=wɛ́t tə ɬx̣=í·l=əxʸ//, /'*Who is standing there?, Who's there?*'/, attested by AC (8/15/70), <**léwe kwe tewát aswá ptámethox?**>, //lə́wə kʷə tə=wɛ́t ʔɛ-s=wɛ́ ptɛ́=məT-axʸ//, /'*Who are you that's asking me this?*'/, syntactic comment: syntax is unusual with aswá, attested by AC (9/29/71), <**léwe tewát?**>, //ləwə tə=wɛ́t//, /'*Who are you?*'/, attested by AC (8/15/70), <**(wát, tewát, stám) (kw'a, ta') skwíx?**>, //(wɛ́t, tə=wɛ́t, s=tɛ́m) (k'ʷ-ɛ, t-ɛʔ) s=kʷíxʸ//, /'*What's your name?*'/, attested by BHTTC (10/3/76), <**tewát te sqwmáy?**>, //tə=wɛ́t tə s=qʷəm=ɛ́y//, /'*Whose dog?*'/, literally /'who is? the dog'/, attested by AC (12/8/71), <**chel ō lhq'élexw wetewátes.**>, //c-əl ʔəw ɬ=q'ə́l=l-əxʷ wə-tə=wɛ́t-əs//, /'*I know who it is.*'/, attested by EB.

<**tewátes**>, df //tə=wɛ́t=əs//, PRON /'*somebody, anybody*'/, (<**=es**> meaning uncertain), syntactic analysis: nominal, attested by EB (12/16/75, 1/12/76), AC (12/8/71), Deming (3/29/79), example: <**ístexwchelcha ò í kw'e tewátes.**>, //ʔí=sT-əxʷ-c-əl-cɛ ʔà ʔí k'ʷə tə=wɛ́t=əs//, /'*I'll leave it with somebody.*'/, attested by EB, <**ốwechel líl kw'étslexw tewát[es].**>, //ʔówə-c-əl lí-l k'ʷə́c=l-əxʷ tə=wɛ́t[=əs]//, /'*I didn't see anybody.*'/, attested by EB, <**tewátes t'we sqwmáy.**>, //tə=wɛ́t=əs t'wə s=qʷəm=ɛ́y//, /'*(It must be) somebody's dog.*'/, literally /'it is somebody must be is dog'/, attested by AC, <**líyetsel málqlexw kw'e tewátes?**>, //lí-ə-c-əl mɛ́lq=l-əxʷ k'ʷə tə=wɛ́t=əs//, /'*Did I forget anybody? (forget s-o)*'/, attested by Deming, <**tewátesò kw'e emí sq'ó.**>, //tə=wɛ́t=əs-à k'ʷə ʔəmí s=q'á//, /'*Anybody can come along.*'/, literally /'it's just anybody that come be with'/, attested by EB, <**lép'exes te xeytl'á:ls mékw' tewátes.**>, //lə́p'=əxʸ-əs tə x̣iƛ'=ɛ́·ls mə́k'ʷ tə=wɛ́t=əs//, /'*The grizzly ate anybody. (eat s-o/s-th)*'/, attested by Elders Group (3/29/77).

<**kw'ewátes**>, df //k'ʷə=wɛ́t=əs//, PRON ['*something*'], (<**kw'e=**> *the (abstract, remote)*), (<**=es**> meaning unclear), syntactic analysis: nominal, attested by AD (5/1/79), example: <**áxwethòm kw'ewátes.**>, //ʔɛ́xʷ=əT-àm k'ʷə=wɛ́t=əs//, /'*Someone will give you something.*'/, literally /'you are given something'/, attested by AD.

<**mekw'ewátes ~ mekw'ewát**>, cpds //mək'ʷ=wɛ́t=əs ~ mək'ʷ=wɛ́t//, PRON /'*everybody, everyone*'/, root <**mékw'**> *all, every*, root <**wát**> *who?, who*, (<**=es**> meaning unclear), syntactic analysis: nominal, attested by Elders Group (3/29/77), others, example: <**mekw'ewát lép'exes te xeytl'áls. ~ lép'exes te xeytl'á:ls mekw'ewátes.**>, //mək'ʷ=wɛ́t lə́p'=əxʸ-əs tə x̣íƛ'=ɛ́ls ~ lə́p'=əxʸ-əs tə x̣iƛ'=ɛ́·ls mək'ʷ=wɛ́t=əs//, /'*The grizzly ate everybody.*'/, attested by Elders Group.

<**kw'elhwát**>, df //k'ʷə(=)ɬ=wɛ́t//, PRON /'*who else?, who (of several)?, (anybody else (AC))*'/, (<**kw'e(=)lh=**> meaning unclear unless <**kw'élh**> *spill*), syntactic analysis: interrogative verb, Elder's comment: "this word is short for kw'elh tewát", attested by EB (4/28/78), also /'*anybody else*'/, attested by AC (12/10/71), example: <**qas kw'elhwát?**>, //qɛ-s k'ʷəɬ=wɛ́t//, /'*and who else?, and who (of several)?*'/, attested by EB, <**ōwéta kw'elhwát tél:exw welís alétsa te sléxwelh.**>, //ʔowə= ´tɛ k'ʷəɬ=wɛ́t tə́l=l-əxʷ wə-lí-s ʔɛlə́cɛ tə s=lə́xʷ=wəɬ//, /'*Nobody knows where the canoe is.*'/, literally /'there is not anybody else know it if- is there -it is where? the canoe'/, usage: Story of the Flood, attested by AC.

<**swótle**>, df //s=wɛ[=Aá=]t=lə//, PRON /'*somebody, someone*'/, (<**s=**> *nominalizer*), (<**ó=ablaut**>

derivational), probably **<=lə>** *this, here* probably as in **<te'íle>** *this*, phonology: ablaut, syntactic analysis: nominal, attested by AC (10/23/71), AD (3/6/79), IHTTC (8/8/77), example: **<skwíxs te swótle>**, //s=kʷíxʸ-s tə s=wɛ[=Aá=]t=lə//, /'*somebody's name*'/, literally /'name -of the somebody'/, attested by AC, **<óxwestchexw te'íle x̱éltel kw'e swótle.>**, //ʔɛ[=Aá=]xʷ=əs=T-c-əxʷ tə=ʔí=lə x̣i[=Aə́=]l=təl k'ʷə s=wɛ[=Aá=]t=lə//, /'*Give this pencil to someone.*'/, attested by AD, **<éy t'wa meythómes kw'e swótl'e.>**, //ʔɛ́y t'wɛ mɛy=T-ámə-əs k'ʷə s=wɛ[=Aá=]t=lə//, /'*It would be good if someone helps you.*'/, attested by IHTTC.

<=wát>, da //=wɛ́t//, NUM /'*(whoever, one out of)*'/, CJ, syntactic analysis: lexical suffix; found in **<mekw'wát ~ mekw'át>**, //mək'ʷ=(w)ɛ́t//, /'*somebody*'/, from **<mékw'>** *everybody, all* and **<wát>**, free root //wɛ́t//, PRON /'*who?, who*'/.

<wá:ta>, CJ /'*is there none?, isn't there any?*'/, *see* éwe ~ ő́we.

<wáth'>, free root //wɛ́θ'//, ABFC ['*pry*'], MC, syntactic analysis: intransitive verb, comment: not attested but must occur in light of the following word.

<wóweth'>, cts //wɛ[-AáC$_1$ə-]θ'//, ABFC ['*prying*'], MC, (**<ó-ablaut plus -R1->** *continuative*), phonology: ablaut, reduplication, syntactic analysis: transitive verb, attested by IHTTC (8/25/77).

<shxwoweth'ílep or **shxwwoweth'ílep>**, dnom //sxʷ=wɛ[=AaC$_1$ə=]θ'=íləp//, TOOL ['*shovel*'], LAND, literally /'something for prying earth'/, (**<shxw=>** *something for*), lx **<=ílep>** *earth, dirt*, phonology: ablaut, reduplication, syntactic analysis: nominal, attested by IHTTC (8/25/77), contrast **<lepál>** *shovel*.

<swáweth'>, strs //s=wɛ́[=C$_1$ə=]θ'//, MC ['*(be) locked with a stick*'], (**<s=>** *stative*), (**<=R1=>** *resultative*), phonology: reduplication, syntactic analysis: adjective/adjectival verb, attested by Elders Group (1/25/78).

<wáth'et>, pcs //wɛ́θ'=əT//, MC /'*pry s-th, lock s-th (the Indian way/barred/wedged), pry s-th up, lever it up*'/, ABFC, (**<=et>** *purposeful control transitivizer*), syntactic analysis: transitive verb, attested by Elders Group (1/25/78), EB (4/27/76), IHTTC (8/25/77), comment: , Salish cognate: Squamish /wác'-an/ *lever up; pry loose (tr.)* K69:89, historical/comparative detail: should one compare this word with weth'át *teases-o* (i.e. *sort of pry someone*)? following Kuipers who relates the two Squamish cognates to each other.

<xwewáth'et>, df //xʷə=wɛ́θ'=əT//, pcs, MC ['*unlock it*'], possibly **<xwe=>** *un-*, syntactic analysis: transitive verb, attested by Elders Group (1/25/78).

<shxwéth'tel or **shxwwéth'tel>**, dnom //sxʷ=wɛ[=Aə́=]θ'=təl//, MC /'*a latch, Indian lock*'/, BLDG, ASM ['a latch fastened in the middle or on one end, or loose which slides through'], see illustration, (**<shxw=>** *nominalizer, something for/that*), (**<é-ablaut>** *resultative or durative*), lx **<=tel>** *device to*, phonology: ablaut, consonant merger, syntactic analysis: nominal, attested by IHTTC (8/22/77).

<wáth'elh>, ds //wɛ́θ'=(əw)əɬ//, BSK ['*to weave slats (like a th'ő́wex̱ basket or bulrush mat or inner or middle cedar bark)*'], literally /'pry/bar/lock basket/vessel'/, probably **<=elh** (probably ~ **=ewelh)>** *basket, vessel, canoe*, Elder's comment: "perhaps also to weave wool but AD believes they have different weaves for wool, each of which is named [twine, twill, etc.] (AD 6/8/79)", syntactic analysis: intransitive verb, attested by AD (6/18/79).

<wáweth'elh>, cts //wɛ́[-C$_1$ə-]θ'=əɬ//, BSK ['*weaving slats*'], (**<-R1->** *continuative*), phonology: reduplication, syntactic analysis: intransitive verb, attested by AD (6/8/79).

<wá:th'elh ~ wáth'elh>, dnom //wɛ́[=·=]θ'=əɬ ~ wɛ́θ'=əɬ//, BSK /'*bulrush mat, reed mat, mat (of cattail/roots/bulrushes, etc.), (wall mat (Elders Group 11/12/75)*'/, ASM ['usually used for a foot mat (Deming)'], possibly **<=:=>** *derivational*, possibly **<=elh>** *according to the ways of the, in the way of the, traditional*, phonology: possible lengthening, syntactic analysis: nominal, attested by Elders Group (9/10/75, 4/23/80), Deming (4/17/80), also <**wáts'elh**>, //wɛ́c'=əɬ//, also /'*wall mat*'/, attested by Elders Group (11/12/75), also <**wáts'elh**>, //wɛ́c'=əɬ//, also /'*reed mat*'/, attested by TM (Elders Group 4/23/80).

<**wáth'elh**>, BSK ['*to weave slats (like a th'ō̄we<u>x</u> basket or bulrush mat or inner or middle cedar bark)*'], *see* wáth'.

<**wá:th'elh ~ wáth'elh**>, BSK /'*bulrush mat, reed mat, mat (of cattail/roots/bulrushes, etc.), (wall mat (Elders Group 11/12/75)*'/, *see* wáth'.

<**wáth'et**>, MC /'*pry s-th, lock s-th (the Indian way/barred/wedged), pry s-th up, lever it up*'/, *see* wáth'.

<**wáts'et**>, probable stem //wɛ́c'(=)ət// meaning unknown

<**swáts'et**>, df //s=wɛ́c'ət//, FIRE /'*torch (made from pitch) (SJ and MV), (bark shield for fire* (Elders Group 3/6/78)*)*'/, (<**s=**> *nominalizer, something to*), root meaning unknown, syntactic analysis: nominal, attested by SJ and MV (Deming 3/2/77), Salish cognate: Squamish /sxʷáčit/ *torch* W73:271, K67:294, also /'*bark shield for fire*'/, attested by Elders Group (3/8/78).

<**wáweth'elh**>, BSK ['*weaving slats*'], *see* wáth'.

<**wá:y**>, possibly root //wɛ́·y or wi[=Aɛ́·=]y//, SOC /'*(be) found out (something you were trying to hide), to be discovered (something secret)*'/, EFAM, possibly <**á:-ablaut**> *resultative*, phonology: possible ablaut, syntactic analysis: intransitive verb, attested by IHTTC (7/5/77), Salish cognate: Skagit dial. of Lushootseed root /wíʔ-/ *announce in a loud voice* as in /wíʔ-əd/ *shout, announce in a loud voice, holler [tr.]* H76:553,56, Squamish root /wáy/ as in /wáy-at/ *reveal, make public (tr.)* K69:89.

<**wá:yt**>, pcs //wɛ́·y=T or wi[=Aɛ́·=]y=T//, SOC ['*warn s-o*'], EFAM, possibly <**á:-ablaut**> *resultative*, (<**=t**> *purposeful control transitivizer*), phonology: possible ablaut, possible clipping, syntactic analysis: transitive verb, attested by IHTTC (7/5/77), compare with perhaps <**yó:t**> *warn s-o* (poss. clipping?), Salish cognate: Squamish /wáy-at/ *reveal, make public (tr.)* K69:89 (vs. Squamish /yá-nʔ/ *warn (tr.)* K67:382 and root /yuh/ *take care, be careful* K67:383), Lushootseed /wíʔ-əd/ *shout, announce in a loud voice, holler* H76:553,56, Skagit dial. /wíʔ-ad/ *yell, call out loudly, telephone* H76:420, also /'*warning (of an attack)*'/, attested by Deming and/or JL and/or NP (Fish Camp 7/19/79), example: <**lílh me wá:ytem.**>, //lí-ɬ mə wɛ́·y=T-əm//, /'*He was warned.*'/, attested by JL and/or NP and/or Deming (Fish Camp 7/19/79).

<**wíyt**>, pcs //wɛ[=Aə́=]y=T or wɛ[=Aí=]y=T or wíy=T//, SOC /'*go warn s-o in secret, go tell s-o in secret*'/, EFAM, possibly <**é-ablaut** or **í-ablaut**> *resultative*?, (<**-t**> *purposeful control transitivizer*), phonology: possible ablaut, syntactic analysis: transitive verb, attested by Elders Group (4/28/76); found in <**wíythòmè**>, //wɛ[=Aə́=]y=T-ámə//, /'*warn you*'/, attested by Elders Group, example: <**le wíyt.**>, //lə wɛ[=Aə́=]y=T//, /'*Go tell/warn someone in secret.*'/, attested by Elders Group.

<**wá(:)y**>, possible root //wɛ́(·)y//, meaning uncertain

<**shxwewá(:)y**>, df //sxʷ=(h)ə-wɛ́(·)y//, KIN ['*parent*'], (<**shxw=**> *something for/that, someone for/that*), root meaning unknown, unless <**wá:y**> *found out (something you were trying to hide), discovered (something secret)* (also as in wá:yt *warn s-o*)–as parents are always doing both, <shxw=> *nominalizer for continuative*, probably <he-> *continuative*, syntactic analysis: nominal, attested by AC (11/10/71), other sources: H-T <tEcswe'> (macron over e) ([tə šswé(y)] /tə s(xʷ)wɛ́y/) *parent*, example: <**yéthestes te mestíyexw te sqwà:ls te sí:les or s<u>x</u>wewá(:)ys.**>, //yə́θəs=T-əs tə məstíyəxʷ tə s=qʷɛ̀·l-s tə sí·lə-s or sxʷ=wɛ́(·)y-s//, /'*He told the people the words of his grandfather or his parent.*'/, usage: contemporary text, attested by AC (11/10/71), Salish cognate: Nooksack <swálay7 ~ shwálay> (NKF1.1206; NKF3.2231; NKF2.1981).

<**shxwwáli**>, pln //sxʷ=wɛ́[=lə=]y//, KIN /'*parents, relations (ancestors?)*'/, (<**=le=**> *plural*), phonology: infixed plural, syntactic analysis: nominal, attested by AC (8/15/70, 9/29/71, 11/10/71), other sources: ES /šxʷwɛ̀lí/ (CwMs /šxʷwɛ́li/) *parents, ancestors*, H-T <cwa'li> (macron over a)(p.395) ~ <swca'li> (macron or umlaut over a) *parents*, Salish cognate: Nooksack <swálay7 ~ shwálay> (NKF1.1206; NKF3.2231; NKF2.1981).

<**wáy**>, bound root //wɛ́y// *daylight, day*

<**wáyel**>, incs //wɛ́y=əl//, WETH /'*get daylight, become day*'/, lx <**=el**> *go, come, get, become, inceptive*, syntactic analysis: intransitive verb, attested by AC, Elders Group (9/17/75), example: <**lulh me wáyel.**>, //lə-uɬ mə wɛ́y=əl//, /'*Its' getting daylight.*'/, literally /'past -already come/start to get daylight'/, attested by AC (8/8/70); found in <**wáyelcha**>, //wɛ́y=əl-cɛ//, /'*it's tomorrow*'/, literally /'it will come/go/get day(light)'/, attested by AC (10/6/71), example: <**álhche(xw) qelát wá:yel ~ óscha qelát wá:yel**>, //ʔɛ́ɬ-cɛ qəlɛ́t wɛ́·y=əl ~ ʔás-cɛ qəlɛ́t wɛ́·y=əl//, /'*day after tomorrow*'/, literally /'? -future again become day'/, attested by Elders Group (9/17/75).

<**swáyel ~ swáyél ~ swàyèl**>, dnom //s=wɛ́y=əl//, WETH /'*day, daytime, sky, weather, (horizon (BJ))*'/, TIME ['*day*'], (<**s=**> *nominalizer*), phonology: optional updrifting, optional downdrifting, syntactic analysis: nominal, attested by AC, BJ (5/10/64), DM (12/4/64), IHTTC (8/10/77), Deming (1/18/79, 3/31/77), Elders Group (3/3/76, 3/2/77), DC (12/19/78), other sources: ES /swɛ́yə̀l/ *day, sky*, also <**kw'e chíchelh**>, //k'ʷə cí[=C$_1$ə=]ɬ//, also /'*sky*'/, literally /'what (remote) is high up'/, Elder's comment: "others use swàyèl *day* for *sky*", attested by EB (2/16/76), also <**swá:yél ~ swà:yèl ~ swáyél ~ swàyèl**>, //s=wɛ́(·)y=əl//, also /'*horizon, sky, day*'/, attested by BJ (12/5/64), example: <**Q: stámelh swàyèl kw'e cheláqelhelh? A.: yiláwelhàt.**>, //s=tɛ́m-əɬ s=wɛ́y=əl k'ʷə cəlɛ́q=əɬ-əɬ. yilɛ́w=əɬɛ̀t//, /'*Q.: What day was yesterday? A.: Monday.*'/, literally /'is what? -past day the (abstract/remote/invisible) yesterday'/, attested by IHTTC, <**éy swàyèl, méle.**>, //ʔɛ́y s=wɛ́y=əl mélə//, /'*Good day, child.*'/, attested by Deming, <**Q.: stám swàyèl tlówàyèl? A: (yiláwelhàt., sthemélts., slhíxws., sx̱e'óthels., slhq'átses., t'óqw'tem., sx̱ax̱elhát.)**>, //s=tɛ́m s=wɛ́y=əl təlá=wɛ́y=əl. (yilɛ́w=əɬɛ̀t, s=θəm=ə́lc, s=ɬíxʷ=s, s=x̣əʔáθəl=s, s=ɬq'ɛ́=cəs=s, t'áq'ʷ=T=əm, s=x̣ɛ́=C$_1$ə=əɬɛ̀t)//, /'*Q.: What day is today? A. (Monday., Tuesday., Wednesday., Thursday., Friday., Saturday., Sunday.)*'/, attested by IHTTC (8/10/77), <**lhíxw swáyel**>, //ɬíxʷ s=wɛ́y=əl//, /'*three days*'/, attested by Elders Group (3/2/77), <**Q.: stámcha swàyèl wàyèlès? A.: sx̱e'óthels.**>, //s=tɛ́m-cɛ s=wɛ́y=əl wɛ̀y=ə̀l=ə̀s. s=x̣əʔáθəl=s//, /'*Q.: What day is tomorrow? A.: Thursday.*'/, literally /'is what? -future day tomorrow. thursday'/, attested by IHTTC, <**x̱éytl' te swáyel.**>, //x̣í·ƛ' tə s=wɛ́y=əl//, /'*The day is cold., (The weather is cold.)*'/, attested by Deming, <**kw'ókw'es te swáyel.**>, //k'ʷɛ[=AáC$_1$ə=]s tə s=wɛ́y=əl//, /'*The day is hot.*'/, attested by Deming, <**(le, ulh) kw'ósthet te swáyel.**>, //(lə, ʔuɬ) k'ʷɛ́s=θət tə s=wɛ́y=əl//, /'*The day is getting warm.*'/, literally /'(past, already) got warm the day'/, attested by Deming, <**tl'emx̱wx̱éylem te swáyel.**>, //ƛ'əm=x̣ʷ=x̣(əl)=íl=əm tə s=wɛ́y=əl or ƛ'əm=x̣ʷ=x̣ə[=Aí=]l=əm tə s=wɛ́y=əl//, /'*The day is hailing.*'/, dialects: *Chill.*, attested by Deming, <**mótl' te swáyel.**>, //máƛ' tə s=wɛ́y=əl//, /'*The weather is bad.*'/, from <**mótl'**> *stumped*, attested by Elders Group (3/3/76), <**íxwcha selchím té swàyèl.**>, //ʔíxʷ-cɛ səlcím tə s=wɛ́y=əl//, /'*I wonder what the weather will be like?*'/, literally /'I wonder -future is how the day/weather'/, attested by DC (12/19/78).

<**seswá:yél**>, pln //C$_1$ə=swɛ́·yə́l//, TIME ['*days*'], (irregular), (<**R5-**> *plural*), phonology: reduplication of prefix permitted because in a power song, syntactic analysis: nominal, usage: taken from a power song, attested by CT, EB (9/18/78).

<**téxwswàyel ~ texwswàyèl ~ texwswáyél**>, ds //təxʷ=s=wɛ́y=əl//, TIME /'*midday, noon*'/, (<**texw=**> *mid-*), phonology: optional downdrifting, optional updrifting, syntactic analysis: adverb/adverbial verb, attested by Elders Group (3/1/76), AD (4/28/78), DM (12/4/64), Deming

(1/25/79), example: <**(lámescha, xwewáscha) texwswàyèl**>, //(lɛ́m-əs-cɛ, xʷ=(ʔ)əwə=ɛs-cɛ) təxʷ=s=wɛ́y=əl//, /'*before noon*'/, literally /'(when it will go, when it will be not yet) noon'/, attested by AD, <**yiláw texwswáyel**>, //yilɛ́w təxʷ=s=wɛ́y=əl//, /'*after noon (minutes after twelve o'clock a.m.), afternoon*'/, attested by Elders Group, DM, <**yéyilaw texwswáyel**>, //C$_1$ə= ´=yilɛw təxʷ=s=wɛ́y=əl//, /'*a little after noon, later on in the afternoon*'/, attested by Elders Group, <**texwwáyél s'álhtel**>, //təxʷ=s=wɛ́y=əl s=ʔɛ́ɬ=T-əl//, /'*noon meal*'/, literally /'mid-day something to= eat =purposely -with each other'/, attested by Deming.

<**tlówàyèl ~ tlowáyél**>, ds //t(ə=)lá=wɛ́y=əl//, TIME ['*today*'], (<**tló=**> *this*), possibly <**te=**> *the (present)*, possibly <**ló**> *here*, phonology: optional downshifting/downdrifting, updrifting, possible vowel-loss, syntactic analysis: adverb/adverbial verb, nominal?, attested by IHTTC (8/10/77), Deming (3/31/77), Elders Group (1/19/77), example: <**stám swàyèl tlówàyèl?**>, //s=tɛ́m s=wɛ́y=əl tlá=wɛ́y=əl//, /'*What day is today?*'/, attested by IHTTC, <**ewéte tl'emx̱wéyle tlowáyél.**>, //ʔəwə= ´tə ƛ'əm=x̣ʷ=íl=ə tlá=wɛ́y=əl//, /'*There's no hail today.*'/, attested by Deming, <**yeláwel x̱éytl' tlówàyèl telí cheláqelh(elh).**>, //yəlɛ́w=əl x̣í·yƛ' tlá=wɛ́y=əl təlí cəlɛ́q=əɬ(-əɬ)//, /'*Today is colder than yesterday.*'/, literally /'go past cold today from/than yesterday'/, attested by Elders Group, <**l stl'í kw'els qw'él:ém te sth'óqwi tlowáyel.**>, //l s=ƛ'í k'ʷə-l-s q'ʷə́l·=əm tə s=θ'áqʷi tla=wɛ́yəl//, /'*I want to barbecue salmon today.*'/, attested by AC.

<**wáyeles ~ wáyélés ~ wàyèlès**>, ds //wɛ́y=əl=əs//, TIME ['*tomorrow*'], lx <**=es**> *cyclic period*, phonology: optional updrifting, optional downdrifting, syntactic analysis: adverb/adverbial verb, attested by DM (12/4/64), BJ (5/10/64), Deming (1/18/79), IHTTC (8/10/77), EB (5/1/78), Elders Group (3/19/75), also <**wáyeles ~ wáy:eles ~ wáy:élés ~ wày:èlès**>, //wɛ́y=əl=əs ~ wɛ́·y=əl=əs//, phonology: length transfer to following consonant, attested by AC (8/6/70, 10/15/71, 11/13/71), example: <**lámtsel wáy:eles.**>, //lɛ́=m-c-əl wɛ́·y=əl=əs//, /'*I'll go tomorrow.*'/, attested by AC, <**látselcha xwelí wáy:eles.**>, //lɛ́-c-əl-cɛ xʷə=lí wɛ́·y=əl=əs//, /'*I'll be there tomorrow.*'/, literally /'I'm going to -future get there tomorrow'/, attested by AC, <**álhtelchexwcha wáy:élés.**>, //ʔɛ́ɬ=T-əl-c-əxʷ-cɛ wɛ́·y=əl=əs//, /'*You'll eat tomorrow.*'/, attested by AC (11/13/71), <**(álhtelchètchà, álhteltsèlchà) wày:èlès.**>, //(ʔɛ́ɬ=T-əl-c-ət-cɛ, ʔɛ́ɬ=T-əl-c-əl-cɛ) wɛ́·y=əl=əs//, /'*(We'll eat, I'll eat) tomorrow.*'/, attested by AC (11/13/71), <**álhtelchapcha wáy:eles.**>, //ʔɛ́ɬ=T-əl-c-ɛp-cɛ wɛ́·y=əl=əs//, /'*You (plural) will eat tomorrow.*'/, attested by AC (11/13/71), <**li a sqwá:lewel kwes xwe'í:s wéy:eles?**>, //li-ə ʔɛ s=qʷɛ̀·l=əwəl kʷ-əs xʷə=ʔí·-s wɛ́·y=əl=əs//, /'*Do you think they'll come (get here) tomorrow?*'/, attested by AC (9/18/71), <**kw'etslométselcha wàyèles.**>, //k'ʷəc=l-amə-c-əl-cɛ wɛ́y=əl=əs//, /'*I'll see you tomorrow.*'/, attested by Deming, <**lámtselcha látelh(es) wáyélés.**>, //lɛ́=m-c-əl-cɛ lɛ́t=əɬ(-əs) wɛ́y=əl=əs//, /'*I'll go early tomorrow morning. (early morning)*'/, attested by EB, <**lámes slát wáyeles**>, //lɛ́m-əs s=lát wɛ́y=əl=əs//, /'*(when it goes to) tomorrow night*'/, attested by Elders Group (3/19/75).

<**wáyeles ~ wáyélés ~ wàyèlès**>, TIME ['*tomorrow*'], *see* wáyel.

<**wá:yt**>, SOC ['*warn s-o*'], *see* wá:y.

<**we=**>, da //wə=//, TIME ['*suddenly*'], syntactic analysis: derivational prefix; found in <**welhéq'**>, //wə=ɬə́q'//, /'*sound of a spank on a bottom*'/, attested by AD (2/19/79), <**wets'étl'**>, //wə=c'ə́ƛ' or wə=c'i[=Aə́=]ƛ'//, /'*drop, fall*'/, literally /'suddenly get short?'/ or possibly root as in <**c'ƛ'ə́m**> *jump*, <**wets'á:**>, //wə=c'ɛ́·//, /'*get to the top or summit of a mountain*'/, literally /'suddenly be astride'/, root <**ts'á:**> *top, on top*

<**we= ~ u= ~ uw= ~ ew= ~ =ew ~ =w ~ =u**>, da //wə= ~ ʔu= ~ ʔuw= ~ ʔəw= ~ =əw ~ =w ~ =u//, EFAM ['*contrastive*'], syntactic analysis: derivational prefix or suffix, also <**u= ~ uw= ~ =u**>, //ʔu= ~ ʔuw= ~ =u//, also <**ew= ~ =ew**>, //ʔəw= ~ =əw//, also <**=w**>, //=w//; found in <**su**>, //s-ew//, /'*so*'/,

<tú(:)tl'ò>, //tə=w=ƛ'á or tə=ú=ƛ'á//, /'*that's him, he's the one*'/, **<thú(:)tl'ò>**, //θə=w=ƛ'á or θə=ú=ƛ'á//, /'*that's her, she's the one*'/, **<yutl'ó:lem>**, //yə=w=ƛ'á=lə=m or yə=ú=ƛ'á=lə=m//, /'*that's them, they are the ones*'/, **<welh ~ ulh>**, //wə=ɬ ~ ʔu=ɬ//, /'*already*'/, (**<-lh>** past tense), **<we'ól ~ we'ólew ~ we'ólwe>**, //wə=ʔál ~ wə=ʔál=əw ~ wə=ʔál wə=//, /'*too (overly)*'/, attested by AC, others, also **<ólewe>**, //ʔál(ə)=wə//, attested by EB, others, example: **<we'ólwe qé<u>x</u> te slhé<u>x</u>welhchas>**, //wə=ʔál wə=qə́x̣ tə s=ɬə́x̣ʷ=əɬcɛ-s//, /'*an awful lot of spit, too much spit*'/, attested by AC, **<ólewe lóp<u>x</u>wem>**, //ʔál=wə lápx̣ʷ=əm//, /'*(making) too much noise*'/, attested by EB, **<ólewe xwétes tl'esu míq'.>**, //ʔál=wə xʷə́təs ƛ'ə-s-u míq'//, /'*It was too heavy and it sank. (sink)*'/, **<we'ólwe qwe'íqweqws ta (<u>x</u>éltel, <u>x</u>wé:ylem).>**, //wə=ʔál wə=qʷəʔíqʷ=əqʷ-s t-ɛ (x̣ə́l=təl, x̣ʷí·ləm)//, /'*Your (pen/pencil, rope) is too thin/narrow.*'/, attested by JL; found in **<wiyóth>**, //wə=yáθ//, /'*always*'/, **<welóy>**, //wə=láy//, /'*only, just*'/, example: **<ts'áts'elew kw'ókw'es tlòwáyél.>**, //c'ɛ́[=C_1ə=]l=əw k'ʷɛ[=Aá=C_1ə=]s təlá=wɛ́yəl//, /'*It's really hot today.*'/, attested by EB,

<we->, (**<wə->**), MOOD /'*subjunctive, when, if*'/, syntactic analysis: ip, syntactic comment: requires the same word to be affixed with subordinate subject pronoun set (=al, =exw, =es, =et, =ap ~ =elep)(these pronouns lose their initial vowel after verbs ending in <i>), attested by Elders Group, EB, CT and HT, IHTTC, AC, Deming, others; found in **<wekw'á:yàl>**, //wə-k'ʷɛ́·y-ɛ̀l//, /'*if I get hungry*'/, attested by Elders Group (6/28/78), example: **<éy t'we kw'el sqwálewel we'emís.>**, //ʔɛ́y t'wə k'ʷə-l s=qʷɛ̀l=əwəl wə-ʔəmí-s//, /'*I'll be glad if he comes.*'/, attested by Elders Group (2/16/77), **<(we<u>x</u>éytl'exw, we'íxw <u>x</u>éytl') hókwexlha ta' kopú.>**, //(wə-x̣í·ƛ'-əxʷ, wə-ʔí-xʷ x̣í·ƛ') hákʷ=əxʸ-ɬɛ t-ɛʔ kapú//, /'*If you're cold put on your coat.*'/, attested by EB (5/25/76), **<welís thét ta sqwálewel>**, //wə-lí-s θə́t t-ɛ s=qʷɛ̀l=əwəl//, /'*if you think that, if your mind says so*'/, literally /'if- aux -it say that the -your mind'/, attested by EB (4/18/78), **<welí[s] kw'e li te éqwelets te thqát éwe lís eyém.>**, //wə-lí[-s] k'ʷə li tə ʔə́qʷ=ələc-s tə θqɛ́t ʔə́wə lí-s ʔɛy=ə́m//, /'*If it's on the back of the tree it's not as strong.*'/, attested by CT and HT (6/21/76), **<éwe stl'ís kw'es maytólxws welámet sőwq'tòlè.>**, //ʔə́wə s=ƛ'í-s-s k'ʷ-əs mɛy=T-álxʷ-s wə-lɛ́=m-ət séwq'=T-álə//, /'*He doesn't want to help us when we go find you folks. (search for s-o)*'/, dialects: *Chill.*, attested by IHTTC (8/22/77), also **<éwe stl'íses kws maytóxwes welámet súwq'tòlè.>**, //ʔə́wə s=ƛ'í-s-əs kʷ-s mɛy=T-áxʷ-əs wə-lɛ́=m-ət sə́wq'=T-álə//, dialects: *Cheh.*, attested by EB (IHTTC 8/22/77), also **<éwe stl'íses maytóxwes welámet súwq'tòlè.>**, //ʔə́wə s=ƛ'í-s-əs mɛy=T-áxʷ-əs wə-lɛ́=m-ət sə́wq'=T-álə//, dialects: *Tait*, attested by SP and AK and AD (IHTTC 8/22/77), **<éy t'wa meythómet.>**, //ʔɛ́y t'wɛ mɛy=T-áməət//, /'*It would be good if we help you.*'/, attested by IHTTC (8/8/77), comment: this example shows that we- can sometimes be omitted with no loss of meaning if the subordinate (subjunctive?) pronouns are used.

<wé>, free root //wə́//, EFAM ['*Is that okay?*'], Elder's comment: "a question word used at the end of a sentence to ask if it's okay, not very common", syntactic analysis: particle, syntactic comment: tag-question, attested by AD (11/19/79).

<wék'>, possible root or stem //wə́k'// or //wə́q'=K// meaning unknown

<swék'>, df //s=wə́k' or s=wə́q'=K//, SOCT /'*a dandy, someone who overdresses, a show-off, comedian, someone who always cracks jokes, smart-alec; proud*'/, ASM ['used mainly of someone who overdresses and acts funny about it (usually a younger person), sometimes with a little envy or pride in the person, sometimes with a person who does something smart that the elders are proud of (AD)'], (**<s=>** *nominalizer*), root meaning unknown, possibly **<=K (fronting** or **palatalization)>** *diminutive*, phonology: possible fronting, syntactic analysis: nominal, attested by Elders Group (3/19/75), EB (2/27/76), Deming (6/15/78), AD (1/10/79), also **<swék'elets>**, //s=wə́k'=ələc or s=wə́q'=K=ələc//, attested by Elders Group (3/19/75), EB (2/27/76, 6/16/76), Deming (6/15/78), AD (1/18/79),, also /'*smart ass*'/, attested by Deming (6/15/78), also **<swék'ten>**, //s=wə́k'=tən//, also /*'show-off'*/, attested by Elders Group (2/8/78), also /*'brave man'*/, attested by HP (Elders Group 2/8/78).

<**Swék'ten**>, ds //s=wə́k'=tən//, N [*'Hank Pennier's nickname'*], lx <**=ten**> (Downriver Halkomelem for <**=tel**> *something to, device to, male name ending)*, syntactic analysis: nominal, attested by Elders Group (2/8/78).

<**wel**>, possibly root //wəl//, QUAL /*'really, real'*/, ASM ['used before color terms by TG and NP to distinguish very dark shades, except for /p'ə́q'/ where it points out the focus'], possibly <**we=**> *contrastive*, possibly root <**el**> *just*, syntactic analysis: adverb/adverbial verb, attested by Elders Group (2/5/75, 3/29/78), TG (8/19/87), NP (8/20/87), see charts by Rob MacLaury, example: <**tsel wel ő westexw.**>, //c-əl wəl ʔówə=sT-əx^w//, /*'I really say no.'*/, attested by Elders Group (3/29/78), <**ts'áts'el wel the'í:t**>, //c'ɛ́[=C_1ə=]l wəl θəʔí·t//, /*'It's really true.'*/, literally /'it's very/really really true'/, attested by Elders Group (2/5/75).

<**weltá:lt**>, df //wɛ́·l=tə[=M2=]l=T//, HUNT /*'spring snare [s-th], [a?] spring snare'*/, *see* <**wá:l**> *throw*.

<**welék'**>, possibly root //wələ́k' or w[=əl=]ə́q'=K//, EZ /*'little green frog, little green tree frog, (Pacific tree toad)'*/, [*'Hyla regilla'*], possibly root <**wéq'**> *frog croak*, possibly <**=el=**> *plural*, probably <**=K (fronting)**> *diminutive*, phonology: probable fronting, possible infixed plural, syntactic analysis: noun, nominal, attested by Elders Group (2/27/80, 3/1/72, 12/15/76), contrast <**weq'iyethílem**> *a kind of frog*, Salish cognate: Lushootseed /wáq'waq' ~ wəlís ~ wəq'íq'/ *an unidentified kind of small frog* and /swə́ləq'/ *Frog talk; specifically what Frog would sing to her baby to try to get him to stop crying* H76:546,550,452, example: <**qwà:l te welék'.**>, //q^{w}ɛ̀·l tə w[=əl=]ə́q'=K//, /*'The frog croaks., The frog talks.'*/, LANG, ABFC, attested by Elders Group (12/15/76).

<**welék'es**>, dnom //w[=əl=]ə́q'=K=əs//, TIME [*'the month/moon beginning in March'*], literally /'little frog season'/, Elder's comment: "when the little frogs begin to sing or talk", lx <**=es**> *cyclic period*, syntactic analysis: adverb/adverbial verb, nominal?, attested by Elders Group (3/12/75, 2/5/75), contrast <**we<u>x</u>és**> *frog*, also <**wó<u>x</u>es**>, //wə[=Aá=]x̣=əs//, attested by Elders Group (2/5/75).

<**welék'es**>, TIME [*'the month/moon beginning in March'*], *see* welék'.

<**welékwsa**>, us //wələ́k^{w}sɛ//, EB /*'poison fern that grows in swampy places, (*prob. *water hemlock, poison hemlock)'*/, ['probably *Cicuta douglasii*'], ASM ['poisonous water hemlock looks like a fern and grows in swampy places'], syntactic analysis: nominal, attested by Elders Group (2/26/75).

<**welé<u>x</u>**>, EZ /*'frog, (if generic may include Pacific tree toad* and perhaps the introduced species*: bullfrog, green frog, red-legged frog, western spotted frog, and the tailed toad)'*/, *see* we<u>x</u>és.

<**welóy**>, CJ /*'be only (contrastive), be just (contrastive)'*/, *see* lóy.

<**Welqémex**>, PLN [*'Greenwood Island'*], *see* qám.

<**wélwelàm ~ wélwelà:m**>, chrs //wə́l=C_1əC_2=ə[=Aɛ̀=]m or wɛ́(·)l=C_1əC_2=ə[=M3=]m//, durs, SD /*'to echo, (echoing (Elders Group 10/27/76)'*/, possibly root <**wál ~ wá:l**> *throw*, (<**=R2**> *characteristic*), possibly <**á(:)-ablaut**> *durative*, possibly <**metathesis type 3**> *derivational*, phonology: reduplication, ablaut or metathesis type 3, downstepping, syntactic analysis: intransitive verb, attested by Elders Group (3/15/72), other sources: JH /wə̀lwəlé·m/ *echo*, Salish cognate: Squamish /wálam/ *toecho* W73:88, K69:89, Nooksack /wúlæ̀ʔæ̀m/ *to echo* Amoss 1961, also <**welwelá:m**>, //wəl=C_1əC_2=ə[=Aɛ́·=]m or wɛ́·l=C_1əC_2=ə[=M3=]m//, attested by Deming (5/24/79), also <**wélwelà:m**>, //wə́l=C_1əC_2=ə[=Aɛ́·=]m or wɛ́·l=C_1əC_2=ə[=M3=]m//, also /*'echoing'*/, attested by Elders Group (10/27/76).

<**swélwelàm**>, dnom //s=wə́l=C_1əC_2=ə[=Aɛ́=]m or s=wɛ́l=C_1əC_2=ə[=M3=]m//, SD ['*an echo*'], (<**s=**> *nominalizer*), phonology: reduplication, ablaut or metathesis type 3, syntactic analysis: nominal, attested by Elders Group (3/72).

<**wélweleq**>, bound stem //wə́l=C_1əC_2=ələq//, possibly root <**wál ~ wá:l**> *throw*, probably <**=R2**> *characteristic*, possibly <**=eleq**> *waves*

<**swélweleq**>, df //s=wə́l=C_1əC_2=ələq//, WATR ['*a kind of ice*'], (semological comment: perhaps of a special kind, word used in a song sung by CT), (<**s=**> *nominalizer*), possibly root <**wál ~ wá:l**> *throw*, probably <**=R2**> *characteristic*, possibly <**=eleq**> *waves*, prob. lit. "something (ice) that the waves characteristically throw", phonology: reduplication, syntactic analysis: nominal, attested by CT, EB and AD (9/19/78), example: <**swélweleqtsel á'a**>, //s=wə́l=C_1əC_2=ələq-c-əl ʔɛ́ʔɛ//, /'*I am ice, yes.*'/, usage: song, attested by CT.

<**welh ~ ulh ~ =ulh**>, possibly root //wəɬ or wə-ɬ ~ ʔu-ɬ ~ =u-ɬ//, TIME ['*already*'], probably root <**we ~ ʔəw ~ ʔu**> *contrastive*, probably <**-lh**> *past tense*, phonology: vocalization, syntactic analysis: adverb/adverbial verb, attested by EB, AC, Deming, Elders Group, others, Salish cognate: Saanich and Samish dialects of NSt /k^{w}ɬ/ *already* G86:59, example: <**ulh là:m.**>, //ʔu-ɬ lɛ́=m//, /'*He's already gone.*'/, phonology: downdrifting, emphatic lengthening, attested by EB (2/2/76), <**látsel welh**>, //lɛ́-c-əl wəɬ//, /'*I already did*'/, dialects: *Chill./Sardis*, attested by EB (6/7/76), also <**láchulh**>, //lɛ́-c(əl)-u-ɬ//, phonology: unusual pronoun allomorph (-ts for -tsel) also found in Nooksack, dialects: *Cheh.*, attested by EB (6/7/76), <**lulh syíyexw.**>, //lə-u-ɬ s=yə[=(Aí)=C_1ə=]x^w//, /'*It's already unwrapped.*'/, (semological comment: see also *untie, unravel, unwind, fall apart, come apart, come loose, break down*, all meanings of the same root), attested by Deming (6/22/78), <**welh tu méq'**>, //wəɬ t=u mə́q'//, /'*nearly full (of food)*'/, literally /'already sort of filled (of food)'/, attested by EB (2/6/76), <**welh tu léts' ~ xwálhqey léts'**>, //wəɬ t=u lə́c' ~ x^{w}ɛ́lq=əy lə́c'//, /'*near full (of a container)*'/, literally /'already somewhat full ~ almost/nearly full'/, attested by EB, <**welh tu ítet**>, //wəɬ t=u ʔítət//, /'*nearly asleep*'/, literally /'already sort of asleep'/, attested by EB, <**stowlh ley kwíkwemel**>, //s=t=(əʔ)ɛ=(Aa)-wɬ lɛ -yə(=) k^{w}í[=C_1ə=]m=əl//, /'*already turning red*'/, literally /'(prob.) like - already going -in motion getting red'/, attested by AD (8/6/79), <**th'exwmetólxwchexw, lálh tstulh t-sós.**>, //θ'əx^w=məT-álx^w-c-əx^w, lɛ́-ɬ c-t-u-ɬ ts(=)ás//, /'*Pity us, we are getting unfortunate.*'/, phonology: ulh phonetically attached to preposed pronoun, attested by Elders Group (TM, DF, or NP).

<**=welh ~ =wílh**>, da //=wəɬ ~ =wíɬ//, EFAM /'*in the mind, -minded, disposition*'/, syntactic analysis: lexical suffix, derivational suffix; found in <**lexwqélwelh**>, //ləx^w=qə́l=wəɬ//, /'*cranky, crabby, dirty-minded*'/, literally /'always bad/dirty -minded'/, <**xwe'éywelh**>, //x^{w}ə=ʔɛ́y=wəɬ//, /'*kind, generous*'/, literally /'become good -minded/in disposition'/, <**xwqélwelh**>, //x^w=qə́l=wəɬ//, /'*stingy*'/, <**sqelwílhmet**>, //s=qəl=wíɬ=məT//, /'*hate s-o*'/, also <**=wílh**>, //=wíɬ//.

<**welhchí:ws**>, EFAM ['*real tired*'], *see* lhchí:ws.

<**welhéleq'**>, SD /'*fall splat, (make the) sound of a spank or slap*'/, *see* welhéq'.

<**welhíth**>, TIME ['*a long time ago*'], *see* híth.

<**welhí:thelh ~ welhíthelh**>, TIME ['*a long time ago*'], *see* híth.

<**wép**>, TVMO ['*overloaded*'], *see* wíp or wép.

<**wep'éth' ~ wep'áth'**>, WETH /'*come out (of sun), come up (of sun)*'/, *see* p'eth'.

<**weq'iyethílem**>, mdls //wəq'=əyəθəl=íl=əm//, EZ ['*a kind of frog*'], possibly root <**wéq'**> *frog croak*, lx <**=eyethel ~ =ó:ythel**> *on the jaw, on the lips, music*, (<**=íl**> *go, come, get, become*), (<**=em**> *middle voice*), syntactic analysis: nominal, attested by Elders at Katz Class (BHTTC, T.G.,

P.D.Peters) (10/5/76), contrast <**welék'**> *little green tree frog, (Pacific tree toad)*, Salish cognate: Lushootseed /wáq’waq’ ~ wəlís ~ wəq’íq’/ *an unidentified kind of small frog* and /swə́ləq’/ *Frog talk; specifically what Frog would sing to her baby to try to get him to stop crying* H76:546,550,452.

<**wétexel**>, bound stem //wə́tə=x^{y}əl or wə́t=əx^{y}=əl//, root meaning unknown.

<**swétexel**>, df //s=wə́tə=x^{y}əl or s=wə́t=əx^{y}=əl//, WETH ['*rainbow*'], (<**s=**> *nominalizer*), root meaning unknown, probably <**=xel**> *precipitation; on the leg*, or possibly <**=ex**> *upright, vertical*, and <**=el**> *go, come, get, become*, comment: =ex=el is less likely because there is good evidence these two suffixes co-occur in the opposite order (=íl=ex) as in lhx̲ílex *stand* and qw'eyílex *dance*, syntactic analysis: nominal, dialects: *Cheh. or Tait*, attested by Elders Group (4/2/75), Deming (3/31/77).

<**wet'émeqw'**>, SD /'*splash (the sound and the action), [splash suddenly], splash once*'/, *see* t'émeqw'.

<**wéthweth**>, EZ ['*spotted sandpiper*'], *see* wíth.

<**weth'át**>, pcs //wɛ́θ’=ə[=Aɛ́=]T or wəθ’=ə[=Aɛ́=]T//, durs, SOC ['*tease s-o*'], EFAM, literally possibly /'purposely pry/lever someone for a long time'/, probably root <**wáth'**> as in <**wáth'et**> *pry s-th up, lever it*, (<**á=ablaut**> *durative*), (<**=et**> *purposeful control transitivizer*), phonology: ablaut, possible vowel-reduction, syntactic analysis: transitive verb, attested by EB (3/29/76), DC and Ben James and AD (12/19/78), Salish cognate: Squamish root /wac’ ~ wəc’/ *tease, pry loose, lever up' as in /wə-wc’-át/ tease (tr.)* W73:263, K69:89, Sechelt /wác’-at/ *to tease* T77:35 but not Sechelt /wát’-at/ *to lever up, pry up* T77:30-31 and B86:289, also <**ewth'át**>, //ʔə(=)wɛθ’=ə[=Aɛ́=]T//, dialects: *Tait, Cheh.*, attested by IHTTC (9/2/77), also <**hewth'át**>, //hə=wɛθ’=ə[=Aɛ́=]T//, dialects: *Sumas (Kilgard)*, attested by JS (IHTTC 9/2/77), comment: but this form may be continuative (see example below), example: <**l stl'í kw'els weth'át.**>, //l s=ƛ’í k’^{w}-əl-s wɛθ’=ə[=Aɛ́=]T//, /'*I want to tease someone.*'/, attested by DC and Ben James and AD (12/19/78).

<**hewth'át**>, cts //hə-wɛθ’=ə[=Aɛ́=]T//, durs, SOC ['*teasing s-o*'], EFAM, (<**he-**> *continuative*), phonology: ablaut, vowel-loss, he- continuative is used regularly before roots beginning in w, y, l, or m, syntactic analysis: transitive verb, attested by AC (10/21/71), EB (3/29/76), also <**hí:wth'àt**>, //hí·=wɛθ’=ə[=Aɛ́=]T//, dialects: *Sumas (Kilgard)*, attested by JS (IHTTC 9/2/77), also <**í:wth'àt**>, //ʔí·=wɛθ’=ə[=Aɛ́=]T//, dialects: *Tait, some Cheh.*, attested by IHTTC (9/2/77), example: <**hóytlha kw'es hewth'át.**>, //hay=T-ɬɛ k’^{w}-əs hə-wɛθ’=ə[=Aɛ́=]T//, /'*Stop teasing him.*'/, comment: <**kw'a's**> might be more proper here, attested by EB (3/29/76), <**latlh hewth'át.**>, //lɛ-tɬ hə-wɛθ’=ə[=Aɛ́=]T//, /'*Go tease him.*'/, (semological comment: continuatives are sometimes used like this), attested by JS (IHTTC (9/2/77).

<**hewth'eláq**>, chrs //hə-wɛθ’=ələ[=Aɛ́=]q//, durs, cts, SOC ['*teasing*'], (semological comment: probably mistranslated for *a teaser*), (<**he-**> *continuative*), (<**=eleq**> *someone who habitually*), (<**á-ablaut**> *durative*), phonology: ablaut, syntactic analysis: intransitive verb??, nominal?, attested by BHTTC (10/2/76).

<**í:wthelàq**>, chrs //ʔí·=wɛθ’=ələ[=Aɛ́=]q//, durs, cts, SOC /'*a teaser, somebody that teases to get one's goat*'/, literally /'someone who habitually is teasing/prying/levering'/, phonology: ablaut, downstepping, syntactic analysis: nominal, attested by IHTTC (9/2/77).

<**wetl'éleqw**>, SD /'*a shot, explosion*'/, *see* tl'ál ~ tl'á:l.

<**wets'á:**>, DIR ['*get to the top or summit of a mountain*'], *see* ts'á:.

<**wets'á:lómet**>, TVMO ['*bring oneself to a summit (of a mountain)*'], *see* ts'á:.

<**wets'étl' ~ wech'étl'**>, possibly root //wəc’ə́ƛ’ or wə=c’ə́ƛ’ or wə=c’i[=Aə́=]ƛ’//, TVMO /'*fell of its own accord (of an object from a height or from upright), drop down (object/person, from a shelf,*

bridge, cliff, etc.), fall off/, possibly <**we=**> *suddenly*, possibly root <**ts'étl'** or **ts'ítl'**> *short*, possibly <**é-ablaut on root i**> *resultative or derivational*, phonology: possible ablaut, syntactic analysis: intransitive verb, attested by EB (12/15/75), AC, Elders Group (3/72), HT (6/8/76), CT (6/8/76), example: <**le wech'étl'.**>, //lə wə(=)c'ə́ƛ'//, /'*He dropped down., He fell off.*'/, attested by AC (10/13/71), <**me wets'étl'.**>, //mə wə(=)c'ə́ƛ'//, /'*It dropped (from a shelf, for ex.).*'/, attested by EB, <**le wets'étl' te stl'ítl'qelh li te shxwt'álh.**>, //lə wə(=)c'ə́ƛ' tə s=C_1í=ƛ'əq=əɬ li tə sxʷ=t'ɛ́ɬ//, /'*A child drops off a bridge.*'/, attested by HT, <**le wets'étl' te qó: li te qw'eléqel.**>, //lə wə(=)c'ə́ƛ' tə qá· li tə q'ʷələ́qəl//, /'*a drop-off, The water drops off a cliff.*'/, attested by CT.

<**wets'étl'lexw**>, ncs //wə(=)c'ə́ƛ'=l-əxʷ//, ABDF ['*drop s-th by accident*'], (<**=l**> *non-control transitivizer, accidentally, happen to, manage to*), (<**-exw**> *third person object*), syntactic analysis: transitive verb, attested by EB (2/9/76).

<**wets'étl'lexw**>, ABDF ['*drop s-th by accident*'], *see* wets'étl' ~ wech'étl'.

<**wéwe**>, bound root or stem //wə́wə// meaning unknown

<**shxwéwe**>, df //sxʷ=wə́wə or s=xʷəw=ə or sxʷ=wə́=C_1ə or sxʷ=wə́w=ə//, EZ ['*cougar*'], ['*Felis concolor oregonensis*'], probably <**shxw=**> *something for/that*, possibly <**s=**> *nominalizer, something to*, root meaning unknown, possibly from Chinook Jargon (see below), possibly <**=e**> *living entity*, possibly <**=R1**> *continuative or resultative or derivational*, phonology: possible reduplication, syntactic analysis: nominal, attested by IHTTC (7/26/77), AC (8/7/70, 9/30/71), Elders Group (3/1/72), ME (11/21/72 tape)), other sources: ES /šxʷə́w·a ~ xʷƛ'ə́qtələc/ *cougar*, JH /sxʷú·wè/ *cougar*, H-T <cwō'wa> *cougar, panther (Felis concolor)*, Salish cognate: Squamish /(n-)s-wúʔwu/ *cougar, mountain lion* W73:68, K67:307, Lushootseed (EK, LL, ESi) /s-wəwáʔ/ ~ (JC) /s-wə́wəʔ/ *cougar* and perhaps (EK) /swəw'wáʔ/ *little cougar* H76:551, Chinook Jargon <swaawa> *panther* Johnson 1978:382, also <**swéwe**>, //s=wə́w(=)ə or s=wə́=C_1ə//, attested by NP (IHTTC 7/26/77), also <**shxwewéwe**>, //sxʷ=wə́w(=)ə or sxʷ=wə́=C_1ə//, attested by AK and SP (IHTTC 7/26/77), AK (11/21/72 tape).

<**Shxwewéwe**>, dnom //sxʷ=wə́w(=)ə or sxʷ=wə́=C_1ə//, PLN ['*next slough entering Harrison River above Xemó:leqw*'], Elder's comment: "means *coyote*", comment: probably error for "means *cougar*", phonology: possible reduplication, syntactic analysis: nominal, attested by EL (3/1/78), also <**Shxwúwélem**>, //sxʷ=wú=C_1ə=´=əl=əm or sxʷ=wə́=C_1ə=´=əl=əm//, phonology: possible stress-shift, attested by EL (Chehalis place names boat trip 6/27/78).

<**wexés**>, us //wəxʸə́s or wə=xʸə́s or wəxʸ=ə[=´=]s//, DIR ['*(come) out of thick bushes*'], TVMO, possibly <**we=**> *suddenly*, root meaning unknown unless root as in wíwexem *frayed (of a rope)*, possibly <**=es**> *on the face*, possibly <=´=> *derivational*, syntactic analysis: intransitive verb, attested by IHTTC (7/5/77), example: <**me wexés**>, //mə wə(=)xʸə́s//, /'*come out of thick bushes*'/, attested by IHTTC.

<**we<u>x</u>és**>, df //wəx̣=ə[=´=]s//, EZ /'*frog, (if generic may include Pacific tree toad* and perhaps the introduced species*: bullfrog, green frog, red-legged frog, western spotted frog, and the tailed toad)*'/, ['if generic includes families *Ranidae* and *Bufonidae* and may include *Hyla regilla* and perhaps the introduced species: *Rana catesbeiana, Rana clamitans, Rana aurora aurora, Rana pretiosa pretiosa*, and *Ascaphus truei*, if not generic then includes only members of family *Ranidae* and/or family *Bufonidae*'], SD ['*the sound a frog makes (IHTTC only)*'], root meaning uncertain but form is exactly same as word meaning *out of thick bushes*, possibly <**=es**> *on the face*, possibly <=´=> *derivational*, syntactic analysis: noun, nominal, attested by Elders Group (2/5/75), contrast <**pípehò:m**> *frog*, contrast <**weq'iyethílem**> *a kind of frog*, contrast <**welék'**> *little green tree frog, (Pacific tree toad)*, Salish cognate: Squamish /wəx̣ə́s/ *frog* W73:108, K67:377 and *frog (members of family Ranidae and family Bufonidae)* Bouchard and Kennedy 1976:119-120, Sechelt /wəx̣ə́s/ *frog* T77:9, also /'*the sound*

a frog makes'/, attested by IHTTC (8/10/77).

<**Wex̲ésem ~ Lexwwex̲ésem**>, ds //wəx̣ə́s=əm ~ ləx^{w}=wəx̣ə́s=əm//, PLN ['*Bill Bristol Island*'], (<**lexw=**> *always*), (<**=em**> *place to have/get*), syntactic analysis: nominal, attested by AD and SP (perhaps from MP) (IHTTC 7/8/77), Elders on American Bar place names trip (AD and AK) (6/26/78), Elders at Katz Class (BHTTC 10/5/76), source: place names reference file #46.

<**wóx̲es**>, df //wə[=Aá=]x̣=əs//, TIME ['*month beginning in March*'], (semological comment: named after *frog croaking* or *frog*), (<**ó-ablaut**> *derivational*), possibly <**=es**> *cyclic period*, phonology: ablaut, syntactic analysis: nominal, attested by IHTTC (8/10/77), Elders Group (2/5/75), contrast <**welék'es**> *moon beginning in March*, Salish cognate: possibly Squamish /wə́ɬx̣s/ *time of the last snow when the frogs come to life, probably March* W73:108, K67:377.

<**welé x̲**>, df //w[=əl=]ə́x̣//, EZ /'*frog, (if generic may include Pacific tree toad* and perhaps the introduced species*: bullfrog, green frog, red-legged frog, western spotted frog, and the tailed toad)*'/, ['if generic includes families *Ranidae* and *Bufonidae* and may include *Hyla regilla* and perhaps the introduced species: *Rana catesbeiana, Rana clamitans, Rana aurora aurora, Rana pretiosa pretiosa*, and *Ascaphus truei*, if not generic then includes only members of family *Ranidae* and/or family *Bufonidae*'], possibly <**=el=**> *plural*, root meaning unknown, phonology: possible infixed plural, syntactic analysis: nominal, attested by Elders Group (2/27/80).

<**Wex̲ésem ~ Lexwwex̲ésem**>, PLN ['*Bill Bristol Island*'], *see* wex̲és.

<**wex̲ó:mō:lh**>, cpds //wəx̣=x̣ɛ[=Aá=]·m=óɬ or wə=x̣ɛ[=Aá=]·m=ó:ɬ//, EZ /'*big frog (even bigger than pípehò:m and cries like a baby), (*probably *bullfrog,* possibly *green frog)*'/, probably ['*Rana catesbeiana*'], possibly ['*Rana clamitans*'], (semological comment: both the species mentioned have alarm cries described in Green and Campbell 1984 as screams and wails, both are now common in the Stó:lō area though introduced from the east by the White man), literally possibly /'frog weep/cry baby (or) suddenly weep/cry baby'/, probably root <**x̲à:m**> *cry, weep*, possibly root <**wex̲**> meaning uncertain but found in words for *frog* and *croak*, possibly <**we=**> *suddenly*, <**=óllh**> *young, offspring/child*, possibly <**ō-ablaut**> *derivational*, phonology: ablaut, possible consonant-loss (l before lh), syntactic analysis: nominal, attested by AD (7/6/79).

<**we'ól ~ ól(e)we ~ ólew**>, NUM /'*too (overly), very much*'/, *see* òl ~ -òl ~ -ò ~ el.

<**wí: ~ wíy**>, probable root //wíy ~ wɛ́·y// *warn*, compare **wá:y**.

<**Swí:lhcha ~ Swíylhcha**>, df //s=wíy=ɬcɛ//, PLN ['*Cultus Lake*'], ASM ['because of stl'áleqem creatures thought to inhabit Cultus Lake it was avoided except by those training for power, several kinds of stl'áleqems were reported to live in the lake, a bear-like creature that dwelled underwater and ate all but the bones of men lowered into the lake on ropes, and creatures seen in small muddy swirls of water which then gave the person seeing them <**xó:lís**> (fatal soul-loss sickness after seeing stl'áleqem creatures)'], ASM ['a creek that runs from Cultus Lake into Chilliwack River is called Sweltzer Creek, an early spelling of Swíylhcha, perhaps by a White man with a British or American r-less dialect'], (<**s=**> *nominalizer*), probably root <**wíy ~ wá:y**> *warn*, lx <**=élhcha ~ =lhcha**> *unclear liquid*, syntactic analysis: nominal, attested by AC (8/14/70), others, other sources: Gibbs, H-T02

<**wíp**>, bound root //wíp or wə́p *load with something heavy*//, Salish cognate: Squamish root /wip/ as in /wi-wip-áy-qs-n-m/ *be hanging down (ab. small objects, e.g., icicles, leaves)' (formally a passive of a verb in /-nəx^{w}/ not recorded by itself) K67:379.*

<**wép**>, rsls //wi[=Aə́=]p//, TVMO ['*overloaded*'], DESC, HUNT, ASM ['in packing on one's back, can't lift it, have to leave some meat if packing meat'], (<**é-ablaut on root i**> *resultative*), phonology: ablaut, syntactic analysis: adjective/adjectival verb, attested by IHTTC (7/5/77),

example: <**tsel wép.**>, //c-əl wi[=Aə́=]p//, /'*I'm overloaded.*'/, attested by IHTTC.

<**swíp**>, stvi //s=wə[=Aí=]p//, TVMO ['*(be) loaded with a heavy pack*'], HUNT, (<**s=**> *stative*), syntactic analysis: adjective/adjectival verb, attested by IHTTC (7/5/77).

<**swewíp**>, df //s=C_1ə=wip//, TVMO ['*more than one person heavily loaded with packs*'], HUNT, possibly <**s=**> *nominalizer or stative*, (<**R5=**> *plural*), phonology: reduplication, syntactic analysis: nominal?, adjective/adjectival verb?, attested by IHTTC (7/5/77).

<**swepwíp**>, plv //s=C_1əC_2=wíp//, TVMO ['*each had a heavy pack*'], HUNT, literally /'many have heavy load, many are loaded heavily'/, (<**s=**> *stative*), (<**R3=**> *plural agent*), phonology: reduplication, syntactic analysis: adjective/adjectival verb, attested by IHTTC (7/5/77).

<**wí:q ~ wíq**>, bound root //wí·q ~ wíq *widen, spread*//, Salish cognate: possibly Squamish root /wiq'/ *open (ab. container)* as in /wiq'-c-ánʔ ~ wiq'-c-nʔ/ *pull, force open (tr.)* and /wíq'-c-m/ *pull open one's mouth (with one's hands) (itr.)* K69:90, possibly Lushootseed /gʷə́q'/ *open, opening, clearing* H76:171, historical/comparative detail: Halkomelem appear to have lost glottalization from q' if these forms are cognate.

<**wí:qet**>, pcs //wí·q=əT//, CAN /'*spread s-th, widen s-th*'/, MC, ASM ['for ex. a canoe by dropping hot stones in it while it is filled with water'], (<**=et**> *purposeful control transitivizer*), syntactic analysis: transitive verb, attested by Elders Group (9/10/75).

<**wíqes**>, ds //wíq=əs//, ABFC ['*to yawn*'], literally /'widen on the face'/, lx <**=es**> *on the face*, syntactic analysis: intransitive verb, attested by Elders Group.

<**wíweqes**>, cts //wí[-C_1ə-]q=əs//, ABFC ['*yawning*'], (<**-R1-**> *continuative*), phonology: reduplication, syntactic analysis: intransitive verb, attested by AC (8/15/70).

<**wíqes**>, ABFC ['*to yawn*'], *see* wí:q ~ wíq.

<**wí:qet**>, CAN /'*spread s-th, widen s-th*'/, *see* wí:q ~ wíq.

<**wíth**>, bound root //wíθ meaning prob. imitative//.

<**wéthweth**>, chrs //wi[=Aə́=]θ=C_1əC_2//, EZ ['*spotted sandpiper*'], ['*Actitis macularia*'], literally (probably) /'characteristically (goes) weeth'/, ASM ['the call of the spotted sandpiper is described by Udvardy 1977 as "weet-weet-weet", thus probably the name (G79:16)'], (<**é-ablaut**> *derivational*), (<**=R2**> *characteristic*), phonology: reduplication, ablaut, syntactic analysis: nominal, attested by AK and/or SP and/or AD (Raft Trip 8/30/77), Salish cognate: Squamish /wəcwíc/ *spotted sandpiper (Actitis macularia)* or possibly *pectoral sandpiper (Calidris melantotos)* or *western sandpiper (Ereunetas mauri)* Bouchard and Kennedy 1976:78 versus /s-p'ə-p'láč'/ *snipe* W73:241, K69:56, contrast <**sqasíya ~ sqathíya ~ sq'asíya ~ skasíya**> *common snipe, Wilson's snipe (Capella gallinago)* after Hill-Tout's <skasi'a> (umlaut over first a, macron over i) *snipe*, also EZ /'*snipe, (Wilson's snipe or common snipe)*'/, ['*Capella gallinago*'], Elder's comment: "rather than wíthiya (EL and JL)", attested by EL and JL (9/15/78), Elders Group (6/4/75, 2/11/76, 2/18/76).

<**wóthiya**>, ds //wi[=Aá=]θ=iyɛ//, EZ ['*female spotted sandpiper*'], ['*Actitis macularia*'], (<**ó-ablaut**> *derivational*), lx <**=iya**> *affectionate diminutive*, phonology: ablaut, syntactic analysis: nominal, attested by AK and/or SP and/or AD (Raft Trip on Fraser R. from X̲elhálh to Alhqá:yem 8/30/77), also <**wíthiya**>, //wíθ=iyɛ//, also EZ ['*snipe (large or small)*'], ['*Capella gallinago*'], attested by BJ (12/5/64).

<**wí:we ~ wíwe**>, stem //wí(·)wə or wí(·)w=ə or C_1í=wə or wí(·)=C_1ə// *eulachon, oolachen, candle-fish*

<**swí:we ~ swíwe**>, df //s=wí(·)wə or s=wí(·)w=ə or s=C_1í=wə or s=wí(·)=C_1ə//, EZ /'*eulachon, oolachen, candle-fish*'/, ['*Thaleichthys pacificus*'], ASM ['small oily fish that run in great numbers up the Fraser River in spring, they are caught at the mouth of the Fraser in April and upriver at

Chehalis till about May 10th, the extracted oil was a great delicacy and was used much as butter is by Whites, it was traded and obtained by trade both among the Stó:lō, the fish was also dried and smoked and eaten fresh (delicious pan-fried with a little bread crumbs, eaten bones and all since the bones are so fine), cold weather forces the run too deep in the river for them to be dipped, they are caught nowadays with wire mesh dippers but formerly with special scoops which had their own name'], MED ['if a person rubs eulachon oil on his head he will go crazy (this is one tradition)'], (<**s=**> *nominalizer*), root meaning unknown, possibly <**=e**> *living thing*, possibly <**R4=**> *diminutive*, possibly <**=R1**> *diminutive or continuative or resultative*, phonology: possible reduplication, syntactic analysis: nominal, attested by AC (8/29/70, 11/17/71), BJ (12/5/64), Elders Group (3/1/72), other sources: ES /swí·wə/ and JH /swí·wè/ *eulachon*, H-T <swe'Ewa> (macron over e) *oolachan (Thaleichthys pacificus)*, Salish cognate: Squamish /sx̣^{w}íwʔač/ *eulachon, candlefish* K69:60, also <**swí:wa**>, //s=C_1í=wɛ//, attested by DM (12/4/64), also <**swí'we**>, //s=wíʔwə or s=C_1í=ʔ=wə or s=wí[=ʔ=]=C_1ə//, dialects: *Matsqui*, attested by Deming (5/6/76), example: <**latset qó:lem te swíwe.**>, //lɛ-c-ət qá·=əl=əm tə s=wíwə//, /'*Let's scoop oolachens.*'/, attested by Deming (5/6/76).

<**temwíwe**> or possibly <**temswíwe**>, ds //təm=wíwə or təm=s=wíwə//, TIME /'*month beginning in April at the mouth of the Fraser, May-June (Jenness:Sepass), oolachen moon*'/, literally /'time to get eulachon, eulachon time/season'/, (<**tem=**> *time, season, time to*), (semological comment: the form without s= may be a verb *get eulachons*), phonology: possible reduplication, syntactic analysis: nominal?, adverb/adverbial verb?, attested by Elders Group (3/12/75), also <**temxwíwe ~ temwíwe**>, //təm=x^{w}íwə ~ təm=wíwə//, source: Jenness's field notes on William Sepass of Sardis (months from Sepass's calendar).

<**wíweles**>, probable stem //C_1í=wələs or wí[=C_1ə=]ləs//, root meaning unknown unless related to the root **wiq** in **swíqe** *man.*

<**swíweles ~ swíwles**>, df //s=C_1í=wələs or s=wí[=C_1ə=]ləs//, HAT /'*adolescent boy (about 10 to 15 yrs. old), teenaged boy, young man (teenager)*'/, (<**s=**> *nominalizer*), possibly <**R4=**> *diminutive*, possibly <**=R1=**> *derivational*, root meaning unknown, phonology: reduplication, syntactic analysis: nominal, attested by AC (8/15/70, 10/23/71), CT (6/8/76), Elders Group (10/1/75), other sources: ES /swíw·ləs/ *adolescent boy*, H-T <swe'wilus> (macron over e) *youth* and <swa'wilus> (macron over a) *youths (coll.)*, Salish cognate: Lushootseed /s-wəlús/ *young man of noble parentage* H76:551, example: <**q'á:mis te swíweles**>, //q'ɛ́·m(=)iy-s tə s=C_1í=wələs//, /'*the girl's boyfriend*'/, literally /'girl -his/her the boy'/, comment: misglossed, should be *the boy's girlfriend*, attested by Elders Group (10/1/75).

<**swóweles**>, pln //s=wi[=Aá=][=C_1ə=]ləs//, HAT ['*lots of adolescent/teenaged boys*'], (<**ó-ablaut**> *plural*), phonology: ablaut, reduplication, syntactic analysis: nominal, attested by AC (10/21/71), others.

<**wíweqes**>, ABFC ['*yawning*'], *see* wí:q ~ wíq.

<**wiweqw'óthet**>, FSH ['*jerk-lining for sturgeon in a canoe*'], *see* wṓqw' ~ wéqw'.

<**wíx**>, bound stem //wíx^y// meaning uncertain

<**wíwexem**>, rsls //wí[=C_1ə=]x^y=əm//, incs, DESC ['*frayed (of a rope)*'], (<**=R1=**> *resultative*), (<**=em**> *have, get, inceptive*), phonology: reduplication, syntactic analysis: adjective/adjectival verb, attested by AHTTC (2/8/80), compare <**wexés**> *(come) out of thick bushes*?.

<**wiyálhò**>, ASP ['*(just) started (to do something)*'], *see* yalh.

<**wíyeka**>, N /'*little man (nickname for a person), (sonny boy (MV and DF))*'/, *see* swíyeqe ~ swíyqe ~ swí:qe.

<**wíyeq ~ wíyq ~ wí:q**>, probable bound root //wíyəq ~ wíyq ~ wí·q// *male*, also see alternative analysis of this root under <**wáq ~ wiq**>, bound root //wɛ́q ~ wiq// *male*, above (where etymologies for <**swáqeth**>, df //s=wɛ́q(=)əθ or s=wi[=Aɛ́=]q=ə(=)θ//, KIN ['*husband*'], literally (possibly) /'someone that's a male spouse' and its derivations are found. The vowel of the original root is either <**a**> or <**i**>.

<**swíyeqe ~ swíyqe ~ swí:qe**>, df //s=wí·q=ə//, HAT ['*man (15 years and up)*'], EZ ['*male (creature)*'], EB ['*male (plant)*'], (<**s=**> *nominalizer*), possibly root <**wí:q**> *male*, possibly <**=e**> *living entity*, syntactic analysis: nominal, attested by AC (11/24/71, etc.), BJ (5/10/64), Elders Group (3/15/72), many others, other sources: ES /swə́y·qɛ/ (MsCw /swə́yʔqɛ/) *man*, Salish cognate: Squamish /swíʔqa/ *man* W73:172, K67:300, and from G82: dialects of NSt (Lummi) /swə́yʔqəʔ/, (Saanich) /swə́yʔqe/ (P70) ~ /swíʔqɛ/ (B74a), (Songish) /swáyʔqe(ʔ)/, (Sooke) /swə́yqəʔ/, (Samish) VU /swə́y'əqa/ ~ LD /swə́y'qaʔ/, and of SSt (Clallam) /swə́yʔqəʔ/ all *man, male*, historical/comparative detail: historical evidence and the derived form <**wiyeka**> /wí·q=K=ɛ/ *little man* both suggest the final vowel once was /=ɛ/ in Upriver Halkomelem, example: <**iyómex swí:qe**>, //ʔiy=áməxʸ s=wí·q=ə//, /'*handsome man*'/, attested by AC (12/8/71), <**swí(y)eqe kw'e mél:es**>, //s=wí·q=ə k'ʷə mə́l·ɛ-s//, /'*a son, (his/her/its/their child is male)*'/, literally /'is male the (remote) his/her/its/their offspring'/, attested by AC (10/23/71), <**(qél, híkw, i'axwíl) swíyeqe**>, //(qə́l, híkʷ, C_1í=ʔɛxʷ(=)íl) s=wí·q=ə//, /'*(bad, big, little) man*'/, attested by AC (8/4/70), <**talúwe swíyeqe.**>, //tɛ=lə́wə s=wí·q=ə//, /'*You are a man.*'/, attested by Elders Group (3/15/72).

<**sí:wí:qe**>, pln //s=í·=wí·q=ə or s=hí·=wí·q=ə//, HAT /'*men, males*'/, EZ, EB, (<**-(h)í:=**> **between s= and w...**> *plural*), phonology: infixed plural, possible consonant merger, syntactic analysis: nominal, attested by AC (10/21/71), others, other sources: H-T <siwe'Eka> (macron over i and over e) *men (collect.)*.

<**swíwíqe**>, dmn //s=C_1í=wíq=ə//, HAT /'*little man, small man*'/, (<**R4=**> *diminutive*), phonology: reduplication, syntactic analysis: nominal, attested by EB (11/1/78).

<**swiqe'ál** or **swiyeqe'ál**>, df //s=wiq=ə=ʔɛ́l//, EB ['*male part of male plant*'], ASM ['unclear whether this refers just to the stamen (male pollen producing part of a flower) or more'], lx <**='ál**> *part (of a plant)*?, comment: the glottal stop <**'**> /ʔ/ appears to belong to the suffix since in <**slheli'ál**> there is one present and <**slháli**> usually has an allomorph with final <**y**> before vowel initial consonants; found in <**slheliyó:llh**> *girl*, syntactic analysis: nominal, attested by IHTTC (9/23/77), compare with <**slheli'ál**> *female part of a female plant.*

<**swiyeqe'ó:llh**>, ds //s=wí·q=ə=ʔá·lɬ//, HAT ['*boy (from 5 to 10 yrs.)*'], lx <**='ó:llh ~ ó:llh**> *child, offspring, young*, syntactic analysis: nominal, attested by EB (2/16/76), AC (10/23/71), BJ (5/10/64), other sources: H-T <sweEka'tl> (macron over e and a) *boy*, also /'*boy (from baby to 4 or 5 yrs.)*'/, dialects: *Chill.*, attested by EB (2/16/76).

<**siwíqe'ó:llh** or **siwí:qe'ó:llh**>, pln //s=[=i=]wí·q=ə=ʔá·lɬ//, HAT ['*boys*'], (<**=(h)i= between s= and w... or y...**> *plural*), phonology: infixed plural, syntactic analysis: nominal, attested by AC (10/23/71).

<**swiwiqe'ó:llh**>, dmn //s=C_1í=wiq=ə=ʔá·lɬ//, HAT ['*boy (from baby to 4 or 5 years)*'], (<**R4=**> *diminutive*), phonology: reduplication, syntactic analysis: nominal, dialects: *Cheh.*, attested by EB (2/16/76)

<**wíyeka**>, dmn //wí·q[=K=]=ɛ//, N /'*little man (nickname for a person), (sonny boy (MV and DF))*'/, SOCT, (<**=K= (fronting)**> *diminutive*), phonology: fronting, syntactic analysis: noun, nominal, attested by IHTTC (8/23/77), also <**wí'ke**>, //wíʔq[=K=]=ə//, also /'*sonny boy*'/, attested by MV and EF (Deming 4/27/78).

<**wiyóth kwsu éys te sqwálewels te lólets'e**>, EFAM /'*optimist, a person whose thoughts are always*

good'/, *see* wiyóth.

<**wiyóth kwsu qéls te sqwálewels te lólets'e**>, EFAM /'*pessimist, a person whose thoughts are always bad*'/, *see* wiyóth.

<**wíyt**>, SOC /'*go warn s-o in secret, go tell s-o in secret*'/, *see* wá:y.

<**wóchmel**>, free root //wácməl//, SOCT ['*watchman*'], borrowed from English <watchman>, syntactic analysis: noun, nominal, attested by Elders Group (1/7/76).

<**Wolích**>, PLN /'*Wahleach whistle stop on Seabird Island where Wayne Bobb lived in 1977, (*now also *Wahleach Lake (man-made) [EB])*'/, *see* x̲wále ~ x̲wá:le.

<**wóq**>, bound root //wáq// *glow, blaze*, or possibly related to //wí·q ~ wíq//, bound root *widen, spread*
<**wóweqem**>, cts //wá[-C_1ə-]q=əm//, FIRE /'*glowing of coals not quite gone out yet, red blaze of a fire (DM)*'/, root meaning unknown, (<**-R1-**> *continuative*), probably <**=em**> *have, get, intransitive*, phonology: reduplication, syntactic analysis: intransitive verb, attested by Elders Group (1/16/80), Salish cognate: perhaps Lushootseed (Skagit dial.) /g^wəq/ ~ (Snohomish dial.) /gəq/ *sunshine, brightness* as in /ʔəs-g^wə́q/ *the sun is shining* H76:155, also /'*red blaze of a fire*'/, attested by DM (12/4/64).

<**Wóshetem**>, free root //wášətəm//, PLN /'*Washington (state), Washington (D.C.)*'/, probably borrowed from English <Washington>, syntactic analysis: noun, nominal, attested by Deming Elders (3/15/79)(SJ, MC, MV, LG), Salish cognate: Lushootseed /wášətəb/ *Washington* H76:546.

<**wó:thel**>, df //wá=áθəl//, FOOD ['*share a meal*'], SOC, root meaning unknown unless <**wá:**> *continue* as in yewá: *along* and syewá:l *ancestors*, probably <**=óthel ~ =ó:thel**> *in the mouth*, phonology: possible vowel merger, syntactic analysis: intransitive verb, attested by Deming (12/15/77), Salish cognate: possibly? Squamish /wə́ʔu/ *continue, carry on* W73:67, K67:377, possibly? Lushootseed /wáwəx^w/ *join in eating (the food is put on the table and people pick out what they want...)* H76:548, example: <**michap wó:thel sq'eq'ó talhlímelh.**>, //mi-c-ɛp wá=áθəl s=C_1ə=q'á tɛ=ɬlíməɬ//, /'*Come and share (our meal) with us.*'/, attested by Deming.

<**wóthiya**>, EZ ['*female spotted sandpiper*'], *see* wíth.

<**wóweqem**>, cts //wá[-C_1ə-]q=əm//, FIRE /'*glowing of coals not quite gone out yet, red blaze of a fire (DM)*'/, see under root <**woq**>

<**Wowés**>, possibly root or stem //wawə́s or wa[=R1=][=´=]s//, PLN ['*place across the Fraser River from Union Bar*'], ASM ['there's a White settlement there now'], (semological comment: may have something to do with across or opposite), possibly root possibly root <**was**> or stem <**wowés**> *opposite* as perhaps in <**wowis=st=eleq**> *jealous* perhaps literally *made opposite for awhile habitually*, possibly <**=R1=**> *resultative or derivational*, possibly <=´=> *derivational*, more likely clipped form from <**Iwówes**> /**ʔi=wá[=R1=]s**/ *Union Bar*, phonology: possible reduplication, possible stress-shift, syntactic analysis: nominal, compare <**Iwówes**> /**ʔi=wá[=R1=]s**/ *Union Bar*, compare also <**Ó:ywoses**> *west side of Fraser River at Emory Creek* (perhaps <á(:)y=wós=es> /ʔɛ́·y=was=əs/ with <a → o> /ɛ → a/ automatic before <**=es**> *face*), attested by Elders Group (7/6/77), source: place names reference file #15.

<**wóweth'**>, ABFC ['*prying*'], *see* wáth'.

<**wówí:ls**>, ECON ['*(be scramble-giving)*'], *see* wál or wá:l.

<**wowistéleq**>, df //wɛ[=C_1ə=Ai=]s=sT=ələq//, EFAM /'*jealous, (envious (EB))*'/, ASM ['for ex. either of a rival or of one's spouse'], literally (possibly??) /'made opposite for awhile (durative) habitually'/, possibly root <**was**> *opposite*, possibly <**=R1=**> *resultative or continuative*, possibly <**i-ablaut on e**>

durative, possibly <**=st**> *causative control transitivizer*, possibly <**=éleq**> *habitually*, phonology: possible reduplication, possible ablaut, possible consonant merger, syntactic analysis: intransitive verb, attested by Elders Group (3/3/76), Salish cognate: the affix in: Squamish /pistə́nʔaq/ *jealous* W73:152, K69:43, Samish dial. of NSt /pəstə́nəq/ *jealous* G86:79, and possibly in Lushootseed /s-pipídəq/ *jealous* H76:300, also <**wòwistéleq**>, //wá[=C_1əAi=]s=sT=ə́ləq//, also /'*jealous, envious*'/, attested by EB (1/7/76), example: <**tsel wowistéleq.**>, //c-əl wa[=C_1əAi=]s=sT=ə́ləq//, /'*I'm jealous (either of a rival or of my spouse).*'/, attested by Elders Group.

<**wowistéleqmet**>, iecs //wa[=C_1ə=Ai=]s=sT=ə́ləq=məT//, EFAM ['*be jealous of s-o*'], (<**=met**> *indirect effect non-control transitivizer*), phonology: possible reduplication, possible ablaut, possible consonant merger, syntactic analysis: transitive verb, attested by Elders Group (3/3/76), example: <**tsel wowistéleqmet te swótle.**>, //c-əl wa[=C_1ə=Ai=]s=sT=ə́ləq=məT tə s=wɛ[=Aá=]t=lə//, /'*I'm jealous of somebody.*'/, attested by Elders Group.

<**wowistéleqmet**>, EFAM ['*be jealous of s-o*'], *see* wowistéleq.

<**wó*x*es**>, TIME ['*month beginning in March*'], *see* we*x*és.

<**wố:l**>, probably root //wó·l or wə́[=R1=]l//, EB /'*bulrush, tule*'/, ['*Scirpus acutus*'], ASM ['round/cylindrical reeds (rather than flat like cattails) which were used for mats but less common that cattails, can be found at Hicks Lake'], possibly <**=R1=**> meaning unclear, phonology: possible reduplication, syntactic analysis: noun, nominal, attested by BJ (12/5/64, 5/10/64), Elders Group (7/2/75), LJ via AD (6/18/79), other sources: ES /wə́w·l/ (Ms /wí·lʔ/, Cw /wə́lʔ/) *tule*, JH /wú·l/ *tule*, Salish cognate: Lushootseed /ʔúlal/ *cattail* H76:682, Squamish /wəl/ *bulrush* (single stemmed plant which can be peeled like corn (inside part used for making mats, outside part split and braided used for the ends of this rain- proof mat) K69:89, also probably /'*green reeds that always grow with bulrushes*'/, attested by AC (11/19/71), also /'*jointed reed or rush used for whistle*'/, attested by AC (9/10/71), also <**wố:l ~ wú:l**>, //wó·l//, also /'*cattail rush*'/, attested by SJ (Deming 4/17/80).

<**wố:lalh**>, df //wó·l=ɛɬ//, WV ['*bulrush mat*'], BSK, HHG, possibly <**=alh**> perhaps *weaving, mat*, syntactic analysis: noun, nominal, attested by AK (Elders Group 1/23/80), comment: AK agreed on this pronunciation but did not pronounce it herself, other sources: ES /wə́w·lɛɬ/ (CwMs /wí·lʔɛɬ/) *tule mat*.

<**wố:lalh**>, WV ['*bulrush mat*'], *see* wố:l.

<**wốqw' ~ wéqw'**>, free root //wóq'ʷ ~ wə́q'ʷ//, ABDF ['*to drown*'], also DIR ['*(drift downriver)*'], syntactic analysis: intransitive verb, attested by Elders Group (3/72, 3/26/75), AC (8/7/70), EB (1/26/76), others, Salish cognate: Squamish /wúq'ʷ/ *go downstream* W73:83, K67:379, K69:89, Nooksack /wóq'ʷ/ *drift* Amoss 1961, Twana /wúq'ʷ/ *drift*, Lummi dial. of NSt /wəq'ʷ-íl-əŋ/ *(go) downstream; south*, Songish dial. of NSt /kʷə́q'ʷ/ *downriver*, Clallam /kʷə́q'ʷ-i/ *go downstream* all cognate set #32 in G82:13, Samish dial. of NSt (VU) /wáq'ʷ-əɬ/ ~ (LD) /wáq'ʷ-ɬ/ *downstream* G86:64, historical/comparative detail: the main meaning of the Upriver Halkomelem differs from those of the cognates, and the Halkomelem vowel should not be that same as in the cognate forms in Squamish, Nooksack and Twana (Proto-Central Salish *u becomes Upriver Halkomelem /a/), these irregularities may show the form was borrowed into Halkomelem, example: <**le wốqw'.**>, //lə wóq'ʷ//, /'*He drowned.*'/, syntactic comment: ambiguous past, attested by AC (8/7/70), <**mốkw' wốqw'.**>, //mók'ʷ wóq'ʷ//, /'*All drowned.*'/, attested by AC (8/7/70), <**le wốqw' tl'esu s'í:kw'.**>, //lə wóq'ʷ ƛ'ə=s=u s=ʔí·k'ʷ//, /'*He was drowned and lost.*'/, attested by EB (1/26/76).

<**wōqw'wốqw'**>, plv //C_1əC_2=wóq'ʷ//, WATR ['*a flood*'], literally /'many drown (or) many downriver'/, (<**R3=**> *plural*), phonology: reduplication, e → ō, syntactic analysis: nominal?, attested by Elders Group (3/15/72).

<**wṓqw'et**>, pcs //wóq’^{w}=əT//, WATR [*'drop s-th into the water'*], (<**=et**> *purposeful control transitivizer*), syntactic analysis: transitive verb, attested by AD and NP (4/11/80), also <**wéqw'et**>, //wə́q’^{w}=əT//, also /*'throw s-th into the water'*/, attested by EB (3/1/76).

<**wōqw'ílem ~ wōqw'éylem ~ wōqw'ílém ~ wōqw'éylém**>, mdls //wóq’^{w}=íl=əm//, incs, DIR /*'go downstream, go downriver, down the river'*/, WATR, CAN, TVMO, (<**=íl**> *go, come, get, become*), (<**=em**> *middle voice*), phonology: optional updrifting, syntactic analysis: intransitive verb, attested by EB (12/15/75), TG (Elders Group 3/1/72).

<**héwqw'elem ~ hṓwqw'elem**>, cts //hə́-wq’^{w}=əl=əm//, DIR /*'(going) downstream, drift downstream, (drifting downstream)'*/, WATR, CAN, TVMO, (<**hé-**> *continuative* before resonants), phonology: vowel-loss in root after stressed prefix, vowel-reduction in suffix, syntactic analysis: intransitive verb, attested by Elders Group (3/1/72, 6/16/76).

<**xwōqw'éylem**>, incs //x^{w}ə=wq’^{w}=íl=əm ~ x^{w}=wq’^{w}=íl=əm//, DIR /*'go in the direction of the water, go downriver'*/, WATR, CAN, TVMO, possibly <**xwe=**> *get, become*, possibly <**xw=**> *toward*, phonology: vowel-loss in root between prefix and stressed suffix, vocalization of ew or w to ō, syntactic analysis: intransitive verb, attested by EB (3/1/76, 4/26/76), also /*'going downstream'*/, attested by AC (8/25/70), example: <**le xwōqw'éylem thel méle.**>, //lə x^{w}ə=wq’^{w}=íl=əm θ-əl mə́lə//, /*'My daughter went downstream.'*/, attested by EB (4/26/76), <**latsel xwōqw'éylem.**>, //lɛ-c-əl x^{w}=wq’^{w}=íl=əm//, /*'I'm going downstream.'*/, attested by AC.

<**yexwṓqw'elem**>, mos //yə=x^{w}=hə́-wq’^{w}=əl=əm//, incs, mdls, TVMO [*'travelling by going downriver'*], DIR, WATR, CAN, (<**ye=**> *travelling by, while moving along*), (<**xwe=**> *get, become*), (<**hé-**> *continuative*), (<**=el ~ =íl**> *go, come, get, become*), (<**=em**> *middle voice*), phonology: vowel-loss in root after stressed prefix, vowel-loss in prefix before stressed prefix, vocalization of éw to ō, vowel-reduction/allomorph in suffix, consonant merger, syntactic analysis: adverb/adverbial verb, attested by EB (6/7/76).

<**sōqw'á<u>x</u>el**>, dnom //s=wō[=M1=]q’^{w}=ɛ́x̣əl//, BLDG [*'lower [downriver] end of house (inside or outside)'*], DIR, (<**s=**> *nominalizer*), lx <**=á<u>x</u>el**> *end (of building), side, part*, phonology: metathesis, syntactic analysis: nominal, attested by Elders Group (8/25/76).

<**ōqw'íles ~ ōqw'éyles**>, df //wō[=M1=]q’^{w}=íl=əs or ʔə=wq’^{w}=íl=əs//, PLN /*'mouth of Hunter Creek, (Restmore Caves* (Wells)*)'*/, Elder's comment: literally /'facing downriver'/, possibly <**he= ~ hé=**> *continuative*?, possibly <**=íl**> *go, come, get, become*, probably <**=es**> *on the face*, (<**zero**> *nominalizer*), comment: i.e. a verb used over time as place name becoming a nominal/noun, phonology: vocalization of w to ō or e → ō, syntactic analysis: nominal, attested by IHTTC (8/5/77 incl. AK, TG, AD but not SP on that day), source: place names reference file #184, also <**Uqw'íles**>, //wq’^{w}=íl=əs//, also /*'Restmore Caves'*/, literally /'watching downriver'/, (semological comment: so named after an Indian murderer who lived there and killed people coming upriver till he was killed by an organized group of Indian people (Duff 1952)), phonology: metathesis, source: Wells 1965 (lst ed.):15.

<**sōqw'ólwelh**>, stvi //s=wō[=M1=]q’^{w}=álwəɬ//, DIR [*'(be) downstream below something'*], WATR, literally /'be on the downriver side'/, (<**s=**> *stative*), lx <**=ólwelh**> *on the side*, phonology: metathesis, syntactic analysis: adverb/adverbial verb, attested by AC (8/25/70), example: <**sōqw'ólwelh te syáyeq'.**>, //s=wq’^{w}=álwəɬ tə s=yɛ́[=C$_{1}$ə=]q’//, /*'(It's) downriver past the log.'*/, literally /'the log is on the downriver side'/, attested by AC.

<**xwōqw'ṓ:lh**>, df //x^{w}=wō[=M1=]q’^{w}=ówəɬ or x^{w}=wq’^{w}=ó·ɬ//, TVMO [*'drifting back downriver (like spawned-out salmon)'*], DIR, WATR, possibly <**xw=**> *toward*?, possibly <**xwe=**> *get, become*, probably <**=ṓwelh**> *canoe, vessel*, possibly <**=ṓ:lh**> *large fish*?? or> *offspring*??, phonology: metathesis, syntactic analysis: intransitive verb, attested by Deming (4/1/76).

<**wiweqw'óthet**>, dmv //C_1í=wəq’^{w}=ə[=Aá=]T-ət//, pcs, rfls, durs, FSH [*'jerk-lining for sturgeon in a canoe'*], CAN, ASM ['sitting in a canoe holding a rope anchored onshore with rocks on one end and with sturgeon-sized gaff hooks on the other end in the water'], literally /'drifting oneself purposely downriver a little for a (long) while'/, (<**R4=**> *diminutive*), (<**=et**> *purposeful control transitivizer*), (<**ó-ablaut**> *durative*), (<**-et**> *reflexive*), phonology: ablaut, syntactic analysis: intransitive verb, attested by BHTTC (11/10/76).

<**wṓqw'elh**>, bound stem //wóq’^{w}=əɬ//, possibly *downriver weaving.*

<**swṓqw'elh**>, df //s=wóq’^{w}=əɬ//, WV */'woven goat-wool blanket, (twilled weave (JL))'/*, ASM ['sometimes woven mixed with dog wool and/or cottonwood fluff, the wool was often whitened with baked diatomaceous earth (st'ewṓkw'), several different weaves were used in the surviving examples and newly made blankets including a twilled weave and a twined weave, there are several excellent books on this weaving now called Salish weaving, the original blankets were very highly valued and were used as money in potlatches and in trade with Hudson's Bay Co. (a practice which H.B.C. also used with their own trade blankets), according to AC the goat-wool blankets were only used as a cape and never slept on, the goat wool was obtained from mountain goats killed but more was obtained by Stó:lō people following goat trails and picking hairs left in the bushes where goats frequented (example those which they ate from)'], (<**s=**> *nominalizer*), root possibly <**wṓqw' ~ wéqw'**> *drift downriver*, lx <**=elh**> *weaving, mat* as in <**wṓl=á:lh**> *bulrush/tule mat*, possibly lit. /'downriver weaving'/, syntactic analysis: nominal, attested by Elders Group (3/1/72), AC (10/23/71, 12/4/71), DM (12/4/64), many others, Salish cognate: Squamish /swúq’^{w}aɬ/ *Indian blanket* W73:39, K67:299, Samish dial. of NSt /swə́wq’^{w}əɬ/ [swóq’^{w}əɬ] *goat wool blanket* G86:83, also */'twilled weave'/*, attested by JL (Elders Group 8/8/79), example: <**tsel thíyt te swṓqw'elh telí te sáys te p'eq'élqel.**>, //c-əl θíy=T tə s=wóq’^{w}=əɬ təlí tə sɛ́y-s tə p’əq’=ə́lqəl//, */'I made a blanket of (from) the wool of the mountain goat.'/*, attested by AC (12/4/71).

<**wṓqw'et**>, WATR [*'drop s-th into the water'*], *see* wṓqw' ~ wéqw'.

<**wōqw'ílem ~ wōqw'éylem ~ wōqw'ílém ~ wōqw'éylém**>, DIR */'go downstream, go downriver, down the river'/*, *see* wṓqw' ~ wéqw'.

<**wōqw'wṓqw'**>, WATR [*'a flood'*], *see* wṓqw' ~ wéqw'.

X

<**x=**>, da or bound root //x^{y}=//, ANA ['*genital*'], syntactic analysis: derivational prefix/lexical suffix or bound root; found in <**xá:welh**>, //x^{y}=ɛ́·wəɬ//, /'*vagina, vulva*'/, lx <**=á:welh**> *canoe, boat, vessel, dish*, <**sxéle**>, //s=x^{y}=ɛ[=Aə́=]lɛ or s=x^{y}ə́l=ɛlɛ//, /'*penis*'/, possibly <**=álá**> *container*, possibly root <**xel**> *roll, rotate*, <**xíwe**>, //x^{y}=íwɛ or x^{y}íwə//, /'*urinate (of a woman)*'/, possibly <**=íwa**> *cord*, <**xátl'**>, //x^{y}(=)ɛ́ƛ'//, /'*have an erection*'/, perhaps <**sxáye**>, //s=x^{y}(ɛ)=iyɛ(=M2)//, /'*co-wife, younger co-wives*'/, perhaps root < **xóp'**>, //x^{y}(=)áp'//, /'*squat*'/.

<**xálxwthet**>, ABFC ['*cool off (of a person)*'], *see* xó:lxwem.

<**xálh ~ xá:lh**>, free root //x^{y}ɛ́ɬ ~ x^{y}ɛ́·ɬ//, LAND ['*road*'], SOC, BLDG ['*door*'], syntactic analysis: noun, nominal, attested by AC (8/13/70, 10/1/71, 9/30/71), Elders Group (3/72, 3/2/77), EB, others, other sources: ES /x^{y}ɛ́·ɬ/ (Cw /šɛ́ɬ/, Ms /x^{y}ɛ́ɬ/) *road (trail)*, JH /xé·ɬ/ *road, path*, Salish cognate: cognate set #8 in Galloway 1988, PCS *x^{y}wáɬ *trail, way; doorway*, Se /šáwɬ/, Sq /šuáɬ/, Nk (PA61, G84a:SJ, G84b:LT:LG) /šǽɬ/, Nk (G83b:PA:GS) /x^{y}ǽɬ/ (Hk accent), Lm /sóɬ/, Smb (LD, VU, TB) SnSg So(E69) /sáɬ/, So (TTE74) /sóɬ/, Cl /súɬ/, Ld /šə́g^{w}ɬ/, Ld (Suttles65) /šág^{w}ɬ/, Tw (Suttles65) /šuwʔáɬ/, example: <**yíyeq te xálh**>, //yí[-C$_{1}$ə-]q tə x^{y}ɛ́ɬ//, /'*snowing on the road*'/, literally /'the road is falling snow'/, attested by AC (9/30/71), <**lám te sle'ólwelhs té xàlh.**>, //lɛ́=m tə s=ləʔ=álwəɬ-s tə x^{y}ɛ́ɬ//, /'*He went across the road.*'/, phonology: sentence stress, attested by EB.

<**kyóxàlh** or **kyóxàlh**>, cpds //k^{y}á=x^{y}ɛ[= ̀=]ɬ or k^{y}á x^{y}ɛ́ɬ//, CAN ['*railroad*'], root <**kyó**> *car*, root <**xálh**> *road*, possibly <= ̀=> *derivational*, phonology: possible stress-shift or sentence stress, syntactic analysis: nominal or nominal phrase with modifier(s), attested by Elders Group (3/2/77).

<**xáxlh**>, dmn //x^{y}ɛ[=C$_{1}$ə=]ɬ//, LAND /'*path, trail*'/, SOC, (<**=R1=**> *diminutive*), phonology: reduplication, syntactic analysis: noun, nominal, attested by Elders Group (3/2/77), AC (8/13/70).

<**xá:m**>, free root //x^{y}ɛ́·m//, CAN ['*get a canoe stuck on a rock or something*'], WATR, literally /'get shallowed'/, syntactic analysis: intransitive verb, attested by IHTTC (7/19/77).

<**sxáxem**>, strs //s=x^{y}ɛ́[=C$_{1}$ə=]m//, WATR ['*shallow*'], (<**s=**> *stative*), (<**=R1=**> *resultative*), phonology: reduplication, syntactic analysis: adjective/adjectival verb, attested by IHTTC (7/19/77), EB (12/4/75), BJ (5/10/64, 12/5/64).

<**sxáxem**>, dnom //s=x^{y}ɛ́[=C$_{1}$ə=]m//, WATR ['*shallow water*'], (<**s=**> *nominalizer*), (<**=R1=**> *resultative or continuative*), phonology: reduplication, syntactic analysis: nominal, attested by Elders Group (3/26/75).

<**Xáméles**>, ds //xɛ́m=ə[= ́=]l=əs//, PLN /'*island off of Wahleach Island, island at bridge on river side on east end of Seabird Island*'/, literally /'get stuck in the river on the face [of the island]'/, (<**=el**> *come, go, get, become*), possibly <= ́=> *derivational*, lx <**=es**> *on the face*, phonology: possible stress-shift, syntactic analysis: nominal, attested by IHTTC (8/5/77), AK (8/30/77), source: place names reference file #183.

<**Xemó:leqw**>, ds //x^{y}ɛm=á·[=lə=]q^{w}//, PLN ['*Leon's Slough on Harrison River*'], ASM ['just above Shxwpópélem and below Híqelem, east of Q'iq'ewetó:lthel'], literally /'shallow with many fish'/, lx <**=ó:qw**> *fish (head)*, (<**=le=**> *plural*), phonology: infixed plural, vowel-reduction in root before stressed suffix, syntactic analysis: nominal, attested by EL (9/27/77, 3/1/78, 6/27/78 Harrison R. Boat trip), source: place names reference file #299.

<**xá:mthet ~ xómthet**>, incs //x^{y}ɛ́·m=θət ~ x^{y}ɛ[=Aá=]m=θət//, WATR ['*getting shallow*'], (<**=thet**> *get, become*), possibly <**ó-ablaut**> optional before <**=thet**>, phonology: optional ablaut, syntactic

analysis: intransitive verb, attested by IHTTC (7/19/77), also <**xó:mthet ~ xómthet**>, //xʸɛ[=Aá=]·m=θət ~ xʸɛ[=Aá=]m=θət//, also /'*got shallow*'/, attested by EB (12/4/75).

<**Xáméles**>, PLN /'*island off of Wahleach Island, island at bridge on river side on east end of Seabird Island*'/, *see* xá:m.

<**xá:mthet ~ xómthet**>, WATR ['*getting shallow*'], *see* xá:m.

<**xáqlhelem**>, SPRD ['*(be) sighing (of a spirit-dancer)*'], *see* xeqlhálém.

<**xaqxeqlhálem**>, SPRD ['*sighing over and over (of a spirit-dancer before or after dancing)*'], *see* xeqlhálém.

<**xáq'**>, bound root //xʸɛ́q' *hang open*//.

<**xáq'em**>, mdls //xʸɛ́q'=əm//, ABFC ['*open one's mouth*'], (<**=em**> *middle voice*), syntactic analysis: intransitive verb, attested by Elders Group (2/6/80).

<**xáxeq'em**>, cts //xʸɛ́[-C_1ə-]q'=əm//, ABFC ['*opening one's mouth*'], (<**-R1-**> *continuative*), phonology: reduplication, syntactic analysis: intransitive verb, attested by Elders Group (2/6/80).

<**xixq'á:m ~ xixq'ám**>, durs //xʸɛ[-C_1ə-]q'=ə[=Aɛ́(·)=]m//, ABFC ['*mouth open*'], (<**-R1-**> *resultative*), (<**á(:)-ablaut**> *durative*), phonology: reduplication, ablaut, syntactic analysis: adjective/adjectival verb, attested by Elders Group (4/16/75), EB (5/25/76), example: <**lóyexwa xixq'ámes?**>, //láy=yəxʷ=ɛ xʸɛ[-C_1ə-]q'=ə[=Aɛ́=]m-əs//, /'*Does he/she have to have his/her mouth open?*'/, attested by EB.

<**xeq'ó:thet**>, df //xʸɛ́q'[=M1=]=θət or xʸɛq'=ə[=Aɛ́·=]T-ət//, MC ['*hang something up*'], probably <**metathesis**> *non-continuative*, probably <**á:-ablaut**> *durative*, probably <**=thet**> *get, become*, possibly <**=et**> *purposeful control transitivizer*, possibly <**-et**> *reflexive*??, (semological comment: there is a semantic element of *purposeful control* in this stem but not *reflexive* unless it is mistranslated for *hang oneself*), phonology: á → ó before =thet automatically, syntactic analysis: intransitive verb, attested by EB (12/15/75).

<**xáq'em**>, ABFC ['*open one's mouth*'], *see* xáq'.

<**xá:t**>, free root //xʸɛ́·t//, HUNT ['*bullet*'], FSH /'*sinker, (fish) weight*'/, LAND ['*lead*'], MC ['*lead weight*'], syntactic analysis: noun, nominal, attested by CT (6/8/76), Elders Group (2/19/75), Salish cognate: Squamish /šát/ *ammunition, shot* W73, historical/comparative detail: if the Squamish form is borrowed from English /šát/ *shot* then the Halkomelem form was either borrowed from another Salish language word /šát/ and made to fit the regular sound correspondences non-Upriver Halkomelem /š/ = Upriver Halkomelem /xʸ/ and non-Nooksack/Halkomelem/Northern Straits /a/ = Halkomelem /ɛ/ Nooksack /æ/ and Northern Straits /e/; or the Halkomelem form may have come from Nooksack or Northern Straits which had in turn borrowed it from another Salish language and done the same thing, also <**xát**>, //xʸɛ́t//, attested by Deming (5/20/76), EB (2/6/76).

<**xetáléqetel**>, ds //xʸɛt=ɛ́lə́q=təl//, FSH ['*sinker line*'], literally /'lead/weight/sinker (in the) waves device'/, lx <**=áléq**> *waves*, lx <**=tel**> *device*, phonology: possible updrifting, syntactic analysis: nominal, attested by CT (6/8/76).

<**xátl'**>, free root //xʸɛ́ƛ'//, ABFC /'*get erect (of penis only), have an erection*'/, possibly root <**xá**> *genital*, possibly <**=tl'**> meaning unknown unless *stiff, hard*, phonology: sound symbolism?, syntactic analysis: intransitive verb, attested by JL (7/20/79 Fish Camp), other sources: JH /xá·ƛ'/ *to have an erection*.

<**sxtl'í:qw**>, ds //s=xʸ(ɛ)ƛ'=í·qʷ//, ANA ['*head of the penis*'], literally /'the top of the head of an erection'/, (<**s=**> *nominalizer*), lx <**=í:qw**> *top of the head*, (semological comment: somatic suffixes usually drop the locative *on* feature in independent body part words), phonology: vowel-loss in root

before stressed suffix, syntactic analysis: nominal, attested by DM (JH), other sources: JH /sxƛ'í·qʷ/ *head of penis*, contrast <**shxw'á:q'**> *foreskin* (JH66:11 also from DM).

<**xáweleq**>, EB ['*carrot-like plant used for green dye*'], *see* xáwéq.

<**xá:welh**>, free stem //xʸ=ɛ́·wəɬ or xʸɛ́=ɛ́wəɬ//, ANA /'*woman's genitals, vulva, vagina*'/, possibly root <**xá ~ x**> *genital*, probably not root <**xáw**> *bone*, possibly <**=áwelh ~ =ő́welh ~ =ewelh**> *vessel, dish, canoe*, phonology: possible vowel merger, sound-symbolism?, syntactic analysis: noun, nominal, attested by Elders Group (8/20/75), other sources: ES ChMs /xʸɛ́wəɬ/ (-wəɬ *vessel*)(Cw /šɛ́wəɬ/) *vulva*, Salish cognate: not Squamish /sc'uhnc'/ *vulva* W73:280, K69:57, compare <**xíwe**> *urinate (of a woman)*, also <**sxáwelh**>, //s=xʸɛ́(=ə)wəɬ//, attested by JL (7/20/79 Fish Camp).

<**xawelhíqw**>, ds //xʸ=ɛ́·wəɬ=íqʷ or xʸɛ́=ɛ́wəɬ=íqʷ//, ANA /'*clitoris*'/, lx <**=íqw**> *top of the head*, Elders Group

<**xáwéq**>, ds //xʸɛ́w=əq or xʸəw=ɛ́[=M2=]q//, EB /'*wild carrot (*possibly *spring gold or wild carraway), domestic carrot (both that planted and that gone wild)*'/, possibly ['*Lomatium utriculatum* or *Perideridiae gairdneri*, also *Daucus carota*'], probably root <**xáw**> *bone* probably root as in cognates from other languages, possibly <**=eq ~ =áq**> *in the penis*, possibly <**metathesis**> *derivational*, phonology: possible metathesis, updrifting, syntactic analysis: noun, nominal, attested by BJ (12/5/64), other sources: ES /xʸɛ́wə́q/ *wild carrot, carrot*, H-T <Hia'wEk> (macron on i and a) *carrot (native root resembling)*, Salish cognate: Squamish /šáwaq/ *carrot* and perhaps root /šawʔ/ *bone* W73:53, K67:323, Lushootseed (Southern dialects) /šágʷəq/, (Northern dialects) /šəgʷáq/ *carrot* and perhaps /šáw'/ *bone* H76:455-457, also <**xá:wéq**>, //xʸɛ́·w=əq//, attested by AC (11/17/71).

<**xáweq kíks seplíl**>,FOOD /'*carrot cake*'/, (lit. carrot + cake + bread), (attested by RG,EH 6/16/98 to SN, edited by BG with RG,EH 6/26/00)

<**xáweq sqe'óleqw**>, FOOD /'*carrot juice*'/, (lit. carrot + fruit juice), (attested by RG,EH 6/16/98 to SN, edited by BG with RG,EH 6/26/00)

<**xíxewíyeq** or **xíxewíq**>, dmpn //C_1í=xɛw(=)ə[=Aí=]q//, EB ['*little carrots*'], (<**R4=**> *diminutive*), possibly <**í-ablaut**> *plural*?, phonology: reduplication, ablaut, syntactic analysis: nominal, attested by AK and SP (7/13/75).

<**xaweqá:l**>, ds //xɛw(=)əq=ɛ́·l//, EB /'*yarrow, also parsely fern*'/, ['*Achillea millefolium*, also *Cryptogramma crispa*'], MED ['drink yarrow tea for medicine if you are going to eat taboo food, eating salmon or deer meat are taboo for a boy or girl going through puberty, for a widow or widower, and for someone who has just lost his parents or lost a child, one gets raw inside if he eats salmon or deer at such a time and breaks the taboo (AD), also medicine to stimulate or speed childbirth (MC), also both yarrow and parsely fern are tuberculosis medicine'], lx <**=á:l**> *similar to, -like, or part/portion*, syntactic analysis: nominal, attested by AD (3/5/79), also <**xaweqál**>, //xʸɛw(=)əq=ɛ́l//, attested by MC and SJ (Deming 2/10/77).

<**xáweleq**>, df //xʸɛ́w=ə[=lə=]q or xʸɛ́w=əl=əq//, EB ['*carrot-like plant used for green dye*'], ['(unidentified)'], possibly <**=le=**> *plural*, possibly <**=el**> *-like, similar to*, phonology: possible infixed plural, syntactic analysis: nominal, attested by JL (3/31/78).

<**Xíxewqèyl** or **Xíxewqì:l ~ Xewqéyl** or **Xewqí:l**>, ds //C_1í=xʸɛw(=)əq=í·l ~ xʸɛw(=)əq=í·l//, PLN ['*slough about mid-point in Seabird Island where xáweleq plant grew*'], ASM ['slough located outside the track along the river, on the east side'], (<**R4=**> *diminutive*), (<**=í:l**> *come, go, get, become*), phonology: optional reduplication, vowel-loss in suffix before stressed suffix, syntactic analysis: nominal, attested by JL (3/31/78), also <**Xixewqéyls** or **Xixewqí:ls**>, //C_1í=xɛw(=)əq=í·ls//, also /'*place on the south side of Seabird Island nearly opposite Xáméles Island, carrot-like plants used for green dye used to grow there*'/, attested by JL (Seabird Is. trip

4/3/78).

<**xaweqá:l**>, EB /'*yarrow, also parsely fern*'/, *see* xáwéq.

<**xáxeq'em**>, ABFC ['*opening one's mouth*'], *see* xáq'.

<**xáxlh**>, LAND /'*path, trail*'/, *see* xálh ~ xá:lh.

<**xaxt'ó:les**>, df //C_1ε=xət'=á·ləs or x^yə[=C_1ə=]t'=á·ləs//, EB /'*trillium, B.C. easter lily*'/, ['*Trillium ovatum*'], MED ['take twin trillium root (root of trillium which has a double flower, wash it, scald it, set it on your eyes to take off cataracts*)*'], ABDF ['*cataracts*'], possibly root <**xét ~ xet'**> *swim (of fish)*, possibly <**R8=** or **=R1=**> *derivational*, lx <**=ó:les**> *on the eye*, phonology: reduplication, syntactic analysis: nominal, attested by Elders Group (9/17/75), AD and NP (1/23/80), EB (3/2/76).

<**xá:y ~ xà:y**>, free root //x^yέ·y ~ x^yὲ·y//, ANAF /'*gills, also "boot" (boot-shaped organ attached to fish gill)*'/, syntactic analysis: noun, nominal, attested by Deming (4/1/76), Elders Group (6/11/75), Salish cognate: Squamish /šáʔyay/ *gills (of fish)* W73:116, K67:323, Lushootseed (LG) /s-x̣áy'ay'/ ~ (EK, LL) /s-x̣əyay'/ *gills* H76:586.

<**sxiyí:ws**>, ds //s=x^yεy=í·ws or s=x^yε[=Aə=]y=í·ws or s=x^yε[=Ai=]y=í·ws//, ABDF ['*smallpox*'], literally (probably) /'like fish scales on the skin/body'/, (<**s=**> *nominalizer*), lx <**=í:ws**> *on the skin, on the body*, possibly <**e-ablaut** or **i-ablaut**> *derivational,* (or perhaps) *like*, phonology: possibly ablaut, syntactic analysis: nominal, attested by BJ (12/5/64), contrast <**spél:exw**> *chickenpox* (CT 10/15/73).

<**xáye**>, possible bound root or stem //x^yέ(=i)yə//, meaning unknown

<**sxáye**>, df //s=x^yέ(=i)yə//, KIN /'*a husband's younger wives, co-wife*'/, (<**s=**> *nominalizer*), possibly root <**xá**> *genital*, possibly <**=iye**> *affectionate diminutive*, phonology: possible vowel merger, syntactic analysis: nominal, attested by AC (8/15/70), other sources: ES /sx^yá·yε/ *co-wife*, Salish cognate: Squamish /šáʔyu/ *co-wife; screech owl; corpse; lie dead* W73:289, K67:323, Samish dial. of NSt /sáyeʔ/ *two wives, co-wives, husband of ex-wife, wife of ex-husband* G86:79.

<**xá:ysem**>, df //xέ·ys=əm//, EZ ['*ant*'], ['order *Hymenoptera*, family *Formicidae*'], root meaning unknown, possibly <**=em**> *have/get or middle voice*, syntactic analysis: nominal, attested by AC (12/4/71), BJ (12/5/64), others, other sources: ES /x^yà·ysəm/ *ant*, JH /xéysəm/ *ant*, H-T <yha'isEm> (macron over a and i) *ant (Formica sp.)*.

<**xá'at**>, pcs //x^yέʔ=əT or x^yέʔ=ə[=Aε=]T//, ABFC ['*hold s-o in one's arms*'], (<**=et**> *purposeful control transitivizer*), phonology: possible a-ablaut phonological echo, syntactic analysis: transitive verb, attested by EB (5/21/76).

<**xe'át**>, cts //x^yέʔ=ə[-M2-]T//, ABFC /'*holding s-o in one's arms, (holding a baby in one's arms [Elder's Group])*'/, (<**metathesis type 2**> *continuative*), phonology: metathesis, syntactic analysis: transitive verb, attested by EB (5/21/76), also /'*holding a baby in one's arms*'/, attested by Elders Group (5/19/76), example: <**xe'át tel méle**>, //x^yέʔ=ə[-M2-]T t-əl mélə//, /'*holding my child in my arms*'/, attested by Elders Group (5/19/76).

<**xixe'át**>, dmv //C_1í=x^yέʔ=ə[-M2-]T//, ABFC ['*holding a wee baby in one's arms*'], (<**R4=**> *diminutive*), phonology: reduplication, metathesis, syntactic analysis: transitive verb, attested by EB (5/21/76); found in <**xixe'átes.**>, //C_1í=x^yέʔ=ə[-M2-]T-əs//, /'*He's holding a wee baby in his arms.*'/, attested by EB.

<**xchápth ~ schápth**>, us //x^ycέpθ ~ scέpθ//, KIN /'*uncle's wife, aunt's husband, parent's sibling's spouse, uncle by marriage, aunt by marriage*'/, syntactic analysis: noun, nominal, attested by AC (11/16/71), others, other sources: ES ChMs /x^ycέpθ/ and JH /xcépθ/ both *parent's sibling's spouse*, H-T <sQutca'pEts ~ cutca'pEtc> (macron over both u, umlaut over both a) *aunt's husband, uncle's wife,*

Salish cognate: Cowichan /cɛ́pθ/ *parent's sibling's spouse* (ES), Sechelt /čápc/ *parent's sibling, parent's sibling's spouse,* MCx /čɛ́pθ/ *uncle, aunt* (Davis 1970, 1981p.c.) ~ MCx /čiyɛ́pθ/ *parent's sibling, parent's sibling's spouse* (Suttles 1965), NSt /séčs/ *uncle, aunt* TTE74, Clallam /cáčc/ *parent's sibling, parent's sibling's spouse* TTE74, all in G82:40, cognate set #194, also Samish dial. of NSt /séčs/ *parent's sibling* as well as Samish /šx^{w}séčs/ *parent's sibling's spouse* G86:79, example: **<semíkw' tel schápth>**, //sə=mə[=Aí=]k'^{w} t-əl scɛ́pθ//, /'*all of my uncle's wives*'/, attested by AC (11/16/71).**<=xel>**, da //=x^{y}əl//, ANA /'*on the foot or leg, in the foot or leg, tail of fish, leg of other animate creatures*'/, WETH /'*precipitation, ray of light*'/, LT, syntactic analysis: lexical affix, derivational suffix; found in **<lhékw'xel>**, //ɬə́k'^{w}=x^{y}əl//, /'*to trip, stumble*'/, literally /'hook on foot'/, **<th'èx̲wxélém>**, //θ'ə̀x̣^{w}=x^{y}ə́l=əm//, /'*wash one's feet*'/, **<sléx̲xel>**, //s=lə́x̣=x^{y}əl//, /'*toe*'/, **<sxéts'xel>**, //s=x^{y}ə́c'=x^{y}əl//, /'*splinter or sliver in foot*'/, **<lhéts'xel>**, //ɬə́c'=x^{y}əl//, /'*cut on the foot*'/, **<qwémxwxel>**, //q^{w}ə́m=x^{w}=x^{y}əl//, /'*ankle*'/, literally /'lump of foot'/, **<sth'émxel>**, //sθ'ə́m=x^{y}əl//, /'*shin*'/, literally /'bone in leg'/, **<sq'epólqwtelxel>**, //sq'əp=áləq^{w}=təl=x^{y}əl//, /'*kneecap*'/, **<lekwxá:l>**, //lək^{w}=x^{y}ə[=Aɛ́·=]l//, /'*broke a leg*'/, **<qwlhí:yxel>**, //q^{w}ɬ=í·y=x^{y}əl//, /'*shoe(s)*'/, literally /'driftwood on foot'/, **<thelíwáxel ~ tselíwáxel>**, //θəl=íwɛ́=x^{y}əl ~ cəl=íwɛ́=x^{y}əl//, /'*snowshoe(s)*'/, **<láxel>**, //lɛ́=x^{y}əl//, /'*fishing platform (for still-dip-netting)*'/, **<xwó:mxelem>**, //x^{w}á·m=x^{y}əl=əm//, /'*run*'/, **<xwemxá:lem>**, //x^{w}əm=x^{y}ɛ́·l=əm orx̣^{w}əm=x^{y}ə[=Aɛ́·=]l=əm//, /'*running*'/, (semological comment: some speakers of Tait and Chehalis dialects say the glosses are reversed on the last two words), root **<x̲wém>** *hurry, be fast,* phonology: fronting, **<sqwelqwélxel>**, //s=C$_1$əC$_2$=q^{w}ə́l=x^{y}əl//, /'*tuft(s) of hair on a horse's legs*'/, **<sx̲épxel>**, //sx̣ə́p=x^{y}əl//, /'*fish tail*'/, **<tl'emtl'émxel>**, //C$_1$əC$_2$=ƛ'ə́m=x^{y}əl//, /'*grasshopper*'/, literally /'repeatedly jumping foot or leg'/, **<pítxel>**, //pít=x^{y}əl//, /'*salamander*'/, **<tl'élx̲xel>**, //ƛ'ə́l=x̣=x^{y}əl//, /'*spring salmon (generic)*'/, literally /'spotted foot'/, **<slhémxel>**, //s=ɬə́m=x^{y}əl//, /'*dew*'/, literally /'moisture precipitation/moisture on the foot'/, **<sq'óxel>**, //sq'á=x^{y}əl//, /'*partner*'/, literally /'together in foot'/, **<stheqelxélém>**, //sθəqəl=x^{y}ə́l=əm//, /'*rainbow*'/.

<xél>, bound root //x^{y}ə́l *roll, rotate*//.

<xélétst>, pcs //x^{y}ə́l=əc=T//, TVMO ['*roll s-th over*'], MC, possibly **<=ets>** *on the back,* (**<=t>** *purposeful control transitivizer*), phonology: updrifting, possible consonant merger, syntactic analysis: transitive verb, attested by Elders Group (5/26/76), Salish cognate: possibly Squamish /ší-šiʔč/ *round (around)* W73:219, K67:324, example: **<xélétst te syáyeq'>**, //x^{y}ə́l=əc=T tə s=yɛ́[=C$_1$ə=]q'//, /'*roll a log over*'/, attested by Elders Group.

<xéletsem>, mdls //x^{y}ə́l=əc=əm//, TVMO /'*rolling over; wheeled* '/, **<=em>** *middle voice,* attested by RG & EH (4/9/99 Ling332)

<xéletsem shxwqeyqex̲óthet>, cpds //x^{y}ə́l=əc=əm /s(=)x^{w}=qi[=C$_1$ə=]x̣=ɛ[=Aá=]T=ət//, GAM //'*roller skates, roller blade skates*'//, lit. "wheeled/rolling skate", attested by RG & EH (4/9/99 Ling332), *see* xél or qíx.

<xelókw' ~ xeló:kw'>, df //x^{y}əl=ák'^{w} ~ x^{y}əl=á·k'^{w}//, SH /'*round, full (of the moon)*'/, possibly **<=ókw'>** meaning uncertain, compare **<st'elákw'>** *circular, round and flat,* syntactic analysis: adjective/adjectival verb, attested by EB (2/6/76), AC (9/15/71, 10/1/71, 10/8/71), other sources: ES /x^{y}əlá·k'^{w}/ *round,* JH /xə́lək'^{w}/ *round,* Salish cognate: Squamish /šiʔúk'^{w}/ *round, compact* W73:219, K67:325, also **<xelákw'>**, //x^{y}əl=ɛ́k'^{w}//, attested by CT (6/8/76), example: **<lulh xeló:kw' te skw'exós.>**, //lə=uɬ x^{y}əl=á·k'^{w} tə s=k'^{w}əx^{y}=ás//, /'*The moon is full.*'/, attested by AC (10/1/71).

<xixwelókw'>, dmn //C$_1$í=x^{y}[=W=]əl=ák'^{w}//, SH /'*small bundle, small package*'/, MC, literally /'little round'/, (**<R4=>** *diminutive*), (**<=W= (labialization) of x> automatic with some roots beginning with <x>** (as in Musqueam (Suttles 7.2.1))), phonology: labialization, syntactic analysis: nominal, attested by AC (10/1/71).

<xelkw'ó:ls>, ds //x^{y}əl=á(·)k'^{w}=M1=á(·)ls//, SH /'*(spherical), round (of ball, apple, potato, rock, full* *moon, but not of a pear)'*/, possibly <**metathesis type 1**> *non-continuative*?, lx <**=ó:ls ~ =óls**> *spherical object (esp. ball, fruit, rock)*, phonology: vowel merger, syntactic analysis: adjective/adjectival verb, nominal?, attested by AC (10/1/71, 8/6/70), EB (2/9/76), CT (6/8/76).

<**xelókw'els**>, ds //x^{y}əl=ɛ[=Aá=]k'^{w}=á[=Aə=]ls//, SH /'*really round, (perfectly spherical?)*'/, possibly <**ó-ablaut**> *continuative*, possibly <**e-ablaut**> *durative*, phonology: ablaut, syntactic analysis: adjective/adjectival verb, attested by CT (6/8/76).

<**xíxelkwòls**>, dmn //C$_1$í=x^{y}əl=á(·)k'^{w}=M1=á(·)ls//, PE /'*cotton balls*'/, lit. "little rolled balls", <R4=> *diminutive*, attested by RG & EH (4/10/99 Ling332).

<**xíxelkwòls s'álqsel**>, cpds /C$_1$í=x^{y}əl=á(·)k'^{w}=M1=á(·)ls s=ʔɛ́l=qsəl//, PE /'*Q-tips*'/, lit. "little rolled balls - on a point", (<**s=**> *nominalizer*), probably root <**'ál**> *pole, shaft, length*?, lx <**=qsel**> *on the nose, on the point*, attested by RG & EH (4/10/99 Ling332).

<**xelékw't**>, pcs //x^{y}əl=a[=Aə́=]k'^{w}=T//, TVMO /'*roll s-th (like a log), (roll it up [AC])*'/, (<**é-ablaut**> *durative*), (<**=t**> *purposeful control transitivizer*), phonology: ablaut, syntactic analysis: transitive verb, attested by EB (2/9/76), also /'*roll it up*'/, attested by AC (9/15/71); found in <**xelékw'tlha.**>, //x^{y}əl=a[=Aə́=]k'^{w}=T-ɬɛ//, /'*Roll it up.*'/, attested by AC, compare <**xwélekw't**> *roll it up*.

<**xelkw'ámeth'**>, ds //x^{y}əl=(ɛ)k'^{w}=ɛ́məθ'//, SH ['*round (of a pole)*'], lx <**=ámeth'**> *long thin object (pole, rope, thread, etc.)*, phonology: vowel-loss before stressed suffix, syntactic analysis: adjective/adjectival verb, attested by CT (6/8/76).

<**sxéltsep**>, ds //s=x^{y}ə́l=(ə́l)cəp//, FIRE ['*firedrill*'], TOOL, ASM ['stick rotated on kindling to start sparks and fire, the stick was often long-leaf willow'], literally /'something to rotate (on) firewood'/, (<**s=**> *nominalizer*), lx <**=élchep ~ =éltsep** or **=tsep ~ =chep**> *firewood, wood*, phonology: possible syllable-loss, syntactic analysis: nominal, attested by Deming (4/6/78), Elders Group (3/15/72), other sources: ES /sx^{y}ə́lcəs/ (Ms /sx^{y}ə́lcəp/, Cw /šə́lcəp/) *firedrill*, Salish cognate: Squamish /ší-čəp/ [šə́yčəp] *firedrill* W73:101, K69:69.

<**xéltsepelhp**>, ds //x^{y}ə́l=cəp=əɬp//, EB /'*long-leaf willow, Sitka willow*'/, ['*Salix lasiandra*'], MED ['used for medicine of some kind'], literally /'firedrill tree'/, lx <**=elhp**> *tree, plant*, syntactic analysis: nominal, attested by EL (9/27/77), contrast <**ts'ats'í:ts'etl' sts'ó:lha x̲wá:lá:lhp**> *long-leaf willow, Sitka willow*, contrast <**x̲wá:lá:lhp**> *willow*, contrast <**tl'áqt sts'ó:lha x̲wá:lá:lhp**> *short-leaf willow, Pacific willow.*

<**sxélts' ~ sxél:ts'**>, ds //s=x^{y}ə́l=lc'//, ANAB /'*feather (any kind), (fine feathers [EB], small feathers [IHTTC], lots of feathers [EB])*'/, literally /'something to rotate around in circles'/, (semological comment: could be so named after the fact that such feathers rotate slowly as they fall to earth or after their use in the sx̲wóyx̲wey dance where they are fastened to spin around on the headdress, fine feathers were sometimes stuck to grease on spirit-dancers and were also thrown all over ceremonially from a bag when a new spirit-dancer dances in public for the first time (EB 1/8/76)), (<**s=**> *something to, nominalizer*), lx <**=elts'**> *around in circles*, phonology: consonant merger, syntactic analysis: nominal, attested by AC (8/13/70, 9/10/71), Elders Group (3/15/72), other sources: ES /sx^{y}ílc' ~ sƛ̓'p'ɛ́·lqəl/ feather, Salish cognate: possibly Samish dial. of NSt /šə́ləč'/ *go around in a circle, to circle* G86:82, also /'*fine feather(s)*'/, attested by EB (5/25/76), also /'*small feathers*'/, attested by IHTTC (9/19/77), also /'*lots of feathers*'/, attested by EB (1/8/76).

<**xélcha**>, bound root //x^{y}ə́lcɛ *catch fish*//.

<**chxélcha**>, izs //c=x^{y}ə́lcɛ//, FSH /'*to catch (fish, game, birds)*'/, HUNT, (<**ch= ~ ts=**> *intransitivizer*), syntactic analysis: intransitive verb, attested by Deming (5/26/76), EB (1/8/76), Salish cognate: Sechelt /šə́nču/ *to catch (animal in trap)* T77:26, example: <**chxélcha te sth'óqwí.**>, //c=x^{y}ə́lcɛ tə s=θ'áq^{w}i//, /'*He caught a fish.*'/, attested by EB (1/8/76), <**chxélche**>, [čx^{y}ílčʌ], '*catch a fish*',

attested by (EH,RG) 7/27/99 (SU transcription, tape 3).

<**chxólcho**>, ctvi [čxʸálča] (BG: final vowel prob. mistranscribed for <**a**> /ɛ/), FSH /'*always catching fish*'/ (BG: the *always* is probably not required, overemphasizing *continuative*), HUNT, attested by (EH,RG) 7/27/99 (SU transcription, tape 3), <*chexelcho>, [čɪxʸɪlča], *'catching fish' (EH,RG) 7/27/99 (SU transcription, tape 3)

<**sxélcha ~ sxélche**>, dnom //s=xʸə́lcɛ ~ s=xʸə́lcə//, FSH /'*one's catch (fish, game, etc.)*'/, HUNT, (<**s=**> *nominalizer*), syntactic analysis: nominal, attested by BHTTC (8/30/76), EB (1/8/76, 12/15/75, 6/23/78), example: <**qéx̱ te sxélchas.**>, //qə́x̣ tə s=xʸə́lcɛ-s//, /'*His catch is big.*'/, literally /'is many/much the his catch'/, attested by EB (1/8/76), <**stám kw' sth'óqwi a sxélcha?**>, //s=tɛ́m k'ʷə s=θ'áqʷi ʔɛ s=xʸə́lcɛ//, /'*What kind of fish did you catch?*'/, literally /'is what? the (remote) fish your catch'/, attested by EB (12/15/75), <**chelà:lqwlha te sxélchas.**>, //cəlɛ̀·l=qʷɬɛ tə s=xʸə́lcɛ-s//, /'*He sure caught a lot.*'/, literally /'is sure a lot the his catch'/, attested by EB (6/23/78).

<**xéle**>, possible root or stem //xʸə́l(=)ə or xʸ=ɛ[=Aə́=]=lə or or xʸə́l=ɛlə//, meaning uncertain

<**sxéle**>, df //s=xʸə́lə or s=xʸɛ[=Aə́=](=)lə//, ANA ['*penis*'], (<**s=**> *nominalizer, something to*), possibly root <**x ~ xá**> *genital*, possibly root <**xel**> *roll, rotate*?, possibly <**é-ablaut**> *derivational*, phonology: possible ablaut, syntactic analysis: nominal, attested by Elders Group (8/20/75), BJ (12/5/64), other sources: ES /xʸɛ́lə/ (Ms /xʸə́lə/, Cw /šə́lə/) *penis*, Salish cognate: Squamish /šə́lʔ/ *penis* W73:196, K69:69, Lushootseed /šəláʔ/ *penis* H76:458.

<**Sxéle**>, df //s=xʸə́lə//, PLN ['*Penis Rock near Cheam View*'], (semological comment: shaped like a penis, probably turned to stone by the Transformer in a story (see Boas 1895)), syntactic analysis: nominal.

<**xéle'ò:les**>, ds //xʸə́lə=ʔá·ləs//, ABDF ['*sty in the eye*'], literally perhaps /'penis on the eye'/, (semological comment: perhaps so named for the physical resemblance), possibly root <**xéle**> *penis*, or perhaps literally /'roll/rotate on the eye'/, with root <**xél**> *roll, rotate*, lx <**=ó:les ~ ='ó:les**> *on the eye*, phonology: downstepping, syntactic analysis: nominal, attested by HP (Elders Group 9/22/76).

<**xelékw't**>, TVMO /'*roll s-th (like a log), (roll it up [AC])*'/, *see* xél.

<**xéletsem**>, mdls //xʸə́l=əc=əm//, TVMO /'*rolling over; wheeled*'/, *see* xél.

<**xéletsem shxwqeyqex̱óthet**>, cpds //xʸə́l=əc=əm /s(=)xʷ=qi[=C$_1$ə=]x̣=ɛ[=Aá=]T=ət//, GAM //'*roller skates, roller blade skates*'//, lit. "wheeled/rolling skate", *see* xél or qíx.

<**xélétst**>, TVMO ['*roll s-th over*'], *see* xél.

<**xéle'ò:les**>, ABDF ['*sty in the eye*'], *see* sxéle.

<**xelkw'ámeth'**>, SH ['*round (of a pole)*'], *see* xél.

<**xelkw'ó:ls**>, SH /'*(spherical), round (of ball, apple, potato, rock, full moon, but not of a pear)*'/, *see* xél.

<**xelókw' ~ xeló:kw'**>, SH /'*round, full (of the moon)*'/, *see* xél.

<**xelókw'els**>, SH /'*really round, (perfectly spherical?)*'/, *see* xél.

<**xéltsepelhp**>, EB /'*long-leaf willow, Sitka willow*'/, *see* xél.

<**xemá:l**>, bound root or stem //xʸəmɛ́·l// *have an enemy, hold a grudge*

<**sxemá:l**>, df //s=xʸəmɛ́·l//, SOC ['*enemy*'], (<**s=**> *nominalizer*), syntactic analysis: nominal, attested by AC (8/15/70), BJ (12/5/64), Elders Group (3/72, 3/23/77), other sources: ES /sʸəmɛ́l/ *enemy*, Salish cognate: Squamish /šmán/ *enemy* W73:90, K67:323, Lushootseed /šəbád/ *enemy* H76:457, example: <**híkw l sxemà:l.**>, //híkʷ l s=xʸəmɛ́·l//, /'*He's my big enemy., I hate that person.*'/,

phonology: sentence-stress, attested by JL (5/5/75).

<**sxelmá:l**>, pln //s=x^{y}ə[=lə=]mɛ́·l//, SOC ['*enemies*'], (<**=le=**> *plural*), phonology: infixed plural, vowel-loss in infix before stressed syllable, syntactic analysis: nominal, attested by JL (5/5/75), example: <**híkw l sxelmá:l yithá.**>, //hík^w l s=x^{y}ə[=lə=]mɛ́·l yə=θɛ́//, /'*My enemies there are big., I hate more than one person there.*'/, attested by JL.

<**xixemó:ltel**>, pcs //x^{y}ə[-C_1ə-]mɛ[=Aá=]·l=t-əl//, rcps, cts, SOC ['*holding a grudge against each other*'], (<**-R1-**> *continuative*), (<**ó-ablaut automatic on á before =tel**>), (<**=t**> *purposeful control transitivizer*), (<**-el**> *reciprocal*), phonology: vowel raising of e →i between x and x, a →o before =tel automatic,reduplication, syntactic analysis: intransitive verb, attested by Elders Group (3/23/77).

<**Xemó:leqw**>, PLN ['*Leon's Slough on Harrison River*'], *see* xá:m.

<**xepá:ltel**>, CARV ['*wood-carving knife*'], *see* xíp.

<**xepólst**>, HARV ['*peel s-th (esp. fruit or vegetable root or a vegetable like squash or a round object)*'], *see* xíp.

<**xépqst**>, TOOL ['*sharpen it (of a point)*'], *see* xíp.

<**xéq**>, free root //x^{y}ə́q//, TIB ['*be complete*'], syntactic analysis: adjective/adjectival verb, attested by Elders Group, Salish cognate: Squamish /šə́q/ *be finished, be completed, over* W73:100, K67:323, example: <**le xéq.**>, //lə x^{y}ə́q//, /'*It's complete.*'/, attested by Elders Group (3/15/72).

<**xeqláxw**>, ncs //x^{y}əq=l-ə[=Aɛ́=]x^w//, durs, TIB ['*complete s-th*'], (<**=l**> *non-control transitivizer*), (<**á-ablaut on inflectional suffix**> *durative*), phonology: ablaut, syntactic analysis: transitive verb, attested by Elders Group (3/15/72), example: <**tsel xeqláxw.**>, //c-əl xəq=l-ə[=Aɛ́=]x^w//, /'*I completed it.*'/, attested by Elders Group, <**lichxw xeqláxw?**>, //li-c-x^w x^{y}əq=l-ə[=Aɛ́=]x^w//, /'*Did you complete it?*'/, attested by Elders Group.

<**xeqláxw**>, TIB ['*complete s-th*'], *see* xéq.

<**xeqlhálém**>, mdls //x^{y}əq=ɬɛ́l=əm//, SPRD /'*to sigh (of a spirit-dancer), make a loud (breathy) noise*'/, ABFC, literally perhaps /'complete/finish in one's windpipe (or) high in one's windpipe'/, possibly root <**xeq**> /x^{y}əq/ *complete*, lx <**=lhál**> *in the windpipe, throat (air-passage)*, (<**=em**> *middle voice*), phonology: updrifting, syntactic analysis: intransitive verb, attested by Deming (3/30/78), Salish cognate: Squamish /šəq-ɬál-m/ *be out of breath* K67:323, possibly Lushootseed root /šə́q/ *up, high* H76:459.

<**xáqlhelem**>, cts //x^{y}əq=ɬɛ[-M2-]l=əm//, SPRD ['*(be) sighing (of a spirit-dancer)*'], ABFC, (<**metathesis type 2**> *continuative*), phonology: metathesis type 2, syntactic analysis: intransitive verb, attested by Deming (3/30/78).

<**xaqxeqlhálem**>, df //C_1əC_2=x^{y}əq=ɬɛ́l=əm or x^{y}əq=C_1əC_2=ɬɛ́l=əm//, SPRD ['*sighing over and over (of a spirit-dancer before or after dancing)*'], ABFC, possibly <**R3=**> *plural action*, possibly <**=R2**> *characteristic*, phonology: xaq... probably mistranscribed for xeq..., syntactic analysis: intransitive verb, attested by Deming (3/30/78), EB (8/4/78).

<**xeq'ó:thet**>, MC ['*hang something up*'], *see* xáq'.

<**xetáléqetel**>, FSH ['*sinker line*'], *see* xá:t.

<**xetàm ~ xtàm**>, mdls //x^{y}ət=ə[=Aɛ́=]m or x^{y}ɛ́t=M1=əm//, ABFC ['*swim (of fish)*'], possibly <**á-ablaut on suffix**> *durative*, possibly <**metathesis type 1**> *non-continuative*, (<**=em**> *middle voice*), phonology: metathesis or ablaut, syntactic analysis: intransitive verb, attested by AD and NP (1/21/80), Salish cognate: Squamish /štám/ *dive* and root /šat ~ šət/ *dive* as also in /šə-št-ámʔ/ *dive*

head down, /nəxʷ-šə́t-št-am/ *a diver*, and /šát-št-am/ *golden-eye duck* (the Upriver Halkomelem form for this duck /lɛ́qləqəm/ also means *diving characteristically*) W73:81, K67:323, K69:69.

<**xétem**>, cts //xʸə́t=əm or xʸɛ[-Aə́-]t=əm//, ABFC /'*swimming (of fish), (swim (of a fish) [EB])*'/, possibly <**é-ablaut**> *continuative*, phonology: possible ablaut, syntactic analysis: intransitive verb, attested by AD and NP (1/23/80), BJ (12/5/64, new transcript, old p.306) NP (12/6/73), Elders Group (4/26/78), also /'*swim (of a fish)*'/, attested by BHTTC (8/31/76), also <**xét'em**>, //xʸə́t'=əm or xʸɛ[-Aə́-]t'=əm//, also /'*swim (of a fish)*'/, attested by EB (3/2/76), example: <**le xétem te sthóqwi.**>, //lə xʸə́t=əm tə s=θáqʷi//, /'*The salmon is travelling.*'/, attested by BJ, <**xétem te sth'ó:qwi.**>, //xə́t=əm tə s=θ'á·qʷi//, /'*The fish are swimming.*'/, attested by NP (12/6/73).

<**xétem**>, ABFC /'*swimming (of fish), (swim (of a fish) [EB])*'/, *see* xetàm ~ xtàm.

<**xetqwewí:lt**>, pcs //xʸət(=)qʷ=iwəl=í·l=T or xʷ[=F=]at(=)qʷ=iwəl=í·l=T//, incs, SH ['*hollow it out*'], root meaning unknown unless xwót(=)qw=iwel *hollow*, possibly <**=F= (fronting)**> *diminutive*, lx <**=í:l**> *go, come, get, become*, (<**=t**> *purposeful control transitivizer*), phonology: possible fronting, vowel-reduction or allomorph, syllable-loss, syntactic analysis: transitive verb, attested by AD (3/6/79), Salish cognate: Saanich dial. of NSt /šətqʷ-kʷíl-ət/ *to hollow s-th out* B74a:65.

<**xét'**>, free root //xʸə́t'//, DESC /'*slack, loose (of a pack)*'/, syntactic analysis: adjective/adjectival verb, attested by IHTTC (7/19/77).

<**xet'éla**>, df //xʸət'=ə́lɛ//, DESC /'*loose (of a pack), slack (of a pack), too low (of a pack)*'/, literally /'slack by the side of the head'/, (semological comment: so named because packs were usually carried by tumpline around the head, now extended to back-packs too), lx <**=éla**> *on the side of the head, by the ear, on the temples, by the cheek*, syntactic analysis: adjective/adjectival verb, attested by IHTTC (7/19/77), example: <**xet'éla tel schí:m.**>, //xʸət'=ə́lɛ t-əl s=cə[=Aí·=]m//, /'*My pack is slack., My pack is loose (the straps are loose).*'/, attested by IHTTC.

<**xet'éla**>, DESC /'*loose (of a pack), slack (of a pack), too low (of a pack)*'/, *see* xét'.

<**xéth' ~ xéts'**>, bound? root, doublet //xʸə́θ' ~ xʸə́c'// *get a sliver*

<**xéth'ches**>, ds //xʸə́θ'=cəs//, ABDF ['*get a sliver in one's hand*'], lx <**=ches ~ =tses**> *on the hand*, syntactic analysis: intransitive verb, compare <**xéts'ches**> *get a splinter/sliver in the hand*, attested by Elders Group (4/16/75), Salish cognate: Lushootseed root /š(i)c'(i)/ *stick into, stick through, sheathe, insert* as in /šíc'-id/ *stick it into* H76:463, historical/comparative detail: doublet with xéts'ches which is cognate with a Squamish root.

<**xéts'ches**>, ds //xʸə́c'=cəs//, ABDF ['*get a sliver or splinter in the hand*'], lx <**=ches ~ =tses**> *on the hand*, syntactic analysis: intransitive verb, compare <**xéth'ches**> *get a sliver in one's hand*, attested by BJ (12/5/64 new transcript, old p.333), Salish cognate: Squamish /sč'-ač/ *splinter, slivver (in finger)* W73:246, K67:288 (prob. error for /šč'-ač/) prob. from Squamish root /šíč'/ *be all around, amidst, surrounded by* K67:324, K69:69-70.

<**xéts'xel**>, ds //xʸə́c'=xʸəl//, ABDF ['*get a sliver or splinter in the foot*'], lx <**=xel**> *on the foot*, syntactic analysis: intransitive verb, attested by BJ (12/5/64 new transcript, old p.333).

<**xets'í:lem**>, EB ['*go through the woods*'], *see* xí:ts' ~ xíts' ~ xets'.

<**xets'ő:wes**>, CAN ['*(one person) puts away his paddles (and canoe and gear for winter)*'], *see* xits' ~ xets'.

<**xets'ő wesem**>, CAN ['*store away one's paddles*'], *see* xits' ~ xets'.

<**xets'ő:westel**>, CAN /'*everybody put away (fishing gear, canoe and) paddles (for winter), put away each other's paddles [and canoes and gear] for winter*'/, *see* xits' ~ xets'.

<**xets'ő:westel ~ xets'őwestel**>, TIME /'*moon or month beginning in November, (put away each other's paddles), (sometimes the moon beginning in October, depending on the weather [Elders Group 3/12/75], (moon or month beginning in January [Elders Group 2/5/75])*'/, *see* xits' ~ xets'.

<**xe'át**>, ABFC /'*holding s-o in one's arms, (holding a baby in one's arms [Elder's Group])*'/, *see* xá'at.

<**xíleqw**>, possibly root //xʸíl(=)əqʷ//, MC /'*to search through, to rummage*'/, ABFC, possibly root <**xél**> *roll, rotate*, possibly <**=eqw**> *on top (of the head)*, syntactic analysis: intransitive verb, attested by IHTTC (7/5/77), Salish cognate: Lushootseed root /šil(i)/ 'come out from under, emerge; dig around to uncover s-th' as in /ʔu-šíl-id/ 'dig around to find [uncover] it' H76:465-466.

<**xíleqwt**>, pcs //xʸíl(=)əqʷ=T//, MC /'*search through it, rummage through it, search s-o (like Customs officials)*'/, ABFC, (<**=t**> *purposeful control transitivizer*), syntactic analysis: transitive verb, attested by IHTTC (7/5/77); found in <**xíleqwthòmè**>, //xʸíləqʷ=T-ámə//, /'*search you*'/, attested by IHTTC.

<**xíxeleqwt**>, cts //xʸí[-C$_1$ə-]l(=)əqʷ=T//, MC /'*searching it, digging through it*'/, ABDF, (<**-R1-**> *continuative*), phonology: reduplication, syntactic analysis: transitive verb, attested by IHTTC (7/5/77).

<**xíleqwt**>, MC /'*search through it, rummage through it, search s-o (like Customs officials)*'/, *see* xíleqw.

<**xíp**>, bound root //xʸíp *plane (with a plane), trim, taper, peel outer layer with knife or plane*//.

<**xípet**>, pcs //xʸíp=əT//, CARV /'*plane it (with a plane), trim it, taper it (about wood, like slats or roots for baskets, poles for houseposts/totem poles, paddles), taper it (with knife or plane), peel it (a fruit, etc.), whittle it, strip or peel bark off of it, scrape it (of carrots), (carve it, peel it [AC])*'/, HARV, FOOD, BSK, CAN, MC, (<**=et**> *purposeful control transitivizer*), syntactic analysis: transitive verb, attested by EB (4/27/76, 1/8/76), Deming (4/30/80), CT and HT (6/21/76), MH (Deming 1/4/79), other sources: H-T <Hi'pit> (macron over i) 'to peel bark, etc.', contrast JH /θà·lá·st/ *to bark, peel* and /ɬə́q'ʷ/ 'to be peeled', also <**xí:pet**>, //xʸí·p=əT//, also /'*carve it, peel it*'/, attested by AC (9/1/71, 11/24/71), example: <**xí:pet te (p'elyí:ws, slá:y, kwémlexw)**>, //xʸí·p=əT tə (p'əl=y=í·ws, s=lɛ́·y, kʷə́mləxʷ)//, /'*peel the (bark of a tree, bark of a fir tree, root of a tree)*'/, attested by AC (11/24/71), <**le xi:petes.**>, //lə xʸi·p=əT-əs//, /'*He carved it.*'/, attested by AC (9/1/71), <**te sqewá:meth's te thqát, tl'ó tl'émexw xípet.**>, //tə s=qɛ́·w=ə[=M2=]məθ'-s tə θqɛ́t, ƛ'á ƛ'ə́m-əxʷ xʸíp=əT//, /'*The sunny side of a tree, that's the part you strip off*'/, attested by CT and HT, <**xípet te xáwéq**>, //xʸíp=əT tə xʸɛ́w=əq//, /'*scrape the carrots*'/, attested by MH (Deming 1/4/79).

<**xepólst**>, pcs //xʸip=áls=T//, HARV ['*peel s-th (esp. fruit or vegetable root or a vegetable like squash or a round object)*'], lx <**=óls ~ =ó:ls**> *fruit, ball, rock, round object*, (<**=t**> *purposeful control transitivizer*), phonology: vowel-reduction in root, syntactic analysis: transitive verb, attested by AC (11/24/71), other sources: H-T <Hipa'lst> (macron over a) *to peel roots, etc.*, also <**xepó:lst**>, //xʸip=á·ls=T//, also /'*peel it (like potatoes, etc.)*'/, attested by Deming (4/10/80), example: <**xepólst te (qwe'óp, sqá:wth)**>, //xʸip=áls=T tə (qʷəʔáp, s=qɛ́·w(=)θ)//, /'*peel (apples, potatoes)*'/, attested by AC.

<**sxíxep**>, dnom //s=xʸí[=C$_1$ə=]p//, TOOL ['*a planer*'], (<**s=**> *nominalizer*), (<**=R1=**> *continuative*), phonology: reduplication, syntactic analysis: nominal, attested by Elders Group (3/26/75, early fall 1976).

<**sqw'emóx̱w sxíxep**>, cpds //s=q'ʷəm=ə[=Aá=]x̣ʷ s=xʸí[=C$_1$ə=]p//, CAN ['*bent U-shaped plane with handle on each end for canoe-making*'], TOOL, <**sqw'emóx̱w**>, ABFC ['*(be) doubled up in bed on one's side with knees drawn up*'], CAN ['*bent U-shaped plane with handle on each end for*

canoe-making'], *see* qw'ómx̲w. (<**s=**> *stative*), (<**ó-ablaut**> *resultative*), (<**s=**> *nominalizer*), (<**=R1=**> *continuative*), phonology: ablaut, reduplication, syntactic analysis: nominal phrase with modifier(s), attested by Elders Group (early fall 1976).

<**sqw'emóx̲w xíxepels**>, cpds //s=q'^{w}əm=ə[=Aá=]x̣^{w} x^{y}í[=C$_1$ə=]p=əls//, sas, CAN ['*bent U-shaped plane with handle on each end for canoe-making*'], TOOL, <**sqw'emóx̲w**>, ABFC ['*(be) doubled up in bed on one's side with knees drawn up*'], CAN ['*bent U-shaped plane with handle on each end for canoe-making*'], *see* qw'ómx̲w. (<**s=**> *stative*), (<**ó-ablaut**> *resultative*),(<**=R1=**> *continuative*), (<**=els**> *structured activity continuative device for*), phonology: ablaut, reduplication, syntactic analysis: nominal phrase with modifier(s), attested by Elders Group (early fall 1976).

<**xepá:ltel**>, df //x^{y}ip=ɛ́·l(=)təl//, CARV ['*wood-carving knife*'], TOOL, root <**xip**> *plane, trim, peel outer layer with knife/plane*, possibly <**=á:l** or **=á:ltel**> meaning uncertain, probably <**=tel**> *device to*, syntactic analysis: nominal, attested by EB (5/25/76), CAN ['*U-shaped or horseshoe-shaped knife (or plane) for scraping out canoe*'], TOOL, attested by Elders Group (2/27/80).

<**xépqst**>, rsls //x^{y}i[=Aə́=]p=qs=T//, pcs, TOOL ['*sharpen it (of a point)*'], (<**é-ablaut on root i**> *resultative*), lx <**=qs**> *on the nose, point*, (<**=t**> *purposeful control transitivizer*), phonology: ablaut, syntactic analysis: transitive verb, attested by Elders Group (5/26/76).

<**xípet**>, CARV /'*plane it (with a plane), trim it, taper it (about wood, like slats or roots for baskets, poles for houseposts/totem poles, paddles), taper it (with knife or plane), peel it (a fruit, etc.), whittle it, strip or peel bark off of it, scrape it (of carrots), (carve it, peel it [AC])*'/, *see* xíp.

<**xíq**>, bound root //x^{y}íq//, *lift up and out, squeeze up and out*

<**xíqt**>, pcs //x^{y}íq=T//, ABFC /'*take it out of a box, pull it out of a box*'/, MC, probably root <**xíq**> *lift up and out, squeeze up and out*, (<**=t**> *purposeful control transitivizer*), syntactic analysis: transitive verb, attested by Elders Group (5/26/76), Salish cognate: Lushootseed root /šəq/ 'high, up' as in /šə́q-əd/ //šə́q=t// 'lift it up' H76:459.

<**sxíxeq?** or **sxíxeq'?**>, df //s=x^{y}í[=C$_1$ə=]q or s=C$_1$í=x^{y}ɛq'//, EB ['*a kind of blueberry*'], (<**s=**> *nominalizer, something to/that*), possibly root <**xiq**> *lift up and out, squeeze up and out, high, up*, (semological comment: possibly so named if this is the same blueberry as <**sx̲wéxixeq ~ sx̲w'éxixeq**> because the latter grows on a small bush on summits high up in the mountains), possibly <**R4=**> *diminutive*, possibly root <**xaq'**> *hang open* possibly root as in <**xeq'ó:thet**> *hang up*, phonology: reduplication, syntactic analysis: nominal, compare <**sx̲wéxixeq ~ sx̲w'éxixeq**> *small sweet high mountain*

<**sx̲wéxixeq ~ sx̲w'éxixeq**>, df //s=x̣^{w}ə́x^{y}ix^{y}əq ~ s=x̣^{w}ʔə́x^{y}ix^{y}əq or s=x̣^{w}(ʔ)ə́=C$_1$í=x^{y}əq or s=x̣^{w}(ʔ)ə́=x^{y}i[=C$_1$ə=]q or s=x̣^{w}(ʔ)ə́x^y=əC$_2$=əq//, EB /'*small gray mountain blueberry on a low plant, dwarf blueberry*'/, ['*Vaccinium caespitosum*'], ASM ['the sweetest kind, grows at summit, often very short'], (<**s=**> *nominalizer, something to/that*), possibly root <**xiq**> *lift up and out, squeeze up and out*, compare <**xixqelísem**> *toothpaste*, compare <**xíq=t**> *take/pull s-th out of a box*, comment: possibly compound, possibly <**R4=**> *diminutive*, possibly <**=R1=**> *diminutive or derivational*, possibly <**=R6=**> *derivational*, phonology: reduplication, syntactic analysis: nominal, attested by CT, Elders Group and Deming (Mt. Baker trip 9/3/75), other sources: Duff 1952: /swɪxɪx^{y}uk/ *gray (huckle)berries*, also <**sxíxeq** or **sxíxeq'**>, //s=x^{y}í[=C$_1$ə=]q or s=x^{y}í[=C$_1$ə=]q'//, also /'*a kind of blueberry*'/, attested by Elders Group (7/10/75), also <**xwe'éxixeq**>, //x^{w}ə=ʔə́=x^{y}i[=C$_1$ə=]q or x^{w}əʔə́=C$_1$í=x^{y}əq//, EB ['*blueberry*'], also /'*dwarf blueberry or Cascade blueberry*'/, also /'*(Vaccinium caespitosum* or *Vaccinium deliciosum)*'/, attested by Elders Group (3/1/72), also <**swéxixeq**>, //s=wə́=x^{y}i[=C$_1$ə=]q//, also /'*mountain or swamp blueberry (unsure)*'/, attested by AC (11/19/71, 11/22/71), also <**swéxixeq'**>, //s=wə́=x^{y}i[=C$_1$ə=]q'//, also /'*blueberry*'/, attested by AC (11/24/71).

<**xixqelísem?**>, mdls //xí[=C_1ə=]q=əlís=əm//, PE ['*toothpaste*(?)'], literally perhaps /'squeezing up and out on one's teeth/tooth'/, <**xíq**> *squeeze up and out, lift up and out,* lx <**=elís**> *on the tooth,* (<**=em**> *middle voice*), possibly <**zero**> *nominalization,* phonology: reduplication, syntactic analysis: nominal, Elder's comment: "unsure of form and meaning", attested by Elders Group (6/1/77).

<**xítem**>, df //x^{y}ít=əm//, EFAM ['*wish for someone's food*'], FOOD, possibly <**=em**> *middle voice,* possibly <**=em**> *intransitivizer/have/get,* syntactic analysis: intransitive verb, attested by IHTTC (7/5/77), Salish cognate: Squamish /šítim-minʔ/ 'covet (tr.)' as in /na wa šítim-minʔ-tas ta na wa húyʔstax^w/ *He was wishing he could have some of what you are eating.* K69:69.

<**xíxetem**>, cts //x^{y}í[-C_1ə-]t=əm//, EFAM ['*wishing for someone's food (esp. when in sight)*'], FOOD, (<**-R1-**> *continuative*), phonology: reduplication, syntactic analysis: intransitive verb, attested by BHTTC (8/31/76), Elders Group (3/23/77).

<**xixtímestexw** or **xixtímstexw**>, caus //x^{y}i[=C_1ə=]t=(əm)=ím=sT-əx^w or x^{y}i[-C_1ə-]t=ə[=Aí=]m=sT-əx^w//, EFAM ['*tempt s-o (with sex or lust)*'], ABFC, literally perhaps /'purposely causing s-o repeatedly to wish for someone's food/spouse (or perhaps) purposely causing s-o for a long time to wish for someone's food/spouse'/, (<**=R1=**> *continuative*), possibly <**=ím**> *repeatedly,* possibly <**í-ablaut on suffix e**> *durative,* (<**=st**> *causative control transitivizer*), (<**-exw**> *third person object*), phonology: reduplication, ablaut or syllable-loss, syntactic analysis: transitive verb, attested by Elders Group (3/23/77).

<**xits' ~ xets'**>, bound root //x^{y}ic' ~ x^{y}əc' *tuck, put away, store away*//.

<**xíts'et**>, pcs //x^{y}íc'=əT//, MC /'*store it away (wedged-in up off ground), put s-th away for winter, stow s-th away*'/, ASM ['of pencil in ear, of paddles in the woods or in a split pole or in a crack in a plank house'], (<**=t**> *purposeful control transitivizer*), syntactic analysis: transitive verb, attested by IHTTC (7/19/77), also <**xets'ét**>, //x^{y}ə́c'=M1=T//, possibly <**metathesis type 2**> *non-continuative,* phonology: possible metathesis, attested by Elders Group (1/22/75).

<**xixets'eláx̱el**>, rsls //x^{y}i[=C_1ə=]c'=əlɛx̣əl//, ABFC ['*have something under one arm*'], literally /'tucked/stored on the arm'/, (<**=R1=**> *resultative*), lx <**=eláx̱el**> *on the arm,* phonology: reduplication, syntactic analysis: adjective/adjectival verb, attested by IHTTC (7/19/77).

<**xixets'eláx̱em**>, mdls //x^{y}i[=C_1ə=]c'=əlɛ́x̣(əl)=əm//, rsls, ABFC ['*put one's hands under one's arms*'], literally /'tuck oneself in one's arm'/, (<**=em**> *middle voice*), phonology: reduplication, syllable-loss of el before =em, syntactic analysis: intransitive verb, attested by IHTTC (7/19/77).

<**xets'ő:wes**>, ds //x^{y}ic'=ó·wəs or x^{y}i[=Aə=]c'=ó·wəs//, CAN ['*(one person) puts away his paddles (and canoe and gear for winter)*'], literally /'tuck/stow/store away canoe paddle'/, possibly <**e-ablaut**> *derivational,* lx <**=ő:wes**> *canoe paddle,* phonology: probable vowel-reduction, syntactic analysis: intransitive verb, attested by Elders Group (3/12/75), example: <**xets'ő:wes te Rudy.**>, //x^{y}ic'=ó·wəs tə Rudy//, /'*Rudy put away his (gear, canoe, and) paddles.*'/, attested by Elders Group.

<**xets'őwesem**>, mdls //x^{y}ic'=ó·wəs=əm//, CAN ['*store away one's paddles*'], (<**=em**> *middle voice*), syntactic analysis: intransitive verb, attested by IHTTC (7/19/77), example: <**latsel xets'őwesem.**>, //lɛ-c-əl x^{y}ic'=ówəs=əm//, /'*I'm going to store away my paddle.*'/, attested by IHTTC.

<**xets'ő:westel**>, rcps //x^{y}ic'=ó·wəs=T-əl//, pcs, CAN /'*everybody put away (fishing gear, canoe and) paddles (for winter), put away each other's paddles [and canoes and gear] for winter*'/, (<**=t**> *purposeful control transitivizer*), (<**-et**> *reciprocal*), phonology: vowel-reduction, syntactic analysis: intransitive verb, attested by Elders Group (3/12/75).

<**xets'ő:westel ~ xets'őwestel**>, ds //x^{y}ic'=ó(·)wəs=təl//, TIME /'*moon or month beginning in*

November, (put away each other's paddles), (sometimes the moon beginning in October, depending on the weather [Elders Group [3/12/75], (moon or month beginning in January [Elders Group 2/5/75])'/, literally /'put away each other's paddles'/, Elder's comment: "the word for November means *store everything away, get everything ready for winter* (AC though she did not remember the word)", probably <**zero**> *nominalizer*, syntactic analysis: nominal, attested by Elders Group (1/22/75, 3/12/75, 3/28/79), AC (8/14/70, 10/8/71), other sources: Jenness's field notes of interviews and calendar of Wm. Sepass of Sardis can be transliterated as /xʸəc'=ówəs=təl/ *November-December, time to put paddles away*, also /'*moon beginning in January*'/, attested by Elders Group (2/5/75).

<**xí:ts' ~ xíts' ~ xets'**>, bound root //xʸí(·)c' ~ xʸəc' *amidst the woods/bush/vegetation*//, Salish cognate: probably Squamish root /šič'/ *be all around* as in /šič'-án/ *circle around (tr.)* K67:324 and /ʔə(s)-ší-šč'/ *surrounded by, esp. amidst vegetation, in the bush* K69:69-70, perhaps also?? Lushootseed root /šic'(i)/ *stick through, stick in, sheathe, insert* H76:463-463, comment: a connection with root xíts' *tuck away, ...* seems possible.

<**sxí:xets' ~ sxíxets'**>, df //s=xí·[=C_1ə=]c'//, EB /'*(be in the) woods, (amidst bush or vegetation, be tucked away?)*'/, possibly <**s=**> *stative or nominalizer*, possibly <**=R1=**> *resultative or continuative*, phonology: reduplication, syntactic analysis: nominal, attested by AC (8/11/70, 9/10/71), EB (3/9/76), ME (tape 11/21/72), other sources: ES /sxʸí·xʸəc'/ *woods*, Salish cognate: Squamish /ʔə(s)-ší-šč'/ 'surrounded by, esp. 'amidst vegetation, in the bush' K69:69-70, example: <**qwóqwel li te sxíxets'**>, //qʷɛ[-AáC_1ə]l li tə s=xʸí[=C_1ə=]c'//, /'*(used to) always talk in the bush*'/, literally /'be talking in the woods/bush/vegetation'/, attested by ME.

<**xets'í:lem**>, mdls //xʸic'=í·l=əm or xʸí·c'=ə[=M2=]l=əm or xʸəc'=í·l=əm//, incs, EB ['*go through the woods*'], TVMO, literally /'go/come/get oneself amidst the woods/bush/vegetation'/, (<**=í:l ~ =íl ~ =el**> *go, come, get, become*), (<**=em**> *middle voice*), phonology: vowel-reduction or possible metathesis, syntactic analysis: intransitive verb, attested by AC (9/10/71), example: <**tsel la xets'í:lem tl'olsuw kw'étslexw te spáth.**>, //c-əl lɛ (or lə) xʸic'=í·l=əm ƛ'a-l-s=əw k'ʷéc=l-əxʷ tə s=pɛ́θ//, /'*I went through the woods and I saw the bear.*'/, attested by AC.

<**xets'á:ls**>, sas //xʸic'=ɛ́·ls//, HARV /'*cut wood (with a saw), saw wood, (cut wood to store away)*'/, possibly root <**xits' ~ xets'**> *tuck, put away, store away* or <**xí:ts' ~ xíts' ~ xets'**> *amidst the woods/brush/vegetation*, (<**=á:ls**> *structured activity non-continuative*), phonology: vowel-reduction before stressed suffix and in non-continuative, syntactic analysis: intransitive verb, compare root perhaps <**xits' ~ xets'**> *store away* or perhaps <**sxí:xets'**> *the woods, (thick vegetation)*, attested by EB (3/9/76).

<**xíxets'els**>, cts //xʸí[-C_1ə-]c'=əls//, sas, HARV /'*cutting wood (with a saw), sawing wood*'/, (<**-R1-**> *continuative*), phonology: reduplication, syntactic analysis: intransitive verb, attested by EB (3/9/76).

<**xíts'**> or <**xets'**>, probable bound root //xʸíc'// or //xʸəc'//

<**xíxets'em**>, df //xʸí[-C_1ə-]c'=əm or [C_1í=xʸəc'=əm//, SM /'*stinking (smell of outhouse or pig farm), (to stink [Elders Group 11/10/76, AC 9/1/71])*'/, root meaning unknown, possibly <**-R1-**> *continuative*, possibly <**=R1=**> *resultative or derivational*, possibly <**=em**> *have, get, intransitivizer*, phonology: reduplication, syntactic analysis: adjective/adjectival verb, attested by Elders Group (12/10/75), EB (8/14/78), also /'*to stink*'/, attested by Elders Group (11/10/76), AC (9/1/71).

<**xts'ímthet**>, df //xʸic'=ím=θət or xʸic'=ə[=Aí=]m=θət or xʸic'=ím=T-ət//, SM ['*(have/get a) strong stink*'], possibly <**=ím**> *repeatedly*, possibly <**=em**> *have/get/intransitivizer*, possibly <**í-ablaut on e in suffix**> *durative*, probably <**=thet**> *get, become*, possibly <**=t**> *purposeful control*

transitivizer, possibly <**-et**> *reflexive*, phonology: possible ablaut, syntactic analysis: intransitive verb, attested by Elders Group (6/16/76).

<**xíts'et**>, MC /'*store it away (wedged-in up off ground), put s-th away for winter, stow s-th away*'/, *see* xits' ~ xets'.

<**xíwe**>, possibly root or stem //x^{y}íwə or x^{y}=íwə//, ABFC ['*urinate*'], possibly root <**x**> *genital*, possibly <**=íwe**> meaning uncertain unless *cord*??, syntactic analysis: intransitive verb, attested by BHTTC (8/25/76), AD (1/15/79), Salish cognate: in part Lushootseed /tiwáʔ/ *urinate (female)* in contrast to Lushootseed /sʔəx̣^{w}áʔ ~ sx̣^{w}áʔ/ *urinate (male)* H76:504, 452, Samish dial. of NSt /šəšíwaʔ/ *urinate; penis[?]* G86:75, also /'*urinate (of a man?)*'/, attested by BHTTC (8/25/76), also /'*urinate (used for male or female)*'/, attested by AD (1/15/79); found in <**xíwechexw.**>, //x^{y}íwə-c-əx^{w}//, /'*Urinate.*'/, usage: said to a child, for ex., attested by AD (1/15/79).

<**xíxwe**>, cts //x^{y}(=)í[-C_1ə-]wə//, ABFC ['*urinating*'], ASM ['used of animals doing it (dogs, horses, for ex.)'], (<**-R1-**> *continuative*), phonology: vowel-loss, consonant merger, x reduplication as xw in some roots as in Musqueam (Suttles consonant alternation1984:7.2.1, p.13 of ms. ch.7), syntactic analysis: intransitive verb, attested by AD (1/15/79).

<**xiwe'áléx̱eth**>, ds //x(=)iwə=ʔɛ́ləx̣əθ//, ABDF /'*wet the bed, (urinate in the bed)*'/, lx <**=áléx̱eth'**> *bed*, phonology: th prob. mistranscribed for th', syntactic analysis: intransitive verb, attested by AD (1/15/79).

<**xíxewe'áléx̱eth'**>, cts //x(=)í[-C_1ə-]wə=ʔɛ́ləx̣əθ'//, ABDF ['*wetting his/her bed*'], (<**-R1-**> *continuative*), phonology: no x reduplication as xw here, syntactic analysis: intransitive verb, attested by JL (Fish Camp 7/20/79).

<**xiwe'áléx̱eth**>, ABDF /'*wet the bed, (urinate in the bed)*'/, *see* xíwe.

<**xíxeleqwt**>, MC /'*searching it, digging through it*'/, *see* xíleqw.

<**xíxeles**>, probable stem //x^{y}í[=C_1ə=]l(=)əs//, root meaning unknown

<**sxíxeles**>, stvi //s=x^{y}í[=C_1ə=]l(=)əs//, EFAM /'*insistant, persistant (like a child pressing to go along), bull-headed, doesn't mind, does just the opposite, (stubborn, contrary)*'/, (<**s=**> *stative*), (<**=R1=**> *continuative or resultative*), possibly <**=es**> *in the face*, phonology: reduplication, syntactic analysis: adjective/adjectival verb, attested by IHTTC (8/8/77), Deming (3/15/79--SJ, MC, MV, LG), Salish cognate: Squamish /ʔə(s)-ší-šiʔus/ *stubborn* W73:256, K69:92.

<**xíxemel ~ xíxemal**>, df //C_1í=x^{y}ɛm=əl or x^{y}ɛ[=Aí=][-C_1ə-]m=əl//, FSH /'*drift-netting, catching fish with one or two canoes drifting downstream with a net in deep water*'/, possibly root <**xám**> *shallow* if the net is held shallow, possibly <**R1=**> *diminutive or continuative*, possibly <**-R1-**> *continuative*, possibly <**í-ablaut**> *derivational*, lx <**=el**> *come, go, get, become*, phonology: reduplication, possible ablaut, possible vowel-reduction, syntactic analysis: intransitive verb, attested by DM (12/4/64 new transcript, new pp.188-189), Salish cognate: perhaps Squamish /šə́maʔn/ *fish with dipnet (itr.)* beside /šə́maʔn-tn/ *dip net'* W73:184, K69:69 (not Squamish /səyx̣-áʔ-m/ *use a driftnet'* K69:61), perhaps Lushootseed /šə́bəd/ *a fishing net like a basket with a wide opening but narrows to a point so the fish can't turn around; used in creeks; made from cedar boughs; a bag net* H76:457.

<**xixemó:ltel**>, SOC ['*holding a grudge against each other*'], *see* sxemá:l.

blueberry, dwarf blueberry (Vaccinium caespitosum).

<**xíxetem**>, EFAM ['*wishing for someone's food (esp. when in sight)*'], *see* xítem.

<**xixets'eláx̱el**>, ABFC ['*have something under one arm*'], *see* xits' ~ xets'.

<**xixets'eláx̱em**>, ABFC ['*put one's hands under one's arms*'], *see* xits' ~ xets'.

<**xíxets'els**>, HARV /'*cutting wood (with a saw), sawing wood*'/, *see* xets'á:ls.

<**xíxewe'álé<u>x</u>eth'**>, ABDF ['*wetting his/her bed*'], *see* xíwe.

<**xíxewíyeq** or **xíxewíq**>, EB ['*little carrots*'], *see* xáwéq.

<**xixe'át**>, ABFC ['*holding a wee baby in one's arms*'], *see* xá'at.

<**xixkw'ó:m**>, ABFC ['*swimming (be in swimming)*'], *see* xókw' ~ xó:kw'.

<**xíxpò:m**>, SD /'*whistle with pursed lips, whistling*'/, *see* xó:pem.

<**xixqelísem?**>, mdls //xí[=C$_1$ə=]q=əlís=əm//, PE ['*toothpaste*(?)'], literally perhaps /'squeezing up and out on one's teeth/tooth'/, with root <**xíq**> *squeeze up and out, lift up and out*, lx <**=elís**> *on the tooth*, (<**=em**> *middle voice*), possibly <**zero**> *nominalization*, phonology: reduplication, syntactic analysis: nominal, Elder's comment: "unsure of form and meaning", attested by Elders Group (6/1/77).

<**xixq'á:m ~ xixq'ám**>, ABFC ['*mouth open*'], *see* xáq'.

<**xixtímestexw** or **xixtímstexw**>, EFAM ['*tempt s-o (with sex or lust)*'], *see* xítem.

<**xixxweláwa**>, df //x^{y}i[=C$_1$ə=]wə=əlɛ́wɛ or C$_1$í=x^{y}ɛw=əlɛ́wɛ//, ANAF ['*fish air-bladder*'], possibly root <**xíwe**> *urinate (of female)* or <**xaw**> *bone*, possibly <**=R1=**> *continuative or resultative*, possibly <**R4=**> *diminutive*, possibly <**=eláwa**> *bladder/long thing*, phonology: reduplication, possible x reduplication as xw, syntactic analysis: nominal, attested by Elders Group (4/28/76), Salish cognate: perhaps in part Squamish /pláwaʔ/ *air-bladder of fish (used as container for oil)* K69:42 [my analysis, possibly Squamish root /pəh/ *blow*], and Samish /šəpəlíwəʔ/ *fish eggs hung in an air bladder'* G86:78, perhaps in part Salish lexical affix /-ewa/ *long things'* Haeberlin (Thompson) 1974:231, suffix 6.19.

<**xíxwe**>, ABFC ['*urinating*'], *see* xíwe.

<**xixwelókw'**>, SH /'*small bundle, small package*'/, *see* xél.

<**xókw' ~ xó:kw'**>, bound root //x^{y}ák'^{w} ~ x^{y}á·k'^{w} *bathe*//.

<**sxókw'**>, dnom //s=x^{y}ák'^{w}//, TIME ['*fourth day after a death (when everyone washes up (bathes))*'], REL, SOC, ASM ['after a death the body was prepared by special people and kept in the house for visitors to pay their respects, nowadays this is done by undertakers, on the fourth day there is now a funeral and burial, if there is a ritual burning ceremony it is done four days after the burial'], possibly <**s=...=es**> *day, cyclic period* possibly with <**=es**> lost, possibly <**s=**> *nominalizer, something to*, syntactic analysis: nominal, attested by IHTTC (7/15/77).

<**xó:kw'em**>, mdls //x^{y}á·k'^{w}=əm//, ABFC ['*to bathe*'], (<**=em**> *middle voice*), syntactic analysis: intransitive verb, attested by AC (9/7/71), IHTTC (8/29/77--SP, EB, AK, NP), other sources: JH /xá·k'^{w}əm/ *to bathe*, Salish cognate: Squamish /šúk'^{w}-um/ *bathe (itr.)* W73:15, K67:324, example: <**wiyóth kws tsésetémet kws xó:kw'ems.**>, //wə=yáθ k^w-s cə́s=əT-əm-ət k^w-s x^{y}á·k'^{w}=əm-s//, /'*He was always sent to bathe.*'/, attested by IHTTC.

<**xóxekw'em**>, cts //x^{y}á[-R-]k'^{w}=əm//, ABFC ['*bathing*'], (<**-R1-**> *continuative*), phonology: reduplication, syntactic analysis: intransitive verb, attested by AC (9/7/71), IHTTC (8/29/77--SP, EB, AK, NP), example: <**wiyóth kws tsésetémet kws xóxekw'ems**>, //wə=yáθ k^w-s cə́s=əT-əm-ət k^w-s x^{y}á[-C$_1$ə-]k'^{w}=əm-s//, /'*He was always sent to bathe.*'/, attested by IHTTC.

<**shxwxóxekw'em**>, dnom //sx^w=x^{y}á[=C$_1$ə=]k'^{w}=əm//, BLDG ['*bathtub*'], literally /'something for bathing oneself'/, (<**shxw=**> *something for*), phonology: reduplication, syntactic analysis: nominal, attested by Elders Group (6/1/77), AD (8/80), example: <**lí slíts' te shxwxóxekw'em?**>, //lí s=lə[=Aí=]c' tə sx^w=x^{y}á[=C$_1$ə=]k'^{w}=əm//, /'*Is the bathtub full?*'/,

attested by AD.

<**xókw'emá:lá**>, dnom //xʸák'ʷ=əm=ɛ́·lɛ́//, BLDG ['*bathtub*'], literally /'container of bathe oneself'/, lx <**=á:lá**> *container of*, syntactic analysis: nominal, attested by BHTTC (9/1/76).

<**xixkw'ó:m**>, durs //C_1í=xʸakʷ=ə[=Aá·=]m or C_1í=xʸá·k'ʷ=ə[-M1-]m//, dmv, cts, ABFC ['*swimming (be in swimming)*'], PLAY ['*playing in water*'], (<**R4=**> *diminutive*), probably <**ó:-ablaut**> *durative*, possibly <**metathesis**> *continuative*, phonology: reduplication, ablaut or metathesis, probable vowel-reduction, syntactic analysis: intransitive verb, attested by AC, Deming (8/4/77), contrast <**t'í:ts'em**> *swim (the crawl, etc.)*, other sources: ES /xʸəxʸk'ʷá·m/ *swim (be in swimming)*, Suttles ca1984:7.5 and 7.5.1 has Musqueam /xʸixʸk'ʷám'/ *be in swimming* (p.132) as a durative progressive (= my durative continuative) as well as durative diminutives (p.135) which have similar forms, example: <**ílh xíxkw'ò:m.**>, //ʔí-ɬ C_1í=xʸak'ʷ=ə[=Aá·=]m//, /'*They were swimming.*'/, attested by AC (9/7/71).

<**xó:kw'et**>, pcs //xʸá·k'ʷ=əT//, ABFC /'*(bathe s-o, give s-o a bath), make s-o take a bath*'/, (semological comment: the subject is in full control with =et so the translation *make s-o take a bath* is probably not as accurate as *bathe s-o, give s-o a bath*), (<**=et**> *purposeful control transitivizer*), syntactic analysis: transitive verb, attested by AC, Salish cognate: Squamish /šúk'ʷ-ut/ *bathe (tr.)* W73:15, K67:324, example: <**lalh(a) xó:kw'et.**>, //lɛ-ɬ(ɛ) xʸá·k'ʷ=əT//, /'*(Go give him/her a bath.), Make him take a bath.*'/, attested by AC (10/21/71).

<**xó:kw'em**>, ABFC ['*to bathe*'], *see* xókw' ~ xó:kw'.

<**xókw'emá:lá**>, BLDG ['*bathtub*'], *see* xókw' ~ xó:kw'.

<**xó:kw'et**>, ABFC /'*(bathe s-o, give s-o a bath), make s-o take a bath*'/, *see* xókw' ~ xó:kw'.

<**xó:l**>, bound root //xʸá·l *bore a hole, drill a hole*//.

<**xó:lt**>, pcs //xʸá·l=T//, TOOL ['*to bore a hole*'], (<**=t**> *purposeful control transitivizer*), syntactic analysis: transitive verb, attested by Elders Group (3/1/72 tape), Salish cognate: Squamish /šúy-uy-ʔn/ *make holes with an awl (tr.)* W73:142, K67:324, K69:69, example: <**tsel xó:lt.**>, //c-əl xʸá·l=T//, /'*I bore (a hole).*'/, attested by Elders Group.

<**sxoxwí:ls**>, dnom //s=xʸa[=C_1ə=]l=əls//, sas, TOOL /'*a borer, an auger*'/, (<**s=**> *nominalizer*), (<**=R1=**> *continuative*), (<**=í:ls ~ =əls**> *structured activity continuative device to*), phonology: reduplication, x reduplicated as xw in some roots as in Musqueam (Suttles consonant alternation1984:7.2.1 [p.13 of ch.7]), el→íy before =els or syllable-loss (el before =els or =í:ls), syntactic analysis: nominal, attested by Elders Group (3/1/72 tape).

<**sxoxwő:ls**>, sas //s=xʸa[-C_1ə-]l=əls//, cts, TOOL /'*boring a hole*'/, possibly <**s=**> *stative*, (<**-R1-**> *continuative*), (<**=els**> *structured activity continuative*), phonology: reduplication, x reduplicated as xw, el→éw or ő́w before els, syntactic analysis: intransitive verb, attested by Elders Group (3/1/72 tape).

<**xó:lelhp**>, df //xʸá·l=əɬp//, EB /'*plant with three black berries always joined together,* (possibly *black twinberry)*'/, ['possibly *Lonicera involucrata*'], ASM ['not medicine for xó:lí:s so far as known--I asked to see if the two words might have the same root, there are few plants with joined black berries in the area so *black twinberry* seems the likeliest identification'], root meaning unknown unless xó:l *bore a hole*, lx <**=elhp**> *plant, tree*, syntactic analysis: nominal, attested by IHTTC (at Victoria Curriculum Conference 11/2-5/77), Salish cognate: Cowichan /šá·l'əɬp/ *red-osier dogwood (Cornus stolonifera) Turner and Bell 1971:81 though this species is not related to black twinberry and in fact has white berries used to induce vomiting by the Saanich and Stó:lō (Upriver Halkomelem th'e<u>x</u>wíyelhp).*

<**xó:lé<u>x</u>wem**>, WETH ['*getting real drafty*'], *see* xó:lxwem.

<**xò:lí:s**>, us //xʸà·lí·s//, ABDF ['*a fatal kind of shock on seeing a stl'áleqem (supernatural creature)*'], ASM ['symptoms can include vomiting until a person dies, soul-loss, (after seeing a sílhqey) twisting up horribly and dying, insanity (after seeing a sasquatch)'], root meaning unknown unless <**xó:l**> *bore a hole, drill a hole*, possibly <**=es**> *face*, possibly <**-Aí:-**> *durative*, syntactic analysis: intransitive verb, attested by Elders Group (2/19/75).

<**xó:lt**>, TOOL ['*to bore a hole*'], *see* xó:l.

<**xó:lxwem**>, izs //xʸá·lxʷ=əm//, TAST /'*have a menthol taste, (have a cool taste)*'/, semantic environment ['menthol cigarettes, medicine'], root meaning unknown, (<**=em**> *have, get, intransitivizer*), syntactic analysis: intransitive verb, attested by SJ (Deming, on elders trip to Banff 8/25/78), also <**xó:lxwem ~ xó:lx̱wem**>, //xʸá·lxʷ=əm ~ xʸá·lx̣ʷ=əm//, also SM /'*(have a) menthol smell, (be) strong-smelling (of medicine)*'/, attested by Deming (1/31/80), also <**xó:lx̱wem**>, //xá·lx̣ʷ=əm//, WETH, also /'*get drafty [cool?]*'/, attested by Deming (3/31/77), example: <**xó:lxwem te st'élmexw.**>, //xʸá·lxʷ=əm tə s=t'ə́lməxʷ//, /'*The medicine has a menthol taste.*'/, attested by SJ (8/25/78), <**ts'áts'el xó:lx̱wem**>, //c'ɛ́[=C₁ə=]l xʸá·lx̣ʷ=əm//, /'*real strong smelling (of medicine)*'/, attested by Deming (1/31/77).

<**xó:lx̱wem**>, izs //xá·lx̣ʷ=əm//, WETH ['*get drafty*'], (<**=em**> *have, get, intransitivizer*), syntactic analysis: intransitive verb, attested by Deming (3/31/77), example: <**me xó:lx̱wem.**>, //mə xʸá·lx̣ʷ=əm//, /'*(It) gets drafty.*'/, attested by Deming (3/31/77).

<**xó:léx̱wem**>, cts //xʸá·l[-ə́-]x̣ʷ=əm//, WETH ['*getting real drafty*'], (<**-é-**> *continuative*), phonology: é-infix which is rare, syntactic analysis: intransitive verb, attested by Deming (3/31/77), example: <**me xó:léx̱wem.**>, //mə xʸá·l[-ə́-]x̣ʷ=əm//, /'*(It is) getting real drafty.*'/, attested by Deming (3/31/77).

<**xálxwthet**>, incs //xʸa[=Aɛ́=]lxʷ=θət//, ABFC ['*cool off (of a person)*'], possibly <**á-ablaut**> meaning unknown, (<**=thet**> *get, become, inceptive*), phonology: possible ablaut of o→a before =thet, syntactic analysis: intransitive verb, attested by Elders Group (5/19/76).

<**xó:lx̱wem**>, WETH ['*get drafty*'], *see* xó:lxwem.

<**xólh**>, bound root //xʸáɬ *look*//, Salish cognate: Lushootseed (Northern dial.) root /šuɬ/ *see, look* as in /ʔu-šúɬ/ *look around*, /šúɬ/ *look(ing)*, /ʔə(s)šúšɬəbid/ *looking for s-o (to come), expecting s-o* H76:469-471.

<**xólhmet ~ xólhemet**>, iecs //xʸáɬ=məT//, SOC /'*look after s-o, protect s-o, take care of s-o*'/, (<**=met**> *indirect effect non-control transitivizer*), syntactic analysis: transitive verb, attested by EB (2/6/76), Elders Group (4/28/76, 6/16/76), Salish cognate: Lushootseed /ʔə(s)-šúšɬ-əbid/ *looking for s-o (to come), expecting s-o* H76:469-471, example: <**te xólhmet kwe tsméle**>, //tə xʸáɬ=məT kʷə c=mə́lə//, SOC ['*mid-wife (helps to deliver babies)*'], literally /'the one who looks after the one who gives birth'/, attested by CT and HT (6/21/76).

<**xóxelhmet**>, cts //xʸá[-C₁ə-]ɬ=məT//, SOC /'*looking after s-o, taking care of s-o*'/, (<**-R1-**> *continuative*), phonology: reduplication, syntactic analysis: transitive verb, attested by EB, also <**xó:lhmet**>, //xʸá[-·-]ɬ=məT//, (<**-:-**> *continuative*), phonology: lengthening?, attested by TG (4/75), example: <**xóxelhmet the tsméle**>, //xʸá[-C₁ə-]ɬ=məT θə c=mə́lə//, /'*looking after someone having a baby*'/, literally /'looking after s-o the (female) have a child'/, attested by EB (2/6/76), <**tsel xó:lhmethòme.**>, //c-əl xʸá·ɬ=məT-ámə//, /'*I'm looking after you., I'm taking care of you.*'/, attested by TG (4/75).

<**xólhmethet ~ xó:lhmethet**>, rfls //xʸá(·)ɬ=məT-ət//, SOC /'*take care of oneself, look after oneself, be careful*'/, (<**-et**> *reflexive*), syntactic analysis: intransitive verb, attested by Elders Group

(3/1/72, 4/28/76, 5/19/76, 6/16/76); found in <**xólhemethetchexw.**>, //x^yáɬ=məT-ət-c-əx^w//, /'*Take care of yourself.*'/, attested by Elders Group (4/28/76), EB, <**xólhmethetchxwò.**>, //x^yáɬ=məT-ət-c-x^w-à//, /'*Be careful., Take care.*'/, attested by Elders Group (5/19/76), <**xólhmethetlha.**>, //x^yáɬ=məT-ət-ɬɛ//, /'*Be careful.*'/, usage: said to person who has tripped and hurt himself (for ex.), attested by Elders Group (5/19/76).

<**xó:lhmethet**>, cts //x^yá[-·-]ɬ=məT-ət//, SOC ['*taking care of oneself*'], (<**-:-**> *continuative*), phonology: lengthening, syntactic analysis: intransitive verb, attested by TG (4/75); found in <**xó:lhmethettsel.**>, //x^yá[-·-]ɬ=məT-ət-c-əl//, /'*I'm taking care of myself.*'/, attested by TG.

<**xolhmílh** or **xolhmíylh**>, ds //x^yaɬ=m(əT)=íylh//, SOC ['*to babysit someone else's kids (children)*'], literally /'look after a child'/, lx <**=iylh ~ =áylh**> *child*, phonology: syllable-loss of et in =met before stressed lexical affix which functions as object, syntactic analysis: intransitive verb, attested by AD and AK (Trip to Five-Mile Creek 4/30/79).

<**xolhemílh** or **xolhemíylh**>, cts //x^yaɬ=[-ə-]m(əT)=íyɬ//, SOC ['*babysitting*'], (<**-e-**> *continuative*), phonology: infixed e, syllable-loss, syntactic analysis: intransitive verb, attested by Elders Group (3/13/80).

<**xólhemìlh ~ xòlhemí:lh** or **xòlhemí:ylh**>, dnom //x^ya[=´=]ɬ=ə=m=íyɬ//, SOC /'*babysitter (for kids, etc.)*'/, SPRD /'*babysitter (for new spirit-dancers), any of the workers who help in initiating a spirit-dancer, (initiator or helper of spirit-dancers)*'/, possibly <**=´=**> *nominalizer*?, phonology: stress-shift, downstepping, syntactic analysis: nominal, attested by Elders Group (4/28/76, 3/1/72), also <**xolhemílh**>, //x^yaɬ=ə=m(əT)=íyɬ//, attested by AD (1/19/79), RG & EH (4/10/99 Ling332), example: <**tsel xolhemílh.**>, //c-əl x^yaɬ=ə=m(əT)=íyɬ//, /'*I'm a babysitter.*'/, attested by AD (1/19/79).

<**xolhemílh** or **xolhemíylh**>, SOC ['*babysitting*'], *see* xólh.

<**xólhemìlh ~ xòlhemí:lh** or **xòlhemí:ylh**>, SOC /'*babysitter (for kids, etc.)*'/, *see* xólh.

<**xólhmet ~ xólhemet**>, SOC /'*look after s-o, protect s-o, take care of s-o*'/, *see* xólh.

<**xó:lhmethet**>, SOC ['*taking care of oneself*'], *see* xólh.

<**xólhmethet ~ xó:lhmethet**>, SOC /'*take care of oneself, look after oneself, be careful*'/, *see* xólh.

<**xolhmílh** or **xolhmíylh**>, SOC ['*to babysit someone else's kids (children)*'], *see* xólh.

<**xó:pem**>, ds //x^yá·p=əm//, SD ['*to whistle*'], MUS, LANG, (<**=em**> *middle voice or have/get/intransitivizer*), syntactic analysis: intransitive verb, attested by EB (12/12/75), Salish cognate: Squamish /šúpn/ *to whistle* W73:287, K67:324.

<**xíxpò:m**>, dmv //C_1í=x^yá·p=ə[=M2=]m or C_1í=x^yap=ə[=Aá·=]m//, SD /'*whistle with pursed lips, whistling*'/, MUS, LANG, (<**R4=**> *diminutive*), possibly <**metathesis**> *derivational*, possibly <**ó:-ablaut**> *durative*, phonology: reduplication, metathesis or ablaut, downstepping, syntactic analysis: intransitive verb, attested by Deming (7/27/78), EB (12/12/75, 5/4/76), MV (Deming 5/4/78), *<**xíxpò:m te st'ílem**> rejected, //C_1í=x^yá·p=ə[=M1=]m tə s=t'íl=əm//, /'*whistling the song*'/, Elder's comment: "one just can say xíxpò:m", attested by EB (5/4/76), example: <**ő́wechxw swiyeqáxw, qe xixpó:mchexw.**>, //ʔówə-c-x^w s=wíqə-ɛ́x^w qə C_1í=x^yá·p=ə[=M2=]m-c-əx^w//, /'*You're not a man but you're whistling.*'/, usage: a saying to young girls around puberty to stop them from whistling, Elder's comment: "her grandmother told her this", attested by MV (Deming 5/4/78).

<**xópethet**>, ABFC ['*squat*'], *see* xóp'.

<**xóp'**>, bound root //x^yáp' *squat*//.

<**sxóxep**> or better <**sxóxep'**>, strs //s=x^yá[=C_1ə=]p'//, ABFC ['*(be) squatting*'], (<**s=**> *stative*),

(<=**R1**=> *resultative or continuative*), phonology: reduplication, p probably mistranscribed for p', syntactic analysis: adjective/adjectival verb, attested by IHTTC (9/1/77), Salish cognate: Cowichan /šəšáʔp'-nəc/ *to squat* B74c:77, Saanich dial. of NSt /šəšáʔp'-əwəc/ *to squat* B74a:77.

<**xópethet**>, or better <**xóp'ethet**>, df //xʸáp'=θət//, ABFC ['*squat*'], possibly <=**ethet**> *get, become, inceptive*, phonology: p probably mistranscribed for p', syntactic analysis: intransitive verb, attested by IHTTC; found in <**xópethetlha.**>, //xʸáp'=θət-ɬɛ//, /'*Squat.*'/, attested by IHTTC (9/1/77).

<**xóp'em**>, mdls //xʸáp'=əm//, ABFC /'*squat*'/, <=**em**> *middle voice*, attested by RG & EH (4/9/99 Ling332)

<**xóxekw'em**>, ABFC ['*bathing*'], *see* xókw' ~ xó:kw'.

<**xóxelhmet**>, SOC /'*looking after s-o, taking care of s-o*'/, *see* xólh.

<**xts'ímthet**>, SM ['*(have/get a) strong stink*'], *see* xíxets'em.

XW

<**xw=**>, da //x^{w}=//, DIR *toward(s), for*, see under <shxw=> and also found in: <**xwth'í:t**>, df //x^{w}=θ'íy=T//, SOC /*'thank s-o (for a cure, for pall-bearing, a ceremony, being a witness)'*/ (see under root <ch'it>), <**xwch'alech'á:ls**>, sas //x^{w}=C$_{1}$ɛ[=lə=]=c'ɛ́=ɛ́ls//, FOOD [*'put on the stove (water/food)'*], HHG, literally /'(towards) many things put on top of in a structured activity'/ (see under root <ch'a(:)>); Salish cognate: Nk //x^{w}=// *towards*, Galloway, Adams & Renteria 2004a.

<**xw=**>, da //x^{w}=//, ANA /*'on the vulva, in the vagina'*/, syntactic analysis: derivational prefix, comment: <**xw=**> *on the vulva, in the vagina* is rarely attested in material I have gathered (probably due to my not having asked for forms containing it and due to the modesty used by the elders in translating those they gave me); another complicating factor in recognizing it is the fact that there are other prefixes with the same shape (**xw=** *always*, **xw(e)=** *become, get*, **xw=** used after s= *nominalizer*, **xw=** meaning uncertain but used esp. with words suffixed with **=ó:s ~ =es** *on the face* and some other body part suffixes;, comment: other forms with this suffix include three place names: 1.) <**Xwth'kw'ém**> (/x^{w}=θ'k'^{w}=ə́m/) *small creek near American Bar used to heal sores* said to mean *sores* but is not the same as the word for *sores* and may mean literally *place to bring sores in the vagina/vulva*; 2.) <**Xwyélés ~ Lexwyélés**> *rock up the Harrison River from the old Chehalis Indian cemetery which also has marks near it called Tracks of Mink* (<**Sx̲éyeltels te Sqayéx̲iya**>); this place is the subject of a story told in Boas (Bertz translation, 1980 version:34) about a woman with this name, who had teeth in her vagina and bit off Mink's right hand (so his tracks can still be seen where he ran out of her house) and was soon transformed into rock by the Transformer,<**X̲á:ls**>; thus the name probably means literally *(always) teeth in the vagina* since <**yélés**> means *teeth* and <**le=**> means *always*; 3.) <**Xwth'ístel**> *place across the Fraser River from Q'alelíktel,* where the root is <**th'ís=tel ~ ts'ís=tel**> *horn, antler.*, Salish cognate: Musqueam /x^{w}-$_{3}$/ *vulva; inward, inhering; possessing* (probably several homophonous suffixes)--Suttles ca1984:13.4.7 gives some very clear examples: /x^{w}-θí/ *big vulva* from /θí/ *big*, /x^{w}-ʔə́y'/ *clean vulva* from /ʔə́y'/ *good, clean* /x^{w}=k^{w}ən-ét/ *put one's hand on a woman's vulva* (from /k^{w}ən-ét/ (*grasp s-o/s-th with one's hand*), /š=x^{w}=q^{w}ín/ *woman's pubic hair* from /q^{w}ín/ *body hair* as in /q^{w}ín=əws/ *body hair* and /q^{w}ín=eq/ *male pubic hair*, and possibly /x^{w}-mə́q'^{w}/ *miscarry* from /mə́q'^{w}/ *burst*, and as in <**xwpelákw**>, //x^{w}=pələ[=Aɛ́=]k^{w}//, /*'peek under a woman's skirt, (catch sight of a woman's vulva/vagina)'*/, attested by Elders Group (9/21/77), also possibly as in <**xwpóysekel**>, ds //x^{w}=páysəkəl//, /*'to bicycle (of a woman), ride a bicycle (of a woman)'*/, attested by RG & EH (4/9/99 Ling332).

<**xw=**>, da //x^{w}=//, ANA [*'pertaining to the head'*], (semological comment: mainly used sporadically with body part suffixes of the head <**=es**> *on the face*, <**=eqw**> *on top of the head*, <**=ó:thel**> *on the mouth*, perhaps <**=eqel**> *of the throat* and <**=á:lí:ya**> *of the ear*), syntactic analysis: derivational prefix, lexical affix; found in <**xwthó:qw**>, //x^{w}=θ=á·q^{w}//, /*'big head'*/, root <**th= ~ thi ~ the**> *big*, <**xwthó:s**>, //x^{w}=θ=á·s//, /*'big face'*/, root <**th= ~ thi ~ the**> *big*, <**xwthó:thel**>, //x^{w}=θ=á·θəl//, /*'big mouth'*/, root <**th= ~ thi ~ the**> *big*, <**xwtl'ó:qtes**>, //x^{w}=ƛ'á·qt=əs//, /*'long face, morose'*/, <**xwpopó:s**>, //x^{w}=pap=á·s//, /*'hair all over the face'*/, <**xwmékwetht ~ mékwetht**>, //(x^{w}=)mə́k^{w}=əθ=t//, /*'kiss s-o'*/, <**xwmékwethel ~ mékwethel**>, //(x^{w}=)mə́k^{w}=əθəl//, /*'kiss s-o on the lips (mouth)'*/, root <**mékw**> *stout*, <**xwlíyémés**>, //x^{w}=líyə́m=əs//, /*'smile'*/, root <**líyém**> *laugh*, <**shxw'óthestses**>, //s=x^{w}=ʔáθəs=cəs//, /*'palm of hand'*/, root <**s'óthes**> *face*, <**shxw'óthesxel**>, //s=x^{w}=ʔáθəs=x^{y}əl//, /*'sole of foot'*/, <**xwt'óxwestses**>, //x^{w}=t'áx^{w}=əs=cəs//, /*'hollow of the hand'*/, root <**t'óxw**> *going downriver*, (<**=es**> *on the face*), (<**=tses**> *of the hand*), <**xwt'óxwesxel**>,

//xʷ=t'áxʷ=əs=xʸəl//, /'arch of the foot'/, <**xwmélkw'es**>, //xʷ=mə́lk'ʷ=əs//, /'get hit in the face by s-th falling'/, <**xwlalá:**>, //xʷ=lɛlɛ́·//, /'listen hard'/, <**xwlalá:m**>, //xʷ=lɛlɛ́·=m//, /'listen'/, possibly root <**l**> meaning unknown, possibly <**=alá:**> may be related to somatic suffix <**=á:lí:ya**> *in the ear*, possibly <**shxwthí:qel**>, //s=xʷ=θí·=qəl//, /'loud voice'/, root <**thí:**> *big*, (<**=eqel**> *in the throat*), possibly <**shxw'í:le**>, //s=xʷ=ʔí·lə//, /'side of head ~ cheek'/, root meaning unknown.

<**xw= ~ lexw=** ~ (rarely) **le=**>, da //**ləxʷ= ~ xʷ= ~ (rarely) lə=**//, TIME ['*always*'], syntactic analysis: derivational prefix; found in <**lexw'éy ~ xw'éywelh**>, //ləxʷ=ʔɛ́y ~ xʷ=ʔɛ́y=wəɬ//, /'*generous, always good*'/, <**lexwqélwelh**>, //ləxʷ=qə́ɬ=wəɬ//, /'*cranky, crabby, dirty-minded*'/ (root <**qél**> *bad; dirty)*, <**lexwmálqewelh**>, //ləxʷ=mɛ́lq=əwəɬ//, /'*forgetful; passed out (if drunk)*'/, <**lexwslhám**>, //ləxʷ=s=ɬɛ́m//, /'*always choking on liquid*'/, also <**lexwshxwlhám**>, //ləxʷ=sxʷ=ɬɛ́m//, /'*choking on liquid*'/, <**lexwstl'ép**>, //ləxʷ=s=ƛ'ə́p//, /'*always deep*'/, (<**s=**> *stative*), <**Lkwṓxwethem**>, //l(ə)=kʷóxʷəθ=əm//, /'*Six-Mile Creek and bay on west side of Harrison Lake*'/, literally /'always coho place or always catch coho since this is a coho spawning ground'/, attested by EL, <**Lexwyó:qwem ~ Xwyó:qwem**>, //ləxʷ=yá·qʷ=əm ~ xʷ=yá·qʷ=əm//, /'*mountain above Union Bar,* also prob. *Trafalgar Flat below it*'/, literally /'always (smells of) rotten fish (since spawned out salmon, yó:qwem, collect in the river nearby)'/, attested by SP, <**Xwchí:yò:m**>, PLN /'*Cheam Island (my name for an island in the Fraser River across from Cheam Indian Reserve #2), Cheam village, Cheam Indian Reserve #1*'/, literally /'always a place to get strawberries '/.

<**=xw ~ =exw**>, da //=xʷ ~ =əxʷ//, SH /'*lump-like, round*'/, syntactic analysis: lexical suffix, also <**=exw**>, //=əxʷ//; found in <**(s)th'emxweláx̱el**>, //(s=)θ'am=xʷ=əlɛ́x̣əl//, /'*an elbow*'/, <**th'eméxwelets**>, //θ'ɛm=ə[=´=]xʷ=ələc//, /'*downriver end/point of island*'/, literally /'tide out round/lump-like at the bottom'/, <**ts'él:exw**>, //c'ə́l·=əxʷ//, /'*turn back into a quiet slough from the river*'/, root <**ts'él(:)**> *turn*, <**sts'épxwel**>, //s=c'ə́p=xʷ=əl//, /'*wart*'/, root <**ts'ép**> *dirty*.

<**xwa ~ xwe**>, free root //xʷɛ ~ xʷə//, ASP /'*become, get*'/, see under allomorph <**xwe**> *become, get*.

<**xwá**>, free root //xʷɛ́//, ABDF /'*starve, be starving, be famished, (be extremely hungry [Deming,JL])*'/, FOOD, Elder's comment: "worse than <**kw'à:y**> *be hungry*", syntactic analysis: intransitive verb, attested by EB (2/9/76, 12/19/75), Elders Group (3/72), Salish cognate: Squamish /xʷəh/ *be totally starved, be in state of extreme exhaustion, have passed out from hunger, (extreme)* and /xʷiʔús/ *be very hungry* W73:251,146, K69:78-79, K67:350, also /'*be hungry, (be extremely hungry)*'/, attested by Deming (2/7/80), JL, example: <**tsel welh xwá.**>, //c-əl wə=ɬ xʷɛ́//, /'*I'm starving.*'/, literally /'I already starve.'/, attested by Elders Group (3/72), <**le xwá tutl'o qesu le q'ó:y.**>, //lə xʷɛ́ t=u=ƛ'a qə-s-u lə q'á·y//, /'*He starved and so he died.*'/, *<**le kw'à:y tutl'o qesu le q'ó:y.**> rejected by EB (2/9/76), <**me xwá**>, //mə xʷɛ́//, /'*to be hungry*'/, literally /'come to starve, start to starve'/, attested by JL, <**latsellh xwá. ~ látsullh xwá.**>, //lɛ-c-əl-ɬ xʷɛ́ ~ lɛ́-c-u-ɬ xʷɛ́//, /'*I am hungry.*'/, literally /'I was going to starve. ~ I was already going to starve.'/, attested by Deming.

<**xwexwá**>, cts //C_1ə-xʷɛ́//, ABDF ['*starving*'], FOOD, (<**R5-**> *continuative*), phonology: reduplication, syntactic analysis: intransitive verb, attested by Deming (2/7/80), others, Salish cognate: Saanich dial. of NSt /c-xʷəxʷíiŋ/ *to starve* B74a:78.

<**temxwá**>, ds //təm=xʷɛ́//, TIME ['*famine*'], FOOD, literally /'time to starve'/, (<**tem=**> *time*), syntactic analysis: nominal, *<**temkw'à:y**> rejected by EB (2/9/76).

<**xwát**>, pcs //xʷɛ́=T//, TVMO /'*lessen it (of someone's load), halve it, make s-th lighter (in weight), lessen it (like when someone's pack is too heavy)*'/, MC, root meaning unknown unless <**xwá**> *starve*, (<**=t**> *purposeful control transitivizer*), syntactic analysis: transitive verb, attested by Deming (2/7/80), AD (11/19/79, 2/28/80), Salish cognate: possibly Squamish /xʷát-anʔ/ *make less (heavy), take off from (tr.)* K69:78, possibly Lushootseed /xʷác-ad/ *take s-th off to lighten it*

H76:555, example: <**tu xwátchexw.**>, //tu xʷɛ́=T-c-əxʷ//, /'*Make it lighter (in weight).*'/, literally /'a little/somewhat you lighten s-th in weight'/, attested by AD.

<**xwátem**>, pcs //xʷɛ́=T-əm//, SPRD /'*somebody is made to fast, he is starved (purposely)*'/, FOOD, (<**=t**> *purposeful control transitivizer*), (<**-em**> *passive third person patient (object)*), syntactic analysis: transitive verb-passive, attested by Deming (2/7/80).

<**xwexwátem**>, cts //C_1ə-xʷɛ́=T-əm//, SPRD /'*fasting*'/, SOC, <**R5-**> *continuative*, attested by RG & EH (4/10/99 Ling332).

<**xwóthet**>, pcrs //xʷɛ[=Aá=]=T-ət//, ABDF /'*to abstain from food, to fast, starve oneself*'/, FOOD, (<**=t**> *purposeful control transitivizer*), (<**-et**> *reflexive*), phonology: a→o automatically before =thet, syntactic analysis: intransitive verb, attested by Elders Group (1/30/80), Salish cognate: Squamish /xʷiʔús-cut/ *starve oneself* W73:251, K69:78-79, also <**xwáthet**>, //xʷɛ́=T-ət//, also /'*make oneself famished*'/, attested by EB (12/19/75), example: <**tsel xwáthet.**>, //c-əl xʷɛ́=T-ət//, /'*I made myself famished.*'/, attested by EB (12/19/75).

<**xwexwóthet**>, cts //C_1ə-xʷɛ[=Aá=]=T-ət//, ABDF /'*starving oneself, being on a "crash" diet*'/, FOOD, (<**R5-**> *continuative*), phonology: reduplication, ablaut, syntactic analysis: intransitive verb, attested by Elders Group (1/30/80).

<**xwà:lx**>, pcis //xʷɛ̀=əl=xʸ//, ABFC /'*lift up s-th, lift [s-th], hoist [s-th] up*'/, (<**=el**> *go, come, get, become*), (<**=x**> *purposeful control transitivizer inanimate object preferred*), phonology: vowel merger, syntactic analysis: transitive verb, attested by JL (5/5/75), also <**xwàlx**>, //xʷɛ̀=əl=xʸ//, attested by EB (12/17/75), RG & EH (4/9/99 Ling332), example: <**xwálx**>, //xʷɛ́=əl=xʸ//, attested by AC, <**le xwálxes te xwétes (leplós, lesák, smá:lt).**>, //lə xʷɛ́=əl=xʸ-əs tə xʷə́təs (ləplás, ləsɛ́k, s=mɛ́·lt)//, /'*He liefted the heavy (plank, sack, rock).*'/, attested by AC (10/31/71), <**tl'olsuw xwálx tel chálex sta'á te shxwélméxwelh sqwàl kw'els thét-s "Hello."**>, //ƛ'a-l-s-uw xʷɛ́=əl=xʸ t-əl cɛ́ləxʸ s=t=ɛʔɛ́ s=xʷə́lméxʷ=əɬ s=qʷɛ̀·l k'ʷ-əl-s θə́t-s "Hello."//, /'*And I lifted my hand like the Indian way to say "Hello."*'/, usage: recent narrative, attested by AC (11/10/71), <**xwálx tel chálex tl'olsu thét "hóy siyá:ya."**>, //xʷɛ́=əl=xʸ t-əl cɛ́ləxʸ ƛ'a-l-s-uw θə́t "háy s=yɛ̀·yɛ."//, /'*Raising my hand then I said, "Hello, friends."*'/, usage: recent narrative, attested by AC (11/10/71).

<**shxwélchep**>, df //s=xʷ(=)ə́lcəp or /s=xʷɛ̀l=ə́lcəp//, FIRE /'*home-made lantern (using candle in a can with a hole in it, etc.), jack-o-lantern*'/, LT, HHG, (<**s=**> *nominalizer, something to*), possibly <**shxw=**> *nominalizer, something for*, root probably same as in <**xwà:lx**> *lift up s-th, lift [s-th], hoist [s-th] up*'/, lx <**=élchep**> *firewood*, phonology: loss of transitivizer <**=x**>, syntactic analysis: nominal, attested by TG (Elders Group 2/6/80), contrast <**swáchet**> *lantern, torch*, Salish cognate: Squamish /sxʷáčit/ *torch, light, lamp* only with Halkomelem <**swáchet**> *lantern, torch*, not with <**shxwélchep**>.

<**xwóxwe**>, rsls //xʷɛ=AáC_1ə//, DESC /'*light (weight), lightweight*'/, SOCT ['*fast runner*'], (<**ó-ablaut and =R1=**> *resultative*), phonology: ablaut, reduplication, syntactic analysis: adjective/adjectival verb, also nominal, attested by IHTTC (9/13/77), EB (12/19/75), AC (8/6/70, 8/29/70), Salish cognate: Squamish /ʔáʔxʷa/ *light (ab. weight), swift* W73:162, K67:392, Lushootseed /xʷəʔáʔxʷəʔ/ *light weight* H76:562, Sechelt /xʷíxʷxʷa/ *light of weight* T77:21, Sechelt /xʷíxʷa/ *light of weight* B77:53, Samish dial. of NSt /xʷəxʷéw'xʷə/ *lightweight* G86:91, Saanich dial. of NSt /xʷəxʷáwxʷə/ *lightweight* B74a:44.

<**shxwóxwel**>, incs //s=xʷɛ=AáC_1ə=əl//, ABFC /'*to lift, raise*'/, literally /'go/get to be lightweight'/, (<**s=**> *stative*), (<**=el**> *go, come, get, become*), phonology: ablaut, reduplication, syntactic analysis: intransitive verb, attested by AD and NP (1/23/80).

<**shxwóxwelstexw**>, caus //s=xʷɛ[=AáC_1ə=]=əl=sT-əxʷ//, ABFC /'*keep it in the air, lift s-th/s-o*

off the floor'/, SPRD [*'lift s-o (of a spirit dancer being initiated)'*], (<**s=**> *stative*), (<**ó-ablaut plus =R1=**> *resultative*), (<**=el**> *go, come, get, become*), (<**=st**> *causative control transitivizer*), (<**-exw**> *third person object*), phonology: ablaut, reduplication, vowel merger, syntactic analysis: transitive verb, attested by AD and NP (1/23/80), also <**shxwó:xwelstexw**>, //s=x^{w}ɛ[=Aá·C$_{1}$ə=]=əl=sT-əx^{w}//, also /*'holding s-th up'*/, attested by JL (5/5/75).

<**xwá:lq**>, free root //x^{w}ɛ̀·lq//, QUAL [*'almost'*], ABDF [*'to almost die'*], syntactic analysis: adverb/adverbial verb, attested by EB (1/9/76), compare possibly <**x̲wíleqlexw**> *almost kill s-o (accidentally/managed to)*, Salish cognate: prob. not Lushootseed /x̣^{w}úl-ud/ *put it near* H76:620, ASM ['almost'], example: <**xwá:lqtsel líl lá:m.**>, //x^{w}ɛ̀·lq-c-əl lí-l lɛ̀·=m//, /*'I almost went.'*/, attested by EB, <**xwá:lqchexw lám, étl'?**>, //x^{w}ɛ̀·lq-c-əx^{w} lɛ̀=m, ʔə́ƛ̓'//, /*'You almost went, didn't you?'*/, syntactic analysis: tag-question, attested by EB, ASM ['almost die']; found in <**xwá:lqtsel.**>, //x^{w}ɛ̀·lq-c-əl//, /*'I almost died., I almost did.'*/, attested by EB.

<**xwá:lqi ~ xwálqey**>, df //x^{w}ɛ̀·lq=i ~ x^{w}ɛ́lq=əy//, QUAL [*'almost'*], syntactic analysis: adverb/adverbial verb, attested by EB (1/9/76, 2/6/76), example: <**xwá:lq i tós te kyó.**>, //x^{w}ɛ̀·lq=i tás tə k^{y}á//, /*'He almost got hit by a car.'*/, attested by EB (1/9/76), <**xwálqey léts' ~ wélh tu léts'**>, //x^{w}ɛ́lq=əy lə́c' ~ wə́=ɬ tu lə́c'//, /*'(It's) near full (of a container).'*/, attested by EB (2/6/76).

<**xwá:lqi ~ xwálqey**>, QUAL [*'almost'*], *see* xwá:lq.

<**xwà:lx**>, ABFC /*'lift up s-th, lift [s-th], hoist [s-th] up'*/, *see* xwá.

<**xwát**>, TVMO /*'lessen it (of someone's load), halve it, make s-th lighter (in weight), lessen it (like when someone's pack is too heavy)'*/, *see* xwá.

<**xwátem**>, SOC /*'somebody is made to fast, he is starved (purposely)'*/, *see* xwá.

<**Xwatóy**>, N /*'Female Salmonberry Bird, (Female Swainson's Thrush)'*/, *see* xwét.

<**xwathtálém**>, WETH /*'getting cloudy, clouding up'*/, *see* thá:t.

<**xwáth'**>, bound root //x^{w}ɛ́θ' *rock, teeter*//.

<**xwáth'em**>, mdls //x^{w}ɛ́θ'=əm//, ABFC [*'to rock'*], TVMO, (<**=em**> *middle voice or intransitivizer*), syntactic analysis: intransitive verb, attested by IHTTC (9/7/77), Salish cognate: probably Saanich dial. of NSt /x^{w}ə́θ'-əŋ/ *to stagger*, possibly Lushootseed /x^{w}íc'ic'ab/ *balance, teeter, stagger* H76:562.

<**xwixweth'álem**>, dmv //C$_{1}$í-x^{w}ɛ́θ'=ə[=M2=]l=əm//, ABFC [*'rocking'*], TVMO, (<**R4-**> *diminutive*), (semological comment: diminutive verbs are always continuative as well as in Musqueam (Suttles ca1984:ch.7)), possibly <**á-ablaut**> *durative*, possibly <**metathesis**> *derivational*, phonology: reduplication, metathesis or ablaut and vowel-reduction, downstepping, syntactic analysis: intransitive verb, attested by Elders Group (6/1/77), compare <**shxwth'ámqels**> *scissors*, also <**xwíxweth'àlem**>, //C$_{1}$í-x^{w}ɛ́θ'-ə[=M2=]l=əm or x^{w}i[-C$_{1}$ə-]θ'=ə[=Aɛ́=]l=əm//, also /*'rocking'*/, PLAY [*'teeter-totter'*], attested by IHTTC (9/7/77).

<**xwíxweth'àlem sch'áletstel**>, cpds //C$_{1}$í-x^{w}ɛθ'=ə[=Aɛ́=]l=əm s=c'ɛ́=ləc=təl//, HHG [*'a rocking chair'*], literally /'rocking chair'/, phonology: reduplication, metathesis or ablaut, syntactic analysis: nominal phrase with modifier(s), attested by IHTTC (9/7/77), also <**xwixweth'álem (sh)xwch'áletstel**>, //C$_{1}$í-x^{w}ɛ́θ'=ə[=Aɛ́=]l=əm (s)x^{w}=c'ɛ́=ləc=təl//, attested by Elders Group (6/1/77).

<**Xwíxweth'àlem**>, ds //C$_{1}$í-x^{w}ɛ́θ'=ə[=Aɛ́=]l=əm//, PLN [*'stone underwater Teeter-totter near X̲elháլh'*], ASM ['turned to stone by X̲à:ls'], phonology: reduplication, metathesis or ablaut, syntactic analysis: nominal, attested by IHTTC (9/7/77).

<**shxwth'ámqels**>, dnom //s=x^{w}ɛ́θ'=ə[=M2=]m=q=əls//, sas, TOOL ['*scissors*'], HHG, (<**s=** or **shxw=**> *nominalizer*), root <**xwáth'**> *teeter, rock*, <**=em**> *intransitivizer/have/get or middle voice*, possibly <**metathesis**> *continuative*, lx <**=q**> *closable container*, (<**=els**> *structured activity continuative device for*), phonology: possible metathesis, syntactic analysis: nominal, attested by Elders Group (2/11/76).

<**shxwth'ámqels qw'x̱wéltses/qw'x̱wélches**>, cpds //s=x^{w}ɛ́θ'=ə[=M2=]m=q=əls q'^{w}ix̣^{w}=ə[=´=]l=cəs or q'^{w}ə́x̣^{w}=ə[=M2=]l=cəs//, PE /'*fingernail clippers*'/, lit. "scissors for the fingernails", <**shxw=**> *nominalizer*), root <**xwáth'**> *teeter, rock*, <**=em**> *intransitivizer/have/get or middle voice*, possibly <**metathesis**> *continuative*, lx <**=q**> *closable container*, (<**=els**> *structured activity continuative device for*),. <**qw'íx̱w**> *dark brown*, <**=el=**> *plural*, <**=tses**> *on the hand*, attested by RG & EH (4/10/99 Ling332)

<**xwixweth'áletstel**>, df //C$_1$í-x^{w}ɛ́θ'=ə[=Aɛ́=]ləc=təl//, HHG ['*a rocking chair*'], literally /'device for rocking on the bottom duratively'/, (<**R4-**> *continuative*), (<**á-ablaut**> *durative*), lx <**=elets**> *on the bottom, on the rump*, lx <**=tel**> *device for*, phonology: reduplication, ablaut, syntactic analysis: nominal, attested by EB (2/28/78).

<**xwóxwth'**>, bound stem //x^{w}ɛ[=AaC$_1$ə=]θ'//, ABFC *teetered/rocked*

<**shxwóxwth'**>, strs //s=x^{w}ɛ[=AaC$_1$ə=]θ'//, EFAM /'*be crazy, be insane*'/, literally /'be teetered/rocked'/, (<**s=**> *stative*), (<**ó-ablaut plus =R1=**> *resultative*), phonology: ablaut, reduplication, syntactic analysis: adjective/adjectival verb, attested by Elders Group (3/3/76), EB (1/7/76), other sources: JH /sx̣^{w}áx̣^{w}c'/ *to be insane*, Salish cognate: prob. not Sechelt /x^{w}áx^{w}-wiwan-íl-əm/ *crazy* B77:56, not Saanich /sx^{w}áʔx^{w}ək'^{w}/ *crazy* B74a:46 nor Samish /sx^{w}éʔx^{w}ək'^{w}/ *to be crazy* G86a:76, also <**shxwó:xwth'**>, //s=x^{w}ɛ[=Aá·C$_1$ə=]θ'//, attested by EB (12/12/75), AC (11/11/71).

<**shxwixwóxwth'**>, dmv //s=C$_1$í=x^{w}ɛ[=AáC$_1$ə=]θ'//, EFAM /'*(be) stupid, not all there (mentally), (be) a little crazy*'/, literally /'a little bit teetered/rocked'/, (<**R4=**> *diminutive*), phonology: double reduplication, ablaut, syntactic analysis: adjective/adjectival verb, attested by AC (11/11/71), Elders Group (3/3/76), example: <**tu shxwixwóxwth'**>, //tu s=C$_1$í=x^{w}ɛ[=AáC$_1$ə=]θ'//, /'*a little bit crazy*'/, (semological comment: tu *a little bit, sort of*), attested by Elders Group.

<**xwoxwth'áleq[w]thom**>, pcs //x^{w}ɛ[=C$_1$ə=]θ'=a[=M2=]ləq^{w}=T-àm//, EFAM /'*you're crazy in the head, you're sick in the head*'/, literally /'you were purposely made teetering/crazy in the head'/, comment: q prob. mistranscribed for qw, (<**metathesis**> *derivational*), lx <**=óleqw**> *in the head*, (<**=t**> *purposeful control transitivizer*), (<**-òm**> *passive second person object/patient*), phonology: reduplication, metathesis, syntactic analysis: transitive verb, attested by Elders Group (1/16/80).

<**xwó:xwth'tem**>, pcs //x^{w}ɛ[=Aá·C$_1$ə=]θ'=T=əm//, EFAM ['*sexy*'], literally /'purposely get teetered/crazy'/, (<**=t**> *purposeful control transitivizer*), (<**=em**> *intransitivizer/have/get or ?middle voice*), phonology: ablaut, reduplication, syntactic analysis: intransitive verb, attested by EB (12/12/75).

<**xwoxwth'í:lem**>, mdls //x^{w}ɛ[=AaC$_1$ə=]θ'=í·l=əm//, SOCT /'*prostitute, whore*'/, literally /'(someone that) goes/comes/brings/gets oneself sexy (teetered/crazy)'/, (<**=í:l**> *go, come, get, become*), (<**=em**> *middle voice*), (<**zero**> *nominalizer*), phonology: ablaut, reduplication, zero nominalizer, syntactic analysis: nominal, attested by Elders Group (3/21/77).

<**xwáth'em**>, ABFC ['*to rock*'], *see* xwáth'.

<**Xwawíthí:m**>, df //x^{w}ɛ=wíθ=í·m//, PLN ['*place above Yale*'], possibly <**xwa=**> *become*, possibly root

<**wíth**> perhaps *call of sandpiper*, (<**=í:m**> *repeatedly*), syntactic analysis: nominal, attested by IHTTC (8/29/77)(those Tait speakers present incl. SP and AK).

<**xwá:ye**>, bound root or stem //x^{w}ɛ́·yə// *in the middle, in the center*

<**shxwá:ye**>, stvi //s=x^{w}ɛ́·yə//, DIR /'*be in the middle, be in the center*'/, (<**s=**> *stative*), syntactic analysis: adverb/adverbial verb, attested by Elders Group (8/20/75), example: <**tsel shxwá:ye.**>, //c-əl s=x^{w}ɛ́·yə//, /'*I'm in the middle/center.*'/, attested by Elders Group.

<**shxwá:ytses**>, dnom //s=x^{w}ɛ́·yə=cəs//, ANA /'*second finger, middle finger*'/, literally /'something to be in the middle on the hand'/, (<**s=**> *nominalizer, something to*), lx <**=tses**> *on the hand*, phonology: vowel-loss, syntactic analysis: nominal, attested by Elders Group (8/20/75).

<**xwayólem**>, df //x^{w}=ɛy=ál=əm//, SOC ['*gift one really makes use of*'], possibly <**xw=**> *always*, possibly root <**ey**> *good*, possibly <**=ól**> *just*, possibly <**=em**> *have/get/intransitivizer*, syntactic analysis: nominal, attested by Elders Group (4/21/76 esp. TG).

<**xwchém:és**>, TVMO ['*they met*'], *see* chó:m.

<**xwchém:est**>, TVMO ['*meet s-o*'], *see* chó:m.

<**Xwchí:yò:m**>, PLN /'*Cheam Island (my name for an island in the Fraser River across from Cheam Indian Reserve #2), Cheam village, Cheam Indian Reserve #1*'/, *see* schí:ya.

<**xwchókwel**>, TVMO /'*where is s-o going?, where is s-o travelling?, where is s-o headed for?*'/, *see* chá:l or chó:l.

<**xwch'alech'á:ls**>, FOOD ['*put on the stove (water/food)*'], *see* ts'á:.

<**xwch'áletsem**>, ABFC ['*have a seat*'], *see* ts'á:.

<**xwe=**>, da //x^{w}ə=//, ASP /'*become, get*'/, syntactic analysis: derivational prefix, lexical affix; found in <**xwe'éyem**>, //x^{w}ə=ʔɛ́y=əm//, /'*clear (of river water)*'/, root <**éy**> *good*, <**xwehíwel**>, //x^{w}ə=híwəl//, /'*go upstream*'/, root <**ahíw**> *upstream*, <**xwewqw'éylém**>, //x^{w}ə=wq'^{w}=ɛ́yl=ə́m//, /'*go downstream*'/, root <**wő̧qw'**> *drift downstream; drown*, <**xwtití:m**>, //x^{w}=tiyt=í·m//, /'*eddy water*'/, literally /'go upstream repeatedly'/, <**xwechá:l ~ xwchá:l**>, //x^{w}(ə)=cɛ́·l//, /'*where is someone going?*'/ (see root in <**chó:lt**> *follow behind someone)*, <**xwechókwel ~ xwchókwel**>, //x^{w}(ə)=cák^{w}əl//, /'*where is s-o headed?.*'/.

<**xwe ~ xwa**>, free root //x^{w}ə ~ x^{w}ɛ//, ASP /'*become, get*'/, syntactic analysis: auxiliary verb, syntactic comment: works as a prefix also with the same meaning, attested by EB, Elders Group, example: <**iyá:qtes te spó:l tl'ésu mé xwe swíyeqe.**>, //ʔiyɛ́·q=T-əs tə s=pá·l ƛ'a-s-u mə x^{w}ə s=wíq=ə//, /'*He changed a crow into a man.*'/, literally /'he changes it the crow and so it comes to become man'/, attested by EB (1/16/76), <**iyóqthet te skwówech esu xwe mestíyexw.**>, //ʔiyɛ[=Aá=]q=T-ət tə s=k^{w}áw(=)əc ʔə-s-u x^{w}ə məstíyəx^{w}//, /'*The sturgeon changed into a person.*'/, literally /'he changed himself the sturgeon and so become person'/, attested by EB (4/28/78), <**mé xwé híkw te thqá:t.**>, //mə x^{w}ə hík^{w} tə θqɛ́·t//, /'*The tree has gotten big (and tall).*'/, attested by EB (12/1/75), <**le xwá éy.**>, //lə x^{w}ɛ́ ʔɛ́y//, /'*It got better.*'/, attested by Elders Group (3/9/77); found in <**xwe'í:**>, //x^{w}ə=ʔí·//, /'*get here, arrive*'/, literally /'get/become here'/, attested by AC, many others, example: <**yalhtsel xwe'í:.**>, //yɛ=ɬ-c-əl x^{w}ə=ʔí·//, /'*I got back., (I just now got here/arrived.)*'/, attested by AC (9/1/71), <**lulh xwe'í te (swíwe, sthóqwi, kwő̧xweth).**>, //lə-uɬ x^{w}ə=ʔi tə (s=wíwə, s=θáq^{w}i, k^{w}óx^{w}=əθ)//, /'*The (eulachons, fish, cohos) are here now/running.*'/, attested by AC (11/17/71), <**li a sqwá:lewel kwes xwe'i:s wáy:eles?**>, //li ʔɛ s=q^{w}ɛ̀·l=iwəl k^{w}-əs x^{w}ə=ʔí·-s wɛ́y·əl=əs//, /'*Do you think they'll come tomorrow?*'/, attested by AC (9/18/71).

<**xwechà:l**>, TVMO /'*where did he go?, where is he/she/etc.?*'/, *see* chá:l ~ chó:l.

<**xwehíwel**>, DIR ['*go upstream*'], *see* ahíw.

<**xwehó**> or <qwehá>, possible root or stem //xʷəh// meaning uncertain or //qʷəhɛ́// *go through a tunnel/hole*

<**shxwehóméllhelh**>, df //s=xʷəh=áməl=ɬəɬ or sxʷ=qʷəhɛ=áməl=ɬəɬ//, ANA ['*adam's apple*'], literally perhaps /'something that goes through a tunnel/hole part in the windpipe/throat'/, (<**shxw=** or **s=**> *something that*), possibly root <**qwehá**> *go through a tunnel/hole*, possibly root <**xweh**> meaning uncertain, lx <**=óméł**> *part of (body)*, lx <**=lhelh**> *in the windpipe/throat*, phonology: possible vowel merger, possible consonant merger, syntactic analysis: nominal, attested by Elders Group (8/20/75).

<**xwekw'á:ls**>, SOC /'*to drag (for a body in the river, for ex.)*'/, *see* xwókw' ~ xwekw'ó.

<**xwékw'est**>, ABFC ['*dragging s-o/s-th*'], *see* xwókw' ~ xwekw'ó.

<**xwekw'ó:st**>, ABFC ['*drag s-th/s-o*'], *see* xwókw' ~ xwekw'ó.

<**xwekw'ót**>, ABFC ['*drag s-th/s-o*'], *see* xwókw' ~ xwekw'ó.

<**xwel**>, free root //xʷəl//, QUAL ['*still*'], phonology: unstressed/low tone, syntactic analysis: adverb/adverbial verb, syntactic comment: usually preposed to the word it modifies, attested by AC, Deming (6/22/78), EB, CT and HT (6/21/76), Elders Group (3/29/78), AH (Deming 2/8/79), Salish cognate: perhaps Lushootseed /x̣ʷul'/ *merely, just that and nothing else* (adverb, usually preposed) H76:620, example: <**li xwel emí te slháqwems?**>, //li xʷəl ʔə=mí tə s=ɬɛ́qʷ=əm-s//, /'*Is he/she still breathing?*'/, literally /'does it still come the his/her breath'/, attested by AC (8/14/70), <**lí xwel áyelexw?**>, //lí xʷəl ʔɛ́y=ləxʷ//, /'*Is he still alive?*'/, attested by AC (8/15/70), <**xwel x̲ex̲é:yls**>, //xʷəl C_1ə-x̣íl=əls//, /'*still writing*'/, attested by Deming, <**xwel isá:le.**>, //xʷəl ʔisɛ́·lə//, /'*There's only two., There's just two.*'/, literally /'there's still two'/, attested by EB (5/12/78), <**xwel qéx̲.**>, //xʷəl qə́x̣//, /'*There's still lots.*'/, attested by EB (5/12/78), <**le xwel totí:ltes té sqwéltels.**>, //lə xʷəl tá[-C_1ə-]l=í·l=T-əs tə s=qʷɛ[=Aə́=]l=təl-s//, /'*He's still learning his language.*'/, attested by CT and HT (6/21/76), <**lúw xwel ő̃westexw.**>, //lə=əw xʷəl ʔówə=sT-əxʷ//, /'*He's still denying someone.*'/, attested by Elders Group, <**xwel í te lhíxw sléxwelh.**>, //xʷəl ʔí tə ɬíxʷ s=lə́xʷ=wəɬ//, /'*Three canoes are still here.*'/, attested by AH (Deming 2/8/79), <**xwel sts'ets'á te stiqí:w.**>, //xʷəl s=C_1əC_2=c'ɛ́ tə s=tiqí·w//, /'*He's still astride the horse.*'/, attested by EB (3/1/76), <**xwel x̲éyth' te sqw'él.**>, //xʷəl x̣í:θ' tə s=q'ʷə́l//, /'*Your cooking is not done.*'/, literally /'still is uncooked/unripe the cooking'/, attested by Elders Group (3/5/80), <**xwel tsqwá:y.**>, //xʷəl c=qʷɛ́·y//, /'*It's still green.*'/, attested by Deming (SJ esp. 5/3/79).

<**xwelá ~ xwelám ~ xwlá ~ xwlám**>, DIR /'*toward, towards, for*'/, *see* la.

<**xwélalà:m ~ xwélalàm**>, ABFC ['*listening*'], *see* xwlalá:.

<**xwelált**>, TIME ['*become evening*'], *see* lá:t.

<**xweláltelh**>, TIME ['*last night*'], *see* lá:t.

<**xwelám**>, df //xʷ(ə)=lɛ́=m//, DIR ['*toward*'], possibly <**xw=**> *toward*, possibly <**xwe=**> *get, become*, possibly root <**lá(=m)**> *go to, going to*, (<**=m**> *middle voice*), syntactic analysis: preposition/prepositional verb, attested by EB, others, see under stem <**lá=m**> *go to, going to*, Salish cognate: in part perhaps Nooksack /txʷ=/ or /xʷ=/ both *toward* Galloway, Adams & Renteria 2004a, perhaps Lushootseed //dxʷ-ʔal// /txʷəl/ *toward* H76:148, example: <**tiyéléstchexw ta' q'éwe xwelám te t'ómél.**>, //tiy=ə[= ´=]l=əs=T-c-əxʷ t-ɛʔ q'ə́wə xʷ(ə)=lɛ́=m tə t'áməl//, /'*Lean your cane against the wall.*'/, literally /'you lean it purposely your cane toward the wall'/, attested by EB.

<**xwélchep**> or <**xw**>, possible stem or root //xʷɛ́l=ə́lcəp// *lift/hoist firewood*

<**shxwélchep**>, df //s=xʷ(=)ə́lcəp or /s=xʷɛ́l=ə́lcəp//, FIRE /'*home-made lantern (using candle in a can with a hole in it, etc.), jack-o-lantern*'/, LT, HHG, (<**s=**> *nominalizer, something to*), possibly <**shxw=**> *nominalizer, something for*, root probably same as in <**xwà:lx**> *lift up s-th, lift [s-th], hoist [s-th] up*'/, lx <**=élchep**> *firewood*, syntactic analysis: nominal, attested by TG (Elders Group 2/6/80), contrast <**swáchet**> *lantern, torch*, Salish cognate: Squamish /sxʷáčit/ *torch, light, lamp* only with Halkomelem <**swáchet**> *lantern, torch*, not with <**shxwélchep**>.

<**xwélekw'**>, free root or stem //xʷə́l(=)ək'ʷ//, SH ['*to wrap*'], root meaning uncertain unless <xwà:l> *lift*, lx <**=kw' ~ =ekw'**> *round, around in circles*, syntactic analysis: intransitive verb, attested by Deming (6/22/78), Salish cognate: Lushootseed /xʷəlk'ʷ/ *wrap around; intoxicated* H76:560, also <**xwélkw'**>, free root //xʷə́lk'ʷ//, WATR, also /'*to eddy*'/, (semological comment: probably in context of /*water, to wrap around* → *to eddy*), attested by EB (3/22/76).

<**xwélekw't**>, pcs //xʷə́l=ək'ʷ=T//, SH ['*wrap s-th*'], ABFC, (<**=t**> *purposeful control transitivizer*), syntactic analysis: transitive verb, attested by Deming (6/22/78), contrast <**xélekw't**> *roll it*, Salish cognate: Lushootseed /xʷə́lək'ʷ-əd/ *wrap it up* H76:560.

<**xwelxwélekw't**>, plv //C_1əC_2=xʷə́l=ək'ʷ=T//, SH /'*wrap it again, rewrap it, (correction by AD:) roll it up (of a mat, carpet, etc.)*'/, ABFC, (<**R3=**> *plural action*), phonology: reduplication, syntactic analysis: transitive verb, attested by Deming (6/22/78), AD (3/10/80).

<**shxwelókw'**>, strs //s=xʷəl=ə[=Aá=]k'ʷ//, SH ['*(be) wrapped*'], DESC, (<**s=**> *stative*), (<**ó-ablaut**> *resultative*), phonology: ablaut, syntactic analysis: adjective/adjectival verb, attested by Deming (6/22/78).

<**xwelókw'stexw ~ shxwelókw'stexw**>, caus //(s=)xʷəl=ə[=Aá=]k'ʷ=sT-əxʷ//, SH ['*keep it wrapped*'], (<**=st**> *causative control transitivizer*), (<**-exw**> *third person object*), phonology: ablaut, syntactic analysis: transitive verb, attested by Deming (6/22/78).

<**xwelkw'ím**>, rpts //xʷəl=ək'ʷ=ím//, WATR ['*eddy (in water)*'], lx <**=ím**> *repeatedly*, syntactic analysis: intransitive verb, nominal??, attested by Elders Group (3/72).

<**xwélekw't**>, SH ['*wrap s-th*'], *see* xwélekw'.

<**xwelemő̂welh ~ xwlemő̂welh**>, TVMO ['*get hit on the back*'], *see* ló:m ~ lóm.

<**xwelí ~ xwlí**>, DIR /'*get there, arrive there, reach there*'/, *see* lí.

<**xwelí**> or <**eli(y)**>, possible root //xʷəlí// meaning uncertain or //ʔəli(y)// *dream, vision* or //ʔɛ́y// *keep on going* (root of /ʔɛ́y(=)ləxʷ/ *be alive, healthy, live*).

<**shxwelí**>, df //s=xʷəlí or sxʷ=ʔəli= ´//, REL /'*soul, spirit of a living person*'/, possibly <**s=**> *nominalizer, something to*, possibly <**shxw=**> *something for/that, nominalizer*, possibly root <**eli**> *dream* (as in <**élíyá**>, df //ʔə́lí(?=í)yɛ́//, REL /'*to dream, have a vision*'/), possibly <**= ´**> *derivational*, phonology: possible stress-shift, syntactic analysis: nominal, attested by BJ (12/5/64 new transcript old p.328), Elders Group (11/19/75), other sources: ES /šxʷəlí ~ sxʷáyəlxʷ/ (CwMs /šxʷəlí/) *life, soul*, Salish cognate: Sechelt /sxʷʔáy'i/ *soul, life spirit* B77:32, Samish dial. of NSt /səlí/ *soul* G86a:81, Saan. dial. of NSt /səlí/ *soul* (vs. /ʔéy'le/ *life spirit* B74a:26 which is cognate perhaps with Squamish /s-ʔáy-nəxʷ/ *life, spirit* W73:162, K67:303, K69:94 and Upriver Halkomelem /ʔɛ́y(=)ləxʷ/ *be alive, healthy, live*).

<**xwelí:ls**>, DIR /'*get to, reach there*'/, *see* lí.

<**xwelítem**>, us //xʷəlítəm or xʷə(=)lí(=)t(=)əm//, SOCT /'*White person, (Caucasian), White man*'/, root meaning uncertain but suggested by two elders to be <**xwá**>, free root //xʷɛ́//, ABDF /'*starve, be*

starving, be famished, (be extremely hungry since the first Whites were often in this state when they arrived, always asking about food, etc.; another elder suggested the word was related to the Chinook Jargon word for *bullet* (which I cannot find in Johnson 1978), syntactic analysis: nominal, attested by AC, BJ (12/5/64), BHTTC (11/19/76), Elders Group, Deming, others, other sources: ES /xʷəlítəm/ *white man*, Salish cognate: Squamish /xʷalítn/ *White person* W73:288, K67:349, Sechelt /xʷalítn/ *White person* T77:17, Saanich dial. of NSt /xʷnítəm/ *White person* B74a:30, Samish dial. of NSt (VU) /xʷənítəm ~ xʷənítəm'/ *White person* G86a:80, Lushootseed /xʷəltəb/ *Caucasian* H76:561, comparative note: the inconsistency in l vs. n and final n vs. m among the seeming cognates probably show diffusion, example: **<lichxw we'éy 'el qwóqwel kw'es me kwetxwílem te xwelítem?>**, //li-c-xʷ wə=ʔɛ́y ʔəl qʷɛ[-AáC_1ə-]l k'ʷ-əs mə kʷətɛxʷ=íl=əm tə xʷəlítəm//, /'*Were you still talking when the White man came in? (come inside)*'/, attested by AC (9/30/71).

<**xwelitemáwtxw**>, ds //xʷəlítəm=ɛ́wtxʷ//, BLDG ['*lumber house*'], literally /'White man house/building'/, lx <**=áwtxw**> *house, building*, syntactic analysis: nominal, attested by Elders Group (6/28/78).

<**xwelítemelh**>, ds ///xʷəlítəm=əɬɬ//, SOCT /'according to the White man, White man fashion'/, lx <=elh> *according to the ways of, -style, -fashion*; found in <**xwelítemelh skw'ő:lmexwelhp**>, EB /'*Himalaya blackberry bush, evergreen blackberry bush*'/, *see* skw'ő:lmexw

<**xwelítemelh sókw'**>, EB /'*celery*'/, FOOD, (lit. white man style inner core of cow parsnip (i.e., yó:le), (attested by RG,EH 6/16/98 to SN, edited by BG with RG,EH 6/26/00)

<**xwelítemelh x̲eyeslótel** (or) **kw'ókw'es kwémlexw s'élhtel**>, EB /'*ginger*'/, FOOD (lit. white man style + wild ginger (or) hot + root + food), (attested by RG,EH 6/16/98 to SN, edited by BG with RG,EH 6/26/00)

<**xwelítemelh yó:le**>, EB /'*asparagus*'/, FOOD, (lit. white man style + cow parsnip), (attested by RG,EH 6/16/98 to SN, edited by BG with RG,EH 6/26/00)

<**xwelítemelh sqwà:l**>, LANG /'*English language*'/, attested by RG & EH (4/10/99 Ling332)

<**shxwelítemelh méxts'el**>, cpds //s=xʷəlítəm=əɬ méxʸ(=)c'(=)əl//, EZ ['*common bedbug*'], ['*Cimex lectularius*'], ABDF, literally /'Whiteman style/kind of louse'/, (<**s=**> *stative*), lx <**=elh**> *style, kind of, in the fashion of*, syntactic analysis: adjective/adjectival verb nominal, attested by BHTTC, Elders Group, Deming.

<**xwelítemqel**>, ds //xʷəlítəm=qəl//, LANG /'*the White man's language, the English language*'/, lx <**=qel**> *language*, syntactic analysis: nominal, attested by AC (10/6/71, 11/10/71), RG & EH (4/10/99 Ling332), example: <**mőkw' xwelítemqel.**>, //mə́k'ʷ xʷəlítəm=qəl//, /'*They all spoke English.*'/, literally /'everybody White man language'/, attested by AC (11/10/71).

<**xwelitemáwtxw**>, BLDG ['*lumber house*'], *see* xwelítem.

<**xwelítemelh skw'ő:lmexwelhp**>, EB /'*Himalaya blackberry bush, evergreen blackberry bush*'/, *see* skw'ő:lmexw.

<**xwelítemqel**>, LANG /'*the White man's language, the English language*'/, *see* xwelítem.

<**Xwelíwiya**>, dmn //xʷəlíw=iyɛ//, N ['*Seagull*'], ASM ['name of a character in a story'], root meaning unknown, (<**=iya**> *affectionate diminutive*), syntactic analysis: nominal, attested by Deming (4/12/79), see under stem <**Qwolíwiya**.

<**xwelkw'ím**>, WATR ['*eddy (in water)*'], *see* xwélekw'.

<**xwélmexw**>, df //xʷə́l(=)məxʷ or xʷə[=´=]l=məxʷ//, SOCT /'*Indian person, (North American) Indian*'/, root meaning unknown unless xwel *still*, lx <**=mexw**> *person, people*, possibly <=´=> *derivational*,

phonology: possible stress-shift, syntactic analysis: nominal, attested by AC (11/10/71, 12/7/71), EB (11/26/75, 1/9/76, 2/13/78), others, other sources: ES /xʷə́lmə́xʷ/ *Indian*, JH /xʷílmə̀xʷ/ *Indian*, H-T <Qu'l'muq> (macron over second u) *Indian*, Salish cognate: Saanich dial. of NSt /(ʔə)xʷílŋəxʷ/ *Indian* B74a:30, not Squamish /s-tə́l-məxʷ/ *Indian* W73:149, K67:281, not Lushootseed /ʔáciɬtəbixʷ/ *person; Indian* H76:643, not Sechelt /s-qál-mixʷ/ *Indian* T77:17, not Samish dial. of NSt /ʔəɬtélŋəxʷ/ *people, tribe* G86a:105, also <**xwélméxw** or **xwèlmèxw**>, //xʷə́l=məxʷ//, phonology: updrifting, downdrifting, attested by EB, also <**xwémlexw**>, //xʷə́l=m[=M1=]əxʷ//, attested by TM, example: <**lám te xwélmexw las ehá:we té tl'alqtéle li te thá.**>, //lɛ́=m tə xʷə́l=məxʷ lɛ-s ʔəhɛ́·wə təƛ̕'ɛ[=lə=]qt=ə́lə li tə θɛ́//, /'*Indians go hunting deer there.*'/, attested by AC (12/7/71), <**t'it'elemetes the xwélmexw q'á:mi te pésk'a st'í:lem.**>, //t'í[-C_1ə-]l=əməT-əs θə xʷə́l=məxʷ q'ɛ́·m=iy tə pə́sk'ɛ s=t'í·l=əm//, /'*The adolescent Indian girl sings the hummingbird song.*'/, attested by EB (2/13/78) approved this sentence constructed by a class member, <**qélchap xwélmexw.**>, //qə́l-c-ɛp xʷə́l=məxʷ//, /'*You're bad people.*'/, literally /'you're bad Indian people'/, attested by EB (11/26/75), <**qél yé xwèlmèxw.**>, //qə́l yə xʷə̀lmə́xʷ (or xʷə̀lmə̀xʷ)//, /'*The people are bad., (They are) bad people.*'/, literally /'is/are bad the (plural human) Indian person'/, attested by EB (11/26/75), <**lhéq'elh x̱ét'e yé xwèlmèxw.**>, //ɬə́q'=əɬ x̣ə́t'ə yə xʷə́l=məxʷ//, /'*The people used to say.*'/, attested by EB (1/9/76). Contrast <**ó:wqw'elmexw** or **ó:wkw'elmexw**>, *a group of people, a tribe of people, several tribes.*

<**ts'xwélmexw ~ ts'xwílmexw**>, df //c'=xʷə́lməxʷ or c'xʷ=xʷə́lməxʷ or c'xʷ=ə́lməxʷ ~ c'íxʷ[=M1=]=əl(=)məxʷ//, SOCT [*'friends'*], probably root <**xwelmexw**>, possibly root or compounded <**ts'íxw ~ th'íxw**> *pity, help*, possibly <**ts= ~ ch= ~ ts'=**> *stative (with color terms), have, get (elsewhere)*, possibly <**metathesis**> *derivational*, possibly <**=el=**> *plural*, lx <**=élmexw**> *people* or lx <**=mexw**> *person*, phonology: possible metathesis, syntactic analysis: nominal, attested by RP and NP (5/4/76).

<**xwelmexwáwtxw**>, ds //xʷəlməxʷ=ɛ́wtxʷ//, BLDG /'*longhouse, smokehouse (for spirit-dancing, etc.), Indian house, plank house*'/, literally /'Indian house/building'/, lx <**=áwtxw**> *house, building*, syntactic analysis: nominal, attested by AC (8/8/70), Elders Group (1/8/75, 11/12/75, 1/21/76, 6/28/78).

<**xwelméxwqel**>, ds //xʷəlmə́xʷ=qəl//, LANG /'*an Indian language, talk Indian*'/, lx <**=qel**> *language*, phonology: possible stress-shift, syntactic analysis: nominal; intransitive verb?, attested by AC (10/6/71, 11/13/71), others, example: <**tl'os'ésuw xwelméxwqel li tethá sew qwàl te lólets'e.**>, //ƛ̕'a-s-ə́s-əw xʷəlmə́xʷ=qəl li tə=θɛ́ s-əw qʷɛ̀l tə C_1á=ləc'ə//, /'*Then the announcer/master of ceremonies speaks in Indian there.*'/, literally /'then he contrastive talks Indian in there so spoke the one person'/, attested by AC (11/10/71).

<**xwelmexwáwtxw**>, BLDG /'*longhouse, smokehouse (for spirit-dancing, etc.), Indian house, plank house*'/, *see* xwélmexw.

<**xwelméxwqel**>, LANG /'*an Indian language, talk Indian*'/, *see* xwélmexw.

<**xwelókw'stexw ~ shxwelókw'stexw**>, SH [*'keep it wrapped'*], *see* xwélekw'.

<**xwélp'**>, df //xʷə́l=p'//, ABFC [*'to fan'*], root meaning unknown, lx <**=p'**> *on itself*, syntactic analysis: intransitive verb, attested by IHTTC (7/5/77).

<**xwélp'es**>, ds //xʷə́l=p'=əs//, ABFC [*'to fan in the face'*], lx <**=es**> *on the face*, syntactic analysis: intransitive verb, attested by IHTTC (7/5/77).

<**xwélp't**>, pcs //xʷə́l=p'=T//, ABFC /'*fan s-o, brush s-o with a branch*'/, ASM ['brushing s-o/s-th with a bough is sometimes done by ritualists or shamans to brush away unwanted spirits from a person or place'], (<**=t**> *purposeful control transitivizer*), syntactic analysis: transitive verb, attested by

IHTTC (7/5/77); found in <**xwélp'tem**>, //x^{w}ə́l=p'=T-əm//, /'*(s-o was) brushed with branch*'/, attested by IHTTC (7/5/77).

<**xwélp'tel**>, dnom //x^{w}ə́l=p'=təl//, HHG ['*a fan*'], ASM ['originally made of grouse tail tied open at base and dried; I was given one of these at a Fish Camp'], lx <**=tel**> *device to*, syntactic analysis: nominal, attested by IHTTC (7/6/77).

<**xwélp'es**>, ABFC ['*to fan in the face*'], *see* xwélp'.

<**xwélp't**>, ABFC /'*fan s-o, brush s-o with a branch*'/, *see* xwélp'.

<**xwélp'tel**>, HHG ['*a fan*'], *see* xwélp'.

<**xwélwels**>, probable bound stem //x^{w}ə́lw(=)əls//, meaning uncertain

<**shxwélwels**>, df //s=x^{w}ə́lw(=)əls//, sas, HHG ['*container*'], (<**s=**> *something that*), root meaning unknown, (<**=els**> *structured activity continuative nominal*), syntactic analysis: nominal, attested by CT and HT (6/21/76), Salish cognate: perhaps Lushootseed /sk^{w}ədúlč/ *container* (LG) from root /k^{w}əd(á)/ *take, get, hold* H76:246, example: <**lhq'átseqel shxwélwels**>, //ɬq'ɛ́=cs=əqəl s=x^{w}ə́lw=əls//, /'*five containers*'/, attested by CT and HT.

<**xwelxwélekw't**>, SH /'*wrap it again, rewrap it, (correction by AD:) roll it up (of a mat, carpet, etc.)*'/, *see* xwélekw'.

<**xwém ~ x̱wém**>, free root //x^{w}ə́m ~x̣^{w}ə́m//, TVMO /'*be fast, hurry*'/, see under stem <**x̱wém**> *be fast, hurry*.

<**xwemá**>, MC ['*open*'], *see* má ~ má'-.

<**xwemá:qet**>, HHG /'*take a cover off, take it off (a cover of a container), open it (bottle, box, kettle, book, etc.)*'/, *see* má ~ má'-.

<**xwemá:t**>, MC ['*open it*'], *see* má ~ má'-.

<**xwématsel ~ xwémetsel**>, bound stem //x^{w}ə́m=əcəl// or //qwómetsel// *lump on the back*

<**shxwématsel ~ shxwémetsel**>, df //s=x^{w}ə́m=əcəl//or //shxw=qwómetsel//, EZ /'*fisher, an animal close to a mink, animal like an otter*'/, ['*Martes pennanti pennanti*'], (<**s=**> *nominalizer, something to*), possibly root <**kwém**> *lump*, possibly root <**xwem**> *fast* or <qwem> *lump*, lx <**=etsel**> *on the back, on the surface, on top*, phonology: possible spirantization, syntactic analysis: nominal, attested by Elders Group (9/1/76, 3/21/79), other sources: H-T <Cwo'mEtsEl> *otter*, Salish cognate: possibly? Thompson /n=wan=íkn'/ *fisher* B74c:9, also (probably) /'*wolverine*'/, attested by Elders Group (2/11/76), also <**shxwémétsel**>, //s=x^{w}ə́m=ə́cəl//, also EZ ['*wolverine*'], ['*Gulo luscus luscus*'], Elder's comment: "so named because it has a hunch-back", attested by ME (11/21/72 tape) (compare <**sqwómetsel**>, stvi //s=q^{w}ám=əcəl//, ABDF ['*get hunchbacked*']),

<**xwéma'à:ls**>, BLDG ['*doorman*'], *see* má ~ má'-.

<**xwema'à:ls**>, BLDG ['*open the door*'], *see* má ~ má'-.

<**xwémlexw**>, ncs //x^{w}ə́m=l-əx^{w} or x^{w}ə=mɛ́=l-əx^{w}//, SOC ['*did s-o a favor*'], root meaning uncertain but perhaps from <**xwemá**> *open*, (<**=l**> *non-control transitivizer (accidentally, manage to)*), (<**-exw**> *third person object*), phonology: possible vowel loss, syntactic analysis: transitive verb, attested by Deming (5/6/76); found in <**xwemlóx**>, //x^{w}əm=l-áx^{y}//, /'*did me a favor*'/, dialects: *Chill.*, attested by Deming (5/6/76), also <**xwemlómx**>, //x^{w}əm=l-ámx^{y}//, attested by Deming (5/6/76).

<**shxwémlexw**>, stvi //s=x^{w}ə́m=l-əx^{w} or s=x^{w}ə=mɛ́=l-əx^{w}//, SOC ['*did s-o a favor*'], (<**s=**> *stative*), syntactic analysis: transitive verb, attested by IHTTC (9/16/77), TM/DF/NP/TG (Elders Group 3/22/78), Deming (5/6/76); found in <**shxwemlóxchexw.**>, //s=x^{w}əm=l-áx^{y}-c-əx^{w}//, /'*You did me a*

favor., Thank you.'/, attested by IHTTC, <**(sh)xwemlómxchexw.**>, //(s=)xʷəm=l-ámxʸ-c-əxʷ//, /'*You did me a favor.*'/, dialects: *Matsqui*, attested by Deming, example: <**Le th'exwstélemet ó siyám. Maytólxwchexw. Th'exwmetólxwchexw, lálh tstulh t-sós. Qéx̲ te shxwhókwixtset. Shxwemlólxwchexw. Yalhixw kw'a's hóy.**>, //lə θ'əxʷ=sT-ə́ləmət ʔá s=iy=ɛ́m. mɛy=T-álxʷ-c-əxʷ. θ'əxʷ=məT-álxʷ-c-əxʷ, lɛ́-ɬ c-t-uɬ tsás. qə́x̣ tə sxʷ=hákʷ=əxʸ-c-ət. s=xʷəm=l-álxʷ-c-əxʷ. yɛɬ-i-xʷ k'ʷ-ɛʔ-s háy//, /'*Pity us, oh Lord. Help us. Pity us, we're getting unfortunate. We'll use it in many ways. You did us a favor. Thank you.*'/, usage: words or prayer said to plants before picking for medicine, bark, etc., attested by TM/DF/NP (Elders Group 3/22/78).

<**xwemlí:kw**>, possible bound stem //xʷəmlí·kʷ//, root meaning unknown unless related to xweml- as in xwémlexw *do s-o a favor*

<**shxwemlí:kw**>, df //s=xʷəmlí·kʷ//, KIN /'*parent's cousin, parent's sibling, uncle, aunt*'/, (<**s=**> *nominalizer*), root meaning unknown, syntactic analysis: nominal, attested by Elders Group (6/8/77), AC (9/29/71, 11/16/71), other sources: ES /šxʷəmlí·kʷ/ *parent's sibling*, H-T <sQumEle'k·Q ~ cwumEle'k·Q> (macron over both e) *uncle* and <t'scumEle'k·Q> (macron over e) *aunt* and <lek·Q> (macron over e) *uncle/aunt (term of address).*

<**shxwemlá:lekw**>, pln //s=xʷəmli[=Aɛ́·=lə=]kʷ//, KIN /'*uncles (all of them), aunts (all of them)*'/, (<**á:-ablaut and =le= infix**> *plural (collective)*), phonology: ablaut, infixed =le=, syntactic analysis: nominal, attested by AC (9/29/71), example: <**tl'ó a shxwemlá:lekw.**>, //ƛ'á ʔɛ s=xʷəmli[=Aɛ́·=lə=]kʷ//, /'*That's your uncles/aunts.*'/, attested by AC.

<**xwemthiy**>, possible bound stem //xwəm=θiy-//, meaning unknown unless related to root in shxwemlí:kw *parent's cousin, parent's sibling, uncle, aunt.*

<**shxwemthiyà:lh**>, //s=xʷəm=θiy=ɛ̀·ɬ or /s=xʷəm=qθiy=ɛ̀·ɬ//, /'*deceased uncle or aunt or grandparent or someone responsible for you directly or indirectly*'/, <**=à:lh ~ =elh**> *late (deceased);, past tense*, perhaps compare <**qethiyálh**>, df //qəθiy=ɛ́ɬ//, KIN /'*deceased uncle, deceased grand-uncle*'/. phonology: possible consonant loss of <**q**> between <**m**> of prefix and <**th**> of root, compare Samish dial. of N. Straits LD /qsəčé·ɬ/ (VU /qsəčéləɬ/) *deceased parent's sibling* G86:79, Lushootseed /qəsíʔ/ *uncle, male sibling of either parent while that parent is living* H76:382 (which show that <**qethiyálh**> has root <qethiy> with basic meaning of *uncle* + =álh *deceased, past tense)*, as does possibly <**shxwemthiyà:lh**>.

<**shxwemxwemthiyá:lh**>, //s=C_1əC_2=xʷəm=qθiy=ɛ́·ɬ//, /'*deceased uncles or aunts or grandparents responsible for someone*'/,

<**xwemxálem**>, ds //x̣ʷ[=K=]əm=xʸə[=Aɛ́=]l=əm//, ABFC ['*to run*'], see under root <**x̲wém ~ xwém**> *be fast, hurry.*

<**xwémxel**>, WETH /'*raining hard, pouring rain, (raining fast)*'/, *see* x̲wém ~ xwém *be fast, hurry.*

<**xweqw'él:a**>, df //xʷ[=F=]əq'ʷ=ə́l·ɛ//, EB ['*scouring rush*'], ['*Equisetum hiemale*'], literally perhaps /'hang-over'/, ASM ['(each round reed comes up alone, jointed pink and black at joints when young, green with black joints when older); can break the reed at the joints and suck water from them (Elders Group)'], root meaning uncertain but probably <**x̲wíqw'**>, bound root //x̣ʷíq'ʷ *tie up and hang, tie around*//, as in <**x̲wíqw'esem**> *hang oneself*, lx <**=él:a**> *in the temples*, compare <**xweqw'éle'á:ltel**> *hang-over medicine; small-flowered alumroot*, phonology: probable fronting, syntactic analysis: nominal, attested by Elders Group (7/2/75), Salish cognate: perhaps Squamish root /x̣ʷəq'ʷ ~x̣ʷiq'ʷ/ *be tied* as in /x̣ʷíq'ʷ-us-m/ *hang oneself* W73:129, K69:87.

<**xweqw'ele'á:ltel**>, df //xʷ[=F=]əq'ʷ=əlɛ=ʔɛ́·l(=)təl//, MED ['*hang-over medicine*'], EB /'*small-flowered alumroot,* (and possibly) *smooth Heuchera*'/, ['*Heuchera micrantha*, and possibly *Heuchera glabra* or hybrid'], MED ['used as medicine for hang-over, for "thrush" (white coating in

a baby's mouth), and for trenchmouth'], literally perhaps /'hung/tied around-in the temples medicine'/, root probably <**x̲wíqw'**>, bound root //x̣ʷíq'ʷ *tie up and hang, tie around*//, lx <**=el:a**> *in the temples*, lx <**=á:ltel**> *medicine*, phonology: probably fronting, compare <**th'el='á:ltel**> *heart medicine* for the same suffix, phonology: epenthetic glottal stop, syntactic analysis: nominal, attested by SP and AK (7/13/75).

<**xweqw'ele'á:ltel**>, MED ['*hang-over medicine*'], *see* xweqw'él:a.

<**xwéqw'ethet**>, ABFC /'*crawling (as of snake, seal, slug, snail), (dragging oneself)*'/, *see* xwókw' ~ xwekw'ó.

<**Xweqw'oyíqw**>, df //xʷəq'ʷ=ayíqʷ or xʷə=q'ʷay=íqʷ//, PLN ['*Echo Island in Harrison Lake*'], ASM ['this island is in the southern end of the lake and is so named in English because one can hear one's voice echo from the island from a point/points on the western shore of the island, especially at <**X̲wix̲we'áqel**> *Echo Point* (which means *imitating the voice* in Halkomelem), there are also rocks shaped like a bear and a horned owl at Echo Point'], possibly lx <xwe=> *become*, root meaning unknown unless <qw'óy> an old form of <q'óy> *die*, or possibly <**x̲wíqw'**>, bound root //x̣ʷíq'ʷ *tie up and hang, tie around*// instead , lx <**=oyíqw**> meaning uncertain or more likely <=íqw> *on top of the head*, semantic comment: possible if reference is to the two stone heads of bear and owl there or to a place of ritually tying headbands around the top of the head, syntactic analysis: nominal, attested by EL (Chehalis trip with EB and NP also 9/27/77), source: place names file reference #313, also <**Xwōqw'oyíqw**>, //xʷəq'ʷ=ayíqʷ or xʷə=q'ʷay=íqʷ//, attested by EL (3/1/78 Stó:lō Sítel tape), also <**Xweqwoyíqw**>, //xʷəqʷ=ayíqʷ or xʷə=qʷay=íqʷ// (poss. lit. **'**become yellow on top of the head**'**–this etymology not suggested by an elder), attested by EL (Harrison River and Lake placenames boat trip 6/27/78), also <**Xwōqwiyáqw**>, //xʷəqʷ=iyɛ́qʷ//, comment: probably mistranscribed though possibly metathesis of last two vowels, source: place names file reference #120, attested by EL with Elders Group (Harrison Lake boat trip to Port Douglas 6/18/75).

<**xwesá:lews**>, EB ['*leaves falling*'], *see* xwís.

<**xwét**>, free root //xʷə́t//, EZ /'*Swainson's thrush, the salmonberry bird*'/, ['*Hylocichla ustulata ustulata*'], ASM ['this bird is famed for pecking holes in berry baskets to get salmonberries, it hangs out near salmonberry bushes (and has a call that sounds very much like a single "xwét" whistled), also identified from photos in Udvardy (by Deming elders), in a story this is the name of their call too, it makes these calls when the salmonberries are ripe, always eats berries, punches holes in berry baskets (IHTTC)'], SD ['*call of the Swainson's thrush*'], syntactic analysis: noun, nominal, attested by Deming (5/24/79), LG and SJ (Deming 4/12/79), IHTTC (8/23/77), Salish cognate: Squamish /xʷə́t/ *Swainson's thrush* B78:18 and Kennedy and Bouchard 1976:97-99, Lushootseed /s-xʷə́t/ *thrush, salmonberry bird* H76:562.

<**Xwét**>, free root //xʷə́t//, N /'*Male Salmonberry Bird, (Male Swainson's Thrush)*'/, ASM ['also the name of its call'], usage: name in a story, syntactic analysis: noun, nominal, attested by IHTTC (8/23/77).

<**Xwatóy**>, ds //xʷə[=Aɛ=]t=áy(ɛ)//, N /'*Female Salmonberry Bird, (Female Swainson's Thrush)*'/, SD ['*the call of the female Swainson's thrush*'], usage: name in a story, (<**a-ablaut**> *derivational*), possibly <**=óya**> *affectionate diminutive, female name ending*, possibly <**=óy**> meaning uncertain, phonology: possible ablaut, possible vowel-loss, syntactic analysis: nominal, attested by IHTTC (8/23/77).

<**Xwét**>, N /'*Male Salmonberry Bird, (Male Swainson's Thrush)*'/, *see* xwét.

<**xwetáqt**>, pcs //xʷə=tɛ́q=T or xʷɛ́t=ə[=M2=]q=T//, ABFC /'*put it down, take it down (s-th on the wall*

for ex.)'/, HHG, probably <**xwe=**> *become*, probably root <**táq**> *close*, possibly root <**xwát**> *make it lighter, lessen the load, take it off someone's pack*, possibly <**=eq**> meaning unclear, possibly <**metathesis type 2**> *derivational*, <**=t**> *purposeful control transitivizer*, phonology: possible metathesis, syntactic analysis: transitive verb, attested by AK and most others (Elders Group 3/26/80).

<**xwetá:yeqel**>, LANG /*'answering, replying, answering back*'/, *see* tiy.

<**xwétes ~ xwét:es**>, free root //x^{w}ə́təs ~ x^{w}ə́t·əs//, DESC [*'heavy'*], syntactic analysis: adjective/adjectival verb, attested by Elders Group (3/15/72), AC (8/6/70, 10/1/71, 8/29/70, 10/6/71, 10/21/71), AD, other sources: ES (CwMsCh) /x^{w}ə́təs/ *heavy*, Salish cognate: not cognate with Squamish, Sechelt, Saanich and Samish dials. of NSt /x̣ə́m/ *heavy* nor with Lushootseed /x̣ə́b/ *heavy*, example: <**lí: xwét:es?**>, //lí-ə x^{w}ə́t·əs//, /*'Is it heavy?'*/, attested by AC (10/21/71), <**híkw xwétes mestíyexw**>, //hík^{w} x^{w}ə́təs məstíyəx^{w}//, /*'big heavy person'*/, attested by AC (10/21/71), <**xwét:es syó:ys**>, //x^{w}ə́t·əs s=yá·ys//, /*'heavy work (as in manual labor)'*/, attested by AC (8/29/70), <**qelátstexwchexw esu las tu xwe xwétes.**>, //qəlɛ́t=sT-əx^{w}-c-əx^{w} ʔə-s-u lɛ-s tu x^{w}ə x^{w}ə́təs//, /*'Add more [to it] and make it heavier.'*/, literally /'you add more/cause it to be again so it goes to a little get/become heavy'/, attested by AD, <**xwét:es te sqwétxem.**>, //x^{w}ə́t·əs tə s=q^{w}ə́tx^{y}=əm//, /*'The fog is heavy.'*/, attested by AC (10/6/71).

<**xwetiyéqel**>, LANG /*'answer, reply, (answer back [BHTTC])'*/, *see* tiy.

<**xwétkw'em**>, CLO [*'denim cloth'*], *see* xwót'kw'em.

<**xwétkw'emáyiws**>, CLO /*'denim pants, jeans'*/, *see* xwót'kw'em.

<**xwétkw'emélwet**>, CLO [*'denim clothes'*], *see* xwót'kw'em.

<**Xwétxel** or **X̲wétxel**>, df //x^{w}ə́t=x^{y}əl or x̣^{w}a[=Aə́=]tix^{y}=(x^{y})əl//, PLN [*'Whetkyel village east of Little Mountain by Agassiz'*], root meaning unknown unless <**xwét**> *Swainson's thrush* or <**xwétes**> *heavy* or the same root as in <**sx̲wotíx**> *helldiver, pied-billed grebe*?, possibly lx <**=xel**> *on the foot, precipitation*, possibly <**=el**> *go, come, get, become*, possibly <**é-ablaut**> *resultative or derivational*, phonology: possible ablaut, possible consonant merger, syntactic analysis: nominal, source: Wells 1965 (lst ed.):23 <HWET-kyel> (with dash through k) *Whetkyel, village east of Little Mt. by Agassiz.*

<**xweth'**>, probable bound root //x^{w}ə́θ'// *twist, sprain*

<**xweth'éqw'tses**>, df //x^{w}ə́θ'=ə[=M2=]q'^{w}=cəs or x^{w}ɛθ'=ə[=´=]q'^{w}=cəs//, rsls, ABDF [*'sprained wrist'*], ANA [*'wrist or hand joint'*], root <**xweth'**> *twist, sprain*, lx <**=eqw'**> *around in a circle, lump*, probably <**metathesis** or **stress-shift**> *resultative*, lx <**=tses**> *on the hand*, phonology: metathesis or stress-shift, possible vowel-reduction, syntactic analysis: nominal; adjective/adjectival verb, attested by Elders Group (7/27/75), Salish cognate: Squamish /s-x̣^{w}ə́c'q'^{w}/ *joint, cut, place of division* as also in /s-x̣^{w}əc'q'^{w}-áč/ *wrist* and /x̣^{w}əc'q'^{w}=án/ *cut off (tr.)* W73:153,294, K67:298,371, Sechelt /x̣^{w}ə́c'-x̣^{w}əc'-q'^{w}/ *joints* T77:14, and the same =qw' suffix in Lushootseed /p'əs-q'^{w}-əg^{w}ás/ *joint* and /s-p'əs-q'^{w}-šad/ *ankle* and /p'əs-q'^{w}-əg^{w}ás-ačiʔ/ *wrist* H76:358, historical/comparative detail: the cognates make one wonder if xw here is mistranscribed for x̲w.

<**xweth'éqw'xel**>, df //x^{w}ə́θ'=ə[=M2=]q'^{w}=x^{y}əl//, ABDF [*'sprained ankle'*], ANA [*'ankle joint'*], root meaning unknown, lx <**=eqw'**> *around in a circle, lump*, probably <**metathesis**> *resultative*, lx <**=xel**> *on the foot*, phonology: metathesis, syntactic analysis: nominal; adjective/adjectival verb, Elder's comment: "xwtl'elétsxel is wrong", attested by Elders Group (7/27/75, 10/8/75), Salish cognate: affixes in Lushootseed /s-p'əs-q'^{w}-šád/ *ankle* H76:358 and Squamish /p'álq'^{w}-šn/ *sprain one's ankle* W73:6, K67:252.

<**xwetskwí:lem**>, TVMO [*'(go) far away'*], *see* chó:kw.

<**xwéts'xel**>, df //xʷə́c'=xʸəl//, WETH /'*stop raining, stop snowing*'/, root meaning uncertain (but in cognates it alone means *stop raining*, lx <**=xel**> *precipitation*, syntactic analysis: intransitive verb, attested by Elders Group (6/8/77), Stanley Jones (6/25/75), Deming (3/31/77), Salish cognate: Squamish /xʷáč'/ *stop raining* and perhaps /xʷəč'šíʔ/ *interspace, space between* as in /txʷ-xʷəč'šiʔ/ *move to the space between* W73:254, K67:349,348, Lushootseed /xʷáč'/ (VH /x̣ʷáč'/) *stop raining* as in /ʔu-xʷáč'(əxʷ)/ *it stopped raining* H76:555, Saanich dial. of NSt /xʷéθ'sən/ *to stop raining* B74a:79, Samish dial. of NSt (VU) /xʷéc'-sən ~ xʷéθ'-sən/ *to stop raining* G86a:64, also for -xel Sechelt /č'áwšən/ (metathesized root?) *to stop raining* B77:93, example: <**lulh xwéts'xel.**>, //lə-uɬ xʷə́c'=xʸəl//, /'*It's stopped raining.*'/, attested by Deming, for a song to stop the rain see under <**x̱é::yq'**>.

<**xwewá**>, CJ /'*not yet be, be not yet*'/, *see* éwe ~ ő́we.

<**xwewá:**>, CJ /'*isn't s-o yet?, isn't it yet?, hasn't s-o yet?*'/, *see* éwe ~ ő́we.

<**xwewáth'et**>, MC ['*unlock it*'], *see* wáth'.

<**xwéwes**>, us //xʷə́wəs//, EFAM /'*Sure., Exactly.*'/, syntactic analysis: interjection, Elder's comment: "possibly Skagit", attested by RP (2/27/76).

<**xwéweslexw**>, ncs //xʷə́wəs=l-əxʷ//, FOOD ['*beat s-o out of food*'], SOC, unless <**xw=ʔə́wə=**> *become not*, (<**=l**> *non-control transitivizer, accidentally/managed to*), (<**-exw**> *third person object*), syntactic analysis: transitive verb, attested by Elders Group (3/3/76), Salish cognate: perhaps Squamish /xʷíʔ-nəxʷ/ ("not-lack control (tr.)") *lose, have lost* K67:349, example: <**le xwōweslóxes.**>, //lə xʷəwəs=l-áxʸ-əs//, /'*He beat me out of food.*'/, attested by Elders Group; found in <**xweweslò:m.**>, //xʷəwəs=l-à·m//, /'*I got beat out of food.*'/, syntactic analysis: passive, attested by Elders Group.

<**xwexwá**>, ABDF ['*starving*'], *see* xwá.

<**xwéxwemxelí:m**>, ABFC ['*running on and off*'], *see* x̱wém ~ xwém.

<**xwexwílex**>, TVMO /'*got up with a quick motion, got up quickly*'/, *see* xwílex.

<**xwexwíye**>, df //xʷəxʷ=íyɛ orx̣ʷ[=K=]əx̣ʷ[=K=]ɛ[=Aí=]y=ə//, EZ /'*salmonberry worm, (*prob. *larvae of moths or butterflies or two-winged flies)*'/, ['probably larvae of *Lepidoptera or Diptera*, possibly larvae of order *Lepidoptera*, family *Tortricidae*'], ASM ['unidentified larvae found inside the cap of the salmonberry when picked late in the season'], root meaning unknown unless related to <**x̱wex̱wá:ye**> *fly*, possibly <**=íya**> *affectionate(?) diminutive*, possibly <**=K= (fronting)**> *diminutive or derivational*, phonology: possible fronting, syntactic analysis: nominal, attested by Elders Group (3/12/75), Deming (3/15/79 incl. SJ, MC, MV, LG).

<**xwexwó:s**>, bound root or stem //xʷəxʷ(=)á·s//, meaning uncertain

<**shxwexwó:s**>, df //s=xʷəxʷ(=)á·s or sxw=xwí[=Aó:=]s//, EZ ['*thunderbird*'], WETH ['*thunder*'], POW, ASM ['thunderbird is a huge bird, a stl'áleqem creature which causes all the effects of thunderstorms, he lives in caves in certain mountains, these caves are said to be covered with sparkly mica from his living there and are sometimes sought out by those questing for great spirit power (the power of the thunderbird)'], (semological comment: the weather effects are expressed through the metaphor THUNDERSTORM EFFECTS ARE ACTIONS OF THUNDERBIRD; found in examples below), (<**s=**> *nominalizer, something to*), root meaning unknown but compare the root in <**xwíset ~ xwítset**> *shake s-th (tree or bush) for fruit or leaves, comb a bush (for berries), shake s-th (a mat or blanket for ex.)*, since thunder does shake things and causes thunder when he shakes his wings, possibly <**=ó:s**> *in the face*, syntactic analysis: nominal, attested by Deming (3/31/77),

BJ (12/5/64), MV (Deming 5/4/78), others, other sources: ES /šxʷəwxʷá·s/ (CwMs /šxʷəwxʷáʔs/) *thunderbird*, Salish cognate: Saanich dial. of NSt /sxʷəxʷáʔs/ *thunderbird* B74a:4, Samish dial. of NSt /sxʷəxʷáʔas ~ sx̣ʷəx̣ʷáʔas/ *thunderbird* G86a:70, not Lushootseed /s-x̣ʷə́qʷəb/ *thunderbird* H76:613, example: <**lómetes te shxwexwó:s.**>, //lám=əT-əs tə s=xʷəxʷ(=)á·s//, WETH, /'*Lightning strikes., A thunderbolt (strikes)., (Thunder throws and hits s-th.)*'/, literally /'thunderbird throws and hits s-th'/, attested by MV (Deming 5/4/78), <**me séx̱we te shxwexwó:s.**>, //mə sə́x̣ʷə tə s=xʷəxʷ(=)á·s//, WETH, /'*It's raining., Thunder is urinating.*'/, literally /'thunderbird starts to urinate'/, attested by Deming (3/31/77), <**qwíx̱tes te tl'qá:ls te shxwexwó:s.**>, //qʷíy=x̣=T-əs tə ƛ'q'ɛ́·l-s tə s=xʷəxʷ(=)á·s//, WETH, /'*to thunder, Thunder shakes his wings.*'/, literally /'he shakes s-th the his wings the thunderbird'/, attested by Deming (3/31/77), <**qwíx̱tes te lhéptels te shxwexwó:s.**>, //qʷíy=x̣=T-əs tə ɬə́p=təl-s tə s=xʷəxʷ(=)á·s//, WETH, /'*to lightning, Thunder moves or shakes his eyelashes.*'/, literally /'he moves/shakes the his eyelashes the thunderbird'/, attested by Deming (3/31/77), Salish cognate: Saanich dial. of NSt /qʷə́y'x̣sət tθə sxʷəxʷáʔs/ *thunderstorm* B74a:4, Samish dial. of NSt /qʷə́yəx̣sət tə sxʷəxʷáʔas/ *have a thunderstorm* ("thunderbird is shaking himself") G86a:63, Salish cognates in metaphor: Squamish /t'x̣-áyʔus-m/ *open one's eyes, lightning* W73:190, K67:268, Samish dial. of NSt /k'ʷəléčil tə sxʷəxʷáʔas/ *lightning* ("thunderbird is opening his eyes") G86a:63, <**x̱éleq't te shxwexwó:s.**>, //x̣ə́ləq'=T tə s=xʷəxʷ(=)á·s//, WETH, /'*to lightning, have lightning, Thunder opens his eyes.*'/, literally /'thunderbird opens his eyes'/, attested by Deming (3/31/77), BJ (12/5/64), Deming (1974), <**x̱élx̱eleq't te shxwexwó:s.**>, //x̣ə́l[=C_1əC_2=]əq'=T tə s=xʷəxʷ(=)á·s//, WETH, /'*having lightning, Thunder is opening his eyes.*'/, literally /'thunderbird is opening his eyes'/, attested by Deming (3/31/77).

<**Xwexwó:stel**>, ds //xʷəxʷ(=)á·s=təl//, PLN ['*mountain shaped like a thunderbird across the Fraser River from Q'ów (the "howl") mountain*'], ASM ['it is shaped like a thunderbird (shxwexwó:s) and it fought with Q'ów mountain till the X̱ex̱éyls (Transformers) turned them to stone, Xwexwó:stel is a shape on the face of the mountain just west next to Th'áth'ele (q.v.) on the south side of the Fraser River'], literally /'thunder(bird) device/thing to'/, lx <**=tel**> *device to, thing to*, syntactic analysis: nominal, attested by AD (3/7/78), AD and Evangeline Pete (6/26/78).

<**Xwexwó:stel**>, PLN ['*mountain shaped like a thunderbird across the Fraser River from Q'ów (the "howl") mountain*'], *see* shxwexwó:s.

<**xwexwóthet**>, ABDF /'*starving oneself, being on a "crash" diet*'/, *see* xwá.

<**xwéylemt te télmels**>, SCH /'*measure the knowledge, give a test*'/, MC, *see* x̱wéylémt.

<**xwéytheqel**>, LANG /'*interpreting, (telling on someone [EB])*'/, *see* yéth.

<**xwe'éyem ~ xw'éyem**>, WATR /'*be clear (of water), be smooth (AC)*'/, *see* éy ~ éy:.

<**xwe'í**>, TVMO /'*arrive, arriving, come here, have come, get here, get back, come in (in a race)*'/, *see* í.

<**xwe'ílòmèt**>, TVMO ['*manage to get here*'], *see* í.

<**xwe'í:lstexw**>, TVMO ['*bring s-o/s-th here*'], *see* í.

<**xwe'í:qw'wí:ls ~ xwe'íyeqw'wí:ls**>, HHG ['*drying dishes*'], *see* íqw'.

<**xwe'ít**>, us //xʷəʔít//, MOOD /'*what happened?, what is it?, why?*'/, syntactic analysis: interrogative verb, attested by Elders Group (2/5/75), other sources: JH /xʷəʔí·t/ *what happened?*, contrast <**tl'okwselchí:m**> *why?*, compare <**xwe'í:t**> *what is s-o doing?*, Salish cognate: remotely possible is N. Lushootseed /ʔəx̣íd/ *what act/state, why not (do s-th)* (S. Lushootseed /x̣íd/) as in /ʔu-ʔəx̣íd/ *what happened?, what did you do?* and /yəx̣i ʔuʔəx̣íd/ *why?* H76:662-663 (if cognate this would require

metathesis historically of the first two consonants and labialization historically of /x̣/ or delabialization of /x̣ʷ/), ASM ['what happened?'], example: <**chxwe'ít?**>, //c-xʷ xʷəʔít//, /'*What happened to you?*'/, phonology: consonant merger, attested by Elders Group (2/5/75), ASM ['what is it?'], attested by CT (6/8/76), ASM ['why?'], also <**xwe'ít ~ xw'ít**>, //xʷəʔít ~ xʷʔít//, attested by EB, <**xw'ít kw'a's ő́we líxw lám?**>, //xʷʔít k'ʷ-ɛʔ-s ʔówə lí-xʷ lɛ́=m//, /'*Why didn't you go?*'/, semantic environment Elder's comment: "used when no one depended on her but she just changed her mind", attested by EB (5/26/76), <**xw'ít kwá?**>, //xʷʔít kʷɛ́//, /'*Why do you?, What for?*'/, literally /'why anyway'/, attested by EB (1/9/76), <**xw'ít kwses x̱tá t(e)thá?**>, //xʷʔít kʷ-s-əs x̣tɛ́ tə=θɛ́//, /'*Why did he do that?*'/, attested by EB (1/9/76), <**xwe'ít kwa tl'o'a sulh thíyt?**>, //xʷəʔít kʷɛ́ ƛ'a ʔɛ s-uɬ θíy=T//, /'*Why did you make it?*'/, attested by EB (1/9/76), also <**tl'ókwselchí:ms kw'as lé thìyt?**>, //ƛ'á=kʷ=səlcí·m-s k'ʷ-ɛ-s lə θíy=T//, attested by AC (1973: p.121), <**xw'ít kw'a's ő́welh ...?**>, //xʷʔít k'ʷ-ɛʔ-s ʔówə-ɬ ...//, /'*Why don't you ...*'/, attested by EB (4/27/76), <**xwe'ít kw'a's ő́welh lháq'et ta' kopú?**>, //xʷəʔít k'ʷ-ɛʔ-s ʔówə-ɬ ɬɛ́q'=əT t-ɛʔ kapú//, /'*Why don't you put down your coat?*'/, attested by EB (4/27/76).

<**xwe'í:t**>, cts //xʷəʔí[-·-]t//, MOOD /'*what is s-o doing?, what is s-o saying?, what is he/she/it doing/saying?*'/, TIB, LANG, semantic environment ['an answer to such a question is also *continuative*, such as <**ó:met.**> *He/She is sitting.* or <**lhx̱é:ylex.**> *He/She is standing.*'], LANG ['*what s-o is saying*'], semantic environment ['subordinate subjunctive'], (<-:-> *continuative*), phonology: lengthening, syntactic analysis: intransitive verb, attested by AC, Elders Group (2/5/75), EF (Deming class 5/18/78), IHTTC (9/15/77), NP (10/26/75), BHTTC (10/21/76), AD (12/18/78, 1/8/80), EB (9/20/78), MV (Deming 5/4/78), also <**xwe'ít**>, //xʷəʔít//, attested by AD and EB (11/10/78), also <**xwe'íyet**>, //xʷəʔí[-·-]t or xʷəʔíyət//, attested by AC (9/15/71), EF (Deming 5/18/78), ASM ['what is s-o doing?'], example: <**xwe'í:tchexw?**>, //xʷəʔí[-·-]t-c-əxʷ//, /'*What are you doing?*'/, attested by AC (9/15/71), <**echexw xwe'í:t? ~ chexw xwe'í:t?**>, //(ʔə)-c-əxʷ xʷəʔí[-·-]t//, /'*What are you doing?*'/, attested by AC (12/8/71), <**í:lhchexw xwe'íyet?**>, //ʔí·-ɬ-c-əxʷ xʷəʔí[-·-]t//, /'*What were you doing?*'/, attested by AC (9/15/71), <**tsel xwe'í:t?**>, //c-əl xʷəʔí[-·-]t//, /'*What am I doing?*'/, attested by NP (10/26/75), <**Q. Achexw xwe'í:t? A. Atsel lhí:m.**>, //ʔɛ-c-əxʷ xʷəʔí[-·-]t? ʔɛ-c-əl ɬí·m.//, /'*What are you doing? I'm picking.*'/, attested by BHTTC (10/21/76), <**chxwe'í:t?**>, //c-xʷ xʷəʔi[-·-]t//, /'*What are you doing?, What are you saying?*'/, attested by Elders Group (2/5/75), <**ílh xwe'í:t?**>, //ʔí-ɬ xʷəʔí[-·-]t//, /'*What did he do?*'/, attested by AD (1/8/80), <**Q. ílhchexw xwe'í:t? A. ílhtsel lhí:m.**>, //ʔí-ɬ-c=əxʷ xʷəʔí[-·-]t? ʔí-ɬ-c-əl ɬí·m.//, /'*What were you doing? I was picking.*'/, attested by BHTTC (10/21/76), <**xwe'í:t yalh ta' skwó:y(e)x̱thet?**>, //xʷəʔí[-·-]t yɛɬ t-ɛʔ s=kʷi[-Aá·-]y(=)x̣=T-ət//, /'*What are you doing?*'/, literally /'what are they doing now your doings'/, attested by AD (12/18/79), <**ólechexw óle xwe'í:t?**>, //ʔálə-c-əxʷ ʔálə xʷəʔí[-·-]t//, /'*What are you doing? (angrily), (What on earth are you doing?)*'/, literally /'you are true/right true/right what is s-o doing? (or) truly truly what are you doing?'/, attested by Deming Evening Class (EF/MV/others 5/18/78), ASM ['what is s-o saying?'], <**chxw kwoyálh xwe'í:t?**>, //c-xʷ kʷɛ yɛɬ xʷəʔí[-·-]t//, /'*What are you saying now?*'/, attested by EB (9/20/78), <**óle xwe'í:t?**>, //ʔálə xʷəʔí[-·-]t//, /'*What did he say?*'/, literally /'really/truly what is he saying?'/, attested by MV (Deming 5/4/78), <**xwe'í:t ta sqwálewel?**>, //xʷəʔí[-·-]t t-ɛ s=qʷɛ́l=əwəl//, /'*What are you thinking about?*'/, literally /'what are they saying? your thoughts/talk in the mind'/, attested by AC (10/15/71), also <**xwe'í:t kw'a sqwáléwel?**>, //x̣ʷəʔí[-·-]t k'ʷ-ɛ s=qʷɛl=əwəl//, also /'*What are you thinking?*'/, attested by AC (8/28/70), ASM ['what s-o is saying'], <**mő́kw'tset ő́welh teló:met welí:xw xwe'í:t.**>, //mok'ʷ-c-ət ʔówə-ɬ təl=l-ámət wə-lí·-xʷ xʷəʔí[-·-]t//, /'*We don't understand what you're saying.*'/, attested by AC (10/6/71), <**ōwéta slhéq'elexw wexwe'í:tes kw'el sqwà:l.**>, //ʔowə=´tɛ s=ɬ[=ə́=]=q'ɛl=l-əxʷ wə-xʷəʔí[-·-]t-əs k'ʷ-əl s=qʷɛ̀·l//, /'*I didn't know what to say.*'/, attested by AC (11/10/71).

<**xwe'ítixw** or **xwe'ít yexw**>, cpds //xʷəʔít=yəxʷ or xʷəʔít yəxʷ//, MOOD /'*I wonder what s-o will do?, I wonder what I will do?*'/, root <**xwe'ít**> *what is it?, what happened?, why, (what does s-o do?),* root <**yexw**> *I wonder*, phonology: vowel-loss in postclitic, vocalization of y between consonants, syntactic analysis: interrogative verb, attested by EB and AD (11/10/78), AD (12/18/78), Salish cognate: Saan. and Samish dials. of NSt /yəxʷ/ (postposed/enclitic) *conjectural, must be, I wonder* G86a:59, also <**(yexw xwe'ít)**>, //ʔixw xʷəʔít (or) yəxʷ xʷəʔít//, attested by EB and AD (11/10/78), example: <**xwe'ítixwcha tútl'ò?**>, //xʷəʔít=yəxʷ-cɛ t=ú=ƛ'à//, /'*I wonder what he'll do?*'/, attested by AD (12/18/78); found in <**xwe'ítixwtselcha?**>, //xʷəʔít=yəxʷ-c-əl-cɛ//, /'*I wonder what I'll do?*'/, attested by AD (12/18/78), <**xwe'ítixwtsetcha?**>, //xʷəʔít=yəxʷ-c-ət-cɛ//, /'*I wonder what we'll do?*'/, attested by AD (12/18/78), <**xwe'ítixwchexwcha?**>, //xʷəʔít=yəxʷ-c-əxʷ-cɛ//, /'*I wonder what you'll do?*'/, attested by AD (12/18/78), <**xwe'ítixwchapcha?**>, //xʷəʔít=yəxʷ-c-ɛp-cɛ//, /'*I wonder what you folks will do?*'/, attested by AD (12/18/78), example: <**ixwtsel xwe'ít?** or **yexwtsel xwe'ít?**>, //yəxʷ-c-əl xʷəʔít//, /'*I wonder what shall I do?*'/, attested by AD and EB (11/10/78).

<**xwe'í:t**>, MOOD /'*what is s-o doing?, what is s-o saying?, what is he/she/it doing/saying?*'/, *see* xwe'ít.

<**xwe'ítixw** or **xwe'ít yexw**>, MOOD /'*I wonder what s-o will do?, I wonder what I will do?*'/, *see* xwe'ít.

<**xwe'ít'et**>, ds //xʷə=ʔa[=Aí=]t'=əT//, incs, pcs, HUNT /'*draw a bow, cock a gun, (draw it (of a bow), cock it (of a gun))*'/, SOC, (<**xwe=**> *get, become, inceptive*), (<**í-ablaut**> *derivational* perhaps aspectual), root <**ót'**> *stretch*, (<**=et**> *purposeful control transitivizer*), phonology: ablaut, syntactic analysis: transitive verb, attested by Elders Group (2/19/75), *see* root ót'.

<**xwe'íwelmet**>, iecs //xʷə=ʔíwəl=məT//, EFAM ['*pay attention to s-o*'], literally /'get/become in the mind toward s-o'/, (semological comment: with negation can be translated as *ignore s-o*), root <**xwe**> *get, become*, lx <**=(')íwel**> *in the mind*, (<**=met**> *indirect effect non-control transitivizer*), phonology: epenthetic glottal stop between vowels at morpheme boundary, syntactic analysis: transitive verb, attested by SJ (5/3/78), AD and EB (11/10/78), also <**xwel'íwelmet**>, //xʷəl=ʔíwəl=məT//, comment: the first <**l**>/l/ is omitted when this word is attested the following day by both AD and EB (11/10/78) and the derivation makes sense without it but not with it; also <**l'**>/lʔ/ is tolerated only when produced by reduplication; so it seem most likely that the first <**l**> is in error or mistranscribed, attested by EB (11/9/78), <**li xwe'íwelmetem?**>, //li-ə xʷə=ʔíwəl=məT-əm//, /'*Are they paying attention to him?*'/, attested by AD and EB (11/10/78), example: <**kw'á:y kws ő̲wes xwe'íwelméthóxes.**>, //k'ʷɛ́·y kʷ-s ʔówə-s xʷə=ʔíwəl=məT-áxʸ-əs//, /'*She can't do that, not pay any attention to me.*'/, literally /'it can't be that she not pay attention to me'/, usage: story of Mink and Miss Pitch, attested by SJ (5/3/78), <**ő̲welh xwel'íwelmétes.**>, //ʔówə-ɬ xʷə(l)=ʔíwəl=məT-əs//, /'*She ignored him., She didn't pay any attention to him.*'/, attested by EB (11/9/78).

<**Xwe'íweqw'óthel**>, df //xʷə(=)ʔíwəq'ʷ=áθəl//, PLN /'*slough facing south [east] across from Chehalis, B.C.*'/, possibly <**xwe=**> *get, become*, root meaning unknown, lx <**=óthel**> *in the mouth, in the mouth of a river*, syntactic analysis: nominal, attested by EL (3/1/78 Stó:lō Sítel tape).

<**xwe'í:yá:qepem**>, mdls //xʷə=ʔi[=´·=]yɛ́·q=əp=əm//, LANG ['*to joke*'], literally /'get/become changed on one's end/bottom/rump'/, (semological comment: this could be a humorous reference to rump or more likely to the fact that what one says involves a change at the end of the sentence or story (which is what surprises the listener and causes the humor)), (<**xwe=**> *get, become*), root <**iyá:q**> *to change*, (<**=´:=**> *resultative*), lx <**=ep**> *on the end, on the bottom, on the rump*, (<**=em**> *middle voice*), syntactic analysis: intransitive verb, attested by JL (5/5/75), Salish cognate: Cowichan dial. of Halkomelem /xʷiy'ɛ́qəpəm/ *to joke* B74b:66, Saanich dial. of NSt /xʷiy'éqəč/ *to joke* B74a:66, also

<**xwe'íyáqepem**>, //xʷə=ʔíyɛ́q=əp=əm//, attested by AD (3/6/79), also *see* iyá:q.

<**xwíkw'**>, bound root //xʷík'ʷ *gray, grey*//, comment: using derived forms of the root as a modifier of other color terms the following combinations were given by AK: tsxwíkw' (tskwím, sts'óla, tsqwáy, qálq, semth'íl, tsméth') (once glossed *light* before tsqwáy); tsxwíxwekw' (qálq, tsqwáy, tsméth'); xwíxwekw' (tsqwáy, tsqwáy, tsméth', qwiqwóyáls); sxwíxwekw' tsqwáy; tsxwíxwekw'el (tsméth', tsqw'íx̱w "like dark brown"); xwíxwekw'el (sts'óla, qálq, tsqwáy).

<**tsxwíkw'**>, ds //c=xʷík'ʷ//, LT /'*(have/be) gray, (have/be) grey*'/, ASM ['squares circled on the color chart of Berlin and Kay (1969) (rows top to bottom = B-I, columns left to right = 1-40, side column of white to black = 0); individual speakers circled the following squares for tsxwíkw': TM: B0, C0, D0; EL: C0; AK: G0, H0; TG (with RP): I13, I14, I15, I16, I17, I18, I19; NP (xwíxwekw'el): H12, H13, H14;'], ASM ['the following color terms are used by AK before tsxwíkw' to specify shades of the color: p'(e)q'íl'], (<**ts=** ~ **ch=**> *have, stative with colors*), syntactic analysis: adjective/adjectival verb, chart by Rob MacLaury, attested by TM (Elders Group 2/14/79), EL (2/20/79), AK (1/24/79), Deming (5/3/79), (esp. SJ), Salish cognate: Squamish root /-xʷík'ʷ ~ xʷə́k'ʷ/ *grey* as in /xʷək'ʷ-xʷík'ʷ/ *grey* and /xʷíxʷik'ʷ/ *small [grey] blueberry* W73:124, K67:348, 350, also <**chxwíkw'**>, //c=xʷík'ʷ//, attested by BHTTC (9/9/76), example: <**tsxwíkw' te stqóye.**>, //c=xʷík'ʷ tə s=tqáyə//, /'*The wolf is gray.*'/, attested by Deming (5/3/79), <**tsxwíkw' te slek'iyáp.**>, //c=xʷík'ʷ tə s=lək'iy(=)ɛ́p//, /'*The coyote is gray.*'/, attested by Deming (5/3/79, esp. SJ).

<**tsxwíkw'ómex**>, ds //c=xʷík'ʷ=áməxʸ//, LT /'*[looks gray, gray-looking]*'/, (<**ts=**> *have, get, stative with colors*), (<**=ómex**> *looks, -looking, in color*), syntactic analysis: adjective/adjectival verb, attested by NP, see charts by Rob MacLaury.

<**xwíxwekw'**>, cts //xʷí[=C₁ə=]k'ʷ//, LT ['*[being gray]*'], (<**=R1=**> *continuative*), syntactic analysis: adjective/adjectival verb, attested by NP, see charts by Rob MacLaury.

<**tsxwíxwekw'**>, cts //c=xʷí[=C₁ə=]k'ʷ//, LT ['*[be getting gray]*'], (<**ts=**> *have, get, stative with colors*), (<**=R1=**> *continuative*), syntactic analysis: adjective/adjectival verb, attested by TG, see charts by Rob MacLaury.

<**xwíkw'el**>, incs //xʷík'ʷ=əl//, LT /'*be faded (of clothes), (get/become) faded, (go or get or become gray)*'/, (<**=el**> *go, come, get, become*), syntactic analysis: adjective/adjectival verb, attested by CT (6/8/76), example: <**la xwíkw'el te kopú.**>, //lɛ (or lə) xʷík'ʷ=əl tə kapú//, /'*The coat is faded.*'/, attested by CT.

<**xwíxwekw'el**>, cts //xʷí[=C₁ə=]k'ʷ=əl//, LT /'*(grayish, getting gray)*'/, semantic environment ['not of hair'], literally /'going/getting/becoming gray'/, (<**=R1=**> *continuative*), phonology: reduplication, syntactic analysis: adjective/adjectival verb, chart by Rob MacLaury, ASM ['squares circled on the color chart of Berlin and Kay (1969) (rows top to bottom = B-I, columns left to right = 1-40, side column of white to black = 0); NP circled the following squares for xwíxwekw'el: H12, H13, H14'], contrast <**x̱ólemthet**> *turn gray (of hair)*, attested by NP (Elders Group 2/7/79, 1987).

<**tsxwíxwekw'el**>, strs //c=xʷí[=C₁ə=]k'ʷ=əl//, LT ['*grayish*'], semantic environment ['not of hair'], literally /'be getting/becoming gray'/, (<**ts=** ~ **ch=**> *have, stative with colors*), syntactic analysis: adjective/adjectival verb, chart by Rob MacLaury, attested by JL (5/8/79).

<**xwíxwekw'**>, df //xʷí[=C₁ə=]k'ʷ//, EB /'*gray mountain blueberry which looks like sx̱wéxixeq but is sweeter, oval-leaved blueberry, could also be Cascade blueberry*'/, ['*Vaccinium ovalifolium*, possibly also *Vaccinium deliciosum*'], root <**xwíkw'**> *gray*, (semological comment: so named because the berry is more gray than blue, actually blue with a whitish dusting or coating on the berry that grays the color to grayish-blue), (<**=R1=**> *continuative or resultative or derivational*),

(<**zero**> *nominalizer*), phonology: reduplication, zero nominalization, syntactic analysis: nominal, attested by Elders Group (9/10/75), TM (3/24/76), others, Salish cognate: Squamish /x^{w}í-x^{w}ik'^{w}/ *oval-leaved blueberry (Vaccinium ovalifolium), also domestic blueberry (Vaccinium spp.)* Bouchard and Turner 1976:94-95, T72:11, from root /x^{w}ík'^{w}/ *gray* K67:250, Lushootseed (Snohomish dial.) /šúʔšuk'^{w}/ *an unidentified blueberry* from root /šúk'^{w}/ *powder, gray* as in /ʔə(s)-šúk'^{w}-il/ *become gray, light gray* and /x̣i-šúk'^{w}/ *gray* H76:468, Thompson /x^{w}íx^{w}ak'/ *oval-leaved blueberry, "grey blueberry", Vaccinium ovalifolium, also commercial blueberries* Turner, Thompson, Thompson & York 1973ms.:37.

<**xwíkw'el**>, LT */'be faded (of clothes), (get/become) faded, (go or get or become gray)'/, see* xwíkw'.

<**xwílex**>, df //x^{w}íy=el=əx^y//, ABFC */'stand up, rise from a seat'/*, literally /'go/come get upright'/, probably root <**xwe**> *become, get* (normally a prefix however), (<**=el ~ =íl**> *go, come, get, become*), lx <**=ex**> *upright*, phonology: vowel merger, syntactic analysis: intransitive verb, attested by IHTTC (9/15/77).

<**xwexwílex**>, rsls //x^{w}ə[=C_1ə=]=íl=əx^y or C_1ə=x^{w}íy=əl=əx^y//, TVMO */'got up with a quick motion, got up quickly'/*, possibly <**R5=** or **=R1=**> *resultative*, phonology: updrifting, syntactic analysis: intransitive verb, attested by Elders Group (3/1/72), example: <**le xwexwílex.**>, //lə x^{w}ə[=C_1ə=]=íl=əx^y//, */'got up with a quick motion'/*, literally /'he/she got up with a quick motion'/, attested by Elders Group, <**chexw me xwexwílex.**>, //c-əx^w mə x^{w}ə[=C_1ə=]=íl=əx^y//, */'You're already standing., You got up quick.'/*, attested by Elders Group.

<**xwiléxmet** or **xwíléxmet**>, iecs //x^{w}iy=əl=əx^y=məT or x^{w}ə=íl=əx^y=məT//, SOC [*'stand up for s-o (respected)'*], ABFC, (<**=met**> *indirectly effecting non-control transitivizer*), phonology: vowel merger, updrifting, syntactic analysis: transitive verb, attested by IHTTC (9/15/77).

<**xwiléxmet** or **xwíléxmet**>, SOC [*'stand up for s-o (respected)'*], *see* xwílex.

<**xwíq**>, us //x^{w}íq//, SOC [*'someone's turn'*], syntactic analysis: intransitive verb?, attested by no name/date but early 1979, Salish cognate: prob. not Squamish /x^{w}i-ʔq/ *have its bottom exposed* from root /x^{w}əy ~ x^{w}í/ *appear* K69:78 nor root in Squamish /(ʔə)s-x^{w}í-x^{w}iq/ *lively, happy, gay* K67:294, K69:92,78, but perhaps Squamish /x^{w}ík'/ *have the pointer in the slahal game guess wrong* K69:78.

<**xwíqw**>, bound root //x^{w}íq^w *press and rub*//.

<**xwíqwet**>, pcs //x^{w}íq^w=əT//, ABFC [*'press and rub s-th'*], CLO [*'iron s-th'*], (<**=et**> *purposeful control transitivizer*), syntactic analysis: transitive verb, attested by Elders Group (6/1/77), Deming (4/26/79), Salish cognate: Lushootseed root /x^{w}ik^w(i)/ *scrape, rub hard* as in /x^{w}ík^w-id/ //x^{w}ík^w-it// *scrape it, rub it, rub it hard* H76:563.

*<**shxwíxweqwels**>, dnom //sx^w=x^{w}í[=C_1ə=]q^w=əls//, sas, cts, HHG ['*an iron*'], CLO, literally* /'something for pressing and rubbing hard as a structured activity device'/, (<**sx^w=**> *something for, nominalizer*), (<**=R1=**> *continuative*), (<**=els**> *structured activity continuative device*), phonology: reduplication, probable consonant merger, syntactic analysis: nominal, attested by Elders Group (6/1/77).

<**shxwqwó:lthels**>, df //s(x^w)=x^{w}iq^w=á·lθ(əl)=əls//, CARV [*'a wood carving'*], literally perhaps /'something pressed and rubbed hard on the knee as a structured activity'/, (semological comment: nice confirmation of such an etymology was provided by watching one of the last expert carvers work, Joe Lorenzetto (see photo Galloway 1980:131a)),(<**s=** or **shxw=**> *nominalizer, something that*), root <**xwíqw**> *press and rub hard*, lx <**=ó:lthel**> *on the knee*, (<**=els**> *structured activity continuative device*), phonology: syllable-loss, possible consonant merger, syntactic analysis: nominal, attested by DM (12/4/64 new transcript old p.258), TG (4/23/75).

<**xwíqwet**>, ABFC [*'press and rub s-th'*], *see* xwíqw.

<**xwís**>, free root //xʷís//, EB /*'fall off (of leaves, berries)'*/, syntactic analysis: intransitive verb, attested by EB (3/29/76), also <**xwí:s**>, //xʷí·s or xʷíy=əs//, also EB /*'open (of peas, beans)'*/, possibly root <**xwíy**> *awake, wake, arise*, possibly <**=es**> *on the face*, attested by AC (11/24/71), example: <**lulh xwí·s**>, //lə=uɬ xʷís (or) lə=uɬ xʷíy=əs//, /*'all opened (of beans or peas)'*/, attested by AC.

<**xwíset ~ xwítset**>, pcs //xʷís=əT ~ xʷíc=əT//, HARV /*'shake s-th (tree or bush) for fruit or leaves, comb a bush (for berries), shake s-th (a mat or blanket for ex.)'*/, (<**=et**> *purposeful control transitivizer*), *phonology: the root apparently has a variant,* <**xwíts**> *syntactic analysis: transitive* verb, attested by Elders Group (5/5/76, 3/5/80), EB (3/29/76, 4/27/76), Salish cognate: Lushootseed root /xʷís(i)/ *brush off (e.g. rug, tablecloth)* as in /xʷís-id/ *brush it off (e.g. rug, tablecloth)* (not used for brushing off clothes one has on) H76:564, 535, also Lushootseed /xʷə́c-əd/ *take (clothing) off* and the same root also in /xʷc-áb/ *empty* H76:559-560.

<**xwesá:lews**>, ds //xʷis=ɛ́·ləws or xʷi[-Aə-]s=ɛ́·ləws//, EB [*'leaves falling'*], possibly <**e-ablaut**> *continuative or durative or resultative*, lx <**=á:lews**> *leaf*, phonology: vowel reduction or ablaut, syntactic analysis: intransitive verb, attested by BHTTC (10/14/76).

<**telxwítsel**>, df //təl=xʷíc=əl//, TIME [*'toward November'*], literally /'from get/become fall(en) (of leaves)'/, probably <**tel=**> *from*, root <**xwíts**> *fall (of leaves/berries)*, (<**=el**> *go, come, get, become*), syntactic analysis: adverb/adverbial verb, attested by Elders Group (3/19/75), example: <**lulh telxwítsel.**>, //lə=uɬ təl=xʷíc=əl//, /*'Leaves are falling., towards November'*/, attested by Elders Group.

<**xwíset ~ xwítset**>, HARV /*'shake s-th (tree or bush) for fruit or leaves, comb a bush (for berries), shake s-th (a mat or blanket for ex.)'*/, *see* xwís.

<**xwítel**>, bound stem //xʷíy=təl//, probably *wake up device*

<**shxwítel**>, dnom //s=xʷíy=təl//, HHG /*'chamberpot, potty-chair, urinal'*/, (<**s=**> *nominalizer*), probably root <**xwíy**> *wake up*, lx <**=tel**> *device for*, syntactic analysis: nominal, attested by Elders Group (8/20/75).

<**xwíxet**>, ABFC [*'wake s-o up'*], *see* xwíy ~ xʷí.

<**xwíxwekw'**>, LT [*'[being gray]'*], *see* xwíkw'.

<**xwíxwekw'**>, EB /*'gray mountain blueberry which looks like sx̲wéxixeq but is sweeter, oval-leaved blueberry, could also be Cascade blueberry'*/, *see* xwíkw'.

<**xwíxwekw'el**>, LT /*'(grayish, getting gray)'*/, *see* xwíkw'.

<**xwixwekw'elátsem**>, CAN /*'automobile, car'*/, *see* xwókw' ~ xwekw'ó.

<**xwixwekw'ósxelem ~ xwekw'ósxelem**>, ABDF [*'dragging one's feet'*], *see* xwókw' ~ xwekw'ó.

<**xwíxwel**>, df //C_1í=xʷəl or xʷí[=C_1ə=]l or C_1í=xʷ[=K=]ɛl//, EB /*'shrub, small bush (for ex. growing on river edge, or like vine maple or thimbleberry or willow), brush, underbrush'*/, root meaning unknown unless related to root x̲wál *willow*, possibly <**R4=**> *diminutive*, possibly <**=R1=**> *diminutive or derivational*, possibly <**=K= (fronting)**> *derivational or diminutive*, phonology: reduplication, possible fronting, syntactic analysis: noun, nominal, attested by AC (11/22/71), Elders Group (4/7/76), other sources: ES /xʷíxʷəl/ *underbrush*, H-T <Qi'QEl> (macron over i) *bush (small), shrub* (vs. H-T <tsu'tsakut> *bush (big)* (/θə́θəqət/ *little tree*)), Salish cognate: Squamish /xʷí-xʷlʔ/ *branches* ("little trees") W73:43, K67:350, also <**x̲wíx̲wel**>, //C_1í=x̲ʷəl//, attested by AC (11/26/71).

<**Xwíxweth'àlem**>, PLN [*'stone underwater Teeter-totter near X̲elhálh'*], *see* xwáth'.

<**xwixweth'álem**>, ABFC ['*rocking*'], *see* xwáth'.

<**xwíxweth'àlem sch'áletstel**>, HHG ['*a rocking chair*'], *see* xwáth'.

<**xwixweth'áletstel**>, HHG ['*a rocking chair*'], *see* xwáth'.

<**xwíy ~ xʷí**>, free root //xʷíy//, ABFC ['*wake up*'], syntactic analysis: intransitive verb, attested by AC, example: <**le xwí.**>, //lə xʷí(y)//, /'*He woke up.*'/, attested by AC (8/15/70); found in <**xwíylha. ~ xwí:lha.**>, //xʷíy-ɬɛ//, /'*Wake up.*'/, attested by AC (9/7/71).

<**shxwexwí**>, strs //s=C_1ə=xʷíy//, ABFC ['*be awake*'], (<**s=**> *stative*), (<**R5=**> *resultative*), phonology: reduplication, syntactic analysis: adjective/adjectival verb, attested by EB (12/19/75), AC (8/15/70), example: <**lí we shxwexwí?**>, //li=ə wə=s=C_1ə=xʷíy//, /'*Is he [really] awake?*'/, attested by EB, <**le shxwexwí.**>, //lə s=C_1ə=xʷíy//, /'*He has awakened.*'/, attested by AC.

<**shxwíyxwiy ~ shxwíxwiy**>, chrs //s=xʷíy=C_1əC_2//, stvi, ABFC ['*(be) easy to wake up*'], (<**s=**> *stative*), (<**=R2**> *characteristic*), phonology: reduplication, syntactic analysis: adjective/adjectival verb, attested by IHTTC (8/8/77).

<**xwíyt**>, pcs //xʷíy=T//, ABFC ['*wake s-o up*'], (<**=t**> *purposeful control transitivizer*), syntactic analysis: transitive verb, attested by JL and NP and Deming (Fish Camp 7/19/79), Salish cognate: Saanich dial. of NSt /xʷə́č-ət/ *to wake s-o up* B74a:82; found in <**xwíytem.**>, //xʷíy=T-əm//, /'*He was woken up.*'/, syntactic analysis: passive, attested by JL and NP and Deming.

<**xwíythet ~ xwíthet**>, pcrs //xʷíy=T-ət//, ABFC /'*wake up (oneself), (wake oneself purposely)*'/, (<**=t**> *purposeful control transitivizer*), (<**-et**> *reflexive*), syntactic analysis: intransitive verb, attested by AC (8/15/70), JL and NP and Deming (Fish Camp 7/19/79), EB (12/12/75), Salish cognate: Samish dial. of NSt (VU) /xʷəčə́sət/, (LD) /xʷəčə́st/ //xʷə́č=M1=sət// *wake up* G86a:76, Saanich dial. of NSt /xʷə́čəsət/ *wake up (oneself)* B74a:82, example: <**tsel me xwíythet.**>, //c-əl mə xʷíy=T-ət//, /'*I woke myself up.*'/, attested by EB; found in <**xwíythetlha.**>, //xʷíy=T-ət-ɬɛ//, /'*Wake up.*'/, attested by EB, <**xwíythetchap.**>, //xʷíy=T-ət-c-ɛp//, /'*Wake up you guys.*'/, attested by AD (8/80).

<**xwíxet**>, pcs //xʷíy=əxʸ=əT//, ABFC ['*wake s-o up*'], probably <**=ex**> *upright*, (<**=et**> *purposeful control transitivizer*), syntactic analysis: transitive verb, attested by EB (12/12/75); found in <**xwíxetlha.**>, //xʷíy=əxʸ=əT-ɬɛ//, /'*Wake him up.*'/, attested by EB, example: <**welh iyólem kwe'ás xwíxet; wulh ólew híth kws ítet-s.**>, //wəɬ ʔiy=ál=əm kʷə-ʔɛ-s xʷíy=əxʸ=əT; wə=uɬ ʔál=əw híθ kʷ-s ʔítət-s//, /'*It's alright for you to wake him up; he's already slept too long.*'/, attested by EB.

<**xwiyós**>, ds //xʷiy=ás//, ABFC ['*alert*'], EFAM, literally /'awake in the face'/, lx <**=ós**> *in the face*, syntactic analysis: adjective/adjectival verb, attested by AD and EB (9/21/78).

<**shxwixwiyós** or **shxwiyxwiyós**>, chrs //s=xʷiy=C_1əC_2=ás//, stvi, EFAM ['*wide-awake*'], literally /'be characteristically alert/awake in the face'/, (<**s=**> *stative*), (<**=R2**> *characteristic*), lx <**=ós**> *in the face*, phonology: reduplication, syntactic analysis: adjective/adjectival verb, attested by AD (8/80); found in <**shxwixwiyóstsel.**>, //s=xʷiy=C_1əC_2=ás-c-əl//, /'*I'm wide awake.*'/, attested by AD.

<**shxwiyxwiyós**>, dnom //s=xʷiy=C_1əC_2=ás//, chrs, EFAM ['*early-bird*'], ABFC, literally /'someone that is characteristically alert/wakes up in the face'/, (<**s=**> *nominalizer, someone that*), root <**xwiy**> *wake up*, (<**=R2**> *characteristic*), lx <**=ós**> *in the face*, phonology: reduplication, syntactic analysis: nominal, attested by IHTTC (8/8/77).

<**xwiyáxkel**>, bound stem (borrowing) //xʷiyɛ́xʸkʸəl//, probably *rack of horns*, root meaning unkonwn

<**shxwiyáxkel**>, df //s=xʷiyɛ́xʸkʸəl//, EZ /'*(moose, British Columbia moose), elk*'/, ['*(Alces alces andersoni)*'], (semological comment: the translation as *elk* is among the younger generation of

elders since all the really old speakers and cognates in the other Salish languages show that q'óyíyets is *elk* and this term is *moose*), (<**s=**> *nominalizer*), syntactic analysis: nominal, probably borrowed from Thompson (Lytton dial.) /laxʷáyaxkn/ *moose* B74c:8 (vs. Lytton dial. /sqʷáy'axkn/ *horn, antler* B74c:22, attested by Elders Group (9/1/76), BHTTC (2/5/75, 8/31/76), also <**kwiyáxqel**>, //kʷiyÉ›xʸ=qəl//, also /'*moose, rack of horns*'/, ANAA ['*rack of horns*'], attested by AL (Elders Group 3/1/72), Salish cognate: Thompson (Lytton dial.) /laxʷáyaxkn/ *moose* B74c:8 (vs. Lytton dial. /sqʷáy'axkn/ *horn, antler* B74c:22, also <**kwiyáxchel**>, //kʷiyÉ›xʸ=cəl//, also /'*moose, rack of horns*'/, ANAA ['*rack of horns*'], attested by SP (Elders Group 3/1/72), Salish cognate: Thompson (Lytton dial.) /laxʷáyaxkn/ *moose* B74c:8 (vs. Lytton dial. /sqʷáy'axkn/ *horn, antler* B74c:22.

<**xwíyeqwela**>, FIRE ['*black soot*'], *see* yéqw.

<**xwiyétheqel**>, LANG /'*to interpret, (tell on someone [EB])*'/, *see* yéth.

<**xwiyétheqet**>, LANG ['*interpret for s-o*'], *see* yéth.

<**xwiyó:leqw**>, DIR ['*(become/get) upside down*'], *see* yél or perhaps yá:l.

<**xwiyó:leqwt**>, DIR ['*turn s-o upside down*'], *see* yél or perhaps yá:l.

<**xwiyós**>, ABFC ['*alert*'], *see* xwíy ~ xʷí.

<**xwiyótheqel**>, MUS /'*(have a) high pitch (voice or melody), (have a) sharp voice*'/, *see* éy ~ éy:.

<**xwíyt**>, ABFC ['*wake s-o up*'], *see* xwíy ~ xʷí.

<**xwíythet ~ xwíthet**>, ABFC /'*wake up (oneself), (wake oneself purposely)*'/, *see* xwíy ~ xʷí.

<**xwkw'ókw'etsest**>, ABFC ['*staring at s-o*'], *see* kw'áts ~ kw'éts.

<**xwlalá:**>, df //xʷ=lÉ›lÉ›́(=)· or xʷ=lÉ›lÉ›́(-)·//, ABFC /'*straining to listen, really listening, listening hard, trying to listen, (listen [AC])*'/, possibly <**xw=**> *become, get*, possibly <**=:**> *durative or continuative*, phonology: possible lengthening, syntactic analysis: intransitive verb, attested by EB (12/17/75), also <**xwlalá**>, //xʷ=lÉ›lÉ›́//, RG & EH (4/10/99 Ling332), Salish cognate: Nooksack /ʔolænǽ/ *hear* Amoss 1961, possibly Squamish (in part) /txʷ-áyaʔn/ *listen*, W73, also <**xwlalá**>, //xʷ=lÉ›lÉ›́//, ABFC ['*just listening (not talking)*'], syntactic analysis: intransitive verb, attested by IHTTC (9/15/77), also <**xwlála**>, //xʷ=lÉ›́lÉ›//, also /'*listening*'/, attested by AC (9/18/71), also /'*listen*'/, attested by AC (9/8/71), example: <**sh:, tsel xwlalá:.**>, //š:, c-əl xʷ=lÉ›lÉ›́(=)·//, /'*Shh, I'm trying to listen.*'/, attested by EB; found in <**xwlalá:lha.**>, //xʷ=lÉ›lÉ›́·-ɬÉ›//, /'*Listen., You listen.*'/, attested by AC.

<**xwlalá:m ~ xwlalám**>, mdls //xʷ=lÉ›́lÉ›·=əm//, ABFC /'*listen, hark, listen to something particular*'/, (<**=em**> *middle voice or intransitivizer/have/get*), phonology: vowel merger, syntactic analysis: intransitive verb, attested by Elders Group (3/15/72), IHTTC (9/15/77), EB (12/17/75), RG & EH (4/10/99 Ling332), Salish cognate: PCS cognate set 61 in G82:17 quotes these: Saanich dial. of NSt /ləlén'-əŋ/ *listen* (vs. /csel'én/ *to hear*), Songish dial. of NSt /léʔn-əŋ/ *to hear* (can be followed by resultative -é,i.e. /leʔn-é-ŋ/, Sooke dial. of NSt /yə-y-ŋʔ-sát/ *listening*, Cowichan dial. of Halkomelem /xʷiyən'é·m/ *listen*; found in <**xwlalá:mlha.**>, //xʷ=lÉ›lÉ›́[-·-]=əm-ɬÉ›//, /'*Listen.*'/, attested by EB, also <**xwlalámlha.**>, //xʷ=lÉ›lÉ›́=əm-ɬÉ›//, attested by IHTTC, <**xwlalámalha.**>, //xʷ=lÉ›lÉ›́=m-É›ɬÉ›//, /'*Listen, you people.*'/, attested by IHTTC, <**xwlálámchexw.**>, //xʷ=lÉ›lÉ›́=əm-c-əxʷ.//, /'*You're called to witness.*'/, literally /'you listen'/, usage: in ceremonies in the longhouse, semantic environment ['usually follows calling out the Indian name of the person called to witness a ceremony (bestowing an Indian name, removing a new dancer's headdress, thanking people who helped initiate a dancer or helped in some other way, etc.)'], attested by Elder Roberts (Bill Roberts) (Deming 4/20/78), <**xwlalá:mchelcha.**>, //xʷ=lÉ›lÉ›́·=əm-c-əl-cÉ›//, /'*I'll listen.*'/, attested by EB,

example: <**õwelh xwlalà:m.**>, //ʔówə-ɬ xʷ=lɛlɛ́·=əm//, /'*He never listens.*'/, attested by EB.

<**xwélalà:m ~ xwélalàm**>, cts //xʷ[-ə́-]lɛlɛ́·=əm ~ xʷ[-ə́-]lɛlɛ́=əm//, ABFC ['*listening*'], (<**-é-**> *continuative*), phonology: infixed schwa, vowel merger, syntactic analysis: intransitive verb, attested by EB (12/17/75, 4/2/76).

<**xwlalá:met**>, iecs //xʷ=lɛlɛ́·=məT//, ABFC ['*listen to s-o*'], (<**=met**> *indirect effect non-control transitivizer*), syntactic analysis: transitive verb, attested by EB (12/17/75), also <**xwlalámet**>, //xʷ=lɛlɛ́=məT//, attested by AC (9/18/71), CT (6/8/76), example: <**tsel xwlalá:met.**>, //c-əl xʷ=lɛlɛ́·=məT//, /'*I listened to him.*'/, attested by EB, <**lichexw xwlalámethóx?**>, //li-c-əxʷ xʷ=lɛlɛ́=məT-áxʸ//, /'*Are you listening to me?*'/, attested by AC; found in <**xwlalámethóxlha.**>, //xʷ=lɛlɛ́=məT-áxʸ-ɬɛ//, /'*Listen to me.*'/, attested by AC, <**xwlálámethò:m.**>, //xʷ=lɛlɛ́=məT-à·m//, /'*You are listened to.*'/, attested by CT.

<**xwlalámstexw ~ xwlalástexw**>, caus //xʷ=lɛlɛ́=əm=sT-əxʷ ~ /xʷ=lɛlɛ́=sT-əxʷ//, SOC ['*make s-o listen*'], SPRD /'*call s-o to witness, call s-o to listen*'/, REL, (<**=st**> *causative control transitivizer*), (<**-exw**> *third person object*), phonology: vowel merger, syntactic analysis: transitive verb, attested by IHTTC, Elders Group, RG & EH (4/10/99 Ling332); found in <**xwlalámsthòm.**>, //xʷ=lɛlɛ́=m=sT-à·m//, /'*You are made to listen., You are called to witness/listen.*'/, attested by IHTTC (9/15/77), Elders Group (6/8/77), <**xwelalámsthòxes**>, //xʷ=lɛlɛ́=m=sT-àxʸ-əs//, SPRD /'*he/she calle me to witness*'/, attested by RG & EH (4/10/99 Ling332), <**xwelalástem ~ xwelalámstem**>, //xʷ=lɛlɛ́=sT-əm ~ /xʷ=lɛlɛ́=m=sT-əm//, SPRD /'*they call him/her/them to witness*'/, lit. "he/she/they is/are caused to listen", attested by RG & EH (4/10/99 Ling332), <**xwelalástem tútl'ò**>, //xʷ=lɛlɛ́=sT-əm t=ə́w=ƛ'a//, SPRD /'*he is (called) to witness*'/, attested by RG & EH (4/10/99 Ling332)

<**xwlalá:m ~ xwlalám**>, ABFC /'*listen, hark, listen to something particular*'/, *see* xwlalá:.

<**xwlalá:met**>, ABFC ['*listen to s-o*'], *see* xwlalá:.

<**xwlalá(m)stexw**>, SOC ['*make s-o listen*'], *see* xwlalá:.

<**xwléts'eqel**>, LANG ['*different language*'], *see* láts'.

<**xwlí**>, possible stem //xʷ=lí//, but *also see main entry under* lí.

<**shxwlí**>, dnom //sxʷ=lí//, DIR /'*(place, location), where s-o is at*'/, literally /'something that's at (or) place where s-o is at'/, (<**s= ~ shxw=**> *something that, nominalizer*), possibly <**xw=**> *located at, from(?)*, probably root <**lí**> *be at, in, on; be there*, syntactic analysis: nominal, attested by JL (Elders Group (3/29/78), Salish cognate: Lushootseed in part /diʔ/ *to, at the side of, in* H76:138, perhaps Squamish /naʔ/ *be on, at (location, time); be there: be absent* K67:312, example: <**kwxõmexws ta' shxwlí**>, //kʷəxʸ=óməxʷ-s t-ɛʔ s=xʷ=lí//, /'*place name, name of the place where you come from*'/, attested by JL also *see main entry under* lí.

<**õwéta xwlí:s**>, cpds //ʔowə= ́tɛ xʷ=lí-s//, EFAM /'*it doesn't matter, it's useless*'/, literally /'where it's at is nothing'/, syntactic analysis: vp, attested by Deming (1/18/79).

<**ewétò shxwlís**>, cpds //ʔəwə= ́tɛ-à s=xʷ=lí-s//, EFAM /'*useless, no special use, ordinary*'/, literally /'where it's at is just nothing'/, syntactic analysis: vp, attested by Elders Group (4/2/80), example: <**le ewétò shxwlís st'ìlèm.**>, //lə ʔəwə= ́tɛ-à s=xʷ=lí-s s=t'íl=əm//, /'*It was just an ordinary song., It was a useless song., It was a song of no special use.*'/, attested by Elders Group.

<**ewéta shxwlístexw**>, caus //ʔəwə= ́tɛ s=xʷ=lí=sT-əxʷ//, cpds, EFAM /'*not care about s-o, have no use for s-o, be impassive*'/, literally /'cause s-o to be at nothing'/, (<**=st**> *causative control transitivizer*), (<**-exw**> *third person object*), syntactic analysis: vneg nominal=transitive verb, attested by Elders Group (4/6/77), example: <**ewéta shxwlístexw tewátes.**>, //ʔəwə= ́tɛ

s=xʷ=lí=sT-əxʷ tə=wɛ́t=əs//, /'*He doesn't care about anyone., He's got no use for anyone., He's impassive.*'/, attested by Elders Group.

<**xwlíyémés**>, ABFC ['*to smile*'], *see* líyém ~ leyém.

<**xwló:yemes**>, ABFC ['*smiling*'], *see* líyém ~ leyém.

<**xwlhépelets**>, ABDF /'*sat down (with a plop?), [slip off on one's bottom or chair]*'/, *see* x̲wlhép.

<**xwmá:m** or **lexwmá:m**>, DESC /'*open (of a bottle, basket, etc.)*'/, *see* má ~ má'-.

<**xwmath'elqéylémt**>, EFAM ['*tell a lie for s-o*'], *see* máth'el.

<**xwmá:x**>, MC /'*open it (door, gate, anything)*'/, *see* má ~ má'-.

<**xwmékwàthel**>, ABDF ['*he got kissed*'], *see* mékw.

<**xwmékwàthem**>, ABDF ['*kiss*'], *see* mékw.

<**xwmékwàtht**>, ABDF /'*kiss s-th, (kiss s-o [Deming, IHTTC])*'/, *see* mékw.

<**xwmítsesem**>, ABFC ['*pass s-th (by hand)*'], *see* mí ~ mé ~ me.

<**xwókwesem**>, izs //xʷákʷ(=)əs=əm//, SM ['*smells like urine*'], root meaning unknown, possibly <**=es**> *on the face*, (<**=em**> *have/get/intransitive or middle voice*), syntactic analysis: intransitive verb, attested by Elders Group (5/25/77), compare perhaps <**xwóxweqw'em**> *bad-smelling*, Salish cognate: perhaps Lushootseed /xʷásəb/ *the smell of urine* H76:558 (this cognate would point to an UHk mistransciption–that the form should be <**xwóxwesem**>), prob. not Lushootseed /xʷák'ʷəb/ *smell of s-th burning (usu. feathers)* H76:557.

<**xwókw' ~ xwekw'ó**>, bound root //xʷák'ʷ *drag*//.

<**xwekw'ót**>, pcs //xʷák'ʷ-M1=əT//, ABFC ['*drag s-th/s-o*'], (<**metathesis type 1**> *non-continuative*), (<**=et**> *purposeful control transitivizer*), phonology: metathesis, syntactic analysis: transitive verb, attested by AD (3/5/79), Elders Group (3/72), EB (5/3/76), Salish cognate: Squamish /xʷúk'ʷ-n/ *drag, pull (tr.)* W73:84, K67:349, also <**xweqwót**>, //xʷáqʷ=M1=T//, comment: qw prob. mistranscribed for kw', attested by AC (8/11/70), also <**xwókw'et**>, //xʷák'ʷ=əT//, attested by Elders Group (3/72), example: <**xwekw'ótes tl' Bill the Málí.**>, //xʷák'ʷ=M1=T-əsƛ' Bill θə mɛ́lí//, /'*Bill drags Mary.*'/, *<**xwekw'á:ls te Bill the Málí.**> rejected by EB (5/3/76), <**xweqwótes te syáyas.**>, //xʷáqʷ=M1=T-əs tə s=yɛ́yɛ-s//, /'*He dragged his friend.*'/, attested by AC.

<**xwó:kw'thet**>, pcrs //xʷá[=·=]k'ʷ=T-ət//, ABFC ['*drag oneself*'], (<**=:=**> meaning unclear), (<**-et**> *reflexive*), phonology: lengthening, syntactic analysis: intransitive verb, attested by Elders Group (3/72), also <**xwóqw'ethet**>, //xʷáq'ʷ=əT-ət//, also ABFC /'*crawl (as of a snake, seal, slug, snail)*'/, (semological comment: a snake doesn't ts'átem *crawl (on legs)*), comment: qw' may be alternative to kw' rather than mistranscription here, also different is the non-metathesized non-continuative form here unlike for most of the Coqualeetza Elders Group, attested by Deming (1/31/80).

<**xwéqw'ethet**>, cts //xʷa[-Aə́-]q'ʷ=əT-ət//, ABFC /'*crawling (as of snake, seal, slug, snail), (dragging oneself)*'/, (<**é-ablaut**> *continuative*), phonology: ablaut, syntactic analysis: intransitive verb, attested by Deming (1/31/80), example: <**xwéqw'ethet te (áshxw, q'oyátl'iya, álhqey).**>, //xʷa[-Aə́-]q'ʷ=əT-ət tə (ʔɛ́sxʷ, q'ayɛ́ƛ'=iyɛ, ʔɛ́ɬq=əy)//, /'*The (seal, snail/slug, snake) is crawling.*'/, attested by Deming (1/31/80).

<**xwekw'á:ls**>, sas //xʷak'ʷ-M1=ɛ́(·)ls//, SOC /'*to drag (for a body in the river, for ex.)*'/, (<**metathesis type 1**> *non-continuative*), (<**=á:ls ~ =áls**> *structured activity continuative*), phonology: metathesis, vowel merger, syntactic analysis: intransitive verb, attested by EB (5/3/76), also

<**xweqwá:ls**>, //x^{w}aq^w=M1=ɛ́(·)ls//, also /'*to drag (for ex. wood, logs, persons)*'/, attested by AC (8/11/70), example: <**xwekw'á:ls te Bill.**>, //x^{w}ak'^{w}=M1=ɛ́(·)ls tə Bill//, /'*Bill went to drag.*'/, attested by EB (5/3/76).

<**xwóqw'el**>, incs //x^{w}áq'^{w}=əl//, ABFC ['*drag*'], comment: qw' prob. mistranscribed for kw', (<**=el**> *go, come, get, become*), syntactic analysis: intransitive verb, attested by Elders Group (10/1/75).

<**xwekw'ó:st**>, ds //x^{w}ák'^{w}-M1=əs=T or x^{w}ák'^{w}-M1=á·s=T//, pcs, ABFC ['*drag s-th/s-o*'], literally /'drag s-o/s-th purposely on the face'/, (<**metathesis type 1**> *non-continuative*), lx <**=es ~ =ó:s**> *on the face*, (<**=t**> *purposeful control transitivizer*), phonology: metathesis, vowel merger, syntactic analysis: transitive verb, attested by Elders Group (3/72), EB (5/3/76), Salish cognate: Saanich dial. of NSt /x^{w}k'^{w}ást/ *to drag s-th* B74a:61, also <**xwekw'óst**>, //x^{w}ák'^{w}=M1=əs=T//, attested by AD (3/5/79), RG & EH (4/9/99 Ling332); found in <**xwekw'ó:stem.**>, //x^{w}ák'^{w}=M1=əs=T-əm//, /'*Someone was dragged.*'/, attested by EB, example: <**lámtsel xwekw'óst.**>, //lɛ́=m-c-əl x^{w}ák'^{w}=M1=əs=T//, /'*I'm going to drag it.*'/, attested by AD.

<**xwékw'est**>, cts //x^{w}a[-Aə́-]k'^{w}=əs=T//, ABFC ['*dragging s-o/s-th*'], (<**é-ablaut**> *continuative*), phonology: ablaut, syntactic analysis: transitive verb, attested by Elders Group (3/72), AD (3/5/79), also <**xwéqwest ~ xwéqw'est**>, //x^{w}a[-Aə́-]q^w=əs=T ~ x^{w}a[-Aə́-]q'^{w}=əs=T//, attested by AC (8/11/70).

<**xwixwekw'ósxelem ~ xwekw'ósxelem**>, mdls //C$_1$í=x^{w}ak'^{w}=(M1=)ás=x^{y}əl=əm//, dmv, ABDF ['*dragging one's feet*'], literally /'dragging the face of one's foot (sole) a little'/, (<**R4=**> *diminutive action*), (semological comment: as in Musqueam (Suttles ca1984:ch.7) verb diminutives are always also continuative), lx <**=ós**> *on the face*, lx <**=xel**> *of the foot*, (semological comment: these two suffixes combine semantically to produce *on the sole of the foot* (the independent word for *sole of foot*, shxw'óthesxel,is also literally *the face of the foot*)), (<**=em**> *middle voice*), phonology: reduplication, possibly metathesis, syntactic analysis: intransitive verb, attested by Elders Group (10/27/76).

<**xwókw'eletsem**>, mdls //x^{w}ák'^{w}=ələc=əm//, cts, ABDF ['*dragging one's behind or rump or bottom*'], lx <**=elets**> *on the bottom, on the rump*, (semological comment: lack of metathesis type 1 yields *continuative* here), (<**=em**> *middle voice*), syntactic analysis: intransitive verb, attested by Elders Group (3/15/72), example: <**xwókw'eletsem lhíxw só:les**>, //x^{w}ák'^{w}=ələc=əm ɬí-x^w səl=á·[=M2=]s//, /'*dragging your behind when you're drunk*'/, attested by Elders Group (3/15/72).

<**xwókw'eletsem**>, ds //x^{w}ák'^{w}=ələc=əm//, CAN /'*high-bow canoe, high-bow river canoe, streetcar, tram, taxi, car, automobile*'/, literally /'dragging one's rump/bottom'/, ASM ['thirty or forty feet long, four feet wide, made by the Chilliwacks and others for travel to salt water, it had a projecting bow (see drawing Elders Group 1/28/76) and was used for everything'], (<**zero**> *nominalizer*), syntactic analysis: nominal, attested by DM (12/4/64 new transcript new p.167), Elders Group (3/15/72, 3/1/76) Deming (1/31/80), also <**xwóqw'eletsem**>, //x^{w}áq'^{w}=ələc=əm//, attested by Elders Group (10/1/75, 1/28/76).

<**xwixwekw'elátsem**>, dmn //C$_1$í=x^{w}ak'^{w}=ələ[=Aɛ́=]c=əm//, durs, CAN /'*automobile, car*'/, literally /'dragging its bottom a little, dragging its little bottom'/, (semological comment: perhaps referring to the tailpipe?), (<**R4=**> *diminutive*), (<**á-ablaut**> *derivational or durative*), phonology: reduplication, ablaut, syntactic analysis: nominal, attested by IHTTC (7/28/77), contrast <**to<u>x</u>wemíwel**> *car, automobile*, contrast <**kyó:**> *car, automobile.*

<**shxweqw'élqstel**>, df //s=x^{w}əq'^{w}=ə́ləqs=təl//, CLO ['*nose-ring*'], PE, literally /'(prob.) something to drag on the nose device'/, (<**s=**> *something to, nominalizer*), probably root <**xwokw'**> *drag*, comment: qw' may be Chill. variant pronunciation for kw' as in *drag*, lx <**=éleqs**> *on the nose*, lx

<**=tel**> *device, device to, something to*, phonology: vowel-reduction in root, syntactic analysis: nominal, attested by DM (12/4/64 new transcript new pp.180-181).

<**shxwékw'thelh sq'éytes**>, cpds //s=xʷək'ʷ=θəɬ s=q'ít=əs// (sic for <**shxwékw'lhelh sqéytes**>, cpds //s=x ʷək'ʷ=ɬəɬ s=q'ít=əs//), CLO /'*kerchief*'/, lit. /"dragged on the throat headband"/, <**s=**> nominalizer, <**xwekw'**> *drag*, <**=élhelh ~ =lhelh** ~ poss. **=elhlelh**> *in the windpipe, throat*, <**s=**> nominalizer, <**qít**> *tied*, <**=es**> *on the face*, attested by RG & EH (4/10/99 Ling332)

<**xwókw'**>, bound root //xʷák'ʷ *numb*//.

<**shxwóxwekw'**>, strs //s=xʷá[=C_1ə=]k'ʷ//, ABDF ['*numb (can also be used joking of a drunk)*'], (<**s=**> *stative*), (<**=R1=**> *resultative*), phonology: reduplication, syntactic analysis: adjective/adjectival verb, attested by EB (7/6/76), IHTTC (8/8/77), Salish cognate: Squamish /ʔəs-xʷá-xʷk'ʷ/ *drunk* with the same root in /xʷák'ʷ-i/ //xʷák'ʷ=iy// *get drunk* and /xʷák'ʷ-i-šn/ *have pins and needles in one's leg* (but vs. /tnúɬ/ *numb*) W73:86, K69:78, K67:349, Sechelt /s-xʷák'ʷil/ *drunk* T77:22, B77:54 (vs. Sechelt /č'áč'áɬ/ *numb* B77:56), Saanich dial. of NSt /s-xʷəxʷék'ʷ-təŋ/ *drunk* and /sxʷéʔxʷək'ʷ/ *crazy* B74aa:44, 46, Samish dial. of NSt (LD) /s-xʷəxʷík'ʷtŋ/ *drunk*, and perhaps Lushootseed /xʷák'ʷil/ *tired* H76:557.

<**xwókw'eltem**>, df //xʷák'ʷ=əl=təm or xʷák'ʷ=əl=T-əm//, ABDF /'*numb, made numb*'/, (<**=el**> *go, come, get, become*), possibly <**=tem**> *past participle*, possibly <**=T**> *purposeful control transitivizer*, possibly <**=em**> *intransivizer, have, get*, syntactic analysis: adjective/adjectival verb, attested by EB (12/4/75, 7/6/76), example: <**ley xwókw'eltem.**>, //lə yə=xʷák'ʷ=əl=təm//, ABDF, /'*getting numb, going to sleep (of foot or other parts)*'/, attested by EB.

<**xwókw'elxel**>, ds //xʷák'ʷ=əl=xʸəl//, ABDF /'*numb in the foot, the foot is asleep*'/, lx <**=xel**> *on the foot*, syntactic analysis: adjective/adjectival verb, attested by EB (7/6/76).

<**xwókw'eltel**>, ds //xʷák'ʷ=ɛltəl or xʷák'ʷ=əl=təl//, EB ['*big-leaved avens*'], ['*Geum macrophyllum*'], MED ['*numbing medicine*'], ASM ['part rubbed on as a numbing medicine, also eaten by the ruffed grouse'], lx <**=altel**> *medicine*, possibly <**=el**> *come, go, get, become*, possibly <**=tel**> *something to, device to*, syntactic analysis: nominal.

<**xwókw'eletsem**>, ABDF ['*dragging one's behind or rump or bottom*'], *see* xwókw' ~ xwekw'ó.

<**xwókw'eletsem**>, CAN /'*high-bow canoe, high-bow river canoe, streetcar, tram, taxi, car, automobile*'/, *see* xwókw' ~ xwekw'ó.

<**xwókw'eltel**>, EB ['*big-leaved avens*'], *see* xwókw'.

<**xwókw'eltem**>, ABDF /'*numb, made numb*'/, *see* xwókw'.

<**xwókw'elxel**>, ABDF /'*numb in the foot, the foot is asleep*'/, *see* xwókw'.

<**xwó:kw'thet**>, ABFC ['*drag oneself*'], *see* xwókw' ~ xwekw'ó.

<**Xwoqwsemó:leqw**>, df //xʷə([=Aa=])=qʷəs=əm=ə[-Aá·-]ləqʷ//, PLN ['*basin lake near top of Cheam Peak*'], ASM ['also called hole at foot of Cheam Peak, both translations make sense because the lake, of about 30- to 40-foot diameter, is located at the base of the peak (at 4800 ft.) just below where it starts the final sharp ascent to the 6913ft. summit from a long meadowed ridge at about the 5800ft. level, when I made the climb with two friends about 1982 and camped on the meadow overnight we could see the lake from the meadow and it was very tempting to use it to wash up, we started down but it proved a lot further than it looked (1000 ft. down) though reachable with some care, certainly it was used for just such purposes by the Stó:lō people who camped and picked blueberries on the meadows there (the blueberries are still delicious for breakfast there)'], Elder's comment: "it means *washing one's head*", literally perhaps /'place to get dropped into the water on top of the head/hair'/,

(semological comment: perhaps so named because one could easily fall head-first into the little lake since the mountain around it has slippery vegetation and is moderately steep), possibly <**xwe=**> *get, become*, possibly <**o-ablaut**> *continuative or derivational*, possibly root <**qwes**> *fall in the water, drop in the water*, possibly <**=em**> *place to have/get or intransitivizer or middle voice*, lx <**=eleqw**> *on top of the head, on the hair*, possibly <**ó:-ablaut**> *durative* or *derivational*, possibly <**zero**> *nominalizer*, phonology: possible vowel-loss, possible ablaut, zero nominalizer, syntactic analysis: nominal, attested by CT (1973), source: place names reference file #274 and #274a. Compare <**xwóyeqwem**> (or perhaps) <**xwáyeqwem**>, mdls //xʷáy=əqʷ=əm or xʷɛ́y=əqʷ=əm//, ABFC ['*wash one's head and hair*'], root meaning unknown unless related to <xwíqw=et> (<xwíyqw=et>) *press and rub it, iron it*<**xwóqw'**> or more likely <**xwáqw'**>, bound root //xʷáq'ʷ// or //xʷɛ́q'ʷ// *bad smell (of s-th burning?)*(see Lushootseed cognate)

<**xwóqw'el**>, ABFC ['*drag*'], *see* xwókw' ~ xwekw'ó.

<**Xwóqw'ilwets?**>, df //xʷáq'ʷ=il(=)wəc//, PLN ['*village near Katz*'], root meaning unknown unless <**xwóqw'**> *bad-smelling* or <**xwókw'**> *numb*, possibly <**=il**> *go, come, get, become*, possibly <**=ewets**> *on the back*, syntactic analysis: nominal, source: Wells 1965 (lst ed.):25 <WHAH-kw.ayl-wihts> *village near Katz.*

<**xwótekwem**>, FIRE ['*(have/get) a sudden flame*'], *see* xwótkwem.

<**xwótkw ~ xwótqw**>, bound root or stem //xʷát(=)kʷ ~ xʷát(=)qʷ or xʷɛ[=Aá=]t(=)kʷ/qʷ// *dig out, hollow out*, possibly root <**xwát**> *lighten (in weight)*??, possibly <**ó=ablaut**> *resultative*, possibly <**=kw**> *round, in circles*,

<**shxwótkw**>, strs //s=xʷɛ[=Aá=]t(=)kʷ//, SH /'*(be) dug out, (be hollowed out)*'/, (<**s=**> *stative*), possibly root <**xwát**> *lighten (in weight)*??, possibly <**ó=ablaut**> *resultative*, possibly <**=kw**> *round, in circles*, phonology: possible ablaut, syntactic analysis: adjective/adjectival verb, attested by EB (7/6/76).

<**shxwótkwewel**>, stvi //s=xʷát(=)kʷ=iwəl or s=xʷɛ[=Aá=]t(=)kʷ=əwəl//, SH ['*hollow (of tree or log)*'], (<**s=**> *stative*), lx <**=iwel ~ =ewel**> *in the insides*, phonology: possible ablaut, vowel reduction or allomorph, syntactic analysis: adjective/adjectival verb, attested by Elders Group (3/15/72), CT (6/8/76), also <**shxwótqwewel**>, //s=xʷát(=)qʷ=iwəl or s=xʷát(=)qʷ=əwəl//, attested by AD (3/6/79).

<**xetqwewí:lt**>, pcs //xʸət(=)qʷ=iwəl=í·l=T or xʷ[=F=]at(=)qʷ=iwəl=í·l=T//, incs, SH ['*hollow it out*'], root meaning unknown unless <**xwót(=)qw=iwel**> *hollow*, possibly <**=F= (fronting)**> *diminutive*, lx <**=í:l**> *go, come, get, become*, (<**=t**> *purposeful control transitivizer*), phonology: possible fronting, vowel-reduction or allomorph, syllable-loss, syntactic analysis: transitive verb, attested by AD (3/6/79), Salish cognate: Saanich dial. of NSt /šətqʷ-kʷíl-ət/ *to hollow s-th out* B74a:65.

<**xwótkwem**>, df //xʷátkʷ=əm//, FIRE /'*(to) flame, (have/get) a flame, to blaze*'/, root meaning unknown, (<**=em**> *have/get/intransitivizer or middle voice*), syntactic analysis: intransitive verb, attested by Elders Group (10/27/76, 1/16/80), EB (5/26/76), Salish cognate: Squamish /xʷə́tkʷ-m ~ xʷə́-xʷətkʷ-m/ *to flame* W73:102, K69:78, prob. not Lushootseed root /x̣ʷikʷ(i)/ in /ʔu-x̣ʷíkʷi-cut/ *(the fire) blazed up* H76:616.

<**xwótekwem**>, cts //xʷát[-ə-]kʷ=əm//, FIRE ['*(have/get) a sudden flame*'], possibly <**-e-**> *continuative*, phonology: infixed schwa, syntactic analysis: intransitive verb, attested by EB (5/26/76).

<**xwótqwem**>, df //xʷátqʷ=əm//, SD /'*make the sound of water splashing or dripping fast, (make the sound of a waterfall, make the sound of pouring rain dripping or splashing in puddles loudly)*'/,

WATR, root meaning unknown, (<**=em**> *intransitivizer/have/get or middle voice*), syntactic analysis: intransitive verb, attested by LG (Deming 4/17/80), Salish cognate: Nooksack /xʷátqʷəm/ *make the sound of a waterfall/loud splashing of falling water* (BG field notes), possible connection with Lushootseed root /xʷít'- ~ xʷt'-/ *fall/drop from a height* as in /s-xʷət'/ *waterfall* and /ʔu-xʷít'-il/ *fall (from a high place)* H76:564, possible connection with Sechelt and Mainland Comox /x̣ʷax̣ʷát'q'ím/ *thunderstorm*?? T77:8, B75prelim:4, also SD [*'sound of boiling water'*], attested by AD (4/21/80), also /*'dripping fast'*/, attested by SJ (Deming 4/17/80).

<**shxwótqwelwetem**>, ds //s=xʷátqʷ=əlwət=əm//, HHG [*'washboard'*], CLO, literally /'something to sound loud splashing water on one's clothes (or) something to have/get the sound of loud splashing water on clothes'/, (<**s=**> *nominalizer, something to*), probably root <**xwótqw**> *sound of loud splashing water*, lx <**=elwet**> *clothes*, probably <**=em**> *middle voice or intransitivizer/have/get*, syntactic analysis: nominal, attested by BHTTC (9/1/76).

<**xwót'kw'em**>, df //xʷát'k'ʷ=əm or xʷá[=t'=]k'ʷ=əm//, SD /*'(have/get) soft rustling (of material), shuffling (sound)'*/, possibly <**=t'=**> *sound*??, possibly root <**xwókw'**> *drag* possibly root as in <**xwekw'ót**> *drag s-th/s-o*, (<**=em**> *intransitivizer/have/get*), phonology: possible infixed lexical affix??, syntactic analysis: intransitive verb, attested by Elders Group (10/27/76), contrast <**xwótq'esílem**> *raven's trilling sound (like hoarse woman's voice)*, Salish cognate: infix perhaps also in Squamish /c'ət'q'-m/ *a drop falls* cognate with Upriver Halkomelem /θ'q'ə́m/ *to drip* W73:85, K69:54.

<**xwót'kw'emxel**>, ds //xʷát'k'ʷ=əm=xʸəl//, ABDF /*'drag one's foot, to shuffle (the feet)'*/, possibly root <**xwókw'**> *drag* possibly root as in <**xwekw'ót**> *drag s-th/s-o*, possibly <**=t'=**> *sound*??, (<**=em**> *intransitivizer/have/get*), lx <**=xel**> *on the foot*, syntactic analysis: intransitive verb, attested by Elders Group (10/27/76).

<**xwétkw'em**>, df //xʷa[=Aə́=]t'[=G=]k'ʷ=əm//, CLO [*'denim cloth'*], literally /'place to have/get shuffling/rustling sound'/, Elder's comment: "refers to the sound it makes", (<**é-ablaut**> *derivational*), possibly <**=G= (deglottalization)**> *derivational* or mistranscribed, possibly <**=em**> *place to have/get*, phonology: possible ablaut, possible deglottalization, syntactic analysis: nominal, attested by BHTTC (late 10/76).

<**xwétkw'emáyiws**>, ds //xʷa[=Aə́=]t[=G=]k'ʷ=əm=ɛ́y(=)iws//, CLO /*'denim pants, jeans'*/, lx <**=áyiws**> *pants* lx <**from =áy**> *bark/wool/covering and =iws> on the body*, phonology: possible ablaut, possible deglottalization, syntactic analysis: nominal, attested by BHTTC (late 10/76).

<**xwétkw'emélwet**>, ds //xʷa[=Aə́=]t[=G=]k'ʷ=əm=ə́lwət//, CLO [*'denim clothes'*], lx <**=ə́lwət**> *clothes*, phonology: possible ablaut, possible deglottalization, syntactic analysis: nominal, attested by BHTTC (late 10/76).

<**xwót'kw'emxel**>, ABDF /*'drag one's foot, to shuffle (the feet)'*/, *see* xwót'kw'em.

<**xwot'q'esílem**>, df //xʷat'q'(=)əs=íl=əm or xʷa[=t'=]q'=əs=íl=əm//, SD [*'a trilling sound a raven makes'*], EZ, LANG, ASM ['sounds like a hoarse woman's voice, it means someone will give you something if you hear it'], Elder's comment: "it means <**áxwethòm kw'ewátes**> (*someone will give you something*)", root meaning unknown, possibly <**=t'=**> *sound*??, possibly <**=es**> *on the face*, lx <**=íl**> *go, come, get, become*, (<**=em**> *intransitivizer/have/get or middle voice*), phonology: possible infixed lexical affix??, syntactic analysis: intransitive verb, attested by AK (Trip to Five-Mile Creek 4/30/79), AD (5/1/79).

<**xwóthet**>, ABDF /*'to abstain from food, to fast, starve oneself'*/, *see* xwá.

<**xwóxw**>, possible root //xʷáxʷ//, meaning unknown

<**shxwóxw**>, df //s=x^{w}áx^{w}//, EB /'*rabbit, (varying hare,* perhaps now also the introduced *eastern cottontail)*'/, ['*Lepus americanus cascadensis and Lepus americanus washingtoni*, now perhaps *Sylvilagus floridanus mearnsi*'], (<**s=**> *nominalizer*), root meaning unknown, syntactic analysis: nominal, dialects: *Tait*, attested by AK (11/21/72), Salish cognate: probably not Squamish /sx^{w}ax^{w}/ *pigmy owl, saw-whet owl (Aegolius acadicus)* K67:294, Kennedy and Bouchard 1976:85.

<**xwóxwe**>, DESC /'*light (weight), lightweight*'/, *see* xwá.

<**xwóxweqw'em**>, izs //x^{w}á[=C$_1$ə=]q'^{w}=əm//, SM ['*bad-smelling*'], root meaning unknown, possibly <**=R1=**> *continuative or resultative*, possibly <**=em**> *intransitivizer/have/get or middle voice*, perhaps compare <**xwókwesem**> *smells like urine*, phonology: reduplication, syntactic analysis: adjective/adjectival verb, attested by Deming (3/23/78), Salish cognate: perhaps Lushootseed /x^{w}ák'^{w}əb/ *smellof s-th burning (usu. feathers)* H76:557.

<**xwóxweyem**>, ECON ['*selling*'], *see* xwóyem.

<**xwoxweyíwel**>, EFAM /'*be happy, being happy*'/, *see* xwoyíwel ~ xwoyíwél.

<**xwoxwiyómet**>, ECON ['*selling it*'], *see* xwóyem.

<**xwoxwiyómethet ~ xoxwiyómethet**>, pcrs //x̣^{w}[=K=]ə[-C$_1$ə-]yɛ[=Aá=]m=əT-ət or x^{w}a[-C$_1$ə-]y=ə[=Aá=]m=əT-ət//, cts, durs, LANG /'*denying an accusation, clearing oneself*'/, literally /'telling a story purposely on oneself for a long time'/ or possibly /'selling oneself on purpose for a long time'/, possibly root <**xwóy=em**> *sell*, or root <**x̲wiyám**> *tell a story*, or root <**xoy=em**> meaning unknown, possibly <**=K= (fronting)**> *derivational*, (<**-R1-**> *continuative*), (<**ó-ablaut**> *durative*), (<**=et**> *purposeful control transitivizer*), (<**-et**> *reflexive*), phonology: reduplication, ablaut, possible fronting, comment: originally transcribed as xoxwiyómethet but x must be in error for xw in light of the cognates and the Halkomelem forms which are likely to show the same root; however it is possible that an otherwise unknown root <**xoy(=)em**> is the root here since a number of roots beginning in <**x**> have -R1- reduplication with <**xwe**> instead of <**xe**>, see <xixwewe> *urinating* from <xíwe> *urinate* and <xoxwwí:ls> *a borer*, syntactic analysis: intransitive verb, attested by IHTTC (7/19/77), Salish cognate: Squamish /x^{w}íyin-cút/ *deny (a lie)* B78:74, Mainland Comox /x̣^{w}áʔíʔəsčit/ *to deny (a lie)* B75prelim.:72.

<**xwoxwth'áleq[w]thom**>, EFAM /'*you're crazy in the head, you're sick in the head*'/, *see* xwáth'.

<**xwoxwth'í:lem**>, SOCT /'*prostitute, whore*'/, *see* xwáth'.

<**xwó:xwth'tem**>, EFAM ['*sexy*'], *see* xwáth'.

<**xwóyem**>, izs //x^{w}áy=əm//, ECON ['*sell*'], (<**=em**> *intransitivizer/have/get*), syntactic analysis: intransitive verb, attested by EB (1/30/76, 5/4/76), Salish cognate: Squamish /x̣^{w}úyum/ *sell (itr.)* W73:226, K67:349, Lushootseed /x^{w}úyub/ *sell* H76:573.

<**xwóxweyem**>, cts //x^{w}á[-C$_1$ə-]y=əm//, ECON ['*selling*'], (<**-R1-**> *continuative*), phonology: reduplication, syntactic analysis: intransitive verb, attested by EB (5/4/76).

<**xwóymét ~ xwó:ymét**>, pcs //x^{w}áy=əm=əT//, ECON ['*sell s-th*'], (<**=em**> *intransitivizer/have/get*), (<**=et**> *purposeful control transitivizer*), possibly <**=met**> *indirect effect non-control transitivizer*, phonology: updrifting, vowel-loss, syntactic analysis: transitive verb, attested by EB (2/2/76, 1/30/76, 5/4/76), example: <**xwóymetes tutl'o te sth'óqwi.**>, //x^{w}áy=əm=əT-əs t=u=ƛ'a tə s=θ'áq^{w}(=)i//, /'*He sold the fish.*'/, *<**xwóyem tutl'o te sth'óqwi.**> rejected by EB (5/4/76).

<**xwoxwiyómet**>, cts //x^{w}a[-C$_1$ə-]y=ə[=Aá=]m=əT//, ECON ['*selling it*'], (<**-R1-**> *continuative*), possibly <**ó-ablaut**> *durative*, phonology: reduplication, possible ablaut, syntactic analysis: transitive verb, attested by EB (2/2/76).

<**shxwimá:le ~ shxwiymála ~ shxwímàlà**>, dnom //s=xʷ(a)y=(ə)m=ɛ́(·)lɛ́//, BLDG ['*a store (commercial establishment)*'], ECON, literally /'container of something to sell'/, lx <**=á:la ~ =ála ~ =àlà**> *container of*, phonology: double vowel-loss, vowel-reduction, vocalization of y, updrifting, downstepping, syntactic analysis: nominal, attested by AC (9/18/71), Elders Group (7/27/75, 1/21/76).

<**xwóyeqwem**> (or perhaps) <**xwáyeqwem**>, mdls //xʷáy=əqʷ=əm or xʷɛ́y=əqʷ=əm//, ABFC ['*wash one's head and hair*'], root meaning unknown unless related to <**xwíqw=et**> (<**xwíyqw=et**>) *press and rub it, iron it*, lx <**=eqw**> *on top of the head, on the hair*, (<**=em**> *middle voice*), syntactic analysis: intransitive verb, attested by AC (11/11/71), Salish cognate: Squamish /xʷáyʔ-qʷ-mʔ/ *wash one's head* W73:282, K67:349, example: <**latsel xwóyeqwem.**>, //lɛ-c-əl xʷáy=əqʷ=əm//, /'*I'm going to wash my head.*'/, attested by AC.

<**xwóyeqw'em**>, df //xʷáyəq'ʷ=əm//, ABDF /'*(have/get) wheezing, rattling breath*'/, root meaning unknown, (<**=em**> *have/get/intransitivizer or middle voice*), syntactic analysis: intransitive verb, attested by Elders Group (12/15/76).

<**xwóyeqw'emíles**>, ds //xʷóyəq'ʷ=əm=íləs//, ABDF /'*wheezing in the chest, rattling in the chest*'/, lx <**=íles**> *in the chest*, syntactic analysis: intransitive verb, attested by Elders Group (12/15/76).

<**xwóyeqw'emíles**>, ABDF /'*wheezing in the chest, rattling in the chest*'/, *see* xwóyeqw'em.

<**xwoyíwel ~ xwoyíwél**>, df //xʷay=íwəl or xʷ=(ʔ)ɛ[=Aa=]y=íwəl//, EFAM /'*become glad, become happy, happy inside*'/, literally /'(probably) become good in the insides/mind'/, possibly <**xwe=**> *get, become*, possibly root <**éy**> *be good*, possibly <**o-ablaut**> *derivational*, lx <**=íwel**> *in the mind, in the insides*, phonology: optional updrifting, possible ablaut, syntactic analysis: adjective/adjectival verb, attested by Elders Group (3/15/72, 4/16/75, 7/9/75, 2/16/77, 3/2/77), EB (12/16/75), Deming (5/18/78), compare <**xwóywél**> *thrill* (possibly an alternate pronunciation and translation for <**xwoyíwel**>**?**, possibly a distinct word**)**, Salish cognate: probably not Squamish /(ʔə)s-xʷí-xʷiq/ *happy, lively, gay* W73:130, K67:294, K69:59, 92, example: <**(xwoyíwel, éy) tel sqwálewel.**>, //(xʷ=(ʔ)ɛ[=Aa=]y=íwəl, ʔɛ́y) t-əl s=qʷɛ̀l=iwəl//, /'*I'm happy.*'/, literally /'my thoughts/feelings are happy/glad'/, attested by Elders Group (4/16/75), <**xwoyíwel kw'el sqwá:lewel.**>, //xʷ=(ʔ)ɛ[=Aa=]y=íwəl k'ʷ-əl s=qʷɛ̀·l=iwəl//, /'*I'm happy.*'/, attested by Elders Group (2/16/77), <**ts'áts'eltsel xwoyíwel tel sqwálewel kw'els me xwe'í sq'ó talhluwep (éy l sí:yáye, l sí:yáye sí:yám).**>, //c'ɛ́[=C_1ə=]l-c-əl xʷ=(ʔ)ɛ[=Aa=]y=íwəl t-əl s=qʷɛ̀l=iwəl k'ʷ-əl-s mə xʷə=ʔí s=q'á tɛ=ɬ=luwə=p (ʔɛ́y l s=í=ɛ́y=i[=M2=]yɛ, l s=í=ɛ́y=i[=M2=]yɛ s=í=ɛ́y=ə́[=M2=]m)//, /'*I'm very happy to come here at this gathering my (good friends, dear friends).*'/, usage: public speaking, attested by Deming (5/18/78), <**xwoyíwel á skwó:l telówà:yel.**>, //xʷ=(ʔ)ɛ[=Aa=]y=íwəl ʔɛ s=kʷá·l təlá=wɛ̀·yəl//, /'*Happy Birthday to you.*'/, literally /'your birth this day is happy'/, attested by Elders Group (7/9/75), <**xwoyíwel kw'els lám.**>, //xʷ=(ʔ)ɛ[=Aa=]y=íwəl k'ʷ-əl-s lɛ́=m//, /'*I'm happy/glad to go.*'/, attested by Elders Group (3/2/77).

<**xwoxweyíwel**>, cts //xʷa[-C_1ə-]y=íwəl ~ xʷa[-C_1ə-]y=í·wəl//, EFAM /'*be happy, being happy*'/, (<**-R1-**> *continuative* or *resultative* or both to account for both translations), phonology: reduplication, syntactic analysis: adjective/adjectival verb, Elder's comment: "she doesn't use xwoyíwel", attested by EB (12/16/75, 2/13/78, 3/19/76); found in <**xwoxweyí:weltsel.**>, //xʷa[-C_1ə-]y=í·wəl-c-əl//, /'*I'm happy.*'/, attested by EB (3/19/76), example: <**xwoxweyí:wel tel sqwálewel.**>, //xʷa[-C_1ə-]y=í·wəl t-əl s=qʷɛ̀l=iwəl//, /'*I'm happy.*'/, literally /'my thoughts/feeling are becoming happy'/, attested by EB (3/19/76).

<**xwoyíwelmet**>, iecs //xʷ=(ʔ)ɛ[=Aa=]y=íwəl=məT//, EFAM ['*happy to see s-o*'], literally /'become good in the insides toward s-o'/, (<**=met**> *indirect effect non-control transitivizer*), phonology:

possible ablaut, syntactic analysis: transitive verb, attested by Elders Group (2/16/77).

<**xwoyíwelstexw**>, caus //x^{w}=(ʔ)ɛ[=Aa=]y=íwəl=sT-əx^{w}//, EFAM /'*make s-o happy, cheer s-o up*'/, literally /'make/cause s-o to become good in the insides'/, (<**=st**> *causative control transitivizer*), (<-**exw**> *third person object*), phonology: possible ablaut, syntactic analysis: transitive verb, attested by Elders Group (2/16/77).

<**xwoyíwelmet**>, EFAM ['*happy to see s-o*'], *see* xwoyíwel ~ xwoyíwél.

<**xwoyíwelstexw**>, EFAM /'*make s-o happy, cheer s-o up*'/, *see* xwoyíwel ~ xwoyíwél.

<**xwóykwem**>, df //x^{w}áyk^{w}=əm//, TVMO /'*shaking bushes (of animal or person unseen, for ex.)*'/, root meaning unknown, possibly lx <=kw> *in circles*, possibly <**=em**> *intransitivizer/have/get or middle voice*, syntactic analysis: intransitive verb, attested by IHTTC (7/19/77), compare <**xwóyqwem**> *shaky and weak*, compare <**x̲wóyqwesem**> *one's head is shaking constantly (like with disease)*, compare <**xwóyqw'esem**> *wobbly*, compare <**xwóyeqwthòm**> *you're shaking all over*.

<**xwóymét ~ xwó:ymét**>, ECON ['*sell s-th*'], *see* xwóyem.

<**xwóyqw**> or more likely just <**xwóy**>, probable root //x^{w}áy// *shaky* or possibly //x^{w}áyqw// *shaky*

<**xwóyqwem**>, mdls //x^{w}áyqw=əm//, ABDF ['*(get) shaky and weak*'], root meaning unknown, (<**=em**> *middle voice*), syntactic analysis: intransitive verb, attested by IHTTC (7/19/77), compare <**xwóykwem**> *shaking bushes (of animal or person unseen for ex.)*, compare <**x̲wóyqwesem**> *one's head is shaking constantly (like with disease)*, compare <**xwóyqw'esem**> *wobbly*, compare <**xwóyeqwthòm**> *you're shaking all over*, Salish cognate: possibly Squamish /x̣^{w}áy/ *become senseless, paralyzed; faint; perish* (if a doublet with Upriver Halkomelem /x̣^{w}ɛ́y/ *perish in a group, die in a group*) K67:371.

<**x̲wóyqwesem**>, mdls //x̣^{w}áyq^{w}=əs=əm//, ABDF ['*one's head is shaking constantly (like with disease)*'], root meaning unknown, lx <**=es**> *on the face*, (<**=em**> *middle voice*), syntactic analysis: intransitive verb, attested by IHTTC (9/16/77), compare <**xwóyqwem**> *shaky and weak*, compare <**xwóykwem**> *shaking bushes (of animal or person unseen for ex.)*, compare <**xwóyqw'esem**> *wobbly*, compare <**xwóyeqwthòm**> *you're shaking all over*.

<**xwóyeqwthòm**>, pcs //x^{w}áyəq^{w}=T-àm//, if, ABDF ['*you're shaking all over*'], literally /'you are shaken all over'/, root meaning unknown, probably <**=t**> *purposeful control transitivizer*, (<**-òm**> *passive second person object/patient*), syntactic analysis: transitive verb, syntactic comment: passive, attested by Elders Group (1/16/80), compare <**xwóyqwem**> *shaky and weak*, compare <**xwóykwem**> *shaking bushes (of animal or person unseen for ex.)*, compare <**x̲wóyqwesem**> *one's head is shaking constantly (like with disease)*, compare <**xwóyqw'esem**> *wobbly*.

<**xwóyqw'esem**>, mdls //x^{w}áyq'^{w}=əs=əm//, ABDF ['*wobbly*'], probable bound root <**xwóy**> //x^{w}áy// *shaky*, lx <**=qw' ~ =eqw'**> *around in circles*, lx <**=es**> *on the face*, (<**=em**> *middle voice*), syntactic analysis: intransitive verb, attested by Deming (4/26/79), compare <**x̲wóyqwesem**> *one's head is shaking constantly (like with disease)*, compare <**xwóyqwem**> *shaky and weak*, compare <**xwóykwem**> *shaking bushes (of animal or person unseen for ex.)*, compare <**xwóyeqwthòm**> *you're shaking all over*, also <**xwáyq'esem**>, //x^{w}ɛ́yq'=əs=əm//, attested by Elders Group (5/3/78), example: <**xwóyqw'esem s'í:mex**>, //x^{w}áyq'^{w}=əs=əm s=ʔí[=·=]m=əx^{y}//, /'*a wobbly walk*'/, attested by Deming (4/26/79), also <**xwáyq'esem s'ímex**>, //x^{w}ɛ́yq'=əs=əm s=ʔím=əx^{y}//, attested by Elders Group (5/3/78).

<**xwóywél**>, ds //x^{w}=(ʔ)ɛ[=Aá=]y=iwəl or x^{w}áy(=)wəl or x^{w}ə=Aá=yəw=əl//, EFAM /'*(get a) thrill, (to) thrill*'/, probably bound root <**xwóy**> //x^{w}áy// *shaky*, possibly <**xwe=**> *get, become*, possibly <**ó-ablaut**> *derivational*, possibly root <**éy**> *good*, possibly root <**yew**> *feel spiritual power*, probably

<**=íwel ~ =ewel**> *on the insides, in the mind,* less likely <**=el**> *go, come, get, become,* phonology: possible ablaut, possible vowel-loss in root, syntactic analysis: intransitive verb, attested by BHTTC (late 10/76).

<**xwpóysekel**>, ds //x^{w}=páysəkəl//, TVMO /'*to cycle, ride a bicycle*'/, *see* póysekel.

<**xwő:qel ~ xwőwqel ~ xwéwqel**>, possible bound stem //x^{w}ów=qəl ~ x^{w}ə́w=qəl or x̣^{w}[=F=]i[=Aə́=]w=qəl//, meaning uncertain

<**shxwő:qel ~ shxwőwqel ~ shxwéwqel**>, df //s=x^{w}ów=(ə)qəl ~ s=x^{w}ə́w=(ə)qəl or s=x̣^{w}[=F=]i[=Aə́=]w=(ə)qəl//, EZ /'*whistling swan,* probably also *trumpeter swan*'/, ['*Olor columbianus,* probably also *Olor buccinator*'], literally perhaps /'something that's whistling in the throat'/, (<**s=** or **sxw=**> *nominalizer, something that*), possibly root <**xwíw** or **x̲wíw**> *whistle* (a root otherwise unattested in UHk but Lushootseed has such a root, see below), possibly <**=F= (fronting)**> *diminutive*?, possibly <**é-ablaut**> *continuative or derivational,* lx <**=(e)qel**> *in the throat,* phonology: possible ablaut, possible fronting, syntactic analysis: nominal, attested by BJ (12/5/64), Elders Group (6/4/75), other sources: ES /sx^{w}ə́wqəl/ *whistling swan,* H-T <cwō'kEl> *swan (white)(Olor columbianus),* Salish cognate: Squamish /(s)x^{w}ə́wqn/ *white swan, whistling swan* W73:258, K67:294, K69:59 and *whistling swan (Olor columbianus) and trumpeter swan (Olor buccinator)* Kennedy and Bouchard 1976:67-68, Sechelt /x^{w}úqin/ *swan* T77:11, Mainland Comox /híwqin/ *swan* B75prelim.:16, Saanich dial. of NSt /sx^{w}ə́wqən/ *swan* B74a:14, Lushootseed root /x̣^{w}íw/ and /x̣^{w}íw-əl/ *to whistle* H76:618, also <**sx̲wőqw'qel**>, //s=x̣^{w}oq'^{w}=qəl or s=x̣^{w}ə́q'^{w}=qəl//, attested by Elders Group (2/18/76).

<**Xwōqwiyáqw**>, us //x^{w}oq^{w}iyɛ́q^{w} or x^{w}oq^{w}=ɛ́y(=)i[=M2=]q^{w}//, PLN ['*Echo Island in southern quarter of Harrison Lake*'], ASM ['about three miles long, south of Cascade Peninsula and about three miles north of Harrison Hot Springs'], syntactic analysis: nominal, attested by Elders Group (6/18/75 on boat trip to Port Douglas), comment: very noisy motor on boat, name from EL may have been mistranscribed, contrast <**X̲wōx̲we'áqel ~ Xwōxwe'áqel**> *Echo Island,* compare and *see* <**Xweqw'oyíqw**> which may be a more correct form for this name.

<**xwōqw'éylem**>, DIR /'*go in the direction of the water, go downriver*'/, *see* wőqw' ~ wéqw'.

<**xwōqw'ő:ls**>, df //x^{w}oq'^{w}=ó·ls orx̣^{w}[=F=]oq'^{w}=ó·ls//, EB /'*arrowleaf, wapato, Indian potato*'/, ['*Sagittaria latifolia*'], ASM ['underwater tubers formerly harvested at Pitt Meadows, Sumas Lake, Kawkawa Lake and probably other areas, they grow in water with the arrowhead shaped leaves sticking out of the water on long stalks, Susan Jimmie's mother and grandmother used to go out to Sumas Lake by Kilgard just about mid-March and get these arrowleaf potatoes, they were sweet and were also called q'áq'et'em sqá:wth ("sweet potato"); they also dried them and when you soaked them in water they would puff right up again (SJ); they grow around Pitt Lake, can be dug in fall in two ways: Mandy Charnley remembers they were dug with a pick-ax in mudflats when the water went down and Evangeline Pete remembers they were loosened with the toes while hanging onto the canoe they'd float to the surface (Elders Group 7/21/76)'], possibly root <**x̲wóqw'**> *pole a canoe,* possibly <**=F= (fronting)**> *diminutive,* lx <**=ó:ls**> *roughly spherical/round object, fruit, tuber, ball, rock,* possibly <**ő:-ablaut**> *derivational,* phonology: possibly the second <**ő**> shows the form is borrowed from a language like Nooksack or Squamish which has /o/ or /u/ (respectively) corresponding to Upriver Halkomelem /a/ historically (as in this suffix), syntactic analysis: nominal, attested by SJ (3/17/77), Elders Group (7/21/76), Deming (6/21/79), other sources: Suttles 1955:27 Katzie dial. of Downriver Halkomelem /x̣^{w}aq'^{w}ól?s/ *wapato (Sagittaria latifolia),* Salish cognate: Squamish /x̣^{w}ə-x^{w}ək'^{w}əl?s/ (stress unknown) *a kind of potato* (recording doubtful) W73:203, K67:371, Squamish /x̣^{w}ux^{w}uk'^{w}úlc/ (said borrowed from the Fraser River people [Halkomelem]) *Indian potato, arrowleaf*

(not found in the Squamish area and obtained by trade from the Stó:lō people)(Sagittaria latifolia) Bouchard and Turner 1976:40-42, Thompson (Lytton dial.) /q'^{w}aq'^{w}úl's/ *wapato, arrow-leaf (Sagittaria latifolia) (lower valey wild potato, grew in Chilliwack area, brought to Spuzzum in big baskets for trade)* Turner, Thompson, Thompson & York 1973ms:11.

<**xwōqw'ṓ:lh**>, TVMO [*'drifting back downriver (like spawned-out salmon)'*], *see* wṓqw' ~ wéqw'.

<**shxwōqw'ṓ:lh**>, df //s=x^{w}e=wq'^{w}=ó·ɬ//, EZ [*'August run spring salmon that go up Silver Creek (near Hope)'*], ['August Silver Creek run of *Oncorhynchus tshawytscha*'], (<**s=**> *nominalizer, something to*), lit. *something that's drifting back downriver (like spawned-out salmon)*, possibly <**=ṓ:lh**> meaning uncertain, syntactic analysis: nominal, attested by Elders Group (3/26/75).

<**Xwōxwe'áqel**>, ds //C$_{1}$ə-x̣^{w}[=F=](=)əʔɛ́=əqəl//, PLN [*'Echo Island in Harrison Lake'*], see under stem <**x̲wix̲we'á**> *imitate.*

<**xwp**> or <**xwép**>, bound root //x^{w}p// or //x^{w}ə́p//, ABFC /*'pick up from the ground or floor'*/

<**xwpét**>, pcs //x^{w}ə́p-M1=T// or //x^{w}p=əT//, ABFC [*'pick s-th up from the ground or floor'*], (possibly <**metathesis type 1**> *non-continuative*), (<**=t** ~ **=et**> *purposeful control transitivizer*), phonology: poss. metathesis, syntactic analysis: transitive verb, attested by EB (1/26/76), also <**x̲wpét**>, //x̣^{w}ə́p-M1=T// or //x̣^{w}p=əT//, attested by RG & EH (4/9/99 Ling332), example: <**xwpétlha ta' kopú.**>, //x^{w}p=ə́T-ɬɛ t-ɛʔ kapú// or //x^{w}ə́p=M1=T-ɬɛ t-ɛʔ kapú//, /*'Pick up your coat (from the floor).'*/, attested by EB.

<**xwpósem**>, vis or mdls //x^{w}p=ós=əm//, SPRD //*'show a picture at a memorial ceremony'*//, morphosememic development (SMM), semantic comment: from literally /'pick up a face from the ground/floor'/ ['since at a memorial ceremony, framed pictures of those remembered are lifted up and carried around the longhouse at spirit dances or separate memorial ceremonies; such ceremonies are done for recently deceased as well as every few years for loved ones who passed away years earlier'], attested by RG & EH (4/10/99 Ling332), examaple: <**me xwpósem te hákw'elesem**>, /mə x^{w}p=ós=əm tə hɛ́k'^{w}=ələs=əm/, /'come show a picture of those remembered'/, attested by RG & EH (4/10/99 Ling332)

<**xwpelákw**>, CLO [*'peek under a woman's skirt'*], *see* pél:ékw.

<**xwpét**>, pcs //x^{w}ə́p-M1=T// or //x^{w}p=əT//, ABFC [*'pick s-th up from the ground or floor'*], *see* xwp.

<**xwpopó:s**>, ANA /*'(have a) hairy face, (have) hair on the face, (have a woolly face)'*/, *see* pá:pa.

<**xwqwó:lthels**>, bound stem //x^{w}íq^{w}=á·lθ(əl)=əls//, *press and rub hard on the knee as a structured activity, see* **xwíqw** *press and rub.*

<**shxwqwó:lthels**>, df //s(x^{w})=x^{w}iq^{w}=á·lθ(əl)=əls//, CARV [*'a wood carving'*], literally /'something pressed and rubbed hard on the knee as a structured activity'/, (semological comment: nice confirmation of such an etymology was provided by watching one of the last expert carvers work, Joe Lorenzetto (see photo Galloway 1980:131a)),(<**s=** or **shxw=**> *nominalizer, something that*), root <**xwíqw**> *press and rub hard*, lx <**=ó:lthel**> *on the knee*, (<**=els**> *structured activity continuative device*), phonology: syllable-loss, possible consonant merger, syntactic analysis: nominal, attested by DM (12/4/64 new transcript old p.258), TG (4/23/75).

<**xwtáq**>, SH /*'(get closed, become closed)'*/, *see* téq.

<**xwtélqet**>, LANG [*'repeat s-th (verbally)'*], *see* tél ~ tá:l ~ tiy.

<**xwtetáq**>, BLDG [*'be closed'*], *see* téq.

<**xwtí:chest ~ xwtí(:)ychest**>, SOC [*'got even with s-o'*], *see* tiy.

<**xwtíyches**>, SOC [*'fight back'*], *see* tiy.

<**xwt'át'ekwel**>, CSTR /*'bridge, cable crossing'*/, *see* t'ákwel.

<**xwt'ót'epels ~ shxwt'ót'epels**>, TOOL [*'adze (for making canoes and pit-house ladders)'*], *see* t'óp.

<**xwt'ó:welh**>, ABDF [*'your back is sprained'*], *see* t'ó.

<**xwt'óxwestses**>, ANA [*'hollow of hand'*], *see* t'óxw.

<**xwt'óxwesxel**>, ANA [*'arch of foot'*], *see* t'óxw.

<**xwthó:s**>, ANA [*'(have) a big face'*], *see* thi ~ tha ~ the ~ thah ~ theh.

<**xwthó:thel**>, ANA [*'(have) a big mouth'*], *see* thi ~ tha ~ the ~ thah ~ theh.

<**Xwth'ístel**>, PLN [*'a place across the Fraser River from the rock named Q'aleliktel'*], *see* th'ís.

<**xwth'í:t**>, SOC /*'thank s-o (for a cure, for pall-bearing, a ceremony, being a witness)'*/, *see* ts'ít ~ ch'í:t.

<**Xwth'kw'ém**>, PLN [*'medicine spring on the Fraser River beach about a half mile above (north) of the American Bar beach'*], *see* th'ekw' or th'íkw'.

<**xwtl'óqtes**>, ANA [*'(have a) long face'*], *see* tl'áqt.

<**xwúxwe**>, possible root or stem //x^{w}i[=Aə́=]=C$_1$ə or s=x^{w}i[=Aú=]=C$_1$ə//, root meaning unknown

<**shxwúxwe**>, stvi //s=x^{w}i[=Aə́=]=C$_1$ə or s=x^{w}i[=Aú=]=C$_1$ə//, EFAM /*'(be) ambitious, (be) willing'*/, (<**s=**> *stative*), possibly root <**xwi(y)**> *awake, alert*, possibly <**=R1**> *continuative or resulttive or derivational*, possibly <**é-ablaut** or **ú-ablaut**> *durative*, phonology: possible ablaut, reduplication, syntactic analysis: adjective/adjectival verb, attested by Elders Group (1/21/76), compare <**xwiyós**> *alert*, compare <**shxwixwiyós**> *early-bird*, Salish cognate: Squamish /s-x^{w}ə́-x^{w}aʔ/ *diligent, good worker* W73:79, K67:294, Samish dial. of NSt /s-x^{w}ə́y'x^{w}əy'/ *diligent; lively* from root /x^{w}əy ~ x^{w}əč'/ *wake* as in /s-x^{w}áy'-əɬ/ *awake* and /x^{w}əčə́-sət/ *wake up* G86:90, 76.

<**Xwyélés ~ Lexwyélés**>, PLN [*'rock up the Harrison River from the old Chehalis Indian cemetery'*], *see* yél:és.

<**xw'elyó:les**>, ABFC [*'(have) good sight'*], *see* éy ~ éy:.

<**xw'éyeqel**>, ABFC [*'(have) a clear voice'*], *see* éy ~ éy:.

<**xw'éywelh ~ xwe'éywelh ~ xwe'éy:welh**>, EFAM /*'good-hearted, kind-hearted, kind, generous, helpful, easy-going, good-natured'*/, *see* éy ~ éy:.

<**xw'ílámálá ~ xw'ílàmàlà**>, ANA /*'shoulder (name of body part, unpossessed)'*/, *see* ílàm.

<**xw'ilamő́welh**>, CAN /*'carry a canoe on one's shoulders, to portage'*/, *see* ílàm.

<**xw'í:lmet**>, TVMO [*'reach s-o here'*], *see* í.

<**xw'í:ls**>, TVMO [*'manage to get to s-o here'*], *see* í.

<**xw'í'àlh**>, LANG [*'talk quietly'*], *see* éy ~ éy:.

X̲

<**x̲::**>, free root //x̣:// or //x̣··//, EFAM /'*(glad greeting sound, also sound to show pride in accomplishment)*'/, semantic environment ['the oldest generations (grandparents of 1976's elders) used to say this as they patted kids under the chin with palm upright'], syntactic analysis: interjection, attested by BHTTC (10/13/76).

<**=x̲ ~ =ex̲**>, da //=x̣ ~ =əx̣//, DIR /'*distributive, all over, all around*'/, syntactic analysis: lexical suffix, also <**=ex̲**>, //=əx̣//; found in <**á:lx̲em**>, //ʔɛ́·l=x̣=əm//, /'*(make) a murmur, to murmur*'/ (compare <**ó:lthet**> *to groan)*, <**kwíyx̲**>, //kʷíy=x̣//, /'*to move*'/ (compare <**kwíyx̲t**> *move s-th* and <**kwíyx̲thet**> *move, move itself, move oneself)*, <**skw'álx̲**> (perhaps), //s=k'ʷɛ́l=x̣//, /'*immature bald eagle*'/, <**lőwéx̲ ~ léwéx̲**>, //lə́w=əx̣//, /'*rib, ribs*'/ (compare <**lew=**> *put inside a hole)*, <**lhépx̲lexw**>, //ɬə́p=x̣=l-əxʷ//, /'*blink them (one's eyes)*'/ (compare <**lhép**> *fold skin, close with skin* and <**lhéplexw**> *blink)*, <**lhétx̲tem**>, //ɬə́t=x̣=T-əm//, /'*tremble*'/ (compare <**lhátx̲tem**> *be trembling, shiver)*, <**spélhx̲el**>, //s=p'[=D=]ə́ɬ=x̣=əl//, /'*prairie, grassy open land*'/ (compare possibly <**p'élh**> *flatten)*, <**Qétex̲em**>, //qɛ[=Aə́=]t=əx̣=əm//, /'*mountain on west side of Fraser R. above American Bar which had a steaming pond at the top*'/ (compare <**qát ~ qá:t**> *cook or heat or warm with steam)*, <**qí:wx̲ ~ qéywx̲ ~ qá:wx̲**>, //qí·w=x̣ ~ qɛ́·w=x̣//, /'*steelhead trout*'/ (compare perhaps <**qá:w**> *rest*?), <**qétx̲t**>, //qə́t=x̣=T or qɛ[=Aə́=]t=x̣=T//, /'*feel s-o/s-th with fingers*'/ (compare perhaps <**qát**> *warm or heat with steam*?), <**q'etx̲áls**>, //q'ət=x̣=ɛ́ls//, /'*to rattle (cans, etc., to wake newlyweds), to shivaree (someone)*'/ (compare <**q'et**> *rattling sound, scraping sound)*, <**q'átx̲em**>, //q'ə[-Aɛ́-]t=x̣=əm//, /'*scraping sound (as metal on dishes, etc.), rattling sound*'/, <**sq'éth'x̲**>, //s=q'ə́θ'=x̣//, /'*dung, (scattered excrement or droppings?)*'/ (compare <**sq'éth'**> *dung, shit)*, <**q'oyéx̲ ~ q'eyéx̲ ~ q'éyex̲em ~ q'oyéx̲em**>, //q'əy=ə[=´=]x̣(=əm)//, /'*whirlpool*'/ (compare <**q'ey**> *wind around, tie, knot)*, <**sq'x̲áp**>, //səq'=x̣=ɛ́p//, /'*stump of a tree (still rooted)*'/ (compare <**seq'**> *split, crack,* and <**=áp**> *in the dirt, ground)*, <**qwítx̲**>, //qʷít=x̣//, /'*Pacific dogwood flower*'/ (root meaning unknown), <**qwá:yx̲t**>, //qʷɛ́·y=x̣=T//, /'*shake s-th*'/ (compare <**qwá:yx̲thet**> *it shook (itself), shaking, bobbing around* and <**qwíyx̲t**> *(shaking s-th)* probably also <**kwíyx̲**> *move)*, <**t'áyx̲**>, //t'ɛ́y=x̣//, /'*be envious*'/ (compare <**t'áy**> *emotionally upset* as in <**táyeq'**> *angry* and <**st'ó:yx̲w**> *brooding*), <**th'álx̲em**>, //θ'ɛ́l=x̣=əm//, /'*transparent, can be seen through (skin, curtain, etc.), translucent*'/, <**th'átx̲em ~ ts'átx̲em**>, //θ'ɛ́t=x̣=əm ~ c'ɛ́t=x̣=əm//, /'*clinking, tinkling*'/, <**tl'á:lx̲em**>, //ƛ'ɛ́·l=x̣=əm//, /'*(have/get a) crackle and pop (log in fire, firecrackers, etc.)*'/ (compare <**tl'ál ~ tl'á:l**> *sharp sound)*, <**tl'eltl'élx̲**>, //C_1əC_2=ƛ'ə́l=x̣//, /'*spotted with circles or round dots*'/ (compare <**tl'él**> *spotted, speckled)*, <**tl'emx̲wx̲éylem**>, //ƛ'əm=x̣ʷ=x̣=í:l=əm//, /'*to hail, be hailing*'/ (compare with <**tl'ém**> *(make) short hard crack or snap noise or sound,* <**=x̲w**> *lump, spherical or round object,* and <**=í:l**> *come, go, get, become)*, <**tl'épx̲t**>, //ƛ'ə́p=x̣=T//, /'*sow s-th, drop or spread seed in rills, scatter s-th*'/ (compare <**tl'ép**> *down, below, deep)*, <**stl'ápx̲**>, //s=ƛ'ə[=Aɛ́=]p=x̣//, /'*be scattered all over*'/ (compare <**tl'ép**> *down, below, deep)*, <**tl'ápex̲em**>, //ƛ'ə[=Aɛ́=]p=əx̣=əm//, /'*fall down and scatter, drop and scatter*'/, <**tl'x̲áx̲el**>, //ƛ'ɛ́xʸ-M1=x̣=əT orƛ'ɛ́xʸ-M1=ɛ́x̣əl//, /'*burst open, split open of its own accord*'/ (compare <**tl'éx**> *rip apart, split apart)*, <**tl'xáx̲et**>, //ƛ'ɛ́xʸ-M1=x̣=əT//, /'*to split s-th open (like a deer or fish)*'/, <**sts'épx̲**>, //s=c'ə́p=x̣//, /'*be dirty*'/ (compare <**ts'ép**> *dirty)*, <**ts'epx̲élqsel**> *(have a) dirty nose,* <**ts'épx̲es**> *(have a) dirty face,* <**ts'épx̲tses**> *(have) dirty hands,* <**ts'epí:wel**> *(have a) dirty rump,* <**ts'ápex̲el**>, //c'ə[=Aɛ=]p=əx̣=əl//, /'*it got rusty*'/ (compare <**ts'ép**> *dirty)*, <**ts'ékwx̲t**>, //c'ə́kʷ=x̣=T//, /'*fry s-th*'/, <**x̲éylex̲**>, //x̣í=əl=əx̣ or x̣əy=əl=əx̣//, /'*to war, go to war*'/ (compare root <**x̲éy** or **x̲íy**> *against or fight)*, <**yélx̲t**>, //yə́l=x̣=T//, /'*look for s-th/s-o*'/

(compare root <**yél**> *turn*), <**yá:lx̲**>, //yə́[=Aɛ́·=]l=x̣//, /'*search*'/ (compare <**á:-ablaut**> *durative.*

<**x̲ahá:met**>, ABFC /'*cried for s-th, (be crying for s-th/s-o)*'/, *see* x̲à:m ~ x̲á:m.

<**x̲álew**>, free root //x̣ɛ́ləw//, FOOD /'*big serving spoon, spoon with handle about ten to 12 inches long, ladle, (spoon carved from mountain goat horn)*'/, (semological comment: Joe Lorenzetto (JL) was probably the last Stó:lō carver who made mountain goat horn spoons), TOOL, HHG, PE, ANAF ['*spoon-shaped bone back of upper lip of sturgeon*'], ASM ['can be used for a little spoon in fact, there is a tradition that the bones of the sturgeon can be used as models of every kind of tool, (the others may have been named after the tools like this one?)'], syntactic analysis: noun, nominal, attested by Elders Group (4/2/75, 4/5/78, 9/21/77, 1/28/76), other sources: ES Cowichan dial. of Halkomelem /x̣ɛ́ləw/ *spoon*, Salish cognate: Squamish /x̣áʔlu/ *spoon made of wild sheep's horn* K67:368.

<**x̲alwéla**>, ds //x̣ɛləw=ə́lɛ orx̣ɛləw=ɛ[=Aə́=]lɛ//, [x̣ɛlwílɛ], FSH ['*horn rings for dip-nets*'], literally perhaps /'container for ladle/spoon/dipper'/, ASM ['made from mountain goat horn or in latter days from cow horn, these hold the net to the frame and when a string holding them all is loosened they slide shut holding the fish inside'], probably root <**x̲álew**> *ladle, spoon*, probably <**=ála**> *container for*, probably <**é-ablaut**> *derivational*, phonology: probable ablaut, vowel-loss in root, syntactic analysis: nominal, attested by Elders Group (3/26/75).

<**x̲álqem**>, df //x̣ə[-Aɛ́-]l(=)q=əm//, cts, TVMO /'*rolling, moving [around in circles]*'/, (<**á-ablaut**> *continuative*), possibly <**=q**> meaning unknown, probably <**=em**> *have/get/intransitivizer or middle voice*, phonology: probable ablaut, syntactic analysis: intransitive verb, attested by SJ (Deming 8/10/78), compare <**x̲é(l)lhchem**> *swim, (to dog-paddle)* with same root, Salish cognate: Squamish /x̣ə́lq'-m/ *roll or fall down (from a raised position)* beside /x̣lq'-án/ *roll down off, knock down off (tr.)* W73:218, K67:367, 366. Compare also <**x̲élqes**>, ABFC ['*to wave (the hand)*']

<**x̲álqem pékcha ~ x̲álqem x̲wíthiya**>, cpds //x̣ə[-Aɛ́-]lq=əm pə́kcɛ ~ x̣ə[-Aɛ́-]lq=əmx̣ʷíθ=iyɛ//, PLAY /'*moving picture, movie*'/, literally /'moving [around in circles]/rolling picture ~ moving [around in circles]/rolling likeness/photo/carving of person or animal'/, phonology: ablaut, syntactic analysis: nominal phrase with modifier(s), attested by SJ (Deming 8/10/78).

<**xelx̲álqem**>, plv //C_1əC_2=x̣ə[-Aɛ́-]lq=əm//, TVMO /'*moving, (many moving around in circles, moving around in circles many times)*'/, (<**R3=**> *plural subject/action*), phonology: reduplication, probable ablaut, syntactic analysis: intransitive verb, attested by Elders Group (6/1/77).

<**xelx̲álqem**>, dnom //C_1əC_2=x̣ə[-Aɛ́-]lq=əm//, PLAY ['*movie(s)*'], literally /'many moving around in circles, moving around in circles many times'/, (<**R3=**> *plural subject/action*), (<**zero**> *nominalizer*), phonology: reduplication, probable ablaut, zero nominalizer, syntactic analysis: nominal, attested by Elders Group (6/1/77).

<**xelx̲ólqemóles**>, df //C_1əC_2=x̣ə[=Aá=]lq=əm=áləs or C_1əC_2=x̣ɛ[=Aá=]lq=əm=áləs//, ABFC ['*roll one's eyes*'], (<**R3=**> *plural action*), possibly <**ó-ablaut**> meaning uncertain here, lx <**=óles**> *on the eyes, in the eyes*, phonology: ó-ablaut on root a, syntactic analysis: intransitive verb, attested by Elders Group (4/23/80).

<**x̲álqem pékcha ~ x̲álqem x̲wíthiya**>, PLAY /'*moving picture, movie*'/, *see* x̲álqem.

<**X̲á:ls ~ X̲à:ls**>, sas //x̣i=ɛ́·ls//, N ['*Transformer*'], REL, ASM ['this is the most common name for the Transformer, the origin of the Transformers is told in Dan Milo's story of Black Bear['s Children] and Grizzly Bear (Wells (Maud, Galloway, Weeden eds.) 1987:89-90), in which Grizzly Bear murders Black Bear (both female) and eats Black Bear, Black Bear's children (4 brothers + 1 sister) discover this and flee, eventually pursuading a man to drown Grizzly Bear while crossing a river, after other adventures the children wander off to the land of the horizon and return as Transformers,

accompanied by Mink, a sexual mischief-maker, Boas 1895 (Bertz 1977) tells many of the stories of the wanderings and transformations of the Transformers from the Upriver Halkomelem area as well as other areas'], probably bound root <**x̱í**> ~ <**x̱éy**> *against, change, transform*, (<**=á:ls**> *structured activity non-continuative*), literally /'transform as a structured activity'/,(<**zero**> *nominalizer*), phonology: zero nominalizer, vowel merger, syntactic analysis: nominal, attested by AC, Elders Group, Deming, DM, BJ, others, other sources: ES /x̣əx̣ɛ́·ls/ (CwMs /x̣ɛ́·ls/) *world changer*, Boas 1895 (Bertz 1977 translation), H-T, Wells (Maud, Galloway, Weeden eds.) 1987:89-90, etc., Salish cognate: Squamish /s-x̣áyʔs/ *mythical Transformer, World Changer* K67:297, not Lushootseed /dúkʷibəɬ/ *Transformer* H76:143, Samish dial. of NSt /x̣éʔel's/ *the Transformer* G86:70, Sechelt /wáx̣als/ *Transformer* T77:15 (the /wá-/ may be cognate with UHk <we=>/wə=/ *suddenly*). Also see less common name: <**X̱éyt**>, ds //x̣í(y)=T or x̣ə́y=T//, N ['*Transformer*'], REL, (from <**x̱í**> ~ <**x̱éy**> *against, change, transform*), ASM ['this is another [less common] name for the Transformer, more common names are X̱á:ls ~ X̱à:ls and X̱ex̱á:ls for all the Transformers (he and his 3 siblings), for the root of <**X̱éyt**> see <**x̱í**> ~ <**x̱éy**> *against, change, transform* and <**x̱ít**> ~ <**x̱éyt**>, pcs //x̣í(y)=T or x̣ə́y=T//, IDOC /'*transform s-th/s-o, change s-th/s-o*'/, REL, ASM ['used when passing something (food, clothing, belongings) over a fire at a burning to feed the dead, and other spiritual transformations']

<**X̱ex̱á:ls**>, dmpn //C_1ə=xi=ɛ́·ls//, N ['*the Transformers*'], ASM ['used of talking of the siblings (and Mink?)'], (<**R5=**> *diminutive plural or plural*), (<**=á:ls**> *structured activity non-continuative*), (<**zero**> *nominalizer*), phonology: reduplication, zero nominalizer, vowel merger, syntactic analysis: nominal, attested by AC, Elders Group, others, other sources: ES /x̣əx̣ɛ́·ls/ (CwMs /x̣ɛ́·ls/) *world changer*, Boas 1895 (Bertz 1977 translation), H-T.

<**x̱alwéla**>, FSH ['*horn rings for dip-nets*'], *see* **x̱**álew.

<**x̱à:m** ~ **x̱á:m**>, free root or stem //x̣ɛ̀·m ~x̣ɛ́·m(=m) or possibly x̣ɛ́·h=m//, ABFC /'*weep, cry, weeping, crying*'/, may have <=(e)m> *middle voice* and phonology: cluster simplification <**mm → :m**> or <**hm → m** >, syntactic analysis: intransitive verb, attested by AC (8/14/70, 10/21/71), Elders Group (3/29/78), EB (1/30/76), other sources: ES /x̣ɛ̀·m/ *cry*, Salish cognate: Squamish /x̣əh-m ~ x̣ám/ *to cry, [also in sent. exx.] crying* W73:72, K67:367, K69:85, Lushootseed //x̣áhəb// *cry* realized as /x̣áab/ *cry, crying* H76:577, also <**x̱ám**>, //x̣ɛ́m//, also /'*weep, cry*'/, attested by Deming (3/16/78); found in <**x̱á:mtsel.**>, //x̣ɛ́·m-c-əl//, /'*I cry.*'/, dialects: *rare in Sardis dial., not said in Tait and Cheh. dialects*, attested by BHTTC (10/21/76), example: <**xwewá lís x̱à:m.**>, //xʷ=(ʔ)əwə=ɛ́ lí-sx̣ɛ̀·m.//, /'*He hasn't cried yet.*'/, attested by AD (3/31/78), <**xwewá lís x̱à:m?**>, //xʷ=ʔəwə-ə lí-sx̣ɛ̀·m//, /'*Hasn't he cried yet?*'/, attested by AD (3/31/78), <**x̱íyet qetl'ésu x̱á:ms**>, //x̣íy=əT qə-ƛ'ə́-s-u x̣ɛ́·m-s//, /'*fight him till he cries*'/, attested by AC (10/21/71), <**hewth'átlha qetl'ésu x̱á:ms.**>, //hə=wɛ́θ'=ə[=M2=]T-ɬɛ qə-ƛ'ə́-s-ux̣ɛ́·m-s//, /'*Tease him (be teasing s-o) till he cries.*'/, attested by AC (10/21/71).

<**x̱á:m**>, cts //x̣ɛ́[-·-]m//, ABFC /'*crying, weeping*'/, (<**-:-**> *continuative*), phonology: possible lengthening or tone change (mid-pitch-stress/mid tone → high-pitch-stress/high tone) though speakers are not always consistent in either contrast, syntactic analysis: intransitive verb, attested by Deming (3/16/78), BHTTC (10/21/76), example: <**x̱à:m yéxwtselcha.**>, //x̣ɛ̀·m yə́xʷ-c-əl-cɛ//, /'*I'm expecting to cry.*'/, literally /'I will expect to cry.'/, attested by BHTTC (10/21/76), <**tsel x̱à:m.**>, //c-əlx̣ɛ̀·m//, /'*I'm crying.*'/, attested by BHTTC (10/21/76), <**Q. Lílhachexw x̱à:m? A. Ílhtsel x̱à:m.**>, //lí-ɬ-ə-c-əxʷx̣ɛ̀·m? í-ɬ-c-əlx̣ɛ̀·m//, /'*Q. Were you crying? A. I was crying.*'/, attested by BHTTC (10/21/76).

<**x̱emx̱ám**>, plv //C_1əC_2=x̣ɛ́m//, ABFC ['*lots of people crying*'], (<**R3=**> *plural subject continuative?*), phonology: reduplication, syntactic analysis: intransitive verb, attested by Deming

(3/16/78).

<**x̲ex̲á:m**>, cts //C_1ə=x̣ɛ́·m//, plv, ABFC ['*crying a lot*'], (<**R5=**> *continuative (and plural action)*), phonology: reduplication, syntactic analysis: intransitive verb, attested by Elders Group (3/29/78).

<**X̲ex̲ám Smá:lt**>, cpds //C_1ə=x̣ɛ́m s=mɛ́·lt//, PLN ['*rock in the Fraser River near Scowlitz where a woman was crying a lot*'], ASM ['there is a story explaining this, DF knows it'], literally /'crying a lot rock'/, syntactic analysis: intransitive verb (as adjective/adjectival verb) nominal, attested by DF (Elders Group 11/9/77), other sources: Wells 1965 (lst ed.):15 <hah-HAHM> *rock in Fraser R. near Scowlitz.*

<**xíx̲à:m ~ x̲éyx̲à:m**>, dmv //C_1í=x̣ɛ̀·m or C_1í=x̣ɛ̀[-·-]m//, ABFC /'*sobbing, crying a little, (to sob [EB])*'/, (<**R4=**> *diminutive action*), phonology: reduplication, syntactic analysis: intransitive verb, attested by DF and NP (Elders Group 4/26/78), also /'*to sob*'/, attested by EB (1/30/76).

<**x̲á:met**>, iecs //x̣ɛ́m=məT//, ABFC ['*cry for s-o/s-th*'], SOC, (<**=met**> *indirect effect non-control transitivizer*), phonology: consonant merger (mm → :m), syntactic analysis: transitive verb, attested by BHTTC (10/14/7), EB (3/1/76), Elders Group (3/15/72), other sources: JH /x̣é·mət/ *to cry for*; found in <**x̲á:metes.**>, //x̣ɛ́m=məT-əs//, /'*He cried for him.*'/, attested by EB, example: <**x̲á:metes kwa.**>, //x̣ɛ́m=məT-əs kʷɛ//, /'*He cried for him (in regret)(after being mean to him).*'/, attested by EB; found in <**x̲ámetòlèm.**>, //x̣ɛ́m=məT-àlə̀m//, /'*You folks are being cried about., You folks are lonely.*'/, attested by BHTTC, example: <**le x̲á:metòlèm.**>, //ləx̣ɛ́m=məT-àlə̀m//, no translation given(He cried for you folks., He was crying for you folks.), attested by Elders Group (3/15/72 tape).

<**x̲ahá:met**>, df //C_1ɛ=x̣[-B-]ɛ́m=məT or C_1ə-x̣[-B-]ɛ́m=məT//, ABFC /'*cried for s-th, (be crying for s-th/s-o)*'/, SOC, possibly <**R8=**> *resultative or continuative*, possibly <**R5-**> *continuative or plural action continuative*, phonology: -B- (backing, x̲ → h) optional dissimilation (historically this actually reflects a root <xah> as seen in cognates of <**x̲à:m ~ x̲á:m**> above), reduplication, consonant merger (mm → :m), syntactic analysis: transitive verb, attested by AC (10/21/71), example: <**x̲ahá:métes te qwe'óp.**>, //C_1ɛ=x̣[-B-]ɛ́m=məT-əs tə qʷəʔáp//, /'*He cried for the apple.*'/, phonology: updrifting, attested by AC.

<**x̲ehó:methet**>, rcps //C_1ɛ=x̣[-B-]ɛ[-Aá-]m=məT-ət//, [x̣(ə)há·məθət], iecs, ABFC /'*cry for oneself, (crying for oneself)*'/, EFAM ['*sorry for oneself*'], (<**R8=**> *resultative or continuative*), phonology: reduplication, vowel-loss in prefix, backing and ó-ablaut of root a automatic before =thet, consonant merger, syntactic analysis: intransitive verb, syntactic comment: reflexive of indirect effect non-control transitivizer, attested by AC (10/21/71), other sources: JH /x̣á·məθət/ *to cry for oneself.*

<**x̲á:mlexw**>, ncs //x̣ɛ́·m=l-əxʷ//, EFAM ['*make s-o cry (accidentally or manage to)*'], ABFC, SOC, (<**=l**> *non-control transitivizer (accidentally, manage to)*), (<**-exw**> *third person object*), syntactic analysis: transitive verb, attested by BHTTC (10/21/76), example: <**achap x̲á:mlòx.**>, //ʔɛ-c-ɛpx̣ɛ́·m=l-áxʸ//, /'*You folks made me cry.*'/, attested by BHTTC.

<**ts'elhx̲à:m**>, ds //c'əɬ=x̣ɛ̀·m//, SOC /'*cry with someone, a person one cries with (related or not), unrelated grandparents of a deceased grandchild, etc.*'/, ASM ['example two grandparents of a deceased grandchild could be called this'], KIN /'*different grandparents of a deceased grandchild, etc.*'/, (<**ts'elh=**> *nearby*), syntactic analysis: nominal, attested by Elders Group (6/8/77).

<**x̲amélmel**>, ds //x̣ɛm=ə́lməl//, EFAM /'*want to cry, feel like crying*'/, lx <**=élmel**> *in the mind, want to, feel like,* syntactic analysis: intransitive verb, attested by Elders Group (4/26/78).

<**X̲emó:th'iya**>, df //x̣ɛm=á·θ'(=)iyɛ//, PLN ['*small peak next to Mount Cheam*'], N ['*youngest sister of*

Lhílheqey (Mount Cheam) that cries'], ASM ['so named because she cries because she can't see the Fraser River, a lot of creeks run together down down her (esp. when it rains), two other sisters (neighboring peaks) of Mt. Cheam are Olóxwelwet and Ts'símtelòt'], root <**x̲ám**> *cry*, lx <**=ó:th'**> meaning unknown unless related to <**=th'**> (probably) ['*small portion*'], lx <**=iya**> *affectionate diminutive; female name ending,* phonology: vowel-reduction, syntactic analysis: nominal, attested by AC and CT (1973), IHTTC (8/23/77), source: place names reference file #126.

<**sx̲ómes**>, dnom //s=x̣ɛ́[=Aá=]m=əs//, SOC //'a gift in memory from someone gone'//, PE, SPRD, lit./ "something - wept - on the face"/, <**s=**> *nominalizer*, <**=es**> *on the face*, phonology: automatic <**a**> → <**o**> before <=**es**> face, attested by RG & EH (4/10/99 Ling332).

<**x̲amélmel**>, EFAM /'*want to cry, feel like crying*'/, *see* x̲à:m ~ x̲á:m.

<**x̲á:met**>, ABFC ['*cry for s-o/s-th*'], *see* x̲à:m ~ x̲á:m.

<**x̲á:meth**>, possible stem //x̣ɛ́·m(=)aθ//, root meaning unknown, more likely root is <**sáx̲**> *bitter* (see entry immediately below)

<**sx̲á:meth**>, df //s=x̣ɛ́·m=aθ// or /sɛ́x̣[=M1=]=əm=aθ//, EB ['*cottonwood sap or cambium*'], ['cambium/sap of *Populus balsamifera trichocarpa*'], ASM ['the sweet cambium was scraped or licked off of the inside of peeled bark and eaten fresh, but (according to Turner 1975:226) soured or fermented very quickly when exposed to air'], probably <**s=**> *nominalizer*, possibly root <**x̲à:m ~ x̲á:m**> *weep* (stem *tears in the mouth*?), or more likely same root as in <**sásex̲em**> *bitter* as the cambium is sweet but turns bitter if exposed to air too long, probably <**=óth ~ =eth ~ =óthel**> *in the mouth*, syntactic analysis: nominal, attested by Elders Group, see main entry under <**sx̲á:meth**> under the letter S.

<**x̲á:mlexw**>, EFAM ['*make s-o cry (accidentally or manage to)*'], *see* x̲à:m ~ x̲á:m.

<**x̲ám'x̲em'**>, chrs //x̣ɛ́m'=C_1əC_2//, EB /'*gray lacy lichen or tree moss (real fine like hair, grows on maples)*'/, ['*unidentified*'], root meaning unknown, (<**=R2**> *characteristic*), probably Nooksack language or borrowed from it or Matsqui dial. -- Upriver Halkomelem doesn't have glottalized <m'>/m'/, phonology: reduplication, syntactic analysis: nominal, attested by SJ (Deming 5/24/79).

<**x̲ápkw'els**>, FOOD ['*crackers*'], (lit. crunching noise structured activity [thing]), *see* x̲ep'ékw'

<**x̲ápkw'em**>, SD /'*make a crunching or crackling noise, crunching (gnawing) sound*'/, *see* x̲ep'ékw'.

<**x̲áp'kw'els**>, ABFC /'*chewing with a crunch, nibbling, gnawing*'/, *see* x̲ep'ékw'.

<**x̲áp'kw't ~ (sic) x̲ápkwt**>, ABFC /'*gnawing s-th, be gnawing on s-th*'/, *see* x̲ep'ékw'.

<**x̲áp'kw'tem**>, df //x̣ə[-Aɛ́-]p'(=)k'ʷ=təm//, ABDF ['*be aching (of bones)*'], literally possibly /'have crunched/cracked (of bones)'/, (<**á-ablaut**> *continuative or resultative*), (<**=tem**> *past participle* or *stative*), syntactic analysis: intransitive verb, attested by AD (2/28/79), also <**x̲á:p'qwtem**>, //x̣ə[-Aɛ́·-]p'qʷ=təm (or x̣ə[-Aɛ́·-]p'=k'ʷ=təm)//, also ABDF /'*(have/get) rheumatism, aching*'/, attested by NP (10/26/75), Salish cognate: in part Squamish /x̣əp'k'ʷ-íws-n-t-m/ *be rheumatic* K67:366, in part Saanich dial. of NSt /x̣əpk'ʷ-íkʷəs-t-əŋ/ *rheumatism* B74a:25, example: <**ő̃wechexw lámexwcha xwa siyólexwe a'áchewlh x̲áp'kw'tem ta' sth'éth'elòm.**>, //ʔówə-c-əxʷ lɛ́=m-əxʷ-cɛ xʷɛ s=yáləxʷ=ə ʔɛʔɛ́-cɛ-wɬ x̣ə[-Aɛ́-]p'k'ʷ=təm t-ɛʔ s=C_1əAə́=θ'[=əl=]á·m//, /'*You're not going to get old until (unless) your bones are aching.*'/, usage: saying or proverb, attested by AD (2/28/79), <**x̲á:p'qwtem tel sth'ó:m.**>, //x̣ə[-Aɛ́·-]p'=qʷ=təm t-əl s=θ'á·m//, /'*My bones are aching.*'/, attested by NP (10/26/75), *see* x̲ep'ékw'.

<**x̲áp'qw'em**>, df //x̣ə[-Aɛ́-]p'=q'ʷ=əm or x̣ə[-Aɛ́-]p'=k'ʷ=B=əm//, ABDF /'*it aches (like of bones),*

(be aching (of bones))'/, probably <**á-ablaut**> *resultative or continuative*, possibly <**=qw'**> *around in circles*' or <**=kw'**> *round, around in circles*, possibly <**=B (backing)**> *derivational*, (<**=em**> *middle voice or intransitivizer/have/get),* phonology: possible ablaut, possible backing, possible dissimilation from x̱ápkw'em *make a crunching sound*, comment: the phonetic similarity and the fact that aching bones often make the same sound as in *crunching (of bones, etc.)* makes the connection of the forms with <**kw'**> and <**qw'**> very pursuasive, there is also the same variation in glottalization and fronting/backing in both the aching words and the crunching words here, so I list them under the same root as does Kuipers for the Squamish forms, syntactic analysis: intransitive verb, attested by AD (2/28/79), Salish cognate: Squamish /x̣əp'k'ʷ-án-t-m/ *to hurt, ache* K67:66 , *see* x̱ep'ékw'.

<**x̱ás**>, bound root //x̣ɛ́s *make up the mind, determine*//.

<**sx̱áx̱as**>, strs //s=x̣ɛ́[=C₁ə=]s//, EFAM /'*(be) determined, got your mind made up*'/, (<**s=**> *stative*), (<**=R1=**> *resultative*), phonology: reduplication, syntactic analysis: adjective/adjectival verb, attested by BHTTC (11/10/76).

<**x̱ásel**>, incs //x̣ɛ́s=əl//, EFAM ['*(get) determined*'], (<**=el**> *go, come, get, become*), syntactic analysis: intransitive verb, attested by Elders Group (3/2/77).

<**x̱asélmet**>, df //x̣ɛs=ə́lməl=əT orx̣ɛs=ə[=´=]l=məT//, EFAM /'*determined (about s-th), have to do it, got to do it*'/, possibly <**=élmel**> *in the mind, feel like, want to*, possibly <**=el**> *go, come, get, become*, possibly <**= ´=**> *derivational*, possibly <**=et**> *purposeful control transitivizer*, possibly <**=met**> *indirect effect non-control transitivizer*, phonology: possible stress-shift, possible syllable-loss (el before =et), syntactic analysis: transitive verb, attested by BHTTC (11/10/76), Elders Group (3/2/77).

<**sx̱ax̱esélmet**>, dnom //s=x̣ɛ[=C₁ə=]s=ə́lməl=əT//, EFAM ['*determination*'], (<**s=**> *nominalizer*), (<**=R1=**> *resultative or continuative*), phonology: reduplication, probable syllable-loss, syntactic analysis: nominal, attested by BHTTC (11/10/76).

<**x̱asáxw**>, us //x̣ɛsɛ́xʷ//, ABDF ['*(have a) harelip*'], syntactic analysis: intransitive verb?, attested by BHTTC (8/31/76).

<**x̱asélmet**>, EFAM /'*determined (about s-th), have to do it, got to do it*'/, *see* x̱ás.

<**x̱átqem ~ x̱étqem**>, izs //x̣ɛ́tq=əm ~ x̣ə́tq=əm//, TCH ['*rough (like corduroy)*'], root meaning unknown, (<**=em**> *intransitivizer, get, have*), syntactic analysis: adjective/adjectival verb, attested by BHTTC (late 10/76).

<**x̱át'kw'els**>, CARV /'*carving wood, whittling*'/, *see* x̱et'kw'á:ls.

<**x̱áth' ~ x̱e'áth'**>, bound root //x̣ɛθ' ~x̣[=əʔɛ́=]əθ' *measure, mark a measurement*//, (<**=e'á=**> *comparative*), Salish cognate: Lushootseed /x̣ə́c'/ *counter used in bone game* [one is won with each correct guess of each bone] H76:589, compare perhaps <**x̱e'óthel**> *four*??.

<**sx̱e'áth'**>, dnom //s=x̣[=əʔɛ́=]θ'//, DESC /'*a measure, a true mark*'/, (<**s=**> *nominalizer*), syntactic analysis: nominal, attested by EB (4/2/76), Salish cognate: Lushootseed /x̣ə́c'/ *counter used in bone game* H76:589, Sechelt /x̣əʔac'-át/ *to measure* T77:30.

<**sx̱e'áth'**>, stvi //s=x̣[=əʔɛ́=]θ'//, HARV ['*spotted (marked and located)*'], HUNT, DESC, TVMO, (<**s=**> *stative*), syntactic analysis: adjective/adjectival verb, attested by CT (6/8/76).

<**sx̱e'áth'tel**>, dnom //s=x̣[=əʔɛ́=]θ'=təl//, DESC /'*measuring device*'/, <s=> *nominalizer* or <s=> *stative*, <=tel> *device, thing to*, semantic comment: [it is unclear whether this term is derived from <**sx̱e'áth'**> *a measure, a true mark* or from <**sx̱e'áth'**>,*spotted (marked and located)*, especially in the compound derived from it, the literal meaning would be resp. /"measure device, device to

measure"/ or /"device to measure (mark and locate)"/ since a map is already marked and located and measured, also if this word means *a measure device* it could also mean *ruler, tape measure,* etc.], attested by RG & EH (4/10/99 Ling332)

<**sx̲e'áth'tels té tèmèxw**>, cpds //s=x̣[=əʔɛ́=]θ'=təl-s tə́ tə̀mə̀xʷ//, PLN /'*map* '/, lit./ "measuring device of the earth"/, phonological comment: the tone marked on the article <te> reflects the frequent updrift from low to high tone before mid tones, attested by RG & EH (4/10/99 Ling332)

<**x̲e'áth'stexw**>, caus //x̣[=əʔɛ́=]θ'=sT-əxʷ//, HARV /'*mark s-th, blaze it (of a trail), get/have s-th spotted (marked and located), make note of s-th*'/, HUNT, TVMO, DESC, (<**=st**> *causative control transitivizer*), (<**-exw**> *third person object*), syntactic analysis: transitive verb, attested by CT (6/8/76), also <**sx̲e'áth'stexw**>, //s=x̣[=əʔɛ́=]θ'=sT-əxʷ//, (<**s=**> *stative*), attested by AD (3/6/80), example: <**lichxw x̲e'áth'stexw?**>, //lí-c-xʷx̣[=əʔɛ́=]θ'=st-əxʷ//, /'*Did you have it spotted (marked and located)?*'/, attested by CT, <**sx̲e'áth'stexwchxw ta' xálh.**>, //s=x̣[=əʔɛ́=]θ'=sT-əxʷ-c-xʷ t-ɛʔ xʸɛ́ɬ//, /'*Mark your trail., Blaze your trail.*'/, attested by AD, <**sx̲e'áth'stexwchexw shxwlís kw'as kwá:lx.**>, //s=x̣[=əʔɛ́=]θ'=sT-əxʷ-c-əxʷ sxʷ=lí-s k'ʷ-ɛ-s kʷɛ́·l=xʸ//, /'*Make note of where you hide it.*'/, attested by AD, <**sx̲e'áth'stexwchxw kw'as le qéylemt.**>, //s=x̣[=əʔɛ́=]θ'=sT-əxʷ-c-xʷ k'ʷ-ɛ-s lə qí·l=əm=T//, /'*Make note of where you put it.*'/, literally /'you make note of/mark it that you past store s-th away'/, attested by AD.

<**x̲á:th't ~ x̲áth't**>, pcs //x̣ɛ́·θ'=T ~x̣ɛ́θ'=T//, DESC /'*put a mark on it (like water level of river), mark it, weigh it, (measure it)*'/, (<**=t**> *purposeful control transitivizer*), syntactic analysis: transitive verb, attested by EB (4/2/76, 5/5/76).

<**X̲áth'aq**>, df //x̣ɛ́θ'=ɛq//, PLN ['*Hatzic*'], ASM ['name of an unidentified plant which grew there lots (SP and AK)'], Elder's comment to David Rozen: "it means *measuring the penis*", literally /'mark on the penis, measure the penis'/, (semological comment: Hatzic Lake has a penis-shaped peninsula which could be connected with a story?), lx <**=aq**> *on the penis*, (<**zero**> *nominalizer*), phonology: zero nominalizer, syntactic analysis: nominal, attested by SP and AK (6/27/75), David Rozen, source: place names file reference #121.

<**x̲áth'tel**>, dnom //x̣ɛ́θ'=təl//, DESC /'*a mark to show where something is, a marker (to show a trail, something buried, a grave)*'/, TVMO, REL, lx <**=tel**> *something to, nominalizer*, syntactic analysis: nominal, attested by Elders Group (2/27/80).

<**x̲á:th'etstel**>, dnom //x̣ɛ́·θ'=əc=təl//, REL ['*grave pole*'], ASM ['carved post often an effigy or likeness of the person (a standing human body), formerly put in grave houses (see Barbeau photo)'], Barbeau photo in Galloway 1980, lx <**=ets**> *on the back*, lx <**=tel**> *device to*, syntactic analysis: nominal, attested by CT (6/8/76).

<**X̲áth'aq**>, PLN ['*Hatzic*'], *see* **x̲**áth' ~ **x̲**e'áth'.

<**x̲á:th'etstel**>, REL ['*grave pole*'], *see* **x̲**áth' ~ **x̲**e'áth'.

<**x̲á:th't ~ x̲áth't**>, DESC /'*put a mark on it (like water level of river), mark it, weigh it, (measure it)*'/, *see* **x̲**áth' ~ **x̲**e'áth'.

<**x̲áth'tel**>, DESC /'*a mark to show where something is, a marker (to show a trail, something buried, a grave)*'/, *see* **x̲**áth' ~ **x̲**e'áth'.

<**x̲átl'**>, free root //x̣ɛ́ƛ'//, WETH /'*rough (of wind or water), turbulent (of wind or water), real swift (of water)*'/, WATR, EFAM, syntactic analysis: adjective/adjectival verb, attested by Elders Group (4/2/75), Deming (3/31/77), Salish cognate: Lushootseed /x̣áƛ'/ *difficult* (in exx. meaning *hard work, impassable brushy place*) also in /x̣áƛ'-il/ *argument that ends in a fight* and /ʔu-x̣áƛ'=il/ *argue, talk rough, fight verbally* H76:583, also <**x̲á:tl'**>, //x̣ɛ́·ƛ'//, attested by EB (12/4/75), Elders Group

(3/26/75), compare possibly <**x̱eytl'áls** or **x̱itl'áls**> *grizzly bear* with same root??.

<**x̱otl'thet**>, incs //x̣ɛ[=Aá=]ƛ'=θət//, WETH ['*be windy*'], (<=**thet**> *get, become*), phonology: ó-ablaut on root a automatic before =thet, syntactic analysis: intransitive verb, attested by Elders Group (4/2/75), Deming (3/31/77), example: <**x̱ótl'thet te swáyel.**>, //x̣ɛ[=Aá=]ƛ'=θət tə s=wɛ́yəl//, /'*The day is windy.*'/, attested by Elders Group, <**x̱ótl'thet tlowáyél.**>, //x̣ɛ[=Aá=]ƛ'=θət təla=wɛ́yə́l//, /'*It's windy today.*'/, attested by Deming.

<**x̱áts'et**>, us //x̣ɛ́c'ət//, EB ['*fireweed*'], ['*Epilobium angustifolium*'], ASM ['peeled shoots are eaten raw in spring before they flower, a good vegetable but somewhat slimy, late summer seed fluff was gathered and mixed sometimes with dog wool and mountain goat wool for blankets'], syntactic analysis: noun, nominal, attested by Elders Group (5/7/75), AC (11/26/71 forgot name), Salish cognate: Squamish /x̣áč't/ *fireweed* W73:101, K67:368.

<**x̱á:ws**>, free root //x̣ɛ́·ws//, DESC ['*new*'], EB ['*fresh*'], FOOD, syntactic analysis: adjective/adjectival verb, attested by AC (8/6/70), AD (10/9/79), other sources: ES /x̣ɛ́·ws/ *new*, Salish cognate: Squamish /x̣áwʔs/ *new, fresh (ab. food)* W73:184, K67:368, Lushootseed (Skagit dial.) /x̣áw's/ *new, fresh* H76:584, also <**x̱áws**>, //x̣ɛ́ws//, attested by EB (12/1/75, 1/7/76, 8/14/78), Elders Group (3/15/72), <**tex̱wò x̱á:ws.**>, //təx̣ʷ-àx̣ɛ́·ws//, /'*(It's) brand new.*'/, literally /'just lately/after a short while new'/, attested by AD, example: <**eyéschxwò ta' x̱áws syó:ys**>, //ʔɛy=ə́s-c-xʷ-à t-ɛʔx̣ɛ́ws s=yá·ys//, /'*Have fun in your new work.*'/, attested by EB (8/14/78).

<**x̱awsólkwlh** or **x̱awsó:lkwlh**>, ds //x̣ɛws=álkʷɬ or x̣ɛws=á·lkʷɬ//, SPRD ['*new spirit-dancer*'], ASM ['in first through third year of dancing'], literally /'new spirit power'/, lx <**=ólkwlh** or **=ó:lkwlh**> *spirit power*, syntactic analysis: nominal, attested by IHTTC (8/22/77), RG & EH (4/10/99 Ling332), Salish cognate: Squamish /x̣əws-álkʷɬ/ *new dancer* W73:184, K69:85, Lushootseed /x̣áw's-ul'qʷɬ/ *a new dancer* H76:584, also <**x̱awsólxw**>, //x̣ɛws=álxʷ//, attested by EB (5/12/78).

<**x̱awsó:lh**>, ds //x̣ɛws=á·ɬ orx̣ɛws=á·lɬ//, SPRD /'*new dancer (new spirit-dancer), (new) baby (in spirit-dancing)*'/, literally /'new baby'/, ASM ['a person being initiated into spirit-dancing in his first year is called by this term in Upriver Halq'eméylem and called a "baby" in English, during the initiation he/she is kept isolated in a longhouse away from his home community, made to fast and purify him/herself, bathe in streams, hear drumming, and after several weeks is sent out in the woods in certain spiritual locations on a quest for his/her guardian spirit or spirit power'], he/she gets a vision/dream of the creature or thing with this power and acquires its spirit song and spirit dance, during the initiation he/she also has to wear a special wool or bark hat over his head and face and is trained in the rituals and beliefs of the spirit dancing society, when he/she has a spirit song which drummers can drum to he/she begins travelling extensively to spirit dance gatherings in various locations, until his hat is ritually removed at the end of the first season he is still called a "baby" and is protected and watched by "babysitters" (see xólhemíylh), lx <**=ó:llh** ~ **=ó:lh** ~ **=áylh** ~ **=i(y)lh**> *baby*, syntactic analysis: nominal, attested by AD (2/20/80).

<**x̱awsólkwlh** or **x̱awsó:lkwlh**>, SPRD ['*new spirit-dancer*'], *see* **x̱**á:ws.

<**x̱awsó:lh**>, SPRD /'*new dancer (new spirit-dancer), (new) baby (in spirit-dancing)*'/, *see* **x̱**á:ws.

<**x̱áx̱e**>, rsls //x̣ɛ́=C₁ə//, REL /'*sacred, holy, (taboo)*'/, (<**=R1**> *resultative*), phonology: reduplication, syntactic analysis: adjective/adjectival verb, attested by IHTTC (8/11/77), EB (12/18/75), Salish cognate: Lushootseed /x̣áx̣aʔ/ *forbid* and /s-x̣áʔx̣aʔ/ *great, sacred* H76:584.

<**X̱áx̱e Slát**>, cpds //x̣ɛ́=C₁ə s=lɛ́t//, CH /'*Christmas Eve, night before Christmas*'/, TIME, literally /'sacred/holy night'/, syntactic analysis: nominal phrase with modifier(s), attested by IHTTC.

<**X̱áx̱e Smestí:yexw**>, cpds //x̣ɛ́=C₁ə s=məstí·yəxʷ//, CH /'*Holy Spirit, Holy Ghost*'/, literally

/'holy/sacred spirit'/, syntactic analysis: nominal phrase with modifier(s), attested by EB.

<**Sx̱áx̱e**>, dnom //s=x̣ɛ́=C_1ə//, PLN /'*Morris Creek (near Chehalis, B.C.), Morris Lake (near Chehalis)*'/, literally /'something to be sacred/taboo'/, ASM ['there is a story which explains this told on the perhaps untranscribed tape of the 8/24/77 Elders Meeting by DF, perhaps the same story as related below under Sx̱áx̱e Smá:lt *Morris Mountain*'], (<**s=**> *nominalizer, something to*), phonology: reduplication, syntactic analysis: nominal, attested by DF (Elders Group 8/24/77), EL (with NP and EB) (Chehalis trip 9/27/77), source: place names file reference #239 (Morris Creek) and #239a (Morris Lake).

<**sx̱áx̱e**>, strs //s=x̣ɛ́=C_1ə//, REL /'*(be) sacred, holy*'/, ASM ['can be used with any religion, Salish, Christian, etc.'], (<**s=**> *stative*), phonology: reduplication, syntactic analysis: adjective/adjectival verb, attested by Elders Group (2/10/75), DF (Elders Group 8/24/77 and 1/16/79), EL (with NP and EB) (Chehalis trip 9/27/77), Salish cognate: Lushootseed /s-x̣áʔx̣aʔ/ *great, sacred* H76:584.

<**Sx̱áx̱e Smá:lt**>, cpds //s=x̣ɛ́=C_1ə s=mɛ́·lt//, PLN ['*Morris Mountain (near Chehalis)*'], ASM ['it grew in the flood and the Chehalis people climbed it and were saved, nowadays you can go there if you know where and ask for rain or for a man, etc., there is a special tree there where a kind of blowing sound was always heard, a powerful place (DF)'], literally /'sacred mountain'/, syntactic analysis: nominal phrase with modifier(s), attested by DF (Elders Group 1/16/79).

<**sx̱ax̱elh(l)át ~ sx̱ex̱elh(l)at**>, ds //s=x̣ɛ=C_1ə=(ə)ɬ(l)ɛ́t//, REL ['*Sunday (sacred day)*'], TIME, literally /'sacred day'/, lx <**=elhát** or **=elhlát**> *day*, phonology: possible consonant merger, syntactic analysis: nominal, attested by Elders Group (3/19/75), IHTTC (8/10/77), others, Salish cognate: Lushootseed /x̣áx̣aʔ-əɬdát/ *Sunday ("great/sacred day")* H76:586, example: <**Q. stám swàyèl tlówàyèl? A. Sx̱ax̱elhát.**>, //s=tɛ́m s=wɛ̀yə̀l təlá=wɛ̀yə̀l? s=xɛ=C_1ə=əɬɛ́t//, /'*Q. What day is today? A. Sunday.*'/, attested by IHTTC.

<**x̱áx̱emilàlèm ~ x̱áx̱milàlèm**>, df //x̣ɛ́=C_1ə=əm=il=l-ɛ̀lə̀m//, if, REL /'*confession, to go to confession, to confess*'/, literally apparently /'I am managed to be made to go get sacred/taboo'/, comment: no derivational suffixes are known which combine to form =(e)milàlèm but =l-àlèm occurs as *first person passive of non-control transitive verbs* and here yields a very plausible meaning, *they managed to/happened to make me, I was managed/happened to be made to*, =íl is also likely since one must *go, come, get to* Catholic confessions, =em is the only remaining suffix possible (the intransitivizer could occur in this position) and *have, get* is also semantically plausible with the root x̱áx̱e *sacred, taboo*, especially with the sense of *get taboo* because one is confessing to things one has done which are taboo in Catholic religion;, comment: if this derivation is right, there should be a form, <**x̱áx̱emílexw**> /x̣ɛ́=R1=əm=íl=l-əx^w/ *(manage/happen) to get s-o to go to confession*, or there once was such a form and the first person passive of it has been petrified or crystallized with the meaning given by today's elders, *to confess, go to confession*, if the form is not petrified and <**x̱áx̱emílexw**> can still be used, then the translation for <**x̱áx̱emilàlèm**> should be corrected here to something like *they got me to go to confession* or *I go to confession*, root <**x̱áx̱e**> *sacred, holy, taboo*, possibly <**=em**> *intransitivizer, have, get*, possibly root <**=íl**> *go, come, get, become*, probably <**=l**> *non-control transitivizer (manage to/happen to/accidentally)*, probably <**-èlàm**> *passive first person patient/object*, phonology: probable consonant-loss or consonant merger (=il=l → il), the retention of unstressed i is made more likely before stressed object pronoun endings as in first person passive, with =íl retaining stress only before the unstressed third person object -exw, syntactic analysis: transitive verb-passive, attested by IHTTC (9/9/77), AD (9/29/77).

<**x̱ax̱esyúwes** or **x̱ax̱e syúwes**>, cpds //x̣ɛ=C_1ə=s=yúwə=s ~ x̣ɛ=C_1ə=s=yówə=s orx̣ɛ=C_1ə s=yówə=s//, EZ /'*bluejay, Steller's jay (sacred fortune-teller)*'/, ['*Cyanocitta stelleri paralia* and

Cyanocitta stelleri annectens'], literally /'sacred fortune-teller'/, ASM ['so named because it predicts good news when it cries <**q'ey q'ey q'ey**>, and bad news when it cries <**chéke chéke chéke chéke**> in high notes'], lx <**=s**> meaning unclear here, contrast <**kwá:y**> *bluejay, Steller's jay*, syntactic analysis: nominal, syntactic comment: perhaps a true compound or perhaps two words, attested by Elders Group (4/16/75).

<**sx̲ax̲e'áylh**>, cpds //s=x̣ɛ=C_1ə=ʔɛ́yɬ//, HUMC ['*deformed baby*'], literally /'sacred baby or taboo baby'/, ASM ['in pre-contact times such babies were usually left to die on certain mountains, such as T'ámiyahò:y (Mount McGuire), thus the literal meaning taboo baby is more likely than sacred baby'], (<**s=**> *nominalizer or stative*), lx //=ʔɛ́yɬ//<**='áylh**> *baby*, phonology: epenthetic glottal stop, syntactic analysis: nominal, attested by Deming (3/15/79 incl. SJ, MC, MV, LG).

<**sx̲ex̲ómṓlh**>, df //s=x̣ɛ=C_1ə=phám=ówɬ or s=x̣ə[=C_1əAá=]m=óɬ//, EZ ['*huge pretty frog with supernatural powers*'], (<**s=**> *nominalizer*), root <**x̲áx̲e**> *sacred, holy, taboo*, compounded with root <pehóm> *frog*, <**=óllh**> *young, offspring/child*, possibly <**ō-ablaut**> *derivational* (possibly borrowed from a Salish language with **/u/** or **/o/**), phonology: probable reduplication, possible ablaut, probable consonant loss and vowel merger, syntactic analysis: nominal, attested by BHTTC (11/24/76).

<**x̲áx̲ekw'**>, possibly root //x̣ɛ́x̣ək'ʷ orx̣ɛ́[=R1=](=)k'ʷ or R7=x̣ək'ʷ//, EB /'*bulb or root called wild artichoke, Jerusalem artichoke*'/, ['*Helianthus tuberosus*'], ASM ['has edible bulb (tuber) which could be eaten raw or cooked, used to dry them, there used to be lots at Uncle Dave's place at Seabird Island (David Charles, husband of Mary Charles) and some also grew by Chehalis'], (semological comment: the Jerusalem artichoke flowers in September and is best harvested in late fall or after the first cold snap, it is native to central North America but through cultivation by both Indians and non-Indians it has now spread and gone wild in most areas of North America, the English name is a corruption of the Italian word for sunflower since it is a member of the sunflower family, it has a yellow, daisy-like flower and grows up to ten feet tall, it was identified from a sample gathered on Seabird Island), possibly root <**x̲ákw'**> meaning unknown, possibly root <**x̲ékw'**> *wedged in*, (semological comment: the root meaning *wedged in* is possible since the tubers often grow in clumps which appear wedged together, such a name could remind a person how they might find the tubers when digging for them), possibly <**=R1=**> *resultative or continuative*, possibly <**R7=**> meaning uncertain, possibly <**zero**> *nominalizer*, phonology: possible reduplication, possible zero nominalizer, syntactic analysis: nominal, attested by Elders Group (9/22/76).

<**x̲ax̲elts'elísem**>, ABDF ['*grinding one's teeth*'], *see* **x̲**élts'.

<**x̲áx̲elts'íwélém**>, SH ['*is getting twisted*'], *see* **x̲**élts'.

<**x̲áx̲emilàlèm ~ x̲áx̲milàlèm**>, REL /'*confession, to go to confession, to confess*'/, *see* **x̲áx̲**e.

<**X̲áx̲e Slát**>, CH /'*Christmas Eve, night before Christmas*'/, *see* **x̲áx̲**e.

<**X̲áx̲e Smestí:yexw**>, CH /'*Holy Spirit, Holy Ghost*'/, *see* **x̲áx̲**e.

<**x̲áx̲esxèlem**>, HUNT ['*setting a trap*'], *see* **x̲**ésxel.

<**x̲ax̲esyúwes** or **x̲ax̲e syúwes**>, EZ /'*bluejay, Steller's jay (sacred fortune-teller)*'/, *see* **x̲áx̲**e.

<**x̲ehó:methet**>, ABFC /'*cry for oneself, (crying for oneself)*'/, *see* **x̲**à:m ~ **x̲**á:m.

<**x̲ékw'**>, free root //x̣ə́k'ʷ//, SH ['*it gets narrow or wedged in*'], ASM ['like if one is crawling and gets stuck, also used if one's clothes are too tight and one is wedged in them'], syntactic analysis: intransitive verb, attested by Elders Group (4/16/75), example: <**le x̲ékw'.**>, //lə x̣ə́k'ʷ//, /'*It got*

narrow., He/She/It got wedged in.'/, attested by Elders Group.

<**sx̱ex̱ákw'**>, strs //s=x̣ə[=C_1ɛ́(·)=]k'ʷ//, SH /'*(be) squeezed in, jammed up, tight*'/, (<**s=**> *stative*), (<**=R9=**> *resultative*), phonology: reduplication, syntactic analysis: adjective/adjectival verb, attested by Deming (11/1/79).

<**sx̱ex̱ákw'**>, dnom //s=x̣ə[=C_1ɛ́(·)=]k'ʷ//, LAND /'*canyon (narrow, walled in with rock)*'/, literally /'something that's squeezed/wedged/jammed in'/, (<**s=**> *nominalizer*), (<**=R9=**> *resultative*), phonology: reduplication, syntactic analysis: nominal, attested by Elders Group (4/16/75).

<**x̱ex̱ekw'íwel ~ x̱ax̱ekw'íwel**>, ds //x̣ə[=C_1ɛ́(·)=]k'ʷ=íwəl//, ABDF /'*get constipated, "bound up"*'/, literally /'wedged in/jammed up in the insides/rectum'/, (<**=R1=**> *resultative*), lx <**=íwel**> *in the rectum, in the insides*, phonology: reduplication, vowel-reduction, syntactic analysis: adjective/adjectival verb, attested by Elders Group (3/3/76), contrast <**ts'iyxwíwel**> *constipated, "bound up"* (lit. "got dry in the rectum"), example: <**x̱ex̱ekw'íwelchapcha. x̱ex̱ekw'íwelchapcha. hálp'exexw te alíle. hálp'exexw te alíle.**>, //x̣ə[=C_1ɛ́(·)=]k'ʷ=íwəl-c-ɛp-cɛ. x̣ə[=C_1ɛ́(·)=]k'ʷ=íwəl-c-ɛp-cɛ. hɛ́-ləp'=əxʸ-əxʷ tə ʔɛlílə. hɛ́-ləp'=əxʸ-əxʷ tə ʔɛlílə.//, phonology: if 1 represents do, 2 re, 3 mi, 4 fa, 5 so, 6 la, 7 ti, 8 do (here in a major scale), this song is sung to the following pitches on each syllable: 3 5 5 8 6 5. 3 5 5 8 6 5. 3 3 1 1 1 2 1. 3 3 1 1 1 2 1. For the rhythms now, if 1 = whole rest, 2 = half note, 4 = quarter note, 8 = eighth note, 16 = sixteenth note, the rhythms of each verse are: 8 8 8 8 4 4 1. 8 8 8 8 4 4 1. 8 8 8 16 16 4 4 1. 8 8 8 16 16 4 4 1., /'*You'll get constipated. You'll get constipated. If you eat salmonberries. If you eat salmonberries.*'/, usage: a berry-picking song, attested by EF (Deming 9/21/78).

<**x̱ekw'óles**>, df //x̣ək'ʷ=áləs//, ANA /'*fish backbone (not dried), (backbone of any creature [Elders Group 7/27/75])*'/, possibly root <**x̱ekw'**> *wedge in, jam in, get narrow/tight*, possibly <**=óles**> *on the eyes, in looks*, probably <**zero**> *nominalizer*, phonology: probably zero nominalizer, syntactic analysis: nominal, attested by Elders Group (4/28/76), contrast <**sx̱éwe**> *dried fish backbone*, compare <**x̱ekw'ólesewíts**> *backbone (of human or other creatures), spine*, other sources: ES /sx̣k'ʷá·lə́s/ *backbone*, JH /sx̣k'ʷá·ləs/ *backbone*, H-T <s'q'wa'lis> (macron over a) *spine of fish, fish bone* (vs. <s'q'wa'lisEwe'ts> (macron over a and e) *spine (of the body)*, Salish cognate: perhaps the root in Lushootseed /x̣k'ʷ-áp/ *the back part of a chicken that is eaten* derived from root /x̣ək'ʷ(u)/ *turn it over face down* as also in /ʔu-x̣ə́k'ʷ čəd/ *I turned over* and /x̣k'ʷ-ud/ *turn it over* H76:592, also /'*backbone (of any creature)*'/, attested by Elders Group (7/27/75).

<**x̱ekw'ólesewíts**>, ds //x̣ək'ʷ=áləs=əwíc//, ANA /'*backbone (of human or other creatures), spine (human or other creature)*'/, lx <**=ewíts**> *on the back*, syntactic analysis: nominal, attested by Elders Group (7/27/75), contrast <**shxwth'omewíts**> *backbone (of any creature)*.

<**x̱ekw'ólesewíts**>, ANA /'*backbone (of human or other creatures), spine (human or other creature)*'/, *see* x̱ekw'óles.

<**x̱él:**>, bound root //x̣ə́l// *move, around in circle,* below are listed some possible derivations, see under the forms themselves for full entries and forms derived from them

<**x̱él:e**>, bound rootor stem //x̣ə́l·(=)ə//, probably root <**x̱él:**> *move, move around in circles*, probably lx <**=e ~ =a**> *living thing*

<**x̱éleq't**>, us //x̣ə́ləq't//, ABFC ['*open one's eyes*']

<**x̱élqes**>, df //x̣ə́l(=)q(=)əs//, ABFC ['*to wave (the hand)*'], SOC, possibly root <**x̱él**> *to mark, make a mark/sign*, possibly root <**x̱ál(=q)**> or <<**x̱él(=q)**>> *move around in circles, roll*, possibly <**=q**> meaning uncertain unless <**=q**> *closable container*, possibly <**=es**> *on the face, round object*??, syntactic analysis: intransitive verb, attested by Deming (6/21/79)

<**x̱álqem**>, cts, TVMO /'*rolling, moving [around in circles]*'/

<**x̱élts'**>, free stem //x̣ə́lc' or x̣ə́l=c' or x̣ə́l=(əl)c'//, TVMO ['*to twist*'], possibly root <**x̱él**> *move, around in circle,* possibly <**=elts'** or **=ts'**> *twist, turn around*, phonology: possible syllable-loss of **el** after **...él**, possible sound symbolism, syntactic analysis: intransitive verb, attested by Elders Group (6/9/76), Salish cognate: Saanich dial. of NSt /x̣ə́ləč'-sət/ *turn oneself around* B74a:81, also for PCS suffix */=əlč' ~ =lč' ~ =č'/ *twist, turn around* see cognate set #215 in Galloway 1982.

<**x̱élts't**>, pcs //x̣ə́l=c'=T//, ABFC /twist it/, TVMO, <=t> *purposeful control transitivizer*, attested by RG & EH (4/9/99 Ling332)

<**x̱álx̱elts't**>, plv //$C_1V_1C_2$=x̣ə́l=c'=T (or) C_1ə[=Aɛ́=]C_2=x̣ə́l=c'=T//, poss. also cts, ABFC /'*twist it around (a few times)*'/, either <**R13=**> or <**R3- plus ablaut**> *plural continuative* or *plural* resp., attested by RG & EH (4/9/99 Ling332)

<**x̱élts'thet**>, rfls //x̣ə́l=c'=T-et/, ABFC /'*turn around*'/, <**-et**> *reflexive*, attested by RG & EH (4/9/99 Ling332)

<**x̱élhchem**>, mdls //x̣ə́(l)=ɬc(ɛ)=əm//, ABFC /'*swim, (tread water), (wading in deep water [LJ], swimming [Elders Group])*'/, literally /'(probably) move oneself around in circles in water'/, probably root <**x̱él**> *move around in circles, roll*, lx <**=(e)lhcha**> *in water, unclear liquid*, (<**=em**> *middle voice*), phonology: consonant merger, vowel-loss (twice), syntactic analysis: intransitive verb, dialects: *Cheh.*, attested by RM (4/23/76), contrast <**t'íts'em**> *swim*, also /'*wading in deep water*'/, attested by LJ (Elders Group 4/26/78), also /'*swimming*'/, dialects: *Cheh.*, attested by Elders Group (4/5/78), contrast <**t'ít'ets'em**> *swimming under the waer when diving*.

<**x̱él ~ x̱é:yl** (or better) **x̱í:l**>, bound root //x̣əl ~ x̣í·l *mark, paint marks, write*//.

<**x̱é:ylt**>, pcs //x̣í·l=T//, SCH ['*write s-th*'], REL /'*paint s-o, (paint marks on s-th/s-o)*'/, (<**=t**> *purposeful control transitivizer*), phonology: possible ablaut, syntactic analysis: transitive verb, attested by EB (12/12/75, 4/27/76), AC (11/10/71, 11/30/71), IHTTC (8/24/77), Elders Group (10/1/75), Salish cognate: Squamish /x̣ə́lʔ-t/ *write (tr.)* beside /x̣ə́lʔ/ *write (itr.)* W73:294, K67:367, Lushootseed root /x̣ál(a)/ *mark, write, decorate* as in /x̣ál-ad/ *write s-th* and /dxʷ-x̣ál-əs-əb-əxʷ/ *mark/paint one's face* H76:579-580, example: <**etsel x̱é:ylt.**>, //ʔə-c-əl x̣í·l=T//, /'*I wrote it.*'/, attested by AC, <**álthe le x̱é:ylt.**>, //ʔɛ́lθə lə x̣í·l=T//, /'*(It's me that wrote it.)*'/, attested by AC, <**x̱é:yltlha ta' skwíx.**>, //x̣í·l=T-ɬɛ t-ɛʔ s=kʷíxʸ//, /'*Write your name.*'/, attested by EB, <**x̱é:yltchexw lá te pípe.**>, //x̣í·l=T-c-əxʷ lɛ́ tə pípə//, /'*Write it down on paper.*'/, attested by Elders Group, <**x̱é:yltes te sqwà:ls te swas "chief".**>, //x̣í·l=T-əs tə s=qʷɛ̀·l-s tə s=wɛ́-s "chief"//, /'*He wrote the words of his "chief".*'/, attested by AC.

<**x̱é:ylthet**>, pcrs //x̣í·l=T-ət//, REL ['*paint one's body*'], literally /'paint marks on oneself purposely'/, (<**-et**> *reflexive*), syntactic analysis: intransitive verb, attested by EB (4/27/76).

<**x̱ex̱é:ylt**>, cts //C_1ə-x̣í·l=T//, SCH ['*writing s-th*'], (<**R5-**> *continuative*), phonology: reduplication, syntactic analysis: transitive verb, attested by AC (11/30/71), example: <**tsel x̱ex̱é:ylt.**>, //c-əl C_1ə-x̣í·l=T//, /'*I'm writing it.*'/, attested by AC.

<**(x̱é:yllhts(e)t)**>, bens //x̣í·l-ɬc=T//, SCH ['*write for s-o*'], (<**-lhts**> *benefactive*), (<**=t**> *purposeful control transitivizer*), syntactic analysis: transitive verb, attested by IHTTC; found in <**x̱é:yllhtsthòx**>, //x̣í·l-ɬc=T-áxʸ//, /'*write for me*'/, attested by IHTTC (8/24/77).

<**sx̱ex̱é:yl**>, strs //s=C_1ə=x̣í·l//, SCH ['*already written*'], (<**s=**> *stative*), (<**R5=**> *resultative*), phonology: reduplication, syntactic analysis: adjective/adjectival verb, attested by IHTTC (8/24/77).

<**sx̱éylstexw**>, caus //s=x̣í·l=sT-əxʷ//, SCH ['*got s-th written down*'], (<**s=**> *stative*), (<**=st**> *causative control transitivizer*), (<**-exw**> *third person object*), syntactic analysis: transitive verb, attested by

LJ (4/7/78), example: <**tl'ó kwe lixw éw sx̱éylstexw te "Hooknose"?**>, //ƛ'á kʷə li-xʷ ʔəw s=x̣í·l=sT-əxʷ tə "Hooknose"//, /'*Have you got it written down "Hooknose"?*'/, attested by Lizzie Johnson (History tape #34 4/7/78).

<**x̱elá:ls**>, sas //x̣il=ɛ́·ls or x̣əl=ɛ́·ls//, SCH ['*writing (while doing it)*'], (<**=á:ls**> *structured activity non-continuative*), (semological comment: the translation seems continuative but may only reflect the structured activity sense of the meaning, that is, done for a while or as a temporary occupation), phonology: vowel-reduction or allomorph, syntactic analysis: intransitive verb, attested by IHTTC (8/24/77).

<**sx̱elá:ls**>, dnom //s=x̣il=ɛ́·ls or s=x̣əl=ɛ́·ls//, SCH ['*writings*'], (<**s=**> *nominalizer, something to*), syntactic analysis: nominal, attested by Deming (6/31/79), also SOC ['*mail?*'], Elder's comment: "unsure", attested by Deming (1/25/79).

<**x̱ex̱é:yls**>, sas //C_1ə-x̣í·l=əls//, cts, SCH ['*writing (while doing it as a structured activity)*'], (<**R5-**> *continuative*), (<**=els**> *structured activity continuative*), phonology: reduplication, syllable-loss (el after í:l), syntactic analysis: intransitive verb, attested by IHTTC (8/24/77), EB (1/16/76), Deming (6/22/78), example: <**xwel x̱ex̱é:yls**>, //xʷəl C_1ə-x̣í·l=əls//, /'*still writing*'/, attested by Deming (6/22/78).

<**sx̱ex̱é:yls**>, sas //s=C_1ə=x̣í·l=əls//, dnom, SCH /'*something one writes with, (writing implement)*'/, literally /'something that is a tool for writing as a structured activity'/, (<**s=**> *something that, nominalizer*), (<**R5=**> *continuative*), (<**=els**> *structured activity continuative tool for*), phonology: reduplication, *syllable-loss,* syntactic analysis: nominal, attested by IHTTC (8/24/77), contrast <**x̱éltel**> *something one writes with, (writing implement), pen, pencil.*

<**Sx̱elá:wtxw**>, ds //s=x̣il=ɛ́·wtxʷ ~ s=x̣əl=ɛ́·wtxʷ//, PLN /'*Schelowat, a village at the bend in Hope Slough at Annis Rd. where there was a painted or marked house*'/, ASM ['a village just across Hope Slough from where the Melody Cafe was in 1964 (HE 10/8/64), between Rosedale and Cheam (AC)'], literally /'marked/painted house'/, (<**s=**> *nominalizer*), lx <**=á:wtxw**> *house*, syntactic analysis: nominal, attested by HE (10/8/64 tape, our new transcription), AC (1973), Elders Group (7/20/77), other sources: Wells 1965 (lst ed.):23, Wells 1966, source: place names file reference #80, #284.

<**x̱élesem**>, vis //x̣i[=Aə́=]l=əs=əm//, PE //'(pictured, marked, painted)'//, or possibly mdls, possibly <**é-ablaut on root i**> *resultative or durative or derivational*, lx <**=es**> *face*, phonology: possible ablaut, syntactic analysis: intransitive verb or middle verb, example: <**mestíyexw x̱élesem**>, //məstíyəxʷ x̣ə́l=əs=əm// 09or //məstíyəxʷ x̣i[=Aə́=]l=əs=əm//, //'picture of a person'//,lit. /'person pictured'/, attested by RG & EH (4/10/99 Ling332)

<**sx̱éles**>, df //s=x̣i[=Aə́=]l=əs or s=x̣ə́l=əs//, BSK ['*design on basket*'], ASM ['these were also called by what they looked like: arrowhead (t'exelá), ladder (skw'íytel), mountain, lightning, village, river, and many more'], literally /'something (to get) marked/painted on the face'/,(<**s=**> *nominalizer, something to*), possibly <**é-ablaut on root i**> *resultative or durative or derivational*, lx <**=es**> *on the face*, phonology: possible ablaut, syntactic analysis: nominal, attested by IHTTC (8/24/77), Elders Group (6/11/75), also PE ['*picture, design*'], attested by RG & EH (4/10/99 Ling332), Salish cognate: Lushootseed /dxʷ-x̣ál-us-əb-əxʷ/ *mark or paint one's face* shows the cognate root /x̣al(u)/ *mark, write, decorate* and suffix H76:580.

<**sx̱elx̱éles**>, pln //s=C_1əC_2=x̣ə́l=əs or s=C_1əC_2=x̣i[=Aə́=]l=əs//, BSK /'*designs on basket, basket designs*'/, (<**R3=**> *plural*), phonology: reduplication, possible ablaut, syntactic analysis: nominal, attested by IHTTC (8/24/77).

<**sx̱elx̱éles te syó:qwem**>, cpds //s=C_1əC_2=x̣ə́l=əs-s tə s=yá·qʷ=əm//, WETH ['*rays of light*'], LT ['*sunbeams*'], literally /'designs of the sun'/, ASM ['NP was told that sunbeams are like fingers

and not to touch them or your fingers will get long, AD was told "don't grab for dust in a sunbeam or you'll be grabby"'], syntactic analysis: nominal phrase with modifier(s), attested by Elders Group (4/16/75), NP and AD (4/11/80).

<**x̱elx̱élest**>, pcs //C_1əC_2=x̣ə́l=əs=T or C_1əC_2=x̣i[=Aə́=]l=əs=T//, BSK ['*decorate it with different designs*'], MC, (<**R3=**> *plural action*), possibly <**é-ablaut on root i**> *derivational or durative or resultative,* lx <**=es**> *on the face*, (<**=t**> *purposeful control transitivizer*), phonology: reduplication, possible ablaut, syntactic analysis: transitive verb, attested by IHTTC (8/24/77).

<**x̱élestexw**>, caus //pcs //x̣ə́l=əs=sT-əx^w//, SPRD //'*show a picture*'//, REL, MC, <**=st**> *causative*, <**-exw**> *3rd person object*, attested by RG & EH (4/10/99 Ling332)

<**X̱elíqel**>, ds //x̣íl=ə[=M2=]qəl//, PLN ['*steep rock wall that used to have Indian writing at first C.P.R. tunnel above Haig*'], literally /'mark/write/paint marks on the cliff/throat'/, ASM ['there ued to be Indian writing here, the rock is steep right down to the river, perhaps even overhanging'], (<**metathesis**> *derivational*), lx <**=eqel**> *on the cliff, on the throat*, (<**zero**> *nominalizer*), phonology: metathesis, zero nominalizer, syntactic analysis: nominal, attested by IHTTC (8/24/77), source: place names file reference #229.

<**Sx̱é:ylmet** or **sx̱é:ylmet**>, ds //s=x̣í·l=əm=ət or s=x̣í·l=əm=a[=Aə=]t//, EZ ['*male black bear with white spot [or mark] on the chest*'], ['*Ursus americanus altifrontalis* with white spot on chest'], N, (semological comment: perhaps both a name and the word for a bear with such a mark), literally /'something/someone that gets/has marked/painted male name'/, (<**s=**> *nominalizer, something/someone that*), (<**=em**> *have, get, intransitivizer*), lx <**=et**> *male name*, syntactic analysis: nominal, attested by ME (11/21/72 tape).

<**Sx̱éylmòt** or **sx̱éylmòt**>, ds //s=x̣í·l=əm=àt//, EZ ['*female black bear with white spot [or mark] on the chest*'], ['*Ursus americanus altifrontalis* with white spot on chest'], N, (semological comment: perhaps both a name and the word for a bear with such a mark), literally /'something/someone that gets/has marked/painted female name'/, (<**s=**> *nominalizer, something/someone that*), (<**=em**> *have, get, intransitivizer*), lx <**=òt**> *female name*, syntactic analysis: nominal, attested by ME (11/21/72 tape).

<**sx̱elpéla**>, df //s=x̣əl=ɛp=ə́lɛ or s=x̣əl=p'=ə́lɛ//, ANAH ['*sideburn(s)*'], (<**s=**> *nominalizer, something to*), root <**x̱el**> *mark, decorate*, possibly <**=ap**> *on the bottom*, possibly <**=p'**> *on itself*, lx <**=éla**> *on the side of the head, temple, cheek*, phonology: possible vowel-loss, possible mistranscription of p for p', syntactic analysis: nominal, attested by Elders Group (8/20/75).

<**sx̱élqs**>, ds //s=x̣ə́l=qs//, DESC ['*a stripe (on the nose or point)*'], LT, (<**s=**> *nominalizer*), lx <**=qs**> *on the nose, on the point*, syntactic analysis: nominal, attested by JL (5/8/79), Salish cognate: Lushootseed /ʔəs-x̣ál'-x̣əl/ *speckled, striped* H76:580. Squamish /n-x̣ə́-x̣lʔ-č/ *having marks on the back, a stripe on the back* K69:85, example: <**sx̱élqs te kw'síts**>, //s=x̣ə́l=qs-s tə k'^{w}əs=íc//, /'*the stripe of the rainbow trout*'/, attested by JL (5/8/79).

<**sx̱élx̱elqs**>, pln //s=x̣ə́l=C_1əC_2=qs//, DESC ['*stripes (on the nose or point)*'], LT, (<**=R2**> *plural* here though usually *characteristic*), comment: perhaps mistranscribed for sx̱elx̱élqs /s=R3=x̣ə́lqs/, phonology: reduplication, syntactic analysis: nominal, attested by JL (5/8/79), example: <**sx̱élx̱elqs te kw'síts**>, //s=x̣ə́l=C_1əC_2=qs-s tə k'^{w}əs=íc//, comment: perhaps mistranscribed for sx̱elx̱élqs /s=R3=x̣ə́lqs/, /'*the stripes of the rainbow trout*'/, attested by JL (5/8/79).

<**x̱élq'eqs**>, df //x̣ə́l=q'=əqs or x̣i[=Aə́=][=lə=]q'=əqs//, EZ /'*bluebill duck, (identified from photos as) lesser scaup*'/, ['*Aythys affinis*'], literally /'marked/stripe on something else on the nose (or) scratched (leaving marks) plural on something else on the nose'/, Elder's comment: "the name means

it has a stripe on its nose", possibly root <**x̲él**> *mark, paint a mark, stripe*, possibly root <**x̲í=q'**> *scratch and leave mark*, possibly <**é-ablaut**> *resultative*, possibly <**=le=**> *plural*, lx <**=q'**> *on something else*, lx <**=eqs**> *on the nose*, (<**zero**> *nominalizer*), phonology: possible infixed plural, possible ablaut, zero nominalizer, syntactic analysis: nominal, attested by EL (9/15/78).

<**x̲éltel**>, ds //x̣ə́l=təl//, SCH /'*pencil, pen, something to write with, (device to write or paint or mark with)*'/, literally /'something/device to write/paint marks/mark'/, lx <**=tel**> *device to, something to*, syntactic analysis: nominal, attested by Elders Group (2/19/75, 1/19/77), EB (3/1/76), AC, others, Salish cognate: Squamish /x̣ə́lʔ-tn/ *pencil* W73:196, K67:367, Lushootseed /x̣ál-təd/ *writing utensil, pencil, pen* H76:579, example: <**méstexw ta' x̲éltel.**>, //mi=Aə́=sT-əxʷ t-ɛʔ x̣ə́l=təl//, /'*Give me your pencil.*'/, literally /'cause s-th to have come your pencil/writing device'/, attested by EB (3/1/76), <**yeláwel tl'áqt tel x̲éltel telí ta swá.**>, //yəlɛ́w=əlƛ̓'ɛ́qt t-əl x̣ə́l=təl təlí t-ɛ s=wɛ́//, /'*My pencil is longer than yours.*'/, attested by Elders Group (1/19/77), <**we'ólwe qwe'íqweqws ta x̲éltel.**>, //wə=ʔál wə=qʷəʔíqʷ=əqʷ-s t-ɛ x̣ə́l=təl//, /'*Your pen/pencil is too thin/narrow.*'/, attested by JL (7/13/79).

<**x̲elá:ls**>, SCH ['*writing (while doing it)*'], *see* **x̲**él ~ **x̲**é:yl (or better) **x̲**í:l.

<**x̲él:e**>, bound rootor stem //x̣əl·(=)ə//, probably root <**x̲él:**> *move, move around in circles*, probably lx <**=e ~ =a**> *living thing*

<**sx̲él:e**>, dnom //s=x̣ə́l·ə//, ANA /'*leg, foot*'/, (<**s=**> *nominalizer*), syntactic analysis: nominal, attested by AC (8/15/70, 9/10/71, 11/11/71), SJ, EB (1/7/76), Elders Group (1/24/79), BJ (5/10/64), other sources: ES /sx̣ə́l·ə/ (CwMs /sx̣ə́nʔə/) *foot (leg)*, H-T <sqE'la> *leg (whole)*, Cowichan /sx̣ə́n·ɛ/ Amy Cooper (9/10/71), example: <**tsel lekwláxw tel sx̲él:e.**>, //c-əl ləkʷ=l-ə[=Aɛ́=]xʷ t-əl s=x̣ə́l·ə//, /'*I broke my foot/leg. (break s-th (sticklike) accidentally)*'/, attested by AC (11/11/71), <**selí:kw te sx̲él:es.**>, //s=lə[=Aí·=]kʷ tə s=x̣ə́l·ə-s (or) s=(h)ə=lə[=Aí·=]kʷ tə s=x̣ə́l·ə-s//, /'*Her leg is broken. (break)*'/, attested by AC (11/11/71), <**yexw x̲élh te sx̲él:es tl'oses yelhyó:qwt.**>, //yəxʷ x̣ə́ɬ tə s=x̣ə́l·ə-s ƛ̓'a-s-əs yə=ɬiyá·qʷt//, /'*His leg must hurt, he's [travelling] behind.*'/, attested by EB (1/7/76), <**x̲élh tel sx̲él:e.**>, //x̣ə́ɬ t-əl s=x̣ə́l·ə//, /'*My foot hurts.*'/, attested by Elders Group (1/24/79), <**téqlexw tel sx̲él:e.**>, //tə́qləxʷ t-əl s=x̣ə́l·ə//, /'*My foot aches.*'/, attested by SJ.

<**sx̲ex̲éyle** or **sx̲ex̲íle**>, pln //s=C_1ə=x̣ə[=Aí=]l·ə or s=x̣ə[=C_1əAí=]l·ə//, ANAH /'*(both human) legs, (both) feet*'/, possibly <**R5=** or **=R1=**> *plural*, possibly <**í-ablaut**> *resultative or durative or automatic*, possibly <**í-ablaut**> automatic with *plural* here, phonology: reduplication, ablaut, length-loss, syntactic analysis: nominal, attested by EB and TM (Elders Group 2/13/80), AD (2/80).

<**sx̲ex̲é:yle** or **sx̲ex̲í:le**>, df //s=C_1ə=x̣ə[=Aí=][=·=]l·ə or s=x̣ə[=C_1əAí=][=·=]l·ə//, ANAH /'*whole leg, (whole of both legs)*'/, possibly <**R5=** or **=R1=**> *plural*, possibly <**í-ablaut**> *resultative or durative or automatic*, possibly <**í-ablaut**> automatic with *plural* here, possibly <**=:=**> *augmentative/emphatic*, phonology: reduplication, ablaut, lengthening, syntactic analysis: nominal, attested by JL (7/13/79), example: <**tl'áleqt ta' sx̲ex̲é:yle.**>, //ƛ̓'ɛ́[=lə=]qt t-ɛʔ s=x̣ə[=C_1əAí=·=]l·ə//, /'*Your leg is long.*'/, comment: mistranslated, should be *Your legs are long.* since the verb is clearly pluralized too with =le=, attested by JL.

<**sx̲elx̲éyle**>, pln //s=C_1əC_2=x̣ə[=Aí=]l·ə//, ANA /'*legs (more than two, for ex. non-human)*'/, (<**R3=**> *plural (many)*), possibly <**í-ablaut**> *resultative or durative or automatic*, possibly <**í-ablaut**> automatic with *plural* here, phonology: reduplication, ablaut, length-loss, syntactic analysis: nominal, attested by EB and TG (Elders Group 2/13/80), AD, example: <**tl'álxchxw te sx̲elx̲éyles te letàm.**>, //ƛ̓'ɛ́l=xʸ-c-xʷ tə s=C_1ə=x̣ə[=Aí=]l·ə-s tə lətɛ̀m//, /'*Put the legs (back) on the table.*'/,

literally /'you attach -s-th the legs of the table'/, attested by AD.

<**sx̲éyeltel ~ sx̲í:ltel**>, df //s=x̣ə[=Aí=]l·ə=təl//, ABFC /'*footprint, tracks*'/, (<**s=**> *nominalizer*), root <**x̣ə́l·ə**> *foot, leg,* possibly <**í-ablaut**> *resultative or durative or automatic,* lx <**=tel**> *something, device,* phonology: ablaut, vowel-loss, length movement automatic between consonants to before the first cluster member, syntactic analysis: nominal, attested by AC (11/26/71), DM (12/4/64), Salish cognate: Squamish /n-x̣ə́nʔə-tn/ *tracks, footprints* from /s-x̣ə́nʔ/ *foot, leg* W73:272, K69:63.

<**Sx̲éyeltels Te Sqoyéx̲iya**>, cpds //s=x̣ə[=Aí=]l·ə=təl-s tə s=qayə́x̣=iyɛ//, PLN /'*the Tracks of Mink, holes shaped like a mink's tracks toward the base of the rock-face called Xwyélés or Lexwyélés*'/, literally /'track(s)/footprint(s) of the Mink'/, (semological comment: see under Xwyélés for the story explaining both the rock and the footprints, the rock is on the Harrison River, we photographed the rock and its tracks on a boat trip with EL to document placenames), phonology: ablaut, length movement, syntactic analysis: nominal phrase with modifier(s), attested by EL (6/27/78 on boat trip up Harrison River).

<**x̲éleq't**>, us //x̣ə́ləq't//, ABFC ['*open one's eyes*'], (semological comment: with this meaning one would expect a middle voice form with a lexical suffix for *on the eye(s),* instead we get a form that looks more like a purposeful control transitive but is not one--it doesn't take the third person subject suffix -es which all purposeful control transitives do-- see examples below), possibly root <**x̲él:**> *move, move around in circles,* syntactic analysis: intransitive verb?, attested by Deming, BJ, example: <**x̲éleq't te shxwexwó:s.**>, //x̣ə́ləq't tə s=xʷəxʷá·s//, /'*to lightning, have lightning, Thunder(bird) opens his eyes.*'/, POW, attested by Deming (1974, 3/31/77), BJ (12/5/64).

<**x̲élx̲eleq't**>, df //x̣ə́l[=C_1əC_2=]əq't//, ABFC ['*opening one's eyes*'], (<**=R2=**> *characteristic or continuative*), phonology: reduplication, syntactic analysis: intransitive verb?, attested by Deming, Elders Group (7/9/75), example: <**x̲élx̲eleq't te shxwexwó:s.**>, //x̣ə́l[=C_1əC_2=]əq't tə s=xʷəxʷá·s//, /'*having lightning, Thunder(bird) is opening his eyes.*'/, attested by Deming (3/31/77).

<**x̲éleq't te shxwexwó:s.**>, //x̣ə́ləq't tə s=xʷəxʷá·s//, WETH /'*to lightning, have lightning, Thunder(bird) opens his eyes.*'/, POW, attested by Deming (1974, 3/31/77), BJ (12/5/64), *see* x̲éleq't.

<**X̲elíqel**>, PLN ['*steep rock wall that used to have Indian writing at first C.P.R. tunnel above Haig*'], *see* x̲él ~ x̲é:yl (or better) x̲í:l.

<**x̲elóx̲cha**>, WATR ['*little lakes*'], *see* x̲ó:tsa ~ x̲ó:cha.

<**x̲élqes**>, df //x̣ə́l(=)q(=)əs//, ABFC ['*to wave (the hand)*'], SOC, possibly root <**x̲él**> *to mark, make a mark/sign,* possibly root <**x̲él:**> *move, move around in circles,* possibly <**=q**> meaning uncertain unless <**=q**> *closable container,* possibly <**=ó:s ~ =ós ~ =es**> *on the face, face of the hand or foot, round object*??, syntactic analysis: intransitive verb, attested by Deming (6/21/79). Compare also <**x̲álqem**>, cts, TVMO /'*rolling, moving [around in circles]*'/

<**x̲élqesà:ls**>, sas //x̣ə́l(=)q(=)əs=ɛ̀·ls//, ABFC ['*to wave (one's arms)*'], SOC, (<**=à:ls**> *structured activity continuative*), (semological comment: <**=els**> *structured activity non-continuative* would fit the meaning here better than <**=à:ls**>), phonology: downstepping, syntactic analysis: intransitive verb, attested by AD (5/1/79).

<**x̲ólqesà:ls**>, cts //x̣ə[-Aá-]l(=)q(=)əs=ɛ̀·ls//, ABFC ['*waving (one's arms)*'], SOC, (<**ó-ablaut**> *continuative*), (<**=à:ls**> *structured activity continuative*), phonology: ablaut, downstepping, syntactic analysis: intransitive verb, attested by AD (5/1/79, 5/8/79).

<**x̲élqest**>, pcs //x̣ə́l(=)q(=)əs=T//, ABFC ['*wave at s-o*'], SOC, (<**=t**> *purposeful control transitivizer*), syntactic analysis: transitive verb, attested by Elders Group (5/5/76); found in <**x̲élqestlha.**>,

//x̣ə́l(=)q(=)əs=T-ɬɛ//, /'*Wave at somebody., (Wave at him/her/them.)*'/, attested by Elders Group.

<**x̲élqesà:ls**>, ABFC ['*to wave (one's arms)*'], *see* **x̲**élqes.

<**x̲élqest**>, ABFC ['*wave at s-o*'], *see* **x̲**élqes.

<**x̲éltel**>, SCH /'*pencil, pen, something to write with, (device to write or paint or mark with)*'/, *see* **x̲**él ~ **x̲**é:yl (or better) **x̲**í:l.

<**x̲élts'**>, possibly free root or stem //x̣ə́lc' or x̣ə́l(:)=c' or x̣ə́l(:)=(əl)c'//, TVMO ['*to twist*'], possibly root <**x̲él**:> *move, move around in circle*, possibly <**=elts'** or **=ts'**> *twist, turn around*, phonology: possible syllable-loss of **el** after ...**él**, possible sound symbolism, syntactic analysis: intransitive verb, attested by Elders Group (6/9/76), Salish cognate: Saanich dial. of NSt /x̣ə́ləč'-sət/ *turn oneself around* B74a:81, also for PCS suffix */=əlč' ~ =lč' ~ =č'/ *twist, turn around* see cognate set #215 in Galloway 1982.

<**sx̲á:lts'**>, strs //s=x̣ə[=Aɛ́·=]l=(əl)c'//, DIR /'*(be) turned around, turned the wrong way*'/, (<**s=**> *stative*), (<**á:-ablaut**> *resultative*), phonology: ablaut, possible syllable-loss, syntactic analysis: adjective/adjectival verb, attested by EB (5/25/76).

<**sx̲á:lts'emeth'**>, strs //s=x̣ə[=Aɛ́·=]l=c'=əməθ'//, ds, EB ['*grown twisted (of a tree)*'], lx <**=emeth'**> *standing, upright, in height*, phonology: ablaut, possible syllable-loss, syntactic analysis: adjective/adjectival verb, attested by CT (6/8/76).

<**sx̲álts'xel**>, ds //s=x̣ə[=Aɛ́=]l=c'=xʸəl//, ABFC ['*(have the) legs crossed*'], ASM ['if you cross your legs all the time you'll get twisted with cramped hips and an s-shaped back so you can't get up (EF)'], literally /'be twisted on the leg(s)'/, lx <**=xel**> *on the leg/foot*, phonology: ablaut, possible syllable-loss, syntactic analysis: adjective/adjectival verb, attested by Deming (4/26/79 incl. EF).

<**sx̲álts'ewel**>, ds //s=x̣ə[=Aɛ́=]l=c'=iwəl//, ABFC ['*be twisted*'], literally /'be twisted in the insides'/, lx <**=ewel ~ =íwel**> *in the insides*, phonology: ablaut, vowel-reduction, syntactic analysis: adjective/adjectival verb, attested by CT (6/8/76), example: <**sx̲álts'ewel te álhqey.**>, //s=x̣ə[=Aɛ́=]l=c'=iwəl tə ʔɛ́ɬq=əy//, /'*The snake is twisted.*'/, attested by CT.

<**sx̲ó:lts'iyethel**>, ds //s=x̣ə[=Aɛ́=·Aá=·]l=c'=iyəθəl//, ABDF ['*to have a crooked jaw*'], literally /'be twisted on the jaw'/, ASM ['people sometimes get that way when a ghost bumps them'], lx <**=iyethel**> *on the jaw*, phonology: double ablaut, ó:-ablaut on á: in root automatic before =iyethel?, syntactic analysis: adjective/adjectival verb, attested by EB (5/25/76).

<**x̲élts't**>, pcs //x̣ə́l=c'=T//, TVMO /'*twist s-th/s-o, turn it around, turn s-o, turn s-th (for ex. a page)*'/, DIR, (<**=t**> *purposeful control transitivizer*), syntactic analysis: transitive verb, attested by Elders Group (6/9/76, 5/26/76, 5/5/76, 3/16/77), EB (4/28/78); found in <**x̲élts'tes, ~ x̲élts'thetes.**>, //x̣ə́l=c'=T-əs ~ x̣ə́l=c'=T-ət-əs(?)//, /'*He turned it around.*'/, attested by EB (4/28/78), example: <**x̲élts't te pípe lám te lhq'á:tses.**>, //x̣ə́l=c'=T tə pípə lɛ́m tə ɬq'ɛ́·t=cəs//, /'*Turn to page five., Turn the page to page five.*'/, literally /'turn the paper go to five'/, attested by Elders Group (3/16/77).

<**x̲élts'tem**>, df //x̣ə́l=c'=T=əm or x̣ə́l=c'=T-əm or x̣ə́l=təm//, EFAM /'*be twisted (mentally), he's twisted (mentally)*'/, possibly <**=t**> *purposeful control transitivizer*, possibly <**=em**> *intransitivizer/have/get or middle voice*, possibly <**=tem**> *past participle*, syntactic analysis: adjective/adjectival verb, attested by Elders Group (1/16/79).

<**x̲élts'thet**>, pcrs //x̣ə́l=c'=T-ət//, ABFC /'*turn oneself around, turn (oneself) around*'/, TVMO, DIR, (<**=t**> *purposeful control transitivizer*), (<**=et**> *reflexive*), syntactic analysis: intransitive verb, attested by Elders Group (8/25/76), EB (4/28/78).

<**x̲ax̲elts'elísem**>, mdls //C_1ɛ́-x̣əl=c'=əlís=əm//, ABDF ['*grinding one's teeth*'], (<**R7-**> *continuative*),

lx <**=elís**> *on the tooth/teeth*, (<**=em**> *middle voice*), phonology: reduplication, syntactic analysis: intransitive verb, attested by Elders Group (5/19/76).

<**x̱élts'es**>, ds //x̣ə́l=(əl)c'=əs//, TVMO ['*twist by the head*'], literally /'twist on the face'/, syntactic analysis: intransitive verb, attested by Elders Group (6/9/76).

<**x̱élts'est**>, pcs //x̣ə́l=c'=əs=T//, TVMO ['*twist s-o/s-th by the head*'], (<**=t**> *purposeful control transitivizer*), syntactic analysis: transitive verb, attested by Elders Group (6/9/76).

<**x̱élts'esem**>, mdls //x̣ə́l=c'=əs=əm//, ABFC ['*turn one's head*'], (<**=em**> *middle voice*), syntactic analysis: intransitive verb, attested by IHTTC (9/16/77).

<**x̱elts'íwélém**>, df //x̣əl=c'=íwə́l=əm or x̣əl=c'=íwəl=əm//, SH ['*get twisted [inside]*'], EB, lx <**=íwel** or **=íwél**> *on the insides*, (<**=em**> *middle voice or have/get/intransitivizer*), phonology: updrifting, syntactic analysis: intransitive verb, attested by CT (6/8/76), compare <**sx̱álts'ewel**> *be twisted*, example: <**le x̱elts'íwélém.**>, //lə x̣əl=c'=íwəl=əm//, /'*It got twisted.*'/, attested by CT, <**le x̱elts'íwélém te thqát.**>, //lə x̣əl=c'=íwəl=əm tə θqɛ́t//, /'*The tree is twisted.*'/, attested by CT.

<**x̱áx̱elts'íwélém**>, cts //C_1ɛ́-x̣əl=c'=íwəl=əm//, SH ['*is getting twisted*'], (<**R7-**> *continuative*), phonology: reduplication, syntactic analysis: intransitive verb, attested by CT (6/8/76), example: <**le x̱áx̱elts'íwélém.**>, //lə C_1ɛ́-x̣əl=c'=íwəl=əm//, /'*It's getting twisted.*'/, attested by CT.

<**x̱élts'es**>, TVMO ['*twist by the head*'], *see* **x̱**élts'.

<**x̱élts'esem**>, ABFC ['*turn one's head*'], *see* **x̱**élts'.

<**x̱élts'est**>, TVMO ['*twist s-o/s-th by the head*'], *see* **x̱**élts'.

<**x̱elts'íwélém**>, SH ['*get twisted [inside]*'], *see* **x̱**élts'.

<**x̱élts't**>, TVMO /'*twist s-th/s-o, turn it around, turn s-o, turn s-th (for ex. a page)*'/, *see* **x̱**élts'.

<**x̱élts'tem**>, EFAM /'*be twisted (mentally), he's twisted (mentally)*'/, *see* **x̱**élts'.

<**x̱élts'thet**>, ABFC /'*turn oneself around, turn (oneself) around*'/, *see* **x̱**élts'.

<**x̱elx̱álqem**>, TVMO /'*moving, (many moving around in circles, moving around in circles many times)*'/, *see* **x̱**álqem.

<**x̱elx̱álqem**>, PLAY ['*movie(s)*'], *see* **x̱**álqem.

<**x̱élx̱eleq't**>, ABFC ['*opening one's eyes*'], *see* **x̱**éleq't.

<**x̱élx̱eleq't te shxwexwó:s.**>, //x̣əl[=C_1əC_2=]əq't tə s=x^{w}əx^{w}á·s//, WETH /'*having lightning, Thunder(bird) is opening his eyes.*'/, POW, attested by Deming (3/31/77), *see* **x̱**éleq't.

<**x̱elx̱élest**>, BSK ['*decorate it with different designs*'], *see* **x̱**él ~ **x̱**é:yl (or better) **x̱**í:l.

<**x̱elx̱ólqemóles**>, ABFC ['*roll one's eyes*'], *see* **x̱**álqem.

<**x̱élh**>, free root //x̣ə́ɬ//, ABDF /'*hurt, be hurt, (ache [Elders Group 3/1/72], to really hurt (more than an ache) [AD])*'/, EFAM, syntactic analysis: intransitive verb, attested by Deming (6/15/78), Elders Group (2/16/76), LJ (Elders Group 6/28/78), Salish cognate: Lushootseed root /x̣əɬ/ *sick* as in /ʔəs-x̣ə́ɬ/ *be sick, hurt* H76:593, root in Squamish /x̣ɬán/ *epidemic/ K69:84,* also /'*to really hurt (more than an ache)*'/, attested by AD (2/28/79), also /'*ache*'/, attested by Elders Group (3/1/72), example: <**x̱élh tel s'íles lhíl kw'à:y.**>, //x̣ə́ɬ t-əl s=ʔíləs ɬí-l k'^{w}ɛ̀·y//, /'*My chest hurts when I get hungry.*'/, attested by LJ.

<**x̱élh (te, kw'e) sqwálewel**>, cpds //x̣ə́ɬ (tə, k'^{w}ə) s=q^{w}ɛ́l=iwəl//, EFAM /'*be sorry, the feelings are hurt*'/, literally /'the (present/unspecified, abstract) thoughts/feeling are hurt'/, syntactic analysis: intransitive verb demonstrative article nominal, attested by Deming (6/15/78), Elders Group

(2/19/75, 4/16/75, 2/16/76, 6/28/78), CT (6/8/76), example: <**x̲élh tel sqwálewel. ~ x̲élh kw'el sqwálewel.**>, //x̣ə́ɬ (t-əl, k'ʷ-əl) s=qʷɛ̀l=iwəl//, /'*I'm sorry., My feelings are hurt.*'/, attested by Elders Group, <**x̲élh kw'a sqwá:lewel.**>, //x̣ə́ɬ k'ʷ-ɛ s=qʷɛ̀·l=əwəl//, /'*You are sorry., You mourn.*'/, attested by CT (6/8/76), <**wálh me x̲élh kw'a' sqwálewel lhíxw me p'élh?**>, //ʔəwə-ə-ɬ mə x̣ə́ɬ k'ʷ-ɛʔ s=qʷɛ̀l=iwəl ɬí-xʷ mə p'ə́ɬ//, /'*Do you ever feel sorry when you sober up?*'/, literally /'is it never? (is not -yes/no-question -past) come/become be hurt your feelings/thoughts when -you become sober'/, attested by Elders Group (6/28/78).

<**x̲ex̲élh**>, cts //C₁ə-x̣ə́ɬ//, ABDF /'*(be) hurting, be aching*'/, EFAM, (<**R5-**> *continuative*), phonology: reduplication, syntactic analysis: intransitive verb, attested by Elders Group (11/9/77, 12/7/77).

<**x̲ex̲élh te sqwálewel**>, cpds //C₁ə-x̣ə́ɬ tə s=qʷɛ̀l=iwəl//, EFAM ['*be feeling sorry*'], literally /'are hurting the thoughts/feelings'/, phonology: reduplication, down-drifting, vowel-reduction, syntactic analysis: intransitive verb demonstrative article nominal, attested by Elders Group (11/9/77).

<**x̲ex̲élh**>, rsls //C₁ə=x̣ə́ɬ//, ABDF ['*"sored up"*'], (<**R5=**> *resultative*), phonology: reduplication, syntactic analysis: intransitive verb, probably adjective/adjectival verb, attested by EB (Elders Group 4/26/78).

<**sx̲élh**>, dnom //s=x̣ə́ɬ//, ABDF /'*a wound, (a hurt?)*'/, (<**s=**> *nominalizer*), syntactic analysis: nominal, attested by EB (12/16/75), example: <**me i'éyel tel sx̲élh.**>, //mə C₁əC₂=ʔɛ́y=əl t-əl s=x̣ə́ɬ//, /'*My wound healed.*'/, literally /'(be)come get better my wound/hurt'/, attested by EB.

<**x̲élhlexw**>, ncs //x̣ə́ɬ=l-əxʷ//, ABDF /'*hurt s-o [accidentally, happen to, manage to]*'/, (<**=l**> *non-control transitivizer*), (<**-exw**> *third person object*), syntactic analysis: transitive verb, attested by Elders Group (4/26/78); found in <**x̲élhlòx**>, //x̣ə́ɬ=l-áxʸ//, /'*hurt me*'/, phonology: downstepping, attested by Elders Group.

<**x̲elhláxw**>, durs //x̣əɬ=l-ə[=Aɛ́=]xʷ//, ABDF /'*hurt s-o/s-th [for awhile, accidentally]*'/, (<**á-ablaut**> *durative*), phonology: ablaut, syntactic analysis: transitive verb, attested by AC (11/11/71), example: <**tsel x̲elhláxw tel sx̲éyes.**>, //c-əl x̣əɬ=l-ə[=Aɛ́=]xʷ t-əl s=x̣ə́y(=)əs//, /'*I hurt my head.*'/, attested by AC.

<**x̲ex̲élhlexw**>, cts //C₁ə-x̣ə́ɬ=l-əxʷ//, ABDF /'*(be) hurting s-o [accidentally, happening to/managing to]*'/, Elder's comment: "unsure", (<**R5-**> *continuative*), syntactic analysis: transitive verb, attested by NP (Elders Group 4/26/78).

<**x̲lhét**>, pcs //x̣ə́ɬ=M1=T//, SOC ['*beat s-o up*'], literally /'hurt s-o on purpose'/, (<**metathesis type 1**> *non-continuative*), (<**=t**> *purposeful control transitivizer*), phonology: metathesis, syntactic analysis: transitive verb, attested by Elders Group (1/25/78), EB (12/17/75, 12/19/75); found in <**x̲lhétes.**>, //x̣ə́ɬ=M1=T-əs//, /'*S-o beat s-o up., (He/She/They beat him/her/it/them up.)*'/, attested by EB (12/17/75), <**x̲lhétem.**>, //x̣ə́ɬ=M1=T-əm//, /'*He got beat up.*'/, attested by EB (12/19/75).

<**x̲lhá:léqel ~ x̲elháléqel**>, ds //x̣əɬ=ɛ́(·)lə́qəl//, ABDF ['*(have a) headache*'], lx <**=á:léqel**> *on the skull, on the front of the head*, possibly <**=á(:)-ablaut**> *durative*, syntactic analysis: intransitive verb, attested by BJ (12/5/64), Elders Group (3/1/72), compare <**tesáléqel**> *bump one's head.*

<**x̲elhálwes**>, ds //x̣əɬ=ɛ́lwəs or x̣əɬ=ə[=Aɛ́=]lwəs//, ABDF /'*have a pain in the stomach, (have a stomach-ache), one's stomache hurts*'/, lx <**=élwes (~? =álwes)**> *in the stomach*, probably <**á-ablaut**> *durative*, phonology: probable ablaut, syntactic analysis: intransitive verb, attested by Elders Group (1/24/79); found in <**x̲elhálwestsel.**>, //x̣əɬ=ə[=Aɛ́=]lwəs-c-əl//, /'*My stomach hurts., I have a pain in the stomach.*'/, attested by Elders Group.

<**x̲elhwílh**>, df //x̣əɬ=wə[=Aí=]ɬ//, ds, EFAM /'*to disappoint, (be disappointed)*'/, lx <**=welh**> *in disposition, -minded*, (<**í-ablaut**> *durative or resultative*), phonology: ablaut, syntactic analysis:

intransitive verb, attested by Elders Group (3/72).

<**x̲elhwílhlexw**>, ncs //x̣əɬ=wə[=Aí=]ɬ=l-əxʷ//, EFAM ['*disappoint s-o*'], (<**=l**> *non-control transitivizer*), (<**-exw**> *third person object*), phonology: ablaut, syntactic analysis: transitive verb, attested by Deming (4/27/78), EB (1/20/76), Elders Group (3/72), example: <**tsel x̲elhwílhlòmè.**>, //c-əl x̣əɬ=wə[=Aí=]ɬ=l-ámə//, /'*I disappointed you.*'/, phonology: downstepping, updrifting, attested by EB, <**latsel x̲elhwílhlòmè.**>, //lɛ-c-əl x̣əɬ=wə[=Aí=]ɬ=ɬ-ámə//, /'*I'm going to disappoint you.*'/, attested by EB, <**chexw x̲elhwílhlòx.**>, //c-əxʷ x̣əɬ=wə[=Aí=]ɬ=l-áxʸ//, /'*You disappointed me.*'/, attested by Elders Group (3/72).

<**X̲elhlálh ~ X̲elhálh**>, ds //x̣əɬ=ɛ́lə=M2=ɬ//, PLN ['*former village directly across the Fraser River from Yale*'], Elder's comment: literally /'injured people'/, ASM ['so named because a lot of people were hurt by a big war or fight with west coast raiders (AK), alternatively so named because XeXáls (the Transformers) turned so many to stone here'], lx <**=ále**> *people*, (<**metathesis**> *derivational*), (<**=lh**> *past tense*), phonology: metathesis, vowel-loss, optional consonant merger, syntactic analysis: nominal, attested by AK and SP (Fish Camp 8/2/77), AK/SP/AD (Raft trip 9/13/77), IHTTC (8/11/77), other sources: Wells 1965 (lst ed.):25, source: place names file reference #4a.

<**x̲lhélets**>, ds //x̣əɬ=ə́ləc//, ABDF ['*tired on the rump*'], literally /'sore on the bottom/rump'/, lx <**=élets**> *on the bottom, on the rump*, phonology: vowel-loss, syntactic analysis: adjective/adjectival verb, attested by SJ (3/17/77).

<**x̲lhém**>, df //x̣əɬ=ə́m//, ABDF ['*to be tired*'], literally /'hurt/sore in strength'/, lx <**=ém**> *in strength*, phonology: vowel-loss, syntactic analysis: adjective/adjectival verb, attested by EB (12/12/75, 1/7/76), Deming (1/31/80), example: <**x̲lhém tel sx̲elx̲éyle.**>, //x̣əɬ=ə́m t-əl s=C_1əC_2=x̣ə[=Aí=]lə//, /'*My legs are tired.*'/, attested by Deming.

<**x̲lhém:et**>, iecs //x̣əɬ=ə́m=məT//, EFAM /'*tired of s-th, bored with s-th*'/, ABDF, literally /'hurt in strength toward s-th'/, (<**=met**> *indirect effect non-control transitivizer*), phonology: consonant merger (mm → m:), vowel-loss, syntactic analysis: transitive verb, attested by Elders Group (2/16/77), synonym <**lhchí:wsmet**>.

<**sx̲élhx̲elh**>, dnom //s=x̣ə́ɬ=C_1əC_2//, chrs, ANAF /'*tiny fin above tail of fish,* (perhaps *spines above tail of some fish*)'/, literally perhaps /'something to characteristically hurt'/, ASM ['perhaps so named because they are often sharp'], (<**s=**> *nominalizer*), (<**=R2**> *characteristic*), phonology: reduplication, syntactic analysis: nominal, attested by Elders Group (4/28/76).

<**x̲elhálwes**>, ABDF /'*have a pain in the stomach, (have a stomach-ache), one's stomache hurts*'/, *see* **x̲**élh.

<**x̲élhchem**>, mdls //x̣ə́(l:)=ɬc(ɛ)=əm//, ABFC /'*swim, (tread water), (wading in deep water [LJ], swimming [Elders Group])*'/, literally /'(probably) move oneself around in circles in water'/, probably root <**x̲él:**> *move around in circles, roll*, lx <**=(e)lhcha**> *in water, unclear liquid*, (<**=em**> *middle voice*), phonology: consonant merger, vowel-loss (twice), syntactic analysis: intransitive verb, dialects: *Cheh.*, attested by RM (4/23/76), contrast <**t'íts'em**> *swim*, also /'*wading in deep water*'/, attested by LJ (Elders Group 4/26/78), also /'*swimming*'/, dialects: *Cheh.*, attested by Elders Group (4/5/78), contrast <**t'ít'ets'em**> *swimming under the waer when diving.*

<**x̲ólhchem**>, cts //x̣ə[-Aá-]l=ɬc(ɛ)=əm//, ABFC /'*swimming (of dog, deer, animal), (dog-paddling)*'/, (<**ó-ablaut**> *continuative*), comment: in **x̲**álqem *moving [around in circles], rolling* root **x̲**él has á-ablaut *continuative*, phonology: ablaut, consonant merger, vowel-loss (twice), syntactic analysis: intransitive verb, attested by Elders Group (4/26/78).

<**X̲elhlálh ~ X̲elhálh**>, PLN ['*former village directly across the Fraser River from Yale*'], *see* **x̲**élh.

<**x̲elhláxw**>, ABDF /*'hurt s-o/s-th [for awhile, accidentally]'*/, *see* x̲élh.

<**x̲élhlexw**>, ABDF /*'hurt s-o [accidentally, happen to, manage to]'*/, *see* x̲élh.

<**x̲élh (te, kw'e) sqwálewel**>, EFAM /*'be sorry, the feelings are hurt'*/, *see* x̲élh.

<**x̲elhwílh**>, EFAM /*'to disappoint, (be disappointed)'*/, *see* x̲élh.

<**x̲elhwílhlexw**>, EFAM [*'disappoint s-o'*], *see* x̲élh.

<**X̲emó:th'iya**>, PLN [*'small peak next to Mount Cheam'*], *see* x̲à:m ~ x̲á:m.

<**x̲emx̲ám**>, ABFC [*'lots of people crying'*], *see* x̲à:m ~ x̲á:m.

<**x̲émx̲em**>, chrs //x̣ə́m=C_1əC_2//, EB /*'giant horsetail, also common horsetail, (mushroom [AC])'*/, [*'Equisetum telmateia, Equisetum arvense'*], ASM ['pollen cone and probably also the shoots of the giant horsetail were eaten in spring, water could be sucked from jointed fragments also'], root meaning unknown, (<**=R2**> *characteristic*), phonology: reduplication, syntactic analysis: nominal, attested by Deming, Salish cognate: Cowichan dial. of Halkomelem /sx̣ə́mʔx̣əmʔ/ and Saanich dial. of NSt /sx̣ə́mx̣əm/ both *scouring rush (E. arvense [sic? E. hiemale?]) and giant horsetail (E. telmateia)* Turner and Bell 1971:68, Squamish /s-x̣ə́m-x̣m/ *horsetail (bot.)* W73:144, K69:80 or *scouring rush (E. hiemale), common horsetail (E. arvense), and giant horsetail (E. telmateia)* Bouchard and Turner 1976:14-15, and possibly showing the ancient root Columbian /x̣ə́m'/ *be dry* Kinkade 1981:47 since horsetail was used as a source of water (this is not Kinkade's idea, only mine), also /*'mushroom'*/, attested by AC (11/26/71).

<**x̲emx̲ímels ~ x̲emx̲íméls**>, EZ /*'chicken hawk (red-tailed hawk), hawk (large and small varieties)'*/, *see* x̲ím.

<**x̲epá:y ~ x̲epáy ~ x̲pá:y**>, EB [*'western red cedar wood'*], *see* **sx̲íp**.

<**x̲épchest**>, pcs //x̣ə́p=cəs=T//, ABFC [*'snatch it from s-o'*], root meaning unknown, lx <**=ches ~ =ches**> *on the hand*, (<**=t**> *purposeful control transitivizer*), syntactic analysis: transitive verb, attested by Elders Group (3/24/76), Salish cognate: possibly Lushootseed root in /x̣əp-ús-əb/ *lift head up, straighten up* H76:597; found in <**x̲epchesthóxes.**>, //x̣əp=cəs=T-áxʸ-əs//, /*'He snatched it from me.'*/, attested by Elders Group.

<**x̲épeqw** (or **x̲ép'eqw?** or **x̲ép'ekw'?**)>, possible stem //x̣ə́p=əqʷ or x̣ə́p'=D=əqʷ (or x̣ə́p'=əqʷ or x̣ə[=´=]p'ək'ʷ)//, root meaning uncertain, perhaps *crispy* or *crunchy*

<**sx̲épeqw** (or **sx̲ép'eqw?** or **sx̲ép'ekw'?**)>, dnom //s=x̣ə́p=əqʷ or s=x̣ə́p'=D=əqʷ (or s=x̣ə́p'=əqʷ or s=x̣ə[=´=]p'ək'ʷ)//, ANAF [*'edible gristle inside fish head (nose gristle)'*], literally (perhaps) /'something crispy/to chew with a crunch in the top of the head'/, ASM ['eaten as a delicacy'], (<**s=**> *nominalizer, something to*), root meaning unknown unless <x̲ép'(=kw')> *chew with a crunch*, possibly <**=D (deglottaliza-tion)**> *derivational*, lx <**=eqw**> *on top of the head*, compare <x̲ep'ékw'> *make a crunch underfoot*, compare <**x̲ep'kw'=á:ls**> *chew with a crunch*, phonology: possible deglottalization, syntactic analysis: nominal, attested by Deming (4/1/76), Salish cognate: Lushootseed /sx̣ə́p'(ə)k'ʷ ~ sx̣ə́p'k'ʷ-əs/ *edible cartilage in front part of fish nose* from root as in /x̣ə́p'k'ʷ-əd/ *chew s-th hard that makes noise* H76:598, Squamish /sx̣p'ə́k'ʷ/ *cartilage* W73:53, K69:59 from root /x̣əp'/ *to split, break, crack* as also in /x̣ə́p'-nəxʷ/ *have broken, break accid. (tr.)* and /s-x̣ə́p'-šn/ *fish tail* (lit. "split leg") but especially this root with root extension /-k'ʷ/ as in /x̣əp'k'ʷ-ánʔ/ *chew up (tr.)(so that the object cracks)* and /x̣əp'k'ʷ-án-t-m/ *to hurt, ache* and /x̣əp'k'ʷ-íws-n-t-m/ *be rheumatic* K69:84, K67:366.

<**x̲épkw'em**>, TCH /*'brittle, crisp'*/, *see* x̲ep'ékw'.

<**x̱épxel** (or **x̱ép'xel)**>, dnom //x̣ə́p=xʸəl or x̣ə́p'=D=xʸəl (or x̣ə́p'=xʸəl)//, meaning uncertain if not *chew on the foot with a crunch*

<**sx̱épxel** (or **sx̱ép'xel)**>, dnom //s=x̣ə́p=xʸəl or s=x̣ə́p'=D=xʸəl (or s=x̣ə́p'=xʸəl)//, ANAF [*'fish tail'*], literally perhaps /'something to chew with a crunch on the foot (tail)'/, ASM ['eaten often when cooked crisply'], (<**s=**> *nominalizer, something to*), root meaning unknown unless <**x̱ép'(=kw')**> *chew with a crunch*, possibly <**=D (deglottalization)**> *derivational*, lx <**=xel**> *on the foot (tail)*, compare <x̱ep'ékw'> *make a crunch underfoot*, compare <**x̱ep'kw'=á:ls**> *chew with a crunch*, phonology: possible deglottalization, syntactic analysis: nominal, attested by AC (8/13/70, 9/18/71), Deming (4/1/76), other sources: ES /sx̣ə́pxʸəl/ (but Ms /sx̣ə́p'xʸən/, Cw /sx̣ə́p'šən/ glottalized) *fish tail*, Salish cognate: Squamish /s-x̣ə́p'-šn/ *fish tail* from root /x̣əp'/ *split, break, crack* as also in /x̣ə́p'-nəxʷ/ *have broken, break accidentally (tr.)* W73:102, K67:297, 367, also Squamish /sx̣əp'šən/ *caudal peduncle or "narrow section near tail of fish"* Kennedy and Bouchard 1976:38-39.

<**x̱epx̱epkw't**>, ABFC [*'chewed it up'*], *see* x̱ep'ékw'.

<**x̱epyúwelh**>, HHG [*'cedar trough (to serve food)'*], *see* sx̱íp.

<**x̱ep'ékw'**>, possibly root //x̣əp'ə́k'ʷ or x̣ə́p'=ə[=M2=]k'ʷ//, SD /*'make a crunch underfoot (bones, nut, glass, etc.), make a crunch'*/, root meaning unknown unless as in Squamish cognate, possibly <**=ekw'**> meaning unclear unless *round, around*, possibly <**metathesis**> *derivational*, phonology: possible metathesis, syntactic analysis: intransitive verb, attested by IHTTC (9/2/77), Salish cognate: Lushootseed /x̣ə́p'k'ʷ-əd/ *chew s-th hard that makes noise* H76:598, Squamish /x̣əp'k'ʷ-ánʔ/ *chew up (tr.)(so that the object cracks)* from root /x̣əp'/ *to split, break, crack* as also in /x̣ə́p'-nəxʷ/ *have broken, break accid. (tr.)* and /s-x̣ə́p'-šn/ *fish tail* (lit. "split leg") but especially with root extension /-k'ʷ/ K69:84, K67:366.

<**x̱ep'kw'á:ls**>, sas //x̣əp'(=)k'ʷ=ɛ́·ls//, ABFC [*'chew with a crunch'*], SD, FOOD, (<**=á:ls**> *structured activity non-continuative*), syntactic analysis: intransitive verb, attested by IHTTC (9/2/77).

<**x̱áp'kw'els**>, cts //x̣ə[-Aɛ́-]p'(=)k'ʷ=əls//, sas, ABFC /*'chewing with a crunch, nibbling, gnawing'*/, SD, FOOD, (<**á-ablaut**> *continuative*), (<**=els**> *structured activity continuative*), syntactic analysis: intransitive verb, attested by IHTTC (9/2/77), Elders Group (1/21/76), *<**x̱áp'kw'els te Bill te kyá:lti.**> rejected, */'Bill's chewing up/gnawing the candy.'/ rejected by EB (5/3/76).

<**x̱ápkw'els**>, dnom //x̣ə[-Aɛ́-]p'(=)k'ʷ=əls// FOOD *crackers* (lit. crunching noise structured activity [thing]), nominal alloseme of the continuative stem just above (attested by RG,EH 6/16/98 to SN, edited by BG with RG,EH 6/26/00)

<**x̱ép'kw't ~ x̱épkw't ~ (sic) x̱épkwt**>, pcs //x̣ə́p'(=)k'ʷ=T ~ x̣ə́p'=D=k'ʷ=T//, ABFC /*'gnaw s-th, chew s-th [crunchy]'*/, FOOD, SD, (<**=t**> *purposeful control transitivizer*), phonology: deglottalization, dissimilation, syntactic analysis: transitive verb, attested by EB (5/3/76, 12/5/75), example: <**x̱épkw'tes te kyá:lti.**>, //x̣ə́p'=D=k'ʷ=T-əs tə kʸɛ́·lti//, /*'He chewed the candy.'*/, attested by EB (5/3/76).

<**x̱áp'kw't ~ (sic) x̱ápkwt**>, cts //x̣ə[-Aɛ́-]p'=D=k'ʷ=T//, ABFC /*'gnawing s-th, be gnawing on s-th'*/, FOOD, SD, (<**á-ablaut**> *continuative*), phonology: ablaut, deglottalization, dissimilation, syntactic analysis: transitive verb, attested by EB (12/15/75), example: <**x̱ápkwtes te sqwemáy te sth'ó:m.**>, //x̣ə[-Aɛ́-]p'=D=k'ʷ=T-əs tə s=qʷəm=ɛ́y tə s=θ'á·m//, /*'The dog is gnawing on a bone.'*/, attested by EB.

<**x̱epx̱epkw't**>, plv //$C_1əC_2$=x̣əp'=D=k'ʷ=T//, ABFC [*'chewed it up'*], FOOD, SD, (<**R3=**> *plural action, completive*), phonology: reduplication, deglottalization, dissimilation, syntactic analysis: transitive verb, attested by EB (5/3/76), example: <**x̱epx̱épkw'tes te kyá:lti.**>,

//C₁əC₂=x̣əp'=D=k'ʷ=T-əs tə kʸɛ́·lti//, /'*He chewed up the candy.*'/, attested by EB.

<**x̱épkw'em**>, izs //x̣ə́p'=D=k'ʷ=əm//, TCH /'*brittle, crisp*'/, (<**=D (deglottalization)**> *derivational*), (<**=em**> *intransitivizer, have, get*), phonology: deglottalization, dissimilation, syntactic analysis: adjective/adjectival verb, attested by HT and CT (6/8/76), SP (BHTTC late 10/76), also <**x̱ép'kw'em**>, //x̣ə́p'=k'ʷ=əm//, also /'*crisp*'/, attested by EB and TG (BHTTC late 10/76).

<**x̱ápkw'em**>, cts //x̣ə[-Aɛ́-]p'=D=k'ʷ=əm//, SD /'*make a crunching or crackling noise, crunching (gnawing) sound*'/, semantic environment ['like ice breaking or chewing apples or peanuts'], (<**á-ablaut**> *continuative*), phonology: ablaut, deglottalization, dissimilation, syntactic analysis: intransitive verb, synonym <**tl'ámqw'els**>, attested by EB (3/12/76), BHTTC (11/11/76 or 11/12/76).

<**x̱ep'ewíts**>, ABDF ['*marked on the back*'], *see* **x̱íp**'.

<**x̱ep'í:tsel**>, ds //x̣i(=)p'=í·c(-)əl or x̣i[=Aə=](=)p'=í·cəl//, EZ /'*chipmunk with two stripes, Northwestern chipmunk, also Townsend chipmunk*'/, ['*Eutamias amoenus (affinis?), Eutamias townsendi*'], literally /'(get) scratched on the back'/, ASM ['when they come out in winter and shake their mats or mattresses and blankets, that's when the last snow has wide flakes'], Elder's comment: "he may have gotten his scratched back from grizzly bear in a story (Elders Group 3/21/79)", root <**x̱ip' ~ x̱ey=p'**> *scratch and leave mark (on itself)*, probably <**e-ablaut**> *resultative*, lx <**=í(:)tsel**> *on the back, on the surface, on the top,* or lx <**=ewíts ~ =íts ~ =ích ~ =ech**> *on the back, on the back of something* (first allomorph possibly has <**=ew**> *on the body,* see that main entry under allomorph <**=ewíts**>) plus <-el> *come, go, get, inceptive*, (<**zero**> *nominalizer*), phonology: ablaut or vowel-reduction, zero nominalizer, syntactic analysis: nominal, attested by ME (11/21/72 tape), compare <**s-x̱éyp'**> *line*, other sources: JH /x̣əp'í·cəl/ *chipmunk.*

<**x̱ex̱p'í:tsel ~ x̱ex̱p'ítsel ~ sx̱ex̱p'í:tsel**>, ds //(s=)x̣i[=Aə=C₁ə=](=)p'=í(·)c'əl//, [(s)x̣əx̣p'í(·)c'əl], EZ /'*chipmunk with more than two stripes, Northwestern chipmunk, Townsend chipmunk*'/, ['*Eutamias amoenus felix* (has more than two stripes), Eutamias townsendi, perhaps also *Eutamias amoenus affinis*'], literally /'(something) (got) scratched several times on the back'/, (<**s=**> *nominalizer*), (<**e-ablaut**> *resultative*), (<**=R1=**> *plural*), phonology: ablaut, reduplication, syntactic analysis: nominal, attested by Elders Group (3/21/79), AK (11/21/72 tape), other sources: ES /cicəpyáθəl/ (CwMs /x̣əx̣p'ícən/) *chipmunk*, Salish cognate: Squamish /s-x̣ə-x̣p'-í-čn/ *chipmunk* W73:59, K69:60 and *Northwestern chipmunk (Eutamias amoenus felix)* Kennedy and Bouchard 1976:2, Skagit dial. of Lushootseed /x̣íx̣ip'ič'/ *chipmunk* H76:604.

<**x̱ep'kw'á:ls**>, ABFC ['*chew with a crunch*'], *see* x̱ep'ékw'.

<**x̱ép'kw't ~ x̱épkw't ~ (sic) x̱épkwt**>, ABFC /'*gnaw s-th, chew s-th [crunchy]*'/, *see* x̱ep'ékw'.

<**x̱éq**>, bound root //x̣ə́q *straddle*//.

<**x̱eqét**>, pcs //x̣ə́q-M1=T//, ABFC /'*straddle s-th (log, fish, etc.)*'/, **(metathesis type 1** *non-continuative*), (<**=t**> *purposeful control transitivizer*), phonology: metathesis, epenthetic schwa (e), syntactic analysis: transitive verb, attested by IHTTC (8/29/77), Salish cognate: Lushootseed root /x̣əq/ *wrap around* as in /x̣ə́q-əd/ *wrap string/cloth around it, tie it, wind it around* H76:598.

<**Lex̱ex̱éq**>, df //lə(xʷ)=C₁ə=x̣ə́q//, PLN ['*Luckakuck Creek*'], ASM ['in what is now Sardis, B.C., it flows on the east side of Vedder Road in front of former Edenbank farm, before contact it got its name as a kind of cuss-word people would say since they had to cross it by a slippery log which they wound up straddling (either by accident or design) (DM)'], literally /'always straddled (or) always straddling'/, (<**lexw= ~ xw=** ~ (rarely) **le=**> *always*), (<**R5=**> *resultative or continuative*), phonology: reduplication, syntactic analysis: nominal, attested by DM (1/8/62 new transcript

Wells tapes), IHTTC (8/29/77), other sources: Wells 1965 (lst ed.), Wells 1966, source: place names file reference #90.

<**xeqét**>, ABFC */'straddle s-th (log, fish, etc.)'/, see* xéq.

<**xeq'**>, free root //x̣ə́q'//, DESC ['*narrow (of rocky passage)*'], syntactic analysis: adjective/adjectival verb, attested by Elders Group (7/9/75).

<**xeq'át**>, df //x̣əq'=ə[=Aɛ́=]t//, LAND */'flat smooth and bare rock, a [rock] bluff, a bluff (straight up)'/*, possibly <**=et**> *past participle*?? as in <=t=em> *past participle* where <**=em**> is probably *intransitivizer/have/get*, perhaps <á-ablaut> is *durative*, syntactic analysis: nominal, attested by BHTTC (10/21/76), Elders Group (3/15/72, 4/2/75).

<**sxeq'xéq'et**>, df //s=C_1əC_2=x̣ə́q'=ət//, LAND ['*a little bluff (of rock)*'], (<**s=**> *nominalizer*), possibly <**R3=**> *plural or ?diminutive*, comment: the meaning is *diminutive* (the translation *little*) but this type of reduplication is rarely attested for any meaning but *plural*, phonology: reduplication, syntactic analysis: nominal, attested by Elders Group (4/2/75).

<**Xeq'átelets**>, ds //x̣əq'=ə[=Aɛ́=]t=ələc//, PLN ['*place in Fraser River two miles above American Bar with narrow rock*'], ASM ['so named because the smooth flat bare rock walls get so narrow here that the river gets only four or five feet high Nov.-Feb. and you can see the bottom'], probably root <**xeq'át**> *smooth flat bare rock*, possibly root <**xéq'**> *narrow*, possibly <**=et**> perhaps *past participle*, possibly <**á-ablaut**> *resultative or continuative*, lx <**=elets**> *on the bottom*, phonology: probable ablaut, syntactic analysis: nominal, attested by Elders Group (7/9/75, 7/13/77), SP and AK (Fish Camp 8/2/77), source: place names file reference #54 and #132.

<**xeq'át**>, LAND */'flat smooth and bare rock, a [rock] bluff, a bluff (straight up)'/, see* xeq'.

<**Xeq'átelets**>, PLN ['*place in Fraser River two miles above American Bar with narrow rock*'], *see* xeq'.

<**xést'el**>, us //x̣ə́st'əl//, EZ */'nits, louse eggs'/*, ['eggs of the order *Phthiraptera* (lice), esp. eggs of *Pediculus humanus* (human lice) and perhaps of other parasites'], syntactic analysis: nominal, attested by CT (6/21/76), Deming (2/7/80), Salish cognate: Squamish /x̣əst'ánʔ/ *nits* W73:185, K69:84, Lushootseed /x̣əst'ád/ *nit* H76:598.

<**xésxel**>, df //x̣ə́s=x^{y}əl//, HUNT */'metal trap, any trap, (also deadfall trap)'/*, root meaning unknown unless cognate with Squamish root below for *contract, shrink, cramp*, lx <**=xel**> *on the foot*, syntactic analysis: nominal, attested by Elders Group (11/26/75, 10/20/76), other sources: ES /x̣ə́sx^{y}əl/ (Ms /x̣ə́sx^{y}ən/, Cw /x̣ə́ššən/) *deadfall*, Salish cognate: Squamish /x̣ə́s-šn/ *big trap with stone, deadfall* W73:272, K67:367 perhaps from Squamish root /x̣is/ *shrink, contract, cramp* as in /x̣ís-inʔ-t-m/ *shrink* K69:86, K67:369, Samish dial. of NSt /x̣ə́šən'/ *trap, deadfall trap* G86:85.

<**xáxesxèlem**>, izs //C_1ɛ́-x̣əs=x^{y}əl=əm//, cts, HUNT ['*setting a trap*'], (<**R7-**> *continuative*), (<**=em**> *intransitivizer/have/get*), phonology: reduplication, updrifting, syntactic analysis: intransitive verb, attested by Elders Group (10/20/76), IHTTC (8/15/77), Salish cognate: Squamish /x̣əs-šn-ʔám/ *to trap (itr.)* K67:367.

<**Xaxesxélem**>, ds //C_1ɛ́=x̣əs=x^{y}ə[=´=]l=əm//, PLN ['*mountain [north] across from Lizzie Johnson's place on Seabird Island*'], literally /'place to be having set traps'/, (<**R7=**> *continuative or resultative*), (<**=´= (stress-shift)**> *derivational*), (<**=em**> *place to have/get*), phonology: reduplication, stress-shift, syntactic analysis: nominal, attested by IHTTC (8/15/77), source: place names file reference #191.

<**xét'**> or <**xt'**>, bound root //x̣ə́t'// or //x̣t'// *evil spell.*

<**xt'ét**>, pcs //x̣ə́t'=M1=T//, IDOC */'cast a spell on s-o, put a spell on s-o, shoot power into s-o'/*, ASM

['such power is shot invisibly by Indian doctors and can only be removed usually by another Indian doctor, when it is removed it is sometimes found to be a piece of bone, sometimes it is an invisible spirit that is cast out by the curing Indian doctor/shaman'], (<**metathesis type 1**> *non-continuative*), (<**=t**> *purposeful control transitivizer*), phonology: metathesis, syntactic analysis: transitive verb, attested by Elders Group (2/25/76), other sources: ES ChMsCw /x̣t'ə́t/ *shoot power (into victim)*, Salish cognate: Squamish root /x̣ət'/ *evil charm* as in /x̣t'-ə́t/ *put an evil spell on s-o (tr.)* and /ʔəs-x̣ə́t'-x̣ət'/ *bewitched* K69:84.

<**x̲t'áls** or **x̲t'á:ls**>, sas //x̣ə́t'=M1=ɛ́(·)ls//, IDOC /'*cast a spell, throw a spell, put on a spell, shoot power*'/, (<**metathesis type 1**> *non-continuative*), (<**=á:ls ~ =áls**> *structured activity non-continuative*), phonology: metathesis, syntactic analysis: intransitive verb, attested by Elders Group (2/25/76), Salish cognate: Samish dial. of NSt (LD) /x̣t'=ə́ləʔ/ *shoot power into s-o (done by an Indian doctor)* with /=ə́ləʔ/ *structured activity non-continuative* G86:81.

<**x̲ét'e**>, possibly root //x̣ə́t'ə or x̣ə́tʔ(ə) or x̣ə́təʔ-M1//, cts, LANG /'*be saying, say, said*'/, the first two etymologies show <**lack of metathesis type 1**> *continuative ~ resultative,* the third shows the root <xéte'> with <**metathesis type 1**> *continuative ~ resultative*; elders didn't relate the *say/sing* verb with <**t'**> to the *do/doing* verb with <**t**>, I have shown them related here (as Suttles does for Musqueam) but have put them in the current entry under <**x̲ét'e**> since it comes before <**x̲tá: ~ x̲tá**> in the alphabet (the latter *do/doing* set is found under <**x̲tá: ~ x̲tá**> cross-referenced back here as main entry, phonology: consonant merger (//tʔ// → /t'/), epenthetic schwa, syntactic analysis: intransitive verb, attested by JL, EB, AC, others, Salish cognate: Musqueam dial. of Halkomelem /x̣ə́t'ə/ *be saying, be doing* as irregular progressive [= my continuative] of /x̣tɛ́ʔ/ *do* Suttles ca1984ms:ch. 7 p.96 [my numbering] or section 7.2.11, Squamish /táʔ-šit/ *do for s-o, make for s-o* W73:81, K67:264, comment: Suttles' analysis for Musqueam is plausible for Upriver Halkomelem too because of three facts: 1) x̲ét'e is once translated as *be doing this* (see fifth example below) as well as *be saying, said,* 2) the Upriver causative form /x̣ə́t'əstəxʷ/ is translated both as *telling s-o, told s-o* (showing both the use as *continuative* and as *resultative*) and also as *did s-th* (see example below), and 3) a number of roots with /ə́/ <é> have continuatives with the unmodified (unmetathesized) root and non-continuatives with <**metathesis type 1**> *non-continuative*, if the root is //x̣ə́tʔ// then the addition of metathesis type 1 would produce /x̣tə́ʔ/ with apparently ɛ́-ablaut then added (the only irregularity) producing the Musqueam /x̣tɛ́ʔ/ and Upriver /x̣tɛ́/ *do* (/ʔ/ becomes optional length in Upriver Halkomelem after vowel at word end), example: <**tl'e kwses x̲ét'e á:lhtel, "tl'óts'a Siyó:ylexwe Smált tethá."**>, //ƛ̓a kʷ-s-əs x̣ə́t'ə ʔɛ́·ɬ=təl, ƛ̓á-c'ɛ s=yá·[=C₁ə=]ləxʷ=ə s=mɛ́lt tə=θɛ́//, /'*That's what they said, "That's Siyó:ylexwe Mountain there."*'/, attested by JL (4/7/78 Coqualeetza History Department tape #34), <**lhéq'elh x̲ét'e yé xwèlmèxw**>, //ɬə́q'-əɬ x̣ə́t'ə yə xʷə̀l=məxʷ//, /'*the people used to say*'/, attested by EB (1/9/76), <**osu x̲ét'e skw'áy kw'es í:kw's wátes kw'e me séweq't te sléxwelh.**>, //ʔa-s-u x̣ə́t'ə s=k'ʷɛ́y k'ʷ-əs ʔí·k'ʷ-s wɛ́t=əs k'ʷə mə sə́wəq'=T tə s=lə́xʷ=wəɬ//, /'*So [they said] it won't be lost whoever comes to look for (it) the canoe.*'/, usage: Story of the Flood, attested by AC (12/7/71), <**ō te x̲ét'etò.**>, //ʔo tə x̣ə́t'ə tà (or) ʔo tə x̣ə́t'ə=t-à//, /'*Oh the talking.*'/, semantic environment ['said when fed up with someone talking too much'], usage: saying, comment: if <**tò**> is not a morpheme here then perhaps the form has <**=t**> *past participle* to derive *the talking* with <**-ò**> *just* being phonetically suffixed after that as usual, for <**tò**>/tà/ compare Lushootseed /ta/ *(emphatic particle)* Hess 1976:472 perhaps, attested by EB (4/27/76); found in <**wex̲et'áxwcha**>, //wə-x̣ət'ə-ɛ́xʷ-cɛ//, /'*when you will be doing this, When you get older you'll be doing this.*'/, usage: saying often used by grandparents or parents of 1979's elders when showing children how to do something, attested by AD (11/22/79).

<**x̲ét'estexw**>, caus //x̣ə́t'ə=sT-əxʷ//, LANG /'*told s-o/s-th, be telling s-o/s-th, did s-th, (be doing s-th)*'/, (<**=st**> *causative control transitivizer*), (<**-exw**> *third person object*), syntactic analysis:

transitive verb, attested by IHTTC (8/9/77, 8/29/77), AC (12/7/71), LJ (4/7/78 History Dept. tape #34), AL (Elders Group 3/72, Heritage Proj. tape 33, lesson VII), Elders Group (2/19/75), AD (11/22/79); found in <**x̱et'esthóxes.**>, *//x̣ət'ə=sT-áxʸ-əs//*, */'He told me.'/*, attested by IHTTC (8/9/77), example: <**x̱ét'esthò:m kw'as éy mestíyexw.**>, *//x̣ə́t'ə=sT-à·m k'ʷ-ɛ-s ʔɛ́y məstíyəxʷ//*, */'They told you you are a good person.'/*, literally /'you were told that you are good person'/, attested by IHTTC (8/29/77), <**òsu x̱ét'estexwes te mestíyex kwses hí:kwthetcha te qó:.**>, *//ʔà-s-u x̣ə́t'ə=sT-əxʷ-əs tə məstíyəxʷ kʷ-s-əs hí[=·=]kʷ=θət-cɛ tə qá·//*, */'So he tells the people that the water will get [real] big or rise.'/*, usage: Story of the Flood, attested by AC (12/7/71), <**x̱ét'estxwes te stó:les te Paul Webster ...**>, *//x̣ə́t'ə=sT-əxʷ-əs tə s=tá·ləs-s tə Paul Webster ...//*, */'Paul Webster's wife said ...'/*, attested by LJ (4/7/78), <**x̱ét'estexwes yí o qwóqwel t'éqoya.**>, *//x̣ə́t'ə=sT-əxʷ-əs yə ʔa qʷɛ[-C_1əAá-]l t'ə́q=oyɛ//*, */'Some people say "t'éqoya" [for dirty].'/*, literally /'some (the ones) just talking told it little fart'/, attested by AL (Elders Group 3/72); found in <**x̱ét'estem.**>, *//x̣ə́t'ə=sT-əm//*, */'So they say., They say., It is said., (can be used while gesturing to mean) It is done., They did it.'/*, literally /'it is said/done (by them [unspecified people])'/, attested by Elders Group (2/19/75), AD (11/22/79), example: <**esésu tl'ó x̱ét'estem --, stám kw'e yalh ...**>, *//ʔə-s-əs-u ƛ'á x̣ə́t'ə=sT-əm, s=tɛ́m k'ʷə yɛɬ ...//*, */'And they said that's --, now what was it? ...'/*, usage: talking to oneself, attested by LJ (4/7/78), <**x̱ét'estem kw'e lò.**>, *//x̣ə́t'ə=sT-əm k'ʷə là//*, */'It's done this way.'/*, attested by AD (11/22/79).

<**x̱tá: ~ x̱tá**>, if *//x̣ə[-M1-]t[-Aɛ́-]ʔ//*, [x̣tǽ· ~ x̣tǽ], TIB */'do, do this'/*, root <**x̱ét'(e)**> *be saying, say, said, (be doing)*, (<**metathesis type 1**> *non-continuative*), probably <**á-ablaut**> allomorphic, phonology: metathesis, ablaut allomorphic, syntactic analysis: intransitive verb, attested by AD (3/10/80), EB (1/9/76), Salish cognate: Squamish /táʔ-šit/ *do for s-o, make for s-o* W73:81, K67:264, perhaps Lushootseed /ta/ *(emphatic particle)* H76:472, example: <**x̱tá(:)chexw kw'e lò.**>, *//x̣ə[-M1-]t[-Aɛ́-]ʔ-c-əxʷ k'ʷə là//*, */'Go like this.'/*, literally /'You do (this) this.'/, attested by AD (3/10/80), <**xw'ít kwses x̱tá(:) t(e)thá?**>, *//xʷʔít kʷ-s-əs x̣ə[-M1-]t[-Aɛ́-]ʔ tə=θɛ́//*, */'Why did he do that?'/*, attested by EB (1/9/76); found in <**x̱tá(:)tsa kw'e lò**>, *//x̣ə[-M1-]t[-Aɛ́-]ʔ-cɛ k'ʷə là//*, no translation given, literally /'it will do this'/, attested by AD (3/10/80).

<**sx̱tá(:)**>, strs *//s=x̣ə[-M1-]t[-Aɛ́-]ʔ//*, QUAL */'the same kind, the same, (said that way, done that way)'/*, (<**s=**> *stative*), syntactic analysis: adjective/adjectival verb, attested by AD (3/10/80), Salish cognate: Musqueam /sx̣t'é ~ sx̣t'éʔ ~ sx̣ət'éʔ/ *said that way, so-called, done that way, the same, prepared* resultative of /x̣té/ *do* Suttles ca1984: ch.7, p.153, section 7.7.4, example: <**tl'ó ò sx̱tá(:).**>, *//ƛ'á ʔà s=x̣ə[-M1-]t[-Aɛ́-]ʔ//*, */'This is the same kind.'/*, attested by AD, <**ō sx̱tá(:) ò te skwíxs.**>, *//ʔəw s=x̣ə[-M1-]t[-Aɛ́-]ʔ ʔà tə s=kʷíxʸ-s//*, */'It's got the same name.'/*, literally /'contrastive/really said that way/the same just the its name (or) It's really just the same name.'/, attested by AD.

<**sx̱tá(:)stexw**>, caus *//s=x̣ə[-M1-]t[-Aɛ́-]ʔ=sT-əxʷ//*, TIB *['do it this way']*, (<**=st**> *causative control transitivizer*), (<**-exw**> *third person object*), syntactic analysis: transitive verb, attested by AD (3/10/80); found in <**sx̱tá(:)stexwchexw.**>, *//s=x̣ə[-M1-]t[-Aɛ́-]ʔ=sT-əxʷ-c-əxʷ//*, */'Do it this way.'/*, attested by AD.

<**x̱tá:stexw**>, caus *//x̣ə[-M1-]t[-Aɛ́-]ʔ=sT-əxʷ//*, TIB */'do it, do s-th'/*, (<**=st**> *causative control transitivizer*), (<**-exw**> *third person object*), phonology: this is the one form where length is clearly attested for the glottal stop in the Musqueam cognate forms, syntactic analysis: transitive verb, attested by Elders Group (2/26/75), example: <**skw'áy kw'els x̱tá:stexw.**>, *//s=k'ʷɛ́y k'ʷ-əl-s x̣ə[-M1-]t[-Aɛ́-]ʔ=sT-əxʷ//*, */'I can't do it.'/*, attested by Elders Group.

<**x̱t'ét**>, pcs *//x̣ə́t'=M1=T//*, IDOC */'cast a spell on s-o, put a spell on s-o, shoot power into s-o'/*, ASM ['such power is shot invisibly by Indian doctors and can only be removed usually by another

Indian doctor, when it is removed it is sometimes found to be a piece of bone, sometimes it is an invisible spirit that is cast out by the curing Indian doctor/shaman'], (<**metathesis type 1**> *non-continuative*), (<**=t**> *purposeful control transitivizer*), phonology: metathesis, syntactic analysis: transitive verb, attested by Elders Group (2/25/76), other sources: ES ChMsCw /x̣t’ə́t/ *shoot power (into victim)*, Salish cognate: Squamish root /x̣ət’/ *evil charm* as in /x̣t’-ə́t/ *put an evil spell on s-o (tr.)* and /ʔəs-x̣ə́t’-x̣ət’/ *bewitched* K69:84.

<**x̲t'áls** or **x̲t'á:ls**>, sas //x̣ə́t’=M1=ɛ́(·)ls//, IDOC /'*cast a spell, throw a spell, put on a spell, shoot power*'/, (<**metathesis type 1**> *non-continuative*), (<**=á:ls ~ =áls**> *structured activity non-continuative*), phonology: metathesis, syntactic analysis: intransitive verb, attested by Elders Group (2/25/76), Salish cognate: Samish dial. of NSt (LD) /x̣t’=ə́ləʔ/ *shoot power into s-o (done by an Indian doctor)* with /=ə́ləʔ/ *structured activity non-continuative* G86:81.

<**x̲ét'estexw**>, LANG /'*told s-o/s-th, be telling s-o/s-th, did s-th, (be doing s-th)*'/, *see* x̲ét'e.

<**x̲et'kw'á:ls**>, sas //x̣ət’k’ʷ=ɛ́·ls//, CARV /'*carve wood, whittle*'/, (<**=á:ls**> *structured activity non-continuative*), syntactic analysis: intransitive verb, attested by Elders Group (1/21/76), EB (5/12/76), Salish cognate: Sechelt root in /x̣ət’k’ʷ-ə́m/ *to carve* and /x̣ət’k’ʷ-át/ *to carve (tr.)* T77:26, B77:69, Mainland Comox root in /x̣ə́t’k’ʷ-əʔəm/ *to carve, put a design on something* B75prelim.:69, Saanich dial. of NSt root in /x̣t’ə́k’ʷ-əŋ/ *to carve* B74a:57, Samish dial. of NSt root in /x̣ə́t’k’ʷ-ŋ/ *carving (a pole, etc.)* G86:92.

<**x̲át'kw'els**>, cts //x̣ə[-Aɛ́-]t’k’ʷ=əls//, sas, CARV /'*carving wood, whittling*'/, (<**á-ablaut**> *continuative*), (<**=els**> *structured activity continuative*), phonology: ablaut, syntactic analysis: intransitive verb, attested by EB (5/12/76).

<**x̲ét'kw'els**>, dnom //x̣ə[=´=]t’k’ʷ=əls//, sas, CARV ['*a carving*'], (<=´=> *continuative or resultative*), (<**=els**> *structured activity continuative nominal*), phonology: stress-shift, syntactic analysis: nominal, attested by Elders Group (1/28/76).

<**x̲ét'kw'els**>, CARV ['*a carving*'], *see* x̲et'kw'á:ls.

<**x̲éth**>, probably root //x̣ə́θ or θə́x̣=M2 *shove, push*//.

<**x̲thét**>, pcs //x̣ə́θ-M1=T//, ABFC ['*shove s-th*'], (<**metathesis type 1**> *non-continuative*), (<**=t**> *purposeful control transitivizer*), phonology: metathesis, syntactic analysis: transitive verb, attested by EB (1/30/76), compare <**thx̲ét**> *push s-th/s-o, shove s-th/s-o*, comment: x̲thét may be a metathesis of thx̲ét (idiolectal or dialectal) or it may be a survival of the Lushootseed cognate with a semantic reversal (not uncommon in historical semantic developments), other sources: ES /θx̣ə́t/ *push*, Salish cognate: Lushootseed root /x̣əc/ *pull out, extract* as in /x̣ə́c-əd/ *pull(ing) it out* H76:588-589, cognates with the form if metathesized from attested thx̲ét include: Squamish /cx̣ə́-t/ *push (a person)* W73:207, K67:273-274, *shove* B78:91 and Samish dial. of NSt /sx̣ə́t/ *push/shove s-o/s-th* beside /sə́x̣t/ *pushing it* G86:96.

<**x̲ethós**>, ds //x̣əθ=ás//, PLAY ['*to bet*'], ECON, literally /'shove money'/, lx <**=ós**> *dollars, money, round objects, on the face, cyclic period*, syntactic analysis: intransitive verb, attested by EB (3/8/76), Elders Group (2/11/76), Salish cognate: perhaps Squamish /cuás-m/ *bet* beside /cuás-min/ *bet s-o (tr.)* W73:37, K69:53, Colville Okanagan /x̣c-x̣ca-m/ *bet* M87:297, example: <**ílhchel x̲ethós.**>, //ʔí-ɬ-c-əl x̣əθ=ás//, /'*I bet [past tense].*'/, attested by EB, <**isólescha kw'els x̲ethós.**>, //ʔisɛ[=Aá=]l=əs-cɛ k’ʷ-əl-s x̣əθ=ás//, /'*I'll bet two dollars.*'/, literally /'it will be two dollars that I bet (shove money)'/, attested by EB, <**ílhchel x̲ethós (tel tá:le., te isó:les.)**>, //ʔí-ɬ-c-əl x̣əθ=ás (t-əl tɛ́·lə, tə ʔisɛ[=Aá·=]l=əs)//, /'*I bet (my money., two dollars.)*'/, attested by EB.

<**x̲thémés**>, df //x̣ə́θ-M1=m=əs//, PLAY ['*betting money*'], Elder's comment: "unsure", (semological comment: such a form would more likely mean *bet money*), (<**metathesis type 1**> *non-*

continuative), lx <**=es**> *money, dollars*, phonology: metathesis, syntactic analysis: intransitive verb, attested by EB (2/2/76), Salish cognate: Colville Okanagan /x̣c-x̣ca-m/ *bet* M87:297.

<**xeth'ét**>, pcs //x̣ə́θ[='=]-M1=T//x̣ə́θ'-M1=T//, ABFC [*'push s-th (in)'*], (<**metathesis type 1**> *non-continuative*), (<**=t**> *purposeful control transitivizer*), phonology: either glottalized allomorph or infixed <='=>glottal stop or <=**G**=>glottalization *derivational*, metathesis, syntactic analysis: transitive verb, attested by AC (8/6/70, 10/13/71), other sources: JH /xəθ'ə́t/ *to push in*; found in <**xeth'étes.**>, //x̣ə́θ'=M1=T-əs//, /*'He pushed it.'*/, attested by AC (10/15/71).

<**xethelálh**>, NUM [*'four times'*], *see* **x**e'ó:thel ~ **x**e'óthel.

<**xethelsxá**>, NUM [*'forty'*], *see* **x**e'ó:thel ~ **x**e'óthel.

<**xethelsxále**>, NUM [*'forty people'*], *see* **x**e'ó:thel ~ **x**e'óthel.

<**xethelsxó:s**>, TIME [*'forty days'*], *see* **x**e'ó:thel ~ **x**e'óthel.

<**xethí:le ~ xethíle**>, NUM [*'four people'*], *see* **x**e'ó:thel ~ **x**e'óthel.

<**xethílemets'**>, NUM /*'four ropes, four threads, four sticks, four poles, (four long thin objects)'*/, *see* **x**e'ó:thel ~ **x**e'óthel.

<**xethíleqel**>, NUM [*'four containers'*], *see* **x**e'ó:thel ~ **x**e'óthel.

<**xethíléqw**>, NUM [*'four fish'*], *see* **x**e'ó:thel ~ **x**e'óthel.

<**xethíles**>, NUM /*'four dollars, ((also) four blankets [Boas])'*/, *see* **x**e'ó:thel ~ **x**e'óthel.

<**xethílews**>, NUM [*'four birds'*], *see* **x**e'ó:thel ~ **x**e'óthel.

<**xethí:lhp** or **xethíyelhp**>, NUM [*'four trees'*], *see* **x**e'ó:thel ~ **x**e'óthel.

<**xethlá:wes**>, NUM /*'four paddles, four paddlers'*/, *see* **x**e'ó:thel ~ **x**e'óthel.

<**xethós**>, PLAY [*'to bet'*], *see* **x**éth.

<**xéth'xeth'**>, EFAM /*'cranky, quick-tempered'*/, *see* **x**íth' ~ **x**éyth'.

<**xéwe**>, probable bound root or stem //x̣ə́wə//, meaning unknown

<**sxéwe**>, dnom //s=x̣ə́wə//, FOOD [*'dried fish backbone (with meat left on it)'*], ASM ['the meat is what is dried'], (<**s=**> *nominalizer, something to*), syntactic analysis: nominal, attested by Elders Group (3/15/72, 4/28/76), Deming (4/1/76), BJ (12/5/64), DM (12/4/64), other sources: ES /sx̣ə́wə/ (CwMs /sx̣ə́ʔwə/) *fish backbone*, Salish cognate: Sechelt /sx̣ə́wa/ *backbone* T77:14, Squamish /s-x̣ə́wʔ/ *dried salmon backbone* W73:221, K67:297, perhaps also /s-xʷáw-inas/ *breastbone* K67:298, example: <**kw'íkw'ets' te sxéwe**>, //k'ʷí[=C_1ə=]c' tə s=x̣ə́wə//, /*'the fish backbone [got butchered] (with meat on)'*/, attested by DM (12/4/64).

<**Xexá:ls**>, N [*'the Transformers'*], *see* **x**ít.

<**xexá:m**>, ABFC [*'crying a lot'*], *see* **x**à:m ~ **x**á:m.

<**Xexám Smá:lt**>, PLN [*'rock in the Fraser River near Scowlitz where a woman was crying a lot'*], *see* **x**à:m ~ **x**á:m.

<**xexekw'íwel ~ xaxekw'íwel**>, ABDF /*'get constipated, "bound up"'*/, *see* **x**ékw'.

<**xéxel**>, df //x̣ə́x̣(=)əl or x̣ə́[=C_1ə=]l//, WETH /*'frost, get frosty'*/, possibly <**=el**> *go, come, get, become*, possibly <**=R1=**> *continuative or resultative*, phonology: possible reduplication, syntactic analysis: intransitive verb?, attested by BJ (12/5/64). Elders Group (4/2/75), Deming (3/31/77), other sources: ES /x̣ɛ́x̣əl/ (CwMs /x̣ə́x̣ən/) *frost*, Salish cognate: Squamish /x̣ə́-x̣nʔ/

frost W73:109, K67:367 beside /x̣ə-x̣nʔ-án-t-m/ *freezing (of the ground)* K67:367, example: <**me x̲éx̲el te témexw.**>, //mə x̣ə́x̣=əl tə tə́məxʷ//, /'*The ground gets frosty.*'/, attested by Deming.

<**x̲ex̲élh**>, ABDF /'*(be) hurting, be aching*'/, *see* **x̲**élh.

<**x̲ex̲élh**>, ABDF ['"*sored up*"'], *see* **x̲**élh.

<**x̲ex̲élhlexw**>, ABDF /'*(be) hurting s-o [accidentally, happening to/managing to]*'/, *see* **x̲**élh.

<**x̲ex̲élh te sqwálewel**>, EFAM ['*be feeling sorry*'], *see* **x̲**élh.

<**x̲ex̲éyet**>, SOC ['*beating s-o up*'], *see* **x̲**éyet.

<**x̲ex̲é:yls**>, SCH ['*writing (while doing it as a structured activity)*'], *see* **x̲**él ~ **x̲**é:yl (or better) **x̲**í:l.

<**x̲ex̲é:ylt**>, SCH ['*writing s-th*'], *see* **x̲**él ~ **x̲**é:yl (or better) **x̲**í:l.

<**X̲ex̲éyth'elhp**>, PLN ['*place on the east side of Seabird Island*'], *see* **x̲**íth'.

<**x̲ex̲éyx̲e**>, EFAM ['*being ashamed*'], *see* **x̲**éy**x̲**e ~ **x̲**í**x̲**e.

<**x̲ex̲e'ó:thel**>, NUM ['*four to each*'], *see* **x̲**e'ó:thel ~ **x̲**e'óthel.

<**x̲ex̲p'ítsel sisemó:ye**>, EZ ['*yellow-jacket bee*'], *see* sisemó:ya ~ sisemóya ~ sisemóye ~ sísemòye.

<**x̲ex̲p'í:tsel ~ x̲ex̲p'ítsel ~ sx̲ex̲p'í:tsel**>, EZ /'*chipmunk with more than two stripes, Northwestern chipmunk, Townsend chipmunk*'/, *see* **x̲**ep'í:tsel.

<**x̲ex̲q'elá:lhp**>, df //x̣i[=C₁ə=](=)q'=əlɛ=əɬp or x̣i[=C₁ə=](=)q'=əlɛ=ɛ́ɬp//, EB /'*False Solomon's seal, Twisted-stalk, rosy-flowered Twisted-stalk, star-flowered Solomon's seal*'/, ['*Smilacina racemosa, Streptopus amplexifolius, Streptopus roseus curvipes, Smilacina stellata*'], MED ['False Solomon's seal is used as medicine for dandruff, its roots are also medicine in a sweatbath for swollen legs'], literally /'scratching an itch on the temples/side of the head plant'/, (semological comment: clearly named for its use as dandruff medicine), root <**x̲i(=)q'**> *scratch an itch (on something else)*, lx <**=q'**> *on something else*, (<**=R1=**> *continuative*), lx <**=ela**> *on the temples, on the side of the head*, lx <**=elhp ~ =álhp**> *plant, tree*, phonology: reduplication, vowel-reduction, vowel merger, syntactic analysis: nominal, attested by not recorded on file slip, contrast <**sth'í:ms te álhqey**> *snakeberry (incl. False Solomon's seal, Twisted-stalk, rosy-flowered Twisted-stalk, star-flowered Solomon's seal, and Hooker's fairy bells)*, note that Gunther 1973:25 gives the Quileute word which means "snake plant" and notes that the Quileute believe that garter snakes and water snakes ate the berries), Salish cognate: probably not Colville Okanagan /q'ixʸán/ *False Solomon's seal, star-flowered Solomon's seal* Turner, Bouchard and Kennedy 1980:48 since this would require historical metathesis of the root consonants and Halkomelem /x̣/ corresponding to Okanagan /xʸ/ and Turner, Bouchard and Kennedy give an etymology as "marked foot" with the /-xʸán/ as *foot*.

<**x̲éyes ~ x̲éy:es**>, probable bound stem //x̣ə́y(·)=əs//, root meaning uncertain unless *against*, thus stem meaning might be "against the face"

<**sx̲éyes ~ sx̲éy:es**>, df //s=x̣ə́y(·)=əs//, ANA ['*head (of any living thing)*'], (<**s=**> *nominalizer, something to*), possibly <**=es**> *on the face*, syntactic analysis: nominal, attested by AC (8/14/70, 9/18/71, 11/11/71), BJ (5/10/64 old vs. new transcription new p.108, 12/5/64 old vs. new transcript old p.306), Elders Group (3/72), IHTTC (9/7/77), other sources: ES /sx̣áy·əs/ *head*, JH /sx̣ə́yəs/ *head*, H-T <sqai'yus> *head*, Salish cognate: Lushootseed /s-x̣əy'ús/ *head* H76:599 vs. /s-x̣áy'us/ (LL) *boiled salmon heads* ~ (ESi) *head* H76:600, also <**sx̲óyes ~ sx̲óy:es**>, //s=x̣áy(·)=əs//, also /'*fish head*'/, attested by AC (8/13/70), BJ (12/5/64 old transcript), Deming (4/1/76), also /'*head*'/, attested by LJ (Elders Group 6/28/78), Elders Group (3/1/72), example: <**tsel x̲elhláxw tel**

sx̲éyes.>, //c-əl x̣əɬ=l-ə[=Aɛ́=]x^{w} t-əl s=x̣ə́yəs//, /'*I hurt my head. (hurt s-th accidentally)*'/, attested by AC (11/11/71), <**sx̲óy:es te sth'óqwi**>, //s=x̣áy·əs-s tə s=θ'áq^{w}=i//, /'*head of a salmon*'/, <**sx̲éy:es te (músmes, sthóqwi, mestíyexw)**>, //s=x̣ə́y·əs-s tə (mús=C_1əC_2, s=θáq^{w}=i, məstíyəx^{w})//, /'*head of a (cow, fish, person)*'/, attested by AC (9/18/71), <**sá:lth'tem tel sx̲éyes.**>, //sə[=Aɛ́·=]l=θ'=təm t-əl s=x̣ə́yəs//, /'*My head is dizzy.*'/, attested by Elders Group (3/72), <**lhéq' me sélts'tem tel sx̲óyes lhíl áx̲eth.**>, //ɬə́q' mə sə́l=c'=təm t-əl s=x̣áyəs ɬí-l ʔɛ́x̣əθ//, /'*Sometimes my head spins when I lay down.*'/, attested by LJ (Elders Group 6/28/78), <**sáyem tel sx̲óyes.**>, //sɛ́y=əm t-əl s=x̣áyəs//, /'*My head is hurt.*'/, attested by Elders Group (3/1/72).

<**Sx̲éyes te Sx̲wó:yx̲wey**>, cpds //s=x̣ə́yəs-s tə s=x̣^{w}ɛ[=Aá·=]y=C_1əC_2//, PLN ['*rock that was a sx̲wó:yx̲wey head (mask) turned to stone at X̲elhlálh*'], literally /'head of the sx̲wó:yx̲wey'/, syntactic analysis: nominal phrase with modifier(s), attested by IHTTC (9/7/77).

<**x̲éyeslótel**>, df //x̣ə́y=əs=əl=ə[=Aá=]təl//, EB ['*wild ginger*'], ['*Asarum caudatum*'], Elder's comment: literally /'facing each other'/ (go/get against each other on the face durative), ASM ['a few people flavored meats with the roots'], (semological comment: so named because of the paired leaves that face each other), MED ['for medicine to prevent colic or gas in babies, pour hot water over the whole plant, then cool it some and bathe the baby, wild ginger also used for heart medicine'], contrast <**th'alátel**> *wild ginger (lit. heart medicine)*, probably root <**x̲éy ~ x̲íy**> *against*, lx <**=es**> *on the face*, (<**=el**> *go, come, get, become*), (<**=(e)tel**> *reciprocal, each other*), (<**ó-ablaut in inflection**> *durative*), (<**zero**> *nominalizer*), phonology: ablaut, vowel-loss, zero nominalizer, syntactic analysis: nominal, attested by Elders Group (raft trip slide identifications 9/13/77).

<**xwelítemelh x̲eyeslótel** (or) **kw'ókw'es kwémlexw s'élhtel**>, EB /'*ginger*'/, FOOD /'*ginger*'/, (lit. white man style + wild ginger (or) hot + root + food), (attested by RG,EH 6/16/98 to SN, edited by BG with RG,EH 6/26/00)

<**x̲éyet**>, pcs //x̣íy=əT or x̣ə́y=əT//, SOC /'*beat s-o up, kick s-o in fight, lick s-o (in fight), spank s-o, fight s-o (till he cries for ex.), fight s-o in anger, fight s-o back*'/, possibly root <**x̲éy**> *against*, (<**=et**> *purposeful control transitivizer*), syntactic analysis: transitive verb, attested by AD (12/17/79), Elders Group (1/25/78, 2/19/75), EB (12/19/75), AC (10/21/71, etc.), Salish cognate: Squamish /x̣ə́y-n/ *stop people (obj.) from fighting/arguing/gambling (tr.)* W73:99, K67:368; found in <**x̲eyethométselcha.**>, //x̣əy=əT-ámə-c-əl-cɛ//, /'*I'll beat you [up]., I'll lick you.*'/, attested by Elders Group (2/19/75), example: <**x̲éyet ta' mímele.**>, //x̣ə́y=əT t-ɛʔ C_1í=mələ//, /'*Spank your child.*'/, attested by EB, <**iyó:lem kw'as x̲éyet.**>, //ʔiy=á·l=əm k'^{w}-ɛ-s x̣ə́y=əT//, /'*It's alright for you to spank him.*'/, attested by EB, <**x̲éyet qetl'ésu x̲á:ms**>, //x̣ə́y=əT qə=ƛ'ə́=s=ux̣ɛ̀·m-s//, /'*fight him till he cries (cry)*'/, attested by AC; found in <**x̲éyetlha.**>, //x̣ə́y=əT-ɬɛ//, /'*Fight back.*'/, attested by AC (8/11/70), example: <**le x̲éyethóxes.**>, //lə x̣ə́y=əT-áx^{y}-əs//, /'*He fought me in anger., He hit me.*'/, attested by AC (8/27/73), <**lhexwá:lh kwses x̲éyethòxes.**>, //ɬix^{w}=ɛ́·ɬ k^{w}-s-əs x̣ə́y=əT-áx^{y}-əs//, /'*Three times he hit me.*'/, attested by AC (8/4/70).

<**x̲ex̲éyet**>, cts //C_1ə-x̣ə́y=əT//, SOC ['*beating s-o up*'], (<**R5-**> *continuative*), phonology: reduplication, syntactic analysis: transitive verb, attested by Elders Group (1/25/78).

<**X̲éyteleq**>, chrs //x̣ə́y=əT=ələq//, N ['*name of an old man from Kilgard who was a strong warrior (fighter)*'], ASM ['he once punched through a man's chest in battle, he was also a strong Indian dancer (spirit dancer)'], N ['*now also the name of Ambrose Silver*'], literally /'someone (male name) who usually fights/wins a fight'/, lx <**=eleq**> *someone who usually, occupational; male name*, phonology: vowel-loss, syntactic analysis: nominal, attested by Elders Group (4/21/76).

<**x̲eyímelets**>, EB ['*roots of a tree when it floats downriver*'], *see* xím.

<**x̲éylém**>, ABFC ['*growl (of an animal)*'], *see* x̲ílém.

<**x̲é:yles**>, ABFC ['*made it (if laxative finally works)*'], *see* **x̲**ilés.

<**X̲éylés**>, PLN /'*place by Albert Cooper's house on Chilliwack River Road near Vedder Crossing, former village where a slide is now on north bank of Chilliwack River opposite Liumchen Creek*'/, *see* x̲ílés.

<**x̲é:yllhts(e)t**>, SCH ['*write for s-o*'], *see* **x̲**í:l.

<**x̲é:ylt**>, SCH ['*write s-th*'], *see* **x̲**í:l.

<**x̲é:ylthet**>, REL ['*paint one's body*'], *see* **x̲**í:l.

<**X̲éylx̲el(e)mòs**> ~ <**X̲ílx̲el(e)mòs**>, chrs //x̣í(·)l=C_1əC_2=əm=ás or x̣ə[=Aí=]l=C_1əC_2=əm=ás//, PLN ['*one of the two rocks of Lady Franklin Rock*'], *see* X̲ílx̲el(e)mòs.

<**x̲éymem**>, ABFC ['*grab a handful*'], *see* **x̲**ím.

<**x̲éymet**>, ABFC ['*grab s-th/s-o*'], *see* **x̲**ím.

<**x̲éymleqwt**>, ABFC /'*pull s-o's hair, grab s-o's hair*'/, *see* **x̲**ím.

<**x̲éyp'eqsel**>, ABDF ['*scraped on the nose*'], *see* **x̲**íp'.

<**x̲éyp'es**>, ABDF ['*scraped on the face*'], *see* **x̲**íp'.

<**x̲éyp** <**x̲wíqw'el**> *sleet, silver thaw* **et**>, ABFC /'*scratch s-o/s-th and leave a mark, rake it, claw it, scrape it*'/, *see* **x̲íp**'.

<**x̲è::yq'**> ABFC /'*snore sound*'/, free root //x̣ì:q'// [x̣è:q'], ASM ['found in a song to stop the rain, sung by CT (Mrs. Cecilia Thomas of Seabird Island) on a tape recorded by a visiting ethnomusicologist Albert Friesen from Univ. of Michigan [Coqualeetza or the Sto:lo Archives may have a copy of the tape which EB and I used to transcribe and learn the song from], CT learned it from an aunt of Elizabeth Herrling who got it in a dream, CT said it is not a winter spirit-song, but cautioned you have to really believe in it or it won't work; the words are <**X̲ét'e yalh, teló spò:l, kw'els őwe telí'àl, telúwe Syoqwíl, x̲è::yq', x̲è::yq', x̲è::yq', x̲è::yq'**.> sung to the melody 113$^{\flat}$, 113$^{\flat}$, 13$^{\flat}$13$^{\flat}$3$^{\flat}$, 13$^{\flat}$111, 2, 2, 2, 2. (1=do, 2=re, 3=mi, 4=fa, 5=so major) and rhythm: .5 .5 .5 2, .5 .5 2, 1 .5 .5 .5 .5 2, .5 .5 .5 .5 2‿1, 2.5.5, 2.5.5. 2.5.5., 2.5.5 (.5=eighth note, 1=quarter note, 1.5=dotted quarter note, 2=half note, 2.5=dotted half note 2.5.5=double dotted half note [length of 7 eighths]). The words mean, *That crow says now, that I'm not from you Sun, snore, snore, snore, snore.*' which may be about the rain crow that brings rain. The author (BG) learned it and by the year 2000 had used it 52 times (it worked 50 of those times, stopping the rain in about half an hour; on June 12 or 19, 2000 (after 2 weeks of rain and while it was still raining--as it has to be to work) I sung it at an Elders Meeting at Coqualeetza/Sto:lo Nation while teaching an advanced Halkomelem Class through SFU, Linguistics 432.2, Elizabeth Herrling and some of my students sang it along with me, I was loaned a drum also [drum beats are steady quarter notes] and we sang the song the traditional four times; before we finished the fourth repetition, I heard some of the staff and elders whispering, "look!, look outside! the rain's stopped and the sun's coming out!" I have only used it a few times in Saskatchewan and it worked about 2 out of 3 times in that Province.], attested by CT about 1976; the word is similar to the verb <**x̲wíqw'em**> *to snore* but lacks the <**=em**> middle voice and unrounds and unglottalizes the consonants; the way it is used in the song is as the *sound of snoring*.

<**x̲éyq'et**>, ABFC /'*scratch it (like of an itch), (itch it)*'/, *see* **x̲**íq'.

<**X̲éyt**>, N ['*Transformer*'], *see* **x̲**ít.

<**X̲éyteleq**>, N [*'name of an old man from Kilgard who was a strong warrior (fighter)'*], *see* x̲éyet.

<**x̲éytet**>, LANG /*'snap at s-o (verbally or in arguing), growl at s-o (with words)'*/, *see* **x̲í**tem.

<**x̲éyth'elhp**>, EB /*'alder tree, red alder'*/, *see* **x̲í**th'.

<**x̲é:ytl'thet**>, WETH [*'getting colder'*], *see* **x̲í**:tl'.

<**x̲éytl'thet**>, WETH [*'get cold'*], *see* **x̲í**:tl'.

<**x̲eywésem** or **x̲éywésem**>, EFAM /*'to scowl, make a bad face or a scowl'*/, *see* **x̲í**wel.

<**x̲éywét**>, LANG /*'advise s-o not to do something bad, (advise s-o against s-th), advise s-o to change, stop s-o from doing something'*/, *see* **x̲í**wel.

<**x̲éyx̲ekw'els**>, ABFC /*'chewing (something hard, like apple)'*/, *see* **x̲í**kw'et.

<**x̲éyx̲ekw'et**>, ABFC [*'be chewing s-th hard'*], *see* **x̲í**kw'et.

<**x̲éyx̲elexw**>, EFAM /*'(accidentally) make s-o ashamed, insult s-o (accidentally or manage to)'*/, *see* x̲éyx̲e ~ **x̲íx̲**e.

<**x̲éyx̲elex̲**>, SOC /*'war, (warring), fighting a war'*/, *see* **x̲íléx̲**.

<**x̲éyx̲elòmèt**>, EFAM /*'to shame oneself [accidentally], (get) embarrassed, (become ashamed of oneself?)'*/, *see* x̲éyx̲e ~ **x̲íx̲**e.

<**x̲éyx̲emels**>, EB [*'burdock'*], *see* **x̲í**m.

<**x̲éyx̲emels ch'ech'éqw'**>, EB [*'burdock'*], *see* **x̲í**m.

<**x̲éyx̲ep'els**>, ABFC /*'scratch, (scratching as a structured activity)'*/, *see* **x̲íp**'.

<**x̲éyx̲ep'ílep**>, HARV /*'a rake, a harrow'*/, *see* **x̲í**p'.

<**x̲éyx̲eq'els**>, ABFC [*'scratching'*], *see* **x̲í**q'.

<**x̲eyx̲eq'qéylem**>, ABFC [*'scratching one's head'*], *see* **x̲í**q'.

<**x̲éyx̲esel**>, EFAM /*'getting spooked, being afraid that bad spirits are around, spooky feeling'*/, *see* **x̲í**sel.

<**x̲éyx̲esem**>, EFAM [*'creepy'*], *see* **x̲í**sel.

<**x̲éyx̲estexw**>, EFAM [*'make s-o ashamed'*], *see* **x̲íx̲**e.

<**x̲éyx̲etem**>, LANG [*'growling (with words)'*], *see* **x̲í**tem.

<**x̲éyx̲etet**>, LANG [*'snapping at s-o (verbally or in arguing)'*], *see* **x̲í**tem.

<**x̲éyx̲ethet**>, EFAM [*'shame oneself (purposely)'*], *see* **x̲íx̲**e.

<**x̲eyx̲ets'émthet**>, ABDF [*'(get) real itching'*], *see* **x̲í**th' ~ **x̲é**yth'.

<**x̲éyx̲ewet**>, LANG /*'advising s-o not to do something, advising him to change'*/, *see* **x̲í**wel.

<**x̲e'áth'stexw**>, HARV /*'mark s-th, blaze it (of a trail), get/have s-th spotted (marked and located), make note of s-th'*/, *see* **x̲**áth' ~ **x̲**e'áth'.

<**x̲e'ó:thel ~ x̲e'óthel**>, df //x̣əʔ=á(·)θəl or x̣əʔá(·)θ=əl or x̣=əʔɛ́=áθəl//, NUM [*'four'*], root meaning unknown unless related to that in <**x̲**e'áth'> *measure, mark a measure*, possibly <**=ó(:)thel**> *in the mouth*, possibly <**=el**> *go, come, get, become*, possibly <**=e'á**> *comparative*, phonology: possible vowel merger, syntactic analysis: num, adjective/adjectival verb, attested by AC (8/4/70, 10/8/71), CT (9/5/73), NP (12/6/73), BJ (5/10/64), others, other sources: ES /x̣aʔáθəl/ (CwMs /x̣aʔáθən/) *four*, Salish cognate: Squamish /x̣aʔúcn/ *four (objects)* W73:107, K67:369, example: <**ts'kw'éx qas te**

x̲e'ó:thel>, //c'=k'ʷə́xʸ qɛ-s tə x̣əʔ=á·θəl//, /'*twenty-four*'/, attested by CT, <**ó:pel qas (te, kw'e) x̲e'ó:thel**>, //ʔá·pəl qɛ-s (tə, k'ʷə) x̣əʔ=á·θəl//, /'*fourteen*'/, attested by AC (8/4/70), CT (9/5/73), <**tl'o yóswe lí:s x̲e'ótheles láts'ewets mestíyexw le q'ép li tethá.**>, //ƛ'á yáswə lí·-s x̣əʔ=áθəl-əs lɛ́c'=əwəc məstíyəxʷ lə q'ə́p li təθɛ́//, /'*There was maybe four hundred people gathered there.*'/, usage: narrative, attested by AC (11/10/71), <**tsel áxwet mékw' te sqwéqwemiy te x̲e'ó:thel sth'ò:m.**>, //c-əl ʔɛ́xʷ=əT mə́k'ʷ t-ɛ s=C₁íAə́=qʷəm=ɛy tə x̣əʔ=á·θəl s=θ'à·m//, /'*I gave all your dogs four bones.*'/, literally /'I give s-o/s-th food all the puppies the four bone'/, attested by AC (11/30/71).

<**x̲ex̲e'ó:thel**>, ds //C₁ə=x̣əʔ=á·θəl//, NUM ['*four to each*'], (<**R5=**> *distributive*), Elder's comment: "never heard the other numbers done like this, maybe lhéchelesem (Nooksack language)", phonology: reduplication, syntactic analysis: adjective/adjectival verb, attested by AC (11/30/71), Salish cognate: perhaps Squamish /x̣ə-x̣aʔúcn/ *four (persons)* W73:107, K67:367.

<**x̲ethelálh**>, ds //x̣(ʔ)=aθəl=ɛ́ɬ orx̣(ʔ)=əθəl=ɛ́ɬ//, NUM ['*four times*'], TIME, numc //=álh *times, occasions*//, phonology: vowel-loss, consonant merger or consonant-loss, vowel-reduction or allomorph, syntactic analysis: adverb/adverbial verb, attested by Elders Group (3/19/75), AC (8/4/70, 8/8/70, 10/8/71), Salish cognate: Squamish /x̣ʷucn-áɬ-n-cut/ *make a fourth attempt* W73:107, K69:86, example: <**x̲ethlálh kwses x̲éyethòxes.**>, //x̣(ʔ)=əθəl=ɛ́ɬ kʷ-s-əs x̣íy=əT-áxʸ-əs//, /'*Four times he hit me.*'/, attested by AC (8/4/70).

<**x̲ethlá:wes**>, ds //x̣(ʔ)=əθəl=ɛ́·wəs//, NUM /'*four paddles, four paddlers*'/, CAN, numc //=ōwes ~ =ṓwes ~ =á:wes *paddles*//, phonology: vowel-loss, consonant-loss or consonant merger, vowel-reduction, syntactic analysis: nominal, attested by Elders Group (7/27/75).

<**x̲ethelsxá**>, ds //x̣(ʔ)=əθəl=(əl)sxʸɛ́//, NUM ['*forty*'], numc //=elsxá *times ten*//, phonology: vowel-loss, consonant-loss or consonant merger, vowel-reduction, syntactic analysis: adjective/adjectival verb, attested by AC (8/4/70), CT (9/5/73), Mary Charles (9/5/73), BJ (12/5/64 new transcript old p.336), DM (12/4/64 new transcript old p.262), Salish cognate: Squamish /x̣ucn-aɬšáʔ ~ x̣əcn-aɬšáʔ/ *forty* W73:107, K67:212.

<**x̲ethelsxále**>, ds //x̣(ʔ)=əθəl=(əl)sxʸɛ́=ɛ́lə//, NUM ['*forty people*'], HUMC, numc //=ále *people*//, phonology: vowel-loss, consonant-loss or consonant merger, vowel-reduction, vowel merger, syntactic analysis: nominal, attested by Elders Group (3/19/75).

<**x̲ethelsxó:s**>, ds //x̣(ʔ)=əθəl=(əl)sxʸɛ́=á·s or x̣(ʔ)=əθəl=(əl)sxʸɛ́=Aá=ás//, TIME ['*forty days*'], literally /'forty cyclic periods'/, ECON ['*forty dollars*'], NUM, numc //=ó:s ~ =ós ~ =es *cyclic period, round objects, dollars, on the face*//, phonology: vowel-loss, consonant-loss or consonant merger, vowel-reduction, vowel merger, possible ablaut automatic of a before =es/=ós, syntactic analysis: adjective/adjectival verb, nominal, attested by DM (12/4/64), AC (11/30/71), example: <**x̲ethelsxó:s swà:yel**>, //x̣(ʔ)=əθəl=(əl)sxʸɛ́=á·s tə s=wɛ̀·yəl//, /'*forty days*'/, attested by DM (12/4/64).

<**x̲ethí:le ~ x̲ethíle**>, ds //x̣(ʔ)=əθə[=Aí=](l)=ɛlə//, NUM ['*four people*'], HUMC, (semological comment: includes counting sasquatches), numc //=ale *people*//, phonology: vowel-loss, consonant-loss or consonant merger, vowel-reduction, ablaut, consonant-loss or consonant-shift, vowel merger, syntactic analysis: adjective/adjectival verb, nominal, attested by Elders Group (3/19/75, 1/30/80), AC (10/8/71, 11/30/71); found in <**x̲ethílétset**>, //x̣(ʔ)=əθə[=Aí=](l)=ɛlə-c-ət//, /'*(There's) four of us.*'/, literally /'we are four people'/, attested by AC (10/8/71), example: <**x̲ethí:le te siwíqe qa lólets'e the slhálí.**>, //x̣(ʔ)=əθə[=Aí=](l)=ɛlə tə s[=i=]wíq=ə qɛ C₁á=ləc'ə θə s=ɬɛ́l=í//, /'*(There's four men and one woman.)*'/, attested by AC (11/30/71), <**x̲ethíle sásq'ets**>, //x̣(ʔ)=əθə[=Aí=](l)=ɛlə sɛ́sq'əc//, /'*four sasquatches*'/, attested by Elders Group (1/30/80).

<**x̲ethí:lhp** or **x̲ethíyelhp**>, ds //x̣(ʔ)=əθə[=Aí=]l=əɬp or x̣(ʔ)=əθəl=əɬp//, NUM ['*four trees*'], EB,

numc //=elhp *tree*//, phonology: vowel-loss, consonant-loss or consonant merger, vowel-reduction, ablaut, el →íy automatically before =elhp, syntactic analysis: adjective/adjectival verb, nominal, attested by Elders Group (3/19/75).

<**x̲ethílemets'**>, ds //x̣(ʔ)=əθə[=Aí=]l=əməcʼ//, NUM /'*four ropes, four threads, four sticks, four poles, (four long thin objects)*'/, HHG, lx <**=emets'**> *long thin objects, ropes, threads, sticks, poles*, phonology: vowel-loss, consonant-loss or consonant merger, vowel-reduction, ablaut, syntactic analysis: adjective/adjectival verb, nominal?, attested by AD (4/12/78), other sources: Boas 1890 Scowlitz ms..

<**x̲ethíleqel**>, ds //x̣(ʔ)=əθə[=Aí=]l=əqəl//, NUM ['*four containers*'], HHG, lx <**=eqel**> *container, throat, speech*, phonology: vowel-loss, consonant-loss or consonant merger, vowel-reduction, ablaut, syntactic analysis: adjective/adjectival verb, nominal?, attested by AD (4/12/78).

<**x̲ethíléqw**>, ds //x̣(ʔ)=əθə[=Aí=]l=əqʷ//, NUM ['*four fish*'], EZ, lx <**=eqw**> *fish*, phonology: vowel-loss, consonant-loss or consonant merger, vowel-reduction, ablaut, updrifting, syntactic analysis: adjective/adjectival verb, nominal?, attested by BHTTC (8/24/76).

<**x̲ethíles**>, ds //x̣(ʔ)=əθə[=Aí=]l=əs//, NUM /'*four dollars, ((also) four blankets [Boas])*'/, ECON, lx <**=es**> *dollars*, phonology: vowel-loss, consonant-loss or consonant merger, vowel-reduction, ablaut, syntactic analysis: adjective/adjectival verb, nominal?, attested by AC (8/4/70, 10/6/71, 10/8/71), AD (4/12/78), other sources: Boas 1890 Scowlitz ms., also /'*four blankets, four dollars*'/, attested by Boas 1890 Scowlitz ms..

<**x̲ethílews**>, ds //x̣(ʔ)=əθə[=Aí=]l=əws//, NUM ['*four birds*'], EZ, lx <**=ews**> *birds, (on the body/skin)*, phonology: vowel-loss, consonant-loss or consonant merger, vowel-reduction, ablaut, syntactic analysis: adjective/adjectival verb, nominal?, attested by Elders Group (3/29/77).

<**x̲e'otheláyiws**>, ds //x̣əʔ=aθəl=ɛ́y(=)iws//, NUM ['*four pants*'], CLO, lx <**=áy(=)iws**> *pants*, syntactic analysis: adjective/adjectival verb, nominal?, attested by AD (4/12/78).

<**x̲e'óthelmó:t ~ x̲e'óthelmò:t**>, ds //x̣əʔ=áθəl=má·t ~ x̣əʔ=áθəl=mà·t//, NUM /'*four kinds, (four piles [Elders Group 7/27/75])*'/, (semological comment: *piles* may have been corrected to *kinds* by the IHTTC translation), lx <**=mó:t ~ =mò:t**> *kinds*, syntactic analysis: adjective/adjectival verb, nominal?, attested by IHTTC (7/28/77), Elders Group (7/27/75), also /'*four piles*'/, attested by Elders Group (7/27/75).

<**x̲(e)'othelòls**>, ds //x̣(ə)ʔ=aθəl=àls//, NUM ['*four fruit in a group or cluster (as they grow on a plant)*'], EB, lx <**=òls ~ =ó:ls**> *fruit, spherical objects, rocks*, syntactic analysis: adjective/adjectival verb, nominal?, attested by AD (4/12/78).

<**x̲e'othelő́welh**>, ds //x̣əʔ=aθəl=ówəɬ//, NUM /'*four canoes, four boats*'/, CAN, lx <**=ő́welh**> *canoe, vessel*, syntactic analysis: adjective/adjectival verb, nominal?, attested by AD (4/12/78).

<**sx̲e'óthels**>, ds //s=x̣əʔ=áθəl=s//, TIME /'*Thursday, four o'clock, (fourth cyclic period)*'/, NUM, literally /'fourth cyclic period'/, lx <**s=...=s**> *cyclic period, -th day; -th hour, o'clock*, syntactic analysis: nominal, attested by Elders Group (3/19/75), IHTTC (8/10/77), AC (10/6/71), Salish cognate: Squamish /s-x̣áʔúcn-s/ *Thursday* K67:369, ASM ['Thursday'], example: <**Q. stám swàyèl tlówàyèl? A. sx̲e'óthels.**>, //s=tɛ́m s=wɛ̀yəl təlá=wɛ̀yə̀l? s=x̣əʔ=áθəl=s//, /'*Q. What day is today? A. Thursday.*'/, attested by IHTTC, ASM ['four o'clock'], <**wetéses te sx̲e'ó:thels**>, //wə-tə́s-əs tə s=x̣əʔ=á·θəl=s//, /'*when it gets to four o'clock*'/, attested by AC.

<**x̲e'otheláyiws**>, NUM ['*four pants*'], *see* **x̲**e'ó:thel ~ **x̲**e'óthel.

<**x̲e'óthelmó:t ~ x̲e'óthelmò:t**>, NUM /'*four kinds, (four piles [Elders Group 7/27/75])*'/, *see* **x̲**e'ó:thel ~ **x̲**e'óthel.

<**x(e)'othelòls**>, NUM [*'four fruit in a group or cluster (as they grow on a plant)'*], *see* xe'ó:thel ~ xe'óthel.

<**xe'othelṓwelh**>, NUM /*'four canoes, four boats'*/, *see* xe'ó:thel ~ xe'óthel.

<**xí(y) ~ xéy**>, possibly root //x̣í(y) ~ x̣ə́y *against, (change, transform)*//, comment: this may be a root (or sound symbolic), with single consonants added to form free form stems, many of the single consonants may be suffixes with isolatable meanings (like <**=q'**> and <**=p'**>) but some may be merely stem extenders which have no consistent meanings with other roots, <**xí(y) ~ xéy**> *against* works for many (if not most) Upriver Halq'eméylem words it appears in, thus it seems present in: **<xéy=et>** *beat up s-o, spank s-o, lick s-o (in fight)*, **<xéy=kw'=et>** *chew it hard*, **<xéy=l=ém>** *growl (of animal)*, **<xéy=l=ém>** *growl (of a person), snap*, **<xéy=l=és>** *steep drop- off*, **<xéy=l=ex>** *to war* (=(e)x *distributive*), **<xéy=m=et>** *grab s-o/s-th*, **<xí=p' ~ xéy=p'>** *scratch and leave mark, line*, **<xíq' ~ xéy=q'>** *scratch to itch*, **<xí=s=el ~ xéy=s=el>** *get a spooked feeling*, **<xí=t>** *transform it, change it*, **<xéy=th'>** *raw, unripe ("against food")*, **<s=xí[=xe=]th'>** *look angry without talking, look disappointed*, **<xéy=th'=el>** *got impatient*, **<xí[=xe=]=th'=em>** *itchy*, **<xey=w=és=em>** *scowl*, **<xéy=w=ét>** *advise s-o against doing something bad, stop s-o from doing something bad*, **<xéyxe>** *be ashamed*; that includes almost every root beginning with this sequence, though **<xéytl'>** *cold* seems not to fit; the same root or sound-symbolic **<xi>** *against* seems to also fit almost every /x̣ə/-initial root in Hess 1976 (including many cognates with the Halkomelem forms listed just above); the Lushootseed form is not related to the prefix /x̣i-/ used with Lushootseed color terms; Squamish may also have a cognate root; because its status as a root in Halkomelem is not yet clear I have shown words which may contain it as separate entries rather than all sub-entries under one root, this also should make the words easier to look up, Salish cognate: Lushootseed /x̣i/ [*against*] as in: /x̣ib(i)/ *grab with pressure (as a hawk would do), claw*, /x̣icil/ *angry*, prob. /x̣ic'/ *raw (meat)*, /x̣íc'il/ *shame, guilt*, /x̣ídib/ *growl*, /x̣ídub/ *catch s-o doing s-th wrong*, /x̣ik'ʷ/ *ugly, mean, rough; strange appearance*, /x̣ílix̣/ *war, battle, fight*, /x̣iƛ'(i)/ *fell a tree*, /x̣ip'(i)/ *scratch (and leave a mark) (derivative: (Skagit)* /x̣íx̣əp'ič'/ *chipmunk*), /x̣iq'(i)/ *scratch, esp. to relieve an itch*, poss. /x̣it'ahəb/ *squat*?, /x̣íx̣ə/ *shame*, /x̣ix̣q'/ *get the best of s-o, compete; refuse* H76, similarly Squamish root /x̣əy- ~ x̣i-/ which Kuipers suggests means *cause to stop (fighting, being a nuisance, etc.)* K69:84, K67:368.

<**xíkwel**> ~ <**xéykwel**>, possible bound stem //x̣í(y)kʷ=əl//, meaning uncertain, or an alternate analysis would have root <**sx**> (medial vowel deleted before stressed suffix) + <=íkwel> (not attested elsewhere but perhaps a doublet with UHk <=íwel> *on the insides*–very appropriate in a word meaning *gizzards*

<**sxíkwel**> ~ <**sxéykwel**>, df //s=x̣í(y)kʷ=əl or sx̣=íkʷəl//, ANA ['*gizzards*'], (<**s=**> *nominalizer, something to*), root meaning unknown, lx <**=el**> *go, come, get, become*, syntactic analysis: nominal, attested by Maggie Pennier (Elders Group 1/24/79), example: <**sxéykwels te chékel**>, //s=x̣í(y)kʷ=əl-s tə cə́kəl//, /*'chicken('s) gizzards'*/, attested by Maggie Pennier.

<**xíkwel**> ~ <**xéykwel**>, possible bound stem //x̣í(y)kʷ=əl//, meaning uncertain, or an alternate analysis would have root <sx> (medial vowel deleted before stressed suffix) + <=íkwel> (not attested elsewhere but perhaps a doublet with UHk <=íwel> *on the insides*, or the red potatoes could possibly resemble *gizzards*, thus

<**sxíkwel**> ~ <**sxéykwel**>, df //s=x̣í(y)kʷ=əl or sx̣=íkʷəl//, EB /*'wild red potatoes that pigs eat, (probably Jerusalem artichoke)'*/, ASM ['a tall plant with big leaves, some grew at American Bar in the 1920's'], ['probably *Helianthus tuberosus*'], (<**s=**> *nominalizer, something to*), root meaning unknown, lx <**=el**> *go, come, get, become*, syntactic analysis: nominal, attested by LJ via AD (6/18/79).

<**x̲íkw'**> ~ <**x̲éykw'**>, stem or root //x̣í=k'^{w}// or //x̣ík'^{w}// *chew*

<**x̲éykw'et**>, pcs //x̣í=k'^{w}=əT or x̣ík'^{w}=əT//, ABFC /'*chew it (s-th hard, apple, pill)*'/, possibly root <**x̲í**> *against*, possibly <**=kw'**> *around in circles*, (<**=et**> *purposeful control transitivizer*), syntactic analysis: transitive verb, attested by EB (5/18/76), Salish cognate: Squamish /x̣ík'^{w}-in/ *chew (not at regular meal),munch (tr.?)* W73:57, K69:84.

<**x̲éyx̲ekw'et**>, cts //x̣í[-C_1ə-]k'^{w}=əT//, ABFC ['*be chewing s-th hard*'], (<**-R1-**> *continuative*), phonology: reduplication, syntactic analysis: transitive verb, attested by EB (5/3/76), example: <**x̲éyx̲ekw'etes te thíthqet.**>, //x̣í[-C_1ə-]k'^{w}=əT-əs tə C_1í=θəqɛt//, /'*He (for ex. a beaver) is chewing a small tree.*'/, attested by EB.

<**x̲éyx̲ekw'els**>, sas //x̣í[-C_1əC_2-](=)k'^{w}=əls//, cts, ABFC /'*chewing (something hard, like apple)*'/, (<**-R1-**> *continuative*), (<**=els**> *structured activity continuative*), phonology: reduplication, syntactic analysis: intransitive verb, attested by EB (5/3/76).

<**x̲ílém**> ~ <**x̲éylém**>, df //x̣í(y)=l=əm//, ABFC ['*growl (of an animal)*'], possibly root <**x̲éy**> *against*, possibly <**=l**> meaning unknown, possibly <**=em**> *middle voice or intransitivizer/have/get*, phonology: possible vowel merger, updrifting, syntactic analysis: intransitive verb, attested by Elders Group (5/19/76, 12/15/76), Salish cognate: Squamish /x̣íʔn-m/ *growl* W73:125, K67:369, Saanich dial. of NSt /x̣íx̣ən-əŋ/ *to growl [growling]* B74a:64, also <**x̲é:ylem**>, //x̣í·l=əm or x̣íy=l=əm//, attested by CT (6/8/76).

<**x̲ílep**> ~ <**x̲éylep**>, df //x̣í=íləp or x̣ə[=Aí=](y)=íləp//, LAND ['*swept ground*'], probably root <**x̲íy ~ x̲éy**> *against or scratch*, possibly <**í-ablaut**> *resultative*, possibly root <**íx̲w**> *sweep* (unlikely since it would require otherwise unmotivated metathesis and delabialization), lx <**=ílep**> *ground, dirt*, phonology: possible ablaut, possible vowel merger, syntactic analysis: adjective/adjectival verb?, nominal?, attested by Deming (11/1/79).

<**x̲ílés**> ~ <**x̲éylés**>, df //x̣ə́y(=)əl=əs or x̣í(=)l=ə[=´=]s//, LAND /'*steep drop-off, a drop-off, very steep slope, steep shore, steep riverbank, a slide*'/, root meaning unknown unless <**x̲éy**> *against*, possibly <**=el**> *go, come, get, become*, possibly <**=es**> *on the face*, possibly <**=´=**> *derivational*, phonology: possible stress-shift or updrifting, possible vowel-loss, syntactic analysis: nominal, attested by CT (6/8/76, 6/21/76), Elders Group (4/2/75, 8/24/77), Salish cognate: prob. not Squamish /s-x^{w}əh-áyʔus/ *dropoff (for ex. at bottom of beach)* W73:85, K69:78.

<**X̲éylés**>, df //x̣ə́y(=)l=əs//, PLN /'*place by Albert Cooper's house on Chilliwack River Road near Vedder Crossing, former village where a slide is now on north bank of Chilliwack River opposite Liumchen Creek*'/, literally /'slide, steep slope'/, syntactic analysis: nominal, attested by Elders Group (8/24/77), AC, other sources: Wells 1965 (lst ed.):19, source: place names reference file #222.

<**x̲é:yles**>, df //x̣í[=·=]y=əl=əs//, ABFC ['*made it (if laxative finally works)*'], literally perhaps /'really dropped off or slid'/, possibly <**=:=**> *emphatic*, phonology: possible lengthening, syntactic analysis: intransitive verb, attested by Elders Group (3/3/76), example: <**tsel x̲é:yles.**>, //c-əl x̣í[=·=]y=əl=əs//, /'*I made it (if laxative finally works).*'/, attested by Elders Group.

<**x̲í:les**> ~ <**x̲é:ylés**>, ABFC ['*made it (if laxative finally works)*'], *see* **x̲**ílés.

<**x̲íléx̲**> ~ <**x̲éyléx̲**>, ds //x̣í=(ə)l=ə[=´=]x̣//, SOC /'*to war, go to war*'/, literally /'go against all around/distributive (or) go fight all around'/, possibly root <**x̲éy ~ x̲í**> *against or fight*, (<**=el**> *go, come, get, become*), (<**=x̲ ~ =ex̲**> *distributive, all around*), possibly <**=´=**> *derivational*, phonology: consonant-loss, updrifting or stress-shift, syntactic analysis: intransitive verb, attested by Elders Group (2/27/80), EB (5/5/76), compare <**x̲éy=et**> *to fight s-o, beat s-o up*, Salish cognate:

Lushootseed /x̣ílix̣/ *war, battle, fight* H76:603, Squamish /x̣ə́yx̣ ~ x̣íʔx̣/ *war* beside /x̣əyx̣=ə́wiɬ/ *war canoe* W73:281, K67:368 and Squamish /x̣əyx̣-qín-m/ *war whoop* W73:281, K69:85, example: <**le x̱éyléx̱.**>, //lə x̣ə́y=əl=ə[=´=]x̣//, /'*He went to war.*'/, attested by EB.

<**x̱éyx̱elex̱**>, cts //x̣í[-C_1ə-]=l=əx̣//, SOC /'*war, (warring), fighting a war*'/, (<**-R1-**> *continuative*), phonology: reduplication, syntactic analysis: intransitive verb, attested by Elders Group (11/26/75), EB (5/5/76).

<**x̱í:llhts(e)t**> ~ <**x̱é:yllhts(e)t**>, SCH ['*write for s-o*'], *see* **x̱**í:l..

<**x̱í:lt**> ~ <**x̱é:ylt**>, SCH ['*write s-th*'], *see* **x̱**í:l.

<**x̱í:lthet**> ~ <**x̱é:ylthet**>, REL ['*paint one's body*'], *see* **x̱**í:l.

<**X̱ílx̱el(e)mòs**> ~ <**X̱éylx̱el(e)mòs**>, chrs //x̣í(·)l=C_1əC_2=əm=ás or x̣ə[=Aí=]l=C_1əC_2=əm=ás//, PLN ['*one of the two rocks of Lady Franklin Rock*'], literally perhaps /'characteristically have marks on the face'/, Elder's comment: ASM ['the other of the rocks has a name too, it too was once a man but changed to rock by X̱à:ls and thrown in the river, X̱éylx̱elemòs was said to have had multiple eyes in his forehead (thus perhaps the name)'], N ['*name of a man changed to rock by X̱à:ls and thrown in the river*'], probably root <**x̱éyl ~ x̱í:l ~ x̱él**> *mark, write,* (<**=R2**> *characteristic*), probably <**=em**> *intransitivizer/have/get,* lx <**=ós**> *on the face,* phonology: reduplication, possible ablaut, downstepping, syntactic analysis: nominal, attested by JL (12/14/77), other sources: Boas 1895 (Indianische Sagen ..., 1977 Bertz translation):28 records the story (forms in angle brackets within square brackets are in Stó:lō orthography; those outside square brackets here are in Boas's orthography): "<Qe'lqElEmas> [macron over e], the first of the <QEtla'tl> (macron over a) [the village of <**X̱elhlálh**> /x̣əɬ=lɛ́=ɬ/, across from Yale], was very powerful. His tribe were all river monsters. Once <Qals> [umlaut over a][<**X̱à:ls**> /x̣ɛ̀·ls/, the Transformer] came to him. The three brothers crossed the river to visit him while their sister stayed on the opposite shore. They managed to cross the river, which is very dangerous at this spot, without mishap., But when they came to [<**X̱éylx̱el(e)mòs**>] he called his tribe, and when [<**X̱à:ls**>] saw the dreadful forms he fainted. [<**X̱éylx̱el(e)mòs**>] took a magic potion out of his basket, sprinkled it over him and so revived him. <Sk·Ela'o>[macron over a] [<**Sqeláw**> /s=qəlɛ́w/ *beaver*], the brother of [<**X̱éylx̱el(e)mòs**>], was the first chief of the <Spe'yim> [<**Spíyem**> /s=píy=əm/] ([Spuzzum], the southernmost village of the Ntlakyapamuq [Thompson]). When he saw that [<**X̱à:ls**>] came to his brother, he dug an underground passage to his house to be able to help him in case of need. [could this be the name of the other rock of Lady Franklin Rock?].

<**x̱ilx̱elemós**> ~ <**x̱eylx̱elemós**>, chrs //x̣il=C_1əC_2=əm=ás or x̣ə[=Ai=]l=C_1əC_2=əm=ás//, WETH ['*fleecy wave clouds that look like sheep*'], literally perhaps /'characteristically have marks on the face'/, probably root <**x̱éyl ~ x̱í:l ~ x̱él**> *mark, write,* (<**=R2**> *characteristic*), probably <**=em**> *intransitivizer/have/get,* lx <**=ós**> *on the face,* phonology: reduplication, possible ablaut, syntactic analysis: nominal, attested by Elders Group (4/2/75), AC.

<**x̱ím**> ~ <**x̱éym**>, bound probable root //x̣ím or x̣í=m *grab*//, Salish cognate: Lushootseed root /x̣ib(i)/ *grab with pressure (as a hawk would do), claw* H76:600. Squamish root /x̣im/ as in /x̣ím-inʔ/ *grab s-o by the hair, pull s-o's hair (tr.)* and /x̣ám-i/ *grab and hold on to (itr.)* W73:122, K67:367, 369.

<**x̱éymem**>, izs //x̣í(=)m=əm//, ABFC ['*grab a handful*'], (<**=em**> *intransitivizer, get, have*), syntactic analysis: intransitive verb, attested by IHTTC (8/31/77).

<**x̱éymet**>, pcs //x̣í(=)m=əT//, ABFC ['*grab s-th/s-o*'], (<**=et**> *purposeful control transitivizer*), syntactic analysis: transitive verb, attested by EB (12/15/75), Elders Group (7/9/75); found in <**x̱eymethóme**>, //x̣im=əT-ámə//, /'*grab you*'/, attested by Elders Group.

<**x̲éymleqwt**>, pcs //x̣í(=)m=ləq^w=T//, ds, ABFC /'*pull s-o's hair, grab s-o's hair*'/, literally /'grab s-o on the hair'/, lx <**=(e)leqw**> *on the hair*, (<**=t**> *purposeful control transitivizer*), syntactic analysis: transitive verb, attested by EB (12/15/75), Elders Group (7/9/75); found in <**x̲éymleqwthò:m.**>, //x̣í(=)m=ləq^w=T-à·m//, /'*Your hair was grabbed or pulled., (s-o) pulled/grabbed your hair.*'/, attested by Elders Group.

<**x̲éyx̲emels**>, dnom //x̣í[=C_1ə=]m=əls//, cts, sas, EB ['*burdock*'], ['*Arctium minus*'], literally /'something grabbing'/, ASM ['introduced by non-Indians, named after the qualities of the burrs'], (<**=R1=**> *continuative*), (<**=els**> *structured activity continuative nominal*), phonology: reduplication, syntactic analysis: nominal, attested by Elders Group (7/2/75, 7/23/75).

<**x̲éyx̲emels ch'ech'éqw'**>, cpds //x̣í[=C_1ə=]m=əls C_1ə=c'ə́q'^{w}//, EB ['*burdock*'], ['*Arctium minus*'], literally /'grabbing little thorns'/, (<**=R1=**> *continuative*), (<**=els**> *structured activity continuative nominal*), (<**R5=**> *diminutive (plural?)),* phonology: reduplication, syntactic analysis: nominal phrase with modifier(s), attested by Elders Group (7/23/75).

<**x̲emx̲ímels ~ x̲emx̲íméls**>, sas //C_1əC_2=x̣ím=əls//, dnom, EZ /'*chicken hawk (red-tailed hawk), hawk (large and small varieties)*'/, ['*Buteo jamaicensis, Buteo* genus and *Accipiter* genus'], literally /'something grabbing many times/things as a structured activity'/, Elder's comment: "it means it scoops down and grabs (AC)", (<**R3=**> *plural action/object*), (<**=els**> *structured activity continuative nominal*), phonology: reduplication, optional updrifting, syntactic analysis: nominal, attested by AC (12/4/71), BJ (12/5/64), Elders Group (6/4/75, 2/18/76), other sources: ES /x̣əmx̣íməls/ *hawk*, H-T <Humqe'mEls> (macron over e) *hawk (Accipiter sp.)(large)* and <HeqEmqe'mEls> (macrons over both e) *hawk (Accipiter sp.)(small)* and <se'kElEtc> (macron over e) *hawk (Accipiter sp.)*, Salish cognate: Lushootseed /x̣íbx̣ib/ *chicken-hawk; generic term for bird of prey* H76:601, not Squamish /sx̣íp'im/ *chicken hawk* K69:60 and Kennedy and Bouchard 1976:72 *Cooper's hawk, sharp-shinned hawk, marsh hawk, red-tailed hawk*, also /'*hawk (large)*'/, attested by Elders Group (3/1/72).

<**x̲ix̲emx̲íméls**>, dmn //C_1í=C_1əC_2=x̣í(=)m=əls//, EZ ['*little hawk*'], ['probably of *Accipiter* genus'], (<**R4=**> *diminutive*), (<**R3=**> *plural action/object*), phonology: double reduplication, optional updrifting, syntactic analysis: nominal, attested by BHTTC (11/15/76), also <**x̲wix̲emx̲éyméls**>, //C_1í=C_1əC_2=x̣í(=)m=əls//, also /'*small hawk*'/, comment: **x̲**w probably mistranscribed for **x̲**, attested by Elders Group (3/1/72).

<**x̲eyímelets**>, df //x̣í[=·=]m=ələc//, EB ['*roots of a tree when it floats downriver*'], root <**xéym**> *grab*, possibly <**=:=**> *derivational*, lx <**=elets**> *on the bottom*, (<**zero**> *nominalizer*), phonology: possible lengthening, zero nominalizer, syntactic analysis: nominal, attested by Elders Group (5/2/79).

<**x̲ímem**> ~ <**x̲éymem**>, ABFC ['*grab a handful*'], *see* **x̲í**m.

<**x̲ímet**> ~ <**x̲éymet**>, ABFC ['*grab s-th/s-o*'], *see* **x̲**ím.

<**x̲ímleqwt**>, ~ <**x̲éymleqwt**> ABFC /'*pull s-o's hair, grab s-o's hair*'/, *see* **x̲**ím.

<**x̲íp**> ~ <**x̲éyp**>, possibly root //x̣ip or x̣í=p'=D//, TVMO ['*miss*'], CAN, ASM ['like to not make it over a wave or ripple and go back downstream'], possibly root <**x̲í ~ x̲éy**> *against*, possibly <**=p'**> *on something else*, possibly root <**x̲íp'**> *scratch and leave mark*, possibly <**=D (deglottalization)**> *derivational*, phonology: possible deglottalization, syntactic analysis: intransitive verb, attested by BHTTC (8/30/76), Salish cognate: perhaps Squamish /x̣íp'/ *get nipped, scratched, touched (by something flying by)* K67:369.

<**x̲íp**> ~ <**x̲éyp**>, possibly root //x̣ip or x̣í=p'=D//, prob. related to <**x̲íp'**> *scratch and leave mark*
<**sx̲íp**> ~ <**sx̲éyp**>, df //s=x̣í(=)p or s=x̣í=p'=D//, LT ['*a line*'], (<**s=**> *nominalizer, something to/that*),

possibly root <**x̱í**> *against*, possibly <**=p**> meaning unknown, probably <**=p'**> *on something else*, possibly root <**x̱íp'**> *scratch and leave mark*, possibly <**=D (deglottalization)**> *derivational (resultative?)*, phonology: possible deglottalization, syntactic analysis: nominal, attested by Elders Group (6/1/77), compare <**sx̱éyx̱ep'**> *a stripe*, compare <**x̱éyp'=et**> *scratch it and leave mark, scrape it, rake it*, example: <**thékw' sx̱éyp**>, //θə́k'ʷ s=x̣í(=)p//, /'*straight line*'/, attested by Elders Group.

<**sx̱éyx̱ep**>, pln //s=x̣í[=C₁ə=]p//, LT ['*lines*'], (<**=R1=**> *plural*), phonology: reduplication, syntactic analysis: nominal, attested by Elders Group (6/1/77).

<**sx̱éypx̱ep**>, pln //s=x̣íp=C₁əC₂//, LT ['*lots of lines*'], (<**=R2**> *plural*), phonology: reduplication, syntactic analysis: nominal, attested by Elders Group (6/1/77).

<**x̱epá:y ~ x̱epáy ~ x̱pá:y**>, ds //x̣i[=Aə=]p=ɛ́·y or x̣i=p'=D=ɛ́·y//, EB ['*western red cedar wood*'], ['*Thuja plicata*'], literally /'(probably) lined bark'/, probably root <**x̱í(=)p**> *line*, probably <**e-ablaut on root i**> *resultative*, lx <**=á:y**> *bark*, phonology: probable ablaut, optional vowel-loss, syntactic analysis: nominal, attested by AC (8/11/70, 8/25/70, 9/10/71, 11/19/71), BJ (5/10/64, 12/5/64), Elders Group (3/72 tape 33), other sources: ES /x̣pá·y/ (CwMs /x̣pɛ́y/) *red cedar (as material)*, JH /x̣péy/ *red cedar*, H-T <Hapai> (umlaut over first a, macron over second) *cedar (Thuja gigantea)*, Salish cognate: Squamish /x̣p-áyʔ/ *cedar* W73:55, K67:366, root in Lushootseed /x̣páyʔəc/ *cedar tree* H76:606, example: <**x̱epáy kwémléxw ~ kwémlexws te x̱epáy**>, //x̣i[=Aə=]p=ɛ́·y kʷə́mlə́xʷ ~ kʷə́mləxʷ-s tə x̣i[=Aə=]p=ɛ́·y//, /'*(red) cedar root*'/, attested by AC (8/25/70, 9/10/71), <**x̱epá:y ló:thel**>, //x̣i[=Aə=]p=ɛ́·y lá·θəl//, /'*(red) cedar dish*'/, attested by Elders Group (3/72).

<**x̱pá:yelhp ~ x̱páyelhp**>, ds //x̣i[=Aə=]p=ɛ́·y=əɬp//, EB ['*western red cedar tree*'], ['*Thuja plicata*'], lx <**=elhp**> *tree*, phonology: probable ablaut, optional vowel-loss, syntactic analysis: nominal, attested by BJ (12/5/64), Elders Group (1/29/75, 7/23/75), CT and HT (6/8/76), example: <**p'elyi:ws te x̱páyelhp**>, //p'əl=əy=í·ws-s tə x̣i[=Aə=]p=ɛ́·y=əɬp//, /'*outer red cedar bark*'/, literally /'bark of the red cedar tree'/, attested by CT and HT.

<**x̱epyúwelh**>, ds //x̣əp=ɛy=ówəɬ//, HHG ['*cedar trough (to serve food)*'], FOOD, lx <**=ówelh ~ =úwelh**> *vessel, canoe*, phonology: vowel-loss, syntactic analysis: nominal, attested by Elders Group (3/72 tape 33).

<**x̱pó:ys**>, ds //x̣əp=ɛ[=Aá=]·y=əs//, BSK /'*wide cedar (sapling) strips or slats from young cedar trunks, cedar slat work (basketry)*'/, literally /'red cedar wood on the face'/, lx <**=es**> *on the face*, phonology: ó-ablaut automatic before =es, vowel-loss (twice), syntactic analysis: nominal, attested by Elders Group (3/24/76, 6/11/75).

<**x̱pá:ytses ~ x̱páytses**>, ds //x̣əp=ɛ́·y=cəs//, EB /'*(red) cedar limb, (red) cedar bough*'/, ['*Thuja plicata*'], literally /'red cedar hand'/, ASM ['red cedar boughs are used by ritualists to sweep out the corners of a longhouse or to brush people to get rid of ghosts in cleansing ceremonies, they are also used under bedding in camping to sweeten the smell and keep away pests as well as soften the ground one sleeps on (done for ex. at the fish drying camps by elders)'], lx <**=tses**> *(on the) hand, bough*, phonology: vowel-loss, optional length-loss, syntactic analysis: nominal, attested by EB (2/6/76), Elders Group (7/23/75), HT and CT (6/8/76).

<**x̱íp'**> ~ <**x̱éyp'**>, possibly root //x̣í(=)p' *scratch and leave mark*//, root <**x̱í**> *against*, possibly <**=p'**> *on something else*, (semological comment: the meaning of this suffix everywhere else is *on itself* but in this root it seems to have switched meanings with =q' *on something else*).

<**x̱éyp'et**>, pcs //x̣í=p'=əT//, ABFC /'*scratch s-o/s-th and leave a mark, rake it, claw it, scrape it, rake it*'/, ASM ['for ex. scratch s-o/s-th as a cat would scratch s-o'], (<**=et**> *purposeful control*

transitivizer), syntactic analysis: transitive verb, attested by AD (10/10/79), EB (4/27/76, 3/2/76), other sources: ES /x̣Ɛyp'ət/ *scratch*, Salish cognate: Lushootseed /x̣íp'-id/ *scratch it and leave a mark* H76:604, Squamish /x̣íp'-in/ *scratch (tr.)* W73:224, K67:369, also <**x̱ípet**>, //x̣í=p'=D=əT//, [x̣épət], comment: p may be misrecorded for p', attested by AC (8/24/70, 10/13/71), example: <**x̱éyp'et te sch'ólha**>, //x̣í(=)p'=əT tə s=c'áɬɛ//, /'*rake the leaves (leaf)*'/, attested by AD.

<**sx̱éyx̱ep'**>, rsls //s=x̣í[=C_1ə=](=)p'//, dnom, LT ['*a stripe*'], (<**s=**> *nominalizer*), (<**=R1=**> *resultative*), phonology: reduplication, syntactic analysis: nominal, attested by AD (10/10/79).

<**x̱éyx̱ep'els**>, sas //x̣í[-C_1ə-](=)p'=əls//, cts, ABFC /'*scratch, (scratching as a structured activity)*'/, (<-**R1-**> *continuative*), (<**=els**> *structured activity continuative*), phonology: reduplication, syntactic analysis: intransitive verb, attested by Elders Group (3/15/72).

<**x̱éyp'eqsel**>, ds //x̣í(=)p'=əqsəl//, ABDF ['*scraped on the nose*'], lx <**=eqsel**> *on the nose*, syntactic analysis: intransitive verb, prob. adjective/adjectival verb, attested by JL (5/5/75).

<**x̱éyp'es**>, ds //x̣í(=)p'=əs//, ABDF ['*scraped on the face*'], lx <**=es**> *on the face*, syntactic analysis: intransitive verb, prob. adjective/adjectival verb, attested by JL (5/5/75).

<**x̱ep'ewíts**>, ds //x̣i(=)p'=əwíc//, ABDF ['*marked on the back*'], LT, lx <**=ewíts**> *on the back*, phonology: vowel-reduction, syntactic analysis: intransitive verb, prob. adjective/adjectival verb, attested by AD (10/10/79).

<**sx̱eyx̱ep'ewíts ~ sx̱eyx̱ep'ōwíts**>, strs //s=x̣i[=C_1ə=](=)p'=əwíc//, LT ['*striped on back*'], (<**s=**> *stative*), (<**=R1=**> *resultative*), lx <**=ewíts**> *on the back*, phonology: reduplication, syntactic analysis: adjective/adjectival verb, attested by ME (11/21/72 tape).

<**x̱éyx̱ep'ílep**>, ds //x̣í[=C_1ə=](=)p'=íləp//, HARV /'*a rake, a harrow*'/, TOOL, literally /'scratching dirt and leaving a mark'/, (<**=R1=**> *continuative*), lx <**=ílep**> *dirt, ground*, (<**zero**> *nominalizer*), phonology: reduplication, zero nominalizer, syntactic analysis: nominal, attested by Elders Group (3/15/72).

<**x̱íp'eqsel**> ~ <**x̱éyp'eqsel**>, ABDF ['*scraped on the nose*'], *see* **x̱íp'**.

<**x̱íp'es**> ~ <**x̱éyp'es**>, ABDF ['*scraped on the face*'], *see* **x̱íp'**.

<**x̱íp'et**> ~ <**x̱éyp'et**>, ABFC /'*scratch s-o/s-th and leave a mark, rake it, claw it, scrape it*'/, *see* **x̱íp'**.

<**x̱íqeya**> ~ <**x̱éyqeya**>, df //x̣ə[=Aí=]q=əyɛ or x̣íq=əyɛ//, EZ /'*old salmon (ready to die, spotted)*'/, possibly root <**x̱éq**> *straddle*, (semological comment: if correct perhaps becaue dying salmon often straddle (lie over) rocks), possibly <**í-ablaut**> *resultative*, lx <**=eya**> *affectionate diminutive*, phonology: possible ablaut, syntactic analysis: nominal, attested by Elders Group (4/28/76).

<**x̱íq'**> ~ <**x̱éyq'**>, stem or root //x̣í(=)q' *scratch (like of an itch)*//, root <**x̱í**> *against*, possibly <**=q'**> *on itself*, (semological comment: the meaning of this suffix everywhere else is *on something else* but in this root it seems to have switched meanings with =p' *on itself*), Salish cognate: Lushootseed root /x̣iq'/ *scratch, esp. to relieve an itch* H76:604, Squamish /x̣íq'/ *be scratched* as also in /x̣íq'-in-cut/ *scratch oneself* and /x̣íq'-q^w-mʔ/ *scratch one's head* W73:224-225, K67:369, K69:86.

<**x̱éyq'et**>, pcs //x̣í(=)q'=əT//, ABFC /'*scratch it (like of an itch), (itch it)*'/, (<**=et**> *purposeful+ control transitivizer*), syntactic analysis: transitive verb, attested by EB (3/2/76), Salish cognate: in part Squamish /x̣íq'-in/ *scratch* W73:224-225, K67:369, Lushootseed /x̣íq'-id/ //x̣íq'=it// *scratch it to relieve an itch* H76:604.

<**x̱éyx̱eq'els**>, cts //x̣í[-C_1ə-](=)q'=əls//, sas, ABFC ['*scratching*'], (<**-R1-**> *continuative*), (<**=els**> *structured activity continuative*), phonology: reduplication, syntactic analysis: intransitive verb, attested by EB (3/2/76).

<**xeyxeq'qéylem**>, cts //x̣i[-C_1ə-](=)q'=qəl=íl=əm or x̣i[-C_1ə-](=)q'=qə[=Aí=]l=əm//, [x̣ex̣əq'qéləm], mdls, ABFC [*'scratching one's head'*], ASM ['a stick made of wood of the wild rose was sometimes used to scratch in the hair'], (<**-R1-**> *continuative*), lx <**=qel**> *on the head, in the head*, possibly <**í-ablaut**> *durative*, possibly <**=íl**> *go, come, get, become*, (<**=em**> *middle voice*), phonology: reduplication, ablaut or syllable-loss, syntactic analysis: intransitive verb, attested by IHTTC (7/15/77).

<**xíq'et**> ~ <**xéyq'et**>, ABFC /*'scratch it (like of an itch), (itch it)'*/, *see* **x**íq'.

<**xís**> ~ <**xéys**>, stem or root //x̣í(=)əs or x̣í(=)s//, *spooky feeling, creepy feeling*

<**xéysel**>, df //x̣í(=)əs=əl or x̣í(=)s=əl//, EFAM /*'get a spooky or spooked feeling, afraid that bad spirits are around, get spooked, fear something behind'*/, possibly root <**xéy ~ xí**> *against*, possibly <**=es**> *on the face*, possibly <**=s**> meaning unknown, (<**=el**> *go, come, get, become*), phonology: probable vowel merger, syntactic analysis: intransitive verb, attested by Elders Group (3/15/72, 3/3/76, 3/2/77), RP and EB (2/12/76), Salish cognate: perhaps Lushootseed root /x̣əc/ *fear* as in /ʔəs-x̣ə́c/ *be afraid* H76:587, or perhaps Squamish root /x̣is/ *shrink, contract, cramp* or Squamish /x̣iʔ-x̣í-s/ *feign at (tr.)* and /x̣íʔ-x̣i-s/ *make a feigning movement at, make believe (tr.)* W73:98, K67:368, 370, K69:86.

<**xéyxesel**>, cts //x̣í[-C_1ə-](=)əs=əl//, EFAM /*'getting spooked, being afraid that bad spirits are around, spooky feeling'*/, (<**-R1-**> *continuative*), phonology: reduplication, vowel merger, syntactic analysis: intransitive verb, attested by RP and EB (2/12/76), Elders Group (3/15/72, 4/16/75).

<**xéyxesem**>, df //x̣í[=C_1ə=]=əs=əm//, EFAM [*'creepy'*], (<**=R1=**> *resultative or continuative*), (<**=em**> *have/get/intransitivizer or middle voice*), phonology: reduplication, vowel merger, syntactic analysis: intransitive verb, attested by EB (3/1/76).

<**xít**> ~ <**xéyt**>, pcs //x̣í(y)=T or x̣ə́y=T//, IDOC /*'transform s-th/s-o, change s-th/s-o'*/, REL, ASM ['used when passing something (food, clothing, belongings) over a fire at a burning to feed the dead (it makes them usable both by the spirits of the deceased owner when the things are put into the fire and by living friends and relatives present after the remainder is passed over the fire a certain number of times while the ritualist speaks to the departed spirits), also used when an Indian doctor/shaman sprinkles water, and when Xá:ls (the Transformer) or Xexéyls (the Transformers) transform someone into rock or creatures'], possibly root <**xí(y) ~ xéy**> *against*, (<**=t**> *purposeful control transitivizer*), syntactic analysis: transitive verb, attested by Elders Group (2/27/80).

<**Xéyt**>, ds //x̣í(y)=T or x̣ə́y=T//, N [*'Transformer'*], REL, ASM ['this is another [less common] name for the Transformer, more common names are Xá:ls ~ Xà:ls and for he and his 3 siblings (2 brothers + one sister), Xexá:ls; the origin of the Transformers is told in Dan Milo's story of Black Bear['s Childeren] and Grizzly Bear, in which Grizzly Bear murders Black Bear (both mothers) and eats Black Bear, Black Bear's children discover this and flee, eventually pursuading a man to drown Grizzly Bear while crossing a river, after other adventures the children wander off to the land of the horizon and return as Transformers, accompanied by Mink, a sexual mischief-maker, Boas 1895 (Bertz 1977) tells many of the stories of the wanderings and transformations of the Transformers from the Upriver Halkomelem area as well as other areas'], literally /'transform s-th/s-o, change s-th/s-o'/, (<**zero**> *nominalizer*), phonology: zero nominalizer, syntactic analysis: nominal, attested by AD (4/27/79), contrast <**Xá:ls ~ Xà:ls**> *the Transformer*, contrast <**Xexá:ls**> *the Transformers*, comment: both these forms derive from the same root as does <xéyt> (perhaps <xéy> *against* but they are listed under both xéyt and Xá:ls to make them easier to find.

<**xiyxéyt** or **xeyxéyt**>, df //C_1í=x̣í(y)=T or C_1əC_2=x̣íy=T//, IDOC /*'transform it more, pass it over the*

fire more (at a burning)'/, REL, possibly <**R4=**> *diminutive*, possibly <**R3=**> *plural action*, phonology: reduplication, syntactic analysis: transitive verb, attested by Elders Group (2/27/80); found in <**x̲i(y)x̲éytchexw.**>, //C_1í=x̣í(y)=T-c-əxʷ or C_1əC_2=x̣íy=T-c-əxʷ//, /'*Transform it more., Pass it over the fire more (at a burning).*'/, attested by Elders Group.

<**x̲ít**> or <**x̲éyt**>, //x̣íy(=)t// or //x̣ít// *growl*

<**x̲éytem**>, df //x̣í=T=əm or x̣í(=)t=əm//, LANG /'*growl (of people, with words), speak gruffly*'/, EFAM, possibly root <**x̲éy ~ x̲í**> *against*, contrast <**x̲éy(=)t**> *beat s-o up*, contrast <**x̲éy(=)t**> *transform s-o, change s-o*, possibly <**=t**> meaning unknown, possibly <**=em**> *middle voice or intransitivizer/have/get*, possibly <**=em**> *speak a language from* possibly as in <**halq'eméylem**> *Halkomelem language, speak Halkomelem* and <**lhéchelesem**> *Nooksack language, speak Nooksack*, (semological comment: this last suffix =em *speak a language from* may just be a special case of *place to have/get* used with the prime tribal village name since the language names where this use is attested (Halkomelem, Nooksack, and Straits all have a cognate suffix and use for their language names) all have stems which are village names most centrally located in the language territory, i.e. /ləq'ɛməl/ *Nicomen village, near Deroche, B.C.*, /ɬəč'ǽlos/ *village in what is now Everson, Wash.*, and /lək'ʷəŋən/ *village on what is now the Songhees reserve in the city of Victoria, B.C.*), syntactic analysis: intransitive verb, attested by EB (4/26/76, 12/15/75, Salish cognate: perhaps Lushootseed /x̣íd-ib/ *growl* H76:602, though that is more likely cognate with Upriver Halkomelem /x̣í(y)=l=əm/ *growl (of animal)* and Squamish /x̣íʔn-m/ *growl (of animal)*, W73, Lushootseed /d/ usu. corresp. to Downriver Halkomelem /n/, Squamish /n/ but Hess 1976 notes that Lushootseed //-t// transitivizer is usually realized as Lushootseed /d/.

<**x̲éyx̲etem**>, cts //x̣í[-C_1ə-](=)t=əm//, izs, LANG ['*growling (with words)*'], (<**-R1-**> *continuative*), (<**=em**> *intransitivizer, have, get*), phonology: reduplication, syntactic analysis: intransitive verb, attested by EB (12/15/75).

<**x̲éytet**>, pcs //x̣í(=)t=əT//, LANG /'*snap at s-o (verbally or in arguing), growl at s-o (with words)*'/, EFAM, (<**=et**> *purposeful control transitivizer*), syntactic analysis: transitive verb, attested by IHTTC (8/9/77), EB (12/15/75); found in <**x̲eytethóxes.**>, //x̣i(=)t=əT-áxʸ-əs//, /'*He snapped at me (verbally or in arguing)., He growled at me (with words).*'/, attested by IHTTC, EB.

<**x̲éyx̲etet**>, cts //x̣í[-C_1ə-](=t)=əT//, LANG ['*snapping at s-o (verbally or in arguing)*'], (<**-R1-**> *continuative*), phonology: reduplication, syntactic analysis: transitive verb, attested by IHTTC (8/9/77); found in <**x̲eyx̲etethóxes.**>, //x̣i[-C_1ə-](=)t=əT-áxʸ-əs//, /'*He was snapping at me (verbally or in arguing).*'/, attested by IHTTC.

<**x̲ítet**> ~ <**x̲éytet**>, LANG /'*snap at s-o (verbally or in arguing), growl at s-o (with words)*'/, *see* **x̲í**tem.

<**x̲íth'**> ~ <**x̲éyth'**>, ds //x̣í=θ'//, EB ['*unripe*'], FOOD /'*raw, uncooked*'/, possibly root <**x̲éy ~ x̲í**> *against*, possibly <**=th'**> *food, small portion*, compare <**lhémth'**> *pick at food* where <**lhem ~ lhím**> is *pick*, syntactic analysis: adjective/adjectival verb, attested by Elders Group (3/5/80), AC (9/1/71), Salish cognate: Lushootseed /x̣íc'/ *raw (meat)* vs. /qʷúx̣ʷadəb/ *unripe* H76:602, root in Squamish /x̣c'-áyʔ/ *unfinished canoe hull* K69:84, root in Cowichan and Musqueam /x̣əθ'ɛyʔ/ (vs. Chilliwack /pə́qsəwə́ɬ/) *unfinished hull* ES ["uncooked tree/bark" because it hasn't yet had red-hot rocks and water applied to burn out the core for a canoe], example: <**le xwel x̲éyth'.**>, //lə xʷəl x̣í=θ'//, /'*They're on the unripe side.*'/, literally /'past third person subject still unripe'/, attested by AC, <**xwel x̲éyth' te sqw'el.**>, //xʷəl x̣í·θ' tə s=q'ʷə́l//, /'*Your cooking is not done.*'/, literally /'still is uncooked the cooking'/, attested by Elders Group (3/5/80).

<**x̲éyth'elhp**>, ds //x̣í=θ'=əɬp//, EB /'*alder tree, red alder*'/, ['*Alnus rubra*'], literally /'unripe tree'/, (semological comment: perhaps so named since the bark and wood turn deep red or orange when

exposed to moist air (Turner 1979:190)), ASM ['bark used to dye bitter cherry bark black for basketry designs, wood used green to smoke fish, spoons and dishes carved out of the wood'], lx <**=elhp**> *tree*, syntactic analysis: nominal, attested by Elders Group (3/72, 3/1/72), Deming (6/21/79), AC (11/19/71, 11/26/71), other sources: ES /x̣ɛ́·yθ'əɬp/ *alder*, H-T <He'tsElp> (macron over e) *alder tree (Alnus rubra)*, Salish cognate: Sechelt /x̣íx̣ic'-ay/ *alder* T77:11.

<**X̱ex̱éyth'elhp**>, pln //C_1ə=x̣í=θ'=əɬp//, PLN [*'place on the east side of Seabird Island'*], ASM ['place going [east] toward the river at Wahleach where lots of alders were, it was located at the south point of the little bay due east of Wahleach railroad stop, Xixewqéyls another place name pointed out by JL (referring to a carrot-like plant/yarrow that grew there and was used for dye) is located at the north end of the little bay, another possible location for X̱ex̱éyth'elhp is at the south point of the biggest bay on the east side of Seabird (south of the little bay) but that would mean that the reference to Wahleach is totally wrong, JL likely came across the Fraser by canoe from his home in the Peters Reserve with his grandmother to reach these places'], literally /'many (little) alder trees'/, (<**R5=**> *plural or diminutive plural*), syntactic analysis: nominal, attested by JL (4/1/78), IHTTC (8/15/77), Elders Group (8/31/77), source: place names reference file #196 and #266.

<**x̱íth'**> ~ <**x̱éyth'**>, bound root or stem //x̣í(=)θ' *to itch (need to scratch)*//, probably root <**x̱i=** ~ **x̱ey=**> *against* + lx <**=th'**> (probably) *small portion*, Salish cognate: Squamish root /x̣íc'/ *itch* as in /x̣íc'-im/ *itch* and /x̣í-x̣ic'-m ~ x̣ə́-x̣ic'-m/ *itch* W73:152, K67:367, 369, 370.

<**x̱íx̱eth'em**>, df //x̣í[=C_1ə=](=)θ'=əm//, ABDF [*'itchy'*], (<**=R1=**> *continuative or resultative*), (<**=em**> *intransitivizer/have/get or middle voice*), phonology: reduplication, syntactic analysis: adjective/adjectival verb, attested by BHTTC (late 10/76), Salish cognate: Squamish /x̣í-x̣ic'-m ~ x̣ə́-x̣ic'-m/ *itch* W73:152, K67:367, 369, 370, also <**x̱éyx̱ets'em**>, //x̣í[=C_1ə=](=)c'=əm//, also /*'to itch'*/, attested by JL (5/5/75).

<**x̱eyx̱ets'émthet**>, incs //x̣í[=C_1ə=](=c')=ə[=´=]m=θət//, ABDF [*'(get) real itching'*], (<**=thet**> *get, become*), phonology: reduplication, stress-shift automatic before =thet? or allomorphic, syntactic analysis: intransitive verb, attested by JL (5/5/75).

<**x̱íth' ~ x̱éyth'**>, root or stem //x̣í(=)θ' ~ x̣ə́y(=)θ' *impatient* or *itchy, impatient*//, probably root <**x̱i=** ~ **x̱ey=**> *against* + lx <**=th'**> (probably) *small portion*, probably same root as preceding root <**x̱íth'**> ~ <**x̱éyth'**>, bound root or stem //x̣í(=)θ' *to itch (need to scratch)*//.

<**x̱íth'el ~ x̱éyth'el**>, incs //x̣ə[=Aí=]θ'=əl or x̣í(=)θ'=əl//, EFAM [*'got impatient'*], literally perhaps /'got an itch'/, possibly <**í-ablaut of root e**> *resultative*, (<**=el**> *go, come, get, become*), phonology: possible ablaut, syntactic analysis: intransitive verb, attested by Elders Group (3/16/77), Salish cognate: possibly Lushootseed /x̣íc-il/ *angry* which has derivative /x̣íc-il-əb/ *grumpy, kind of angry* H76:601-602.

<**x̱éth'x̱eth'**>, chrs //x̣ə́θ'=C_1əC_2//, EFAM /*'cranky, quick-tempered'*/, literally perhaps /'characteristically itchy'/, (<**=R2**> *characteristic*), phonology: reduplication, syntactic analysis: adjective/adjectival verb, attested by IHTTC (7/26/77 except EB), also <**sx̱éth'x̱eth'**>, //s=x̣ə́θ'=C_1əC_2//, (<**s=**> *stative*), attested by EB (IHTTC 7/26/77).

<**sx̱éyx̱eth'**>, strs //s=x̣í[=C_1ə=](=)θ' or s=x̣ə[=AíC_1ə=]θ'//, EFAM [*'disappointed and angry-looking without talking'*], (<**s=**> *stative*), possibly root <**x̱éy**> *against*, possibly root <**x̱éyth'**> *itch*, (<**=R1= (perhaps with í-ablaut)**> *resultative*), possibly <**=th'**> *small portion*, phonology: reduplication, possible ablaut, syntactic analysis: adjective/adjectival verb, attested by EB (6/14/76), Salish cognate: prob. Lushootseed root /x̣íc'-il/ *shame, guilt* as in /ʔəs-x̣íc'-il/ *be guilty* and /ʔəs-x̣íc'-il-us/ *contorted, distorted face from bad feelings* and /x̣íc'-il-àyucid/ *shame in the mouth* related to root

/x̣íx̣i/ *shamɛ* and /x̣ídub/ *catch s-o doing something wrong* H76:602, perhaps Squamish /x̣íc'-i/ *bring shame upon oneself (so that one has to blush)* W73:228, K69:85 vs. Squamish root /ʔix̣/ → /s-ʔíx̣-i/ *shame* (metathesis?) K67:305, W73:228.

<**sx̲eyx̲eth'ó:ythel**>, ds //s=x̣í[=C_1ə=](=)θ'=á·yθəl or s=x̣ə[=AíC_1ə=]θ'=á·yθəl//, strs, ABDF /'*ugly expression in mouth, ugly grin*'/, EFAM, lx <**=ó:ythel**> *on the lips/jaw*, phonology: reduplication, possible ablaut, syntactic analysis: adjective/adjectival verb, attested by Elders Group (3/3/76).

<**x̲íth'el ~ x̲éyth'el**>, EFAM ['*got impatient*'], *see* **x̲**íth' ~ **x̲**éyth'.

<**x̲íth'elhp**> ~ <**x̲éyth'elhp**>, EB /'*alder tree, red alder*'/, *see* **x̲**íth'.

<**x̲í:tl'**> ~ <**x̲éytl'**>, free root //x̣í·ƛ'//, TCH ['*be cold*'], WETH, semantic environment ['of water, food, weather, ground, etc.'], syntactic analysis: adjective/adjectival verb, attested by AC (8/4/70, 9/8/71, 10/1/71), EB (12/1/75), Deming (3/31/77), Elders Group (1/19/77), BJ (5/10/64), other sources: ES /x̣ɛ́·yƛ'/ *cold*, JH /x̣í·ƛ'/ *cold*, Salish cognate: no cognates found in dictonaries/word lists of MCx, Se, Sq, San, Sam, Ld, Nk, Th, Cm, however Ld does have /ƛ'áx̣/ *feel cold* (Bates, Hess & Hilbert 1994:152) which is probably cognate through historical metathesis, example: <**x̲éytl' te swáyel.**>, //x̣í·ƛ' tə s=wɛ́yəl//, /'*The day is cold.*'/, attested by Deming, <**x̲é:ytl' te témexw.**>, //x̣í·ƛ' tə tə́məxʷ//, /'*The ground is cold.*'/, attested by AC, <**yeláwel x̲éytl' tlówàyèl telí kw'e cheláqelh(elh).**>, //yəlɛ́w=əl x̣í·ƛ' təlá=wɛ̀yə̀l təlí k'ʷə cəlɛ́q(=)əɬ(-əɬ)//, /'*Today is colder than yesterday.*'/, attested by Elders Group.

<**x̲éytl'thet**>, incs //x̣í·ƛ'=θət//, WETH ['*get cold*'], (<**=thet**> *get, become*), phonology: the root vowel cannot be /ɛ/ because /ɛ/ → /a/ automatically (<**a**> → <**o**>) before <=**thet**> and there is no such change here, syntactic analysis: intransitive verb, attested by AD (4/21/80), EB (2/16/76), example: <**hókwextselcha te'íle hólem swéta welámescha x̲éytl'thet.**>, //hákʷ=əxʸ-c-əl-cɛ tə=ʔí=la hál=əm sʷə́tɛ wə-lɛ́=m-əs-cɛ x̣í·ƛ'=θət//, /'*I'll wear/put on this warm sweater when it gets cold. (wear s-th, put on s-th)*'/, attested by AD.

<**x̲é:ytl'thet**>, cts //x̣í·[-·-]ƛ'=θət or x̣í[-·-]yƛ'=θət//, WETH ['*getting colder*'], (<**-:-**> *continuative (or) augmentative*), phonology: lengthening, syntactic analysis: intransitive verb, attested by EB (2/16/76), example: <**ulh me x̲é:ytl'thet.**>, //ʔuɬ mə x̣í·[-·-]ƛ'=θət//, /'*It's getting colder.*'/, other sources: Gibbs' *autumn*, attested by EB, <**me x̲é:ytl'thet.**>, //mə x̣í·[-·-]ƛ'=θət//, /'*(It's) winter.*'/, literally /'become/come/start to be getting colder'/, attested by EB.

<**temx̲é:ytl'thet**>, ds //təm=x̣í·[=·=]ƛ'=θət//, TIME ['*winter*'], literally /'time for getting colder'/, (<**tem=**> *season for, time for*), syntactic analysis: adverb/adverbial verb, attested by DM (12/4/64).

<**temx̲éytl'**>, ds //təm=x̣í·ƛ'//, TIME ['*winter*'], literally /'season/time for cold'/, (<**tem=**> *season for, time for*), syntactic analysis: adverb/adverbial verb, attested by Elders Group (3/12/75), AC (8/14/70, 10/8/71), others.

<**sx̲éytl'**>, dnom //s=x̣í·ƛ'//, TIME ['*winter*'], literally /'the cold'/, (<**s=**> *nominalizer*), syntactic analysis: nominal, attested by AC (10/8/71).

<**x̲itl'áls ~ x̲itl'á:ls**> ~ <**x̲eytl'áls ~ x̲eytl'á:ls**>, df //x̣ɛ[=y=]ƛ'=ɛ́·ls//, sas, EZ ['*grizzly bear*'], ['*Ursus arctos horribilis*'], ASM ['they turn right when they first come out of their cave, they were not eaten since they sometimes eat humans (parts have been found in their stomaches), they are hard to kill -- must be shot in the ear (all this from ME who calls them **x̲á**x̲e *sacred, taboo*'], possibly root <**x̲áytl'**> <**x̲óytl' ~ x̲ó:yt**> *cranky, aggressive, ready to fight, violent*, comment: <**x̲áytl'**> if the root is a bound form, attested elsewhere only before <**=thet**> (which automatically changes any root <**a**> to <**o**>as in <**x̲óytl'thet**>), possibly root <**x̲átl'**> *rough, turbulent (of wind/water)*, compare <**x̲óytl' ~ x̲ó:ytl'**>

below, possibly <**=y=**> epenthetic, possibly <**=á:ls**> *structured activity non-continuative nominal*,thus a possible literal meaning of /'cranky/aggressive/ready to fight/violent as a structured activity'/ syntactic analysis: nominal, attested by Mrs. Margaret Jim (Mrs. August Jim) and JL and AC (10/62 Wells tape new transcript), AK (11/21/72 tape), ME (11/21/72 tape), Elders Group (3/29/77), JL and EB and Maggie Pennier and HT and Lawrence James and DF and AG and NP (Elders Group 6/7/78), BJ (5/10/64 Wells tapes new transcript new p.121), contrast <**kw'í:tsel**> *grizzly bear (DF: small grizzly)*, comment: kw'í:tsel was used also by DF and NP and HT (Elders Group 6/7/78) and by DM (Wells tapes new transcripts) and BJ (5/10/64 Wells tapes new transcript new p.121), also /'*large grizzly bear*'/, attested by DF (6/7/78), also <**x̲eytl'álth**>, //x̣ɛyƛ'=ɛ́lθ//, attested by Deming (3/11/76), comment: perhaps mistranscribed, example: <**lép'exes te x̲eytl'áls (mekw'ewátes, mékw' tewátes).**>, //lə́p'=əx^{y}-əs təx̣ɛyƛ'=ɛ́ls (mək'^{w}=əwɛ́t=əs, mə́k'^{w} tə=wɛ́t=əs)//, /'*The grizzly ate everybody/anybody. (eat s-o/s-th)*'/, attested by Elders Group (3/29/77), <**mekw'ewát lép'exes te x̲eytl'áls.**>, //mək'^{w}=əwɛ́t lə́p'=əx^{y}-əs təx̣ɛyƛ'=ɛ́ls//, /'*The grizzly ate everybody.*'/, attested by Elders Group (3/29/77).

<**x̲ítl'thet**>, ~ <**x̲éytl'thet**> WETH ['*get cold*'], *see* **x̲**í:tl'.

<**x̲í:tl'thet**> ~ <**x̲é:ytl'thet**>, WETH ['*getting colder*'], *see* **x̲**í:tl'.

<**x̲íwel**> ~ <**x̲éywel**>, bound root //x̣í=íwə́l or x̣í=íwəl or x̣í=əwəl *against in the mind* or *shame in the mind*//, compare root <**x̲éy ~ x̲í**> *against*, compare <**x̣íx̲e**> *be ashamed.*

<**x̲éywét**>, pcs //x̣í=íw(əl)=əT or x̣í=íwə́(l)=T or x̣í=əw(əl)=əT//, LANG /'*advise s-o not to do something bad, (advise s-o against s-th), advise s-o to change, stop s-o from doing something*'/, SOC, (<**=et ~ =t**> *purposeful control transitivizer*), phonology: vowel merger, regular syllable-loss (of el before =et), possible updrifting, syntactic analysis: transitive verb, attested by EB (12/19/75, 3/8/76), Elders Group (1/25/78); found in <**x̲éywétes.**>, //x̣í=íwə́l=əT-əs//, /'*He advises him to not to do something., He advises him to change., He advises him to do something.*'/, attested by EB.

<**x̲éyx̲ewet**>, cts //x̣í[-C$_1$ə-]=íw(əl)=əT//, LANG /'*advising s-o not to do something, advising him to change*'/, SOC, (<**-R1-**> *continuative*), phonology: reduplication, syntactic analysis: transitive verb, attested by EB (12/19/75, 3/8/76).

<**x̲eywésem** or **x̲éywésem**>, mdls //x̣í=íwə́(l)=əs=əm or x̣í=əw(əl)=ə[=´=]s=əm//, EFAM /'*to scowl, make a bad face or a scowl*'/, ABFC, SOC, literally /'against/shame in the mind on one's face'/, lx <**=es**> *on the face*, possibly <**=´=**> *derivational*, phonology: possible stress-shift, syllable-loss, syntactic analysis: intransitive verb, attested by Elders Group (5/3/78).

<**sx̲éyx̲ewes**>, stvi //s=x̣í[-C$_1$ə-]=əw(əl)=əs or s=x̣í[=C$_1$ə=]=əw(əl)=əs//, EFAM /'*(be) scowling (if mad or ate something sour), ((made a) funny (strange) face [Elders Group 1/21/76])*'/, ABFC, SOC, (<**s=**> *stative*), possibly <**-R1-**> *continuative*, possibly <**=R1=**> *resultative*, phonology: reduplication, syllable-loss, syntactic analysis: adjective/adjectival verb, attested by Elders Group (5/3/78), also /'*(made a) funny face (strange)*'/, attested by Elders Group (1/21/76).

<**x̲iwésem** or **x̲íwésem**> ~ <**x̲eywésem** or **x̲éywésem**>, EFAM /'*to scowl, make a bad face or a scowl*'/, *see* **x̲**íwel.

<**x̲íwét**> ~ <**x̲éywét**>, LANG /'*advise s-o not to do something bad, (advise s-o against s-th), advise s-o to change, stop s-o from doing something*'/, *see* **x̲í**wel.

<**x̲íx̲à:m ~ x̲éyx̲à:m**>, ABFC /'*sobbing, crying a little, (to sob [EB])*'/, *see* **x̲**à:m ~ **x̲**á:m.

<**x̲íx̲e** ~ **x̲éyx̲e**>, rsls //x̣í=C$_1$ə//, EFAM ['*ashamed*'], (<**=R1**> *resultative*), phonology: reduplication, syntactic analysis: adjective/adjectival verb, attested by Elders Group (3/1/72, 1/25/78), Salish

cognate: Lushootseed /x̣íx̣i/ *shame* and /ʔəs-x̣íx̣i/ *be ashamed* H76:605-606, Saanich dial. of NSt /x̣íx̣əxə/ *to be ashamed* B74a:54, perhaps root in Squamish /x̣íc'-i/ *bring shame upon oneself (e.g. so that one has to blush)* and perhaps metathesized root /ʔíx̣/ *shame* in /s-ʔíx̣-i/ *shame* W73:228, K67:305, 399, K69:85, example: <**tsel me x̲éyx̲e.**>, //c-əl mə x̣í=C_1ə//, /'*I am ashamed., I am getting ashamed.*'/, attested by Elders Group (3/1/72).

<**x̲ex̲éyx̲e**>, cts //C_1ə-x̣í=C_1ə//, EFAM ['*being ashamed*'], (<**R5-**> *continuative*), (<**=R1**> *resultative*), phonology: double reduplication, grammatical comment: continuative resultatives are quite rare, syntactic analysis: adjective/adjectival verb, attested by Elders Group (1/25/78).

<**x̲éyx̲elexw**>, ncs //x̣í=C_1ə=l-əx^{w}//, EFAM /'*(accidentally) make s-o ashamed, insult s-o (accidentally or manage to)*'/, (<**=l**> *non-control transitivizer*), (<**-exw**> *third person object*), phonology: reduplication, syntactic analysis: transitive verb, attested by EB (12/16/75), Elders Group (6/7/78); found in <**xeyx̲elóxes.**>, //x̣í=C_1ə=l-áx^{y}-əs//, /'*He (accidentally) made me ashamed.*'/, attested by Elders Group, example: <**tsel x̲éyx̲elexw tel siyá:ye.**>, //c-əl x̣í=C_1ə=l-əx^{w} t-əl s=yɛ·yə//, /'*I insulted my friend.*'/, attested by EB.

<**x̲éyx̲elòmèt**>, ncrs //x̣í=C_1ə=l-àmə̀t//, EFAM /'*to shame oneself [accidentally], (get) embarrassed, (become ashamed of oneself?)*'/, (<**-òmèt**> *reflexive*), phonology: reduplication, syntactic analysis: intransitive verb, attested by Elders Group (10/6/76, 3/1/72).

<**x̲éyx̲ethet**>, pcrs //x̣í=C_1ə=T-ət//, EFAM ['*shame oneself (purposely)*'], (<**=t**> *purposeful control transitivizer*) + (<**-et**> *reflexive*), or instead possibly <**=thet**> *get, become*, phonology: reduplication, syntactic analysis: intransitive verb, attested by Elders Group (3/1/72), example: <**tsel x̲éyx̲ethet.**>, //c-əl x̣í=C_1ə=T-ət//, /'*I shamed myself.*'/, attested by Elders Group.

<**x̲éyx̲estexw**>, caus //x̣í=C_1ə=sT-əx^{w}//, EFAM ['*make s-o ashamed*'], (<**=st**> *causative control transitivizer*), (<**-exw**> *third person object*), phonology: reduplication, syntactic analysis: transitive verb, attested by EB (12/16/75), Elders Group (6/7/78); found in <**x̲eyx̲esthóxes.**>, //x̣í=C_1ə=sT-áx^{y}-əs//, /'*He made me ashamed.*'/, attested by Elders Group, example: <**tsel x̲éyx̲estexw.**>, //c-əl x̣í=C_1ə=sT-əx^{w}//, /'*I made him ashamed.*'/, attested by EB; found in <**x̲éyx̲esthò:m.**>, //x̣í=C_1ə=sT-à·m//, /'*S-o made you ashamed.*'/, attested by EB (12/16/75).

<**x̲íx̲ekw'els**> ~ <**x̲éyx̲ekw'els**>, ABFC /'*chewing (something hard, like apple)*'/, *see* **x̲**íkw'et.

<**x̲íx̲ekw'et**> ~ <**x̲éyx̲ekw'et**>, ABFC ['*be chewing s-th hard*'], *see* **x̲**íkw'et.

<**x̲íx̲elexw**> ~ <**x̲éyx̲elexw**>, EFAM /'*(accidentally) make s-o ashamed, insult s-o (accidentally or manage to)*'/, *see* **x̲íx̲**e.

<**x̲íx̲elex̲**> ~ <**x̲éyx̲elex̲**>, SOC /'*war, (warring), fighting a war*'/, *see* **x̲**ilé**x̲**.

<**x̲íx̲elòmèt**> ~ <**x̲éyx̲elòmèt**>, EFAM /'*to shame oneself [accidentally], (get) embarrassed, (become ashamed of oneself?)*'/, *see* **x̲íx̲**e.

<**x̲íx̲emels**> ~ <**x̲éyx̲emels**>, EB ['*burdock*'], *see* **x̲**ím.

<**x̲íx̲emels ch'ech'éqw'**> ~ <**x̲éyx̲emels ch'ech'éqw'**>, EB ['*burdock*'], *see* **x̲**ím.

<**x̲ix̲emx̲íméls**>, EZ ['*little hawk*'], *see* **x̲í**m.

<**x̲íx̲ep'els**> ~ <**x̲éyx̲ep'els**>, ABFC /'*scratch, (scratching as a structured activity)*'/, *see* **x̲**íp'.

<**x̲íx̲ep'ílep**> ~ <**x̲éyx̲ep'ílep**>, HARV /'*a rake, a harrow*'/, *see* **x̲**íp'.

<**x̲íx̲eq'els**> ~ <**x̲éyx̲eq'els**>, ABFC ['*scratching*'], *see* **x̲**íq'.

<**x̲ix̲eq'qéylem**> ~ <**x̲eyx̲eq'qéylem**>, ABFC ['*scratching one's head*'], *see* **x̲**íq'.

<**x̲íx̲esel**> ~ <**x̲éyx̲esel**>, EFAM /'*getting spooked, being afraid that bad spirits are around, spooky feeling*'/, *see* x̲ísel.

<**x̲íx̲esem**> ~ <**x̲éyx̲esem**>, EFAM ['*creepy*'], *see* x̲ísel.

<**x̲íx̲estexw**> ~ <**x̲éyx̲estexw**>, EFAM ['*make s-o ashamed*'], *see* x̲íx̲e.

<**x̲íx̲etem**> ~ <**x̲éyx̲etem**>, LANG ['*growling (with words)*'], *see* x̲ítem.

<**x̲íx̲etet**> ~ <**x̲eyx̲etet**>, LANG ['*snapping at s-o (verbally or in arguing)*'], *see* x̲ítem.

<**x̲íx̲ethet**> ~ <**x̲éyx̲ethet**>, EFAM ['*shame oneself (purposely)*'], *see* x̲íx̲e.

<**x̲íx̲eth'em**>, ABDF ['*itchy*'], *see* x̲íth' ~ x̲éyth'.

<**x̲ix̲ets'émthet**> ~ <**x̲eyx̲ets'émthet**>, ABDF ['*(get) real itching*'], *see* x̲íth' ~ x̲éyth'.

<**x̲íx̲ewet**> ~ <**x̲éyx̲ewet**>, LANG /'*advising s-o not to do something, advising him to change*'/, *see* x̲íwel.

<**x̲iyx̲éyt** or **x̲eyx̲éyt**>, IDOC /'*transform it more, pass it over the fire more (at a burning)*'/, *see* x̲ít.

<**x̲lhá:léqel ~ x̲elháléqel**>, ABDF ['*(have a) headache*'], *see* x̲élh.

<**x̲lhélets**>, ABDF ['*tired on the rump*'], *see* x̲élh.

<**x̲lhém**>, ABDF ['*to be tired*'], *see* x̲élh.

<**x̲lhém:et**>, EFAM /'*tired of s-th, bored with s-th*'/, *see* x̲élh.

<**x̲lhét**>, SOC ['*beat s-o up*'], *see* x̲élh.

<**x̲ólem**>, izs //x̣ál=əm//, LT /'*gray (of hair), grey (of hair)*'/, possibly root <**x̲ál ~ x̲él ~ x̲íl (x̲éyl)**> *mark, paint, write*, possibly <**ó-ablaut**> *resultative or durative*, probably <**=em**> *intransitivizer, have, get*, syntactic analysis: adjective/adjectival verb, attested by AC (8/4/70).

<**sx̲ó:lem**>, strs //s=x̣á·l=əm//, LT /'*(be) real gray (of hair), (grey hair)*'/, <**s=**> *stative*, or possibly <**s=**> *nominalizer*, possibly <**=:=**> *augmentative* or *resultative*, syntactic analysis: adjective/adjectival verb or nominal, attested by AC (10/6/71), Salish cognate: MCx /x̣ʷúwəm/ *grey hair* B75prelim.:28, Sechelt /sx̣ʷúlum/ *grey hair* T77:14, Squamish /s-x̣ʷúyum/ *grey hair* W73:124, K69:86, Saanich dial. of NSt /s-x̣áləm-əs/ *grey hair* B74a:22, Samish dial. of NSt /s-x̣áləm-əs/ *grey hair* G86:75.

<**x̲olémthet**>, incs //x̣al=ə[-´-]m=θət//, cts, ABDF ['*turning gray (in hair)*'], (<**-´-**> *continuative*), (<**=thet**> *get, become*), phonology: stress-shift, syntactic analysis: intransitive verb, attested by AC (8/4/70, 8/29/70), example: <**lulh x̲olémthet.**>, //lə-uɬ x̣al=ə[-´-]m=θət//, /'*He's turning gray (his hair).*'/, literally /'he already is turning gray'/, attested by AC (8/4/70).

<**x̲ó:lemthet**>, rsls //x̣á[=·=]l=əm=θət//, ABDF ['*really turned gray (of hair)*'], (<**=:=**> *resultative*), (<**=thet**> *get, become*), phonology: lengthening, syntactic analysis: intransitive verb, attested by AC (10/6/71).

<**x̲olémthet**>, ABDF ['*turning gray (in hair)*'], *see* x̲ólem.

<**x̲ó:lemthet**>, ABDF ['*really turned gray (of hair)*'], *see* x̲ólem.

<**x̲ó:letsa**>, WATR ['*many lakes*'], *see* x̲ó:tsa ~ x̲ó:cha.

<**X̲ó:letsa Smá:lt**>, PLN ['*mountain right back of Yale town reserve with two big lakes and many small ones*'], *see* x̲ó:tsa ~ x̲ó:cha.

<**x̲ólqesà:ls**>, ABFC ['*waving (one's arms)*'], *see* x̲élqes.

<**x̲ólhchem**>, ABFC /*'swimming (of dog, deer, animal), (dog-paddling)'*/, *see* x̲élhchem.

<**x̲ó:qel ~ x̲óqel**>, df //x̣á=əqəl//, EZ ['*marten*'], ['*Martes americana caurina*'], Elder's comment: "has yellowish fur, more-so than mink", ASM ['it has a dark [deep-colored] chest because it and Weasel and maybe Squirrel all got burnt in a story [prob. involving the Transformer] (Elders Group 3/21/79), the marten is said to live up high in the mountains, to eat squirrels, climb trees, and steal food'], root meaning unknown unless *yellow/orange* or *dark [deep-colored]*, lx <**=eqel**> *on the throat*, (semological comment: so named probably due to the yellow or orange patch on its throat and breast, the color is especially deep orange and extensive in this subspecies from the coast (Cowan and Guiget 1965), the body fur is a richer brown inclining toward cinnamon in color), phonology: probable vowel merger, syntactic analysis: nominal, attested by AK (11/21/72), ME (11/21/72 tape), Elders Group (2/11/76, 9/1/76, 3/21/79), other sources: JH /x̣á·qəl/ *marten*, ES /x̣á·qəl ~ sq'ɛ̂·ƛ̓'/ (CwMs /x̣áʔqən/) *otter* (but I have /sq'ɛ̂·ƛ̓'/ only for *otter*), Salish cognate: Squamish /x̣^{w}úʔqin/ *marten* W73:174, K69:86.

<**x̲otl'thet**>, WETH ['*be windy*'], *see* x̲átl'.

<**x̲ó:tsa ~ x̲ó:cha**>, free root //x̣á·cɛ//, WATR ['*lake*'], syntactic analysis: noun, nominal, attested by AC (8/14/70, 10/13/71), BJ (5/10/64, 12/5/64), EB, other sources: ES /x̣ácə̀/ (Cw /x̣ácɛʔ/, Ms /x̣ácaʔ/) *lake*, Salish cognate: PCS /*x̣áčuʔ/ *lake* cognate set #79 in G82 includes: Squamish and Lushootseed /x̣áčuʔ/ *lake* [W73:156, K67:368, H76:577], Nooksack /x̣ǽčò/ *lake* Amoss 1961, SanSg /x̣áčə/, Sg (Suttles 1965) /x̣áčaʔ/, Sooke /x̣áčəʔ/ E69, all *lake*, historical/comparative detail: note that Halkomelem has metathesized the vowels in this word and Upriver Halkomelem has also included its reflex (length) of the final glottal stop in the metathesis (its length is now medial), example: <**lám kw'e sle'óthels te x̲ó:tsa.**>, //lɛ́=m k'^{w}ə s=l=əʔɛ=áθəl-s tə x̣á·cɛ//, /*'He went across the lake.'*/, attested by EB.

<**x̲óx̲tsa ~ x̲óx̲cha**>, dmn //x̣á[=C_1ə=]cɛ//, WATR /*'small lake, pond'*/, (<**=R1=**> *diminutive*), phonology: reduplication, length-loss before reduplication, syntactic analysis: noun, nominal, attested by Elders Group (5/28/75), AC (10/23/71), JL (4/7/78 History Dept. tape 34), example: <**esésu x̲óx̲cha the'ít tethá lí te chóleqwmels.**>, //ʔə-s-əs-u x̣á[=C_1ə=]cɛ θəʔít tə=θɛ́ li tə cáləq^{w}=məls//, /*'It's really a (little) lake there on the side away from the river'*/, attested by JL.

<**x̲elóx̲cha**>, dmpn //x̣[=əl=]á[=C_1ə=]cɛ//, WATR ['*little lakes*'], (<**=el=**> *plural*), phonology: infixed plural, reduplication, length-loss before reduplication, syntactic analysis: noun, nominal, attested by JL (4/7/78).

<**x̲ó:letsa**>, pln //x̣á·[=lə=]cɛ//, WATR ['*many lakes*'], (<**=le=**> *plural*), phonology: infixed plural, syntactic analysis: noun, nominal, attested by IHTTC (7/8/77), SP and AK (Fish Camp 8/2/77), Elders Group (9/13/77).

<**X̲ó:letsa Smá:lt**>, cpds //x̣ǽ·[=lə=]cɛ s=mɛ́·lt//, PLN ['*mountain right back of Yale town reserve with two big lakes and many small ones*'], ASM ['it is on the C.P.R. side, Frozen Lake is one of several lakes on that mountain'], literally /'many lakes mountain'/, phonology: infixed plural, syntactic analysis: nominal phrase with modifier(s), attested by IHTTC (7/8/77), SP and AK (Fish Camp 8/2/77), Elders Group (9/13/77), source: place names reference file #34.

<**Sx̲óchaqel**>, ds //s=x̣ácɛ=qəl//, PLN ['*Chilliwack Lake*'], literally /'lake at the head (of the river) (BJ, Elders Group 8/24/77)'/, (<**s=**> *nominalizer, something that*), root <**x̲ócha**> *lake*, lx <**=qel**> *on the head, at the head of a river*, syntactic analysis: nominal, attested by BJ, CT (1973), Elders Group (5/28/75, 8/24/77), other sources: Wells 1965 (lst ed.), Wells 1966, source: place names reference file #165 and #226.

<**x̱ots'oyíqw**>, df //x̣ac'ay=íqʷ//, FOOD [*'barbecued fish head'*], FSH, root meaning unknown (not likely <**x̱íth'**> ~ <**x̱éyth'**> *unripe, raw, uncooked* or <**x̱íth'**> ~ <**x̱éyth'**> *itch),* (possibly <**x̱áth' ~ x̱e'áth'**>, *measure, mark a measurement* or root in <**x̱áts'et**> *fireweed* whose bark/covering is peeled and the shoots then eaten raw), possibly lx <**=á:y ~ =ey ~ =iy**> *bark, wood, plant, covering (*whose <a> may have gone to <o> before suffixes pertaining to the face or head [thus perhaps the root vowel as well] or may just be the <ey> allomorph), this may make sense since the barbecued skin of the fish head is and eaten when crispy , lx <**=íqw**> *on the top of the head*, phonology: possible <**ts'-th'**> etymological variation as attested elsewhere, syntactic analysis: nominal, attested by MH (Deming 1/4/79).

<**x̱ots'oyíqw slhóp**>, cpds //x̣ac'ay=íqʷ s=ɬáp//, FOOD [*'fish head soup'*], phonology: some speakers use slhóp' for *soup, stew*, syntactic analysis: nominal phrase with modifier(s), attested by MH (Deming 1/4/79).

<**x̱óx̱tsa ~ x̱óx̱cha**>, WATR /*'small lake, pond'*/, *see* x̱ó:tsa ~ x̱ó:cha.

<**x̱óyes ~ q'óyes**>, bound root or stem //x̣áyəs ~ q'áyəs//, meaning unknown

<**sx̱óyeseqw ~ sq'óyeseqw**>, df //s=x̣áyəs=əqʷ ~ s=q'áyəs=əqʷ//, CLO [*'soft feathers put in oiled hair for dancing'*], probably <**s=**> *nominalizer*, possibly stem or root in <**s=x̱óyes**> ~ <**sx̱éyes ~ sx̱éy:es**> *'head (of any living thing)*, secont allomorph possibly root <**q'óyes**> meaning unknown, lx <**=eqw**> *on the hair*, syntactic analysis: nominal, attested by Elders Group (2/5/75).

<**x̱óytl' ~ x̱ó:ytl'**>, bound root or stem //x̣á(·)yƛ'//, meaning unknown unless related to <**x̱átl'**> *rough, turbulent (of wind/water)*, prob. same root as in <**x̱itl'áls ~ x̱itl'á:ls**> ~ <**x̱eytl'áls ~ x̱eytl'á:ls**>, df //x̣ɛ[=y=]ƛ'=ɛ́·ls//, sas, EZ [*'grizzly bear'*], [*'Ursus arctos horribilis'*].

<**sx̱óytl'thet ~ sx̱ó:ytl'thet**>, stvi //s=x̣á(·)yƛ'=T-ət or s=x̣á(·)yƛ'=θət or s=x̣ɛ[=Aá=y=]ƛ'=T-ət or s=x̣ɛ[=Aá=y=]ƛ'=θət//, EFAM /*'(be) aggressive, cranky, ready to fight, (be) violent, hot-headed'*/, Elder's comment: "this is also what they call grizzly bears", (<**s=**> *stative*), probably root <**x̱átl'**> *rough, turbulent (of wind/water)*, possibly <**=y=**> meaning unknown, comment: =y= is not attested elsewhere and may be epenthetic, possibly <**=t**> *purposeful control transitivizer*, possibly <**-et**> *reflexive*, possibly <**=thet**> *get, become*, phonology: probable ablaut (a → o automatic before =thet), possible epenthetic y, syntactic analysis: adjective/adjectival verb, attested by EB (10/19/77, 12/19/75), Elders Group (3/1/72, 3/23/77).

<**x̱pá:yelhp ~ x̱páyelhp**>, EB [*'western red cedar tree'*], *see* sx̱íp.

<**x̱pá:ytses ~ x̱páytses**>, EB /*'(red) cedar limb, (red) cedar bough'*/, *see* sx̱íp.

<**x̱pó:ys**>, BSK /*'wide cedar (sapling) strips or slats from young cedar trunks, cedar slat work (basketry)'*/, *see* sx̱íp.

<**x̱tá:stexw**>, TIB /*'do it, do s-th'*/, *see* x̱ét'e.

<**x̱tá: ~ x̱tá**>, TIB /*'do, do this'*/, *see* x̱ét'e.

<**x̱t'**>,or <**x̱ét'**> bound root//x̣t'// or //x̣ə́t'// *evil spell* or more likely merely root <**x̱ét'e**> //x̣ə́t'ə or x̣ə́tʔ(ə) or x̣ə́təʔ-M1//, cts, LANG /*'be saying, say, said'*/, since a spell is *said,* see also under <**x̱ét'e**>

<**x̱t'ét**>, pcs //x̣ə́t'=M1=T//, IDOC /*'cast a spell on s-o, put a spell on s-o, shoot power into s-o'*/, ASM ['such power is shot invisibly by Indian doctors and can only be removed usually by another Indian doctor, when it is removed it is sometimes found to be a piece of bone, sometimes it is an invisible spirit that is cast out by the curing Indian doctor/shaman'], (<**metathesis type 1**> *non-continuative*), (<**=t**> *purposeful control transitivizer*), phonology: metathesis, syntactic analysis: transitive verb, attested by Elders Group (2/25/76), other sources: ES ChMsCw /x̣t'ə́t/ *shoot power (into victim),*

Salish cognate: Squamish root /xət'/ *evil charm* as in /xt'-ə́t/ *put an evil spell on s-o (tr.)* and /ʔəs-xə́t'-xət'/ *bewitched* K69:84.

<**x̱t'áls** or **x̱t'á:ls**>, sas //xə́t'=M1=Ɛ́(·)ls//, IDOC /'*cast a spell, throw a spell, put on a spell, shoot power*'/, (<**metathesis type 1**> *non-continuative*), (<**=á:ls ~ =áls**> *structured activity non-continuative*), phonology: metathesis, syntactic analysis: intransitive verb, attested by Elders Group (2/25/76), Salish cognate: Samish dial. of NSt (LD) /xt'=ələʔ/ *shoot power into s-o (done by an Indian doctor)* with /=ələʔ/ *structured activity non-continuative* G86:81.

<**x̱t'áls** or **x̱t'á:ls**>, IDOC /'*cast a spell, throw a spell, put on a spell, shoot power*'/, *see* **x̱**ét'.

<**x̱t'ét**>, IDOC /'*cast a spell on s-o, put a spell on s-o, shoot power into s-o*'/, *see* **x̱**ét'.

<**x̱thémés**>, PLAY ['*betting money*'], *see* **x̱**éth.

<**x̱thét**>, ABFC ['*shove s-th*'], *see* **x̱**éth.

X̲W

<**=x̲w**>, da //=x̣ʷ//, SH /'*round, around*'/, syntactic analysis: lexical suffix; found in <**qw'emétx̲w**>, //q'ʷəm(=)ə́t=x̣ʷ//, /'*water lily, door knob*'/, <**tl'emx̲wx̲í:lem**>, //ƛ'əm=x̣ʷ=x̣=í·l=əm//, /'*hail*'/, <**qweméx̲weth'**>, //qʷə́m=M1=x̣ʷ=əθ'//, /'*lumpy clay*'/, <**qw'émx̲wtses**>, //q'ʷə́m=x̣ʷ=cəs//, /'*wrist*'/, <**melmólx̲w**>, //C_1əC_2=mál=x̣ʷ//, /'*greasy; mixed up*'/, <**qwí(y)x̲w**>, //qʷə́y=x̣ʷ//, /'*miss a shot*'/, literally /'move around'/, <**spá:lx̲w ~ spá:lxw**>, //s=pi[=Aɛ́·=]l=x̣ʷ//, /'*underground food, edible corms/tubers/bulbs, camas*'/, <**mélhx̲wel**>, //mə́ɬ=x̣ʷ=əl//, /'*Indian plum, June plum*'/, <**th'ó:yx̲wem**>, //θ'á·y=x̣ʷ=əm//, /'*(get) nervous, (get) excited*'/, <**yélx̲w**>, //yə́l=x̣ʷ//, /'*smooth (of boulder for ex.)*'/, <**yó:lx̲wtem**>, //yə[=Aá·=]l=x̣ʷ=təm//, /'*delirious*'/, literally /'be in a state of turning over around in circles'/.

<**x̲wálá:lhp ~ x̲wá:lá:lhp**>, EB /'*willow (includes especially short-leaf willow or Sitka willow,* also *long-leaf willow or Pacific willow,* and *red willow bush)*'/, *see* **x̲**wále ~ **x̲**wá:le.

<**x̲wále ~ x̲wá:le**>, bound root //x̣ʷɛ́lə ~x̣ʷɛ́·lə perhaps *willow*//.

<**x̲wálá:lhp ~ x̲wá:lá:lhp**>, df //x̣ʷɛ́(·)lə=ɛ́ɬp//, EB /'*willow (includes especially short-leaf willow or Sitka willow,* also *long-leaf willow or Pacific willow,* and *red willow bush)*'/, ['especially *Salix sitchensis*, also *Salix lasiandra*, and possibly other *Salix species*'], MED ['good medicine for sores, make tea from the inner bark to gargle with for mouth sores, also scald last year's leaves and use on open sore (EB)'], root meaning unknown unless *willow* or unless *reef net* as in the Samish cognate, lx <**=álhp ~ =elhp**> *tree, plant*, phonology: vowel merger, syntactic analysis: nominal, attested by AC (11/19/71, 11/26/71), BJ (12/5/64 new transcript old p.300), EL (Chehalis trip 9/27/77), SJ (Deming 9/21/78), EB, JL (Fish Camp 7/19/79), other sources: ES /x̣ʷɛlɛ́·ɬp/ (CwMs /x̣ʷɛ́lɛʔɛɬp/) *willow*, JH /x̣ʷalé·ɬp/ *willow tree*, H-T <Qa'ilalp> (macron over first a) *willow*, Salish cognate: Squamish /x̣ʷáy-ʔay/ *willow* K69:86 and *Sitka willow (Salix sitchensis),* and probably *other willows (such as S. hookeriana and S. scouleriana)* Bouchard and Turner 1976:122, Lushootseed /s-x̣ʷáluʔ(əč) ~x̣ʷəx̣ʷálu(ač)/ *willow (tree)* H76:608, Samish dial. of NSt /s-x̣ʷəlé-eɬč ~ s-x̣ʷəlí-ʔiɬč/ *willow ("reef net plant") from /s-x̣ʷáləʔ/ reef-net* G86:85, Saanich dial. of NSt /sx̣ʷəlíʔiɬč/ *willow* B74a:15, Mainland Comox /sə́x̣ʷay/ *willow, red willow* B75prelim.:19, contrast <**xéltsepelhp**> *long-leaf willow, Pacific willow (Salix lasiandra),* attested by EL, also /'*white willow*'/, attested by SJ, example: <**x̲wá:lá:lhp theqát**>, //x̣ʷɛ́·lə=ɛ́ɬp θəqɛ́t//, /'*willow tree*'/, attested by AC (11/26/71), <**x̲wíx̲wel x̲wá:lá:lhp**>, //C_1í=x̣ʷəl (orx̣ʷí[=C_1ə=]l)x̣ʷɛ́·lə=ɛ́ɬp//, /'*willow bush*'/, attested by AC (11/26/71), <**ts'ats'í:ts'etl' stsó:lha x̲wá:lá:lhp**>, //C_1ɛ=c'í[=·=C_1ə=]ƛ' s=cá·ɬɛx̣ʷɛ́·lə=ɛ́ɬp//, EB /'*short leaf willow, (Sitka willow)*'/, ['*Salix sitchensis*'], attested by AC (11/26/71), <**tl'áqt stsó:lha x̲wá:lá:lhp**>, //ƛ'ɛ́qt s=cá·ɬɛx̣ʷɛ́·lə=ɛ́ɬp//, EB /'*long leaf willow, (Pacific willow)*'/, ['*Salix lasiandra*'], attested by AC (11/26/71).

<**x̲wóx̲welá:lhp**>, dmn //x̣ʷɛ[=AáC₁ə=]lə=ɛ́ɬp//, EB /'*a small willow tree, a low willow*'/, (<**ó-ablaut** and **=R1=**> *diminutive, small*), phonology: ablaut, reduplication, syntactic analysis: nominal, attested by BJ (12/5/64 Wells tapes new transcript old p.300).

<**X̲wóx̲welá:lhp**>, ds //x̣ʷɛ[=AáC₁ə=]lə=ɛ́ɬp//, PLN ['*a village by Yale along Yale Creek*'], ASM ['an area on the upriver [of the Fraser R., i.e. north] side of Yale Creek where there were lots of willows and a settlement till washed out by the high flood of 1897'], literally /'a small willow tree, a low willow'/, phonology: ablaut, reduplication, syntactic analysis: nominal, attested by BJ (12/5/64 Wells tapes new transcript old p.300), IHTTC (7/8/77 MP via AD and SP in writing

and verbally), Elders Group (7/6/77, 9/13/77 and AK and SP and AD on Raft trip), other sources: Wells 1965 (lst ed.):25, source: place names reference file #4.

<**Xwolích ~ Xwelích**>, ds //x̣ʷalə=íc orx̣ʷɛ[=Aa=]lə=íc ~ x̣ʷɛ(=Aə=)lə=íc//, PLN /'*place at Ruby Creek where Paul Webster lived some years ago, now Wahleach Island Indian Reserve #2 and area at mouth of Mahood Creek*'/, ASM ['across the Fraser River from O'hamil, across from shingle mill, at log house at end of road to river turn right'], Elder's comment: "name means lots of willows there", literally /'willow on the back'/, lx <**=ich**> *on the back*, phonology: vowel merger, possible ablaut, syntactic analysis: nominal, attested by IHTTC (8/31/77, 8/15/77), AK/SP/AD (Raft trip 8/30/77), Elders on place names trip to Seabird Island (EB, JL, AD, others) (4/3/78), Elders Group (7/13/77 on this day at least the following attended and gave some place names: LJ, SP, AG, DF), source: place names reference file #65a and #65.

<**Wolích**>, ds //xʷ[w]alíc//, PLN /'*Wahleach whistle stop on Seabird Island where Wayne Bobb lived in 1977, (*now also *Wahleach Lake (man-made)* [EB])'/, ASM ['named after Xwolích (may not be an old name)'], phonology: irregular change of xw to w, syntactic analysis: nominal, attested by LJ (IHTTC 8/15/77), source: place names reference file #195, also /'*Wahleach Lake*'/, ASM ['the lake is an articifial one, recently dammed, the name probably refers to the creek [if Indians had any hand in choosing it]'], attested by EB (12/8/75).

<**xwástel**>, ds //x̣ʷɛ́s=təl orx̣ʷə[=Aɛ́=]s=təl//, PE /'*solid grease, suet, lump of grease, (stomach fat [CT])*'/, ASM ['cooked in a ball so it wouldn't crumble, could be carried in one's purse or bag, used like face cream to clean face, mixed with paint for spirit dancing face paint, etc.'], HUNT, FOOD /'*lard, shortening*'/, bound root <**xwás** or **xwés**> *produce grease, produce animal fat*, probably <**á-ablaut**> *derivational*, lx <**=tel**> *device to, something (to)*, syntactic analysis: nominal, attested by Elders Group (3/16/77), MH (Deming 1/4/79), contrast <**slós**> *fat*, comment: MH reports <**slós**> is also *lard, shortening*, Salish cognate: Squamish /x̣ʷə́s/ *be fat* and /x̣ʷás-tn/ *hardened grease, fat* beside /x̣ʷəs-íʔ/ *get fat* W73:97, 123, K67:371, K69:86, Lushootseed /x̣ʷə́s/ *fat* beside /s-x̣ʷə́s/ *grease* and /ʔu-x̣ʷəs-il-d/ *fatten s-o/s-th up* H76:613-614, Sechelt /s-x̣ʷə́s/ *grease, fat* T77:14, also /'*stomach fat*'/, attested by CT (6/8/76), example: <**xwástels te (spá:th, áshxw, tl'elqtéle, p'q'élqel, músmes)**>, //x̣ʷə[=Aɛ́=]s=təl-s tə (s=pɛ́·θ, ʔɛ́sxʷ, ƛ'ɛ[=lə=]qt=ələ, p'əq'=ə́lqəl, mús=C_1əC_2)//, /'*solid (bear, seal, deer, mountain goat, beef/cow) grease*'/, literally /'solid grease -its/-of the (bear, etc.)'/, usage: in careful speech, attested by Elders Group (3/16/77), also <**(spá:th, áshxw, tl'elqtéle, p'q'élqel, músmes) xwástel**>, //(s=pɛ́·θ, ʔɛ́sxʷ,ƛ'ɛ[=lə=]qt=ə́lɛ, p'əq'=ə́lqəl, mús=C_1əC_2) x̣ʷə[=Aɛ́=]s=təl//, usage: rapid speech, not as good as the forms preceding such as xwástels te spá:th, syntactic comment: this may point out that such nominal(as adjective) nominal phrases in general are tolerated in fast speech but not preferred in careful speech, attested by Elders Group (3/16/77).

<**xwà:y ~ xwá:y**>, free root //x̣ʷɛ̀·y ~x̣ʷɛ́·y//, ABDF /'*perish together, many die (in famine, sickness, fire), all die, get wiped out*'/, syntactic analysis: intransitive verb, attested by EB (1/26/76), SP (8/28/75), Salish cognate: PCS cognate set 29a in Galloway 1982:12 includes: Squamish /x̣ʷáy/ *perish, faint, become senseless, become paralyzed* W73:196, K67:370, Nooksack /x̣ʷǽy/ *die*, Sechelt /x̣ʷáy(ʔ)/ *already dead* and /x̣ʷáyat/ *kill them (two) on purpose*, Mainland Comox /x̣ʷáy/ *everybody's dead, several perish*, Sooke dial. of NSt /x̣ʷə́y/ *they are dead* and /x̣ʷéč-t/ *wipe them out* and /x̣ʷčé-t-ŋ/ *they were slaughtered, killed off*, beside Squamish /x̣ʷáy-at/ *slaughter, wipe out (tr.)* K69:86.

<**xwó:y**>, df //x̣ʷɛ[=Aá]·y//, ABDF ['*they all died*'], possibly <**ó-ablaut of root a**> *resultative*, phonology: possible ablaut, syntactic analysis: intransitive verb, attested by SP (8/28/75), example: <**le xwó:y. ~ le xwá:y.**>, //lə x̣ʷɛ[=Aá=]·y ~ ləx̣ʷɛ́·y//, /'*They all died.*'/, attested by SP.

<**Sxwoyehá:lá**>, df //s=x̣ʷɛ[=Aa=]y=ə=(h)ɛ́·lɛ́//, PLN ['*Squia-ala (now Chilliwack Indian Reserve #7)*'], ASM ['at the junction of old Chilliwack River and Koquapilt Slough, so named because

many were killed together by canoe raiders and they were buried in a pit (Elders Group 7/20/77), Squia-a-ala is the (D.I.A.) spelling used for the present reserve name'], literally perhaps /'something that's a container of people who all died together'/, (<**s=**> *nominalizer, something to*), possibly <**=e**> *entity, being*, lx <**=á:lá ~ =há:lá ~ =à(:)là**> *container of*, phonology: possible ablaut, epenthetic h, syntactic analysis: nominal, attested by Elders Group (7/20/77, 1/15/75), source: place names reference file #82, other sources: Wells 1965 (lst ed.):19, also <**Sx̱wá:yehà:là**>, //s=x̣ʷɛ̀·y=ə=hɛ̀·lɛ̀//, attested by CT (1973), also <**Sx̱wayehále**>, //s=x̣ʷɛ[=Aa=]y=ə=hɛ́lɛ//, attested by BJ (5/10/64 Wells tapes new transcript new p.142, 144-146).

<**Sx̱woyímelh**>, ds //s=x̣ʷɛ[=Aa=]y(=əm)=ím=əɬ//, PLN ['*New Westminster*'], literally /'nominalizer/something that many died together repeatedly in past'/, Elder's comment: "means *place where lots of people died, (or) all died*", ASM ['named from x̱wó:y *all died* because two innocent Indian men were hung there, and one, before the rope was put around his neck, told the people that because he was innocent many would die after him; soon after, a fire burned down New Westminster, killing a number of people including the judge; this happened when all the buildings, fences, and sidewalks were wooden, about 1860 or so (SP)'], (<**s=**> *nominalizer*), possibly <**=em**> *place to have/get*, (<**=ím**> *repeatedly*), (<**=elh**> *past tense*), phonology: ablaut, syntactic analysis: nominal, attested by Elders Group (7/6/77), SP (8/28/75), source: place names reference file #24, other sources: Wells 1965 (lst ed.):15.

<**Sx̱wóx̱wiymelh**>, ds //s=x̣ʷɛ[=AáC_1ə=]y=əm=əɬ//, PLN ['*village near and above [upriver from] Katz where 36 pit-houses were wiped out in an epidemic*'], ASM ['people died right in their pit-houses, only one family was saved because it took to the mountains [in winter], the place is near Evangeline Pete's place near Katz'], literally /'place where all/many died in past'/, (<**s=**> *nominalizer*), (<**ó-ablaut plus =R1=**> *resultative*), (<**=em**> *place to have/get*), (<**=elh**> *past tense*), phonology: reduplication, ablaut, vowel-loss, syntactic analysis: nominal, attested by Elders Group (7/6/77), SP (8/28/75), source: place names reference file #23, Elders at Katz Class (TG/AG/PDP/SP? 10/5/76).

<**x̱wá:yt**>, pcs //x̣ʷɛ̀·y=T//, SOC ['*kill them*'], (<**=t**> *purposeful control transitivizer*), syntactic analysis: transitive verb, attested by Deming (2/7/80).

<**x̱wōx̱wáye ~ x̱wex̱wáye ~ x̱wōx̱wá:ye**>, df //C_1ə=x̣ʷɛ́(·)y=ə//, EZ /'*blowfly, big fly, (little fly (one of them) [Elders Group 2/19/75])*'/, ['order *Diptera*, family *Calliphoridae*'], ASM ['(this is the fly that develops from maggots in carrion, the family includes the *bluebottle fly* and *greenbottle fly* with metallic irridescent coloring on their backs)'], (semological comment: may be so named (from root x̱wáy) since they would be especially numerous around those who died in a group), possibly <**R5=**> *diminutive*, possibly root <**x̱wá(:)y**> *many die*, possibly <**=e**> *living thing/entity*, phonology: reduplication, syntactic analysis: nominal, attested by Elders Group (3/1/72), EB (11/24/75), other sources: H-T <qōQai'a> *fly (Musca sarcophaga sp.)*, Salish cognate: Squamish root in /ʔáx̣ʷáyʔ/ *house-fly, black fly* W73:104, K67:392 and *housefly (family Muscidae,* prob. *Musca domestica and Musca autumnalis* Kennedy and Bouchard 1976:115, Lushootseed /x̣ʷəx̣ʷáyu/ *fly (insect)* H76:615, Sechelt /x̣ʷax̣ʷayúʔ/ *black fly* T77:9, Mainland Comox /x̣ʷáx̣ʷáyím'/ *housefly* B75prelim.:12, also /'*little fly (one of them)*'/, attested by Elders Group (2/19/75), also EZ ['*black flies*'], ['family *Simulidae*'], ASM ['(unlike blowflies and house-flies, black flies have a humpback appearance, they are abundant near water (laid on water plants or wet rocks) and females can attack in clouds and bite warm-blooded creatures)'], attested by Elders Group (7/20/77), example: <**t'ít'elem te (qwá:l, sisemó:ya, x̱wex̱wiyáye, x̱wex̱wá:ya).**>, //t'í[-C_1ə-]l=əm tə (qʷɛ̀·l, C_1í=səm=á·yɛ, C_1ə=x̣ʷɛ́y=i[=M2=]yɛ, C_1ə=x̣ʷɛ̀·y=ə)//, /'*The (mosquito, bee, smaller fly, larger fly) is buzzing.*'/,

literally /'the (mosquito, bee, smaller fly, larger fly) is singing'/, attested by AD and TG (8/22/72, 8/23/72).

<**X̱wōx̱wá:ye**>, ds //C_1ə=x̣ʷɛ́·y=ə//, PLN /'*village on east bank of Sweltzer Creek (above Sx̱woyehá:lá), (creek by the village of the same name [X̱wōx̱wá:ye] [Wells])*'/, ASM ['name of village on Soowahlie creek (Sweltzer Creek), as soon as you pass the church at Soowahlie and cross the bridge it's on the left by a round rock (BJ 12/5/64), this is above (upriver from) Sx̱woyehá:lá (Squia-ala in D.I.A. spelling for that reserve name)'], Elder's comment: "the name means black flies (Elders Group) or blow-flies (BJ)", phonology: reduplication, syntactic analysis: nominal, attested by Elders Group (7/20/77), source: place names reference file #91, other sources: Wells 1965 (lst ed.):19, also /'*creek by village of same name [X̱wōx̱wá:ye]*'/, source: Wells 1966, also <**X̱wix̱wiyáye**>, //C_1í=x̣ʷɛ́y=i[=M2=]yɛ//, attested by BJ (12/5/64).

<**x̱wiyáye**>, dmn //x̣ʷɛ́y=i[=M2=]yɛ//, EZ ['*a fly*'], ['family uncertain'], (<**=iye ~ =iya**> *diminutive*), probably <**metathesis**> *derivational*, phonology: probable metathesis, syntactic analysis: nominal, attested by Deming (3/15/79 incl. SJ, MC, MV, LG).

<**x̱wex̱wiyáye ~ x̱wix̱wiyáye**>, dmn //C_1ə=x̣ʷɛ́y=i[=M2=]yɛ ~ C_1í=ʷɛ́y=i[=M2=]yɛ//, EZ ['*house-fly*'], ['family *Muscidae, Musca domestica* and prob. *Musca autumnalis*'], ASM ['a well-known spirit song of Charlie Sampson of Chilliwack Landing (Sqwá) was called the fly song; AC recalled the words as: x̱wix̱wiyáyetsel. x̱wix̱wiyáyetsel. (*I am the fly. I am the fly.) with melody: 5 5 5 3 5 5-3 3 3 2 2-3 (1=do, 2=re, 3=mi, 4=fa, 5=so major) and rhythm: 1.5 .5 1 1 2, .5-1 .5 1 1 1-1 (.5=eighth note, 1=quarter note, 1.5=dotted quarter note, 2=half note, dashes are glissandi or glides)'],* (<**R5=** or **R4=**> *diminutive*), phonology: reduplication, probable metathesis, syntactic analysis: nominal, attested by Elders Group (3/1/72), AD and TG (8/22/72, 8/23/72), Deming (3/15/79 incl. SJ, MC, MV, LG), AC (8/13/70), AC, NP (1/20/76), other sources: ES /x̣ʷəx̣ʷəyá:yɛ/ *fly*, H-T <Qōqwiáya> (macrons over both a) *fly (Musca domestica)*, also <**x̱wix̱wiyáye**>, //C_1í=ʷɛ́y=i[=M2=]yɛ//, also EZ /'*a fly, blow-fly*'/, ['order *Diptera*, family *Calliphoridae*'], attested by BJ (12/5/64), example: <**t'ít'elem te (qwá:l, sisemó:ya, x̱wex̱wiyáye, x̱wex̱wá:ya).**>, //t'í[-C_1ə-]l=əm tə (qʷɛ́·l, C_1í=səm=á·yɛ, C_1ə=x̣ʷɛ́y=i[=M2=]yɛ, C_1ə=x̣ʷɛ́·y=ə)//, /'*The (mosquito, bee, smaller fly, larger fly) is buzzing.*'/, literally /'the (mosquito, bee, smaller fly, larger fly) is singing'/, attested by AD and TG (8/22/72, 8/23/72).

<**x̱wiyx̱wiyáye**>, pln //C_1əC_2=x̣ʷɛ́y=i[=M2=]yɛ//, EZ /'*a lot of flies, big blow-flies*'/, ['order *Diptera*, family *Calliphoridae*'], (<**R3=**> *plural*), phonology: reduplication, syntactic analysis: nominal, attested by Elders Group (2/19/75), AC (9/1/71).

<**x̱wá:yt**>, SOC ['*kill them*'], *see* x̱wà:y ~ x̱wá:y.

<**x̱weló:y**>, possibly root //x̣ʷəlá·y *stagger?*//.

<**x̱wex̱weló:ystem**>, caus //x̣ʷə[-C_1ə-]lá·y=sT-əm//, cts, ABDF ['*staggering around*'], literally possibly? /'*s-o was being caused to stagger*'/, (<**-R1-**> *continuative*), possibly root <**x̱weló:y**> *stagger*, (<**=st**> *causative control transitivizer*), (<**-em**> *passive*), phonology: reduplication, syntactic analysis: transitive verb-passive, attested by Elders Group (5/26/76), contrast <**yitá:lstem**> *staggering around* under root <**tél ~ tá:l**> *repeat, respond.*

<**x̱wex̱weló:ysthòm**>, caus //x̣ʷə[=C_1ə=]lá·y=sT-à·m//, rsls, if, ABDF ['*you get staggered*'], (<**=R1=**> *resultative*), (<**=st**> *causative control transitivizer*), (<**-ò:m**> *passive second person patient/object*), phonology: reduplication, syntactic analysis: intransitive verb-passive, attested by Elders Group (5/26/76), contrast <**telsthòm**> *you get staggered* under root <**tél ~ tá:l**> *repeat, respond.*

<**x̱wélhepxel**>, ABDF ['*slipping off with a foot*'], *see* x̱wlhép.

<**x̲welhx̲wélhepxel**>, ABDF /'*slip with both feet, lose balance on both feet*'/, *see* x̲wlhép.

<**x̲wém ~ xwém**>, free root //x̣ʷə́m ~ xʷə́m//, TVMO /'*hurry, hurry up, be quick, be fast, move faster, quickly*'/, phonology: xwém is possibly mistranscribed for x̲wém, though x̲wemxálem ~ xwemxálem *run* also shows the same variation (or mistranscription), syntactic analysis: adverb/adverbial verb, attested by BJ (5/10/64 new p.123, 12/5/64), AC, EB, Elders Group (10/27/76), EB/Deming/IHTTC (fall 1977), Salish cognate: Samish and Saanich dials. of NSt /x̣ʷə́ŋ/ *fast, hurry* G86:90 and B74a:42, Squamish root /x̣ʷam ~x̣ʷəm/ *rushing current, swiftly moving water* as in /x̣ʷám ~x̣ʷə́m/ *run swiftly (ab. water)* W73:220, K67:371; found in <**x̲wémlha.**>, //x̣ʷə́m-ɬɛ//, /'*Hurry up., Run. (ordering)*'/, (<**-lha**> *ordering imperative*), attested by EB (5/5/78), <**x̲wémtlh.**>, //x̣ʷə́m=tɬ//, /'*Hurry up (coaxing).*'/, (<**-tlh**> *coaxing imperative*), attested by EB (5/5/78), <**xwémalha.**>, //xʷə́m-ɛɬɛ//, /'*Hurry up (you folks)., Run. (ordering)*'/, (<**-alha**> *ordering imperative you pl.*), attested by AC (9/7/71), example: <**xwémlha latst lhí:m kw'e alí:le.**>, //xʷə́m-ɬɛ lɛ-c-ət ɬí·m k'ʷə ʔɛlí·lə//, /'*Hurry up, let's pick salmonberries. (be picking)*'/, attested by AC (11/24/71), <**tu xwémlha.**>, //tu xʷə́m-ɬɛ//, /'*Move a little faster.*'/, attested by EB/Deming/IHTTC (fall 1977), <**kwélhtu x̲wém**>, //kʷə́ɬtux̣ʷə́m//, /'*very fast*'/, attested by EB (12/19/75), <**x̲wém kw'els kw'qwémésthòm.**>, //x̣ʷə́m k'ʷ-əl-s k'ʷəqʷ=ə́m=əsT-àm//, /'*I can knock you down fast. (you are knocked down/clubbed)*'/, attested by Elders Group (10/27/76), <**lalh áyel xwém. ~ xwém lalh áyel.**>, //lɛ-ɬ ʔɛ́y=əl xʷə́m ~ xʷə́m lɛ-ɬ ʔɛ́y=əl//, /'*Go away quickly.*'/, attested by AC (11/30/71).

<**lex̲wõ:m ~ lex̲wõm**>, df //lə(xʷ)=x̣ʷə[=Aó(·)=]m//, WATR /'*rapids, fast water, clear water, flowing fast, going fast, swift (water)*'/, (<**lexw= ~ (very rarely) le=**> *always*), (<**ó(:)-ablaut**> *derivational*), phonology: õ-ablaut rare, possible consonant merger, syntactic analysis: nominal, adjective/adjectival verb, attested by BJ (12/5/64), Elders Group (3/15/72, 3/26/75), other sources: ES /ləx̣ʷə́w·m/ (Ms /x̣ʷə́ym/, Cw /x̣ʷəwm/) *rapids, rushing current in sea or river*, example: <**lex̲wõm te qó:.**>, //lə(xʷ)=x̣ʷə[=Aó·=]m tə qá·//, /'*swift water, (The water is swift.)*'/, attested by Elders Group (3/26/75).

<**x̲wemx̲wém**>, ds //C₁əC₂=x̣ʷə́m//, TVMO /'*hurry up, faster*'/, (<**R3=**> *comparative or augmentative or plural*), phonology: reduplication, syntactic analysis: adverb/adverbial verb, attested by Elders Group (1/30/80), example: <**x̲wemx̲wém õw òl.**>, //C₁əC₂=x̣ʷə́m ʔəw ʔàl//, /'*"More faster.", even faster, (still faster)*'/, attested by Elders Group.

<**x̲wemx̲wemeléqel**>, chrs //x̣ʷəm=C₁əC₂=əl=ə́qəl//, LANG ['*talk fast*'], literally /'(go/get) characteristically fast in speech'/, (<**=R2**> *characteristic*), (<**=el**> *go, come, get, become*), lx <**=éqel**> *in the throat, in speech, language*, phonology: reduplication, comment: word originally mistranscribed as x̲wemx̲wemeléqep but =eléqep would mean *taste, smell* and must be error for =eléqel *in speech*, syntactic analysis: intransitive verb, attested by Elders Group (11/10/76).

<**x̲weméthel**>, ds //x̣ʷə́m=ə[=M2=]θəl//, FOOD /'*eat fast, eating fast, hurry to eat*'/, BPI ['*(have a) quick mouth*'], lx <**=ethel ~ =óthel**> *in the mouth*, (<**metathesis**> *continuative or derivational*), phonology: metathesis, syntactic analysis: intransitive verb, prob. adjective/adjectival verb, attested by Elders Group (3/15/72); found in <**x̲wémethellha.**>, //x̣ʷə́m'=ə[=M2=]θəl-ɬɛ//, /'*Eat fast.*'/, attested by EB/Deming/IHHTC (fall 1977), example: <**x̲wémethellh álhtel.**>, //x̣ʷə́m=ə[=M2=]θəl-tɬ ʔɛ́ɬ=təl//, /'*Hurry to come eat [a meal].*'/, attested by NP (6/4/80).

<**x̲wémetses**>, ds //x̣ʷə́m=əcəs//, TVMO /'*pick fast, (do fast with the hands)*'/, literally /'hurry/be fast in the hand'/, lx <**=tses ~ =etses**> *in the hand*, syntactic analysis: intransitive verb, attested by EB/Deming/IHTTC (fall 1977), example: <**tu x̲wémetseslha.**>, //tux̣ʷə́m=əcəs-ɬɛ//, /'*Pick fast.*'/, attested by EB/Deming/IHTTC (fall 1977).

<**xwémxel**>, ds //x̣ʷ[=F=]ə́m=xʸəl//, WETH /'*raining hard, pouring rain, (raining fast)*'/, literally /'fast

precipitation'/, possibly **<=F= (fronting)>** *derivational*, lx **<=xel>** *precipitation (rain, snow, sleet, etc.)*, phonology: possible fronting or allomorph, syntactic analysis: intransitive verb, attested by Deming, others, see under stem **<xwémxel**, example: **<xwémxel li te s'átl'q.>**, //x̣ʷ[=F=]əm=xʸəl li tə s=ʔɛ́ƛ'q//, /'*It's raining hard outside.*'/, attested by Deming (3/31/77).

<xwemxálém ~ x̱wemxálém>, mdls //x̣ʷ[=F=]əm=xʸə[=Aɛ́=]l=əm ~x̣ʷəm=xʸə[=Aɛ́=]l=əm//, ABFC ['*run*'], ASM ['of people or animals'], literally /'hurry/be fast on one's foot'/, possibly **<=F= (fronting)>** *derivational*, (**<á-ablaut>** *derivational*), lx **<=xel>** *on the foot*, (**<=em>** *middle voice*), phonology: ablaut, fronting, updrifting, syntactic analysis: intransitive verb, attested by BHTTC, IHTTC, EB, AC (8/7/70, 9/7/71), BJ (5/10/64), also <xwemxálem>, without updrifting, //x̣ʷ[=F=]əm=xʸə[=Aɛ́=]l=əm//, attested by RG & EH (4/9/99 Ling332); found in **<xwemxálémlha.>**, //x̣ʷ[=F=]əm=xʸə[=Aɛ́=]l=əm-ɬɛ//, /'*Run.*'/, attested by BHTTC (10/13/76), example: **<xwemxálémlha la(m) te steqtál.>**, //x̣ʷ[=F=]əm=xʸə[=Aɛ́=]l=əm-ɬɛ lɛ(=m) tə s=tɛ́q=tə[=M2=]l//, /'*Run to the door.*'/, attested by IHTTC (9/15/77), **<tsel t'át kw'els xwemxálém kw'e la me t'éqw' tel slhákw'em.>**, //c-əl t'ɛ́=T k'ʷ-əl-sx̣ʷ[=F=]əm=xʸə[=Aɛ́=]l=əm k'ʷə lɛ mə t'ə́q'ʷ t-əl s=ɬɛ́k'ʷ=əm//, /'*I tried to run but I ran out of breath.*'/, attested by EB (12/12/75).

<x̱wó:mxelem ~ xwó:mxelem ~ x̱wómxelem ~ xwómxelem>, cts //xʷə[-Aá(·)-]m=xʸəl=əm ~x̣ʷ[=F=]ə[-Aá(·)-]m=xʸəl=əm//, ABFC /'*running, run[ing] around*'/, SOC ['*a runner*'], PLAY, (**<ó(:)-ablaut>** *continuative*), phonology: ablaut, fronting, syntactic analysis: intransitive verb, attested by AC (10/13/71), BHTTC (10/13/76), EB (1/30/76, 2/6/76), Elders Group (2/76), example: **<xwómxelem qetl'osésu lhékw'xel qetl'osésu (wets'étl', tsélq) qetl'osésu lekwxál.>**, //x̣ʷ[=F=]ə[-Aá-]m=xʸəl=əm qə-ƛ'a-s-ə́s-u ɬə́k'ʷ=xʸəl qə-ƛ'a-s-ə́s-u (wə=c'ə́ cə́lq) qə-ƛ'a-s-ə́s-u ləkʷ=xʸə[=Aɛ́]l//, /'*He was running and he tripped and fell and broke his leg. (fall, break a leg)*'/, attested by AC (10/13/71), **<tl'ó te xwómxelem.>**, //ƛ'á təx̣ʷ[=F=]ə[-Aá-]m=xʸəl=əm//, /'*That's the runner.*'/, literally /'that's the one running'/, syntactic comment: relative clause with verb rather than xwómxelem being a derived nominal, attested by Elders Group (2/76).

<xwéxwemxelí:m>, dmpv //C_1í=Aə́=x̣ʷ[=F=]əm=xʸəl=əm=í·m or C_1í=Aə́=x̣ʷ[=F=]əm=xʸəl=ə[=Aí·=]m//, [xʷʊ́xʷəmxʸɪlí·m], ABFC ['*running on and off*'], (**<R4=>** *diminutive*), (**<é-ablaut on R4=>** *plural of diminutive*), probably **<=í:m>** *repeatedly*, possibly **<í:-ablaut on suffix e>** *durative*, phonology: reduplication, ablaut, fronting, syllable-loss or ablaut, syntactic analysis: intransitive verb, attested by BHTTC (10/13/76).

<x̱wemx̱wlí:m>, df //x̣ʷəm=x̣ʷ=əl=í·m or xʷəm=x̣ʷ=əl=ə[-Aí·-]m, less likely x̣ʷəm=xʸəl=əm=í·m or x̣ʷəm=xʸəl=ə[=Aí·=]m or $C_1əC_2$=x̣ʷ[=əl=]əm=í·m//, ABFC ['*hurrying*'], comment: ...**x̱**wl... possibly error for ...xl... or assimilation, possibly **<R3=>** *plural*, possibly **<=x̱w>** *all around*, possibly **<=el=>** *plural*, possibly **<=í:m>** *repeatedly* or **<í:-ablaut on suffix e>** *durative*, phonology: syllable-loss or assimilation, ablaut, possible infixed plural, syntactic analysis: intransitive verb, attested by EB (12/18/75).

<x̱weméthel>, FOOD /'*eat fast, eating fast, hurry to eat*'/, *see* **x̱**wém ~ xwém.

<x̱wémetses>, TVMO /'*pick fast, (do fast with the hands)*'/, *see* **x̱**wém ~ xwém.

<x̱wemx̱wém>, TVMO /'*hurry up, faster*'/, *see* **x̱**wém ~ xwém.

<x̱wemx̱wemeléqel>, LANG ['*talk fast*'], *see* **x̱**wém ~ xwém.

<x̱wemx̱wlí:m>, ABFC ['*hurrying*'], *see* **x̱**wém ~ xwém.

<x̱wés>, bound root //x̣ʷə́s *river splits around a rock*//.

<Sx̱wesálh>, df //s=xʷəs=ɛ́ɬ or s=xʷəs=ə[=Aɛ́=]ɬ//, PLN /'*place above Yale where the Fraser River splits around a rock, island above Steamboat Island (latter just below Five-Mile Creek)*'/, (**<s=>**

nominalizer), possibly <**=álh**> meaning unclear, possibly <**=elh**> *past tense*, possibly <**á-ablaut**> *durative or derivational*, phonology: possible ablaut, SP and AK not sure of the name but gave location, syntactic analysis: nominal, attested by IHTTC with elders at Place Names Meeting (8/23/77), SP and AK (Fish Camp 8/2/77), source: place names reference file #134 and #217, also <**X̲wesálh**>, //x̣ʷəs=ɛ́ɬ orx̣ʷəs=ə[=Aɛ́=]ɬ//, attested by IHTTC with elders (8/23/77), source: place names reference file #217.

<**x̲wét**>, free root //x̣ʷə́t//, SH /'*to tear, it rips*'/, syntactic analysis: intransitive verb, attested by EB (1/30/76, 3/30/76), Elders Group (5/16/80), Salish cognate: Lushootseed (Southern dial.) /x̣ʷə́t/ as in /ʔəs-x̣ʷə́t/ *it's torn* H76:614, and perhaps Sechelt /xʷə́ʔ-at/ *to tear off/apart* T77:34, example: <**x̲wét te s'íth'ems.**>, //x̣ʷə́t tə s=ʔíθ'ə=m-s//, /'*Her dress tears.*'/, comment: correcting her previous translation (Her dress is torn.), attested by EB (2/6/76, 3/30/76).

<**x̲wtát**>, pcs //x̣ʷət=ə[=Aɛ́=]t//, durs, SH /'*rip it up, tear it up, rip s-th, tear s-th*'/, semantic environment ['about cloth, paper, buckskin, leaves, anything'], (<**=et**> *purposeful control transitivizer*), (<**á-ablaut on e in suffix**> *durative*), phonology: ablaut, syntactic analysis: transitive verb, attested by Elders Group (5/14/80), Deming (3/25/76), EB (2/6/76); found in <**x̲wtátes.**>, //x̣ʷət=ə[=Aɛ́=]T-əs//, /'*He tore it.*'/, attested by EB (2/6/76).

<**x̲wetx̲wét**>, plv //C_1əC_2=x̣ʷə́t//, SH ['*torn up (in pieces)* (or prob. better) *(tear up (in many pieces))*'], (semological comment: some entries from this date with resultative translations were corrected by the speaker at a later date to leave out the resultative translation, this example was not mentioned the second time but probably needs the same correction (torn up → tear up)), (<**R3=**> *plural action/object*), phonology: reduplication, syntactic analysis: intransitive verb, attested by EB (2/6/76).

<**sx̲wex̲wéyt** or **sx̲wex̲wít**>, strs //s=C_1ə=x̣ʷə[=Aí=]t//, SH ['*torn*'], (<**s=**> *stative*), possibly <**R5= í-ablaut**> *resultative*, possibly <**=R1= í-ablaut**> *resultative*, phonology: reduplication, ablaut, syntactic analysis: adjective/adjectival verb, attested by EB (3/30/76).

<**x̲wetíwél**>, ds //x̣ʷət=íwə́l//, CLO ['*rip on the bottom or insides*'], lx <**=íwél**> *in the insides, in the rectum,* (now also) *on the bottom*, syntactic analysis: intransitive verb, attested by Elders Group (5/14/80), example: <**x̲wetíwél te seqíws**>, //x̣ʷət=íwə́l tə səq=íws//, /'*rip one's pants*'/, attested by Elders Group.

<**x̲wetíwél**>, CLO ['*rip on the bottom or insides*'], *see* **x̲**wét.

<**x̲wetx̲wét**>, SH ['*torn up (in pieces)* (or prob. better) *(tear up (in many pieces))*'], *see* **x̲**wét.

<**x̲wétl'**>, probable bound root //x̣ʷə́ƛ'//, probably *rolled*

<**sx̲wétl'qel**>, df //s=x̣ʷə́ƛ'=qəl//, HHG /'*pillow, rolled bulrush mat*'/, ASM ['often the tails of cat-tail rushes were used to stuff pillows and mattresses'], (<**s=**> *nominalizer, something to*), root meaning unknown unless x̲wétl' *rolled*, lx <**=qel**> *on the head*, syntactic analysis: nominal, attested by AC (9/10/71), Elders Group (2/27/80), TG (4/75), other sources: JH /sxʷx̣ʷə́ƛ'əqə̀l/ *pillow*, Salish cognate: Sechelt /x̣ʷəƛ'-qín/ *pillow, cushion* T77:18, Lushootseed /x̣ʷəƛ't/ *pillow* H76:613, also <**shxwétl'qel (**or **shxwx̲wétl'qel?)**>, //sxʷ=x̣ʷə́ƛ'=qəl//, attested by Elders Group (3/1/72), comment: xw may be mistranscribed for xwx̲w.

<**sx̲wetl'qelá:la**>, ds //s=x̣ʷəƛ'=qəl=ɛ́·lɛ//, HHG /'*pillow slip, pillow-case*'/, lx <**=á:la**> *container of/for*, syntactic analysis: nominal, attested by AC (9/10/71), Elders Group (3/1/72), also <**shxwetl'qelá:la (**or **shxwx̲wetl'qelá:la?)**>, //sxʷ=x̣ʷəƛ'=qəl=ɛ́·lɛ//, attested by Elders Group (3/1/72), comment: xw may be mistranscribed for xwx̲w.

<**x̲wewe**>, probable root //x̣ʷəw// or //x̣ʷɛ́w// or most likely //x̣ʷ[=F=]əw(=)ə//, perhaps same root in

<**shxwéwe**>, df //sxʷ=wə́wə or s=xʷəw=ə or sxʷ=wə́=C_1ə or sxʷ=wə́w=ə//, EZ ['*cougar*'], ['*Felis concolor oregonensis*']

<**sx̲wewál**>, df //s=x̣ʷəwɛ́l or s=x̣ʷɛ́w=ə[=M2=]l or more likely x̣ʷ[=F=]əw(=)ə=ɛ́l//, EZ ['*fox*'], ['*Vulpes fulva cascadensis*'], (<**s=**> *nominalizer, something to*), stem possibly <**xwéwe**> as in *cougar*, and with <**=á:l**> *similar to, -like, or part/portion* may mean "cougar-like", if not then possibly <**metathesis**> *derivational*, phonology: possible fronting or metathesis, syntactic analysis: nominal, attested by ME (11/21/72 tape), Elders Group (4/16/75), Salish cognate: Thompson /x̣ʷʕʷayxʷ/ *fox* B74c:9, Columbian /sxʷə́ʕʷxʷʕʷ/ *fox* K81:68 (where /ʕʷ/ is labialized pharyngeal stop found in some Interior and Tsamosan Salish languages), also <**shwál**>, //s(xʷ)wɛ́l//, attested by HP (3/3/76).

<**x̲wex̲weló:ystem**>, ABDF ['*staggering around*'], *see* **x̲**weló:y.

<**x̲wex̲weló:ysthòm**>, ABDF ['*you get staggered*'], *see* **x̲**weló:y.

<**x̲wex̲we'á**>, df //x̣ʷəx̣ʷ=əʔɛ or C_1ə=x̣ʷ=əʔɛ́//, SOC /'*copy, imitate*'/, root meaning unknown, lx <**=e'á**> *comparative, (like)*, possibly <**R5=**> *derivational?*, phonology: possible reduplication, syntactic analysis: intransitive verb, attested by AD (3/6/79), Salish cognate: Squamish /x̣ʷə-x̣ʷáʔ/ *imitate* K69:86, Saanich dial. of NSt /x̣ʷəx̣ʷáʔ/ *imitate* B74a:66, example: <**sta yálh ulh x̲wex̲we'á.**>, //s=t(=əʔ)ɛ́ yɛɬ ʔuɬ x̣ʷəx̣ʷ=əʔɛ́//, /'*Now he imitates., Now he copies.*'/, attested by AD.

<**x̲wix̲we'á**>, cts //x̣ʷə[-Ai-]x̣ʷ=əʔɛ́ or C_1í-x̣ʷ=əʔɛ́//, SOC ['*imitating*'], possibly <**í-ablaut**> *continuative*, possibly <**R4-**> *continuative* (unusual use of R4), phonology: ablaut or reduplication, syntactic analysis: intransitive verb, attested by EB (4/26/76).

<**x̲wex̲we'át**>, pcs //x̣ʷəx̣ʷ=əʔɛ́=T or C_1ə=x̣ʷ=əʔɛ́=T//, SOC /'*copy s-o, imitate s-o*'/, (<**=t**> *purposeful control transitivizer*), syntactic analysis: transitive verb, attested by AD (3/6/79), Elders Group (4/6/77).

<**x̲wix̲we'át**>, cts //x̣ʷə[-Ai-]x̣ʷ=əʔɛ́=T or C_1í-x̣ʷ=əʔɛ́=T//, SOC /'*imitating s-o, copying s-o*'/, possibly <**í-ablaut**> *continuative*, possibly <**R4-**> *continuative* (unusual use of R4), phonology: ablaut or reduplication, syntactic analysis: transitive verb, attested by Elders Group (4/6/77), EB (4/26/76, 5/3/76); found in <**x̲wix̲we'áthométsel.**>, //x̣ʷə[-Ai-]x̣ʷ=əʔɛ́=T-ámə-c-əl//, /'*I'm imitating you.*'/, attested by EB (4/26/76), <**x̲wix̲we'áthò:m.**>, //x̣ʷə[-Ai-]x̣ʷ=əʔɛ́=T-à·m//, /'*You were imitated., They imitated you., (You were being imitated.)*'/, attested by EB (4/26/76), example: <**x̲wix̲we'átes te spá:th.**>, //x̣ʷə[-Ai-]x̣ʷ=əʔɛ́=T-əs tə s=pɛ́θ//, /'*He's imitating a bear.*'/, attested by EB (5/3/76), <**x̲wix̲we'átem kw cheláqelhelh.**>, //x̣ʷə[-Ai-]x̣ʷ=əʔɛ́=T-əm kʷ cəlɛ́q(=)əɬ=əɬ//, /'*He was imitated yesterday., They imitated him yesterday., (They were imitating him yesterday.)*'/, attested by EB (4/26/76).

<**X̲wix̲we'áqel ~ Xwixwe'áqel ~ Xwōxwe'áqel**>, ds //x̣ʷə[=Ai=]x̣ʷ=əʔɛ́=əqəl ~ C_1í-xʷ[=F=]=əʔɛ́=əqəl ~ C_1ə=xʷ[=F=]=əʔɛ́=əqəl//, PLN /'*Echo Point on Echo Island, Echo Bay on Echo Island*'/, literally /'imitating a voice'/, ASM ['the island is in Harrison Lake, the bay is on the west side of the island by Chítmexw and Spá:th rocks on the island'], Elder's comment: so named because if you talk slow here you can hear the echo of your own voice talking back to you, possibly <**=F= (fronting)**> *derivational*, lx <**=eqel**> *in the throat, speech, voice*, (<**zero**> *nominalizer*), phonology: ablaut or reduplication, optional fronting, zero nominalizer, syntactic analysis: nominal, attested by EL (3/1/78 tape, 6/27/78 boat trip).

<**x̲wix̲we'ó:s**>, ds //x̣ʷə[=Ai=]x̣ʷ=əʔɛ́=ás ~ C_1í-x̣ʷ=əʔɛ́=á·s//, SOC ['*making a face*'], literally /'copying/imitating on the face'/, lx <**=ó:s ~ =ós ~ =es**> *on the face*, phonology: ablaut or reduplication, vowel merger, syntactic analysis: intransitive verb, attested by Elders Group (1/21/76).

<**x̲wex̲we'át**>, SOC /'*copy s-o, imitate s-o*'/, *see* x̲wex̲we'á.

<**x̲wex̲wiyáye ~ x̲wix̲wiyáye**>, EZ ['*house-fly*'], *see* x̲wōx̲wáye ~ x̲wex̲wáye ~ x̲wōx̲wá:ye.

<**x̲wéychesem** (or better) **x̲wíythesem**>, PE ['*get one's picture taken*'], *see* x̲wíyth.

<**x̲wéyx̲weleqw** or **x̲wí:x̲weleqw**>, EZ ['*small bird*'], *see* x̲wí:leqw ~ x̲wé:yleqw ~ x̲wéyleqw.

<**x̲we'ít**>, us //x̣ʷəʔít//, TOOL ['*a wedge*'], syntactic analysis: noun, nominal, attested by CT (6/8/76), Elders Group (2/5/75), other sources: ES (ChMsCw) /x̣ʷəʔít/ *wedge*, JH /x̣ʷəʔí·t/ *a wooden wedge*, Salish cognate: Squamish /x̣ʷəʔít/ *wedge* W73:286, K67:371, Sechelt /s-x̣ʷəʔít/ *wedge* T77:19.

<**x̲wík'**>, perhaps bound root or stem //x̣ʷík' or x̣ʷiq'=F//, meaning unknown unless whole word is onomatopoeic

<**sx̲wík'**>, df //s=x̣ʷík' or s=x̣ʷiq'=F//, EZ /'*winter robin, bush robin, varied thrush*'/, ['*Ixoreus naevius naevius*'], SD ['*call of the winter robin or varied thrush*'], ASM ['the varied thrush stays in the Stó:lō area all winter, unlike the American robin'], (<**s=**> *nominalizer*), possibly <**=F (fronting)**> *diminutive*, phonology: sound symbolism, possible fronting, syntactic analysis: nominal, attested by EL (9/15/78), Elders Group (3/19/75, 2/18/76, 5/14/80), Salish cognate: perhaps Squamish /sx̣ʷíš/ *varied thrush (Ixoreus naevius)* K69:60 and Kennedy and Bouchard 1976:97-98, perhaps Lushootseed /s-x̣ʷíʔ ~ s-x̣ʷəx̣ʷí/ *unidentified kind of small bird whose myth name is* /s-pícx̣ʷ/ H76:619, not Sechelt /tik'-tik'-šín/ *thrush* T77:11, also <**x̲wéyk'** or **x̲wík'**>, //x̣ʷík'//, attested by Elders Group (6/4/75).

<**x̲wéylem ~ x̲wé:ylem ~ x̲wí:lem**>, df //x̣ʷí·l=əm//, WV /'*rope, twine, string, thread*'/, HARV, HUNT, EB ['*stringy fibers (as on cow parsnip)*'], root meaning unknown, possibly <**=em**> *intransitivizer/have/get*, syntactic analysis: noun, nominal, attested by AC, Elders Group (2/19/75, 4/5/78), IHTTC (7/19/77), JL (7/13/79), other sources: ES /x̣ʷéy·ləm/ (CwMs /x̣ʷéyʔləmʔ/) *rope*, Salish cognate: Squamish /x̣ʷíʔlm/ *rope* W73:219, K67:372, Samish dial. of NSt VU /x̣ʷéyləm'/, LD /x̣ʷéy'ləm'/ *rope* beside /x̣ʷəx̣ʷey'ləm'/ *string, twine* G86:86, and PCS cognate set #105 in G82 includes: Nooksack /xʷíylìm/ *rope* A61, Sechelt /x̣ʷílm/ *rope* beside /x̣ʷí-x̣ʷəlm/ *string, twine* T77:19, also Sechelt /x̣ʷíləm/ *rope* B80pc and B83pc, Skagit dial. of Lushootseed /x̣ʷíləb/ *thread* H76:616 [note? Lushootseed root /x̣ʷíl'/ *lost, turned around*], Twana /x̣ʷíləb/ *thread* NT79 & NT82, Lummi dial. of NSt /x̣ʷíʔləm/ *rope, thread* (Demers 1982 p.c.), Saanich dial. of NSt /x̣ʷíl'əm/ *rope*, Songish and Clallam /x̣ʷiʔləm/ *rope*, example: <**p'áth'tsel. alétsa kwthel x̲wéylem?**>, //p'έθ'-c-əl. ʔεlécε kʷθ-əl x̣ʷí·ləm//, /'*I'm going to sew. Where is my thread?*'/, literally /'I sew (present as immediate future) where is it the (near but not visible) -my thread'/, attested by AC (9/30/71), <**x̲wéylems te stiqíw**>, //x̣ʷí·ləm-s tə s=tiqíw//, /'*the horse's rope*'/, attested by AC (9/30/71), <**selá kw'as q'í(y)set te x̲wéylem.**>, //s=(hə=)lέ k'ʷ-ε-s q'í(y)s=əT tə x̣ʷí·ləm//, /'*Tie the rope tight.*'/, literally /'(it) is tight that you tie s-th the rope'/, attested by AC (9/30/71), <**le hó:kwexes thel tà:l te x̲wéylem kwses p'ewí:tes tel s'í:th'em.**>, //lə há·kʷ=əxʸ-əs θ-əl tὲ·l təx̣ʷí·ləm kʷ-s-əs p'əw=ə[=Aí·=]T-əs t-əl s=ʔí·θ'ə=m//, /'*My mother used the thread to patch up my dress.*'/, literally /'past use s-th the (female present) -my mother the thread that she/he patch s-th up the (present/unspecified) dress/clothing'/, attested by AC (9/21/71), <**líqwet te x̲wéylem**>, //líqʷ=əT təx̣ʷí·ləm//, /'*let out a rope (let it out (of rope))*'/, literally /'loosen it the rope'/, attested by IHTTC (7/19/77), <**x̲wéylems te téx̲wets**>, //x̣ʷí·ləm-s tə tə́x̣ʷ(=)əc//, /'*bowstring*'/, literally /'its string the bow'/, attested by Elders Group (4/5/78), <**we'ólwe qwe'íqweqws ta x̲wé:ylem.**>, //wə=ʔál wə=qʷəʔíqʷ=əqʷ-s t-εx̣ʷí·ləm//, /'*Your rope is too thin/narrow.*'/, attested by JL.

<**x̲wéylémt**>, pcs //x̣ʷí·l(=)əm=T//, DESC /'*weigh s-th, (*(also) *measure s-th* [EB]*)*'/, possibly root <**x̲wéylem**> *rope*, pcs //=t *purposeful control transitivizer*//, phonology: updrifting, syntactic analysis:

transitive verb, attested by CT and HT (6/21/76), also /'*measure s-th, weigh s-th*'/, attested by EB, example: <**x̱wéylémt kwstámes**>, //x̣ʷí·ləm=T kʷ=s=tɛm=əs//, /'*weigh something*'/, attested by CT and HT.

<**xwéylemt te télmels**> or better <**x̱wéylemt te télmels**>, cpds //x̣ʷí·l(=)əm=T tə ta[=Aə́=]l=(əl)məl-s//, SCH /'*measure the knowledge, give a test*'/, <**télmel**>, //ta[=Aə́=]l=(əl)məl//, *the mind, someone's own knowledge*, <**é-ablaut**> *resultative*, lx <**=mel**> *part, portion* or lx <**=élmel**> *in the mind*, attested by RG & EH (4/10/99 Ling332)

<**x̱wíleqlexw**>, ncs //x̣ʷíləq=l-əxʷ or xʷ[=Q=]ɛ[=Aí=]l[=ə=]q=l-əxʷ//, df, SOC ['*almost kill s-o*'], root meaning unknown, Elder's comment: "may come from xwá:lq *almost*", comment: derivation from xwá:lq would require several unusual processes: backing, í-ablaut of root a, and =e= infixing, possibly <**=Q= (backing)**> *derivational*?, possibly <**í-ablaut**> *derivational*, possibly <**=e=**> *plural*? or> *derivational*, (<**=l**> *non-control transitivizer*), (<**-exw**> *third person object*), phonology: possible backing, possible ablaut, possible infixed e (schwa), syntactic analysis: transitive verb, attested by EB (2/21/78); found in <**x̱wíleqlóxes.**>, //x̣ʷíləq=l-áxʸ-əs//, /'*He almost killed me.*'/, attested by EB.

<**x̱wilx̱wíleqlexw** or **x̱welx̱wíleqlexw**>, plv //C_1əC_2=x̣ʷíləq=l-əxʷ//, SOC ['*repeatedly almost kill s-o*'], (<**R3=**> *plural action*), phonology: reduplication, syntactic analysis: transitive verb, attested by EB (2/21/78, 4/25/78), example in the words to EB's grandmother's thunder spirit song: <**x̱wilx̱wileqlóxes kw'e x̱wéyleqws kw'e chíchelh. ~ x̱wílx̱wiliqlómxes kw'e x̱wéyleqws kw'e chíchelh.**>, //C_1əC_2=x̣ʷiləq=l-áxʸ-əs k'ʷəx̣ʷí·l(=)əqʷ-s k'ʷə cí[=C_1ə=]ɬ//, /'*The thunderbird repeatedly almost killed me.*'/, literally /'he repeatedly almost kills me the (remote/distant) big bird of the (remote) high up/height'/, (semological comment: notice the idiom used for *thunderbird*, lit. "the bird bird of the remote high up/height", EB's granny also had three other spirit songs besides this thunder song, a wolf song, a crying song, and one other, the words to the crying song were: <**ye'éyò selá:we**> (not translated but <**selá:we**> is *lonely*, <**ye=**> *moving along*, <**éy**> *good*, <**-ò**> *just*)), usage: spirit songs, attested by EB.

<**x̱wí:leqw ~ x̱wé:yleqw ~ x̱wéyleqw**>, possibly root //x̣ʷí·l(=)əqʷ orx̣ʷí=ələqʷ//, EZ /'*big bird, (large bird (of any kind)), any waterfowl*'/, possibly <**=eqw ~ =eleqw**> *on top of the head*, phonology: possible vowel merger, syntactic analysis: noun, nominal, dialects: *Cheh.*, attested by Elders Group (2/5/75, 2/19/75, 6/4/75, 2/18/76), EB (2/21/78. 4/25/78), contrast <**mó:qw**> *large bird; duck, waterfowl* (Chill. dialect), Salish cognate: Squamish /x̣ʷílʔəqʷ/ *duck (generic),* (for LM includes: *ducks* and also *scoter, grebes, cormorant, murre, murrelet,* and *smaller loons)* K67:372, K69:87.

<**x̱wéyx̱weleqw** or **x̱wí:x̱weleqw**>, dmn //x̣ʷí·[=C_1ə=]ləqʷ or C_1í=x̣ʷiləqʷ//, EZ ['*small bird*'], probably <**R4=** or **=R1=**> *diminutive*, phonology: reduplication, syntactic analysis: nominal, attested by Elders Group (2/5/75).

<**x̱wilx̱wíleqlexw** or **x̱welx̱wíleqlexw**>, SOC ['*repeatedly almost kill s-o*'], *see* x̱wíleqlexw.

<**x̱wíqel**>, probable bound stem //x̣ʷíq(=)əl or x̣ʷə[=Aí=]q=əl//, meaning uncertain

<**sx̱wíqel**>, df //s=x̣ʷíq(=)əl or s=x̣ʷə[=Aí=]q=əl//, WETH ['*tree bent to ground with ice and frozen*'], EB, (<**s=**> *stative or nominalizer*), root meaning unknown but if <**q**> is error for <**qw'**> then the root means *tied and hanging down* and this is an alternate pronunciation of <**x̱wíqw'el**> *sleet, silver thaw*, probably <**í-ablaut on root e**> *resultative*, probably <**=el**> *come, go, get, become*, phonology: possible ablaut, syntactic analysis: nominal, adjective/adjectival verb?, attested by Elders Group (2/8/78), compare <**x̱wíqw'el**> *sleet, silver thaw*.

<**x̱wíqw'**>, bound root //x̣ʷíq'ʷ *tie up and hang, tie around*//, Salish cognate: Squamish root /x̣ʷiq'ʷ ~x̣ʷəq'ʷ/ *be tied* as in /x̣ʷíq'ʷ-inʔ/ *tie up, connect (tr.)* K67:372 and /x̣ʷíq'ʷ-us-n/ *hang (a person)(tr.)* K69:87.

<**sx̲wíx̲weqw'**>, strs //s=x̣ʷí[=C$_1$ə=]q’ʷ//, FSH ['*(hung up in a fish net)*'], HUNT, CLO, MC, (<**s=**> *stative*), (<**=R1=**> *resultative*), phonology: reduplication, syntactic analysis: adjective/adjectival verb, attested by Elders Group (2/11/76), example: <**ewéta sx̲wíx̲weqw'.**>, //ʔəwə= ́tɛ s=x̣ʷí[=C$_1$ə=]q’ʷ//, /'*There's no fish on your net.*'/, literally /'(there) is nothing hung up in a fish net'/, attested by Elders Group.

<**x̲wíqw'est**>, pcs //x̣ʷíq’ʷ=əs=T//, SOC /'*put a rope around s-o/s-th's neck, put a leash on s-th, hang s-o*'/, ASM ['can be done to a person, dog, horse, etc., doesn't necessarily hurt them, the meaning of hanging to kill was brought by the non-Indian post- contact'], literally /'tie s-o/s-th purposely around on the face (to hang down)'/, lx <**=es**> *on the face*, (<**=t**> *purposeful control transitivizer*), syntactic analysis: transitive verb, attested by AD (3/6/79), Elders Group (4/16/75), other sources: JH /x̣ʷí·q’ʷəst/ *to hang a person*, Salish cognate: Squamish /x̣ʷíq’ʷ-us-n/ *hang (a person)(tr.)* K69:87.

<**x̲wíqw'esem**>, mdls //x̣ʷíq’ʷ=əs=əm//, SOC /'*hang oneself, (hung by a rope [AC])*'/, literally /'tie oneself around on the face to hang down'/, lx <**=es**> *on the face*, (<**=em**> *middle voice*), syntactic analysis: intransitive verb, attested by Elders Group (3/5/80), also /'*hung by a rope*'/, attested by AC (8/28/70).

<**sx̲wéqw'lhelh**>, ds //s=x̣ʷi[=Aə́=]q’ʷ=ɬəɬ//, CLO /'*scarf, neckerchief*'/, literally /'something that is tied around on the throat to hang down'/, (<**s=**> *nominalizer, something that*), (<**é-ablaut on root i**> *resultative*), lx <**=lhelh**> *on the throat, on the front of the neck*, phonology: ablaut, syntactic analysis: nominal, attested by Elders Group (9/24/75), Salish cognate: Sechelt /s-x̣ʷú-x̣ʷq’ʷ-ɬaɬ/ *kerchief* T77:18, Samish dial. of NSt /s-x̣ʷíx̣ʷq’ʷ-ɬnəɬ/ *anything one has on one's neck (cloth, neckerchief, necklace, etc.)* G86:84, also <**xweqw'éllhelh**>, //x̣ʷ(=F=)i[=Aə=]q’ʷ=ə́lɬəɬ//, also /'*scarf, necktie*'/, possibly <**=F= (fronting)**> *diminutive or derivational*, phonology: possible fronting, ablaut, attested by MP and SP and EB (Elders Group 2/1/78), also /'*necktie, bowtie*'/, Elder's comment: "can't remember the word for *necktie, bowtie*", attested by BHTTC (10/21/76).

<**sx̲wéqw'ellhelh**>, ds //s=x̣ʷi[=Aə́=]q’ʷ=əlɬəɬ//, CLO ['*necklace*'], literally /'something that is tied around on the throat to hang down'/, (<**s=**> *nominalizer, something that*), (<**é-ablaut on root i**> *resultative*), lx <**=éllhelh**> *on the throat, on the front of the neck*, phonology: ablaut, syntactic analysis: nominal, attested by Elders Group (11/26/75), Salish cognate: Sechelt /s-x̣ʷú-x̣ʷq’ʷ-ɬaɬ/ *kerchief* T77:18, Samish dial. of NSt /s-x̣ʷíx̣ʷq’ʷ-ɬnəɬ/ *anything one has on one's neck (cloth, neckerchief, necklace, etc.)* G86:84.

<**x̲wíqw'el**>, incs //x̣ʷíq’ʷ=əl//, WETH /'*to sleet, have a silver thaw*'/, ASM ['sleet is freezing rain, silver thaw is a thaw which melts and refreezes'], literally /'go/come/get/become tie around and hang down'/, (semological comment: *to sleet* uses the active *go/come* meaning, *have a silver thaw* usesthe *get/become* meaning of =el), syntactic analysis: intransitive verb, attested by Deming (3/31/77).

<**x̲wí:qw'el**>, cts //x̣ʷí[-·-]q’ʷ=əl//, WETH /'*sleeting, be sleeting*'/, (<**-:-**> *continuative*), phonology: lengthening, syntactic analysis: intransitive verb, attested by Elders Group (4/16/75), example: <**x̲wí:qw'el te swáyel.**>, //x̣ʷí[-·-]q’ʷ=əl tə s=wɛ́yəl//, /'*It's sleeting., The day is sleeting.*'/, attested by Elders Group (4/16/75).

<**x̲wíqw'el**>, WETH /'*to sleet, have a silver thaw*'/, *see* **x̲**wíqw'.

<**x̲wí:qw'el**>, WETH /'*sleeting, be sleeting*'/, *see* **x̲**wíqw'.

<**x̲wíqw'em ~ x̲wí:qw'em**>, df //x̣ʷíq’ʷ=əm ~x̣ʷí·q’ʷ=əm//, ABFC ['*to snore*'], (<**=em**> *middle voice or intransitivizer/have/get*), syntactic analysis: intransitive verb, attested by Elders Group (4/16/75, 3/5/80), other sources: JH /x̣ʷí·q’ʷəm/ *to snore, snoring* JH66:22,15, Salish cognate: Mainland Comox /x̣ʷúq’ʷt/ *to snore* B75prelim.:91, Sechelt /x̣ʷúq’ʷ-t/ *to snore* T77:33, Squamish /x̣ʷúq’ʷ-n/ *to snore* K67:372, not Lushootseed /x̣ʷálitut/ *to snore* H76:608 which appears to be a compound of

/ʔítut/ *to sleep* perhaps with /x̣ʷal'/ *lack control.*

<**x̲wíx̲weqw'em**>, cts //x̣ʷí[-C_1ə-]q'ʷ=əm//, ABFC ['*snoring*'], (<**-R1-**> *continuative*), phonology: reduplication, syntactic analysis: intransitive verb, attested by Elders Group (4/16/75, 3/5/80), AC (8/28/70).

<**x̲wíqw'esem**>, SOC /'*hang oneself, (hung by a rope [AC])*'/, *see* **x̲**wíqw'.

<**x̲wíqw'est**>, SOC /'*put a rope around s-o/s-th's neck, put a leash on s-th, hang s-o*'/, *see* **x̲**wíqw'.

<**x̲wítl'**>, probable root or stem //x̣ʷíƛ'//, meaning unknown

<**sx̲wítl'**>, df //s(=)x̣ʷíƛ'//, EZ /'*catbird (has black head), rufous-sided towhee*'/, ['*Pipilo erythrophthalmus*'], ASM ['rufous-sided towhee was identified by EL from pictures in David Marshall (1973): Familiar Birds of Northwest Forests, Fields and Gardens and called the catbird by EL who said it is called the catbird in English because it calls like a cat meowing; there is also another bird in the Stó:lō territory marginally, the gray catbird (Dumetella carolinensis) according to Udvardy 1977 which makes mewing calls but has only a black cap; the rufous-sided towhee has an entirely black head, makes a call described by Udvardy (1977:598) as an "inquisitive meewww?" and a song he describes for the Pacific coast variety/dialect as "to-wheeeee", "a buzzy trill", these descriptions fit resp. the cat's meow description given by EL and the Stó:lō name itself sx̲wítl' which could perhaps resemble a buzzy trilled to-wheeeee (x̲w and tl' providing the buzz and the s= then rounding of x̲w providing the first "to-" like sound)'], possibly <**s=**> *nominalizer, something to,* phonology: probable sound symbolism, onomatopoeia, syntactic analysis: nominal, attested by Deming (4/12/79), EL (9/15/78), Salish cognate: not Saanich dial. of NSt /sx̣éeš/ *catbird* B74a:14, but in Squamish the *rufous-sided towhee* (name forgotten) was also called the *catbird* (Kennedy and Bouchard 1976:100), possibly Lushootseed /sx̣ʷəx̣ʷiʔ ~ sx̣ʷiʔ/ *an unidentified kind of small bird* H76:619.

<**x̲wíx̲weqw'em**>, ABFC ['*snoring*'], *see* **x̲**wíqw'em ~ **x̲**wí:qw'em.

<**x̲wix̲we'á**>, SOC ['*imitating*'], *see* **x̲**we**x̲**we'á.

<**X̲wix̲we'áqel ~ Xwixwe'áqel ~ Xwōxwe'áqel**>, PLN /'*Echo Point on Echo Island, Echo Bay on Echo Island*'/, *see* **x̲**we**x̲**we'á.

<**x̲wix̲we'át**>, SOC /'*imitating s-o, copying s-o*'/, *see* **x̲**we**x̲**we'á.

<**x̲wix̲we'ó:s**>, SOC ['*making a face*'], *see* **x̲**we**x̲**we'á.

<**x̲wíx̲wiyá:m**>, LANG ['*to recite or tell a fairy tale*'], *see* **x̲**wiyám.

<**x̲wix̲wíyem**>, df //C_1í=x̣ʷíy=əm or C_1əC_2=x̣ʷíy=əm or C_1í=xʷíy=əm//, EFAM ['*nervous while walking on something narrow*'], possibly <**R4=**> *diminutive or resultative*, possibly <**R3=**> *plural*, probably root <**xwiy**> *wake, awake*, possibly root <**x̲wíy**> meaning unknown, phonology: possible mistranscription of x̲w for xw, syntactic analysis: intransitive verb, attested by IHTTC (9/7/77), Salish cognate: probably not Squamish /x̣ʷáʔ=ilwəs/ *become excited, become disturbed* W73:92, K69:86.

<**x̲wiyám**>, possibly root //x̣ʷiyɛ́(·)m orx̣ʷiy=ə[=Aɛ́(·)=]m//, LANG ['*tell a story [legendary]*'], PLAY, SOC, possibly <**=em**> *intransitivizer, have, get*, possibly <**á(:)-ablaut on suffix e**> *durative*, (semological comment: durative meaning is plausible because the legendary stories told were often very long with many episodes), phonology: possible ablaut, syntactic analysis: intransitive verb, attested by Deming (3/15/79) (SJ, MC, MV, LG), Salish cognate: Southern Lushootseed /s-x̣ʷiʔáb/ *traditional story, myth* H76:619, Squamish /x̣ʷə-x̣ʷi-ʔámʔ/ *tell a story (itr.)* beside /x̣ʷə-x̣ʷi-ʔús-n/ *tell a story to (tr.)* and /s-x̣ʷə-x̣ʷi-ʔámʔ/ *non-realistic story, a myth* W73:254, K67:298, 371; found in <**x̲wiyámlha.**>, //x̣ʷiy=ə[=Aɛ́=]m-ɬɛ//, /'*Tell a story.*'/, attested by Deming (3/15/79).

<**x̱wíx̱wiyá:m**>, df //C_1í=x̣ʷiy=ə[=Aɛ́·=]m//, LANG [*'to recite or tell a fairy tale'*], PLAY, SOC, possibly <**R4=**> *diminutive*, phonology: reduplication, syntactic analysis: intransitive verb, attested by EB (1/30/76).

<**x̱wiyex̱wiyám** or **x̱wiyx̱wiyá(:)m**>, plv //C_1əC_2=x̣ʷiy=ə[=Aɛ́(·)=]m//, LANG [*'(be) telling stories [legendary]'*], PLAY, SOC, (semological comment: pluralized verbs are always *continuative* as well (as in Musqueam, Suttles ca1984: chapter 7)), (<**R3=**> *plural continuative*), phonology: reduplication, syntactic analysis: intransitive verb, attested by AC (8/24/70), example: <**x̱wiyex̱wiyám te siyólexwe.**>, //C_1əC_2=x̣ʷiy=ə[=Aɛ́(·)=]m tə s=yáləxʷ=ə//, /*'The old man is telling stories.'*/, attested by AC.

<**sx̱wiyám**>, dnom //s=x̣ʷiy=ə[=Aɛ́=]m//, LANG /*'story, (myth, legend)'*/, PLAY, SOC, (<**s=**> *nominalizer, something to/that*), phonology: possible ablaut, syntactic analysis: nominal, dialects: *Chill.*, attested by SJ and MC and MV (Deming 3/15/79), other sources: ES /sx̣ʷəyɛ́·m/ (CwMs /sx̣ʷəyʔɛ́mʔ/) *myth*, Salish cognate: Southern Lushootseed /s-x̣ʷiʔáb/ *traditional story, myth* H76:619.

<**sx̱wex̱wiyám ~ sx̱wō̱x̱wiyá:m**>, dmn //s=C_1ə=x̣ʷiy=ə[=Aɛ́(·)=]m//, LANG /*'child's fable, story, fairy tale, child's story'*/, PLAY, SOC, (<**R5=**> *diminutive*), phonology: reduplication, possible ablaut, syntactic analysis: nominal, attested by EB (1/30/76), SJ and MC and MV (Deming 3/15/79), AC (9/1/71, 11/10/71, 11/11/71, 8/24/70), CT (9/5/73, 9/15/73), Mary Charles (9/5/73), Elders Group (1/7/76), contrast <**sqwélqwel**> *true story, narrative, news*, example: <**ő̱we lis the'í:t sta'á kw'e sx̱wō̱x̱wiyám.**>, //ʔówə li-s θəʔí·t s=t=ɛʔɛ́ k'ʷə s=C_1ə=x̣ʷiy=ə[=Aɛ́=]m//, /*'It's not true but it's like a fable.'*/, attested by AC (11/11/71), <**le hóy te sx̱wō̱x̱wiyám.**>, //lə háy tə s=C_1ə=x̣ʷiy=ə[=Aɛ́=]m//, /*'He end[ed] a story., He finish[ed] a story.'*/, attested by Elders Group.

<**sx̱wolex̱wiyám**>, pln //s=C_1á=lə=x̣ʷiy=ə[=Aɛ=]m or s=C_1ə[=Aa=lə=]=x̣ʷiy=ə[=Aɛ́=]m//, HAT [*'ancient people over a hundred years old'*], ASM ['they can't move, just lay there in the pit-house, they take liquids, in spring the family digs out the roof to get them out into the sun'], literally perhaps /'legend people'/, possibly <**R10=**> *person* (as in <**lólets'e**> *one person*?) or more likely <**=le=**> *plural*), possibly <**o-ablaut**> *derivational*, probably <**á-ablaut**> *durative*, phonology: reduplication, infixed plural, ablaut, syntactic analysis: nominal, attested by BHTTC (9/9/76).

<**x̱wiyáye**>, EZ [*'a fly'*], *see* **x̱**wō̱**x̱**wáye ~ **x̱**we**x̱**wáye ~ **x̱**wō̱**x̱**wá:ye.

<**x̱wiyex̱wiyám** or **x̱wiyx̱wiyá(:)m**>, LANG [*'(be) telling stories [legendary]'*], *see* **x̱**wiyám.

<**x̱wíyth**>, bound root //x̣ʷíyθ *have a likeness made*//.

<**x̱wíythi**>, ds //x̣ʷíyθ(=)iy//, CARV /*'carved outside post on longhouse, totem pole'*/, (semological comment: probably *have a likeness made of a person or creature on wood* since these were the principal things carved on Stó:lō houseposts or poles, funeral boxes, grave poles, spindle whorls, masks), possibly <**=iy**> *bark, [old meaning] tree*, syntactic analysis: noun?, intransitive verb?, attested by DM (12/4/64), TG (4/23/75).

<**sx̱wíythi ~ sx̱wéythi**>, df //s=x̣ʷíyθ(=)i(y)//, PE /*'likeness, portrait, photograph, photo, statue'*/, (semological comment: the word may have also included likenesses painted on drums, houses, skins, rocks, etc. since it now includes photographs), (<**s=**> *nominalizer, something to*), syntactic analysis: nominal, attested by Elders Group (3/19/75), TG (4/23/75).

<**sx̱wéythiyes ~ sx̱wíythiyes**>, ds //s=x̣ʷíyθ=iy=əs//, CLO /*'headdress, face costume, mask'*/, lx <**=es**> *on the face*, syntactic analysis: nominal, attested by Elders Group (3/19/75), TG (4/23/75).

<**x̱wéychesem** (or better) **x̱wíythesem**>, mdls //x̣ʷíyθ=əs=əm//, PE [*'get one's picture taken'*], literally

/'get a likeness of one's/a face'/, lx <**=es**> *of the face*, (<**=em**> *middle voice or intransitivizer/have/get*), phonology: ch probably mistranscribed for th (esp. in light of x̲wiyx̲wiythiyósem *motion pictures, movies*) but could also be an artifact of legitimate ts/ch ~ th (incomplete sound shift in this word for the speaker/speakers giving the word), syntactic analysis: intransitive verb, attested by Elders Group (6/28/78).

<**x̲wiyx̲wiythiyósem**>, df //C_1əC_2=x̣ʷiyθ=iy(=)ás=əm or x̣ʷiy[=C_1əC_2=]θ=iy(=)ás=əm//, PLAY /'*movies, motion pictures*'/, possibly <**R3=**> *plural*, possibly <**=R2=**> *characteristic*, root <**x̲wiyth**> *(have/get a) likeness*, probably <**=iyós**> *around in circles*, possibly <**=ós**> *of the face*, (<**=em**> *place to have/get*), phonology: reduplication, syntactic analysis: nominal, attested by Elders Group (4/21/76).

<**x̲wíythi**>, CARV /'*carved outside post on longhouse, totem pole*'/, see x̲wíyth.

<**x̲wiyx̲wiyáye**>, EZ /'*a lot of flies, big blow-flies*'/, see x̲wōx̲wáye ~ x̲wex̲wáye ~ x̲wōx̲wá:ye.

<**x̲wiyx̲wiythiyósem**>, PLAY /'*movies, motion pictures*'/, see x̲wíyth.

<**x̲wlhép**>, df //x̣ʷɬ(=)ə́p orx̣ʷə́ɬ[=M1=]p or xʷ[=B=]ə=ɬə́p//, ABDF /'*slip off (one's feet, hands, bottom), lose balance*'/, possibly <**=ép**> *on the bottom*, possibly <**metathesis type 1**> *non-continuative*, possibly <**xwe=**> *become, get*, possibly <**=B= (backing)**> *derivational*, phonology: possible metathesis, possible backing, phonology: x̲w could be mistranscribed for xw, see xwlhépelets *sit down (with a plop?), [slip off one's chair]*, all derived forms below with x̲w were elicited at the same class meeting, syntactic analysis: intransitive verb, attested by BHTTC (8/30/76), compare <**elhápt**> *slip it out (what a woman says to a man)*, Salish cognate: probably Squamish /ɬúp/ *be way off, be out of reach, be away from the edge* as also in /ɬúp-n/ *put away (tr.)* and /ɬúp-cut/ *move away* K67:329-330.

<**x̲wlhépxel**>, df //x̣ʷə́ɬ[=M1=]p=xʸəl orx̣ʷ[=B=]ə=ɬə́p=xʸəl//, ABDF /'*slip off with a foot, lose balance [on feet]*'/, lx <**=xel**> *on the foot*, phonology: possible metathesis, possible backing, phonology: x̲w could be mistranscribed for xw, see xwlhépelets *sit down (with a plop?), [slip off one's chair]*, syntactic analysis: intransitive verb, attested by BHTTC (8/30/76).

<**x̲wélhepxel**>, df //x̣ʷə́ɬəp=xʸəl orx̣ʷ[=B=]ə́=ɬəp=xʸəl//, ABDF ['*slipping off with a foot*'], (<**lack of metathesis**> *continuative*), lx <**=xel**> *on the foot*, phonology: possible backing, phonology: x̲w could be mistranscribed for xw, see xwlhépelets *sit down (with a plop?), [slip off one's chair]*, syntactic analysis: intransitive verb, attested by BHTTC (8/30/76).

<**x̲welhx̲wélhepxel**>, df //C_1əC_2=x̣ʷə́ɬəp=xʸəl or C_1əC_2=x̣ʷ[=B=]ə́=ɬəp=xʸəl//, ABDF /'*slip with both feet, lose balance on both feet*'/, (<**R3=**> *plural*), lx <**=xel**> *on the foot*, phonology: reduplication, possible backing, phonology: x̲w could be mistranscribed for xw, see xwlhépelets *sit down (with a plop?), [slip off one's chair]*, syntactic analysis: intransitive verb, attested by BHTTC (8/30/76).

<**x̲wlhépches**>, df //x̣ʷə́ɬ[=M1=]p=cəs orx̣ʷ[=B=]ə=ɬə́p=cəs//, ABDF /'*slip off the hands, slip out of the hands*'/, lx <**=ches ~ =tses**> *on the hand*, phonology: possible metathesis, possible backing, phonology: x̲w could be mistranscribed for xw, see xwlhépelets *sit down (with a plop?), [slip off one's chair]*, syntactic analysis: intransitive verb, attested by BHTTC (8/30/76).

<**xwlhépelets**>, df //xʷə́ɬ[=M1=]p=ələc or x̣ʷ[=F=]ə=ɬə́p=ələc//, ABDF /'*sat down (with a plop?), [slip off on one's bottom or chair]*'/, literally /'slip off on one's rump'/, lx <**=elets**> *on the rump, on the bottom*, phonology: possible metathesis, possible fronting, syntactic analysis: intransitive verb, attested by Elders Group (4/5/78).

<**x̲wlhépches**>, ABDF /'*slip off the hands, slip out of the hands*'/, see x̲wlhép.

<**x̱wlhépxel**>, ABDF */'slip off with a foot, lose balance [on feet]'/*, *see* **x̱**wlhép.

<**X̱wolích ~ X̱welích**>, PLN */'place at Ruby Creek where Paul Webster lived some years ago, now Wahleach Island Indian Reserve #2 and area at mouth of Mahood Creek'/*, *see* **x̱**wále ~ **x̱**wá:le.

<**x̱wó:qw'**>, probably root //x̣ʷá·q'ʷ//, EZ */'sawbill duck, fish-duck, common merganser (larger), American merganser'/*, [*'Mergus merganser'*], syntactic analysis: noun, nominal, attested by AC (12/4/71), BJ (12/5/64), EL (9/15/78), Elders Group (2/18/76), EB (2/13/78), other sources: ES /x̣ʷá·q'ʷ/ *sawbill*, JH /x̣á·q'ʷ/ (sic) *merganser*, Salish cognate: Mainland Comox /x̣ʷúʔq'ʷ/ *sawbill duck* B75prelim.:16, Squamish /x̣ʷúhq'ʷ/ *merganser, sawbill duck* K69:86 or better /x̣ʷúuq'ʷ/ *common merganser (Mergus merganser) and red-breasted merganser (M. serrator), sawbill duck* Kennedy and Bouchard 1976:71, Saanich dial. of NSt /x̣ʷáʔaq'ʷ/ *sawbill duck* B74a:14, example: <**qwóqwel te x̱wó:qw'.**>, //qʷɛ[=AáC₁ə=]l təx̣ʷá·q'ʷ//, */'The sawbill is talking.'/*, attested by AC (12/4/71), <**th'ó:kws te x̱wó:qw' qas te léts'e pésk'a.**>, //θ'ákʷs təx̣ʷá·q'ʷ qɛ-s tə lə́c'ə pə́sk'ɛ//, */'There are seven sawbill ducks and one hummingbird.'/*, attested by EB (2/13/78 approved this sentence constructed by class member).

<**x̱wóqw'**>, bound root //x̣ʷáq'ʷ *pole a canoe*//.

<**x̱wóqw'et**>, pcs //x̣ʷáq'ʷ=əT//, CAN [*'to pole a canoe'*], (<**=et**> *purposeful control transitivizer*), syntactic analysis: transitive verb, attested by Elders Group (3/26/75, 10/1/75), Salish cognate: Squamish root in /x̣ʷúq'ʷ-cut/ *to pole up (in a canoe)* K67:372.

<**x̱wóx̱weqw'et**>, cts //x̣ʷá[-C₁ə-]q'ʷ=əT//, CAN [*'poling a canoe'*], (<**-R1-**> *continuative*), phonology: reduplication, syntactic analysis: transitive verb, attested by Elders Group (3/26/75).

<**sx̱wő̄qw'tel**>, ds //s=x̣ʷa[=Aó=]q'ʷ=təl or s=x̣ʷa[=Aə́=]q'ʷ=təl//, CAN [*'canoe pole'*], literally /'device to pole a canoe'/, (<**s=**> *nominalizer, something to*), (<**ő̄-ablaut** or **é-ablaut**> *derivational*), lx <**=tel**> *device to, something to*, phonology: ablaut, syntactic analysis: nominal, attested by BJ (5/10/64), DM (12/4/64), AC (12/7/71), Elders Group (3/1/72, 3/26/75), EB, other sources: ES /sx̣ʷə́q'ʷtəl/ *canoe pole*, Salish cognate: Squamish /s-x̣ʷúq'ʷ-tn/ *canoe pole* K67:372, example: <**kw'étslexwes te sléxwelh, sq'émel, qas te sx̱wő̄qw'tel.**>, //k'ʷɛ[=Aə́=]c=l-əxʷ-əs tə s=lə́xʷ=wəɬ, s=q'ə́m(=)əl, qɛ-s tə s=x̣ʷa[=Aó=]q'ʷ=təl//, */'He saw a canoe, a paddle, and a canoe pole. (see s-th/s-o)'/*, attested by EB.

<**x̱wóqw'et**>, CAN [*'to pole a canoe'*], *see* **x̱**wóqw'.

<**x̱wotíx**>, probable bound root //x̣ʷatíxʸ//, meaning uncertain

<**sx̱wotíx**>, df //s=x̣ʷatíxʸ//, EZ */'hell-diver, pied-billed grebe'/*, [*'Podilymbus podiceps'*], ASM ['comes up the Fraser in the fall, a marsh bird, has hind legs way back, is a diver'], probably <**s=**> *nominalizer*, root meaning unknown, syntactic analysis: nominal, attested by BJ (12/5/64), Elders Group (2/11/76, 6/4/75), other sources: ES /sx̣ʷatì·xʸ/ *hell-diver*, Salish cognate: Lushootseed /x̣ʷətís/ *silver diver, "regular" diver (larger bird than the "small diver")* H76:614, Samish dial. of NSt /sx̣ʷtís/ *black diver (has white front)* G86:67, Saanich dial. of NSt /sxʷtís/ *black diver* B74a:14.

<**x̱wótl'aqw**>, possible bound stem //x̣ʷáƛ'ɛqʷ//, possible from root <**x̱wétl'**> *rolled up*

<**Sx̱wótl'aqwem**>, df //s=x̣ʷáƛ'ɛqʷ=əm//, PLN */'Emory Creek,* also *village at mouth of Emory Creek on both sides of the creek'/*, Elder's comment: literally /'water always boiling up rough'/, possibly <**s=**> *nominalizer, something to/that*, possibly root <**x̱wétl'**> *rolled up* possibly root <**as in sx̱wétl'qel**> *pillow, rolled up bulrush mat*, possibly <**ó-ablaut**> *resultative or continuative or derivational*, possibly <**=eqw**> *on top of the head* or more likely <**=aqw**> *around in circles*, .probably <**=em**> *intransitivizer, have, get*, syntactic analysis: nominal, attested by Elders Group (7/6/77 incl. Maggie Pennier, Mary Peters, CT, LJ), SP/AK/AD (Raft trip 8/30/77), source: place

names reference file #9, also <**Sx̱wótl'áqw'em**>, //s=x̣ʷáƛ'ɛ́q'ʷ=əm//, attested by Elders Group (7/9/75).

<**x̱wóx̱welá:lhp**>, EB /'*a small willow tree, a low willow*'/, *see* **x̱wále ~ x̱wá:le**.

<**X̱wóx̱welá:lhp**>, PLN ['*a village by Yale along Yale Creek*'], *see* **x̱wále ~ x̱wá:le**.

<**x̱wóx̱weqw'et**>, CAN ['*poling a canoe*'], *see* **x̱wóqw'**.

<**x̱wó:y**>, ABDF ['*they all died*'], *see* **x̱wà:y ~ x̱wá:y**.

<**x̱wóy**>, probably bound root or stem //x̣ʷáy or x̣ʷɛ́[=Aá=]y//, probably *shaking constantly*

<**sx̱wóyéleqw**>, df //s=x̣ʷáy=ə́ləqʷ or s=x̣ʷɛ́[=Aá=]y=ələqʷ//, CLO ['*(special head-dress)*'], SPRD, possibly <**s=**> *nominalizer, something to*, possibly root <**x̱wóy**> *shaking constantly* as in <**x̱wóyqwesem**> *one's head is shakingconstantly (like with disease)*, (semological comment: this is plausible since new dancers must almost constantly shake their staffs at dances and this also shakes their heads), possibly root <**x̱wáy**> *die in a group, all die*, (semological comment: this is plausible since new dancers are regarded as babies, newly reborn), lx <**=eleqw**> *on top of the head, on the hair*, phonology: possible ó-ablaut on root á automatic before suffixes of the head, syntactic analysis: nominal, attested by Elders Group (11/26/75).

<**sx̱wóyéleqws te x̱awsólkwlh**>, cpds //s=x̣ʷɛ́[=Aá=]y=ələqʷ-s təx̣ɛws=álkʷɬ//, CLO ['*new spirit-dancer's head-dress or [cedar-bark] hat*'], SPRD, literally /'special head-dress of the new guardian spirit'/, syntactic analysis: nominal phrase with modifier(s), attested by Elders Group (11/26/75, 3/16/78).

<**x̱wóyqwesem**>, mdls //x̣ʷáyqʷ=əs=əm//, ABDF ['*one's head is shaking constantly (like with disease)*'], root meaning unknown, lx <**=es**> *on the face*, (<**=em**> *middle voice or intransitivizer/have/get*), syntactic analysis: intransitive verb, attested by IHTTC (9/16/77).

<**sx̱wó:yx̱wey ~ sx̱wóyx̱wey**>, df //s=x̣ʷá(·)y=C_1əC_2 or s=x̣ʷɛ[=Aá=]·y=C_1əC_2//, REL /'*sx̱wóyx̱wey ceremony featuring a masked dance, the sx̱wóyx̱wey mask and dance*'/, ASM ['the wooden mask has protruding pegs for eyes and a carved protruding tongue, ears are often carved at the top and feathers and spinners fastened to the top, cloth drapes over the back of the head of the dancer, the dancer carries a hoop from which dangle large pectin shells which are rattled, during the dance a chorus of women sing the special song, the dance is done by prescribed numbers of dancers all similarly costumed, the right to do the dance is inherited through the female line, the dance may be put on at special ceremonies such as birth, marriage, death, cleansing or opening a longhouse, it is the only Stó:lō masked dance and the only mask they use, I saw the dance used at the opening of a new long-house for spirit-dancing in Chehalis, B.C.'], (<**s=**> *nominalizer, something to*), possibly root <**x̱wóy**> *shaking constantly* as in <**x̱wóyqwesem**> *one's head is shaking constantly (like with disease)*, (semological comment: this is plausible since the pectin shell rattles are shaken as a feature of the dance and the headresses also to make the flickers whirl), possibly root <**x̱wáy**> *die in a group, all die*, (semological comment: this is plausible since the mask and dance were said to originate with people who lived underwater in Kawkawa Lake (near Hope) and danced to try to save their people who were dying en masse of a leprosy-like disease), possibly <**ó-ablaut**> *derivational*, (<**=R2**> *characteristic*), phonology: reduplication, possible ablaut, syntactic analysis: nominal, attested by AC, Elders Group, DM, BJ, Salish cognate: Squamish /s-x̣ʷáyʔ-x̣ʷay/ *mask* K67:298, 372 (the vowel shows the word is borrowed from Halkomelem).

<**Sx̱wó:yx̱wey ~ Sx̱wóyx̱wey**>, df //s=x̣ʷá(·)y=C_1əC_2 or s=x̣ʷɛ[=Aá=]·y=C_1əC_2//, PLN /'*rock shaped like a man's head with a sx̱wó:yx̱wey mask on a point near the head of Harrison River, the point also called Spook's Point*'/, ASM ['located across the Harrison River from Skwtéxwqel point, both

points are near the outlet of Harrison Lake which forms the head (start) of Harrison River'], syntactic analysis: nominal, attested by EL (9/27/77, 3/1/78, 6/27/78), source: place names reference file #288.

<**Sx̱éyes te Sx̱wó:yx̱wey**>, cpds //s=x̣ə́yəs-s tə s=x̣ʷá(·)y=C_1əC_2//, PLN ['*a sx̱wó:yx̱wey head turned to stone on land at X̱elhlálh somewhere*'], literally /'the head of the sx̱wó:yx̱wey'/, syntactic analysis: nominal phrase with modifier(s), attested by IHTTC (9/7/77).

<**Sx̱wó:yx̱weyla ~ Sx̱wóyx̱weyla**>, ds //s=x̣ʷá(·)y=C_1əC_2=ɛlɛ//, PLN ['*village above Yakweakwioose on both sides of the Chilliwack River*'], ASM ['the river changed course around the turn of the century [1900] and now goes west from Vedder Crossing, the location of the old village site is near Higginson Rd., above Chilliwack Indian Reserve #8, where the Anglican church is now [1964]'], literally /'container of the sx̱wó:yx̱wey mask, home of the sx̱wó:yx̱wey mask'/, ASM ['so named presumably because one of the early owners of the mask lived there'], lx <**=álá ~ =àlà**> *container of/for*, phonology: reduplication, syntactic analysis: nominal, attested by BJ (12/5/64), other sources: Wells 1965 (lst ed.):19, source: place names reference file #175 and #176.

<**X̱wő:leqw**>, df //x̣ʷó·l=əqʷ//, PLN ['*Whonnock village*'], ASM ['a downriver Halkomelem-speaking village on the north side of the Fraser River'], root meaning unknown, possibly <**=eqw**> *on top of the head, on the hair*, syntactic analysis: nominal, attested by DF (Elders Group 4/23/80).

<**x̱wős**>, probable bound root //x̣ʷó(·)s//, *foam*

<**sx̱wősem ~ sx̱wő:sem ~ sx̱ő(:)sem**>, ds //s=x̣ʷó(·)s(=)əm//, EB ['*soapberry*'], ['*Shepherdia canadensis*'], FOOD /'*Indian ice-cream, whipped soapberry foam*'/, ASM ['the berries do not grow in Stó:lō territory but were obtained by trade with the Thompsons and others, the berries if rubbed between the hands will produce a white foam or froth, in aboriginal times (and still rarely today) the berries (or a syrup from them) were whipped up in special soapberry baskets kept grease-free, they were whipped up with special cedar whisks and the foam was eaten on special small flat paddle-shaped soapberry spoons, nowadays soapberries are more often whipped up with an electric beater in modern bowls kept grease-free (or the foam is inhibited), it is usually sweetened with sugar now, though in the old days other berries or other sweetening agents were added'], (<**s=**> *nominalizer, something to*), borrowed from Thompson /s-x̣ʷús-əm/ *soapberry* from root /x̣ʷús/ *foam* Turner 1973ms:34, phonology: optional partial delabialization before the <**ō**>/o/, we can tell this vowel is not from <**ew**>/əw/ because of the Musqueam and Cowichan cognates which have a different vowel and no <**w**>/w/, syntactic analysis: nominal, attested by AC (8/11/70, 11/24/71, 9/18/71), BJ (12/5/64), OW (Deming 1/4/79), other sources: ES /sx̣ʷə́wsəm/ (CwMs /sx̣ʷɛ́səm/) *soapberry*, Salish cognate: Thompson /s-x̣ʷús-əm/ *soapberry* from root /x̣ʷús/ *foam* Turner 1973ms:34, Squamish /s-x̣ʷús-m/ *soapberry* beside /x̣ʷús-um/ *prepare soapberries* K69:60, Lushootseed /s-x̣ʷúsəb ~ s-x̣ʷásəb/ *soapberry. Indian ice cream* H76:611, 623, Saanich dial. of NSt /sx̣ʷésəm/ *soapberry* B74a:15, Samish dial. of NSt /sx̣ʷésəm ~ sx̣ʷésəŋ/ *soapberry* G86:71, also <**x̱ősem**>, //x̣ʷósəm//, attested by MH (Deming 1/4/79).

<**sx̱wōsemálá**>, ds //s=x̣ʷosəm=ɛ́lɛ́//, BSK /'*soapberry basket, Indian ice-cream basket*'/, FOOD, ASM ['a tall basket with round bottom for whipping soapberries'], lx <**=álá**> *container for*, syntactic analysis: nominal, attested by Elders Group (3/24/76).

<**X̱wōx̱wá:ye**>, PLN /'*village on east bank of Sweltzer Creek (above Sx̱woyehá:lá), (creek by the village of the same name [X̱wōx̱wá:ye] [Wells])*'/, *see* x̱wōx̱wáye ~ x̱wex̱wáye ~ x̱wōx̱wá:ye.

<**x̱wőx̱wtha**> or <**x̱wéth**>, possible bound stem //x̣ʷə́[=C_1ə=]θ=ɛ//, root meaning unknown

<**sx̱wőx̱wtha**>, df //s=x̣ʷə́[=C_1ə=]θ=ɛ//, EZ /'*song sparrow,* also *brown sparrow,* (could include any or all of the following which occur in the Stó:lō area: *Savannah sparrow, vesper sparrow, lark*

sparrow, tree sparrow, chipping sparrow, Harris sparrow, fox sparrow, white-crowned sparrow, golden-crowned sparrow, and song sparrow) (type of brown wren [BHTTC 11/15/76], *larger wren (but smaller than robin)* [Elders Group 2/18/76]*)*'/, ['*Melospiza melodia morphna*, (perhaps any/all of the following: *Passerculus sandwichensis brooksi, Pooecetes gramineus, Chondestes grammacus, Spizella arborea, Spizella passerina, Zonotrichia querula, Passerella iliaca, Zonotrichia leucophrys, Zonotrichia atricapilla, Melospiza melodia morphna)*'], (<**s=**> *nominalizer, something to/that*), possibly <**=R1=**> *continuative/resultative*, root meaning unknown, possibly <**=a**> *living creature*, phonology: possible reduplication, syntactic analysis: nominal, attested by JL (9/15/78), Salish cognate: perhaps Squamish /s-x̣ʷíx̣ʷ/ *sparrow* K69:60 and *Savannah sparrow (Passerculus sandwichensis)* Kennedy and Bouchard 1976:100, probably Lushootseed /s-x̣ʷə́x̣ʷc'q'ʷ/ *river snipe (a small blackish diver and good swimmer, it eats trout eggs; it's mostly in creeks and rivers; in mythology he is a tricky sort of guy; he makes up lies to scare people ....)* H76:615, also <**sx̱wṓx̱wcha**>, //s=x̣ʷə́[=C_1ə=]c=ɛ//, attested by EL (9/15/78), also <**sx̱wéthx̱weth**>, //s=x̣ʷə́θ=C_1əC_2//, also /'*sparrow*'/, (<**=R2**> *characteristic*), dialects: *Katzie (downriver dial.)*, attested by Elders Group (6/4/75), comment: this apparently shows the root is **x̱**wéth, also /'*type of brown wren*'/, attested by BHTTC (11/15/76), also /'*larger wren (but smaller than robin)*'/, dialects: *Tait*, attested by Elders Group (2/18/76), also <**sx̱wṓx̱wlha**>, //s=x̣ʷə́[=C_1ə=]ɬ=ɛ//, also /'*larger wren (but smaller than robin)*'/, dialects: *Cheh.*, attested by Elders Group (2/18/76).

<**x̱wpét**>, //x̣ʷə́p-M1=T// or //x̣ʷp=əT//, ABFC ['*pick s-th up from the ground or floor*'], *see* <**xwpét**> under xwp.

<**x̱wtát**>, SH /'*rip it up, tear it up, rip s-th, tear s-th*'/, *see* **x̱**wét.

Y

<**yákw'**>, free root //yɛ́k’^{w}//, ECON ['*hire*'], syntactic analysis: intransitive verb, attested by Elders Group (3/15/72), EB (6/7/76), Salish cognate: Lushootseed /ják’^{w}adiʔ/ *invite* H76:211, example: <**láchulh yákw'.**>, //lɛ́-c(-əl)-uɬ yɛ́k’^{w}//, /'*I already hired., I've already hired.*'/, grammatical comment: zero optional as first person subject marker, attested by EB, Elders Group, also <**látsel welh le yákw'. ~ láchulh le yákw'.**>, //lɛ́-c-əl wəɬ lə yɛ́k’^{w} ~ lɛ́-c(-əl)-uɬ lə yɛ́·k’^{w}//, attested by Elders Group, <**látselcha yákw'.**>, //lɛ́-c-əl-cɛ yɛ́k’^{w}//, /'*I'm going to hire.*'/, attested by Elders Group.

<**yákw'emet ~ yékw'emet**>, iecs //yɛ́k’^{w}=məT ~ yɛ[=Aə́=]k’^{w}=məT//, ECON ['*hire s-o*'], (<**é-ablaut**> *derivational*), (<**=met**> *indirect effect non-control transitivizer*), phonology: optional ablaut, epenthetic e or syllabic m, syntactic analysis: transitive verb, syntactic comment: this form would be indistinguishable from a form with =em *intransitivizer* followed by =et *purposeful control transitivizer* but the latter seems unlikely since yákw' is used as an intransitive by itself (yákw'em is not yet attested), (semological comment: semantically, *to hire* (esp. if the meaning was originally *invite* as in the Lushootseed cognate and as in pre-contact days without money) does not involve full control over the person hired, only indirect control (or non-control since the person may quit, work slowly, etc.)), attested by Elders Group (3/15/72), contrast <**híyqwt**> *coax s-o, persuade s-o, invite s-o, (recuit s-o)* which is unrelated in form; found in <**yékw'emetes.**>, //yɛ[=Aə́=]k’^{w}=məT-əs//, /'*He hires someone.*'/, attested by Elders Group, example: <**látsel welh yákw'emethòmè. ~ láchulh yákw'emethòmè.**>, //lɛ́-c-əl wəɬ yɛ́k’^{w}=məT-ámə ~ lɛ́-c(-əl)-uɬ yɛ́k’^{w}=məT-ámə//, /'*I've already hired you.*'/, phonology: ...thòmè may show the pronoun object is -óme ~ -òmè, grammatical comment: zero optional as first person subject marker, attested by Elders Group, <**líchxw welh yékw'emet?**>, //lí-c-x^w wəɬ yɛ[=Aə́=]k’^{w}=məT//, /'*Did you already hire someone?*'/, attested by Elders Group, <**látselcha yékw'emet wáyélés.**>, //lɛ́-c-əl-cɛ yɛ[=Aə́=]k’^{w}=məT wɛ́yəl=əs//, /'*I'm going to hire someone tomorrow.*'/, phonology: updrifting, attested by Elders Group, <**látselcha yékw'emethòmè**>, //lɛ́-c-əl-cɛ yɛ[=Aə́=]k’^{w}=məT-ámə//, /'*I will hire you.*'/, attested by Elders Group; found in <**yekw'emethométsel. ~ yékw'emethométsel.**>, //yɛ[=Aə́=]k’^{w}=məT-ámə-c-əl or yɛ[=Aə́=]k’^{w}=məT-àmə̀-c-əl//, /'*I hire you., I'll hire you (now).*'/, (semological comment: a performative), attested by Elders Group.

<**yáyekw'emet**>, cts //yɛ́[-C_1ə-]k’^{w}=məT//, ECON ['*hiring s-o*'], (<**-R1-**> *continuative*), phonology: reduplication, syntactic analysis: transitive verb, attested by Elders Group (3/15/72); found in <**yáyekw'emetes.**>, //yɛ́[-C_1ə-]k’^{w}=məT-əs//, /'*He's hiring someone.*'/, attested by Elders Group.

<**yákw'emet ~ yékw'emet**>, ECON ['*hire s-o*'], *see* yákw'.

<**yál**> or <**yel**>, probable root //yɛ́l// meaning unknown unless *glide* or //yəl// *turn*

<**yáyelem**>, cts //yɛ́[-C_1ə-]l=əm//, ABFC /'*sailing (of a bird), gliding on the wind*'/, (<**-R1-**> *continuative*), (<**=em**> *middle voice or intransitivizer/have/get*), phonology: reduplication, syntactic analysis: intransitive verb, attested by SJ (Deming 8/10/78), Salish cognate: perhaps Squamish /yəl-aʔn/ *wing* with possible root /yəl/ *turn* as in /s-ilʔánm/ *year* K67:380, Nooksack <ay yálam> *(one bird) to fly in circles (like a hawk sailing above prey)(*NKF2.1861), prob. not Squamish /yáwap/ *sail* K67:382.

<**yalkw'ólhem** or **yelkw'wólhem**>, SOC /'*close up a meeting, wind up a meeting, complete a meeting*'/, *see* yókw' ~ yóqw'.

<**yá:lx̲**>, SOC ['*search*'], *see* yél or perhaps yá:l.

<**yá:lx̲t**>, SOC ['*search for s-th*'], *see* yél or perhaps yá:l.

<**yalh**>, free root //yɛɬ//, ASP /'*as usual, this time, now, the first time*'/, syntactic analysis: adverb/adverbial verb, attested by EB (1/9/76), LJ (4/7/78 History Dept. tape #34), Elders Group (2/8/78), Salish cognate: Musqueam dial. of Halkomelem /yéɬ/ (/yɛ́ɬ/ in ES orthog.) *only now, only then* (Suttles ca1984:4.3.1 and 18.4.14), Squamish /yaɬ/ *at last; after than, then* W73:3, K67:382, Saanich dial. of NSt /čəɬ/ *(particle) immediate past* in G86:60 from M86, possibly Lushootseed /yáʔɬ/ *(adverb) unrealized wish, be unable, want to but can't* H76:628, probably not Lushootseed /jəɬ/ *(modal particle) so it would seem, must be* H76:219-220, example: <**esésu tl'ó x̲ét'estem, stám kw'e yalh ...**>, //ʔə-s-ə́s-u ƛ'á x̣ə́t'ə=sT-əm, s=tɛ́m k'ʷə yɛɬ ...//, /'*And they said that's--, now what is it?...*'/, attested by LJ, <**yalhtsel sqw'él:ém**>, //yɛɬ-c-əl s=q'ʷə́l=əm//, /'*the first time I barbecued*'/, syntactic comment: notice the attachment of the subject pronoun to yalh as with adverb/adverbial verb's rather than particles, attested by Elders Group, <**yalhs'es me lhémexw.**>, //yɛɬ-s-ʔəs mə ɬə́məxʷ//, /'*It just started to rain.*'/, attested by Deming (3/31/77); Salish cognate: Musqueam /yéɬ/ *only now, only then* Suttles ca 1985:4.3.1, 18.4.14

<**yálhò**>, ds //yɛ́ɬ=à//, ASP /'*begin, start, (be) just started, just began, be just begun*'/, literally /'just now, just the first time, just this time'/, (<**=ò**> *just*), syntactic analysis: adverb/adverbial verb, attested by Elders Group (3/24/76, 2/8/78), EB (12/19/75), Deming (3/31/77), example: <**yálhòls yó:ys ~ yálhels yó:ys.**>, //yɛ́ɬ=à-l-s yá·ys//, /'*I started work., I started to work.*'/, literally /'is just now/is just begun my work'/, *<**yálhò tsel (s)yó:ys.**> rejected, syntactic comment: subject is expressed by possessive pronoun preceding -s subordinate clause nominalizer which nominalizes the following verb phrase so it can be possessed, attested by Elders Group (2/8/78), also <**yálhòlse le yóys.**>, //yɛ́ɬ=à-l-s lə yóys//, phonology: epenthetic e, attested by EB (Elders Group 2/8/78), <**yalhels yó:ys tloqá:ys.**>, //yɛ́ɬ=à-l-s yá·ys tla=qɛ́·ys//, /'*I just started working [this instant].*'/, attested by Elders Group (2/8/78), <**yálhòlse ts'qw'ő́wélh.**>, //yɛ́ɬ-à-l-s c'əq'ʷ=ówəɬ//, /'*I started to make a basket.*'/, phonology: epenthetic e, attested by EB (12/19/75), <**yálho'ó kw'e'asé ts'qw'ő́welh.**>, //yɛ́ɬ=a-ʔɛ k'ʷə-ʔɛ-s c'əq'ʷ=ówəɬ//, /'*You just start(ed) to make a basket.*'/, phonology: epenthetic e, yálho'ó perhaps mistranscribed for yálhò'á, syntactic comment: unusual double subject marking but both with possessive pronouns, attested by EB (12/19/75).

<**wiyálhò**>, ds //wə=yɛ́ɬ=à//, ASP ['*(just) started (to do something)*'], (<**we=**> *contrastive*), syntactic analysis: adverb/adverbial verb, attested by Elders Group (3/24/76), example: <**wiyálhòlses thíyt.**>, //wə=yɛ́ɬ-à-l-s-əs θíy=T//, /'*I just started to make it*'/, attested by Elders Group.

<**yálhò**>, ASP /'*begin, start, (be) just started, just began, be just begun*'/, *see* yalh.

<**Yálhxetel**>, df //yɛ́ɬ=xʸə(l)=təl or ye=o[=Aɛ́=]ɬ=xʸə(l)=təl//, PLN /'*island or point on north side of first slough north of the mouth of Chehalis River, (next slough and point above Mímex̲wel [EL 3/1/78])*'/, ASM ['the main canoe landing for Chehalis, the biggest landing at Chehalis, a point located about 100 yards further up Harrison River from the first slough (**Mímex̲wel**) above (north of) Chehalis River mouth (EL), near the end of present Chehalis Reserve Road by old church, the second slough north of Chehalis River it was where they had floats and beached their canoes (EB)'], possibly <**ye=**> *travelling by, in motion or (the) plural human*, root meaning unknown unless ólh *get aboard a canoe*, possibly <**á-ablaut**> *derivational*, possibly <**=xel**> *on the foot*, possibly <**=tel**> *device, something to*, phonology: consonant-loss (l on =xel before =tel), syntactic analysis: nominal, attested by DF and EB (3/3/76), EL (3/1/78), EB (12/8/75), EL with NP and EB (Chehalis place names trip 9/27/77), IHTTC (8/25/77), source: place names reference file #105 and #110, also /'*next slough and point above Mímex̲wel*'/, attested by EL (3/1/78).

<**yálh yuw kw'a's hò:y**>, LANG /'*I thank you (deeply), I thank you (deeply)., Thank you.*'/, *see* hò:y ~

hó:y ~ hóy.

<**yáq'**>, free root //yɛ́q'//, EB ['*to fall (about a tree)*'], syntactic analysis: intransitive verb, attested by Elders Group (3/72), Salish cognate: Squamish /yáq'/ *fall down* as also in /yáq'-an/ *cause to fall down (tr.)* K67:382, example: <**le yáq'.**>, //lə yɛ́q'//, /'*It fell (of a tree).*'/, attested by Elders Group.

<**syáyeq'**>, dnom //s=yɛ́[=C_1ə=]q'//, rsls, EB ['*log*'], literally /'something that has fallen (of a tree)'/, (<**s=**> *nominalizer*), (<**=R1=**> *resultative*), phonology: reduplication, syntactic analysis: nominal, attested by AC (8/26/70, 11/16/71), other sources: H-T <s'ya'uk> (umlaut over a) *log (in the forest)* vs. <kwEtla'i> (umlaut over a) *log (in the water).*

<**syáq'yeq'**>, pln //s=yɛ́q'=C_1əC_2//, EB ['*a lot of logs*'], (<**=R2**> *plural* but usually *characteristic*), phonology: reduplication, syntactic analysis: nominal, attested by JL (5/5/75).

<**yáq'et**>, pcs //yɛ́q'=əT//, HARV /'*to fall it (a tree), to fell a tree, to fall a tree*'/, (<**=et**> *purposeful control transitivizer*), syntactic analysis: transitive verb, attested by Elders Group (3/15/72, 3/19/75).

<**yáyeq'et**>, cts //yɛ́[-C_1ə-]q'=əT//, HARV /'*falling it, falling a tree*'/, (<**-R1-**> *continuative*), phonology: reduplication, syntactic analysis: transitive verb, attested by Elders Group (3/15/72), example: <**yáyeq'etes te thqát.**>, //yɛ́[-C_1ə-]q'=əT-əs tə θqɛ́t//, /'*He's falling a tree.*'/, attested by Elders Group.

<**yéq'lexw ~ yéq'elexw**>, ncs //yɛ[=Aə́=]q'=l-əx^w//, HARV /'*managed to fell a tree, (managed to fall it)*'/, (<**é-ablaut**> *resultative*), (<**=l**> *non-control transitivizer*), (<**-exw**> *third person object*), phonology: ablaut, optional epenthetic e, syntactic analysis: transitive verb, attested by Elders Group (3/15/7).

<**yeq'á:ls**>, sas //yəq'=ɛ́·ls//, HARV ['*fall a tree*'], (<**=á:ls**> *structured activity non-continuative*), phonology: vowel-reduction, syntactic analysis: intransitive verb, attested by IHTTC (9/2/77).

<**yáyeq'els**>, cts //yɛ́[-C_1ə-]q'=əls//, sas, HARV /'*falling (a tree), be falling trees*'/, (<**-R1-**> *continuative*), (<**=els**> *structured activity continuative*), phonology: reduplication, syntactic analysis: intransitive verb, attested by Elders Group (3/15/72), EB, IHTTC (9/2/77).

<**yáyeq'els**>, dnom //yɛ́[=C_1ə=]q'=əls//, sas, HARV /'*a faller, a logger*'/, (<**=R1=**> *continuative*), (<**=els**> *structured activity continuative nominal*), phonology: reduplication, syntactic analysis: nominal, attested by IHTTC (9/2/77).

<**yáq'et**>, HARV /'*to fall it (a tree), to fell a tree, to fall a tree*'/, *see* yáq'.

<**yá:t**>, free root //yɛ́·t//, ABDF /'*to vomit, throw up*'/, syntactic analysis: intransitive verb, attested by AC (8/14/70), other sources: ES /yɛ́·t/ (circumflex over ɛ) (Cw /yɛ́ʔɛt/) *vomit*, Salish cognate: Squamish /yaʔt/ *vomit* and /yə́-yaʔt/ *vomit continuously* K67:382, 381.

<**yáyet ~ yáyat**>, rsls //yɛ́[-C_1ə-]t//, ABDF ['*vomiting*'], (<**-R1-**> *resultative* or *continuative*), phonology: reduplication, syntactic analysis: intransitive verb, attested by AC (8/14/70), Salish cognate: Squamish /yə́-yaʔt/ *vomit continuously* K67:381.

<**syá:ttel**>, dnom //s=yɛ́·t=təl//, MED ['*throw-up medicine*'], ASM ['medicine to make one throw up'], (<**s=**> *nominalizer*), lx <**=tel**> *device, something, medicine*, syntactic analysis: nominal, attested by Elders Group (7/23/75).

<**héyetélmel**>, cts //hɛ́-yɛt=ə́lməl//, ABDF ['*nauseated*'], literally /'vomiting in the mind, think about/feel like vomiting'/, (<**hé- ~ há-**> *continuative*), lx <**=élmel**> *in the mind, think about, feel like*, syntactic analysis: intransitive verb.

<**yá:tel**>, probable bound root or stem //yɛ́·t(=)əl or s=yɛ́·(yə)=təl//, root possibly <yá: or yá:ye> *be*

friend, relative, <=tel> may be *reciprocal* or *someone for*

<**syá:tel**>, dnom //s=yɛ́·t(=)əl or s=yɛ́·=təl//, SOCT /'*widow, widower*'/, (<**s=**> *nominalizer*), root meaning unknown unless <**yá:**> *to be friend* as in root <**yá:ya**>, stem <**syá:ya**> *friend*, possibly <**=el**> *go, come, get, become*, possibly <**=tel**> *something that, someone to*, syntactic analysis: nominal, attested by NP (10/10/75), Elders Group (3/13/80), other sources: ES /syɛ̂təl/ (CwMs /syɛ̂ʔtən/) *widow, widower*, Salish cognate: Squamish /syáʔtn/ *widow(er)* K67:300, perhaps Squamish root /yaʔ/ *tight, shut or tied tightly* as in /yáʔ-n/ *put on, hold, tie tightly (tr.)* and /yáʔ-ya/ *tight* and /yáʔ-ya-c/ *stoppered tightly (ab. bottle)* K67:381 (however this would require a doublet in Halkomelem since this root in Squamish is more clearly cognate with the root in Upriver Halkomelem /selá/ //s=hə-lɛ́// *tight*).

<**yatílém**>, incs //yɛt=íl=əm//, SOC /'*become a widow, become a widower*'/, (<**=íl**> *go, come, get, become*), (<**=em**> *intransitivizer, have, get*), phonology: updrifting, syntactic analysis: intransitive verb, attested by Elders Group (3/13/80).

<**yatílém**>, SOC /'*become a widow, become a widower*'/, *see* syá:tel.

<**yátl'q'els**>, MC ['*painting*'], *see* yétl'.

<**yátl'q't**>, ABFC ['*rubbing it*'], *see* yétl'.

<**ya<u>x</u> ~ á<u>x</u>**>, free root //yɛx̣ ~ ʔɛ́x̣//, EFAM ['*bad*'], usage: baby-talk, said to a child of crawling age to teach him something is bad, syntactic analysis: interjection, attested by AD.

<**yá<u>x</u>q' ~ iyá<u>x</u>q'**>, possible bound root or stem //(i)yɛ́x̣q'//, root meaning unknown, initial <i> probably epenthetic, the derived form is lit. "something for doing X as a structured activity" and the stem or root here expresses what the pouch does, the doing X part, possibly <**=q'**> *on something else, within something else*, leaving root or stem <**yáx**> meaning unknown (only <**yéxch ~ yéxts**>, free root //yə́x̣c *give as a gift*// comes close in shape), or less likely <**ye-**> *travelling along while (doing X)*, leaving root or stem <**<u>x</u>áq'**> if there is derivational metathesis or if not <**<u>x</u>q'**>, roots attested so far which have these two consonants are <**<u>x</u>eq'**>, free root //x̣ə́q'//, DESC ['*narrow (of rocky passage)*'], <**<u>x</u>íq'**> ~ <**<u>x</u>éyq'**>, possibly root //x̣í(=)q' *scratch (like of an itch)*//, and none of these seem convincing semantically.

<**shxwyá<u>x</u>q'els ~ shxwiyá<u>x</u>q'els**>, dnom //sx^{w}=yɛ́x̣q'=əls//, sas, HUNT ['*pouch (like for gunpowder)*'], PE, (<**shxw=**> *something for*), root meaning unknown, (<**=els**> *structured activity continuative nominal/tool for*), syntactic analysis: nominal, attested by DM (12/4/64 Wells tape new transcript new p.180).

<**yá:ya**>, possibly root //yɛ́·yɛ or ʔɛ́y=M1=iyɛ or ʔɛ́y=M2=R2 *be friends, relatives*//.

<**siyá:ya ~ siyáya ~ syá:ya ~ siyá(:)ye**>, dnom //s=yɛ́·yɛ or s=ʔɛ́y=M1=iyɛ or s=ʔɛ́y=M2=C_1əC_2//, SOC ['*friend, relative*'], (<**s=**> *nominalizer, someone that*), possibly <**=e**> *person, being*, possibly <**á:-ablaut**> *derivational*, possibly root <**ey ~ iy** (before suffixes)> *good* or <**yá:ya**> perhaps *be friends, relatives*, possibly <**=iya**> *affectionate diminutive*, possibly <**M1 or M2 metathesis**> *derivational*, possibly <**=R2**> *characteristic*, comment: this etymology yields stem yá:ya, phonology: consonant-loss of glottal stop, reduplication, possible metathesis, possible vowel merger, syntactic analysis: nominal, attested by AC (many occasions), BJ (5/10/64, 12/5/64), Deming (12/15/77), others, example: <**siyám l siyáye,**>, //s=iy=ɛ́m l s=ʔiy=C_1əC_2[=Aɛ́·=]=ə//, /'*My dear friends,*'/, usage: speeches, attested by Deming, <**we'ólwel stl'í l siyá:ye.**>, //wə=ʔál-wə-l s=ƛ'í l s=ʔiy=C_1əC_2[=Aɛ́·=]=ə//, /'*I like my friend a lot.*'/, attested by EB, other sources: ES /syɛ́·yɛ/ (CwMs /syɛ́ʔyɛʔ/) *friend, relative*, H-T <sie'ya> (macrons over i and e) *companion, comrade*, Salish cognate: Squamish /s-yáyʔ/ *friend; be related to, be on friendly terms with* [s-

nominalizer vs. s- *stative*] K67:300, W73:214, K69:60, Lushootseed /s-yáyaʔ/ (perhaps /s-yáʔyaʔ/) *relative, friend* H76:627, example: <**tl'ó:l siyá:ya.**>, //ƛ'á-əl s=yɛ́·yɛ//, /'*That's my friend.*'/, attested by AC (9/29/71), <**lhwélep l siyáya**>, //ɬ=lə́w[=M2=]ə=p l s=yɛ́·yɛ//, /'*You people are my friends.*'/, attested by AC (9/29/71), also <**talhwélep l siyáye**>, //tɛ=ɬ=lə́w[=M2=]ə=p l s=yɛ́yə//, also /'*you people my friends*'/, attested by Deming (12/15/77), <**siyáyes te stá:xwelh.**>, //s=yɛ́·yɛ-s tə s=tɛ́·x^{w}=əɬ//, /'*Children are his friends.*'/, attested by AC (9/29/71).

<**sí:yá:ya**>, pln //s=C_1əC_2=yɛ́·yɛ or s=í·=yɛ́·yɛ or s=hə́=yɛ́·yɛ or /s=ʔi[=´·=]y=C_1əC_2[=Aɛ́·=]=ə//, SOC ['*friends, lots of friends*'], possibly <**R3=**> *plural*, possibly <**í:=**> *plural*, possibly <**hé=**> *plural*, phonology: vowel-loss and vocalization of y, could also now be analyzed as lengthening and stress-insertion (as in sí:yá:m, the plural of siyá:m *respected leader, chief*; this process is also used to form continuatives occasionally; found in sí:yá:met *flirting with s-o*) but here can be anaylzed as reduplication, s(i) →sí: plurals, historical/comparative detail: the Lushootseed cognate shows what is probably the ultimate origin of all the plurals of s(i)=y... words → sí:y..., that is prefixed reduplication, considering Cowichan and Musqueam with glottal stop as the second root consonant (corresponding regularly to length in Chilliwack), Proto-Halkomelem had a plural form //*s=R3=yɛ́ʔyɛʔ// or //*s=yəʔ=yɛ́ʔyɛʔ// which apparently lost the first vowel and vocalized the /y/ to /i/ between consonants (both frequent processes), then upriver glottal stop before consonant was changed to length and final glottal stop was dropped (also regular), leaving Upriver Halq'eméylem with /sí·yɛ́·yɛ/, the vocalization happens also in the Squamish cognate but not in the Lushootseed cognate, syntactic analysis: nominal, attested by EB, AC, Deming (5/18/78), others, Salish cognate: Squamish /s-í-yayʔ/ *friends* K67:300, Lushootseed /syə̀yáʔyaʔ/ *friends, relations* H76:627, example: <**ts'áts'eltsel xwoyíwel tel sqwálewel kw'els me xwe'í sq'o talhlúwep l sí:yáye sí:yám.**>, //c'ɛ́[=C_1ə=]l-c-əl x^{w}=ɛ[=Aa=]y=íwəl t-əl s=q^{w}ɛ̀l=əwəl k'^{w}-əl-s mə x^{w}ə=ʔí s=q'á tɛ=ɬ=lúwə=p l s=C_1əC_2=yɛ́·yɛ s=i[=´·=]y=ɛ́·m//, /'*I'm very happy to come here at this gathering my dear friends.*'/, usage: speech, attested by Deming (5/18/78).

<**yáyetel** (prob. also **yáyatel)**>, rcps //yɛ́yɛ=təl//, pcs, SOC /'*they've made friends, (make friends with each other)*'/, (<**=tel**> *reciprocal*), syntactic analysis: intransitive verb, attested by AC (11/16/71), other sources: perhaps ES /yáytəl/ *blood relatives*, Salish cognate: verbal use of the same root cognate in Squamish /yáy-nəwʔas/ *become friends* K69:91.

<**yóyatel**>, cts //yɛ[-Aá-]yɛ=təl//, rcps, SOC /'*they're making friends, (making friends with each other)*'/, (<**ó-ablaut on root a**> *continuative*), phonology: ablaut, syntactic analysis: intransitive verb, attested by AC (11/16/71).

<**yáyekw'emet**>, ECON ['*hiring s-o*'], *see* yákw'.

<**yáyelem**>, ABFC /'*sailing (of a bird), gliding on the wind*'/, *see* **yal**

<**yáyeq'els**>, HARV /'*falling (a tree), be falling trees*'/, *see* yáq'.

<**yáyeq'els**>, HARV /'*a faller, a logger*'/, *see* yáq'.

<**yáyeq'et**>, HARV /'*falling it, falling a tree*'/, *see* yáq'.

<**yáyetel** (prob. also **yáyatel)**>, SOC /'*they've made friends, (make friends with each other)*'/, *see* yá:ya.

<**yáyet ~ yáyat**>, ABDF ['*vomiting*'], *see* yá:t.

<**yáysele ~ yéysele**>, HUMC ['*two people*'], *see* isá:le ~ isále ~ isá:la.

<**ye=**>, da //yə=//, DEM ['*nominalizer plural*'], phonology: probably phonologically prefixed because in some cases the <**e**> merges with a following consonant (for ex. =w) to form a new vowel (as in yutló:lem *it's them*), syntactic analysis: derivational prefix, syntactic comment: a number of verbs

(demonstrative, interrogative, pronominal) can serve a nominal or pronominal function when phonologically prefixed with ye=; found in <**yutl'ó:lem**>, //yə=w=ƛ'á(·)[=lə=]=m//, /'*it's them, they are the ones*'/.

<**ye= ~ yi= ~ í**>, da //yə= ~ yi= ~ ʔi//, TVMO /'*travelling by, in motion, while moving along, while travelling along*'/, syntactic analysis: derivational prefix, Salish cognate: Samish dial. of NSt /ʔiʔ- ~ ʔi- ~ yi-/ *in motion, while moving* G86:56; found in <**yeló:lh**>, //yə=ʔ[=əl=]á·ɬ//, /'*travelling by canoe, travelling by car/boat/train*'/, literally /'travelling along aboard (a canoe, nowadays also a car/boat/train)'/, <**ye'í:mex ~ yi'í:mex**>, //yə=ʔí[-·-]m=əxʸ//, /'*travelling by foot, travelling on foot*'/, literally /'travelling along walking'/, <**yets'ets'á:**>, //yə=C_1ə=c'ɛ·//, /'*travelling by horse*'/, literally /'travelling along astride'/, <**yexwéwqw'elem**>, //yə=xʷə=´=wəq'ʷ=əl=əm//, /'*travelling by going downriver*'/, literally /'travelling along going downriver'/, <**yex̲wóx̲weqw'et**>, //yə=x̣ʷá[-C_1ə-]q'ʷ=əT//, /'*poling along in a canoe (in quiet water), travelling by poling a canoe*'/, literally /'travelling along poling a canoe'/.

<**ye ~ yi**>, free root //yə ~ yi//, DEM ['*the (plural [usually human])*'], syntactic analysis: demonstrative article, attested by EB, Elders Group, AC, others, Salish cognate: Lushootseed /ʔi-/ *(derivational prefix) collective* for ex. in /ʔi-sčə́txʷəd/ *bears*, /ʔi-qyúuqs/ *group of seagulls*, and /ʔi-ƛ'úb/ *enough* H76:666, example: <**ye (xwélmexw, mestíyexw, qwóqwel)**>, //yə (xʷə́l=məxʷ, məstíyəxʷ, qʷɛ[-Aá-]l)//, /'*the (Indians/people, people, speakers)*'/, literally /'the (plural) (Indian, person, speaking)'/, <**ye líkw' kw'e Kamloops, ye líkw' mő́kw' shxwtelís li te B.C.**>, //yə lík'ʷ k'ʷə Kamloops, yə lík'ʷ mók'ʷ sxʷ=təlí-s li tə B.C.//, /'*some from Kamloops, some from all over B.C.*'/, usage: narrative of recent gathering, attested by AC (11/10/71), <**qesu lá:m ye lí:kw'.**>, //qə-s-u lɛ́·=m yə lí·k'ʷ//, /'*And so a few went.*'/, usage: story of the Flood, attested by AC (12/7/71), <**xwey'éyelhs ye qweqwà:l**>, //xʷ=C_1əC_2=ʔɛ́y=əɬ-s yə C_1ə=qʷɛ̀·l//, /'*[they are (many)] talking good*'/, literally /'they (many) are in good/clear voice the (pl.) [ones] talking (public speaking)'/, attested by JL (Elders Group 8/29/79), <**kw'étslexwes te swíyeqe mékw' yi slhellhálí**>, //k'ʷə́c=l-əxʷ-əs tə s=wíq=ə mə́k'ʷ yi s=C_1əC_2=ɬɛ́l=i//, /'*The men saw all the women.*'/, attested by Elders Group, <**lemlémetchxw mékw' ye tskwí:m l á:wkw'.**>, //C_1əC_2=lə́m=əT-c-xʷ mə́k'ʷ yə c=kʷí·m l ʔɛ́·wk'ʷ//, /'*Fold all my red clothes.*'/, attested by Elders Group, <**lemlémetchxw mékw' yel á:wkw'.**>, //C_1əC_2=lə́m=əT-c-xʷ mə́k'ʷ yə-l ʔɛ́·wk'ʷ//, /'*Fold all my clothes.*'/, attested by Elders Group, <**le q'ep'lóxes wiyóthe kwsu háléms ye mímelha.**>, //lə q'əp'=l-áxʸ-əs wi=yáθ-ə kʷ-s-u hɛ́-lɛ=m-s yə mí[-C_1ə-]ɬɛ//, /'*He got me addicted to (hooked on) always going to spirit dances. (get s-o addicted, get s-o hooked)*'/, attested by EB, <**tl'ó tàls yithá.**>, //ƛ'á tɛ̀l-s yi=θɛ́//, /'*That's their mother.*'/, attested by AC (8/28/70), <**álhtelcha yithá wéyeles.**>, //ʔɛ́ɬ=təl-cɛ yi=θɛ́ wɛ́yəl=əs//, /'*They'll eat tomorrow.*'/, attested by AC (11/13/71).

<**yékw'et**>, SH /'*break up s-th by crumpling, crush it up, rub it together fast (to soften or clean), rub it to soften it (of plants, etc.), fluff it (inner cedar bark to soften it)*'/, *see* yókw' ~ yóqw'.

<**yekw'ó:lh**> or perhaps <**yekw'wó:lh**>, CAN ['*one's canoe is broken up*'], *see* yókw' ~ yóqw'.

<**yekw'ólhem**> or perhaps <**yekw'wólhem**>, CAN ['*break(ing) the canoe*'], *see* yókw' ~ yóqw'.

<**yél ~ yá:l**>, bound root //yə́l ~ yɛ́·l *turn*//, Salish cognate: Squamish root /yəl/ *turn* as in /yə́l-aʔn/ *wing* and /s-ilʔánm/ *year* K67:380, Lushootseed root /jal-/ [dzál-] *reverse the side of, turn over, turn around, go around/over some obstruction* as in /jál-q-əd/ *turn it over*, /jál-q-us/ *turn face to opposite direction/, /jal-jəl-q/ turn around several times/, /jál-qs/ go around a point,* [and probably] /s-jál-č'/ (Skagit) ~ /s-jál-c'/ (Snohomish) *year, turning of the seasons* H76:212-213.

<**yélqw't**>, pcs //ye[=Aá·=]l=q'ʷ=T//, SOC /'*upset bed, mess s-th up*'/, VALJ, probably root <**yel**> *turn*, possibly <**ó:-ablaut**> *durative or resultative*, possibly <**=qw'**> *around in circles*, (<**=t**> *purposeful*

control transitivizer), phonology: possible ablaut, syntactic analysis: transitive verb, attested by Elders Group (6/1/77).

<**yó:lqw'**>, ds //ye[=Aá·=]l=q'^{w}//, SOC /'*make a mess, mess up*'/, VALJ, probably root <**yel**> *turn*, possibly <**ó:-ablaut**> *durative or resultative*, possibly <**=qw'**> *around in circles*, phonology: possible ablaut, syntactic analysis: intransitive verb, attested by Elders Group (6/1/77).

<**yó:lqw'es**>, ds //ye[=Aá·=]l=q'^{w}=əs//, SOC ['*make a real mess*'], VALJ, probably root <**yel**> *turn*, possibly <**ó:-ablaut**> *durative or resultative*, possibly <**=es**> *on the face*?, phonology: possible ablaut, syntactic analysis: intransitive verb, attested by Elders Group (6/1/77).

<**xwiyó:leqw**>, ds //x^{w}ə=yə[=Aá·=]l=əq^w//, DIR ['*(become/get) upside down*'], (<**xwe=**> *become, get*), possibly <**ó:-ablaut**> *durative or resultative*, lx <**=eqw**> *on top of the head*, phonology: possible ablaut, syntactic analysis: intransitive verb, adjective/adjectival verb?, attested by Elders Group (5/5/76).

<**xwiyó:leqwt**>, pcs //x^{w}ə=yə[=Aá·=]l=əq^w=T//, DIR ['*turn s-o upside down*'], (<**=t**> *purposeful control transitivizer*), phonology: possible ablaut, syntactic analysis: transitive verb, attested by Elders Group (5/5/76), compare perhaps <**yó:lx̲wtem**> *delirious*, compare perhaps <**syó:letsep**> *wave (of water)*.

<**yélx̲t**>, pcs //yə́l=x̣=T//, SOC ['*look for s-th/s-o*'], root <**yél**> *turn*, lx <**=x̲**> *distributive, all over*, (<**=t**> *purposeful control transitivizer*), syntactic analysis: intransitive verb, attested by EB (3/1/76), Salish cognate: Squamish /yə́lx̣/ *look for (itr.)* and /yə́lx̣-t/ *look for (tr.)* K67:380; found in <**yélx̲tchexw.**>, //yə́l=x̣=T-c-əx^w//, /'*Look for s-th/s-o., You look for s-th/s-o.*'/, attested by EB.

<**yá:lx̲t**>, durs //yə[=Aɛ́·=]l=x̣=T//, SOC ['*search for s-th*'], (<**á:-ablaut**> *resultative*), syntactic analysis: transitive verb, attested by EB (1/30/76).

<**yá:lx̲**>, durs //yə[=Aɛ́·=]l=x̣//, SOC ['*search*'], root <**yél**> *turn*, (<**á:-ablaut**> *durative*), lx <**=x̲**> *distributive, all over*, phonology: ablaut, syntactic analysis: intransitive verb, attested by EB (1/30/76).

<**yelá:w ~ yeláw ~ yiláw**>, possibly root //yəlɛ́(·)w or yəl=ɛ́(·)w or yil=ɛ́(·)w//, DIR /'*be over, past (passed)*'/, TIME, possibly root <**yel**> *turn*, possibly <**=á(:)w**> meaning unknown, syntactic analysis: adverb/adverbial verb, attested by Elders Group (3/19/75), EB (1/26/76), Salish cognate: Lushootseed /yəláw'/ *proceed* H76:630, example: <**yiláw te syáyeq'**>, //yilɛ́w tə s=yɛ́[=C_1ə=]q'//, /'*over the log*'/, attested by Elders Group, <**yiláw texwswáyel**>, //yilɛ́w təx^w=s=wɛ́yəl//, /'*afternoon (minutes after 12 noon)*'/, attested by Elders Group, <**chxw la yelá:w.**>, //c-x^w lɛ yəlɛ́·w//, /'*You passed by.*'/, literally /'you went past'/, attested by EB, <**alht'éqw' syiláws te slhéms**>, //ʔɛɬ=t'ə́q'^{w} s-yilɛ́w-s tə s=ɬə́m=s//, /'*half an hour past eleven o'clock, thirty minutes after 11:00*'/, literally /'half (portion broken (of string) of what's passed of the eleventh hour'/, attested by Elders at Fish Camp (7/19/78).

<**yéyilaw ~ yíyelaw**>, dmv //C_1í=yilɛ́w ~ C_1í=yəlɛ́w//, DIR /'*a little past, a little after*'/, TIME, (<**R4=**> *diminutive*), phonology: reduplication, syntactic analysis: adverb/adverbial verb, attested by Elders Group (3/1/76), SJ (Deming 1/20/77), example: <**yéyilaw texwswáyel**>, //C_1í=yilɛw təx^w=s=wɛ́yəl//, /'*a little after noon, later on in the afternoon*'/, attested by Elders Group, <**yíyelaw te slhíxws**>, //C_1í=yəlɛw tə s=ɬíx^w=s//, /'*past three o'clock*'/, Elder's comment: "this is as close as the old people got to minutes", attested by SJ.

<**yelá:wt**>, pcs //yəlɛ́·w=T//, TVMO ['*pass by s-o*'], DIR, (<**=t**> *purposeful control transitivizer*), syntactic analysis: transitive verb, attested by EB (1/26/76), example: <**lam o yelá:wthò:m.**>, //lɛ́=m ʔà yəlɛ́·w=T-à·m//, /'*You were passed by., He passed you by.*'/, literally /'he goes just you are passed by'/, attested by EB.

<**yelá:wx**>, pcis //yəlɛ́·w=x^y//, TVMO ['*to pass by s-th/s-o*'], DIR, (<**=x**> *purposeful control transitivizer inanimate object preferred*), syntactic analysis: transitive verb, attested by EB (1/26/76), example: <**lam o yelá:wxóxes; ő̱we is ye qwélsthóxes.**>, //lɛ=m ʔà yəlɛ́·w=x^y-áx^y-əs ʔə́wə ʔi-s yə q^wɛ[=Aə́=]l=sT-áx^y-əs//, /'*He just passed by me; he didn't speak to me. (speak to s-o)*'/, attested by EB.

<**yeláwel**>, incs //yəlɛ́w=əl//, TVMO /'*just past, over*'/, (<**=el**> *go, come, get, become*), syntactic analysis: adverb/adverbial verb, attested by Elders Group (1/19/77), Salish cognate: Saanich dial. of NSt /čəl'éwəl/ *to pass by* B74a:70.

<**yilawelhát ~ yiláwelhàt ~ syiláwelhàt**>, ds //yilɛ́w=əɬ(=)lɛ́t//, TIME ['*Monday (day past)*'], literally /'day after [Sunday] ~ something past day'/, (<**s=**> *nominalizer*), lx <**=elh(=)lát**> *day, past (tense) night*, phonology: consonant merger (lhl → lh), optional downstepping, syntactic analysis: nominal, attested by Elders Group (3/19/75), IHTTC (8/10/77), EB (5/1 or 2/78), example: <**lámtselcha kw'e syiláwelhàt.**>, //lɛ́=m-c-əl-cɛ k'ʷə s=yilɛ́w=əɬ=lɛ́t//, /'*I'm going to go on Monday., I'll go on Monday.*'/, attested by EB.

<**yeláwel**>, TVMO /'*just past, over*'/, *see* yelá:w ~ yeláw ~ yiláw.

<**yelá:wt**>, TVMO ['*pass by s-o*'], *see* yelá:w ~ yeláw ~ yiláw.

<**yelá:wx**>, TVMO ['*to pass by s-th/s-o*'], *see* yelá:w ~ yeláw ~ yiláw.

<**yél:és**>, possibly root //yə́l·ə́s or y=əlí[=Aə́=]s//, ANA /'*tooth, teeth*'/, possibly <**=elís**> *of the tooth*, possibly <**é-ablaut on affix**> *durative or derivational*, phonology: possible ablaut, possible lengthening (of resonant between two stressed vowels, updrifting, syntactic analysis: noun, nominal, attested by AC (8/14/70, 9/10/71), BJ (5/10/64), EB, other sources: ES /yə́lə́s/ *tooth*, Proto-Central Salish */yənís ~ yə́nis/ *tooth*, Salish cognate: PCS cognate set #18 in G88 (#145 in G82) includes: MCx /ǰə́nəs/ [ǰínɪs], Pt /yə́nəs/ [yínɪs] ~ /yənís/ (Boas 1886 Pentlatch.field notes <yini's>), Se /yə́nis/, Sq /yənís/ K67:380, CwMs /yə́nəs/ ES, Nk /yənís/ A61, G84a:SJ, NStCl /čə́nəs/, Ld /ǰədís/ H76:217, Tw /yədís ~ yə́dis/ all *tooth*, example: <**líye sá:yem ta yél:és?**>, //lí-ə sɛ́·y=əm t-ɛ yə́l·ə́s//, /'*Have you got a toothache?, Does your tooth hurt?*'/, attested by AC (9/10/71), <**kw'óqw lí te yél:és**>, //k'ʷáqʷ lí tə yə́l·ə́s//, /'*hit with a stick-like object on the teeth*'/, attested by EB (1/12/76).

<**Xwyélés ~ Lexwyélés**>, ds //x^w=yə́lə́s ~ lə(x^w)=x^w=yə́lə́s//, PLN ['*rock up the Harrison River from the old Chehalis Indian cemetery*'], ASM ['it also has marks near it called *Tracks of Mink* (**S<u>x</u>éyeltels te Sqayé<u>x</u>iya**); this place is the subject of a story told in Boas (Bertz translation, 1980 version:34) about a woman with this name who had teeth in her vagina and bit off Mink's right hand (so his tracks can still be seen where he ran out of her house) and was soon transformed into rock by the Transformer, <u>X</u>á:ls;'], literally /'(always) teeth in the vagina'/, lx <**xw=**> *in the vagina, on the vulva*, (<**lexw= ~ xw= ~ le=**> *always*), phonology: possible consonant merger, syntactic analysis: nominal, attested by EL (3/1/78, 6/27/78).

<**yélyelesem**>, chrs //yə́l[=C_1əC_2=]əs=əm//, ABDF /'*(have) a steady toothache, have a toothache*'/, (<**=R2=**> *characteristic*), (<**=em**> *intransitivizer, have, get*), possibly <**=em**> *middle voice*, phonology: reduplication, syntactic analysis: intransitive verb, attested by Elders Group (3/3/76, 9/1/76, 1/24/79), also <**yelyélés**>, //C_1əC_2=yə́lə́s//, also /'*toothache*'/, attested by AH and LG (Deming 5/8/80); found in <**yélyelesemtsel.**>, //yə́l[=C_1əC_2=]əs=əm-c-əl//, /'*I have a toothache.*'/, attested by Elders Group (1/24/79).

<**yelyelísem**>, ds //C_1əC_2=y=əlís=əm or C_1əC_2=yə́lə[=Aí=]s=əm//, WETH ['*(have/get) many icicles*'], WATR, literally /'have/get many teeth(-like objects)'/, (<**R3=**> *plural (collective)*), lx <**=elís ~ =élés**> *(of the) tooth*, possibly <**í= on é in root**> *resultative*, possibly <**=em**>

intransitivizer/have/get, possibly <**=em**> *place to have/get*, phonology: reduplication, possible ablaut, syntactic analysis: intransitive verb?, nominal?, attested by Elders Group (4/16/75).

<**syalyelísem**>, dnom //s=C_1əC_2[=Aɛ=]yələ[=Aí=]s=əm or s=C_1əC_2[=Aɛ=]y=əlís=əm//, WETH ['*icicles*'], WATR, (<**s=**> *nominalizer*), possibly <**a-ablaut**> *derivational*, phonology: reduplication, ablaut, possible double ablaut, syntactic analysis: nominal, attested by Deming (3/31/77), Elders Group (4/16/75).

<**yelòlèm**>, df //yəl=ál(=)əm//, TIME ['*(have/get a year)*'], possibly root <**yel ~ yil**> *turn*, possibly <**=em**> *intransitivizer, have, get*, phonology: downdrifting, updrifting, syntactic analysis: intransitive verb?, attested by Elders Group (5/26/76), compare root <**yál**> *turn around, reverse sides*??, example: <**émi yelòlèm**>, //ʔəmí yəl=áləm//, /'*the coming year*'/, attested by Elders Group, <**áschew émi yelòlèm**>, //ʔɛ́scəw ʔəmí yəl=áləm//, /'*the next coming year, next year that's coming*'/, attested by Elders Group.

<**syílòlèm ~ siló:lém ~ sílòlèm**>, dnom //s=yíl(=)ál(=)əm ~ s=(y)il=á·l(=)əm//, TIME ['*year*'], (<**s=**> *nominalizer, something to/that*), possibly root <**yel ~ yil**> *turn*, possibly <**=em**> *intransitivizer, have, get*, phonology: downstepping, updrifting, syntactic analysis: nominal, attested by AC (8/14/70, 10/8/71), Elders Group (5/26/76, 3/12/75, 3/26/75, 4/16/75), EB (1/12/76), BHTTC (10/2/76), other sources: ES /syilá·ləm/ *year*, Salish cognate: Squamish /s-il-ʔánm/ *year* poss. from root /yəl/ *turn* W73:294, K67:305, 380, Lushootseed /s-jə́l-č'/ (Skagit dial.) ~ /s-ǰə́l-c'/ (Snohomish dial.) *year, turning of seasons* H76:213-214, example: <**léts'e siló:lém**>, //lə́c'ə s=yil=á·ləm//, /'*one year*'/, attested by AC, also <**léts'e syilòlèm**>, //lə́c'ə s=yil=áləm//, attested by DM (12/4/64 Wells tapes new transcript old p.261), <**lulh kw'íl silólém?**>, //lə-uɬ k'ʷíl s=yil=áləm//, /'*How old is he?, How many years is he?*'/, literally /'past (third person obj.) -already is how many? year'/, attested by AC, <**lhí:xw siló:lém**>, //ɬí·xʷ s=yil=á·ləm//, /'*three years*'/, attested by AC, <**x̱áws silólem**>, //x̣ɛ́ws s=yil=áləm//, /'*(white man's) New Year*'/, attested by Elders Group (3/12/75), <**isále silólem**>, //ʔisɛ́lə s=yil=áləm//, /'*two years*'/, attested by Elders Group (3/26/75), <**lhq'átses syilólém**>, //ɬq'ɛ́t=cəs s=yil=áləm//, /'*five years*'/, attested by EB (1/12/76), <**t'x̱emelsxá qas te t'x̱ém syilólem kwseselh kwó:l**>, //t'x̣əm=əlsxʸɛ́ qɛ-s tə t'x̣ə́m s=yil=áləm kʷ-s-əs-əɬ kʷá·l//, /'*sixty-sixth year since her birth*'/, attested by Elders Group (4/16/75), <**welh kw'íl syilólem kw'as yóyes?**>, //wəɬ k'ʷíl s=yil=áləm k'ʷ-ɛ-s yá[-C_1ə-]s//, /'*How many years have you been working?*'/, attested by BHTTC (10/2/76).

<**yeló:lh**>, TVMO /'*to travel by canoe,* (nowadays also) *travel by airplane, travel by train, travel by car*'/, *see* ó:lh.

<**yélqw't**>, SOC /'*upset bed, mess s-th up*'/, *see* yél or perhaps yá:l.

<**yélt**>, us //yə́lt//, LAND ['*(have a) small earth slide (small landslide)*'], root possibly <**yel**> *turn*?? with stative <**-t**>??, syntactic analysis: intransitive verb?, nominal??, dialects: *Cheh.*, attested by Elders Group (4/2/75).

<**syélt**>, dnom //s=yə́lt//, LAND ['*large rock slide that includes trees and other debris*'], (<**s=**> *nominalizer, something to/that*), syntactic analysis: nominal, dialects: *Seabird Is.*, attested by Elders Group (4/2/75), contrast <**syéx̱w**> *rock-slide* (Katz dial.).

<**yélth**>, free root //yə́lθ//, ABDF ['*to poison*'], SOC, root possibly related to <**yel**> *turn*??, possible lx <**=th**> *in mouth*??, syntactic analysis: intransitive verb, attested by AC (11/24/71), Deming (6/21/79).

<**yéltht**>, pcs //yə́lθ=T//, SOC ['*poison s-o/s-th on purpose*'], (<**=t**> *purposeful control transitivizer*), syntactic analysis: transitive verb, attested by AC (11/24/71), Deming (6/21/79); found in <**yélth:ò:m**>, //yə́lθ=T-à·m//, /'*you'll get poisoned, (s-o) poison(ed) you*'/, phonology: consonant

merger, attested by AC.

<**yélthṯ**>, SOC [*'poison s-o/s-th on purpose'*], *see* yélth.

<**yélx̱t**>, SOC [*'look for s-th/s-o'*], *see* yél or perhaps yá:l.

<**yélx̱w**>, possibly root //yə́lx̣ʷ or yə́l=x̣ʷ//, TCH /*'smooth (of boulder, for ex.)'*/, DESC, possibly <**=x̱w**> *lump-like*, syntactic analysis: adjective/adjectival verb, attested by BHTTC (late 10/76).

<**yélyelesem**>, ABDF /*'(have) a steady toothache, have a toothache'*/, *see* yél:és.

<**yelyelísem**>, WETH [*'(have/get) many icicles'*], *see* yél:és.

<**yelhyó:qwt**>, TIME /*'be last (in travelling), be behind (in travelling)'*/, *see* lhiyó:qwt.

<**yém ~ yem**>, bound root //yə́m ~ yəm (perhaps) *stretch around the middle*//.

<**yemáwéstel**>, df //yəm=ɛ́wə́s=təl//, BSK [*'wide cedar root strips for baskets'*], ASM ['the part that was wrapped around fine bundled strips called shxwth'á:lhtel'], literally perhaps /'device to stretch around the middle of (basket?)'/, lx <**=áwés**> meaning unknown unless here *basket* (though usually *paddle)*, lx <**=tel**> *device, something to*, syntactic analysis: nominal, attested by Elders Group (6/11/75).

<**yémqetel**>, df //yə́m=qə(l)=təl//, BSK /*'buckskin straps, lid for berry basket'*/, HARV, ASM ['the lid consisted of buckskin straps tied zigzag across the top'], KIN [*'buckskin straps for tying a baby in its cradle or basket'*], literally perhaps /'device to stretch around the middle on the head'/, (semological comment: perhaps named after packstraps made of buckskin), probably <**=qel**> *on the head*, lx <**=tel**> *device, something to*, phonology: consonant-loss (l before =tel), syntactic analysis: nominal, attested by Elders Group (6/11/75).

<**shxwyémtel ~ shxwiyémtel**>, df //sxʷ=yə́m=təl//, CLO /*'belt, (necklace?? [DM])'*/, literally perhaps /'device that stretches around the middle'/, (<**shxw=**> *something for/that*), lx <**=tel**> *device, something to*, syntactic analysis: nominal, attested by TG (Elders Group 3/1/72), Elders Group (8/20/75), AC (10/23/71), Salish cognate: Squamish /nəxʷ-yə́mʔ-tn/ *belt* K67:311, also /*'necklace (?)'*/, Elder's comment: "unsure", attested by DM (12/4/64).

<**yémxtel**>, dnom //yə́m=xʸ(əl)=**təl**//, CLO /*'shoelace, shoe-lace'*/, literally perhaps /'device that stretches around the middle on the foot'/, lx <**=xel**> *on the foot*, lx <**=tel**> *device, something to,* phonology: syllable-loss (el before =tel), syntactic analysis: nominal, attested by DC (Elders Group 4/23/80), also <**yémxetel**>, //yə́m=xʸə(l)=təl//, phonology: consonant-loss (l before =tel), attested by EB (1/6/76), example: <**q'áp'et ta' yémxetel.**>, //q'ɛ́p'=əT t-ɛʔ yə́m=xʸə(l)=təl//, /*'Tie your shoelace.'*/, literally /'tie s-th your shoelace'/, attested by EB.

<**syémyem**>, chrs //s=yə́m=C$_1$əC$_2$//, stvi, ABFC [*'to be pregnant'*], literally perhaps /'to be characteristically stretched around the middle'/, (<**s=**> *stative*), (<**=R2**> *characteristic(ally)*), phonology: reduplication, syntactic analysis: adjective/adjectival verb, attested by EB (1/30/76), Elders Group (10/1/75).

<**yemáwéstel**>, BSK [*'wide cedar root strips for baskets'*], *see* yém ~ yem.

<**yémqetel**>, BSK /*'buckskin straps, lid for berry basket'*/, *see* yém ~ yem.

<**yémq't**>, pcs //yə́m(=)q'=T//, TCH /*'rub (oil or water) in s-th to clean or soften, rub s-th to soften or clean it, (shaping a stone hammer with abrasion?, shaping?, mixing paint?, pressing together or crushing? [BHTTC 9/2/76])'*/, ASM ['for ex. after dipping it in water, like washing clothes (MC)'], root meaning unknown unless <**yém ~ yem**> *stretch around the middle*, possibly <**=q'**> *on something else, within something else*, (<**=t**> *purposeful control transitivizer*), syntactic analysis: transitive verb,

attested by AD (5/1/79), Deming (4/26/79), also /*'rub s-th to soften or clean it, for ex. after dipping it in water, like washing clothes*'/, attested by MC (Deming 4/26/79), also /*'shaping a stone hammer with abrasion?, shaping?, mixing paint?, pressing together or crushing?*'/, (semological comment: these may all be proper translations since shaping a stone hammer (or other things) with abrasion involves keeping it wet with water so it doesn't get too hot, mixing paint certainly involves rubbing liquid in the pigment, *pressing s-th together/crushing it* if in oil or water would also fit), attested by BHTTC (9/2/76).

<**yémxtel**>, CLO /*'shoelace, shoe-lace*'/, *see* yém ~ yem.

<**yeqelsxá:y**>, WETH [*'first snow*'], *see* yíq.

<**yeqílem ~ eqéylem**>, mdls //yəq=íl=əm~ ʔəq=íl=əm//, incs, TVMO /*'crawl underneath, (go underneath)*'/, (<**=íl**> *go, come, get, become*), (<**=em**> *middle voice*), syntactic analysis: intransitive verb, attested by EB, Salish cognate: Squamish /yəqə́y/ *to creep* and /y-iʔqə́y/ *creeping* K67:380; Lushootseed /dzəqíl/<jəqíl> *crawl, have head down* H76:221, example: <**le eqéylem lá te lálem**>, //lə ʔəq=íl=əm lɛ́ tə lɛ́ləm//, /*'He crawled under the house.*'/, literally /'he past crawl/go under go to the house'/, attested by EB.

<**Híqelem** or **Híyqelem**>, cts //hə-yq=íl=əm//, PLN /*'creek and bay on Harrison River just below the old native Chehalis Cemetery, on the east side of Harrison River*'/, literally /'going underneath'/, ASM ['so named because one used to have to go under a big log there in one's canoe; the log is rotten away now; this is the creek or bay above Sqiqemló and also above Xemó:leqw but across the river from Xemó:leqw'], (<he-> *continuative*), photo taken 6/27/78, phonology: consonant alternation, most likely the root is ʔəq (EB) ~ yəq (EL), syntactic analysis: nominal, attested by EL, source: place name file reference #297.

<**(Yeqyeqámen)**>, df //yəq=C_1əC_2=ɛ́məl//, PLN [*'an old course of Atchelitz Creek*'], possibly root <**yeq**> *crawl under*, possibly <**=R2**> *characteristic*, lx <**=ámel**> *part/portion (of the body, geographic features)*, phonology: possible reduplication, n is either misrecorded or a downriver pronunciation of an upriver place name, syntactic analysis: nominal, compare <**hí(y)qelem**> *crawl under*, source: Wells 1965 (lst ed.):13, Salish cognate: perhaps Squamish root /yəq-ə́y/ *to creep* K67:380 which is cognate with Upriver Halkomelem /hí-yq=əl=əm/ *crawl under*.

<**yéq'**>, bound root //yə́q' *file, abrade*//, Salish cognate: Squamish root /yəq' ~ yaq'/ *be polished (ab. stone), be sharpened (ab. knife)* as in /yáq'-an2/ *sharpen (by filing)* and /yəq'-mín/ *filings* (Coeur d'Alene cognate also cited /yaq'/ *file, whet*) K69:91, K67:382, Lushootseed root /jəq'/ [dzəq'] *grind, sharpen* as in /jə́q'-əd/ *grind it, sharpen it* H76:221.

<**yeq'à:ls**>, sas //yəq'=ɛ̀·ls//, MC [*'to file [abrasively]*'], CARV, TOOL, (<**=á:ls ~ =à:ls**> *structured activity non-continuative*), phonology: possible downshifting, syntactic analysis: intransitive verb, attested by Elders Group (3/15/72).

<**hiyeq'á:l**>, ds //hi=yəq'=ɛ́·l//, SOCT /*'a filer, someone that's filing (with a file)*'/, (<**hi- ~ he-**> *continuative*), lx <**=á:l**> *someone that, something that*, syntactic analysis: nominal, attested by IHTTC (9/2/77).

<**shxwíyq'el** or **shxwíq'el**>, ds //sx^w=hí-yəq'=əl//, TOOL [*'a file*'], literally /'something for going to file'/, (<**shxw=**> *something for*), (<**hí-**> *continuative*), (<**=el**> *go, come, get, become*), phonology: consonant merger, vowel-loss, syntactic analysis: nominal, attested by Elders Group (Fish Camp 7/11/78).

<**héyeq'et ~ héyq'et**>, pcs //hə́-yəq'=əT//, cts, MC [*'filing s-th*'], TOOL, (<**hé- ~ hí- ~ há-**> *continuative*), (<**=et**> *purposeful control transitivizer*), phonology: optional vowel-loss, syntactic

analysis: transitive verb, attested by Elders Group (3/15/72); found in <**héyeq'etes. ~ héyq'etes.**>, //hə́-yəq'=əT-əs//, /'*He's filing it.*'/, attested by Elders Group.

<**yéq'es**>, df //yə́q'=əs//, MC ['*to file*'], lx <**=es**> *on the face, round thing*, syntactic analysis: intransitive verb, attested by Elders Group (3/15/72).

<**héyq'es**>, cts //hə́-yəq'=əs//, MC ['*filing*'], (<**he-**> *continuative*), syntactic analysis: intransitive verb, attested by Elders Group (3/15/72).

<**yéq'est**>, pcs //yə́q'=əs=T//, TOOL ['*grind or sharpen s-th (of edged tools)*'], literally /'file purposely on the face of s-th'/, (<**=t**> *purposeful control transitivizer*), syntactic analysis: transitive verb, attested by Elders Group (3/15/72, 5/26/76), Salish cognate: Squamish /nəxʷ-iq'-ús-n/ *sharpen (tr.)* from root /yəq'/ *be sharpened* K67:382, example: <**yéq'est te lháts'tel**>, //yə́q'=əs=T tə ɬi[=Aɛ=]c'=təl//, /'*sharpen a knife*'/, attested by Elders Group (5/26/76).

<**yeq'á:ls**>, HARV ['*fall a tree*'], *see* yáq'.

<**yeq'à:ls**>, MC ['*to file [abrasively]*'], *see* yéq'.

<**yéq'es**>, MC ['*to file*'], *see* yéq'.

<**yéq'est**>, TOOL ['*grind or sharpen s-th (of edged tools)*'], *see* yéq'.

<**yéq'lexw ~ yéq'elexw**>, HARV /'*managed to fell a tree, (managed to fall it)*'/, *see* yáq'.

<**yeq'pó:s** (prob. error or variant for **yeqp'ó:s**)>, ABFC ['*(travelling/moving) stooped over*'], *see* qep'.

<**yéqw**>, free root //yə́qʷ//, FIRE /'*burned, to burn, scorch*'/, syntactic analysis: intransitive verb, attested by Elders Group (3/15/72), EB (1/30/76), AC (8/8/70, 9/15/71), Salish cognate: Squamish /yəqʷ- ~ (h)iʔqʷ-/ *fire* as in /yə́qʷ-lčp/ *put wood on the fire* and /hiʔqʷín/ *light, torch, candle* K67:381, Saanich dial. of NSt /čə́qʷ/ *any fire, flame* B74a:7, Samish dial. of NSt /čə́qʷ/ *to burn* G86:66, example: <**yéqw te lálem.**>, //yə́qʷ tə lɛ́ləm//, /'*The house burned.*'/, attested by AC (8/8/70), <**le yéqw.**>, //lə yə́qʷ//, /'*It burned.*'/, attested by AC (8/6/70, 8/14/70), also /'*It is burnt.*'/, attested by Elders Group (3/15/72), <**le yéqw te lálem.**>, //lə yə́qʷ tə lɛ́ləm//, /'*The house is burnt.*'/, attested by AC (8/6/70), <**xwá:lqey yèqw**>, //xʷɛ́·lqəy yə́qʷ//, /'*nearly burned*'/, attested by EB (2/6/76), also <**xwá:lqeyèqw**>, //xʷɛ́·lqə(y)yə́qʷ//, phonology: word-boundary loss, consonant merger, usage: fast speech, attested by EB (2/6/76).

<**héyeqw**>, cts //hɛ́-yəqʷ//, FIRE ['*be burning*'], (<**hé- ~ há- ~ hí-**> *continuative*), syntactic analysis: intransitive verb, attested by Elders Group (3/15/72), AC, also <**híyeqw**>, //hí-yəqʷ//, attested by EB (12/15/75, 2/6/76), example: <**héyeqw kw'e tsóleqw.**>, //hɛ́-yəqʷ k'ʷə cáləqʷ//, /'*The backwoods is burning.*'/, attested by AC (8/14/70), <**xwel héyeqw.**>, //xʷəl hɛ́-yəqʷ//, /'*It's [still] burning.*'/, attested by AC (8/6/70), <**u xwel híyeqw.**>, //ʔu xʷəl hí-yəqʷ//, /'*It's still burning.*'/, attested by EB (12/15/75).

<**héyeqw**>, dnom //hɛ́=yəqʷ//, FIRE /'*fire, ((*also*) flame* [EB, Elders Group]*)*'/, ASM ['any kind, wood, forest, etc.'], (<**hé- ~ há- ~ hí-**> *continuative* or *resultative*), (<**zero**> *nominalizer*), syntactic analysis: nominal, attested by Elders Group (3/15/72), BJ (5/10/64), DM (12/4/64), AC (8/14/70, 9/8/71), EF (8/10/79 at ICSL), other sources: ES /hɛ́·yəqʷ/ *fire*, also <**híyeqw**>, //hí=yəqʷ//, also /'*flame, fire*'/, attested by EB (12/15/75, 2/6/76), Elders Group (1/7/76, 4/23/80), example: <**eyém te híyeqw.**>, //ʔɛy=ə́m tə hí=yəqʷ//, /'*The fire is burning strong.*'/, literally /'is strong the fire'/, attested by EB (2/6/76), <**le tl'ékw'el te héyeqw.**>, //lə ƛ'ə́k'ʷ=əl tə hɛ́=yəqʷ//, /'*The fire went out.*'/, literally /'past go out (of fire) the fire'/, attested by EB (11/27/75), <**welh tl'ékw'el te híyeqw.**>, //wəɬ ƛ'ə́k'ʷ=əl tə hí=yəqʷ//, /'*The fire has gone out.*'/, literally /'already go out the fire'/, attested by EB (12/15/75), <**tl'ékw'elt te híyeqw**>, //ƛ'ə́k'ʷ=əl=T tə hí=yəqʷ//, /'*Put out a fire.*'/,

literally /'put it out (of fire)'/, attested by Elders Group (1/7/76), <**tesét te héyeqw**>, //tə́s=M1=T tə hɛ́=yəq^{w}//, /'*Go towards the fire.*'/, literally /'go towards s-th the fire'/, attested by EF (8/10/79 at the Salish Conference/ICSL).

<**elíyliyem te híyqw.**>, cpds //ʔəlíy=C_1əC_2=əm tə hí=yəq^{w}//, FIRE ['*the fire is laughing*'], ASM ['this is said when the fire is <**pá:yts'em**> *sparking* and it tells you you'll have a visitor who laughs when he comes'], literally /'be characteristically laughing the fire'/, (<**e=**> meaning-unknown>), (<**=R2**> *characteristically or plural*), phonology: reduplication, syntactic analysis: sentence, attested by Elders Group (4/23/80).

<**yéqwt**>, pcs //yə́q^{w}=T//, FIRE /'*burn s-th, light s-th*'/, (<**=t**> *purposeful control transitivizer*), syntactic analysis: transitive verb, attested by CT and HT (6/21/76), example: <**éx̲qst te máches qesu yéqwt kw'e sísq' or kw'estámés**>, //ʔə́x̣=qs=T tə mɛ́cəs qə-s-u yə́q^{w}=T k'^{w}ə sí[=C_1ə=]q' or k'^{w}ə=s=tɛ́m=əs//, /'*strike the match and light the kindling or something (strike it (of a match), scrape it)*'/, attested by CT.

<**híyeqwt**>, cts //hí-yəq^{w}=T//, FIRE ['*burning s-th*'], (<**hí-**> *continuative*), syntactic analysis: transitive verb, attested by Elders Group (3/15/72); found in <**híyeqwtem.**>, //hí-yəq^{w}=T-əm//, /'*it is being burned*'/, attested by Elders Group.

<**híyeqwtem siyólh**>, cpds //hí-yəq^{w}=T-əm s=yáɬ//, FIRE ['*firewood*'], literally /'wood being burned'/, syntactic analysis: nominal phrase with modifier(s), attested by Elders Group (3/15/72).

<**yéqwelht**>, bens //yə́q^{w}=əɬ(c)=T//, FIRE ['*burn it for s-o*'], (<**=elhts ~ =elh**> *benefactive*), (<**=t**> *purposeful control transitivizer*), syntactic analysis: transitive verb, attested by EB (3/1/76), example: <**tsel yéqwelht**>, //c-əl yə́q^{w}=əɬ(c)=T//, /'*I burned it for someone.*'/, attested by EB; found in <**yeqwelhthóxchexw.**>, //yəq^{w}=əɬ(c)=T-áx^{y}-c-əx^{w}//, /'*You burn it for me.*'/, attested by EB (3/1/76).

<**Syéqw**>, dnom //s=yə́q^{w}//, [syʊ́q^{w}], PLN ['*village site (burned) on Atchelitz Creek*'], ASM ['located north of the present Vedder River, about at South Sumas, said to mean *burned over place*'], literally /'something that burned'/, (<**s=**> *nominalizer, something that*), syntactic analysis: nominal, source: Wells 1966 <s'YOOK-q>.

<**yíyeqw**>, df //C_1í=yəq^{w} or yə[=Aí=C_1ə=]q^{w}//, FIRE /'*fire (out of control), forest fire burning, fire burning*'/, probably <**R4=**> *diminutive*, possibly <**í-ablaut**> *derivational*, possibly <**=R1=**> *continuative*, phonology: reduplication, syntactic analysis: intransitive verb, attested by Elders Group (6/11/75).

<**Syíyeqw**>, dnom //s=C_1í=yəq^{w}//, PLN ['*burnt mountain across from American Bar*'], ASM ['in front of Qw'éywelh, on the CN (east) side of the Fraser R.'], Elder's comment: "means burnt mountain", literally /'something that burned in a forest fire'/, (<**s=**> *nominalizer*), phonology: reduplication, syntactic analysis: nominal, attested by SP and AD from MP (IHTTC 7/8/77), source: place names reference file #29a and #31, also /'*burnt place at summit of X̲ó:letsa Smá:lt (which is above Yale)*'/, attested by SP and AK (Fish Camp 8/2/77).

<**yeqwyéqw**>, plv //C_1əC_2=yə́q^{w}//, FIRE /'*house on fire, house fire*'/, literally /'many burning'/, phonology: reduplication, syntactic analysis: intransitive verb, attested by Elders Group (3/15/72).

<**Yeqwyeqwí:ws**>, plv //C_1əC_2=yəq^{w}=í·ws//, PLN /'*Yakweakwioose, next village above Scowkale, village near Sardis on the old Chilliwack River course, now Chilliwack Indian Reserve #9*'/, ASM ['by some accounts this village was repeatedly burnt out (Elders Group 7/20/77), by another the grass burned there yearly (AC 1973), during Hill-Tout's field work on Upriver Halkomelem (ca 1898-1902) the chief of the village was Qw'atíseltel (Chief Louie) (Elders Group 1/15/75 recalled

his name after hearing attempts to pronounce the name Hill-Tout recorded as <Qate'selta> [circumflex over first a, macron over first e]), "Yakweakwioose" is the spelling used by the Dept. of Indian Affairs and the Indian band itself for the reserve now'], literally /'house fires on the covering/body/skin'/, Elder's comment: "the name means *burnt out (of houses)* since just the houses, not the people, were burnt out (BJ 12/5/64)", (semological comment: the stem seems to be the one meaning *house fire* but the suffix can only be one meaning *on the body/skin/covering*, that makes no sense at present unless perhaps by covering is meant the grass that AC reported burned every year as well), lx <**=í:ws**> *on the body, on the skin, on the covering*, (<**zero**> *nominalizer*), phonology: reduplication, zero nominalizer, syntactic analysis: nominal, attested by BJ (5/10/64, 12/5/64), Elders Group (7/20/77), AC (1973), other sources: Wells 1965 (lst ed.):19, Wells 1966, source: place names reference file #88.

<**syeqwyíqw**>, df //s=C_1əC_2=yə[=Aí=]qʷ//, LT ['*burnt color*'], (<**s=**> *stative*), (<**R3=**> *plural or derivational*), (<**í-ablaut**> *durative*), phonology: reduplication, ablaut, syntactic analysis: adjective/adjectival verb, historical/comparative detail: the pattern of ablaut and reduplication for this derived color term is exactly the same as for some colors terms in Nooksack, Squamish, and perhaps other Salish languages (Squamish and Nooksack /xʷək'ʷxʷík'ʷ/ *gray* from root /xʷək'ʷ/ *gray* for ex., as well as the words for *red*, *black*, etc.), attested by ME (11/21/72).

<**heyeqwá:la**>, ds //hɛ=yəqʷ=ɛ́·lɛ//, FIRE ['*fireplace*'], literally /'container of fire/burning'/, (<**hɛ=**> *continuative or resultative*), lx <**=á:la**> *container of*, syntactic analysis: nominal, attested by Elders Group (5/3/78), Salish cognate: Saanich dial. of NSt /s-čə́qʷ-uʔs-elə/ *fireplace* B74a:32.

<**shxwhéyqwela ~ shxwhéyqwala**>, ds //sxʷ=hɛ́=yəqʷ=ɛlɛ//, FIRE ['*firepit in house*'], literally /'container of something for burning'/, (<**shxw=**> *something for*), phonology: vowel-loss, vowel-reduction, syntactic analysis: nominal, attested by DM (12/4/64 new transcript Wells tapes new p.175).

<**xwíyeqwela**>, df //xʷe=hí=yəqʷ=ɛlɛ or xʷə[=´=]=yəqʷ=ɛlɛ//, FIRE ['*black soot*'], possibly <**xw=**> *always*, possibly <**xwe=**> *become*, possibly <**hí-**> *continuative or resultative*, possibly <=´=> *derivational*, lx <**=ala**> *container of*, phonology: possible vowel-loss, possible consonant merger, possible stress-shift, vowel-reduction, syntactic analysis: nominal, attested by DM (12/4/64 new transcript new p.176).

<**yeqwá:ls**>, sas //yəqʷ=ɛ́·ls//, REL /'*have a ritual burning ceremony, have a burning, feed the dead, (food offered to the dead [at a ritual burning] [EB 5/25/76])*'/, FIRE, literally /'burn as a structured activity'/, ASM ['the burning ceremony is held four days after burial of a dead person, at dawn; also one year after the last burning or death, done at sunset; it is done by a ritualist (RM, DF, and some others), the favorite food and drink of the deceased is prepared by the family and passed over a fire by the ritualist while he calls the spirit or ghost of the deceased in a special language (falsetto, often with ends of words not finished, sometimes with special songs), half of each plate of food or drink is scraped into the fire by the ritualist, who can usually tell when the spirit comes and takes it, (RM described the spirit as looking like faint sparkles when it comes and snatches the food),'], the spirits of other relatives dead longer are often feed similarly from plates and glasses (with their names attached nowadays), the outdoor fire is built specially and the witnesses (family and friends of the departed) are instructed to stand quietly around the fire but out of a line between the fire and the nearby graveyard where the deceased were buried, people can get ghosted or have their souls taken by the spirits or get a twisted jaw if bumped by the spirits coming to get food, children are kept away because they are especially vulnerable, the ceremony is quite moving and powerful,, some of the newly deceased's favorite possessions are also burned on the fire and some are passed through the fire/smoke and then saved out, after the dead have all been fed the witnesses are allowed to eat

the remaining half-plates of food and are given the possessions to be distributed, if follow-up burnings are not held or not held often enough (yearly) bereft family members may sometimes be haunted or ghosted, usually another burning ceremony should then be arranged to feed the hungry spirit so that the ghosted person can stop seeing the ghost of his relative or hearing sounds made by the ghost, (<**=á:ls**> *structured activity*), syntactic analysis: intransitive verb, attested by BJ (12/5/64), IHTTC (8/4/77), also /'*food offered to the dead [at a ritual burning]*'/, attested by EB (5/25/76).

<**syeqwá:ls**>, dnom //s=yəqʷ=ɛ́·ls//, sas, REL /'*clothing, food, and possessions burned and given away when a person dies, (possessions and food burned and given away at a burning)*'/, FIRE, literally /'something to burn as a structured activity'/, (<**s=**> *nominalizer, something to*), syntactic analysis: nominal, attested by AC (9/15/71).

<**híyeqwels**>, cts //hí=yəqʷ=əls//, sas, REL /'*the one who burns [at a burning ceremony], (ritualist at a burning)*'/, FIRE, literally /'someone burning as a structured activity'/, (<**hí=**> *continuative*), (<**=els**> *structured activity continuative nominal*), syntactic analysis: nominal, attested by BJ (12/5/64), EB (6/9/76).

<**yéqwelchep ~ yéqweltsep**>, ds //yə́qʷ=əlcəp//, FIRE /'*build a fire, make a fire, make the fire, (stoke the fire)*'/, literally /'burn firewood'/, lx <**=elchep ~ =élchep**> *firewood*, syntactic analysis: intransitive verb, attested by EB (1/7/76), AC (8/14/70), Elders Group (3/15/72), AD (8/80), Salish cognate: Squamish /yə́qʷ-lčp/ *put wood on the fire* K67:381; found in <**yéqweltsepchexw.**>, //yə́qʷ=əlcəp-c-əxʷ//, /'*Make a fire., Light a fire.*'/, attested by AD.

<**híyqwelchep**>, cts //hí-yəqʷ=əlcəp//, FIRE /'*making the fire, building the fire, (stoking a fire)*'/, literally /'burning firewood'/, (<**hí-**> *continuative*), syntactic analysis: intransitive verb, attested by NP and AD (AHTTC 2/22/80), example: <**Líwlh la tl'ékw'el te híyeqw? Li s'ú:met te stó:les (te lò?, te híyqwelchep?)**>, //li-ə-uɬ lə ƛ'ə́k'ʷ=əl tə hí=yəqʷ? li-ə s=ʔə[=Aú·=]mət tə s=tá·ləs (tə là, tə hí-yəqʷ=əlcəp)?//, /'*Is the fire already gone out? Is the wife lazy (here?, who makes the fire?)*'/, usage: sayings in the smokehouse (during spirit-dancing season) if no one keeps the fire stoked, attested by NP and AD (AHTTC 2/22/80).

<**yéqwelchept**>, pcs //yə́qʷ=əlcəp=T//, FIRE ['*make a fire for s-o*'], (<**=t**> *purposeful control transitivizer*), syntactic analysis: transitive verb, attested by EB (3/1/76); found in <**yèqwelchepthóxlha.**>, //yə́qʷ=əlcəp=T-áxʸ-ɬɛ//, /'*Make a fire for me.*'/, attested by EB.

<**yeqwí:l ~ yeqwì:l**>, durs //yəqʷ=ə[=Aí·=]l//, HHG /'*an electric light, coal-oil lamp, lamp*'/, LT, literally /'durative go burn'/, (<**=el**> *go, come, get, become*), (<**í:-ablaut on e in suffix**> *durative*), (<**zero**> *nominalizer*), phonology: ablaut, zero nominalizer, syntactic analysis: nominal, attested by Elders Group (3/16/77), EB (12/17/75), Salish cognate: Sechelt /hiyqʷíʔn/ *lamp, light, torch* T77:18, Squamish /hiʔqʷín/ *light, torch, candle* K67:381, example: <**yéqw te yeqwí:l**>, //yə́qʷ tə yəqʷ=ə[=Aí·=]l//, /'*light the lantern, light the lamp*'/, attested by EB.

<**yeqwí:lem ~ yeqwéylem**>, incs //yəqʷ=ə[=Aí·=]l=əm//, LT /'*make a light, turn the light on, light the lamp*'/, HHG, (<**=em**> *intransitivizer, have, get*), phonology: ablaut, syntactic analysis: intransitive verb, attested by Elders Group (3/15/72), AD (8/80); found in <**yeqwí:lemchexw.**>, //yəqʷ=ə[=Aí·=]l=əm-c-əxʷ//, /'*Make a light., Turn the light on., Light the lamp.*'/, attested by AD.

<**yeqwí:ls**>, sas //yəqʷ=ɛ[=Aí=]·ls//, durs, LT ['*make a light*'], HHG, (<**=á:ls**> *structured activity non-continuative*), (<**í-ablaut**> *durative or derivational*), phonology: ablaut, syntactic analysis: intransitive verb, attested by Elders Group, synonym <**táwelt**>.

<**yeqwí:les**>, ds //yəqʷ=í·ləs//, ABDF ['*have heartburn*'], literally /'burn in the chest'/, lx <**=í:les**> *in*

the chest, syntactic analysis: intransitive verb, attested by EB (12/15/75), Elders Group (3/3/76), MH (Deming 1/4/79), Salish cognate: Mainland Comox /jɑ^íkʷám-ín'əs/ *indigestion* B75prelim:32, Saanich dial. of NSt /čqʷ-ínəs/ *indigestion* B74a:25, example: <**tsel yeqwí:les.**>, //c-əl yəqʷ=í·ləs//, /'*I have heartburn.*'/, attested by MH (Deming 1/4/79).

<**yeqwílep**>, ds //yəqʷ=íləp//, EB ['*burnt (i.e. dry) grass*'], literally /'burnt ground'/, lx <**=ílep ~ =élep**> *ground*, syntactic analysis: nominal, attested by Elders Group (5/16/79).

<**Yeqwílmet ~ Syeqwílmetxw**>, ds //yəqʷ=íl=mət ~ s=yəqʷ=íl=mətxʷ//, N ['*Male Grizzly Bear*'], literally /'get burnt male name ~ something that got burnt male name (house)'/, ASM ['names in bears' language, a bear or any animal will not hurt you if you stand and call its proper name, but you have to watch the fur of the bear and must get the right name and say it just right or you'd better run, these names describe the burnt look to the grizzly's fur'], (<**s=**> *nominalizer, something to/that*), root <**yeqw**> *burnt*, (<**=íl**> *go, come, get, become*), lx <**=met**> *male name*, lx <**=metxw**> *male name (house/dynasty)*, syntactic analysis: nominal, attested by ME (11/21/72 tape).

<**Yeqwílmetelòt**>, ds //yəqʷ=íl=mət=əlàt//, N ['*Female Grizzly Bear*'], literally /'get burnt female name'/, ASM ['name in bears' language, a bear or any animal will not hurt you if you stand and call its proper name, but you have to watch the fur of the bear and must get the right name and say it just right or you'd better run, these names describe the burnt look to the grizzly's fur'], root <**yeqw**> *burnt*, (<**=íl**> *go, come, get, become*), lx <**=met**> *male name*, lx <**=elòt**> *female name*, syntactic analysis: nominal, attested by ME (11/21/72 tape).

<**syéqwlhàlà**>, df //s=yə́qʷ=ɬ=ɛ́lɛ̀//, FIRE /'*firepit, fireplace*'/, literally perhaps /'container of what was burnt'/, (<**s=**> *nominalizer, something to*), possibly <**=lh**> *past tense*?, lx <**=álá**> *container of*, phonology: downstepping, syntactic analysis: nominal, attested by Elders Group (3/15/72), also <**yeqwálá**>, //yəqʷ=ɛ́lɛ́//, attested by RP (Elders Group 3/15/72).

<**syeqwlhá:ltel**>, df //s=yəqʷ=ɬ=ɛ́·ltəl or s=yəqʷ=ɬɛ́·l=təl//, FIRE /'*tinder, material used to start a fire with (fine dried cedar bark)*'/, (<**s=**> *nominalizer, something to*), possibly <**=lh**> *past tense*, possibly <**=á:ltel**> *medicine for*, possibly <**=lhá:l**> *in the windpipe*, possibly <**=tel**> *device, something to*, syntactic analysis: nominal, attested by Elders Group (3/15/72).

<**syó:qwem**>, dnom //s=yə[=Aá·=]qʷ=əm//, WETH ['*sun*'], (<**s=**> *nominalizer, something to/that*), (<**ó:-ablaut**> *derivational*), possibly <**=em**> *intransitivizer, have, get*, possibly <**=em**> *place to have/get*, phonology: probable ablaut, syntactic analysis: nominal, attested by AC (9/8/71, 8/14/70), BJ (5/10/64, 12/5/64), Deming, MP and AD, SP/AK/AD (Raft trip 8/30/77), other sources: ES /syá·qʷəm/ *sun*, Salish cognate: Sechelt /s-yá-yqʷ/ *sun* T77:7, example: <**lulh me pél:ekw te syó:qwem.**>, //lə-uɬ mə pə́l·əkʷ tə s=yə[=Aá·=]qʷ=əm//, /'*The sun has come out.*'/, attested by Deming (3/31/77).

<**spéxwqels te syóqwem sp'áq'em**>, EB /'*sunflower seeds'/,* FOOD, (lit. small airborne seed of + the + sun + flower), (attested by RG,EH 6/16/98 to SN, edited by BG with RG,EH 6/26/00)

<**sx̱elx̱éles te syó:qwem**>, cpds //s=C_1əC_2=x̣ə́l=əs-s tə s=yá·qʷ=əm//, WETH ['*rays of light*'], LT ['*sunbeams*'], literally /'designs of the sun'/, ASM ['NP was told that sunbeams are like fingers and not to touch them or your fingers will get long, AD was told "don't grab for dust in a sunbeam or you'll be grabby"'], syntactic analysis: nominal phrase with modifier(s), attested by Elders Group (4/16/75), NP and AD (4/11/80).

<**tále te syó:qwem**>, cpds //tɛ́lə(-s) tə s=yə[=Aá·=]qʷ=əm//, EZ /'*metallic blue-green beetle, "June bug"*, probably *metallic wood-boring beetle,* or possibly *some types of long-horn beetle which are metallic green with reddish legs*'/, ['probably order *Coleoptera*, family *Buprestidae*, genus *Buprestis*, or possibly family *Cerambycidae*, genus *Gaurotes*'], literally /'money (of) the sun'/,

ASM ['it's good luck to find and keep one'], (irregular)dropping of -s *possessive* may be *derivational* here to separate the idiom from the literal phrase, phonology: ablaut, consonant-loss, syntactic analysis: nominal phrase with modifier(s), attested by SP or AK or AD (Raft Trip from X̱elhálh to Alhqá:yem 8/30/77).

<**yeqwá:ls**>, REL /'*have a ritual burning ceremony, have a burning, feed the dead, (food offered to the dead [at a ritual burning] [EB 5/25/76])*'/, *see* yéqw.

<**yéqwelchep ~ yéqweltsep**>, FIRE /'*build a fire, make a fire, make the fire, (stoke the fire)*'/, *see* yéqw.

<**yéqwelchept**>, FIRE ['*make a fire for s-o*'], *see* yéqw.

<**yéqwelht**>, FIRE ['*burn it for s-o*'], *see* yéqw.

<**Yéqwelhtax̱ ~ Yéqwelhta**>, free root //yə́qʷəɬtax̣ ~ yə́qʷəɬta//, SOCT /'*Yuculta Kwakiutl people, southern Kwakiutl people from Cape Mudge north who raided the Salish people*'/, ASM ['Yuculta is the Dept. of Indian Affairs spelling for a reserve at Cape Mudge on an island near Campbell River on Vancouver Island, the Kwakiutl people from here for a ways north were aggressive raiders during the 19th century and perhaps earlier, their descendants now are members of 12 or 13 bands, they raided the Stó:lō numerous times as far up as Yale, many Stó:lō villages were relocated further up the Chilliwack R. and lookouts were posted, numerous stories were told about battles, deaths, ambushes, and slave-taking, the Stó:lō made a few return raids as well'], borrowed from Kwakw'ala /yíqʷəɬtax̣/ *village at Cape Mudge*, syntactic analysis: nominal, attested by BJ (12/5/64), BHTTC (11/19/76), Salish cognate: Squamish /yíqʷiɬtax̣/ *North people, people from Campbell R. north* K67:381, K69:90, Nooksack /yóqʷəɬtəx̣/ *people from the North (esp. southern Kwakiutl raiders)* A78:10.

<**yeqwí:lem ~ yeqwéylem**>, LT /'*make a light, turn the light on, light the lamp*'/, *see* yéqw.

<**yeqwílep**>, EB ['*burnt (i.e. dry) grass*'], *see* yéqw.

<**yeqwí:les**>, ABDF ['*have heartburn*'], *see* yéqw.

<**Yeqwílmet ~ Syeqwílmetxw**>, N ['*Male Grizzly Bear*'], *see* yéqw.

<**Yeqwílmetelòt**>, N ['*Female Grizzly Bear*'], *see* yéqw.

<**yeqwí:l ~ yeqwì:l**>, HHG /'*an electric light, coal-oil lamp, lamp*'/, *see* yéqw.

<**yeqwí:ls**>, LT ['*make a light*'], *see* yéqw.

<**yéqwt**>, FIRE /'*burn s-th, light s-th*'/, *see* yéqw.

<**yeqwyéqw**>, FIRE /'*house on fire, house fire*'/, *see* yéqw.

<**Yeqwyeqwí:ws**>, PLN /'*Yakweakwioose, next village above Scowkale, village near Sardis on the old Chilliwack River course, now Chilliwack Indian Reserve #9*'/, *see* yéqw.

<**yét'**> or <**yít'**>, possile root //yet'// meaning uncertain or perhaps //yit'// *melt, thaw*

<**Siyét'e**>, df //s=yi[=Aə́=]t'=ə//, PLN /'*village now at north end of Agassiz-Rosedale bridge, now Tseatah Indian Reserve #2 (of Cheam band)*'/, ASM ['located on a slough, former village site and area of north shore of Fraser River across from Cheam Island'], (<**s=**> *nominalizer, something to/that*), possibly root <**yít'**> as in <**yít'=em**> *thaw, melt*, possibly <**é-ablaut on root i**> *resultative*, possibly <**=e**> *living thing*, so perhaps lit. "thawed person/people", phonology: possible ablaut, syntactic analysis: nominal, attested by AK (8/30/77), JL and AD and AK (4/7/78), source: place names reference file #256, also <**Siyét'o**>, //s=yə́t'=a//, source: Wells 1965 (lst ed.):23, Duff 1952, also <**Siyét'a**>, //s=yə́t'=ɛ//, attested by HE (10/8/64).

<**yet'qw'íwsem**>, mdls //yət'=q'ʷ=íws=əm or ya[=Aə́=]t'=q'ʷ=íws=əm//, ABFC ['*lather one's body*'],

PE, possibly root <**yít'**> *melt*, (semological comment: perhaps this root since soap does seem to melt into lather), possibly root <**yót' ~ yót**> *rub*? as in shxwiyòtqw'ewí:ls> *dishcloth*, possibly <**é-ablaut of root i**> *resultative*, lx <**=qw'**> *around in circles*, lx <**=íws**> *on the body, on the skin*, (<**=em**> *middle voice*), phonology: possible ablaut, syntactic analysis: intransitive verb, attested by JL (Fish Camp 7/20/79).

<**yéth**>, bound root //yə́θ *tell what happened , report*//, Salish cognate: Lushootseed root /yəc-/ *tell, report, inform; news* as in //yəc-t// *tell s-o* and /ʔu-yə́c-c čəxʷ/ *you told me* and /yə́c-əb/ *tell* and /yə́c-əb-txʷ/ *tell s-o* H76:628-629, Squamish root /yəc/ as in /s-yə́c/ *story (realistic)* and /s-yə́c-m/ *news, information* K67:300 and /yə́c-m/ *tell, report (tr.)* K67:380.

<**yéthest**>, pcs //yə́θ=əs=T//, LANG /'*tell s-o something that happened, tell s-o (bring something out)*'/, possibly <**=es**> meaning uncertain, (<**=t**> *purposeful control transitivizer*), syntactic analysis: transitive verb, attested by AC, EB (4/29/76), AD (12/17/79), example: <**láchxw yéthest tha tál.**>, //lɛ́-c-xʷ yə́θ=əs=T θ-ɛ tɛ́l//, /'*Go tell your mother.*'/, attested by AC (8/28/70), <**líchxw yéthest?**>, //lí-c-xʷ yə́θ=əs=T//, /'*Do you tell it?*'/, attested by AC (9/20/71), <**tsel yéthest.**>, //c-əl yə́θ=əs=T//, /'*I told it.*'/, attested by AC (9/30/71), <**le yéthesthóxes.**>, //lə yə́θ=əs=T-áxʸ-əs or lə yə́θ=sT-áxʸ-əs//, /'*He told me.*'/, attested by AC (8/28/70).

<**yéthestexw**>, caus //yə́θ=sT-əxʷ or yə́θ=əs=sT-əxʷ//, no translation given, literally /'cause s-o to tell what happened'/, (<**=st**> *causative control transitivizer*), phonology: possible consonant merger, syntactic analysis: transitive verb, attested by Ed and Delphine Kelly (12/10/71).

<**yétheqet**>, pcs //yə́θ=əq(əl)=T or yə́θ=əqə(l)=T//, ds, LANG ['*teach s-o a language*'], lx <**=eqel**> *in speech, in the throat*, (<**=et ~ =t**> *purposeful control transitivizer*), phonology: possible syllable-loss (el before =t), possible consonant-loss (l before =t), syntactic analysis: transitive verb, attested by IHTTC (9/21/77).

<**xwiyétheqel**>, ds //xʷ=yə́θ=əqəl//, LANG /'*to interpret, (tell on someone [EB])*'/, literally /'(probably) always tell what happened in speech/language'/, (<**xw=**> *always*), lx <**=eqel**> *in speech, in language*, syntactic analysis: intransitive verb, attested by AC (9/15/71, 10/6/71), also /'*tell on someone*'/, attested by EB (3/7/78), example: <**latsel xwiyétheqel.**>, //lɛ-c-əl xʷ=yə́θ=əqəl//, /'*I'll go and interpret.*'/, attested by AC (9/15/71), <**lí a stl'í kw'as xwiyétheqel?**>, //lí ʔɛ s=ƛ'í k'ʷ-ɛ-s xʷ=yə́θ=əqəl//, /'*Do you want to interpret?*'/, attested by AC (10/6/71).

<**xwéytheqel**>, cts //xʷ[-ə́-]=yəθ=əqəl or xʷ=yə́[-M1-]θ=əqəl//, LANG /'*interpreting, (telling on someone [EB])*'/, (<**é-infix** or **metathesis**> *continuative*), phonology: infixed schwa or metathesis, possible vowel-loss, syntactic analysis: intransitive verb, attested by AC (9/15/71), also <**xwíytheqel**>, //xʷ[-ə́-]=yəθ=əqəl or xʷ=yə́[-M1-]θ=əqəl//, also /'*telling on someone*'/, attested by EB (3/7/78), example: <**ílh le xwéytheqel.**>, //ʔí-ɬ lə xʷ=yə́[-M1-]θ=əqəl//, /'*He was interpreting.*'/, attested by AC, <**ílhtsel xwéytheqel.**>, //ʔí-ɬ-c-əl xʷ=yə́[-M1-]θ=əqəl//, /'*I was interpreting.*'/, attested by AC.

<**xwiyétheqet**>, pcs //xʷ=yə́θ=əq(əl)=əT or xʷ=yə́θ=əqə(l)=T//, LANG ['*interpret for s-o*'], literally /'interpret s-o'/, (<**=et ~ =t**> *purposeful control transitivizer*), phonology: possible syllable-loss (el before =t), possible consonant-loss (l before =t), syntactic analysis: transitive verb, attested by AC (10/6/71), example: <**metlh xwiyetheqethóx.**>, //mə-tɬ xʷ=yə́θ=əq(əl)=əT-áxʸ//, /'*Come and interpret for me.*'/, attested by AC, <**lí a stl'í kw'as xwiyétheqethóx?**>, //lí ʔɛ s=ƛ'í k'ʷ-ɛ-s xʷ=yə́θ=əq(əl)=əT-áxʸ//, /'*Do you want to interpret for me?*'/, literally /'is it your want that-you interpret me'/, attested by AC, <**lí a stl'í kw'es álthes xwiyétheqethò:m?**>, //lí ʔɛ s=ƛ'í k'ʷ-əs ʔɛ́lθə-s xʷ=yə́θ=əq(əl)=əT-à·m//, /'*Do you want me to interpret for you?*'/, literally /'is it your want that-it it is me you are interpreted'/, attested by AC.

<**lexwshxwiyétheqel**>, ds //ləxʷs=xʷə=yə́θ=əqəl or ləxʷ=sxʷ=yə́θ=əqəl//, LANG /'*a gossip, person that always gossips*'/, literally /'person that always becomes/gets to tell what happened in speech (or) always someone for telling what happened in speech'/, (<**lexws=**> *person that always*), possibly <**lexw=**> *always*, possibly <**xwe=**> *get, become*, syntactic analysis: nominal, attested by EB (3/9/76), AC (9/15/71).

<**yethéleqw**>, ABDF ['*(have a) pointed head*'], *see* éy ~ éy:.

<**yétheqet**>, LANG ['*teach s-o a language*'], *see* yéth.

<**yéthest**>, LANG /'*tell s-o something that happened, tell s-o (bring something out)*'/, *see* yéth.

<**yéthestexw**>, LANG ['*cause s-o to tell what happened*'], *see* yéth.

<**yétl'**>, bound root //yə́ƛ' *rub*//.

<**yétl'q't**>, pcs //yə́ƛ'=q'=T//, ABFC /'*rub s-th/s-o, smear s-th, (paint s-th)*'/, MC, lx <**=q'**> *on something else*, (<**=t**> *purposeful control transitivizer*), syntactic analysis: transitive verb, attested by IHTTC (7/18/77), Elders Group (4/28/76, 5/26/76), compare <**yótl'et**> *shine s-th*, other sources: ES (CwMsCh) /yíƛ'q't/ *rub*, Salish cognate: Squamish /yəƛ'q'/ *rub, paint* as in /yəƛ'q'-ánʔ/ *rub, paint (tr.)* K67:380.

<**yátl'q't**>, cts //yə[-Aɛ́-]ƛ'=q'=T//, ABFC ['*rubbing it*'], MC ['*painting it*'], (<**á-ablaut**> *continuative*), phonology: ablaut, syntactic analysis: transitive verb, attested by Elders Group (4/28/76), EB (4/28/76), example: <**yátl'q't tel lálem**>, //yə[-Aɛ́-]ƛ'=q'=T t-əl lɛ́ləm//, /'*painting my house*'/, attested by EB.

<**yátl'q'els**>, sas //yə[-Aɛ́-]ƛ'=q'=əls//, cts, MC ['*painting*'], (<**á-ablaut**> *continuative*), (<**=els**> *structured activity continuative*), phonology: ablaut, syntactic analysis: intransitive verb, attested by IHTTC (7/18/77), EB (4/28/76).

<**syátl'q'els**>, dnom //s=yə[-Aɛ́-]ƛ'=q'=əls//, sas, MC ['*paint (nominal)*'], literally /'something man-made (tool) for painting'/, (<**s=**> *nominalizer*), (<**=els**> *structured activity continuative nominal/tool for*), phonology: ablaut, syntactic analysis: nominal, attested by IHTTC (7/18/77), DM (12/4/64), also <**shxwiyáth'qels**>, probably mistranscribed for <**shxwiyátl'q'els**>, //sxʷ=yɛ́θ'q=əls or sxʷ=yə[=Aɛ́=]ƛ'=q'=əls//, also /'*paint (for walls, etc.)*'/, attested by Elders Group (5/25/77), example: <**(tsq'éyx̱, tskwí:m, eyó:les) siyátl'q'els ~ (tsq'éyx̱, tskwí:m, eyó:les) tsq'éyx̱ siyáth'qels**>, //(c=q'íx̣, c=kʷí·m, ʔɛy=á·ləs) s=yə[=Aɛ́=]ƛ'=q'=əls ~ (c=q'íx̣, c=kʷí·m, ʔɛy=á·ləs) sxʷ=yɛ́θ'q=əls//, /'*(black, red, yellow) paint*'/, attested by DM (12/4/64 Wells tapes, new transcript, new p.181).

<**s(i)yátl'qels te qw'x̱wéltses**>, cpds ///s=yə[-Aɛ́-]ƛ'=q'=əls-s tə q'ʷix̣ʷ=ə[=´=]l=cəs//, PE /'*nail polish*'/ (lit. "paint for (of) the fingernail"), attested by RG & EH (4/10/99 Ling332)

<**yétl'q'esem**>, mdls //yə́ƛ'=q'=əs=əm//, PE ['*put paint on one's face*'], REL, lx <**=q'**> *on something else*, lx <**=es**> *on the face*, (<**=em**> *middle voice, one's own*), syntactic analysis: intransitive verb, attested by IHTTC (7/18/77).

<**yétl'q'est**>, pcs //yə́ƛ'=q'=əs=T//, ABFC ['*smear something on s-o's face [purposely]*'], PE, lx <**=q'**> *on something else*, lx <**=es**> *on the face*, (<**=t**> *purposeful control transitivizer*), syntactic analysis: transitive verb, attested by Elders Group (5/26/76); found in <**yétl'q'esthométsel.**>, //yə́ƛ'=q'=əs=T-ámə-c-əl//, /'*I smear something on your face.*'/, attested by Elders Group.

<**yétl'q'íws**>, ds //yə́ƛ'=q'=íws//, PE ['*put paint on the body*'], lx <**=q'**> *on something else*, lx <**=íws**> *on the body*, syntactic analysis: intransitive verb, attested by IHTTC (7/18/77).

<**yétl'q'esem**>, PE ['*put paint on one's face*'], *see* yétl'.

<**yétl'q'est**>, ABFC [*'smear something on s-o's face [purposely]'*], *see* yétl'.

<**yétl'q'íws**>, PE [*'put paint on the body'*], *see* yétl'.

<**yétl'q't**>, ABFC /*'rub s-th/s-o, smear s-th, (paint s-th)'*/, *see* yétl'.

<**yets'ets'á**>, TVMO /*'to travel by horse, already riding a horse'*/, *see* ts'á:.

<**yéw: ~ yéw**>, bound root //yə́w(·) *communicate with a spirit or spirits*//, Salish cognate: Squamish root /yəw(ʔ)/ approximate meaning: *spiritual power* K67:381.

<**syéw:e ~ syéwe ~ syő:we ~ syú:we**>, df //s=yə́w·=ə ~ s=yə́w=ə//, REL /*'fortune-teller, seer, person who can see things in the future, female witch'*/, literally perhaps /'someone (living thing) to communicate with a spirit'/, (<**s=**> *nominalizer, someone to/that*), possibly <**=e**> *living thing*, syntactic analysis: nominal, attested by BJ (12/5/64), Elders Group (11/19/75), EB (2/11/76, 4/24/78, 5/25/76), AC (11/16/71), other sources: ES /syə́w·ə/ (CwMs /syə́wʔə/) *seer*, Salish cognate: Squamish /ʔəs-yə́wʔ/ *seer, fortune-teller* K67:381, Nooksack /syóʔwæ/ *seer (usually a woman)* A78:15-16, Saanich dial. of NSt /syə́w'ə/ *seer (forecasts the future)* B74a:26, possibly Southern Lushootseed /jə́gʷə/ *a kind of monster* H76:217, 317.

<**hí:ywes**>, pncs //hí-yəw=əs//, REL [*'predicting the future'*], (<**hí-**> *continuative*), (<**=es**> *psychological non-control transitivizer*), syntactic analysis: transitive verb, attested by Elders Group (3/28/79).

<**syúwél ~ syéw:el**>, dnom //s=yə́w·=əl//, SPRD /*'an Indian dancer's spirit power; spirit power song'*/, ASM ['the spirit that comes to a person training to be a spirit dancer, it appears to him in a dream unbidden or more often sought out on a spirit quest in the woods, the spirit may be a creature or even an inanimate object but it sings a song and does a characteristic dance in the dream, the new dancer, when he comes to, practices both with drummers who help him do it the same way each time and who learn it and thereafter drum it and can sing it with him (no one else can sing it) during spirit dancing season'], (<**s=**> *nominalizer, something to*), root <**yéw:**> *communicate with a spirit*, (<**=el**> meaning uncertain, perhaps *device*), historical/comparative detail: not the =el meaning *go/come/get/become* since that is cognate with =el in Cowichan, Musqueam, and other Salish languages, the cognates for this word instead have =en which Suttles (ca1984:14.6.8) says in Musqueam (/-ən ~ -ən'/) may be a lexical suffix meaning something like *instrument*, phonology: updrifting, syntactic analysis: nominal, attested by Elders Group (2/25/76), EB (3/31/78), AD (3/31/78), AC (10/15/71, 9/29/71), BJ (12/5/64), Salish cognate: Squamish /s-yə́w-an/ *[spirit] song* from root /yəw(ʔ)/ *spiritual power* beside /yəwʔ-ín-m/ *sing (tr.)* and /yəwʔ=ínʔ-c/ *understand (speech)* K67:300,381, Lushootseed /yáwdəb/ *spirit power song* beside /ɬu-yáwdəb/ *sing one's power* H76:627, Samish dial. of NSt /syə́wən/ *spirit song (and its dance)* G86:81, Nooksack /syóʔwən/ *spirit power, guardian spirit; spirit song and dance* A78:49ff, example: <**le t'ít'elem te syéw:els te sí:les.**>, //lə t'í[-C_1ə-]]=əm tə s=yə́w·=əl-s tə sí·lə-s//, /*'She's singing her grandmother's [spirit] song.'*/, attested by AC, <**ewá:lh t'ílemesthòm té syùwels?**>, //ʔəwə-ə-əɬ t'íl=əm=sT-àm tə s=yúw=əl-s//, /*'Does he ever sing you his spirit song?'*/, literally /'was it not/never? you were sung for the his spirit song'/, phonology: sentence pitch on article and downstepping, attested by EB, <**éwelh t'ílemesthò:m té syùwèls.**>, //ʔə́wə-əɬ t'íl=əm=sT-à·m tə s=yúw=əl-s//, /*'He never sang you his spirit song.'*/, literally /'it was not/never you were sung for the his spirit song'/, phonology: sentence pitch on article and downstepping, attested by AD, <**t'át'emet te syő́wels**>, //t'ɛ́=C_1ə-=məT tə s=yúw=əl-s//, /*'singer for someone (at spirit dance)'*/, lit. /"trying-conserning-it/s-o the spirit-song-his/her"/, attested by RG & EH (4/10/99 Ling332).

<**yewí:lt**>, pcs //yəw=í·l=T or yəw=ə[=Aí·=l=T//, REL [*'casting an evil spell on s-o'*], (<**=í:l** meaning

uncertain but perhaps *come, go, get* or perhaps <=Aí:=> *durative* or, historical/comparative detail: Musqueam cognate has /-í·n/ meaning uncertain (Suttles ca1984:14.6.9), (<**=t**> *purposeful control transitivizer*), syntactic analysis: transitive verb, attested by EB (5/25/76), contrast <**x̲t'ét**> *put/cast a spell on s-o*.

<**syiwí:l ~ syewí:l**>, df //s=yə[=Ai=]w=í·l or s=yəw=ə[=Aí·=]l//, REL /'*a sung spell, power to help or harm people or to do [ritual] burning, power to do witchcraft and predict the future, an evil spell, (magic spell) (someone who has power to take things out of a person or put things in [by magic] [Elders Group 2/25/76], ritualist [Elders Group 1/21/76], witch [EB 4/25/78])*'/, ASM ['the spell is usually inherited, "if you don't sing it right maybe you'll go crazy"'], (<**s=**> *nominalizer, something to*), (<**=í:l**> meaning uncertain, perhaps *come, go, get*–stressed full-grade of <**=el**>), historical/comparative detail: Musqueam cognate has /-í·n/ meaning uncertain (Suttles ca1984:14.6.9), probably <**í:-ablaut of suffix e**> *durative*, phonology: ablaut, syntactic analysis: nominal, attested by BJ (12/5/64), Elders Group (11/19/75), EB (5/25/76), other sources: ES /syəwí·n/ (CwMs /syəʔwínʔ/) *inherited spell*, Salish cognate: Squamish /siwʔínʔ/ *magic power* K69:62, Nooksack /siwínʔ/ *magic spell* A78:16, also REL ['*someone who has power to take things out of a person or put things in [by magic]*'], attested by Elders Group (2/25/76), also REL ['*ritualist*'], attested by Elders Group (1/21/76), also /'*witch*'/, attested by EB (4/25/78).

<**yewí:lmet**>, iecs //yəw=í·l=məT//, REL /'*(cast a spell for s-o, use a magical power for s-o)*'/, semantic environment ['of a fortune-teller, shaman (Indian doctor, medicine man), ritualist'], (<**=í:l** meaning uncertain, perhaps *come, go, get*–stressed full-grade of <**=el**> or <**í:-ablaut of suffix e**> *durative*), historical/comparative detail: Musqueam cognate has /-í·n/ meaning uncertain (Suttles ca1984:14.6.9), (<**=met**> *indirect effect non-control transitivizer*), syntactic analysis: transitive verb, attested by BJ (12/5/64).

<**yiwí:leqw**>, ds //yiw=í·l=əq^{w}//, REL ['*medicine song [sung by shaman]*'], literally perhaps /'use a magical power/sung spell on the hair'/, ASM ['spells were often cast upon people by shamans in the person's absence by using some of the person's hair (obtained without his/her knowledge), thus for spells on a person to love someone, to get sick, etc.'], , perhaps *come, go, get*–stressed full-grade of <**=el**> or <**í:-ablaut of suffix e**> *durative*), historical/comparative detail: Musqueam cognate has /-í·n/ meaning uncertain (Suttles ca1984:14.6.9), lx <**=eqw**> *on the hair, on top of the head*, syntactic analysis: nominal, attested by BJ (12/5/64).

<**syiwí:leqw**>, ds //s=yiw=í·l=əq^{w}//, REL /'*war-whoop, (*(probably) *a sung spell before battle)*'/, SOC, literally perhaps /'something that is a sung spell on the head/hair'/, (semological comment: if the meaning of head rather than hair is used it may refer to the occasional practice of cutting off enemies heads as battle trophies), (<**s=**> *nominalizer, something to*), (<**=í:l** , perhaps *come, go, get*–stressed full-grade of <**=el**> or <**í:-ablaut of suffix e**> *durative*), historical/comparative detail: Musqueam cognate has /-í·n/ meaning uncertain (Suttles ca1984:14.6.9), lx <**=eqw**> *on the hair, on top of the head*, syntactic analysis: nominal, attested by BJ (12/5/64).

<**heywí:leqw**>, df //hɛ=yew=í·l=əq^{w}//, REL /'*a category of religious songs including sx̲wó:yx̲wey songs and burning songs, a burning song*'/, ASM ['the burning song is sung six days after a person dies at which time a ritualist burns his clothes and food (BJ)'], (<**he=**> *continuative or plural*), phonology: vowel-loss, syntactic analysis: nominal, attested by BJ (12/5/64 new transcript old pp.323-324).

<**syő́wméxwtses**>, df //s=yə́w=mə[=´=]x^{w}=cəs//, REL ['*large rattle used at spirit-dances*'], PE, ASM ['used only by someone who inherited the power to use it, old examples in museums are made with horn or leather enclosing the hard objects inside that rattle, often mountain goat/dog wool braids were fastened around the edges to hang down, usually D-shaped with the handle

attached to the middle of the rounded sewn-together bottom'], (<**s=**> *nominalizer, something to/that*), possibly root <**yéw ~ yíw**> *call/get a spirit/power*, possibly <**=mexw**> *person, people*, possibly <**=´=**> *derivational*, lx <**=tses**> *on the hand*, phonology: stress-shift, syntactic analysis: nominal, attested by BJ (12/5/64 new transcript old p.320), Salish cognate: Sechelt /yɛl-míxʷ-čis/ *rattle* T77:18, also <**syilméxwtses**>, //s-yil=mə[=´=]xʷ=cəs//, also /'*a rattle*'/, attested by Elders Group (2/5/75).

<**yewá:**>, df //yə=wɛ́·//, TVMO ['*along*'], possibly <**ye=**> *travelling along, while in motion*, possibly root <**wá:**> meaning uncertain, perhaps *continue*, syntactic analysis: adverb/adverbial verb, attested by AC (8/23/73), Salish cognate: Squamish root /wa(ʔ) ~ wə-/ as in the predicative clitic /wa/ *continuous/ and in /wə́ʔ-u/ continue, carry on* and /wə́ʔ-u-s/ *continue, carry on (tr.)* K67:378, perhaps Lushootseed /yəháw' ~ yáwʔ/ *proceed, go ahead* H76:630 with metathesis, example: <**wátsa lamál yewá:?**>, //ʔəwə-ə-cɛ lɛ=m-ɛ́l yə=wɛ́·//, /'*Can I go along?, Will you take me along?*'/, literally /'will it not be? I go along'/, attested by AC, <**látsel yewá:.**>, //lɛ́-c-əl yə=wɛ́·//, /'*I'm going [along] with you.*'/, literally /'I'm going along'/, attested by AC.

<**yewá:l**>, possibly root //yəwɛ́·l or yə=wɛ́·=əl//, NUM ['*first*'], possibly <**ye=**> *along*, possibly root <**wá:**> *continue*, possibly <**=el**> *go, come, get, become*, phonology: possible vowel merger, syntactic analysis: adverb/adverbial verb, attested by Elders Group (7/9/75), AC (10/13/71), EB (4/14/78), MV (Deming 5/4/78), Salish cognate: Squamish /yawʔánʔ/ *first, before, ahead, former* as also in /s-yawʔánʔ/ *place of origin; ancestry*and also perhaps related to root /hiwʔ/ *forward, ahead* K67:382, 300, Lushootseed /yawʔ ~ yəháw'/ *proceed, go ahead* H76:630, example: <**yewál qw'él te elíle.**>, //yəwɛ́l q'ʷə́l tə ʔəlílə//, /'*The salmonberry is first ripe.*'/, attested by EB, <**álthe yewál me xwe'í.**>, //ʔɛ́lθə yəwɛ́l mə xʷə=ʔí//, /'*I came first.*'/, literally /'it's me first come to arrive'/, attested by Elders Group, <**tl'ó yewá:lelh ts'lhimexóstels.**>, //ƛ'á yəwɛ́·l-əɬ c'əɬ=(ʔ)im=əxʸ=ás=təl-s//, /'*That's the first one he was going with [romantically]., That's the first one he was going for a walk with.*'/, attested by MV, <**me stetís kwthe yewá:l.**>, //mə s=C_1ə=tə[=Aí=]s kʷθə yəwɛ́·l//, /'*He came close to the first.*'/, attested by AC (10/13/71).

<**syewá:l ~ syewál**>, dnom //s=yəwɛ́·l or s=yə=wɛ́·=əl ~ s=yəwɛ́l//, KIN ['*ancestors*'], literally /'someone that is first (or) someone to be first'/, (<**s=**> *nominalizer, someone to/that*), phonology: possible vowel merger, syntactic analysis: nominal, attested by IHTTC (9/13/77), AC (9/29/71), EB (2/27/76), other sources: ES /syəwɛ́·l/ *ancestors, lineage*, Salish cognate: Squamish /s-yawʔánʔ/ *place of origin; ancestry* K67:382, example: <**tl'ól syewá:l.**>, //ƛ'á-l s=yəwɛ́·l//, /'*That's my ancestors.*'/, attested by AC.

<**syewá:lelh ~ syewálelh**>, if //s=yəwɛ́·l-əɬ//, KIN ['*departed ancestors*'], (<**-elh**> *past tense*), syntactic analysis: nominal, attested by EB (2/27/76), IHTTC (9/13/77), example: <**sqwà:ls ta' syuwá:lelh**>, //s=qʷɛ̀·l-s t-ɛʔ s=yəwɛ́·l-əɬ//, /'*words of your ancestors*'/, attested by EB, <**shxwtelís te syewálelh**>, //sxʷ=təlí-s tə s=yəwɛ́l-əɬ//, /'*where the past ancestors came from (where s-o comes from)*'/, attested by Elders Group (3/29/78).

<**syesyewálelh**>, pln //s=C_1ə=s=yə(=)wɛ́=əl-əɬ//, KIN /'*ancestors past, (all one's ancestors)*'/, (irregular), (<**R5=s=**> *plural*), comment: the reduplication of a prefix is not attested in any other word and seems like an error but several members of the Elders Group were certain of the form, phonology: reduplication, reduplication of prefix, syntactic analysis: nominal, attested by Elders Group (3/29/78), example: <**stó:lō syesyewálelh**>, //s=tá·l=əw s=C_1ə=s=yəwɛ́·l-əɬ//, /'*Stó:lō ancestors, Stalo ancestors*'/, attested by Elders Group.

<**yewá:lmels ~ iwá:lmels**>, df //yə(=)wɛ́·(=)əl=əm=əls or yə(=)wɛ́·(=)əl=məl=əs ~ ʔi-ywɛ́·l=əm=əls//, TIME ['*before*'], possibly <**=em**> *intransitivizer/have/get*, possibly <**=els**>

structured activity continuative, possibly <**(h)i-**> *continuative* before y, possibly <**=mel**> *part, portion*, possibly <**=es**> *cyclic time period*, phonology: possible vowel-loss, syntactic analysis: adverb/adverbial verb, attested by AC, DM (12/4/64), others, example: <**yewálmels kw'e tseláqelh(elh)**>, //yəwɛ́l=məl=əs k'ʷə cəlɛ́q=əɬ(-əɬ)//, /'*the day before yesterday*'/, attested by AC (10/15/71), also <**léts'e swáyel iwá:lmels kw'e cheláqelhelh**>, //lə́c'ə s=wɛ́yəl ʔi-ywɛ́·l=məls k'ʷə cəlɛ́q=əɬ-əɬ//, attested by DM (12/4/64), <**wá:lxchexw yewá:lmels kw'as wets'étl'.**>, //wɛ́·l=xʸ-c-əxʷ yəwɛ́·l=məls k'ʷ-ɛ-s wə=c'ə́ƛ'//, /'*Throw it before you fall.*'/, attested by AC (10/13/71), <**lulh qwáyel te s'óthes yuwá:lmels kwses melqí:wsem.**>, //lə-uɬ qʷɛ́y=əl tə s=ʔáθ=əs-s yəwɛ́·l=məls kʷ-s-əs mɛlq=í·ws=əm//, /'*Her face is turning green before she faints.*'/, attested by AC (11/17/71), <**iwá:lmels kws xwe'í:s te sth'ó:qwi**>, //ʔi-ywɛ́·l=məls kʷ-s xʷə=ʔí·-s tə s=θ'áqʷi//, /'*before the salmon come (arrive)*'/, attested by DM (12/4/64).

<**yewá:lmels ~ iwá:lmels**>, TIME ['*before*'], *see* yewá:l.

<**yewí:lmet**>, REL /'*(cast a spell for s-o, use a magical power for s-o)*'/, *see* yéw: ~ yéw.

<**yewí:lt**>, REL ['*casting an evil spell on s-o*'], *see* yéw: ~ yéw.

<**yexw**>, free root //yəxʷ//, EFAM ['*I wonder*'], syntactic analysis: mpcl, attested by AD (3/10/80), Salish cognate: Saanich dial. of NSt /yəxʷ/ postposed modal particle, *conjectural*, often translated as *I wonder* or by *must be (not obligation/necessity)* Montler 1986:208-209, Samish dial. of NSt /yəxʷ/ (identical to Saanich in meaning, syntactic class, and function) G84a:59, example: <**tl'ó: yexw**>, //ƛ'á-ə yəxʷ//, /'*I wonder if., (Is it that, I wonder?)*'/, attested by AD (3/10/80), <**x̲à:m yéxwtselcha.**>, //x̣ɛ̀·m yə́xʷ-c-əl-cɛ//, /'*I'm expecting to cry.(?)*'/, Elder's comment: "unsure of translation", attested by BHTTC (10/21/76).

<**yexwő̃qw'elem**>, TVMO ['*travelling by going downriver*'], *see* wő̃qw' ~ wéqw'.

<**yéx̲ch ~ yéx̲ts ~ yéx̲cha ~ yéx̲tsa**>, free root //yə́x̣cɛ *give as a gift*//.

<**syéx̲cha ~ syéx̲tsa**>, dnom //s=yə́x̣cɛ//, SOC /'*a gift*'/, <s=> *nominalizer*, attested by RG & EH (4/10/99 Ling332)

<**yéx̲chet ~ yéx̲tset**>, pcs //yə́x̣c=əT//, SOC ['*give a gift to s-o*'], (<**=et**> *purposeful control transitivizer*), syntactic analysis: transitive verb, attested by AC (9/7/71), Elders Group (3/15/72, 4/16/75), other sources: ES /ʔyə́x̣cɛt/ *give*, JH /ʔyə́x̣cet/ *give a present*; found in <**yéx̲cetlha.**>, //yə́x̣c=əT-ɬɛ//, /'*Give it to somebody (with you).*'/, attested by AC, <**yéx̲cethóxes.**>, //yə́x̣c=əT-áxʸ-əs//, /'*He gave it to me as a gift., He gave me the gift.*'/, attested by AC, <**yéx̲cethòmè**>, //yə́x̣c=əT-àmə̀//, /'*give to you (as a present), give you something free as a gift*'/, attested by Elders Group (3/15/72, 4/16/75), example: <**yéx̲cethòmétsel te'í:le.**>, //yə́x̣c=əT-àmə́-c-əl tə=ʔí·=lə̀//, /'*I'm giving you this as a gift.*'/, attested by AC.

<**yex̲chí:met**>, df //yəx̣c=í·m=əT or yəx̣c=ə[=Aí·=]məT//, SOC ['*ask for s-th[?]*'], (semological comment: this translation may not be accurate), literally /'give s-th repeatedly as a present[?]'/, possibly <**=í:m**> *repeatedly*, possibly <**=et**> *purposeful control transitivizer*, possibly <**=met**> *indirect effect non-control transitivizer*, possibly <**í:-ablaut on suffix e**> *durative*, phonology: possible ablaut, syntactic analysis: transitive verb, attested by Elders Group (6/16/76); found in <**yex̲chí:métes.**>, //yəx̣c=í·m=əT-əs//, /'*He asked for it.*'/, phonology: updrifting, attested by Elders Group.

<**yéx̲chet ~ yéx̲tset**>, SOC ['*give a gift to s-o*'], *see* yéx̲ch ~ yéx̲ts.

<**yex̲chí:met**>, SOC ['*ask for s-th[?]*'], *see* yéx̲ch ~ yéx̲ts.

<**yéx̲w**>, SH /'*broke down, came (un)loose, came apart, (got) untied, loose, unravelled*'/, *see* yíx̲w.

<**yex̲wá:ls**>, SH ['*breaking (everything)*'], *see* yíx̲w.

<**yéx̲wela**>, df //yə́x̣ʷ=əlɛ//, EZ /'*eagle (generic), (golden eagle [some speakers])*'/, ['*Aquila chrysaetos* and *Haliaeetus leucocephalus*'], ASM ['kids were sometimes teased by telling them eagles will take them'], possibly root <**yéx̲w**> *broke down, came (un)loose, came apart, (got) untied, loose, unravelled*, possibly <**=ela**> *on the temples, on the side of the head, on the cheek*, (<**zero**> *nominalizer*), phonology: zero nominalizer, syntactic analysis: noun, nominal, attested by AC (12/4/71), BJ (5/10/64), Elders Group (3/21/79)(SMN only), other sources: ES /yə́xʷələ/ (Cw /yə́xʷəlɛ/) *eagle (generic)*, JH /yə́xʷəle/ *eagle (generic term)*, Salish cognate: Squamish /yəx̣ʷə́laʔ/ *eagle* K67:381 and *immature bald eagle* Kennedy and Bouchard 1976:73, Lushootseed /yəxʷ(ə)láʔ/ *eagle* H76:633, also /'*golden eagle*'/.

<**yéx̲weletst**>, SH ['*unwrap it*'], *see* yíx̲w.

<**yéx̲wet**>, MC /'*untie s-th, unravel s-th, unwind it, unwrap it, loosen s-th, unlace it*'/, *see* yíx̲w.

<**yéyilaw ~ yíyelaw**>, DIR /'*a little past, a little after*'/, *see* yelá:w ~ yeláw ~ yiláw.

<**ye'íle**>, DIR ['*these*'], *see* í.

<**ye'í:mex**>, TVMO /'*coming by foot, travelling by walking, already walking, travelling on foot*'/, *see* ím.

<**yiláwel kw'a's hò:y**>, LANG /'*thank you very much, Thank you very much.*'/, *see* hò:y ~ hó:y ~ hóy.

<**yilawelhát ~ yiláwelhàt ~ syiláwelhàt**>, TIME ['*Monday (day past)*'], *see* yelá:w ~ yeláw ~ yiláw.

<**yíq**>, free root //yíq//, WETH /'*to snow, (snow falls)*'/, syntactic analysis: intransitive verb, attested by Deming (3/31/77), others, other sources: ES (CwMsCh) /yíq/ *it's snowing*, Salish cognate: Squamish /yíq/ *to snow, it snows* versus /yíʔiq/ //yə́-yiq// *be snowing* K67:383-384, Samish dial. of NSt /číq/ *snow falls* versus (VU) /čéyəq/ //číyəq// *snow is falling* G86:97, example: <**me yíq**>, //mə yíq//, /'*coming to snow, (beginning to snow)*'/, attested by Deming.

<**syíq**>, dnom //s=yíq//, WETH /'*a snow, a snowfall*'/, (<**s=**> *nominalizer*), syntactic analysis: nominal, attested by AC (9/30/71), BJ (5/10/64), example: <**hí:kw te syíq.**>, //hí[=·=]kʷ tə s=yíq//, /'*(It's) a big snow.*'/, literally /'the snowfall is big'/, attested by AC, <**spípew te syíq.**>, //s=pí[=C_1ə=]w tə s=yíq//, /'*The snow is frozen.*'/, *<**spípew te máqa.**> rejected by AC.

<**yíyeq**>, cts //yí[-C_1ə-]q//, WETH /'*(be) snowing, it's snowing, snow is falling*'/, (<**-R1-**> *continuative*), phonology: reduplication, syntactic analysis: intransitive verb, attested by Elders Group (1/7/76, 3/1/76), AC (9/30/71), other sources: ES (CwMsCh) /yíq/ *it's snowing*, JH /yə́·q/ *snowing*, example: <**yíyeq te xálh**>, //yí[-C_1ə-]q tə xʸɛ́ɬ//, /'*(It's) snowing on the road.*'/, attested by AC, <**yí:yeq te smált kw'e xwelá:lt.**>, //yí[=·=][-C_1ə-]q tə s=mɛ́lt k'ʷə xʷə=lɛ́·[=C_1ə=]t//, /'*It was snowing on the mountain last night.*'/, attested by AC.

<**syíyeq**>, df //s=yí[-C_1ə-]q or s=yí[=C_1ə=]q//, WETH /'*falling snow, be snowing*'/, (<**s=**> *nominalizer* or *stative*), possibly <**-R1-**> *continuative*, possibly <**=R1=**> *stative*, phonology: reduplication, syntactic analysis: nominal, adjective/adjectival verb, attested by AC (8/14/70, 9/13/71), IHTTC (7/26/77), example: <**syíyeq te smált.**>, //s=yí[=C_1ə=]q tə s=mɛ́lt//, /'*It's snowing on the mountain.*'/, attested by AC, <**lhálhq'etxel te syíyeq.**>, //ɬɛ[=C_1ə=]q'ət=xʸəl tə s=yí[-C_1ə-]q//, /'*The falling snow has wide flakes/snowflakes.*'/, attested by IHTTC.

<**yeqelsxá:y**>, df //yiq=əlsxʸɛ́=ɛ́y//, WETH ['*first snow*'], lx <**=elsxá**> *times ten, first*, possibly <**=áy**> *covering, wool, bark*, phonology: vowel-reduction, vowel merger, syntactic analysis: intransitive verb, attested by Elders Group (1/22/75).

<**q'elsiyáqem** or **q'elts'yáqem**>, cpds //q'əl=(l)c'=yi[=Aɛ́=]q=əm//, WETH ['*(have/get a) snowdrift*'],

literally (prob.) /'have/get wound around/tangled twisted snow falls'/, root <**q'el**> *wound around, tangled*, lx <**=lts'**> *twisted*, root <**yiq**> *snow falls*, (<**á-ablaut**> *derivational*), (<**=em**> *intransitivizer, have, get*), phonology: probable ablaut, possible consonant merger, syntactic analysis: intransitive verb, attested by Elders Group (4/16/75).

<**sqelyíqem** (or **sq'elyíqem**)>, cpds //s=q'əl=yíq=əm//, WETH ['*a snowdrift*'], literally (prob.) /'something that gets/has tangled/wound around snow falls'/, (<**s=**> *nominalizer, something that*), root <**q'el**> *wound around, tangled*, root <**yiq**> *snow falls*, (<**=em**> *intransitivizer, have, get*), syntactic analysis: nominal, attested by EB (2/15/78).

<**yitá:lstem**>, ABDF ['*staggering around*'], *see* tél ~ tá:l ~ tiy.

<**yít'em**>, ds //yít'=əm//, CST /'*melt, thaw*'/, semantic environment ['of creek, butter, etc., but not of lakes'], (<**=em**> *intransitivizer/have/get or middle voice*), syntactic analysis: intransitive verb, attested by AC (8/14/70), EB (12/10/75), Elders Group (3/14/79), other sources: JH /yét'/ *thaw* versus ES (CwMsCh) /yáx̣^{w}/ *thaw*, compare <**Siyét'a**> *village near Agassiz-Rosedale bridge.*

<**yíyet'em**>, cts //yí[-C_1ə-]t'=əm//, CST ['*be melting*'], (<**-R1-**> *continuative*), phonology: reduplication, syntactic analysis: intransitive verb, attested by Elders Group (3/14/79), example: <**yíyet'em te slós.**>, //yí[-C_1ə-]t'=əm tə s=lás//, /'*The grease is melting.*'/, attested by Elders Group, <**yíyet'em te máqa.**>, //yí[-C_1ə-]t'=əm tə mɛ́qɛ//, /'*The snow is melting.*'/, attested by Elders Group, <**yíyet'em te sx̱wő̃sem.**>, //yí[-C_1ə-]t'=əm tə s=x̣^{w}ós=əm//, /'*The [whipped] soapberries are melting.*'/, attested by Elders Group.

<**yitl'ítl'ew**>, TVMO ['*[travelling along] running away*'], *see* tl'í:w.

<**yí:ts'em**>, probable bound stem //yí·c'=əm//, meaning uncertain

<**syí:ts'em**>, df //s=yí·c'=əm//, LAND ['*sand*'], (<**s=**> *nominalizer, something to/that*), root meaning unknown, (<**=em**> *intransitivizer/have/get*), syntactic analysis: nominal, attested by AC (9/8/71), CT (6/8/76), other sources: ES /səyíc'əm/ (Ms /syíc'əm/) *sand*, also <**siyíts'em**>, //s=yíc'=əm//, attested by AC (8/14/70).

<**syí:ts'emílep**>, ds //s=yí·c'=əm=íləp//, LAND ['*sand bar*'], WATR, literally /'sand ground'/, lx <**=ílep**> *ground, dirt*, syntactic analysis: nominal, attested by CT (6/8/76).

<**yiwí:leqw**>, REL ['*medicine song [sung by shaman]*'], *see* yéw: ~ yéw.

<**yíx̱w**>, free root //yíx̣^{w}//, SH /'*fall apart, come apart (of something man-made)*'/, syntactic analysis: intransitive verb, attested by Elders Group (1/7/75, 1/7/76), EB (4/27/76), Salish cognate: Mainland Comox /číʔx^{w}/ *to come loose* beside /číix^{w}ət/ *to loosen* B75prelim.:81, Lushootseed root /jix̣(i)/ *break down, collapse, break off and fall; be out of order; breakdown of a mechanical device* as in /ʔəs-jíx̣/ *has collapsed (of bridge), is broken (of machine)* and /jíx̣-id/ *break it down* H76:225-226,561 perhaps Sechelt /yáx^{w}/ *to come loose* beside /yáx^{w}-at/ *to loosen* T77:31, example: <**le yíx̱w te sch'áletstel.**>, //lə yíx̣^{w} tə s=c'ɛ́=ləc=təl//, /'*The chair fell apart.*'/, attested by Elders Group (1/7/76).

<**yíx̱wet**>, pcs //yíx̣^{w}=əT//, MC /'*take s-th down, tear down s-th man-made, dismantle s-th, take it apart*'/, SH, (<**=et**> *purposeful control transitivizer*), syntactic analysis: transitive verb, attested by EB (4/26/76, 4/27/76), Deming (4/27/78), Elders Group (4/26/76); found in <**yíx̱wetem.**>, //yíx̣^{w}=əT-əm//, /'*It was torn down (of something man-made)., It was dismantled.*'/, attested by EB (4/27/76), example: <**yíx̱wetchap te siláwtxw.**>, //yíx̣^{w}=əT-c-ɛp tə sil=ɛ́wtx^{w}//, /'*You folks take down the tent.*'/, attested by EB (4/26/76).

<**yéx̱w**>, rsls //yi[=Aə́=]x̣^{w}//, SH /'*broke down, came (un)loose, came apart, (got) untied, loose, unravelled*'/, MC, semantic environment ['(got untied) of shoelace, braid, canoe, etc.'], (<**é-ablaut on root i**> *resultative*), phonology: ablaut, syntactic analysis: intransitive verb, attested by Deming

(6/22/78), EB (12/17/75, 4/27/76, 6/21/76), AHTTC (2/15/80), CT (6/8/76), Salish cognate: Squamish /yə́x̣ʷ/ *untied, loose, free* K69:90 shows the same resultative vowel, Lushootseed root /gəx̣(á)/ *get loose, untie, bail out (of jail)* beside Skagit /gʷə́x̣/ *get loose* and /gəx̣ád/ *untie s-o. bail s-o out of jail* H76:156, example: <**me yéx̱w**>, //mə yə́x̣ʷ//, /'*come loose*'/, attested by CT.

<**yéx̱wet**>, pcs //yi[=Aə́=]x̣ʷ=əT//, MC /'*untie s-th, unravel s-th, unwind it, unwrap it, loosen s-th, unlace it*'/, SH, (<**=et**> *purposeful control transitivizer*), phonology: ablaut, syntactic analysis: transitive verb, attested by Deming (4/27/78, 6/22/78), Elders Group (3/12/75), EB (12/17/75), CT and HT (6/21/76), IHTTC (9/2/77), Salish cognate: Lushootseed /gəx̣ád/ *untie s-o. bail s-o out of jail* H76:156, example: <**yéx̱wet te swéta**>, //yi[=Aə́=]x̣ʷ=əT tə swə́tɛ//, /'*unravel a sweater*'/, attested by CT and HT (6/21/76).

<**híyex̱wet**>, cts //hí-yi[=Aə=]x̣ʷ=əT//, SH ['*unlacing it*'], MC, (<**hí-**> *continuative*), phonology: ablaut, syntactic analysis: transitive verb, attested by IHTTC (9/2/77).

<**syéx̱w**>, dnom //s=yi[=Aə́=]x̣ʷ//, LAND ['*rockslide (that already happened)*'], literally /'something that came loose'/, (<**s=**> *nominalizer, something that*), phonology: ablaut, syntactic analysis: nominal, dialects: *Katz*, attested by Elders Group (4/2/75), AD (AHTTC 2/15/80).

<**syéx̱w**>, strs //s=yi[=Aə́=]x̣ʷ//, SH ['*unravelled*'], MC, (<**s=**> *stative*), phonology: ablaut, syntactic analysis: adjective/adjectival verb, attested by AD (AHTTC 2/15/80).

<**syíyex̱w**>, strs //s=yí[=C$_1$ə=]x̣ʷ//, SH ['*be unwrapped*'], (<**s=**> *stative*), (<**=R1=**> *resultative*), comment: this is an alternate resultative to the one formed by é-ablaut, phonology: reduplication, syntactic analysis: adjective/adjectival verb, attested by Deming (6/22/78), example: <**lulh syíyex̱w.**>, //lə-uɬ s=yí[=C$_1$ə=]x̣ʷ//, /'*It's already unwrapped.*'/, attested by Deming.

<**yex̱wá:ls**>, sas //yix̣ʷ=ɛ́·ls//, SH ['*breaking (everything)*'], MC, (<**=á:ls**> *structured activity non-continuative*), (semological comment: thus the -ing only indicates an activity that was structured and is over, not a continuative activity), phonology: vowel-reduction, syntactic analysis: intransitive verb, attested by Deming (6/22/78).

<**yéx̱weletst**>, ds //yi[=Aə́=]x̣ʷ=ələc=T//, pcs, SH ['*unwrap it*'], MC, literally /'unwrap s-th on the bottom'/, lx <**=elets**> *on the bottom*, (<**=t**> *purposeful control transitivizer*), phonology: ablaut, syntactic analysis: transitive verb, attested by Deming (6/22/78).

<**yíx̱wet**>, MC /'*take s-th down, tear down s-th man-made, dismantle s-th, take it apart*'/, *see* yíx̱w.

<**yíyeq**>, WETH /'*(be) snowing, it's snowing, snow is falling*'/, *see* yíq.

<**yíyeqw**>, FIRE /'*fire (out of control), forest fire burning, fire burning*'/, *see* yéqw.

<**yíyet'em**>, CST ['*be melting*'], *see* yít'em.

<**yókw' ~ yóqw'**>, bound root //yák'ʷ ~ yáq'ʷ *to break (in pieces), smash, crush, crumple*//, Salish cognate: Squamish /yúk'ʷ/ *be smashed* as also in /yúk'ʷ-un/ *smash up (tr.)* and /yúk'ʷ-i/ *be smashed, busted* (for ex. of a bone or a canoe) K69:91, Lushootseed root /juq'ʷ(u)/ *ruin, smash up, shatter* as in /ʔu-júq'ʷ-ud/ *smashing up s-th* (/ʔu-/ *completive*) H76:227.

<**yóqw'em ~ yó:qw'em**>, izs //yá(·)q'ʷ=əm//, SH /'*to break [in pieces], it broke*'/, semantic environment ['for ex. of a plank or a car'], (<**=em**> *intransitivizer, have, get*), syntactic analysis: intransitive verb, attested by AC, example: <**le yó:qw'em te loplós.**>, //lə yá·q'ʷ=əm tə laplás//, /'*The plank broke.*'/, attested by AC (8/6/70).

<**yókw'et**>, pcs //yák'ʷ=əT//, SH ['*break it*'], (<**=et**> *purposeful control transitivizer*), syntactic analysis: transitive verb, attested by Deming (4/27/78), Salish cognate: Musqueam dial. of Halkomelem /yák'ʷət/ *smash it* Suttles ca1984: 7.7.1 (ch.7 p.146), Squamish /yúk'ʷ-un/ *smash up*

(tr.) K69:91, Lushootseed /ʔu-júq'ʷ-ud/ *smashing up s-th* (/ʔu-/ *completive*) H76:227, also **<yóqw'et ~ yó:qw'et>**, //yá(·)q'ʷ=əT//, attested by AC, also **<yákw'et>**, //yɛ́k'ʷ=əT//, attested by EB (3/22/76), example: **<yóqw'et lí te smá:lt>**, //yáq'ʷ=əT lí tə s=mɛ́·lt//, /*'break it on a rock'*/, attested by AC (8/6/70), **<le yó:qw'etes te spí:w.>**, //lə yá·q'ʷ=əT-əs tə s=pí·w//, /*'He broke the ice.'*/, attested by AC (10/13/71); found in **<yákw'etes.>**, //yɛ́k'ʷ=əT-əs//, /*'He broke it.'*/, attested by EB (3/22/76).

<yóyekw'et>, cts //yá[-C_1ə-]k'ʷ=əT//, SH [*'breaking it'*], (<**-R1-**> *continuative*), phonology: reduplication, syntactic analysis: transitive verb, attested by Elders Group (5/19/76).

<yékw'et>, rsls //ya[=Aə́=]k'ʷ=əT//, SH /*'break up s-th by crumpling, crush it up, rub it together fast (to soften or clean), rub it to soften it (of plants, etc.), fluff it (inner cedar bark to soften it)'*/, (<**é-ablaut**> *resultative*), phonology: ablaut, syntactic analysis: transitive verb, attested by AC (8/24/70, 9/7/71), Deming (4/27/78, 4/26/79), Elders Group (9/21/77), Salish cognate: perhaps Lushootseed /čə́jq'ʷ(-əd)/ *rub (it) about (as two pieces of cloth rubbed together); rub bark together (to extract juices for medicine or to make it stringy for making clothing)* H76:93, probably not Squamish /ʔíq'ʷ/ *be rubbed* as also in /ʔíq'ʷ-in/ *rub off* and /ʔíq'ʷ-in=-cut/ *rub oneself off (tr. refl.)* W73:220, K67:399 which is related to the Upriver Halkomelem root /ʔíq'ʷ/ *rub*, though there is clearly some mutual semantic and perhaps phonological influence between roots.

<yekw'ó:lh> or perhaps **<yekw'wó:lh>**, df //yá·k'ʷ=wə[=M2=]ɬ or ya(=Aə=)k'ʷ=wə[=Aá·=]ɬ//, CAN [*'one's canoe is broken up'*], SOC, lx <**=welh**> *canoe*, possibly <**metathesis**> *derivational*, possibly <**e-ablaut**> *resultative*, possibly <**ó:-ablaut on e in suffix**> *durative*, phonology: possible metathesis or ablaut, possible vowel-reduction, consonant merger, syntactic analysis: adjective/adjectival verb, attested by Deming (2/7/80).

<yekw'ólhem> or perhaps **<yekw'wólhem>**, izs //yák'ʷ=wə[=M2=]ɬ=əm or ya(=Aə=)k'ʷ=wə[=Aá=]ɬ=əm//, CAN [*'break(ing) the canoe'*], SPRD /*'have the last spirit dance of the season, have the "sweep up"'*/, literally /'have/get one's canoe broken up'/, (semological comment: so named because spirit-dancing required much travel of participants during the winter dancing season (every weekend nowadays) to different villages and tribes and one had better not break his canoe till the last dance), (semological comment: one of two metaphors focusing on different aspects of the last dance of the season), lx <**=welh**> *canoe*, possibly <**metathesis**> *derivational*, possibly <**e-ablaut**> *resultative*, possibly <**ó:-ablaut on e in suffix**> *durative*, (<**=em**> *intransitivizer, have, get*), phonology: metathesis or ablaut, possible vowel-reduction, consonant merger, syntactic analysis: intransitive verb, attested by RM (4/22/76), contrast <**íx̲wethet**> *have the "sweep up", have the last spirit-dance of the season.*

<yalkw'ólhem or **yelkw'wólhem>**, izs //ya(=Aə=)[=lə=]k'ʷ=wə[=Aá=]ɬ=əm or yə[=lə=]k'ʷwáɬ=əm//, SOC /*'close up a meeting, wind up a meeting, complete a meeting'*/, literally /'many break their canoes'/, (semological comment: a slight extension of the metaphor for the last spirit-dance of the season), (<**=le=**> *plural*), phonology: infixed plural, possible ablaut, vowel-loss, consonant merger, syntactic analysis: intransitive verb, attested by Elders Group (2/25/76).

<yókw'et>, SH [*'break it'*], *see* yókw' ~ yóqw'.

<yóle ~ yóla ~ yó:le>, possibly root //yálə ~ yálɛ ~ yá·lə or yá(·)l=ə ~ yál=ɛ//, EB /*'wild celery, cow parsnip'*/, [*'Heracleum lanatum'*], ASM ['young sprouts are picked in April and May, after stripping the x̲wéylem or string off the outside, the inner part is eaten raw or cooked as a vegetable, best eaten in spring before it flowers and gets tough, the root is used for medicine, the sprout (esp. the inside part) is called sóqw"], possibly **<=e ~ =a>** *living thing*, syntactic analysis: noun, nominal, attested by AC (11/22/71), others, other sources: Duff 1952 /yála/ *cow parsnip*, Salish cognate: Squamish /yúlaʔ/ *Indian rhubarb* K67:383 and *cow parsnip, "Indian rhubarb", Heracleum lanatum* Bouchard and Turner 1976:65, Nooksack /yóʔlǽ/ *wild celery (*prob. *cow parsnip)* A78:7, Lushootseed /yúlaʔ/ *wild celery* H76:636.

<**xwelítemelh yó:le**>, EB /'*asparagus*'/,FOOD, (lit. white man style + cow parsnip), (attested by RG,EH 6/16/98 to SN, edited by BG with RG,EH 6/26/00)&&

<**Slá:yli**>, cpds //s=lɛ́·=yolə=iy//, PLN ['*Cheam View*'], ASM ['place (by whistle stop) on the C.N. (southeast) side of the Fraser below Hope'], Elder's comment: "from yó:le, so named because there was lots of cow parsnip there", <**s=**> *nominalizer or stative*, root <**lá:**> *tight* root <**as in s=e=lá:**> *be tight*, root <**yó:le**> *cow parsnip*, possibly <**=iy**> *bark, (rarely) plant* or possibly as in Nooksack *place*, phonology: vowel-loss, vowel merger, syntactic analysis: nominal, attested by JL (4/7/78 Seabird Is. trip).

<**yó:leseqw ~ yóleseqw**>, CLO ['*hats*'], *see* yó:seqw ~ yóseqw.

<**yó:lexw**>, root or stem //yá·l(=)əxʷ// root meaning probably *turn over (of years)* or *old*

<**siyó:lexwe ~ syó:lexwe ~siyólexwe**>, stvi //s=yá·l(=)əxʷ=ə ~ s=yáləxʷ=ə//, DESC ['*old*'], (<**s=**> *stative*), possibly root <**yó:l**> *turn over (of years)* possibly root as in *year*, possibly <**=exw**> *lump, round, around*, possibly <**=e**> *living thing*, syntactic analysis: adjective/adjectival verb, attested by AC (8/6/70), BJ (5/10/64), other sources: ES /q'ɛʔí·ləm/ (Ms /syáʔləxʷəʔ/, Cw /sʔɛ́ləxʷ/) *old*, (JH has /q'eʔí·ləm/ *old person*), H-T <cia'lEkwa> (macron over i and first a) *old*, comment: AC contrasts /q'ɛʔí·ləm/ semantically as *very old, ancient* (10/23/71, elsewhere), Salish cognate: Saanich dial. of NSt /sʔéləxʷ/ *old* beside /sʔéləxʷsət/ *[get] old (object)* B74a:41, Samish dial. of NSt /sʔéləxʷ/ (TB /ʔesʔéləxʷ/) *old (of tree, person, etc.)* G86:90, example: <**we'ólwe siyólexwe**>, //wə-ʔál wə-s=yáləxʷ=ə//, /'*too old, very old*'/, attested by EB (5/5/78), <**siyólexwe (swíqe, slháli)**>, //s=yáləxʷ=ə (s=wíq=ə, s=ɬɛ́l=iy)//, /'*old (man, woman)*'/, attested by AC (10/23/71), <**siyólexwe (sqwemá:y, lálém)**>, //s=yáləxʷ=ə (s=qʷəm=ɛ́·y, lɛ́ləm)//, /'*old (dog, house)*'/, attested by EB (12/4/75), <**chxw ólewe siyólexwe kw'as sexwe'álexeth'.**>, //c-xʷ ʔál=wə s=yáləxʷ=ə k'ʷ-ɛ-s səx̣ʷə=ʔɛ́ləx̣əθ'//, /'*You're too old to wet your bed.*'/, attested by EB (5/5/78).

<**siyó:lexwe ~ syó:lexwe**>, dnom //s=yá·l(=)əxʷ=ə//, DESC ['*old person*'], (<**s=**> *nominalizer*), possibly root <**yó:l**> *turn over (of years)* possibly root as in <**syeló:lem**> *year*, possibly <**=exw**> *lump, round, around*, possibly <**=e**> *living thing*, syntactic analysis: nominal, attested by AC (8/15/70, 10/15/71, 10/13/71, 10/21/71, 10/31/71), EB (12/1/75), other sources: H-T <cia'lEkwa (tE swe'Eka)> (macrons on i, first a, and e) *old man* and <cia'lEkwa (sE sla'li)> (macrons on both i and on first and last a) *old woman*, Salish cognate: Squamish /s-yúʔ-yuxʷa/ *old person* beside reduplicated plural form /s-í-yʔúxʷa/ prob. //s-í-ʔyúxʷa// *old people* K67:300, root in Saanich dial. of NSt /sʔəlxʷéen/ *elder, old person* B74a:27 and in Samish dial. of NSt /sʔəl'éləxʷ/ *ancestors, elders, old people* G86:79, example: <**stl'í:tl'eqelh te le kw'óqwet te ő̃qwelets te siyólexwe.**>, //s=C_1i=ƛ'əq=əɬ tə lə k'ʷáqʷ=əT tə ʔóqʷ=əlɛc-s tə s=yáləxʷ=ə//, /'*It was a child who hit the old man on the back.*'/, literally /'it is a child who past hit s-o with stick-like obj. the his back/back of the (male) old person'/, attested by AC (10/13/71), <**th'óqwetes te siyólexwe te q'áq'et'em.**>, //θ'áqʷ=əT-əs tə s=yáləxʷ=ə tə q'ɛ́[=C_1ə=]t'=əm//, /'*The old person sucked something sweet.*'/, literally /'he sucks s-th the (gender unspecified) old person that which is sweet'/, attested by AC (10/15/71), <**wiyóth kw'es lhéx̱welhchas te siyólexwe.**>, //wə=yáθ k'ʷ-əs ɬə[-´-]x̣ʷ=əɬcɛ-s tə s=yáləxʷ=ə//, /'*The old man is always spitting.*'/, attested by AC (10/21/71).

<**sí:yólexwe**>, pln //s=hí-yál(=)əxʷ=ə or s=[-í·-]yál(=)əxʷ=ə//, HAT ['*old people*'], possibly <**hí-**>

plural, possibly <**-í:-**> *plural*, phonology: possible consonant merger, possible infixe plural, syntactic analysis: nominal, attested by AC (10/23/71), example: <**qéx̱ te sí:yólexwe**>, //qə́x̣ tə s=[-i·-]yáləxʷ=ə//, /'*(There's) a lot of old people.*'/, attested by AC.

<**siyó:ylexwe**>, dmn //s=yá·[=C₁ə=]ləxʷə//, HAT ['*little old person*'], (<**=R1=**> *diminutive*), phonology: reduplication, syntactic analysis: nominal, attested by EB (11/1/78).

<**Siyó:ylexwe Smá:lt**>, cpds //s=yá·[=C₁ə=]ləxʷə s=mɛ́·lt//, PLN /'*Bear Mountain,* also called *Lhóy''s Mountain*'/, ASM ['the lumpy mountain north of the west end of Seabird Island, Lhóy' was a Thompson Indian from Spuzzum who died about 1942 at about 83 years of age, he was EB's husband Phil Bobb's mother's brother, a number of Thompsons settled years ago on Seabird Island and the reserve there though in the heart of Stó:lō territory was opened to both Thompson and Stó:lō Indians'], literally /'little old person mountain'/, (<**=R1=**> *diminutive*), phonology: reduplication, syntactic analysis: nominal phrase with modifier(s), attested by JL (4/7/78, 4/3/78), IHTTC (8/5/77), example: <**tl'ekwses x̱ét'e á:lhtel, tl'óts'a Siyó:ylexwe Smált tethá.**>, //ƛ'a-kʷ-s-əs x̣ə́t'ə ʔɛ́·ɬ=təl, ƛ'á-c'ɛ s=yǽ·[=C₁ə=]l(=)əxʷ=ə s=mɛ́lt tə=θɛ́//, /'*(Because) that's what they said, that's Little Old Person Mountain there. (reportedly)*'/, attested by JL.

<**yó:letsep**>, probable stem //yá·ləcəp or s=yá·l=cəp//, root probably <**yó:l**> *turn over*

<**syó:letsep**>, df //s=yá·ləcəp or s=yá·l=cəp//, WATR ['*a wave*'], (<**s=**> *nominalizer, something to/that*), probably root <**yó:l**> *turn over*, <**etsep**> is either part of the root or perhaps a rare lx not attested elsewhere in Upriver Halkomelem) <**=etsep**> referring to *currents of water* (see the Lushootseed cognate with ending /čuʔ/, one would expect cognate <=etse> from <=élhcha> *unclear water* or <**=eleq ~ áleq**> *wave*, it may be that the final <p> is influence by unrelated lx <=élchep ~ =éltsep> *firewood* or a mishearing for <m> as in <=em>, however the Nooksack cognate makes it look the the <p> is correct, phonology: possible syllable-loss or consonant merger, syntactic analysis: nominal, dialects: *Tait on Seabird Is.*, attested by Elders Group (3/26/75), CT (6/8/76), other sources: ES /θiθɛ́·ləq/ (CwMs /háʔyəʔləq/) *wave*, Salish cognate: Lushootseed /júlčuʔ/ *wave (of water)* as also in /júlčuʔ-əbəxʷ/ *the waves are getting bigger and running faster* H76:227, possibly Mainland Comox /ǰúw'əkʷ/ *wave* B75prelim.:5 and Sechelt /yúlakʷ/ *wave* T77:8 and Squamish /yú-yaʔ-kʷ/ *wave, current, rapids* as also in /yú-yaʔ-kʷ-m/ *undulate* K67:383, Nooksack <yúnolchup ~ yúl7o7chip> (Galloway & Adams (2007) Classified Word List for Nooksack), also <**syó:lts'ep** (or **syó:ltsep**)>, //s=yá·l=c'=əp or s=yá·l=(əl)cəp//, attested by BJ (12/5/64 new transcript, old p.290), also <**smá:yeleq**>, //s=mɛ́·yə=ələq//, dialects: *Cheh.*, attested by Elders Group (3/26/75), example: <**thitheháleq te syó:letsep.**>, //θí=C₁ə=hɛ́ləq tə s=yá·ləcəp//, /'*The waves are getting bigger.*'/, literally /'be bigger waves the wave'/, attested by Elders Group (3/26/75).

<**yó:lqw'**>, SOC /'*make a mess, mess up*'/, *see* yél or perhaps yá:l.

<**yó:lqw'es**>, SOC ['*make a real mess*'], *see* yél or perhaps yá:l.

<**yó:lx̱wtem**>, df //yá·l(=)x̣ʷ=təm//, ABDF ['*delirious*'], possibly root <**yó:l**> *turn over*, possibly <**=x̱w**> meaning unknown unless *in circles* (not likely *lump* as usual), possibly <**=tem**> *past participle or stative intransitive or adjectival*, syntactic analysis: adjective/adjectival verb, attested by Elders Group (3/23/77).

<**yólh**>, bound root //yáɬ *firewood*//, Salish cognate: Squamish /yúɬ/ *burn (itr.); make a fire (itr.)* as also in /y-íʔuɬ/ //yə́-yəwɬ// *burn (itr.); have a fire burning; fire; firewood*, /yúɬ-un/ *burn (tr.)*, /yúɬ-qs/ *light a pipe; burn one's nose*, /yúɬ-šit/ *burn food or clothes for the dead (tr.)* and /yuɬ-qʷáyʔ-nəwʔas/ *have heartburn* K67:383, K69:91.

<**chiyólh**>, ds //c=yáɬ//, HARV /'*gather firewood (in the woods), get firewood*'/, (<**ch=**> *get, have*), syntactic analysis: intransitive verb, attested by AD (3/5/79), example: <**lámtsel chiyólh.**>, //lɛ́=m-c-əl c=yáɬ//, /'*I'm going to get firewood.*'/, attested by AD, <chiyólh>, [čiyáɬ], 'go out and get wood', attested by EH 6/6/00 (SU transcription, tape 7), '[číčiyáɬ], [čǽyʌl], 'going out and getting wood', EH 6/6/00 (SU transcription, tape 7).

<**chiyóyelh**>, cts //c=yá[-C_1ə-]ɬ//, HARV ['*getting firewood*'], (<**-R1-**> *continuative*), phonology: reduplication, syntactic analysis: intransitive verb, attested by AD (3/5/79), also <**tsyóyelh**>, //c=yá[-C_1ə-]ɬ//, attested by HT (Elders Group 2/6/80).

<**siyólh ~ siyó:lh ~ syólh**>, dnom //s=yáɬ ~ s=yá·ɬ//, HARV /'*wood, firewood*'/, FIRE, (<**s=**> *nominalizer, something to/that*), syntactic analysis: nominal, attested by AC, DM (12/4/64), BJ (12/5/64), EB (12/15/75), IHTTC (7/13/77), Elders Group (3/15/72), HT (6/21/76), other sources: ES /siyá·ɬ/ *wood*, example: <**la lhts'á:ls te siyólh.**>, //lɛ ɬic'=ɛ́·ls tə s=yáɬ//, /'*He's gone cutting wood.*'/, attested by EB (12/11/75), <**le q'pétes te siyó:lh.**>, //lə q'ə́p=M1=T-əs tə s=yá·ɬ//, /'*Someone gathered firewood. (gather s-th)*'/, attested by EB.

<**st'elákw' siyólh**>, cpds //s=t'əlɛ́k'^{w} s=yáɬ//, HUNT ['*circular frame (for tanning hides)*'], syntactic analysis: nominal phrase with modifier(s), attested by HT (6/21/76), example: <**p'áth'et te kw'eléws te sméyeth li te st'elákw' siyólh**>, //p'ɛ́θ'=əT tə k'^{w}əl=ə́w-s tə s=mɛ́yəθ li tə s=t'əlɛ́k'^{w} s=yáɬ//, /'*sew the hide of an animal on a circular frame*'/, attested by HT.

<**syóyelh**>, dmn //s=yá[=C_1ə=]ɬ//, HARV ['*little stick of firewood*'], (<**=R1=**> *diminutive*), phonology: reduplication, syntactic analysis: nominal, attested by IHTTC (7/13/77).

<**syéyelh**>, dmpn //s=C_1íAə́=yaɬ//, HARV ['*lots of little sticks of firewood*'], PLAY /'*slahal scoring sticks, gambling sticks*'/, (<**R4=**> *diminutive*), (<**é-ablaut on R4=**> *plural of diminutive*), phonology: reduplication, ablaut, syntactic analysis: nominal, attested by IHTTC (7/13/77), Deming (7/27/78), Elders Group (3/15/72).

<**shxwyélhtel ~ shxwiyélhtel**>, rsls //sx^w=yo[=Aə́=]ɬ=təl//, dnom, FIRE /'*ashes (cinder-like), cinders (heavy and dirty), embers*'/, (<**shxw=**> *something for*), (<**é-ablaut**> *resultative*), lx <**=tel**> *device, something*, phonology: ablaut, syntactic analysis: nominal, attested by Elders Group (3/1/72), Deming (1/31/80), NP (4/11/80), example: <**tóqweltsep te shxwyélhtel.**>, //táq^w=əlcəp tə sx^w=ya[=Aə́=]ɬ=təl//, /'*The ashes have cooled enough (to handle).*'/, literally /'have cooled enough (to handle) (of firewood)'/, attested by NP.

<**siyólhá:wtxw**>, ds //yáɬ=ɛ́·wtx^w//, BLDG ['*wood-shed*'], FIRE, literally /'(fire)wood building/house'/, syntactic analysis: nominal, attested by EB (5/11/76), AD (1/4/80), also <**yólhá:wtxw**>, //yáɬ=ɛ́·wtx^w//, also /'*food cellar*'/, comment: corrected to *wood-shed* by AD (1/4/80).

<**yó:qw**>, free root //yá·q^w//, FSH ['*rotten fish*'], EZ, syntactic analysis: noun?, nominal?, intransitive verb?, attested by SP and AK (7/13/75), Salish cognate: Lushootseed /yúʔq^w/ *an old salmon that has already spawned and is about to die* H76:636.

<**Lexwyó:qwem**>, ds //ləx^w=yá·q^w=əm//, PLN ['*place on Fraser River between first tunnel and Yale where rotten fish used to (always) pile up*'], ASM ['on the CN (east) side of the river below the mountain called Lexwyó:qwem Smá:lt, in the fall this place always smelled of dead fish since spawned-out ones collected in the river there'], literally /'place to always have/get rotten fish'/, (<**lexw= ~ xw=**> *always*), (<**=em**> *place to have/get*), syntactic analysis: nominal, attested by SP and AK (7/13/75), source: place names reference file #41, also <**Xwyó:qwem**>, //x^w=yá·q^w=əm//, attested by IHTTC (7/8/77), IHTTC and elders (Place Names Meeting 8/23/77).

<**Lexwyó:qwem Smá:lt**>, cpds //ləx^w=yá·q^w=əm s=mɛ́·lt//, PLN ['*mountain on Fraser River between first tunnel and Yale where rotten fish used to (always) pile up*'], ASM ['on the CN (east)

side of the river'], literally /'place to always have/get rotten fish mountain'/, syntactic analysis: nominal phrase with modifier(s), attested by IHTTC (7/8/77), IHTTC and elders (Place Names Meeting 8/23/77), source: place names reference file #42, also <**Xwyóqwem Smált**>, //x^{w}=yá·q^{w}=əm s=mɛ́lt//, ASM ['mountain upriver from Mt. Ogilvie'], attested by AD/AK/others (American Bar trip 6/26/78).

<**yóqw'em**>, mdls //yáq'^{w}=əm//, ABFC ['*to sweat*'], (<**=em**> *middle voice*), syntactic analysis: intransitive verb, attested by AC (8/15/70), Salish cognate: Mainland Comox /ǰíq'^{w}əm/ *to sweat* B75prelim.:94, Sechelt /yáq'^{w}-a *to sweat* T77:34, Squamish /yáq'^{w}-am/ *to sweat; sweat* W73:258, K67:382, Samish dial. of NSt /čáq'^{w}-ŋ/ (VU) *to sweat* beside /čáʔq'^{w}ŋ'/ *sweating* G86:76, historical/comparative detail: irregular correspondence with the stressed vowel: Sq should have /ú/ or Halkomelem /ɛ́/, NSt /é/.

<**yóyeqw'em**>, cts //yá[-C$_1$ə-]q'^{w}=əm//, ABFC ['*sweating*'], (<**-R1-**> *continuative*), phonology: reduplication, syntactic analysis: intransitive verb, attested by BJ (12/5/64), Salish cognate: Squamish /yá-yaq'^{w}am/ *sweat profusely* W73:258, K67:382.

<**syó:qw'em**>, dnom //s=yá·q'^{w}=əm//, ANA ['*sweat [noun]*'], (<**s=**> *nominalizer*), syntactic analysis: nominal, attested by BJ (12/5/64).

<**yóqw'em ~ yó:qw'em**>, SH /'*to break [in pieces], it broke*'/, *see* yókw' ~ yóqw'.

<**yó:seqw ~ yóseqw**>, df //yá(·)s=əq^{w}//, CLO ['*hat*'], root meaning unknown, lx <**=eqw**> *on top of the head, on the hair*, syntactic analysis: noun, nominal, attested by AC (10/6/71, 10/21/71, 10/23/71), DM (12/4/64), BJ (5/10/64), Elders Group (3/15/72), other sources: ES /yá·sàq^{w}/ (CwMs /yáʔsaq^{w}/) *hat*, Salish cognate: Squamish /yásaʔq^{w}/ *head-cover used by medicine man; hat* K69:382, Saanich dial. of NSt /sčə́saʔq^{w}/ *hat* B74a:34, Samish dial. of NSt /yásaʔq^{w}ŋ/ *put on one's hat* G86:84, example: <**qé<u>x</u> te yó:seqw**>, //qə́x̣ tə yá·s=əq^{w}//, /'*a lot of hats*'/, attested by AC.

<**yó:yseqw ~ yóyseqw**>, dmn //yá(·)[=C$_1$ə=]s=əq^{w}//, CLO ['*small hat*'], (<**=R1=**> *diminutive*), phonology: reduplication, syntactic analysis: noun, nominal, attested by Elders Group (3/15/72), IHTTC (8/25/77), EL with NP and EB and AD (Chehalis trip 9/27/77), EL (3/1/78, 6/27/78).

<**Yó:yseqw**>, dmn //yá·[=C$_1$ə=]s=əq^{w}//, PLN ['*rock that looks like a little hat on west (Chehalis) side of Harrison River above mouth of Morris Creek*'], ASM ['below Ts'éqwela and across from Lexwyélés'], literally /'little hat'/, (<**=R1=**> *diminutive*), phonology: reduplication, syntactic analysis: noun, nominal, attested by IHTTC (8/25/77), EL with NP and EB and AD (Chehalis trip 9/27/77), EL (3/1/78, 6/27/78), source: place names reference file #289.

<**yó:leseqw ~ yóleseqw**>, pln //yá·[=lə=]s=əq^{w} ~ yá[=lə=]s=əq^{w}//, CLO ['*hats*'], (<**=le=**> *plural*), phonology: infixed plural, syntactic analysis: noun, nominal, attested by Elders Group (3/15/72).

<**siyó:yseqw**>, strs //s=yá·[=C$_1$ə=]s=əq^{w} or s=yá·[-C$_1$ə-]s=əq^{w}//, CLO ['*be wearing a hat*'], (<**s=**> *stative*), (<**=R1=**> *resultative*), possibly <**-R1-**> *continuative*, phonology: reduplication, syntactic analysis: adjective/adjectival verb, attested by AC (10/23/71).

<**yóseqwem**>, mdls //yás=əq^{w}=əm//, CLO ['*put on one's hat*'], (<**=em**> *middle voice*), syntactic analysis: intransitive verb, attested by AD (4/15/80), Salish cognate: Samish dial. of NSt (LD) /yásaʔq^{w}=ŋ/ *put on one's hat* G86:84.

<**yóseqwem**>, CLO ['*put on one's hat*'], *see* yó:seqw ~ yóseqw.

<**yóswe ~ yó:swe**>, possibly root //yá(·)swə or yá(·)s=wə or yə=s=wá(·)=M2//, MOOD /'*maybe, perhaps, I don't know (if), may (possibly)*'/, syntactic analysis: particle, attested by Elders Group (10/6/76), AC (10/8/71, 11/10/71, 12/8/71), Deming (1/18/79), EB, IHTTC (incl. all: SP, NP, AD, AK, DC, EB 8/22/77), Salish cognate: perhaps in part Saanich dial. of NSt /wáw'ə/ *maybe* B74a:49

beside /ʔiʔ-wəwə/ *perhaps, maybe* M86, G86:59, and Samish dial. of NSt /ʔi-wáwaʔ/ *perhaps, maybe* G86:60 and Mainland Comox /gúgúhúy'/ *maybe* B75prelim:59 (which would correspond to a hypothetical Halkomelem /wawahá·y/ by the regular sound correspondences), example: <**yóswe kw'els lám te'á'altha.**>, //yás=wə k'ʷ-əl-s lɛ́=m tɛ=C_1ɛ́=ʔɛlθɛ//, /'*Perhaps I may go.*'/, attested by EB (2/16/76), <**yóswe kw'á'as lám telő wé.**>, //yás=wə k'ʷ-ɛ́ʔɛ-s lɛ́=m tɛ=lə́wə//, /'*Perhaps you may go.*'/, attested by EB (2/16/76), <**yóswe kws lám tútl'ò.**>, //yás=wə kʷ-s lɛ́=m tə́=w=ƛ'á//, /'*Perhaps he may go.*'/, attested by EB (2/16/76), <**yóswe 'á**>, //yás=wə ʔɛ́//, /'*Maybe yes.*'/, attested by EB (4/23/76), <**yóswetsel líl welà:m.**>, //yás=wə-c-əl lí-l wə-lɛ̀·=m//, /'*I might go.*'/, attested by Elders Group (10/6/76), <**yó:swe weskw'áyes kw'els lám.**>, //yá·swə wə-s=k'ʷɛ́y-əs k'ʷ-əl-s lɛ́=m//, /'*I don't know if I can go., Maybe it's impossible for me to go., (Maybe I can't go.)*'/, attested by SP, NP, AD, AK, and DC (IHTTC 8/22/77), also <**yó:swe skw'áyes kw'els lám.**>, //yá·swə s=k'ʷɛ́y-əs k'ʷ-əl-s lɛ́=m//, attested by AD, AK, DC, and EB (IHTTC 8/22/77), <**yóswe welámá:l.**>, //yós=wə wə-lɛ́m-ɛ́·l//, /'*I might go.*'/, attested by AC (12/8/71), <**yóswe tl'ós máls, yóswe tl'ós sí:les.**>, //yáswə ƛ'á-s mɛ́l-s, yáswə ƛ'á-s sí·lə-s//, /'*Maybe it's his father, or maybe it's his grandfather.*'/, usage: recent narrative, attested by AC (11/10/71).

<**yó:t ~ yót**>, pcs //yá·=T ~ yá=T//, LANG ['*warn s-o*'], SOC, (<**=t**> *purposeful control transitivizer*), syntactic analysis: transitive verb, attested by Elders Group (10/1/75), NP (Elders Group 4/26/78), contrast <**wá:yt**> *warn s-o*, Salish cognate: Squamish /yúh ~ yəh/1 *be careful, take care* as also in /yúh/ *careful* and esp. /yá-nʔ/ *warn (tr.)* W73:281,53, K67:282,283, historical/comparative detail: Upriver Halkomelem /wɛ́·y=T/ *warn s-o* and Squamish cognate /wáy-at/ *reveal s-th, make s-th public, make an announcement about s-o/s-th* (K69:89) though partially similar in shape and meaning are probably not related, example: <**tsel yó:t te stá:x̲welh.**>, //c-əl yá·=T tə s=tɛ́·x̣ʷ=əɬ//, /'*I warned the children.*'/, attested by Elders Group (10/1/75).

<**hé:yó:t**>, cts //hɛ́-yá·=T//, LANG ['*warning s-o*'], SOC, (<**há- ~ hé- ~ hí-**> *continuative*), phonology: the root retains its stress here even after the stressed prefix probably to dissimilate from the continuative of yá:t *vomit* which is probably <**héyet**> as seen in <**héyetélmel**> *nauseated*, lengthening on prefix here may be mistranscribed, syntactic analysis: transitive verb, attested by Elders Group (10/1/75, 4/28/76), example: <**hé:yó:t te stá:x̲welh**>, //hɛ́-yá·=T tə s=tɛ́·x̣ʷ=əɬ//, /'*warning the children*'/, attested by Elders Group (10/1/75).

<**héyót**>, rsls //hɛ́=yá(·)=T//, LANG ['*warned s-o*'], SOC, (<**há= ~ hé=**> *resultative*), syntactic analysis: transitive verb, attested by Elders Group (4/28/76), example: <**(chulh ~ chel ulh) héyóthòmè.**>, //(c-uɬ ~ c-əl ʔuɬ) hə́-yá=T-àmə̀//, /'*I warned you.*'/, attested by Elders Group.

<**siyót**>, stvi //s=yá=T//, SOC ['*beware*'], literally perhaps /'be warned of s-o/s-th'/, (<**s=**> *stative*), (semological comment: performative), syntactic analysis: prob. transitive verb, attested by Elders Group (4/26/78); found in <**siyótchxwò.**>, //s=yá=T-c-xʷ-à//, /'*Beware.*'/, literally /'you just be warned of s-o/s-th'/, attested by Elders Group.

<**yot'**> ~ <**yet'**>, possible root //yat' or yət'// perhaps *rub* or *scrub*

<**yet'qw'íwsem**>, mdls //yət'=q'ʷ=íws=əm or ya[=Aə́=]t'=q'ʷ=íws=əm//, ABFC ['*lather one's body*'], PE, possibly root <**yít'**> *melt*, (semological comment: perhaps this root since soap does seem to melt into lather), possibly root <**yót' ~ yót**> *rub*? as in <**shxwiyòtqw'ewí:ls**> *dishcloth*, possibly <**é-ablaut of root i**> *resultative*, lx <**=qw'**> *around in circles*, lx <**=íws**> *on the body, on the skin*, (<**=em**> *middle voice*), phonology: possible ablaut, syntactic analysis: intransitive verb, attested by JL (Fish Camp 7/20/79).

<**shxwiyòtqw'ewí:ls** or better **shxwyòt'qw'ewí:ls**>, df //sxʷ=yát=q'ʷ=əwí·ls or sxʷ=yát'=q'ʷ=əwí·ls//, HHG ['*dishcloth*'], literally perhaps /'something for rubbing around in circles on dishes'/, (<**shxw=**>

something for), possibly root <**yót** or **yót'**> *rub*?, lx <**=qw'**> *around in circles*, lx <**=ewí:ls**> *dishes*, syntactic analysis: nominal, attested by Elders Group (6/1/77), AD (8/80), example: <**alétsa te shxwiyòtqw'ewí:ls?**>, //ʔɛlə́cɛ tə sxʷ=yát=q'ʷ=əwí·ls//, /'*Where is the dishcloth?*'/, attested by AD (8/80).

<**Yó:yt'elwet**>, df //yá·[=C_1ə=]t'=əlwət//, N ['*Old Mary of Chehalis*'], ASM ['she had a smokehouse in Chehalis between that of Old Phillip and that of Paul August (EL and EB (3/1/78), a little upriver from Yálhxetel'], literally perhaps /'rubbing clothes'/, possibly root <**yó:t'**> *rub*?, possibly <**=R1=**> *continuative*, lx <**=elwet**> *female name ending;* also *clothes*, phonology: reduplication, syntactic analysis: nominal, attested by EL and EB (3/1/78).

<**yóth**>, probable root //yáθ// *always*

<**wiyóth**>, ds //wə=yáθ//, TIME /'*always, all the time, (*(also) *often, over and over [TG])*'/, (<**we=** ~ **=we** ~ **=ew** ~ **=u**> *contrastive*), root <**yóth**> *always*, phonology: vowel-raising (ey → iy unstressed), syntactic analysis: adverb/adverbial verb, attested by Elders Group (3/1/72, 2/16/77), AC, EB (Elders Group 4/26/78), AD (1/23/79), Salish cognate: Nooksack /mæ-yúc/ *always* PA61, Samish dial. of NSt /yás/ *always* G86, also /'*always, often, over and over*'/, attested by TG (4/75), example: <**wiyóths kw'es í:wólems te stá:xwelh, t'ít'elem kw'es í:wólems.**>, //wə=yáθ-s k'ʷ-əs ʔi[-´·-]wál=əm-s tə s=tɛ́·xʷ=əɬ, t'í[-C_1ə-]l=əm k'ʷ-əs ʔi[-´·-]wál=əm-s//, /'*The children are playing all the time, singing as they're playing.*'/, attested by AC (10/15/71), <**wiyóth kw'es lhéx̲welhchas te siyólexwe.**>, //wə=yáθ k'ʷ-əs ɬə́x̣ʷ=əɬcɛ-s tə s=yáləxʷ=ə//, /'*The old man is always spitting.*'/, attested by AC (10/21/71), <**tl'ó wiyóth mamíyet.**>, //ƛ'á wə=yáθ mɛ[-C_1ə-´-]y=T//, /'*He is always helping.*'/, literally /'That one always is helping s-o'/, attested by AC (10/23/71), <**wiyóth welólets'e è**>, //wə=yáθ wə=C_1á=ləc'ə ʔə̀//, /'*always alone*'/, attested by AC (12/8/71), <**wiyóth kws xwtatíyeqels.**>, //wə=yáθ kʷ-s xʷ=C_1ɛ=tíy=əqəl-s//, /'*He's always answering back.*'/, attested by EB, <**wiyóth è kws yóyes.**>, //wə=yáθ ʔə̀ kʷ-s yá[-C_1ə-]s//, /'*He works every day.*'/, literally /'always just that he is working'/, attested by AD.

<**wiyóth kwsu éys te sqwálewels te lólets'e**>, cpds //wə=yáθ kʷ-s-u ʔɛ́y-s tə s=qʷɛ̀l=əwəl-s tə C_1á=ləc'ə//, EFAM /'*optimist, a person whose thoughts are always good*'/, literally /'always that -they/it -contrastive be good -they the thoughts -his the one person'/, syntactic analysis: sentence, attested by Elders Group (2/16/77).

<**wiyóth kwsu qéls te sqwálewels te lólets'e**>, cpds //wə=yáθ kʷ-s-u qə́l-s tə s=qʷɛ̀l=əwəl-s tə C_1á=ləc'ə//, EFAM /'*pessimist, a person whose thoughts are always bad*'/, literally /'always that -they/it -contrastive be bad -they the thoughts -his the one person'/, syntactic analysis: sentence, attested by Elders Group (2/16/77).

<**kw'ō wiyóth(cha) ò ~ kw'ō hélémcha ò**>, cpds //k'ʷ-əw wə=yáθ(-cɛ) ʔà ~ k'ʷ-əw hə́-lɛ[=Aə́=]m-cɛ ʔà//, TIME ['*forever*'], literally /'what really (will be) just always ~ what really will be just going on'/, syntactic analysis: subordinate clause, attested by Elders Group.

<**yóthet**>, pcrs //yá=T-ət//, TVMO ['*to back up (walk or move backwards)*'], semantic environment ['of a person (yourself), horse, canoe, car, etc.'], (<**=t**> *purposeful control transitivizer*), (<**-et**> *reflexive*), syntactic analysis: intransitive verb, attested by BHTTC (9/2/76), SJ (Deming 4/17/80), Salish cognate: Musqueam /yáʔ=t/ *back it up* Suttles ca1984 7.2.4 (ch.7 p.53), historical/comparative detail: is the Musqueam form related to Upriver /yó:t/ *warn s-o* or homophonous?, also <**yó'thet**>, //yáʔ=T-ət//, dialects: *Sumas/Matsqui*, attested by Deming (4/17/80), also <**yó'tset**>, //yáʔ=c-ət//, dialects: *unknown*, attested by Tillie Sampson (=Matilda Sampson) (Deming 4/17/80).

<**héyethet ~ héythet**>, cts //hɛ́-ya=T-ət//, TVMO ['*backing up*'], (<**hé- ~ hɛ́-**> *continuative*), phonology: vowel-reduction ~ vowel-loss, syntactic analysis: intransitive verb, attested by BHTTC

(9/2/76), Salish cognate: Musqueam /hə́y'ət ~ həy'áʔt/ *back it up* Suttles ca1984 7.2.4.

<**yótl'et ~ yótl'at**>, pcs //yáƛ'=əT or yə[=Aá=]ƛ'=əT ~ yə[=Aá=]ƛ'=ə[=Aɛ=]T//, HHG [*'shine it'*], probably root <**yetl'**> *rub* probably root as in <**yetl'-q'-t**> *rub it, paint it*, possibly <**ó-ablaut**> *derivational*, (<**=et**> *purposeful control transitivizer*), possibly <**a-ablaut on e in suffix**> *durative*, phonology: ablaut, syntactic analysis: transitive verb, attested by Elders Group (6/16/76), example: <**yótl'at ta' spú:l.**>, //yə[=Aá=]ƛ'=ə[=Aɛ=]T t-ɛʔ s=pú·l//, /*'shine your spoon'*/, attested by Elders Group (5/26/76), <**yótl'at te qwlhíxel**>, //yə[=Aá=]ƛ'=ə[=Aɛ=]T tə qʷəɬ=ə[=´=]y=xʸəl//, /*'shine the shoe'*/, attested by Elders Group (5/26/76).

<**yó:wthet**>, LANG [*'bragging'*], *see* yú:w.

<**yó<u>x</u>w**>, free root //yáx̣ʷ//, WATR [*'to thaw'*], syntactic analysis: intransitive verb, attested by NP (Fish Camp 7/11/78), other sources: ES (CwMsCh) /yáx̣ʷ/ *thaw*, Salish cognate: Mainland Comox /ǰíx̣ʷ/ *to melt (as ice)* beside /ǰáx̣ʷ-ət/ *th [tr.]* B75prelim.:82,95, Sechelt /yáx̣ʷ/ *to melt, thaw* T77:31, Squamish root /yáx̣ʷ/ *melt, thaw* as in /yáx̣ʷ-iʔ/ *to thaw* and /yáx̣ʷ-an/ *melt (tr.)* W73:176, K69:91, Lushootseed root /ǰáx̣ʷ(a)/ as in /ʔu-ǰáx̣ʷ/ *thaw, melt* and /ǰáx̣ʷ-at-əb/ *it was thawed* H76:217, Saanich dial. of NSt /čáx̣ʷ/ *to thaw* beside /čáx̣ʷ-əŋ/ *to melt (as ice)* B74a:80, 69, Samish dial. of NSt /čáx̣ʷ-əŋ/ *to melt* G86:95, Thompson /zʔaxʷ/ *to melt (as ice)* beside /zaʔáxʷ/ *to thaw* B74c:64,76, Columbian /saʔx̣ʷ/ *melt* beside /sáx̣ʷ-ən/ *I melt it* K81:77.

<**yóyatel**>, SOC /*'they're making friends, (making friends with each other)'*/, *see* yá:ya.

<**yóyekw'et**>, SH [*'breaking it'*], *see* yókw' ~ yóqw'.

<**yóyeqw'em**>, ABFC [*'sweating'*], *see* yóqw'em.

<**yóyes**>, SOC /*'working, be working'*/, *see* yó:ys.

<**yó:ys**>, free root //yá·ys//, SOC [*'to work'*], syntactic analysis: intransitive verb, attested by AC, IHTTC (9/2/77), Elders Group (2/8/78, 6/28/78), others, other sources: ES /yá·ys/ (CwMs /ʔyáys/) *work*, JH /ʔyá·ys/ *work*, Salish cognate: Lushootseed /yáyus/ *work* may belong here or may be cognate with the continuative Upriver Halkomelem /yáyəs/ *working* (Lushootseed /ʔu-yáyus/ *working* uses /ʔu-/ *continuative*) H76:627, Saanich dial. of NSt /čéy/ *to work* B74a:83, example: <**la yó:ys.**>, //lɛ yá·ys//, /*'He's gone to work.'*/, attested by AC (8/24/70), <**lí a stl'í: kw'as yó:ys?**>, //lí ʔɛ s=ƛ'í· k'ʷ-ɛ-s yá·ys//, /*'Do you want to work?'*/, attested by AC (10/6/71), <**yalhtsel yó:ys**>, //yɛɬ-c-əl yá·ys//, /*'the first time I worked'*/, literally perhaps /'I started to work'/, attested by Elders Group (2/8/78), <**lhíl yó:ys**>, //ɬí-l yá·ys//, /*'when I worked'*/, attested by Elders Group (6/28/78), <**yálhòls yó:ys ~ yálhels yó:ys**>, //yɛ́ɬ-à-l-s yá·ys ~ yɛ́ɬ-əl-s yá·ys//, /*'I started work., I started to work.'*/, *<**yálhò tsel yó:ys**> rejected by Elders Group (2/8/78), also <**yálhòlse le yó:ys**>, //yɛ́ɬ-àl-s-ə lə yá·ys//, attested by EB (Elders Group 2/8/78), <**yalhels yó:ys tloqá:ys. ~ yalhel syó:ys tloqá:ys.**>, //yɛɬ-əl-s yá·ys təla=qɛ́·ys//, /*'I just started working.'*/, literally /'I started work now.'/, attested by Elders Group (2/8/78).

<**yóyes**>, cts //yá[-C_1ə-](y)s//, SOC /*'working, be working'*/, (semological comment: usually with continuatives I do not show the *be* in the English translation because be + -ing is required by English not by Halkomelem, it would be just as valid a translation to show all Halkomelem continuatives translated in English with be + -ing as does Suttles 1984a), (<**-R1-**> *continuative*), phonology: reduplication, irregular consonant-loss of the second root consonant is a slight phonetic change in this case (/yáyəys > yáyəs/) but brings the continuative in line with most C1VC2 root continuatives and so assimilates to the predominant continuative pattern, syntactic analysis: intransitive verb, attested by IHTTC (9/2/77), AC (8/24/70), Elders Group, EB, Salish cognate: Samish dial. of NSt (VU) /čéʔe(y)/ //čé[-ʔ-yə-]y// *working* G86:98, example: <**la yóyes.**>, //lɛ yá[-

C_1ə-](y)s//, /'*He's working.*'/, attested by AC, <**ílh yóyes.**>, //ʔí-ɬ yá[-C_1ə-](y)s//, /'*He was working.*'/, attested by AC, <**ílhtsel yóyes.**>, //ʔíɬ-c-əl yá[-C_1ə-](y)s//, /'*I was working.*'/, attested by Elders Group (2/8/78), <**yóyes te swéta**>, //yá[-C_1ə-](y)s tə s=wə́tɛ//, /'*working on a sweater*'/, attested by Elders Group (3/14/79), <**yóyes o qew lát ò.**>, //yá[-C_1ə-](y)s ʔà qə-w lɛ́t ʔà//, /'*She works all day.*'/, literally /'she/he/it is just working until just evening'/, attested by EB (Elders Group 1/24/79).

<**lexwsyóyes ~ lexwsiyó:yes**>, ds //ləx^{w}s=yá[= ·=][-C_1ə-](y)s//, SOC ['*[someone] always working*'], (<**lexws=**> *someone who is always*), (<**=:=**> *emphatic*), phonology: lengthening, syntactic analysis: nominal, attested by EB (6/14/76).

<**shxweyó:yes** or better **shxwyó:yes**>, ds //sx^w=yá[= ·=C_1ə=](y)s//, TOOL ['*tool*'], literally /'something for really working'/, (<**shxw=**> *something for*), (<**=:=**> *emphatic*), phonology: lengthening, syntactic analysis: nominal, attested by EB (5/25/76), Salish cognate: Lushootseed /səx^w-u-yáyus/ *tool, what you work with* where /səx^w-/ is a derivational prefix meaning *an agent or functioning device that habitually performs an act associated with the stem* and /ʔu-/ is *continuative* H76:444, 443, also <**sxwyó:yes**>, //sx^w=yá[= ·=C_1ə=](y)s//, WV, also /'*loom*'/, Elder's comment: "Mary Peters called a loom just <**sxwyó:yes**>", phonology: some Tait speakers (TG for ex.) lack the allophone [š] before /x^w/ (<**sh**> before <**xw**>), it is unclear whether TG (who was in the BHTTC or Beginning Halkomelem Teacher Training Course) gave the form or whether some other speaker gave it to accurately reflect Mary's pronunciation, but Mary may have been present that day as a visitor to the class with her daughter EP, attested by BHTTC (8/23/76).

<**syó:ys**>, dnom //s=yá·ys//, SOC ['*work*'], (<**s=**> *nominalizer*), syntactic analysis: nominal, attested by EB, AC, Elders Group, others, example: <**éwe ís tl'í syó:ys.**>, //ʔə́wə ʔí-s ƛ'í s=yá·ys//, /'*It's easy work., It's not hard work.*'/, attested by EB (12/19/75), <**schewétmet te syó:ys.**>, //s=cəwa[=Aə́=]t=məT tə syá·ys(-s)//, /'*He's good at that/(his) work.*'/, literally /'be good at/know how to do s-th the work (-his)'/, attested by Elders Group (3/3/76), <**eyéschxwò ta' x̱áws syó:ys.**>, //ʔɛy=ə́s-c-x^w-à t-ɛʔx̣ɛ́ws s=yá·ys//, /'*Have fun in your new work.*'/, literally /'you just have fun your new work'/, usage: used for farewell to a departing staff member, attested by EB (8/14/78), <**stám kw'a syó:ys?**>, //s=tɛ́m k'^{w}-ɛ s=yá·ys//, /'*What's your work?*'/, attested by AC (11/17/71), <**qéx̱ syó:ys yutl'ólem, tíméthet syó:ys, qayalhs'es le xwe'í: kw'the ílh la tl'epí:l.**>, //qə́x̣ s=yá·ys-s yə=w=ƛ'á[=lə=]m, tím=əT-ət s=yá·ys-s, qɛ yɛ́ɬ-s-ʔə-s lə x^{w}ə=ʔí· k'^{w}θə ʔí-ɬ lɛ ƛ'əp=í·l//, /'*They had a lot of work, hard work, before the one that went down arrived [back up]. (descend, go down)*'/, semantic environment ['an Indian was lowered down a cliff to a cave then hauled back up having found artifacts in the cave below Mómet'es from the time of the Flood'], usage: Story of the Flood, attested by AC (12/7/71).

<**yó:yseqw ~ yóyseqw**>, CLO ['*small hat*'], *see* yó:seqw ~ yóseqw.

<**Yó:yseqw**>, PLN ['*rock that looks like a little hat on west (Chehalis) side of Harrison River above mouth of Morris Creek*'], *see* yó:seqw ~ yóseqw.

<**Yó:yt'elwet**>, df //yá·[=C_1ə=]t'=əlwət//, N ['*Old Mary of Chehalis*']

<**yúkw'es**>, us //yúk'^{w}əs//, SOC ['*busy at home all the time*'], syntactic analysis: adjective/adjectival verb?, attested by IHTTC (9/2/77).

<**Yù:l**>, us //yù·l//, PLN ['*island in river on which Yune's Cannery was built*'], ASM ['in the river between Tsawwassen and Fraser River that goes by Lulu Island, Yune is not a non-Indian name, it is from Yù:l (properly Downriver Yù:n) which is the Indian name of the island'], syntactic analysis: nominal, attested by Elders Group (4/23/80), also <**Yù:n**>, //yù·n//, dialects: *Downriver Halkomelem*,

attested by Elders Group (4/23/80).

<**yutl'étl'elòm**>, PRON /*'(that's) them (lots of little ones), they (many small ones)*'/, *see* tl'ó ~ tl'o.

<**yutl'ó:lem**>, PRON /*'that's them (gender unspecified), they, them*'/, *see* tl'ó ~ tl'o.

<**yú:w**>, free root //yә́w·//, LANG ['*(said when praising something beautiful)*'], EFAM, phonology: vowel-raising (//ә́w·// → /ú·w/), syntactic analysis: interjection, attested by Elders Group (5/19/76), perhaps also used in <**yálh yuw kw'a's hò:y**>, LANG /*'I thank you (deeply), I thank you (deeply)., Thank you.*'/, *see* hò:y ~ hó:y ~ hóy; Salish cognate: Lushootseed /yú(ʔ)/ slang for /háʔɬ/ *good* as in /pút yu su-lәllícut ʔә tiʔәʔ šiq^{w}s/ *His hat was changing (colors) very prettily,* H76:636, Squamish root in /yә́w-t/ *to praise (tr.), brag about (tr.)* and /yә́w-cut/ *brag (lit. praise oneself)* K69:90.

<**yó:wthet**>, pcrs //yә[-Aá-]w·=T-әt//, cts, LANG ['*bragging*'], EFAM, (<**ó-ablaut**> *continuative*), (<**=t**> *purposeful control transitivizer*), (<**-et**> *reflexive),* phonology: ablaut, syntactic analysis: intransitive verb, attested by Elders Group (5/3/78), Salish cognate: Squamish /yә́w-t/ *to praise (tr.), brag about (tr.)* and esp. /yә́w-cut/ *brag (lit. praise oneself)* K69:90, example: <**lichxw yó:wthet?**>, //li-c-x^{w} yә[-Aá-]w·=T-әt//, /*'Are you bragging?*'/, attested by Elders Group (5/3/78)

<**yú:wqwlha**>, df //yә́w·=q^{w}ɬɛ//, EFAM /*'how beautiful., be really beautiful*'/, possibly <**=qwlha**> *emphatic*, syntactic analysis: interjection, attested by EB (5/18/76), example: <**yú:wqwlha ta' qwlhíxel.**>, //yә́w·=q^{w}ɬɛ t-ɛʔ q^{w}әɬ=ә[=´=]y=x^{y}әl//, /*'You've got really beautiful shoes.*'/, literally /'is really beautiful your shoe'/, attested by EB.

<**yú:wqwlha**>, EFAM /*'how beautiful., be really beautiful*'/, *see* yú:w.

' or ’

Either form of the apostrophe here stands for what is known in linguistics as a glottal stop when it appears after a vowel. When it appears after a consonant it stands for what is known in linguistics as glottalization; when it occurs after consonants it is treated as part of the characters that make up that letter in the Stó:lō writing system. Only on very rare cases, in Upriver Halkomelem, does glottal stop occur after a consonant when that consonant is also found glottalized in other words; to show an actual glottal stop follows such a plain consonant, they are separated with a dash, as in <**ets-'ets**> *stutter*.

While glottal stop is rare at the end of a word and before consonants in Upriver Halkomelem (most have changed to length), glottal stop actually occurs as the onset of every word spelled with an initial vowel in the Stó:lō writing system. Since it is predictable there, it is not written there. The same is true for most root forms beginning in this dictionary; any written with an initial vowel begin with a glottal stop when they occur word initially; some also have the glottal stop when prefixed, as in <**s'ith'em**> *clothes.* Some never occur word intially and do not have a glottal stop when prefixed. When reduplicated those roots which have an initial glottal stop, also copy it as C1 (consonant 1 of the root).

Since the apostrophe is not written at the start of words and roots with initial glottal stop, there are no entries needed for this letter in the Stó:lō orthography. In the other dialect groups of Halkomelem, Downriver Halkomelem and Island Halkomelem, glottal stop can occur after most if not all consonants and is much more frequent. Thus a separate symbol is needed in those dialects for glottal stop, so that glottalized consonants and consonant followed by glottal stop can be shown correctly and separately. Tesó:s te mestíyexw!

In some cases a glottal stop is added to separate a vowel final root or stem and a vowel initial suffix, but more often the vowels are allowed to merge and combine according to rules described in Galloway 1977 and 1993. In the international phonetic alphabet, glottal stop is written with a question mark without the dot. Below are two examples. The first shows a reduplicated stem with the glottal stop reduplicated. The second example shows a suffix which sometimes uses glottal stop to separate it from a root or stem which ends in a vowel. In both cases I have spelled the stem or stuffix with an apostrophe to show how it works, but in the dictionary and writing system normally, the initial glottal stop or apostrophe will always be left off. Thus will be found under the letter <**a**> under <**al'álíy**> and the suffix will be found under <**=ó:ylha**> in the letter <**o**>.

<**'al'álíy**> (normally written <**al'álíy**>), VALJ ['*all good*'], *see* éy ~ éy:.

<**=(')ó:ylha**> (normally written <**=ó:ylha**>), da //=(ʔ)á·yɬɛ//, EB ['*(wooden?)*'], perhaps originally a compound with root <**yo:lh**> *cut tree, log* plus metathesis yielding <**=o:ylh**> plus <**=e ~ =a**> *living entity*, could less plausibly be seen as <**=á:y**> *bark, plant, wool, covering*, possibly <**=lh**> *past tense*, syntactic analysis: lexical suffix, compare <**=ó:ylh ~ =iylh**> *(bed?)*??; found in <**mimele'ó:ylha**>, //C_1í=mələ=ʔ=á·yɬɛ//, /'*doll*'/ (from <**mímele**> *baby, tiny child* (with <**R4=**> *diminutive* + <**méle**> *child*); <**=ó:ylh=a**> should be compared to <**s=yó:lh**> *firewood, wood* and <**s=yó:ylh**> *little firewood, little stick of wood* and <**=a**> *living thing* contrast <**=iylh**> *child or young*. In my data the word for *doll* is the only example.

' or '

Either form of the apostrophe here stands for what is known in linguistics as a glottal stop when it appears after a vowel. When it appears after a consonant it stands for what is known in linguistics as glottalization; when it occurs after consonants it is treated as part of the characters that make up that letter in the Stó:lō writing system. Only on very rare cases, in Upriver Halkomelem, does glottal stop occur after a consonant when that consonant is also found glottalized in other words; to show an actual glottal stop follows such a plain consonant, they are separated with a dash, as in <ets-'ets> stutter.

While glottal stop is rare at the end of a word and before consonants in Upriver Halkomelem (most have changed to length), glottal stop actually occurs as the onset of every word spelled with an initial vowel in the Stó:lō writing system. Since it is predictable there, it is not written there. The same is true for most root forms beginning in this dictionary; any written with an initial vowel begin with a glottal stop when they occur word initially; some also have the glottal stop when prefixed, as in <s'ith'em> clothes. Some never occur word initially and do not have a glottal stop when prefixed. When reduplicated those roots which have an initial glottal stop also copy it as C1 (consonant 1 of the root).

Since the apostrophe is not written at the start of words and roots with initial glottal stop, there are no entries needed for this letter in the Stó:lō orthography. In the other dialect groups of Halkomelem, Downriver Halkomelem and Island Halkomelem, glottal stop can occur after most if not all consonants and is much more frequent. Thus a separate symbol is needed in those dialects for glottal stop, so that glottalized consonants and consonant followed by glottal stop can be shown correctly and separately. Tsesóts'e mestiyexw!

In some cases a glottal stop is added to separate a vowel final root or stem and a vowel initial suffix, but more often the vowels are allowed to merge and combine according to rules described in Galloway 1977 and 1993. In the international phonetic alphabet, glottal stop is written with a question mark without the dot. Below are two examples. The first shows a reduplicated stem with the glottal stop reduplicated. The second example shows a suffix which sometimes uses glottal stop to separate it from a root or stem which ends in a vowel. In both cases I have spelled the stem or suffix with an apostrophe to show how it works, but in the dictionary and writing system normally the initial glottal stop or apostrophe will always be left off. Thus will be found under the letter <a> under <al'ály> and the suffix will be found under <=ó:ylha> in the letter <o>.

<'al'ály> (normally written <al'ály>), VAL [[illegible]], good], see ey ~ éy.

<=' ó:ylha> (normally written <=ó:ylha>), da //=(ʔ)á·yɬe//, LS [[illegible]], perhaps originally a compound with root <yálh> cut tree, log plus metathesis yielding <=ó:ylh> plus <=e> ~ <=a> living thing, could less plausibly be seen as <=á:y> bark, plant, wool, covering, possibly <=lh> past tense, syntactic analysis: lexical suffix, compare <=ó:ylh> [illegible] found in <mimele'ó:ylha>, [illegible] (from <mimele> [illegible], [illegible] should be compared to <=ó:lh> [illegible] and <=ó:ylh> little tree/wood, [illegible] and <=e> living thing contrast <=ó:lh> child or young, in my data the word for [illegible] is the only example.

Galloway: Upriver Halkomelem Dictionary

English-to-Halq'eméylem Index

a

a

the (distant and out of sight, remote), (definite but distant and out of sight, remote), the (abstract), a (remote, abstract), some, (indefinite):: kw'e.
the (male, present, visible), the (gender or presence and visibility unspecified), a (male, present and visible), a (gender or presence and visibility unspecified):: te, te.

abandon

leave s-o, leave s-th, go away from s-o/s-th, abandon s-o, leave s-o behind:: áyeles < á:y.

Abies amabilis or Abies grandis

prob. Abies lasiocarpa, if sample is mistaken poss. Abies amabilis or Abies grandis, if term balsam is mistaken poss. a variety of Pseudotsuga menziesii:: q'et'emá:yelhp < q'át'em.

Abies grandis:: t'ó:xw ~ t'óxw ~ t'óx̲w.

branch of probably Abies grandis:: t'óx̲wtses < t'ó:xw ~ t'óxw ~ t'óx̲w.
prob. Abies lasiocarpa, if sample is mistaken poss. Abies amabilis or Abies grandis, if term balsam is mistaken poss. a variety of Pseudotsuga menziesii:: q'et'emá:yelhp < q'át'em.
probably Abies grandis:: t'ó:xw ~ t'óxw ~ t'óx̲w.

Abies lasiocarpa

prob. Abies lasiocarpa, if sample is mistaken poss. Abies amabilis or Abies grandis, if term balsam is mistaken poss. a variety of Pseudotsuga menziesii:: q'et'emá:yelhp < q'át'em.

able

be alright, be okay, it's alright, it's okay, can, be able, it's enough, be right, be correct, that's right:: iyólem ~ iyó:lem < éy ~ éy:.

aboard

be aboard, be in (a conveyance):: eló:lh < ó:lh.
get in a canoe, get aboard:: ó:lh.
get s-th aboard (a canoe, car, conveyance):: eló:lhstexw < ó:lh.
put s-th/s-o aboard, put it on-board:: ó:lhstexw < ó:lh.

about

be singing about s-o/s-th:: t'ít'elemet < t'íl.
sing about s-o/s-th:: t'ílemet < t'íl.
think s-o is talking or laughing about one:: tl'ostélmét < tl'óst or tl'óstexw.

above

be above, be high, top, up above, way high:: chíchelh < =chílh ~ chílh=.
high, upper, above:: =chílh ~ chílh=.
over, in the air over, above:: stselhsó:lwelh < =chílh ~ chílh=.

abrasion

rub (oil or water) in s-th to clean or soften, rub s-th to soften or clean it, (shaping a stone hammer with abrasion?, shaping?, mixing paint?, pressing together or crushing? [BHTTC 9/2/76]):: yémq't.

absent)

agent (human, gender unspecified, absent):: tl'.
by (agent. human, gender unspecified, absent):: tl'.

absent) (CONT'D)

that's her (absent):: kwsú:tl'ò < kw.
that's her (absent), she (absent):: kwsú:tl'ò < tl'ó ~ tl'o.
that's him (absent), that's her (absent), it's him (absent), it's her (absent):: kwthú:tl'ò < kw, kwthú:tl'ò < kw, kwthú:tl'ò < kw.
that's him (absent), that's her (absent), it's him/her (absent), he (absent), she (absent):: kwthú:tl'ò < tl'ó ~ tl'o.
that's them (absent, not present):: kwthú:tl'òlem < kw.
that's them (absent, not present), they (absent):: kwthú:tl'òlem < tl'ó ~ tl'o.

absent-minded

(be) absent-minded, forgetful:: q'thá:mtem < q'thá:m.

abstain

to abstain from food, to fast, starve oneself:: xwóthet < xwá.

abstract

that (abstract subordinating conjunction):: kw'e.
the (distant and out of sight, remote), (definite but distant and out of sight, remote), the (abstract), a (remote, abstract), some, (indefinite):: kw'e.
the (present, not visible, gender unspecified), the (remote, abstract):: kwe < kw.
(there), (action distant or abstract):: lí ~ lí: ~ li.
the (remote, not visible, abstract), some (indefinite):: kw.

Acarina

class Arachnida, order Acarina, Dermacentor andersoni, and probably Ixodes pacificus:: t'pí.
class Arachnida, order Acarina, probably Ixodes pacificus and Dermacentor andersoni resp.:: méth'elhqìwèl < méth'elh.

accept

discriminate against s-o, not accept s-o:: memí:lt < mí:lt.
not accept s-o, discriminate against s-o:: memí:lt < mí:lt.
not want s-o, not accept s-o, discriminate against s-o:: mí:lt.
pretending to be good, want to be accepted:: éystelómet ~ éy:stelómet < éy ~ éy:.
take s-th, accept s-th, get s-th, fetch s-th, pick s-th up:: kwú:t.

accident

drop s-th by accident:: wets'étl'lexw < wets'étl' ~ wech'étl'.

accidentally

accidentally hurt an old injury of s-o, (accidentally reinjure s-o):: qélhlexw < qélh.
(accidentally) make s-o ashamed, insult s-o (accidentally or manage to):: x̲éyx̲elexw < x̲éyx̲e ~ x̲íx̲e.
(be) hurting s-o [accidentally, happening to/managing to]:: x̲ex̲élhlexw < x̲élh.
break s-th (stick-like) (accidentally):: lekwlá:xw < lékw.
drop s-th (accidentally):: tsélqlexw < tsélq ~ chélq.
drop s-th (accidentally), let s-o go:: kwò:lxw < kwá:.
frightened s-o [accidentally], [happened/managed to] frighten s-o:: th'ith'íkw'elexw < th'íkw' or th'ekw'.
hit s-o unintentionally, hit s-o accidentally:: kw'óqwlexw < kw'óqw.
hit with an arrow accidentally:: ts'eqw'eláxw < ts'éqw'.
hurt s-o [accidentally, happen to, manage to]:: x̲élhlexw < x̲élh.

accidentally (CONT'D)

hurt s-o/s-th [for awhile, accidentally]:: x̲elhláxw < x̲élh.
kill s-th/s-o accidentally, (happen to or manage to kill s-th/s-o):: q'eyléxw < q'ó:y ~ q'óy.
make s-o ashamed [happen to or accidentally or manage to]:: lháylexw < lháy.
make s-o cry (accidentally or manage to):: x̲á:mlexw < x̲à:m ~ x̲á:m.
non-control reflexive, happen to or manage to or accidentally do to oneself:: =l=ómet or =l-ómet ~ =l=ó:met.
non-control transitivizer, accidentally, happen to, manage to do to s-o/s-th:: =l.
scare s-o accidentally:: sí:silexw < síy.
step on it accidentally:: óméléxw < i┐ m.
to shame oneself [accidentally], (get) embarrassed, (become ashamed of oneself?):: xéyx̲elòmèt < x̲éyx̲e ~ x̲íx̲e.
touch s-o accidentally, bump s-o, bumped s-o:: téslexw < tós.

Accipiter

Buteo jamaicensis, Buteo genus and Accipiter genus:: x̲emx̲ímels ~ x̲emx̲íméls < x̲éym.
probably of Accipiter genus:: x̲ix̲emx̲íméls < x̲éym.

accompany

accompanying s-o:: q'eq'exí:lt < q'ó.
accompany s-o, go with s-o:: sq'ó:t ~ sq'ót < q'ó.
accompany s-o, go with s-o, go along with s-o:: q'exí:lt < q'ó.
accompany s-o little or elderly:: q'eq'exí:lt < q'ó.

accomplishment)

(glad greeting sound, also sound to show pride in accomplishment):: x̲::.

according to

according to the ways of the, in the way of the:: =elh.

accordion :: ót'etem qweló:ythetel < qwà:l.

accumulating)

it's snowing, (snow is accumulating):: mámeqe < máqa ~ máqe.

Acer circinatum

Acer circinatum, Acer glabrum var. douglasii or Acer douglasii:: sí:ts'elhp.

Acer douglasii

Acer circinatum, Acer glabrum var. douglasii or Acer douglasii:: sí:ts'elhp.

Acer glabrum var. douglasii

Acer circinatum, Acer glabrum var. douglasii or Acer douglasii:: sí:ts'elhp.

Acer macrophyllum:: q'emő:lhp ~ q'emőwelhp < sq'émél.

ache

be aching (of bones):: x̲áp'kw'tem < x̲ep'ékw'.
(be) hurting, be aching:: x̲ex̲élh < x̲élh.
(be) sore, (be) hurting all the time, painful, aching:: sáyém < sáyem.
(have a) headache:: x̲lhá:léqel ~ x̲elháléqel < x̲élh.
have a pain in the stomach, (have a stomach-ache), one's stomache hurts:: x̲elhálwes < x̲élh.

ache (CONT'D)

(have) a steady toothache, have a toothache:: yélyelesem < yél:és.
(have/get) rheumatism, aching:: x̱áp'kw'tem < x̱ep'ékw'.
hurt, be hurt, (ache [Elders Group 3/1/72], to really hurt (more than an ache) [AD]):: x̱élh.
it aches (like of bones), (be aching (of bones)):: x̱áp'qw'em < x̱ep'ékw'.
it aches of arthritis:: chálh.
it's aching of arthritis:: cháchelh < chálh.
to hurt again (as when a painful place is bumped and hurts again or as when a pain inside one's body returns again), (to ache [SJ]):: téqlexw.

Achillea millefolium
Achillea millefolium, also Cryptogramma crispa:: xaweqá:l < xáwéq.

Achlys triphylla:: lhxwáléws < lhí:xw.

Acipenser transmontanus:: skwó:wech ~ skwówech.

acknowledge
acknowledge oneself:: telómelthet < tól.

acorn
nut of hazelnut bush, acorn, any nut, walnut, peanut, etc.:: sth'í:tsem < th'éts.

Acrididae
order Orthoptera family Acrididae or perhaps family Tettigoniidae:: tl'emékw' < tl'ámkw'em, tl'emékw' < tl'ém, tl'emtl'émxel < tl'ém, ts'áts'etl'em < ts'tl'ám ~ ts'tl'ém, ts'ats'etl'í:m < ts'tl'ám ~ ts'tl'ém, ts'í:ts'á:tl'em < ts'tl'ám ~ ts'tl'ém.

across :: st'át'elh < t'álh.
be across, be on the other side of:: sle'ó:thel < le'á.
bring s-th/s-o across a river, (ferry s-o/s-th over):: t'kwíléstexw < t'ákwel.
carry a packstrap slung across the chest (over one shoulder and under one arm):: st'át'elhíles < t'álh.

across the Fraser River from Union Bar
place across the Fraser River from Union Bar:: Wowés.

act
acting smart:: smímts'el < máth'el.

Actaea rubra
Actaea rubra if red baneberry is correct identification:: í:lwelh.

Actitis macularia:: wéthweth < wíth, wóthiya < wíth.

adam's apple:: shxwehóméllhelh.

add
add some, add it, (do it again [AD]):: ts'xwót, ts'xwót.
add some water [to s-th]:: ch'exwélhchat < ts'xwót.
do it again, add more (to s-th):: qelátstexw < qelát.
put s-th with (something), add s-th (to something), include s-th:: q'ót < q'ó.

add (CONT'D)

trickling, dribbling, water bubbling up in a river, add water to a container, water running under:: kw'átem.

addict

contract a disease, catch a disease, get addicted:: q'áp'.
he passes on a disease to s-o, he gets s-o addicted:: q'ep'lóxes < q'áp'.

admire

admire s-th/s-o:: thélmet.
admiring s-o/s-th:: tháthelmet < thélmet.

admit

admitting s-o/s-th, letting s-o/s-th in, bringing s-o/s-th inside:: kwétexwt < kwetáxw.
bring s-o/s-th in (to a house/enclosure), take s-o/s-th in(inside a house/enclosure), admit s-o (into a house/enclosure), let s-o/s-th in (to a house/enclosure), put s-o/s-th in (inside a house/enclosure:: kwetáxwt < kwetáxw.

adolescent

adolescent male (before he changes to a man, about 13, when his voice changes, etc.):: tumiyáth'.
adolescent virgin girl, young girl (about ten to fifteen years), girl (from ten till she becomes a woman):: q'á:mi ~ q'á:miy.
(young) girls, lots of (adolescent) girls:: q'á:lemi ~ q'á:lemey < q'á:mi ~ q'á:miy.

adolescent boy

adolescent boy (about 10 to 15 yrs. old), teenaged boy, young man (teenager):: swíweles ~ swíwles.

adopt

adopt a child:: txwmelám < méle ~ mél:a, txwméla ~ texwméla < méle ~ mél:a.
adopted child:: smelám < méle ~ mél:a.

adult

small adult cow:: múmesmes < músmes.
small adult cows, (small adult cattle):: melúmesmes < músmes.

advise

advise s-o, teach s-o, show s-o:: íwest < íwes.
showing s-o (how to do it), teaching s-o, advising s-o, guiding s-o, directing s-o:: í:west < íwes.

adze :: st'et'eméls ~ st'et'ebéls < t'ém.

adze (for making canoes and pit-house ladders):: xwt'ót'epels ~ shxwt'ót'epels < t'óp.
adze with handle for canoe-making, elbow-adze:: hálíytel < hà:y.
adzing, chopping, chopping with an adze:: t'et'éméls < t'ém.
to chop with an adze, to chop, to adze, an adze:: t'eméls < t'ém.
U-shaped or horseshoe-shaped knife for scraping out an adzed canoe:: sqw'emqw'emóx̲w < qw'ómx̲w.

Aegolius acadicus)

Glaucidium gnoma swarthi (or Glaucidium gnoma grinnelli) and Cryptoglaux acadia

Aegolius acadicus) (CONT'D)
acadia (or Aegolius acadicus):: spopeleqwíth'a ~ spopeleqwíth'e < poleqwíth'a.

affectionate
affectionate diminutive:: =iya ~ =óya.

afraid
afraid to try:: qelélwes < qél.
animal or bird one is afraid of and can't see, powerful creature, supernatural creature:: stl'á:leqem.
be afraid, be scared, be nervous:: sí:si < síy.
be afraid of s-th/s-o:: sí:simet < síy.
coward, person that's always afraid:: lexwsí:si < síy.
get a spooky or spooked feeling, afraid that bad spirits are around, get spooked, fear something behind:: x̲éysel.
getting spooked, being afraid that bad spirits are around, spooky feeling:: x̲éyx̲esel < x̲éysel.

after
a little past, a little after:: yéyilaw ~ yíyelaw < yelá:w ~ yeláw ~ yiláw.
be last, be behind, after:: lhiyó:qwt.
later, after a while, later on, wait a while:: téx̲w.

after-birth:: s'ó:qw.

again :: ew.
add some, add it, (do it again [AD]):: ts'xwót.
again, another, more:: qelát.
do it again, add more (to s-th):: qelátstexw < qelát.
next, again:: atse.
to hurt again (as when a painful place is bumped and hurts again or as when a pain inside one's body returns again), (to ache [SJ]):: téqlexw.
wrap it again, rewrap it, (correction by AD:) roll it up (of a mat, carpet, etc.):: xwelxwélekw't < xwélekw'.

against
holding a grudge against each other:: xixemó:ltel < sxemá:l.
lean s-th against something:: tiyélést < tiy.

Agassiz (B.C.)
the whole Agassiz (B.C.) area (JL), Agassiz Mountain (AK), place near Agassiz where Hamersley Hopyards were (possibly some other speakers):: Alámex.
Whetkyel village east of Little Mountain by Agassiz:: Xwétxel or X̲wétxel.

Agassiz Mountain:: Alámex Smámelt < Alámex.
Agassiz Mountain (or more likely Mount Woodside):: Sqwehíwel < qwá.
the whole Agassiz (B.C.) area (JL), Agassiz Mountain (AK), place near Agassiz where Hamersley Hopyards were (possibly some other speakers):: Alámex.
village on north bank of the Fraser River above Agassiz Mountain:: Tsítsqem.
Wahleach Bluff, a lookout mountain with rock sticking out over a bluff, also the lookout point on Agassiz Mountain:: Kw'okw'echíwel < kw'áts ~ kw'éts.

Agassiz-Rosedale bridge
village now at north end of Agassiz-Rosedale bridge, now Tseatah Indian Reserve #2 (of Cheam band):: Siyét'e.

agate
jade (nephrite) (used for sharpening [chopping] stones), any agate (can be used as flint to strike a spark):: t'émq'ethel.

agent
agent (human, gender unspecified, absent):: tl'.
by (agent. human, gender unspecified, absent):: tl'.

aggressive
(be) aggressive, cranky, ready to fight, (be) violent, hot-headed:: sx̲óytl'thet ~ sx̲ó:ytl'thet.

ago
a long time ago:: welhíthelh < híth, welhí:thelh < híth, welhíth < híth.
long ago:: wet'ót'.
recently, just now, lately, (at one recent moment), not long ago:: qá:ys.

agree :: éyeles < éy ~ éy:.

aid
help s-o, defend s-o, protect s-o, aid s-o:: má:yt ~ máyt < máy.

aim
aiming it:: momí:yt < mó:yt.
aim it:: mó:yt.
point at, aim:: mót'es.

air
keep it in the air, lift s-th/s-o off the floor:: shxwóxwelstexw < xwá.

air-bladder
fish air-bladder:: xixxweláwa.

airborne)
get hit (by s-th thrown or airborne):: ló:m ~ lóm.

airplane :: lhólhekw' stim:ő̃t < lhó:kw' ~ lhókw', lhólhekw' stimő̃t < stim:ő̃:t.
to travel by canoe, (nowadays also) travel by airplane, travel by train, travel by car:: yeló:lh < ó:lh.

Aix sponsa:: qwiwílh.

akimbo)
put hands on both hips, (put hands akimbo):: piypiyólwelhem < píy.

Albert Flat
village or settlement on the west side of the Fraser River at Emory Creek by Frank Malloway's fish camp, Albert Flat (Yale Indian Reserve #5):: Ó:ywoses.

Alces alces andersoni)

Alces alces andersoni)
    (Alces alces andersoni):: shxwiyáxkel.

alder
    alder tree, red alder:: x̱éyth'elhp < x̱éyth'.
    a yellowish glow at night given off by old birch and alder:: qwéth'.
    small mountain alder:: wásewey.

Alectoria (Bryoria)

Alectoria (Bryoria)
    possibly Letharia vulpina or Alectoria (Bryoria) species or Usnea species:: mex̱t'éles.

Alectoria fremontii:: sqwelíp.

alert :: xwiyós < xwíy ~ x[illegible]í.

alfalfa sprouts:: tsqwá:y spéxwqel < qwá:y, píxw
    (lit. green + fine airborne seed)

algae
    green pond slime or river slime, algae:: stíxem < tíxem.

Alium cepa:: éniyels.

alive
    be alive, be living, be in good health, be healthy, be well:: áylexw ~ áyelexw.
    come alive, come back to life, get better (from sickness), get well, revive:: áylexw ~ áyelexw.
    keep s-o/s-th alive:: á:yelexwstexw < áylexw ~ áyelexw.

all
    all, every:: mékw' ~ mṓkw'.
    all good:: 'al'álíy < éy ~ éy:.
    all of them (people):: semíkw' < mékw' ~ mṓkw'.
    always, all the time, ((also) often, over and over [TG]):: wiyóth.
    ancestors past, (all one's ancestors):: syesyewálelh < yewá:l.
    (be) all bundled up:: stl'etl'íqw'.
    busy at home all the time:: yúkw'es.
    cut it all up:: t'eqw't'éqw'et < t'éqw'.
    perish together, many die (in famine, sickness, fire), all die, get wiped out:: x̱wà:y ~ x̱wá:y.
    (take all of themselves, pick themselves all up):: mōkw'éthet < mékw' ~ mṓkw', mōkw'éthet < mékw' ~ mṓkw'.
    take it all, pick it all up:: mekw'ét ~ mōkw'ét ~ mōkw'ót < mékw' ~ mṓkw'.
    they all died:: x̱wó:y < x̱wà:y ~ x̱wá:y.
    uncles (all of them), aunts (all of them):: sxwemlá:lekw < shxwemlí:kw.

all around
    distributive, all over, all around:: =x̱ ~ =ex̱.

allergic
    prickly (from fir bark, wool, or something one is allergic to), irritant, have an allergic

allergic (CONT'D)
reaction (to fir powder or cedar bark):: th'íth'ekwem < th'íkw.

Allison's
a place on Chilliwack River, a little above Anderson Flat and Allison's (between Tamihi Creek and Slesse Creek), a village at deep water between Tamihi Creek and Slesse Creek:: Iy'óythel < éy ~ éy:.

Allium acuminatum
Allium cernuum, prob. also Allium acuminatum:: st'áxet.

Allium cernuum
Allium cernuum, prob. also Allium acuminatum:: st'áxet.

all over
(be) scattered all over:: stl'ápx̲ < tl'ép.
distributive, all over, all around:: =x̲ ~ =ex̲.
(get) lots of water all over since it's raining so hard, really getting rainy:: t'emt'émqw'xel < t'émeqw'.
you'll get punched all over:: th'óleqw'esthòm < th'í:qw'et.
you're shaking all over:: xwóyeqwthòm.

almost :: xwá:lq, xwá:lqi ~ xwálqey < xwá:lq.
almost kill s-o:: x̲wíleqlexw.
(be) partially blind, almost blind:: qelsílém < qél.
going to piss right away, almost piss oneself, (have an urgent or extreme or painful need to urinate):: ts'áléqel.
repeatedly almost kill s-o:: x̲wilx̲wíleqlexw or x̲welx̲wíleqlexw < x̲wíleqlexw.
to almost die:: xwá:lq.

Alnus rubra:: x̲éyth'elhp < x̲éyth'.

Alnus tenuifolia:: wásewey.

alone :: ilólets'e ~ hilólets'e < léts'a ~ léts'e.
leave s-o alone, stop pestering s-o:: kwikwe'át < kwá:.
one person, be alone:: lólets'e < léts'a ~ léts'e.

along :: yewá:.
accompany s-o, go with s-o, go along with s-o:: q'exí:lt < q'ó.
along, together, be included, with:: sq'eq'ó < q'ó.
along, with, together with:: sq'ó < q'ó.
jumping along, jumping up and down:: ts'ats'etl'í:m < ts'tl'ám ~ ts'tl'ém.
to sing along or follow in singing a spirit song:: t'à:m.
travelling by, in motion, while moving along, while travelling along:: ye= ~ yi= ~ i┐.
(while) travelling along, in motion:: ye=.

Alopius vulpinus
perhaps Cetorhinus maximus, Hexanchus griseus, Alopius vulpinus, and/or others:: q'ellhomelétsel < q'ellhólemètsel.

already :: welh ~ ulh ~ =ulh.

already (CONT'D)

already written:: sx̱ex̱é:yl < x̱él ~ x̱é:yl ~ x̱í:l
(be) cooked, (be) already cooked:: sqw'eqw'í:l < qw'él.
coming by foot, travelling by walking, already walking, travelling on foot:: ye'í:mex < i┐m.
he/she/it was (already), they were (already):: lulh < le.
now I, (now I'm already):: tl'ékwálsulh < tl'ó ~ tl'o.

alright

be alright, be okay, it's alright, it's okay, can, be able, it's enough, be right, be correct, that's right:: iyólem ~ iyó:lem < éy ~ éy:.
be alright, be well, be fine, be okay:: éy òl ~ éyòl ~ éyò < éy ~ éy:.
be fine (in health), be alright (in health), be well:: we'éy òl ~ we'éyòl ~ we'éyò ~ u éyò ~ u'éyò < éy ~ éy:.

alumroot

small-flowered alumroot, and possibly smooth Heuchera:: qw'eléqetel < qw'eléqel, xweqw'ele'á:ltel < xweqw'él:a.

always :: lexw= ~ xw=, lexw= ~ xw= ~ (rarely) le=.

always, all the time, ((also) often, over and over [TG]):: wiyóth.
a person that always:: lexws= < lexw= ~ xw= ~ (rarely) le=.
a person that always hunts, hunter:: lexws=há:wa < háwe.
a person that always sings:: lexwst'í:lem < t'íl.
a person that's always lazy:: lexws'ú:met < emét.
(be) always scared:: lexwsí:si ~ xwsí:si < síy.
be always sickly:: q'é:yq'ey < q'ó:y ~ q'óy.
coward, person that's always afraid:: lexwsí:si < síy.
deeper, always deep:: lexwstl'ép < tl'ép.
mountain on Fraser River between first tunnel and Yale where rotten fish used to (always) pile up:: Lexwyó:qwem Smá:lt < yó:qw.
optimist, a person whose thoughts are always good:: wiyóth kwsu éys te sqwálewels te lólets'e < wiyóth.
person who is always lazy:: lexws'í:ts'el < í:ts'el.
pessimist, a person whose thoughts are always bad:: wiyóth kwsu qéls te sqwálewels te lólets'e < wiyóth.
place on Fraser River between first tunnel and Yale where rotten fish used to (always) pile up:: Lexwyó:qwem < yó:qw.
[someone] always working:: lexwsyóyes ~ lexwsiyó:yes < yó:ys.
someone that always:: lexws=.
sometimes?, always?:: lheq.

Alwís

name of second creek below (here south of) Suka Creek (as of 8/30/77), creek called Alwís's Bow-line:: Alwís Lhqéletel.

Amadis

Cultus Lake Mountain, actually Mount Amadis or International Ridge:: Swílhcha Smá:lt < Swílhcha.

amazement)

(expression of amazement):: hó'ì'.

ambitious
(be) ambitious, (be) willing:: shxwúxwe.
(be) willing to do one's work, (ambitious [BHTTC]):: lexws'ó:les.

Ambystoma gracile decorticatum
Ensatina eschscholtzi and Plethodon vehiculum and possibly also: Ambystoma macrodactylum macrodactylum, Ambystoma gracile gracile, and possibly Ambystoma gracile decorticatum:: pí:txel.

Ambystoma gracile gracile
Ensatina eschscholtzi and Plethodon vehiculum and possibly also: Ambystoma macrodactylum macrodactylum, Ambystoma gracile gracile, and possibly Ambystoma gracile decorticatum:: pí:txel.

Ambystoma macrodactylum macrodactylum
Ensatina eschscholtzi and Plethodon vehiculum and possibly also: Ambystoma macrodactylum macrodactylum, Ambystoma gracile gracile, and possibly Ambystoma gracile decorticatum:: pí:txel.

Amelanchier alnifolia:: sk'ak'áxwe, ts'esláts, ts'eslátselhp < ts'esláts.

America
America, United States:: Pástel.

American :: Pástel.

American Bar
burnt mountain across from American Bar:: Syíyeqw < yéqw.
medicine spring on the Fraser River beach about a half mile above (north) of the American Bar beach:: Xwth'kw'ém < th'ekw' or th'íkw'.
Mill Creek (at American Bar), Puckat Creek on map also:: Peqwchṓ:lthel Stótelō < péqw.
mountain across the Fraser River from American Bar:: Qw'íywelh or Qw'éywelh.
mountain on the west (C.P.R.) side of the Fraser River above American Bar which had a steaming pond at the top, (year-round village at mouth of American Creek on west bank of the Fraser River [Duff]):: Qétex̲em < qá:t.
place in Fraser River two miles above American Bar with narrow rock:: X̲eq'átelets < x̲eq'.
village at American Bar, village on west bank of Fraser River at American Creek, American Bar Reserve:: Peqwchṓ:lthel ~ Peqwechṓ:lthel < péqw.

American Creek
mountain on the west (C.P.R.) side of the Fraser River above American Bar which had a steaming pond at the top, (year-round village at mouth of American Creek on west bank of the Fraser River [Duff]):: Qétex̲em < qá:t.
village at American Bar, village on west bank of Fraser River at American Creek, American Bar Reserve:: Peqwchṓ:lthel ~ Peqwechṓ:lthel < péqw.
year-round village at mouth of American Creek on west bank of the Fraser River:: Qétex̲em < qá:t.

amidst
(be in the) woods, (amidst bush or vegetation, be tucked away?):: sxí:xets' ~ sxíxets' < xí:ts' ~ xíts' ~ xets'.

amount
give an equal share or amount to s-o, give (food?) to s-o, share with s-o:: áxwest < áxw.

amusement
be fun, have (lots of) fun, have amusement, having lots of fun, be pleasant:: íyes ~ éyes < éy ~ éy:.

Anas acuta
Anas americana (~ Mareca americana), prob. also Anas penelope (~ Mareca penelope), (Anas acuta [BJ]):: sése.

Anas americana
Anas americana (~ Mareca americana), prob. also Anas penelope (~ Mareca penelope), (Anas acuta [BJ]):: sése.

Anas penelope
Anas americana (~ Mareca americana), prob. also Anas penelope (~ Mareca penelope), (Anas acuta [BJ]):: sése.

Anas platyrhynchos
Anas platyrhynchos, perhaps generic for duck:: teléqsel ~ tel:éqsel.

ancestor
ancestors:: syewá:l ~ syewál < yewá:l.
ancestors past, (all one's ancestors):: syesyewálelh < yewá:l.
departed ancestors:: syewá:lelh ~ syewálelh < yewá:l.
parents, relations (ancestors?):: shxwwáli < shxwewá(:)y.

anchor :: mesíyeltel ~ mesí:ltel.
homemade anchor, kilik, calik, (killick):: skw'éstel.

anchor-line
anchor-line, mooring-line, bow-line, what is used to tie up a canoe:: lhqéletel < lhqé:ylt.

ancient
ancient people over a hundred years old:: sx̲wolex̲wiyám < x̲wiyám.
getting ancient, getting old:: q'e'ílém < q'a'í:lem ~ q'e'í:lem.
very old, ancient, get ancient, be ancient:: q'a'í:lem ~ q'e'í:lem.

and :: qas < qe.
and, but, or:: qe.
and so, and then:: qesu < qe, qetl'osu ~ qetl'esu < qe.
and so (he, she, it, they):: qetl'osésu ~ qetl'os'ésu < tl'ó ~ tl'o, tl'osésu ~ tl'os'ésu < tl'ó ~ tl'o.
and then (he, she, it):: tl'esu < tl'ó ~ tl'o.

Anderson Flat
a place on Chilliwack River, a little above Anderson Flat and Allison's (between Tamihi Creek and Slesse Creek), a village at deep water between Tamihi Creek and Slesse Creek:: Iy'óythel < éy ~ éy:.

angel :: lisós.

anger

snap one's eyes at s-o [in anger or disgust]:: th'éplexwlexw (or perhaps th'ép'lexwlexw) < th'éplexw (or perhaps th'ép'lexw).

Anglican

Englishman, English, Canadian, Canada, Anglican:: kelchóch ~ kyelchóch.

angry

being angry, continue to be angry, angry, mad, roused, stirred up:: t'át'eyeq' ~ t'át'iyeq' < t'ay.
disappointed and angry-looking without talking:: sx̲éyx̲eth' < x̲íth' ~ x̲éyth'.
get angry, get mad, be angry:: t'áyeq' < t'ay.

Anguis fragilis

Anguis fragilis:: aleqá:y < álhqey ~ álhqay.

angular

angular or perpendicular extension:: =áx̲el ~ =ex̲el.

animal

a biter (animal, fish, etc.), a thing that is (always) biting:: ch'ech'émels < ts'ámet ~ ch'ámet.
animal or bird one is afraid of and can't see, powerful creature, supernatural creature:: stl'á:leqem.
animal tripe (stomach, upper and lower), bowel:: spéxw.
catch an animal, get an animal:: kwélest < kwél.
fisher (mink-like animal):: thswál.
flesh (human, non-human), meat (of dried fish, animal, or bird):: slhíqw.
furry on the whole body (of an animal):: siysá:yiws < sá:y.
(game) animal, (meat):: sméyeth ~ sméyéth.
growing (of animals, children, etc.):: ts'íts'esem < ts'ísem.
growl (of an animal):: x̲éylém < x̲éykw'et.
(have) animal smell (of bear, skunk, dog, etc.), (have) animal stink, (have) human smell (of underarm, body odor, etc.), (have) body odor:: pápeth'em.
horn of an animal:: th'ístel < th'ís.
[left] front leg quarter of deer or other animal:: sth'ikweláx̲el < th'íkwe.
let oneself fall, drop oneself down (by parachute, rope, etc., said of little birds trying to fly out of nest, little animals trying to get down and let themselves fall):: chólqthet < tsélq ~ chélq.
little animal(s):: smímiyàth < sméyeth ~ sméyéth.
runt of litter, smallest pup or kitten or animal in litter:: th'íth'kw'oya < sth'ékw', th'íth'kw' < sth'ékw'.
shaking bushes (of animal or person unseen, for ex.):: xwóykwem.
sneaking after an animal:: tl'ítl'ets'élqem < tl'í:ts'.
spear animals by torchlight:: lex̲éywa ~ lex̲íwa.
spotted with irregular shaped blobs (like if mud-spattered, used of dogs, deer, and other animals so marked):: st'á:lq.
swimming (of dog, deer, animal), (dog-paddling):: x̲ólhchem < x̲élhchem.
tail (of animal, bird):: stl'ep'él:ets ~ stl'ep'élets.
to escape (as an animal from a trap), got away from something that trapped a person or

animal (CONT'D)

animal:: tl'ewlómét ~ tl'ōwlómét < tl'í:w.
to rot, rotten (of fruit, animal, flora, fauna, food):: th'óqw'em ~ th'ó:qw'em.
tracking an animal:: chokwelélqem < chó:kw.
unidentified animal with marks on its face, perhaps badger or wolverine:: sqoyép.
wool, fur, animal hair:: sá:y.

animate
that's (an animate being), it's (usually animate):: tl'ó ~ tl'o.

ankle
ankle joint:: xweth'éqw'xel.
ankle (the lump part):: qwémx̲wxel < qwó:m ~ qwóm ~ qwem.
leg got sprained, (sprain one's ankle [JL]):: ts'lhéqw'xel < ts'lhóqw'.
legs crossed, cross one's ankles (either sitting or standing) [prob. error], (ankles crossed (either sitting or standing)):: q'eyáweth'xel < q'ey ~ q'i.
sprained ankle:: xweth'éqw'xel.

Annis Rd.
Schelowat, a village at the bend in Hope Slough at Annis Rd. where there was a painted or marked house:: Sx̲elá:wtxw < x̲él ~ x̲é:yl ~ x̲í:l

announce
speaker at a gathering, announcer at a gathering:: lheqqwóqwel or lheq qwóqwel < qwà:l.

announcer
speaker at a gathering, announcer at a gathering:: lheqqwóqwel or lheq qwóqwel < qwà:l.

annoy
annoyed:: th'íwél, th'íwél < ts'íw.
annoyed s-o, bothered s-o, pestered s-o:: th'íwélstexw < th'íwél, th'íwélstexw < ts'íw.
annoyed with s-th, annoyed by s-o, tired of s-o:: ts'íwélmét < ts'íw.
being annoyed:: th'íth'ewel < th'íwél.
to be fed up [with s-o/s-th], (annoyed with s-o/s-th):: th'íwélmét < th'íwél.

another
again, another, more:: qelát.
another room, different room:: láts'ewtxw < láts'.
(be) true to one another:: the'íttel < the'í:t.
helping one another, (helper [Elders Group]):: momíyelhtel < máy.
help out, go help, pitch in, help one another:: móylhtel < máy.
purposeful control reciprocal, (perhaps just) reciprocal, (do purposely to) each other, (do purposely to) one another:: =t=el.

ant :: xá:ysem.

anthill
lots of anthills:: qwemqwó:mth' < qwó:m ~ qwóm ~ qwem.

anus
in the rump, in the anus, in the rectum, in the bottom, on the insides, inside parts, core, inside the head:: =í:wel ~ =íwel ~ =ewel.

any

is there none?, isn't there any?:: wá:ta < éwe ~ őwe.

anybody

everybody, everyone, (anybody [Elders Group 3/1/72]):: mekw'ewát < mékw' ~ mőkw'.
somebody, anybody:: tewátes < wát.
who else?, who (of several)?, (anybody else (AC)):: kw'elhwát < wát.

anything

whatever it is, what it is, it is anything, it is something:: stámés < tám.

anyway

anyway, ever, (new information as in NStraits):: kwá.
try to do something (no matter what, anyway):: iyálewethet < éy ~ éy:.

apart

break (of ground), crack apart (of its own accord) (of ground), ripped:: tl'éx.
broke down, came (un)loose, came apart, (got) untied, loose, unravelled:: yéx̲w < yíx̲w.
fall apart, come apart (of something man-made):: yíx̲w.
rip it apart:: tl'xát < tl'éx.
take s-th down, tear down s-th man-made, dismantle s-th, take it apart:: yíx̲wet < yíx̲w.

Apidae

order Hymenoptera, superfamily Apoidea, family Apidae, including Apis mellifera (introduced), also family Bombidae and family Vespidae and possibly bee-like members of family Syrphidae (order Diptera):: sisemó:ya ~ sisemóya ~ sisemóye ~ sísemòye.

Apis mellifera

order Hymenoptera, superfamily Apoidea, family Apidae, including Apis mellifera (introduced), also family Bombidae and family Vespidae and possibly bee-like members of family Syrphidae (order Diptera):: sisemó:ya ~ sisemóya ~ sisemóye ~ sísemòye.

Apocynum androsaemifolium

Apocynum androsaemifolium, possibly also Apocynum cannabinum:: méthelh.

Apocynum cannabinum

Apocynum androsaemifolium, possibly also Apocynum cannabinum:: méthelh.

Apoidea

order Hymenoptera, superfamily Apoidea, family Apidae, including Apis mellifera (introduced), also family Bombidae and family Vespidae and possibly bee-like members of family Syrphidae (order Diptera):: sisemó:ya ~ sisemóya ~ sisemóye ~ sísemòye.

appear

appear, come into view, rise into view:: pél:ékw.

appearance

in looks, -looking, in appearance:: =ó:mex ~ =óméx ~ =òmèx ~ =ómex ~ =omex ~ =emex.
what does it look like?, what does he/she look like?, (how is he/she/it in appearance or looks?), (what color is it? [NP]):: selchímomex < selchí:m ~ selchím.

apple)
    chewing (something hard, like apple):: x̲éyx̲ekw'els < x̲éykw'et.
    chew it (s-th hard, apple, pill):: x̲éykw'et.
    crabapple, (now) domesticated apple:: qwe'óp.
    crabapple tree, domestic apple tree:: qwe'ó:pelhp < qwe'óp.
    (spherical), round (of ball, apple, potato, rock, full moon, but not of a pear):: xelkw'ó:ls < xél.

apple juice:: qwe’óp sqe’óleqw < qwe’óp, qó:
    (lit. apple + fruit juice)

apprehend
    (emprisoned), put in jail, grounded, restricted, caught, apprehended:: qíq'.

approach
    approach, get near, get closer, reach, go up to, get up to:: tés.
    approaching, getting near, getting closer:: tetés < tés.
    approach (your nets for ex.):: ts'íméIthet < ts'íméI ~ ts'ímel.
    get close, approach, get near, nearly, (go close, come close):: ts'íméI ~ ts'ímel.
    get close to s-o/s-th, approach s-th/s-o:: ts'íméImet < ts'íméI ~ ts'ímel.

April
    hungry time (about mid-April to mid-May), famine (Elders 3/72):: temkw'à:y < kw'à:y.
    month beginning in April at the mouth of the Fraser, May-June (Jenness:Sepass), oolachen moon:: temwíwe (or possibly) temswíwe < swí:we ~ swíwe.
    month or moon of March to April, grass moon:: sox̲wí:les < só:x̲wel ~ sóx̲wel.
    time of the baby sockeye's coming, early spring (usually April), April moon:: temkwíkwexel.

April-fool
    fooling s-o, (fool s-o as a joke, April-fool s-o [Deming]):: q'íq'elstá:xw < q'á:l.

apron :: í:pel.
    dog-hair blanket dancing apron (DM 12/4/64):: kw'eléw ~ kw'elṓw.
    loincloth, dog-hair apron, dog-hair mat:: sthíyep.

Aquila chrysaetos:: ts'ésqel.
    Aquila chrysaetos and Haliaeetus leucocephalus:: yéx̲wela.

Arachnida
    class Arachnida, order Acarina, Dermacentor andersoni, and probably Ixodes pacificus:: t'pí.
    class Arachnida, order Acarina, probably Ixodes pacificus and Dermacentor andersoni resp.:: méth'elhqìwèl < méth'elh.
    class Arachnida, order Araneida, also order Phalangida:: q'ésq'esetsel < q'ey ~ q'i.
    class Arachnida, order Phalangida:: tl'áleqtxel q'esq'ésetsel < q'ey ~ q'i, tl'áleqtxel q'ésq'esetsel < tl'áqt.

Araneida
    class Arachnida, order Araneida, also order Phalangida:: q'ésq'esetsel < q'ey ~ q'i.

arch

arch of foot:: xwt'óxwesxel < t'óxw.

Archilochus alexandri

possibly Trochilidae family, probably including Selasphorus rufus, Archilochus alexandri, and Stellula calliope:: pésk'a.

Arctium minus:: x̲éyx̲emels ch'ech'éqw' < x̲éym, x̲éyx̲emels < x̲éym.

Arctostaphylos uva-ursi

Arctostaphylos uva-ursi, (intro.) Pisum sativum, (intro.) Phaseolus vulgaris, and probably Vicea gigantea:: tl'íkw'el.

Ardea herodias

Ardea herodias especially subspecies fannini:: sméqw'o ~ smṓqw'o.

area)

Cowichan (people, dialect, area):: Qewítsel < qew.
Saanich reserves area:: Sáléch.
Salkaywul, an area with big cracked cedar trees on Hope Slough above Schelowat (Chilliwack I.R. #1) (Sx̲eláwtxw):: Salq'íwel < séq'.
Sumas village and area from present-day Kilgard to Fraser River, Sumas village (on both sides of the Fraser at the east end of Sumas Mt.), (Devil's Run (below Láx̲ewey), the area between Sumas Mt. and Fraser River [Elders Group 7/13/77], Sumas River (probably requires Stó:lō river or Stótelō creek to follow) [Wells 1965], Sumas Lake (probably requires X̲ótsa lake after Semáth for this meaning) [Elders Group 7/13/77]):: Smá:th ~ Semá:th ~ Semáth.
Victoria, B.C., city of Victoria area, Fort Victoria:: Sth'ó:mes.
village or area on north side of Suka Creek (which is on the east side of the Fraser River:: Kwókwxwemels < kwoxw.

area up the mountainside

an area up the mountainside from Ñwox̲welálhp (Yale):: Chelqwílh ~ Chelqwéylh < chá:l or chó:l.

aren't

isn't?, aren't?, don't?, doesn't?, (be not?):: ewá ~ ōwá ~ wá < éwe ~ ṓwe.

Arion aster

also Limax maximus and Arion aster:: q'oyátl'iye.

arise

sit, sit down, sit up, arise (from lying or sitting), get up (from lying down, from bed or chair):: emét.

arm :: t'á:lew ~ t'álew.
armband:: q'ep'eláx̲tel < q'áp'.
break an arm:: lekweláx̲el < lékw.
carry a packstrap or both packstraps over the shoulder(s) and under the arm(s):: sq'iwq'ewíles < q'e:yw ~ q'í:w.
carry s-th/s-o on one's arm:: s'ókw'(e)stexw < ókw'.
cross one's arms (but not fold one's arms across chest) [prob. error], (arms crossed [but not

arm (CONT'D)

folded across chest):: q'eyáweth'eláx̲el < q'ey ~ q'i.
cut one's arm:: lhets'elá:x̲el < lhíts' ~ lhí:ts'.
have something under one arm:: xixets'eláx̲el < xits' ~ xets'.
hit on the arm:: kw'eqwelá:x̲el < kw'óqw.
hold both arms (or wings) outstretched, (stretch out one's arms/wings):: tex̲eláx̲elem < tex̲.
holding a wee baby in one's arms:: xixe'át < xá'at.
holding s-o in one's arms, (holding a baby in one's arms [Elder's Group]):: xe'át < xá'at.
hold s-o in one's arms:: xá'at.
I got hard (of arm, leg, penis, etc.):: tl'x̲wòlèm < tl'éx̲w.
left arm:: sth'íkwechís < th'íkwe.
lying on one's stomach with head down on one's arms:: qiqep'eyósem < qep'.
on the arm, in the arm, on or in the wing:: =eláx̲el.
point of elbow, arm bone:: th'emeláx̲el < hth'b.txt.
put one's hands under one's arms:: xixets'eláx̲em < xits' ~ xets'.
right arm:: siyachís < éy ~ éy:, s'iyláx̲el < éy ~ éy:.
skin of the arm:: kw'elōwáx̲el < kw'eléw ~ kw'elṓw.
square, corner, arm with elbow out:: st'eláx̲el.
strawberry birthmark on the arm:: schíyeláx̲el < schí:ya.
stretch out the wings, stretch out the arm(s):: tex̲eláx̲el < tex̲.
to be arm in arm (like escorting someone), to take an arm (of someone):: s'ókw'ches < ókw'.
to wave (one's arms):: x̲élqesà:ls < x̲élqes.
waving (one's arms):: x̲ólqesà:ls < x̲élqes.

Armadillidium vulgare

class Crustacea, order Isopoda, Armadillidium vulgare:: k'ák'elha.

armband

armband:: q'ep'eláx̲tel < q'áp'.

arm in arm

to be arm in arm (like escorting someone), to take an arm (of someone):: s'ókw'ches < ókw'.

armpit :: shxw'íláx̲el.

around

around the outside of the house:: sélts'ex̲el < sél or sí(:)l.
beach in front of old Scowlitz village, the point the Harrison River goes around by Kilby's store:: Sq'iq'ewílem < q'éw ~ q'ew.
(be) turned around, turned the wrong way:: sx̲á:lts' < x̲élts'.
(circle) around the fire once and return to the start, make one circle in longhouse:: sélts' < sél or sí(:)l.
distributive, all over, all around:: =x̲ ~ =ex̲.
feeling around:: qátx̲els < qétx̲t.
go around a bend in the river, go around a turn, go around something in one's way:: q'ewílem < q'éw ~ q'ew.
go around a bend (in water):: q'éwlets ~ q'ówlets < q'éw ~ q'ew.
go around (a point, a bend, a curve, etc.) in the water, make a U-turn (in the water, could use today on land with a car):: q'ówletsem < q'éw ~ q'ew.
go around inside the longhouse counter-clockwise:: selts'elwílem < sél or sí(:)l.

around (CONT'D)

go around s-th in the water:: q'ówletst < q'éw ~ q'ew.
go over or around (hill, rock, river, etc.):: q'ál.
has come around (of a cyclic period of time):: séqsel.
hug s-o around:: qwemchíwet < qwem.
it shook (shakes itself), shaking, bobbing around:: qwá:yx̲thet < qwá:y.
location around a house, part:: =mel.
moving, (many moving around in circles, moving around in circles many times):: x̲elx̲álqem < x̲álqem.
on the side of the head, on the temples, around the ear, on the cheek:: =éla.
pass around to give away (at a dance for example):: lhít'es < lhít'.
pass it around (papers, berries, anything):: lhít'et < lhít'.
pass it around to s-o:: lhít'est < lhít'.
(perhaps) around in circles:: =qw' ~ =eqw'.
(perhaps) round, around in circles:: =kw' ~ =ekw'.
place above Yale where the Fraser River splits around a rock, island above Steamboat Island (latter just below Five-Mile Creek):: Sx̲wesálh < x̲wés.
put a rope around s-o/s-th's neck, put a leash on s-th, hang s-o:: x̲wíqw'est < x̲wíqw'.
rags wound around the legs in the cold or to protect from mosquitoes, (leggings):: q'élq'xetel < q'ál.
rolling, moving [around in circles]:: x̲álqem.
round, around:: =x̲w.
running, run[ing] around:: x̲wó:mxelem ~ xwó:mxelem ~ x̲wómxelem ~ xwómxelem < x̲wém ~ xwém.
staggering around:: x̲wex̲weló:ystem < x̲weló:y, yitá:lstem < tél ~ tá:l ~ tiy.
swivel one's hips (as in the Hawaiian hula for ex.) (shake one's bottom around):: qwayx̲élechem < qwá:y.
turn around a bend, go around a bend, turn around (to go back), turn around a corner:: q'ewqé:ylém ~ q'ewqéylém (better q'ewqí:lem) < q'éw ~ q'ew.
turn (oneself) around, make a U-turn:: ts'elqéylém < ts'el.
turn oneself around, turn (oneself) around:: x̲élts'thet < x̲élts'.
turn s-th around:: ts'elqéylt or ts'elqí:lt < ts'el.
twist s-th/s-o, turn it around, turn s-o, turn s-th (for ex. a page):: x̲élts't < x̲élts'.
twist, turn around, around in circles:: =ts' ~ =elts' ~ =á:lts'.
village on east bank of Fraser River below Siwash Creek (Aseláw), now Yale Indian Reserves 19 and 20, named because of a big rock in the area that the trail had to pass (go around), also the name of the rock:: Q'alelíktel < q'ál.

arrive

arrive, arriving, come here, have come, get here, get back, come in (in a race):: xwe'í < í.
get there, arrive there, reach there:: xwelí ~ xwlí < lí.
just came, (just arrived):: tátsel.

arrow :: ts'eqw'eláx < ts'éqw'.

arrow, gun:: sakweláx ~ sekweláx < kwél.
arrow pouch, (a quiver for arrows):: th'esélatel.
be hit (with arrow, bullet, anything shot that you've aimed), got shot, (got pierced), got poked into, got wounded (with gun or arrow):: ts'éqw'.
blunt-headed arrow:: s-hótl'eqw.
hit with an arrow accidentally:: ts'eqw'eláxw < ts'éqw'.
miss s-th (in shooting at it with arrow, spear or gun):: qwíx̲wet < qwíx̲w.
pointer to show direction (like in a trail) (could be an arrow or stick or mark in the ground):: shxwmót'estel < mót'es.
to miss a shot (an arrow, spear or gun):: qwíx̲w.

arrowhead :: t'exelá.
(perhaps) copper, (hard metal that looks like gold but isn't, maybe copper [Elders at Katz Class 10/5/76], metal found in mines and used for arrowheads [Elders Group 5/28/75], gold [EB]):: sqw'él.

arrowleaf :: sqeqewíthelh < sqáwth ~ sqá:wth.
arrowleaf, wapato, Indian potato:: xwōqw'ṓ:ls.
potato (generic), including three or four kinds of wild potato: arrowleaf or wapato, Jerusalem artichoke, blue camas, and qíqemxel (so far unidentified plant), besides post-contact domestic potato:: sqáwth ~ sqá:wth.

arthritis
it aches of arthritis:: chálh.
it's aching of arthritis:: cháchelh < chálh.

Arthropoda
probably class Arthropoda:: sth'ékw'.

artichoke
bulb or root called wild artichoke, Jerusalem artichoke:: x̲áx̲ekw'.
potato (generic), including three or four kinds of wild potato: arrowleaf or wapato, Jerusalem artichoke, blue camas, and qíqemxel (so far unidentified plant), besides post-contact domestic potato:: sqáwth ~ sqá:wth.
wild red potatoes that pigs eat, (probably Jerusalem artichoke):: sx̲éykwel.
wild red potato (grew at American Bar in the 1920's), possibly Jerusalem artichoke:: sx̲éykwel.

article
nominalizer (female present and visible or presence or proximity unspecified), demonstrative article:: the=.
nominalizer (male or gender unspecified, present and visible or presence or proximity unspecified), demonstrative article:: ta=, te=.

Aruncus sylvester:: chochkwó:les < chó:kw.

as
when (simultaneous subordinating conjunction), as:: kw'e.

Asarum caudatum:: x̲éyeslótel, th'alátel < th'á:lá ~ th'ála ~ th'á:le ~ th'ále.

Ascaphus truei
if generic includes families Ranidae and Bufonidae and may include Hyla regilla and perhaps the introduced species: Rana catesbeiana, Rana clamitans, Rana aurora aurora, Rana pretiosa pretiosa, and Ascaphus truei, if not generic then includes only members of family Ranidae and/or family Bufonidae:: wex̲és, weléx̲ < wex̲és.

ash
ashes (cinder-like), cinders (heavy and dirty), embers:: shxwiyélhtel ~ shxwyélhtel < yólh.
fine ashes floating up from a fire:: tqwó:chep < tóqweltsep.
fine white ashes:: sts'á:s ~ sts'ás.
mountain ash berries, (perhaps also) mountain ash tree:: qwíqwelh.
sparks, red hot ashes thrown out:: qw'á:ychep < qw'á:y.

ashamed

(accidentally) make s-o ashamed, insult s-o (accidentally or manage to):: xéyx̲elexw < x̲éyx̲e ~ x̲íx̲e.
ashamed of s-th:: lhístexw < lháy.
be ashamed:: x̲éyx̲e ~ x̲íx̲e.
being ashamed:: x̲ex̲éyx̲e < x̲éyx̲e ~ x̲íx̲e.
be shamed:: lháy.
feel embarrassed and shy because ashamed, be ashamed:: lhistélémét < lháy.
make s-o ashamed:: x̲éyx̲estexw < x̲éyx̲e ~ x̲íx̲e.
make s-o ashamed [happen to or accidentally or manage to]:: lháylexw < lháy.

ashamed (CONT'D)

to shame oneself [accidentally], (get) embarrassed, (become ashamed of oneself?):: x̲éyx̲elòmèt < x̲éyx̲e ~ x̲íx̲e.

ash color :: sts'á:s ~ sts'ás.

ashes)

baked (in ashes), baked (in a stove):: s'ótheqw < ótheqw.
bake s-th in ashes, bake s-th in a stove:: ótheqwt < ótheqw.
to roast potatoes in hot sand or ashes, bake in ashes, bake in stove:: ótheqw.

ashore

drift ashore:: qwélh.
pull ashore in a canoe, land a canoe:: lhà:l.

Asio otus

possibly also the following other horned owls found in the area: long-eared owl Asio otus and spotted owl Strix occidentalis:: chítmexw.

ask

ask about s-o:: petá:mes < petá:m.
ask a favor, ask pity, beseech:: th'exwstélémét < th'íxw ~ th'éxw.
(ask for a favor or pity for s-o):: th'exwstí:lmet < th'íxw ~ th'éxw.
ask for s-th[?]:: yex̲chí:met < yéx̲ch ~ yéx̲ts.
asking about s-o, asking after s-o:: pétemes < petá:m.
begging for a favor, asking for help:: th'íth'exwstélémét < th'íxw ~ th'éxw.

asleep

fall asleep:: itetlómet < ítet, léqw.
nodding (falling asleep):: létqw'estem.
numb in the foot, the foot is asleep:: xwókw'elxel < xwókw'.
sleep, go to sleep, asleep:: ítet.
sleeping, asleep:: í:tet < ítet.

asparagus:: xwelítemelh yó:le < xwelítem, yó:le (lit. white man style + cow parsnip)

aspen

poplar, Lombardy poplar (intro.), also black cottonwood and perhaps trembling aspen which may have rarely occurred on the eastern and northeastern edges of Stó:lō territory:: p'elp'álq'emá:lews ~ p'elp'àlq'emá:lews < p'álq'em.

aspen (CONT'D)
"poplar", probably includes black cottonwood and trembling aspen (though trembling aspen is rare in Upriver Halq'eméylem territory):: th'estíyelhp < th'ís, th'ex̲tíyelhp < th'éx̲.

ass
butt, ass, rump, buttocks:: slhél:éts ~ slhél:ets ~ slhéléts ~ slhélets < lhél.
(have a) sloppy ass:: slhelp'íwel < lhél.
stick it up someone's rump:: t'ekwíwet < t'ékw.
(stuck in the rectum), stuck in the ass:: st'ekwíwel < t'ékw.

asthma
roots (resembling eyes looking at you) of a kind of plant that's good for asthma:: qelémes < qélém ~ qél:ém.

astonish
be surprised, astonished:: lewálh.

astride
be astride, be sitting on:: sts'ets'á < ts'á:.
they came on (top of):: ch'alech'á (~ ts'alets'á) < ts'á:.

as usual
as usual, this time, now, the first time:: yalh.

at
at home, be living (somewhere), stay:: tl'eláxw ~ tl'láxw < tl'élexw.
be in, in, be on, on, be at, at, before (an audience), (untranslated):: lí ~ li.
(place, location), where s-o is at:: shxwlí.
where it's at, where it's from:: shxwlí < lí ~ li.

Atchelitz
Atchelitz Creek, an old Chilliwack River channel:: Áthelets < áthelets.
Atchelitz village and now Chilliwack Indian reserve #8:: Áthelets < áthelets.

Atchelitz Creek
an old course of Atchelitz Creek:: (Yeqyeqámen).
a tributary of Atchelitz Creek:: Kwōkwa'áltem ?.
village site (burned) on Atchelitz Creek:: Syéqw < yéqw.

attach
put s-th on (of a design on a dress, of a shirt, shoes, etc.), attach it, stick it on, fasten it:: tl'álx < tl'ál.
to be attached, to be fixed or fastened, be put on:: stl'átl'el < tl'ál.

attempt
make an attempt (to do something difficult, like running rapids in a canoe, mountain-climbing, winning a game, etc.), give it a try:: t'óthet < t'á.
try it, attempt it:: t'át ~ t'á:t < t'á.

attention
pay attention to s-o:: xwe'íwelmet.

auger

a borer, an auger:: sxoxwí:ls < xó:l.
borer to make holes, auger:: sqweqwá:ls ~ shxwqweqwá:ls < qwá.

augmentative

comparative or augmentative:: =R1= or =C1e=.
plural or augmentative:: R11= or C1V1=.

August

August run spring salmon that go up Silver Creek (near Hope):: shxwōqw'ṓ:lh.
coho salmon time, August to September:: temkwṓxweth < kwṓxweth.
July to August, (big spring salmon time):: temth'oló:lh < sth'olólh.
sockeye moon, month to get sockeye salmon (begins with first quarter after black moon in July, lasts into August), July to August, (June to July [Jenness: WS]):: temthéqi < sthéqi ~ sthéqey.

aunt

parent's cousin, parent's sibling, uncle, aunt:: shxwemlí:kw.
uncle, aunt:: kwiyó:s.
uncles (all of them), aunts (all of them):: sxwemlá:lekw < shxwemlí:kw.
uncle's wife, aunt's husband, parent's sibling's spouse, uncle by marriage, aunt by marriage:: xchápth ~ schápth.

aunt's husband

uncle's wife, aunt's husband, parent's sibling's spouse, uncle by marriage, aunt by marriage:: xchápth ~ schápth.

Auricularia

Fomes sp. including Fomes applanatus and probably others, possibly Polyporus sp., possibly Ganoderma sp., prob. also jelly fungi of Tremella and maybe Auricularia and Dacrymyces species, especially Tremella mesenterica (Yellow trembler) which is abundant only on the red alder and is reddish-orange matching the color, translucence and shape of those eaten by some of the Stó:lō elders, the jelly fungi could possibly have a different name from the bracket fungus:: s'ómó:qwes.

automobile

automobile, car:: tox̱wemíwel < tóx̱w, xwixwekw'elátsem < xwókw' ~ xwekw'ó.
car, automobile:: kyó.
high-bow canoe, high-bow river canoe, streetcar, tram, taxi, car, automobile:: xwókw'eletsem < xwókw' ~ xwekw'ó.

autumn

autumn, fall (season):: temhilálxw < híl.

auxiliary

(auxiliary verb), ([may also imply] here):: í.

avalanche lily

blue camas, yellow dog-tooth violet = yellow avalanche lily:: sk'ámets ~ sk'ámeth.

Avena fatua

both Avena sativa and Avena fatua:: ṓts.

Avena sativa
both Avena sativa and Avena fatua:: ő̄ts.

avens
big-leaved avens:: th'ith'kwimelálews, th'ith'kwimelálews < th'íkw, xwókw'eltel < xwókw'.

avocado:: thós sth'emíwel sékwluwi < thi, th'em, sékwluwi
(lit. big round + pit + soft smooth texture)

awake
be awake:: shxwexwí < xwíy ~ x í.
wide-awake:: shxwixwiyós or shxwiyxwiyós < xwíy ~ x í.

aware
become aware (said for ex. of a child about three years or so, or of realizing how something is done), come to one's senses, sober up:: p'élh.

away
(an Indian doctor or shaman) working, curing, chasing the bad things away:: lhálhewels < lhá:w.
be on the other side of, be on the side facing away:: sle'ólwelh < le'á.
be tucked away, put away so well you can't find it, be solid:: slá ~ selá ~ slá: (probably).
be watchful, be facing away:: sle'ó:les < le'á.
carried away:: títiyex̱w < tíyex̱w, tíyex̱w.
elope, run away together:: chó:mtel < chó:m.
everybody put away (fishing gear, canoe and) paddles (for winter), put away each other's paddles [and canoes and gear] for winter:: xets'ő̄:westel < xits' ~ xets'.
get away, leave, (perhaps just) away:: á:yel < á:y.
get carried away and sleepy from eating too rich food:: melmelő̄ws < mál ~ mél.
go away (as away from the fire):: tsx̱éylém or tsx̱ílém.
go away from the river:: chó:m.
leave s-o, leave s-th, go away from s-o/s-th, abandon s-o, leave s-o behind:: áyeles < á:y.
(one person) puts away his paddles (and canoe and gear for winter):: xets'ő̄:wes < xits' ~ xets'.
part away from the river, side away from the river:: chóleqwmel < chá:l or chó:l.
preserved fish, preserved meat, dried fish, dried meat (usually fish), smoked salmon, wind-dried salmon (old word), what is stored away, what is put away:: sq'éyle.
put away, (it has been put away):: q'éylòm.
put s-th away, save s-th (food for ex.):: qéylemt ~ qé:ylemt < qéylem ~ qé:ylem ~ qí(:)lem.
run away:: lhá:w.
running away:: tl'ítl'ew < tl'í:w.
s-o has been put away (in grave-house or buried), he's/she's been buried:: qéylemtem ~ qé:ylemtem < qéylem ~ qé:ylem ~ qí(:)lem.
s-o/s-th has been put away:: qéylemtem ~ qé:ylemtem < qéylem ~ qé:ylem ~ qí(:)lem.
store away one's paddles:: xets'ő̄wesem < xits' ~ xets'.
store it away (wedged-in up off ground), put s-th away for winter, stow s-th away:: xítse't < xits' ~ xets'.
take it off (of a table for example), take it away (from something), take it off (of eyeglasses, of skin off an animal), take s-o off/away (from something), take s-th out (a tooth for ex.):: máx < má ~ má'-.
to escape (as an animal from a trap), got away from something that trapped a person or

away (CONT'D)

animal:: tl'ewlómét ~ tl'ōwlómét < tl'í:w.
to escape (of a man or a slave), run away:: tl'í:w.
[travelling along] running away:: yitl'ítl'ew < tl'í:w.
turn away, turn one's face away:: qelésem < qél.
turn one's face, (turn one's body away [IHTTC]):: ts'ólesem ~ ts'ólésem < ts'el.

away from
away from the shore, toward the river:: chúchu ~ chúwchuw ~ chéwchew < cháchew ~ cháchu.
from away from the river:: telchó:leqwtel < chá:l or chó:l.
in the backwoods, toward the woods, away from the river, in the bush:: chó:leqw < chá:l or chó:l.

awhile
hurt s-o/s-th [for awhile, accidentally]:: x̲elhláxw < x̲élh.

awl
awl (any kind):: stl'eqówtel.

axe
big axe, double-bladed heavy axe:: kw'óqweletstel ~ kw'óqwletstel < kw'óqw.
chop one's foot (with axe), [get chopped on the foot (with axe)]:: t'émxel < t'ém.
chop wood (with an axe), split wood:: th'iqw'élchep or th'iyqw'éltsep < th'íyeqw'.
little hatchet, little axe:: kw'qwém < kw'óqw.

Aythya valisineria:: lamélwelh.

Aythys affinis:: x̲élq'eqs.

Ay-wa-wis
village at Union Bar, now also Hope Indian Reserve #5 (#15 in Duff 1952), Ay-wa-wis:: Iwówes.

baby :: sqá:qele ~ sqáqele < sqá:q.
a swing, a little treadle they swing the babies on:: q'éyt'o ~ q'éyt'e.
baby basket, cradle basket, basketry cradle:: p'ó:th'es ~ p'óth'es.
baby basket rock just below main bay and sand bar of Lexwtl'átl'ekw'em (Klaklacum, Indian Reserve #12, first village and reserve south of American Creek), on the west side of the Fraser River:: Lexwp'oth'esála ~ Xwp'oth'esála < p'ó:th'es ~ p'óth'es.
baby bottle:: sqemó'álá < qemó:.
baby chicks:: chelichkelsó:llh < chékel.
baby elk, (young elk):: q'oyíyetsó:llh < q'oyíyets or q'oyí:ts.
baby frog, probably also tadpole:: pipehó:mó:llh < peh or pó(:)h.
baby horse:: steqiwó:llh < stiqíw.
baby (kin), child (kin) (up to about eigit years old):: mímele < méle ~ mél:a.
baby sockeye salmon:: skwíkwexel.
baby wren, little or young wren:: t'át'emiya < t'ámiya.
buckskin straps for tying a baby in its cradle or basket:: yémqetel < yém ~ yem.
child (post-baby to pre-adolescent), child (under 12), (young [BJ]):: stl'ítl'eqelh ~ stl'í:tl'eqelh.
child, young, baby:: =ílh ~ =íylh ~ =éylh ~ =elh ~ =á(:)ylh.

baby (CONT'D)

deformed baby:: sxaxe'áylh < xáxe, t'ámiya.
fawn, baby deer:: st'ít'ele < st'él'e.
giving birth, having a child, having a baby:: tsméla < méle ~ mél:a.
have given birth, already had a child, had a baby, (delivered):: sémele < méle ~ mél:a.
hermaphrodite (person with organs of both sexes), hermaphrodite baby:: t'ámiya.
holding a wee baby in one's arms:: xixe'át < xá'at.
holding s-o in one's arms, (holding a baby in one's arms [Elder's Group]):: xe'át < xá'at.
hush a baby from crying, (hush s-o (a baby) from crying):: ch'exwí:lt < ts'áxw.
last baby (youngest baby), the last-born, a child cranky and jealous of an expected brother or sister:: óqw'a < óqw'.
new dancer (new spirit-dancer), (new) baby (in spirit-dancing):: xawsó:lh < xá:ws.
pacify a baby, pacify it (a baby), sing or hum to a baby to quiet it, sing to it (a zaby), (sing a lullaby to it):: tl'ó:t.
rabbit: snowshoe/varying hare, now probably also eastern cottontail rabbit (introduced), (baby rabbit, small rabbit or hare [Elders Group]):: sqíqewàth < sqewáth.
smallest peak just below Mount Cheam (on left of Mt. Cheam looking south), Lhílheqey's (Mt. Cheam's) baby (located about where her breast would be on the left hand side facing her):: Óyewòt.
soft spot on (top of) a baby's head, fontanel:: sqe'éleqw < qí: ~ qí'.
swing for baby cradle:: séqtel < seqíws ~ seqí:ws.
time of the baby sockeye's coming, early spring (usually April), April moon:: temkwíkwexel.
water pygmies, water baby:: s'ó:lmexw.
younger deer, baby horse, younger cow, fawn, colt, calf:: st'él'e.

babysit

babysitter (for kids, etc.):: xólhemìlh ~ xòlhemí:lh < xólh.
babysitter (for new spirit-dancers), any of the workers who help in initiating a spirit-dancer, (initiator or helper of spirit-dancers):: xólhemìlh ~ xòlhemí:lh < xólh.
babysitting:: xolhemílh < xólh.
baby-sitting, the one baby-sitting, baby-sitter:: á:lmelh < álmelh.
to baby-sit one's own children:: álmelh.
to babysit someone else's kids (children):: xolhmílh < xólh.

back

arrive, arriving, come here, have come, get here, get back, come in (in a race):: xwe'í < í.
back end of a house (inside or outside), back part of a house:: stselqwáxel < chá:l or chó:l.
backing up:: héyethet ~ héythet < yóthet.
back (of a tree) (the side away from the rising sun):: óqwelets.
back of the body, the whole back:: óqwelets.
(be) with one's back towards something or someone:: schewíts.
break one's spine, break one's back, have a humpback/hunchback:: lekwewíts < lékw.
bringing it back:: q'éyq'elstexw < q'ó:lthet.
bring s-o/s-th back:: ámeq't.
carrying on one's back, packing on one's back:: chmà:m < chám.
carry s-th on one's back, pack s-th on one's back:: chámet < chám.
drifting backwards in two canoes with net between to catch sturgeon, (drift-netting), backing up (of canoe, train):: tewláts.
fight back:: xwtíyches < tiy.
get hit on the back:: xwelemṓwelh ~ xwlemṓwelh, xwelemṓwelh ~ xwlemṓwelh < ló:m ~ lóm.
get hunchbacked:: sqwómetsel < qwó:m ~ qwóm ~ qwem.

back (CONT'D)

give it back, bring it back, return s-th:: q'élstexw < q'ó:lthet.
have one's hands behind one's back:: sq'eth'ewíts ~ sq'eth'ōwíts < q'áth'.
hit on the back:: kw'qwewíts < kw'óqw.
hunchback, humpback, lump on the back:: skwómàtsel (sqwómàtsel) < qwó:m ~ qwóm ~ qwem.
(in) back of a house:: tselqwáx̱el < chá:l or chó:l.
in back of a house, behind a house:: tselqwáx̱elmel < chá:l or chó:l.
it got smashed in the back end or rear end:: téslatstem < tós.
lie down on one's back:: kw'aqálém < kw'e'í ~ kw"í ~ kw'í.
lie on one's back, on his back:: kw'e'íyeqel ~ kw'e'íqel < kw'e'í ~ kw"í ~ kw'í.
lying on one's back:: kw'e'í:qel < kw'e'í ~ kw"í ~ kw'í.
marked on the back:: x̱ep'ewíts < x̱éyp'.
neck, (back of head and back of neck [EB], nape of the neck [Elders Group 5/3/78]):: tépsem.
on the back:: =ewíts ~ =íts ~ =ích ~ =ech.
on the back of the head, back of the neck:: =épsem.
pack on one's back, carry on one's back:: chámem < chám.
piggy-back:: méwiya.
put one's hands behind one's back:: q'eth'ōwítsem < q'áth'.
put one's head back (tilt one's face up):: q'óx̱esem.
return, come back, go back:: q'ó:lthet.
revive s-o, bring s-o back to life, heal s-o, (EB) give s-o medicine to make him better?:: á:yelexwt < áylexw ~ áyelexw.
save s-o, (EB) bring s-o back to life:: á:yelexwlexw < áylexw ~ áyelexw.
skin of the back:: kw'elōwíts < kw'eléw ~ kw'elṓw.
sloppy back:: slhellhélp'elets < lhél.
sprain the back:: ts'lhéqw'ewíts < ts'lhóqw'.
striped on back:: sx̱eyx̱ep'ewíts ~ sx̱eyx̱ep'ōwíts < x̱éyp'.
the back (on the body), (lower back [Deming]):: slhéq'ōwelh < lheq'át ~ lhq'á:t.
to back up (walk or move backwards):: yóthet.
to the back (near the wall), on the inside (on a bed toward the wall):: lhelhá:l.
travelling by and packing on his back (might be said of a passer-by):: iychmà:m ~ iytsmà:m < chám.
turn back into a quiet slough from the river, be going into a slough from the river:: ts'élexw < ts'el.
your back is sprained:: xwt'ó:welh < t'ó.

back and forth

back and forth, (go or come back and forth):: q'elq'í:lthet ~ q'elq'éylthet < q'ó:lthet.

backbone

backbone (of human or other creatures), spine (human or other creature):: x̱ekw'ólesewíts < x̱ekw'óles.
cord, muscle, tendon, nerve cord by backbone:: tl'e'ímél ~ tl'e'í:mel.
dried fish backbone (with meat left on it):: sx̱éwe.
fish backbone (not dried), (backbone of any creature [Elders Group 7/27/75]):: x̱ekw'óles.
(someone's) spine, (someone's) backbone:: th'omewích ~ th'ó:bewíts < sth'ó:m.
the spine, the backbone:: shxwth'omewíts < sth'ó:m.

back up

drifting backwards in two canoes with net between to catch sturgeon, (drift-netting),

back up (CONT'D)

backing up (of canoe, train):: tewláts.

backward

(be) tight, (leaning backwards [EB]):: sq'áq'eth' < q'áth'.
drifting backwards in two canoes with net between to catch sturgeon, (drift-netting), backing up (of canoe, train):: tewláts.
to back up (walk or move backwards):: yóthet.

backwater

slough, backwater, ((also) eddy [AC]):: sts'élexw < ts'el.

backwoods

in the backwoods, toward the woods, away from the river, in the bush:: chó:leqw < chá:l or chó:l.
(maybe) the backwoods side:: stselqwóthel < chá:l or chó:l.

(bad) :: áx̲ ~ yáx̲.

bad-looking (of log or board not of a person), rough:: qelímó:les < qél.
bad morning breath:: qeléqep látelh slhákw'em < qél.
bad-smelling:: xwóxweqw'em.
be bad (of water, person, anything), be dirty (of house, clothes, person, etc.):: qél.
be naughty, be bad (a menace) (but not quite as bad as qél):: qíqel < qél.
dirty (weather), bad weather, storm:: qél:em ~ qél:ém or leqél:e(´)m < qél.
get a spooky or spooked feeling, afraid that bad spirits are around, get spooked, fear something behind:: x̲éysel.
getting spooked, being afraid that bad spirits are around, spooky feeling:: x̲éyx̲esel < x̲éysel.
have a bad smell:: qeléqep < qél.
it smells, give off a smell, smell bad:: hóqwem < hóqw.
look bad, look mean:: qelóméx < qél.
pessimist, a person whose thoughts are always bad:: wiyóth kwsu qéls te sqwálewels te lólets'e < wiyóth.
said to a child of crawling age to teach him something is bad:: yax̲ ~ áx̲.
(said when something smells bad):: éxw.
smell bad, (have a) bad fragrance, (have a) bad smell:: qéleqep < qél.
strong smell, bad stink, smell that can't be located:: simáléqep < éy ~ éy:.
taste bad:: qéleqep < qél.
(this cry of a bluejay [Steller's jay] warns you of bad news):: chéke chéke chéke chéke.
to scowl, make a bad face or a scowl:: x̲eywésem or x̲éywésem < x̲éywel.
turn bad, (get) spoiled (of clothes for ex.), (get) dirty:: qelqéyl or qelqí:l < qél.
turn bad in smell, smells like it's turned bad:: qelqéyláléqep < qél.

badger

a spirit power of a kw'őxweqs dancer, (perhaps wolverine or badger spirit power):: sqoyép < sqoyép.
badger or wolverine:: melmélkw'es sqoyép < sqoyép.
unidentified animal with marks on its face, perhaps badger or wolverine:: sqoyép.
yellow badger, possibly wolverine:: sqoyép ~ melmélkw'es sqoyép.

badminton

a fairly flat clearing on a mountain in Morris Valley where they used to play ts'its'eqweló:l or Indian badminton:: Ts'éqwela ~ Th'éqwela < ts'éqw ~ th'éqw.

bag

container for left-overs taken home from feast, doggie bag:: meq'ethále < méq'.
skunk's stink bag, skunk's stink sac:: spú'amal ~ spú'emel < pú'.
skunk's stink bag (stink sac):: skwukwtisláts.
suitcase (Deming), luggage (Deming), clothing container, clothes bag, trunk (for clothes), etc.:: áwkw'emálá < á:wkw'.

bagel

donut, bagel:: sqweqwá seplíl < seplíl ~ seplí:l.

bag net

bag net, sack net:: lesák swéltel < swéltel.
to bag net, to sack net, to still-dip with two canoes:: thqá:lem.

bail

a bailer, canoe bailer:: lhéltel < lhí:lt ~ lhílt.
bail, (bail s-th):: lhí:lt ~ lhílt.
bailing:: lhalhí:lt < lhí:lt ~ lhílt.
bailing (a canoe, etc.), bail oneself:: lhí:lthet ~ lhílthet < lhí:lt ~ lhílt.

bait

bait (for fishing):: má:la ~ má:le.
bait (for trapline):: má:la ~ má:le.
baiting s-th (fish-line):: mamá:lat < má:la ~ má:le.
baiting s-th (trap):: mamá:lat < má:la ~ má:le.
bait it for s-o:: má:lalht < má:la ~ má:le.
bait s-th (a trap for animals or birds):: má:lat < má:la ~ má:le.
bait s-th (fish-line, fish-hook, fish-trap):: má:lat < má:la ~ má:le.
fishing basket, bait basket:: shxwmálahá:lá < má:la ~ má:le.

bake

baked (in ashes), baked (in a stove):: s'ótheqw < ótheqw.
bakery:: qw'elemáwtxw < qw'él.
bake s-th in ashes, bake s-th in a stove:: ótheqwt < ótheqw.
bake underground, (steam-cook underground, cook in a steam-pit):: qetás < qá:t.
baking (bread esp.):: thá:yém < thíy.
baking over an open fire, roasting over an open fire, barbecuing, cooking in an oven:: qw'eqw'élém < qw'él.
baking underground:: qétes < qá:t.
barbecue, bake (meat, vegetables, etc.) in open fire, bake over fire, roast over open fire, bake under hot sand, bake in oven, cook in oven, (boiled down (as jam) [CT, HT]):: qw'élém < qw'él.
barbecued food, (salmon bake [Deming]):: sqw'él:ém < qw'él.
barbecued, roasted, (baked (in an oven) [DC]):: s=qw'elém < qw'él.
roast potatoes, baked potatoes:: s'ótheqw < ótheqw.
stuff steam-cooked underground, what is baked underground:: sqetás < qá:t.
to bake (bread, other food):: thíyém < thíy.
to roast potatoes in hot sand or ashes, bake in ashes, bake in stove:: ótheqw.

baked potato:: s'ótheqw < ótheqw (lit. something + baked)

Baker

Mount Baker:: Kwelxá:lxw < kwél.

bakery

bakery:: qw'elemáwtxw < qw'él.

Balaenoptera borealis

perhaps generic, most likely includes all local balleen whales, i.e., suborder Mysticeti, especially Balaenoptera physalus and Megaptera novaeangliae, possibly Eschrichtius glaucus, Balaenoptera borealis, Balaenoptera acutorostrata, Sibbaldus musculus, Eubalaena sieboldi, could include the following toothed whales (suborder Odontoceti): Physeter catodon, possibly Berardius bairdi, Mesoplodon stejnegeri, Ziphius cavirostrus:: qwél:és ~ qwélés.

Balaenoptera physalus

perhaps generic, most likely includes all local balleen whales, i.e., suborder Mysticeti, especially Balaenoptera physalus and Megaptera novaeangliae, possibly Eschrichtius glaucus, Balaenoptera borealis, Balaenoptera acutorostrata, Sibbaldus musculus, Eubalaena sieboldi, could include the following toothed whales (suborder Odontoceti): Physeter catodon, possibly Berardius bairdi, Mesoplodon stejnegeri, Ziphius cavirostrus:: qwél:és ~ qwélés.

balance

slip off (one's feet, hands, bottom), lose balance:: x̲wlhép.
slip off with a foot, lose balance [on feet]:: x̲wlhépxel < x̲wlhép.
slip with both feet, lose balance on both feet:: x̲welhx̲wélhepxel < x̲wlhép.

bald

bald-headed:: th'óqweleqw.
bald rock, bare rock:: ts'qó:ls.
(be) bald-headed:: sth'ó:qweleqw < th'óqweleqw.

bald eagle

bald eagle (mature with white head):: sp'óq'es < p'éq'.
immature bald eagle:: skw'álx̲.

baldpate

widgeon (duck), American widgeon or baldpate, probably also the European widgeon, (pintail duck [BJ]):: sése.

ball

(be) rolled up in a ball (twine, yarn, etc.):: sqw'ómx̲wes < qw'ómx̲w.
five spherical objects, five fruit, five rocks, five balls (five fruit in a group (as they grow on a plant) [AD]):: lhq'atsesóls < lheq'át ~ lhq'á:t.
roll s-th up in a ball:: qw'ómx̲west < qw'ómx̲w.
roughly spherical object(s), ball:: =ó:ls.
small balls of snow on one's feet:: qwelqwélxel < qwélxel.
(spherical), round (of ball, apple, potato, rock, full moon, but not of a pear):: xelkw'ó:ls < xél.

balleen

whale (perhaps generic), could include the following balleen whales: common finback whale, humpback whale, possibly gray whale, Sei/Pollack whale, Minke whale, blue whale, Pacific right

balleen (CONT'D)

whale, could include the following toothed whales: sperm whale, poss. Baird beaked whale, Stejneger beaked whale, Cuvier whale:: qwél:és ~ qwélés.

balsam fir

balsam fir (has sweet sap or cambium, grows at higher altitudes, called larch by some, "balsam" is a popular name for trees of the genus Abies), from a sample taken prob. subalpine fir, if sample is mistaken poss. Pacific silver fir or grand fir, if the term balsam is mistaken too, poss. a variety of Douglas fir:: q'et'emá:yelhp < q'át'em.

banana:: pelále

banana bread:: pelále seplíl < pelále, seplíl (lit. banana + bread)

band

armband:: q'ep'eláx̲tel < q'áp'.
headband, headband made out of cedar bark woven by widow or widower when mourning:: qítes ~ qéytes < qít.
new spirit dancer's headband:: qítes ~ qéytes < qít.
waistband of a skirt:: qéttel < qít.
woven headband of packstrap, tumpline:: q'sí:ltel < q'ey ~ q'i.

baneberry

short unidentified plant, about 3 ft. tall with red berries like a short mountain ash, the berries are bitter but the plant is used as medicine, possibly red baneberry:: í:lwelh.

bang

make a banging sound:: kwótx̲wem ~ kwótxwem.
[make a bang, make a sudden hard thump sound]:: kw'péx̲w.
(make the) sound of a spank on a bottom, (fall down with a bang [Elders Group 5/19/76]):: welhéq'.

bank

a river bank caving in:: péqweles < péqw.
bank (money house, money building):: tale'áwtxw < tá:le ~ tále.
broken off in pieces (like a river-bank):: peqwpéqw < péqw.
Katz river-bank, Ruby Creek settlement, village on north bank of Fraser River just below (west of) the mouth of Ruby Creek:: Spópetes < pó:t.
riverbank, bank of a river:: semlóthel.
steep drop-off, a drop-off, very steep slope, steep shore, steep riverbank, a slide:: x̲éylés.
the whole riverbank on the CPR (west) side of the Fraser River just south of Strawberry Island and just north of Peqwchṓ:lthel:: Selch'éle < sél or sí(:)l.

Bar

a hunter turned to stone now located below Hemhémetheqw near Hill's Bar on the east bank of the Fraser River:: Tewít < tewít.
a little bay in the Fraser River a quarter mile east of Iwówes (Union Bar, Aywawwis):: Qíqemqèmèl < qém:el.
a rock shaped like a dog on the east shore of the Fraser River near Hill's Bar and below Tewít (a rock shaped like a human hunter):: Sqwemá:y (?) < qwem.
a turn in the Fraser River on the CPR (northwest) side two miles east of American Bar, Texas Bar bend in the Fraser River:: Sq'ewílem < q'éw ~ q'ew.

Bar (CONT'D)

elk (or) moose turned to stone in the Fraser River by Hill's Bar:: Q'oyíyets ~ Q'oyí:ts < q'oyíyets or q'oyí:ts.
flat rocks (bedrock) with holes at Hill's Bar where they used to make smótheqw (prepared fish oil) from sockeye heads:: Hemhémetheqw < mótheqw or metheqw.
Hill's Bar:: Qwíth'qweth'iyósem < qwéth'.
Hill's Bar (a stretch of shoreline between Yale and Hope, on the east side of the Fraser river):: Qw'elóqw' < qw'él.
Hill's Bar (between Yale and Hope), Fraser River where it goes over Hill's Bar on the CN (east) side:: Qw'áléts.
Mill Creek (at American Bar), Puckat Creek on map also:: Peqwchő:lthel Stótelō < péqw.
spear-shaped rock on beach on the Fraser near Hill's Bar:: Tá:lh < tá:lh.
village at American Bar, village on west bank of Fraser River at American Creek, American Bar Reserve:: Peqwchő:lthel ~ Peqwechő:lthel < péqw.

bar

a slough on Harrison River north side by the mouth of Chehalis River which has a knee-shaped sandbar at its mouth, this is the next slough above (upriver from) Meth'á:lmexwem:: Q'iq'ewetó:lthel < q'éw ~ q'ew.
pry s-th, lock s-th (the Indian way/barred/wedged), pry s-th up, lever it up:: wáth'et < wáth'.
sand bar:: syí:ts'emílep < syí:ts'em.

barbecue

baking over an open fire, roasting over an open fire, barbecuing, cooking in an oven:: qw'eqw'élém < qw'él.
barbecue, bake (meat, vegetables, etc.) in open fire, bake over fire, roast over open fire, bake under hot sand, bake in oven, cook in oven, (boiled down (as jam) [CT, HT]):: qw'élém < qw'él.
barbecued fish head:: x̲ots'oyíqw.
barbecued food, (salmon bake [Deming]):: sqw'él:ém < qw'él.
barbecued, roasted, (baked (in an oven) [DC]):: s=qw'elém < qw'él.
barbecue stick, cooking stick (split stick for barbecuing salmon),:: pí:kwel.
barbecue sticks, (split roasting stick):: qw'éltel < qw'él.

bare

bald rock, bare rock:: ts'qó:ls.
flat smooth and bare rock, a [rock] bluff, a bluff (straight up):: x̲eq'át < x̲eq'.
(have a) bare foot:: semáxel < má ~ má'-.

Bare Bluffs

Bare Bluffs, a steep slope on the west side of Harrison Lake:: Lhó:leqwet.

bark

bark at s-o/s-th:: tl'éwt < tl'éw.
bark house:: sokw'emáwtxw < sókw'.
barking:: tl'áwels < tl'éw.
barking a lot, lots of barking:: tl'éwtl'ewels < tl'éw.
bark (of any tree):: p'alyí:ws ~ p'alyíws ~ p'elyíws.
bark (of tree, bush, etc.):: p'elyú:s ~ p'alyú:s or p'elyíws ~ p'alyíws.
bark, wood, plant:: =á:y ~ =ey ~ =iy.
blackened bitter cherry bark:: pélel.
break up s-th by crumpling, crush it up, rub it together fast (to soften or clean), rub it to

bark (CONT'D)

soften it (of plants, etc.), fluff it (inner cedar bark to soften it):: yékw'et < yókw' ~ yóqw'.
cedar bark mat:: slhqw'á:y < lhéqw'.
cedar bark skirt:: lhqw'áy < lhéqw', sèqw'emí:ws < síqw'em.
cherry bark (for baskets):: st'elém < t'elém.
cottonwood bark driftwood (it was used to carve toy canoes), cottonwood driftwood used for carving toy canoes:: qwémélép ~ qwemélep.
fir bark:: slá:y < lá:y.
get dust or bark in both eyes:: thq'elq'ó:les < théq'.
get dust or bark in one eye:: thq'ó:les < théq'.
headband, headband made out of cedar bark woven by widow or widower when mourning:: qítes ~ qéytes < qít.
inner cedar bark:: slewí < léw.
inner cedar bark (maybe error), (birch bark [AHTTC]):: sèqw'emí:ws < síqw'em.
new spirit-dancer's head-dress or [cedar-bark] hat:: sx̲wóyéleqws te x̲awsólkwlh < sx̲wóyéleqw.
outer cedar bark:: sókw'em < sókw'.
peel bark (as structured activity):: lheqw'á:ls < lhéqw'.
peel cedar bark:: síqw'em.
peeling bark:: lhólheqw'els < lhéqw'.
peel it (bark off a tree), bark it, (de-bark it), pull itdown (of bark, board, etc.), pull it up (of bark, board):: lheqw'ó:t < lhéqw'.
plane it (with a plane), trim it, taper it (about wood, like slats or roots for baskets, poles for houseposts/totem poles, paddles), taper it (with knife or plane), peel it (a fruit, etc.), whittle it, strip or peel bark off of it, scrape it (of carrots), (carve it, peel it [AC]):: xípet < xíp.
prickly (from fir bark, wool, or something one is allergic to), irritant, have an allergic reaction (to fir powder or cedar bark):: th'íth'ekwem < th'íkw.
rough (of wood), lumpy (of ground, bark, etc.):: smelhmélhqw.
skin or bark pulls off:: síkw'em < síkw'.
tinder, material used to start a fire with (fine dried cedar bark):: syeqwlhá:ltel < yéqw.
tiny slivers of fir bark, fir bark powder:: sth'íkwem < th'íkw.
to bark:: tl'ewéls < tl'éw.

bark-peeler

bark-peeler:: lhéqw'ewsà:ls < lhéqw'.

bark shield for fire

torch (made from pitch) (SJ and MV), (bark shield for fire (Elders Group 3/6/78)):: swáts'et.

barn

barn, (hay house, grass building):: sox̲weláwtxw < só:x̲wel ~ sóx̲wel.

barrel

barrel, probably also tub:: q'eyós < q'ey ~ q'i.

base

base of a tree:: shxw'étselets < áthelets.
base of mountain or something high:: shxw'étselets < áthelets.
hull of berry (inside left after the berry is picked), "stem" or base of berry left after the berry is picked:: th'ép'oyeqw ~ th'épeyeqw.

basin

basin lake near top of Cheam Peak:: Xwoqwsemó:leqw.

basket

a lot of baskets:: sá:letel ~ sá:ltel < sí:tel ~ sítel.
baby basket, cradle basket, basketry cradle:: p'ó:th'es ~ p'óth'es.
baby basket rock just below main bay and sand bar of Lexwtl'átl'ekw'em (Klaklacum, Indian Reserve #12, first village and reserve south of American Creek), on the west side of the Fraser River:: Lexwp'oth'esála ~ Xwp'oth'esála < p'ó:th'es ~ p'óth'es.
basket (any kind):: sí:tel ~ sítel.
baskets:: sá'eltel < sí:tel ~ sítel.
basket-weaving:: sch'eqw'ṓwelh < ts'éqw'.
berry-basket:: sth'ímàlà ~ sth'ímà:la < sth'í:m ~ sth'ì:m.
buckskin straps for tying a baby in its cradle or basket:: yémqetel < yém ~ yem.
buckskin straps, lid for berry basket:: yémqetel < yém ~ yem.
cedar sapling basket:: tl'pát.
cedar slat basket, cedar sapling basket:: th'ṓwex̲ ~ th'ṓwéx̲.
cherry bark (for baskets):: st'elém < t'elém.
clothes basket:: shxw'awkw'ála < á:wkw'.
coiled bottom of a basket before the sides are on:: skwélets < kwél.
design on basket:: sx̲éles < x̲él ~ x̲é:yl ~ x̲í:l
designs on basket, basket designs:: sx̲elx̲éles < x̲él ~ x̲é:yl ~ x̲í:l
face of a basket, (design on a basket):: =ó:s ~ =ós ~ =es.
fine cedar root strips for baskets:: shxwth'á:lhtel.
fishing basket, bait basket:: shxwmálahá:lá < má:la ~ má:le.
grass scalded and bleached white for basketry imbrication (designs), sometimes called white straw grass, probably blue-joint reed-grass:: th'á:x̲ey ~ th'áx̲ey < th'áx̲.
little basket:: sí:stel < sí:tel ~ sítel.
little baskets:: selístel < sí:tel ~ sítel.
little berry basket:: kw'álhem, lí:latses < elíle, skw'álhem < kw'élh.
making a basket, (weaving a cedar root basket):: th'éqw'ōwelh ~ (probably ts'éqw'ōwelh) < ts'éqw'.
plane it (with a plane), trim it, taper it (about wood, like slats or roots for baskets, poles for houseposts/totem poles, paddles), taper it (with knife or plane), peel it (a fruit, etc.), whittle it, strip or peel bark off of it, scrape it (of carrots), (carve it, peel it [AC]):: xípet < xíp.
soapberry basket, Indian ice-cream basket:: sx̲wōsemálá < sx̲wōsem ~ sx̲wṓ:sem ~ sx̲ṓ(:)sem.
stink-egg basket, stink salmon egg basket:: kw'ōle'álá < kw'ṓ:la ~ kw'ú:la.
storage basket (for oil, fruit, clothes), burial basket for twins, round basket (any size, smaller at top), clay jug (to store oil or fruit):: skwá:m ~ skwám < kwá:m ~ kwám.
throw s-o down hard (like a wrestler), tap s-th (a container's bottom) [hard] on something to make the contents settle (like berry basket):: th'esét ~ th'sét < th'és.
to weave a cedar root basket:: ts'eqw'ṓ:welh ~ ts'eqw'ṓwelh ~ ch'eqw'ṓwelh < ts'éqw'.
water basket:: shxwqó:m < qó:.
wide cedar root strips for baskets:: yemáwéstel < yém ~ yem.
wide cedar (sapling) strips or slats from young cedar trunks, cedar slat work (basketry):: x̲pó:ys < sx̲éyp.

bat :: skw'elyáx̲el.

bat, may include any/all of the following which occur in the Stó:lō area: western big-eared bat, big brown bat, silver-haired bat, hoary bat, California myotis, long-eared myotis, little brown myotis, long-legged myotis, Yuma myotis, and possibly the keen myotis:: p'íp'eth'elàx̲el ~ p'ip'eth'eláx̲el < p'í:.
may include any or all of the following (all of which occur in the area): western big-eared

bat (CONT'D)

bat, big brown bat, silver-haired bat, hoary bat, California myotis, long-eared myotis, little brown myotis, long-legged myotis, Yuma myotis, and possibly the keen myotis, respectively:: skw'elyáx̲el.
young bat:: skw'íkw'elyàx̲el < skw'elyáx̲el.

bath)
(bathe s-o, give s-o a bath), make s-o take a bath:: xó:kw'et < xókw' ~ xó:kw'.

bathe
(bathe s-o, give s-o a bath), make s-o take a bath:: xó:kw'et < xókw' ~ xó:kw'.
bathing:: xóxekw'em < xókw' ~ xó:kw'.
fourth day after a death (when everyone washes up (bathes)):: sxókw' < xókw' ~ xó:kw'.
to bathe:: xó:kw'em < xókw' ~ xó:kw'.

bathroom
outhouse, toilet, bathroom:: atl'qeláwtxw < átl'q.

bathtub :: shxwxóxekw'em < xókw' ~ xó:kw', xókw'emá:lá < xókw' ~ xó:kw'.

battle)
war-whoop, ((probably) a sung spell before battle):: syiwí:leqw < yéw: ~ yéw.

Bay
Echo Point on Echo Island, Echo Bay on Echo Island:: X̲wix̲we'áqel ~ Xwixwe'áqel ~ Xwōxwe'áqel < x̲wex̲we'á.
Pretty's Bay on Harrison River:: Sásq'etstel < sásq'ets.

bay :: sméya.
a little bay in the Fraser River a quarter mile east of Iwówes (Union Bar, Aywawwis):: Qíqemqèmèl < qém:el.
a little bay or eddy on Harrison River about two miles downriverfrom Chehalis:: Skw'á:lx̲w.
bay at upper end of Íyém (Yale Indian Reserve #22):: Qémelets < qám.
bay at upper end of Yale Indian Reserve #2 (Four-and-a-half Mile Creek) (near the northern end of Stó:lō territory):: Sqemqémelets < qám.
Haig bay, a calm place on the west (C.P.R.) side of the Fraser River by the Haig railroad stop, below and across from Hope:: Sqám ~ Sqà:m < qám.
largest deepest bay on Harrison River (between Victor McDonald's place and Morris Mt.):: Híkw Sméya < híkw.
name of a seal bay on Harrison River just before Pretty's house going to Chehalis:: Áshxwetel < áshxw.
Six-Mile Creek and bay on west side of Harrison Lake:: Lkwṓxwethem < kwṓxweth.

be
a net is set, be set (of a net by canoe, not of a pole net):: semíliyel < mí:l ~ míl.
be aching (of bones):: x̲áp'kw'tem < x̲ep'ékw'.
be ashamed:: x̲éyx̲e ~ x̲íx̲e.
be brown:: tsqw'íx̲w < qw'íx̲w.
be chewing s-th hard:: x̲éyx̲ekw'et < x̲éykw'et.
be considerate:: sts'íts'exw.
be cut:: slhíts' < lhíts' ~ lhí:ts'.
be deep, be very deep, be deep water:: shxwtl'ép < tl'ép.
be drunk, got drunk:: só:les < sél or sí(:)l.

be (CONT'D)

be dry, get dry, to dry:: ts'íyxw ~ ts'éyxw ~ ch'íyxw.
(be) dug out, (be hollowed out):: shxwótkw < xwótkw ~ xwótqw.
be dumbfounded, be surprised, be stupified, be speechless:: slholhekw'íwel ~ slholhekw'í:wel < lhó:kw' ~ lhókw'.
be feeling sorry:: x̱ex̱élh te sqwálewel < x̱élh.
be fixed, be fixed up properly:: sthethíy < thíy.
be from where?:: tel'alétse ~ tel:étse < tel=.
be gathered together:: sq'eq'íp < q'ép.
[be getting black]:: sq'íq'ex̱el < q'íx̱.
[be getting brown]:: sqw'íqw'ex̱wel < qw'íx̱w.
be greedy:: sqél:éxw < qél:éxw ~ qel(:)éxw.
be happy, being happy:: xwoxweyíwel < xwoyíwel ~ xwoyíwél.
be hit (with arrow, bullet, anything shot that you've aimed), got shot, (got pierced), got poked into, got wounded (with gun or arrow):: ts'éqw'.
be hopping:: ts'áts'ets'tl'ím < ts'tl'ám ~ ts'tl'ém.
(be) hurting, be aching:: x̱ex̱élh < x̱élh.
be in a hurry:: s'ówth < áwth.
be in a state of -ness:: =tem.
being angry, continue to be angry, angry, mad, roused, stirred up:: t'át'eyeq' ~ t'át'iyeq' < t'ay.
being ashamed:: x̱ex̱éyx̱e < x̱éyx̱e ~ x̱íx̱e.
being homesick:: t'ót'ekw'élmel < t'ó:kw'.
being similar:: st'at'á < t.
being tickled, (having tickling, getting tickling), tickley:: sá:yt'em ~ sayít'em < síyt'.
be inside a pit-house:: sqemí:l < sqémél.
be in the middle, be in the center:: shxwá:ye.
be light (illuminated):: státewel < táw.
be like, be similar to, be the same as, be a kind of:: sta'á ~ ste'á < t.
be married:: smamalyí < malyí.
be melting:: yíyet'em < yít'em.
be near, be close to, be beside, be next to:: stetís < tés.
be on top of:: sts'ets'á < ts'á:.
be overcome with pleasurable feelings after eating great salmon or a great meal:: ts'éqw'.
be over, past (passed):: yelá:w ~ yeláw ~ yiláw.
be patient, Be patient.:: tl'épstexw ta' sqwálewel. < tl'ép.
be really tangled, it's really tangled:: sq'á:lq' < q'ál.
be skinny:: chtíth < títh ~ tí:th.
be skinny, be thin:: stíth ~ stí:th < títh ~ tí:th.
be sorry, the feelings are hurt:: x̱élh (te, kw'e) sqwálewel < x̱élh.
(be) sunk:: smímeq' < míq'.
be tangled (on something):: sq'álq' < q'ál.
be twisted:: sx̱álts'ewel < x̱élts'.
be twisted (mentally), he's twisted (mentally):: x̱élts'tem < x̱élts'.
be under an umbrella:: sq'elóts'eqw < q'el.
be unwrapped:: syíyex̱w < yíx̱w.
be wearing a hat:: siyó:yseqw < yó:seqw ~ yóseqw.
be yellow, be green:: tsqwá:y < qwá:y.
continuative, be -ing:: -R1- or -C1e-, R5- or C1e-, R8= or C1a=, =R9= or =C1á(:)=.
get angry, get mad, be angry:: t'áyeq' < t'ay.
get stuck in the mud, get mired, be mired, get muddy:: t'ékw.
have, get, stative or be with colors:: ts= ~ ts'.

be (CONT'D)

having labor pains, being in labor in childbirth:: ts'áts'elem.
how beautiful., be really beautiful:: yú:wqwlha < yú:w.
hurry, hurry up, be quick, be fast, move faster, quickly:: x̲wém ~ xwém.
[looks a state of going brown, be getting brown-looking]:: sqw'íqw'ex̲welomex < qw'íx̲w.
seven, to be seven:: th'ó:kws.
sleeting, be sleeting:: x̲wí:qw'el < x̲wíqw'.
stative, be:: s=.
to be attached, to be fixed or fastened, be put on:: stl'átl'el < tl'ál.
working, be working:: yóyes < yó:ys.

beach

beach in front of old Scowlitz village, the point the Harrison River goes around by Kilby's store:: Sq'iq'ewílem < q'éw ~ q'ew.
beach on east side of Harrison Lake across from Long Island where there are lots of flat rocks, most of which have holes in them:: Sqweqwehíwel < qwá.
beach, shore:: cháchew ~ cháchu.
go out from the beach (if in a canoe):: tó:l ~ tò:l.
soft (knee-shaped) cliff on a beach:: =ó:lthel.

bead :: th'eth'x̲éyt or th'eth'x̲ít < th'ex̲ét.
little tiny beads:: ts'ets'emíkw.
prayer beads:: lesúpli.

beak

(have a) hook nose, beak nose, Roman nose, (be bent-nosed):: sqémqsel < qém.

beam :: shxwt'ólhestel < t'álh.
cross-beam (in a house):: st'álh < t'álh, t'élhmel < t'álh.
sunbeams:: sx̲elx̲éles te syó:qwem < yéqw.
beams (of longhouse, all of them), houseposts:: stíqw'teqw' < tíqw'.

bean

kinnikinnick berry, bearberry, Indian tobacco, domestic pea, domestic green bean, and probably giant vetch berry:: tl'íkw'el.
kinnikinnick plant, domestic pea-vine, domestic bean-vine, giant vetch vine:: tl'ikw'íyelhp < tl'íkw'el.
open (of peas, beans):: xwís.
bean sprouts:: ts'íts'esem tl'íkw'els (lit. growing up + bean) < ts'ís, tl'íkw'el
kidney beans:: tskwimómex tl'íkw'el (lit. dark red in appearance + bean) < kwím, tl'íkw'el
lima beans:: thós sp'eq'í:l tl'íkw'el (lit. big round + off-white + bean) < thí, p'éq', tl'íkw'el

Bear

Female Grizzly Bear:: Yeqwílmetelòt < yéqw.
Male Grizzly Bear:: Yeqwílmet ~ Syeqwílmetxw < yéqw.

bear

bear cub:: spathó:llh < pá:th.
bear dung:: spàthélets < pá:th.
bear (generic), esp. black bear, also includes brown bear, bear with a white breast, and grizzly bear though these all have separate names:: spá:th < pá:th.
bear-shaped rock up on cliff on south side above Echo Point bay on Echo Island in

bear (CONT'D)

Harrison Lake:: Spá:th < pá:th.
bear trap:: pathúyel < pá:th.
brown bear:: spá:th < pá:th, tskwímelqel < kwí:m.
female black bear with white spot [or mark] on the chest:: Sx̲éylmòt or sx̲éylmòt < x̲él ~ x̲é:yl ~ x̲í:l.
grizzly bear:: x̲eytl'áls ~ x̲eytl'á:ls, kw'í:tsel.
male black bear with white spot [or mark] on the chest:: Sx̲é:ylmet or sx̲é:ylmet < x̲él ~ x̲é:yl ~ x̲í:l.
to be born:: kwól ~ kwó:l.
white-breasted bear, a bear with white on the breast, (brown bear with a white chest [AK]):: ts'aweyí:les < ts'áwi or ts'áwiy.

bearberry
kinnikinnick berry, bearberry, Indian tobacco, domestic pea, domestic green bean, and probably giant vetch berry:: tl'íkw'el.

beard
hair on the chin or jaw, beard, mustache:: qwiliyéthel < qwíl ~ qwel.

Bear Mountain
Bear Mountain, also called Lhóy"s Mountain:: Siyó:ylexwe Smá:lt < siyó:lexwe ~ syó:lexwe ~siyólexwe

beat
a drum, small stick used to drum or beat time to songs in slahal game:: q'ówet.
beating (s-o/s-th), thrashing (s-o/s-th):: qw'óqw'eqwet < qw'óqw.
beating s-o/s-th with a stick, hitting s-o/s-th with a stick, clubbing it:: kw'ókw'eqwet < kw'óqw.
beating s-o up:: x̲ex̲éyet < x̲éyet.
beat s-o out of food:: (xwéweslexw).
beat or hit s-o/s-th with a stick, hit s-th (on purpose), hit s-o intentionally:: kw'óqwet < kw'óqw.
beat s-o up:: x̲lhét < x̲élh.
beat s-o up, kick s-o in fight, lick s-o (in fight), spank s-o, fight s-o (till he cries for ex.), fight s-o in anger, fight s-o back:: x̲éyet.
beat up s-o as a lesson till he learns or gives up, teach s-o a lesson:: lepét < lép.
slow beat:: t'íw ~ t'í:w.
smash s-th to pieces (hard pitch, splintery wood, a glass), break s-th to pieces, beat s-th/s-o to a pulp:: th'ő:wt
stick for beating blankets or clothes or mat, blanket-beater, clothes-beater, mat-beater, rug-beater:: kw'ekw'qwá:lth'átel < kw'óqw.

beater
soapberry beater, stick for whipping up soapberries or Indian ice cream:: th'amawéstel or th'emawéstel < th'ím ~ th'í:m.
stick for beating blankets or clothes or mat, blanket-beater, clothes-beater, mat-beater, rug-beater:: kw'ekw'qwá:lth'átel < kw'óqw.

beautiful.:: éyqwlha < éy ~ éy:, qélqwlha < qél.
good-looking, beautiful, pretty, handsome, looks good:: iyó:mex ~ iyóméx ~ iyómex < éy ~ éy:.
how beautiful., be really beautiful:: yú:wqwlha < yú:w, yú:wqwlha < yú:w.

Beaver
Beaver (name in a story):: Qelá:wiya < sqelá:w.

beaver :: sqelá:w.
  little beaver:: sqiqelá:w < sqelá:w.

Beaver Creek
  Beaver Creek (at U.S.-Canada boundary line):: Sqelá:w (Stótelō) < sqelá:w.

beaver dam:: teqáp or teqíp < téq.

Beaver Lake
  Beaver Lake or Hanging Lake:: Sqelá:w (X̲óx̲tsa) < sqelá:w.

because
  because (he, she, it, they):: tl'okw'es ~ tl'okwses ~ tl'ekwses < tl'ó ~ tl'o.

become
  become aware (said for ex. of a child about three years or so, or of realizing how something is done), come to one's senses, sober up:: p'élh.
  become a widow, become a widower:: yatílém < syá:tel.
  become, get:: xwa ~ xwe, xwe=, xwe ~ xwa.
  become glad, become happy, happy inside:: xwoyíwel ~ xwoyíwél.
  be faded (of clothes), (get/become) faded, (go or get or become gray):: xwíkw'el < xwíkw'.
  [be get/go/become red]:: tskwímel < kwí:m.
  get, (become), turn, go:: =thet.
  (get closed, become closed):: xwtáq < téq.
  go, come, get, become:: =í:l ~ =i┐l ~ =el.
  gone blue, (go blue, get blue, become blue):: meth'í:l < méth'.
  got red, became red, gone red:: kwí:mel < kwí:m.
  lose heart, become disappointed, become discouraged:: qelqéyl or qelqí:l < qél, qelqéyl or qelqí:l < qél.

bed :: pí:t, shxw'áx̲eth < áx̲eth.
  bed, (child, young):: =á(:)ylh ~ =á(:)lh ~ =elh (~ =iylh ~ =ó:llh ?).
  (be) doubled up in bed on one's side with knees drawn up:: sqw'emóx̲w < qw'ómx̲w.
  beds:: shxw'álex̲eth(') < áx̲eth.
  boards put under bed if moved outside:: lhex̲ōwéstel < lhá:x̲ ~ lháx̲.
  fix oneself in bed:: tl'ó:thet < tl'ó:t.
  make a bed, make (straighten up) a bed, make one's bed:: thiyá:lhem ~ thiyálhem < thíy.
  mattress, mats used in beds, (diaper(s) [AC]):: slhá:wel.
  platform (in house, etc.), bed platform, platform in bottom of canoe, flooring (the planks):: lálwes.
  riverbed:: stolōwálá < tó:l ~ tò:l.
  roll over in bed, turn over in bed:: ts'ó:lex̲eth' < ts'el.
  sofa, couch, chesterfield, place where one's sitting, (bed [AC, MC (Katzie)]):: shxw'ó:met < emét.
  to the back (near the wall), on the inside (on a bed toward the wall):: lhelhá:l.
  upset bed, mess s-th up:: yélqw't < yél or perhaps yá:l.
  wet one's head (sic?), (wet one's bed repeatedly):: lhélqwelhem < lhél.
  wet the bed, (urinate in the bed):: sex̲we'áléx̲eth' < séx̲we, xiwe'áléx̲eth < xíwe.
  wetting his/her bed:: xíxewe'áléx̲eth' < xíwe.

bedbug
    common bedbug:: lhelhq'etíwel < lheq'át ~ lhq'á:t, shxwelítemelh méxts'el < méxts'el.

bedroom
    bedroom, hotel:: itetáwtxw < ítet, pí:tawtxw < pí:t.

bee
    bee, honeybee, hornet, wasp:: sisemó:ya ~ sisemóya ~ sisemóye ~ sísemòye.
    bumblebee:: mékwmekw < mékw.
    yellow-jacket bee:: x̲ex̲p'ítsel sisemó:ye < sisemó:ya ~ sisemóya ~ sisemóye ~ sísemòye.

beef
    cow, bull, beef:: músmes.

beer :: p'óp'eqw'em < p'óqw'em.

beer parlor
    liquor store, beer parlor (AC):: lamáwtxw < lám.

beets:: tskwím shxw'ólewù < kwím, shxw'ólewù
    (lit. red + turnip)

beetle
    ladybug, ladybird beetle:: slhálhlí < slhá:lí.
    metallic blue-green beetle, "June bug", probably metallic wood-boring beetle, or possibly some types of long-horn beetle which aremetallic green with reddish legs:: tále te syó:qwem < tá:le ~ tále, tále te syó:qwem < yéqw.

before :: yewá:lmels ~ iwá:lmels < yewá:l.
    be in, in, be on, on, be at, at, before (an audience), (untranslated):: lí ~ li.

beg
    beggar:: lexwshxwmó:mel < shxwmó:l.
    begging:: shxwmómel < shxwmó:l.
    begging for a favor, asking for help:: th'íth'exwstélémét < th'íxw ~ th'éxw.
    to beg:: shxwmó:l.
    type of bird that begs for bones or food with the song: paspes(y)í(:)tsel kw'e sth'ò:m th'ò:m th'ò:m, probably a song sparrow:: paspesítsel ~ paspasyí:tsel ~ pespesí:tsel < pas ~ pes.

begin
    begin(ning) to, start(ing) to, inceptive:: mí ~ mé ~ me.
    begin, start, (be) just started, just began, be just begun:: yálhò < yalh.
    feel like singing a spirit song, be in a trance making sighsand crying sounds before singing a spirit song, be in the beginning of a trance before the spirit song is recognizable (the motions and sounds, crying out or wailing before singing):: lhéch.

behind
    be last, be behind, after:: lhiyó:qwt.
    be last (in travelling), be behind (in travelling):: yelhyó:qwt < lhiyó:qwt.
    be with behind facing toward something (like a fire):: sle'álets < le'á.
    dragging one's behind or rump or bottom:: xwókw'eletsem < xwókw' ~ xwekw'ó.

behind (CONT'D)

drag out behind:: tóx̲wem < tóx̲w.
feel creepy, fear something behind one:: sísem < síy.
feeling creepy, fearing something behind one:: sísesem < síy.
follow after, coming behind (the one ahead knows):: chokwelélqem < chó:kw.
follow behind s-o, trail s-o:: chokwí:lt < chó:kw.
follow s-th/s-o (on foot, in a car, or on a horse, for ex.), follow behind s-o:: chó:lt < chá:l or chó:l.
forget s-th, forget s-o, forget s-th behind:: málqlexw ~ málqelexw < mál ~ mél.
get a spooky or spooked feeling, afraid that bad spirits are around, get spooked, fear something behind:: x̲éysel.
go out of sight (behind something), disappear [behind something], [get in shade]:: t'á:l.
(have a) dirty behind, (dirty in the rump, dirty in the rectum):: ts'epí:wel < ts'épx̲.
have one's hands behind one's back:: sq'eth'ewíts ~ sq'eth'ōwíts < q'áth'.
hit on the behind (with a stick-like object):: kw'qwélets < kw'óqw.
in back of a house, behind a house:: tselqwáx̲elmel < chá:l or chó:l.
kick s-o in the behind, kick s-o in the rump:: lamá'íwét < lemá'.
leave s-o, leave s-th, go away from s-o/s-th, abandon s-o, leave s-o behind:: áyeles < á:y.
put one's hands behind one's back:: q'eth'ōwítsem < q'áth'.

being

being annoyed:: th'íth'ewel < th'íwél.
being nervous, being excited, (getting nervous/excited):: th'óyéx̲wem < th'ó:yx̲wem.
having labor pains, being in labor in childbirth:: ts'áts'elem.
someone is being pinched:: th'ith'lhákw'etem < th'lhákw'.

belch

belching:: qwóqwets'et < qwáts'et.
to belch, to burp:: qwáts'et.

believe :: q'á:l.

believe s-o, trust s-o:: q'élmet < q'á:l.
believing:: q'áq'el < q'á:l.
believing s-o:: q'áq'elmet < q'á:l.
doubting s-o/s-th, be not believing s-o/s-th:: mameth'élexw < máth'el.
doubt s-o, not believe s-th/s-o:: meth'éléxw < máth'el.

bell

bellringer:: tíltel mál < tí:ltel.
to rattle (of dishes or anything else loose), jingle (of money or any metal shaken), peal or toll (of a bell), make the sound of a bell, to ring (of a bell, telephone, in the ears):: th'á:tsem < th'éts or th'á(:)ts.
to ring a bell:: tí:ltel.

bellringer

bellringer:: tíltel mál < tí:ltel.

belly

belly fin:: th'étmel.
belly, stomach:: kw'él:a ~ kw'éla.

belly-button

belly-button, navel:: mőx̲woya ~ mőx̲weya ~ méx̲weya.
little belly-button:: mímx̲woya < mőx̲woya ~ mőx̲weya ~ méx̲weya.
ruptured belly button, ruptured navel:: lhéx̲welòw < lhex̲w.

belong

chief's, (belonging to a chief, in the style of a chief):: siyómelh < siyám ~ (rare) siyá:m.
(one's) own, belongs to (one):: swá.

belongings

belongings (AC):: á:wkw'.

below

"a little below":: stutuwóthel ~ stewtewóthel.
a little below the mouth of a creek or slough:: chichewóthel < cháchew ~ cháchu.
(be) below, (be) underneath, (be) at the bottom of a pile or stack:: stl'epólwelh ~ stl'pólwelh < tl'ép.
(be) downstream below something:: sōqw'ólwelh < wőqw' ~ wéqw'.
deep down, below, down below, low:: tl'ép.
downriver, down that way, downriver below:: lhósex̲el < lhós.
go down, go down below, get low:: tl'pí:l ~ tl'epí:l < tl'ép.

belt

belt, (necklace?? [DM]):: shxwyémtel ~ shxwiyémtel < yém ~ yem.
tighten it (a belt, a pack, etc.):: q'íxwet.

bench

chair, bench, seat, something to sit on:: ch'áletstel ~ sch'á(:)letstel ~ shxwch'áletstel < ts'á:.

bend

a bend in a river, a curve of a lake:: sq'ówqel < q'éw ~ q'ew.
a bend in a road:: sq'ówqel < q'éw ~ q'ew.
a turn in the Fraser River on the CPR (northwest) side two miles east of American Bar, Texas Bar bend in the Fraser River:: Sq'ewílem < q'éw ~ q'ew.
be bent, be crooked:: spópiy < pó:y.
(be) bent, (perhaps bent round):: sqóqem < qém.
bending lots of things, bending them (lots of things):: piypó:yt < pó:y.
bending over:: qép'esem < qep'.
bending s-th:: pópeyt ~ pópiyt < pó:y.
bend s-th:: pó:yt < pó:y.
bent over?:: stl'ítl'em.
be supple, be easy to bend:: met'mét'.
go around a bend in the river, go around a turn, go around something in one's way:: q'ewílem < q'éw ~ q'ew.
go around a bend (in water):: q'éwlets ~ q'ówlets < q'éw ~ q'ew.
go around (a point, a bend, a curve, etc.) in the water, make a U-turn (in the water, could use today on land with a car):: q'ówletsem < q'éw ~ q'ew.
(have a) hook nose, beak nose, Roman nose, (be bent-nosed):: sqémqsel < qém.
limber, supple, bend easily (of a person):: leqw'ímőws.
put one's head down, bend, bend over, bend over with one's head down, stoop down:: qep'ósem < qep'.

bend (CONT'D)

tree bent to ground with ice and frozen:: sx̲wíqel.
turn around a bend, go around a bend, turn around (to go back), turn around a corner:: q'ewqé:ylém ~ q'ewqéylém (better q'ewqí:lem) < q'éw ~ q'ew.

benefactive

benefactive, do for s-o, malefactive, do on s-o:: -lhts.

bent

bent U-shaped plane with handle on each end for canoe-making:: sqw'emóx̲w sxíxep < xíp, sqw'emóx̲w xíxepels < xíp.

Berardius bairdi

perhaps generic, most likely includes all local balleen whales, i.e., suborder Mysticeti, especially Balaenoptera physalus and Megaptera novaeangliae, possibly Eschrichtius glaucus, Balaenoptera borealis, Balaenoptera acutorostrata, Sibbaldus musculus, Eubalaena sieboldi, could include the following toothed whales (suborder Odontoceti): Physeter catodon, possibly Berardius bairdi, Mesoplodon stejnegeri, Ziphius cavirostrus:: qwél:és ~ qwélés.

Berberis aquifolium:: th'ő:lth'iyelhp.

Berberis nervosa:: selíy, selíyelhp < selíy.

bereft

pitiful, (bereft, poor):: selá:wa.

berry :: =ó:me.

a kind of blueberry:: sxíxeq? or sxíxeq'?.
a sprout or shoot (esp. of the kinds peeled and eaten in spring), sweet green inner shoots, green berry shoots, salmonberry shoots, wild raspberry shoots and greens, salmonberry sprouts, blackcap shoots, thimbleberry shoots, wild rhubarb shoots, fern shoots:: stháthqiy.
berry-basket:: sth'ímàlà ~ sth'ímà:la < sth'í:m ~ sth'ì:m.
berry, berries, (fruit [AC, AD]):: sth'í:m ~ sth'ì:m.
berry plant:: th'í:melhp < sth'í:m ~ sth'ì:m.
berry juice:: sth'í:m sqe'óleqw < th'í:m, qó:
blackberry, berry of the wild trailing blackberry, berry of evergreen blackberry (intro.), berry of Himalaya blackberry (intro.), respectively:: skw'ő:lmexw.
blackberry (fruit), (before contact, only) wild trailing blackberry, (now also) evergreen blackberry, (now also) Himalaya blackberry:: skw'ő:lmexw.
blackcap berry:: tselqó:mé < tsélq.
blackcap berry or berries:: tselqó:me ~ tselqómo < tsélq ~ chélq.
black hawthorn berry, blackhaw berries:: máts'el.
blue elderberry:: th'í:kwekw ~ th'í:qweqw.
bog blueberry, tall swamp blueberry:: mó:lsem ~ mólsem.
bog cranberry:: qwemchó:ls < qwà:m ~ qwám.
buckskin straps, lid for berry basket:: yémqetel < yém ~ yem.
dried saskatoon berries:: sk'ak'áxwe.
fall off (of leaves, berries):: xwís.
fresh saskatoon berry, service-berry, June berry:: ts'esláts.
gooseberry:: t'á:mxw.
gray mountain blueberry which looks like sx̲wéxixeq but is sweeter, oval-leaved blueberry, could also be Cascade blueberry:: xwíxwekw' < xwíkw'.

berry (CONT'D)

hull of berry (inside left after the berry is picked), "stem" or base of berry left after the berry is picked:: th'ép'oyeqw ~ th'épeyeqw.
Japanese wineberry:: th'elíth'eplexw ~ ts'elíts'eplexw (or perhaps ts'elíts'ep'lexw) < th'éplexw (or perhaps th'ép'lexw).
kinnikinnick berry, bearberry, Indian tobacco, domestic pea, domestic green bean, and probably giant vetch berry:: tl'íkw'el.
little berry basket:: kw'álhem, skw'álhem < kw'élh.
mountain ash berries, (perhaps also) mountain ash tree:: qwíqwelh.
pick berries, pick off (leaves, fruit, vegetables, hops), (pluck off, harvest):: lhím.
plant with three black berries always joined together, (possibly black twinberry):: xó:lelhp.
possibly high-bush cranberry, more likely squashberry:: kwúkwewels.
prickly swamp currant, swamp gooseberry:: th'kw'íwíyelhp < th'ekw' or th'íkw'.
red elderberry:: sth'íwéq'.
red elderberry (the berry):: sth'íwéq'.
red-flowering currant berry, Indian currant berry, probably also stink currant berry also called skunk currant berry:: sp'á:th'.
red huckleberry:: sqá:la, sqá:le.
salal berry:: t'áqe.
salmonberry (the berry itself):: elíle.
shiny black mountain huckleberry, also called a mountain blueberry by the speakers:: kwxwó:mels < kwoxw.
short gray bog blueberries with berries in bunches, probably the Canada blueberry also known as velvet-leaf blueberry, this term is for both the fruit and the plant:: lhewqí:m.
short Oregon grape berry:: selíy.
smallest gray swamp blueberries, smallest variety of Canada blueberry:: lhelhewqí:m < lhewqí:m.
small gray mountain blueberry on a low plant, dwarf blueberry:: sx̱wéxixeq ~ sx̱w'éxixeq.
"snakeberry", includes False Solomon's seal, star-flowered Solomon's seal, and probably Twisted-stalk (2 spp.) and Hooker's fairy bells:: sth'íms te álhqey < sth'í:m ~ sth'i:m.
snowberry:: pepq'éyò:s < p'éq'.
snowberry plant:: qewówelhp.
soapberry:: sx̱wősem ~ sx̱wő:sem ~ sx̱ő(:)sem.
spread them out to dry (berries, bulrushes, etc.):: ts'íyxwt ~ ts'éyxwt < ts'íyxw ~ ts'éyxw ~ ch'íyxw.
swamp gooseberry, prickly swamp currant:: ts'qw'í:wíyelhp.
tall gray mountain blueberry, probably Alaska blueberry:: léth'ilets.
tall Oregon grape berry:: th'ő:lth'iyelhp sth'í:m ~ sth'í:ms te th'ő:lth'iyelhp < th'ő:lth'iyelhp.
thimbleberry:: t'qwém.
to cup water in one's hands, to cup berries in one's hands:: qéltsesem < qó:.
touch s-o purposely, squish it (of berries, etc.), smash s-th, mash it (berries, potatoes, carrots, etc.), bump it:: tóset < tós.
whitecap berry, white blackcap berry:: p'éq' tselqó:me < tsélq ~ chélq.
wild red raspberry, domestic red raspberry:: s'ó:ytheqw < éy ~ éy:.

berry basket

little berry basket:: lí:latses < elíle.

beseech

ask a favor, ask pity, beseech:: th'exwstélémét < th'íxw ~ th'éxw.

beside

be near, be close to, be beside, be next to:: stetís < tés.

best

(be) bragging, extravagant in claims, bull-headed, claims he's the best:: sqoyéx̲iya < sqáyéx̲ ~ sqayéx̲.
be totally independent, doing the best one can:: óyó:lwethet < éy ~ éy:.
manage by oneself (in food or travel), try to do it by oneself, try to be independent, do the best one can:: iyóleméthet < éy ~ éy:.
my dear, (little best friend, little dear friend, etc.):: q'éyq'eleq ~ (better) q'íq'eleq < q'ó.
pal, best friend, dear friend, chum:: q'óleq ~ q'e'óléq < q'ó.

better

be good, good, well, nice, fine, better, better (ought to), it would be good if, may it be good, let it be good, happy, glad, clean, well-behaved, polite, virgin, popular, comfortable (with furniture, other things?),:: éy ~ éy:.
come alive, come back to life, get better (from sickness), get well, revive:: áylexw ~ áyelexw.
making s-th better, repairing s-th once discarded:: p'áp'ekw'et < p'ákw'.
recover, be better:: i'éyel < éy ~ éy:.
repair s-th once discarded, make s-th better, fix s-th up, repair s-th:: p'ákw'et < p'ákw'.
revive s-o, bring s-o back to life, heal s-o, (EB) give s-o medicine to make him better?:: á:yelexwt < áylexw ~ áyelexw.

Betula papyriforma commutata:: sékw'emiy < síkw'.

between

middle (in age or spatial position), between:: alxwítsel.
put s-th between the teeth, put it in one's mouth, bite on s-th (not into it):: ts'ámet ~ ch'ámet.

beware :: siyót < yó:t ~ yót.

bicycle

a bicycle:: póysekel.
to cycle, ride a bicycle:: xwpóysekel < póysekel.

big

be big, be large, be high (of floodwater), rise (of floodwater):: híkw.
be big (of a fire), the fire is big, the fire is going strong, big fire:: thó:lchep ~ thó:ltsep < thi ~ tha ~ the ~ thah ~ theh.
(be) larger, bigger:: thíthe < thi ~ tha ~ the ~ thah ~ theh.
be very big:: hí:kw ~ hí::kw < híkw.
big bird:: thehíws < thi ~ tha ~ the ~ thah ~ theh.
big bird, (large bird (of any kind)), any waterfowl:: x̲wí:leqw ~ x̲wé:yleqw ~ x̲wéyleqw.
big-bodied people, (have big bodies):: thíthehí:ws < thi ~ tha ~ the ~ thah ~ theh.
big ears, (have big ears):: thithehá:lí:ya < thi ~ tha ~ the ~ thah ~ theh.
big penis, (have a big penis):: thá:q < thi ~ tha ~ the ~ thah ~ theh.
big person (of females), big lady:: thékwàl.
big tree, (be big of a tree or plant):: sthá:lhp < thi ~ tha ~ the ~ thah ~ theh, sthá:lhp < thi ~ tha ~ the ~ thah ~ theh.
big voice (usually deep):: thíwelh < thi ~ tha ~ the ~ thah ~ theh.

big (CONT'D)

big waves, (have big waves):: thitheháleq < thi ~ tha ~ the ~ thah ~ theh.
get big, rise (of floodwater):: híkwthet < híkw.
(have) a big face:: xwthó:s < thi ~ tha ~ the ~ thah ~ theh.
have a big head:: thó:qw < thi ~ tha ~ the ~ thah ~ theh.
(have a) big mouth:: thehó:ythel < thi ~ tha ~ the ~ thah ~ theh, xwthó:thel < thi ~ tha ~ the ~ thah ~ theh.
(have a) big neck:: thahápsem < thi ~ tha ~ the ~ thah ~ theh.
(have a) big nose:: sméqsel < méqsel.
(have a) big rump:: thehíwel < thi ~ tha ~ the ~ thah ~ theh.
(have a) big rump, (have a) big "bum" (bottom):: thahélets < thi ~ tha ~ the ~ thah ~ theh.
(have a) real big foot, (have a) huge foot:: thí:thaxel < thi ~ tha ~ the ~ thah ~ theh.
(have) big eyes:: thithehó:les < thi ~ tha ~ the ~ thah ~ theh.
(have) big feet:: thíthexel < thi ~ tha ~ the ~ thah ~ theh.
(have) big hand(s):: thíthetses < thi ~ tha ~ the ~ thah ~ theh.
(have) big heads (of a bunch of fish for ex.):: thítheqw < thi ~ tha ~ the ~ thah ~ theh.
(have) sloppy ears, big ears:: slhellhelp'á:lí:ya < lhél.
longhouse for spirit-dancers, the big house, smokehouse (for spirit-dancing):: stháwtxw < thi ~ tha ~ the ~ thah ~ theh.
rising, getting big:: hahíkwthet < híkw.
something big (and round) (for ex. big fruit, big rocks, etc.):: thíthes < thi ~ tha ~ the ~ thah ~ theh.
stout (of a person), thick (of a tree), thick around, coarse (of a rope), big (fat) (of a person). big (in girth):: mékw, mékw.

Big Dipper

Big Dipper, (the Elk):: Q'oyíyets ~ Q'oyí:ts < q'oyíyets or q'oyí:ts.

bile

gall-bladder, gall, bile, have bile trouble, be jaundiced, bilious:: lelets' ~ laléts'.

bilious

gall-bladder, gall, bile, have bile trouble, be jaundiced, bilious:: leléts' ~ laléts'.

bill

bird's bill:: t'óp'els < t'óp', t'ót'ep'els < t'óp'.

Billy Harris's Slough

slough called Billy Harris's Slough or Louie's Slough, the next slough east of Yálhxetel and west of Q'iq'ewetó:lthel:: Meth'á:lméxwem ~ Mth'á:lmexwem.

bind

tie it up, bind it, tie it (parcel, broken shovel handle, belt, two ropes together):: q'áp'et ~ q'á:p'et < q'áp'.

birch

a yellowish glow at night given off by old birch and alder:: qwéth'.
birch, western white birch:: sékw'emiy < síkw'.
inner cedar bark (maybe error), (birch bark [AHTTC]):: sèqw'emí:ws < síqw'em.
place where a grove of birches stood/stand near the Kickbush place on Chilliwack River Road in Sardis, (village at junction of Semmihault Creek and Chilliwack River [Wells 1965 (lst ed.):19]) :: Sekw'sekw'emá:y < síkw'.

Bird

Female Salmonberry Bird, (Female Swainson's Thrush):: Xwatóy < xwét.
Male Salmonberry Bird, (Male Swainson's Thrush):: Xwét < xwét.

bird

animal or bird one is afraid of and can't see, powerful creature, supernatural creature:: stl'á:leqem.
big bird:: thehíws < thi ~ tha ~ the ~ thah ~ theh.
big bird, (large bird (of any kind)), any waterfowl:: x̲wí:leqw ~ x̲wé:yleqw ~ x̲wéyleqw.
bird's bill:: t'óp'els < t'óp', t'ót'ep'els < t'óp'.
call of a little bird (chickadee?):: ts'í:ts'tlemeth' < ts'í:tl' ~ ts'ítl'.
common nighthawk, (rain bird [Elders Group]):: pí:q'.
eight birds:: tqatsíws < tqá:tsa.
five birds:: lhq'atssí:ws < lheq'át ~ lhq'á:t.
flesh (human, non-human), meat (of dried fish, animal, or bird):: slhíqw.
four birds:: x̲ethílews < x̲e'ó:thel ~ x̲e'óthel.
gray or brown-gray chichadee-sized bird which calls t'ú' or tsk tsk in maple woods near American Bar:: t'ú'.
larger bird (any kind, generic), waterfowl, duck, (mallard [Cheh. dial.]):: mó:qw.
let oneself fall, drop oneself down (by parachute, rope, etc., said of little birds trying to fly out of nest, little animals trying to get down and let themselves fall):: chólqthet < tsélq ~ chélq.
nine birds:: tuxwíws < tú:xw.
one bird:: lets'íws < léts'a ~ léts'e.
sailing (of a bird), gliding on the wind:: yáyelem.
seven birds:: th'ekwsíws < th'ó:kws.
six birds (dead or alive):: t'x̲emṓws < t'éx̲.
small bird:: x̲wéyx̲weleqw or x̲wí:x̲weleqw < x̲wí:leqw ~ x̲wé:yleqw ~ x̲wéyleqw.
small bird (any kind, generic):: mí:meqw ~ mímeqw < mó:qw.
Swainson's thrush, the salmonberry bird:: xwét.
tail (of animal, bird):: stl'ep'él:ets ~ stl'ep'élets.
ten birds:: epálōws < ó:pel, opelíws < ó:pel.
three birds:: lhxwíws < lhí:xw.
thunderbird:: shxwexwó:s.
to catch (fish, game, birds):: chxélcha < xélcha.
two birds:: iselíws < isá:le ~ isále ~ isá:la, islóqw < isá:le ~ isále ~ isá:la.
type of bird that begs for bones or food with the song: paspes(y)í(:)tsel kw'e sth'ò:m th'ò:m th'ò:m, probably a song sparrow:: paspesítsel ~ paspasyí:tsel ~ pespesí:tsel < pas ~ pes.

birth

after-birth:: s'ó:qw.
giving birth, having a child, having a baby:: tsméla < méle ~ mél:a.
have given birth, already had a child, had a baby, (delivered):: sémele < méle ~ mél:a.
having labor pains, being in labor in childbirth:: ts'áts'elem.

birthmark

strawberry birthmark on the arm:: schíyeláx̲el < schí:ya.

bit

a little bit, small bit, a few:: emímel ~ amí:mel.
a small person (old or young) is picking or trying to pick, an inexperienced person is picking or trying to pick, picking a little bit, someone who can't pick well is picking:: lhilhím < lhím.

bit (CONT'D)

(be a) little bit proud, [a little] proud:: smámth'el < máth'el.
small (AC, BJ), little (AC), a little bit (Deming: EF, MC, Cheh.: EB):: axwíl.

bite

a bite:: sq'éykw' < q'éykw' or q'í:kw'.
a biter (animal, fish, etc.), a thing that is (always) biting:: ch'ech'émels < ts'ámet ~ ch'ámet.
a thing that bites:: ch'emá:ls < ts'ámet ~ ch'ámet.
bite into s-th/s-o, bite s-th, bite s-o:: q'éykw'et ~ q'í:kw'et < q'éykw' or q'í:kw'.
biting into s-th/s-o, biting s-o/s-th:: q'éyq'ekw'et < q'éykw' or q'í:kw'.
biting on s-th:: ch'mát < ts'ámet ~ ch'ámet.
put s-th between the teeth, put it in one's mouth, bite on s-th (not into it):: ts'ámet ~ ch'ámet.
to snap (one's fingers, a louse when one bites it, etc.):: tl'eméqw < tl'ém.

bitter :: títex̲em.

be bitter (like of cascara bark or medicine or rancid peanuts):: sásex̲em ~ sá:sex̲em < sáx̲em.
bitter, rancid:: chíchex̲em.
got rancid, got bitter:: chx̲í:mthet < chíchex̲em.

black

be black:: tsq'éyx̲ ~ tsq'íx̲ ~ ts'q'éyx̲ ~ ts'q'íx̲ < q'íx̲.
[be getting black]:: sq'íq'ex̲el < q'íx̲, tsq'íq'ex̲el < q'íx̲.
black eye, bruised eye:: st'it'eqó:les < t'íq.
black paint:: ts'q'éyx̲ témelh < témélh.
get black:: q'íx̲el < q'íx̲.
[getting black]:: q'íq'ex̲el < q'íx̲.
paint one's face red or black (spirit dancer, Indian doctor, ritualist, etc.):: lhíx̲esem < lhá:x̲ ~ lháx̲.
plant with three black berries always joined together, (possibly black twinberry):: xó:lelhp.
scorch s-th, blacken s-th with fire, heat it up (near a fire), burning a canoe with pitchwood to remove splinters and burn on black pitch):: qw'á:yt < qw'á:y.
spread red or black paint on s-th(?)/s-o:: lhíx̲et < lhá:x̲ ~ lháx̲.
to paint red or black (spirit dancer, Indian doctor, etc.):: lhíx̲ < lhá:x̲ ~ lháx̲.

blackberry

blackberry, berry of the wild trailing blackberry, berry of evergreen blackberry (intro.), berry of Himalaya blackberry (intro.), respectively:: skw'ṓ:lmexw, skw'ṓ:lmexw.
blackberry (fruit), (before contact, only) wild trailing blackberry, (now also) evergreen blackberry, (now also) Himalaya blackberry:: skw'ṓ:lmexw.
blackberry juice:: sqw'ṓ:lmexw sqe'óleqw < qw'ṓ:lmexw, qó:
blackberry vine, blackberry bush:: skw'ṓ:lmexwelhp < skw'ṓ:lmexw.
Himalaya blackberry bush, evergreen blackberry bush:: xwelítemelh skw'ṓ:lmexwelhp < skw'ṓ:lmexw.
trailing blackberry vine:: shxwelméxwelh skw'ṓ:lmexwelhp < skw'ṓ:lmexw.

blackbird

blackbird, Brewer's blackbird, or smaller crow, i.e., northwestern crow:: q'eláq'a.

blackboard)

blackboard)
  eraser (for pencil or blackboard):: shxwe'íqw'els < íqw'.

blackcap
  a sprout or shoot (esp. of the kinds peeled and eaten in spring), sweet green inner shoots, green berry shoots, salmonberry shoots, wild raspberry shoots and greens, salmonberry sprouts, blackcap shoots, thimbleberry shoots, wild rhubarb shoots, fern shoots:: stháthqiy.
  blackcap berry:: tselqó:mé < tsélq.
  blackcap berry or berries:: tselqó:me ~ tselqómo < tsélq ~ chélq.
  blackcap bush:: tselqó:má:lhp < tsélq ~ chélq.
  blackcap plant:: tselqó:má:lhp < tsélq.
  whitecap berry, white blackcap berry:: p'éq' tselqó:me < tsélq ~ chélq.

blacken
  blackened bitter cherry bark:: pélel.
  scorch s-th, blacken s-th with fire, heat it up (near a fire), burning a canoe with pitchwood to remove splinters and burn on black pitch):: qw'á:yt < qw'á:y.

blackfish
  killer whale, blackfish:: q'ellhólemètsel.

black fly
  gnat, probably includes non-biting midges, biting midges, and (biting) black flies:: pepx̲wíqsel < píxw.

blackhaw
  black hawthorn berry, blackhaw berries:: máts'el.

bladder :: séx̲watel ~ séx̲wàtel < séx̲we, sex̲we'álá < séx̲we.
  fish air-bladder:: xixxweláwa.

blade
  shoulder-blade:: kweq'tál.

Blaine
  White Rock, B.C., Blaine, Wash.:: P'eq'ó:ls < p'éq'.

blank
  splitting wood (esp. blanks and bolts):: póqwels < péqw.

blanket
  blanket (modern), covering:: léx̲wtel < lex̲w.
  blanket robe:: tl'exwewítstel < tl'xw ~ tl'exw.
  cover s-o with a blanket, cover s-th, cover s-th/s-o up:: léx̲wet < lex̲w.
  eight Indian blankets [Boas], eight dollars:: tqó:tsó:s < tqá:tsa.
  four dollars, ((also) four blankets [Boas]):: x̲ethíles < x̲e'ó:thel ~ x̲e'óthel.
  nine dollars, (nine Indian blankets [Boas]):: tú:xwes < tú:xw.
  one dollar, one Indian blanket (Boas):: léts'es < léts'a ~ léts'e.
  pile it up (blankets, rocks, anything):: ts'itóléstexw.
  seven dollars, (seven Indian blankets or dollars [Boas]):: th'ókwses < th'ó:kws.
  shake s-th (tree or bush) for fruit or leaves, comb a bush (for berries), shake s-th (a mat or blanket for ex.):: xwíset ~ xwítset < xwís.

blanket (CONT'D))

six dollars, (six Indian blankets [Boas]):: t'xém:es ~ t'xémés < t'éx.
spread it out (of blanket, net, book, etc.):: tlhét ~ tlhát ~ telhét < télh.
square dressing room or shelter of blankets where sxwóyxwey dancers change before doing the sxwóyxwey dance:: q'eléts'tel < q'el.
stick for beating blankets or clothes or mat, blanket-beater, clothes-beater, mat-beater, rug-beater:: kw'ekw'qwá:lth'átel < kw'óqw.
ten dollars, (ten Indian blankets [Boas]):: epóles < ó:pel.
three dollars, three tokens of wealth, three blankets (Boas), three cyclic periods:: lhí:xwes < lhí:xw.
two dollars, [Boas] two Indian blankets:: isó:les < isá:le ~ isále ~ isá:la.
woven goat-wool blanket, (twilled weave (JL)):: swṓqw'elh.

blanket-beater

stick for beating blankets or clothes or mat, blanket-beater, clothes-beater, mat-beater, rug-beater:: kw'ekw'qwá:lth'átel < kw'óqw.

blast

(make) a blast or boom (and the earth shakes afterward):: làtém.

blaze

(be) blazed (of a mark in a tree), chipped (of mark in tree):: st'ót'ep < t'óp.
glowing of coals not quite gone out yet, red blaze of a fire (DM):: wóweqem.
mark s-th, blaze it (of a trail), get/have s-th spotted (marked and located), make note of s-th:: xe'áth'stexw < xáth' ~ xe'áth'.
(to) flame, (have/get) a flame, to blaze:: xwótkwem.

bleach

grass scalded and bleached white for basketry imbrication (designs), sometimes called white straw grass, probably blue-joint reed-grass:: th'á:xey ~ th'áxey < th'áx.

bleed :: choléxwem.

bleeding:: chó:lxwem < choléxwem.
bleeding nose, (be/have bleeding in the nose):: sthxwélqsel < thóxw or théxw.
have a nose bleed:: thxwómélqsel < thóxw or théxw.
having a nose bleed:: thóxwemélqsel < thóxw or théxw.

bless

bless s-th/s-o:: plíst.

blind

(be) blind, (be) completely blind:: qéyxes ~ qíxes.
(be) partially blind, almost blind:: qelsílém < qél.

blinders

window shades, blinds, blinders (on a horse, etc.):: t'oléstel < t'á:l.

blinds

window shades, blinds, blinders (on a horse, etc.):: t'oléstel < t'á:l.

blink :: lhéplexw < lhép.

blinking one's eyes repeatedly:: lhéplhepxlexw < lhép.

blInk (CONT'D))

blink one's eyes:: lhépx̲lexw < lhép.
shut one's eyes, close one's eyes, (blink [EB]):: th'éplexw (or perhaps th'ép'lexw).
shutting one's eyes repeatedly, (blinking [EB]):: th'épth'eplexw (or perhaps th'ép'th'ep'lexw) < th'éplexw (or perhaps th'ép'lexw).

blister :: qó:tsó:m < qó:.

blob
spotted with irregular shaped blobs (like if mud-spattered, used of dogs, deer, and other animals so marked):: st'á:lq.

blood :: scholéx̲wem < choléxwem, stháthiyel.

bloom
bloom or (plant) fuzz (spore, pollen, seed fluff) after it bursts:: spekw'ém < pékw' ~ péqw'.
just starting to flower, blooming, (flowering):: p'áp'eq'em < p'áq'em.
to bloom, to flower:: p'áq'em.

blow
blow, blow s-th:: pó:t.
blowing (of an Indian doctor on a patient):: pópex̲wels < póx̲w.
blowing spray (humorously said of a child teething):: pópex̲wels < póx̲w.
blown:: pepó:tem < pó:t.
blow (spray) on a patient (of an Indian doctor or shaman), blow spray on s-o/s-th (of a shaman, a person ironing, a child teething):: póx̲wet < póx̲w.
blow (wind):: pehá:ls < peh or pó(:)h.
flute, wind instrument, blown musical instrument:: pepó:tem < pó:t.
stop blowing (of the wind):: chémq ~ tsémq.
to drop or blow plant fluff (like dandelions, fireweed, cottonwood, etc.), to blow (of dusty or flaky stuff like wood dust, dandruff, maybe seeds):: pípexwem < píxw.
when plant fuzz blows:: pókw'em < pékw' ~ péqw'.

blow-fly
a fly, blow-fly:: x̲wex̲wiyáye ~ x̲wix̲wiyáye < x̲wōx̲wáye ~ x̲wex̲wáye ~ x̲wōx̲wá:ye.
a lot of flies, big blow-flies:: x̲wiyx̲wiyáye < x̲wōx̲wáye ~ x̲wex̲wáye ~ x̲wōx̲wá:ye.
blowfly, big fly, (little fly (one of them) [Elders Group 2/19/75]):: x̲wōx̲wáye ~ x̲wex̲wáye ~ x̲wōx̲wá:ye.

blubber
seal fat, seal blubber:: sqwló.

blue
[be a little blue]:: tsmímeth' < méth'.
[be in a state of get blue]:: smeth'íl < méth', tsmeth'íl < méth'.
[be in a state of getting blue]:: semth'íl < méth'.
blue, be blue, have blue:: tsméth' < méth'.
gone blue, (go blue, get blue, become blue):: meth'í:l < méth'.
(have) blue eyes:: ts'meth'ó:les < méth'.
(have) marble eyes, (have) blue eyes:: mopeló:les.
[looks blue, blue-looking]:: tsméth'òmèx < méth'.

blueberry

a kind of blueberry:: sxíxeq? or sxíxeq'?.
bog blueberry bush:: mólsemelhp < mó:lsem ~ mólsem.
bog blueberry, tall swamp blueberry:: mó:lsem ~ mólsem, mó:lsem ~ mólsem.
gray mountain blueberry which looks like sx̲wéxixeq but is sweeter, oval-leaved blueberry, could also be Cascade blueberry:: xwíxwekw' < xwíkw'.
shiny black mountain huckleberry, also called a mountain blueberry by the speakers:: kwxwó:mels < kwoxw.
short gray bog blueberries with berries in bunches, probably the Canada blueberry also known as velvet-leaf blueberry, this term is for both the fruit and the plant:: lhewqí:m, lhewqí:m.
smallest gray swamp blueberries, smallest variety of Canada blueberry:: lhelhewqí:m < lhewqí:m.
small gray mountain blueberry on a low plant, dwarf blueberry:: sx̲wéxixeq ~ sx̲w'éxixeq.
tall gray mountain blueberry, probably Alaska blueberry:: léth'ilets, léth'ilets.

bluebill duck

bluebill duck, (identified from photos as) lesser scaup:: x̲élq'eqs.

Bluejay :: Sqéyiya.

bluejay

bluejay, Steller's jay:: kwá:y.
bluejay, Steller's jay (sacred fortune-teller):: x̲ax̲esyúwes or x̲ax̲e syúwes < x̲áx̲e.
cry of a bluejay [Steller's jay] that means good news:: q'ey, q'ey, q'ey.
(this cry of a bluejay [Steller's jay] warns you of bad news):: chéke chéke chéke chéke.

Bluff

Wahleach Bluff, a lookout mountain with rock sticking out over a bluff, also the lookout point on Agassiz Mountain:: Kw'okw'echíwel < kw'áts ~ kw'éts.

bluff

a little bluff (of rock):: sx̲eq'x̲éq'et < x̲eq'.
flat smooth and bare rock, a [rock] bluff, a bluff (straight up):: x̲eq'át < x̲eq'.
lying, telling a lie, (bluffing [BHTTC]):: mameth'álem < máth'el.
Mount Ogilvie or a round peak or bluff on Mt. Ogilvie where mountain goats live, the mountain or peak or bluff resembles big breasts:: Qwemth'í:les < qwó:m ~ qwóm ~ qwem.
to bluff, pretend one knows something, (be) stuck up:: math'álem < máth'el.

Bluffs

Bare Bluffs, a steep slope on the west side of Harrison Lake:: Lhó:leqwet.

blunder

make a mistake, blunder:: mélmel < mál ~ mél.

blunt

(be) blunt (edge or point), dull (of edge/point):: qelóth < qél.
blunt (end of canoe pole):: témkwes.
blunt-headed arrow:: s-hótl'eqw.
blunt (of poles):: témqweqsel.

blush

one's face is red, one is blushing:: kwelkwímelésem < kwí:m.

board

bad-looking (of log or board not of a person), rough:: qelímó:les < qél.
board for stretching squirrel or skunk hides, etc.:: tépelhállh < tpólh.
boards in a canoe bottom:: lhex̱ōwéstel < lhá:x̱ ~ lháx̱.
boards put under bed if moved outside:: lhex̱ōwéstel < lhá:x̱ ~ lháx̱.
(have a) flat head, (have cranial deformation by cradle-board):: sp'íp'elheqw < p'ílh.
plank, board, lumber:: loplós ~ leplós.
put s-th/s-o aboard, put it on-board:: ó:lhstexw < ó:lh.
sticking out through a hole (like a toe out of a sock, knee out of a hole in pants, a nail driven clear through the other side of a board), come out into the open:: qwōhóls (or perhaps) qwehóls < qwá.

boat :: pṓt.

a boom on a boat:: ts'eqw'elítsetel.
a canoe or boat cut off short in the rear (because the stern couldn't be repaired):: t'qw'á:lats < t'éqw'.
a ferry (canoe, boat, ferryboat):: shxwt'át'ekwels < t'ákwel.
bow of canoe or boat:: =ó:s ~ =ós ~ =es.
canoe, boat:: =ṓ:welh ~ =ṓwelh ~ =ōwelh ~ =ewelh ~ =á:welh ~ =welh ~ =ewí:l.
eight canoes, eight boats:: tqátsa'ṓwelh ? < tqá:tsa.
five canoes belonging to one person, five boats:: lhq'atsesṓwelh ~ lhq'atseséwelh < lheq'át ~ lhq'á:t.
four canoes, four boats:: x̱e'othelṓwelh < x̱e'ó:thel ~ x̱e'óthel.
mast on a canoe or boat:: spotelálá < pó:t.
nine canoes, nine boats:: tuxwṓwelh < tú:xw.
one canoe, one boat:: lets'ṓwelh < léts'a ~ léts'e.
row-boat:: pṓtṓwelh < pṓt.
seven canoes, seven boats:: th'okwsṓwelh < th'ó:kws.
six canoes, six boats:: t'x̱emṓwelh < t'éx̱.
steamboat:: stim:ṓ:t.
ten canoes, ten boats:: opelṓwelh < ó:pel.
three canoes, three wagons, three conveyances (any form of transportation), three boats:: lhxwó:lh < lhí:xw.
two canoes, two boats:: islṓwelh ? or isṓwelh ? < isá:le ~ isále ~ isá:la.

bob

it shook (shakes itself), shaking, bobbing around:: qwá:yx̱thet < qwá:y.
to bob:: pepélekwes < pél:ékw.

Bobb

Wahleach whistle stop on Seabird Island where Wayne Bobb lived in 1977, (now also Wahleach Lake (man-made) [EB]):: Wolích < x̱wále ~ x̱wá:le.

Bobcat :: Sqelóts'emes < sqets'ómes.

bobcat :: sqets'ómes.

body

big-bodied people, (have big bodies):: thíthehí:ws < thi ~ tha ~ the ~ thah ~ theh.
body (while alive):: slexwíws.
breast bone, part of human body between breast bone and ribs:: th'x̲áméł.
club on the body:: kw'qwí:ws < kw'óqw.
furry on the whole body (of an animal):: siysá:yiws < sá:y.
ghost, corpse, dead body:: spoleqwíth'a < poleqwíth'a.
grease one's body:: melxwíwsem < mélxw.
hair anywhere on the body (arms, legs, chest, underarms, etc.):: qwilṓws < qwíl ~ qwel.
hair on the body:: sqwelqwílōws ~ sqwelqwéylōws < qwíl ~ qwel.
lather one's body:: yet'qw'íwsem.
left side of the body:: sth'ekwe'í:ws < th'íkwe.
one side of the body (between arm and hip):: slheq'ó:lwelh < lheq'át ~ lhq'á:t.
on the body, on the skin, on the covering:: =í:ws ~ =ews.
on the body, on top of itself:: =á:w ~ =í:w ~ =ew.
paint one's body:: x̲é:ylthet < x̲él ~ x̲é:yl ~ x̲í:l
put paint on the body:: yétl'q'íws < yétl'.
relieved (in one's body):: ts'elxwí:wsem < ts'el.
ten bodies:: opelíws < ó:pel.
to drag (for a body in the river, for ex.):: xwekw'á:ls < xwókw' ~ xwekw'ó.
to whip all over the body with cedar boughs:: kw'oqwchí:ws < kw'óqw.
turn one's face, (turn one's body away [IHTTC]):: ts'ólesem ~ ts'ólésem < ts'el.
wash one's body:: th'ex̲wíwsem < th'éx̲w or th'óx̲w.
yellow-bodied:: tsqwayíws < qwá:y.

body odor

(have) animal smell (of bear, skunk, dog, etc.), (have) animal stink, (have) human smell (of underarm, body odor, etc.), (have) body odor:: pápeth'em.

bog

Labrador tea, "Indian tea", "swamp tea":: mó:qwem.
(sphagnum) bog, marsh:: mó:qwem.

boil

a boil:: sqw'echém.
barbecue, bake (meat, vegetables, etc.) in open fire, bake over fire, roast over open fire, bake under hot sand, bake in oven, cook in oven, (boiled down (as jam) [CT, HT]):: qw'élém < qw'él.
be boiled:: sqwóls < qwó:ls.
boiling (currently):: lhó:tqwem < lhot.
boiling, making boil, (cooking in boiling liquid):: qwó:ls.
boiling s-th:: qwó:lst < qwó:ls.
boil it for me:: qwelselhtsthó:x < qwó:ls.
boil s-th:: qwélst < qwó:ls.
boil water:: lhótqwem < lhot.
pot to boil in:: lhámkiya.
pot to boil in, iron pot, smaller iron pot:: lhémkiya ~ lhámkiya < lhém.
something to boil in:: sh(xw)qwó:ls < qwó:ls.
sound of boiling water:: xwótqwem.
to boil:: lhetqwá:ls < lhot.
to boil, make boil:: qwéls < qwó:ls.
water kettle, boiler pan (for canning, washing clothes or dishes):: qowletsá:ls < qew.

boiler pan
water kettle, boiler pan (for canning, washing clothes or dishes):: qowletsá:ls < qew.

bolt
splitting wood (esp. blanks and bolts):: póqwels < péqw.

Bombidae
family Bombidae, Bombus spp.:: mékwmekw < mékw.
order Hymenoptera, superfamily Apoidea, family Apidae, including Apis mellifera (introduced), also family Bombidae and family Vespidae and possibly bee-like members of family Syrphidae (order Diptera):: sisemó:ya ~ sisemóya ~ sisemóye ~ sísemòye.

Bombus spp.
family Bombidae, Bombus spp.:: mékwmekw < mékw.

Bonasa umbellus sabini:: skwéth' ~ skwéth'kweth', sqwéth', stíxwem.

bone :: sth'ó:m.
backbone (of human or other creatures), spine (human or other creature):: x̲ekw'ólesewíts < x̲ekw'óles.
be aching (of bones):: x̲áp'kw'tem < x̲ep'ékw'.
bone marrow:: slésxel < ló:s ~ lós.
bones:: sth'emth'ó:m < sth'ó:m.
breast bone, part of human body between breast bone and ribs:: th'x̲ámél.
collarbone:: (s)tl'lhíléstel < t'álh.
dried fish backbone (with meat left on it):: sx̲éwe.
fish backbone (not dried), (backbone of any creature [Elders Group 7/27/75]):: x̲ekw'óles.
it aches (like of bones), (be aching (of bones)):: x̲áp'qw'em < x̲ep'ékw'.
make a crunch underfoot (bones, nut, glass, etc.):: x̲ep'ékw'.
point of elbow, arm bone:: th'emeláx̲el < hth'b.txt.
small bones:: sth'eth'eló:m < sth'ó:m.
(someone's) spine, (someone's) backbone:: th'omewích ~ th'ó:bewíts < sth'ó:m.
spoon-shaped bone back of upper lip of sturgeon:: x̲álew.
the spine, the backbone:: shxwth'omewíts < sth'ó:m.
wrist, wrist bone (on outer side of wrist, little finger side, lump of wrist):: qwémx̲wtses < qwó:m ~ qwóm ~ qwem.

book
spread it out (of blanket, net, book, etc.):: tlhét ~ tlhát ~ telhét < télh.

boom
a boom on a boat:: ts'eqw'elítsetel.
(make) a blast or boom (and the earth shakes afterward):: làtém.

boot
gills, also "boot" (boot-shaped organ attached to fish gill):: xá:y ~ xà:y.
gumboots, rubber boots:: kw'ekw'íxwxel < kw'íxw.

boot-shaped organ
gills, also "boot" (boot-shaped organ attached to fish gill):: xá:y ~ xà:y.

bore

a borer, an auger:: sxoxwí:ls < xó:l.
bored:: ts'íts'ewel < ts'íw.
borer to make holes, auger:: sqweqwá:ls ~ shxwqweqwá:ls < qwá.
tired of s-th, bored with s-th:: x̲lhém:et < x̲élh.
tired of s-th, bored with s-th:: lhchí:wsmet < lhchí:ws.
to bore a hole:: xó:lt < xó:l.

born

first-born:: schí:lh < =chílh ~ chílh=.
last baby (youngest baby), the last-born, a child cranky and jealous of an expected brother or sister:: óqw'a < óqw'.
to be born:: kwól ~ kwó:l.

borrow :: chélhta.

be borrowed:: schókwelelh.
borrowing:: chókwelhta (or chókwellhta) < schókwelelh.
get credit, borrow (money for ex.), (getting credit, borrowing):: qw'íméls.
lend it to s-o, let s-o borrow it:: chélhtat ~ chélhtet < chélhta.

boss :: shxwsiyám < siyám ~ (rare) siyá:m.

chief, leader, respected person, boss, rich, dear:: siyá:m < éy ~ éy:.
respected leader, chief, upper-class person, boss, master, your highness:: siyám ~ (rare) siyá:m.

both

both burned, (many got burned):: kw'áles < kw'ás.
both cheeks:: shxw'el'íle < shxw'íle ~ shxw'í:le.
both eyebrows:: themthómél < thómél.
both heels, two heels, (heel):: th'etselétsxel < th'éts.
(both human) legs, (both) feet:: sx̲ex̲éyle or sx̲ex̲íle < sx̲él:e.
chin, jaw (of fish, human, etc.), (lips (both), cheek, side of the face [DM]):: ts'emxó:ythel.
get dust or bark in both eyes:: thq'elq'ó:les < théq'.
got (both) shoes on wrong feet:: sts'ókw'elxel < sts'ó:kw'xel.
heel, (both heels):: th'elétsxel < th'éts.
hold both arms (or wings) outstretched, (stretch out one's arms/wings):: tex̲eláx̲elem < tex̲.
slip with both feet, lose balance on both feet:: x̲welhx̲wélhepxel < x̲wlhép.
whole leg, (whole of both legs):: sx̲ex̲é:yle or sx̲ex̲í:le < sx̲él:e.

bother

annoyed s-o, bothered s-o, pestered s-o:: th'íwélstexw < th'íwél, th'íwélstexw < ts'íw.

bottle :: shxwlámá:lá < lám.

baby bottle:: sqemó'álá < qemó:.
nursing bottle:: sqemálá < qemó:.

bottle-opener

an opener, can-opener, bottle-opener:: shxwéma'ám < má ~ má'-, shxwémeqel < má ~ má'-, shxwémeqèyls < má ~ má'-.

bottom

(be) below, (be) underneath, (be) at the bottom of a pile or stack:: stl'epólwelh ~ stl'pólwelh < tl'ép.
bottom of a tree, trunk of a tree:: s'aléts.
coiled bottom of a basket before the sides are on:: skwélets < kwél.
deep bottom (of a river, lake, water, canoe, anything):: stl'epláts < tl'ép.
dragging one's behind or rump or bottom:: xwókw'eletsem < xwókw' ~ xwekw'ó.
foundation of a house, bottom of a tree:: s'alétsmel < s'aléts.
(have a) big rump, (have a) big "bum" (bottom):: thahélets < thi ~ tha ~ the ~ thah ~ theh.
(have a) skinny butt, (be skinny on the rump or bottom):: sth'émlets < sth'ó:m.
hole in the bottom (of bucket, etc.):: sqwálats < qwá.
in the rump, in the anus, in the rectum, in the bottom, on the insides, inside parts, core, inside the head:: =í:wel ~ =íwel ~ =ewel.
it got smashed in the back end or rear end:: téslatstem < tós.
(make the) sound of a spank on a bottom, (fall down with a bang [Elders Group 5/19/76]):: welhéq'.
on the bottom (of anything):: =élets ~ =lets.
on the rump, on the bottom, on the buttock(s):: =élets ~ =lets.
(probably) tickle the bottom of someone's feet, (tickle s-o on the foot):: sét'xt < síyt'.
rip on the bottom or insides:: x̲wetíwél < x̲wét.
sat down (with a plop?), [slip off on one's bottom or chair]:: xwlhépelets < x̲wlhép.
slide on one's seat, (sliding on one's bottom):: qíqex̲életsem ~ qéyqex̲életsem < qíx̲em ~ (less good spelling) qéyx̲em.
slip off (one's feet, hands, bottom), lose balance:: x̲wlhép.
spread one's legs (sitting for example), (be spread in the bottom):: spapx̲íwel < páx̲.
swivel one's hips (as in the Hawaiian hula for ex.) (shake one's bottom around):: qwayx̲élechem < qwá:y.
take it off from the bottom of s-th (a pack for ex.):: mexlátst < má ~ má'-.
the bottom (of a waterfall, body of water, basket, anything):: áthelets.
to still-dip, rest dip-net on bottom (of river):: thqá:lem.
touching bottom (of a canoe or a person):: tesláts < tós.
warming your bum, (be warming the bottom or rump):: sqewálets < qew.
warm it up (on the bottom):: qówletst < qew.
warm one's rump, warm one's bottom:: qewéletsem < qew.

bough

fir boughs, needle of any other conifer than spruce:: qwélatses.
limb or bough of tree:: =tses ~ =ches.
(red) cedar limb, (red) cedar bough:: x̲pá:ytses ~ x̲páytses < sx̲éyp.
to whip all over the body with cedar boughs:: kw'oqwchí:ws < kw'óqw.

boulder

place on mountain above Ruby Creek where there's lots of boulders all over the mountain lined up in rows:: Thíthesem < thi ~ tha ~ the ~ thah ~ theh.

bounce

bumping or bouncing hard on the rump:: th'esth'esélets < th'és.
jumping up and down or bouncing up and down (of an Indian doctor training):: hélmethet < lá:m.

"bound up"

get constipated, "bound up":: x̲ex̲ekw'íwel ~ x̲ax̲ekw'íwel < x̲ékw'.

Bovis
genus Bovis:: músmes.

bow
bow of a canoe:: q'lhól.
bow of canoe or boat:: =ó:s ~ =ós ~ =es.
bow (weapon):: té<u>x</u>wets.
draw a bow, cock a gun:: xwe'ít'et.
draw a bow, cock a gun, (draw it (of a bow), cock it (of a gun)):: xwe'ít'et < ót'.
high-bow canoe, high-bow river canoe, streetcar, tram, taxi, car, automobile:: xwókw'eletsem < xwókw' ~ xwekw'ó.

bowel
animal tripe (stomach, upper and lower), bowel:: spéxw.

bowel movement
have a bowel movement, defecate, to shit:: ó'.

bowl
grease bowl:: shxwlósàlà < ló:s ~ lós.
sugar bowl:: shúkwe'àlà < súkwe ~ súkwa ~ shúkwe.

Bow-line
name of second creek below (here south of) Suka Creek (as of 8/30/77), creek called Alwís's Bow-line:: Alwís Lhqéletel.

bow-line
anchor-line, mooring-line, bow-line, what is used to tie up a canoe:: lhqéletel < lhqé:ylt.

bowman)
pull in once with a canoe paddle wide or slow, pull in in turning (a canoe paddling stroke done by a bowman):: lhímes.

box
be box-shaped:: kw'elókw'exwóles < kw'óxwe.
(be) too tight (of shoes, clothes, trap, box), tight (of a dress one can't get into), too tight to get into (of dress, car, box of cards, etc.):: stl'etl'íq' < tl'íq'.
box, trunk, grave box (old-style, not buried), coffin, casket:: kw'óxwe.
dry storage box in tree or on top of pole (for salmon and other dried provisions):: póqw'elh < pó:qw' ~ póqw'.
fire box or fire platform and fire shield for torch-lighting or pit-lamping fire:: tl'áts'eq.
It's boxed., It's in a box.:: skw'ókw'exwe < kw'óxwe.
(mice) chewing (a wall, box, etc.):: ts'átxwels ~ ch'átxwels.
one's hand jammed (in a trap, under a box, etc.):: tl'í:q'etses < tl'íq'.
take it out of a box, pull it out of a box:: xíqt.

box lunch
(food) provisions for a trip, box lunch:: sáwel.

boy

adolescent boy (about 10 to 15 yrs. old), teenaged boy, young man (teenager):: swíweles ~ swíwles.
boy (from 5 to 10 yrs.):: swiyeqe'ó:llh < swíyeqe ~ swíyqe ~ swí:qe.
boy (from baby to 4 or 5 years):: swiwiqe'ó:llh < swíyeqe ~ swíyqe ~ swí:qe.
boys:: siwíqe'ó:llh or siwí:qe'ó:llh < swíyeqe ~ swíyqe ~ swí:qe.
changing in voice (of a boy):: qw'iqw'elá:mqel ~ qw'iqw'elámqel < qw'íl.
little man (nickname for a person), (sonny boy (MV and DF)):: wíyeka < swíyeqe ~ swíyqe ~ swí:qe.
lots of adolescent/teenaged boys:: swóweles < swíweles ~ swíwles.
to change (of a boy's voice at puberty):: qw'elá:m < qw'íl.

boy-friend

sweetheart, person of the opposite sex that one is running around with, girl-friend, boy-friend:: ts'elh'á:y < ts'elh=.

bra :: sqemálá < qemó:.

brace

put one's hand on s-th to brace oneself, brace oneself on s-th/s-o:: píyet < píy.

bracelet :: th'ómetsel < sth'ó:m.

Brachyura

probably the tribe Brachyura (a tribe is intermediate between a family and a suborder):: á:yx̲.

bracken

bracken fern root, rhizome of bracken fern:: sá:q.
bracken fern (top, part above ground):: ptákwem.

bracket fungus:: s'ómó:qwes.

bracket fungus, (possibly also some jelly fungi like yellow trembler):: s'ómó:qwes.

brag

(be) bragging, extravagant in claims, bull-headed, claims he's the best:: sqoyéx̲iya < sqáyéx̲ ~ sqayéx̲.

braid

a braid:: st'amxá:lts' < t'ámex.
to braid (hair):: t'ámex.

brain :: sméth'elheqw, sméth'qel.

branch

break off branches of berries:: lekwátssá:ls < lékw.
fan s-o, brush s-o with a branch:: xwélp't < xwélp'.
fine needles of hoarfrost on a branch:: pú:ches ~ púwches, pú:ches ~ púwches < pí:w.
heart of a root, seed, nut (kernel), core of plant or seedling, core (of tree, branch, any growing thing), pith (of bush), seed or pit [U.S.] or pip [Cdn.] of a fruit:: sth'emí:wel ~ sth'emíwel ~ sth'emíwél < sth'ó:m.
tree limb, branch (of tree), (knot on a tree [CT]):: sts'á:xt.
white fir branch:: t'óx̲wtses < t'ó:xw ~ t'óxw ~ t'óx̲w.

brant
smaller goose, brant, (black brant), for the smaller goose possibly also the cackling goose and lesser Canada goose:: tl'ákw'x̲el.

Branta bernicla
Branta bernicla, (Branta nigricans), possibly also Branta canadensis minima and Branta canadensis (leucopareia or parvipes):: tl'ákw'x̲el.

Branta canadensis:: áx̲e.

Branta canadensis canadensis:: tl'x̲wốmálqel ~ tl'ax̲wốmálqel.

Branta canadensis (leucopareia or parvipes)
Branta bernicla, (Branta nigricans), possibly also Branta canadensis minima and Branta canadensis (leucopareia or parvipes):: tl'ákw'x̲el.

Branta canadensis minima
Branta bernicla, (Branta nigricans), possibly also Branta canadensis minima and Branta canadensis (leucopareia or parvipes):: tl'ákw'x̲el.

Branta nigricans)
Branta bernicla, (Branta nigricans), possibly also Branta canadensis minima and Branta canadensis (leucopareia or parvipes):: tl'ákw'x̲el.

Brassica campestris:: shxw'ólewù.

Brassica oleracea:: kápech.

brave
(be) brave:: iyálewes < éy ~ éy:.

bread
baking (bread esp.):: thá:yém < thíy.
bread, flour:: seplíl ~ seplí:l.
cover s-o, cover s-th (like yeast bread):: tl'x̲wét (or probably tl'xwét) < tl'xw ~ tl'exw.
banana bread:: pelále seplíl < pelále, seplíl
moss bread:: sqwelíp.
potato bread:: sqáwth seplíl < qáwth, seplíl
sourdough bread:: t'át'ets'em seplíl (lit. sour + bread)< t'áts', seplíl
to bake (bread, other food):: thíyém < thíy.

break
all broken up (of sticks or bones, of the bones of a person who got in an accident):: lékwlekw < lékw.
be broken (of stick-like object):: selí:kw < lékw.
break a leg, (have/get) a broken leg:: lekwxá:l ~ lekwxál < lékw.
break an arm:: lekweláx̲el < lékw.
breaking (everything):: yex̲wá:ls < yíx̲w.
breaking it:: yóyekw'et < yókw' ~ yóqw'.
break(ing) the canoe:: yekw'ólhem or perhaps yekw'wólhem < yókw' ~ yóqw'.
break it:: yókw'et < yókw' ~ yóqw'.

break (CONT'D))

break it in pieces with one's hands:: peqwpéqwet < péqw.
break (of a flexible object like a rope, string or breath), it broke:: t'éqw'.
break (of a stick-like object):: lékw.
break off:: pqwá:ls < péqw.
break off branches of berries:: lekwátssá:ls < lékw.
break (of ground), crack apart (of its own accord) (of ground), ripped:: tl'éx.
break one's neck:: lekwépsem < lékw.
break one's spine, break one's back, have a humpback/hunchback:: lekwewíts < lékw.
break s-th in two (with one's hands), break it in half (with one's hands only), break off a piece of s-th:: peqwót < péqw.
break s-th (stick-like):: lekwát < lékw.
break s-th (stick-like) (accidentally):: lekwlá:xw < lékw.
break up s-th by crumpling, crush it up, rub it together fast (to soften or clean), rub it to soften it (of plants, etc.), fluff it (inner cedar bark to soften it):: yékw'et < yókw' ~ yóqw'.
broke down, came (un)loose, came apart, (got) untied, loose, unravelled:: yéx̲w < yíx̲w.
broken off in pieces (like a river-bank):: peqwpéqw < péqw.
Chehalis River mouth (below the highway bridge, where land is breaking up into sand bars), (an opening one could get through in a canoe in high water near Chehalis {IHTTC 8/25/77], small creek (branch of Chehalis River) several hundred yards up Chehalis River from where the road goes from old Chehalis village site to Chehalis River [EL 9/27/77]):: Spōqwṓwelh ~ Speqwṓ:lh < péqw.
dead and broken [of a plant]:: st'ápiy < t'ápiy.
her hand is broken, his hand is broken:: selkwá:tses < lékw.
I broke my fast:: le hóystexw tel sxwexwá < hò:y ~ hó:y ~ hóy.
one's canoe is broken up:: yekw'ó:lh or perhaps yekw'wó:lh < yókw' ~ yóqw'.
she broke her hand, he broke his hand:: lekwátses < lékw.
smash s-th to pieces (hard pitch, splintery wood, a glass), break s-th to pieces, beat s-th/s-o to a pulp:: th'ṓ:wt.
split off, break off, break a piece off, break in two, split in two:: péqw.
to break [in pieces], it broke:: yóqw'em ~ yó:qw'em < yókw' ~ yóqw'.

break wind

to pass gas, break wind, to fart:: pú'.

breast

breast bone, part of human body between breast bone and ribs:: th'x̲ámél.
breast, nipple, milk:: sqemó: < qemó:.
Mount Ogilvie or a round peak or bluff on Mt. Ogilvie where mountain goats live, the mountain or peak or bluff resembles big breasts:: Qwemth'í:les < qwó:m ~ qwóm ~ qwem.
squeezing the breast of s-o/s-th, milking s-o/s-th:: p'ip'eth'élmet < p'í:.
suckle, suck milk from a breast:: qemó:.
white-breasted bear, a bear with white on the breast, (brown bear with a white chest [AK]):: ts'aweyí:les < ts'áwi or ts'áwiy.

breath

bad morning breath:: qeléqep látelh slhákw'em < qél.
break (of a flexible object like a rope, string or breath), it broke:: t'éqw'.
breath (noun):: slhákw'em.
cut off one's breath:: t'eqw'lhálém < t'éqw'.
(have/get) wheezing, rattling breath:: xwóyeqw'em.
out of breath and over-tired and over-hungry:: pqwíles < péqw.

breath (CONT'D))

run out (of breath):: t'éqw'.
to sigh (of a spirit-dancer), make a loud (breathy) noise:: xeqlhálém.

breathe

breathing:: pexwelhálém < pexwlhálém.
breathe in:: sot'elhàlèm.
to breathe (once):: pexwlhálém.
breathe out:: péxwelhàlèm < péxw.
to sigh, breathe out whew:: hóxwethílém.

bridge :: shxwt'álh < t'álh.

bridge, cable crossing:: xwt'át'ekwel < t'ákwel.
bridge of nose:: sth'émqsel < hth'b.txt.
fell of its own accord (of an object from a height or from upright), drop down (object/person, from a shelf, bridge, cliff, etc.), fall off:: wets'étl' ~ wech'étl'.

bright

bright (in color):: tstáwél ~ táwél < táw.

bring

admitting s-o/s-th, letting s-o/s-th in, bringing s-o/s-th inside:: kwétexwt < kwetáxw.
bringing it back:: q'éyq'elstexw < q'ó:lthet.
bring it down (from upstairs or from upper shelf, etc.):: tl'pí:lx ~ tl'pì:lx < tl'ép.
bring it out for the first time (of a spirit-song):: p'í:t < p'í:.
bring oneself to a climax, to climax, to orgasm, masturbate:: wets'á:lómet < ts'á:.
bring oneself to a summit (of a mountain):: wets'á:lómet < ts'á:.
bring s-o/s-th back:: ámeq't.
bring s-o/s-th here:: xwe'í:lstexw < í.
bring s-o/s-th in (to a house/enclosure), take s-o/s-th in(inside a house/enclosure), admit s-o (into a house/enclosure), let s-o/s-th in (to a house/enclosure), put s-o/s-th in (inside a house/enclosure:: kwetáxwt < kwetáxw.
bring s-th, brought s-th:: ma'eméstexw ~ máméstexw < mí ~ mé ~ me.
bring s-th, fetch s-th, get s-th (bring it), give it to s-o(as s-th fetched, not as a gift):: méstexw < mí ~ mé ~ me.
bring s-th/s-o across a river, (ferry s-o/s-th over):: t'kwíléstexw < t'ákwel.
bring s-th/s-o outside (purposely):: atl'qílt < átl'q.
bring s-th to someone:: le'áméstexw < mí ~ mé ~ me.
give it back, bring it back, return s-th:: q'élstexw < q'ó:lthet.
revive s-o, bring s-o back to life, heal s-o, (EB) give s-o medicine to make him better?:: á:yelexwt < áylexw ~ áyelexw.
save s-o, (EB) bring s-o back to life:: á:yelexwlexw < áylexw ~ áyelexw.

bring in

bring in firewood, bring wood in:: kwtxwéltsep ~ kwetxwéltsep < kwetáxw.

bring s-o food

give s-o food, bring s-o food, pass food to s-o:: áxwet.

brisket

inside brisket of meat (deer, etc.):: th'x̲éyles or th'x̲íles.
outside brisket of meat:: qw'íwelh.

Bristol Island
  Bill Bristol Island:: We<u>x</u>ésem ~ Lexwwe<u>x</u>ésem < we<u>x</u>és.

brittle
  brittle, crisp:: <u>x</u>épkw'em < <u>x</u>ep'ékw'.

broccoli:: tsqwá:y p'áp'eq'em kápech < qwá:y, p'áq', kápech
  (lit. green + flowering/flowered + cabbage)

broke
  be broke [financially]:: stesó:s < t-sós ~ tesós.

brome grass
  a grass that grows with berries in fields and everywhere and has seeds that stick in one's throat when eaten with berries, probably a type of brome grass, likely California brome grass, possibly sweet cicely:: táqalh.

Bromus
  probably a Bromus sp., likely Bromus carinatus, possibly Osmorhiza chilensis and Osmorhiza purpurea,:: táqalh.

Bromus carinatus
  probably a Bromus sp., likely Bromus carinatus, possibly Osmorhiza chilensis and Osmorhiza purpurea,:: táqalh.

brooch
  brooch, pin (ornament pinned to clothing):: ts'eqw'eléstel < ts'éqw'.

brood
  brooding:: st'á:y<u>x</u>w < t'ay.
  sit on eggs, to hatch eggs, to brood eggs:: tl'xwá:ylhem < tl'xw ~ tl'exw.

broom :: é<u>x</u>wtel < í<u>x</u>w.

brother
  (be) brother and sister, (be siblings to each other), (be) first cousin to each other:: qeló:qtel < sqá:q.
  brother-in-law's wife, (spouse's sibling's spouse), (step-sibling, step-brother, step-sister [AC]):: slets'éleq < láts'.
  girl's younger brother (pet name):: iyá:q, iyá:q.
  great grandparent, great grandchild, sibling or (up to fourth) cousin of great grandparent, great grandchild of brother or sister or (up to fourth) cousin:: sts'ó:meqw.
  half-sibling, half-brother, half-sister:: lets'ő̄w(e)yelh ~ slets'ő̄weyelh < láts'.
  husband's brothers, (perhaps also wife's sisters?, spouse's siblings?, sibling's spouses?):: smetmátexwtel < smátexwtel.
  husband's brother, wife's sister, spouse's sibling (cross-sex), brother-in-law, sister-in-law, sibling's spouse (cross-sex):: smátexwtel.
  nephew, niece, sibling's child (child of sister or brother or cousin (up to and including fourth cousin) [Elders Group]):: stí:wel.
  older sibling, elder cousin (child of older sibling of one's parent, grandchild of older sibling of one's grandparent, great grandchild of older sibling of one's great grandparent), cousin of senior line, older brother, older sister:: sétl'atel < sétl'a ~ sétl'o.

brother (CONT'D))

sibling, brother, sister:: álex.
(siblings), brothers:: el'álex < álex.
spouse's sibling, sibling's spouse (cross sex), for ex., husband's brother, (wife's sister, woman's sister's husband, man's brother's wife):: smátexwtel.
to make a sign with its foot it wants a younger brother or younger sister:: oqw'exélem < óqw'.
younger sibling, younger brother, younger sister, child of younger sibling of one's parent, "younger" cousin (could even be fourth cousin [through younger sibling of one's great great grandparent]):: sqá:q.
younger, younger sibling, cousin of a junior line (cousin by an ancestor younger than the speaker's), junior cousin (child of a younger sibling of one's parent, (great) grandchild of a younger sibling of one's(great) grandparent), younger brother, younger sister:: sóseqwt ~ (rarely) só:seqwt.

brother-in-law
husband's brother, wife's sister, spouse's sibling (cross-sex), brother-in-law, sister-in-law, sibling's spouse (cross-sex):: smátexwtel.

brother-in-law's wife
brother-in-law's wife, (spouse's sibling's spouse), (step-sibling, step-brother, step-sister [AC]):: slets'éleq < láts'.

brother's wife
sister-in-law, husband's sister, brother's wife, wife's sister (EB):: shxw'álex < álex.
spouse's sibling, sibling's spouse (cross sex), for ex., husband's brother, (wife's sister, woman's sister's husband, man's brother's wife):: smátexwtel.

brown :: tsqw'iqw'ex̲w < qw'íx̲w.
(be) a dark color (of clothes, complexions, etc.), (dark gray, dark brown):: stl'ítl'esel < stl'ítl'es.
be brown:: tsqw'íx̲w < qw'íx̲w.
[be getting brown]:: sqw'íqw'ex̲wel < qw'íx̲w, tsqw'íqw'ex̲wel < qw'íx̲w.
be red, red, reddish-brown, copper-colored:: tskwí:m < kwí:m.
brown bear:: tskwímelqel < kwí:m.
(brownish):: qw'íqw'ex̲w < qw'íx̲w.
[getting brown]:: qw'íqw'ex̲wel < qw'íx̲w.
have reddish-brown fur, have reddish-brown animal hair:: tskwímelqel < kwí:m.
have red hair, have reddish-brown hair:: tskwí:meqw < kwí:m.
[looks a state of going brown, be getting brown-looking]:: sqw'íqw'ex̲welomex < qw'íx̲w.

brownish)
(tan, brownish):: p'íp'ex̲wel, sp'íp'ex̲wel < p'íp'ex̲wel.

bruise
a bruise:: st'ít'eqel < t'íq.
be bruised:: t'íqel < t'íq.
black eye, bruised eye:: st'it'eqó:les < t'íq.

brussels sprouts:: mémeles kápech < méle, kápech
(lit. many little children of + cabbage)

brush

brush one's teeth:: th'ex̲wélesem < th'éx̲w or th'óx̲w.
brush s-th off, brush it (by hand or with branches):: píxwet < píxw.
fan s-o, brush s-o with a branch:: xwélp't < xwélp'.
shrub, small bush (for ex. growing on river edge, or like vine maple or thimbleberry or willow), brush, underbrush:: xwíxwel.

Bryophyta

phylum Bryophyta:: qwà:m ~ qwám.

Bryoria) species

possibly Letharia vulpina or Alectoria (Bryoria) species or Usnea species:: mex̲t'éles.

bubble

foaming, bubbling, foamy:: p'óp'eqw'em < p'óqw'em.
trickling, dribbling, water bubbling up in a river, add water to a container, water running under:: kw'átem.

Bubo virginianus

Bubo virginianus occidentalis, Bubo virginianus saturatus, and perhaps other Bubo virginianus subspecies:: chítmexw.

Bubo virginianus occidentalis

Bubo virginianus occidentalis, Bubo virginianus saturatus, and perhaps other Bubo virginianus subspecies:: chítmexw.

Bubo virginianus saturatus

Bubo virginianus occidentalis, Bubo virginianus saturatus, and perhaps other Bubo virginianus subspecies:: chítmexw.

Bucephala clangula

probably Bucephala clangula and Bucephala islandica:: láqleqem < léqem.

Bucephala islandica

probably Bucephala clangula and Bucephala islandica:: láqleqem < léqem.

bucket

collected rain-water drops in a bucket:: th'q'emelétsem < th'q'ém ~ th'eq'ém.
pail, bucket, kettle (BJ, Gibbs):: skw'ó:wes ~ skw'ówes.

buckskin

buckskin clothes:: míyethélwét < sméyeth ~ sméyéth.
buckskin, rawhide, tanned buckskin:: áx̲elqel.
buckskin straps for tying a baby in its cradle or basket:: yémqetel < yém ~ yem.
buckskin straps, lid for berry basket:: yémqetel < yém ~ yem.

bud

flower of wild rose, hip or bud of wild rose, including: Nootka rose, probably also dwarf or woodland rose and swamp rose, possibly (from Hope east) prickly rose:: qá:lq.

bufflehead (duck)

a white-headed duck, [could be bufflehead, snow goose, emperor goose, poss. oldsquaw, or hooded merganser, other duck-like birds with white heads do not occur in the Stó:lō area and the emperor goose would be only an occasional visitor]:: skemí'iya.

Bufo boreas boreas

family Ranidae and family Bufonidae, esp. Bufo boreas boreas and recent introductions Rana catesbeiana and Rana clamitans, and Ascaphus truei, Rana aurora aurora, and Rana pretiosa pretiosa:: pípehò:m < peh or pó(:)h.

Bufonidae

if generic includes families Ranidae and Bufonidae and may include Hyla regilla and perhaps the introduced species: Rana catesbeiana, Rana clamitans, Rana aurora aurora, Rana pretiosa pretiosa, and Ascaphus truei, if not generic then includes only members of family Ranidae and/or family Bufonidae:: wex̲és, weléx̲ < wex̲és.

bug

common bedbug:: lhelhq'etíwel < lheq'át ~ lhq'á:t, shxwelítemelh méxts'el < méxts'el.
ladybug, ladybird beetle:: slhálhlí < slhá:lí.
little bug:: sth'ékw'oye < sth'ékw'.
metallic blue-green beetle, "June bug", probably metallic wood-boring beetle, or possibly some types of long-horn beetle which aremetallic green with reddish legs:: tále te syó:qwem < tá:le ~ tále, tále te syó:qwem < yéqw.
worm, bug:: sth'ékw'.

build

build a fire, make a fire, make the fire, (stoke the fire):: yéqwelchep ~ yéqweltsep < yéqw.
build a house (make a house):: thiyéltxwem < thíy.
making the fire, building the fire, (stoking a fire):: híyqwelchep < yéqw.

building)

bank (money house, money building):: tale'áwtxw < tá:le ~ tále.
barn, (hay house, grass building):: sox̲weláwtxw < só:x̲wel ~ sóx̲wel.
building, house:: =á:wtxw ~ =áwtxw ~ =ewtxw ~ =(á)ltxw ~ =(el)txw.
church house, the church (building):: ts'ahéyelhá:wtxw < ts'ahéyelh.
Indian dance-house, "smoke-house", (spirit-dance building):: smilha'áwtxw < mílha.
plank building:: s'iltexwím < s'í:ltexw.
three houses, (three buildings):: lhxwá:wtxw < lhí:xw.

bulb

bulb or root called wild artichoke, Jerusalem artichoke:: x̲áx̲ekw'.
unidentified plant with round bulbs that look and taste like potatoes, round root like potatoes that used to be eaten and tastes like potatoes:: qíqemxel ~ qéyqemxel < qém.

bull

cow, bull, beef:: músmes.

bullet :: xá:t.

be hit (with arrow, bullet, anything shot that you've aimed), got shot, (got pierced), got poked into, got wounded (with gun or arrow):: ts'éqw'.

bullfrog

big frog (even bigger than pípehò:m and cries like a baby), (probably bullfrog, possibly green frog):: wex̲ó:mṓ:lh.

big pretty frog, bullfrog with colors on his back:: pehó:mṓ:lh < peh or pó(:)h.

frog, (esp. Northwestern toad, if generic also includes the tree toad and recent introductions the bullfrog and green frog, and the tailed toad, red-legged frog, and western spotted frog), (if generic may also include water frog that lives in springs and keeps the water cold [Halq'eméylem name unknown to Elders Group on 1/30/80], and a huge pretty frog (bigger than pípehò:m) that has supernatural powers and cries like a baby [sx̲ex̲ómṓlh ~ wex̲ó:mṓ:lh]), (big frog with warts [AD]):: pípehò:m < peh or pó(:)h.

frog, (if generic may include Pacific tree toad and perhaps the introduced species: bullfrog, green frog, red-legged frog, western spotted frog, and the tailed toad):: wex̲és, weléx̲ < wex̲és.

bullhead

bullhead, (brown bullhead):: smó:tx̲w ~ smótx̲w.

bull-headed

(be) bragging, extravagant in claims, bull-headed, claims he's the best:: sqoyéx̲iya < sqáyéx̲ ~ sqayéx̲.

insistant, persistant (like a child pressing to go along), bull-headed, doesn't mind, does just the opposite, (stubborn, contrary):: sxíxeles.

bulrush

bulrush mat:: wṓ:lalh < wṓ:l.

bulrush mat, reed mat, mat (of cattail/roots/bulrushes, etc.), (wall mat (Elders Group 11/12/75):: wá:th'elh ~ wáth'elh < wáth'.

bulrush, tule:: wṓ:l.

cattail, cattail rush or reed, (bulrush [AC, BJ]):: sth'á:qel.

pillow, rolled bulrush mat:: sx̲wétl'qel.

spread them out to dry (berries, bulrushes, etc.):: ts'íyxwt ~ ts'éyxwt < ts'íyxw ~ ts'éyxw ~ ch'íyxw.

"bum"

(have a) big rump, (have a) big "bum" (bottom):: thahélets < thi ~ tha ~ the ~ thah ~ theh.

warming your bum, (be warming the bottom or rump):: sqewálets < qew.

bumblebee :: mékwmekw < mékw.

bump

bumped on the head:: teséleqw < tós.

bump, get hit by something moving (for ex. by a car):: tós.

bumping or bouncing hard on the rump:: th'esth'esélets < th'és.

bump the head:: tesálèqel < tós.

bump them together:: testéstexw < tós.

tapping it (with something), mashing s-th, grinding s-th, be bumping s-o:: tóteset < tós.

to hurt again (as when a painful place is bumped and hurts again or as when a pain inside one's body returns again), (to ache [SJ]):: téqlexw.

touch s-o accidentally, bump s-o, bumped s-o:: téslexw < tós.

touch s-o purposely, squish it (of berries, etc.), smash s-th, mash it (berries, potatoes, carrots, etc.), bump it:: tóset < tós.

bun

(have the) hair in a bun:: sq'éth'ep < q'áth'.

bunch

a whole bunch having fun:: eyó:sthet ~ iyósthet < éy ~ éy:.
bunch of rabbits:: sqweqwewáth < qwá.
(have) big heads (of a bunch of fish for ex.):: thítheqw < thi ~ tha ~ the ~ thah ~ theh.
little crows, small crows, bunch of small crows, (bunch of northwestern crows):: spepelól ~ spepeló:l < spó:l.
(more than one) entering a house, going in (of a whole bunch):: kwetexwí:lem < kwetáxw.

bunch of little ones

a bunch of little ones:: emémel < emímel ~ amí:mel.

bundle

(be) all bundled up:: stl'etl'íqw'.
small bundle, small package:: xixwelókw' < xél.

Buprestidae

probably order Coleoptera, family Buprestidae, genus Buprestis, or possibly family Cerambycidae, genus Gaurotes:: tále te syó:qwem < tá:le ~ tále, tále te syó:qwem < yéqw.

Buprestis

probably order Coleoptera, family Buprestidae, genus Buprestis, or possibly family Cerambycidae, genus Gaurotes:: tále te syó:qwem < tá:le ~ tále, tále te syó:qwem < yéqw.

burdock :: x̲éyx̲emels ch'ech'éqw' < x̲éym, x̲éyx̲emels < x̲éym.

burial

burial grove of Scowkale:: Tl'átl'elh ?.
storage basket (for oil, fruit, clothes), burial basket for twins, round basket (any size, smaller at top), clay jug (to store oil or fruit):: skwá:m ~ skwám < kwá:m ~ kwám.

burl

lump on a tree, burl:: smétsa.

burn

be burning:: héyeqw < yéqw.
both burned, (many got burned):: kw'áles < kw'ás.
burned in the throat:: kw'és=qel < kw'ás.
burned (of rocks), scorched (of rocks):: qw'óqw'iy < qw'á:y.
burned on the finger or hand, burnt the hand, a hand got burnt:: kw'éstses < kw'ás.
burned on the foot:: kw'ésxel < kw'ás.
burned on the lips:: kw'esó:ythel < kw'ás.
burned on the rump:: kw'esélets < kw'ás.
burned, to burn, scorch:: yéqw.
burning s-th:: híyeqwt < yéqw.
burn it for s-o:: yéqwelht < yéqw.
burn s-th, light s-th:: yéqwt < yéqw.
burnt color:: syeqwyíqw < yéqw.

burn (CONT'D))

burnt (i.e. dry) grass:: yeqwílep < yéqw.
burnt mountain across from American Bar:: Syíyeqw < yéqw.
clothing, food, and possessions burned and given away when a person dies, (possessions and food burned and given away at a burning):: syeqwá:ls < yéqw.
fire (out of control), forest fire burning, fire burning:: yíyeqw < yéqw.
get burned (of human or creature):: kw'ás.
have a ritual burning ceremony, have a burning, feed the dead, (food offered to the dead [at a ritual burning] [EB 5/25/76]):: yeqwá:ls < yéqw.
have heartburn:: yeqwí:les < yéqw.
(portion not burnt up, burnt or gone out completely portion):: th'ex̲míl < th'éx̲.
scorch s-th, blacken s-th with fire, heat it up (near a fire), burning a canoe with pitchwood to remove splinters and burn on black pitch):: qw'á:yt < qw'á:y.
stop burning (of a burn), go down (of swelling):: t'esí:l < t'ás.
the one who burns [at a burning ceremony], (ritualist at a burning):: híyeqwels < yéqw.
to scald s-th/s-o, burn s-th/s-o [with hot liquid]:: th'áx̲et < th'áx̲.
village site (burned) on Atchelitz Creek:: Syéqw < yéqw.

burning

a category of religious songs including sx̲wó:yx̲wey songs and burning songs, a burning song:: heywí:leqw < yéw: ~ yéw.
a sung spell, power to help or harm people or to do [ritual] burning, power to do witchcraft and predict the future, an evil spell, (magic spell) (someone who has power to take things out of a person or put things in [by magic] [Elders Group 2/25/76], ritualist [Elders Group 1/21/76], witch [EB 4/25/78]):: syiwí:l ~ syewí:l < yéw: ~ yéw.
clothing, food, and possessions burned and given away when a person dies, (possessions and food burned and given away at a burning):: syeqwá:ls < yéqw.
have a ritual burning ceremony, have a burning, feed the dead, (food offered to the dead [at a ritual burning] [EB 5/25/76]):: yeqwá:ls < yéqw.
the one who burns [at a burning ceremony], (ritualist at a burning):: híyeqwels < yéqw.
transform it more, pass it over the fire more (at a burning):: x̲iyx̲éyt or x̲eyx̲éyt < x̲éyt.

burp

to belch, to burp:: qwáts'et.

burst

bloom or (plant) fuzz (spore, pollen, seed fluff) after it bursts:: spekw'ém < pékw' ~ péqw'.
burst, burst out, (get) smash(ed) (something round and filled):: méqw' ~ mőqw'.
burst open, split open of its own accord (like a dropped watermelon):: tl'xáx̲el < tl'éx.
it burst (of spores or seed fluff):: pekw'ém < pékw' ~ péqw'.

bury

(be) buried:: spapí:l < pél (perhaps ~ pí:l by now).
bury s-th, plant s-th:: pí:lt < pél (perhaps ~ pí:l by now).
s-o has been put away (in grave-house or buried), he's/she's been buried:: qéylemtem ~ qé:ylemtem < qéylem ~ qé:ylem ~ qí(:)lem.

bush

bark (of tree, bush, etc.):: p'elyú:s ~ p'alyú:s or p'elyíws ~ p'alyíws.
(be in the) woods, (amidst bush or vegetation, be tucked away?):: sxí:xets' ~ sxíxets' < xí:ts' ~ xíts' ~ xets'.
blackberry vine, blackberry bush:: skw'ő:lmexwelhp < skw'ő:lmexw.

bush (CONT'D))

blackcap bush:: tselqó:má:lhp < tsélq ~ chélq.
blue elderberry bush, blue elderberry tree:: th'íkwekwelhp < th'í:kwekw ~ th'í:qweqw.
bog blueberry bush:: mólsemelhp < mó:lsem ~ mólsem.
gooseberry bush:: t'á:mxwelhp < t'á:mxw.
hazelnut bush or tree:: sth'í:tsemelhp < sth'í:tsem.
hazelnut tree or bush:: sth'í:tsemelhp < th'éts.
heart of a root, seed, nut (kernel), core of plant or seedling, core (of tree, branch, any growing thing), pith (of bush), seed or pit [U.S.] or pip [Cdn.] of a fruit:: sth'emí:wel ~ sth'emíwel ~ sth'emíwél < sth'ó:m.
Himalaya blackberry bush, evergreen blackberry bush:: xwelítemelh skw'ṓ:lmexwelhp < skw'ṓ:lmexw.
Indian currant bush, red-flowering currant bush, prob. also stink currant bush:: sp'á:th'elhp < sp'á:th'.
Indian plum bush:: mélhx̲welelhp < mélhx̲wel.
in the backwoods, toward the woods, away from the river, in the bush:: chó:leqw < chá:l or chó:l.
red elderberry bush:: sth'íwéq'elhp < sth'íwéq'.

red huckleberry bush:: sqá:lá:lhp ~ qá:lá:lhp < sqá:la.
red huckleberry plant or bush:: qá:lá:lhp < sqá:le.
salal bush:: t'áqà:lhp < t'áqe.
saskatoon bush, service-berry bush:: ts'eslátselhp < ts'esláts.
shake s-th (tree or bush) for fruit or leaves, comb a bush (for berries), shake s-th (a mat or blanket for ex.):: xwíset ~ xwítset < xwís.
shaking bushes (of animal or person unseen, for ex.):: xwóykwem.
short Oregon grape bush:: selíyelhp < selíy.
shrub, small bush (for ex. growing on river edge, or like vine maple or thimbleberry or willow), brush, underbrush:: xwíxwel.
tall Oregon grape bush:: th'ṓ:lth'iyelhp.
thick crowded tight bushes, bushes growing wide from narrow roots or base:: sq'epláts < q'ép.
thimbleberry plant or bush:: t'qwémelhp < t'qwém.
wild rose bush, including: Nootka rose, probably also dwarf or woodland rose and swamp rose, possibly (from Hope east) prickly rose:: qá:lqelhp < qá:lq.

bushes

(come) out of thick bushes:: wexés.

bush robin

winter robin, bush robin, varied thrush:: sx̲wík'.

bush-tit

chickadee: black-capped chickadee, probably also chestnut-backed chickadee, possibly also the least bush-tit:: skíkek < sqá:q.
chickadee: black-capped chickadee, prob. also chestnut-backed chickadee, poss. also least bush-tit:: méxts'el.

bushy

bushy hair:: stíx̲eqw ~ stí:x̲eqw.
(have) bushy and uncombed hair:: chílheqw < =chílh ~ chílh=.

busy

busy at home all the time:: yúkw'es.

but

and, but, or:: qe.

butcher

butchering:: kw'íkw'ets' < kw'íts'.
cleaning or butchering a fish or animal:: kw'íkw'ets'els < kw'íts'.
cut open and butcher it, clean it (of fish or animal):: kw'íts'et < kw'íts'.
fish butchering knife:: kw'éts'tel < kw'íts'.
sides of butchered salmon with knife marks in them:: kw'íkw'ets' < kw'íts'.

Buteo

Buteo jamaicensis, Buteo genus and Accipiter genus:: x̲emx̲ímels ~ x̲emx̲íméls < x̲éym.

Buteo jamaicensis

Buteo jamaicensis, Buteo genus and Accipiter genus:: x̲emx̲ímels ~ x̲emx̲íméls < x̲éym.

butt

butt, ass, rump, buttocks:: slhél:éts ~ slhél:ets ~ slhéléts ~ slhélets < lhél.
cigarette butt:: th'ex̲míls te sp'ótl'em < th'éx̲.
(have a) skinny butt, (be skinny on the rump or bottom):: sth'émlets < sth'ó:m.

butter :: péte.

butter dish:: péte'àlà < péte.

butterfly :: sesx̲á, smímeyàth ~ smímoyàth.

(butterfly (generic) [AC]):: lholeqwót.
butterfly (medium- and small-sized):: ep'ó:yethel? or epó:yethel?.
probably butterfly with white spot, (perhaps white butterfly), if the name applies to one or more predominantly white butterflies it could include the following which occur in the Stó:lō area: Clodius parnassian butterfly, Phoebus' parnassian butterfly, pale tiger swallowtail butterfly, white pine butterfly, checkered white butterfly, veined white butterfly, albino females of alfalfa sulphur butterfly:: p'ip'eq'eyós < p'éq'.
salmonberry worm, (prob. larvae of moths or butterflies or two-winged flies):: xwexwíye.

buttock

butt, ass, rump, buttocks:: slhél:éts ~ slhél:ets ~ slhéléts ~ slhélets < lhél.
on the rump, on the bottom, on the buttock(s):: =élets ~ =lets.

button :: lheq(e)léstel < lhéq.

be buttoned:: slheq(e)lí:s < lhéq.
(be) tight-fitting (of clothes, can't be quite buttoned):: spex̲elís < páx̲.
button it:: lheqlíst < lhéq.
button (up):: lheq(e)lí:sem < lhéq.

buttoned)

(be) tight-fitting (of clothes, can't be quite buttoned):: spepíx̲ < páx̲.

buy
buy (as structured activity), He bought (as structured activity).:: alqá:ls ~ alqáls < iléq.
buying (as structured activity), He's buying (it) [as structured activity].:: íleqels < iléq.
buy it for s-o:: iléqelhtst < iléq.
buy s-th:: iléqet < iléq.

buzz
buzzing (of insects):: t'ít'elem < t'íl.
buzz (of insects):: t'ílém ~ t'ílem < t'íl.

by
by (agent. human, gender unspecified, absent):: tl'.
coming by foot, travelling by walking, already walking, travelling on foot:: ye'í:mex < ím.
get separated (by distance), be by themselves, be separate:: halts'elí.
go travelling by way of, go via:: ley ~ lay < la.
pass by s-o:: yelá:wt < yelá:w ~ yeláw ~ yiláw.
to pass by s-th/s-o:: yelá:wx < yelá:w ~ yeláw ~ yiláw.
to travel by canoe, (nowadays also) travel by airplane, travel by train, travel by car:: yeló:lh < ó:lh.
travelling by, in motion, while moving along, while travelling along:: ye= ~ yi= ~ i┐.

by way of
by way of:: telál.
go through (somewhere), go via (somewhere), go by way of:: lhe'á.

cabbage :: kápech.
skunk cabbage:: ts'ó:kw'e ~ ch'ó:kw'e ~ ts'ó:kw'a.

cabin
little house, cabin (say 12 ft. x 10 ft. or less), small home, storage house (small shed-like house, enclosed with door), outhouse (slang), toilet (slang):: lílem < lá:lém.
log cabin:: t'mí:wsà:ls < t'ém.
log house, log-cabin:: lokáwtxw < lók ~ làk.

cable crossing
bridge, cable crossing:: xwt'át'ekwel < t'ákwel.

cake:: kíks
carrot cake:: xáweq kíks seplíl (lit. carrot + cake + bread)< xáweq, kíks, seplíl
lemon cake:: t'át'ets'em qwíqwòyèls kíks seplíl < t'áts', qwá:y, kíks, seplíl (lit. lemon (itself from sour little yellowish fruit) + cake + bread)

Calamagrostis canadensis
probably Calamagrostis canadensis:: th'á:xey ~ th'áxey < th'áx.

calf
calf:: músmesò:llh < músmes.
calf (of the leg):: q'átl'elxel.
younger deer, baby horse, younger cow, fawn, colt, calf:: st'él'e.

California:: kalipõli.

calik

homemade anchor, kilik, calik, (killick):: skw'éstel.

call

call (by voice), shout, yell, holler:: tà:m.
(calling a chicken):: chek chek chek.
call of a little bird (chickadee?):: ts'í:ts'tlemeth' < ts'í:tl' ~ ts'ítl'.
call of the chickadee:: swí:tì.
call of the Swainson's thrush:: xwét.
call of the winter robin or varied thrush:: sx̲wík'.
call s-o (by voice), holler at s-o, shout at s-o, shout at s-o:: tà:met ~ tàmet < tà:m.
call s-o to witness, call s-o to listen:: xwlalámstexw < xwlalá:.
gray or brown-gray chichadee-sized bird which calls t'ú' or tsk tsk in maple woods near American Bar:: t'ú'.
he/she called me to witness:: xwelalámsthòxes < xwlalá:.
make a high hooting call (maybe only of spirits):: hó:kwt.
the call of the female Swainson's thrush:: Xwatóy < xwét.
they call him/her/them to witness (lit. "he/she/they is/are caused to listen"):: xwelalástem ~ xwelalámstem < xwlalá:.

Calliphoridae

order Diptera, family Calliphoridae:: x̲wex̲wiyáye ~ x̲wix̲wiyáye < x̲wōx̲wáye ~ x̲wex̲wáye ~ x̲wōx̲wá:ye, x̲wiyx̲wiyáye < x̲wōx̲wáye ~ x̲wex̲wáye ~ x̲wōx̲wá:ye, x̲wōx̲wáye ~ x̲wex̲wáye ~ x̲wōx̲wá:ye.

calm

be calm:: slílexwelh.
be calm (of water or wind), (get calm (wind/water), calm down (wind/water), be smooth (of water) [AC, LH]):: qám.
calm (of water), smooth (of water), (when the river is) quiet or calm:: p'ep'ákwem < p'ékw.
calm water (calmer than sqám):: sqáqem < qám.
(get) calm, (become) calm, peaceful:: líqwel < líqw.
get calm (of wind):: qametólém ~ qametólem < qám.
Haig bay, a calm place on the west (C.P.R.) side of the Fraser River by the Haig railroad stop, below and across from Hope:: Sqám ~ Sqà:m < qám.
place in Katz or Ruby Creek, may be name for Charlie Joe's place near Katz at the mouth of a creek where the water is always calm:: sqemélwélh ~ sqemélwelh < qám.
slackened down, calmed down:: líqwem < líqw.
(the wind) is calm, calm (of wind):: qémxel < qám.

Calvatia

probably Calvatia gigantea and Lycoperdon perlatum/gemmatum and possibly other Calvatia or Lycoperdon spp.:: pópkw'em < pékw' ~ péqw'.

Calvatia gigantea

probably Calvatia gigantea and Lycoperdon perlatum/gemmatum and possibly other Calvatia or Lycoperdon spp.:: pópkw'em < pékw' ~ péqw'.

camas

blue camas, (any edible underground vegetable food [SP], vegetable root(s) [MH]):: spá:lxw.

camas (CONT'D))

blue camas, yellow dog-tooth violet = yellow avalanche lily:: sk'ámets ~ sk'ámeth.
potato (generic), including three or four kinds of wild potato: arrowleaf or wapato, Jerusalem artichoke, blue camas, and qíqemxel (so far unidentified plant), besides post-contact domestic potato:: sqáwth ~ sqá:wth.

Camassia leichtlinii

Camassia quamash and Camassia leichtlinii:: spá:lxw.
including: Sagittaria latifolia, Helianthus tuberosus, Camassia quamash (and Camassia leichtlinii), and unidentified plant, besides Solanum tuberosum:: sqáwth ~ sqá:wth.
resp. Camassia leichtlinii and Camassia quamash, Erythronium grandiflorum:: sk'ámets ~ sk'ámeth.

Camassia quamash

Camassia quamash and Camassia leichtlinii:: spá:lxw.
including: Sagittaria latifolia, Helianthus tuberosus, Camassia quamash (and Camassia leichtlinii), and unidentified plant, besides Solanum tuberosum:: sqáwth ~ sqá:wth.
resp. Camassia leichtlinii and Camassia quamash, Erythronium grandiflorum:: sk'ámets ~ sk'ámeth.

cambium

black cottonwood cambium (soft matter between the bark and the wood):: sx̲á:meth.
cottonwood sap, cottonwood cambium:: ts'its'emá:welh.
cottonwood sap or cambium:: sx̲á:meth.

Cameleats

Chilliwack Mountain, village of Cameleats on west end of Chilliwack Mountain:: Qwemí(:)líts.

camp

a camp:: q'élmel < q'el.
camp and rest:: qelá:wthet < qá:w.
to camp, (camping [BHTTC]):: q'élém < q'el.

Camp River

Camp Slough, Camp River:: S'alxwítsel < alxwítsel.

Camp Slough

Camp Slough, Camp River:: S'alxwítsel < alxwítsel.

can

be alright, be okay, it's alright, it's okay, can, be able, it's enough, be right, be correct, that's right:: iyólem ~ iyó:lem < éy ~ éy:.
be totally independent, doing the best one can:: óyó:lwethet < éy ~ éy:.
manage by oneself (in food or travel), try to do it by oneself, try to be independent, do the best one can:: iyólewéthet < éy ~ éy:.
metal can (in U.S. English), a tin (in Canadian English):: q'éx̲q'x̲el < q'(e)x̲.
water kettle, boiler pan (for canning, washing clothes or dishes):: qowletsá:ls < qew.

Canada

Englishman, English, Canadian, Canada, Anglican:: kelchóch ~ kyelchóch.

Canada goose
    big Canada goose, big honker:: tl'x̱wṓmálqel ~ tl'ax̱wṓmálqel.

Canadian
    Englishman, English, Canadian, Canada, Anglican:: kelchóch ~ kyelchóch.

canary-grass
    reed canary-grass:: ts'á:yas te th'á:x̱ey < th'áx̱.

candle
    point or tip of a long object (pole, tree, knife, candle, land):: =eqs ~ =éqsel ~ =élqsel ~ =elqs.

candle-fish
    eulachon, oolachen, candle-fish:: swí:we ~ swíwe.

candy :: kálti.

cane
    cane, staff:: q'éwe.
    new spirit dancer's cane:: q'ewú:w < q'éwe.

Canis familiaris:: sqwemá:y ~ sqwmá:y ~ sqwemáy < qwem.

Canis latrans lestes:: sk'ek'iyáp ~ slek'iyáp, slek'iyáp.

Canis lupus columbianus
    Canis lupus fuscus [tentative], Canis lupus columbianus:: stqó:ya ~ stqó:ye ~ stqó:yá.

Canis lupus fuscus [tentative]
    Canis lupus fuscus [tentative], Canis lupus columbianus:: stqó:ya ~ stqó:ye ~ stqó:yá.

Cannery
    island in river on which Yune's Cannery was built:: Yù:l.

Cannibal
    Cannibal Ogress, Wild Cannibal Woman:: Th'ṓwx̱iya < th'ṓwex̱ ~ th'ṓwéx̱.

cannot locate
    smell that one cannot locate, strong stink:: simáléqep.

canoe :: =ólh.
    a bailer, canoe bailer:: lhéltel < lhí:lt ~ lhílt.
    a canoe or boat cut off short in the rear (because the stern couldn't be repaired):: t'qw'á:lats < t'éqw'.
    adze (for making canoes and pit-house ladders):: xwt'ót'epels ~ shxwt'ót'epels < t'óp.
    adze with handle for canoe-making, elbow-adze:: hálíytel < hà:y.
    a ferry (canoe, boat, ferryboat):: shxwt'át'ekwels < t'ákwel.
    all the equipment for making a canoe, canoe-making equipment:: halíyches < hà:y.
    anchor-line, mooring-line, bow-line, what is used to tie up a canoe:: lhqéletel < lhqé:ylt.
    be how many canoes?:: kw'ilṓwelh < kw'í:l ~ kw'íl.

canoe (CONT'D))

big high-bowed canoe from the Coast, Nootka war canoe, huge canoe:: q'ex̲wṓ:welh ~ q'ex̲wṓwelh.
blunt (end of canoe pole):: témkwes.
boards in a canoe bottom:: lhex̲ōwéstel < lhá:x̲ ~ lháx̲.
bow of a canoe:: q'lhól.
bow of canoe or boat:: =ó:s ~ =ós ~ =es.
break(ing) the canoe:: yekw'ólhem or perhaps yekw'wólhem < yókw' ~ yóqw'.
canoe (any kind), car, vehicle (any kind):: sléxwelh.
canoe, boat:: =ṓ:welh ~ =ṓwelh ~ =ōwelh ~ =ewelh ~ =á:welh ~ =welh ~ =ewí:l.
canoe paddle:: sq'émél.
canoe paddle, paddler(s):: =ṓwes ~ =ṓ:wes ~ =á:wes ~ =ewes.
canoe pole:: sx̲wṓqw'tel < x̲wóqw'.
canoe shed:: slexwelháwtxw < sléxwelh.
canoe with shovel-nose at both ends, same as tl'elá:y:: sqwéthem < qweth.
canoe-work, canoe-making:: s=há:y < hà:y.
carry a canoe on one's shoulders, to portage:: xw'ilamṓwelh < ílàm.
caulking a canoe, plugging a canoe:: t'ékwōwelh < t'ékw.
come with s-o (in a canoe for ex.):: q'ewí:lt < q'éw ~ q'ew.
cottonwood bark driftwood (it was used to carve toy canoes), cottonwood driftwood used for carving toy canoes:: qwémélép ~ qwemélep.
crosspieces in a canoe, (thwarts):: lhex̲elwélhtel < lhá:x̲ ~ lháx̲.
deep bottom (of a river, lake, water, canoe, anything):: stl'epláts < tl'ép.
double-ended canoe:: púpt < pṓt.
drifting backwards in two canoes with net between to catch sturgeon, (drift-netting), backing up (of canoe, train):: tewláts.
drift-netting, catching fish with one or two canoes drifting downstream with a net in deep water:: xíxemel ~ xíxemal.
eight canoes, eight boats:: tqátsa'ṓwelh ? < tqá:tsa.
everybody put away (fishing gear, canoe and) paddles (for winter), put away each other's paddles [and canoes and gear] for winter:: xets'ṓ:westel < xits' ~ xets'.
five canoes belonging to one person, five boats:: lhq'atsesṓwelh ~ lhq'atseséwelh < lheq'át ~ lhq'á:t.
four canoes, four boats:: x̲e'othelṓwelh < x̲e'ó:thel ~ x̲e'óthel.
get a canoe stuck on a rock or something:: xá:m.
get in a canoe, get aboard:: ó:lh.
get off (a canoe or conveyance), get out of a canoe, (disembark):: qw'í:m, qw'í:m.
get s-th aboard (a canoe, car, conveyance):: eló:lhstexw < ó:lh.
go out from the beach (if in a canoe):: tó:l ~ tò:l.
group of canoes travelling upstream (moving to camp for fish-drying for ex.):: istéytiyel.
high-bow canoe, high-bow river canoe, streetcar, tram, taxi, car, automobile:: xwókw'eletsem < xwókw' ~ xwekw'ó.
inside or core of a plant or fruit (or canoe or anything):: =í:wel ~ =íwel ~ =ewel.
make a canoe, making a canoe:: hà:y.
make it hollow (of canoe, log, etc.):: thiyeqwewí:lt < thíy.
making a canoe:: hahà:y < hà:y.
mast on a canoe or boat:: spotelálá < pó:t.
nine canoes, nine boats:: tuxwṓwelh < tú:xw.
one canoe, one boat:: lets'ṓwelh < léts'a ~ léts'e.
(one person) puts away his paddles (and canoe and gear for winter):: xets'ṓ:wes < xits' ~ xets'.
one's canoe is broken up:: yekw'ó:lh or perhaps yekw'wó:lh < yókw' ~ yóqw'.
patch a canoe:: lhéqōwelh ~ lhéqwōwelh < lhéq.
poling a canoe:: x̲wóx̲weqw'et < x̲wóqw'.

canoe (CONT'D))

pry (a canoe paddling stroke when the canoe is hard to turn):: lhímesem < lhímes.
pry with paddle in stern to turn a canoe sharply, pry (canoe stroke done by a sternman):: q'á:lets.
pull ashore in a canoe, land a canoe:: lhà:l.
pulling a canoe through rough water by a rope in the front:: tx̲wő́welh < tóx̲w.
pulling a canoe through rough water by a rope in the front, pulling a canoe with a rope:: tóx̲wesem < tóx̲w.
pull in once with a canoe paddle wide or slow, pull in in turning (a canoe paddling stroke done by a bowman):: lhímes.
push out from shore (in canoe):: thex̲ósem < théx̲.
racing-canoe:: táyewelh < tá:y.
racing in a canoe, canoe-racing (while you're doing it):: tátey < tá:y.
raid s-o in canoes:: sléxwelhmet < sléxwelh.
scorch s-th, blacken s-th with fire, heat it up (near a fire), burning a canoe with pitchwood to remove splinters and burn on black pitch):: qw'á:yt < qw'á:y.
set a net (by canoe), set one's net, fish with a net, (submerge a net):: míliyel < mí:l ~ míl.
seven canoes, seven boats:: th'okwső́welh < th'ó:kws.
short canoe:: ts'ítl'ewelh < ts'í:tl' ~ ts'ítl'.
shovel-nose canoe:: tl'elá:y.
six canoes, six boats:: t'x̲emő́welh < t'éx̲.
small canoe:: slílxwelh < sléxwelh.
steer a canoe:: tháyelets.
stern of canoe, stern-man among paddlers:: iláq.
ten canoes, ten boats:: opelő́welh < ó:pel.
three canoes, three wagons, three conveyances (any form of transportation), three boats:: lhxwó:lh < lhí:xw.
tie it up (of a canoe):: lhqé:ylt.
tip over (of a canoe):: qwélh.
tippy (of a canoe):: kw'éth'em < kw'eth'ém.
to bag net, to sack net, to still-dip with two canoes:: thqá:lem.
to fasten s-th by tying, tie up s-th (like canoe, horse, laces, nets, cow, shoelaces), tie it:: q'éyset ~ q'í(:)set < q'ey ~ q'i.
to paddle, paddling a canoe (in rough water):: éxel.
to pole a canoe:: x̲wóqw'et < x̲wóqw'.
to race in a canoe:: tá:y.
to travel by canoe, (nowadays also) travel by airplane, travel by train, travel by car:: yeló:lh < ó:lh.
touching bottom (of a canoe or a person):: tesláts < tós.
two canoes, two boats:: islő́welh ? or iső́welh ? < isá:le ~ isále ~ isá:la.
unloading a canoe, taking things out of a canoe:: qw'íméls < qw'í:m.
U-shaped or horseshoe-shaped knife for scraping out an adzed canoe:: sqw'emqw'emóx̲w < qw'ómx̲w.
U-shaped or horseshoe-shaped knife (or plane) for scraping out canoe:: xepá:ltel < xíp.

canoe-making

bent U-shaped plane with handle on each end for canoe-making:: sqw'emóx̲w sxíxep < xíp, sqw'emóx̲w xíxepels < xíp.

can-opener

an opener, can-opener, bottle-opener:: shxwéma'ám < má ~ má'-, shxwémeqel < má ~ má'-, shxwémeqèyls < má ~ má'-.

can't
    (be) tight-fitting (of clothes, can't be quite buttoned):: spepíx̲ < páx̲.
    impossible, can't be:: kw'á:y ~ kw'áy.
    it is impossible, it can't be, it never is:: skw'á:y < kw'á:y ~ kw'áy.

can't reach:: sq'thá:mtses < q'thá:m.
    can't reach (with hand):: q'thá:mtses < q'thá:m.

can't see
    (have/be) dirty water, (not clear, unclear, can't see the bottom (of water) [EL]):: mímexwel.

canvas-back duck:: lamélwelh.

canyon
    canyon area on Chehalis Creek just above (upriver or north from) the main highway bridge (esp. the first cliff on the east side) [means one-legged]:: Páléxel ~ Paléxel.
    canyon (narrow, walled in with rock):: sx̲ex̲ákw' < x̲ékw'.

cape :: lópōs.

Capella gallinago:: wéthweth < wíth, wóthiya < wíth.

Cape Mudge
    Yuculta Kwakiutl people, southern Kwakiutl people from Cape Mudge north who raided the Salish people:: Yéqwelhtax̲ ~ Yéqwelhta.

capsize
    tip over, capsize:: kw'élh.

car
    automobile, car:: tox̲wemíwel < tóx̲w, xwixwekw'elátsem < xwókw' ~ xwekw'ó.
    (be) too tight (of shoes, clothes, trap, box), tight (of a dress one can't get into), too tight to get into (of dress, car, box of cards, etc.):: stl'etl'íq' < tl'íq'.
    canoe (any kind), car, vehicle (any kind):: sléxwelh.
    car, automobile:: kyó.
    get in a conveyance, get in a car, mount a horse:: ó:lh.
    get s-th aboard (a canoe, car, conveyance):: eló:lhstexw < ó:lh.
    get wedged (by falling tree, for ex.), got run over (by car, train, etc.):: tl'íq'.
    go around (a point, a bend, a curve, etc.) in the water, make a U-turn (in the water, could use today on land with a car):: q'ówletsem < q'éw ~ q'ew.
    high-bow canoe, high-bow river canoe, streetcar, tram, taxi, car, automobile:: xwókw'eletsem < xwókw' ~ xwekw'ó.
    run over it (with car), spread it (for ex. on bread with knife), put it up (of wallpaper), (stick it on), stick s-th closed (with pitch for ex.):: tl'íq't < tl'íq'.
    to travel by canoe, (nowadays also) travel by airplane, travel by train, travel by car:: yeló:lh < ó:lh.

card
    a carder (for carding wool):: shxwtéxelqèyls < tex.
    card wool, comb s-th, (carding/combing s-th (wool/hair)):: téxelqèylt < tex.

care

care about s-o/s-th:: shxwlístexw < lí ~ li.
carry it carefully, handle it with care:: sts'áts'elstexw < ts'á:.
look after s-o, protect s-o, take care of s-o:: xólhmet ~ xólhemet < xólh.
looking after s-o, taking care of s-o:: xóxelhmet < xólh.
not care about s-o, have no use for s-o, be impassive:: ewéta shxwlístexw < shxwlí.
take care of oneself, look after oneself, be careful:: xólhmethet ~ xó:lhmethet < xólh.
taking care of oneself:: xó:lhmethet < xólh.

careful

be careful:: thehíthet < thehít, tu s'éy ~ u s'éyò < éy ~ éy:.
take care of oneself, look after oneself, be careful:: xólhmethet ~ xó:lhmethet < xólh.

carefully

carry it carefully, handle it with care:: sts'áts'elstexw < ts'á:.

caress

caressing s-o:: ótqwt < etqwt.
caress s-o:: etqwt.

carp :: scheláka.

carpet

wrap it again, rewrap it, (correction by AD:) roll it up (of a mat, carpet, etc.):: xwelxwélekw't < xwélekw'.

carraway)

wild carrot (possibly spring gold or wild carraway), domestic carrot (both that planted and that gone wild):: xáwéq.

carried away

carried away:: tíyex̲w.
get carried away and sleepy from eating too rich food:: ló:metsel < ló:m ~ lóm, melmelṓws < mál ~ mél.
get carried away (emotionally):: théqw'.

carrot

carrot cake:: xáweq kíks seplíl (lit. carrot + cake + bread) < xáweq, kíks, seplíl
carrot juice:: xáweq sqe'óleqw < xáweq, qó:
carrot-like plant used for green dye:: xáweleq < xáwéq.
little carrots:: xíxewíyeq or xíxewíq < xáwéq.
plane it (with a plane), trim it, taper it (about wood, like slats or roots for baskets, poles for houseposts/totem poles, paddles), taper it (with knife or plane), peel it (a fruit, etc.), whittle it, strip or peel bark off of it, scrape it (of carrots), (carve it, peel it [AC]):: xípet < xíp.
touch s-o purposely, squish it (of berries, etc.), smash s-th, mash it (berries, potatoes, carrots, etc.), bump it:: tóset < tós.
wild carrot (possibly spring gold or wild carraway), domestic carrot (both that planted and that gone wild):: xáwéq.

carry

carried away:: títiyex̲w < tíyex̲w, tíyex̲w.
carry a canoe on one's shoulders, to portage:: xw'ilamṓwelh < ílàm.

carry (CONT'D))

carry a packstrap around the shoulders and across the chest at the collarbone:: s'íteyí:les.
carry a packstrap or both packstraps over the shoulder(s) and under the arm(s):: sq'iwq'ewíles < q'e:yw ~ q'í:w.
carry a packstrap slung across the chest (over one shoulder and under one arm):: st'át'elhíles < t'álh.
carry[ing] a packstrap around the head:: chmaméleqw < chám.
carrying on one's back, packing on one's back:: chmà:m < chám.
carrying s-th/s-o on one's back, packing it on one's back:: chmá:t < chám.
carry it carefully, handle it with care:: sts'áts'elstexw < ts'á:.
carry on one's shoulder:: ílàm.
carry s-o:: kwelát < kwél.
carry s-th on one's back, pack s-th on one's back:: chámet < chám.
carry s-th on one's shoulder:: í:lá:mt < ílàm.
carry s-th/s-o on one's arm:: s'ókw'(e)stexw < ókw'.
get carried away (emotionally):: théqw'.
pack on one's back, carry on one's back:: chámem < chám.
water (someone) carried, (water fetched/gotten):: sqó:m < qó:.

carve

a carving:: x̲ét'kw'els < x̲et'kw'á:ls.
a wood carving:: shxwqwó:lthels, shxwqwó:lthels.
big serving spoon, spoon with handle about ten to 12 inches long, ladle, (spoon carved from mountain goat horn):: x̲álew.
carved outside post on longhouse, totem pole:: x̲wíythi < x̲wíyth.
carve stone, work in stone:: t'eléx̲ot < t'éléx̲.
carve wood, whittle:: x̲et'kw'á:ls.
carving wood, whittling:: x̲át'kw'els < x̲et'kw'á:ls.
plane it (with a plane), trim it, taper it (about wood, like slats or roots for baskets, poles for houseposts/totem poles, paddles), taper it (with knife or plane), peel it (a fruit, etc.), whittle it, strip or peel bark off of it, scrape it (of carrots), (carve it, peel it [AC]):: xípet < xíp.
wood-carving knife:: xepá:ltel < xíp.

carving

a wood carving:: shxwqwó:lthels.

cascara

be bitter (like of cascara bark or medicine or rancid peanuts):: sásex̲em ~ sá:sex̲em < sáx̲em.
cascara tree:: q'á:yx̲elhp.

case

clothes container, suitcase, clothes case:: áwkw'emálá < á:wkw'.
pillow slip, pillow-case:: sx̲wetl'qelá:la < sx̲wétl'qel.
tool case:: á:wkw'mal < á:wkw'.

casket

box, trunk, grave box (old-style, not buried), coffin, casket:: kw'óxwe.

cast

(cast a spell for s-o, use a magical power for s-o):: yewí:lmet < yéw: ~ yéw.
cast a spell on s-o, put a spell on s-o, shoot power into s-o:: x̲t'ét < x̲ét'.
cast a spell, throw a spell, put on a spell, shoot power:: x̲t'áls or x̲t'á:ls < x̲ét'.
casting an evil spell on s-o:: yewí:lt < yéw: ~ yéw.

caste
(have a) white caste over the eye, (have a) cataract:: p'eq'ó:les < p'éq'.

Castor canadensis leucodontus:: sqelá:w, sqiqelá:w < sqelá:w.

castrate
castrated, he was castrated:: ma'elétstem < má ~ má'-.

cat
domestic cat:: pús.
kitten:: púpsò:llh < pús.

cataract
cataracts:: xaxt'ó:les.
(have a) white caste over the eye, (have a) cataract:: p'eq'ó:les < p'éq'.
(have) one white eye, (have a cataract on one eye):: sqwelxwó:lés.

catbird
catbird (has black head), rufous-sided towhee:: sxwítl'.

catch
catch an animal, get an animal:: kwélest < kwél.
catching a fish by hook, hooking s-th, gaffing a fish:: lhílhekw'et < lhíkw' ~ lhí:kw'.
catch it:: kwút < kwú:t.
catch s-o:: qíq'et < qíq'.
catch up with someone:: chél:exw < chá:l ~ chó:l.
contract a disease, catch a disease, get addicted:: q'áp'.
drifting backwards in two canoes with net between to catch sturgeon, (drift-netting), backing up (of canoe, train):: tewláts.
drift-netting, catching fish with one or two canoes drifting downstream with a net in deep water:: xíxemel ~ xíxemal.
(emprisoned), put in jail, grounded, restricted, caught, apprehended:: qíq'.
get s-th, catch s-th, have s-th, find s-th:: kwélexw ~ kwél:exw < kwél.
hook fish, catch fish (by hook), to gaff-hook fish:: lhekw'á:ls < lhíkw' ~ lhí:kw'.
November, time to catch salmon:: temth'ó:qwi < sth'ó:qwi ~ sth'óqwi.
one's catch (fish, game, etc.):: sxélcha ~ sxélche < xélcha.
see s-o/s-th, catch sight of s-th/s-o:: kw'étslexw < kw'áts ~ kw'éts.
to catch (fish, game, birds):: chxélcha < xélcha.
to hook, to catch (by horns or thorns):: lhíkw' ~ lhí:kw'.

catechism :: katkasyéthem.

category
a category of religious songs including sxwó:yxwey songs and burning songs, a burning song:: heywí:leqw < yéw: ~ yéw.

caterpillar:: smímexàlh.
inchworm, (caterpillar of the geometrid moth family):: q'álq'elp'í:w < q'ál, q'alq'elő:wsem < q'ál.

Cathartes aura:: éq"eq'esem.

Catharus guttatus
respectively Hylocichla guttata or Catharus guttatus, or possibly Hylocichla minima or Catharus minimus:: slhólho.

Catharus minimus
respectively Hylocichla guttata or Catharus guttatus, or possibly Hylocichla minima or Catharus minimus:: slhólho.

Catholic :: Káthlek.

Catostomus catostomus
probably Catostomus catostomus:: skwímeth < kwí:m.

Catostomus macrocheilus
probably Catostomus macrocheilus:: q'óx̲el.
prob. Catostomus macrocheilus:: qw'á:ts.

cat-tail
cat-tail, cattail reed:: sth'á:qel.
cattail, cattail rush or reed, (bulrush [AC, BJ]):: sth'á:qel.
cattail mat (large or small):: solá:ts.
fine airborne seed(s) (not used of plum or apple seed(s) or the hard seeds -- sth'emíwél is used for those) (used for dandelion seeds, cottonwood seeds, etc., tail of a cat-tail reed, (plant fluff (possibly including tail of cat-tail rush) [Elders Group 2/27/80]):: spéxwqel ~ spéx̲wqel < píxw.

cattail/roots/bulrushes
bulrush mat, reed mat, mat (of cattail/roots/bulrushes, etc.), (wall mat (Elders Group 11/12/75):: wá:th'elh ~ wáth'elh < wáth'.

cattle)
small adult cows, (small adult cattle):: melúmesmes < músmes.

Caucasian)
White person, (Caucasian), White man:: xwelítem.

cauliflower:: p'éq' sp'áq'em kápech < p'éq', p'áq', kápech
(lit. white + flower + cabbage)

caulk
caulking a canoe, plugging a canoe:: t'ékwōwelh < t'ékw.

causative
causative control transitivizer:: =st.

cause
(make that s-th (instead), cause that to be s-th (instead)):: tl'óst or tl'óstexw.

cautious
(be) cautious:: st'émt'em < t'ám.

cave :: kwelqéylém ~ kwelqílém.

cave (CONT'D))

a river bank caving in:: péqweles < péqw.
caves:: kwelkwelqéylém < kwelqéylém ~ kwelqílém.
mountain with caves that is behind Hunter Creek (in 1976-1977 they blasted this mountain where it was beside Trans-Canada Highway #1 to shorten the highway past it):: Tómtomiyeqw.

Caves

mouth of Hunter Creek, (Restmore Caves (Wells)):: ōqw'íles ~ ōqw'éyles < wṓqw' ~ wéqw'.
Restmore Caves [Wells]), (mouth of Hunter Creek [IHTTC]):: Uqw'íles.

cedar

cedar bark mat:: slhqw'á:y < lhéqw'.
cedar bark skirt:: lhqw'áy < lhéqw', sèqw'emí:ws < síqw'em.
cedar limb rope (slitted):: stélwél.
cedar pole:: sókw'émelhp < sókw'.
cedar sapling basket:: tl'pát.
cedar slat basket, cedar sapling basket:: th'ṓwex̲ ~ th'ṓwéx̲.
cedar trough (to serve food):: x̲epyúwelh < sx̲éyp.
fine cedar root strips for baskets:: shxwth'á:lhtel.
fine cedar root weaving, fine cedar root work:: sts'éqw' ~ sch'éqw' < ts'éqw'.
headband, headband made out of cedar bark woven by widow or widower when mourning:: qítes ~ qéytes < qít.
inner cedar bark:: slewí < léw.
inner cedar bark (maybe error), (birch bark [AHTTC]):: sèqw'emí:ws < síqw'em.
making a basket, (weaving a cedar root basket):: th'éqw'ōwelh ~ (probably ts'éqw'ōwelh) < ts'éqw'.
outer cedar bark:: sókw'em < sókw'.
peel cedar bark:: síqw'em.
prickly (from fir bark, wool, or something one is allergic to), irritant, have an allergic reaction (to fir powder or cedar bark):: th'íth'ekwem < th'íkw.
(red) cedar limb, (red) cedar bough:: x̲pá:ytses ~ x̲páytses < sx̲éyp.
small float for nets (made from singed cedar):: qwōqwá:l ~ qweqwá:l.
tinder, material used to start a fire with (fine dried cedar bark):: syeqwlhá:ltel < yéqw.
to weave a cedar root basket:: ts'eqw'ṓ:welh ~ ts'eqw'ṓwelh ~ ch'eqw'ṓwelh < ts'éqw'.
western red cedar tree:: x̲pá:yelhp ~ x̲páyelhp < sx̲éyp.
western red cedar wood:: x̲epá:y ~ x̲epáy ~ x̲pá:y < sx̲éyp.
wide cedar root strips for baskets:: yemáwéstel < yém ~ yem.
wide cedar (sapling) strips or slats from young cedar trunks, cedar slat work (basketry):: x̲pó:ys < sx̲éyp.
yellow cedar:: pó:xeleqw.
young cedar:: súsekw'.
young (red) cedar:: shxwt'ám:etsel.

cedar-bark]

new spirit-dancer's head-dress or [cedar-bark] hat:: sx̲wóyéleqws te x̲awsólkwlh < sx̲wóyéleqw.

ceiling :: skwetxwós < kwetáxw.

roof, shake(s) on roof, shingle(s) on roof, ceiling:: síqetsel < seqíws ~ seqí:ws.

celery:: xwelítemelh sókw' < xwelítem, sókw'

(lit. white man style + inner core of cow parsnip (i.e., yó:le)
wild celery, cow parsnip:: yóle ~ yóla ~ yó:le.

cellar

root cellar, (root house [AD]}:: spepíláwtxw < pél (perhaps ~ pí:l by now).

cent

a half dollar, fifty cents:: lhséq' < séq'.
ten cents, dime:: mí:t ~ mít.

center

be in the middle, be in the center:: shxwá:ye.
core of a rock, center of a rock, core of anything, heart of anything inanimate:: sth'emí:wel ~ sth'emíwel ~ sth'emíwél < sth'ó:m.
crown of head, center of the top of the head where the hair starts:: sq'eyx̲éleqw.

centipede

centipede, and poss. millipede:: lhets'íméls te pítxel < lhts'ímél.

Centre Creek:: Stahiyáq?? or Stiyáq?? or St'ahiyáq?? or Stahí:q??.

village across from or a little above the mouth of Centre Creek into Chilliwack River:: Swóyel.

Cerambycidae

probably order Coleoptera, family Buprestidae, genus Buprestis, or possibly family Cerambycidae, genus Gaurotes:: tále te syó:qwem < tá:le ~ tále, tále te syó:qwem < yéqw.

Ceratopogonidae

order Diptera, probably families Chiromidae, Ceratopogonidae, and Simuliidae:: pepx̲wíqsel < píxw.

ceremony

have a ritual burning ceremony, have a burning, feed the dead, (food offered to the dead [at a ritual burning] [EB 5/25/76]):: yeqwá:ls < yéqw.
name s-o (in a ceremony):: kwíxet < kwí:x ~ kwíx.
sx̲wóyx̲wey ceremony featuring a masked dance, the sx̲wóyx̲wey mask and dance:: sx̲wó:yx̲wey ~ sx̲wóyx̲wey.
thank s-o (for a cure, for pall-bearing, a ceremony, being a witness):: xwth'í:t < ts'ít ~ ch'í:t.
the one who burns [at a burning ceremony], (ritualist at a burning):: híyeqwels < yéqw.

certainly

(polite imperative?, (polite) certainly, (polite) of course):: òwelh ~ -òwèlh.

Cervus canadensis nelsoni

Cervus canadensis roosevelti, perhaps also Cervus canadensis nelsoni:: q'oyíyets or q'oyí:ts.

Cervus canadensis roosevelti

Cervus canadensis roosevelti, perhaps also Cervus canadensis nelsoni:: q'oyíyets or q'oyí:ts.

Cestoidea

order Cestoidea, esp. Taenia solium:: sqwó:qwetl'í:wèl.

Cetorhinus maximus

perhaps Cetorhinus maximus, Hexanchus griseus, Alopius vulpinus, and/or others:: q'ellhomelétsel < q'ellhólemètsel.

chair

a rocking chair:: xwíxweth'àlem sch'áletstel < xwáth', xwixweth'áletstel < xwáth'.
chair, bench, seat, something to sit on:: ch'áletstel ~ sch'á(:)letstel ~ shxwch'áletstel < ts'á:.
chamberpot, potty-chair, urinal:: shxwítel.
(make/have a) squeaking sound (of a tree, of a chair, of shoes), squeaking (of shoes, trees), (creaking):: qá:ytl'em.
missed the chair in sitting down, missed one's chair:: sépelets.
sat down (with a plop?), [slip off on one's bottom or chair]:: xwlhépelets < x̲wlhép.

Chamaecyparis nootkatensis:: pó:xeleqw.

chamberpot

chamberpot, potty-chair, urinal:: shxwítel.

change :: iyá:q.

change course (of a river):: táyéqel.
change it (money) for s-o:: iyóqelhtsthet < iyá:q.
change it (of money):: iyáqest < iyá:q.
change (money):: siyóqelhtsthet < iyá:q.
change oneself (purposely), change oneself into something else, change s-th on oneself:: iyóqthet < iyá:q.
change s-o/s-th (into something else), transform s-o/s-th:: iyá:qt ~ iyáqt < iyá:q.
change s-th (mental/emotional):: iyá:q.
change s-th (physically), replace:: iyá:qt ~ iyáqt < iyá:q.
change s-th (purposely), change s-o, transform s-o/s-th, trade s-th, replace s-th:: iyá:qt ~ iyáqt < iyá:q.
changing in voice (of a boy):: qw'iqw'elá:mqel ~ qw'iqw'elámqel < qw'íl.
to change (of a boy's voice at puberty):: qw'elá:m < qw'íl.
transform s-th/s-o, change s-th/s-o:: x̲éyt.

channel

a channel between an island and the main shore a) across Harrison River from where the Phillips smokehouse was at Chehalis village (slightly downriver from the mouth of Chehalis R. into Harrison R.), also b) at Harrison Lake where the hatchery was:: Lheltá:lets ~ Lheltálets < lhà:l.
a channel that makes an island, inside channel:: lheltálets < lhà:l.
go through a channel:: lheltáletsem < lhà:l.

char)

speckled trout, (prob. brook trout, also called speckled char):: sp'íp'ehà:th' ~ sp'íp'ehàth' < sp'á:th'.

characteristic:: =R12 or =C1V1.

characteristic, inherent continuative:: =R2 or =C1eC2.

characteristically]

be crooked [characteristically]:: spóypiy < pó:y.

charcoal
black coals, charcoal:: p'áts't.

charge
charging (of an angry grizzly for ex.):: á:lqem, i'á:lqem < á:lqem.

Charles
a place just past the west end of Seabird Island, towards Agassiz, AK's grandfather only translated it as Hamersley's (see Hamersley's hopyards), it was located at the west end of Seabird Island i.e. property between Dan Thomas's and Uncle Dave Charles's places, across from Sqémelets [Elders on Seabird Is. trip 6/20/78]):: Qwoméx̲weth' < qwó:m ~ qwóm ~ qwem.

chase
(an Indian doctor or shaman) working, curing, chasing the bad things away:: lhálhewels < lhá:w.
chase it away, (chase s-o/s-th away):: wálhet.
chase s-o, chase s-th, chasing s-o/s-th:: á:ystexw < á:y.
go after s-th/s-o, chase s-o/s-th (not stopping or slowing tillit's caught):: eyát < á:y.
He's chasing them/it repeatedly.:: iy'iyátes < á:y.

chase s-o to have sex:: á:ystexw < á:y.

Cheam)
a mountain facing Chilliwack and adjacent to Mt. Cheam, theoldest sister of Lhílheqey (Mount Cheam):: Oló:xwelwet.
another small peak just to the right of the Mount Cheam summit peak as one faces south, she is another daughter of Lhílheqey (Mt. Cheam):: S'óyewòt < Óyewòt.
Cheam Island (my name for an island in the Fraser River across from Cheam Indian Reserve #2), Cheam village, Cheam Indian Reserve #1:: Xwchí:yò:m < schí:ya, Xwchí:yò:m < schí:ya, Xwchí:yò:m < schí:ya.
creek between Popkum and Cheam, also a location near Popkum, (must be second of two creeks above Popkum that cross Highway #1 [JL 4/7/78]):: sthamí:l.
Mt. Cheam:: Lhílheqey.
one (second) of two creeks just above Popkum which cross Highway #1, (creek between Popkum and Cheam, also a place near Popkum [AC]):: Sthamí:l < themá.
other sister of Lhílheqey or Mount Cheam:: Ts'símteló:t < ts'ísem.
smallest peak just below Mount Cheam (on left of Mt. Cheam looking south), Lhílheqey's (Mt. Cheam's) baby (located about where her breast would be on the left hand side facing her):: Óyewòt.
small peak next to Mount Cheam:: X̲emó:th'iya < x̲à:m ~ x̲á:m.
village now at north end of Agassiz-Rosedale bridge, now Tseatah Indian Reserve #2 (of Cheam band):: Siyét'e.
youngest sister of Lhílheqey (Mount Cheam) that cries:: Ñemó:th'iya < x̲à:m ~ x̲á:m.

Cheam Creek
Cheam Creek on north side below Ford Creek:: Sqwe'óp (?) < qwe'óp.

Cheam Lake
village on east bank of Fraser River near the outlet from Cheam Lake, Popkum Indian village:: Pópkw'em < pékw' ~ péqw'.

Cheam Peak
basin lake near top of Cheam Peak:: Xwoqwsemó:leqw.
the hole (lake) at the foot of Cheam Peak on the south side:: Sqwá:p < qwá.

Cheam View:: Slá:yli < yóle ~ yóla ~ yó:le.
Penis Rock near Cheam View:: Sxéle < sxéle.

cheap
be cheap:: semyó: ~ semyó.

cheat
cheating s-o:: íhóyt < ehó:yt.
cheat s-o (in slahal for ex.):: ehó:yt.

check
check a net or trap (for animal):: kw'echú:yel < kw'áts ~ kw'éts.
check a net or trap (for fish):: kw'echú:yel < kw'áts ~ kw'éts.

cheek :: slheqwéla < slhíqw.
both cheeks:: shxw'el'íle < shxw'íle ~ shxw'í:le.
cheek, cheek-bone:: shxw'íle ~ shxw'í:le.
chin, jaw (of fish, human, etc.), (lips (both), cheek, side of the face [DM]):: ts'emxó:ythel.
fish cheeks:: thipéle, possibly th'ipéle.
on the side of the head, on the temples, around the ear, on the cheek:: =éla.
sitting on one cheek of the rump:: tewálehélets < tewále.

cheek-bone
cheek, cheek-bone:: shxw'íle ~ shxw'í:le.

cheeky
cheeky, rough (of a person in conduct):: lhálts'.

cheer
make s-o happy, cheer s-o up:: xwoyíwelstexw < xwoyíwel ~ xwoyíwél.

cheese:: chí:s
tl'éxw ts'íyxw sqemó: < tl'éx̱w, ts'íyxw, qemó:
(lit. cheese or hard + dry + milk)

Chehalis
Chehalis village on Harrison River, the Heart Rock for which Chehalis, B.C. was named (at the mouth of Chehalis River):: Ts'a'í:les < ts'á:.
Morris Creek (near Chehalis, B.C.), Morris Lake (near Chehalis):: Sx̱áx̱e < x̱áx̱e.
Morris Mountain (near Chehalis):: Sx̱áx̱e Smá:lt < x̱áx̱e.
October moon, time to smoke Chehalis spring salmon:: tempó:kw' < pó:qw' ~ póqw'.
slough facing south [east] across from Chehalis, B.C.:: Xwe'íweqw'óthel.
small Chehalis spring salmon:: pepqw'ólh < pó:qw' ~ póqw'.

Chehalis Creek
canyon area on Chehalis Creek just above (upriver or north from) the main highway bridge (esp. the first cliff on the east side) [means one-legged]:: Páléxel ~ Paléxel.

Chehalis Creek (CONT'D))
Fraser River, (Chehalis Creek, Chehalis River [Elders Group, EL/EB/NP]):: Stó:lō < tó:l ~ tò:l.
silver spring salmon that came up Harrison River and Chehalis Creek, (first spring salmon [Deming]):: sqwéx̲em < qwéx̲em.
Statlu Creek, one of the main tributaries of Chehalis Creek:: stótelō < tó:l ~ tò:l.

Chehalis Indian cemetery
rock up the Harrison River from the old Chehalis Indian cemetery:: Xwyélés ~ Lexwyélés < yél:és.

Chehalis Lake
spring salmon which goes to Chehalis Lake in May then returns to salt water:: sth'olólh.

Chehalis River
a slough on Harrison River north side by the mouth of Chehalis River which has a knee-shaped sandbar at its mouth, this is the next slough above (upriver from) Meth'á:lmexwem:: Q'iq'ewetó:lthel < q'éw ~ q'ew.
Chehalis River mouth (below the highway bridge, where land is breaking up into sand bars), (an opening one could get through in a canoe in high water near Chehalis {IHTTC 8/25/77], small creek (branch of Chehalis River) several hundred yards up Chehalis River from where the road goes from old Chehalis village site to Chehalis River [EL 9/27/77]):: Spōqwṓwelh ~ Speqwṓ:lh < péqw, Spōqwṓwelh ~ Speqwṓ:lh < péqw.
Chehalis village on Harrison River, the Heart Rock for which Chehalis, B.C. was named (at the mouth of Chehalis River):: Ts'a'í:les < ts'á:.
Harrison River spring salmon, Harrison River chinook salmon, big Chehalis River spring salmon, (preserved (smoked?) meat [AC: Tait dialect]):: pó:qw' ~ póqw'.
heart-shaped island near the mouth of Chehalis River that beat like a heart:: Th'álátel ~ Th'á:lá ~ Th'ála < th'á:lá ~ th'ála ~ th'á:le ~ th'ále.
island or point on north side of first slough north of the mouth of Chehalis River, (next slough and point above Mímex̲wel [EL 3/1/78]):: Yálhxetel.
late fall Harrison River and Chehalis River sockeye salmon (last run, kind of red):: qwechíwiya.
late fall sockeye salmon (last run on Harrison River and Chehalis River, kind of red):: sqwó:yxw.
place near mouth of Chehalis River where they had a mass burial during a smallpox epidemic:: Smimstiyexwálá ~ Smímstíyexwá:le < mestíyexw.
west fork of stream which goes into Chehalis River above Páléxel:: Th'ámxwelqs.

cherry
blackened bitter cherry bark:: pélel.
cherry bark (for baskets):: st'elém < t'elém.
choke cherry:: lhex̲wlhéx̲w < lhex̲w.
wild cherry tree, bitter cherry tree:: t'elémelhp < t'elém.

chest)
(be) doubled up (a person with knees up to his chest), all doubled over:: sqw'emqw'emóx̲w < qw'ómx̲w.
carry a packstrap around the shoulders and across the chest at the collarbone:: s'íteyí:les.
carry a packstrap slung across the chest (over one shoulder and under one arm):: st'át'elhíles < t'álh.
chest (human or animal thorax):: s'í:les ~ s'í:lés.
cools one's chest inside:: th'elhílésem < th'álh.
female black bear with white spot [or mark] on the chest:: Sx̲éylmòt or sx̲éylmòt < x̲él ~ x̲é:yl ~ x̲í:l.

chest) (CONT'D))

have a hot drink, warm one's chest inside:: qatílésem < qá:t.
hit on the chest:: kw'qwí:les < kw'óqw.
male black bear with white spot [or mark] on the chest:: Sx̲é:ylmet or sx̲é:ylmet < x̲él ~ x̲é:yl ~ x̲í:l.
on the chest, in the chest:: =í:les.
skin of the chest:: kw'elōwíles < kw'eléw ~ kw'elṓw.
wheezing in the chest, rattling in the chest:: xwóyeqw'emíles < xwóyeqw'em.

chesterfield
sofa, couch, chesterfield, place where one's sitting, (bed [AC, MC (Katzie)]):: shxw'ó:met < emét.

chew :: th'ám < th'a.
be chewing s-th hard:: x̲éyx̲ekw'et < x̲éykw'et.
chewed it up:: x̲epx̲epkw't < x̲ep'ékw'.
chewing:: th'á:m ~ ts'á:m < th'a.
chewing (gum):: th'eth'ám < th'a.
chewing (something hard, like apple):: x̲éyx̲ekw'els < x̲éykw'et.
chewing s-th:: th'eth'át < th'a.
chewing with a crunch, nibbling, gnawing:: x̲áp'kw'els < x̲ep'ékw'.
chew it (s-th hard, apple, pill):: x̲éykw'et.
chew s-th:: th'át < th'a.
chew with a crunch:: x̲ep'kw'á:ls < x̲ep'ékw'.
gnaw s-th, chew s-th [crunchy]:: x̲ép'kw't ~ x̲épkw't ~ (sic) x̲épkwt < x̲ep'ékw'.
(mice) chewing (a wall, box, etc.):: ts'átxwels ~ ch'átxwels.

chick
baby chicks:: chelichkelsó:llh < chékel.

chickadee
call of a little bird (chickadee?):: ts'í:ts'tlemeth' < ts'í:tl' ~ ts'ítl'.
call of the chickadee:: swí:tì.
chickadee: black-capped chickadee, probably also chestnut-backed chickadee, possibly also the least bush-tit:: skíkek < sqá:q.
chickadee: black-capped chickadee, prob. also chestnut-backed chickadee, poss. also least bush-tit:: méxts'el.

chicken :: chékel.
baby chicks:: chelichkelsó:llh < chékel.
(calling a chicken):: chek chek chek.
chicken drumstick:: sx̲éles te chékel < x̲éle, chékel (lit. leg of + the + chicken)
chicken dung:: chèkelélets < chékel.
roast chicken:: sqw'élem chékel < qw'él, chékel (lit. roasted/barbecued + chicken)

chicken hawk
chicken hawk (red-tailed hawk), hawk (large and small varieties):: x̲emx̲ímels ~ x̲emx̲íméls < x̲éym.

chickenpox
(have) smallpox, measles, chickenpox:: pelkwí:ws < pél:ékw.

chief

chief, leader, respected person, boss, rich, dear:: siyá:m < éy ~ éy:.
chief's, (belonging to a chief, in the style of a chief):: siyómelh < siyám ~ (rare) siyá:m.
respected leader, chief, upper-class person, boss, master, your highness:: siyám ~ (rare) siyá:m.
respected leaders, chiefs, upper-class people:: sí:yá:m < siyám ~ (rare) siyá:m.

child

adopt a child:: txwmelám < méle ~ mél:a, txwméla ~ texwméla < méle ~ mél:a.
adopted child:: smelám < méle ~ mél:a.
already had children:: semsémele < méle ~ mél:a.
baby (kin), child (kin) (up to about eigit years old):: mímele < méle ~ mél:a.
bed, (child, young):: =á(:)ylh ~ =á(:)lh ~ =elh (~ =iylh ~ =ó:llh ?).
blowing spray (humorously said of a child teething):: pópex̲wels < póx̲w.
blow (spray) on a patient (of an Indian doctor or shaman), blow spray on s-o/s-th (of a shaman, a person ironing, a child teething):: póx̲wet < póx̲w.
child (of someone, kinterm), offspring, son, daughter:: méle ~ mél:a.
child (post-baby to pre-adolescent), child (under 12), (young [BJ]):: stl'ítl'eqelh ~ stl'í:tl'eqelh.
children (generic):: stá:xwelh.
children (kinterm, someone's), sons, daughters:: mámele < méle ~ mél:a.
children (not one's own necessarily, generic):: stá:xwelh.
child, young, baby:: =ílh ~ =íylh ~ =éylh ~ =elh ~ =á(:)ylh.
girl child, girl (from 5 to 10 years or so):: slheliyó:llh < slhá:lí.
giving birth, having a child, having a baby:: tsméla < méle ~ mél:a.
growing (of animals, children, etc.):: ts'íts'esem < ts'ísem.
have given birth, already had a child, had a baby, (delivered):: sémele < méle ~ mél:a.
her deceased children, (his deceased children):: mameláselh < méle ~ mél:a.
illegitimate child:: skáslekem.
insistant, persistant (like a child pressing to go along), bull-headed, doesn't mind, does just the opposite, (stubborn, contrary):: sxíxeles.
it smells (said to child):: úx̲.
last baby (youngest baby), the last-born, a child cranky and jealous of an expected brother or sister:: óqw'a < óqw'.
nephew, niece, sibling's child (child of sister or brother or cousin (up to and including fourth cousin) [Elders Group]):: stí:wel.
nephews, nieces, sibling's children:: statí:wel < stí:wel.
older sibling, elder cousin (child of older sibling of one's parent, grandchild of older sibling of one's grandparent, great grandchild of older sibling of one's great grandparent), cousin of senior line, older brother, older sister:: sétl'atel < sétl'a ~ sétl'o.
poor little one, you poor thing (said to a child):: t'ó:t'.
reject someone as a spouse or partner for one's child:: qá:lmílh < qéylem ~ qé:ylem ~ qí(:)lem.
reject someone as a spouse or partner for your child:: qá:lmílh.
said to a child of crawling age to teach him something is bad:: yax̲ ~ áx̲.
step-child:: texwmélem < méle ~ mél:a.
step-children:: texwmámelem < méle ~ mél:a.
teachings for children, what is taught to one's children:: s'iwesá:ylhem < íwes.
to babysit someone else's kids (children):: xolhmílh < xólh.
younger sibling, younger brother, younger sister, child of younger sibling of one's parent, "younger" cousin (could even be fourth cousin [through younger sibling of one's great great

grandparent]):: sqá:q.

childbirth

having labor pains, being in labor in childbirth:: ts'áts'elem.

child of deceased sibling

child of deceased sibling, child of deceased brother/sister:: swelmáylh ~ swelméylh < swálém.

child's in-law

children's in-laws:: skw'ekw'ílwes < skw'élwés.

child's spouse's parent, child's spouse's sibling, child's in-laws:: skw'élwés.

child's spouse

child's spouse, son-in-law, daughter-in-law, (man's) sister's husband:: schiwtálh.

sons-in-law, daughters-in-law, children's spouses:: schí:wetálh < schiwtálh.

child's spouse's parent

child's spouse's parent, child's spouse's sibling, child's in-laws:: skw'élwés.

child's spouse's sibling

child's spouse's parent, child's spouse's sibling, child's in-laws:: skw'élwés.

chill

be chilled (of a person), got cold (of a person):: th'óth'elhem < th'álh.

Chilliwack

Chilliwack Indian people:: Sts'elxwíqw ~ Ts'elxwíqw ~ Ts'elxwéyeqw < ts'el.

Squia-ala (now Chilliwack Indian Reserve #7):: Sxwoyehá:lá < xwà:y ~ xwá:y.

Tzeachten, a (recent) settlement on the upper reaches of the lower Chilliwack River, now Chilliwack Indian Reserve #13 near Sardis:: Ch'iyáqtel < sts'iyáq.

Yakweakwioose, next village above Scowkale, village near Sardis on the old Chilliwack River course, now Chilliwack Indian Reserve #9:: Yeqwyeqwí:ws < yéqw.

Chilliwack Indian Reserve

Kwakwawapilt village and reserve (Chilliwack Indian Reserve #6):: Qweqwe'ópelhp < qwe'óp.

Scowkale, sometimes misspelled Skulkayn, now Chilliwack Indian Reserves #10 and #11:: Sq'ewqé(:)yl ~ Sq'ewqí:l < q'éw ~ q'ew.

Chilliwack Lake:: Sxóchaqel < xó:tsa ~ xó:cha.

Chilliwack Mountain

Chilliwack Mountain, village of Cameleats on west end of Chilliwack Mountain:: Qwemí(:)líts.

Chilliwack River:: Sts'elxwíqw ~ Ts'elxwíqw ~ Ts'elxwéyeqw < ts'el.

an old course of the Chilliwack River, now Vedder River:: Lhewálmel < lhá:w.

a place on Chilliwack River, a little above Anderson Flat and Allison's (between Tamihi Creek and Slesse Creek), a village at deep water between Tamihi Creek and Slesse Creek:: Iy'óythel < éy ~ éy:.

Chilliwack River (CONT'D))

creek with its mouth on the south side of Chilliwack River and above the mouth of Middle Creek:: Sch'iyáq < sts'iyáq.

place by Albert Cooper's house on Chilliwack River Road near Vedder Crossing, former village where a slide is now on north bank of Chilliwack River opposite Liumchen Creek:: X̱éylés < x̱éylés.

Semmihault Creek, a stream from the east joining the old Chilliwack River near the Chilliwack airport:: Smiyó:llh?.

Soowahlie village (where Sweltzer Creek met Chilliwack River), Soowahlie Reserve near Vedder Crossing:: Th'ewá:lí < th'éw.

Sweltzer Creek (the stream from Cultus Lake to Chilliwack River at Soowahlie):: Swílhcha Stótelō < Swílhcha.

Tzeachten, a (recent) settlement on the upper reaches of the lower Chilliwack River, now Chilliwack Indian Reserve #13 near Sardis:: Ch'iyáqtel < sts'iyáq.

village above Yakweakwioose on both sides of the Chilliwack River:: Sx̱wó:yx̱weyla ~ Sx̱wóyx̱weyla < sx̱wó:yx̱wey ~ sx̱wóyx̱wey.

village across from or a little above the mouth of Centre Creek into Chilliwack River:: Swóyel.

village at junction of Ryder Lake Creek and Chilliwack River:: T'ept'ṓp.

village on a small flat a little above Vedder Crossing, on the north side of Chilliwack River:: Th'óth'emels < th'óméls.

Watery Eaves, a famous longhouse and early village on a flat area on Chilliwack River just a quarter mile upriver/east above Vedder Crossing:: Qoqoláx̱el < qó:.

Yakweakwioose, next village above Scowkale, village near Sardis on the old Chilliwack River course, now Chilliwack Indian Reserve #9:: Yeqwyeqwí:ws < yéqw.

Chilliwack River Road

place where a grove of birches stood/stand near the Kickbush place on Chilliwack River Road in Sardis, (village at junction of Semmihault Creek and Chilliwack River [Wells 1965 (lst ed.):19]):: Sekw'sekw'emá:y < síkw'.

Chilopoda

class Chilopoda and poss. class Diplopoda:: lhets'íméls te pítxel < lhts'ímél.

Chimaphila umbellata:: chéchelex < chálex.

chin

chin, jaw (of fish, human, etc.), (lips (both), cheek, side of the face [DM]):: ts'emxó:ythel.

hair on the chin or jaw, beard, mustache:: qwiliyéthel < qwíl ~ qwel.

hit on the mouth, [hit on the chin, hit on the lip, hit on the jaw]:: kw'qwó:ythel < kw'óqw.

on the lips, on the jaw, on the chin:: =ó:ythel.

skin of the mouth, (prob. also skin of the chin or jaw or lips):: kw'elōwó:ythel < kw'eléw ~ kw'elṓw.

china

long china platter:: qwsó:les.

Chinese

Chinese person:: chá:lmel.

Chinese language:: chálmelqel < chá:lmel.

chinook salmon
Harrison River spring salmon, Harrison River chinook salmon, big Chehalis River spring salmon, (preserved (smoked?) meat [AC: Tait dialect]):: pó:qw' ~ póqw'.
spring salmon (generic), (Chinook salmon):: tl'élx̲xel ~ tl'álx̲xel < tl'él.
white Fraser River spring salmon that goes upriver with the redspring salmon, (white Fraser River chinook salmon):: speqá:s.

chip
(be) blazed (of a mark in a tree), chipped (of mark in tree):: st'ót'ep < t'óp.
to chip it (like wood):: t'ópet < t'óp.
wood chips:: t'ámel (or) t'ém:el < t'ém.

chipmunk :: tsitsepyóthel.
chipmunk, i.e., Northwestern chipmunk and Townsend chipmunk:: qwémxel < qwem.
chipmunk with more than two stripes, Northwestern chipmunk, Townsend chipmunk:: x̲ex̲p'í:tsel ~ x̲ex̲p'ítsel ~ sx̲ex̲p'í:tsel < x̲ep'í:tsel.
chipmunk with two stripes, Northwestern chipmunk, also Townsend chipmunk:: x̲ep'í:tsel.

Chiromidae
order Diptera, probably families Chiromidae, Ceratopogonidae, and Simuliidae:: pepx̲wíqsel < píxw.

Chiroptera
order Chiroptera, family Vespertilionidae:: skw'elyáx̲el.
order Chiroptera, family Vespertilionidae, may include any or all of the following: Corynorhinus townsendi townsendi, Eptesicus fuscus bernardinus, Lasionycteris noctivagans, Lasiurus cinereus, Myotis californicus caurinus, Myotis evotis pacificus, Myotis lucifugus alascensis, Myotis volans longicrus, Myotis yumanensis saturatus, and possibly Myotis keeni keeni:: p'íp'eth'eláx̲el ~ p'ip'eth'eláx̲el < p'í:.

chisel
a chisel:: t'et'émels < t'ém.

Choate Creek
Choate Creek on the west (C.P.R,) side of the Fraser River:: St'élxweth' stótelō < St'élxweth'.
village near the mouth of Choate Creek, (Choate Creek [AK, SP/AD], (Stullawheets village on a hill on the east bank of the Fraser River near the mouth of Suka Creek [elders on American Bar Trip (AD/AK/?)]):: St'élxweth'.

chocolate lily:: stl'éleqw'.

choke
(be) choked with smoke:: p'eltl'ómelh < p'ótl'em.
choke on bone or s-th solid:: áq'elh.
choke on food, get choked on food:: t'kwíles ~ t'ekwíles < t'ékw.
choke on water, choked on liquid:: lexwslhém ~ lexwslhám < lhém.
choke s-o/s-th:: p'ith'lhált < p'í:.
getting choked on food:: t'ékweles < t'ékw.

Chondestes grammacus
Melospiza melodia morphna, (perhaps any/all of the following: Passerculus sandwichensis

Chondestes grammacus (CONT'D))
brooksi, Pooecetes gramineus, Chondestes grammacus, Spizella arborea, Spizella passerina, Zonotrichia querula, Passerella iliaca, Zonotrichia leucophrys, Zonotrichia atricapilla, Melospiza melodia morphna):: sx̲wṓx̲wtha.

choose
pick it, choose it, sort it, (choose s-o/s-th):: míset < mís.

chop
adzing, chopping, chopping with an adze:: t'et'éméls < t'ém.
chop one's foot (with axe), [get chopped on the foot (with axe)]:: t'émxel < t'ém.
chop one's hand, [get chopped on the hand]:: t'émches < t'ém.
chopped in different places:: st'amt'í:m (or better) st'emt'í:m < t'ém.
chopping the ground (with hoe or mattock):: t'et'émélep < t'ém.
chop s-th in different places:: t'emt'émet < t'ém.
chop wood, split wood, (chop/split s-th wood):: séq'et < séq'.
chop wood (with an axe), split wood:: th'iqw'élchep or th'iyqw'éltsep < th'íyeqw'.
jade (nephrite) (used for sharpening [chopping] stones), any agate (can be used as flint to strike a spark):: t'émq'ethel.
smooth a log by chopping:: t'mí:ws < t'ém.
to chop with an adze, to chop, to adze, an adze:: t'eméls < t'ém.
wood chips:: t'ámel (or) t'ém:el < t'ém.

Chordeiles minor minor:: pí:q'.

Christ
Jesus Christ:: Síthikwi.

Christmas
Christmas day:: swáyels te Chíchelh Siyám < =chílh ~ chílh=.
Christmas Eve, night before Christmas:: X̲áx̲e Slát < x̲áx̲e.

Chrysops
family Tabanidae, genus Chrysops:: lheméléts'.

chum
ma'am, female friend, chum (female), little girl:: iyés < éy ~ éy:.
pal, best friend, dear friend, chum:: q'óleq ~ q'e'óléq < q'ó.
sir, male friend, chum (male), sonny:: iyéseq < éy ~ éy:.

chum salmon
dog salmon, chum salmon:: kw'ó:lexw.

Church
to pray, have a church service, (a Church (organization, not building) [Elders Group]):: ts'ahéyelh.

church
church house, the church (building):: ts'ahéyelhá:wtxw < ts'ahéyelh, ts'ahéyelhá:wtxw < ts'ahéyelh.
to pray, have a church service, (a Church (organization, not building) [Elders Group]):: ts'ahéyelh.

Cicadidae

probably mostly family Gryllidae, but perhaps family Prophalanopsidae, also perhaps singing groups such as family Tettigoniidae (order Orthoptera) or Cicadidae (order Hemiptera):: tó:lthíwa < tó:l ~ tò:l.

cicely

a grass that grows with berries in fields and everywhere and has seeds that stick in one's throat when eaten with berries, probably a type of brome grass, likely California brome grass, possibly sweet cicely:: táqalh.

Cicuta douglasii

probably Cicuta douglasii:: welékwsa.

cigar :: sikó.

cigarette :: sikelít.

cigarette butt:: th'ex̲míls te sp'ótl'em < th'éx̲.

Cimex lectularius:: shxwelítemelh méxts'el < méxts'el.

Cimex lectularius (order Hemiptera, family Cimicidae):: lhelhq'etíwel < lheq'át ~ lhq'á:t.

Cinclus mexicanus

Cinclus mexicanus:: smélx̲weth'.

cinder

ashes (cinder-like), cinders (heavy and dirty), embers:: shxwiyélhtel ~ shxwyélhtel < yólh.

circle

a circle:: st'elákw' < t'elákw'.

(circle) around the fire once and return to the start, make one circle in longhouse:: sélts' < sél or sí(:)l.

circular frame (for tanning hides):: st'elákw' siyólh < yólh.

go in a semi-circle (or part of a circle) with the current:: selch'éle < sél or sí(:)l.

go in full circle with the current:: sá:lch'ōwelh < sél or sí(:)l.

(in a) circle:: =iyó:s.

lower circle under eye:: stl'epó:lemelh ~ stl'epó:les < tl'ép.

moving, (many moving around in circles, moving around in circles many times):: x̲elx̲álqem < x̲álqem.

(perhaps) around in circles:: =qw' ~ =eqw'.

(perhaps) round, around in circles:: =kw' ~ =ekw'.

rolling, moving [around in circles]:: x̲álqem.

spotted with circles or round dots:: tl'eltl'élx̲ < tl'él.

twist, turn around, around in circles:: =ts' ~ =elts' ~ =á:lts'.

upper circle over the eye, probably upper eyelid:: chelhó:lemelh < =chílh ~ chílh=, schelhó:les < =chílh ~ chílh=.

circular

circular frame (for tanning hides):: st'elákw' siyólh < yólh.

circular objects:: =ó:s ~ =ós ~ =es.

circular, round and flat:: st'elákw' < t'elákw'.

Cirseum arvense
  Cirseum vulgare, Cirseum arvense, and probably Cirseum edule, Cirseum brevistylum:: ts'eqw'ts'eqw' < ts'éqw'.

Cirseum brevistylum
  Cirseum vulgare, Cirseum arvense, and probably Cirseum edule, Cirseum brevistylum:: ts'eqw'ts'eqw' < ts'éqw'.

Cirseum edule
  Cirseum vulgare, Cirseum arvense, and probably Cirseum edule, Cirseum brevistylum:: ts'eqw'ts'eqw' < ts'éqw'.

Cirseum vulgare
  Cirseum vulgare, Cirseum arvense, and probably Cirseum edule, Cirseum brevistylum:: ts'eqw'ts'eqw' < ts'éqw'.

Citrus aurantium
  especially Citrus sinensis, also Citrus aurantium:: qwiqwóyáls ~ qwiqwóyéls ~ qwiqwòyàls < qwá:y.

Citrus limon:: tsqwá:y < qwá:y.

Citrus sinensis
  especially Citrus sinensis, also Citrus aurantium:: qwiqwóyáls ~ qwiqwóyéls ~ qwiqwòyàls < qwá:y.

claim
  (be) bragging, extravagant in claims, bull-headed, claims he's the best:: sqoyéx̲iya < sqáyéx̲ ~ sqayéx̲.

clam
  clam, butter clam, fresh-water clam, fresh-water mussel:: s'óx̲we, s'óx̲we.
  dried big clams threaded onto a string of inner cedar bark (obtained in trade):: swà:m.
  (horse clam):: swà:m.

clap
  clap one's hands, clap once with hands:: lhéqw'tsesem < lhóqw'et.
  clapping with (one's) hands:: lhólheqw'tsesem < lhóqw'et.

class
  high class people:: semelá:lh < smelá:lh.
  low class person, [person on the lowest economic class]:: stít-sòs < t-sós ~ tesós.
  respected leader, chief, upper-class person, boss, master, your highness:: siyám ~ (rare) siyá:m.
  respected leaders, chiefs, upper-class people:: sí:yá:m < siyám ~ (rare) siyá:m.
  respected person, (high class person [EB]):: smelá:lh.

claw
  fingernail, nail of finger, claw:: qw'ex̲wéltses.
  scratch s-o/s-th and leave a mark, rake it, claw it, scrape it:: x̲éyp'et < x̲éyp'.

clay

diatomaceous earth (could be mixed with things to whiten them--for ex. dog and goat wool), white clay for white face paint (for pure person spirit-dancers), white powder from mountains, white clay they make powder from to lighten goat and dog wool for blankets, powder, talc, white face paint:: st'ewő́kw'.

hard clay, hard earth, smooth (hard) earth:: síq'.

lumpy clay:: qwóméx̲weth' < qwó:m ~ qwóm ~ qwem.

name of place with clay at the edge of the river at some location:: S'áqwemx̲weth' < qwó:m ~ qwóm ~ qwem.

red ochre, (clay colored reddish by oxides of iron):: témélh.

storage basket (for oil, fruit, clothes), burial basket for twins, round basket (any size, smaller at top), clay jug (to store oil or fruit):: skwá:m ~ skwám < kwá:m ~ kwám.

clean

be good, good, well, nice, fine, better, better (ought to), it would be good if, may it be good, let it be good, happy, glad, clean, well-behaved, polite, virgin, popular, comfortable (with furniture, other things?),:: éy ~ éy:.

break up s-th by crumpling, crush it up, rub it together fast (to soften or clean), rub it to soften it (of plants, etc.), fluff it (inner cedar bark to soften it):: yékw'et < yókw' ~ yóqw'.

clean hands:: éyetses < éy ~ éy:.

clean [in everything: clothes, house, person, etc.], clean in one's person and what one owns:: eyétses < éy ~ éy:.

cleaning or butchering a fish or animal:: kw'íkw'ets'els < kw'íts'.

clean it (of table, land, etc.):: tí:lt.

clean one's face:: ep'ósem < á:p' ~ áp'.

clean one's nose:: meqsélem < méqsel.

cut open and butcher it, clean it (of fish or animal):: kw'íts'et < kw'íts'.

is clean, good:: éy ~ éy:.

(perhaps) (be) clean (of a house):: sts'ets'íx̲ < th'x̲ét.

(possibly) clean out brush from a graveyard or the ceremony of graveyard cleaning:: stselqwá:ls < chá:l or chó:l.

(possibly) to clean s-th:: th'x̲ét.

rub (oil or water) in s-th to clean or soften, rub s-th to soften or clean it, (shaping a stone hammer with abrasion?, shaping?, mixing paint?, pressing together or crushing? [BHTTC 9/2/76]):: yémq't.

clear

be clear (of water), be smooth (AC):: xwe'éyem ~ xw'éyem < éy ~ éy:.

be in clear voice, be in good voice, be in good health, healthy:: shxw'éyelh < éy ~ éy:.

clear it (of land):: tí:lt.

clear up (of weather), turn fine (after a hard storm):: iyílem < éy ~ éy:.

(have) a clear voice:: xw'éyeqel < éy ~ éy:.

(have/be) dirty water, (not clear, unclear, can't see the bottom (of water) [EL]):: mímexwel.

rapids, fast water, clear water, flowing fast, going fast, swift (water):: lex̲wő́:m ~ lex̲wő́m < x̲wém ~ xwém.

to clear land:: tí:lthet < tí:lt.

clearing

a fairly flat clearing on a mountain in Morris Valley where they used to play ts'its'eqweló:l or Indian badminton:: Ts'éqwela ~ Th'éqwela < ts'éqw ~ th'éqw.

cleft
    cleft in back of the neck:: t'ayéq'psem < t'ay.

cleft palate
    cleft palate, harelip:: qiqewótheló:ythel < sqewáth.

Clethrionomys gapperi cascadensis
    may include any or all of the following which occur in this area: creeping vole Microtus oregoni serpens, long-tail vole Microtus longicaudus macrurus, mountain heather vole Phenacomys intermedius oramontis, boreal redback vole Clethrionomys gapperi cascadensis, Norway rat (intro.) Rattus norvegicus, and perhaps roof rat Rattus rattus, also includes bushy-tailed wood rat (packrat) Neotoma cinerea occidentalis which has its own name below:: há:wt.
    prob. the introduced Rattus norvegius, native species possiblyincluding any/all of these four: Microtus oregoni serpens, Microtus longicaudus macrurus, Phenacomys intermedius oramontis, and Clethrionomys gapperi cascadensis, possibly also the introduced Rattus rattus:: ts'á:txwels < ts'átxwels ~ ch'átxwels.

cliff
    cliff, vertical rock face:: qw'eléqel.
    fell of its own accord (of an object from a height or from upright), drop down (object/person, from a shelf, bridge, cliff, etc.), fall off:: wets'étl' ~ wech'étl'.
    soft (knee-shaped) cliff on a beach:: =ó:lthel.
    throat of a cliff or mountain:: =eqel.

climax
    bring oneself to a climax, to climax, to orgasm, masturbate:: wets'á:lómet < ts'á:.
    to climax, come (sexually), ejaculate:: qw'lhòlèm or qw'lhlòlèm.

climb
    climb a mountain, climb a hill, go up a mountain or hill:: kw'íyeqel < kw'í ~ kw'íy, kw'íyeqel < kw'í ~ kw'íy.
    climb, get up a vertical surface:: kw'í ~ kw'íy.
    climbing, rising:: kw'ekw'í < kw'í ~ kw'íy.

clink
    clinking, tinkling (of glass, ice in glass, glasses together, dishes together, metal together):: ts'átx̲em ~ th'átx̲em.
    (have) clinking (of glass or dishes or metal), (have) tinkling sound (of glass, ice in glass, glasses together):: th'átx̲em ~ ts'átx̲em.

clippers
    nail clippers (lit. "scissors for the fingernails"):: shxwth'ámqels qw'x̲wéltses/qw'x̲wélches < xwáth', qw'ex̲w.

clitoris
    clitoris:: xawelhíqw < xá:welh

clock :: lhók.
    eight o'clock:: steqá:tsas < tqá:tsa.
    eleven o'clock:: slhéms < lhém.

clock (CONT'D)

Friday, five o'clock:: Slhq'átses < lheq'át ~ lhq'á:t.
hour, o'clock, day of week:: s=...=s.
nine o'clock:: stú:xws < tú:xw.
o'clock:: s= =s.
seven o'clock:: sth'ó:kws < th'ó:kws.
six o'clock:: st'x̲éms < t'éx̲.
ten o'clock, (tenth hour):: s'ó:pels < ó:pel.
three o'clock (< the third hour):: slhíxws < lhí:xw.
Thursday, four o'clock, (fourth cyclic period):: sx̲e'óthels < x̲e'ó:thel ~ x̲e'óthel.
two o'clock, two hours:: isáles < isá:le ~ isále ~ isá:la.

(closable container):: =q

close
a lot of trees close together (young), thicket:: théqet < theqát ~ thqá:t.
approach, get near, get closer, reach, go up to, get up to:: tés.
approaching, getting near, getting closer:: tetés < tés.
be closed:: xwtetáq < téq.
be near, be close to, be beside, be next to:: stetís < tés.
close by itself:: téq.
close s-th:: tqát < téq.
close s-th (for ex. a box), put a lid on s-th (for ex. a pot), cover it with a lid:: qp'á:qet < qep'.
close together, (narrow? [MV]):: tl'éts' < tl'í:ts'.
close up a meeting, wind up a meeting, complete a meeting:: yalkw'ólhem or yelkw'wólhem < yókw' ~ yóqw'.
closing one's eyes, shutting one's eyes:: th'íth'eplexw (or perhaps th'íth'ep'lexw) < th'éplexw (or perhaps th'ép'lexw).
come close, come near, come sit in (with a group):: teséthet ~ tséthet < tés.
get close, approach, get near, nearly, (go close, come close):: ts'ímél ~ ts'ímel.
(get closed, become closed):: xwtáq < téq.
get close to s-o/s-th, approach s-th/s-o:: ts'ímélmet < ts'ímél ~ ts'ímel.
getting close:: ts'íts'emel < ts'ímél ~ ts'ímel.
(have) one eye closed:: lheq'ó:les.
lots of eyes being closed:: th'elíth'eplexw ~ ts'elíts'eplexw (or perhaps ts'elíts'ep'lexw) < th'éplexw (or perhaps th'ép'lexw).
pair of twins, pair of closest friends:: sq'eq'e'óleq < q'ó.
run over it (with car), spread it (for ex. on bread with knife), put it up (of wallpaper), (stick it on), stick s-th closed (with pitch for ex.):: tl'íq't < tl'íq'.
shut one's eyes, close one's eyes, (blink [EB]):: th'éplexw (or perhaps th'ép'lexw).

cloth :: sí:l.
be wearing a loincloth:: sthiyáp < sthíyep.
cloth or warm material to wrap around the foot, stockings:: chóxwxel.
denim cloth:: xwétkw'em < xwót'kw'em.
dishcloth:: shxwiyòtqw'ewí:ls.
face-cloth:: shxwíqw'estel < íqw'.
loincloth, dog-hair apron, dog-hair mat:: sthíyep.
needle (for sewing cloth, for mat-making):: p'éth'tel < p'áth'.

clothes :: á:wkw', =íth'a ~ =íth'e.

clothes (CONT'D)

(be) a dark color (of clothes, complexions, etc.), (dark gray, dark brown):: stl'ítl'esel < stl'ítl'es.

be faded (of clothes), (get/become) faded, (go or get or become gray):: xwíkw'el < xwíkw'.

(be) tight-fitting (of clothes, can't be quite buttoned):: spex̲elís < páx̲, spepíx̲ < páx̲.

(be) too tight (of shoes, clothes, trap, box), tight (of a dress one can't get into), too tight to get into (of dress, car, box of cards, etc.):: stl'etl'íq' < tl'íq'.

be worn out (of clothes for ex.), be old (of clothes), smashed up when dropped, dissolved:: th'éw.

buckskin clothes:: míyethélwét < sméyeth ~ sméyéth.

clothes basket:: shxw'awkw'ála < á:wkw'.

clothes, clothing (esp. Indian clothing, men's or women's), something to wear, dress, gown:: s'íth'em < íth'a.

clothes container, suitcase, clothes case:: áwkw'emálá < á:wkw', áwkw'emálá < á:wkw'.

clothes store:: awkw'áwtxw < á:wkw'.

clothes store, clothing store:: ith'emáwtxw < íth'a.

denim clothes:: xwétkw'emélwet < xwót'kw'em.

patch s-th (of clothes, nets), patch s-th up:: p'ōwíyt ~ p'ewíyt < p'ewíy ~ p'ōwíy.

peel it off (clothes):: lhqw'íwst < lhéqw'.

slide down (of clothes):: lhósem < lhós.

stick for beating blankets or clothes or mat, blanket-beater, clothes-beater, mat-beater, rug-beater:: kw'ekw'qwá:lth'átel < kw'óqw.

suitcase (Deming), luggage (Deming), clothing container, clothes bag, trunk (for clothes), etc.:: áwkw'emálá < á:wkw'.

take off one's clothes, undress:: lhōwth'ám < lhewíth'a.

take someone's food or clothes:: kwétxwt.

two garments, two (items of) clothes:: islélwet < isá:le ~ isále ~ isá:la.

washing one's clothes:: th'éx̲welwetem < th'éx̲w or th'óx̲w.

wash one's clothes:: th'x̲welwétem < th'éx̲w or th'óx̲w.

water kettle, boiler pan (for canning, washing clothes or dishes):: qowletsá:ls < qew.

clothing

clothes, clothing (esp. Indian clothing, men's or women's), something to wear, dress, gown:: s'íth'em < íth'a.

clothes store, clothing store:: ith'emáwtxw < íth'a.

clothing, food, and possessions burned and given away when a person dies, (possessions and food burned and given away at a burning):: syeqwá:ls < yéqw.

clothing, material:: =íth'a < íth'a.

garment, clothing:: =elwet ~ =élwet.

suitcase (Deming), luggage (Deming), clothing container, clothes bag, trunk (for clothes), etc.:: áwkw'emálá < á:wkw'.

upper clothing, clothing on upper half of the body:: chlhíth'a < =chílh ~ chílh=.

warm (of clothing):: hólem.

cloud :: shxw'áthtel < thá:t.

be steaming (in many places), be cloudy with rain-clouds:: pelpólx̲wem < poléx̲wem.

fleecy wave clouds that look like sheep:: x̲eylx̲elemós.

(get a) ray of sun between clouds:: qeyqeyx̲elósem < qéyqeyx̲elà.

getting cloudy, clouding up:: xwathtálém < thá:t.

clove-hitch

spear pole knot hitch (two half-hitches), clove-hitch knot:: ts'sítsim.

clover

clover, prob. both white clover and red clover:: lhő:me.

club

beating s-o/s-th with a stick, hitting s-o/s-th with a stick, clubbing it:: kw'ókw'eqwet < kw'óqw.
clubbed on the back of the neck, clubbed on the back of the head:: kw'qwépsem < kw'óqw.
clubbing many times, hitting many times:: kw'elqwál < kw'óqw.
club on the body:: kw'qwí:ws < kw'óqw.
hit s-o on the head, club him on the head:: kw'qwéleqwt < kw'óqw.
hit with a stick-like object, clubbed:: kw'óqw.
salmon club:: kw'óqwestel < kw'óqw.
sturgeon club, fish club (for salmon, sturgeon, etc.):: slá:meth.
war club, club for any purpose:: kw'óqwestel < kw'óqw.

cluster]

eight fruit in a group [or cluster] (as they grow on a plant):: tqòtsòls < tqá:tsa.
four fruit in a group or cluster (as they grow on a plant):: x̱(e)'othelòls < x̱e'ó:thel ~ x̱e'óthel.
nine fruit in a group or cluster (as they grow on a plant):: tuxwòls < tú:xw.
seven fruit in a group or cluster (as they grow on a plant):: th'ekwòls < th'ó:kws.
three fruit in a cluster (as they grow on a plant):: lhexwòls < lhí:xw.

coal

black coals, charcoal:: p'áts't.

coal-oil lamp

an electric light, coal-oil lamp, lamp:: yeqwí:l ~ yeqwì:l < yéqw.

coarse

(have) coarse hair:: mekwélqel < mékw.
stout (of a person), thick (of a tree), thick around, coarse (of a rope), big (fat) (of a person). big (in girth):: mékw.

coat :: kopú.

coax

coaxing imperative plural:: -atlha.
coaxing imperative singular:: -tlh ~ -lh.

Coccinellidae)

order Coleoptera, family Coccinellidae):: slhálhlí < slhá:lí.

cock

draw a bow, cock a gun:: xwe'ít'et.
draw a bow, cock a gun, (draw it (of a bow), cock it (of a gun)):: xwe'ít'et < ót'.

cock-eyed
    cross-eyed, prob. also cock-eyed:: skw'íts'òlès.

cod
    ling-cod:: á:yt ~ é:yt, mechó:s.

coffee :: kópi.

coffee mate
    powdered milk/coffee mate:: ts'áyxw s-qemó < ts'áyxw, qemó (lit. dry + milk)

coffee-pot:: kópi'álá < kópi.

coffin
    box, trunk, grave box (old-style, not buried), coffin, casket:: kw'óxwe.

coho salmon
    coho net:: kwṓxwethtel < kwṓxweth.
    coho salmon, silver salmon:: kwṓxweth.
    coho salmon time, August to September:: temkwṓxweth < kwṓxweth.
    small (fully grown) coho salmon, [kokanee]:: sth'ímiya < sth'í:m ~ sth'ì:m.

coil
    be coiled (ready to strike for ex. of a snake):: sq'elá:w < q'ál.
    (be) coiling (ready to strike) (of a snake):: sq'elq'elá:w < q'ál.
    coiled bottom of a basket before the sides are on:: skwélets < kwél.
    coiled up méthelh rope for fishing (for sturgeon and spring salmon):: ts'tíxem.
    coil it, wind it up (of string, rope, yarn):: q'élq't < q'ál.

Colaptes cafer cafer
    Colaptes cafer cafer and rarely Colaptes cafer collaris, (if large is correct Dryocopus pileatus [AK], if small is correct, probably Sphyrapicus (varius) ruber or possibly Dryobates villosus harrisi and Dryobates villosus orius or Dryobates pubescens (esp.) gairdneri some zoologists replace the genus Dryobates with Dendrocopos, others with Picoides):: th'íq.

Colaptes cafer collaris
    Colaptes cafer cafer and rarely Colaptes cafer collaris, (if large is correct Dryocopus pileatus [AK], if small is correct, probably Sphyrapicus (varius) ruber or possibly Dryobates villosus harrisi and Dryobates villosus orius or Dryobates pubescens (esp.) gairdneri some zoologists replace the genus Dryobates with Dendrocopos, others with Picoides):: th'íq.

cold
    a cough, a cold with a cough:: stó:qw'em < tó:qw'em.
    be chilled (of a person), got cold (of a person):: th'óth'elhem < th'álh.
    be cold:: x̲éytl' ~ x̲í:tl'.
    (cold (of a person) or get cooled down, get cold):: th'ólhem < th'álh.
    freezing, freezing cold:: pípewels < pí:w.
    get cold:: x̲éytl'thet < x̲éytl' ~ x̲í:tl'.
    getting colder:: x̲é:ytl'thet < x̲éytl' ~ x̲í:tl'.
    (have) fingers so cold they can't bend:: memekwóyetses < mékw.

cold (CONT'D)

(have/get) a head cold:: th'ólhem sq'óq'ey < th'álh.
north-east wind, north wind, east wind, cold wind:: só:tets.
one's hand sticks to something (in cold, to honey, to glue, etc.):: t'elémtses < t'elém.

Coleoptera

order Coleoptera, family Coccinellidae):: slhálhlí < slhá:lí.
probably order Coleoptera, family Buprestidae, genus Buprestis, or possibly family Cerambycidae, genus Gaurotes:: tále te syó:qwem < tá:le ~ tále, tále te syó:qwem < yéqw.

Colias erytheme

if the name applies to one or more predominantly white butterflies it could include the following which occur in the Stó:lō area: family Papilionidae: Parnassius clodius, Parnassius phoebus Papilio eurymedon, family Pieridae: Neophasia menapia, Pieris occidentalis, Pieris napi, albino females of Colias erytheme:: p'ip'eq'eyós < p'éq'.

collarbone:: (s)tl'lhíléstel < t'álh.

collect

collect, collect money, take a collection, gather:: q'pá:ls < q'ép.
collected rain-water drops in a bucket:: th'q'emelétsem < th'q'ém ~ th'eq'ém.
collected rain-water from a drip:: th'q'émelets ~ ts'q'émelets < th'q'ém ~ th'eq'ém.
collect, gather:: q'pém < q'ép.
collecting:: q'ápels < q'ép.
collecting s-th, gathering s-th:: q'ápt or q'ápet < q'ép.
gather s-th, pick up s-th (stuff that's scattered about), collect s-th, gather it up, pick them up (already gathered or not):: q'pét < q'ép.
to gather (of people esp.), to collect:: q'ép.

collection

collect, collect money, take a collection, gather:: q'pá:ls < q'ép.

collective)

elders (many collective):: siyelyólexwa < siyólexwe.
plural, (usually) many in a group, collective:: R3= or C1eC2=.
(rare) plural, (usually) many in a group, collective:: R5= or C1e=, =R6= or =eC2=, R7= or C1á=, R8= or C1a=.

color

ash color:: sts'á:s ~ sts'ás.
(be) a dark color (of clothes, complexions, etc.), (dark gray, dark brown):: stl'ítl'esel < stl'ítl'es.
bright (in color):: tstáwél ~ táwél < táw.
burnt color:: syeqwyíqw < yéqw.
have, get, stative or be with colors:: ts= ~ ts'.
in color:: =ó:mex ~ =ómėx ~ =òmèx ~ =ómex ~ =omex ~ =emex.
(many) different colors:: lets'ló:ts'tel < láts'.
orange (fruit), especially mandarin orange (the fruit), also domestic orange, (also orange (color)):: qwiqwóyáls ~ qwiqwóyéls ~ qwiqwòyàls < qwá:y.
red ochre color, color of red clay of iron oxide used for religious paint and face paint:: témélh.
rose color:: qá:lq.

color (CONT'D)

stative (with color terms), have, get (elsewhere):: ts= ~ ch=.
what does it look like?, what does he/she look like?, (how is he/she/it in appearance or looks?), (what color is it? [NP]):: selchímomex < selchí:m ~ selchím.

colt

colt:: statiqíwò:llh < stiqíw.
younger deer, baby horse, younger cow, fawn, colt, calf:: st'él'e.

Columba fasciata

including Columba fasciata, Zenaidura macroura, possibly Ectopistes migratorius, also Columbia livia (introduced):: hemó:.

Columbia livia

including Columba fasciata, Zenaidura macroura, possibly Ectopistes migratorius, also Columbia livia (introduced):: hemó:.

comb

card wool, comb s-th, (carding/combing s-th (wool/hair)):: téxelqèylt < tex.
comb (for hair):: lhts'ímél.
combing one's hair:: téxelqéylem < tex.
comb one's hair, comb one's own hair:: texqéylem < tex.
comb s-o's hair:: texqé:ylt < tex.
fine comb:: lhémxts'el < méxts'el.
(louse-comb):: lhémxts'el < méxts'el, lhémxts'eltel < méxts'el.
real fine-tooth comb:: lhémxts'eltel < méxts'el.
shake s-th (tree or bush) for fruit or leaves, comb a bush (for berries), shake s-th (a mat or blanket for ex.):: xwíset ~ xwítset < xwís.

come :: emí: ~ emí < mí ~ mé ~ me.

appear, come into view, rise into view:: pél:ékw.
arrive, arriving, come here, have come, get here, get back, come in (in a race):: xwe'í < í.
back and forth, (go or come back and forth):: q'elq'í:lthet ~ q'elq'éylthet < q'ó:lthet.
become aware (said for ex. of a child about three years or so, or of realizing how something is done), come to one's senses, sober up:: p'élh.
broke down, came (un)loose, came apart, (got) untied, loose, unravelled:: yéx̱w < yíx̱w.
come, came, He came., She came.:: ma'emí ~ ma'mí < mí ~ mé ~ me.
come close, come near, come sit in (with a group):: teséthet ~ tséthet < tés.
come, coming, come to, coming to:: mí ~ mé ~ me.
come near me, (sic? for make me get near):: tesésthòx < tés.
come near s-o, (come to s-o):: emíls < mí ~ mé ~ me.
come out (of hair) (like hair in a comb):: qw'ém.
come out (of sun), come up (of sun):: wep'éth' ~ wep'áth' < p'eth'.
come to after fainting, (revive after fainting):: p'elhíws < p'élh.
come to see s-o/s-th, visit s-o:: kw'átset < kw'áts ~ kw'éts.
Come (urging one person).:: míthelh < mí ~ mé ~ me.
come with s-o:: sq'ómet < q'ó.
come with s-o (in a canoe for ex.):: q'ewí:lt < q'éw ~ q'ew.
coming by foot, travelling by walking, already walking, travelling on foot:: ye'í:mex < i┐m.
coming with s-o:: sq'eq'ómet < q'ó.
fall apart, come apart (of something man-made):: yíx̱w.

come (CONT'D)

follow after, coming behind (the one ahead knows):: chokwelélqem < chó:kw.
get close, approach, get near, nearly, (go close, come close):: ts'ímél ~ ts'ímel, ts'ímél ~ ts'ímel.
go, come, get, become:: =í:l ~ =i┐ l ~ =el.
go with, come with, be partner with:: q'axí:l < q'ó.
has come around (of a cyclic period of time):: séqsel.
just came, (just arrived):: tátsel.
just come out on (of sun):: p'eth'.
just coming out of the earth (of plants for ex.):: qwósem.
return, come back, go back:: q'ó:lthet.
sticking out through a hole (like a toe out of a sock, knee out of a hole in pants, a nail driven clear through the other side of a board), come out into the open:: qwōhóls (or perhaps) qwehóls < qwá.
they came on (top of):: ch'alech'á (~ ts'alets'á) < ts'á:.
tide coming in, water coming in, water coming up (ocean tide or river):: qém:el.
to climax, come (sexually), ejaculate:: qw'lhòlèm or qw'lhlòlèm.
to float, come up to the surface, rise to the surface, to surface:: p'ékw.
watch for s-o to come, be on the watch for s-o:: qw'óqw'elhmet < qw'ólh or qw'álh.
where s-o came from:: shxwtelí < tel=.

come alive

come alive, come back to life, get better (from sickness), get well, revive:: áylexw ~ áyelexw.

come back to life

come alive, come back to life, get better (from sickness), get well, revive:: áylexw ~ áyelexw.

comedian

a dandy, someone who overdresses, a show-off, comedian, someone who always cracks jokes, smart-alec:: swék'.

come in

go in (a house/enclosure), come in, come inside, enter a house or enclosure:: kwetxwí:lem < kwetáxw.

come off :: má ~ má'-.

it peeled off, comes off:: lhéqw'.

come out

come out (of sun), come up (of sun):: wep'éth' ~ wep'áth' < p'eth'.
just come out on (of sun):: p'eth'.

come to

come, coming, come to, coming to:: mí ~ mé ~ me.
come to after fainting, (revive after fainting):: p'elhíws < p'élh.

come up

(be) Spring, [cyclic period] when everything comes up:: kw'íyles ~ kw'éyles < kw'í ~ kw'íy.
(be) Spring, [time or season] when everything comes up:: temkw'éyles < kw'í ~ kw'íy.

come up (CONT'D)

come out (of sun), come up (of sun):: wep'éth' ~ wep'áth' < p'eth'.
place where the sun comes up:: swep'áth' < p'eth'.

comfort
comfort s-o, sympathize with s-o:: smámekw'et < mákw'a.

comfortable:: éy ~ éy:.
be good, good, well, nice, fine, better, better (ought to), it would be good if, may it be good, let it be good, happy, glad, clean, well-behaved, polite, virgin, popular, comfortable (with furniture, other things?),:: éy ~ éy:.

command
command imperative second person plural:: -alha.
command imperative second person singular:: -lha.

Commodore)
Indian name of Mary Amy (Lorenzetto) (Commodore) Cooper:: Óyewòt.
name of a fierce old warrior from Sumas, an ancestor of the Commodore family:: Qwá:l < qwá:l.

communion :: lekaléstel.

Comox language
Sliammon people, Sliammon dialect (of the Comox language, Mainland Comox):: Sloyámén.

companion
companion, other part:: sq'ó < q'ó.

comparative
comparative or augmentative:: =R1= or =C1e=.

complete
be complete:: xéq.
close up a meeting, wind up a meeting, complete a meeting:: yalkw'ólhem or yelkw'wólhem < yókw' ~ yóqw'.
complete s-th:: xeqláxw < xéq.

completely
go out completely (of fire):: th'éx̲.
(portion not burnt up, burnt or gone out completely portion):: th'ex̲míl < th'éx̲.

complexion
(be) a dark color (of clothes, complexions, etc.), (dark gray, dark brown):: stl'ítl'esel < stl'ítl'es.

comprehend)
find s-th out, understand s-th, learn s-th, realize s-th, now know what s-th is like, read (and comprehend) s-th, understand s-o:: tél:exw ~ (in rapid speech) télexw < tól.

cone
pine-cone:: sts'ék'.

confess
    confession, to go to confession, to confess:: x̱áx̱emilàlèm ~ x̱áx̱milàlèm < x̱áx̱e.

confident
    know oneself, be confident:: lheq'elómet < q'á:l.

confuse
    confused:: melmílets' < mál ~ mél.

conifer
    fir boughs, needle of any other conifer than spruce:: qwélatses.

conscience
    conscience, spirit (which can be lost temporarily), soul, life-spirit, power of one's will:: smestíyexw < mestíyexw.

considerate
    be considerate:: sts'íts'exw, sts'íts'exw < th'íxw ~ th'éxw.
    (be) considerate of each other:: sts'its'exwtel < sts'íts'exw, sts'íts'exwtel < th'íxw ~ th'éxw.

constant
    keep the fire at a constant temperature:: txwéltsep.

constantly
    one's head is shaking constantly (like with disease):: x̱wóyqwesem, x̱wóyqwesem.

constipated:: t'kwíwel < t'ékw.
    get constipated, "bound up":: x̱ex̱ekw'íwel ~ x̱ax̱ekw'íwel < x̱ékw'.
    really constipated:: ch'iyxwíwel < ts'íyxw ~ ts'éyxw ~ ch'íyxw.

consumption
    hog fennel, Indian consumption plant:: q'ex̱mí:l.

contact
    (get) a disease gotten by contacting a frog, a skin eruption, also the same disease as the man got in Kawkawa Lake in the Sx̱wó:yx̱wey story, (perhaps also) leprosy:: qw'ő:m.

container :: shxwélwels.
    (closable container):: =q.
    clothes container, suitcase, clothes case:: áwkw'emálá < á:wkw'.
    container for left-overs taken home from feast, doggie bag:: meq'ethále < méq'.
    container for, receptacle for:: =á:lá ~ =álá ~ =àlà ~ =ela.
    container(s):: =eqel.
    eight containers:: tqátsáleqel < tqá:tsa.
    empty container (like bottles esp. if there's lots):: shxwema'ámel < má ~ má'-.
    five containers:: lhq'átseqel < lheq'át ~ lhq'á:t.
    four containers:: x̱ethíleqel < x̱e'ó:thel ~ x̱e'óthel.
    nine containers:: tuxwáleqel < tú:xw.
    one container:: léts'eqel < léts'a ~ léts'e.
    seven containers:: th'ekwsáleqel < th'ó:kws.
    six containers:: t'x̱émeqel < t'éx̱.

container (CONT'D)

small container:: a'axwíleqel < axwíl, mímeleqel.
small containers (a number of them):: mémeleqel < mímeleqel.
suitcase (Deming), luggage (Deming), clothing container, clothes bag, trunk (for clothes), etc.:: áwkw'emálá < á:wkw'.
take a cover off, take it off (a cover of a container), open it (bottle, box, kettle, book, etc.):: xwemá:qet < má ~ má'-.
ten containers:: opeláleqel < ó:pel.
the inside (of a container):: skwetxwewílh < kwetáxw.
thirty containers:: lhexwelsxáleqel < lhí:xw.
three containers:: lhíxweqel < lhí:xw.
twenty containers:: ts'kw'exáleqel < ts'kw'éx.
two containers:: isáleqel < isá:le ~ isále ~ isá:la.
vessel, (container):: =ṓ:welh ~ =ṓwelh ~ =ōwelh ~ =ewelh ~ =á:welh ~ =welh ~ =ewí:l.

continuative

characteristic, inherent continuative:: =R2 or =C1eC2.
continuative, be -ing:: -R1- or -C1e-, R5- or C1e-, R8= or C1a=, =R9= or =C1á(:)=.
continuative, resultative:: há- ~ hé-.
diminutive, little (of subject, object, agent, patient or action), small, (all diminutive verbs are also continuative):: R4= or C1í=, =R6= or =eC2=, R7= or C1á=.
plural continuative:: R13= or C1V1C2=.
structured activity continuative, structured activity continuative nominal or tool or person:: =els.

continue

being angry, continue to be angry, angry, mad, roused, stirred up:: t'át'eyeq' ~ t'át'iyeq' < t'ay.
continuing on singing:: t'élt'elem < t'íl.

continuous

be dripping, (have) continuous dripping, water dropping:: th'áq'em < th'q'ém ~ th'eq'ém.
continuous shooting or popping sounds:: tl'éltl'eleqw' < tl'ál ~ tl'á:l.
(making a) continuous rustling noise (of paper or silk or material), rustling (of leaves, paper, a sharp sound):: sá:wts'em < sawéts'em.

contract

contract a disease, catch a disease, get addicted:: q'áp'.

contrary)

insistant, persistant (like a child pressing to go along), bull-headed, doesn't mind, does just the opposite, (stubborn, contrary):: sxíxeles.

contrastive:: we= ~ u= ~ uw= ~ ew= ~ =ew ~ =w ~ =u.

be only (contrastive), be just (contrastive):: welóy < lóy.
then (action following a previous action, contrastive), so (contrastive):: su.

control

causative control transitivizer:: =st.
purposeful control reciprocal, (perhaps just) reciprocal, (do purposely to) each other, (do purposely to) one another:: =t=el.
purposeful control reflexive, do purposely to oneself:: =thet.

control (CONT'D)

purposeful control transitivizer, do purposely to s-o/s-th:: =t ~ =et.
purposeful control transitivizer inanimate object preferred:: =ex.

conveyance)

be aboard, be in (a conveyance):: eló:lh < ó:lh.
get in a conveyance, get in a car, mount a horse:: ó:lh.
get off (a canoe or conveyance), get out of a canoe, (disembark):: qw'í:m.
get s-th aboard (a canoe, car, conveyance):: eló:lhstexw < ó:lh.
three canoes, three wagons, three conveyances (any form of transportation), three boats:: lhxwó:lh < lhí:xw.

convulsion

(have) fits, convulsions:: q'áq'etl'.

cook

bake underground, (steam-cook underground, cook in a steam-pit):: qetás < qá:t.
baking over an open fire, roasting over an open fire, barbecuing, cooking in an oven:: qw'eqw'élém < qw'él.
barbecue, bake (meat, vegetables, etc.) in open fire, bake over fire, roast over open fire, bake under hot sand, bake in oven, cook in oven, (boiled down (as jam) [CT, HT]):: qw'élém < qw'él.
barbecue stick, cooking stick (split stick for barbecuing salmon),:: pí:kwel.
(be) cooked, (be) already cooked:: sqw'eqw'í:l < qw'él.
boiling, making boil, (cooking in boiling liquid):: qwó:ls.
cooked fish head:: sth'óqwes < sth'ó:qwi ~ sth'óqwi.
cooked (over fire):: qw'él.
cooking, (cooking) food:: skwúkw < kwúkw.
cook s-th:: qw'élt < qw'él.
dish, big cooking and serving trough used in longhouse, feast dish, plate (of wood or basketry), (platter), tray:: ló:thel.
fish eggs, salmon eggs, roe, (cooked salmon eggs [JL]):: qéléx̲.
getting cooked:: qw'eqwél < qw'él.
not cooked enough (of fish), [undercooked]:: lálekw'em.
something that's cooked:: sqw'éls < qw'él.
stuff steam-cooked underground, what is baked underground:: sqetás < qá:t.
(the) cooking:: sqw'él < qw'él.
(the) cooking, (soup, stew [DM, CT]):: sqwéls < qwó:ls.
to cook, cooking:: kwúkw.

cookhouse

cookhouse, kitchen:: kwukwáwtxw < kwúkw.

cool

(cold (of a person) or get cooled down, get cold):: th'ólhem < th'álh.
cool down enough to touch (or handle or work with):: tóqweltsep.
cool down (of a person):: th'álh.
cooling it (of food):: títemí:lt < temí:lt.
cooling off (of food):: titemí:lthet < temí:lt.
cool it (of food):: temí:lt.
cool off (of a person):: xálxwthet < xó:lxwem.
cool off (of food):: temí:lthet < temí:lt.
cool oneself:: th'ólhethet < th'álh.

cool (CONT'D)

cool oneself off:: th'álhethet < th'álh.
cools one's chest inside:: th'elhílésem < th'álh.
(have?) a cool drink:: th'elhílésem < th'álh, th'elhqéylem or th'elhqílem ~ th'elhqílém < th'álh.
have a menthol taste, (have a cool taste):: xó:lxwem.
it is cool [of weather], (be) cool (of a place):: sth'áth'elh < th'álh.

Cooper
Indian name of Mary Amy (Lorenzetto) (Commodore) Cooper:: Óyewòt.
place by Albert Cooper's house on Chilliwack River Road near Vedder Crossing, former village where a slide is now on north bank of Chilliwack River opposite Liumchen Creek::X̲éylés < x̲éylés.

coordinated outfit
dancer's uniform, (any) coordinated outfit:: s-hóyews < hóyiws.

copper :: qwíqwi ~ qwíyqwiy.
big copper pot:: ts'qw'ṓstel ~ ts'qw'ṓwstel.
(perhaps) copper, (hard metal that looks like gold but isn't, maybe copper [Elders at Katz Class 10/5/76], metal found in mines and used for arrowheads [Elders Group 5/28/75], gold [EB]):: sqw'él, sqw'él.

copper-colored
be red, red, reddish-brown, copper-colored:: tskwí:m < kwí:m.

copy
copy, imitate:: x̲wex̲we'á.
copy s-o, imitate s-o:: x̲wex̲we'át < x̲wex̲we'á.
imitating s-o, copying s-o:: x̲wix̲we'át < x̲wex̲we'á.

Coqualeetza
Coqualeetza stream esp. where it joins Luckakuck Creek, later Coqualeetza (residential school, then hospital, then Indian cultural centre and Education Training Centre):: Kw'eqwálíth'a < kw'óqw.

Coqualeetza stream
Coqualeetza stream esp. where it joins Luckakuck Creek, later Coqualeetza (residential school, then hospital, then Indian cultural centre and Education Training Centre):: Kw'eqwálíth'a < kw'óqw.

Coquihalla River:: Kw'ikw'iyá:la < kw'íy.
maybe the same place as Sqw'ex̲wáq (pool where Kawkawa Creek comes into the Coquihalla River and where the water pygmies lived):: Skw'íkw'x̲weq (or better, Sqw'íqw'x̲weq) < Sqw'ex̲wáq.
pool where Kawkawa Creek comes into the Coquihalla River:: Sqw'ex̲wáq.

Coquitlam :: Kwíkwetl'em.
Coquitlam Indian people:: Kwíkwetl'em.

cord
cord, muscle, tendon, nerve cord by backbone:: tl'e'ímél ~ tl'e'í:mel.
(poss.) cord, rope:: =í:wa ~ =í:wá: ~ =el=a┐ wa.

cord (CONT'D)
spinal rope inside sturgeon, (sturgeon spinal cord):: qw'ólhla.

corduroy)
rough (like corduroy):: x̲átqem ~ x̲étqem.

core
core of a rock, center of a rock, core of anything, heart of anything inanimate:: sth'emí:wel ~ sth'emíwel ~ sth'emíwél < sth'ó:m.
heart of a root, seed, nut (kernel), core of plant or seedling, core (of tree, branch, any growing thing), pith (of bush), seed or pit [U.S.] or pip [Cdn.] of a fruit:: sth'emí:wel ~ sth'emíwel ~ sth'emíwél < sth'ó:m, sth'emí:wel ~ sth'emíwel ~ sth'emíwél < sth'ó:m.
inside or core of a plant or fruit (or canoe or anything):: =í:wel ~ =íwel ~ =ewel.
in the rump, in the anus, in the rectum, in the bottom, on the insides, inside parts, core, inside the head:: =í:wel ~ =íwel ~ =ewel.

cork line
float line, cork line:: qwōqwá:l ~ qweqwá:l.

corn :: kwól.
white sweet corn:: p'éq' q'áq'et'em kwó:l < p'éq', q'át', kwó:l (lit. white + sweet + corn)

Corner
Cottonwood Corner:: Kwó:le.

corner
square, corner, arm with elbow out:: st'elá̲xel.
turn around a bend, go around a bend, turn around (to go back), turn around a corner:: q'ewqé:ylém ~ q'ewqéylém (better q'ewqí:lem) < q'éw ~ q'ew.

Cornus nuttallii:: qwítx̲, qwítx̲elhp < qwítx̲.

Cornus stolonifera:: th'ex̲wíyelhp.

corpse
ghost, corpse, dead body:: spoleqwíth'a < poleqwíth'a.

correct
be alright, be okay, it's alright, it's okay, can, be able, it's enough, be right, be correct, that's right:: iyólem ~ iyó:lem < éy ~ éy:.
(meaning uncertain), (perhaps right, correct):: mà.
right (correct):: leq'á:lh < léq'.

Corvus brachyrhynchos
Corvus brachyrhynchos, (Corvus corax [EF, some Deming elders]):: spó:l.

Corvus caurinus:: spelól < spó:l, spepelól ~ spepeló:l < spó:l.
Euphagus cyanocephalus, or Corvus caurinus:: q'eláq'a.
prob. Corvus caurinus:: spopelál < spó:l.

Corvus corax

Corvus corax:: skéweqs < sqéweqs, sqéweqs, sqéweqs.
Corvus brachyrhynchos, (Corvus corax [EF, some Deming elders]):: spó:l.

Corylus cornuta:: sth'í:tsem, sth'í:tsemelhp < sth'í:tsem, sth'í:tsemelhp < th'éts.

Corynorhinus townsendi townsendi
Corynorhinus townsendi townsendi, Eptesicus fuscus bernardinus, Lasionycteris noctivagans, Lasiurus cinereus, Myotis californicus caurinus, Myotis evotis pacificus, Myotis lucifugus alascensis, Myotis volans longicrus, Myotis yumanensis saturatus, and possibly Myotis keeni keeni:: skw'elyáx̲el.
order Chiroptera, family Vespertilionidae, may include any or all of the following: Corynorhinus townsendi townsendi, Eptesicus fuscus bernardinus, Lasionycteris noctivagans, Lasiurus cinereus, Myotis californicus caurinus, Myotis evotis pacificus, Myotis lucifugus alascensis, Myotis volans longicrus, Myotis yumanensis saturatus, and possibly Myotis keeni keeni:: p'íp'eth'elàx̲el ~ p'ip'eth'eláx̲el < p'í:.

cost
cost ten dollars:: epoléstexw < ó:pel.

(costume) :: =ómet ?.
dancer's uniform, (any) coordinated outfit:: s-hóyews < hóyiws.
dancing costume:: slewómet ~ lewómet.
headdress, face costume, mask:: sx̲wéythiyes ~ sx̲wíythiyes < x̲wíyth.
spirit-dancing costume, wool hat for spirit-dancer (Deming):: s-hóyiws.
trimmings on uniform (paddles, etc.):: stl'íitl'ets < tl'íts ~ tl'ích.

cotton balls
cotton balls (lit. "little rolled balls"):: xíxelkwòls < xél.
cotton balls (lit. "plant fluff - ball"):: pípexwem pó:l < píxw, pó:l.

cottontail
big rabbit, older rabbit, big/older snowshoe/varying hare, now probably also big/older eastern cottontail rabbit (introduced):: sqiqewóthel < sqewáth, sqwiqweyóthel.
(larger) rabbit: snowshoe or varying hare, now probably also eastern cottontail rabbit (introduced):: sqewáth.
rabbit: snowshoe/varying hare, now probably also eastern cottontail rabbit (introduced), (baby rabbit, small rabbit or hare [Elders Group]):: sqíqewàth < sqewáth.
rabbit, (varying hare, perhaps now also the introduced eastern cottontail):: shxwóxw.

cottonwood
black cottonwood cambium (soft matter between the bark and the wood):: sx̲á:meth.
black cottonwood tree:: chewṓ:lhp < cháchew ~ cháchu.
cottonwood bark driftwood (it was used to carve toy canoes), cottonwood driftwood used for carving toy canoes:: qwémélép ~ qwemélep.
cottonwood sap, cottonwood cambium:: ts'its'emá:welh.
cottonwood sap or cambium:: sx̲á:meth.
poplar, Lombardy poplar (intro.), also black cottonwood and perhaps trembling aspen which may have rarely occurred on the eastern and northeastern edges of Stó:lō territory:: p'elp'álq'emá:lews ~ p'elp'àlq'emá:lews < p'álq'em.
"poplar", probably includes black cottonwood and trembling aspen (though trembling aspen is rare in Upriver Halq'eméylem territory):: th'estíyelhp < th'ís, th'ex̲tíyelhp < th'éx̲.

cottonwood (CONT'D)

to drop or blow plant fluff (like dandelions, fireweed, cottonwood, etc.), to blow (of dusty or flaky stuff like wood dust, dandruff, maybe seeds):: pípexwem < píxw.

Cottonwood Beach

Cottonwood Beach (in the southern quarter of Harrison Lake):: Chewő:lhp < cháchew ~ cháchu.

Cottonwood Corner:: Kwó:le.

couch

sofa, couch, chesterfield, place where one's sitting, (bed [AC, MC (Katzie)]):: shxw'ó:met < emét.

cougar :: shxwéwe.

cough

a cough, a cold with a cough:: stó:qw'em < tó:qw'em.
coughing:: tóteqw'em < tó:qw'em.
to cough:: tó:qw'em.

count :: kw'xá:m < kw'áx.
be counted:: skw'ekw'íx < kw'áx.
counting:: kw'áxem < kw'áx.
counting them, counting s-th:: kw'áxt < kw'áx.
count them, count s-th:: kw'xát < kw'áx.

counter-clockwise

go around inside the longhouse counter-clockwise:: selts'elwílem < sél or sí(:)l.

courage

courage (lit. in the stomach):: =á:lwes ~ =élwes.
in the stomach, in courage:: =álwes ~ =élwes.

course

an old course of Atchelitz Creek:: (Yeqyeqámen).
change course (of a river):: táyéqel.

cousin

(be) brother and sister, (be siblings to each other), (be) first cousin to each other:: qeló:qtel < sqá:q.
grandparent, grandparent's sibling, grandparent's first cousin:: sí:le.
great grandparent, great grandchild, sibling or (up to fourth) cousin of great grandparent, great grandchild of brother or sister or (up to fourth) cousin:: sts'ó:meqw, sts'ó:meqw.
great great grandparent, great great grandchild, sibling or cousin (up to fourth) of great great grandparent/-child:: th'ép'ayeqw ~ th'épayeqw.
great great great great grandparent, great great great great grandchild, sibling or cousin (up to fourth) of great great great great grandparent or -child:: tómiyeqw.
nephew, niece, sibling's child (child of sister or brother or cousin (up to and including fourth cousin) [Elders Group]):: stí:wel.
older sibling, elder cousin (child of older sibling of one's parent, grandchild of older sibling of one's grandparent, great grandchild of older sibling of one's great grandparent), cousin of senior line,

cousin (CONT'D)

older brother, older sister:: sétl'atel < sétl'a ~ sétl'o, sétl'atel < sétl'a ~ sétl'o.

older siblings, elder cousins (first/second/third cousins by an older sibling of one's ancestor):: sá:tl'atel < sétl'a ~ sétl'o.

parent's cousin, parent's sibling, uncle, aunt:: shxwemlí:kw.

sibling/cousin of great great grand-parent/-child:: ékwiyeqw.

sibling/cousin of great great great grandparent/-child:: ékwiyeqw.

younger siblings, "younger" cousins (first, second, or third cousins [whose connecting ancestor is younger than ego's]):: sqelá:q < sqá:q.

younger sibling, younger brother, younger sister, child of younger sibling of one's parent, "younger" cousin (could even be fourth cousin [through younger sibling of one's great great grandparent]):: sqá:q.

younger, younger sibling, cousin of a junior line (cousin by an ancestor younger than the speaker's), junior cousin (child of a younger sibling of one's parent, (great) grandchild of a younger sibling of one's(great) grandparent), younger brother, younger sister:: sóseqwt ~ (rarely) só:seqwt, sóseqwt ~ (rarely) só:seqwt.

cover

a cover, lid:: qp'á:letstel < qep'.

blanket (modern), covering:: léx̲wtel < lex̲w.

close s-th (for ex. a box), put a lid on s-th (for ex. a pot), cover it with a lid:: qp'á:qet < qep'.

cover it (s-th open):: qp'á:letset < qep'.

cover oneself up:: léx̲wethet < lex̲w.

cover s-o, cover s-th (like yeast bread):: tl'x̲wét (or probably tl'xwét) < tl'xw ~ tl'exw.

cover s-o with a blanket, cover s-th, cover s-th/s-o up:: léx̲wet < lex̲w.

take a cover off, take it off (a cover of a container), open it (bottle, box, kettle, book, etc.):: xwemá:qet < má ~ má'-.

you get covered on the mouth (by a flying squirrel at night for ex.):: qep'ó:ythòm < qep'.

covering

floor, floor mat, floor covering, linoleum, rug:: lhex̲éyléptel < lhá:x̲ ~ lháx̲.

on the body, on the skin, on the covering:: =í:ws ~ =ews.

thick plank for side of house, thick shake for longhouse roof, covering over hole in roof of pit-house:: s'í:ltexw.

cow

calf:: músmesò:llh < músmes.

cow, bull, beef:: músmes.

small adult cow:: múmesmes < músmes.

small adult cows, (small adult cattle):: melúmesmes < músmes.

to fasten s-th by tying, tie up s-th (like canoe, horse, laces, nets, cow, shoelaces), tie it:: q'éyset ~ q'í(:)set < q'ey ~ q'i.

younger deer, baby horse, younger cow, fawn, colt, calf:: st'él'e.

coward

coward, person that's always afraid:: lexwsí:si < síy.

cowboy :: káwpōy.

cowboy hat:: kawpōyóweq(w) < káwpōy.

(make) a whoop, a cowboy's whoop:: q'exelám.

Cowichan
Cowichan (people, dialect, area):: Qewítsel < qew.

co-wife
a husband's younger wives, co-wife:: sxáye.

cow parsnip
cow parsnip sprout (especially the edible inside part):: sóqw'.
stringy fibers (as on cow parsnip):: x̲wéylem ~ x̲wé:ylem ~ x̲wí:lem.
wild celery, cow parsnip:: yóle ~ yóla ~ yó:le.

coyote :: sk'ek'iyáp ~ slek'iyáp, slek'iyáp.
little coyote:: lilk'eyáp < slek'iyáp.

crab :: á:yx̲.

crabapple
crabapple, (now) domesticated apple:: qwe'óp.
crabapple tree, domestic apple tree:: qwe'ó:pelhp < qwe'óp.
(have) sound of popping small round things (snowberries, herring eggs as when eating them, rice krispies, crabapples, cranberries, etc.), (have a crunching sound (as of grasshopper, rice krispies)):: tl'ámkw'em, tl'ámkw'em < tl'ém.

crabby
(be) cranky, crabby, dirty-minded:: lexwqélwelh < qél.

crack
a crack:: sisíq' < séq'.
a cracked mountain where the pipeline crosses the Fraser River between Hope and Agassiz:: Sisíq' < séq'.
break (of ground), crack apart (of its own accord) (of ground), ripped:: tl'éx.
lots of cracks:: seq'síq' < séq'.
plugging a hole or leak or crack in anything:: t'ót'ekwels < t'ékw.
Salkaywul, an area with big cracked cedar trees on Hope Slough above Schelowat (Chilliwack I.R. #1) (Sx̲eláwtxw):: Salq'íwel < séq'.
split s-th, crack s-th:: seq'át ~ sq'át < séq'.
to crack, to split (of its own accord), ((also) cracked, a crack [AC]):: séq'.

crackers:: x̲ápkw'els < x̲épekw'
(lit. crunching noise structured activity [thing])

crackle
crackling and popping (of a log in fire or firecrackers):: tl'áléx̲em < tl'ál ~ tl'á:l.
crunchy (loud when eating), crackling (noise when eating):: tl'ámqw'els < tl'ém.
crunchy (loud when eating), crackling (sound or noise when eating):: tl'ámqw'els < tl'ámkw'em.
(have/get a) crackle and pop (sound of a log in a fire or of firecrackers):: tl'á:lx̲em < tl'ál ~ tl'á:l.
make a crunching or crackling noise, crunching (gnawing) sound:: x̲ápkw'em < x̲ep'ékw'.

cradle
baby basket, cradle basket, basketry cradle:: p'ó:th'es ~ p'óth'es.
buckskin straps for tying a baby in its cradle or basket:: yémqetel < yém ~ yem.
(have a) flat head, (have cranial deformation by cradle-board):: sp'íp'elheqw < p'ílh.
swing for baby cradle:: séqtel < seqíws ~ seqí:ws.

Crago vulgaris
suborder Natantia, probably Crago and other genera, especially Crago vulgaris, Pandalus danae were identified by AD from a photo as the kind AD's parents got dried from the Chinese and called by this name:: homò:y.

cramp
cramped:: q'á:lp'tem < q'élptem ~ q'élp'tem.
cramping:: q'áq'elptem < q'élptem ~ q'élp'tem.
getting a cramp:: q'elq'élp'tem < q'élptem ~ q'élp'tem.
to have cramps, get a cramp, to be cramped:: q'élptem ~ q'élp'tem.

cranberry
cranberry juice:: kwúkwewels sqe'óleqw (or) qwemchó:ls sqe'óleqw) < kwúkwewels, qwà:m, qó:
(lit. high-bush cranberry + fruit juice (or better:) bog cranberry + fruit juice)
bog cranberry:: qwemchó:ls < qwà:m ~ qwám.
(have) sound of popping small round things (snowberries, herring eggs as when eating them, rice krispies, crabapples, cranberries, etc.), (have a crunching sound (as of grasshopper, rice krispies)):: tl'ámkw'em, tl'ámkw'em < tl'ém.
possibly high-bush cranberry, more likely squashberry:: kwúkwewels.

crane
(be) pigeon-toed, (sandhill crane toed:: slímiyeqwxel < slí:m.
great blue heron, (often called) "crane":: sméqw'o ~ smő́qw'o.
sandhill crane:: slí:m.

cranefly
cranefly, leatherjacket (immature cranefly):: spelwálh qwá:l < qwá:l, tl'áleqtxel qwá:l < qwá:l.
cranefly, "leatherjacket" (insect):: tl'áleqtxel qwá:l < tl'áqt.

cranial deformation
(have a) flat head, (have cranial deformation by cradle-board):: sp'íp'elheqw < p'ílh.

cranky :: t'it'á:yeq' < t'ay.
(be) aggressive, cranky, ready to fight, (be) violent, hot-headed:: sx̲óytl'thet ~ sx̲ó:ytl'thet.
(be) cranky, crabby, dirty-minded:: lexwqélwelh < qél.
cranky, quick-tempered:: x̲éth'x̲eth' < x̲íth' ~ x̲éyth'.
last baby (youngest baby), the last-born, a child cranky and jealous of an expected brother or sister:: óqw'a < óqw'.

Crataegus douglasii:: máts'el, mats'íyelhp < máts'el.

crawl :: ts'tá:m.
crawl (as of a snake, seal, slug, snail):: xwó:kw'thet < xwókw' ~ xwekw'ó.
crawling:: ts'átem < ts'tá:m.

crawl (CONT'D)

crawling (as of snake, seal, slug, snail), (dragging oneself):: xwéqw'ethet < xwókw' ~ xwekw'ó.
crawl through (like through a fence):: qwahéylém ~ qwahí:lém < qwá.
crawl underneath, (go underneath):: eqílem ~ eqéylem.
swimming, (swimming under the water after diving (Cheh.) [Elders Group], swimming with crawl strokes, etc. [Deming]):: t'ít'etsem ~ t'ít'echem < t'ítsem.
swim (of a person), swim (with crawl strokes, etc.):: t'ítsem.

crayon:: mamelehá:yelh x̲éltel < méle ~ mél:a.

crazy
be crazy, be insane:: shxwóxwth' < xwáth'.
(be) stupid, not all there (mentally), (be) a little crazy:: shxwixwóxwth' < xwáth'.
you're crazy in the head, you're sick in the head:: xwoxwth'áleq[w]thom < xwáth'.

creak
(make/have a) squeaking sound (of a tree, of a chair, of shoes), squeaking (of shoes, trees), (creaking):: qá:ytl'em.

creature)
a fatal kind of shock on seeing a stl'áleqem (supernatural creature):: xò:lí:s.
animal or bird one is afraid of and can't see, powerful creature, supernatural creature:: stl'á:leqem.
backbone (of human or other creatures), spine (human or other creature):: x̲ekw'ólesewíts < x̲ekw'óles.
(little supernatural creature), little stl'áleqem:: stl'ítl'leqem < stl'á:leqem.
lots of stl'áleqems, (lots of supernatural creatures):: stl'eltl'áléqem < stl'á:leqem.
two supernatural creatures:: yáysele ~ yéysele < isá:le ~ isále ~ isá:la.

credit
get credit:: íx̲em.
get credit, borrow (money for ex.), (getting credit, borrowing):: qw'íméls.
lend money to s-o, [give s-o credit]:: ex̲ímt < íx̲em.
to put on credit ??:: ex̲ímels < íx̲em.

Creek
a neck of land on the west side of Harrison Lake just north of Twenty-Mile Creek and across from the north tip of Long Island:: Shxwtépsem < tépsem.
an old course of Atchelitz Creek:: (Yeqyeqámen).
a place on Chilliwack River, a little above Anderson Flat and Allison's (between Tamihi Creek and Slesse Creek), a village at deep water between Tamihi Creek and Slesse Creek:: Iy'óythel < éy ~ éy:, Iy'óythel < éy ~ éy:.
Atchelitz Creek, an old Chilliwack River channel:: Áthelets < áthelets.
a tributary of Atchelitz Creek:: Kwōkwa'áltem ?.
August run spring salmon that go up Silver Creek (near Hope):: shxwōqw'ō:lh.
Beaver Creek (at U.S.-Canada boundary line):: Sqelá:w (Stótelō) < sqelá:w.
canyon area on Chehalis Creek just above (upriver or north from) the main highway bridge (esp. the first cliff on the east side) [means one-legged]:: Páléxel ~ Paléxel.
Centre Creek:: Stahiyáq?? or Stiyáq?? or St'ahiyáq?? or Stahí:q??.
Cheam Creek on north side below Ford Creek:: Sqwe'óp (?) < qwe'óp.
Choate Creek on the west (C.P.R,) side of the Fraser River:: St'élxweth' stótelō <

Creek (CONT'D)

St'élxweth'.

creek from Hicks Lake [sic? from Deer Lake] that's actually three creeks all leaving from the lake, probably Mahood Creek, (also Hick's Mountain [LJ]):: Sílhíxw < lhí:xw.

Emory Creek, also village at mouth of Emory Creek on both sides of the creek:: Sx̲wótl'aqwem.

Five-Mile Creek:: Lohíts ~ Lahíts ~ Lahích ~ Slahích.

Ford Creek, (=Foley Creek?):: Ets'íts'a or Eth'íth'a or Ets'íth'a, Ets'íts'a or Eth'íth'a or Ets'íth'a.

Ford Lake (sic Foley Lake), Ford Creek (sic Foley Creek) on north side of Chilliwack River below Post Creek:: Lasisélhp?.

Fraser River, (Chehalis Creek, Chehalis River [Elders Group, EL/EB/NP]):: Stó:lō < tó:l ~ tò:l.

Gordon Creek:: Sókw'ech Stó:lō < sókw'.

Hatchery Creek, tributary of Sweltzer Creek (which drains Cultus Lake):: Stṓtelō < tó:l ~ tò:l.

Hicks Creek:: Péps? or Píps?.

Katz river-bank, Ruby Creek settlement, village on north bank of Fraser River just below (west of) the mouth of Ruby Creek:: Spópetes < pó:t.

Lackaway village, Lackaway Creek:: Lá:x̲ewey.

Little Matsqui Creek:: Stótlōtel < tó:l ~ tò:l.

Luckakuck Creek:: Lex̲ex̲éq < x̲éq.

Mary Ann Creek, village at mouth of Mary Ann Creek into the Fraser (in Yale, B.C., Yale Town Indian Reserve #1):: Sése.

Matsqui village, (Matsqui Creek [Wells]):: Máthxwi.

maybe the same place as Sqw'ex̲wáq (pool where Kawkawa Creek comes into the Coquihalla River and where the water pygmies lived):: Skw'íkw'x̲weq (or better, Sqw'íqw'x̲weq) < Sqw'ex̲wáq.

Middle Creek:: Lóyaqwe'áth'? or Lóyaqwe'áts'?, Lóyeqw'e'áts (most likely) or Lóyaqwe'áts' or Lóyaqwe'áth', Nesókwech ~ Nasókwach.

Mill Creek (at American Bar), Puckat Creek on map also:: Peqwchṓ:lthel Stótelō < péqw.

monument at Saddle Rock at Five Mile Creek:: Sólkweyem?? or Solkw'í:m??.

Morris Creek (near Chehalis, B.C.), Morris Lake (near Chehalis):: Sx̲áx̲e < x̲áx̲e.

mouth of Weaver Creek:: Lhemqwó:tel < lhém.

Mt. MacFarlane Creek:: possibly Chéchem.

north and south sides of the mouth of Five-Mile Creek:: Lexwts'ístel < th'ís.

place where a grove of birches stood/stand near the Kickbush place on Chilliwack River Road in Sardis, (village at junction of Semmihault Creek and Chilliwack River [Wells 1965 (lst ed.):19]):: Sekw'sekw'emá:y < síkw'.

place where Yale Creek divides (forks) above the highway bridge over the creek:: T'ít'x̲elhchò:m < t'éx̲.

pool where Kawkawa Creek comes into the Coquihalla River:: Sqw'ex̲wáq.

Post Creek:: Kwṓkwelem ?.

(probably) Mahood Creek and Johnson Slough, (possibly) Wahleach River or Hicks Creek (creek at bridge on east end of Seabird Island [AK]):: Qwōhòls < qwá.

(probably) Slollicum Creek:: Stl'áleqem Stótelō < stl'á:leqem.

Restmore Caves [Wells]), (mouth of Hunter Creek [IHTTC]):: Uqw'íles.

Ruby Creek (the creek not the village):: St'ít'x̲oya < t'éx̲.

Ryder Lake Creek:: T'ept'ṓp Stótelō < T'ept'ṓp.

Sakwi Creek, a stream that joins Weaver Creek about one-third mile above the salmon hatchery:: Qeywéx̲em < qí:wx̲ ~ qéywx̲ ~ qá:wx̲ ~ qáwx̲.

Semmihault Creek, a stream from the east joining the old Chilliwack River near the Chilliwack airport:: Smiyó:llh?.

Silver Creek, Silver Hope Creek:: Tl'íkw'elem < tl'íkw'el.

Creek (CONT'D)

silver spring salmon that came up Harrison River and Chehalis Creek, (first spring salmon [Deming]):: sqwéx̲em < qwéx̲em.
Siwash Creek, on the CN (east) side of the Fraser River:: Aseláw Stótelō < Aseláw.
Six-Mile Creek and bay on west side of Harrison Lake:: Lkwṓxwethem < kwṓxweth.
Skwellepil Creek:: Skwálepel < kwà:l.
Sowaqua Creek:: Swókwel < swókwel.
Spuzzum village (on south bank of Spuzzum Creek at its mouth onto the Fraser River), also Spuzzum Creek:: Spíyem.
Statlu Creek, one of the main tributaries of Chehalis Creek:: stótelō < tó:l ~ tò:l, stótelō < tó:l ~ tò:l.
Suka Creek (on east side of Fraser River above Hope):: Skwíyò Stó:lō < Skwíyò.
Sweltzer Creek (the stream from Cultus Lake to Chilliwack River at Soowahlie):: Swílhcha Stótelō < Swílhcha.
Tamihi Creek:: T'ami(ye)hóy (Stótelō) < t'ámiya.
the first creek above Hemlock Valley road which also crosses the road to Morris Valley, also the name for Pretty Creek:: Lhemqwótel Stótelō < lhém.
Upper Sumas Creek:: Tátelín??.
village across from or a little above the mouth of Centre Creek into Chilliwack River:: Swóyel.
village at American Bar, village on west bank of Fraser River at American Creek, American Bar Reserve:: Peqwchṓ:lthel ~ Peqwechṓ:lthel < péqw.
village at junction of Ryder Lake Creek and Chilliwack River:: T'ept'ṓp.
village at mouth of Stulkawhits Creek on Fraser River:: Lexwtl'íkw'elem < tl'íkw'el.
village just below (on the south side of) Suka Creek, on the CN side (east side) of the Fraser River across from Dogwood Valley:: Skwíyò.
village near the mouth of Choate Creek, (Choate Creek [AK, SP/AD], (Stullawheets village on a hill on the east bank of the Fraser River near the mouth of Suka Creek [elders on American Bar Trip (AD/AK/?)]):: St'élxweth', St'élxweth'.
village on both sides of Liumchen Creek, Liumchen Creek, Liumchen Mountain:: Loyú:mthel ~ Loyúmthel.
wide place at the mouth of the east (upriver) branch of Jones Creek:: Swílth'.
winter village on flat at mouth of Gordon Creek:: Sókw'ech ~ Sókw'ets < sókw'.

creek

a creek probably on the CPR side (west side) of the Fraser River between Yale and Strawberry Island:: Mélx̲weth' < smélx̲weth'.
a fork in a creek:: st'éx̲ < t'éx̲.
a little below the mouth of a creek or slough:: chichewóthel < cháchew ~ cháchu.
Chehalis River mouth (below the highway bridge, where land is breaking up into sand bars), (an opening one could get through in a canoe in high water near Chehalis {IHTTC 8/25/77], small creek (branch of Chehalis River) several hundred yards up Chehalis River from where the road goes from old Chehalis village site to Chehalis River [EL 9/27/77]):: Spōqwṓwelh ~ Speqwṓ:lh < péqw.
creek between Popkum and Cheam, also a location near Popkum, (must be second of two creeks above Popkum that cross Highway #1 [JL 4/7/78]):: sthamí:l.
creek from Hicks Lake [sic? from Deer Lake] that's actually three creeks all leaving from the lake, probably Mahood Creek, (also Hick's Mountain [LJ]):: Sílhíxw < lhí:xw.
creek, little river, small creek, small river:: stótelō ~ stó:telō < tó:l ~ tò:l.
creek near Green Point on east side of Harrison Lake:: Lhewálh.
creek that runs into Yale Creek about two miles up (above the mouth of Yale Creek into the Fraser River):: Kwátexw.

creek (CONT'D)

creek with its mouth on the south side of Chilliwack River and above the mouth of Middle Creek:: Sch'iyáq < sts'iyáq.
end of a falling section of land, end of a level stretch of land, (head of a creek or island [Elders Group]):: lhéq'qel.
head of a creek or island:: lheqel ~ lhequl.
lots of little creeks:: stételō < tó:l ~ tò:l.
name of second creek below (here south of) Suka Creek (as of 8/30/77), creek called Alwís's Bow-line:: Alwís Lhqéletel.
old lake above Smith Falls, Smith Falls creek (which enters Cultus Lake at its northeast corner):: Slhílhets' < lhíts' ~ lhí:ts'.
one (second) of two creeks just above Popkum which cross Highway #1, (creek between Popkum and Cheam, also a place near Popkum [AC]):: Sthamí:l < themá.
(probably) Mahood Creek and Johnson Slough, (possibly) Wahleach River or Hicks Creek (creek at bridge on east end of Seabird Island [AK]):: Qwōhòls < qwá.
rough (of a river or creek):: qw'íwelh.
smaller creek:: stútlō < tó:l ~ tò:l.
Sumas village and area from present-day Kilgard to Fraser River, Sumas village (on both sides of the Fraser at the east end of Sumas Mt.), (Devil's Run (below Láx̲ewey), the area between Sumas Mt. and Fraser River [Elders Group 7/13/77], Sumas River (probably requires Stó:lō river or Stótelō creek to follow) [Wells 1965], Sumas Lake (probably requires X̲ótsa lake after Semáth for this meaning) [Elders Group 7/13/77]):: Smá:th ~ Semá:th ~ Semáth.
the first creek above Hemlock Valley road which also crosses the road to Morris Valley, also the name for Pretty Creek:: Lhemqwótel Stótelō < lhém.
to drain (of a pond), (get) dried up (of creek, empty cup, etc.):: t'óqwel.
tributary, small creek that goes into a bigger river:: sqwá < qwá.
village on east bank of Sweltzer Creek (above Sx̲woyehá:lá), (creek by the village of the same name [X̲wōx̲wá:ye] [Wells]):: X̲wōx̲wá:ye < x̲wōx̲wáye ~ x̲wex̲wáye ~ x̲wōx̲wá:ye.

creepy :: x̲éyx̲esem < x̲éysel.
feel creepy, fear something behind one:: sísem < síy.
feeling creepy, fearing something behind one:: sísesem < síy.

cricket :: tó:lthíwa < tó:l ~ tò:l.

cripple
be lame (esp. if deformed), be a cripple, to limp, have a limp:: slékwlets ~ slékwelets < lékw.

crisp
brittle, crisp:: x̲épkw'em < x̲ep'ékw'.

crochet
a hook for crocheting:: lhílhekw'els < lhíkw' ~ lhí:kw'.

crooked
be bent, be crooked:: spópiy < pó:y.
be crooked [characteristically]:: spóypiy < pó:y.
(have a) crooked hand:: spíytses < pó:y.
(have a) crooked leg, (be a) crooked-legged person:: spipíyxel < pó:y.
to have a crooked jaw:: sx̲ó:lts'iyethel < x̲élts'.
went crooked:: póythet < pó:y.

crooked-legged

crooked-legged
  (have a) crooked leg, (be a) crooked-legged person:: spipíyxel < pó:y.

Cross)
  crossing oneself, (making the sign of the Cross):: pá:yewsem < pó:y.
  make the sign of the Cross, (cross oneself):: píyewsem ~ píwsem < pó:y.

cross
  across:: st'át'elh < t'álh.
  a cross, grave cross, gravestone, cross one hangs up:: lakwwí:l.
  bring s-th/s-o across a river, (ferry s-o/s-th over):: t'kwíléstexw < t'ákwel.
  cross a river, cross a road, cross over:: t'ákwel.
  crossing oneself, (making the sign of the Cross):: pá:yewsem < pó:y.
  crossing over:: t'át'ekwel < t'ákwel.
  cross one's arms (but not fold one's arms across chest) [prob. error], (arms crossed [but not folded across chest]):: q'eyáweth'eláx̲el < q'ey ~ q'i.
  cross one's hands [prob. error], (hands crossed):: q'eyáweth'ches < q'ey ~ q'i.
  cross one's legs:: q'eyáweth'xelem < q'ey ~ q'i.
  dirty, (have a cross face [EB]):: qelés < qél.
  (have the) legs crossed:: sx̲álts'xel < x̲élts'.
  legs crossed, cross one's ankles (either sitting or standing) [prob. error], (ankles crossed (either sitting or standing)):: q'eyáweth'xel < q'ey ~ q'i.
  make the sign of the Cross, (cross oneself):: píyewsem ~ píwsem < pó:y.
  small cross:: lílakw'wì:l < lakwwí:l.
  something used to cross over a river, ferry, place good for crossing:: xwt'át'ekwel < t'ákwel.
  the only safe place to cross a river:: shxwtitós or shxwtiytós.

cross-beam
  cross-beam (in a house):: st'álh < t'álh, t'élhmel < t'álh.

cross-eyed
  cross-eyed, prob. also cock-eyed:: skw'íts'òlès.

Crossing
  Promontory Mountain by Vedder Crossing:: Stitó:s ~ Stitó:s.

crossing
  bridge, cable crossing:: xwt'át'ekwel < t'ákwel.

cross-legged
  sitting cross-legged:: silílh.

crosspiece
  crosspieces in a canoe, (thwarts):: lhex̲elwélhtel < lhá:x̲ ~ lhác̲.
  fish-spreader for drying fish, cross-piece for drying fish, salmon stretcher:: t'á:ts'.

cross sex)
  spouse's sibling, sibling's spouse (cross sex), for ex., husband's brother, (wife's sister, woman's sister's husband, man's brother's wife):: smátexwtel.

Crotalus viridus oreganus:: th'éx̲tel < th'éx̲.

crouch down:: tl'ípethet < tl'ép.

Crow
Raven, (Mister Raven or Mister Crow? [AK 1/16/80]):: Skwówéls.

crow :: spopelál < spó:l.
big crow, common crow, also known as western crow or American crow, (raven [EF, some Deming elders]):: spó:l.
blackbird, Brewer's blackbird, or smaller crow, i.e., northwestern crow:: q'eláq'a.
howling (of a dog), crowing (of a rooster):: q'ówem < q'á:w.
large red-necked woodpecker, large red-headed woodpecker, rain crow (black with red comb on head) (AC), pileated woodpecker:: temélhépsem < témélh.
little crows, small crows, bunch of small crows, (bunch of northwestern crows):: spepelól ~ spepeló:l < spó:l.
smaller crow, northwestern crow:: spelól < spó:l.

crowd
crowding together:: q'ópthet < q'ép.
crowd s-o out:: plhét < pélh.
crowd together, gather together, people gather:: q'péthet < q'ép.
get crowded:: pélh.
get crowded out:: pelhpélh < pélh.
(someone) standing in the middle of a crowd:: s-hómkwstem.
thick crowded tight bushes, bushes growing wide from narrow roots or base:: sq'epláts < q'ép.

crown
crown of head:: sqw'óteleqw.
crown of head, center of the top of the head where the hair starts:: sq'eyx̲éleqw.

crumple
break up s-th by crumpling, crush it up, rub it together fast (to soften or clean), rub it to soften it (of plants, etc.), fluff it (inner cedar bark to soften it):: yékw'et < yókw' ~ yóqw'.

crunch
chewing with a crunch, nibbling, gnawing:: x̲áp'kw'els < x̲ep'ékw'.
chew with a crunch:: x̲ep'kw'á:ls < x̲ep'ékw'.
crunchy (loud when eating), crackling (noise when eating):: tl'ámqw'els < tl'ém.
crunchy (loud when eating), crackling (sound or noise when eating):: tl'ámqw'els < tl'ámkw'em.
gnaw s-th, chew s-th [crunchy]:: x̲ép'kw't ~ x̲épkw't ~ (sic) x̲épkwt < x̲ep'ékw'.
(have) sound of popping small round things (snowberries, herring eggs as when eating them, rice krispies, crabapples, cranberries, etc.), (have a crunching sound (as of grasshopper, rice krispies)):: tl'ámkw'em, tl'ámkw'em < tl'ém.
make a crunching or crackling noise, crunching (gnawing) sound:: x̲ápkw'em < x̲ep'ékw'.
make a crunch underfoot (bones, nut, glass, etc.):: x̲ep'ékw'.

crush
break up s-th by crumpling, crush it up, rub it together fast (to soften or clean), rub it to soften it (of plants, etc.), fluff it (inner cedar bark to soften it):: yékw'et < yókw' ~ yóqw'.

crush (CONT'D)

crush (of berries), smash (of berries), squish (of berries, etc.), to mash:: tósem < tós.
many get crushed, get all crushed, many smashed (round and filled):: meqw'méqw' < méqw' ~ mṓqw'.
rub (oil or water) in s-th to clean or soften, rub s-th to soften or clean it, (shaping a stone hammer with abrasion?, shaping?, mixing paint?, pressing together or crushing? [BHTTC 9/2/76]):: yémq't.

cry

cried for s-th, (be crying for s-th/s-o):: x̲ahá:met < x̲à:m ~ x̲á:m.
cry for oneself, (crying for oneself):: x̲ehó:methet < x̲à:m ~ x̲á:m.
cry for s-o/s-th:: x̲á:met < x̲à:m ~ x̲á:m.
crying a lot:: x̲ex̲á:m < x̲à:m ~ x̲á:m.
crying, weeping:: x̲á:m < x̲à:m ~ x̲á:m.
cry of a bluejay [Steller's jay] that means good news:: q'ey, q'ey, q'ey.
cry with someone, a person one cries with (related or not), unrelated grandparents of a deceased grandchild, etc.:: ts'elhx̲à:m < x̲à:m ~ x̲á:m.
easy to cry, (cries easily):: qe'álts ~ qiqe'álts < qó:.
feel like singing a spirit song, be in a trance making sighsand crying sounds before singing a spirit song, be in the beginning of a trance before the spirit song is recognizable (the motions and sounds, crying out or wailing before singing):: lhéch.
hush a baby from crying, (hush s-o (a baby) from crying):: ch'exwí:lt < ts'áxw.
lots of people crying:: x̲emx̲ám < x̲à:m ~ x̲á:m.
make one's mouth like one's going to cry:: pespesó:ythílem < pas ~ pes.
make s-o cry (accidentally or manage to):: x̲á:mlexw < x̲à:m ~ x̲á:m.
rock in the Fraser River near Scowlitz where a woman was crying a lot:: X̲ex̲ám Smá:lt < x̲à:m ~ x̲á:m.
screaming, crying (of a baby):: kwekwchám < kwátsem ~ kwáchem.
sobbing after crying:: qésqesí:l < qásel.
sobbing, crying a little, (to sob [EB]):: xíx̲à:m ~ x̲éyx̲à:m < x̲à:m ~ x̲á:m.
(this cry of a bluejay [Steller's jay] warns you of bad news):: chéke chéke chéke chéke.
tired out from crying:: qesqesí:lqel < qásel, qsí:lthet < qásel.
want to cry, feel like crying:: x̲amélmel < x̲à:m ~ x̲á:m.
weep, cry, weeping, crying:: x̲à:m ~ x̲á:m.
youngest sister of Lhílheqey (Mount Cheam) that cries:: Ñemó:th'iya < x̲à:m ~ x̲á:m.

Cryptoglaux acadia acadia

Glaucidium gnoma swarthi (or Glaucidium gnoma grinnelli) and Cryptoglaux acadia acadia (or Aegolius acadicus):: spopeleqwíth'a ~ spopeleqwíth'e < poleqwíth'a.

Cryptogramma crispa

Achillea millefolium, also Cryptogramma crispa:: xaweqá:l < xáwéq.

crystal :: th'áth'elh.

cub

bear cub:: spathó:llh < pá:th.

cucumber :: kwúkwemels.

Cucumis sativus:: kwúkwemels.

Culicidae
family Culicidae, also included as a type of "mosquito" in family Tipulidae:: qwá:l.

Cultus Lake:: Swí:lhcha ~ Swíylhcha.
Cultus Lake, (also village at Cultus Lake near Hatchery Creek [Wells (lst ed.):19]):: Swílhcha.
Cultus Lake Mountain, actually Mount Amadis or International Ridge:: Swílhcha Smá:lt < Swílhcha.
Hatchery Creek, tributary of Sweltzer Creek (which drains Cultus Lake):: Stṓtelō < tó:l ~ tò:l.
Sweltzer Creek (the stream from Cultus Lake to Chilliwack River at Soowahlie):: Swílhcha Stótelō < Swílhcha.

cup :: lepót, lopót.
handle of a cup:: q'ṓ:l (or better) qw'ṓ:l.
to cup water in one's hands, to cup berries in one's hands:: qéltsesem < qó:.

cupboard
any kind of cupboard:: shxwlathílé < ló:thel.

cure
(an Indian doctor or shaman) working, curing, chasing the bad things away:: lhálhewels < lhá:w.
cure s-o, heal s-o by Indian doctoring:: lhá:wet < lhá:w.
curing s-o (as an Indian doctor):: lhálhewet < lhá:w.
heal, be cured:: lhá:w.
thank s-o (for a cure, for pall-bearing, a ceremony, being a witness):: xwth'í:t < ts'ít ~ ch'í:t.

curious
be curious:: kw'ókw'eleqw.

curl
curly hair, (be curly-haired(?), have curly hair(?)):: sq'elq'élp'eqw < q'ál.
curly hair, (have curly hair(?)):: sq'elq'élp'es < q'ál, sq'ó:lp'eqw < q'ál.

currant
flower of the red-flowering currant:: qwelíyes.
Indian currant bush, red-flowering currant bush, prob. also stink currant bush:: sp'á:th'elhp < sp'á:th', sp'á:th'elhp < sp'á:th', sp'á:th'elhp < sp'á:th'.
prickly swamp currant, swamp gooseberry:: th'kw'íwíyelhp < th'ekw' or th'íkw'.
red-flowering currant berry, Indian currant berry, probably also stink currant berry also called skunk currant berry:: sp'á:th', sp'á:th'.
swamp gooseberry, prickly swamp currant:: ts'qw'í:wíyelhp.

current
go in a semi-circle (or part of a circle) with the current:: selch'éle < sél or sí(:)l.
go in full circle with the current:: sá:lch'ōwelh < sél or sí(:)l.

curve
a bend in a river, a curve of a lake:: sq'ówqel < q'éw ~ q'ew.

curve (CONT'D)

go around (a point, a bend, a curve, etc.) in the water, make a U-turn (in the water, could use today on land with a car):: q'ówletsem < q'éw ~ q'ew.

cushion :: lháx̲eletstel < lhá:x̲ ~ lháx̲, shxwthéletstel < thél.

Customs officials)

search through it, rummage through it, search s-o (like Customs officials):: xíleqwt < xíleqw.

cut

a canoe or boat cut off short in the rear (because the stern couldn't be repaired):: t'qw'á:lats < t'éqw'.
a cut on the hand:: shxwlhéts'tses < lhíts' ~ lhí:ts'.
be cut:: slhíts' < lhíts' ~ lhí:ts'.
cut (grass, hay):: lhéch'elechá:ls < lhíts' ~ lhí:ts'.
cut it all up:: t'eqw't'éqw'et < t'éqw'.
cut it (wood, lawn, etc.):: t'eqw'ót < t'éqw'.
cut off one's breath:: t'eqw'lhálém < t'éqw'.
cut off the tip of one's nose:: lhts'élqsel < lhíts' ~ lhí:ts'.
cut one's arm:: lhets'elá:x̲el < lhíts' ~ lhí:ts'.
cut one's foot:: lhéts'xel < lhíts' ~ lhí:ts'.
cut one's hair:: lhíts'eqwem < lhíts' ~ lhí:ts'.
cut on one's hand, (cut one's finger [EB}):: lhéts'ches < lhíts' ~ lhí:ts'.
cut on the mouth:: lhts'ó:ythel < lhíts' ~ lhí:ts'.
cut open and butcher it, clean it (of fish or animal):: kw'íts'et < kw'íts'.
cut something off for s-o:: lhíts'elhtset < lhíts' ~ lhí:ts'.
cut s-th (string or rope):: tl'qw'ót.
cut s-th (with anything: knife, saw, scythe, etc.), cut s-o:: lhí:ts'et < lhíts' ~ lhí:ts'.
cutting (grass, hay):: lhílhech'elchá:ls < lhíts' ~ lhí:ts'.
cutting them up (of logs):: t'ot'qw'íth'et < t'éqw'.
cutting wood (with a saw), sawing wood:: xíxets'els < xets'á:ls.
cut wood (with a saw), saw wood, (cut wood to store away):: xets'á:ls.
fish cut real thin for wind-drying but without cross cuts, dried fish cut differently than slhíts'es:: st'ál.
get cut:: lhíts' ~ lhí:ts'.
(get the) top cut off:: t'eqw'qéyl or t'eqw'qí:l < t'éqw'.
sawing wood, cutting wood with a saw:: lhílhets'els < lhíts' ~ lhí:ts'.
to cut wood (with a saw), saw wood, (to cut [as structured activity] [Deming}):: lhts'á:ls < lhíts' ~ lhí:ts', lhts'á:ls < lhíts' ~ lhí:ts'.

cute. :: ák'.

cute, a little one is good, good (of s-th little):: í'iy < éy ~ éy:.
cute little one:: á'iy ~ 'á'iy < éy ~ éy:.
good (of little ones), cute (of many of them):: é'iy ~ á'iy < éy ~ éy:.

cut-grass

sharp grass, cut-grass:: pxá:y.

Cyanocitta stelleri annectens

Cyanocitta stelleri paralia and Cyanocitta stelleri annectens:: x̲ax̲esyúwes or x̲ax̲e syúwes < x̲áx̲e, kwá:y.

Cyanocitta stelleri paralia
Cyanocitta stelleri paralia and Cyanocitta stelleri annectens:: x̲ax̲esyúwes or x̲ax̲e syúwes < x̲áx̲e, kwá:y.

cycle
to cycle, ride a bicycle:: xwpóysekel < póysekel.

cyclic period]
(be) Spring, [cyclic period] when everything comes up:: kw'íyles ~ kw'éyles < kw'í ~ kw'íy.
cyclic period, moon, season:: =ó:s ~ =ós ~ =es.
(fifty cyclic periods [DM]):: lhèq'etselsxó:s ~ lhéq'etselsxó:s < lheq'át ~ lhq'á:t.
has come around (of a cyclic period of time):: séqsel.
one cyclic period:: léts'es < léts'a ~ léts'e.
thirty cyclic periods:: lhexwelhsxó:s < lhí:xw.
three dollars, three tokens of wealth, three blankets (Boas), three cyclic periods:: lhí:xwes < lhí:xw.
Thursday, four o'clock, (fourth cyclic period):: sx̲e'óthels < x̲e'ó:thel ~ x̲e'óthel.

Cyperaceae
family Gramineae and possibly family Cyperaceae (sedges):: só:x̲wel ~ sóx̲wel.

Cyprinus carpio:: scheláka.

dab
dab it on:: ts'ep'ét.

Dacrymyces
Fomes sp. including Fomes applanatus and probably others, possibly Polyporus sp., possibly Ganoderma sp., prob. also jelly fungi of Tremella and maybe Auricularia and Dacrymyces species, especially Tremella mesenterica (Yellow trembler) which is abundant only on the red alder and is reddish-orange matching the color, translucence and shape of those eaten by some of the Stó:lō elders, the jelly fungi could possibly have a differnet name from the bracket fungus:: s'ómó:qwes.

daddy long-legs
daddy long-legs, harvestman spider:: tl'áleqtxel q'ésq'esetsel < tl'áqt.
daddy long-legs (spider), harvestman spider:: tl'áleqtxel q'esq'ésetsel < q'ey ~ q'i.

dam
beaver dam:: teqáp or teqíp < téq.

damp
pour water on s-th to keep it damp:: kw'lhó:st < kw'élh.
smelling damp, rank:: qwóqwelem.

dance
a kind of spirit-dance done after the syúwel (spirit power) hasleft a dancer but the dancer still needs to dance:: qw'éx̲weqs.
an experienced spirit dancer:: sts'eláxwem.
a non-spirit-dancer:: st'ólkwlh.

dance (CONT'D)

a spirit-dance, a winter-dance:: smílha < mílha.
a spirit power of a kw'ṓxweqs dancer, (perhaps wolverine or badger spirit power):: sqoyép < sqoyép.
babysitter (for new spirit-dancers), any of the workers who help in initiating a spirit-dancer, (initiator or helper of spirit-dancers):: xólhemìlh ~ xòlhemí:lh < xólh.
dance-hall:: qw'eyilexáwtxw < qw'eyílex ~ qw'eyíléx.
dancing costume:: slewómet ~ lewómet.
(doing) spirit-dancing, winter-dancing (when they're in action):: mímelha < mílha.
have the last spirit dance of the season, have the "sweep up":: yekw'ólhem or perhaps yekw'wólhem < yókw' ~ yóqw'.
having fun at a non-spiritual dance:: oyewílem.
his/her dance:: sqw'eyílexs < qw'eyílex ~ qw'eyíléx.
Indian dance-house, "smoke-house", (spirit-dance building):: smilha'áwtxw < mílha.
invite s-o (to come eat, dance etc.) (any number), invite s-o to a feast:: tl'e'áxet < tl'e'á ~ tl'á'.
inviting (to come eat, dance), to give a potlatch, (give a feast or gathering), to invite to a feast, invite to a potlatch:: tl'etl'áxel < tl'e'á ~ tl'á'.
lift s-o (of a spirit dancer being initiated):: shxwóxwelstexw < xwá.
longhouse for spirit-dancers, the big house, smokehouse (for spirit-dancing):: stháwtxw < thi ~ tha ~ the ~ thah ~ theh.
longhouse, smokehouse (for spirit-dancing, etc.), Indian house, plank house:: xwelmexwáwtxw < xwélmexw.
new spirit dancer's headband:: qítes ~ qéytes < qít.
non-spirit-dancers (lots of them):: st'elt'ólkwlh < st'ólkwlh.
soft (down) feathers put in oiled hair for dancing:: sq'óyeseqw ~ sx̲óyeseqw < sq'óyes.
soft feathers put in oiled hair for dancing:: sx̲óyeseqw ~ sq'óyeseqw.
spirit power, spirit-dancer:: =ó:lkwlh.
square dressing room or shelter of blankets where sx̲wóyx̲wey dancers change before doing the sx̲wóyx̲wey dance:: q'eléts'tel < q'el.
sx̲wóyx̲wey ceremony featuring a masked dance, the sx̲wóyx̲wey mask and dance:: sx̲wó:yx̲wey ~ sx̲wóyx̲wey.
(the) spirit-dancing:: smímelha < mílha.
to spirit-dance, to spirit-dance (of a group), have aspirit-dance, to winter-dance:: mílha.

dance-house

Indian dance-house, "smoke-house", (spirit-dance building):: smilha'áwtxw < mílha.

dancer

an Indian dancer's spirit power:: syúwél ~ syéw:el < yéw: ~ yéw.
dancer's uniform, (any) coordinated outfit:: s-hóyews < hóyiws.
new dancer (new spirit-dancer), (new) baby (in spirit-dancing):: x̲awsó:lh < x̲á:ws.
new spirit-dancer:: x̲awsólkwlh or x̲awsó:lkwlh < x̲á:ws.
new spirit-dancer's head-dress or [cedar-bark] hat:: sx̲wóyéleqws te x̲awsólkwlh < sx̲wóyéleqw.
paint one's face red or black (spirit dancer, Indian doctor, ritualist, etc.):: lhíx̲esem < lhá:x̲ ~ lháx̲.
to paint red or black (spirit dancer, Indian doctor, etc.):: lhíx̲ < lhá:x̲ ~ lháx̲.

dancing

spirit-dancing costume, wool hat for spirit-dancer (Deming):: s-hóyiws.

dancing apron

dog-hair blanket dancing apron (DM 12/4/64):: kw'eléw ~ kw'elốw.

dancing costume

dancing costume:: slewómet ~ lewómet.

dandelion :: qwáyúwél < qwá:y.

to drop or blow plant fluff (like dandelions, fireweed, cottonwood, etc.), to blow (of dusty or flaky stuff like wood dust, dandruff, maybe seeds):: pípexwem < píxw.

dandruff

(have) dandruff:: lheqw'lhéqw'eqw < lhéqw'.

to drop or blow plant fluff (like dandelions, fireweed, cottonwood, etc.), to blow (of dusty or flaky stuff like wood dust, dandruff, maybe seeds):: pípexwem < píxw.

dandy

a dandy, someone who overdresses, a show-off, comedian, someone who always cracks jokes, smart-alec:: swék'.

danger.

close to danger., danger., stop.:: í' ~ i'.

dangerous

scare oneself (in being reckless), scare oneself (do something one knows is dangerous and get scared even more than expected):: sí:silómet ~ sí:silòmèt < síy.

dark

(be) a dark color (of clothes, complexions, etc.), (dark gray, dark brown):: stl'ítl'esel < stl'ítl'es.

(be) dark (as at night):: thá:t.

get dark:: thetí:l < thá:t.

getting dark:: lálàt < lá:t.

dark glasses)

eyeglasses, (probably dark glasses):: st'óle'oléstel < t'á:l.

Daucus carota

possibly Lomatium utriculatum or Perideridiae gairdneri, also Daucus carota:: xáwéq.

daughter

another small peak just to the right of the Mount Cheam summit peak as one faces south, she is another daughter of Lhílheqey (Mt. Cheam):: S'óyewòt < Óyewòt.

child (of someone, kinterm), offspring, son, daughter:: méle ~ mél:a.

children (kinterm, someone's), sons, daughters:: mámele < méle ~ mél:a.

daughter-in-law

child's spouse, son-in-law, daughter-in-law, (man's) sister's husband:: schiwtálh.

relative of deceased spouse, mother/brother/sister/cousin/relative of deceased husband, dead spouse's relative or sibling, daughter-in-law if son dies:: ts'á:ya.

sons-in-law, daughters-in-law, children's spouses:: schí:wetálh < schiwtálh.

David

(Indian name of) David (of Cultus Lake):: Seláq'oyatel.

day :: swáyel ~ swáyél ~ swàyèl < wáyel.

be what day?:: skw'íles < kw'í:l ~ kw'íl.

day, daytime, sky, weather, (horizon (BJ)):: swáyel ~ swáyél ~ swàyèl < wáyel.

day before yesterday:: lhulhá

day of the week:: =elhlát ~ =lhát.

days:: seswá:yél < wáyel.

eight days of northeast wind:: unknown.

forty days:: x̲ethelsxó:s < x̲e'ó:thel ~ x̲e'óthel.

four days of northeast wind:: unknown.

fourth day after a death (when everyone washes up (bathes)):: sxókw' < xókw' ~ xó:kw'.

get daylight, become day:: wáyel.

hour, o'clock, day of week:: s=...=s.

Monday (day past):: yilawelhát ~ yiláwelhàt ~ syiláwelhàt < yelá:w ~ yeláw ~ yiláw.

Sunday (sacred day):: sx̲ax̲elh(l)át ~ sx̲ex̲elh(l)at < x̲áx̲e.

-th day of the week:: s= =s.

today, this day:: tlowáyél ~ tlówàyèl < ló.

Wednesday (< the third day):: slhíxws < lhí:xw.

day-dream

(be) in a daze, day-dreaming:: stekwtákw.

daylight

get daylight, become day:: wáyel.

daytime

day, daytime, sky, weather, (horizon (BJ)):: swáyel ~ swáyél ~ swàyèl < wáyel.

daze

(be) in a daze, day-dreaming:: stekwtákw.

dead

be dead:: sq'óq'ey < q'ó:y ~ q'óy.

dead and broken [of a plant]:: st'ápiy < t'ápiy.

die, be dead, be paralyzed:: q'ó:y ~ q'óy.

ghost, corpse, dead body:: spoleqwíth'a < poleqwíth'a.

have a ritual burning ceremony, have a burning, feed the dead, (food offered to the dead [at a ritual burning] [EB 5/25/76]):: yeqwá:ls < yéqw.

it's dead (of a tree):: t'ápiythet < t'ápiy.

it's going dead (of a tree):: t'ópiythet < t'ápiy.

lost and presumed dead, perish:: s'í:kw' < íkw' ~ í:kw'.

deadfall

a prop used to trip a deadfall trap:: tpólhtel < tpólh.

deadfall trap:: tl'iq'áwtxw < tl'íq'.

metal trap, any trap, (also deadfall trap):: x̲ésxel.

snare, deadfall:: s'eweltá:l < íwel.

deaf

deaf
deaf, deaf (but can hear a little):: tl'ékwela.

dear :: siyám ~ (rare) siyá:m.
chief, leader, respected person, boss, rich, dear:: siyá:m < éy ~ éy:.
dear friends:: q'e'ó:leq < q'ó.
hubby, dear husband, pet term for husband:: swóweqeth < swáqeth.
my dear, (little best friend, little dear friend, etc.):: q'éyq'eleq ~ (better) q'íq'eleq < q'ó.
pal, best friend, dear friend, chum:: q'óleq ~ q'e'óléq < q'ó.

death
fourth day after a death (when everyone washes up (bathes)):: sxókw' < xókw' ~ xó:kw'.

de-bark
peel it (bark off a tree), bark it, (de-bark it), pull itdown (of bark, board, etc.), pull it up (of bark, board):: lheqw'ó:t < lhéqw'.

debris
large rock slide that includes trees and other debris:: syélt < yélt.

debt
repay, pay a debt:: léwlets ~ lőwlets.

deceased
deceased one:: stewéqel.
deceased ones, late ones:: stáweqel < stewéqel.
deceased uncle, deceased grand-uncle:: qethiyálh.
departed ancestors:: syewá:lelh ~ syewálelh < yewá:l.
elders past, deceased old people:: siyolexwálh < siyólexwe.
her deceased children, (his deceased children):: mameláselh < méle ~ mél:a.
late (deceased), past tense:: =à:lh ~ =elh.
lost (deceased):: sóstem < sát.
that was her (deceased):: kwsú:tl'ò:lh < kw.
that was her (deceased), she (deceased):: kwsú:tl'ò:lh < tl'ó ~ tl'o.
that was him (deceased), he (deceased):: kw'ú:tl'ò:lh < tl'ó ~ tl'o.
that was them (deceased):: kwthú:tl'òlèmèlh < kw.
that was them (deceased), they (deceased):: kwthú:tl'ò:lèmèlh < tl'ó ~ tl'o.
(word used when showing a picture of the deceased at a memorial ceremony, and telling the family to dry their tears) his/her face/their faces are dried:: th'éyx̲westem < ts'íyxw ~ ts'éyxw ~ ch'íyxw.

deceased spouse
relative of deceased spouse:: th'á:ya.
relative of deceased spouse, mother/brother/sister/cousin/relative of deceased husband, dead spouse's relative or sibling, daughter-in-law if son dies:: ts'á:ya.
to marry a sibling of one's deceased spouse:: th'áyá:m < ts'á:ya.

deceive
fool s-o, deceive s-o, (lie to s-o [SJ]):: q'elstá:xw < q'á:l.

December
- about December, (January to February [Billy Sepass]):: meqó:s < máqa ~ máqe.
- moon or month beginning in February, (November to December, time when ice forms [and sticks] [Billy Sepass in Jenness]):: temtl'í:q'es < tl'íq'.

decide
- think, ponder, study, decide:: tó:lthet < tól.

decorate
- decorate it with different designs:: x̱elx̱élest < x̱él ~ x̱é:yl ~ x̱í:l

deep
- be deep:: stl'ép < tl'ép.
- be deep, be very deep, be deep water:: shxwtl'ép < tl'ép.
- big voice (usually deep):: thíwelh < thi ~ tha ~ the ~ thah ~ theh.
- deep bottom (of a river, lake, water, canoe, anything):: stl'epláts < tl'ép.
- deep down, below, down below, low:: tl'ép.
- deeper, always deep:: lexwstl'ép < tl'ép.
- drift-netting, catching fish with one or two canoes drifting downstream with a net in deep water:: xíxemel ~ xíxemal.
- (make s-th deep or low):: tl'épstexw < tl'ép.
- swim, (tread water), (wading in deep water [LJ], swimming [Elders Group]):: x̱élhchem.

deer
- black-tailed deer:: tl'alqtéle ~ tl'elqtéle < tl'áqt.
- deer (Columbia blacktail or Coast), mule deer:: tl'alqtéle ~ tl'elqtéle < tl'áqt.
- deer hooves:: kwóxwemal , < kwoxw.
- deer-skin moccasin:: stl'éqxel.
- fawn, baby deer:: st'ít'ele < st'él'e.
- inside brisket of meat (deer, etc.):: th'x̱éyles or th'x̱íles.
- [left] front leg quarter of deer or other animal:: sth'íkweláx̱el < th'íkwe.
- swimming (of dog, deer, animal), (dog-paddling):: x̱ólhchem < x̱élhchem.
- to split s-th open (like deer or fish):: tl'xáx̱et < tl'éx.
- white-tailed deer:: tl'alqtéle ~ tl'elqtéle < tl'áqt.
- younger deer, baby horse, younger cow, fawn, colt, calf:: st'él'e.

deer fly :: lhemélétsʼ.

defecate
- have a bowel movement, defecate, to shit:: ó'.
- made it (if laxative finally works):: x̱é:yles < x̱éylés.
- mess in one's pants (shit in one's pants):: ó'ayiwsem < ó'.

defend
- help s-o, defend s-o, protect s-o, aid s-o:: má:yt ~ máyt < máy.
- weapon (arrow, club, etc.), something used to defend oneself:: hí:tel ~ hí:ytel < iyó:tel.

definite
- the (distant and out of sight, remote), (definite but distant and out of sight, remote), the (abstract), a (remote, abstract), some, (indefinite):: kw'e.

deformation

(have a) flat head, (have cranial deformation by cradle-board):: sp'íp'elheqw < p'ílh.

deformed

deformed baby:: sx̱ax̱e'áylh < x̱áx̱e, t'ámiya.

delay

delay oneself:: iy'eyómthet < óyém.
delay s-o:: oyómt < óyém, q'éylómstexw < q'éylòm.
delay s-o, slow s-o down:: oyémstexw < óyém.

delirious :: yó:lx̱wtem.

deliver

have given birth, already had a child, had a baby, (delivered):: sémele < méle ~ mél:a.

Deming

Deming (Wash.), South Fork of Nooksack River and village nearest Deming:: xwe'éyem ~ xw'éyem < éy ~ éy:.

demonstrative

nominalizer (female present and visible or presence or proximity unspecified), demonstrative article:: the=.
nominalizer (male or gender unspecified, present and visible or presence or proximity unspecified), demonstrative article:: ta=, te=.

den

house, home, den, lodge, hive:: lá:lém.

Dendragapus obscurus fuliginosus:: mí:t'.

Dendrocopos

Colaptes cafer cafer and rarely Colaptes cafer collaris, (if large is correct Dryocopus pileatus [AK], if small is correct, probably Sphyrapicus (varius) ruber or possibly Dryobates villosus harrisi and Dryobates villosus orius or Dryobates pubescens (esp.) gairdneri some zoologists replace the genus Dryobates with Dendrocopos, others with Picoides):: th'íq.
probably Sphyrapicus (varius) ruber and/or possibly Dryobates villosus harrisi and Dryobates villosus orius or(downy woodpecker) Dryobates pubescens (gairdneri esp.), forMunro and Cowan's Dryobates genus Peterson uses Dendrocopos andUdvardy uses Picoides:: qw'opx̱wiqsélem < qw'ópx̱w.

denim

denim cloth:: xwétkw'em < xwót'kw'em.
denim clothes:: xwétkw'emélwet < xwót'kw'em.
denim pants, jeans:: xwétkw'emáyiws < xwót'kw'em.

deny it :: őwestexw ~ éwestexw < éwe ~ őwe.

departed

departed ancestors:: syewá:lelh ~ syewálelh < yewá:l.

depend
    depending on someone:: tehí:lewel.

dependent
    (probably also) subordinate or dependent (with passive):: -èt.

Depot Creek
    Depot Creek (off upper Chilliwack River):: possibly Chechíx̲em < chíchex̲em.

Dermacentor andersoni
    class Arachnida, order Acarina, Dermacentor andersoni, and probably Ixodes pacificus:: t'pí.
    class Arachnida, order Acarina, probably Ixodes pacificus and Dermacentor andersoni resp.:: méth'elhqiwèl < méth'elh.

Deroche
    a place near Deroche, B.C., just east of Lakahahmen Indian Reserve #10 (which is registered with D.I.A. as Skweam):: Skwiyó:m < Skwíyò.
    place across the Fraser River from Deroche:: P'eq'ó:les < p'éq'.

descendant
    head of descendants:: =eqw ~ =(e)leqw ~ =íqw ~ =ó:qw.

design
    decorate it with different designs:: x̲elx̲élest < x̲él ~ x̲é:yl ~ x̲í:l
    design on basket:: sx̲éles < x̲él ~ x̲é:yl ~ x̲í:l
    designs on basket, basket designs:: sx̲elx̲éles < x̲él ~ x̲é:yl ~ x̲í:l
    face of a basket, (design on a basket):: =ó:s ~ =ós ~ =es.
    picture, design:: sx̲éles < x̲él ~ x̲é:yl ~ x̲í:l.
    put s-th on (of a design on a dress, of a shirt, shoes, etc.), attach it, stick it on, fasten it:: tl'álx < tl'ál.

desire
    desire s-th, desire s-o, wish for s-th/s-o:: témex.
    desiring s-th:: téméx < témex.
    want, desire, like, need:: stl'í ~ stl'í: < tl'í ~ tl'í:.

desk :: letám.
    table, desk:: letám.

destroy
    spoil s-th, destroy s-th:: qelqé:ylt or qelqí:lt < qél.

determination
    determination:: sx̲ax̲esélmet < x̲ás.

determined
    (be) determined, got your mind made up:: sx̲áx̲as < x̲ás.
    determination:: sx̲ax̲esélmet < x̲ás.
    determined (about s-th), have to do it, got to do it:: x̲asélmet < x̲ás.
    (get) determined:: x̲ásel < x̲ás.

develop
    (get or develop a) sprain, to sprain:: ts'lhóqw'.

device
    device, implement, thing used for:: =tel.
    device, tool:: =í:ls.
    device, tool, thing for doing something [as a structured activity]), person doing something [as structured activity]:: =els.
    pencil, pen, something to write with, (device to write or paint or mark with):: x̱éltel < x̱él ~ x̱é:yl ~ x̱í:l

devil
    devil, Satan:: líyóm.

devil's club
    devil's club plant:: qwó:pelhp.

Devil's Run:: Líyómxetel < líyóm.
    Sumas village and area from present-day Kilgard to Fraser River, Sumas village (on both sides of the Fraser at the east end of Sumas Mt.), (Devil's Run (below Láx̱ewey), the area between Sumas Mt. and Fraser River [Elders Group 7/13/77], Sumas River (probably requires Stó:lō river or Stótelō creek to follow) [Wells 1965], Sumas Lake (probably requires X̱ótsa lake after Semáth for this meaning) [Elders Group 7/13/77]):: Smá:th ~ Semá:th ~ Semáth.

dew :: lhémtel < lhém, slhémlhem < lhém, slhémxel < lhém.

dialect
    Cowichan (people, dialect, area):: Qewítsel < qew.
    Kwantlen people, Kwantlen dialect of Downriver Halkomelem:: Qw'ó:ltl'el.
    Pilalt tribe, Pilalt people, Pilalt dialect, (Pilalt, village at west end of Little Mountain by Agassiz [Wells, Duff]):: Pelólhxw.
    Sliammon people, Sliammon dialect (of the Comox language, Mainland Comox):: Sloyámén.

diaper :: sqelá:lh < qél.
    mattress, mats used in beds, (diaper(s) [AC]):: slhá:wel.

diarrhea
    get diarrhea:: tl'xátem < tl'éx.

diatomaceous earth
    diatomaceous earth (could be mixed with things to whiten them--for ex. dog and goat wool), white clay for white face paint (for pure person spirit-dancers), white powder from mountains, white clay they make powder from to lighten goat and dog wool for blankets, powder, talc, white face paint:: st'ewṓkw'.

Dicamptodon ensatus:: tseyí:yex̱.
    prob. Dicamptodon ensatus, poss. also Taricha granulosa granulosa, prob. also Gerrhonotis coeruleus principis:: seyíyex̱.

Dickinson
    nickname for Nat Dickinson:: Pepx̲wíqsel < píxw.

dictionary:: tóltí:lqel < tól.

did
    never did, he/she/they never did:: őwethelh < éwe ~ őwe.

didn't
    wasn't?, weren't?, didn't?:: ewá:lh ~ wá:lh < éwe ~ őwe.
    weren't ever?, wasn't ever?, didn't ever?, does s-o ever?, never used to, not going to (but did anyway) [perhaps in the sense of never usually do X but did this time]:: ewá:lh ~ wá:lh < éwe ~ őwe.

die
    clothing, food, and possessions burned and given away when a person dies, (possessions and food burned and given away at a burning):: syeqwá:ls < yéqw.
    die, be dead, be paralyzed:: q'ó:y ~ q'óy.
    (have) quieter water, died down a little:: sqám < qám.
    in-laws or relatives when the connecting link dies:: ts'its'á:ya < ts'á:ya.
    old salmon (ready to die, spotted):: x̲éyqeya.
    perish together, many die (in famine, sickness, fire), all die, get wiped out:: x̲wà:y ~ x̲wá:y.
    they all died:: x̲wó:y < x̲wà:y ~ x̲wá:y.
    to almost die:: xwá:lq.

diet
    starving oneself, being on a "crash" diet:: xwexwóthet < xwá.

different :: láts'.
    a different kind:: lets'emót < láts'.
    another room, different room:: láts'ewtxw < láts'.
    be different:: selá:ts' < láts'.
    chopped in different places:: st'amt'í:m (or better) st'emt'í:m < t'ém.
    chop s-th in different places:: t'emt'émet < t'ém.
    decorate it with different designs:: x̲elx̲élest < x̲él ~ x̲é:yl ~ x̲í:l
    different person, stranger:: lets'ő:mexw < láts'.
    different tribe, different people, strangers:: lets'ó:lmexw < láts'.
    drifting a net in different places:: qwáseliyel < qwés.
    look different:: lelts'ó:méx < láts'.
    (many) different colors:: lets'ló:ts'tel < láts'.
    two different things:: selélets' < láts'.

difficult
    (be) difficult, hard (of work, etc.):: tl'í ~ tl'í:.
    make an attempt (to do something difficult, like running rapids in a canoe, mountain-climbing, winning a game, etc.), give it a try:: t'óthet < t'á.

dig :: thiyeqwá:ls ~ thiyqwá:ls < thíy.
    (be) dug out, (be hollowed out):: shxwótkw < xwótkw ~ xwótqw.
    digging:: thóyeqwels < thíy.
    digging stick:: shxwthóyeqwels < thíy, sqá:lex̲ ~ sqálex̲.
    dig it, dig s-th, dig for s-th:: thíyeqwt or thíyqwt < thíy.

dig (CONT'D)

searching it, digging through it:: xíxeleqwt < xíleqw.

digest

food settled (in the stomach), food is settled (in the stomach), (be settled (of food in the stomach), be comfortably digested (of food)):: qsákw'.

digging stick

digging stick:: shxwthóyeqwels < thíy, sqá:lex̲ ~ sqálex̲.

dim

dim it:: sóyt < sóy.
(get) dusk, (get dim):: só:yel < sóy.

dime

ten cents, dime:: mí:t ~ mít.

diminutive

affectionate diminutive:: =iya ~ =óya.
diminutive, little (of subject, object, agent, patient or action):: =R1= or =C1e=.
diminutive, little (of subject, object, agent, patient or action), small, (all diminutive verbs are also continuative):: R4= or C1í=, =R6= or =eC2=, R7= or C1á=.
diminutive, small, little:: R5= or C1e=.

dingy

(dingy white, off-white):: stl'ítl'es.

dip

a waiting dip-net with frame and string trap:: thqálem < thqá:lem.
dipping water:: qóqelem < qó:.
go in the water, walk slowly into the water, (dip oneself in the water [HT]:: mí:lthet < mí:l ~ míl.
holding on to a thqálem, waiting dip-netting, still-dipping:: théqelem < thqá:lem.
place where one fishes by waiting with a dip-net, dip-net fishing place, place where one still-dips:: sthqálem < thqá:lem.
to bag net, to sack net, to still-dip with two canoes:: thqá:lem.
to dip a net, (dipping a net):: qóqelets < qó:.
to dip water, get water, fetch water, pack water:: qó:m < qó:.
to scoop, to dip, dip water:: qó:lem < qó:.
to still-dip, rest dip-net on bottom (of river):: thqá:lem.

Diplopoda

class Chilopoda and poss. class Diplopoda:: lhets'íméls te pítxel < lhts'ímél.

dip-net

a dip-net, (a scoop net [CT]):: q'emó:stel < q'emós ~ q'emó:s.
a waiting dip-net with frame and string trap:: thqálem < thqá:lem.
dip-netting, fishing with a scoop net, (harpooning fish at night [DM 12/4/64]):: q'íq'emó:s ~ q'éyq'emó:s < q'emós ~ q'emó:s.
holding on to a thqálem, waiting dip-netting, still-dipping:: théqelem < thqá:lem.
horn rings for dip-nets:: x̲alwéla < x̲álew.
place where one fishes by waiting with a dip-net, dip-net fishing place, place where one

dip-net (CONT'D)

still-dips:: sthqálem < thqá:lem.
to dip-net:: q'emós ~ q'emó:s.
to dip-net, a dip-net:: qó:lets < qó:.
to still-dip, rest dip-net on bottom (of river):: thqá:lem.

Dipper

Big Dipper, (the Elk):: Q'oyíyets ~ Q'oyí:ts < q'oyíyets or q'oyí:ts.

dipper (bird):: smélx̲weth'.

Diptera

order Diptera, family Calliphoridae:: x̲wex̲wiyáye ~ x̲wix̲wiyáye < x̲wōx̲wáye ~ x̲wex̲wáye ~ x̲wōx̲wá:ye, x̲wiyx̲wiyáye < x̲wōx̲wáye ~ x̲wex̲wáye ~ x̲wōx̲wá:ye, x̲wōx̲wáye ~ x̲wex̲wáye ~ x̲wōx̲wá:ye.
order Diptera, family Tipulidae:: spelwálh, tl'áleqtxel qwá:l < tl'áqt.
order Diptera, probably families Chiromidae, Ceratopogonidae, and Simuliidae:: pepx̲wíqsel < píxw.
order Hymenoptera, superfamily Apoidea, family Apidae, including Apis mellifera (introduced), also family Bombidae and family Vespidae and possibly bee-like members of family Syrphidae (order Diptera):: sisemó:ya ~ sisemóya ~ sisemóye ~ sísemòye.
probably larvae of Lepidoptera or Diptera, possibly larvae of order Lepidoptera, family Tortricidae:: xwexwíye.

direct

directing, training, teaching, guiding:: í:wes < íwes.
showing s-o (how to do it), teaching s-o, advising s-o, guiding s-o, directing s-o:: í:west < íwes.
teach how to do something, teach, guide, direct, show:: íwes.

direction of the water

go in the direction of the water, go downriver:: xwōqw'éylem < wốqw' ~ wéqw'.

dirt

a lot of dirt:: sqel:ép ~ sqél:ep < qél.
(be) dirty:: chmítl' < mótl', mótl'.
dirt, ground:: =ílép ~ =í:lep ~ =éylép ~ =elep ~ =áp ~ =íp ~ =ép.
dirty, filthy:: t'íqqwlha < t'íq.
hill (dirt, includes both sides of hill), little hill:: skwókwep ~ skwokwepílep.

dirty :: t'éqoya < t'íq.

ashes (cinder-like), cinders (heavy and dirty), embers:: shxwiyélhtel ~ shxwyélhtel < yólh.
be bad (of water, person, anything), be dirty (of house, clothes, person, etc.):: qél.
(be) cranky, crabby, dirty-minded:: lexwqélwelh < qél.
(be) dirty:: chmítl' < mótl', mótl', qél:em ~ qél:ém or leqél:e(´)m < qél, sts'épx̲ < ts'épx̲.
(be) dirty (in everything) (in one's clothes, house, person):: qelétses < qél.
dirty, filthy:: t'íqqwlha < t'íq.
dirty, (have a cross face [EB]):: qelés < qél.
dirty (weather), bad weather, storm:: qél:em ~ qél:ém or leqél:e(´)m < qél.
(have a) dirty face:: ts'épx̲es < ts'épx̲.
(have a) dirty nose:: ts'epx̲élqsel < ts'épx̲.
(have/be) dirty water, (not clear, unclear, can't see the bottom (of water) [EL]):: mímexwel.

dirty (CONT'D)

(have) dirty feet:: ts'épx̲el < ts'épx̲.
(have) dirty hands:: qéletses < qél, ts'epx̲tses < ts'épx̲.
puddle that's always dirty, dirty pond, stagnant pool of water, (it never dries out [AK]):: th'qwélhcha.
turn bad, (get) spoiled (of clothes for ex.), (get) dirty:: qelqéyl or qelqí:l < qél.

dirty behind

(have a) dirty behind, (dirty in the rump, dirty in the rectum):: ts'epí:wel < ts'épx̲.

dirty-minded

(be) cranky, crabby, dirty-minded:: lexwqélwelh < qél.

disappear

disappear, drop out of sight, (to fade [Elders Group 3/72]):: théxw ~ théx̲w.
disappearing:: thethéx̲w < théxw ~ théx̲w.
disappear (purposely):: thexwó:thet < théxw ~ théx̲w.
go out of sight (behind something), disappear [behind something], [get in shade]:: t'á:l.

disappoint

disappointed and angry-looking without talking:: sx̲éyx̲eth' < x̲íth' ~ x̲éyth'.
disappoint s-o:: x̲elhwílhlexw < x̲élh.
lose heart, become disappointed, become discouraged:: qelqéyl or qelqí:l < qél.
to disappoint, (be disappointed):: x̲elhwílh < x̲élh.

discard

repair s-th once discarded, make s-th better, fix s-th up, repair s-th:: p'ákw'et < p'ákw'.
throw s-th away, discard s-th, throw s-o away, discard s-o:: íkw'et < íkw' ~ í:kw'.

discarded

making s-th better, repairing s-th once discarded:: p'áp'ekw'et < p'ákw'.

discourage

lose heart, become disappointed, become discouraged:: qelqéyl or qelqí:l < qél.

discover

(be) found out (something you were trying to hide), to be discovered (something secret):: wá:y.
discover s-th, find s-th:: thex̲láxw.

discriminate

discriminate against s-o, not accept s-o:: memí:lt < mí:lt.
not accept s-o, discriminate against s-o:: memí:lt < mí:lt.
not want s-o, not accept s-o, discriminate against s-o:: mí:lt.

disease

contract a disease, catch a disease, get addicted:: q'áp'.
(get) a disease gotten by contacting a frog, a skin eruption, also the same disease as the man got in Kawkawa Lake in the Sx̲wó:yx̲wey story, (perhaps also) leprosy:: qw'ṓ:m.
(have a) chronic skin disease marked by reddish skin and itching, have "seven-year itch":: lhóth'.
he passes on a disease to s-o, he gets s-o addicted:: q'ep'lóxes < q'áp'.

disease (CONT'D)

one's head is shaking constantly (like with disease):: x̱wóyqwesem, x̱wóyqwesem.
scabies (a skin disease), ("seven-year itch", itch lasting seven years [Deming 2/7/80]):: slhóth' < lhóth'.

disembark)
get off (a canoe or conveyance), get out of a canoe, (disembark):: qw'í:m.

disgust
disgusted:: qelqálém < qél.
(said when you are disgusted):: éx̱.
snap one's eyes at s-o [in anger or disgust]:: th'éplexwlexw (or perhaps th'ép'lexwlexw) < th'éplexw (or perhaps th'ép'lexw).
yechh., (expression of disgust used by some elders on seeing or smelling something disgusting):: áq'.

dish :: =ṓ:welh ~ =ṓwelh ~ =ōwelh ~ =ewelh ~ =á:welh ~ =welh ~ =ewí:l.
big wooden dish (often two feet long), feast dish, wooden platter, (big stirring spoon [LJ], carved wooden spoon, big wooden spoon [AC, BJ, DM]):: qwelhyṓwelh ~ qwelhliyṓwelh ~ qwelhlyúwelh < qwélh.
butter dish:: péte'àlà < péte.
clinking, tinkling (of glass, ice in glass, glasses together, dishes together, metal together):: ts'átx̱em ~ th'átx̱em.
dish, big cooking and serving trough used in longhouse, feast dish, plate (of wood or basketry), (platter), tray:: ló:thel, ló:thel.
dishcloth:: shxwiyòtqw'ewí:ls.
dishes:: =ewí:ls.
dish towel:: shxw'áp'ewí:ls < a┐ :p' ~ a┐ p', shxwiqw'ewí:ls < íqw'.
dry dishes, wipe off dishes:: iqw'wí:ls < íqw'.
drying dishes:: xwe'í:qw'wí:ls ~ xwe'íyeqw'wí:ls < íqw'.
dry them (dishes), dry s-th (dish):: eqw'ewílt < íqw'.
(have) clinking (of glass or dishes or metal), (have) tinkling sound (of glass, ice in glass, glasses together):: th'átx̱em ~ ts'átx̱em.
help oneself to food, serve oneself, serve oneself food (with a ladle), serve oneself a meal (food), (put on a dish [CT, HT]):: lhá:x̱em ~ lháx̱em < lhá:x̱ ~ lháx̱.
long feast dish:: qwethíles < qweth.
maple dish:: q'emṓ:lhpíwelh < sq'émél.
to rattle (of dishes or anything else loose), jingle (of money or any metal shaken), peal or toll (of a bell), make the sound of a bell, to ring (of a bell, telephone, in the ears):: th'á:tsem < th'éts or th'á(:)ts.
washing dishes:: th'óx̱wí:ls < th'éx̱w or th'óx̱w.
wash the dishes:: th'ex̱wewíls ~ th'ex̱wwí:ls ~ th'x̱wwí:ls ~ th'x̱wí:ls < th'éx̱w or th'óx̱w.
water kettle, boiler pan (for canning, washing clothes or dishes):: qowletsá:ls < qew.

dishcloth
dishcloth:: shxwiyòtqw'ewí:ls.

dish-pan
sink, dish-pan:: shxwth'ox̱wewí:ls < th'éx̱w or th'óx̱w.

dish-towel:: shxw'áp'ewí:ls < áp'.

dislike
  be disliked:: qélsem < qél.
  dislike s-o/s-th, to not like s-o/s-th:: qélstexw < qél.

dismantle
  take s-th down, tear down s-th man-made, dismantle s-th, take it apart:: yíx̲wet < yíx̲w.

Disporum hookerii
  respectively Smilacina racemosa, Smilacina stellata, Streptopus amplexifolius (and Streptopus roseus), and Disporum hookerii:: sth'íms te álhqey < álhqey ~ álhqay.
  Smilacina racemosa, Smilacina stellata, and probably Streptopus amplexifolius, Streptopus roseus, and Disporum hookerii:: sth'íms te álhqey < sth'í:m ~ sth'i:m.

disposition
  in the mind, -minded, disposition:: =welh ~ =wílh.

dissolve
  be worn out (of clothes for ex.), be old (of clothes), smashed up when dropped, dissolved:: th'éw.

distance
  a sound heard starting up again in the distance:: eháléqep < ehó.
  far, be far away, far off, way in the distance:: chó:kw.
  (made) a faint sound carried by the air, sound within hearingdistance, sound within earshot:: eháléqep < ehó.

distant
  keep on hearing a distant sound:: sasetáleqep < sát.
  (make) a distant sound:: stáléqep < sát.
  the (distant and out of sight, remote), (definite but distant and out of sight, remote), the (abstract), a (remote, abstract), some, (indefinite):: kw'e.
  (there), (action distant or abstract):: lí ~ lí: ~ li.

distribute:: kweléqelh.
  distribute to s-o:: kweléqelh(t)st < kweléqelh.

distributive
  distributive, all over, all around:: =x̲ ~ =ex̲.
  distributive, to each:: R5= or C1e=.

dive
  a diver:: hálqem < léqem, leqléqem < léqem.
  dive (already in water), go underwater, sink oneself down:: leqàlèm < léqem.
  dive, dive in:: léqem.
  diving:: hálqem < léqem.
  goldeneye duck (probably both the common goldeneye duck and the Barrow goldeneye duck), (a kind of diving duck [Elders Group]):: láqleqem < léqem.

divide
  divide something in half with s-o:: tseléqelhtst.
  place where Yale Creek divides (forks) above the highway bridge over the creek:: T'ít'x̲elhchò:m < t'éx̲.

dizzy

(be) dizzy:: sá:lts'tem < sél or sí(:)l, sélts'tem < sél or sí(:)l.
(get) dizzy, get drunk:: séles < sél or sí(:)l.

do

add some, add it, (do it again [AD]):: ts'xwót.
a doing:: skwó:yex̲thet ~ skwó:yx̲thet < kwíyx̲.
benefactive, do for s-o, malefactive, do on s-o:: -lhts.
be totally independent, doing the best one can:: óyó:lwethet < éy ~ éy:.
determined (about s-th), have to do it, got to do it:: x̲asélmet < x̲ás.
did s-o a favor:: (shxwémlexw) < (xwémlexw), (xwémlexw).
do, do this:: x̲tá: ~ x̲tá < x̲ét'e.
do I have to?, does one have to?:: lóyéxwa < lóy.
do it again, add more (to s-th):: qelátstexw < qelát.
do it, do it oneself:: iyálewet ~ eyálewet < éy ~ éy:.
do it, do s-th:: x̲tá:stexw < x̲ét'e.
do it harder:: tímet.
do it this way:: sx̲tá(:)stexw < x̲ét'e.
do s-th oneself:: iyálewet < éy ~ éy:.
do s-th well:: sthí:ystexw < thíy.
exert oneself, make a big effort, do with all one's might, [do] as hard as possible, do it harder (used if already paddling for ex.):: tíméthet < tímet.
insistant, persistant (like a child pressing to go along), bull-headed, doesn't mind, does just the opposite, (stubborn, contrary):: sxíxeles.
I wonder what s-o will do?, I wonder what I will do?:: xwe'ítixw or xwe'ít yexw < xwe'ít.
make s-th, fix s-th, do s-th:: thíyt < thíy.
manage by oneself (in food or travel), try to do it by oneself, try to be independent, do the best one can:: iyólewéthet < éy ~ éy:.
non-control reflexive, make oneself do something, keep oneself doing something:: =st=èlèmèt or =st-èlèmèt ~ =st-elómet.
pick fast, (do fast with the hands):: x̲wémetses < x̲wém ~ xwém.
scare oneself (in being reckless), scare oneself (do something one knows is dangerous and get scared even more than expected):: sí:silómet ~ sí:silòmèt < síy.
studying s-th, thinking about s-th, learning s-th, training for s-th, trying to do s-th:: totí:lt < tól.
try to do something (no matter what, anyway):: iyálewethet < éy ~ éy:.
what is s-o doing?, what is s-o saying?, what is he/she/it doing/saying?:: xwe'í:t < xwe'ít.

dock

wild rhubarb, western dock, common yellow dock, domestic rhubarb:: t'emó:sa.

doctor

(an Indian doctor or shaman) working, curing, chasing the bad things away:: lhálhewels < lhá:w.
blowing (of an Indian doctor on a patient):: pópex̲wels < póx̲w.
blow (spray) on a patient (of an Indian doctor or shaman), blow spray on s-o/s-th (of a shaman, a person ironing, a child teething):: póx̲wet < póx̲w.
cure s-o, heal s-o by Indian doctoring:: lhá:wet < lhá:w.
curing s-o (as an Indian doctor):: lhálhewet < lhá:w.
hand rattle of Indian doctor or shaman:: kwóxwemal ~ kwóxwmal < kwoxw.
Indian doctor at work, shaman at work, healer:: lhalhewéleq < lhá:w.

doctor (CONT'D)

Indian doctor, shaman, medicine man, Indian doctor's spirit power (Elders Group 11/19/75):: shxwlá:m < lá:m.
Indian red paint (used by spirit dancers, ritualists, and Indian doctors or shamans):: témélh.
jumping up and down or bouncing up and down (of an Indian doctor training):: hélmethet < lá:m.
jump up and down (of Indian doctor training):: lemóthet < lá:m.
paint one's face red or black (spirit dancer, Indian doctor, ritualist, etc.):: lhíx̲esem < lhá:x̲ ~ lháx̲.
place of training to become an Indian doctor (pit made from repeated jumping every year on the same spot):: shxwlemóthetále < lá:m.
spirit power of an Indian doctor or shaman:: slá:m < lá:m.
to paint red or black (spirit dancer, Indian doctor, etc.):: lhíx̲ < lhá:x̲ ~ lháx̲.

Doctor's Point
a stone like a statue at Harrison Lake, probably Doctor's Point:: Skoyá:m ~ Skeyá:m.
Doctor's Point on northwest shore Harrison Lake:: Lhx̲é:ylex < lhéx̲.

dodge
get out of the way, get off the way, dodge:: íyeqthet < iyá:q.

does
weren't ever?, wasn't ever?, didn't ever?, does s-o ever?, never used to, not going to (but did anyway) [perhaps in the sense of never usually do X but did this time]:: ewá:lh ~ wá:lh < éwe ~ ṓwe.

doesn't
isn't?, aren't?, don't?, doesn't?, (be not?):: ewá ~ ōwá ~ wá < éwe ~ ṓwe.
unless he, if he doesn't:: ewás < éwe ~ ṓwe.

dog :: sqwemá:y ~ sqwmá:y ~ sqwemáy < qwem.
a lot of (small) dogs, puppies:: sqwéqwemay < qwem.
a rock shaped like a dog on the east shore of the Fraser River near Hill's Bar and below Tewít (a rock shaped like a human hunter):: Sqwemá:y (?) < qwem.
dog house:: sqwemayáwtxw < qwem.
dog wool:: sqwemá:yalqel < qwem.
dog wool fibre:: qweqwemeylíth'e < qwem.
howling (of a dog), crowing (of a rooster):: q'ówem < q'á:w.
puppy:: sqwíqwemay < qwem.
small puppy:: sqwíqwemeyò:llh < qwem.
swimming (of dog, deer, animal), (dog-paddling):: x̲ólhchem < x̲élhchem.

dogbane
grass or fibre for nets or twine, spreading dogbane, possibly also Indian hemp:: méthelh.

doggie bag
container for left-overs taken home from feast, doggie bag:: meq'ethále < méq'.

dog-hair
dog-hair blanket dancing apron (DM 12/4/64):: kw'eléw ~ kw'elṓw.
loincloth, dog-hair apron, dog-hair mat:: sthíyep.

Dog Mountain
    Dog Mountain above Katz Reserve:: Q'á:w < q'á:w.

dog-paddle
    swimming (of dog, deer, animal), (dog-paddling):: x̲ólhchem < x̲élhchem.

dog salmon
    dog salmon, chum salmon:: kw'ó:lexw.
    September to October, dog salmon time:: temkw'ó:lexw < kw'ó:lexw.
    smokehouse, house for smoking fish:: kw'olexwáwtxw < kw'ó:lexw.

dog-tooth violet
    blue camas, yellow dog-tooth violet = yellow avalanche lily:: sk'ámets ~ sk'ámeth.

dogwood
    Pacific dogwood flower, flowering dogwood flower:: qwítx̲.
    Pacific dogwood, flowering dogwood:: qwítx̲elhp < qwítx̲.
    red-osier dogwood, (also called "red willow" [SJ, EL]):: th'ex̲wíyelhp.

Dogwood Valley
    village just below (on the south side of) Suka Creek, on the CN side (east side) of the Fraser River across from Dogwood Valley:: Skwíyò.

doll :: mimele'ó:ylha < méle ~ mél:a.

dollar
    a half dollar, fifty cents:: lhséq' < séq'.
    cost ten dollars:: epoléstexw < ó:pel.
    eight dollars:: tqó:tsó:s < tqá:tsa.
    eighty dollars:: téqetselsx̲ós < tqá:tsa.
    fifty dollars:: lhèq'etselsxó:s ~ lhéq'etselsxó:s < lheq'át ~ lhq'á:t.
    five dollars:: lhq'ó:tses < lheq'át ~ lhq'á:t.
    forty dollars:: x̲ethelsxó:s < x̲e'ó:thel ~ x̲e'óthel.
    four dollars, ((also) four blankets [Boas]):: x̲ethíles < x̲e'ó:thel ~ x̲e'óthel.
    lots of money, (many dollars):: qx̲ó:s < qéx̲.
    money, dollar(s):: =ó:s ~ =ós ~ =es.
    nine dollars, (nine Indian blankets [Boas]):: tú:xwes < tú:xw.
    ninety dollars:: tú:xwelsxó:s < tú:xw.
    one dollar, one Indian blanket (Boas):: léts'es < léts'a ~ léts'e.
    seven dollars, (seven Indian blankets or dollars [Boas]):: th'ókwses < th'ó:kws.
    seventy dollars:: th'èkwetselsxó:s < th'ó:kws.
    six dollars, (six Indian blankets [Boas]):: t'x̲ém:es ~ t'x̲émés < t'éx̲.
    sixty dollars:: t'x̲émelsxós < t'éx̲.
    ten dollars, (ten Indian blankets [Boas]):: epóles < ó:pel.
    thirty dollars:: lhexwelsxó:s < lhí:xw.
    three dollars, three tokens of wealth, three blankets (Boas), three cyclic periods:: lhí:xwes < lhí:xw.
    twenty dollars:: ts'kw'xó:s < ts'kw'éx.
    two dollars, [Boas] two Indian blankets:: isó:les < isá:le ~ isále ~ isá:la.

dolly varden
    dolly varden trout:: thex̲ó:th.

done
    finish eating, be done eating:: hó:ythel < hò:y ~ hó:y ~ hóy.
    finish, stop, quit, get done, be finished, have enough, be done, be ready:: hò:y ~ hó:y ~ hóy.

don't
    isn't?, aren't?, don't?, doesn't?, (be not?):: ewá ~ ōwá ~ wá < éwe ~ ṓwe.

don't know
    maybe, perhaps, I don't know (if), may (possibly):: yóswe ~ yó:swe.

donut, doughnut, bagel:: sqweqwá seplíl < qwá, seplíl
    (lit. be got a hole/with a hole + bread)

door :: xálh ~ xá:lh.
    door, doorway, door of a big (communal) house or longhouse:: steqtá:l < téq.
    open the door:: xwema'à:ls < má ~ má'-.

door-knob :: qw'emétx̲w.

doorman :: xwéma'à:ls < má ~ má'-.

doorway
    door, doorway, door of a big (communal) house or longhouse:: steqtá:l < téq.

dorsal
    dorsal fin (long fin in back):: q'áwetsel.

dot
    spotted with circles or round dots:: tl'eltl'élx̲ < tl'él.

double
    all doubled up:: sqwemqwemóx̲w.
    (be) doubled up (a person with knees up to his chest), all doubled over:: sqw'emqw'emóx̲w < qw'ómx̲w.
    (be) doubled up in bed on one's side with knees drawn up:: sqw'emóx̲w < qw'ómx̲w.

double-ended
    double-ended canoe:: púpt < pṓt.

double-headed
    supernatural double-headed snake:: sílhqey < isá:le ~ isále ~ isá:la.

doubt
    doubting s-o/s-th, be not believing s-o/s-th:: mameth'élexw < máth'el.
    doubt s-o, not believe s-th/s-o:: meth'éléxw < máth'el.
    Really. (said in doubt):: kw'è: < kw'é.

dough

make it thin (of dough, etc.):: th'eth'emí:lstexw < th'eth'emí:l.
press s-th down (like yeast dough):: qéytl't ~ qí(y)tl't.
shake s-th down, pack s-th down, push s-th down, knead s-th (esp. of bread dough), press it down (like yeast bread):: qeth'ét.

doughnut, donut:: sqweqwá seplíl < qwá, seplíl
(lit. be got a hole/with a hole + bread)

Douglas

Douglas fir log or wood:: ts'sá:y.
(Douglas) fir tree:: ts'sá:yelhp < ts'sá:y.
Lillooet people, Port Douglas (also Lillooet) people:: sth'kwólh.

dove

pigeon, dove, including band-tailed pigeon, mourning dove, and possibly passenger pigeon, also (introduced) domestic pigeon, rock dove:: hemó:.

down

(become/get) upside down:: xwiyó:leqw < yél or perhaps yá:l.
bring it down (from upstairs or from upper shelf, etc.):: tl'pí:lx ~ tl'pì:lx < tl'ép.
broke down, came (un)loose, came apart, (got) untied, loose, unravelled:: yéx̲w < yíx̲w.
deep down, below, down below, low:: tl'ép.
down feathers, real fine feathers:: sq'óyes.
downriver, down that way:: lhelhós < lhós.
downriver, down that way, downriver below:: lhósex̲el < lhós.
face down, (upside-down [Deming]):: qep'ós < qep', qep'ós < qep'.
fall, fall off, drop, drop off, drop or fall down (of person):: tsélq ~ chélq.
fell of its own accord (of an object from a height or from upright), drop down (object/person, from a shelf, bridge, cliff, etc.), fall off:: wets'étl' ~ wech'étl'.
go down, go down below, get low:: tl'pí:l ~ tl'epí:l < tl'ép.
go down hill, go down from anything:: tl'pílém < tl'ép.
go down(hill) to the water, go towards the river:: t'óxw.
go down (of swelling):: t'esí:l < t'ás.
go down to the river:: chóxw.
go out into the river, go down to the river, walk down to the river:: tó:l ~ tò:l.
(have) pants sliding down:: lhosemáyiws < lhós.
jumping along, jumping up and down:: ts'ats'etl'í:m < ts'tl'ám ~ ts'tl'ém.
knock s-o down:: kw'qwémést(exw?) < kw'óqw.
laying down, putting down:: lhálheq'els < lháq'.
lay it down, put it down:: lháq'et < lháq'.
let oneself fall, drop oneself down (by parachute, rope, etc., said of little birds trying to fly out of nest, little animals trying to get down and let themselves fall):: chólqthet < tsélq ~ chélq.
lie down:: lhóq'ethet < lháq'.
lower it down, (lower s-th down):: tl'pí:lt ~ tl'épelt < tl'ép.
lower s-th down:: tl'épt < tl'ép, tl'pí:lstexw < tl'ép.
lying down on one's stomach:: qíqep'yó:lha ~ qéyqep'yó:lha < qep'.
lying on one's stomach with head down on one's arms:: qiqep'eyósem < qep'.
press s-th down (like yeast dough):: qéytl't ~ qí(y)tl't.
put it down, take it down (s-th on the wall for ex.):: xwetáqt.
put one's head down, bend, bend over, bend over with one's head down, stoop down::

down (CONT'D)

qep'ósem < qep'.
put them down (several objects):: lháleq'et < lháq'.
putting it down:: lhálheq'et < lháq'.
sat down (with a plop?), [slip off on one's bottom or chair]:: xwlhépelets < x̲wlhép.
shake s-th down, pack s-th down, push s-th down, knead s-th (esp. of bread dough), press it down (like yeast bread):: qeth'ét.
sit, sit down, sit up, arise (from lying or sitting), get up (from lying down, from bed or chair):: emét.
sitting, sitting down, sitting up:: ó:met ~ ó'emet < emét.
slide down (of clothes):: lhósem < lhós.
soft (down) feathers put in oiled hair for dancing:: sq'óyeseqw ~ sx̲óyeseqw < sq'óyes.
stop burning (of a burn), go down (of swelling):: t'esí:l < t'ás.
take s-th down, tear down s-th man-made, dismantle s-th, take it apart:: yíx̲wet < yíx̲w.
throw s-o down hard (like a wrestler), tap s-th (a container's bottom) [hard] on something to make the contents settle (like berry basket):: th'esét ~ th'sét < th'és.
throw s-o down [hard] on the rump:: th'eséletst < th'és.
to fall down and scatter, drop and scatter:: tl'ápex̲em < tl'ép.
to go down (of water), subside (of water), the tide goes out or down, (be going out (of tide) [BJ]):: th'à:m ~ th'ám.
tracks going down to the river:: tó:lxel < tó:l ~ tò:l.
turn s-o upside down:: xwiyó:leqwt < yél or perhaps yá:l.
turn s-th upside-down:: qep'óst < qep'.

down feathers

down feathers, real fine feathers:: sq'óyes.

downhill

go down(hill) to the water, go towards the river:: t'óxw.

downriver)

(also drift downriver):: wṓqw' ~ wéqw'.
downriver, down that way:: lhelhós < lhós.
downriver, down that way, downriver below:: lhósex̲el < lhós.
downriver, (from downriver):: tellhó:s < lhós.
drifting back downriver (like spawned-out salmon):: xwōqw'ṓ:lh < wṓqw' ~ wéqw'.
go downstream, go downriver, down the river:: wōqw'ílem ~ wōqw'éylem ~ wōqw'ílém ~ wōqw'éylém < wṓqw' ~ wéqw'.
go in the direction of the water, go downriver:: xwōqw'éylem < wṓqw' ~ wéqw'.
lower [downriver] end of house (inside or outside):: sōqw'áx̲el < wṓqw' ~ wéqw'.
roots of a tree when it floats downriver:: x̲eyímelets.
travelling by going downriver:: yexwṓqw'elem < wṓqw' ~ wéqw'.

Downriver Halkomelem

Kwantlen people, Kwantlen dialect of Downriver Halkomelem:: Qw'ó:ltl'el.

downstream

(be) downstream below something:: sōqw'ólwelh < wṓqw' ~ wéqw'.
go downstream, go downriver, down the river:: wōqw'ílem ~ wōqw'éylem ~ wōqw'ílém ~ wōqw'éylém < wṓqw' ~ wéqw'.
(going) downstream, drift downstream, (drifting downstream):: héwqw'elem ~ hṓwqw'elem < wṓqw' ~ wéqw'.

down the river
go downstream, go downriver, down the river:: wōqw'ílem ~ wōqw'éylem ~ wōqw'ílém ~ wōqw'éylém < wṓqw' ~ wéqw'.

drafty
get drafty:: xó:lx̲wem < xó:lxwem.
getting real drafty:: xó:léx̲wem < xó:lxwem.

drag :: xwóqw'el < xwókw' ~ xwekw'ó.
crawling (as of snake, seal, slug, snail), (dragging oneself):: xwéqw'ethet < xwókw' ~ xwekw'ó.
dragging one's behind or rump or bottom:: xwókw'eletsem < xwókw' ~ xwekw'ó.
dragging one's feet:: xwixwekw'ósxelem ~ xwekw'ósxelem < xwókw' ~ xwekw'ó.
dragging s-o/s-th:: xwékw'est < xwókw' ~ xwekw'ó.
drag oneself:: xwó:kw'thet < xwókw' ~ xwekw'ó.
drag one's foot, to shuffle (the feet):: xwót'kw'emxel < xwót'kw'em.
drag out behind:: tóx̲wem < tóx̲w.
drag s-o:: xwekw'óst < xwókw' ~ xwekw'ó.
drag s-th/s-o:: xwekw'ó:st < xwókw' ~ xwekw'ó, xwekw'ót < xwókw' ~ xwekw'ó.
to drag (for a body in the river, for ex.):: xwekw'á:ls < xwókw' ~ xwekw'ó.

dragonfly :: lhílhló:ya.

drain
to drain (of a pond), (get) dried up (of creek, empty cup, etc.):: t'óqwel.

draw
draw a bow, cock a gun:: xwe'ít'et.
draw a bow, cock a gun, (draw it (of a bow), cock it (of a gun)):: xwe'ít'et < ót'.

drawing
picture, photo, (drawing, etc.):: pékcha.

drawn up
(be) doubled up in bed on one's side with knees drawn up:: sqw'emóx̲w < qw'ómx̲w.

dream
a dream:: s'élíyá < élíyá.
(be) in a daze, day-dreaming:: stekwtákw.
dream, dreaming:: el'èliyà < élíyá.
dreaming:: el'èliyà < élíyá.
dreaming about s-o/s-th:: el'éliyemet < élíyá.
spirit dream, vision, (any) dream:: s'élíyá < élíyá.
to dream, dreaming:: élíyá.
to dream, have a vision:: élíyá, élíyá.

dreaming :: el'èliyà < élíyá.
dream, dreaming:: el'èliyà < élíyá.

dress
a dress, woman's dress:: slewíws.

dress(CONT'D)

(be) too tight (of shoes, clothes, trap, box), tight (of a dress one can't get into), too tight to get into (of dress, car, box of cards, etc.):: stl'etl'íq' < tl'íq'.
clothes, clothing (esp. Indian clothing, men's or women's), something to wear, dress, gown:: s'íth'em < íth'a.
put on a dress:: eth'íwsem < íth'a.
square dressing room or shelter of blankets where sx̱wóyx̱wey dancers change before doing the sx̱wóyx̱wey dance:: q'eléts'tel < q'el.
thin (of material like a dress, also of a string):: th'eth'emí:l.
to dress, get dressed:: íth'em < íth'a.

dressing room
square dressing room or shelter of blankets where sx̱wóyx̱wey dancers change before doing the sx̱wóyx̱wey dance:: q'eléts'tel < q'el.

dribble
trickling, dribbling, water bubbling up in a river, add water to a container, water running under:: kw'átem.

dried
to drain (of a pond), (get) dried up (of creek, empty cup, etc.):: t'óqwel.

dried fish
fish cut real thin for wind-drying but without cross cuts, dried fish cut differently than slhíts'es:: st'ál.

drift
(also drift downriver):: wṓqw' ~ wéqw'.
a snowdrift:: sqelyíqem (or sq'elyíqem) < yíq.
drift ashore:: qwélh.
drifting a net in different places:: qwáseliyel < qwés.
drifting back downriver (like spawned-out salmon):: xwōqw'ṓ:lh < wṓqw' ~ wéqw'.
drifting backwards in two canoes with net between to catch sturgeon, (drift-netting), backing up (of canoe, train):: tewláts.
drifting (drift-netting):: lhólhes < lhós.
dry snow coming in (drifting), fine snow that leaks into a house:: sqwelxómé ~ sqwelxóme < qwélxel.
dry snow (that can drift):: sqwélxem < qwélxel.
(going) downstream, drift downstream, (drifting downstream):: héwqw'elem ~ hṓwqw'elem < wṓqw' ~ wéqw'.
(have/get a) snowdrift:: q'elsiyáqem or q'elts'yáqem < yíq.
set a net and drift with it:: qwsá:wiyel < qwés.
throw a net into water (to drift, not to set), throw a net out, (gill net [TG]):: qwsá:yel < qwés.

drift-net
drifting backwards in two canoes with net between to catch sturgeon, (drift-netting), backing up (of canoe, train):: tewláts.
drifting (drift-netting):: lhólhes < lhós.
drift-netting, catching fish with one or two canoes drifting downstream with a net in deep water:: xíxemel ~ xíxemal.
slough where people used to drift-net by Martin Harris's place at Seabird Island:: Titáwlechem < tewláts.
to drift-net, to fish with drift-net:: lhós.

driftwood :: qwlhá:y < qwélh.
cottonwood bark driftwood (it was used to carve toy canoes), cottonwood driftwood used for carving toy canoes:: qwémélép ~ qwemélep.
lots of little pieces of driftwood:: qwéqwelhi(y) < qwélh.

drill
firedrill:: sxéltsep < xél.
fire-drill, stick spun to start fire:: sí:lcheptel < sél or sí(:)l.
make a hole in s-th, drill a hole in s-th:: qwát < qwá.

drink
a drink:: sqó:qe < qó:.
drink s-th:: qó:qet < qó:.
drink without using hands:: homiyósem.
(have?) a cool drink:: th'elhílésem < th'álh, th'elhqéylem or th'elhqílem ~ th'elhqílém < th'álh.
have a hot drink, warm one's chest inside:: qatílésem < qá:t.
to drink:: qó:qe < qó:.

drip
be dripping, (have) continuous dripping, water dropping:: th'áq'em < th'q'ém ~ th'eq'ém.
collected rain-water from a drip:: th'q'émelets ~ ts'q'émelets < th'q'ém ~ th'eq'ém.
make the sound of water splashing or dripping fast, (make the sound of a waterfall, make the sound of pouring rain dripping or splashing in puddles loudly):: xwótqwem.
to drip (once), water drops once, a drop of water, a drip:: th'q'ém ~ th'eq'ém.

drive
driver (of car, wagon, etc.):: kwelósel < kwél.

Drop)
Rainbow Falls on Harrison Lake, (Sturgeon's Drop):: Tsólqthet te Skwówech < tsélq ~ chélq.

drop
be dripping, (have) continuous dripping, water dropping:: th'áq'em < th'q'ém ~ th'eq'ém.
collected rain-water drops in a bucket:: th'q'emelétsem < th'q'ém ~ th'eq'ém.
disappear, drop out of sight, (to fade [Elders Group 3/72]):: théxw ~ théx̲w.
drop a net into water:: qwesú:yel < qwés.
drop it on purpose:: tsélqt < tsélq ~ chélq.
drop oneself into a seat, throw oneself on the floor or ground in a tantrum, throw a tantrum:: kw'qweméthet < kw'óqw.
drop s-th (accidentally):: tsélqlexw < tsélq ~ chélq.
drop s-th (accidentally), let s-o go:: kwò:lxw < kwá:.
drop s-th by accident:: wets'étl'lexw < wets'étl' ~ wech'étl'.
drop s-th into the water:: wő̄qw'et < wő̄qw' ~ wéqw'.
drop s-th (of a bunch of apples, etc. that one is carrying):: tsélqòlèm < tsélq ~ chélq.
fall, fall off, drop, drop off, drop or fall down (of person):: tsélq ~ chélq.
fall on one's forehead, drop on one's forehead, fall onto one's head:: méleqw (or) leméleqw.
fell of its own accord (of an object from a height or from upright), drop down (object/person, from a shelf, bridge, cliff, etc.), fall off:: wets'étl' ~ wech'étl'.

drop (CONT'D)
let go of s-th/s-o, drop s-th, set s-o free, turn s-o/s-th loose:: kwá:t ~ kwát < kwá:.
let oneself fall, drop oneself down (by parachute, rope, etc., said of little birds trying to fly out of nest, little animals trying to get down and let themselves fall):: chólqthet < tsélq ~ chélq.
(make a) ringing sound when something drops:: ts'tés.
ringing sound when something drops (spoon, metal ashtray or something heavy):: ts'tés.
sow s-th, drop or spread seed in rills, scatter s-th, (sowing s-th [AC]):: tl'épx̲t < tl'ép.
to drip (once), water drops once, a drop of water, a drip:: th'q'ém ~ th'eq'ém.
to drop or blow plant fluff (like dandelions, fireweed, cottonwood, etc.), to blow (of dusty or flaky stuff like wood dust, dandruff, maybe seeds):: pípexwem < píxw.
to fall down and scatter, drop and scatter:: tl'ápex̲em < tl'ép.

drop-off
steep drop-off, a drop-off, very steep slope, steep shore, steep riverbank, a slide:: x̲éylés.

droppings
dung, (scattered excrement?, fecal droppings?):: sq'éth'x̲ < sq'éth'.

drown
to drown:: wố qw' ~ wéqw'.

drum
a drum, small stick used to drum or beat time to songs in slahal game:: q'ówet.
drum for s-o:: q'ewételhtst < q'ówet, q'ewétt < q'ówet.
drumming:: q'ewétem < q'ówet.
drumstick (for drum):: pumí:l.
frame for stretching hides, frame (for drying hides, etc.), frame for a drum:: tpélhtel ~ tepélhtel < tpólh.
to drum, a drum:: q'owét < q'ówet.

drumstick
drumstick (for drum):: pumí:l.
chicken drumstick:: sx̲éles te chékel < x̲éle, chékel
(lit. leg of + the + chicken)

drunk
be drunk, got drunk:: só:les < sél or sí(:)l.
(get) dizzy, get drunk:: séles < sél or sí(:)l.
get s-o drunk:: séleslexw < sél or sí(:)l.
numb (can also be used joking of a drunk):: shxwóxwekw' < xwókw'.
to fall on something (of a drunk):: qwélh.

dry
(be) dried:: sch'á:yxw < ts'íyxw ~ ts'éyxw ~ ch'íyxw.
be dry, get dry, to dry:: ts'íyxw ~ ts'éyxw ~ ch'íyxw.
burnt (i.e. dry) grass:: yeqwílep < yéqw.
dried fish:: schá:lhtel ~ stsá:lhtel < =chílh ~ chílh=.
dried fish backbone (with meat left on it):: sx̲éwe.
dried meat:: sch'á:yxwels < ts'íyxw ~ ts'éyxw ~ ch'íyxw.
dry dishes, wipe off dishes:: iqw'wí:ls < íqw'.
dry herring eggs:: sts'ámex.
drying:: ts'áyxw < ts'íyxw ~ ts'éyxw ~ ch'íyxw.

dry (CONT'D)

drying dishes:: xwe'í:qw'wí:ls ~ xwe'íyeqw'wí:ls < íqw'.
drying s-th:: ch'áyxwt < ts'íyxw ~ ts'éyxw ~ ch'íyxw.
dry in the throat:: ch'íyxweqel < ts'íyxw ~ ts'éyxw ~ ch'íyxw.
dry snow coming in (drifting), fine snow that leaks into a house:: sqwelxómé ~ sqwelxóme < qwélxel.
dry snow (that can drift):: sqwélxem < qwélxel.
dry s-th:: ts'íyxwt ~ ts'éyxwt < ts'íyxw ~ ts'éyxw ~ ch'íyxw.
dry storage box in tree or on top of pole (for salmon and other dried provisions):: póqw'elh < pó:qw' ~ póqw'.
dry them (dishes), dry s-th (dish):: eqw'ewílt < íqw'.
fish cut real thin for wind-drying but without cross cuts, dried fish cut differently than slhíts'es:: st'ál.
fish-drying rack:: shxwch'á:yxwels < ts'íyxw ~ ts'éyxw ~ ch'íyxw.
fish drying rack (for wind-drying):: sí:.
fish ready for drying:: chachí:lhtel ~ chachíyelhtel < =chílh ~ chílh=.
fish-spreader for drying fish, cross-piece for drying fish, salmon stretcher:: t'á:ts'.
frame for stretching hides, frame (for drying hides, etc.), frame for a drum:: tpélhtel ~ tepélhtel < tpólh.
gone soft and spoiled (of dried fish):: th'íth'eqel < sth'í:qel.
hang fish (especially salmon) for drying:: chálhtel < =chílh ~ chílh=.
hanging lots of fish to dry:: chachí:lhtel ~ chachíyelhtel < =chílh ~ chílh=.
my throat is dry:: ts'iyxweqthàlèm < ts'íyxw ~ ts'éyxw ~ ch'íyxw.
preserved fish, preserved meat, dried fish, dried meat (usually fish), smoked salmon, wind-dried salmon (old word), what is stored away, what is put away:: sq'éyle.
puddle that's always dirty, dirty pond, stagnant pool of water, (it never dries out [AK]):: th'qwélhcha.
spread them out to dry (berries, bulrushes, etc.):: ts'íyxwt ~ ts'éyxwt < ts'íyxw ~ ts'éyxw ~ ch'íyxw.
their faces/his/her face are dried (a word used when showing a picture of the deceased at a memorial ceremony, and telling the family to dry their tears):: th'éyx̱westem < ts'íyxw ~ ts'éyxw ~ ch'íyxw.
time to dry fish, first of July (at Yale), October (at Chehalis):: temchálhtel < =chílh ~ chílh=.
tinder, material used to start a fire with (fine dried cedar bark):: syeqwlhá:ltel < yéqw.
to drain (of a pond), (get) dried up (of creek, empty cup, etc.):: t'óqwel.

Dryobates pubescens
Colaptes cafer cafer and rarely Colaptes cafer collaris, (if large is correct Dryocopus pileatus [AK], if small is correct, probably Sphyrapicus (varius) ruber or possibly Dryobates villosus harrisi and Dryobates villosus orius or Dryobates pubescens (esp.) gairdneri some zoologists replace the genus Dryobates with Dendrocopos, others with Picoides):: th'íq.

Dryobates pubescens (gairdneri esp.)
probably Sphyrapicus (varius) ruber and/or possibly Dryobates villosus harrisi and Dryobates villosus orius or(downy woodpecker) Dryobates pubescens (gairdneri esp.), for Munro and Cowan's Dryobates genus Peterson uses Dendrocopos andUdvardy uses Picoides:: qw'opx̱wiqsélem < qw'ópx̱w.

Dryobates villosus harrisi
Colaptes cafer cafer and rarely Colaptes cafer collaris, (if large is correct Dryocopus pileatus [AK], if small is correct, probably Sphyrapicus (varius) ruber or possibly Dryobates villosus harrisi and Dryobates villosus orius or Dryobates pubescens (esp.) gairdneri some zoologists replace the genus Dryobates with Dendrocopos, others with Picoides):: th'íq.
probably Sphyrapicus (varius) ruber and/or possibly Dryobates villosus harrisi and Dryobates villosus orius

Dryobates villosus harrisi (CONT'D)
or(downy woodpecker) Dryobates pubescens (gairdneri esp.), forMunro and Cowan's Dryobates genus Peterson uses Dendrocopos andUdvardy uses Picoides:: qw'opx̲wiqsélem < qw'ópx̲w.

Dryobates villosus orius
Colaptes cafer cafer and rarely Colaptes cafer collaris, (if large is correct Dryocopus pileatus [AK], if small is correct, probably Sphyrapicus (varius) ruber or possibly Dryobates villosus harrisi and Dryobates villosus orius or Dryobates pubescens (esp.) gairdneri some zoologists replace the genus Dryobates with Dendrocopos, others with Picoides):: th'íq.
probably Sphyrapicus (varius) ruber and/or possibly Dryobates villosus harrisi and Dryobates villosus orius or(downy woodpecker) Dryobates pubescens (gairdneri esp.), forMunro and Cowan's Dryobates genus Peterson uses Dendrocopos andUdvardy uses Picoides:: qw'opx̲wiqsélem < qw'ópx̲w.

Dryocopus pileatus:: temélhépsem < témélh, t'ot'ep'íqselem < t'óp'.
Colaptes cafer cafer and rarely Colaptes cafer collaris, (if large is correct Dryocopus pileatus [AK], if small is correct, probably Sphyrapicus (varius) ruber or possibly Dryobates villosus harrisi and Dryobates villosus orius or Dryobates pubescens (esp.) gairdneri some zoologists replace the genus Dryobates with Dendrocopos, others with Picoides):: th'íq.

Dryopteris austriaca
probably Dryopteris austriaca:: th'ékwa.

duck
a white-headed duck, [could be bufflehead, snow goose, emperor goose, poss. oldsquaw, or hooded merganser, other duck-like birds with white heads do not occur in the Stó:lō area and the emperor goose would be only an occasional visitor]:: skemí'iya.
bluebill duck, (identified from photos as) lesser scaup:: x̲élq'eqs.
canvas-back duck:: lamélwelh.
goldeneye duck (probably both the common goldeneye duck and the Barrow goldeneye duck), (a kind of diving duck [Elders Group]):: láqleqem < léqem.
larger bird (any kind, generic), waterfowl, duck, (mallard [Cheh. dial.]):: mó:qw.
mallard, duck:: teléqsel ~ tel:éqsel.
sawbill duck, fish-duck, common merganser (larger), American merganser:: x̲wó:qw'.
to duck:: kwóyethet.
wood duck (makes nest in tree):: qwiwílh.

duel
rock above Yale where Ñá:ls gritted his teeth and scratched rocks as he duelled with a medicine man across the Fraser:: Th'ex̲elís < th'ex̲elís.

dull
(be) blunt (edge or point), dull (of edge/point):: qelóth < qél.

dumbfounded
be dumbfounded, be surprised, be stupified, be speechless:: slholhekw'íwel ~ slholhekw'í:wel < lhó:kw' ~ lhókw'.
be startled, be dumbfounded, be shocked, be stupified, be speechless, be overwhelmed:: lholhekw'íwel ~ lholhkw'íwel < lhó:kw' ~ lhókw'.

dung
bear dung:: spàthélets < pá:th.
chicken dung:: chèkelélets < chékel.

dung (CONT'D)

dung, excrement, feces:: s'óq.
dung, (excrement, feces), shit:: sq'éth'.
dung, feces, shit:: s'ó' < ó'.
dung, (scattered excrement?, fecal droppings?):: sq'éth'x̲ < sq'éth'.

dusk

(get) dusk, (get dim):: só:yel < sóy.
getting dusk:: lhó:yel.

dust :: pó:lqw'em < pékw' ~ péqw'.
dust (is flying):: pékw'em < pékw' ~ péqw'.
get dust or bark in both eyes:: thq'elq'ó:les < théq'.
get dust or bark in one eye:: thq'ó:les < théq'.
smoke puffing out, (puff out (dust, powder, plant spores, seed fluff, light snow, smoke), form puffs of dust):: pékw' ~ péqw'.
the dust flew, it's dusty:: pekw'ém < pékw' ~ péqw'.
to drop or blow plant fluff (like dandelions, fireweed, cottonwood, etc.), to blow (of dusty or flaky stuff like wood dust, dandruff, maybe seeds):: pípexwem < píxw.

dusty

the dust flew, it's dusty:: pekw'ém < pékw' ~ péqw'.

dye

carrot-like plant used for green dye:: xáweleq < xáwéq.

each

distributive, to each:: R5= or C1e=.
each (person):: ta'elólets'e < léts'a ~ léts'e.
four to each:: x̲ex̲e'ó:thel < x̲e'ó:thel ~ x̲e'óthel.
he's holding s-th in each hand:: s'i'á:ytses < á:y.

each other)

(be) brother and sister, (be siblings to each other), (be) first cousin to each other:: qeló:qtel < sqá:q.
(be) considerate of each other:: sts'its'exwtel < sts'íts'exw, sts'íts'exwtel < th'íxw ~ th'éxw.
everybody put away (fishing gear, canoe and) paddles (for winter), put away each other's paddles [and canoes and gear] for winter:: xets'ṓ:westel < xits' ~ xets'.
going with each other [romantically], going for a walk with each other:: ts'lhimexóstel < ts'elh=.
go with each other (romantically), go for a walk with each other (romantically):: ts'lhimexóstel < i┐ m.
holding a grudge against each other:: xixemó:ltel < sxemá:l.
moon or month beginning in November, (put away each other's paddles), (sometimes the moon beginning in October, depending on the weather [Elders Group [3/12/75], (moon or month beginning in January [Elders Group 2/5/75]):: xets'ṓ:westel ~ xets'ṓwestel < xits' ~ xets'.
purposeful control reciprocal, (perhaps just) reciprocal, (do purposely to) each other, (do purposely to) one another:: =t=el.
they're making friends, (making friends with each other):: yóyatel < yá:ya.
they've made friends, (make friends with each other):: yáyetel (prob. also yáyatel) < yá:ya.
to meet (each other):: q'eqótel < q'ó.
wink at each other, ((maybe) squint [EB]):: th'ikwóstel < th'iykw'.

each other) (CONT'D)
winking at each other:: th'ith'ikwóstel < th'iykw'.

eager
(be) eager, enthused:: secheláts.

eagle
bald eagle (mature with white head):: sp'óq'es < p'éq'.
eagle (generic), (golden eagle [some speakers]):: yéx̲wela.
golden eagle:: ts'ésqel.
immature bald eagle:: skw'álx̲.

"Eagle Falls"
"Eagle Falls" on the west side of Harrison Lake, probably Walian Creek falls:: Kwótxwem Stó:lō < kwótx̲wem ~ kwótxwem.

ear :: q'ő:l (or better) qw'ő:l.
big ears, (have big ears):: thithehá:lí:ya < thi ~ tha ~ the ~ thah ~ theh.
ear lobe:: stl'epá:lí:ya ~ stl'epá:liya < tl'ép.
ear-splitting:: seq'á:lí:ya < séq'.
hair in the ears:: sqwelqwelá:lí:ya < qwíl ~ qwel.
(have) ringing in the ear:: th'atsemá:lí:ya < th'éts or th'á(:)ts.
(have) sloppy ears, big ears:: slhellhelp'á:lí:ya < lhél.
hit on the ear, hit on the temple (side of the head):: kw'qwá:lí:ya < kw'óqw.
on the ear, in the ear:: =á:lí:ya.
on the side of the head, on the temples, around the ear, on the cheek:: =éla.
pierced ear:: sqwehá:liya < qwá.
punched on the ear:: th'qw'á:lí:ye < th'í:qw'et.
put something in the ear (to block hearing), (plug the ear):: t'ekwá:lí:ya < t'ékw.
top of the ear:: schelhá:liya < =chílh ~ chílh=.
to rattle (of dishes or anything else loose), jingle (of money or any metal shaken), peal or toll (of a bell), make the sound of a bell, to ring (of a bell, telephone, in the ears):: th'á:tsem < th'éts or th'á(:)ts.

early
be early morning, early morning:: lá:telh < lá:t.
early, right away:: txwém.

early-bird:: shxwiyxwiyós < xwíy ~ x[illegible]í.

ear-ring :: ts'qw'élá < ts'éqw'.

earshot
(made) a faint sound carried by the air, sound within hearingdistance, sound within earshot:: eháléqep < ehó.

ear-splitting
ear-splitting:: seq'á:lí:ya < séq'.

earth
a large portion of the earth:: slháq'emex.
diatomaceous earth (could be mixed with things to whiten them--for ex. dog and goat

earth (CONT'D)

wool), white clay for white face paint (for pure person spirit-dancers), white powder from mountains, white clay they make powder from to lighten goat and dog wool for blankets, powder, talc, white face paint:: st'ewő̃kw'.
earth, ground, land, the earth, the world:: tém:éxw ~ tem:éxw ~ ~ tèm:èxw ~ témexw.
hard clay, hard earth, smooth (hard) earth:: síq'.
(have a) small earth slide (small landslide):: yélt.
just coming out of the earth (of plants for ex.):: qwósem.

earthworm

earthworm (esp. the most common introduced in B.C.):: sth'ékw's te téméxw < sth'ékw'.

easily)

easy to cry, (cries easily):: qe'álts ~ qiqe'álts < qó:.

east

(be) upstream, east (in some contexts):: ahíw.
north-east wind, north wind, east wind, cold wind:: só:tets.

Easter lily

trillium, B.C. Easter lily:: xaxt'ó:les.

easy

(be) easy to wake up:: shxwíyxwiy ~ shxwíxwiy < xwíy ~ x[illegible]í.
easy to cry, (cries easily):: qe'álts ~ qiqe'álts < qó:.
(have) good eyes, (have) good sight, soft on the eyes, easy on the eyes:: eyólés ~ eyó:les < éy ~ éy:.
it's easy, be easy, easy (to get):: lí:leq.

easy-going

good-hearted, kind-hearted, kind, generous, helpful, easy-going, good-natured:: xw'éywelh ~ xwe'éywelh ~ xwe'éy:welh < éy ~ éy:.

easy to bend

be supple, be easy to bend:: met'mét'.

eat

(be) full (from eating), (get filled (from eating) [AC]):: méq'.
be overcome with pleasurable feelings after eating great salmon or a great meal:: ts'éqw'.
crunchy (loud when eating), crackling (noise when eating):: tl'ámqw'els < tl'ém.
crunchy (loud when eating), crackling (sound or noise when eating):: tl'ámqw'els < tl'ámkw'em.
eat (a meal):: álhtel.
eat fast, eating fast, hurry to eat:: x̲weméthel < x̲wém ~ xwém.
eating (a meal):: í:lhtel < álhtel.
eating s-th (short of a meal):: hálp'ex < lép'ex.
eat s-th (short of a social meal):: lép'ex.
fill oneself up (by eating):: meq'lómet < méq'.
finish eating, be done eating:: hó:ythel < hò:y ~ hó:y ~ hóy.
get carried away and sleepy from eating too rich food:: ló:metsel < ló:m ~ lóm, melmelő̃ws < mál ~ mél.
give me s-th (to eat):: áxw < áxw.
invite s-o (to come eat, dance etc.) (any number), invite s-o to a feast:: tl'e'áxet < tl'e'á ~ tl'á'.

eat (CONT'D)

inviting (to come eat, dance), to give a potlatch, (give a feast or gathering), to invite to a feast, invite to a potlatch:: tl'etl'áxel < tl'e'á ~ tl'á'.

someone who is greedy, someone who eats all the time, (glutton):: sqel:éxw < qél:éxw ~ qel(:)éxw.

throw different leftovers together for a meal, throw a meal together, eat a snack:: p'ekw'ethílem < p'ákw'.

Eaves

Watery Eaves, a famous longhouse and early village on a flat area on Chilliwack River just a quarter mile upriver/east above Vedder Crossing:: Qoqolá x̲el < qó:.

Eayem)

pool down from Tillie Gutierrez's grandfather's fish-drying rack at Íyem (Eayem):: qemqémel ~ qemqémél < qém:el.

Echinodontium tinctorium

(perhaps) Echinodontium tinctorium:: témélh.

echo

an echo:: swélwelàm < wélwelàm ~ wélwelà:m.

to echo, (echoing (Elders Group 10/27/76):: wélwelàm ~ wélwelà:m.

Echo Bay

Echo Point on Echo Island, Echo Bay on Echo Island:: X̲wix̲we'áqel ~ Xwixwe'áqel ~ Xwōxwe'áqel < x̲wex̲we'á.

Echo Island

bear-shaped rock up on cliff on south side above Echo Point bay on Echo Island in Harrison Lake:: Spá:th < pá:th.

Echo Island in Harrison Lake:: Xweqw'oyíqw, Xwōxwe'áqel.

Echo Island in southern quarter of Harrison Lake:: Xwōqwiyáqw.

Echo Point on Echo Island, Echo Bay on Echo Island:: X̲wix̲we'áqel ~ Xwixwe'áqel ~ Xwōxwe'áqel < x̲wex̲we'á.

Echo Point

bear-shaped rock up on cliff on south side above Echo Point bay on Echo Island in Harrison Lake:: Spá:th < pá:th.

Echo Point on Echo Island, Echo Bay on Echo Island:: X̲wix̲we'áqel ~ Xwixwe'áqel ~ Xwōxwe'áqel < x̲wex̲we'á.

horned owl-shaped rock (beside Spá:th, a bear-shaped rock) up on a cliff on the south side above Echo Point bay on Echo Island in Harrison Lake:: Chítmexw < chítmexw.

eclipse

an eclipse (of sun or moon):: t'ó:ltel ~ t'óltel < t'á:l.

eclipse s-th:: t'á(:)lt < t'á:l.

Ectopistes migratorius

including Columba fasciata, Zenaidura macroura, possibly Ectopistes migratorius, also Columbia livia (introduced):: hemó:.

-ed (also see past and past tense)
resultative, -ed, have -en (usually results in a past tense or past participle translation in English):: =R1= or =C1e=, R5= or C1e=, R8= or C1a=, =R9= or =C1á(:)=.

eddy
a little bay or eddy on Harrison River about two miles downriverfrom Chehalis:: Skw'á:lx̲w.
eddy (in water):: xwelkw'ím < xwélekw'.
eddy water (where you set nets), [to eddy repeatedly?]:: xwtitím or xwtiytím.
slough, backwater, ((also) eddy [AC]):: sts'élexw< ts'el.

edge :: =óth.
(be) blunt (edge or point), dull (of edge/point):: qelóth < qél.
be sharp, have a sharp edge:: eyó:th ~ iyóth < éy ~ éy:.
edge of the world:: sóyéx̲el < sóy.
embroidery, trimming (stitches on an edge):: stl'ítl'ets < tl'íts ~ tl'ích.
grind or sharpen s-th (of edged tools):: yéq'est < yéq'.
lie? with surface facing up, sticking up, on the side? or edge?:: kw'e'í ~ kw''í ~ kw'í.

edible
blue camas, (any edible underground vegetable food [SP], vegetable root(s) [MH]):: spá:lxw.
edible gristle inside fish head (nose gristle):: sx̲épeqw (or sx̲ép'eqw? or sx̲ép'ekw'?).

Edward
King Edward:: Kíl Ítewet < kelchóch ~ kyelchóch.

Edwards
place of moss-covered stones at upper end of Hope Slough not far from Harry Edwards' home (as of 1964):: Qwómqwemels < qwà:m ~ qwám.

eek.
yipes., eek.:: alelí'.

eel
eel, Pacific lamprey, western brook lamprey:: kwótawi ~ kwótewi.

effort
exert oneself, make a big effort, do with all one's might, [do] as hard as possible, do it harder (used if already paddling for ex.):: tíméthet < tímet.

egg
egg (of bird, fowl):: mámelehò:llh < méle ~ mél:a.
fish eggs, salmon eggs, roe, (cooked salmon eggs [JL]):: qélé x̲.
(have) sound of popping small round things (snowberries, herring eggs as when eating them, rice krispies, crabapples, cranberries, etc.), (have a crunching sound (as of grasshopper, rice krispies)):: tl'ámkw'em, tl'ámkw'em < tl'ém.
nits, louse eggs:: x̲ést'el.
salmon after spawning when its eggs are loose:: t'iléqel.
sit on eggs, to hatch eggs, to brood eggs:: tl'xwá:ylhem < tl'xw ~ tl'exw.
stink-eggs:: kw'ő:la ~ kw'ú:la.
stink-egg basket, stink salmon egg basket:: kw'ōle'álá < kw'ő:la ~ kw'ú:la.

egg (CONT'D)
to take all the loose eggs out of s-th (a salmon):: pethíwet ~ pethíwét < páthet.

eight :: tqá:tsa.
eight birds:: tqatsíws < tqá:tsa.
eight canoes, eight boats:: tqátsa'ṓwelh ? < tqá:tsa.
eight containers:: tqátsáleqel < tqá:tsa.
eight days of northeast wind:: unknown.
eight dollars:: tqó:tsó:s < tqá:tsa.
eight fish:: teqatsíqw < tqá:tsa.
eight fruit in a group [or cluster] (as they grow on a plant):: tqòtsòls < tqá:tsa.
eight Indian blankets [Boas], eight dollars:: tqó:tsó:s < tqá:tsa.
eight o'clock:: steqá:tsas < tqá:tsa.
eight people:: teqátsa'ále < tqá:tsa.
eight ropes, eight threads, eight sticks, eight poles:: tqátsámets' < tqá:tsa.
eight times:: tqatsálh < tqá:tsa.
eighty:: teqtselhsxá < tqá:tsa.

eighty
eighty:: teqtselhsxá < tqá:tsa.
eighty dollars:: téqetselsx̲ós < tqá:tsa.
eighty people:: teqetselsxá:le < tqá:tsa.

ejaculate :: méqw' ~ mṓqw'.
to climax, come (sexually), ejaculate:: qw'lhòlèm or qw'lhlòlèm.

elastic
(be) stretchy, (be) elastic:: ét"et' < ót'.

elbow
an elbow, elbow (the name of it):: th'emxwelábx̲el < hth'b.txt.
leaning the face on the hand with elbow propped:: piyósem < píy.
point of elbow, arm bone:: th'emeláx̲el < hth'b.txt.
skinned elbow:: th'eqeláx̲el < th'áq ~ ts'áq or ts'éq ~ th'éq.
(someone's) elbow:: sth'emxweláx̲el < hth'b.txt.
square, corner, arm with elbow out:: st'eláx̲el.

Elbow Lake mountain
next mountain above (north/upriver from) Títxwemqsel (Wilson's Point or Grouse Point), possibly Elbow Lake mountain [north of Harrison Mills, on west side of the Harrison River],
Willoughby's Point [opposite Lhá:lt, but does this mean across Harrison R. as I first thought and show on the topographic map "Harrison Lake 92H/5" where I have pencilled in all Chehalis place names) or does it mean on the opposite, i.e. south end of the same bay where Lhá:lt starts, i.e. both on the west side of Harrison R. as are Títxwemqsel and Elbow Lake mountain?]:: Kw'íkw'exwelhp < kw'íxw.

elder
elders (many collective):: siyelyólexwa < siyólexwe.
elders past, deceased old people:: siyolexwálh < siyólexwe.
old people, elders:: sí:yólexwe < siyólexwe.
old person, an elder:: siyólexwe < siyólexwe.

elderberry
 blue elderberry:: th'í:kwekw ~ th'í:qweqw.
 blue elderberry bush, blue elderberry tree:: th'íkwekwelhp < th'í:kwekw ~ th'í:qweqw.
 red elderberry:: sth'íwéq'.
 red elderberry bush:: sth'íwéq'elhp < sth'íwéq'.
 red elderberry (the berry):: sth'íwéq'.

elder cousin
 older sibling, elder cousin (child of older sibling of one's parent, grandchild of older sibling of one's grandparent, great grandchild of older sibling of one's great grandparent), cousin of senior line, older brother, older sister:: sétl'atel < sétl'a ~ sétl'o.
 older siblings, elder cousins (first/second/third cousins by an older sibling of one's ancestor):: sá:tl'atel < sétl'a ~ sétl'o.

elderly
 accompany s-o little or elderly:: q'eq'exí:lt < q'ó.

electric
 an electric light, coal-oil lamp, lamp:: yeqwí:l ~ yeqwì:l < yéqw.

eleven
 eleven o'clock:: slhéms < lhém.

Elk)
 Big Dipper, (the Elk):: Q'oyíyets ~ Q'oyí:ts < q'oyíyets or q'oyí:ts.

elk
 baby elk, (young elk):: q'oyíyetsó:llh < q'oyíyets or q'oyí:ts.
 elk (or) moose turned to stone in the Fraser River by Hill's Bar:: Q'oyíyets ~ Q'oyí:ts < q'oyíyets or q'oyí:ts.
 elk, Roosevelt elk, perhaps also (introduced) Rocky Mountain elk:: q'oyíyets or q'oyí:ts.
 (moose, British Columbia moose), elk:: shxwiyáxkel.

Elk Creek Falls:: Skw'íkw'ets'tel.
 Elk Creek Falls on west side of Elk Mountain:: possibly Chelchálíth.

elope
 elope, run away together:: chó:mtel < chó:m.
 elope with s-o or meet up with s-o:: chémlexw ~ chemléxw < chó:m.

else
 on something else, within ssomething else:: =q'.
 who else?, who (of several)?, (anybody else (AC)):: kw'elhwát < wát, kw'elhwát < wát.

embarrass
 feel embarrassed and shy because ashamed, be ashamed:: lhistélémét < lháy.
 feeling embarrassed:: lholhistélemet < lháy.
 to shame oneself [accidentally], (get) embarrassed, (become ashamed of oneself?):: x̲éyx̲elòmèt < x̲éyx̲e ~ x̲íx̲e.

ember

ashes (cinder-like), cinders (heavy and dirty), embers:: shxwiyélhtel ~ shxwyélhtel < yólh.

embroider

embroidering:: tl'ítl'echels < tl'íts ~ tl'ích.
embroider it, embroider s-th:: tl'íchet < tl'íts ~ tl'ích.
embroidery, trimming (stitches on an edge):: stl'ítl'ets < tl'íts ~ tl'ích.

Emory Creek

Emory Creek, also village at mouth of Emory Creek on both sides of the creek:: Sx̲wótl'aqwem.
village or settlement on the west side of the Fraser River at Emory Creek by Frank Malloway's fish camp, Albert Flat (Yale Indian Reserve #5):: Ó:ywoses.

emphasis)

it's you, you are the one. you (focus or emphasis):: léwe.

emphatic :: R7= or C1á=.

emprison

(emprisoned), put in jail, grounded, restricted, caught, apprehended:: qíq'.

empty

be empty:: shxwemám < má ~ má'-.
empty container (like bottles esp. if there's lots):: shxwema'ámel < má ~ má'-.
ran out (of food, money, etc.), have no more, be finished (offood), (be empty (of container of supplies) [EB: Cheh., Tait]):: ő:wkw'.

-en

resultative, -ed, have -en (usually results in a past tense or past participle translation in English):: =R1= or =C1e=, R5= or C1e=, R8= or C1a=, =R9= or =C1á(:)=.

enclosure

be inside a house, be inside an enclosure:: skwetáxw < kwetáxw.
go in (a house/enclosure), come in, come inside, enter a house or enclosure:: kwetxwí:lem < kwetáxw.

end

back end of a house (inside or outside), back part of a house:: stselqwáx̲el < chá:l or chó:l.
blunt (end of canoe pole):: témkwes.
canoe with shovel-nose at both ends, same as tl'elá:y:: sqwéthem < qweth.
end of a falling section of land, end of a level stretch of land, (head of a creek or island [Elders Group]):: lhéq'qel.
end or side of a house (inside/outside):: =áx̲el ~ =ex̲el.
front end of a house (inside or outside):: chuchuwáx̲el < cháchew ~ cháchu.
it got smashed in the back end or rear end:: téslatstem < tós.
join two poles together, splice it together (of a rope), (join together on the ends):: t'qwíqst.
lower [downriver] end of house (inside or outside):: sōqw'áx̲el < wőqw' ~ wéqw'.
point of land at the end of an island:: sth'eméxwelets.
tilt s-th, lift s-th up at one end or one side, tilt s-th sideways:: tewá:let < tewále.
to split roots from the wrong end (small end):: séx̲w.
upper end of house (inside or outside):: stiytáx̲el or stitáx̲el < tiyt.

end (CONT'D)

upper end of Seabird Island, village at the upper end of Seabird Island, Maria Slough separating Seabird Island from north shore of Fraser River, now used for Seabird Island as a whole:: Sq'éwqel ~ Sq'ówqel < q'éw ~ q'ew.

west or downriver end of Seabird Island:: Sth'eméxwelets < sth'eméxwelets.

ended

double-ended canoe:: púpt < pőt.

enemy :: sxemá:l.

enemies:: sxelmá:l < sxemá:l.

engine

engine, motor:: í:lchel.

English

Englishman, English, Canadian, Canada, Anglican:: kelchóch ~ kyelchóch.

English language:: xwelítemqel < xwelítem, xwelítemelh sqwà:l < xwelítem.

Englishman

Englishman, English, Canadian, Canada, Anglican:: kelchóch ~ kyelchóch.

Enhydra lutris lutris

Lutra canadensis pacifica, perhaps also Enhydra lutris lutris:: sq'á:tl'.

enjoy

he was fun, he was enjoyed, they enjoyed him:: eyéstem < éy ~ éy:.

like s-o [his/her personality], like s-th [its taste, its idea], be interested in s-th/s-o, enjoy s-o sexually:: éystexw ~ éy:stexw < éy ~ éy:.

enough

be alright, be okay, it's alright, it's okay, can, be able, it's enough, be right, be correct, that's right:: iyólem ~ iyó:lem < éy ~ éy:.

finish, stop, quit, get done, be finished, have enough, be done, be ready:: hò:y ~ hó:y ~ hóy.

Ensatina eschscholtzi

Ensatina eschscholtzi and Plethodon vehiculum and possibly also: Ambystoma macrodactylum macrodactylum, Ambystoma gracile gracile, and possibly Ambystoma gracile decorticatum:: pí:txel.

enter

go in (a house/enclosure), come in, come inside, enter a house or enclosure:: kwetxwí:lem < kwetáxw.

(more than one) entering a house, going in (of a whole bunch):: kwetexwí:lem < kwetáxw.

entertain

entertaining s-o:: t'at'íyelt < t'íyelt or t'í:lt.

entertain s-o:: t'íyelt or t'í:lt.

enthused
(be) eager, enthused:: secheláts.

Entosphenus tridentatus
Entosphenus tridentatus, Lampetra richardsoni:: kwótawi ~ kwótewi.

envious
be envious:: t'áyx̲ < t'ay.
jealous, (envious (EB)):: wowistéleq.

epidemic
village near and above [upriver from] Katz where 36 pit-houses were wiped out in an epidemic:: Sx̲wóx̲wiymelh < x̲wà:y ~ x̲wá:y.

Epilobium angustifolium:: x̲áts'et.

Eptesicus fuscus bernardinus
Corynorhinus townsendi townsendi, Eptesicus fuscus bernardinus, Lasionycteris noctivagans, Lasiurus cinereus, Myotis californicus caurinus, Myotis evotis pacificus, Myotis lucifugus alascensis, Myotis volans longicrus, Myotis yumanensis saturatus, and possibly Myotis keeni keeni:: skw'elyáx̲el.
order Chiroptera, family Vespertilionidae, may include any or all of the following: Corynorhinus townsendi townsendi, Eptesicus fuscus bernardinus, Lasionycteris noctivagans, Lasiurus cinereus Myotis californicus caurinus, Myotis evotis pacificus, Myotis lucifugus alascensis, Myotis volans longicrus, Myotis yumanensis saturatus, and possibly Myotis keeni keeni:: p'íp'eth'elàx̲el ~ p'ip'eth'eláx̲el < p'í:.

equal
give an equal share or amount to s-o, give (food?) to s-o, share with s-o:: áxwest < áxw.

equipment
all the equipment for making a canoe, canoe-making equipment:: halíyches < hà:y.

Equisetum arvense
Equisetum telmateia, Equisetum arvense:: x̲émx̲em.

Equisetum hiemale:: xweqw'él:a.

Equisetum telmateia
Equisetum telmateia, Equisetum arvense:: x̲émx̲em.

Equus asinus
hybrid between a horse Equus caballus and an ass Equus asinus:: miyúl.

Equus caballus:: stiqíw.
hybrid between a horse Equus caballus and an ass Equus asinus:: miyúl.

-er
one who, -er, one who does as an occupation:: =éleq.

erase

erase
    scrape it (of hide or anything), scrape s-o, erase it:: íx̲et < íx̲.

eraser
    eraser (for pencil or blackboard):: shxwe'íqw'els < íqw'.

erect
    get erect (of penis only), have an erection:: xátl'.
    upright, erect:: =ex.

Erethizon dorsatum nigrescens:: swatíya.

errand)
    send s-o to do/get something, send s-o for something, (send s-o on an errand):: tsesá:t ~ tssá:t ~ tsesát ~ tssát < tsesá ~ tssá or tsás.
    s-o was being sent [on errands]:: tsésetem < tsesá ~ tssá or tsás.

Errock
    Lake Errock:: Qwíqwex̲em < qwéx̲em.

eruption
    (get) a disease gotten by contacting a frog, a skin eruption, also the same disease as the man got in Kawkawa Lake in the Sx̲wó:yx̲wey story, (perhaps also) leprosy:: qw'ṓ:m.

Erythronium grandiflorum
    resp. Camassia leichtlinii and Camassia quamash, Erythronium grandiflorum:: sk'ámets ~ sk'ámeth.

escape
    escape (from slavery for ex.), get out (from being snowed in or snagged in river for ex.):: kwólòmèt < kwá:.
    escape, get out:: kwálòmèt < kwá:.
    start to struggle, start to flip around to escape (fish esp.):: kwetl'éthet < kwá:.
    to escape (as an animal from a trap), got away from something that trapped a person or animal:: tl'ewlómét ~ tl'ōwlómét < tl'í:w.
    to escape (of a man or a slave), run away:: tl'í:w.

Eschrichtius glaucus
    perhaps generic, most likely includes all local balleen whales, i.e., suborder Mysticeti, especially Balaenoptera physalus and Megaptera novaeangliae, possibly Eschrichtius glaucus, Balaenoptera borealis, Balaenoptera acutorostrata, Sibbaldus musculus, Eubalaena sieboldi, could include the following toothed whales (suborder Odontoceti): Physeter catodon, possibly Berardius bairdi, Mesoplodon stejnegeri, Ziphius cavirostrus:: qwél:és ~ qwélés.

Esilao
    Esilao village, Siwash Creek village:: Aseláw.
    mountain above Esilao, Siwash Creek Mountain:: Aseláw Smált < Aseláw.

esophagus
    in the throat, in the esophagus, in the voice:: =eqel.

especially
  make it especially for s-o:: swástexw < swá.

Eubalaena sieboldi
  perhaps generic, most likely includes all local balleen whales, i.e., suborder Mysticeti, especially Balaenoptera physalus and Megaptera novaeangliae, possibly Eschrichtius glaucus, Balaenoptera borealis, Balaenoptera acutorostrata, Sibbaldus musculus, Eubalaena sieboldi, could include the following toothed whales (suborder Odontoceti): Physeter catodon, possibly Berardius bairdi, Mesoplodon stejnegeri, Ziphius cavirostrus:: qwél:és ~ qwélés.

eulachon
  eulachon oil:: tl'í:na.
  eulachon, oolachen, candle-fish:: swí:we ~ swíwe.
  to scoop (for ex. oolachens, eulachons):: qó:lem < qó:.

Euphagus cyanocephalus
  Euphagus cyanocephalus, or Corvus caurinus:: q'eláq'a.

Eutamias amoenus
  Eutamias amoenus, Eutamias townsendi:: tsitsepyóthel.

Eutamias amoenus (affinis
  Eutamias amoenus (affinis?), Eutamias townsendi:: x̲ep'í:tsel.
  Eutamias amoenus felix, Eutamias amoenus affinis?, Eutamias townsendi:: qwémxel < qwem.
  Eutamias amoenus felix (has more than two stripes), Eutamias townsendi, perhaps also Eutamias amoenus affinis:: x̲ex̲p'í:tsel ~ x̲ex̲p'ítsel ~ sx̲ex̲p'í:tsel < x̲ep'í:tsel.

Eutamias amoenus felix
  Eutamias amoenus felix, Eutamias amoenus affinis?, Eutamias townsendi:: qwémxel < qwem.
  Eutamias amoenus felix (has more than two stripes), Eutamias townsendi, perhaps also Eutamias amoenus affinis:: x̲ex̲p'í:tsel ~ x̲ex̲p'ítsel ~ sx̲ex̲p'í:tsel < x̲ep'í:tsel.

Eutamias townsendi
  Eutamias amoenus (affinis?), Eutamias townsendi:: x̲ep'í:tsel.
  Eutamias amoenus, Eutamias townsendi:: tsitsepyóthel.
  Eutamias amoenus felix, Eutamias amoenus affinis?, Eutamias townsendi:: qwémxel < qwem.
  Eutamias amoenus felix (has more than two stripes), Eutamias townsendi, perhaps also Eutamias amoenus affinis:: x̲ex̲p'í:tsel ~ x̲ex̲p'ítsel ~ sx̲ex̲p'í:tsel < x̲ep'í:tsel.

even
  got even with s-o:: xwtí:chest ~ xwtí(:)ychest < tiy.
  to be even:: slíq' < léq'.

evening
  become evening:: xwelált < lá:t.

ever
  anyway, ever, (new information as in NStraits):: kwá.

ever (CONT'D)

forever:: kw'ō wiyóth(cha) ò ~ kw'ō hélémcha ò < wiyóth.
never, not ever:: éwelh < éwe ~ ő́we.
weren't ever?, wasn't ever?, didn't ever?, does s-o ever?, never used to, not going to (but did anyway) [perhaps in the sense of never usually do X but did this time]:: ewá:lh ~ wá:lh < éwe ~ ő́we.
whatever it is, what it is, it is anything, it is something:: stámés < tám.
whenever:: lhéq'es < lhéq'.
whenever, whenever it is:: temtámes < tám.

every
all, every:: mékw' ~ mő́kw'.

everybody
everybody, everyone:: mekw'ewátes ~ mekw'ewát < wát.
everybody, everyone, (anybody [Elders Group 3/1/72]):: mekw'ewát < mékw' ~ mő́kw'.

everyone
everybody, everyone:: mekw'ewátes ~ mekw'ewát < wát.
everybody, everyone, (anybody [Elders Group 3/1/72]):: mekw'ewát < mékw' ~ mő́kw'.

everything:: mekw'stám ~ mōkw'rtám < mékw' ~ mő́kw'.
breaking (everything):: yexwá:ls < yíxw.

evidential)
maybe, I guess, I'm uncertain, must be (evidently), (evidential), have to (I guess):: t'wa ~ t'we.
so they say, (reportedly, reportative, evidential?):: -ts'á.

evidently)
maybe, I guess, I'm uncertain, must be (evidently), (evidential), have to (I guess):: t'wa ~ t'we.

evil
a sung spell, power to help or harm people or to do [ritual] burning, power to do witchcraft and predict the future, an evil spell, (magic spell) (someone who has power to take things out of a person or put things in [by magic] [Elders Group 2/25/76], ritualist [Elders Group 1/21/76], witch [EB 4/25/78]):: syiwí:l ~ syewí:l < yéw: ~ yéw.
casting an evil spell on s-o:: yewí:lt < yéw: ~ yéw.

exactly)
just, (exactly):: =ò:l ~ =ól ~ =ò ~ ò ~ ó:l.
right (in the sense of exactly or just):: ate.
Sure., Exactly.:: xwéwes.

examine
look at s-th/s-o, examine s-o/s-th:: kw'átset < kw'áts ~ kw'éts.

excite
startled s-o, (excited s-o [Elders Group 3/2/77]):: lhkw'íwel:exw < lhó:kw' ~ lhókw'.

excited
being nervous, being excited, (getting nervous/excited):: th'óyéxwem < th'ó:yxwem.

excited (CONT'D)

(get/become) nervous, (get/become) excited:: th'ó:yx̲wem.

excrement

dung, excrement, feces:: s'óq.
dung, (excrement, feces), shit:: sq'éth'.
dung, (scattered excrement?, fecal droppings?):: sq'éth'x̲ < sq'éth'.

excuse

Excuse me.:: qw'óqw'elex̲thòx < qw'óqw'elex̲.
Excuse us.:: qw'óqw'elex̲tòlè < qw'óqw'elex̲.

exert

exert oneself, make a big effort, do with all one's might, [do] as hard as possible, do it harder (used if already paddling for ex.):: tíméthet < tímet.

expect :: kw'étskw'ets < kw'áts ~ kw'éts.
expect s-o:: kw'étskw'etsmet < kw'áts ~ kw'éts.

expensive :: tl'í ~ tl'í:.
make s-th expensive:: tl'ístexw < tl'í ~ tl'í:.

experienced

an experienced spirit dancer:: sts'eláxwem.

expert

expert hunter (who comes back with game every time he hunts), good hunter:: tewít.

explode

a shot, explosion:: wetl'éleqw < tl'ál ~ tl'á:l.
explode:: tl'eléqw < tl'ál ~ tl'á:l.
(to spark), explode with sparks and make sparky noises:: páyéts'em.

expression

ugly expression in mouth, ugly grin:: sx̲eyx̲eth'ó:ythel < x̲íth' ~ x̲éyth'.

extension

angular or perpendicular extension:: =áx̲el ~ =ex̲el.

extinguish

to extinguish it, put it out (a fire):: tl'ékw'elt < tl'ékw'el.

extract

lemon extract:: tsqwá:yem < qwá:y.
use, extract, extract a portion:: lh- ~ lhé-.
vanilla, (vanilla extract):: ts'q'éyx̲em < q'íx̲.

extravagant

(be) bragging, extravagant in claims, bull-headed, claims he's the best:: sqoyéx̲iya < sqáyéx̲ ~ sqayéx̲.

extreme

going to piss right away, almost piss oneself, (have an urgent or extreme or painful need to

extreme (CONT'D)

urinate):: ts'áléqel.

extremely)

(be) very, (extremely), really:: ts'áts'el.

eye

be fading (of eyesight):: stselá:l.
(be) swollen on the eye, (have a) swollen eye:: schxwó:les < chxw= ~ =chíxw, schxwó:les < chxw= ~ =chíxw.
black eye, bruised eye:: st'it'eqó:les < t'íq, st'it'eqó:les < t'íq.
blinking one's eyes repeatedly:: lhéplhepxlexw < lhép.
blink one's eyes:: lhépxlexw < lhép.
closing one's eyes, shutting one's eyes:: th'íth'eplexw (or perhaps th'íth'ep'lexw) < th'éplexw (or perhaps th'ép'lexw).
cross-eyed, prob. also cock-eyed:: skw'íts'òlès.
eye (of human, animal, fish, etc.):: qélém ~ qél:ém.
eyes:: qeqéylém ~ qeqéylem ~ (qeqílém) < qélém ~ qél:ém.
get dust or bark in both eyes:: thq'elq'ó:les < théq'.
get dust or bark in one eye:: thq'ó:les < théq'.
(have a) white caste over the eye, (have a) cataract:: p'eq'ó:les < p'éq'.
(have) big eyes:: thithehó:les < thi ~ tha ~ the ~ thah ~ theh.
(have) blue eyes:: ts'meth'ó:les < méth'.
(have) good eyes, (have) good sight, soft on the eyes, easy on the eyes:: eyólés ~ eyó:les < éy ~ éy:.
(have) marble eyes, (have) blue eyes:: mopeló:les.
(have) one eye closed:: lheq'ó:les.
(have) one white eye, (have a cataract on one eye):: sqwelxwó:lés.
(have) quick eyes, (have) peeping-Tom eyes:: aliyólés < éy ~ éy:.
have red eyes:: tskwimó:les < kwí:m.
hit in the eye (on the eyelid):: kw'qwó:les ~ kw'qwóles < kw'óqw.
lots of eyes:: qelqélem < qélém ~ qél:ém.
lots of eyes being closed:: th'elíth'eplexw ~ ts'elíts'eplexw (or perhaps ts'elíts'ep'lexw) < th'éplexw (or perhaps th'ép'lexw).
lower circle under eye:: stl'epó:lemelh ~ stl'epó:les < tl'ép.
one's eyes are watering:: qo'qo'ólésem < qó:.
on the eye(s), in the eye(s), on the eyelid(s):: =ó:les.
open both one's eyes real wide:: pexó:lésem < páx.
opening one's eyes:: xélxeleq't < xéleq't.
open one's eyes:: xéleq't.
poke oneself in the eye (with finger, stick, etc.):: telkwó:lésem.
pupil of the eye:: q'eyxóles < q'íx.
roll one's eyes:: xelxólqemóles < xálqem.
roots (resembling eyes looking at you) of a kind of plant that's good for asthma:: qelémes < qélém ~ qél:ém.
shading one's eyes from the sun with the hand (looking into the sun):: xwtóxesem.
shut one's eyes, close one's eyes, (blink [EB]):: th'éplexw (or perhaps th'ép'lexw).
shutting one's eyes repeatedly, (blinking [EB]):: th'épth'eplexw (or perhaps th'ép'th'ep'lexw) < th'éplexw (or perhaps th'ép'lexw).
snap one's eyes at s-o [in anger or disgust]:: th'éplexwlexw (or perhaps th'ép'lexwlexw) < th'éplexw (or perhaps th'ép'lexw).
sty in the eye:: xéle'ò:les < sxéle.

eye (CONT'D)

tear (from eye):: qe'ó:les < qó:.
twitch, flutter (of one's eye, hand, skin, etc.):: lhawét'em < lhá:w.
upper circle over the eye, probably upper eyelid:: chelhó:lemelh < =chílh ~ chílh=, schelhó:les < =chílh ~ chílh=.

eyebrow :: thómél.
both eyebrows:: themthómél < thómél.

eyeglasses:: skw'echó:steló:les < kw'áts ~ kw'éts.
eyeglasses, (probably dark glasses):: st'óle'oléstel < t'á:l.

eyelash
eyelid, eyelash:: lhéptel < lhép.

eyelid
eyelid, eyelash:: lhéptel < lhép.
hit in the eye (on the eyelid):: kw'qwó:les ~ kw'qwóles < kw'óqw.
on the eye(s), in the eye(s), on the eyelid(s):: =ó:les.
spread the eyelids open with the fingers (done to oneself or to someone else), (probably also spread s-th apart):: páx̱et < páx̱.
upper circle over the eye, probably upper eyelid:: chelhó:lemelh < =chílh ~ chílh=, schelhó:les < =chílh ~ chílh=.

eyesight)
be fading (of eyesight):: stselá:l.
eyesight, sight:: skw'áts < kw'áts ~ kw'éts.

face :: s'ó:thes ~ s'óthes.
a tear (on the face):: sqó:s < qó:.
be facing toward:: le'ós < le'á.
be on the other side of, be on the side facing away:: sle'ólwelh < le'á.
(be) scowling (if mad or ate something sour), ((made a) funny (strange) face [Elders Group 1/21/76]):: sx̱éyx̱ewes < x̱éywel.
be watchful, be facing away:: sle'ó:les < le'á.
be with behind facing toward something (like a fire):: sle'álets < le'á.
chin, jaw (of fish, human, etc.), (lips (both), cheek, side of the face [DM]):: ts'emxó:ythel.
cliff, vertical rock face:: qw'eléqel.
diatomaceous earth (could be mixed with things to whiten them--for ex. dog and goat wool), white clay for white face paint (for pure person spirit-dancers), white powder from mountains, white clay they make powder from to lighten goat and dog wool for blankets, powder, talc, white face paint:: st'ewő̗kw'.
dirty, (have a cross face [EB]):: qelés < qél.
face down, (upside-down [Deming]):: qep'ós < qep'.
face of a basket, (design on a basket):: =ó:s ~ =ós ~ =es.
face of a mountain:: =ó:s ~ =ós ~ =es.
face of the moon:: =ó:s ~ =ós ~ =es.
face up:: kw'e'ós < kw'e'í ~ kw''í ~ kw'í.
facing up, head sticking up:: kw'ekw'e'íqw ~ kw'ekw'íqw < kw'e'í ~ kw''í ~ kw'í.
get hit in the face:: xwmélkw'es.
(have) a big face:: xwthó:s < thi ~ tha ~ the ~ thah ~ theh.
(have a) dirty face:: ts'épx̱es < ts'épx̱.

face (CONT'D)

(have a) hairy face, (have) hair on the face, (have a woolly face):: xwpopó:s < pá:pa.
(have a) long face:: xwtl'óqtes < tl'áqt.
(have a) speckled face, (have) freckles:: tl'eltl'élx̲os < tl'él.
(have a) wide face:: lhq'ó:tes < lheq'át ~ lhq'á:t.
(have a) wrinkled face:: lhélp'es < lhél.
(have a) wrinkled face with many wrinkles:: lhellhélp'es < lhél.
headdress, face costume, mask:: sx̲wéythiyes ~ sx̲wíythiyes < x̲wíyth.
hit on the face (several times):: melmélkw'es < xwmélkw'es.
hit s-o in the face, punch s-o in the face:: th'í:qw'est < th'í:qw'et.
leaning the face on the hand with elbow propped:: piyósem < píy.
long face:: stl'óqtes < tl'áqt.
looking sad, (making a sour face [MV, EF]):: sló:ltes.
making a face:: x̲wix̲we'ó:s < x̲wex̲we'á.
one's face is red, one is blushing:: kwelkwímelésem < kwí:m.
on the face, face of the hand or foot, opened surface of a salmon:: =ó:s ~ =ós ~ =es.
paint one's face red or black (spirit dancer, Indian doctor, ritualist, etc.):: lhíx̲esem < lhá:x̲ ~ lháx̲.
powdered on the face:: st'ewíqw'es < st'ewőkw'.
punched in the face:: th'qw'ó:s < th'í:qw'et.
put one's head back (tilt one's face up):: q'óx̲esem.
put paint on one's face:: yétl'q'esem < yétl'.
put (white) paint on one's face:: t'ewőkw'esem < st'ewőkw'.
(rain or sweat) trickling down one's face:: kw'tómés < kw'átem.
scraped on the face:: x̲éyp'es < x̲éyp'.
scratch s-o on the face:: t'lhóqw'est < t'élheqw' ~ t'lhóqw'.
sit facing a river and watch it, sit on a riverbank and sunbathe:: chichewós < cháchew ~ cháchu.
smear something on s-o's face [purposely]:: yétl'q'est < yétl'.
spill (on the face?):: kw'lhó:s < kw'élh.
splash on the face:: lhéltes < lhél.
splash s-o in the face, squirt s-o in the face:: lhélest < lhél.
to fan in the face:: xwélp'es < xwélp'.
to powder one's face, put powder on one's face:: t'ewőkw'esem < st'ewőkw'.
to scowl, make a bad face or a scowl:: x̲eywésem or x̲éywésem < x̲éywel.
turn away, turn one's face away:: qelésem < qél.
turn one's face towards:: ó:sem.
turn one's face, (turn one's body away [IHTTC]):: ts'ólesem ~ ts'ólésem < ts'el.
washing one's face, washing his/her face:: th'éx̲wesèm < th'éx̲w or th'óx̲w.
wash one's face:: th'ex̲wó:sem ~ th'ex̲wósem < th'éx̲w or th'óx̲w.
wet one's face:: lhélqesem < lhél.
wipe one's face:: íqw'esem < íqw', óp'esem < áp'.

face-cloth:: shxwíqw'estel < íqw'.

facing

facing towards, facing me (sic?):: ehó:les.

fade

be faded (of clothes), (get/become) faded, (go or get or become gray):: xwíkw'el < xwíkw'.
be fading (of eyesight):: stselá:l.
disappear, drop out of sight, (to fade [Elders Group 3/72]):: théxw ~ théx̲w.

fade (CONT'D)

get rubbed off, to smudge (a line), to smear, to fade (of material):: íqw'em < íqw'.

faint

(made) a faint sound carried by the air, sound within hearingdistance, sound within earshot:: ehéléqep < ehó.
pass out, faint:: t'eqw'élhelh < t'éqw'.
to faint:: melqí:wsem < mál ~ mél.

fairy bells

"snakeberry", includes False Solomon's seal, star-flowered Solomon's seal, and probably Twisted-stalk (2 spp.) and Hooker's fairy bells:: sth'íms te álhqey < sth'í:m ~ sth'ì:m.

fall

a faller, a logger:: yáyeq'els < yáq'.
a snow, a snowfall:: syíq < yíq.
(be) snowing, it's snowing, snow is falling:: yíyeq < yíq.
fall and roll:: hílém < híl.
fall apart, come apart (of something man-made):: yíx̲w.
fall asleep:: itetlómet < ítet, léqw.
fall a tree:: yeq'á:ls < yáq'.
fallen snow, (year):: máqa ~ máqe.
fall, fall off, drop, drop off, drop or fall down (of person):: tsélq ~ chélq.
falling:: chá:lq < tsélq.
falling (a tree), be falling trees:: yáyeq'els < yáq'.
falling it, falling a tree:: yáyeq'et < yáq'.
falling snow, be snowing:: syíyeq < yíq.
fall in the water, fall overboard (of one person):: qwés.
fall off (of its own accord, of petals or seed fluff):: píxw.
fall off (of leaves, berries):: xwís.
fall off (of petals or seed fluff):: píxwem < píxw.
fall on one's forehead, drop on one's forehead, fall onto one's head:: méleqw (or) leméleqw.
fall splat, (make the) sound of a spank or slap:: welhéleq' < welhéq'.
fell of its own accord (of an object from a height or from upright), drop down (object/person, from a shelf, bridge, cliff, etc.), fall off:: wets'étl' ~ wech'étl'.
hair is falling out, losing one's hair:: qw'eméqel < qw'ém.
leaves falling:: xwesá:lews < xwís.
let oneself fall, drop oneself down (by parachute, rope, etc., said of little birds trying to fly out of nest, little animals trying to get down and let themselves fall):: chólqthet < tsélq ~ chélq.
(make the) sound of a spank on a bottom, (fall down with a bang [Elders Group 5/19/76]):: welhéq'.
managed to fell a tree, (managed to fall it):: yéq'lexw ~ yéq'elexw < yáq'.
slip and fall hard (either a person or something he's carrying):: th'esáp < th'és.
to fall (about a tree):: yáq'.
to fall down and scatter, drop and scatter:: tl'ápex̲em < tl'ép.
to fall it (a tree), to fell a tree, to fall a tree:: yáq'et < yáq'.
to fall (of a person, waterfall, etc.), stumble:: tsélq.
to fall on something (of a drunk):: qwélh.
to snow, (snow falls):: yíq.

fall (season)
autumn, fall (season):: temhilálxw < híl.

falls
"Eagle Falls" on the west side of Harrison Lake, probably Walian Creek falls:: Kwótxwem Stó:lō < kwótx̲wem ~ kwótxwem.
Elk Creek Falls:: Skw'íkw'ets'tel.
Rainbow Falls (on Harrison Lake's southeast side):: Tsólqthet te Skwówech < skwó:wech ~ skwówech.
Rainbow Falls on Harrison Lake, (Sturgeon's Drop):: Tsólqthet te Skwówech < tsélq ~ chélq.
waterfall, falls:: skwél.

False Solomon's seal
False Solomon's seal, Twisted-stalk, rosy-flowered Twisted-stalk, star-flowered Solomon's seal:: x̲ex̲q'elá:lhp.
"snakeberry", including False Solomon's seal, star-flowered Solomon's seal, and probably Twisted-stalk and Hooker's fairy bells:: sth'íms te álhqey < álhqey ~ álhqay.
"snakeberry", includes False Solomon's seal, star-flowered Solomon's seal, and probably Twisted-stalk (2 spp.) and Hooker's fairy bells:: sth'íms te álhqey < sth'í:m ~ sth'i:m.

family
rock figure near the rocks shaped like a family underwater:: Th'elíth'eqes.
smallest of a litter or family:: th'akw'ó:y < sth'ékw', th'ith'kw'ó:y < sth'ékw'.

famine :: temxwá < xwá.
hungry time (about mid-April to mid-May), famine (Elders 3/72):: temkw'à:y < kw'à:y.
perish together, many die (in famine, sickness, fire), all die, get wiped out:: x̲wà:y ~ x̲wá:y.

famished
starve, be starving, be famished, (be extremely hungry [Deming,JL]):: xwá.

fan
a fan:: xwélp'tel < xwélp'.
fan s-o, brush s-o with a branch:: xwélp't < xwélp'.
to fan:: xwélp'.
to fan in the face:: xwélp'es < xwélp'.

fancy
fancy lining:: shxwthí:lestel.

fang
(have) sharp teeth, (have) fangs:: silís < éy ~ éy:.

far
(being far?):: chóchekw < chó:kw.
far, be far away, far off, way in the distance:: chó:kw.
from far away:: telchókw < chó:kw.
go far away:: chekwílem < chó:kw, xwetskwí:lem < chó:kw.

fart :: p'ehí ~ p'ehéy.

fart (CONT'D)

a fart:: spú' < pú'.
fart on the rump, (a show-off):: pú'elets < pú'.
to fart, pass gas:: téq'.
to pass gas, break wind, to fart:: pú'.

fast

be fast, hurry:: xwém ~ x̲wém.
eat fast, eating fast, hurry to eat:: x̲weméthel < x̲wém ~ xwém.
fasting:: xwexwátem < xwá.
fasting for Lent, prob. also Lent:: kyal:ám.
fast runner:: xwóxwe < xwá.
howling fast:: q'ówel < q'á:w.
hurry, hurry up, be quick, be fast, move faster, quickly:: x̲wém ~ xwém.
hurry up, faster:: x̲wemx̲wém < x̲wém ~ xwém.
I broke my fast (lit. "past - cause to finish it - my - starving"), -le hóystexw tel sxwexwá
make the sound of water splashing or dripping fast, (make the sound of a waterfall, make the sound of pouring rain dripping or splashing in puddles loudly):: xwótqwem.
pick fast, (do fast with the hands):: x̲wémetses < x̲wém ~ xwém.
raining hard, pouring rain, (raining fast):: xwémxel < x̲wém ~ xwém.
rapids, fast water, clear water, flowing fast, going fast, swift (water):: lex̲wố:m ~ lex̲wốm < x̲wém ~ xwém.
somebody is made to fast, he is starved (purposely):: xwátem < xwá.
to abstain from food, to fast, starve oneself:: xwóthet < xwá.
to hurry, hurry up, move fast:: ówthet < áwth.

fasten

put s-th on (of a design on a dress, of a shirt, shoes, etc.), attach it, stick it on, fasten it:: tl'álx < tl'ál.
to be attached, to be fixed or fastened, be put on:: stl'átl'el < tl'ál.
to fasten s-th by tying, tie up s-th (like canoe, horse, laces, nets, cow, shoelaces), tie it:: q'éyset ~ q'í(:)set < q'ey ~ q'i.

fat

a rock along Harrison River which looks like layers of seal fat all along its bottom:: Skwló ~ Sqwló < skwló ~ sqwló.
be fat:: ló:s ~ lós.
fat, grease, lard, (oil [EB], shortening [MH]):: sló:s ~ slós < ló:s ~ lós.
fatty salmon head:: lésleseqw < ló:s ~ lós.
get fat, put on weight, getting fat:: ló:sthet ~ lósthet < ló:s ~ lós.
seal fat:: skwló ~ sqwló.
Seal Fat Rock on Harrison River just upriver from Th'éqwela (place by Morris Lake where Indian people used to play Indian badminton), this rock has what resembles seal fat all around it:: Skwló ~ Sqwló < sqwló.
seal fat, seal blubber:: sqwló.
solid grease, suet, lump of grease, (stomach fat [CT]):: x̲wástel.
stout (of a person), thick (of a tree), thick around, coarse (of a rope), big (fat) (of a person). big (in girth):: mékw.

fatal

a fatal kind of shock on seeing a stl'áleqem (supernatural creature):: xò:lí:s.

father :: má:l ~ mál.
 little father:: smà:l < má:l ~ mál.
 name of Chief Albert Louie's father:: T'íxwelátse ~ Tíxwelátsa.

father-in-law
 mother-in-law, father-in-law, spouse's parent, parent-in-law:: skw'ílhew.

Father's Mother
 Grandma, Father's Mother (nickname):: táta < tá:l ~ tà:l ~ tál.

fauna
 to rot, rotten (of fruit, animal, flora, fauna, food):: th'óqw'em ~ th'ó:qw'em.

favor
 ask a favor, ask pity, beseech:: th'exwstélémét < th'íxw ~ th'éxw.
 (ask for a favor or pity for s-o):: th'exwstí:lmet < th'íxw ~ th'éxw.
 begging for a favor, asking for help:: th'íth'exwstélémét < th'íxw ~ th'éxw.
 did s-o a favor:: (shxwémlexw) < (xwémlexw), (xwémlexw).

fawn
 fawn, baby deer:: st'ít'ele < st'él'e.
 younger deer, baby horse, younger cow, fawn, colt, calf:: st'él'e.

fear
 be afraid, be scared, be nervous:: sí:si < síy.
 feel creepy, fear something behind one:: sísem < síy.
 feeling creepy, fearing something behind one:: sísesem < síy.
 get a spooky or spooked feeling, afraid that bad spirits are around, get spooked, fear something behind:: x̱éysel.

feast
 a feast:: stl'etl'áxel < tl'e'á ~ tl'á'.
 big wooden dish (often two feet long), feast dish, wooden platter, (big stirring spoon [LJ], carved wooden spoon, big wooden spoon [AC, BJ, DM]):: qwelhyőwelh ~ qwelhliyőwelh ~ qwelhlyúwelh < qwélh.
 container for left-overs taken home from feast, doggie bag:: meq'ethále < méq'.

 feast left-overs, left-overs of food (which guests can take home):: sméq'eth < méq'.
 invite s-o (to come eat, dance etc.) (any number), invite s-o to a feast:: tl'e'áxet < tl'e'á ~ tl'á'.
 inviting (to come eat, dance), to give a potlatch, (give a feast or gathering), to invite to a feast, invite to a potlatch:: tl'etl'áxel < tl'e'á ~ tl'á'.
 long feast dish:: qwethíles < qweth.

feast dish
 dish, big cooking and serving trough used in longhouse, feast dish, plate (of wood or basketry), (platter), tray:: ló:thel.

feather :: =álqel ~ =élqel.
 down feathers, real fine feathers:: sq'óyes.
 feather (any kind), (fine feathers [EB], small feathers [IHTTC], lots of feathers [EB])::

feather (CONT'D)

sxélts' ~ sxél:ts' < xél.
long feather (from wing):: stl'p'álqel.
soft (down) feathers put in oiled hair for dancing:: sq'óyeseqw ~ sx̲óyeseqw < sq'óyes.
soft feathers put in oiled hair for dancing:: sx̲óyeseqw ~ sq'óyeseqw.
wing, (big feather [IHTTC]):: stl'q'á:l.

February

about December, (January to February [Billy Sepass]):: meqó:s < máqa ~ máqe.
month beginning with first sliver of moon in February, (time things stick to the hand (in cold)):: temt'elémtses < t'elém.
month or moon that begins in February:: Qwémxel < qwem.
moon of February to March, (torch season):: peló:qes < peló:qel.
moon or month beginning in February, (November to December, time when ice forms [and sticks] [Billy Sepass in Jenness]):: temtl'í:q'es < tl'íq'.

feces

dung, excrement, feces:: s'óq.
dung, (excrement, feces), shit:: sq'éth'.
dung, feces, shit:: s'ó' < ó'.
dung, (scattered excrement?, fecal droppings?):: sq'éth'x̲ < sq'éth'.

fed up

to be fed up [with s-o/s-th], (annoyed with s-o/s-th):: th'íwélmét < th'íwél.

feed

have a ritual burning ceremony, have a burning, feed the dead, (food offered to the dead [at a ritual burning] [EB 5/25/76]):: yeqwá:ls < yéqw.

feel

be feeling sorry:: x̲ex̲élh te sqwálewel < x̲élh.
feel creepy, fear something behind one:: sísem < síy.
feel embarrassed and shy because ashamed, be ashamed:: lhistélémét < lháy.
feeling around:: qátx̲els < qétx̲t.
feeling creepy, fearing something behind one:: sísesem < síy.
feeling embarrassed:: lholhistélemet < lháy.
feeling sorry for oneself:: tesestélemet < t-sós ~ tesós.
feel it with fingertips:: p'átl'et.
feel like going:: halemélmel < la.
feel like singing a spirit song, be in a trance making sighsand crying sounds before singing a spirit song, be in the beginning of a trance before the spirit song is recognizable (the motions and sounds, crying out or wailing before singing):: lhéch.
feel one's head, (feel the head):: qetx̲éleqw < qétx̲t.
feel s-th/s-o with fingers, feel s-th, feel s-o:: qétx̲t.
hurting, feeling sore, (feel[ing] pain [BJ]):: táteqlexw < téqlexw.
the feeling, something's feel:: qétx̲mel < qétx̲t.
thoughts, feelings:: sqwá:lewel ~ sqwálewel ~ sqwà(:)lewel < qwà:l.
to pity s-o, feel sorry for s-o:: th'éxwmet < th'íxw ~ th'éxw.
to tingle (like arm waking up from numbness), (have/get a) stinging feeling:: thátkwem.
want to cry, feel like crying:: x̲amélmel < x̲à:m ~ x̲á:m.
want to pee, (want to urinate, feel like one has to urinate):: síyt'eqem < síyt'.

feeling
be overcome with pleasurable feelings after eating great salmon or a great meal:: ts'éqw'.
get a spooky or spooked feeling, afraid that bad spirits are around, get spooked, fear something behind:: x̲éysel.
getting spooked, being afraid that bad spirits are around, spooky feeling:: x̲éyx̲esel < x̲éysel.
thoughts, feelings:: sqwá:lewel ~ sqwálewel ~ sqwà(:)lewel < qwà:l.

feelings
be sorry, the feelings are hurt:: x̲élh (te, kw'e) sqwálewel < x̲élh.
strong feelings, mad all the time but won't fight:: simíwél < éy ~ éy:.

feet
(both human) legs, (both) feet:: sx̲ex̲éyle or sx̲ex̲íle < sx̲él:e.

Felis concolor oregonensis:: shxwéwe.

Felis domestica:: púpsò:llh < pús, pús.

fell
managed to fell a tree, (managed to fall it):: yéq'lexw ~ yéq'elexw < yáq'.
to fall it (a tree), to fell a tree, to fall a tree:: yáq'et < yáq'.

Female
Female Grizzly Bear:: Yeqwílmetelòt < yéqw.
Female Salmonberry Bird, (Female Swainson's Thrush):: Xwatóy < xwét.

female :: slhá:lí, slhá:lí.
big person (of females), big lady:: thékwàl.
female black bear with white spot [or mark] on the chest:: Sx̲éylmòt or sx̲éylmòt < x̲él ~ x̲é:yl ~ x̲í:l
female name:: =elhót, =elò:t ~ =eló:t, =emòt, =ewòt, =òt ~ =ò:t.
female name (garment):: =elwet ~ =élwet.
female part of female plant:: slheli'ál < slhá:lí.
fortune-teller, seer, person who can see things in the future, female witch:: syéw:e ~ syéwe ~ syő:we ~ syú:we < yéw: ~ yéw.
nominalizer (female present and visible or presence or proximity unspecified), demonstrative article:: the=.
that's her, she (present or presence unspecified), her (present or presence unspefified), that (female):: thú:tl'ò < tl'ó ~ tl'o.
that's them (female), they (female), them (female):: thutl'ó:lem < tl'ó ~ tl'o.
the (female, near but not visible), (female, near but not in sight) (translated by gender specific words in English, like aunt, etc.):: kwse < kw.
the (female, present and visible), the (female, unspecified presence and/or unspecified visibility):: the.
woman, female:: slhá:lí.

fence :: q'eléx̲el < q'ál.
(be) fenced in:: sq'eláx̲el < q'ál.
fence it:: q'elx̲á:lt < q'ál.
fence s-th in:: q'eléx̲elt < q'ál.

fennel
hog fennel, Indian consumption plant:: q'exmí:l.

ferment
fermenting:: t'eth'ó:mthet < t'áth'.
sour (unripe or half-ripe fruit, lemon, Oregon grape, fermenting fruit):: t'át'eth'em < t'áth'.

fern
a sprout or shoot (esp. of the kinds peeled and eaten in spring), sweet green inner shoots, green berry shoots, salmonberry shoots, wild raspberry shoots and greens, salmonberry sprouts, blackcap shoots, thimbleberry shoots, wild rhubarb shoots, fern shoots:: stháthqiy.
bracken fern root, rhizome of bracken fern:: sá:q.
bracken fern (top, part above ground):: ptákwem.
licorice fern:: st'uslóye, tl'asíp, t'usló:ye.
mountain fern with a wide top (used by flower shops), probably spiny wood-fern:: th'ékwa, th'ékwa.
poison fern that grows in swampy places, (prob. water hemlock, poison hemlock):: welékwsa.
sword fern:: sthxá:lem.
yarrow, also parsely fern:: xaweqá:l < xáwéq.

ferry
a ferry (canoe, boat, ferryboat):: shxwt'át'ekwels < t'ákwel.
a ferryman:: t'át'ekwels < t'ákwel.
bring s-th/s-o across a river, (ferry s-o/s-th over):: t'kwíléstexw < t'ákwel.
something used to cross over a river, ferry, place good for crossing:: xwt'át'ekwel < t'ákwel.

ferryboat
a ferry (canoe, boat, ferryboat):: shxwt'át'ekwels < t'ákwel.

ferryman
a ferryman:: t'át'ekwels < t'ákwel.

fetch
bring s-th, fetch s-th, get s-th (bring it), give it to s-o(as s-th fetched, not as a gift):: méstexw < mí ~ mé ~ me.
get, fetch:: kwél:em ~ kwélem < kwél.
take s-th, accept s-th, get s-th, fetch s-th, pick s-th up:: kwú:t.
to dip water, get water, fetch water, pack water:: qó:m < qó:.
water (someone) carried, (water fetched/gotten):: sqó:m < qó:.

few
a few little rats:: haheláwt < há:wt.
a few mice:: kw'elókw't'el < kw'át'el.
a little bit, small bit, a few:: emímel ~ amí:mel.

fiber
processed fiber:: (=)l=íth'e < íth'a.
stringy fibers (as on cow parsnip):: xwéylem ~ xwé:ylem ~ xwí:lem.

fibre
dog wool fibre:: qweqwemeylíth'e < qwem.
grass or fibre for nets or twine, spreading dogbane, possibly also Indian hemp:: méthelh.
stringy fibers (as on cow parsnip):: x̲wéylem ~ x̲wé:ylem ~ x̲wí:lem.

fifty :: lhéq'etselsxà < lheq'át ~ lhq'á:t.
a half dollar, fifty cents:: lhséq' < séq'.
(fifty cyclic periods [DM]):: lhèq'etselsxó:s ~ lhéq'etselsxó:s < lheq'át ~ lhq'á:t.
fifty dollars:: lhèq'etselsxó:s ~ lhéq'etselsxó:s < lheq'át ~ lhq'á:t.
fifty people:: lheq'etselsxále < lheq'át ~ lhq'á:t.

fight
(be) aggressive, cranky, ready to fight, (be) violent, hot-headed:: sx̲óytl'thet ~ sx̲ó:ytl'thet.
beat s-o up, kick s-o in fight, lick s-o (in fight), spank s-o, fight s-o (till he cries for ex.), fight s-o in anger, fight s-o back:: x̲éyet.
fight back:: xwtíyches < tiy.
fighting:: ó:ytel < iyó:tel.
name of an old man from Kilgard who was a strong warrior (fighter):: X̲elhálh
to fight:: iyó:tel.
to separate people fighting, to split up people fighting:: memáx < má ~ má'-.
war, (warring), fighting a war:: x̲éyx̲elex̲ < x̲éylex̲.

figure
good figure, good shape:: eyámeth' < éy ~ éy:.
rock figure near the rocks shaped like a family underwater:: Th'elíth'eqes.

file
a file:: shxwíq'el or shxwíyq'el < yéq'.
a filer, someone that's filing (with a file):: hiyeq'á:l < yéq'.
filing:: héyq'es < yéq'.
filing s-th:: héyeq'et ~ héyq'et < yéq'.
to file:: yéq'es < yéq'.
to file (abrasively):: lhth'óméls < th'óméls, yeq'à:ls < yéq'.
whetstone, a file, sandstone:: th'óméls.

fill
be full:: selíts' ~ slíts' < léts'.
(be) full (from eating), (get filled (from eating) [AC]):: méq'.
burst, burst out, (get) smash(ed) (something round and filled):: méqw' ~ ḿőqw'.
fill (of container):: léts'.
fill oneself, fill oneself up:: lets'éthet < léts'.
fill oneself up (by eating):: meq'lómet < méq'.
fill s-th (with liquid or solid), fill it up:: lets'ét < léts'.
squish s-th round and filled, smash s-th round and filled:: méqw'et < méqw' ~ ḿőqw'.

filthy
dirty, filthy:: t'íqqwlha < t'íq.

fin :: =étmel ?.
belly fin:: th'étmel.
dorsal fin (long fin in back):: q'áwetsel.

fin (CONT'D)

fin, neck fin, i.e. pectoral fin:: q'étmel.
tiny fin above tail of fish, (perhaps spines above tail of some fish):: sxélhxelh < xélh.

find

(be) found:: smő̄kw' or semő̄kw' < mékw' ~ mő̄kw'.
discover s-th, find s-th:: thexláxw.
find a seat, have a seat, sit down:: ch'álechem < ts'á:.
find it, pick it up:: mékw'et ~ mő̄kw'et < mékw' ~ mő̄kw'.
find s-th :: kwélexw ~ kwél:exw < kwél.
find s-th out, understand s-th, learn s-th, realize s-th, now know what s-th is like, read (and comprehend) s-th, understand s-o:: tél:exw ~ (in rapid speech) télexw < tól.
get s-th, catch s-th, have s-th, find s-th:: kwélexw ~ kwél:exw < kwél.

find it funny:: í'istexw < éy ~ éy:.

find out

find s-th out, understand s-th, learn s-th, realize s-th, now know what s-th is like, read (and comprehend) s-th, understand s-o:: tél:exw ~ (in rapid speech) télexw < tól.
(be) found out (something you were trying to hide), to be discovered (something secret):: wá:y.

fine :: éy ~ éy:.

be alright, be well, be fine, be okay:: éy òl ~ éyòl ~ éyò < éy ~ éy:.
be fine (in health), be alright (in health), be well:: we'éy òl ~ we'éyòl ~ we'éyò ~ u éyò ~ u'éyò < éy ~ éy:.
be good, good, well, nice, fine, better, better (ought to), it would be good if, may it be good, let it be good, happy, glad, clean, well-behaved, polite, virgin, popular, comfortable (with furniture, other things?),:: éy ~ éy:.
clear up (of weather), turn fine (after a hard storm):: iyílem < éy ~ éy:.
dry snow coming in (drifting), fine snow that leaks into a house:: sqwelxómé ~ sqwelxóme < qwélxel.
feather (any kind), (fine feathers [EB], small feathers [IHTTC], lots of feathers [EB]):: sxélts' ~ sxél:ts' < xél.
fine ashes floating up from a fire:: tqwó:chep < tóqweltsep.
fine cedar root strips for baskets:: shxwth'á:lhtel.
fine cedar root weaving, fine cedar root work:: sts'éqw' ~ sch'éqw' < ts'éqw'.
fine (in health):: ō éy ~ ōw'éy < éy ~ éy:.
fine snow:: qwelqwélxel < qwélxel.
fine white ashes:: sts'á:s ~ sts'ás.
fog appearing on the water, (fine snow [AK]):: qwelqwélxel < qwélxel.
got stormy with lots of fine snow in the air:: qwálxtem < qwélxel.
(have) fine hair:: kweleleselqel.
(maybe) fine mist of fog or rain, ((perhaps) getting foggy [EB]):: qweqweqwtí:mxel < qwétxem.
real fine snow:: qwelxómé < qwélxel.
tinder, material used to start a fire with (fine dried cedar bark):: syeqwlhá:ltel < yéqw.

fine-tooth comb

real fine-tooth comb:: lhémxts'eltel < méxts'el.

finger

finger :: sléx̲tses < léx̲.
burned on the finger or hand, burnt the hand, a hand got burnt:: kw'éstses < kw'ás.
cut on one's hand, (cut one's finger [EB}):: lhéts'ches < lhíts' ~ lhí:ts'.
feel s-th/s-o with fingers, feel s-th, feel s-o:: qétx̲t.
finger ring:: siyálémtses.
first finger, index finger:: mét'esemél < mót'es, mót'estel < mót'es, mót'estses < mót'es.
get squeezed (in hand or fingers):: p'íth'em < p'í:.
(have) fingers so cold they can't bend:: memekwóyetses < mékw.
index finger, pointing finger:: mómet'es < mót'es, mómet'es < mót'es.
knuckles (all the joints of the hand and fingers):: qwemqwémx̲wtses < qwó:m ~ qwóm ~ qwem.
little finger, fourth finger:: soseqwtóletses < sóseqwt ~ (rarely) só:seqwt.
on the hand or finger, in the hand or finger:: =tses ~ =ches.
pick food by one's fingers (before a meal):: lhámth't < lhím.
picking food by the fingers before the meal:: lhémth' < lhím.
poke oneself in the eye (with finger, stick, etc.):: telkwó:lésem.
second finger, index finger:: stl'eqtóletses < tl'áqt.
second finger, middle finger:: shxwá:ytses < shxwá:ye.
snap one's fingers:: tl'eméqwtses < tl'ém.
third finger:: malyítses < malyí, sts'ats'íts'etl'tses < ts'í:tl' ~ ts'ítl'.
to snap (one's fingers, a louse when one bites it, etc.):: tl'eméqw < tl'ém.

fingernail
fingernail, nail of finger, claw:: qw'ex̲wéltses.
fingernail clippers (lit. "scissors for the fingernails"):: shxwth'ámqels qw'x̲wéltses/qw'x̲wélches < xwáth', qw'ex̲w.
in-grown finger-nail:: kyépetses < kyépe=.
split s-th open (with fingernail):: thíts'et.

fingertips
feel it with fingertips:: p'átl'et.

finish
finish eating, be done eating:: hó:ythel < hò:y ~ hó:y ~ hóy.
finished, over:: hà:m.
finish it (of food):: ú:kw't < ő́wkw'.
finish, stop, quit, get done, be finished, have enough, be done, be ready:: hò:y ~ hó:y ~ hóy, hò:y ~ hó:y ~ hóy.
ran out (of food, money, etc.), have no more, be finished (offood), (be empty (of container of supplies) [EB: Cheh., Tait]):: ő́wkw'.

fir
balsam fir (has sweet sap or cambium, grows at higher altitudes, called larch by some, "balsam" is a popular name for trees of the genus Abies), from a sample taken prob. subalpine fir, if sample is mistaken poss. Pacific silver fir or grand fir, if the term balsam is mistaken too, poss. a variety of Douglas fir:: q'et'emá:yelhp < q'át'em.
Douglas fir:: lá:yelhp < lá:y.
Douglas fir log or wood:: ts'sá:y.
(Douglas) fir tree:: ts'sá:yelhp < ts'sá:y.
fir bark:: slá:y < lá:y.
fir boughs, needle of any other conifer than spruce:: qwélatses.

fir (CONT'D)

grand fir, white fir:: t'ó:xw ~ t'óxw ~ t'óx̲w, t'ó:xw ~ t'óxw ~ t'óx̲w.
pitchwood (esp. fir, pine, spruce):: kw'íxwelhp < kw'íxw.
prickly (from fir bark, wool, or something one is allergic to), irritant, have an allergic reaction (to fir powder or cedar bark):: th'íth'ekwem < th'íkw.
tiny slivers of fir bark, fir bark powder:: sth'íkwem < th'íkw.
white fir branch:: t'óx̲wtses < t'ó:xw ~ t'óxw ~ t'óx̲w.
white fir, probably grand fir:: t'ó:xw ~ t'óxw ~ t'óx̲w.

fire

baking over an open fire, roasting over an open fire, barbecuing, cooking in an oven:: qw'eqw'élém < qw'él.
barbecue, bake (meat, vegetables, etc.) in open fire, bake over fire, roast over open fire, bake under hot sand, bake in oven, cook in oven, (boiled down (as jam) [CT, HT]):: qw'élém < qw'él.
be big (of a fire), the fire is big, the fire is going strong, big fire:: thó:lchep ~ thó:ltsep < thi ~ tha ~ the ~ thah ~ theh.
build a fire, make a fire, make the fire, (stoke the fire):: yéqwelchep ~ yéqweltsep < yéqw.
(circle) around the fire once and return to the start, make one circle in longhouse:: sélts' < sél or sí(:)l.
cooked (over fire):: qw'él.
crackling and popping (of a log in fire or firecrackers):: tl'áléx̲em < tl'ál ~ tl'á:l.
fine ashes floating up from a fire:: tqwó:chep < tóqweltsep.
fire, ((also) flame [EB, Elders Group]):: héyeqw < yéqw.
fire box or fire platform and fire shield for torch-lighting or pit-lamping fire:: tl'áts'eq.
fire-drill, stick spun to start fire:: sí:lcheptel < sél or sí(:)l.
fire (out of control), forest fire burning, fire burning:: yíyeqw < yéqw.
firepit, fireplace:: syéqwlhàlà < yéqw.
fireplace:: heyeqwá:la < yéqw.
fire poker:: shxwthó:yeltsep < thíy.
firewood:: =élchep ~ =éltsep.
fix a fire, straighten the fire up, stoke the fire:: thiyéltsep < thíy.
go away (as away from the fire):: tsx̲éylém or tsx̲ílém.
go out completely (of fire):: th'éx̲.
go out (of fire, flame or lamp):: tl'ékw'el.
(have/get a) crackle and pop (sound of a log in a fire or of firecrackers):: tl'á:lx̲em < tl'ál ~ tl'á:l.
heat it up, warm it up, smoke s-th over a fire:: pákw'et.
heat up (on fire, stove):: qewletsá:ls < qew.
(he) light(s) s-th on fire, (he) set s-th on fire:: sétqtstes.
house on fire, house fire:: yeqwyéqw < yéqw.
keep the fire at a constant temperature:: txwéltsep.
make a fire for s-o:: yéqwelchept < yéqw.
making the fire, building the fire, (stoking a fire):: híyqwelchep < yéqw.
perish together, many die (in famine, sickness, fire), all die, get wiped out:: x̲wà:y ~ x̲wá:y.
scorch s-th, blacken s-th with fire, heat it up (near a fire), burning a canoe with pitchwood to remove splinters and burn on black pitch):: qw'á:yt < qw'á:y.
the fire is laughing:: elíyliyem te híyqw. < yéqw.
tinder, material used to start a fire with (fine dried cedar bark):: syeqwlhá:ltel < yéqw.
toast it by a fire (of smoked fish):: kw'áset < kw'ás.
to extinguish it, put it out (a fire):: tl'ékw'elt < tl'ékw'el.
torch (made from pitch) (SJ and MV), (bark shield for fire (Elders Group 3/6/78)):: swáts'et.

fire (CONT'D)

to toast by a fire (of smoke-cured fish, dried fish), get toasted by fire (of smoke-dried fish):: kw'ásem < kw'ás.
transform it more, pass it over the fire more (at a burning):: x̲iyx̲éyt or x̲eyx̲éyt < x̲éyt.
warming up by a fire:: qéwethet < qew.
warm up by a fire:: qewéthet < qew.

firecracker
crackling and popping (of a log in fire or firecrackers):: tl'áléx̲em < tl'ál ~ tl'á:l.
(have/get a) crackle and pop (sound of a log in a fire or of firecrackers):: tl'á:lx̲em < tl'ál ~ tl'á:l.
popping (of firecrackers):: tl'eltl'ó:lqwem < tl'ál ~ tl'á:l.

firedrill :: sxéltsep < xél.
fire-drill, stick spun to start fire:: sí:lcheptel < sél or sí(:)l.

firepit
firepit, fireplace:: syéqwlhàlà < yéqw.
firepit in house:: shxwhéyqwela < yéqw.

fireplace
firepit, fireplace:: syéqwlhàlà < yéqw.
fireplace:: heyeqwá:la < yéqw.

fireweed :: x̲áts'et.
to drop or blow plant fluff (like dandelions, fireweed, cottonwood, etc.), to blow (of dusty or flaky stuff like wood dust, dandruff, maybe seeds):: pípexwem < píxw.

firewood :: híyeqwtem siyólh < yéqw.
bring in firewood, bring wood in:: kwtxwéltsep ~ kwetxwéltsep < kwetáxw.
firewood:: =élchep ~ =éltsep.
gather firewood (in the woods), get firewood:: chiyólh < yólh.
getting firewood:: chiyóyelh < yólh.
little stick of firewood:: syóyelh < yólh.
lots of little sticks of firewood:: syéyelh < yólh.
split firewood:: th'iyeqw'á:ls < th'íyeqw'.
split it (firewood):: th'íyeqw't < th'íyeqw'.
splitting firewood:: th'óyeqw'els < th'íyeqw'.
wood, firewood:: siyólh ~ siyó:lh ~ syólh < yólh.

firmly
firmly planted in ground (can't be pulled out):: slálets < slá ~ selá ~ slá: (probably).

first :: yewá:l.
a rock in the creek at the upriver end of Seabird Island that was a girl washing after her first period:: The Théthex̲w or Thethéthex̲w < thethíx̲w.
as usual, this time, now, the first time:: yalh.
first finger, index finger:: mét'esemél < mót'es, mót'estel < mót'es, mót'estses < mót'es.
first snow:: yeqelsxá:y < yíq.
first time:: =elhsxá ~ =elsxá.
girl at puberty, (girl's first period):: thethíx̲w.
silver spring salmon that came up Harrison River and Chehalis Creek, (first spring salmon

first (CONT'D)

[Deming]):: sqwéx̲em < qwéx̲em.

first-born:: schí:lh < =chílh ~ chílh=.

first month

first month ?:: mímele < méle ~ mél:a.

first person plural

first person plural patient or object of passive:: -òlèm.
first person plural subjunctive subject:: -et.
us, first person plural object:: -ólxw ~ -óxw.

first person singular

first person singular patient or object of passive:: -àlèm.
first person singular subjunctive subject:: -ál.
me, first person singular object:: -óx.
my, first person singular possessive pronoun, first person subordinate subject:: -el ~ -l ~ l.

first time

bring it out for the first time (of a spirit-song):: p'í:t < p'í:.

fish

a biter (animal, fish, etc.), a thing that is (always) biting:: ch'ech'émels < ts'ámet ~ ch'ámet.
a fisherman, a man that goes out fishing:: sth'óth'eqwi < sth'ó:qwi ~ sth'óqwi.
a fish that's going to spawn:: chewélhem ~ tsewélhem ~ tsōwélhem < cháchew ~ cháchu.
a group making (fish) oil:: hemhémetheqw < mótheqw or metheqw.
bait s-th (fish-line, fish-hook, fish-trap):: má:lat < má:la ~ má:le.
barbecued fish head:: x̲ots'oyíqw.
catching a fish by hook, hooking s-th, gaffing a fish:: lhílhekw'et < lhíkw' ~ lhí:kw'.
coiled up méthelh rope for fishing (for sturgeon and spring salmon):: ts'tíxem.
cooked fish head:: sth'óqwes < sth'ó:qwi ~ sth'óqwi.
dip-netting, fishing with a scoop net, (harpooning fish at night [DM 12/4/64]):: q'íq'emó:s ~ q'éyq'emó:s < q'emós ~ q'emó:s.
dried fish:: schá:lhtel ~ stsá:lhtel < =chílh ~ chílh=.
dried fish backbone (with meat left on it):: sx̲éwe.
drift-netting, catching fish with one or two canoes drifting downstream with a net in deep water:: xíxemel ~ xíxemal.
edible gristle inside fish head (nose gristle):: sx̲épeqw (or sx̲ép'eqw? or sx̲ép'ekw'?).
eight fish:: teqatsíqw < tqá:tsa.
everybody put away (fishing gear, canoe and) paddles (for winter), put away each other's paddles [and canoes and gear] for winter:: xets'ṓ:westel < xits' ~ xets'.
fish air-bladder:: xixxweláwa.
fish (any kind), (salmon (any kind, not trout or sturgeon) [AC]):: sth'ó:qwi ~ sth'óqwi.
fish backbone (not dried), (backbone of any creature [Elders Group 7/27/75]):: x̲ekw'óles.
fish butchering knife:: kw'éts'tel < kw'íts'.
fish cheeks:: thipéle, possibly th'ipéle.
fish cut real thin for wind-drying but without cross cuts, dried fish cut differently than slhíts'es:: st'ál, st'ál.
fish-drying rack:: shxwch'á:yxwels < ts'íyxw ~ ts'éyxw ~ ch'íyxw.
fish drying rack (for wind-drying):: sí:.

fish (CONT'D)

fish eggs, salmon eggs, roe, (cooked salmon eggs [JL]):: qéléx̲.
fish gall-bladder, (animal and bird gall-bladder [AC], gall-bladder (of fish, frog, animal, human) [Elders Group 2/27/80]):: mésel.
fish (=heads):: =eqw ~ =(e)leqw ~ =íqw ~ =ó:qw.
fish head soup:: x̲ots'oyíqw slhóp < x̲ots'oyíqw.
fish heart:: mélqw.
fishing basket, bait basket:: shxwmálahá:lá < má:la ~ má:le.
fishing by a line, line-fishing, trout-fishing, fishing with a pole (for trout):: qw'iqw'emó:thel ~ qw'íqw'emó:thel < qw'emó:thel.
fishing line:: qw'emóthetel < qw'emó:thel.
fishing platform:: láxel.
fishing pole:: qw'óqw'iy.
fish ready for drying:: chachí:lhtel ~ chachíyelhtel < =chílh ~ chílh=.
fish scales:: sts'álts'.
fish slime, slime (of any kind, from fish, algae, etc.):: stíxem < tíxem.
fish-spreader for drying fish, cross-piece for drying fish, salmon stretcher:: t'á:ts'.
fish tail:: sx̲épxel (or sx̲ép'xel).
fish trap, weir:: sts'iyáq.
five fish:: lhq'atsesíqw < lheq'át ~ lhq'á:t.
flat rocks (bedrock) with holes at Hill's Bar where they used to make smótheqw (prepared fish oil) from sockeye heads:: Hemhémetheqw < mótheqw or metheqw.
flesh (human, non-human), meat (of dried fish, animal, or bird):: slhíqw.
float (for fishing net):: p'ekwtál < p'ékw.
four fish:: x̲ethíléqw < x̲e'ó:thel ~ x̲e'óthel.
(gaff) hook fisherman, a hooker:: thehímélh.
gills, also "boot" (boot-shaped organ attached to fish gill):: xá:y ~ xà:y.
gone soft and spoiled (of dried fish):: th'íth'eqel < sth'í:qel.
"grayling", probably mountain whitefish:: spó:ltsep.
hang fish (especially salmon) for drying:: chálhtel < =chílh ~ chílh=.
hanging lots of fish to dry:: chachí:lhtel ~ chachíyelhtel < =chílh ~ chílh=.
(have) big heads (of a bunch of fish for ex.):: thítheqw < thi ~ tha ~ the ~ thah ~ theh.
hide-away that a fish makes:: t'esítsmels < t'ás.
hook fish, catch fish (by hook), to gaff-hook fish:: lhekw'á:ls < lhíkw' ~ lhí:kw'.
(hung up in a fish net):: sx̲wíx̲weqw' < x̲wíqw'.
jumping (of fish):: mámeq'em < máq'em.
killer whale, blackfish:: q'ellhólemètsel.
little roundmouth suckerfish, probably longnose sucker:: skwímeth < kwí:m.
little suckerfish with big salmon-like mouth, prob. largescale sucker:: qw'á:ts.
long thin slices of fish removed to dry from slhíts'es (wind-driedsalmon):: slhíqwetsel < slhíqw.
mountain on Fraser River between first tunnel and Yale where rotten fish used to (always) pile up:: Lexwyó:qwem Smá:lt < yó:qw.
nine fish:: tuxwíqw < tú:xw.
not cooked enough (of fish), [undercooked]:: lálekw'em.
one's catch (fish, game, etc.):: sxélcha ~ sxélche < xélcha.
on the foot or leg, in the foot or leg, tail of fish, leg of other animate creatures:: =xel.
place on Fraser River between first tunnel and Yale where rotten fish used to (always) pile up:: Lexwyó:qwem < yó:qw.
place where one fishes by waiting with a dip-net, dip-net fishing place, place where one still-dips:: sthqálem < thqá:lem.
prepared fish oil (usually sockeye oil):: smótheqw < mótheqw or metheqw.

fish (CONT'D)

preserved fish, preserved meat, dried fish, dried meat (usually fish), smoked salmon, wind-dried salmon (old word), what is stored away, what is put away:: sq'éyle.
prong of spear, prong of fish spear:: qáthexw.
rotten fish:: yó:qw.
salmon weir, fish trap:: ch'iyáqtel < sts'iyáq.
set a net (by canoe), set one's net, fish with a net, (submerge a net):: míliyel < mí:l ~ míl.
seven fish:: th'okwsíqw ~ th'okwsesíqw < th'ó:kws.
sinker, (fish) weight:: xá:t.
skin of fish head without gristle:: t'áwleqw.
smokehouse, house for smoking fish:: kw'olexwáwtxw < kw'ó:lexw.
soaking dried fish:: lhálqi < lhél.
spear (any kind), spear (for fish or war), fish-spear, telescopic spear for sturgeon, harpoon, detachable harpoon points:: tá:lh.
spear fish by torchlight, to torchlight, to pit-lamp:: lex̲éywa ~ lex̲íwa.
spearing fish by torchlight:: hálx̲eywa ~ hálx̲iwa < lex̲éywa ~ lex̲íwa.
spearing fish, spearing (fish):: thá:q'els < théq'.
spear it (a fish), stab s-o/s-th with something sharp, pierce s-o/s-th, prick s-o (with a pin, for ex.), poke s-o (with a pin, etc.):: thq'ét < théq'.
steelhead fishing place on the Fraser River below Lhílhkw'elqs, at Hogg Slough:: Qéywex̲em < qí:wx̲ ~ qéywx̲ ~ qá:wx̲ ~ qáwx̲.
straddle s-th (log, fish, etc.):: x̲eqét < x̲éq.
sturgeon club, fish club (for salmon, sturgeon, etc.):: slá:meth.
sucker fish, especially big sucker or elephant sucker, probably largescale sucker:: q'óx̲el.
swimming (of fish), (swim (of a fish) [EB]):: xétem < xetàm ~ xtàm.
swim (of fish):: xetàm ~ xtàm.
three fish:: lhíxweqw < lhí:xw.
time to dry fish, first of July (at Yale), October (at Chehalis):: temchálhtel < =chílh ~ chílh=.
tiny fin above tail of fish, (perhaps spines above tail of some fish):: sx̲élhx̲elh < x̲élh.
toast it by a fire (of smoked fish):: kw'áset < kw'ás.
to catch (fish, game, birds):: chxélcha < xélcha.
to drift-net, to fish with drift-net:: lhós.
to fish:: tsth'óqwi < sth'ó:qwi ~ sth'óqwi.
to fish with a pole or rod, to fish by a line:: qw'emó:thel.
to jump (of fish):: máq'em.
to soak (fish, beans, dried fruit, only food, not of cedar roots), rehydrate dried food, soak dried fish:: lhélqi < lhél.
to spear fish:: thq'á:ls < théq'.
to split s-th open (like deer or fish):: tl'xáx̲et < tl'éx.
to toast by a fire (of smoke-cured fish, dried fish), get toasted by fire (of smoke-dried fish):: kw'ásem < kw'ás.
two fish:: iselíqw < isá:le ~ isále ~ isá:la.

fish-drying

group of canoes travelling upstream (moving to camp for fish-drying for ex.):: istéytiyel.

fish-duck

sawbill duck, fish-duck, common merganser (larger), American merganser:: x̲wó:qw'.

fisher

fisher, an animal close to a mink, animal like an otter:: shxwématsel ~ shxwémetsel.

fisher (CONT'D)

fisher (mink-like animal):: thswál.

fisherman

a fisherman, a man that goes out fishing:: sth'óth'eqwi < sth'ó:qwi ~ sth'óqwi.

fishhawk

osprey, fishhawk:: th'éxwth'exw < th'íxw ~ th'éxw.

fish-hook

small fish-hook (for trout, etc.), trolling hook:: kw'ōwiyékw ~ kw'ōyékw.

fishing line

fishing line:: qw'emóthetel < qw'emó:thel.

fishing pole

fishing pole:: qw'óqw'iy.

fish smokehouse:: chalhteláwtxw < =chílh ~ chílh=.

fish-spreader

fish-spreader for drying fish, cross-piece for drying fish, salmon stretcher:: t'á:ts'.

fist

punch s-o/s-th, hit s-o/s-th with fist:: th'í:qw'et.

fit

(be) tight-fitting (of clothes, can't be quite buttoned):: spex̲elís < páx̲, spepíx̲ < páx̲.
(have) fits, convulsions:: q'áq'etl'.

five :: lheq'á:tses ~ lheq'átses ~ lhq'á(:)tses < lheq'át ~ lhq'á:t.
five birds:: lhq'atssí:ws < lheq'át ~ lhq'á:t.
five canoes belonging to one person, five boats:: lhq'atsesṓwelh ~ lhq'atseséwelh < lheq'át ~ lhq'á:t.
five containers:: lhq'átseqel < lheq'át ~ lhq'á:t.
five dollars:: lhq'ó:tses < lheq'át ~ lhq'á:t.
five fish:: lhq'atsesíqw < lheq'át ~ lhq'á:t.
five garments:: lhq'atsesélwet < lheq'át ~ lhq'á:t.
five houses belonging to one person:: lhq'atsesáwtxw < lheq'át ~ lhq'á:t.
five kinds, five piles (perhaps a loose translation):: lhq'átsesmó:t < lheq'át ~ lhq'á:t.
five little ones, five young (animal or human):: lhq'atses'ó:llh < lheq'át ~ lhq'á:t.
five paddles, (by extension) five paddlers:: lhq'átsesṓwes < lheq'át ~ lhq'á:t.
five (pairs of) pants:: lhq'atseséyiws < lheq'át ~ lhq'á:t.
five people:: lhq'átsále < lheq'át ~ lhq'á:t.
five ropes, five threads, five sticks, five poles:: lhq'átssámets' < lheq'át ~ lhq'á:t.
five spherical objects, five fruit, five rocks, five balls (five fruit in a group (as they grow on a plant) [AD]):: lhq'atsesóls < lheq'át ~ lhq'á:t.
five times:: lhq'atses'álh < lheq'át ~ lhq'á:t.
five trees:: lhq'atsesálhp < lheq'át ~ lhq'á:t.
Friday, five o'clock:: Slhq'átses < lheq'át ~ lhq'á:t.

Five-Mile Creek

Five-Mile Creek:: Lohíts ~ Lahíts ~ Lahích ~ Slahích.
monument at Saddle Rock at Five Mile Creek:: Sólkweyem?? or Solkw'í:m??.
north and south sides of the mouth of Five-Mile Creek:: Lexwts'ístel < th'ís.

fix
be fixed, be fixed up properly:: sthethíy < thíy.
fix a fire, straighten the fire up, stoke the fire:: thiyéltsep < thíy.
fixing s-th, making s-th:: thá:yt < thíy.
fix oneself in bed:: tl'ó:thet < tl'ó:t.
fix oneself up:: thíythet < thíy.
made, fixed, repaired:: thíy.
make it for s-o, fix it for s-o:: thiyélhtset ~ thiyélhchet < thíy.
make s-th, fix s-th, do s-th:: thíyt < thíy.
making it for s-o, fixing it for s-o:: tháyelhtset < thíy.
repair s-th once discarded, make s-th better, fix s-th up, repair s-th:: p'ákw'et < p'ákw'.
to be attached, to be fixed or fastened, be put on:: stl'átl'el < tl'ál.

fizz
fizzing:: t'ayíts'em.

flabby
(have) flabby lips, (have) sloppy lips:: slhelp'ó:ythel < lhél.

flakes
have wide snowflakes:: lhálhq'etxel < lheq'át ~ lhq'á:t.

flame
fire, ((also) flame [EB, Elders Group]):: héyeqw < yéqw.
flame (noun):: sts'ó:ltsep < ts'á: ~ ch'á:.
go out (of fire, flame or lamp):: tl'ékw'el.
(have/get) a sudden flame:: xwótekwem < xwótkwem.
(to) flame, (have/get) a flame, to blaze:: xwótkwem.

flannelette
flannelette, velvet, woolly material, fluffy material, soft material:: pá:píth'a < pá:pa.

flashlight
any kind of light that one carries, torch (made from pitch), lantern, lamp, flashlight:: slá<u>x</u>et < lá<u>x</u>et.

flat
a fairly flat clearing on a mountain in Morris Valley where they used to play ts'its'eqweló:l or Indian badminton:: Ts'éqwela ~ Th'éqwela < ts'éqw ~ th'éqw.
(be) flat:: sp'íp'elh < p'ílh.
(be) flattened:: sp'ap'ílh < p'ílh.
flat smooth and bare rock, a [rock] bluff, a bluff (straight up):: <u>x</u>eq'át < <u>x</u>eq'.
flattening it:: p'íp'elhet < p'ílh.
flatten it:: p'ílhat < p'élh.
flatten s-th, flatten it:: p'ílhet < p'ílh.
(have a) flat head, (have cranial deformation by cradle-board):: sp'íp'elheqw < p'ílh.
(have a) flat nose:: sp'íp'elheqsel ~ sp'élhqsel < p'ílh.

flat (CONT'D)

level, flat:: léq'.
level ground, flat (of ground):: leq'éylep ~ leq'ílep < léq'.
village on a small flat a little above Vedder Crossing, on the north side of Chilliwack River:: Th'óth'emels < th'óméls.

flea

jumping flea:: t'ót'elhem.

fleecy

fleecy wave clouds that look like sheep:: x̲eylx̲elemós.

flesh

flesh (human, non-human), meat (of dried fish, animal, or bird):: slhíqw.

flexible

break (of a flexible object like a rope, string or breath), it broke:: t'éqw'.

flicker

red-shafted flicker (woodpecker), medium-sized woodpecker with red under the wing, (pileated woodpecker [AK] (but this is a large bird), small red-headed woodpecker [probably red-breasted sapsucker, possibly hairy woodpecker or downy woodpecker] [Elders Group 3/1/72}):: th'íq.

flint :: máxet.

jade (nephrite) (used for sharpening [chopping] stones), any agate (can be used as flint to strike a spark):: t'émq'ethel.

flip

flipping around (of fish), struggling (of anything alive trying to get free):: kwótl'thet < kwá:.
start to struggle, start to flip around to escape (fish esp.):: kwetl'éthet < kwá:.
turn s-th/s-o over, flip it over (of fish for ex.), turn it inside out:: chaléwt.

flirt

flirting with s-o:: sí:yá:met < siyám ~ (rare) siyá:m.

float

be floating:: p'ep'ákw ~ p'ap'ákw < p'ékw, sp'ep'ákw' < p'ékw.
fine ashes floating up from a fire:: tqwó:chep < tóqweltsep.
float (for fishing net):: p'ekwtál < p'ékw.
lots of floats:: p'íp'ekwtà:l < p'ékw.
roots of a tree when it floats downriver:: x̲eyímelets.
small float for nets (made from singed cedar):: qwōqwá:l ~ qweqwá:l.
to float, come up to the surface, rise to the surface, to surface:: p'ékw.

float line

float line, cork line:: qwōqwá:l ~ qweqwá:l.

flood

a flood:: wōqw'wṓqw' < wṓqw' ~ wéqw'.

floodwater) (CONT'D)

floodwater)

be big, be large, be high (of floodwater), rise (of floodwater):: híkw.
get big, rise (of floodwater):: híkwthet < híkw.

floor

drop oneself into a seat, throw oneself on the floor or ground in a tantrum, throw a tantrum:: kw'qweméthet < kw'óqw.
floor, floor mat, floor covering, linoleum, rug:: lhex̲éyléptel < lhá:x̲ ~ lháx̲.
floor (of longhouse or anywhere):: lhx̲éyléptel < lhá:x̲ ~ lháx̲.
floor mat, rug:: thélxetel < thél.
pick s-th up from the ground or floor:: xwpét.
platform (in house, etc.), bed platform, platform in bottom of canoe, flooring (the planks):: lálwes.
sloping floor, (tilted):: tewále.

flora

to rot, rotten (of fruit, animal, flora, fauna, food):: th'óqw'em ~ th'ó:qw'em.

flounder

halibut, flounder (prob. starry flounder):: p'éwiy ~ p'ṓwiy < p'ewíy ~ p'ōwíy.

flour

bread, flour:: seplíl ~ seplí:l.

flow :: kw'élh.

be flowing:: kw'ekw'élh < kw'élh.
overflowed:: p'í:ltem < p'í:l or p'él.
overflows:: p'eléts'tem < p'í:l or p'él.
rapids, fast water, clear water, flowing fast, going fast, swift (water):: lex̲wṓ:m ~ lex̲wṓm < x̲wém ~ xwém.

flower :: =oyes, sp'á:q'em < p'áq'em.

flower of the red-flowering currant:: qwelíyes.
flower of wild rose, hip or bud of wild rose, including: Nootka rose, probably also dwarf or woodland rose and swamp rose, possibly (from Hope east) prickly rose:: qá:lq.
just starting to flower, blooming, (flowering):: p'áp'eq'em < p'áq'em.
little flowers:: sp'eláp'q'em < p'áq'em.
Pacific dogwood flower, flowering dogwood flower:: qwítx̲.
"snake's flower", prob. same plant as "snakeberry", q.v.:: sp'áq'ems te álhqey < álhqey ~ álhqay.
to bloom, to flower:: p'áq'em.

fluff)

bloom or (plant) fuzz (spore, pollen, seed fluff) after it bursts:: spekw'ém < pékw' ~ péqw'.
break up s-th by crumpling, crush it up, rub it together fast (to soften or clean), rub it to soften it (of plants, etc.), fluff it (inner cedar bark to soften it):: yékw'et < yókw' ~ yóqw'.
fall off (of its own accord, of petals or seed fluff):: píxw.
fall off (of petals or seed fluff):: píxwem < píxw.
fine airborne seed(s) (not used of plum or apple seed(s) or the hard seeds -- sth'emíwél is used for those) (used for dandelion seeds, cottonwood seeds, etc., tail of a cat-tail reed, (plant fluff (possibly including tail of cat-tail rush) [Elders Group 2/27/80]):: spéxwqel ~ spéx̲wqel < píxw.

fluff) (CONT'D)

- flannelette, velvet, woolly material, fluffy material, soft material:: pá:píth'a < pá:pa.
- it burst (of spores or seed fluff):: pekw'ém < pékw' ~ péqw'.
- smoke puffing out, (puff out (dust, powder, plant spores, seed fluff, light snow, smoke), form puffs of dust):: pékw' ~ péqw'.
- to drop or blow plant fluff (like dandelions, fireweed, cottonwood, etc.), to blow (of dusty or flaky stuff like wood dust, dandruff, maybe seeds):: pípexwem < píxw.
- when plant fuzz blows:: pókw'em < pékw' ~ péqw'.
- woolly, fluffy:: pá:pa.

fluffy

- flannelette, velvet, woolly material, fluffy material, soft material:: pá:píth'a < pá:pa.
- woolly, fluffy:: pá:pa.

flute

- flute, wind instrument, blown musical instrument:: pepó:tem < pó:t.

flutter

- twitch, flutter (of one's eye, hand, skin, etc.):: lhawét'em < lhá:w.
- twitching (of one's eye, hand, skin, etc.), fluttering:: lhá:wt'em < lhá:w.

fly

- a fly:: x̲wiyáye < x̲wōx̲wáye ~ x̲wex̲wáye ~ x̲wōx̲wá:ye.
- a fly, blow-fly:: x̲wex̲wiyáye ~ x̲wix̲wiyáye < x̲wōx̲wáye ~ x̲wex̲wáye ~ x̲wōx̲wá:ye.
- a lot of flies, big blow-flies:: x̲wiyx̲wiyáye < x̲wōx̲wáye ~ x̲wex̲wáye ~ x̲wōx̲wá:ye.
- black flies:: x̲wōx̲wáye ~ x̲wex̲wáye ~ x̲wōx̲wá:ye.
- blowfly, big fly, (little fly (one of them) [Elders Group 2/19/75]):: x̲wōx̲wáye ~ x̲wex̲wáye ~ x̲wōx̲wá:ye.
- deer fly:: lhemélets'.
- dust (is flying):: pékw'em < pékw' ~ péqw'.
- flying:: lhólhekw' < lhó:kw' ~ lhókw'.
- gnat, probably includes non-biting midges, biting midges, and (biting) black flies:: pepx̲wíqsel < píxw.
- house-fly:: x̲wex̲wiyáye ~ x̲wix̲wiyáye < x̲wōx̲wáye ~ x̲wex̲wáye ~ x̲wōx̲wá:ye.
- let oneself fall, drop oneself down (by parachute, rope, etc., said of little birds trying to fly out of nest, little animals trying to get down and let themselves fall):: chólqthet < tsélq ~ chélq.
- salmonberry worm, (prob. larvae of moths or butterflies or two-winged flies):: xwexwíye.
- sand-fly, no-see-um fly, biting midge:: pxwíqs < píxw.
- the dust flew, it's dusty:: pekw'ém < pékw' ~ péqw'.
- to fly:: lhó:kw' ~ lhókw'.

flying squirrel:: sqépò:thèl < qep'.

- you get covered on the mouth (by a flying squirrel at night for ex.):: qep'ó:ythòm < qep'.

foam :: sp'óp'eqw'em < p'óqw'em, sp'óqw'em < p'óqw'em.

- foaming, bubbling, foamy:: p'óp'eqw'em < p'óqw'em.
- Indian ice-cream, whipped soapberry foam:: sx̲wṓsem ~ sx̲wṓ:sem ~ sx̲ṓ(:)sem.
- to foam:: p'óqw'em.

foamy

- foaming, bubbling, foamy:: p'óp'eqw'em < p'óqw'em.

focus

- it's you, you are the one. you (focus or emphasis):: léwe.

fog

fog appearing on the water, (fine snow [AK]):: qwelqwélxel < qwélxel.
fog, mist:: sqwétxem < qwétxem.
get fog on the water, (get steam (of the ground) [DC]):: qwélxel.
getting foggy:: qwétxem.
(maybe) fine mist of fog or rain, ((perhaps) getting foggy [EB]):: qweqweqwtí:mxel < qwétxem.

fold

folding lots of things, fold s-th several times or many times:: lemlémet < lémet.
fold s-th (once):: lémet.

Foley Creek

Ford Creek, (=Foley Creek?):: Ets'íts'a or Eth'íth'a or Ets'íth'a.
Ford Lake (sic Foley Lake), Ford Creek (sic Foley Creek) on north side of Chilliwack River below Post Creek:: Lasisélhp?.

Foley Lake)

Ford Lake (sic Foley Lake), Ford Creek (sic Foley Creek) on north side of Chilliwack River below Post Creek:: Lasisélhp?.

follow

follow after, coming behind (the one ahead knows):: chokwelélqem < chó:kw.
follow behind s-o, trail s-o:: chokwí:lt < chó:kw.
follow, follow along after (the one ahead knows):: chó:lqem < chá:l or chó:l.
following s-o:: chokwú:lt < chó:kw.
following tracks:: tátelxel < tá:lxel.
follow s-o:: sq'exí:lmet < q'ó.
follow s-th/s-o (on foot, in a car, or on a horse, for ex.), follow behind s-o:: chó:lt < chá:l or chó:l.
follow tracks:: tá:lxel.
go following s-o:: chochí:lt < chá:l or chó:l.
little partner, little person who follows or goes with one:: sq'iq'exí:l ~ q'iq'exí:l < q'ó.
lots following:: chelchó:lqem < chá:l or chó:l.
to sing along or follow in singing a spirit song:: t'à:m.
tracking, following prints:: kw'ókw'etsxel < kw'áts ~ kw'éts.

Fomes

Fomes sp. including Fomes applanatus and probably others, possibly Polyporus sp., possibly Ganoderma sp., prob. also jelly fungi of Tremella and maybe Auricularia and Dacrymyces species, especially Tremella mesenterica (Yellow trembler) which is abundant only on the red alder and is reddish-orange matching the color, translucence and shape of those eaten by some of the Stó:lō elders, the jelly fungi could possibly have a differnet name from the bracket fungus:: s'ómó:qwes.
Fomes spp.:: s'ómó:qwes.

Fomes applanatus

Fomes sp. including Fomes applanatus and probably others, possibly Polyporus sp., possibly Ganoderma sp., prob. also jelly fungi of Tremella and maybe Auricularia and Dacrymyces species, especially Tremella mesenterica (Yellow trembler) which is abundant only on the red alder and is reddish-orange matching the color, translucence and shape of those eaten by some

Fomes applanatus (CONT'D)

of the Stó:lō elders, the jelly fungi could possibly have a different name from the bracket fungus:: s'ómó:qwes.

fontanel

soft spot on (top of) a baby's head, fontanel:: sqe'éleqw < qí: ~ qí'.

food :: s'álhtel < álhtel.

barbecued food, (salmon bake [Deming]):: sqw'él:ém < qw'él.

beat s-o out of food:: (xwéweslexw).

blue camas, (any edible underground vegetable food [SP], vegetable root(s) [MH]):: spá:lxw.

cedar trough (to serve food):: x̲epyúwelh < sx̲éyp.

choke on food, get choked on food:: t'kwíles ~ t'ekwíles < t'ékw.

clothing, food, and possessions burned and given away when a person dies, (possessions and food burned and given away at a burning):: syeqwá:ls < yéqw.

cooking, (cooking) food:: skwúkw < kwúkw.

cooling it (of food):: títemí:lt < temí:lt.

cooling off (of food):: titemí:lthet < temí:lt.

cool it (of food):: temí:lt.

cool off (of food):: temí:lthet < temí:lt.

feast left-overs, left-overs of food (which guests can take home):: sméq'eth < méq'.

finish it (of food):: ú:kw't < ṓwkw'.

(food) given:: áxwe ~ s'áxwe < áxw, s'áxwem < áxw.

(food) provisions for a trip, box lunch:: sáwel.

food settled (in the stomach), food is settled (in the stomach), (be settled (of food in the stomach), be comfortably digested (of food)):: qsákw'.

get carried away and sleepy from eating too rich food:: ló:metsel < ló:m ~ lóm, melmelṓws < mál ~ mél.

getting choked on food:: t'ékweles < t'ékw.

give an equal share or amount to s-o, give (food?) to s-o, share with s-o:: áxwest < áxw.

give s-o food:: áxwet < áxw.

give s-o food, bring s-o food, pass food to s-o:: áxwet, áxwet, áxwet.

giving (food):: á:xwem < áxw.

have a ritual burning ceremony, have a burning, feed the dead, (food offered to the dead [at a ritual burning] [EB 5/25/76]):: yeqwá:ls < yéqw.

help oneself to food, serve oneself, serve oneself food (with a ladle), serve oneself a meal (food), (put on a dish [CT, HT]):: lhá:x̲em ~ lháx̲em < lhá:x̲ ~ lháx̲.

leftover food, scraps:: sq'éylòm < q'éylòm.

manage by oneself (in food or travel), try to do it by oneself, try to be independent, do the best one can:: iyólewéthet < éy ~ éy:.

pick food by one's fingers (before a meal):: lhámth't < lhím.

picking food by the fingers before the meal:: lhémth' < lhím.

ran out (of food, money, etc.), have no more, be finished (offood), (be empty (of container of supplies) [EB: Cheh., Tait]):: ṓwkw'.

run out of food, be out of food:: ú:kw'elets < ṓwkw'.

share food with s-o:: áxwet.

stingy of food, refuse (somebody something):: kw'íyà:m < kw'íy.

take left-over food:: méq'etsem < méq'.

take someone's food or clothes:: kwétxwt.

to abstain from food, to fast, starve oneself:: xwóthet < xwá.

to bake (bread, other food):: thíyém < thíy.

to rot, rotten (of fruit, animal, flora, fauna, food):: th'óqw'em ~ th'ó:qw'em.

food (CONT'D)
to soak (fish, beans, dried fruit, only food, not of cedar roots), rehydrate dried food, soak dried fish:: lhélqi < lhél.
warming up food:: t'álkw'els < t'álqw' or t'élqw'.
warm up (food, tea, etc.):: t'elkw'á:ls < t'álqw' or t'élqw'.
wish for someone's food:: xítem.
wishing for someone's food (esp. when in sight):: xíxetem < xítem.

fool
fooling s-o, (fool s-o as a joke, April-fool s-o [Deming]):: q'íq'elstá:xw < q'á:l.
fool s-o, deceive s-o, (lie to s-o [SJ]):: q'elstá:xw < q'á:l.

foot
all the joints of the foot and toes:: qwemqwémx̲wxel < qwó:m ~ qwóm ~ qwem.
arch of foot:: xwt'óxwesxel < t'óxw.
be lame, (be) sick on the foot, (have) a sick foot, (have) a hurt foot:: q'óq'eyxel < q'ó:y ~ q'óy.
(both human) legs, (both) feet:: sx̲ex̲éyle or sx̲ex̲íle < sx̲él:e.
burned on the foot:: kw'ésxel < kw'ás.
bushy hair on horses' legs (tufts like on Clydesdale breed), tufts of fur on horse's feet:: qwelqwélxel < qwíl ~ qwel.
chop one's foot (with axe), [get chopped on the foot (with axe)]:: t'émxel < t'ém.
cloth or warm material to wrap around the foot, stockings:: chóxwxel.
coming by foot, travelling by walking, already walking, travelling on foot:: ye'í:mex < i┐m.
cut one's foot:: lhéts'xel < lhíts' ~ lhí:ts'.
dragging one's feet:: xwixwekw'ósxelem ~ xwekw'ósxelem < xwókw' ~ xwekw'ó.
drag one's foot, to shuffle (the feet):: xwót'kw'emxel < xwót'kw'em.
footprint, tracks:: sx̲éyeltel ~ sx̲í:ltel < sx̲él:e.
get a shoe on the wrong foot:: sts'ó:kw'xel.
get a sliver or splinter in the foot:: xéts'xel.
(get a) sprained foot, leg got out of joint:: plhéqw'xel ~ p'lhéqw'xel.
got (both) shoes on wrong feet:: sts'ókw'elxel < sts'ó:kw'xel.
(have a) bare foot:: semáxel < má ~ má'-.
(have a) real big foot, (have a) huge foot:: thí:thaxel < thi ~ tha ~ the ~ thah ~ theh.
(have) big feet:: thíthexel < thi ~ tha ~ the ~ thah ~ theh.
(have) dirty feet:: ts'épx̲el < ts'épx̲.
have wide feet:: lhálhq'etxel < lheq'át ~ lhq'á:t.
hit on the leg, [hit on the foot]:: kw'éqwxel < kw'óqw.
leg, foot:: sx̲él:e.
make a crunch underfoot (bones, nut, glass, etc.):: x̲ep'ékw'.
mat, (foot mat):: ṓkw'xatel.
numb in the foot, the foot is asleep:: xwókw'elxel < xwókw'.
on the foot or leg, in the foot or leg, tail of fish, leg of other animate creatures:: =xel.
(probably) tickle the bottom of someone's feet, (tickle s-o on the foot):: sét'xt < síyt'.
slip off (one's feet, hands, bottom), lose balance:: x̲wlhép.
slip off with a foot, lose balance [on feet]:: x̲wlhépxel < x̲wlhép.
slipping off with a foot:: x̲wélhepxel < x̲wlhép.
slip with both feet, lose balance on both feet:: x̲welhx̲wélhepxel < x̲wlhép.
small balls of snow on one's feet:: qwelqwélxel < qwélxel.
sole (of the foot), (instep [AC, DM]):: shxw'óthesxel ~ shxwe'óthesxel < s'ó:thes ~ s'óthes.

foot (CONT'D)

something to tie the feet:: q'ép'xetel (unless q'épxetel is correct) < q'áp'.
suction sound of feet pulling out of mud:: t'áxwqem.
to make a sign with its foot it wants a younger brother or younger sister:: oqw'exélem < óqw'.
top of the foot:: tslhítselxel < =chílh ~ chílh=.
wash one's feet:: th'èx̲wxél:ém < th'éx̲w or th'óx̲w.

footprint

footprint, tracks:: sx̲éyeltel ~ sx̲í:ltel < sx̲él:e.
tracking, following prints:: kw'ókw'etsxel < kw'áts ~ kw'éts.

for

benefactive, do for s-o, malefactive, do on s-o:: -lhts.
burn it for s-o:: yéqwelht < yéqw.
(cast a spell for s-o, use a magical power for s-o):: yewí:lmet < yéw: ~ yéw.
cried for s-th, (be crying for s-th/s-o):: x̲ahá:met < x̲à:m ~ x̲á:m.
cry for s-o/s-th:: x̲á:met < x̲à:m ~ x̲á:m.
fry it for s-o:: ts'ékwx̲elhtst < ts'ékwx̲t.
make a fire for s-o:: yéqwelchept < yéqw.
make it for s-o, fix it for s-o:: thiyélhtset ~ thiyélhchet < thíy.
making it for s-o, fixing it for s-o:: tháyelhtset < thíy.
pluck it for me:: qw'emōwselhtsthó:x < qw'ém.
sing it for s-o:: t'ílemelhtst < t'íl.
toward, towards, for:: xwelá ~ xwelám ~ xwlá ~ xwlám < la.
write for s-o:: (x̲é:yllhts(e)t) < x̲él ~ x̲é:yl ~ x̲í:l

Ford Creek

Ford Creek, (=Foley Creek?):: Ets'íts'a or Eth'íth'a or Ets'íth'a.

Ford Creek (sic Foley Creek)

Ford Lake (sic Foley Lake), Ford Creek (sic Foley Creek) on north side of Chilliwack River below Post Creek:: Lasisélhp?.

Ford Lake (sic Foley Lake)

Ford Lake (sic Foley Lake), Ford Creek (sic Foley Creek) on north side of Chilliwack River below Post Creek:: Lasisélhp?.

forehead :: sqw'éméls.

fall on one's forehead, drop on one's forehead, fall onto one's head:: méleqw (or) leméleqw.
(have a) wide forehead:: lheq'tò:ls < lheq'át ~ lhq'á:t.

forest

fire (out of control), forest fire burning, fire burning:: yíyeqw < yéqw.
trees, thicket, timber, woods, forest:: theqthéqet < theqát ~ thqá:t.

forever :: kw'ō wiyóth(cha) ò ~ kw'ō hélémcha ò < wiyóth.

forget :: malqelómet < mál ~ mél.

(be) absent-minded, forgetful:: q'thá:mtem < q'thá:m.
forget s-th, forget s-o, forget s-th behind:: málqlexw ~ málqelexw < mál ~ mél.

forget (CONT'D)

forgetting (s-th/s-o):: mámelqlexw < mál ~ mél.
forgot s-th, have forgotten s-th, forgot s-o/s-th in one's mind:: málqeles < mál ~ mél.

forgetful :: lexwmálqewelh < mál ~ mél, shxwmelmálq < mál ~ mél.
forgetful, mixed up (mentally, emotionally):: melmelqwìwèl < mál ~ mél.

for goodness sakes.:: eyeléwthelh < éy ~ éy:.

for granted
take s-o for granted:: tl'exwló:st.

fork :: sts'ó:qw'els < ts'éqw'.
a fork in a creek:: st'éx̲ < t'éx̲.
a fork in a road (or trail):: st'éx̲ < t'éx̲.
a fork in a tree:: st'éx̲ < t'éx̲.
fork in a tree?:: st'ex̲láts < t'éx̲.
fork in tree, fork in tree roots:: st'it'x̲óyaq < t'éx̲.
forks in stream:: t'x̲éthet < t'éx̲.
place where Yale Creek divides (forks) above the highway bridge over the creek:: T'ít'x̲elhchò:m < t'éx̲.
poke it, pin s-th, pick it up (on sharp pointed object), pick s-th up on a fork (or other sharp object):: ts'qw'ét < ts'éqw'.
west fork of stream which goes into Chehalis River above Páléxel:: Th'ámxwelqs.

Formicidae
order Hymenoptera, family Formicidae:: xá:ysem.

fortune-teller)
bluejay, Steller's jay (sacred fortune-teller):: x̲ax̲esyúwes or x̲ax̲e syúwes < x̲áx̲e.
fortune-teller, seer, person who can see things in the future, female witch:: syéw:e ~ syéwe ~ syő:we ~ syú:we < yéw: ~ yéw.
seer, fortune-teller, person that senses the future:: síwe ~ syéwe < síw.

Fort Victoria
Victoria, B.C., city of Victoria area, Fort Victoria:: Sth'ó:mes.

forty
forty:: x̲ethelsxá < x̲e'ó:thel ~ x̲e'óthel.
forty days:: x̲ethelsxó:s < x̲e'ó:thel ~ x̲e'óthel.
forty dollars:: x̲ethelsxó:s < x̲e'ó:thel ~ x̲e'óthel.
forty people:: x̲ethelsxále < x̲e'ó:thel ~ x̲e'óthel.

Fort Yale
Yale, Fort Yale:: Puchí:l.

found
(be) found:: smőkw' or semőkw' < mékw' ~ mőkw'.

foundation
foundation of a house, bottom of a tree:: s'alétsmel < s'aléts.

found out

(be) found out (something you were trying to hide), to be discovered (something secret):: wá:y.

four :: x̱e'ó:thel ~ x̱e'óthel.

forty:: x̱ethelsxá < x̱e'ó:thel ~ x̱e'óthel.
four birds:: x̱ethílews < x̱e'ó:thel ~ x̱e'óthel.
four canoes, four boats:: x̱e'othelṓwelh < x̱e'ó:thel ~ x̱e'óthel, x̱e'othelṓwelh < x̱e'ó:thel ~ x̱e'óthel.
four containers:: x̱ethíleqel < x̱e'ó:thel ~ x̱e'óthel.
four days of northeast wind:: unknown.
four dollars, ((also) four blankets [Boas]):: x̱ethíles < x̱e'ó:thel ~ x̱e'óthel.
four fish:: x̱ethíléqw < x̱e'ó:thel ~ x̱e'óthel.
four fruit in a group or cluster (as they grow on a plant):: x̱(e)'othelòls < x̱e'ó:thel ~ x̱e'óthel.
four kinds, (four piles [Elders Group 7/27/75]):: x̱e'óthelmó:t ~ x̱e'óthelmò:t < x̱e'ó:thel ~ x̱e'óthel.
four paddles, four paddlers:: x̱ethlá:wes < x̱e'ó:thel ~ x̱e'óthel.
four pants:: x̱e'otheláyiws < x̱e'ó:thel ~ x̱e'óthel.
four people:: x̱ethí:le ~ x̱ethíle < x̱e'ó:thel ~ x̱e'óthel.
four ropes, four threads, four sticks, four poles, (four long thin objects):: x̱ethílemets' < x̱e'ó:thel ~ x̱e'óthel.
four times:: x̱ethelálh < x̱e'ó:thel ~ x̱e'óthel.
four to each:: x̱ex̱e'ó:thel < x̱e'ó:thel ~ x̱e'óthel.
four trees:: x̱ethí:lhp or x̱ethíyelhp < x̱e'ó:thel ~ x̱e'óthel.
Thursday, four o'clock, (fourth cyclic period):: sx̱e'óthels < x̱e'ó:thel ~ x̱e'óthel.

Four-and-a-half Mile Creek)

bay at upper end of Yale Indian Reserve #2 (Four-and-a-half Mile Creek) (near the northern end of Stó:lō territory):: Sqemqémelets < qám.

fourth

fourth day after a death (when everyone washes up (bathes)):: sxókw' < xókw' ~ xó:kw'.
little finger, fourth finger:: soseqwtóletses < sóseqwt ~ (rarely) só:seqwt.
Thursday, four o'clock, (fourth cyclic period):: sx̱e'óthels < x̱e'ó:thel ~ x̱e'óthel.

fowl

big bird, (large bird (of any kind)), any waterfowl:: x̱wí:leqw ~ x̱wé:yleqw ~ x̱wéyleqw.
larger bird (any kind, generic), waterfowl, duck, (mallard [Cheh. dial.]):: mó:qw.

fox :: sx̱wewál.

Fragaria vesca

Fragaria vesca, Fragaria virginiana:: schí:ya.

Fragaria virginiana

Fragaria vesca, Fragaria virginiana:: schí:ya.

fragrance

fragrance, smell, odor:: =áléqep ~ =áleqep.
have a fragrance, have a good smell, smell good:: eyáléqep ~ iyáléqep < éy ~ éy:.
smell bad, (have a) bad fragrance, (have a) bad smell:: qéleqep < qél.

frame

a waiting dip-net with frame and string trap:: thqálem < thqá:lem.

frame (CONT'D)

circular frame (for tanning hides):: st'elákw' siyólh < yólh.
frame for stretching hides, frame (for drying hides, etc.), frame for a drum:: tpélhtel ~ tepélhtel < tpólh.

Franklin

one of the two rocks of Lady Franklin Rock:: X̱éylx̱el(e)mòs.

Fraser River

a hunter turned to stone now located below Hemhémetheqw near Hill's Bar on the east bank of the Fraser River:: Tewít < tewít.
a little bay in the Fraser River a quarter mile east of Iwówes (Union Bar, Aywawwis):: Qíqemqèmèl < qém:el.
another rough place in the Fraser River (Tait area):: Sq'ólep'ex̱w < Sq'íp'ex̱w.
a place across the Fraser River from the rock named Q'alelíktel:: Xwth'ístel < th'ís.
a real rough place in the Fraser River impassible in a canoe (in the Tait area, prob. between Spuzzum and Yale):: Sq'íp'ex̱w.
a stretch of water in the Fraser River on the C.N. side by Strawberry Island:: Kwetl'kwótl'thetōws < kwá:.
a turn in the Fraser River between Ruby Creek and Katz (about a mile upriver from the mouth of Ruby Creek and Ruby Creek I.R. #9 (called Lukseetsis-sum on maps and D.I.A. records, see Lexwthíthesem)), also the name of a village at this spot, spelled Skawahlook, Indian Reserve #1, on topographical maps and D.I.A. records:: Sq'ewá:lxw < q'éw ~ q'ew.
a turn in the Fraser River on the CPR (northwest) side two miles east of American Bar, Texas Bar bend in the Fraser River:: Sq'ewílem < q'éw ~ q'ew.
elk (or) moose turned to stone in the Fraser River by Hill's Bar:: Q'oyíyets ~ Q'oyí:ts < q'oyíyets or q'oyí:ts.
former village directly across the Fraser River from Yale:: X̱elhlálh ~ X̱elhálh < x̱élh.
Fraser River, (Chehalis Creek, Chehalis River [Elders Group, EL/EB/NP]):: Stó:lō < tó:l ~ tò:l.
Fraser River (way out at the end), mouth of the Fraser River:: Chuchuwálets < cháchew ~ cháchu.
Hill's Bar (between Yale and Hope), Fraser River where it goes over Hill's Bar on the CN (east) side:: Qw'áléts.
large whirlpool in the Fraser River just above Hill's Bar and near the west (CPR) side:: Hémq'eleq < méq'.
medicine spring on the Fraser River beach about a half mile above (north) of the American Bar beach:: Xwth'kw'ém < th'ekw' or th'íkw'.
mountain on Fraser River between first tunnel and Yale where rotten fish used to (always) pile up:: Lexwyó:qwem Smá:lt < yó:qw.
mountain shaped like a thunderbird across the Fraser River from Q'ów (the "howl") mountain:: Xwexwó:stel < shxwexwó:s.
place above Yale where the Fraser River splits around a rock, island above Steamboat Island (latter just below Five-Mile Creek):: Sx̱wesálh < x̱wés.
place in Fraser River two miles above American Bar with narrow rock:: X̱eq'átelets < x̱eq'.
place in Fraser River where there's an underwater spring of cold water:: Mimexwílem < mímexwel.
place on Fraser River between first tunnel and Yale where rotten fish used to (always) pile up:: Lexwyó:qwem < yó:qw.
place on the Fraser River above Yale where there are whirlpools:: Q'eyq'éyex̱em < q'ey ~ q'i.
rock in the Fraser River near Scowlitz where a woman was crying a lot:: X̱ex̱ám Smá:lt < x̱à:m ~ x̱á:m.

Fraser River (CONT'D)

small shoreline ridge on the Fraser River and all along the river around the larger mountain across the Trans-Canada Highway from Jones Hill:: Sqayéx̲iya Smált ~ Sqáqeyex̲iya Smált < sqáyéx̲ ~ sqayéx̲.

steelhead fishing place on the Fraser River below Lhílhkw'elqs, at Hogg Slough:: Qéywex̲em < qí:wx̲ ~ qéywx̲ ~ qá:wx̲ ~ qáwx̲.

Stó:lō people, Halkomelem-speaking people living along the Fraser River or its tributaries from Five Mile Creek above Yale downriver to the mouth of the Fraser:: Stó:lō < tó:l ~ tò:l.

the whole riverbank on the CPR (west) side of the Fraser River just south of Strawberry Island and just north of Peqwchő:lthel:: Selch'éle < sél or sí(:)l.

unnamed mountain on the northwest side of the Fraser River between Hope and Yale which has white mineral deposits visible from the river:: Lexwp'ép'eq'es < p'éq'.

village at American Bar, village on west bank of Fraser River at American Creek, American Bar Reserve:: Peqwchő:lthel ~ Peqwechő:lthel < péqw.

village just below (on the south side of) Suka Creek, on the CN side (east side) of the Fraser River across from Dogwood Valley:: Skwíyò.

village on north bank of the Fraser River above Agassiz Mountain:: Tsítsqem.

frayed

frayed (of a rope):: wíwexem.

freckle

(have a) speckled face, (have) freckles:: tl'eltl'élx̲os < tl'él.

free)

flipping around (of fish), struggling (of anything alive trying to get free):: kwótl'thet < kwá:.

let go of s-th/s-o, drop s-th, set s-o free, turn s-o/s-th loose:: kwá:t ~ kwát < kwá:.

freeze

be frozen:: spípew < pí:w.

freezer:: shxwpípewels < pí:w.

freeze s-th/s-o:: píwet < pí:w.

freezing, freezing cold:: pípewels < pí:w.

to freeze:: pewá:ls < pí:w.

tree bent to ground with ice and frozen:: sx̲wíqel.

French

Frenchman, French person:: pálchmel.

French fries:: slós qwóls sqá:wth < lós, qwóls, qá:wth
(lit. fat + boiled + potato)

Frenchman

Frenchman, French person:: pálchmel.

fresh :: x̲á:ws.

be fresh (of water), be tasteless:: th'áwém ~ th'áwem.

fresh-water

clam, butter clam, fresh-water clam, fresh-water mussel:: s'óx̲we.

Friday

Friday, five o'clock:: Slhq'átses < lheq'át ~ lhq'á:t.

friend :: siyá:ya ~ siyáya ~ syá:ya ~ siyá(:)ye < yá:ya, siyá:ye ~ siyáye.

dear friends:: q'e'ó:leq < q'ó.

friends:: sí:yá:ya < yá:ya, ts'xwélmexw ~ ts'xwílmexw < xwélmexw.

lots of friends:: sí:yá:ye < siyá:ye ~ siyáye.

ma'am, female friend, chum (female), little girl:: iyés < éy ~ éy:.

my dear, (little best friend, little dear friend, etc.):: q'éyq'eleq ~ (better) q'íq'eleq < q'ó.

pair of twins, pair of closest friends:: sq'eq'e'óleq < q'ó.

pal, best friend, dear friend, chum:: q'óleq ~ q'e'óléq < q'ó.

sir, male friend, chum (male), sonny:: iyéseq < éy ~ éy:.

sweetheart, person of the opposite sex that one is running around with, girl-friend, boy-friend:: ts'elh'á:y < ts'elh=.

they're making friends, (making friends with each other):: yóyatel < yá:ya.

they've made friends, (make friends with each other):: yáyetel (prob. also yáyatel) < yá:ya.

fries

French fries:: slós qwóls sqá:wth < lós, qwóls, qá:wth (lit. fat + boiled + potato)

frighten

frightened s-o [accidentally], [happened/managed to] frighten s-o:: th'ith'íkw'elexw < th'íkw' or th'ekw'.

get frightened:: th'eth'íkw'thet < th'íkw' or th'ekw'.

Fritillaria camschatcensis:: =oyes.

similar to Fritillaria lanceolata but different, probably Fritillaria camschatcensis:: péth'oyes.

Fritillaria lanceolata:: stl'éleqw'.

similar to Fritillaria lanceolata but different, probably Fritillaria camschatcensis:: péth'oyes.

frog

a kind of frog:: weq'iyethílem.

baby frog, probably also tadpole:: pipehó:mó:llh < peh or pó(:)h.

big frog (even bigger than pípehò:m and cries like a baby), (probably bullfrog, possibly green frog):: wex̲ó:mő:lh.

big pretty frog, bullfrog with colors on his back:: pehó:mő:lh < peh or pó(:)h, pehó:mő:lh < peh or pó(:)h.

frog, (esp. Northwestern toad, if generic also includes the tree toad and recent introductions the bullfrog and green frog, and the tailed toad, red-legged frog, and western spotted frog), (if generic may also include water frog that lives in springs and keeps the water cold [Halq'eméylem name unknown to Elders Group on 1/30/80], and a huge pretty frog (bigger than pípehò:m) that has supernatural powers and cries like a baby [sx̲ex̲ómőlh ~ wex̲ó:mő:lh]), (big frog with warts [AD]):: pípehò:m < peh or pó(:)h.

frog, (if generic may include Pacific tree toad and perhaps the introduced species: bullfrog, green frog, red-legged frog, western spotted frog, and the tailed toad):: wex̲és, weléx̲ < wex̲és.

frogs:: pepípehò:m < peh or pó(:)h.

(get) a disease gotten by contacting a frog, a skin eruption, also the same disease as the frog (CONT'D)

man got in Kawkawa Lake in the Sx̲wó:yx̲wey story, (perhaps also) leprosy:: qw'ő:m.
huge pretty frog with supernatural powers:: sx̲ex̲ómőlh.
little green frog, little green tree frog, (Pacific tree toad):: welék'.
the sound a frog makes (IHTTC only):: wex̲és.

"frog leaf"
common plantain, ribbed plantain, called "frog leaf":: pipehomá:lews < peh or pó(:)h.

from :: tel=, tel=.
be from:: telí < tel=.
be from where?:: tel'alétse ~ tel:étse < tel=.
downriver, (from downriver):: tellhó:s < lhós.
from away from the river:: telchó:leqwtel < chá:l or chó:l.
from far away:: telchókw < chó:kw.
from upriver:: teltíyt < tiyt.
go out from the beach (if in a canoe):: tó:l ~ tò:l.
where is he/she/it from?, from where?:: tel'alétsa < alétsa.
where it's at, where it's from:: shxwlí < lí ~ li.
where s-o came from:: shxwtelí < tel=.

front :: átheqel.
front end of a house (inside or outside):: chuchuwáx̲el < cháchew ~ cháchu.
front, in front of:: axelés.
front leg:: t'á:lew ~ t'álew.
front of a house:: axelésmel < axelés.
[left] front leg quarter of deer or other animal:: sth'ikweláx̲el < th'íkwe.
on the front of the neck, in the windpipe, in the trachea:: =lhelh ~ =lhál.
undress in front of someone, strip-tease:: lhuwth'ím < lhewíth'a.

front of the neck:: shxw'állhelh.

frost
fine needles of hoarfrost on a branch:: pú:ches ~ púwches, pú:ches ~ púwches < pí:w.
frost, get frosty:: x̲éx̲el.

fruit :: =ó:ls, =ó:ls.
berry, berries, (fruit [AC, AD]):: sth'í:m ~ sth'i:m.
eight fruit in a group [or cluster] (as they grow on a plant):: tqòtsòls < tqá:tsa.
five spherical objects, five fruit, five rocks, five balls (five fruit in a group (as they grow on a plant) [AD]):: lhq'atsesóls < lheq'át ~ lhq'á:t, lhq'atsesóls < lheq'át ~ lhq'á:t.
four fruit in a group or cluster (as they grow on a plant):: x̲(e)'othelòls < x̲e'ó:thel ~ x̲e'óthel.
fruit juice:: sqe'éleqw < qó:.
heart of a root, seed, nut (kernel), core of plant or seedling, core (of tree, branch, any growing thing), pith (of bush), seed or pit [U.S.] or pip [Cdn.] of a fruit:: sth'emí:wel ~ sth'emíwel ~ sth'emíwél < sth'ó:m.
Indian plum (the fruit), (also called) June plum:: mélhx̲wel.
inside or core of a plant or fruit (or canoe or anything):: =í:wel ~ =íwel ~ =ewel.
juicy fruit:: sqe'ó:ls < qó:.
nine fruit in a group or cluster (as they grow on a plant):: tuxwòls < tú:xw.
one fruit (as it grows singly on a plant):: lets'òls ~ léts'òls < léts'a ~ léts'e.
orange (fruit), especially mandarin orange (the fruit), also domestic orange, (also orange

fruit (CONT'D)

(color)):: qwiqwóyáls ~ qwiqwóyéls ~ qwiqwòyàls < qwá:y.
peel s-th (esp. fruit or vegetable root or a vegetable like squash or a round object):: xepólst < xíp.
pick berries, pick off (leaves, fruit, vegetables, hops), (pluck off, harvest):: lhím.
plane it (with a plane), trim it, taper it (about wood, like slats or roots for baskets, poles for houseposts/totem poles, paddles), taper it (with knife or plane), peel it (a fruit, etc.), whittle it, strip or peel bark off of it, scrape it (of carrots), (carve it, peel it [AC]):: xípet < xíp.
seven fruit in a group or cluster (as they grow on a plant):: th'ekwòls < th'ó:kws.
shake s-th (tree or bush) for fruit or leaves, comb a bush (for berries), shake s-th (a mat or blanket for ex.):: xwíset ~ xwítset < xwís.
six fruit in a group (as they grow on a plant):: t'x̲emòls < t'éx̲.
something big (and round) (for ex. big fruit, big rocks, etc.):: thíthes < thi ~ tha ~ the ~ thah ~ theh.
sour (unripe or half-ripe fruit, lemon, Oregon grape, fermenting fruit):: t'át'eth'em < t'áth'.
ten fruit in a group (as they grow on a plant), (ten attached fruit):: opelòls < ó:pel, opelòls < ó:pel.
three fruit in a cluster (as they grow on a plant):: lhexwòls < lhí:xw.
to rot, rotten (of fruit, animal, flora, fauna, food):: th'óqw'em ~ th'ó:qw'em.
two fruit in a group (as they grow on a plant):: isòls ? < isá:le ~ isále ~ isá:la.

fry

(already) fried:: sts'ákwx̲ ~ sch'ákwx̲ < ts'ékwx̲t.
(be) frying s-th:: ts'ákwx̲t < ts'ékwx̲t.
frying:: ts'ákwx̲els < ts'ékwx̲t.
frying pan:: ts'ákwx̲els < ts'ékwx̲t.
fry it for s-o:: ts'ékwx̲elhtst < ts'ékwx̲t.
fry s-th:: ts'ékwx̲t.
to fry (as a structured activity):: ts'ekwx̲á:ls ~ ts'ekwx̲áls < ts'ékwx̲t.

frying pan

frying pan:: ts'ákwx̲els < ts'ékwx̲t.

fuck

have intercourse, fuck:: kw'átl'.
have intercourse with s-o, fuck s-o:: kw'átl'et < kw'átl'.

full

(be) full (from eating), (get filled (from eating) [AC]):: méq'.
round, full (of the moon):: xelókw' ~ xeló:kw' < xél.

fun

be fun, have (lots of) fun, have amusement, having lots of fun, be pleasant:: íyes ~ éyes < éy ~ éy:.
having fun:: í:yó:sem < éy ~ éy:.
having fun at a non-spiritual dance:: oyewílem.
having lots of fun, it's a lot of fun:: í'eyó:stem < éy ~ éy:.
he was fun, he was enjoyed, they enjoyed him:: eyéstem < éy ~ éy:.
making fun of s-o, (ridiculing s-o):: lhílhàth't < lhílhàth'.
making fun, (ridiculing):: lhílhàth'.

funeral
    have a funeral:: qéylemà:ls < qéylem ~ qé:ylem ~ qí(:)lem.

fungus
    bracket fungus:: s'ómó:qwes.
    bracket fungus, (possibly also some jelly fungi like yellow trembler):: s'ómó:qwes.
    (perhaps) red rock fungus used for Indian paint, (perhaps) Indian paint fungus:: témélh.

funny
    (be) scowling (if mad or ate something sour), ((made a) funny (strange) face [Elders Group 1/21/76]):: sx̲éyx̲ewes < x̲éywel.
    find it funny:: í'istexw < éy ~ éy:.

fur
    bushy hair on horses' legs (tufts like on Clydesdale breed), tufts of fur on horse's feet:: qwelqwélxel < qwíl ~ qwel.
    furry on the whole body (of an animal):: siysá:yiws < sá:y.
    have reddish-brown fur, have reddish-brown animal hair:: tskwímelqel < kwí:m.
    wool, fur:: =á:y ~ =ey ~ =iy.
    wool, fur, animal hair:: sá:y.

future
    a sung spell, power to help or harm people or to do [ritual] burning, power to do witchcraft and predict the future, an evil spell, (magic spell) (someone who has power to take things out of a person or put things in [by magic] [Elders Group 2/25/76], ritualist [Elders Group 1/21/76], witch [EB 4/25/78]):: syiwí:l ~ syewí:l < yéw: ~ yéw.
    fortune-teller, seer, person who can see things in the future, female witch:: syéw:e ~ syéwe ~ syő:we ~ syú:we < yéw: ~ yéw.
    go, go to, going, going to, go(ing) to (in future), be gone:: lám < la.
    go, go to, going, going to, (go somewhere else to do the action), going to (in future):: la.
    predicting the future:: hí:ywes < yéw: ~ yéw.
    seer, fortune-teller, person that senses the future:: síwe ~ syéwe < síw.

future tense:: -cha.

fuzz
    bloom or (plant) fuzz (spore, pollen, seed fluff) after it bursts:: spekw'ém < pékw' ~ péqw'.
    when plant fuzz blows:: pókw'em < pékw' ~ péqw'.

gable
    peak of house, gable or plank over smokehole:: sq'eyx̲éleqw.

gaff
    catching a fish by hook, hooking s-th, gaffing a fish:: lhílhekw'et < lhíkw' ~ lhí:kw'.
    (gaff) hook fisherman, a hooker:: thehímélh.
    gaffing:: lhílhekw'els < lhíkw' ~ lhí:kw'.
    gaff it (a fish):: lhíkw'et < lhíkw' ~ lhí:kw'.

gaff-hook
    gaff-hook (a large pole-mounted hook):: lhékw'tel < lhíkw' ~ lhí:kw'.
    gaff-hooking (all the time, catching a lot):: lhákw'els < lhíkw' ~ lhí:kw'.

gaff-hook (CONT'D)

hook fish, catch fish (by hook), to gaff-hook fish:: lhekw'á:ls < lhíkw' ~ lhí:kw'.
spear, shaft (of spear/harpoon/gaff-hook), gaff-hook pole:: s'álem, s'álem.

gait

gait, a walk:: s'ímex < i┐ m.

gall

gall-bladder, gall, bile, have bile trouble, be jaundiced, bilious:: leléts' ~ laléts'.

gall-bladder

animal and bird gall-bladder:: mél:eqw.
fish gall-bladder, (animal and bird gall-bladder [AC], gall-bladder (of fish, frog, animal, human) [Elders Group 2/27/80]):: mésel.
gall-bladder, gall, bile, have bile trouble, be jaundiced, bilious:: leléts' ~ laléts'.

gallop

galloping:: kwekwó:thet < kwá:.
to gallop:: kwó:thet < kwá:.

game

a drum, small stick used to drum or beat time to songs in slahal game:: q'ówet.
(have a) paralyzed hand, game hand:: slhéx̲tses < lhéx̲.
(have a) paralyzed leg, game leg:: slhéx̲xel < lhéx̲.
one's catch (fish, game, etc.):: sxélcha ~ sxélche < xélcha.
to catch (fish, game, birds):: chxélcha < xélcha.

Ganoderma

Fomes sp. including Fomes applanatus and probably others, possibly Polyporus sp., possibly Ganoderma sp., prob. also jelly fungi of Tremella and maybe Auricularia and Dacrymyces species, especially Tremella mesenterica (Yellow trembler) which is abundant only on the red alder and is reddish-orange matching the color, translucence and shape of those eaten by some of the Stó:lō elders, the jelly fungi could possibly have a differnet name from the bracket fungus:: s'ómó:qwes.

garbage

garbage, trash:: sqel:ép ~ sqél:ep < qél.

garden

the planting, seeds to plant, what is planted (sown), garden:: spí:ls < pél (perhaps ~ pí:l by now).
weeds in a garden:: ts'esémelep ~ ts'esémelép < ts'ísem.

garlic:: séyem éliyels < éy, éliyels
(lit. strong + [domestic] onion)

garment)

female name (garment):: =elwet ~ =élwet.
five garments:: lhq'atseséIwet < lheq'át ~ lhq'á:t.
garment, clothing:: =elwet ~ =élwet.
two garments, two (items of) clothes:: islélwet < isá:le ~ isále ~ isá:la.

garter

garter :: sq'ep'ó:lthetel < q'áp', sq'pólthetel < q'ép.

gas

to fart, pass gas:: téq'.
to pass gas, break wind, to fart:: pú'.

Gasterosteus aculeatus

possibly Gasterosteus aculeatus:: smó:tx̲w ~ smótx̲w.

Gastropoda

probably most members of the class Gastropoda:: q'oyátl'iye.

gather

a gathering, a meeting:: sq'ép < q'ép.
be gathered together:: sq'eq'íp < q'ép.
collect, collect money, take a collection, gather:: q'pá:ls < q'ép.
collect, gather:: q'pém < q'ép.
collecting s-th, gathering s-th:: q'ápt or q'ápet < q'ép.
crowd together, gather together, people gather:: q'péthet < q'ép.
gather firewood (in the woods), get firewood:: chiyólh < yólh.
gathering (of people):: q'áp < q'ép.
gather s-th, pick up s-th (stuff that's scattered about), collect s-th, gather it up, pick them up (already gathered or not):: q'pét < q'ép.
October to November, (wood gathering time):: tsélcheptel?.
to gather (of people esp.), to collect:: q'ép.

gathering)

inviting (to come eat, dance), to give a potlatch, (give a feast or gathering), to invite to a feast, invite to a potlatch:: tl'etl'áxel < tl'e'á ~ tl'á'.
speaker at a gathering, announcer at a gathering:: lheqqwóqwel or lheq qwóqwel < qwà:l.

Gaultheria shallon:: t'áqe.

Gaurotes

probably order Coleoptera, family Buprestidae, genus Buprestis, or possibly family Cerambycidae, genus Gaurotes:: tále te syó:qwem < tá:le ~ tále, tále te syó:qwem < yéqw.

Gavia arctica

Gavia immer, possibly also Gavia stellata, possibly also Gavia arctica:: swókwel.

Gavia immer

Gavia immer, possibly also Gavia stellata, possibly also Gavia arctica:: swókwel.

Gavia stellata

Gavia immer, possibly also Gavia stellata, possibly also Gavia arctica:: swókwel.

gear

everybody put away (fishing gear, canoe and) paddles (for winter), put away each other's paddles [and canoes and gear] for winter:: xets'ő:westel < xits' ~ xets'.
(one person) puts away his paddles (and canoe and gear for winter):: xets'ő:wes < xits' ~ xets'.

gee.

gee.

gee., good grief., well. (said when surprised), goodness., gee whiz.:: átsele.

gender

nominalizer (male or gender unspecified, present and visible or presence or proximity unspecified), demonstrative article:: ta=, te=.

the (male, present, visible), the (gender or presence and visibility unspecified), a (male, present and visible), a (gender or presence and visibility unspecified):: te.

nominalizer (female present and visible or presence or proximity unspecified), demonstrative article:: the=.

that's her, she (present or presence unspecified), her (present or presence unspefified), that (female):: thú:tl'ò < tl'ó ~ tl'o.

that's them (female), they (female), them (female):: thutl'ó:lem < tl'ó ~ tl'o.

the (female, near but not visible), (female, near but not in sight) (translated by gender specific words in English, like aunt, etc.):: kwse < kw.

the (female, present and visible), the (female, unspecified presence and/or unspecified visibility):: the.

gender unspecified

agent (human, gender unspecified, absent):: tl'.

by (agent. human, gender unspecified, absent):: tl'.

that's them (gender unspecified), they, them:: yutl'ó:lem < tl'ó ~ tl'o.

the (male or gender unspecified, near but not in sight):: kwthe < kw.

the (present, not visible, gender unspecified), the (remote, abstract):: kwe < kw.

generalize

generalize, reminisce:: lale'úlem.

generous :: lexw'éy < éy ~ éy:.

good-hearted, kind-hearted, kind, generous, helpful, easy-going, good-natured:: xw'éywelh ~ xwe'éywelh ~ xwe'éy:welh < éy ~ éy:.

genitals :: x=.

(have) hemorrhoids, (have) open sores on genitals or rump:: th'kw'íwel < th'ekw' or th'íkw'.

on the penis, in the penis, on the genitals, on the male:: =á:q ~ =aq ~ =eq.

on the woman's genitals, on the vulva, in the vagina:: xw= .

penis:: sx/éle.

woman's genitals, vulva, vagina:: xá:welh, .

Geometridae

order Lepidoptera, caterpillar of family Geometridae:: q'alq'elő:wsem < q'ál.

order Lepidoptera, caterpillar of the family Geometridae:: q'álq'elp'í:w < q'ál.

order Lepidoptera (esp. incl. grey moths of families Noctuidae, Geometridae, and Lymantriidae):: . lholeqwót.

George

King George:: Kíl Chóch < kelchóch ~ kyelchóch.

German

German person:: chá:mel ?.

Gerrhonotis coeruleus principis

prob. Dicamptodon ensatus, poss. also Taricha granulosa granulosa, prob. also Gerrhonotis coeruleus principis:: seyíyex̲.

get

approach, get near, get closer, reach, go up to, get up to:: tés, tés.
approaching, getting near, getting closer:: tetés < tés.
arrive, arriving, come here, have come, get here, get back, come in (in a race):: xwe'í < í.
be chilled (of a person), got cold (of a person):: th'óth'elhem < th'álh.
become, get:: xwa ~ xwe, xwe=, xwe ~ xwa.
(be) determined, got your mind made up:: sx̲áx̲as < x̲ás.
be drunk, got drunk:: só:les < sél or sí(:)l.
be dry, get dry, to dry:: ts'íyxw ~ ts'éyxw ~ ch'íyxw.
be faded (of clothes), (get/become) faded, (go or get or become gray):: xwíkw'el < xwíkw'.
[be getting black]:: sq'íq'ex̲el < q'íx̲.
[be getting brown]:: sqw'íqw'ex̲wel < qw'íx̲w.
[be getting/going a little red]:: skwekwíkwemel < kwí:m, tskwekwíkwemel < kwí:m.
[be getting red, be going red]:: skwíkwemel < kwí:m.
be getting shorter:: ts'íts'etl'thet < ts'í:tl' ~ ts'ítl'.
be hit (with arrow, bullet, anything shot that you've aimed), got shot, (got pierced), got poked into, got wounded (with gun or arrow):: ts'éqw'.
being tickled, (having tickling, getting tickling), tickley:: sá:yt'em ~ sayít'em < síyt'.
bring s-th, fetch s-th, get s-th (bring it), give it to s-o(as s-th fetched, not as a gift):: méstexw < mí ~ mé ~ me.
bump, get hit by something moving (for ex. by a car):: tós.
catch an animal, get an animal:: kwélest < kwél.
choke on food, get choked on food:: t'kwíles ~ t'ekwíles < t'ékw.
chop one's foot (with axe), [get chopped on the foot (with axe)]:: t'émxel < t'ém.
chop one's hand, [get chopped on the hand]:: t'émches < t'ém.
(cold (of a person) or get cooled down, get cold):: th'ólhem < th'álh.
come near me, (sic? for make me get near):: tesésthòx < tés.
frost, get frosty:: x̲éx̲el.
gather firewood (in the woods), get firewood:: chiyólh < yólh.
get a canoe stuck on a rock or something:: xá:m.
get a hole:: qwá.
get angry, get mad, be angry:: t'áyeq' < t'ay.
get a shoe on the wrong foot:: sts'ó:kw'xel.
get a sliver in one's hand:: xéth'ches.
get a sliver or splinter in the foot:: xéts'xel.
get a sliver or splinter in the hand:: xéts'ches.
get a spooky or spooked feeling, afraid that bad spirits are around, get spooked, fear something behind:: x̲éysel.
(get a) thrill, (to) thrill:: xwóywél.
get away, leave, (perhaps just) away:: á:yel < á:y.
get a wife:: tscháxw < chá:xw.
get, (become), turn, go:: =thet.
get better (from sickness), get well, revive, come alive, come back to life,:: áylexw ~ áyelexw.
get big, rise (of floodwater):: híkwthet < híkw.
get black:: q'íx̲el < q'íx̲.
get burned (of human or creature):: kw'ás.

get (CONT'D)

get calm (of wind):: qametólém ~ qametólem < qám.
get carried away and sleepy from eating too rich food:: ló:metsel < ló:m ~ lóm, melmelṓws < mál ~ mél.
get carried away (emotionally):: théqw'.
get close, approach, get near, nearly, (go close, come close):: ts'ímél ~ ts'ímel.
(get closed, become closed):: xwtáq < téq.
get close to s-o/s-th, approach s-th/s-o:: ts'ímélmet < ts'ímél ~ ts'ímel.
get cold:: x̲éytl'thet < x̲éytl' ~ x̲í:tl'.
get constipated, "bound up":: x̲ex̲ekw'íwel ~ x̲ax̲ekw'íwel < x̲ékw'.
get credit, borrow (money for ex.), (getting credit, borrowing):: qw'íméls.
get crowded:: pélh.
get crowded out:: pelhpélh < pélh.
get cut:: lhíts' ~ lhí:ts'.
get dark:: thetí:l < thá:t.
get diarrhea:: tl'xátem < tl'éx.
(get) dizzy, get drunk:: séles < sél or sí(:)l.
get drafty:: xó:lx̲wem < xó:lxwem.
(get) dusk, (get dim):: só:yel < sóy.
get dust or bark in both eyes:: thq'elq'ó:les < théq'.
get dust or bark in one eye:: thq'ó:les < théq'.
get erect (of penis only), have an erection:: xátl'.
get fat, put on weight, getting fat:: ló:sthet ~ lósthet < ló:s ~ lós.
get, fetch:: kwél:em ~ kwélem < kwél.
get fog on the water, (get steam (of the ground) [DC]):: qwélxel.
get frightened:: th'eth'íkw'thet < th'íkw' or th'ekw'.
get hit (by s-th thrown or airborne):: ló:m ~ lóm.
get hit in the face:: xwmélkw'es.
get hit on the back:: xwelemṓwelh ~ xwlemṓwelh, xwelemṓwelh ~ xwlemṓwelh < ló:m ~ lóm.
get hurt:: má:kwlh.
get juicy of its own accord:: qó:lhthet < qó:.
get light:: táwel < táw.
get mad at oneself:: qelqelí:lthet < qél.
get off (a canoe or conveyance), get out of a canoe, (disembark):: qw'í:m.
get offended, get irritated:: qwox̲wlómét < qwóx̲wlexw.
get one's picture taken:: x̲wéychesem (or better) x̲wíythesem < x̲wíyth.
get on top of something:: ts'ílem < ts'á:.
(get or develop a) sprain, to sprain:: ts'lhóqw'.
get outside:: átl'qel < átl'q.
get quiet (of wind), stop (of wind):: chó:ythet.
get ready:: hilékw.
get red, become red, go red:: tskwímel < kwí:m
(get) shaky and weak:: xwóyqwem.
get skinny:: títhel < títh ~ tí:th.
get s-o drunk:: séleslexw < sél or sí(:)l.
get s-o's name, manage to get s-o's name:: kwíxelexw ~ kwéxwelexw < kwí:x ~ kwíx.
get splashed:: lhá:ltem < lhél.
get squeezed (in hand or fingers):: p'íth'em < p'í:.
get s-th aboard (a canoe, car, conveyance):: eló:lhstexw < ó:lh.
get s-th, catch s-th, have s-th, find s-th:: kwélexw ~ kwél:exw < kwél.
get stuck:: t'elém.
get stuck in the mud, get mired, be mired, get muddy:: t'ékw.

get (CONT'D)

get sweetened:: q'et'ómthet < q'át'em.
get there, arrive there, reach there:: xwelí ~ xwlí < lí.
getting a cramp:: q'elq'élp'tem < q'élptem ~ q'élp'tem.
getting ancient, getting old:: q'e'ílém < q'a'í:lem ~ q'e'í:lem.
[getting black]:: q'íq'ex̲el < q'íx̲.
[getting brown]:: qw'íqw'ex̲wel < qw'íx̲w.
getting choked on food:: t'ékweles < t'ékw.
getting close:: ts'íts'emel < ts'ímél ~ ts'ímel.
getting cloudy, clouding up:: xwathtálém < thá:t.
getting colder:: x̲é:ytl'thet < x̲éytl' ~ x̲í:tl'.
getting cooked:: qw'eqwél < qw'él.
getting dusk:: lhó:yel.
getting firewood:: chiyóyelh < yólh.
getting foggy:: qwétxem.
getting mouldy in taste or smell:: pópeqwem < póqw.
getting ready to go:: hí:lekw ~ hílekw < hilékw.
getting real drafty:: xó:léx̲wem < xó:lxwem.
getting ripe:: qw'eqwél < qw'él.
getting shallow:: xá:mthet ~ xómthet < xá:m.
getting spooked, being afraid that bad spirits are around, spooky feeling:: x̲éyx̲esel < x̲éysel.
getting to like somebody:: i'é:ymet < éy ~ éy:.
getting to the summit of a mountain:: hewts'á: < ts'á:.
getting warmer:: léqwem.
getting yellow, turning yellow, turning green:: qwóqweyel ~ qwóqwiyel < qwá:y.
get to the top or summit of a mountain:: wets'á: < ts'á:.
get tripped, to trip:: lhékw'qsel < lhíkw' ~ lhí:kw'.
get twisted [inside]:: x̲elts'íwélém < x̲élts'.
get used to s-th/s-o:: tl'éltl'elmet < tl'élexw.
get warm (of weather):: kw'ósthet < kw'ás.
get weak:: qelámthet < qél.
get weak (from laughing, walking, working too long, sickness):: qiqelá:mthet < qél.
get wedged (by falling tree, for ex.), got run over (by car, train, etc.):: tl'íq'.
get white:: p'eq'í:l < p'éq'.
go, come, get, become:: =í:l ~ =i┐l ~ =el.
go down, go down below, get low:: tl'pí:l ~ tl'epí:l < tl'ép.
gone blue, (go blue, get blue, become blue):: meth'í:l < méth'.
got (both) shoes on wrong feet:: sts'ókw'elxel < sts'ó:kw'xel.
got even with s-o:: xwtí:chest ~ xwtí(:)ychest < tiy.
got rancid, got bitter:: chx̲í:mthet < chíchex̲em.
got red, became red, gone red:: kwí:mel < kwí:m.
got stormy with lots of fine snow in the air:: qwálxtem < qwélxel.
got up with a quick motion, got up quickly:: xwexwíléx < xwíléx.
got warm:: líqwem < léqwem.
(grayish, getting gray):: xwíxwekw'el < xwíkw'.
have, get, stative or be with colors:: ts= ~ ts'.
he passes on a disease to s-o, he gets s-o addicted:: q'ep'lóxes < q'áp'.
I got hard (of arm, leg, penis, etc.):: tl'x̲wòlèm < tl'éx̲w.
is getting twisted:: x̲áx̲elt'íwélém < x̲élts'.
it gets narrow or wedged in:: x̲ékw'.
it got rusty:: ts'ápex̲el.
it got smashed in the back end or rear end:: téslatstem < tós.

get (CONT'D)

it's getting red:: kwíkwemel < kwí:m.
leg got sprained, (sprain one's ankle [JL]):: ts'lhéqw'xel < ts'lhóqw'.
[looks a state of going brown, be getting brown-looking]:: sqw'íqw'ex̲welomex < qw'íx̲w.
(make/have a) sound getting softer:: théxweleqep < théxw ~ théx̲w.
male name, (prob.) repeatedly gets wives/houses:: =ímeltxw.
manage to get here:: xwe'ílòmèt < í.
many get crushed, get all crushed, many smashed (round and filled):: meqw'méqw' < méqw' ~ mṍqw'.
mark s-th, blaze it (of a trail), get/have s-th spotted (marked and located), make note of s-th:: x̲e'áth'stexw < x̲áth' ~ x̲e'áth'.
scratching repeatedly to get in:: t'elht'élheqw'els < t'élheqw' ~ t'lhóqw'.
scratching to get in (?):: t'élheqw'els < t'élheqw' ~ t'lhóqw'.
send s-o to do/get something, send s-o for something, (send s-o on an errand):: tsesá:t ~ tssá:t ~ tsesát ~ tssát < tsesá ~ tssá or tsás.
sensible, wise, (get sensible, get wise):: q'e'í:les ~ q'e'í:lés.
stative (with color terms), have/get (elsewhere):: ch=, ts= ~ ch=.
take s-th, accept s-th, get s-th, fetch s-th, pick s-th up:: kwú:t.
to dip water, get water, fetch water, pack water:: qó:m < qó:.
to escape (as an animal from a trap), got away from something that trapped a person or animal:: tl'ewlómét ~ tl'ōwlómét < tl'í:w.
to get skinned, peel the skin off:: ts'ó:l.
to have cramps, get a cramp, to be cramped:: q'élptem ~ q'élp'tem.
to ride [along], hook a ride, get a ride, send oneself:: lépetsel < lépets.
to stumble, get staggered:: télstem < tél ~ tá:l ~ tiy.
turning yellow, getting yellow, turning green:: qwóyel < qwá:y.
turn yellow, got yellow:: qwáyel < qwá:y.
very old, ancient, get ancient, be ancient:: q'a'í:lem ~ q'e'í:lem.
want to get a wife, He wants to get a wife.:: scháchxwelmel < chá:xw.
water (someone) carried, (water fetched/gotten):: sqó:m < qó:.
you get covered on the mouth (by a flying squirrel at night for ex.):: qep'ó:ythòm < qep'.
you get staggered:: x̲wex̲weló:ysthòm < x̲weló:y.
you'll get punched all over:: th'óleqw'esthòm < th'í:qw'et.

get in

get in a canoe, get aboard:: ó:lh.
get in a conveyance, get in a car, mount a horse:: ó:lh.

get out

escape (from slavery for ex.), get out (from being snowed in or snagged in river for ex.):: kwólòmèt < kwá:.
escape, get out:: kwálòmèt < kwá:.

get out of the way

get out of the way, get off the way, dodge:: íyeqthet < iyá:q.

get s-th :: kwélexw ~ kwél:exw < kwél.

get to

get to, reach there:: xwelí:ls < lí.
made it to shore, get to shore:: lhál:omet < lhà:l.
manage to get to s-o here:: xw'í:ls < í.

get up
climb, get up a vertical surface:: kw'í ~ kw'íy.
sit, sit down, sit up, arise (from lying or sitting), get up (from lying down, from bed or chair):: emét.

get well
come alive, come back to life, get better (from sickness), get well, revive:: áylexw ~ áyelexw.

Geum macrophyllum:: th'ith'kwimelálews, th'ith'kwimelálews < th'íkw, xwókw'eltel < xwókw'.

Ghost
Holy Spirit, Holy Ghost:: X̲áx̲e Smestí:yexw < x̲áx̲e.

ghost
ghost, corpse, dead body:: spoleqwíth'a < poleqwíth'a.
to ghost s-o, (to haunt s-o):: poleqwíth'et < poleqwíth'a.

gift
a gift:: syéx̲cha ~ syéx̲tsa < yéx̲ch ~ yéx̲ts ~ yéx̲cha ~ yéx̲tsa.
a gift in memory from someone gone (lit. "something - wept - in the face"):: sx̲ómes < x̲à:m ~ x̲á:m.
gift one really makes use of:: xwayólem.
give a gift to s-o:: yéx̲chet ~ yéx̲tset < yéx̲ch ~ yéx̲ts.

gill
gills, also "boot" (boot-shaped organ attached to fish gill):: xá:y~ xà:y.

gill net :: qwsá:yel < qwés.
net (any kind, for any purpose), fish net, gill-net (Elders Group 11/26/75)):: swéltel.
net shuttle and net-measure, gill-net measure, (loom [Elders Group]):: t'élhtsestel < t'álh.
throw a net into water (to drift, not to set), throw a net out, (gill net [TG]):: qwsá:yel < qwés.

ginger:: xwelítemelh x̲eyeslótel < xwelítem, x̲eyes
(lit. white man style + wild ginger)
kw'ókw'es kwémlexw s'élhtel < kw'ós, kwémlexw, álhtel
(lit. hot + root + food)
wild ginger:: x̲éyeslótel, th'alátel < th'á:lá ~ th'ála ~ th'á:le ~ th'ále.

girl
adolescent virgin girl, young girl (about ten to fifteen years), girl (from ten till she becomes a woman):: q'á:mi ~ q'á:miy, q'á:mi ~ q'á:miy.
a rock in the creek at the upriver end of Seabird Island that was a girl washing after her first period:: The Théthex̲w or Thethéthex̲w < thethíx̲w.
girl at puberty, (girl's first period):: thethíx̲w.
girl child, girl (from 5 to 10 years or so):: slheliyó:llh < slhá:lí, slheliyó:llh < slhá:lí.
girl (from baby to 4 or 5 yrs.):: slhelhliyó:llh < slhá:lí.
little girl (perhaps four years), young girl, (girl from five to ten years [EB]):: q'áq'emi < q'á:mi ~ q'á:miy.
lots of little girls:: q'eq'elá:mi < q'á:mi ~ q'á:miy.
ma'am, female friend, chum (female), little girl:: iyés < éy ~ éy:.

girl (CONT'D)

(young) girls, lots of (adolescent) girls:: q'á:lemi ~ q'á:lemey < q'á:mi ~ q'á:miy.

girl-friend

sweetheart, person of the opposite sex that one is running around with, girl-friend, boy-friend:: ts'elh'á:y < ts'elh=.

girth)

stout (of a person), thick (of a tree), thick around, coarse (of a rope), big (fat) (of a person). big (in girth):: mékw.

give :: á:m (?).

(bathe s-o, give s-o a bath), make s-o take a bath:: xó:kw'et < xókw' ~ xó:kw'.
bring s-th, fetch s-th, get s-th (bring it), give it to s-o(as s-th fetched, not as a gift):: méstexw < mí ~ mé ~ me.
clothing, food, and possessions burned and given away when a person dies, (possessions and food burned and given away at a burning):: syeqwá:ls < yéqw.
(food) given:: áxwe ~ s'áxwe < áxw, s'áxwem < áxw.
give a gift to s-o:: yéx̲chet ~ yéx̲tset < yéx̲ch ~ yéx̲ts.
give an equal share or amount to s-o, give (food?) to s-o, share with s-o:: áxwest < áxw.
give him/her ten dollars:: epoléstexw < ó:pel.
give it back, bring it back, return s-th:: q'élstexw < q'ó:lthet.
give it to me:: óxw < áxw.
give it to s-o, give to s-o:: óxwest < áxw.
give me s-th (to eat):: áxw < áxw.
give s-o food:: áxwet < áxw.
give s-o light:: láx̲et.
giving (food):: á:xwem < áxw.
giving it to s-o:: ó:xwest < áxw.
inviting (to come eat, dance), to give a potlatch, (give a feast or gathering), to invite to a feast, invite to a potlatch:: tl'etl'áxel < tl'e'á ~ tl'á'.
make an attempt (to do something difficult, like running rapids in a canoe, mountain-climbing, winning a game, etc.), give it a try:: t'óthet < t'á.
measure the knowledge (give a test):: xwéylemt te télmels < x̲wéylémt, tól.
pass around to give away (at a dance for example):: lhít'es < lhít'.
revive s-o, bring s-o back to life, heal s-o, (EB) give s-o medicine to make him better?:: á:yelexwt < áylexw ~ áyelexw.

give away

to scramble-give, throw money/blankets/poles to a crowd, give away at a big (winter) dance [by throwing]:: wá:ls < wál or wá:l.

give birth

giving birth, having a child, having a baby:: tsméla < méle ~ mél:a.
have given birth, already had a child, had a baby, (delivered):: sémele < méle ~ mél:a.

give s-o food

give s-o food, bring s-o food, pass food to s-o:: áxwet.

give up

beat up s-o as a lesson till he learns or gives up, teach s-o a lesson:: lepét < lép.
learn a lesson, give up:: lép.

gizzards

gizzards :: sx̲éykwel.

glad

become glad, become happy, happy inside:: xwoyíwel ~ xwoyíwél.
be good, good, well, nice, fine, better, better (ought to), it would be good if, may it be good, let it be good, happy, glad, clean, well-behaved, polite, virgin, popular, comfortable (with furniture, other things?),:: éy ~ éy:.
(glad greeting sound, also sound to show pride in accomplishment):: x̲::.

glass :: ts'áwi or ts'áwiy.
clinking, tinkling (of glass, ice in glass, glasses together, dishes together, metal together):: ts'átx̲em ~ th'átx̲em.
(have) clinking (of glass or dishes or metal), (have) tinkling sound (of glass, ice in glass, glasses together):: th'átx̲em ~ ts'átx̲em.
make a crunch underfoot (bones, nut, glass, etc.):: x̲ep'ékw'.
smash s-th to pieces (hard pitch, splintery wood, a glass), break s-th to pieces, beat s-th/s-o to a pulp:: th'ő:wt.

glasses

eyeglasses:: skw'echó:steló:les < kw'áts ~ kw'éts.
eyeglasses, (probably dark glasses):: st'óle'oléstel < t'á:l, st'óle'oléstel < t'á:l.

Glaucidium gnoma grinnelli)

Glaucidium gnoma swarthi (or Glaucidium gnoma grinnelli) and Cryptoglaux acadia acadia (or Aegolius acadicus):: spopeleqwíth'a ~ spopeleqwíth'e < poleqwíth'a.

Glaucidium gnoma swarthi

Glaucidium gnoma swarthi (or Glaucidium gnoma grinnelli) and Cryptoglaux acadia acadia (or Aegolius acadicus):: spopeleqwíth'a ~ spopeleqwíth'e < poleqwíth'a.
Glaucidium gnoma swarthi, some also call order Lepidoptera by this name:: spopeleqwíth'a ~ spopeleqwíth'e < poleqwíth'a.

Glaucomys sabrinus fuliginosus

Glaucomys sabrinus oregonensis and from Hope north Glaucomys sabrinus fuliginosus:: sqépò:thèl < qep'.

Glaucomys sabrinus oregonensis

Glaucomys sabrinus oregonensis and from Hope north Glaucomys sabrinus fuliginosus:: sqépò:thèl < qep'.

glide

sailing (of a bird), gliding on the wind:: yáyelem.

glitter

shine like a reflection, reflect, glitter, sparkle:: p'álq'em.
shining, (glittering, sparkling (with many reflections)):: p'elp'álq'em < p'álq'em.
to glitter:: tl'á:wq'em.

gloomy

(be) gloomy:: qéylés < qél.

glove :: th'qwó:lecha ~ th'qwó:letse.
 mittens, gloves:: th'qwó:letses < th'qwó:lecha ~ th'qwó:letse.

glow
 a yellowish glow at night given off by old birch and alder:: qwéth'.
 glowing of coals not quite gone out yet, red blaze of a fire (DM):: wóweqem.

glue :: shxwt'elémels < t'elém.
 flat organ in sturgeon which was skinned off and boiled down for glue:: mát.
 one's hand sticks to something (in cold, to honey, to glue, etc.):: t'elémtses < t'elém.

glug
 glug glug glug:: klekleklék perhaps.

glutton)
 someone who is greedy, someone who eats all the time, (glutton):: sqel:éxw < qél:éxw ~ qel(:)éxw.

gnat
 gnat, probably includes non-biting midges, biting midges, and (biting) black flies:: pepx̲wíqsel < píxw.

gnaw
 chewing with a crunch, nibbling, gnawing:: x̲áp'kw'els < x̲ep'ékw'.
 gnawing s-th, be gnawing on s-th:: x̲áp'kw't ~ (sic) x̲ápkwt < x̲ep'ékw'.
 gnaw s-th, chew s-th [crunchy]:: x̲ép'kw't ~ x̲épkw't ~ (sic) x̲épkwt < x̲ep'ékw'.
 make a crunching or crackling noise, crunching (gnawing) sound:: x̲ápkw'em < x̲ep'ékw'.

go
 accompany s-o, go with s-o:: sq'ó:t ~ sq'ót < q'ó.
 accompany s-o, go with s-o, go along with s-o:: q'exí:lt < q'ó.
 approach, get near, get closer, reach, go up to, get up to:: tés.
 back and forth, (go or come back and forth):: q'elq'í:lthet ~ q'elq'éylthet < q'ó:lthet.
 beach in front of old Scowlitz village, the point the Harrison River goes around by Kilby's store:: Sq'iq'ewílem < q'éw ~ q'ew.
 be big (of a fire), the fire is big, the fire is going strong, big fire:: thó:lchep ~ thó:ltsep < thi ~ tha ~ the ~ thah ~ theh.
 be faded (of clothes), (get/become) faded, (go or get or become gray):: xwíkw'el < xwíkw'.
 [be getting/going a little red]:: skwekwíkwemel < kwí:m, tskwekwíkwemel < kwí:m.
 [be getting red, be going red]:: skwíkwemel < kwí:m.
 be on one's way, be going:: hálém < la.
 (be) slow, (be) late, go slow:: óyém.
 confession, to go to confession, to confess:: x̲áx̲emilàlèm ~ x̲áx̲milàlèm < x̲áx̲e.
 crawl underneath, (go underneath):: eqílem ~ eqéylem.
 dive (already in water), go underwater, sink oneself down:: leqàlèm < léqem.
 drop s-th (accidentally), let s-o go:: kwò:lxw < kwá:.
 feel like going:: halemélmel < la.
 get, (become), turn, go:: =thet.
 get close, approach, get near, nearly, (go close, come close):: ts'ímél ~ ts'ímel.
 [get/go/become red]:: tskwímel < kwí:m.
 go around a bend in the river, go around a turn, go around something in one's way::

go (CONT'D)

q'ewílem < q'éw ~ q'ew.
go around a bend (in water):: q'éwlets ~ q'ówlets < q'éw ~ q'ew.
go around (a point, a bend, a curve, etc.) in the water, make a U-turn (in the water, could use today on land with a car):: q'ówletsem < q'éw ~ q'ew.
go around inside the longhouse counter-clockwise:: selts'elwílem < sél or sí(:)l.
go around s-th in the water:: q'ówletst < q'éw ~ q'ew.
go away (as away from the fire):: tsx̱éylém or tsx̱ílém.
go away from the river:: chó:m.
go, come, get, become:: =í:l ~ =i┐l ~ =el.
go down, go down below, get low:: tl'pí:l ~ tl'epí:l < tl'ép.
go down hill, go down from anything:: tl'pílém < tl'ép.
go down(hill) to the water, go towards the river:: t'óxw.
go down (of swelling):: t'esí:l < t'ás.
go downstream, go downriver, down the river:: wōqw'ílem ~ wōqw'éylem ~ wōqw'ílém ~ wōqw'éylém < wṓqw' ~ wéqw'.
go down to the river:: chóxw.
go far away:: chekwílem < chó:kw, xwetskwí:lem < chó:kw.
go following s-o:: chochí:lt < chá:l or chó:l.
go for a walk, take a stroll, stroll:: imexósem < i┐m.
go, go to, going, going to, go(ing) to (in future), be gone:: lám < la, lám <la.
go, go to, going, going to, (go somewhere else to do the action), going to (in future):: la, la.
go in a semi-circle (or part of a circle) with the current:: selch'éle < sél or sí(:)l.
go in full circle with the current:: sá:lch'ōwelh < sél or sí(:)l.
going out(side) with a light:: láx̱etem < láx̱et.
going to piss right away, almost piss oneself, (have an urgent or extreme or painful need to urinate):: ts'áléqel.
going towards the river or water:: t'ót'exw < t'óxw.
going with each other [romantically], going for a walk with each other:: ts'lhimexóstel < ts'elh=.
go in the direction of the water, go downriver:: xwōqw'éylem < wṓqw' ~ wéqw'.
go in the water, walk slowly into the water, (dip oneself in the water [HT]:: mí:lthet < mí:l ~ míl.
gone blue, (go blue, get blue, become blue):: meth'í:l < méth'.
gone soft and spoiled (of dried fish):: th'íth'eqel < sth'í:qel.
go out completely (of fire):: th'éx̱.
go out from the beach (if in a canoe):: tó:l ~ tò:l.
go out into the river, go down to the river, walk down to the river:: tó:l ~ tò:l.
go out (of fire, flame or lamp):: tl'ékw'el.
go out of sight (behind something), disappear [behind something], [get in shade]:: t'á:l.
go over or around (hill, rock, river, etc.):: q'ál.
go through:: qwehá < qwá.
go through a channel:: lheltáletsem < lhà:l.
go through (somewhere), go via (somewhere), go by way of:: lhe'á.
go through the woods:: xets'í:lem < xí:ts' ~ xíts' ~ xets'.
go travelling by way of, go via:: ley ~ lay < la.
go upstream:: xwehíwel < ahíw.
go with, come with, be partner with:: q'axí:l < q'ó.
go with each other (romantically), go for a walk with each other (romantically):: ts'lhimexóstel < i┐m.
he's gone (mentally):: hélemémstem < la.

go (CONT'D)

it's going dead (of a tree):: t'ópiythet < t'ápiy.
it went into him/her (of spirit power):: thex̲we'í:ls.
leave s-o, leave s-th, go away from s-o/s-th, abandon s-o, leave s-o behind:: áyeles < á:y.
let go of s-th/s-o, drop s-th, set s-o free, turn s-o/s-th loose:: kwá:t ~ kwát < kwá:.
little partner, little person who follows or goes with one:: sq'iq'exí:l ~ q'iq'exí:l < q'ó.
[looks a state of going brown, be getting brown-looking]:: sqw'íqw'ex̲welomex < qw'íx̲w.
(more than one) entering a house, going in (of a whole bunch):: kwetexwí:lem < kwetáxw.
place to go to:: shxwlàm < la.
(portion not burnt up, burnt or gone out completely portion):: th'ex̲míl < th'éx̲.
return, come back, go back:: q'ó:lthet.
slow down, go slow:: silíxw.
stop burning (of a burn), go down (of swelling):: t'esí:l < t'ás.
to go down (of water), subside (of water), the tide goes out or down, (be going out (of tide) [BJ]):: th'à:m ~ th'ám.
to war, go to war:: x̲éyléx̲.
tracks going down to the river:: tó:lxel < tó:l ~ tò:l.
travelling (without a destination), going out:: leq'á:l(e)q'el ~ leq'á:lqel < leq'áleq'el (~ leq'áleqel (rare)).
turn around a bend, go around a bend, turn around (to go back), turn around a corner:: q'ewqé:ylém ~ q'ewqéylém (better q'ewqí:lem) < q'éw ~ q'ew.
turn back into a quiet slough from the river, be going into a slough from the river:: ts'élexw < ts'el.
village on east bank of Fraser River below Siwash Creek (Aseláw), now Yale Indian Reserves 19 and 20, named because of a big rock in the area that the trail had to pass (go around), also the name of the rock:: Q'alelíktel < q'ál.
wandering, where someone goes:: shxwélem ~ shxwélém < la.
went crooked:: póythet < pó:y.
where did he go?, where is he/she/etc.?:: xwechà:l < chá:l or chó:l.
where is s-o going?, where is s-o travelling?, where is s-o headed for?:: xwchókwel < chákw.

go after s-th/s-o

go after s-th/s-o, chase s-o/s-th (not stopping or slowing tillit's caught):: eyát < á:y.

go and (do s-th)

going to (future), will go and (do s-th):: la.

goat

big serving spoon, spoon with handle about ten to 12 inches long, ladle, (spoon carved from mountain goat horn):: x̲álew.
male mountain goat:: sí:lá:kw
mountain goat:: p'q'élqel < p'éq'.

goatsbeard (plant):: chochkwó:les < chó:kw.

God

God, the Lord:: Chíchelh Siyá:m ~ Chíchelh Siyám < =chílh ~ chílh=.

go in

go in (a house/enclosure), come in, come inside, enter a house or enclosure:: kwetxwí:lem < kwetáxw.

go(ing) to

go, go to, going, going to, go(ing) to (in future), be gone:: lám < la.
go, go to, going, going to, (go somewhere else to do the action), going to (in future):: la.

goiter

lump on person (or creature), goiter:: smétsa.

gold :: kú:l.

(perhaps) copper, (hard metal that looks like gold but isn't, maybe copper [Elders at Katz Class 10/5/76], metal found in mines and used for arrowheads [Elders Group 5/28/75], gold [EB]):: sqw'él.

goldeneye duck

goldeneye duck (probably both the common goldeneye duck and the Barrow goldeneye duck), (a kind of diving duck [Elders Group]):: láqleqem < léqem.

gone (mentally)

he's gone (mentally):: héleméstem < la.

good

all good:: 'al'álíy < éy ~ éy:.
be good at s-th:: schewétmet < schewót.
be good, good, well, nice, fine, better, better (ought to), it would be good if, may it be good, let it be good, happy, glad, clean, well-behaved, polite, virgin, popular, comfortable (with furniture other things?),:: éy ~ éy:.
be in clear voice, be in good voice, be in good health, healthy:: shxw'éyelh < éy ~ éy:.
cute, a little one is good, good (of s-th little):: í'iy < éy ~ éy:, í'iy < éy ~ éy:.
good figure, good shape:: eyámeth' < éy ~ éy:.
good-looking, beautiful, pretty, handsome, looks good:: iyó:mex ~ iyóméx ~ iyómex < éy ~ éy:.
good (of little ones), cute (of many of them):: é'iy ~ á'iy < éy ~ éy:.
good tasting (savory, not sweet), tasty:: ts'áts'esem.
have a fragrance, have a good smell, smell good:: eyáléqep ~ iyáléqep < éy ~ éy:.
(have) good eyes, (have) good sight, soft on the eyes, easy on the eyes:: eyólés ~ eyó:les < éy ~ éy:.
(have) good sight:: xw'elyó:les < éy ~ éy:.
having lots of fun, having a good time:: eyó:sthet ~ iyósthet < éy ~ éy:.
is clean, good:: éy ~ éy:.
it would be good:: éy ~ éy:.
more than one is good, good (of many things or people):: álíy ~ 'álíy < éy ~ éy:.
nice, well-behaved, good:: éy ~ éy:.
optimist, a person whose thoughts are always good:: wiyóth kwsu éys te sqwálewels te lólets'e < wiyóth.
pretending to be good, want to be accepted:: éystelómet ~ éy:stelómet < éy ~ éy:.
smart, know how, good at it:: schewót.
starting to smell good:: iyáléqepthet < éy ~ éy:.
what s-o/s-th is good for:: shxw'éy < éy ~ éy:.

good-for-nothing

be always lazy, be a lazybones, be stupid, be a good-for-nothing:: s'ú:met < emét.

good grief.
    gee., good grief., well. (said when surprised), goodness., gee whiz.:: átsele.

good health
    be alive, be living, be in good health, be healthy, be well:: áylexw ~ áyelexw.
    be in good health, be healthy:: shxw'éyelh < éy ~ éy:.

good-hearted
    good-hearted, kind-hearted, kind, generous, helpful, easy-going, good-natured:: xw'éywelh ~ xwe'éywelh ~ xwe'éy:welh < éy ~ éy:.

good-looking:: eyelhómex < éy ~ éy:.
    good-looking, beautiful, pretty, handsome, looks good:: iyó:mex ~ iyóméx ~ iyómex < éy ~ éy:.

good-natured
    good-hearted, kind-hearted, kind, generous, helpful, easy-going, good-natured:: xw'éywelh ~ xwe'éywelh ~ xwe'éy:welh < éy ~ éy:.

goodness.
    for goodness sakes.:: eyeléwthelh < éy ~ éy:.
    gee., good grief., well. (said when surprised), goodness., gee whiz.:: átsele.
    oh for goodness sakes., well. (in surprise):: lá:la.
    oh my goodness.:: qéléméx ~ ő qèlèmèx ~ ló qèlèmèx.

good news
    cry of a bluejay [Steller's jay] that means good news:: q'ey, q'ey, q'ey.

Goodyera oblongifolia:: pepepó:tem ~ pépepò:tem ~ pepepótem < pó:t.

goose
    a white-headed duck, [could be bufflehead, snow goose, emperor goose, poss. oldsquaw, or hooded merganser, other duck-like birds with white heads do not occur in the Stó:lō area and the emperor goose would be only an occasional visitor]:: skemí'iya.
    big Canada goose, big honker:: tl'x̲wőmálqel ~ tl'ax̲wőmálqel.
    Canada goose:: áx̲e.
    smaller goose, brant, (black brant), for the smaller goose possibly also the cackling goose and lesser Canada goose:: tl'ákw'x̲el.

gooseberry:: t'á:mxw.
    gooseberry bush:: t'á:mxwelhp < t'á:mxw.
    gooseberry time, the month or moon (first sliver) that starts in June:: temt'á:mxw < t'á:mxw.
    prickly swamp currant, swamp gooseberry:: th'kw'íwíyelhp < th'ekw' or th'íkw'.
    swamp gooseberry, prickly swamp currant:: ts'qw'í:wíyelhp.

goose-shaped rock
    a goose-shaped rock near Hamisley Mt. and near Hooknose Mountain or Lhílhkw'elqs, west of Agassiz, B.C.:: Áx̲etel < áx̲e.

Gordon Creek:: Sókw'ech Stó:lō < sókw'.
  winter village on flat at mouth of Gordon Creek:: Sókw'ech ~ Sókw'ets < sókw'.

gosh.
  oh my gosh.:: éyelew < éy ~ éy:.

Goshen, Wash. :: Kúshen.

got to
  determined (about s-th), have to do it, got to do it:: x̲asélmet < x̲ás.

go up
  climb a mountain, climb a hill, go up a mountain or hill:: kw'íyeqel < kw'í ~ kw'íy.

gown
  clothes, clothing (esp. Indian clothing, men's or women's), something to wear, dress, gown:: s'íth'em < íth'a.

grab
  grab a handful:: x̲éymem < x̲éym.
  grab s-th/s-o:: x̲éymet < x̲éym.
  pull s-o's hair, grab s-o's hair:: x̲éymleqwt < x̲éym.

grace)
  It's you to thank the Lord, (Please say grace):: lúwe ts'ít te Chíchelh Siyám < =chílh ~ chílh=.

Gramineae
  family Gramineae and possibly family Cyperaceae (sedges):: só:x̲wel ~ sóx̲wel.

grammophone
  musical instrument, grammophone, phonograph, record player:: qweló:ythetel ~ qwelóyethetel < qwà:l.

grampa :: sísi < sí:le.
  grandfather (affectionate), (grampa):: máma < má:l ~ mál.

Grampus rectipinna
  Grampus rectipinna also known as Orcinus rectipinna:: q'ellhólemètsel.

grandchild
  grandchild, grandchild of sibling, grandchild of cousin (esp. in the old days):: í:meth.
  grandchildren:: em'í:meth < í:meth.
  great grandchildren, great grandparents:: sts'ólemeqw < sts'ó:meqw.
  great grandparent, great grandchild, sibling or (up to fourth) cousin of great grandparent, great grandchild of brother or sister or (up to fourth) cousin:: sts'ó:meqw.
  great great grandchild:: ékwiyeqw.
  great great grandchildren:: th'eth'í:payeqw < th'ép'ayeqw ~ th'épayeqw.
  great great grandparent, great great grandchild, sibling or cousin (up to fourth) of great great grandparent/-child:: th'ép'ayeqw ~ th'épayeqw.
  older sibling, elder cousin (child of older sibling of one's parent, grandchild of older sibling

grandchild (CONT'D)

of one's grandparent, great grandchild of older sibling of one's great grandparent), cousin of senior line older brother, older sister:: sétl'atel < sétl'a ~ sétl'o.

younger, younger sibling, cousin of a junior line (cousin by an ancestor younger than the speaker's), junior cousin (child of a younger sibling of one's parent, (great) grandchild of a younger sibling of one's(great) grandparent), younger brother, younger sister:: sóseqwt ~ (rarely) só:seqwt.

grandchild of cousin

grandchild, grandchild of sibling, grandchild of cousin (esp. in the old days):: í:meth.

grandchild of sibling

grandchild, grandchild of sibling, grandchild of cousin (esp. in the old days):: í:meth.

grandfather

grandfather (affectionate), (grampa):: máma < má:l ~ mál.

grandmother (pet name), grandfather (pet name), granny, grandpa:: sísele < sí:le.

Grandma

Grandma, Father's Mother (nickname):: táta < tá:l ~ tà:l ~ tál.

grandmother

grandmother (pet name), grandfather (pet name), granny, grandpa:: sísele < sí:le.

grandpa

grandmother (pet name), grandfather (pet name), granny, grandpa:: sísele < sí:le.

grandparent

grandparent, grandparent's sibling, grandparent's first cousin:: sí:le.

grandparents:: selsí:le < sí:le.

great grandchildren, great grandparents:: sts'ólemeqw < sts'ó:meqw.

great grandparent, great grandchild, sibling or (up to fourth) cousin of great grandparent, great grandchild of brother or sister or (up to fourth) cousin:: sts'ó:meqw.

great great grandparent:: ékwiyeqw.

great great grandparent, great great grandchild, sibling or cousin (up to fourth) of great great grandparent/-child:: th'ép'ayeqw ~ th'épayeqw.

grandparent/-child

great great great grandparent/-child:: ékwiyeqw.

grandparents of a deceased grandchild

cry with someone, a person one cries with (related or not), unrelated grandparents of a deceased grandchild, etc.:: ts'elhx̲à:m < x̲à:m ~ x̲á:m.

grand-uncle

deceased uncle, deceased grand-uncle:: qethiyálh.

Granite Mountain

Granite Mountain, the second mountain back of X̲óletsa, northwest of Kwelkwelqéylem:: Th'emth'ómels < th'óméls.

granny

grandmother (pet name), grandfather (pet name), granny, grandpa:: sísele < sí:le.

grape:: qelíps
    grape juice:: qelíps sqe'óleqw < qelíps, qó:

grapefruit:: sásex̲em qwíyqwòyèls < sáx̲, qwá:y
    (lit. bitter + orange fruit/little yellowish fruit)
    grapefruit juice:: sásex̲em qwíyqwòyèls sqe'óleqw < sáx̲, qwá:y, qó:

grasp:: tl'kwót.
    hold s-th (in one's grasp), holding s-th (in one's grasp), have s-th, grasp s-th:: kwelát < kwél.

grass
    a grass growing between Yale and Emory Creek used for fish-nets:: méthelh.
    a grass that grows with berries in fields and everywhere and has seeds that stick in one's throat when eaten with berries, probably a type of brome grass, likely California brome grass, possibly sweet cicely:: táqalh.
    a grass which grows at a meadow above Duncan's place at Chehalis which was dried, twined, and used for making fish nets:: méthelh.
    a kind of marsh grass which grows near the foot of Agassiz Mountain may have also been called méthelh and used like it by the Chehalis people:: méthelh.
    a special kind of grass used for making fish nets that grows at Hedley and was traded for in bundles:: méthelh.
    barn, (hay house, grass building):: sox̲weláwtxw < só:x̲wel ~ sóx̲wel.
    burnt (i.e. dry) grass:: yeqwílep < yéqw.
    cut (grass, hay):: lhéch'elechá:ls < lhíts' ~ lhí:ts'.
    cutting (grass, hay):: lhílhech'elchá:ls < lhíts' ~ lhí:ts'.
    grass (every kind) (wild and now domestic types), hay:: só:x̲wel ~ sóx̲wel.
    grass or fibre for nets or twine, spreading dogbane, possibly also Indian hemp:: méthelh.
    grass scalded and bleached white for basketry imbrication (designs), sometimes called white straw grass, probably blue-joint reed-grass:: th'á:x̲ey ~ th'áx̲ey < th'áx̲.
    month or moon of March to April, grass moon:: sox̲wí:les < só:x̲wel ~ sóx̲wel.
    plants, grass:: =eletsá:ls, =elesà:ls.
    prairie, grassy open land, (grassy valley [EB, Gibbs, Elders Group]}:: spélhx̲el.
    reed canary-grass:: ts'á:yas te th'á:x̲ey < th'áx̲.
    sharp grass, cut-grass:: pxá:y.

grasshopper:: tl'emtl'émxel, tl'emtl'émxel < tl'ém.
    grasshopper (ordinary), perhaps longhorned grasshopper:: tl'emtl'émxel, ts'áts'etl'em < ts'tl'ám ~ ts'tl'ém, ts'ats'etl'í:m < ts'tl'ám ~ ts'tl'ém, ts'í:ts'á:tl'em < ts'tl'ám ~ ts'tl'ém.
    grasshopper, (possibly the longhorned grasshopper):: tl'emékw' < tl'ámkw'em, tl'emékw' < tl'ém.
    (have) sound of popping small round things (snowberries, herring eggs as when eating them, rice krispies, crabapples, cranberries, etc.), (have a crunching sound (as of grasshopper, rice krispies)):: tl'ámkw'em, tl'ámkw'em < tl'ém.

grave
    a cross, grave cross, gravestone, cross one hangs up:: lakwwí:l.
    a mark to show where something is, a marker (to show a trail, something buried, a grave):: x̲áth'tel < x̲áth' ~ x̲e'áth'.
    grave pole:: x̲á:th'etstel < x̲áth' ~ x̲e'áth'.

grave box
    box, trunk, grave box (old-style, not buried), coffin, casket:: kw'óxwe.

grave-house
    s-o has been put away (in grave-house or buried), he's/she's been buried:: qéylemtem ~ qé:ylemtem < qéylem ~ qé:ylem ~ qí(:)lem.

gravel
    gravel, sand smaller than pebbles:: th'ex̲ét.

gravestone
    a cross, grave cross, gravestone, cross one hangs up:: lakwwí:l.

graveyard :: smekw'e'ála < mákw'a.
    (possibly) clean out brush from a graveyard or the ceremony of graveyard cleaning:: stselqwá:ls < chá:l or chó:l.

gray (also see under "grey" below)
    (be) a dark color (of clothes, complexions, etc.), (dark gray, dark brown):: stl'ítl'esel < stl'ítl'es.
    be faded (of clothes), (get/become) faded, (go or get or become gray):: xwíkw'el < xwíkw'.
    [be getting gray]:: tsxwíxwekw' < xwíkw'.
    [being gray]:: xwíxwekw' < xwíkw'.
    (be) real gray (of hair), (grey hair):: sx̲ó:lem < x̲ólem.
    grayish:: tsxwíxwekw'el < xwíkw'.
    (grayish, getting gray):: xwíxwekw'el < xwíkw'.
    gray mountain blueberry which looks like sx̲wéxixeq but is sweeter, oval-leaved blueberry, could also be Cascade blueberry:: xwíxwekw' < xwíkw'.
    gray (of hair), grey (of hair):: x̲ólem.
    (have/be) gray, (have/be) grey:: tsxwíkw' < xwíkw'.
    [looks gray, gray-looking]:: tsxwíkw'o┐ mex < xwíkw'.
    really turned gray (of hair):: x̲ó:lemthet < x̲ólem.
    turning gray (in hair):: x̲olémthet < x̲ólem.

grayback
    body louse, grayback:: p'éq' méxts'el < méxts'el.

grayish
    grayish:: tsxwíxwekw'el < xwíkw'.
    (grayish, getting gray):: xwíxwekw'el < xwíkw'.

"grayling"
    "grayling", probably mountain whitefish:: spó:ltsep.

grease
    fat, grease, lard, (oil [EB], shortening [MH]):: sló:s ~ slós < ló:s ~ lós.
    grease bowl:: shxwlósàlà < ló:s ~ lós.
    grease one's body:: melxwíwsem < mélxw.
    grease s-th:: ló:st < ló:s ~ lós.
    grease s-th/s-o, oil s-th/s-o, rub something on s-th/s-o:: mélxwt < mélxw.
    greasy-headed:: lésleseqw < ló:s ~ lós.
    solid grease, suet, lump of grease, (stomach fat [CT]):: x̲wástel.

great (CONT'D)

great

be great, be important:: hí:kw ~ hí::kw < híkw.
be overcome with pleasurable feelings after eating great salmon or a great meal:: ts'éqw'.
great great grandparent:: ékwiyeqw.
great great great grandparent/-child:: ékwiyeqw.

great grandchild

great grandchildren, great grandparents:: sts'ólemeqw < sts'ó:meqw.
great grandparent, great grandchild, sibling or (up to fourth) cousin of great grandparent, great grandchild of brother or sister or (up to fourth) cousin:: sts'ó:meqw.
older sibling, elder cousin (child of older sibling of one's parent, grandchild of older sibling of one's grandparent, great grandchild of older sibling of one's great grandparent), cousin of senior line, older brother, older sister:: sétl'atel < sétl'a ~ sétl'o.
younger, younger sibling, cousin of a junior line (cousin by an ancestor younger than the speaker's), junior cousin (child of a younger sibling of one's parent, (great) grandchild of a younger sibling of one's(great) grandparent), younger brother, younger sister:: sóseqwt ~ (rarely) só:seqwt.

great grandparent

great grandchildren, great grandparents:: sts'ólemeqw < sts'ó:meqw.
great grandparent, great grandchild, sibling or (up to fourth) cousin of great grandparent, great grandchild of brother or sister or (up to fourth) cousin:: sts'ó:meqw.

great great grandchild

great great grandchildren:: th'eth'í:payeqw < th'ép'ayeqw ~ th'épayeqw.
great great grandparent, great great grandchild, sibling or cousin (up to fourth) of great great grandparent/-child:: th'ép'ayeqw ~ th'épayeqw.

great great grandparent

great great grandparent, great great grandchild, sibling or cousin (up to fourth) of great great grandparent/-child:: th'ép'ayeqw ~ th'épayeqw.

great great great great grandchild

great great great great grandparent, great great great great grandchild, sibling or cousin (up to fourth) of great great great great grandparent or -child:: tómiyeqw.

great great great great grandparent

great great great great grandparent, great great great great grandchild, sibling or cousin (up to fourth) of great great great great grandparent or -child:: tómiyeqw.

grebe

hell-diver, pied-billed grebe:: sx̲wotíx.

greedy

be greedy:: sqél:éxw < qél:éxw ~ qel(:)éxw.
someone who is greedy, someone who eats all the time, (glutton):: sqel:éxw < qél:éxw ~ qel(:)éxw.

green

be yellow, be green:: tsqwá:y < qwá:y.
carrot-like plant used for green dye:: xáweleq < xáwéq.
getting yellow, turning yellow, turning green:: qwóqweyel ~ qwóqwiyel < qwá:y.

green (CONT'D)
[have/get/be in a state of going a little yellow or green]:: tsqwíqweyel < qwá:y.
[having/getting/being in a state of yellow or green]:: tsqwóqwey < qwá:y.
leaf-green:: sts'ó:lha ~ sch'ó:lha ~ sts'ólha.
[looks yellow or green, yellow/green-looking]:: tsqwáyòmèx < qwá:y.
[stative/be getting yellow, stative/be getting green]:: tsqwóqwiyel < qwá:y.
turning yellow, getting yellow, turning green:: qwóyel < qwá:y.

greens
a sprout or shoot (esp. of the kinds peeled and eaten in spring), sweet green inner shoots, green berry shoots, salmonberry shoots, wild raspberry shoots and greens, salmonberry sprouts, blackcap shoots, thimbleberry shoots, wild rhubarb shoots, fern shoots:: stháthqiy.

Greenwood Island:: Welqémex < qám.

greet
greet s-o, thank s-o:: ts'ít ~ ch'í:t.

greeting
(glad greeting sound, also sound to show pride in accomplishment):: x̲::.

grey (also see under "gray" above)
(be) real gray (of hair), (grey hair):: sx̲ó:lem < x̲ólem.
gray (of hair), grey (of hair):: x̲ólem.
(have/be) gray, (have/be) grey:: tsxwíkw' < xwíkw'.
really turned gray (of hair):: x̲ó:lemthet < x̲ólem.
turning gray (in hair):: x̲olémthet < x̲ólem.

grin
ugly expression in mouth, ugly grin:: sx̲eyx̲eth'ó:ythel < x̲íth' ~ x̲éyth'.

grind
grinding one's teeth:: x̲ax̲elts'elísem < x̲élts'.
grind or sharpen s-th (of edged tools):: yéq'est < yéq'.
mashing, grinding (stones, something hard):: tótesem < tós.
tapping it (with something), mashing s-th, grinding s-th, be bumping s-o:: tóteset < tós.

gristle
edible gristle inside fish head (nose gristle):: sx̲épeqw (or sx̲ép'eqw? or sx̲ép'ekw'?).
skin of fish head without gristle:: t'áwleqw.

grit
rock above Yale where Ñá:ls gritted his teeth and scratched rocks as he duelled with a medicine man across the Fraser:: Th'ex̲elís < th'ex̲elís.

Grizzly Bear
Female Grizzly Bear:: Yeqwílmetelòt < yéqw.
Male Grizzly Bear:: Yeqwílmet ~ Syeqwílmetxw < yéqw.

grizzly bear:: kw'í:tsel, x̲eytl'áls ~ x̲eytl'á:ls

groan

keeps on groaning:: i'ó:lthet ò < ó:lthet.
to groan:: ó:lthet.

groceries :: s'álhtel < álhtel.

ground

be lying on the ground:: slhálheq' < lháq'.
break (of ground), crack apart (of its own accord) (of ground), ripped:: tl'éx.
chopping the ground (with hoe or mattock):: t'et'émélep < t'ém.
dirt, ground:: =ílép ~ =í:lep ~ =éylép ~ =elep ~ =áp ~ =íp ~ =ép.
drop oneself into a seat, throw oneself on the floor or ground in a tantrum, throw a tantrum:: kw'qweméthet < kw'óqw.
earth, ground, land, the earth, the world:: tém:éxw ~ tem:éxw ~ ~ tèm:èxw ~ témexw.
(emprisoned), put in jail, grounded, restricted, caught, apprehended:: qíq'.
firmly planted in ground (can't be pulled out):: slálets < slá ~ selá ~ slá: (probably).
get fog on the water, (get steam (of the ground) [DC]):: qwélxel.
hard ground:: tl'x̲wéylep or tl'x̲wílep < tl'éx̲w.
hole in the ground, trench (if discussing length):: shxwthó:yqw < thíy.
level ground, flat (of ground):: leq'éylep ~ leq'ílep < léq'.
lying on the ground:: lhálheq' < lháq'.
pick s-th up from the ground or floor:: xwpét.
rough (of wood), lumpy (of ground, bark, etc.):: smelhmélhqw.
sloping ground:: tewálehílép < tewále.
sprout(ing) up, stick(ing) its head out of the ground (of a plant):: qw'íles < qw'íl.
steep hill, sloping ground:: sqotemí:lep ~ sqoteméylep.
store it away (wedged-in up off ground), put s-th away for winter, stow s-th away:: xítse't < xits' ~ xets'.
swept ground:: x̲éylep.
tree bent to ground with ice and frozen:: sx̲wíqel.

"groundhog"

hoary marmot, (also known as) "mountain groundhog", "groundhog", or "whistler", poss. also yellow-bellied marmot:: sqwíqw.

group

a group:: sq'eq'íp < q'ép.
a group making (fish) oil:: hemhémetheqw < mótheqw or metheqw.
a group of people, a tribe of people, several tribes:: ó:wqw'elmexw or ó:wkw'elmexw.
a group separating themselves from another group:: halts'elíthet < halts'elí.
four fruit in a group or cluster (as they grow on a plant):: x̲(e)'othelòls < x̲e'ó:thel ~ x̲e'óthel.
group of canoes travelling upstream (moving to camp for fish-drying for ex.):: istéytiyel.
nine fruit in a group or cluster (as they grow on a plant):: tuxwòls < tú:xw.
plural, (usually) many in a group, collective:: R3= or C1eC2=.
(rare) plural, (usually) many in a group, collective:: R5= or C1e=, =R6= or =eC2=, R7= or C1á=, R8= or C1a=.
six fruit in a group (as they grow on a plant):: t'x̲emòls < t'éx̲.

grouse

blue grouse, blue-billed grouse:: mí:t', mí:t'.
ruffed grouse, (also known as) willow grouse:: sqwéth'.

grouse (CONT'D)
willow grouse (a local name for ruffed grouse), ruffed grouse:: stíxwem, stíxwem.
willow grouse, ruffed grouse:: skwéth' ~ skwéth'kweth'.

Grouse Point
Wilson's Point (on Harrison River), (also called) Grouse Point:: Títxwemqsel < stíxwem.

grove
burial grove of Scowkale:: Tl'átl'elh ?.
place where a grove of birches stood/stand near the Kickbush place on Chilliwack River Road in Sardis, (village at junction of Semmihault Creek and Chilliwack River [Wells 1965 (lst ed.):19]):: Sekw'sekw'emá:y < síkw'.

grow
growing (of animals, children, etc.):: ts'íts'esem < ts'ísem.
growing [s-o] up, (raising s-o):: ts'símt < ts'ísem.
growing up:: kw'ekw'ém < kw'ém.
grown twisted (of a tree):: sx̲á:lts'emeth' < x̲élts'.
grow up:: kw'ém.
to grow:: ts'ísem.

growl
growling (of one's stomach):: kw'ó:yx̲wem.
growl (of an animal):: x̲éylém < x̲éykw'et.

grudge
hold a grudge, hate:: sqelwílh < qél.
holding a grudge against each other:: xixemó:ltel < sxemá:l.

grunt :: ésqthet.

Grus canadensis tabida:: slí:m.

Gryllidae
probably mostly family Gryllidae, but perhaps family Prophalanopsidae, also perhaps singing groups such as family Tettigoniidae (order Orthoptera) or Cicadidae (order Hemiptera):: tó:lthíwa < tó:l ~ tò:l.

guardian spirit
guardian spirit, spirit power:: =ó:lkwlh.

guess
maybe, I guess, I'm uncertain, must be (evidently), (evidential), have to (I guess):: t'wa ~ t'we.
to guess, make a guess:: st'e'áwel ~ st'áwel, st'e'áwel ~ st'áwel < t.

guide
a guide:: í:wesà:ls < íwes.
directing, training, teaching, guiding:: í:wes < íwes.
guiding:: í:weséleq < íwes.
showing s-o (how to do it), teaching s-o, advising s-o, guiding s-o, directing s-o:: í:west < íwes.

guide (CONT'D)

teach how to do something, teach, guide, direct, show:: íwes.

gull

seagull (generic), gull, certainly including the glaucous-winged gull, and possibly including any or all of the following species which occur in the Stó:lō area: Bonaparte's gull, short-billed gull, ring-billed gull, California gull, herring gull:: slílōwya.

seagull (possibly generic), certainly including the glaucus-winged gull, and possibly including any or all of the following which occur in the Upriver Halkomelem-speaking area: Bonaparte's gull, short-billed gull, ring-billed gull, California gull, herring gull:: qw'elíteq.

gullet

throat (inside part), gullet, voice:: sqelxwá:le ~ sqelxwále < qél:éxw ~ qel(:)éxw.

Gulo luscus luscus:: shxwématsel ~ shxwémetsel.

perhaps Taxidea taxus taxus or Gulo luscus luscus:: sqoyép.

Taxidea taxus taxus or Gulo luscus luscus:: melmélkw'es sqoyép < sqoyép.

Taxidea taxus taxus, possibly Gulo luscus luscus:: sqoyép ~ melmélkw'es sqoyép.

gum)

chewing (gum):: th'eth'ám < th'a.

gummy (sticky):: tl'ítl'eq'el < tl'íq'.

pitch, sap, gum, chewing gum:: kw'íxw, kw'íxw.

gumboots

gumboots, rubber boots:: kw'ekw'íxwxel < kw'íxw.

gummy

gummy (sticky):: tl'ítl'eq'el < tl'íq'.

gums :: slheqwél:es < slhíqw.

gun

arrow, gun:: sakwelá̱x ~ sekwelá̱x < kwél.

be hit (with arrow, bullet, anything shot that you've aimed), got shot, (got pierced), got poked into, got wounded (with gun or arrow):: ts'éqw'.

draw a bow, cock a gun:: xwe'ít'et.

draw a bow, cock a gun, (draw it (of a bow), cock it (of a gun)):: xwe'ít'et < ót'.

miss s-th (in shooting at it with arrow, spear or gun):: qwíx̲wet < qwíx̲w.

spray gun:: spópex̲welsà:ls < póx̲w.

to miss a shot (an arrow, spear or gun):: qwíx̲w.

gunpowder)

pouch (like for gunpowder):: shxwyáx̲q'els ~ shxwiyáx̲q'els.

gurgle

(have) sound of water sloshing around inside (a bottle, etc.) or gurgling:: qw'át'ts'em.

gut

guts, intestines:: q'eq'éy < q'ey ~ q'i.

Gutierrez

pool down from Tillie Gutierrez's grandfather's fish-drying rack at Íyem (Eayem):: qemqémel ~ qemqémél < qém:el.

guts

insides (animal or human or other?), (internal organs, guts, etc.), (stomach [inside] [DM]):: sts'elxwíwel < ts'el.

Haig

rocky place between two CPR tunnels above and about half a mile east of Haig:: Popeleqwith'á:m ~ Lexwpopeleqwith'á:m < poleqwíth'a.

steep rock wall that used to have Indian writing at first C.P.R. tunnel above Haig:: X̲elíqel < x̲él ~ x̲é:yl ~ x̲í:l

Haig bay

Haig bay, a calm place on the west (C.P.R.) side of the Fraser River by the Haig railroad stop, below and across from Hope:: Sqám ~ Sqà:m < qám.

hail

hailing (weather):: kw'ekw'xwós < kw'xwós.

hail when it comes in sheets:: kw'íkw'xwòs < kw'xwós.

the hail:: skw'ekw'xwós < kw'xwós, tl'emx̲wéyle < tl'ém.

to hail, be hailing:: tl'emx̲wxéylem or tl'emx̲wxílem < tl'ém.

to hail (weather):: kw'xwós.

hair

(be) real gray (of hair), (grey hair):: sx̲ó:lem < x̲ólem.

bushy hair:: stíx̲eqw ~ stí:x̲eqw.

bushy hair on horses' legs (tufts like on Clydesdale breed), tufts of fur on horse's feet:: qwelqwélxel < qwíl ~ qwel.

combing one's hair:: téxelqéylem < tex.

comb one's hair, comb one's own hair:: texqéylem < tex.

comb s-o's hair:: texqé:ylt < tex.

come out (of hair) (like hair in a comb):: qw'ém.

crown of head, center of the top of the head where the hair starts:: sq'eyx̲éleqw.

curly hair, (be curly-haired(?), have curly hair(?)):: sq'elq'élp'eqw < q'ál.

curly hair, (have curly hair(?)):: sq'elq'élp'es < q'ál, sq'ó:lp'eqw < q'ál.

cut one's hair:: lhíts'eqwem < lhíts' ~ lhí:ts'.

gray (of hair), grey (of hair):: x̲ólem.

hair anywhere on the body (arms, legs, chest, underarms, etc.):: qwilṓws < qwíl ~ qwel.

hair in the ears:: sqwelqwelá:lí:ya < qwíl ~ qwel.

hair in the nose:: sqwelqwélqsel < qwíl ~ qwel.

hair is falling out, losing one's hair:: qw'eméqel < qw'ém.

hair (of the head):: má:qel.

hair on the body:: sqwelqwílōws ~ sqwelqwéylōws < qwíl ~ qwel.

hair on the chin or jaw, beard, mustache:: qwiliyéthel < qwíl ~ qwel.

(have a) hairy face, (have) hair on the face, (have a woolly face):: xwpopó:s < pá:pa.

(have a) part in the hair, to part (hair):: kw'éts'eles < kw'íts'.

(have) bushy and uncombed hair:: chílheqw < =chílh ~ chílh=.

(have) coarse hair:: mekwélqel < mékw.

(have) fine hair:: kweleleselqel.

hair (CONT'D)

have reddish-brown fur, have reddish-brown animal hair:: tskwímelqel < kwí:m.
have red hair, have reddish-brown hair:: tskwí:meqw < kwí:m.
(have the) hair in a bun:: sq'éth'ep < q'áth'.
loincloth, dog-hair apron, dog-hair mat:: sthíyep.
oil one's hair, oil one's head:: mélxweqwem < mélxw, melxwqwéylém < mélxw.
on top of the head, on the hair:: =eqw ~ =(e)leqw ~ =íqw ~ =ó:qw.
part the hair on the right side (left side as people look at you), have the hair parted on the right side:: kelchochéleqw < kelchóch ~ kyelchóch.
pubic hair:: qwéyleq ~ qwíleq < qwíl ~ qwel.
pull out (hair):: qw'emét < qw'ém.
pull s-o's hair, grab s-o's hair:: x̲éymleqwt < x̲éym.
really turned gray (of hair):: x̲ó:lemthet < x̲ólem.
singe the hairs off skin:: kw'síws < kw'ás.
soft (down) feathers put in oiled hair for dancing:: sq'óyeseqw ~ sx̲óyeseqw < sq'óyes.
soft feathers put in oiled hair for dancing:: sx̲óyeseqw ~ sq'óyeseqw.
tickled (by a hair, by a light touch):: sá:yx̲wem.
to part one's hair:: kw'éts'elesem < kw'íts'.
turning gray (in hair):: x̲olémthet < x̲ólem.
wash one's hair, wash one's head:: th'ex̲wíqwem < th'éx̲w or th'óx̲w.
wash one's head and hair:: xwóyeqwem (or perhaps) xwáyeqwem.
wool, fur, animal hair:: sá:y.

hairy
(have a) hairy face, (have) hair on the face, (have a woolly face):: xwpopó:s < pá:pa.

half :: alht'éqw' < t'éqw', lhséq' < séq'.
a half dollar, fifty cents:: lhséq' < séq'.
break s-th in two (with one's hands), break it in half (with one's hands only), break off a piece of s-th:: peqwót < péqw.
divide something in half with s-o:: tseléqelhtst.
lessen it (of someone's load), halve it, make s-th lighter (in weight), lessen it (like when someone's pack is too heavy):: xwát < xwá.

half-breed:: lhséq' < séq'.

half-brother
half-sibling, half-brother, half-sister:: lets'ṓw(e)yelh ~ slets'ṓweyelh < láts'.

half-hitch
spear pole knot hitch (two half-hitches), clove-hitch knot:: ts'sítsim.

half-sibling
half-sibling, half-brother, half-sister:: lets'ṓw(e)yelh ~ slets'ṓweyelh < láts'.

half-sister
half-sibling, half-brother, half-sister:: lets'ṓw(e)yelh ~ slets'ṓweyelh < láts'.

Haliaeetus leucocephalus:: skw'álx̲, sp'óq'es < p'éq'.
Aquila chrysaetos and Haliaeetus leucocephalus:: yéx̲wela.

halibut

halibut, flounder (prob. starry flounder):: p'éwiy ~ p'ṓwiy < p'ewíy ~ p'ōwíy.

Halkomelem

Kwantlen people, Kwantlen dialect of Downriver Halkomelem:: Qw'ó:ltl'el.

Stó:lō people, Halkomelem-speaking people living along the Fraser River or its tributaries from Five Mile Creek above Yale downriver to the mouth of the Fraser:: Stó:lō < tó:l ~ tò:l.

Upriver Halkomelem language, to speak Upriver Halkomelem:: Hálq'eméylem < Leq'á:mél.

hall

dance-hall:: qw'eyilexáwtxw < qw'eyílex ~ qw'eyíléx.

halve

lessen it (of someone's load), halve it, make s-th lighter (in weight), lessen it (like when someone's pack is too heavy):: xwát < xwá.

Hamersley

a place just past the west end of Seabird Island, towards Agassiz, AK's grandfather only translated it as Hamersley's (see Hamersley's hopyards), it was located at the west end of Seabird Island i.e. property between Dan Thomas's and Uncle Dave Charles's places, across from Sqémelets [Elders on Seabird Is. trip 6/20/78]):: Qwoméx̲weth' < qwó:m ~ qwóm ~ qwem.

Hamersley Hopyards

the whole Agassiz (B.C.) area (JL), Agassiz Mountain (AK), place near Agassiz where Hamersley Hopyards were (possibly some other speakers):: Alámex.

Hamersly Hopyard Hill

Hook-nose, Hook-nose Mountain, Hamersly Hopyard Hill:: Lhílhkw'eleqs ~ Lhílhkw'elqs < lhíkw' ~ lhí:kw'.

hammer

hammer, stone hand hammer, sledge hammer:: shxwtélhtses < télhches.

hit on the hand with a hammer:: télhches.

nail s-th, hammer s-th:: hám:et.

rub (oil or water) in s-th to clean or soften, rub s-th to soften or clean it, (shaping a stone hammer with abrasion?, shaping?, mixing paint?, pressing together or crushing? [BHTTC 9/2/76]):: yémq't.

hand :: chálėx.

a cut on the hand:: shxwlhéts'tses < lhíts' ~ lhí:ts'.

(be) left-handed:: sth'íkwetses < th'íkwe.

(be) sick on the hand, (have) a sick hand, (have) a hurt hand:: q'óq'eytses < q'ó:y ~ q'óy.

break it in pieces with one's hands:: peqwpéqwet < péqw.

break s-th in two (with one's hands), break it in half (with one's hands only), break off a piece of s-th:: peqwót < péqw.

burned on the finger or hand, burnt the hand, a hand got burnt:: kw'éstses < kw'ás.

can't reach (with hand):: q'thá:mtses < q'thá:m.

chop one's hand, [get chopped on the hand]:: t'émches < t'ém.

clap one's hands, clap once with hands:: lhéqw'tsesem < lhóqw'et.

clapping with (one's) hands:: lhólheqw'tsesem < lhóqw'et.

clean hands:: éyetses < éy ~ éy:.

hand (CONT'D)

cross one's hands [prob. error], (hands crossed):: q'eyáweth'ches < q'ey ~ q'i.
cut on one's hand, (cut one's finger [EB}):: lhéts'ches < lhíts' ~ lhí:ts'.
get a sliver in one's hand:: xéth'ches.
get a sliver or splinter in the hand:: xéts'ches.
get squeezed (in hand or fingers):: p'íth'em < p'í:.
grab a handful:: x̲éymem < x̲éym.
hammer, stone hand hammer, sledge hammer:: shxwtélhtses < télhches.
hands:: chelchálέx < chálέx.
(have a) crooked hand:: spíytses < pó:y.
(have a) paralyzed hand, game hand:: slhéx̲tses < lhéx̲.
(have) big hand(s):: thíthetses < thi ~ tha ~ the ~ thah ~ theh.
(have) dirty hands:: qéletses < qél, ts'epx̲tses < ts'épx̲.
have one's hands behind one's back:: sq'eth'ewíts ~ sq'eth'ōwíts < q'áth'.
her hand is broken, his hand is broken:: selkwá:tses < lékw.
he's holding s-th in each hand:: s'i'á:ytses < á:y.
hit on the hand with a hammer:: télhches.
holding a hand:: kwelátses < kwél.
holding the hand of s-o:: kwelátsest < kwél.
hollow of hand:: xwt'óxwestses < t'óxw.
knocking with one's hand:: kwókwexwetsesem < kwoxw.
knuckles (all the joints of the hand and fingers):: qwemqwémx̲wtses < qwó:m ~ qwóm ~ qwem.
leaning the face on the hand with elbow propped:: piyósem < píy.
left-handed:: th'íkwetses < th'íkwe.
lying on one side with one's head propped up on one hand:: piypiyáleqálem < píy.
month beginning with first sliver of moon in February, (time things stick to the hand (in cold)):: temt'elémtses < t'elém.
one's hand sticks to something (in cold, to honey, to glue, etc.):: t'elémtses < t'elém.
on the hand or finger, in the hand or finger:: =tses ~ =ches.
palm (of the hand):: shxw'óthestses ~ shxwe'óthestses < s'ó:thes ~ s'óthes.
pass s-th (by hand):: xwmítsesem < mí ~ mé ~ me.
pick fast, (do fast with the hands):: x̲wémetses < x̲wém ~ xwém.
put a hand on one hip:: piypiyólwelh < píy.
put hands on both hips, (put hands akimbo):: piypiyólwelhem < píy.
put one's hand on s-th to brace oneself, brace oneself on s-th/s-o:: píyet < píy.
put one's hands behind one's back:: q'eth'ōwítsem < q'áth'.
put one's hands under one's arms:: xixets'eláx̲em < xits' ~ xets'.
right hand:: s'eyí:wtses < éy ~ éy:.
shading one's eyes from the sun with the hand (looking into the sun):: xwtóx̲esem.
shake hands:: kwelétses < kwél.
shake hands with s-o:: kwelétsest < kwél.
shaking a lot of hands:: kwéletsesà:ls < kwél.
shaking hands:: kweltssà:ls < kwél.
shaking the hand of s-o, shaking his hand:: kwéletsest < kwél.
she broke her hand, he broke his hand:: lekwátses < lékw.
slip off the hands, slip out of the hands:: x̲wlhépches < x̲wlhép.
spindle for spinning wool, a hand spinner:: sélseltel < sél or sí(:)l.
to cup water in one's hands, to cup berries in one's hands:: qéltsesem < qó:.
to wave (the hand):: x̲élqes.
twitch, flutter (of one's eye, hand, skin, etc.):: lhawét'em < lhá:w.
wash one's hands:: th'ex̲wá:tsesem < th'éx̲w or th'óx̲w.

hand (CONT'D)

wrist or hand joint:: xweth'éqw'tses.

handkerchief for nose:: áp'eqselem < á:p' ~ áp'.

handle

carry it carefully, handle it with care:: sts'áts'elstexw < ts'á:.
cool down enough to touch (or handle or work with):: tóqweltsep.
handle of a cup:: q'ő:l (or better) qw'ő:l.
handle of a knife, knife-handle:: lhà:ts'telálá < lhíts' ~ lhí:ts'.
handle of a spoon:: skwélemel < kwél.
long-handled stirring spoon:: shxwqwáylhechàls < qwá:y.

handsome

good-looking, beautiful, pretty, handsome, looks good:: iyó:mex ~ iyóméx ~ iyómex < éy ~ éy:.

hang

be slack, loose, too loose, hanging loose (of a slackened rope):: slí:leqw < líqw.
hang fish (especially salmon) for drying:: chálhtel < =chílh ~ chílh=.
hanging lots of fish to dry:: chachí:lhtel ~ chachíyelhtel < =chílh ~ chílh=.
hang on (grab and hang on):: kwelà:ls < kwél.
hang oneself, (hung by a rope [AC]):: x̲wíqw'esem < x̲wíqw'.
hang onto s-o:: kwú:ls < kwél.
hang something up:: xeq'ó:thet < xáq'.
hang s-th on a line, hang s-th on a nail, hang s-th up:: q'é:ywet (or better) q'í:wet < q'e:yw ~ q'í:w.
hang s-th (on a nail or hat hanger), hook it back on (of a stitch lost in knitting):: ókw'est < ókw'.
(have) snot hanging from the nose:: slholh(e)x̲wélqsel < lhex̲w.
(hung) under:: síq < seqíws ~ seqí:ws.
(hung up in a fish net):: sx̲wíx̲weqw' < x̲wíqw'.
put a rope around s-o/s-th's neck, put a leash on s-th, hang s-o:: x̲wíqw'est < x̲wíqw'.
smoking salmon, (hanging fish up to smoke):: chá:lhtel < =chílh ~ chílh=.
spinning (while hanging), (twirling):: ts'á:lq'em < ts'el.

Hanging Lake

Beaver Lake or Hanging Lake:: Sqelá:w (X̲óx̲tsa) < sqelá:w.

happen

what happened?, what is it?, why?:: xwe'ít.

happen to

frightened s-o [accidentally], [happened/managed to] frighten s-o:: th'ith'íkw'elexw < th'íkw' or th'ekw'.
happen to smell s-th:: hóqwlexw ~ héqwlexw < hóqw.
(happen to) surprise s-o:: lewálhlexw < lewálh.
hurt s-o [accidentally, happen to, manage to]:: x̲élhlexw < x̲élh.
kill s-th/s-o accidentally, (happen to or manage to kill s-th/s-o):: q'eyléxw < q'ó:y ~ q'óy.
make s-o ashamed [happen to or accidentally or manage to]:: lháylexw < lháy.
non-control reflexive, happen to or manage to or accidentally do to oneself:: =l=ómet or =l-ómet ~ =l=ó:met.

happen to (CONT'D)

non-control transitivizer, accidentally, happen to, manage to do to s-o/s-th:: =l.

happy

become glad, become happy, happy inside:: xwoyíwel ~ xwoyíwél.
be good, good, well, nice, fine, better, better (ought to), it would be good if, may it be good, let it be good, happy, glad, clean, well-behaved, polite, virgin, popular, comfortable (with furniture, other things?),:: éy ~ éy:.
be happy, being happy:: xwoxweyíwel < xwoyíwel ~ xwoyíwél.
happy to see s-o:: xwoyíwelmet < xwoyíwel ~ xwoyíwél.
make s-o happy, cheer s-o up:: xwoyíwelstexw < xwoyíwel ~ xwoyíwél.

hard

be chewing s-th hard:: x̲éyx̲ekw'et < x̲éykw'et.
(be) difficult, hard (of work, etc.):: tl'í ~ tl'í:.
(be) hard, stiff (material), strong (of rope, material, not of a person), tough:: tl'éx̲w.
bumping or bouncing hard on the rump:: th'esth'esélets < th'és.
chewing (something hard, like apple):: x̲éyx̲ekw'els < x̲éykw'et.
chew it (s-th hard, apple, pill):: x̲éykw'et.
do it harder:: tímet.
exert oneself, make a big effort, do with all one's might, [do] as hard as possible, do it harder (used if already paddling for ex.):: tíméthet < tímet.
(get) lots of water all over since it's raining so hard, really getting rainy:: t'emt'émqw'xel < t'émeqw'.
hard clay, hard earth, smooth (hard) earth:: síq'.
hard ground:: tl'x̲wéylep or tl'x̲wílep < tl'éx̲w.
I got hard (of arm, leg, penis, etc.):: tl'x̲wòlèm < tl'éx̲w.
[make a bang, make a sudden hard thump sound]:: kw'péx̲w.
mashing, grinding (stones, something hard):: tótesem < tós.
(perhaps) copper, (hard metal that looks like gold but isn't, maybe copper [Elders at Katz Class 10/5/76], metal found in mines and used for arrowheads [Elders Group 5/28/75], gold [EB]):: sqw'él.
raining hard, pouring rain, (raining fast):: xwémxel < x̲wém ~ xwém.
slip and fall hard (either a person or something he's carrying):: th'esáp < th'és.
stiff, hard:: th'éts.
straining to listen, really listening, listening hard, trying to listen, (listen [AC]):: xwlalá:.
throw s-o down hard (like a wrestler), tap s-th (a container's bottom) [hard] on something to make the contents settle (like berry basket):: th'esét ~ th'sét < th'és.
throw s-o down [hard] on the rump:: th'eséletst < th'és.
to harden:: tl'ex̲wéthet < tl'éx̲w.
to harden (of pitch, wax, etc.), (harden s-th):: th'etsét < th'éts.
too hard to eat:: th'éts.

harden

to harden:: tl'ex̲wéthet < tl'éx̲w.

"hardhack"

oceanspray plant, "ironwood", "hardhack":: qáthelhp < qáthexw.
pink spirea, "hardhack":: t'áts'elhp < t'á:ts'.

hare

big rabbit, older rabbit, big/older snowshoe/varying hare, now probably also big/older

hare (CONT'D)

eastern cottontail rabbit (introduced):: sqiqewóthel < sqewáth, sqwiqweyóthel.
jackrabbit, also big or older rabbit (snowshoe/varying hare):: sqwíqweyóthel < qwá.
(larger) rabbit: snowshoe or varying hare, now probably also eastern cottontail rabbit (introduced):: sqewáth.
rabbit: snowshoe/varying hare, now probably also eastern cottontail rabbit (introduced), (baby rabbit, small rabbit or hare [Elders Group]):: sqíqewàth < sqewáth.
rabbit, (varying hare, perhaps now also the introduced eastern cottontail):: shxwóxw.

harelip
cleft palate, harelip:: qiqewótheló:ythel < sqewáth.
(have a) harelip:: x̱asáxw.

hark
listen, hark, listen to something particular:: xwlalá:m ~ xwlalám < xwlalá:.

harm
a sung spell, power to help or harm people or to do [ritual] burning, power to do witchcraft and predict the future, an evil spell, (magic spell) (someone who has power to take things out of a person or put things in [by magic] [Elders Group 2/25/76], ritualist [Elders Group 1/21/76], witch [EB 4/25/78]):: syiwí:l ~ syewí:l < yéw: ~ yéw.

harpoon
dip-netting, fishing with a scoop net, (harpooning fish at night [DM 12/4/64]):: q'íq'emó:s ~ q'éyq'emó:s < q'emós ~ q'emó:s.
spear (any kind), spear (for fish or war), fish-spear, telescopic spear for sturgeon, harpoon, detachable harpoon points:: tá:lh.
spear, shaft (of spear/harpoon/gaff-hook), gaff-hook pole:: s'álem.

Harris
slough called Billy Harris's Slough or Louie's Slough, the next slough east of Yálhxetel and west of Q'iq'ewetó:lthel:: Meth'á:lméxwem ~ Mth'á:lmexwem.
slough where people used to drift-net by Martin Harris's place at Seabird Island:: Titáwlechem < tewláts.

Harrison Bay:: Leqémél < qém:el.

Harrison Bay bridge
longest dirt point sticking out on Harrison River about a quarter mile above Harrison Bay bridge:: Tl'éqteqsel < tl'áqt.

Harrison Hot Springs
Harrison Hot Springs:: Qwó:ls < qwó:ls.

Harrison Lake
a neck of land on the west side of Harrison Lake just north of Twenty-Mile Creek and across from the north tip of Long Island:: Shxwtépsem < tépsem.
a stone like a statue at Harrison Lake, probably Doctor's Point:: Skoyá:m ~ Skeyá:m.
Bare Bluffs, a steep slope on the west side of Harrison Lake:: Lhó:leqwet.
beach on east side of Harrison Lake across from Long Island where there are lots of flat rocks, most of which have holes in them:: Sqweqwehíwel < qwá.
bear-shaped rock up on cliff on south side above Echo Point bay on Echo Island in

Harrison Lake (CONT'D)

Harrison Lake:: Spá:th < pá:th.

Cottonwood Beach (in the southern quarter of Harrison Lake):: Chewṓ:lhp < cháchew ~ cháchu.

Doctor's Point on northwest shore Harrison Lake:: Lhx̲é:ylex < lhéx̲.

"Eagle Falls" on the west side of Harrison Lake, probably Walian Creek falls:: Kwótxwem Stó:lō < kwótx̲wem ~ kwótxwem.

Echo Island in Harrison Lake:: Xweqw'oyíqw, Xwōxwe'áqel.

Echo Island in southern quarter of Harrison Lake:: Xwōqwiyáqw.

horned owl-shaped rock (beside Spá:th, a bear-shaped rock) up on a cliff on the south side above Echo Point bay on Echo Island in Harrison Lake:: Chítmexw < chítmexw.

Long Island (in Harrison Lake):: Híkw Tl'tsás < híkw.

place just south of Doctor's Point on Harrison Lake northwest side:: S'ót'o < ót'.

Rainbow Falls (on Harrison Lake's southeast side):: Tsólqthet te Skwówech < skwó:wech ~ skwówech.

Rainbow Falls on Harrison Lake, (Sturgeon's Drop):: Tsólqthet te Skwówech < tsélq ~ chélq.

Rainbow Falls on the east side of Harrison Lake:: Tsólqthet te Skwówech < tsélq.

Sasquatch rock on Harrison River or Harrison Lake:: Sásq'ets (probably) < sásq'ets.

Six-Mile Creek and bay on west side of Harrison Lake:: Lkwṓxwethem < kwṓxweth.

Whale Point at the southwest end of Harrison Lake:: Qwél:és < qwél:és ~ qwélés.

Harrison River

a channel between an island and the main shore a) across Harrison River from where the Phillips smokehouse was at Chehalis village (slightly downriver from the mouth of Chehalis R. into Harrison R.), also b) at Harrison Lake where the hatchery was:: Lheltá:lets ~ Lheltálets < lhà:l.

a little bay or eddy on Harrison River about two miles downriverfrom Chehalis:: Skw'á:lx̲w.

a nice place near Morris Creek on the (right?) side of Harrison River [IHTTC 8/25/77]):: Lhó:leqwet.

a point or bald hill on Harrison River where people waited to spear silver spring salmon:: Chth'éylem < chth'éylem.

a rock along Harrison River which looks like layers of seal fat all along its bottom:: Skwló ~ Sqwló < skwló ~ sqwló.

a slough on Harrison River north side by the mouth of Chehalis River which has a knee-shaped sandbar at its mouth, this is the next slough above (upriver from) Meth'á:lmexwem:: Q'iq'ewetó:lthel < q'éw ~ q'ew.

beach in front of old Scowlitz village, the point the Harrison River goes around by Kilby's store:: Sq'iq'ewílem < q'éw ~ q'ew.

Chehalis village on Harrison River, the Heart Rock for which Chehalis, B.C. was named (at the mouth of Chehalis River):: Ts'a'í:les < ts'á:.

Harrison River spring salmon, Harrison River chinook salmon, big Chehalis River spring salmon, (preserved (smoked?) meat [AC: Tait dialect]):: pó:qw' ~ póqw'.

largest deepest bay on Harrison River (between Victor McDonald's place and Morris Mt.):: Híkw Sméya < híkw.

late fall Harrison River and Chehalis River sockeye salmon (last run, kind of red):: qwechíwiya.

late fall sockeye salmon (last run on Harrison River and Chehalis River, kind of red):: sqwó:yxw.

Leon's Slough on Harrison River:: Xemó:leqw < xá:m.

longest dirt point sticking out on Harrison River about a quarter mile above Harrison Bay bridge:: Tl'éqteqsel < tl'áqt.

next slough on north side of Harrison River above (east of) Smímstíyexwá:le, a muddy

Harrison River (CONT'D)

slough where fish spawn, right across from Johnny Leon's place at Chehalis and about 100 yards downstream (west) of Yálhxetel:: Mímex̲wel (or prob. better, Mímexwel) < mímexwel.

point of land on Harrison River (somewhere between Lheltá:lets and Híqelem) where during a famine the old people scooped minnows and boiled them to make soup:: Sqíqemlò < sqíqemlò.

point on west side of Harrison River on which or across from which Sx̲wó:yx̲wey is located (the rock formation resembling a sx̲wó:yx̲wey mask):: Skwtéxwqel < kwetáxw.

Pretty's Bay on Harrison River:: Sásq'etstel < sásq'ets.

rock shaped like a man's head with a sx̲wó:yx̲wey mask on a point near the head of Harrison River, the point also called Spook's Point:: Sx̲wó:yx̲wey ~ Sx̲wóyx̲wey < sx̲wó:yx̲wey ~ sx̲wóyx̲wey.

rock shaped like a man's nose on the north side of Harrison River:: Méqsel < méqsel.

rock that looks like a little hat on west (Chehalis) side of Harrison River above mouth of Morris Creek:: Yó:yseqw < yó:seqw ~ yóseqw.

rock up the Harrison River from the old Chehalis Indian cemetery:: Xwyélés ~ Lexwyélés < yél:és.

Sasquatch rock on Harrison River or Harrison Lake:: Sásq'ets (probably) < sásq'ets.

Seal Fat Rock on Harrison River just upriver from Th'éqwela (place by Morris Lake where Indian people used to play Indian badminton), this rock has what resembles seal fat all around it:: Skwló ~ Sqwló < sqwló.

silver spring salmon that came up Harrison River and Chehalis Creek, (first spring salmon [Deming]):: sqwéx̲em < qwéx̲em.

slough on west side of Harrison River, the first slough upriver from Q'iq'ewetó:lthel and first slough below Xemó:leqw:: Shxwpópélem.

Wilson's Point (on Harrison River), (also called) Grouse Point:: Títxwemqsel < stíxwem.

harrow

a rake, a harrow:: x̲éyx̲ep'ílep < x̲éyp'.

harvest)

pick berries, pick off (leaves, fruit, vegetables, hops), (pluck off, harvest):: lhím.

pick s-th, (harvest s-th):: lhemét < lhím.

harvestman spider

daddy long-legs, harvestman spider:: tl'áleqtxel q'ésq'esetsel < tl'áqt.

daddy long-legs (spider), harvestman spider:: tl'áleqtxel q'esq'ésetsel < q'ey ~ q'i.

hasn't

isn't s-o yet?, isn't it yet?, hasn't s-o yet?:: xwewá: < éwe ~ ṓwe.

hat :: =ó(:)weqw, yó:seqw ~ yóseqw.

be wearing a hat:: siyó:yseqw < yó:seqw ~ yóseqw.

cowboy hat:: kawpōyóweq(w) < káwpōy.

hats:: yó:leseqw ~ yóleseqw < yó:seqw ~ yóseqw.

new spirit-dancer's head-dress or [cedar-bark] hat:: sx̲wóyéleqws te x̲awsólkwlh < sx̲wóyéleqw.

put on one's hat:: yóseqwem < yó:seqw ~ yóseqw.

rock that looks like a little hat on west (Chehalis) side of Harrison River above mouth of Morris Creek:: Yó:yseqw < yó:seqw ~ yóseqw.

small hat:: yó:yseqw ~ yóyseqw < yó:seqw ~ yóseqw.

spirit-dancing costume, wool hat for spirit-dancer (Deming):: s-hóyiws.

hatch

sit on eggs, to hatch eggs, to brood eggs:: tl'xwá:ylhem < tl'xw ~ tl'exw.

hatchery

a channel between an island and the main shore a) across Harrison River from where the Phillips smokehouse was at Chehalis village (slightly downriver from the mouth of Chehalis R. into Harrison R.), also b) at Harrison Lake where the hatchery was:: Lheltá:lets ~ Lheltálets < lhà:l.

Hatchery Creek

Cultus Lake, (also village at Cultus Lake near Hatchery Creek [Wells (lst ed.):19]):: Swílhcha.

Hatchery Creek, tributary of Sweltzer Creek (which drains Cultus Lake):: Stṓtelō < tó:l ~ tò:l.

hatchet

little hatchet, little axe:: kw'qwém < kw'óqw.

hate :: sqeltí:l < qél.

hate s-o:: sqelwílhmet ~ qelwílhmet < qél.

hold a grudge, hate:: sqelwílh < qél.

Hatzic :: X̲áth'aq < x̲áth' ~ x̲e'áth'.

haunt

be haunted:: séyí:m < síy.

to ghost s-o, (to haunt s-o):: poleqwíth'et < poleqwíth'a.

have

find a seat, have a seat, sit down:: ch'álechem < ts'á:.

get erect (of penis only), have an erection:: xátl'.

get s-th, catch s-th, have s-th, find s-th:: kwélexw ~ kwél:exw < kwél.

have a big head:: thó:qw < thi ~ tha ~ the ~ thah ~ theh.

have a cool drink:: th'elhqéylem or th'elhqílem ~ th'elhqílém < th'álh.

have a hot drink, warm one's chest inside:: qatílésem < qá:t.

have a menthol taste, (have a cool taste):: xó:lxwem.

have a nose bleed:: thxwómélqsel < thóxw or théxw.

have a pain in the stomach, (have a stomach-ache), one's stomache hurts:: x̲elhálwes < x̲élh.

have a seat:: xwch'áletsem < ts'á:.

(have) blue eyes:: ts'meth'ó:les < méth'.

have, get, stative or be with colors:: ts= ~ ts'.

have heartburn:: yeqwí:les < yéqw.

have one's hands behind one's back:: sq'eth'ewíts ~ sq'eth'ōwíts < q'áth'.

have pain, to hurt:: sáyem.

have something under one arm:: xixets'eláx̲el < xits' ~ xets'.

have s-th :: kwélexw ~ kwél:exw < kwél.

have the last spirit dance of the season, have the "sweep up":: yekw'ólhem or perhaps yekw'wólhem < yókw' ~ yóqw'.

have worms, he got worms:: th'eth'ekw'íwetem < sth'ékw'.

having a nose bleed:: thóxwemélqsel < thóxw or théxw.

having labor pains, being in labor in childbirth:: ts'áts'elem.

hold s-th (in one's grasp), holding s-th (in one's grasp), have s-th, grasp s-th:: kwelát < kwél.

have (CONT'D)

I'd rather have (s-th), I'd prefer (s-th) (make that s-th instead):: tl'óst or tl'óstexw.
mark s-th, blaze it (of a trail), get/have s-th spotted (marked and located), make note of s-th:: x̲e'áth'stexw < x̲áth' ~ x̲e'áth'.
resultative, -ed, have -en (usually results in a past tense or past participle translation in English):: =R1= or =C1e=, R5= or C1e=, R8= or C1a=, =R9= or =C1á(:)=.
stative (with color terms), have, get (elsewhere):: ts= ~ ch=.
to have a crooked jaw:: sx̲ó:lts'iyethel < x̲élts'.
to have cramps, get a cramp, to be cramped:: q'élptem ~ q'élp'tem.

have a baby

giving birth, having a child, having a baby:: tsméla < méle ~ mél:a.

have a child

already had children:: semsémele < méle ~ mél:a.
giving birth, having a child, having a baby:: tsméla < méle ~ mél:a.
have given birth, already had a child, had a baby, (delivered):: sémele < méle ~ mél:a.

have/get

stative (with color terms), have/get (elsewhere):: ch=.

have to

determined (about s-th), have to do it, got to do it:: x̲asélmet < x̲ás.
do I have to?, does one have to?:: lóyéxwa < lóy.
maybe, I guess, I'm uncertain, must be (evidently), (evidential), have to (I guess):: t'wa ~ t'we.
want to pee, (want to urinate, feel like one has to urinate):: síyt'eqem < síyt'.

having

having labor pains, being in labor in childbirth:: ts'áts'elem.

hawk

chicken hawk (red-tailed hawk), hawk (large and small varieties):: x̲emx̲ímels ~ x̲emx̲íméls < x̲éym, x̲emx̲ímels ~ x̲emx̲íméls < x̲éym.
little hawk:: x̲ix̲emx̲íméls < x̲éym.

hawthorn

black hawthorn berry, blackhaw berries:: máts'el.
black hawthorn tree:: mats'íyelhp < máts'el.

hay

barn, (hay house, grass building):: sox̲weláwtxw < só:x̲wel ~ sóx̲wel.
cut (grass, hay):: lhéch'elechá:ls < lhíts' ~ lhí:ts'.
cutting (grass, hay):: lhílhech'elchá:ls < lhíts' ~ lhí:ts'.
grass (every kind) (wild and now domestic types), hay:: só:x̲wel ~ sóx̲wel.
haying time:: temsóx̲wel < só:x̲wel ~ sóx̲wel.

haying

haying time:: temsóx̲wel < só:x̲wel ~ sóx̲wel.

hazelnut

hazelnut bush or tree:: sth'í:tsemelhp < sth'í:tsem.

hazelnut (CONT'D)

hazelnut (the nut), any nut:: sth'í:tsem.
hazelnut tree or bush:: sth'í:tsemelhp < th'éts.
nut of hazelnut bush, acorn, any nut, walnut, peanut, etc.:: sth'í:tsem < th'éts.

he

and so (he, she, it, they):: qetl'osésu ~ qetl'os'ésu < tl'ó ~ tl'o, tl'osésu ~ tl'os'ésu < tl'ó ~ tl'o.
and then (he, she, it):: tl'esu < tl'ó ~ tl'o.
because (he, she, it, they):: tl'okw'es ~ tl'okwses ~ tl'ekwses < tl'ó ~ tl'o.
he (present or presence unspecified), he's the one that, it's him that, she or it (present or presence unspecified), that or this (immediately before nominal):: tú:tl'ò ~ tútl'ò ~ tútl'o < tl'ó ~ tl'o.
that he, that she, that it, that they:: kws ...-s ~ kwses ~ kw'es ...-s < kw.
that's a little one (male, about one to five years old), he (little):: tú:tl'òtl'èm < tl'ó ~ tl'o.
that's him (absent), that's her (absent), it's him/her (absent), he (absent), she (absent):: kwthú:tl'ò < tl'ó ~ tl'o.
that was him (deceased), he (deceased):: kw'ú:tl'ò:lh < tl'ó ~ tl'o.

head

a sxwó:yxwey head turned to stone on land at Xelhlálh somewhere:: Sxéyes te Sxwó:yxwey < sxwó:yxwey ~ sxwóyxwey.
at the head or source of a river, the inside head or inlet of a river:: =qel.
bald-headed:: th'óqweleqw.
barbecued fish head:: xots'oyíqw.
(be) bald-headed:: sth'ó:qweleqw < th'óqweleqw.
bumped on the head:: teséleqw < tós.
bump the head:: tesálèqel < tós.
carry[ing] a packstrap around the head:: chmaméleqw < chám.
clubbed on the back of the neck, clubbed on the back of the head:: kw'qwépsem < kw'óqw.
cooked fish head:: sth'óqwes < sth'ó:qwi ~ sth'óqwi.
crown of head:: sqw'óteleqw.
crown of head, center of the top of the head where the hair starts:: sq'eyxéleqw.
edible gristle inside fish head (nose gristle):: sxépeqw (or sxép'eqw? or sxép'ekw'?).
end of a falling section of land, end of a level stretch of land, (head of a creek or island [Elders Group]):: lhéq'qel.
facing up, head sticking up:: kw'ekw'e'íqw ~ kw'ekw'íqw < kw'e'í ~ kw''í ~ kw'í.
fall on one's forehead, drop on one's forehead, fall onto one's head:: méleqw (or) leméleqw.
fatty salmon head:: lésleseqw < ló:s ~ lós.
feel one's head, (feel the head):: qetxéleqw < qétxt.
fish head soup:: xots'oyíqw slhóp < xots'oyíqw.
greasy-headed:: lésleseqw < ló:s ~ lós.
have a big head:: thó:qw < thi ~ tha ~ the ~ thah ~ theh.
(have a) flat head, (have cranial deformation by cradle-board):: sp'íp'elheqw < p'ílh.
(have a) headache:: xlhá:léqel ~ xelháléqel < xélh.
(have a) pointed head:: yethéleqw < éy ~ éy:.
(have) big heads (of a bunch of fish for ex.):: thítheqw < thi ~ tha ~ the ~ thah ~ theh.
(have/get) a head cold:: th'ólhem sq'óq'ey < th'álh.
head of a creek or island:: lheqel ~ lhequl.
head of an island:: =qel.
head (of any living thing):: sxéyes ~ sxéy:es.

head (CONT'D)

head of a river:: =eqw ~ =(e)leqw ~ =íqw ~ =ó:qw.
head of descendants:: =eqw ~ =(e)leqw ~ =íqw ~ =ó:qw.
head of the penis:: sxtl'í:qw < xátl'.
hit on the ear, hit on the temple (side of the head):: kw'qwá:lí:ya < kw'óqw.
hit on the top of the head:: kw'qwéleqw < kw'óqw.
hit s-o on the head, club him on the head:: kw'qwéleqwt < kw'óqw.
in the head:: =áléqel, =qel, =qéyl ~ =qel.
in the rump, in the anus, in the rectum, in the bottom, on the insides, inside parts, core, inside the head:: =í:wel ~ =íwel ~ =ewel.
lying on one side with one's head propped up on one hand:: piypiyáleqálem < píy.
lying on one's stomach with head down on one's arms:: qiqep'eyósem < qep'.
neck, (back of head and back of neck [EB], nape of the neck [Elders Group 5/3/78]):: tépsem.
nodding one's head:: líleqwesem < líqw.
nod one's head, nod one's head (up and down for yes for ex.):: líqwesem < líqw.
oil his/her/its head:: mélxweqwt < mélxw.
oil one's hair, oil one's head:: mélxweqwem < mélxw, melxwqwéylém < mélxw.
one's head is shaking constantly (like with disease):: x̲wóyqwesem, x̲wóyqwesem.
on the back of the head, back of the neck:: =épsem.
on the side of the head, on the temples, around the ear, on the cheek:: =éla.
on top of the head, on the hair:: =eqw ~ =(e)leqw ~ =íqw ~ =ó:qw.
pertaining to the head:: xw=.
put one's head back (tilt one's face up):: q'óx̲esem.
put one's head down, bend, bend over, bend over with one's head down, stoop down:: qep'ósem < qep'.
put one's head to one side, lay on one side of the head:: lexósem < lex.
rock shaped like a man's head with a sx̲wó:yx̲wey mask on a point near the head of Harrison River, the point also called Spook's Point:: Sx̲wó:yx̲wey ~ Sx̲wóyx̲wey < sx̲wó:yx̲wey ~ sx̲wóyx̲wey.
rock that was a sx̲wó:yx̲wey head (mask) turned to stone at X̲elhlálh:: Sx̲éyes te Sx̲wó:yx̲wey < sx̲éyes ~ sx̲éy:es.
scratching one's head:: x̲eyx̲eq'qéylem < x̲éyq'.
shake one's head side to side (as in saying no):: kwíythesem.
shaking one's head side to side (as in saying no):: kwóythesem < kwíythesem.
skin of fish head without gristle:: t'áwleqw.
skin of the head, scalp:: kw'elṓweqw < kw'eléw ~ kw'elṓw.
soak one's head:: mí:leqwem < mí:l ~ míl, mí:leqwthet < mí:l ~ míl.
soft spot on (top of) a baby's head, fontanel:: sqe'éleqw < qí: ~ qí'.
(special head-dress):: sx̲wóyéleqw.
sprout(ing) up, stick(ing) its head out of the ground (of a plant):: qw'íles < qw'íl.
temples (on head):: th'iyaméle or th'iyaméla.
top of the head, scalp:: t'émleqw < t'ém.
turn one's head:: x̲élts'esem < x̲élts'.
twist by the head:: x̲élts'es < x̲élts'.
twist s-o/s-th by the head:: x̲élts'est < x̲élts'.
wash one's hair, wash one's head:: th'ex̲wíqwem < th'éx̲w or th'óx̲w.
wash one's head and hair:: xwóyeqwem (or perhaps) xwáyeqwem.
wet one's head (sic?), (wet one's bed repeatedly):: lhélqwelhem < lhél.
where is s-o going?, where is s-o travelling?, where is s-o headed for?:: xwchókwel < chákw.
you're crazy in the head, you're sick in the head:: xwoxwth'áleq[w]thom < xwáth'.

headache

(have a) headache:: x̲lhá:léqel ~ x̲elháléqel < x̲élh.

headband

headband, headband made out of cedar bark woven by widow or widower when mourning:: qítes ~ qéytes < qít.
new spirit dancer's headband:: qítes ~ qéytes < qít.
woven headband of packstrap, tumpline:: q'sí:ltel < q'ey ~ q'i.

headdress

headdress, face costume, mask:: sx̲wéythiyes ~ sx̲wíythiyes < x̲wíyth.
new spirit-dancer's head-dress or [cedar-bark] hat:: sx̲wóyéleqws te x̲awsólkwlh < sx̲wóyéleqw.
(special head-dress):: sx̲wóyéleqw.

headed

supernatural double-headed snake:: sílhqey < isá:le ~ isále ~ isá:la.

heal

cure s-o, heal s-o by Indian doctoring:: lhá:wet < lhá:w.
heal, be cured:: lhá:w.
Indian doctor at work, shaman at work, healer:: lhalhewéleq < lhá:w.
it healed up, (to heal up):: q'éytl'thet < q'éytl'.
revive s-o, bring s-o back to life, heal s-o, (EB) give s-o medicine to make him better?:: á:yelexwt < áylexw ~ áyelexw.

healer

Indian doctor at work, shaman at work, healer:: lhalhewéleq < lhá:w.

health

be alive, be living, be in good health, be healthy, be well:: áylexw ~ áyelexw.
be fine (in health), be alright (in health), be well:: we'éy òl ~ we'éyòl ~ we'éyò ~ u éyò ~ u'éyò < éy ~ éy:.
be in clear voice, be in good voice, be in good health, healthy:: shxw'éyelh < éy ~ éy:.
be in good health, be healthy:: shxw'éyelh < éy ~ éy:.
fine (in health):: ō éy ~ ōw'éy < éy ~ éy:.

healthy

be alive, be living, be in good health, be healthy, be well:: áylexw ~ áyelexw.
be in clear voice, be in good voice, be in good health, healthy:: shxw'éyelh < éy ~ éy:.
be in good health, be healthy:: shxw'éyelh < éy ~ éy:.

hear

hearing (about):: sísewel < síw.
hearing, (hear [Elders Group, EB]):: ts'íts'lhà:m ~ ts'its'lhá:m ~ ts'ets'lhà:m < ts'lhà:m, ts'íts'lhà:m ~ ts'its'lhá:m ~ ts'ets'lhà:m < ts'lhà:m.
hearing s-th/s-o:: ts'its'lhá:met ~ ts'íts'lhámet < ts'lhà:m.
hear s-o/s-th:: ts'lhá:met < ts'lhà:m.
keep on hearing a distant sound:: sasetáleqep < sát.
sense something (that will happen), hear about it:: síwélmét ~ síwélmet < síw.
to hear:: ts'lhà:m.

heart :: th'á:lá ~ th'ála ~ th'á:le ~ th'ále.
  core of a rock, center of a rock, core of anything, heart of anything inanimate:: sth'emí:wel ~ sth'emíwel ~ sth'emíwél < sth'ó:m.
  fish heart:: mélqw.
  heart of a root, seed, nut (kernel), core of plant or seedling, core (of tree, branch, any growing thing), pith (of bush), seed or pit [U.S.] or pip [Cdn.] of a fruit:: sth'emí:wel ~ sth'emíwel ~ sth'emíwél < sth'ó:m.
  heart-shaped island near the mouth of Chehalis River that beat like a heart:: Th'álátel ~ Th'á:lá ~ Th'ála < th'á:lá ~ th'ála ~ th'á:le ~ th'ále.
  heart-shaped mountain on the CN (south) side of the Fraser River east of Mt. Cheam:: Th'áth'ele < th'á:lá ~ th'ála ~ th'á:le ~ th'ále.
  lose heart, become disappointed, become discouraged:: qelqéyl or qelqí:l < qél.

heartburn
  have heartburn:: yeqwí:les < yéqw.

Heart Rock
  Chehalis village on Harrison River, the Heart Rock for which Chehalis, B.C. was named (at the mouth of Chehalis River):: Ts'a'í:les < ts'á:.

heart-shaped island
  heart-shaped island near the mouth of Chehalis River that beat like a heart:: Th'álátel ~ Th'á:lá ~ Th'ála < th'á:lá ~ th'ála ~ th'á:le ~ th'ále.

heart-shaped mountain
  heart-shaped mountain on the CN (south) side of the Fraser River east of Mt. Cheam:: Th'áth'ele < th'á:lá ~ th'ála ~ th'á:le ~ th'ále.

heat :: skw'ókw'es < kw'ás.
  heat it up, warm it up, smoke s-th over a fire:: pákw'et.
  heat up (on fire, stove):: qewletsá:ls < qew.
  scorch s-th, blacken s-th with fire, heat it up (near a fire), burning a canoe with pitchwood to remove splinters and burn on black pitch):: qw'á:yt < qw'á:y.
  shimmering (in heat):: pó:lex̱wem < poléx̱wem.

heaven :: chíchelh téméxw < =chílh ~ chílh=.

heavily
  more than one person heavily loaded with packs:: swewíp < wíp or wép.

heavy :: xwétes ~ xwét:es.
  (be) loaded with a heavy pack:: swíp < wíp or wép.
  each had a heavy pack:: swepwíp < wíp or wép.
  ringing sound when something drops (spoon, metal ashtray or something heavy):: ts'tés.
  too heavy to lift:: éw.

heel
  both heels, two heels, (heel):: th'etselétsxel < th'éts.
  heel, (both heels):: th'elétsxel < th'éts.

height
  fell of its own accord (of an object from a height or from upright), drop down (object/person, from a shelf, bridge, cliff, etc.), fall off:: wets'étl' ~ wech'étl'.
  upright, standing, height, stature, pole:: =ámets' ~ =ámeth' ~ =ó:meth' ~ =emeth'.

Helianthus tuberosus:: x̲áx̲ekw'.
  including: Sagittaria latifolia, Helianthus tuberosus, Camassia quamash (and Camassia leichtlinii), and unidentified plant, besides Solanum tuberosum:: sqáwth ~ sqá:wth.
  possibly Helianthus tuberosus:: sx̲éykwel.
  probably Helianthus tuberosus:: sx̲éykwel.

hell-diver
  hell-diver, pied-billed grebe:: sx̲wotíx.

hello :: láw.

help
  a helper:: míytel < máy.
  a sung spell, power to help or harm people or to do [ritual] burning, power to do witchcraft and predict the future, an evil spell, (magic spell) (someone who has power to take things out of a person or put things in [by magic] [Elders Group 2/25/76], ritualist [Elders Group 1/21/76], witch [EB 4/25/78]):: syiwí:l ~ syewí:l < yéw: ~ yéw.
  begging for a favor, asking for help:: th'íth'exwstélémét < th'íxw ~ th'éxw.
  helping:: mamíyet < máy.
  helping one another, (helper [Elders Group]):: momíyelhtel < máy.
  help oneself to food, serve oneself, serve oneself food (with a ladle), serve oneself a meal (food), (put on a dish [CT, HT]):: lhá:x̲em ~ lháx̲em < lhá:x̲ ~ lháx̲.
  help out, go help, pitch in, help one another:: móylhtel < máy.
  help s-o, defend s-o, protect s-o, aid s-o:: má:yt ~ máyt < máy.

helper
  babysitter (for new spirit-dancers), any of the workers who help in initiating a spirit-dancer, (initiator or helper of spirit-dancers):: xólhemìlh ~ xòlhemí:lh < xólh.

helpful
  good-hearted, kind-hearted, kind, generous, helpful, easy-going, good-natured:: xw'éywelh ~ xwe'éywelh ~ xwe'éy:welh < éy ~ éy:.

helpless
  pitiful person, helpless person, person unable to do anythingfor himself:: skw'ékw'ith < skw'iyéth.

Hemhémetheqw
  a hunter turned to stone now located below Hemhémetheqw near Hill's Bar on the east bank of the Fraser River:: Tewít < tewít.

hemlock
  hemlock tree, Western hemlock:: mélemélhp.
  poison fern that grows in swampy places, (prob. water hemlock, poison hemlock):: welékwsa.

hemorrhoid

(have) hemorrhoids, (have) open sores on genitals or rump:: th'kw'íwel < th'ekw' or th'íkw'.

hemp

grass or fibre for nets or twine, spreading dogbane, possibly also Indian hemp:: méthelh.

her

her deceased children, (his deceased children):: mameláselh < méle ~ mél:a.
him, her, it, them, third person object:: -exw.
his, her, its, their, third person possessive pronoun, third person subordinate subject:: -s.
that's her (absent):: kwsú:tl'ò < kw.
that's her (absent), she (absent):: kwsú:tl'ò < tl'ó ~ tl'o.
that's her, she (present or presence unspecified), her (present or presence unspefified), that (female):: thú:tl'ò < tl'ó ~ tl'o.
that's him (absent), that's her (absent), it's him (absent), it's her (absent):: kwthú:tl'ò < kw.
that's him (absent), that's her (absent), it's him/her (absent), he (absent), she (absent):: kwthú:tl'ò < tl'ó ~ tl'o.
that was her (deceased):: kwsú:tl'ò:lh < kw.
that was her (deceased), she (deceased):: kwsú:tl'ò:lh < tl'ó ~ tl'o.

Heracleum lanatum:: sóqw', yóle ~ yóla ~ yó:le.

herd

herd of horses:: steliqíw < stiqíw.

here :: ló.

arrive, arriving, come here, have come, get here, get back, come in (in a race):: xwe'í < í.
(auxiliary verb), ([may also imply] here):: í.
bring s-o/s-th here:: xwe'í:lstexw < í.
here, be here:: íkw'elò ~ ikw'eló ~ íkw'elo < í.
here, be here, be in (i.e. here):: í.
here, this place:: íkw'eló ~ íkw'elo < ló.
leave s-th here:: íchelstexw < í.
leave this here, leave s-th here:: ístexw ó < í.
manage to get here:: xwe'ílòmèt < í.
manage to get to s-o here:: xw'í:ls < í.
reach s-o here:: xw'í:lmet < í.
stay here, stay, remain at a place:: í ò < í.
stay right here, staying right here:: í ò kw'eló < í.
this (speaker is holding it), this one, this thing here:: te'íle ~ te'í:le < í.

hermaphrodite

hermaphrodite (person with organs of both sexes), hermaphrodite baby:: t'ámiya.

heron

great blue heron:: smṓqw'o.
great blue heron, (often called) "crane":: sméqw'o ~ smṓqw'o.
(heron nesting area which was the) upriver end of Herrling Island in Fraser River just below Popkum, also the name of the village or settlement on Herrling Island:: Smémeqw'o < sméqw'o ~ smṓqw'o.

herring
dry herring eggs:: sts'ámex.

Herrling Island
(heron nesting area which was the) upriver end of Herrling Island in Fraser River just below Popkum, also the name of the village or settlement on Herrling Island:: Smémeqw'o < sméqw'o ~ smṓqw'o.

he/she/it
he/she/it was (already), they were (already):: lulh < le.

Heuchera
Heuchera micrantha and possibly Heuchera glabra or hybrid:: qw'eléqetel < qw'eléqel.
small-flowered alumroot, and possibly smooth Heuchera:: qw'eléqetel < qw'eléqel, xweqw'ele'á:ltel < xweqw'él:a.

Heuchera glabra
Heuchera micrantha, and possibly Heuchera glabra or hybrid:: xweqw'ele'á:ltel < xweqw'él:a.

Heuchera micrantha
Heuchera micrantha and possibly Heuchera glabra or hybrid:: qw'eléqetel < qw'eléqel, xweqw'ele'á:ltel < xweqw'él:a.

hew
hew (stone, wood, anything):: t'élex̲è:yls < t'éléx̲.

Hexanchus griseus
perhaps Cetorhinus maximus, Hexanchus griseus, Alopius vulpinus, and/or others:: q'ellhomelétsel < q'ellhólemètsel.

hiccough
something like a hiccough ?:: há:kw'elem ?.
to hiccough, hiccup:: hék'elh ~ hékw'elh.

hiccup
to hiccough, hiccup:: hék'elh ~ hékw'elh.

Hicks Creek:: Péps? or Píps?.
(probably) Mahood Creek and Johnson Slough, (possibly) Wahleach River or Hicks Creek (creek at bridge on east end of Seabird Island [AK]):: Qwōhòls < qwá.

Hick's Mountain
creek from Hicks Lake [sic? from Deer Lake] that's actually three creeks all leaving from the lake, probably Mahood Creek, (also Hick's Mountain [LJ]):: Sílhíxw < lhí:xw.

Hicks Rd.
lake in back of Paul Webster's old place on Hicks Rd. near Jones Creek:: Th'qwélhcha < th'qwélhcha.

hide

hide
a hiding:: shxwkwál < kwà:l.
board for stretching squirrel or skunk hides, etc.:: tépelhállh < tpólh.
circular frame (for tanning hides):: st'elákw' siyólh < yólh.
frame for stretching hides, frame (for drying hides, etc.), frame for a drum:: tpélhtel ~ tepélhtel < tpólh.
hide an object, hide s-th:: kwà:lx < kwà:l.
hide-away that a fish makes:: t'esítsmels < t'ás.
hide it for s-o:: kwá:lxelht < kwà:l.
hiding an object:: kwokwí:lx < kwà:l.
hiding an object real well:: kwókwelx < kwà:l.
hiding, hiding oneself:: kwekwí:l ~ kwokwí:l < kwà:l.
hiding place, refuge, hide-out:: kwokwílàlà < kwà:l.
several places where there were pit-houses in which to hide from enemy raids (place to hide):: Skwokwílàla < kwà:l.
skin, hide (with/without hair or fur), pelt, sinew:: kw'eléw ~ kw'elő̄w.
someone's hiding, (a child is hiding ?):: kwekwí:lh < kwà:l.
something hidden away:: skwálepel < kwà:l.
to hide, hide oneself:: kwà:l.

hide-away
hide-away that a fish makes:: t'esítsmels < t'ás.

hiding place

hiding place
hiding place, refuge, hide-out:: kwokwílàlà < kwà:l.

high
be above, be high, top, up above, way high:: chíchelh < =chílh ~ chílh=.
be big, be large, be high (of floodwater), rise (of floodwater):: híkw.
(have a) high pitch (voice or melody), (have a) sharp voice:: xwiyótheqel < éy ~ éy:.
(have a) high voice:: chélhqel < =chílh ~ chílh=.
high, upper, above:: =chílh ~ chílh=.
high water time (yearly, usually in June), June:: temqó: ~ temqoqó: < qó:.
make a high hooting call (maybe only of spirits):: hó:kwt.

high-bow
high-bow canoe, high-bow river canoe, streetcar, tram, taxi, car, automobile:: xwókw'eletsem < xwókw' ~ xwekw'ó.

high-bowed
big high-bowed canoe from the Coast, Nootka war canoe, huge canoe:: q'ex̲wő:welh ~ q'ex̲wőwelh.

high class
high class people:: semelá:lh < smelá:lh.
respected person, (high class person [EB]):: smelá:lh.

highness
respected leader, chief, upper-class person, boss, master, your highness:: siyám ~ (rare) siyá:m.

hide tide

high tide :: me lets'léts' < léts'.

Hill

Hook-nose, Hook-nose Mountain, Hamersly Hopyard Hill:: Lhílhkw'eleqs ~ Lhílhkw'elqs < lhíkw' ~ lhí:kw'.

hill :: sqotemílep.

a point or bald hill on Harrison River where people waited to spear silver spring salmon:: Chth'éylem < chth'éylem.

climb a mountain, climb a hill, go up a mountain or hill:: kw'íyeqel < kw'í ~ kw'íy.

go down hill, go down from anything:: tl'pílém < tl'ép.

go over or around (hill, rock, river, etc.):: q'ál.

hill (dirt, includes both sides of hill), little hill:: skwókwep ~ skwokwepílep.

little stone, pebble, little rock hill, small rock mountain (like in the Fraser River in the canyon):: smámelet < smá:lt.

lots of little streams (like the kind coming down a hill after a rain):: teltelewá:m < tó:l ~ tò:l.

side hills or tilted hills northwest of Ñó:letsa near Yale:: Tewtewá:la ~ Tutuwále < tewále.

side hills, tilted hills, slopes:: tewtewá:la ~ tutuwále < tewále.

steep hill, sloping ground:: sqotemí:lep ~ sqoteméylep.

steep (of road, hill, etc.), (very steep slope [Elders Group]):: théq.

Hill's Bar:: Qwíth'qweth'iyósem < qwéth'.

a hunter turned to stone now located below Hemhémetheqw near Hill's Bar on the east bank of the Fraser River:: Tewít < tewít.

a rock shaped like a dog on the east shore of the Fraser River near Hill's Bar and below Tewít (a rock shaped like a human hunter):: Sqwemá:y (?) < qwem.

elk (or) moose turned to stone in the Fraser River by Hill's Bar:: Q'oyíyets ~ Q'oyí:ts < q'oyíyets or q'oyí:ts.

flat rocks (bedrock) with holes at Hill's Bar where they used to make smótheqw (prepared fish oil) from sockeye heads:: Hemhémetheqw < mótheqw or metheqw.

Hill's Bar (a stretch of shoreline between Yale and Hope, on the east side of the Fraser river):: Qw'elóqw' < qw'él.

Hill's Bar (between Yale and Hope), Fraser River where it goes over Hill's Bar on the CN (east) side:: Qw'áléts.

large whirlpool in the Fraser River just above Hill's Bar and near the west (CPR) side:: Hémq'eleq < méq'.

spear-shaped rock on beach on the Fraser near Hill's Bar:: Tá:lh < tá:lh.

him

he (present or presence unspecified), he's the one that, it's him that, she or it (present or presence unspecified), that or this (immediately before nominal):: tú:tl'ò ~ tútl'ò ~ tútl'o < tl'ó ~ tl'o.

him, her, it, them, third person object:: -exw.

him (there, near but not visible), that one:: kwethá ~ kwe thá < kw.

that's him (absent), that's her (absent), it's him (absent), it's her (absent):: kwthú:tl'ò < kw.

that's him (absent), that's her (absent), it's him/her (absent), he (absent), she (absent):: kwthú:tl'ò < tl'ó ~ tl'o.

that was him (deceased), he (deceased):: kw'ú:tl'ò:lh < tl'ó ~ tl'o.

hind

hind leg:: lheq'láts < lheq'át ~ lhq'á:t.
small hind quarters:: lhílheq'làts < lheq'át ~ lhq'á:t.

Hindu

a Hindu, an East Indian:: híltu.
a small Hindu, a small East Indian:: híheltu < híltu.

hip :: sts'émlets < sth'ó:m.
be lame (in hip, esp. from birth):: skw'í:lets < kw'í ~ kw'íy.
flower of wild rose, hip or bud of wild rose, including: Nootka rose, probably also dwarf or woodland rose and swamp rose, possibly (from Hope east) prickly rose:: qá:lq.
hip, hips:: lheq'láts < lheq'át ~ lhq'á:t.
limp in the hip:: hálkweletsem < lékw.
put a hand on one hip:: piypiyólwelh < píy.
put hands on both hips, (put hands akimbo):: piypiyólwelhem < píy.
small hips:: lhílheq'làts < lheq'át ~ lhq'á:t.
swivel one's hips (as in the Hawaiian hula for ex.) (shake one's bottom around):: qwayx̱élechem < qwá:y.

Hippoglossus stenolepis

Hippoglossus stenolepis, prob. Platichthys stellatus:: p'éwiy ~ p'ṓwiy < p'ewíy ~ p'ōwíy.

hire :: yákw'.
hire s-o:: yákw'emet ~ yékw'emet < yákw'.
hiring s-o:: yáyekw'emet < yákw'.

his

her deceased children, (his deceased children):: mameláselh < méle ~ mél:a.
his, her, its, their, third person possessive pronoun, third person subordinate subject:: -s.

hissing :: lhálheqem < lháqem.

hit

beating s-o/s-th with a stick, hitting s-o/s-th with a stick, clubbing it:: kw'ókw'eqwet < kw'óqw.
beat s-o/s-th with a stick, hit s-o/s-th with a stick, hit s-th (on purpose), hit s-o intentionally:: kw'óqwet < kw'óqw.
be hit (with arrow, bullet, anything shot that you've aimed), got shot, (got pierced), got poked into, got wounded (with gun or arrow):: ts'éqw'.
bump, get hit by something moving (for ex. by a car):: tós.
clubbing many times, hitting many times:: kw'elqwál < kw'óqw.
get hit (by s-th thrown or airborne):: ló:m ~ lóm.
get hit in the face:: xwmélkw'es.
get hit on the back:: xwelemṓwelh ~ xwlemṓwelh, xwelemṓwelh ~ xwlemṓwelh < ló:m ~ lóm.
hit in the eye (on the eyelid):: kw'qwó:les ~ kw'qwóles < kw'óqw.
hit it (what was aimed for):: lómet < ló:m ~ lóm.
hit on the arm:: kw'eqwelá:x̱el < kw'óqw.
hit on the back:: kw'qwewíts < kw'óqw.
hit on the behind (with a stick-like object):: kw'qwélets < kw'óqw.
hit on the chest:: kw'qwí:les < kw'óqw.

hit (CONT'D)

hit on the ear, hit on the temple (side of the head):: kw'qwá:lí:ya < kw'óqw.
hit on the face (several times):: melmélkw'es < xwmélkw'es.
hit on the hand with a hammer:: télhches.
hit on the leg, [hit on the foot]:: kw'éqwxel < kw'óqw.
hit on the mouth, [hit on the chin, hit on the lip, hit on the jaw]:: kw'qwó:ythel < kw'óqw, kw'qwó:ythel < kw'óqw.
hit on the top of the head:: kw'qwéleqw < kw'óqw.
hit s-o in the face, punch s-o in the face:: th'í:qw'est < th'í:qw'et.
hit s-o on the head, club him on the head:: kw'qwéleqwt < kw'óqw.
hit s-o unintentionally, hit s-o accidentally:: kw'óqwlexw < kw'óqw.
hit with an arrow accidentally:: ts'eqw'eláxw < ts'éqw'.
hit with a stick-like object, clubbed:: kw'óqw.
it hit (what was aimed for):: lóm < ló:m ~ lóm.
punch s-o/s-th, hit s-o/s-th with fist:: th'í:qw'et.
throw and hit s-th/s-o, strike s-th/s-o (with something thrown):: ló:met ~ lómet < ló:m ~ lóm.
throwing and hitting s-th:: lólemet < ló:m ~ lóm.
whip once (with stick), got hit:: qw'óqw.

hitch)

something that you hook onto (like a trailer hitch):: s'óqw' < óqw'.
spear pole knot hitch (two half-hitches), clove-hitch knot:: ts'sítsim.

hive

house, home, den, lodge, hive:: lá:lém.

hoarfrost

fine needles of hoarfrost on a branch:: pú:ches ~ púwches, pú:ches ~ púwches < pí:w.

hoe :: lopyúws, shxwt'et'emélep < t'ém, shxwthóyeqwels < thíy.

chopping the ground (with hoe or mattock):: t'et'émélep < t'ém.

hog fennel

hog fennel, Indian consumption plant:: q'ex̱mí:l.

Hogg Slough

steelhead fishing place on the Fraser River below Lhílhkw'elqs, at Hogg Slough:: Qéywex̱em < qí:wx̱ ~ qéywx̱ ~ qá:wx̱ ~ qáwx̱.

hoist

lift up s-th, lift [s-th], hoist [s-th] up:: xwà:lx < xwá.

hold

he's holding s-th in each hand:: s'i'á:ytses < á:y.
hold a grudge, hate:: sqelwílh < qél.
hold both arms (or wings) outstretched, (stretch out one's arms/wings):: tex̱eláx̱elem < tex̱.
holding a grudge against each other:: xixemó:ltel < sxemá:l.
holding a hand:: kwelátses < kwél.
holding a wee baby in one's arms:: xixe'át < xá'at.
holding on to a thqálem, waiting dip-netting, still-dipping:: théqelem < thqá:lem.
holding s-o in one's arms, (holding a baby in one's arms [Elder's Group]):: xe'át < xá'at.

hold (CONT'D)

holding the hand of s-o:: kwelátsest < kwél.
hold it:: kwelát < kwél.
hold it steady, (hold s-th steady):: tl'eláxwstexw < tl'élexw.
hold s-o in one's arms:: xá'at.
hold s-th (in one's grasp), holding s-th (in one's grasp), have s-th, grasp s-th:: kwelát < kwél.
pot-holder:: kwéltsestel < kwél.
someone small is holding (holds) it:: kwikwelát < kwél.

hole

a hole:: sqweqwá < qwá.
beach on east side of Harrison Lake across from Long Island where there are lots of flat rocks, most of which have holes in them:: Sqweqwehíwel < qwá.
borer to make holes, auger:: sqweqwá:ls ~ shxwqweqwá:ls < qwá.
get a hole:: qwá.
hole (in roof, tunnel, pants, mountain, at bottom of some lakes), tunnel:: sqwahíwel < qwá.
hole in the bottom (of bucket, etc.):: sqwálats < qwá.
hole in the ground, trench (if discussing length):: shxwthó:yqw < thíy.
knothole:: sts'axtálá < sts'á:xt.
make a hole in s-th, drill a hole in s-th:: qwát < qwá.
natural holes or tunnels east of Iwówes and above Lhilheltálets that water came out of after rain:: Sqwelíqwehíwel ~ Sqwelíqwehiwèl < qwá.
plugging a hole or leak or crack in anything:: t'ót'ekwels < t'ékw.
plug it (a hole, leak):: t'ekwót < t'ékw.
smokehole:: sp'otl'emá:látel < p'ótl'em.
sticking out through a hole (like a toe out of a sock, knee out of a hole in pants, a nail driven clear through the other side of a board), come out into the open:: qwōhóls (or perhaps) qwehóls < qwá.
the hole (lake) at the foot of Cheam Peak on the south side:: Sqwá:p < qwá.
the Tracks of Mink, holes shaped like a mink's tracks toward the base of the rock-face called Xwyélés or Lexwyélés:: Sx̲éyeltels Te Sqoyéx̲iya < sx̲él:e.
to bore a hole:: xó:lt < xó:l.

holler

a holler, (a yell, a shout):: stà:m < tà:m.
call (by voice), shout, yell, holler:: tà:m.
call s-o (by voice), holler at s-o, shout at s-o, shout at s-o:: tà:met ~ tàmet < tà:m.
shouting repeatedly, hollering repeatedly, yelling (repeatedly):: tatí:m < tà:m.
to scream, holler (of a spirit-dancer):: kwátsem ~ kwáchem.

hollow

(be) dug out, (be hollowed out):: shxwótkw < xwótkw ~ xwótqw.
(be) hollow:: sqwa'í:wel < qwá.
hollow it out:: xetqwewí:lt.
hollow of hand:: xwt'óxwestses < t'óxw.
hollow (of tree or log):: shxwótkwewel < xwótkw ~ xwótqw.
make it hollow (of canoe, log, etc.):: thiyeqwewí:lt < thíy.

Holodiscus discolor:: qáthelhp < qáthexw.

holy
(be) sacred, holy:: sx̲áx̲e < x̲áx̲e.
sacred, holy, (taboo):: x̲áx̲e.

Holy Ghost
Holy Spirit, Holy Ghost:: X̲áx̲e Smestí:yexw < x̲áx̲e.

Holy Spirit
Holy Spirit, Holy Ghost:: X̲áx̲e Smestí:yexw < x̲áx̲e.

home
at home, be living (somewhere), stay:: tl'eláxw ~ tl'láxw < tl'élexw.
(be) homesick:: t'ekw'élmél < t'ó:kw'.
being homesick:: t'ót'ekw'élmel < t'ó:kw'.
busy at home all the time:: yúkw'es.
(get/go) home:: t'ó:kw'.
house, home, den, lodge, hive:: lá:lém.
little house, cabin (say 12 ft. x 10 ft. or less), small home, storage house (small shed-like house, enclosed with door), outhouse (slang), toilet (slang):: lílem < lá:lém.
take s-o home:: t'ékw'stexw ~ t'ókw'stexw < t'ó:kw'.
to stay at home:: álwem.

homesick
(be) homesick:: t'ekw'élmél < t'ó:kw'.
being homesick:: t'ót'ekw'élmel < t'ó:kw'.

honey :: meláses te sisemóye < meláses.
one's hand sticks to something (in cold, to honey, to glue, etc.):: t'elémtses < t'elém.

honeybee
bee, honeybee, hornet, wasp:: sisemó:ya ~ sisemóya ~ sisemóye ~ sísemòye.

honeycomb :: mámelehà:yèlhs te sisemóye < méle ~ mél:a.

honeysuckle
orange honeysuckle:: q'éyt'o ~ q'í:t'o.

Honey (term of address)
Honey (term of address to one's spouse), Husband, Wife:: láw.

honker
big Canada goose, big honker:: tl'x̲wṓmálqel ~ tl'ax̲wṓmálqel.

hoof
deer hoof rattle of spirit-dancer (stick with deer hoof rattles tied onto it):: kwóxwemal ~ kwóxwmal < kwoxw.
hoof, esp. deer hoof (off deer or attached to stick as rattle):: kw'óxwemel < kw'óxwe.

hook
a hook for crocheting:: lhílhekw'els < lhíkw' ~ lhí:kw'.
bait s-th (fish-line, fish-hook, fish-trap):: má:lat < má:la ~ má:le.

hook (CONT'D)

catching a fish by hook, hooking s-th, gaffing a fish:: lhílhekw'et < lhíkw' ~ lhí:kw'.
gaff-hook (a large pole-mounted hook):: lhékw'tel < lhíkw' ~ lhí:kw'.
(gaff) hook fisherman, a hooker:: thehímélh.
hang s-th (on a nail or hat hanger), hook it back on (of a stitch lost in knitting):: ókw'est < ókw'.
(have a) hook nose, beak nose, Roman nose, (be bent-nosed):: sqémqsel < qém.
hook fish, catch fish (by hook), to gaff-hook fish:: lhekw'á:ls < lhíkw' ~ lhí:kw'.
hook onto s-th:: thehít.
hook s-th (by horns):: lhíkw'et < lhíkw' ~ lhí:kw'.
small fish-hook (for trout, etc.), trolling hook:: kw'ōwiyékw ~ kw'ōyékw.
something that you hook onto (like a trailer hitch):: s'óqw' < óqw'.
to hook, to catch (by horns or thorns):: lhíkw' ~ lhí:kw'.
to ride [along], hook a ride, get a ride, send oneself:: lépetsel < lépets.

Hooker's fairy bells

"snakeberry", includes False Solomon's seal, star-flowered Solomon's seal, and probably Twisted-stalk (2 spp.) and Hooker's fairy bells:: sth'íms te álhqey < sth'í:m ~ sth'ì:m.
"snakeberry", including False Solomon's seal, star-flowered Solomon's seal, and probably Twisted-stalk and Hooker's fairy bells:: sth'íms te álhqey < álhqey ~ álhqay.

hooking

gaff-hooking (all the time, catching a lot):: lhákw'els < lhíkw' ~ lhí:kw'.

Hook-nose

Hook-nose, Hook-nose Mountain, Hamersly Hopyard Hill:: Lhílhkw'eleqs ~ Lhílhkw'elqs < lhíkw' ~ lhí:kw'.

hoot

make a high hooting call (maybe only of spirits):: hó:kwt.

hop

be hopping:: ts'áts'ets'tl'ím < ts'tl'ám ~ ts'tl'ém.
grasshopper (ordinary), perhaps longhorned grasshopper:: tl'emtl'émxel, ts'áts'etl'em < ts'tl'ám ~ ts'tl'ém, ts'ats'etl'í:m < ts'tl'ám ~ ts'tl'ém, ts'í:ts'á:tl'em < ts'tl'ám ~ ts'tl'ém.
jump, hop (once):: ts'tl'ám ~ ts'tl'ém.
jumping, hopping:: ts'á:tl'em ~ ch'á:tl'em ~ ts'átl'em < ts'tl'ám ~ ts'tl'ém.

Hope

Hope Indian Reserve #12 (Klaklacum):: Tl'átl'ekw'em ~ Lexwtl'átl'ekw'em.
Lake of the Woods (small lake across the Fraser R. from Hope, B.C.):: Q'alelíktel < q'ál.
village on the site of Hope, modern Hope, B.C.:: Ts'qó:ls < ts'qó:ls.

hope :: taméxw ~ staméxw.

Hope Mountain:: St'ámiya < t'ámiya.

Hope River

village at west end of Little Mountain (Mount Shannon) on Hope Slough, also a name for Hope Slough or Hope River:: Sqwá:la < qwá.

Hope Slough

Hope Slough

place of moss-covered stones at upper end of Hope Slough not far from Harry Edwards' home (as of 1964):: Qwómqwemels < qwà:m ~ qwám.

Salkaywul, an area with big cracked cedar trees on Hope Slough above Schelowat (Chilliwack I.R. #1) (Sx̲eláwtxw):: Salq'íwel < séq'.

Schelowat, a village at the bend in Hope Slough at Annis Rd. where there was a painted or marked house:: Sx̲elá:wtxw < x̲él ~ x̲é:yl ~ x̲í:l

Skwali, a village north of Hope Slough and Skwah:: Skwáli.

village at east end of Little Mountain on Hope Slough, upper end of Mount Shannon [DM]:: Qwolíwiya or Ñwolíwiya.

village at west end of Little Mountain (Mount Shannon) on Hope Slough, also a name for Hope Slough or Hope River:: Sqwá:la < qwá.

hops

domestic hops:: hóps.

pick berries, pick off (leaves, fruit, vegetables, hops), (pluck off, harvest):: lhím.

Hopyard Hill

Hook-nose, Hook-nose Mountain, Hamersly Hopyard Hill:: Lhílhkw'eleqs ~ Lhílhkw'elqs < lhíkw' ~ lhí:kw'.

horizon

day, daytime, sky, weather, (horizon (BJ)):: swáyel ~ swáyél ~ swàyèl < wáyel.

horn)

big serving spoon, spoon with handle about ten to 12 inches long, ladle, (spoon carved from mountain goat horn):: x̲álew.

horn of an animal:: th'ístel < th'ís.

horn rings for dip-nets:: x̲alwéla < x̲álew.

rack of horns:: shxwiyáxkel.

horned owl

horned owl, great horned owl:: chítmexw.

hornet

bee, honeybee, hornet, wasp:: sisemó:ya ~ sisemóya ~ sisemóye ~ sísemòye.

horse :: stiqíw.

baby horse:: steqiwó:llh < stiqíw.

bushy hair on horses' legs (tufts like on Clydesdale breed), tufts of fur on horse's feet:: qwelqwélxel < qwíl ~ qwel.

colt:: statiqíwò:llh < stiqíw.

get in a conveyance, get in a car, mount a horse:: ó:lh.

herd of horses:: steliqíw < stiqíw.

little horse:: stiteqíw < stiqíw.

to fasten s-th by tying, tie up s-th (like canoe, horse, laces, nets, cow, shoelaces), tie it:: q'éyset ~ q'í(:)set < q'ey ~ q'i.

to travel by horse, already riding a horse:: yets'ets'á < ts'á:.

younger deer, baby horse, younger cow, fawn, colt, calf:: st'él'e.

horseshoe-shaped
  U-shaped or horseshoe-shaped knife for scraping out an adzed canoe:: sqw'emqw'emóx̲w < qw'ómx̲w.
  U-shaped or horseshoe-shaped knife (or plane) for scraping out canoe:: xepá:ltel < xíp.

horsetail
  giant horsetail, also common horsetail, (mushroom [AC]):: x̲émx̲em.

hospital :: q'oq'eyá:wtxw < q'ó:y ~ q'óy.

hot
  be hot, be warm:: kw'ókw'es < kw'ás.
  have a hot drink, warm one's chest inside:: qatílésem < qá:t.
  hot on the rump, hot seat:: kw'esélets < kw'ás.
  sparks, red hot ashes thrown out:: qw'á:ychep < qw'á:y.
  to scald s-th/s-o, burn s-th/s-o [with hot liquid]:: th'áx̲et < th'áx̲.
  woven mat to put hot plates on:: lháx̲tsestel < lhá:x̲ ~ lháx̲.

hotel
  bedroom, hotel:: itetáwtxw < ítet, pí:tawtxw < pí:t.

hot-headed
  (be) aggressive, cranky, ready to fight, (be) violent, hot-headed:: sx̲óytl'thet ~ sx̲ó:ytl'thet.

Hot Springs
  Harrison Hot Springs:: Qwó:ls < qwó:ls.

hour
  be what hour?, be what time?:: skw'í:ls < kw'í:l ~ kw'íl.
  hour, o'clock, day of week:: s=...=s.
  ten o'clock, (tenth hour):: s'ó:pels < ó:pel.
  three o'clock (< the third hour):: slhíxws < lhí:xw.
  two o'clock, two hours:: isáles < isá:le ~ isále ~ isá:la.

house
  adze (for making canoes and pit-house ladders):: xwt'ót'epels ~ shxwt'ót'epels < t'óp.
  around the outside of the house:: sélts'ex̲el < sél or sí(:)l.
  back end of a house (inside or outside), back part of a house:: stselqwáx̲el < chá:l or chó:l, stselqwáx̲el < chá:l or chó:l.
  bank (money house, money building):: tale'áwtxw < tá:le ~ tále.
  bark house:: sokw'emáwtxw < sókw'.
  barn, (hay house, grass building):: sox̲weláwtxw < só:x̲wel ~ sóx̲wel.
  be inside a house, be inside an enclosure:: skwetáxw < kwetáxw.
  be inside a pit-house:: sqemí:l < sqémél.
  build a house (make a house):: thiyéltxwem < thíy.
  building, house:: =á:wtxw ~ =áwtxw ~ =ewtxw ~ =(á)ltxw ~ =(el)txw.
  carved outside post on longhouse, totem pole:: x̲wíythi < x̲wíyth.
  church house, the church (building):: ts'ahéyelhá:wtxw < ts'ahéyelh.
  (circle) around the fire once and return to the start, make one circle in longhouse:: sélts' < sél or sí(:)l.
  cookhouse, kitchen:: kwukwáwtxw < kwúkw.

house (CONT'D)

cross-beam (in a house):: st'álh < t'álh, t'élhmel < t'álh.
dog house:: sqwemayáwtxw < qwem.
door, doorway, door of a big (communal) house or longhouse:: steqtá:l < téq.
end or side of a house (inside/outside):: =áx̱el ~ =ex̱el.
firepit in house:: shxwhéyqwela < yéqw.
five houses belonging to one person:: lhq'atsesáwtxw < lheq'át ~ lhq'á:t.
foundation of a house, bottom of a tree:: s'alétsmel < s'aléts.
front end of a house (inside or outside):: chuchuwáx̱el < cháchew ~ cháchu.
front of a house:: axelésmel < axelés.
go in (a house/enclosure), come in, come inside, enter a house or enclosure:: kwetxwí:lem < kwetáxw.
house, home, den, lodge, hive:: lá:lém.
house on fire, house fire:: yeqwyéqw < yéqw.
house-post, post:: sqáqeltel.
houses:: lalàlèm < lá:lém.
(in) back of a house:: tselqwáx̱el < chá:l or chó:l.
in back of a house, behind a house:: tselqwáx̱elmel < chá:l or chó:l.
Indian dance-house, "smoke-house", (spirit-dance building):: smilha'áwtxw < mílha.
little house, cabin (say 12 ft. x 10 ft. or less), small home, storage house (small shed-like house, enclosed with door), outhouse (slang), toilet (slang):: lílem < lá:lém.
location around a house, part:: =mel.
log house, log-cabin:: lokáwtxw < lók ~ làk.
longhouse for spirit-dancers, the big house, smokehouse (for spirit-dancing):: stháwtxw < thi ~ tha ~ the ~ thah ~ theh.
longhouse, smokehouse (for spirit-dancing, etc.), Indian house, plank house:: xwelmexwáwtxw < xwélmexw.
lower [downriver] end of house (inside or outside):: sōqw'áx̱el < wṓqw' ~ wéqw'.
lumber house:: xwelitemáwtxw < xwelítem.
male name, (prob.) repeatedly gets wives/houses:: =ímeltxw.
(more than one) entering a house, going in (of a whole bunch):: kwetexwí:lem < kwetáxw.
on top of the house:: chélhmel < =chílh ~ chílh=.
opposite side of house on inside:: lheq'ewílh.
peak of house:: sq'eyth'éleqw.
peak of house, gable or plank over smokehole:: sq'eyx̱éleqw.
pit-house, keekwillie house, semi-subterranean house:: sqémél, sqémél.
plank house:: shxwhṓ:wtewelh, s'iltexwáwtxw ~ iltexwáwtxw < s'í:ltexw.
root cellar, (root house [AD]}:: spepíláwtxw < pél (perhaps ~ pí:l by now).
root house:: spélmàlà < pél (perhaps ~ pí:l by now).
Schelowat, a village at the bend in Hope Slough at Annis Rd. where there was a painted or marked house:: Sx̱elá:wtxw < x̱él ~ x̱é:yl ~ x̱í:l
schoolhouse:: iwesáwtxw < íwes, skwuláwtxw < skwú:l.
shakes on house, roof:: síqetseláwtxw < seqíws ~ seqí:ws.
smokehouse, house for smoking fish:: kw'olexwáwtxw < kw'ó:lexw.
s-o has been put away (in grave-house or buried), he's/she's been buried:: qéylemtem ~ qé:ylemtem < qéylem ~ qé:ylem ~ qí(:)lem.
sweathouse:: qetíwstel < qá:t.
the outside part of a house:: s'átl'qmel < átl'q.
thick plank for side of house, thick shake for longhouse roof, covering over hole in roof of pit-house:: s'í:ltexw.
three houses, (three buildings):: lhxwá:wtxw < lhí:xw.

house (CONT'D)

two houses:: islá:wtxw < isá:le ~ isále ~ isá:la.
upper end of house (inside or outside):: stiytáx̲el or stitáx̲el < tiyt.
upper part or top of a house, upper part or top of a pit-house:: tslháltxw < =chílh ~ chílh=.
Watery Eaves, a famous longhouse and early village on a flat area on Chilliwack River just a quarter mile upriver/east above Vedder Crossing:: Qoqoláx̲el < qó:.

house-fly :: x̲wex̲wiyáye ~ x̲wix̲wiyáye < x̲wōx̲wáye ~ x̲wex̲wáye ~ x̲wōx̲wá:ye.

house-post
beams (of longhouse, all of them), houseposts:: stíqw'teqw' < tíqw'.
house-post, post:: sqáqeltel.
plane it (with a plane), trim it, taper it (about wood, like slats or roots for baskets, poles for houseposts/totem poles, paddles), taper it (with knife or plane), peel it (a fruit, etc.), whittle it, strip or peel bark off of it, scrape it (of carrots), (carve it, peel it [AC]):: xípet < xíp.

how
how beautiful., be really beautiful:: yú:wqwlha < yú:w.
how does it smell?, How does it smell?:: selchímáléqep < selchí:m ~ selchím.
how is it?, be how?:: selchí:m ~ selchím.
(probably) how is s-o/s-th?:: schákwel < chákw.
smart, know how, good at it:: schewót.
what does it look like?, what does he/she look like?, (how is he/she/it in appearance or looks?), (what color is it? [NP]):: selchímomex < selchí:m ~ selchím.
what does it sound like?, What does it sound like?, (how does it sound?):: selchí:meleqel < selchí:m ~ selchím.

howl
howling:: q'ó:w < q'á:w.
howling fast:: q'ówel < q'á:w.
howling (of a dog), crowing (of a rooster):: q'ówem < q'á:w.
many are howling:: q'eq'ówel < q'á:w.
to howl:: q'á:w.

how many
are how many?:: kw'í:l ~ kw'íl.
be how many canoes?:: kw'ilṓwelh < kw'í:l ~ kw'íl.
how many paddles?:: kw'ilṓwes < kw'í:l ~ kw'íl.
how many people?:: kw'ílà < kw'í:l ~ kw'íl.
how many times:: kw'elálh < kw'í:l ~ kw'íl.
how many trees:: kw'í:là:lhp ~ kw'ílà:lhp < kw'í:l ~ kw'íl.

how much
be how much money?:: kw'í:les ~ kw'íles < kw'í:l ~ kw'íl.

hubby
hubby, dear husband, pet term for husband:: swóweqeth < swáqeth.

huckleberry
red huckleberry:: kw'óqwtses < kw'óqw, sqá:la, sqá:le.
red huckleberry bush:: sqá:lá:lhp ~ qá:lá:lhp < sqá:la.
red huckleberry plant or bush:: qá:lá:lhp < sqá:le.

hucklesberry (CONT'D)

shiny black mountain huckleberry, also called a mountain blueberry by the speakers:: kwxwó:mels < kwoxw.

hug :: qelwíls.
hug s-o:: qelwílst < qelwíls.
hug s-o around:: qwemchíwet < qwem.

huge
(have a) real big foot, (have a) huge foot:: thí:thaxel < thi ~ tha ~ the ~ thah ~ theh.

hula
swivel one's hips (as in the Hawaiian hula for ex.) (shake one's bottom around):: qwayx̲élechem < qwá:y.

hull
hull of berry (inside left after the berry is picked), "stem" or base of berry left after the berry is picked:: th'ép'oyeqw ~ th'épeyeqw.

hum
pacify a baby, pacify it (a baby), sing or hum to a baby to quiet it, sing to it (a zaby), (sing a lullaby to it):: tl'ó:t.

human
agent (human, gender unspecified, absent):: tl'.
backbone (of human or other creatures), spine (human or other creature):: x̲ekw'ólesewíts < x̲ekw'óles.
by (agent. human, gender unspecified, absent):: tl'.
(have) animal smell (of bear, skunk, dog, etc.), (have) animal stink, (have) human smell (of underarm, body odor, etc.), (have) body odor:: pápeth'em.
the (plural [usually human]):: ye ~ yi.

humid
sultry, humid:: s-hómkw.

hummingbird
hummingbird, prob. including rufous hummingbird, black-chinned hummingbird, and calliope hummingbird:: pésk'a, pésk'a, pésk'a.

humpback
hunchback, humpback, lump on the back:: skwómàtsel (sqwómàtsel) < qwó:m ~ qwóm ~ qwem.

humpback/hunchback
break one's spine, break one's back, have a humpback/hunchback:: lekwewíts < lékw.

humpback salmon
humpback salmon, pink salmon, humpy:: hő:liya.
small-sized humpback salmon:: húheliya < hő:liya.

humpy
humpback salmon, pink salmon, humpy:: hő:liya.

Humulus lupulus:: hóps.

hunchback
  break one's spine, break one's back, have a humpback/hunchback:: lekwewíts < lékw.
  get hunchbacked:: sqwómetsel < qwó:m ~ qwóm ~ qwem.
  hunchback, humpback, lump on the back:: skwómàtsel (sqwómàtsel) < qwó:m ~ qwóm ~ qwem.

hundred
  ancient people over a hundred years old:: sx̲wolex̲wiyám < x̲wiyám.
  hundred, one hundred:: lá:ts'ewets ~ láts'ewets < láts'.

hungry
  be hungry:: kw'ókw'iy < kw'à:y.
  get hungry:: kw'à:y.
  hungry time (about mid-April to mid-May), famine (Elders 3/72):: temkw'à:y < kw'à:y.
  out of breath and over-tired and over-hungry:: pqwíles < péqw.
  starve, be starving, be famished, (be extremely hungry [Deming,JL]):: xwá.

hunt
  a person that always hunts, hunter:: lexws=há:wa < háwe.
  expert hunter (who comes back with game every time he hunts), good hunter:: tewít.
  hunting:: há:we < háwe.
  to hunt:: háwe.

hunter
  a hunter turned to stone now located below Hemhémetheqw near Hill's Bar on the east bank of the Fraser River:: Tewít < tewít.
  expert hunter (who comes back with game every time he hunts), good hunter:: tewít.

Hunter Creek
  mountain with caves that is behind Hunter Creek (in 1976-1977 they blasted this mountain where it was beside Trans-Canada Highway #1 to shorten the highway past it):: Tómtomiyeqw.
  mouth of Hunter Creek, (Restmore Caves (Wells)):: ōqw'íles ~ ōqw'éyles < wṓqw' ~ wéqw'.
  Restmore Caves [Wells]), (mouth of Hunter Creek [IHTTC]):: Uqw'íles.

hurry
  be fast, hurry:: xwém ~ x̲wém.
  be in a hurry:: s'ówth < áwth.
  eat fast, eating fast, hurry to eat:: x̲weméthel < x̲wém ~ xwém.
  hurry, hurry up, be quick, be fast, move faster, quickly:: x̲wém ~ xwém.
  hurrying:: x̲wemx̲wlí:m < x̲wém ~ xwém.
  hurry up, faster:: x̲wemx̲wém < x̲wém ~ xwém.
  to hurry, hurry up, move fast:: ówthet < áwth.

hurt
  accidentally hurt an old injury of s-o, (accidentally reinjure s-o):: qélhlexw < qélh.
  a wound, (a hurt?):: sx̲élh < x̲élh.
  (be) hurting, be aching:: x̲ex̲élh < x̲élh.
  (be) hurting s-o [accidentally, happening to/managing to]:: x̲ex̲élhlexw < x̲élh.
  be lame, (be) sick on the foot, (have) a sick foot, (have) a hurt foot:: q'óq'eyxel < q'ó:y ~ q'óy.

hurt (CONT'D)

(be) sick on the hand, (have) a sick hand, (have) a hurt hand:: q'óq'eytses < q'ó:y ~ q'óy.
(be) sore, (be) hurting all the time, painful, aching:: sáyém < sáyem.
be sorry, the feelings are hurt:: x̲élh (te, kw'e) sqwálewel < x̲élh.
get hurt:: má:kwlh.
have a pain in the stomach, (have a stomach-ache), one's stomache hurts:: x̲elhálwes < x̲élh.
have pain, to hurt:: sáyem.
hurt, be hurt, (ache [Elders Group 3/1/72], to really hurt (more than an ache) [AD]):: x̲élh.
hurting, feeling sore, (feel[ing] pain [BJ]):: táteqlexw < téqlexw.
hurt inside:: qélh.
hurt s-o [accidentally, happen to, manage to]:: x̲élhlexw < x̲élh.
hurt, sore:: nána.
hurt s-o/s-th [for awhile, accidentally]:: x̲elhláxw < x̲élh.
to hurt again (as when a painful place is bumped and hurts again or as when a pain inside one's body returns again), (to ache [SJ]):: téqlexw.

Husband

Honey (term of address to one's spouse), Husband, Wife:: láw.

husband :: swáqeth.

child's spouse, son-in-law, daughter-in-law, (man's) sister's husband:: schiwtálh.
hubby, dear husband, pet term for husband:: swóweqeth < swáqeth.
married woman, got a husband, got married to a husband:: swóweqeth < swáqeth.
married women, ((plural) got husbands):: swóqeweqeweth (or better) swóq-weqeth < swáqeth.
spouse's sibling, sibling's spouse (cross sex), for ex., husband's brother, (wife's sister, woman's sister's husband, man's brother's wife):: smátexwtel.
uncle's wife, aunt's husband, parent's sibling's spouse, uncle by marriage, aunt by marriage:: xchápth ~ schápth.

husband's brother

husband's brothers, (perhaps also wife's sisters?, spouse's siblings?, sibling's spouses?):: smetmátexwtel < smátexwtel.
husband's brother, wife's sister, spouse's sibling (cross-sex), brother-in-law, sister-in-law, sibling's spouse (cross-sex):: smátexwtel.
spouse's sibling, sibling's spouse (cross sex), for ex., husband's brother, (wife's sister, woman's sister's husband, man's brother's wife):: smátexwtel.

husband's sister

sister-in-law, husband's sister, brother's wife, wife's sister (EB):: shxw'álex < álex.

hush

hush a baby from crying, (hush s-o (a baby) from crying):: ch'exwí:lt < ts'áxw.

hut

puberty hut:: sqíqemel < sqémél.

Hyla regilla:: welék'.

if generic includes families Ranidae and Bufonidae and may include Hyla regilla and perhaps the introduced species: Rana catesbeiana, Rana clamitans, Rana aurora aurora, Rana pretiosa pretiosa, and Ascaphus truei, if not generic then includes only members of family Ranidae and/or family Bufonidae:: wex̲és, weléx̲ < wex̲és.

Hylocichla guttata
respectively Hylocichla guttata or Catharus guttatus, or possibly Hylocichla minima or Catharus minimus:: slhólho.

Hylocichla minima
respectively Hylocichla guttata or Catharus guttatus, or possibly Hylocichla minima or Catharus minimus:: slhólho.

Hylocichla ustulata ustulata:: xwét.

Hymenoptera
order Hymenoptera, family Formicidae:: xá:ysem.
order Hymenoptera, superfamily Apoidea, family Apidae, including Apis mellifera (introduced), also family Bombidae and family Vespidae and possibly bee-like members of family Syrphidae (order Diptera):: sisemó:ya ~ sisemóya ~ sisemóye ~ sísemòye.

I
I guess, I'm uncertain, maybe, must be (evidently), (evidential), have to (I guess):: t'wa ~ t'we.
I got hard (of arm, leg, penis, etc.):: tl'x̲wòlèm < tl'éx̲w.
I (non-subordinate subject):: -tsel ~ (very rarely) -chel ~ tsel.
it's me, that's me, I do, I am:: áltha ~ álthe.
it's me., that's me., I do, I am (ls emphatic):: á'altha < áltha ~ álthe.
I wonder:: yexw.
I wonder what s-o will do?, I wonder what I will do?:: xwe'ítixw or xwe'ít yexw < xwe'ít.
me (after prepositional verbs), I (after prepositional verbs):: tl'á'altha < áltha ~ álthe.
me, I:: ta'áltha < áltha ~ álthe.
me myself, I myself (emphatic):: ta'á'altha < áltha ~ álthe.
so then I:: tl'olsu < tl'ó ~ tl'o.

ice :: spí:w < pí:w.
a kind of ice:: swélweleq.
clinking, tinkling (of glass, ice in glass, glasses together, dishes together, metal together):: ts'átx̲em ~ th'átx̲em.
fine little marble-sized pieces of ice:: sth'ṓwsem or sth'éwsem.
(have) clinking (of glass or dishes or metal), (have) tinkling sound (of glass, ice in glass, glasses together):: th'átx̲em ~ ts'átx̲em.
tree bent to ground with ice and frozen:: sx̲wíqel.

ice-cream
Indian ice-cream, whipped soapberry foam:: sx̲wṓsem ~ sx̲wṓ:sem ~ sx̲ṓ(:)sem.
soapberry basket, Indian ice-cream basket:: sx̲wōsemálá < sx̲wṓsem ~ sx̲wṓ:sem ~ sx̲ṓ(:)sem.
soapberry beater, stick for whipping up soapberries or Indian ice cream:: th'amawéstel or th'emawéstel < th'ím ~ th'í:m.

icicle
(have/get) many icicles:: yelyelísem < yél:és.
icicles:: syalyelísem < yél:és.

Ictalurus nebulosus:: smó:tx̲w ~ smótx̲w.

idea]

like s-o [his/her personality], like s-th [its taste, its idea], be interested in s-th/s-o, enjoy s-o sexually:: éystexw ~ éy:stexw < éy ~ éy:.
someone's own knowledge, someone's own idea:: stélmel < tól.

if)

maybe, perhaps, I don't know (if), may (possibly):: yóswe ~ yó:swe.
subjunctive, when, if:: we-.

if not

unless he, if he doesn't:: ewás < éwe ~ ō̃we.

I guess

maybe, I guess, I'm uncertain, must be (evidently), (evidential), have to (I guess):: t'wa ~ t'we.

illegitimate

illegitimate child:: skáslekem.

illuminate

be light, (be lit up), be illuminated:: státew ~ státōw < táw.
be light (illuminated):: státewel < táw.

imbrication

grass scalded and bleached white for basketry imbrication (designs), sometimes called white straw grass, probably blue-joint reed-grass:: th'á:x̲ey ~ th'áx̲ey < th'áx̲.

imitate

copy, imitate:: x̲wex̲we'á.
copy s-o, imitate s-o:: x̲wex̲we'át < x̲wex̲we'á.
imitating:: x̲wix̲we'á < x̲wex̲we'á.
imitating s-o, copying s-o:: x̲wix̲we'át < x̲wex̲we'á.

impassible

a real rough place in the Fraser River impassible in a canoe (in the Tait area, prob. between Spuzzum and Yale):: Sq'íp'ex̲w.

impassive

not care about s-o, have no use for s-o, be impassive:: ewéta shxwlístexw < shxwlí.

impatient

got impatient:: x̲íth'el ~ x̲éyth'el < x̲íth' ~ x̲éyth'.

imperative

coaxing imperative plural:: -atlha.
coaxing imperative singular:: -tlh ~ -lh.
command imperative second person plural:: -alha.
command imperative second person singular:: -lha.
polite imperative:: áwélh ~ (-)àwèlh, -lhqwe.
(polite imperative?, (polite) certainly, (polite) of course):: òwelh ~ -òwèlh.

implement
    device, implement, thing used for:: =tel.

important
    be great, be important:: hí:kw ~ hí::kw < híkw.

impossible
    impossible, can't be:: kw'á:y ~ kw'áy.
    it is impossible, it can't be, it never is:: skw'á:y < kw'á:y ~ kw'áy.

I'm uncertain
    maybe, I guess, I'm uncertain, must be (evidently), (evidential), have to (I guess):: t'wa ~ t'we.

in
    admitting s-o/s-th, letting s-o/s-th in, bringing s-o/s-th inside:: kwétexwt < kwetáxw.
    be aboard, be in (a conveyance):: eló:lh < ó:lh.
    be in, in, be on, on, be at, at, before (an audience), (untranslated):: lí ~ li.
    be inside (a hollow object), be in (a hollow object):: slíw < léw.
    be in the middle, be in the center:: shxwá:ye.
    bring in firewood, bring wood in:: kwtxwéltsep ~ kwetxwéltsep < kwetáxw, kwtxwéltsep ~ kwetxwéltsep < kwetáxw.
    bring s-o/s-th in (to a house/enclosure), take s-o/s-th in(inside a house/enclosure), admit s-o (into a house/enclosure), let s-o/s-th in (to a house/enclosure), put s-o/s-th in (inside a house/enclosure:: kwetáxwt < kwetáxw.
    get in a canoe, get aboard:: ó:lh.
    go in (a house/enclosure), come in, come inside, enter a house or enclosure:: kwetxwí:lem < kwetáxw, kwetxwí:lem < kwetáxw.
    here, be here, be in (i.e. here):: í.
    in back of a house, behind a house:: tselqwáx̲elmel < chá:l or chó:l.
    (more than one) entering a house, going in (of a whole bunch):: kwetexwí:lem < kwetáxw.
    put it in (and leave it), stick it into s-th hollow:: léwex < léw.
    put s-th between the teeth, put it in one's mouth, bite on s-th (not into it):: ts'ámet ~ ch'ámet.
    scratching repeatedly to get in:: t'elht'élheqw'els < t'élheqw' ~ t'lhóqw'.
    scratching to get in (?):: t'élheqw'els < t'élheqw' ~ t'lhóqw'.

inanimate
    core of a rock, center of a rock, core of anything, heart of anything inanimate:: sth'emí:wel ~ sth'emíwel ~ sth'emíwél < sth'ó:m.

inanimate object preferred
    purposeful control transitivizer inanimate object preferred:: =ex.

inceptive
    begin(ning) to, start(ing) to, inceptive:: mí ~ mé ~ me.

inchworm
    inchworm, (caterpillar of the geometrid moth family):: q'álq'elp'í:w < q'ál, q'alq'elṓ:wsem < q'ál.

include

along, together, be included, with:: sq'eq'ó < q'ó.
join, (include oneself purposely):: q'ó:thet < q'ó.
put s-th with (something), add s-th (to something), include s-th:: q'ót < q'ó.

indefinite)

the (distant and out of sight, remote), (definite but distant and out of sight, remote), the (abstract), a (remote, abstract), some, (indefinite):: kw'e.
the (remote, not visible, abstract), some (indefinite):: kw.

independent

be totally independent, doing the best one can:: óyó:lwethet < éy ~ éy:.
manage by oneself (in food or travel), try to do it by oneself, try to be independent, do the best one can:: iyólewéthet < éy ~ éy:.
subject of independent clause, non-subordinate subject:: ts- ~ ch-.

index finger

first finger, index finger:: mét'esemél < mót'es, mót'estel < mót'es, mót'estses < mót'es.
index finger, pointing finger:: mómet'es < mót'es.
second finger, index finger:: stl'eqtóletses < tl'áqt.

Indian

a Hindu, an East Indian:: híltu.
arrowleaf, wapato, Indian potato:: xwōqw'ṓ:ls.
a small Hindu, a small East Indian:: híheltu < híltu.
Indian person, (North American) Indian:: xwélmexw.
longhouse, smokehouse (for spirit-dancing, etc.), Indian house, plank house:: xwelmexwáwtxw < xwélmexw.

Indian consumption plant

hog fennel, Indian consumption plant:: q'ex̱mí:l.

Indian currant

Indian currant bush, red-flowering currant bush, prob. also stink currant bush:: sp'á:th'elhp < sp'á:th'.
red-flowering currant berry, Indian currant berry, probably also stink currant berry also called skunk currant berry:: sp'á:th'.

Indian dance-house

Indian dance-house, "smoke-house", (spirit-dance building):: smilha'áwtxw < mílha.

Indian doctor

(an Indian doctor or shaman) working, curing, chasing the bad things away:: lhálhewels < lhá:w.
cure s-o, heal s-o by Indian doctoring:: lhá:wet < lhá:w.
curing s-o (as an Indian doctor):: lhálhewet < lhá:w.
Indian doctor at work, shaman at work, healer:: lhalhewéleq < lhá:w.
Indian doctor, shaman, medicine man, Indian doctor's spirit power (Elders Group 11/19/75):: shxwlá:m < lá:m.
Indian red paint (used by spirit dancers, ritualists, and Indian doctors or shamans):: témélh.

Indian doctor (CONT'D)

jumping up and down or bouncing up and down (of an Indian doctor training):: hélmethet < lá:m.

jump up and down (of Indian doctor training):: lemóthet < lá:m.

paint one's face red or black (spirit dancer, Indian doctor, ritualist, etc.):: lhíx̱esem < lhá:x̱ ~ lháx̱.

place of training to become an Indian doctor (pit made from repeated jumping every year on the same spot):: shxwlemóthetále < lá:m.

spirit power of an Indian doctor or shaman:: slá:m < lá:m.

to paint red or black (spirit dancer, Indian doctor, etc.):: lhíx̱ < lhá:x̱ ~ lháx̱.

Indian hemp

grass or fibre for nets or twine, spreading dogbane, possibly also Indian hemp:: méthelh.

Indian ice-cream

Indian ice-cream, whipped soapberry foam:: sx̱wṓsem ~ sx̱wṓ:sem ~ sx̱ṓ(:)sem.

soapberry basket, Indian ice-cream basket:: sx̱wōsemálá < sx̱wṓsem ~ sx̱wṓ:sem ~ sx̱ṓ(:)sem.

soapberry beater, stick for whipping up soapberries or Indian ice cream:: th'amawéstel or th'emawéstel < th'ím ~ th'í:m.

Indian paint fungus

(perhaps) red rock fungus used for Indian paint, (perhaps) Indian paint fungus:: témélh.

Indian plum

Indian plum bush:: mélhx̱welelhp < mélhx̱wel.

Indian plum (the fruit), (also called) June plum:: mélhx̱wel.

"Indian tea"

Labrador tea, "Indian tea", "swamp tea":: mó:qwem.

Indian tobacco

kinnikinnick berry, bearberry, Indian tobacco, domestic pea, domestic green bean, and probably giant vetch berry:: tl'íkw'el.

indirect effect

indirect effect non-control reflexive:: =methet.

indirect effect non-control transitivizer:: =met.

inexperienced

a small person (old or young) is picking or trying to pick, an inexperienced person is picking or trying to pick, picking a little bit, someone who can't pick well is picking:: lhilhím < lhím.

influence

pulled, influenced:: thékw'.

-ing

continuative, be -ing:: -R1- or -C1e-, R5- or C1e-, R8= or C1a=, =R9= or =C1á(:)=.

in-grown

in-grown finger-nail:: kyépetses < kyépe=.

in-grown toe-nail:: kyépe=xel < kyépe=.

in half

break s-th in two (with one's hands), break it in half (with one's hands only), break off a piece of s-th:: peqwót < péqw.

inherent

characteristic, inherent continuative:: =R2 or =C1eC2.
plural, inherent plural:: =R2 or =C1eC2.

initiate

babysitter (for new spirit-dancers), any of the workers who help in initiating a spirit-dancer, (initiator or helper of spirit-dancers):: xólhemìlh ~ xòlhemí:lh < xólh.
lift s-o (of a spirit dancer being initiated):: shxwóxwelstexw < xwá.

injure

accidentally hurt an old injury of s-o, (accidentally reinjure s-o):: qélhlexw < qélh.

-in-law :: sexw=.

child's spouse's parent, child's spouse's sibling, child's in-laws:: skw'élwés.
in-laws or relatives when the connecting link dies:: ts'its'á:ya < ts'á:ya.
in-laws (?), parents-in-law, spouse's parents:: skw'álhew < skw'ílhew.

inlet

at the head or source of a river, the inside head or inlet of a river:: =qel.

inner

inner cedar bark:: slewí < léw.
inner cedar bark (maybe error), (birch bark [AHTTC]):: sèqw'emí:ws < síqw'em.
inner lining, inner side:: skwetxwó:lwelh < kwetáxw.

in one's way

go around a bend in the river, go around a turn, go around something in one's way:: q'ewílem < q'éw ~ q'ew.

insane

be crazy, be insane:: shxwóxwth' < xwáth'.

insect

buzzing (of insects):: t'ít'elem < t'íl.
buzz (of insects):: t'ílém ~ t'ílem < t'íl.

inside

admitting s-o/s-th, letting s-o/s-th in, bringing s-o/s-th inside:: kwétexwt < kwetáxw.
at the head or source of a river, the inside head or inlet of a river:: =qel.
become glad, become happy, happy inside:: xwoyíwel ~ xwoyíwél.
be inside (a hollow object), be in (a hollow object):: slíw < léw.
be inside a house, be inside an enclosure:: skwetáxw < kwetáxw.
be inside a pit-house:: sqemí:l < sqémél.
bring s-o/s-th in (to a house/enclosure), take s-o/s-th in(inside a house/enclosure), admit s-o (into a house/enclosure), let s-o/s-th in (to a house/enclosure), put s-o/s-th in (inside a house/enclosure:: kwetáxwt < kwetáxw.
get twisted [inside]:: x̲elts'íwélém < x̲élts'.

inside (CONT'D)

go around inside the longhouse counter-clockwise:: selts'elwílem < sél or sí(:)l.
go in (a house/enclosure), come in, come inside, enter a house or enclosure:: kwetxwí:lem < kwetáxw.
(have) sound of water sloshing around inside (a bottle, etc.) or gurgling:: qw'át'ts'em.
hurt inside:: qélh.
inside or core of a plant or fruit (or canoe or anything):: =í:wel ~ =íwel ~ =ewel.
in the rump, in the anus, in the rectum, in the bottom, on the insides, inside parts, core, inside the head:: =í:wel ~ =íwel ~ =ewel.
keep s-o/s-th inside:: kwetáxwstexw < kwetáxw.
leave s-o/s-th inside:: skwetáxwstexw < kwetáxw.
put it in (and leave it), stick it into s-th hollow:: léwex < léw.
roof of the mouth, inside of upper lip, palate:: chelhqí:l ~ chelhqéyl < =chílh ~ chílh=.
the inside (of a container):: skwetxwewílh < kwetáxw.
to hurt again (as when a painful place is bumped and hurts again or as when a pain inside one's body returns again), (to ache [SJ]):: téqlexw.
to rattle s-th inside:: kwétxwt < kwótx̲wem ~ kwótxwem.
to the back (near the wall), on the inside (on a bed toward the wall):: lhelhá:l.

inside out

be turned inside out:: schelá:w < chaléwt.
turn s-th/s-o over, flip it over (of fish for ex.), turn it inside out:: chaléwt.

insides

insides (animal or human or other?), (internal organs, guts, etc.), (stomach [inside] [DM]):: sts'elxwíwel < ts'el.
in the rump, in the anus, in the rectum, in the bottom, on the insides, inside parts, core, inside the head:: =í:wel ~ =íwel ~ =ewel.
rip on the bottom or insides:: x̲wetíwél < x̲wét.

insistant

insistant, persistant (like a child pressing to go along), bull-headed, doesn't mind, does just the opposite, (stubborn, contrary):: sxíxeles.

instant

now, this moment, this instant:: tloqá:ys < ló.
now, this moment, this instant, (right now):: tloqá:ys < qá:ys.

instead)

I'd rather have (s-th), I'd prefer (s-th) (make that s-th instead):: tl'óst or tl'óstexw.
(make that s-th (instead), cause that to be s-th (instead)):: tl'óst or tl'óstexw.

instep

sole (of the foot), (instep [AC, DM]):: shxw'óthesxel ~ shxwe'óthesxel < s'ó:thes ~ s'óthes.

instrument

flute, wind instrument, blown musical instrument:: pepó:tem < pó:t, pepó:tem < pó:t.
musical instrument, grammophone, phonograph, record player:: qweló:ythetel ~ qwelóyethetel < qwà:l.
playing a musical instrument:: qwiqwelóythetel < qwà:l.

insult
(accidentally) make s-o ashamed, insult s-o (accidentally or manage to):: x̲éyx̲elexw < x̲éyx̲e ~ x̲íx̲e.

intentionally
beat s-o/s-th with a stick, hit s-o/s-th with a stick, hit s-th (on purpose), hit s-o intentionally:: kw'óqwet < kw'óqw.

intercourse
have intercourse, fuck:: kw'átl'.
have intercourse with s-o, fuck s-o:: kw'átl'et < kw'átl'.
making love, having intercourse:: pipelá:ls < pél (perhaps ~ pí:l by now).
thinking about having intercourse:: kw'okw'etl'élmel < kw'átl'.

interest
like s-o [his/her personality], like s-th [its taste, its idea], be interested in s-th/s-o, enjoy s-o sexually:: éystexw ~ éy:stexw < éy ~ éy:.

internal organs
insides (animal or human or other?), (internal organs, guts, etc.), (stomach [inside] [DM]):: sts'elxwíwel < ts'el.

International Ridge
Cultus Lake Mountain, actually Mount Amadis or International Ridge:: Swílhcha Smá:lt < Swílhcha.

interrogative:: -á.
interrogative, yes/no question:: -e.
is that okay? (interrogative tag-question):: é.
weren't ever?, wasn't ever?, didn't ever?, does s-o ever?, never used to, not going to (but did anyway) [perhaps in the sense of never usually do X but did this time]:: ewá:lh ~ wá:lh < éwe ~ őwe.

intestine
guts, intestines:: q'eq'éy < q'ey ~ q'i.

in the way
be in the way:: leq'á:lh < léq'.

into
go out into the river, go down to the river, walk down to the river:: tó:l ~ tò:l.
it went into him/her (of spirit power):: thex̲we'í:ls.
put it in (and leave it), stick it into s-th hollow:: léwex < léw.

in two
break s-th in two (with one's hands), break it in half (with one's hands only), break off a piece of s-th:: peqwót < péqw.
split off, break off, break a piece off, break in two, split in two:: péqw.

invite
invite s-o (to come eat, dance etc.) (any number), invite s-o to a feast:: tl'e'áxet < tl'e'á ~ tl'á', tl'e'áxet < tl'e'á ~ tl'á'.
inviting (to come eat, dance), to give a potlatch, (give a feast or gathering), to invite to a

invite (CONT'D)
feast, invite to a potlatch:: tl'etl'áxel < tl'e'á ~ tl'á'.

Iridoprocne bicolor
especially Iridoprocne bicolor and Riparia riparia:: qw'sí:tsel.

iron
an iron:: shxwíxweqwels < xwíqw.
blow (spray) on a patient (of an Indian doctor or shaman), blow spray on s-o/s-th (of a shaman, a person ironing, a child teething):: póx̲wet < póx̲w.
iron s-th:: xwíqwet < xwíqw.
iron (the metal), silver:: chíkmel.
pot to boil in, iron pot, smaller iron pot:: lhémkiya ~ lhámkiya < lhém.

"ironwood"
oceanspray plant, "ironwood", "hardhack":: qáthelhp < qáthexw.

irritate
get offended, get irritated:: qwox̲wlómét < qwóx̲wlexw.
prickly (from fir bark, wool, or something one is allergic to), irritant, have an allergic reaction (to fir powder or cedar bark):: th'íth'ekwem < th'íkw.

is
is there none?, isn't there any?:: wá:ta < éwe ~ ṓwe.

-ish :: =el.

Island
a lumpy mountain back of Seabird Island:: Sqwemqwómx̲w < qwó:m ~ qwóm ~ qwem.
a neck of land on the west side of Harrison Lake just north of Twenty-Mile Creek and across from the north tip of Long Island:: Shxwtépsem < tépsem.
a place just past the west end of Seabird Island, towards Agassiz, AK's grandfather only translated it as Hamersley's (see Hamersley's hopyards), it was located at the west end of Seabird Island i.e. property between Dan Thomas's and Uncle Dave Charles's places, across from Sqémelets [Elders on Seabird Is. trip 6/20/78]):: Qwoméx̲weth' < qwó:m ~ qwóm ~ qwem.
bear-shaped rock up on cliff on south side above Echo Point bay on Echo Island in Harrison Lake:: Spá:th < pá:th.
Cheam Island (my name for an island in the Fraser River across from Cheam Indian Reserve #2), Cheam village, Cheam Indian Reserve #1:: Xwchí:yò:m < schí:ya.
Echo Island in Harrison Lake:: Xweqw'oyíqw, Xwōxwe'áqel.
Echo Island in southern quarter of Harrison Lake:: Xwōqwiyáqw.
Echo Point on Echo Island, Echo Bay on Echo Island:: X̲wix̲we'áqel ~ Xwixwe'áqel ~ Xwōxwe'áqel < x̲wex̲we'á.
Greenwood Island:: Welqémex < qám.
(heron nesting area which was the) upriver end of Herrling Island in Fraser River just below Popkum, also the name of the village or settlement on Herrling Island:: Smémeqw'o < sméqw'o ~ smṓqw'o.
island off of Wahleach Island, island at bridge on river side on east end of Seabird Island:: Xáméles < xá:m, Xáméles < xá:m.
Long Island (in Harrison Lake):: Híkw Tl'tsás < híkw.
Lulu Island:: Lhewqí:m Tl'chás < lhewqí:m.
Nicomen Island (in the Fraser River near Deroche), also a specific place on northeast end

Island (CONT'D)

of Nicomen Island where lots of people used to gather [now Sumas Indian Reserve #10]:: Leq'á:mél.
place above Yale where the Fraser River splits around a rock, island above Steamboat Island (latter just below Five-Mile Creek):: Sx̲wesálh < x̲wés.
place on the east side of Seabird Island:: X̲ex̲éyth'elhp < x̲éyth'.
(probably) Mahood Creek and Johnson Slough, (possibly) Wahleach River or Hicks Creek (creek at bridge on east end of Seabird Island [AK]):: Qwōhòls < qwá.
Queen's Island:: Qemlólhp < sq'émél.
slough about mid-point in Seabird Island where xáweleq plant grew:: Xíxewqèyl or Xíxewqì:l ~ Xewqéyl or Xewqí:l < xáwéq.
slough where people used to drift-net by Martin Harris's place at Seabird Island:: Titáwlechem < tewláts.
upper end of Seabird Island, village at the upper end of Seabird Island, Maria Slough separating Seabird Island from north shore of Fraser River, now used for Seabird Island as a whole:: Sq'éwqel ~ Sq'ówqel < q'éw ~ q'ew.
west or downriver end of Seabird Island:: Sth'eméxwelets < sth'eméxwelets.

island :: tl'chá:s ~ tl'tsá:s.

end of a falling section of land, end of a level stretch of land, (head of a creek or island [Elders Group]):: lhéq'qel.
head of a creek or island:: lheqel ~ lhequl.
head of an island:: =qel.
heart-shaped island near the mouth of Chehalis River that beat like a heart:: Th'álátel ~ Th'á:lá ~ Th'ála < th'á:lá ~ th'ála ~ th'á:le ~ th'ále.
island in front of Iwówes (Elders Group 7/9/75):: Lhilheltálets < lhà:l.
island in river on which Yune's Cannery was built:: Yù:l.
island off of Wahleach Island, island at bridge on river side on east end of Seabird Island:: Xáméles < xá:m.
island or point on north side of first slough north of the mouth of Chehalis River, (next slough and point above Mímex̲wel [EL 3/1/78]):: Yálhxetel.
place above Yale where the Fraser River splits around a rock, island above Steamboat Island (latter just below Five-Mile Creek):: Sx̲wesálh < x̲wés.
point of geog. features like island or mountain or land:: =eqs ~ =éqsel ~ =élqsel ~ =elqs.
point of land at the end of an island:: sth'eméxwelets.

isn't

isn't?, aren't?, don't?, doesn't?, (be not?):: ewá ~ ōwá ~ wá < éwe ~ ő́we.
isn't s-o yet?, isn't it yet?, hasn't s-o yet?:: xwewá: < éwe ~ ő́we.
is there none?, isn't there any?:: wá:ta < éwe ~ ő́we.

Isolillock Mountain

Isolillock Mountain (near Silver Creek):: Tl'ítl'xeleqw.

Is that okay

Is that okay?:: wé.
is that okay? (interrogative tag-question):: é.

it

and so (he, she, it, they):: qetl'osésu ~ qetl'os'ésu < tl'ó ~ tl'o, tl'osésu ~ tl'os'ésu < tl'ó ~ tl'o.
and then (he, she, it):: tl'esu < tl'ó ~ tl'o.
because (he, she, it, they):: tl'okw'es ~ tl'okwses ~ tl'ekwses < tl'ó ~ tl'o.

it (CONT'D)

he (present or presence unspecified), he's the one that, it's him that, she or it (present or presence unspecified), that or this (immediately before nominal):: tú:tl'ò ~ tútl'ò ~ tútl'o < tl'ó ~ tl'o.
he/she/it was (already), they were (already):: lulh < le.
him, her, it, them, third person object:: -exw.
that he, that she, that it, that they:: kws ...-s ~ kwses ~ kw'es ...-s < kw.

itch

(get) real itching:: x̲eyx̲ets'émthet < x̲íth' ~ x̲éyth'.
(have a) chronic skin disease marked by reddish skin and itching, have "seven-year itch":: lhóth'.
itchy:: x̲íx̲eth'em < x̲íth' ~ x̲éyth'.
scabies (a skin disease), ("seven-year itch", itch lasting seven years [Deming 2/7/80]):: slhóth' < lhóth'.
scratch it (like of an itch), (itch it):: x̲éyq'et < x̲éyq'.

its

his, her, its, their, third person possessive pronoun, third person subordinate subject:: -s.
that's (an animate being), it's (usually animate):: tl'ó ~ tl'o.
that's him (absent), that's her (absent), it's him (absent), it's her (absent):: kwthú:tl'ò < kw.
that's him (absent), that's her (absent), it's him/her (absent), he (absent), she (absent):: kwthú:tl'ò < tl'ó ~ tl'o.

itself)

it shook (shakes itself), shaking, bobbing around:: qwá:yx̲thet < qwá:y.
moving, moving oneself/itself:: kwó:yxthet ~ kwó:yex̲thet ~ kwó:yxethet < kwíyx̲.
on itself, within itself:: =p'.
on the body, on top of itself:: =á:w ~ =í:w ~ =ew.
tangled on its own/itself:: q'elq'élp' < q'ál.

Iwówes

island in front of Iwówes (Elders Group 7/9/75):: Lhilheltálets < lhà:l.
natural holes or tunnels east of Iwówes and above Lhilheltálets that water came out of after rain:: Sqwelíqwehíwel ~ Sqwelíqwehìwèl < qwá.

Ixodes pacificus

class Arachnida, order Acarina, Dermacentor andersoni, and probably Ixodes pacificus:: t'pí.
class Arachnida, order Acarina, probably Ixodes pacificus and Dermacentor andersoni resp.:: méth'elhqìwèl < méth'elh.

Ixoreus naevius naevius:: sx̲wík'.

Íyém

bay at upper end of Íyém (Yale Indian Reserve #22):: Qémelets < qám.
pool down from Tillie Gutierrez's grandfather's fish-drying rack at Íyem (Eayem):: qemqémel ~ qemqémél < qém:el.

Jack

Indian name of Old Jack (of Yakweakwioose or perhaps Scowkale):: T'eláqw'tel < t'álqw' or t'élqw'.

jack

jack
jack spring salmon with black nose:: tl'elxálōwelh or tl'elxálōllh < tl'él.

jacket
jacket, vest:: cháket.
small jacket:: cháchket < cháket.

jack-o-lantern
home-made lantern (using candle in a can with a hole in it, etc.), jack-o-lantern:: shxwélchep.

jackrabbit
jackrabbit, also big or older rabbit (snowshoe/varying hare):: sqwíqweyóthel < qwá.

jade
jade (nephrite) (used for sharpening [chopping] stones), any agate (can be used as flint to strike a spark):: t'émq'ethel.

jail :: qíq'áwtxw < qíq'.
(emprisoned), put in jail, grounded, restricted, caught, apprehended:: qíq'.

jam)
barbecue, bake (meat, vegetables, etc.) in open fire, bake over fire, roast over open fire, bake under hot sand, bake in oven, cook in oven, (boiled down (as jam) [CT, HT]):: qw'élém < qw'él.
(be) squeezed in, jammed up, tight:: sx̲ex̲ákw' < x̲ékw'.
one's hand jammed (in a trap, under a box, etc.):: tl'í:q'etses < tl'íq'.

jampile
jampile, log-jam:: steqtéq < téq.

January
about December, (January to February [Billy Sepass]):: meqó:s < máqa ~ máqe.
moon or month beginning in November, (put away each other's paddles), (sometimes the moon beginning in October, depending on the weather [Elders Group [3/12/75], (moon or month beginning in January [Elders Group 2/5/75]):: xets'ő:westel ~ xets'őwestel < xits' ~ xets'.

Japanese
Japanese person:: chaplí.

Japanese wineberry:: th'elíth'eplexw ~ ts'elíts'eplexw (or perhaps ts'elíts'ep'lexw) < th'éplexw (or perhaps th'ép'lexw).

jaundice
gall-bladder, gall, bile, have bile trouble, be jaundiced, bilious:: lelets' ~ laléts'.

jaw
chin, jaw (of fish, human, etc.), (lips (both), cheek, side of the face [DM]):: ts'emxó:ythel.
hair on the chin or jaw, beard, mustache:: qwiliyéthel < qwíl ~ qwel.
(have a) twisted mouth, twisted jaw:: pó:yethel < pó:y.
hit on the mouth, [hit on the chin, hit on the lip, hit on the jaw]:: kw'qwó:ythel < kw'óqw.
on the lip or jaw:: =ó:ythel ~ =eyéthel ~ =eyth(íl).

jaw (CONT'D)

on the lips, on the jaw, on the chin:: =ó:ythel.
skin of the mouth, (prob. also skin of the chin or jaw or lips):: kw'elōwó:ythel < kw'eléw ~ kw'elṓw.
to have a crooked jaw:: sx̲ó:lts'iyethel < x̲élts'.

jay
bluejay, Steller's jay:: kwá:y.
bluejay, Steller's jay (sacred fortune-teller):: x̲ax̲esyúwes or x̲ax̲e syúwes < x̲áx̲e.
cry of a bluejay [Steller's jay] that means good news:: q'ey, q'ey, q'ey.
(this cry of a bluejay [Steller's jay] warns you of bad news):: chéke chéke chéke chéke.
whiskey jack, Canada jay:: sáwel < sáwel.

jealous
be jealous of s-o:: wowistéleqmet < wowistéleq.
jealous, (envious (EB)):: wowistéleq.
last baby (youngest baby), the last-born, a child cranky and jealous of an expected brother or sister:: óqw'a < óqw'.

jeans
denim pants, jeans:: xwétkw'emáyiws < xwót'kw'em.

jerk-lining
jerk-lining for sturgeon in a canoe:: wiweqw'óthet < wṓqw' ~ wéqw'.

Jerusalem artichoke
bulb or root called wild artichoke, Jerusalem artichoke:: x̲áx̲ekw'.
potato (generic), including three or four kinds of wild potato: arrowleaf or wapato, Jerusalem artichoke, blue camas, and qíqemxel (so far unidentified plant), besides post-contact domestic potato:: sqáwth ~ sqá:wth.
wild red potatoes that pigs eat, (probably Jerusalem artichoke):: sx̲éykwel.
wild red potato (grew at American Bar in the 1920's), possibly Jerusalem artichoke:: sx̲éykwel.

Jesus Christ:: Síthikwi.

jingle
to rattle (of dishes or anything else loose), jingle (of money or any metal shaken), peal or toll (of a bell), make the sound of a bell, to ring (of a bell, telephone, in the ears):: th'á:tsem < th'éts or th'á(:)ts.

Joe
nickname of Freddie Joe:: sépelets.
place in Katz or Ruby Creek, may be name for Charlie Joe's place near Katz at the mouth of a creek where the water is always calm:: sqemélwélh ~ sqemélwelh < qám.

jog
jog, to trot (animal or person):: lhapxálem.

Johnson
mountain [north] across from Lizzie Johnson's place on Seabird Island:: X̲ax̲esxélem < x̲ésxel.

Johnson Slough

(probably) Mahood Creek and Johnson Slough, (possibly) Wahleach River or Hicks Creek (creek at bridge on east end of Seabird Island [AK]):: Qwōhòls < qwá.

join

join, (include oneself purposely):: q'ó:thet < q'ó.
join s-th together:: lheqtó:léstexw < lhéq.
join two poles together, splice it together (of a rope), (join together on the ends):: t'qwíqst.
put them together, (join them together):: q'ótelt ~ q'ótòlt < q'ó.

joint

all the joints of the foot and toes:: qwemqwémx̲wxel < qwó:m ~ qwóm ~ qwem.
ankle joint:: xweth'éqw'xel.
(get a) sprained foot, leg got out of joint:: plhéqw'xel ~ p'lhéqw'xel.
knuckles (all the joints of the hand and fingers):: qwemqwémx̲wtses < qwó:m ~ qwóm ~ qwem.
wrist or hand joint:: xweth'éqw'tses.

joke

a dandy, someone who overdresses, a show-off, comedian, someone who always cracks jokes, smart-alec:: swék'.
fooling s-o, (fool s-o as a joke, April-fool s-o [Deming]):: q'íq'elstá:xw < q'á:l.

Jones Creek

lake in back of Paul Webster's old place on Hicks Rd. near Jones Creek:: Th'qwélhcha < th'qwélhcha.
wide place at the mouth of the east (upriver) branch of Jones Creek:: Swílth'.

Jones Hill

small shoreline ridge on the Fraser River and all along the river around the larger mountain across the Trans-Canada Highway from Jones Hill:: Sqayéx̲iya Smált ~ Sqáqeyex̲iya Smált < sqáyéx̲ ~ sqayéx̲.

journey

travel (to a destination), be on a journey:: leq'áleq'el (~ leq'áleqel (rare)).

jug

storage basket (for oil, fruit, clothes), burial basket for twins, round basket (any size, smaller at top), clay jug (to store oil or fruit):: skwá:m ~ skwám < kwá:m ~ kwám.

juice :: qó:lhcha < qó:.
fruit juice:: sqe'éleqw < qó:.
get juicy of its own accord:: qó:lhthet < qó:.
juicy fruit:: sqe'ó:ls < qó:.
unclear liquid, water, juice:: =elhcha.
apple juice:: qwe'óp sqe'óleqw < qwe'óp, qó:
blackberry juice:: sqw'ő:lmexw sqe'óleqw < qw'ő:lmexw, qó:
carrot juice:: xáweq sqe'óleqw < xáweq, qó:
cranberry juice:: kwúkwewels sqe'óleqw (or better: qwemchó:ls sqe'óleqw)< kwúkwewels, qwà:m ~ qwám, qó:
(lit. high-bush cranberry + fruit juice (or better:) bog cranberry + fruit juice)

juice (CONT'D)

grape juice:: qelíps sqe'óleqw < qelíps, qó:
grapefruit juice:: sásex̲em qwíyqwòyèls sqe'óleqw < sáx̲, qwá:y,, qó:
(lit. grapefruit [itself bitter + yellow fruit] + fruit juice)
lemon-lime juice:: t'át'ets'em qwíyqwòyèls qas te t'át'ets'em tsqwáyqwòyèls sqe'óleqw < t'áts', qwá:y, qó:
(lit. lemon fruit [itself < sour little yellowish fruit] + and + the + lime fruit [itself < sour greenish fruit]+ fruit juice)
orange juice:: qwíyqwòyèls sqe'óleqw < qwá:y, qó:
pineapple juice:: st'elt'elíqw qwe'óp sqe'óleqw < t'el, qwe'óp, qó:
(lit. pineapple [itself from bumpy and prickly + apple] + fruit juice)
raspberry juice:: s'óytheqw sqe'óleqw < éy, qó:
soapberry juice:: sx̲wṓsem sqe'óleqw < x̲wṓs, qó:
strawberry juice:: schíya sqe'óleqw < chíya, qó:
tomato juice:: temítō sqe'óleqw < temítō, qó:
V8 juice:: smómeleqw spíls s'élhtel sqe'óleqw < móleqw, píl, álhtel, qó:
(lit. mixed + planted + food + fruit juice)
vegetable juice:: spíls s'élhtel sqe'óleqw < píl, álhtel, qó:
(lit. planted + food + fruit juice)

juicy

get juicy of its own accord:: qó:lhthet < qó:.
juicy fruit:: sqe'ó:ls < qó:.

July

(first lunar month beginning in) July, (tenth month):: epóléstel < ó:pel.
first of July:: temchálhtel < =chílh ~ chílh=.
July to August, (big spring salmon time):: temth'oló:lh < sth'olólh.
month or moon beginning in July:: temqwá:l < qwá:l.
sockeye moon, month to get sockeye salmon (begins with first quarter after black moon in July, lasts into August), July to August, (June to July [Jenness: WS]):: temthéqi < sthéqi ~ sthéqey, temthéqi < sthéqi ~ sthéqey.
time to dry fish, first of July (at Yale), October (at Chehalis):: temchálhtel < =chílh ~ chílh=.

jump

jump at s-o:: ts'tl'émet < ts'tl'ám ~ ts'tl'ém.
jump, hop (once):: ts'tl'ám ~ ts'tl'ém.
jumping:: ts'áts'etl'em < ts'tl'ám ~ ts'tl'ém.
jumping along, jumping up and down:: ts'ats'etl'í:m < ts'tl'ám ~ ts'tl'ém.
jumping, hopping:: ts'á:tl'em ~ ch'á:tl'em ~ ts'átl'em < ts'tl'ám ~ ts'tl'ém.
jumping (of fish):: mámeq'em < máq'em.
jumping up and down or bouncing up and down (of an Indian doctor training):: hélmethet < lá:m.
jump up and down (of Indian doctor training):: lemóthet < lá:m.
place of training to become an Indian doctor (pit made from repeated jumping every year on the same spot):: shxwlemóthetále < lá:m.
to jump (of fish):: máq'em.
water jumping (as it goes over a rough bottom in a river):: kwetl'kwótl'thetōws < kwá:.

June

gooseberry time, the month or moon (first sliver) that starts in June:: temt'á:mxw < t'á:mxw.
high water time (yearly, usually in June), June:: temqó: ~ temqoqó: < qó:.

June (CONT'D)

month beginning in April at the mouth of the Fraser, May-June (Jenness:Sepass), oolachen moon:: temwíwe (or possibly) temswíwe < swí:we ~ swíwe.

sockeye moon, month to get sockeye salmon (begins with first quarter after black moon in July, lasts into August), July to August, (June to July [Jenness: WS]):: temthéqi < sthéqi ~ sthéqey.

June berry

fresh saskatoon berry, service-berry, June berry:: ts'esláts.

"June bug"

metallic blue-green beetle, "June bug", probably metallic wood-boring beetle, or possibly some types of long-horn beetle which aremetallic green with reddish legs:: tále te syó:qwem < tá:le ~ tále, tále te syó:qwem < yéqw.

June plum

Indian plum (the fruit), (also called) June plum:: mélhx̱wel.

junior

younger, younger sibling, cousin of a junior line (cousin by an ancestor younger than the speaker's), junior cousin (child of a younger sibling of one's parent, (great) grandchild of a younger sibling of one's(great) grandparent), younger brother, younger sister:: sóseqwt ~ (rarely) só:seqwt.

junior line

younger, younger sibling, cousin of a junior line (cousin by an ancestor younger than the speaker's), junior cousin (child of a younger sibling of one's parent, (great) grandchild of a younger sibling of one's(great) grandparent), younger brother, younger sister:: sóseqwt ~ (rarely) só:seqwt.

juniper

(possibly the name for) common juniper or creeping juniper:: th'el'á:ltel < th'á:lá ~ th'ála ~ th'á:le ~ th'ále.

Juniperus communis:: th'el'á:ltel < th'á:lá ~ th'ála ~ th'á:le ~ th'ále.

just

begin, start, (be) just started, just began, be just begun:: yálhò < yalh.
be only (contrastive), be just (contrastive):: welóy < lóy.
be only, just:: lóy.
just came, (just arrived):: tátsel.
just, (exactly):: =ò:l ~ =ól ~ =ò ~ ò ~ ó:l.
just like:: st'ó'o ~ st'á ò < t.
just listening (not talking):: xwlalá:.
just (simply, merely):: òl ~ -òl ~ -ò ~ el.
(just) started (to do something):: wiyálhò < yalh.

just now

recently, just now, lately, (at one recent moment), not long ago:: qá:ys.

Kateseslie

Kateseslie, a spring-water stream east of Coqualeetza, part of the Kw'eqwá:líth'a [property or stream?] that went through Sardis and came out to the Cottonwood Corner:: Katsesló:y.

Katz

a mountain above Evangeline Pete's place at Katz:: Sesíq' < séq'.

Katz (CONT'D)

Dog Mountain above Katz Reserve:: Q'á:w < q'á:w.
Katz river-bank, Ruby Creek settlement, village on north bank of Fraser River just below (west of) the mouth of Ruby Creek:: Spópetes < pó:t.
place in Katz or Ruby Creek, may be name for Charlie Joe's place near Katz at the mouth of a creek where the water is always calm:: sqemélwélh ~ sqemélwelh < qám.
village near and above [upriver from] Katz where 36 pit-houses were wiped out in an epidemic:: Sx̲wóx̲wiymelh < x̲wà:y ~ x̲wá:y.
village near Katz:: (Xwóqw'ilwets?).

Katzie

Katzie village:: Q'éyts'i(y).

Katz Landing

village at what's now Katz Reserve, Katz Landing:: Chowéthel < cháchew ~ cháchu.

Katz Reserve

village at what's now Katz Reserve, Katz Landing:: Chowéthel < cháchew ~ cháchu.

Kawkawa Creek

maybe the same place as Sqw'ex̲wáq (pool where Kawkawa Creek comes into the Coquihalla River and where the water pygmies lived):: Skw'íkw'x̲weq (or better, Sqw'íqw'x̲weq) < Sqw'ex̲wáq.
pool where Kawkawa Creek comes into the Coquihalla River:: Sqw'ex̲wáq.

Kawkawa Lake

(get) a disease gotten by contacting a frog, a skin eruption, also the same disease as the man got in Kawkawa Lake in the Sx̲wó:yx̲wey story, (perhaps also) leprosy:: qw'ő:m.
Kawkawa Lake (near Hope, B.C.):: Q'éwq'ewe < q'á:w.
trail and steep slope on the west shore of Kawkawa Lake where the trail went up and over a steep hill and then down:: Sq'éywetselem ~ Sq'éywetsélém < q'e:yw ~ q'í:w.

keekwillie

pit-house, keekwillie house, semi-subterranean house:: sqémél.

keep

keep it in the air, lift s-th/s-o off the floor:: shxwóxwelstexw < xwá.
keep it wrapped:: xwelókw'stexw ~ shxwelókw'stexw < xwélekw'.
keep s-o/s-th alive:: á:yelexwstexw < áylexw ~ áyelexw.
keep s-o/s-th inside:: kwetáxwstexw < kwetáxw.
keep the fire at a constant temperature:: txwéltsep.
non-control reflexive, make oneself do something, keep oneself doing something:: =st=èlèmèt or =st-èlèmèt ~ =st-elómet.

keep on

keep on going:: á:y.
keep on hearing a distant sound:: sasetáleqep < sát.
keeps on groaning:: i'ó:lthet ò < ó:lthet.

kerchief :: tl'xwíqwtel < tl'xw ~ tl'exw, shxwékw'thelh sq'éytes < xwókw' ~ xwekw'ó.

kernel)

heart of a root, seed, nut (kernel), core of plant or seedling, core (of tree, branch, any growing thing), pith (of bush), seed or pit [U.S.] or pip [Cdn.] of a fruit:: sth'emí:wel ~ sth'emíwel ~ sth'emíwél < sth'ó:m

ketchup:: temítō smelmólkw (lit. tomato + spread) < temítō, mólkw

ketchup/stewed tomatoes:: stósem temíitō (lit. smashed + tomato) < tós, temíitō

kettle

pail, bucket, kettle (BJ, Gibbs):: skw'ó:wes ~ skw'ówes.

water kettle, boiler pan (for canning, washing clothes or dishes):: qowletsá:ls < qew.

key :: leklí ~ lekelí.

lock it with a key:: lekelít ~ xwleklít < leklí ~ lekelí.

kick :: lema'à:ls < lemá'.

beat s-o up, kick s-o in fight, lick s-o (in fight), spank s-o, fight s-o (till he cries for ex.), fight s-o in anger, fight s-o back:: x̱éyet.

kicking:: hálma'à:ls < lemá'.

kick s-o in the behind, kick s-o in the rump:: lamá'íwét < lemá'.

kick s-th around:: lemlemá:t < lemá'.

kick s-th/s-o:: lemá:t < lemá'.

Kickbush

place where a grove of birches stood/stand near the Kickbush place on Chilliwack River Road in Sardis, (village at junction of Semmihault Creek and Chilliwack River [Wells 1965]):: Sekw'sekw'emá:y < síkw'.

kick s-o out:: atl'qílt < átl'q.

kid :: mímstiyexw < mestíyexw.

babysitter (for kids, etc.):: xólhemìlh ~ xòlhemí:lh < xólh.

kids:: mamastiyexw (or better) mémestiyexw < mestíyexw.

that's them (little kids), they (little kids):: tl'étl'elò:m < tl'ó ~ tl'o.

to babysit someone else's kids (children):: xolhmílh < xólh.

kidnap

kidnap s-o, run away with s-o:: tl'ṓwstexw < tl'í:w.

kidney

kidneys:: smeltáléqel < smá:lt.

kidney beans:: tskwimómex tl'íkw'el (lit. dark red in appearance + bean) < kwim, tl'íkw'el

Kilby's store

beach in front of old Scowlitz village, the point the Harrison River goes around by Kilby's store:: Sq'iq'ewílem < q'éw ~ q'ew.

Kilgard

Kilgard village on Upper Sumas River:: Kw'ekw'e'í:qw ~ Kw'ekw'e'íqw ~ Kw'ekw'í:qw < kw'e'í ~ kw''í ~ kw'í.

Sumas village and area from present-day Kilgard to Fraser River, Sumas village (on both sides of the Fraser at the east end of Sumas Mt.), (Devil's Run (below Láx̱ewey), the area

Kilgard (CONT'D)

between Sumas Mt. and Fraser River [Elders Group 7/13/77], Sumas River (probably requires Stó:lō river or Stótelō creek to follow) [Wells 1965], Sumas Lake (probably requires X̲ótsa lake after Semáth for this meaning) [Elders Group 7/13/77]):: Smá:th ~ Semá:th ~ Semáth.

kilik

homemade anchor, kilik, calik, (killick):: skw'éstel.

kill

almost kill s-o:: x̲wíleqlexw.
killing s-th:: q'óq'eyt < q'ó:y ~ q'óy.
kill oneself:: q'óythet < q'ó:y ~ q'óy.
kill s-o (purposely):: q'ó:yt < q'ó:y ~ q'óy.
kill s-th (purposely):: q'ó:yt < q'ó:y ~ q'óy.
kill s-th/s-o accidentally, (happen to or manage to kill s-th/s-o):: q'eyléxw < q'ó:y ~ q'óy.
kill them:: x̲wá:yt < x̲wà:y ~ x̲wá:y.
repeatedly almost kill s-o:: x̲wilx̲wíleqlexw or x̲welx̲wíleqlexw < x̲wíleqlexw.

killer whale

killer whale, blackfish:: q'ellhólemètsel.

killick)

homemade anchor, kilik, calik, (killick):: skw'éstel.

kind

a different kind:: lets'emót < láts'.
be like, be similar to, be the same as, be a kind of:: sta'á ~ ste'á < t.
five kinds, five piles (perhaps a loose translation):: lhq'átsesmó:t < lheq'át ~ lhq'á:t.
four kinds, (four piles [Elders Group 7/27/75]):: x̲e'óthelmó:t ~ x̲e'óthelmò:t < x̲e'ó:thel ~ x̲e'óthel.
good-hearted, kind-hearted, kind, generous, helpful, easy-going, good-natured:: xw'éywelh ~ xwe'éywelh ~ xwe'éy:welh < éy ~ éy:.
one kind, one pile:: lets'emó:t < léts'a ~ léts'e.
piles, kinds:: =mó:t.
the same kind, the same:: sx̲tá(:) < x̲ét'e.
three kinds, three piles of things:: lhixwmó:t < lhí:xw.
two kinds:: isálemó:t < isá:le ~ isále ~ isá:la.

kind-hearted

good-hearted, kind-hearted, kind, generous, helpful, easy-going, good-natured:: xw'éywelh ~ xwe'éywelh ~ xwe'éy:welh < éy ~ éy:.

kindling :: sísq' < séq'.

kind of

(be) kind of lazy:: s'i'omó:met < emét.

King Edward:: Kíl Ítewet < kelchóch ~ kyelchóch.

kingfisher

kingfisher, belted kingfisher:: th'etséla < th'éts.

King George:: Kíl Chóch < kelchóch ~ kyelchóch.

kinnikinnick
  kinnikinnick berry, bearberry, Indian tobacco, domestic pea, domestic green bean, and probably giant vetch berry:: tl'íkw'el.
  kinnikinnick plant, domestic pea-vine, domestic bean-vine, giant vetch vine:: tl'ikw'íyelhp < tl'íkw'el.

kiss :: xwmékwàthem < mékw.
  he got kissed:: xwmékwàthel < mékw.
  kiss s-o:: mṓkweset < mékw.
  kiss s-th, (kiss s-o [Deming, IHTTC]):: xwmékwàtht < mékw.
  to kiss, kiss on the lips:: mékweth ~ mékwethel < mékw.

kitchen :: kéchel.
  cookhouse, kitchen:: kwukwáwtxw < kwúkw.

kitten
  kitten:: púpsò:llh < pús.
  runt of litter, smallest pup or kitten or animal in litter:: th'íth'kw'oya < sth'ékw', th'íth'kw' < sth'ékw'.

Klaklacum
  baby basket rock just below main bay and sand bar of Lexwtl'átl'ekw'em (Klaklacum, Indian Reserve #12, first village and reserve south of American Creek), on the west side of the Fraser River:: Lexwp'oth'esála ~ Xwp'oth'esála < p'ó:th'es ~ p'óth'es.
  Hope Indian Reserve #12 (Klaklacum):: Tl'átl'ekw'em ~ Lexwtl'átl'ekw'em.

knead
  shake s-th down, pack s-th down, push s-th down, knead s-th (esp. of bread dough), press it down (like yeast bread):: qeth'ét.

knee
  a slough on Harrison River north side by the mouth of Chehalis River which has a knee-shaped sandbar at its mouth, this is the next slough above (upriver from) Meth'á:lmexwem:: Q'iq'ewetó:lthel < q'éw ~ q'ew.
  (be) doubled up (a person with knees up to his chest), all doubled over:: sqw'emqw'emóx̲w < qw'ómx̲w.
  (be) doubled up in bed on one's side with knees drawn up:: sqw'emóx̲w < qw'ómx̲w.
  kneecap:: qep'tá:lém < qep', sq'epóleqwtelxel (perhaps error for sqep'óleqwtelxel) < qep'.
  knee (naming it, the name of it):: qep'ó:lthetel < qep'.
  knee (someone's):: sqep'ó:lthetel < qep'.
  on the knee:: =ó:lthel.
  skinned knee(s):: th'qó:lthel < th'áq ~ ts'áq or ts'éq ~ th'éq.
  soft (knee-shaped) cliff on a beach:: =ó:lthel.
  sticking out through a hole (like a toe out of a sock, knee out of a hole in pants, a nail driven clear through the other side of a board), come out into the open:: qwōhóls (or perhaps) qwehóls < qwá.
  thigh, leg above the knee:: spatálép ~ spatálep.

kneecap
  kneecap:: qep'tá:lém < qep', sq'epóleqwtelxel (perhaps error for sqep'óleqwtelxel) < qep'.

kneel

kneel down:: th'q'elhx̲ám < th'q'elhx̲á:m.
kneeling:: th'q'álhx̲e [or th'q'álhx̲em] < th'q'elhx̲á:m.
make s-o kneel:: th'q'elhx̲oméstexw < th'q'elhx̲á:m.
to kneel, kneel down:: th'q'elhx̲á:m.
they made them/him/her kneel down:: th'eq'elhsx̲á:m < th'q'elhx̲á:m.

knife :: lhá:ts'tel < lhíts' ~ lhí:ts'.
cut s-th (with anything: knife, saw, scythe, etc.), cut s-o:: lhí:ts'et < lhíts' ~ lhí:ts'.
fish butchering knife:: kw'éts'tel < kw'íts'.
handle of a knife, knife-handle:: lhà:ts'telálá < lhíts' ~ lhí:ts'.
plane it (with a plane), trim it, taper it (about wood, like slats or roots for baskets, poles for houseposts/totem poles, paddles), taper it (with knife or plane), peel it (a fruit, etc.), whittle it, strip or peel bark off of it, scrape it (of carrots), (carve it, peel it [AC]):: xípet < xíp.
pocket knife:: hálkw < lékw.
point or tip of a long object (pole, tree, knife, candle, land):: =eqs ~ =éqsel ~ =élqsel ~ =elqs.
run over it (with car), spread it (for ex. on bread with knife), put it up (of wallpaper), (stick it on), stick s-th closed (with pitch for ex.):: tl'íq't < tl'íq'.
U-shaped or horseshoe-shaped knife for scraping out an adzed canoe:: sqw'emqw'emóx̲w < qw'ómx̲w.
U-shaped or horseshoe-shaped knife (or plane) for scraping out canoe:: xepá:ltel < xíp.
wood-carving knife:: xepá:ltel < xíp.

knit

hang s-th (on a nail or hat hanger), hook it back on (of a stitch lost in knitting):: ókw'est < ókw'.

knock

knocking on s-th:: kwókwexwet < kwoxw.
knocking, rapping:: kwókwexwels < kwoxw.
knocking, rapping (in the distance), tapping:: kwókwexwem < kwoxw.
knocking with one's hand:: kwókwexwetsesem < kwoxw.
knock (once), rap:: kwxwà:ls < kwoxw.
knock on s-th:: kwóxwet < kwoxw.
knock s-o down:: kw'qwémést(exw?) < kw'óqw.

knot)

loosen it (of a knot):: kw'étxwt.
spear pole knot hitch (two half-hitches), clove-hitch knot:: ts'sítsim.
tree limb, branch (of tree), (knot on a tree [CT]):: sts'á:xt.

knothole :: sts'axtálá < sts'á:xt.

know

acknowledge oneself:: telómelthet < tól.
find s-th out, understand s-th, learn s-th, realize s-th, now know what s-th is like, read (and comprehend) s-th, understand s-o:: tél:exw ~ (in rapid speech) télexw < tól.
know oneself, be confident:: lheq'elómet < q'á:l.
know s-th, know s-o:: lheq'él:exw ~ lhq'él:exw ~ lhq'élexw < q'á:l.
maybe, perhaps, I don't know (if), may (possibly):: yóswe ~ yó:swe.

know (CONT'D)
not know how to:: sqe'íyeqel ~ sqe'í:qel.
smart, know how, good at it:: schewót.
someone's own knowledge, someone's own idea:: stélmel < tól.
the mind, someone's own knowledge:: télmel < tól.

knowledge
measure the knowledge (give a test):: xwéylemt te télmels < x̲wéylémt, tól.
someone's own knowledge, someone's own idea:: stélmel < tól.
the mind, someone's own knowledge:: télmel < tól.

knuckle
knuckles (all the joints of the hand and fingers):: qwemqwémx̲wtses < qwó:m ~ qwóm ~ qwem.

kokanee]
small (fully grown) coho salmon, [kokanee]:: sth'ímiya < sth'í:m ~ sth'ì:m.

Kwakiutl
Yuculta Kwakiutl people, southern Kwakiutl people from Cape Mudge north who raided the Salish people:: Yéqwelhtax̲ ~ Yéqwelhta.

Kwakwawapilt
Kwakwawapilt village and reserve (Chilliwack Indian Reserve #6):: Qweqwe'ópelhp < qwe'óp.

Kwantlen
Kwantlen, Langley, B.C.:: Qw'ó:ltl'el.
Kwantlen people, Kwantlen dialect of Downriver Halkomelem:: Qw'ó:ltl'el.

Kwelkwelqéylem
Granite Mountain, the second mountain back of X̲óletsa, northwest of Kwelkwelqéylem:: Th'emth'ómels < th'óméls.

kw'ő̃xweqs dance
a spirit power of a kw'ő̃xweqs dancer, (perhaps wolverine or badger spirit power):: sqoyép < sqoyép.

labor
having labor pains, being in labor in childbirth:: ts'áts'elem.

Labrador tea
Labrador tea, "Indian tea", "swamp tea":: mó:qwem.

lace
shoelace, shoe-lace:: yémxtel < yém ~ yem.
to fasten s-th by tying, tie up s-th (like canoe, horse, laces, nets, cow, shoelaces), tie it:: q'éyset ~ q'í(:)set < q'ey ~ q'i.

lack
lack, need:: =le or =ele.

Lackaway
    Lackaway village, Lackaway Creek:: Lá:x̲ewey.

Lackaway Creek
    Lackaway village, Lackaway Creek:: Lá:x̲ewey.

Lactuca muralis:: lhelelméxwtel < lhél, qetelméxwtel < qá:t.

ladder
    adze (for making canoes and pit-house ladders):: xwt'ót'epels ~ shxwt'ót'epels < t'óp.
    ladder, notched cedar pole ladder, rope ladder (pre-contact or later), modern ladder:: skw'íytel < kw'í ~ kw'íy.

ladle
    big serving spoon, spoon with handle about ten to 12 inches long, ladle, (spoon carved from mountain goat horn):: x̲álew.
    help oneself to food, serve oneself, serve oneself food (with a ladle), serve oneself a meal (food), (put on a dish [CT, HT]):: lhá:x̲em ~ lháx̲em < lhá:x̲ ~ lháx̲.
    to ladle:: qó:lem < qó:.

lady
    big person (of females), big lady:: thékwàl.
    little ladies:: slhelhlíli < slhá:lí.

ladybird beetle
    ladybug, ladybird beetle:: slhálhlí < slhá:lí.

ladybug
    ladybug, ladybird beetle:: slhálhlí < slhá:lí.

Lady Franklin Rock
    one of the two rocks of Lady Franklin Rock:: X̲éylx̲el(e)mòs.

Laidlaw
    village now called Ohamil Reserve or Laidlaw:: Shxw'ōwhámél ~ Shxw'ōhámél.

Lakahahmen
    a place near Deroche, B.C., just east of Lakahahmen Indian Reserve #10 (which is registered with D.I.A. as Skweam):: Skwiyó:m < Skwíyò.

Lake
    a channel between an island and the main shore a) across Harrison River from where the Phillips smokehouse was at Chehalis village (slightly downriver from the mouth of Chehalis R. into Harrison R.), also b) at Harrison Lake where the hatchery was:: Lheltá:lets ~ Lheltálets < lhà:l.
    a neck of land on the west side of Harrison Lake just north of Twenty-Mile Creek and across from the north tip of Long Island:: Shxwtépsem < tépsem.
    a stone like a statue at Harrison Lake, probably Doctor's Point:: Skoyá:m ~ Skeyá:m.
    Bare Bluffs, a steep slope on the west side of Harrison Lake:: Lhó:leqwet.
    beach on east side of Harrison Lake across from Long Island where there are lots of flat rocks, most of which have holes in them:: Sqweqwehíwel < qwá.
    Beaver Lake or Hanging Lake:: Sqelá:w (X̲óx̲tsa) < sqelá:w.

Lake (CONT'D)

Chilliwack Lake:: Sx̱óchaqel < x̱ó:tsa ~ x̱ó:cha.
Cottonwood Beach (in the southern quarter of Harrison Lake):: Chewő:lhp < cháchew ~ cháchu.
Cultus Lake, (also village at Cultus Lake near Hatchery Creek [Wells (lst ed.):19]):: Swílhcha.
Doctor's Point on northwest shore Harrison Lake:: Lhx̱é:ylex < lhéx̱.
Ford Lake (sic Foley Lake), Ford Creek (sic Foley Creek) on north side of Chilliwack River below Post Creek:: Lasisélhp?.
(get) a disease gotten by contacting a frog, a skin eruption, also the same disease as the man got in Kawkawa Lake in the Sx̱wó:yx̱wey story, (perhaps also) leprosy:: qw'ő:m.
Hatchery Creek, tributary of Sweltzer Creek (which drains Cultus Lake):: Stőtelō < tó:l ~ tò:l.
horned owl-shaped rock (beside Spá:th, a bear-shaped rock) up on a cliff on the south side above Echo Point bay on Echo Island in Harrison Lake:: Chítmexw < chítmexw.
Kawkawa Lake (near Hope, B.C.):: Q'éwq'ewe < q'á:w.
Lake Errock:: Qwíqwex̱em < qwéx̱em.
Lake of the Woods:: Shxwqó:m < qó:.
Lake of the Woods (small lake across the Fraser R. from Hope, B.C.):: Q'alelíktel < q'ál.
Lindeman Lake:: Tl'aqewólem??.
Lindeman Lake or Post Lake:: (possibly) Schewíts < cháchew ~ cháchu, (possibly) Schewíts < cháchew ~ cháchu.
Morris Creek (near Chehalis, B.C.), Morris Lake (near Chehalis):: Sx̱áx̱e < x̱áx̱e.
place just south of Doctor's Point on Harrison Lake northwest side:: S'ót'o < ót'.
(probably) Slollicum Lake:: Stl'áleqem X̱ótsa < stl'á:leqem.
probably Texas Lake:: St'élxweth' X̱ótsa < St'élxweth'.
Rainbow Falls (on Harrison Lake's southeast side):: Tsólqthet te Skwówech < skwó:wech ~ skwówech.
Rainbow Falls on the east side of Harrison Lake:: Tsólqthet te Skwówech < tsélq.
Ryder Lake:: T'ept'őp (X̱ótsa) < T'ept'őp.
Schkam Lake near Haig:: Sqám < qám.
spring salmon which goes to Chehalis Lake in May then returns to salt water:: sth'olólh.
Sumas Prairie west (on the west side of Sumas Lake):: Sx̱elálets??.
Sumas village and area from present-day Kilgard to Fraser River, Sumas village (on both sides of the Fraser at the east end of Sumas Mt.), (Devil's Run (below Láx̱ewey), the area between Sumas Mt. and Fraser River [Elders Group 7/13/77], Sumas River (probably requires Stó:lō river or Stótelō creek to follow) [Wells 1965], Sumas Lake (probably requires X̱ótsa lake after Semáth for this meaning) [Elders Group 7/13/77]):: Smá:th ~ Semá:th ~ Semáth.
Sweltzer Creek (the stream from Cultus Lake to Chilliwack River at Soowahlie):: Swílhcha Stótelō < Swílhcha.
Tamihi Lake:: T'ami(ye)hóy (X̱ótsa) < t'ámiya.
trail and steep slope on the west shore of Kawkawa Lake where the trail went up and over a steep hill and then down:: Sq'éywetselem ~ Sq'éywetsélém < q'e:yw ~ q'í:w.
Wahleach whistle stop on Seabird Island where Wayne Bobb lived in 1977, (now also Wahleach Lake (man-made) [EB]):: Wolích < x̱wále ~ x̱wá:le.
Whale Point at the southwest end of Harrison Lake:: Qwél:és < qwél:és ~ qwélés.

lake :: x̱ó:tsa ~ x̱ó:cha.
a bend in a river, a curve of a lake:: sq'ówqel < q'éw ~ q'ew.
basin lake near top of Cheam Peak:: Xwoqwsemó:leqw.
deep bottom (of a river, lake, water, canoe, anything):: stl'epláts < tl'ép.
lake in back of Paul Webster's old place on Hicks Rd. near Jones Creek:: Th'qwélhcha <

lake (CONT'D)

th'qwélhcha.
little lakes:: x̲elóx̲cha < x̲ó:tsa ~ x̲ó:cha.
many lakes:: x̲ó:letsa < x̲ó:tsa ~ x̲ó:cha.
mountain right back of Yale town reserve with two big lakes and many small ones:: X̲ó:letsa Smá:lt < x̲ó:tsa ~ x̲ó:cha.
old lake above Smith Falls, Smith Falls creek (which enters Cultus Lake at its northeast corner):: Slhílhets' < lhíts' ~ lhí:ts'.
small lake, pond:: x̲óx̲tsa ~ x̲óx̲cha < x̲ó:tsa ~ x̲ó:cha.
stagnant water lake or ponds at the downriver end of Skw'átets or Peters Reserve near Laidlaw:: Th'qwélhcha < th'qwélhcha.
Sumas village and area from present-day Kilgard to Fraser River, Sumas village (on both sides of the Fraser at the east end of Sumas Mt.), (Devil's Run (below Láx̲ewey), the area between Sumas Mt. and Fraser River [Elders Group 7/13/77], Sumas River (probably requires Stó:lō river or Stótelō creek to follow) [Wells 1965], Sumas Lake (probably requires X̲ótsa lake after Semáth for this meaning) [Elders Group 7/13/77]):: Smá:th ~ Semá:th ~ Semáth.
the hole (lake) at the foot of Cheam Peak on the south side:: Sqwá:p < qwá.

Lake Errock:: Qwíqwex̲em < qwéx̲em.

Lake of the Woods:: Shxwqó:m < qó:.
Lake of the Woods (small lake across the Fraser R. from Hope, B.C.):: Q'alelíktel < q'ál.

lamb
little lamb:: mímetú < metú.

lame
be lame, (be) sick on the foot, (have) a sick foot, (have) a hurt foot:: q'óq'eyxel < q'ó:y ~ q'óy.
be lame (esp. if deformed), be a cripple, to limp, have a limp:: slékwlets ~ slékwelets < lékw.
be lame (in hip, esp. from birth):: skw'í:lets < kw'í ~ kw'íy.

lamp
an electric light, coal-oil lamp, lamp:: yeqwí:l ~ yeqwì:l < yéqw.
any kind of light that one carries, torch (made from pitch), lantern, lamp, flashlight:: sláx̲et < láx̲et.
go out (of fire, flame or lamp):: tl'ékw'el.
make a light, turn the light on, light the lamp:: yeqwí:lem ~ yeqwéylem < yéqw.

Lampetra richardsoni
Entosphenus tridentatus, Lampetra richardsoni:: kwótawi ~ kwótewi.

lamprey
eel, Pacific lamprey, western brook lamprey:: kwótawi ~ kwótewi, kwótawi ~ kwótewi.

land
a neck of land on the west side of Harrison Lake just north of Twenty-Mile Creek and across from the north tip of Long Island:: Shxwtépsem < tépsem.
a sx̲wó:yx̲wey head turned to stone on land at X̲elhlálh somewhere:: Sx̲éyes te Sx̲wó:yx̲wey < sx̲wó:yx̲wey ~ sx̲wóyx̲wey.
clean it (of table, land, etc.):: tí:lt.
clear it (of land):: tí:lt.

land (CONT'D)

earth, ground, land, the earth, the world:: tém:éxw ~ tem:éxw ~ ~ tèm:èxw ~ témexw.
end of a falling section of land, end of a level stretch of land, (head of a creek or island [Elders Group]):: lhéq'qel.
neck of land:: =épsem.
point of geog. features like island or mountain or land:: =eqs ~ =éqsel ~ =élqsel ~ =elqs.
point of land at the end of an island:: sth'eméxwelets.
point or tip of a long object (pole, tree, knife, candle, land):: =eqs ~ =éqsel ~ =élqsel ~ =elqs.
prairie, grassy open land, (grassy valley [EB, Gibbs, Elders Group]}:: spélhx̲el.
pull ashore in a canoe, land a canoe:: lhà:l.
to clear land:: tí:lthet < tí:lt.
to land s-th (from water):: lhá:lt < lhà:l.

landslide)
(have a) small earth slide (small landslide):: yélt.

Langley
Kwantlen, Langley, B.C.:: Qw'ó:ltl'el.

language:: sqwéltel < qwà:l
Chinese language:: chálmelqel < chá:lmel.
English language:: xwelítemqel < xwelítem, xwelítemelh sqwà:l < xwelítem.
Nooksack language:: Lhéchelesem
Sliammon people, Sliammon dialect (of the Comox language, Mainland Comox):: Sloyámén.
Upriver Halkomelem language, to speak Upriver Halkomelem:: Hálq'eméylem < Leq'á:mél.

lantern
any kind of light that one carries, torch (made from pitch), lantern, lamp, flashlight:: sláx̲et < láx̲et.
home-made lantern (using candle in a can with a hole in it, etc.), jack-o-lantern:: shxwélchep.

larch
balsam fir (has sweet sap or cambium, grows at higher altitudes, called larch by some, "balsam" is a popular name for trees of the genus Abies), from a sample taken prob. subalpine fir, if sample is mistaken poss. Pacific silver fir or grand fir, if the term balsam is mistaken too, poss. a variety of Douglas fir:: q'et'emá:yelhp < q'át'em.

lard
fat, grease, lard, (oil [EB], shortening [MH]):: sló:s ~ slós < ló:s ~ lós.
lard, shortening:: x̲wástel.

large
be big, be large, be high (of floodwater), rise (of floodwater):: híkw.
(be) larger, bigger:: thíthe < thi ~ tha ~ the ~ thah ~ theh.
big bird, (large bird (of any kind)), any waterfowl:: x̲wí:leqw ~ x̲wé:yleqw ~ x̲wéyleqw.
large rock slide that includes trees and other debris:: syélt < yélt.

large portion
a large portion of the earth:: slháq'emex.

Larus
possibly genus Larus, certainly including Larus glaucescens and possibly any/all of the following: Larus philadelphia, Larus canus, Larus delawarensis, Larus californicus, Larus argentatus:: qw'elíteq.
possibly genus Larus, certainly including Larus glaucescens, possibly including any/all of the following (respectively): Larus philadelphia, Larus canus, Larus delawarensis, Larus californicus, Larus argentatus:: slílōwya.

Larus argentatus
possibly genus Larus, certainly including Larus glaucescens and possibly any/all of the following: Larus philadelphia, Larus canus, Larus delawarensis, Larus californicus, Larus argentatus:: qw'elíteq.
possibly genus Larus, certainly including Larus glaucescens, possibly including any/all of the following (respectively): Larus philadelphia, Larus canus, Larus delawarensis, Larus californicus, Larus argentatus:: slílōwya.

Larus californicus
possibly genus Larus, certainly including Larus glaucescens and possibly any/all of the following: Larus philadelphia, Larus canus, Larus delawarensis, Larus californicus, Larus argentatus:: qw'elíteq.
possibly genus Larus, certainly including Larus glaucescens, possibly including any/all of the following (respectively): Larus philadelphia, Larus canus, Larus delawarensis, Larus californicus, Larus argentatus:: slílōwya.

Larus canus
possibly genus Larus, certainly including Larus glaucescens and possibly any/all of the following: Larus philadelphia, Larus canus, Larus delawarensis, Larus californicus, Larus argentatus:: qw'elíteq.
possibly genus Larus, certainly including Larus glaucescens, possibly including any/all of the following (respectively): Larus philadelphia, Larus canus, Larus delawarensis, Larus californicus, Larus argentatus:: slílōwya.

Larus delawarensis
possibly genus Larus, certainly including Larus glaucescens and possibly any/all of the following: Larus philadelphia, Larus canus, Larus delawarensis, Larus californicus, Larus argentatus:: qw'elíteq.
possibly genus Larus, certainly including Larus glaucescens, possibly including any/all of the following (respectively): Larus philadelphia, Larus canus, Larus delawarensis, Larus californicus, Larus argentatus:: slílōwya.

Larus glaucescens
possibly genus Larus, certainly including Larus glaucescens and possibly any/all of the following: Larus philadelphia, Larus canus, Larus delawarensis, Larus californicus, Larus argentatus:: qw'elíteq.
possibly genus Larus, certainly including Larus glaucescens, possibly including any/all of the following (respectively): Larus philadelphia, Larus canus, Larus delawarensis, Larus californicus, Larus argentatus:: slílōwya.

Larus philadelphia
possibly genus Larus, certainly including Larus glaucescens and possibly any/all of the following: Larus philadelphia, Larus canus, Larus delawarensis, Larus californicus, Larus

Larus philadelphia (CONT'D)

argentatus:: qw'elíteq.

possibly genus Larus, certainly including Larus glaucescens, possibly including any/all of the following (respectively): Larus philadelphia, Larus canus, Larus delawarensis, Larus californicus, Larus argentatus:: slílōwya.

larvae

salmonberry worm, (prob. larvae of moths or butterflies or two-winged flies):: xwexwíye.

Lasionycteris noctivagans

Corynorhinus townsendi townsendi, Eptesicus fuscus bernardinus, Lasionycteris noctivagans, Lasiurus cinereus, Myotis californicus caurinus, Myotis evotis pacificus, Myotis lucifugus alascensis, Myotis volans longicrus, Myotis yumanensis saturatus, and possibly Myotis keeni keeni:: skw'elyáx̲el.

order Chiroptera, family Vespertilionidae, may include any or all of the following: Corynorhinus townsendi townsendi, Eptesicus fuscus bernardinus, Lasionycteris noctivagans, Lasiurus cinereus, Myotis californicus caurinus, Myotis evotis pacificus, Myotis lucifugus alascensis, Myotis volans longicrus, Myotis yumanensis saturatus, and possibly Myotis keeni keeni:: p'íp'eth'elàx̲el ~ p'ip'eth'eláx̲el < p'í:.

Lasiurus cinereus

Corynorhinus townsendi townsendi, Eptesicus fuscus bernardinus, Lasionycteris noctivagans, Lasiurus cinereus, Myotis californicus caurinus, Myotis evotis pacificus, Myotis lucifugus alascensis, Myotis volans longicrus, Myotis yumanensis saturatus, and possibly Myotis keeni keeni:: skw'elyáx̲el.

order Chiroptera, family Vespertilionidae, may include any or all of the following: Corynorhinus townsendi townsendi, Eptesicus fuscus bernardinus, Lasionycteris noctivagans, Lasiurus cinereus, Myotis californicus caurinus, Myotis evotis pacificus, Myotis lucifugus alascensis, Myotis volans longicrus, Myotis yumanensis saturatus, and possibly Myotis keeni keeni:: p'íp'eth'elàx̲el ~ p'ip'eth'eláx̲el < p'í:.

last

be last, be behind, after:: lhiyó:qwt.

be last (in travelling), be behind (in travelling):: yelhyó:qwt < lhiyó:qwt.

have the last spirit dance of the season, have the "sweep up":: yekw'ólhem or perhaps yekw'wólhem < yókw' ~ yóqw'.

last baby (youngest baby), the last-born, a child cranky and jealous of an expected brother or sister:: óqw'a < óqw'.

last year:: spelwálh.

the last time:: ílhulhòy < hò:y ~ hó:y ~ hóy.

last-born

last baby (youngest baby), the last-born, a child cranky and jealous of an expected brother or sister:: óqw'a < óqw'.

last night:: xweláltelh < lá:t.

latch

a latch, Indian lock:: shxwéth'tel or shxwwéth'tel < wáth'.

late

(be) slow, (be) late, go slow:: óyém.

deceased ones, late ones:: stáweqel < stewéqel.

late (deceased), past tense:: =à:lh ~ =elh.

late in the night:: lhóp.

lately
  recently, just now, lately, (at one recent moment), not long ago:: qá:ys.

later :: -à.
  a little later (??):: keke'át < ká(t) ~ ke'át.
  later, after a while, later on, wait a while:: téx̲w.
  wait, be later:: ká(t) ~ ke'át.

lather
  lather one's body:: yet'qw'íwsem.

laugh
  laughing:: lá:yem ~ láyem < líyém ~ leyém.
  laughter:: alíliyem ~ elíliyem < líyém ~ leyém.
  lots of laughing, (many are laughing [AC]):: líyliyem < líyém ~ leyém.
  the fire is laughing:: elíyliyem te híyqw. < yéqw.
  think s-o is talking or laughing about one:: tl'ostélmét < tl'óst or tl'óstexw.
  think someone is talking or laughing about oneself:: tl'emstélemet ~ tl'emstélémét < tl'émstexw, tl'ostélmet.
  to laugh:: líyém ~ leyém.

launch
  launch s-th/s-o into the water, push s-o/s-th into the water, throw it in the water:: qwsét < qwés.

lawn
  cut it (wood, lawn, etc.):: t'eqw'ót < t'éqw'.

laxative
  made it (if laxative finally works):: x̲é:yles < x̲éylés.

lay
  laying down, putting down:: lhálheq'els < lháq'.
  lay it down, put it down:: lháq'et < lháq'.
  put one's head to one side, lay on one side of the head:: lexósem < lex.
  turn it on its side, lay it on its side:: lexét < lex.

lazy
  a person that's always lazy:: lexws'ú:met < emét.
  be always lazy, be a lazybones, be stupid, be a good-for-nothing:: s'ú:met < emét.
  (be) kind of lazy:: s'i'omó:met < emét.
  person who is always lazy:: lexws'í:ts'el < í:ts'el.
  temporarily lazy:: í:ts'el.

lazybones
  be always lazy, be a lazybones, be stupid, be a good-for-nothing:: s'ú:met < emét.

lead :: xá:t.
  lead weight:: xá:t.

leader

chief, leader, respected person, boss, rich, dear:: siyá:m < éy ~ éy:.
respected leader, chief, upper-class person, boss, master, your highness:: siyám ~ (rare) siyá:m.
respected leaders, chiefs, upper-class people:: sí:yá:m < siyám ~ (rare) siyá:m.
warrior, (leader of a raiding party [CT]):: stó:méx.

leaf :: =á:lews, sts'ó:lha ~ sch'ó:lha ~ sts'ólha.
common plantain, ribbed plantain, called "frog leaf":: pipehomá:lews < peh or pó(:)h.
fall off (of leaves, berries):: xwís.
leaf, leaves:: =á:lews.
leaves:: =á:lxw.
leaves falling:: xwesá:lews < xwís.
long leaf willow, (Pacific willow):: x̲wálá:lhp ~ x̲wá:lá:lhp < x̲wále ~ x̲wá:le.
(making a) continuous rustling noise (of paper or silk or material), rustling (of leaves, paper, a sharp sound):: sá:wts'em < sawéts'em.
one leaf:: lets'álews < léts'a ~ léts'e.
pick berries, pick off (leaves, fruit, vegetables, hops), (pluck off, harvest):: lhím.
shake s-th (tree or bush) for fruit or leaves, comb a bush (for berries), shake s-th (a mat or blanket for ex.):: xwíset ~ xwítset < xwís.
short leaf willow, (Sitka willow):: x̲wálá:lhp ~ x̲wá:lá:lhp < x̲wále ~ x̲wá:le.
ten leaves:: epálōws < ó:pel.
three leaves:: lhxwálews < lhí:xw.
two leaves:: islálews < isá:le ~ isále ~ isá:la.
vanilla leaf:: lhxwáléws < lhí:xw.

leaf-green:: sts'ó:lha ~ sch'ó:lha ~ sts'ólha.

leak

dry snow coming in (drifting), fine snow that leaks into a house:: sqwelxómé ~ sqwelxóme < qwélxel.
leaking:: p'íp'ex̲w < p'íx̲w.
plugging a hole or leak or crack in anything:: t'ót'ekwels < t'ékw.
plug it (a hole, leak):: t'ekwót < t'ékw.
to leak:: p'íx̲w.

lean

be leaning:: slóli, slóliyes ~ slólí:s < slóli.
(be) tight, (leaning backwards [EB]):: sq'áq'eth' < q'áth'.
leaning:: tiyó:les < tiy.
leaning over (something):: q'í:wethet < q'e:yw ~ q'í:w.
leaning the face on the hand with elbow propped:: piyósem < píy.
leaning to one side:: sló:litses < slóli.
lean s-th against something:: tiyélést < tiy.

learn

beat up s-o as a lesson till he learns or gives up, teach s-o a lesson:: lepét < lép.
find s-th out, understand s-th, learn s-th, realize s-th, now know what s-th is like, read (and comprehend) s-th, understand s-o:: tél:exw ~ (in rapid speech) télexw < tól.
learn a lesson, give up:: lép.
studying s-th, thinking about s-th, learning s-th, training for s-th, trying to do s-th:: totí:lt < tól.

leash

put a rope around s-o/s-th's neck, put a leash on s-th, hang s-o:: x̲wíqw'est < x̲wíqw'.

"leatherjacket" (insect)

cranefly, "leatherjacket" (immature cranefly):: spelwálh qwá:l < qwá:l, tl'áleqtxel qwá:l < qwá:l.

cranefly, "leatherjacket" (insect):: tl'áleqtxel qwá:l < tl'áqt.

leave

get away, leave, (perhaps just) away:: á:yel < á:y.

leave s-o, leave s-th, go away from s-o/s-th, abandon s-o, leave s-o behind:: áyeles < á:y.

leave s-o/s-th inside:: skwetáxwstexw < kwetáxw.

leave s-th here:: íchelstexw < í.

leave this here, leave s-th here:: ístexw ó < í.

leave alone

leave s-o alone, stop pestering s-o:: kwikwe'át < kwá:.

Ledum groenlandicum:: mó:qwem.

left

(be) left-handed:: sth'íkwetses < th'íkwe.

left arm:: sth'íkwechís < th'íkwe.

[left] front leg quarter of deer or other animal:: sth'ikweláx̲el < th'íkwe.

left-handed:: th'íkwetses < th'íkwe.

left (of a side):: th'íkwe.

left side of the body:: sth'ekwe'í:ws < th'íkwe.

the left, the left side:: sth'íkwe < th'íkwe.

left-over

container for left-overs taken home from feast, doggie bag:: meq'ethále < méq'.

feast left-overs, left-overs of food (which guests can take home):: sméq'eth < méq'.

leftover food, scraps:: sq'éylòm < q'éylòm.

leftovers, scraps (not taken home as smeq'óth is):: qelmí:lthel < qéylem ~ qé:ylem ~ qí(:)lem.

take left-over food:: méq'etsem < méq'.

throw different leftovers together for a meal, throw a meal together, eat a snack:: p'ekw'ethílem < p'ákw'.

leg

(both human) legs, (both) feet:: sx̲ex̲éyle or sx̲ex̲íle < sx̲él:e.

break a leg, (have/get) a broken leg:: lekwxá:l ~ lekwxál < lékw.

bushy hair on horses' legs (tufts like on Clydesdale breed), tufts of fur on horse's feet:: qwelqwélxel < qwíl ~ qwel.

calf (of the leg):: q'átl'elxel.

canyon area on Chehalis Creek just above (upriver or north from) the main highway bridge (esp. the first cliff on the east side) [means one-legged]:: Páléxel ~ Paléxel.

cross one's legs:: q'eyáweth'xelem < q'ey ~ q'i.

daddy long-legs (spider), harvestman spider:: tl'áleqtxel q'esq'ésetsel < q'ey ~ q'i.

front leg:: t'á:lew ~ t'álew.

leg (CONT'D)

(get a) sprained foot, leg got out of joint:: plhéqw'xel ~ p'lhéqw'xel.
has short legs:: ts'eléletl'xel < ts'í:tl' ~ ts'ítl'.
(have a) crooked leg, (be a) crooked-legged person:: spipíyxel < pó:y.
(have a) paralyzed leg, game leg:: slhéx̲xel < lhéx̲.
(have the) legs crossed:: sx̲álts'xel < x̲élts'.
hind leg:: lheq'láts < lheq'át ~ lhq'á:t.
hit on the leg, [hit on the foot]:: kw'éqwxel < kw'óqw.
I got hard (of arm, leg, penis, etc.):: tl'x̲wòlèm < tl'éx̲w.
[left] front leg quarter of deer or other animal:: sth'ikweláx̲el < th'íkwe.
leg, foot:: sx̲él:e.
leg got sprained, (sprain one's ankle [JL]):: ts'lhéqw'xel < ts'lhóqw'.
legs crossed, cross one's ankles (either sitting or standing) [prob. error], (ankles crossed (either sitting or standing)):: q'eyáweth'xel < q'ey ~ q'i.
legs (more than two, for ex. non-human):: sx̲elx̲éyle < sx̲él:e.
long legs, long-legged:: tl'áleqtxel < tl'áqt.
on the foot or leg, in the foot or leg, tail of fish, leg of other animate creatures:: =xel.
overstretch one's legs when walking with too big a step:: t'íw ~ t'ì:w.
rags wound around the legs in the cold or to protect from mosquitoes, (leggings):: q'élq'xetel < q'ál.
spread apart s-o's legs:: px̲íwét < páx̲.
spread one's legs (sitting for example), (be spread in the bottom):: spapx̲íwel < páx̲.
thigh, leg above the knee:: spatálép ~ spatálep.
whole leg, (whole of both legs):: sx̲ex̲é:yle or sx̲ex̲í:le < sx̲él:e.

legged

(have a) crooked leg, (be a) crooked-legged person:: spipíyxel < pó:y.

leggings)

rags wound around the legs in the cold or to protect from mosquitoes, (leggings):: q'élq'xetel < q'ál.

lemon:: t'át'ets'em qwíyqwòyèls < t'áth' ~ t'áts', qwá:y. (lit. sour + orange fruit/little yellowish fruit)

lemon (post-contact):: tsqwá:y < qwá:y.
lemon cake:: t'át'ets'em qwíqwòyèls kíks seplíl < t'áth' ~ t'áts', qwá:y, kíks, seplíl. (lit. lemon (itself from sour little yellowish fruit) + cake + bread)
lemon extract:: tsqwá:yem < qwá:y.
lemonade:: t'át'ets'em qwíyqwòyèls sqe'óleqw < t'áth' ~ t'áts', qwá:y, qó:. (lit. lemon [itself < sour little yellow fruit] + fruit juice)
lemon-lime juice:: t'át'ets'em qwíyqwòyèls qas te t'át'ets'em tsqwáyqwòyèls sqe'óleqw < t'áth' ~ t'áts', qwá:y, qó:.(lit. lemon fruit [itself < sour little yellowish fruit] + and + the + lime fruit [itself < sour + greenish fruit]+ fruit juice)
sour (unripe or half-ripe fruit, lemon, Oregon grape, fermenting fruit):: t'át'eth'em < t'áth'.

lend

lend it to s-o, let s-o borrow it:: chélhtat ~ chélhtet < chélhta.
lend money to s-o, [give s-o credit]:: ex̲ímt < íx̲em.
lend s-o money:: ex̲ímstexw < íx̲em.

length

length:: stl'eqtí:m < tl'áqt.

Lent

Lent
    fasting for Lent, prob. also Lent:: kyal:ám.

Leon
    next slough on north side of Harrison River above (east of) Smímstíyexwá:le, a muddy slough where fish spawn, right across from Johnny Leon's place at Chehalis and about 100 yards downstream (west) of Yálhxetel:: Mímex̲wel (or prob. better, Mímexwel) < mímexwel.

Leon's Slough
    Leon's Slough on Harrison River:: Xemó:leqw < xá:m.

Lepidoptera
    Glaucidium gnoma swarthi, some also call order Lepidoptera by this name:: spopeleqwíth'a ~ spopeleqwíth'e < poleqwíth'a.
    order Lepidoptera:: sesx̲á, smímeyàth ~ smímoyàth.
    order Lepidoptera, caterpillar of family Geometridae:: q'alq'elő:wsem < q'ál.
    order Lepidoptera, caterpillar of the family Geometridae:: q'álq'elp'í:w < q'ál.
    order Lepidoptera (esp. incl. grey moths of families Noctuidae, Geometridae, and Lymantriidae):: lholeqwót.
    probably larvae of Lepidoptera or Diptera, possibly larvae of order Lepidoptera, family Tortricidae:: xwexwíye.

Lepidoptera or Diptera
    probably larvae of Lepidoptera or Diptera, possibly larvae of order Lepidoptera, family Tortricidae:: xwexwíye.

leprosy
    (get) a disease gotten by contacting a frog, a skin eruption, also the same disease as the man got in Kawkawa Lake in the Sx̲wó:yx̲wey story, (perhaps also) leprosy:: qw'ő:m.

Lepus americanus cascadensis
    Lepus americanus cascadensis and Lepus americanus washingtoni, now perhaps Sylvilagus floridanus mearnsi:: shxwóxw.
    Lepus americanus cascadensis and Lepus americanus washingtoni, now probably also Sylvilagus floridanus mearnsi:: sqewáth, sqiqewóthel < sqewáth, sqwiqweyóthel.
    Lepus americanus cascadensis and Lepus americanus washingtoni, now prob. also Sylvilagus floridanus mearnsi:: sqíqewàth < sqewáth.
    Lepus townsendi, also big or older Lepus americanus cascadensis and Lepus americanus washingtoni:: sqwíqweyóthel < qwá.

Lepus americanus washingtoni
    Lepus americanus cascadensis and Lepus americanus washingtoni, now perhaps Sylvilagus floridanus mearnsi:: shxwóxw.
    Lepus americanus cascadensis and Lepus americanus washingtoni, now probably also Sylvilagus floridanus mearnsi:: sqewáth, sqiqewóthel < sqewáth, sqwiqweyóthel.
    Lepus americanus cascadensis and Lepus americanus washingtoni, now prob. also Sylvilagus floridanus mearnsi:: sqíqewàth < sqewáth.
    Lepus townsendi, also big or older Lepus americanus cascadensis and Lepus americanus washingtoni:: sqwíqweyóthel < qwá.

Lepus townsendi
  Lepus townsendi, also big or older Lepus americanus cascadensis and Lepus americanus washingtoni:: sqwíqweyóthel < qwá.

less
  lessen it (of someone's load), halve it, make s-th lighter (in weight), lessen it (like when someone's pack is too heavy):: xwát < xwá.

lessen
  lessen it (of someone's load), halve it, make s-th lighter (in weight), lessen it (like when someone's pack is too heavy):: xwát < xwá.

lesson
  beat up s-o as a lesson till he learns or gives up, teach s-o a lesson:: lepét < lép.
  learn a lesson, give up:: lép.

let
  admitting s-o/s-th, letting s-o/s-th in, bringing s-o/s-th inside:: kwétexwt < kwetáxw.
  be good, good, well, nice, fine, better, better (ought to), it would be good if, may it be good, let it be good, happy, glad, clean, well-behaved, polite, virgin, popular, comfortable (with furniture, other things?),:: éy ~ éy:.
  bring s-o/s-th in (to a house/enclosure), take s-o/s-th in(inside a house/enclosure), admit s-o (into a house/enclosure), let s-o/s-th in (to a house/enclosure), put s-o/s-th in (inside a house/enclosure:: kwetáxwt < kwetáxw.
  lend it to s-o, let s-o borrow it:: chélhtat ~ chélhtet < chélhta.
  let oneself fall, drop oneself down (by parachute, rope, etc., said of little birds trying to fly out of nest, little animals trying to get down and let themselves fall):: chólqthet < tsélq ~ chélq.

let go
  drop s-th (accidentally), let s-o go:: kwò:lxw < kwá:.
  let go of s-th/s-o, drop s-th, set s-o free, turn s-o/s-th loose:: kwá:t ~ kwát < kwá:.

Letharia vulpina
  possibly Letharia vulpina or Alectoria (Bryoria) species or Usnea species:: mex̱t'éles.

let it be :: éy ~ éy:.

let out
  slacken it, let it out (of a rope), loosen it, (lower it (prob. of s-th suspended):: líqwet < líqw.

lettuce
  wall lettuce:: lhelelméxwtel < lhél, qetelméxwtel < qá:t.

level
  level, flat:: léq'.
  level ground, flat (of ground):: leq'éylep ~ leq'ílep < léq'.
  put a mark on it (like water level of river), mark it, weigh it, (measure it):: x̱á:th't ~ x̱áth't < x̱áth' ~ x̱e'áth'.

lever

pry s-th, lock s-th (the Indian way/barred/wedged), pry s-th up, lever it up:: wáth'et < wáth'.

Lhilheltálets

natural holes or tunnels east of Iwówes and above Lhilheltálets that water came out of after rain:: Sqwelíqwehíwel ~ Sqwelíqwehìwèl < qwá.

Lhílheqey

another small peak just to the right of the Mount Cheam summit peak as one faces south, she is another daughter of Lhílheqey (Mt. Cheam):: S'óyewòt < Óyewòt.

youngest sister of Lhílheqey (Mount Cheam) that cries:: Ñemó:th'iya < x̱à:m ~ x̱á:m.

Lhóy'

Bear Mountain, also called Lhóy''s Mountain:: Siyó:ylexwe Smá:lt < siyó:lexwe ~ syó:lexwe ~siyólexwe.

Lhóy''s Mountain

Bear Mountain, also called Lhóy''s Mountain:: Siyó:ylexwe Smá:lt < siyó:lexwe ~ syó:lexwe ~siyólexwe.

liar

a little liar:: shxwmámth'elqel < máth'el.

liar:: shxwmáth'elqel < máth'el.

lice

lots of lice:: mexméxts'el < méxts'el.

lichen

black tree lichen, black tree "moss":: sqwelíp.

gray lacy lichen or tree moss (real fine like hair, grows on maples):: x̱ám'x̱em'.

gray or green tree "moss" (lichen) hanging on tree limbs, possibly wolf lichen or other species:: mex̱t'éles.

lick

beat s-o up, kick s-o in fight, lick s-o (in fight), spank s-o, fight s-o (till he cries for ex.), fight s-o in anger, fight s-o back:: x̱éyet.

licking it:: th'íth'emet < th'ím ~ th'í:m.

lick s-th (with tongue):: th'ímet ~ ts'í:met < th'ím ~ th'í:m.

licorice fern:: st'uslóye, tl'asíp, t'usló:ye.

lid

a cover, lid:: qp'á:letstel < qep'.

buckskin straps, lid for berry basket:: yémqetel < yém ~ yem.

close s-th (for ex. a box), put a lid on s-th (for ex. a pot), cover it with a lid:: qp'á:qet < qep'.

lie

a little liar:: shxwmámth'elqel < máth'el.

be lying on the ground:: slhálheq' < lháq'.

lie (CONT'D)
fool s-o, deceive s-o, (lie to s-o [SJ]):: q'elstá:xw < q'á:l.
liar:: shxwmáth'elqel < máth'el.
lie down:: lhóq'ethet < lháq'.
lie down on one's back:: kw'aqálém < kw'e'í ~ kw''í ~ kw'í.
lie on one's back, on his back:: kw'e'íyeqel ~ kw'e'íqel < kw'e'í ~ kw''í ~ kw'í.
lie? with surface facing up, sticking up, on the side? or edge?:: kw'e'í ~ kw''í ~ kw'í.
lying down on one's stomach:: qíqep'yó:lha ~ qéyqep'yó:lha < qep'.
lying on its side:: slíx < lex.
lying on one's back:: kw'e'í:qel < kw'e'í ~ kw''í ~ kw'í.
lying on one side with one's head propped up on one hand:: piypiyáleqálem < píy.
lying on one's stomach with head down on one's arms:: qiqep'eyósem < qep'.
lying on the ground:: lhálheq' < lháq'.
lying, telling a lie, (bluffing [BHTTC]):: mameth'álem < máth'el.
tell a lie for s-o:: xwmath'elqéylémt < máth'el.
to lie (prevaricate):: math'elqéylem < máth'el.

lie down :: áx̲eth.
little baby lying down:: i'ax̲íth < áx̲eth.
lying down:: á:x̲eth < áx̲eth.

life
come alive, come back to life, get better (from sickness), get well, revive:: áylexw ~ áyelexw.
revive s-o, bring s-o back to life, heal s-o, (EB) give s-o medicine to make him better?:: á:yelexwt < áylexw ~ áyelexw.
save s-o, (EB) bring s-o back to life:: á:yelexwlexw < áylexw ~ áyelexw.

life-spirit
conscience, spirit (which can be lost temporarily), soul, life-spirit, power of one's will:: smestíyexw < mestíyexw.

lift
keep it in the air, lift s-th/s-o off the floor:: shxwóxwelstexw < xwá.
lift s-o (of a spirit dancer being initiated):: shxwóxwelstexw < xwá.
lift up s-th, lift [s-th], hoist [s-th] up:: xwà:lx < xwá, xwà:lx < xwá.
tilt s-th, lift s-th up at one end or one side, tilt s-th sideways:: tewá:let < tewále.
to lift, raise:: shxwóxwel < xwá.
too heavy to lift:: éw.

light
an electric light, coal-oil lamp, lamp:: yeqwí:l ~ yeqwì:l < yéqw.
any kind of light that one carries, torch (made from pitch), lantern, lamp, flashlight:: sláx̲et < láx̲et.
be light, (be lit up), be illuminated:: státew ~ státōw < táw.
be light (illuminated):: státewel < táw.
burn s-th, light s-th:: yéqwt < yéqw.
get light:: táwel < táw.
give s-o light:: láx̲et.
going out(side) with a light:: láx̲etem < láx̲et.
(he) light(s) s-th on fire, (he) set s-th on fire:: sétqtstes.
lessen it (of someone's load), halve it, make s-th lighter (in weight), lessen it (like when someone's pack is too heavy):: xwát < xwá.

light (CONT'D)
light s-th, make a light (of s-th), turn it on (a light):: táwelt < táw.
light up s-th/s-o, shine a light on s-th/s-o:: táwet < táw.
light (weight), lightweight:: xwóxwe < xwá.
make a light:: yeqwí:ls < yéqw.
make a light, turn the light on, light the lamp:: yeqwí:lem ~ yeqwéylem < yéqw.
precipitation, ray of light:: =xel.
rays of light:: sx̲elx̲éles te syó:qwem < x̲él ~ x̲é:yl ~ x̲í:l
tickled (by a hair, by a light touch):: sá:yx̲wem.
tip-toeing, (walking lightly, sneaking):: t'et'ásxelem < t'ás.
walk lightly, sneak:: t'ásxelem < t'ás.

lighten
diatomaceous earth (could be mixed with things to whiten them--for ex. dog and goat wool), white clay for white face paint (for pure person spirit-dancers), white powder from mountains, white clay they make powder from to lighten goat and dog wool for blankets, powder, talc, white face paint:: st'ewṓkw'.

like
a little, a little like, slightly:: tu.
be like, be similar to, be the same as, be a kind of:: sta'á ~ ste'á < t.
dislike s-o/s-th, to not like s-o/s-th:: qélstexw < qél.
getting to like somebody:: i'é:ymet < éy ~ éy:.
just like:: st'ó'o ~ st'á ò < t.
like s-o [his/her personality], like s-th [its taste, its idea], be interested in s-th/s-o, enjoy s-o sexually:: éystexw ~ éy:stexw < éy ~ éy:.
love, like:: stl'ítl'el < tl'í ~ tl'í:.
not like s-th any more:: qelqélexw < qél.
sound like (in voice):: staqí:l < t.
to love s-o, like s-o:: tl'íls ~ tl'í:ls < tl'í ~ tl'í:.
to resemble, look like, (similar-looking):: st'at'ó:mex < t.
want, desire, like, need:: stl'í ~ stl'í: < tl'í ~ tl'í:.
what does it look like?, what does he/she look like?, (how is he/she/it in appearance or looks?), (what color is it? [NP]):: selchímomex < selchí:m ~ selchím.
what does it sound like?, What does it sound like?, (how does it sound?)::selchí:meleqel < selchí:m ~selchím

likeness
likeness, portrait, photograph, photo, statue:: sx̲wíythi ~ sx̲wéythi < x̲wíyth.

Lilium columbianum:: sx̲ameléxwthelh < sáx̲em.

Lillooet
Lillooet people, Port Douglas (also Lillooet) people:: sth'kwólh.

lily
blue camas, yellow dog-tooth violet = yellow avalanche lily:: sk'ámets ~ sk'ámeth.
chocolate lily:: stl'éleqw'.
plant similar to stl'éleqw' (chocolate lily) but different, (probably rice root):: péth'oyes.
tiger lily:: sx̲ameléxwthelh < sáx̲em.
trillium, B.C. easter lily:: xaxt'ó:les.
water-lily, yellow pond lily:: qw'emétx̲w.

lima beans

lima beans:: thós sp'eq'í:l tl'íkw'el < thí, p'éq', tl'íkw'el
(lit. big round + off-white + bean)

Limax maximus
also Limax maximus and Arion aster:: q'oyátl'iye.

limb
cedar limb rope (slitted):: stélwél.
limb (of tree):: sts'éxttses < sts'á:xt.
limb or bough of tree:: =tses ~ =ches.
prop up a limb with a Y-shaped stick, (prop s-th up (of a limb, with a Y-shaped stick)):: ts'qw'ít or th'qw'it.
(red) cedar limb, (red) cedar bough:: x̲pá:ytses ~ x̲páytses < sx̲éyp.
tree limb, branch (of tree), (knot on a tree [CT]):: sts'á:xt.

limber
limber, supple, bend easily (of a person):: leqw'ímṓws.

lime:: t'át'ets'em tsqwáyqwòyèls (lit. sour + greenish fruit) < t'áts', qwá:y

limp
be lame (esp. if deformed), be a cripple, to limp, have a limp:: slékwlets ~ slékwelets < lékw.
limp in the hip:: hálkweletsem < lékw.

Lindeman Creek
Lindeman Creek below Chilliwack Lake, on the north side of Chilliwack River::
(possibly) Schewíts < cháchew ~ cháchu.

Lindeman Lake:: Tl'aqewólem??.
Lindeman Lake or Post Lake:: (possibly) Schewíts < cháchew ~ cháchu.

line
a line:: sx̲éyp.
anchor-line, mooring-line, bow-line, what is used to tie up a canoe:: lhqéletel < lhqé:ylt.
bait s-th (fish-line, fish-hook, fish-trap):: má:lat< má:la ~ má:le.
fishing by a line, line-fishing, trout-fishing, fishing with a pole (for trout)::
qw'iqw'emó:thel ~ qw'íqw'emó:thel < qw'emó:thel.
fishing line:: qw'emóthetel < qw'emó:thel.
float line, cork line:: qwōqwá:l ~ qweqwá:l, qwōqwá:l ~ qweqwá:l.
hang s-th on a line, hang s-th on a nail, hang s-th up:: q'é:ywet (or better) q'í:wet < q'e:yw
~ q'í:w.
lines:: sx̲éyx̲ep < sx̲éyp.
lots of lines:: sx̲éypx̲ep < sx̲éyp.
older sibling, elder cousin (child of older sibling of one's parent, grandchild of older sibling
of one's grandparent, great grandchild of older sibling of one's great grandparent), cousin of senior line,
older brother, older sister:: sétl'atel < sétl'a ~ sétl'o.
sinker line:: xetáléqetel < xá:t.
to fish with a pole or rod, to fish by a line:: qw'emó:thel.
younger, younger sibling, cousin of a junior line (cousin by an ancestor younger than the
speaker's), junior cousin (child of a younger sibling of one's parent, (great) grandchild of a younger sibling
of one's(great) grandparent), younger brother, younger sister:: sóseqwt ~ (rarely) só:seqwt.

line-fishing
    fishing by a line, line-fishing, trout-fishing, fishing with a pole (for trout):: qw'iqw'emó:thel ~ qw'íqw'emó:thel < qw'emó:thel.

ling-cod :: á:yt ~ é:yt, mechó:s.

lining
    fancy lining:: shxwthí:lestel.
    inner lining, inner side:: skwetxwó:lwelh < kwetáxw.

linoleum
    floor, floor mat, floor covering, linoleum, rug:: lhex̲éyléptel < lhá:x̲ ~ lháx̲.

lip
    burned on the lips:: kw'esó:ythel < kw'ás.
    chin, jaw (of fish, human, etc.), (lips (both), cheek, side of the face [DM]):: ts'emxó:ythel.
    (have a) harelip:: x̲asáxw.
    (have) flabby lips, (have) sloppy lips:: slhelp'ó:ythel < lhél.
    (have) pursed lips when pouting:: smóst'iyethel.
    (have the) mouth round and open with rounded lips:: sqwoqwtó:ythel < qwá.
    (have) thick lips:: pelhtó:ythel < plhá:t.
    hit on the mouth, [hit on the chin, hit on the lip, hit on the jaw]:: kw'qwó:ythel < kw'óqw.
    lower lip:: stl'epóyethel < tl'ép.
    on the lip or jaw:: =ó:ythel ~ =eyéthel ~ =eyth(íl).
    on the lips, on the jaw, on the chin:: =ó:ythel.
    red part of the lips, (both) lips:: lhepteló:ythel < lhép.
    roof of the mouth, inside of upper lip, palate:: chelhqí:l ~ chelhqéyl < =chílh ~ chílh=.
    skin of the mouth, (prob. also skin of the chin or jaw or lips):: kw'elōwó:ythel < kw'eléw ~ kw'elṓw.
    to kiss, kiss on the lips:: mékweth ~ mékwethel < mékw.
    upper lip:: schelhóyethel < =chílh ~ chílh=.
    whistle with pursed lips, whistling:: xíxpò:m < xó:pem.

lipstick :: témélh.

liquid
    choke on water, choked on liquid:: lexwslhém ~ lexwslhám < lhém.
    liquid in the mouth:: qe'ó:ythel < qó:.
    to scald s-th/s-o, burn s-th/s-o [with hot liquid]:: th'áx̲et < th'áx̲.
    to stir (a liquid), stir (mixing ingredients):: qwáylhechàls < qwá:y.
    unclear liquid, water, juice:: =elhcha.

liquor
    liquor, rum:: lám.
    liquor store, beer parlor (AC):: lamáwtxw < lám.

listen
    call s-o to witness, call s-o to listen:: xwlalámstexw < xwlalá:.
    he/she called me to witness:: xwelalámsthòxes < xwlalá:.
    just listening (not talking):: xwlalá:.
    listen, hark, listen to something particular:: xwlalá:m ~ xwlalám < xwlalá:.

listen (CONT'D)

listening:: xwélalà:m ~ xwélalàm < xwlalá:.
listen to s-o:: xwlalá:met < xwlalá:.
make s-o listen:: xwlalámstexw < xwlalá:.
straining to listen, really listening, listening hard, trying to listen, (listen [AC]):: xwlalá:.
they call him/her/them to witness (lit. "he/she/they is/are caused to listen"):: xwelalástem ~ xwelalámstem < xwlalá:.

litter

runt of litter, smallest pup or kitten or animal in litter:: th'íth'kw'oya < sth'ékw', th'íth'kw' < sth'ékw'.
smallest of a litter or family:: th'akw'ó:y < sth'ékw', th'ith'kw'ó:y < sth'ékw'.

little

accompany s-o little or elderly:: q'eq'exí:lt < q'ó.
a few little rats:: haheláwt < há:wt.
a little, a little like, slightly:: tu, tu.
a little below the mouth of a creek or slough:: chichewóthel < cháchew ~ cháchu.
a little bit, small bit, a few:: emímel ~ amí:mel.
a little bluff (of rock):: sx̲eq'x̲éq'et < x̲eq'.
a little liar:: shxwmámth'elqel < máth'el.
a little past, a little after:: yéyilaw ~ yíyelaw < yelá:w ~ yeláw ~ yiláw.
a small person (old or young) is picking or trying to pick, an inexperienced person is picking or trying to pick, picking a little bit, someone who can't pick well is picking:: lhilhím < lhím.
baby wren, little or young wren:: t'át'emiya < t'ámiya.
(be a) little bit proud, [a little] proud:: smámth'el < máth'el.
[be a little blue]:: tsmímeth' < méth'.
[be getting/going a little red]:: skwekwíkwemel < kwí:m, tskwekwíkwemel< kwí:m.
(be) stupid, not all there (mentally), (be) a little crazy:: shxwixwóxwth' < xwáth'.
blowfly, big fly, (little fly (one of them) [Elders Group 2/19/75]):: x̲wōx̲wáye ~ x̲wex̲wáye ~ x̲wōx̲wá:ye.
creek, little river, small creek, small river:: stótelō ~ stó:telō < tó:l ~ tò:l.
cute, a little one is good, good (of s-th little):: í'iy < éy ~ éy:, í'iy < éy~ éy:.
cute little one:: á'iy ~ 'á'iy < éy ~ éy:.
diminutive, little (of subject, object, agent, patient or action):: =R1= or =C1e=.
diminutive, little (of subject, object, agent, patient or action), small, (all diminutive verbs are also continuative):: R4= or C1í=, =R6= or =eC2=, R7= or C1á=.
diminutive, small, little:: R5= or C1e=.
five little ones, five young (animal or human):: lhq'atses'ó:llh < lheq'át ~ lhq'á:t.
good (of little ones), cute (of many of them):: é'iy ~ á'iy < éy ~ éy:.
[have/get/be in a state of going a little yellow or green]:: tsqwíqweyel < qwá:y.
(have) quieter water, died down a little:: sqám < qám.
hill (dirt, includes both sides of hill), little hill:: skwókwep ~ skwokwepílep.
little animal(s):: smímiyàth < sméyeth ~ sméyéth.
little baby lying down:: i'ax̲íth < áx̲eth.
little basket:: sí:stel < sí:tel ~ sítel.
little baskets:: selístel < sí:tel ~ sítel.
little beaver:: sqiqelá:w < sqelá:w.
little belly-button:: mímx̲woya < mṓx̲woya ~ mṓx̲weya ~ méx̲weya.
little bug:: sth'ékw'oye < sth'ékw'.
little carrots:: xíxewíyeq or xíxewíq < xáwéq.
little coyote:: lilk'eyáp < slek'iyáp.
little crows, small crows, bunch of small crows, (bunch of northwestern crows):: spepelól

little (CONT'D)

~ spepeló:l < spó:l.
little father:: smà:l < má:l ~ mál.
little finger, fourth finger:: soseqwtóletses < sóseqwt ~ (rarely) só:seqwt.
little flowers:: sp'eláp'q'em < p'áq'em.
little girl (perhaps four years), young girl, (girl from five to ten years [EB]):: q'áq'emi < q'á:mi ~ q'á:miy.
little hawk:: x̲ix̲emx̲íméls < x̲éym.
little horse:: stiteqíw < stiqíw.
little house, cabin (say 12 ft. x 10 ft. or less), small home, storage house (small shed-like house, enclosed with door), outhouse (slang), toilet (slang):: lílem < lá:lém.
little ladies:: slhelhlíli < slhá:lí.
little lakes:: x̲elóx̲cha < x̲ó:tsa ~ x̲ó:cha.
little lamb:: mímetú < metú.
little old person:: siyó:ylexwe < siyó:lexwe ~ syó:lexwe ~siyólexwe.
little partner, little person who follows or goes with one:: sq'iq'exí:l ~ q'iq'exí:l < q'ó.
little pig:: kwíkweshú < kweshú.
little skunk:: sth'íth'peq < sth'épeq.
little sled:: shxwqeyqex̲elátsem ~ shxwqiqex̲elátsem < qíx̲em ~ (less good spelling) qéyx̲em.
little, small:: emémel < emímel ~ amí:mel.
little smart one:: schéchewòt < schewót.
little stick of firewood:: syóyelh < yólh.
little stone, pebble, little rock hill, small rock mountain (like in the Fraser River in the canyon):: smámelet < smá:lt.
(little supernatural creature), little stl'áleqem:: stl'ítl'leqem < stl'á:leqem.
little tiny beads:: ts'ets'emíkw.
little tree:: thí:thqet < theqát ~ thqá:t.
little tree[s]:: thétheqet < theqát ~ thqá:t.
little wives:: stételes < stó:les.
little woman, small woman:: slhálhli < slhá:lí.
lots of little creeks:: stételō < tó:l ~ tò:l.
lots of little girls:: q'eq'elá:mi < q'á:mi ~ q'á:miy.
lots of little pieces of driftwood:: qwéqwelhi(y) < qwélh.
lots of little red:: tskwékwelim < kwí:m.
lots of little sticks of firewood:: syéyelh < yólh.
lots of little streams (like the kind coming down a hill after a rain):: teltelewá:m < tó:l ~ tò:l.
ma'am, female friend, chum (female), little girl:: iyés < éy ~ éy:.
meadow, (little prairie):: spáplhx̲el < spélhx̲el.
my dear, (little best friend, little dear friend, etc.):: q'éyq'eleq ~ (better) q'íq'eleq < q'ó.
poor little one, you poor thing (said to a child):: t'ó:t'.
rock that looks like a little hat on west (Chehalis) side of Harrison River above mouth of Morris Creek:: Yó:yseqw < yó:seqw ~ yóseqw.
scared a little:: sesí:si < síy.
scrubby little ones, (little ugly ones):: qéqelelhó:mex < qél.
short pants, little pants, underpants:: siseqíws ~ síseqíws < seqíws ~ seqí:ws.
small (AC, BJ), little (AC), a little bit (Deming: EF, MC, Cheh.: EB):: axwíl.
small (in quantity), a little:: emémel < emímel ~ amí:mel.
small little plants:: sts'éts'esem < ts'ísem.
small (smaller than axwíl), little:: í:'axwì:l ~ í:'axwí:l < axwíl.
sobbing, crying a little, (to sob [EB]):: x̲íx̲à:m ~ x̲éyx̲à:m < x̲à:m ~ x̲á:m.
that's a little one (male, about one to five years old), he (little):: tú:tl'òtl'èm < tl'ó ~ tl'o.

little (CONT'D)
that's them (little kids), they (little kids):: tl'étl'elò:m < tl'ó ~ tl'o.
that's them (little ones) (male?):: tutl'étl'elò:m < tl'ó ~ tl'o.
(that's) them (lots of little ones), they (many small ones):: yutl'étl'elòm < tl'ó ~ tl'o.
three little people:: lhelhxwále < lhí:xw.

little man
little man (nickname for a person), (sonny boy (MV and DF)):: wíyeka < swíyeqe ~ swíyqe ~ swí:qe.
little man, small man:: swíwíqe < swíyeqe ~ swíyqe ~ swí:qe.

Little Matsqui Creek:: Stótlōtel < tó:l ~ tò:l.

Little Mountain
village at east end of Little Mountain on Hope Slough, upper end of Mount Shannon [DM]:: Qwolíwiya or Ñwolíwiya.
village at west end of Little Mountain (Mount Shannon) on Hope Slough, also a name for Hope Slough or Hope River:: Sqwá:la < qwá.
Whetkyel village east of Little Mountain by Agassiz:: Xwétxel or X̲wétxel.

little ones
a bunch of little ones:: emémel < emímel ~ amí:mel.

Liumchen
village on both sides of Liumchen Creek, Liumchen Creek, Liumchen Mountain:: Loyú:mthel ~ Loyúmthel.

Liumchen Creek
place by Albert Cooper's house on Chilliwack River Road near Vedder Crossing, former village where a slide is now on north bank of Chilliwack River opposite Liumchen Creek:: X̲éylés <
village on both sides of Liumchen Creek, Liumchen Creek, Liumchen Mountain:: Loyú:mthel ~ Loyúmthel.

Liumchen Mountain
village on both sides of Liumchen Creek, Liumchen Creek, Liumchen Mountain:: Loyú:mthel ~ Loyúmthel.

live
at home, be living (somewhere), stay:: tl'eláxw ~ tl'láxw < tl'élexw.
be alive, be living, be in good health, be healthy, be well:: áylexw ~ áyelexw.

liver :: stsél:ém.

living
soul, spirit of a living person:: shxwelí.

living-room
(could be used for) living-room:: ó:metáwtxw < emét.

living thing:: =e ~ =a.

lizard

big gray lizard, (Pacific giant salamander):: tseyí:yex̲.

big gray rock lizard, probably Pacific giant salamander which is cognate in Squamish, possibly also the Pacific coast newt which is commonest in B.C. and also is found in this area, prob. also the northern alligator lizard:: seyíyex̲.

slow-worm ("a slow-moving foot-long snake"), actually a species of blind legless lizard:: aleqá:y < álhqey ~ álhqay.

small red or brown "lizard", red salamander and western red-backed salamander, and possibly also the following brown species attested in the area: long-toed salamander, northwestern salamander, and possibly the British Columbia salamander:: pí:txel.

load

(be) loaded with a heavy pack:: swíp < wíp or wép.

lessen it (of someone's load), halve it, make s-th lighter (in weight), lessen it (like when someone's pack is too heavy):: xwát < xwá.

more than one person heavily loaded with packs:: swewíp < wíp or wép.

loaded

overloaded:: wép < wíp or wép.

lobe

ear lobe:: stl'epá:lí:ya ~ stl'epá:liya < tl'ép.

locate

mark s-th, blaze it (of a trail), get/have s-th spotted (marked and located), make note of s-th:: x̲e'áth'stexw < x̲áth' ~ x̲e'áth'.

spotted (marked and located):: sx̲e'áth' < x̲áth' ~ x̲e'áth'.

location

creek between Popkum and Cheam, also a location near Popkum, (must be second of two creeks above Popkum that cross Highway #1 [JL 4/7/78]):: sthamí:l.

location around a house, part:: =mel.

(place, location), where s-o is at:: shxwlí.

locative

locative, on the:: =el ~ =a(:)l ~ =o(:)l.

(possibly an old) locative:: =el ~ =ál.

lock

a latch, Indian lock:: shxwéth'tel or shxwwéth'tel < wáth'.

(be) locked with a stick:: swáweth' < wáth'.

lock it with a key:: lekelít ~ xwleklít < leklí ~ lekelí.

pry s-th, lock s-th (the Indian way/barred/wedged), pry s-th up, lever it up:: wáth'et < wáth'.

lodge

house, home, den, lodge, hive:: lá:lém.

log :: syáyeq' < yáq'.

a faller, a logger:: yáyeq'els < yáq'.

a lot of logs:: syáq'yeq' < yáq'.

log (CONT'D)

bad-looking (of log or board not of a person), rough:: qelímó:les < qél.
crackling and popping (of a log in fire or firecrackers):: tl'áléx̲em < tl'ál ~ tl'á:l.
cutting them up (of logs):: t'ot'qw'íth'et < t'éqw'.
Douglas fir log or wood:: ts'sá:y.
(have/get a) crackle and pop (sound of a log in a fire or of firecrackers):: tl'á:lx̲em < tl'ál ~ tl'á:l.
hollow (of tree or log):: shxwótkwewel < xwótkw ~ xwótqw.
log cabin:: t'mí:wsà:ls < t'ém.
logging:: ts-hélàk < lók ~ làk.
log house, log-cabin:: lokáwtxw < lók ~ làk.
make it hollow (of canoe, log, etc.):: thiyeqwewí:lt < thíy.
roll s-th (like a log), (roll it up [AC]):: xelékw't < xél.
smooth a log by chopping:: t'mí:ws < t'ém.
straddle s-th (log, fish, etc.):: x̲eqét < x̲éq.

log cabin

log cabin:: t'mí:wsà:ls < t'ém.
log house, log-cabin:: lokáwtxw < lók ~ làk.

log-jam

jampile, log-jam:: steqtéq < téq.

loincloth

be wearing a loincloth:: sthiyáp < sthíyep.
loincloth, dog-hair apron, dog-hair mat:: sthíyep.

Lomatium nudicaule:: q'ex̲mí:l.

Lomatium utriculatum

possibly Lomatium utriculatum or Perideridiae gairdneri, also Daucus carota:: xáwéq.

lonesome

(being) lonesome (refers to someone else):: t'etí:l < t'í:l.
be lonesome for s-o, miss s-o:: t'í:lmet ~ t'ílmet < t'í:l.
(be) lonesome (referring to oneself):: t'í:l.

long

a long time ago:: welhíthelh < híth, welhí:thelh < híth, welhíth < híth.
a long time, it's a long time:: híth.
(be) long, tall (of tree, anything):: tl'áqt.
daddy long-legs (spider), harvestman spider:: tl'áleqtxel q'esq'ésetsel < q'ey ~ q'i.
four ropes, four threads, four sticks, four poles, (four long thin objects):: x̲ethílemets' < x̲e'ó:thel ~ x̲e'óthel.
(have a) long face:: xwtl'óqtes < tl'áqt.
(have a) long neck:: tl'éqtepsem < tl'áqt.
length:: stl'eqtí:m < tl'áqt.
long ago:: wet'ót'.
longest dirt point sticking out on Harrison River about a quarter mile above Harrison Bay bridge:: Tl'éqteqsel < tl'áqt.
long face:: stl'óqtes < tl'áqt.
long feather (from wing):: stl'p'álqel.
long leaf willow, (Pacific willow):: x̲wálá:lhp ~ x̲wá:lá:lhp < x̲wále ~ x̲wá:le.

long (CONT'D)

long legs, long-legged:: tl'áleqtxel < tl'áqt.
point or tip of a long object (pole, tree, knife, candle, land):: =eqs ~ =éqsel ~ =élqsel ~ =elqs.
(seven long objects), seven ropes, seven threads, seven sticks, seven poles:: th'okwsámets' < th'ó:kws.
(six long objects), six ropes, six threads, six sticks, six poles:: t'x̲émemets' < t'éx̲.
three ropes, three threads, three sticks, three poles, (three long narrow objects):: lhxwámeth' < lhí:xw.

longhouse
carved outside post on longhouse, totem pole:: x̲wíythi < x̲wíyth.
(circle) around the fire once and return to the start, make one circle in longhouse:: sélts' < sél or sí(:)l.
dish, big cooking and serving trough used in longhouse, feast dish, plate (of wood or basketry), (platter), tray:: ló:thel.
door, doorway, door of a big (communal) house or longhouse:: steqtá:l < téq.
go around inside the longhouse counter-clockwise:: selts'elwílem < sél or sí(:)l.
longhouse for spirit-dancers, the big house, smokehouse (for spirit-dancing):: stháwtxw < thi ~ tha ~ the ~ thah ~ theh.
longhouse, smokehouse (for spirit-dancing, etc.), Indian house, plank house:: xwelmexwáwtxw < xwélmexw.
main rafters of longhouse:: sh(xw)kw'ekw'í < kw'í ~ kw'íy.
thick plank for side of house, thick shake for longhouse roof, covering over hole in roof of pit-house:: s'í:ltexw.
Watery Eaves, a famous longhouse and early village on a flat area on Chilliwack River just a quarter mile upriver/east above Vedder Crossing:: Qoqoláx̲el < qó:.

Long Island
a neck of land on the west side of Harrison Lake just north of Twenty-Mile Creek and across from the north tip of Long Island:: Shxwtépsem < tépsem.
beach on east side of Harrison Lake across from Long Island where there are lots of flat rocks, most of which have holes in them:: Sqweqwehíwel < qwá.
Long Island (in Harrison Lake):: Híkw Tl'tsás < híkw.

longnose sucker
little roundmouth suckerfish, probably longnose sucker:: skwímeth < kwí:m.

Lonicera ciliosa:: q'éyt'o ~ q'í:t'o.

Lonicera involucrata
possibly Lonicera involucrata:: xó:lelhp.

look
Look., See.:: kw'é.
look after s-o, protect s-o, take care of s-o:: xólhmet ~ xólhemet < xólh.
look at one's face:: kw'echó:sem < kw'áts ~ kw'éts.
look at s-th/s-o, examine s-o/s-th:: kw'átset < kw'áts ~ kw'éts.
look bad, look mean:: qelóméx < qél.
look different:: lelts'ó:méx < láts'.
look for s-th/s-o:: yélx̲t < yél or perhaps yá:l.
looking after s-o, taking care of s-o:: xóxelhmet < xólh.

look (CONT'D)

looking at s-th/s-o:: kw'ókw'etset < kw'áts ~ kw'éts.
looking sad, (making a sour face [MV, EF]):: sló:ltes.
[looks a state of going brown, be getting brown-looking]:: sqw'íqw'ex̲welomex < qw'íx̲w.
[looks blue, blue-looking]:: tsméth'òmèx < méth'.
Look., See.:: kw'é.
[looks purple, purple-looking]:: st'áwelòmèx < st'áwel.
[looks red, red-looking]:: tskwimómex < kwí:m.
[looks rose, rose-looking]:: qálqomex < qá:lq.
[looks white, white-looking]:: p'eq'óméx < p'éq'.
[looks yellow or green, yellow/green-looking]:: tsqwáyòmèx < qwá:y.
shading one's eyes from the sun with the hand (looking into the sun):: xwtóx̲esem.
stare at someone's face, look at s-o's face, stare at s-o, look at s-o:: kw'ótsest < kw'áts ~ kw'éts.
take care of oneself, look after oneself, be careful:: xólhmethet ~ xó:lhmethet < xólh.
to resemble, look like, (similar-looking):: st'at'ó:mex < t.
what does it look like?, what does he/she look like?, (how is he/she/it in appearance or looks?), (what color is it? [NP]):: selchímomex < selchí:m ~ selchím.
worried, sad, looking sad:: st'á:yx̲w < t'ay.

-looking

bad-looking (of log or board not of a person), rough:: qelímó:les < qél.
disappointed and angry-looking without talking:: sx̲éyx̲eth' < x̲íth' ~ x̲éyth'.
in looks, -looking, in appearance:: =ó:mex ~ =óméx ~ =òmèx ~ =ómex ~ =omex ~ =emex.
[looks a state of going brown, be getting brown-looking]:: sqw'íqw'ex̲welomex < qw'íx̲w.
[looks blue, blue-looking]:: tsméth'òmèx < méth'.
[looks gray, gray-looking]:: tsxwíkw'o┐mex < xwíkw'.
[looks purple, purple-looking]:: st'áwelòmèx < st'áwel.
[looks red, red-looking]:: tskwimómex < kwí:m.
[looks rose, rose-looking]:: qálqomex < qá:lq.
[looks white, white-looking]:: p'eq'óméx < p'éq'.
[looks yellow or green, yellow/green-looking]:: tsqwáyòmèx < qwá:y.
to resemble, look like, (similar-looking):: st'at'ó:mex < t.

lookout

Wahleach Bluff, a lookout mountain with rock sticking out over a bluff, also the lookout point on Agassiz Mountain:: Kw'okw'echíwel < kw'áts ~ kw'éts.

looks

in looks, -looking, in appearance:: =ó:mex ~ =óméx ~ =òmèx ~ =ómex ~ =omex ~ =emex.
[looks gray, gray-looking]:: tsxwíkw'o┐mex < xwíkw'.

looks good

good-looking, beautiful, pretty, handsome, looks good:: iyó:mex ~ iyóméx ~ iyómex < éy ~ éy:.

loom :: t'élhtel < t'álh.

a loom:: t'lhéses < t'álh.
net shuttle and net-measure, gill-net measure, (loom [Elders Group]):: t'élhtsestel < t'álh.

Loon

Female Loon:: Q'ewq'eweló:t < q'á:w.
Male Loon:: Q'ewq'ewelátsa < q'á:w.

loon

common loon, possibly also red-throated loon (though that has a separate name in Squamish), possibly also arctic loon:: swókwel.

loose

be slack, loose, too loose, hanging loose (of a slackened rope):: slí:leqw < líqw.
broke down, came (un)loose, came apart, (got) untied, loose, unravelled:: yéx̲w < yíx̲w.
let go of s-th/s-o, drop s-th, set s-o free, turn s-o/s-th loose:: kwá:t ~ kwát < kwá:.
loose (of a pack), slack (of a pack), too low (of a pack):: xet'éla < xét'.
salmon after spawning when its eggs are loose:: t'iléqel.
slack, loose (of a pack):: xét'.
to rattle (of dishes or anything else loose), jingle (of money or any metal shaken), peal or toll (of a bell), make the sound of a bell, to ring (of a bell, telephone, in the ears):: th'á:tsem < th'éts or th'á(:)ts.
untie s-th, unravel s-th, unwind it, unwrap it, loosen s-th, unlace it:: yéx̲wet < yíx̲w.

loosen

loosen it (of a knot):: kw'étxwt.
slacken it, let it out (of a rope), loosen it, (lower it (prob. of s-th suspended):: líqwet < líqw.

Lophodytes cucullatus:: thíyéqel.

Lophortyx californicus

Oreortyx pictus, possibly also Lophortyx californicus:: kwéyl.

Lord

God, the Lord:: Chíchelh Siyá:m ~ Chíchelh Siyám < =chílh ~ chílh=.
It's you to thank the Lord, (Please say grace):: lúwe ts'ít te Chíchelh Siyám < =chílh ~ chílh=.

Lorenzetto)

Indian name of Mary Amy (Lorenzetto) (Commodore) Cooper:: Óyewòt.

lose

become lost, get lost:: íkw' ~ í:kw'.
hair is falling out, losing one's hair:: qw'eméqel < qw'ém.
lose s-th:: ókw'elexw < íkw' ~ í:kw'.
lose (s-th, an object, etc.):: ekw'ólem < íkw' ~ í:kw'.
lose s-th/s-o:: théxwlexw < théxw ~ théx̲w.
lost (deceased):: sóstem < sát.
lost one's voice:: stqá:qel < téq.
slip off (one's feet, hands, bottom), lose balance:: x̲wlhép.
slip off with a foot, lose balance [on feet]:: x̲wlhépxel < x̲wlhép.
slip with both feet, lose balance on both feet:: x̲welhx̲wélhepxel < x̲wlhép.

lose heart

lose heart, become disappointed, become discouraged:: qelqéyl or qelqí:l < qél.

lost

become lost, get lost:: íkw' ~ í:kw'.
lost and presumed dead, perish:: s'í:kw' < íkw' ~ í:kw'.
lost (deceased):: sóstem < sát.

lot(s)

a lot got rubbed off:: ó:leqw' < íqw'.
a lot of baskets:: sá:letel ~ sá:ltel < sí:tel ~ sítel.
a lot of dirt:: sqel:ép ~ sqél:ep < qél.
a lot of flies, big blow-flies:: x̲wiyx̲wiyáye < x̲wōx̲wáye ~ x̲wex̲wáye ~ x̲wōx̲wá:ye.
a lot of logs:: syáq'yeq' < yáq'.
a lot of people:: qx̲álets < qéx̲.
a lot of rocks:: smelmá:lt < smá:lt.
a lot of (small) dogs, puppies:: sqwéqwemay < qwem.
a lot of trees close together (young), thicket:: théqet < theqát ~ thqá:t.
barking a lot, lots of barking:: tl'éwtl'ewels < tl'éw.
be many, be a lot of, lots of, much:: qéx̲.
bending lots of things, bending them (lots of things):: piypó:yt < pó:y.
crying a lot:: x̲ex̲á:m < x̲à:m ~ x̲á:m.
feather (any kind), (fine feathers [EB], small feathers [IHTTC], lots of feathers [EB]):: sxélts' ~ sxél:ts' < xél.
folding lots of things, fold s-th several times or many times:: lemlémet < lémet.
(get) lots of water all over since it's raining so hard, really getting rainy:: t'emt'émqw'xel < t'émeqw'.
hanging lots of fish to dry:: chachí:lhtel ~ chachíyelhtel < =chílh ~ chílh=.
having lots of fun, it's a lot of fun:: í'eyó:stem < éy ~ éy:.
it's sure a lot:: chelà:lqwlha < chelà:l.
[lot of] trout:: th'eth'qwá:y < sth'eqwá:y.
lots of people crying:: x̲emx̲ám < x̲à:m ~ x̲á:m.
rock in the Fraser River near Scowlitz where a woman was crying a lot:: X̲ex̲ám Smá:lt < x̲à:m ~ x̲á:m.
shaking a lot of hands:: kwéletsesà:ls < kwél.
splitting wood, (splitting it (a lot of wood):: seq'séq'et < séq'.
to perish (of a lot of people):: s'ekw''í:kw' < íkw' ~ í:kw'.
what a lot., it's sure a lot:: chelà:l.
lots following:: chelchó:lqem < chá:l or chó:l.
lots of anthills:: qwemqwó:mth' < qwó:m ~ qwóm ~ qwem.
lots of cracks:: seq'síq' < séq'.
lots of eyes:: qelqélem < qélém ~ qél:ém.
lots of eyes being closed:: th'elíth'eplexw ~ ts'elíts'eplexw (or perhaps ts'elíts'ep'lexw) < th'éplexw (or perhaps th'ép'lexw).
lots of floats:: p'íp'ekwtà:l < p'ékw.
lots of friends:: sí:yá:ye < siyá:ye ~ siyáye.
lots of laughing, (many are laughing [AC]):: líyliyem < líyém ~ leyém.
lots of lice:: mexméxts'el < méxts'el.
lots of lines:: sx̲éypx̲ep < sx̲éyp.
lots of little creeks:: stételō < tó:l ~ tò:l.
lots of little girls:: q'eq'elá:mi < q'á:mi ~ q'á:miy.
lots of little pieces of driftwood:: qwéqwelhi(y) < qwélh.

lot(s) (CONT'D)

lots of little red:: tskwékwelim < kwí:m.
lots of little sticks of firewood:: syéyelh < yólh.
lots of little streams (like the kind coming down a hill after a rain):: teltelewá:m < tó:l ~ tò:l.
lots of lumps (any size):: sqwemqwó:mx̲w < qwó:m ~ qwóm ~ qwem.
lots of minnows:: qéqemlò < sqíqemlò.
lots of money, (many dollars):: qx̲ó:s < qéx̲.
(lots of people are) proud, (many are proud):: smá:leth'el ~ smá:lth'el < máth'el.
lots of people crying:: x̲emx̲ám < x̲à:m ~ x̲á:m.
lots of people picking:: lhemlhí:m < lhím.
lots of people visiting (one another):: lá:leqel.
lots of sores, (possibly) rash:: sth'ekw'th'ékw' < th'ekw' or th'íkw'.
lots of squares:: st'elt'eláx̲el < st'eláx̲el.
lots of stl'áleqems, (lots of supernatural creatures):: stl'eltl'áléqem < stl'á:leqem.
lots of times:: qx̲álh < qéx̲.
make s-th lots, make lots of s-th:: qéx̲stexw < qéx̲.
non-spirit-dancers (lots of them):: st'elt'ólkwlh < st'ólkwlh.
place on mountain above Ruby Creek where there's lots of boulders all over the mountain lined up in rows:: Thíthesem < thi ~ tha ~ the ~ thah ~ theh.
splashing, splashing (lots of times):: t'ó:mqw'em < t'émeqw'.
spotted with lots of [irregular] spots:: st'elt'élq < st'á:lq.
squeaking (of lots of mice):: th'eth'elá:ykwem < th'á:ykwem.
(that's) them (lots of little ones), they (many small ones):: yutl'étl'elòm < tl'ó ~ tl'o.
(young) girls, lots of (adolescent) girls:: q'á:lemi ~ q'á:lemey < q'á:mi ~ q'á:miy.

loud

a loud voice:: sthí:qel < thi ~ tha ~ the ~ thah ~ theh.
(be) loud:: shxwtl'ó:s.
be loud in sound, a loud sound (?):: chqwáléqep.
crunchy (loud when eating), crackling (noise when eating):: tl'ámqw'els < tl'ém.
crunchy (loud when eating), crackling (sound or noise when eating):: tl'ámqw'els < tl'ámkw'em.
loud (of a voice):: sthí:qel < thi ~ tha ~ the ~ thah ~ theh.
make the sound of water splashing or dripping fast, (make the sound of a waterfall, make the sound of pouring rain dripping or splashing in puddles loudly):: xwótqwem.
to sigh (of a spirit-dancer), make a loud (breathy) noise:: xeqlhálém.

Louie

name of Chief Albert Louie's father:: T'íxwelátse ~ Tíxwelátsa.

Louie's Slough

slough called Billy Harris's Slough or Louie's Slough, the next slough east of Yálhxetel and west of Q'iq'ewetó:lthel:: Meth'á:lméxwem ~ Mth'á:lmexwem.

louse

body louse, grayback:: p'éq' méxts'el < méxts'el.
human louse: head louse, (secondarily) body louse, and possibly crab louse, (unclear if animal lice are included):: méxts'el.
lots of lice:: mexméxts'el < méxts'el.
(louse-comb):: lhémxts'el < méxts'el, lhémxts'eltel < méxts'el.
to snap (one's fingers, a louse when one bites it, etc.):: tl'eméqw < tl'ém.

louse-comb)
(louse-comb):: lhémxts'el < méxts'el, lhémxts'eltel < méxts'el.

louse egg
nits, louse eggs:: x̲ést'el.

love
love, like:: stl'ítl'el < tl'í ~ tl'í:.
making love, having intercourse:: pipelá:ls < pél (perhaps ~ pí:l by now).
to love s-o, like s-o:: tl'íls ~ tl'í:ls < tl'í ~ tl'í:.

low
a small willow tree, a low willow:: x̲wóx̲welá:lhp < x̲wále ~ x̲wá:le.
deep down, below, down below, low:: tl'ép.
go down, go down below, get low:: tl'pí:l ~ tl'epí:l < tl'ép.
loose (of a pack), slack (of a pack), too low (of a pack):: xet'éla < xét'.
low class person, [person on the lowest economic class]:: stít-sòs < t-sós ~ tesós.
lower s-th down:: tl'épt < tl'ép.
(make s-th deep or low):: tl'épstexw < tl'ép.
small gray mountain blueberry on a low plant, dwarf blueberry:: sx̲wéxixeq ~ sx̲w'éxixeq.

lower
lower circle under eye:: stl'epó:lemelh ~ stl'epó:les < tl'ép.
lower [downriver] end of house (inside or outside):: sōqw'áx̲el < wốqw' ~ wéqw'.
lower it down, (lower s-th down):: tl'pí:lt ~ tl'épelt < tl'ép.
lower lip:: stl'epóyethel < tl'ép.
lower s-th down:: tl'épt < tl'ép, tl'pí:lstexw < tl'ép.
slacken it, let it out (of a rope), loosen it, (lower it (prob. of s-th suspended):: líqwet < líqw.

Lower Sumas River
Sumas Mountain (also Tuckquail, a village on both sides of Lower Sumas River [Wells]):: T'ex̲qé:yl or T'ex̲qí:l < t'éx̲.

Luckakuck Creek:: Lex̲ex̲éq < x̲éq.

luggage
suitcase (Deming), luggage (Deming), clothing container, clothes bag, trunk (for clothes), etc.:: áwkw'emálá < á:wkw'.

luke-warm
warm, luke-warm:: t'álqw'em < t'álqw' or t'élqw'.

lullaby
pacify a baby, pacify it (a baby), sing or hum to a baby to quiet it, sing to it (a zaby), (sing a lullaby to it):: tl'ó:t.
sing a lullaby to s-o:: tétemest.

Lulu Island:: Lhewqí:m Tl'chás < lhewqí:m.

lumber
    lumber house:: xwelitemáwtxw < xwelítem.
    plank, board, lumber:: loplós ~ leplós.

Lumbricus terrestris
    esp. Lumbricus terrestris:: sth'ékw's te téméxw < sth'ékw'.

Lummi
    Lummi (person, people):: Lém:i ~ Lexwlém:i.

Lummi Reserve:: Lém:i ~ Lexwlém:i.

lump :: qwó:mth' < qwó:m ~ qwóm ~ qwem.
    a lumpy mountain back of Seabird Island:: Sqwemqwómx̲w < qwó:m ~ qwóm ~ qwem.
    ankle (the lump part):: qwémx̲wxel < qwó:m ~ qwóm ~ qwem.
    hunchback, humpback, lump on the back:: skwómàtsel (sqwómàtsel) < qwó:m ~ qwóm ~ qwem.
    lots of lumps (any size):: sqwemqwó:mx̲w < qwó:m ~ qwóm ~ qwem.
    lump-like, round:: =xw ~ =exw.
    lump on a tree, burl:: smétsa.
    lump on person (or creature), goiter:: smétsa.
    lumpy clay:: qwóméx̲weth' < qwó:m ~ qwóm ~ qwem.
    solid grease, suet, lump of grease, (stomach fat [CT]):: x̲wástel.
    wrist, wrist bone (on outer side of wrist, little finger side, lump of wrist):: qwémx̲wtses < qwó:m ~ qwóm ~ qwem.

lumpy
    rough (of wood), lumpy (of ground, bark, etc.):: smelhmélhqw.

lunch
    a small lunch:: sásewel < sáwel.
    (food) provisions for a trip, box lunch:: sáwel.

lung
    lung, lungs (both):: sp'élxwem.

lust)
    tempt s-o (with sex or lust):: xixtímestexw or xixtímstexw < xítem.

Lutra canadensis pacifica
    Lutra canadensis pacifica, perhaps also Enhydra lutris lutris:: sq'á:tl'.

Lycoperdon
    probably Calvatia gigantea and Lycoperdon perlatum/gemmatum and possibly other Calvatia or Lycoperdon spp.:: pópkw'em < pékw' ~ péqw'.

Lycoperdon perlatum/gemmatum
    probably Calvatia gigantea and Lycoperdon perlatum/gemmatum and possibly other Calvatia or Lycoperdon spp.:: pópkw'em < pékw' ~ péqw'.

Lymantriidae)
    order Lepidoptera (esp. incl. grey moths of families Noctuidae, Geometridae, and Lymantriidae)::

Lymantriidae) (CONT'D)
lholeqwót.

Lynx
Racoon (name in a story), (Lynx [JL]):: Smelő' < mélés.

lynx
Canada lynx:: chő:wqwela.

Lynx canadensis canadensis:: chő:wqwela.

Lynx rufus fasciatus:: sqets'ómes.

Lysichitum americanum:: ts'ó:kw'e ~ ch'ó:kw'e ~ ts'ó:kw'a.

ma'am
ma'am, female friend, chum (female), little girl:: iyés < éy ~ éy:.

MacFarlane Creek
Mt. MacFarlane Creek:: possibly Chéchem.

machine :: meshí:l.
sewing machine:: shxwp'áp'eth' < p'áth'.
spindle for spinning wool, a hand spinner, a spinning machine:: shxwqáqelets' < qálets'.
washtub, washing machine:: shxwth'éx̲welwetem < th'éx̲w or th'óx̲w.

Mack
also the words of Mack's spirit song:: Á:yiya.
Mack (EB's great grandfather):: Á:yiya.

mad
being angry, continue to be angry, angry, mad, roused, stirred up:: t'át'eyeq' ~ t'át'iyeq' < t'ay.
(be) scowling (if mad or ate something sour), ((made a) funny (strange) face [Elders Group 1/21/76]):: sx̲éyx̲ewes < x̲éywel.
get angry, get mad, be angry:: t'áyeq' < t'ay.
get mad at oneself:: qelqelí:lthet < qél.
strong feelings, mad all the time but won't fight:: simíwél < éy ~ éy:.

maggot(s) :: á:pel.

magic
a sung spell, power to help or harm people or to do [ritual] burning, power to do witchcraft and predict the future, an evil spell, (magic spell) (someone who has power to take things out of a person or put things in [by magic] [Elders Group 2/25/76], ritualist [Elders Group 1/21/76], witch [EB 4/25/78]):: syiwí:l ~ syewí:l < yéw: ~ yéw, syiwí:l ~ syewí:l < yéw: ~ yéw.
(cast a spell for s-o, use a magical power for s-o):: yewí:lmet < yéw: ~ yéw.
someone who has power to take things out of a person or put things in [by magic]:: syiwí:l ~ syewí:l < yéw: ~ yéw.

magpie
black-billed magpie:: álel.

Mahood Creek

creek from Hicks Lake [sic? from Deer Lake] that's actually three creeks all leaving from the lake, probably Mahood Creek, (also Hick's Mountain [LJ]):: Sílhíxw < lhí:xw.

place at Ruby Creek where Paul Webster lived some years ago, now Wahleach Island Indian Reserve #2 and area at mouth of Mahood Creek:: X̲wolích ~ X̲welích < x̲wále ~ x̲wá:le.

(probably) Mahood Creek and Johnson Slough, (possibly) Wahleach River or Hicks Creek (creek at bridge on east end of Seabird Island [AK]):: Qwōhòls < qwá.

mail

mail?:: sx̲elá:ls < x̲él ~ x̲é:yl ~ x̲í:l

make

(accidentally) make s-o ashamed, insult s-o (accidentally or manage to):: x̲éyx̲elexw < x̲éyx̲e ~ x̲íx̲e.

a group making (fish) oil:: hemhémetheqw < mótheqw or metheqw.

all the equipment for making a canoe, canoe-making equipment:: halíyches < hà:y.

(bathe s-o, give s-o a bath), make s-o take a bath:: xó:kw'et < xókw' ~ xó:kw'.

(be) determined, got your mind made up:: sx̲áx̲as < x̲ás.

borer to make holes, auger:: sqweqwá:ls ~ shxwqweqwá:ls < qwá.

build a fire, make a fire, make the fire, (stoke the fire):: yéqwelchep ~ yéqweltsep < yéqw.

build a house (make a house):: thiyéltxwem < thíy.

canoe-work, canoe-making:: s=há:y < hà:y.

(circle) around the fire once and return to the start, make one circle in longhouse:: sélts' < sél or sí(:)l.

come near me, (sic? for make me get near):: tesésthòx < tés.

crossing oneself, (making the sign of the Cross):: pá:yewsem < pó:y.

exert oneself, make a big effort, do with all one's might, [do] as hard as possible, do it harder (used if already paddling for ex.):: tíméthet < tímet.

fixing s-th, making s-th:: thá:yt < thíy.

go around (a point, a bend, a curve, etc.) in the water, make a U-turn (in the water, could use today on land with a car):: q'ówletsem < q'éw ~ q'ew.

I'd rather have (s-th), I'd prefer (s-th) (make that s-th instead):: tl'óst or tl'óstexw.

lessen it (of someone's load), halve it, make s-th lighter (in weight), lessen it (like when someone's pack is too heavy):: xwát < xwá.

light s-th, make a light (of s-th), turn it on (a light):: táwelt < táw.

looking sad, (making a sour face [MV, EF]):: sló:ltes.

made, fixed, repaired:: thíy.

made it (if laxative finally works):: x̲é:yles < x̲éylés.

made it to shore, get to shore:: lhál:omet < lhà:l.

[make a bang, make a sudden hard thump sound]:: kw'péx̲w.

make a bed, make (straighten up) a bed, make one's bed:: thiyá:lhem ~ thiyálhem < thíy.

make a canoe, making a canoe:: hà:y.

make a crunching or crackling noise, crunching (gnawing) sound:: x̲ápkw'em < x̲ep'ékw'.

make a crunch underfoot (bones, nut, glass, etc.):: x̲ep'ékw'.

make a fire for s-o:: yéqwelchept < yéqw.

make a hole in s-th, drill a hole in s-th:: qwát < qwá.

make a light:: yeqwí:ls < yéqw.

make a light, turn the light on, light the lamp:: yeqwí:lem ~ yeqwéylem < yéqw.

make a mess, mess up:: yó:lqw' < yél or perhaps yá:l.

make a mistake, blunder:: mélmel < mál ~ mél.

make an attempt (to do something difficult, like running rapids in a canoe, mountain-climbing, winning a game, etc.), give it a try:: t'óthet < t'á.

make (CONT'D)

make a real mess:: yó:lqw'es < yél or perhaps yá:l.
make it especially for s-o:: swástexw < swá.
make it for s-o, fix it for s-o:: thiyélhtset ~ thiyélhchet < thíy.
make it hollow (of canoe, log, etc.):: thiyeqwewí:lt < thíy.
make it strong, make him/her/them strong:: eyémstexw < éy ~ éy:.
make it thin (of dough, etc.):: th'eth'emí:lstexw < th'eth'emí:l.
make noise, be noisy, (a noise [EB], making noise [EB]):: ló:px̲wem.
make oneself useful:: p'óp'ekw'ethet < p'ákw'.
make one's mouth like one's going to cry:: pespesó:ythílem < pas ~ pes.
make s-o ashamed:: x̲éyx̲estexw < x̲éyx̲e ~ x̲íx̲e.
make s-o ashamed [happen to or accidentally or manage to]:: lháylexw < lháy.
make s-o cry (accidentally or manage to):: x̲á:mlexw < x̲à:m ~ x̲á:m.
make s-o happy, cheer s-o up:: xwoyíwelstexw < xwoyíwel ~ xwoyíwél.
make s-o kneel:: th'q'elhx̲oméstexw < th'q'elhx̲á:m.
make s-o listen:: xwlalámstexw < xwlalá:.
make s-o sick:: q'óq'eystexw < q'ó:y ~ q'óy.
make s-o well:: i'éyelstexw < éy ~ éy:.
make s-th be noisy, make noise with s-th:: lópx̲wemstexw < ló:px̲wem.
(make s-th deep or low):: tl'épstexw < tl'ép.
make s-th expensive:: tl'ístexw < tl'í ~ tl'í:.
make s-th, fix s-th, do s-th:: thíyt < thíy.
make s-th lots, make lots of s-th:: qéx̲stexw < qéx̲.
make s-th thick:: plhátstexw < plhá:t.
(make that s-th (instead), cause that to be s-th (instead)):: tl'óst or tl'óstexw.
make the sign of the Cross, (cross oneself):: píyewsem ~ píwsem < pó:y.
make the sound of water splashing or dripping fast, (make the sound of a waterfall, make the sound of pouring rain dripping or splashing in puddles loudly):: xwótqwem.
making a canoe:: hahà:y < hà:y.
making a face:: x̲wix̲we'ó:s < x̲wex̲we'á.
making fun, (ridiculing):: lhílhàth'.
making it for s-o, fixing it for s-o:: tháyelhtset < thíy.
making love, having intercourse:: pipelá:ls < pél (perhaps ~ pí:l by now).
making noise:: lópex̲wem < ló:px̲wem, lópex̲wemstexw < ló:px̲wem.
making s-o slow:: silíxwstexw < silíxw.
making s-th better, repairing s-th once discarded:: p'áp'ekw'et < p'ákw'.
making the fire, building the fire, (stoking a fire):: híyqwelchep < yéqw.
mark s-th, blaze it (of a trail), get/have s-th spotted (marked and located), make note of s-th:: x̲e'áth'stexw < x̲áth' ~ x̲e'áth'.
non-control reflexive, make oneself do something, keep oneself doing something:: =st=èlèmèt or =st-èlèmèt ~ =st-elómet.
numb, made numb:: xwókw'eltem < xwókw'.
repair s-th once discarded, make s-th better, fix s-th up, repair s-th:: p'ákw'et < p'ákw'.
revive s-o, bring s-o back to life, heal s-o, (EB) give s-o medicine to make him better?:: á:yelexwt < áylexw ~ áyelexw.
sparking, sparkling, exploding with sparks and making sparky noises, making sparky noises:: pá:yts'em < páyéts'em.
they're making friends, (making friends with each other):: yóyatel < yá:ya.
they've made friends, (make friends with each other):: yáyetel (prob. also yáyatel) < yá:ya.
to guess, make a guess:: st'e'áwel ~ st'áwel, st'e'áwel ~ st'áwel < t.
to make a sign with its foot it wants a younger brother or younger sister:: oqw'exélem < óqw'.

make (CONT'D)

to scowl, make a bad face or a scowl:: x̲eywésem or x̲éywésem < x̲éywel.
to sigh (of a spirit-dancer), make a loud (breathy) noise:: xeqlhálém.
turn (oneself) around, make a U-turn:: ts'elqéylém < ts'el.
weaving (for ex. a tumpline), mending a net, making a net:: q'éyq'esetsel < q'ey ~ q'i.

make a canoe

make a canoe, making a canoe:: hà:y.

Male

Male Grizzly Bear:: Yeqwílmet ~ Syeqwílmetxw < yéqw.
Male Salmonberry Bird, (Male Swainson's Thrush):: Xwét < xwét.

male

adolescent male (before he changes to a man, about 13, when his voice changes, etc.):: tumiyáth'.
male black bear with white spot [or mark] on the chest:: Sx̲é:ylmet or sx̲é:ylmet < x̲él ~ x̲é:yl ~ x̲í:l
male (creature):: swíyeqe ~ swíyqe ~ swí:qe.
male name:: =elácha, =elálexw ~ =elàlèx̲w, =eleq, =éylém ~ =ílém, =iyetel, =thet.
male name, (prob.) repeatedly gets wives/houses:: =ímeltxw.
male name version of Olóxwelwet:: Olóxwiyetel < Oló:xwelwet.
male part of male plant:: swiqe'ál or swiyeqe'ál < swíyeqe ~ swíyqe ~ swí:qe.
male (plant):: swíyeqe ~ swíyqe ~ swí:qe.
men, males:: sí:wí:qe < swíyeqe ~ swíyqe ~ swí:qe.
nominalizer (male or gender unspecified, present and visible or presence or proximity unspecified), demonstrative article:: ta=, te=.
on the penis, in the penis, on the genitals, on the male:: =á:q ~ =aq ~ =eq.
that's a little one (male, about one to five years old), he (little):: tú:tl'òtl'èm < tl'ó ~ tl'o.
that's them (little ones) (male?):: tutl'étl'elò:m < tl'ó ~ tl'o.
that's them (male), they (male), them (male):: tutl'ó:lem < tl'ó ~ tl'o.
the (male or gender unspecified, near but not in sight):: kwthe < kw.
the (male, present and visible or presence and visibilityunspecified):: te.
the (male, present, visible), the (gender or presence and visibility unspecified), a (male, present and visible), a (gender or presence and visibility unspecified):: te.

malefactive

benefactive, do for s-o, malefactive, do on s-o:: -lhts.

male friend

sir, male friend, chum (male), sonny:: iyéseq < éy ~ éy:.

mallard

larger bird (any kind, generic), waterfowl, duck, (mallard [Cheh. dial.]):: mó:qw.
mallard, duck:: teléqsel ~ tel:éqsel.

Malloway

village or settlement on the west side of the Fraser River at Emory Creek by Frank Malloway's fish camp, Albert Flat (Yale Indian Reserve #5):: Ó:ywoses.

Malus malus)

Pyrus fusca, Pyrus malus (= Malus malus):: qwe'óp.

man

adolescent boy (about 10 to 15 yrs. old), teenaged boy, young man (teenager):: swíweles ~ swíwles.
little man (nickname for a person), (sonny boy (MV and DF)):: wíyeka < swíyeqe ~ swíyqe ~ swí:qe.
little man, small man:: swíwíqe < swíyeqe ~ swíyqe ~ swí:qe.
man (15 years and up):: swíyeqe ~ swíyqe ~ swí:qe.
man with two wives:: islá:ltexw < isá:le ~ isále ~ isá:la.
men, males:: sí:wí:qe < swíyeqe ~ swíyqe ~ swí:qe.
name of an old man from Kilgard who was a strong warrior (fighter):: X̲éyteleq < x̲éyet.
to escape (of a man or a slave), run away:: tl'í:w.

manage (to)

(accidentally) make s-o ashamed, insult s-o (accidentally or manage to):: x̲éyx̲elexw < x̲éyx̲e ~ x̲íx̲e.
frightened s-o [accidentally], [happened/managed to] frighten s-o:: th'ith'íkw'elexw < th'íkw' or th'ekw'.
get s-o's name, manage to get s-o's name:: kwíxelexw ~ kwéxwelexw < kwí:x ~ kwíx.
hurt s-o [accidentally, happen to, manage to]:: x̲élhlexw < x̲élh.
kill s-th/s-o accidentally, (happen to or manage to kill s-th/s-o):: q'eyléxw < q'ó:y ~ q'óy.
make s-o ashamed [happen to or accidentally or manage to]:: lháylexw < lháy.
make s-o cry (accidentally or manage to):: x̲á:mlexw < x̲à:m ~ x̲á:m.
manage by oneself (in food or travel), try to do it by oneself, try to be independent, do the best one can:: iyólewéthet < éy ~ éy:.
managed to fell a tree, (managed to fall it):: yéq'lexw ~ yéq'elexw < yáq'.
manage to get here:: xwe'ílòmèt < í.
manage to get to s-o here:: xw'í:ls < í.
non-control reflexive, happen to or manage to or accidentally do to oneself:: =l=ómet or =l-ómet ~ =l=ó:met.
non-control transitivizer, accidentally, happen to, manage to do to s-o/s-th:: =l.

man-made)

fall apart, come apart (of something man-made):: yíx̲w.
take s-th down, tear down s-th man-made, dismantle s-th, take it apart:: yíx̲wet < yíx̲w.

many

are how many?:: kw'í:l ~ kw'íl.
be how many canoes?:: kw'ilő̃welh < kw'í:l ~ kw'íl.
be many, be a lot of, lots of, much:: qéx̲.
be steaming (in many places), be cloudy with rain-clouds:: pelpólx̲wem < poléx̲wem.
clubbing many times, hitting many times:: kw'elqwál < kw'óqw.
elders (many collective):: siyelyólexwa < siyólexwe.
folding lots of things, fold s-th several times or many times:: lemlémet < lémet.
good (of little ones), cute (of many of them):: é'iy ~ á'iy < éy ~ éy:.
(have a) wrinkled face with many wrinkles:: lhellhélp'es < lhél.
(have/get) many icicles:: yelyelísem < yél:és.
how many paddles?:: kw'ilő̃wes < kw'í:l ~ kw'íl.
how many people?:: kw'ílà < kw'í:l ~ kw'íl.
how many times:: kw'elálh < kw'í:l ~ kw'íl.
how many trees:: kw'í:là:lhp ~ kw'ílà:lhp < kw'í:l ~ kw'íl.
lots of laughing, (many are laughing [AC]):: líyliyem < líyém ~ leyém.
lots of money, (many dollars):: qx̲ó:s < qéx̲.
(lots of people are) proud, (many are proud):: smá:leth'el ~ smá:lth'el < máth'el.

many (CONT'D)

many are howling:: q'eq'ówel < q'á:w.
(many) different colors:: lets'ló:ts'tel < láts'.
many get crushed, get all crushed, many smashed (round and filled):: meqw'méqw' < méqw' ~ mṓqw'.
many lakes:: x̲ó:letsa < x̲ó:tsa ~ x̲ó:cha.
(many small rocks):: smemá:lt < smá:lt.
more than one is good, good (of many things or people):: álíy ~ 'álíy < éy ~ éy:.
mountain right back of Yale town reserve with two big lakes and many small ones:: X̲ó:letsa Smá:lt < x̲ó:tsa ~ x̲ó:cha.
moving, (many moving around in circles, moving around in circles many times):: x̲elx̲álqem < x̲álqem.
perish together, many die (in famine, sickness, fire), all die, get wiped out:: x̲wà:y ~ x̲wá:y.
plural, (usually) many in a group, collective:: R3= or C1eC2=.
(rare) plural, (usually) many in a group, collective:: R5= or C1e=, =R6= or =eC2=, R7= or C1á=, R8= or C1a=.
shining, (glittering, sparkling (with many reflections)):: p'elp'álq'em < p'álq'em.
small containers (a number of them):: mémeleqel < mímeleqel.
(that's) them (lots of little ones), they (many small ones):: yutl'étl'elòm < tl'ó ~ tl'o.
torn up (in pieces) (or prob. better) (tear up (in many pieces)):: x̲wetx̲wét < x̲wét.
wetting many things:: lhóleqwet < lhéqw.

many times
whipping s-o/s-th many times:: qw'ó:leqwet < qw'óqw.

map:: sx̲e'áth'tels té tèmèxw (lit. "measuring device of the earth") < x̲áth' ~ x̲e'áth'.

maple
broad-leaf maple:: q'emṓ:lhp ~ q'emṓwelhp < sq'émél.
maple dish:: q'emṓ:lhpíwelh < sq'émél.
vine maple, Douglas maple:: sí:ts'elhp.

marble
(have) marble eyes, (have) blue eyes:: mopeló:les.

marble-sized
fine little marble-sized pieces of ice:: sth'ṓwsem or sth'éwsem.

March
month beginning in March:: wóx̲es < wex̲és.
(month beginning in) March, ((birds) making music):: qweloythí:lem < qwà:l.
month or moon of March to April, grass moon:: sox̲wí:les < só:x̲wel ~ sóx̲wel.
moon of February to March, (torch season):: peló:qes < peló:qel.
the month/moon beginning in March:: welék'es < welék'.

Mareca americana)
Anas americana (~ Mareca americana), prob. also Anas penelope (~ Mareca penelope), (Anas acuta [BJ]):: sése.

Mareca penelope)
Anas americana (~ Mareca americana), prob. also Anas penelope (~ Mareca penelope), (Anas acuta [BJ]):: sése.

Maria Slough

upper end of Seabird Island, village at the upper end of Seabird Island, Maria Slough separating Seabird Island from north shore of Fraser River, now used for Seabird Island as a whole:: Sq'éwqel ~ Sq'ówqel < q'éw ~ q'ew.

wide place in Maria Slough (just north of Lougheed Highway bridge), west mouth of Maria Slough:: Sqémelech < qám.

marijuana

marijuana, "pot", "weed", weed:: ts'esémelep ~ ts'esémelép < ts'ísem.

mark

a mark to show where something is, a marker (to show a trail, something buried, a grave):: x̲áth'tel < x̲áth' ~ x̲e'áth'.

a measure, a true mark:: sx̲e'áth' < x̲áth' ~ x̲e'áth'.

(be) blazed (of a mark in a tree), chipped (of mark in tree):: st'ót'ep < t'óp.

female black bear with white spot [or mark] on the chest:: Sx̲éylmòt or sx̲éylmòt < x̲él ~ x̲é:yl ~ x̲í:l

male black bear with white spot [or mark] on the chest:: Sx̲é:ylmet or sx̲é:ylmet < x̲él ~ x̲é:yl ~ x̲í:l

marked on the back:: x̲ep'ewíts < x̲éyp'.

mark s-th, blaze it (of a trail), get/have s-th spotted (marked and located), make note of s-th:: x̲e'áth'stexw < x̲áth' ~ x̲e'áth'.

paint s-o, (paint marks on s-th/s-o):: x̲é:ylt < x̲él ~ x̲é:yl ~ x̲í:l

pencil, pen, something to write with, (device to write or paint or mark with):: x̲éltel < x̲él ~ x̲é:yl ~ x̲í:l

pointer to show direction (like in a trail) (could be an arrow or stick or mark in the ground):: shxwmót'estel < mót'es.

put a mark on it (like water level of river), mark it, weigh it, (measure it):: x̲á:th't ~ x̲áth't < x̲áth' ~ x̲e'áth', x̲á:th't ~ x̲áth't < x̲áth' ~ x̲e'áth'.

Schelowat, a village at the bend in Hope Slough at Annis Rd. where there was a painted or marked house:: Sx̲elá:wtxw < x̲él ~ x̲é:yl ~ x̲í:l

scratch s-o/s-th and leave a mark, rake it, claw it, scrape it:: x̲éyp'et < x̲éyp'.

spotted (marked and located):: sx̲e'áth' < x̲áth' ~ x̲e'áth'.

unidentified animal with marks on its face, perhaps badger or wolverine:: sqoyép.

marmot

hoary marmot, (also known as) "mountain groundhog", "groundhog", or "whistler", poss. also yellow-bellied marmot:: sqwíqw.

Rocky Mountain pika, hoary marmot, rock-rabbit:: sk'í:l.

Marmota caligata cascadensis

Marmota caligata cascadensis, poss. also Marmota flaviventris avara:: sqwíqw.

Marmota flaviventris avara

Marmota caligata cascadensis, poss. also Marmota flaviventris avara:: sqwíqw.

marriage

separated in marriage:: skwekwó:tel < kwá:.

uncle's wife, aunt's husband, parent's sibling's spouse, uncle by marriage, aunt by marriage:: xchápth ~ schápth.

married woman

married woman, got a husband, got married to a husband:: swóweqeth < swáqeth.

married woman (CONT'D)
married women, ((plural) got husbands):: swóqeweqeweth (or better) swóq-weqeth < swáqeth.

marrow :: tétesxel.
bone marrow:: slésxel < ló:s ~ lós.

marry
be married:: smamalyí < malyí.
got married to a wife:: scháchexw < chá:xw.
married woman, got a husband, got married to a husband:: swóweqeth < swáqeth.
married women, ((plural) got husbands):: swóqeweqeweth (or better) swóq-weqeth < swáqeth.
marry, get married:: malyí.
to marry a sibling of one's deceased spouse:: th'áyá:m < ts'á:ya.

marsh
big marsh below old Pretty's place and above modern Scowlitz:: Lhá:lt < lhà:l.
Labrador tea, "Indian tea", "swamp tea":: mó:qwem.
(sphagnum) bog, marsh:: mó:qwem.

marten :: x̲ó:qel ~ x̲óqel.

Martes americana caurina:: x̲ó:qel ~ x̲óqel.

Martes pennanti pennanti:: shxwématsel ~ shxwémetsel, thswál.

Mary
Old Mary of Chehalis:: Yó:yt'elwet.

Mary Ann Creek
Mary Ann Creek, village at mouth of Mary Ann Creek into the Fraser (in Yale, B.C., Yale Town Indian Reserve #1):: Sése.
mountain west of Ñó:letsa, (mountain north of Sése (Mary Ann Creek), shortcut to Ñó:letsa [Elders Group (Fish Camp 9/29-31/77)]):: Tl'átl'eq'xélém < tl'aq' ~ tl'q'.
village between Yale Creek and Mary Ann Creek on the CP side (west bank of the Fraser R.) where lots of cottonwoods grow/grew (near Yale, B.C.):: Lexwchéwõlhp < cháchew ~ cháchu.

mash
crush (of berries), smash (of berries), squish (of berries, etc.), to mash:: tósem < tós.
mashing, grinding (stones, something hard):: tótesem < tós.
tapping it (with something), mashing s-th, grinding s-th, be bumping s-o:: tóteset < tós.
touch s-o purposely, squish it (of berries, etc.), smash s-th, mash it (berries, potatoes, carrots, etc.), bump it:: tóset < tós.

mask :: slhewó:stel.
headdress, face costume, mask:: sx̲wéythiyes ~ sx̲wíythiyes < x̲wíyth.
mask covering the face (lit. "face is inside"):: skwetóxwes < .
mask over the eyes:: sq'eyq'tóles < q'ey ~ q'i.
rock shaped like a man's head with a sx̲wó:yx̲wey mask on a point near the head of Harrison River, the point also called Spook's Point:: Sx̲wó:yx̲wey ~ Sx̲wóyx̲wey < sx̲wó:yx̲wey ~ sx̲wóyx̲wey.

mask (CONT'D)

sxwóyxwey ceremony featuring a masked dance, the sxwóyxwey mask and dance:: sxwó:yxwey ~ sxwóyxwey.

masked dance:: skwetóxwes sqw'eyílex < kwetáxw.

sxwóyxwey ceremony featuring a masked dance, the sxwóyxwey mask and dance:: sxwó:yxwey ~ sxwóyxwey.

Mass

Mass, (to say Mass?):: lomá:s ~ lemá:s.

saying Mass:: lílemas < lomá:s ~ lemá:s.

mast

mast on a canoe or boat:: spotelálá < pó:t.

master

respected leader, chief, upper-class person, boss, master, your highness:: siyám ~ (rare) siyá:m.

masturbate

bring oneself to a climax, to climax, to orgasm, masturbate:: wets'á:lómet < ts'á:.

mat

bulrush mat:: wő:lalh < wő:l.

bulrush mat, reed mat, mat (of cattail/roots/bulrushes, etc.), (wall mat (Elders Group 11/12/75):: wá:th'elh ~ wáth'elh < wáth'.

cattail mat (large or small):: solá:ts.

cedar bark mat:: slhqw'á:y < lhéqw'.

floor, floor mat, floor covering, linoleum, rug:: lhexéyléptel < lhá:x ~ lháx.

floor mat, rug:: thélxetel < thél.

loincloth, dog-hair apron, dog-hair mat:: sthíyep.

mat, (foot mat):: őkw'xatel.

mattress, mats used in beds, (diaper(s) [AC]):: slhá:wel.

needle (for sewing cloth, for mat-making):: p'éth'tel < p'áth'.

pillow, rolled bulrush mat:: sxwétl'qel.

shake s-th (tree or bush) for fruit or leaves, comb a bush (for berries), shake s-th (a mat or blanket for ex.):: xwíset ~ xwítset < xwís.

stick for beating blankets or clothes or mat, blanket-beater, clothes-beater, mat-beater, rug-beater:: kw'ekw'qwá:lth'átel < kw'óqw.

woven mat to put hot plates on:: lháxtsestel < lhá:x ~ lháx.

wrap it again, rewrap it, (correction by AD:) roll it up (of a mat, carpet, etc.):: xwelxwélekw't < xwélekw'.

match

match, matches:: máches.

material)

(be) hard, stiff (material), strong (of rope, material, not of a person), tough:: tl'éxw.

clothing, material:: =íth'a < íth'a.

cloth or warm material to wrap around the foot, stockings:: chóxwxel.

flannelette, velvet, woolly material, fluffy material, soft material:: pá:píth'a < pá:pa.

(have/get) a rustling noise (not continuous) (of paper, silk, or other material), (to rustle):: sawéts'em.

material) (CONT'D)
(have/get) soft rustling (of material), shuffling (sound):: xwót'kw'em.
(making a) continuous rustling noise (of paper or silk or material), rustling (of leaves, paper, a sharp sound):: sá:wts'em < sawéts'em.
strong (of material):: tl'x̲wíth'a < tl'éx̲w.
thin (of material like a dress, also of a string):: th'eth'emí:l.
trimmings (of material), sawdust, shavings:: lhéts'emel < lhíts' ~ lhí:ts'.

(material for)
(material for)?:: =lh ?.

math:: mekw'stám skw'xám/mekw'stám skw'áxem (lit. "everything in numbers") < kw'áx ~ kw'x ~ kw'xá.

Matsqui
Matsqui village, (Matsqui Creek [Wells]):: Máthxwi.

Matsqui Creek
Little Matsqui Creek:: Stótlōtel < tó:l ~ tò:l.

matter
it doesn't matter, it's useless:: ōwéta xwlí:s < shxwlí.

mattock :: mátek.
chopping the ground (with hoe or mattock):: t'et'émélep < t'ém.

mattress
mattress, mats used in beds, (diaper(s) [AC]):: slhá:wel.

May)
hungry time (about mid-April to mid-May), famine (Elders 3/72):: temkw'à:y < kw'à:y.
salmonberry time, (usually) May:: tem'elíle < elíle.

may
maybe, perhaps, I don't know (if), may (possibly):: yóswe ~ yó:swe.

maybe
maybe, I guess, I'm uncertain, must be (evidently), (evidential), have to (I guess):: t'wa ~ t'we.
maybe, perhaps, I don't know (if), may (possibly):: yóswe ~ yó:swe.

may it be good
be good, good, well, nice, fine, better, better (ought to), it would be good if, may it be good, let it be good, happy, glad, clean, well-behaved, polite, virgin, popular, comfortable (with furniture, other things?),:: éy ~ éy:.

May-June
month beginning in April at the mouth of the Fraser, May-June (Jenness:Sepass), oolachen moon:: temwíwe (or possibly) temswíwe < swí:we ~ swíwe.

McGuire
Mount McGuire, (Tamihi Mountain [BJ]):: T'amiyahó:y < t'ámiya.

me

it's me, that's me, I do, I am:: áltha ~ álthe.
it's me., that's me., I do, I am (ls emphatic):: á'altha < áltha ~ álthe.
me (after prepositional verbs), I (after prepositional verbs):: tl'á'altha < áltha ~ álthe.
me, first person singular object:: -óx.
me, I:: ta'áltha < áltha ~ álthe.
me myself, I myself (emphatic):: ta'á'altha < áltha ~ álthe.

meadow

meadow, (little prairie):: spáplhx̲el < spélhx̲el.

meal

be overcome with pleasurable feelings after eating great salmon or a great meal:: ts'éqw'.
eat (a meal):: álhtel.
eating (a meal):: í:lhtel < álhtel.
help oneself to food, serve oneself, serve oneself food (with a ladle), serve oneself a meal (food), (put on a dish [CT, HT]):: lhá:x̲em ~ lháx̲em < lhá:x̲ ~ lháx̲.
pass s-th (at a meal for ex.):: sátet < sát.
share a meal:: wó:thel.
throw different leftovers together for a meal, throw a meal together, eat a snack:: p'ekw'ethílem < p'ákw'.

mean

look bad, look mean:: qelóméx < qél.

measles

(have) measles:: kw'sí:ws.
(have) smallpox, measles, chickenpox:: pelkwí:ws < pél:ékw.

measure

a measure, a true mark:: sx̲e'áth' < x̲áth' ~ x̲e'áth'.
measuring device:: sx̲e'áth'tel < x̲áth' ~ x̲e'áth'.
map (lit. "measuring device of the earth"):: sx̲e'áth'tels té tèmèxw < x̲áth' ~ x̲e'áth'.
measure the knowledge (give a test):: xwéylemt te télmels < x̲wéylémt, tól.
net shuttle and net-measure, gill-net measure, (loom [Elders Group]):: t'élhtsestel < t'álh.
net shuttle, mesh-measure (usually part of the shuttle):: shxwq'éyq'esetsel < q'ey ~ q'i.
put a mark on it (like water level of river), mark it, weigh it, (measure it):: x̲á:th't ~ x̲áth't < x̲áth' ~ x̲e'áth'.
weigh s-th, ((also) measure s-th [EB]):: x̲wéylémt.

meat

dried meat:: sch'á:yxwels < ts'íyxw ~ ts'éyxw ~ ch'íyxw.
flesh (human, non-human), meat (of dried fish, animal, or bird):: slhíqw.
(game) animal, (meat):: sméyeth ~ sméyéth.
Harrison River spring salmon, Harrison River chinook salmon, big Chehalis River spring salmon, (preserved (smoked?) meat [AC: Tait dialect]):: pó:qw' ~ póqw'.
inside brisket of meat (deer, etc.):: th'x̲éyles or th'x̲íles.
outside brisket of meat:: qw'íwelh.
preserved fish, preserved meat, dried fish, dried meat (usually fish), smoked salmon, wind-dried salmon (old word), what is stored away, what is put away:: sq'éyle.
tray for carrying meat:: smèyethálá < sméyeth ~ sméyéth.

medicine

be bitter (like of cascara bark or medicine or rancid peanuts):: sásex̲em ~ sá:sex̲em < sáx̲em.
(have a) menthol smell, (be) strong-smelling (of medicine):: xó:lxwem.
medicine song [sung by shaman]:: yiwí:leqw < yéw: ~ yéw.
medicine spring on the Fraser River beach about a half mile above (north) of the American Bar beach:: Xwth'kw'ém < th'ekw' or th'íkw'.
revive s-o, bring s-o back to life, heal s-o, (EB) give s-o medicine to make him better?:: á:yelexwt < áylexw ~ áyelexw.
short unidentified plant, about 3 ft. tall with red berries like a short mountain ash, the berries are bitter but the plant is used as medicine, possibly red baneberry:: í:lwelh.

medicine man

Indian doctor, shaman, medicine man, Indian doctor's spirit power (Elders Group 11/19/75):: shxwlá:m < lá:m.
rock above Yale where Ñá:ls gritted his teeth and scratched rocks as he duelled with a medicine man across the Fraser:: Th'ex̲elís < th'ex̲elís.

meet

elope with s-o or meet up with s-o:: chémlexw ~ chemléxw < chó:m.
meet s-o:: xwchém:est < chó:m.
they met:: xwchém:és < chó:m.
to meet (each other):: q'eqótel < q'ó.

meeting

a gathering, a meeting:: sq'ép < q'ép.
close up a meeting, wind up a meeting, complete a meeting:: yalkw'ólhem or yelkw'wólhem < yókw' ~ yóqw', yalkw'ólhem or yelkw'wólhem < yókw' ~ yóqw'.

Megaceryle alcyon:: th'etséla < th'éts.

Megaptera novaeangliae

perhaps generic, most likely includes all local balleen whales, i.e., suborder Mysticeti, especially Balaenoptera physalus and Megaptera novaeangliae, possibly Eschrichtius glaucus, Balaenoptera borealis, Balaenoptera acutorostrata, Sibbaldus musculus, Eubalaena sieboldi, could include the following toothed whales (suborder Odontoceti): Physeter catodon, possibly Berardius bairdi, Mesoplodon stejnegeri, Ziphius cavirostrus:: qwél:és ~ qwélés.

Meleagris gallopavo:: slholh(e)x̲wélqsel mó:qw < lhex̲w.

melody)

(have a) high pitch (voice or melody), (have a) sharp voice:: xwiyótheqel < éy ~ éy:.

Melospiza melodia morphna

Melospiza melodia morphna, (perhaps any/all of the following: Passerculus sandwichensis brooksi, Pooecetes gramineus, Chondestes grammacus, Spizella arborea, Spizella passerina, Zonotrichia querula, Passerella iliaca, Zonotrichia leucophrys, Zonotrichia atricapilla, Melospiza melodia morphna):: sx̲wőx̲wtha.
probably Melospiza melodia morphna:: paspesítsel ~ paspasyí:tsel ~ pespesí:tsel < pas ~ pes.

melt

be melting:: yíyet'em < yít'em.

melt (CONT'D)

melt, thaw:: yít'em.

member

member or part (of the body):: =ó:mél ~ =á:mel.
part, member, nick-:: =á:mel.

memorial

(a word used when showing a picture of the deceased at a memorial ceremony, and telling the . family to dry their tears) his/her face/their faces are dried:: th'éyx̲westem < ts'íyxw ~ ts'éyxw ~ ch'íyxw.

memory)

be short (in memory):: q'iq'ethá:m or q'eyq'ethá:m < q'thá:m.
(have a) short memory:: q'thá:m.

men

men, males:: sí:wí:qe < swíyeqe ~ swíyqe ~ swí:qe.

menace)

be naughty, be bad (a menace) (but not quite as bad as qél):: qíqel < qél.

mend

weaving (for ex. a tumpline), mending a net, making a net:: q'éyq'esetsel < q'ey ~ q'i.

menstruate:: qí:w.

a rock in the creek at the upriver end of Seabird Island that was a girl washing after her first period:: The Théthex̲w or Thethéthex̲w < thethíx̲w.
girl at puberty, (girl's first period):: thethíx̲w.
menstruating:: qíqew < qí:w.

mentally)

be twisted (mentally), he's twisted (mentally):: x̲élts'tem < x̲élts'.
he's gone (mentally):: héleméstem < la.

menthol

(have a) menthol smell, (be) strong-smelling (of medicine):: xó:lxwem.
have a menthol taste, (have a cool taste):: xó:lxwem.

Mephitis mephitis spissigrada:: sth'épeq.

baby Mephitis mephitis spissigrada, possibly Spilogale gracilis latifrons:: selíléx̲.

merely)

just (simply, merely):: òl ~ -òl ~ -ò ~ el.

merganser

a white-headed duck, [could be bufflehead, snow goose, emperor goose, poss. oldsquaw, or hooded merganser, other duck-like birds with white heads do not occur in the Stó:lō area and the emperor goose would be only an occasional visitor]:: skemí'iya.
hooded merganser, smaller sawbill:: thíyéqel.
sawbill duck, fish-duck, common merganser (larger), American merganser:: x̲wó:qw'.

Mergus merganser:: x̲wó:qw'.

mesh-measure
net shuttle, mesh-measure (usually part of the shuttle):: shxwq'éyq'esetsel < q'ey ~ q'i.

Mesoplodon stejnegeri
perhaps generic, most likely includes all local balleen whales, i.e., suborder Mysticeti, especially Balaenoptera physalus and Megaptera novaeangliae, possibly Eschrichtius glaucus, Balaenoptera borealis, Balaenoptera acutorostrata, Sibbaldus musculus, Eubalaena sieboldi, could include the following toothed whales (suborder Odontoceti): Physeter catodon, possibly Berardius bairdi, Mesoplodon stejnegeri, Ziphius cavirostrus:: qwél:és ~ qwélés.

mess
make a mess, mess up:: yó:lqw' < yél or perhaps yá:l.
make a real mess:: yó:lqw'es < yél or perhaps yá:l.
mess in one's pants (shit in one's pants):: ó'ayiwsem < ó'.
upset bed, mess s-th up:: yélqw't < yél or perhaps yá:l.

message
send somebody off with a message:: tssálem < tsesá ~ tssá or tsás.
the messenger:: (kw)the tátí:m < tà:m.

messenger
the messenger:: (kw)the tátí:m < tà:m.

metal
clinking, tinkling (of glass, ice in glass, glasses together, dishes together, metal together):: ts'átx̱em ~ th'átx̱em.
(have) clinking (of glass or dishes or metal), (have) tinkling sound (of glass, ice in glass, glasses together):: th'átx̱em ~ ts'átx̱em.
(perhaps) copper, (hard metal that looks like gold but isn't, maybe copper [Elders at Katz Class 10/5/76], metal found in mines and used for arrowheads [Elders Group 5/28/75], gold [EB]):: sqw'él.
ringing sound when something drops (spoon, metal ashtray or something heavy):: ts'tés.
to rattle (of dishes or anything else loose), jingle (of money or any metal shaken), peal or toll (of a bell), make the sound of a bell, to ring (of a bell, telephone, in the ears):: th'á:tsem < th'éts or th'á(:)ts.

metallic
metallic blue-green beetle, "June bug", probably metallic wood-boring beetle, or possibly some types of long-horn beetle which aremetallic green with reddish legs:: tále te syó:qwem < tá:le ~ tále, tále te syó:qwem < yéqw.

méthelh
coiled up méthelh rope for fishing (for sturgeon and spring salmon):: ts'tíxem.

Methodist :: Máthedes.

Microtus longicaudus macrurus
may include any or all of the following which occur in this area: creeping vole Microtus oregoni serpens, long-tail vole Microtus longicaudus macrurus, mountain heather vole Phenacomys intermedius oramontis, boreal redback vole Clethrionomys gapperi cascadensis, Norway rat (intro.) Rattus norvegicus, and perhaps roof rat Rattus rattus, also includes

Microtus longicaudus macrurus (CONT'D)

bushy-tailed wood rat (packrat) Neotoma cinerea occidentalis which has its own name below:: há:wt.
prob. the introduced Rattus norvegius, native species possiblyincluding any/all of these four: Microtus oregoni serpens, Microtus longicaudus macrurus, Phenacomys intermedius oramontis, and Clethrionomys gapperi cascadensis, possibly also the introduced Rattus rattus:: ts'á:txwels < ts'átxwels ~ ch'átxwels.

Microtus oregoni serpens

may include any or all of the following which occur in this area: creeping vole Microtus oregoni serpens, long-tail vole Microtus longicaudus macrurus, mountain heather vole Phenacomys intermedius oramontis, boreal redback vole Clethrionomys gapperi cascadensis, Norway rat (intro.) Rattus norvegicus, and perhaps roof rat Rattus rattus, also includes bushy-tailed wood rat (packrat) Neotoma cinerea occidentalis which has its own name below:: há:wt.
prob. the introduced Rattus norvegius, native species possiblyincluding any/all of these four: Microtus oregoni serpens, Microtus longicaudus macrurus, Phenacomys intermedius oramontis, and Clethrionomys gapperi cascadensis, possibly also the introduced Rattus rattus:: ts'á:txwels < ts'átxwels ~ ch'átxwels.

mid- :: téx̱w, texw=.

midday

midday, noon:: téxwswàyel ~ texwswàyèl ~ texwswáyél < wáyel.

middle

be in the middle, be in the center:: shxwá:ye.
middle (in age or spatial position), between:: alxwítsel.
out in the middle of the river:: chuchuwó:ythel < cháchew ~ cháchu.
second finger, middle finger:: shxwá:ytses < shxwá:ye.
(someone) standing in the middle of a crowd:: s-hómkwstem.

Middle Creek:: Lóyaqwe'áth'? or Lóyaqwe'áts'?, Lóyeqw'e'áts (most likley) or Lóyaqwe'áts' or Lóyaqwe'áth', Nesókwech ~ Nasókwach.

creek with its mouth on the south side of Chilliwack River and above the mouth of Middle Creek:: Sch'iyáq < sts'iyáq.

midge

gnat, probably includes non-biting midges, biting midges, and (biting) black flies:: pepx̱wíqsel < píxw.
sand-fly, no-see-um fly, biting midge:: pxwíqs < píxw.

midget :: st'éps ~ st'epsóye, ts'ékw'iya.

midget, small people:: s'ó:lmexw.
(probably) tiny midget:: t'it'epsó:ye < st'éps ~ st'epsóye.

mid-wife

mid-wife (helps to deliver babies):: xólhmet ~ xólhemet < xólh.

might

exert oneself, make a big effort, do with all one's might, [do] as hard as possible, do it harder (used if already paddling for ex.):: tíméthet < tímet.

milk

breast, nipple, milk:: sqemó: < qemó:.

milk (CONT'D)

powdered milk/coffee mate:: ts'áyxw sqemó < ts'íyxw, qemó (lit. dry + milk)
squeezing the breast of s-o/s-th, milking s-o/s-th:: p'ip'eth'élmet < p'í:.
suckle, suck milk from a breast:: qemó:.

Milky Way
The Milky Way:: Te Lewómet < slewómet ~ lewómet.

Mill Creek
Mill Creek (at American Bar), Puckat Creek on map also:: Peqwchṓ:lthel Stótelō < péqw.

millipede
centipede, and poss. millipede:: lhets'íméls te pítxel < lhts'íméĺ.

milt
milt, salmon milt:: tl'qw'á:y.

Míme͟xwel
island or point on north side of first slough north of the mouth of Chehalis River, (next slough and point above Míme͟xwel [EL 3/1/78]):: Yálhxetel.

mind
(be) determined, got your mind made up:: s͟xá͟xas < ͟xás.
in the mind:: =élmél.
in the mind, -minded, disposition:: =welh ~ =wílh.
the mind, someone's own knowledge:: télmel < tól.

-minded
(be) cranky, crabby, dirty-minded:: lexwqélwelh < qél.
in the mind, -minded, disposition:: =welh ~ =wílh.

mines
(perhaps) copper, (hard metal that looks like gold but isn't, maybe copper [Elders at Katz Class 10/5/76], metal found in mines and used for arrowheads [Elders Group 5/28/75], gold [EB]):: sqw'él.

minister
priest, minister:: leplít.

Mink
Mink (name in some stories):: sqáyé͟x ~ sqayé͟x.
Mink (name in stories), pet name of Mink:: Sqayé͟xiya ~ Sqáyè͟xiya < sqáyé͟x ~ sqayé͟x.
the Tracks of Mink, holes shaped like a mink's tracks toward the base of the rock-face called Xwyélés or Lexwyélés:: S͟xéyeltels Te Sqoyé͟xiya < s͟xél:e.

mink :: chachí:q'el, sqáyé͟x ~ sqayé͟x.

minnow :: sqíqemlò, ts'ókw.
lots of minnows:: qéqemlò < sqíqemlò.
point of land on Harrison River (somewhere between Lheltá:lets and Híqelem) where during a famine the old people scooped minnows and boiled them to make soup:: Sqíqemlò < sqíqemlò.

mire
    get stuck in the mud, get mired, be mired, get muddy:: t'ékw.

mirror :: skw'echó:stel < kw'áts ~ kw'éts.
    mirror, (probably small mirror):: skw'ikw'echó:sem < kw'áts ~ kw'éts.

mischievious
    be rowdy, be a nuisance, be mischievious:: qwélqwel < qwà:l.

miss :: x̲éyp.
    be lonesome for s-o, miss s-o:: t'í:lmet ~ t'ílmet < t'í:l.
    missed the chair in sitting down, missed one's chair:: sépelets.
    miss s-th (in shooting at it with arrow, spear or gun):: qwíx̲wet < qwíx̲w.
    to miss a shot (an arrow, spear or gun):: qwíx̲w.

missing
    (have a) tooth missing, (have) teeth missing (any number), (be) toothless:: slhémoqel < lhém.

mist
    fog, mist:: sqwétxem < qwétxem.
    (maybe) fine mist of fog or rain, ((perhaps) getting foggy [EB]):: qweqweqwtí:mxel < qwétxem.

mistake
    make a mistake, blunder:: mélmel < mál ~ mél.
    mistake in splitting roots by making them uneven:: t'ats'ex̲elí:m < t'á:ts'.

Mister Raven
    Raven, (Mister Raven or Mister Crow? [AK 1/16/80]):: Skwówéls.

mistress
    wife (not respectful), the "old lady", "squaw", mistress:: chá:xw.

mitten
    mittens, gloves:: th'qwó:letses < th'qwó:lecha ~ th'qwó:letse.

mix
    forgetful, mixed up (mentally, emotionally):: melmelqwìwèl < mál ~ mél.
    mixed (of anything, vegetables, brains, etc.):: smómeleqw < mál ~ mél.
    mixed up:: memílets' < mál ~ mél, memílets' < mí:l ~ míl.
    mix s-th, put them together:: q'etóléstexw < q'ó.
    really mixed s-th up:: melmóléqwet < mál ~ mél.
    rub (oil or water) in s-th to clean or soften, rub s-th to soften or clean it, (shaping a stone hammer with abrasion?, shaping?, mixing paint?, pressing together or crushing? [BHTTC 9/2/76]):: yémq't.

moccasin :: sqélxel.
    deer-skin moccasin:: stl'éqxel.

mock orange:: sth'élhp.

molasses

molasses :: meláses.

mole :: speláwél < pél (perhaps ~ pí:l by now).

Mom
Mother (the speaker's), Mom, Mum:: tátel < tá:l ~ tà:l ~ tál, tà:t, tát or tàt < tá:l ~ tà:l ~ tál.

moment
now, this moment, this instant:: tloqá:ys < ló.
now, this moment, this instant, (right now):: tloqá:ys < qá:ys.
recently, just now, lately, (at one recent moment), not long ago:: qá:ys.

Monday
Monday (day past):: yilawelhát ~ yiláwelhàt ~ syiláwelhàt < yelá:w ~ yeláw ~ yiláw.

money :: tá:le ~ tále.
bank (money house, money building):: tale'áwtxw < tá:le ~ tále.
be how much money?:: kw'í:les ~ kw'íles < kw'í:l ~ kw'íl.
be short (of money or other things):: sq'thà:m < q'thá:m.
change it (money) for s-o:: iyóqelhtsthet < iyá:q.
change it (of money):: iyáqest < iyá:q.
change (money):: siyóqelhtsthet < iyá:q.
collect, collect money, take a collection, gather:: q'pá:ls < q'ép.
get credit, borrow (money for ex.), (getting credit, borrowing):: qw'íméls.
lend money to s-o, [give s-o credit]:: ex̲ímt < íx̲em.
lend s-o money:: ex̲ímstexw < íx̲em.
lots of money, (many dollars):: qx̲ó:s < qéx̲.
money, dollar(s):: =ó:s ~ =ós ~ =es.
ran out (of food, money, etc.), have no more, be finished (offood), (be empty (of container of supplies) [EB: Cheh., Tait]):: ṍwkw'.
to rattle (of dishes or anything else loose), jingle (of money or any metal shaken), peal or toll (of a bell), make the sound of a bell, to ring (of a bell, telephone, in the ears):: th'á:tsem < th'éts or th'á(:)ts.

monster
something scary, monster:: chí'.

month :: skw'exó:s ~ skw'xó:s.
(first lunar month beginning in) July, (tenth month):: epóléstel < ó:pel.
first month ?:: mímele < méle ~ mél:a.
gooseberry time, the month or moon (first sliver) that starts in June:: temt'á:mxw < t'á:mxw.
(month beginning in) March, ((birds) making music):: qweloythí:lem < qwà:l.
month beginning with first sliver of moon in February, (time things stick to the hand (in cold)):: temt'elémtses < t'elém.
month or moon beginning in July:: temqwá:l < qwá:l.
month or moon in November:: telxwíts.
month or moon of March to April, grass moon:: sox̲wí:les < só:x̲wel ~ sóx̲wel.
month or moon that begins in February:: Qwémxel < qwem.
moon or month beginning in February, (November to December, time when ice forms [and sticks] [Billy Sepass in Jenness]):: temtl'í:q'es < tl'íq'.

month (CONT'D)

month beginning in March:: wóx̲es < wex̲és.
the month/moon beginning in March:: welék'es < welék'.
moon or month beginning in November, (put away each other's paddles), (sometimes the moon beginning in October, depending on the weather [Elders Group [3/12/75], (moon or month beginning in January [Elders Group 2/5/75]):: xets'ṓ:westel ~ xets'ṓwestel < xits' ~ xets'.
(perhaps) month:: =á:lts' ~ =á:lth'ts.
sockeye moon, month to get sockeye salmon (begins with first quarter after black moon in July, lasts into August), July to August, (June to July [Jenness: WS]):: temthéqi < sthéqi ~ sthéqey.
third month since:: lhxwá:lth'ts < lhí:xw.

monument

monument at Saddle Rock at Five Mile Creek:: Sólkweyem?? or Solkw'í:m??.

moon :: skw'exó:s ~ skw'xó:s.

an eclipse (of sun or moon):: t'ó:ltel ~ t'óltel < t'á:l.
cyclic period, moon, season:: =ó:s ~ =ós ~ =es.
face of the moon:: =ó:s ~ =ós ~ =es.
gooseberry time, the month or moon (first sliver) that starts in June:: temt'á:mxw < t'á:mxw.
month beginning in April at the mouth of the Fraser, May-June (Jenness:Sepass), oolachen moon:: temwíwe (or possibly) temswíwe < swí:we ~ swíwe.
month beginning with first sliver of moon in February, (time things stick to the hand (in cold)):: temt'elémtses < t'elém.
month or moon beginning in July:: temqwá:l < qwá:l.
month or moon in November:: telxwíts.
month or moon of March to April, grass moon:: sox̲wí:les < só:x̲wel ~ sóx̲wel.
month or moon that begins in February:: Qwémxel < qwem.
moon of February to March, (torch season):: peló:qes < peló:qel.
moon or month beginning in February, (November to December, time when ice forms [and sticks] [Billy Sepass in Jenness]):: temtl'í:q'es < tl'íq'.
moon or month beginning in November, (put away each other's paddles), (sometimes the moon beginning in October, depending on the weather [Elders Group [3/12/75], (moon or month beginning in January [Elders Group 2/5/75]):: xets'ṓ:westel ~ xets'ṓwestel < xits' ~ xets'.
moon (possibly one of the quarters):: lhqá:lts'.
October moon, time to smoke Chehalis spring salmon:: tempó:kw' < pó:qw' ~ póqw'.
round, full (of the moon):: xelókw' ~ xeló:kw' < xél.
sockeye moon, month to get sockeye salmon (begins with first quarter after black moon in July, lasts into August), July to August, (June to July [Jenness: WS]):: temthéqi < sthéqi ~ sthéqey.
(spherical), round (of ball, apple, potato, rock, full moon, but not of a pear):: xelkw'ó:ls < xél.
the month/moon beginning in March:: welék'es < welék'.
time of the baby sockeye's coming, early spring (usually April), April moon:: temkwíkwexel.
worn out (used when quarter moon is nearly invisible), (set (of the sun)):: th'éx̲.

mooring-line

anchor-line, mooring-line, bow-line, what is used to tie up a canoe:: lhqéletel < lhqé:ylt.

moose

elk (or) moose turned to stone in the Fraser River by Hill's Bar:: Q'oyíyets ~ Q'oyí:ts < q'oyíyets or q'oyí:ts.

moose (CONT'D)

(moose, British Columbia moose), elk:: shxwiyáxkel.

more

again, another, more:: qelát.
do it again, add more (to s-th):: qelátstexw < qelát.
ran out (of food, money, etc.), have no more, be finished (offood), (be empty (of container of supplies) [EB: Cheh., Tait]):: ő̈wkw'.
transform it more, pass it over the fire more (at a burning):: x̲iyx̲éyt or x̲eyx̲éyt < x̲éyt.

more than one

more than one is good, good (of many things or people):: álíy ~ 'álíy < éy ~ éy:.

morning

be early morning, early morning:: lá:telh < lá:t.
bad morning breath:: qeléqep látelh slhákw'em < qél.

morose

(be) morose:: xwtl'óqtes < tl'áqt.

Morris Creek

Morris Creek (near Chehalis, B.C.), Morris Lake (near Chehalis):: Sx̲áx̲e < x̲áx̲e.
rock that looks like a little hat on west (Chehalis) side of Harrison River above mouth of Morris Creek:: Yó:yseqw < yó:seqw ~ yóseqw.

Morris Lake

Morris Creek (near Chehalis, B.C.), Morris Lake (near Chehalis):: Sx̲áx̲e < x̲áx̲e.

Morris Lake Mountain:: Sth'éqwela < ts'éqw ~ th'éqw.

Morris Mountain

Morris Mountain (near Chehalis):: Sx̲áx̲e Smá:lt < x̲áx̲e.

Morris Valley

a fairly flat clearing on a mountain in Morris Valley where they used to play ts'its'eqweló:l or Indian badminton:: Ts'éqwela ~ Th'éqwela < ts'éqw ~ th'éqw.

mosquito

mosquito, (also included as a type of "mosquito" is the cranefly):: qwá:l.
rags wound around the legs in the cold or to protect from mosquitoes, (leggings):: q'élq'xetel < q'ál.
to smudge (make smoke to get rid of mosquitoes):: p'tl'ómt < p'ótl'em.

moss

a multi-colored moss:: Q'éyts'i(y).
black tree lichen, black tree "moss":: sqwelíp.
gray lacy lichen or tree moss (real fine like hair, grows on maples):: x̲ám'x̲em'.
have a mossy smell:: qwomáléqep < qwà:m ~ qwám.
moss (any kind, on rocks or trees):: qwà:m ~ qwám.
place of moss-covered stones at upper end of Hope Slough not far from Harry Edwards' home (as of 1964):: Qwómqwemels < qwà:m ~ qwám.
pretty white lacy moss:: máqelhp < má:qel.

moss bread:: sqwelíp.

"moss" (lichen)

gray or green tree "moss" (lichen) hanging on tree limbs, possibly wolf lichen or other species:: mex̱t'éles.

moth

inchworm, (caterpillar of the geometrid moth family):: q'álq'elp'í:w < q'ál, q'alq'elő:wsem < q'ál.

moth (esp, the grey one that comes out at night):: lholeqwót.

pygmy owl, some also call the moth (big ones or little ones) by this name:: spopeleqwíth'a ~ spopeleqwíth'e < poleqwíth'a.

salmonberry worm, (prob. larvae of moths or butterflies or two-winged flies):: xwexwíye.

Mother

Grandma, Father's Mother (nickname):: táta < tá:l ~ tà:l ~ tál.

Mother (the speaker's), Mom, Mum:: tátel < tá:l ~ tà:l ~ tál, tà:t, tát or tàt < tá:l ~ tà:l ~ tál.

mother :: tá:l ~ tà:l ~ tál.

mother-in-law

mother-in-law, father-in-law, spouse's parent, parent-in-law:: skw'ílhew.

motion

got up with a quick motion, got up quickly:: xwexwíléx < xwíléx.

travelling by, in motion, while moving along, while travelling along:: ye= ~ yi= ~ i┐.

(while) travelling along, in motion:: ye=.

motor

engine, motor:: í:lchel.

mould

(be) mouldy smelling:: popeqwemáléqep < póqw.

get mouldy:: póqwthet < póqw.

getting mouldy in taste or smell:: pópeqwem < póqw.

mould (on food, clothes, etc.):: spópeqw < póqw.

mount

get in a conveyance, get in a car, mount a horse:: ó:lh.

mounting a horse, mounting a person:: ts'ílém < ts'á:.

Mountain

Agassiz Mountain:: Alámex Smámelt < Alámex.

Agassiz Mountain (or more likely Mount Woodside):: Sqwehíwel < qwá.

Bear Mountain, also called Lhóy"s Mountain:: Siyó:ylexwe Smá:lt < siyó:lexwe ~ syó:lexwe ~siyólexwe.

Chilliwack Mountain, village of Cameleats on west end of Chilliwack Mountain:: Qwemí(:)líts.

creek from Hicks Lake [sic? from Deer Lake] that's actually three creeks all leaving from the lake, probably Mahood Creek, (also Hick's Mountain [LJ]):: Sílhíxw < lhí:xw.

Cultus Lake Mountain, actually Mount Amadis or International Ridge:: Swílhcha Smá:lt

Mountain (CONT'D)

< Swílhcha.
Dog Mountain above Katz Reserve:: Q'á:w < q'á:w.
Granite Mountain, the second mountain back of X̲óletsa, northwest of Kwelkwelqéylem:: Th'emth'ómels < th'óméls.
Hook-nose, Hook-nose Mountain, Hamersly Hopyard Hill:: Lhílhkw'eleqs ~ Lhílhkw'elqs < lhíkw' ~ lhí:kw'.
Hope Mountain:: St'ámiya < t'ámiya.
Isolillock Mountain (near Silver Creek):: Tl'ítl'xeleqw.
Morris Lake Mountain:: Sth'éqwela < ts'éqw ~ th'éqw.
Morris Mountain (near Chehalis):: Sx̲áx̲e Smá:lt < x̲áx̲e.
mountain above Esilao, Siwash Creek Mountain:: Aseláw Smált < Aseláw.
Mount McGuire, (Tamihi Mountain [BJ]):: T'amiyahó:y < t'ámiya.
Promontory Mountain by Vedder Crossing:: Stitó:s ~ Stitó:s.
Sumas Mountain (also Tuckquail, a village on both sides of Lower Sumas River [Wells]):: T'ex̲qé:yl or T'ex̲qí:l < t'éx̲.
the whole Agassiz (B.C.) area (JL), Agassiz Mountain (AK), place near Agassiz where Hamersley Hopyards were (possibly some other speakers):: Alámex.
Three Creeks Mountain:: Lhelhxwáyeleq < lhí:xw.
village at east end of Little Mountain on Hope Slough, upper end of Mount Shannon [DM]:: Qwolíwiya or Ñwolíwiya.
village at west end of Little Mountain (Mount Shannon) on Hope Slough, also a name for Hope Slough or Hope River:: Sqwá:la < qwá.
village on both sides of Liumchen Creek, Liumchen Creek, Liumchen Mountain:: Loyú:mthel ~ Loyúmthel.
Yale Mountain:: Popelehó:ys.

mountain

a cracked mountain where the pipeline crosses the Fraser River between Hope and Agassiz:: Sisíq' < séq'.
a fairly flat clearing on a mountain in Morris Valley where they used to play ts'its'eqweló:l or Indian badminton:: Ts'éqwela ~ Th'éqwela < ts'éqw ~ th'éqw.
a lumpy mountain back of Seabird Island:: Sqwemqwómx̲w < qwó:m ~ qwóm ~ qwem.
a mountain above Evangeline Pete's place at Katz:: Sesíq' < séq'.
a mountain facing Chilliwack and adjacent to Mt. Cheam, theoldest sister of Lhílheqey (Mount Cheam):: Oló:xwelwet.
a mountain just south of Yale Mountain (Popelehó:ys) with a big hole like a tunnel in it above the highway at Yale:: Tekwóthel ~ Tkwóthel.
base of mountain or something high:: shxw'étselets < áthelets.
bring oneself to a summit (of a mountain):: wets'á:lómet < ts'á:.
burnt mountain across from American Bar:: Syíyeqw < yéqw.
climb a mountain, climb a hill, go up a mountain or hill:: kw'íyeqel < kw'í ~ kw'íy.
face of a mountain:: =ó:s ~ =ós ~ =es.
getting to the summit of a mountain:: hewts'á: < ts'á:.
get to the top or summit of a mountain:: wets'á: < ts'á:.
Granite Mountain, the second mountain back of X̲óletsa, northwest of Kwelkwelqéylem:: Th'emth'ómels < th'óméls.
heart-shaped mountain on the CN (south) side of the Fraser River east of Mt. Cheam:: Th'áth'ele < th'á:lá ~ th'ála ~ th'á:le ~ th'ále.
little stone, pebble, little rock hill, small rock mountain (like in the Fraser River in the canyon):: smámelet < smá:lt.
mountain across the Fraser River from American Bar:: Qw'íywelh or Qw'éywelh.

mountain (CONT'D)

mountain behind (west of) Tkwóthel near Yale (on the CPR side):: Lewóxwemey or Lewóx̲wemey.

mountain in back of Restmore Lodge (or some say way back of Mt. Cheam):: Smímkw' < mékw' ~ mṓkw'.

mountain [north] across from Lizzie Johnson's place on Seabird Island:: X̲ax̲esxélem < x̲ésxel.

mountain on Fraser River between first tunnel and Yale where rotten fish used to (always) pile up:: Lexwyó:qwem Smá:lt < yó:qw.

mountain on the west (C.P.R.) side of the Fraser River above American Bar which had a steaming pond at the top, (year-round village at mouth of American Creek on west bank of the Fraser River [Duff]):: Qétex̲em < qá:t.

mountain right back of Yale town reserve with two big lakes and many small ones:: X̲ó:letsa Smá:lt < x̲ó:tsa ~ x̲ó:cha.

mountain shaped like a thunderbird across the Fraser River from Q'ów (the "howl") mountain:: Xwexwó:stel < shxwexwó:s.

mountain west of Ñó:letsa, (mountain north of Sése (Mary Ann Creek), shortcut to Ñó:letsa [Elders Group (Fish Camp 9/29-31/77)]):: Tl'átl'eq'xélém < tl'aq' ~ tl'q'.

mountain with caves that is behind Hunter Creek (in 1976-1977 they blasted this mountain where it was beside Trans-Canada Highway #1 to shorten the highway past it):: Tómtomiyeqw.

name of the first mountain northwest of Ñó:letsa Smá:lt (Ñó:letsa Smá:lt a mountain with Frozen Lake as one of several lakes on it):: Kwelkwelqéylém < kwelqéylém ~ kwelqílém.

next mountain above (north/upriver from) Títxwemqsel (Wilson's Point or Grouse Point), possibly Elbow Lake mountain [north of Harrison Mills, on west side of the Harrison River], Willoughby's Point [opposite Lhá:lt, but does this mean across Harrison R. as I first thought and show on the topographic map "Harrison Lake 92H/5" where I have pencilled in all Chehalis place names) or does it mean on the opposite, i.e. south end of the same bay where Lhá:lt starts, i.e. both on the west side of Harrison R. as are Títxwemqsel and Elbow Lake mountain?]:: Kw'íkw'exwelhp < kw'íxw.

peak of mountain:: sq'eyth'éleqw.

place on mountain above Ruby Creek where there's lots of boulders all over the mountain lined up in rows:: Thíthesem < thi ~ tha ~ the ~ thah ~ theh.

point of geog. features like island or mountain or land:: =eqs ~ =éqsel ~ =élqsel ~ =elqs.

small sharp mountain high above Ñelhálh and across the Fraser River from Yale:: Mómet'es < mót'es.

stone, rock (any size), mountain:: smá:lt.

the mountain above Suka Creek:: Skwíyò Smált < Skwíyò.

the summit (of a mountain):: swets'a'á < ts'á:.

third mountain behind Ñó:letsa and northwest of Th'emth'ómels:: Tskwím Smált < kwí:m.

throat of a cliff or mountain:: =eqel.

unnamed mountain on the northwest side of the Fraser River between Hope and Yale which has white mineral deposits visible from the river:: Lexwp'ép'eq'es < p'éq'.

Wahleach Bluff, a lookout mountain with rock sticking out over a bluff, also the lookout point on Agassiz Mountain:: Kw'okw'echíwel < kw'áts ~ kw'éts.

mountain ash

mountain ash berries, (perhaps also) mountain ash tree:: qwíqwelh.

mountainside

an area up the mountainside from Ñwox̲welálhp (Yale):: Chelqwílh ~ Chelqwéylh < chá:l or chó:l.

Mount Amadis
  Cultus Lake Mountain, actually Mount Amadis or International Ridge:: Swílhcha Smá:lt < Swílhcha.

Mount Baker:: Kwelxá:lxw < kwél.

Mount Cheam)
  a mountain facing Chilliwack and adjacent to Mt. Cheam, theoldest sister of Lhílheqey (Mount Cheam):: Oló:xwelwet.
  another small peak just to the right of the Mount Cheam summit peak as one faces south, she is another daughter of Lhílheqey (Mt. Cheam):: S'óyewòt < Óyewòt.
  other sister of Lhílheqey or Mount Cheam:: Ts'símteló:t < ts'ísem.
  smallest peak just below Mount Cheam (on left of Mt. Cheam looking south), Lhílheqey's (Mt. Cheam's) baby (located about where her breast would be on the left hand side facing her):: Óyewòt.
  small peak next to Mount Cheam:: X̲emó:th'iya < x̲à:m ~ x̲á:m.
  youngest sister of Lhílheqey (Mount Cheam) that cries:: Ñemó:th'iya < x̲à:m ~ x̲á:m.

Mount McGuire
  Mount McGuire, (Tamihi Mountain [BJ]):: T'amiyahó:y < t'ámiya.

Mount Ogilvie:: Qemqemó < qemó:.
  Mount Ogilvie or a round peak or bluff on Mt. Ogilvie where mountain goats live, the mountain or peak or bluff resembles big breasts:: Qwemth'í:les < qwó:m ~ qwóm ~ qwem.

Mount Shannon
  village at east end of Little Mountain on Hope Slough, upper end of Mount Shannon [DM]:: Qwolíwiya or Ñwolíwiya.
  village at west end of Little Mountain (Mount Shannon) on Hope Slough, also a name for Hope Slough or Hope River:: Sqwá:la < qwá.

Mount Woodside)
  Agassiz Mountain (or more likely Mount Woodside):: Sqwehíwel < qwá.

mourn
  headband, headband made out of cedar bark woven by widow or widower when mourning:: qítes ~ qéytes < qít.

mouse
  a few mice:: kw'elókw't'el < kw'át'el.
  (mice) chewing (a wall, box, etc.):: ts'átxwels ~ ch'átxwels.
  mouse, probably includes at least: white-footed deer mouse, cascade deer mouse, and the post-contact house mouse, respectively:: kw'át'el.
  northwest jumping mouse:: sétsetets.
  rat, vole (short-tailed mouse), may include any or all of the following which occur in this area: creeping vole, long-tail vole, mountain heather vole, boreal redback vole, Norway rat (intro.), and perhaps roof rat, also includes bushy-tailed wood rat (packrat) which has its own name below:: há:wt.
  squeaking (of lots of mice):: th'eth'elá:ykwem < th'á:ykwem.
  squeak (of a mouse):: th'á:ykwem.

mouth :: thó:thel ~ thóthel.
  a little below the mouth of a creek or slough:: chichewóthel < cháchew ~ cháchu.
  cut on the mouth:: lhts'ó:ythel < lhíts' ~ lhí:ts'.

mouth (CONT'D)

Fraser River (way out at the end), mouth of the Fraser River:: Chuchuwálets < cháchew ~ cháchu.
(go) wash one's mouth out:: th'ex̲wqéylem or th'ex̲wqílem < th'éx̲w or th'óx̲w, th'x̲woythílem < th'éx̲w or th'óx̲w.
(have a) big mouth:: thehó:ythel < thi ~ tha ~ the ~ thah ~ theh, xwthó:thel < thi ~ tha ~ the ~ thah ~ theh.
(have a) quick mouth:: x̲weméthel < x̲wém ~ xwém.
have a round mouth:: kwamó:ythel < kwá:m ~ kwám.
(have a) twisted mouth, twisted jaw:: pó:yethel < pó:y.
(have the) mouth round and open with rounded lips:: sqwoqwtó:ythel < qwá.
(have) trench mouth:: qw'eléqel.
hit on the mouth, [hit on the chin, hit on the lip, hit on the jaw]:: kw'qwó:ythel < kw'óqw.
liquid in the mouth:: qe'ó:ythel < qó:.
make one's mouth like one's going to cry:: pespesó:ythílem < pas ~ pes.
mouth of Weaver Creek:: Lhemqwó:tel < lhém.
mouth open:: xixq'á:m ~ xixq'ám < xáq'.
on the mouth, in the mouth:: =ó:thel ~ =(e)thel.
opening one's mouth:: xáxeq'em < xáq'.
open one's mouth:: xáq'em < xáq'.
put s-th between the teeth, put it in one's mouth, bite on s-th (not into it):: ts'ámet ~ ch'ámet.
roof of the mouth, inside of upper lip, palate:: chelhqí:l ~ chelhqéyl < =chílh ~ chílh=.
shut your mouth, (shut one's mouth):: t'ekwó:ythí:lem < t'ékw.
skin of the mouth, (prob. also skin of the chin or jaw or lips):: kw'elōwó:ythel < kw'eléw ~ kw'elṓw.
ugly expression in mouth, ugly grin:: sx̲eyx̲eth'ó:ythel < x̲íth' ~ x̲éyth'.
wide place at the mouth of the east (upriver) branch of Jones Creek:: Swílth'.
you get covered on the mouth (by a flying squirrel at night for ex.):: qep'ó:ythòm < qep'.

mouthwash:: th'ex̲wílésem < th'éx̲w ~ th'óx̲w.

move

bump, get hit by something moving (for ex. by a car):: tós.
group of canoes travelling upstream (moving to camp for fish-drying for ex.):: istéytiyel.
hurry, hurry up, be quick, be fast, move faster, quickly:: x̲wém ~ xwém.
move, move itself, move oneself:: kwíyx̲thet < kwíyx̲.
move over:: sex̲éylem or sex̲ílem < síx̲.
move s-th:: kwíyx̲t < kwíyx̲.
move s-th over:: síx̲et < síx̲.
moving, (many moving around in circles, moving around in circles many times):: x̲elx̲álqem < x̲álqem.
moving, moving oneself/itself:: kwó:yxthet ~ kwó:yex̲thet ~ kwó:yxethet < kwíyx̲.
moving (one's residence):: seló:lh < ó:lh.
rolling, moving [around in circles]:: x̲álqem.
(shaking, quaking, moving oneself):: qwíyx̲thet < qwá:y.
to back up (walk or move backwards):: yóthet.
to hurry, hurry up, move fast:: ówthet < áwth.
to move:: kwíyx̲.
travelling by, in motion, while moving along, while travelling along:: ye= ~ yi= ~ i┐.
(travelling/moving) stooped over:: yeq'pó:s (prob. error or variant for yeqp'ó:s) < qep'.
(while) travelling along, in motion:: ye=.
widen it, move it wider:: léx̲et < léx̲.

Mt. Cheam :: Lhílheqey.

Mt. MacFarlane Creek:: possibly Chéchem.

much
 be how much money?:: kw'í:les ~ kw'íles < kw'í:l ~ kw'íl.
 be many, be a lot of, lots of, much:: qéx̲.
 too (overly), very much:: we'ól ~ ól(e)we ~ ólew < òl ~ -òl ~ -ò ~ el.

mud :: st'ekwt'ékw < t'ékw, sth'íth'eqel < sth'í:qel.
 get stuck in the mud, get mired, be mired, get muddy:: t'ékw.
 muddy:: t'ékwt'ekw < t'ékw, th'íth'eqel < sth'í:qel.
 mud, wet mud:: sth'í:qel.
 spotted with irregular shaped blobs (like if mud-spattered, used of dogs, deer, and other animals so marked):: st'á:lq.
 suction sound of feet pulling out of mud:: t'áxwqem.

muddy
 next slough on north side of Harrison River above (east of) Smímstíyexwá:le, a muddy slough where fish spawn, right across from Johnny Leon's place at Chehalis and about 100 yards downstream (west) of Yálhxetel:: Mímex̲wel (or prob. better, Mímexwel) < mímexwel.

Mudge
 Yuculta Kwakiutl people, southern Kwakiutl people from Cape Mudge north who raided the Salish people:: Yéqwelhtax̲ ~ Yéqwelhta.

mule :: miyúl.

Mum
 Mother (the speaker's), Mom, Mum: tátel < tá:l ~ tà:l ~ tál

murder
 got murdered:: skwálṓws < kwà:l.
 murdering, murderer (of more than one):: kwókwelōws ~ kwókwelews < kwà:l.
 murder s-o:: kwelkwálówst ~ kwelkwáléwst < kwà:l.
 to murder:: kwáléws ~ kwálṓws < kwà:l, kwelkwálóws ~ kwelkwáléws < kwà:l.

Musca autumnalis
 family Muscidae, Musca domestica and prob. Musca autumnalis:: x̲wex̲wiyáye ~ x̲wix̲wiyáye < x̲wōx̲wáye ~ x̲wex̲wáye ~ x̲wōx̲wá:ye.

Musca domestica
 family Muscidae, Musca domestica and prob. Musca autumnalis:: x̲wex̲wiyáye ~ x̲wix̲wiyáye < x̲wōx̲wáye ~ x̲wex̲wáye ~ x̲wōx̲wá:ye.

Muscidae
 family Muscidae, Musca domestica and prob. Musca autumnalis:: x̲wex̲wiyáye ~ x̲wix̲wiyáye < x̲wōx̲wáye ~ x̲wex̲wáye ~ x̲wōx̲wá:ye.

muscle
 cord, muscle, tendon, nerve cord by backbone:: tl'e'ímél ~ tl'e'í:mel.

muscle (CONT'D)
(have/get) sore muscles:: q'éyq'ey ~ q'íq'i < q'ey ~ q'i.
tighten up (tense one's muscles, for ex.):: tl'ótl'ethet < tl'óth'et.

mushroom
big all-white edible mushroom:: q'ém:és ~ q'ém:es.
giant horsetail, also common horsetail, (mushroom [AC]):: x̲émx̲em.

music :: =ó:ythel ~ =eyéthel ~ =eyth(íl).
flute, wind instrument, blown musical instrument:: pepó:tem < pó:t.
(month beginning in) March, ((birds) making music):: qweloythí:lem < qwà:l.
musical instrument, grammophone, phonograph, record player:: qweló:ythetel ~ qwelóyethetel < qwà:l.
playing a musical instrument:: qwiqwelóythetel < qwà:l.

musical instrument
flute, wind instrument, blown musical instrument:: pepó:tem < pó:t.

muskrat :: sq'élhq'elh.

Mus musculus domesticus
Peromyscus maniculatus, Peromyscus oreas, and Mus musculus domesticus:: kw'át'el.

Musqueam
a village or place at Musqueam (now in Vancouver):: Málí.

Musqueam village:: Xwméthkwiyem.

mussel
clam, butter clam, fresh-water clam, fresh-water mussel:: s'óx̲we.

must
maybe, I guess, I'm uncertain, must be (evidently), (evidential), have to (I guess):: t'wa ~ t'we.

mustache
hair on the chin or jaw, beard, mustache:: qwiliyéthel < qwíl ~ qwel.

Mustela erminea (fallenda and invicta)
Mustela erminea (fallenda and invicta) and Mustela frenata (altifrontalis and nevadensis):: lhets'á:m.

Mustela frenata (altifrontalis and nevadensis)
Mustela erminea (fallenda and invicta) and Mustela frenata (altifrontalis and nevadensis):: lhets'á:m.

Mustela vison energumenos:: chachí:q'el, sqáyéx̲ ~ sqayéx̲.

my :: l ~ -l ~ -el.
my, first person singular possessive pronoun, first person subordinate subject:: -el ~ -l ~ l.

my goodness.
oh my goodness.:: qélémèx ~ ő qèlèmèx ~ ló qèlèmèx.

my gosh.
  oh my gosh.:: éyelew < éy ~ éy:.

myotis
  bat, may include any/all of the following which occur in the Stó:lō area: western big-eared bat, big brown bat, silver-haired bat, hoary bat, California myotis, long-eared myotis, little brown myotis, long-legged myotis, Yuma myotis, and possibly the keen myotis:: p'íp'eth'elàx̲el ~ p'ip'eth'eláx̲el < p'í:.
  may include any or all of the following (all of which occur in the area): western big-eared bat, big brown bat, silver-haired bat, hoary bat, California myotis, long-eared myotis, little brown myotis, long-legged myotis, Yuma myotis, and possibly the keen myotis, respectively:: skw'elyáx̲el.

Myotis californicus caurinus
  Corynorhinus townsendi townsendi, Eptesicus fuscus bernardinus, Lasionycteris noctivagans, Lasiurus cinereus, Myotis californicus caurinus, Myotis evotis pacificus, Myotis lucifugus alascensis, Myotis volans longicrus, Myotis yumanensis saturatus, and possibly Myotis keeni keeni:: skw'elyáx̲el.
  order Chiroptera, family Vespertilionidae, may include any or all of the following: Corynorhinus townsendi townsendi, Eptesicus fuscus bernardinus, Lasionycteris noctivagans, Lasiurus cinereus, Myotis californicus caurinus, Myotis evotis pacificus, Myotis lucifugus alascensis, Myotis volans longicrus, Myotis yumanensis saturatus, and possibly Myotis keeni keeni:: p'íp'eth'elàx̲el ~ p'ip'eth'eláx̲el < p'í:.

Myotis evotis pacificus
  Corynorhinus townsendi townsendi, Eptesicus fuscus bernardinus, Lasionycteris noctivagans, Lasiurus cinereus, Myotis californicus caurinus, Myotis evotis pacificus, Myotis lucifugus alascensis, Myotis volans longicrus, Myotis yumanensis saturatus, and possibly Myotis keeni keeni:: skw'elyáx̲el.
  order Chiroptera, family Vespertilionidae, may include any or all of the following: Corynorhinus townsendi townsendi, Eptesicus fuscus bernardinus, Lasionycteris noctivagans, Lasiurus cinereus, Myotis californicus caurinus, Myotis evotis pacificus, Myotis lucifugus alascensis, Myotis volans longicrus, Myotis yumanensis saturatus, and possibly Myotis keeni keeni:: p'íp'eth'elàx̲el ~ p'ip'eth'eláx̲el < p'í:.

Myotis keeni keeni
  Corynorhinus townsendi townsendi, Eptesicus fuscus bernardinus, Lasionycteris noctivagans, Lasiurus cinereus, Myotis californicus caurinus, Myotis evotis pacificus, Myotis lucifugus alascensis, Myotis volans longicrus, Myotis yumanensis saturatus, and possibly Myotis keeni keeni:: skw'elyáx̲el.
  order Chiroptera, family Vespertilionidae, may include any or all of the following: Corynorhinus townsendi townsendi, Eptesicus fuscus bernardinus, Lasionycteris noctivagans, Lasiurus cinereus, Myotis californicus caurinus, Myotis evotis pacificus, Myotis lucifugus alascensis, Myotis volans longicrus, Myotis yumanensis saturatus, and possibly Myotis keeni keeni:: p'íp'eth'elàx̲el ~ p'ip'eth'eláx̲el < p'í:.

Myotis lucifugus
  Corynorhinus townsendi townsendi, Eptesicus fuscus bernardinus, Lasionycteris noctivagans, Lasiurus cinereus, Myotis californicus caurinus, Myotis evotis pacificus, Myotis lucifugus alascensis, Myotis volans longicrus, Myotis yumanensis saturatus, and possibly Myotis keeni keeni:: skw'elyáx̲el.
  order Chiroptera, family Vespertilionidae, may include any or all of the following: Corynorhinus townsendi townsendi, Eptesicus fuscus bernardinus, Lasionycteris noctivagans, Lasiurus cinereus, Myotis californicus caurinus, Myotis evotis pacificus, Myotis lucifugus alascensis, Myotis volans longicrus, Myotis yumanensis saturatus, and possibly Myotis keeni keeni:: p'íp'eth'elàx̲el ~ p'ip'eth'eláx̲el < p'í:.

Myotis lucifugus alascensis
   Corynorhinus townsendi townsendi, Eptesicus fuscus bernardinus, Lasionycteris noctivagans, Lasiurus cinereus, Myotis californicus caurinus, Myotis evotis pacificus, Myotis lucifugus alascensis, Myotis volans longicrus, Myotis yumanensis saturatus, and possibly Myotis keeni keeni:: skw'elyáx̲el.
   order Chiroptera, family Vespertilionidae, may include any or all of the following: Corynorhinus townsendi townsendi, Eptesicus fuscus bernardinus, Lasionycteris noctivagans, Lasiurus cinereus, Myotis californicus caurinus, Myotis evotis pacificus, Myotis lucifugus alascensis, Myotis volans longicrus, Myotis yumanensis saturatus, and possibly Myotis keeni keeni:: p'íp'eth'elàx̲el ~ p'ip'eth'eláx̲el < p'í:.

Myotis volans longicrus
   Corynorhinus townsendi townsendi, Eptesicus fuscus bernardinus, Lasionycteris noctivagans, Lasiurus cinereus, Myotis californicus caurinus, Myotis evotis pacificus, Myotis lucifugus alascensis, Myotis volans longicrus, Myotis yumanensis saturatus, and possibly Myotis keeni keeni:: skw'elyáx̲el.
   order Chiroptera, family Vespertilionidae, may include any or all of the following: Corynorhinus townsendi townsendi, Eptesicus fuscus bernardinus, Lasionycteris noctivagans, Lasiurus cinereus, Myotis californicus caurinus, Myotis evotis pacificus, Myotis lucifugus alascensis, Myotis volans longicrus, Myotis yumanensis saturatus, and possibly Myotis keeni keeni:: p'íp'eth'elàx̲el ~ p'ip'eth'eláx̲el < p'í:.

Myotis yumanensis saturatus
   Corynorhinus townsendi townsendi, Eptesicus fuscus bernardinus, Lasionycteris noctivagans, Lasiurus cinereus, Myotis californicus caurinus, Myotis evotis pacificus, Myotis lucifugus alascensis, Myotis volans longicrus, Myotis yumanensis saturatus, and possibly Myotis keeni keeni:: skw'elyáx̲el.
   order Chiroptera, family Vespertilionidae, may include any or all of the following: Corynorhinus townsendi townsendi, Eptesicus fuscus bernardinus, Lasionycteris noctivagans, Lasiurus cinereus, Myotis californicus caurinus, Myotis evotis pacificus, Myotis lucifugus alascensis, Myotis volans longicrus, Myotis yumanensis saturatus, and possibly Myotis keeni keeni:: p'íp'eth'elàx̲el ~ p'ip'eth'eláx̲el < p'í:.

myself
   me myself, I myself (emphatic):: ta'á'altha < áltha ~ álthe.

Mysticeti
   perhaps generic, most likely includes all local balleen whales, i.e., suborder Mysticeti, especially Balaenoptera physalus and Megaptera novaeangliae, possibly Eschrichtius glaucus, Balaenoptera borealis, Balaenoptera acutorostrata, Sibbaldus musculus, Eubalaena sieboldi, could include the following toothed whales (suborder Odontoceti): Physeter catodon, possibly Berardius bairdi, Mesoplodon stejnegeri, Ziphius cavirostrus:: qwél:és ~ qwélés.

nail
   a metal nail:: th'éstel < th'ís.
   fingernail, nail of finger, claw:: qw'ex̲wéltses.
   hang s-th on a line, hang s-th on a nail, hang s-th up:: q'é:ywet (or better) q'í:wet < q'e:yw ~ q'í:w.
   hang s-th (on a nail or hat hanger), hook it back on (of a stitch lost in knitting):: ókw'est < ókw'.
   nail it:: th'íset < th'ís.
   nail s-th, hammer s-th:: hám:et.
   pull out a nail, (pull it out (a metal nail)):: th'ót.
   sticking out through a hole (like a toe out of a sock, knee out of a hole in pants, a nail

nail (CONT'D)

driven clear through the other side of a board), come out into the open:: qwōhóls (or perhaps) qwehóls < qwá.

toenail:: qw'x̲wélxel.

nail clippers:: shxwth'ámqels qw'x̲wéltses/qw'x̲wélches (lit. "scissors for the fingernails") < xwáth', qw'ex̲w.

nail polish:: siyátl'qels te qw'x̲wéltses (lit' "paint for the fingernail") < yétl', qw'ex̲w.

naked

be naked:: lhewíth'a.

name

Beaver (name in a story):: Qelá:wiya < sqelá:w.
female name:: =elhót, =elò:t ~ =eló:t, =emòt, =ewòt, =òt ~ =ò:t.
female name (garment):: =elwet ~ =élwet.
get s-o's name, manage to get s-o's name:: kwíxelexw ~ kwéxwelexw < kwí:x ~ kwíx.
girl's younger brother (pet name):: iyá:q, iyá:q.
Grandma, Father's Mother (nickname):: táta < tá:l ~ tà:l ~ tál.
grandmother (pet name), grandfather (pet name), granny, grandpa:: sísele < sí:le.
Indian name of Old Jack (of Yakweakwioose or perhaps Scowkale):: T'eláqw'tel < t'álqw' or t'élqw'.
knee (naming it, the name of it):: qep'ó:lthetel < qep'.
male name:: =elácha, =elálexw ~ =elàlèx̲w, =eleq, =éylém ~ =ílém, =iyetel, =thet.
male name, (prob.) repeatedly gets wives/houses:: =ímeltxw.
male name version of Olóxwelwet:: Olóxwiyetel < Oló:xwelwet.
Mink (name in some stories):: sqáyéx̲ ~ sqayéx̲.
Mink (name in stories), pet name of Mink:: Sqayéx̲iya ~ Sqáyèx̲iya < sqáyéx̲ ~ sqayéx̲.
name of a fierce old warrior from Sumas, an ancestor of the Commodore family:: Qwá:l < qwá:l.
name of a man from Yale who had seven wives:: Líqwetem < líqw.
name of an old man from Kilgard who was a strong warrior (fighter):: X̲éyteleq < x̲éyet.
name of Chief Albert Louie's father:: T'íxwelátse ~ Tíxwelátsa.
name s-o (in a ceremony):: kwíxet < kwí:x ~ kwíx.
naming:: kwexáls < kwí:x ~ kwíx.
nickname:: kwekwxá:mel < kwí:x ~ kwíx.
nickname for someone who is proud:: slék'.
nickname of Freddie Joe:: sépelets.
now also the name of Ambrose Silver:: Ñéyteleq < x̲éyet.
personal name:: skwí:x ~ skwíx < kwí:x ~ kwíx.
pet name:: =R1= or =C1e=.
place-name, name of a place:: kwxő:mexw < kwí:x ~ kwíx.
Pussy Willow (name in stories):: Qweqwemeytá:ye < qwem.
Skunk (name in story):: S'épek ~ Í'pek ~ S'í'pek < sth'épeq.
Who are they naming?:: tewát kw'e kwíkwexetem < kwí:x ~ kwíx.
Who was named?:: tewát kw'e kwíxetem < kwí:x ~ kwíx.
younger sibling (pet name):: ká:k ~ kyá:ky < sqá:q.

naming ceremony:: skwíkwexetem < kwí:x ~ kwíx.

nape

neck, (back of head and back of neck [EB], nape of the neck [Elders Group 5/3/78]):: tépsem.

nape (CONT'D)

skin of the nape of the neck:: kw'elōwépsem < kw'eléw ~ kw'elṓw.

narrow

(be) narrow:: qweqwís.
canyon (narrow, walled in with rock):: sx̲ex̲ákw' < x̲ékw'.
close together, (narrow? [MV]):: tl'éts' < tl'í:ts'.
it gets narrow or wedged in:: x̲ékw'.
narrow (of rocky passage):: x̲eq'.
nervous while walking on something narrow:: x̲wix̲wíyem.
place in Fraser River two miles above American Bar with narrow rock:: X̲eq'átelets < x̲eq'.
three ropes, three threads, three sticks, three poles, (three long narrow objects):: lhxwámeth' < lhí:xw.

Nat

nickname for Nat Dickinson:: Pepx̲wíqsel < píxw.

Natantia

suborder Natantia, probably Crago and other genera, especially Crago vulgaris, Pandalus danae were identified by AD from a photo as the kind AD's parents got dried from the Chinese and called by this name:: homò:y.

naughty

be naughty, be bad (a menace) (but not quite as bad as qél):: qíqel < qél.

nauseated :: héyetélmel < yá:t.

navel

belly-button, navel:: mṓx̲woya ~ mṓx̲weya ~ méx̲weya.
ruptured belly button, ruptured navel:: lhéx̲welòw < lhex̲w.

near

approach, get near, get closer, reach, go up to, get up to:: tés.
approaching, getting near, getting closer:: tetés < tés.
be near, be close to, be beside, be next to:: stetís < tés.
(be) near me:: stetisthóx ~ stetísthó:x < tés.
come close, come near, come sit in (with a group):: teséthet ~ tséthet < tés.
come near me, (sic? for make me get near):: tesésthòx < tés.
come near s-o, (come to s-o):: emíls < mí ~ mé ~ me.
get close, approach, get near, nearly, (go close, come close):: ts'ímél ~ ts'ímel.
near neighbors:: ts'ellhxwílmexw < ts'elh=.
the (female, near but not visible), (female, near but not in sight) (translated by gender specific words in English, like aunt, etc.):: kwse < kw.
to the back (near the wall), on the inside (on a bed toward the wall):: lhelhá:l.

near but not in sight)

the (male or gender unspecified, near but not in sight):: kwthe < kw.

near but not visible)

him (there, near but not visible), that one:: kwethá ~ kwe thá < kw.

nearly

get close, approach, get near, nearly, (go close, come close):: ts'ímél ~ ts'ímel.

neck

a neck of land on the west side of Harrison Lake just north of Twenty-Mile Creek and across from the north tip of Long Island:: Shxwtépsem < tépsem.
break one's neck:: lekwépsem < lékw.
cleft in back of the neck:: t'ayéq'psem < t'ay.
clubbed on the back of the neck, clubbed on the back of the head:: kw'qwépsem < kw'óqw.
fin, neck fin, i.e. pectoral fin:: q'étmel.
front of the neck:: shxw'állhelh.
(have a) big neck:: thahápsem < thi ~ tha ~ the ~ thah ~ theh.
(have a) long neck:: tl'éqtepsem < tl'áqt.
(have a) small neck, (have a) scrawny neck:: qwe'íqwepsem < qwe'íqw.
large red-necked woodpecker, large red-headed woodpecker, rain crow (black with red comb on head) (AC), pileated woodpecker:: temélhépsem < témélh.
neck, (back of head and back of neck [EB], nape of the neck [Elders Group 5/3/78]):: tépsem.
neck of land:: =épsem.
on the back of the head, back of the neck:: =épsem.
on the front of the neck, in the windpipe, in the trachea:: =lhelh ~ =lhál.
put a rope around s-o/s-th's neck, put a leash on s-th, hang s-o:: x̲wíqw'est < x̲wíqw'.
skin of the nape of the neck:: kw'elōwépsem < kw'eléw ~ kw'elṓw.

neckerchief

scarf, neckerchief:: sx̲wéqw'lhelh < x̲wíqw'.

necklace :: sx̲wéqw'ellhelh < x̲wíqw'.
belt, (necklace?? [DM]):: shxwyémtel ~ shxwiyémtel < yém ~ yem.

need

going to piss right away, almost piss oneself, (have an urgent or extreme or painful need to urinate):: ts'áléqel.
lack, need:: =le or =ele.
want, desire, like, need:: stl'í ~ stl'í: < tl'í ~ tl'í:.

needle

fine needles of hoarfrost on a branch:: pú:ches ~ púwches, pú:ches ~ púwches < pí:w.
fir boughs, needle of any other conifer than spruce:: qwélatses.
needle (for sewing cloth, for mat-making):: p'éth'tel < p'áth'.
needle of plant, (thorn):: p'éth'tel < p'áth'.
needle of spruce:: ts'ets'éqw' < ts'éqw'.

Negro :: q'éyx̲eya < q'íx̲, qw'íx̲wes < qw'íx̲w.
small Negro:: qw'íqw'x̲wes < qw'íx̲w.

neighbor :: ts'élhxwélmexw < ts'elh=.
near neighbors:: ts'ellhxwílmexw < ts'elh=.

Neophasia menapia

if the name applies to one or more predominantly white butterflies it could include the following which occur in the Stó:lō area: family Papilionidae: Parnassius clodius, Parnassius phoebus, Papilio eurymedon, family Pieridae: Neophasia menapia, Pieris occidentalis, Pieris napi, albino females

Neophasia menapia (CONT'D)
of Colias erytheme:: p'ip'eq'eyós < p'éq'.

Neotoma cinerea occidentalis:: qélqel há:wt < há:wt.
may include any or all of the following which occur in this area: creeping vole Microtus oregoni serpens, long-tail vole Microtus longicaudus macrurus, mountain heather vole Phenacomys intermedius oramontis, boreal redback vole Clethrionomys gapperi cascadensis, Norway rat (intro.) Rattus norvegicus, and perhaps roof rat Rattus rattus, also includes bushy-tailed wood rat (packrat) Neotoma cinerea occidentalis which has its own name below:: há:wt.

nephew
nephew, niece, sibling's child (child of sister or brother or cousin (up to and including fourth cousin) [Elders Group]):: stí:wel.
nephews, nieces, sibling's children:: statí:wel < stí:wel.

nephrite)
jade (nephrite) (used for sharpening [chopping] stones), any agate (can be used as flint to strike a spark):: t'émq'ethel.

nerve
cord, muscle, tendon, nerve cord by backbone:: tl'e'ímél ~ tl'e'í:mel.

nervous
be afraid, be scared, be nervous:: sí:si < síy.
being nervous, being excited, (getting nervous/excited):: th'óyéx̲wem < th'ó:yx̲wem.
(get/become) nervous, (get/become) excited:: th'ó:yx̲wem.
nervous while walking on something narrow:: x̲wix̲wíyem.

-ness
be in a state of -ness:: =tem.

nest :: smìmelehollhála < méle ~ mél:a.

net
a dip-net, (a scoop net [CT]):: q'emó:stel < q'emós ~ q'emó:s.
a net is set, be set (of a net by canoe, not of a pole net):: semíliyel < mí:l ~ míl.
a set net, a stationary net:: semláliyel < mí:l ~ míl.
a waiting dip-net with frame and string trap:: thqálem < thqá:lem.
bag net, sack net:: lesák swéltel < swéltel.
check a net or trap (for animal):: kw'echú:yel < kw'áts ~ kw'éts.
check a net or trap (for fish):: kw'echú:yel < kw'áts ~ kw'éts.
coho net:: kwőxwethtel < kwőxweth.
dip-netting, fishing with a scoop net, (harpooning fish at night [DM 12/4/64]):: q'íq'emó:s ~ q'éyq'emó:s < q'emós ~ q'emó:s.
drifting a net in different places:: qwáseliyel < qwés.
drifting backwards in two canoes with net between to catch sturgeon, (drift-netting), backing up (of canoe, train):: tewláts.
drifting (drift-netting):: lhólhes < lhós.
drift-netting, catching fish with one or two canoes drifting downstream with a net in deep water:: xíxemel ~ xíxemal.
drop a net into water:: qwesú:yel < qwés.
eddy water (where you set nets), [to eddy repeatedly?]:: xwtitím or xwtiytím.

net (CONT'D)

float (for fishing net):: p'ekwtál < p'ékw.
gill net:: qwsá:yel < qwés.
grass or fibre for nets or twine, spreading dogbane, possibly also Indian hemp:: méthelh.
holding on to a thqálem, waiting dip-netting, still-dipping:: théqelem < thqá:lem.
horn rings for dip-nets:: x̲alwéla < x̲álew.
(hung up in a fish net):: sx̲wíx̲weqw' < x̲wíqw'.
net (any kind, for any purpose), fish net, gill-net (Elders Group 11/26/75)):: swéltel.
net (for ducks, fish):: swéltel.
net shuttle and net-measure, gill-net measure, (loom [Elders Group]):: t'élhtsestel < t'álh, t'élhtsestel < t'álh.
net shuttle, mesh-measure (usually part of the shuttle):: shxwq'éyq'esetsel < q'ey ~ q'i.
net, trap:: =á:yel ~ =iyel ~ =ú:yel.
patch s-th (of clothes, nets), patch s-th up:: p'ōwíyt ~ p'ewíyt < p'ewíy ~ p'ōwíy.
place where one fishes by waiting with a dip-net, dip-net fishing place, place where one still-dips:: sthqálem < thqá:lem.
set a net and drift with it:: qwsá:wiyel < qwés.
set a net (by canoe), set one's net, fish with a net, (submerge a net):: míliyel < mí:l ~ míl.
slough where people used to drift-net by Martin Harris's place at Seabird Island:: Titáwlechem < tewláts.
small float for nets (made from singed cedar):: qwōqwá:l ~ qweqwá:l.
sockeye net:: sthéqeytel < sthéqi ~ sthéqey.
spread it out (of blanket, net, book, etc.):: tlhét ~ tlhát ~ telhét < télh.
spring salmon net:: tl'elxéltel (or tl'elx̲xéltel) < tl'él.
throw a net into water (to drift, not to set), throw a net out, (gill net [TG]):: qwsá:yel < qwés.
to bag net, to sack net, to still-dip with two canoes:: thqá:lem.
to dip a net, (dipping a net):: qóqelets < qó:.
to dip-net:: q'emós ~ q'emó:s.
to dip-net, a dip-net:: qó:lets < qó:.
to drift-net, to fish with drift-net:: lhós.
to fasten s-th by tying, tie up s-th (like canoe, horse, laces, nets, cow, shoelaces), tie it:: q'éyset ~ q'í(:)set < q'ey ~ q'i.
to still-dip, rest dip-net on bottom (of river):: thqá:lem.
tying a net:: q'ésetsel < q'ey ~ q'i.
weaving (for ex. a tumpline), mending a net, making a net:: q'éyq'esetsel < q'ey ~ q'i.

net-measure
net shuttle and net-measure, gill-net measure, (loom [Elders Group]):: t'élhtsestel < t'álh.

nettle
stinging nettle:: th'éx̲th'ex̲ < th'éx̲.

Neurotrichus gibbsi
family Talpidae, especially Scapanus orarius orarius, also Neurotrichus gibbsi:: speláwél < pél (perhaps ~ pí:l by now).

never
it is impossible, it can't be, it never is:: skw'á:y < kw'á:y ~ kw'áy.
never did, he/she/they never did:: ṓwethelh < éwe ~ ṓwe.
never, not ever:: éwelh < éwe ~ ṓwe.
never used to:: ewá:lh ~ wá:lh < éwe ~ ṓwe.

never (CONT'D)

weren't ever?, wasn't ever?, didn't ever?, does s-o ever?, never used to, not going to (but did anyway) [perhaps in the sense of never usually do X but did this time]:: ewá:lh ~ wá:lh < éwe ~ őwe, ewá:lh ~ wá:lh < éwe ~ őwe.

never dry

puddle that's always dirty, dirty pond, stagnant pool of water, (it never dries out [AK]):: th'qwélhcha.

never used to:: ewá:lh ~ wá:lh < éwe ~ őwe.

never usually do X but did this time]

not going to (but did anyway), [perhaps in the sense of: never usually do X but did this time]:: ewá:lh ~ wá:lh < éwe ~ őwe.

new :: x̲á:ws.

babysitter (for new spirit-dancers), any of the workers who help in initiating a spirit-dancer, (initiator or helper of spirit-dancers):: xólhemìlh ~ xòlhemí:lh < xólh.

new dancer (new spirit-dancer), (new) baby (in spirit-dancing):: x̲awsó:lh < x̲á:ws.

new spirit-dancer:: x̲awsólkwlh or x̲awsó:lkwlh < x̲á:ws.

new information

anyway, ever, (new information as in NStraits):: kwá.

newlyweds)

to rattle (cans, etc. to wake newlyweds), to shivaree (someone):: q'etx̲áls < q'et.

news

cry of a bluejay [Steller's jay] that means good news:: q'ey, q'ey, q'ey.

(this cry of a bluejay [Steller's jay] warns you of bad news):: chéke chéke chéke chéke.

new spirit-dancer

new dancer (new spirit-dancer), (new) baby (in spirit-dancing):: x̲awsó:lh < x̲á:ws.

new spirit-dancer:: x̲awsólkwlh or x̲awsó:lkwlh < x̲á:ws.

new spirit dancer's cane:: q'ewú:w < q'éwe.

new spirit-dancer's head-dress or [cedar-bark] hat:: sx̲wóyéleqws te x̲awsólkwlh < sx̲wóyéleqw.

new spirit dancer's cane:: q'ewú:w < q'éwe.

new spirit-dancer's head-dress or [cedar-bark] hat:: sx̲wóyéleqws te x̲awsólkwlh < sx̲wóyéleqw.

newt

big gray rock lizard, probably Pacific giant salamander which is cognate in Squamish, possibly also the Pacific coast newt which is commonest in B.C. and also is found in this area, prob. also the northern alligator lizard:: seyíyex̲.

New Westminster:: Sx̲woyímelh < x̲wà:y ~ x̲wá:y.

Reserve near New Westminster, B.C., (South Westminster [DF]):: Qiqá:yt.

next

be near, be close to, be beside, be next to:: stetís < tés.

next, again:: atse.

person next to one:: stetísmels < tés.

nibble
  chewing with a crunch, nibbling, gnawing:: x̲áp'kw'els < x̲ep'ékw'.

nice
  be good, good, well, nice, fine, better, better (ought to), it would be good if, may it be good, let it be good, happy, glad, clean, well-behaved, polite, virgin, popular, comfortable (with furniture, other things?),:: éy ~ éy:.
  nice, well-behaved, good:: éy ~ éy:.

nick- :: =ó:mél ~ =á:mel.
  part, member, nick-:: =á:mel.

nickname :: kwekwxá:mel < kwí:x ~ kwíx.
  Grandma, Father's Mother (nickname):: táta < tá:l ~ tà:l ~ tál.
  Hank Pennier's nickname:: Swék'ten < swék'.
  little man (nickname for a person), (sonny boy (MV and DF)):: wíyeka < swíyeqe ~ swíyqe ~ swí:qe.
  nickname for Nat Dickinson:: Pepx̲wíqsel < píxw.
  nickname for someone who is proud:: slék'.
  nickname of Freddie Joe:: sépelets.
  nickname of Louie Punch:: Píx̲eya < píx̲eya.

Nicomen Island
  Nicomen Island (in the Fraser River near Deroche), also a specific place on northeast end of Nicomen Island where lots of people used to gather [now Sumas Indian Reserve #10]:: Leq'á:mél.

niece
  nephew, niece, sibling's child (child of sister or brother or cousin (up to and including fourth cousin) [Elders Group]):: stí:wel.
  nephews, nieces, sibling's children:: statí:wel < stí:wel.

night :: slá:t ~ slát < lá:t.
  a yellowish glow at night given off by old birch and alder:: qwéth'.
  Christmas Eve, night before Christmas:: X̲áx̲e Slát < x̲áx̲e.
  last night:: xweláltelh < lá:t.
  late in the night:: lhóp.

nighthawk
  common nighthawk, (rain bird [Elders Group]):: pí:q'.

nightmare
  have a nightmare, to sleep-walk:: píx̲eya.
  having a nightmare:: pepíx̲eya < píx̲eya.

nine :: tú:xw.
  nine birds:: tuxwíws < tú:xw.
  nine canoes, nine boats:: tuxwṓwelh < tú:xw.
  nine containers:: tuxwáleqel < tú:xw.
  nine dollars, (nine Indian blankets [Boas]):: tú:xwes < tú:xw.
  nine fish:: tuxwíqw < tú:xw.
  nine fruit in a group or cluster (as they grow on a plant):: tuxwòls < tú:xw.

nine (CONT'D)

nine o'clock:: stú:xws < tú:xw.
nine people:: tuxwále < tú:xw.
nine ropes, nine threads, nine sticks, nine poles:: tuxwámets' < tú:xw.
nine times:: tú:xwà:lh < tú:xw.
ninety:: tú:xwelsxá ~ tù:xwelsxá < tú:xw.

ninety

ninety:: tú:xwelsxá ~ tù:xwelsxá < tú:xw.
ninety dollars:: tú:xwelsxó:s < tú:xw.
ninety people:: tuxwelsxá:le < tú:xw.

nipple

breast, nipple, milk:: sqemó: < qemó:.

nit

nits, louse eggs:: x̱ést'el.

no

no, not be, be not:: éwe ~ őwe.
say no:: éwe ~ őwe, őwestexw ~ éwestexw < éwe ~ őwe.
shake one's head side to side (as in saying no):: kwíythesem.
shaking one's head side to side (as in saying no):: kwóythesem < kwíythesem.
there's none, there's nothing, there's nobody, there's no, be none, be nothing, be nobody:: ewéta < éwe ~ őwe.

nobody

there's none, there's nothing, there's nobody, there's no, be none, be nothing, be nobody:: ewéta < éwe ~ őwe.

Noctuidae

order Lepidoptera (esp. incl. grey moths of families Noctuidae, Geometridae, and Lymantriidae):: lholeqwót.

nod

nodding (falling asleep):: létqw'estem.
nodding one's head:: líleqwesem < líqw.
nod one's head, nod one's head (up and down for yes for ex.):: líqwesem < líqw, líqwesem < líqw.

no good

it's no good:: óx̱.
nuisance, something that's no good:: sqel:ép ~ sqél:ep < qél.

noise

(have/get) a rustling noise (not continuous) (of paper, silk, or other material), (to rustle):: sawéts'em.
make a crunching or crackling noise, crunching (gnawing) sound:: x̱ápkw'em < x̱ep'ékw'.
(make a) rumbling noise:: titómelest.
(make/have a) scratching noise:: t'lhóqw'els < t'élheqw' ~ t'lhóqw'.
make noise, be noisy, (a noise [EB], making noise [EB]):: ló:px̱wem.
make s-th be noisy, make noise with s-th:: lópx̱wemstexw < ló:px̱wem.

noise (CONT'D)

(making a) continuous rustling noise (of paper or silk or material), rustling (of leaves, paper, a sharp sound):: sá:wts'em < sawéts'em.
making noise:: lópex̲wem < ló:px̲wem, lópex̲wemstexw < ló:px̲wem.
sparking, sparkling, exploding with sparks and making sparky noises, making sparky noises:: pá:yts'em < páyéts'em.
splash (the noise and the action):: t'émeqw'.
to sigh (of a spirit-dancer), make a loud (breathy) noise:: xeqlhálém.
(to spark), explode with sparks and make sparky noises:: páyéts'em.

noisy

make noise, be noisy, (a noise [EB], making noise [EB]):: ló:px̲wem.
make s-th be noisy, make noise with s-th:: lópx̲wemstexw < ló:px̲wem.

no matter what

try to do something (no matter what, anyway):: iyálewethet < éy ~ éy:.

nominal

structured activity continuative, structured activity continuative nominal or tool or person:: =els.

(nominalizer):: s=, =em.

nominalizer (female present and visible or presence or proximity unspecified), demonstrative article:: the=.
nominalizer (male or gender unspecified, present and visible or presence or proximity unspecified), demonstrative article:: ta=, te=.
nominalizer plural:: ye=.
nominalizer, something for, someone for, something that:: shxw=.
nominalizer, something to, something that, someone to/that:: s=.

no more

ran out (of food, money, etc.), have no more, be finished (offood), (be empty (of container of supplies) [EB: Cheh., Tait]):: ő wkw'.

non-continuative

structured activity non-continuative:: =á:ls.

non-control

indirect effect non-control reflexive:: =methet.
indirect effect non-control transitivizer:: =met.
non-control reflexive, happen to or manage to or accidentally do to oneself:: =l=ómet or =l-ómet ~ =l=ó:met.
non-control reflexive, make oneself do something, keep oneself doing something:: =st=èlèmèt or =st-èlèmèt ~ =st-elómet.
non-control transitivizer, accidentally, happen to, manage to do to s-o/s-th:: =l.
psychological non-control transitivizer:: =eles ~ =les.

none

is there none?, isn't there any?:: wá:ta < éwe ~ őwe.
there's none, there's nothing, there's nobody, there's no, be none, be nothing, be nobody:: ewéta < éwe ~ őwe.

non-human)
    legs (more than two, for ex. non-human):: sx̲elx̲éyle < sx̲él:e.

non-spirit-dancer
    a non-spirit-dancer:: st'ólkwlh.
    non-spirit-dancers (lots of them):: st'elt'ólkwlh < st'ólkwlh.
    people without paint on face (non-spirit dancers):: s'ep'ó:s < á:p' ~ áp'.

non-spiritual dance
    having fun at a non-spiritual dance:: oyewílem.

non-subordinate subject)
    I (non-subordinate subject):: -tsel ~ (very rarely) -chel ~ tsel.
    subject of independent clause, non-subordinate subject:: ts- ~ ch-.
    we (non-subordinate subject), our:: -tset ~ -chet.

noodles:: ts'íyxw stotekwtíqw seplíl < ts'íyxw, tokwt, seplíl
(lit. dry + stringy hair + bread)

Nooksack
    Nooksack language:: Lhéchelesem
    Nooksack people:: Lexwsá:q < sá:q.

Nooksack River
    Deming (Wash.), South Fork of Nooksack River and village nearest Deming:: xwe'éyem ~ xw'éyem < éy ~ éy:.
    place in Whatcom County, Washington, (Nooksack River [AC or CT]):: Lexwsá:q < sá:q.

noon
    midday, noon:: téxwswàyel ~ texwswàyèl ~ texwswáyél < wáyel.

Nootka
    big high-bowed canoe from the Coast, Nootka war canoe, huge canoe:: q'ex̲wő:welh ~ q'ex̲wőwelh.

north
    north-east wind, north wind, east wind, cold wind:: só:tets.

northeast
    eight days of northeast wind:: unknown.
    four days of northeast wind:: unknown.
    north-east wind, north wind, east wind, cold wind:: só:tets.

nose :: méqsel.
    a stripe (on the nose or point):: sx̲élqs < x̲él ~ x̲é:yl ~ x̲í:l
    bleeding nose, (be/have bleeding in the nose):: sthxwélqsel < thóxw or théxw.
    bridge of nose:: sth'émqsel < hth'b.txt.
    canoe with shovel-nose at both ends, same as tl'elá:y:: sqwéthem < qweth.
    clean one's nose:: meqsélem < méqsel.
    cut off the tip of one's nose:: lhts'élqsel < lhíts' ~ lhí:ts'.
    edible gristle inside fish head (nose gristle):: sx̲épeqw (or sx̲ép'eqw? or sx̲ép'ekw'?).
    (get/have a) runny nose:: lhx̲wélqsel < lhex̲w.

nose (CONT'D)

- hair in the nose:: sqwelqwélqsel < qwíl ~ qwel.
- (have a) big nose:: sméqsel < méqsel.
- (have a) dirty nose:: ts'epx̲élqsel < ts'épx̲.
- (have a) flat nose:: sp'íp'elheqsel ~ sp'élhqsel < p'ílh.
- (have a) hook nose, beak nose, Roman nose, (be bent-nosed):: sqémqsel < qém.
- have a nose bleed:: thxwómélqsel < thóxw or théxw.
- (have a) scabby nose:: ts'eqw'élqsel < ts'éqw'.
- (have a) swollen nose:: chxwélqsel < chxw= ~ =chíxw.
- (have a) thin (point or nose):: qwe'íqweqs < qwe'íqw.
- (have) snot hanging from the nose:: slholh(e)x̲wélqsel < lhex̲w.
- having a nose bleed:: thóxwemélqsel < thóxw or théxw.
- Hook-nose, Hook-nose Mountain, Hamersly Hopyard Hill:: Lhílhkw'eleqs ~ Lhílhkw'elqs < lhíkw' ~ lhí:kw'.
- on the nose, in the nose:: =eqs ~ =éqsel ~ =élqsel ~ =elqs.
- punched on the nose:: th'qw'élqsel < th'í:qw'et.
- rock shaped like a man's nose on the north side of Harrison River:: Méqsel < méqsel.
- scraped on the nose:: x̲éyp'eqsel < x̲éyp'.
- stripes (on the nose or point):: sx̲élx̲elqs < x̲él ~ x̲é:yl ~ x̲í:l
- tip or point of one's nose:: s'álqsel.

no-see-um fly

- sand-fly, no-see-um fly, biting midge:: pxwíqs < píxw.

nose-ring :: shxweqw'élqstel.

no special use

- useless, no special use, ordinary:: ewétò shxwlís < shxwlí.

not

- isn't?, aren't?, don't?, doesn't?, (be not?):: ewá ~ ōwá ~ wá < éwe ~ őwe.
- never, not ever:: éwelh < éwe ~ őwe.
- no, not be, be not:: éwe ~ őwe.
- not cooked enough (of fish), [undercooked]:: lálekw'em.
- not yet be, be not yet:: xwewá < éwe ~ őwe.
- unless he, if he doesn't:: ewás < éwe ~ őwe.
- wasn't?, weren't?, didn't?:: ewá:lh ~ wá:lh < éwe ~ őwe.
- weren't ever?, wasn't ever?, didn't ever?, does s-o ever?, never used to, not going to (but did anyway) [perhaps in the sense of never usually do X but did this time]:: ewá:lh ~ wá:lh < éwe ~ őwe.

not accept

- discriminate against s-o, not accept s-o:: memí:lt < mí:lt.
- not accept s-o, discriminate against s-o:: memí:lt < mí:lt.
- not want s-o, not accept s-o, discriminate against s-o:: mí:lt.

not all there

- (be) stupid, not all there (mentally), (be) a little crazy:: shxwixwóxwth' < xwáth'.

not believe

- doubting s-o/s-th, be not believing s-o/s-th:: mameth'élexw < máth'el.
- doubt s-o, not believe s-th/s-o:: meth'éléxw < máth'el.

not care

not care about s-o, have no use for s-o, be impassive:: ewéta shxwlístexw < shxwlí.

not clear

(have/be) dirty water, (not clear, unclear, can't see the bottom (of water) [EL]):: mímexwel.

note

mark s-th, blaze it (of a trail), get/have s-th spotted (marked and located), make note of s-th:: x̲e'áth'stexw < x̲áth' ~ x̲e'áth'.

not ever

never, not ever:: éwelh < éwe ~ ṓwe.

not going to (but did anyway)

not going to (but did anyway), [perhaps in the sense of: never usually do X but did this time]:: ewá:lh ~ wá:lh < éwe ~ ṓwe.

nothing

there's none, there's nothing, there's nobody, there's no, be none, be nothing, be nobody:: ewéta < éwe ~ ṓwe.

notice

notice s-o/s-th:: qw'óqw'elhlexw < qw'ólh or qw'álh.

not in sight)

the (female, near but not visible), (female, near but not in sight) (translated by gender specific words in English, like aunt, etc.):: kwse < kw.

the (male or gender unspecified, near but not in sight):: kwthe < kw.

not know

not know how to:: sqe'íyeqel ~ sqe'í:qel.

not like

dislike s-o/s-th, to not like s-o/s-th:: qélstexw < qél.

not like s-th any more:: qelqélexw < qél.

not long ago

recently, just now, lately, (at one recent moment), not long ago:: qá:ys.

not matter

it doesn't matter, it's useless:: ōwéta xwlí:s < shxwlí.

not mind

insistant, persistant (like a child pressing to go along), bull-headed, doesn't mind, does just the opposite, (stubborn, contrary):: sxíxeles.

no to s-o

tell s-o to say no to s-o:: ṓwestexw ~ éwestexw < éwe ~ ṓwe.

not present)
  that's them (absent, not present):: kwthú:tl'òlem < kw.
  that's them (absent, not present), they (absent):: kwthú:tl'òlem < tl'ó ~ tl'o.

not showing
  (the) shade (of a tree for ex.), something that's not showing:: st'á:t'el < t'á:l.

not talkative
  be shy, be not talkative, quiet (of a person):: p'áp'xwem.

not talking)
  just listening (not talking):: xwlalá:.

not used
  part not used (like seeds of cantelope, core of apple, blood in fish, etc.), worst part:: sqéls < qél.

not visible)
  him (there, near but not visible), that one:: kwethá ~ kwe thá < kw.
  the (female, near but not visible), (female, near but not in sight) (translated by gender specific words in English, like aunt, etc.):: kwse < kw.
  the (present, not visible, gender unspecified), the (remote, abstract):: kwe < kw.
  the (remote, not visible, abstract), some (indefinite):: kw.

not want
  not want s-o:: mí:lt.
  not want s-o, not accept s-o, discriminate against s-o:: mí:lt.

no use
  not care about s-o, have no use for s-o, be impassive:: ewéta shxwlístexw < shxwlí.

November
  month or moon in November:: telxwíts.
  moon or month beginning in February, (November to December, time when ice forms [and sticks] [Billy Sepass in Jenness]):: temtl'í:q'es < tl'íq'.
  moon or month beginning in November, (put away each other's paddles), (sometimes the moon beginning in October, depending on the weather [Elders Group [3/12/75], (moon or month beginning in January [Elders Group 2/5/75]):: xets'ő:westel ~ xets'őwestel < xits' ~ xets'.
  November, time to catch salmon:: temth'ó:qwi < sth'ó:qwi ~ sth'óqwi.
  October to November, (wood gathering time):: tsélcheptel?.
  toward November:: telxwítsel < xwís.

now
  as usual, this time, now, the first time:: yalh.
  now I, (now I'm already):: tl'ékwálsulh < tl'ó ~ tl'o.
  now, this moment, this instant:: tloqá:ys < ló.
  now, this moment, this instant, (right now):: tloqá:ys < qá:ys.
  recently, just now, lately, (at one recent moment), not long ago:: qá:ys.

nuisance
  be rowdy, be a nuisance, be mischievious:: qwélqwel < qwà:l.

nuisance (CONT'D)

nuisance, something that's no good:: sqel:ép ~ sqél:ep < qél.

numb

numb (can also be used joking of a drunk):: shxwóxwekw' < xwókw'.
numb in the foot, the foot is asleep:: xwókw'elxel < xwókw'.
numb, made numb:: xwókw'eltem < xwókw'.
to tingle (like arm waking up from numbness), (have/get a) stinging feeling:: thátkwem.

number :: skw'exá:m < kw'áx.

Nuphar polysepalum:: qw'emétx̲w.

nut:: sth'ítsem < th'éts
(lit. something to get hardened, since the shell of nuts has to harden before they are edible)
hazelnut (the nut), any nut:: sth'í:tsem < th'éts.
heart of a root, seed, nut (kernel), core of plant or seedling, core (of tree, branch, any growing thing), pith (of bush), seed or pit [U.S.] or pip [Cdn.] of a fruit:: sth'emí:wel ~ sth'emíwel ~ sth'emíwél < sth'ó:m.
make a crunch underfoot (bones, nut, glass, etc.):: x̲ep'ékw'.
nut of hazelnut bush, acorn, any nut, walnut, peanut, etc.:: sth'í:tsem < th'éts.

Nyctea scandiaca:: sqwṓqweqw.

oak

oak tree, garry oak:: p'xwélhp.

oar :: pōtṓwes < pṓt.

oats

oats, both domestic oats and wild oats:: ṓts, ṓts, ṓts.

obey

obey s-o:: iyó:lemstexw < éy ~ éy:.

object

first person plural patient or object of passive:: -òlèm.
first person singular patient or object of passive:: -àlèm.
four ropes, four threads, four sticks, four poles, (four long thin objects):: x̲ethílemets' < x̲e'ó:thel ~ x̲e'óthel.
him, her, it, them, third person object:: -exw.
me, first person singular object:: -óx.
purposeful control transitivizer inanimate object preferred:: =ex.
roughly spherical object(s), ball:: =ó:ls.
second person singular patient or object of passive:: -ò:m.
third person patient or object of passive:: -em.
us, first person plural object:: -ólxw ~ -óxw.
you (pl.), second person plural object:: -óle.
you (sg.), second person singular object:: -óme.

object of preposition

independent object of preposition:: tl'a- ~ tl'e- ~ tl'-.
us (nominalized object of preposition), to us, with us:: tl'elhlímelh < lhlímelh.

object of preposition (CONT'D)
you folks (object of preposition), to you folks, with you folks:: tl'alhwélep < lhwélep.
you (sg.) (object of preposition):: tl'eléwe ~ tl'léwe < léwe.

occasions
times, occasions:: =álh ~ =áxw ~ =á.

occupation
one who, -er, one who does as an occupation:: =éleq.

ocean
sea, ocean, salt water:: kw'ótl'kwa.

oceanspray
oceanspray plant, "ironwood", "hardhack":: qáthelhp < qáthexw.

Ochotona princeps brunnescens:: sk'í:l.

ochre
red ochre, (clay colored reddish by oxides of iron):: témélh.
red ochre color, color of red clay of iron oxide used for religious paint and face paint:: témélh.

o'clock :: s= =s.
eight o'clock:: steqá:tsas < tqá:tsa.
eleven o'clock:: slhéms < lhém.
Friday, five o'clock:: Slhq'átses < lheq'át ~ lhq'á:t.
hour, o'clock, day of week:: s=...=s.
nine o'clock:: stú:xws < tú:xw.
seven o'clock:: sth'ó:kws < th'ó:kws.
six o'clock:: st'x̲éms < t'éx̲.
ten o'clock, (tenth hour):: s'ó:pels < ó:pel.
three o'clock (< the third hour):: slhíxws < lhí:xw.
Thursday, four o'clock, (fourth cyclic period):: sx̲e'óthels < x̲e'ó:thel ~ x̲e'óthel.
two o'clock, two hours:: isáles < isá:le ~ isále ~ isá:la.

October :: temchálhtel < =chílh ~ chílh=.
moon or month beginning in November, (put away each other's paddles), (sometimes the moon beginning in October, depending on the weather [Elders Group [3/12/75], (moon or month beginning in January [Elders Group 2/5/75]):: xets'ṓ:westel ~ xets'ṓwestel < xits' ~ xets'.
October moon, time to smoke Chehalis spring salmon:: tempó:kw' < pó:qw' ~ póqw'.
October to November, (wood gathering time):: tsélcheptel?.
September to October, dog salmon time:: temkw'ó:lexw < kw'ó:lexw.
time to dry fish, first of July (at Yale), October (at Chehalis):: temchálhtel < =chílh ~ chílh=.

Octopus
probably genus Octopus, the Squamish cognate is identified as Octopus apollyon:: sqéymeqw'.

octopus :: sqéymeqw'.

Octopus apollyon

Octopus apollyon
probably genus Octopus, the Squamish cognate is identified as Octopus apollyon:: sqéymeqw'.

Odlum
maybe also the whirlpool by Odlum on the same side but below Hope [AD, AK, SP (American Bar place names trip 6/26/78)]:: Hémq'eleq < méq'.
name of place right across from Bristol Island, also called Odlum:: Petéyn.

Odocoileus hemionis columbianus
Odocoileus hemionis columbianus, Odocoileus hemionis hemionis:: tl'alqtéle ~ tl'elqtéle < tl'áqt.

Odocoileus hemionis hemionis
Odocoileus hemionis columbianus, Odocoileus hemionis hemionis:: tl'alqtéle ~ tl'elqtéle < tl'áqt.

Odocoilus hemionis:: tl'alqtéle ~ tl'elqtéle < tl'áqt.

Odocoilus virginianus:: tl'alqtéle ~ tl'elqtéle < tl'áqt.

Odonata
order Odonata:: lhílhló:ya.

Odontoceti):
perhaps generic, most likely includes all local balleen whales, i.e., suborder Mysticeti, especially Balaenoptera physalus and Megaptera novaeangliae, possibly Eschrichtius glaucus, Balaenoptera borealis, Balaenoptera acutorostrata, Sibbaldus musculus, Eubalaena sieboldi, could include the following toothed whales (suborder Odontoceti): Physeter catodon, possibly Berardius bairdi, Mesoplodon stejnegeri, Ziphius cavirostrus:: qwél:és ~ qwélés.

odor
fragrance, smell, odor:: =áléqep ~ =áleqep.
(have) animal smell (of bear, skunk, dog, etc.), (have) animal stink, (have) human smell (of underarm, body odor, etc.), (have) body odor:: pápeth'em.

of course)
(polite imperative?, (polite) certainly, (polite) of course):: òwelh ~ -òwèlh.

off
come off:: má ~ má'-.
get off (a canoe or conveyance), get out of a canoe, (disembark):: qw'í:m.
keep it in the air, lift s-th/s-o off the floor:: shxwóxwelstexw < xwá.
sat down (with a plop?), [slip off on one's bottom or chair]:: xwlhépelets < x̲wlhép.
slip off (one's feet, hands, bottom), lose balance:: x̲wlhép.
slip off the hands, slip out of the hands:: x̲wlhépches < x̲wlhép.
slip off with a foot, lose balance [on feet]:: x̲wlhépxel < x̲wlhép.
slipping off with a foot:: x̲wélhepxel < x̲wlhép.
take it off from the bottom of s-th (a pack for ex.):: mexlátst < má ~ má'-.
take it off (of a table for example), take it away (from something), take it off (of eyeglasses, of skin off an animal), take s-o off/away (from something), take s-th out (a tooth for ex.)::

off (CONT'D)

máx < má ~ má'-.
taking s-th off:: hámex < má ~ má'-.

offend
get offended, get irritated:: qwox̲wlómét < qwóx̲wlexw.
offend s-o:: qwóx̲wlexw.

offer
have a ritual burning ceremony, have a burning, feed the dead, (food offered to the dead [at a ritual burning] [EB 5/25/76]):: yeqwá:ls < yéqw.

off ground)
store it away (wedged-in up off ground), put s-th away for winter, stow s-th away:: xítse't < xits' ~ xets'.

officials)
search through it, rummage through it, search s-o (like Customs officials):: xíleqwt < xíleqw.

offspring :: =ó:llh ~ =óllh ~ =elh ~ ='ó:llh.
child (of someone, kinterm), offspring, son, daughter:: méle ~ mél:a.

off-white)
(dingy white, off-white):: stl'ítl'es.

of (partitive):: telí < tel=.

often
always, all the time, ((also) often, over and over [TG]):: wiyóth.

Ogilvie
Mount Ogilvie:: Qemqemó < qemó:.
Mount Ogilvie or a round peak or bluff on Mt. Ogilvie where mountain goats live, the mountain or peak or bluff resembles big breasts:: Qwemth'í:les < qwó:m ~ qwóm ~ qwem.

Ogress
Cannibal Ogress, Wild Cannibal Woman:: Th'ṓwx̲iya < th'ṓwex̲ ~ th'ṓwéx̲.

Ohamil
village now called Ohamil Reserve or Laidlaw:: Shxw'ōwhámél ~ Shxw'ōhámél.

oh for goodness sakes.
oh for goodness sakes., well. (in surprise):: lá:la.

oh my goodness.:: qéléméx ~ ṓ qèlèmèx ~ ló qèlèmèx.

oh my gosh.:: éyelew < éy ~ éy:.

oh-oh. :: a'á.

oil

a group making (fish) oil:: hemhémetheqw < mótheqw or metheqw.
(be) oiled:: smólxw < mélxw.
(be) oily (?):: smelmólxw < mélxw.
eulachon oil:: tl'í:na.
fat, grease, lard, (oil [EB], shortening [MH]):: sló:s ~ slós < ló:s ~ lós.
flat rocks (bedrock) with holes at Hill's Bar where they used to make smótheqw (prepared fish oil) from sockeye heads:: Hemhémetheqw < mótheqw or metheqw.
grease s-th/s-o, oil s-th/s-o, rub something on s-th/s-o:: mélxwt < mélxw.
oil his/her/its head:: mélxweqwt < mélxw.
oil one's hair, oil one's head:: mélxweqwem < mélxw, melxwqwéylém < mélxw.
prepared fish oil (usually sockeye oil):: smótheqw < mótheqw or metheqw.
rub (oil or water) in s-th to clean or soften, rub s-th to soften or clean it, (shaping a stone hammer with abrasion?, shaping?, mixing paint?, pressing together or crushing? [BHTTC 9/2/76]):: yémq't.
soft (down) feathers put in oiled hair for dancing:: sq'óyeseqw ~ sx̲óyeseqw < sq'óyes.
soft feathers put in oiled hair for dancing:: sx̲óyeseqw ~ sq'óyeseqw.

okay :: tl'ótl'em.

be alright, be okay, it's alright, it's okay, can, be able, it's enough, be right, be correct, that's right:: iyólem ~ iyó:lem < éy ~ éy:.
be alright, be well, be fine, be okay:: éy òl ~ éyòl ~ éyò < éy ~ éy:.
Is that okay?:: wé.
is that okay? (interrogative tag-question):: é.

old :: siyólexwe, siyó:lexwe ~ syó:lexwe ~siyólexwe.

ancient people over a hundred years old:: sx̲wolex̲wiyám < x̲wiyám.
an old course of Atchelitz Creek:: (Yeqyeqámen).
a small person (old or young) is picking or trying to pick, an inexperienced person is picking or trying to pick, picking a little bit, someone who can't pick well is picking:: lhilhím < lhím.
be worn out (of clothes for ex.), be old (of clothes), smashed up when dropped, dissolved:: th'éw.
elders past, deceased old people:: siyolexwálh < siyólexwe.
getting ancient, getting old:: q'e'ílém < q'a'í:lem ~ q'e'í:lem.
little old person:: siyó:ylexwe < siyó:lexwe ~ syó:lexwe ~siyólexwe.
old people:: sí:yólexwe < siyó:lexwe ~ syó:lexwe ~siyólexwe.
old people, elders:: sí:yólexwe < siyólexwe.
old person:: siyó:lexwe ~ syó:lexwe < siyó:lexwe ~ syó:lexwe ~siyólexwe.
old person, an elder:: siyólexwe < siyólexwe.
old salmon (ready to die, spotted):: x̲éyqeya.
very old, ancient, get ancient, be ancient:: q'a'í:lem ~ q'e'í:lem.

older brother

older sibling, elder cousin (child of older sibling of one's parent, grandchild of older sibling of one's grandparent, great grandchild of older sibling of one's great grandparent), cousin of senior line, older brother, older sister:: sétl'atel < sétl'a ~ sétl'o.

older sibling

older sibling, elder cousin (child of older sibling of one's parent, grandchild of older sibling of one's grandparent, great grandchild of older sibling of one's great grandparent), cousin of senior line, older brother, older sister:: sétl'atel < sétl'a ~ sétl'o.

older sibling (CONT'D)

older siblings, elder cousins (first/second/third cousins by an older sibling of one's ancestor):: sá:tl'atel < sétl'a ~ sétl'o.

older sister

older sibling, elder cousin (child of older sibling of one's parent, grandchild of older sibling of one's grandparent, great grandchild of older sibling of one's great grandparent), cousin of senior line, older brother, older sister:: sétl'atel < sétl'a ~ sétl'o.

oldest

oldest (sibling):: séltl'o < sétl'a ~ sétl'o.

Old Jack

Indian name of Old Jack (of Yakweakwioose or perhaps Scowkale):: T'eláqw'tel < t'álqw' or t'élqw'.

"old lady"

wife (not respectful), the "old lady", "squaw", mistress:: chá:xw.

oldsquaw

a white-headed duck, [could be bufflehead, snow goose, emperor goose, poss. oldsquaw, or hooded merganser, other duck-like birds with white heads do not occur in the Stó:lō area and the emperor goose would be only an occasional visitor]:: skemí'iya.

Olor buccinator

Olor columbianus, probably also Olor buccinator:: shxwő:qel ~ shxwőwqel ~ shxwéwqel.

Olor columbianus

Olor columbianus, probably also Olor buccinator:: shxwő:qel ~ shxwőwqel ~ shxwéwqel.

on :: í, lí.

be across, be on the other side of:: sle'ó:thel < le'á.
(being/put) on the top shelf:: ts'ech'ó:lwelh < ts'á:.
be in, in, be on, on, be at, at, before (an audience), (untranslated):: lí ~ li.
benefactive, do for s-o, malefactive, do on s-o:: -lhts.
be on the other side of, be on the side facing away:: sle'ólwelh < le'á.
be on top of:: sts'ets'á < ts'á:.
coming by foot, travelling by walking, already walking, travelling on foot:: ye'í:mex < i┐m.
lie on one's back, on his back:: kw'e'íyeqel ~ kw'e'íqel < kw'e'í ~ kw"í ~ kw'í.
locative, on the:: =el ~ =a(:)l ~ =o(:)l.
on something else, within ssomething else:: =q'.
put on the stove (water/food):: xwch'alech'á:ls < ts'á:.
put s-th on (of a design on a dress, of a shirt, shoes, etc.), attach it, stick it on, fasten it:: tl'álx < tl'ál.
they came on (top of):: ch'alech'á (~ ts'alets'á) < ts'á:.

on and off

running on and off:: xwéxwemxelí:m < x̲wém ~ xwém.

on-board

put s-th/s-o aboard, put it on-board:: ó:lhstexw < ó:lh.

once
    once, one time:: lets'áxw < léts'a ~ léts'e.

Oncorhynchus gorbuscha:: hő:liya, húheliya < hő:liya.

Oncorhynchus keta:: kw'ó:lexw.

Oncorhynchus kisutch:: kwőxweth.
    small fully grown Oncorhynchus kisutch:: sth'ímiya < sth'í:m ~ sth'i:m.

Oncorhynchus nerka:: skwíkwexel, sqwó:yxw, sthéqi ~ sthéqey, tsésqey.
    late fall Harrison/Chehalis River run of Oncorhynchus nerka:: qwechíwiya.

Oncorhynchus tschawytscha:: pó:qw' ~ póqw', spó:x̲em ~ spéx̲em.

Oncorhynchus tshawytscha:: speqá:s, sqwéx̲em < qwéx̲em, sth'olólh, tl'elxálōwelh or tl'elxálōllh < tl'él, tl'élx̲xel ~ tl'álx̲xel < tl'él.
    August Silver Creek run of Oncorhynchus tshawytscha:: shxwōqw'ő:lh.

Ondatra zibethica osoyoosensis:: sq'élhq'elh.

one :: léts'a ~ léts'e.
    deceased one:: stewéqel.
    deceased ones, late ones:: stáweqel < stewéqel.
    (have) one white eye, (have a cataract on one eye):: sqwelxwó:lés.
    he (present or presence unspecified), he's the one that, it's him that, she or it (present or presence unspecified), that or this (immediately before nominal):: tú:tl'ò ~ tútl'ò ~ tútl'o < tl'ó ~ tl'o.
    him (there, near but not visible), that one:: kwethá ~ kwe thá < kw.
    it is us, we are the ones, we ourselves:: lhlímelh.
    more than one is good, good (of many things or people):: álíy ~ 'álíy < éy ~ éy:.
    once, one time:: lets'áxw < léts'a ~ léts'e.
    one bird:: lets'íws < léts'a ~ léts'e.
    one canoe, one boat:: lets'ő welh < léts'a ~ léts'e.
    one container:: léts'eqel < léts'a ~ léts'e.
    one cyclic period:: léts'es < léts'a ~ léts'e.
    one dollar, one Indian blanket (Boas):: léts'es < léts'a ~ léts'e.
    one fruit (as it grows singly on a plant):: lets'òls ~ léts'òls < léts'a ~ léts'e.
    one kind, one pile:: lets'emó:t < léts'a ~ léts'e.
    one leaf:: lets'álews < léts'a ~ léts'e.
    one paddle, one paddler:: lets'á:wes < léts'a ~ léts'e.
    one pair of pants:: lets'áyiws < léts'a ~ léts'e.
    one person, be alone:: lólets'e < léts'a ~ léts'e.
    one rope, one thread, one stick, one pole:: lets'ámeth' < léts'a ~ léts'e.
    one round object:: léts'es < léts'a ~ léts'e.
    one side of the body (between arm and hip):: slheq'ó:lwelh < lheq'át ~ lhq'á:t.
    one tree:: sléts'elhp < léts'a ~ léts'e.
    one who, -er, one who does as an occupation:: =éleq.
    take one step:: tiqxálém ~ tiyqxálém.
    that's a little one (male, about one to five years old), he (little):: tú:tl'òtl'èm < tl'ó ~ tl'o.
    that's them (little ones) (male?):: tutl'étl'elò:m < tl'ó ~ tl'o.
    (that's) them (lots of little ones), they (many small ones):: yutl'étl'elòm < tl'ó ~ tl'o.

one (CON'TD)
the one who burns [at a burning ceremony], (ritualist at a burning):: híyeqwels < yéqw.
think s-o is talking or laughing about one:: tl'ostélmét < tl'óst or tl'óstexw.
(whoever, one out of):: =wát.

one another
(be) true to one another:: the'íttel < the'í:t.
helping one another, (helper [Elders Group]):: momíyelhtel < máy.
help out, go help, pitch in, help one another:: móylhtel < máy.
purposeful control reciprocal, (perhaps just) reciprocal, (do purposely to) each other, (do purposely to) one another:: =t=el.

one-legged
canyon area on Chehalis Creek just above (upriver or north from) the main highway bridge (esp. the first cliff on the east side) [means one-legged]:: Páléxel ~ Paléxel.

one's
brush one's teeth:: th'ex̲wélesem < th'éx̲w or th'óx̲w.
get one's picture taken:: x̲wéychesem (or better) x̲wíythesem < x̲wíyth.
(go) wash one's mouth out:: th'x̲woythílem < th'éx̲w or th'óx̲w.
grinding one's teeth:: x̲ax̲elts'elísem < x̲élts'.
lather one's body:: yet'qw'íwsem.
nod one's head, nod one's head (up and down for yes for ex.):: líqwesem < líqw.
put on one's hat:: yóseqwem < yó:seqw ~ yóseqw.
put paint on one's face:: yétl'q'esem < yétl'.
scrubby little ones, (little ugly ones):: qéqelelhó:mex < qél.
turn one's face, (turn one's body away [IHTTC]):: ts'ólesem ~ ts'ólésem < ts'el.
washing one's clothes:: th'éx̲welwetem < th'éx̲w or th'óx̲w.
wash one's body:: th'ex̲wíwsem < th'éx̲w or th'óx̲w.
wash one's clothes:: th'x̲welwétem < th'éx̲w or th'óx̲w.
wash one's face:: th'ex̲wó:sem ~ th'ex̲wósem < th'éx̲w or th'óx̲w.
wash one's feet:: th'èx̲wxél:ém < th'éx̲w or th'óx̲w.
wash one's hair, wash one's head:: th'ex̲wíqwem < th'éx̲w or th'óx̲w.
wash one's hands:: th'ex̲wá:tsesem < th'éx̲w or th'óx̲w.
white ones:: p'ép'eq' < p'éq'.
wipe one's face:: íqw'esem < íqw'.

oneself
acknowledge oneself:: telómelthet < tól.
bailing (a canoe, etc.), bail oneself:: lhí:lthet ~ lhílthet < lhí:lt ~ lhílt.
bring oneself to a climax, to climax, to orgasm, masturbate:: wets'á:lómet < ts'á:.
bring oneself to a summit (of a mountain):: wets'á:lómet < ts'á:.
change oneself (purposely), change oneself into something else, change s-th on oneself:: iyóqthet < iyá:q.
cool oneself:: th'ólhethet < th'álh.
cool oneself off:: th'álhethet < th'álh.
cover oneself up:: léx̲wethet < lex̲w.
crawling (as of snake, seal, slug, snail), (dragging oneself):: xwéqw'ethet < xwókw' ~ xwekw'ó.
crossing oneself, (making the sign of the Cross):: pá:yewsem < pó:y.
cry for oneself, (crying for oneself):: x̲ehó:methet < x̲à:m ~ x̲á:m.
delay oneself:: iy'eyómthet < óyém.

oneself (CONT'D)

do it, do it oneself:: iyálewet ~ eyálewet < éy ~ éy:.
do s-th oneself:: iyálewet < éy ~ éy:.
drag oneself:: xwó:kw'thet < xwókw' ~ xwekw'ó.
drop oneself into a seat, throw oneself on the floor or ground in a tantrum, throw a tantrum:: kw'qweméthet < kw'óqw.
exert oneself, make a big effort, do with all one's might, [do] as hard as possible, do it harder (used if already paddling for ex.):: tíméthet < tímet.
feeling sorry for oneself:: tesestélemet < t-sós ~ tesós.
fill oneself, fill oneself up:: lets'éthet < léts'.
fill oneself up (by eating):: meq'lómet < méq'.
fix oneself in bed:: tl'ó:thet < tl'ó:t.
fix oneself up:: thíythet < thíy.
get mad at oneself:: qelqelí:lthet < qél.
hang oneself, (hung by a rope [AC]):: x̲wíqw'esem < x̲wíqw'.
help oneself to food, serve oneself, serve oneself food (with a ladle), serve oneself a meal (food), (put on a dish [CT, HT]):: lhá:x̲em ~ lháx̲em < lhá:x̲ ~ lháx̲.
join, (include oneself purposely):: q'ó:thet < q'ó.
kill oneself:: q'óythet < q'ó:y ~ q'óy.
know oneself, be confident:: lheq'elómet < q'á:l.
let oneself fall, drop oneself down (by parachute, rope, etc., said of little birds trying to fly out of nest, little animals trying to get down and let themselves fall):: chólqthet < tsélq ~ chélq.
make oneself useful:: p'óp'ekw'ethet < p'ákw'.
make the sign of the Cross, (cross oneself):: píyewsem ~ píwsem < pó:y.
manage by oneself (in food or travel), try to do it by oneself, try to be independent, do the best one can:: iyólewéthet < éy ~ éy:.
move, move itself, move oneself:: kwíyx̲thet < kwíyx̲.
moving, moving oneself/itself:: kwó:yxthet ~ kwó:yex̲thet ~ kwó:yxethet < kwíyx̲.
non-control reflexive, happen to or manage to or accidentally do to oneself:: =l=ómet or =l-ómet ~ =l=ó:met.
non-control reflexive, make oneself do something, keep oneself doing something:: =st=èlèmèt or =st-èlèmèt ~ =st-elómet.
pull oneself up, straighten (oneself) up:: thkw'éthet < thékw'.
purposeful control reflexive, do purposely to oneself:: =thet.
rest oneself:: qá:wthet < qá:w.
scare oneself (in being reckless), scare oneself (do something one knows is dangerous and get scared even more than expected):: sí:silómet ~ sí:silòmèt < síy.
separate oneself from a group, separate oneself (from others):: lets'elíthet < halts'elí.
(shaking, quaking, moving oneself):: qwíyx̲thet < qwá:y.
shame oneself (purposely):: x̲éyx̲ethet < x̲éyx̲e ~ x̲íx̲e.
sorry for oneself:: x̲ehó:methet < x̲à:m ~ x̲á:m.
starving oneself, being on a "crash" diet:: xwexwóthet < xwá.
straighten oneself out:: thíythet < thíy, tlhéthet < télh.
stretch oneself:: ót'ethet < ót'.
sweeten oneself:: q'et'ómthet < q'át'em.
take care of oneself, look after oneself, be careful:: xólhmethet ~ xó:lhmethet < xólh.
taking care of oneself:: xó:lhmethet < xólh.
think someone is talking or laughing about oneself:: tl'emstélemet ~ tl'emstélémét < tl'émstexw, tl'ostélmet.
to abstain from food, to fast, starve oneself:: xwóthet < xwá.
to shame oneself [accidentally], (get) embarrassed, (become ashamed of oneself?):: x̲éyx̲elòmèt < x̲éyx̲e ~ x̲íx̲e.

oneself (CONT'D)
to slide (oneself):: qex̱óthet < qíx̱em ~ (less good spelling) qéyx̱em.
turn oneself around, turn (oneself) around:: x̱élts'thet < x̱élts'.
wake up (oneself), (wake oneself purposely):: xwíythet ~ xwíthet < xwíy ~ x[illegible]í.
wipe oneself off:: íqw'ethet < íqw'.

one who
one who, -er, one who does as an occupation:: =éleq.

onion
domestic onion:: éniyels.
wild nodding onion, prob. also Hooker's onion:: st'áxet, st'áxet.

on itself
on itself, within itself:: =p'.

only
be only (contrastive), be just (contrastive):: welóy < lóy.
be only, just:: lóy.
be only remaining:: txwó:ye.
the only safe place to cross a river:: shxwtitós or shxwtiytós.

on one's way
be on one's way, be going:: hálém < la.

oolachen
eulachon, oolachen, candle-fish:: swí:we ~ swíwe.
to scoop (for ex. oolachens, eulachons):: qó:lem < qó:.

oolachen moon
month beginning in April at the mouth of the Fraser, May-June (Jenness:Sepass), oolachen moon:: temwíwe (or possibly) temswíwe < swí:we ~ swíwe.

open :: xwemá < má ~ má'-.
an opener, can-opener, bottle-opener:: shxwéma'ám < má ~ má'-, shxwémeqel < má ~ má'-, shxwémeqèyls < má ~ má'-.
be open (at the top):: shxwemá < má ~ má'-.
burst open, split open of its own accord (like a dropped watermelon):: tl'xáx̱el < tl'éx.
(have the) mouth round and open with rounded lips:: sqwoqwtó:ythel < qwá.
it's open:: shxwemá < má ~ má'-.
mouth open:: xixq'á:m ~ xixq'ám < xáq'.
open both one's eyes real wide:: pex̱ó:lésem < páx̱.
opening one's eyes:: x̱élx̱eleq't < x̱éleq't.
opening one's mouth:: xáxeq'em < xáq'.
open it:: xwemá:t < má ~ má'-.
open it (door, gate, anything):: xwmá:x < má ~ má'-.
open (of a bottle, basket, etc.):: xwmá:m or lexwmá:m < má ~ má'-.
open (of peas, beans):: xwís.
open one's eyes:: x̱éleq't.
open one's mouth:: xáq'em < xáq'.
open the door:: xwema'à:ls < má ~ má'-.
split s-th open (with fingernail):: thíts'et.

open (CONT'D)

spread the eyelids open with the fingers (done to oneself or to someone else), (probably also spread s-th apart):: páx̲et < páx̲.

sticking out through a hole (like a toe out of a sock, knee out of a hole in pants, a nail driven clear through the other side of a board), come out into the open:: qwōhóls (or perhaps) qwehóls < qwá.

take a cover off, take it off (a cover of a container), open it (bottle, box, kettle, book, etc.):: xwemá:qet < má ~ má'-.

to split s-th open (like deer or fish):: tl'xáx̲et < tl'éx.

opened surface

on the face, face of the hand or foot, opened surface of a salmon:: =ó:s ~ =ós ~ =es.

opener

an opener, can-opener, bottle-opener:: shxwéma'ám < má ~ má'-, shxwémeqel < má ~ má'-, shxwémeqèyls < má ~ má'-.

opening

Chehalis River mouth (below the highway bridge, where land is breaking up into sand bars), (an opening one could get through in a canoe in high water near Chehalis {IHTTC 8/25/77], small creek (branch of Chehalis River) several hundred yards up Chehalis River from where the road goes from old Chehalis village site to Chehalis River [EL 9/27/77]):: Spōqwṓwelh ~ Speqwṓ:lh < péqw.

Ophiodon elongatus:: á:yt ~ é:yt, mechó:s.

Oplopanax horridum:: qwó:pelhp.

opposite

insistant, persistant (like a child pressing to go along), bull-headed, doesn't mind, does just the opposite, (stubborn, contrary):: sxíxeles.

opposite side of house on inside:: lheq'ewílh.

optimist

optimist, a person whose thoughts are always good:: wiyóth kwsu éys te sqwálewels te lólets'e < wiyóth.

or :: q'a ~ qa ~ qe.

and, but, or:: qe.

orange :: qwel'qwóyes < qwá:y.

mock orange:: sth'élhp.

orange (fruit), especially mandarin orange (the fruit), also domestic orange, (also orange (color)):: qwiqwóyáls ~ qwiqwóyéls ~ qwiqwòyàls < qwá:y.

oranges:: qwel'qwóyes < qwá:y.

orange juice:: qwíyqwòyèls sqe'óleqw < qwá:y, qó: (lit. orange + fruit juice)

orange loaf:: qwíyqwòyèls seplíl < qwá:y, seplíl (lit. orange fruit + bread)

orange (color):: qwiqwóyáls ~ qwiqwóyéls ~ qwiqwòyàls < qwá:y.

Orcinus rectipinna
    Grampus rectipinna also known as Orcinus rectipinna:: q'ellhólemètsel.

order
    an order (promise of goods/services):: s'ò:m < ò:m.
    to order (food, material, etc.):: ò:m.

ordinary
    useless, no special use, ordinary:: ewétò shxwlís < shxwlí.

Oreamnos americanus americanus:: p'q'élqel < p'éq'.

Oregon grape
    short Oregon grape berry:: selíy.
    short Oregon grape bush:: selíyelhp < selíy.
    sour (unripe or half-ripe fruit, lemon, Oregon grape, fermenting fruit):: t'át'eth'em < t'áth'.
    tall Oregon grape berry:: th'ṓ:lth'iyelhp sth'í:m ~ sth'í:ms te th'ṓ:lth'iyelhp < th'ṓ:lth'iyelhp.
    tall Oregon grape bush:: th'ṓ:lth'iyelhp.

Oreortyx pictus
    Oreortyx pictus, possibly also Lophortyx californicus:: kwéyl.

organ
    flat organ in sturgeon which was skinned off and boiled down for glue:: mát.
    gills, also "boot" (boot-shaped organ attached to fish gill):: xá:y ~ xà:y.

organization
    to pray, have a church service, (a Church (organization, not building) [Elders Group]):: ts'ahéyelh.

organs
    insides (animal or human or other?), (internal organs, guts, etc.), (stomach [inside] [DM]):: sts'elxwíwel < ts'el.

orgasm
    bring oneself to a climax, to climax, to orgasm, masturbate:: wets'á:lómet < ts'á:.

orphan :: swálém.

Orthoptera
    order Orthoptera family Acrididae or perhaps family Tettigoniidae:: tl'emékw' < tl'ámkw'em, tl'emékw' < tl'ém, tl'emtl'émxel, tl'emtl'émxel, tl'emtl'émxel < tl'ém, ts'áts'etl'em < ts'tl'ám ~ ts'tl'ém, ts'ats'etl'í:m < ts'tl'ám ~ ts'tl'ém, ts'í:ts'á:tl'em < ts'tl'ám ~ ts'tl'ém.

Osmaronia cerasiformis:: mélhx̲wel, mélhx̲welelhp < mélhx̲wel.

Osmorhiza chilensis
    probably a Bromus sp., likely Bromus carinatus, possibly Osmorhiza chilensis and Osmorhiza purpurea,:: táqalh.

Osmorhiza purpurea

Osmorhiza purpurea

probably a Bromus sp., likely Bromus carinatus, possibly Osmorhiza chilensis and Osmorhiza purpurea::, táqalh.

osprey

osprey, fishhawk:: th'éxwth'exw < th'íxw ~ th'éxw.

Othello

Othello, (B.C.), a village on the Coquihalla River, on the west side across from the most northwest point above the mouth of Nicolum Creek, up nine miles from Hope on the Kettle Valley Railroad:: Áthelets < áthelets.

other)

(be) brother and sister, (be siblings to each other), (be) first cousin to each other:: qeló:qtel < sqá:q.
(be) considerate of each other:: sts'its'exwtel < sts'íts'exw, sts'íts'exwtel < th'íxw ~ th'éxw.
companion, other part:: sq'ó < q'ó.
going with each other [romantically], going for a walk with each other:: ts'lhimexóstel < ts'elh=.
go with each other (romantically), go for a walk with each other (romantically):: ts'lhimexóstel < i┐m.
holding a grudge against each other:: xixemó:ltel < sxemá:l.
moon or month beginning in November, (put away each other's paddles), (sometimes the moon beginning in October, depending on the weather [Elders Group [3/12/75], (moon or month\ beginning in January [Elders Group 2/5/75]):: xets'ṓ:westel ~ xets'ṓwestel < xits' ~ xets'.
on the other side of the world:: súyéx̲el < sóy.
purposeful control reciprocal, (perhaps just) reciprocal, (do purposely to) each other, (do purposely to) one another:: =t=el.
they're making friends, (making friends with each other):: yóyatel < yá:ya.
they've made friends, (make friends with each other):: yáyetel (prob. also yáyatel) < yá:ya.
to meet (each other):: q'eqótel < q'ó.
wink at each other, ((maybe) squint [EB]):: th'ikwóstel < th'iykw'.
winking at each other:: th'ith'ikwóstel < th'iykw'.

other side

be across, be on the other side of:: sle'ó:thel < le'á.
be on the other side of, be on the side facing away:: sle'ólwelh < le'á.

otter

river otter, perhaps also sea otter:: sq'á:tl'.

Otus asio kennicotti:: spopeleqwíth'a ~ spopeleqwíth'e < poleqwíth'a.

ought to)

be good, good, well, nice, fine, better, better (ought to), it would be good if, may it be good, let it be good, happy, glad, clean, well-behaved, polite, virgin, popular, comfortable (with furniture, other things?),:: éy ~ éy:.

our

ours, our (emphatic):: s'ólh.
we (non-subordinate subject), our:: -tset ~ -chet.

ours

ours, our (emphatic):: s'ólh.

ourselves

it is us, we are the ones, we ourselves:: lhlímelh.

out

come out (of hair) (like hair in a comb):: qw'ém.
get off (a canoe or conveyance), get out of a canoe, (disembark):: qw'í:m.
go out completely (of fire):: th'éx̲.
go out from the beach (if in a canoe):: tó:l ~ tò:l.
go out into the river, go down to the river, walk down to the river:: tó:l ~ tò:l.
go out (of fire, flame or lamp):: tl'ékw'el.
hair is falling out, losing one's hair:: qw'eméqel < qw'ém.
just coming out of the earth (of plants for ex.):: qwósem.
kick s-o out:: atl'qílt < átl'q.
out in the middle of the river:: chuchuwó:ythel < cháchew ~ cháchu.
(portion not burnt up, burnt or gone out completely portion):: th'ex̲míl < th'éx̲.
pull out (hair):: qw'emét < qw'ém.
ran out (of food, money, etc.), have no more, be finished (offood), (be empty (of container of supplies) [EB: Cheh., Tait]):: ṓwkw'.
run out of food, be out of food:: ú:kw'elets < ṓwkw'.
slip it out:: elhápt.
slip off the hands, slip out of the hands:: x̲wlhépches < x̲wlhép.
square, corner, arm with elbow out:: st'eláx̲el.
sticking out through a hole (like a toe out of a sock, knee out of a hole in pants, a nail driven clear through the other side of a board), come out into the open:: qwōhóls (or perhaps) qwehóls < qwá, qwōhóls (or perhaps) qwehóls < qwá.
take it off (of a table for example), take it away (from something), take it off (of eyeglasses, of skin off an animal), take s-o off/away (from something), take s-th out (a tooth for ex.):: máx < má ~ má'-.
take it out of a box, pull it out of a box:: xíqt.
take it out of water:: qw'ímét < qw'í:m.
to extinguish it, put it out (a fire):: tl'ékw'elt < tl'ékw'el.
to go down (of water), subside (of water), the tide goes out or down, (be going out (of tide) [BJ]):: th'à:m ~ th'ám.
unloading a canoe, taking things out of a canoe:: qw'íméls < qw'í:m.

outer

outer cedar bark:: sókw'em < sókw'.

outfit

dancer’s uniform, (any) coordinated outfit:: s-hóyews < hóyiws.

outhouse

little house, cabin (say 12 ft. x 10 ft. or less), small home, storage house (small shed-like house, enclosed with door), outhouse (slang), toilet (slang):: lílem < lá:lém.
outhouse (for solid waste), (shit-house):: wá:cháwtxw.
outhouse, toilet, bathroom:: atl'qeláwtxw < átl'q.
stinking (smell of outhouse or pig farm), (to stink [Elders Group 11/10/76, AC 9/1/71]):: xíxets'em.

out of breath
    out of breath and over-tired and over-hungry:: pqwíles < péqw.

out of control)
    fire (out of control), forest fire burning, fire burning:: yíyeqw < yéqw.

out of joint
    (get a) sprained foot, leg got out of joint:: plhéqw'xel ~ p'lhéqw'xel.

out of sight
    disappear, drop out of sight, (to fade [Elders Group 3/72]):: théxw ~ théx̲w.
    go out of sight (behind something), disappear [behind something], [get in shade]:: t'á:l.
    the (distant and out of sight, remote), (definite but distant and out of sight, remote), the (abstract), a (remote, abstract), some, (indefinite):: kw'e.

out of the way
    get out of the way, get off the way, dodge:: íyeqthet < iyá:q.

out of thick bushes
    (come) out of thick bushes:: wexés.

outside
    around the outside of the house:: sélts'ex̲el < sél or sí(:)l.
    bring s-th/s-o outside (purposely):: atl'qílt < átl'q.
    get outside:: átl'qel < átl'q.
    going out(side) with a light:: láx̲etem < láx̲et.
    outside brisket of meat:: qw'íwelh.
    take it outside (outside of a building or car):: átl'qt < átl'q.
    the outside:: s'átl'q < átl'q.
    the outside part of a house:: s'átl'qmel < átl'q.

outstretched
    hold both arms (or wings) outstretched, (stretch out one's arms/wings):: tex̲eláx̲elem < tex̲.

oven
    baking over an open fire, roasting over an open fire, barbecuing, cooking in an oven:: qw'eqw'élém < qw'él.
    barbecue, bake (meat, vegetables, etc.) in open fire, bake over fire, roast over open fire, bake under hot sand, bake in oven, cook in oven, (boiled down (as jam) [CT, HT]):: qw'élém < qw'él.
    barbecued, roasted, (baked (in an oven) [DC]):: s=qw'elém < qw'él.

over
    always, all the time, ((also) often, over and over [TG]):: wiyóth.
    (be) doubled up (a person with knees up to his chest), all doubled over:: sqw'emqw'emóx̲w < qw'ómx̲w.
    bent over?:: stl'ítl'em.
    be over, past (passed):: yelá:w ~ yeláw ~ yiláw.
    (be) over there, (be) yonder:: lí(:) tí or lí(:)tí.
    (be) scattered all over:: stl'ápx̲ < tl'ép.
    bring s-th/s-o across a river, (ferry s-o/s-th over):: t'kwíléstexw < t'ákwel.
    carry a packstrap or both packstraps over the shoulder(s) and under the arm(s):: sq'iwq'ewíles < q'e:yw ~ q'í:w.

over (CONT'D)

cross a river, cross a road, cross over:: t'ákwel.
crossing over:: t'át'ekwel < t'ákwel.
distributive, all over, all around:: =x̲ ~ =ex̲.
finished, over:: hà:m.
go over or around (hill, rock, river, etc.):: q'ál.
just past, over:: yeláwel < yelá:w ~ yeláw ~ yiláw.
leaning over (something):: q'í:wethet < q'e:yw ~ q'í:w.
move over:: sex̲éylem or sex̲ílem < síx̲.
move s-th over:: síx̲et < síx̲.
over, in the air over, above:: stselhsó:lwelh < =chílh ~ chílh=.
roll over in bed, turn over in bed:: ts'ó:lex̲eth' < ts'el.
something used to cross over a river, ferry, place good for crossing:: xwt'át'ekwel < t'ákwel.
trail and steep slope on the west shore of Kawkawa Lake where the trail went up and over a steep hill and then down:: Sq'éywetselem ~ Sq'éywetsélém < q'e:yw ~ q'í:w.
turn s-th/s-o over, flip it over (of fish for ex.), turn it inside out:: chaléwt.

over and over

always, all the time, ((also) often, over and over [TG]):: wiyóth.
sighing over and over (of a spirit-dancer before or after dancing):: xaqxeqlhálem < xeqlhálém.

overboard

fall in the water, fall overboard (of one person):: qwés.

overcome

be overcome with pleasurable feelings after eating great salmon or a great meal:: ts'éqw'.

overdress

a dandy, someone who overdresses, a show-off, comedian, someone who always cracks jokes, smart-alec:: swék'.

overflow

overflowed:: p'í:ltem < p'í:l or p'él.
overflows:: p'eléts'tem < p'í:l or p'él.

over-hungry

out of breath and over-tired and over-hungry:: pqwíles < péqw.

overload

overloaded:: wép < wíp or wép.

overly

overly ?:: =á: ?.

overripe :: qw'èlqw'èl < qw'él.

overstretch

overstretch one's legs when walking with too big a step:: t'íw ~ t'ì:w.

over-tired
  out of breath and over-tired and over-hungry:: pqwíles < péqw.

overwhelm
  be startled, be dumbfounded, be shocked, be stupified, be speechless, be overwhelmed:: lholhekw'íwel ~ lholhkw'íwel < lhó:kw' ~ lhókw'.

Ovis
  genus Ovis:: metú, mímetú < metú.

owe
  owe s-o:: kwelálhtst < kwél.
  what he owes:: skwelálhchiyelh < kwél.

owl
  also pygmy owl and saw-whet owl:: spopeleqwíth'a ~ spopeleqwíth'e < poleqwíth'a.
  barn owl:: spopeleqwíth'a ~ spopeleqwíth'e < poleqwíth'a.
  horned owl, great horned owl:: chítmexw.
  horned owl-shaped rock (beside Spá:th, a bear-shaped rock) up on a cliff on the south side above Echo Point bay on Echo Island in Harrison Lake:: Chítmexw < chítmexw.
  screech owl especially, probably other small owls as given below but only the screech owl is consistently mentioned by all speakers:: spopeleqwíth'a ~ spopeleqwíth'e < poleqwíth'a.
  small owl, saw-whet owl:: qépkwoya.
  snowy owl, white owl:: sqwő̈qweqw, sqwőqweqw.

own
  comb one's hair, comb one's own hair:: texqéylem < tex.
  (one's) own, belongs to (one):: swá.

pacify
  pacify a baby, pacify it (a baby), sing or hum to a baby to quiet it, sing to it (a zaby), (sing a lullaby to it):: tl'ó:t.

pack
  a pack:: schí:m < chám.
  (be) loaded with a heavy pack:: swíp < wíp or wép.
  carrying on one's back, packing on one's back:: chmà:m < chám.
  carrying s-th/s-o on one's back, packing it on one's back:: chmá:t < chám.
  carry s-th on one's back, pack s-th on one's back:: chámet < chám.
  each had a heavy pack:: swepwíp < wíp or wép.
  lessen it (of someone's load), halve it, make s-th lighter (in weight), lessen it (like when someone's pack is too heavy):: xwát < xwá.
  loose (of a pack), slack (of a pack), too low (of a pack):: xet'éla < xét'.
  more than one person heavily loaded with packs:: swewíp < wíp or wép.
  pack on one's back, carry on one's back:: chámem < chám.
  shake s-th down, pack s-th down, push s-th down, knead s-th (esp. of bread dough), press it down (like yeast bread):: qeth'ét.
  slack, loose (of a pack):: xét'.
  sloppy pack:: slhellhélp'elets < lhél.
  tighten it (a belt, a pack, etc.):: q'íxwet.
  to dip water, get water, fetch water, pack water:: qó:m < qó:.

pack (CONT'D)

to pack:: chím ~ chí:m < chám.
travelling by and packing on his back (might be said of a passer-by):: iychmà:m ~ iytsmà:m < chám.

package
small bundle, small package:: xixwelókw' < xél.

packrat)
may include any or all of the following which occur in this area: creeping vole Microtus oregoni serpens, long-tail vole Microtus longicaudus macrurus, mountain heather vole Phenacomys intermedius oramontis, boreal redback vole Clethrionomys gapperi cascadensis, Norway rat (intro.) Rattus norvegicus, and perhaps roof rat Rattus rattus, also includes bushy-tailed wood rat (packrat) Neotoma cinerea occidentalis which has its own name below:: há:wt.
packrat, i.e. bushy-tailed wood rat:: qélqel há:wt < há:wt.
rat, vole (short-tailed mouse), may include any or all of the following which occur in this area: creeping vole, long-tail vole, mountain heather vole, boreal redback vole, Norway rat (intro.), and perhaps roof rat, also includes bushy-tailed wood rat (packrat) which has its own name below:: há:wt.

packstrap
carry a packstrap around the shoulders and across the chest at the collarbone:: s'íteyí:les.
carry a packstrap or both packstraps over the shoulder(s) and under the arm(s):: sq'iwq'ewíles < q'e:yw ~ q'í:w.
carry a packstrap slung across the chest (over one shoulder and under one arm):: st'át'elhíles < t'álh.
carry[ing] a packstrap around the head:: chmaméleqw < chám.
tumpline, packstrap:: chámatel < chám.
woven headband of packstrap, tumpline:: q'sí:ltel < q'ey ~ q'i.

paddle
canoe paddle:: sq'émél.
canoe paddle, paddler(s):: =ṓwes ~ =ṓ:wes ~ =á:wes ~ =ewes.
everybody put away (fishing gear, canoe and) paddles (for winter), put away each other's paddles [and canoes and gear] for winter:: xets'ṓ:westel < xits' ~ xets'.
five paddles, (by extension) five paddlers:: lhq'átsesṓwes < lheq'át ~ lhq'á:t.
four paddles, four paddlers:: x̲ethlá:wes < x̲e'ó:thel ~ x̲e'óthel.
how many paddles?:: kw'ilṓwes < kw'í:l ~ kw'íl.
moon or month beginning in November, (put away each other's paddles), (sometimes the moon beginning in October, depending on the weather [Elders Group [3/12/75], (moon or month beginning in January [Elders Group 2/5/75]):: xets'ṓ:westel ~ xets'ṓwestel < xits' ~ xets'.
one paddle, one paddler:: lets'á:wes < léts'a ~ léts'e.
(one person) puts away his paddles (and canoe and gear for winter):: xets'ṓ:wes < xits' ~ xets'.
paddles on spirit-dancer's costume, trimmings on uniform (paddles, etc.):: stl'íitl'ets < tl'íts ~ tl'ích.
paddling:: í:xel < éxel.
plane it (with a plane), trim it, taper it (about wood, like slats or roots for baskets, poles for houseposts/totem poles, paddles), taper it (with knife or plane), peel it (a fruit, etc.), whittle it, strip or peel bark off of it, scrape it (of carrots), (carve it, peel it [AC]):: xípet < xíp.
pry (a canoe paddling stroke when the canoe is hard to turn):: lhímesem < lhímes.
pry with paddle in stern to turn a canoe sharply, pry (canoe stroke done by a sternman):: q'á:lets.
pull in once with a canoe paddle wide or slow, pull in in turning (a canoe paddling stroke

paddle (CONT'D)

done by a bowman):: lhímes.
short paddle:: ts'ítl'ōwes or ts'ítl'ewes < ts'í:tl' ~ ts'ítl'.
six paddles, six paddlers:: t'x̲emṓwes < t'éx̲.
soapberry spoon, soapberry paddle, short-handled spoon, flat spoon for sx̲wṓsem:: th'émtel < th'ím ~ th'í:m.
store away one's paddles:: xets'ṓwesem < xits' ~ xets'.
swimming (of dog, deer, animal), (dog-paddling):: x̲ólhchem < x̲élhchem.
ten paddles:: epálōwes < ó:pel.
three paddles, three paddlers:: lhxwṓ:wes < lhí:xw.
to paddle, paddling a canoe (in rough water):: éxel.
two paddles:: islá:wes < isá:le ~ isále ~ isá:la.

paddler

canoe paddle, paddler(s):: =ṓwes ~ =ṓ:wes ~ =á:wes ~ =ewes.
five paddles, (by extension) five paddlers:: lhq'átsesṓwes < lheq'át ~ lhq'á:t.
four paddles, four paddlers:: x̲ethlá:wes < x̲e'ó:thel ~ x̲e'óthel.
one paddle, one paddler:: lets'á:wes < léts'a ~ léts'e.
seven paddlers, seven "pullers":: th'ekwsále < th'ó:kws.
six paddles, six paddlers:: t'x̲emṓwes < t'éx̲.
stern of canoe, stern-man among paddlers:: iláq.
three paddles, three paddlers:: lhxwṓ:wes < lhí:xw.
two paddlers:: islá:wes < isá:le ~ isále ~ isá:la.

page)

twist s-th/s-o, turn it around, turn s-o, turn s-th (for ex. a page):: x̲élts't < x̲élts'.

pail

pail, bucket, kettle (BJ, Gibbs):: skw'ó:wes ~ skw'ówes.

pain

(be) sore, (be) hurting all the time, painful, aching:: sáyém < sáyem.
(be) suffering pain:: s'ṓ:leqw'.
going to piss right away, almost piss oneself, (have an urgent or extreme or painful need to urinate):: ts'áléqel.
have a pain in the stomach, (have a stomach-ache), one's stomache hurts:: x̲elhálwes < x̲élh.
(have/get) throbbing pain:: téxwem.
have pain, to hurt:: sáyem.
having labor pains, being in labor in childbirth:: ts'áts'elem.
hurting, feeling sore, (feel[ing] pain [BJ]):: táteqlexw < téqlexw.
to hurt again (as when a painful place is bumped and hurts again or as when a pain inside one's body returns again), (to ache [SJ]):: téqlexw.

paint

black paint:: ts'q'éyx̲ témelh < témélh.
diatomaceous earth (could be mixed with things to whiten them--for ex. dog and goat wool), white clay for white face paint (for pure person spirit-dancers), white powder from mountains, white clay they make powder from to lighten goat and dog wool for blankets, powder, talc, white face paint:: st'ewṓkw'.
Indian red paint (used by spirit dancers, ritualists, and Indian doctors or shamans):: témélh.
painted people (spirit-dancers):: slhílhex̲es < lhá:x̲ ~ lháx̲.

paint (CONT'D)

painting:: yátl'q'els < yétl'.
painting it:: yátl'q't < yétl'.
paint (nominal):: syátl'q'els < yétl'.
paint one's body:: x̲é:ylthet < x̲él ~ x̲é:yl ~ x̲í:l
paint one's face red or black (spirit dancer, Indian doctor, ritualist, etc.):: lhíx̲esem < lhá:x̲ ~ lháx̲.
paint s-o, (paint marks on s-th/s-o):: x̲é:ylt < x̲él ~ x̲é:yl ~ x̲í:l
pencil, pen, something to write with, (device to write or paint or mark with):: x̲éltel < x̲él ~ x̲é:yl ~ x̲í:l
(perhaps) red rock fungus used for Indian paint, (perhaps) Indian paint fungus:: témélh.
put paint on one's face:: yétl'q'esem < yétl'.
put paint on the body:: yétl'q'íws < yétl'.
put (white) paint on one's face:: t'ewṓkw'esem < st'ewṓkw'.
red paint:: tskwím témelh < témélh.
rub (oil or water) in s-th to clean or soften, rub s-th to soften or clean it, (shaping a stone hammer with abrasion?, shaping?, mixing paint?, pressing together or crushing? [BHTTC 9/2/76]):: yémq't.
rub s-th/s-o, smear s-th, (paint s-th):: yétl'q't < yétl'.
Schelowat, a village at the bend in Hope Slough at Annis Rd. where there was a painted or marked house:: Sx̲elá:wtxw < x̲él ~ x̲é:yl ~ x̲í:l
spread red or black paint on s-th(?)/s-o:: lhíx̲et < lhá:x̲ ~ lháx̲.
to paint red or black (spirit dancer, Indian doctor, etc.):: lhíx̲ < lhá:x̲ ~ lháx̲.
white paint:: p'éq̲' témelh < témélh.

pair

pair of twins, pair of closest friends:: sq'eq'e'óleq < q'ó.

pal

pal, best friend, dear friend, chum:: q'óleq ~ q'e'óléq < q'ó.

palate

cleft palate, harelip:: qiqewótheló:ythel < sqewáth.
roof of the mouth, inside of upper lip, palate:: chelhqí:l ~ chelhqéyl < =chílh ~ chílh=.

pall-bearing

thank s-o (for a cure, for pall-bearing, a ceremony, being a witness):: xwth'í:t < ts'ít ~ ch'í:t.

palm

palm (of the hand):: shxw'óthestses ~ shxwe'óthestses < s'ó:thes ~ s'óthes.

pan

frying pan:: ts'ákwx̲els < ts'ékwx̲t.
sink, dish-pan:: shxwth'ox̲wewí:ls < th'éx̲w or th'óx̲w.
water kettle, boiler pan (for canning, washing clothes or dishes):: qowletsá:ls < qew.

Pandalus danae

suborder Natantia, probably Crago and other genera, especially Crago vulgaris, Pandalus danae were identified by AD from a photo as the kind AD's parents got dried from the Chinese and called by this name:: homò:y.

Pandion haliaetus:: th'éxwth'exw < th'íxw ~ th'éxw.

pant
  panting:: kw'éxalhàlem ~ kw'exelhálém.

pantry :: pélemálá < pél (perhaps ~ pí:l by now).

pants :: =áyiws ~ =éyiws ~ =áyews.
  denim pants, jeans:: xwétkw'emáyiws < xwót'kw'em.
  five (pairs of) pants:: lhq'atseséyiws < lheq'át ~ lhq'á:t.
  four pants:: x̲e'otheláyiws < x̲e'ó:thel ~ x̲e'óthel.
  (have) pants sliding down:: lhosemáyiws < lhós.
  mess in one's pants (shit in one's pants):: ó'ayiwsem < ó'.
  one pair of pants:: lets'áyiws < léts'a ~ léts'e.
  pants, trousers:: seqíws ~ seqí:ws.
  put on one's pants:: seqí:wsem < seqíws ~ seqí:ws.
  short pants, little pants, underpants:: siseqíws ~ síseqíws < seqíws ~ seqí:ws.
  sticking out through a hole (like a toe out of a sock, knee out of a hole in pants, a nail driven clear through the other side of a board), come out into the open:: qwōhóls (or perhaps) qwehóls < qwá.
  three pants:: lhexwáyiws < lhí:xw.
  two pants:: isláyiws < isá:le ~ isále ~ isá:la.
  wet one's pants, (urinate in one's pants):: sex̲we'ayíwsem < séx̲we.

paper :: pípe.
  (have/get) a rustling noise (not continuous) (of paper, silk, or other material), (to rustle):: sawéts'em.
  (making a) continuous rustling noise (of paper or silk or material), rustling (of leaves, paper, a sharp sound):: sá:wts'em < sawéts'em.
  toilet paper:: shxwep'életstel ~ shxwp'életstel < áp'.

Papilio eurymedon
  if the name applies to one or more predominantly white butterflies it could include the following which occur in the Stó:lō area: family Papilionidae: Parnassius clodius, Parnassius phoebus, Papilio eurymedon, family Pieridae: Neophasia menapia, Pieris occidentalis, Pieris napi, albino females of Colias erytheme:: p'ip'eq'eyós < p'éq'.

Papilionidae:
  if the name applies to one or more predominantly white butterflies it could include the following which occur in the Stó:lō area: family Papilionidae: Parnassius clodius, Parnassius phoebus, Papilio eurymedon, family Pieridae: Neophasia menapia, Pieris occidentalis, Pieris napi, albino females of Colias erytheme:: p'ip'eq'eyós < p'éq'.

Papilio spp.:: ep'ó:yethel? or epó:yethel?.

parachute)
  let oneself fall, drop oneself down (by parachute, rope, etc., said of little birds trying to fly out of nest, little animals trying to get down and let themselves fall):: chólqthet < tsélq ~ chélq.

paralyze
  die, be dead, be paralyzed:: q'ó:y ~ q'óy.
  (have a) paralyzed hand, game hand:: slhéx̲tses < lhéx̲.
  (have a) paralyzed leg, game leg:: slhéx̲xel < lhéx̲.

parent :: shxwewá(:)y.
child's spouse's parent, child's spouse's sibling, child's in-laws:: skw'élwés.
having the same parents:: qeqemótel < qemó:.
mother-in-law, father-in-law, spouse's parent, parent-in-law:: skw'ílhew.
older sibling, elder cousin (child of older sibling of one's parent, grandchild of older sibling of one's grandparent, great grandchild of older sibling of one's great grandparent), cousin of senior line, older brother, older sister:: sétl'atel < sétl'a ~ sétl'o.
parents, relations (ancestors?):: shxwwáli < shxwewá(:)y.
step-parent:: tslhilá:m.
younger sibling, younger brother, younger sister, child of younger sibling of one's parent, "younger" cousin (could even be fourth cousin [through younger sibling of one's great great grandparent]):: sqá:q.

parent-in-law
in-laws (?), parents-in-law, spouse's parents:: skw'álhew < skw'ílhew.
mother-in-law, father-in-law, spouse's parent, parent-in-law:: skw'ílhew.

parents
in-laws (?), parents-in-law, spouse's parents:: skw'álhew < skw'ílhew.

parent's cousin
parent's cousin, parent's sibling, uncle, aunt:: shxwemlí:kw.

parent's sibling's spouse
uncle's wife, aunt's husband, parent's sibling's spouse, uncle by marriage, aunt by marriage:: xchápth ~ schápth.

parlor
liquor store, beer parlor (AC):: lamáwtxw < lám.

Parnassius clodius
if the name applies to one or more predominantly white butterflies it could include the following which occur in the Stó:lō area: family Papilionidae: Parnassius clodius, Parnassius phoebus, Papilio eurymedon, family Pieridae: Neophasia menapia, Pieris occidentalis, Pieris napi, albino females of Colias erytheme:: p'ip'eq'eyós < p'éq'.

Parnassius phoebus
if the name applies to one or more predominantly white butterflies it could include the following which occur in the Stó:lō area: family Papilionidae: Parnassius clodius, Parnassius phoebus, Papilio eurymedon, family Pieridae: Neophasia menapia, Pieris occidentalis, Pieris napi, albino females of Colias erytheme:: p'ip'eq'eyós < p'éq'.

parsely fern
yarrow, also parsely fern:: xaweqá:l < xáwéq.

parsnip
cow parsnip sprout (especially the edible inside part):: sóqw'.
stringy fibers (as on cow parsnip):: x̲wéylem ~ x̲wé:ylem ~ x̲wí:lem.
wild celery, cow parsnip:: yóle ~ yóla ~ yó:le.

part

back end of a house (inside or outside), back part of a house:: stselqwáx̲el < chá:l or chó:l.
breast bone, part of human body between breast bone and ribs:: th'x̲ámél.
companion, other part:: sq'ó < q'ó.
female part of female plant:: slheli'ál < slhá:lí.
(have a) part in the hair, to part (hair):: kw'éts'eles < kw'íts'.
location around a house, part:: =mel.
member or part (of the body):: =ó:mél ~ =á:mel.
part away from the river, side away from the river:: chóleqwmel < chá:l or chó:l.
part, member, nick-:: =á:mel.
part not used (like seeds of cantelope, core of apple, blood in fish, etc.), worst part:: sqéls < qél.
part (of a place):: =ó:mél ~ =á:mel.
part, (portion):: tl'émexw.
part the hair on the right side (left side as people look at you), have the hair parted on the right side:: kelchochéleqw < kelchóch ~ kyelchóch.
the outside part of a house:: s'átl'qmel < átl'q.
to part one's hair:: kw'éts'elesem < kw'íts'.
upper part or top of a house, upper part or top of a pit-house:: tslháltxw < =chílh ~ chílh=.

partially

(be) partially blind, almost blind:: qelsílém < qél.

partition

a partition, wall inside:: t'omeliwétel < t'ómel ~ t'ómél.

partitive)

of (partitive):: telí < tel=.

partner :: sq'ó:xel ~ sq'óxel < q'ó.

go with, come with, be partner with:: q'axí:l < q'ó.
little partner, little person who follows or goes with one:: sq'iq'exí:l ~ q'iq'exí:l < q'ó.
partners:: sq'eq'axí:l < q'ó.
reject someone as a spouse or partner for one's child:: qá:lmílh < qéylem ~ qé:ylem ~ qí(:)lem.
reject someone as a spouse or partner for your child:: qá:lmílh.

party

warrior, (leader of a raiding party [CT]):: stó:méx.

Parus atricapillus occidentalis

Parus atricapillus occidentalis, probably also Parus rufescens, possibly also Psaltriparus minimus:: skíkek < sqá:q.
Parus atricapillus occidentalis, prob. Parus rufescens, poss. Psaltriparus minimus:: méxts'el.

Parus rufescens

Parus atricapillus occidentalis, probably also Parus rufescens, possibly also Psaltriparus minimus:: skíkek < sqá:q.
Parus atricapillus occidentalis, prob. Parus rufescens, poss. Psaltriparus minimus:: méxts'el.

pass
be over, past (passed):: yelá:w ~ yeláw ~ yiláw.
he passes on a disease to s-o, he gets s-o addicted:: q'ep'lóxes < q'áp'.
just past, over:: yeláwel < yelá:w ~ yeláw ~ yiláw.
Monday (day past):: yilawelhát ~ yiláwelhàt ~ syiláwelhàt < yelá:w ~ yeláw ~ yiláw.
pass around to give away (at a dance for example):: lhít'es < lhít'.
pass by s-o:: yelá:wt < yelá:w ~ yeláw ~ yiláw.
pass it around (papers, berries, anything):: lhít'et < lhít'.
pass it around to s-o:: lhít'est < lhít'.
pass s-th (at a meal for ex.):: sátet < sát.
pass s-th (by hand):: xwmítsesem < mí ~ mé ~ me.
to pass by s-th/s-o:: yelá:wx < yelá:w ~ yeláw ~ yiláw.
transform it more, pass it over the fire more (at a burning):: x̲iyx̲éyt or x̲eyx̲éyt < x̲éyt.

passage)
narrow (of rocky passage):: x̲eq'.

Passerculus sandwichensis brooksi
Melospiza melodia morphna, (perhaps any/all of the following: Passerculus sandwichensis brooksi, Pooecetes gramineus, Chondestes grammacus, Spizella arborea, Spizella passerina, Zonotrichia querula, Passerella iliaca, Zonotrichia leucophrys, Zonotrichia atricapilla, Melospiza melodia morphna):: sx̲wőx̲wtha.

Passerella iliaca
Melospiza melodia morphna, (perhaps any/all of the following: Passerculus sandwichensis brooksi, Pooecetes gramineus, Chondestes grammacus, Spizella arborea, Spizella passerina, Zonotrichia querula, Passerella iliaca, Zonotrichia leucophrys, Zonotrichia atricapilla, Melospiza melodia morphna):: sx̲wőx̲wtha.

pass food
give s-o food, bring s-o food, pass food to s-o:: áxwet.

pass gas
to fart, pass gas:: téq'.
to pass gas, break wind, to fart:: pú'.

passive
first person plural patient or object of passive:: -òlèm.
first person singular patient or object of passive:: -àlèm.
(probably also) subordinate or dependent (with passive):: -èt.
second person singular patient or object of passive:: -ò:m.
subjunctive of passive:: -èt.
third person patient or object of passive:: -em.

pass out
passed out (if drunk):: lexwmálqewelh < mál ~ mél.
pass out, faint:: t'eqw'élhelh < t'éqw'.

past
a little past, a little after:: yéyilaw ~ yíyelaw < yelá:w ~ yeláw ~ yiláw.
ancestors past, (all one's ancestors):: syesyewálelh < yewá:l.

past (CONT'D)

be over, past (passed):: yelá:w ~ yeláw ~ yiláw.
elders past, deceased old people:: siyolexwálh < siyólexwe.
just past, over:: yeláwel < yelá:w ~ yeláw ~ yiláw.
Monday (day past):: yilawelhát ~ yiláwelhàt ~ syiláwelhàt < yelá:w ~ yeláw ~ yiláw.
recent past third person subject:: le.

paste

stick it on, paste it on (of stamps or anything):: t'elémt < t'elém.

past tense

late (deceased), past tense:: =à:lh ~ =elh.
recent past tense:: á.
wasn't?, weren't?, didn't?:: ewá:lh ~ wá:lh < éwe ~ ṓwe.
weren't ever?, wasn't ever?, didn't ever?, does s-o ever?, never used to, not going to (but did anyway) [perhaps in the sense of never usually do X but did this time]:: ewá:lh ~ wá:lh < éwe ~ ṓwe.

patch

(be) patched:: sp'ewéy < p'ewíy ~ p'ōwíy.
patch a canoe:: lhéqōwelh ~ lhéqwōwelh < lhéq.
patch s-th (of clothes, nets), patch s-th up:: p'ōwíyt ~ p'ewíyt < p'ewíy ~ p'ōwíy.
strawberry vine, strawberry plant, strawberry patch:: schí:yà:lhp < schí:ya.
to patch:: p'ewíy ~ p'ōwíy.
you patch it for me:: p'ṓwiyelhthóxchexw < p'ewíy ~ p'ōwíy.

path

path, trail:: xáxlh < xálh ~ xá:lh.

patient

be patient, Be patient.:: tl'épstexw ta' sqwálewel. < tl'ép.
blowing (of an Indian doctor on a patient):: pópex̲wels < póx̲w.
blow (spray) on a patient (of an Indian doctor or shaman), blow spray on s-o/s-th (of a shaman, a person ironing, a child teething):: póx̲wet < póx̲w.
first person plural patient or object of passive:: -òlèm.
first person singular patient or object of passive:: -àlèm.
second person singular patient or object of passive:: -ò:m.
third person patient or object of passive:: -em.

pay

pay attention to s-o:: xwe'íwelmet.
pay for:: q'áwelhs < q'áwet.
pay s-o:: q'áwet.
repay, pay a debt:: léwlets ~ lṓwlets.

pea

kinnikinnick berry, bearberry, Indian tobacco, domestic pea, domestic green bean, and probably giant vetch berry:: tl'íkw'el.
kinnikinnick plant, domestic pea-vine, domestic bean-vine, giant vetch vine:: tl'ikw'íyelhp < tl'íkw'el.
open (of peas, beans):: xwís.

peaceful

(get) calm, (become) calm, peaceful:: líqwel < líqw.

Peak

basin lake near top of Cheam Peak:: Xwoqwsemó:leqw.
(probably) Slollicum Peak:: Stl'áleqem Smált < stl'á:leqem.
the hole (lake) at the foot of Cheam Peak on the south side:: Sqwá:p < qwá.

peak

another small peak just to the right of the Mount Cheam summit peak as one faces south, she is another daughter of Lhílheqey (Mt. Cheam):: S'óyewòt < Óyewòt.
Mount Ogilvie or a round peak or bluff on Mt. Ogilvie where mountain goats live, the mountain or peak or bluff resembles big breasts:: Qwemth'í:les < qwó:m ~ qwóm ~ qwem.
peak of house:: sq'eyth'éleqw.
peak of house, gable or plank over smokehole:: sq'eyx̲éleqw.
peak of mountain:: sq'eyth'éleqw.
smallest peak just below Mount Cheam (on left of Mt. Cheam looking south), Lhílheqey's (Mt. Cheam's) baby (located about where her breast would be on the left hand side facing her):: Óyewòt.
small peak next to Mount Cheam:: X̲emó:th'iya < x̲à:m ~ x̲á:m.

peal

to rattle (of dishes or anything else loose), jingle (of money or any metal shaken), peal or toll (of a bell), make the sound of a bell, to ring (of a bell, telephone, in the ears):: th'á:tsem < th'éts or th'á(:)ts.

peanut

nut of hazelnut bush, acorn, any nut, walnut, peanut, etc.:: sth'í:tsem < th'éts.

pebble

little stone, pebble, little rock hill, small rock mountain (like in the Fraser River in the canyon):: smámelet < smá:lt.

peck

pecking:: t'ót'ep'els < t'óp'.
peck s-th/s-o:: t'ópet < t'óp.
red-headed woodpecker, (pileated woodpecker):: t'ot'ep'íqselem < t'óp'.
to peck:: t'óp'els < t'óp'.

pectoral

fin, neck fin, i.e. pectoral fin:: q'étmel.

Pediculus capitis

Pediculus capitis, perhaps others of Pediculus humanus:: p'éq' méxts'el < méxts'el.
Pediculus humanus: Pediculus capitis, (secondarily) Pediculus corporis, and possibly Pediculus pubis, (unclear if others of the order Phthiraptera):: méxts'el.

Pediculus corporis

Pediculus humanus: Pediculus capitis, (secondarily) Pediculus corporis, and possibly Pediculus pubis, (unclear if others of the order Phthiraptera):: méxts'el.

Pediculus humanus
eggs of the order Phthiraptera (lice), esp. eggs of Pediculus humanus (human lice) and perhaps of other parasites:: x̲ést'el.
Pediculus capitis, perhaps others of Pediculus humanus:: p'éq' méxts'el < méxts'el.
Pediculus humanus and possibly others of order Phthiraptera:: mexméxts'el < méxts'el.
Pediculus humanus: Pediculus capitis, (secondarily) Pediculus corporis, and possibly Pediculus pubis, (unclear if others of the order Phthiraptera):: méxts'el.

Pediculus pubis
Pediculus humanus: Pediculus capitis, (secondarily) Pediculus corporis, and possibly Pediculus pubis, (unclear if others of the order Phthiraptera):: méxts'el.

pee (see also urinate)
want to pee, (want to urinate, feel like one has to urinate):: síyt'eqem < síyt'.

peek
be peeking:: pelókwes ~ peló:kwes < pél:ékw.
peek under a woman's skirt:: xwpelákw < pél:ékw.

peel
bark-peeler:: lhéqw'ewsà:ls < lhéqw'.
it peeled off, comes off:: lhéqw'.
peel (as a structured activity, for ex. in fixing vegetables):: ts'óls or ts'ó:ls < ts'ó:l.
peel a tree:: lhoqw'esá:ls < lhéqw'.
peel bark (as structured activity):: lheqw'á:ls < lhéqw'.
peel cedar bark:: síqw'em.
peeling bark:: lhólheqw'els < lhéqw'.
peel it (bark off a tree), bark it, (de-bark it), pull itdown (of bark, board, etc.), pull it up (of bark, board):: lheqw'ó:t < lhéqw'.
peel it off (bark of a tree):: lhqw'íwst < lhéqw'.
peel it off (clothes):: lhqw'íwst < lhéqw'.
peel s-th (esp. fruit or vegetable root or a vegetable like squash or a round object):: xepólst < xíp.
plane it (with a plane), trim it, taper it (about wood, like slats or roots for baskets, poles for houseposts/totem poles, paddles), taper it (with knife or plane), peel it (a fruit, etc.), whittle it, strip or peel bark off of it, scrape it (of carrots), (carve it, peel it [AC]):: xípet < xíp.
to get skinned, peel the skin off:: ts'ó:l.

peeler
bark-peeler:: lhéqw'ewsà:ls < lhéqw'.

peeping-Tom
(have) quick eyes, (have) peeping-Tom eyes:: aliyólés < éy ~ éy:.

pelt
skin, hide (with/without hair or fur), pelt, sinew:: kw'eléw ~ kw'elṓw.

pen
pencil, pen, something to write with, (device to write or paint or mark with):: x̲éltel < x̲él ~ x̲é:yl ~ x̲í:l

pencil

eraser (for pencil or blackboard):: shxwe'íqw'els < íqw'.

pencil, pen, something to write with, (device to write or paint or mark with):: x̲éltel < x̲él ~ x̲é:yl ~ x̲í:l

penis :: sxéle.

big penis, (have a big penis):: thá:q < thi ~ tha ~ the ~ thah ~ theh.

foreskin:: shxw'á:q' <

get erect (of penis only), have an erection:: xátl'.

head of the penis:: sxtl'í:qw < xátl'.

I got hard (of arm, leg, penis, etc.):: tl'x̲wòlèm < tl'éx̲w.

on the penis, in the penis, on the genitals, on the male:: =á:q ~ =aq ~ =eq.

press & rub his penis, massage s-o's penis:: xwíqweqt < =á:q ~ =aq ~ =eq

pull s-o's penis:: thekw'áqt < =á:q ~ =aq ~ =eq

she was sucking his penis:: thótheqweqtes < =á:q ~ =aq ~ =eq

tease s-o's penis:: weth'áqt < =á:q ~ =aq ~ =eq

Penis Rock

Penis Rock near Cheam View:: Sxéle < sxéle.

Pennier

Hank Pennier's nickname:: Swék'ten < swék'.

people :: =ále.

a group of people, a tribe of people, several tribes:: ó:wqw'elmexw or ó:wkw'elmexw.

a lot of people:: qx̲álets < qéx̲.

ancient people over a hundred years old:: sx̲wolex̲wiyám < x̲wiyám.

big-bodied people, (have big bodies):: thíthehí:ws < thi ~ tha ~ the ~ thah ~ theh.

Chilliwack Indian people:: Sts'elxwíqw ~ Ts'elxwíqw ~ Ts'elxwéyeqw < ts'el.

Coquitlam Indian people:: Kwíkwetl'em.

Cowichan (people, dialect, area):: Qewítsel < qew.

different tribe, different people, strangers:: lets'ó:lmexw < láts'.

eight people:: teqátsa'ále < tqá:tsa.

eighty people:: teqetselsxá:le < tqá:tsa.

elders past, deceased old people:: siyolexwálh < siyólexwe.

fifty people:: lheq'etselsxále < lheq'át ~ lhq'á:t.

five people:: lhq'átsále < lheq'át ~ lhq'á:t.

forty people:: x̲ethelsxále < x̲e'ó:thel ~ x̲e'óthel.

four people:: x̲ethí:le ~ x̲ethíle < x̲e'ó:thel ~ x̲e'óthel.

high class people:: semelá:lh < smelá:lh.

how many people?:: kw'ílà < kw'í:l ~ kw'íl.

Kwantlen people, Kwantlen dialect of Downriver Halkomelem:: Qw'ó:ltl'el.

Lillooet people, Port Douglas (also Lillooet) people:: sth'kwólh.

lots of people crying:: x̲emx̲ám < x̲à:m ~ x̲á:m.

lots of people picking:: lhemlhí:m < lhím.

Lummi (person, people):: Lém:i ~ Lexwlém:i.

midget, small people:: s'ó:lmexw.

nine people:: tuxwále < tú:xw.

ninety people:: tuxwelsxá:le < tú:xw.

Nooksack people:: Lexwsá:q < sá:q.

old people:: sí:yólexwe < siyó:lexwe ~ syó:lexwe ~siyólexwe.

people (CONT'D)

old people, elders:: sí:yólexwe < siyólexwe.
painted people (spirit-dancers):: slhílhex̲es < lhá:x̲ ~ lháx̲.
people from Semá:th (Sumas village):: Pepá:thxetel < pá:th.
people, person:: =mexw.
people without paint on face (non-dancers):: s'ep'ó:s < á:p' ~ áp'.
Pilalt tribe, Pilalt people, Pilalt dialect, (Pilalt, village at west end of Little Mountain by Agassiz [Wells, Duff]):: Pelólhxw.
Saanich people:: Sáléch.
Salish people:: Sálesh, Syálex.
seven people:: th'ekwsále < th'ó:kws.
seventy people:: th'ekwselsxá:le < th'ó:kws.
Shuswap people:: Shushxwáp.
six people:: t'x̲émele < t'éx̲.
sixty people:: t'x̲emelsxá:le < t'éx̲.
Sliammon people, Sliammon dialect (of the Comox language, Mainland Comox):: Sloyámén.
Squamish people:: Sqwx̲wó:mex, Tellhós < lhós.
Stó:lō people, Halkomelem-speaking people living along the Fraser River or its tributaries from Five Mile Creek above Yale downriver to the mouth of the Fraser:: Stó:lō < tó:l ~ tò:l.
ten people:: epále < ó:pel.
thirty people:: lhxwelhsxále < lhí:xw.
Thompson people:: S'em'oméla < S'omél:a.
three little people:: lhelhxwále < lhí:xw.
three people:: lhxwá:le ~ lhxwále < lhí:xw.
to perish (of a lot of people):: s'ekw"í:kw' < íkw' ~ í:kw'.
twenty people:: ts'ekw'xále < ts'kw'éx.
two people:: yáysele ~ yéysele < isá:le ~ isále ~ isá:la.
Yuculta Kwakiutl people, southern Kwakiutl people from Cape Mudge north who raided the Salish people:: Yéqwelhtax̲ ~ Yéqwelhta.

Peqwchṓ:lthel

the whole riverbank on the CPR (west) side of the Fraser River just south of Strawberry Island and just north of Peqwchṓ:lthel:: Selch'éle < sél or sí(:)l.

perhaps

maybe, perhaps, I don't know (if), may (possibly):: yóswe ~ yó:swe.

Perideridiae gairdneri

possibly Lomatium utriculatum or Perideridiae gairdneri, also Daucus carota:: xáwéq.

period

a rock in the creek at the upriver end of Seabird Island that was a girl washing after her first period:: The Théthex̲w or Thethéthex̲w < thethíx̲w.
(be) Spring, [cyclic period] when everything comes up:: kw'íyles ~ kw'éyles < kw'í ~ kw'íy.
cyclic period, moon, season:: =ó:s ~ =ós ~ =es.
girl at puberty, (girl's first period):: thethíx̲w.
has come around (of a cyclic period of time):: séqsel.
one cyclic period:: léts'es < léts'a ~ léts'e.
Thursday, four o'clock, (fourth cyclic period):: sx̲e'óthels < x̲e'ó:thel ~ x̲e'óthel.

periods
(fifty cyclic periods [DM]):: lhèq'etselsxó:s ~ lhéq'etselsxó:s < lheq'át ~ lhq'á:t.
thirty cyclic periods:: lhexwelhsxó:s < lhí:xw.
three dollars, three tokens of wealth, three blankets (Boas), three cyclic periods:: lhí:xwes < lhí:xw.

perish
lost and presumed dead, perish:: s'í:kw' < íkw' ~ í:kw'.
perish together, many die (in famine, sickness, fire), all die, get wiped out:: x̲wà:y ~ x̲wá:y.
to perish (of a lot of people):: s'ekw"í:kw' < íkw' ~ í:kw'.

Perisoreus canadensis griseus:: sáwel < sáwel.

Peromyscus maniculatus
Peromyscus maniculatus, Peromyscus oreas, and Mus musculus domesticus:: kw'át'el.

Peromyscus oreas
Peromyscus maniculatus, Peromyscus oreas, and Mus musculus domesticus:: kw'át'el.

perpendicular
angular or perpendicular extension:: =áx̲el ~ =ex̲el.

persistant
insistant, persistant (like a child pressing to go along), bull-headed, doesn't mind, does just the opposite, (stubborn, contrary):: sxíxeles.

person :: mestíyexw, R10= or C1ó=, = ´talh.
ancient people over a hundred years old:: sx̲wolex̲wiyám < x̲wiyám.
a person that always:: lexws= < lexw= ~ xw= ~ (rarely) le=.
a person that always hunts, hunter:: lexws=há:wa < háwe.
a person that always sings:: lexwst'í:lem < t'íl.
a person that's always lazy:: lexws'ú:met < emét.
a person that sings all the time (any song), a singer:: st'élt'el < t'íl.
be chilled (of a person), got cold (of a person):: th'óth'elhem < th'álh.
big person (of females), big lady:: thékwàl.
Chinese person:: chá:lmel.
(cold (of a person) or get cooled down, get cold):: th'ólhem < th'álh.
cool off (of a person):: xálxwthet < xó:lxwem.
coward, person that's always afraid:: lexwsí:si < síy.
cry with someone, a person one cries with (related or not), unrelated grandparents of a deceased grandchild, etc.:: ts'elhx̲à:m < x̲à:m ~ x̲á:m.
different person, stranger:: lets'ő:mexw < láts'.
different tribe, different people, strangers:: lets'ó:lmexw < láts'.
eight people:: teqátsa'ále < tqá:tsa.
elders past, deceased old people:: siyolexwálh < siyólexwe.
fifty people:: lheq'etselsxále < lheq'át ~ lhq'á:t.
five people:: lhq'átsále < lheq'át ~ lhq'á:t.
fortune-teller, seer, person who can see things in the future, female witch:: syéw:e ~ syéwe ~ syő:we ~ syú:we < yéw: ~ yéw.
four people:: x̲ethí:le ~ x̲ethíle < x̲e'ó:thel ~ x̲e'óthel.
Frenchman, French person:: pálchmel.

person (CONT'D)

German person:: chá:mel ?.
(have a) crooked leg, (be a) crooked-legged person:: spipíyxel < pó:y.
hermaphrodite (person with organs of both sexes), hermaphrodite baby:: t'ámiya.
high class people:: semelá:lh < smelá:lh.
Indian person, (North American) Indian:: xwélmexw.
Japanese person:: chaplí.
little old person:: siyó:ylexwe < siyó:lexwe ~ syó:lexwe ~siyólexwe.
little partner, little person who follows or goes with one:: sq'iq'exí:l ~ q'iq'exí:l < q'ó.
low class person, [person on the lowest economic class]:: stít-sòs < t-sós ~ tesós.
Lummi (person, people):: Lém:i ~ Lexwlém:i.
nine people:: tuxwále < tú:xw.
ninety people:: tuxwelsxá:le < tú:xw.
old people:: sí:yólexwe < siyó:lexwe ~ syó:lexwe ~siyólexwe.
old people, elders:: sí:yólexwe < siyólexwe.
old person:: siyó:lexwe ~ syó:lexwe < siyó:lexwe ~ syó:lexwe ~siyólexwe.
old person, an elder:: siyólexwe < siyólexwe.
one person, be alone:: lólets'e < léts'a ~ léts'e.
optimist, a person whose thoughts are always good:: wiyóth kwsu éys te sqwálewels te lólets'e < wiyóth.
people, person:: =mexw.
person next to one:: stetísmels < tés.
person who is always lazy:: lexws'í:ts'el < í:ts'el.
pessimist, a person whose thoughts are always bad:: wiyóth kwsu qéls te sqwálewels te lólets'e < wiyóth.
pitiful person, helpless person, person unable to do anythingfor himself:: skw'ékw'ith < skw'iyéth.
quiet down (of a person):: tl'elxwí:wsem < tl'élexw.
respected leader, chief, upper-class person, boss, master, your highness:: siyám ~ (rare) siyá:m.
respected person, (high class person [EB]):: smelá:lh.
Sechelt people, Sechelt person:: Sxixálh.
seer, fortune-teller, person that senses the future:: síwe ~ syéwe < síw.
seven people:: th'ekwsále < th'ó:kws.
shaking bushes (of animal or person unseen, for ex.):: xwóykwem.
short (of a person), shorty:: ts'í:ts'tlemeth' < ts'í:tl' ~ ts'ítl'.
short person, short (in stature):: ch'í:tl'emeth' < ts'í:tl' ~ ts'ítl'.
six people:: t'x̲émele < t'éx̲.
structured activity continuative, structured activity continuative nominal or tool or person:: =els.
sweetheart, person of the opposite sex that one is running around with, girl-friend, boy-friend:: ts'elh'á:y < ts'elh=.
tall (of a person):: tl'eqtámeth' ~ tl'eqtáméth' < tl'áqt.
ten people:: epále < ó:pel.
thirty people:: lhxwelhsxále < lhí:xw.
Thompson Indian, Thompson person:: S'omél:a.
three people:: lhxwá:le ~ lhxwále < lhí:xw.
to escape (as an animal from a trap), got away from something that trapped a person or animal:: tl'ewlómét ~ tl'ōwlómét < tl'í:w.
touching bottom (of a canoe or a person):: tesláts < tós.
twenty people:: ts'ekw'xále < ts'kw'éx.
two people:: yáysele ~ yéysele < isá:le ~ isále ~ isá:la.

personality]
  like s-o [his/her personality], like s-th [its taste, its idea], be interested in s-th/s-o, enjoy s-o sexually:: éystexw ~ éy:stexw < éy ~ éy:.

pessimist
  pessimist, a person whose thoughts are always bad:: wiyóth kwsu qéls te sqwálewels te lólets'e < wiyóth.

pester
  annoyed s-o, bothered s-o, pestered s-o:: th'íwélstexw < th'íwél, th'íwélstexw < ts'íw.
  leave s-o alone, stop pestering s-o:: kwikwe'át < kwá:.

pet
  pet s-th/s-o, stroke s-th/s-o:: p'í:qwt < p'í:.

petal
  fall off (of its own accord, of petals or seed fluff):: píxw.
  fall off (of petals or seed fluff):: píxwem < píxw.

Pete
  a mountain above Evangeline Pete's place at Katz:: Sesíq' < séq'.

Peters
  Squatits village on east bank of Fraser river across from the north end of Seabird Island, Peters Indian Reserves #1, 1a, and 2 on site:: Skw'átets < kw'átem.

Peters Reserve
  stagnant water lake or ponds at the downriver end of Skw'átets or Peters Reserve near Laidlaw:: Th'qwélhcha < th'qwélhcha.

pet name :: =R1= or =C1e=.
  girl's younger brother (pet name):: iyá:q, iyá:q.
  grandmother (pet name), grandfather (pet name), granny, grandpa:: sísele < sí:le.
  Mink (name in stories), pet name of Mink:: Sqayéx̲iya ~ Sqáyèx̲iya < sqáyéx̲ ~ sqayéx̲.
  younger sibling (pet name):: ká:k ~ kyá:ky < sqá:q.

petticoat :: lhiwí:ws.
  underskirt, petticoat:: stl'epá:leq < tl'ép.

Phalangida
  class Arachnida, order Araneida, also order Phalangida:: q'ésq'esetsel < q'ey ~ q'i.
  class Arachnida, order Phalangida:: tl'áleqtxel q'esq'ésetsel < q'ey ~ q'i, tl'áleqtxel q'ésq'esetsel < tl'áqt.

Phalaris arundinacea:: ts'á:yas te th'á:x̲ey < th'áx̲.

Phaseolus vulgaris
  Arctostaphylos uva-ursi, (intro.) Pisum sativum, (intro.) Phaseolus vulgaris, and probably Vicea gigantea:: tl'íkw'el.

Phasianus colchicus:: shxwelítemelh sqwéth' < sqwéth', tl'alqtélets ~ tl'alqtélech < tl'áqt.

pheasant
(probably) (ring-necked) pheasant:: shxwelítemelh sqwéth' < sqwéth'.
ring-necked pheasant:: tl'alqtélets ~ tl'alqtélech < tl'áqt.

Phenacomys intermedius oramontis
may include any or all of the following which occur in this area: creeping vole Microtus oregoni serpens, long-tail vole Microtus longicaudus macrurus, mountain heather vole Phenacomys intermedius oramontis, boreal redback vole Clethrionomys gapperi cascadensis, Norway rat (intro.) Rattus norvegicus, and perhaps roof rat Rattus rattus, also includes bushy-tailed wood rat (packrat) Neotoma cinerea occidentalis which has its own name below:: há:wt.
prob. the introduced Rattus norvegius, native species possiblyincluding any/all of these four: Microtus oregoni serpens, Microtus longicaudus macrurus, Phenacomys intermedius oramontis, and Clethrionomys gapperi cascadensis, possibly also the introduced Rattus rattus:: ts'á:txwels < ts'átxwels ~ ch'átxwels.

Philadelphus gordianus:: sth'élhp.

Phoca vitulina richardi:: áshxw.

phone
ringing, phoning:: th'étsàls < th'éts or th'á(:)ts.
ring s-o up, phone s-o:: th'étst < th'éts or th'á(:)ts.
to rattle (of dishes or anything else loose), jingle (of money or any metal shaken), peal or toll (of a bell), make the sound of a bell, to ring (of a bell, telephone, in the ears):: th'á:tsem < th'éts or th'á(:)ts.

phonograph
musical instrument, grammophone, phonograph, record player:: qweló:ythetel ~ qwelóyethetel < qwà:l.

photo
get one's picture taken:: x̲wéychesem (or better) x̲wíythesem < x̲wíyth.
likeness, portrait, photograph, photo, statue:: sx̲wíythi ~ sx̲wéythi < x̲wíyth.
picture, photo, (drawing, etc.):: pékcha.

photograph
get one's picture taken:: x̲wéychesem (or better) x̲wíythesem < x̲wíyth.
likeness, portrait, photograph, photo, statue:: sx̲wíythi ~ sx̲wéythi < x̲wíyth.
take a picture, to photograph:: pekchá:m < pékcha.

Phthiraptera
eggs of the order Phthiraptera (lice), esp. eggs of Pediculus humanus (human lice) and perhaps of other parasites:: x̲ést'el.
Pediculus humanus and possibly others of order Phthiraptera:: mexméxts'el < méxts'el.
Pediculus humanus: Pediculus capitis, (secondarily) Pediculus corporis, and possibly Pediculus pubis, (unclear if others of the order Phthiraptera):: méxts'el.

Physeter catodon
perhaps generic, most likely includes all local balleen whales, i.e., suborder Mysticeti, especially Balaenoptera physalus and Megaptera novaeangliae, possibly Eschrichtius glaucus,

Physeter catodon (CONT'D)
Balaenoptera borealis, Balaenoptera acutorostrata, Sibbaldus musculus, Eubalaena sieboldi, could include the following toothed whales (suborder Odontoceti): Physeter catodon, possibly Berardius bairdi, Mesoplodon stejnegeri, Ziphius cavirostrus:: qwél:és ~ qwélés.

Pica pica :: álel.

Picea sitchensis:: ts'qw'élhp < ts'éqw'.

pick
a pick:: shxwt'ót'ep'els < t'óp'.
a small person (old or young) is picking or trying to pick, an inexperienced person is picking or trying to pick, picking a little bit, someone who can't pick well is picking:: lhilhím < lhím, lhilhím < lhím.
find it, pick it up:: mékw'et ~ mṓkw'et < mékw' ~ mṓkw'.
gather s-th, pick up s-th (stuff that's scattered about), collect s-th, gather it up, pick them up (already gathered or not):: q'pét < q'ép.
lots of people picking:: lhemlhí:m < lhím.
pick berries, pick off (leaves, fruit, vegetables, hops), (pluck off, harvest):: lhím.
pick fast, (do fast with the hands):: x̲wémetses < x̲wém ~ xwém.
pick food by one's fingers (before a meal):: lhámth't < lhím.
picking (berries, etc.):: lhí:m < lhím.
picking food by the fingers before the meal:: lhémth' < lhím.
picking out:: mímesem < mís.
pick it, choose it, sort it, (choose s-o/s-th):: míset < mís.
pick out, sort:: mísem < mís.
pick s-th, (harvest s-th):: lhemét < lhím.
pick s-th up from the ground or floor:: xwpét.
poke it, pin s-th, pick it up (on sharp pointed object), pick s-th up on a fork (or other sharp object):: ts'qw'ét < ts'éqw'.
something used that one picks up and uses, something second-hand:: smékw'em < mékw' ~ mṓkw'.
(take all of themselves, pick themselves all up):: mōkw'éthet < mékw' ~ mṓkw'.
take it all, pick it all up:: mekw'ét ~ mōkw'ét ~ mōkw'ót < mékw' ~ mṓkw'.
take s-th, accept s-th, get s-th, fetch s-th, pick s-th up:: kwú:t.

pickle :: kwúkwemels (lit. cucumber)
t'át'ets'em kúkumels (lit. sour + cucumber). < t'áts', kwúkwemels or kúkumels

pick up
take s-th, accept s-th, get s-th, fetch s-th, pick s-th up:: kwú:t.

Picoides
Colaptes cafer cafer and rarely Colaptes cafer collaris, (if large is correct Dryocopus pileatus [AK], if small is correct, probably Sphyrapicus (varius) ruber or possibly Dryobates villosus harrisi and Dryobates villosus orius or Dryobates pubescens (esp.) gairdneri some zoologists replace the genus Dryobates with Dendrocopos, others with Picoides):: th'íq.
probably Sphyrapicus (varius) ruber and/or possibly Dryobates villosus harrisi and Dryobates villosus orius or(downy woodpecker) Dryobates pubescens (gairdneri esp.), for Munro and Cowan's Dryobates genus Peterson uses Dendrocopos andUdvardy uses Picoides:: qw'opx̲wiqsélem < qw'ópx̲w.

picture
get one's picture taken:: x̲wéychesem (or better) x̲wíythesem < x̲wíyth.
picture, design:: sx̲éles < x̲él ~ x̲é:yl (or better) x̲í:l.
picture of a person (lit. "person pictured"):: mestíyexw x̲élesem < x̲él ~ x̲é:yl (or better) x̲í:l.
picture, photo, (drawing, etc.):: pékcha.
show a picture:: x̲élestexw < x̲él ~ x̲é:yl (or better) x̲í:l.
show a picture of those remembered:: xwpósem te hákw'elesem < xwp, hákw'eles.
take a picture, to photograph:: pekchá:m < pékcha.
(word used when showing a picture of the deceased at a memorial ceremony, and telling the family to dry their tears) his/her face/their faces are dried:: th'éyx̲westem < ts'íyxw ~ ts'éyxw ~ ch'íyxw.

pie :: pó:y.

piece
break it in pieces with one's hands:: peqwpéqwet < péqw.
break s-th in two (with one's hands), break it in half (with one's hands only), break off a piece of s-th:: peqwót < péqw.
broken off in pieces (like a river-bank):: peqwpéqw < péqw.
lots of little pieces of driftwood:: qwéqwelhi(y) < qwélh.
smash s-th to pieces (hard pitch, splintery wood, a glass), break s-th to pieces, beat s-th/s-o to a pulp:: th'ő:wt.
split off, break off, break a piece off, break in two, split in two:: péqw.
to break [in pieces], it broke:: yóqw'em ~ yó:qw'em < yókw' ~ yóqw'.

pierce
be hit (with arrow, bullet, anything shot that you've aimed), got shot, (got pierced), got poked into, got wounded (with gun or arrow):: ts'éqw'.
pierced ear:: sqwehá:liya < qwá.
spear it (a fish), stab s-o/s-th with something sharp, pierce s-o/s-th, prick s-o (with a pin, for ex.), poke s-o (with a pin, etc.):: thq'ét < théq'.

Pieridae:
if the name applies to one or more predominantly white butterflies it could include the following which occur in the Stó:lō area: family Papilionidae: Parnassius clodius, Parnassius phoebus, Papilio eurymedon, family Pieridae: Neophasia menapia, Pieris occidentalis, Pieris napi, albino females of Colias erytheme:: p'ip'eq'eyós < p'éq'.

Pieris napi
if the name applies to one or more predominantly white butterflies it could include the following which occur in the Stó:lō area: family Papilionidae: Parnassius clodius, Parnassius phoebus, Papilio eurymedon, family Pieridae: Neophasia menapia, Pieris occidentalis, Pieris napi, albino females of Colias erytheme:: p'ip'eq'eyós < p'éq'.

Pieris occidentalis
if the name applies to one or more predominantly white butterflies it could include the following which occur in the Stó:lō area: family Papilionidae: Parnassius clodius, Parnassius phoebus, Papilio eurymedon, family Pieridae: Neophasia menapia, Pieris occidentalis, Pieris napi, albino females of Colias erytheme:: p'ip'eq'eyós < p'éq'.

pig
domestic pig:: kweshú.

pig (CONT'D)

little pig:: kwíkweshú < kweshú.
piglet:: kwekweshú'ò:llh < kweshú.
stinking (smell of outhouse or pig farm), (to stink [Elders Group 11/10/76, AC 9/1/71]):: xíxets'em.

pigeon

pigeon, dove, including band-tailed pigeon, mourning dove, and possibly passenger pigeon, also (introduced) domestic pigeon, rock dove:: hemó:, hemó:, hemó:.

pigeon-toed

(be) pigeon-toed, (sandhill crane toed:: slímiyeqwxel < slí:m.

piggy-back:: méwiya.

pika

Rocky Mountain pika, hoary marmot, rock-rabbit:: sk'í:l.

Pilalt

another village of the Pilalt people:: (possibly) Chuwtí:l < cháchew ~ cháchu.
a village of the Pilalt people:: (probably) Scháchewxel ~ Cháchewxel < cháchew ~ cháchu.
Pilalt tribe, Pilalt people, Pilalt dialect, (Pilalt, village at west end of Little Mountain by Agassiz [Wells, Duff]):: Pelólhxw, Pelólhxw, Pelólhxw.
Pilalt, village at west end of Little Mountain by Agassiz:: Pelólhxw.

pile

a pile:: kwthá.
(be) below, (be) underneath, (be) at the bottom of a pile or stack:: stl'epólwelh ~ stl'pólwelh < tl'ép.
five kinds, five piles (perhaps a loose translation):: lhq'átsesmó:t < lheq'át ~ lhq'á:t.
four kinds, (four piles [Elders Group 7/27/75]):: x̱e'óthelmó:t ~ x̱e'óthelmò:t < x̱e'ó:thel ~ x̱e'óthel.
mountain on Fraser River between first tunnel and Yale where rotten fish used to (always) pile up:: Lexwyó:qwem Smá:lt < yó:qw.
one kind, one pile:: lets'emó:t < léts'a ~ léts'e.
piled up:: skwthá < kwthá.
pile it:: kwthát < kwthá.
pile it up (blankets, rocks, anything):: ts'itóléstexw.
piles, kinds:: =mó:t.
place on Fraser River between first tunnel and Yale where rotten fish used to (always) pile up:: Lexwyó:qwem < yó:qw.
three kinds, three piles of things:: lhixwmó:t < lhí:xw.

pill)

chew it (s-th hard, apple, pill):: x̱éykw'et.

pill-bug :: k'ák'elha.

pillow

pillow, rolled bulrush mat:: sx̱wétl'qel.
pillow slip, pillow-case:: sx̱wetl'qelá:la < sx̱wétl'qel.

pillow-case

pillow slip, pillow-case:: sx̲wetl'qelá:la < sx̲wétl'qel.

pin

brooch, pin (ornament pinned to clothing):: ts'eqw'eléstel < ts'éqw'.

poke it, pin s-th, pick it up (on sharp pointed object), pick s-th up on a fork (or other sharp object):: ts'qw'ét < ts'éqw'.

spear it (a fish), stab s-o/s-th with something sharp, pierce s-o/s-th, prick s-o (with a pin, for ex.), poke s-o (with a pin, etc.):: thq'ét < théq'.

pinch :: ts'elhkw'á:ls < th'lhákw'.

pinching:: ts'álhkw'els < th'lhákw'.

pinch s-th, pinch s-o (and pull the skin):: th'lhákw't < th'lhákw'.

someone is being pinched:: th'ith'lhákw'etem < th'lhákw'.

squeeze s-th/s-o, wring s-th (of clothes), pinch s-th/s-o:: p'íth'et < p'í:.

to pinch:: th'lhákw'.

pine

"jack pine", lodgepole pine:: kw'íkw'exwelhp < kw'íxw.

pine-cone:: sts'ék'.

pine, "yellow" pine, western white pine:: qw'eyíléxelhp < qw'eyílex ~ qw'eyíléx.

pitchwood (esp. fir, pine, spruce):: kw'íxwelhp < kw'íxw.

pineapple:: st'elt'elíqw qwe'óp (lit. bumpy and prickly + apple) < t'el, qwe'óp

pineapple juice:: st'elt'elíqw qwe'óp sqe'óleqw < t'el, qwe'óp, qó: (lit. pineapple [itself from bumpy and prickly + apple] + fruit juice)

pink salmon

humpback salmon, pink salmon, humpy:: hő:liya.

pink spirea

pink spirea, "hardhack":: t'áts'elhp < t'á:ts'.

pintail

widgeon (duck), American widgeon or baldpate, probably also the European widgeon, (pintail duck):: sése.

Pinus contorta:: kw'íkw'exwelhp < kw'íxw.

Pinus monticola:: qw'eyíléxelhp < qw'eyílex ~ qw'eyíléx.

pip

heart of a root, seed, nut (kernel), core of plant or seedling, core (of tree, branch, any growing thing), pith (of bush), seed or pit [U.S.] or pip [Cdn.] of a fruit:: sth'emí:wel ~ sth'emíwel ~ sth'emíwél < sth'ó:m.

pipe

metal pipe:: pó:yp.

pipe (for smoking):: sp'òtl'emálá ~ sp'ótl'emàlà < p'ótl'em.

to smoke a pipe:: lhp'ótl'em < p'ótl'em.

Pipilo erythrophthalmus:: sx̲wítl'.

pipsessewa
Prince's pine, pipsessewa:: chéchelex < chálex.

piss (also see urinate)
going to piss right away, almost piss oneself, (have an urgent/extreme/painful need to urinate):: ts'áléqel.

Pisum sativum
Arctostaphylos uva-ursi, Pisum sativum, Phaseolus vulgaris, & prob.Vicea gigantea::tl'íkw'el.

pit)
bake underground, (steam-cook underground, cook in a steam-pit):: qetás < qá:t.
firepit, fireplace:: syéqwlhàlà < yéqw.
firepit in house:: shxwhéyqwela < yéqw.
heart of a root, seed, nut (kernel), core of plant or seedling, core (of tree, branch, any growing thing), pith (of bush), seed or pit [U.S.] or pip [Cdn.] of a fruit:: sth'emí(:)wel ~sth'emíwél < sth'ó:m.
place of training to become an Indian doctor (pit made from repeated jumping every year on the same spot):: shxwlemóthetále < lá:m.

pitch
(have a) high pitch (voice or melody), (have a) sharp voice:: xwiyótheqel < éy ~ éy:.
pitch, sap, gum, chewing gum:: kw'íxw.
run over it (with car), spread it (for ex. on bread with knife), put it up (of wallpaper), (stick it on), stick s-th closed (with pitch for ex.):: tl'íq't < tl'íq'.
scorch s-th, blacken s-th with fire, heat it up (near a fire), burning a canoe with pitchwood to remove splinters and burn on black pitch):: qw'á:yt < qw'á:y.
smash s-th to pieces (hard pitch, splintery wood, a glass), break s-th to pieces, beat s-th/s-o to a pulp:: th'ő:wt.
to harden (of pitch, wax, etc.), (harden s-th):: th'etsét < th'éts.

pitch in
help out, go help, pitch in, help one another:: móylhtel < máy.

pitchwood
pitchwood (esp. fir, pine, spruce):: kw'íxwelhp < kw'íxw.

pith
heart of a root, seed, nut (kernel), core of plant or seedling, core (of tree, branch, any growing thing), pith (of bush), seed or pit [U.S.] or pip [Cdn.] of a fruit:: sth'emí:wel ~ sth'emíwel ~ sth'emíwél < sth'ó:m.

pit-house
adze (for making canoes and pit-house ladders):: xwt'ót'epels ~ shxwt'ót'epels < t'óp.
be inside a pit-house:: sqemí:l < sqémél.
pit-house, keekwillie house, semi-subterranean house:: sqémél.
thick plank for side of house, thick shake for longhouse roof, covering over hole in roof of pit-house:: s'í:ltexw.
upper part or top of a house, upper part or top of a pit-house:: tslháltxw < =chílh ~ chílh=.
village near and above [upriver from] Katz where 36 pit-houses were wiped out in an epidemic:: Sx̱wóx̱wiymelh < x̱wà:y ~ x̱wá:y.

pitiful

pitiful, (bereft, poor):: selá:wa.
pitiful person, helpless person, person unable to do anythingfor himself:: skw'ékw'ith < skw'iyéth.

pit-lamp

spear fish by torchlight, to torchlight, to pit-lamp:: lexéywa ~ lexíwa.
fire box or fire platform and fire shield for torch-lighting or pit-lamping fire:: tl'áts'eq.

pity :: ts'éxwts'exw (or more correct) th'éxwth'exw < th'íxw ~ th'éxw.
ask a favor, ask pity, beseech:: th'exwstélémét < th'íxw ~ th'éxw.
(ask for a favor or pity for s-o):: th'exwstí:lmet < th'íxw ~ th'éxw.
to pity s-o, feel sorry for s-o:: th'éxwmet < th'íxw ~ th'éxw.

pizza:: st'elákw' sp'íp'elh seplíl < t'el(ákw'), p'ílh, seplíl
(lit. round + flat + bread)

place

a nice place near Morris Creek on the (right?) side of Harrison River [IHTTC 8/25/77]):: Lhó:leqwet.
another rough place in the Fraser River (Tait area):: Sq'ólep'exw < Sq'íp'exw.
a place across the Fraser River from the rock named Q'alelíktel:: Xwth'ístel < th'ís.
a place just past the west end of Seabird Island, towards Agassiz, AK's grandfather only translated it as Hamersley's (see Hamersley's hopyards), it was located at the west end of Seabird Island i.e. property between Dan Thomas's and Uncle Dave Charles's places, across from Sqémelets [Elders on Seabird Is. trip 6/20/78]):: Qwoméxweth' < qwó:m ~ qwóm ~ qwem.
a place near Deroche, B.C., just east of Lakahahmen Indian Reserve #10 (which is registered with D.I.A. as Skweam):: Skwiyó:m < Skwíyò.
a place on Chilliwack River, a little above Anderson Flat and Allison's (between Tamihi Creek and Slesse Creek), a village at deep water between Tamihi Creek and Slesse Creek:: Iy'óythel < éy ~ éy:.
a place probably between Yale and Emory Creek:: Momhiya?.
a real rough place in the Fraser River impassible in a canoe (in the Tait area, prob. between Spuzzum and Yale):: Sq'íp'exw.
a village or place at Musqueam (now in Vancouver):: Málí.
chopped in different places:: st'amt'í:m (or better) st'emt'í:m < t'ém.
chop s-th in different places:: t'emt'émet < t'ém.
drifting a net in different places:: qwáseliyel < qwés.
here, this place:: íkw'eló ~ íkw'elo < ló.
hiding place, refuge, hide-out:: kwokwílàlà < kwà:l.
it is cool [of weather], (be) cool (of a place):: sth'áth'elh < th'álh.
name of place right across from Bristol Island, also called Odlum:: Petéyn.
name of place with clay at the edge of the river at some location:: S'áqwemxweth' < qwó:m ~ qwóm ~ qwem.
Nicomen Island (in the Fraser River near Deroche), also a specific place on northeast end of Nicomen Island where lots of people used to gather [now Sumas Indian Reserve #10]:: Leq'á:mél.
one (second) of two creeks just above Popkum which cross Highway #1, (creek between Popkum and Cheam, also a place near Popkum [AC]):: Sthamí:l < themá.
part (of a place):: =ó:mél ~ =á:mel.
place above Yale:: Xwawíthí:m.
place across the Fraser River from Deroche:: P'eq'ó:les < p'éq'.

place (CONT'D)

place at Ruby Creek where Paul Webster lived some years ago, now Wahleach Island Indian Reserve #2 and area at mouth of Mahood Creek:: X̲wolích ~ X̲welích < x̲wále ~ x̲wá:le.
place by Albert Cooper's house on Chilliwack River Road near Vedder Crossing, former village where a slide is now on north bank of Chilliwack River opposite Liumchen Creek:: X̲éylés <x̲éylés.
place in Fraser River two miles above American Bar with narrow rock:: X̲eq'átelets < x̲eq'.
place in Katz or Ruby Creek, may be name for Charlie Joe's place near Katz at the mouth of a creek where the water is always calm:: sqemélwélh ~ sqemélwelh < qám.
place in Whatcom County, Washington, (Nooksack River [AC or CT]):: Lexwsá:q < sá:q.
place just south of Doctor's Point on Harrison Lake northwest side:: S'ót'o < ót'.
(place, location), where s-o is at:: shxwlí.
place-name, name of a place:: kwxő:mexw < kwí:x ~ kwíx.
place near mouth of Chehalis River where they had a mass burial during a smallpox epidemic:: Smimstiyexwálá ~ Smímstíyexwá:le < mestíyexw.
place of moss-covered stones at upper end of Hope Slough not far from Harry Edwards' home (as of 1964):: Qwómqwemels < qwà:m ~ qwám.
place of training to become an Indian doctor (pit made from repeated jumping every year on the same spot):: shxwlemóthetále < lá:m.
place on Fraser River between first tunnel and Yale where rotten fish used to (always) pile up:: Lexwyó:qwem < yó:qw.
place on mountain above Ruby Creek where there's lots of boulders all over the mountain lined up in rows:: Thíthesem < thi ~ tha ~ the ~ thah ~ theh.
place on the east side of Seabird Island:: X̲ex̲éyth'elhp < x̲éyth'.
place on the Fraser River above Yale where there are whirlpools:: Q'eyq'éyex̲em < q'ey ~ q'i.
place s-th (prob. in water):: mí:lt < mí:l ~ míl.
place to go to:: shxwlàm < la.
place where a grove of birches stood/stand near the Kickbush place on Chilliwack River Road in Sardis, (village at junction of Semmihault Creek and Chilliwack River [Wells 1965 (lst ed.):19]):: Sekw'sekw'emá:y < síkw'.
place where one fishes by waiting with a dip-net, dip-net fishing place, place where one still-dips:: sthqálem < thqá:lem.
place where the sun comes up:: swep'áth' < p'eth'.
place where Yale Creek divides (forks) above the highway bridge over the creek:: T'ít'x̲elhchò:m < t'éx̲.
placing s-th (prob. in water):: hámelet < mí:l ~ míl.
rocky place between two CPR tunnels above and about half a mile east of Haig:: Popeleqwith'á:m ~ Lexwpopeleqwith'á:m < poleqwíth'a.
sofa, couch, chesterfield, place where one's sitting, (bed [AC, MC (Katzie)]):: shxw'ó:met < emét.
someplace, somewhere:: stómchele < tám.
something used to cross over a river, ferry, place good for crossing:: xwt'át'ekwel < t'ákwel.
steelhead fishing place on the Fraser River below Lhílhkw'elqs, at Hogg Slough:: Qéywex̲em < qí:wx̲ ~ qéywx̲ ~ qá:wx̲ ~ qáwx̲.
the only safe place to cross a river:: shxwtitós or shxwtiytós.
wide place at the mouth of the east (upriver) branch of Jones Creek:: Swílth'.
wide place in Maria Slough (just north of Lougheed Highway bridge), west mouth of Maria Slough:: Sqémelech < qám.

place-name

place-name, name of a place:: kwxő:mexw < kwí:x ~ kwíx.
(unidentified placename):: Qw'oqw'íyets or Qw'óqw'iyets.

place to hide)

several places where there were pit-houses in which to hide from enemy raids (place to hide):: Skwokwílàla < kwà:l.

plane

airplane :: lhólhekw' stim:ő:t < lhó:kw' ~ lhókw', lhólhekw' stimőt < stim:ő:t.
a planer:: sxíxep < xíp.
bent U-shaped plane with handle on each end for canoe-making:: sqw'emóx̲w sxíxep < xíp, sqw'emóx̲w xíxepels < xíp.
plane it (with a plane), trim it, taper it (about wood, like slats or roots for baskets, poles for houseposts/totem poles, paddles), taper it (with knife or plane), peel it (a fruit, etc.), whittle it, strip or peel bark off of it, scrape it (of carrots), (carve it, peel it [AC]):: xípet < xíp.
to travel by canoe, (nowadays also) travel by airplane, travel by train, travel by car:: yeló:lh < ó:lh.
U-shaped or horseshoe-shaped knife (or plane) for scraping out canoe:: xepá:ltel < xíp.

plank

longhouse, smokehouse (for spirit-dancing, etc.), Indian house, plank house:: xwelmexwáwtxw < xwélmexw.
peak of house, gable or plank over smokehole:: sq'eyx̲éleqw.
plank, board, lumber:: loplós ~ leplós.
plank building:: s'iltexwím < s'í:ltexw.
plank house:: shxwhő:wtewelh, s'iltexwáwtxw ~ iltexwáwtxw < s'í:ltexw.
platform (in house, etc.), bed platform, platform in bottom of canoe, flooring (the planks):: lálwes.
thick plank for side of house, thick shake for longhouse roof, covering over hole in roof of pit-house:: s'í:ltexw.
top of roof, roof planks:: sts'á:ltexw < ts'á:.

plant

bark, wood, plant:: =á:y ~ =ey ~ =iy.
berry plant:: th'í:melhp < sth'í:m ~ sth'ì:m.
big tree, (be big of a tree or plant):: sthá:lhp < thi ~ tha ~ the ~ thah ~ theh.
blackcap plant:: tselqó:má:lhp < tsélq.
bloom or (plant) fuzz (spore, pollen, seed fluff) after it bursts:: spekw'ém < pékw' ~ péqw'.
break up s-th by crumpling, crush it up, rub it together fast (to soften or clean), rub it to soften it (of plants, etc.), fluff it (inner cedar bark to soften it):: yékw'et < yókw' ~ yóqw'.
bury s-th, plant s-th:: pí:lt < pél (perhaps ~ pí:l by now).
carrot-like plant used for green dye:: xáweleq < xáwéq.
dead and broken [of a plant]:: st'ápiy < t'ápiy.
devil's club plant:: qwó:pelhp.
eight fruit in a group [or cluster] (as they grow on a plant):: tqòtsòls < tqá:tsa.
female part of female plant:: slheli'ál < slhá:lí.
firmly planted in ground (can't be pulled out):: slálets < slá ~ selá ~ slá: (probably).
four fruit in a group or cluster (as they grow on a plant):: x̲(e)'othelòls < x̲e'ó:thel ~ x̲e'óthel.
heart of a root, seed, nut (kernel), core of plant or seedling, core (of tree, branch, any growing thing), pith (of bush), seed or pit [U.S.] or pip [Cdn.] of a fruit:: sth'emí:wel ~ sth'emíwel ~ sth'emíwél < sth'ó:m.
hog fennel, Indian consumption plant:: q'ex̲mí:l.
inside or core of a plant or fruit (or canoe or anything):: =í:wel ~ =íwel ~ =ewel.

plant (CONT'D)

just coming out of the earth (of plants for ex.):: qwósem.
kinnikinnick plant, domestic pea-vine, domestic bean-vine, giant vetch vine:: tl'ikw'íyelhp < tl'íkw'el.
male part of male plant:: swiqe'ál or swiyeqe'ál < swíyeqe ~ swíyqe ~ swí:qe.
needle of plant, (thorn):: p'éth'tel < p'áth'.
nine fruit in a group or cluster (as they grow on a plant):: tuxwòls < tú:xw.
oceanspray plant, "ironwood", "hardhack":: qáthelhp < qáthexw.
plant similar to stl'éleqw' (chocolate lily) but different, (probably rice root):: péth'oyes.
plant with three black berries always joined together, (possibly black twinberry):: xó:lelhp.
red huckleberry plant or bush:: qá:lá:lhp < sqá:le.
roots (resembling eyes looking at you) of a kind of plant that's good for asthma:: qelémes < qélém ~ qél:ém.
salmonberry plant:: elílá:lhp ~ elílà:lhp < elíle.
seven fruit in a group or cluster (as they grow on a plant):: th'ekwòls < th'ó:kws.
short unidentified plant, about 3 ft. tall with red berries like a short mountain ash, the berries are bitter but the plant is used as medicine, possibly red baneberry:: í:lwelh.
six fruit in a group (as they grow on a plant):: t'xemòls < t'éx.
slough about mid-point in Seabird Island where xáweleq plant grew:: Xíxewqèyl or Xíxewqì:l ~ Xewqéyl or Xewqí:l < xáwéq.
small little plants:: sts'éts'esem < ts'ísem.
snowberry plant:: qewówelhp.
sprout(ing) up, stick(ing) its head out of the ground (of a plant):: qw'íles < qw'íl.
strawberry vine, strawberry plant, strawberry patch:: schí:yà:lhp < schí:ya.
the planting, seeds to plant, what is planted (sown), garden:: spí:ls < pél (perhaps ~ pí:l by now).
thimbleberry plant or bush:: t'qwémelhp < t'qwém.
to drop or blow plant fluff (like dandelions, fireweed, cottonwood, etc.), to blow (of dusty or flaky stuff like wood dust, dandruff, maybe seeds):: pípexwem < píxw.
tree, plant:: =elhp.
unidentified plant with round bulbs that look and taste like potatoes, round root like potatoes that used to be eaten and tastes like potatoes:: qíqemxel ~ qéyqemxel < qém.
when plant fuzz blows:: pókw'em < pékw' ~ péqw'.
wild red raspberry plant, domestic red raspberry plant:: s'ó:ytheqwelhp < éy ~ éy:.

Plantago lanceolata

Plantago major and Plantago lanceolata:: slhá:wel.
Plantago major, Plantago lanceolata:: pipehomá:lews < peh or pó(:)h.

Plantago major

Plantago major and Plantago lanceolata:: slhá:wel.
Plantago major, Plantago lanceolata:: pipehomá:lews < peh or pó(:)h.

plantain

common plantain and ribbed plantain:: slhá:wel, slhá:wel.
common plantain, ribbed plantain, called "frog leaf":: pipehomá:lews < peh or pó(:)h, pipehomá:lews < peh or pó(:)h.
rattlesnake plantain:: pepepó:tem ~ pépepò:tem ~ pepepótem < pó:t.

plant fluff

fine airborne seed(s) (not used of plum or apple seed(s) or the hard seeds -- sth'emíwél is

plant fluff (CONT'D)

used for those) (used for dandelion seeds, cottonwood seeds, etc., tail of a cat-tail reed, (plant fluff (possibly including tail of cat-tail rush) [Elders Group 2/27/80]):: spéxwqel ~ spéx̲wqel < píxw.

plants

plants, grass:: =eletsá:ls, =elesà:ls.

plate

dish, big cooking and serving trough used in longhouse, feast dish, plate (of wood or basketry), (platter), tray:: ló:thel.
plates:: lethló:thel < ló:thel.
woven mat to put hot plates on:: lháx̲tsestel < lhá:x̲ ~ lháx̲.

platform

fire box or fire platform and fire shield for torch-lighting or pit-lamping fire:: tl'áts'eq.
fishing platform:: láxel.
platform (in house, etc.), bed platform, platform in bottom of canoe, flooring (the planks):: lálwes.

Platichthys stellatus

Hippoglossus stenolepis, prob. Platichthys stellatus:: p'éwiy ~ p'ṓwiy < p'ewíy ~ p'ōwíy.

platter

big wooden dish (often two feet long), feast dish, wooden platter, (big stirring spoon [LJ], carved wooden spoon, big wooden spoon [AC, BJ, DM]):: qwelhyṓwelh ~ qwelhliyṓwelh ~ qwelhlyúwelh < qwélh.
dish, big cooking and serving trough used in longhouse, feast dish, plate (of wood or basketry), (platter), tray:: ló:thel.
long china platter:: qwsó:les.

play

a fairly flat clearing on a mountain in Morris Valley where they used to play ts'its'eqweló:l or Indian badminton:: Ts'éqwela ~ Th'éqwela < ts'éqw ~ th'éqw.
to play (games, etc.):: ewólem
playful:: lexwsewólem < ewólem.
playing a musical instrument:: qwiqwelóythetel < qwà:l.

playful

playful:: lexwsewólem < ewólem.

pleasant

be fun, have (lots of) fun, have amusement, having lots of fun, be pleasant:: íyes ~ éyes < éy ~ éy:.
(have a) pleasant voice:: iyésqel < éy ~ éy:.

Please

It's you to thank the Lord, (Please say grace):: lúwe ts'ít te Chíchelh Siyám < =chílh ~ chílh=.

pleasure

be overcome with pleasurable feelings after eating great salmon or a great meal:: ts'éqw'.

Plethodon vehiculum
　Ensatina eschscholtzi and Plethodon vehiculum and possibly also: Ambystoma macrodactylum macrodactylum, Ambystoma gracile gracile, and possibly Ambystoma gracile decorticatum:: pí:txel.

plop
　sat down (with a plop?), [slip off on one's bottom or chair]:: xwlhépelets < x̲wlhép.

plow
　a plow:: shxwtl'éxelep < Tl'ítl'xeleqw.

pluck
　pick berries, pick off (leaves, fruit, vegetables, hops), (pluck off, harvest):: lhím.
　pluck it (a bird/fowl):: qw'emṓwst or qw'eméwst < qw'ém.
　pluck it for me:: qw'emōwselhtsthó:x < qw'ém.

plug
　caulking a canoe, plugging a canoe:: t'ékwōwelh < t'ékw.
　plugging a hole or leak or crack in anything:: t'ót'ekwels < t'ékw.
　plug it (a hole, leak):: t'ekwót < t'ékw.
　put something in the ear (to block hearing), (plug the ear):: t'ekwá:lí:ya < t'ékw.

plum
　cultivated plum, plums:: plems.
　Indian plum bush:: mélhx̲welelhp < mélhx̲wel.
　Indian plum (the fruit), (also called) June plum:: mélhx̲wel.

plural :: =le= ~ =el=.
　coaxing imperative plural:: -atlha.
　command imperative second person plural:: -alha.
　first person plural patient or object of passive:: -òlèm.
　first person plural subjunctive subject:: -et.
　nominalizer plural:: ye=.
　plural continuative:: R13= or C1V1C2=.
　plural, inherent plural:: =R2 or =C1eC2, =R2 or =C1eC2.
　plural or augmentative:: R11= or C1V1=.
　plural (rare):: há- ~ hé-.
　plural, (usually) many in a group, collective:: R3= or C1eC2=.
　(rare) plural, (usually) many in a group, collective:: R5= or C1e=, =R6= or =eC2=, R7= or C1á=, R8= or C1a=.
　second person plural subjunctive subject:: -áp ~ -elep.
　the (plural [usually human]):: ye ~ yi.
　us, first person plural object:: -ólxw ~ -óxw.
　you (pl.), second person plural object:: -óle.
　your (pl.), you folks's, second person plural possessive pronoun, second person plural subordinate subject:: -a -elep ~ -a' -elep.

pocket :: s'ehólets < ehó, slheqwe'álá.

Podilymbus podiceps:: sx̲wotíx.

Point
a stone like a statue at Harrison Lake, probably Doctor's Point:: Skoyá:m ~ Skeyá:m.
bear-shaped rock up on cliff on south side above Echo Point bay on Echo Island in Harrison Lake:: Spá:th < pá:th.
Doctor's Point on northwest shore Harrison Lake:: Lhx̲é:ylex < lhéx̲.
Echo Point on Echo Island, Echo Bay on Echo Island:: X̲wix̲we'áqel ~ Xwixwe'áqel ~ Xwōxwe'áqel < x̲wex̲we'á.
next mountain above (north/upriver from) Títxwemqsel (Wilson's Point or Grouse Point), possibly Elbow Lake mountain [north of Harrison Mills, on west side of the Harrison River], Willoughby's Point [opposite Lhá:lt, but does this mean across Harrison R. as I first thought and show on the topographic map "Harrison Lake 92H/5" where I have pencilled in all Chehalis place names) or does it mean on the opposite, i.e. south end of the same bay where Lhá:lt starts, i.e. both on the west side of Harrison R. as are Títxwemqsel and Elbow Lake mountain?]:: Kw'íkw'exwelhp < kw'íxw.
Promontory Point above Vedder Crossing:: Lexwtamílem? < tà:m.
rock shaped like a man's head with a sx̲wó:yx̲wey mask on a point near the head of Harrison River, the point also called Spook's Point:: Sx̲wó:yx̲wey ~ Sx̲wóyx̲wey < sx̲wó:yx̲wey ~ sx̲wóyx̲wey.
Whale Point at the southwest end of Harrison Lake:: Qwél:és < qwél:és ~ qwélés.
Wilson's Point (on Harrison River), (also called) Grouse Point:: Títxwemqsel < stíxwem.

point :: s'eléqs.
a pointer (a stick):: mót'estel < mót'es.
a point or bald hill on Harrison River where people waited to spear silver spring salmon:: Chth'éylem < chth'éylem.
a stripe (on the nose or point):: sx̲élqs < x̲él ~ x̲é:yl ~ x̲í:l
beach in front of old Scowlitz village, the point the Harrison River goes around by Kilby's store:: Sq'iq'ewílem < q'éw ~ q'ew.
(be) blunt (edge or point), dull (of edge/point):: qelóth < qél.
go around (a point, a bend, a curve, etc.) in the water, make a U-turn (in the water, could use today on land with a car):: q'ówletsem < q'éw ~ q'ew.
(have a) pointed head:: yethéleqw < éy ~ éy:.
(have a) thin (point or nose):: qwe'íqweqs < qwe'íqw.
index finger, pointing finger:: mómet'es < mót'es.
island or point on north side of first slough north of the mouth of Chehalis River, (next slough and point above Mímex̲wel [EL 3/1/78]):: Yálhxetel, Yálhxetel.
longest dirt point sticking out on Harrison River about a quarter mile above Harrison Bay bridge:: Tl'éqteqsel < tl'áqt.
point at, aim:: mót'es.
point at s-th:: mót'est < mót'es.
pointer to show direction (like in a trail) (could be an arrow or stick or mark in the ground):: shxwmót'estel < mót'es.
pointing:: mómet'es < mót'es.
point of elbow, arm bone:: th'emeláx̲el < hth'b.txt.
point of geog. features like island or mountain or land:: =eqs ~ =éqsel ~ =élqsel ~ =elqs.
point of land:: s'álqsel.
point of land at the end of an island:: sth'eméxwelets.
point of land on Harrison River (somewhere between Lheltá:lets and Híqelem) where during a famine the old people scooped minnows and boiled them to make soup:: Sqíqemlò < sqíqemlò.
point on west side of Harrison River on which or across from which Sx̲wó:yx̲wey is located (the rock formation resembling a sx̲wó:yx̲wey mask):: Skwtéxwqel < kwetáxw.
point or tip of a long object (pole, tree, knife, candle, land):: =eqs ~ =éqsel ~ =élqsel ~ =elqs.

point (CONT'D)

sharpen it (of a point):: xépqst < xíp.
spear (any kind), spear (for fish or war), fish-spear, telescopic spear for sturgeon, harpoon, detachable harpoon points:: tá:lh.
strike s-th pointed (esp. a match):: éx̲qst < íx̲.
stripes (on the nose or point):: sx̲élx̲elqs < x̲él ~ x̲é:yl ~ x̲í:l
tip or point of one's nose:: s'álqsel.
Wahleach Bluff, a lookout mountain with rock sticking out over a bluff, also the lookout point on Agassiz Mountain:: Kw'okw'echíwel < kw'áts ~ kw'éts.

poison

Pacific rattlesnake, (a poison [LG: Chill.]):: th'éx̲tel < th'éx̲.
poison s-o/s-th on purpose:: yéltht < yélth.
to poison:: yélth.

poison hemlock)

poison fern that grows in swampy places, (prob. water hemlock, poison hemlock):: welékwsa.

poke

be hit (with arrow, bullet, anything shot that you've aimed), got shot, (got pierced), got poked into, got wounded (with gun or arrow):: ts'éqw'.
he/she/it is poking me [purposely]:: ts'eqw'ts'eqw'thóxes < ts'éqw'.
poke it, pin s-th, pick it up (on sharp pointed object), pick s-th up on a fork (or other sharp object):: ts'qw'ét < ts'éqw'.
poke oneself in the eye (with finger, stick, etc.):: telkwó:lésem.
spear it (a fish), stab s-o/s-th with something sharp, pierce s-o/s-th, prick s-o (with a pin, for ex.), poke s-o (with a pin, etc.):: thq'ét < théq'.

poker

fire poker:: shxwthó:yeltsep < thíy.

pole)

blunt (end of canoe pole):: témkwes.
blunt (of poles):: témqweqsel.
canoe pole:: sx̲wőqw'tel < x̲wóqw'.
carved outside post on longhouse, totem pole:: x̲wíythi < x̲wíyth.
cedar pole:: sókw'émelhp < sókw'.
dry storage box in tree or on top of pole (for salmon and other dried provisions):: póqw'elh < pó:qw' ~ póqw'.
eight ropes, eight threads, eight sticks, eight poles:: tqátsámets' < tqá:tsa.
fishing by a line, line-fishing, trout-fishing, fishing with a pole (for trout):: qw'iqw'emó:thel ~ qw'íqw'emó:thel < qw'emó:thel.
fishing pole:: qw'óqw'iy.
five ropes, five threads, five sticks, five poles:: lhq'átssámets' < lheq'át ~ lhq'á:t.
four ropes, four threads, four sticks, four poles, (four long thin objects):: x̲ethílemets' < x̲e'ó:thel ~ x̲e'óthel.
grave pole:: x̲á:th'etstel < x̲áth' ~ x̲e'áth'.
join two poles together, splice it together (of a rope), (join together on the ends):: t'qwíqst.
nine ropes, nine threads, nine sticks, nine poles:: tuxwámets' < tú:xw.
one rope, one thread, one stick, one pole:: lets'ámeth' < léts'a ~ léts'e.
plane it (with a plane), trim it, taper it (about wood, like slats or roots for baskets, poles for houseposts/totem poles, paddles), taper it (with knife or plane), peel it (a fruit, etc.), whittle it, strip or

pole (CONT'D)

peel bark off of it, scrape it (of carrots), (carve it, peel it [AC]):: xípet < xíp.
point or tip of a long object (pole, tree, knife, candle, land):: =eqs ~ =éqsel ~ =élqsel ~ =elqs.
pole ?:: sóskw'em < sókw'.
poling a canoe:: x̲wóx̲weqw'et < x̲wóqw'.
raise it (of a pole):: lhex̲eyléxstexw < lhéx̲.
round (of a pole):: xelkw'ámeth' < xél.
(seven long objects), seven ropes, seven threads, seven sticks, seven poles:: th'okwsámets' < th'ó:kws.
(six long objects), six ropes, six threads, six sticks, six poles:: t'x̲émemets' < t'éx̲.
spear pole knot hitch (two half-hitches), clove-hitch knot:: ts'sítsim.
spear, shaft (of spear/harpoon/gaff-hook), gaff-hook pole:: s'álem.
ten ropes, ten threads, ten sticks, ten poles:: epálemets' < ó:pel.
thin (of tree or pole):: qwe'íqws < qwe'íqw.
three ropes, three threads, three sticks, three poles, (three long narrow objects):: lhxwámeth' < lhí:xw.
to fish with a pole or rod, to fish by a line:: qw'emó:thel.
to pole a canoe:: x̲wóqw'et < x̲wóqw'.
two ropes, two threads, two sticks, two poles, two poles standing up:: isalámeth' < isá:le ~ isále ~ isá:la.
upright, standing, height, stature, pole:: =ámets' ~ =ámeth' ~ =ó:meth' ~ =emeth'.

pole ladder

ladder, notched cedar pole ladder, rope ladder (pre-contact or later), modern ladder:: skw'íytel < kw'í ~ kw'íy.

policeman :: qíqeq'els < qíq'.

polite :: éy ~ éy:.

be good, good, well, nice, fine, better, better (ought to), it would be good if, may it be good, let it be good, happy, glad, clean, well-behaved, polite, virgin, popular, comfortable (with furniture, other things?),:: éy ~ éy:.
polite imperative:: -lhqwe.
(polite imperative?, (polite) certainly, (polite) of course):: òwelh ~ -òwèlh.

pollen

bloom or (plant) fuzz (spore, pollen, seed fluff) after it bursts:: spekw'ém < pékw' ~ péqw'.
when plant fuzz blows:: pókw'em < pékw' ~ péqw'.

Polypodium glycyrrhiza:: st'uslóye, tl'asíp, t'usló:ye.

Polyporus

Fomes sp. including Fomes applanatus and probably others, possibly Polyporus sp., possibly Ganoderma sp., prob. also jelly fungi of Tremella and maybe Auricularia and Dacrymyces species, especially Tremella mesenterica (Yellow trembler) which is abundant only on the red alder and is reddish-orange matching the color, translucence and shape of those eaten by some of the Stó:lō elders, the jelly fungi could possibly have a differnet name from the bracket fungus:: s'ómó:qwes.

Polystichum munitum:: sthx̲á:lem.

pompous)

(be) proud (pompous):: smáth'el < máth'el.

pond

(clean) pond (even if dry):: sqeqó:qel < qó:.
green pond slime or river slime, algae:: stíxem < tíxem.
mountain on the west (C.P.R.) side of the Fraser River above American Bar which had a steaming pond at the top, (year-round village at mouth of American Creek on west bank of the Fraser River [Duff]):: Qétex̲em < qá:t.
puddle that's always dirty, dirty pond, stagnant pool of water, (it never dries out [AK]):: th'qwélhcha.
small lake, pond:: x̲óx̲tsa ~ x̲óx̲cha < x̲ó:tsa ~ x̲ó:cha.
stagnant water lake or ponds at the downriver end of Skw'átets or Peters Reserve near Laidlaw:: Th'qwélhcha < th'qwélhcha.
to drain (of a pond), (get) dried up (of creek, empty cup, etc.):: t'óqwel.

ponder

thinking, pondering, studying, be studying:: totí:lthet < tól.
think, ponder, study, decide:: tó:lthet < tól.

Pooecetes gramineus

Melospiza melodia morphna, (perhaps any/all of the following: Passerculus sandwichensis brooksi, Pooecetes gramineus, Chondestes grammacus, Spizella arborea, Spizella passerina, Zonotrichia querula, Passerella iliaca, Zonotrichia leucophrys, Zonotrichia atricapilla, Melospiza melodia morphna):: sx̲wṍx̲wtha.

pool

maybe the same place as Sqw'ex̲wáq (pool where Kawkawa Creek comes into the Coquihalla River and where the water pygmies lived):: Skw'íkw'x̲weq (or better, Sqw'íqw'x̲weq) < Sqw'ex̲wáq.
pool down from Tillie Gutierrez's grandfather's fish-drying rack at Íyem (Eayem):: qemqémel ~ qemqémél < qém:el.
pool where Kawkawa Creek comes into the Coquihalla River:: Sqw'ex̲wáq.
puddle that's always dirty, dirty pond, stagnant pool of water, (it never dries out [AK]):: th'qwélhcha.

poor

pitiful, (bereft, poor):: selá:wa.
poor little one, you poor thing (said to a child):: t'ó:t'.
poor, unfortunate:: t-sós ~ tesós.

pop

a pop, a shot:: tl'éleqw' < tl'ál ~ tl'á:l.
continuous shooting or popping sounds:: tl'éltl'eleqw' < tl'ál ~ tl'á:l.
crackling and popping (of a log in fire or firecrackers):: tl'áléx̲em < tl'ál ~ tl'á:l.
(have/get a) crackle and pop (sound of a log in a fire or of firecrackers):: tl'á:lx̲em < tl'ál ~ tl'á:l.
(have) sound of popping small round things (snowberries, herring eggs as when eating them, rice krispies, crabapples, cranberries, etc.), (have a crunching sound (as of grasshopper, rice krispies):: tl'ámkw'em, tl'ámkw'em < tl'ém.
popping (of firecrackers):: tl'eltl'ó:lqwem < tl'ál ~ tl'á:l.
soda pop:: sqe'óleqw < qó:.

pop (CONT'D)

(soda) pop:: q'éx̱q'ex̱el sqe'óleqw < q'(e)x̱, qó:
(lit. perhaps: bubbling and fizzy/perhaps: metal can + fruit juice)

Popelehó:ys)
a mountain just south of Yale Mountain (Popelehó:ys) with a big hole like a tunnel in it above the highway at Yale:: Tekwóthel ~ Tkwóthel.

Popkum
creek between Popkum and Cheam, also a location near Popkum, (must be second of two creeks above Popkum that cross Highway #1 [JL 4/7/78]):: sthamí:l.
one (second) of two creeks just above Popkum which cross Highway #1, (creek between Popkum and Cheam, also a place near Popkum [AC]):: Sthamí:l < themá.
village on east bank of Fraser River near the outlet from Cheam Lake, Popkum Indian village:: Pópkw'em < pékw' ~ péqw'.

poplar :: th'estíyelhp < th'ís.
poplar, Lombardy poplar (intro.), also black cottonwood and perhaps trembling aspen which may have rarely occurred on the eastern and northeastern edges of Stó:lō territory:: p'elp'álq'emá:lews ~ p'elp'àlq'emá:lews < p'álq'em, p'elp'álq'emá:lews ~ p'elp'àlq'emá:lews < p'álq'em.
"poplar", probably includes black cottonwood and trembling aspen (though trembling aspen is rare in Upriver Halq'eméylem territory):: th'estíyelhp < th'ís, th'ex̱tíyelhp < th'éx̱.

popular
be good, good, well, nice, fine, better, better (ought to), it would be good if, may it be good, let it be good, happy, glad, clean, well-behaved, polite, virgin, popular, comfortable (with furniture, other things?),:: éy ~ éy:.
is popular:: éy ~ éy:.

Populus
probably genus Populus, probably includes Populus trichocarpa and Populus tremuloides, could include Populus balsamifera but it apparently isn't found in the area, possibly includes non-native Populus nigra:: th'estíyelhp < th'ís, th'ex̱tíyelhp < th'éx̱.

Populus balsamifera trichocarpa:: chewő:lhp < cháchew ~ cháchu.
cambium from Populus balsamifera trichocarpa:: sx̱á:meth.
cambium/sap of Populus balsamifera trichocarpa:: sx̱á:meth.
Populus spp., esp. Populus nigra var. italica, also Populus balsamifera trichocarpa and perhaps Populus tremuloides:: p'elp'álq'emá:lews ~ p'elp'àlq'emá:lews < p'álq'em.
sap or cambium of Populus balsamifera trichocarpa:: ts'its'emá:welh.

Populus nigra
probably genus Populus, probably includes Populus trichocarpa and Populus tremuloides, could include Populus balsamifera but it apparently isn't found in the area, possibly includes non-native Populus nigra:: th'estíyelhp < th'ís, th'ex̱tíyelhp < th'éx̱.

Populus nigra var. italica
Populus spp., esp. Populus nigra var. italica, also Populus balsamifera trichocarpa and perhaps Populus tremuloides:: p'elp'álq'emá:lews ~ p'elp'àlq'emá:lews < p'álq'em.

Populus spp.
  Populus spp., esp. Populus nigra var. italica, also Populus balsamifera trichocarpa and perhaps Populus tremuloides:: p'elp'álq'emá:lews ~ p'elp'àlq'emá:lews < p'álq'em.

Populus tremuloides
  Populus spp., esp. Populus nigra var. italica, also Populus balsamifera trichocarpa and perhaps Populus tremuloides:: p'elp'álq'emá:lews ~ p'elp'àlq'emá:lews < p'álq'em.
  probably genus Populus, probably includes Populus trichocarpa and Populus tremuloides, could include Populus balsamifera but it apparently isn't found in the area, possibly includes non-native Populus nigra:: th'estíyelhp < th'ís, th'ex̲tíyelhp < th'éx̲.

Populus trichocarpa
  probably genus Populus, probably includes Populus trichocarpa and Populus tremuloides, could include Populus balsamifera but it apparently isn't found in the area, possibly includes non-native Populus nigra:: th'estíyelhp < th'ís, th'ex̲tíyelhp < th'éx̲.

porcupine :: swatíya.

portage
  carry a canoe on one's shoulders, to portage:: xw'ilamṓwelh < ílàm.

Port Douglas
  Lillooet people, Port Douglas (also Lillooet) people:: sth'kwólh.

portion
  a large portion of the earth:: slháq'emex.
  part, (portion):: tl'émexw.
  (portion not burnt up, burnt or gone out completely portion):: th'ex̲míl < th'éx̲, th'ex̲míl < th'éx̲.
  (probably) small portion:: =th'.
  use, extract, extract a portion:: lh- ~ lhé-.
  using (a portion):: lh=.

portrait
  likeness, portrait, photograph, photo, statue:: sx̲wíythi ~ sx̲wéythi < x̲wíyth.

possessed)
  shoulder (especially the top), shoulder (someone's, possessed):: shxw'ílámálá ~ shxw'ílàmàlà < ílàm.

possession
  clothing, food, and possessions burned and given away when a person dies, (possessions and food burned and given away at a burning):: syeqwá:ls < yéqw.

possessive pronoun
  his, her, its, their, third person possessive pronoun, third person subordinate subject:: -s.
  my, first person singular possessive pronoun, first person subordinate subject:: -el ~ -l ~ l.
  our, first person plural possessive pronoun, first person plural subordinate subject:: -tset
  your (sgl.), second person singular possessive pronoun, second person subordinate subject:: -a ~ -a'.
  your (pl.), you folks's, second person plural possessive pronoun, second person plural subordinate subject:: -a -elep ~ -a' -elep.

possibly)

maybe, perhaps, I don't know (if), may (possibly):: yóswe ~ yó:swe.

post

carved outside post on longhouse, totem pole:: x̲wíythi < x̲wíyth.
house-post, post:: sqáqeltel.

Post Creek:: Kwṓkwelem ?.

Post Lake

Lindeman Lake or Post Lake:: (possibly) Schewíts < cháchew ~ cháchu.

post office:: pipeháwtxw < pípe.

pot

big copper pot:: ts'qw'ṓstel ~ ts'qw'ṓwstel.
chamberpot, potty-chair, urinal:: shxwítel.
marijuana, "pot", "weed":: ts'esémelep ~ ts'esémelép < ts'ísem.
pot to boil in:: lhámkiya.
pot to boil in, iron pot, smaller iron pot:: lhémkiya ~ lhámkiya < lhém.
small pot:: skw'ékw'ewes < skw'ó:wes ~ skw'ówes.
teapot:: tí'àlà < tí.

potato

arrowleaf, wapato, Indian potato:: xwōqw'ṓ:ls.
potato (generic), including three or four kinds of wild potato: arrowleaf or wapato, Jerusalem artichoke, blue camas, and qíqemxel (so far unidentified plant), besides post-contact domestic potato:: sqáwth ~ sqá:wth.
potato bread:: sqáwth seplíl < qáwth, seplíl
roast potatoes, baked potatoes:: s'ótheqw < ótheqw.
(spherical), round (of ball, apple, potato, rock, full moon, but not of a pear):: xelkw'ó:ls < xél.
to roast potatoes in hot sand or ashes, bake in ashes, bake in stove:: ótheqw.
touch s-o purposely, squish it (of berries, etc.), smash s-th, mash it (berries, potatoes, carrots, etc.), bump it:: tóset < tós.
unidentified plant with round bulbs that look and taste like potatoes, round root like potatoes that used to be eaten and tastes like potatoes:: qíqemxel ~ qéyqemxel < qém.
wild red potatoes that pigs eat, (probably Jerusalem artichoke):: sx̲éykwel.
wild red potato (grew at American Bar in the 1920's), possibly Jerusalem artichoke:: sx̲éykwel.

pot-holder

pot-holder:: kwéltsestel < kwél.

potlatch

a potlatch:: stl'e'áleq < tl'e'á ~ tl'á'.
inviting (to come eat, dance), to give a potlatch, (give a feast or gathering), to invite to a feast, invite to a potlatch:: tl'etl'áxel < tl'e'á ~ tl'á'.

potty-chair

chamberpot, potty-chair, urinal:: shxwítel.

pouch
arrow pouch, (a quiver for arrows):: th'esélatel.
pouch (like for gunpowder):: shxwyáx̲q'els ~ shxwiyáx̲q'els.

pour
make the sound of water splashing or dripping fast, (make the sound of a waterfall, make the sound of pouring rain dripping or splashing in puddles loudly):: xwótqwem.
pouring a liquid:: kw'ókw'elem.
pour s-th out, pour out s-th, spill it:: kw'lhát < kw'élh.
pour water on s-th to keep it damp:: kw'lhó:st < kw'élh.
raining hard, pouring rain, (raining fast):: xwémxel < x̲wém ~ xwém.

pout
(have) pursed lips when pouting:: smóst'iyethel.

powder :: páwta.
be powdered:: spólqw' < pékw' ~ péqw'.
diatomaceous earth (could be mixed with things to whiten them--for ex. dog and goat wool), white clay for white face paint (for pure person spirit-dancers), white powder from mountains, white clay they make powder from to lighten goat and dog wool for blankets, powder, talc, white face paint:: st'ewő kw'.
pouch (like for gunpowder):: shxwyáx̲q'els ~ shxwiyáx̲q'els.
powdered milk/coffee mate:: ts'áyxw sqemó (lit. dry + milk) < ts'íyxw, qemó
powdered on the face:: st'ewíqw'es < st'ewőkw'.
smoke puffing out, (puff out (dust, powder, plant spores, seed fluff, light snow, smoke), form puffs of dust):: pékw' ~ péqw'.
tiny slivers of fir bark, fir bark powder:: sth'íkwem < th'íkw.
to powder one's face, put powder on one's face:: t'ewőkw'esem < st'ewőkw'.

power
an Indian dancer's spirit power:: syúwél ~ syéw:el < yéw: ~ yéw.
a spirit power of a kw'őxweqs dancer, (perhaps wolverine or badger spirit power):: sqoyép < sqoyép.
a sung spell, power to help or harm people or to do [ritual] burning, power to do witchcraft and predict the future, an evil spell, (magic spell) (someone who has power to take things out of a person or put things in [by magic] [Elders Group 2/25/76], ritualist [Elders Group 1/21/76], witch [EB 4/25/78]):: syiwí:l ~ syewí:l < yéw: ~ yéw, syiwí:l ~ syewí:l < yéw: ~ yéw.
(cast a spell for s-o, use a magical power for s-o):: yewí:lmet < yéw: ~ yéw.
cast a spell on s-o, put a spell on s-o, shoot power into s-o:: x̲t'ét < x̲ét'.
cast a spell, throw a spell, put on a spell, shoot power:: x̲t'áls or x̲t'á:ls < x̲ét'.
conscience, spirit (which can be lost temporarily), soul, life-spirit, power of one's will:: smestíyexw < mestíyexw.
guardian spirit, spirit power:: =ó:lkwlh.
huge pretty frog with supernatural powers:: sx̲ex̲ómőlh.
Indian doctor, shaman, medicine man, Indian doctor's spirit power (Elders Group 11/19/75):: shxwlá:m < lá:m.
it went into him/her (of spirit power):: thex̲we'í:ls.
someone who has power to take things out of a person or put things in [by magic]:: syiwí:l ~ syewí:l < yéw: ~ yéw.
spirit power of an Indian doctor or shaman:: slá:m < lá:m.
spirit power, spirit-dancer:: =ó:lkwlh.

powerful

animal or bird one is afraid of and can't see, powerful creature, supernatural creature:: stl'á:leqem.

Prairie

Sumas Prairie west (on the west side of Sumas Lake):: Sx̲elálets??.

prairie)

meadow, (little prairie):: spáplhx̲el < spélhx̲el.
prairie, grassy open land, (grassy valley [EB, Gibbs, Elders Group]}:: spélhx̲el.

pray

(be) praying, (pray [Elders Group]):: ts'í:yelh < ts'ahéyelh, ts'í:yelh < ts'ahéyelh.
prayer:: st'íwiyelh < t'íw ~ t'i:w.
to pray, have a church service, (a Church (organization, not building) [Elders Group]):: ts'ahéyelh.

prayer beads:: lesúpli.

pre-adolescent)

child (post-baby to pre-adolescent), child (under 12), (young [BJ]):: stl'ítl'eqelh ~ stl'í:tl'eqelh.

precipitation

precipitation, ray of light:: =xel.

predict

a sung spell, power to help or harm people or to do [ritual] burning, power to do witchcraft and predict the future, an evil spell, (magic spell) (someone who has power to take things out of a person or put things in [by magic] [Elders Group 2/25/76], ritualist [Elders Group 1/21/76], witch [EB 4/25/78]):: syiwí:l ~ syewí:l < yéw: ~ yéw.
predicting the future:: hí:ywes < yéw: ~ yéw.

prefer

I'd rather have (s-th), I'd prefer (s-th) (make that s-th instead):: tl'óst or tl'óstexw.

pregnant

to be pregnant:: syémyem < yém ~ yem.

prepare

prepared fish oil (usually sockeye oil):: smótheqw < mótheqw or metheqw.

preposition

independent object of preposition:: tl'a- ~ tl'e- ~ tl'-.
me (nominalized object of preposition), to me, with me:: tl'a'áltha ~ tl'e'áltha ~ tl'a'á'altha < áltha.
us (nominalized object of preposition), to us, with us:: tl'elhlímelh < lhlímelh.
you folks (object of preposition), to you folks, with you folks:: tl'alhwélep < lhwélep.
you (sg.) (object of preposition):: tl'eléwe ~ tl'léwe < léwe.

presence)

nominalizer (female present and visible or presence or proximity unspecified),

presence) (CONT'D)

demonstrative article:: the=.

nominalizer (male or gender unspecified, present and visible or presence or proximity unspecified), demonstrative article:: ta=, te=.

the (female, present and visible), the (female, unspecified presence and/or unspecified visibility):: the.

the (male, present, visible), the (gender or presence and visibility unspecified), a (male, present and visible), a (gender or presence and visibility unspecified):: te.

presence unspecified)

he (present or presence unspecified), he's the one that, it's him that, she or it (present or presence unspecified), that or this (immediately before nominal):: tú:tl'ò ~ tútl'ò ~ tútl'o < tl'ó ~ tl'o.

that's her, she (present or presence unspecified), her (present or presence unspefified), that (female):: thú:tl'ò < tl'ó ~ tl'o.

present)

he (present or presence unspecified), he's the one that, it's him that, she or it (present or presence unspecified), that or this (immediately before nominal):: tú:tl'ò ~ tútl'ò ~ tútl'o < tl'ó ~ tl'o.

nominalizer (female present and visible or presence or proximity unspecified), demonstrative article:: the=.

nominalizer (male or gender unspecified, present and visible or presence or proximity unspecified), demonstrative article:: ta=, te=.

that's her, she (present or presence unspecified), her (present or presence unspefified), that (female):: thú:tl'ò < tl'ó ~ tl'o.

the (male, present, visible), the (gender or presence and visibility unspecified), a (male, present and visible), a (gender or presence and visibility unspecified):: te.

the (present, not visible, gender unspecified), the (remote, abstract):: kwe < kw.

present and visible)

the (female, present and visible), the (female, unspecified presence and/or unspecified visibility):: the.

present tense

weren't ever?, wasn't ever?, didn't ever?, does s-o ever?, never used to, not going to (but did anyway) [perhaps in the sense of never usually do X but did this time]:: ewá:lh ~ wá:lh < éwe ~ ṓwe.

preserve

Harrison River spring salmon, Harrison River chinook salmon, big Chehalis River spring salmon, (preserved (smoked?) meat [AC: Tait dialect]):: pó:qw' ~ póqw'.

preserved fish, preserved meat, dried fish, dried meat (usually fish), smoked salmon, wind-dried salmon (old word), what is stored away, what is put away:: sq'éyle.

press

insistant, persistant (like a child pressing to go along), bull-headed, doesn't mind, does just the opposite, (stubborn, contrary):: sxíxeles.

press and rub s-th:: xwíqwet < xwíqw.

press s-th down (like yeast dough):: qéytl't ~ qí(y)tl't.

rub (oil or water) in s-th to clean or soften, rub s-th to soften or clean it, (shaping a stone hammer with abrasion?, shaping?, mixing paint?, pressing together or crushing? [BHTTC 9/2/76]):: yémq't.

shake s-th down, pack s-th down, push s-th down, knead s-th (esp. of bread dough), press it down (like yeast bread):: qeth'ét.

pretend

pretending to be good, want to be accepted:: éystelómet ~ éy:stelómet < éy ~ éy:.
to bluff, pretend one knows something, (be) stuck up:: math'álem < máth'el.

pretty

good-looking, beautiful, pretty, handsome, looks good:: iyó:mex ~ iyóméx ~ iyómex < éy ~ éy:.

Pretty Creek

the first creek above Hemlock Valley road which also crosses the road to Morris Valley, also the name for Pretty Creek:: Lhemqwótel Stótelō < lhém.

Pretty's Bay

Pretty's Bay on Harrison River:: Sásq'etstel < sásq'ets.

prevaricate)

to lie (prevaricate):: math'elqéylem < máth'el.

prick

spear it (a fish), stab s-o/s-th with something sharp, pierce s-o/s-th, prick s-o (with a pin, for ex.), poke s-o (with a pin, etc.):: thq'ét < théq'.

prickly

prickly swamp currant, swamp gooseberry:: th'kw'íwíyelhp < th'ekw' or th'íkw'.

pride

(glad greeting sound, also sound to show pride in accomplishment):: x̲::.

priest

priest, minister:: leplít.

Prince's pine

Prince's pine, pipsessewa:: chéchelex < chálék.

Procyon lotor pacificus:: mélés.

Promontory Mountain

Promontory Mountain by Vedder Crossing:: Stitó:s ~ Stitó:s.

Promontory Point

Promontory Point above Vedder Crossing:: Lexwtamílem? < tà:m.

prong

prong of spear, prong of fish spear:: qáthexw.

prop

a prop:: tpólhtel < tpólh.
a prop used to trip a deadfall trap:: tpólhtel < tpólh.
leaning the face on the hand with elbow propped:: piyósem < píy.
lying on one side with one's head propped up on one hand:: piypiyáleqálem < píy.
prop it up:: tpólht < tpólh.

prop (CONT'D)

propped up:: stpólh < tpólh.
prop up a limb with a Y-shaped stick, (prop s-th up (of a limb, with a Y-shaped stick)):: ts'qw'ít or th'qw'it.

properly

be fixed, be fixed up properly:: sthethíy < thíy.

Prophalanopsidae

probably mostly family Gryllidae, but perhaps family Prophalanopsidae, also perhaps singing groups such as family Tettigoniidae (order Orthoptera) or Cicadidae (order Hemiptera):: tó:lthíwa < tó:l ~ tò:l.

prophet :: élíyá.

propose

to propose to someone:: schéxwmet < chá:xw.

Prosopium williamsoni

probably Prosopium williamsoni:: spó:ltsep.

prostitute

prostitute, whore:: xwoxwth'í:lem < xwáth'.

protect

help s-o, defend s-o, protect s-o, aid s-o:: má:yt ~ máyt < máy.
look after s-o, protect s-o, take care of s-o:: xólhmet ~ xólhemet < xólh.
rags wound around the legs in the cold or to protect from mosquitoes, (leggings):: q'élq'xetel < q'ál.

protrude

stick out (of something), protrude:: st'áqsel.

proud :: síts ~ sích, swék'.

(be a) little bit proud, [a little] proud:: smámth'el < máth'el.
(be) proud:: sp'éqw'.
(be) proud (pompous):: smáth'el < máth'el.
(lots of people are) proud, (many are proud):: smá:leth'el ~ smá:lth'el < máth'el.
nickname for someone who is proud:: slék'.

provisions)

dry storage box in tree or on top of pole (for salmon and other dried provisions):: póqw'elh < pó:qw' ~ póqw'.
(food) provisions for a trip, box lunch:: sáwel.

proximity

nominalizer (female present and visible or presence or proximity unspecified), demonstrative article:: the=.
nominalizer (male or gender unspecified, present and visible or presence or proximity unspecified), demonstrative article:: ta=, te=.

Prunus emarginata:: pélel, t'elémelhp < t'elém.

Prunus spp.:: plems.

Prunus virginiana:: lhex̲wlhéx̲w < lhex̲w.

pry :: wáth'.
  pry (a canoe paddling stroke when the canoe is hard to turn):: lhímesem < lhímes.
  prying:: wóweth' < wáth'.
  pry s-th, lock s-th (the Indian way/barred/wedged), pry s-th up, lever it up:: wáth'et < wáth'.
  pry with paddle in stern to turn a canoe sharply, pry (canoe stroke done by a sternman):: q'á:lets.

Psaltriparus minimus
  Parus atricapillus occidentalis, probably also Parus rufescens, possibly also Psaltriparus minimus:: skíkek < sqá:q.
  Parus atricapillus occidentalis, prob. Parus rufescens, poss. Psaltriparus minimus:: méxts'el.

Pseudotsuga menziesii:: lá:yelhp < lá:y, ts'sá:y, ts'sá:yelhp < ts'sá:y.
  prob. Abies lasiocarpa, if sample is mistaken poss. Abies amabilis or Abies grandis, if term balsam is mistaken poss. a variety of Pseudotsuga menziesii:: q'et'emá:yelhp < q'át'em.

psychological non-control
  psychological non-control transitivizer:: =eles ~ =les.

Pteridum aquilinum:: ptákwem, sá:q.

puberty
  girl at puberty, (girl's first period):: thethíx̲w.
  to change (of a boy's voice at puberty):: qw'elá:m < qw'íl.

puberty hut:: sqíqemel < sqémél.

pubic
  pubic hair:: qwéyleq ~ qwíleq < qwíl ~ qwel.

Puckat Creek
  Mill Creek (at American Bar), Puckat Creek on map also:: Peqwchṓ:lthel Stótelō < péqw.

puddle
  make the sound of water splashing or dripping fast, (make the sound of a waterfall, make the sound of pouring rain dripping or splashing in puddles loudly):: xwótqwem.
  puddle that's always dirty, dirty pond, stagnant pool of water, (it never dries out [AK]):: th'qwélhcha.

puff
  smoke puffing out, (puff out (dust, powder, plant spores, seed fluff, light snow, smoke), form puffs of dust):: pékw' ~ péqw'.

puffball
  puffball, probably giant puffball and gemmed puffball, and possibly other species::

puffball (CONT'D)

pópkw'em < pékw' ~ péqw'.

pull

be straight (of rope but not tree), pulled tight (of rope), stretched tight, tight:: sthethá:kw' < thékw'.
peel it (bark off a tree), bark it, (de-bark it), pull itdown (of bark, board, etc.), pull it up (of bark, board):: lheqw'ó:t < lhéqw', lheqw'ó:t < lhéqw'.
pinch s-th, pinch s-o (and pull the skin):: th'lhákw't < th'lhákw'.
pull ashore in a canoe, land a canoe:: lhà:l.
pulled, influenced:: thékw'.
pulled out (of tooth or teeth), (have one's tooth pulled out):: ma'álésem < má ~ má'-.
pulling a canoe through rough water by a rope in the front:: tx̲wṓwelh < tóx̲w.
pulling a canoe through rough water by a rope in the front, pulling a canoe with a rope:: tóx̲wesem < tóx̲w.
pull in once with a canoe paddle wide or slow, pull in in turning (a canoe paddling stroke done by a bowman):: lhímes.
pull oneself up, straighten (oneself) up:: thkw'éthet < thékw'.
pull out a nail, (pull it out (a metal nail)):: th'ót.
pull out (hair):: qw'emét < qw'ém.
pull skin off s-th (like a bird that's easy to skin):: síkw'et < síkw'.
pull s-o's hair, grab s-o's hair:: x̲éymleqwt < x̲éym.
pull s-th/s-o:: thekw'ét ~ thkw'ét < thékw'.
pull up by the roots:: qw'emét < qw'ém.
skin or bark pulls off:: síkw'em < síkw'.
suction sound of feet pulling out of mud:: t'áxwqem.
take it out of a box, pull it out of a box:: xíqt.

"pullers"

seven paddlers, seven "pullers":: th'ekwsále < th'ó:kws.

pulp

smash s-th to pieces (hard pitch, splintery wood, a glass), break s-th to pieces, beat s-th/s-o to a pulp:: th'ṓ:wt.

pulse :: lhkw'ámṓ(w)s ~ lhkw'ámṓ:s < slhákw'em.

Punch

nickname of Louie Punch:: Píx̲eya < píx̲eya.

punch

hit s-o in the face, punch s-o in the face:: th'í:qw'est < th'í:qw'et.
punched in the face:: th'qw'ó:s < th'í:qw'et.
punched on the ear:: th'qw'á:lí:ye < th'í:qw'et.
punched on the nose:: th'qw'élqsel < th'í:qw'et.
punched s-o on the rump:: th'qw'íwet < th'í:qw'et.
punched s-o on the stomach:: th'qw'álewest < th'í:qw'et.
punch s-o/s-th, hit s-o/s-th with fist:: th'í:qw'et.
you'll get punched all over:: th'óleqw'esthòm < th'í:qw'et.

punish :: lepílítòs.

puny
(be) puny:: stí:tethel < títh ~ tí:th.

pup
runt of litter, smallest pup or kitten or animal in litter:: th'íth'kw'oya < sth'ékw', th'íth'kw' < sth'ékw'.

pupil
pupil of the eye:: q'eyx̲óles < q'íx̲.

puppy
a lot of (small) dogs, puppies:: sqwéqwemay < qwem.
puppy:: sqwíqwemay < qwem.
small puppy:: sqwíqwemeyò:llh < qwem.

purple :: sp'íqw' < p'íqw', st'áwel, tsp'íqw' < p'íqw'.
[be getting/going purple]:: sp'íp'eqw'el < p'íqw'.
[looks purple, purple-looking]:: st'áwelòmèx < st'áwel.

purplish white
(powder white, purplish white?):: st'ewṓkw'.

purpose)
beat s-o/s-th with a stick, hit s-o/s-th with a stick, hit s-th (on purpose), hit s-o intentionally:: kw'óqwet < kw'óqw.
poison s-o/s-th on purpose:: yéltht < yélth.
smell s-th on purpose:: hóqwet < hóqw.

purposeful
purposeful control reciprocal, (perhaps just) reciprocal, (do purposely to) each other, (do purposely to) one another:: =t=el.
purposeful control reflexive, do purposely to oneself:: =thet.
purposeful control transitivizer, do purposely to s-o/s-th:: =t ~ =et.
purposeful control transitivizer inanimate object preferred:: =ex.

purposely)
bring s-th/s-o outside (purposely):: atl'qílt < átl'q.
change oneself (purposely), change oneself into something else, change s-th on oneself:: iyóqthet < iyá:q.
change s-th (purposely), change s-o, transform s-o/s-th, trade s-th, replace s-th:: iyá:qt ~ iyáqt < iyá:q.
disappear (purposely):: thexwó:thet < théxw ~ théx̲w.
drop it on purpose:: tsélqt < tsélq ~ chélq.
he/she/it is poking me [purposely]:: ts'eqw'ts'eqw'thóxes < ts'éqw'.
join, (include oneself purposely):: q'ó:thet < q'ó.
kill s-o (purposely):: q'ó:yt < q'ó:y ~ q'óy.
kill s-th (purposely):: q'ó:yt < q'ó:y ~ q'óy.
poison s-o/s-th on purpose:: yéltht < yélth.
purposeful control reciprocal, (perhaps just) reciprocal, (do purposely to) each other, (do purposely to) one another:: =t=el.
purposeful control reflexive, do purposely to oneself:: =thet.
purposeful control transitivizer, do purposely to s-o/s-th:: =t ~ =et.

purposely) (CONT'D)
shame oneself (purposely):: x̲éyx̲ethet < x̲éyx̲e ~ x̲íx̲e.
smear something on s-o's face [purposely]:: yétl'q'est < yétl'.
somebody is made to fast, he is starved (purposely):: xwátem < xwá.
spoil s-th (purposely):: qelí:lt < qél.
touch s-o purposely, squish it (of berries, etc.), smash s-th, mash it (berries, potatoes, carrots, etc.), bump it:: tóset < tós.
wake up (oneself), (wake oneself purposely):: xwíythet ~ xwíthet < xwíy ~ x í.

purse
wallet, purse:: shxwtále'álá < tá:le ~ tále.
whistle with pursed lips, whistling:: xíxpò:m < xó:pem.

pursed
(have) pursed lips when pouting:: smóst'iyethel.
whistle with pursed lips, whistling:: xíxpò:m < xó:pem.

pus :: méth'elh.

push
launch s-th/s-o into the water, push s-o/s-th into the water, throw it in the water:: qwsét < qwés.
push, (got pushed [EB]):: théx̲.
pushing s-o/s-th:: tháx̲t < théx̲.
push out from shore (in canoe):: thex̲ósem < théx̲.
push s-o/s-th:: thx̲ét ~ thex̲ét < théx̲.
push s-th (in):: x̲eth'ét.
shake s-th down, pack s-th down, push s-th down, knead s-th (esp. of bread dough), press it down (like yeast bread):: qeth'ét.

Pussy Willow
Pussy Willow (name in stories):: Qweqwemeytá:ye < qwem.

pussy willow:: sqweqweméytses < qwem.

put
be tucked away, put away so well you can't find it, be solid:: slá ~ selá ~ slá: (probably).
bring s-o/s-th in (to a house/enclosure), take s-o/s-th in(inside a house/enclosure), admit s-o (into a house/enclosure), let s-o/s-th in (to a house/enclosure), put s-o/s-th in (inside a house/enclosure:: kwetáxwt < kwetáxw.
cast a spell on s-o, put a spell on s-o, shoot power into s-o:: x̲t'ét < x̲ét'.
cast a spell, throw a spell, put on a spell, shoot power:: x̲t'áls or x̲t'á:ls < x̲ét'.
close s-th (for ex. a box), put a lid on s-th (for ex. a pot), cover it with a lid:: qp'á:qet < qep'.
(emprisoned), put in jail, grounded, restricted, caught, apprehended:: qíq'.
everybody put away (fishing gear, canoe and) paddles (for winter), put away each other's paddles [and canoes and gear] for winter:: xets'ő:westel < xits' ~ xets'.
get fat, put on weight, getting fat:: ló:sthet ~ lósthet < ló:s ~ lós.
help oneself to food, serve oneself, serve oneself food (with a ladle), serve oneself a meal (food), (put on a dish [CT, HT]):: lhá:x̲em ~ lháx̲em < lhá:x̲ ~ lháx̲.
laying down, putting down:: lhálheq'els < lháq'.
lay it down, put it down:: lháq'et < lháq'.

put (CONT'D)

mix s-th, put them together:: q'etóléstexw < q'ó.
moon or month beginning in November, (put away each other's paddles), (sometimes the moon beginning in October, depending on the weather [Elders Group [3/12/75], (moon or month beginning in January [Elders Group 2/5/75]):: xets'ṓ:westel ~ xets'ṓwestel < xits' ~ xets'.
(one person) puts away his paddles (and canoe and gear for winter):: xets'ṓ:wes < xits' ~ xets'.
preserved fish, preserved meat, dried fish, dried meat (usually fish), smoked salmon, wind-dried salmon (old word), what is stored away, what is put away:: sq'éyle.
put a hand on one hip:: piypiyólwelh < píy.
put a mark on it (like water level of river), mark it, weigh it, (measure it):: x̲á:th't ~ x̲áth't < x̲áth' ~ x̲e'áth'.
put a rope around s-o/s-th's neck, put a leash on s-th, hang s-o:: x̲wíqw'est < x̲wíqw'.
put away, (it has been put away):: q'éylòm.
put hands on both hips, (put hands akimbo):: piypiyólwelhem < píy.
put it down, take it down (s-th on the wall for ex.):: xwetáqt.
put it in (and leave it), stick it into s-th hollow:: léwex < léw.
put on a dress:: eth'íwsem < íth'a.
put on a shawl:: s'oth'ó:mṓsem < íth'a.
put one's hand on s-th to brace oneself, brace oneself on s-th/s-o:: píyet < píy.
put one's hands behind one's back:: q'eth'ōwítsem < q'áth'.
put one's hands under one's arms:: xixets'eláx̲em < xits' ~ xets'.
put one's head back (tilt one's face up):: q'óx̲esem.
put one's head down, bend, bend over, bend over with one's head down, stoop down:: qep'ósem < qep'.
put one's head to one side, lay on one side of the head:: lexósem < lex.
put on one's hat:: yóseqwem < yó:seqw ~ yóseqw.
put on one's pants:: seqí:wsem < seqíws ~ seqí:ws.
put on one's shoes:: qwelhlixélem ~ qwelhixélem < qwélh.
put on one's socks, (put on one's stockings):: tókelem < stókel.
put on the stove (water/food):: xwch'alech'á:ls < ts'á:.
put paint on one's face:: yétl'q'esem < yétl'.
put paint on the body:: yétl'q'íws < yétl'.
put something in the ear (to block hearing), (plug the ear):: t'ekwá:lí:ya < t'ékw.
put s-th away, save s-th (food for ex.):: qéylemt ~ qé:ylemt < qéylem ~ qé:ylem ~ qí(:)lem.
put s-th between the teeth, put it in one's mouth, bite on s-th (not into it):: ts'ámet ~ ch'ámet.
put s-th on (of a design on a dress, of a shirt, shoes, etc.), attach it, stick it on, fasten it:: tl'álx < tl'ál.
put s-th/s-o aboard, put it on-board:: ó:lhstexw < ó:lh, ó:lhstexw < ó:lh.
put s-th with (something), add s-th (to something), include s-th:: q'ót < q'ó.
put them down (several objects):: lháleq'et < lháq'.
put them together, (join them together):: q'ótelt ~ q'ótòlt < q'ó.
putting it down:: lhálheq'et < lháq'.
put (white) paint on one's face:: t'ewṓkw'esem < st'ewṓkw'.
run over it (with car), spread it (for ex. on bread with knife), put it up (of wallpaper), (stick it on), stick s-th closed (with pitch for ex.):: tl'íq't < tl'íq'.
s-o has been put away (in grave-house or buried), he's/she's been buried:: qéylemtem ~ qé:ylemtem < qéylem ~ qé:ylem ~ qí(:)lem.
s-o/s-th has been put away:: qéylemtem ~ qé:ylemtem < qéylem ~ qé:ylem ~ qí(:)lem.
store it away (wedged-in up off ground), put s-th away for winter, stow s-th away:: xítse't

put (CONT'D)

< xits' ~ xets'.
to be attached, to be fixed or fastened, be put on:: stl'átl'el < tl'ál.
to extinguish it, put it out (a fire):: tl'ékw'elt < tl'ékw'el.
to put on credit ??:: ex̲ímels < íx̲em.
use it, wear it, put it on:: hókwex.

pygmy
maybe the same place as Sqw'ex̲wáq (pool where Kawkawa Creek comes into the Coquihalla River and where the water pygmies lived):: Skw'íkw'x̲weq (or better, Sqw'íqw'x̲weq) < Sqw'ex̲wáq.
water pygmies, water baby:: s'ó:lmexw.

Pyrus fusca
Pyrus fusca, Pyrus malus:: qwe'ó:pelhp < qwe'óp.
Pyrus fusca, Pyrus malus (= Malus malus):: qwe'óp.

Pyrus malus
Pyrus fusca, Pyrus malus:: qwe'ó:pelhp < qwe'óp.
Pyrus fusca, Pyrus malus (= Malus malus):: qwe'óp.

Q'alelíktel
a place across the Fraser River from the rock named Q'alelíktel:: Xwth'ístel < th'ís.

Q'ów
mountain shaped like a thunderbird across the Fraser River from Q'ów (the "howl") mountain:: Xwexwó:stel < shxwexwó:s.

Q-tips (lit. "little rolled balls - [on a] point"):: xíxelkwòls s'álqsel < xél.

quail
mountain quail, possibly also California quail:: kwéyl.

quake
(shaking, quaking, moving oneself):: qwíyx̲thet < qwá:y.

quarter
[left] front leg quarter of deer or other animal:: sth'ikweláx̲el < th'íkwe.
quarter (coin):: kwóte.
small hind quarters:: lhílheq'làts < lheq'át ~ lhq'á:t.

queen :: kwí:l.

Queen's Island:: Qemlólhp < sq'émél.

Queen Victoria:: Kwíl Mektồliya < kwí:l.

Quercus garryana:: p'xwélhp.

question
interrogative, yes/no question:: -e.
weren't ever?, wasn't ever?, didn't ever?, does s-o ever?, never used to, not going to (but

question (CONT'D)

did anyway) [perhaps in the sense of never usually do X but did this time]:: ewá:lh ~ wá:lh < éwe ~ őwe.
yes/no question:: í, lí ~ lí: ~ líye < lí.

quick

got up with a quick motion, got up quickly:: xwexwílék < xwílék.
(have a) quick mouth:: x̲weméthel < x̲wém ~ xwém.
(have) quick eyes, (have) peeping-Tom eyes:: aliyólés < éy ~ éy:.
hurry, hurry up, be quick, be fast, move faster, quickly:: x̲wém ~ xwém.

quick-tempered

cranky, quick-tempered:: x̲éth'x̲eth' < x̲íth' ~ x̲éyth'.

quiet

be shy, be not talkative, quiet (of a person):: p'áp'xwem.
calm (of water), smooth (of water), (when the river is) quiet or calm:: p'ep'ákwem < p'ékw.
get quiet (of wind), stop (of wind):: chó:ythet.
(have) quieter water, died down a little:: sqám < qám.
pacify a baby, pacify it (a baby), sing or hum to a baby to quiet it, sing to it (a zaby), (sing a lullaby to it):: tl'ó:t.
quiet down (of a person):: tl'elxwí:wsem < tl'élexw.
quiet (in movement):: t'ás.
turn back into a quiet slough from the river, be going into a slough from the river:: ts'élexw < ts'el.
walk[ing] silently or quietly:: t'et'ásxel or t'at'ásxel < t'ás.
walk silently, walk quietly:: t'ásxel < t'ás.

quit

finish, stop, quit, get done, be finished, have enough, be done, be ready:: hò:y ~ hó:y ~ hóy.

quiver

arrow pouch, (a quiver for arrows):: th'esélatel.

rabbit

big rabbit, older rabbit, big/older snowshoe/varying hare, now probably also big/older eastern cottontail rabbit (introduced):: sqiqewóthel < sqewáth, sqwiqweyóthel.
bunch of rabbits:: sqweqwewáth < qwá.
jackrabbit, also big or older rabbit (snowshoe/varying hare):: sqwíqweyóthel < qwá.
(larger) rabbit: snowshoe or varying hare, now probably also eastern cottontail rabbit (introduced):: sqewáth.
rabbit: snowshoe/varying hare, now probably also eastern cottontail rabbit (introduced), (baby rabbit, small rabbit or hare [Elders Group]):: sqíqewàth < sqewáth.
rabbit, (varying hare, perhaps now also the introduced eastern cottontail):: shxwóxw.

race)

arrive, arriving, come here, have come, get here, get back, come in (in a race):: xwe'í < í.
racing-canoe:: táyewelh < tá:y.
racing in a canoe, canoe-racing (while you're doing it):: tátey < tá:y.
to race in a canoe:: tá:y.

\

racing-canoe
racing-canoe:: táyewelh < tá:y.

rack
fish-drying rack:: shxwch'á:yxwels < ts'íyxw ~ ts'éyxw ~ ch'íyxw.
fish drying rack (for wind-drying):: sí:.
rack of horns:: shxwiyáxkel.

Racoon
Racoon (name in a story), (Lynx [JL]):: Smelṓ' < mélés.

racoon :: mélés.

radishes:: skwekwelím shxw'ólewù < kwím, shxw'ólewù (lit. little red ones + turnip)

raft :: th'táme.

rafter
main rafters of longhouse:: sh(xw)kw'ekw'í < kw'í ~ kw'íy.

ragged
be ragged:: s'ó:lhqw' < lhéqw'.

rags
rags wound around the legs in the cold or to protect from mosquitoes, (leggings):: q'élq'xetel < q'ál.

raid
raid s-o in canoes:: sléxwelhmet < sléxwelh.
warrior, (leader of a raiding party [CT]):: stó:méx.

raiding party
warrior, (leader of a raiding party [CT]):: stó:méx.

railroad :: kyóxàlh < kyó, kyóxàlh or kyóxàlh < xálh ~ xá:lh.
railroad, (railroad track [IHTTC]):: lílṑt.

rain
a rainshower:: lhémt < lhém.
(be) rainy (off and on):: lhémlhemexw < lhém.
common nighthawk, (rain bird [Elders Group]):: pí:q'.
(get) lots of water all over since it's raining so hard, really getting rainy:: t'emt'émqw'xel < t'émeqw', t'emt'émqw'xel < t'émeqw'.
(have) mixed snow and rain together that melts fast, to rain and snow mixed together:: imqáxel ~ hi=mqáxel < máqa ~ máqe, imqáxel ~ hi=mqáxel < máqa ~ máqe.
lots of little streams (like the kind coming down a hill after a rain):: teltelewá:m < tó:l ~ tò:l.
make the sound of water splashing or dripping fast, (make the sound of a waterfall, make the sound of pouring rain dripping or splashing in puddles loudly):: xwótqwem.
(maybe) fine mist of fog or rain, ((perhaps) getting foggy [EB]):: qweqweqwtí:mxel < qwétxem.
raining hard, pouring rain, (raining fast):: xwémxel < x̲wém ~ xwém.
raining, ([having a] rainshower with light wind [BJ]):: lhémexw < lhém.
(rain or sweat) trickling down one's face:: kw'tómés < kw'átem.

rain (CONT'D)

stop raining, stop snowing:: xwéts'xel.
the rain:: slhém:exw ~ slhémexw < lhém.
to rain:: lhéméxw < lhém.

rainbow :: swétexel, sx̲wétexel or sx̲wét'exel, thelqxálém < theqelxélém.
a rainbow:: stheqelxél:ém ~ stheqelxélém < theqelxélém.
(have/get a) rainbow:: theqelxélém.

Rainbow Falls
Rainbow Falls (on Harrison Lake's southeast side):: Tsólqthet te Skwówech < skwó:wech ~ skwówech.
Rainbow Falls on Harrison Lake, (Sturgeon's Drop):: Tsólqthet te Skwówech < tsélq ~ chélq.
Rainbow Falls on the east side of Harrison Lake:: Tsólqthet te Skwówech < tsélq.

rain-clouds
be steaming (in many places), be cloudy with rain-clouds:: pelpólx̲wem < poléx̲wem.

rain crow
large red-necked woodpecker, large red-headed woodpecker, rain crow (black with red comb on head) (AC), pileated woodpecker:: temélhépsem < témélh.

rainshelter:: q'eléts' < q'el.

rainshower
a rainshower:: lhémt < lhém.
raining, ([having a] rainshower with light wind [BJ]):: lhémexw < lhém.

rain-water
collected rain-water drops in a bucket:: th'q'emelétsem < th'q'ém ~ th'eq'ém.
collected rain-water from a drip:: th'q'émelets ~ ts'q'émelets < th'q'ém ~ th'eq'ém.

rainy
(get) lots of water all over since it's raining so hard, really getting rainy:: t'emt'émqw'xel < t'émeqw'.

raise
growing [s-o] up, (raising s-o):: ts'símt < ts'ísem.
raise it (of a pole):: lhex̲eyléxstexw < lhéx̲.
to lift, raise:: shxwóxwel < xwá.

rake
a rake, a harrow:: x̲éyx̲ep'ílep < x̲éyp'.
scratch s-o/s-th and leave a mark, rake it, claw it, scrape it:: x̲éyp'et < x̲éyp'.

Rana aurora aurora
family Ranidae and family Bufonidae, esp. Bufo boreas boreas and recent introductions Rana catesbeiana and Rana clamitans, and Ascaphus truei, Rana aurora aurora, and Rana pretiosa pretiosa:: pípehò:m < peh or pó(:)h.
if generic includes families Ranidae and Bufonidae and may include Hyla regilla and perhaps the introduced species: Rana catesbeiana, Rana clamitans, Rana aurora aurora, Rana pretiosa

Rana aurora aurora (CONT'D)

pretiosa, and Ascaphus truei, if not generic then includes only members of family Ranidae and/or family Bufonidae:: wex̲és, weléx̲ < wex̲és.

Rana catesbeiana

family Ranidae and family Bufonidae, esp. Bufo boreas boreas and recent introductions Rana catesbeiana and Rana clamitans, and Ascaphus truei, Rana aurora aurora, and Rana pretiosa pretiosa:: pípehò:m < peh or pó(:)h.

if generic includes families Ranidae and Bufonidae and may include Hyla regilla and perhaps the introduced species: Rana catesbeiana, Rana clamitans, Rana aurora aurora, Rana pretiosa pretiosa, and Ascaphus truei, if not generic then includes only members of family Ranidae and/or family Bufonidae:: wex̲és, weléx̲ < wex̲és.

probably Rana catesbeiana, possibly Rana clamitans:: wex̲ó:mő:lh.

Rana catesbeiana, and prob. Rana clamitans:: pehó:mő:lh < peh or pó(:)h.

Rana clamitans

family Ranidae and family Bufonidae, esp. Bufo boreas boreas and recent introductions Rana catesbeiana and Rana clamitans, and Ascaphus truei, Rana aurora aurora, and Rana pretiosa pretiosa:: pípehò:m < peh or pó(:)h.

if generic includes families Ranidae and Bufonidae and may include Hyla regilla and perhaps the introduced species: Rana catesbeiana, Rana clamitans, Rana aurora aurora, Rana pretiosa pretiosa, and Ascaphus truei, if not generic then includes only members of family Ranidae and/or family Bufonidae:: wex̲és, weléx̲ < wex̲és.

probably Rana catesbeiana, possibly Rana clamitans:: wex̲ó:mő:lh.

Rana catesbeiana, and prob. Rana clamitans:: pehó:mő:lh < peh or pó(:)h.

Rana pretiosa pretiosa

family Ranidae and family Bufonidae, esp. Bufo boreas boreas and recent introductions Rana catesbeiana and Rana clamitans, and Ascaphus truei, Rana aurora aurora, and Rana pretiosa pretiosa:: pípehò:m < peh or pó(:)h.

if generic includes families Ranidae and Bufonidae and may include Hyla regilla and perhaps the introduced species: Rana catesbeiana, Rana clamitans, Rana aurora aurora, Rana pretiosa pretiosa, and Ascaphus truei, if not generic then includes only members of family Ranidae and/or family Bufonidae:: wex̲és, weléx̲ < wex̲és.

rancid

be bitter (like of cascara bark or medicine or rancid peanuts):: sásex̲em ~ sá:sex̲em < sáx̲em.

bitter, rancid:: chíchex̲em.

got rancid, got bitter:: chx̲í:mthet < chíchex̲em.

Ranidae

family Ranidae and family Bufonidae, esp. Bufo boreas boreas and recent introductions Rana catesbeiana and Rana clamitans, and Ascaphus truei, Rana aurora aurora, and Rana pretiosa pretiosa:: pípehò:m < peh or pó(:)h.

if generic includes families Ranidae and Bufonidae and may include Hyla regilla and perhaps the introduced species: Rana catesbeiana, Rana clamitans, Rana aurora aurora, Rana pretiosa pretiosa, and Ascaphus truei, if not generic then includes only members of family Ranidae and/or family Bufonidae:: wex̲és, weléx̲ < wex̲és.

rank

smelling damp, rank:: qwóqwelem.

rap

knocking, rapping:: kwókwexwels < kwoxw.
knocking, rapping (in the distance), tapping:: kwókwexwem < kwoxw.
knock (once), rap:: kwxwà:ls < kwoxw.

rapid

(make a) rapid repeated sound usually on wood:: qw'ópx̲wem < qw'ópx̲w.

rapids

rapids, fast water, clear water, flowing fast, going fast, swift (water):: lex̲wố:m ~ lex̲wốm < x̲wém ~ xwém.

rash

lots of sores, (possibly) rash:: sth'ekw'th'ékw' < th'ekw' or th'íkw'.

raspberry

a sprout or shoot (esp. of the kinds peeled and eaten in spring), sweet green inner shoots, green berry shoots, salmonberry shoots, wild raspberry shoots and greens, salmonberry sprouts, blackcap shoots, thimbleberry shoots, wild rhubarb shoots, fern shoots:: stháthqiy.
wild red raspberry, domestic red raspberry:: s'ó:ytheqw < éy ~ éy:.
wild red raspberry plant, domestic red raspberry plant:: s'ó:ytheqwelhp < éy ~ éy:.
raspberry juice:: s'óytheqw sqe'óleqw < éy, qó:
(lit. raspberry + fruit juice)

rat

a big rat (prob. the introduced Norway rat, probably native species of large vole which may include any or all of the following that are found in the area: creeping vole, long-tail vole, mountain heather vole, boreal redback vole), possibly also the introduced roof rat:: ts'á:txwels < ts'átxwels ~ ch'átxwels.
a few little rats:: haheláwt < há:wt.
packrat, i.e. bushy-tailed wood rat:: qélqel há:wt < há:wt.
rat, vole (short-tailed mouse), may include any or all of the following which occur in this area: creeping vole, long-tail vole, mountain heather vole, boreal redback vole, Norway rat (intro.), and perhaps roof rat, also includes bushy-tailed wood rat (packrat) which has its own name below:: há:wt.
small rat, small vole:: hiháwt < há:wt.

rather

I'd rather have (s-th), I'd prefer (s-th) (make that s-th instead):: tl'óst or tl'óstexw.

rattle

deer hoof rattle of spirit-dancer (stick with deer hoof rattles tied onto it):: kwóxwemal ~ kwóxwmal < kwoxw.
hand rattle of Indian doctor or shaman:: kwóxwemal ~ kwóxwmal < kwoxw.
(have/get) wheezing, rattling breath:: xwóyeqw'em.
large rattle used at spirit-dances:: syốwméxwtses.
rattling s-th:: q'átx̲(e)t < q'et.
scraping sound (like scraping food off dishes), rattling (of dishes, metal pots, wagon on gravel):: q'átx̲em < q'et.
to rattle (cans, etc. to wake newlyweds), to shivaree (someone):: q'etx̲áls < q'et.
to rattle (of dishes or anything else loose), jingle (of money or any metal shaken), peal or

rattle (CONT'D)

toll (of a bell), make the sound of a bell, to ring (of a bell, telephone, in the ears):: th'á:tsem < th'éts or th'á(:)ts.
to rattle s-th inside:: kwétxwt < kwótx̲wem ~ kwótxwem.
wheezing in the chest, rattling in the chest:: xwóyeqw'emíles < xwóyeqw'em.

rattlesnake
Pacific rattlesnake, (a poison [LG: Chill.]):: th'éx̲tel < th'éx̲.

Rattus norvegicus
may include any or all of the following which occur in this area: creeping vole Microtus oregoni serpens, long-tail vole Microtus longicaudus macrurus, mountain heather vole Phenacomys intermedius oramontis, boreal redback vole Clethrionomys gapperi cascadensis, Norway rat (intro.) Rattus norvegicus, and perhaps roof rat Rattus rattus, also includes bushy-tailed wood rat (packrat) Neotoma cinerea occidentalis which has its own name below:: há:wt.

Rattus norvegius
prob. the introduced Rattus norvegius, native species possiblyincluding any/all of these four: Microtus oregoni serpens, Microtus longicaudus macrurus, Phenacomys intermedius oramontis, and Clethrionomys gapperi cascadensis, possibly also the introduced Rattus rattus:: ts'á:txwels < ts'átxwels ~ ch'átxwels.

Rattus rattus
may include any or all of the following which occur in this area: creeping vole Microtus oregoni serpens, long-tail vole Microtus longicaudus macrurus, mountain heather vole Phenacomys intermedius oramontis, boreal redback vole Clethrionomys gapperi cascadensis, Norway rat (intro.) Rattus norvegicus, and perhaps roof rat Rattus rattus, also includes bushy-tailed wood rat (packrat) Neotoma cinerea occidentalis which has its own name below:: há:wt.
prob. the introduced Rattus norvegius, native species possiblyincluding any/all of these four: Microtus oregoni serpens, Microtus longicaudus macrurus, Phenacomys intermedius oramontis, and Clethrionomys gapperi cascadensis, possibly also the introduced Rattus rattus:: ts'á:txwels < ts'átxwels ~ ch'átxwels.

Raven :: Skwówéls.
Raven, (Mister Raven or Mister Crow? [AK 1/16/80]):: Skwówéls.

raven :: skéweqs < sqéweqs, sqéweqs, sqéweqs.
a trilling sound a raven makes:: xwot'q'esílem.
big crow, common crow, also known as western crow or American crow, (raven [EF, some Deming elders]):: spó:l.

ravine :: stl'éxs < Tl'ítl'xeleqw.

raw
raw, uncooked:: x̲éyth'.

rawhide
buckskin, rawhide, tanned buckskin:: áx̲elqel.

ray
(get a) ray of sun between clouds:: qeyqeyx̲elósem < qéyqeyx̲elà.
precipitation, ray of light:: =xel.

ray (CONT'D)

rays of light:: sxelxéles te syó:qwem < xél ~ xé:yl ~ xí:l

reach :: tssátses < tsesá ~ tssá or tsás, séttsesem.

approach, get near, get closer, reach, go up to, get up to:: tés.

can't reach:: sq'thá:mtses < q'thá:m.

can't reach (with hand):: q'thá:mtses < q'thá:m.

get there, arrive there, reach there:: xwelí ~ xwlí < lí.

get to, reach there:: xwelí:ls < lí.

reach s-o here:: xw'í:lmet < í.

reaction

prickly (from fir bark, wool, or something one is allergic to), irritant, have an allergic reaction (to fir powder or cedar bark):: th'íth'ekwem < th'íkw.

read

find s-th out, understand s-th, learn s-th, realize s-th, now know what s-th is like, read (and comprehend) s-th, understand s-o:: tél:exw ~ (in rapid speech) télexw < tól.

reading:: kwexáls < kwí:x ~ kwíx.

read it:: kwíxet < kwí:x ~ kwíx.

read it (see well enough to read it):: kw'átset < kw'áts ~ kw'éts.

ready

(be) aggressive, cranky, ready to fight, (be) violent, hot-headed:: sxóytl'thet ~ sxó:ytl'thet.

be coiled (ready to strike for ex. of a snake):: sq'elá:w < q'ál.

(be) coiling (ready to strike) (of a snake):: sq'elq'elá:w < q'ál.

be ready:: s-hí:lekw ~ s-hílekw < hilékw.

finish, stop, quit, get done, be finished, have enough, be done, be ready:: hò:y ~ hó:y ~ hóy.

get ready:: hilékw.

getting ready to go:: hí:lekw ~ hílekw < hilékw.

real

(have a) real big foot, (have a) huge foot:: thí:thaxel < thi ~ tha ~ the ~ thah ~ theh.

make a real mess:: yó:lqw'es < yél or perhaps yá:l.

really, real:: wel.

real tired:: welhchí:ws < lhchí:ws.

turning to real yellow:: qwáyewel < qwá:y.

realize

find s-th out, understand s-th, learn s-th, realize s-th, now know what s-th is like, read (and comprehend) s-th, understand s-o:: tél:exw ~ (in rapid speech) télexw < tól.

Really.

Really. (said in doubt):: kw'è: < kw'é.

really

(be/get) really worried:: th'áth'iyekw.

be really:: áth'el.

be really tangled, it's really tangled:: sq'á:lq' < q'ál.

(be) very, (extremely), really:: ts'áts'el.

gift one really makes use of:: xwayólem.

really (CONT'D)

how beautiful., be really beautiful:: yú:wqwlha < yú:w.
really mixed s-th up:: melmóléqwet < mál ~ mél.
really, real:: wel.
really round, (perfectly spherical?):: xelókw'els < xél.
really turned gray (of hair):: x̲ó:lemthet < x̲ólem.
straining to listen, really listening, listening hard, trying to listen, (listen [AC]):: xwlalá:.

rear

a canoe or boat cut off short in the rear (because the stern couldn't be repaired):: t'qw'á:lats < t'éqw'.
it got smashed in the back end or rear end:: téslatstem < tós.

recently

recently, just now, lately, (at one recent moment), not long ago:: qá:ys.

receptacle

container for, receptacle for:: =á:lá ~ =álá ~ =àlà ~ =ela.

reciprocal

purposeful control reciprocal, (perhaps just) reciprocal, (do purposely to) each other, (do purposely to) one another:: =t=el.

reckless)

scare oneself (in being reckless), scare oneself (do something one knows is dangerous and get scared even more than expected):: sí:silómet ~ sí:silòmèt < síy.

record player

musical instrument, grammophone, phonograph, record player:: qweló:ythetel ~ qwelóyethetel < qwà:l.

recover

recover, be better:: i'éyel < éy ~ éy:.

rectum)

(have a) dirty behind, (dirty in the rump, dirty in the rectum):: ts'epí:wel < ts'épx̲.
(have a) wide rump, (wide in the rectum):: lheq'tíwél < lheq'át ~ lhq'á:t.
in the rump, in the anus, in the rectum, in the bottom, on the insides, inside parts, core, inside the head:: =í:wel ~ =íwel ~ =ewel.
stick it up someone's rump:: t'ekwíwet < t'ékw.
(stuck in the rectum), stuck in the ass:: st'ekwíwel < t'ékw.

red]

[be especially red]:: tskwí:m < kwí:m.
[be extra specially red]:: tskwí::m < kwí:m.
[be get/go/become red]:: tskwímel < kwí:m.
[be getting/going a little red]:: skwekwíkwemel < kwí:m, tskwekwíkwemel < kwí:m.
[be getting red, be going red]:: skwíkwemel < kwí:m.
[being red]:: tskwíkwem < kwí:m.
be red, red, reddish-brown, copper-colored:: tskwí:m < kwí:m.
got red, became red, gone red:: kwí:mel < kwí:m.
have red eyes:: tskwimó:les < kwí:m.

red] (CONT'D)

have red hair, have reddish-brown hair:: tskwí:meqw < kwí:m.
Indian red paint (used by spirit dancers, ritualists, and Indian doctors or shamans):: témélh.
it's getting red:: kwíkwemel < kwí:m.
[looks red, red-looking]:: tskwimómex < kwí:m.
lots of little red:: tskwékwelim < kwí:m.
one's face is red, one is blushing:: kwelkwímelésem < kwí:m.
paint one's face red or black (spirit dancer, Indian doctor, ritualist, etc.):: lhíx̲esem < lhá:x̲ ~ lháx̲.
sparks, red hot ashes thrown out:: qw'á:ychep < qw'á:y.
spread red or black paint on s-th(?)/s-o:: lhíx̲et < lhá:x̲ ~ lháx̲.
to paint red or black (spirit dancer, Indian doctor, etc.):: lhíx̲ < lhá:x̲ ~ lháx̲.

red baneberry
short unidentified plant, about 3 ft. tall with red berries like a short mountain ash, the berries are bitter but the plant is used as medicine, possibly red baneberry:: í:lwelh.

reddish :: tskwíkwemel < kwí:m.
(have a) chronic skin disease marked by reddish skin and itching, have "seven-year itch":: lhóth'.
red ochre, (clay colored reddish by oxides of iron):: témélh.

reddish-brown
be red, red, reddish-brown, copper-colored:: tskwí:m < kwí:m.
have reddish-brown fur, have reddish-brown animal hair:: tskwímelqel < kwí:m.
have red hair, have reddish-brown hair:: tskwí:meqw < kwí:m.

red-flowering currant
red-flowering currant berry, Indian currant berry, probably also stink currant berry also called skunk currant berry:: sp'á:th'.

red-necked
large red-necked woodpecker, large red-headed woodpecker, rain crow (black with red comb on head) (AC), pileated woodpecker:: temélhépsem < témélh.

red ochre
red ochre, (clay colored reddish by oxides of iron):: témélh.
red ochre color, color of red clay of iron oxide used for religious paint and face paint:: témélh.

red paint:: tskwím témelh < témélh.

"red willow"
red-osier dogwood, (also called "red willow" [SJ, EL]):: th'ex̲wíyelhp.

reed
bulrush mat, reed mat, mat (of cattail/roots/bulrushes, etc.), (wall mat (Elders Group 11/12/75):: wá:th'elh ~ wáth'elh < wáth'.
cat-tail, cattail reed:: sth'á:qel.

reed canary-grass:: ts'á:yas te th'á:x̲ey < th'áx̲.

reed-grass
grass scalded and bleached white for basketry imbrication (designs), sometimes called white straw grass, probably blue-joint reed-grass:: th'á:x̲ey ~ th'áx̲ey < th'áx̲.

reflect
shine like a reflection, reflect, glitter, sparkle:: p'álq'em.
shining, (glittering, sparkling (with many reflections)):: p'elp'álq'em < p'álq'em.

reflexive :: =et or -et.
indirect effect non-control reflexive:: =methet.
non-control reflexive, happen to or manage to or accidentally do to oneself:: =l=ómet or =l-ómet ~ =l=ó:met.
non-control reflexive, make oneself do something, keep oneself doing something:: =st=èlèmèt or =st-èlèmèt ~ =st-elómet.
purposeful control reflexive, do purposely to oneself:: =thet.

refuge
hiding place, refuge, hide-out:: kwokwílàlà < kwà:l.

refuse
refuse s-o something:: kw'íyat < kw'íy.
stingy of food, refuse (somebody something):: kw'íyà:m < kw'íy.

rehydrate
to soak (fish, beans, dried fruit, only food, not of cedar roots), rehydrate dried food, soak dried fish:: lhélqi < lhél.

reinjure
accidentally hurt an old injury of s-o, (accidentally reinjure s-o):: qélhlexw < qélh.

reject
reject (a person):: qá:lh.
reject someone as a spouse or partner for one's child:: qá:lmílh < qéylem ~ qé:ylem ~ qí(:)lem.
reject someone as a spouse or partner for your child:: qá:lmílh.

relations (ancestors
parents, relations (ancestors?):: shxwwáli < shxwewá(:)y.

relative
in-laws or relatives when the connecting link dies:: ts'its'á:ya < ts'á:ya.
relative (of any kind):: sts'ó:.

relative of deceased spouse:: th'á:ya.
relative of deceased spouse, mother/brother/sister/cousin/relative of deceased husband, dead spouse's relative or sibling, daughter-in-law if son dies:: ts'á:ya.

relax:: tl'elxwí:wsem < tl'élexw.
relaxed [in the throat]:: qáwlhelh < qá:w.
relaxing, resting:: qaqíw < qá:w.

release it:: kwát < kwá:.

relieve
- relieved (in one's body):: ts'elxwí:wsem < ts'el.

religious
- a category of religious songs including sx̲wó:yx̲wey songs and burning songs, a burning song:: heywí:leqw < yéw: ~ yéw.

relish:: sth'íth'eqw kúkumels (lit. chopped + cucumber) < th'íqw, kwúkwemels or kúkumels

remain
- be only remaining:: txwó:ye.
- stay here, stay, remain at a place:: í ò < í.

remember :: há:kw'elem ?.
- remembering s-o, remembering s-th:: há:kw'eles < hákw'eles.
- remember s-o, remember s-th:: hákw'eles.
- show a picture of those remembered:: xwpósem te hákw'elesem < xwp, hákw'eles.

reminisce
- generalize, reminisce:: lale'úlem.

remote)
- the (distant and out of sight, remote), (definite but distant and out of sight, remote), the (abstract), a (remote, abstract), some, (indefinite):: kw'e.
- the (present, not visible, gender unspecified), the (remote, abstract):: kwe < kw.
- the (remote, not visible, abstract), some (indefinite):: kw.

remove
- scorch s-th, blacken s-th with fire, heat it up (near a fire), burning a canoe with pitchwood to remove splinters and burn on black pitch):: qw'á:yt < qw'á:y.

repair
- made, fixed, repaired:: thíy.
- making s-th better, repairing s-th once discarded:: p'áp'ekw'et < p'ákw'.
- repair s-th once discarded, make s-th better, fix s-th up, repair s-th:: p'ákw'et < p'ákw'.

repay
- repay, pay a debt:: léwlets ~ lṓwlets.

repeat
- (make a) rapid repeated sound usually on wood:: qw'ópx̲wem < qw'ópx̲w.

repeatedly:: =í:m.
- blinking one's eyes repeatedly:: lhéplhepx̲lexw < lhép.
- male name, (prob.) repeatedly gets wives/houses:: =ímeltxw.
- repeatedly almost kill s-o:: x̲wilx̲wíleqlexw or x̲welx̲wíleqlexw < x̲wíleqlexw.
- scratching repeatedly to get in:: t'elht'élheqw'els < t'élheqw' ~ t'lhóqw'.
- shouting repeatedly, hollering repeatedly, yelling (repeatedly):: tatí:m < tà:m.
- shutting one's eyes repeatedly, (blinking [EB]):: th'épth'eplexw (or perhaps th'ép'th'ep'lexw) < th'éplexw (or perhaps th'ép'lexw).
- wet one's head (sic?), (wet one's bed repeatedly):: lhélqwelhem < lhél.

replace
change s-th (physically), replace:: iyá:qt ~ iyáqt < iyá:q.
change s-th (purposely), change s-o, transform s-o/s-th, trade s-th, replace s-th:: iyá:qt ~ iyáqt < iyá:q.

reportative
so they say, (reportedly, reportative, evidential?):: -ts'á.

reportedly
so they say, (reportedly, reportative, evidential?):: -ts'á.

resemble
to resemble, look like, (similar-looking):: st'at'ó:mex < t.

Reserve
a place near Deroche, B.C., just east of Lakahahmen Indian Reserve #10 (which is registered with D.I.A. as Skweam):: Skwiyó:m < Skwíyò.
a turn in the Fraser River between Ruby Creek and Katz (about a mile upriver from the mouth of Ruby Creek and Ruby Creek I.R. #9 (called Lukseetsis-sum on maps and D.I.A. records, see Lexwthíthesem)), also the name of a village at this spot, spelled Skawahlook, Indian Reserve #1, on topographical maps and D.I.A. records:: Sq'ewá:lxw < q'éw ~ q'ew.
bay at upper end of Íyém (Yale Indian Reserve #22):: Qémelets < qám.
bay at upper end of Yale Indian Reserve #2 (Four-and-a-half Mile Creek) (near the northern end of Stó:lō territory):: Sqemqémelets < qám.
Cheam Island (my name for an island in the Fraser River across from Cheam Indian Reserve #2), Cheam village, Cheam Indian Reserve #1:: Xwchí:yò:m < schí:ya.
Hope Indian Reserve #12 (Klaklacum):: Tl'átl'ekw'em ~ Lexwtl'átl'ekw'em.
Kwakwawapilt village and reserve (Chilliwack Indian Reserve #6):: Qweqwe'ópelhp < qwe'óp.
Lummi Reserve:: Lém:i ~ Lexwlém:i.
Mary Ann Creek, village at mouth of Mary Ann Creek into the Fraser (in Yale, B.C., Yale Town Indian Reserve #1):: Sése.
Nicomen Island (in the Fraser River near Deroche), also a specific place on northeast end of Nicomen Island where lots of people used to gather [now Sumas Indian Reserve #10]:: Leq'á:mél.
place at Ruby Creek where Paul Webster lived some years ago, now Wahleach Island Indian Reserve #2 and area at mouth of Mahood Creek:: X̲wolích ~ X̲welích < x̲wále ~ x̲wá:le.
Reserve near New Westminster, B.C., (South Westminster [DF]):: Qiqá:yt.
Scowkale, sometimes misspelled Skulkayn, now Chilliwack Indian Reserves #10 and #11:: Sq'ewqé(:)yl ~ Sq'ewqí:l < q'éw ~ q'ew.
Skwah village, now Skwah Reserve:: Sqwehá < qwá.
Skwah village, now Skwah Reserve, also known as Wellington Reserve:: Sqwá < qwá.
Soowahlie village (where Sweltzer Creek met Chilliwack River), Soowahlie Reserve near Vedder Crossing:: Th'ewá:lí < th'éw.
Squatits village on east bank of Fraser river across from the north end of Seabird Island, Peters Indian Reserves #1, 1a, and 2 on site:: Skw'átets < kw'átem.
Squia-ala (now Chilliwack Indian Reserve #7):: Sx̲woyehá:lá < x̲wà:y ~ x̲wá:y.
Tzeachten, a (recent) settlement on the upper reaches of the lower Chilliwack River, now Chilliwack Indian Reserve #13 near Sardis:: Ch'iyáqtel < sts'iyáq.
village at American Bar, village on west bank of Fraser River at American Creek, American Bar Reserve:: Peqwchṓ:lthel ~ Peqwechṓ:lthel < péqw.
village at outlet of old Chilliwack River on Fraser River, now known as Skway reserve (Chilliwack Indian

Reserve (CONT'D)

Reserve #5):: Shxwhá:y < hà:y.
village at Union Bar, now also Hope Indian Reserve #5 (#15 in Duff 1952), Ay-wa-wis:: Iwówes.
village now at north end of Agassiz-Rosedale bridge, now Tseatah Indian Reserve #2 (of Cheam band):: Siyét'e.
village now called Ohamil Reserve or Laidlaw:: Shxw'ōwhámél ~ Shxw'ōhámél.
village on east bank of Fraser River below Siwash Creek (Aseláw), now Yale Indian Reserves 19 and 20, named because of a big rock in the area that the trail had to pass (go around), also the name of the rock:: Q'alelíktel < q'ál.
village or settlement on the west side of the Fraser River at Emory Creek by Frank Malloway's fish camp, Albert Flat (Yale Indian Reserve #5):: Ó:ywoses.
Yakweakwioose, next village above Scowkale, village near Sardis on the old Chilliwack River course, now Chilliwack Indian Reserve #9:: Yeqwyeqwí:ws < yéqw.

residence)
moving (one's residence):: seló:lh < ó:lh.

respect
chief, leader, respected person, boss, rich, dear:: siyá:m < éy ~ éy:.
respected leader, chief, upper-class person, boss, master, your highness:: siyám ~ (rare) siyá:m.
respected leaders, chiefs, upper-class people:: sí:yá:m < siyám ~ (rare) siyá:m.
respected person, (high class person [EB]):: smelá:lh.
respect s-o:: ólhet.
stand up for s-o (respected):: xwiléxmet or xwíléxmet < xwílex.

rest
camp and rest:: qelá:wthet < qá:w.
relaxing, resting:: qaqíw < qá:w.
rest oneself:: qá:wthet < qá:w.
to rest:: qá:w.
to still-dip, rest dip-net on bottom (of river):: thqá:lem.

restaurant:: alhteláwtxw < álhtel.

Restmore Caves
mouth of Hunter Creek, (Restmore Caves (Wells)):: ōqw'íles ~ ōqw'éyles < wōqw' ~ wéqw'.
Restmore Caves [Wells]), (mouth of Hunter Creek [IHTTC]):: Uqw'íles.

restrict
(emprisoned), put in jail, grounded, restricted, caught, apprehended:: qíq'.

resultative
continuative, resultative:: há- ~ hé-.
resultative, -ed, have -en (usually results in a past tense or past participle translation in English):: =R1= or =C1e=, R5= or C1e=, R8= or C1a=, =R9= or =C1á(:)=.

return
(circle) around the fire once and return to the start, make one circle in longhouse:: sélts' < sél or sí(:)l.

return (CONT'D)

give it back, bring it back, return s-th:: q'élstexw < q'ó:lthet.
return, come back, go back:: q'ó:lthet.
to hurt again (as when a painful place is bumped and hurts again or as when a pain inside one's body returns again), (to ache [SJ]):: téqlexw.

reveal s-th:: atl'qílt < átl'q.

revive

come alive, come back to life, get better (from sickness), get well, revive:: áylexw ~ áyelexw.
come to after fainting, (revive after fainting):: p'elhíws < p'élh.
revive s-o, bring s-o back to life, heal s-o, (EB) give s-o medicine to make him better?:: á:yelexwt < áylexw ~ áyelexw.

rewrap it

wrap it again, rewrap it, (correction by AD:) roll it up (of a mat, carpet, etc.):: xwelxwélekw't < xwélekw'.

Rhamnus purshiana:: q'á:yx̲elhp.

rheumatism

(have/get) rheumatism, aching:: x̲áp'kw'tem < x̲ep'ékw'.

Rheum hybridum

Rumex occidentalis, Rheum hybridum:: t'emó:sa.

rhizome

bracken fern root, rhizome of bracken fern:: sá:q.

rhubarb

a sprout or shoot (esp. of the kinds peeled and eaten in spring), sweet green inner shoots, green berry shoots, salmonberry shoots, wild raspberry shoots and greens, salmonberry sprouts, blackcap shoots, thimbleberry shoots, wild rhubarb shoots, fern shoots:: stháthqiy.
wild rhubarb, western dock, common yellow dock, domestic rhubarb:: t'emó:sa, t'emó:sa.

rib

breast bone, part of human body between breast bone and ribs:: th'x̲ámél.
on the rib(s):: =őwéx̲.
rib, ribs:: lőwéx̲ ~ lewéx̲.

Ribes

Ribes spp., Ribes divaricatum, Ribes lobbii, possibly others:: t'á:mxw.

Ribes bracteosum

Ribes sanguineum, probably also Ribes bracteosum:: sp'á:th'.
Ribes sanguineum, prob. also Ribes bracteosum:: sp'á:th'elhp < sp'á:th'.

Ribes divaricatum

Ribes spp., Ribes divaricatum, Ribes lobbii, possibly others:: t'á:mxw.

Ribes lacustre:: th'kw'íwíyelhp < th'ekw' or th'íkw'.

Ribes lobbii

Ribes spp., Ribes divaricatum, Ribes lobbii, possibly others:: t'á:mxw.

Ribes sanguineum:: =oyes.

flower of Ribes sanguineum:: qwelíyes.

Ribes sanguineum, probably also Ribes bracteosum:: sp'á:th'.

Ribes sanguineum, prob. also Ribes bracteosum:: sp'á:th'elhp < sp'á:th'.

rice krispies)

(have) sound of popping small round things (snowberries, herring eggs as when eating them, rice krispies, crabapples, cranberries, etc.), (have a crunching sound (as of grasshopper, rice krispies)):: tl'ámkw'em, tl'ámkw'em < tl'ém.

rice root)

plant similar to stl'éleqw' (chocolate lily) but different, (probably rice root):: péth'oyes.

rich

chief, leader, respected person, boss, rich, dear:: siyá:m < éy ~ éy:.

get carried away and sleepy from eating too rich food:: ló:metsel < ló:m ~ lóm, melmelőws < mál ~ mél.

rich, wealthy:: siyám ~ (rare) siyá:m.

ride

ride (on):: sts'ets'á < ts'á:.

riding with someone, (riding along):: hálpetsel < lépets.

they came on (top of):: ch'alech'á (~ ts'alets'á) < ts'á:.

to ride [along], hook a ride, get a ride, send oneself:: lépetsel < lépets.

to travel by horse, already riding a horse:: yets'ets'á < ts'á:.

Ridge

Cultus Lake Mountain, actually Mount Amadis or International Ridge:: Swílhcha Smá:lt < Swílhcha.

ridge

small shoreline ridge on the Fraser River and all along the river around the larger mountain across the Trans-Canada Highway from Jones Hill:: Sqayéx̱iya Smált ~ Sqáqeyex̱iya Smált < sqáyéx̱ ~ sqayéx̱.

ridicule

making fun of s-o, (ridiculing s-o):: lhílhàth't < lhílhàth'.

making fun, (ridiculing):: lhílhàth'.

right

be alright, be okay, it's alright, it's okay, can, be able, it's enough, be right, be correct, that's right:: iyólem ~ iyó:lem < éy ~ éy:.

(meaning uncertain), (perhaps right, correct):: mà.

right arm:: siyachís < éy ~ éy:, s'iyláx̱el < éy ~ éy:.

right hand:: s'eyí:wtses < éy ~ éy:.

right (in the sense of exactly or just):: ate.

stay right here, staying right here:: í ò kw'eló < í.

right away

early, right away:: txwém.

right away (CONT'D)

going to piss right away, almost piss oneself, (have an urgent or extreme or painful need to urinate):: ts'áléqel.

right (correct):: leq'á:lh < léq'.

right now)

now, this moment, this instant, (right now):: tloqá:ys < qá:ys.

right side:: s'eyí:ws < éy ~ éy:.

part the hair on the right side (left side as people look at you), have the hair parted on the right side:: kelchochéleqw < kelchóch ~ kyelchóch.

right-side up

turn s-th right-side up:: kw'ethí:lt (possible error for kw'eth'í:lt).

ring

bellringer:: tíltel mál < tí:ltel.
ear-ring:: ts'qw'élá < ts'éqw'.
finger ring:: siyálémtses.
(have) ringing in the ear:: th'atsemá:lí:ya < th'éts or th'á(:)ts.
horn rings for dip-nets:: x̲alwéla < x̲álew.
(make a) ringing sound when something drops:: ts'tés.
nose-ring:: shxweqw'élqstel.
ringing, phoning:: th'étsàls < th'éts or th'á(:)ts.
ringing sound when something drops (spoon, metal ashtray or something heavy):: ts'tés.
ring s-o up, phone s-o:: th'étst < th'éts or th'á(:)ts.
to rattle (of dishes or anything else loose), jingle (of money or any metal shaken), peal or toll (of a bell), make the sound of a bell, to ring (of a bell, telephone, in the ears):: th'á:tsem < th'éts or th'á(:)ts.
to ring a bell:: tí:ltel.

rip

break (of ground), crack apart (of its own accord) (of ground), ripped:: tl'éx.
rip it apart:: tl'xát < tl'éx.
rip it up, tear it up, rip s-th, tear s-th:: x̲wtát < x̲wét.
rip on the bottom or insides:: x̲wetíwél < x̲wét.
to tear, it rips:: x̲wét.

Riparia riparia

especially Iridoprocne bicolor and Riparia riparia:: qw'sí:tsel.

ripe

getting ripe:: qw'eqwél < qw'él.
overripe:: qw'èlqw'èl < qw'él.
ripe, ripened:: qw'él.

rise

appear, come into view, rise into view:: pél:ékw.
be big, be large, be high (of floodwater), rise (of floodwater):: híkw.
climbing, rising:: kw'ekw'í < kw'í ~ kw'íy.
get big, rise (of floodwater):: híkwthet < híkw.

rise (CONT'D)

got up with a quick motion, got up quickly:: xwexwíléx < xwíléx.
rise, swell:: p'ò:m.
rising, getting big:: hahíkwthet < híkw.
sit, sit down, sit up, arise (from lying or sitting), get up (from lying down, from bed or chair):: emét.
stand up, rise from a seat:: xwíléx.
to float, come up to the surface, rise to the surface, to surface:: p'ékw.

ritual]

a sung spell, power to help or harm people or to do [ritual] burning, power to do witchcraft and predict the future, an evil spell, (magic spell) (someone who has power to take things out of a person or put things in [by magic] [Elders Group 2/25/76], ritualist [Elders Group 1/21/76], witch [EB 4/25/78]):: syiwí:l ~ syewí:l < yéw: ~ yéw.
have a ritual burning ceremony, have a burning, feed the dead, (food offered to the dead [at a ritual burning] [EB 5/25/76]):: yeqwá:ls < yéqw.

ritualist :: syiwí:l ~ syewí:l < yéw: ~ yéw.

a sung spell, power to help or harm people or to do [ritual] burning, power to do witchcraft and predict the future, an evil spell, (magic spell) (someone who has power to take things out of a person or put things in [by magic] [Elders Group 2/25/76], ritualist [Elders Group 1/21/76], witch [EB 4/25/78]):: syiwí:l ~ syewí:l < yéw: ~ yéw.
Indian red paint (used by spirit dancers, ritualists, and Indian doctors or shamans):: témélh.
paint one's face red or black (spirit dancer, Indian doctor, ritualist, etc.):: lhíx̲esem < lhá:x̲ ~ lháx̲.
the one who burns [at a burning ceremony], (ritualist at a burning):: híyeqwels < yéqw.

River

a channel between an island and the main shore a) across Harrison River from where the Phillips smokehouse was at Chehalis village (slightly downriver from the mouth of Chehalis R. into Harrison R.), also b) at Harrison Lake where the hatchery was:: Lheltá:lets ~ Lheltálets < lhà:l.
a little bay in the Fraser River a quarter mile east of Iwówes (Union Bar, Aywawwis):: Qíqemqèmèl < qém:el.
a nice place near Morris Creek on the (right?) side of Harrison River [IHTTC 8/25/77]):: Lhó:leqwet.
an old course of the Chilliwack River, now Vedder River:: Lhewálmel < lhá:w, Lhewálmel < lhá:w.
another rough place in the Fraser River (Tait area):: Sq'ólep'ex̲w < Sq'íp'ex̲w.
a place on Chilliwack River, a little above Anderson Flat and Allison's (between Tamihi Creek and Slesse Creek), a village at deep water between Tamihi Creek and Slesse Creek:: Iy'óythel < éy ~ éy:.
a real rough place in the Fraser River impassible in a canoe (in the Tait area, prob. between Spuzzum and Yale):: Sq'íp'ex̲w.
a slough on Harrison River north side by the mouth of Chehalis River which has a knee-shaped sandbar at its mouth, this is the next slough above (upriver from) Meth'á:lmexwem:: Q'iq'ewetó:lthel < q'éw ~ q'ew.
a turn in the Fraser River between Ruby Creek and Katz (about a mile upriver from the mouth of Ruby Creek and Ruby Creek I.R. #9 (called Lukseetsis-sum on maps and D.I.A. records, see Lexwthíthesem)), also the name of a village at this spot, spelled Skawahlook, Indian Reserve #1, on topographical maps and D.I.A. records:: Sq'ewá:lxw < q'éw ~ q'ew.
a turn in the Fraser River on the CPR (northwest) side two miles east of American Bar,

River (CONT'D)

Texas Bar bend in the Fraser River:: Sq'ewílem < q'éw ~ q'ew.

beach in front of old Scowlitz village, the point the Harrison River goes around by Kilby's store:: Sq'iq'ewílem < q'éw ~ q'ew.

Chehalis River mouth (below the highway bridge, where land is breaking up into sand bars), (an opening one could get through in a canoe in high water near Chehalis {IHTTC 8/25/77], small creek (branch of Chehalis River) several hundred yards up Chehalis River from where the road goes from old Chehalis village site to Chehalis River [EL 9/27/77]):: Spōqwṓwelh ~ Speqwṓ:lh < péqw, Spōqwṓwelh ~ Speqwṓ:lh < péqw.

Chilliwack River:: Sts'elxwíqw ~ Ts'elxwíqw ~ Ts'elxwéyeqw < ts'el.

Coquihalla River:: Kw'ikw'iyá:la < kw'íy.

creek with its mouth on the south side of Chilliwack River and above the mouth of Middle Creek:: Sch'iyáq < sts'iyáq.

elk (or) moose turned to stone in the Fraser River by Hill's Bar:: Q'oyíyets ~ Q'oyí:ts < q'oyíyets or q'oyí:ts.

Fraser River, (Chehalis Creek, Chehalis River [Elders Group, EL/EB/NP]):: Stó:lō < tó:l ~ tò:l.

Harrison River spring salmon, Harrison River chinook salmon, big Chehalis River spring salmon, (preserved (smoked?) meat [AC: Tait dialect]):: pó:qw' ~ póqw'.

heart-shaped island near the mouth of Chehalis River that beat like a heart:: Th'álátel ~ Th'á:lá ~ Th'ála < th'á:lá ~ th'ála ~ th'á:le ~ th'ále.

Hill's Bar (between Yale and Hope), Fraser River where it goes over Hill's Bar on the CN (east) side:: Qw'áléts.

large whirlpool in the Fraser River just above Hill's Bar and near the west (CPR) side:: Hémq'eleq < méq'.

late fall Harrison River and Chehalis River sockeye salmon (last run, kind of red):: qwechíwiya.

late fall sockeye salmon (last run on Harrison River and Chehalis River, kind of red):: sqwó:yxw.

Leon's Slough on Harrison River:: Xemó:leqw < xá:m.

maybe the same place as Sqw'ex̲wáq (pool where Kawkawa Creek comes into the Coquihalla River and where the water pygmies lived):: Skw'íkw'x̲weq (or better, Sqw'íqw'x̲weq) < Sqw'ex̲wáq.

next slough on north side of Harrison River above (east of) Smímstíyexwá:le, a muddy slough where fish spawn, right across from Johnny Leon's place at Chehalis and about 100 yards downstream (west) of Yálhxetel:: Míme x̲wel (or prob. better, Mímexwel) < mímexwel.

place above Yale where the Fraser River splits around a rock, island above Steamboat Island (latter just below Five-Mile Creek):: Sx̲wesálh < x̲wés.

place in Fraser River where there's an underwater spring of cold water:: Mimexwílem < mímexwel.

place in Whatcom County, Washington, (Nooksack River [AC or CT]):: Lexwsá:q < sá:q.

place on Fraser River between first tunnel and Yale where rotten fish used to (always) pile up:: Lexwyó:qwem < yó:qw.

place on the Fraser River above Yale where there are whirlpools:: Q'eyq'éyex̲em < q'ey ~ q'i.

pool where Kawkawa Creek comes into the Coquihalla River:: Sqw'ex̲wáq.

(probably) Mahood Creek and Johnson Slough, (possibly) Wahleach River or Hicks Creek (creek at bridge on east end of Seabird Island [AK]):: Qwōhòls < qwá.

rock in the Fraser River near Scowlitz where a woman was crying a lot:: X̲ex̲ám Smá:lt < x̲à:m ~ x̲á:m.

Seal Fat Rock on Harrison River just upriver from Th'éqwela (place by Morris Lake where Indian people used to play Indian badminton), this rock has what resembles seal fat all around it:: Skwló ~ Sqwló < sqwló.

River (CONT'D)

Semmihault Creek, a stream from the east joining the old Chilliwack River near the Chilliwack airport:: Smiyó:llh?.

silver spring salmon that came up Harrison River and Chehalis Creek, (first spring salmon [Deming]):: sqwéx̱em < qwéx̱em.

slough on west side of Harrison River, the first slough upriver from Q'iq'ewetó:lthel and first slough below Xemó:leqw:: Shxwpópélem.

steelhead fishing place on the Fraser River below Lhílhkw'elqs, at Hogg Slough:: Qéywex̱em < qí:wx̱ ~ qéywx̱ ~ qá:wx̱ ~ qáwx̱.

Stó:lō people, Halkomelem-speaking people living along the Fraser River or its tributaries from Five Mile Creek above Yale downriver to the mouth of the Fraser:: Stó:lō < tó:l ~ tò:l.

Sumas village and area from present-day Kilgard to Fraser River, Sumas village (on both sides of the Fraser at the east end of Sumas Mt.), (Devil's Run (below Láx̱ewey), the area between Sumas Mt. and Fraser River [Elders Group 7/13/77], Sumas River (probably requires Stó:lō river or Stótelō creek to follow) [Wells 1965], Sumas Lake (probably requires X̱ótsa lake after Semáth for this meaning) [Elders Group 7/13/77]):: Smá:th ~ Semá:th ~ Semáth.

Sweltzer Creek (the stream from Cultus Lake to Chilliwack River at Soowahlie):: Swílhcha Stótelō < Swílhcha.

the whole riverbank on the CPR (west) side of the Fraser River just south of Strawberry Island and just north of Peqwchṓ:lthel:: Selch'éle < sél or sí(:)l.

village at American Bar, village on west bank of Fraser River at American Creek, American Bar Reserve:: Peqwchṓ:lthel ~ Peqwechṓ:lthel < péqw.

village at junction of Ryder Lake Creek and Chilliwack River:: T'ept'ṓp.

village at west end of Little Mountain (Mount Shannon) on Hope Slough, also a name for Hope Slough or Hope River:: Sqwá:la < qwá.

west fork of stream which goes into Chehalis River above Páléxel:: Th'ámxwelqs.

Wilson's Point (on Harrison River), (also called) Grouse Point:: Títxwemqsel < stíxwem.

river :: stó:lō < tó:l ~ tò:l.

a bend in a river, a curve of a lake:: sq'ówqel < q'éw ~ q'ew.

(also drift downriver):: wṓqw' ~ wéqw'.

at the head or source of a river, the inside head or inlet of a river:: =qel.

away from the shore, toward the river:: chúchu ~ chúwchuw ~ chéwchew < cháchew ~ cháchu.

bring s-th/s-o across a river, (ferry s-o/s-th over):: t'kwíléstexw< t'ákwel.

calm (of water), smooth (of water), (when the river is) quiet or calm:: p'ep'ákwem < p'ékw.

change course (of a river):: táyéqel.

creek, little river, small creek, small river:: stótelō ~ stó:telō < tó:l ~ tò:l.

cross a river, cross a road, cross over:: t'ákwel.

deep bottom (of a river, lake, water, canoe, anything):: stl'epláts < tl'ép.

downriver, down that way:: lhelhós < lhós.

downriver, down that way, downriver below:: lhósex̱el < lhós.

downriver, (from downriver):: tellhó:s < lhós.

from away from the river:: telchó:leqwtel < chá:l or chó:l.

from upriver:: teltíyt < tiyt.

go around a bend in the river, go around a turn, go around something in one's way:: q'ewílem < q'éw ~ q'ew.

go away from the river:: chó:m.

go down(hill) to the water, go towards the river:: t'óxw.

go downstream, go downriver, down the river:: wōqw'ílem ~ wōqw'éylem ~ wōqw'ílém ~ wōqw'éylém < wṓqw' ~ wéqw'.

river (CONT'D)

go down to the river:: chóxw.
going towards the river or water:: t'ót'exw < t'óxw.
go out into the river, go down to the river, walk down to the river:: tó:l ~ tò:l.
go over or around (hill, rock, river, etc.):: q'ál.
green pond slime or river slime, algae:: stíxem < tíxem.
head of a river:: =eqw ~ =(e)leqw ~ =íqw ~ =ó:qw.
in the backwoods, toward the woods, away from the river, in the bush:: chó:leqw < chá:l or chó:l.
name of place with clay at the edge of the river at some location:: S'áqwemx̲weth' < qwó:m ~ qwóm ~ qwem.
out in the middle of the river:: chuchuwó:ythel < cháchew ~ cháchu.
part away from the river, side away from the river:: chóleqwmel < chá:l or chó:l.
put a mark on it (like water level of river), mark it, weigh it, (measure it):: x̲á:th't ~ x̲áth't < x̲áth' ~ x̲e'áth'.
riverbank, bank of a river:: semlóthel.
riverbed:: stolōwálá < tó:l ~ tò:l.
roots of a tree when it floats downriver:: x̲eyímelets.
rough (of a river or creek):: qw'íwelh.
sit facing a river and watch it, sit on a riverbank and sunbathe:: chichewós < cháchew ~ cháchu.
something used to cross over a river, ferry, place good for crossing:: xwt'át'ekwel < t'ákwel.
Sumas village and area from present-day Kilgard to Fraser River, Sumas village (on both sides of the Fraser at the east end of Sumas Mt.), (Devil's Run (below Láx̲ewey), the area between Sumas Mt. and Fraser River [Elders Group 7/13/77], Sumas River (probably requires Stó:lō river or Stótelō creek to follow) [Wells 1965], Sumas Lake (probably requires X̲ótsa lake after Semáth for this meaning) [Elders Group 7/13/77]):: Smá:th ~ Semá:th ~ Semáth.
the only safe place to cross a river:: shxwtitós or shxwtiytós.
tide coming in, water coming in, water coming up (ocean tide or river):: qém:el.
to drag (for a body in the river, for ex.):: xwekw'á:ls < xwókw' ~ xwekw'ó.
to still-dip, rest dip-net on bottom (of river):: thqá:lem.
tracks going down to the river:: tó:lxel < tó:l ~ tò:l.
turn back into a quiet slough from the river, be going into a slough from the river:: ts'élexw < ts'el.
upriver, up that way, (way upriver [RP, EB]):: títex̲el or tíytex̲el < tiyt.

river-bank)

broken off in pieces (like a river-bank):: peqwpéqw < péqw.
Katz river-bank, Ruby Creek settlement, village on north bank of Fraser River just below (west of) the mouth of Ruby Creek:: Spópetes < pó:t.
riverbank, bank of a river:: semlóthel.
sit facing a river and watch it, sit on a riverbank and sunbathe:: chichewós < cháchew ~ cháchu.
steep drop-off, a drop-off, very steep slope, steep shore, steep riverbank, a slide:: x̲éylés.
the whole riverbank on the CPR (west) side of the Fraser River just south of Strawberry Island and just north of Peqwchṓ:lthel:: Selch'éle < sél or sí(:)l.

riverbed

riverbed:: stolōwálá < tó:l ~ tò:l.

road :: xálh ~ xá:lh.

road (CONT'D)

a bend in a road:: sq'ówqel < q'éw ~ q'ew.
a fork in a road (or trail):: st'éx̲ < t'éx̲.
cross a river, cross a road, cross over:: t'ákwel.
railroad:: kyóxàlh or kyóxàlh < xálh ~ xá:lh.
steep (of road, hill, etc.), (very steep slope [Elders Group]):: théq.

roar

roaring (of falls, for ex.), rumbling (of falls, thunder, quake, rockslide, etc.):: kwóte x̲wem < kwótx̲wem ~ kwótxwem.
to rumble, to roar:: kwótx̲wem ~ kwótxwem.

roast

baking over an open fire, roasting over an open fire, barbecuing, cooking in an oven:: qw'eqw'élém < qw'él.
barbecue, bake (meat, vegetables, etc.) in open fire, bake over fire, roast over open fire, bake under hot sand, bake in oven, cook in oven, (boiled down (as jam) [CT, HT]):: qw'élém < qw'él.
barbecued, roasted, (baked (in an oven) [DC]):: s=qw'elém < qw'él.
barbecue sticks, (split roasting stick):: qw'éltel < qw'él.
roast chicken:: sqw'élem chékel (lit. roasted/barbecued + chicken) < qw'él, chékel
roast potatoes, baked potatoes:: s'ótheqw < ótheqw.
to roast potatoes in hot sand or ashes, bake in ashes, bake in stove:: ótheqw.

rob

steal from s-o, rob s-o, short-change s-o:: qá:lt < qá:l.

robe

blanket robe:: tl'exwewítstel < tl'xw ~ tl'exw.

robin

American robin:: skw'okw'qá:q ~ skw'okw'qáq ~ skw'ōkw'qáq.
call of the winter robin or varied thrush:: sx̲wík'.
winter robin, bush robin, varied thrush:: sx̲wík'.

Rock

Chehalis village on Harrison River, the Heart Rock for which Chehalis, B.C. was named (at the mouth of Chehalis River):: Ts'a'í:les < ts'á:.
monument at Saddle Rock at Five Mile Creek:: Sólkweyem?? or Solkw'í:m??.
one of the two rocks of Lady Franklin Rock:: X̲éylx̲el(e)mòs.
Penis Rock near Cheam View:: Sxéle < sxéle.
Saddle Rock above Yale:: Ts'ístel < th'ís.
Seal Fat Rock on Harrison River just upriver from Th'éqwela (place by Morris Lake where Indian people used to play Indian badminton), this rock has what resembles seal fat all around it:: Skwló ~ Sqwló < sqwló.
White Rock, B.C.:: P'eq'ó:ls.
White Rock, B.C., Blaine, Wash.:: P'eq'ó:ls < p'éq'.

rock)

a little bluff (of rock):: sx̲eq'x̲éq'et < x̲eq'.
a lot of rocks:: smelmá:lt < smá:lt.
a rock along Harrison River which looks like layers of seal fat all along its bottom:: Skwló ~ Sqwló < skwló ~ sqwló.

rock (CONT'D)

a rocking chair:: xwíxweth'àlem sch'áletstel < xwáth', xwixweth'áletstel < xwáth'.

a rock in the creek at the upriver end of Seabird Island that was a girl washing after her first period:: The Théthex̱w or Thethéthex̱w < thethíx̱w.

a rock shaped like a dog on the east shore of the Fraser River near Hill's Bar and below Tewít (a rock shaped like a human hunter):: Sqwemá:y (?) < qwem.

a snake rock in the Fraser River just north of Strawberry Island which had snakes sunning themselves and covering the rock:: Alhqá:yem < álhqey ~ álhqay.

a sx̱wó:yx̱wey head turned to stone on land at X̱elhlálh somewhere:: Sx̱éyes te Sx̱wó:yx̱wey < sx̱wó:yx̱wey ~ sx̱wóyx̱wey.

baby basket rock just below main bay and sand bar of Lexwtl'átl'ekw'em (Klaklacum, Indian Reserve #12, first village and reserve south of American Creek), on the west side of the Fraser River:: Lexwp'oth'esála ~ Xwp'oth'esála < p'ó:th'es ~ p'óth'es.

bald rock, bare rock:: ts'qó:ls, ts'qó:ls.

bear-shaped rock up on cliff on south side above Echo Point bay on Echo Island in Harrison Lake:: Spá:th < pá:th.

burned (of rocks), scorched (of rocks):: qw'óqw'iy < qw'á:y.

canyon (narrow, walled in with rock):: sx̱ex̱ákw' < x̱ékw'.

cliff, vertical rock face:: qw'eléqel.

core of a rock, center of a rock, core of anything, heart of anything inanimate:: sth'emí:wel ~ sth'emíwel ~ sth'emíwél < sth'ó:m.

five spherical objects, five fruit, five rocks, five balls (five fruit in a group (as they grow on a plant) [AD]):: lhq'atsesóls < lheq'át ~ lhq'á:t.

flat rocks (bedrock) with holes at Hill's Bar where they used to make smótheqw (prepared fish oil) from sockeye heads:: Hemhémetheqw < mótheqw or metheqw.

flat smooth and bare rock, a [rock] bluff, a bluff (straight up):: x̱eq'át < x̱eq'.

four rocks in the Fraser River by Peqwchő:lthel (American Bar) that are shaped like rumps:: Slhélets < lhél.

get a canoe stuck on a rock or something:: xá:m.

go over or around (hill, rock, river, etc.):: q'ál.

horned owl-shaped rock (beside Spá:th, a bear-shaped rock) up on a cliff on the south side above Echo Point bay on Echo Island in Harrison Lake:: Chítmexw < chítmexw.

large rock slide that includes trees and other debris:: syélt < yélt.

little stone, pebble, little rock hill, small rock mountain (like in the Fraser River in the canyon):: smámelet < smá:lt.

(many small rocks):: smemá:lt < smá:lt.

name of a seal-shaped rock formerly on the Harrison or Chehalis River:: Áshxwetel < áshxw.

narrow (of rocky passage):: x̱eq'.

pile it up (blankets, rocks, anything):: ts'itóléstexw.

place above Yale where the Fraser River splits around a rock, island above Steamboat Island (latter just below Five-Mile Creek):: Sx̱wesálh < x̱wés.

place in Fraser River two miles above American Bar with narrow rock:: X̱eq'átelets < x̱eq'.

rock above Yale where Ñá:ls gritted his teeth and scratched rocks as he duelled with a medicine man across the Fraser:: Th'ex̱elís < th'ex̱elís.

rock figure near the rocks shaped like a family underwater:: Th'elíth'eqes.

rocking:: xwixweth'álem < xwáth'.

rock in the Fraser River near Scowlitz where a woman was crying a lot:: X̱ex̱ám Smá:lt < x̱à:m ~ x̱á:m.

rocks:: =ó:ls.

rock shaped like a man's head with a sx̱wó:yx̱wey mask on a point near the head of Harrison River, the point also called Spook's Point:: Sx̱wó:yx̱wey ~ Sx̱wóyx̱wey < sx̱wó:yx̱wey ~ sx̱wóyx̱wey.

rock (CONT'D)

rock shaped like a man's nose on the north side of Harrison River:: Méqsel < méqsel.
rock that looks like a little hat on west (Chehalis) side of Harrison River above mouth of Morris Creek:: Yó:yseqw < yó:seqw ~ yóseqw.
rock that was a sx̲wó:yx̲wey head (mask) turned to stone at X̲elhlálh:: Sx̲éyes te Sx̲wó:yx̲wey < sx̲éyes ~ sx̲éy:es.
rock up the Harrison River from the old Chehalis Indian cemetery:: Xwyélés ~ Lexwyélés < yél:és.
Sasquatch rock on Harrison River or Harrison Lake:: Sásq'ets (probably) < sásq'ets.
something big (and round) (for ex. big fruit, big rocks, etc.):: thíthes < thi ~ tha ~ the ~ thah ~ theh.
spear-shaped rock on beach on the Fraser near Hill's Bar:: Tá:lh < tá:lh.
(spherical), round (of ball, apple, potato, rock, full moon, but not of a pear):: xelkw'ó:ls < xél.
steep rock wall that used to have Indian writing at first C.P.R. tunnel above Haig:: X̲elíqel < x̲él ~ x̲é:yl ~ x̲í:l
stone, rock (any size), mountain:: smá:lt.
the Tracks of Mink, holes shaped like a mink's tracks toward the base of the rock-face called Xwyélés or Lexwyélés:: Sx̲éyeltels Te Sqoyéx̲iya < sx̲él:e.
to rock:: xwáth'em < xwáth'.
village on east bank of Fraser River below Siwash Creek (Aseláw), now Yale Indian Reserves 19 and 20, named because of a big rock in the area that the trail had to pass (go around), also the name of the rock:: Q'alelíktel < q'ál.

rocking chair

a rocking chair:: xwíxweth'àlem sch'áletstel < xwáth', xwixweth'áletstel < xwáth'.

rock-rabbit

Rocky Mountain pika, hoary marmot, rock-rabbit:: sk'í:l.

rockslide

rockslide (that already happened):: syéx̲w < yíx̲w.

rod

to fish with a pole or rod, to fish by a line:: qw'emó:thel.

roe

fish eggs, salmon eggs, roe, (cooked salmon eggs [JL]):: qéléx̲.

roll

(be) rolled up in a ball (twine, yarn, etc.):: sqw'ómx̲wes < qw'ómx̲w.
fall and roll:: hílém < híl.
moving, (many moving around in circles, moving around in circles many times):: x̲elx̲álqem < x̲álqem.
pillow, rolled bulrush mat:: sx̲wétl'qel.
rolling down:: hel-hílém < híl.
rolling, moving [around in circles]:: x̲álqem.
roll oneself (over and over usually):: hí:lthet < híl.
roll one's eyes:: x̲elx̲ólqemóles < x̲álqem.
roll over in bed, turn over in bed:: ts'ó:lex̲eth' < ts'el.
roll s-o over, roll s-th over:: hí:lt < híl.
roll s-th (like a log), (roll it up [AC]):: xelékw't < xél.
roll s-th over:: xélétst < xél.

roll (CONT'D)

roll s-th up in a ball:: qw'ómx̲west < qw'ómx̲w.
wrap it again, rewrap it, (correction by AD:) roll it up (of a mat, carpet, etc.):: xwelxwélekw't < xwélekw'.

roller

roller blade skates, roller skates (lit. "wheeled/rolling skate"):: xéletsem shxwqeyqex̲óthet < xél, qíx̲ ~ qéyx̲.
roller skates, roller blade skates (lit. "wheeled/rolling skate"):: xéletsem shxwqeyqex̲óthet < xél, qíx̲ ~ qéyx̲.

Roman

(have a) hook nose, beak nose, Roman nose, (be bent-nosed):: sqémqsel < qém.

romantically]

going with each other [romantically], going for a walk with each other:: ts'lhimexóstel < ts'elh=.
go with each other (romantically), go for a walk with each other (romantically):: ts'lhimexóstel < i┐m.

roof

roof of the mouth, inside of upper lip, palate:: chelhqí:l ~ chelhqéyl < =chílh ~ chílh=.
roof, shake(s) on roof, shingle(s) on roof, ceiling:: síqetsel < seqíws ~ seqí:ws.
shakes on house, roof:: síqetseláwtxw < seqíws ~ seqí:ws.
thick plank for side of house, thick shake for longhouse roof, covering over hole in roof of pit-house:: s'í:ltexw.
top of roof, roof planks:: sts'á:ltexw < ts'á:.

room

another room, different room:: láts'ewtxw < láts'.
(could be used for) living-room:: ó:metáwtxw < emét.
square dressing room or shelter of blankets where sx̲wóyx̲wey dancers change before doing the sx̲wóyx̲wey dance:: q'eléts'tel < q'el.

rooster :: lúste.

howling (of a dog), crowing (of a rooster):: q'ówem < q'á:w.

root :: kwémléxw ~ kwemléxw ~ kwémlexw ~ kwèmlèxw.

blue camas, (any edible underground vegetable food [SP], vegetable root(s) [MH]):: spá:lxw.
bracken fern root, rhizome of bracken fern:: sá:q.
bulb or root called wild artichoke, Jerusalem artichoke:: x̲áx̲ekw'.
fine cedar root strips for baskets:: shxwth'á:lhtel.
fine cedar root weaving, fine cedar root work:: sts'éqw' ~ sch'éqw' < ts'éqw'.
fork in tree, fork in tree roots:: st'it'x̲óyaq < t'éx̲.
heart of a root, seed, nut (kernel), core of plant or seedling, core (of tree, branch, any growing thing), pith (of bush), seed or pit [U.S.] or pip [Cdn.] of a fruit:: sth'emí:wel ~ sth'emíwel ~ sth'emíwél < sth'ó:m.
making a basket, (weaving a cedar root basket):: th'éqw'ōwelh ~ (probably ts'éqw'ōwelh) < ts'éqw'.
mistake in splitting roots by making them uneven:: t'ats'ex̲elí:m < t'á:ts'.
peel s-th (esp. fruit or vegetable root or a vegetable like squash or a round object):: xepólst < xíp.
plane it (with a plane), trim it, taper it (about wood, like slats or roots for baskets, poles for

root (CONT'D)

houseposts/totem poles, paddles), taper it (with knife or plane), peel it (a fruit, etc.), whittle it, strip or peel bark off of it, scrape it (of carrots), (carve it, peel it [AC]):: xípet < xíp.

pull up by the roots:: qw'emét < qw'ém.

root cellar, (root house [AD]}:: spepíláwtxw < pél (perhaps ~ pí:l by now).

root house:: spélmàlà < pél (perhaps ~ pí:l by now).

root? or trunk?:: =óyaq.

roots of a tree when it floats downriver:: x̲eyímelets.

roots (resembling eyes looking at you) of a kind of plant that's good for asthma:: qelémes < qélém ~ qél:ém.

to split roots from the wrong end (small end):: séx̲w.

to weave a cedar root basket:: ts'eqw'ő:welh ~ ts'eqw'őwelh ~ ch'eqw'őwelh < ts'éqw'.

unidentified plant with round bulbs that look and taste like potatoes, round root like potatoes that used to be eaten and tastes like potatoes:: qíqemxel ~ qéyqemxel < qém.

wide cedar root strips for baskets:: yemáwéstel < yém ~ yem.

roots/bulrushes

bulrush mat, reed mat, mat (of cattail/roots/bulrushes, etc.), (wall mat (Elders Group 11/12/75):: wá:th'elh ~ wáth'elh < wáth'.

rope

(be) hard, stiff (material), strong (of rope, material, not of a person), tough:: tl'éx̲w.

be straight (of rope but not tree), pulled tight (of rope), stretched tight, tight:: sthethá:kw' < thékw'.

break (of a flexible object like a rope, string or breath), it broke:: t'éqw'.

cedar limb rope (slitted):: stélwél.

coiled up méthelh rope for fishing (for sturgeon and spring salmon):: ts'tíxem.

cut s-th (string or rope):: tl'qw'ót.

eight ropes, eight threads, eight sticks, eight poles:: tqátsámets' < tqá:tsa.

five ropes, five threads, five sticks, five poles:: lhq'átssámets' < lheq'át ~ lhq'á:t.

four ropes, four threads, four sticks, four poles, (four long thin objects):: x̲ethílemets' < x̲e'ó:thel ~ x̲e'óthel.

hang oneself, (hung by a rope [AC]):: x̲wíqw'esem < x̲wíqw'.

join two poles together, splice it together (of a rope), (join together on the ends):: t'qwíqst.

let oneself fall, drop oneself down (by parachute, rope, etc., said of little birds trying to fly out of nest, little animals trying to get down and let themselves fall):: chólqthet < tsélq ~ chélq.

nine ropes, nine threads, nine sticks, nine poles:: tuxwámets' < tú:xw.

one rope, one thread, one stick, one pole:: lets'ámeth' < léts'a ~ léts'e.

(poss.) cord, rope:: =í:wa ~ =í:wá: ~ =el=a┐ wa.

pulling a canoe through rough water by a rope in the front:: tx̲wőwelh < tóx̲w.

pulling a canoe through rough water by a rope in the front, pulling a canoe with a rope:: tóx̲wesem < tóx̲w.

put a rope around s-o/s-th's neck, put a leash on s-th, hang s-o:: x̲wíqw'est < x̲wíqw'.

rope, twine, string, thread:: x̲wéylem ~ x̲wé:ylem ~ x̲wí:lem.

(seven long objects), seven ropes, seven threads, seven sticks, seven poles:: th'okwsámets' < th'ó:kws.

(six long objects), six ropes, six threads, six sticks, six poles:: t'x̲émemets' < t'éx̲.

spinal rope inside sturgeon, (sturgeon spinal cord):: qw'ólhla.

ten ropes, ten threads, ten sticks, ten poles:: epálemets' < ó:pel.

three ropes, three threads, three sticks, three poles, (three long narrow objects):: lhxwámeth' < lhí:xw.

two ropes, two threads, two sticks, two poles, two poles standing up:: isalámeth' < isá:le ~ isále ~ isá:la.

rope ladder
ladder, notched cedar pole ladder, rope ladder (pre-contact or later), modern ladder:: skw'íytel < kw'í ~ kw'íy.

Rosa acicularis
including: Rosa nutkana, probably also Rosa pisocarpa and Rosa gymnocarpa, possibly (from Hope east) Rosa acicularis:: qá:lq.
including: Rosa nutkana, probably also Rosa pisocarpa and Rosa gymnocarpa, possibly Rosa acicularis:: qá:lqelhp < qá:lq.

Rosa gymnocarpa
including: Rosa nutkana, probably also Rosa pisocarpa and Rosa gymnocarpa, possibly (from Hope east) Rosa acicularis:: qá:lq.
including: Rosa nutkana, probably also Rosa pisocarpa and Rosa gymnocarpa, possibly Rosa acicularis:: qá:lqelhp < qá:lq.

Rosa nutkana
including: Rosa nutkana, probably also Rosa pisocarpa and Rosa gymnocarpa, possibly (from Hope east) Rosa acicularis:: qá:lq.
including: Rosa nutkana, probably also Rosa pisocarpa and Rosa gymnocarpa, possibly Rosa acicularis:: qá:lqelhp < qá:lq.

Rosa pisocarpa
including: Rosa nutkana, probably also Rosa pisocarpa and Rosa gymnocarpa, possibly (from Hope east) Rosa acicularis:: qá:lq.
including: Rosa nutkana, probably also Rosa pisocarpa and Rosa gymnocarpa, possibly Rosa acicularis:: qá:lqelhp < qá:lq.

rose
flower of wild rose, hip or bud of wild rose, including: Nootka rose, probably also dwarf or woodland rose and swamp rose, possibly (from Hope east) prickly rose:: qá:lq.
[looks rose, rose-looking]:: qálqomex < qá:lq.
rose color:: qá:lq.
smell like a rose:: qelqósem < qá:lq.
wild rose bush, including: Nootka rose, probably also dwarf or woodland rose and swamp rose, possibly (from Hope east) prickly rose:: qá:lqelhp < qá:lq.

rot
(have) a rotten smell:: th'óth'eqw'emáléqep < th'óqw'em ~ th'ó:qw'em.
(have) a rotten taste:: th'óth'eqw'emáléqep < th'óqw'em ~ th'ó:qw'em.
mountain on Fraser River between first tunnel and Yale where rotten fish used to (always) pile up:: Lexwyó:qwem Smá:lt < yó:qw.
place on Fraser River between first tunnel and Yale where rotten fish used to (always) pile up:: Lexwyó:qwem < yó:qw.
rotted:: th'qw'ó:mthet < th'óqw'em ~ th'ó:qw'em.
rotten:: th'óth'eqw'em < th'óqw'em ~ th'ó:qw'em.
rotten fish:: yó:qw.
rotten wood:: pqwá:y < póqw.
rotting:: th'óth'eqw'em < th'óqw'em ~ th'ó:qw'em.
to rot, rotten (of fruit, animal, flora, fauna, food):: th'óqw'em ~ th'ó:qw'em.

rouge :: sméts', sméts'.

rough

another rough place in the Fraser River (Tait area):: Sq'ólep'ex̲w < Sq'íp'ex̲w.
a real rough place in the Fraser River impassible in a canoe (in the Tait area, prob. between Spuzzum and Yale):: Sq'íp'ex̲w.
bad-looking (of log or board not of a person), rough:: qelímó:les < qél.
cheeky, rough (of a person in conduct):: lhálts'.
pulling a canoe through rough water by a rope in the front:: tx̲wőwelh < tóx̲w.
pulling a canoe through rough water by a rope in the front, pulling a canoe with a rope:: tóx̲wesem < tóx̲w.
rough (like corduroy):: x̲átqem ~ x̲étqem.
rough (of a river or creek):: qw'íwelh.
rough (of wind or water), turbulent (of wind or water), real swift (of water):: x̲átl'.
rough (of wood), lumpy (of ground, bark, etc.):: smelhmélhqw.

round)

(be) bent, (perhaps bent round):: sqóqem < qém.
burst, burst out, (get) smash(ed) (something round and filled):: méqw' ~ mőqw'.
circular, round and flat:: st'elákw' < t'elákw'.
have a round mouth:: kwamó:ythel < kwá:m ~ kwám.
(have) sound of popping small round things (snowberries, herring eggs as when eating them, rice krispies, crabapples, cranberries, etc.), (have a crunching sound (as of grasshopper, rice krispies)):: tl'ámkw'em, tl'ámkw'em < tl'ém.
(have the) mouth round and open with rounded lips:: sqwoqwtó:ythel < qwá.
lump-like, round:: =xw ~ =exw.
many get crushed, get all crushed, many smashed (round and filled):: meqw'méqw' < méqw' ~ mőqw'.
Mount Ogilvie or a round peak or bluff on Mt. Ogilvie where mountain goats live, the mountain or peak or bluff resembles big breasts:: Qwemth'í:les < qwó:m ~ qwóm ~ qwem.
peel s-th (esp. fruit or vegetable root or a vegetable like squash or a round object):: xepólst < xíp.
(perhaps) round:: =ekw ~ =íkw.
(perhaps) round, around in circles:: =kw' ~ =ekw'.
really round, (perfectly spherical?):: xelókw'els < xél.
round, around:: =x̲w.
round, full (of the moon):: xelókw' ~ xeló:kw' < xél.
round (of a pole):: xelkw'ámeth' < xél.
something big (and round) (for ex. big fruit, big rocks, etc.):: thíthes < thi ~ tha ~ the ~ thah ~ theh.
(spherical), round (of ball, apple, potato, rock, full moon, but not of a pear):: xelkw'ó:ls < xél.
spotted with circles or round dots:: tl'eltl'élx̲ < tl'él.
squish s-th round and filled, smash s-th round and filled:: méqw'et < méqw' ~ mőqw'.
storage basket (for oil, fruit, clothes), burial basket for twins, round basket (any size, smaller at top), clay jug (to store oil or fruit):: skwá:m ~ skwám < kwá:m ~ kwám.
tiny round things:: emémeles < emímel ~ amí:mel.
unidentified plant with round bulbs that look and taste like potatoes, round root like potatoes that used to be eaten and tastes like potatoes:: qíqemxel ~ qéyqemxel < qém.

round object
one round object:: léts'es < léts'a ~ léts'e.

rouse
being angry, continue to be angry, angry, mad, roused, stirred up:: t'át'eyeq' ~ t'át'iyeq' < t'ay.

row-boat :: pőtőwelh < pőt.

rowdy
be rowdy, be a nuisance, be mischievious:: qwélqwel < qwà:l.

rub
a lot got rubbed off:: ó:leqw' < íqw'.
break up s-th by crumpling, crush it up, rub it together fast (to soften or clean), rub it to soften it (of plants, etc.), fluff it (inner cedar bark to soften it):: yékw'et < yókw' ~ yóqw'.
get rubbed off, to smudge (a line), to smear, to fade (of material):: íqw'em < íqw'.
grease s-th/s-o, oil s-th/s-o, rub something on s-th/s-o:: mélxwt < mélxw.
press and rub s-th:: xwíqwet < xwíqw.
rubbing it:: yátl'q't < yétl'.
rub (oil or water) in s-th to clean or soften, rub s-th to soften or clean it, (shaping a stone hammer with abrasion?, shaping?, mixing paint?, pressing together or crushing? [BHTTC 9/2/76]):: yémq't.
rub s-th off, wipe s-th:: íqw'et < íqw'.
rub s-th/s-o, smear s-th, (paint s-th):: yétl'q't < yétl'.

rubber
gumboots, rubber boots:: kw'ekw'íxwxel < kw'íxw.

Rubus idaeus malanolasius:: s'ó:ytheqw < éy ~ éy:.

Rubus idaeus var. strigosus:: s'ó:ytheqw < éy ~ éy:.

Rubus laciniatus
before contact, only Rubus ursinus, now also Rubus laciniatus, and Rubus procerus:: skw'ő:lmexw.
Rubus procerus, Rubus laciniatus:: xwelítemelh skw'ő:lmexwelhp < skw'ő:lmexw.
Rubus ursinus, Rubus laciniatus (intro.), Rubus procerus (intro.):: skw'ő:lmexw.
Rubus ursinus, Rubus laciniatus, Rubus procerus:: skw'ő:lmexwelhp < skw'ő:lmexw.

Rubus leucodermis:: tselqó:má:lhp < tsélq ~ chélq, tselqó:mé < tsélq, tselqó:me ~ tselqómo < tsélq ~ chélq.
Rubus leucodermis, albino variety:: p'éq' tselqó:me < tsélq ~ chélq.

Rubus parviflorus:: t'qwém.

Rubus phoenicolasius:: th'elíth'eplexw ~ ts'elíts'eplexw (or perhaps ts'elíts'ep'lexw) < th'éplexw (or perhaps th'ép'lexw).

Rubus procerus
before contact, only Rubus ursinus, now also Rubus laciniatus, and Rubus procerus:: skw'ő:lmexw.
Rubus procerus, Rubus laciniatus:: xwelítemelh skw'ő:lmexwelhp < skw'ő:lmexw.
Rubus ursinus, Rubus laciniatus (intro.), Rubus procerus (intro.):: skw'ő:lmexw.

Rubus procerus (CONT'D)
  Rubus ursinus, Rubus laciniatus, Rubus procerus:: skw'ő:lmexwelhp < skw'ő:lmexw.

Rubus spectabilis:: elíle.

Rubus ursinus:: shxwelméxwelh skw'ő:lmexwelhp < skw'ő:lmexw.
  before contact, only Rubus ursinus, now also Rubus laciniatus, and Rubus procerus:: skw'ő:lmexw.
  Rubus ursinus, Rubus laciniatus (intro.), Rubus procerus (intro.):: skw'ő:lmexw.
  Rubus ursinus, Rubus laciniatus, Rubus procerus:: skw'ő:lmexwelhp < skw'ő:lmexw.

Ruby Creek
  Katz river-bank, Ruby Creek settlement, village on north bank of Fraser River just below (west of) the mouth of Ruby Creek:: Spópetes < pó:t.
  place at Ruby Creek where Paul Webster lived some years ago, now Wahleach Island Indian Reserve #2 and area at mouth of Mahood Creek:: X̲wolích ~ X̲welích < x̲wále ~ x̲wá:le.
  place in Katz or Ruby Creek, may be name for Charlie Joe's place near Katz at the mouth of a creek where the water is always calm:: sqemélwélh ~ sqemélwelh < qám.
  place on mountain above Ruby Creek where there's lots of boulders all over the mountain lined up in rows:: Thíthesem < thi ~ tha ~ the ~ thah ~ theh.
  railway tunnel just past (east of) Ruby Creek:: T'ít'emt'ámex.
  Ruby Creek (the creek not the village):: St'ít'x̲oya < t'éx̲.
  village above Ruby Creek:: Sxowál?? or Xowál??.

rudder :: shxwtháyelets < tháyelets, tháyeletstel < tháyelets.

rug :: lháx̲xetel < lhá:x̲ ~ lháx̲.
  floor, floor mat, floor covering, linoleum, rug:: lhex̲éyléptel < lhá:x̲ ~ lháx̲.
  floor mat, rug:: thélxetel < thél.

rug-beater
  stick for beating blankets or clothes or mat, blanket-beater, clothes-beater, mat-beater, rug-beater:: kw'ekw'qwá:lth'átel < kw'óqw.

ruler
  measuring device, ruler:: sx̲e'áth'tel < x̲áth' ~ x̲e'áth'.

rum
  liquor, rum:: lám.

rumble
  (make a) rumbling noise:: titómelest.
  roaring (of falls, for ex.), rumbling (of falls, thunder, quake, rockslide, etc.):: kwótex̲wem < kwótx̲wem ~ kwótxwem.
  to rumble, to roar:: kwótx̲wem ~ kwótxwem.

Rumex acetosella:: t'át'eth'em < t'áth'.

Rumex occidentalis
  Rumex occidentalis, Rheum hybridum:: t'emó:sa.

rummage
  search through it, rummage through it, search s-o (like Customs officials):: xíleqwt < xíleqw.

rummage (CONT'D)

to search through, to rummage:: xíleqw.

rump

bumping or bouncing hard on the rump:: th'esth'esélets < th'és.
burned on the rump:: kw'esélets < kw'ás.
butt, ass, rump, buttocks:: slhél:éts ~ slhél:ets ~ slhéléts ~ slhélets < lhél.
dragging one's behind or rump or bottom:: xwókw'eletsem < xwókw' ~ xwekw'ó.
fart on the rump, (a show-off):: pú'elets < pú'.
four rocks in the Fraser River by Peqwchṓ:lthel (American Bar) that are shaped like rumps:: Slhélets < lhél.
(have a) big rump:: thehíwel < thi ~ tha ~ the ~ thah ~ theh.
(have a) big rump, (have a) big "bum" (bottom):: thahélets < thi ~ tha ~ the ~ thah ~ theh.
(have a) dirty behind, (dirty in the rump, dirty in the rectum):: ts'epí:wel < ts'épx̲.
(have a) skinny butt, (be skinny on the rump or bottom):: sth'émlets < sth'ó:m.
(have a) sloppy rump:: slhellhelp'élets < lhél.
(have a) wide rump, (wide in the rectum):: lheq'tíwél < lheq'át ~ lhq'á:t.
(have) hemorrhoids, (have) open sores on genitals or rump:: th'kw'íwel < th'ekw' or th'íkw'.
hit on the behind (with a stick-like object):: kw'qwélets < kw'óqw.
hot on the rump, hot seat:: kw'esélets < kw'ás.
in the rump, in the anus, in the rectum, in the bottom, on the insides, inside parts, core, inside the head:: =í:wel ~ =íwel ~ =ewel.
kick s-o in the behind, kick s-o in the rump:: lamá'íwét < lemá'.
on the rump, on the bottom, on the buttock(s):: =élets ~ =lets.
punched s-o on the rump:: th'qw'íwet < th'í:qw'et.
rump (slang):: stl'ep'él:ets ~ stl'ep'élets.
sitting on one cheek of the rump:: tewálehélets < tewále.
stick it up someone's rump:: t'ekwíwet < t'ékw.
throw s-o down [hard] on the rump:: th'eséletst < th'és.
tired on the rump:: x̲lhélets < x̲élh.
warming your bum, (be warming the bottom or rump):: sqewálets < qew.
warm one's rump, warm one's bottom:: qewéletsem < qew.

Run

Devil's Run:: Líyómxetel < líyóm.
Sumas village and area from present-day Kilgard to Fraser River, Sumas village (on both sides of the Fraser at the east end of Sumas Mt.), (Devil's Run (below Láx̲ewey), the area between Sumas Mt. and Fraser River [Elders Group 7/13/77], Sumas River (probably requires Stó:lō river or Stótelō creek to follow) [Wells 1965], Sumas Lake (probably requires X̲ótsa lake after Semáth for this meaning) [Elders Group 7/13/77]):: Smá:th ~ Semá:th ~ Semáth.

run :: xwemxálém ~ x̲wemxálém < x̲wém ~ xwém.
a runner:: x̲wó:mxelem ~ xwó:mxelem ~ x̲wómxelem ~ xwómxelem < x̲wém ~ xwém.
August run spring salmon that go up Silver Creek (near Hope):: shxwōqw'ṓ:lh.
elope, run away together:: chó:mtel < chó:m.
fast runner:: xwóxwe < xwá.
(get/have a) runny nose:: lhx̲wélqsel < lhex̲w.
get wedged (by falling tree, for ex.), got run over (by car, train, etc.):: tl'íq'.
kidnap s-o, run away with s-o:: tl'ṓwstexw < tl'í:w.
late fall Harrison River and Chehalis River sockeye salmon (last run, kind of red):: qwechíwiya.

run (CONT'D)

late fall sockeye salmon (last run on Harrison River and Chehalis River, kind of red):: sqwó:yxw.
run away:: lhá:w.
running after s-o, running after s-th:: chichelót < chá:l or chó:l.
running away:: tl'ítl'ew < tl'í:w.
running on and off:: xwéxwemxelí:m < x̲wém ~ xwém.
running, run[ing] around:: x̲wó:mxelem ~ xwó:mxelem ~ x̲wómxelem ~ xwómxelem < x̲wém ~ xwém.
run out (of breath):: t'éqw'.
run over it (with car), spread it (for ex. on bread with knife), put it up (of wallpaper), (stick it on), stick s-th closed (with pitch for ex.):: tl'íq't < tl'íq'.
sweetheart, person of the opposite sex that one is running around with, girl-friend, boy-friend:: ts'elh'á:y < ts'elh=.
to escape (of a man or a slave), run away:: tl'í:w.
to run:: xwemxálem.
[travelling along] running away:: yitl'ítl'ew < tl'í:w.
trickling, dribbling, water bubbling up in a river, add water to a container, water running under:: kw'átem.

runny

(get/have a) runny nose:: lhx̲wélqsel < lhex̲w.

run out

ran out (of food, money, etc.), have no more, be finished (offood), (be empty (of container of supplies) [EB: Cheh., Tait]):: ốwkw'.
run out of food, be out of food:: ú:kw'elets < ốwkw'.

runt

runt of litter, smallest pup or kitten or animal in litter:: th'íth'kw'oya < sth'ékw', th'íth'kw' < sth'ékw'.

rupture

ruptured belly button, ruptured navel:: lhéx̲welòw < lhex̲w.

rush

pillow, rolled bulrush mat:: sx̲wétl'qel.
scouring rush:: xweqw'él:a.

rust

(be) rusty:: sts'ápex̲el < ts'ápex̲el.
it got rusty:: ts'ápex̲el.

rustle)

(have/get) a rustling noise (not continuous) (of paper, silk, or other material), (to rustle):: sawéts'em.
(have/get) soft rustling (of material), shuffling (sound):: xwót'kw'em.
(making a) continuous rustling noise (of paper or silk or material), rustling (of leaves, paper, a sharp sound):: sá:wts'em < sawéts'em.

Ryder Lake:: T'ept'ốp (X̲ótsa) < T'ept'ốp.

Ryder Lake Creek:: T'ept'ṓp Stótelō < T'ept'ṓp.
    village at junction of Ryder Lake Creek and Chilliwack River:: T'ept'ṓp.

Saanich
    Saanich people:: Sálech.
    Saanich reserves area:: Sálech.

sac
    skunk's stink bag, skunk's stink sac:: spú'amal ~ spú'emel < pú'.
    skunk's stink bag (stink sac):: skwukwtisláts.

sack :: lesák.

sack net
    bag net, sack net:: lesák swéltel < swéltel.
    to bag net, to sack net, to still-dip with two canoes:: thqá:lem.

sacred
    (be) sacred, holy:: sx̲áx̲e < x̲áx̲e.
    bluejay, Steller's jay (sacred fortune-teller):: x̲ax̲esyúwes or x̲ax̲e syúwes < x̲áx̲e.
    sacred, holy, (taboo):: x̲áx̲e.
    Sunday (sacred day):: sx̲ax̲elh(l)át ~ sx̲ex̲elh(l)at < x̲áx̲e.

sad
    looking sad, (making a sour face [MV, EF]):: sló:ltes.
    worried, sad, looking sad:: st'á:yx̲w < t'ay.

Saddle Rock
    monument at Saddle Rock at Five Mile Creek:: Sólkweyem?? or Solkw'í:m??.
    Saddle Rock above Yale:: Ts'ístel < th'ís.

safe
    the only safe place to cross a river:: shxwtitós or shxwtiytós.

Sagittaria latifolia:: sqeqewíthelh < sqáwth ~ sqá:wth, xwōqw'ṓ:ls.
    including: Sagittaria latifolia, Helianthus tuberosus, Camassia quamash (and Camassia leichtlinii), and unidentified plant, besides Solanum tuberosum:: sqáwth ~ sqá:wth.

sail
    (a) sail:: pótel < pó:t.
    sailing (of a bird), gliding on the wind:: yáyelem.

Sakwi Creek
    Sakwi Creek, a stream that joins Weaver Creek about one-third mile above the salmon hatchery:: Qeywéx̲em < qí:wx̲ ~ qéywx̲ ~ qá:wx̲ ~ qáwx̲.

salal
    salal berry:: t'áqe.
    salal bush:: t'áqà:lhp < t'áqe.

salamander)

big gray lizard, (Pacific giant salamander):: tseyí:yex̲.

big gray rock lizard, probably Pacific giant salamander which is cognate in Squamish, possibly also the Pacific coast newt which is commonest in B.C. and also is found in this area, prob. also the northern alligator lizard:: seyíyex̲.

small red or brown "lizard", red salamander and western red-backed salamander, and possibly also the following brown species attested in the area: long-toed salamander, northwestern salamander, and possibly the British Columbia salamander:: pí:txel.

Salish

Salish people:: Sálesh, Syálex.

saliva

spit, saliva:: slhx̲wélhcha < lhex̲w.

Salix

Salix species, possibly Salix hookeriana or Salix sitchensis or any Salix?:: sqweqweméytses < qwem.

Salix hookeriana

Salix species, possibly Salix hookeriana or Salix sitchensis or any Salix?:: sqweqweméytses < qwem.

Salix lasiandra:: x̲wálá:lhp ~ x̲wá:lá:lhp < x̲wále ~ x̲wá:le, xéltsepelhp < xél.

especially Salix sitchensis, also Salix lasiandra, and possiblyother Salix species:: x̲wálá:lhp ~ x̲wá:lá:lhp < x̲wále ~ x̲wá:le.

Salix sitchensis:: x̲wálá:lhp ~ x̲wá:lá:lhp < x̲wále ~ x̲wá:le.

especially Salix sitchensis, also Salix lasiandra, and possiblyother Salix species:: x̲wálá:lhp ~ x̲wá:lá:lhp < x̲wále ~ x̲wá:le.

Salix species, possibly Salix hookeriana or Salix sitchensis or any Salix?:: sqweqweméytses < qwem.

Salix species

especially Salix sitchensis, also Salix lasiandra, and possiblyother Salix species:: x̲wálá:lhp ~ x̲wá:lá:lhp < x̲wále ~ x̲wá:le.

Salkaywul

Salkaywul, an area with big cracked cedar trees on Hope Slough above Schelowat (Chilliwack I.R. #1) (Sx̲eláwtxw):: Salq'íwel < séq'.

Salmo

genera Salvelinus and Salmo:: sth'eqwá:y.

Salmo clarki clarki:: spó:ltsep.

Salmo gairdneri, prob. also Salmo clarki clarki:: kw'síts.

Salmo gairdneri:: qí:wx̲ ~ qéywx̲ ~ qá:wx̲ ~ qáwx̲.

Salmo gairdneri, prob. also Salmo clarki clarki:: kw'síts.

salmon

a point or bald hill on Harrison River where people waited to spear silver spring salmon:: Chth'éylem < chth'éylem.

August run spring salmon that go up Silver Creek (near Hope):: shxwōqw'ṓ:lh.

baby sockeye salmon:: skwíkwexel.

barbecued food, (salmon bake [Deming]):: sqw'él:ém < qw'él.

barbecue stick, cooking stick (split stick for barbecuing salmon),:: pí:kwel.

coho salmon, silver salmon:: kwṓxweth.

coho salmon time, August to September:: temkwṓxweth < kwṓxweth.

coiled up méthelh rope for fishing (for sturgeon and spring salmon):: ts'tíxem.

dog salmon, chum salmon:: kw'ó:lexw.

dry storage box in tree or on top of pole (for salmon and other dried provisions):: póqw'elh < pó:qw' ~ póqw'.

early (March) spring salmon:: spó:x̲em ~ spéx̲em.

fatty salmon head:: lésleseqw < ló:s ~ lós.

fish (any kind), (salmon (any kind, not trout or sturgeon) [AC]):: sth'ó:qwi ~ sth'óqwi.

fish eggs, salmon eggs, roe, (cooked salmon eggs [JL]):: qéléx̲.

fish-spreader for drying fish, cross-piece for drying fish, salmon stretcher:: t'á:ts'.

Harrison River spring salmon, Harrison River chinook salmon, big Chehalis River spring salmon, (preserved (smoked?) meat [AC: Tait dialect]):: pó:qw' ~ póqw', pó:qw' ~ póqw'.

humpback salmon, pink salmon, humpy:: hṓ:liya.

jack spring salmon with black nose:: tl'elxálōwelh or tl'elxálōllh < tl'él.

July to August, (big spring salmon time):: temth'oló:lh < sth'olólh.

late fall Harrison River and Chehalis River sockeye salmon (last run, kind of red):: qwechíwiya.

late fall sockeye salmon (last run on Harrison River and Chehalis River, kind of red):: sqwó:yxw.

milt, salmon milt:: tl'qw'á:y.

November, time to catch salmon:: temth'ó:qwi < sth'ó:qwi ~ sth'óqwi.

October moon, time to smoke Chehalis spring salmon:: tempó:kw' < pó:qw' ~ póqw'.

old salmon (ready to die, spotted):: x̲éyqeya.

on the face, face of the hand or foot, opened surface of a salmon:: =ó:s ~ =ós ~ =es.

preserved fish, preserved meat, dried fish, dried meat (usually fish), smoked salmon, wind-dried salmon (old word), what is stored away, what is put away:: sq'éyle.

salmon after spawning when its eggs are loose:: t'iléqel.

salmon after spawning, with no more eggs:: kwómexw.

September to October, dog salmon time:: temkw'ó:lexw < kw'ó:lexw.

sides of butchered salmon with knife marks in them:: kw'íkw'ets' < kw'íts'.

silver spring salmon that came up Harrison River and Chehalis Creek, (first spring salmon [Deming]):: sqwéx̲em < qwéx̲em.

small Chehalis spring salmon:: pepqw'ólh < pó:qw' ~ póqw'.

small (fully grown) coho salmon, [kokanee]:: sth'ímiya < sth'í:m ~ sth'ì:m.

small salmon (generic):: sth'óth'eqwi < sth'ó:qwi ~ sth'óqwi.

small-sized humpback salmon:: húheliya < hṓ:liya.

small sockeye salmon:: thíthqey < sthéqi ~ sthéqey, tsésqey.

smokehouse, house for smoking fish:: kw'olexwáwtxw < kw'ó:lexw.

smoking salmon, (hanging fish up to smoke):: chá:lhtel < =chílh ~ chílh=.

sockeye moon, month to get sockeye salmon (begins with first quarter after black moon in July, lasts into August), July to August, (June to July [Jenness: WS]):: temthéqi < sthéqi ~ sthéqey.

sockeye salmon:: sthéqi ~ sthéqey.

spearing sqwéx̲em (silver spring salmon) in clear water after waiting for them::

salmon (CONT'D)

chth'éylem.
spring salmon (generic), (Chinook salmon):: tl'élx̲xel ~ tl'álx̲xel < tl'él, tl'élx̲xel ~ tl'álx̲xel < tl'él.
spring salmon net:: tl'elxéltel (or tl'elx̲xéltel) < tl'él.
spring salmon which goes to Chehalis Lake in May then returns to salt water:: sth'olólh.
stink-egg basket, stink salmon egg basket:: kw'ōle'álá < kw'ő:la ~ kw'ú:la.
to take all the loose eggs out of s-th (a salmon):: pethíwet ~ pethíwét < páthet.
white Fraser River spring salmon that goes upriver with the redspring salmon, (white Fraser River chinook salmon):: speqá:s.
wind-dried opened and scored salmon:: slhíts'es < lhíts' ~ lhí:ts'.

salmonberry
a sprout or shoot (esp. of the kinds peeled and eaten in spring), sweet green inner shoots, green berry shoots, salmonberry shoots, wild raspberry shoots and greens, salmonberry sprouts, blackcap shoots, thimbleberry shoots, wild rhubarb shoots, fern shoots:: stháthqiy.
salmonberry plant:: elílá:lhp ~ elílà:lhp < elíle.
salmonberry (the berry itself):: elíle.
salmonberry time, (usually) May:: tem'elíle < elíle.
Swainson's thrush, the salmonberry bird:: xwét.

Salmonberry Bird
Female Salmonberry Bird, (Female Swainson's Thrush):: Xwatóy < xwét.
Male Salmonberry Bird, (Male Swainson's Thrush):: Xwét < xwét.

salmonberry worm
salmonberry worm, (prob. larvae of moths or butterflies or two-winged flies):: xwexwíye.

salmon club:: kw'óqwestel < kw'óqw.

Salpinctes obsoletus
Troglodytes troglodytes pacificus, may also include (esp.)Thryomanes bewickii, Telmatodytes palustris paludicola, Troglodytes aedon,and Salpinctes obsoletus:: t'ámiya.

salt :: tl'álhem.
salty:: tl'átl'elhem < tl'álhem.
smells like salt, (have/get a salt smell):: tl'alhémáleqep < tl'álhem.

salt water
sea, ocean, salt water:: kw'ótl'kwa.

Salvelinus
genera Salvelinus and Salmo:: sth'eqwá:y.

Salvelinus fontinalis
probably Salvelinus fontinalis:: sp'íp'ehà:th' ~ sp'íp'ehàth' < sp'á:th'.

Salvelinus malma:: thex̲ó:th.

Salvelinus namaycush:: slókwech.

Sambucus cerulea:: th'í:kwekw ~ th'í:qweqw.

Sambucus racemosa

Sambucus racemosa:: sth'íwéq', sth'íwéq', sth'íwéq'elhp < sth'íwéq'.

same
be like, be similar to, be the same as, be a kind of:: sta'á ~ ste'á < t.
the same kind, the same:: sx̲tá(:) < x̲ét'e.

sand :: syí:ts'em.
barbecue, bake (meat, vegetables, etc.) in open fire, bake over fire, roast over open fire, bake under hot sand, bake in oven, cook in oven, (boiled down (as jam) [CT, HT]):: qw'élém < qw'él.
gravel, sand smaller than pebbles:: th'ex̲ét.
sand bar:: syí:ts'emílep < syí:ts'em.
to roast potatoes in hot sand or ashes, bake in ashes, bake in stove:: ótheqw.

sandbar
a slough on Harrison River north side by the mouth of Chehalis River which has a knee-shaped sandbar at its mouth, this is the next slough above (upriver from) Meth'á:lmexwem:: Q'iq'ewetó:lthel < q'éw ~ q'ew.

sand-fly
sand-fly, no-see-um fly, biting midge:: pxwíqs < píxw.

sandhill crane:: slí:m.
(be) pigeon-toed, (sandhill crane toed:: slímiyeqwxel < slí:m.

sandpiper
female spotted sandpiper:: wóthiya < wíth.
spotted sandpiper:: wéthweth < wíth.

sandstone
whetstone, a file, sandstone:: th'óméls.

sap
cottonwood sap, cottonwood cambium:: ts'its'emá:welh.
cottonwood sap or cambium:: sx̲á:meth.
pitch, sap, gum, chewing gum:: kw'íxw.

sapling
cedar sapling basket:: tl'pát.
cedar slat basket, cedar sapling basket:: th'ṓwex̲ ~ th'ṓwéx̲.
wide cedar (sapling) strips or slats from young cedar trunks, cedar slat work (basketry):: x̲pó:ys < sx̲éyp.

sapsucker
red-shafted flicker (woodpecker), medium-sized woodpecker with red under the wing, (pileated woodpecker [AK] (but this is a large bird), small red-headed woodpecker [probably red-breasted sapsucker, possibly hairy woodpecker or downy woodpecker] [Elders Group 3/1/72}):: th'íq.
small red-headed woodpecker, probably red-breasted sapsucker, and/or possibly the hairy woodpecker or downy woodpecker:: qw'opx̲wiqsélem < qw'ópx̲w.

Sardis
Tzeachten, a (recent) settlement on the upper reaches of the lower Chilliwack River, now Chilliwack Indian Reserve #13 near Sardis:: Ch'iyáqtel < sts'iyáq.

Sardis (CONT'D)

Yakweakwioose, next village above Scowkale, village near Sardis on the old Chilliwack River course, now Chilliwack Indian Reserve #9:: Yeqwyeqwí:ws < yéqw.

Sardis Park

a spring water stream with source at present-day Sardis Park, Soowahlihl:: (Th'ewálí:l) < th'éw.

saskatoon

dried saskatoon berries:: sk'ak'áxwe.
fresh saskatoon berry, service-berry, June berry:: ts'esláts.
saskatoon bush, service-berry bush:: ts'eslátselhp < ts'esláts.

Sasquatch

Sasquatch rock on Harrison River or Harrison Lake:: Sásq'ets (probably) < sásq'ets.

sasquatch :: sásq'ets.

Satan

devil, Satan:: líyóm.

Saturday :: t'óqw'tem < t'éqw'.

save

put s-th away, save s-th (food for ex.):: qéylemt ~ qé:ylemt < qéylem ~ qé:ylem ~ qí(:)lem.
save s-o, (EB) bring s-o back to life:: á:yelexwlexw < áylexw ~ áyelexw.

sauce

soy sauce:: chólmelelh tl'álhem < chólmel, tl'álhem (lit. Chinese style + salt)

savory

good tasting (savory, not sweet), tasty:: ts'áts'esem.

saw :: shxwlhílhets'els < lhíts' ~ lhí:ts'.
cut s-th (with anything: knife, saw, scythe, etc.), cut s-o:: lhí:ts'et < lhíts' ~ lhí:ts'.
cutting wood (with a saw), sawing wood:: xíxets'els < xets'á:ls.
cut wood (with a saw), saw wood, (cut wood to store away):: xets'á:ls.
sawing wood:: lhilhts'óltsep < lhíts' ~ lhí:ts'.
sawing wood, cutting wood with a saw:: lhílhets'els < lhíts' ~ lhí:ts'.
to cut wood (with a saw), saw wood, (to cut [as structured activity] [Deming}):: lhts'á:ls < lhíts' ~ lhí:ts'.

sawbill

hooded merganser, smaller sawbill:: thíyéqel.
sawbill duck, fish-duck, common merganser (larger), American merganser:: x̲wó:qw'.

sawdust

trimmings (of material), sawdust, shavings:: lhéts'emel < lhíts' ~ lhí:ts'.

Saxidomus giganteus:: s'óx̲we.

say
saying Mass:: lílemas < lomá:s ~ lemá:s.
say. (said to get someone's attention):: láw.
so they say, (reportedly, reportative, evidential?):: -ts'á.
what is s-o doing?, what is s-o saying?, what is he/she/it doing/saying?:: xwe'í:t < xwe'ít.

say grace)
It's you to thank the Lord, (Please say grace):: lúwe ts'ít te Chíchelh Siyám < =chílh ~ chílh=.

say no :: éwe ~ őwe, őwestexw ~ éwestexw < éwe ~ őwe.
tell s-o to say no to s-o:: őwestexw ~ éwestexw < éwe ~ őwe.

scab
(have a) scabby nose:: ts'eqw'élqsel < ts'éqw'.

scabies
scabies (a skin disease), ("seven-year itch", itch lasting seven years [Deming 2/7/80]):: slhóth' < lhóth'.

scald
grass scalded and bleached white for basketry imbrication (designs), sometimes called white straw grass, probably blue-joint reed-grass:: th'á:x̲ey ~ th'áx̲ey < th'áx̲.
to scald s-th/s-o, burn s-th/s-o [with hot liquid]:: th'áx̲et < th'áx̲.

scale
fish scales:: sts'álts'.

scalp
skin of the head, scalp:: kw'előweqw < kw'eléw ~ kw'előw.
top of the head, scalp:: t'émleqw < t'ém.

Scapanus orarius orarius
family Talpidae, especially Scapanus orarius orarius, also Neurotrichus gibbsi:: speláwél < pél (perhaps ~ pí:l by now).

scar
a scar:: sq'éytl' or sq'ítl' < q'éytl'.

scare
be afraid, be scared, be nervous:: sí:si < síy.
(be) always scared:: lexwsí:si ~ xwsí:si < síy.
coward, person that's always afraid:: lexwsí:si < síy.
He's scaring them.:: sisistáxwes. < síy.
scared a little:: sesí:si < síy.
scare oneself (in being reckless), scare oneself (do something one knows is dangerous and get scared even more than expected):: sí:silómet ~ sí:silòmèt < síy.
scare s-o accidentally:: sí:silexw < síy.

scarf
scarf, neckerchief:: sx̲wéqw'lhelh < x̲wíqw'.

scary

something scary, monster:: chí'.

scatter

(be) scattered all over:: stl'ápx̲ < tl'ép.
scatter s-th:: páthet.
sow s-th, drop or spread seed in rills, scatter s-th, (sowing s-th [AC]):: tl'épx̲t < tl'ép.
to fall down and scatter, drop and scatter:: tl'ápex̲em < tl'ép.

scaup

bluebill duck, (identified from photos as) lesser scaup:: x̲élq'eqs.

Schelowat

Salkaywul, an area with big cracked cedar trees on Hope Slough above Schelowat (Chilliwack I.R. #1) (Sx̲eláwtxw):: Salq'íwel < séq'.
Schelowat, a village at the bend in Hope Slough at Annis Rd. where there was a painted or marked house:: Sx̲elá:wtxw < x̲él ~ x̲é:yl ~ x̲í:l

Schizothaerus capax

Tersus capax ~ Schizothaerus capax:: swà:m.

Schkam Lake

Schkam Lake near Haig:: Sqám < qám.

school :: skwú:l.

schoolhouse:: iwesáwtxw < íwes, skwuláwtxw < skwú:l.

Scirpus acutus:: wṓ:l.

Scirpus microcarpus:: pxá:y.

scissors :: shxwth'ámqels.

scoop

a dip-net, (a scoop net [CT]):: q'emó:stel < q'emós ~ q'emó:s.
dip-netting, fishing with a scoop net, (harpooning fish at night [DM 12/4/64]):: q'íq'emó:s ~ q'éyq'emó:s < q'emós ~ q'emó:s.
scoop s-th:: qó:lt < qó:.
to scoop (for ex. oolachens, eulachons):: qó:lem < qó:.
to scoop, to dip, dip water:: qó:lem < qó:.

scorch

burned (of rocks), scorched (of rocks):: qw'óqw'iy < qw'á:y.
burned, to burn, scorch:: yéqw.
scorch s-th, blacken s-th with fire, heat it up (near a fire), burning a canoe with pitchwood to remove splinters and burn on black pitch):: qw'á:yt < qw'á:y.

score

wind-dried opened and scored salmon:: slhíts'es < lhíts' ~ lhí:ts'.

scouring rush
    scouring rush:: xweqw'él:a.

Scowkale
    burial grove of Scowkale:: Tl'átl'elh ?.
    Scowkale, sometimes misspelled Skulkayn, now Chilliwack Indian Reserves #10 and #11:: Sq'ewqé(:)yl ~ Sq'ewqí:l < q'éw ~ q'ew.

scowl
    (be) scowling (if mad or ate something sour), ((made a) funny (strange) face [Elders Group 1/21/76]):: sx̲éyx̲ewes < x̲éywel.
    to scowl, make a bad face or a scowl:: x̲eywésem or x̲éywésem < x̲éywel.

Scowlitz
    beach in front of old Scowlitz village, the point the Harrison River goes around by Kilby's store:: Sq'iq'ewílem < q'éw ~ q'ew.
    old Scowlitz village:: Sq'éwlets ~ Sq'ówlets < q'éw ~ q'ew.
    rock in the Fraser River near Scowlitz where a woman was crying a lot:: X̲ex̲ám Smá:lt < x̲à:m ~ x̲á:m.

scramble
    scramble-giving, a scramble:: swá:ls < wál or wá:l.

scramble-give
    (be scramble-giving):: wówí:ls < wál or wá:l.
    scramble-giving, a scramble:: swá:ls < wál or wá:l.
    to scramble-give, throw money/blankets/poles to a crowd, give away at a big (winter) dance [by throwing]:: wá:ls < wál or wá:l.

scrap
    leftover food, scraps:: sq'éylòm < q'éylòm.
    leftovers, scraps (not taken home as smeq'óth is):: qelmí:lthel < qéylem ~ qé:ylem ~ qí(:)lem.

scrape
    plane it (with a plane), trim it, taper it (about wood, like slats or roots for baskets, poles for houseposts/totem poles, paddles), taper it (with knife or plane), peel it (a fruit, etc.), whittle it, strip or peel bark off of it, scrape it (of carrots), (carve it, peel it [AC]):: xípet < xíp.
    scraped on the face:: x̲éyp'es < x̲éyp'.
    scraped on the nose:: x̲éyp'eqsel < x̲éyp'.
    scrape hair off it, scrape hide off of it:: álq't.
    scrape it (of hide or anything), scrape s-o, erase it:: íx̲et < íx̲.
    scrape where skin comes off, skinned:: ts'áq < th'áq ~ ts'áq or ts'éq ~ th'éq.
    scraping it:: í:x̲et < íx̲.
    scraping sound (like scraping food off dishes), rattling (of dishes, metal pots, wagon on gravel):: q'átx̲em < q'et.
    scratch, get scratched, scrape, get scraped:: íx̲.
    scratch s-o/s-th and leave a mark, rake it, claw it, scrape it:: x̲éyp'et < x̲éyp'.
    U-shaped or horseshoe-shaped knife for scraping out an adzed canoe:: sqw'emqw'emóx̲w < qw'ómx̲w.
    U-shaped or horseshoe-shaped knife (or plane) for scraping out canoe:: xepá:ltel < xíp.

scratch

(make/have a) scratching noise:: t'lhóqw'els < t'élheqw' ~ t'lhóqw'.
scratch around:: exwá:ls.
scratch, get scratched, scrape, get scraped:: íx̲.
scratching:: x̲éyx̲eq'els < x̲éyq'.
scratching around:: íxwels < exwá:ls.
scratching one's head:: x̲eyx̲eq'qéylem < x̲éyq'.
scratching repeatedly to get in:: t'elht'élheqw'els < t'élheqw' ~ t'lhóqw'.
scratching to get in (?):: t'élheqw'els < t'élheqw' ~ t'lhóqw'.
scratch it (like of an itch), (itch it):: x̲éyq'et < x̲éyq'.
scratch on s-th:: t'élheqw'et < t'élheqw' ~ t'lhóqw'.
scratch, (scratching as a structured activity):: x̲éyx̲ep'els < x̲éyp'.
scratch s-o on the face:: t'lhóqw'est < t'élheqw' ~ t'lhóqw'.
scratch s-o/s-th and leave a mark, rake it, claw it, scrape it:: x̲éyp'et < x̲éyp'.
scratch s-th up:: t'elht'élheqw'et < t'élheqw' ~ t'lhóqw'.

scrawny

be scrawny, be thin:: qwe'íqweqw < qwe'íqw.
(have a) small neck, (have a) scrawny neck:: qwe'íqwepsem < qwe'íqw.

scream

a scream:: skwátsem ~ skwáchem < kwátsem ~ kwáchem.
screaming, crying (of a baby):: kwekwchám < kwátsem ~ kwáchem.
to scream, holler (of a spirit-dancer):: kwátsem ~ kwáchem.

screw

a screw:: sklú.

scrubby

scrubby little ones, (little ugly ones):: qéqelelhó:mex < qél.

scythe

cut s-th (with anything: knife, saw, scythe, etc.), cut s-o:: lhí:ts'et < lhíts' ~ lhí:ts'.

sea

sea, ocean, salt water:: kw'ótl'kwa.

Seabird Island

a lumpy mountain back of Seabird Island:: Sqwemqwómx̲w < qwó:m ~ qwóm ~ qwem.
a place just past the west end of Seabird Island, towards Agassiz, AK's grandfather only translated it as Hamersley's (see Hamersley's hopyards), it was located at the west end of Seabird Island i.e. property between Dan Thomas's and Uncle Dave Charles's places, across from Sqémelets [Elders on Seabird Is. trip 6/20/78]):: Qwoméx̲weth' < qwó:m ~ qwóm ~ qwem.
a rock in the creek at the upriver end of Seabird Island that was a girl washing after her first period:: The Théthex̲w or Thethéthex̲w < thethíx̲w.
island off of Wahleach Island, island at bridge on river side on east end of Seabird Island:: Xáméles < xá:m.
mountain [north] across from Lizzie Johnson's place on Seabird Island:: X̲ax̲esxélem < x̲ésxel.
place on the east side of Seabird Island:: X̲ex̲éyth'elhp < x̲éyth'.
(probably) Mahood Creek and Johnson Slough, (possibly) Wahleach River or Hicks Creek (creek at bridge on east end of Seabird Island [AK]):: Qwōhòls < qwá.

Seabird Island (CONT'D)
slough about mid-point in Seabird Island where xáweleq plant grew:: Xíxewqèyl or Xíxewqì:l ~ Xewqéyl or Xewqí:l < xáwéq.
slough where people used to drift-net by Martin Harris's place at Seabird Island:: Titáwlechem < tewláts.
upper end of Seabird Island, village at the upper end of Seabird Island, Maria Slough separating Seabird Island from north shore of Fraser River, now used for Seabird Island as a whole:: Sq'éwqel ~ Sq'ówqel < q'éw ~ q'ew.
Wahleach whistle stop on Seabird Island where Wayne Bobb lived in 1977, (now also Wahleach Lake (man-made) [EB]):: Wolích < x̲wále ~ x̲wá:le.
west or downriver end of Seabird Island:: Sth'eméxwelets < sth'eméxwelets.

Seagull :: Xwelíwiya.

seagull
seagull (generic):: á:we.
seagull (generic), gull, certainly including the glaucous-winged gull, and possibly including any or all of the following species which occur in the Stó:lō area: Bonaparte's gull, short-billed gull, ring-billed gull, California gull, herring gull:: slílōwya.
seagull (possibly generic), certainly including the glaucus-winged gull, and possibly including any or all of the following which occur in the Upriver Halkomelem-speaking area: Bonaparte's gull, short-billed gull, ring-billed gull, California gull, herring gull:: qw'elíteq.

seal
a rock along Harrison River which looks like layers of seal fat all along its bottom:: Skwló ~ Sqwló < skwló ~ sqwló.
crawl (as of a snake, seal, slug, snail):: xwó:kw'thet < xwókw' ~ xwekw'ó.
crawling (as of snake, seal, slug, snail), (dragging oneself):: xwéqw'ethet < xwókw' ~ xwekw'ó.
hair seal:: áshxw.
name of a seal bay on Harrison River just before Pretty's house going to Chehalis:: Áshxwetel < áshxw.
name of a seal-shaped rock formerly on the Harrison or Chehalis River:: Áshxwetel < áshxw.
seal fat:: skwló ~ sqwló.
Seal Fat Rock on Harrison River just upriver from Th'éqwela (place by Morris Lake where Indian people used to play Indian badminton), this rock has what resembles seal fat all around it:: Skwló ~ Sqwló < sqwló.
seal fat, seal blubber:: sqwló.

Seal Fat Rock
Seal Fat Rock on Harrison River just upriver from Th'éqwela (place by Morris Lake where Indian people used to play Indian badminton), this rock has what resembles seal fat all around it:: Skwló ~ Sqwló < sqwló.

search :: yá:lx̲ < yél or perhaps yá:l.
search for s-o:: sō̗:q't ~ séwq't ~ sú:q't ~ súwq't.
search for s-th:: yá:lx̲t < yél or perhaps yá:l.
searching it, digging through it:: xíxeleqwt < xíleqw.
search through it, rummage through it, search s-o (like Customs officials):: xíleqwt < xíleqw.
to search through, to rummage:: xíleqw.

season]

(be) Spring, [time or season] when everything comes up:: temkw'éyles < kw'í ~ kw'íy.
cyclic period, moon, season:: =ó:s ~ =ós ~ =es.
moon of February to March, (torch season):: peló:qes < peló:qel.
spring (season), (time to sprout up):: temqw'íles ~ temqw'éyles < qw'íl.
time for, time to, season of:: tem=.
time, season:: tem=.

seat

chair, bench, seat, something to sit on:: ch'áletstel ~ sch'á(:)letstel ~ shxwch'áletstel < ts'á:.
drop oneself into a seat, throw oneself on the floor or ground in a tantrum, throw a tantrum:: kw'qweméthet < kw'óqw.
find a seat, have a seat, sit down:: ch'álechem < ts'á:.
have a seat:: xwch'áletsem < ts'á:.
hot on the rump, hot seat:: kw'esélets < kw'ás.
slide on one's seat, (sliding on one's bottom):: qíqex̲életsem ~ qéyqex̲életsem < qíx̲em ~ (less good spelling) qéyx̲em.
stand up, rise from a seat:: xwílé x.

Sechelt

Sechelt people, Sechelt person:: Sxixálh.

second

creek between Popkum and Cheam, also a location near Popkum, (must be second of two creeks above Popkum that cross Highway #1 [JL 4/7/78]):: sthamí:l.
one (second) of two creeks just above Popkum which cross Highway #1, (creek between Popkum and Cheam, also a place near Popkum [AC]):: Sthamí:l < themá.
second finger, index finger:: stl'eqtóletses < tl'áqt.
second finger, middle finger:: shxwá:ytses < shxwá:ye.

second-hand

second-hand store:: mékw'emáwtxw < mékw' ~ mőkw'.
something used that one picks up and uses, something second-hand:: smékw'em < mékw' ~ mőkw'.
use second-hand:: mékw'em < mékw' ~ mőkw'.

second person plural

command imperative second person plural:: -alha.
second person plural subjunctive subject:: -áp ~ -elep.
you (pl.), second person plural object:: -óle.
your (pl.), you folks's, second person plural possessive pronoun, second person plural subordinate subject:: -a -elep ~ -a' -elep.

second person singular

command imperative second person singular:: -lha.
second person singular patient or object of passive:: -ò:m.
second person singular subjunctive subject:: -exw.
you (sg.), second person singular object:: -óme.
you (sg.) (subject of an independent clause), second person singular:: -chexw, -chxw.
your (sg.), second person sg. possessive pronoun, second person sg. subordinate subject pronoun:: -a'.

secret

go warn s-o in secret, go tell s-o in secret:: wíyt < wá:y.

section

end of a falling section of land, end of a level stretch of land, (head of a creek or island [Elders Group]):: lhéq'qel.

secure

be tight, be secured tightly:: slá ~ selá ~ slá: (probably).

See.

Look., See.:: kw'e.

see

be fading (of eyesight):: stselá:l.
come to see s-o/s-th, visit s-o:: kw'átset < kw'áts ~ kw'ets.
fortune-teller, seer, person who can see things in the future, female witch:: syéw:e ~ syéwe ~ syṓ:we ~ syú:we < yéw: ~ yéw.
happy to see s-o:: xwoyíwelmet < xwoyíwel ~ xwoyíwél.
(have/be) dirty water, (not clear, unclear, can't see bottom (of water) [EL]):: mímexwel.
Look., See.:: kw'é.
seeing s-o:: kw'ókw'etslexw < kw'áts ~ kw'ets
seeing s-o (i.e. visiting s-o):: kw'ókw'etset < kw'áts ~ kw'ets.
see s-o/s-th, catch sight of s-th/s-o:: kw'étslexw < kw'áts ~ kw'ets.
transparent, can be seen through (skin, curtain, etc.), translucent:: th'álx̲em.

seed

a grass that grows with berries in fields and everywhere and has seeds that stick in one's throat when eaten with berries, probably a type of brome grass, likely California brome grass, possibly sweety cicely:: táqalh.
bloom or (plant) fuzz (spores, pollen, seed fluff) after it bursts:: spekw'ém.< pékw' ~ péqw'.
fine airborne seed(s) (not used of plum or apple seed(s) or the hard seeds – sth'emíwel is used for those) (used for dandelion seeds, cottonwood seeds, etc., tail of a cat-tail reed, (plant fluff (possibly including tail of cat-tail rush) [Elders Group 2/27/80]):: spéxwqel ~ spéx̲wqel < píxw.
heart of a root, seed, nut (kernel), core of plant or seedling, core (of tree, branch, any growing thing), pith (of bush), seed or pit [U.S.] or pip [Cdn.] of a fruit:: sth'emí:wel ~ sth'emíwel ~ sth'emíwél < sth'ó:m.
sow s-th, drop or spread see in rills, scatter s-th, (sowing s-th [AC]):: tl'épx̲t < tl'ép.
sunflower seeds:: spéxwqels te syóqwem sp'áq'em < píxw, yéqw, p'áq' (lit. small airborne seed of + the + sun + flower).
the planting, seeds to plant, what is planted (sown), garden:: spí:ls < pél (perhaps ~ pí:l by now).
to drop or blow plant fluff (like dandelions, fireweed, cottonwood, etc.), to blow (of dusty or flaky stuff like wood dust, dandruff, maybe seeds):: pípexwem < píxw.

seer

fortune-teller, seer, person who can see things in the future, female witch:: syéw:e ~ syéwe ~ syṓ:we ~ syú:we < yéw: ~ yéw.
seer, fortune-teller, person that senses the future:: síwe ~ syéwe < síw.

Selasphorus rufus
possibly Trochilidae family, probably including Selasphorus rufus, Archilochus alexandri, and Stellula calliope:: pésk'a.

S<u>x</u>eláwtxw)
Salkaywul, an area with big cracked cedar trees on Hope Slough above Schelowat (Chilliwack I.R. #1) (S<u>x</u>eláwtxw):: Salq'íwel < séq'.

sell :: xwóyem.
selling:: xwóxweyem < xwóyem.
selling it:: xwoxwiyómet < xwóyem.
sell s-th:: xwóymét ~ xwó:ymét < xwóyem.

Semiahmoo
Semiahmoo, White Rock, B.C.:: Semyó:me ~ Sam(i)yó:me < semyó: ~ semyó.

semi-circle
go in a semi-circle (or part of a circle) with the current:: selch'éle < sél or sí(:)l.

semi-subterranean
pit-house, keekwillie house, semi-subterranean house:: sqémél.

Semmihault Creek
place where a grove of birches stood/stand near the Kickbush place on Chilliwack River Road in Sardis, (village at junction of Semmihault Creek and Chilliwack River [Wells 1965 (lst ed.):19]):: Sekw'sekw'emá:y < síkw'.
Semmihault Creek, a stream from the east joining the old Chilliwack River near the Chilliwack airport:: Smiyó:llh?.

send :: lépets.
send (a person) for something:: tssàlèm < tsesá ~ tssá or tsás.
send somebody off with a message:: tssálem < tsesá ~ tssá or tsás.
send s-o to do/get something, send s-o for something, (send s-o on an errand):: tsesá:t ~ tssá:t ~ tsesát ~ tssát < tsesá ~ tssá or tsás.
send s-th:: lépetst < lépets.
something sent:: slépets < lépets.
s-o was being sent [on errands]:: tsésetem < tsesá ~ tssá or tsás.
to ride [along], hook a ride, get a ride, send oneself:: lépetsel < lépets.

senior line
older sibling, elder cousin (child of older sibling of one's parent, grandchild of older sibling of one's grandparent, great grandchild of older sibling of one's great grandparent), cousin of senior line, older brother, older sister:: sétl'atel < sétl'a ~ sétl'o.

sense
become aware (said for ex. of a child about three years or so, or of realizing how something is done), come to one's senses, sober up:: p'élh.
seer, fortune-teller, person that senses the future:: síwe ~ syéwe < síw.
sense something (that will happen), hear about it:: síwélmét ~ síwélmet < síw.

sensible

sensible, wise, (get sensible, get wise):: q'e'í:les ~ q'e'í:lés.

separate

a group separating themselves from another group:: halts'elíthet < halts'elí.
get separated (by distance), be by themselves, be separate:: halts'elí.
separated in marriage:: skwekwó:tel < kwá:.
separate oneself from a group, separate oneself (from others):: lets'elíthet < halts'elí.
to separate people fighting, to split up people fighting:: memáx < má ~ má'-.
to separate things or objects:: alts'elít < halts'elí.

September

coho salmon time, August to September:: temkwő xweth < kwőxweth.
September to October, dog salmon time:: temkw'ó:lexw < kw'ó:lexw.

serve

be served:: slhálhex̲ < lhá:x̲ ~ lháx̲.
cedar trough (to serve food):: x̲epyúwelh < sx̲éyp.
dish, big cooking and serving trough used in longhouse, feast dish, plate (of wood or basketry), (platter), tray:: ló:thel.
help oneself to food, serve oneself, serve oneself food (with a ladle), serve oneself a meal (food), (put on a dish [CT, HT]):: lhá:x̲em ~ lháx̲em < lhá:x̲ ~ lháx̲, lhá:x̲em ~ lháx̲em < lhá:x̲ ~ lháx̲, lhá:x̲em ~ lháx̲em < lhá:x̲ ~ lháx̲.
serve oneself (mainly soup and liquids):: kw'á:lem.
serve you (food):: áxwethòmè < áxw.

service

to pray, have a church service, (a Church (organization, not building) [Elders Group]):: ts'ahéyelh.

service-berry

fresh saskatoon berry, service-berry, June berry:: ts'esláts.
saskatoon bush, service-berry bush:: ts'eslátselhp < ts'esláts.

set

a net is set, be set (of a net by canoe, not of a pole net):: semíliyel < mí:l ~ míl.
a set net, a stationary net:: semláliyel < mí:l ~ míl.
eddy water (where you set nets), [to eddy repeatedly?]:: xwtitím or xwtiytím.
(he) light(s) s-th on fire, (he) set s-th on fire:: sétqtstes.
set a net and drift with it:: qwsá:wiyel < qwés.
set a net (by canoe), set one's net, fish with a net, (submerge a net):: míliyel < mí:l ~ míl.
set a snare trap:: íweltàlem < íwel.
setting a trap:: x̲áx̲esxèlem < x̲ésxel.
worn out (used when quarter moon is nearly invisible), (set (of the sun)):: th'éx̲.

set free

let go of s-th/s-o, drop s-th, set s-o free, turn s-o/s-th loose:: kwá:t ~ kwát < kwá:.

settle

food settled (in the stomach), food is settled (in the stomach), (be settled (of food in the stomach), be comfortably digested (of food)):: qsákw'.

settle (CONT'D)

throw s-o down hard (like a wrestler), tap s-th (a container's bottom) [hard] on something to make the contents settle (like berry basket):: th'esét ~ th'sét < th'és.

settlement

(heron nesting area which was the) upriver end of Herrling Island in Fraser River just below Popkum, also the name of the village or settlement on Herrling Island:: Smémeqw'o < sméqw'o ~ smốqw'o.

Katz river-bank, Ruby Creek settlement, village on north bank of Fraser River just below (west of) the mouth of Ruby Creek:: Spópetes < pó:t.

Tzeachten, a (recent) settlement on the upper reaches of the lower Chilliwack River, now Chilliwack Indian Reserve #13 near Sardis:: Ch'iyáqtel < sts'iyáq.

village or settlement on the west side of the Fraser River at Emory Creek by Frank Malloway's fish camp, Albert Flat (Yale Indian Reserve #5):: Ó:ywoses.

seven

seven birds:: th'ekwsíws < th'ó:kws.
seven canoes, seven boats:: th'okwsốwelh < th'ó:kws.
seven containers:: th'ekwsáleqel < th'ó:kws.
seven dollars, (seven Indian blankets or dollars [Boas]):: th'ókwses < th'ó:kws.
seven fish:: th'okwsíqw ~ th'okwsesíqw < th'ó:kws.
seven fruit in a group or cluster (as they grow on a plant):: th'ekwòls < th'ó:kws.
(seven long objects), seven ropes, seven threads, seven sticks, seven poles:: th'okwsámets' < th'ó:kws.
seven o'clock:: sth'ó:kws < th'ó:kws.
seven paddlers, seven "pullers":: th'ekwsále < th'ó:kws.
seven people:: th'ekwsále < th'ó:kws.
seven times:: th'ekwsálh < th'ó:kws.
seven, to be seven:: th'ó:kws.
seventy:: th'èkwetselhsxá < th'ó:kws.

seventy

seventy:: th'èkwetselhsxá < th'ó:kws.
seventy dollars:: th'èkwetselsxó:s < th'ó:kws.
seventy people:: th'ekwselsxá:le < th'ó:kws.

"seven-year itch"

(have a) chronic skin disease marked by reddish skin and itching, have "seven-year itch":: lhóth'.

scabies (a skin disease), ("seven-year itch", itch lasting seven years [Deming 2/7/80]):: slhóth' < lhóth'.

several

a group of people, a tribe of people, several tribes:: ó:wqw'elmexw or ó:wkw'elmexw.
put them down (several objects):: lháleq'et < lháq'.
several (people, animals) (exact number unknown):: kw'í:làs ~ kw'ílàs < kw'í:l ~ kw'íl.

several times

folding lots of things, fold s-th several times or many times:: lemlémet < lémet.
hit on the face (several times):: melmélkw'es < xwmélkw'es.

sew :: p'áth'.
(be) sewed (already):: sp'áp'eth' < p'áth'.

sew (CONT'D)

needle (for sewing cloth, for mat-making):: p'éth'tel < p'áth'.
sewing:: p'áp'eth' < p'áth'.
sewing machine:: shxwp'áp'eth' < p'áth'.
sew s-th, sew it:: p'áth'et < p'áth'.

sewing machine
sewing machine:: shxwp'áp'eth' < p'áth'.

sex
bring oneself to a climax, to climax, to orgasm, masturbate:: wets'á:lómet < ts'á:.
chase s-o to have sex:: á:ystexw < á:y.
ejaculate :: méqw' ~ mőqw'.
have intercourse, fuck:: kw'átl'.
have intercourse with s-o, fuck s-o:: kw'átl'et < kw'átl'.
hermaphrodite (person with organs of both sexes), hermaphrodite baby:: t'ámiya.
like s-o [his/her personality], like s-th [its taste, its idea], be interested in s-th/s-o, enjoy s-o sexually:: éystexw ~ éy:stexw < éy ~ éy:.
making love, having intercourse:: pipelá:ls < pél (perhaps ~ pí:l by now).
sexy:: xwó:xwth'tem < xwáth'.
tempt s-o (with sex or lust):: xixtímestexw or xixtímstexw < xítem.
thinking about having intercourse:: kw'okw'etl'élmel < kw'átl'.
to climax, come (sexually), ejaculate:: qw'lhòlèm or qw'lhlòlèm.
turned on sexually:: témex.

shade
a shade:: st'ált'exw < t'á:l.
go out of sight (behind something), disappear [behind something], [get in shade]:: t'á:l.
shading one's eyes from the sun with the hand (looking into the sun):: xwtóx̲esem.
(the) shade (of a tree for ex.), something that's not showing:: st'á:t'el < t'á:l.
window shades, blinds, blinders (on a horse, etc.):: t'oléstel < t'á:l.

shadow :: qéyqeyx̲elà.

shaft
spear, shaft (of spear/harpoon/gaff-hook), gaff-hook pole:: s'álem.

shake
(get) shaky and weak:: xwóyqwem.
it shook (shakes itself), shaking, bobbing around:: qwá:yx̲thet < qwá:y.
one's head is shaking constantly (like with disease):: x̲wóyqwesem, x̲wóyqwesem.
roof, shake(s) on roof, shingle(s) on roof, ceiling:: síqetsel < seqíws ~ seqí:ws.
shake hands:: kwelétses < kwél.
shake hands with s-o:: kwelétsest < kwél.
shake one's head side to side (as in saying no):: kwíythesem.
shakes on house, roof:: síqetseláwtxw < seqíws ~ seqí:ws.
(shake s-th):: qwá:yx̲(e)t < qwá:y.
shake s-th down, pack s-th down, push s-th down, knead s-th (esp. of bread dough), press it down (like yeast bread):: qeth'ét.
shake s-th (tree or bush) for fruit or leaves, comb a bush (for berries), shake s-th (a mat or blanket for ex.):: xwíset ~ xwítset < xwís.
shaking a lot of hands:: kwéletsesà:ls < kwél.

shake (CONT'D)

shaking bushes (of animal or person unseen, for ex.):: xwóykwem.
shaking hands:: kweltssà:ls < kwél.
shaking one's head side to side (as in saying no):: kwóythesem < kwíythesem.
(shaking, quaking, moving oneself):: qwíyx̲thet < qwá:y.
(shaking s-th):: qwíyx̲(e)t < qwá:y.
shaking the hand of s-o, shaking his hand:: kwéletsest < kwél.
swivel one's hips (as in the Hawaiian hula for ex.) (shake one's bottom around):: qwayx̲élechem < qwá:y.
thick plank for side of house, thick shake for longhouse roof, covering over hole in roof of pit-house:: s'í:ltexw.
to rattle (of dishes or anything else loose), jingle (of money or any metal shaken), peal or toll (of a bell), make the sound of a bell, to ring (of a bell, telephone, in the ears):: th'á:tsem < th'éts or th'á(:)ts.
you're shaking all over:: xwóyeqwthòm.

Shakers :: Shéykes.

shallow :: sxáxem < xá:m.
getting shallow:: xá:mthet ~ xómthet < xá:m.
shallow water:: sxáxem < xá:m.
wading in shallow water:: sísex̲wem < síx̲wem.

shaman)
(an Indian doctor or shaman) working, curing, chasing the bad things away:: lhálhewels < lhá:w.
blowing (of an Indian doctor on a patient):: pópex̲wels < póx̲w.
blow (spray) on a patient (of an Indian doctor or shaman), blow spray on s-o/s-th (of a shaman, a person ironing, a child teething):: póx̲wet < póx̲w.
hand rattle of Indian doctor or shaman:: kwóxwemal ~ kwóxwmal < kwoxw.
Indian doctor at work, shaman at work, healer:: lhalheweléq < lhá:w.
Indian doctor, shaman, medicine man, Indian doctor's spirit power (Elders Group 11/19/75):: shxwlá:m < lá:m.
Indian red paint (used by spirit dancers, ritualists, and Indian doctors or shamans):: témélh.
medicine song [sung by shaman]:: yiwí:leqw < yéw: ~ yéw.
spirit power of an Indian doctor or shaman:: slá:m < lá:m.

shame
(accidentally) make s-o ashamed, insult s-o (accidentally or manage to):: x̲éyx̲elexw < x̲éyx̲e ~ x̲íx̲e.
be ashamed:: x̲éyx̲e ~ x̲íx̲e.
being ashamed:: x̲ex̲éyx̲e < x̲éyx̲e ~ x̲íx̲e.
be shamed:: lháy.
make s-o ashamed:: x̲éyx̲estexw < x̲éyx̲e ~ x̲íx̲e.
make s-o ashamed [happen to or accidentally or manage to]:: lháylexw < lháy.
shame oneself (purposely):: x̲éyx̲ethet < x̲éyx̲e ~ x̲íx̲e.
to shame oneself [accidentally], (get) embarrassed, (become ashamed of oneself?):: x̲éyx̲elòmèt < x̲éyx̲e ~ x̲íx̲e.

Shannon
village at east end of Little Mountain on Hope Slough, upper end of Mount Shannon [DM]:: Qwolíwiya or Ñwolíwiya.
village at west end of Little Mountain (Mount Shannon) on Hope Slough, also a name for

Shannon (CONT'D)

Hope Slough or Hope River:: Sqwá:la < qwá.

shape

be box-shaped:: kw'elókw'exwóles < kw'óxwe.
good figure, good shape:: eyámeth' < éy ~ éy:.
rub (oil or water) in s-th to clean or soften, rub s-th to soften or clean it, (shaping a stone hammer with abrasion?, shaping?, mixing paint?, pressing together or crushing? [BHTTC 9/2/76]):: yémq't.

shaped

U-shaped or horseshoe-shaped knife for scraping out an adzed canoe:: sqw'emqw'emóx̲w < qw'ómx̲w.

share

give an equal share or amount to s-o, give (food?) to s-o, share with s-o:: áxwest < áxw.
share a meal:: wó:thel.
share food with s-o:: áxwet.

shark

shark, [perhaps basking shark, six-gill shark, thresher shark, and/or others, probably generic]:: q'ellhomelétsel < q'ellhólemètsel.

sharp

be a sharp sound, have a sharp sound, make a sharp sound:: eyotháléqep < éy ~ éy:.
be sharp, have a sharp edge:: eyó:th ~ iyóth < éy ~ éy:.
grind or sharpen s-th (of edged tools):: yéq'est < yéq'.
(have a) high pitch (voice or melody), (have a) sharp voice:: xwiyótheqel < éy ~ éy:.
(have) sharp teeth, (have) fangs:: silís < éy ~ éy:.
(making a) continuous rustling noise (of paper or silk or material), rustling (of leaves, paper, a sharp sound):: sá:wts'em < sawéts'em.
poke it, pin s-th, pick it up (on sharp pointed object), pick s-th up on a fork (or other sharp object):: ts'qw'ét < ts'éqw'.
sharpen it (of a point):: xépqst < xíp.
sharp grass, cut-grass:: pxá:y.
spear it (a fish), stab s-o/s-th with something sharp, pierce s-o/s-th, prick s-o (with a pin, for ex.), poke s-o (with a pin, etc.):: thq'ét < théq'.

sharpen

jade (nephrite) (used for sharpening [chopping] stones), any agate (can be used as flint to strike a spark):: t'émq'ethel.

shave

shave (the face):: ex̲ó:ythelem < íx̲.
shaving:: íx̲iyethílem < íx̲.

shavings

trimmings (of material), sawdust, shavings:: lhéts'emel < lhíts' ~ lhí:ts'.

shawl

big shawl:: s'oth'ó:mes < íth'a.
put on a shawl:: s'oth'ó:mõsem < íth'a.

she

and so (he, she, it, they):: qetl'osésu ~ qetl'os'ésu < tl'ó ~ tl'o, tl'osésu ~ tl'os'ésu < tl'ó ~ tl'o.
and then (he, she, it):: tl'esu < tl'ó ~ tl'o.
because (he, she, it, they):: tl'okw'es ~ tl'okwses ~ tl'ekwses < tl'ó ~ tl'o.
he (present or presence unspecified), he's the one that, it's him that, she or it (present or presence unspecified), that or this (immediately before nominal):: tú:tl'ò ~ tútl'ò ~ tútl'o < tl'ó ~ tl'o.
he/she/it was (already), they were (already):: lulh < le.
that he, that she, that it, that they:: kws ...-s ~ kwses ~ kw'es ...-s < kw.
that's her (absent), she (absent):: kwsú:tl'ò < tl'ó ~ tl'o.
that's her, she (present or presence unspecified), her (present or presence unspefified), that (female):: thú:tl'ò < tl'ó ~ tl'o.
that's him (absent), that's her (absent), it's him/her (absent), he (absent), she (absent):: kwthú:tl'ò < tl'ó ~ tl'o.
that was her (deceased), she (deceased):: kwsú:tl'ò:lh < tl'ó ~ tl'o.

shed

canoe shed:: slexwelháwtxw < sléxwelh.
little house, cabin (say 12 ft. x 10 ft. or less), small home, storage house (small shed-like house, enclosed with door), outhouse (slang), toilet (slang):: lílem < lá:lém.
wood-shed:: siyólhá:wtxw < yólh.

sheep

domestic sheep:: metú.
sheep wool:: metú:lqel ~ metú:'álqel < metú.

sheet

hail when it comes in sheets:: kw'íkw'xwòs < kw'xwós.
sheets:: síts.

shelf :: shxwch'ech'áls < ts'á:.
(being/put) on the top shelf:: ts'ech'ó:lwelh < ts'á:.
fell of its own accord (of an object from a height or from upright), drop down (object/person, from a shelf, bridge, cliff, etc.), fall off:: wets'étl' ~ wech'étl'.

shell

shell (shiny part):: ts'áwi or ts'áwiy.

shelter

a shelter:: st'ált'exw < t'á:l.
rainshelter:: q'eléts' < q'el.
sheltered:: st'ált'exw < t'á:l.
square dressing room or shelter of blankets where sx̲wóyx̲wey dancers change before doing the sx̲wóyx̲wey dance:: q'eléts'tel < q'el.

Shepherdia canadensis:: sx̲wṓsem ~ sx̲wṓ:sem ~ sx̲ṓ(:)sem.

shh :: sht ~ sh:t.

shield

fire box or fire platform and fire shield for torch-lighting or pit-lamping fire:: tl'áts'eq.

shield (CONT'D)
torch (made from pitch) (SJ and MV), (bark shield for fire (Elders Group 3/6/78)):: swáts'et.

shimmer
shimmering (in heat):: pó:lex̲wem < poléx̲wem.

shin :: sth'émxel < hth'b.txt.

shine
light up s-th/s-o, shine a light on s-th/s-o:: táwet < táw.
shell (shiny part):: ts'áwi or ts'áwiy.
shine it:: yótl'et ~ yótl'at.
shine like a reflection, reflect, glitter, sparkle:: p'álq'em.
shining, (glittering, sparkling (with many reflections)):: p'elp'álq'em < p'álq'em.
shiny:: ts'á:lts'em.

shingle
roof, shake(s) on roof, shingle(s) on roof, ceiling:: síqetsel < seqíws ~ seqí:ws.

shirt :: stl'pí:wel ~ tl'pí:wel < tl'ép.
put s-th on (of a design on a dress, of a shirt, shoes, etc.), attach it, stick it on, fasten it:: tl'álx < tl'ál.

shit
dung, (excrement, feces), shit:: sq'éth'.
dung, feces, shit:: s'ó' < ó'.
have a bowel movement, defecate, to shit:: ó'.
mess in one's pants (shit in one's pants):: ó'ayiwsem < ó'.

shit-house)
outhouse (for solid waste), (shit-house):: wá:cháwtxw.

shivaree
to rattle (cans, etc. to wake newlyweds), to shivaree (someone):: q'etx̲áls < q'et.

shiver
be trembling, shiver:: lhátx̲tem < lhétx̲tem.

shock
a fatal kind of shock on seeing a stl'áleqem (supernatural creature):: xò:lí:s.
be startled, be dumbfounded, be shocked, be stupified, be speechless, be overwhelmed:: lholhekw'íwel ~ lholhkw'íwel < lhó:kw' ~ lhókw'.

shoe :: qwlhí:xel ~ qwelhí:xel < qwélh.
(be) too tight (of shoes, clothes, trap, box), tight (of a dress one can't get into), too tight to get into (of dress, car, box of cards, etc.):: stl'etl'íq' < tl'íq'.
get a shoe on the wrong foot:: sts'ó:kw'xel.
got (both) shoes on wrong feet:: sts'ókw'elxel < sts'ó:kw'xel.
(make/have a) squeaking sound (of a tree, of a chair, of shoes), squeaking (of shoes, trees), (creaking):: qá:ytl'em.
put on one's shoes:: qwelhlixélem ~ qwelhixélem < qwélh.

shoe (CONT'D)

put s-th on (of a design on a dress, of a shirt, shoes, etc.), attach it, stick it on, fasten it:: tl'álx < tl'ál.

shoelace

shoelace, shoe-lace:: yémxtel < yém ~ yem.
to fasten s-th by tying, tie up s-th (like canoe, horse, laces, nets, cow, shoelaces), tie it:: q'éyset ~ q'í(:)set < q'ey ~ q'i.

shoo :: sh.

shoot

a sprout or shoot (esp. of the kinds peeled and eaten in spring), sweet green inner shoots, green berry shoots, salmonberry shoots, wild raspberry shoots and greens, salmonberry sprouts, blackcap shoots, thimbleberry shoots, wild rhubarb shoots, fern shoots:: stháthqiy.
be hit (with arrow, bullet, anything shot that you've aimed), got shot, (got pierced), got poked into, got wounded (with gun or arrow):: ts'éqw'.
cast a spell on s-o, put a spell on s-o, shoot power into s-o:: x̲t'ét < x̲ét'.
cast a spell, throw a spell, put on a spell, shoot power:: x̲t'áls or x̲t'á:ls < x̲ét'.
continuous shooting or popping sounds:: tl'éltl'eleqw' < tl'ál ~ tl'á:l.
miss s-th (in shooting at it with arrow, spear or gun):: qwíx̲wet < qwíx̲w.
shoot (gun, etc.):: kweléx ~ kwel:éx < kwél.
shooting:: ákwelex < kwél.
shoot s-th/s-o:: kweléxt < kwél.
to miss a shot (an arrow, spear or gun):: qwíx̲w.
to shoot, shoot (with bow and arrow):: kweléx ~ kwel:éx < kwél.

shore

away from the shore, toward the river:: chúchu ~ chúwchuw ~ chéwchew < cháchew ~ cháchu.
beach, shore:: cháchew ~ cháchu.
drift ashore:: qwélh.
made it to shore, get to shore:: lhál:omet < lhà:l, lhál:omet < lhà:l.
push out from shore (in canoe):: thex̲ósem < théx̲.
steep drop-off, a drop-off, very steep slope, steep shore, steep riverbank, a slide:: x̲éylés.

shoreline

Hill's Bar (a stretch of shoreline between Yale and Hope, on the east side of the Fraser river):: Qw'elóqw' < qw'él.

short :: ts'í:ts'etl' < ts'í:tl' ~ ts'ítl'.
a canoe or boat cut off short in the rear (because the stern couldn't be repaired):: t'qw'á:lats < t'éqw'.
be getting shorter:: ts'íts'etl'thet < ts'í:tl' ~ ts'ítl'.
be short (in memory):: q'iq'ethá:m or q'eyq'ethá:m < q'thá:m.
be short (of money or other things):: sq'thà:m < q'thá:m.
has short legs:: ts'eléletl'xel < ts'í:tl' ~ ts'ítl'.
(have a) short memory:: q'thá:m.
short canoe:: ts'ítl'ewelh < ts'í:tl' ~ ts'ítl'.
shorter:: ts'ats'í:ts'etl' ~ ts'ats'íts'etl' < ts'í:tl' ~ ts'ítl'.
short leaf willow, (Sitka willow):: x̲wálá:lhp ~ x̲wá:lá:lhp < x̲wále ~ x̲wá:le.
short (of a person), shorty:: ts'í:ts'tlemeth' < ts'í:tl' ~ ts'ítl'.

short (CONT'D)

short paddle:: ts'ítl'ōwes or ts'ítl'ewes < ts'í:tl' ~ ts'ítl'.
short pants, little pants, underpants:: siseqíws ~ síseqíws < seqíws ~ seqí:ws.
short person, short (in stature):: ch'í:tl'emeth' < ts'í:tl' ~ ts'ítl'.
takes short steps:: ts'tl'étl'xel < ts'í:tl' ~ ts'ítl'.

short-change
steal from s-o, rob s-o, short-change s-o:: qá:lt < qá:l.

shortcut :: tl'atl'eq'xélém < tl'aq' ~ tl'q'.
a shortcut:: tl'ítl'q'ey < tl'aq' ~ tl'q'.
mountain west of Ñó:letsa, (mountain north of Sése (Mary Ann Creek), shortcut to Ñó:letsa [Elders Group (Fish Camp 9/29-31/77)]):: Tl'átl'eq'xélém < tl'aq' ~ tl'q'.
take a shortcut:: tl'itl'q'oyám < tl'aq' ~ tl'q'.

shortening
fat, grease, lard, (oil [EB], shortening [MH]):: sló:s ~ slós < ló:s ~ lós.
lard, shortening:: x̲wástel.

shot
a pop, a shot:: tl'éleqw' < tl'ál ~ tl'á:l.
a shot, explosion:: wetl'éleqw < tl'ál ~ tl'á:l.
to miss a shot (an arrow, spear or gun):: qwíx̲w.

shoulder
carry a canoe on one's shoulders, to portage:: xw'ilamṓwelh < ílàm.
carry a packstrap or both packstraps over the shoulder(s) and under the arm(s):: sq'iwq'ewíles < q'e:yw ~ q'í:w.
carry on one's shoulder:: ílàm.
carry s-th on one's shoulder:: í:lá:mt < ílàm.
shoulder (especially the top), shoulder (someone's, possessed):: shxw'ílámálá ~ shxw'ílàmàlà < ílàm.
shoulder (name of body part, unpossessed):: xw'ílámálá ~ xw'ílàmàlà < ílàm.

shoulder-blade:: kweq'tál.

shout)
a holler, (a yell, a shout):: stà:m < tà:m.
call (by voice), shout, yell, holler:: tà:m.
call s-o (by voice), holler at s-o, shout at s-o, shout at s-o:: tà:met ~ tàmet < tà:m.
shouting repeatedly, hollering repeatedly, yelling (repeatedly):: tatí:m < tà:m.

shove
shove s-th:: x̲thét < x̲éth.

shovel :: lepál, shxwoweth'ílep or shxwwoweth'ílep < wáth'.
shovel, spade:: lopál.

shovel-nose
canoe with shovel-nose at both ends, same as tl'elá:y:: sqwéthem < qweth.
shovel-nose canoe:: tl'elá:y.

show

advise s-o, teach s-o, show s-o:: íwest < íwes.

a mark to show where something is, a marker (to show a trail, something buried, a grave):: x̲áth'tel < x̲áth' ~ x̲e'áth'.

showing his/her teeth:: th'ex̲elís.

showing s-o (how to do it), teaching s-o, advising s-o, guiding s-o, directing s-o:: í:west < íwes.

teach how to do something, teach, guide, direct, show:: íwes

show a picture (at a memorial ceremony)

show a picture:: x̲élestexw < x̲él ~ x̲é:yl (or better) x̲í:l.

show a picture of those remembered:: xwpósem te hákw'elesem < xwp, hákw'eles.

(word used when showing a picture of the deceased at a memorial ceremony, and telling the family to dry their tears) his/her face/their faces are dried:: th'éyx̲westem < ts'íyxw ~ ts'éyxw ~ ch'íyxw.

shower

a rainshower:: lhémt < lhém.

raining, ([having a] rainshower with light wind [BJ]):: lhémexw < lhém.

show-off :: pú'elets < pú'.

a dandy, someone who overdresses, a show-off, comedian, someone who always cracks jokes, smart-alec:: swék'.

fart on the rump, (a show-off):: pú'elets < pú'.

shrimp :: homò:y.

shrink :: q'élp'thet < q'élp't.

shrink s-th:: q'élp't.

shrub

shrub, small bush (for ex. growing on river edge, or like vine maple or thimbleberry or willow), brush, underbrush:: xwíxwel.

shuffle

drag one's foot, to shuffle (the feet):: xwót'kw'emxel < xwót'kw'em.

(have/get) soft rustling (of material), shuffling (sound):: xwót'kw'em.

Shuswap

Shuswap people:: Shushxwáp.

shut

closing one's eyes, shutting one's eyes:: th'íth'eplexw (or perhaps th'íth'ep'lexw) < th'éplexw (or perhaps th'ép'lexw).

shut one's eyes, close one's eyes, (blink [EB]):: th'éplexw (or perhaps th'ép'lexw).

shutting one's eyes repeatedly, (blinking [EB]):: th'épth'eplexw (or perhaps th'ép'th'ep'lexw) < th'éplexw (or perhaps th'ép'lexw).

shut your mouth, (shut one's mouth):: t'ekwó:ythí:lem < t'ékw.

shuttle

net shuttle and net-measure, gill-net measure, (loom [Elders Group]):: t'élhtsestel < t'álh.

net shuttle, mesh-measure (usually part of the shuttle):: shxwq'éyq'esetsel < q'ey ~ q'i.

shy
be shy, be not talkative, quiet (of a person):: p'áp'xwem.
feel embarrassed and shy because ashamed, be ashamed:: lhistélémét < lháy.

Sibbaldus musculus
perhaps generic, most likely includes all local balleen whales, i.e., suborder Mysticeti, especially Balaenoptera physalus and Megaptera novaeangliae, possibly Eschrichtius glaucus, Balaenoptera borealis, Balaenoptera acutorostrata, Sibbaldus musculus, Eubalaena sieboldi, could include the following toothed whales (suborder Odontoceti): Physeter catodon, possibly Berardius bairdi, Mesoplodon stejnegeri, Ziphius cavirostrus:: qwél:és ~ qwélés.

sibling
(be) brother and sister, (be siblings to each other), (be) first cousin to each other:: qeló:qtel < sqá:q.
brother-in-law's wife, (spouse's sibling's spouse), (step-sibling, step-brother, step-sister [AC]):: slets'éleq < láts'.
child's spouse's parent, child's spouse's sibling, child's in-laws:: skw'élwés.
grandparent, grandparent's sibling, grandparent's first cousin:: sí:le.
great grandparent, great grandchild, sibling or (up to fourth) cousin of great grandparent, great grandchild of brother or sister or (up to fourth) cousin:: sts'ó:meqw.
great great grandparent, great great grandchild, sibling or cousin (up to fourth) of great great grandparent/-child:: th'ép'ayeqw ~ th'épayeqw.
great great great great grandparent, great great great great grandchild, sibling or cousin (up to fourth) of great great great great grandparent or -child:: tómiyeqw.
half-sibling, half-brother, half-sister:: lets'ṓw(e)yelh ~ slets'ṓweyelh < láts'.
husband's brothers, (perhaps also wife's sisters?, spouse's siblings?, sibling's spouses?):: smetmátexwtel < smátexwtel.
older sibling, elder cousin (child of older sibling of one's parent, grandchild of older sibling of one's grandparent, great grandchild of older sibling of one's great grandparent), cousin of senior line, older brother, older sister:: sétl'atel < sétl'a ~ sétl'o.
older siblings, elder cousins (first/second/third cousins by an older sibling of one's ancestor):: sá:tl'atel < sétl'a ~ sétl'o.
oldest (sibling):: séltl'o < sétl'a ~ sétl'o.
parent's cousin, parent's sibling, uncle, aunt:: shxwemlí:kw.
relative of deceased spouse, mother/brother/sister/cousin/relative of deceased husband, dead spouse's relative or sibling, daughter-in-law if son dies:: ts'á:ya.
sibling, brother, sister:: álex.
(siblings), brothers:: el'álex < álex.
small younger sibling:: sqiqáq < sqá:q.
spouse's sibling, sibling's spouse (cross sex), for ex., husband's brother, (wife's sister, woman's sister's husband, man's brother's wife):: smátexwtel.
to marry a sibling of one's deceased spouse:: th'áyá:m < ts'á:ya.
younger sibling (pet name):: ká:k ~ kyá:ky < sqá:q.
younger siblings, "younger" cousins (first, second, or third cousins [whose connecting ancestor is younger than ego's]):: sqelá:q < sqá:q.
younger sibling, younger brother, younger sister, child of younger sibling of one's parent, "younger" cousin (could even be fourth cousin [through younger sibling of one's great great grandparent]):: sqá:q, sqá:q.
younger, younger sibling, cousin of a junior line (cousin by an ancestor younger than the speaker's), junior cousin (child of a younger sibling of one's parent, (great) grandchild of a younger sibling of one's(great) grandparent), younger brother, younger sister:: sóseqwt ~ (rarely) só:seqwt.

sibling (CONT'D)

youngest (sibling):: se'ó:seqwt < sóseqwt ~ (rarely) só:seqwt.

sibling/cousin

sibling/cousin of great great grand-parent/-child:: ékwiyeqw.
sibling/cousin of great great great grandparent/-child:: ékwiyeqw.

sibling (cross-sex)

husband's brother, wife's sister, spouse's sibling (cross-sex), brother-in-law, sister-in-law, sibling's spouse (cross-sex):: smátexwtel.

sibling's child

nephew, niece, sibling's child (child of sister or brother or cousin (up to and including fourth cousin) [Elders Group]):: stí:wel.
nephews, nieces, sibling's children:: statí:wel < stí:wel.

sibling's spouse

husband's brothers, (perhaps also wife's sisters?, spouse's siblings?, sibling's spouses?):: smetmátexwtel < smátexwtel.
spouse's sibling, sibling's spouse (cross sex), for ex., husband's brother, (wife's sister, woman's sister's husband, man's brother's wife):: smátexwtel.
uncle's wife, aunt's husband, parent's sibling's spouse, uncle by marriage, aunt by marriage:: xchápth ~ schápth.

sibling's spouse (cross-sex)

husband's brother, wife's sister, spouse's sibling (cross-sex), brother-in-law, sister-in-law, sibling's spouse (cross-sex):: smátexwtel.

sick

be always sickly:: q'é:yq'ey < q'ó:y ~ q'óy.
(be) homesick:: t'ekw'élmél < t'ó:kw'.
being homesick:: t'ót'ekw'élmel < t'ó:kw'.
be lame, (be) sick on the foot, (have) a sick foot, (have) a hurt foot:: q'óq'eyxel < q'ó:y ~ q'óy.
be sick:: q'óq'ey < q'ó:y ~ q'óy.
(be) sick on the hand, (have) a sick hand, (have) a hurt hand:: q'óq'eytses < q'ó:y ~ q'óy.
make s-o sick:: q'óq'eystexw < q'ó:y ~ q'óy.
sickness:: sq'óq'ey < q'ó:y ~ q'óy.
you're crazy in the head, you're sick in the head:: xwoxwth'áleq[w]thom < xwáth'.

sickness

perish together, many die (in famine, sickness, fire), all die, get wiped out:: x̲wà:y ~ x̲wá:y.

side

be across, be on the other side of:: sle'ó:thel < le'á.
(be) doubled up in bed on one's side with knees drawn up:: sqw'emóx̲w < qw'ómx̲w.
be on the other side of, be on the side facing away:: sle'ólwelh < le'á.
end or side of a house (inside/outside):: =áx̲el ~ =ex̲el.
first warmed side of a tree, sunny side of a tree:: sqewá:meth' < qew.
inner lining, inner side:: skwetxwó:lwelh < kwetáxw.
leaning to one side:: sló:litses < slóli.
left (of a side):: th'íkwe.

side (CONT'D)

left side of the body:: sth'ekwe'í:ws < th'íkwe.
lie? with surface facing up, sticking up, on the side? or edge?:: kw'e'í ~ kw''í ~ kw'í.
lying on its side:: slíx < lex.
lying on one side with one's head propped up on one hand:: piypiyáleqálem < píy.
(maybe) the backwoods side:: stselqwóthel < chá:l or chó:l.
one side of the body (between arm and hip):: slheq'ó:lwelh < lheq'át ~ lhq'á:t.
one side of the body (probably someone's):: s'í:lwelh < í:lwelh.
on the other side of the world:: súyéx̲el < sóy.
on the side of the head, on the temples, around the ear, on the cheek:: =éla.
opposite side of house on inside:: lheq'ewílh.
part away from the river, side away from the river:: chóleqwmel < chá:l or chó:l.
put one's head to one side, lay on one side of the head:: lexósem < lex.
side hills or tilted hills northwest of Ñó:letsa near Yale:: Tewtewá:la ~ Tutuwále < tewále.
side hills, tilted hills, slopes:: tewtewá:la ~ tutuwále < tewále.
side (of the body):: í:lwelh.
sides of butchered salmon with knife marks in them:: kw'íkw'ets' < kw'íts'.
side, -ward:: =ó:lwelh.
the left, the left side:: sth'íkwe < th'íkwe.
tilt s-th, lift s-th up at one end or one side, tilt s-th sideways:: tewá:let < tewále.
turn it on its side, lay it on its side:: lexét < lex.
warm side:: sqewós < qew.

sideburn(s):: sx̲elpéla < x̲él ~ x̲é:yl ~ x̲í:l

side of the head)
hit on the ear, hit on the temple (side of the head):: kw'qwá:lí:ya < kw'óqw.

side to side
shake one's head side to side (as in saying no):: kwíythesem.
shaking one's head side to side (as in saying no):: kwóythesem < kwíythesem.

sidewalk
what one walks on (trail, board sidewalk, cement sidewalk, etc.):: shxw'ímex < i┐m.

sideways
tilt s-th, lift s-th up at one end or one side, tilt s-th sideways:: tewá:let < tewále.

sigh
(be) sighing (of a spirit-dancer):: xáqlhelem < xeqlhálém.
feel like singing a spirit song, be in a trance making sighsand crying sounds before singing a spirit song, be in the beginning of a trance before the spirit song is recognizable (the motions and sounds, crying out or wailing before singing):: lhéch.
sighing over and over (of a spirit-dancer before or after dancing):: xaqxeqlhálem < xeqlhálém.
to sigh, breathe out whew:: hóxwethílém.
to sigh (of a spirit-dancer), make a loud (breathy) noise:: xeqlhálém.

sight
be fading (of eyesight):: stselá:l.
disappear, drop out of sight, (to fade [Elders Group 3/72]):: théxw ~ théx̲w.

sight (CONT'D)

eyesight, sight:: skw'áts < kw'áts ~ kw'éts.
go out of sight (behind something), disappear [behind something], [get in shade]:: t'á:l.
(have) good eyes, (have) good sight, soft on the eyes, easy on the eyes:: eyólés ~ eyó:les < éy ~ éy:.
(have) good sight:: xw'elyó:les < éy ~ éy:.
see s-o/s-th, catch sight of s-th/s-o:: kw'étslexw < kw'áts ~ kw'éts.
the (female, near but not visible), (female, near but not in sight) (translated by gender specific words in English, like aunt, etc.):: kwse < kw.
the (male or gender unspecified, near but not in sight):: kwthe < kw.

sign

crossing oneself, (making the sign of the Cross):: pá:yewsem < pó:y.
make the sign of the Cross, (cross oneself):: píyewsem ~ píwsem < pó:y.
to make a sign with its foot it wants a younger brother or younger sister:: oqw'exélem < óqw'.

silent

walk[ing] silently or quietly:: t'et'ásxel or t'at'ásxel < t'ás.
walk silently, walk quietly:: t'ásxel < t'ás.

silk

(have/get) a rustling noise (not continuous) (of paper, silk, or other material), (to rustle):: sawéts'em.
(making a) continuous rustling noise (of paper or silk or material), rustling (of leaves, paper, a sharp sound):: sá:wts'em < sawéts'em.

Silver

now also the name of Ambrose Silver:: Ñéyteleq < x̱éyet.

silver

iron (the metal), silver:: chíkmel.

Silver Creek

August run spring salmon that go up Silver Creek (near Hope):: shxwōqw'ṓ:lh.
Isolillock Mountain (near Silver Creek):: Tl'ítl'xeleqw.
Silver Creek, Silver Hope Creek:: Tl'íkw'elem < tl'íkw'el.

silver salmon

coho salmon, silver salmon:: kwṓxweth.

silver spring salmon)

spearing sqwéx̱em (silver spring salmon) in clear water after waiting for them:: chth'éylem.

silver thaw

to sleet, have a silver thaw:: x̱wíqw'el < x̱wíqw'.

similar

being similar:: st'at'á < t.
be like, be similar to, be the same as, be a kind of:: sta'á ~ ste'á < t.
to resemble, look like, (similar-looking):: st'at'ó:mex < t.

simply
  just (simply, merely):: òl ~ -òl ~ -ò ~ el.

Simulidae
  family Simuliidae:: x̲wōx̲wáye ~ x̲wex̲wáye ~ x̲wōx̲wá:ye.
  order Diptera, probably families Chiromidae, Ceratopogonidae, and Simuliidae:: pepx̲wíqsel < píxw.

simultaneous
  when (simultaneous subordinating conjunction), as:: kw'e.

sinew
  skin, hide (with/without hair or fur), pelt, sinew:: kw'eléw ~ kw'elṓw.

sing :: t'ílém ~ t'ílem < t'íl.
  a person that always sings:: lexwst'í:lem < t'íl.
  a person that sings all the time (any song), a singer:: st'élt'el < t'íl.
  a sung spell, power to help or harm people or to do [ritual] burning, power to do witchcraft and predict the future, an evil spell, (magic spell) (someone who has power to take things out of a person or put things in [by magic] [Elders Group 2/25/76], ritualist [Elders Group 1/21/76], witch [EB 4/25/78]):: syiwí:l ~ syewí:l < yéw: ~ yéw.
  be singing about s-o/s-th:: t'ít'elemet < t'íl.
  continuing on singing:: t'élt'elem < t'íl.
  feel like singing a spirit song, be in a trance making sighsand crying sounds before singing a spirit song, be in the beginning of a trance before the spirit song is recognizable (the motions and sounds, crying out or wailing before singing):: lhéch.
  pacify a baby, pacify it (a baby), sing or hum to a baby to quiet it, sing to it (a zaby), (sing a lullaby to it):: tl'ó:t.
  sing about s-o/s-th:: t'ílemet < t'íl.
  sing a lullaby to s-o:: tétemest.
  sing for s-o, (cause s-o to sing?):: t'ílemestexw < t'íl.
  singing:: t'ít'elem < t'íl.
  sing it for s-o:: t'ílemelhtst < t'íl.
  to sing along or follow in singing a spirit song:: t'à:m.
  war-whoop, ((probably) a sung spell before battle):: syiwí:leqw < yéw: ~ yéw.

singe
  singe the hairs off skin:: kw'síws < kw'ás.
  small float for nets (made from singed cedar):: qwōqwá:l ~ qweqwá:l.

singer
  a person that sings all the time (any song), a singer:: st'élt'el < t'íl.
  singer for someone:: t'át'emet te syṓwels < t'á, yéw: ~ yéw.

single-file
  walking single-file:: chichelóqtel < chá:l or chó:l.

singular
  coaxing imperative singular:: -tlh ~ -lh.
  command imperative second person singular:: -lha.
  first person singular patient or object of passive:: -àlèm.
  first person singular subjunctive subject:: -ál.

singular (CONT'D)

me, first person singular object:: -óx.
my, first person singular possessive pronoun, first person subordinate subject:: -el ~ -l ~ l.
second person singular patient or object of passive:: -ò:m.
second person singular subjunctive subject:: -exw.
you (sg.), second person singular object:: -óme.

sink

(be) sunk:: smímeq' < míq'.
be underwater, sink to the bottom:: míq'.
dive (already in water), go underwater, sink oneself down:: leqàlèm < léqem.
sink, dish-pan:: shxwth'ox̲wewí:ls < th'éx̲w or th'óx̲w.
sink s-th, sink it:: míq'et < míq'.

sinker

sinker, (fish) weight:: xá:t.
sinker line:: xetáléqetel < xá:t.

Siphonaptera

order Siphonaptera:: t'ót'elhem.

sir :: iyéseq < éy ~ éy:.
sir, male friend, chum (male), sonny:: iyéseq < éy ~ éy:.

sister

a mountain facing Chilliwack and adjacent to Mt. Cheam, theoldest sister of Lhílheqey (Mount Cheam):: Oló:xwelwet.
(be) brother and sister, (be siblings to each other), (be) first cousin to each other:: qeló:qtel < sqá:q.
brother-in-law's wife, (spouse's sibling's spouse), (step-sibling, step-brother, step-sister [AC]):: slets'éleq < láts'.
great grandparent, great grandchild, sibling or (up to fourth) cousin of great grandparent, great grandchild of brother or sister or (up to fourth) cousin:: sts'ó:meqw.
half-sibling, half-brother, half-sister:: lets'ő w(e)yelh ~ slets'ő weyelh < láts'.
husband's brothers, (perhaps also wife's sisters?, spouse's siblings?, sibling's spouses?):: smetmátexwtel < smátexwtel.
husband's brother, wife's sister, spouse's sibling (cross-sex), brother-in-law, sister-in-law, sibling's spouse (cross-sex):: smátexwtel.
nephew, niece, sibling's child (child of sister or brother or cousin (up to and including fourth cousin) [Elders Group]):: stí:wel.
older sibling, elder cousin (child of older sibling of one's parent, grandchild of older sibling of one's grandparent, great grandchild of older sibling of one's great grandparent), cousin of senior line, older brother, older sister:: sétl'atel < sétl'a ~ sétl'o.
other sister of Lhílheqey or Mount Cheam:: Ts'símteló:t < ts'ísem.
sibling, brother, sister:: álex.
sister-in-law, husband's sister, brother's wife, wife's sister (EB):: shxw'álex < álex, shxw'álex < álex.
sisters-in-law:: shxw'el'álex < álex.
spouse's sibling, sibling's spouse (cross sex), for ex., husband's brother, (wife's sister, woman's sister's husband, man's brother's wife):: smátexwtel.
to make a sign with its foot it wants a younger brother or younger sister:: oqw'exélem < óqw'.

sister (CONT'D)

younger sibling, younger brother, younger sister, child of younger sibling of one's parent, "younger" cousin (could even be fourth cousin [through younger sibling of one's great great grandparent]):: sqá:q.

younger, younger sibling, cousin of a junior line (cousin by an ancestor younger than the speaker's), junior cousin (child of a younger sibling of one's parent, (great) grandchild of a younger sibling of one's(great) grandparent), younger brother, younger sister:: sóseqwt ~ (rarely) só:seqwt.

youngest sister of Lhílheqey (Mount Cheam) that cries:: Ñemó:th'iya < x̲à:m ~ x̲á:m.

sister-in-law

husband's brother, wife's sister, spouse's sibling (cross-sex), brother-in-law, sister-in-law, sibling's spouse (cross-sex):: smátexwtel.

sister-in-law, husband's sister, brother's wife, wife's sister (EB):: shxw'álex < álex.

sisters

husband's brothers, (perhaps also wife's sisters?, spouse's siblings?, sibling's spouses?):: smetmátexwtel < smátexwtel.

sister's husband

child's spouse, son-in-law, daughter-in-law, (man's) sister's husband:: schiwtálh.

spouse's sibling, sibling's spouse (cross sex), for ex., husband's brother, (wife's sister, woman's sister's husband, man's brother's wife):: smátexwtel.

sit

be astride, be sitting on:: sts'ets'á < ts'á:.

chair, bench, seat, something to sit on:: ch'áletstel ~ sch'á(:)letstel ~ shxwch'áletstel < ts'á:.

come close, come near, come sit in (with a group):: teséthet ~ tséthet < tés.

find a seat, have a seat, sit down:: ch'álechem < ts'á:.

He sat., She sat.:: ma'emét < emét.

legs crossed, cross one's ankles (either sitting or standing) [prob. error], (ankles crossed (either sitting or standing)):: q'eyáweth'xel < q'ey ~ q'i.

missed the chair in sitting down, missed one's chair:: sépelets.

sat down (with a plop?), [slip off on one's bottom or chair]:: xwlhépelets < x̲wlhép.

sit facing a river and watch it, sit on a riverbank and sunbathe:: chichewós < cháchew ~ cháchu.

sit on eggs, to hatch eggs, to brood eggs:: tl'xwá:ylhem < tl'xw ~ tl'exw.

sit, sit down, sit up, arise (from lying or sitting), get up (from lying down, from bed or chair):: emét.

sitting cross-legged:: silílh.

sitting on one cheek of the rump:: tewálehélets < tewále.

sitting, sitting down, sitting up:: ó:met ~ ó'emet < emét.

sofa, couch, chesterfield, place where one's sitting, (bed [AC, MC (Katzie)]):: shxw'ó:met < emét.

Siwash Creek

Siwash Creek, on the CN (east) side of the Fraser River:: Aseláw Stótelō < Aseláw.

Siwash Creek Mountain

mountain above Esilao, Siwash Creek Mountain:: Aseláw Smált < Aseláw.

Siwash Creek village
    Esilao village, Siwash Creek village:: Aseláw.

six   :: t'x̲ém < t'éx̲.
    six birds (dead or alive):: t'x̲emőws < t'éx̲.
    six canoes, six boats:: t'x̲emőwelh < t'éx̲, t'x̲emőwelh < t'éx̲.
    six containers:: t'x̲émeqel < t'éx̲.
    six dollars, (six Indian blankets [Boas]):: t'x̲ém:es ~ t'x̲émés < t'éx̲.
    six fruit in a group (as they grow on a plant):: t'x̲emòls < t'éx̲.
    (six long objects), six ropes, six threads, six sticks, six poles:: t'x̲émemets' < t'éx̲.
    six o'clock:: st'x̲éms < t'éx̲.
    six paddles, six paddlers:: t'x̲emőwes < t'éx̲.
    six people:: t'x̲émele < t'éx̲.
    six times:: t'x̲emálh < t'éx̲.
    sixty:: t'x̲emelsxá < t'éx̲.

Six-Mile Creek
    Six-Mile Creek and bay on west side of Harrison Lake:: Lkwőxwethem < kwőxweth.

sixty
    sixty:: t'x̲emelsxá < t'éx̲.
    sixty dollars:: t'x̲émelsxós < t'éx̲.
    sixty people:: t'x̲emelsxá:le < t'éx̲.

sizzle
    sizzling:: ch'áwq'em.

Skawahlook
    a turn in the Fraser River between Ruby Creek and Katz (about a mile upriver from the mouth of Ruby Creek and Ruby Creek I.R. #9 (called Lukseetsis-sum on maps and D.I.A. records, see Lexwthíthesem)), also the name of a village at this spot, spelled Skawahlook, Indian Reserve #1, on topographical maps and D.I.A. records:: Sq'ewá:lxw < q'éw ~ q'ew.

skid
    slip, skid:: qíx̲em ~ (less good spelling) qéyx̲em.

skim
    skim it off:: pálétst.

skin
    buckskin straps for tying a baby in its cradle or basket:: yémqetel < yém ~ yem.
    buckskin straps, lid for berry basket:: yémqetel < yém ~ yem.
    deer-skin moccasin:: stl'éqxel.
    (get) a disease gotten by contacting a frog, a skin eruption, also the same disease as the man got in Kawkawa Lake in the Sx̲wó:yx̲wey story, (perhaps also) leprosy:: qw'ő:m.
    (get/have) white spots on the skin:: th'íq.
    get skinned:: síkw'.
    (have a) chronic skin disease marked by reddish skin and itching, have "seven-year itch":: lhóth'.
    (have?) white spotted skin:: sp'íq' < p'éq'.
    on the body, on the skin, on the covering:: =í:ws ~ =ews.

skin (CONT'D)

pinch s-th, pinch s-o (and pull the skin):: th'lhákw't < th'lhákw'.
pull skin off s-th (like a bird that's easy to skin):: síkw'et < síkw'.
scabies (a skin disease), ("seven-year itch", itch lasting seven years [Deming 2/7/80]):: slhóth' < lhóth'.
scrape where skin comes off, skinned:: ts'áq < th'áq ~ ts'áq or ts'éq ~ th'éq.
singe the hairs off skin:: kw'síws < kw'ás.
skin, hide (with/without hair or fur), pelt, sinew:: kw'eléw ~ kw'elṓw.
skinned elbow:: th'eqeláx̱el < th'áq ~ ts'áq or ts'éq ~ th'éq.
skinned knee(s):: th'qó:lthel < th'áq ~ ts'áq or ts'éq ~ th'éq.
skin of fish head without gristle:: t'áwleqw.
skin of the arm:: kw'elōwáx̱el < kw'eléw ~ kw'elṓw.
skin of the back:: kw'elōwíts < kw'eléw ~ kw'elṓw.
skin of the chest:: kw'elōwíles < kw'eléw ~ kw'elṓw.
skin of the head, scalp:: kw'elṓweqw < kw'eléw ~ kw'elṓw.
skin of the mouth, (prob. also skin of the chin or jaw or lips):: kw'elōwó:ythel < kw'eléw ~ kw'elṓw, kw'elōwó:ythel < kw'eléw ~ kw'elṓw.
skin of the nape of the neck:: kw'elōwépsem < kw'eléw ~ kw'elṓw.
skin of the throat:: kw'elṓwlhelh < kw'eléw ~ kw'elṓw.
skin or bark pulls off:: síkw'em < síkw'.
to get skinned, peel the skin off:: ts'ó:l.
tough skin:: tl'x̱wíws < tl'éx̱w.
twitch, flutter (of one's eye, hand, skin, etc.):: lhawét'em < lhá:w.

skinny
be skinny:: chtíth < títh ~ tí:th.
be skinny, be thin:: stíth ~ stí:th < títh ~ tí:th.
get skinny:: títhel < títh ~ tí:th.
(have a) skinny butt, (be skinny on the rump or bottom):: sth'émlets < sth'ó:m.

skip (rope):: ts'tl'émetst < ts'tl'ám ~ ts'tl'ém.

skirt :: tl'ítl'eptel < tl'ép.
cedar bark skirt:: lhqw'áy < lhéqw', sèqw'emí:ws < síqw'em.
peek under a woman's skirt:: xwpelákw < pél:ékw.
underskirt, petticoat:: stl'epá:leq < tl'ép.
waistband of a skirt:: qéttel < qít.

Skowkale (also mispelled Scowkale and Skulkayn by Indian Affairs in past)
a spring-water stream south of Skowkale:: Temélhem < témélh.

Skulkayn
Scowkale, sometimes misspelled Skulkayn, now Chilliwack Indian Reserves #10 and #11:: Sq'ewqé(:)yl ~ Sq'ewqí:l < q'éw ~ q'ew.

Skunk
Skunk (name in story):: S'épek ~ Í'pek ~ S'í'pek < sth'épeq.

skunk
baby striped skunk (before it gets stripes), possibly spotted skunk:: selíléx̱.
board for stretching squirrel or skunk hides, etc.:: tépelhállh < tpólh.
little skunk:: sth'íth'peq < sth'épeq.

skunk (CONT'D)

skunk's stink bag, skunk's stink sac:: spú'amal ~ spú'emel < pú'.
skunk's stink bag (stink sac):: skwukwtisláts.
striped skunk:: sth'épeq.

skunk cabbage:: ts'ó:kw'e ~ ch'ó:kw'e ~ ts'ó:kw'a.

skunk currant
red-flowering currant berry, Indian currant berry, probably also stink currant berry also called skunk currant berry:: sp'á:th'.

Skwah
Skwah village, now Skwah Reserve:: Sqwehá < qwá.
Skwah village, now Skwah Reserve, also known as Wellington Reserve:: Sqwá < qwá.

Skwali
Skwali, a village north of Hope Slough and Skwah:: Skwáli.

Skway
village at outlet of old Chilliwack River on Fraser River, now known as Skway reserve (Chilliwack Indian Reserve #5):: Shxwhá:y < hà:y.

Skweam)
a place near Deroche, B.C., just east of Lakahahmen Indian Reserve #10 (which is registered with D.I.A. as Skweam):: Skwiyó:m < Skwíyò.

Skwellepil Creek:: Skwálepel < kwà:l.

Skw'átets
stagnant water lake or ponds at the downriver end of Skw'átets or Peters Reserve near Laidlaw:: Th'qwélhcha < th'qwélhcha.

sky
day, daytime, sky, weather, (horizon (BJ)):: swáyel ~ swáyél ~ swàyèl < wáyel.

slack
be slack, loose, too loose, hanging loose (of a slackened rope):: slí:leqw < líqw.
loose (of a pack), slack (of a pack), too low (of a pack):: xet'éla < xét'.
slack, loose (of a pack):: xét'.

slacken
be slack, loose, too loose, hanging loose (of a slackened rope):: slí:leqw < líqw.
slackened down, calmed down:: líqwem < líqw.
slacken it, let it out (of a rope), loosen it, (lower it (prob. of s-th suspended):: líqwet < líqw.

slahal
a drum, small stick used to drum or beat time to songs in slahal game:: q'ówet.
guess it, [make] a point in slahal:: t'ámet < <t'ám
guesser (in slahal):: t'át'emes < t'ám
play slahal, play the bone-game:: lehà:l.
slahal bone(s):: th'ómtsestel < th'ó:m

slahal (CONT'D)

slahal game, the bone-game, (slahal sticks, gambling sticks [BJ])'/:: slehà:l < lehà:l.
slahal scoring sticks, gambling sticks, lots of little sticks of firewood:: syéyelh < yólh

slap

fall splat, (make the) sound of a spank or slap:: welhéleq' < welhéq'.
slapping s-o:: lhólheqw'et < lhóqw'et.
slap s-o/s-th:: lhóqw'et.

slat

cedar slat basket, cedar sapling basket:: th'ṓwex̲ ~ th'ṓwéx̲.
plane it (with a plane), trim it, taper it (about wood, like slats or roots for baskets, poles for houseposts/totem poles, paddles), taper it (with knife or plane), peel it (a fruit, etc.), whittle it, strip or peel bark off of it, scrape it (of carrots), (carve it, peel it [AC]):: xípet < xíp.
slat(s):: =ṓwéx̲.
to weave slats (like a th'ṓwex̲ basket or bulrush mat or inner or middle cedar bark):: wáth'elh < wáth'.
weaving slats:: wáweth'elh < wáth'.
wide cedar (sapling) strips or slats from young cedar trunks, cedar slat work (basketry):: x̲pó:ys < sx̲éyp.

slave :: skw'iyéth.
to escape (of a man or a slave), run away:: tl'í:w.

sled

little sled:: shxwqeyqex̲elátsem ~ shxwqiqex̲elátsem < qíx̲em ~ (less good spelling) qéyx̲em.

sledge hammer

hammer, stone hand hammer, sledge hammer:: shxwtélhtses < télhches.

sleep

fall asleep:: itetlómet < ítet, léqw.
get carried away and sleepy from eating too rich food:: ló:metsel < ló:m ~ lóm, melmelṓws < mál ~ mél.
nodding (falling asleep):: létqw'estem.
numb in the foot, the foot is asleep:: xwókw'elxel < xwókw'.
sleep, go to sleep, asleep:: ítet.
sleeping, asleep:: í:tet < ítet.
sleepy:: ítetem < ítet.
sleepy-head:: lexwshxw'í:tet < ítet.

sleep-walk

have a nightmare, to sleep-walk:: píx̲eya.

sleepy

get carried away and sleepy from eating too rich food:: ló:metsel < ló:m ~ lóm, melmelṓws < mál ~ mél.

sleet

sleeting, be sleeting:: x̲wí:qw'el < x̲wíqw'.
to sleet, have a silver thaw:: x̲wíqw'el < x̲wíqw'.

sleigh :: slí.

Slesse Creek
a place on Chilliwack River, a little above Anderson Flat and Allison's (between Tamihi Creek and Slesse Creek), a village at deep water between Tamihi Creek and Slesse Creek:: Iy'óythel < éy ~ éy:.

Sliammon
Sliammon people, Sliammon dialect (of the Comox language, Mainland Comox):: Sloyámén.

slice
long thin slices of fish removed to dry from slhíts'es (wind-driedsalmon):: slhíqwetsel < slhíqw.

slide
(have a) small earth slide (small landslide):: yélt.
(have) pants sliding down:: lhosemáyiws < lhós.
large rock slide that includes trees and other debris:: syélt < yélt.
place by Albert Cooper's house on Chilliwack River Road near Vedder Crossing, former village where a slide is now on north bank of Chilliwack River opposite Liumchen Creek:: X̲éylés < x̲éylés.
rockslide (that already happened):: syéx̲w < yíx̲w.
slide down (of clothes):: lhósem < lhós.
slide it:: qéyx̲et < qíx̲ ~ qéyx̲.
slide on one's seat, (sliding on one's bottom):: qíqex̲életsem ~ qéyqex̲életsem < qíx̲em ~ (less good spelling) qéyx̲em.
slippery, sliding:: qíqex̲em < qíx̲em ~ (less good spelling) qéyx̲em.
steep drop-off, a drop-off, very steep slope, steep shore, steep riverbank, a slide:: x̲éylés.
to slide:: qéyx̲em < qíx̲ ~ qéyx̲.

to slide (oneself):: qex̲óthet < qíx̲em ~ (less good spelling) qéyx̲em.

slightly
a little, a little like, slightly:: tu.

slime
fish slime, slime (of any kind, from fish, algae, etc.):: stíxem < tíxem.
green pond slime or river slime, algae:: stíxem < tíxem.
slimy:: títexem < tíxem.

slingshot
slingshot (of the stretched kind):: ó:t' < ót'.
whirled slingshot:: sts'élqes < ts'el.

slip
pillow slip, pillow-case:: sx̲wetl'qelá:la < sx̲wétl'qel.
sat down (with a plop?), [slip off on one's bottom or chair]:: xwlhépelets < x̲wlhép.
slip and fall hard (either a person or something he's carrying):: th'esáp < th'és.
slip it out:: elhápt.
slip off (one's feet, hands, bottom), lose balance:: x̲wlhép.
slip off the hands, slip out of the hands:: x̲wlhépches < x̲wlhép.
slip off with a foot, lose balance [on feet]:: x̲wlhépxel < x̲wlhép.

slip (CONT'D)

slippery, sliding:: qíqex̲em < qíx̲em ~ (less good spelling) qéyx̲em.
slipping off with a foot:: x̲wélhepxel < x̲wlhép.
slip, skid:: qíx̲em ~ (less good spelling) qéyx̲em.
slip with both feet, lose balance on both feet:: x̲welhx̲wélhepxel < x̲wlhép.

slit

cedar limb rope (slitted):: stélwél.

sliver

get a sliver in one's hand:: xéth'ches.
get a sliver or splinter in the foot:: xéts'xel.
get a sliver or splinter in the hand:: xéts'ches.
tiny slivers of fir bark, fir bark powder:: sth'íkwem < th'íkw.

Slollicum Creek

(probably) Slollicum Creek:: Stl'áleqem Stótelō < stl'á:leqem.

Slollicum Lake

(probably) Slollicum Lake:: Stl'áleqem X̲ótsa < stl'á:leqem.

Slollicum Peak

(probably) Slollicum Peak:: Stl'áleqem Smált < stl'á:leqem.

slope

a slope:: tewélehàm < tewále.
Bare Bluffs, a steep slope on the west side of Harrison Lake:: Lhó:leqwet.
side hills, tilted hills, slopes:: tewtewá:la ~ tutuwále < tewále.
sloping floor, (tilted):: tewále.
sloping ground:: tewálehílép < tewále.
steep drop-off, a drop-off, very steep slope, steep shore, steep riverbank, a slide:: x̲éylés.
steep hill, sloping ground:: sqotemí:lep ~ sqoteméylep.
steep (of road, hill, etc.), (very steep slope [Elders Group]):: théq.
steep slope (but less steep than théq):: theqílep < théq.
trail and steep slope on the west shore of Kawkawa Lake where the trail went up and over a steep hill and then down:: Sq'éywetselem ~ Sq'éywetsélém < q'e:yw ~ q'í:w.

sloping

steep hill, sloping ground:: sqotemí:lep ~ sqoteméylep.

sloppy

(have a) sloppy ass:: slhelp'íwel < lhél.
(have a) sloppy rump:: slhellhelp'élets < lhél.
(have) flabby lips, (have) sloppy lips:: slhelp'ó:ythel < lhél.
(have) sloppy ears, big ears:: slhellhelp'á:lí:ya < lhél.
sloppy back:: slhellhélp'elets < lhél.
sloppy pack:: slhellhélp'elets < lhél.
ugly, sloppy (in dress, walk, etc.):: qélelhóméx < qél.

slosh

(have) sound of water sloshing around inside (a bottle, etc.) or gurgling:: qw'át'ts'em.

Slough

Slough

Leon's Slough on Harrison River:: Xemó:leqw < xá:m.
place of moss-covered stones at upper end of Hope Slough not far from Harry Edwards' home (as of 1964):: Qwómqwemels < qwà:m ~ qwám.
(probably) Mahood Creek and Johnson Slough, (possibly) Wahleach River or Hicks Creek (creek at bridge on east end of Seabird Island [AK]):: Qwōhòls < qwá.
Salkaywul, an area with big cracked cedar trees on Hope Slough above Schelowat (Chilliwack I.R. #1) (Sx̲eláwtxw):: Salq'íwel < séq'.
Skwali, a village north of Hope Slough and Skwah:: Skwáli.
slough called Billy Harris's Slough or Louie's Slough, the next slough east of Yálhxetel and west of Q'iq'ewetó:lthel:: Meth'á:lméxwem ~ Mth'á:lmexwem.
steelhead fishing place on the Fraser River below Lhílhkw'elqs, at Hogg Slough:: Qéywex̲em < qí:wx̲ ~ qéywx̲ ~ qá:wx̲ ~ qáwx̲.
upper end of Seabird Island, village at the upper end of Seabird Island, Maria Slough separating Seabird Island from north shore of Fraser River, now used for Seabird Island as a whole:: Sq'éwqel ~ Sq'ówqel < q'éw ~ q'ew.
village at east end of Little Mountain on Hope Slough, upper end of Mount Shannon [DM]:: Qwolíwiya or Ñwolíwiya.
village at west end of Little Mountain (Mount Shannon) on Hope Slough, also a name for Hope Slough or Hope River:: Sqwá:la < qwá.
wide place in Maria Slough (just north of Lougheed Highway bridge), west mouth of Maria Slough:: Sqémelech < qám.

slough

a little below the mouth of a creek or slough:: chichewóthel < cháchew ~ cháchu.
a slough on Harrison River north side by the mouth of Chehalis River which has a knee-shaped sandbar at its mouth, this is the next slough above (upriver from) Meth'á:lmexwem:: Q'iq'ewetó:lthel < q'éw ~ q'ew.
island or point on north side of first slough north of the mouth of Chehalis River, (next slough and point above Mímex̲wel [EL 3/1/78]):: Yálhxetel, Yálhxetel.
next slough entering Harrison River above Xemó:leqw:: Shxwewéwe < shxwéwe.
next slough on north side of Harrison River above (east of) Smímstíyexwá:le, a muddy slough where fish spawn, right across from Johnny Leon's place at Chehalis and about 100 yards downstream
slough about mid-point in Seabird Island where xáweleq plant grew:: Xíxewqèyl or Xíxewqì:l ~ Xewqéyl or Xewqí:l < xáwéq.
slough, backwater, ((also) eddy [AC]):: sts'élexw < ts'el.
slough called Billy Harris's Slough or Louie's Slough, the next slough east of Yálhxetel and west of Q'iq'ewetó:lthel:: Meth'á:lméxwem ~ Mth'á:lmexwem.
slough facing south [east] across from Chehalis, B.C.:: Xwe'íweqw'óthel.
slough just east of T'ít'emt'ámex (which is at the railway tunnel north of Ruby Creek), slough near Sq'ewá:lxw and just eastof Silhíxw (which is creek from Hick's Lake):: Lexwskw'owőwelh.
slough on west side of Harrison River, the first slough upriver from Q'iq'ewetó:lthel and first slough below Xemó:leqw:: Shxwpópélem.
slough west of Yálhxetel:: Mímex̲wel (or prob. better, Mímexwel) < mímexwel.
slough where people used to drift-net by Martin Harris's place at Seabird Island:: Titáwlechem < tewláts.
turn back into a quiet slough from the river, be going into a slough from the river:: ts'élexw < ts'el.

slow

(be) slow, (be) late, go slow:: óyém.
(be) slower:: íy'eyòm < óyém.
delay s-o, slow s-o down:: oyémstexw < óyém.
making s-o slow:: silíxwstexw < silíxw.
pull in once with a canoe paddle wide or slow, pull in in turning (a canoe paddling stroke done by a bowman):: lhímes.
slow beat:: t'íw ~ t'ì:w.
slow down, go slow:: silíxw.
to walk slow:: i'oyóm or i'eyóm < óyém.

slow-worm

slow-worm ("a slow-moving foot-long snake"), actually a species of blind legless lizard:: aleqá:y < álhqey ~ álhqay.

slug

crawl (as of a snake, seal, slug, snail):: xwó:kw'thet < xwókw' ~ xwekw'ó.
crawling (as of snake, seal, slug, snail), (dragging oneself):: xwéqw'ethet < xwókw' ~ xwekw'ó.
snail, slug:: q'oyátl'iye.

slung

carry a packstrap slung across the chest (over one shoulder and under one arm):: st'át'elhíles < t'álh.

small

a little bit, small bit, a few:: emímel ~ amí:mel.
a lot of (small) dogs, puppies:: sqwéqwemay < qwem.
a small Hindu, a small East Indian:: híheltu < híltu.
a small lunch:: sásewel < sáwel.
a small person (old or young) is picking or trying to pick, an inexperienced person is picking or trying to pick, picking a little bit, someone who can't pick well is picking:: lhilhím < lhím.
a small willow tree, a low willow:: x̲wóx̲welá:lhp < x̲wále ~ x̲wá:le.
creek, little river, small creek, small river:: stótelō ~ stó:telō < tó:l ~ tò:l.
diminutive, little (of subject, object, agent, patient or action), small, (all diminutive verbs are also continuative):: R4= or C1í=, =R6= or =eC2=, R7= or C1á=.
diminutive, small, little:: R5= or C1e=.
feather (any kind), (fine feathers [EB], small feathers [IHTTC], lots of feathers [EB]):: sxélts' ~ sxél:ts' < xél.
(have a) small earth slide (small landslide):: yélt.
(have a) small neck, (have a) scrawny neck:: qwe'íqwepsem < qwe'íqw.
he (a small child) is wearing it.:: híhòkwexes < hókwex.
little crows, small crows, bunch of small crows, (bunch of northwestern crows):: spepelól ~ spepeló:l < spó:l.
little house, cabin (say 12 ft. x 10 ft. or less), small home, storage house (small shed-like house, enclosed with door), outhouse (slang), toilet (slang):: lílem < lá:lém.
little, small:: emémel < emímel ~ amí:mel.
little stone, pebble, little rock hill, small rock mountain (like in the Fraser River in the canyon):: smámelet < smá:lt.
little woman, small woman:: slhálhli < slhá:lí.
(many small rocks):: smemá:lt < smá:lt.

small (CONT'D)

midget, small people:: s'ó:lmexw.
(probably) small portion:: =th'.
rabbit: snowshoe/varying hare, now probably also eastern cottontail rabbit (introduced), (baby rabbit, small rabbit or hare [Elders Group]):: sqíqewàth < sqewáth.
runt of litter, smallest pup or kitten or animal in litter:: th'íth'kw'oya < sth'ékw', th'íth'kw' < sth'ékw'.
shrub, small bush (for ex. growing on river edge, or like vine maple or thimbleberry or willow), brush, underbrush:: xwíxwel.
small (AC, BJ), little (AC), a little bit (Deming: EF, MC, Cheh.: EB):: axwíl.
small adult cow:: múmesmes < músmes.
small adult cows, (small adult cattle):: melúmesmes < músmes.
small bird:: x̲wéyx̲weleqw or x̲wí:x̲weleqw < x̲wí:leqw ~ x̲wé:yleqw ~ x̲wéyleqw.
small bones:: sth'eth'eló:m < sth'ó:m.
small bundle, small package:: xixwelókw' < xél.
small canoe:: slílxwelh < sléxwelh.
small Chehalis spring salmon:: pepqw'ólh < pó:qw' ~ póqw'.
small container:: a'axwíleqel < axwíl, mímeleqel.
small containers (a number of them):: mémeleqel < mímeleqel.
small cross:: lílakw'wì:l < lakwwí:l.
smaller creek:: stútlō < tó:l ~ tò:l.
smallest of a litter or family:: th'akw'ó:y < sth'ékw', th'ith'kw'ó:y < sth'ékw'.
small float for nets (made from singed cedar):: qwōqwá:l ~ qweqwá:l.
small (fully grown) coho salmon, [kokanee]:: sth'ímiya < sth'í:m ~ sth'i:m.
small hat:: yó:yseqw ~ yóyseqw < yó:seqw ~ yóseqw.
small hind quarters:: lhílheq'làts < lheq'át ~ lhq'á:t.
small hips:: lhílheq'làts < lheq'át ~ lhq'á:t.
small (in quantity), a little:: emémel < emímel ~ amí:mel.
small jacket:: cháchket < cháket.
small lake, pond:: x̲óx̲tsa ~ x̲óx̲cha < x̲ó:tsa ~ x̲ó:cha.
small little plants:: sts'éts'esem < ts'ísem.
small Negro:: qw'íqw'x̲wes < qw'íx̲w.
small owl, saw-whet owl:: qépkwoya.
small peak next to Mount Cheam:: X̲emó:th'iya < x̲à:m ~ x̲á:m.
small pot:: skw'ékw'ewes < skw'ó:wes ~ skw'ówes.
small puppy:: sqwíqwemeyò:llh < qwem.
small rat, small vole:: hiháwt < há:wt.
small salmon (generic):: sth'óth'eqwi < sth'ó:qwi ~ sth'óqwi.
small-sized humpback salmon:: húheliya < hő:liya.
small (smaller than axwíl), little:: í:'axwì:l ~ í:'axwí:l < axwíl.
small sockeye salmon:: thíthqey < sthéqi ~ sthéqey, tsésqey.
small tree:: a'axwíyelhp < axwíl.
small waterfall:: skwíkwel < skwél.
small younger sibling:: sqiqáq < sqá:q.
someone small is holding (holds) it:: kwikwelát < kwél.
(that's) them (lots of little ones), they (many small ones):: yutl'étl'elòm < tl'ó ~ tl'o.
tributary, small creek that goes into a bigger river:: sqwá < qwá.

small man

little man, small man:: swíwíqe < swíyeqe ~ swíyqe ~ swí:qe.

smallpox :: sxiyí:ws < xá:y ~ xà:y.

smallpox (CONT'D)

(have) smallpox:: spelékw < pél:ékw.
(have) smallpox, measles, chickenpox:: pelkwí:ws < pél:ékw.

smart

acting smart:: smímts'el < máth'el.
little smart one:: schéchewòt < schewót.
smart-alec:: smámth'eqel < máth'el.
smarten up:: q'e'ílésthet < q'e'í:les ~ q'e'í:lés.
smarten up, sober up:: p'elhéthet < p'élh.
smart, know how, good at it:: schewót.
think one(self) is smart:: mamts'ólthet < máth'el.

smart-alec

a dandy, someone who overdresses, a show-off, comedian, someone who always cracks jokes, smart-alec:: swék'.
smart-alec:: smámth'eqel < máth'el.

smarten up

smarten up:: q'e'ílésthet < q'e'í:les ~ q'e'í:lés.

smarty :: p'ehí ~ p'ehéy.

smash

be worn out (of clothes for ex.), be old (of clothes), smashed up when dropped, dissolved:: th'éw.
burst, burst out, (get) smash(ed) (something round and filled):: méqw' ~ mṓqw'.
crush (of berries), smash (of berries), squish (of berries, etc.), to mash:: tósem < tós.
it got smashed in the back end or rear end:: téslatstem < tós.
many get crushed, get all crushed, many smashed (round and filled):: meqw'méqw' < méqw' ~ mṓqw'.
smash s-th to pieces (hard pitch, splintery wood, a glass), break s-th to pieces, beat s-th/s-o to a pulp:: th'ṓ:wt.
squish s-th round and filled, smash s-th round and filled:: méqw'et < méqw' ~ mṓqw'.
touch s-o purposely, squish it (of berries, etc.), smash s-th, mash it (berries, potatoes, carrots, etc.), bump it:: tóset < tós.

smear

get rubbed off, to smudge (a line), to smear, to fade (of material):: íqw'em < íqw'.
rub s-th/s-o, smear s-th, (paint s-th):: yétl'q't < yétl'.
smear something on s-o's face [purposely]:: yétl'q'est < yétl'.

smell

a smell:: s-hóqwem < hóqw.
bad-smelling:: xwóxweqw'em.
(be) mouldy smelling:: popeqwemáléqep < póqw.
fragrance, smell, odor:: =áléqep ~ =áleqep.
getting mouldy in taste or smell:: pópeqwem < póqw.
giving off a smell, to smell:: hó:qwem < hóqw.
happen to smell s-th:: hóqwlexw ~ héqwlexw < hóqw.
have a bad smell:: qeléqep < qél.
have a fragrance, have a good smell, smell good:: eyáléqep ~ iyáléqep < éy ~ éy:.

smell (CONT'D)

(have a) menthol smell, (be) strong-smelling (of medicine):: xó:lxwem.
have a mossy smell:: qwomáléqep < qwà:m ~ qwám.
(have) animal smell (of bear, skunk, dog, etc.), (have) animal stink, (have) human smell (of underarm, body odor, etc.), (have) body odor:: pápeth'em, pápeth'em.
(have an) underarm smell:: qw'ox̲wemáléqep.
(have) a rotten smell:: th'óth'eqw'emáléqep < th'óqw'em ~ th'ó:qw'em.
(have a) smoky smell:: p'op'etl'á:leqem < p'ótl'em, sp'otl'emáleqep < p'ótl'em.
(have a) sweet smell:: q'áq'et'emáléqep < q'át'em.
how does it smell?, How does it smell?:: selchímáléqep < selchí:m ~ selchím.
it smells, give off a smell, smell bad:: hóqwem < hóqw.
it smells (said to child):: úx̲.
(said when something smells bad):: éxw.
smell bad, (have a) bad fragrance, (have a) bad smell:: qéleqep < qél.
smelling damp, rank:: qwóqwelem.
smelling, sniffing (of an animal like a dog, etc.):: hóqwels < hóqw.
smelling s-th:: hó:qwet < hóqw, hó:qwlexw < hóqw.
smell like a rose:: qelqósem < qá:lq.
smells like salt, (have/get a salt smell):: tl'alhémáleqep < tl'álhem.
smells like urine:: xwókwesem.
smell s-th on purpose:: hóqwet < hóqw.
smell that one cannot locate, strong stink:: simáléqep.
starting to smell good:: iyáléqepthet < éy ~ éy:.
stinking (smell of outhouse or pig farm), (to stink [Elders Group 11/10/76, AC 9/1/71]):: xíxets'em.
strong smell, bad stink, smell that can't be located:: simáléqep < éy ~ éy:.
turn bad in smell, smells like it's turned bad:: qelqéyláléqep < qél.

Smilacina racemosa

respectively Smilacina racemosa, Smilacina stellata, Streptopus amplexifolius (and Streptopus roseus), and Disporum hookerii:: sth'íms te álhqey < álhqey ~ álhqay.
Smilacina racemosa, Smilacina stellata, and probably Streptopus amplexifolius, Streptopus roseus, and Disporum hookerii:: sth'íms te álhqey < sth'í:m ~ sth'ì:m.
Smilacina racemosa, Streptopus amplexifolius, Streptopus roseus curvipes, Smilacina stellata:: x̲ex̲q'elá:lhp.

Smilacina stellata

respectively Smilacina racemosa, Smilacina stellata, Streptopus amplexifolius (and Streptopus roseus), and Disporum hookerii:: sth'íms te álhqey < álhqey ~ álhqay.
Smilacina racemosa, Smilacina stellata, and probably Streptopus amplexifolius, Streptopus roseus, and Disporum hookerii:: sth'íms te álhqey < sth'í:m ~ sth'ì:m.
Smilacina racemosa, Streptopus amplexifolius, Streptopus roseus curvipes, Smilacina stellata:: x̲ex̲q'elá:lhp.

smile

smiling:: xwló:yemes < líyém ~ leyém.
to smile:: xwlíyémés < líyém ~ leyém.

Smith Falls creek

old lake above Smith Falls, Smith Falls creek (which enters Cultus Lake at its northeast corner):: Slhílhets' < lhíts' ~ lhí:ts'.

smoke :: sp'ó:tl'em ~ sp'ótl'em < p'ótl'em.
(be) choked with smoke:: p'eltl'ómelh < p'ótl'em.
(have a) smoky smell:: p'op'etl'á:leqem < p'ótl'em, sp'otl'emáleqep < p'ótl'em.
heat it up, warm it up, smoke s-th over a fire:: pákw'et.
October moon, time to smoke Chehalis spring salmon:: tempó:kw' < pó:qw' ~ póqw'.
pipe (for smoking):: sp'òtl'emálá ~ sp'ótl'emàlà < p'ótl'em.
preserved fish, preserved meat, dried fish, dried meat (usually fish), smoked salmon, wind-dried salmon (old word), what is stored away, what is put away:: sq'éyle.
smokehouse, house for smoking fish:: kw'olexwáwtxw < kw'ó:lexw.
smoke puffing out, (puff out (dust, powder, plant spores, seed fluff, light snow, smoke), form puffs of dust):: pékw' ~ péqw', pékw' ~ péqw'.
smoking:: p'ó:p'etl'em ~ p'op'etl'em < p'ótl'em.
smoking salmon, (hanging fish up to smoke):: chá:lhtel < =chílh ~ chílh=.
to smoke:: p'ótl'em.
to smoke a pipe:: lhp'ótl'em < p'ótl'em.
to smudge (make smoke to get rid of mosquitoes):: p'tl'ómt < p'ótl'em.

smokehole :: sp'otl'emá:látel < p'ótl'em.
peak of house, gable or plank over smokehole:: sq'eyx̱éleqw.

smokehouse
fish smokehouse:: chalhteláwtxw < =chílh ~ chílh=.
Indian dance-house, "smoke-house", (spirit-dance building):: smilha'áwtxw < mílha.
longhouse for spirit-dancers, the big house, smokehouse (for spirit-dancing):: stháwtxw < thi ~ tha ~ the ~ thah ~ theh.
longhouse, smokehouse (for spirit-dancing, etc.), Indian house, plank house:: xwelmexwáwtxw < xwélmexw.
smokehouse, house for smoking fish:: kw'olexwáwtxw < kw'ó:lexw.

smoky
(have a) smoky smell:: p'op'etl'á:leqem < p'ótl'em, sp'otl'emáleqep < p'ótl'em.

smooth
be calm (of water or wind), (get calm (wind/water), calm down (wind/water), be smooth (of water) [AC, LH]):: qám.
be clear (of water), be smooth (AC):: xwe'éyem ~ xw'éyem < éy ~ éy:.
calm (of water), smooth (of water), (when the river is) quiet or calm:: p'ep'ákwem < p'ékw.
flat smooth and bare rock, a [rock] bluff, a bluff (straight up):: x̱eq'át < x̱eq'.
hard clay, hard earth, smooth (hard) earth:: síq'.
smooth a log by chopping:: t'mí:ws < t'ém.
smooth (of boulder, for ex.):: yélx̱w.
smooth (of pole, stick, or wood):: eyámeth' < éy ~ éy:.
smooth (of wood):: ey'ó:les < éy ~ éy:.

smudge
get rubbed off, to smudge (a line), to smear, to fade (of material):: íqw'em < íqw'.
to smudge (make smoke to get rid of mosquitoes):: p'tl'ómt < p'ótl'em.

snack
throw different leftovers together for a meal, throw a meal together, eat a snack::

snack (CONT'D)

p'ekw'ethílem < p'ákw'.

snag

snagged, tangled on something, something gets tangled up (like a net):: q'elq'élq' < q'ál.

snail)

crawl (as of a snake, seal, slug, snail):: xwó:kw'thet < xwókw' ~ xwekw'ó.
crawling (as of snake, seal, slug, snail), (dragging oneself):: xwéqw'ethet < xwókw' ~ xwekw'ó.
snail, slug:: q'oyátl'iye.

snake)

be coiled (ready to strike for ex. of a snake):: sq'elá:w < q'ál.
(be) coiling (ready to strike) (of a snake):: sq'elq'elá:w < q'ál.
crawl (as of a snake, seal, slug, snail):: xwó:kw'thet < xwókw' ~ xwekw'ó.
crawling (as of snake, seal, slug, snail), (dragging oneself):: xwéqw'ethet < xwókw' ~ xwekw'ó.
snake (generic):: álhqey ~ álhqay.
strike (of a snake) at s-o:: ts'tl'émet < ts'tl'ám ~ ts'tl'ém.
supernatural double-headed snake:: sílhqey < isá:le ~ isále ~ isá:la.
two-headed supernatural snake:: sílhqey < álhqey ~ álhqay.

"snakeberry"

"snakeberry", includes False Solomon's seal, star-flowered Solomon's seal, and probably Twisted-stalk (2 spp.) and Hooker's fairy bells:: sth'íms te álhqey < sth'í:m ~ sth'i:m.
"snakeberry", including False Solomon's seal, star-flowered Solomon's seal, and probably Twisted-stalk and Hooker's fairy bells:: sth'íms te álhqey < álhqey ~ álhqay.

snake rock

a snake rock in the Fraser River just north of Strawberry Island which had snakes sunning themselves and covering the rock:: Alhqá:yem < álhqey ~ álhqay.

"snake's flower"

"snake's flower", prob. same plant as "snakeberry", q.v.:: sp'áq'ems te álhqey < álhqey ~ álhqay.

snap

snap one's eyes at s-o [in anger or disgust]:: th'éplexwlexw (or perhaps th'ép'lexwlexw) < th'éplexw (or perhaps th'ép'lexw).
snap one's fingers:: tl'eméqwtses < tl'ém.
to snap (one's fingers, a louse when one bites it, etc.):: tl'eméqw < tl'ém.

snare

set a snare trap:: íweltàlem < íwel.
snare, deadfall:: s'eweltá:l < íwel.
snare, snare trap:: s'eweltá:l < íwel.
spring snare:: s'eweltá:l < íwel, s'eweltá:l < íwel, t'í:tsel.
spring snare [s-th], [a?] spring snare:: weltá:lt.

snare trap

spring snare trap:: s'eweltá:l < íwel.

snatch
    snatch it from s-o:: x̲épchest.

sneak
    sneaking after an animal:: tl'ítl'ets'élqem < tl'í:ts'.
    sneaking in:: tl'ítl'ets'élqem < tl'í:ts'.
    sneaking up to s-o:: tl'í:tl'ets'et < tl'í:ts'.
    sneak up to s-o/s-th:: tl'í:ts'et < tl'í:ts'.
    tip-toeing, (walking lightly, sneaking):: t'et'ásxelem < t'ás.
    to sneak along, (sneaking along):: tl'ítl'ets' < tl'í:ts'.
    walk lightly, sneak:: t'ásxelem < t'ás.

sneeze
    to sneeze:: hásem, háshuw.

sniff
    smelling, sniffing (of an animal like a dog, etc.):: hóqwels < hóqw.
    sniff (a person, like with a cold, etc.):: lhotqsélem < lhot.
    sniffing (a person, like with a cold, etc.):: lholhetqsélem < lhot.

snipe
    snipe (large or small):: wóthiya < wíth.
    snipe, (Wilson's snipe or common snipe):: wéthweth < wíth, wéthweth < wíth.

snore
    snoring:: x̲wíx̲weqw'em < x̲wíqw'em ~ x̲wí:qw'em.
    to snore:: x̲wíqw'em ~ x̲wí:qw'em.

snot :: sméteqsel ~ smetóqsel.
    (be) snotty:: smetméteqsel ~ smatmáteqsel < sméteqsel ~ smetóqsel.
    (have) snot hanging from the nose:: slholh(e)x̲wélqsel < lhex̲w.

snow
    a snow, a snowfall:: syíq < yíq.
    a snowdrift:: sqelyíqem (or sq'elyíqem) < yíq.
    (be) snowing, it's snowing, snow is falling:: yíyeq < yíq.
    dry snow coming in (drifting), fine snow that leaks into a house:: sqwelxómé ~ sqwelxóme < qwélxel.
    dry snow (that can drift):: sqwélxem < qwélxel.
    fallen snow, (year):: máqa ~ máqe.
    falling snow, be snowing:: syíyeq < yíq.
    fine snow:: qwelqwélxel < qwélxel.
    first snow:: yeqelsxá:y < yíq.
    fog appearing on the water, (fine snow [AK]):: qwelqwélxel < qwélxel.
    got stormy with lots of fine snow in the air:: qwálxtem < qwélxel.
    (have/get a) snowdrift:: q'elsiyáqem or q'elts'yáqem < yíq.
    (have) mixed snow and rain together that melts fast, to rain and snow mixed together:: imqáxel ~ hi=mqáxel < máqa ~ máqe, imqáxel ~ hi=mqáxel < máqa ~ máqe.
    it's snowing, (snow is accumulating):: mámeqe < máqa ~ máqe.
    real fine snow:: qwelxómé < qwélxel.
    small balls of snow on one's feet:: qwelqwélxel < qwélxel.

snow (CONT'D)

smoke puffing out, (puff out (dust, powder, plant spores, seed fluff, light snow, smoke), form puffs of dust):: pékw' ~ péqw'.
stop raining, stop snowing:: xwéts'xel.
to snow, (snow falls):: yíq.

snowberry :: pepq'éyò:s < p'éq'.
snowberry plant:: qewówelhp.

snowdrift
a snowdrift:: sqelyíqem (or sq'elyíqem) < yíq.
(have/get a) snowdrift:: q'elsiyáqem or q'elts'yáqem < yíq.

snowflake
have wide snowflakes:: lhálhq'etxel < lheq'át ~ lhq'á:t.

snowshoe
snowshoes:: thelí:wá:xel < thél.

so
and so, and then:: qesu < qe, qetl'osu ~ qetl'esu < qe.
and so (he, she, it, they):: qetl'osésu ~ qetl'os'ésu < tl'ó ~ tl'o, tl'osésu ~ tl'os'ésu < tl'ó ~ tl'o.
so then I:: tl'olsu < tl'ó ~ tl'o.
so then you:: tl'o'asu < tl'ó ~ tl'o.
then (action following a previous action, contrastive), so (contrastive):: su.

soak
soaked (right through):: th'eq'mítem < th'q'ém ~ th'eq'ém.
soaked, wet:: lhélq < lhél.
soaking dried fish:: lhálqi < lhél.
soak it:: lhélqit ~ lhélqeyt < lhél.
soak one's head:: mí:leqwem < mí:l ~ míl, mí:leqwthet < mí:l ~ míl.
to soak (fish, beans, dried fruit, only food, not of cedar roots), rehydrate dried food, soak dried fish:: lhélqi < lhél, lhélqi < lhél.

soap :: sṓp, sp'óp'eqw'em < p'óqw'em.

soapberry :: sxwṓsem ~ sxwṓ:sem ~ sxṓ(:)sem.
soapberry basket, Indian ice-cream basket:: sxwōsemálá < sxwṓsem ~ sxwṓ:sem ~ sxṓ(:)sem.
soapberry beater, stick for whipping up soapberries or Indian ice cream:: th'amawéstel or th'emawéstel < th'ím ~ th'í:m.
soapberry juice:: sxwṓsem sqe'óleqw < xwṓs, qó:
(lit. soapberry + fruit juice)
soapberry spoon, soapberry paddle, short-handled spoon, flat spoon for sxwṓsem:: th'émtel < th'ím ~ th'í:m.

soapberry foam
Indian ice-cream, whipped soapberry foam:: sxwṓsem ~ sxwṓ:sem ~ sxṓ(:)sem.

sob
sobbing after crying:: qésqesí:l < qásel.

sob (CONT'D)
sobbing, crying a little, (to sob [EB]):: x̲íx̲à:m ~ x̲éyx̲à:m < x̲à:m ~ x̲á:m.

sober
become aware (said for ex. of a child about three years or so, or of realizing how something is done), come to one's senses, sober up:: p'élh.
(be) sober:: sp'ap'ílh < p'élh.
smarten up, sober up:: p'elhéthet < p'élh.
sober s-o up:: p'ílhat < p'élh.

sock
put on one's socks, (put on one's stockings):: tókelem < stókel.
sticking out through a hole (like a toe out of a sock, knee out of a hole in pants, a nail driven clear through the other side of a board), come out into the open:: qwōhóls (or perhaps) qwehóls < qwá.
stocking, socks:: stókel.

sockeye salmon
baby sockeye salmon:: skwíkwexel.
flat rocks (bedrock) with holes at Hill's Bar where they used to make smótheqw (prepared fish oil) from sockeye heads:: Hemhémetheqw < mótheqw or metheqw.
late fall Harrison River and Chehalis River sockeye salmon (last run, kind of red):: qwechíwiya.
late fall sockeye salmon (last run on Harrison River and Chehalis River, kind of red):: sqwó:yxw.
prepared fish oil (usually sockeye oil):: smótheqw < mótheqw or metheqw.
small sockeye salmon:: thíthqey < sthéqi ~ sthéqey, tsésqey.
sockeye moon, month to get sockeye salmon (begins with first quarter after black moon in July, lasts into August), July to August, (June to July [Jenness: WS]):: temthéqi < sthéqi ~ sthéqey.
sockeye net:: sthéqeytel < sthéqi ~ sthéqey.
sockeye salmon:: sthéqi ~ sthéqey.
time of the baby sockeye's coming, early spring (usually April), April moon:: temkwíkwexel.

soda
soda pop:: sqe'óleqw < qó:.

sofa
sofa, couch, chesterfield, place where one's sitting, (bed [AC, MC (Katzie)]):: shxw'ó:met < emét.

soft :: líqw'em, qí:qe ~ qéyqe ~ qíqe < qí: ~ qí'.
break up s-th by crumpling, crush it up, rub it together fast (to soften or clean), rub it to soften it (of plants, etc.), fluff it (inner cedar bark to soften it):: yékw'et < yókw' ~ yóqw'.
flannelette, velvet, woolly material, fluffy material, soft material:: pá:píth'a < pá:pa.
gone soft and spoiled (of dried fish):: th'íth'eqel < sth'í:qel.
(have/get) soft rustling (of material), shuffling (sound):: xwót'kw'em.
(have) good eyes, (have) good sight, soft on the eyes, easy on the eyes:: eyólés ~ eyó:les < éy ~ éy:.
(make/have a) sound getting softer:: théxweleqep < théxw ~ théx̲w.
rub (oil or water) in s-th to clean or soften, rub s-th to soften or clean it, (shaping a stone hammer with abrasion?, shaping?, mixing paint?, pressing together or crushing? [BHTTC 9/2/76])::

soft (CONT'D)

yémq't.
soft feathers put in oiled hair for dancing:: sx̱óyeseqw ~ sq'óyeseqw.
soft (knee-shaped) cliff on a beach:: =ó:lthel.
soft spot on (top of) a baby's head, fontanel:: sqe'éleqw < qí: ~ qí'.
splat, sound of something wet and soft dropped, to splatter:: wet'éleq.

soggy
(go/get/become) soggy:: tl'ítl'eqel.

Solanum tuberosum
including: Sagittaria latifolia, Helianthus tuberosus, Camassia quamash (and Camassia leichtlinii), and unidentified plant, besides Solanum tuberosum:: sqáwth ~ sqá:wth.

sole
sole (of the foot), (instep [AC, DM]):: shxw'óthesxel ~ shxwe'óthesxel < s'ó:thes ~ s'óthes.

solid
be tucked away, put away so well you can't find it, be solid:: slá ~ selá ~ slá: (probably).

solid grease
solid grease, suet, lump of grease, (stomach fat [CT]):: x̱wástel.

Solomon's seal
False Solomon's seal, Twisted-stalk, rosy-flowered Twisted-stalk, star-flowered Solomon's seal:: x̱ex̱q'elá:lhp.
"snakeberry", includes False Solomon's seal, star-flowered Solomon's seal, and probably Twisted-stalk (2 spp.) and Hooker's fairy bells:: sth'íms te álhqey < sth'í:m ~ sth'ì:m, sth'íms te álhqey < sth'í:m ~ sth'ì:m.
"snakeberry", including False Solomon's seal, star-flowered Solomon's seal, and probably Twisted-stalk and Hooker's fairy bells:: sth'íms te álhqey < álhqey ~ álhqay.

some
add some, add it, (do it again [AD]):: ts'xwót.
add some water [to s-th]:: ch'exwélhchat < ts'xwót.
the (distant and out of sight, remote), (definite but distant and out of sight, remote), the (abstract), a (remote, abstract), some, (indefinite):: kw'e.
the (remote, not visible, abstract), some (indefinite):: kw.

somebody
somebody, anybody:: tewátes < wát.
somebody, someone:: swótle < wát.

someone
a dandy, someone who overdresses, a show-off, comedian, someone who always cracks jokes, smart-alec:: swék'.
a filer, someone that's filing (with a file):: hiyeq'á:l < yéq'.
a sung spell, power to help or harm people or to do [ritual] burning, power to do witchcraft and predict the future, an evil spell, (magic spell) (someone who has power to take things out of a person or put things in [by magic] [Elders Group 2/25/76], ritualist [Elders Group 1/21/76], witch [EB 4/25/78]):: syiwí:l ~ syewí:l < yéw: ~ yéw.
knee (someone's):: sqep'ó:lthetel < qep'.

someone (CONT'D)

nominalizer, something for, someone for, something that:: shxw=.
nominalizer, something to, something that, someone to/that:: s=.
somebody, someone:: swótle < wát.
[someone] always working:: lexwsyóyes ~ lexwsiyó:yes < yó:ys.
someone that always:: lexws=.
someone who has power to take things out of a person or put things in [by magic]:: syiwí:l ~ syewí:l < yéw: ~ yéw.
someone who is greedy, someone who eats all the time, (glutton):: sqel:éxw < qél:éxw ~ qel(:)éxw.

someone for

nominalizer, something for, someone for, something that:: shxw=.

someone's)

(someone's) elbow:: sth'emxweláx̲el < hth'b.txt.
(someone's) spine, (someone's) backbone:: th'omewích ~ th'ó:bewíts < sth'ó:m.

someone to/someone that

nominalizer, something to, something that, someone to/that:: s=.

someplace

someplace, somewhere:: stómchele < tám.

something :: kw'ewátes < wát.

chair, bench, seat, something to sit on:: ch'áletstel ~ sch'á(:)letstel ~ shxwch'áletstel < ts'á:.
clothes, clothing (esp. Indian clothing, men's or women's), something to wear, dress, gown:: s'íth'em < íth'a.
nuisance, something that's no good:: sqel:ép ~ sqél:ep < qél.
on something else, within ssomething else:: =q'.
pencil, pen, something to write with, (device to write or paint or mark with):: x̲éltel < x̲él ~ x̲é:yl ~ x̲í:l
something big (and round) (for ex. big fruit, big rocks, etc.):: thíthes < thi ~ tha ~ the ~ thah ~ theh.
something hidden away:: skwálepel < kwà:l.
something one writes with, (writing implement):: sx̲ex̲é:yls < x̲él ~ x̲é:yl ~ x̲í:l
something sent:: slépets < lépets.
something that's cooked:: sqw'éls < qw'él.
something that you hook onto (like a trailer hitch):: s'óqw' < óqw'.
something to boil in:: sh(xw)qwó:ls < qwó:ls.
something to tie the feet:: q'ép'xetel (unless q'épxetel is correct) < q'áp'.
something used to cross over a river, ferry, place good for crossing:: xwt'át'ekwel < t'ákwel.
(the) shade (of a tree for ex.), something that's not showing:: st'á:t'el < t'á:l.
whatever it is, what it is, it is anything, it is something:: stámés < tám.

something for

nominalizer, something for, someone for, something that:: shxw=.

something that

nominalizer, something to, something that, someone to/that:: s=.

something to
nominalizer, something to, something that, someone to/that:: s=.

something used
something used that one picks up and uses, something second-hand:: smékw'em < mékw' ~ mő̃kw'.

sometimes :: láts.
is it sometimes?:: lhéq'e < lhéq'.
sometimes?, always?:: lheq.
sometimes, (yes [RM]):: lhéq'.
when, (sometimes [EB]):: lhí.

somewhere
someplace, somewhere:: stómchele < tám.

son
child (of someone, kinterm), offspring, son, daughter:: méle ~ mél:a.
children (kinterm, someone's), sons, daughters:: mámele < méle ~ mél:a.

song
a category of religious songs including sx̲wó:yx̲wey songs and burning songs, a burning song:: heywí:leqw < yéw: ~ yéw.
a drum, small stick used to drum or beat time to songs in slahal game:: q'ówet.
also the words of Mack's spirit song:: Á:yiya.
bring it out for the first time (of a spirit-song):: p'í:t < p'í:.
feel like singing a spirit song, be in a trance making sighsand crying sounds before singing a spirit song, be in the beginning of a trance before the spirit song is recognizable (the motions and sounds, crying out or wailing before singing):: lhéch.
medicine song [sung by shaman]:: yiwí:leqw < yéw: ~ yéw.
song (non-religious):: stñílém < t'íl.
songs:: st'elt'ílém < t'íl.
spirit power song:: syúwél ~ syéw:el < yéw: ~ yéw.
to sing along or follow in singing a spirit song:: t'à:m.
type of bird that begs for bones or food with the song: paspes(y)í(:)tsel kw'e sth'ò:m th'ò:m th'ò:m, probably a song sparrow:: paspesítsel ~ paspasyí:tsel ~ pespesí:tsel < pas ~ pes.

son-in-law
child's spouse, son-in-law, daughter-in-law, (man's) sister's husband:: schiwtálh.
sons-in-law, daughters-in-law, children's spouses:: schí:wetálh < schiwtálh.

sonny :: iyéseq < éy ~ éy:.
sir, male friend, chum (male), sonny:: iyéseq < éy ~ éy:.
little man (nickname for a person), (sonny boy (MV and DF)):: wíyeka < swíyeqe ~ swíyqe ~ swí:qe.

soot
black soot:: xwíyeqwela < yéqw.

Soowahlie
Soowahlie village (where Sweltzer Creek met Chilliwack River), Soowahlie Reserve near

Soowahlie (CONT'D)

Vedder Crossing:: Th'ewá:lí < th'éw.
Sweltzer Creek (the stream from Cultus Lake to Chilliwack River at Soowahlie):: Swílhcha Stótelō < Swílhcha.

Soowahlihl

a spring water stream with source at present-day Sardis Park, Soowahlihl:: (Th'ewálí:l) < th'éw.

Sorbus sitchensis:: qwíqwelh.

sore

a sore, open sore(s):: sth'eth'íkw' < th'ekw' or th'íkw'.
(be) sore, (be) hurting all the time, painful, aching:: sáyém < sáyem.
(have/get) sore muscles:: q'éyq'ey ~ q'íq'i < q'ey ~ q'i.
(have) hemorrhoids, (have) open sores on genitals or rump:: th'kw'íwel < th'ekw' or th'íkw'.
hurting, feeling sore, (feel[ing] pain [BJ]):: táteqlexw < téqlexw.
hurt, sore:: nána.
lots of sores, (possibly) rash:: sth'ekw'th'ékw' < th'ekw' or th'íkw'.
"sored up":: x̲ex̲élh < x̲élh.

sorrel)

sourgrass, (sheep sorrel):: t'át'eth'em < t'áth'.

sorry

be feeling sorry:: x̲ex̲élh te sqwálewel < x̲élh.
be sorry, the feelings are hurt:: x̲élh (te, kw'e) sqwálewel < x̲élh.
feeling sorry for oneself:: tesestélemet < t-sós ~ tesós.
sorry for oneself:: x̲ehó:methet < x̲à:m ~ x̲á:m.
to pity s-o, feel sorry for s-o:: th'éxwmet < th'íxw ~ th'éxw.

sort

pick it, choose it, sort it, (choose s-o/s-th):: míset < mís.
pick out, sort:: mísem < mís.

so they say

so they say, (reportedly, reportative, evidential?):: -ts'á.

soul

conscience, spirit (which can be lost temporarily), soul, life-spirit, power of one's will:: smestíyexw < mestíyexw.
soul, spirit of a living person:: shxwelí.

sound :: =áléqep ~ =áleqep.

a pop, a shot:: tl'éleqw' < tl'ál ~ tl'á:l.
a shot, explosion:: wetl'éleqw < tl'ál ~ tl'á:l.
a sound heard starting up again in the distance:: eháléqep < ehó.
a trilling sound a raven makes:: xwot'q'esílem.
be a sharp sound, have a sharp sound, make a sharp sound:: eyotháléqep < éy ~ éy:.
be loud in sound, a loud sound (?):: chqwáléqep.
clinking, tinkling (of glass, ice in glass, glasses together, dishes together, metal together)::

sound (CONT'D)

ts'átx̲em ~ th'átx̲em.
continuous shooting or popping sounds:: tl'éltl'eleqw' < tl'ál ~ tl'á:l.
crackling and popping (of a log in fire or firecrackers):: tl'áléx̲em < tl'ál ~ tl'á:l.
crunchy (loud when eating), crackling (noise when eating):: tl'ámqw'els < tl'ém.
crunchy (loud when eating), crackling (sound or noise when eating):: tl'ámqw'els < tl'ámkw'em.
explode:: tl'eléqw < tl'ál ~ tl'á:l.
fall splat, (make the) sound of a spank or slap:: welhéleq' < welhéq'.
feel like singing a spirit song, be in a trance making sighsand crying sounds before singing a spirit song, be in the beginning of a trance before the spirit song is recognizable (the motions and sounds, crying out or wailing before singing):: lhéch.
(glad greeting sound, also sound to show pride in accomplishment):: x̲::.
(have a) steady sound that's been stopped for a while:: thxwáléqep < théxw ~ théx̲w.
(have) clinking (of glass or dishes or metal), (have) tinkling sound (of glass, ice in glass, glasses together):: th'átx̲em ~ ts'átx̲em.
(have/get a) crackle and pop (sound of a log in a fire or of firecrackers):: tl'á:lx̲em < tl'ál ~ tl'á:l.
(have/get) a rustling noise (not continuous) (of paper, silk, or other material), (to rustle):: sawéts'em.
(have/get) soft rustling (of material), shuffling (sound):: xwót'kw'em.
(have) sound of popping small round things (snowberries, herring eggs as when eating them, rice krispies, crabapples, cranberries, etc.), (have a crunching sound (as of grasshopper, rice krispies)):: tl'ámkw'em, tl'ámkw'em < tl'ém.
(have) sound of water sloshing around inside (a bottle, etc.) or gurgling:: qw'át'ts'em.
keep on hearing a distant sound:: sasetáleqep < sát.
(made) a faint sound carried by the air, sound within hearingdistance, sound within earshot:: ehálé qep < ehó.
make a banging sound:: kwótx̲wem ~ kwótxwem.
[make a bang, make a sudden hard thump sound]:: kw'péx̲w.
make a crunching or crackling noise, crunching (gnawing) sound:: x̲ápkw'em < x̲ep'ékw'.
(make) a distant sound:: stáléqep < sát.
(make a) rapid repeated sound usually on wood:: qw'ópx̲wem < qw'ópx̲w.
(make a) ringing sound when something drops:: ts'tés.
(make/have a) scratching noise:: t'lhóqw'els < t'élheqw' ~ t'lhóqw'.
(make/have a) sound getting softer:: théxweleqep < théxw ~ théx̲w.
(make/have a) squeaking sound (of a tree, of a chair, of shoes), squeaking (of shoes, trees), (creaking):: qá:ytl'em.
(make the) sound of a spank on a bottom, (fall down with a bang [Elders Group 5/19/76]):: welhéq'.
make the sound of water splashing or dripping fast, (make the sound of a waterfall, make the sound of pouring rain dripping or splashing in puddles loudly):: xwótqwem.
(making a) continuous rustling noise (of paper or silk or material), rustling (of leaves, paper, a sharp sound):: sá:wts'em < sawéts'em.
popping (of firecrackers):: tl'eltl'ó:lqwem < tl'ál ~ tl'á:l.
ringing sound when something drops (spoon, metal ashtray or something heavy):: ts'tés.
scraping sound (like scraping food off dishes), rattling (of dishes, metal pots, wagon on gravel):: q'átx̲em < q'et.
sound like (in voice):: staqí:l < t.
sound of boiling water:: xwótqwem.
splash (the noise and the action):: t'émeqw'.
splash (the sound and the action), [splash suddenly], splash once:: wet'émeqw' <

sound (CONT'D)

t'émeqw'.
splat, sound of something wet and soft dropped, to splatter:: wet'éleq.
squeak (of a mouse):: th'á:ykwem.
suction sound of feet pulling out of mud:: t'áxwqem.
the sound a frog makes (IHTTC only):: wex̲és.
to rattle (of dishes or anything else loose), jingle (of money or any metal shaken), peal or toll (of a bell), make the sound of a bell, to ring (of a bell, telephone, in the ears):: th'á:tsem < th'éts or th'á(:)ts.
to sigh (of a spirit-dancer), make a loud (breathy) noise:: xeqlhálém.
what does it sound like?, What does it sound like?, (how does it sound?):: selchí:meleqel < selchí:m ~ selchím.

soup
fish head soup:: x̲ots'oyíqw slhóp < x̲ots'oyíqw.
soup, (stew):: slhóp'.
(the) cooking, (soup, stew [DM, CT]):: sqwéls < qwó:ls.

sour)
(be) scowling (if mad or ate something sour), ((made a) funny (strange) face [Elders Group 1/21/76]):: sx̲éyx̲ewes < x̲éywel.
looking sad, (making a sour face [MV, EF]):: sló:ltes.
sour (unripe or half-ripe fruit, lemon, Oregon grape, fermenting fruit):: t'át'eth'em < t'áth'.

source
at the head or source of a river, the inside head or inlet of a river:: =qel.

sourdough bread:: t'át'ets'em seplíl (lit. sour + bread) < t'áts', seplíl

sourgrass
sourgrass, (sheep sorrel):: t'át'eth'em < t'áth'.

south
south wind:: tellhelhó:s < lhós.

South Fork of Nooksack River and village nearest Deming
Deming (Wash.), South Fork of Nooksack River & village:: xwe'éyem ~ xw'éyem < éy ~ éy:.

South Westminster
Reserve near New Westminster, B.C., (South Westminster [DF]):: Qiqá:yt.

south wind
south wind, warm wind:: schéxwem.

sow
sow s-th, drop or spread seed in rills, scatter s-th, (sowing s-th [AC]):: tl'épx̲t < tl'ép.
the planting, seeds to plant, what is planted (sown), garden:: spí:ls < pél (perhaps ~ pí:l by now).

Sowaqua Creek:: Swókwel < swókwel.

soy sauce:: chólmelelh tl'álhem (lit. Chinese style + salt) < chólmel, tl'álhem spade

shovel, spade:: lopál.

spaghetti:: tl'áqt ts'íyxw seplíl (lit. long + dry + bread) < tl'áqt, ts'íyxw, seplíl

Spaniard :: spayṓ:l.

spank

beat s-o up, kick s-o in fight, lick s-o (in fight), spank s-o, fight s-o (till he cries for ex.), fight s-o in anger, fight s-o back:: x̲éyet.
fall splat, (make the) sound of a spank or slap:: welhéleq' < welhéq'.
(make the) sound of a spank on a bottom, (fall down with a bang [Elders Group 5/19/76]):: welhéq'.
spank s-o:: kw'eqwíwét < kw'óqw.

spark)

jade (nephrite) (used for sharpening [chopping] stones), any agate (can be used as flint to strike a spark):: t'émq'ethel.
lots of sparks going up at the same time:: pá:yth'em < páyéts'em.
sparking, sparkling, exploding with sparks and making sparky noises, making sparky noises:: pá:yts'em < páyéts'em.
sparks, red hot ashes thrown out:: qw'á:ychep < qw'á:y.
(to spark), explode with sparks and make sparky noises:: páyéts'em, páyéts'em.
to spark (with a pop):: tl'á:lx̲em < tl'ál ~ tl'á:l.

sparkle

shine like a reflection, reflect, glitter, sparkle:: p'álq'em.
shining, (glittering, sparkling (with many reflections)):: p'elp'álq'em < p'álq'em.
sparking, sparkling, exploding with sparks and making sparky noises, making sparky noises:: pá:yts'em < páyéts'em.
sparkling (with reflections):: pá:yts'em < páyéts'em.

sparrow

song sparrow, also brown sparrow, (could include any or all of the following which occur in the Stó:lō area: Savannah sparrow, vesper sparrow, lark sparrow, tree sparrow, chipping sparrow, Harris sparrow, fox sparrow, white-crowned sparrow, golden-crowned sparrow, and song sparrow) (type of brown wren [BHTTC 11/15/76], larger wren (but smaller than robin) [Elders Group 2/18/76]):: sx̲wṓx̲wtha, sx̲wṓx̲wtha.
type of bird that begs for bones or food with the song: paspes(y)í(:)tsel kw'e sth'ò:m th'ò:m th'ò:m, probably a song sparrow:: paspesítsel ~ paspasyí:tsel ~ pespesí:tsel < pas ~ pes.

spatter

spotted with irregular shaped blobs (like if mud-spattered, used of dogs, deer, and other animals so marked):: st'á:lq.

spawn

a fish that's going to spawn:: chewélhem ~ tsewélhem ~ tsōwélhem < cháchew ~ cháchu.
be spawning:: chewélhem ~ tsewélhem ~ tsōwélhem < cháchew ~ cháchu.
salmon after spawning when its eggs are loose:: t'iléqel.
salmon after spawning, with no more eggs:: kwómexw.
spawning:: théwelhem < cháchew ~ cháchu.
spawning (in action when you see them):: théwelhem < cháchew ~ cháchu.

spawn (CONT'D)

to spawn:: chewélhem ~ tsewélhem ~ tsōwélhem < cháchew ~ cháchu.

speak

being spoken to (of babies in spirit dancing):: qwṓ:lqwelstem < qwà:l.
speak, talk, give a speech:: qwà:l.
speaking, speaker; :: qwóqwel < qwà:l.
speaking to a lot of people/at a gathering:: qwṓ:lqwel < qwà:l.

speaker

speaker; speaking:: qwóqwel < qwà:l.
speaker at a gathering, announcer at a gathering:: lheqqwóqwel or lheq qwóqwel < qwà:l.

spear

a point or bald hill on Harrison River where people waited to spear silver spring salmon:: Chth'éylem < chth'éylem.
miss s-th (in shooting at it with arrow, spear or gun):: qwíx̱wet < qwíx̱w.
prong of spear, prong of fish spear:: qáthexw.
spear animals by torchlight:: lex̱éywa ~ lex̱íwa.
spear (any kind), spear (for fish or war), fish-spear, telescopic spear for sturgeon, harpoon, detachable harpoon points:: tá:lh.
spear fish by torchlight, to torchlight, to pit-lamp:: lex̱éywa ~ lex̱íwa.
spearing fish by torchlight:: hálx̱eywa ~ hálx̱iwa < lex̱éywa ~ lex̱íwa.
spearing fish, spearing (fish):: thá:q'els < théq'.
spearing sqwéx̱em (silver spring salmon) in clear water after waiting for them:: chth'éylem.
spearing s-th:: tháq't < théq'.
spear it (a fish), stab s-o/s-th with something sharp, pierce s-o/s-th, prick s-o (with a pin, for ex.), poke s-o (with a pin, etc.):: thq'ét < théq'.
spear pole knot hitch (two half-hitches), clove-hitch knot:: ts'sítsim.
spear, shaft (of spear/harpoon/gaff-hook), gaff-hook pole:: s'álem.
spear-shaped rock on beach on the Fraser near Hill's Bar:: Tá:lh < tá:lh.
to miss a shot (an arrow, spear or gun):: qwíx̱w.
to spear fish:: thq'á:ls < théq'.

spear/harpoon/gaff-hook)

spear, shaft (of spear/harpoon/gaff-hook), gaff-hook pole:: s'álem.

special

make it especially for s-o:: swástexw < swá.

speckle

(have a) speckled face, (have) freckles:: tl'eltl'élx̱os < tl'él.

speechless

be dumbfounded, be surprised, be stupified, be speechless:: slholhekw'íwel ~ slholhekw'í:wel < lhó:kw' ~ lhókw'.
be startled, be dumbfounded, be shocked, be stupified, be speechless, be overwhelmed:: lholhekw'íwel ~ lholhkw'íwel < lhó:kw' ~ lhókw'.

spell

a sung spell, power to help or harm people or to do [ritual] burning, power to do witchcraft

spell (CONT'D)

and predict the future, an evil spell, (magic spell) (someone who has power to take things out of a person or put things in [by magic] [Elders Group 2/25/76], ritualist [Elders Group 1/21/76], witch [EB 4/25/78]):: syiwí:l ~ syewí:l < yéw: ~ yéw.
(cast a spell for s-o, use a magical power for s-o):: yewí:lmet < yéw: ~ yéw.
cast a spell on s-o, put a spell on s-o, shoot power into s-o:: x̲t'ét < x̲ét'.
cast a spell, throw a spell, put on a spell, shoot power:: x̲t'áls or x̲t'á:ls < x̲ét'.
casting an evil spell on s-o:: yewí:lt < yéw: ~ yéw.
war-whoop, ((probably) a sung spell before battle):: syiwí:leqw < yéw: ~ yéw.

sperm :: sq'óq'ey < q'ó:y ~ q'óy.

sphagnum)
(sphagnum) bog, marsh:: mó:qwem.

spherical
five spherical objects, five fruit, five rocks, five balls (five fruit in a group (as they grow on a plant) [AD]):: lhq'atsesóls < lheq'át ~ lhq'á:t.
really round, (perfectly spherical?):: xelókw'els < xél.
roughly spherical object(s), ball:: =ó:ls.
(spherical), round (of ball, apple, potato, rock, full moon, but not of a pear):: xelkw'ó:ls < xél.

Sphyrapicus (varius) ruber
Colaptes cafer cafer and rarely Colaptes cafer collaris, (if large is correct Dryocopus pileatus [AK], if small is correct, probably Sphyrapicus (varius) ruber or possibly Dryobates villosus harrisi and Dryobates villosus orius or Dryobates pubescens (esp.) gairdneri some zoologists replace the genus Dryobates with Dendrocopos, others with Picoides):: th'íq.
probably Sphyrapicus (varius) ruber and/or possibly Dryobates villosus harrisi and Dryobates villosus orius or(downy woodpecker) Dryobates pubescens (gairdneri esp.), forMunro and Cowan's Dryobates genus Peterson uses Dendrocopos andUdvardy uses Picoides:: qw'opx̲wiqsélem < qw'ópx̲w.

spider :: q'ésq'esetsel < q'ey ~ q'i.
daddy long-legs, harvestman spider:: tl'áleqtxel q'ésq'esetsel < tl'áqt.
daddy long-legs (spider), harvestman spider:: tl'áleqtxel q'esq'ésetsel < q'ey ~ q'i.

spill
pour s-th out, pour out s-th, spill it:: kw'lhát < kw'élh.
spill (on the face?):: kw'lhó:s < kw'élh.
tip over, spill (of liquid or solid), spilled, spill accidentally:: kw'élh.

Spilogale gracilis latifrons
baby Mephitis mephitis spissigrada, possibly Spilogale gracilis latifrons:: selílé x̲.

spin
fire-drill, stick spun to start fire:: sí:lcheptel < sél or sí(:)l.
it's twined (like rolled on thigh and twisted, spun):: sí:ltem < sél or sí(:)l.
spindle for spinning wool, a hand spinner:: sélseltel < sél or sí(:)l.
spindle for spinning wool, a hand spinner, a spinning machine:: shxwqáqelets' < qálets'.
spinning (while hanging), (twirling):: ts'á:lq'em < ts'el.
spinning, whirling:: siselts'iyósem < sél or sí(:)l.

spin (CONT'D)

spinning wool:: qáqelets' < qálets'.
spin wool or twine:: qálets'.
wool spinner, spindle for spinning wool, spinning stick:: sélsel < sél or sí(:)l.

spinal

spinal rope inside sturgeon, (sturgeon spinal cord):: qw'ólhla.

spindle

spindle for spinning wool, a hand spinner:: sélseltel < sél or sí(:)l.
spindle for spinning wool, a hand spinner, a spinning machine:: shxwqáqelets' < qálets'.
wool spinner, spindle for spinning wool, spinning stick:: sélsel < sél or sí(:)l.

spine

backbone (of human or other creatures), spine (human or other creature):: x̲ekw'ólesewíts < x̲ekw'óles.
break one's spine, break one's back, have a humpback/hunchback:: lekwewíts < lékw.
(someone's) spine, (someone's) backbone:: th'omewích ~ th'ó:bewíts < sth'ó:m.
the spine, the backbone:: shxwth'omewíts < sth'ó:m.

spines

tiny fin above tail of fish, (perhaps spines above tail of some fish):: sx̲élhx̲elh < x̲élh.

spinner

spindle for spinning wool, a hand spinner:: sélseltel < sél or sí(:)l.
wool spinner, spindle for spinning wool, spinning stick:: sélsel < sél or sí(:)l.

spinning machine

spindle for spinning wool, a hand spinner, a spinning machine:: shxwqáqelets' < qálets'.

Spiraea douglasii:: t'áts'elhp < t'á:ts'.

spirea

pink spirea, "hardhack":: t'áts'elhp < t'á:ts'.

Spirit

Holy Spirit, Holy Ghost:: X̲áx̲e Smestí:yexw < x̲áx̲e.

spirit :: smímstiyexw < mestíyexw.

an Indian dancer's spirit power:: syúwél ~ syéw:el < yéw: ~ yéw.
a spirit power of a kw'őxweqs dancer, (perhaps wolverine or badger spirit power):: sqoyép < sqoyép.
conscience, spirit (which can be lost temporarily), soul, life-spirit, power of one's will:: smestíyexw < mestíyexw.
get a spooky or spooked feeling, afraid that bad spirits are around, get spooked, fear something behind:: x̲éysel.
getting spooked, being afraid that bad spirits are around, spooky feeling:: x̲éyx̲esel < x̲éysel.
guardian spirit, spirit power:: =ó:lkwlh, =ó:lkwlh.
soul, spirit of a living person:: shxwelí.

spirit-dance

a kind of spirit-dance done after the syúwel (spirit power) hasleft a dancer but the dancer

spirit-dance (CONT'D)

still needs to dance:: qw'éx̲weqs.
an experienced spirit dancer:: sts'eláxwem.
a non-spirit-dancer:: st'ólkwlh.
a spirit-dance, a winter-dance:: smílha < mílha.
babysitter (for new spirit-dancers), any of the workers who help in initiating a spirit-dancer, (initiator or helper of spirit-dancers):: xólhemilh ~ xòlhemí:lh < xólh.
(be) sighing (of a spirit-dancer):: xáqlhelem < xeqlhálém.
diatomaceous earth (could be mixed with things to whiten them--for ex. dog and goat wool), white clay for white face paint (for pure person spirit-dancers), white powder from mountains, white clay they make powder from to lighten goat and dog wool for blankets, powder, talc, white face paint:: st'ewŏ́kw'.
(doing) spirit-dancing, winter-dancing (when they're in action):: mímelha < mílha.
have the last spirit dance of the season, have the "sweep up":: yekw'ólhem or perhaps yekw'wólhem < yókw' ~ yóqw'.
Indian dance-house, "smoke-house", (spirit-dance building):: smilha'áwtxw < mílha.
Indian red paint (used by spirit dancers, ritualists, and Indian doctors or shamans):: témélh.
large rattle used at spirit-dances:: syŏ́wméxwtses.
lift s-o (of a spirit dancer being initiated):: shxwóxwelstexw < xwá.
longhouse for spirit-dancers, the big house, smokehouse (for spirit-dancing):: stháwtxw < thi ~ tha ~ the ~ thah ~ theh.
longhouse, smokehouse (for spirit-dancing, etc.), Indian house, plank house:: xwelmexwáwtxw < xwélmexw.
new spirit dancer's headband:: qítes ~ qéytes < qít.
non-spirit-dancers (lots of them):: st'elt'ólkwlh < st'ólkwlh.
sighing over and over (of a spirit-dancer before or after dancing):: xaqxeqlhálem < xeqlhálém.
(the) spirit-dancing:: smímelha < mílha.
to sigh (of a spirit-dancer), make a loud (breathy) noise:: xeqlhálém.
to spirit-dance, to spirit-dance (of a group), have aspirit-dance, to winter-dance:: mílha.
to sweep up, the sweep-up (last spirit dance of season in a given longhouse):: íx̲wethet < íx̲w.

spirit-dancer

deer hoof rattle of spirit-dancer (stick with deer hoof rattles tied onto it):: kwóxwemal ~ kwóxwmal < kwoxw, kwetsmí:l, kwechmí:l < kwáchem ~ kwátsem..
his/her dance:: sqw'eyílexs < qw'eyílex ~ qw'eyíléx.
new dancer (new spirit-dancer), (new) baby (in spirit-dancing):: x̲awsó:lh < x̲á:ws.
new spirit-dancer:: x̲awsólkwlh or x̲awsó:lkwlh < x̲á:ws.
new spirit dancer's cane:: q'ewú:w < q'éwe.
new spirit-dancer's head-dress or [cedar-bark] hat:: sx̲wóyéleqws te x̲awsólkwlh < sx̲wóyéleqw.
paint one's face red or black (spirit dancer, Indian doctor, ritualist, etc.):: lhíx̲esem < lhá:x̲ ~ lháx̲.
people without paint on face (non-dancers):: s'ep'ó:s < á:p' ~ áp'.
spirit-dancer's paint:: témelh < témélh.
spirit-dancer's uniform, (any) coordinated outfit:: s-hóyews < hóyiws.
spirit power song:: syúwél ~ syéw:el < yéw: ~ yéw.
spirit power, spirit-dancer:: =ó:lkwlh.
the painted people (dancers):: slhílhex̲es < lhá:x̲ ~ lháx̲.
to paint red or black (spirit dancer, Indian doctor, etc.):: lhíx̲ < lhá:x̲ ~ lháx̲.
to scream, holler (of a spirit-dancer):: kwátsem ~ kwáchem.
trimmings on uniform (paddles, etc.):: stl'íitl'ets < tl'íts ~ tl'ích.

spirit-dancing
dog-hair blanket dancing apron (DM 12/4/64):: kw'eléw ~ kw'elṓw.
spirit-dancing costume, wool hat for spirit-dancer (Deming):: s-hóyiws.

spirit dream
spirit dream, vision, (any) dream:: s'élíyá < élíyá.

spirit power
guardian spirit, spirit power:: =ó:lkwlh.
Indian doctor, shaman, medicine man, Indian doctor's spirit power (Elders Group 11/19/75):: shxwlá:m < lá:m.
it went into him/her (of spirit power):: thex̲we'í:ls.
spirit power of an Indian doctor or shaman:: slá:m < lá:m.
spirit power, spirit-dancer:: =ó:lkwlh.

spirit song
also the words of Mack's spirit song:: Á:yiya.
bring it out for the first time (of a spirit-song):: p'í:t < p'í:.
feel like singing a spirit song, be in a trance making sighsand crying sounds before singing a spirit song, be in the beginning of a trance before the spirit song is recognizable (the motions and sounds, crying out or wailing before singing):: lhéch.
to sing along or follow in singing a spirit song:: t'à:m.

Spirogyra spp.:: stíxem < tíxem.

spit
spit it out, spit it up:: lhex̲wót ~ lhx̲wó:t < lhex̲w.
spit, saliva:: slhx̲wélhcha < lhex̲w.
spitting:: lhéx̲welhcha < lhex̲w.
to spit:: lhx̲wélhcha < lhex̲w.

Spizella arborea
Melospiza melodia morphna, (perhaps any/all of the following: Passerculus sandwichensis brooksi, Pooecetes gramineus, Chondestes grammacus, Spizella arborea, Spizella passerina, Zonotrichia querula, Passerella iliaca, Zonotrichia leucophrys, Zonotrichia atricapilla, Melospiza melodia morphna):: sx̲wṓx̲wtha.

Spizella passerina
Melospiza melodia morphna, (perhaps any/all of the following: Passerculus sandwichensis brooksi, Pooecetes gramineus, Chondestes grammacus, Spizella arborea, Spizella passerina, Zonotrichia querula, Passerella iliaca, Zonotrichia leucophrys, Zonotrichia atricapilla, Melospiza melodia morphna):: sx̲wṓx̲wtha.

splash :: lhélt < lhél.
get splashed:: lhá:ltem < lhél.
make the sound of water splashing or dripping fast, (make the sound of a waterfall, make the sound of pouring rain dripping or splashing in puddles loudly):: xwótqwem.
splashing, splashing (lots of times):: t'ó:mqw'em < t'émeqw'.
splash on the face:: lhéltes < lhél.
splash s-o in the face, squirt s-o in the face:: lhélest < lhél.
splash s-o with water, spray s-o with water:: lhéltest < lhél.

splash (CONT'D)

splash (the noise and the action):: t'émeqw'.
splash (the sound and the action), [splash suddenly], splash once:: wet'émeqw' < t'émeqw'.

splat

fall splat, (make the) sound of a spank or slap:: welhéleq' < welhéq'.
splat, sound of something wet and soft dropped, to splatter:: wet'éleq.

splatter

splat, sound of something wet and soft dropped, to splatter:: wet'éleq.

splice

join two poles together, splice it together (of a rope), (join together on the ends):: t'qwíqst.

splinter

get a sliver or splinter in the foot:: xéts'xel.
get a sliver or splinter in the hand:: xéts'ches.
scorch s-th, blacken s-th with fire, heat it up (near a fire), burning a canoe with pitchwood to remove splinters and burn on black pitch):: qw'á:yt < qw'á:y.

split

barbecue sticks, (split roasting stick):: qw'éltel < qw'él.
burst open, split open of its own accord (like a dropped watermelon):: tl'xáx̱el < tl'éx.
chop wood, split wood, (chop/split s-th wood):: séq'et < séq'.
chop wood (with an axe), split wood:: th'iqw'élchep or th'iyqw'éltsep < th'íyeqw'.
ear-splitting:: seq'á:lí:ya < séq'.
mistake in splitting roots by making them uneven:: t'ats'ex̱elí:m < t'á:ts'.
place above Yale where the Fraser River splits around a rock, island above Steamboat Island (latter just below Five-Mile Creek):: Sx̱wesálh < x̱wés.
split firewood:: th'iyeqw'á:ls < th'íyeqw'.
split it (firewood):: th'íyeqw't < th'íyeqw'.
split off, break off, break a piece off, break in two, split in two:: péqw.
split s-th, crack s-th:: seq'át ~ sq'át < séq'.
split s-th open (with fingernail):: thíts'et.
splitting firewood:: th'óyeqw'els < th'íyeqw'.
splitting wood (esp. blanks and bolts):: póqwels < péqw.
splitting wood, (splitting it (a lot of wood):: seq'séq'et < séq'.
to crack, to split (of its own accord), ((also) cracked, a crack [AC]):: séq'.
to separate people fighting, to split up people fighting:: memáx < má ~ má'-.
to split roots from the wrong end (small end):: séx̱w.
to split s-th open (like deer or fish):: tl'xáx̱et < tl'éx.

spoil

gone soft and spoiled (of dried fish):: th'íth'eqel < sth'í:qel.
spoiling s-th:: qelqelí:lt < qél.
spoil s-th, destroy s-th:: qelqé:ylt or qelqí:lt < qél.
spoil s-th (purposely):: qelí:lt < qél.
turn bad, (get) spoiled (of clothes for ex.), (get) dirty:: qelqéyl or qelqí:l < qél.

spook

get a spooky or spooked feeling, afraid that bad spirits are around, get spooked, fear

spook (CONT'D)

something behind:: x̲éysel.

getting spooked, being afraid that bad spirits are around, spooky feeling:: x̲éyx̲esel < x̲éysel.

Spook's Point

rock shaped like a man's head with a sx̲wó:yx̲wey mask on a point near the head of Harrison River, the point also called Spook's Point:: Sx̲wó:yx̲wey ~ Sx̲wóyx̲wey < sx̲wó:yx̲wey ~ sx̲wóyx̲wey.

spoon

big serving spoon, spoon with handle about ten to 12 inches long, ladle, (spoon carved from mountain goat horn):: x̲álew.

big wooden dish (often two feet long), feast dish, wooden platter, (big stirring spoon [LJ], carved wooden spoon, big wooden spoon [AC, BJ, DM]):: qwelhyő̃welh ~ qwelhliyő̃welh ~ qwelhlyúwelh < qwélh.

handle of a spoon:: skwélemel < kwél.

long-handled stirring spoon:: shxwqwáylhechàls < qwá:y.

(metal) spoon:: spú:l.

ringing sound when something drops (spoon, metal ashtray or something heavy):: ts'tés.

soapberry spoon, soapberry paddle, short-handled spoon, flat spoon for sx̲wő̃sem:: th'émtel < th'ím ~ th'í:m.

spoon-shaped bone back of upper lip of sturgeon:: x̲álew.

spore

bloom or (plant) fuzz (spore, pollen, seed fluff) after it bursts:: spekw'ém < pékw' ~ péqw'.

it burst (of spores or seed fluff):: pekw'ém < pékw' ~ péqw'.

smoke puffing out, (puff out (dust, powder, plant spores, seed fluff, light snow, smoke), form puffs of dust):: pékw' ~ péqw'.

when plant fuzz blows:: pókw'em < pékw' ~ péqw'.

spot

female black bear with white spot [or mark] on the chest:: Sx̲éylmòt or sx̲éylmòt < x̲él ~ x̲é:yl ~ x̲í:l

(get/have) white spots on the skin:: th'íq.

(have?) white spots:: sp'eq'p'íq' < p'éq'.

(have?) white spotted skin:: sp'íq' < p'éq'.

male black bear with white spot [or mark] on the chest:: Sx̲é:ylmet or sx̲é:ylmet < x̲él ~ x̲é:yl ~ x̲í:l

mark s-th, blaze it (of a trail), get/have s-th spotted (marked and located), make note of s-th:: x̲e'áth'stexw < x̲áth' ~ x̲e'áth'.

old salmon (ready to die, spotted):: x̲éyqeya.

soft spot on (top of) a baby's head, fontanel:: sqe'éleqw < qí: ~ qí'.

spotted:: stl'eqtl'éq.

spotted (marked and located):: sx̲e'áth' < x̲áth' ~ x̲e'áth'.

spotted with circles or round dots:: tl'eltl'élx̲ < tl'él.

spotted with irregular shaped blobs (like if mud-spattered, used of dogs, deer, and other animals so marked):: st'á:lq.

spotted with lots of [irregular] spots:: st'elt'élq < st'á:lq.

spouse)

brother-in-law's wife, (spouse's sibling's spouse), (step-sibling, step-brother, step-sister [AC]):: slets'éleq < láts'.

child's spouse, son-in-law, daughter-in-law, (man's) sister's husband:: schiwtálh.

child's spouse's parent, child's spouse's sibling, child's in-laws:: skw'élwés.

spouse (CONT'D)

husband's brothers, (perhaps also wife's sisters?, spouse's siblings?, sibling's spouses?):: smetmátexwtel < smátexwtel.
reject someone as a spouse or partner for one's child:: qá:lmílh < qéylem ~ qé:ylem ~ qí(:)lem.
reject someone as a spouse or partner for your child:: qá:lmílh.
relative of deceased spouse:: th'á:ya.
relative of deceased spouse, mother/brother/sister/cousin/relative of deceased husband, dead spouse's relative or sibling, daughter-in-law if son dies:: ts'á:ya.
sons-in-law, daughters-in-law, children's spouses:: schí:wetálh < schiwtálh.
spouse's sibling, sibling's spouse (cross sex), for ex., husband's brother, (wife's sister, woman's sister's husband, man's brother's wife):: smátexwtel.
steal someone's spouse:: ts'eláltxw < ts'el.
to marry a sibling of one's deceased spouse:: th'áyá:m < ts'á:ya.
uncle's wife, aunt's husband, parent's sibling's spouse, uncle by marriage, aunt by marriage:: xchápth ~ schápth.

spouse (cross-sex)
husband's brother, wife's sister, spouse's sibling (cross-sex), brother-in-law, sister-in-law, sibling's spouse (cross-sex):: smátexwtel.

spouse's parent
in-laws (?), parents-in-law, spouse's parents:: skw'álhew < skw'ílhew.
mother-in-law, father-in-law, spouse's parent, parent-in-law:: skw'ílhew.

spouse's sibling
husband's brothers, (perhaps also wife's sisters?, spouse's siblings?, sibling's spouses?):: smetmátexwtel < smátexwtel.
spouse's sibling, sibling's spouse (cross sex), for ex., husband's brother, (wife's sister, woman's sister's husband, man's brother's wife):: smátexwtel.

spouse's sibling (cross-sex)
husband's brother, wife's sister, spouse's sibling (cross-sex), brother-in-law, sister-in-law, sibling's spouse (cross-sex):: smátexwtel.

spouse's sibling's spouse)
brother-in-law's wife, (spouse's sibling's spouse), (step-sibling, step-brother, step-sister [AC]):: slets'éleq < láts'.

sprain
(get a) sprained foot, leg got out of joint:: plhéqw'xel ~ p'lhéqw'xel.
(get or develop a) sprain, to sprain:: ts'lhóqw'.
leg got sprained, (sprain one's ankle [JL]):: ts'lhéqw'xel < ts'lhóqw'.
sprained ankle:: xweth'éqw'xel.
sprained wrist:: xweth'éqw'tses.
sprain, (getting sprained?):: t'ot'á < t'ó.
sprain the back:: ts'lhéqw'ewíts < ts'lhóqw'.
to sprain:: t'ó.
your back is sprained:: xwt'ó:welh < t'ó.

spray :: lhó:ltes < lhél.
blowing spray (humorously said of a child teething):: pópe<u>x</u>wels < pó<u>x</u>w.

spray (CONT'D)

blow (spray) on a patient (of an Indian doctor or shaman), blow spray on s-o/s-th (of a shaman, a person ironing, a child teething):: póx̲wet < póx̲w.
splash s-o with water, spray s-o with water:: lhéltest < lhél.
spray gun:: spópex̲welsà:ls < póx̲w.
spraying (as a structured activity):: lhá:ltelechá:ls < lhél.

spread

fish-spreader for drying fish, cross-piece for drying fish, salmon stretcher:: t'á:ts'.
run over it (with car), spread it (for ex. on bread with knife), put it up (of wallpaper), (stick it on), stick s-th closed (with pitch for ex.):: tl'íq't < tl'íq'.
sow s-th, drop or spread seed in rills, scatter s-th, (sowing s-th [AC]):: tl'épx̲t < tl'ép.
spread apart s-o's legs:: px̲íwét < páx̲.
spread it out (of blanket, net, book, etc.):: tlhét ~ tlhát ~ telhét < télh.
spread one's legs (sitting for example), (be spread in the bottom):: spapx̲íwel < páx̲.
spread red or black paint on s-th(?)/s-o:: lhíx̲et < lhá:x̲ ~ lháx̲.
spread s-th, widen s-th:: wí:qet < wí:q ~ wíq.
spread the eyelids open with the fingers (done to oneself or to someone else), (probably also spread s-th apart):: páx̲et < páx̲.
spread them out to dry (berries, bulrushes, etc.):: ts'íyxwt ~ ts'éyxwt < ts'íyxw ~ ts'éyxw ~ ch'íyxw.

Spring

(be) Spring, [cyclic period] when everything comes up:: kw'íyles ~ kw'éyles < kw'í ~ kw'íy.
(be) Spring, [time or season] when everything comes up:: temkw'éyles < kw'í ~ kw'íy.

spring

a spring water stream near Yakweakwioose:: Thíthx̲ < thíx̲.
a spring-water stream south of Skowkale:: Temélhem < témélh.
a sprout or shoot (esp. of the kinds peeled and eaten in spring), sweet green inner shoots, green berry shoots, salmonberry shoots, wild raspberry shoots and greens, salmonberry sprouts, blackcap shoots, thimbleberry shoots, wild rhubarb shoots, fern shoots:: stháthqiy.
Harrison Hot Springs:: Qwó:ls < qwó:ls.
medicine spring on the Fraser River beach about a half mile above (north) of the American Bar beach:: Xwth'kw'ém < th'ekw' or th'íkw'.
place in Fraser River where there's an underwater spring of cold water:: Mimexwílem < mímexwel.
spring (season), (time to sprout up):: temqw'íles ~ temqw'éyles < qw'íl.
spring tide (when a river first rises in May):: qó:.
spring (water source):: thíx̲.
time of the baby sockeye's coming, early spring (usually April), April moon:: temkwíkwexel.

spring gold

wild carrot (possibly spring gold or wild carraway), domestic carrot (both that planted and that gone wild):: xáwéq.

spring salmon

a point or bald hill on Harrison River where people waited to spear silver spring salmon:: Chth'éylem < chth'éylem.
August run spring salmon that go up Silver Creek (near Hope):: shxwōqw'ṓ:lh.

spring salmon (CONT'D)
coiled up méthelh rope for fishing (for sturgeon and spring salmon):: ts'tíxem.
early (March) spring salmon:: spó:x̱em ~ spéx̱em.
Harrison River spring salmon, Harrison River chinook salmon, big Chehalis River spring salmon, (preserved (smoked?) meat [AC: Tait dialect]):: pó:qw' ~ póqw'.
jack spring salmon with black nose:: tl'elxálōwelh or tl'elxálōllh < tl'él.
July to August, (big spring salmon time):: temth'oló:lh < sth'olólh.
October moon, time to smoke Chehalis spring salmon:: tempó:kw' < pó:qw' ~ póqw'.
silver spring salmon that came up Harrison River and Chehalis Creek, (first spring salmon [Deming]):: sqwéx̱em < qwéx̱em.
small Chehalis spring salmon:: pepqw'ólh < pó:qw' ~ póqw'.
spearing sqwéx̱em (silver spring salmon) in clear water after waiting for them:: chth'éylem.
spring salmon (generic), (Chinook salmon):: tl'élx̱xel ~ tl'álx̱xel < tl'él.
spring salmon net:: tl'elxéltel (or tl'elx̱xéltel) < tl'él.
spring salmon which goes to Chehalis Lake in May then returns to salt water:: sth'olólh.
white Fraser River spring salmon that goes upriver with the redspring salmon, (white Fraser River chinook salmon):: speqá:s.

spring snare (trap):: s'eweltá:l < íwel, s'eweltá:l < íwel.
spring snare [s-th], [a?] spring snare:: weltá:lt.

spring water
a spring water stream with source at present-day Sardis Park, Soowahlihl:: (Th'ewálí:l) < th'éw.

sprinkle
(get sprinkled):: lhá:ltem < lhél.
sprinkle it (usually by hand):: lhélt < lhél.
starting to sprinkle, start sprinkling:: lhálétem < lhél.

sprout
a sprout or shoot (esp. of the kinds peeled and eaten in spring), sweet green inner shoots, green berry shoots, salmonberry shoots, wild raspberry shoots and greens, salmonberry sprouts, blackcap shoots, thimbleberry shoots, wild rhubarb shoots, fern shoots:: stháthqiy.
alfalfa sprouts:: tsqwá:y spéxwqel < qwá:y, píxw
(lit. green + fine airborne seed)
bean sprouts:: ts'íts'esem tl'íkw'els < ts'ís, tl'íkw'els
(lit. growing up + bean)
brussel(s) sprouts:: mémeles kápech < mél:e, kápech
(lit. many little children of + cabbage)
cow parsnip sprout (especially the edible inside part):: sóqw'.
spring (season), (time to sprout up):: temqw'íles ~ temqw'éyles < qw'íl.
sprouted up, sprouting up:: qwáqel.
sprout(ing) up, stick(ing) its head out of the ground (of a plant):: qw'íles < qw'íl.
to sprout (from root):: kw'íqel < kw'í ~ kw'íy.

spruce
needle of spruce:: ts'ets'éqw' < ts'éqw'.
pitchwood (esp. fir, pine, spruce):: kw'íxwelhp < kw'íxw.
spruce tree, Sitka spruce:: ts'qw'élhp < ts'éqw'.

Spuzzum :: Spíyem.

Spuzzum (CONT'D)
Spuzzum village (on south bank of Spuzzum Creek at its mouth onto the Fraser River), also Spuzzum Creek:: Spíyem.

Spuzzum Creek
Spuzzum village (on south bank of Spuzzum Creek at its mouth onto the Fraser River), also Spuzzum Creek:: Spíyem.

Squamish
Squamish people:: Sqwx̲wó:mex.
Squamish people:: Tellhós < lhós.

square
lots of squares:: st'elt'eláx̲el < st'eláx̲el.
square, corner, arm with elbow out:: st'eláx̲el.

squash
peel s-th (esp. fruit or vegetable root or a vegetable like squash or a round object):: xepólst < xíp.

squashberry
possibly high-bush cranberry, more likely squashberry:: kwúkwewels.

squat :: xópethet < xóp'.
(be) squatting:: sxóxep < xóp'.

Squatits
Squatits village on east bank of Fraser river across from the north end of Seabird Island, Peters Indian Reserves #1, 1a, and 2 on site:: Skw'átets < kw'átem.

"squaw"
wife (not respectful), the "old lady", "squaw", mistress:: chá:xw.

squeak
(make/have a) squeaking sound (of a tree, of a chair, of shoes), squeaking (of shoes, trees), (creaking):: qá:ytl'em.
squeaking (of lots of mice):: th'eth'elá:ykwem < th'á:ykwem.
squeak (of a mouse):: th'á:ykwem.

squeal
squealing (like a pig for ex.):: kwíkwekwchá:m < kwátsem ~ kwáchem.
to squeal on someone:: qwélqwelàtstem < qwà:l.

squeeze
(be) squeezed in, jammed up, tight:: sx̲ex̲ákw' < x̲ékw'.
get squeezed (in hand or fingers):: p'íth'em < p'í:.
squeeze s-th/s-o, wring s-th (of clothes), pinch s-th/s-o:: p'íth'et < p'í:.
squeezing out:: p'íp'eth'em < p'í:.
squeezing s-th/s-o:: p'íp'eth'et < p'í:.
squeezing the breast of s-o/s-th, milking s-o/s-th:: p'ip'eth'élmet < p'í:.

Squia-ala

Squia-ala (now Chilliwack Indian Reserve #7):: Sx̲woyehá:lá < x̲wà:y ~ x̲wá:y.

squint

wink at each other, ((maybe) squint [EB]):: th'ikwóstel < th'iykw'.

Squirrel

Douglas squirrel, possibly a character name, i.e. Squirrel:: skwóye or Skwóye.

squirrel

board for stretching squirrel or skunk hides, etc.:: tépelhállh < tpólh.
Douglas squirrel:: sqwéth'elh.
Douglas squirrel, possibly a character name, i.e. Squirrel:: skwóye or Skwóye.
flying squirrel:: sqépò:thèl < qep'.
squirrel, Douglas squirrel:: skwóye.
you get covered on the mouth (by a flying squirrel at night for ex.):: qep'ó:ythòm < qep'.

squirt

splash s-o in the face, squirt s-o in the face:: lhélest < lhél.
to squirt:: wet'éléth'.

squish

crush (of berries), smash (of berries), squish (of berries, etc.), to mash:: tósem < tós.
squish it up:: mítl'et.
squish s-th round and filled, smash s-th round and filled:: méqw'et < méqw' ~ mṓqw'.
touch s-o purposely, squish it (of berries, etc.), smash s-th, mash it (berries, potatoes, carrots, etc.), bump it:: tóset < tós.

stab

spear it (a fish), stab s-o/s-th with something sharp, pierce s-o/s-th, prick s-o (with a pin, for ex.), poke s-o (with a pin, etc.):: thq'ét < théq'.

stack

(be) below, (be) underneath, (be) at the bottom of a pile or stack:: stl'epólwelh ~ stl'pólwelh < tl'ép.

staff

cane, staff:: q'éwe.

stagger

staggering (after you trip for ex.):: tá:lstem < tél ~ tá:l ~ tiy.
staggering around:: x̲wex̲weló:ystem < x̲weló:y, yitá:lstem < tél ~ tá:l ~ tiy.
to stumble, get staggered:: télstem < tél ~ tá:l ~ tiy.
you get staggered:: x̲wex̲weló:ysthòm < x̲weló:y.

stagnant

puddle that's always dirty, dirty pond, stagnant pool of water, (it never dries out [AK]):: th'qwélhcha.
stagnant water lake or ponds at the downriver end of Skw'átets or Peters Reserve near Laidlaw:: Th'qwélhcha < th'qwélhcha.

stake

stake it (for ex. of a horse):: lóqwet.

stamp

stick it on, paste it on (of stamps or anything):: t'elémt < t'elém.

stand

legs crossed, cross one's ankles (either sitting or standing) [prob. error], (ankles crossed (either sitting or standing)):: q'eyáweth'xel < q'ey ~ q'i.
(someone) standing in the middle of a crowd:: s-hómkwstem.
standing up:: lhex̲é:ylex < lhéx̲.
stand up:: lhex̲éyléx < lhéx̲.
stand up (by oneself):: lhx̲eylexlómet < lhéx̲.
stand up for s-o (respected):: xwiléxmet or xwíléxmet < xwíléx.
stand up, rise from a seat:: xwíléx.
two ropes, two threads, two sticks, two poles, two poles standing up:: isalámeth' < isá:le ~ isále ~ isá:la.
upright, standing, height, stature, pole:: =ámets' ~ =ámeth' ~ =ó:meth' ~ =emeth'.

star :: kwósel.

stare

stare at someone's face, look at s-o's face, stare at s-o, look at s-o:: kw'ótsest < kw'áts ~ kw'éts.
staring:: kw'okw'etsíls < kw'áts ~ kw'éts.
staring at s-o:: xwkw'ókw'etsest < kw'áts ~ kw'éts.

star-flowered Solomon's seal

"snakeberry", including False Solomon's seal, star-flowered Solomon's seal, and probably Twisted-stalk and Hooker's fairy bells:: sth'íms te álhqey < álhqey ~ álhqay.

start

a sound heard starting up again in the distance:: ehálé qep < ehó.
begin, start, (be) just started, just began, be just begun:: yálhò < yalh.
begin(ning) to, start(ing) to, inceptive:: mí ~ mé ~ me.
fire-drill, stick spun to start fire:: sí:lcheptel < sél or sí(:)l.
(just) started (to do something):: wiyálhò < yalh.
(probably) start to (no citation gloss, just in context):: ésta.
starting to smell good:: iyáléqepthet < éy ~ éy:.
starting to sprinkle, start sprinkling:: lhálétem < lhél.
start, started:: iyóthet.
start to struggle, start to flip around to escape (fish esp.):: kwetl'éthet < kwá:.
tinder, material used to start a fire with (fine dried cedar bark):: syeqwlhá:ltel < yéqw.

startle

be startled, be dumbfounded, be shocked, be stupified, be speechless, be overwhelmed:: lholhekw'íwel ~ lholhkw'íwel < lhó:kw' ~ lhókw'.
startled s-o, (excited s-o [Elders Group 3/2/77]):: lhkw'íwel:exw < lhó:kw' ~ lhókw'.

starve

somebody is made to fast, he is starved (purposely):: xwátem < xwá.

starve (CONT'D)
starve, be starving, be famished, (be extremely hungry [Deming,JL]):: xwá.
starving:: xwexwá < xwá.
starving oneself, being on a "crash" diet:: xwexwóthet < xwá.
to abstain from food, to fast, starve oneself:: xwóthet < xwá.

state
be in a state of -ness:: =tem.

stationary
a set net, a stationary net:: semláliyel < mí:l ~ míl.

stative :: s=.
have, get, stative or be with colors:: ts= ~ ts'.
stative, be:: s=.
stative (with color terms), have/get (elsewhere):: ch=, ts= ~ ch=.

Statlu Creek
Statlu Creek, one of the main tributaries of Chehalis Creek:: stótelō < tó:l ~ tò:l.

statue
a stone like a statue at Harrison Lake, probably Doctor's Point:: Skoyá:m ~ Skeyá:m.
likeness, portrait, photograph, photo, statue:: sx̲wíythi ~ sx̲wéythi < x̲wíyth.

stature)
short person, short (in stature):: ch'í:tl'emeth' < ts'í:tl' ~ ts'ítl'.
upright, standing, height, stature, pole:: =ámets' ~ =ámeth' ~ =ó:meth' ~ =emeth'.

stay
at home, be living (somewhere), stay:: tl'eláxw ~ tl'láxw < tl'élexw.
stay here, stay, remain at a place:: í ò < í.
stay in one place:: tl'eláxwelets < tl'élexw.
stay right here, staying right here:: í ò kw'eló < í.
to stay at home:: álwem.

steady
(have a) steady sound that's been stopped for a while:: thxwáléqep < théxw ~ théx̲w.
(have) a steady toothache, have a toothache:: yélyelesem < yél:és.
hold it steady, (hold s-th steady):: tl'eláxwstexw < tl'élexw.

steak:: tsétsmel sméyeth < tséts, méyeth
(lit. cut off + meat)

steal :: qá:l.
steal from s-o, rob s-o, short-change s-o:: qá:lt < qá:l.
stealing:: qáqel < qá:l.
steal someone's spouse:: ts'eláltxw < ts'el.

stealthy
be stealthy:: t'et'ás < t'ás.

steam
  bake underground, (steam-cook underground, cook in a steam-pit):: qetás < qá:t.
  baking underground:: qétes < qá:t.
  be steaming (in many places), be cloudy with rain-clouds:: pelpólx̱wem < poléx̱wem.
  get fog on the water, (get steam (of the ground) [DC]):: qwélxel.
  mountain on the west (C.P.R.) side of the Fraser River above American Bar which had a steaming pond at the top, (year-round village at mouth of American Creek on west bank of the Fraser River [Duff]):: Qétex̱em < qá:t.
  steaming:: pó:lex̱wem < poléx̱wem.
  steaming it:: pó:lxwt < poléx̱wem.
  steam s-th:: poléxwt < poléx̱wem.
  to steam, start to steam:: poléx̱wem, poléx̱wem.

steamboat :: stim:ṓ:t.

Steamboat Island
  place above Yale where the Fraser River splits around a rock, island above Steamboat Island (latter just below Five-Mile Creek):: Sx̱wesálh < x̱wés.

steam-cook
  bake underground, (steam-cook underground, cook in a steam-pit):: qetás < qá:t.

steam-cooked
  stuff steam-cooked underground, what is baked underground:: sqetás < qá:t.

steam-pit)
  bake underground, (steam-cook underground, cook in a steam-pit):: qetás < qá:t.

steelhead (trout)
  steelhead fishing place on the Fraser River below Lhílhkw'elqs, at Hogg Slough:: Qéywex̱em < qí:wx̱ ~ qéywx̱ ~ qá:wx̱ ~ qáwx̱.
  steelhead trout:: qí:wx̱ ~ qéywx̱ ~ qá:wx̱ ~ qáwx̱.

steep
  Bare Bluffs, a steep slope on the west side of Harrison Lake:: Lhó:leqwet.
  steep drop-off, a drop-off, very steep slope, steep shore, steep riverbank, a slide:: x̱éylés.
  steep hill, sloping ground:: sqotemí:lep ~ sqoteméylep.
  steep (of road, hill, etc.), (very steep slope [Elders Group]):: théq.
  steep rock wall that used to have Indian writing at first C.P.R. tunnel above Haig:: X̱elíqel < x̱él ~ x̱é:yl ~ x̱í:l
  steep slope (but less steep than théq):: theqílep < théq.

steer
  steer a canoe:: tháyelets.

Steller's jay
  bluejay, Steller's jay:: kwá:y.
  bluejay, Steller's jay (sacred fortune-teller):: x̱ax̱esyúwes or x̱ax̱e syúwes < x̱áx̱e.
  (this cry of a bluejay [Steller's jay] warns you of bad news):: chéke chéke chéke chéke.

Stellula calliope
possibly Trochilidae family, probably including Selasphorus rufus, Archilochus alexandri, and Stellula calliope:: pésk'a.

"stem"
hull of berry (inside left after the berry is picked), "stem" or base of berry left after the berry is picked:: th'ép'oyeqw ~ th'épeyeqw.

step- :: texw=.
overstretch one's legs when walking with too big a step:: t'íw ~ t'i:w.
step on it accidentally:: óméléxw < i┐ m.
step on s-th, step on it:: ímet < i┐ m.
step over something:: kw'élwelh.
take one step:: tiqxálém ~ tiyqxálém.
takes short steps:: ts'tl'étl'xel < ts'í:tl' ~ ts'ítl'.
taking a step:: té:yqxálem < tiqxálém ~ tiyqxálém.

step-brother
brother-in-law's wife, (spouse's sibling's spouse), (step-sibling, step-brother, step-sister [AC]):: slets'éleq < láts'.

step-child:: texwmélem < méle ~ mél:a.
step-children:: texwmámelem < méle ~ mél:a.

step-parent:: tslhilá:m.

step-sibling
brother-in-law's wife, (spouse's sibling's spouse), (step-sibling, step-brother, step-sister [AC]):: slets'éleq < láts'.

step-sister
brother-in-law's wife, (spouse's sibling's spouse), (step-sibling, step-brother, step-sister [AC]):: slets'éleq < láts'.

stern
a canoe or boat cut off short in the rear (because the stern couldn't be repaired):: t'qw'á:lats < t'éqw'.
pry with paddle in stern to turn a canoe sharply, pry (canoe stroke done by a sternman):: q'á:lets.
stern of canoe, stern-man among paddlers:: iláq.

stew)
soup, (stew):: slhóp'.
(the) cooking, (soup, stew [DM, CT]):: sqwéls < qwó:ls.

stewed tomatoes
ketchup/stewed tomatoes:: stósem temíitō < tós, temíitō (lit. smashed + tomato)

stick
a drum, small stick used to drum or beat time to songs in slahal game:: q'ówet.

stick (CONT'D)

a grass that grows with berries in fields and everywhere and has seeds that stick in one's throat when eaten with berries, probably a type of brome grass, likely California brome grass, possibly sweet cicely:: táqalh.

barbecue stick, cooking stick (split stick for barbecuing salmon),:: pí:kwel.

barbecue sticks, (split roasting stick):: qw'éltel < qw'él.

beating s-o/s-th with a stick, hitting s-o/s-th with a stick, clubbing it:: kw'ókw'eqwet < kw'óqw.

beat s-o/s-th with a stick, hit s-o/s-th with a stick, hit s-th (on purpose), hit s-o intentionally:: kw'óqwet < kw'óqw.

be broken (of stick-like object):: selí:kw < lékw.

break (of a stick-like object):: lékw.

break s-th (stick-like):: lekwát < lékw.

break s-th (stick-like) (accidentally):: lekwlá:xw < lékw.

digging stick:: shxwthóyeqwels < thíy, sqá:lex̲ ~ sqálex̲.

drumstick (for drum):: pumí:l.

eight ropes, eight threads, eight sticks, eight poles:: tqátsámets' < tqá:tsa.

facing up, head sticking up:: kw'ekw'e'íqw ~ kw'ekw'íqw < kw'e'í ~ kw''í ~ kw'í.

fire-drill, stick spun to start fire:: sí:lcheptel < sél or sí(:)l.

five ropes, five threads, five sticks, five poles:: lhq'átssámets' < lheq'át ~ lhq'á:t.

four ropes, four threads, four sticks, four poles, (four long thin objects):: x̲ethílemets' < x̲e'ó:thel ~ x̲e'óthel.

get a canoe stuck on a rock or something:: xá:m.

get stuck:: t'elém.

get stuck in the mud, get mired, be mired, get muddy:: t'ékw.

gummy (sticky):: tl'ítl'eq'el < tl'íq'.

little stick of firewood:: syóyelh < yólh.

lots of little sticks of firewood:: syéyelh < yólh.

month beginning with first sliver of moon in February, (time things stick to the hand (in cold)):: temt'elémtses < t'elém.

moon or month beginning in February, (November to December, time when ice forms [and sticks] [Billy Sepass in Jenness]):: temtl'í:q'es < tl'íq'.

nine ropes, nine threads, nine sticks, nine poles:: tuxwámets' < tú:xw.

one rope, one thread, one stick, one pole:: lets'ámeth' < léts'a ~ léts'e.

one's hand sticks to something (in cold, to honey, to glue, etc.):: t'elémtses < t'elém.

pointer to show direction (like in a trail) (could be an arrow or stick or mark in the ground):: shxwmót'estel < mót'es.

poke oneself in the eye (with finger, stick, etc.):: telkwó:lésem.

prop up a limb with a Y-shaped stick, (prop s-th up (of a limb, with a Y-shaped stick)):: ts'qw'ít or th'qw'it.

put it in (and leave it), stick it into s-th hollow:: léwex < léw.

put s-th on (of a design on a dress, of a shirt, shoes, etc.), attach it, stick it on, fasten it:: tl'álx < tl'ál.

run over it (with car), spread it (for ex. on bread with knife), put it up (of wallpaper), (stick it on), stick s-th closed (with pitch for ex.):: tl'íq't < tl'íq'.

(seven long objects), seven ropes, seven threads, seven sticks, seven poles:: th'okwsámets' < th'ó:kws.

(six long objects), six ropes, six threads, six sticks, six poles:: t'x̲émemets' < t'éx̲.

soapberry beater, stick for whipping up soapberries or Indian ice cream:: th'amawéstel or th'emawéstel < th'ím ~ th'í:m.

sprout(ing) up, stick(ing) its head out of the ground (of a plant):: qw'íles < qw'íl.

stick for beating blankets or clothes or mat, blanket-beater, clothes-beater, mat-beater, rug-beater:: kw'ekw'qwá:lth'átel < kw'óqw.

stick (CONT'D)

sticking out through a hole (like a toe out of a sock, knee out of a hole in pants, a nail driven clear through the other side of a board), come out into the open:: qwōhóls (or perhaps) qwehóls < qwá.
stick it on, paste it on (of stamps or anything):: t'elémt < t'elém.
stick it up someone's rump:: t'ekwíwet < t'ékw.
stick out (of something), protrude:: st'áqsel.
stick out one's tongue, (stick it out (the tongue)):: lháléqet.
(stuck in the rectum), stuck in the ass:: st'ekwíwel < t'ékw.
ten ropes, ten threads, ten sticks, ten poles:: epálemets' < ó:pel.
three ropes, three threads, three sticks, three poles, (three long narrow objects):: lhxwámeth' < lhí:xw.
two ropes, two threads, two sticks, two poles, two poles standing up:: isalámeth' < isá:le ~ isále ~ isá:la.
whip once (with stick), got hit:: qw'óqw.
wool spinner, spindle for spinning wool, spinning stick:: sélsel < sél or sí(:)l.

stickleback

stickleback, possibly threespine stickleback:: smó:tx̲w ~ smótx̲w.

stick-like object)

hit on the behind (with a stick-like object):: kw'qwélets < kw'óqw.
hit with a stick-like object, clubbed:: kw'óqw.

stiff

(be) hard, stiff (material), strong (of rope, material, not of a person), tough:: tl'éx̲w.
be stiff (of arm or foot):: slhelháx̲ < lhéx̲.
stiff, hard:: th'éts.
stiff (of body):: lhx̲étem < lhéx̲.

still :: xwel.

still (of water):: qó:mthet < qám.

still-dip

a waiting dip-net with frame and string trap:: thqálem < thqá:lem.
holding on to a thqálem, waiting dip-netting, still-dipping:: théqelem < thqá:lem.
place where one fishes by waiting with a dip-net, dip-net fishing place, place where one still-dips:: sthqálem < thqá:lem.
to bag net, to sack net, to still-dip with two canoes:: thqá:lem.
to still-dip, rest dip-net on bottom (of river):: thqá:lem.

sting

stinging nettle:: th'éx̲th'ex̲ < th'éx̲.
sting s-o/s-th:: kweléxt < kwél.
to tingle (like arm waking up from numbness), (have/get a) stinging feeling:: thátkwem.

stingy :: qélwelh < qél.

be stingy:: skw'íkw'iy ~ skw'íkw'i < kw'íy.
stingy of food, refuse (somebody something):: kw'íyà:m < kw'íy.

stink

(have) animal smell (of bear, skunk, dog, etc.), (have) animal stink, (have) human smell (of

stink (CONT'D)

underarm, body odor, etc.), (have) body odor:: pápeth'em.
(have/get a) strong stink:: xts'ímthet < xíxets'em.
skunk's stink bag (stink sac):: skwukwtisláts.
smell that one cannot locate, strong stink:: simáléqep.
stink-egg basket, stink salmon egg basket:: kw'ōle'álá < kw'ṓ:la ~ kw'ú:la.
stinking (smell of outhouse or pig farm), (to stink [Elders Group 11/10/76, AC 9/1/71]):: xíxets'em.
strong smell, bad stink, smell that can't be located:: simáléqep < éy ~ éy:.

stink bag
skunk's stink bag, skunk's stink sac:: spú'amal ~ spú'emel < pú'.
skunk's stink bag (stink sac):: skwukwtisláts.

stink currant
red-flowering currant berry, Indian currant berry, probably also stink currant berry also called skunk currant berry:: sp'á:th'.

stink-egg
stink-egg basket, stink salmon egg basket:: kw'ōle'álá < kw'ṓ:la ~ kw'ú:la.
stink-eggs:: kw'ṓ:la ~ kw'ú:la.

stink sac
skunk's stink bag, skunk's stink sac:: spú'amal ~ spú'emel < pú'.
skunk's stink bag (stink sac):: skwukwtisláts.

stir
being angry, continue to be angry, angry, mad, roused, stirred up:: t'át'eyeq' ~ t'át'iyeq' < t'ay.
big wooden dish (often two feet long), feast dish, wooden platter, (big stirring spoon [LJ], carved wooden spoon, big wooden spoon [AC, BJ, DM]):: qwelhyṓwelh ~ qwelhliyṓwelh ~ qwelhlyúwelh < qwélh.
long-handled stirring spoon:: shxwqwáylhechàls < qwá:y.
to stir (a liquid), stir (mixing ingredients):: qwáylhechàls < qwá:y.

stitch
embroidery, trimming (stitches on an edge):: stl'ítl'ets < tl'íts ~ tl'ích.
hang s-th (on a nail or hat hanger), hook it back on (of a stitch lost in knitting):: ókw'est < ókw'.

stl'áleqem
a fatal kind of shock on seeing a stl'áleqem (supernatural creature):: xò:lí:s.

stocking
cloth or warm material to wrap around the foot, stockings:: chóxwxel.
put on one's socks, (put on one's stockings):: tókelem < stókel.
stockings:: chóxwxel.
stocking, socks:: stókel.

stoke
build a fire, make a fire, make the fire, (stoke the fire):: yéqwelchep ~ yéqweltsep < yéqw.
fix a fire, straighten the fire up, stoke the fire:: thiyéltsep < thíy.

stoke (CONT'D)

making the fire, building the fire, (stoking a fire):: híyqwelchep < yéqw.

Stó:lō

Stó:lō people, Halkomelem-speaking people living along the Fraser River or its tributaries from Five Mile Creek above Yale downriver to the mouth of the Fraser:: Stó:lō < tó:l ~ tò:l.

stomach

animal tripe (stomach, upper and lower), bowel:: spéxw.
belly, stomach:: kw'él:a ~ kw'éla.
courage (lit. in the stomach):: =á:lwes ~ =élwes.
food settled (in the stomach), food is settled (in the stomach), (be settled (of food in the stomach), be comfortably digested (of food)):: qsákw'.
growling (of one's stomach):: kw'ó:yx̲wem.
(have an) upset stomach:: p'eléts'tem < p'í:l or p'él.
have a pain in the stomach, (have a stomach-ache), one's stomache hurts:: x̲elhálwes < x̲élh.
insides (animal or human or other?), (internal organs, guts, etc.), (stomach [inside] [DM]):: sts'elxwíwel < ts'el.
in the stomach, in courage:: =álwes ~ =élwes.
in the stomach, on the stomach:: =á:lwes ~ =élwes.
lying down on one's stomach:: qíqep'yó:lha ~ qéyqep'yó:lha < qep'.
lying on one's stomach with head down on one's arms:: qiqep'eyósem < qep'.
on the stomach or ventral surface of a body:: =(e)yó:lhe.
punched s-o on the stomach:: th'qw'álewest < th'í:qw'et.
solid grease, suet, lump of grease, (stomach fat [CT]):: x̲wástel.

stomach-ache)

have a pain in the stomach, (have a stomach-ache), one's stomache hurts:: x̲elhálwes < x̲élh.

stone

a hunter turned to stone now located below Hemhémetheqw near Hill's Bar on the east bank of the Fraser River:: Tewít < tewít.
a stone like a statue at Harrison Lake, probably Doctor's Point:: Skoyá:m ~ Skeyá:m.
a sx̲wó:yx̲wey head turned to stone on land at X̲elhlálh somewhere:: Sx̲éyes te Sx̲wó:yx̲wey < sx̲wó:yx̲wey ~ sx̲wóyx̲wey.
carve stone, work in stone:: t'eléx̲ot < t'éléx̲.
elk (or) moose turned to stone in the Fraser River by Hill's Bar:: Q'oyíyets ~ Q'oyí:ts < q'oyíyets or q'oyí:ts.
hammer, stone hand hammer, sledge hammer:: shxwtélhtses < télhches.
hew (stone, wood, anything):: t'élex̲è:yls < t'éléx̲.
jade (nephrite) (used for sharpening [chopping] stones), any agate (can be used as flint to strike a spark):: t'émq'ethel.
little stone, pebble, little rock hill, small rock mountain (like in the Fraser River in the canyon):: smámelet < smá:lt.
mashing, grinding (stones, something hard):: tótesem < tós.
place of moss-covered stones at upper end of Hope Slough not far from Harry Edwards' home (as of 1964):: Qwómqwemels < qwà:m ~ qwám.
rub (oil or water) in s-th to clean or soften, rub s-th to soften or clean it, (shaping a stone hammer with abrasion?, shaping?, mixing paint?, pressing together or crushing? [BHTTC 9/2/76]):: yémq't.
stone, rock (any size), mountain:: smá:lt.
stone underwater Teeter-totter near Ñelhálh:: Xwíxweth'àlem < xwáth'.

stone (CONT'D)

whetstone, a file, sandstone:: th'óméls.

stoop

put one's head down, bend, bend over, bend over with one's head down, stoop down:: qep'ósem < qep'.
(travelling/moving) stooped over:: yeq'pó:s (prob. error or variant for yeqp'ó:s) < qep'.

stop :: tl'élexw.

close to danger., danger., stop.:: í' ~ i'.
finish, stop, quit, get done, be finished, have enough, be done, be ready:: hò:y ~ hó:y ~ hóy.
get quiet (of wind), stop (of wind):: chó:ythet.
(have a) steady sound that's been stopped for a while:: thxwáléqep < théxw ~ théx̲w.
stop blowing (of the wind):: chémq ~ tsémq.
stop burning (of a burn), go down (of swelling):: t'esí:l < t'ás.
stopped:: tl'eláxw ~ tl'láxw < tl'élexw.
stop raining, stop snowing:: xwéts'xel.
stop s-th:: tl'eléxwstexw < tl'élexw.
Wahleach whistle stop on Seabird Island where Wayne Bobb lived in 1977, (now also Wahleach Lake (man-made) [EB]):: Wolích < x̲wále ~ x̲wá:le.

stop pestering

leave s-o alone, stop pestering s-o:: kwikwe'át < kwá:.

storage

dry storage box in tree or on top of pole (for salmon and other dried provisions):: póqw'elh < pó:qw' ~ póqw'.
little house, cabin (say 12 ft. x 10 ft. or less), small home, storage house (small shed-like house, enclosed with door), outhouse (slang), toilet (slang):: lílem < lá:lém.
storage basket (for oil, fruit, clothes), burial basket for twins, round basket (any size, smaller at top), clay jug (to store oil or fruit):: skwá:m ~ skwám < kwá:m ~ kwám.
stored, in storage:: qeyqelémtem < qéylem ~ qé:ylem ~ qí(:)lem.

store

a store (commercial establishment):: shxwimá:le ~ shxwimála ~ shxwímàlà < xwóyem.
clothes store:: awkw'áwtxw < á:wkw'.
clothes store, clothing store:: ith'emáwtxw < íth'a.
cut wood (with a saw), saw wood, (cut wood to store away):: xets'á:ls.
liquor store, beer parlor (AC):: lamáwtxw < lám.
preserved fish, preserved meat, dried fish, dried meat (usually fish), smoked salmon, wind-dried salmon (old word), what is stored away, what is put away:: sq'éyle.
second-hand store:: mékw'emáwtxw < mékw' ~ mő́kw'.
store away one's paddles:: xets'ő́wesem < xits' ~ xets'.
stored, in storage:: qeyqelémtem < qéylem ~ qé:ylem ~ qí(:)lem.
store it away (wedged-in up off ground), put s-th away for winter, stow s-th away:: xítse't < xits' ~ xets'.

storm

dirty (weather), bad weather, storm:: qél:em ~ qél:ém or leqél:e(´)m < qél.
got stormy with lots of fine snow in the air:: qwálxtem < qwélxel.

story

(get) a disease gotten by contacting a frog, a skin eruption, also the same disease as the man got in Kawkawa Lake in the Sx̲wó:yx̲wey story, (perhaps also) leprosy:: qw'ő:m.

stout

stout (of a person), thick (of a tree), thick around, coarse (of a rope), big (fat) (of a person). big (in girth):: mékw.

stove :: stú:p.

baked (in ashes), baked (in a stove):: s'ótheqw < ótheqw.
bake s-th in ashes, bake s-th in a stove:: ótheqwt < ótheqw.
heat up (on fire, stove):: qewletsá:ls < qew.
pot-bellied stove, cook-stove:: kwúkwstú:p < stú:p.
put on the stove (water/food):: xwch'alech'á:ls < ts'á:.
to roast potatoes in hot sand or ashes, bake in ashes, bake in stove:: ótheqw.

stow

store it away (wedged-in up off ground), put s-th away for winter, stow s-th away:: xítse't < xits' ~ xets'.

straddle

straddle s-th (log, fish, etc.):: x̲eqét < x̲éq.

straight :: thékw'.

be straight (of rope but not tree), pulled tight (of rope), stretched tight, tight:: sthethá:kw' < thékw'.
pull oneself up, straighten (oneself) up:: thkw'éthet < thékw'.
straightened out, got straight(ened):: télh.
straighten oneself out:: tlhéthet < télh.

straighten

fix a fire, straighten the fire up, stoke the fire:: thiyéltsep < thíy.
make a bed, make (straighten up) a bed, make one's bed:: thiyá:lhem ~ thiyálhem < thíy.
straighten oneself out:: thíythet < thíy.

strain

straining to listen, really listening, listening hard, trying to listen, (listen [AC]):: xwlalá:.
to strain s-th (for ex. fruit):: pethíwet ~ pethíwét < páthet.

strange)

(be) scowling (if mad or ate something sour), ((made a) funny (strange) face [Elders Group 1/21/76]):: sx̲éyx̲ewes < x̲éywel.

stranger

different person, stranger:: lets'ő:mexw < láts'.
different tribe, different people, strangers:: lets'ó:lmexw < láts'.

strap

buckskin straps for tying a baby in its cradle or basket:: yémqetel < yém ~ yem.
buckskin straps, lid for berry basket:: yémqetel < yém ~ yem.
carry a packstrap or both packstraps over the shoulder(s) and under the arm(s)::

strap (CONT'D)

sq'iwq'ewíles < q'e:yw ~ q'í:w.

strawberry

also domestic strawberry:: schí:ya.
strawberry birthmark on the arm:: schíyeláx̲el < schí:ya.
strawberry juice:: schíya sqe'óleqw (lit. strawberry + fruit juice) < chíya, qó:
strawberry vine, strawberry plant, strawberry patch:: schí:yà:lhp < schí:ya.
wild strawberry:: schí:ya.

Strawberry Island

also the name of the village on Strawberry Island:: Alhqá:yem < álhqey ~ álhqay.
a stretch of water in the Fraser River on the C.N. side by Strawberry Island:: Kwetl'kwótl'thetōws < kwá:.
the whole riverbank on the CPR (west) side of the Fraser River just south of Strawberry Island and just north of Peqwchṓ:lthel:: Selch'éle < sél or sí(:)l.

stream

a spring water stream near Yakweakwioose:: Thíthx̲ < thíx̲.
a spring-water stream south of Skowkale:: Temélhem < témélh.
a spring water stream with source at present-day Sardis Park, Soowahlihl:: (Th'ewálí:l) < th'éw.
Coqualeetza stream esp. where it joins Luckakuck Creek, later Coqualeetza (residential school, then hospital, then Indian cultural centre and Education Training Centre):: Kw'eqwálíth'a < kw'óqw.
forks in stream:: t'x̲éthet < t'éx̲.
Kateseslie, a spring-water stream east of Coqualeetza, part of the Kw'eqwá:líth'a [property or stream?] that went through Sardis and came out to the Cottonwood Corner:: Katsesló:y.
lots of little streams (like the kind coming down a hill after a rain):: teltelewá:m < tó:l ~ tò:l.
west fork of stream which goes into Chehalis River above Páléxel:: Th'ámxwelqs.

streetcar

high-bow canoe, high-bow river canoe, streetcar, tram, taxi, car, automobile:: xwókw'eletsem < xwókw' ~ xwekw'ó.

strength :: =á:m ~ =ém.

(be) weak (in strength, also in taste [TM]):: qiqelá:m ~ qiqelà:m < qél.

Streptopus amplexifolius

respectively Smilacina racemosa, Smilacina stellata, Streptopus amplexifolius (and Streptopus roseus), and Disporum hookerii:: sth'íms te álhqey < álhqey ~ álhqay.
Smilacina racemosa, Smilacina stellata, and probably Streptopus amplexifolius, Streptopus roseus, and Disporum hookerii:: sth'íms te álhqey < sth'í:m ~ sth'ì:m.
Smilacina racemosa, Streptopus amplexifolius, Streptopus roseus curvipes, Smilacina stellata:: x̲ex̲q'elá:lhp.

Streptopus roseus

respectively Smilacina racemosa, Smilacina stellata, Streptopus amplexifolius (and Streptopus roseus), and Disporum hookerii:: sth'íms te álhqey < álhqey ~ álhqay.
Smilacina racemosa, Smilacina stellata, and probably Streptopus amplexifolius, Streptopus roseus, and Disporum hookerii:: sth'íms te álhqey < sth'í:m ~ sth'ì:m.

Streptopus roseus curvipes

Smilacina racemosa, Streptopus amplexifolius, Streptopus roseus curvipes, Smilacina stellata:: x̲ex̲q'elá:lhp.

stretch :: ót'.

be straight (of rope but not tree), pulled tight (of rope), stretched tight, tight:: sthethá:kw' < thékw'.
(be) stretchy, (be) elastic:: ét"et' < ót'.
board for stretching squirrel or skunk hides, etc.:: tépelhállh < tpólh.
fish-spreader for drying fish, cross-piece for drying fish, salmon stretcher:: t'á:ts'.
frame for stretching hides, frame (for drying hides, etc.), frame for a drum:: tpélhtel ~ tepélhtel < tpólh.
hold both arms (or wings) outstretched, (stretch out one's arms/wings):: tex̲eláx̲elem < tex̲.
overstretch one's legs when walking with too big a step:: t'íw ~ t'í:w.
slingshot (of the stretched kind):: ó:t' < ót'.
stretched?? (said after giving another word meaning stretched):: lhétemet.
stretch it (stretch out someone's arms or wings):: tx̲ét < tex̲.
stretch oneself:: ót'ethet < ót'.
stretch out the wings, stretch out the arm(s):: tex̲eláx̲el < tex̲.
stretch s-th out, stretch it:: ót'et < ót'.

strike

be coiled (ready to strike for ex. of a snake):: sq'elá:w < q'ál.
(be) coiling (ready to strike) (of a snake):: sq'elq'elá:w < q'ál.
strike (of a snake) at s-o:: ts'tl'émet < ts'tl'ám ~ ts'tl'ém.
strike s-th pointed (esp. a match):: éx̲qst < íx̲.
throw and hit s-th/s-o, strike s-th/s-o (with something thrown):: ló:met ~ lómet < ló:m ~ lóm.

string

a waiting dip-net with frame and string trap:: thqálem < thqá:lem.
break (of a flexible object like a rope, string or breath), it broke:: t'éqw'.
cut s-th (string or rope):: tl'qw'ót.
rope, twine, string, thread:: x̲wéylem ~ x̲wé:ylem ~ x̲wí:lem.
stringy fibers (as on cow parsnip):: x̲wéylem ~ x̲wé:ylem ~ x̲wí:lem.
thin (of material like a dress, also of a string):: th'eth'emí:l.

strip

fine cedar root strips for baskets:: shxwth'á:lhtel.
plane it (with a plane), trim it, taper it (about wood, like slats or roots for baskets, poles for houseposts/totem poles, paddles), taper it (with knife or plane), peel it (a fruit, etc.), whittle it, strip or Peel bark off of it, scrape it (of carrots), (carve it, peel it [AC]):: xípet < xíp.
wide cedar root strips for baskets:: yemáwéstel < yém ~ yem.
wide cedar (sapling) strips or slats from young cedar trunks, cedar slat work (basketry):: x̲pó:ys < sx̲éyp.

stripe

a stripe:: sx̲éyx̲ep' < x̲éyp'.
a stripe (on the nose or point):: sx̲élqs < x̲él ~ x̲é:yl ~ x̲í:l
chipmunk with more than two stripes, Northwestern chipmunk, Townsend chipmunk:: x̲ex̲p'í:tsel ~ x̲ex̲p'ítsel ~ sx̲ex̲p'í:tsel < x̲ep'í:tsel.
chipmunk with two stripes, Northwestern chipmunk, also Townsend chipmunk:: x̲ep'í:tsel.

stripe (CONT'D)

striped on back:: sx̲eyx̲ep'ewíts ~ sx̲eyx̲ep'ōwíts < x̲éyp'.
(stripes) :: =eth ?.
stripes (on the nose or point):: sx̲élx̲elqs < x̲él ~ x̲é:yl ~ x̲í:l

strip-tease
undress in front of someone, strip-tease:: lhuwth'ím < lhewíth'a.

Strix occidentalis
possibly also the following other horned owls found in the area: long-eared owl Asio otus and spotted owl Strix occidentalis:: chítmexw.

stroke
pet s-th/s-o, stroke s-th/s-o:: p'í:qwt < p'í:.
pry (a canoe paddling stroke when the canoe is hard to turn):: lhímesem < lhímes.
pry with paddle in stern to turn a canoe sharply, pry (canoe stroke done by a sternman):: q'á:lets.
pull in once with a canoe paddle wide or slow, pull in in turning (a canoe paddling stroke done by a bowman):: lhímes.
swimming, (swimming under the water after diving (Cheh.) [Elders Group], swimming with crawl strokes, etc. [Deming]):: t'ít'etsem ~ t'ít'echem < t'ítsem.
swim (of a person), swim (with crawl strokes, etc.):: t'ítsem.

stroll
go for a walk, take a stroll, stroll:: imexósem < i┐ m.

strong :: sáyém < sáyem.
be big (of a fire), the fire is big, the fire is going strong, big fire:: thó:lchep ~ thó:ltsep < thi ~ tha ~ the ~ thah ~ theh.
(be) hard, stiff (material), strong (of rope, material, not of a person), tough:: tl'éx̲w.
be strong:: eyém ~ iyém < éy ~ éy:.
be strong (of animates or inanimates):: kw'ómkw'em.
(have a) menthol smell, (be) strong-smelling (of medicine):: xó:lxwem.
(have/get a) strong stink:: xts'ímthet < xíxets'em.
make it strong, make him/her/them strong:: eyémstexw < éy ~ éy:.
smell that one cannot locate, strong stink:: simáléqep.
strong feelings, mad all the time but won't fight:: simíwél < éy ~ éy:.
strong (of material):: tl'x̲wíth'a < tl'éx̲w.
strong smell, bad stink, smell that can't be located:: simáléqep < éy ~ éy:.

structured activity])
device, tool, thing for doing something [as a structured activity]), person doing something [as structured activity]:: =els.
structured activity continuative, structured activity continuative nominal or tool or person:: =els.
structured activity non-continuative:: =á:ls.

struggle
flipping around (of fish), struggling (of anything alive trying to get free):: kwótl'thet < kwá:.
start to struggle, start to flip around to escape (fish esp.):: kwetl'éthet < kwá:.

stubborn

(be) stubborn:: sepsáp.
insistant, persistant (like a child pressing to go along), bull-headed, doesn't mind, does just the opposite, (stubborn, contrary):: sxíxeles.

stuck

get stuck:: t'elém.
get stuck in the mud, get mired, be mired, get muddy:: t'ékw.
(stuck in the rectum), stuck in the ass:: st'ekwíwel < t'ékw.

stuck up

to bluff, pretend one knows something, (be) stuck up:: math'álem < máth'el.

study

studying s-th, thinking about s-th, learning s-th, training for s-th, trying to do s-th:: totí:lt < tól.
study it:: tó:lt < tól.
thinking, pondering, studying, be studying:: totí:lthet < tól, totí:lthet < tól.
think, ponder, study, decide:: tó:lthet < tól.

stuff

stuff steam-cooked underground, what is baked underground:: sqetás < qá:t.

Stulkawhits Creek

village at mouth of Stulkawhits Creek on Fraser River:: Lexwtl'íkw'elem < tl'íkw'el.

Stullawheets

village near the mouth of Choate Creek, (Choate Creek [AK, SP/AD], (Stullawheets village on a hill on the east bank of the Fraser River near the mouth of Suka Creek [elders on American Bar Trip (AD/AK/?)]):: St'élxweth'.

stumble

to fall (of a person, waterfall, etc.), stumble:: tsélq.
to stumble, get staggered:: télstem < tél ~ tá:l ~ tiy.

stump

(be) stumped:: mótl'.
stump (of a tree [still rooted]):: sq'x̲áp.

stupid

be always lazy, be a lazybones, be stupid, be a good-for-nothing:: s'ú:met < emét.
(be) stupid, not all there (mentally), (be) a little crazy:: shxwixwóxwth' < xwáth'.

stupidity)

wrapped up (in stupidity):: s'i'hó < ehó.

stupified

be dumbfounded, be surprised, be stupified, be speechless:: slholhekw'íwel ~ slholhekw'í:wel < lhó:kw' ~ lhókw'.
be startled, be dumbfounded, be shocked, be stupified, be speechless, be overwhelmed:: lholhekw'íwel ~ lholhkw'íwel < lhó:kw' ~ lhókw'.

stupify

be dumbfounded, be surprised, be stupified, be speechless:: slholhekw'íwel ~ slholhekw'í:wel < lhó:kw' ~ lhókw'.

Sturgeon

Rainbow Falls on Harrison Lake, (Sturgeon's Drop):: Tsólqthet te Skwówech < tsélq ~ chélq.

sturgeon

coiled up méthelh rope for fishing (for sturgeon and spring salmon):: ts'tíxem.

drifting backwards in two canoes with net between to catch sturgeon, (drift-netting), backing up (of canoe, train):: tewláts.

flat organ in sturgeon which was skinned off and boiled down for glue:: mát.

jerk-lining for sturgeon in a canoe:: wiweqw'óthet < wṓqw' ~ wéqw'.

spear (any kind), spear (for fish or war), fish-spear, telescopic spear for sturgeon, harpoon, detachable harpoon points:: tá:lh.

spinal rope inside sturgeon, (sturgeon spinal cord):: qw'ólhla.

spoon-shaped bone back of upper lip of sturgeon:: x̲álew.

sturgeon club, fish club (for salmon, sturgeon, etc.):: slá:meth.

sturgeon, white sturgeon:: skwó:wech ~ skwówech.

sty

sty in the eye:: xéle'ò:les < sxéle.

style

chief's, (belonging to a chief, in the style of a chief):: siyómelh < siyám ~ (rare) siyá:m.

subject

first person plural subjunctive subject:: -et.

first person singular subjunctive subject:: -ál.

his, her, its, their, third person possessive pronoun, third person subordinate subject:: -s.

I (non-subordinate subject):: -tsel ~ (very rarely) -chel ~ tsel.

my, first person singular possessive pronoun, first person subordinate subject:: -el ~ -l ~ l.

recent past third person subject:: le.

second person plural subjunctive subject:: -áp ~ -elep.

second person singular subjunctive subject:: -exw.

subject of independent clause, non-subordinate subject:: ts- ~ ch-, ts- ~ ch-.

third person subject (of transitive verbs):: -es.

third person subjunctive subject:: -es.

we (non-subordinate subject), our:: -tset ~ -chet.

your (pl.), you folks's, second person plural possessive pronoun, second person plural subordinate subject:: -a -elep ~ -a' -elep.

subjunctive

first person plural subjunctive subject:: -et.

first person singular subjunctive subject:: -ál.

second person plural subjunctive subject:: -áp ~ -elep.

second person singular subjunctive subject:: -exw.

subjunctive of passive:: -èt.

subjunctive, when, if:: we-.

third person subjunctive subject:: -es.

submerge

set a net (by canoe), set one's net, fish with a net, (submerge a net):: míliyel < mí:l ~ míl.

subordinate

his, her, its, their, third person possessive pronoun, third person subordinate subject:: -s.
my, first person singular possessive pronoun, first person subordinate subject:: -el ~ -l ~ l.
(probably also) subordinate or dependent (with passive):: -èt.
your (pl.), you folks's, second person plural possessive pronoun, second person plural subordinate subject:: -a -elep ~ -a' -elep.

subordinating conjunction)

that (abstract subordinating conjunction):: kw'e.
when (simultaneous subordinating conjunction), as:: kw'e.

subside

to go down (of water), subside (of water), the tide goes out or down, (be going out (of tide) [BJ]):: th'à:m ~ th'ám.

suck

be sucking s-th:: th'óth'eqwet < th'óqwet.
suckle, suck milk from a breast:: qemó:.
suck s-th:: th'óqwet.

sucker

little roundmouth suckerfish, probably longnose sucker:: skwímeth < kwí:m.
sucker fish, especially big sucker or elephant sucker, probably largescale sucker:: q'óx̲el.

suckerfish

little roundmouth suckerfish, probably longnose sucker:: skwímeth < kwí:m.
little suckerfish with big salmon-like mouth, prob. largescale sucker:: qw'á:ts.
sucker fish, especially big sucker or elephant sucker, probably largescale sucker:: q'óx̲el.

suckle

suckle, suck milk from a breast:: qemó:.
suckling:: qéqemó: < qemó:.

suction

suction sound of feet pulling out of mud:: t'áxwqem.

sudden

(have/get) a sudden flame:: xwótekwem < xwótkwem.
[make a bang, make a sudden hard thump sound]:: kw'péx̲w.

suddenly :: we=, we=.

splash (the sound and the action), [splash suddenly], splash once:: wet'émeqw' < t'émeqw'.

suet

solid grease, suet, lump of grease, (stomach fat [CT]):: x̲wástel.

suffer
(be) suffering pain:: s'ő:leqw'.

sugar :: súkwe ~ súkwa ~ shúkwe.
sugar bowl:: shúkwe'àlà < súkwe ~ súkwa ~ shúkwe.
sugar it:: súkwet ~ shúkwet < súkwe ~ súkwa ~ shúkwe.

suitcase :: áwkw'emálá < á:wkw'.
clothes container, suitcase, clothes case:: áwkw'emálá < á:wkw'.
suitcase (Deming), luggage (Deming), clothing container, clothes bag, trunk (for clothes), etc.:: áwkw'emálá < á:wkw'.

Suka Creek
Suka Creek (on east side of Fraser River above Hope):: Skwíyò Stó:lō < Skwíyò.
the mountain above Suka Creek:: Skwíyò Smált < Skwíyò.
village just below (on the south side of) Suka Creek, on the CN side (east side) of the Fraser River across from Dogwood Valley:: Skwíyò.
village near the mouth of Choate Creek, (Choate Creek [AK, SP/AD], (Stullawheets village on a hill on the east bank of the Fraser River near the mouth of Suka Creek [elders on American Bar Trip (AD/AK/?)]):: St'élxweth'.
village or area on north side of Suka Creek (which is on the east side of the Fraser River:: Kwókwxwemels < kwoxw.

sultry
sultry, humid:: s-hómkw.

Sumas
Nicomen Island (in the Fraser River near Deroche), also a specific place on northeast end of Nicomen Island where lots of people used to gather [now Sumas Indian Reserve #10]:: Leq'á:mél.
people from Semá:th (Sumas village):: Pepá:thxetel < pá:th.

Sumas Creek
Upper Sumas Creek:: Tátelín??.

Sumas Lake
a village at the south end of former Sumas Lake on the mountain:: Snaníth.
Sumas village and area from present-day Kilgard to Fraser River, Sumas village (on both sides of the Fraser at the east end of Sumas Mt.), (Devil's Run (below Lá<u>x</u>ewey), the area between Sumas Mt. and Fraser River [Elders Group 7/13/77], Sumas River (probably requires Stó:lō river or Stótelō creek to follow) [Wells 1965], Sumas Lake (probably requires <u>X</u>ótsa lake after Semáth for this meaning) [Elders Group 7/13/77]):: Smá:th ~ Semá:th ~ Semáth.

Sumas Mountain
Sumas Mountain (also Tuckquail, a village on both sides of Lower Sumas River [Wells]):: T'e<u>x</u>qé:yl or T'e<u>x</u>qí:l < t'é<u>x</u>.

Sumas Prairie
Sumas Prairie west (on the west side of Sumas Lake):: S<u>x</u>elálets??.

Sumas River

Sumas Mountain (also Tuckquail, a village on both sides of Lower Sumas River [Wells]):: T'ex̲qé:yl or T'ex̲qí:l < t'éx̲.

Sumas village and area from present-day Kilgard to Fraser River, Sumas village (on both sides of the Fraser at the east end of Sumas Mt.), (Devil's Run (below Láx̲ewey), the area between Sumas Mt. and Fraser River [Elders Group 7/13/77], Sumas River (probably requires Stó:lō river or Stótelō creek to follow) [Wells 1965], Sumas Lake (probably requires X̲ótsa lake after Semáth for this meaning) [Elders Group 7/13/77]):: Smá:th ~ Semá:th ~ Semáth.

village on both sides of the Lower Sumas River:: Lexwchmóqwem?.

Sumas village

Sumas village and area from present-day Kilgard to Fraser River, Sumas village (on both sides of the Fraser at the east end of Sumas Mt.), (Devil's Run (below Láx̲ewey), the area between Sumas Mt. and Fraser River [Elders Group 7/13/77], Sumas River (probably requires Stó:lō river or Stótelō creek to follow) [Wells 1965], Sumas Lake (probably requires X̲ótsa lake after Semáth for this meaning) [Elders Group 7/13/77]):: Smá:th ~ Semá:th ~ Semáth.

summer :: kw'ósthet < kw'ás, temkw'ókw'es < kw'ás.

summit

bring oneself to a summit (of a mountain):: wets'á:lómet < ts'á:.
getting to the summit of a mountain:: hewts'á: < ts'á:.
get to the top or summit of a mountain:: wets'á: < ts'á:.
the summit (of a mountain):: swets'a'á < ts'á:.

sun :: syó:qwem < yéqw.

an eclipse (of sun or moon):: t'ó:ltel ~ t'óltel < t'á:l.
come out (of sun), come up (of sun):: wep'éth' ~ wep'áth' < p'eth'.
first warmed side of a tree, sunny side of a tree:: sqewá:meth' < qew.
(get a) ray of sun between clouds:: qeyqeyx̲elósem < qéyqeyx̲elà.
just come out on (of sun):: p'eth'.
place where the sun comes up:: swep'áth' < p'eth'.
shading one's eyes from the sun with the hand (looking into the sun):: xwtóx̲esem.
sunbeams:: sx̲elx̲éles te syó:qwem < yéqw.
sunning oneself:: ch'ich'ewós.
worn out (used when quarter moon is nearly invisible), (set (of the sun)):: th'éx̲.

sunbathe

sit facing a river and watch it, sit on a riverbank and sunbathe:: chichewós < cháchew ~ cháchu.

sunbeams

sunbeams:: sx̲elx̲éles te syó:qwem < yéqw.

Sunday

Sunday (sacred day):: sx̲ax̲elh(l)át ~ sx̲ex̲elh(l)at < x̲áx̲e.

sunflower seeds:: spéxwqels te syóqwem sp'áq'em < píxw, yéqw. p'áq'
(lit. small airborne seed of + the + sun + flower)

sunny side
    first warmed side of a tree, sunny side of a tree:: sqewá:meth' < qew.

sunset :: sóyéx̲el < sóy.

supernatural creature)
    a fatal kind of shock on seeing a stl'áleqem (supernatural creature):: xò:lí:s.
    animal or bird one is afraid of and can't see, powerful creature, supernatural creature:: stl'á:leqem.
    huge pretty frog with supernatural powers:: sx̲ex̲ómőlh.
    (little supernatural creature), little stl'áleqem:: stl'ítl'leqem < stl'á:leqem.
    lots of stl'áleqems, (lots of supernatural creatures):: stl'eltl'áléqem < stl'á:leqem.
    two-headed supernatural snake:: sílhqey < álhqey ~ álhqay.
    two supernatural creatures:: yáysele ~ yéysele < isá:le ~ isále ~ isá:la.

supple
    be supple, be easy to bend:: met'mét'.
    limber, supple, bend easily (of a person):: leqw'ímőws.

Sure.
    Sure., Exactly.:: xwéwes.

sure
    it's sure a lot:: chelà:lqwlha < chelà:l.
    what a lot., it's sure a lot:: chelà:l.

surface
    on the face, face of the hand or foot, opened surface of a salmon:: =ó:s ~ =ós ~ =es.
    on the stomach or ventral surface of a body:: =(e)yó:lhe.
    to float, come up to the surface, rise to the surface, to surface:: p'ékw.

surprise :: lhekw'í:wel < lhó:kw' ~ lhókw'.
    be dumbfounded, be surprised, be stupified, be speechless:: slholhekw'íwel ~ slholhekw'í:wel < lhó:kw' ~ lhókw'.
    be surprised:: ts'éq'.
    be surprised, astonished:: lewálh.
    be surprised by s-th/s-o:: lewálhmet < lewálh.
    (happen to) surprise s-o:: lewálhlexw < lewálh.
    oh for goodness sakes., well. (in surprise):: lá:la.
    surprised:: q'éq'ewes.

suspect
    suspect, be suspicious:: t'ót'emethet < t'ám.

suspenders:: q'ewí:lestel < q'e:yw ~ q'í:w.

suspicious
    suspect, be suspicious:: t'ót'emethet < t'ám.

Swainson's thrush
    call of the Swainson's thrush:: xwét.

Swainson's thrush (CONT'D)

Female Salmonberry Bird, (Female Swainson's Thrush):: Xwatóy < xwét.
Male Salmonberry Bird, (Male Swainson's Thrush):: Xwét < xwét.
Swainson's thrush, the salmonberry bird:: xwét.
the call of the female Swainson's thrush:: Xwatóy < xwét.

swallow

swallow, espcially tree swallow and bank swallow, poss. others found in the area such as violet-green swallow?, barn swallow?, cliff swallow? and rough-winged swallow?:: qw'sí:tsel.
swallowing s-th:: hémq'et < méq'.
swallow s-th, swallow it:: méq'et < méq'.

swamp

swamp gooseberry, prickly swamp currant:: ts'qw'í:wíyelhp.

"swamp tea"

Labrador tea, "Indian tea", "swamp tea":: mó:qwem.

swan

whistling swan, probably also trumpeter swan:: shxwő:qel ~ shxwőwqel ~ shxwéwqel, shxwő:qel ~ shxwőwqel ~ shxwéwqel.

sweat)

(rain or sweat) trickling down one's face:: kw'tómés < kw'átem.
sweathouse:: qetíwstel < qá:t.
sweating:: yóyeqw'em < yóqw'em.
sweat [noun]:: syó:qw'em < yóqw'em.
to sweat:: yóqw'em.

sweater :: swéta.

sweathouse

sweathouse:: qetíwstel < qá:t.

sweep

be swept:: s'íx̲w < íx̲w.
sweep it:: íx̲wet < íx̲w.
swept ground:: x̲éylep.
to sweep up, the sweep-up (last spirit dance of season in a given longhouse):: íx̲wethet < íx̲w.

"sweep up"

have the last spirit dance of the season, have the "sweep up":: yekw'ólhem or perhaps yekw'wólhem < yókw' ~ yóqw'.
to sweep up, the sweep-up (last spirit dance of season in a given longhouse):: íx̲wethet < íx̲w.

sweet

(be) sweet:: q'áq'et'em < q'át'em.
get sweetened:: q'et'ómthet < q'át'em.
(have a) sweet smell:: q'áq'et'emáléqep < q'át'em.
sweeten oneself:: q'et'ómthet < q'át'em.
white sweet corn:: p'éq' q'áq'et'em kwó:l (lit. white + sweet + corn) < p'éq', q'át', kwó:l

sweet cicely

a grass that grows with berries in fields and everywhere and has seeds that stick in one's throat when eaten with berries, probably a type of brome grass, likely California brome grass, possibly sweet cicely:: táqalh.

sweetheart

sweetheart, person of the opposite sex that one is running around with, girl-friend, boy-friend:: ts'elh'á:y < ts'elh=.

swell

(be) swollen:: chechíxw < chxw= ~ =chíxw, p'e'ómthet < p'ò:m.

(be) swollen on the eye, (have a) swollen eye:: schxwó:les < chxw= ~ =chíxw.

be swollen, swelled up (EB), swelling (AC):: chxwétem < chxw= ~ =chíxw.

go down (of swelling):: t'esí:l < t'ás.

(have a) swollen nose:: chxwélqsel < chxw= ~ =chíxw.

rise, swell:: p'ò:m.

stop burning (of a burn), go down (of swelling):: t'esí:l < t'ás.

to swell (of a body part):: chxw= ~ =chíxw.

Sweltzer Creek

Hatchery Creek, tributary of Sweltzer Creek (which drains Cultus Lake):: Stṓtelō < tó:l ~ tò:l.

Soowahlie village (where Sweltzer Creek met Chilliwack River), Soowahlie Reserve near Vedder Crossing:: Th'ewá:lí < th'éw.

Sweltzer Creek (the stream from Cultus Lake to Chilliwack River at Soowahlie):: Swílhcha Stótelō < Swílhcha.

village on east bank of Sweltzer Creek (above Sx̲woyehá:lá), (creek by the village of the same name [X̲wōx̲wá:ye] [Wells]):: X̲wōx̲wá:ye < x̲wōx̲wáye ~ x̲wex̲wáye ~ x̲wōx̲wá:ye.

swift

rapids, fast water, clear water, flowing fast, going fast, swift (water):: lex̲wṓ:m ~ lex̲wṓm < x̲wém ~ xwém.

rough (of wind or water), turbulent (of wind or water), real swift (of water):: x̲átl'.

swim

swimming (be in swimming):: xixkw'ó:m < xókw' ~ xó:kw'.

swimming (of dog, deer, animal), (dog-paddling):: x̲ólhchem < x̲élhchem.

swimming (of fish), (swim (of a fish) [EB]):: xétem < xetàm ~ xtàm, xétem < xetàm ~ xtàm.

swimming, (swimming under the water after diving (Cheh.) [Elders Group], swimming with crawl strokes, etc. [Deming]):: t'ít'etsem ~ t'ít'echem < t'ítsem.

swim (of a person), swim (with crawl strokes, etc.):: t'ítsem.

swim (of fish):: xetàm ~ xtàm.

swim, (tread water), (wading in deep water [LJ], swimming [Elders Group]):: x̲élhchem.

swing

a swing, a little treadle they swing the babies on:: q'éyt'o ~ q'éyt'e.

swing for baby cradle:: séqtel < seqíws ~ seqí:ws.

swinging:: q'éyq'et'e < q'éyt'o ~ q'éyt'e.

swivel

swivel one's hips (as in the Hawaiian hula for ex.) (shake one's bottom around):: qwayx̲élechem < qwá:y.

swollen

(be) swollen:: chechíxw < chxw= ~ =chíxw, p'e'ómthet < p'ò:m.
(be) swollen on the eye, (have a) swollen eye:: schxwó:les < chxw= ~ =chíxw, schxwó:les < chxw= ~ =chíxw.
be swollen, swelled up (EB), swelling (AC):: chxwétem < chxw= ~ =chíxw.
(have a) swollen nose:: chxwélqsel < chxw= ~ =chíxw.

sword fern:: sthx̲á:lem.

Sx̲woyehá:lá)

village on east bank of Sweltzer Creek (above Sx̲woyehá:lá), (creek by the village of the same name [X̲wōx̲wá:ye] [Wells]):: X̲wōx̲wá:ye < x̲wōx̲wáye ~ x̲wex̲wáye ~ x̲wōx̲wá:ye.

Sx̲wó:yx̲wey

(get) a disease gotten by contacting a frog, a skin eruption, also the same disease as the man got in Kawkawa Lake in the Sx̲wó:yx̲wey story, (perhaps also) leprosy:: qw'ṓ:m.

sx̲wó:yx̲wey

a category of religious songs including sx̲wó:yx̲wey songs and burning songs, a burning song:: heywí:leqw < yéw: ~ yéw.
a sx̲wó:yx̲wey head turned to stone on land at X̲elhlálh somewhere:: Sx̲éyes te Sx̲wó:yx̲wey < sx̲wó:yx̲wey ~ sx̲wóyx̲wey.
rock shaped like a man's head with a sx̲wó:yx̲wey mask on a point near the head of Harrison River, the point also called Spook's Point:: Sx̲wó:yx̲wey ~ Sx̲wóyx̲wey < sx̲wó:yx̲wey ~ sx̲wóyx̲wey.
rock that was a sx̲wó:yx̲wey head (mask) turned to stone at X̲elhlálh:: Sx̲éyes te Sx̲wó:yx̲wey < sx̲éyes ~ sx̲éy:es.
sx̲wóyx̲wey ceremony featuring a masked dance, the sx̲wóyx̲wey mask and dance:: sx̲wó:yx̲wey ~ sx̲wóyx̲wey.

sx̲wóyx̲wey dance

square dressing room or shelter of blankets where sx̲wóyx̲wey dancers change before doing the sx̲wóyx̲wey dance:: q'eléts'tel < q'el.

sx̲wṓsem

soapberry spoon, soapberry paddle, short-handled spoon, flat spoon for sx̲wṓsem:: th'émtel < th'ím ~ th'í:m.

Sylvilagus floridanus mearnsi

Lepus americanus cascadensis and Lepus americanus washingtoni, now perhaps Sylvilagus floridanus mearnsi:: shxwóxw.
Lepus americanus cascadensis and Lepus americanus washingtoni, now probably also Sylvilagus floridanus mearnsi:: sqewáth, sqiqewóthel < sqewáth, sqwiqweyóthel.
Lepus americanus cascadensis and Lepus americanus washingtoni, now prob. also Sylvilagus floridanus mearnsi:: sqíqewàth < sqewáth.

sympathize

comfort s-o, sympathize with s-o:: smámekw'et < mákw'a.

Symphoricarpos albus
Symphoricarpos albus:: =oyes, pepq'éyò:s < p'éq', qewówelhp.

Syrphidae
order Hymenoptera, superfamily Apoidea, family Apidae, including Apis mellifera (introduced), also family Bombidae and family Vespidae and possibly bee-like members of family Syrphidae (order Diptera):: sisemó:ya ~ sisemóya ~ sisemóye ~ sísemòye.

Tabanidae
family Tabanidae, genus Chrysops:: lhemélétsʼ.

table :: letám.
clean it (of table, land, etc.):: tí:lt.
table, desk:: letám.

taboo)
sacred, holy, (taboo):: x̲áx̲e.

tadpole
baby frog, probably also tadpole:: pipehó:mó:llh < peh or pó(:)h.

Taenia solium
order Cestoidea, esp. Taenia solium:: sqwó:qwetl'í:wèl.

tag-question)
is that okay? (interrogative tag-question):: é.

tail
fine airborne seed(s) (not used of plum or apple seed(s) or the hard seeds -- sth'emíwél is used for those) (used for dandelion seeds, cottonwood seeds, etc., tail of a cat-tail reed, (plant fluff (possibly including tail of cat-tail rush) [Elders Group 2/27/80]):: spéxwqel ~ spéx̲wqel < píxw.
fish tail:: sx̲épxel (or sx̲ép'xel).
on the foot or leg, in the foot or leg, tail of fish, leg of other animate creatures:: =xel.
tail (of animal, bird):: stl'ep'él:ets ~ stl'ep'élets.
tiny fin above tail of fish, (perhaps spines above tail of some fish):: sx̲élhx̲elh < x̲élh.
to wag its tail:: tl'ap'élatsem < stl'ep'él:ets ~ stl'ep'élets.
weasel, one or both of the following which are in the area: short-tailed weasel and long-tailed weasel:: lhets'á:m.

take
(bathe s-o, give s-o a bath), make s-o take a bath:: xó:kw'et < xókw' ~ xó:kw'.
bring s-o/s-th in (to a house/enclosure), take s-o/s-th in(inside a house/enclosure), admit s-o (into a house/enclosure), let s-o/s-th in (to a house/enclosure), put s-o/s-th in (inside a house/enclosure:: kwetáxwt < kwetáxw.
collect, collect money, take a collection, gather:: q'pá:ls < q'ép.
get one's picture taken:: x̲wéychesem (or better) x̲wíythesem < x̲wíyth.
look after s-o, protect s-o, take care of s-o:: xólhmet ~ xólhemet < xólh.
looking after s-o, taking care of s-o:: xóxelhmet < xólh.
put it down, take it down (s-th on the wall for ex.):: xwetáqt.
(take all of themselves, pick themselves all up):: mōkw'éthet < mékw' ~ mṓkw'.
take a picture, to photograph:: pekchá:m < pékcha.
take a shortcut:: tl'itl'q'oyám < tl'aq' ~ tl'q'.

take (CONT'D)

take care of oneself, look after oneself, be careful:: xólhmethet ~ xó:lhmethet < xólh.
take it all, pick it all up:: mekw'ét ~ mōkw'ét ~ mōkw'ót < mékw' ~ mṓkw'.
take it off from the bottom of s-th (a pack for ex.):: mexlátst < má ~ má'-.
take it out of a box, pull it out of a box:: xíqt.
take it out of water:: qw'ímét < qw'í:m.
take it outside (outside of a building or car):: átl'qt < átl'q.
take left-over food:: méq'etsem < méq'.
take off one's clothes, undress:: lhōwth'ám < lhewíth'a.
take one step:: tiqxálém ~ tiyqxálém.
take s-o for granted:: tl'exwló:st.
take s-o home:: t'ékw'stexw ~ t'ókw'stexw < t'ó:kw'.
take someone's food or clothes:: kwétxwt.
takes short steps:: ts'tl'étl'xel < ts'í:tl' ~ ts'ítl'.
take s-th, accept s-th, get s-th, fetch s-th, pick s-th up:: kwú:t.
take s-th down, tear down s-th man-made, dismantle s-th, take it apart:: yíx̲wet < yíx̲w.
taking a step:: té:yqxálem < tiqxálém ~ tiyqxálém.
taking care of oneself:: xó:lhmethet < xólh.
to be arm in arm (like escorting someone), to take an arm (of someone):: s'ókw'ches < ókw'.
to take all the loose eggs out of s-th (a salmon):: pethíwet ~ pethíwét < páthet.
unloading a canoe, taking things out of a canoe:: qw'íméls < qw'í:m.

take away

take it off (of a table for example), take it away (from something), take it off (of eyeglasses, of skin off an animal), take s-o off/away (from something), take s-th out (a tooth for ex.):: máx < má ~ má'-.

take off

take a cover off, take it off (a cover of a container), open it (bottle, box, kettle, book, etc.):: xwemá:qet < má ~ má'-.
take it off from the bottom of s-th (a pack for ex.):: mexlátst < má ~ má'-.
take it off (of a table for example), take it away (from something), take it off (of eyeglasses, of skin off an animal), take s-o off/away (from something), take s-th out (a tooth for ex.):: máx < má ~ má'-.
taking s-th off:: hámex < má ~ má'-.

take out

take it off (of a table for example), take it away (from something), take it off (of eyeglasses, of skin off an animal), take s-o off/away (from something), take s-th out (a tooth for ex.):: máx < má ~ má'-.
take it out (outside/outside of a container) atl'qéylt < átl'q.
take-out food:: atl'qéylt s'álhtel < átl'q.

talc

diatomaceous earth (could be mixed with things to whiten them--for ex. dog and goat wool), white clay for white face paint (for pure person spirit-dancers), white powder from mountains, white clay they make powder from to lighten goat and dog wool for blankets, powder, talc, white face paint:: st'ewṓkw'.

talk

think s-o is talking or laughing about one:: tl'ostélmét < tl'óst or tl'óstexw.

talk (CONT'D)

think someone is talking about s-o:: tl'émstexw.
think someone is talking or laughing about oneself:: tl'emstélemet ~ tl'emstélémét < tl'émstexw, tl'ostélmet.

talkative

be shy, be not talkative, quiet (of a person):: p'áp'xwem.

tall

(be) long, tall (of tree, anything):: tl'áqt.
tall (of a person):: tl'eqtámeth' ~ tl'eqtáméth' < tl'áqt.
tall (of tree):: tl'eqtíwél < tl'áqt.

Talpidae

family Talpidae, especially Scapanus orarius orarius, also Neurotrichus gibbsi:: speláwél < pél (perhaps ~ pí:l by now).

tame

(be) tame:: qw'óqw'el.

Tamiasciurus douglasi mollipilosus:: skwóye, sqwéth'elh.

Tamihi

Tamihi village at the mouth of Tamihi Creek:: T'emiyéq(w) ?? < t'ámiya.

Tamihi Creek:: T'ami(ye)hóy (Stótelō) < t'ámiya.

a place on Chilliwack River, a little above Anderson Flat and Allison's (between Tamihi Creek and Slesse Creek), a village at deep water between Tamihi Creek and Slesse Creek:: Iy'óythel < éy ~ éy:.
Tamihi village at the mouth of Tamihi Creek:: T'emiyéq(w) ?? < t'ámiya.

Tamihi Lake:: T'ami(ye)hóy (X̱ótsa) < t'ámiya.

Tamihi Mountain

Mount McGuire, (Tamihi Mountain [BJ]):: T'amiyahó:y < t'ámiya.

tan

be yellowish, be tan:: sqwóqweyel ~ sqwóqwiyel < qwá:y.
circular frame (for tanning hides):: st'elákw' siyólh < yólh.
(tan, brownish):: p'íp'ex̱wel, sp'íp'ex̱wel < p'íp'ex̱wel.

tangle

be really tangled, it's really tangled:: sq'á:lq' < q'ál.
be tangled (on something):: sq'álq' < q'ál.
snagged, tangled on something, something gets tangled up (like a net):: q'elq'élq' < q'ál.
tangled on its own/itself:: q'elq'élp' < q'ál.

tansy

tansy (possible name):: sthxwélqseltel < thóxw or théxw.

tantrum

drop oneself into a seat, throw oneself on the floor or ground in a tantrum, throw a

tantrum (CONT'D)

tantrum:: kw'qweméthet < kw'óqw.

tap

knocking, rapping (in the distance), tapping:: kwókwexwem < kwoxw.
tapping it (with something), mashing s-th, grinding s-th, be bumping s-o:: tóteset < tós.
throw s-o down hard (like a wrestler), tap s-th (a container's bottom) [hard] on something to make the contents settle (like berry basket):: th'esét ~ th'sét < th'és.

taper

plane it (with a plane), trim it, taper it (about wood, like slats or roots for baskets, poles for houseposts/totem poles, paddles), taper it (with knife or plane), peel it (a fruit, etc.), whittle it, strip or peel bark off of it, scrape it (of carrots), (carve it, peel it [AC]):: xípet < xíp, xípet < xíp.

tapeworm :: sqwó:qwetl'í:wèl.

Taraxacum officinale:: qwáyúwél < qwá:y.

Taricha granulosa granulosa

prob. Dicamptodon ensatus, poss. also Taricha granulosa granulosa, prob. also Gerrhonotis coeruleus principis:: seyíyex̲.

taste :: t'á, t'ets'élmel < t'á.

(be) weak (in strength, also in taste [TM]):: qiqelá:m ~ qiqelà:m < qél.
getting mouldy in taste or smell:: pópeqwem < póqw.
good tasting (savory, not sweet), tasty:: ts'áts'esem.
have a menthol taste, (have a cool taste):: xó:lxwem.
(have) a rotten taste:: th'óth'eqw'emáléqep < th'óqw'em ~ th'ó:qw'em.
like s-o [his/her personality], like s-th [its taste, its idea], be interested in s-th/s-o, enjoy s-o sexually:: éystexw ~ éy:stexw < éy ~ éy:.
taste bad:: qéleqep < qél.
taste s-th, try s-th:: t'át ~ t'á:t < t'á.
(the) taste:: st'a'áleqep < t'á.

tasteless

be fresh (of water), be tasteless:: th'áwém ~ th'áwem.
to be tasteless:: th'áth'ewem < th'áwém ~ th'áwem.

tasty

good tasting (savory, not sweet), tasty:: ts'áts'esem.

tattletale:: smó:tx̲w ~ smótx̲w.

taxi

high-bow canoe, high-bow river canoe, streetcar, tram, taxi, car, automobile:: xwókw'eletsem < xwókw' ~ xwekw'ó.

Taxidea taxus taxus

perhaps Taxidea taxus taxus or Gulo luscus luscus:: sqoyép.
Taxidea taxus taxus or Gulo luscus luscus:: melmélkw'es sqoyép < sqoyép.
Taxidea taxus taxus, possibly Gulo luscus luscus:: sqoyép ~ melmélkw'es sqoyép.

Taxus brevifolia

Taxus brevifolia:: téx̲wetselhp < téx̲wets.

tea :: tí.
Labrador tea, "Indian tea", "swamp tea":: mó:qwem.
teapot:: tí'àlà < tí.
warm up (food, tea, etc.):: t'elkw'á:ls < t'álqw' or t'élqw'.

teach
advise s-o, teach s-o, show s-o:: íwest < íwes.
beat up s-o as a lesson till he learns or gives up, teach s-o a lesson:: lepét < lép.
directing, training, teaching, guiding:: í:wes < íwes.
showing s-o (how to do it), teaching s-o, advising s-o, guiding s-o, directing s-o:: í:west < íwes.
teach how to do something, teach, guide, direct, show:: íwes.
teachings for children, what is taught to one's children:: s'iwesá:ylhem < íwes.
training, teaching, upbringing:: s'í:wes < íwes.

teacher :: skwúkwelstèleq < skwú:l.

teapot
teapot:: tí'àlà < tí.

tear
a tear (on the face):: sqó:s < qó:.
rip it up, tear it up, rip s-th, tear s-th:: x̲wtát < x̲wét.
take s-th down, tear down s-th man-made, dismantle s-th, take it apart:: yíx̲wet < yíx̲w.
tear (from eye):: qe'ó:les < qó:.
torn:: sx̲wex̲wéyt or sx̲wex̲wít < x̲wét.
torn up (in pieces) (or prob. better) (tear up (in many pieces)):: x̲wetx̲wét < x̲wét.
to tear, it rips:: x̲wét.
(word used when showing a picture of the deceased at a memorial ceremony, and telling the family .to dry their tears) his/her face/their faces are dried:: th'éyx̲westem < ts'íyxw ~ ts'éyxw ~ ch'íyxw.

tease
a teaser, somebody that teases to get one's goat:: í:wthelàq < weth'át.
tease s-o:: weth'át.
teasing:: hewth'eláq < weth'át.
teasing s-o:: hewth'át < weth'át.

teenage
adolescent boy (about 10 to 15 yrs. old), teenaged boy, young man (teenager):: swíweles ~ swíwles.

Teeter-totter
stone underwater Teeter-totter near Ñelhálh:: Xwíxweth'àlem < xwáth'.

teeth
(have) sharp teeth, (have) fangs:: silís < éy ~ éy:.

teething)
blowing spray (humorously said of a child teething):: pópex̲wels < póx̲w.

teething (CONT'D)

blow (spray) on a patient (of an Indian doctor or shaman), blow spray on s-o/s-th (of a shaman, a person ironing, a child teething):: póx̲wet < póx̲w.

telephone

ringing, phoning:: th'étsàls < th'éts or th'á(:)ts.
ring s-o up, phone s-o:: th'étst < th'éts or th'á(:)ts.
to rattle (of dishes or anything else loose), jingle (of money or any metal shaken), peal or toll (of a bell), make the sound of a bell, to ring (of a bell, telephone, in the ears):: th'á:tsem < th'éts or th'á(:)ts.

tell

go warn s-o in secret, go tell s-o in secret:: wíyt < wá:y.
lying, telling a lie, (bluffing [BHTTC]):: mameth'álem < máth'el.
tell a lie for s-o:: xwmath'elqéylémt < máth'el.
telling on s-o:: qwelqwélés < qwà:l.

tell s-o to say no to s-o:: ṓwestexw ~ éwestexw < éwe ~ ṓwe.

Telmatodytes palustris paludicola

Troglodytes troglodytes pacificus, may also include (esp.)Thryomanes bewickii, Telmatodytes palustris paludicola, Troglodytes aedon,and Salpinctes obsoletus:: t'ámiya.

temper

cranky, quick-tempered:: x̲éth'x̲eth' < x̲íth' ~ x̲éyth'.

temperature

keep the fire at a constant temperature:: txwéltsep.

temple

hit on the ear, hit on the temple (side of the head):: kw'qwá:lí:ya < kw'óqw.
on the side of the head, on the temples, around the ear, on the cheek:: =éla.
temples (on head):: th'iyaméle or th'iyaméla.

tempt

tempt s-o (with sex or lust):: xixtímestexw or xixtímstexw < xítem.

ten :: ó:pel.

cost ten dollars:: epoléstexw < ó:pel.
(first lunar month beginning in) July, (tenth month):: epóléstel < ó:pel.
ten birds:: epálōws < ó:pel, opelíws < ó:pel.
ten bodies:: opelíws < ó:pel.
ten canoes, ten boats:: opelṓwelh < ó:pel.
ten cents, dime:: mí:t ~ mít.
ten containers:: opeláleqel < ó:pel.
ten dollars, (ten Indian blankets [Boas]):: epóles < ó:pel.
ten fruit in a group (as they grow on a plant), (ten attached fruit):: opelòls < ó:pel.
ten leaves:: epálōws < ó:pel.
ten o'clock, (tenth hour):: s'ó:pels < ó:pel.
ten paddles:: epálōwes < ó:pel.
ten people:: epále < ó:pel.
ten ropes, ten threads, ten sticks, ten poles:: epálemets' < ó:pel.

ten (CONT'D)

ten times:: opelálh < ó:pel.
times ten, -ty (multiple of ten):: =elhsxá ~ =elsxá.

tender
be tender (in emotions):: chácha.

tendon
cord, muscle, tendon, nerve cord by backbone:: tl'e'ímél ~ tl'e'í:mel.

tense
tighten up (tense one's muscles, for ex.):: tl'ótl'ethet < tl'óth'et.

tent :: siláwtxw ~ sí:láwtxw < sí:l.

tenth
ten o'clock, (tenth hour):: s'ó:pels < ó:pel.

Tersus capax
Tersus capax ~ Schizothaerus capax:: swà:m.

test
test him/her if he/she is strong) t'át ew esu éyem < t'á.
test it, taste it, try it:: t'át < t'á.
test s-o--measure the knowledge (give a test):: xwéylemt te télmels < x̲wéylémt, tól.

testicle :: mátsel.
on the testicles:: =elétsel ~ =átsel.
testicles:: mámetsel < mátsel.

Tettigoniidae
order Orthoptera family Acrididae or perhaps family Tettigoniidae:: tl'emékw' < tl'ámkw'em, tl'emékw' < tl'ém, tl'emtl'émxel, tl'emtl'émxel, tl'emtl'émxel < tl'ém, ts'áts'etl'em < ts'tl'ám ~ ts'tl'ém, ts'ats'etl'í:m < ts'tl'ám ~ ts'tl'ém, ts'í:ts'á:tl'em < ts'tl'ám ~ ts'tl'ém.
probably mostly family Gryllidae, but perhaps family Prophalanopsidae, also perhaps singing groups such as family Tettigoniidae (order Orthoptera) or Cicadidae (order Hemiptera):: tó:lthíwa < tó:l ~ tò:l.

Tewít
a rock shaped like a dog on the east shore of the Fraser River near Hill's Bar and below Tewít (a rock shaped like a human hunter):: Sqwemá:y (?) < qwem.

Texas Bar
a turn in the Fraser River on the CPR (northwest) side two miles east of American Bar, Texas Bar bend in the Fraser River:: Sq'ewílem < q'éw ~ q'ew.

Texas Lake
probably Texas Lake:: St'élxweth' X̲ótsa < St'élxweth'.

-th
-th day of the week:: s= =s.

Thaleichthys pacificus:: swí:we ~ swíwe.

than

than :: telí < tel=.

thank

greet s-o, thank s-o:: ts'ít ~ ch'í:t.
It's you to thank the Lord, (Please say grace):: lúwe ts'ít te Chíchelh Siyám < =chílh ~ chílh=.
thank s-o (for a cure, for pall-bearing, a ceremony, being a witness):: xwth'í:t < ts'ít ~ ch'í:t.

that

he (present or presence unspecified), he's the one that, it's him that, she or it (present or presence unspecified), that or this (immediately before nominal):: tú:tl'ò ~ tútl'ò ~ tútl'o < tl'ó ~ tl'o, tú:tl'ò ~ tútl'ò ~ tútl'o < tl'ó ~ tl'o.
him (there, near but not visible), that one:: kwethá ~ kwe thá < kw.
(make that s-th (instead), cause that to be s-th (instead)):: tl'óst or tl'óstexw.
that (abstract subordinating conjunction):: kw'e.
that he, that she, that it, that they:: kws ...-s ~ kwses ~ kw'es ...-s < kw.
that's her (absent):: kwsú:tl'ò < kw.
that's her, she (present or presence unspecified), her (present or presence unspefified), that (female):: thú:tl'ò < tl'ó ~ tl'o.
that's him (absent), that's her (absent), it's him (absent), it's her (absent):: kwthú:tl'ò < kw.
that's them (absent, not present):: kwthú:tl'òlem < kw.
that was her (deceased):: kwsú:tl'ò:lh < kw.
that was her (deceased), she (deceased):: kwsú:tl'ò:lh < tl'ó ~ tl'o.
that was him (deceased), he (deceased):: kw'ú:tl'ò:lh < tl'ó ~ tl'o.
that was them (deceased):: kwthú:tl'òlèmèlh < kw.
that was them (deceased), they (deceased):: kwthú:tl'ò:lèmèlh < tl'ó ~ tl'o.

that's

that's a little one (male, about one to five years old), he (little):: tú:tl'òtl'èm < tl'ó ~ tl'o.
that's (an animate being), it's (usually animate):: tl'ó ~ tl'o.
that's her (absent), she (absent):: kwsú:tl'ò < tl'ó ~ tl'o.
that's her, she (present or presence unspecified), her (present or presence unspefified), that (female):: thú:tl'ò < tl'ó ~ tl'o.
that's him (absent), that's her (absent), it's him/her (absent), he (absent), she (absent):: kwthú:tl'ò < tl'ó ~ tl'o.
that's them (absent, not present), they (absent):: kwthú:tl'òlem < tl'ó ~ tl'o.
that's them (female), they (female), them (female):: thutl'ó:lem < tl'ó ~ tl'o.
that's them (gender unspecified), they, them:: yutl'ó:lem < tl'ó ~ tl'o.
that's them (little kids), they (little kids):: tl'étl'elò:m < tl'ó ~ tl'o.
that's them (little ones) (male?):: tutl'étl'elò:m < tl'ó ~ tl'o.
that's them (male), they (male), them (male):: tutl'ó:lem < tl'ó ~ tl'o.

that which

what, which, that which, the one that/who:: te.

thaw

melt, thaw:: yít'em.
to sleet, have a silver thaw:: x̲wíqw'el < x̲wíqw'.
to thaw:: yóx̲w.

the

the (distant and out of sight, remote), (definite but distant and out of sight, remote), the (abstract), a (remote, abstract), some, (indefinite):: kw'e, kw'e.
the (female, near but not visible), (female, near but not in sight) (translated by gender specific words in English, like aunt, etc.):: kwse < kw.
the (female, present and visible), the (female, unspecified presence and/or unspecified visibility):: the.
the (male or gender unspecified, near but not in sight):: kwthe < kw.
the (male, present, visible), the (gender or presence and visibility unspecified), a (male, present and visible), a (gender or presence and visibility unspecified):: te, te.
the (plural [usually human]):: ye ~ yi.
the (present, not visible, gender unspecified), the (remote, abstract):: kwe < kw.
the (remote, not visible, abstract), some (indefinite):: kw.

their

his, her, its, their, third person possessive pronoun, third person subordinate subject:: -s.

them

bump them together:: testéstexw < tós.
him, her, it, them, third person object:: -exw.
kill them:: x̲wá:yt < x̲wà:y ~ x̲wá:y.
that's them (absent, not present):: kwthú:tl'òlem < kw.
that's them (absent, not present), they (absent):: kwthú:tl'òlem < tl'ó ~ tl'o.
that's them (female), they (female), them (female):: thutl'ó:lem < tl'ó ~ tl'o.
that's them (gender unspecified), they, them:: yutl'ó:lem < tl'ó ~ tl'o.
that's them (little kids), they (little kids):: tl'étl'elò:m < tl'ó ~ tl'o.
that's them (little ones) (male?):: tutl'étl'elò:m < tl'ó ~ tl'o.
(that's) them (lots of little ones), they (many small ones):: yutl'étl'elòm < tl'ó ~ tl'o.
that's them (male), they (male), them (male):: tutl'ó:lem < tl'ó ~ tl'o.
that was them (deceased):: kwthú:tl'òlèmèlh < kw.
that was them (deceased), they (deceased):: kwthú:tl'ò:lèmèlh < tl'ó ~ tl'o.
they (known to the speaker), them (known to the speaker):: á:lhtel.

themselves

get separated (by distance), be by themselves, be separate:: halts'elí.
(take all of themselves, pick themselves all up):: mōkw'éthet < mékw' ~ mṓkw'.

then

and so, and then:: qesu < qe, qetl'osu ~ qetl'esu < qe.
and then (he, she, it):: tl'esu < tl'ó ~ tl'o.
so then I:: tl'olsu < tl'ó ~ tl'o.
so then you:: tl'o'asu < tl'ó ~ tl'o.
then (action following a previous action, contrastive), so (contrastive):: su.

the one that/who

what, which, that which, the one that/who:: te.

Th'éqwela

Seal Fat Rock on Harrison River just upriver from Th'éqwela (place by Morris Lake where Indian people used to play Indian badminton), this rock has what resembles seal fat all around it:: Skwló ~ Sqwló < sqwló.

there

(be) over there, (be) yonder:: lí(:) tí or lí(:)tí.
be there:: lí.
get there, arrive there, reach there:: xwelí ~ xwlí < lí.
get to, reach there:: xwelí:ls < lí.
is there none?, isn't there any?:: wá:ta < éwe ~ ŏ́we.
(there), (action distant or abstract):: lí ~ lí: ~ li.
there (nearby):: thá.

there's

there's none, there's nothing, there's nobody, there's no, be none, be nothing, be nobody:: ewéta < éwe ~ ŏ́we.

these

these:: ye'íle < í.

they)

and so (he, she, it, they):: qetl'osésu ~ qetl'os'ésu < tl'ó ~ tl'o, tl'osésu ~ tl'os'ésu < tl'ó ~ tl'o.
because (he, she, it, they):: tl'okw'es ~ tl'okwses ~ tl'ekwses < tl'ó ~ tl'o.
he/she/it was (already), they were (already):: lulh < le.
that he, that she, that it, that they:: kws ...-s ~ kwses ~ kw'es ...-s < kw.
that's them (absent, not present), they (absent):: kwthú:tl'òlem < tl'ó ~ tl'o.
that's them (female), they (female), them (female):: thutl'ó:lem < tl'ó ~ tl'o.
that's them (gender unspecified), they, them:: yutl'ó:lem < tl'ó ~ tl'o.
that's them (little kids), they (little kids):: tl'étl'elò:m < tl'ó ~ tl'o.
(that's) them (lots of little ones), they (many small ones):: yutl'étl'elòm < tl'ó ~ tl'o.
that's them (male), they (male), them (male):: tutl'ó:lem < tl'ó ~ tl'o.
that was them (deceased), they (deceased):: kwthú:tl'ò:lèmèlh < tl'ó ~ tl'o.
they came on (top of):: ch'alech'á (~ ts'alets'á) < ts'á:.
they (known to the speaker), them (known to the speaker):: á:lhtel.

thick

be thick:: plhá:t.
(have) thick lips:: pelhtó:ythel < plhá:t.
make s-th thick:: plhátstexw < plhá:t.
stout (of a person), thick (of a tree), thick around, coarse (of a rope), big (fat) (of a person). big (in girth):: mékw.

thick bushes

(come) out of thick bushes:: wexés.

thicket

a lot of trees close together (young), thicket:: théqet < theqát ~ thqá:t.
trees, thicket, timber, woods, forest:: theqthéqet < theqát ~ thqá:t.

thief :: qélqel < qá:l.

thigh

thigh, leg above the knee:: spatálép ~ spatálep.

thimbleberry:: t'qwém.
  a sprout or shoot (esp. of the kinds peeled and eaten in spring), sweet green inner shoots, green berry shoots, salmonberry shoots, wild raspberry shoots and greens, salmonberry sprouts, blackcap shoots, thimbleberry shoots, wild rhubarb shoots, fern shoots:: stháthqiy.
  thimbleberry plant or bush:: t'qwémelhp < t'qwém.

thin
  be scrawny, be thin:: qwe'íqweqw < qwe'íqw.
  be skinny, be thin:: stíth ~ stí:th < títh ~ tí:th.
  fish cut real thin for wind-drying but without cross cuts, dried fish cut differently than slhíts'es:: st'ál.
  four ropes, four threads, four sticks, four poles, (four long thin objects):: x̲ethílemets' < x̲e'ó:thel ~ x̲e'óthel.
  (have a) thin (point or nose):: qwe'íqweqs < qwe'íqw.
  make it thin (of dough, etc.):: th'eth'emí:lstexw < th'eth'emí:l.
  thin (of material like a dress, also of a string):: th'eth'emí:l.
  thin (of tree or pole):: qwe'íqws < qwe'íqw.

thing :: =´ta.
  a biter (animal, fish, etc.), a thing that is (always) biting:: ch'ech'émels < ts'ámet ~ ch'ámet.
  a thing that bites:: ch'emá:ls < ts'ámet ~ ch'ámet.
  device, tool, thing for doing something [as a structured activity]), person doing something [as structured activity]:: =els.
  living thing:: =e ~ =a.
  poor little one, you poor thing (said to a child):: t'ó:t'.
  three things:: lhelhíxw ~ lhíxw < lhí:xw.
  tiny round things:: emémeles < emímel ~ amí:mel.
  two different things:: selélets' < láts'.
  two things:: islá < isá:le ~ isále ~ isá:la.

thing used for
  device, implement, thing used for:: =tel.

think :: sta'á:wel < t.
  studying s-th, thinking about s-th, learning s-th, training for s-th, trying to do s-th:: totí:lt < tól.
  thinking about having intercourse:: kw'okw'etl'élmel < kw'átl'.
  thinking about s-th:: st'awélmet < t.
  thinking of something, (thinking):: qwoqwelíwel < qwà:l.
  thinking, pondering, studying, be studying:: totí:lthet < tól.
  think one(self) is smart:: mamts'ólthet < máth'el.
  think, ponder, study, decide:: tó:lthet < tól.
  think s-o is talking or laughing about one:: tl'ostélmét < tl'óst or tl'óstexw.
  think someone is talking about s-o:: tl'émstexw.
  think someone is talking or laughing about oneself:: tl'emstélemet ~ tl'emstélémét < tl'émstexw, tl'ostélmet.
  thoughts, feelings:: sqwá:lewel ~ sqwálewel ~ sqwà(:)lewel < qwà:l.

third
  third month since:: lhxwá:lth'ts < lhí:xw.
  three o'clock (< the third hour):: slhíxws < lhí:xw.

third finger

third finger:: malyítses < malyí, sts'ats'íts'etl'tses < ts'í:tl' ~ ts'ítl'.

third person

him, her, it, them, third person object:: -exw.
his, her, its, their, third person possessive pronoun, third person subordinate subject:: -s.
recent past third person subject:: le.
third person patient or object of passive:: -em.
third person subject (of transitive verbs):: -es.
third person subjunctive subject:: -es.

thirsty

be thirsty:: lhqó:la ~ lhqó:le < qó:.
be thirsty, get thirsty:: tsqó:le < qó:.

thirty :: lhèxwelsxá < lhí:xw.
thirty containers:: lhexwelsxáleqel < lhí:xw.
thirty cyclic periods:: lhexwelhsxó:s < lhí:xw.
thirty dollars:: lhexwelsxó:s < lhí:xw.
thirty people:: lhxwelhsxále < lhí:xw.

this :: teló= ~ tlo┐=.
as usual, this time, now, the first time:: yalh.
do, do this:: x̲tá: ~ x̲tá < x̲ét'e.
do it this way:: sx̲tá(:)stexw < x̲ét'e.
he (present or presence unspecified), he's the one that, it's him that, she or it (present or presence unspecified), that or this (immediately before nominal):: tú:tl'ò ~ tútl'ò ~ tútl'o < tl'ó ~ tl'o.
here, this place:: íkw'eló ~ íkw'elo < ló.
leave this here, leave s-th here:: ístexw ó < í.
now, this moment, this instant:: tloqá:ys < ló.
now, this moment, this instant, (right now):: tloqá:ys < qá:ys.
these:: ye'íle < í.
this (speaker is holding it), this one, this thing here:: te'íle ~ te'í:le < í.
this (speaker is not holding it but is close enough to touch it):: te í ~ te'í < í.
today, this day:: tlowáyél ~ tlówàyèl < ló.

thistle

Scotch thistle, (includes two introduced thistles and probably two native ones, from samples gathered, pressed and examined: Scotch thistle, Canada thistle, probably montane edible thistle and Indian thistle):: ts'eqw'ts'eqw' < ts'éqw'.

Thomas

(also name of the late) Mrs. Cecilia Thomas of Seabird Island:: Ts'símteló:t < ts'ísem.
a place just past the west end of Seabird Island, towards Agassiz, AK's grandfather only translated it as Hamersley's (see Hamersley's hopyards), it was located at the west end of Seabird Island i.e. property between Dan Thomas's and Uncle Dave Charles's places, across from Sqémelets [Elders on Seabird Is. trip 6/20/78]):: Qwoméx̲weth' < qwó:m ~ qwóm ~ qwem.

Thompson

Thompson Indian, Thompson person:: S'omél:a.
Thompson people:: S'em'oméla < S'omél:a.

thorn)

needle of plant, (thorn):: p'éth'tel < p'áth'.

thought

optimist, a person whose thoughts are always good:: wiyóth kwsu éys te sqwálewels te lólets'e < wiyóth.

pessimist, a person whose thoughts are always bad:: wiyóth kwsu qéls te sqwálewels te lólets'e < wiyóth.

thoughts, feelings:: sqwá:lewel ~ sqwálewel ~ sqwà(:)lewel < qwà:l.

thousand :: táwsel.

thrash

beating (s-o/s-th), thrashing (s-o/s-th):: qw'óqw'eqwet < qw'óqw.

thread

eight ropes, eight threads, eight sticks, eight poles:: tqátsámets' < tqá:tsa.

five ropes, five threads, five sticks, five poles:: lhq'átssámets' < lheq'át ~ lhq'á:t.

four ropes, four threads, four sticks, four poles, (four long thin objects):: x̲ethílemets' < x̲e'ó:thel ~ x̲e'óthel.

nine ropes, nine threads, nine sticks, nine poles:: tuxwámets' < tú:xw.

one rope, one thread, one stick, one pole:: lets'ámeth' < léts'a ~ léts'e.

rope, twine, string, thread:: x̲wéylem ~ x̲wé:ylem ~ x̲wí:lem.

(seven long objects), seven ropes, seven threads, seven sticks, seven poles:: th'okwsámets' < th'ó:kws.

(six long objects), six ropes, six threads, six sticks, six poles:: t'x̲émemets' < t'éx̲.

ten ropes, ten threads, ten sticks, ten poles:: epálemets' < ó:pel.

three ropes, three threads, three sticks, three poles, (three long narrow objects):: lhxwámeth' < lhí:xw.

two ropes, two threads, two sticks, two poles, two poles standing up:: isalámeth' < isá:le ~ isále ~ isá:la.

three :: lhí:xw.

plant with three black berries always joined together, (possibly black twinberry):: xó:lelhp.

third month since:: lhxwá:lth'ts < lhí:xw.

three birds:: lhxwíws < lhí:xw.

three canoes, three wagons, three conveyances (any form of transportation), three boats:: lhxwó:lh < lhí:xw.

three containers:: lhíxweqel < lhí:xw.

three dollars, three tokens of wealth, three blankets (Boas), three cyclic periods:: lhí:xwes < lhí:xw.

three fish:: lhíxweqw < lhí:xw.

three fruit in a cluster (as they grow on a plant):: lhexwòls < lhí:xw.

three houses, (three buildings):: lhxwá:wtxw < lhí:xw.

three kinds, three piles of things:: lhixwmó:t < lhí:xw.

three leaves:: lhxwálews < lhí:xw.

three little people:: lhelhxwále < lhí:xw.

three o'clock (< the third hour):: slhíxws < lhí:xw.

three paddles, three paddlers:: lhxwő:wes < lhí:xw.

three pants:: lhexwáyiws < lhí:xw.

three people:: lhxwá:le ~ lhxwále < lhí:xw.

three ropes, three threads, three sticks, three poles, (three long narrow objects):: lhxwámeth' < lhí:xw.

three (CONT'D)

three things:: lhelhíxw ~ lhíxw < lhí:xw.
three times, thrice:: lhxwá:lh < lhí:xw.
three trees:: lhxwá:lhp < lhí:xw.

Three Creeks Mountain:: Lhelhxwáyeleq < lhí:xw.

thrice

three times, thrice:: lhxwá:lh < lhí:xw.

thrill

(get a) thrill, (to) thrill:: xwóywél.

throat

a grass that grows with berries in fields and everywhere and has seeds that stick in one's throat when eaten with berries, probably a type of brome grass, likely California brome grass, possibly sweet cicely:: táqalh.
burned in the throat:: kw'és=qel < kw'ás.
dry in the throat:: ch'íyxweqel < ts'íyxw ~ ts'éyxw ~ ch'íyxw.
in the throat, in the esophagus, in the voice:: =eqel.
my throat is dry:: ts'iyxweqthàlèm < ts'íyxw ~ ts'éyxw ~ ch'íyxw.
relaxed [in the throat]:: qáwlhelh < qá:w.
skin of the throat:: kw'elṓwlhelh < kw'eléw ~ kw'elṓw.
throat (inside part), gullet, voice:: sqelxwá:le ~ sqelxwále < qél:éxw ~ qel(:)éxw.
throat of a cliff or mountain:: =eqel.

throb

(have/get) throbbing pain:: téxwem.

through

crawl through (like through a fence):: qwahéylém ~ qwahí:lém < qwá.
go through:: qwehá < qwá.
go through a channel:: lheltáletsem < lhà:l.
go through (somewhere), go via (somewhere), go by way of:: lhe'á.
go through the woods:: xets'í:lem < xí:ts' ~ xíts' ~ xets'.
sticking out through a hole (like a toe out of a sock, knee out of a hole in pants, a nail driven clear through the other side of a board), come out into the open:: qwōhóls (or perhaps) qwehóls < qwá.

throw

cast a spell, throw a spell, put on a spell, shoot power:: x̲t'áls or x̲t'á:ls < x̲ét'.
drop oneself into a seat, throw oneself on the floor or ground in a tantrum, throw a tantrum:: kw'qweméthet < kw'óqw.
get hit (by s-th thrown or airborne):: ló:m ~ lóm.
launch s-th/s-o into the water, push s-o/s-th into the water, throw it in the water:: qwsét < qwés.
sparks, red hot ashes thrown out:: qw'á:ychep < qw'á:y.
throw and hit s-th/s-o, strike s-th/s-o (with something thrown):: ló:met ~ lómet < ló:m ~ lóm.
throw a net into water (to drift, not to set), throw a net out, (gill net [TG]):: qwsá:yel < qwés.
throw different leftovers together for a meal, throw a meal together, eat a snack:: p'ekw'ethílem < p'ákw'.

throw (CONT'D)

throwing and hitting s-th:: lólemet < ló:m ~ lóm.
throw s-o down hard (like a wrestler), tap s-th (a container's bottom) [hard] on something to make the contents settle (like berry basket):: th'esét ~ th'sét < th'és.
throw s-o down [hard] on the rump:: th'eséletst < th'és.
throw s-th (a rock, etc.), throw it (to someone):: wá:lx < wál or wá:l.
throw s-th away, discard s-th, throw s-o away, discard s-o:: íkw'et < íkw' ~ í:kw'.
to scramble-give, throw money/blankets/poles to a crowd, give away at a big (winter) dance [by throwing]:: wá:ls < wál or wá:l.

throw up
to vomit, throw up:: yá:t.

Thrush)
Female Salmonberry Bird, (Female Swainson's Thrush):: Xwatóy < xwét.
Male Salmonberry Bird, (Male Swainson's Thrush):: Xwét < xwét.

thrush
brown thrush (could be hermit thrush, or possibly gray-cheeked thrush):: slhólho.
call of the Swainson's thrush:: xwét.
call of the winter robin or varied thrush:: sx̲wík'.
Swainson's thrush, the salmonberry bird:: xwét.
the call of the female Swainson's thrush:: Xwatóy < xwét.
winter robin, bush robin, varied thrush:: sx̲wík'.

thrust s-th:: thxwót.

Thryomanes bewickii
Troglodytes troglodytes pacificus, may also include (esp.)Thryomanes bewickii, Telmatodytes palustris paludicola, Troglodytes aedon,and Salpinctes obsoletus:: t'ámiya.

thud
thudding (of footsteps or horses hooves on ground):: kwómkwem < kwém.
to thud (dull, outside):: kwém.

Thuja plicata:: x̲epá:y ~ x̲epáy ~ x̲pá:y < sx̲éyp, x̲pá:yelhp ~ x̲páyelhp < sx̲éyp, x̲pá:ytses ~ x̲páytses < sx̲éyp, súsekw'.
Thuja plicata:: sókw'em < sókw'.

thumb :: mekwó:méltses < mékw.

thump
[make a bang, make a sudden hard thump sound]:: kw'péx̲w.

thunder :: shxwexwó:s.

thunderbird:: shxwexwó:s.
mountain shaped like a thunderbird across the Fraser River from Q'ów (the "howl") mountain:: Xwexwó:stel < shxwexwó:s.

Thursday
Thursday (a less common name):: smős < mős.

Thursday (CONT'D)

Thursday, four o'clock, (fourth cyclic period):: sx̲e'óthels < x̲e'ó:thel ~ x̲e'óthel.

thwarts)

crosspieces in a canoe, (thwarts):: lhex̲elwélhtel < lhá:x̲ ~ lháx̲.

tick

tick, wood tick, and probably Pacific Coast tick:: t'pí.
tick, woodtick, probably Pacific Coast tick and the wood tick:: méth'elhqìwèl < méth'elh.

tickle

being tickled, (having tickling, getting tickling), tickley:: sá:yt'em ~ sayít'em < síyt'.
(probably) tickle the bottom of someone's feet, (tickle s-o on the foot):: sét'xt < síyt'.
tickled (by a hair, by a light touch):: sá:yx̲wem.
tickle s-o:: síyt't ~ sí:t't < síyt'.
tickling:: sá:yt'els < síyt'.
tickling s-o:: sá:yt't < síyt'.

tide

high tide:: me lets'léts' < léts'.
spring tide (when a river first rises in May):: qó:.
(the) tide:: sqém:el < qém:el.
tide coming in, water coming in, water coming up (ocean tide or river):: qém:el.
to go down (of water), subside (of water), the tide goes out or down, (be going out (of tide) [BJ]):: th'à:m ~ th'ám.

tie

anchor-line, mooring-line, bow-line, what is used to tie up a canoe:: lhqéletel < lhqé:ylt.
buckskin straps for tying a baby in its cradle or basket:: yémqetel < yém ~ yem.
something to tie the feet:: q'ép'xetel (unless q'épxetel is correct) < q'áp'.
tie it up, bind it, tie it (parcel, broken shovel handle, belt, two ropes together):: q'áp'et ~ q'á:p'et < q'áp'.
tie it up (of a canoe):: lhqé:ylt.
to fasten s-th by tying, tie up s-th (like canoe, horse, laces, nets, cow, shoelaces), tie it:: q'éyset ~ q'í(:)set < q'ey ~ q'i.
tying a net:: q'ésetsel < q'ey ~ q'i.
tying it:: q'éyq'eset < q'ey ~ q'i.
tying it up:: q'áq'ep'et < q'áp'.
tying up:: q'áq'ep'els < q'áp'.

tiger lily:: sx̲ameléxwthelh < sáx̲em.

tight

(be) squeezed in, jammed up, tight:: sx̲ex̲ákw' < x̲ékw'.
be straight (of rope but not tree), pulled tight (of rope), stretched tight, tight:: sthethá:kw' < thékw'.
be tight, be secured tightly:: slá ~ selá ~ slá: (probably).
(be) tight, (leaning backwards [EB]):: sq'áq'eth' < q'áth'.
(be) too tight (of shoes, clothes, trap, box), tight (of a dress one can't get into), too tight to get into (of dress, car, box of cards, etc.):: stl'etl'íq' < tl'íq'.
tighten it (a belt, a pack, etc.):: q'íxwet.
tighten it up, wind it up:: tl'óth'et.

tighten
    tighten it up, wind it up:: tl'óth'et.
    tighten up (tense one’s muscles, for ex.):: tl’ótl’ethet < tl'óth'et.

tight-fitting
    (be) tight-fitting (of clothes, can't be quite buttoned):: spex̲elís < páx̲, spepíx̲ < páx̲.

till
    until, till, while:: qew ~ qwō ~ qe ... u/ew < qe.

tilt
    put one's head back (tilt one's face up):: q'óx̲esem.
    side hills or tilted hills northwest of Ñó:letsa near Yale:: Tewtewá:la ~ Tutuwále < tewále.
    side hills, tilted hills, slopes:: tewtewá:la ~ tutuwále < tewále.
    sloping floor, (tilted):: tewále.
    tilt s-th, lift s-th up at one end or one side, tilt s-th sideways:: tewá:let < tewále.

timber
    trees, thicket, timber, woods, forest:: theqthéqet < theqát ~ thqá:t.

time
    a drum, small stick used to drum or beat time to songs in slahal game:: q'ówet.
    a long time ago:: welhíthelh < híth, welhí:thelh < híth, welhíth < híth.
    a long time, it's a long time:: híth.
    always, all the time, ((also) often, over and over [TG]):: wiyóth.
    as usual, this time, now, the first time:: yalh.
    (be) Spring, [time or season] when everything comes up:: temkw'éyles < kw'í ~ kw'íy.
    be what hour?, be what time?:: skw'í:ls < kw'í:l ~ kw'íl.
    bring it out for the first time (of a spirit-song):: p'í:t < p'í:.
    busy at home all the time:: yúkw'es.
    coho salmon time, August to September:: temkwṓxweth < kwṓxweth.
    first time:: =elhsxá ~ =elsxá.
    gooseberry time, the month or moon (first sliver) that starts in June:: temt'á:mxw < t'á:mxw.
    has come around (of a cyclic period of time):: séqsel.
    having lots of fun, having a good time:: eyó:sthet ~ iyósthet < éy ~ éy:.
    haying time:: temsóx̲wel < só:x̲wel ~ sóx̲wel.
    high water time (yearly, usually in June), June:: temqó: ~ temqoqó: < qó:.
    hungry time (about mid-April to mid-May), famine (Elders 3/72):: temkw'à:y < kw'à:y.
    July to August, (big spring salmon time):: temth'oló:lh < sth'olólh.
    month beginning with first sliver of moon in February, (time things stick to the hand (in cold)):: temt'elémtses < t'elém.
    moon or month beginning in February, (November to December, time when ice forms [and sticks] [Billy Sepass in Jenness]):: temtl'í:q'es < tl'íq'.
    November, time to catch salmon:: temth'ó:qwi < sth'ó:qwi ~ sth'óqwi.
    October moon, time to smoke Chehalis spring salmon:: tempó:kw' < pó:qw' ~ póqw'.
    October to November, (wood gathering time):: tsélcheptel?.
    once, one time:: lets'áxw < léts'a ~ léts'e.
    salmonberry time, (usually) May:: tem'elíle < elíle.
    September to October, dog salmon time:: temkw'ó:lexw < kw'ó:lexw.

time (CONT'D)

six times:: t'x̲emálh < t'éx̲.
spring (season), (time to sprout up):: temqw'íles ~ temqw'éyles < qw'íl.
the last time:: ílhulhòy < hò:y ~ hó:y ~ hóy.
time for, time to, season of:: tem=.
time of the baby sockeye's coming, early spring (usually April), April moon:: temkwíkwexel.
time, season:: tem=.
time to dry fish, first of July (at Yale), October (at Chehalis):: temchálhtel < =chílh ~ chílh=.

times

clubbing many times, hitting many times:: kw'elqwál < kw'óqw.
eight times:: tqatsálh < tqá:tsa.
first time:: =elhsxá ~ =elsxá.
five times:: lhq'atses'álh < lheq'át ~ lhq'á:t.
folding lots of things, fold s-th several times or many times:: lemlémet < lémet.
four times:: x̲ethelálh < x̲e'ó:thel ~ x̲e'óthel.
hit on the face (several times):: melmélkw'es < xwmélkw'es.
how many times:: kw'elálh < kw'í:l ~ kw'íl.
lots of times:: qx̲álh < qéx̲.
moving, (many moving around in circles, moving around in circles many times):: x̲elx̲álqem < x̲álqem.
nine times:: tú:xwà:lh < tú:xw.
seven times:: th'ekwsálh < th'ó:kws.
splashing, splashing (lots of times):: t'ó:mqw'em < t'émeqw'.
ten times:: opelálh < ó:pel.
three times, thrice:: lhxwá:lh < lhí:xw.
times, occasions:: =álh ~ =áxw ~ =á.
times ten, -ty (multiple of ten):: =elhsxá ~ =elsxá.
twice, two times:: themá.
whipping s-o/s-th many times:: qw'ó:leqwet < qw'óqw.

tin

metal can (in U.S. English), a tin (in Canadian English):: q'éx̲q'x̲el < q'(e)x̲.

tinder

tinder, material used to start a fire with (fine dried cedar bark):: syeqwlhá:ltel < yéqw.

tingle

to tingle (like arm waking up from numbness), (have/get a) stinging feeling:: thátkwem.

tinkle

clinking, tinkling (of glass, ice in glass, glasses together, dishes together, metal together):: ts'átx̲em ~ th'átx̲em.

tiny

little tiny beads:: ts'ets'emíkw.
(probably) tiny midget:: t'it'epsó:ye < st'éps ~ st'epsóye.
tiny round things:: emémeles < emímel ~ amí:mel.

tip

cut off the tip of one's nose:: lhts'élqsel < lhíts' ~ lhí:ts'.

tip (CONT'D)

point or tip of a long object (pole, tree, knife, candle, land):: =eqs ~ =éqsel ~ =élqsel ~ =elqs.
tip (from horizontal or vertical):: kw'élh.
tip or point of one's nose:: s'álqsel.
tip over, capsize:: kw'élh.
tip over (of a canoe):: qwélh.
tip over, spill (of liquid or solid), spilled, spill accidentally:: kw'élh.
tippy (of a canoe):: kw'éth'em < kw'eth'ém.
to tip (of canoe, etc.):: kw'eth'ém.

tip-toe
tip-toeing, (walking lightly, sneaking):: t'et'ásxelem < t'ás.

Tipulidae
family Tipulidae:: spelwálh qwá:l < qwá:l, tl'áleqtxel qwá:l < qwá:l.
order Diptera, family Tipulidae:: spelwálh, tl'áleqtxel qwá:l < tl'áqt.

tire
annoyed with s-th, annoyed by s-o, tired of s-o:: ts'íwélmét < ts'íw.
real tired:: welhchí:ws < lhchí:ws.
tired:: lhchí:ws, qásel.
tired of s-th, bored with s-th:: x̲lhém:et < x̲élh.
tired of waiting:: q'sém.
tired on the rump:: x̲lhélets < x̲élh.
tired out:: qsí:l < qásel.
tired out from crying:: qesqesí:lqel < qásel, qsí:lthet < qásel.
to be tired:: x̲lhém < x̲élh.

tired
out of breath and over-tired and over-hungry:: pqwíles < péqw.
real tired:: welhchí:ws < lhchí:ws.
tired:: lhchí:ws.
tired of s-th, bored with s-th:: lhchí:wsmet < lhchí:ws.

to
come, coming, come to, coming to:: mí ~ mé ~ me.
come near s-o, (come to s-o):: emíls < mí ~ mé ~ me.
distributive, to each:: R5= or C1e=.
go, go to, going, going to, go(ing) to (in future), be gone:: lám < la.
go, go to, going, going to, (go somewhere else to do the action), going to (in future):: la.
to the back (near the wall), on the inside (on a bed toward the wall):: lhelhá:l.
us (nominalized object of preposition), to us, with us:: tl'elhlímelh < lhlímelh.
you folks (object of preposition), to you folks, with you folks:: tl'alhwélep < lhwélep.

toad
frog, (esp. Northwestern toad, if generic also includes the tree toad and recent introductions the bullfrog and green frog, and the tailed toad, red-legged frog, and western spotted frog), (if generic may also include water frog that lives in springs and keeps the water cold [Halq'eméylem name unknown to Elders Group on 1/30/80], and a huge pretty frog (bigger than pípehò:m) that has supernatural powers and cries like a baby [sx̲ex̲ómőlh ~ wex̲ó:mő:lh]), (big frog with warts [AD]):: pípehò:m < peh or pó(:)h.
frog, (if generic may include Pacific tree toad and perhaps the introduced species: bullfrog,

toad (CONT'D)

green frog, red-legged frog, western spotted frog, and the tailed toad):: wex̲és, welée̲x̲ < wex̲és.
little green frog, little green tree frog, (Pacific tree toad):: welék'.

toast
toast it by a fire (of smoked fish):: kw'áset < kw'ás.
to toast by a fire (of smoke-cured fish, dried fish), get toasted by fire (of smoke-dried fish):: kw'ásem < kw'ás.

tobacco :: sp'ó:tl'em ~ sp'ótl'em < p'ótl'em.
kinnikinnick berry, bearberry, Indian tobacco, domestic pea, domestic green bean, and probably giant vetch berry:: tl'íkw'el.

today :: tlówàyèl ~ tlowáyél < wáyel.
today, this day:: tlowáyél ~ tlówàyèl < ló.

toe :: slé̲x̲xel < lé̲x̲.
all the joints of the foot and toes:: qwemqwémx̲wxel < qwó:m ~ qwóm ~ qwem.
(be) pigeon-toed, (sandhill crane toed:: slímiyeqwxel < slí:m.
(big) toe:: mekwó:mélxel < mékw.
sticking out through a hole (like a toe out of a sock, knee out of a hole in pants, a nail driven clear through the other side of a board), come out into the open:: qwōhóls (or perhaps) qwehóls < qwá.

toenail :: qw'x̲wélxel.
in-grown toe-nail:: kyépe=xel < kyépe=.

together
along, together, be included, with:: sq'eq'ó < q'ó.
along, with, together with:: sq'ó < q'ó.
a lot of trees close together (young), thicket:: théqet < theqát ~ thqá:t.
be gathered together:: sq'eq'íp < q'ép.
bump them together:: testéstexw < tós.
clinking, tinkling (of glass, ice in glass, glasses together, dishes together, metal together):: ts'átx̲em ~ th'átx̲em.
close together, (narrow? [MV]):: tl'éts' < tl'í:ts'.
crowding together:: q'ópthet < q'ép.
crowd together, gather together, people gather:: q'péthet < q'ép.
elope, run away together:: chó:mtel < chó:m.
join s-th together:: lheqtó:léstexw < lhéq.
join two poles together, splice it together (of a rope), (join together on the ends):: t'qwíqst.
mix s-th, put them together:: q'etóléstexw < q'ó.
perish together, many die (in famine, sickness, fire), all die, get wiped out:: x̲wà:y ~ x̲wá:y.
put them together, (join them together):: q'ótelt ~ q'ótòlt < q'ó.

toilet
little house, cabin (say 12 ft. x 10 ft. or less), small home, storage house (small shed-like house, enclosed with door), outhouse (slang), toilet (slang):: lílem < lá:lém.
outhouse, toilet, bathroom:: atl'qeláwtxw < átl'q.
toilet paper:: shxwep'életstel ~ shxwp'életstel < áp'.

toll
to rattle (of dishes or anything else loose), jingle (of money or any metal shaken), peal or toll (of a bell), make the sound of a bell, to ring (of a bell, telephone, in the ears):: th'á:tsem < th'éts or th'á(:)ts.

tomorrow :: wáyeles ~ wáyélés ~ wàyèlès < wáyel.

tongue :: téxwthelh.
on the tongue:: =éxwthelh.
stick out one's tongue, (stick it out (the tongue)):: lhálêqet.

too :: we'ól ~ ól(e)we ~ ólew < òl ~ -òl ~ -ò ~ el.
(be) too tight (of shoes, clothes, trap, box), tight (of a dress one can't get into), too tight to get into (of dress, car, box of cards, etc.):: stl'etl'íq' < tl'íq'.
too heavy to lift:: éw.
too (overly), very much:: we'ól ~ ól(e)we ~ ólew < òl ~ -òl ~ -ò ~ el.

tool :: shxweyó:yes < yó:ys.
device, tool:: =í:ls.
grind or sharpen s-th (of edged tools):: yéq'est < yéq'.
structured activity continuative, structured activity continuative nominal or tool or person:: =els.
tool case:: á:wkw'mal < á:wkw'.

tooth
brush one's teeth:: th'exwélesem < th'éxw or th'óxw.
grinding one's teeth:: xaxelts'elísem < xélts'.
(have) a steady toothache, have a toothache:: yélyelesem < yél:és.
(have a) tooth missing, (have) teeth missing (any number), (be) toothless:: slhémoqel < lhém.
(have) sharp teeth, (have) fangs:: silís < éy ~ éy:.
on the teeth or tooth:: =elís ~ =él:es.
pulled out (of tooth or teeth), (have one's tooth pulled out):: ma'álésem < má ~ má'-.
put s-th between the teeth, put it in one's mouth, bite on s-th (not into it):: ts'ámet ~ ch'ámet.
rock above Yale where Ñá:ls gritted his teeth and scratched rocks as he duelled with a medicine man across the Fraser:: Th'exelís < th'exelís.
showing his/her teeth:: th'exelís.
tooth, teeth:: yél:és.

toothache
(have) a steady toothache, have a toothache:: yélyelesem < yél:és.

toothless
(have a) tooth missing, (have) teeth missing (any number), (be) toothless:: slhémoqel < lhém.

toothpaste
toothpaste(?):: xixqelísem?.

top :: =qéyl ~ =qel.

top (CONT'D)

be above, be high, top, up above, way high:: chíchelh < =chílh ~ chílh=.
(being/put) on the top shelf:: ts'ech'ó:lwelh < ts'á:.
be on top of:: sts'ets'á < ts'á:.
crown of head, center of the top of the head where the hair starts:: sq'eyx̱éleqw.
get on top of something:: ts'ílem < ts'á:.
(get the) top cut off:: t'eqw'qéyl or t'eqw'qí:l < t'éqw'.
get to the top or summit of a mountain:: wets'á: < ts'á:.
on the body, on top of itself:: =á:w ~ =í:w ~ =ew.
on top (for ex. of a tree):: =qéyl ~ =qel.
on top of the head, on the hair:: =eqw ~ =(e)leqw ~ =íqw ~ =ó:qw.
on top of the house:: chélhmel < =chílh ~ chílh=.
they came on (top of):: ch'alech'á (~ ts'alets'á) < ts'á:.
top of roof, roof planks:: sts'á:ltexw < ts'á:.
top of the ear:: schelhá:liya < =chílh ~ chílh=.
top of the foot:: tslhítselxel < =chílh ~ chílh=.
upper part or top of a house, upper part or top of a pit-house:: tslháltxw < =chílh ~ chílh=.

top of the head

hit on the top of the head:: kw'qwéleqw < kw'óqw.
top of the head, scalp:: t'émleqw < t'ém.

torch :: peló:qel.

any kind of light that one carries, torch (made from pitch), lantern, lamp, flashlight:: sláx̱et < láx̱et.
moon of February to March, (torch season):: peló:qes < peló:qel.
torch (made from pitch) (SJ and MV), (bark shield for fire (Elders Group 3/6/78)):: swáts'et.

torchlight

spear animals by torchlight:: lex̱éywa ~ lex̱íwa.
spear fish by torchlight, to torchlight, to pit-lamp:: lex̱éywa ~ lex̱íwa.
spearing fish by torchlight:: hálx̱eywa ~ hálx̱iwa < lex̱éywa ~ lex̱íwa.

torch-lighting

fire box or fire platform and fire shield for torch-lighting or pit-lamping fire:: tl'áts'eq.

torn

torn:: sx̱wex̱wéyt or sx̱wex̱wít < x̱wét.

Tortricidae

probably larvae of Lepidoptera or Diptera, possibly larvae of order Lepidoptera, family Tortricidae:: xwexwíye.

totem pole

carved outside post on longhouse, totem pole:: x̱wíythi < x̱wíyth.

touch

cool down enough to touch (or handle or work with):: tóqweltsep.
tickled (by a hair, by a light touch):: sá:yx̱wem.
touching bottom (of a canoe or a person):: tesláts < tós.
touch s-o accidentally, bump s-o, bumped s-o:: téslexw < tós.
touch s-o purposely, squish it (of berries, etc.), smash s-th, mash it (berries, potatoes,

carrots, etc.), bump it:: tóset < tós.

tough

(be) hard, stiff (material), strong (of rope, material, not of a person), tough:: tl'éx̲w.
tough skin:: tl'x̲wíws < tl'éx̲w.

toward :: xwelám.

away from the shore, toward the river:: chúchu ~ chúwchuw ~ chéwchew < cháchew ~ cháchu.
be facing toward:: le'ós < le'á.
(be) with one's back towards something or someone:: schewíts.
go down(hill) to the water, go towards the river:: t'óxw.
going towards the river or water:: t'ót'exw < t'óxw.
in the backwoods, toward the woods, away from the river, in the bush:: chó:leqw < chá:l or chó:l.
to the back (near the wall), on the inside (on a bed toward the wall):: lhelhá:l.
toward, towards, for:: xwelá ~ xwelám ~ xwlá ~ xwlám < la.
turn one's face towards:: ó:sem.

towel

dish-towel:: shxw'áp'ewí:ls < áp', shxw'áp'ewí:ls < a˥ :p' ~ a˥ p', shxwiqw'ewí:ls < íqw'.
large towel:: shxw'óp'estel < áp'.

towhee

catbird (has black head), rufous-sided towhee:: sx̲wítl'.

town :: tówel.

toy

cottonwood bark driftwood (it was used to carve toy canoes), cottonwood driftwood used for carving toy canoes:: qwémélép ~ qwemélep.

trachea

on the front of the neck, in the windpipe, in the trachea:: =lhelh ~ =lhál.

track

following tracks:: tátelxel < tá:lxel.
follow tracks:: tá:lxel.
footprint, tracks:: sx̲éyeltel ~ sx̲í:ltel < sx̲él:e.
railroad, (railroad track [IHTTC]):: lílȍt.
the Tracks of Mink, holes shaped like a mink's tracks toward the base of the rock-face called Xwyélés or Lexwyélés:: Sx̲éyeltels Te Sqoyéx̲iya < sx̲él:e.
tracking an animal:: chokwelélqem < chó:kw.
tracking, following prints:: kw'ókw'etsxel < kw'áts ~ kw'éts.
tracks going down to the river:: tó:lxel < tó:l ~ tò:l.

Tracks of Mink

the Tracks of Mink, holes shaped like a mink's tracks toward the base of the rock-face called Xwyélés or Lexwyélés:: Sx̲éyeltels Te Sqoyéx̲iya < sx̲él:e.

trade

change s-th (purposely), change s-o, transform s-o/s-th, trade s-th, replace s-th:: iyá:qt ~

trade (CONT'D)

iyáqt < iyá:q.
trade with s-o:: iyáqelhtst < iyá:q, iyáqestexw < iyá:q.

trail)

a fork in a road (or trail):: st'éx̲ < t'éx̲.
a mark to show where something is, a marker (to show a trail, something buried, a grave):: x̲áth'tel < x̲áth' ~ x̲e'áth'.
follow behind s-o, trail s-o:: chokwí:lt < chó:kw.
mark s-th, blaze it (of a trail), get/have s-th spotted (marked and located), make note of s-th:: x̲e'áth'stexw < x̲áth' ~ x̲e'áth'.
path, trail:: xáxlh < xálh ~ xá:lh.
trail and steep slope on the west shore of Kawkawa Lake where the trail went up and over a steep hill and then down:: Sq'éywetselem ~ Sq'éywetsélém < q'e:yw ~ q'í:w.
what one walks on (trail, board sidewalk, cement sidewalk, etc.):: shxw'ímex < i┐ m.

trailer hitch)

something that you hook onto (like a trailer hitch):: s'óqw' < óqw'.

train

directing, training, teaching, guiding:: í:wes < íwes.
drifting backwards in two canoes with net between to catch sturgeon, (drift-netting), backing up (of canoe, train):: tewláts.
get wedged (by falling tree, for ex.), got run over (by car, train, etc.):: tl'íq'.
jumping up and down or bouncing up and down (of an Indian doctor training):: hélmethet < lá:m.
jump up and down (of Indian doctor training):: lemóthet < lá:m.
place of training to become an Indian doctor (pit made from repeated jumping every year on the same spot):: shxwlemóthetále < lá:m.
studying s-th, thinking about s-th, learning s-th, training for s-th, trying to do s-th:: totí:lt < tól.
to travel by canoe, (nowadays also) travel by airplane, travel by train, travel by car:: yeló:lh < ó:lh.
training:: kw'ekw'íythet < kw'í ~ kw'íy.
training, teaching, upbringing:: s'í:wes < íwes.

tram

high-bow canoe, high-bow river canoe, streetcar, tram, taxi, car, automobile:: xwókw'eletsem < xwókw' ~ xwekw'ó.

trance

feel like singing a spirit song, be in a trance making sighsand crying sounds before singing a spirit song, be in the beginning of a trance before the spirit song is recognizable (the motions and sounds, crying out or wailing before singing):: lhéch.

transform

change s-o/s-th (into something else), transform s-o/s-th:: iyá:qt ~ iyáqt < iyá:q.
change s-th (purposely), change s-o, transform s-o/s-th, trade s-th, replace s-th:: iyá:qt ~ iyáqt < iyá:q.
transform it more, pass it over the fire more (at a burning):: x̲iyx̲éyt or x̲eyx̲éyt < x̲éyt.
transform s-th/s-o, change s-th/s-o:: x̲éyt.

Transformer

Transformer:: X̲á:ls ~ X̲à:ls < x̲éyt, X̲éyt < x̲éyt.
the Transformers:: X̲ex̲á:ls < x̲éyt.

transitive
third person subject (of transitive verbs):: -es.

transitivizer
causative control transitivizer:: =st.
indirect effect non-control transitivizer:: =met.
non-control transitivizer, accidentally, happen to, manage to do to s-o/s-th:: =l.
psychological non-control transitivizer:: =eles ~ =les.
purposeful control transitivizer, do purposely to s-o/s-th:: =t ~ =et.
purposeful control transitivizer inanimate object preferred:: =ex.

translucent
transparent, can be seen through (skin, curtain, etc.), translucent:: th'álx̲em.

transparent
(be) transparent:: sth'óth'elh < th'áth'elh.
transparent, can be seen through (skin, curtain, etc.), translucent:: th'álx̲em.

transportation)
three canoes, three wagons, three conveyances (any form of transportation), three boats:: lhxwó:lh < lhí:xw.

trap
a prop used to trip a deadfall trap:: tpólhtel < tpólh.
a waiting dip-net with frame and string trap:: thqálem < thqá:lem.
bait s-th (a trap for animals or birds):: má:lat < má:la ~ má:le.
bait s-th (fish-line, fish-hook, fish-trap):: má:lat < má:la ~ má:le.
bear trap:: pathúyel < pá:th.
(be) too tight (of shoes, clothes, trap, box), tight (of a dress one can't get into), too tight to get into (of dress, car, box of cards, etc.):: stl'etl'íq' < tl'íq'.
check a net or trap (for animal):: kw'echú:yel < kw'áts ~ kw'éts.
check a net or trap (for fish):: kw'echú:yel < kw'áts ~ kw'éts.
deadfall trap:: tl'iq'áwtxw < tl'íq'.
fish trap, weir:: sts'iyáq.
metal trap, any trap, (also deadfall trap):: x̲ésxel.
one's hand jammed (in a trap, under a box, etc.):: tl'í:q'etses < tl'íq'.
salmon weir, fish trap:: ch'iyáqtel < sts'iyáq.
set a snare trap:: íweltàlem < íwel.
setting a trap:: x̲áx̲esxèlem < x̲ésxel.
snare, snare trap:: s'eweltá:l < íwel.
spring snare trap:: s'eweltá:l < íwel.
to escape (as an animal from a trap), got away from something that trapped a person or animal:: tl'ewlómét ~ tl'ōwlómét < tl'í:w.
trap, net:: =á:yel ~ =iyel ~ =ú:yel.

trash
garbage, trash:: sqel:ép ~ sqél:ep < qél.

travel

be last (in travelling), be behind (in travelling):: yelhyó:qwt < lhiyó:qwt.
coming by foot, travelling by walking, already walking, travelling on foot:: ye'í:mex < i┐m.
go travelling by way of, go via:: ley ~ lay < la.
group of canoes travelling upstream (moving to camp for fish-drying for ex.):: istéytiyel.
manage by oneself (in food or travel), try to do it by oneself, try to be independent, do the best one can:: iyólewéthet < éy ~ éy:.
to travel by canoe, (nowadays also) travel by airplane, travel by train, travel by car:: yeló:lh < ó:lh.
to travel by horse, already riding a horse:: yets'ets'á < ts'á:.
travelling by and packing on his back (might be said of a passer-by):: iychmà:m ~ iytsmà:m < chám.
travelling by, in motion, while moving along, while travelling along:: ye= ~ yi= ~ i┐.
(travelling/moving) stooped over:: yeq'pó:s (prob. error or variant for yeqp'ó:s) < qep'.
travelling (without a destination), going out:: leq'á:l(e)q'el ~ leq'á:lqel < leq'áleq'el (~ leq'áleqel (rare)).
travel (to a destination), be on a journey:: leq'áleq'el (~ leq'áleqel (rare)).
where is s-o going?, where is s-o travelling?, where is s-o headed for?:: xwchókwel < chákw.
(while) travelling along, in motion:: ye=.

travelling

travelling by going downriver:: yexwőqw'elem < wőqw' ~ wéqw'.

travelling along

(while) travelling along, in motion:: ye=.

tray

dish, big cooking and serving trough used in longhouse, feast dish, plate (of wood or basketry), (platter), tray:: ló:thel.
tray for carrying meat:: smèyethálá < sméyeth ~ sméyéth.

treadle

a swing, a little treadle they swing the babies on:: q'éyt'o ~ q'éyt'e.

tread water)

swim, (tread water), (wading in deep water [LJ], swimming [Elders Group]):: x̱élhchem.

tree :: theqát ~ thqá:t.

a fork in a tree:: st'éx̱ < t'éx̱.
alder tree, red alder:: x̱éyth'elhp < x̱éyth'.
a lot of trees close together (young), thicket:: théqet < theqát ~ thqá:t.
a small willow tree, a low willow:: x̱wóx̱welá:lhp < x̱wále ~ x̱wá:le.
bark (of tree, bush, etc.):: p'elyú:s ~ p'alyú:s or p'elyíws ~ p'alyíws.
(be) blazed (of a mark in a tree), chipped (of mark in tree):: st'ót'ep < t'óp.
(be) long, tall (of tree, anything):: tl'áqt.
big tree, (be big of a tree or plant):: sthá:lhp < thi ~ tha ~ the ~ thah ~ theh, sthá:lhp < thi ~ tha ~ the ~ thah ~ theh.
black hawthorn tree:: mats'íyelhp < máts'el.
blue elderberry bush, blue elderberry tree:: th'íkwekwelhp < th'í:kwekw ~ th'í:qweqw.
bottom of a tree, trunk of a tree:: s'aléts.

tree (CONT'D)

cascara tree:: q'á:yx̲elhp.
crabapple tree, domestic apple tree:: qwe'ó:pelhp < qwe'óp.
(Douglas) fir tree:: ts'sá:yelhp < ts'sá:y.
dry storage box in tree or on top of pole (for salmon and other dried provisions):: póqw'elh < pó:qw' ~ póqw'.
fall a tree:: yeq'á:ls < yáq'.
falling (a tree), be falling trees:: yáyeq'els < yáq'.
falling it, falling a tree:: yáyeq'et < yáq'.
first warmed side of a tree, sunny side of a tree:: sqewá:meth' < qew.
five trees:: lhq'atsesálhp < lheq'át ~ lhq'á:t.
fork in a tree?:: st'ex̲láts < t'éx̲.
fork in tree, fork in tree roots:: st'it'x̲óyaq < t'éx̲.
foundation of a house, bottom of a tree:: s'alétsmel < s'aléts.
four trees:: x̲ethí:lhp or x̲ethíyelhp < x̲e'ó:thel ~ x̲e'óthel.
get wedged (by falling tree, for ex.), got run over (by car, train, etc.):: tl'íq'.
gray lacy lichen or tree moss (real fine like hair, grows on maples):: x̲ám'x̲em'.
grown twisted (of a tree):: sx̲á:lts'emeth' < x̲élts'.
hazelnut bush or tree:: sth'í:tsemelhp < sth'í:tsem.
hazelnut tree or bush:: sth'í:tsemelhp < th'éts.
heart of a root, seed, nut (kernel), core of plant or seedling, core (of tree, branch, any growing thing), pith (of bush), seed or pit [U.S.] or pip [Cdn.] of a fruit:: sth'emí:wel ~ sth'emíwel ~ sth'emíwél < sth'ó:m.
hemlock tree, Western hemlock:: mélemélhp.
hollow (of tree or log):: shxwótkwewel < xwótkw ~ xwótqw.
how many trees:: kw'í:là:lhp ~ kw'ílà:lhp < kw'í:l ~ kw'íl.
it's dead (of a tree):: t'ápiythet < t'ápiy.
it's going dead (of a tree):: t'ópiythet < t'ápiy.
large rock slide that includes trees and other debris:: syélt < yélt.
limb (of tree):: sts'éxttses < sts'á:xt.
limb or bough of tree:: =tses ~ =ches.
little tree:: thí:thqet < theqát ~ thqá:t.
little tree[s]:: thétheqet < theqát ~ thqá:t.
(make/have a) squeaking sound (of a tree, of a chair, of shoes), squeaking (of shoes, trees), (creaking):: qá:ytl'em.
managed to fell a tree, (managed to fall it):: yéq'lexw ~ yéq'elexw < yáq'.
mountain ash berries, (perhaps also) mountain ash tree:: qwíqwelh.
oak tree, garry oak:: p'xwélhp.
one tree:: sléts'elhp < léts'a ~ léts'e.
on top (for ex. of a tree):: =qéyl ~ =qel.
peel a tree:: lhoqw'esá:ls < lhéqw'.
peel it off (bark of a tree):: lhqw'íwst < lhéqw'.
point or tip of a long object (pole, tree, knife, candle, land):: =eqs ~ =éqsel ~ =élqsel ~ =elqs.
roots of a tree when it floats downriver:: x̲eyímelets.
shake s-th (tree or bush) for fruit or leaves, comb a bush (for berries), shake s-th (a mat or blanket for ex.):: xwíset ~ xwítset < xwís.
small tree:: a'axwíyelhp < axwíl.
spruce tree, Sitka spruce:: ts'qw'élhp < ts'éqw'.
stump (of a tree [still rooted]):: sq'x̲áp.
tall (of tree):: tl'eqtíwél < tl'áqt.
thin (of tree or pole):: qwe'íqws < qwe'íqw.

tree (CONT'D)

three trees:: lhxwá:lhp < lhí:xw.
to fall (about a tree):: yáq'.
to fall it (a tree), to fell a tree, to fall a tree:: yáq'et < yáq'.
tree bent to ground with ice and frozen:: sx̲wíqel.
tree limb, branch (of tree), (knot on a tree [CT]):: sts'á:xt.
tree, plant:: =elhp.
trees, thicket, timber, woods, forest:: theqthéqet < theqát ~ thqá:t.
two trees:: isá:lhp ~ s'isá:lhp < isá:le ~ isále ~ isá:la.
western red cedar tree:: x̲pá:yelhp ~ x̲páyelhp < sx̲éyp.
wild cherry tree, bitter cherry tree:: t'elémelhp < t'elém.
yew tree, Pacific yew:: téx̲wetselhp < téx̲wets.

tremble :: lhétx̲tem.
be trembling, shiver:: lhátx̲tem < lhétx̲tem.

trembler)
bracket fungus, (possibly also some jelly fungi like yellow trembler):: s'ómó:qwes.

Tremella
Fomes sp. including Fomes applanatus and probably others, possibly Polyporus sp., possibly Ganoderma sp., prob. also jelly fungi of Tremella and maybe Auricularia and Dacrymyces species, especially Tremella mesenterica (Yellow trembler) which is abundant only on the red alder and is reddish-orange matching the color, translucence and shape of those eaten by some of the Stó:lō elders, the jelly fungi could possibly have a differnet name from the bracket fungus:: s'ómó:qwes.

Tremella mesenterica
Fomes sp. including Fomes applanatus and probably others, possibly Polyporus sp., possibly Ganoderma sp., prob. also jelly fungi of Tremella and maybe Auricularia and Dacrymyces species, especially Tremella mesenterica (Yellow trembler) which is abundant only on the red alder and is reddish-orange matching the color, translucence and shape of those eaten by some of the Stó:lō elders, the jelly fungi could possibly have a differnet name from the bracket fungus:: s'ómó:qwes.

trench
hole in the ground, trench (if discussing length):: shxwthó:yqw < thíy.

trench mouth
(have) trench mouth:: qw'eléqel.

tribe
a group of people, a tribe of people, several tribes:: ó:wqw'elmexw or ó:wkw'elmexw.
different tribe, different people, strangers:: lets'ó:lmexw < láts'.
Pilalt tribe, Pilalt people, Pilalt dialect, (Pilalt, village at west end of Little Mountain by Agassiz [Wells, Duff]):: Pelólhxw.

tributary
a tributary of Atchelitz Creek:: Kwōkwa'áltem ?.
Hatchery Creek, tributary of Sweltzer Creek (which drains Cultus Lake):: Stṓtelō < tó:l ~ tò:l.
Statlu Creek, one of the main tributaries of Chehalis Creek:: stótelō < tó:l ~ tò:l.
tributary, small creek that goes into a bigger river:: sqwá < qwá.

trickle
    (rain or sweat) trickling down one's face:: kw'tómés < kw'átem.
    trickling, dribbling, water bubbling up in a river, add water to a container, water running under:: kw'átem.

Trifolium pratense
    prob. both Trifolium repens and Trifolium pratense:: lhő:me.

Trifolium repens
    prob. both Trifolium repens and Trifolium pratense:: lhő:me.

trill
    a trilling sound a raven makes:: xwot'q'esílem.

trillium
    trillium, B.C. easter lily:: xaxt'ó:les.

Trillium ovatum:: xaxt'ó:les.

trim
    embroidery, trimming (stitches on an edge):: stl'ítl'ets < tl'íts ~ tl'ích.
    plane it (with a plane), trim it, taper it (about wood, like slats or roots for baskets, poles for houseposts/totem poles, paddles), taper it (with knife or plane), peel it (a fruit, etc.), whittle it, strip or peel bark off of it, scrape it (of carrots), (carve it, peel it [AC]):: xípet < xíp.

trimmings
    trimmings (of material), sawdust, shavings:: lhéts'emel < lhíts' ~ lhí:ts'.
    trimmings on uniform (paddles, etc.):: stl'íitl'ets < tl'íts ~ tl'ích.

trip
    a prop used to trip a deadfall trap:: tpólhtel < tpólh.
    (food) provisions for a trip, box lunch:: sáwel.
    get tripped, to trip:: lhékw'qsel < lhíkw' ~ lhí:kw'.
    staggering (after you trip for ex.):: tá:lstem < tél ~ tá:l ~ tiy.
    to trip:: lhékw'xel < lhíkw' ~ lhí:kw'.
    to trip s-o:: lhékw'xet < lhíkw' ~ lhí:kw'.

tripe :: spéxw.
    animal tripe (stomach, upper and lower), bowel:: spéxw.

Trochilidae
    possibly Trochilidae family, probably including Selasphorus rufus, Archilochus alexandri, and Stellula calliope:: pésk'a.

Troglodytes aedon
    Troglodytes troglodytes pacificus, may also include (esp.)Thryomanes bewickii, Telmatodytes palustris paludicola, Troglodytes aedon,and Salpinctes obsoletus:: t'ámiya.

Troglodytes troglodytes pacificus
    Troglodytes troglodytes pacificus, may also include (esp.)Thryomanes bewickii, Telmatodytes palustris paludicola, Troglodytes aedon,and Salpinctes obsoletus:: t'ámiya.

troll

small fish-hook (for trout, etc.), trolling hook:: kw'ōwiyékw ~ kw'ōyékw.

trot

to trot (animal or person), jog:: lhapxálem.

trouble

gall-bladder, gall, bile, have bile trouble, be jaundiced, bilious:: lelléts' ~ laléts'.

trough

cedar trough (to serve food):: x̲epyúwelh < sx̲éyp.
dish, big cooking and serving trough used in longhouse, feast dish, plate (of wood or basketry), (platter), tray:: ló:thel.

trousers

pants, trousers:: seqíws ~ seqí:ws.

trout

cut-throat trout, coastal cut-troat trout:: spó:ltsep.
dolly varden trout:: thex̲ó:th.
[lot of] trout:: th'eth'qwá:y < sth'eqwá:y.
rainbow trout, prob. also coastal cutthroat trout:: kw'síts.
speckled trout, (prob. brook trout, also called speckled char):: sp'íp'ehà:th' ~ sp'íp'ehàth' < sp'á:th', sp'íp'ehà:th' ~ sp'íp'ehàth' < sp'á:th'.
steelhead trout:: qí:wx̲ ~ qéywx̲ ~ qá:wx̲ ~ qáwx̲.
trout (any kind), trout (generic):: sth'eqwá:y.
white trout, (if not rainbow or cutthroat trout, probably lake trout also called grey trout):: slókwech.

trout-fishing

fishing by a line, line-fishing, trout-fishing, fishing with a pole (for trout):: qw'iqw'emó:thel ~ qw'íqw'emó:thel < qw'emó:thel.

true

a measure, a true mark:: sx̲e'áth' < x̲áth' ~ x̲e'áth'.
be true, it's true, be truly:: the'í:t.
(be) true to one another:: the'íttel < the'í:t.

trunk

bottom of a tree, trunk of a tree:: s'aléts.
box, trunk, grave box (old-style, not buried), coffin, casket:: kw'óxwe.
root? or trunk?:: =óyaq.
suitcase (Deming), luggage (Deming), clothing container, clothes bag, trunk (for clothes), etc.:: áwkw'emálá < á:wkw'.
wide cedar (sapling) strips or slats from young cedar trunks, cedar slat work (basketry):: x̲pó:ys < sx̲éyp.

trust

believe s-o, trust s-o:: q'élmet < q'á:l.

try

afraid to try:: qelélwes < qél.

try (CONT'D)

a small person (old or young) is picking or trying to pick, an inexperienced person is picking or trying to pick, picking a little bit, someone who can't pick well is picking:: lhilhím < lhím.
make an attempt (to do something difficult, like running rapids in a canoe, mountain-climbing, winning a game, etc.), give it a try:: t'óthet < t'á.
manage by oneself (in food or travel), try to do it by oneself, try to be independent, do the best one can:: iyólewéthet < éy ~ éy:.
straining to listen, really listening, listening hard, trying to listen, (listen [AC]):: xwlalá:.
studying s-th, thinking about s-th, learning s-th, training for s-th, trying to do s-th:: totí:lt < tól.
taste s-th, try s-th:: t'át ~ t'á:t < t'á.
trying it:: t'et'át < t'á.
try it, attempt it:: t'át ~ t'á:t < t'á.
try to do something (no matter what, anyway):: iyálewethet < éy ~ éy:.

Tseatah
village now at north end of Agassiz-Rosedale bridge, now Tseatah Indian Reserve #2 (of Cheam band):: Siyét'e.

ts'its'eqweló:l
a fairly flat clearing on a mountain in Morris Valley where they used to play ts'its'eqweló:l or Indian badminton:: Ts'éqwela ~ Th'éqwela < ts'éqw ~ th'éqw.

Tsuga heterophylla:: mélemélhp.

tub
barrel, probably also tub:: q'eyós < q'ey ~ q'i.
bathtub:: shxwxóxekw'em < xókw' ~ xó:kw', xókw'emá:lá < xókw' ~ xó:kw'.
washtub, washing machine:: shxwth'éx̲welwetem < th'éx̲w or th'óx̲w.

tuberculosis
(have) tuberculosis:: toteqw'ó:mestem < tó:qw'em.

tuck
(be in the) woods, (amidst bush or vegetation, be tucked away?):: sxí:xets' ~ sxíxets' < xí:ts' ~ xíts' ~ xets'.
be tucked away, put away so well you can't find it, be solid:: slá ~ selá ~ slá: (probably).

Tuckquail
Sumas Mountain (also Tuckquail, a village on both sides of Lower Sumas River [Wells]):: T'ex̲qé:yl or T'ex̲qí:l < t'éx̲.

Tuesday :: sthémelts ~ sthemélts < themá.

tuft
bushy hair on horses' legs (tufts like on Clydesdale breed), tufts of fur on horse's feet:: qwelqwélxel < qwíl ~ qwel.

tule
bulrush, tule:: wő:l.

tumpline

tumpline, packstrap:: chámatel < chám.
weaving (for ex. a tumpline), mending a net, making a net:: q'éyq'esetsel < q'ey ~ q'i.
woven headband of packstrap, tumpline:: q'sí:ltel < q'ey ~ q'i.

tunnel

a mountain just south of Yale Mountain (Popelehó:ys) with a big hole like a tunnel in it above the highway at Yale:: Tekwóthel ~ Tkwóthel.
hole (in roof, tunnel, pants, mountain, at bottom of some lakes), tunnel:: sqwahíwel < qwá.
mountain on Fraser River between first tunnel and Yale where rotten fish used to (always) pile up:: Lexwyó:qwem Smá:lt < yó:qw.
natural holes or tunnels east of Iwówes and above Lhilheltálets that water came out of after rain:: Sqwelíqwehíwel ~ Sqwelíqwehìwèl < qwá.
place on Fraser River between first tunnel and Yale where rotten fish used to (always) pile up:: Lexwyó:qwem < yó:qw.
railway tunnel just past (east of) Ruby Creek:: T'ít'emt'ámex.
steep rock wall that used to have Indian writing at first C.P.R. tunnel above Haig:: X̱elíqel < x̱él ~ x̱é:yl ~ x̱í:l

turbulent

rough (of wind or water), turbulent (of wind or water), real swift (of water):: x̱átl'.

Turdus migratorius caurinus:: skw'okw'qá:q ~ skw'okw'qáq ~ skw'ōkw'qáq.

turkey

wild turkey:: slholh(e)x̱wélqsel mó:qw < lhex̱w.

turn

a turn in the Fraser River between Ruby Creek and Katz (about a mile upriver from the mouth of Ruby Creek and Ruby Creek I.R. #9 (called Lukseetsis-sum on maps and D.I.A. records, see Lexwthíthesem)), also the name of a village at this spot, spelled Skawahlook, Indian Reserve #1, on topographical maps and D.I.A. records:: Sq'ewá:lxw < q'éw ~ q'ew.
a turn in the Fraser River on the CPR (northwest) side two miles east of American Bar, Texas Bar bend in the Fraser River:: Sq'ewílem < q'éw ~ q'ew.
(be) turned around, turned the wrong way:: sx̱á:lts' < x̱élts'.
be turned inside out:: schelá:w < chaléwt.
clear up (of weather), turn fine (after a hard storm):: iyílem < éy ~ éy:.
get, (become), turn, go:: =thet.
getting yellow, turning yellow, turning green:: qwóqweyel ~ qwóqwiyel < qwá:y.
go around a bend in the river, go around a turn, go around something in one's way:: q'ewílem < q'éw ~ q'ew.
go around (a point, a bend, a curve, etc.) in the water, make a U-turn (in the water, could use today on land with a car):: q'ówletsem < q'éw ~ q'ew.
light s-th, make a light (of s-th), turn it on (a light):: táwelt < táw.
make a light, turn the light on, light the lamp:: yeqwí:lem ~ yeqwéylem < yéqw.
pry (a canoe paddling stroke when the canoe is hard to turn):: lhímesem < lhímes.
pry with paddle in stern to turn a canoe sharply, pry (canoe stroke done by a sternman):: q'á:lets.
pull in once with a canoe paddle wide or slow, pull in in turning (a canoe paddling stroke done by a bowman):: lhímes.

turn (CONT'D)

really turned gray (of hair):: x̲ó:lemthet < x̲ólem.
roll over in bed, turn over in bed:: ts'ó:lex̲eth' < ts'el.
someone's turn:: xwíq.
turn around:: x̲élts'thet < x̲él:.
turn around a bend, go around a bend, turn around (to go back), turn around a corner:: q'ewqé:ylém ~ q'ewqéylém (better q'ewqí:lem) < q'éw ~ q'ew.
turn away, turn one's face away:: qelésem < qél.
turn back into a quiet slough from the river, be going into a slough from the river:: ts'élexw < ts'el.
turn bad, (get) spoiled (of clothes for ex.), (get) dirty:: qelqéyl or qelqí:l < qél.
turn bad in smell, smells like it's turned bad:: qelqéyláléqep < qél.
turned on sexually:: témex.
turning gray (in hair):: x̲olémthet < x̲ólem.
turning to real yellow:: qwáyewel < qwá:y.
turning yellow, getting yellow, turning green:: qwóyel < qwá:y.
turn it on its side, lay it on its side:: lexét < lex.
turn (oneself) around, make a U-turn:: ts'elqéylém < ts'el, ts'elqéylém < ts'el.
turn oneself around, turn (oneself) around:: x̲élts'thet < x̲élts'.
turn one's face towards:: ó:sem.
turn one's face, (turn one's body away [IHTTC]):: ts'ólesem ~ ts'ólésem < ts'el, ts'ólesem ~ ts'ólésem < ts'el.
turn one's head:: x̲élts'esem < x̲élts'.
turn s-o upside down:: xwiyó:leqwt < yél or perhaps yá:l.
turn s-th around:: ts'elqéylt or ts'elqí:lt < ts'el.
turn s-th right-side up:: kw'ethí:lt (possible error for kw'eth'í:lt).
turn s-th/s-o over, flip it over (of fish for ex.), turn it inside out:: chaléwt, chaléwt.
turn s-th upside-down:: qep'óst < qep'.
turn yellow, got yellow:: qwáyel < qwá:y.
twist s-th/s-o, turn it around, turn s-o, turn s-th (for ex. a page):: x̲élts't < x̲élts', x̲élts't < x̲élts', x̲élts't < x̲élts'.
twist, turn around, around in circles:: =ts' ~ =elts' ~ =á:lts'.

turnip
domestic turnip:: shxw'ólewù.

turn loose
let go of s-th/s-o, drop s-th, set s-o free, turn s-o/s-th loose:: kwá:t ~ kwát < kwá:.

turn the tables on s-o:: leq'éltsest < léq'.

turtle:: slálem álhqey < lá:lém, álhqey ~ álhqay.

tweezers:: p'íp'eth'tel < p'í:.

twenty :: ts'kw'éx.
twenty containers:: ts'kw'exáleqel < ts'kw'éx.
twenty dollars:: ts'kw'xó:s < ts'kw'éx.
twenty people:: ts'ekw'xále < ts'kw'éx.

Twenty-Mile Creek
a neck of land on the west side of Harrison Lake just north of Twenty-Mile Creek and

Twenty-Mile Creek (CONT'D)
across from the north tip of Long Island:: Shxwtépsem < tépsem.

twice
twice, two times:: themá.

twilled weave
woven goat-wool blanket, (twilled weave (JL)):: swṓqw'elh.

twin
pair of twins, pair of closest friends:: sq'eq'e'óleq < q'ó.
twins:: sts'iyáye.

twinberry)
plant with three black berries always joined together, (possibly black twinberry):: xó:lelhp.

twine
(be) rolled up in a ball (twine, yarn, etc.):: sqw'ómx̱wes < qw'ómx̱w.
grass or fibre for nets or twine, spreading dogbane, possibly also Indian hemp:: méthelh.
it's twined (like rolled on thigh and twisted, spun):: sí:ltem < sél or sí(:)l.
rope, twine, string, thread:: x̱wéylem ~ x̱wé:ylem ~ x̱wí:lem.
spin wool or twine:: qálets'.

twined
it's twined (like rolled on thigh and twisted, spun):: sí:ltem < sél or sí(:)l.
twined weave:: s'o(')elexw?.

twins
storage basket (for oil, fruit, clothes), burial basket for twins, round basket (any size, smaller at top), clay jug (to store oil or fruit):: skwá:m ~ skwám < kwá:m ~ kwám.

twirl
spinning (while hanging), (twirling):: ts'á:lq'em < ts'el.

twist
be twisted:: sx̱álts'ewel < x̱élts'.
be twisted (mentally), he's twisted (mentally):: x̱élts'tem < x̱élts'.
get twisted [inside]:: x̱elts'íwélém < x̱élts'.
grown twisted (of a tree):: sx̱á:lts'emeth' < x̱élts'.
(have a) twisted mouth, twisted jaw:: pó:yethel < pó:y.
is getting twisted:: x̱áx̱elt'íwélém < x̱élts'.
to twist:: x̱élts'.
twist by the head:: x̱élts'es < x̱élts'.
twist it:: x̱élts't < x̱él:.
twist it around (a few times):: x̱álx̱elts't < x̱él:.
twist s-o/s-th by the head:: x̱élts'est < x̱élts'.
twist s-th/s-o, turn it around, turn s-o, turn s-th (for ex. a page):: x̱élts't < x̱élts'.
twist, turn around, around in circles:: =ts' ~ =elts' ~ =á:lts'.

Twisted-stalk
False Solomon's seal, Twisted-stalk, rosy-flowered Twisted-stalk, star-flowered Solomon's seal:: x̱ex̱q'elá:lhp.

Twisted-stalk (CONT'D)

"snakeberry", includes False Solomon's seal, star-flowered Solomon's seal, and probably Twisted-stalk (2 spp.) and Hooker's fairy bells:: sth'íms te álhqey < sth'í:m ~ sth'i:m.
"snakeberry", including False Solomon's seal, star-flowered Solomon's seal, and probably Twisted-stalk and Hooker's fairy bells:: sth'íms te álhqey < álhqey ~ álhqay.

twitch
twitch, flutter (of one's eye, hand, skin, etc.):: lhawét'em < lhá:w.
twitching:: th'á:ykw'em < th'iykw'.
twitching (of one's eye, hand, skin, etc.), fluttering:: lhá:wt'em < lhá:w.

two :: isá:le ~ isále ~ isá:la.
break s-th in two (with one's hands), break it in half (with one's hands only), break off a piece of s-th:: peqwót < péqw.
man with two wives:: islá:ltexw < isá:le ~ isále ~ isá:la.
split off, break off, break a piece off, break in two, split in two:: péqw.
twice, two times:: themá.
two birds:: iselíws < isá:le ~ isále ~ isá:la, islóqw < isá:le ~ isále ~ isá:la.
two canoes, two boats:: islṓwelh ? or isṓwelh ? < isá:le ~ isále ~ isá:la.
two containers:: isáleqel < isá:le ~ isále ~ isá:la.
two different things:: selélets' < láts'.
two dollars, [Boas] two Indian blankets:: isó:les < isá:le ~ isále ~ isá:la.
two fish:: iselíqw < isá:le ~ isále ~ isá:la.
two fruit in a group (as they grow on a plant):: isòls ? < isá:le ~ isále ~ isá:la.
two garments, two (items of) clothes:: islélwet < isá:le ~ isále ~ isá:la, islélwet < isá:le ~ isále ~ isá:la.
two houses:: islá:wtxw < isá:le ~ isále ~ isá:la.
two kinds:: isálemó:t < isá:le ~ isále ~ isá:la.
two leaves:: islálews < isá:le ~ isále ~ isá:la.
two o'clock, two hours:: isáles < isá:le ~ isále ~ isá:la.
two paddlers:: islá:wes < isá:le ~ isále ~ isá:la.
two paddles:: islá:wes < isá:le ~ isále ~ isá:la.
two pants:: isláyiws < isá:le ~ isále ~ isá:la.
two people:: yáysele ~ yéysele < isá:le ~ isále ~ isá:la.
two ropes, two threads, two sticks, two poles, two poles standing up:: isalámeth' < isá:le ~ isále ~ isá:la.
two supernatural creatures:: yáysele ~ yéysele < isá:le ~ isále ~ isá:la.
two things:: islá < isá:le ~ isále ~ isá:la.
two trees:: isá:lhp ~ s'isá:lhp < isá:le ~ isále ~ isá:la.

two-headed
supernatural double-headed snake:: sílhqey < isá:le ~ isále ~ isá:la.
two-headed supernatural snake:: sílhqey < álhqey ~ álhqay.

-ty (multiple of ten)
times ten, -ty (multiple of ten):: =elhsxá ~ =elsxá.

Typha latifolia:: sth'á:qel, sth'á:qel.

Tyto alba :: spopeleqwíth'a ~ spopeleqwíth'e < poleqwíth'a.

Tzeachten

Tzeachten, a (recent) settlement on the upper reaches of the lower Chilliwack River, now Chilliwack Indian Reserve #13 near Sardis:: Ch'iyáqtel < sts'iyáq.

ugly

scrubby little ones, (little ugly ones):: qéqelelhó:mex < qél.
ugly expression in mouth, ugly grin:: sx̱eyx̱eth'ó:ythel < x̱íth' ~ x̱éyth'.
ugly, sloppy (in dress, walk, etc.):: qélelhóméx < qél.

umbrella :: q'eléts'éqwtel ~ q'eléts'eqwtel < q'el.
be under an umbrella:: sq'elóts'eqw < q'el.

unable

pitiful person, helpless person, person unable to do anythingfor himself:: skw'ékw'ith < skw'iyéth.

uncertain

maybe, I guess, I'm uncertain, must be (evidently), (evidential), have to (I guess):: t'wa ~ t'we.
(meaning uncertain), (perhaps right, correct):: mà.

uncle

deceased uncle, deceased grand-uncle:: qethiyálh; shxwemthiyálh.
parent's cousin, parent's sibling, uncle, aunt:: shxwemlí:kw.
uncle, aunt:: kwiyó:s.
uncles (all of them), aunts (all of them):: sxwemlá:lekw < shxwemlí:kw.
uncle's wife, aunt's husband, parent's sibling's spouse, uncle by marriage, aunt by marriage:: xchápth ~ schápth.

unclear

(have/be) dirty water, (not clear, unclear, can't see the bottom (of water) [EL]):: mímexwel.
unclear liquid, water, juice:: =elhcha.

uncle's wife

uncle's wife, aunt's husband, parent's sibling's spouse, uncle by marriage, aunt by marriage:: xchápth ~ schápth.

uncombed

(have) bushy and uncombed hair:: chílheqw < =chílh ~ chílh=.

uncooked

raw, uncooked:: x̱éyth'.

uncover

(be) uncovered:: sqw'íqw'el < qw'íl.
uncover it:: qw'í:lt < qw'íl.

under

be under an umbrella:: sq'elóts'eqw < q'el.
carry a packstrap or both packstraps over the shoulder(s) and under the arm(s):: sq'iwq'ewíles < q'e:yw ~ q'í:w.

under (CONT'D)

have something under one arm:: xixets'eláx̲el < xits' ~ xets'.
(hung) under:: síq < seqíws ~ seqí:ws.
lower circle under eye:: stl'epó:lemelh ~ stl'epó:les < tl'ép.
put one's hands under one's arms:: xixets'eláx̲em < xits' ~ xets'.
trickling, dribbling, water bubbling up in a river, add water to a container, water running under:: kw'átem.

underarm
(have) animal smell (of bear, skunk, dog, etc.), (have) animal stink, (have) human smell (of underarm, body odor, etc.), (have) body odor:: pápeth'em.
(have an) underarm smell:: qw'ox̲wemáléqep.

underbrush
shrub, small bush (for ex. growing on river edge, or like vine maple or thimbleberry or willow), brush, underbrush:: xwíxwel.

undercooked]
not cooked enough (of fish), [undercooked]:: lálekw'em.

underfoot
make a crunch underfoot (bones, nut, glass, etc.):: x̲ep'ékw'.

underground
bake underground, (steam-cook underground, cook in a steam-pit):: qetás < qá:t.
baking underground:: qétes < qá:t.
blue camas, (any edible underground vegetable food [SP], vegetable root(s) [MH]):: spá:lxw.
stuff steam-cooked underground, what is baked underground:: sqetás < qá:t.

underneath
(be) below, (be) underneath, (be) at the bottom of a pile or stack:: stl'epólwelh ~ stl'pólwelh < tl'ép.
crawl underneath, (go underneath):: eqílem ~ eqéylem.

underpants
short pants, little pants, underpants:: siseqíws ~ síseqíws < seqíws ~ seqí:ws.

underskirt
underskirt, petticoat:: stl'epá:leq < tl'ép.

understand:: teló:met ~ tel:ómet < tól.
find s-th out, understand s-th, learn s-th, realize s-th, now know what s-th is like, read (and comprehend) s-th, understand s-o:: tél:exw ~ (in rapid speech) télexw < tól.
understand(ing):: toteló:met < tól.
understanding (s-th/s-o):: tótel:exw < tól.

undertaker:: tsmákw'a < mákw'a.

underwater
be underwater, sink to the bottom:: míq'.
dive (already in water), go underwater, sink oneself down:: leqàlèm < léqem.

underwater (CONT'D)

rock figure near the rocks shaped like a family underwater:: Th'elíth'eqes.

undress

take off one's clothes, undress:: lhōwth'ám < lhewíth'a.
undress in front of someone, strip-tease:: lhuwth'ím < lhewíth'a.
undressing:: lhuwth'á:m < lhewíth'a.
undress s-o:: lhuwth'á:mestexw < lhewíth'a.

uneven

mistake in splitting roots by making them uneven:: t'ats'ex̲elí:m < t'á:ts'.

unfortunate

poor, unfortunate:: t-sós ~ tesós.

unidentified

unidentified animal with marks on its face, perhaps badger or wolverine:: sqoyép.
unidentified bird:: t'ú'.
unidentified plant with round bulbs that look and taste like potatoes, round root like potatoes that used to be eaten and tastes like potatoes:: qíqemxel ~ qéyqemxel < qém.

(unidentified placename) [prob. location closest to & southwest of Sqw'á:lets (Hill's Bar) on same side of river]:: Qw'oqw'íyets or Qw'óqw'iyets.

unidentified plant

short unidentified plant, about 3 ft. tall with red berries like a short mountain ash, the berries are bitter but the plant is used as medicine, possibly red baneberry:: í:lwelh.

uniform

trimmings on uniform (paddles, etc.):: stl'íitl'ets < tl'íts ~ tl'ích.

unintentionally

hit s-o unintentionally, hit s-o accidentally:: kw'óqwlexw < kw'óqw.

Union Bar

a little bay in the Fraser River a quarter mile east of Iwówes (Union Bar, Aywawwis):: Qíqemqèmèl < qém:el.
place across the Fraser River from Union Bar:: Wowés.
village at Union Bar, now also Hope Indian Reserve #5 (#15 in Duff 1952), Ay-wa-wis:: Iwówes.

United States

America, United States:: Pástel.

unlace

unlacing it:: híyex̲wet < yíx̲w.
untie s-th, unravel s-th, unwind it, unwrap it, loosen s-th, unlace it:: yéx̲wet < yíx̲w.

unless

unless he, if he doesn't:: ewás < éwe ~ ő we.
until, unless:: a'áchewlh < atse.

unload

unloading a canoe, taking things out of a canoe:: qw'íméls < qw'í:m.

unlock

unlock it:: xwewáth'et < wáth'.

(un)loose

broke down, came (un)loose, came apart, (got) untied, loose, unravelled:: yéx̲w < yíx̲w.

unpossessed)

shoulder (name of body part, unpossessed):: xw'ílámálá ~ xw'ílàmàlà < ílàm.

unravel

broke down, came (un)loose, came apart, (got) untied, loose, unravelled:: yéx̲w < yíx̲w.
unravelled:: syéx̲w < yíx̲w.
untie s-th, unravel s-th, unwind it, unwrap it, loosen s-th, unlace it:: yéx̲wet < yíx̲w.

unripe :: x̲éyth'.

sour (unripe or half-ripe fruit, lemon, Oregon grape, fermenting fruit):: t'át'eth'em < t'áth'.

unseen

shaking bushes (of animal or person unseen, for ex.):: xwóykwem.

unspecified

agent (human, gender unspecified, absent):: tl'.
by (agent. human, gender unspecified, absent):: tl'.
he (present or presence unspecified), he's the one that, it's him that, she or it (present or presence unspecified), that or this (immediately before nominal):: tú:tl'ò ~ tútl'ò ~ tútl'o < tl'ó ~ tl'o.
nominalizer (female present and visible or presence or proximity unspecified), demonstrative article:: the=.
nominalizer (male or gender unspecified, present and visible or presence or proximity unspecified), demonstrative article:: ta=, ta=, te=, te=.
that's her, she (present or presence unspecified), her (present or presence unspefified), that (female):: thú:tl'ò < tl'ó ~ tl'o.
that's them (gender unspecified), they, them:: yutl'ó:lem < tl'ó ~ tl'o.
the (male or gender unspecified, near but not in sight):: kwthe < kw.
the (male, present, visible), the (gender or presence and visibility unspecified), a (male, present and visible), a (gender or presence and visibility unspecified):: te.

unspecified presence

the (female, present and visible), the (female, unspecified presence and/or unspecified visibility):: the.

unspecified visibility)

the (female, present and visible), the (female, unspecified presence and/or unspecified visibility):: the.

untie

broke down, came (un)loose, came apart, (got) untied, loose, unravelled:: yéx̲w < yíx̲w.
untie s-th, unravel s-th, unwind it, unwrap it, loosen s-th, unlace it:: yéx̲wet < yíx̲w.

until

until, till, while:: qew ~ qwō ~ qe ... u/ew < qe.
until, unless:: a'áchewlh < atse.

(untranslated)

be in, in, be on, on, be at, at, before (an audience), (untranslated):: lí ~ li.

unwind

untie s-th, unravel s-th, unwind it, unwrap it, loosen s-th, unlace it:: yéx̲wet < yíx̲w.

unwrap

be unwrapped:: syíyex̲w < yíx̲w.
untie s-th, unravel s-th, unwind it, unwrap it, loosen s-th, unlace it:: yéx̲wet < yíx̲w.
unwrap it:: yéx̲weletst < yíx̲w.

up

approach, get near, get closer, reach, go up to, get up to:: tés.
be above, be high, top, up above, way high:: chíchelh < =chílh ~ chílh=.
(be) all bundled up:: stl'etl'íqw'.
(be) doubled up (a person with knees up to his chest), all doubled over:: sqw'emqw'emóx̲w < qw'ómx̲w.
(be) doubled up in bed on one's side with knees drawn up:: sqw'emóx̲w < qw'ómx̲w.
(be) rolled up in a ball (twine, yarn, etc.):: sqw'ómx̲wes < qw'ómx̲w.
(be) Spring, [cyclic period] when everything comes up:: kw'íyles ~ kw'éyles < kw'í ~ kw'íy.
(be) Spring, [time or season] when everything comes up:: temkw'éyles < kw'í ~ kw'íy.
break up s-th by crumpling, crush it up, rub it together fast (to soften or clean), rub it to soften it (of plants, etc.), fluff it (inner cedar bark to soften it):: yékw'et < yókw' ~ yóqw'.
chewed it up:: x̲epx̲epkw't < x̲ep'ékw'.
climb a mountain, climb a hill, go up a mountain or hill:: kw'íyeqel < kw'í ~ kw'íy.
climb, get up a vertical surface:: kw'í ~ kw'íy.
close up a meeting, wind up a meeting, complete a meeting:: yalkw'ólhem or yelkw'wólhem < yókw' ~ yóqw'.
face up:: kw'e'ós < kw'e'í ~ kw''í ~ kw'í.
facing up, head sticking up:: kw'ekw'e'íqw ~ kw'ekw'íqw < kw'e'í ~ kw''í ~ kw'í.
got up with a quick motion, got up quickly:: xwexwílėx < xwílėx.
(hung up in a fish net):: sx̲wíx̲weqw' < x̲wíqw'.
lie? with surface facing up, sticking up, on the side? or edge?:: kw'e'í ~ kw''í ~ kw'í.
lift up s-th, lift [s-th], hoist [s-th] up:: xwà:lx < xwá.
make a mess, mess up:: yó:lqw' < yél or perhaps yá:l.
one's canoe is broken up:: yekw'ó:lh or perhaps yekw'wó:lh < yókw' ~ yóqw'.
pick s-th up from the ground or floor:: xwpét.
prop it up:: tpólht < tpólh.
pull up by the roots:: qw'emét < qw'ém.
put one's head back (tilt one's face up):: q'óx̲esem.
rip it up, tear it up, rip s-th, tear s-th:: x̲wtát < x̲wét.
roll s-th up in a ball:: qw'ómx̲west < qw'ómx̲w.
run over it (with car), spread it (for ex. on bread with knife), put it up (of wallpaper), (stick it on), stick s-th closed (with pitch for ex.):: tl'íq't < tl'íq'.
sit, sit down, sit up, arise (from lying or sitting), get up (from lying down, from bed or chair):: emét.
sitting, sitting down, sitting up:: ó:met ~ ó'emet < emét.

up (CONT'D)

"sored up":: x̲ex̲élh < x̲élh.
stand up for s-o (respected):: xwiléxmet or xwíléxmet < xwíléx.
store it away (wedged-in up off ground), put s-th away for winter, stow s-th away:: xítse't < xits' ~ xets'.
torn up (in pieces) (or prob. better) (tear up (in many pieces)):: x̲wetx̲wét < x̲wét.
upset bed, mess s-th up:: yélqw't < yél or perhaps yá:l.

up and down
jumping along, jumping up and down:: ts'ats'etl'í:m < ts'tl'ám ~ ts'tl'ém.

upbringing
training, teaching, upbringing:: s'í:wes < íwes.

upper
high, upper, above:: =chílh ~ chílh=.
roof of the mouth, inside of upper lip, palate:: chelhqí:l ~ chelhqéyl < =chílh ~ chílh=.
upper circle over the eye, probably upper eyelid:: chelhó:lemelh < =chílh ~ chílh=, schelhó:les < =chílh ~ chílh=.
upper clothing, clothing on upper half of the body:: chlhíth'a < =chílh ~ chílh=.
upper end of house (inside or outside):: stiytáx̲el or stitáx̲el < tiyt.
upper lip:: schelhóyethel < =chílh ~ chílh=.
upper part or top of a house, upper part or top of a pit-house:: tslháltxw < =chílh ~ chílh=.

upper-class
respected leader, chief, upper-class person, boss, master, your highness:: siyám ~ (rare) siyá:m.
respected leaders, chiefs, upper-class people:: sí:yá:m < siyám ~ (rare) siyá:m.

Upper Sumas Creek:: Tátelín??.

upright
upright, erect:: =ex.
upright, standing, height, stature, pole:: =ámets' ~ =ámeth' ~ =ó:meth' ~ =emeth'.

upriver
from upriver:: teltíyt < tiyt.
upriver, up that way, (way upriver [RP, EB]):: títex̲el or tíytex̲el < tiyt.

upset
upset bed, mess s-th up:: yélqw't < yél or perhaps yá:l.

upset stomach
(have an) upset stomach:: p'eléts'tem < p'í:l or p'él.

upside down
(become/get) upside down:: xwiyó:leqw < yél or perhaps yá:l.
face down, (upside-down [Deming]):: qep'ós < qep'.
turn s-o upside down:: xwiyó:leqwt < yél or perhaps yá:l.
turn s-th upside-down:: qep'óst < qep'.

upstream
(be) upstream, east (in some contexts):: ahíw.
go upstream:: xwehíwel < ahíw.
group of canoes travelling upstream (moving to camp for fish-drying for ex.):: istéytiyel.

up the mountainside
an area up the mountainside from Ñwox̲welálhp (Yale):: Chelqwílh ~ Chelqwéylh < chá:l or chó:l.

up to
approach, get near, get closer, reach, go up to, get up to:: tés.

urgent
going to piss right away, almost piss oneself, (have an urgent or extreme or painful need to urinate):: ts'áléqel.

urinal
chamberpot, potty-chair, urinal:: shxwítel.

urinate :: séx̲we, xíwe.
going to piss right away, almost piss oneself, (have an urgent or extreme or painful need to urinate):: ts'áléqel.
urinating:: seséx̲we < séx̲we, xíxwe < xíwe.
want to pee, (want to urinate, feel like one has to urinate):: síyt'eqem < síyt'.
wet one's pants, (urinate in one's pants):: sex̲we'ayíwsem < séx̲we.
wet the bed, (urinate in the bed):: sex̲we'áléx̲eth' < séx̲we, xiwe'áléx̲eth < xíwe.
wetting his/her bed:: xíxewe'áléx̲eth' < xíwe.

urine :: séx̲we < séx̲we.
smells like urine:: xwókwesem.

Ursus americanus:: spathó:llh < pá:th.

Ursus americanus altifrontalis
Ursus americanus altifrontalis, Ursus americanus cinnamomum:: tskwímelqel < kwí:m.
Ursus americanus altifrontalis with white spot on chest:: Sx̲é:ylmet or sx̲é:ylmet < x̲él ~ x̲é:yl ~ x̲í:l, Sx̲éylmòt or sx̲éylmòt < x̲él ~ x̲é:yl ~ x̲í:l
Ursus americanus cinnamomum, also Ursus americanus altifrontalis:: spá:th < pá:th.
Ursus spp., esp. Ursus americanus altifrontalis:: spá:th < pá:th.
variety of Ursus americanus altifrontalis or Ursus americanus cinnamomum:: ts'aweyí:les < ts'áwi or ts'áwiy.

Ursus americanus cinnamomum
Ursus americanus altifrontalis, Ursus americanus cinnamomum:: tskwímelqel < kwí:m.
Ursus americanus cinnamomum, also Ursus americanus altifrontalis:: spá:th < pá:th.
variety of Ursus americanus altifrontalis or Ursus americanus cinnamomum:: ts'aweyí:les < ts'áwi or ts'áwiy.

Ursus arctos horribilis:: x̲eytl'áls ~ x̲eytl'á:ls, kw'í:tsel.

Ursus spp.
Ursus spp., esp. Ursus americanus altifrontalis:: spá:th < pá:th.

Urtica dioica:: th'éx̲th'ex̲ < th'éx̲.

us
it is us, we are the ones, we ourselves:: lhlímelh.
us, first person plural object:: -ólxw ~ -óxw.
us (nominalized object of preposition), to us, with us:: tl'elhlímelh < lhlímelh.
we, us:: talhlímelh < lhlímelh.

use
gift one really makes use of:: xwayólem.
not care about s-o, have no use for s-o, be impassive:: ewéta shxwlístexw < shxwlí.
use, extract, extract a portion:: lh- ~ lhé-.
use it, wear it, put it on:: hókwex.
useless, no special use, ordinary:: ewétò shxwlís < shxwlí.
use second-hand:: mékw'em < mékw' ~ mṓkw'.
using a (?):: =ám ~ =á (or merely =em).
using (a portion):: lh=.
what use is it?, what use have you got for it?:: stámel < tám.

used
part not used (like seeds of cantelope, core of apple, blood in fish, etc.), worst part:: sqéls < qél.
something used that one picks up and uses, something second-hand:: smékw'em < mékw' ~ mṓkw'.
weren't ever?, wasn't ever?, didn't ever?, does s-o ever?, never used to, not going to (but did anyway) [perhaps in the sense of never usually do X but did this time]:: ewá:lh ~ wá:lh < éwe ~ ṓwe.

used for
device, implement, thing used for:: =tel.

used to :: lhéq'elh < lhéq'.
get used to s-th/s-o:: tl'éltl'elmet < tl'élexw.
never used to:: ewá:lh ~ wá:lh < éwe ~ ṓwe.

useful
make oneself useful:: p'óp'ekw'ethet < p'ákw'.

useless
it doesn't matter, it's useless:: ōwéta xwlí:s < shxwlí.
useless, no special use, ordinary:: ewétò shxwlís < shxwlí.

U-shaped
bent U-shaped plane with handle on each end for canoe-making:: sqw'emóx̲w sxíxep < xíp, sqw'emóx̲w xíxepels < xíp.
U-shaped or horseshoe-shaped knife for scraping out an adzed canoe:: sqw'emqw'emóx̲w < qw'ómx̲w.
U-shaped or horseshoe-shaped knife (or plane) for scraping out canoe:: xepá:ltel < xíp.

Usnea

possibly Letharia vulpina or Alectoria (Bryoria) species or Usnea species:: mex̲t'éles.

usual

as usual, this time, now, the first time:: yalh.

uterus

womb, uterus:: smélàtel < méle ~ mél:a.

U-turn

go around (a point, a bend, a curve, etc.) in the water, make a U-turn (in the water, could use today on land with a car):: q'ówletsem < q'éw ~ q'ew.
turn (oneself) around, make a U-turn:: ts'elqéylém < ts'el.

uvula

uvula (fleshy knob dangling down in throat):: mélqw.
uvula, uvula down in the throat:: mélqweqel ~ smélqweqel < mélqw.

V8 juice:: smómeleqw spíls s'élhtel sqe'óleqw < móleqw, píl, álhtel, qó:
(lit. mixed + planted + food + fruit juice)

Vaccinium alaskaense:: léth'ilets.

Vaccinium caespitosum:: sx̲wéxixeq ~ sx̲w'éxixeq.

Vaccinium deliciosum

Vaccinium ovalifolium, possibly also Vaccinium deliciosum:: xwíxwekw' < xwíkw'.

Vaccinium membranaceum:: kwxwó:mels < kwoxw.

Vaccinium myrtilloides:: lhelhewqí:m < lhewqí:m.
probably Vaccinium myrtilloides:: lhewqí:m.

Vaccinium ovalifolium

Vaccinium ovalifolium, possibly also Vaccinium deliciosum:: xwíxwekw' < xwíkw'.

Vaccinium oxycoccus

Vaccinium oxycoccus, Vaccinium oxycoccus quadripetalus:: qwemchó:ls < qwà:m ~ qwám.

Vaccinium oxycoccus quadripetalus

Vaccinium oxycoccus, Vaccinium oxycoccus quadripetalus:: qwemchó:ls < qwà:m ~ qwám.

Vaccinium parvifolium:: kw'óqwtses < kw'óqw, qá:lá:lhp < sqá:le, sqá:la, sqá:lá:lhp ~ qá:lá:lhp < sqá:la, sqá:le.

Vaccinium uliginosum:: mólsemelhp < mó:lsem ~ mólsem.
probably Vaccinium uliginosum:: mó:lsem ~ mólsem.

vaccuum cleaner (lit. "sucking broom"):: sósetel éx̲wtel < sósetel.

vagina

on the vulva, in the vagina:: xw=.

vagina (CONT'D)

woman's genitals, vulva, vagina:: xá:welh.

valley :: kwesúyex̲el.

prairie, grassy open land, (grassy valley [EB, Gibbs, Elders Group]}:: spélhx̲el.

Vancouver

Vancouver, B.C.:: Lhq'á:lets.

vanilla

vanilla, (vanilla extract):: ts'q'éyx̲em < q'íx̲.

vanilla leaf:: lhxwáléws < lhí:xw.

Vedder Crossing

place by Albert Cooper's house on Chilliwack River Road near Vedder Crossing, former village where a slide is now on north bank of Chilliwack River opposite Liumchen Creek:: X̲éylés < x̲éylés.

Promontory Mountain by Vedder Crossing:: Stitó:s ~ Stitó:s.

Promontory Point above Vedder Crossing:: Lexwtamílem? < tà:m.

Soowahlie village (where Sweltzer Creek met Chilliwack River), Soowahlie Reserve near Vedder Crossing:: Th'ewá:lí < th'éw.

village on a small flat a little above Vedder Crossing, on the north side of Chilliwack River:: Th'óth'emels < th'óméls.

Watery Eaves, a famous longhouse and early village on a flat area on Chilliwack River just a quarter mile upriver/east above Vedder Crossing:: Qoqoláx̲el < qó:.

Vedder River

an old course of the Chilliwack River, now Vedder River:: Lhewálmel < lhá:w.

vegetable

blue camas, (any edible underground vegetable food [SP], vegetable root(s) [MH]):: spá:lxw.

peel (as a structured activity, for ex. in fixing vegetables):: ts'óls or ts'ó:ls < ts'ó:l.

peel s-th (esp. fruit or vegetable root or a vegetable like squash or a round object):: xepólst < xíp.

pick berries, pick off (leaves, fruit, vegetables, hops), (pluck off, harvest):: lhím.

vegetable juice:: spíls s'élhtel sqe'óleqw < píl, álhtel, qó:
(lit. planted + food + fruit juice)

vegetation

(be in the) woods, (amidst bush or vegetation, be tucked away?):: sxí:xets' ~ sxíxets' < xí:ts' ~ xíts' ~ xets'.

vehicle

canoe (any kind), car, vehicle (any kind):: sléxwelh.

veil

a veil:: sxwehóthes < ehó.

vein
　vein, veins:: tétath.

velvet :: témés.
　flannelette, velvet, woolly material, fluffy material, soft material:: pá:píth'a < pá:pa.

ventral surface
　on the stomach or ventral surface of a body:: =(e)yó:lhe.

vertical
　cliff, vertical rock face:: qw'eléqel.

vertical surface
　climb, get up a vertical surface:: kw'í ~ kw'íy.

very
　be very big:: hí:kw ~ hí::kw < híkw.
　(be) very, (extremely), really:: ts'áts'el.
　steep (of road, hill, etc.), (very steep slope [Elders Group]):: théq.
　too (overly), very much:: we'ól ~ ól(e)we ~ ólew < òl ~ -òl ~ -ò ~ el.
　very old, ancient, get ancient, be ancient:: q'a'í:lem ~ q'e'í:lem.

Vespertilionidae
　order Chiroptera, family Vespertilionidae, may include any or all of the following: Corynorhinus townsendi townsendi, Eptesicus fuscus bernardinus, Lasionycteris noctivagans, Lasiurus cinereus, Myotis californicus caurinus, Myotis evotis pacificus, Myotis lucifugus alascensis, Myotis volans longicrus, Myotis yumanensis saturatus, and possibly Myotis keeni keeni:: p'íp'eth'elàx̲el ~ p'ip'eth'eláx̲el < p'í:.

Vespidae
　family Vespidae, genus Vespula, i.e. Vespula spp.:: x̲ex̲p'ítsel sisemó:ye < sisemó:ya ~ sisemóya ~ sisemóye ~ sísemòye.
　order Hymenoptera, superfamily Apoidea, family Apidae, including Apis mellifera (introduced), also family Bombidae and family Vespidae and possibly bee-like members of family Syrphidae (order Diptera):: sisemó:ya ~ sisemóya ~ sisemóye ~ sísemòye.

Vespula
　family Vespidae, genus Vespula, i.e. Vespula spp.:: x̲ex̲p'ítsel sisemó:ye < sisemó:ya ~ sisemóya ~ sisemóye ~ sísemòye, x̲ex̲p'ítsel sisemó:ye < sisemó:ya ~ sisemóya ~ sisemóye ~ sísemòye.

vessel
　vessel, (container):: =ő:welh ~ =őwelh ~ =ōwelh ~ =ewelh ~ =á:welh ~ =welh ~ =ewí:l.

vest
　jacket, vest:: cháket.

vetch
　kinnikinnick berry, bearberry, Indian tobacco, domestic pea, domestic green bean, and probably giant vetch berry:: tl'íkw'el.
　kinnikinnick plant, domestic pea-vine, domestic bean-vine, giant vetch vine:: tl'ikw'íyelhp < tl'íkw'el.

via

go through (somewhere), go via (somewhere), go by way of:: lhe'á.
go travelling by way of, go via:: ley ~ lay < la.

Viburnum edule

possibly Viburnum opulus, more likely Viburnum edule:: kwúkwewels.

Viburnum opulus

possibly Viburnum opulus, more likely Viburnum edule:: kwúkwewels.

Vicea gigantea

Arctostaphylos uva-ursi, (intro.) Pisum sativum, (intro.) Phaseolus vulgaris, and probably Vicea gigantea:: tl'íkw'el.

Victoria

Queen Victoria:: Kwíl Mektốliya < kwí:l.
Victoria, B.C.:: Sth'ó:mes.
Victoria, B.C., city of Victoria area, Fort Victoria:: Sth'ó:mes.

view

appear, come into view, rise into view:: pél:ékw.

village

also the name of the village on Strawberry Island:: Alhqá:yem < álhqey ~ álhqay.
another village of the Pilalt people:: (possibly) Chuwtí:l < cháchew ~ cháchu.
a place on Chilliwack River, a little above Anderson Flat and Allison's (between Tamihi Creek and Slesse Creek), a village at deep water between Tamihi Creek and Slesse Creek:: Iy'óythel < éy ~ éy:.
Atchelitz village and now Chilliwack Indian reserve #8:: Áthelets < áthelets.
a turn in the Fraser River between Ruby Creek and Katz (about a mile upriver from the mouth of Ruby Creek and Ruby Creek I.R. #9 (called Lukseetsis-sum on maps and D.I.A. records, see Lexwthíthesem)), also the name of a village at this spot, spelled Skawahlook, Indian Reserve #1, on topographical maps and D.I.A. records:: Sq'ewá:lxw < q'éw ~ q'ew.
a village at the south end of former Sumas Lake on the mountain:: Snaníth.
a village by Yale along Yale Creek:: X̲wóx̲welá:lhp < x̲wále ~ x̲wá:le.
a village of the Pilalt people:: (probably) Scháchewxel ~ Cháchewxel < cháchew ~ cháchu.
a village or place at Musqueam (now in Vancouver):: Málí.
beach in front of old Scowlitz village, the point the Harrison River goes around by Kilby's store:: Sq'iq'ewílem < q'éw ~ q'ew.
Cheam Island (my name for an island in the Fraser River across from Cheam Indian Reserve #2), Cheam village, Cheam Indian Reserve #1:: Xwchí:yò:m < schí:ya.
Chehalis village on Harrison River, the Heart Rock for which Chehalis, B.C. was named (at the mouth of Chehalis River):: Ts'a'í:les < ts'á:.
Chilliwack Mountain, village of Cameleats on west end of Chilliwack Mountain:: Qwemí(:)líts.
Cultus Lake, (also village at Cultus Lake near Hatchery Creek [Wells (lst ed.):19]):: Swílhcha.
Deming (Wash.), South Fork of Nooksack River and village nearest Deming:: xwe'éyem ~ xw'éyem < éy ~ éy:.
Emory Creek, also village at mouth of Emory Creek on both sides of the creek:: Sx̲wótl'aqwem.

village (CONT'D)

Esilao village, Siwash Creek village:: Aseláw, Aseláw.

former village directly across the Fraser River from Yale:: X̲elhlálh ~ X̲elhálh < x̲élh.

(heron nesting area which was the) upriver end of Herrling Island in Fraser River just below Popkum, also the name of the village or settlement on Herrling Island:: Smémeqw'o < sméqw'o ~ smṓqw'o.

Katzie village:: Q'éyts'i(y).

Katz river-bank, Ruby Creek settlement, village on north bank of Fraser River just below (west of) the mouth of Ruby Creek:: Spópetes < pó:t.

Kilgard village on Upper Sumas River:: Kw'ekw'e'í:qw ~ Kw'ekw'e'íqw ~ Kw'ekw'í:qw < kw'e'í ~ kw''í ~ kw'í.

Kwakwawapilt village and reserve (Chilliwack Indian Reserve #6):: Qweqwe'ópelhp < qwe'óp.

Lackaway village, Lackaway Creek:: Lá:x̲ewey.

Mary Ann Creek, village at mouth of Mary Ann Creek into the Fraser (in Yale, B.C., Yale Town Indian Reserve #1):: Sése.

Matsqui village, (Matsqui Creek [Wells]):: Máthxwi.

mountain on the west (C.P.R.) side of the Fraser River above American Bar which had a steaming pond at the top, (year-round village at mouth of American Creek on west bank of the Fraser River [Duff]):: Qétex̲em < qá:t.

Musqueam village:: Xwméthkwiyem.

old Scowlitz village:: Sq'éwlets ~ Sq'ówlets < q'éw ~ q'ew.

Othello, (B.C.), a village on the Coquihalla River, on the west side across from the most northwest point above the mouth of Nicolum Creek, up nine miles from Hope on the Kettle Valley Railroad:: Áthelets < áthelets.

people from Semá:th (Sumas village):: Pepá:thxetel < pá:th.

Pilalt tribe, Pilalt people, Pilalt dialect, (Pilalt, village at west end of Little Mountain by Agassiz [Wells, Duff]):: Pelólhxw.

Pilalt, village at west end of Little Mountain by Agassiz:: Pelólhxw.

place by Albert Cooper's house on Chilliwack River Road near Vedder Crossing, former village where a slide is now on north bank of Chilliwack River opposite Liumchen Creek:: X̲éylés < x̲éylés.

place where a grove of birches stood/stand near the Kickbush place on Chilliwack River Road in Sardis, (village at junction of Semmihault Creek and Chilliwack River [Wells 1965 (lst ed.):19]):: Sekw'sekw'emá:y < síkw'.

Schelowat, a village at the bend in Hope Slough at Annis Rd. where there was a painted or marked house:: Sx̲elá:wtxw < x̲él ~ x̲é:yl ~ x̲í:l

Skwah village, now Skwah Reserve:: Sqwehá < qwá.

Skwah village, now Skwah Reserve, also known as Wellington Reserve:: Sqwá < qwá.

Skwali, a village north of Hope Slough and Skwah:: Skwáli.

Soowahlie village (where Sweltzer Creek met Chilliwack River), Soowahlie Reserve near Vedder Crossing:: Th'ewá:lí < th'éw.

Spuzzum village (on south bank of Spuzzum Creek at its mouth onto the Fraser River), also Spuzzum Creek:: Spíyem.

Squatits village on east bank of Fraser river across from the north end of Seabird Island, Peters Indian Reserves #1, 1a, and 2 on site:: Skw'átets < kw'átem.

Sumas Mountain (also Tuckquail, a village on both sides of Lower Sumas River [Wells]):: T'ex̲qé:yl or T'ex̲qí:l < t'éx̲.

Sumas village and area from present-day Kilgard to Fraser River, Sumas village (on both sides of the Fraser at the east end of Sumas Mt.), (Devil's Run (below Láx̲ewey), the area between Sumas Mt. and Fraser River [Elders Group 7/13/77], Sumas River (probably requires Stó:lō river or Stótelō creek to follow) [Wells 1965], Sumas Lake (probably requires X̲ótsa lake after Semáth for this

village (CONT'D)

meaning) [Elders Group 7/13/77]):: Smá:th ~ Semá:th ~ Semáth.
Tamihi village at the mouth of Tamihi Creek:: T'emiyéq(w) ?? < t'ámiya.
upper end of Seabird Island, village at the upper end of Seabird Island, Maria Slough separating Seabird Island from north shore of Fraser River, now used for Seabird Island as a whole:: Sq'éwqel ~ Sq'ówqel < q'éw ~ q'ew.
village above Ruby Creek:: Sxowál?? or Xowál??.
village above Yakweakwioose on both sides of the Chilliwack River:: Sx̲wó:yx̲weyla ~ Sx̲wóyx̲weyla < sx̲wó:yx̲wey ~ sx̲wóyx̲wey.
village across from or a little above the mouth of Centre Creek into Chilliwack River:: Swóyel.
village at American Bar, village on west bank of Fraser River at American Creek, American Bar Reserve:: Peqwchṓ:lthel ~ Peqwechṓ:lthel < péqw.
village at east end of Little Mountain on Hope Slough, upper end of Mount Shannon [DM]:: Qwolíwiya or Ñwolíwiya.
village at junction of Ryder Lake Creek and Chilliwack River:: T'ept'ṓp.
village at mouth of Stulkawhits Creek on Fraser River:: Lexwtl'íkw'elem < tl'íkw'el.
village at outlet of old Chilliwack River on Fraser River, now known as Skway reserve (Chilliwack Indian Reserve #5):: Shxwhá:y < hà:y.
village at the confluence of Sweltzer and Soowahlie creeks with Chilliwack River:: Skw'iykw'íylets < kw'í ~ kw'íy.
village at Union Bar, now also Hope Indian Reserve #5 (#15 in Duff 1952), Ay-wa-wis:: Iwówes.
village at west end of Little Mountain (Mount Shannon) on Hope Slough, also a name for Hope Slough or Hope River:: Sqwá:la < qwá.
village at what's now Katz Reserve, Katz Landing:: Chowéthel < cháchew ~ cháchu.
village between Yale Creek and Mary Ann Creek on the CP side (west bank of the Fraser R.) where lots of cottonwoods grow/grew (near Yale, B.C.):: Lexwchéwṓlhp < cháchew ~ cháchu.
village just below (on the south side of) Suka Creek, on the CN side (east side) of the Fraser River across from Dogwood Valley:: Skwíyò.
village near and above [upriver from] Katz where 36 pit-houses were wiped out in an epidemic:: Sx̲wóx̲wiymelh < x̲wà:y ~ x̲wá:y.
village near Katz:: (Xwóqw'ilwets?).
village near the mouth of Choate Creek, (Choate Creek [AK, SP/AD], (Stullawheets village on a hill on the east bank of the Fraser River near the mouth of Suka Creek [elders on American Bar Trip (AD/AK/?)]):: St'élxweth'.
village now at north end of Agassiz-Rosedale bridge, now Tseatah Indian Reserve #2 (of Cheam band):: Siyét'e.
village now called Ohamil Reserve or Laidlaw:: Shxw'ōwhámél ~ Shxw'ōhámél.
village on a small flat a little above Vedder Crossing, on the north side of Chilliwack River:: Th'óth'emels < th'óméls.
village on both sides of Liumchen Creek, Liumchen Creek, Liumchen Mountain:: Loyú:mthel ~ Loyúmthel.
village on both sides of the Lower Sumas River:: Lexwchmóqwem?.
village on east bank of Fraser River below Siwash Creek (Aseláw), now Yale Indian Reserves 19 and 20, named because of a big rock in the area that the trail had to pass (go around), also the name of the rock:: Q'alelíktel < q'ál.
village on east bank of Fraser River near the outlet from Cheam Lake, Popkum Indian village:: Pópkw'em < pékw' ~ péqw'.
village on east bank of Sweltzer Creek (above Sx̲woyehá:lá), (creek by the village of the same name [X̲wōx̲wá:ye] [Wells]):: X̲wōx̲wá:ye < x̲wōx̲wáye ~ x̲wex̲wáye ~ x̲wōx̲wá:ye.
village on north bank of the Fraser River above Agassiz Mountain:: Tsítsqem.

village (CONT'D)

village on the site of Hope, modern Hope, B.C.:: Ts'qó:ls < ts'qó:ls.
village on west bank of old course of Chilliwack River near Tzeachton, also the place nearby where the Stó:lō used to soak dried fish:: Slhálqi < lhél.
village or area on north side of Suka Creek (which is on the east side of the Fraser River:: Kwókwxwemels < kwoxw.
village or settlement on the west side of the Fraser River at Emory Creek by Frank Malloway's fish camp, Albert Flat (Yale Indian Reserve #5):: Ó:ywoses.
village site (burned) on Atchelitz Creek:: Syéqw < yéqw.
village with many pit-houses below Union Bar:: Lhilheltálets < lhà:l.
Watery Eaves, a famous longhouse and early village on a flat area on Chilliwack River just a quarter mile upriver/east above Vedder Crossing:: Qoqoláx̲el < qó:.
Whetkyel village east of Little Mountain by Agassiz:: Xwétxel or X̲wétxel.
Whonnock village:: X̲wṓ:leqw.
winter village on flat at mouth of Gordon Creek:: Sókw'ech ~ Sókw'ets < sókw'.
Yakweakwioose, next village above Scowkale, village near Sardis on the old Chilliwack River course, now Chilliwack Indian Reserve #9:: Yeqwyeqwí:ws < yéqw.
year-round village at mouth of American Creek on west bank of the Fraser River:: Qétex̲em < qá:t.

vine
blackberry vine, blackberry bush:: skw'ṓ:lmexwelhp < skw'ṓ:lmexw.
kinnikinnick plant, domestic pea-vine, domestic bean-vine, giant vetch vine:: tl'ikw'íyelhp < tl'íkw'el.
strawberry vine, strawberry plant, strawberry patch:: schí:yà:lhp < schí:ya.
trailing blackberry vine:: shxwelméxwelh skw'ṓ:lmexwelhp < skw'ṓ:lmexw.

vine maple
vine maple, Douglas maple:: sí:ts'elhp.

Viola :: Poyṓle.

violent
(be) aggressive, cranky, ready to fight, (be) violent, hot-headed:: sx̲óytl'thet ~ sx̲ó:ytl'thet.

Violet :: Póylet.

violet
blue camas, yellow dog-tooth violet = yellow avalanche lily:: sk'ámets ~ sk'ámeth.

virgin :: éy ~ éy:.
adolescent virgin girl, young girl (about ten to fifteen years), girl (from ten till she becomes a woman):: q'á:mi ~ q'á:miy.
be good, good, well, nice, fine, better, better (ought to), it would be good if, may it be good, let it be good, happy, glad, clean, well-behaved, polite, virgin, popular, comfortable (with furniture, other things?),:: éy ~ éy:.

visibility)
the (female, present and visible), the (female, unspecified presence and/or unspecified visibility):: the.
the (male, present, visible), the (gender or presence and visibility unspecified), a (male, present and visible), a (gender or presence and visibility unspecified):: te.

visible)

him (there, near but not visible), that one:: kwethá ~ kwe thá < kw.
nominalizer (female present and visible or presence or proximity unspecified), demonstrative article:: the=.
nominalizer (male or gender unspecified, present and visible or presence or proximity unspecified), demonstrative article:: ta=, te=.
the (female, present and visible), the (female, unspecified presence and/or unspecified visibility):: the.
the (male, present, visible), the (gender or presence and visibility unspecified), a (male, present and visible), a (gender or presence and visibility unspecified):: te.

vision

have a vision before you become an experienced spirit dancer (a sts'eláxwem):: élíyá.
spirit dream, vision, (any) dream:: s'élíyá < élíyá.
to dream, have a vision:: élíyá, élíyá.

visit

be visiting:: làlets'éwtxwem < láts'.
come to see s-o/s-th, visit s-o:: kw'átset < kw'áts ~ kw'éts.
lots of people visiting (one another):: lá:leqel.
seeing s-o (i.e. visiting s-o):: kw'ókw'etset < kw'áts ~ kw'éts.
visit, be on a short visit:: lá:ts'ewtxwem < láts'.

voice :: sqelxwá:le ~ sqelxwále < qél:éxw ~ qel(:)éxw.

a loud voice:: sthí:qel < thi ~ tha ~ the ~ thah ~ theh.
be in clear voice, be in good voice, be in good health, healthy:: shxw'éyelh < éy ~ éy:.
big voice (usually deep):: thíwelh < thi ~ tha ~ the ~ thah ~ theh.
call (by voice), shout, yell, holler:: tà:m.
call s-o (by voice), holler at s-o, shout at s-o, shout at s-o:: tà:met ~ tàmet < tà:m.
changing in voice (of a boy):: qw'iqw'elá:mqel ~ qw'iqw'elámqel < qw'íl.
(have) a clear voice:: xw'éyeqel < éy ~ éy:.
(have a) high pitch (voice or melody), (have a) sharp voice:: xwiyótheqel < éy ~ éy:, xwiyótheqel < éy ~ éy:.
(have a) high voice:: chélhqel < =chílh ~ chílh=.
(have a) pleasant voice:: iyésqel < éy ~ éy:.
in the throat, in the esophagus, in the voice:: =eqel.
lost one's voice:: stqá:qel < téq.
loud (of a voice):: sthí:qel < thi ~ tha ~ the ~ thah ~ theh.
sound like (in voice):: staqí:l < t.
throat (inside part), gullet, voice:: sqelxwá:le ~ sqelxwále < qél:éxw ~ qel(:)éxw.
to change (of a boy's voice at puberty):: qw'elá:m < qw'íl.

vole

a big rat (prob. the introduced Norway rat, probably native species of large vole which may include any or all of the following that are found in the area: creeping vole, long-tail vole, mountain heather vole, boreal redback vole), possibly also the introduced roof rat:: ts'á:txwels < ts'átxwels ~ ch'átxwels.
rat, vole (short-tailed mouse), may include any or all of the following which occur in this area: creeping vole, long-tail vole, mountain heather vole, boreal redback vole, Norway rat (intro.), and perhaps roof rat, also includes bushy-tailed wood rat (packrat) which has its own name below:: há:wt.
small rat, small vole:: hiháwt < há:wt.

vomit
  to vomit, throw up:: yá:t.
  vomiting:: yáyet ~ yáyat < yá:t.

Vulpes fulva cascadensis:: sx̲wewál.

vulture
  turkey vulture:: éq"eq'esem.

vulva
  on the vulva, in the vagina:: xw=.
  woman's genitals, vulva, vagina:: xá:welh.

wade
  swim, (tread water), (wading in deep water [LJ], swimming [Elders Group]):: x̲élhchem.
  to wade:: síx̲wem.
  wading in shallow water:: sísex̲wem < síx̲wem.

waffle:: st'elt'elákw' seplíl < t'el(ákw'), seplíl
  (lit. many squares + bread)

wag
  to wag its tail:: tl'ap'élatsem < stl'ep'él:ets ~ stl'ep'élets.

wagon :: wákel ~ wákyel.
  three canoes, three wagons, three conveyances (any form of transportation), three boats:: lhxwó:lh < lhí:xw.

Wahleach
  place at Ruby Creek where Paul Webster lived some years ago, now Wahleach Island Indian Reserve #2 and area at mouth of Mahood Creek:: X̲wolích ~ X̲welích < x̲wále ~ x̲wá:le.
  (probably) Mahood Creek and Johnson Slough, (possibly) Wahleach River or Hicks Creek (creek at bridge on east end of Seabird Island [AK]):: Qwōhòls < qwá.
  Wahleach whistle stop on Seabird Island where Wayne Bobb lived in 1977, (now also Wahleach Lake (man-made) [EB]):: Wolích < x̲wále ~ x̲wá:le.

Wahleach Bluff
  Wahleach Bluff, a lookout mountain with rock sticking out over a bluff, also the lookout point on Agassiz Mountain:: Kw'okw'echíwel < kw'áts ~ kw'éts.

Wahleach Island
  island off of Wahleach Island, island at bridge on river side on east end of Seabird Island:: Xáméles < xá:m.

wail
  feel like singing a spirit song, be in a trance making sighsand crying sounds before singing a spirit song, be in the beginning of a trance before the spirit song is recognizable (the motions and sounds, crying out or wailing before singing):: lhéch.

waistband
  waistband of a skirt:: qéttel < qít.

wait :: ólmetsel < ólmets.
a waiting dip-net with frame and string trap:: thqálem < thqá:lem.
holding on to a thqálem, waiting dip-netting, still-dipping:: théqelem < thqá:lem.
later, after a while, later on, wait a while:: téx̱w.
place where one fishes by waiting with a dip-net, dip-net fishing place, place where one still-dips:: sthqálem < thqá:lem.
spearing sqwéx̱em (silver spring salmon) in clear water after waiting for them:: chth'éylem.
tired of waiting:: q'sém.
wait, be later:: ká(t) ~ ke'át.
wait for s-o:: ólmetst < ólmets.
waiting:: ó:lmetsel < ólmets.
waiting for s-o:: ó:lmetst < ólmets.

wake
be awake:: shxwexwí < xwíy ~ x í.
(be) easy to wake up:: shxwíyxwiy ~ shxwíxwiy < xwíy ~ x í.
to rattle (cans, etc. to wake newlyweds), to shivaree (someone):: q'etx̱áls < q'et.
to tingle (like arm waking up from numbness), (have/get a) stinging feeling:: thátkwem.
wake s-o up:: xwíxet < xwíy ~ x í, xwíyt < xwíy ~ x í.
wake up:: xwíy ~ x í.
wake up (oneself), (wake oneself purposely):: xwíythet ~ xwíthet < xwíy ~ x í.
wide-awake:: shxwixwiyós or shxwiyxwiyós < xwíy ~ x í.

Walian Creek falls
"Eagle Falls" on the west side of Harrison Lake, probably Walian Creek falls:: Kwótxwem Stó:lō < kwótx̱wem ~ kwótxwem.

walk :: ímex ~ (rare) íméx < i┐ m.
coming by foot, travelling by walking, already walking, travelling on foot:: ye'í:mex < i┐ m.
gait, a walk:: s'ímex < i┐ m.
go for a walk, take a stroll, stroll:: imexósem < i┐ m.
going with each other [romantically], going for a walk with each other:: ts'lhimexóstel < ts'elh=.
go in the water, walk slowly into the water, (dip oneself in the water [HT]:: mí:lthet < mí:l ~ míl.
go out into the river, go down to the river, walk down to the river:: tó:l ~ tò:l.
go with each other (romantically), go for a walk with each other (romantically):: ts'lhimexóstel < i┐ m.
have a nightmare, to sleep-walk:: píx̱eya.
nervous while walking on something narrow:: x̱wix̱wíyem.
overstretch one's legs when walking with too big a step:: t'íw ~ t'ì:w.
tip-toeing, (walking lightly, sneaking):: t'et'ásxelem < t'ás.
to back up (walk or move backwards):: yóthet.
to walk slow:: i'oyóm or i'eyóm < óyém.
walking:: í:mex < i┐ m.
walk[ing] silently or quietly:: t'et'ásxel or t'at'ásxel < t'ás.
walking single-file:: chichelóqtel < chá:l or chó:l.
walk lightly, sneak:: t'ásxelem < t'ás.
walk silently, walk quietly:: t'ásxel < t'ás.

walk (CONT'D)

what one walks on (trail, board sidewalk, cement sidewalk, etc.):: shxw'ímex < i┐ m.

wall

a partition, wall inside:: t'omeliwétel < t'ómel ~ t'ómél.
(mice) chewing (a wall, box, etc.):: ts'átxwels ~ ch'átxwels.
steep rock wall that used to have Indian writing at first C.P.R. tunnel above Haig:: X̲elíqel < x̲él ~ x̲é:yl ~ x̲í:l
to the back (near the wall), on the inside (on a bed toward the wall):: lhelhá:l.
wall (inside or outside):: t'ómel ~ t'ómél.

walled in

canyon (narrow, walled in with rock):: sx̲ex̲ákw' < x̲ékw'.

wallet

wallet, purse:: shxwtále'álá < tá:le ~ tále.

wall lettuce:: lhelelméxwtel < lhél.

wall mat

bulrush mat, reed mat, mat (of cattail/roots/bulrushes, etc.), (wall mat (Elders Group 11/12/75):: wá:th'elh ~ wáth'elh < wáth'.

wallpaper)

run over it (with car), spread it (for ex. on bread with knife), put it up (of wallpaper), (stick it on), stick s-th closed (with pitch for ex.):: tl'íq't < tl'íq'.

walnut

nut of hazelnut bush, acorn, any nut, walnut, peanut, etc.:: sth'í:tsem < th'éts.

wander

wandering, where someone goes:: shxwélem ~ shxwélém < la.

want

not want s-o:: mí:lt.
not want s-o, not accept s-o, discriminate against s-o:: mí:lt.
pretending to be good, want to be accepted:: éystelómet ~ éy:stelómet < éy ~ éy:.
to make a sign with its foot it wants a younger brother or younger sister:: oqw'exélem < óqw'.
want a wife, He wants a wife.:: chxwélmel < chá:xw.
want, desire, like, need:: stl'í ~ stl'í: < tl'í ~ tl'í:.
want to cry, feel like crying:: x̲amélmel < x̲à:m ~ x̲á:m.
want to get a wife, He wants to get a wife.:: scháchxwelmel < chá:xw.
want to pee, (want to urinate, feel like one has to urinate):: síyt'eqem < síyt'.

wapato

arrowleaf, wapato, Indian potato:: xwōqw'ṓ:ls.
potato (generic), including three or four kinds of wild potato: arrowleaf or wapato, Jerusalem artichoke, blue camas, and qíqemxel (so far unidentified plant), besides post-contact domestic potato:: sqáwth ~ sqá:wth.

war

big high-bowed canoe from the Coast, Nootka war canoe, huge canoe:: q'ex̲wő:welh ~ q'ex̲wőwelh.
spear (any kind), spear (for fish or war), fish-spear, telescopic spear for sturgeon, harpoon, detachable harpoon points:: tá:lh.
to war, go to war:: x̲éylé̲x̲.
war, (warring), fighting a war:: x̲éyx̲elex̲ < x̲éylé̲x̲.
war-whoop, ((probably) a sung spell before battle):: syiwí:leqw < yéw: ~ yéw.

war club

war club, club for any purpose:: kw'óqwestel < kw'óqw.

-ward

side, -ward:: =ó:lwelh.

warm

be hot, be warm:: kw'ókw'es < kw'ás.
first warmed side of a tree, sunny side of a tree:: sqewá:meth' < qew.
getting warmer:: léqwem.
get warm (of weather):: kw'ósthet < kw'ás.
got warm:: líqwem < léqwem.
have a hot drink, warm one's chest inside:: qatílésem < qá:t.
heat it up, warm it up, smoke s-th over a fire:: pákw'et.
warming up by a fire:: qéwethet < qew.
warming up food:: t'álkw'els < t'álqw' or t'élqw'.
warming your bum, (be warming the bottom or rump):: sqewálets < qew.
warm it up:: t'élqw't < t'álqw' or t'élqw'.
warm it up (on the bottom):: qówletst < qew.
warm, luke-warm:: t'álqw'em < t'álqw' or t'élqw'.
warm (of clothing):: hólem.
warm one's rump, warm one's bottom:: qewéletsem < qew.
warm side:: sqewós < qew.
warm s-th, warm s-o:: qewét < qew.
warm up by a fire:: qewéthet < qew.
warm up (food, tea, etc.):: t'elkw'á:ls < t'álqw' or t'élqw'.

warn

go warn s-o in secret, go tell s-o in secret:: wíyt < wá:y.
(this cry of a bluejay [Steller's jay] warns you of bad news):: chéke chéke chéke chéke.
warn s-o:: wá:yt < wá:y.

warrior

name of an old man from Kilgard who was a strong warrior (fighter):: X̲éyteleq < x̲éyet.
warrior, (leader of a raiding party [CT]):: stó:méx.

wart :: sts'épxwel ~ sch'épxwel < ts'épx̲.

war-whoop

war-whoop, ((probably) a sung spell before battle):: syiwí:leqw < yéw: ~ yéw.

was

he/she/it was (already), they were (already):: lulh < le.

was (CONT'D)

that was her (deceased):: kwsú:tl'ò:lh < kw.
that was her (deceased), she (deceased):: kwsú:tl'ò:lh < tl'ó ~ tl'o.
that was him (deceased), he (deceased):: kw'ú:tl'ò:lh < tl'ó ~ tl'o.
that was them (deceased):: kwthú:tl'òlèmèlh < kw.
that was them (deceased), they (deceased):: kwthú:tl'ò:lèmèlh < tl'ó ~ tl'o.

wash

(go) wash one's mouth out:: th'ex̲wqéylem or th'ex̲wqílem < th'éx̲w or th'óx̲w, th'x̲woythílem < th'éx̲w or th'óx̲w.
washboard:: shxwótqwelwetem < xwótqwem.
washing dishes:: th'óx̲wí:ls < th'éx̲w or th'óx̲w.
washing one's clothes:: th'éx̲welwetem < th'éx̲w or th'óx̲w.
washing one's face, washing his/her face:: th'éx̲wesèm < th'éx̲w or th'óx̲w.
wash one's body:: th'ex̲wíwsem < th'éx̲w or th'óx̲w.
wash one's clothes:: th'x̲welwétem < th'éx̲w or th'óx̲w.
wash one's face:: th'ex̲wó:sem ~ th'ex̲wósem < th'éx̲w or th'óx̲w.
wash one's feet:: th'èx̲wxél:ém < th'éx̲w or th'óx̲w.
wash one's hair, wash one's head:: th'ex̲wíqwem < th'éx̲w or th'óx̲w.
wash one's hands:: th'ex̲wá:tsesem < th'éx̲w or th'óx̲w.
wash one's head and hair:: xwóyeqwem (or perhaps) xwáyeqwem.
wash s-th:: th'ex̲wót < th'éx̲w or th'óx̲w.
wash the dishes:: th'ex̲wewíls ~ th'ex̲wwí:ls ~ th'x̲wwí:ls ~ th'x̲wí:ls < th'éx̲w or th'óx̲w.
washtub, washing machine:: shxwth'éx̲welwetem < th'éx̲w or th'óx̲w.
water kettle, boiler pan (for canning, washing clothes or dishes):: qowletsá:ls < qew.

washboard

washboard:: shxwótqwelwetem < xwótqwem.

washing machine

washtub, washing machine:: shxwth'éx̲welwetem < th'éx̲w or th'óx̲w.

Washington

Washington (state), Washington (D.C.):: Wóshetem.

washtub

washtub, washing machine:: shxwth'éx̲welwetem < th'éx̲w or th'óx̲w.

wasn't

wasn't?, weren't?, didn't?:: ewá:lh ~ wá:lh < éwe ~ ő̃we.
weren't ever?, wasn't ever?, didn't ever?, does s-o ever?, never used to, not going to (but did anyway) [perhaps in the sense of never usually do X but did this time]:: ewá:lh ~ wá:lh < éwe ~ ő̃we.

wasp

bee, honeybee, hornet, wasp:: sisemó:ya ~ sisemóya ~ sisemóye ~ sísemòye.

watch

sit facing a river and watch it, sit on a riverbank and sunbathe:: chichewós < cháchew ~ cháchu.
watch for s-o to come, be on the watch for s-o:: qw'óqw'elhmet < qw'ólh or qw'álh.

watchful

be watchful, be facing away:: sle'ó:les < le'á.

watchman :: wóchmel.

water :: qó:.

add some water [to s-th]:: ch'exwélhchat < ts'xwót.

a stretch of water in the Fraser River on the C.N. side by Strawberry Island:: Kwetl'kwótl'thetōws < kwá:.

be big, be large, be high (of floodwater), rise (of floodwater):: híkw.

be calm (of water or wind), (get calm (wind/water), calm down (wind/water), be smooth (of water) [AC, LH]):: qám.

be deep, be very deep, be deep water:: shxwtl'ép < tl'ép.

be dripping, (have) continuous dripping, water dropping:: th'áq'em < th'q'ém ~ th'eq'ém.

be fresh (of water), be tasteless:: th'áwém ~ th'áwem.

be underwater, sink to the bottom:: míq'.

boil water:: lhótqwem < lhot.

calm (of water), smooth (of water), (when the river is) quiet or calm:: p'ep'ákwem < p'ékw.

calm water (calmer than sqám):: sqáqem < qám.

choke on water, choked on liquid:: lexwslhém ~ lexwslhám < lhém.

collected rain-water drops in a bucket:: th'q'emelétsem < th'q'ém ~ th'eq'ém.

collected rain-water from a drip:: th'q'émelets ~ ts'q'émelets < th'q'ém ~ th'eq'ém.

deep bottom (of a river, lake, water, canoe, anything):: stl'epláts < tl'ép.

dipping water:: qóqelem < qó:.

dive (already in water), go underwater, sink oneself down:: leqàlèm < léqem.

drift-netting, catching fish with one or two canoes drifting downstream with a net in deep water:: xíxemel ~ xíxemal.

drop a net into water:: qwesú:yel < qwés.

drop s-th into the water:: wṓqw'et < wṓqw' ~ wéqw'.

eddy (in water):: xwelkw'ím < xwélekw'.

eddy water (where you set nets), [to eddy repeatedly?]:: xwtitím or xwtiytím.

fall in the water, fall overboard (of one person):: qwés.

fog appearing on the water, (fine snow [AK]):: qwelqwélxel < qwélxel.

get big, rise (of floodwater):: híkwthet < híkw.

get fog on the water, (get steam (of the ground) [DC]):: qwélxel.

(get) lots of water all over since it's raining so hard, really getting rainy:: t'emt'émqw'xel < t'émeqw'.

go around a bend (in water):: q'éwlets ~ q'ówlets < q'éw ~ q'ew.

go around (a point, a bend, a curve, etc.) in the water, make a U-turn (in the water, could use today on land with a car):: q'ówletsem < q'éw ~ q'ew.

go around s-th in the water:: q'ówletst < q'éw ~ q'ew.

go down(hill) to the water, go towards the river:: t'óxw.

going towards the river or water:: t'ót'exw < t'óxw.

go in the direction of the water, go downriver:: xwōqw'éylem < wṓqw' ~ wéqw'.

go in the water, walk slowly into the water, (dip oneself in the water [HT]:: mí:lthet < mí:l ~ míl, mí:lthet < mí:l ~ míl.

(have/be) dirty water, (not clear, unclear, can't see the bottom (of water) [EL]):: mímexwel.

(have) quieter water, died down a little:: sqám < qám.

(have) sound of water sloshing around inside (a bottle, etc.) or gurgling:: qw'át'ts'em.

water (CONT'D)

high water time (yearly, usually in June), June:: temqó: ~ temqoqó: < qó:.
launch s-th/s-o into the water, push s-o/s-th into the water, throw it in the water:: qwsét < qwés.
make the sound of water splashing or dripping fast, (make the sound of a waterfall, make the sound of pouring rain dripping or splashing in puddles loudly):: xwótqwem.
one's eyes are watering:: qo'qo'ólésem < qó:.
place s-th (prob. in water):: mí:lt < mí:l ~ míl.
placing s-th (prob. in water):: hámelet < mí:l ~ míl.
pour water on s-th to keep it damp:: kw'lhó:st < kw'élh.
puddle that's always dirty, dirty pond, stagnant pool of water, (it never dries out [AK]):: th'qwélhcha.
pulling a canoe through rough water by a rope in the front:: tx̲wṓwelh < tóx̲w.
pulling a canoe through rough water by a rope in the front, pulling a canoe with a rope:: tóx̲wesem < tóx̲w.
put a mark on it (like water level of river), mark it, weigh it, (measure it):: x̲á:th't ~ x̲áth't < x̲áth' ~ x̲e'áth'.
rapids, fast water, clear water, flowing fast, going fast, swift (water):: lex̲wṓ:m ~ lex̲wṓm < x̲wém ~ xwém.
rising, getting big:: hahíkwthet < híkw.
rough (of wind or water), turbulent (of wind or water), real swift (of water):: x̲átl'.
rub (oil or water) in s-th to clean or soften, rub s-th to soften or clean it, (shaping a stone hammer with abrasion?, shaping?, mixing paint?, pressing together or crushing? [BHTTC 9/2/76]):: yémq't.
sea, ocean, salt water:: kw'ótl'kwa.
shallow water:: sxáxem < xá:m.
slough, backwater, ((also) eddy [AC]):: sts'élexw < ts'el.
sound of boiling water:: xwótqwem.
splash s-o with water, spray s-o with water:: lhéltest < lhél.
spring (water source):: thíx̲.
stagnant water lake or ponds at the downriver end of Skw'átets or Peters Reserve near Laidlaw:: Th'qwélhcha < th'qwélhcha.
still (of water):: qó:mthet < qám.
swim, (tread water), (wading in deep water [LJ], swimming [Elders Group]):: x̲élhchem.
take it out of water:: qw'ímét < qw'í:m.
throw a net into water (to drift, not to set), throw a net out, (gill net [TG]):: qwsá:yel < qwés.
tide coming in, water coming in, water coming up (ocean tide or river):: qém:el.
to cup water in one's hands, to cup berries in one's hands:: qéltsesem < qó:.
to dip water, get water, fetch water, pack water:: qó:m < qó:.
to drip (once), water drops once, a drop of water, a drip:: th'q'ém ~ th'eq'ém.
to go down (of water), subside (of water), the tide goes out or down, (be going out (of tide) [BJ]):: th'à:m ~ th'ám.
to scoop, to dip, dip water:: qó:lem < qó:.
trickling, dribbling, water bubbling up in a river, add water to a container, water running under:: kw'átem.
unclear liquid, water, juice:: =elhcha.
wading in shallow water:: sísex̲wem < síx̲wem.
water basket:: shxwqó:m < qó:.
water jumping (as it goes over a rough bottom in a river):: kwetl'kwótl'thetōws < kwá:.
water (someone) carried, (water fetched/gotten):: sqó:m < qó:, sqó:m < qó:.

water baby

  water pygmies, water baby:: s'ó:lmexw.

waterfall

  make the sound of water splashing or dripping fast, (make the sound of a waterfall, make the sound of pouring rain dripping or splashing in puddles loudly):: xwótqwem.

  small waterfall:: skwíkwel < skwél.

  waterfall, falls:: skwél.

waterfowl

  big bird, (large bird (of any kind)), any waterfowl:: x̲wí:leqw ~ x̲wé:yleqw ~ x̲wéyleqw.

  larger bird (any kind, generic), waterfowl, duck, (mallard [Cheh. dial.]):: mó:qw.

water hemlock

  poison fern that grows in swampy places, (prob. water hemlock, poison hemlock):: welékwsa.

water-lily

  water-lily, yellow pond lily:: qw'emétx̲w.

water pygmy

  maybe the same place as Sqw'ex̲wáq (pool where Kawkawa Creek comes into the Coquihalla River and where the water pygmies lived):: Skw'íkw'x̲weq (or better, Sqw'íqw'x̲weq) < Sqw'ex̲wáq.

  water pygmies, water baby:: s'ó:lmexw.

Watery Eaves

  Watery Eaves, a famous longhouse and early village on a flat area on Chilliwack River just a quarter mile upriver/east above Vedder Crossing:: Qoqoláx̲el < qó:.

wave

  a wave:: syó:letsep.

  big waves, (have big waves):: thitheháleq < thi ~ tha ~ the ~ thah ~ theh.

  fleecy wave clouds that look like sheep:: x̲eylx̲elemós.

  to wave (one's arms):: x̲élqesà:ls < x̲élqes.

  to wave (the hand):: x̲élqes.

  wave at s-o:: x̲élqest < x̲élqes.

  waves:: =á:leq ~ =eleq, smá:yeleq.

  waving (one's arms):: x̲ólqesà:ls < x̲élqes.

wax

  to harden (of pitch, wax, etc.), (harden s-th):: th'etsét < th'éts.

way

  according to the ways of the, in the way of the:: =elh.

  be in the way:: leq'á:lh < léq'.

  be on one's way, be going:: hálém < la.

  (be) turned around, turned the wrong way:: sx̲á:lts' < x̲élts'.

  by way of:: telál.

  do it this way:: sx̲tá(:)stexw < x̲ét'e.

  far, be far away, far off, way in the distance:: chó:kw.

way (CONT'D)

get out of the way, get off the way, dodge:: íyeqthet < iyá:q.
go around a bend in the river, go around a turn, go around something in one's way:: q'ewílem < q'éw ~ q'ew.
go travelling by way of, go via:: ley ~ lay < la.
upriver, up that way, (way upriver [RP, EB]):: títex̲el or tíytex̲el < tiyt.

way of

go through (somewhere), go via (somewhere), go by way of:: lhe'á.

we

it is us, we are the ones, we ourselves:: lhlímelh.
we (non-subordinate subject), our:: -tset ~ -chet.
we, us:: talhlímelh < lhlímelh.

weak

(be) weak:: qelá:m < qél.
(be) weak (in strength, also in taste [TM]):: qiqelá:m ~ qiqelà:m < qél.
(get) shaky and weak:: xwóyqwem.
get weak:: qelámthet < qél.
get weak (from laughing, walking, working too long, sickness):: qiqelá:mthet < qél.

wealth

rich, wealthy:: siyám ~ (rare) siyá:m.
three dollars, three tokens of wealth, three blankets (Boas), three cyclic periods:: lhí:xwes < lhí:xw.

weapon

weapon (arrow, club, etc.), something used to defend oneself:: hí:tel ~ hí:ytel < iyó:tel.

wear

be wearing a hat:: siyó:yseqw < yó:seqw ~ yóseqw.
be wearing a loincloth:: sthiyáp < sthíyep.
be worn out (of clothes for ex.), be old (of clothes), smashed up when dropped, dissolved:: th'éw.
clothes, clothing (esp. Indian clothing, men's or women's), something to wear, dress, gown:: s'íth'em < íth'a.
he (a small child) is wearing it.:: híhòkwexes < hókwex.
use it, wear it, put it on:: hókwex.
worn out (used when quarter moon is nearly invisible), (set (of the sun)):: th'éx̲.

weasel

weasel, one or both of the following which are in the area: short-tailed weasel and long-tailed weasel:: lhets'á:m.

weather)

clear up (of weather), turn fine (after a hard storm):: iyílem < éy ~ éy:.
day, daytime, sky, weather, (horizon (BJ)):: swáyel ~ swáyél ~ swàyèl < wáyel.
dirty (weather), bad weather, storm:: qél:em ~ qél:ém or leqél:e(´)m < qél.
get warm (of weather):: kw'ósthet < kw'ás.
it is cool [of weather], (be) cool (of a place):: sth'áth'elh < th'álh.

weave
- basket-weaving:: sch'eqw'ṓwelh < ts'éqw'.
- fine cedar root weaving, fine cedar root work:: sts'éqw' ~ sch'éqw' < ts'éqw'.
- headband, headband made out of cedar bark woven by widow or widower when mourning:: qítes ~ qéytes < qít.
- making a basket, (weaving a cedar root basket):: th'éqw'ōwelh ~ (probably ts'éqw'ōwelh) < ts'éqw'.
- to weave:: q'éysetsel < q'ey ~ q'i.
- to weave a cedar root basket:: ts'eqw'ṓ:welh ~ ts'eqw'ṓwelh ~ ch'eqw'ṓwelh < ts'éqw'.
- to weave slats (like a th'ṓwex basket or bulrush mat or inner or middle cedar bark):: wáth'elh < wáth'.
- twined weave:: s'o(')elexw?.
- tying a net:: q'ésetsel < q'ey ~ q'i.
- weave it:: lhí:lt.
- weaving (for ex. a tumpline), mending a net, making a net:: q'éyq'esetsel < q'ey ~ q'i.
- weaving slats:: wáweth'elh < wáth'.
- woven goat-wool blanket, (twilled weave (JL)):: swṓqw'elh.
- woven headband of packstrap, tumpline:: q'sí:ltel < q'ey ~ q'i.

Weaver Creek
- mouth of Weaver Creek:: Lhemqwó:tel < lhém.
- Sakwi Creek, a stream that joins Weaver Creek about one-third mile above the salmon hatchery:: Qeywéxem < qí:wx ~ qéywx ~ qá:wx ~ qáwx.

web
- web (of spider):: swéltel.

Webster
- lake in back of Paul Webster's old place on Hicks Rd. near Jones Creek:: Th'qwélhcha < th'qwélhcha.
- place at Ruby Creek where Paul Webster lived some years ago, now Wahleach Island Indian Reserve #2 and area at mouth of Mahood Creek:: Xwolích ~ Xwelích < xwále ~ xwá:le.

wedge
- a wedge:: xwe'ít.
- get wedged (by falling tree, for ex.), got run over (by car, train, etc.):: tl'íq'.
- it gets narrow or wedged in:: xékw'.
- pry s-th, lock s-th (the Indian way/barred/wedged), pry s-th up, lever it up:: wáth'et < wáth'.
- store it away (wedged-in up off ground), put s-th away for winter, stow s-th away:: xítse't < xits' ~ xets'.

Wednesday
- Wednesday (< the third day):: slhíxws < lhí:xw.

"weed"
- marijuana, "pot", "weed":: ts'esémelep ~ ts'esémelép < ts'ísem.

weeds :: sqel:ép ~ sqél:ep < qél.
- weeds in a garden:: ts'esémelep ~ ts'esémelép < ts'ísem.

week
    day of the week:: =elhlát ~ =lhát.
    hour, o'clock, day of week:: s=...=s.
    -th day of the week:: s= =s.

weep
    crying, weeping:: x̲á:m < x̲à:m ~ x̲á:m.
    weep, cry, weeping, crying:: x̲à:m ~ x̲á:m.

weigh
    put a mark on it (like water level of river), mark it, weigh it, (measure it):: x̲á:th't ~ x̲áth't < x̲áth' ~ x̲e'áth'.
    weigh s-th, ((also) measure s-th [EB]):: x̲wéylémt.

weight
    get fat, put on weight, getting fat:: ló:sthet ~ lósthet < ló:s ~ lós.
    lead weight:: xá:t.
    lessen it (of someone's load), halve it, make s-th lighter (in weight), lessen it (like when someone's pack is too heavy):: xwát < xwá.
    light (weight), lightweight:: xwóxwe < xwá.
    sinker, (fish) weight:: xá:t.

weir
    fish trap, weir:: sts'iyáq.
    salmon weir, fish trap:: ch'iyáqtel < sts'iyáq.

well :: éy ~ éy:.
    be alive, be living, be in good health, be healthy, be well:: áylexw ~ áyelexw.
    be alright, be well, be fine, be okay:: éy òl ~ éyòl ~ éyò < éy ~ éy:.
    be fine (in health), be alright (in health), be well:: we'éy òl ~ we'éyòl ~ we'éyò ~ u éyò ~ u'éyò < éy ~ éy:.
    be good, good, well, nice, fine, better, better (ought to), it would be good if, may it be good, let it be good, happy, glad, clean, well-behaved, polite, virgin, popular, comfortable (with furniture, other things?),:: éy ~ éy:.
    come alive, come back to life, get better (from sickness), get well, revive:: áylexw ~ áyelexw.
    do s-th well:: sthí:ystexw < thíy.
    gee., good grief., well. (said when surprised), goodness., gee whiz.:: átsele.
    make s-o well:: i'éyelstexw < éy ~ éy:.
    oh for goodness sakes., well. (in surprise):: lá:la.

well-behaved
    be good, good, well, nice, fine, better, better (ought to), it would be good if, may it be good, let it be good, happy, glad, clean, well-behaved, polite, virgin, popular, comfortable (with furniture, other things?),:: éy ~ éy:.
    nice, well-behaved, good:: éy ~ éy:.

Wellington Reserve
    Skwah village, now Skwah Reserve, also known as Wellington Reserve:: Sqwá < qwá.

were
  he/she/it was (already), they were (already):: lulh < le.

weren't
  wasn't?, weren't?, didn't?:: ewá:lh ~ wá:lh < éwe ~ őwe.

weren't ever
  weren't ever?, wasn't ever?, didn't ever?, does s-o ever?, never used to, not going to (but did anyway) [perhaps in the sense of never usually do X but did this time]:: ewá:lh ~ wá:lh < éwe ~ őwe.

west
  west wind:: schéxwem, sqeló:líth'a.

Westminster
  New Westminster:: Sx̲woyímelh < x̲wà:y ~ x̲wá:y.
  Reserve near New Westminster, B.C., (South Westminster [DF]):: Qiqá:yt, Qiqá:yt.

wet
  soaked, wet:: lhélq < lhél.
  splat, sound of something wet and soft dropped, to splatter:: wet'éleq.
  wet, be wet:: lhéqw.
  wet one's face:: lhélqesem < lhél.
  wet one's head (sic?), (wet one's bed repeatedly):: lhélqwelhem < lhél.
  wet one's pants, (urinate in one's pants):: sex̲we'ayíwsem < séx̲we.
  wet s-th:: lhélqt < lhél, lhóqwet < lhéqw.
  wet the bed, (urinate in the bed):: sex̲we'áléx̲eth' < séx̲we, xiwe'áléx̲eth < xíwe.
  wetting his/her bed:: xíxewe'áléx̲eth' < xíwe.
  wetting many things:: lhóleqwet < lhéqw.

whale
  killer whale, blackfish:: q'ellhólemètsel.
  whale (perhaps generic), could include the following balleen whales: common finback whale, humpback whale, possibly gray whale, Sei/Pollack whale, Minke whale, blue whale, Pacific right whale, could include the following toothed whales: sperm whale, poss. Baird beaked whale, Stejneger beaked whale, Cuvier whale:: qwél:és ~ qwélés.

Whale Point
  Whale Point at the southwest end of Harrison Lake:: Qwél:és < qwél:és ~ qwélés.

what
  anchor-line, mooring-line, bow-line, what is used to tie up a canoe:: lhqéletel < lhqé:ylt.
  be what day?:: skw'íles < kw'í:l ~ kw'íl.
  be what hour?, be what time?:: skw'í:ls < kw'í:l ~ kw'íl.
  I wonder what s-o will do?, I wonder what I will do?:: xwe'ítixw or xwe'ít yexw < xwe'ít.
  preserved fish, preserved meat, dried fish, dried meat (usually fish), smoked salmon, wind-dried salmon (old word), what is stored away, what is put away:: sq'éyle.
  stuff steam-cooked underground, what is baked underground:: sqetás < qá:t.
  teachings for children, what is taught to one's children:: s'iwesá:ylhem < íwes.
  the planting, seeds to plant, what is planted (sown), garden:: spí:ls < pél (perhaps ~ pí:l by now).
  what does it look like?, what does he/she look like?, (how is he/she/it in appearance or

what (CONT'D)

looks?), (what color is it? [NP]):: selchímomex < selchí:m ~ selchím, selchímomex < selchí:m ~ selchím.
what does it sound like?, What does it sound like?, (how does it sound?):: selchí:meleqel < selchí:m ~ selchím.
whatever it is, what it is, it is anything, it is something:: stámés < tám.
what happened?, what is it?, why?:: xwe'ít, xwe'ít.
what he owes:: skwelálhchiyelh < kwél.
what is it?, be what?:: stám < tám.
what is s-o doing?, what is s-o saying?, what is he/she/it doing/saying?:: xwe'í:t < xwe'ít.
what one walks on (trail, board sidewalk, cement sidewalk, etc.):: shxw'ímex < i┐m.
what s-o/s-th is good for:: shxw'éy < éy ~ éy:.
what use is it?, what use have you got for it?:: stámel < tám.
what, which, that which, the one that/who:: te.

what a lot.
what a lot., it's sure a lot:: chelà:l.

Whatcom County
place in Whatcom County, Washington, (Nooksack River [AC or CT]):: Lexwsá:q < sá:q.

whatever
whatever it is, what it is, it is anything, it is something:: stámés < tám.

wheeze
(have/get) wheezing, rattling breath:: xwóyeqw'em.
wheezing in the chest, rattling in the chest:: xwóyeqw'emíles < xwóyeqw'em.

when
subjunctive, when, if:: we-.
when (simultaneous subordinating conjunction), as:: kw'e.
when, (sometimes [EB]):: lhí.
when?, when is it?:: temtám < tám.

whenever :: lhéq'es < lhéq'.
whenever, whenever it is:: temtámes < tám.

where
be from where?:: tel'alétse ~ tel:étse < tel=.
(place, location), where s-o is at:: shxwlí.
someplace, somewhere:: stómchele < tám.
wandering, where someone goes:: shxwélem ~ shxwélém < la.
where did he go?, where is he/she/etc.?:: xwechà:l < chá:l or chó:l.
where is he/she/it from?, from where?:: tel'alétsa < alétsa.
where (is it)?:: alétsa.
where is s-o going?, where is s-o travelling?, where is s-o headed for?:: xwchókwel < chákw.
where it's at, where it's from:: shxwlí < lí ~ li.
where s-o came from:: shxwtelí < tel=.

wherever
wherever he's got it:: alétsestxwes < alétsa.

whet
    whetstone, a file, sandstone:: th'óméls.

Whetkyel
    Whetkyel village east of Little Mountain by Agassiz:: Xwétxel or X̲wétxel.

whetstone
    whetstone, a file, sandstone:: th'óméls.

whew
    to sigh, breathe out whew:: hóxwethílém.

which
    what, which, that which, the one that/who:: te, te.

while
    later, after a while, later on, wait a while:: téx̲w.
    travelling by, in motion, while moving along, while travelling along:: ye= ~ yi= ~ i˥.
    until, till, while:: qew ~ qwō ~ qe ... u/ew < qe.
    (while) travelling along, in motion:: ye=.

whip
    a whip:: kw'óqwtel < qw'óqw.
    a whipper:: kw'ókw'qwōwsà:ls < kw'óqw.
    soapberry beater, stick for whipping up soapberries or Indian ice cream:: th'amawéstel or th'emawéstel < th'ím ~ th'í:m.
    to whip all over the body with cedar boughs:: kw'oqwchí:ws < kw'óqw.
    whip it:: qw'óqwet < qw'óqw.
    whip once (with stick), got hit:: qw'óqw.
    whipping s-o/s-th many times:: qw'ó:leqwet < qw'óqw.

whirl
    spinning, whirling:: siselts'iyósem < sél or sí(:)l.
    whirled slingshot:: sts'élqes < ts'el.
    (whirling):: q'eyq'elts'iyósem.

whirlpool :: q'oyéx̲ ~ q'eyéx̲ < q'ey ~ q'i.
    large whirlpool in the Fraser River just above Hill's Bar and near the west (CPR) side:: Hémq'eleq < méq'.
    maybe also the whirlpool by Odlum on the same side but below Hope [AD, AK, SP (American Bar place names trip 6/26/78)]:: Hémq'eleq < méq'.
    place on the Fraser River above Yale where there are whirlpools:: Q'eyq'éyex̲em < q'ey ~ q'i.
    whirlpool (large or small):: q'éyex̲em < q'ey ~ q'i.
    whirlpool that suddenly starts from level water:: q'oyéx̲em < q'ey ~ q'i.

whirlwind :: q'eyq'elts'iyósem spehá:ls, q'eyq'elts'iyósem spehá:ls < q'eyq'elts'iyósem, siselts'iyósem < sél or sí(:)l, skw'elkw'élxel.

whiskey jack
    whiskey jack, Canada jay:: sáwel < sáwel.

whisper

to whisper (once):: lháqem.
whispering:: lhálheqem < lháqem.

whistle

to whistle:: xó:pem.
whistle with pursed lips, whistling:: xíxpò:m < xó:pem.
whistling swan, probably also trumpeter swan:: shxwṓ:qel ~ shxwṓwqel ~ shxwéwqel.

"whistler"

hoary marmot, (also known as) "mountain groundhog", "groundhog", or "whistler", poss. also yellow-bellied marmot:: sqwíqw.

whistle stop

Wahleach whistle stop on Seabird Island where Wayne Bobb lived in 1977, (now also Wahleach Lake (man-made) [EB]):: Wolích < x̲wále ~ x̲wá:le.

white]

[a little white]:: p'íp'eq' < p'éq'.
[be getting a little white]:: tsp'íp'eq'el < p'éq'.
be white:: p'éq'.
diatomaceous earth (could be mixed with things to whiten them--for ex. dog and goat wool), white clay for white face paint (for pure person spirit-dancers), white powder from mountains, white clay they make powder from to lighten goat and dog wool for blankets, powder, talc, white face paint:: st'ewṓkw'.
(dingy white, off-white):: stl'ítl'es.
female black bear with white spot [or mark] on the chest:: Sx̲éylmòt or sx̲éylmòt < x̲él ~ x̲é:yl ~ x̲í:l
fine white ashes:: sts'á:s ~ sts'ás.
(get/have) white spots on the skin:: th'íq.
[get(ing)/go(ing)/becom(ing) a little white]:: p'íp'eq'el < p'éq'.
get white:: p'eq'í:l < p'éq'.
[get whiter, getting white]:: p'áp'eq'el < p'éq'.
grass scalded and bleached white for basketry imbrication (designs), sometimes called white straw grass, probably blue-joint reed-grass:: th'á:x̲ey ~ th'áx̲ey < th'áx̲.
(have a) white caste over the eye, (have a) cataract:: p'eq'ó:les < p'éq'.
(have) one white eye, (have a cataract on one eye):: sqwelxwó:lés.
(have?) white spots:: sp'eq'p'íq' < p'éq'.
(have?) white spotted skin:: sp'íq' < p'éq'.
[looks white, white-looking]:: p'eq'óméx < p'éq'.
male black bear with white spot [or mark] on the chest:: Sx̲é:ylmet or sx̲é:ylmet < x̲él ~ x̲é:yl ~ x̲í:l
(powder white, purplish white?):: st'ewṓkw'.
pretty white lacy moss:: máqelhp < má:qel.
probably butterfly with white spot, (perhaps white butterfly), if the name applies to one or more predominantly white butterflies it could include the following which occur in the Stó:lō area: Clodius parnassian butterfly, Phoebus' parnassian butterfly, pale tiger swallowtail butterfly, white pine butterfly, checkered white butterfly, veined white butterfly, albino females of alfalfa sulphur butterfly:: p'ip'eq'eyós < p'éq'.
put (white) paint on one's face:: t'ewṓkw'esem < st'ewṓkw'.
unnamed mountain on the northwest side of the Fraser River between Hope and Yale which has white mineral deposits visible from the river:: Lexwp'ép'eq'es < p'éq'.
white-breasted bear, a bear with white on the breast, (brown bear with a white chest

white (CONT'D)

[AK]):: ts'aweyí:les < ts'áwi or ts'áwiy.
whitecap berry, white blackcap berry:: p'éq' tselqó:me < tsélq ~ chélq.
white ones:: p'ép'eq' < p'éq'.
white paint:: p'éq' témelh < témélh.

whitecap
whitecap berry, white blackcap berry:: p'éq' tselqó:me < tsélq ~ chélq.

whitefish
"grayling", probably mountain whitefish:: spó:ltsep.

white-headed duck
a white-headed duck, [could be bufflehead, snow goose, emperor goose, poss. oldsquaw, or hooded merganser, other duck-like birds with white heads do not occur in the Stó:lō area and the emperor goose would be only an occasional visitor]:: skemí'iya.

White person
White person, (Caucasian), White man:: xwelítem.

whiter
[get whiter, getting white]:: p'áp'eq'el < p'éq'.

White Rock
Semiahmoo, White Rock, B.C.:: Semyó:me ~ Sam(i)yó:me < semyó: ~ semyó.
White Rock, B.C.:: P'eq'ó:ls.
White Rock, B.C., Blaine, Wash.:: P'eq'ó:ls < p'éq'.

white sweet corn:: p'éq' q'áq'et'em kwó:l (lit. white + sweet + corn) < p'éq', q'át', kwó:l

whittle
carve wood, whittle:: x̲et'kw'á:ls.
carving wood, whittling:: x̲át'kw'els < x̲et'kw'á:ls.
plane it (with a plane), trim it, taper it (about wood, like slats or roots for baskets, poles for houseposts/totem poles, paddles), taper it (with knife or plane), peel it (a fruit, etc.), whittle it, strip or peel bark off of it, scrape it (of carrots), (carve it, peel it [AC]):: xípet < xíp.

who
be who?:: tewát < wát.
fortune-teller, seer, person who can see things in the future, female witch:: syéw:e ~ syéwe ~ syṓ:we ~ syú:we < yéw: ~ yéw.
one who, -er, one who does as an occupation:: =éleq.
the one who burns [at a burning ceremony], (ritualist at a burning):: híyeqwels < yéqw.
what, which, that which, the one that/who:: te.
who else?, who (of several)?, (anybody else (AC)):: kw'elhwát < wát.
who?, who:: wát.

whoever
(whoever, one out of):: =wát.

whole
furry on the whole body (of an animal):: siysá:yiws < sá:y.

whole (CONT'D)

whole leg, (whole of both legs):: sx̲ex̲é:yle or sx̲ex̲í:le < sx̲él:e.

Whonnock

Whonnock village:: X̲wő:leqw.

whoop

(make) a whoop, a cowboy's whoop:: q'exelám.
war-whoop, ((probably) a sung spell before battle):: syiwí:leqw < yéw: ~ yéw.

whore

prostitute, whore:: xwoxwth'í:lem < xwáth'.

why

what happened?, what is it?, why?:: xwe'ít.
why?:: tl'ekwselchíms ~ tl'ekwselchí:ms < selchí:m ~ selchím.

wide

be wide:: lheq'át ~ lhq'á:t.
(have a) wide face:: lhq'ó:tes < lheq'át ~ lhq'á:t.
(have a) wide forehead:: lheq'tò:ls < lheq'át ~ lhq'á:t.
(have a) wide rump, (wide in the rectum):: lheq'tíwél < lheq'át ~ lhq'á:t.
have wide feet:: lhálhq'etxel < lheq'át ~ lhq'á:t.
have wide snowflakes:: lhálhq'etxel < lheq'át ~ lhq'á:t.
open both one's eyes real wide:: pex̲ó:lésem < páx̲.
pull in once with a canoe paddle wide or slow, pull in in turning (a canoe paddling stroke done by a bowman):: lhímes.
thick crowded tight bushes, bushes growing wide from narrow roots or base:: sq'epláts < q'ép.
wide place at the mouth of the east (upriver) branch of Jones Creek:: Swílth'.

wide-awake:: shxwixwiyós or shxwiyxwiyós < xwíy ~ x[illegible]í.

widen

spread s-th, widen s-th:: wí:qet < wí:q ~ wíq.
widen it, move it wider:: léx̲et < léx̲.

wider

widen it, move it wider:: léx̲et < léx̲.

widgeon

widgeon (duck), American widgeon or baldpate, probably also the European widgeon, (pintail duck [BJ]):: sése, sése.

widow

become a widow, become a widower:: yatílém < syá:tel.
headband, headband made out of cedar bark woven by widow or widower when mourning:: qítes ~ qéytes < qít.
widow, widower:: syá:tel.

widower

become a widow, become a widower:: yatílém < syá:tel.

widower (CONT'D)

headband, headband made out of cedar bark woven by widow or widower when mourning:: qítes ~ qéytes < qít.
widow, widower:: syá:tel.

Wife

Honey (term of address to one's spouse), Husband, Wife:: láw.

wife :: stó:les.

a husband's younger wives, co-wife:: sxáye.
brother-in-law's wife, (spouse's sibling's spouse), (step-sibling, step-brother, step-sister [AC]):: slets'éleq < láts'.
get a wife:: tscháxw < chá:xw.
got married to a wife:: schachexw < chá:xw.
little wives:: stételes < stó:les.
male name, (prob.) repeatedly gets wives/houses:: =ímeltxw.
man with two wives:: islá:ltexw < isá:le ~ isále ~ isá:la.
sister-in-law, husband's sister, brother's wife, wife's sister (EB):: shxw'álex < álex.
spouse's sibling, sibling's spouse (cross sex), for ex., husband's brother, (wife's sister, woman's sister's husband, man's brother's wife):: smátexwtel.
uncle's wife, aunt's husband, parent's sibling's spouse, uncle by marriage, aunt by marriage:: xchápth ~ schápth.
want a wife, He wants a wife.:: chxwélmel < chá:xw.
want to get a wife, He wants to get a wife.:: scháchxwelmel < chá:xw.
wife (not respectful), the "old lady", "squaw", mistress:: chá:xw.
wives:: =á:ltxw.

wife's sister

husband's brothers, (perhaps also wife's sisters?, spouse's siblings?, sibling's spouses?):: smetmátexwtel < smátexwtel.
husband's brother, wife's sister, spouse's sibling (cross-sex), brother-in-law, sister-in-law, sibling's spouse (cross-sex):: smátexwtel.
sister-in-law, husband's sister, brother's wife, wife's sister (EB):: shxw'álex < álex.
spouse's sibling, sibling's spouse (cross sex), for ex., husband's brother, (wife's sister, woman's sister's husband, man's brother's wife):: smátexwtel.

will

conscience, spirit (which can be lost temporarily), soul, life-spirit, power of one's will:: smestíyexw < mestíyexw.
going to (future), will go and (do s-th):: la.
I wonder what s-o will do?, I wonder what I will do?:: xwe'ítixw or xwe'ít yexw < xwe'ít.

willing

(be) ambitious, (be) willing:: shxwúxwe.
(be) willing to do one's work, (ambitious [BHTTC]):: lexws'ó:les.

Willoughby's Point

next mountain above (north/upriver from) Títxwemqsel (Wilson's Point or Grouse Point), possibly Elbow Lake mountain [north of Harrison Mills, on west side of the Harrison River], Willoughby's Point [opposite Lhá:lt, but does this mean across Harrison R. as I first thought and show on the topographic map "Harrison Lake 92H/5" where I have pencilled in all Chehalis place names) or does it mean on the opposite, i.e. south end of the same bay where Lhá:lt starts, i.e. both on the west side of

Willoughby's Point (CONT'D)

Harrison R. as are Títxwemqsel and Elbow Lake mountain?]:: Kw'íkw'exwelhp < kw'íxw.

Willow

Pussy Willow (name in stories):: Qweqwemeytá:ye < qwem.

willow

a small willow tree, a low willow:: x̲wóx̲welá:lhp < x̲wále ~ x̲wá:le.
long leaf willow, (Pacific willow):: x̲wálá:lhp ~ x̲wá:lá:lhp < x̲wále ~ x̲wá:le.
long-leaf willow, Sitka willow:: xéltsepelhp < xél.
pussy willow:: sqweqweméytses < qwem.
red-osier dogwood, (also called "red willow" [SJ, EL]):: th'ex̲wíyelhp.
short leaf willow, (Sitka willow):: x̲wálá:lhp ~ x̲wá:lá:lhp < x̲wále ~ x̲wá:le.
willow (includes especially short-leaf willow or Sitka willow, also long-leaf willow or Pacific willow, and red willow bush):: x̲wálá:lhp ~ x̲wá:lá:lhp < x̲wále ~ x̲wá:le.

Wilson's Point

Wilson's Point (on Harrison River), (also called) Grouse Point:: Títxwemqsel < stíxwem.

wind :: spehá:ls < peh or pó(:)h.

be calm (of water or wind), (get calm (wind/water), calm down (wind/water), be smooth (of water) [AC, LH]):: qám.
be windy:: x̲otl'thet < x̲átl'.
blow (wind):: pehá:ls < peh or pó(:)h.
close up a meeting, wind up a meeting, complete a meeting:: yalkw'ólhem or yelkw'wólhem < yókw' ~ yóqw'.
coil it, wind it up (of string, rope, yarn):: q'élq't < q'ál.
eight days of northeast wind:: unknown.
four days of northeast wind:: unknown.
get calm (of wind):: qametólém ~ qametólem < qám.
get quiet (of wind), stop (of wind):: chó:ythet.
north-east wind, north wind, east wind, cold wind:: só:tets.
rags wound around the legs in the cold or to protect from mosquitoes, (leggings):: q'élq'xetel < q'ál.
raining, ([having a] rainshower with light wind [BJ]):: lhémexw < lhém.
rough (of wind or water), turbulent (of wind or water), real swift (of water):: x̲átl'.
sailing (of a bird), gliding on the wind:: yáyelem.
south wind:: tellhelhó:s < lhós.
south wind, warm wind:: schéxwem, schéxwem.
stop blowing (of the wind):: chémq ~ tsémq.
(the wind) is calm, calm (of wind):: qémxel < qám.
tighten it up, wind it up:: tl'óth'et.
to pass gas, break wind, to fart:: pú'.
west wind:: schéxwem, sqeló:líth'a.
whirlwind:: q'eyq'elts'iyósem spehá:ls < q'eyq'elts'iyósem, siselts'iyósem < sél or sí(:)l, skw'elkw'élxel.

wind-dried salmon

long thin slices of fish removed to dry from slhíts'es (wind-driedsalmon):: slhíqwetsel < slhíqw.
wind-dried opened and scored salmon:: slhíts'es < lhíts' ~ lhí:ts'.

wind-dry
fish cut real thin for wind-drying but without cross cuts, dried fish cut differently than slhíts'es:: st'ál.
fish drying rack (for wind-drying):: sí:.
preserved fish, preserved meat, dried fish, dried meat (usually fish), smoked salmon, wind-dried salmon (old word), what is stored away, what is put away:: sq'éyle.

wind instrument
flute, wind instrument, blown musical instrument:: pepó:tem < pó:t.

window :: skw'echó:stel < kw'áts ~ kw'éts.
window shades, blinds, blinders (on a horse, etc.):: t'oléstel < t'á:l.

windpipe
on the front of the neck, in the windpipe, in the trachea:: =lhelh ~ =lhál.

wineberry
Japanese wineberry:: th'elíth'eplexw ~ ts'elíts'eplexw (or perhaps ts'elíts'ep'lexw) < th'éplexw (or perhaps th'ép'lexw).

wing
hold both arms (or wings) outstretched, (stretch out one's arms/wings):: tex̲eláx̲elem < tex̲.
on the arm, in the arm, on or in the wing:: =eláx̲el.
stretch out the wings, stretch out the arm(s):: tex̲eláx̲el < tex̲.
wing, (big feather [IHTTC]):: stl'q'á:l.
wing, whole wing:: tl'q'áláx̲el < stl'q'á:l.

wink
to wink:: th'ikw'ólésem < th'iykw', th'ikw'ósem < th'iykw'.
wink at each other, ((maybe) squint [EB]):: th'ikwóstel < th'iykw'.
winking:: th'ith'ikw'ósem < th'iykw'.
winking at each other:: th'ith'ikwóstel < th'iykw'.

winter :: sx̲éytl' < x̲éytl' ~ x̲í:tl', temx̲éytl' < x̲éytl' ~ x̲í:tl', temx̲é:ytl'thet < x̲éytl' ~ x̲í:tl'.
call of the winter robin or varied thrush:: sx̲wík'.
everybody put away (fishing gear, canoe and) paddles (for winter), put away each other's paddles [and canoes and gear] for winter:: xets'ő:westel < xits' ~ xets'.
(one person) puts away his paddles (and canoe and gear for winter):: xets'ő:wes < xits' ~ xets'.
store it away (wedged-in up off ground), put s-th away for winter, stow s-th away:: xítse't < xits' ~ xets'.

winter-dance
a spirit-dance, a winter-dance:: smílha < mílha.
(doing) spirit-dancing, winter-dancing (when they're in action):: mímelha < mílha.
to spirit-dance, to spirit-dance (of a group), have aspirit-dance, to winter-dance:: mílha.

winter robin
winter robin, bush robin, varied thrush:: sx̲wík'.

wipe

dry dishes, wipe off dishes:: iqw'wí:ls < íqw'.
people without paint on face (non-dancers):: s'ep'ó:s (lit. "wiped on face") < á:p' ~ áp'.
rub s-th off, wipe s-th:: íqw'et < íqw'.
wipe oneself off:: íqw'ethet < íqw'.
wipe one's face:: íqw'esem < íqw', óp'esem < áp'.
wipe s-th:: á:p'et < áp'.
wipe s-th/s-o:: á:p'et ~ áp'et < a┐ :p' ~ a┐ p'.

wiped out

perish together, many die (in famine, sickness, fire), all die, get wiped out:: x̲wà:y ~ x̲wá:y.
village near and above [upriver from] Katz where 36 pit-houses were wiped out in an epidemic:: Sx̲wóx̲wiymelh < x̲wà:y ~ x̲wá:y.

wise

sensible, wise, (get sensible, get wise):: q'e'í:les ~ q'e'í:lés.

wish

desire s-th, desire s-o, wish for s-th/s-o:: témex.
wish for someone's food:: xítem.
wishing for someone's food (esp. when in sight):: xíxetem < xítem.

witch

a sung spell, power to help or harm people or to do [ritual] burning, power to do witchcraft and predict the future, an evil spell, (magic spell) (someone who has power to take things out of a person or put things in [by magic] [Elders Group 2/25/76], ritualist [Elders Group 1/21/76], witch [EB 4/25/78]):: syiwí:l ~ syewí:l < yéw: ~ yéw, syiwí:l ~ syewí:l < yéw: ~ yéw.
fortune-teller, seer, person who can see things in the future, female witch:: syéw:e ~ syéwe ~ syő:we ~ syú:we < yéw: ~ yéw.

with :: í, q'ó.

accompany s-o, go with s-o:: sq'ó:t ~ sq'ót < q'ó.
accompany s-o, go with s-o, go along with s-o:: q'exí:lt < q'ó.
along, together, be included, with:: sq'eq'ó < q'ó.
along, with, together with:: sq'ó < q'ó.
come with s-o:: sq'ómet < q'ó.
come with s-o (in a canoe for ex.):: q'ewí:lt < q'éw ~ q'ew.
coming with s-o:: sq'eq'ómet < q'ó.
cry with someone, a person one cries with (related or not), unrelated grandparents of a deceased grandchild, etc.:: ts'elhx̲à:m < x̲à:m ~ x̲á:m.
going with each other [romantically], going for a walk with each other:: ts'lhimexóstel < ts'elh=.
go with, come with, be partner with:: q'axí:l < q'ó.
little partner, little person who follows or goes with one:: sq'iq'exí:l ~ q'iq'exí:l < q'ó.
put s-th with (something), add s-th (to something), include s-th:: q'ót < q'ó.
sweetheart, person of the opposite sex that one is running around with, girl-friend, boy-friend:: ts'elh'á:y < ts'elh=.
us (nominalized object of preposition), to us, with us:: tl'elhlímelh < lhlímelh.
you folks (object of preposition), to you folks, with you folks:: tl'alhwélep < lhwélep.

within
    on itself, within itself:: =p'.
    on something else, within ssomething else:: =q'.

without talking
    disappointed and angry-looking without talking:: sx̲éyx̲eth' < x̲íth' ~ x̲éyth'.

witness
    call s-o to witness, call s-o to listen:: xwlalámstexw < xwlalá:.
    he/she called me to witness:: xwelalámsthòxes < xwlalá:.
    thank s-o (for a cure, for pall-bearing, a ceremony, being a witness):: xwth'í:t < ts'ít ~ ch'í:t.

wobble
    wobbling on its bottom:: kw'áth'eletsem < kw'eth'ém.
    wobbly:: xwóyqw'esem.

wolf :: stqó:ya ~ stqó:ye ~ stqó:yá.
    wolves:: stelqóye < stqó:ya ~ stqó:ye ~ stqó:yá.

wolverine :: shxwématsel ~ shxwémetsel.
    a spirit power of a kw'őxweqs dancer, (perhaps wolverine or badger spirit power):: sqoyép < sqoyép.
    badger or wolverine:: melmélkw'es sqoyép < sqoyép.
    unidentified animal with marks on its face, perhaps badger or wolverine:: sqoyép.
    yellow badger, possibly wolverine:: sqoyép ~ melmélkw'es sqoyép.

Woman
    Cannibal Ogress, Wild Cannibal Woman:: Th'őwx̲iya < th'őwex̲ ~ th'őwéx̲.

woman
    (a lot of) women:: slhellhá:li < slhá:lí.
    little ladies:: slhelhlíli < slhá:lí.
    little woman, small woman:: slhálhli < slhá:lí.
    married woman, got a husband, got married to a husband:: swóweqeth < swáqeth.
    married women, ((plural) got husbands):: swóqeweqeweth (or better) swóq-weqeth < swáqeth.
    peek under a woman's skirt:: xwpelákw < pél:ékw.
    (post-adolescent) woman, woman (15 yrs. or older):: slhá:lí.
    rock in the Fraser River near Scowlitz where a woman was crying a lot:: X̲ex̲ám Smá:lt < x̲à:m ~ x̲á:m.
    woman, female:: slhá:lí.
    woman's genitals, vulva, vagina:: xá:welh.

womb
    womb, uterus:: smélàtel < méle ~ mél:a.

wonder
    I wonder:: yexw.
    I wonder what s-o will do?, I wonder what I will do?:: xwe'ítixw or xwe'ít yexw < xwe'ít.

wood
    a wood carving:: shxwqwó:lthels, shxwqwó:lthels.

wood (CONT'D)

bark, wood, plant:: =á:y ~ =ey ~ =iy.
big wooden dish (often two feet long), feast dish, wooden platter, (big stirring spoon [LJ], carved wooden spoon, big wooden spoon [AC, BJ, DM]):: qwelhyő́welh ~ qwelhliyő́welh ~ qwelhlyúwelh < qwélh.
bring in firewood, bring wood in:: kwtxwéltsep ~ kwetxwéltsep < kwetáxw.
carve wood, whittle:: x̲et'kw'á:ls.
carving wood, whittling:: x̲át'kw'els < x̲et'kw'á:ls.
chop wood, split wood, (chop/split s-th wood):: séq'et < séq'.
chop wood (with an axe), split wood:: th'iqw'élchep or th'iyqw'éltsep < th'íyeqw'.
cottonwood bark driftwood (it was used to carve toy canoes), cottonwood driftwood used for carving toy canoes:: qwémélép ~ qwemélep.
cut it (wood, lawn, etc.):: t'eqw'ót < t'éqw'.
cutting wood (with a saw), sawing wood:: xíxets'els < xets'á:ls.
cut wood (with a saw), saw wood, (cut wood to store away):: xets'á:ls.
Douglas fir log or wood:: ts'sá:y.
driftwood:: qwlhá:y < qwélh.
firewood:: =élchep ~ =éltsep, híyeqwtem siyólh < yéqw.
gather firewood (in the woods), get firewood:: chiyólh < yólh.
getting firewood:: chiyóyelh < yólh.
hew (stone, wood, anything):: t'élex̲è:yls < t'éléx̲.
little stick of firewood:: syóyelh < yólh.
lots of little pieces of driftwood:: qwéqwelhi(y) < qwélh.
lots of little sticks of firewood:: syéyelh < yólh.
(make a) rapid repeated sound usually on wood:: qw'ópx̲wem < qw'ópx̲w.
October to November, (wood gathering time):: tsélcheptel?.
pitchwood (esp. fir, pine, spruce):: kw'íxwelhp < kw'íxw.
plane it (with a plane), trim it, taper it (about wood, like slats or roots for baskets, poles for houseposts/totem poles, paddles), taper it (with knife or plane), peel it (a fruit, etc.), whittle it, strip or peel bark off of it, scrape it (of carrots), (carve it, peel it [AC]):: xípet < xíp.
rotten wood:: pqwá:y < póqw.
rough (of wood), lumpy (of ground, bark, etc.):: smelhmélhqw.
sawing wood:: lhilhts'óltsep < lhíts' ~ lhí:ts'.
sawing wood, cutting wood with a saw:: lhílhets'els < lhíts' ~ lhí:ts'.
smash s-th to pieces (hard pitch, splintery wood, a glass), break s-th to pieces, beat s-th/s-o to a pulp:: th'ő́:wt.
split firewood:: th'iyeqw'á:ls < th'íyeqw'.
split it (firewood):: th'íyeqw't < th'íyeqw'.
splitting firewood:: th'óyeqw'els < th'íyeqw'.
splitting wood (esp. blanks and bolts):: póqwels < péqw.
splitting wood, (splitting it (a lot of wood)):: seq'séq'et < séq'.
tick, wood tick, and probably Pacific Coast tick:: t'pí.
to chip it (like wood):: t'ópet < t'óp.
to cut wood (with a saw), saw wood, (to cut [as structured activity] [Deming}):: lhts'á:ls < lhíts' ~ lhí:ts'.
western red cedar wood:: x̲epá:y ~ x̲epáy ~ x̲pá:y < sx̲éyp.
wood chips:: t'ámel (or) t'ém:el < t'ém.
wood duck (makes nest in tree):: qwiwílh.
wood, firewood:: siyólh ~ siyó:lh ~ syólh < yólh.
wood-shed:: siyólhá:wtxw < yólh.

wood-carving

wood-carving knife:: xepá:ltel < xíp.

wooden)

(wooden?):: =(')ó:ylha.

woodpecker

large red-necked woodpecker, large red-headed woodpecker, rain crow (black with red comb on head) (AC), pileated woodpecker:: temélhépsem < témélh.

ordinary small woodpecker:: t'ót'ep'els < t'óp'.

red-headed woodpecker, (pileated woodpecker):: t'ot'ep'íqselem < t'óp'.

red-shafted flicker (woodpecker), medium-sized woodpecker with red under the wing, (pileated woodpecker [AK] (but this is a large bird), small red-headed woodpecker [probably red-breasted sapsucker, possibly hairy woodpecker or downy woodpecker] [Elders Group 3/1/72}):: th'íq.

small red-headed woodpecker, probably red-breasted sapsucker, and/or possibly the hairy woodpecker or downy woodpecker:: qw'opx̲wiqsélem < qw'ópx̲w.

woods

(be in the) woods, (amidst bush or vegetation, be tucked away?):: sxí:xets' ~ sxíxets' < xí:ts' ~ xíts' ~ xets'.

go through the woods:: xets'í:lem < xí:ts' ~ xíts' ~ xets'.

in the backwoods, toward the woods, away from the river, in the bush:: chó:leqw < chá:l or chó:l.

trees, thicket, timber, woods, forest:: theqthéqet < theqát ~ thqá:t.

Woodside)

Agassiz Mountain (or more likely Mount Woodside):: Sqwehíwel < qwá.

woodtick

tick, woodtick, probably Pacific Coast tick and the wood tick:: méth'elhqìwèl < méth'elh.

wool :: =álqel ~ =élqel.

a carder (for carding wool):: shxwtéxelqèyls < tex.

card wool, comb s-th, (carding/combing s-th (wool/hair)):: téxelqèylt < tex.

diatomaceous earth (could be mixed with things to whiten them--for ex. dog and goat wool), white clay for white face paint (for pure person spirit-dancers), white powder from mountains, white clay they make powder from to lighten goat and dog wool for blankets, powder, talc, white face paint:: st'ewőkw'.

dog wool:: sqwemá:yalqel < qwem.

dog wool fibre:: qweqwemeylíth'e < qwem.

flannelette, velvet, woolly material, fluffy material, soft material:: pá:píth'a < pá:pa.

prickly (from fir bark, wool, or something one is allergic to), irritant, have an allergic reaction (to fir powder or cedar bark):: th'íth'ekwem < th'íkw.

sheep wool:: metú:lqel ~ metú:'álqel < metú.

spindle for spinning wool, a hand spinner:: sélseltel < sél or sí(:)l.

spindle for spinning wool, a hand spinner, a spinning machine:: shxwqáqelets' < qálets'.

spinning wool:: qáqelets' < qálets'.

spin wool or twine:: qálets'.

wool, fur:: =á:y ~ =ey ~ =iy.

wool, fur, animal hair:: sá:y.

woolly, fluffy:: pá:pa.

wool (CONT'D)

wool spinner, spindle for spinning wool, spinning stick:: sélsel < sél or sí(:)l.

wool hat

spirit-dancing costume, wool hat for spirit-dancer (Deming):: s-hóyiws.

woolly

flannelette, velvet, woolly material, fluffy material, soft material:: pá:píth'a < pá:pa.
(have a) hairy face, (have) hair on the face, (have a woolly face):: xwpopó:s < pá:pa.
woolly, fluffy:: pá:pa.

word

also the words of Mack's spirit song:: Á:yiya.

work :: syó:ys < yó:ys.
(an Indian doctor or shaman) working, curing, chasing the bad things away:: lhálhewels < lhá:w.
(be) difficult, hard (of work, etc.):: tl'í ~ tl'í:.
(be) willing to do one's work, (ambitious [BHTTC]):: lexws'ó:les.
canoe-work, canoe-making:: s=há:y < hà:y.
carve stone, work in stone:: t'eléx̲ot < t'éléx̲.
Indian doctor at work, shaman at work, healer:: lhalhewéleq < lhá:w.
[someone] always working:: lexwsyóyes ~ lexwsiyó:yes < yó:ys.
to work:: yó:ys.
wide cedar (sapling) strips or slats from young cedar trunks, cedar slat work (basketry):: x̲pó:ys < sx̲éyp.
working, be working:: yóyes < yó:ys.

worker

babysitter (for new spirit-dancers), any of the workers who help in initiating a spirit-dancer, (initiator or helper of spirit-dancers):: xólhemìlh ~ xòlhemí:lh < xólh.

world

earth, ground, land, the earth, the world:: tém:éxw ~ tem:éxw ~ ~ tèm:èxw ~ témexw.
edge of the world:: sóyéx̲el < sóy.
on the other side of the world:: súyéx̲el < sóy.

worm

earthworm (esp. the most common introduced in B.C.):: sth'ékw's te téméxw < sth'ékw'.
have worms, he got worms:: th'eth'ekw'íwetem < sth'ékw'.
salmonberry worm, (prob. larvae of moths or butterflies or two-winged flies):: xwexwíye.
slow-worm ("a slow-moving foot-long snake"), actually a species of blind legless lizard:: aleqá:y < álhqey ~ álhqay.
tapeworm:: sqwó:qwetl'í:wèl.
worm, bug:: sth'ékw'.

worn

be worn out (of clothes for ex.), be old (of clothes), smashed up when dropped, dissolved:: th'éw.
worn out (used when quarter moon is nearly invisible), (set (of the sun)):: th'éx̲.

worry

(be/get) really worried:: th'áth'iyekw.

worry (CONT'D)

(be/get) worried about s-o:: th'áth'iyekwémet < th'áth'iyekw.
worried, sad, looking sad:: st'á:yx̲w < t'ay.

worst

part not used (like seeds of cantelope, core of apple, blood in fish, etc.), worst part:: sqéls < qél.

would be good

it would be good:: éy ~ éy:.

wound

a wound, (a hurt?):: sx̲élh < x̲élh.
be hit (with arrow, bullet, anything shot that you've aimed), got shot, (got pierced), got poked into, got wounded (with gun or arrow):: ts'éqw'.

wrap

(be) wrapped:: shxwelókw' < xwélekw'.
cloth or warm material to wrap around the foot, stockings:: chóxwxel.
keep it wrapped:: xwelókw'stexw ~ shxwelókw'stexw < xwélekw'.
to wrap:: xwélekw'.
wrap it again, rewrap it, (correction by AD:) roll it up (of a mat, carpet, etc.):: xwelxwélekw't < xwélekw'.
wrapped up:: s'ehó < ehó.
wrapped up (in stupidity):: s'i'hó < ehó.
wrap s-th:: xwélekw't < xwélekw'.
wrap s-th up (a baby, etc.):: ehó:t < ehó.
wrap s-th up (a present, etc.):: ehó:t < ehó.
wrap up:: ehó.

wren

baby wren, little or young wren:: t'át'emiya < t'ámiya, t'át'emiya < t'ámiya.
little winter wren (a real little bird), wren (likes dense woods and woodpiles), may also include (esp.) Bewick's wren, long-billed marsh wren, house wren, and rock wren (all five possible in the area):: t'ámiya.
song sparrow, also brown sparrow, (could include any or all of the following which occur in the Stó:lō area: Savannah sparrow, vesper sparrow, lark sparrow, tree sparrow, chipping sparrow, Harris sparrow, fox sparrow, white-crowned sparrow, golden-crowned sparrow, and song sparrow) (type of brown wren [BHTTC 11/15/76], larger wren (but smaller than robin) [Elders Group 2/18/76]):: sx̲wṓx̲wtha.

wrestler)

throw s-o down hard (like a wrestler), tap s-th (a container's bottom) [hard] on something to make the contents settle (like berry basket):: th'esét ~ th'sét < th'és.

wring

squeeze s-th/s-o, wring s-th (of clothes), pinch s-th/s-o:: p'íth'et < p'í:.

wrinkle

a wrinkle, (have a wrinkle?):: lhélp' < lhél.
(be) wrinkled:: sq'emq'ámth'.
(have a) wrinkled face:: lhélp'es < lhél.

wrinkle (CONT'D)

(have a) wrinkled face with many wrinkles:: lhellhélp'es < lhél.

wrist

sprained wrist:: xweth'éqw'tses.
wrist or hand joint:: xweth'éqw'tses.
wrist, wrist bone (on outer side of wrist, little finger side, lump of wrist):: qwémx̱wtses < qwó:m ~ qwóm ~ qwem.

write

already written:: sx̱ex̱é:yl < x̱él ~ x̱é:yl ~ x̱í:l
got s-th written down:: sx̱éylstexw < x̱él ~ x̱é:yl ~ x̱í:l
pencil, pen, something to write with, (device to write or paint or mark with):: x̱éltel < x̱él ~ x̱é:yl ~ x̱í:l
something one writes with, (writing implement):: sx̱ex̱é:yls < x̱él ~ x̱é:yl ~ x̱í:l
steep rock wall that used to have Indian writing at first C.P.R. tunnel above Haig:: X̱elíqel < x̱él ~ x̱é:yl ~ x̱í:l
write for s-o:: (x̱é:yllhts(e)t) < x̱él ~ x̱é:yl ~ x̱í:l
write s-th:: x̱é:ylt < x̱él ~ x̱é:yl ~ x̱í:l
writings:: sx̱elá:ls < x̱él ~ x̱é:yl ~ x̱í:l
writing s-th:: x̱ex̱é:ylt < x̱él ~ x̱é:yl ~ x̱í:l
writing (while doing it):: x̱elá:ls < x̱él ~ x̱é:yl ~ x̱í:l
writing (while doing it as a structured activity):: x̱ex̱é:yls < x̱él ~ x̱é:yl ~ x̱í:l

wrong :: kw'á:y ~ kw'áy.

(be) turned around, turned the wrong way:: sx̱á:lts' < x̱élts'.
be wrong:: skw'á:y < kw'á:y ~ kw'áy.
get a shoe on the wrong foot:: sts'ó:kw'xel.
got (both) shoes on wrong feet:: sts'ókw'elxel < sts'ó:kw'xel.
to split roots from the wrong end (small end):: séx̱w.

xáweleq

slough about mid-point in Seabird Island where xáweleq plant grew:: Xíxewqèyl or Xewqí:l < xáwéq.

X̱á:ls

rock above Yale where X̱á:ls gritted his teeth and scratched rocks as he duelled with a medicine man across the Fraser:: Th'ex̱elís < th'ex̱elís.

X̱elhálh ~ X̱elhlálh

stone underwater Teeter-totter near X̱elhálh:: Xwíxweth'àlem < xwáth'.
a sx̱wó:yx̱wey head turned to stone on land at X̱elhlálh somewhere:: Sx̱éyes te Sx̱wó:yx̱wey < sx̱wó:yx̱wey.
rock that was a sx̱wó:yx̱wey head (mask) turned to stone at X̱elhlálh:: Sx̱éyes te Sx̱wó:yx̱wey < sx̱éyes.

X̱óletsa

Granite Mountain, the second mountain back of X̱óletsa, northwest of Kwelkwelqéylem:: Th'emth'ómels < th'óméls.
mountain west of Ñó:letsa, (mountain north of Sése (Mary Ann Creek), shortcut to Ñó:letsa [Elders Group (Fish Camp 9/29-31/77)]):: Tl'átl'eq'xélém < tl'aq' ~ tl'q'.
side hills or tilted hills northwest of Ñó:letsa near Yale:: Tewtewá:la ~ Tutuwále < tewále.

Xwyélés
  the Tracks of Mink, holes shaped like a mink's tracks toward the base of the rock-face called Xwyélés or Lexwyélés:: Sx̱éyeltels Te Sqoyéx̱iya < sx̱él:e.

X̱wox̱welálhp
  an area up the mountainside from X̱wox̱welálhp (Yale):: Chelqwílh ~ Chelqwéylh < chá:l or chó:l.

Yakweakwioose
  a spring water stream near Yakweakwioose:: Thíthx̱ < thíx̱.
  village above Yakweakwioose on both sides of the Chilliwack River:: Sx̱wó:yx̱weyla < sx̱wó:yx̱wey.
  Yakweakwioose, next village above Scowkale, village near Sardis on the old Chilliwack River course, now Chilliwack Indian Reserve #9:: Yeqwyeqwí:ws < yéqw.

Yale)
  an area up the mountainside from Ñwox̱welálhp (Yale):: Chelqwílh ~ Chelqwéylh < chá:l or chó:l.
  a village by Yale along Yale Creek:: X̱wóx̱welá:lhp < x̱wále ~ x̱wá:le.
  former village directly across the Fraser River from Yale:: X̱elhlálh ~ X̱elhálh < x̱élh.
  Mary Ann Creek, village at mouth of Mary Ann Creek into the Fraser (in Yale, B.C., Yale Town Indian Reserve #1):: Sése.
  mountain on Fraser River between first tunnel and Yale where rotten fish used to (always) pile up:: Lexwyó:qwem Smá:lt < yó:qw.
  mountain right back of Yale town reserve with two big lakes and many small ones:: X̱ó:letsa Smá:lt <x̱ó:tsa.
  place above Yale:: Xwawíthí:m.
  place above Yale where the Fraser River splits around a rock, island above Steamboat Island (latter just below Five-Mile Creek):: Sx̱wesálh < x̱wés.
  place on Fraser River between first tunnel and Yale where rotten fish used to (always) pile up:: Lexwyó:qwem < yó:qw.
  side hills or tilted hills northwest of Ñó:letsa near Yale:: Tewtewá:la ~ Tutuwále < tewále.
  Yale, Fort Yale:: Puchí:l.

Yale Creek
  a village by Yale along Yale Creek:: X̱wóx̱welá:lhp < x̱wále ~ x̱wá:le.
  place where Yale Creek divides (forks) above the highway bridge over the creek:: T'ít'x̱elhchò:m < t'éx̱.
  village between Yale Creek and Mary Ann Creek on the CP side (west bank of the Fraser R.) where lots of cottonwoods grow/grew (near Yale, B.C.):: Lexwchéwőlhp < cháchew ~ cháchu.

Yale Indian Reserves 19 and 20
  village on east bank of Fraser River below Siwash Creek (Aseláw), now Yale Indian Reserves 19 and 20, named because of a big rock in the area that the trail had to pass (go around), also the name of the rock:: Q'aleliktel < q'ál.

Yale Mountain:: Popelehó:ys.
  a mountain just south of Yale Mountain (Popelehó:ys) with a big hole like a tunnel in it above the highway at Yale:: Tekwóthel ~ Tkwóthel.

yarn
  (be) rolled up in a ball (twine, yarn, etc.):: sqw'ómx̱wes < qw'ómx̱w.

yarrow
  yarrow, also parsely fern:: xaweqá:l < xáwéq.

yawn
- to yawn:: wíqes < wí:q ~ wíq.
- yawning:: wíweqes < wí:q ~ wíq.

year :: syílòlèm ~ siló:lém ~ sílòlèm < yelòlèm.
- ancient people over a hundred years old:: sx̲wolex̲wiyám < x̲wiyám.
- fallen snow, (year):: máqa ~ máqe.
- (have/get a year):: yelòlèm.
- last year:: spelwálh.

yechh.
- yechh., (expression of disgust used by some elders on seeing or smelling something disgusting):: áq'.

yell
- a holler, (a yell, a shout):: stà:m < tà:m.
- call (by voice), shout, yell, holler:: tà:m.
- shouting repeatedly, hollering repeatedly, yelling (repeatedly):: tatí:m < tà:m.

yellow
- a yellowish glow at night given off by old birch and alder:: qwéth'.
- be yellow, be green:: tsqwá:y < qwá:y.
- be yellowish, be tan:: sqwóqweyel ~ sqwóqwiyel < qwá:y.
- getting yellow, turning yellow, turning green:: qwóqweyel ~ qwóqwiyel < qwá:y.
- [have/get/be in a state of going a little yellow or green]:: tsqwíqweyel < qwá:y.
- [having/getting/being in a state of yellow or green]:: tsqwóqwey < qwá:y.
- [looks yellow or green, yellow/green-looking]:: tsqwáyòmèx < qwá:y.
- [stative/be getting yellow, stative/be getting green]:: tsqwóqwiyel < qwá:y.
- turning to real yellow:: qwáyewel < qwá:y.
- turning yellow, getting yellow, turning green:: qwóyel < qwá:y.
- turn yellow, got yellow:: qwáyel < qwá:y.
- yellow?:: eyólés ~ eyó:les < éy ~ éy:, eyólés ~ eyó:les < éy ~ éy:.
- yellow-bodied:: tsqwayíws < qwá:y.

yellow-jacket
- yellow-jacket bee:: x̲ex̲p'ítsel sisemó:ye < sisemó:ya ~ sisemóya ~ sisemóye ~ sísemòye.

yes :: á:'a.
- nod one's head, nod one's head (up and down for yes for ex.):: líqwesem < líqw.
- sometimes, (yes [RM]):: lhéq'.

yes/no question:: í, lí ~ lí: ~ líye < lí.
- interrogative, yes/no question:: -e.

yesterday
- yesterday, it was yesterday:: cheláqelh.

yet
- isn't s-o yet?, isn't it yet?, hasn't s-o yet?:: xwewá: < éwe ~ őwe.
- not yet be, be not yet:: xwewá < éwe ~ őwe.

yew
    yew tree, Pacific yew:: téx̱wetselhp < téx̱wets.

yipes.
    yipes., eek.:: alelí'.

yogurt:: thepth'epéy t'át'ets'em sqemó < thep(-)th'epéy, t'áts', qemó
    (lit. curdled + sour + milk)(uncertain about initial <th> could be <th'> or both could be <th>)

yoke :: shxw'ílámálá ~ shxw'ílàmàlà < ílàm.

yonder
    (be) over there, (be) yonder:: lí(:) tí or lí(:)tí.

you
    It's you to thank the Lord, (Please say grace):: lúwe ts'ít te Chíchelh Siyám < =chílh ~ chílh=.
    so then you:: tl'o'asu < tl'ó ~ tl'o.
    you get covered on the mouth (by a flying squirrel at night for ex.):: qep'ó:ythòm < qep'.

you all
    it is you (pl.), it is you folks, it is you people, it is you all:: lhwélep.

you folks
    it is you (pl.), it is you folks, it is you people, it is you all:: lhwélep.
    you folks (object of preposition), to you folks, with you folks:: tl'alhwélep < lhwélep.
    you (pl.), you folks, you people:: talhwélep < lhwélep.
    your (pl.), you folks's, second person plural possessive pronoun, second person plural subordinate subject:: -a -elep ~ -a' -elep.

young :: =ó:llh ~ =óllh ~ =elh ~ ='ó:llh.
    adolescent virgin girl, young girl (about ten to fifteen years), girl (from ten till she becomes a woman):: q'á:mi ~ q'á:miy.
    a husband's younger wives, co-wife:: sxáye.
    a lot of trees close together (young), thicket:: théqet < theqát ~ thqá:t.
    a small person (old or young) is picking or trying to pick, an inexperienced person is picking or trying to pick, picking a little bit, someone who can't pick well is picking:: lhilhím < lhím.
    baby elk, (young elk):: q'oyíyetsó:llh < q'oyíyets or q'oyí:ts.
    baby wren, little or young wren:: t'át'emiya < t'ámiya.
    bed, (child, young):: =á(:)ylh ~ =á(:)lh ~ =elh (~ =iylh ~ =ó:llh ?).
    child (post-baby to pre-adolescent), child (under 12), (young [BJ]):: stl'ítl'eqelh ~ stl'í:tl'eqelh.
    child, young, baby:: =ílh ~ =íylh ~ =éylh ~ =elh ~ =á(:)ylh.
    five little ones, five young (animal or human):: lhq'atses'ó:llh < lheq'át ~ lhq'á:t.
    little girl (perhaps four years), young girl, (girl from five to ten years [EB]):: q'áq'emi < q'á:mi ~ q'á:miy.
    wide cedar (sapling) strips or slats from young cedar trunks, cedar slat work (basketry):: x̱pó:ys < sx̱éyp.
    young bat:: skw'íkw'elyàx̱el < skw'elyáx̱el.
    young cedar:: súsekw'.
    younger deer, baby horse, younger cow, fawn, colt, calf:: st'él'e, st'él'e.
    (young) girls, lots of (adolescent) girls:: q'á:lemi ~ q'á:lemey < q'á:mi ~ q'á:miy.

young (CONT'D)

young (red) cedar:: shxwt'ám:etsel.

younger

younger, younger sibling, cousin of a junior line (cousin by an ancestor younger than the speaker's), junior cousin (child of a younger sibling of one's parent, (great) grandchild of a younger sibling of one's(great) grandparent), younger brother, younger sister:: sóseqwt ~ (rarely) só:seqwt.

younger brother

girl's younger brother (pet name):: iyá:q, iyá:q.

to make a sign with its foot it wants a younger brother or younger sister:: oqw'exélem < óqw'.

younger, younger sibling, cousin of a junior line (cousin by an ancestor younger than the speaker's), junior cousin (child of a younger sibling of one's parent, (great) grandchild of a younger sibling of one's(great) grandparent), younger brother, younger sister:: sóseqwt ~ (rarely) só:seqwt.

"younger" cousin

younger sibling, younger brother, younger sister, child of younger sibling of one's parent, "younger" cousin (could even be fourth cousin [through younger sibling of one's great great grandparent]):: sqá:q.

"younger" cousins

younger siblings, "younger" cousins (first, second, or third cousins [whose connecting ancestor is younger than ego's]):: sqelá:q < sqá:q.

younger sibling

small younger sibling:: sqiqáq < sqá:q.

younger sibling (pet name):: ká:k ~ kyá:ky < sqá:q.

younger sibling, younger brother, younger sister, child of younger sibling of one's parent, "younger" cousin (could even be fourth cousin [through younger sibling of one's great great grandparent]):: sqá:q.

younger siblings, "younger" cousins (first, second, or third cousins [whose connecting ancestor is younger than ego's]):: sqelá:q < sqá:q.

younger, younger sibling, cousin of a junior line (cousin by an ancestor younger than the speaker's), junior cousin (child of a younger sibling of one's parent, (great) grandchild of a younger sibling of one's(great) grandparent), younger brother, younger sister:: sóseqwt ~ (rarely) só:seqwt.

younger sister

to make a sign with its foot it wants a younger brother or younger sister:: oqw'exélem < óqw'.

younger, younger sibling, cousin of a junior line (cousin by an ancestor younger than the speaker's), junior cousin (child of a younger sibling of one's parent, (great) grandchild of a younger sibling of one's(great) grandparent), younger brother, younger sister:: sóseqwt ~ (rarely) só:seqwt.

youngest

last baby (youngest baby), the last-born, a child cranky and jealous of an expected brother or sister:: óqw'a < óqw'.

youngest (sibling):: se'ó:seqwt < sóseqwt ~ (rarely) só:seqwt.

youngest sister

youngest sister of Lhílheqey (Mount Cheam) that cries:: Ñemó:th'iya < xà:m ~ xá:m.

you people
    it is you (pl.), it is you folks, it is you people, it is you all:: lhwélep.
    you (pl.), you folks, you people:: talhwélep < lhwélep.

you (pl.)
    it is you (pl.), it is you folks, it is you people, it is you all:: lhwélep.
    you (pl.), second person plural object:: -óle.
    you (pl.), you folks, you people:: talhwélep < lhwélep.

your
    your (sg.), second person sg. possessive pronoun, second person sg. subordinate subject pronoun:: -a'.

your (pl.)
    your (pl.), you folks's, second person plural possessive pronoun, second person plural subordinate subject:: -a -elep ~ -a' -elep.

you (sg.) :: taléwe < léwe.
    it's you, you are the one. you (focus or emphasis):: léwe.
    you (sg.) (object of preposition):: tl'eléwe ~ tl'léwe < léwe.
    you (sg.), second person singular object:: -óme.
    you (sg.) (subject of an independent clause), second peron sg.:: -chexw ~ -chxw.

Y-shaped
    prop up a limb with a Y-shaped stick, (prop s-th up (of a limb, with a Y-shaped stick)):: ts'qw'ít or th'qw'it.

Yuculta
    Yuculta Kwakiutl people, southern Kwakiutl people from Cape Mudge north who raided the Salish people:: Yéqwelhtax ~ Yéqwelhta.

Yune's Cannery
    island in river on which Yune's Cannery was built:: Yù:l.

Zapus trinotatus trinotatus:: sétsetets.

Zea mais :: kwól.

Zenaidura macroura
    including Columba fasciata, Zenaidura macroura, possibly Ectopistes migratorius, also Columbia livia (introduced):: hemó:.

Ziphius cavirostrus
    perhaps generic, most likely includes all local balleen whales, i.e., suborder Mysticeti, especially Balaenoptera physalus and Megaptera novaeangliae, possibly Eschrichtius glaucus, Balaenoptera borealis, Balaenoptera acutorostrata, Sibbaldus musculus, Eubalaena sieboldi, could include the following toothed whales (suborder Odontoceti): Physeter catodon, possibly Berardius bairdi, Mesoplodon stejnegeri, Ziphius cavirostrus:: qwél:és ~ qwélés.

Zonotrichia atricapilla
    Melospiza melodia morphna, (perhaps any/all of the following: Passerculus sandwichensis brooksi, Pooecetes gramineus, Chondestes grammacus, Spizella arborea, Spizella passerina, Zonotrichia querula,

Zonotrichia atricapilla (CONT'D)

Passerella iliaca, Zonotrichia leucophrys, Zonotrichia atricapilla, Melospiza melodia morphna):: sx̲wốx̲wtha.

Zonotrichia leucophrys

Melospiza melodia morphna, (perhaps any/all of the following: Passerculus sandwichensis brooksi, Pooecetes gramineus, Chondestes grammacus, Spizella arborea, Spizella passerina, Zonotrichia querula, Passerella iliaca, Zonotrichia leucophrys, Zonotrichia atricapilla, Melospiza melodia morphna):: sx̲wốx̲wtha.

Zonotrichia querula

Melospiza melodia morphna, (perhaps any/all of the following: Passerculus sandwichensis brooksi, Pooecetes gramineus, Chondestes grammacus, Spizella arborea, Spizella passerina, Zonotrichia querula, Passerella iliaca, Zonotrichia leucophrys, Zonotrichia atricapilla, Melospiza melodia morphna):: sx̲wốx̲wtha.

zucchini:: ts'áyxw kúkumels (could be ts'íyxw kwúkwemels) < ts'íyxw, kwúkwemels or kúkumels (lit. dried + cucumber)